2020 HARRIS ADVERTISING

The **2020 Harris Directories** provides you with the most up-to-date information on the region's most prominent companies. Through offering you multiple ways to look up any specific business within the area, important data can easily be located.
. For reliability and assurance, Harris directories are the source for all pertinent information for all companies in there state.

To **_Highlight_** your company and get the most exposure necessary you can now get full page color advertisements inserted in the front of the book. This gives your company a step up showing all your company's information while remaining competitive with the larger companies. These ad pages are supplied by you and can showcase your company logo's, shareholder letters or any other information you would like the thousands of readers who use the Harris Directories to see.

You also get **_complimentary_** books highlighting your company's information and you can also purchase extra books at a 40% discount.

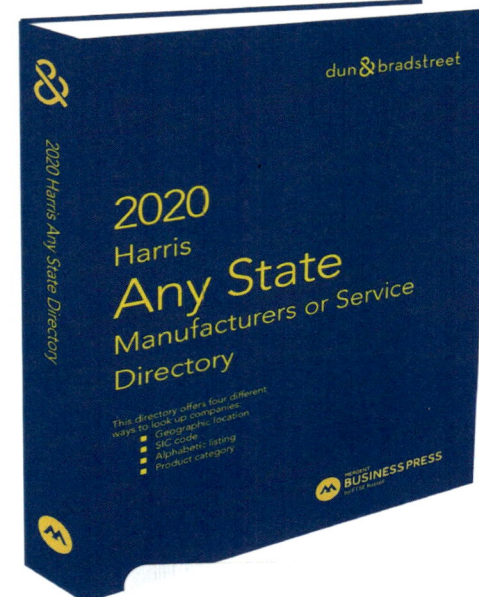

Plan 1

$1,500

1 full page 4 color ad. (Supplied by you)

3 free books (Additional books can be purchased at a 40% discount of regular price)

Plan 2

$2,100

2 full page 4 color ads. (Supplied by you)

5 free books (Additional books can be purchased at a 40% discount of regular price)

Plan 3

$4,000

4 full page color ads. (Supplied by you)

10 Free Book (Additional books can be purchased at 40% discount off original costs)

For additional information or to order please contact

Thomas Wecera at 212-413-7726 thomas.wecera@mergent.com

2020 Harris Illinois Industrial Directory

Published September 2020 next update September 2021

WARNING: Purchasers and users of this directory may not use this directory to compile mailing lists, other marketing aids and other types of data, which are sold or otherwise provided to third parties. Such use is wrongful, illegal and a violation of the federal copyright laws.

CAUTION: Because of the many thousands of establishment listings contained in this directory and the possibilities of both human and mechanical error in processing this information, Mergent Inc. cannot assume liability for the correctness of the listings or information on which they are based. Hence, no information contained in this work should be relied upon in any instance where there is a possibility of any loss or damage as a consequence of any error or omission in this volume.

Publisher
Mergent Inc.
444 Madison Ave
New York, NY 10022

©Mergent Inc All Rights Reserved
2020 Mergent Business Press
ISSN 1080-2614
ISBN 978-1-64141-610-8

TABLE OF CONTENTS

Summary of Contents & Explanatory Notes 4
User's Guide to Listings 6

Geographic Section
County/City Cross-Reference Index 9
Firms Listed by Location City 13

Standard Industrial Classification (SIC) Section
SIC Alphabetical Index 799
SIC Numerical Index 803
Firms Listed by SIC 807

Alphabetic Section
Firms Listed by Firm Name 1031

Product Section
Product Index 1305
Firms Listed by Product Category 1333

SUMMARY OF CONTENTS

Number of Companies 21,530
Number of Decision Makers 44,783
Minimum Number of Employees 3

EXPLANATORY NOTES

How to Cross-Reference in This Directory

Sequential Entry Numbers. Each establishment in the Geographic Section is numbered sequentially (G-0000). The number assigned to each establishment is referred to as its "entry number." To make cross-referencing easier, each listing in the Geographic, SIC, Alphabetic and Product Sections includes the establishment's entry number. To facilitate locating an entry in the Geographic Section, the entry numbers for the first listing on the left page and the last listing on the right page are printed at the top of the page next to the city name.

Source Suggestions Welcome

Although all known sources were used to compile this directory, it is possible that companies were inadvertently omitted. Your assistance in calling attention to such omissions would be greatly appreciated. A special form on the facing page will help you in the reporting process.

Analysis

Every effort has been made to contact all firms to verify their information. The one exception to this rule is the annual sales figure, which is considered by many companies to be confidential information. Therefore, estimated sales have been calculated by multiplying the nationwide average sales per employee for the firm's major SIC/NAICS code by the firm's number of employees. Nationwide averages for sales per employee by SIC/NAICS codes are provided by the U.S. Department of Commerce and are updated annually. All sales—sales (est)—have been estimated by this method. The exceptions are parent companies (PA), division headquarters (DH) and headquarter locations (HQ) which may include an actual corporate sales figure—sales (corporate-wide) if available.

Types of Companies

Descriptive and statistical data are included for companies in the entire state. These comprise manufacturers, machine shops, fabricators, assemblers and printers. Also identified are corporate offices in the state.

Employment Data

The employment figure shown in the Geographic Section includes male and female employees and embraces all levels of the company: administrative, clerical, sales and maintenance. This figure is for the facility listed and does not include other plants or offices. It should be recognized that these figures represent an approximate year-round average. These employment figures are broken into codes A through G and used in the Product and SIC Sections to further help you in qualifying a company. Be sure to check the footnotes on the bottom of pages for the code breakdowns.

Standard Industrial Classification (SIC)

The Standard Industrial Classification (SIC) system used in this directory was developed by the federal government for use in classifying establishments by the type of activity they are engaged in. The SIC classifications used in this directory are from the 1987 edition published by the U.S. Government's Office of Management and Budget. The SIC system separates all activities into broad industrial divisions (e.g., manufacturing, mining, retail trade). It further subdivides each division. The range of manufacturing industry classes extends from two-digit codes (major industry group) to four-digit codes (product).

For example:

Industry Breakdown	Code	Industry, Product, etc.
*Major industry group	20	Food and kindred products
Industry group	203	Canned and frozen foods
*Industry	2033	Fruits and vegetables, etc.

*Classifications used in this directory

Only two-digit and four-digit codes are used in this directory.

Arrangement

1. The **Geographic Section** contains complete in-depth corporate data. This section is sorted by cities listed in alphabetical order and companies listed alphabetically within each city. A County/City Index for referencing cities within counties precedes this section.

> IMPORTANT NOTICE: It is a violation of both federal and state law to transmit an unsolicited advertisement to a facsimile machine. Any user of this product that violates such laws may be subject to civil and criminal penalties, which may exceed $500 for each transmission of an unsolicited facsimile. Mergent Inc. provides fax numbers for lawful purposes only and expressly forbids the use of these numbers in any unlawful manner.

2. The **Standard Industrial Classification (SIC) Section** lists companies under approximately 500 four-digit SIC codes. An alphabetical and a numerical index precedes this section. A company can be listed under several codes. The codes are in numerical order with companies listed alphabetically under each code.

3. The **Alphabetic Section** lists all companies with their full physical or mailing addresses and telephone number.

4. The **Product Section** lists companies under unique Harris categories. An index preceding this section lists all product categories in alphabetical order. Companies can be listed under several categories.

USER'S GUIDE TO LISTINGS

GEOGRAPHIC SECTION

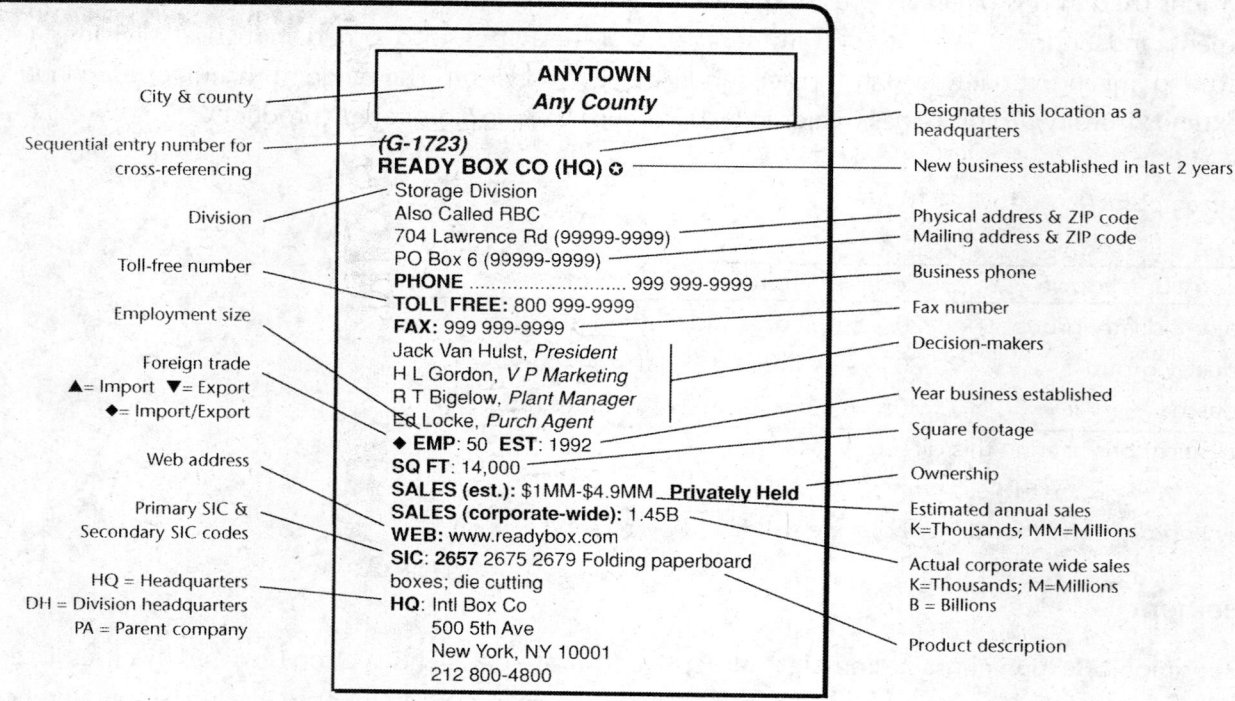

SIC SECTION

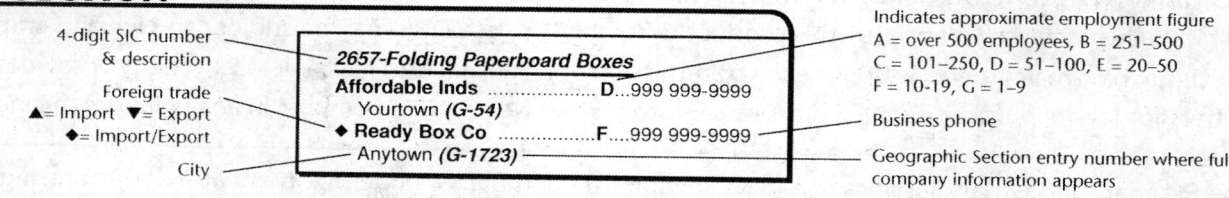

ALPHABETIC SECTION

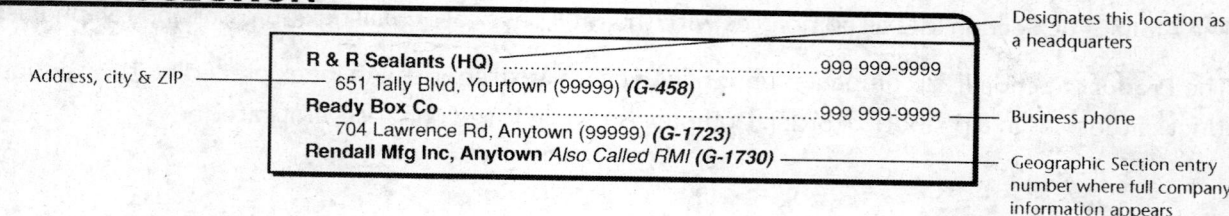

PRODUCT SECTION

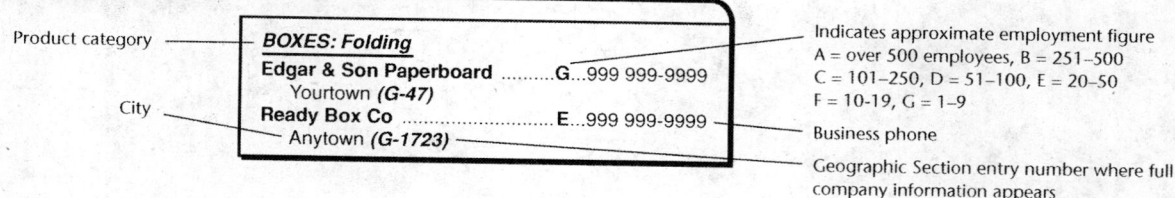

GEOGRAPHIC SECTION
Companies sorted by city in alphabetical order
In-depth company data listed

STANDARD INDUSTRIAL CLASSIFICATIONS
Alphabetical index of classifcation descriptions
Numerical index of classifcation descriptions
Companies sorted by SIC product groupings

ALPHABETIC SECTION
Company listings in alphabetical order

PRODUCT INDEX
Product categories listed in alphabetical order

PRODUCT SECTION
Companies sorted by product and manufacturing service classifications

Illinois
County Map

COUNTY/CITY CROSS-REFERENCE INDEX

Adams
- Camp Point .... (G-2809)
- Clayton .... (G-6909)
- Coatsburg .... (G-6940)
- Fowler .... (G-9742)
- Liberty .... (G-12622)
- Payson .... (G-16317)
- Plainville .... (G-16729)
- Quincy .... (G-16850)
- Ursa .... (G-20004)

Alexander
- Cairo .... (G-2765)
- Mc Clure .... (G-13686)
- Tamms .... (G-19742)

Bond
- Greenville .... (G-10825)
- Mulberry Grove .... (G-14653)
- Pocahontas .... (G-16751)

Boone
- Belvidere .... (G-1644)
- Caledonia .... (G-2768)
- Capron .... (G-2832)
- Garden Prairie .... (G-10236)
- Machesney Park ..... (G-13319)
- Poplar Grove .... (G-16781)

Brown
- Mount Sterling .... (G-14589)
- Timewell .... (G-19797)

Bureau
- Buda .... (G-2500)
- Bureau .... (G-2639)
- Depue .... (G-7716)
- Ladd .... (G-12134)
- Neponset .... (G-15018)
- Ohio .... (G-15845)
- Princeton .... (G-16803)
- Spring Valley .... (G-19307)
- Tiskilwa .... (G-19871)
- Walnut .... (G-20216)

Calhoun
- Batchtown .... (G-1442)
- Hamburg .... (G-10948)
- Hardin .... (G-11016)

Carroll
- Chadwick .... (G-3257)
- Lanark .... (G-12478)
- Milledgeville .... (G-14038)
- Mount Carroll .... (G-14494)
- Savanna .... (G-18403)
- Shannon .... (G-18870)
- Thomson .... (G-19780)

Cass
- Arenzville .... (G-670)
- Ashland .... (G-884)
- Beardstown .... (G-1445)
- Virginia .... (G-20192)

Champaign
- Broadlands .... (G-2410)
- Champaign .... (G-3260)
- Dewey .... (G-7873)
- Fisher .... (G-9667)
- Foosland .... (G-9705)
- Gifford .... (G-10348)
- Homer .... (G-11474)
- Ivesdale .... (G-11756)
- Longview .... (G-13175)
- Mahomet .... (G-13420)
- Ogden .... (G-15837)
- Pesotum .... (G-16599)
- Philo .... (G-16606)
- Rantoul .... (G-16966)
- Sadorus .... (G-18131)
- Saint Joseph .... (G-18317)
- Savoy .... (G-18414)
- Seymour .... (G-18868)
- Thomasboro .... (G-19775)
- Tolono .... (G-19883)
- Urbana .... (G-19972)

Christian
- Assumption .... (G-887)
- Edinburg .... (G-8335)
- Morrisonville .... (G-14350)
- Mount Auburn .... (G-14464)
- Moweaqua .... (G-14651)
- Pana .... (G-16218)
- Taylorville .... (G-19748)

Clark
- Casey .... (G-3198)
- Marshall .... (G-13565)
- Martinsville .... (G-13581)
- West Union .... (G-20690)

Clay
- Clay City .... (G-6902)
- Flora .... (G-9676)
- Ingraham .... (G-11591)
- Louisville .... (G-13178)
- Xenia .... (G-21465)

Clinton
- Albers .... (G-343)
- Aviston .... (G-1178)
- Bartelso .... (G-1252)
- Breese .... (G-2296)
- Carlyle .... (G-2889)
- Damiansville .... (G-7316)
- Germantown .... (G-10330)
- Hoffman .... (G-11402)
- Keyesport .... (G-12043)
- New Baden .... (G-15022)
- Trenton .... (G-19902)

Coles
- Ashmore .... (G-886)
- Charleston .... (G-3397)
- Humboldt .... (G-11522)
- Lerna .... (G-12613)
- Mattoon .... (G-13630)
- Oakland .... (G-15819)

Cook
- Alsip .... (G-406)
- Argo .... (G-673)
- Arlington Heights .... (G-679)
- Bartlett .... (G-1253)
- Bedford Park .... (G-1451)
- Bellwood .... (G-1613)
- Berkeley .... (G-1939)
- Berwyn .... (G-1947)
- Blue Island .... (G-2109)
- Bridgeview .... (G-2317)
- Broadview .... (G-2411)
- Brookfield .... (G-2476)
- Burbank .... (G-2635)
- Burnham .... (G-2644)
- Calumet City .... (G-2772)
- Calumet Park .... (G-2794)
- Chicago .... (G-3461)
- Chicago Heights ..... (G-6728)
- Chicago Ridge .... (G-6788)
- Cicero .... (G-6827)
- Country Club Hills ... (G-7035)
- Countryside .... (G-7043)
- Des Plaines .... (G-7717)
- Dixmoor .... (G-7883)
- Dolton .... (G-7928)
- East Hazel Crest ..... (G-8216)
- Elk Grove Village .... (G-8789)
- Elmwood Park .... (G-9450)
- Evanston .... (G-9485)
- Evergreen Park .... (G-9592)
- Flossmoor .... (G-9698)
- Ford Heights .... (G-9706)
- Forest Park .... (G-9707)
- Forest View .... (G-9730)
- Franklin Park .... (G-9857)
- Glencoe .... (G-10428)
- Glenview .... (G-10517)
- Glenwood .... (G-10639)
- Hanover Park .... (G-10998)
- Harvey .... (G-11069)
- Harwood Heights ..... (G-11101)
- Hazel Crest .... (G-11128)
- Hickory Hills .... (G-11193)
- Hillside .... (G-11324)
- Hodgkins .... (G-11384)
- Hoffman Estates ...... (G-11403)
- Homewood .... (G-11487)
- Indian Head Park ..... (G-11576)
- Inverness .... (G-11592)
- Justice .... (G-11949)
- Kenilworth .... (G-12014)
- La Grange .... (G-12070)
- La Grange Highlands (G-12091)
- La Grange Park .... (G-12094)
- Lansing .... (G-12483)
- Lemont .... (G-12550)
- Lincolnwood .... (G-12809)
- Lynwood .... (G-13291)
- Lyons .... (G-13300)
- Markham .... (G-13548)
- Matteson .... (G-13616)
- Maywood .... (G-13658)
- Mc Cook .... (G-13689)
- Melrose Park .... (G-13816)
- Midlothian .... (G-13989)
- Morton Grove .... (G-14388)
- Mount Prospect .... (G-14509)
- Niles .... (G-15096)
- Norridge .... (G-15228)
- Northbrook .... (G-15328)
- Northfield .... (G-15504)
- Northlake .... (G-15538)
- Oak Forest .... (G-15671)
- Oak Lawn .... (G-15693)
- Oak Park .... (G-15740)
- Olympia Fields .... (G-15896)
- Orland Park .... (G-15931)
- Palatine .... (G-16088)
- Palos Heights .... (G-16181)
- Palos Hills .... (G-16195)
- Palos Park .... (G-16208)
- Park Forest .... (G-16249)
- Park Ridge .... (G-16262)
- Phoenix .... (G-16608)
- Posen .... (G-16789)
- Prospect Heights ..... (G-16835)
- Richton Park .... (G-17027)
- River Forest .... (G-17049)
- River Grove .... (G-17057)
- Riverdale .... (G-17067)
- Riverside .... (G-17080)
- Rolling Meadows ..... (G-17707)
- Rosemont .... (G-17999)
- S Chicago Hts .... (G-18115)
- Sauk Village .... (G-18400)
- Schaumburg .... (G-18423)
- Schiller Park .... (G-18781)
- Skokie .... (G-18911)
- South Holland .... (G-19185)
- Steger .... (G-19486)
- Stickney .... (G-19543)
- Stone Park .... (G-19551)
- Streamwood .... (G-19558)
- Summit Argo .... (G-19676)
- Thornton .... (G-19784)
- Tinley Park .... (G-19798)
- Westchester .... (G-20691)
- Western Springs ..... (G-20718)
- Wheeling .... (G-20834)
- Willow Springs .... (G-21025)
- Wilmette .... (G-21068)
- Winnetka .... (G-21123)
- Worth .... (G-21453)

Crawford
- Annapolis .... (G-590)
- Flat Rock .... (G-9671)
- Oblong .... (G-15824)
- Palestine .... (G-16178)
- Robinson .... (G-17106)

Cumberland
- Greenup .... (G-10819)
- Neoga .... (G-15016)
- Toledo .... (G-19874)

De Witt
- Clinton .... (G-6917)
- Farmer City .... (G-9654)
- Kenney .... (G-12016)

Dekalb
- Cortland .... (G-7015)
- De Kalb .... (G-7429)
- Dekalb .... (G-7664)
- Esmond .... (G-9475)
- Genoa .... (G-10315)
- Hinckley .... (G-11357)
- Kingston .... (G-12055)
- Kirkland .... (G-12059)
- Malta .... (G-13430)
- Sandwich .... (G-18366)
- Somonauk .... (G-19069)
- Sycamore .... (G-19699)
- Waterman .... (G-20297)

Douglas
- Arcola .... (G-645)
- Arthur .... (G-841)
- Atwood .... (G-905)
- Camargo .... (G-2801)
- Tuscola .... (G-19922)
- Villa Grove .... (G-20121)

Dupage
- Addison .... (G-12)
- Aurora .... (G-910)
- Bartlett .... (G-1261)
- Bensenville .... (G-1719)
- Bloomingdale .... (G-1973)
- Burr Ridge .... (G-2647)
- Carol Stream .... (G-2921)
- Clarendon Hills .... (G-6899)
- Darien .... (G-7399)
- Downers Grove .... (G-7948)
- Elmhurst .... (G-9321)
- Eola .... (G-9469)
- Glen Ellyn .... (G-10392)
- Glendale Heights ..... (G-10435)
- Hinsdale .... (G-11360)
- Itasca .... (G-11614)
- Lisle .... (G-12856)
- Lombard .... (G-13033)
- Medinah .... (G-13813)
- Naperville .... (G-14763)
- Oak Brook .... (G-15587)
- Oakbrook Terrace .... (G-15779)
- Roselle .... (G-17938)
- Villa Park .... (G-20126)
- Warrenville .... (G-20228)
- West Chicago .... (G-20528)
- Westmont .... (G-20727)
- Wheaton .... (G-20783)
- Willowbrook .... (G-21028)
- Winfield .... (G-21108)
- Wood Dale .... (G-21146)
- Woodridge .... (G-21269)

Edgar
- Hume .... (G-11526)
- Paris .... (G-16223)

Edwards
- Albion .... (G-346)
- West Salem .... (G-20688)

Effingham
- Altamont .... (G-529)
- Dieterich .... (G-7875)
- Edgewood .... (G-8334)
- Effingham .... (G-8381)
- Mason .... (G-13608)
- Montrose .... (G-14289)
- Shumway .... (G-18903)
- Teutopolis .... (G-19764)
- Watson .... (G-20322)

Fayette
- Farina .... (G-9649)
- Ramsey .... (G-16964)

COUNTY/CITY CROSS-REFERENCE

	ENTRY #

Saint Elmo .... (G-18305)
Saint Peter .... (G-18322)
Shobonier .... (G-18892)
Vandalia .... (G-20010)

Ford
Gibson City .... (G-10335)
Kempton .... (G-12013)
Paxton .... (G-16307)
Piper City .... (G-16625)
Roberts .... (G-17105)

Franklin
Benton .... (G-1917)
Buckner .... (G-2499)
Christopher .... (G-6824)
Ewing .... (G-9602)
Logan .... (G-13032)
Sesser .... (G-18865)
Thompsonville .... (G-19777)
West Frankfort .... (G-20668)
Whittington .... (G-21020)

Fulton
Astoria .... (G-893)
Canton .... (G-2820)
Cuba .... (G-7297)
Ellisville .... (G-9320)
Farmington .... (G-9661)
Lewistown .... (G-12615)
Smithfield .... (G-19063)
Vermont .... (G-20037)

Gallatin
Equality .... (G-9470)
Junction .... (G-11948)
Omaha .... (G-15900)
Ridgway .... (G-17035)
Shawneetown .... (G-18875)

Greene
Carrollton .... (G-3126)
Eldred .... (G-8487)
Greenfield .... (G-10818)
Rockbridge .... (G-17255)
Roodhouse .... (G-17892)
White Hall .... (G-21017)

Grundy
Coal City .... (G-6930)
Mazon .... (G-13681)
Minooka .... (G-14057)
Morris .... (G-14290)
Verona .... (G-20116)

Hamilton
Dahlgren .... (G-7306)
Macedonia .... (G-13317)
Mc Leansboro .... (G-13706)

Hancock
Augusta .... (G-909)
Burnside .... (G-2646)
Carthage .... (G-3134)
Dallas City .... (G-7312)
Hamilton .... (G-10951)
Nauvoo .... (G-15013)
Plymouth .... (G-16750)
Warsaw .... (G-20258)

Hardin
Cave In Rock .... (G-3219)
Rosiclare .... (G-18063)

Henderson
Oquawka .... (G-15906)

Stronghurst .... (G-19633)

Henry
Alpha .... (G-405)
Annawan .... (G-591)
Atkinson .... (G-901)
Cambridge .... (G-2802)
Cleveland .... (G-6912)
Colona .... (G-6975)
Galva .... (G-10226)
Geneseo .... (G-10238)
Kewanee .... (G-12019)
Lynn Center .... (G-13288)
Orion .... (G-15930)
Osco .... (G-15988)

Iroquois
Ashkum .... (G-883)
Chebanse .... (G-3429)
Cissna Park .... (G-6894)
Clifton .... (G-6913)
Crescent City .... (G-7081)
Gilman .... (G-10377)
Loda .... (G-13028)
Martinton .... (G-13589)
Milford .... (G-14033)
Onarga .... (G-15901)
Watseka .... (G-20304)

Jackson
Ava .... (G-1172)
Campbell Hill .... (G-2813)
Carbondale .... (G-2838)
De Soto .... (G-7430)
Gorham .... (G-10682)
Makanda .... (G-13427)
Murphysboro .... (G-14749)
Pomona .... (G-16762)

Jasper
Newton .... (G-15079)
Sainte Marie .... (G-18325)
Wheeler .... (G-20833)
Willow Hill .... (G-21024)

Jefferson
Belle Rive .... (G-1525)
Dix .... (G-7881)
INA .... (G-11575)
Mount Vernon .... (G-14595)
Opdyke .... (G-15904)

Jersey
Dow .... (G-7946)
Elsah .... (G-9458)
Grafton .... (G-10683)
Jerseyville .... (G-11785)
Medora .... (G-13815)

Jo Daviess
East Dubuque .... (G-8174)
Elizabeth .... (G-8786)
Galena .... (G-10163)
Hanover .... (G-10995)
Scales Mound .... (G-18420)
Stockton .... (G-19548)
Warren .... (G-20223)

Johnson
Buncombe .... (G-2628)
Goreville .... (G-10679)
Ozark .... (G-16087)
Vienna .... (G-20117)

Kane
Aurora .... (G-1041)
Batavia .... (G-1338)
Big Rock .... (G-1969)
Burlington .... (G-2640)
Carpentersville .... (G-3090)
Dundee .... (G-8126)
East Dundee .... (G-8186)
Elburn .... (G-8440)
Elgin .... (G-8488)
Geneva .... (G-10249)
Gilberts .... (G-10349)
Hampshire .... (G-10962)
Kaneville .... (G-11954)
Lafox .... (G-12135)
Maple Park .... (G-13459)
North Aurora .... (G-15253)
Pingree Grove .... (G-16621)
Saint Charles .... (G-18140)
Sleepy Hollow .... (G-19061)
South Elgin .... (G-19128)
Sugar Grove .... (G-19637)
Virgil .... (G-20190)
Wasco .... (G-20260)
West Dundee .... (G-20660)

Kankakee
Aroma Park .... (G-839)
Bourbonnais .... (G-2255)
Bradley .... (G-2276)
Essex .... (G-9476)
Grant Park .... (G-10750)
Herscher .... (G-11183)
Kankakee .... (G-11956)
Manteno .... (G-13443)
Momence .... (G-14182)
Saint Anne .... (G-18132)
Union Hill .... (G-19943)

Kendall
Bristol .... (G-2409)
Montgomery .... (G-14229)
Newark .... (G-15074)
Oswego .... (G-15989)
Plano .... (G-16730)
Yorkville .... (G-21471)

Knox
Abingdon .... (G-10)
Dahinda .... (G-7305)
Galesburg .... (G-10184)
Knoxville .... (G-12068)
Maquon .... (G-13477)
Oneida .... (G-15903)
Saint Augustine .... (G-18139)
Wataga .... (G-20286)
Yates City .... (G-21470)

Lake
Abbott Park .... (G-1)
Antioch .... (G-593)
Bannockburn .... (G-1188)
Barrington .... (G-1213)
Beach Park .... (G-1443)
Buffalo Grove .... (G-2502)
Deer Park .... (G-7579)
Deerfield .... (G-7584)
Fox Lake .... (G-9743)
Grayslake .... (G-10758)
Gurnee .... (G-10852)
Hainesville .... (G-10946)
Hawthorn Woods .... (G-11121)

Highland Park .... (G-11250)
Highwood .... (G-11306)
Hoffman Estates .... (G-11472)
Ingleside .... (G-11578)
Inverness .... (G-11599)
Island Lake .... (G-11604)
Kildeer .... (G-12046)
Lake Barrington .... (G-12140)
Lake Bluff .... (G-12168)
Lake Forest .... (G-12218)
Lake Villa .... (G-12345)
Lake Zurich .... (G-12373)
Libertyville .... (G-12624)
Lincolnshire .... (G-12740)
Lindenhurst .... (G-12853)
Long Grove .... (G-13157)
Mettawa .... (G-13977)
Mundelein .... (G-14655)
North Barrington .... (G-15282)
North Chicago .... (G-15290)
Old Mill Creek .... (G-15849)
Park City .... (G-16248)
Port Barrington .... (G-16785)
Riverwoods .... (G-17090)
Round Lake .... (G-18067)
Round Lake Beach .... (G-18087)
Round Lake Heights .... (G-18094)
Round Lake Park .... (G-18095)
Russell .... (G-18114)
South Barrington .... (G-19075)
Vernon Hills .... (G-20038)
Volo .... (G-20196)
Wadsworth .... (G-20207)
Wauconda .... (G-20323)
Waukegan .... (G-20404)
Winthrop Harbor .... (G-21141)
Zion .... (G-21508)

Lasalle
Earlville .... (G-8160)
Grand Ridge .... (G-10688)
La Salle .... (G-12100)
Leland .... (G-12547)
Leonore .... (G-12611)
Lostant .... (G-13176)
Marseilles .... (G-13555)
Mendota .... (G-13933)
Oglesby .... (G-15839)
Ottawa .... (G-16035)
Peru .... (G-16563)
Ransom .... (G-16965)
Seneca .... (G-18858)
Serena .... (G-18863)
Sheridan .... (G-18889)
Streator .... (G-19605)
Tonica .... (G-19887)
Troy Grove .... (G-19920)
Utica .... (G-20005)
Wedron .... (G-20524)

Lawrence
Bridgeport .... (G-2309)
Lawrenceville .... (G-12526)
Saint Francisville .... (G-18313)
Sumner .... (G-19686)

Lee
Amboy .... (G-577)
Compton .... (G-6996)
Dixon .... (G-7887)
Harmon .... (G-11018)
Sublette .... (G-19635)

Livingston
Blackstone .... (G-1970)
Chatsworth .... (G-3425)
Cornell .... (G-7012)
Cullom .... (G-7298)
Dwight .... (G-8156)
Fairbury .... (G-9603)
Flanagan .... (G-9670)
Forrest .... (G-9732)
Pontiac .... (G-16765)
Saunemin .... (G-18402)

Logan
Atlanta .... (G-904)
Elkhart .... (G-9318)
Emden .... (G-9466)
Lincoln .... (G-12728)
Mount Pulaski .... (G-14587)

Macon
Argenta .... (G-671)
Blue Mound .... (G-2142)
Decatur .... (G-7431)
Elwin .... (G-9459)
Harristown .... (G-11032)
Macon .... (G-13404)
Maroa .... (G-13552)
Mount Zion .... (G-14645)
Oreana .... (G-15910)
Warrensburg .... (G-20226)

Macoupin
Benld .... (G-1717)
Brighton .... (G-2400)
Bunker Hill .... (G-2632)
Carlinville .... (G-2867)
Gillespie .... (G-10375)
Girard .... (G-10381)
Mount Olive .... (G-14503)
Palmyra .... (G-16180)
Piasa .... (G-16610)
Staunton .... (G-19474)
Virden .... (G-20184)

Madison
Alhambra .... (G-401)
Alton .... (G-540)
Bethalto .... (G-1964)
Collinsville .... (G-6952)
Cottage Hills .... (G-7028)
Dorsey .... (G-7943)
East Alton .... (G-8162)
Edwardsville .... (G-8343)
Glen Carbon .... (G-10388)
Godfrey .... (G-10646)
Granite City .... (G-10689)
Hamel .... (G-10949)
Hartford .... (G-11034)
Highland .... (G-11204)
Madison .... (G-13405)
Marine .... (G-13498)
Maryville .... (G-13590)
Roxana .... (G-18100)
Saint Jacob .... (G-18316)
South Roxana .... (G-19252)
Troy .... (G-19909)
Venice .... (G-20035)
Wood River .... (G-21259)

Marion
Alma .... (G-404)
Centralia .... (G-3221)
Kinmundy .... (G-12058)

COUNTY/CITY CROSS-REFERENCE

	ENTRY #
Odin	(G-15833)
Patoka	(G-16302)
Salem	(G-18328)
Sandoval	(G-18362)
Walnut Hill	(G-20222)

Marshall
Henry	(G-11162)
Lacon	(G-12125)
Sparland	(G-19254)
Toluca	(G-19885)
Varna	(G-20031)
Washburn	(G-20262)
Wenona	(G-20526)

Mason
Easton	(G-8330)
Havana	(G-11114)
Kilbourne	(G-12044)
Manito	(G-13437)
Mason City	(G-13610)

Massac
Brookport	(G-2498)
Metropolis	(G-13971)

Mcdonough
Blandinsville	(G-1972)
Bushnell	(G-2737)
Colchester	(G-6946)
Good Hope	(G-10670)
Macomb	(G-13388)

Mchenry
Algonquin	(G-365)
Bull Valley	(G-2627)
Cary	(G-3142)
Crystal Lake	(G-7152)
Fox River Grove	(G-9756)
Harvard	(G-11038)
Hebron	(G-11139)
Huntley	(G-11527)
Johnsburg	(G-11800)
Lake In The Hills	(G-12326)
Lakemoor	(G-12471)
Marengo	(G-13478)
Mc Henry	(G-13705)
McCullom Lake	(G-13711)
McHenry	(G-13713)
Oakwood Hills	(G-15821)
Richmond	(G-17006)
Ringwood	(G-17037)
Spring Grove	(G-19262)
Trout Valley	(G-19908)
Union	(G-19937)
Village of Lakewood	(G-20178)
Wonder Lake	(G-21143)
Woodstock	(G-21352)

Mclean
Bloomington	(G-2021)
Carlock	(G-2885)
Chenoa	(G-3432)
Colfax	(G-6950)
Cooksville	(G-7004)
Danvers	(G-7317)
Downs	(G-8112)
Gridley	(G-10843)
Heyworth	(G-11189)
Hudson	(G-11518)
Le Roy	(G-12539)
Lexington	(G-12617)
Normal	(G-15199)

	ENTRY #
Saybrook	(G-18418)
Shirley	(G-18891)
Stanford	(G-19472)
Towanda	(G-19892)

Menard
Athens	(G-896)
Greenview	(G-10823)
Petersburg	(G-16600)

Mercer
Aledo	(G-354)
Alexis	(G-364)
Joy	(G-11947)
Matherville	(G-13614)
New Boston	(G-15026)
New Windsor	(G-15071)
Viola	(G-20180)

Monroe
Columbia	(G-6982)
Fults	(G-10160)
Hecker	(G-11155)
Valmeyer	(G-20009)
Waterloo	(G-20288)

Montgomery
Butler	(G-2749)
Coffeen	(G-6945)
Farmersville	(G-9659)
Fillmore	(G-9665)
Hillsboro	(G-11310)
Litchfield	(G-12959)
Nokomis	(G-15193)
Raymond	(G-16988)

Morgan
Alexander	(G-363)
Chapin	(G-3396)
Concord	(G-6998)
Franklin	(G-9854)
Jacksonville	(G-11757)
Meredosia	(G-13955)
South Jacksonville	(G-19251)
Waverly	(G-20523)
Woodson	(G-21351)

Moultrie
Bethany	(G-1967)
Dalton City	(G-7315)
Lovington	(G-13285)
Sullivan	(G-19659)

Ogle
Byron	(G-2750)
Creston	(G-7101)
Davis Junction	(G-7421)
Forreston	(G-9739)
Kings	(G-12054)
Leaf River	(G-12541)
Mount Morris	(G-14499)
Oregon	(G-15912)
Polo	(G-16755)
Rochelle	(G-17129)
Stillman Valley	(G-19544)
Woosung	(G-21452)

Peoria
Bartonville	(G-1327)
Brimfield	(G-2406)
Chillicothe	(G-6812)
Dunlap	(G-8132)
East Peoria	(G-8249)
Edelstein	(G-8332)

	ENTRY #
Edwards	(G-8336)
Elmwood	(G-9448)
Glasford	(G-10387)
Hanna City	(G-10991)
Mapleton	(G-13468)
Mossville	(G-14452)
Peoria	(G-16372)
Princeville	(G-16825)
Trivoli	(G-19906)
West Peoria	(G-20686)

Perry
Cutler	(G-7304)
Du Quoin	(G-8115)
Pinckneyville	(G-16611)
Tamaroa	(G-19741)

Piatt
Bement	(G-1714)
Cerro Gordo	(G-3256)
Cisco	(G-6891)
La Place	(G-12099)
Mansfield	(G-13442)
Monticello	(G-14277)

Pike
Barry	(G-1248)
Chambersburg	(G-3259)
Detroit	(G-7872)
Griggsville	(G-10849)
Pearl	(G-16318)
Perry	(G-16562)
Pittsfield	(G-16627)
Pleasant Hill	(G-16748)

Pope
Golconda	(G-10665)
Herod	(G-11170)

Pulaski
Grand Chain	(G-10687)
Mounds	(G-14463)
Olmsted	(G-15850)
Ullin	(G-19935)

Putnam
Granville	(G-10754)
Hennepin	(G-11156)
Mark	(G-13545)

Randolph
Baldwin	(G-1184)
Chester	(G-3449)
Coulterville	(G-7029)
Ellis Grove	(G-9319)
Evansville	(G-9590)
Percy	(G-16559)
Red Bud	(G-16991)
Rockwood	(G-17706)
Ruma	(G-18105)
Sparta	(G-19255)
Steeleville	(G-19480)
Tilden	(G-19792)

Richland
Claremont	(G-6898)
Noble	(G-15188)
Olney	(G-15851)

Rock Island
Buffalo Prairie	(G-2626)
Coal Valley	(G-6934)
Cordova	(G-7005)
East Moline	(G-8221)
Hillsdale	(G-11321)

	ENTRY #
Milan	(G-13999)
Moline	(G-14130)
Port Byron	(G-16786)
Reynolds	(G-17005)
Rock Island	(G-17199)
Silvis	(G-18908)
Taylor Ridge	(G-19746)

Saline
Carrier Mills	(G-3123)
Eldorado	(G-8479)
Galatia	(G-10161)
Harrisburg	(G-11019)
Raleigh	(G-16959)
Stonefort	(G-19557)

Sangamon
Auburn	(G-906)
Buffalo	(G-2501)
Chatham	(G-3418)
Dawson	(G-7428)
Divernon	(G-7880)
Glenarm	(G-10425)
Illiopolis	(G-11574)
Mechanicsburg	(G-13811)
New Berlin	(G-15025)
Pawnee	(G-16304)
Pleasant Plains	(G-16749)
Riverton	(G-17089)
Rochester	(G-17163)
Springfield	(G-19313)
Williamsville	(G-21022)

Schuyler
Rushville	(G-18108)

Scott
Winchester	(G-21104)

Shelby
Cowden	(G-7079)
Mode	(G-14067)
Shelbyville	(G-18876)
Sigel	(G-18907)
Tower Hill	(G-19894)
Windsor	(G-21107)

St. Clair
Belleville	(G-1526)
Cahokia	(G-2760)
Caseyville	(G-3210)
Centreville	(G-3255)
Dupo	(G-8135)
East Carondelet	(G-8172)
East Saint Louis	(G-8295)
Fairview Heights	(G-9645)
Freeburg	(G-10088)
Lebanon	(G-12543)
Lenzburg	(G-12610)
Marissa	(G-13543)
Mascoutah	(G-13593)
Millstadt	(G-14041)
National Stock Yards	(G-15012)
New Athens	(G-15019)
O Fallon	(G-15565)
Sauget	(G-18387)
Scott Afb	(G-18856)
Scott Air Force Base	(G-18857)
Smithton	(G-19064)
Swansea	(G-19690)

Stark
Bradford	(G-2273)
Toulon	(G-19890)

	ENTRY #
Wyoming	(G-21457)

Stephenson
Dakota	(G-7311)
Davis	(G-7416)
Freeport	(G-10097)
Kent	(G-12017)
Lena	(G-12597)
Mc Connell	(G-13688)
Orangeville	(G-15908)
Pearl City	(G-16319)
Rock City	(G-17174)
Winslow	(G-21139)

Tazewell
Creve Coeur	(G-7148)
Deer Creek	(G-7571)
Delavan	(G-7715)
East Peoria	(G-8250)
Green Valley	(G-10816)
Hopedale	(G-11516)
Mackinaw	(G-13385)
Minier	(G-14054)
Morton	(G-14352)
North Pekin	(G-15326)
Pekin	(G-16323)
Tremont	(G-19895)
Washington	(G-20265)

Union
Alto Pass	(G-538)
Anna	(G-581)
Cobden	(G-6941)
Dongola	(G-7942)
Jonesboro	(G-11946)

Vermilion
Allerton	(G-403)
Danville	(G-7318)
East Lynn	(G-8220)
Fairmount	(G-9642)
Fithian	(G-9669)
Georgetown	(G-10326)
Henning	(G-11161)
Hoopeston	(G-11505)
Oakwood	(G-15820)
Potomac	(G-16802)
Rossville	(G-18066)
Tilton	(G-19793)
Westville	(G-20778)

Wabash
Allendale	(G-402)
Keensburg	(G-12012)
Mount Carmel	(G-14465)

Warren
Cameron	(G-2808)
Kirkwood	(G-12067)
Monmouth	(G-14214)
Roseville	(G-18062)

Washington
Addieville	(G-11)
Ashley	(G-885)
Nashville	(G-14994)
Okawville	(G-15846)
Richview	(G-17033)
Venedy	(G-20034)

Wayne
Cisne	(G-6892)
Fairfield	(G-9616)
Johnsonville	(G-11811)

COUNTY/CITY CROSS-REFERENCE

	ENTRY #
Mount Erie	(G-14498)
Sims	(G-18910)

White
Carmi	(G-2899)
Crossville	(G-7149)
Enfield	(G-9468)
Grayville	(G-10808)
Norris City	(G-15246)

Whiteside
Coleta	(G-6949)
Deer Grove	(G-7577)
Erie	(G-9472)
Fulton	(G-10151)
Galt	(G-10225)
Lyndon	(G-13286)
Morrison	(G-14340)
Prophetstown	(G-16830)
Rock Falls	(G-17176)
Sterling	(G-19497)
Tampico	(G-19744)

Will
Beecher	(G-1516)
Bolingbrook	(G-2143)
Channahon	(G-3373)
Crest Hill	(G-7083)
Crestwood	(G-7103)
Crete	(G-7134)
Custer Park	(G-7303)
Elwood	(G-9460)
Frankfort	(G-9763)
Homer Glen	(G-11477)
Joliet	(G-11816)
Lockport	(G-12979)
Manhattan	(G-13431)
Mokena	(G-14068)
Monee	(G-14194)
Naperville	(G-14952)
New Lenox	(G-15027)
Peotone	(G-16550)
Plainfield	(G-16639)
Rockdale	(G-17256)
Romeoville	(G-17787)
Shorewood	(G-18893)
University Park	(G-19945)
Wilmington	(G-21095)

Williamson
Carterville	(G-3128)
Creal Springs	(G-7080)
Energy	(G-9467)
Herrin	(G-11171)
Johnston City	(G-11812)
Marion	(G-13499)
Pittsburg	(G-16626)

Winnebago
Cherry Valley	(G-3436)
Durand	(G-8151)
Loves Park	(G-13181)
Machesney Park	(G-13322)
Pecatonica	(G-16320)
Rockford	(G-17275)
Rockton	(G-17692)
Roscoe	(G-17896)
Seward	(G-18867)
South Beloit	(G-19079)
Winnebago	(G-21118)

Woodford
Congerville	(G-6999)
El Paso	(G-8433)
Eureka	(G-9477)
Germantown Hills	(G-10333)
Goodfield	(G-10671)
Metamora	(G-13958)
Minonk	(G-14055)
Roanoke	(G-17098)

GEOGRAPHIC SECTION

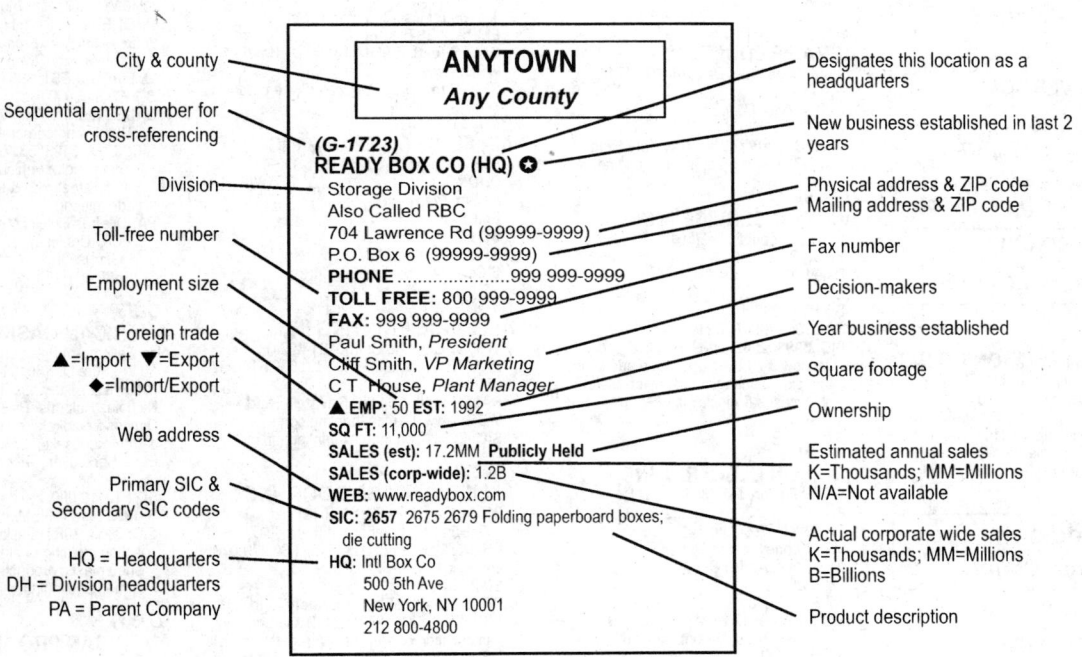

See footnotes for symbols and codes identification.
- This section is in alphabetical order by city.
- Companies are sorted alphabetically under their respective cities.
- To locate cities within a county refer to the County/City Cross Reference Index.

IMPORTANT NOTICE: It is a violation of both federal and state law to transmit an unsolicited advertisement to a facsimile machine. Any user of this product that violates such laws may be subject to civil and criminal penalties which may exceed $500 for each transmission of an unsolicited facsimile. Harris InfoSource provides fax numbers for lawful purposes only and expressly forbids the use of these numbers in any unlawful manner.

Abbott Park
Lake County

(G-1)
ABBOTT LABORATORIES (PA)
Also Called: ABBOTT NUTRITION
100 Abbott Park Rd (60064-3500)
PHONE.....................224 667-6100
Miles D White, *Ch of Bd*
Robert B Ford, *President*
Hubert L Allen, *Exec VP*
John M Capek, *Exec VP*
Lisa D Earnhardt, *Exec VP*
▲ **EMP:** 522 **EST:** 1900
SALES: 31.9B **Publicly Held**
WEB: www.abbott.com
SIC: 2835 3841 3826 2023 In vitro & in vivo diagnostic substances; blood derivative diagnostic agents; hemotology diagnostic agents; microbiology & virology diagnostic products; diagnostic apparatus, medical; medical instruments & equipment, blood & bone work; IV transfusion apparatus; blood testing apparatus; dry, condensed, evaporated dairy products; baby formulas; powdered milk; druggists' preparations (pharmaceuticals)

(G-2)
ABBOTT LABORATORIES INC
200 Abbott Park Rd (60064-3537)
PHONE.....................224 668-2076
Miles D White, *CEO*
Becky Schumacher, *Human Res Mgr*
David Elmore, *Sales Staff*
Ken Miller, *Sales Staff*
Ramani Wonderling, *Manager*
◆ **EMP:** 106

SALES (est): 61.6MM
SALES (corp-wide): 31.9B **Publicly Held**
SIC: 2834 3841 Pharmaceutical preparations; diagnostic apparatus, medical
PA: Abbott Laboratories
100 Abbott Park Rd
Abbott Park IL 60064
224 667-6100

(G-3)
ABBOTT LABS HLTH CARE TR
100 Abbott Park Rd (60064-3502)
PHONE.....................224 667-6100
EMP: 3
SALES: 8MM **Privately Held**
SIC: 2834 Pharmaceutical preparations

(G-4)
ABBOTT NUTRITION MFG INC
200 Abbott Park Rd (60064-3503)
PHONE.....................614 624-6083
EMP: 6
SALES (corp-wide): 31.9B **Publicly Held**
SIC: 2834 Pharmaceutical preparations
HQ: Abbott Nutrition Manufacturing Inc.
2351 N Watney Way Ste C
Fairfield CA 94533
707 399-1100

(G-5)
ABBOTT POINT OF CARE INC
Also Called: Apoc
100 Abbott Park Rd (60064-3502)
PHONE.....................847 937-6100
Rana Van Stan, *Counsel*
Sharon Bracken, *Vice Pres*
Colleen Miller, *Sales Staff*
Connie Carlson, *Payroll Mgr*
Tim Hall, *Program Mgr*
EMP: 180

SALES (corp-wide): 31.9B **Publicly Held**
SIC: 2834 Pharmaceutical preparations
HQ: Abbott Point Of Care Inc.
400 College Rd E
Princeton NJ 08540
609 454-9000

(G-6)
ABBOTT PRODUCTS INC (DH)
100 Abbott Park Rd (60064-3502)
PHONE.....................847 937-6100
Miles D White, *Chairman*
▲ **EMP:** 260 **EST:** 1964
SQ FT: 67,000
SALES (est): 41.5MM
SALES (corp-wide): 31.9B **Publicly Held**
WEB: www.abbott.com
SIC: 2834 8731 Antihistamine preparations; hormone preparations; cough medicines; cold remedies; commercial physical research

(G-7)
ABBOTT UNIVERSAL LLC (HQ)
100 Abbott Park Rd (60064-3502)
PHONE.....................224 667-6100
Miles D White, *Ch of Bd*
Joan Roche, *Engineer*
EMP: 1
SALES (est): 201.4K
SALES (corp-wide): 31.9B **Publicly Held**
SIC: 2834 Druggists' preparations (pharmaceuticals)
PA: Abbott Laboratories
100 Abbott Park Rd
Abbott Park IL 60064
224 667-6100

(G-8)
ABBVIE HOLDINGS INC
Also Called: Abbott Pharmaceutical Corp
100 Abbott Park Rd (60064-3502)
PHONE.....................847 937-7632
Gordon R Solway, *Ch of Bd*
Richard A Gonzalez, *President*
Brian Richmond, *Exec VP*
James E Morrow, *Vice Pres*
Steves H Koehler, *Treasurer*
EMP: 95
SQ FT: 43,000
SALES (est): 13.8MM
SALES (corp-wide): 33.2B **Publicly Held**
SIC: 2834 Thyroid preparations
PA: Abbvie Inc.
1 N Waukegan Rd
North Chicago IL 60064
847 932-7900

(G-9)
ABBVIE INC
200 Abbott Park Rd (60064-3503)
PHONE.....................847 937-4566
Paula J Minnes, *District Mgr*
Erik Axelson, *Counsel*
Daniel Zhang, *Counsel*
Laurie Asbeck-Hickman, *Opers Staff*
Daine Yancey, *Opers Staff*
EMP: 96
SALES (corp-wide): 33.2B **Publicly Held**
WEB: www.abbvie.com
SIC: 2834 Pharmaceutical preparations
PA: Abbvie Inc.
1 N Waukegan Rd
North Chicago IL 60064
847 932-7900

Abingdon
Knox County

(G-10)
JACK BEALL VERTICAL SERVICE IN
109 W Snyder St (61410-1643)
PHONE..................................847 426-7958
EMP: 4
SALES (est): 305.8K **Privately Held**
SIC: 2591 Mfg Drapery Hardware/Blinds

Addieville
Washington County

(G-11)
OTTEN CONSTRUCTION CO INC
786 Old Saint Louis Rd (62214-1608)
PHONE..................................618 768-4310
EMP: 6
SALES: 200K **Privately Held**
SIC: 1521 2452 Single-Family House Construction Mfg Prefabricated Wood Buildings

Addison
Dupage County

(G-12)
355 PALLET SERVICE
704 W Diversey Ave Apt C (60101-3278)
PHONE..................................773 431-6688
Oscar Alonso, *Principal*
EMP: 3
SALES (est): 183.5K **Privately Held**
SIC: 2448 Wood pallets & skids

(G-13)
A & H MANUFACTURING INC
200 W Laura Dr (60101-5014)
PHONE..................................630 543-5900
Habib Abbas, *President*
Fatima Abbas, *Admin Sec*
EMP: 11
SALES (est): 1.8MM **Privately Held**
WEB: www.germakill.com
SIC: 2844 2841 Cosmetic preparations; soap & other detergents

(G-14)
ACCO BRANDS USA LLC
Also Called: G B C Velobind
2171 W Executive Dr # 500 (60101-5625)
PHONE..................................708 280-4702
Dennis L Chandler,
EMP: 35
SALES (corp-wide): 1.9B **Publicly Held**
WEB: www.accobrands.com
SIC: 3579 Binding machines, plastic & adhesive
HQ: Acco Brands Usa Llc
  4 Corporate Dr
  Lake Zurich IL 60047
  800 222-6462

(G-15)
ACCURATE CUSTOM CABINETS INC
115 W Fay Ave (60101-5091)
PHONE..................................630 458-0460
Paul F Steger, *President*
Gary Keller, *Corp Secy*
Camille Scalia, *Bookkeeper*
EMP: 20 EST: 1980
SQ FT: 12,000
SALES (est): 3.4MM **Privately Held**
WEB: www.accuratecustomcabinets.com
SIC: 2522 2521 Cabinets, office: except wood; cabinets, office: wood

(G-16)
ACCURATE FINISHERS
1213 W Capitol Dr 1 (60101-5301)
PHONE..................................630 543-8575
Guillermo Aleman, *Principal*
EMP: 9
SALES (est): 785.2K **Privately Held**
SIC: 3479 Coating of metals & formed products

(G-17)
ACRA PRODUCTS
1820 Kings Point Dr S (60101-1744)
PHONE..................................847 346-9889
Robert Zino, *Principal*
EMP: 3
SALES (est): 275.6K **Privately Held**
SIC: 3724 Aircraft engines & engine parts

(G-18)
ACRYLIC SERVICE INC
1060 W Republic Dr (60101-3133)
PHONE..................................630 543-0336
Dale Damitz, *President*
EMP: 1
SQ FT: 7,200
SALES: 400K **Privately Held**
SIC: 3993 2542 3089 Displays & cutouts, window & lobby; signs, not made in custom sign painting shops; office & store showcases & display fixtures; plastic processing

(G-19)
ADDISON ELECTRIC INC
502 W Factory Rd (60101-4411)
PHONE..................................800 517-4871
Jay Patel, *President*
Mike Kenney, *Sales Mgr*
Jyoti Patel, *Admin Sec*
EMP: 20
SQ FT: 26,000
SALES (est): 17.2MM **Privately Held**
SIC: 5063 7694 Motors, electric; motor controls, starters & relays: electric; electric motor repair

(G-20)
ADDISON INTERIORS COMPANY
711 W Fullerton Ave Ste A (60101-3282)
PHONE..................................630 628-1345
Giovanni Lanera, *President*
Andree Lanera, *Treasurer*
EMP: 3
SQ FT: 7,700
SALES (est): 1.3MM **Privately Held**
SIC: 2512 7641 Upholstered household furniture; upholstery work

(G-21)
ADDISON PRO PLASTICS INC
503 S Westgate St Ste D (60101-4531)
PHONE..................................630 543-6770
Andy Creasor, *President*
EMP: 1
SQ FT: 1,200
SALES (est): 321.9K **Privately Held**
SIC: 5162 3993 Plastics products; signs & advertising specialties

(G-22)
ADVANCED WEIGHING SYSTEMS INC
1433 W Fullerton Ave H (60101-4366)
PHONE..................................630 916-6179
Arthur W Guest, *President*
David Arnold, *Treasurer*
Matt Wade, *Admin Sec*
EMP: 9 EST: 1999
SQ FT: 1,500
SALES (est): 1.5MM **Privately Held**
WEB: www.scaledealer.com
SIC: 3596 5046 Industrial scales; scales, except laboratory

(G-23)
ADVANCED WELDING LTD
760 W Factory Rd (60101-4309)
PHONE..................................708 205-4559
William Meyers, *Managing Prtnr*
Skip Meyers, *Partner*
Skip Robertson, *CTO*
EMP: 17
SQ FT: 2,000
SALES: 3.5MM **Privately Held**
SIC: 7692 Welding repair

(G-24)
AIF INC
Also Called: Absolute Indus Fabricators
1393 W Jeffrey Dr (60101-4331)
PHONE..................................630 495-0077
Ronda Musuraca, *President*
Jeff Howlett, *Engineer*
Jeffrey Howlett, *Engineer*
Joseph F Musuraca, *Admin Sec*
EMP: 32 EST: 1998
SALES (est): 7.9MM **Privately Held**
WEB: www.absolutefab.com
SIC: 3315 Wire & fabricated wire products

(G-25)
AIR FLOW COMPANY INC
850 W Fullerton Ave (60101-3305)
PHONE..................................630 628-1138
Ali Dib, *President*
EMP: 11
SQ FT: 26,000
SALES (est): 2.2MM **Privately Held**
SIC: 3444 Sheet metalwork

(G-26)
ALLIANCE PRINTING INC
1785 W Cortland Ct (60101-4224)
PHONE..................................630 613-9529
EMP: 2
SALES (est): 204.2K **Privately Held**
WEB: www.alliance4printing.com
SIC: 2752 Commercial printing, offset

(G-27)
ALLIED GARAGE DOOR INC
310 W Gerri Ln (60101-5012)
P.O. Box 817, Lombard (60148-0817)
PHONE..................................630 279-0795
Lawrence Parise, *President*
EMP: 40
SALES (est): 2.6MM **Privately Held**
SIC: 1751 5211 2431 3442 Garage door, installation or erection; garage doors, sale & installation; garage doors, overhead: wood; rolling doors for industrial buildings or warehouses, metal

(G-28)
AMAR PLASTICS INC
100 W Industrial Rd (60101-4508)
PHONE..................................630 627-4105
Lakshman Agadi, *President*
Rogelio Bolanos, *Sales Dir*
EMP: 12
SQ FT: 20,000
SALES (est): 1.3MM **Privately Held**
SIC: 3841 Surgical & medical instruments

(G-29)
AMCOR RIGID PACKAGING USA LLC
1035 W Republic Dr (60101-3132)
PHONE..................................630 628-5859
Robert Healy, *Plant Mgr*
Scott Pfaff, *Engineer*
Bob Healy, *Manager*
EMP: 30
SALES (corp-wide): 947.2K **Privately Held**
SIC: 3089 Plastic containers, except foam
HQ: Amcor Rigid Packaging Usa, Llc
  40600 Ann Arbor Rd E # 201
  Plymouth MI 48170

(G-30)
AMERICAN CIRCUIT SYSTEMS INC
712 S Westgate St (60101-5024)
PHONE..................................630 543-4450
Ashok Sheth, *President*
EMP: 40
SQ FT: 10,000
SALES (est): 1.8MM **Privately Held**
SIC: 3672 Printed circuit boards

(G-31)
AMERICAN CNC MACHINE CO INC
749 W Fullerton Ave (60101-3258)
PHONE..................................630 628-6490
Mandy Lanute, *President*
David Masse, *Purch Mgr*
Steve Schenke, *Manager*
EMP: 49
SQ FT: 20,000
SALES (est): 6MM **Privately Held**
SIC: 3599 Machine shop, jobbing & repair

(G-32)
AMERICAN DIESEL TUBE CORP
1240 W Capitol Dr (60101-5375)
PHONE..................................630 628-1830
Jeffrey Mandala, *President*
Juergen Guido, *Owner*
▲ EMP: 10 EST: 1981
SQ FT: 6,000
SALES (est): 1.7MM **Privately Held**
WEB: www.adtcorporation.com
SIC: 3714 3498 3317 5084 Fuel systems & parts, motor vehicle; fabricated pipe & fittings; steel pipe & tubes; engines & parts, diesel
PA: Ditefras Holding Ag
  C/O Urs Heer
  Glarus GL
  556 401-250

(G-33)
AMERICAN GASKET TECH INC
Also Called: Agt Products
10 W Laura Dr (60101-5112)
PHONE..................................630 543-1510
Nicholas Kalouris, *President*
Dimitris Poulokefalos, *Vice Pres*
James Roussakis, *Sales Mgr*
Peter Barkoulies, *Technology*
▲ EMP: 58
SQ FT: 110,000
SALES (est): 13.5MM **Privately Held**
SIC: 3053 3089 Gaskets, all materials; injection molding of plastics; extruded finished plastic products; blister or bubble formed packaging, plastic

(G-34)
AMERICAN PROGRESSIVE CIRCUITS
1772 W Armitage Ct (60101-4207)
PHONE..................................630 495-6900
Shailesh Patel, *President*
Sal C Patel, *VP Opers*
EMP: 25
SQ FT: 17,000
SALES: 1MM **Privately Held**
SIC: 3672 Wiring boards; circuit boards, television & radio printed

(G-35)
ANCHOR PRODUCTS COMPANY
52 W Official Rd (60101-4589)
PHONE..................................630 543-9124
Robert Thrun, *President*
Gary S Thrun, *Vice Pres*
Gary Hampson, *Plant Mgr*
Alexandra Thrun, *QC Mgr*
Gary Thrun, *VP Sls/Mktg*
EMP: 50
SQ FT: 15,000
SALES (est): 12.9MM **Privately Held**
WEB: www.anchorsurgical.com
SIC: 3841 Surgical instruments & apparatus; needles, suture

(G-36)
APSER LABORATORY INC
Also Called: Apser Labs
625 W Factory Rd Ste B (60101-4412)
PHONE..................................630 543-3333
Ansar M Ahmed, *President*
Soofia Ahmed, *Admin Sec*
EMP: 75
SQ FT: 250,000
SALES: 22MM **Privately Held**
SIC: 2834 Pharmaceutical preparations

(G-37)
AR INDUSTRIES
1405 W Bernard Dr Ste C (60101-4341)
PHONE..................................630 543-0282
Anthony Romano, *Owner*
EMP: 3
SALES (est): 261.2K **Privately Held**
SIC: 3999 Manufacturing industries

(G-38)
ARI INDUSTRIES INC
381 S Ari Ct (60101-4353)
PHONE..................................630 953-9100
Kazuo Okazaki, *Ch of Bd*
Daniel Malcolm, *President*
Mark Bolen, *Vice Pres*
Patricia Pondelicek, *Accountant*
Maryjane Banta, *Admin Sec*
▲ EMP: 60 EST: 1954

GEOGRAPHIC SECTION

Addison - Dupage County (G-66)

SQ FT: 52,000
SALES (est): 18.6MM **Privately Held**
SIC: 3823 3357 Industrial process control instruments; nonferrous wiredrawing & insulating
PA: Okazaki Manufacturing Company
3-1-3, Gokodori, Chuo-Ku
Kobe HYO 651-0

(G-39)
ARNEL INDUSTRIES INC
57 W Interstate Rd (60101-4509)
PHONE..................630 543-6500
Edward H Green Jr, *President*
Deborah Green, *Treasurer*
EMP: 30 **EST:** 1958
SQ FT: 75,000
SALES (est): 3.8MM **Privately Held**
WEB: www.newman-green.com
SIC: 3089 3494 Injection molding of plastics; valves & pipe fittings

(G-40)
ARROW SIGN COMPANY INC
415 W Belden Ave Ste F (60101-4933)
PHONE..................630 620-9803
Patrick Palczynski, *President*
EMP: 3
SALES (est): 340K **Privately Held**
SIC: 3993 Signs & advertising specialties

(G-41)
ASPEN MANUFACTURING COMPANY
1001 W Republic Dr Ste 6 (60101-3106)
PHONE..................630 495-0922
Gary Kukla, *President*
EMP: 9
SQ FT: 7,500
SALES (est): 1MM **Privately Held**
SIC: 3452 Bolts, metal

(G-42)
AT&L RESOURCES LLC (DH)
Also Called: Midwest Label Resorces
444 W Interstate Rd (60101-4518)
PHONE..................918 925-0154
Allen Cameron, *President*
Shirley Sminth, *CFO*
Jeffrey Pelcher, *Admin Sec*
EMP: 10 **EST:** 2016
SALES (est): 665.5K
SALES (corp-wide): 105MM **Privately Held**
SIC: 2759 Labels & seals: printing
HQ: Worldwide Printing And Distribution, Inc.
2900 E Apache St
Tulsa OK 74110
918 295-0112

(G-43)
AUTOMATIC SWISS CORPORATION
1130 W National Ave Ste A (60101-3166)
PHONE..................630 543-3888
James Rupprecht, *President*
Peter Witt, *Vice Pres*
David Witt, *Administration*
EMP: 25 **EST:** 1965
SQ FT: 22,500
SALES (est): 5.2MM **Privately Held**
WEB: www.automaticswiss.com
SIC: 3451 Screw machine products

(G-44)
B C DIE & MOLD INC
1046 W Republic Dr (60101-3133)
PHONE..................630 543-5090
William Chesrow Jr, *President*
EMP: 4
SQ FT: 3,600
SALES (est): 432.9K **Privately Held**
SIC: 3544 Dies & die holders for metal cutting, forming, die casting; industrial molds

(G-45)
BALDWIN OXY-DRY CORPORATION (DH)
1210 N Swift Rd (60101-6104)
PHONE..................630 595-3651
Edward T Mc'Loughlin, *Chairman*
Mary Ellen Cahill, *Vice Pres*
Don Gustafson, *Vice Pres*
Martin Haver, *CFO*
▲ **EMP:** 70
SQ FT: 35,000
SALES (est): 16.4MM **Privately Held**
WEB: www.baldwintech.com
SIC: 3555 Printing trades machinery
HQ: Baldwin Technology Company, Inc.
8040 Forsyth Blvd
Saint Louis MO 63105
314 726-2152

(G-46)
BEHABELT USA
2300 W Windsor Ct Ste D (60101-1491)
PHONE..................630 521-9835
Patric Crumley, *Exec VP*
Lauren Magana, *Opers Staff*
Peter Fransemeier, *Exec Dir*
▲ **EMP:** 7 **EST:** 2008
SALES (est): 535.6K **Privately Held**
WEB: www.behabelt.com
SIC: 3052 Rubber & plastics hose & beltings

(G-47)
BELFORD ELECTRONICS INC
1460 W Jeffrey Dr (60101-4343)
PHONE..................630 705-3020
Gary Belford, *Ch of Bd*
Richard Belford, *President*
Michael Belford, *Vice Pres*
Kristin Belford, *Accounts Mgr*
Eric Terez, *Cust Mgr*
▲ **EMP:** 30
SQ FT: 15,000
SALES (est): 8.7MM **Privately Held**
SIC: 5065 3357 Electronic parts; fiber optic cable (insulated)

(G-48)
BERGST SPECIAL TOOLS INC
Also Called: Bergst Engineering
723 W Annorenro Dr (60101-4315)
PHONE..................630 543-1020
Laneta Bergst, *President*
Allen Bergst, *COO*
EMP: 6
SQ FT: 10,000
SALES (est): 750K **Privately Held**
SIC: 3544 3449 Special dies & tools; miscellaneous metalwork

(G-49)
BIBLE TRUTH PUBLISHERS INC
59 W Industrial Rd (60101-4582)
P.O. Box 649 (60101-0649)
PHONE..................630 543-1441
Donald F Rule, *President*
Stephen Rule, *Publisher*
John Kaiser, *Purchasing*
Erika Hintz, *Graphic Designe*
▲ **EMP:** 9 **EST:** 1947
SQ FT: 19,000
SALES (est): 539K **Privately Held**
WEB: www.bibletruthpublishers.com
SIC: 5961 2721 Religious merchandise, mail order; magazines: publishing only, not printed on site

(G-50)
BLACK & DECKER CORPORATION
901 S Rohlwing Rd Ste A (60101-4217)
PHONE..................630 521-1097
Dennis Dallaglio, *General Mgr*
Jeff Persic, *Manager*
EMP: 12
SALES (corp-wide): 14.4B **Publicly Held**
SIC: 3546 Power-driven handtools
HQ: The Black & Decker Corporation
701 E Joppa Rd
Towson MD 21286
410 716-3900

(G-51)
BLACKHAWK MOLDING CO INC (PA)
120 W Interstate Rd (60101-4564)
PHONE..................630 628-6218
Douglas Hidding, *President*
Dale Berg, *General Mgr*
Robert Hidding, *Vice Pres*
Clarence Fellows, *Plant Mgr*
Mike Jones, *Maint Mgr*
◆ **EMP:** 125 **EST:** 1950
SQ FT: 73,000
SALES (est): 27.9MM **Privately Held**
WEB: www.blackhawkmolding.com
SIC: 3089 Molding primary plastic

(G-52)
BLACKHAWK MOLDING CO INC
138 W Interstate Rd (60101-4512)
PHONE..................630 543-3900
Kathy Molnor, *Manager*
EMP: 10
SALES (est): 967.4K
SALES (corp-wide): 27.9MM **Privately Held**
SIC: 3089 Plastic containers, except foam
PA: Blackhawk Molding Co. Inc.
120 W Interstate Rd
Addison IL 60101
630 628-6218

(G-53)
BRADLEY MACHINING INC
136 W Official Rd (60101-4521)
PHONE..................630 543-2875
Edward Youngerman, *President*
Colleen Youngerman, *Admin Sec*
EMP: 10
SALES (est): 1.5MM **Privately Held**
SIC: 3545 3599 3451 Micrometers; machine shop, jobbing & repair; screw machine products

(G-54)
BRAND X-RAY COMPANY
910 S Westwood Ave (60101-4917)
PHONE..................630 543-5331
Jerry Kastic, *President*
David Kassmier, *Admin Sec*
EMP: 16
SQ FT: 3,800
SALES (est): 2.8MM **Privately Held**
SIC: 3844 X-ray apparatus & tubes

(G-55)
BROMINE SYSTEMS INC
1001 W Republic Dr Ste 9 (60101-3106)
PHONE..................331 209-9881
Gregory Johnson, *President*
Ed Schultz, *Partner*
EMP: 3
SALES (est): 450.8K **Privately Held**
SIC: 2899 Water treating compounds

(G-56)
BRUNOS AUTOMOTIVE PRODUCTS
14 W Industrial Rd Ste A (60101-4538)
PHONE..................630 458-0043
Bruno Massel, *President*
EMP: 5
SALES (est): 816.6K **Privately Held**
SIC: 3711 3714 Automobile assembly, including specialty automobiles; motor vehicle parts & accessories

(G-57)
C & C TOOLING INC (PA)
344 W Interstate Rd (60101-4516)
PHONE..................630 543-5523
Jack Corsello, *President*
EMP: 11
SALES (est): 2.2MM **Privately Held**
WEB: www.cctooling.com
SIC: 3545 Machine tool accessories

(G-58)
C CN CHICAGO CORP
421 S Irmen Dr Ste B (60101-4307)
PHONE..................847 671-3319
Sally Jackson, *President*
Sara Wilson, *Exec VP*
EMP: 3
SQ FT: 5,000
SALES (est): 567K **Privately Held**
SIC: 3555 Printing trades machinery

(G-59)
C D TOOLS MACHINING INC
33 W Fullerton Ave (60101-3711)
PHONE..................773 859-2028
Cecylia Dworzynski, *Owner*
Agnieszka K Mendocha, *Administration*
EMP: 5
SALES: 200K **Privately Held**
SIC: 3599 Machine shop, jobbing & repair

(G-60)
C&R DIRECTIONAL BORING
880 S Fiene Dr (60101-5110)
PHONE..................630 458-0055
Russell Cooper, *Owner*
EMP: 2
SALES (est): 362.5K **Privately Held**
SIC: 1381 Directional drilling oil & gas wells

(G-61)
CABOT MCRLECTRONICS POLSG CORP
39 W Official Rd (60101-4532)
PHONE..................630 543-6682
Mark Drzewiecki, *President*
Justin Jones, *Director*
Chip Leen, *General Counsel*
Frances Henderson, *Admin Sec*
EMP: 20
SQ FT: 16,000
SALES (est): 3.3MM
SALES (corp-wide): 1B **Publicly Held**
WEB: www.surfacefinishes.com
SIC: 3827 3544 3829 Optical instruments & lenses; special dies, tools, jigs & fixtures; measuring & controlling devices
PA: Cabot Microelectronics Corporation
870 N Commons Dr
Aurora IL 60504
630 375-6631

(G-62)
CADILLAC TANK MET FBRCTORS INC
225 W Gerri Ln (60101-5009)
P.O. Box 389, Barrington (60011-0389)
PHONE..................630 543-2600
Betty Arnold, *President*
Jack Arnold, *Vice Pres*
EMP: 22 **EST:** 1947
SQ FT: 17,000
SALES (est): 4.5MM **Privately Held**
WEB: www.cadillactank.com
SIC: 3443 Fabricated plate work (boiler shop)

(G-63)
CARDON MOLD FINISHING INC
703 W Annoreno Dr Ste 4 (60101-4323)
PHONE..................630 543-5431
Donald Musial, *President*
Carol Musial, *Corp Secy*
EMP: 4
SQ FT: 1,600
SALES: 300K **Privately Held**
SIC: 3544 3471 Industrial molds; plating & polishing

(G-64)
CAVALLO TOOL SERVICE INC
1714 W Armitage Ct (60101-4207)
PHONE..................630 620-4445
Al Cavallo, *President*
EMP: 6
SALES (est): 744.6K **Privately Held**
SIC: 3541 Machine tools, metal cutting type

(G-65)
CEF INDUSTRIES LLC (DH)
320 S Church St (60101-3750)
PHONE..................630 628-2299
Karin Nelson,
EMP: 114 **EST:** 1946
SQ FT: 83,000
SALES (est): 37.2MM
SALES (corp-wide): 5.2B **Publicly Held**
WEB: www.cefindustries.com
SIC: 3728 3812 Governors, aircraft propeller feathering; landing skis & tracks, aircraft; search & navigation equipment

(G-66)
CENTRAL TOOL SPECIALITIES CO
325 W Factory Rd Ste A (60101-5027)
PHONE..................630 543-6351
Ron Nisson, *President*
Dave Richrath, *Mfg Mgr*
EMP: 8 **EST:** 1962
SQ FT: 7,500

Addison - Dupage County (G-67)   GEOGRAPHIC SECTION

SALES (est): 1.1MM **Privately Held**
WEB: www.centraltoolspecialties.com
SIC: 3544 3469 3354 Special dies & tools; metal stampings; aluminum extruded products

(G-67)
CHAMBERLAIN GROUP INC
1350 N Greenbriar Dr (60101-1037)
PHONE.................................630 705-0300
Gary Chihak, *Branch Mgr*
EMP: 15
SALES (corp-wide): 1.4B **Privately Held**
SIC: 3699 Electrical equipment & supplies
HQ: The Chamberlain Group Inc
    300 Windsor Dr
    Oak Brook IL 60523
    630 279-3600

(G-68)
CHEMQUEST INTERNATIONAL INC
200 W Laura Dr (60101-5014)
PHONE.................................630 628-1900
Habib Abbas, *President*
Fatima Abbas, *Admin Sec*
▲ **EMP:** 37
SQ FT: 113,000
SALES (est): 5MM **Privately Held**
SIC: 2844 Toilet preparations

(G-69)
CHICAGO BREAD COMPANY
Also Called: Boudin Bakery
1405 W Fullerton Ave (60101-4321)
PHONE.................................630 620-1849
Louis J Giraudo, *Ch of Bd*
David Wolsgram, *President*
Gayle Debrosse, *Vice Pres*
Ron Maccarone, *CFO*
Jonathan Bologarsky, *Admin Sec*
EMP: 16
SQ FT: 12,000
SALES (est): 4.3MM **Privately Held**
SIC: 2051 Bakery: wholesale or wholesale/retail combined
HQ: Andre-Boudin Bakeries, Inc.
    50 Francisco St Ste 200
    San Francisco CA 94133
    415 882-1849

(G-70)
CHICAGO PRINT PARTNERS LLC
120 W Laura Dr (60101-5114)
PHONE.................................312 525-2015
Paul Lawless,
EMP: 10
SALES: 2MM **Privately Held**
SIC: 2759 Commercial printing

(G-71)
CHICAGO PRINTING AND EMB INC
60 W Fay Ave (60101-5106)
PHONE.................................630 628-1777
Yousuf Razzak, *President*
Jaaved Razzak, *Admin Sec*
◆ **EMP:** 12
SALES (est): 1.8MM **Privately Held**
WEB: www.yourshirtstore.com
SIC: 7336 2395 2759 7389 Silk screen design; embroidery & art needlework; promotional printing; screen printing; embroidering of advertising on shirts, etc.; T-shirts, custom printed

(G-72)
CHRISTENSEN PRECISION PRODUCTS
1056 W Republic Dr (60101-3133)
PHONE.................................630 543-6525
Karen Palicka, *President*
Ronald Palicka, *Vice Pres*
EMP: 8
SQ FT: 2,600
SALES: 500K **Privately Held**
WEB: www.cppmachineshop.com
SIC: 3444 Sheet metalwork

(G-73)
CLASSIC SHEET METAL INC
1515 W Wrightwood Ct A (60101-3055)
PHONE.................................630 694-0300
Jim Lococo, *President*
Mike Lococo, *COO*
Robert Lococo, *CFO*
Diana Faust, *Administration*
EMP: 50
SQ FT: 90,000
SALES (est): 12.4MM **Privately Held**
WEB: www.classic-sheet-metal.com
SIC: 3444 Sheet metalwork

(G-74)
CLL ENGINEERING LLC
5 W Laura Dr (60101-5111)
PHONE.................................630 628-8393
Steve Franz, *Mng Member*
EMP: 5
SALES (est): 601.3K **Privately Held**
SIC: 3544 Special dies & tools

(G-75)
CNC CHICAGO CORP
421 S Irmen Dr Ste B (60101-4307)
PHONE.................................847 671-3319
Sally Jackson, *Principal*
EMP: 3
SALES (est): 328.2K **Privately Held**
SIC: 3599 Machine shop, jobbing & repair

(G-76)
CNC SWISS INC
761 W Racquet Club Dr A (60101-4317)
PHONE.................................630 543-9595
Jay Borysca, *President*
Boguslaw Siembab, *Principal*
EMP: 5
SALES (est): 611.2K **Privately Held**
SIC: 3599 Machine shop, jobbing & repair

(G-77)
COLUMBIA WOODWORKS CORPORATION
Also Called: Hardwood Furniture & Design
230 W Laura Dr (60101-5014)
PHONE.................................202 526-2387
Garry W Peterson, *President*
Candy Peterson, *Admin Sec*
EMP: 10
SQ FT: 14,000
SALES (est): 1.3MM **Privately Held**
SIC: 2511 Wood household furniture

(G-78)
COMPONENT SALES INCORPORATED
130 S Fairbank St (60101-3120)
PHONE.................................630 543-9666
James R Lovelace II, *President*
Mark Lovelace, *Vice Pres*
Brian Lovelace, *Treasurer*
Tom Lovelace, *Admin Sec*
EMP: 12 **EST:** 1971
SQ FT: 2,500
SALES: 1.4MM **Privately Held**
SIC: 2752 5065 Commercial printing, offset; semiconductor devices; resistors, electronic; electronic parts

(G-79)
COMPUTER MAINTENANCE INC
1433 W Fullerton Ave M (60101-5598)
PHONE.................................630 953-1555
Daniel S Eremenchuk, *President*
George Payciak, *Principal*
Jean Eremenchuk, *Officer*
EMP: 6
SQ FT: 3,500
SALES (est): 590K **Privately Held**
SIC: 7378 5045 7372 Computer peripheral equipment repair & maintenance; computers; printers, computer; prepackaged software

(G-80)
COMPUTERIZED FLEET ANALYSIS
Also Called: Cfa Software
1020 W Fullerton Ave A (60101-4335)
P.O. Box 1309 (60101-8309)
PHONE.................................630 543-1410
Jim Magee, *President*
Michael Ohlinger, *President*
James Magee, *Vice Pres*
EMP: 8 **EST:** 1969
SQ FT: 2,800

SALES (est): 881.4K **Privately Held**
SIC: 7372 Business oriented computer software

(G-81)
CONDOR TOOL & MANUFACTURING
321 W Gerri Ln (60101-5011)
PHONE.................................630 628-8200
Larry Miller, *President*
EMP: 10
SQ FT: 7,500
SALES (est): 1MM **Privately Held**
SIC: 3089 3364 3544 Injection molding of plastics; zinc & zinc-base alloy die-castings; special dies, tools, jigs & fixtures

(G-82)
COSMO FILMS INC (HQ)
775 W Belden Ave Ste D (60101-4944)
PHONE.................................317 790-9547
Sandeep Dutta, *President*
Pradeep Soni, *CFO*
Charles Bohmer, *Human Res Mgr*
Ganesh Girdhari, *Accounts Exec*
Diane Cuzzo, *Sales Staff*
▲ **EMP:** 25 **EST:** 2007
SQ FT: 28,000
SALES: 30MM **Privately Held**
WEB: www.cosmofilms.com
SIC: 3081 Polypropylene film & sheet

(G-83)
CRANE DORRAY CORPORATION
320 S Lombard Rd (60101-3024)
P.O. Box 1465, Elmhurst (60126-8465)
PHONE.................................630 893-7553
Ron Jaeger, *President*
EMP: 8 **EST:** 1981
SQ FT: 3,500
SALES (est): 713.7K **Privately Held**
SIC: 3625 Switches, electric power

(G-84)
CRW FINISHING INC
1470 W Jeffrey Dr (60101-4356)
PHONE.................................630 495-4994
Charles W Calbeck Sr, *President*
Melanie Calbeck, *Corp Secy*
Chuck Calbeck Jr, *Vice Pres*
Jeffrey Bryan, *Manager*
EMP: 20
SQ FT: 18,000
SALES: 5.6MM **Privately Held**
SIC: 3541 3559 Deburring machines; metal finishing equipment for plating, etc.

(G-85)
CUT - TO - SIZE TECHNOLOGY INC
345 S Fairbank St (60101-3137)
PHONE.................................630 543-8328
Mark Karkos, *President*
Maria Karkos, *Admin Sec*
EMP: 20
SQ FT: 31,000
SALES (est): 4.4MM **Privately Held**
SIC: 2541 Store & office display cases & fixtures

(G-86)
DAGGER TOOL CO INC
501 W Interstate Rd (60101-4414)
PHONE.................................630 279-5050
Arthur Tessman Sr, *President*
Mildred Tessman, *Admin Sec*
EMP: 6 **EST:** 1967
SQ FT: 3,000
SALES: 800K **Privately Held**
SIC: 3599 3544 Machine shop, jobbing & repair; special dies, tools, jigs & fixtures

(G-87)
DIAL TOOL INDUSTRIES INC
201 S Church St (60101-3747)
PHONE.................................630 543-3600
Steven Pagliuzza, *President*
Rick Raskow, *Mfg Mgr*
Mario Pagliuzza, *Admin Sec*
Judi Grein, *Admin Asst*
EMP: 100 **EST:** 1955
SQ FT: 40,000
SALES (est): 21.3MM **Privately Held**
WEB: www.dialtool.com
SIC: 3469 3544 Stamping metal for the trade; special dies, tools, jigs & fixtures

(G-88)
DIAMOND EDGE MANUFACTORING
644 W Winthrop Ave (60101-4436)
PHONE.................................630 458-1630
Louis Papamihail, *President*
Roman Buchacz, *Admin Sec*
EMP: 4
SQ FT: 3,500
SALES (est): 673.7K **Privately Held**
SIC: 3541 7699 Machine tools, metal cutting type; industrial tool grinding

(G-89)
DIAMOND SIGN DESIGN
603 W Factory Rd (60101-4400)
PHONE.................................630 543-4900
EMP: 3
SALES (est): 262K **Privately Held**
WEB: www.diamondsignanddesign.com
SIC: 3993 Signs & advertising specialties

(G-90)
DIAMOND TOOL & MOLD INC
1212 W National Ave (60101-3131)
PHONE.................................630 543-7011
Larry Sieber, *President*
Mark Cooper, *Admin Sec*
EMP: 9 **EST:** 1999
SALES: 750K **Privately Held**
WEB: www.diamondtoolandmold.com
SIC: 3544 Industrial molds

(G-91)
DICIANNI GRAPHICS INCORPORATED
421 S Addison Rd (60101-4650)
PHONE.................................630 833-5100
Peter P Dicianni III, *President*
EMP: 12
SQ FT: 2,700
SALES (est): 2MM **Privately Held**
SIC: 2752 7336 Commercial printing, offset; graphic arts & related design

(G-92)
DICKSON/UNIGAGE INC
Also Called: Dickson Company, The
930 S Westwood Ave (60101-4997)
PHONE.................................630 543-3747
Michael Unger, *President*
James F Foley, *Chairman*
Mark T Kohlmeier, *Corp Secy*
Fred Kirsch, *VP Mfg*
Juanita Sinon, *Engineer*
▲ **EMP:** 45
SQ FT: 200,000
SALES (est): 12.6MM **Privately Held**
WEB: www.dicksondata.com
SIC: 3823 5084 3822 3572 Temperature instruments; industrial process type; pressure measurement instruments, industrial; humidity instruments, industrial process type; measuring & testing equipment, electrical; auto controls regulating residntl & coml environmt & applncs; computer storage devices

(G-93)
DIE PROS INC
1233 W Capitol Dr Ste B (60101-3170)
PHONE.................................630 543-2025
Dennis M Lee, *President*
EMP: 4
SQ FT: 2,500
SALES (est): 386.1K **Privately Held**
SIC: 3544 Dies, steel rule; dies & die holders for metal cutting, forming, die casting

(G-94)
DIMENSION MOLDING CORPORATION
777 W Annoreno Dr (60101-4383)
PHONE.................................630 628-0777
Michael Stiglianses, *President*
Brad Saettone, *Maintence Staff*
▲ **EMP:** 40
SALES (est): 6.3MM **Privately Held**
WEB: www.dimensionmold.com
SIC: 3089 Injection molded finished plastic products; injection molding of plastics

▲ = Import ▼ = Export
◆ = Import/Export

GEOGRAPHIC SECTION
Addison - Dupage County (G-125)

(G-95)
DNP ENTERPRISES INC (PA)
1213 W Capitol Dr (60101-5301)
PHONE....................630 628-7210
Mark Poulopoulos, *President*
Deborah Poulopoulos, *Admin Sec*
EMP: 4
SQ FT: 6,000
SALES (est): 454K **Privately Held**
SIC: 3599 Machine & other job shop work

(G-96)
DORAL INC
Also Called: J & F Engineering
344 W Interstate Rd (60101-4516)
PHONE....................630 543-5523
James A Turus, *Owner*
EMP: 3
SQ FT: 5,000
SALES (est): 190.5K **Privately Held**
SIC: 3544 Special dies, tools, jigs & fixtures

(G-97)
DOYLE SIGNS INC (PA)
232 W Interstate Rd (60101-4563)
P.O. Box 1068 (60101-8068)
PHONE....................630 543-9490
Terrence J Doyle, *President*
Larry Spence, *Business Mgr*
Joe Doyle, *Vice Pres*
Joseph T Doyle, *Vice Pres*
Margaret Neander, *Vice Pres*
EMP: 75
SQ FT: 36,800
SALES (est): 15.5MM **Privately Held**
WEB: www.doylesigns.com
SIC: 3993 Neon signs

(G-98)
DPM SOLUTIONS LLC
724 W Racquet Club Dr (60101-4318)
PHONE....................630 285-1170
Alexander Robledo, *Engineer*
EMP: 5 **EST:** 2009
SALES (est): 297.5K **Privately Held**
WEB: www.dpmcncsolutions.com
SIC: 3999 Atomizers, toiletry

(G-99)
DSI SPACEFRAMES INC
509 S Westgate St (60101-4530)
PHONE....................630 607-0045
Thomas Rj Chambers, *President*
▲ **EMP:** 30
SQ FT: 12,000
SALES (est): 8.8MM **Privately Held**
SIC: 3446 3441 Architectural metalwork; fabricated structural metal

(G-100)
DTE ENTERPRISES LLC
Also Called: Dealers Transmission Exchange
2350 W Pinehurst Blvd (60101-6181)
PHONE....................630 307-9355
EMP: 6
SALES (est): 1.4MM **Privately Held**
SIC: 5013 3714 Automotive engines & engine parts; rebuilding engines & transmissions, factory basis

(G-101)
DTI MOLDING TECHNOLOGIES INC
201 S Church St (60101-3747)
PHONE....................630 543-3600
Mario Pagliuzza, *President*
▲ **EMP:** 54
SQ FT: 40,000
SALES (est): 2.5MM **Privately Held**
SIC: 3089 Molding primary plastic

(G-102)
DU ALL PRECISION LLC
1025 W National Ave (60101-3126)
PHONE....................630 543-4243
Kent Niederhofer, *CEO*
EMP: 33
SALES (est): 8.4MM **Privately Held**
SIC: 3599 Machine shop, jobbing & repair

(G-103)
DU PAGE WELDING INC
847 S Westgate St (60101-5025)
PHONE....................630 543-8511
Mark Rose, *President*
Glenn Nelson, *Med Doctor*
▼ **EMP:** 5 **EST:** 1979
SQ FT: 7,300
SALES (est): 350K **Privately Held**
WEB: www.dupagewelding.com
SIC: 7692 Welding repair

(G-104)
DYNAMAC INC
1229 W Capitol Dr (60101-3116)
PHONE....................630 543-0033
Kent Higgins, *President*
Peter Ronge, *Vice Pres*
Paul Flauter, *Prdtn Mgr*
Martin J Keane Sr, *Sales Mgr*
Mariusz Kukielko, *Software Dev*
EMP: 32
SQ FT: 15,000
SALES (est): 6.4MM **Privately Held**
SIC: 3599 Machine shop, jobbing & repair

(G-105)
DYNAMAC MICROWAVE INC
1229 W Capitol Dr (60101-3116)
PHONE....................630 543-0033
Kent Higgins, *Principal*
EMP: 7
SALES (est): 295.8K **Privately Held**
SIC: 3679 Electronic components

(G-106)
E & C CUSTOM PLASTIC INC
466 S Vista Ave (60101-4421)
PHONE....................630 543-3325
Harry Caldwell, *President*
EMP: 30
SALES (est): 5.2MM **Privately Held**
SIC: 3089 Injection molding of plastics

(G-107)
E & T PLASTIC MFG CO INC
Also Called: E & T Plastics of Illinois
140 S Fairbank St (60101-3120)
PHONE....................630 628-9048
Al Bennett, *Manager*
EMP: 10
SALES (corp-wide): 75MM **Privately Held**
WEB: www.e-tplastics.com
SIC: 3089 Extruded finished plastic products
PA: E & T Plastic Manufacturing Co., Inc.
4545 37th St
Long Island City NY 11101
718 729-6226

(G-108)
E-JAY PLASTICS CO
115 W Laura Dr (60101-5113)
PHONE....................630 543-4000
Robert Tyler, *President*
Joan Tyler, *Treasurer*
EMP: 10
SQ FT: 13,000
SALES (est): 1.4MM **Privately Held**
SIC: 3089 3083 Molding primary plastic; laminated plastics plate & sheet

(G-109)
EAGLE CARPET SERVICES LTD
135 S Fairbank St (60101-3119)
PHONE....................956 971-8560
William C Kotlow, *Principal*
Joe Baker, *Principal*
Jim Price, *Principal*
Martin Somen, *Principal*
Charles P Pytlarz, *Admin Sec*
▲ **EMP:** 5
SQ FT: 3,000
SALES (est): 249.4K **Privately Held**
SIC: 2273 Carpets & rugs

(G-110)
EAGLE GEAR & MANUFACTURING CO
740 W Racquet Club Dr (60101-4318)
PHONE....................630 628-6100
Marek Tyrka, *President*
EMP: 12
SALES: 1MM **Privately Held**
SIC: 3599 Machine shop, jobbing & repair

(G-111)
ELCAST MANUFACTURING INC
Also Called: Elcast Lighting
815 W Kay Ave Ste B (60101-4938)
PHONE....................630 628-1992
Peter Biedermann, *President*
Robert Lurski, *Vice Pres*
Dennis Solit, *Natl Sales Mgr*
▲ **EMP:** 20
SALES (est): 2.9MM **Privately Held**
SIC: 3648 3645 Lighting equipment; residential lighting fixtures

(G-112)
ELECTRONIC RESOURCES CORP
817 S Kay Ave Ste 6 (60101-4900)
PHONE....................331 225-3450
David Barrios, *President*
EMP: 4
SALES (est): 502.5K **Privately Held**
SIC: 3672 Printed circuit boards

(G-113)
ELK GROVE RUBBER & PLASTIC CO
99 W Commercial Ave (60101-4501)
PHONE....................630 543-5656
Brian Lovitsch, *President*
Joseph Sabatino, *Vice Pres*
EMP: 15
SQ FT: 8,000
SALES (est): 1.3MM **Privately Held**
SIC: 3061 Mechanical rubber goods

(G-114)
ELLIOTT MACHINE & TOOL CORP
511 W Interstate Rd (60101-4414)
PHONE....................630 543-6755
Jimmy C Mc Namer, *President*
Barbara Mc Namer, *Admin Sec*
EMP: 3 **EST:** 1955
SQ FT: 3,000
SALES (est): 230K **Privately Held**
SIC: 3599 Machine shop, jobbing & repair

(G-115)
ENCON ENVIRONMENTAL CONCEPTS
643 W Winthrop Ave (60101-4435)
PHONE....................630 543-1583
Robert Rusteberg, *President*
EMP: 17 **EST:** 1975
SQ FT: 10,000
SALES (est): 3.5MM **Privately Held**
SIC: 5712 2434 Cabinet work, custom; wood kitchen cabinets

(G-116)
ESSEX GROUP INC
758 W Racquet Club Dr (60101-4318)
PHONE....................630 628-7841
Jessica Utterback, *Manager*
EMP: 69 **Privately Held**
WEB: www.essexgroup.com
SIC: 3357 Building wire & cable, nonferrous
HQ: Essex Group, Inc.
1601 Wall St
Fort Wayne IN 46802
260 461-4000

(G-117)
EUROPEAN ORNAMENTAL IRON WORKS
1786 W Armitage Ct (60101-4207)
PHONE....................630 705-9300
Michael Pietanza, *President*
EMP: 8
SQ FT: 2,400
SALES (est): 800K **Privately Held**
SIC: 1799 3496 3446 3441 Ornamental metal work; miscellaneous fabricated wire products; architectural metalwork; fabricated structural metal; metal household furniture

(G-118)
EXO FABRICATION INC
1140 W Fullerton Ave (60101-4304)
PHONE....................630 501-1136
Leslie E Smiling, *President*
EMP: 6
SALES: 500K **Privately Held**
SIC: 3441 Fabricated structural metal

(G-119)
FCI FLAVORS
1208 N Swift Rd (60101-6104)
PHONE....................630 373-1707
Zack Rumbaugh, *Sales Staff*
Karrie Franklin, *Admin Asst*
EMP: 7
SALES (est): 693.4K **Privately Held**
SIC: 2869 Industrial organic chemicals

(G-120)
FDF ARMATURE INC
220 W Gerri Ln (60101-5010)
PHONE....................630 458-0452
Frank Defrenza, *President*
▲ **EMP:** 8
SQ FT: 7,400
SALES (est): 1.1MM **Privately Held**
SIC: 7694 Rebuilding motors, except automotive

(G-121)
FIBERGLASS SOLUTIONS CORP
436 W Belden Ave (60101-4903)
PHONE....................630 458-0756
Emily A Quiniff, *President*
Gregory Quiniff, *Corp Secy*
Paul Quiniff, *Vice Pres*
EMP: 9 **EST:** 1971
SQ FT: 5,000
SALES (est): 500K **Privately Held**
SIC: 2221 Fiberglass fabrics

(G-122)
FINISHING COMPANY
136 W Commercial Ave (60101-4504)
PHONE....................630 559-0808
JW Carlson, *President*
Joe Gecan, *Prdtn Mgr*
Jeremy Cox, *Accounts Mgr*
EMP: 155
SALES (est): 17.7MM **Privately Held**
SIC: 3471 3479 2851 Anodizing (plating) of metals or formed products; aluminum coating of metal products; colors in oil, except artists'

(G-123)
FLAVOR CONCEPTS INC
1208 N Swift Rd (60101-6104)
PHONE....................630 520-9060
Larry Wadsworth, *President*
David Peterson, *Admin Sec*
EMP: 11
SQ FT: 12,000
SALES (est): 1.8MM **Privately Held**
SIC: 2087 Flavoring extracts & syrups

(G-124)
FLAVORFOCUS LLC
Also Called: Brookside Flavors Ingredients
1210 N Swift Rd (60101-6104)
PHONE....................630 520-9060
Donald L Hawks III, *President*
Richard Nikola, *COO*
William Gambrell, *Vice Pres*
Gaetan Sourceau, *CFO*
Bridget Desalvo, *Human Res Mgr*
EMP: 55
SALES (est): 16.5MM
SALES (corp-wide): 19.2MM **Privately Held**
WEB: www.flavorfocus.com
SIC: 2087 Flavoring extracts & syrups
HQ: Brookside Flavors & Ingredients Llc
201 Tresser Blvd Ste 320
Stamford CT 06901
203 595-4520

(G-125)
FLEXTRON INC
Also Called: Flexible Metal Tubing Conduit
130 W Fay Ave (60101-5108)
PHONE....................630 543-5995
George Wesesku, *President*
Mike Dwyer, *President*
EMP: 14
SQ FT: 13,000
SALES: 1.7MM **Privately Held**
WEB: www.flextroninc.com
SIC: 3599 Hose, flexible metallic

Addison - Dupage County (G-126)

(G-126)
FLOWSERVE CORPORATION
409 S Vista Ave (60101-4420)
PHONE..............................630 543-4240
Brian McAloon, *Technology*
EMP: 30
SALES (corp-wide): 3.9B **Publicly Held**
SIC: 3561 Pumps & pumping equipment
PA: Flowserve Corporation
  5215 N Ocnnor Blvd Ste 23 Connor
  Irving TX 75039
  972 443-6500

(G-127)
FONTELA ELECTRIC INCORPORATED (PA)
1406 W Jeffrey Dr (60101-4356)
PHONE..............................630 932-1600
Antonio Fontela, *President*
Debra C Fontela, *Admin Sec*
EMP: 15
SQ FT: 6,000
SALES (est): 1.3MM **Privately Held**
SIC: 7694 Rebuilding motors, except automotive

(G-128)
FORMAR INC
Also Called: True Dimension
1049 W Republic Dr (60101-3132)
PHONE..............................630 543-1151
Mark Boryscka, *President*
EMP: 12
SQ FT: 12,700
SALES (est): 1.7MM **Privately Held**
SIC: 3451 Screw machine products

(G-129)
FRANCH & SONS TRNSP INC
329 N Mill Rd Unit 108 (60101)
PHONE..............................630 392-3307
Paul M Franch, *President*
EMP: 3
SALES: 400K **Privately Held**
SIC: 2679 7389 Papier mache articles, except statuary & art goods;

(G-130)
FURNEL INC (PA)
350 S Stewart Ave (60101-3310)
PHONE..............................630 543-0885
John P Murzanski, *President*
Matthew Murzanski, *Project Mgr*
EMP: 27
SQ FT: 10,000
SALES (est): 5.4MM **Privately Held**
SIC: 3089 3544 Injection molding of plastics; industrial molds

(G-131)
G BRANCH CORP
409 S Vista Ave Unit B (60101-4420)
PHONE..............................630 458-1909
Grant Branch, *Owner*
EMP: 52
SALES (est): 2MM **Privately Held**
SIC: 3444 Sheet metal specialties, not stamped

(G-132)
G L TOOL AND MANUFACTURING CO
815 S Kay Ave Ste A (60101-4938)
PHONE..............................630 628-1992
Robert Lurski, *President*
Christine Lurski, *Admin Sec*
▲ **EMP:** 16
SQ FT: 11,000
SALES (est): 2.2MM **Privately Held**
SIC: 3471 Finishing, metals or formed products

(G-133)
GALAXY SOURCING INC
15 W Commercial Ave (60101-4501)
PHONE..............................630 532-5003
Shakil Merchant, *President*
Shayan Merchant, *Vice Pres*
▲ **EMP:** 3
SQ FT: 5,000

SALES: 1.5MM **Privately Held**
SIC: 3545 3568 3599 Machine tool attachments & accessories; sprockets (power transmission equipment); pulleys, power transmission; machine shop, jobbing & repair

(G-134)
GALLON INDUSTRIES INC
Also Called: Bm Welding
341 W Factory Rd (60101-5003)
PHONE..............................630 628-1020
Neville Gallon, *President*
Joy Gallon, *Admin Sec*
EMP: 22
SALES (est): 3.8MM **Privately Held**
SIC: 3441 Fabricated structural metal

(G-135)
GARRATT-CALLAHAN COMPANY
340 S La Londe Ave (60101-3394)
PHONE..............................630 543-4411
John Keating, *Branch Mgr*
EMP: 7
SALES (corp-wide): 69.4MM **Privately Held**
SIC: 2899 Water treating compounds
PA: Garratt-Callahan Company
  50 Ingold Rd
  Burlingame CA 94010
  650 697-5811

(G-136)
GENERAL ENGINEERING WORKS
1025 W National Ave (60101-3126)
PHONE..............................630 543-8000
Sue Peters, *President*
John Gassensmith, *Vice Pres*
EMP: 40
SQ FT: 25,000
SALES (est): 7.6MM **Privately Held**
WEB: www.gewinc.com
SIC: 3451 Screw machine products

(G-137)
GENERAL GRINDING CO
1514 W Wrightwood Ct (60101-3071)
PHONE..............................630 543-9088
Ariel Monsivais, *President*
EMP: 7 EST: 1950
SQ FT: 5,000
SALES (est): 894.7K **Privately Held**
SIC: 3599 Machine shop, jobbing & repair; grinding castings for the trade

(G-138)
GENERAL PLATING CO INC
303 W Fay Ave (60101-5007)
PHONE..............................630 543-0088
Josephine Maleski, *President*
Dave Maleski, *Principal*
Jim Maleski, *Vice Pres*
Lisa Maleski, *Admin Sec*
EMP: 7
SQ FT: 5,000
SALES (est): 929.6K **Privately Held**
SIC: 3471 Electroplating of metals or formed products; finishing, metals or formed products

(G-139)
GEORGE HANSEN & CO INC
Also Called: Value Lift
50 W Laura Dr (60101-5115)
PHONE..............................630 628-8700
Sue Hansen, *President*
William Hansen, *President*
Susan Hansen, *CFO*
EMP: 11 EST: 1953
SQ FT: 14,000
SALES: 940K **Privately Held**
WEB: www.value-lift.com
SIC: 3544 Special dies & tools

(G-140)
GIANT FINISHING INC
600 W Factory Rd (60101-4413)
PHONE..............................708 343-6900
Miro Oryszczak, *President*
Paul Podedworney, *Vice Pres*
Ziggy Skirucha, *Treasurer*
Mark Oryszczak, *Admin Sec*
EMP: 5

SALES (est): 1.4MM **Privately Held**
SIC: 3541 Deburring machines

(G-141)
GLC INDUSTRIES INC
Also Called: GLC Engineering
326 W Gerri Ln (60101-5012)
PHONE..............................630 628-5870
George Lambropoulos, *President*
EMP: 20
SQ FT: 12,000
SALES (est): 4.1MM **Privately Held**
SIC: 3444 Sheet metal specialties, not stamped

(G-142)
GLOBAL ABRASIVE PRODUCTS INC
39 W Factory Rd (60101-5101)
PHONE..............................630 543-9466
Boris Andres, *Branch Mgr*
EMP: 40 **Privately Held**
SIC: 2675 Paperboard die-cutting
PA: Global Abrasive Products, Inc.
  62 Mill St
  Lockport NY 14094

(G-143)
GRIND LAP SERVICES INC
1045 W National Ave (60101-3126)
PHONE..............................630 458-1111
John Gallichio, *President*
Marcia Gallichio, *Corp Secy*
EMP: 27 EST: 1977
SQ FT: 27,000
SALES (est): 3MM **Privately Held**
SIC: 7389 3599 Grinding, precision: commercial or industrial; machine shop, jobbing & repair

(G-144)
HAKO MINUTEMAN INC
111 S Rohlwing Rd (60101-3027)
PHONE..............................630 627-6900
Chris Kentop, *Division Mgr*
Christopher Failla, *Business Mgr*
Gigi Deluca, *Safety Mgr*
Michelle Gagliano, *Purchasing*
Dan Barmore, *Finance Mgr*
▲ **EMP:** 2
SALES (est): 472.9K **Privately Held**
WEB: www.minutemanintl.com
SIC: 2752 Commercial printing, offset

(G-145)
HAMMOND SUZUKI USA INC
733 W Annoreno Dr (60101-4315)
PHONE..............................630 543-0277
Manji Suzuki, *President*
Warren Brunsting, *Engineer*
Gregg Gronowski, *Sales Dir*
Thomas Salata, *Sales Staff*
▲ **EMP:** 20
SQ FT: 22,000
SALES (est): 4MM **Privately Held**
SIC: 3651 3931 Speaker systems; organs, all types: pipe, reed, hand, electronic, etc.
PA: Suzuki Musical Instrument Mfg.Co.,Ltd.
  2-25-12, Ryoke, Naka-Ku
  Hamamatsu SZO 430-0

(G-146)
HAUSERMANN ABRADING PROCESS CO
300 W Laura Dr (60101-5016)
PHONE..............................630 543-6688
Marten Hausermann, *President*
Judith L Hausermann, *Treasurer*
Althea Hausermann, *Admin Sec*
EMP: 18 EST: 1977
SQ FT: 24,000
SALES (est): 1.4MM **Privately Held**
SIC: 3541 Grinding, polishing, buffing, lapping & honing machines

(G-147)
HAUSERMANN CONTROLS CO
Also Called: Hausermann Die & Machine
1047 W Compton Pt (60101-2136)
PHONE..............................630 543-6688
Marten Hausermann, *President*
Judith L Hausermann, *Treasurer*
Kimberly Federighi, *Admin Sec*
EMP: 17
SALES (est): 2.4MM **Privately Held**
SIC: 3625 Numerical controls

(G-148)
HCI CABINETRY AND DESIGN INC
305 S Fairbank St (60101-3123)
PHONE..............................630 584-0266
Kris Blaesing, *President*
EMP: 8
SQ FT: 5,000
SALES (est): 1.7MM **Privately Held**
WEB: www.hcicabinet.com
SIC: 5031 2434 1799 Kitchen cabinets; wood kitchen cabinets; kitchen cabinet installation

(G-149)
HERMAN SEEKAMP INC
Also Called: Clyde's Delicious Donuts
1120 W Fullerton Ave (60101-4304)
PHONE..............................630 628-6555
Kent W Bickford, *President*
Willard Bickford, *Chairman*
Kim D Bickford, *Vice Pres*
Nick Tsatsafoulis, *Maint Spvr*
Mike Zdarsky, *Research*
EMP: 115
SQ FT: 54,000
SALES (est): 36.1MM **Privately Held**
WEB: www.clydesdonuts.com
SIC: 2052 2053 2099 2038 Cookies; doughnuts, frozen; food preparations; frozen specialties; doughnuts, except frozen

(G-150)
HIRE-NELSON COMPANY INC
325 W Factory Rd Ste B (60101-5090)
PHONE..............................630 543-9400
Alan Bosworth, *President*
Tony Hernandez, *General Mgr*
Daniel Fors, *Principal*
Kyle Fredrickson, *Principal*
Wayne Juda, *Principal*
EMP: 30 EST: 1977
SQ FT: 25,000
SALES (est): 5.6MM **Privately Held**
WEB: www.hirenelson.com
SIC: 2541 Office fixtures, wood; display fixtures, wood

(G-151)
HOEING DIE & MOLD ENGRAVING
441 W Interstate Rd (60101-4547)
PHONE..............................630 543-0006
Helmut Hoeing, *President*
Barbara Hoeing, *President*
EMP: 3
SQ FT: 3,000
SALES (est): 300K **Privately Held**
SIC: 3479 Engraving jewelry silverware, or metal; etching & engraving

(G-152)
HOPKINS PRINTING & ENVELOPE CO
Also Called: Custom Bindery Services
120 W Laura Dr (60101-5114)
P.O. Box 389 (60101-0389)
PHONE..............................630 543-8227
James Devries, *President*
Donald Campo, *Vice Pres*
Don Campo, *Opers Staff*
Dave Weeks, *Office Mgr*
Jackie Illyes, *Director*
EMP: 13
SQ FT: 15,000
SALES: 2MM **Privately Held**
WEB: www.custom-bindery.com
SIC: 2789 Trade binding services

(G-153)
HOSPITOLOGY PRODUCTS LLC
300 S Lombard Rd (60101-3024)
PHONE..............................630 359-5075
Sujay Kapadia, *Mng Member*
▲ **EMP:** 9
SALES (est): 857.1K **Privately Held**
SIC: 2515 Mattresses & foundations

(G-154)
ILLINOIS SWITCHBOARD CORP
125 W Laura Dr (60101-5178)
PHONE..............................630 543-0910
Don Zastawny, *Ch of Bd*
William Zastawny, *President*

GEOGRAPHIC SECTION

Addison - Dupage County (G-184)

Karen Williams, *CFO*
Karen L Zastawny, *Admin Sec*
EMP: 12
SQ FT: 18,000
SALES (est): 2.5MM **Privately Held**
SIC: 3613 Switchboards & parts, power; panelboards & distribution boards, electric; control panels, electric

(G-155)
INNOVATIVE MAG-DRIVE LLC
409 S Vista Ave (60101-4420)
PHONE..................................630 543-4240
Nick Rentzelos, *Principal*
Matt Moy, *Sales Staff*
EMP: 17
SALES (est): 3.8MM **Privately Held**
SIC: 3568 Power transmission equipment

(G-156)
IVAN SCHWENKER
Also Called: Illinois Pneumatic Tool Co
1480 W Bernard Dr Ste A (60101-4334)
PHONE..................................630 543-7798
Ivan Schwenker, *Owner*
EMP: 3
SQ FT: 4,000
SALES (est): 322.9K **Privately Held**
SIC: 3545 7699 3546 Cutting tools for machine tools; tool repair services; power-driven handtools

(G-157)
J C HOSE & TUBE INC
236 S La Londe Ave Ste C (60101-3342)
PHONE..................................630 543-4747
Linda Chopelas, *President*
John Chopelas, *Admin Sec*
EMP: 5
SQ FT: 5,000
SALES (est): 750K **Privately Held**
SIC: 5074 3492 Plumbing fittings & supplies; hose & tube fittings & assemblies, hydraulic/pneumatic

(G-158)
JASON INCORPORATED
Advance Wire Products
201 S Swift Rd (60101-5621)
PHONE..................................630 627-7000
Todd Merquith, *General Mgr*
EMP: 120
SQ FT: 48,500
SALES (corp-wide): 337.9MM **Publicly Held**
SIC: 3496 3469 3965 Miscellaneous fabricated wire products; metal stampings; fasteners, buttons, needles & pins
HQ: Jason Incorporated
   833 E Michigan St Ste 900
   Milwaukee WI 53202
   414 277-9300

(G-159)
JD NORMAN INDUSTRIES INC (PA)
787 W Belden Ave (60101-4942)
PHONE..................................630 458-3700
Justin D Norman, *President*
Chey Becker-Varto, *Vice Pres*
Elizabeth Kousiakis, *Vice Pres*
Matt Litchfield, *Vice Pres*
Gary Wilhite, *Vice Pres*
▲ **EMP:** 65
SALES (est): 269MM **Privately Held**
WEB: www.jdnorman.com
SIC: 3469 3496 3495 Metal stampings; miscellaneous fabricated wire products; wire springs

(G-160)
JET FINISHERS INC
136 W Commercial Ave (60101-4504)
PHONE..................................847 718-0501
David Allison, *President*
Elois Allison, *Office Mgr*
Curtis Sell, *Admin Sec*
EMP: 53
SQ FT: 52,000
SALES (est): 6.8MM **Privately Held**
SIC: 3479 Coating of metals & formed products

(G-161)
JURA FILMS NORTH AMERICA LLC
230 S Fairbank St (60101-3122)
P.O. Box 1775, Lombard (60148-8775)
PHONE..................................630 261-1226
Carl A Potsch, *Mng Member*
▲ **EMP:** 3
SALES (est): 621.1K **Privately Held**
SIC: 2952 Roofing materials

(G-162)
JVK PRECISION HARD CHROME INC
29 W Commercial Ave (60101-4501)
PHONE..................................630 628-0810
Mary Van Kollenburg, *President*
Mary Beth Van Kollenburg, *President*
James Van Kollenburg, *Treasurer*
Kim Van Kollenberg, *Admin Sec*
EMP: 8
SALES (est): 1MM **Privately Held**
SIC: 3471 Electroplating of metals or formed products

(G-163)
K & C DESIGN AND MANUFACTURING
422 S Irmen Dr (60101-4325)
PHONE..................................630 543-3386
Karen Clark, *Owner*
Keith Clark, *Vice Pres*
EMP: 4 **EST:** 1997
SALES (est): 522K **Privately Held**
WEB: www.kcdesignmfg.com
SIC: 3599 Machine shop, jobbing & repair

(G-164)
K & J SYNTHETIC LUBRICANTS
405 W Myrick Ave (60101-3451)
PHONE..................................630 628-1011
EMP: 6
SALES: 60K **Privately Held**
SIC: 2992 5172 5541 Mfg Lubricating Oils/Greases Whol Petroleum Products Gasoline Service Station

(G-165)
K & P INDUSTRIES INC
Also Called: Addison Electro Polishing Div
1120 W Republic Dr Ste H (60101-3140)
PHONE..................................630 628-6676
Prahlad M Patel, *President*
Kanta P Patel, *Vice Pres*
EMP: 3 **EST:** 1982
SQ FT: 1,100
SALES (est): 240K **Privately Held**
SIC: 3471 Electroplating of metals or formed products

(G-166)
K M I INTERNATIONAL CORP
1411 W Jeffrey Dr (60101-4331)
PHONE..................................630 627-6300
Mohammad Ibrahim, *President*
Karen Fann, *Marketing Staff*
Karen S C Fann, *Admin Sec*
▲ **EMP:** 6
SALES (est): 568.5K **Privately Held**
SIC: 3999 Artificial flower arrangements

(G-167)
KEN MATTHEWS & ASSOCIATES INC
Also Called: Midwest Stucco-Eifs Dist
415 W Belden Ave Ste H (60101-4933)
PHONE..................................630 628-6470
Kenneth L Matthews, *President*
EMP: 3
SQ FT: 7,000
SALES (est): 280K **Privately Held**
SIC: 3275 Plaster & plasterboard, gypsum

(G-168)
KG LIFT INC
1214 W Capitol Dr Ste 8 (60101-5302)
PHONE..................................815 908-1855
Kevin Glass, *President*
EMP: 5 **EST:** 2013
SALES: 300K **Privately Held**
SIC: 3537 Forklift trucks

(G-169)
KIENE DIESEL ACCESSORIES INC
Also Called: Continental Cutoff Machine
325 S Fairbank St (60101-3164)
PHONE..................................630 543-7170
John F Craychee, *President*
Charles W Craychee Jr, *Vice Pres*
Roger Kotalik, *Foreman/Supr*
Alvin Mayo, *Production*
Susan Dejesus, *Sales Staff*
▲ **EMP:** 21
SQ FT: 19,000
SALES (est): 5.3MM **Privately Held**
WEB: www.kienediesel.com
SIC: 3541 3829 3714 Cutoff machines (metalworking machinery); testing equipment: abrasion, shearing strength, etc.; motor vehicle parts & accessories

(G-170)
KIER MFG CO
1450 W Jeffrey Dr (60101-4356)
PHONE..................................630 953-9500
Daniel Kier, *President*
Jim Butkiewicz Jr, *Corp Secy*
Constance Kier, *Shareholder*
EMP: 8 **EST:** 1953
SQ FT: 12,000
SALES (est): 1.3MM **Privately Held**
WEB: www.kiermfg.com
SIC: 3444 3469 Sheet metal specialties, not stamped; stamping metal for the trade

(G-171)
KLEER PAK MFG CO INC
320 S La Londe Ave (60101-3309)
PHONE..................................630 543-0208
Kam Patel, *President*
Gordhan Patel, *Chairman*
Ramesh Gandhi, *Vice Pres*
EMP: 20
SQ FT: 24,000
SALES: 2MM **Privately Held**
SIC: 2673 Food storage & frozen food bags, plastic; plastic bags: made from purchased materials

(G-172)
KLM TOOL COMPANY
930 S Stiles Dr (60101-4913)
PHONE..................................630 458-1700
Kazimerz Laszewicz, *President*
Mike Kazcmarczyk, *Vice Pres*
EMP: 25
SQ FT: 40,000
SALES (est): 3.8MM **Privately Held**
SIC: 3599 Machine shop, jobbing & repair

(G-173)
KMS INDUSTRIES LLC
923 W National Ave (60101-3125)
PHONE..................................331 225-2671
John Mitoraj, *Mng Member*
Greg Klemenswizz,
Robert Sickles,
◆ **EMP:** 4
SQ FT: 18,000
SALES (est): 563.2K **Privately Held**
WEB: www.kmsindustriesllc.com
SIC: 3613 Distribution cutouts

(G-174)
KOHOUT WOODWORK INC
759 W Factory Rd (60101-4308)
PHONE..................................630 628-6257
Steve Kohout, *President*
Esther Kohout, *Vice Pres*
EMP: 5
SALES (est): 607.5K **Privately Held**
SIC: 2499 5031 Decorative wood & woodwork; millwork

(G-175)
KOPIS MACHINE CO INC
329 W Interstate Rd (60101-4559)
PHONE..................................630 543-4138
Floyd Kopis, *President*
Jo Ann Kopis, *Corp Secy*
Vincent Lombardo, *Vice Pres*
Louis Gluth, *VP Sales*
Dawn Kopis, *Office Mgr*
EMP: 28 **EST:** 1956
SQ FT: 9,000
SALES (est): 3.3MM **Privately Held**
WEB: www.kopismachine.com
SIC: 3599 Custom machinery

(G-176)
L A T ENTERPRISE INC
423 W Interstate Rd (60101-4517)
PHONE..................................630 543-5533
Leon A Thill, *President*
Charity Jibala, *Treasurer*
EMP: 3
SQ FT: 5,000
SALES (est): 485.2K **Privately Held**
SIC: 3599 Machine shop, jobbing & repair; custom machinery

(G-177)
LA AUTENTICA MICHOACANA NEVER
507 S Addison Rd (60101-4649)
PHONE..................................630 516-1888
EMP: 3
SALES (est): 296.1K **Privately Held**
SIC: 3421 Table & food cutlery, including butchers'

(G-178)
LAB TEC COSMT BY MARZENA INC
1470 W Bernard Dr (60101-4330)
PHONE..................................630 396-3970
Marzena Savas, *President*
▲ **EMP:** 12
SQ FT: 9,000
SALES (est): 3.4MM **Privately Held**
SIC: 2844 7231 Concentrates, perfume; beauty shops

(G-179)
LABTEC COSMETICS
715 W Racquet Club Dr (60101-4317)
PHONE..................................630 359-4569
EMP: 2
SALES (est): 223.3K **Privately Held**
SIC: 2844 Toilet preparations

(G-180)
LACE TECHNOLOGIES INC
315 S Fairbank St (60101-3123)
PHONE..................................630 528-8083
Charles Han, *President*
EMP: 14
SQ FT: 10,000
SALES (est): 2.4MM **Privately Held**
SIC: 3679 Electronic circuits

(G-181)
LAKESIDE SCREW PRODUCTS INC
1395 W Jeffrey Dr (60101-4331)
PHONE..................................630 495-1606
Zygmunt Soszko, *President*
Shanna Ramirez, *Manager*
EMP: 105 **EST:** 1977
SQ FT: 45,000
SALES (est): 19.3MM **Privately Held**
SIC: 3451 Screw machine products

(G-182)
LENROK INDUSTRIES INC
Also Called: Bramic Industries
542 W Winthrop Ave (60101-4441)
PHONE..................................630 628-1946
Jeffrey Cornell, *Director*
EMP: 6
SALES: 1MM **Privately Held**
SIC: 3599 8742 Machine shop, jobbing & repair; management consulting services

(G-183)
LEWIS ACQUISITION CORP
Also Called: Lewis Plastics
712 W Winthrop Ave (60101-4311)
PHONE..................................773 486-5660
William Lacek, *President*
John Gastaldello, *Maint Mgr*
Mary Wawak, *Admin Sec*
▲ **EMP:** 68
SALES (est): 23.4MM **Privately Held**
SIC: 3089 Injection molding of plastics

(G-184)
LOCKNUT TECHNOLOGY INC
351 S Lombard Rd (60101-3023)
PHONE..................................630 628-5330

Reinhart G Motz, *President*
Carol Motz, *Admin Sec*
▲ **EMP:** 10
SQ FT: 12,000
SALES (est): 2MM **Privately Held**
SIC: 3452 Nuts, metal

(G-185)
LOMBARD SWISS SCREW COMPANY
420 S Rohlwing Rd (60101-4210)
PHONE.................................630 576-5096
Bernard Seewald, *President*
Diana Konecke, *Vice Pres*
Diane Konecke, *Executive*
Karen Calvin, *Admin Sec*
EMP: 40 **EST:** 1972
SQ FT: 27,000
SALES (est): 7.9MM **Privately Held**
SIC: 3451 5072 Screw machine products; screws

(G-186)
LUNDMARK INC
Also Called: Lundmark Wax Co
350 S La Londe Ave (60101-3309)
PHONE.................................630 628-1199
Timothy Burke, *President*
Bill Brennan, *VP Sales*
Mark Walters, *Marketing Staff*
▼ **EMP:** 14
SALES (est): 3.2MM **Privately Held**
SIC: 2842 Specialty cleaning, polishes & sanitation goods

(G-187)
MAC-STER INC
1420 W Bernard Dr (60101-4330)
PHONE.................................847 830-7013
Andrew Sternal, *President*
Christopher Sternal, *Vice Pres*
Ann Sternal, *Admin Sec*
EMP: 10
SALES (est): 1.6MM **Privately Held**
WEB: www.mac-ster.com
SIC: 3444 Forming machine work, sheet metal; metal housings, enclosures, casings & other containers; hoppers, sheet metal; machine guards, sheet metal

(G-188)
MAGNECO INC (HQ)
223 W Interstate Rd (60101-4513)
PHONE.................................630 543-6660
Charles W Connors, *CEO*
EMP: 100
SQ FT: 85,000
SALES (est): 12.9MM
SALES (corp-wide): 65.8MM **Privately Held**
SIC: 3297 Nonclay refractories
PA: Magneco/Metrel, Inc.
223 W Interstate Rd
Addison IL 60101
630 543-6660

(G-189)
MAGNECO INC
206 W Factory Rd (60101-5002)
PHONE.................................630 543-6660
Charles Connors, *Branch Mgr*
EMP: 8
SALES (corp-wide): 65.8MM **Privately Held**
SIC: 3297 Nonclay refractories
HQ: Magneco, Inc
223 W Interstate Rd
Addison IL 60101
630 543-6660

(G-190)
MAGNECO/METREL INC (PA)
223 W Interstate Rd (60101-4513)
PHONE.................................630 543-6660
Charles W Connors Jr, *President*
Charles W Connors, *Chairman*
Madjid Soofi, *Vice Pres*
Don Wilson, *Plant Mgr*
Susan C Malloy, *CFO*
◆ **EMP:** 33 **EST:** 1981
SQ FT: 13,000
SALES: 65.8MM **Privately Held**
SIC: 3567 Industrial furnaces & ovens

(G-191)
MANU-TEC OF ILLINOIS LLC
415 W Belden Ave Ste E (60101-4933)
PHONE.................................630 543-3022
Gene Marino, *CEO*
Tom Kotopka, *President*
EMP: 12
SQ FT: 7,500
SALES: 1.7MM **Privately Held**
SIC: 3672 3679 Printed circuit boards; harness assemblies for electronic use: wire or cable

(G-192)
MARATHON MANUFACTURING INC
110 W Laura Dr (60101-5114)
PHONE.................................630 543-6262
Roy Hall, *President*
Steve Lester, *Engineer*
Mary Hall, *Treasurer*
▲ **EMP:** 30 **EST:** 1996
SQ FT: 20,000
SALES (est): 5.9MM **Privately Held**
WEB: www.marathonmolding.com
SIC: 3089 Injection molding of plastics

(G-193)
MATREX EXHIBITS INC
301 S Church St (60101-3749)
PHONE.................................630 628-2233
Jill D Hebert, *CEO*
Ben Flynn, *Finance*
EMP: 70
SQ FT: 105,000
SALES (est): 10.8MM **Privately Held**
SIC: 7389 3993 Trade show arrangement; exhibit construction by industrial contractors; signs & advertising specialties

(G-194)
MECHANICAL PRODUCTS CORP
330 W Gerri Ln (60101-5092)
PHONE.................................630 543-4842
Frank Marousek, *President*
▲ **EMP:** 10 **EST:** 1963
SQ FT: 10,000
SALES (est): 1.6MM **Privately Held**
WEB: www.mechproducts.com
SIC: 3599 Machine shop, jobbing & repair

(G-195)
MEDGYN PRODUCTS INC
100 W Industrial Rd (60101-4508)
P.O. Box 3126, Oak Brook (60522-3126)
PHONE.................................630 627-4105
Lakshman Agadi, *President*
Susan Bendle, *Finance*
Amar Agadi, *Sales Staff*
Keith Harmon, *Manager*
Aakathi A Singh, *Admin Sec*
▲ **EMP:** 55
SQ FT: 20,000
SALES (est): 17.5MM **Privately Held**
SIC: 5047 3842 Medical equipment & supplies; gynecological supplies & appliances

(G-196)
MEGA CIRCUIT INC
1040 S Westgate St (60101-5022)
PHONE.................................630 543-8460
Kodubhai Patel, *President*
Jim Malavia, *Vice Pres*
Raj Amin, *Director*
Doug Kellerstrass, *Director*
Paresh Patel, *Admin Sec*
▲ **EMP:** 85
SQ FT: 23,000
SALES (est): 13.9MM **Privately Held**
SIC: 3672 Printed circuit boards

(G-197)
MERKEL WOODWORKING INC
300 S Stewart Ave (60101-3310)
PHONE.................................630 458-0700
Bob Merkel, *President*
Debbie Merkel, *Corp Secy*
EMP: 15
SALES: 3MM **Privately Held**
SIC: 2431 Millwork

(G-198)
METAL IMPREGNATING CORP
121 W Official Rd (60101-4520)
P.O. Box 1067 (60101-8067)
PHONE.................................630 543-3443
William Schramm, *President*
Sandee Hendricks, *Corp Secy*
Jeff Schramm, *Assistant VP*
Scott Schramm, *Assistant VP*
Yvonne Schramm, *Vice Pres*
EMP: 8 **EST:** 1960
SQ FT: 6,000
SALES (est): 964.9K **Privately Held**
SIC: 3479 2295 Coating of metals with plastic or resins; coated fabrics, not rubberized

(G-199)
METAL IMPROVEMENT COMPANY LLC
678 W Winthrop Ave (60101-4492)
PHONE.................................630 543-4950
EMP: 20
SALES (corp-wide): 2.4B **Publicly Held**
WEB: www.metalimprovement.com
SIC: 3398 Shot peening (treating steel to reduce fatigue)
HQ: Metal Improvement Company, Llc
80 E Rte 4 Ste 310
Paramus NJ 07652
201 843-7800

(G-200)
METALS AND SERVICES INC
Also Called: Ms
145 N Swift Rd (60101-1447)
PHONE.................................630 627-2900
Carol Gross, *Corp Secy*
Joseph H Baessler, *Vice Pres*
John E Baessler, *Vice Pres*
Mark Baessler, *Vice Pres*
Carol J Gross, *Treasurer*
▲ **EMP:** 70
SQ FT: 106,000
SALES (est): 28.5MM **Privately Held**
SIC: 3444 3449 5051 Sheet metalwork; bars, concrete reinforcing; fabricated steel; steel

(G-201)
MEXACALI SILKSCREEN INC
Also Called: M.S.I.
931 W National Ave (60101-3125)
PHONE.................................630 628-9313
Tino Silva, *President*
EMP: 5
SQ FT: 10,000
SALES (est): 373K **Privately Held**
SIC: 2759 2396 Screen printing; automotive & apparel trimmings

(G-202)
MEXICALI HARD CHROME CORP
502 W Winthrop Ave (60101-4434)
PHONE.................................630 543-0646
Manuel Calvillo, *President*
Raul Calvillo, *Vice Pres*
Trinidad Calvillo, *Vice Pres*
EMP: 27
SQ FT: 12,000
SALES: 1.4MM **Privately Held**
SIC: 3471 Electroplating of metals or formed products

(G-203)
MICA FURNITURE MFG INC
Also Called: Kitchen Design Studio
1130 W Fullerton Ave (60101-4304)
PHONE.................................708 430-1150
Chris Lupa, *President*
Carol Gabdawl, *Vice Pres*
EMP: 8
SQ FT: 6,000
SALES (est): 1.2MM **Privately Held**
SIC: 2434 2511 Wood kitchen cabinets; wood household furniture

(G-204)
MICANAN SYSTEMS INC
721 W Racquet Club Dr (60101-4317)
PHONE.................................630 501-1909
Mike Apergis, *President*
EMP: 2
SALES: 19MM **Privately Held**
SIC: 2431 Garage doors, overhead: wood

(G-205)
MICRO CIRCUIT INC
1225 W National Ave (60101-3130)
PHONE.................................630 628-5760
Govind Patel, *CEO*
Peter Shah, *President*
Nick Sanghani, *Vice Pres*
EMP: 15
SQ FT: 9,000
SALES (est): 1.3MM **Privately Held**
SIC: 3672 Printed circuit boards

(G-206)
MICRO MOLD CORPORATION
777 W Annoreno Dr (60101-4383)
PHONE.................................630 628-0777
Michael Stiglianese, *President*
EMP: 6
SQ FT: 11,000
SALES (est): 867.7K **Privately Held**
WEB: www.micromoldcorp.com
SIC: 3544 Special dies & tools

(G-207)
MICROMATIC SPRING STAMPING INC (PA)
45 N Church St (60101-3802)
PHONE.................................630 607-0141
Walter Prociuk, *President*
Dennis Prociuk, *Vice Pres*
George Zajac, *Plant Mgr*
EMP: 29 **EST:** 1936
SQ FT: 73,000
SALES: 3.5MM **Privately Held**
WEB: www.micromaticspring.com
SIC: 3469 3495 Stamping metal for the trade; wire springs

(G-208)
MID-AMRICA PRTCTIVE CTINGS INC
85 W Industrial Rd (60101-4505)
PHONE.................................630 628-4501
Craig Martin, *President*
Leon S Martin Jr, *Vice Pres*
Neal Mosak, *Sales Staff*
Char Romberg, *Office Mgr*
▲ **EMP:** 2 **EST:** 1973
SQ FT: 10,000
SALES: 10MM **Privately Held**
SIC: 2851 Coating, air curing

(G-209)
MIDWEST CORTLAND INC
235 W Laura Dr (60101-5013)
PHONE.................................847 671-0376
Roy J Urbanek, *President*
Joseph F Urbanek, *Corp Secy*
Thomas Novello Sr, *Vice Pres*
EMP: 20
SQ FT: 30,000
SALES (est): 4.5MM **Privately Held**
WEB: www.midwestcortland.com
SIC: 2631 2675 Paperboard mills; die-cut paper & board

(G-210)
MIDWEST INDEX INC
2121 W Army Trail Rd # 105 (60101-5612)
PHONE.................................847 995-8425
Michael J Gilbert, *President*
John C Eggert, *Vice Pres*
EMP: 73
SQ FT: 29,000
SALES (est): 18MM **Privately Held**
SIC: 3555 2675 Printing trades machinery; die-cut paper & board

(G-211)
MIDWEST LABELS AND DECALS INC (PA)
1235 W Capitol Dr Ste D (60101-3177)
PHONE.................................630 543-7556
Robert Schultz, *President*
EMP: 2
SALES (est): 273.4K **Privately Held**
SIC: 2759 Commercial printing

(G-212)
MIDWEST MACHINE COMPANY LTD
1001 W Republic Dr Ste 13 (60101-3106)
PHONE.................................630 628-0485
Paravel Shunmugavelu, *President*
Vatsaladevi Shunmugavelu, *Admin Sec*

GEOGRAPHIC SECTION

Addison - Dupage County (G-243)

▲ EMP: 4
SQ FT: 2,875
SALES (est): 396K Privately Held
SIC: 3599 Machine shop, jobbing & repair

(G-213)
MIDWEST PLASTIC PRODUCTS
1490 W Bernard Dr Ste C (60101-4337)
PHONE..................................630 262-1095
Dan Hammers, *Prdtn Mgr*
EMP: 7
SALES (est): 1MM Privately Held
WEB: www.midwestplasticproducts.com
SIC: 3089 Injection molding of plastics

(G-214)
MIHA BODYTEC INC
2171 W Executive Dr # 200 (60101-5625)
PHONE..................................833 367-6442
Brian Dillman, *Managing Dir*
Thomas Reil, *CFO*
EMP: 5
SALES (est): 145.4K Privately Held
SIC: 3949 Exercise equipment

(G-215)
MIKES MACHINERY REBUILDERS
125 W Factory Rd (60101-5103)
PHONE..................................630 543-6400
Mike Jajic, *President*
Zorica Jajic, *Vice Pres*
EMP: 6 EST: 1980
SQ FT: 15,000
SALES (est): 750K Privately Held
SIC: 3542 Rebuilt machine tools, metal forming types

(G-216)
MILCO PRECISION MACHINING INC
730 W Annoreno Dr (60101-4316)
PHONE..................................630 628-5730
Fax: 630 628-5731
EMP: 13
SQ FT: 3,600
SALES (est): 2.3MM Privately Held
SIC: 3599 Industrial Machinery, Nec, Nsk

(G-217)
MILPLEX CIRCUITS INC
1772 W Armitage Ct (60101-4207)
PHONE..................................630 250-1580
Sal Patel, *President*
Bhupendra R Patel, *President*
Shashi Patel, *Vice Pres*
Bhasker Patel, *Treasurer*
Ghanshyam G Patel, *Admin Sec*
EMP: 120
SQ FT: 40,000
SALES (est): 14.8MM Privately Held
SIC: 3672 Printed circuit boards

(G-218)
MILPLEX ELECTRONICS INC
1772 W Armitage Ct (60101-4207)
PHONE..................................630 250-1580
Shailesh Patel, *President*
EMP: 25
SALES (est): 2.5MM Privately Held
WEB: www.milplex.com
SIC: 3672 Printed circuit boards

(G-219)
MISTICA FOODS LLC
50 W Commercial Ave (60101-4502)
PHONE..................................630 543-5409
Monika Rose Walas, *President*
Daniel Waligora, *COO*
Geraldine A Smrcina, *CFO*
EMP: 120
SQ FT: 35,000
SALES: 38.4MM Privately Held
SIC: 2013 Sausages & other prepared meats

(G-220)
MITSUBISHI HEAVY INDS AMER INC
Also Called: Machine Tools Div.
1225 N Greenbriar Dr B (60101-6108)
PHONE..................................630 693-4700
Ray Strack, *Branch Mgr*
EMP: 11 Privately Held
SIC: 5084 3599 Industrial machinery & equipment; machine shop, jobbing & repair
HQ: Mitsubishi Heavy Industries America, Inc.
20 Greenway Plz Ste 83
Houston TX 77046
346 308-8800

(G-221)
MOFFAT WIRE & DISPLAY INC
324 S La Londe Ave (60101-3309)
PHONE..................................630 458-8560
Ramesh Gandhi, *President*
Kam Patel, *Vice Pres*
Ruchir Gandhi, *Prdtn Mgr*
Gordhan Patel, *Admin Sec*
EMP: 13
SQ FT: 24,000
SALES (est): 2.7MM Privately Held
SIC: 3496 Miscellaneous fabricated wire products

(G-222)
MOON JUMP INC
1750 W Armitage Ct (60101-4207)
PHONE..................................630 983-0953
Edward Nunez, *Owner*
EMP: 5
SALES (est): 695.9K Privately Held
SIC: 3069 Life jackets, inflatable: rubberized fabric

(G-223)
MORGAN OHARE INC
701 W Factory Rd (60101-4339)
PHONE..................................630 543-6780
Robert Giomi, *President*
Joan Sosinski, *Corp Secy*
EMP: 61 EST: 1981
SQ FT: 70,000
SALES (est): 10MM Privately Held
WEB: www.morganohare.com
SIC: 3471 3398 Electroplating of metals or formed products; tempering of metal

(G-224)
MP MOLD INC
1480 W Bernard Dr Ste C (60101-4334)
PHONE..................................630 613-8086
EMP: 3 EST: 2015
SALES (est): 231.1K Privately Held
SIC: 3544 Industrial molds

(G-225)
N K C INC
751 W Winthrop Ave (60101-4310)
PHONE..................................630 628-9159
Diana Smith, *CEO*
EMP: 2
SQ FT: 2,200
SALES (est): 209.7K Privately Held
SIC: 3599 Machine shop, jobbing & repair

(G-226)
NAL WORLDWIDE HOLDINGS INC
Also Called: Nal.syncreon Addison
1200 N Greenbriar Dr A (60101-1050)
PHONE..................................630 261-3100
Christopher Lyons, *Manager*
EMP: 354
SALES (est): 56.4MM Privately Held
SIC: 3559 Automotive related machinery
PA: Syncreon Technology (Usa) Llc
2851 High Meadow Cir # 250
Auburn Hills MI 48326

(G-227)
NATURES APPEAL MFG CORP
1788 W Whispering Ct (60101-1864)
PHONE..................................630 880-6222
Ralph Jollette, *CEO*
EMP: 8
SALES (est): 194K Privately Held
SIC: 2869 7389 Industrial organic chemicals;

(G-228)
NEWMAN-GREEN INC
57 W Interstate Rd (60101-4509)
PHONE..................................630 543-6500
Edward H Green, *President*
Deborah Green, *Vice Pres*
Diana Bahena, *Sales Staff*
EMP: 80 EST: 1947
SQ FT: 150,000
SALES (est): 12.8MM Privately Held
WEB: www.newman-green.com
SIC: 3499 3494 Aerosol valves, metal; valves & pipe fittings

(G-229)
NITE LITE SIGNS & BALLOONS INC
Also Called: Awesome Amusements Co.
506 S Westgate St (60101-4525)
P.O. Box 377, Saint Charles (60174-0377)
PHONE..................................630 953-2866
Chris Manski, *President*
EMP: 4
SALES (est): 650K Privately Held
SIC: 7312 3993 Poster advertising, outdoor; signs & advertising specialties

(G-230)
OCKERLUND INDUSTRIES INC
1555 W Wrightwood Ct (60101-3034)
PHONE..................................630 620-1269
Guy Ockerlund, *President*
Stan Joray, *Vice Pres*
Tracy Wyatt, *Admin Sec*
▲ EMP: 45
SQ FT: 55,000
SALES (est): 8.8MM Privately Held
SIC: 2653 2441 Corrugated & solid fiber boxes; boxes, wood

(G-231)
OMEGA SIGN & LIGHTING INC
Also Called: Yesco Chicago
100 W Fay Ave (60101-5108)
PHONE..................................630 237-4397
Carmela Menna, *President*
Sam Menna, *Exec Dir*
Hoard Brody, *Executive*
EMP: 38 EST: 2011
SQ FT: 15,000
SALES (est): 4.3MM Privately Held
SIC: 3993 Neon signs

(G-232)
OMG INC
300 S Mitchell Ct (60101-1473)
PHONE..................................413 789-0252
Jose Espinoza, *Warehouse Mgr*
Steve Guzman, *Engineer*
Christine Ingersoll, *Manager*
EMP: 30
SALES (corp-wide): 1.5B Publicly Held
SIC: 3531 Roofing equipment
HQ: Omg, Inc.
153 Bowles Rd
Agawam MA 01001
413 789-0252

(G-233)
PARK PRODUCTS INC
409 W Kay Ave (60101-4904)
PHONE..................................630 543-2474
William Keyser, *President*
Robert Sieloff, *Admin Sec*
EMP: 3
SQ FT: 3,800
SALES (est): 349.5K Privately Held
SIC: 3545 3543 3544 Tools & accessories for machine tools; foundry patternmaking; special dies, tools, jigs & fixtures

(G-234)
PEACOCK COLORS COMPANY INC
1000 W National Ave (60101-3175)
PHONE..................................630 628-1960
Andy Ubhi, *President*
EMP: 20
SQ FT: 20,000
SALES (est): 737.9K Privately Held
SIC: 3089 Injection molding of plastics

(G-235)
PENTEGRA SYSTEMS LLC
780 W Belden Ave Ste A (60101-4939)
PHONE..................................630 941-6000
Edward G Karl, *Mng Member*
Gregory P Augspurger,
Edward Karl,
EMP: 35 EST: 2000
SQ FT: 12,500
SALES (est): 11MM Privately Held
SIC: 1731 3661 Sound equipment specialization; telephones & telephone apparatus

(G-236)
PERFECT MOLD INC
1120 W Republic Dr (60101-3140)
PHONE..................................630 785-6105
Casey Kochanek, *President*
EMP: 3 EST: 1998
SALES (est): 449.1K Privately Held
SIC: 3544 Industrial molds

(G-237)
PERFECT PASTA INC
31 S Fairbank St Ste B (60101-3150)
PHONE..................................630 543-8300
Luigi Bucaro, *President*
Vito Salamone, *Admin Sec*
▲ EMP: 6
SALES (est): 1.6MM Privately Held
WEB: www.perfectpastainc.com
SIC: 2099 Pasta, uncooked: packaged with other ingredients

(G-238)
PHARMACEUTICAL LABS AND CONS I
1010 W Fullerton Ave (60101-4333)
PHONE..................................630 359-3831
EMP: 3
SALES (est): 165.3K Privately Held
SIC: 8734 2834 Testing Laboratory Mfg Pharmaceutical Preparations

(G-239)
PHOENIX PRESS INC
1001 W Republic Dr Ste 15 (60101-3106)
PHONE..................................630 833-2281
Patricia L Danda, *President*
David Conn, *Admin Sec*
EMP: 2
SALES (est): 218.5K Privately Held
SIC: 2752 5963 2741 Commercial printing, lithographic; newspapers, home delivery, not by printers or publishers; patterns, paper: publishing & printing

(G-240)
PIO WOODWORKING INC
1130 W Fullerton Ave (60101-4304)
PHONE..................................630 628-6900
Andrea Faraone, *CEO*
Derek Lofgren, *Principal*
EMP: 2 EST: 2007
SALES (est): 2.3MM Privately Held
WEB: www.pioww.com
SIC: 2431 2521 Woodwork, interior & ornamental; wood office furniture

(G-241)
PIONEER SERVICE INC
542 W Factory Rd (60101-4437)
PHONE..................................630 628-0249
Aneesa Muthana, *President*
Rose Devos, *Business Mgr*
Omar Muthana, *Vice Pres*
Ellen Loome, *Executive Asst*
Bushra Muthana, *Admin Sec*
EMP: 35
SQ FT: 25,000
SALES: 3.5MM Privately Held
SIC: 3451 3541 7389 Screw machine products; machine tools, metal cutting type; grinding, precision: commercial or industrial

(G-242)
PLASTICWORKS INC
712 W Winthrop Ave (60101-4311)
PHONE..................................630 543-1750
Charles L Hackley, *President*
Perry Mascetti, *Vice Pres*
EMP: 10
SQ FT: 2,400
SALES (est): 2MM Privately Held
SIC: 3089 Injection molding of plastics

(G-243)
PLATT INDUSTRIAL CONTROL INC
3n301 Ellsworth Ave (60101-4164)
PHONE..................................630 833-4388
Eileen Plahetka, *President*

Addison - Dupage County (G-244)

EMP: 4
SQ FT: 1,500
SALES (est) 662.9K **Privately Held**
SIC: 3613 Control panels, electric

(G-244)
POKORNEY MANUFACTURING CO
45 N Church St (60101-3802)
PHONE.....................630 458-0406
Carl W Erickson Jr, *President*
Eleanor Erickson, *Corp Secy*
Charles A Erickson, *Vice Pres*
EMP: 8
SQ FT: 15,000
SALES (est) 850K **Privately Held**
WEB: www.pokorney.com
SIC: 3494 3561 Valves & pipe fittings; cylinders, pump

(G-245)
POLYURETHANE PRODUCTS CORP
31 W Industrial Rd (60101-4505)
PHONE.....................630 543-6700
Govind Lakshman, *President*
Malini Lakshman, *Vice Pres*
Ajay Lakshman, *Sales Engr*
▲ EMP: 25
SQ FT: 26,000
SALES (est): 6.3MM **Privately Held**
SIC: 2821 Plastics materials & resins

(G-246)
PORTABLE CMMNCTONS SPCLSTS
901 W Lake St (60101-2078)
PHONE.....................630 458-1800
Nancy Phillips, *President*
Kenneth Phillips, *Vice Pres*
EMP: 6
SQ FT: 6,000
SALES (est): 747.4K **Privately Held**
SIC: 5999 7622 5064 4812 Communication equipment; intercommunication equipment repair; electrical appliances, television & radio; radio telephone communication; receiver-transmitter units (transceiver)

(G-247)
PORTILLOS FOOD SERVICE INC (PA)
380 S Rohlwing Rd (60101-3030)
PHONE.....................630 620-0460
Richard J Portillo, *President*
Sharon Portillo, *Admin Sec*
EMP: 30
SQ FT: 5,000
SALES (est): 26.1MM **Privately Held**
WEB: www.portillos.com
SIC: 5147 2013 Meats, fresh; sausages & other prepared meats

(G-248)
POWER PORT PRODUCTS INC
301 W Interstate Rd (60101-4598)
PHONE.....................630 628-9102
Douglas Murphy, *President*
Christopher Murphy, *Vice Pres*
Sharon Gallo, *Treasurer*
Valeri Picchi, *Admin Sec*
▲ EMP: 20 EST: 1978
SQ FT: 60,000
SALES (est): 5MM **Privately Held**
SIC: 3699 3052 Extension cords; air line or air brake hose, rubber or rubberized fabric

(G-249)
POWER-VOLT INC (PA)
300 W Factory Rd (60101-5004)
P.O. Box 383 (60101-0383)
PHONE.....................630 628-9999
Brij Lal Sharma, *President*
Vijay Sharma, *CPA*
Vijay Kumari Sharma, *Admin Sec*
◆ EMP: 76
SQ FT: 26,000

SALES: 8.5MM **Privately Held**
SIC: 3677 3612 3679 Transformers power supply, electronic type; autotransformers, electric (power transformers); control transformers; distribution transformers, electric; power supplies, all types: static

(G-250)
PRECISION LASER MARKING INC
900 S Kay Ave (60101-4909)
PHONE.....................630 628-8575
Daniel Mahazchek, *President*
Pamela Mahachek, *Admin Sec*
EMP: 8
SQ FT: 5,000
SALES (est): 680.6K **Privately Held**
WEB: www.precisionlasermarking.com
SIC: 3599 Machine shop, jobbing & repair; machine & other job shop work

(G-251)
PRECISION METAL PRODUCTS INC
Also Called: P M P
1209 W Capitol Dr (60101-3116)
PHONE.....................630 458-0100
Mohammed Iqbal, *President*
Richard Smith, *Vice Pres*
EMP: 15
SALES (est): 3.5MM **Privately Held**
SIC: 3444 Sheet metalwork

(G-252)
PRECISION SERVICE MTR INC
121 W Fullerton Ave (60101-3713)
PHONE.....................630 628-9900
Kevin W Zierke, *President*
Lynn E Zierke, *Vice Pres*
EMP: 15
SQ FT: 20,000
SALES (est): 3.5MM **Privately Held**
SIC: 3542 Machine tools, metal forming type

(G-253)
PREMIER MANUFACTURING CORP
35 W Laura Dr (60101-5111)
PHONE.....................847 640-6644
Susan Fischer, *President*
EMP: 15
SQ FT: 10,000
SALES (est): 2.1MM **Privately Held**
WEB: www.premiermfgcorp.com
SIC: 3444 Sheet metalwork

(G-254)
PRESS ON INC
53 S Evergreen Ave (60101-3447)
PHONE.....................630 628-1630
Charles Cernock, *President*
EMP: 1
SALES (est): 250K **Privately Held**
SIC: 2741 Miscellaneous publishing

(G-255)
PRINTING CIRCUIT BOARDS
447 S Vista Ave (60101-4420)
PHONE.....................630 543-3453
Navin Patel, *President*
Rajendra Patel, *Vice Pres*
Arun M Patel, *Admin Sec*
EMP: 15 EST: 1964
SQ FT: 10,000
SALES (est): 3.1MM **Privately Held**
SIC: 3672 Circuit boards, television & radio printed

(G-256)
PRO-QUA INC
305 W Laura Dr (60101-5015)
PHONE.....................630 543-5644
Walter Naziemiec, *President*
EMP: 7
SQ FT: 12,000
SALES (est): 1.1MM **Privately Held**
SIC: 3599 Machine & other job shop work

(G-257)
PROTO PRODUCTIONS INC
840 S Fiene Dr (60101-5119)
PHONE.....................630 628-6626
Kenneth D Hopkins, *President*

Chad Hopkins, *Prdtn Mgr*
EMP: 20
SQ FT: 13,000
SALES (est): 2MM **Privately Held**
SIC: 2541 7389 2542 Display fixtures, wood; exhibit construction by industrial contractors; showcases (not refrigerated): except wood; locker boxes, postal service: except wood

(G-258)
QUAD-METAL INC
1345 W Fullerton Ave (60101-4319)
PHONE.....................630 953-0907
Stanley Sowa Jr, *President*
Matthew Fiore, *Corp Secy*
Matthew G Grieshaber, *Purch Mgr*
EMP: 10
SQ FT: 8,000
SALES (est): 1.4MM **Privately Held**
SIC: 3444 Sheet metal specialties, not stamped

(G-259)
QUALITEK INTERNATIONAL INC
315 S Fairbank St (60101-3171)
PHONE.....................630 628-8083
Phodi Han, *President*
Paul Chadwick, *General Mgr*
Emily Han, *Vice Pres*
Debbie Liguori, *Marketing Staff*
Ong Veronica, *Manager*
▲ EMP: 45 EST: 1980
SQ FT: 45,000
SALES (est): 9.5MM **Privately Held**
SIC: 2899 Fluxes: brazing, soldering, galvanizing & welding

(G-260)
QUALITY BAGS INC
575 S Vista Ave (60101-4422)
PHONE.....................630 543-9800
Leopold Rivera, *CEO*
Eugene Rivera, *President*
Ron Rivera, *Vice Pres*
Glenn Rivera, *Director*
Gloria Rivera, *Admin Sec*
EMP: 11
SQ FT: 17,000
SALES (est): 1.5MM **Privately Held**
SIC: 2671 2759 2673 Plastic film, coated or laminated for packaging; flexographic printing; plastic & pliofilm bags; cellophane bags, unprinted: made from purchased materials

(G-261)
QUALITY FABRICATORS INC (PA)
1035 W Fullerton Ave (60101-3192)
PHONE.....................630 543-0540
Tom A Lovelace, *President*
James R Lovelace, *Principal*
Annette M Loveplace, *Principal*
Brian Lovelace, *COO*
Victor Camacho, *Vice Pres*
EMP: 100
SQ FT: 110,000
SALES (est): 22.3MM **Privately Held**
SIC: 3444 3599 Sheet metalwork; machine shop, jobbing & repair

(G-262)
QUIK IMPRESSIONS GROUP INC
1385 W Jeffrey Dr (60101-4331)
PHONE.....................630 495-7845
Richard Smolke, *CEO*
Robert Spohnolz, *Vice Pres*
Rick Smolke, *Purchasing*
John McGray, *Sales Staff*
Steve McCuiston, *Manager*
EMP: 25 EST: 1995
SALES (est): 5.3MM **Privately Held**
SIC: 2752 Commercial printing, offset

(G-263)
R & R ENGINES AND PARTS INC
Also Called: R&R Engineering
1244 W Capitol Dr Ste 4 (60101-5373)
PHONE.....................630 628-1545
George Bronge, *Partner*
Ray Hartman, *Vice Pres*
EMP: 3
SQ FT: 6,000

SALES (est): 444.9K **Privately Held**
SIC: 3714 Rebuilding engines & transmissions, factory basis

(G-264)
R-M INDUSTRIES INC
38 W Interstate Rd (60101-4510)
PHONE.....................630 543-3071
Richard A Trepanier, *President*
Marie Trepanier, *Admin Sec*
EMP: 10
SQ FT: 3,000
SALES (est): 1.6MM **Privately Held**
SIC: 3599 7692 3443 3398 Machine shop, jobbing & repair; welding repair; fabricated plate work (boiler shop); metal heat treating

(G-265)
RAIMONDE DRILLING CORP
770 W Factory Rd Ste A (60101-4300)
PHONE.....................630 458-0590
Lucille Raimonde, *President*
Anne T Leslie, *President*
Fran Catuto, *Admin Sec*
EMP: 12
SALES (est): 2.4MM **Privately Held**
SIC: 0711 1381 1481 Soil testing services; drilling water intake wells; test boring for nonmetallic minerals

(G-266)
RALPH CODY GRAVROK
Also Called: Witt Disintegrating Service
729 W Fullerton Ave 6f (60101-3260)
PHONE.....................630 628-9570
Ralph Gravrok, *Owner*
EMP: 4
SQ FT: 2,000
SALES (est): 200K **Privately Held**
WEB: www.wittdisintegrating.com
SIC: 7699 3546 3544 Metal reshaping & replating services; power-driven handtools; special dies, tools, jigs & fixtures

(G-267)
RAZNY JEWELERS LTD (PA)
1501 W Lake St Ste 1 (60101-6704)
PHONE.....................630 932-4900
Stanley Razny Jr, *President*
Sally Salcena, *Store Mgr*
Ingrid Razny, *Treasurer*
James Marino, *Sales Staff*
Roberto Martin, *Sales Staff*
◆ EMP: 34 EST: 1964
SQ FT: 8,500
SALES (est): 6.5MM **Privately Held**
WEB: www.razny.com
SIC: 5944 3911 Jewelry, precious stones & precious metals; watches; rings, finger: precious metal; bracelets, precious metal; earrings, precious metal

(G-268)
RCL ELECTRONICS
826 S Iowa Ave (60101-4827)
PHONE.....................630 834-0156
EMP: 3
SALES (est): 140K **Privately Held**
SIC: 3671 Mfg Electron Tubes

(G-269)
RELIABLE CONTAINER INC
210 S Addison Rd (60101-3880)
PHONE.....................630 543-6131
James E Murphy, *President*
Robert E Murphy, *Vice Pres*
Jake Shabez, *Engineer*
Darrel Davis, *Plant Engr*
Dan Wroble, *Sales Staff*
▲ EMP: 41
SQ FT: 65,000
SALES (est): 10.7MM **Privately Held**
SIC: 2653 Boxes, corrugated: made from purchased materials

(G-270)
RELIANCE GEAR CORPORATION
205 W Factory Rd (60101-5001)
PHONE.....................630 543-6640
Matt Mondek, *President*
Ryan Stramel, *Production*
Armando Miranda, *Engineer*
Michael Pacholik, *Engineer*
Sharon Volkovitz, *CFO*

▲ EMP: 56 EST: 1965
SQ FT: 22,000
SALES (est): 18MM
SALES (corp-wide): 994.3MM **Privately Held**
WEB: www.reliancegear.com
SIC: 3566 3568 Gears, power transmission, except automotive; power transmission equipment
HQ: Ashot Ashkelon Industries Ltd.
2 Ezra Yessodi
Ashkelon 78637

(G-271)
RESIN EXCHANGE INC
851 S Westgate St (60101-5025)
PHONE..................630 628-7266
Dan Donnelly, *President*
EMP: 36
SALES (est): 7.9MM **Privately Held**
SIC: 5162 2821 Resins; plastics materials & resins

(G-272)
RESPA PHARMACEUTICALS INC
625 W Factory Rd (60101-4412)
P.O. Box 88222, Carol Stream (60188-0222)
PHONE..................630 543-3333
Paul Hennes, *CEO*
Dorothy Klays, *Principal*
▲ EMP: 42
SQ FT: 300,000
SALES (est): 8.4MM **Privately Held**
SIC: 2834 Pharmaceutical preparations

(G-273)
RF PLASTICS CO
406 W Belden Ave (60101-4903)
PHONE..................630 628-6033
EMP: 5
SQ FT: 6,000
SALES (est): 420K **Privately Held**
SIC: 3089 Injection Molder Of Plastics

(G-274)
RICE PRECISION MACHINING
475 W Interstate Rd (60101-4517)
PHONE..................630 543-7220
Gladys Rice, *Owner*
EMP: 10
SQ FT: 4,800
SALES (est): 1.7MM **Privately Held**
SIC: 3599 Machine shop, jobbing & repair

(G-275)
RIMTEC CORPORATION
211 S Lombard Rd (60101-3021)
PHONE..................630 628-0036
Vijay Kumar Jha, *President*
Vihay Kumar Jha, *President*
Aruna Jha, *Vice Pres*
Ray Johnston, *Production*
Melissa Moore, *Human Resources*
EMP: 12
SQ FT: 12,000
SALES (est): 1.9MM **Privately Held**
SIC: 3625 3568 Electromagnetic clutches or brakes; joints & couplings

(G-276)
ROMTECH MACHINING INC
755 W Factory Rd (60101-4308)
P.O. Box 233 (60101-0233)
PHONE..................630 543-7039
Roman Szymczak, *President*
Christopher Kostecki, *Sales Mgr*
EMP: 5
SQ FT: 5,000
SALES: 1MM **Privately Held**
SIC: 3599 Machine shop, jobbing & repair

(G-277)
ROYAL BOX GROUP LLC
Royal Group Addison, The
654 W Factory Rd (60101-4413)
PHONE..................630 543-4464
Robert Mc Ilvane, *CEO*
Ken Johnson, *General Mgr*
EMP: 50
SALES (corp-wide): 369.4MM **Privately Held**
SIC: 2653 Boxes, corrugated: made from purchased materials
HQ: Royal Box Group, Llc
1301 S 47th Ave
Cicero IL 60804
708 656-2020

(G-278)
RUSH ORDER SIGNS & PRTG LLC
1244 W Capitol Dr Ste B (60101-3178)
PHONE..................630 687-7874
Shahnaz Khan, *Principal*
EMP: 3
SALES (est): 230.8K **Privately Held**
SIC: 2752 Commercial printing, lithographic

(G-279)
RV AIR INC
475 W Interstate Rd (60101-4517)
PHONE..................309 657-4300
Eddie Rice, *CEO*
EMP: 3
SALES (corp-wide): 100K **Privately Held**
SIC: 3564 5075 Filters, air: furnaces, air conditioning equipment, etc.; air filters
PA: Rv Air, Inc.
628 Cleveland St Apt 1407
Clearwater FL 33755
309 657-4300

(G-280)
SAMAD GENERAL SERVICES INC
Also Called: Tamtam Candy
511 N Addison Rd Ste A (60101-6202)
PHONE..................773 593-3332
Mohammed A Aleem, *President*
EMP: 6
SQ FT: 3,000
SALES (est): 300K **Privately Held**
SIC: 5145 5441 2064 Candy; candy; candy & other confectionery products

(G-281)
SANYO SEIKI AMERICA CORP
1417 W Fullerton Ave (60101-4321)
PHONE..................630 876-8270
Koji Yamamae, *Branch Mgr*
EMP: 17 **Privately Held**
SIC: 3061 Mechanical rubber goods
PA: Sanyo Seiki Corporation
125, Kaide
Maniwa OKA 719-3

(G-282)
SCHULTZ BROTHERS INC
1001 W Republic Dr Ste 11 (60101-3106)
PHONE..................630 458-1437
Edward Schultz, *President*
EMP: 4
SQ FT: 3,000
SALES (est): 507.9K **Privately Held**
SIC: 2759 Labels & seals: printing

(G-283)
SECURITY MOLDING INC
255 W Factory Rd (60101-5001)
PHONE..................630 543-8607
Lynn Ricke, *President*
Margaret Ricke, *Corp Secy*
EMP: 17 EST: 1974
SQ FT: 8,000
SALES (est): 2.7MM **Privately Held**
SIC: 3089 Injection molding of plastics

(G-284)
SELECTIVE PLATING INC
240 S Lombard Rd (60101-3022)
PHONE..................630 543-1380
Brian Snodgrass, *President*
Tanja Snodgrass, *Treasurer*
EMP: 20
SQ FT: 10,800
SALES (est): 2.6MM **Privately Held**
SIC: 3471 Electroplating of metals or formed products

(G-285)
SERITEX INC
1052 W Republic Dr (60101-3133)
PHONE..................201 755-3002
Jose Rivera, *President*
EMP: 1 EST: 1996
SALES (est): 400K **Privately Held**
SIC: 2759 Screen printing

(G-286)
SERVICE METAL ENTERPRISES
915 W National Ave (60101-3125)
PHONE..................630 628-1444
Fax: 630 628-1472
EMP: 5
SQ FT: 3,800
SALES (est): 241.5K **Privately Held**
SIC: 3444 Mfg Sheet Metalwork

(G-287)
SF HOLDINGS GROUP LLC
Also Called: Surface Finishes
39 W Official Rd (60101-4532)
PHONE..................630 543-6682
Toby Speechley, *Principal*
EMP: 17
SALES (est): 1.6MM **Privately Held**
SIC: 3599 Machine shop, jobbing & repair

(G-288)
SIERRA MANUFACTURING CORP
480 S Irmen Dr (60101-4354)
PHONE..................630 458-8830
Darius Wozinak, *President*
Mary Kalamaris, *Admin Sec*
EMP: 6 EST: 1971
SALES: 610K **Privately Held**
SIC: 3544 3546 Die sets for metal stamping (presses); cartridge-activated hand power tools

(G-289)
SIGMA COATINGS INC
150 S Church St Ste D (60101-3775)
PHONE..................630 628-5305
Edward Eshoo, *President*
Helena Kasurinen, *Vice Pres*
Thomas Klewer, *Admin Sec*
EMP: 5
SQ FT: 17,000
SALES (est): 524.3K **Privately Held**
SIC: 2891 Adhesives & sealants

(G-290)
SIGNWISE INC
1001 W Republic Dr Ste 16 (60101-3106)
PHONE..................630 932-3204
Kevin Nolan, *President*
Tom Nolan, *Vice Pres*
EMP: 5
SALES (est): 411.2K **Privately Held**
SIC: 3993 Signs, not made in custom sign painting shops

(G-291)
SIKORA AUTOMATION INCORPORATED
845 S Westgate St (60101-5025)
PHONE..................630 833-0298
Alex Fuentes, *President*
EMP: 6
SQ FT: 5,000
SALES (est): 1MM **Privately Held**
SIC: 3599 3829 Machine shop, jobbing & repair; measuring & controlling devices

(G-292)
SONOCO PLASTICS INC
1035 W Republic Dr (60101-3132)
PHONE..................630 628-5859
Jeffrey Di Pasquale, *Branch Mgr*
EMP: 12
SALES (corp-wide): 5.3B **Publicly Held**
SIC: 3082 Unsupported plastics profile shapes
HQ: Sonoco Plastics, Inc.
1 N 2nd St
Hartsville SC 29550
843 383-7000

(G-293)
SOUTHFIELD CORPORATION
799 S Route 53 (60101-4215)
P.O. Box 1123 (60101-8123)
PHONE..................708 563-4056
Ed Zehme, *Branch Mgr*
EMP: 57
SALES (corp-wide): 344.9MM **Privately Held**
SIC: 3273 Ready-mixed concrete
PA: Southfield Corporation
8995 W 95th St
Palos Hills IL 60465
708 344-1000

(G-294)
SPECIALTY NUT & BKY SUP CO INC
1417 W Jeffrey Dr (60101-4331)
PHONE..................630 268-8500
Pasquale Schittino, *President*
Mary Ann Schittino, *Admin Sec*
EMP: 6
SQ FT: 10,000
SALES (est): 680K **Privately Held**
SIC: 2068 5145 Salted & roasted nuts & seeds; nuts, salted or roasted

(G-295)
SPRING R-R CORPORATION
100 W Laura Dr (60101-5114)
PHONE..................630 543-7445
Rick Richter, *CEO*
Randy Richter, *Vice Pres*
Ron Richter, *Opers Mgr*
Ruth Richter, *Treasurer*
EMP: 32
SQ FT: 24,000
SALES (est): 6.1MM **Privately Held**
SIC: 3493 Torsion bar springs

(G-296)
STYLE RITE RESTAURANT EQP CO
578 S Vista Ave (60101-4423)
PHONE..................630 628-0940
Marilyn Loster, *President*
John Loster, *Admin Sec*
EMP: 6
SQ FT: 17,000
SALES (est): 865.3K **Privately Held**
SIC: 3469 5046 Kitchen fixtures & equipment: metal, except cast aluminum; commercial cooking & food service equipment

(G-297)
SUEZ WTS USA INC
Also Called: Hercules Industrial Division
333 S Lombard Rd (60101-3023)
PHONE..................630 543-8480
Brian Vannoni, *Opers-Prdtn-Mfg*
Darren Vitosh, *Executive*
Terry Lupei, *Admin Asst*
EMP: 21
SALES (corp-wide): 94.7MM **Privately Held**
WEB: www.gewater.com
SIC: 2899 Water treating compounds
HQ: Suez Wts Usa, Inc.
4636 Somerton Rd
Trevose PA 19053
215 355-3300

(G-298)
SUNSOURCE HOLDINGS INC (PA)
2301 W Windsor Ct (60101-1460)
PHONE..................630 317-2700
David Sacher, *CEO*
EMP: 3
SALES (est): 165.4MM **Privately Held**
SIC: 3594 Motors: hydraulic, fluid power or air

(G-299)
SUPERIOR SURGICAL INSTRUMEN TS
602 W Lake Park Dr (60101-3221)
PHONE..................630 628-8437
Werner Hausner, *Principal*
EMP: 3
SALES (est): 205.9K **Privately Held**
SIC: 3841 Surgical & medical instruments

(G-300)
SUPERTEK SCIENTIFIC LLC
15 W Commercial Ave (60101-4501)
PHONE..................630 345-3450
Shayan Merchant,
Shakil Merchant,
EMP: 5

Addison - Dupage County (G-301)

SALES (est): 319.1K **Privately Held**
SIC: 3821 3231 3841 3826 Laboratory measuring apparatus; laboratory glassware; surgical & medical instruments; analytical instruments

(G-301)
SWD INC
910 S Stiles Dr (60101-4913)
PHONE..................630 543-3003
Richard A Delawder, *President*
Sharon Delawder, *Treasurer*
Janine Szerszen, *Hum Res Coord*
▲ EMP: 100
SQ FT: 55,000
SALES (est): 19MM **Privately Held**
WEB: www.swdinc.com
SIC: 3471 3965 Finishing, metals or formed products; fasteners, buttons, needles & pins

(G-302)
T & L SHEET METAL INC
555 S Vista Ave (60101-4422)
PHONE..................630 628-7960
Linh Van Le, *President*
Hung Van Le, *Vice Pres*
Tien Van Tran, *Treasurer*
EMP: 10 EST: 1996
SQ FT: 30,000
SALES (est): 1.6MM **Privately Held**
WEB: www.tlsmi.com
SIC: 3444 Sheet metal specialties, not stamped

(G-303)
T/J FABRICATORS INC
2150 W Executive Dr (60101-1487)
PHONE..................630 543-2293
Tom Wisniewski, *CEO*
Robert Wisniewski, *President*
Sharon Smith, *Office Mgr*
Dave Francis, *Technology*
EMP: 65
SQ FT: 104,000
SALES (est): 11.6MM **Privately Held**
SIC: 3444 3599 Sheet metal specialties, not stamped; machine shop, jobbing & repair

(G-304)
TECHNICAL TOOL ENTERPRISE
1550 W Fullerton Ave D (60101-3028)
PHONE..................630 893-3390
EMP: 3 EST: 2007
SALES (est): 240K **Privately Held**
SIC: 3546 3545 3544 Mfg Power-Driven Handtools Mfg Machine Tool Accessories Mfg Dies/Tools/Jigs/Fixtures

(G-305)
TECHNY PRECISION MFG INC
818 S Westwood Ave Ste C (60101-4945)
PHONE..................630 543-7065
Ismet Uzun, *President*
Lucy Uzun, *Executive Asst*
EMP: 10
SQ FT: 18,000
SALES: 750K **Privately Held**
SIC: 3599 Machine shop, jobbing & repair

(G-306)
TFC GROUP LLC
136 W Commercial Ave (60101-4504)
PHONE..................630 559-0808
Robert Salerno, *President*
EMP: 75 EST: 2011
SQ FT: 75,000
SALES: 6MM **Privately Held**
WEB: www.finishingcompany.com
SIC: 3471 Electroplating of metals or formed products; finishing, metals or formed products

(G-307)
THOMAS ELECTRONICS INC
330 S La Londe Ave (60101-3309)
PHONE..................315 923-2051
Fred Klingelhofer, *President*
Dennis Young, *Exec VP*
Tony Valene, *Plant Mgr*
EMP: 25
SALES (corp-wide): 43.9MM **Privately Held**
SIC: 3671 Cathode ray tubes, including rebuilt
PA: Thomas Electronics, Inc
208 Davis Pkwy
Clyde NY 14433
315 923-2051

(G-308)
THREE ANGELS PRINTING SVCS INC
Also Called: 3 Angels
1105 S Westwood Ave (60101-4920)
PHONE..................630 333-4305
EMP: 16
SQ FT: 5,000
SALES (est): 125.6K **Privately Held**
SIC: 2752 Lithographic Commercial Printing

(G-309)
THYBAR CORPORATION (PA)
Also Called: Thycurb Fabricating
913 S Kay Ave (60101-4995)
PHONE..................630 543-5300
Jeffrey Catalano, *President*
Mike Roberts, *Plant Mgr*
Craig Hoffman, *Purchasing*
Mike Lissak, *Engineer*
Patricia Norris, *CFO*
EMP: 32
SQ FT: 40,000
SALES (est): 37.4MM **Privately Held**
WEB: www.thybar.com
SIC: 3444 3441 Sheet metalwork; expansion joints (structural shapes), iron or steel

(G-310)
TJ WIRE FORMING INC
824 S Kay Ave (60101-4907)
PHONE..................630 628-9209
Jerry Krasinski, *President*
EMP: 4
SQ FT: 6,000
SALES (est): 400K **Privately Held**
SIC: 3312 3469 Wire products, steel or iron; metal stampings

(G-311)
TOLERANCES GRINDING CO INC
1020 W National Ave (60101-3127)
PHONE..................630 543-6066
Joseph Dernbach Jr, *President*
EMP: 20 EST: 1964
SQ FT: 8,000
SALES (est): 2.5MM **Privately Held**
WEB: www.tolerancesgrinding.com
SIC: 3599 Machine shop, jobbing & repair

(G-312)
TOOLEX CORPORATION
1204 W Capitol Dr (60101-3117)
PHONE..................630 458-0001
Ron Rogalla, *President*
EMP: 8 EST: 1978
SQ FT: 11,000
SALES: 1MM **Privately Held**
SIC: 3599 Machine shop, jobbing & repair

(G-313)
TOPICAL PHARMACEUTICALS INC
715 W Racquet Club Dr (60101-4317)
PHONE..................630 396-3970
EMP: 15 **Privately Held**
SIC: 2834 Pharmaceutical preparations
PA: Topical Pharmaceuticals Inc.
1470 W Bernard Dr
Addison IL 60101

(G-314)
TOPICAL PHARMACEUTICALS INC (PA)
1470 W Bernard Dr (60101-4330)
PHONE..................630 396-3970
Marzena Savas, *President*
EMP: 5
SQ FT: 15,000
SALES (est): 1.1MM **Privately Held**
SIC: 2834 Pharmaceutical preparations

(G-315)
TOTAL ENGINEERED PRODUCTS INC
908 S Westwood Ave (60101-4917)
PHONE..................630 543-9006
Chris Caliendo, *President*
Christine Caliendo, *Treasurer*
EMP: 3
SQ FT: 3,700
SALES (est): 388.1K **Privately Held**
SIC: 3599 Machine shop, jobbing & repair

(G-316)
TOYO INK INTERNATIONAL CORP
710 W Belden Ave Ste B (60101-4936)
PHONE..................630 930-5100
Fusao Ito, *President*
Isao Kameoka, *Technical Mgr*
David Krakosky, *Sales Staff*
James Honda, *General Counsel*
EMP: 19 **Privately Held**
WEB: www.toyoink.com
SIC: 2893 Printing ink
HQ: Toyo Ink International Corp
1225 N Michael Dr
Wood Dale IL 60191

(G-317)
TRU-NATIVE ENTERPRISES
Also Called: Tru-Native N'Genuity
50 W Commercial Ave (60101-4502)
PHONE..................630 409-3258
Valerie Littlechief, *Principal*
EMP: 2 EST: 2015
SALES (est): 307.4K **Privately Held**
SIC: 5147 2015 Meats & meat products; poultry slaughtering & processing

(G-318)
TRU-TONE FINISHING INC (PA)
128 S Lombard Rd (60101-3020)
PHONE..................630 543-5520
Greg Klemenswicz, *President*
Lori Ard, *General Mgr*
Mike Milam, *Prdtn Mgr*
Juan Espinosa, *Administration*
EMP: 35
SQ FT: 44,000
SALES (est): 6.3MM **Privately Held**
SIC: 3479 7389 Coating of metals & formed products;

(G-319)
TRYSON METAL STAMPG & MFG INC (PA)
311 S Stewart Ave (60101-3340)
PHONE..................630 458-0591
Albert Gursfredi, *Ch of Bd*
Felix Jarczyk, *President*
Leo Maggio, *Director*
EMP: 37
SQ FT: 25,750
SALES (est): 5.5MM **Privately Held**
SIC: 3469 Stamping metal for the trade

(G-320)
TST/IMPRESO INC
450 S Lombard Rd Ste C (60101-4230)
PHONE..................630 775-9555
Mike Schutz, *Plant Mgr*
Bob Mladucky, *Branch Mgr*
EMP: 8
SALES (corp-wide): 115.2MM **Publicly Held**
WEB: www.tstimpreso.com
SIC: 2621 2759 2086 2754 Paper mills; laser printing; water, pasteurized: packaged in cans, bottles, etc.; business form & card printing, gravure
HQ: Tst/Impreso, Inc.
652 Southwestern Blvd
Coppell TX 75019
972 462-0100

(G-321)
U S TOOL & MANUFACTURING CO
1335 W Fullerton Ave (60101-4319)
PHONE..................630 953-1000
Raymond G Foreman, *President*
William Levy, *Vice Pres*
EMP: 20 EST: 1915
SQ FT: 13,500
SALES (est): 1.2MM **Privately Held**
WEB: www.ustoolandmfg.com
SIC: 3714 3429 3643 Motor vehicle engines & parts; manufactured hardware (general); current-carrying wiring devices

(G-322)
ULTRAMATIC EQUIPMENT CO
848 S Westgate St (60101-5087)
PHONE..................630 543-4565
Joe Astronrino, *Manager*
EMP: 20
SALES (corp-wide): 1.3MM **Privately Held**
SIC: 3549 3541 3559 5084 Metalworking machinery; deburring machines; refinery, chemical processing & similar machinery; industrial machinery & equipment; abrasive products
PA: Ultramatic Equipment Co.
8603 E Royal Palm Rd # 260
Scottsdale AZ 85258
480 951-6000

(G-323)
UNISTRUT INTERNATIONAL CORP
Also Called: Unistrut Construction
2171 W Executive Dr # 100 (60101-5625)
PHONE..................630 773-3460
Scott Patchn, *Branch Mgr*
EMP: 70 **Publicly Held**
WEB: www.unistrut.us
SIC: 4226 3993 3444 3443 Special warehousing & storage; signs & advertising specialties; sheet metalwork; fabricated plate work (boiler shop); fabricated structural metal; wood partitions & fixtures
HQ: Unistrut International Corporation
16100 Lathrop Ave
Harvey IL 60426
800 882-5543

(G-324)
UP NORTH PRINTING INC
1050 W Republic Dr (60101-3133)
PHONE..................630 584-8675
William Pickford, *President*
Paula Labash, *Sales Mgr*
EMP: 6
SALES (est): 625.1K **Privately Held**
WEB: www.upnorthprinting.com
SIC: 2752 Commercial printing, offset

(G-325)
V AND L POLISHING CO
341 W Interstate Rd (60101-4515)
PHONE..................630 543-5999
Dan Lavallie, *President*
Virginia Lavallie, *Vice Pres*
EMP: 6
SQ FT: 5,000
SALES: 330K **Privately Held**
SIC: 3471 Polishing, metals or formed products; cleaning, polishing & finishing

(G-326)
VAC-MATIC CORPORATION (PA)
2 S Lincoln Ave (60101-3519)
PHONE..................630 543-4518
Donald C Hundrieser, *President*
James Hundrieser, *Vice Pres*
Anne Hundrieser, *Admin Sec*
EMP: 5
SQ FT: 500
SALES (est): 570.3K **Privately Held**
SIC: 3089 Plastic processing

(G-327)
VEK SCREW MACHINE PRODUCTS
1500 W Wrightwood Ct (60101-3034)
P.O. Box 555 (60101-0555)
PHONE..................630 543-5557
Thelma I Keyworth, *Ch of Bd*
Robert Keyworth, *President*
EMP: 8 EST: 1952
SQ FT: 7,500
SALES (est): 750K **Privately Held**
WEB: www.vekscrewmachineproducts.com
SIC: 3451 3599 Screw machine products; machine & other job shop work

(G-328)
VENUS LABORATORIES INC (PA)
Also Called: Earth Friendly Products
111 S Rohlwing Rd (60101-3027)
PHONE..................630 595-1900
Kelly Vlahakis-Hanks, *CEO*
John Vlahakis, *President*

Joe Janssen, *COO*
Nadereh Afsharmanesh, *Vice Pres*
Craig Harlan, *Vice Pres*
◆ **EMP:** 40
SQ FT: 40,000
SALES (est): 76.7MM **Privately Held**
WEB: www.ecos.com
SIC: 2842 2841 Cleaning or polishing preparations; sanitation preparations; soap & other detergents

(G-329)
VETERAN WIRE AND CABLE LLC
1135 W National Ave (60101-3128)
PHONE 630 327-5849
Christian G Wegener, *President*
EMP: 3
SALES (est): 129.4K **Privately Held**
SIC: 3691 1623 Storage batteries; communication line & transmission tower construction

(G-330)
VFN FIBERGLASS INC
330 W Factory Rd (60101-5004)
PHONE 630 543-0232
Frank Mortensen, *President*
Vic Mortensen, *Vice Pres*
Charmaine Mortensen, *Treasurer*
Gloria Mortensen, *Admin Sec*
EMP: 14
SQ FT: 8,100
SALES (est): 1.1MM **Privately Held**
SIC: 3714 Hoods, motor vehicle

(G-331)
VIS-O-GRAPHIC INC
Also Called: Vis-O-Graphic Printing
1220 W National Ave (60101-3131)
PHONE 630 590-6100
Robert V Dahlke, *President*
Rick Ebel, *Vice Pres*
Jon March, *QC Mgr*
Kellie Slovis, *Controller*
Jacquie Dahlke, *Accounts Exec*
EMP: 30 **EST:** 1945
SQ FT: 10,000
SALES (est): 10.2MM **Privately Held**
WEB: www.visographic.com
SIC: 2752 7336 Commercial printing, offset; graphic arts & related design

(G-332)
WE LOVE SOY INC
Also Called: Chicago Soy Dairy
120 S Fairbank St Unit B (60101-3120)
P.O. Box 666, Glen Ellyn (60138-0666)
PHONE 630 629-9667
Ryan D Howard, *President*
Dan Reed, *Partner*
Joe Conway, *Plant Mgr*
Daniel Ziegler, *Admin Sec*
EMP: 3
SQ FT: 4,400
SALES (est): 593.6K **Privately Held**
SIC: 2024 2064 2022 Ice cream & frozen desserts; marshmallows; imitation cheese

(G-333)
WENESCO INC
930 W National Ave (60101-3125)
P.O. Box 59303, Chicago (60659-0243)
PHONE 773 283-3004
Brian Lowenthal, *President*
Enver Poljak, *Design Engr*
Jon Hernandez, *Sales Mgr*
George Cisneros, *Technical Staff*
EMP: 12
SALES (est): 2.9MM **Privately Held**
WEB: www.wenesco.com
SIC: 3548 2899 Soldering equipment, except hand soldering irons; chemical preparations

(G-334)
WENSCO MICHIGAN CORPORATION
936 W Fullerton Ave (60101-3306)
PHONE 630 333-4440
Judy Nelson, *Principal*
EMP: 16
SALES (corp-wide): 27.7MM **Privately Held**
SIC: 2499 Signboards, wood

PA: Wensco Of Michigan, Corporation
5760 Safety Dr Ne
Belmont MI 49306
616 785-3333

(G-335)
WIKUS SAW TECHNOLOGY CORP
700 W Belden Ave (60101-4941)
PHONE 630 766-0960
Mike Masters, *President*
Martin Mueller, *President*
Kellie Grengs, *Principal*
Dan Miller, *Regional Mgr*
Alberto Faure, *Sales Mgr*
▲ **EMP:** 40 **EST:** 1999
SQ FT: 20,853
SALES (est): 6.7MM
SALES (corp-wide): 63.1MM **Privately Held**
WEB: www.wikussawtech.com
SIC: 3425 Saw blades for hand or power saws
PA: Wikus-Sagenfabrik Wilhelm H. Kullmann Gmbh & Co. Kg
Melsunger Str. 30
Spangenberg 34286
566 350-00

(G-336)
WOODLAND PLASTICS CORP
1340 W National Ave (60101-3149)
PHONE 630 543-1144
Stephen L Sinderson, *President*
Todd Yoesle, *Production*
Nelson L Sinderson, *Admin Sec*
▼ **EMP:** 25
SQ FT: 20,000
SALES (est): 6MM **Privately Held**
SIC: 3089 Injection molding of plastics

(G-337)
WOODLAWN ENGINEERING CO INC
325 W Fay Ave (60101-5078)
PHONE 630 543-3550
Marshall Gordon, *CEO*
Neil Gordon, *President*
Scott Gordon, *Corp Secy*
Jack Hilgenberg, *Vice Pres*
EMP: 20 **EST:** 1956
SQ FT: 25,000
SALES (est): 1MM **Privately Held**
WEB: www.woodlawnengineering.com
SIC: 3444 Sheet metal specialties, not stamped

(G-338)
WORLD WASHER & STAMPING INC
763 W Annoreno Dr (60101-4315)
PHONE 630 543-6749
Dennis L Fielder, *President*
Chester Labno, *Vice Pres*
EMP: 13
SQ FT: 11,800
SALES (est): 1.9MM **Privately Held**
SIC: 3469 Stamping metal for the trade

(G-339)
XENTRIS WIRELESS LLC
1250 N Greenbriar Dr A (60101-1098)
PHONE 844 936-8747
Christina Van Vort, *President*
Allan Bailey, *Chairman*
Ralph Hanan, *Vice Pres*
Vivek Patel, *Engineer*
Paul Blevins, *CFO*
▲ **EMP:** 52
SQ FT: 82,000
SALES (est): 38MM **Privately Held**
SIC: 3663 Cellular radio telephone

(G-340)
ZABIHA HALAL MT PROCESSORS INC
1715 W Cortland Ct (60101-4228)
PHONE 630 620-5000
Mohammad Y Khan, *President*
Sajid Khan, *Vice Pres*
EMP: 1
SALES (est): 233.8K **Privately Held**
WEB: www.fatimabrand.com
SIC: 2011 Meat packing plants

(G-341)
ZITROPACK LTD
240 S La Londe Ave (60101-3307)
PHONE 630 543-1016
Humberto Ortiz, *President*
Ana Ortiz, *Corp Secy*
EMP: 12
SQ FT: 20,000
SALES (est): 3MM **Privately Held**
SIC: 3565 Packaging machinery

(G-342)
ZJ INDUSTRIES INC (PA)
125 W Factory Rd (60101-5103)
PHONE 630 543-6400
Milos Jakic, *President*
Zorica Jajic, *COO*
Zorica Jakic, *Vice Pres*
Nicolas Jakic, *Sales Staff*
EMP: 23 **EST:** 1992
SQ FT: 36,000
SALES (est): 3.1MM **Privately Held**
WEB: www.zjindustriesinc.com
SIC: 3599 Machine shop, jobbing & repair

Albers
Clinton County

(G-343)
ARCHITCTLLY DESIGNED CABINETRY
Also Called: Ad Cabinetry
207 E Dwight St (62215-1042)
PHONE 618 248-5931
Pamela Frost, *President*
EMP: 2 **EST:** 2010
SALES (est): 204.3K **Privately Held**
SIC: 2434 Wood kitchen cabinets

(G-344)
EDS PALLET SERVICE
409 N Commercial St (62215-1379)
P.O. Box 226 (62215-0226)
PHONE 618 248-5386
Ed Wittles, *Owner*
Marvin Wittles, *Owner*
EMP: 10
SALES (est): 1.2MM **Privately Held**
SIC: 2448 Pallets, wood

(G-345)
GATEWAY FUELS INC
5260 State Route 161 (62215-1083)
P.O. Box 255 (62215-0255)
PHONE 618 248-5000
Brian Schrage, *Principal*
EMP: 6 **EST:** 2010
SALES (est): 582.4K **Privately Held**
SIC: 2869 Fuels

Albion
Edwards County

(G-346)
ATARAXIA LLC
Also Called: Gold Leaf
884 Industrial St (62806-9000)
PHONE 618 446-3219
John Dieser, *Opers Staff*
George Archos, *Mng Member*
Ross Morreale, *Officer*
EMP: 35
SALES (est): 3.7MM **Privately Held**
SIC: 2833 Drugs & herbs: grading, grinding & milling

(G-347)
CHAMPION LABORATORIES INC (DH)
200 S 4th St (62806-1313)
PHONE 618 445-6011
Greg Noethlich, *President*
Tim Phillips, *Division Mgr*
Tim Borum, *Regional Mgr*
Dwight Rutledge, *Business Mgr*
John Gaither, *Vice Pres*
◆ **EMP:** 1320

SALES (est): 399.3MM
SALES (corp-wide): 553.7MM **Privately Held**
WEB: www.champlabs.com
SIC: 3714 Filters: oil, fuel & air, motor vehicle

(G-348)
CHAMPION LABORATORIES INC
329 Industrial Dr (62806-1339)
PHONE 618 445-5407
EMP: 12
SALES (corp-wide): 553.7MM **Privately Held**
SIC: 3714 Motor vehicle parts & accessories
HQ: Champion Laboratories, Inc.
200 S 4th St
Albion IL 62806
618 445-6011

(G-349)
EDWARDS COUNTY CONCRETE LLC
327 Industrial Dr (62806-1339)
PHONE 618 445-2711
Jeffrey G Denny, *President*
EMP: 4
SALES (est): 335.9K **Privately Held**
SIC: 3273 Ready-mixed concrete

(G-350)
FARMERS PACKING INC
747 Illinois Route 130 (62806-5209)
PHONE 618 445-3822
David Seisert, *President*
EMP: 10
SALES (est): 838.3K **Privately Held**
SIC: 2011 Meat packing plants

(G-351)
PALLET SOLUTION INC
Hwy 130 N (62806)
P.O. Box 56 (62806-0056)
PHONE 618 445-2316
Julie Kimbrell, *President*
Marcus Charlcraft, *Vice Pres*
EMP: 35
SQ FT: 43,000
SALES: 1.9MM **Privately Held**
SIC: 2448 Pallets, wood

(G-352)
PREMIER TOOL & MACHINE INC
330 Industrial Dr (62806-1348)
PHONE 618 445-9066
David Satava, *President*
Mary Satava, *Vice Pres*
EMP: 4
SQ FT: 6,048
SALES (est): 609.7K **Privately Held**
SIC: 3599 Machine shop, jobbing & repair

(G-353)
T J MARCHE LTD
11 N 5th St (62806-1021)
PHONE 618 445-2314
Cheryl Taylor, *President*
EMP: 5 **EST:** 1974
SQ FT: 2,880
SALES: 300K **Privately Held**
SIC: 7336 3993 2395 Graphic arts & related design; silk screen design; signs & advertising specialties; embroidery & art needlework

Aledo
Mercer County

(G-354)
ALEDO WELDING ENTERPRISES INC
Also Called: Cokel's Welding
1802 Se 3rd St (61231-9450)
PHONE 309 582-2019
Don Yates, *President*
EMP: 5
SQ FT: 4,625
SALES (est): 714.1K **Privately Held**
SIC: 7692 7533 Welding repair; auto exhaust system repair shops

Aledo - Mercer County (G-355) GEOGRAPHIC SECTION

(G-355)
CARDINAL PLATING SOLUTIONS INC
802 Se 19th Ave (61231-9401)
P.O. Box 195 (61231-0195)
PHONE................309 582-6215
Chris Shull, *President*
EMP: 3
SALES (est): 286.6K **Privately Held**
SIC: 3471 Electroplating of metals or formed products

(G-356)
GENERAL GRIND & MACHINE INC
2103 Se 5th St (61231-9473)
P.O. Box 168 (61231-0168)
PHONE................309 582-5959
Mark Bieri, *President*
Mike Shull, *General Mgr*
Schuyler Downey, *Vice Pres*
Alan Edwards, *Plant Mgr*
Doyce Hiscocks, *Purch Mgr*
EMP: 150
SQ FT: 160,000
SALES (est): 44.1MM **Privately Held**
SIC: 3599 Machine shop, jobbing & repair

(G-357)
HENDERSON FAMILY
208 N College Ave (61231-1460)
PHONE................309 236-6783
Leo Henderson Jr, *Principal*
Jason Hessman, *Principal*
EMP: 6
SALES (est): 277.2K **Privately Held**
SIC: 2752 Commercial printing, lithographic

(G-358)
MEMINGER METAL FINISHING INC (PA)
2107 Se 8th St (61231-9406)
P.O. Box 225 (61231-0225)
PHONE................309 582-3363
Patricia Meminger, *President*
Trent Kaufman, *Engineer*
Bruce Meminger, *Admin Sec*
EMP: 11
SALES (est): 2.7MM **Privately Held**
SIC: 3559 3471 Metal finishing equipment for plating, etc.; plating & polishing

(G-359)
RODGER MURPHY
Also Called: Goldsmith, The
103 W Main St (61231-1603)
P.O. Box 142 (61231-0142)
PHONE................309 582-2202
Rodger Murphy, *Owner*
Carla Murphy, *Co-Owner*
EMP: 3
SQ FT: 1,000
SALES: 225K **Privately Held**
SIC: 5944 7631 3911 Jewelry stores; jewelry repair services; jewelry, precious metal

(G-360)
RYANS RUB LLC
402 Se 2nd Ave (61231-1903)
PHONE................773 573-8939
Ryan Latko,
EMP: 3
SALES (est): 91.3K **Privately Held**
SIC: 2099 Seasonings & spices

(G-361)
SHIRT TALES
204 Sw 2nd Ave (61231-1736)
PHONE................309 582-5566
Thomas Ryan, *Partner*
Morgan Ryan, *Partner*
EMP: 2
SALES (est): 279.4K **Privately Held**
SIC: 2759 Screen printing

(G-362)
TIMES RECORD COMPANY
219 S College Ave (61231-1734)
PHONE................309 582-5112
Paul Behan, *President*
Marty Kennedy, *Vice Pres*
Phyllis Lundquist, *Treasurer*
Teresa Welch, *Adv Dir*
EMP: 25 **EST:** 1928
SQ FT: 5,000
SALES (est): 1.2MM **Privately Held**
SIC: 2711 2791 2752 Commercial printing & newspaper publishing combined; typesetting; commercial printing, lithographic

Alexander
Morgan County

(G-363)
RANDY WRIGHT & SON CNSTR
901 E Old 36 (62601-7118)
PHONE................217 478-4171
Randy Wright, *Owner*
EMP: 5 **EST:** 2011
SALES (est): 246.4K **Privately Held**
SIC: 1442 Construction sand & gravel

Alexis
Mercer County

(G-364)
ALEXIS FIRE EQUIPMENT COMPANY
109 E Broadway Ave (61412-5041)
P.O. Box 549 (61412-0549)
PHONE................309 482-6121
Karl Jeffrey Morris, *President*
Daniel Don Reese, *Corp Secy*
Michael Shull, *Vice Pres*
Bob Routt, *Controller*
Dawn Baker, *Accountant*
EMP: 70
SQ FT: 42,000
SALES (est): 16.5MM **Privately Held**
WEB: www.alexisfire.com
SIC: 3711 Fire department vehicles (motor vehicles), assembly of

Algonquin
Mchenry County

(G-365)
A D SKYLIGHTS INC
206 Berg St (60102-3538)
PHONE................847 854-2900
Stefan Szefer, *President*
Jerzy Depczyk, *President*
EMP: 6
SQ FT: 8,000
SALES (est): 500K **Privately Held**
SIC: 3444 Skylights, sheet metal

(G-366)
AVANI SPICES LLC
1690 Stone Ridge Ln (60102-6638)
PHONE................847 532-1075
Avani Amin Carkner, *President*
Robert Shive, *Vice Pres*
EMP: 4
SALES (est): 196.5K **Privately Held**
SIC: 2099 Food preparations

(G-367)
BARTELL CORPORATION
3671 Persimmon Dr (60102-5959)
P.O. Box 5775, Elgin (60121-5775)
PHONE................847 854-3232
John Bartell, *President*
Barbara Bartell, *Vice Pres*
EMP: 7
SALES (est): 461.4K **Privately Held**
SIC: 8711 3549 Machine tool design; assembly machines, including robotic

(G-368)
CANCONEX INC
901 Armstrong St (60102-3548)
P.O. Box 7419 (60102-7419)
PHONE................847 458-9955
James K Atkinson, *President*
EMP: 15
SQ FT: 6,000
SALES (est): 3.2MM **Privately Held**
SIC: 3535 Conveyors & conveying equipment

(G-369)
DIRECT DIMENSION INC (PA)
8195 Pyott Rd (60156-9767)
PHONE................815 479-1936
George Athans, *President*
Leonidas Athans, *Vice Pres*
EMP: 9 **EST:** 1993
SQ FT: 1,500
SALES (est): 2.2MM **Privately Held**
WEB: www.therevolver.info
SIC: 3711 Truck & tractor truck assembly

(G-370)
DISKIN SYSTEMS INC
9550 S Il Route 31 (60102-9724)
PHONE................815 276-7288
Troy Diskin, *President*
Tara Madigan, *Regional Mgr*
Pat Piercen, *Vice Pres*
EMP: 5
SALES (est): 755.9K **Privately Held**
SIC: 3589 Car washing machinery

(G-371)
DMJ GROUP INC
2413 W Algonquin Rd # 227 (60102-9402)
PHONE................847 322-7533
Denise Rognstad, *President*
Jill Rognstad, *Treasurer*
Michelle Chase, *Admin Sec*
EMP: 3
SALES (est): 156.1K **Privately Held**
SIC: 3999 Pet supplies

(G-372)
DVINE WINE CRAFTERS LLC
2380 Esplanade Dr (60102-5449)
PHONE................847 658-4900
Steve Boyer, *Principal*
EMP: 4
SALES (est): 317.6K **Privately Held**
SIC: 2084 Wines

(G-373)
HI TEK TOOL & MACHINING INC
2413 W Algonquin Rd (60102-9402)
PHONE................847 836-6422
Lonnie Alford, *President*
Audrey Alford, *Vice Pres*
EMP: 5
SQ FT: 5,000
SALES (est): 500K **Privately Held**
SIC: 3312 Tool & die steel

(G-374)
INDEPENDENT ANTIQUE RAD MFG
200 Berg St (60102-3538)
PHONE................847 458-7400
Peter Cook, *President*
EMP: 7 **EST:** 1913
SALES (est): 925.4K **Privately Held**
WEB: www.oldradman.com
SIC: 3714 3713 Radiators & radiator shells & cores, motor vehicle; heaters, motor vehicle; truck & bus bodies

(G-375)
J C PRODUCTS INC
1961 Tunbridge Ct (60102-6065)
PHONE................847 208-9616
Jim Chmela, *President*
EMP: 5
SALES (est): 659.8K **Privately Held**
SIC: 3089 Injection molding of plastics

(G-376)
KENMODE TOOL AND ENGRG INC
820 W Algonquin Rd (60102-2482)
PHONE................847 658-5041
Werner Moders, *CEO*
Kurt Moders, *President*
Petra Schindler, *Vice Pres*
Kurt Gascho, *CFO*
Christa Moders, *Treasurer*
◆ **EMP:** 150
SQ FT: 85,000
SALES (est): 47.5MM **Privately Held**
WEB: www.kenmode.com
SIC: 3469 3544 Stamping metal for the trade; special dies & tools

(G-377)
LION TOOL & DIE CO
910 W Algonquin Rd (60102-3578)
P.O. Box 7066 (60102-7066)
PHONE................847 658-8898
Leonard Doerrfeld, *President*
Paul Doerrfeld, *Corp Secy*
EMP: 19
SQ FT: 13,000
SALES (est): 2.6MM **Privately Held**
WEB: www.liontool.com
SIC: 3544 3599 Special dies & tools; machine shop, jobbing & repair

(G-378)
MARSHALL WOLF AUTOMATION INC (PA)
923 S Main St (60102-2735)
PHONE................847 658-8130
Tina Hueppe, *President*
Marc Williams, *Project Mgr*
Fred Swanke, *Sales Engr*
Steve Van Maldegiam, *Sales Engr*
Gregg Nelson, *Marketing Staff*
◆ **EMP:** 20
SALES (est): 15MM **Privately Held**
SIC: 5065 3613 Electronic parts; panelboards & distribution boards, electric

(G-379)
MARTINEZ MANAGEMENT INC
2413 W Algonquin Rd (60102-9402)
PHONE................847 822-7202
Rich Martinez, *President*
EMP: 3
SQ FT: 2,500 **Privately Held**
SIC: 3089 Automotive parts, plastic
PA: Martinez Management, Inc.
800 Blle Trre Pkwy Ste 20
Palm Coast FL 32164

(G-380)
MATERIAL SERVICE CORPORATION
Rr 31 (60102)
P.O. Box 69 (60102-0069)
PHONE................847 658-4559
Frank Anderson, *Manager*
EMP: 27
SALES (corp-wide): 20.8B **Privately Held**
SIC: 3281 1442 Stone, quarrying & processing of own stone products; construction sand & gravel
HQ: Material Service Corporation
2235 Entp Dr Ste 3504
Westchester IL 60154
708 731-2600

(G-381)
MEYER MATERIAL CO MERGER CORP
10500 S Il Route 31 (60102-1641)
PHONE................847 658-7811
Steven Warnke, *Principal*
Gary Floit, *Manager*
EMP: 15
SALES (corp-wide): 4.5B **Privately Held**
SIC: 3273 Ready-mixed concrete
HQ: Meyer Material Company Llc
580 S Wolf Rd
Des Plaines IL 60016
815 331-7200

(G-382)
NEW LIFE PRINTING & PUBLISHING
1508 S Main St (60102-3223)
P.O. Box 7285 (60102-7285)
PHONE................847 658-4111
Monica Brubaker, *President*
Loren Nelson, *Vice Pres*
EMP: 6
SQ FT: 4,000
SALES: 1.5MM **Privately Held**
SIC: 2752 2721 2791 2789 Commercial printing, offset; periodicals; typesetting; bookbinding & related work

(G-383)
OZINGA BROS INC
Also Called: Ozinga Rready Mix
10500 S Il Route 31 (60102-1641)
PHONE................847 783-6500
Brent Horne, *Principal*
EMP: 46

▲ = Import ▼ = Export
◆ = Import/Export

SALES (corp-wide): 434.5MM **Privately Held**
SIC: 3273 Ready-mixed concrete
PA: Ozinga Bros., Inc.
19001 Old Lagrange Rd # 30
Mokena IL 60448
708 326-4200

(G-384)
PROGRESSIVE SOLUTIONS CORP
2848 Corporate Pkwy (60102-2564)
PHONE..................................847 639-7272
Jayson McMahon, *President*
John Marwitz, *Director*
▼ EMP: 5
SQ FT: 7,000
SALES (est): 600K **Privately Held**
SIC: 2899 2841 Chemical preparations; soap & other detergents

(G-385)
RAD SOURCE TECHNOLOGIES INC
8411 Pyott Rd Ste 111 (60156-9704)
PHONE..................................815 477-1291
Richard Adams, *Manager*
EMP: 4
SALES (corp-wide): 2.6MM **Privately Held**
SIC: 3841 Surgical & medical instruments
PA: Rad Source Technologies, Inc.
4907 Golden Pkwy Ste 400
Buford GA 30518
678 765-7900

(G-386)
RAPID MANUFACTURING INC
1320 Chase St Ste 4 (60102-9668)
PHONE..................................847 458-0888
Christine M Janikowski, *President*
Michael E Kilanski, *Corp Secy*
EMP: 4
SQ FT: 6,000
SALES (est): 563K **Privately Held**
SIC: 3544 Special dies & tools

(G-387)
RED RUMI LLC
1020 Estancia Ln (60102-6316)
PHONE..................................847 757-8433
Noman Khan, *Mng Member*
Razi Imam,
Ahmad Salman Mushtaq,
Ibaad Ur Rahman,
EMP: 4
SALES: 300K **Privately Held**
SIC: 2034 Dried & dehydrated fruits

(G-388)
TOOLS FOR INDUSTRY INC
812 Oceola Dr (60102-2972)
P.O. Box 7555 (60102-7555)
PHONE..................................847 658-0455
Glen A Vodicka, *President*
EMP: 2
SALES (est): 295.7K **Privately Held**
SIC: 3541 Machine tools, metal cutting type

(G-389)
TOOLWELD INC
1750 Cumberland Pkwy # 8 (60102-9517)
PHONE..................................847 854-8013
Fred Hild, *President*
Eric Hild, *Treasurer*
EMP: 3
SALES (est): 320.2K **Privately Held**
WEB: www.toolweldmicro.com
SIC: 7692 Welding repair

(G-390)
TSK MNUFACTURING SOLUTIONS LLC
2390 Esplanade Dr 200f (60102-5452)
PHONE..................................847 450-4099
Trent Grimes, *Principal*
EMP: 3
SALES (est): 198.1K **Privately Held**
SIC: 3089 Injection molding of plastics

(G-391)
V C P INC
Also Called: V C P Printing
901 W Algonquin Rd (60102-3573)
PHONE..................................847 658-5090
Herbert Vogt, *President*
Mindy Hack, *Vice Pres*
Scott Coleman, *Prdtn Mgr*
Jeff Alwin, *Foreman/Supr*
Mark Vogt, *Opers Staff*
EMP: 21
SQ FT: 12,000
SALES (est): 3.8MM **Privately Held**
SIC: 2752 2791 7331 Commercial printing, offset; typesetting; direct mail advertising services

(G-392)
VILLAGE VINTNER WINERY BREWRY
2380 Esplanade Dr (60102-5449)
PHONE..................................847 658-4900
Joseph Condo, *Principal*
Steve Boyer, *Director*
EMP: 7 EST: 2012
SALES (est): 746K **Privately Held**
SIC: 2084 Wines

(G-393)
W/S PACKAGING GROUP INC
1310 Zange Dr (60102-2047)
PHONE..................................847 658-7363
John Gorack, *Branch Mgr*
EMP: 5 **Privately Held**
SIC: 2621 5943 Wrapping & packaging papers; stationery stores
HQ: W/S Packaging Group, Inc.
2571 S Hemlock Rd
Green Bay WI 54229
920 866-6300

(G-394)
WAUCONDA TOOL & ENGRG LLC (HQ)
821 W Algonquin Rd (60102-2480)
PHONE..................................847 658-4588
Charles Burnside, *President*
Don Williams, *Vice Pres*
EMP: 55 EST: 1950
SQ FT: 45,000
SALES (est): 19.4MM
SALES (corp-wide): 847.4MM **Publicly Held**
WEB: www.wauconda.com
SIC: 3469 3544 Stamping metal for the trade; special dies, tools, jigs & fixtures
PA: Nn, Inc.
6210 Ardrey Kell Rd # 600
Charlotte NC 28277
980 264-4300

(G-395)
WAYPOINT ENTERPRISES
2328 Stonegate Rd (60102-6654)
PHONE..................................847 551-9213
John St Pierre, *Principal*
EMP: 2 EST: 2010
SALES (est): 230.9K **Privately Held**
WEB: www.waypointent.com
SIC: 3732 Motorboats, inboard or outboard: building & repairing

(G-396)
WHAT WE MAKE INC
Also Called: Furniture Manufacture
207 Berg St (60102-3537)
PHONE..................................331 442-4830
Dan Quinn, *President*
EMP: 7
SQ FT: 11,500
SALES: 950K **Privately Held**
SIC: 2511 Wood household furniture

(G-397)
YOUNG INNOVATIONS INC (HQ)
2260 Wendt St (60102-1400)
PHONE..................................847 458-5400
Dave Sproat, *CEO*
Anthony Davis, *President*
Nichol Schreiber, *Business Mgr*
Brad Amodeo, *Vice Pres*
Dale Carroll, *Opers Staff*
▲ EMP: 93
SQ FT: 113,000

SALES (est): 157.4MM
SALES (corp-wide): 1.3B **Privately Held**
WEB: www.ydnt.com
SIC: 3843 Dental equipment & supplies
PA: The Jordan Company L P
399 Park Ave Fl 30
New York NY 10022
212 572-0800

(G-398)
YOUNG INNOVATIONS INC (PA)
2260 Wendt St (60102-1400)
PHONE..................................847 458-5400
EMP: 57
SALES (est): 51.5MM **Privately Held**
SIC: 3843 Mfg Dental Equipment/Supplies

(G-399)
YOUNG MYDENT LLC
Also Called: Mydent International
2260 Wendt St (60102-1400)
PHONE..................................631 434-3190
Dave Sproat, *President*
EMP: 17
SQ FT: 113,000
SALES (est): 2.8MM
SALES (corp-wide): 1.3B **Privately Held**
SIC: 3843 Dental equipment
HQ: Young Innovations, Inc.
2260 Wendt St
Algonquin IL 60102
847 458-5400

(G-400)
YOUNG OS LLC
2260 Wendt St (60102-1400)
PHONE..................................847 458-5400
Melissa Grillo, *Accounts Mgr*
Dave Hansen, *Accounts Mgr*
Catie Pankow, *Administration*
EMP: 20
SALES (est): 2.2MM **Privately Held**
WEB: www.obtura.com
SIC: 3843 Dental equipment & supplies

Alhambra
Madison County

(G-401)
IDEAL CABINET SOLUTIONS INC
1105 W Main St (62001-2175)
PHONE..................................618 514-7087
Jay Kohlmiller, *President*
EMP: 4
SALES (est): 168.3K **Privately Held**
SIC: 2434 2521 2431 Wood kitchen cabinets; wood office filing cabinets & bookcases; filing cabinets (boxes), office: wood; window trim, wood; moldings & baseboards, ornamental & trim

Allendale
Wabash County

(G-402)
ALLENDALE GRAVEL CO INC
18306 Wabash 18 Ave (62410-2143)
PHONE..................................618 263-3521
James E Litherland Jr, *President*
Sue Murphy, *Corp Secy*
Eric Fields, *Exec Dir*
EMP: 15 EST: 1931
SQ FT: 2,800
SALES (est): 3.7MM **Privately Held**
WEB: www.allendalegravel.com
SIC: 1611 1629 1442 General contractor, highway & street construction; waste water & sewage treatment plant construction; gravel mining

Allerton
Vermilion County

(G-403)
ELEMENT COLLECTION
2731 County Road 100 N (61810-9606)
P.O. Box 81, Urbana (61803-0081)
PHONE..................................217 898-5175
Theodore Gray, *Owner*
EMP: 2
SALES: 200K **Privately Held**
SIC: 2741 Miscellaneous publishing

Alma
Marion County

(G-404)
SUMMERVLLE CONSULTING SVCS LLC
8655 Garrett Rd (62807-1100)
PHONE..................................618 547-7142
Summerville Scott D, *Principal*
EMP: 3 EST: 2015
SALES (est): 205K **Privately Held**
SIC: 3421 Knife blades & blanks

Alpha
Henry County

(G-405)
ALL-FEED PROC & PACKG INC (PA)
210 S 1st St (61413-9480)
PHONE..................................309 629-0001
Timothy Anderson, *President*
▲ EMP: 14
SALES (est): 2MM **Privately Held**
WEB: www.allfeed.com
SIC: 2048 Canned pet food (except dog & cat)

Alsip
Cook County

(G-406)
A & R MACHINE INC
12340 S Keeler Ave (60803-1813)
PHONE..................................708 388-4764
Roman Plewa, *President*
Jane Plewa, *Corp Secy*
Andrew Siemon, *Vice Pres*
EMP: 8
SQ FT: 8,400
SALES (est): 1.5MM **Privately Held**
SIC: 3599 Machine shop, jobbing & repair

(G-407)
A AND P DIRECTIONAL DRLG LLC
11629 S Mayfield Ave (60803-6007)
PHONE..................................708 715-1192
EMP: 8
SALES (corp-wide): 912.6K **Privately Held**
WEB: www.chicagodirectionaldrilling.com
SIC: 1381 Directional drilling oil & gas wells
PA: A And P Directional Drilling Llc
10842 Eleanor Ln
Orland Park IL 60467
708 715-1192

(G-408)
A B S EMBROIDERY INC
4814 W 129th St (60803-3016)
PHONE..................................708 597-7785
William Dawson, *President*
Allen Irvinsks, *Vice Pres*
Scott Parker, *Admin Sec*
EMP: 7
SALES (est): 427.1K **Privately Held**
WEB: www.absembroidery.us
SIC: 2395 Embroidery products, except schiffli machine

Alsip - Cook County (G-409)

(G-409)
A P S GAS TURBINE INC
5324 W 124th St (60803-3205)
PHONE..................................708 262-2939
Stefan Eck, *Principal*
Robert Blue, *Vice Pres*
▲ **EMP:** 2
SALES (est): 244.7K **Privately Held**
SIC: 3511 Gas turbine generator set units, complete

(G-410)
ACCORD CARTON CO
Also Called: Accord Packaging
6155 W 115th St (60803-5153)
PHONE..................................708 272-3050
Robert S Codo, *President*
William M Codo, *Vice Pres*
William Codo, *Vice Pres*
Daisy Gamboa, *Accounting Mgr*
Jim Coen, *Marketing Staff*
EMP: 125
SQ FT: 120,000
SALES (est): 38.7MM **Privately Held**
WEB: www.accordcarton.com
SIC: 2657 2789 2759 Folding paperboard boxes; bookbinding & related work; commercial printing

(G-411)
ACCORD PACKAGING LLC
6155 W 115th St (60803-5153)
PHONE..................................708 272-3050
Ruthie Keefner, *Manager*
EMP: 35
SALES (est): 7.3MM **Privately Held**
SIC: 2631 Container, packaging & boxboard

(G-412)
ACE METAL SPINNING INC
11630 S Mayfield Ave (60803-6010)
PHONE..................................708 389-5635
James J Baur, *President*
George Baur, *Corp Secy*
EMP: 18
SQ FT: 17,000
SALES (est): 3.3MM **Privately Held**
WEB: www.acemetalspinning.com
SIC: 3469 3444 Spinning metal for the trade; sheet metalwork

(G-413)
AIM LLC
Also Called: Aim Mail Centers
11939 S Central Ave Ste B (60803-3400)
PHONE..................................727 544-3000
William G Buckles Jr, *Manager*
William Buckles, *Manager*
EMP: 28
SALES (est): 5.9MM **Privately Held**
SIC: 2221 Fiberglass fabrics

(G-414)
ALSIP MINIMILL LLC
13101 S Pulaski Rd Ste 1 (60803-2026)
PHONE..................................708 625-0098
Carol Nolan, *Purch Mgr*
Nichole Larusso, *Purch Agent*
Wally Lasonde, *Engineer*
Shivamurthy Modgi, *Engineer*
Mike Rubinstin, *CFO*
EMP: 10
SALES (est): 2.5MM **Privately Held**
SIC: 2621 Paper mills

(G-415)
ANIKAM INC
Also Called: Allegra Print & Imaging
12549 S Holiday Dr (60803-3207)
PHONE..................................708 385-0200
Helen Makina, *Ch of Bd*
James Makina, *President*
Steve Makina, *Vice Pres*
Ilene Moran, *Admin Sec*
EMP: 8
SQ FT: 7,500
SALES: 991K **Privately Held**
WEB: www.alsipallegra.com
SIC: 2752 Commercial printing, offset

(G-416)
ANTON-ARGIRES INC
12345 S Latrobe Ave (60803-3210)
PHONE..................................708 388-6250
George Argires, *CEO*
Steven Argires, *Corp Secy*
▲ **EMP:** 6 **EST:** 1949
SQ FT: 6,000
SALES: 3.7MM **Privately Held**
WEB: www.anuts.com
SIC: 5145 2068 Nuts, salted or roasted; salted & roasted nuts & seeds

(G-417)
ARKEMA INC
Also Called: Arkema Coating Resins
12840 S Pulaski Rd (60803-1917)
PHONE..................................708 396-3001
Patrick E Gottschalk, *CEO*
Rory Watts, *Maintence Staff*
EMP: 123
SALES (corp-wide): 120.6MM **Privately Held**
WEB: www.arkema-americas.com
SIC: 2812 Chlorine, compressed or liquefied; caustic soda, sodium hydroxide
HQ: Arkema Inc.
  900 First Ave
  King Of Prussia PA 19406
  610 205-7000

(G-418)
ARKEMA INC
12840 S Pulaski Rd (60803-1917)
PHONE..................................708 385-2188
EMP: 123
SALES (corp-wide): 18.6MM **Privately Held**
SIC: 2812 Mfg Alkalies/Chlorine
HQ: Arkema Inc.
  900 First Ave
  King Of Prussia PA 19406
  610 205-7000

(G-419)
ASAI CHICAGO
12559 S Holiday Dr Ste C (60803-3258)
PHONE..................................708 239-0133
Sam Sarcinelli, *Owner*
EMP: 10
SALES (est): 993.4K **Privately Held**
SIC: 3578 Automatic teller machines (ATM)

(G-420)
B ALLAN GRAPHICS INC
Also Called: Raised Expectations
11629 S Mayfield Ave (60803-6007)
PHONE..................................708 396-1704
Bruce Smith, *President*
Sharon Leja, *Executive Asst*
EMP: 12
SALES (est): 1.5MM **Privately Held**
SIC: 2752 2796 2791 2759 Commercial printing, offset; platemaking services; typesetting; commercial printing; die-cut paper & board

(G-421)
BBC FASTENERS INC
4210 W Shirley Ln (60803-2410)
PHONE..................................708 597-9100
Gerald E Sullivan, *President*
Eugene R Sullivan, *Principal*
James L Dion, *Vice Pres*
Stacy Foster, *Treasurer*
James Dion, *VP Sales*
EMP: 45 **EST:** 1959
SQ FT: 38,000
SALES (est): 13MM **Privately Held**
WEB: www.bbcfasteners.com
SIC: 3452 Bolts, metal; screws, metal; nuts, metal

(G-422)
BEACON INC
12223 S Laramie Ave (60803-3129)
PHONE..................................708 544-9900
Wayne Jagush, *President*
▼ **EMP:** 10
SQ FT: 11,000
SALES (est): 1MM **Privately Held**
SIC: 3556 Food products machinery

(G-423)
BERRY GLOBAL FILMS LLC
12900 S Pulaski Rd (60803-2005)
PHONE..................................708 239-4619
Joe Oliva, *Manager*
Bob Stadler, *Supervisor*
EMP: 70 **Publicly Held**
SIC: 3081 Polyethylene film
HQ: Berry Global Films, Llc
  95 Chestnut Ridge Rd
  Montvale NJ 07645
  201 641-6600

(G-424)
BROTHERS LEAL LLC
12007 S Cicero Ave (60803-2312)
PHONE..................................708 385-4400
Emmanuel Leal, *Principal*
EMP: 5
SALES (est): 680.5K **Privately Held**
WEB: www.brothersleal.net
SIC: 2541 Counter & sink tops

(G-425)
CAKE FACTORY
4018 W 127th St (60803-1923)
PHONE..................................708 897-0872
EMP: 5
SALES (est): 308.5K **Privately Held**
SIC: 2053 Cakes, bakery: frozen

(G-426)
CAPSTONE THERAPEUTICS CORP (PA)
5141 W 122nd St (60803-3102)
PHONE..................................602 286-5520
John M Holliman III, *Chairman*
Les M Taeger, *CFO*
EMP: 2
SQ FT: 1,379
SALES: 2MM **Publicly Held**
SIC: 2834 Pharmaceutical preparations

(G-427)
CHICAGO DRIVE LINE INC
11500 S Central Ave (60803-3417)
PHONE..................................708 385-1900
Roy Frestel, *President*
EMP: 8
SQ FT: 10,000
SALES (est): 1.4MM **Privately Held**
SIC: 3714 7538 5013 Axles, motor vehicle; drive shafts, motor vehicle; general automotive repair shops; motor vehicle supplies & new parts

(G-428)
CHICAGO SHADE MAKERS INC
12617 S Kroll Dr (60803-3221)
PHONE..................................708 597-5590
Garry Nowiszewski, *President*
EMP: 3
SALES: 600K **Privately Held**
SIC: 2591 Window shades

(G-429)
CHICAGO WICKER & TRADING CO
Also Called: Northcape International
5625 W 115th St (60803-5125)
PHONE..................................708 563-2890
Thomas Murray, *President*
William Winzel, *Vice Pres*
Erin Walsh, *CFO*
◆ **EMP:** 45 **EST:** 1999
SQ FT: 89,000
SALES (est): 11.3MM **Privately Held**
SIC: 2511 Wood household furniture

(G-430)
CHISHOLM-BOYD & WHITE
4101 W 126th St Ste 1 (60803-1996)
PHONE..................................708 597-7550
Timothy Yurczak, *Mfg Mgr*
EMP: 2
SALES (est): 211.5K **Privately Held**
SIC: 3542 Machine tools, metal forming type

(G-431)
CHRISTOS WOODWORKING
5865 W 124th St (60803-3501)
PHONE..................................708 975-5045
EMP: 4
SALES (est): 371.3K **Privately Held**
SIC: 2431 Millwork

(G-432)
CIRCLE METAL SPECIALTIES INC
4029 W 123rd St (60803-1872)
PHONE..................................708 597-1700
Robert J Mishka, *President*
Robert Mishka, *Vice Pres*
Robert M Mishka, *Vice Pres*
Michael Mishka, *Treasurer*
Susan Mishka, *Treasurer*
EMP: 25 **EST:** 1965
SQ FT: 21,000
SALES (est): 6.4MM **Privately Held**
WEB: www.circlemetal.com
SIC: 3441 Fabricated structural metal

(G-433)
COCA-COLA REFRESHMENTS USA INC
5321 W 122nd St (60803-3178)
PHONE..................................708 597-6700
Duane Hallstrom, *Vice Pres*
EMP: 220
SALES (corp-wide): 37.2B **Publicly Held**
SIC: 2086 5149 Bottled & canned soft drinks; groceries & related products
HQ: Coca-Cola Refreshments Usa, Inc.
  2500 Windy Ridge Pkwy Se
  Atlanta GA 30339
  770 989-3000

(G-434)
COMET CONECTION INC
Also Called: Comet Press
5040 W 127th St (60803-3213)
P.O. Box 252, Oak Forest (60452-0252)
PHONE..................................312 243-5400
Syed Sharf Alam, *President*
EMP: 4
SQ FT: 1,450
SALES (est): 279.4K **Privately Held**
SIC: 7336 2752 7334 5045 Graphic arts & related design; commercial printing, offset; photocopying & duplicating services; computers, peripherals & software

(G-435)
CROWN CORK & SEAL USA INC
5555 W 115th St (60803-5178)
PHONE..................................708 239-5555
Jim Meyman, *Branch Mgr*
Maureen Jerge, *Executive Asst*
EMP: 150
SALES (corp-wide): 11.6B **Publicly Held**
WEB: www.crowncork.com
SIC: 3411 Metal cans
HQ: Crown Cork & Seal Usa, Inc.
  770 Township Line Rd # 100
  Yardley PA 19067
  215 698-5100

(G-436)
CROWN CORK & SEAL USA INC
11535 S Central Ave (60803-3418)
PHONE..................................708 239-5000
Faroukh Dhunjisha, *Director*
EMP: 118
SALES (corp-wide): 11.6B **Publicly Held**
SIC: 3411 Metal cans
HQ: Crown Cork & Seal Usa, Inc.
  770 Township Line Rd # 100
  Yardley PA 19067
  215 698-5100

(G-437)
CROWN CORK & SEAL USA INC
11535 S Central Ave (60803-3418)
P.O. Box 98106, Chicago (60693-8106)
PHONE..................................708 385-8670
David Lopez, *Design Engr*
EMP: 18
SALES (corp-wide): 11.6B **Publicly Held**
SIC: 3411 Metal cans
HQ: Crown Cork & Seal Usa, Inc.
  770 Township Line Rd # 100
  Yardley PA 19067
  215 698-5100

(G-438)
DART CASTINGS INC
12400 S Lombard Ln (60803-1823)
PHONE..................................708 388-4914
Marek Wolny, *President*
Mark Wolny, *Opers Mgr*
Al Aquino, *Opers Staff*
Teresa Wolny, *Admin Sec*
EMP: 50 **EST:** 1994
SQ FT: 40,000
SALES (est): 11.4MM **Privately Held**
WEB: www.dartcasting.com
SIC: 3363 3364 Aluminum die-castings; zinc & zinc-base alloy die-castings

▲ = Import ▼ = Export
◆ = Import/Export

GEOGRAPHIC SECTION
Alsip - Cook County (G-465)

(G-439)
DAUBERT CROMWELL LLC (PA)
12701 S Ridgeway Ave (60803-1526)
PHONE................................708 293-7750
Martin Simpson, *CEO*
Roy Galman, *COO*
Oscar Abello, *CFO*
Shawn Genz, *Controller*
Natalia Glukhova, *Accountant*
▲ **EMP:** 50
SALES (est): 14.3MM **Privately Held**
SIC: 2671 Packaging paper & plastics film, coated & laminated

(G-440)
DONSON MACHINE COMPANY
12416 S Kedvale Ave (60803-1819)
PHONE................................708 388-0880
Jim Bettinardi, *CEO*
Joseph Bettinardi, *President*
James Bettinardi, *Vice Pres*
Bill Busby, *Director*
▲ **EMP:** 80
SQ FT: 20,000
SALES (est): 18.9MM **Privately Held**
SIC: 3599 Machine shop, jobbing & repair

(G-441)
DORALCO INC
Also Called: Architectural Metal Solutions
5919 W 118th St (60803-3914)
PHONE................................708 388-9324
Matthew Jabaay, *President*
Robert Trainor Jr, *President*
Barbara Blank, *Vice Pres*
Tom O'Malley, *Vice Pres*
Kelly Apuzzo, *Production*
EMP: 50
SQ FT: 18,000
SALES (est): 12MM **Privately Held**
SIC: 1751 3231 Window & door installation & erection; doors, glass; made from purchased glass

(G-442)
DOW CHEMICAL COMPANY
12840 S Pulaski Rd (60803-1917)
PHONE................................708 396-3009
Steve Schoenhold, *Manager*
EMP: 50
SALES (corp-wide): 42.9B **Publicly Held**
SIC: 2869 Industrial organic chemicals
HQ: The Dow Chemical Company
2211 H H Dow Way
Midland MI 48642
989 636-1000

(G-443)
DURO BAG MANUFACTURING COMPANY
12245 S Central Ave (60803-3407)
PHONE................................708 385-8674
Rob Arnold, *Branch Mgr*
EMP: 100
SALES (corp-wide): 2.5B **Privately Held**
SIC: 2673 2674 Plastic bags: made from purchased materials; bags: uncoated paper & multiwall
HQ: Duro Bag Manufacturing Company
7600 Empire Dr
Florence KY 41042
859 371-2150

(G-444)
EDWARD F DATA
Also Called: Jr Sons Welding
12625 S Kroll Dr (60803-3221)
PHONE................................708 597-0158
Edward F Data, *Owner*
EMP: 3
SALES (est): 104.5K **Privately Held**
SIC: 7692 Welding repair

(G-445)
ENGINEERED ABRASIVES INC
Also Called: E A
11631 S Austin Ave (60803-6001)
PHONE................................662 582-4143
Ken Superczynski, *Design Engr*
Michael Wern, *Admin Sec*
Donna Walczak, *Executive Asst*
Michael J Wern, *Admin Sec*
Susan Krueger, *Admin Asst*
◆ **EMP:** 25
SQ FT: 50,000
SALES (est): 7.1MM **Privately Held**
WEB: www.engineeredabrasives.com
SIC: 3629 5084 3549 3541 Blasting machines, electrical; industrial machinery & equipment; metalworking machinery; machine tools, metal cutting type

(G-446)
GC AMERICA INC (HQ)
3737 W 127th St (60803-1542)
PHONE................................708 597-0900
Yutaka Suzuki, *President*
M Dean Porter, *President*
Nancy Franceschi, *District Mgr*
Debbie Iacono, *District Mgr*
Nate Kempf, *District Mgr*
◆ **EMP:** 150 EST: 1928
SQ FT: 80,000
SALES (est): 46.8MM **Privately Held**
WEB: www.gcamerica.com
SIC: 3843 Dental equipment

(G-447)
GC MANUFACTURING AMERICA LLC
3737 W 127th St (60803-1532)
PHONE................................708 597-0900
Steven Fletcher, *President*
Thomas Hawrysz, *Admin Sec*
EMP: 85
SQ FT: 95,000
SALES (est): 46.8MM **Privately Held**
SIC: 3843 Dental equipment & supplies
HQ: Gc America Inc.
3737 W 127th St
Alsip IL 60803
708 597-0900

(G-448)
GRAPHICMARK INC
5659 W 120th St (60803-3449)
PHONE................................708 293-1200
Jim Maz, *President*
EMP: 2
SALES (est): 212.1K **Privately Held**
SIC: 2752 Commercial printing, offset

(G-449)
GRASSO GRAPHICS INC
Also Called: Kwik Kopy Printing
5156 W 125th Pl (60803-3200)
PHONE................................708 489-2060
Salvatore Grasso, *President*
Bert Grasso, *Vice Pres*
Bill Bradshaw, *Sales Associate*
Patricia Grasso, *Admin Sec*
EMP: 8
SALES (est): 1.7MM **Privately Held**
WEB: www.grassographics.com
SIC: 2752 2791 2789 Commercial printing, offset; typesetting; bookbinding & related work

(G-450)
GREIF INC
4300 W 130th St (60803-2003)
P.O. Box 75409, Chicago (60675-5409)
PHONE................................708 371-4777
Janki Brian, *Partner*
Jeffrey Galasso, *Superintendent*
Tony Alvarez, *Production*
Christine Trocellier, *Human Resources*
Michael Barilla, *Technology*
EMP: 35
SALES (corp-wide): 4.6B **Publicly Held**
WEB: www.greif.com
SIC: 2655 Fiber cans, drums & similar products
PA: Greif, Inc.
425 Winter Rd
Delaware OH 43015
740 549-6000

(G-451)
GRIFFITH FOODS GROUP INC (PA)
1 Griffith Ctr (60803-4701)
PHONE................................708 371-0900
D L Griffith, *President*
Michael Plichta, *President*
Deanna Kibelkis, *Vice Pres*
Keith Toomey, *Plant Mgr*
Reginald Plummer, *Production*
◆ **EMP:** 12 EST: 1919
SQ FT: 250,000
SALES: 1B **Privately Held**
WEB: www.griffithfoods.com
SIC: 2099 Seasonings: dry mixes; spices, including grinding

(G-452)
GRIFFITH FOODS INC (DH)
1 Griffith Ctr (60803-4701)
PHONE................................708 371-0900
Brian Griffith, *Ch of Bd*
Donald Bernacchi, *Vice Pres*
Christine Carr, *Vice Pres*
Regina Kump, *Vice Pres*
Steve Lee, *Vice Pres*
▲ **EMP:** 300
SQ FT: 250,000
SALES (est): 167.3MM
SALES (corp-wide): 1B **Privately Held**
SIC: 2099 Seasonings: dry mixes; spices, including grinding

(G-453)
GRIFFITH FOODS WORLDWIDE INC (DH)
Also Called: Griffith Laboratories
12200 S Central Ave (60803-3408)
PHONE................................708 371-0900
Herve De La Vauvre, *President*
Darrell Portz, *Vice Pres*
Kingman Yue, *Vice Pres*
Tim Irwin, *Maint Spvr*
Michelle Ruiz, *Production*
EMP: 3
SQ FT: 250,000
SALES (est): 230.6MM
SALES (corp-wide): 1B **Privately Held**
SIC: 2099 Seasonings: dry mixes; spices, including grinding

(G-454)
HANDS TO WORK RAILROADING
12217 S Cicero Ave (60803-2906)
PHONE................................708 489-9776
Jim Bradley, *Owner*
EMP: 2
SALES (est): 200.4K **Privately Held**
SIC: 2813 5945 Helium; hobbies

(G-455)
HATTAN TOOL COMPANY
4909 W 128th Pl (60803-3011)
PHONE................................708 597-9308
Robert Hattan, *President*
Loretta Hattan, *Admin Sec*
EMP: 9
SQ FT: 7,000
SALES (est): 1.2MM **Privately Held**
SIC: 3599 7692 3544 Machine shop, jobbing & repair; welding repair; special dies, tools, jigs & fixtures

(G-456)
HAWK FASTENER SERVICES
12324 S Laramie Ave (60803-3231)
PHONE................................708 489-2000
Joe Lamantia, *Owner*
▲ **EMP:** 10
SALES (est): 660K **Privately Held**
WEB: www.hawkfastservices.com
SIC: 3965 Fasteners

(G-457)
INDUSTRIAL WELDER REBUILDERS
11700 S Mayfield Ave (60803-3565)
PHONE................................708 371-5688
Arnold Franker, *President*
Margaret Franker, *Vice Pres*
EMP: 5 EST: 1978
SQ FT: 5,050
SALES (est): 929.7K **Privately Held**
SIC: 7699 7692 5084 7629 Welding equipment repair; generators; engines & parts, diesel; electrical repair shops; motors & generators; welding apparatus

(G-458)
IPR SYSTEMS INC
11651 S Mayfield Ave (60803-6007)
PHONE................................708 385-7500
Eugene Tylka, *President*
Caroline M Tylka, *Admin Sec*
EMP: 8
SQ FT: 10,000
SALES: 750K **Privately Held**
SIC: 3679 3677 3674 3612 Rectifiers, electronic; electronic transformers; semiconductors & related devices; transformers, except electric

(G-459)
J & J CARBIDE & TOOL INC
5656 W 120th St (60803-3410)
PHONE................................708 489-0300
Spero Pavlopoulos, *President*
Spero Pavlopoulos, *President*
John Pavlopoulos, *Principal*
Thomas Pavlopoulos, *Vice Pres*
▲ **EMP:** 50 EST: 1966
SQ FT: 20,000
SALES (est): 11.6MM **Privately Held**
WEB: www.jandjcarbide.com
SIC: 3545 3544 Machine tool attachments & accessories; special dies & tools

(G-460)
J & J SNACK FOODS CORP
Also Called: Labriola Baking
3701 W 128th Pl (60803-1514)
PHONE................................708 377-0400
EMP: 235
SALES (corp-wide): 1.1B **Publicly Held**
SIC: 2051 Bread, all types (white, wheat, rye, etc): fresh or frozen; bakery: wholesale or wholesale/retail combined
PA: J & J Snack Foods Corp.
6000 Central Hwy
Pennsauken NJ 08109
856 665-9533

(G-461)
J & L CNC MACHINING INC
12633 S Springfield Ave (60803-1410)
PHONE................................708 388-2090
Jerry Mszal, *Principal*
EMP: 5
SALES (est): 909.4K **Privately Held**
SIC: 3599 Machine shop, jobbing & repair

(G-462)
K C AUDIO
4824 W 129th St (60803-3016)
PHONE................................708 636-4928
Karl Cira, *Owner*
EMP: 2
SALES (est): 306K **Privately Held**
SIC: 3651 Audio electronic systems

(G-463)
KASTALON INC
Also Called: Kastalon Polyurethane Products
4100 W 124th Ct (60803-1876)
PHONE................................708 389-2210
R Bruce Dement, *President*
Joe Krussel, *Plant Engr*
Ted Burke, *Design Engr*
Marta Zwierz, *Design Engr*
Darrell Johanneman, *CFO*
▲ **EMP:** 75 EST: 1963
SQ FT: 50,000
SALES (est): 15.9MM **Privately Held**
WEB: www.kastalon.com
SIC: 2821 Plastics materials & resins

(G-464)
KING METAL CO
4200 W 122nd St (60803-2408)
PHONE................................708 388-3845
Douglas M Heinking, *President*
Mary Ann Heinking, *Admin Sec*
EMP: 6
SQ FT: 5,200
SALES (est): 1.1MM **Privately Held**
SIC: 3446 3441 Ornamental metalwork; fabricated structural metal

(G-465)
KOCSIS BROTHERS MACHINE CO (PA)
11755 S Austin Ave (60803-6002)
PHONE................................708 597-8110
Louis Kocsis, *President*
Louie Kocsis Jr, *Opers Mgr*
Rich Hresan, *Opers Staff*
Jim Selinger, *Production*
Todd Triller, *Purchasing*
▲ **EMP:** 90
SQ FT: 55,000

Alsip - Cook County (G-466)

SALES (est): 21.5MM **Privately Held**
WEB: www.kocsisbros.com
SIC: 3599 Machine shop, jobbing & repair

(G-466)
KOCSIS TECHNOLOGIES INC (PA)
11755 S Austin Ave (60803-6002)
PHONE..............................708 597-4177
Sandra Kocsis, *President*
Louis Kocsis Jr, *Vice Pres*
Mike Vincent, *Mfg Mgr*
Sandra Kocsis-Rogalski, *Engineer*
EMP: 15
SALES (est): 16.9MM **Privately Held**
SIC: 3593 3492 Fluid power actuators, hydraulic or pneumatic; fluid power cylinders, hydraulic or pneumatic; control valves, fluid power: hydraulic & pneumatic

(G-467)
KOCSIS TECHNOLOGIES INC
Also Called: Kocisis Brothers Machine
11755 S Austin Ave (60803-6002)
PHONE..............................708 597-4177
Louis Kocsis Sr, *Manager*
EMP: 5 **Privately Held**
SIC: 3593 3594 3492 Fluid power actuators, hydraulic or pneumatic; fluid power cylinders, hydraulic or pneumatic; hydrostatic drives (transmissions); control valves, fluid power: hydraulic & pneumatic
PA: Kocsis Technologies, Inc.
  11755 S Austin Ave
  Alsip IL 60803

(G-468)
LA CRIOLLA INC
12828 S Ridgeway Ave (60803-1529)
PHONE..............................312 243-8882
Carmen L Maldonado, *President*
Sylvia Maldonado, *Vice Pres*
EMP: 30
SQ FT: 6,000
SALES (est): 6.2MM **Privately Held**
WEB: www.lacriolla.com
SIC: 5149 2099 Spices & seasonings; natural & organic foods; dried or canned foods; food preparations

(G-469)
LOMBARD INVESTMENT COMPANY (PA)
4245 W 123rd St (60803-1805)
PHONE..............................708 389-1060
George Lombard, *President*
John Lombard, *Vice Pres*
EMP: 75
SQ FT: 50,000
SALES: 784.8K **Privately Held**
SIC: 1542 1791 3272 Commercial & office building contractors; precast concrete structural framing or panels, placing of; concrete products, precast

(G-470)
LUTTRELL ENGRAVING INC
Also Called: Lei Graphics
5000 W 128th Pl (60803-3230)
PHONE..............................708 489-3800
Ravon Luttrell, *President*
Christine Luttrell, *Corp Secy*
EMP: 20
SQ FT: 9,916
SALES: 2MM **Privately Held**
WEB: www.leigraphics.com
SIC: 3555 7336 2796 Printing plates; graphic arts & related design; platemaking services

(G-471)
MACHINE CONTROL SYSTEMS INC
12549 S Laramie Ave (60803-3223)
PHONE..............................708 597-1200
William Plummer, *Manager*
EMP: 6
SQ FT: 6,000
SALES (corp-wide): 680.6K **Privately Held**
SIC: 3613 3625 Control panels, electric; generator control & metering panels; relays & industrial controls
PA: Machine Control Systems, Inc
  12424 S Austin Ave
  Palos Heights IL 60463
  708 389-2160

(G-472)
MARTIN EXPLORATION MGT CO (PA)
Also Called: Martin Oil
4501 W 127th St (60803-2609)
PHONE..............................708 385-6500
Carl C Greer, *President*
Harry Vasels, *Vice Pres*
EMP: 9
SQ FT: 3,550
SALES (est): 3.3MM **Privately Held**
SIC: 1382 Oil & gas exploration services

(G-473)
MASTERS & ALLOY LLC
12841 S Pulaski Rd (60803-1916)
PHONE..............................312 582-1880
Nick Muschong,
EMP: 9
SALES (est): 399.8K
SALES (corp-wide): 116.8MM **Privately Held**
SIC: 3313 Alloys, additive, except copper: not made in blast furnaces
PA: Universal Scrap Metals, Inc.
  2500 W Fulton St
  Chicago IL 60612
  312 666-0011

(G-474)
MAUREY INSTRUMENT CORP
5959 W 115th St (60803-5151)
PHONE..............................708 388-9898
Elizabeth Petrus, *President*
Mary Kay Gadomski, *Vice Pres*
EMP: 16 EST: 1952
SQ FT: 10,000
SALES: 1MM **Privately Held**
WEB: www.maureyinstrument.com
SIC: 3825 3676 3625 3621 Potentiometric instruments, except industrial process type; electronic resistors; relays & industrial controls; motors & generators

(G-475)
MAY WOOD INDUSTRIES INC
12636 S Springfield Ave (60803-1411)
PHONE..............................708 489-1515
Nancy Gee, *President*
EMP: 15 EST: 1951
SQ FT: 15,000
SALES: 2.8MM **Privately Held**
SIC: 2431 Millwork

(G-476)
MENASHA PACKAGING COMPANY LLC
11671 S Central Ave (60803)
PHONE..............................708 853-5450
Dennis Graf, *Branch Mgr*
EMP: 300
SALES (corp-wide): 2.2B **Privately Held**
SIC: 2653 Sheets, corrugated: made from purchased materials
HQ: Menasha Packaging Company, Llc
  1645 Bergstrom Rd
  Neenah WI 54956
  920 751-1000

(G-477)
MIDWAY MACHINE & TOOL CO INC
5828 W 117th Pl (60803-6019)
PHONE..............................708 385-3450
John J Koszylko, *President*
EMP: 7
SQ FT: 9,000
SALES (est): 951.6K **Privately Held**
SIC: 3599 7692 Machine shop, jobbing & repair; welding repair

(G-478)
MIDWEST LMINATING COATINGS INC
12650 S Laramie Ave (60803-3226)
PHONE..............................708 653-9500
Philip G Carollo, *President*
John Watkins, *COO*
Jay Carollo, *Vice Pres*
Jo Ann Miller, *Admin Sec*
EMP: 25
SQ FT: 100,000
SALES (est): 6.6MM **Privately Held**
SIC: 2671 3353 3081 2672 Paper coated or laminated for packaging; plastic film, coated or laminated for packaging; foil, aluminum; unsupported plastics film & sheet; coated & laminated paper

(G-479)
MIDWEST MACHINE SERVICE INC
5632 Pleasant Blvd (60803)
PHONE..............................708 229-1122
Ronald Zima, *President*
Jeff Eddington, *Vice Pres*
Mark Larson, *Regl Sales Mgr*
EMP: 15
SQ FT: 2,000
SALES (est): 2MM **Privately Held**
SIC: 3599 7629 Machine shop, jobbing & repair; electrical repair shops

(G-480)
MJT INCORPORATED
Also Called: Ewert, Inc.
5801 W 117th Pl (60803-6018)
PHONE..............................708 597-0059
Marsha J Trosper, *President*
Michael Rockouski, *Vice Pres*
Andy Trosper, *Vice Pres*
EMP: 7
SQ FT: 5,000
SALES (est): 526.9K **Privately Held**
SIC: 3429 Door opening & closing devices, except electrical; keys, locks & related hardware; door locks, bolts & checks; keys & key blanks

(G-481)
MOBILOC LLC
5800 W 117th Pl (60803-6019)
PHONE..............................773 742-1329
Charles Morrissey, *Chairman*
EMP: 9
SALES (est): 673.2K **Privately Held**
SIC: 3699 Security devices

(G-482)
NAEGELE INC
5661 W 120th St (60803-3449)
PHONE..............................708 388-7766
Richard Naegele, *President*
Chuck Naegele, *Engineer*
Ken Hagedorn, *VP Sales*
Mike Philip, *Sales Mgr*
Jon Thompson, *Sales Staff*
◆ EMP: 6
SALES (est): 901.7K **Privately Held**
WEB: www.naegele-inc.com
SIC: 3556 Food products machinery

(G-483)
NELSON SASH SYSTEMS INC
Also Called: Nss Exteriors
4650 W 120th St (60803-2317)
PHONE..............................708 385-5815
Paul Mitoraj, *President*
Charise Mitoraj, *Admin Sec*
EMP: 8
SQ FT: 12,000
SALES: 1.3MM **Privately Held**
SIC: 3442 Window & door frames; sash, door or window: metal

(G-484)
NEW PROCESS STEEL LP
Also Called: N P S
5761 W 118th St (60803-6011)
PHONE..............................708 389-3380
Jason Bates, *Plant Mgr*
Tom Claes, *Sales/Mktg Mgr*
EMP: 63
SALES (corp-wide): 77.3MM **Privately Held**
SIC: 3479 3316 5051 Galvanizing of iron, steel or end-formed products; sheet, steel, cold-rolled: from purchased hot-rolled; metals service centers & offices; steel; sheets, galvanized or other coated; stampings, metal
HQ: New Process Steel, L.P.
  1322 N Post Oak Rd
  Houston TX 77055
  713 686-9631

(G-485)
NUFARM AMERICAS INC (HQ)
Also Called: Nufarm North American Office
11901 S Austin Ave (60803-6013)
PHONE..............................708 377-1330
Brendan Deck, *President*
Greg Hunt, *Managing Dir*
Thomas McDaniel, *Regional Mgr*
Wigbold Nieuwenhuis, *Opers Staff*
Terri Harrop, *Purchasing*
▲ EMP: 60
SQ FT: 15,000
SALES (est): 476.7MM **Privately Held**
WEB: www.nufarm.com
SIC: 2869 2879 Industrial organic chemicals; agricultural chemicals

(G-486)
NUMERICAL CONTROL INCORPORATED
12325 S Keeler Ave (60803-1812)
PHONE..............................708 389-8140
Timothy Gorham, *President*
Douglas Buchler, *President*
EMP: 9 EST: 1965
SQ FT: 6,000
SALES (est): 1.7MM **Privately Held**
SIC: 3569 7699 3613 Assembly machines, non-metalworking; professional instrument repair services; switchgear & switchboard apparatus

(G-487)
NUSEED AMERICAS INC (HQ)
11901 S Austin Ave (60803-6013)
PHONE..............................800 345-3330
Darryl Matthews, *President*
Trygg Olson, *Sales Staff*
Alison Stone, *Manager*
EMP: 22
SALES (est): 3.8MM **Privately Held**
SIC: 2879 Agricultural chemicals

(G-488)
OZINGA CHICAGO READY MIX CON
12660 S Laramie Ave (60803-3226)
PHONE..............................708 479-9050
EMP: 43
SALES (corp-wide): 434.5MM **Privately Held**
SIC: 3273 Ready-mixed concrete
HQ: Ozinga Chicago Ready Mix Concrete, Inc
  2255 S Lumber St
  Chicago IL 60616

(G-489)
PENNANT FOODS
11746 S Austin Ave (60803-6003)
PHONE..............................708 752-8730
EMP: 4
SALES (est): 331.1K **Privately Held**
SIC: 5141 2099 Food brokers; food preparations

(G-490)
PETERSON ELCTR-MSICAL PDTS INC
11601 S Mayfield Ave (60803-6007)
PHONE..............................708 388-3311
Scott Peterson, *President*
Richard Peterson, *Chairman*
Patrick Bovenizer, *Vice Pres*
▲ EMP: 38
SQ FT: 18,000
SALES (est): 7.7MM **Privately Held**
SIC: 3679 3931 Electronic switches; musical instruments

(G-491)
PHOENIX BUSINESS SOLUTIONS LLC
12543 S Laramie Ave (60803-3223)
PHONE..............................708 388-1330
Mike Janousek, *General Mgr*
Jim Kapustiak, *Superintendent*
Nick Banasiak, *Foreman/Supr*
Brian Richardson, *Foreman/Supr*
Bill Stone, *Foreman/Supr*
EMP: 41
SQ FT: 5,000

GEOGRAPHIC SECTION
Alsip - Cook County (G-518)

SALES (est): 9.5MM **Privately Held**
WEB: www.getpbsnow.com
SIC: **1731** 2752 General electrical contractor; advertising posters, lithographed

(G-492)
PINTAS CULTURED MARBLE
5859 W 117th Pl (60803-6018)
PHONE.....................708 385-3360
John A Pinta, *President*
Gerald Pinta, *Vice Pres*
James Pinta, *Vice Pres*
EMP: 26
SQ FT: 42,000
SALES (est): 2.1MM **Privately Held**
SIC: **3281** 2434 2821 Marble, building: cut & shaped; wood kitchen cabinets; plastics materials & resins

(G-493)
PLASTIPAK PACKAGING INC
12325 S Laramie Ave (60803-3206)
PHONE.....................708 385-0721
Perry Dailey, *Branch Mgr*
EMP: 105
SALES (corp-wide): 1.3B **Privately Held**
SIC: **3089** 3085 Pallets, plastic; plastics bottles
HQ: Plastipak Packaging, Inc.
 41605 Ann Arbor Rd E
 Plymouth MI 48170
 734 455-3600

(G-494)
POLMAX LLC
Also Called: Experior Transport
12161 S Central Ave (60803-3405)
PHONE.....................708 843-8300
Tom Dulian, *CEO*
Norbert Loszewski, *President*
Dan Cialdella, *Vice Pres*
Konrad Szczepaniec, *Assoc VP*
Conrad Szccetaniez, *Controller*
EMP: 250
SQ FT: 2,000
SALES (est): 58.5MM **Privately Held**
SIC: **4225** 3829 4111 General warehousing & storage; transits, surveyors'; local & suburban transit

(G-495)
PPG INDUSTRIES INC
Also Called: PPG 5524
5151 W 122nd St (60803-3102)
PHONE.....................708 597-7044
Chris Gallus, *Branch Mgr*
EMP: 4
SALES (corp-wide): 15.1B **Publicly Held**
SIC: **2851** Paints & allied products
PA: Ppg Industries, Inc.
 1 Ppg Pl
 Pittsburgh PA 15272
 412 434-3131

(G-496)
PRAIRIELAND FOOD PRODUCTS CO
3750 W 131st St (60803-1519)
PHONE.....................708 396-8826
Gary Trepina, *President*
Dean Lardner, *Vice Pres*
Tom Musil, *Treasurer*
Victor Sharp Jr, *Admin Sec*
EMP: 5
SQ FT: 10,000
SALES (est): 641K **Privately Held**
SIC: **2096** Potato chips & similar snacks

(G-497)
PRESTONE PRODUCTS CORPORATION
Also Called: Prestone Pdts Kik Cstomer Pdts
13160 S Pulaski Rd (60803-2009)
PHONE.....................708 371-3000
Rob Salas, *Plant Mgr*
EMP: 65
SALES (corp-wide): 3.2MM **Privately Held**
SIC: **2899** Antifreeze compounds
HQ: Prestone Products Corporation
 6250 N River Rd Ste 6000
 Rosemont IL 60018

(G-498)
PROCESS AND CONTROL SYSTEMS
5836 W 117th Pl (60803-6019)
PHONE.....................708 293-0557
John Wojcik, *President*
Jeff Koehler, *Vice Pres*
Jeffery Koehler, *Vice Pres*
Karl Kurgvel, *Vice Pres*
John Frederick, *Admin Sec*
EMP: 17
SQ FT: 10,000
SALES (est): 3.8MM **Privately Held**
SIC: **7371** 3625 Custom computer programming services; control equipment, electric

(G-499)
QUALITY SNACK FOODS INC
Also Called: Q S F
3750 W 131st St (60803-1503)
PHONE.....................708 377-7120
Victor L Sharp Jr, *President*
Gary S Trepina, *Exec VP*
Dean Lardner, *Vice Pres*
Tom Musil, *Site Mgr*
Deborah L Trepina, *Treasurer*
◆ EMP: 70
SQ FT: 25,000
SALES (est): 12.5MM **Privately Held**
SIC: **2096** Potato chips & similar snacks

(G-500)
R K PRECISION MACHINE INC
12512 S Springfield Ave (60803-1409)
PHONE.....................574 293-0231
Tom Rosinski, *President*
EMP: 3
SQ FT: 5,500
SALES (est): 210K **Privately Held**
SIC: **3599** Machine shop, jobbing & repair

(G-501)
RAE PRODUCTS AND CHEM CORP (PA)
11638 S Mayfield Ave (60803-6010)
PHONE.....................708 396-1984
Donna Gruenberg, *President*
Samantha Zickus, *Treasurer*
Samantha Morek, *Admin Sec*
EMP: 6
SQ FT: 46,000
SALES (est): 7MM **Privately Held**
SIC: **5169** 3542 Sealants; marking machines

(G-502)
RELIANCE DENTAL MFG CO
5805 W 117th Pl (60803-6018)
P.O. Box 38, Worth (60482-0038)
PHONE.....................708 597-6694
Robert Faxel, *President*
Richard Faxel, *Vice Pres*
EMP: 7 EST: 1894
SQ FT: 7,500
SALES (est): 840K **Privately Held**
WEB: www.reliancedental.net
SIC: **3843** Dental materials

(G-503)
RESOURCE PLASTICS INC
5623 W 115th St (60803-5125)
PHONE.....................708 389-3558
Bill Steinhaus, *President*
Kim McCormies, *Manager*
EMP: 70
SQ FT: 170,563
SALES (est): 23.2MM **Privately Held**
SIC: **5085** 3089 Industrial supplies; plastic processing

(G-504)
RM LUCAS CO (PA)
Also Called: Lucas Coatings
12400 S Laramie Ave (60803-3209)
PHONE.....................773 523-4300
Robert Barry, *President*
Joe Murphy, *COO*
Barbara B Zahorik, *Purchasing*
Brandon Applegate, *Controller*
Jeff V Pelt, *Sales Mgr*
▼ EMP: 35 EST: 1935
SQ FT: 92,000
SALES (est): 11.9MM **Privately Held**
WEB: www.rmlucas.com
SIC: **2952** 2891 1761 Roofing materials; adhesives & sealants; roofing contractor

(G-505)
ROTH METAL FABRICATORS CORP
3735 W 128th Pl (60803-1514)
PHONE.....................708 371-8300
Donald Wolf, *President*
Jeremy Wolf, *Vice Pres*
Jon Wolf, *Vice Pres*
Beverly Marsek, *Admin Sec*
EMP: 8
SQ FT: 30,000
SALES (est): 1.5MM **Privately Held**
SIC: **3444** 3229 3469 3443 Concrete forms, sheet metal; blocks & bricks, glass; boxes: tool, lunch, mail, etc.: stamped metal; chutes, metal plate; fabricated structural metal

(G-506)
RPI EXTRUSION CO
5623 W 115th St (60803-5125)
PHONE.....................708 389-2584
Robert Murphy, *Owner*
EMP: 5
SALES (est): 576.6K **Privately Held**
SIC: **3089** Extruded finished plastic products

(G-507)
RUSSO WHOLESALE MEAT INC
12306 S Cicero Ave (60803-2908)
PHONE.....................708 385-0500
Frank Russo, *President*
Joseph Russo, *Admin Sec*
EMP: 5 EST: 1995
SQ FT: 2,700
SALES (est): 590.5K **Privately Held**
SIC: **2013** 5147 2045 2033 Sausages & related products, from purchased meat; meats & meat products; pizza mixes: from purchased flour; pizza doughs, prepared: from purchased flour; pizza sauce: packaged in cans, jars, etc.; pizza supplies

(G-508)
S & W MACHINE WORKS INC
12623 S Kroll Dr (60803-3221)
PHONE.....................708 597-6043
Phillip Wisniewski, *President*
William Shalloo, *Admin Sec*
EMP: 6
SQ FT: 3,600
SALES (est): 852.8K **Privately Held**
SIC: **3599** Machine shop, jobbing & repair

(G-509)
SEALMASTER/ALSIP
5844 W 117th Pl (60803-6019)
PHONE.....................708 489-0900
Kyle Arlen, *Manager*
EMP: 3
SALES (est): 226.9K **Privately Held**
SIC: **2951** Asphalt paving mixtures & blocks

(G-510)
SIGN OUTLET INC
5516 W Cal Sag Rd (60803-3309)
PHONE.....................708 824-2222
Darren Rust, *President*
EMP: 4
SQ FT: 3,000
SALES (est): 597.2K **Privately Held**
WEB: www.signoutletusa.com
SIC: **3993** Neon signs

(G-511)
SOTIROS FOODS INC
12560 S Holiday Dr Ste B (60803-3248)
PHONE.....................708 371-0002
Glynn Searl, *President*
EMP: 4
SALES (est): 879.9K **Privately Held**
SIC: **5141** 2099 5149 Food brokers; food preparations; groceries & related products

(G-512)
SOUTHWEST PRINTING CO
12003 S Pulaski Rd (60803-1221)
PHONE.....................708 389-0800
Paul Krueger, *President*

Neva C Krueger, *Treasurer*
EMP: 5
SQ FT: 8,472
SALES (est): 544.5K **Privately Held**
WEB: www.swprints4u.com
SIC: **2752** 2759 Commercial printing, offset; commercial printing

(G-513)
SUBURBAN INDUS TL & MFG CO
11606 S Mayfield Ave (60803-6010)
PHONE.....................708 597-7788
Richard Kovach, *President*
Irene Kovach, *Corp Secy*
Mike Kovach, *Vice Pres*
EMP: 10
SQ FT: 8,000
SALES (est): 1.6MM **Privately Held**
SIC: **3599** Machine shop, jobbing & repair

(G-514)
TAYCORP INC (PA)
Also Called: Taylor Spring Mfg. Co.
5700 W 120th St (60803-3710)
PHONE.....................708 629-0921
John Tyrakowski, *President*
John M Tyrakowski, *President*
Henry Tyrakowski, *Chairman*
Steven C Tyrakowski, *Corp Secy*
Rick Melody, *Research*
▲ EMP: 48 EST: 1950
SQ FT: 16,000
SALES (est): 10.6MM **Privately Held**
WEB: www.taylorspring.com
SIC: **3495** 3677 Wire springs; electronic coils, transformers & other inductors

(G-515)
TAYLORS CANDY INC
4855 W 115th St (60803-2864)
PHONE.....................708 371-0332
Douglas R Taylor, *President*
Gregory D Taylor, *Vice Pres*
EMP: 28
SQ FT: 28,000
SALES (est): 4.6MM **Privately Held**
SIC: **7389** 2064 Packaging & labeling services; candy & other confectionery products; popcorn balls or other treated popcorn products

(G-516)
TMS MANUFACTURING CO
Also Called: Wc Richards
3555 W 123rd St (60803-4125)
PHONE.....................847 353-8000
Steven Murray, *President*
Daniel Johnson, *Vice Pres*
Richard Zilinsky, *CFO*
Bojana Koprivica, *Controller*
EMP: 30 EST: 2010
SALES (est): 350.2K
SALES (corp-wide): 32.1MM **Privately Held**
WEB: www.wcrichards.com
SIC: **2851** Paints & allied products
PA: Terrazzo & Marble Supply Co. Of Illinois
 77 Wheeling Rd
 Wheeling IL 60090
 847 353-8000

(G-517)
UESCO INDUSTRIES INC
Also Called: Service Center
5908 W 118th St (60803-6037)
P.O. Box 489, Worth (60482-0489)
PHONE.....................708 385-7700
EMP: 8
SALES (corp-wide): 8.4MM **Privately Held**
SIC: **3531** 3536 5084 Mfg Construction Machinery Mfg Hoists/Cranes/Monorails Whol Industrial Equipment
PA: Uesco Industries, Inc.
 5908 W 118th St
 Alsip IL 60803
 800 325-8372

(G-518)
UESCO INDUSTRIES INC
Also Called: Uesco Crane
5908 W 118th St (60803-6037)
PHONE.....................800 325-8372
Donald Marks, *President*

Tom Stanek, *Plant Mgr*
Mike Jemilo, *Purch Dir*
Randy Giovannetti, *Parts Mgr*
Jim Jakubal, *Purchasing*
◆ **EMP:** 42
SQ FT: 20,000
SALES (est): 15.5MM **Privately Held**
SIC: 3536 7699 5063 Cranes, overhead traveling; industrial machinery & equipment repair; electrical supplies

(G-519)
UNION CARBIDE CORPORATION
12840 S Pulaski Rd (60803-1999)
PHONE 708 396-3000
Patrick E Gottschalk, *Branch Mgr*
EMP: 57
SALES (corp-wide): 42.9B **Publicly Held**
SIC: 2869 Ethylene oxide
HQ: Union Carbide Corporation
1254 Enclave Pkwy
Houston TX 77077
281 966-2727

(G-520)
VAN LEER CONTAINERS INC (HQ)
4300 W 130th St (60803-2094)
PHONE 708 371-4777
Tony A Riley, *President*
Linda Deady, *Admin Sec*
◆ **EMP:** 150
SQ FT: 415,000
SALES (est): 51.6MM
SALES (corp-wide): 4.6B **Publicly Held**
SIC: 3412 Metal barrels, drums & pails
PA: Greif, Inc.
425 Winter Rd
Delaware OH 43015
740 549-6000

(G-521)
VENTUREDYNE LTD
Scientific Dust Collectors
4101 W 126th St (60803-1901)
PHONE 708 597-7090
Michael Gerardi, *General Mgr*
Donald Marshall, *Materials Mgr*
John Lampos, *Engineer*
Brian Mathews, *Engineer*
Dale Purdy, *Marketing Staff*
EMP: 30
SALES (corp-wide): 146.4MM **Privately Held**
SIC: 3829 Measuring & controlling devices
PA: Venturedyne, Ltd.
600 College Ave
Pewaukee WI 53072
262 691-9900

(G-522)
VERSATILITY TL WORKS MFG INC
Also Called: Vtw
11532 S Mayfield Ave (60803-6009)
PHONE 708 389-8909
Edward Freimuth Jr, *President*
Margarete Freimuth, *Admin Sec*
EMP: 17
SQ FT: 20,000
SALES (est): 4MM **Privately Held**
SIC: 3541 5013 Machine tool replacement & repair parts, metal cutting types; automotive stampings

(G-523)
W & K MACHINING INC
4711 W 120th St (60803-2318)
PHONE 708 430-9000
EMP: 8
SALES (est): 850.1K **Privately Held**
SIC: 3599 Machine shop, jobbing & repair

(G-524)
WEMCO INC
11721 S Austin Ave (60803-6002)
PHONE 708 388-1980
Brandon Goodwin, *President*
William Kuhn, *Vice Pres*
EMP: 17
SQ FT: 12,000
SALES: 1.5MM **Privately Held**
WEB: www.wmcinc.net
SIC: 3556 7699 7692 Food products machinery; industrial machinery & equipment repair; welding repair

(G-525)
WOODWORK REFINED CORPORATION
5917 W 115th St (60803-5151)
PHONE 708 385-7255
William Cavanagh, *President*
Amy C Doan, *Vice Pres*
EMP: 6
SQ FT: 5,800
SALES: 500K **Privately Held**
SIC: 2431 Millwork

(G-526)
WORLDWIDE TILES LTD INC
11708 S Mayfield Ave (60803-3565)
PHONE 708 389-2992
EMP: 3 **EST:** 2004
SALES (est): 180K **Privately Held**
SIC: 3281 5032 Mfg Cut Stone/Products Whol Brick/Stone Material

(G-527)
WORTH STEEL AND MACHINE CO
4001 W 123rd St (60803-1801)
PHONE 708 388-6300
William Bender, *President*
Vita Bender, *President*
Jim Degrado, *General Mgr*
Marge Acevedo, *Principal*
Robert Bender, *Principal*
▲ **EMP:** 25
SQ FT: 45,000
SALES (est): 10.2MM **Privately Held**
SIC: 3547 3316 Rolling mill machinery; bars, steel, cold finished, from purchased hot-rolled

(G-528)
WRAP-ON COMPANY LLC
11756 S Austin Ave (60803-6003)
PHONE 708 496-2150
David McArdle, *President*
Rodney Welty, *Admin Sec*
▲ **EMP:** 25
SQ FT: 50,000
SALES: 3.8MM
SALES (corp-wide): 35.2MM **Privately Held**
WEB: www.wrap-on.com
SIC: 3494 Plumbing & heating valves; pipe fittings
PA: Mcardle Ltd.
142 W Station St
Barrington IL 60010
630 584-6580

Altamont
Effingham County

(G-529)
ALTAMONT NEWS
7 Do It Dr (62411-1135)
P.O. Box 315 (62411-0315)
PHONE 618 483-6176
Omer Siebert, *Partner*
Norma Siebert, *Partner*
EMP: 6 **EST:** 1881
SQ FT: 2,100
SALES (est): 100K **Privately Held**
SIC: 2711 Newspapers: publishing only, not printed on site

(G-530)
ARCHER-DANIELS-MIDLAND COMPANY
Also Called: ADM
601 W Division St (62411-1145)
P.O. Box 247 (62411-0247)
PHONE 618 483-6171
Dennis Schall, *Manager*
EMP: 6
SALES (corp-wide): 64.6B **Publicly Held**
SIC: 2041 5191 2875 Flour & other grain mill products; farm supplies; fertilizers, mixing only
PA: Archer-Daniels-Midland Company
77 W Wacker Dr Ste 4600
Chicago IL 60601
312 634-8100

(G-531)
BETTER NEWS PAPERS INC
Also Called: Altonat
118 N Main St (62411-1448)
P.O. Box 315 (62411-0315)
PHONE 618 483-6176
Mark Hoskins, *Manager*
EMP: 6
SALES (corp-wide): 2.6MM **Privately Held**
SIC: 2711 Newspapers: publishing only, not printed on site; newspapers, publishing & printing
PA: Better News Papers, Inc
314 E Church St Ste 1
Mascoutah IL 62258
618 566-8282

(G-532)
FREDERKING CONSTRUCTION CO
8595 N 300th St (62411-3503)
PHONE 618 483-5031
David W Frederking, *President*
Shane Frederking, *Vice Pres*
Sandy Heyden, *Admin Sec*
EMP: 9 **EST:** 1977
SQ FT: 2,000
SALES (est): 632.4K **Privately Held**
SIC: 1521 1522 1542 2452 New construction, single-family houses; multi-family dwelling construction; nonresidential construction; prefabricated buildings, wood

(G-533)
H & D MOTOR SERVICE
901 W Cumberland Rd (62411-1000)
PHONE 217 342-3262
Robert L Hardiek, *Owner*
EMP: 3 **EST:** 1945
SQ FT: 2,400
SALES (est): 110K **Privately Held**
SIC: 3599 5013 Machine shop, jobbing & repair; automotive supplies & parts; automotive supplies

(G-534)
IRWIN SEATING COMPANY
610 E Cumberland Rd (62411-1640)
P.O. Box 320 (62411-0320)
PHONE 618 483-6157
Win Irwin, *CEO*
Pam Lecrone, *Purchasing*
Steve Grussing, *Manager*
EMP: 120
SALES (corp-wide): 73.7MM **Privately Held**
SIC: 2531 Stadium furniture
HQ: Irwin Seating Company
3251 Fruit Ridge Ave Nw
Grand Rapids MI 49544
616 574-7400

(G-535)
IRWIN TELESCOPIC SEATING CO
610 E Cumberland Rd (62411-1640)
P.O. Box 320 (62411-0320)
PHONE 618 483-6157
Eric Conrad, *President*
Doug Waldo, *Senior VP*
Larry Conner, *Vice Pres*
Damon Duckworth, *Production*
Don Waltrop, *Purch Mgr*
▲ **EMP:** 120
SQ FT: 112,000
SALES (est): 55.7K
SALES (corp-wide): 73.7MM **Privately Held**
SIC: 2531 Stadium furniture
PA: Irwin Seating Holding Company
3251 Fruit Ridge Ave Nw
Grand Rapids MI 49544
616 574-7400

(G-536)
PROMARK ADVERTISING SPECIALTIE
4 N Frontage Rd (62411-3563)
P.O. Box 285 (62411-0285)
PHONE 618 483-6025
Dawn Burrow, *Principal*
EMP: 5

SALES (est): 420.4K **Privately Held**
SIC: 2759 5941 7311 Screen printing; sporting goods & bicycle shops; advertising agencies

(G-537)
RAMSEY WELDING INC
5360 E 900th Ave (62411-2446)
PHONE 618 483-6248
Russell Ramsey, *President*
Rosemary Holland, *Admin Asst*
EMP: 20
SALES: 6MM **Privately Held**
SIC: 7692 Cracked casting repair

Alto Pass
Union County

(G-538)
ALTO VINEYARDS LIMITED (PA)
8515 Highway 127 (62905-2033)
P.O. Box 51 (62905-0051)
PHONE 618 893-4898
Paul Renzaglia, *President*
EMP: 13
SQ FT: 5,000
SALES (est): 2.4MM **Privately Held**
SIC: 5182 2084 Liquor; wines, brandy & brandy spirits

(G-539)
HEDMAN ORCHARD AND VINEYARD
560 Chestnut St (62905-1000)
PHONE 618 893-4923
Anders Hedman, *Owner*
EMP: 4
SALES (est): 383.3K **Privately Held**
SIC: 2084 Wines

Alton
Madison County

(G-540)
ABBOTT MACHINE CO (PA)
700 W Broadway (62002-6104)
P.O. Box 149 (62002-0149)
PHONE 618 465-1898
Rick Abbott, *President*
Robert W Abbott, *Principal*
Michael St Peters, *Corp Secy*
Michael Peters, *Vice Pres*
Deborah Wade, *Admin Sec*
▲ **EMP:** 19
SQ FT: 46,000
SALES: 6MM **Privately Held**
WEB: www.abbottmachineco.com
SIC: 5084 3599 Machine tools & accessories; machine shop, jobbing & repair

(G-541)
ADVANTAGE NEWS
192a Alton Square Mall Dr (62002-5258)
PHONE 618 463-0612
Angie Fulgham, *President*
Fred Pollard, *Editor*
Pamela Isakson, *Accounts Mgr*
Pat Taulbee, *Accounts Mgr*
EMP: 3 **EST:** 2016
SALES (est): 144.3K **Privately Held**
WEB: www.advantagenews.com
SIC: 2711 Newspapers, publishing & printing

(G-542)
AEP INC
1225 Cabin Club Dr (62002-7415)
PHONE 618 466-7668
Peter Kuhn, *Principal*
EMP: 5
SALES (est): 325K **Privately Held**
SIC: 3089 5099 Plastics products; durable goods

(G-543)
ALTON SHEET METAL CORP
801 E Broadway (62002-6404)
P.O. Box 557 (62002-0557)
PHONE 618 462-0609
William N Knetzer, *President*

EMP: 18
SQ FT: 8,000
SALES (est): 3MM **Privately Held**
WEB: www.local268.com
SIC: 1711 3441 Warm air heating & air conditioning contractor; fabricated structural metal

(G-544)
B & B CUSTOM TS & GIFTS
2714 Corner Ct (62002-5328)
PHONE.....................................618 463-0443
Marsha Bennett, *Owner*
Kevan Bennett, *Owner*
EMP: 4
SQ FT: 2,400
SALES (est): 250K **Privately Held**
SIC: 2396 2395 Screen printing on fabric articles; embroidery & art needlework

(G-545)
B D ENTERPRISES
Also Called: B D Sport Photos and Trophies
655 E Broadway (62002)
PHONE.....................................618 462-5861
William Daniels, *Owner*
EMP: 3
SQ FT: 1,600
SALES (est): 80K **Privately Held**
SIC: 7335 5094 2759 Commercial photography; trophies; screen printing

(G-546)
C & L MANUFACTURING ENTPS
Also Called: Industrial Proccess and Sensor
2109 Holland St (62002-3339)
PHONE.....................................618 465-7623
Thomas Lehnen, *President*
Jesse Lehnen, *General Mgr*
EMP: 3 EST: 1923
SQ FT: 1,500
SALES: 100K **Privately Held**
WEB: www.ipscustom.com
SIC: 3269 3829 3357 3315 Pyrometer tubes; thermocouples; nonferrous wire-drawing & insulating; steel wire & related products

(G-547)
CLODFELTER ENGRAVING INC
2109 Holland St (62002-3339)
PHONE.....................................314 968-8418
Marvin Clodfelter, *President*
Teena Schtad, *Vice Pres*
EMP: 8
SQ FT: 4,000
SALES (est): 660K **Privately Held**
SIC: 2796 Engraving on copper, steel, wood or rubber: printing plates; photoengraving plates, linecuts or halftones

(G-548)
COPE & SONS ASPHALT
3510 Thomas Ave (62002-4119)
PHONE.....................................618 462-2207
Joanne Cope, *Owner*
EMP: 3
SALES (est): 161.9K **Privately Held**
SIC: 1771 2951 Blacktop (asphalt) work; asphalt paving mixtures & blocks

(G-549)
COPE PLASTICS INC (PA)
4441 Indl Dr (62002)
P.O. Box 129, Godfrey (62035-0129)
PHONE.....................................618 466-0221
Jane Saale, *CEO*
P Jane Saale, *President*
Jeff Maynard, *COO*
Gene A Appal, *Vice Pres*
James P McCormick, *Vice Pres*
EMP: 100 EST: 1946
SQ FT: 165,000
SALES (est): 246.9MM **Privately Held**
WEB: www.copeplastics.com
SIC: 5162 3599 Plastics sheets & rods; resins, synthetic; plastics products; machine & other job shop work

(G-550)
D & R MACHINE COMPANY INC (PA)
4131 Alby St (62002-4484)
PHONE.....................................618 465-5611
David Gotter, *CEO*
Rene A Gotter, *Vice Pres*
EMP: 7 EST: 1997
SQ FT: 7,000
SALES (est): 2.2MM **Privately Held**
WEB: www.dandrmachineco.com
SIC: 3599 Machine shop, jobbing & repair

(G-551)
D W TERRY WELDING COMPANY
1860 E Broadway (62002-6664)
PHONE.....................................618 433-9722
Erick Terry, *Principal*
EMP: 3
SALES (est): 192.5K **Privately Held**
SIC: 7692 1799 3812 3444 Welding repair; welding on site; search & navigation equipment; sheet metalwork

(G-552)
DIAMOND TEEZ & MORE LLC
4134 Alby St (62002-4478)
P.O. Box 55 (62002-0055)
PHONE.....................................618 579-9876
Cortez Davis, *Mng Member*
EMP: 4 EST: 2018
SALES: 30K **Privately Held**
SIC: 2396 5699 Screen printing on fabric articles; T-shirts, custom printed

(G-553)
DORAS SPINNING WHEEL INC
96 Northport Dr (62002-5940)
PHONE.....................................618 466-1900
Dora Vinson, *President*
Jeffrey S Vinson, *Corp Secy*
Margaret Engemann, *Vice Pres*
EMP: 3
SALES: 60K **Privately Held**
SIC: 2395 Embroidery products, except schiffli machine

(G-554)
EAGLE FORUM (PA)
322 State St Ste 301 (62002-6135)
PHONE.....................................618 462-5415
Phyllis Schlafly, *President*
Ryan Hite, *Comms Dir*
EMP: 6
SALES: 1MM **Privately Held**
SIC: 2731 2721 Pamphlets: publishing only, not printed on site; periodicals

(G-555)
ELECTRONICS BOUTIQUE AMER INC
128 Alton Sq (62002-5917)
PHONE.....................................618 465-3125
David Heasner, *Manager*
EMP: 5 **Publicly Held**
WEB: www.gamestop.com
SIC: 7372 Prepackaged software
HQ: Electronics Boutique Of America Inc.
625 Westport Pkwy
Grapevine TX 76051
817 424-2000

(G-556)
ENERGY SOLUTIONS INC
1520 Worden Ave (62002-4069)
PHONE.....................................618 465-5404
Bill Stoutenborough, *President*
Fay Stoutenborough, *Admin Sec*
EMP: 2
SQ FT: 4,000
SALES (est): 213.1K **Privately Held**
SIC: 1799 3443 Window treatment installation; heat exchangers: coolers (after, inter), condensers, etc.

(G-557)
HANLEY INDUSTRIES INC
3640 Seminary St (62002-5730)
P.O. Box 1058 (62002-1058)
PHONE.....................................618 465-8892
Danny Stahl, *President*
Don Elik, *Project Mgr*
Hubert Presley, *Prdtn Mgr*
Edward Maglasang, *CFO*
Carrie Ross, *Accounting Mgr*
EMP: 80
SQ FT: 75,000
SALES: 7.7MM **Privately Held**
WEB: www.hanleyindustries.com
SIC: 2892 Detonators & detonating caps

(G-558)
HEARST CORPORATION
Also Called: Telegraph, The
219 Piasa St (62002-6232)
PHONE.....................................618 463-2500
Jeff Bergin, *Vice Pres*
EMP: 3
SALES (corp-wide): 8.2B **Privately Held**
SIC: 2711 Newspapers, publishing & printing
PA: The Hearst Corporation
300 W 57th St Fl 42
New York NY 10019
212 649-2000

(G-559)
IMPERIAL MFG GROUP INC
1450 Discovery Pkwy (62002-6504)
PHONE.....................................618 465-3133
Richard Hayes, *Branch Mgr*
EMP: 14
SALES (corp-wide): 243.2MM **Privately Held**
SIC: 5074 3444 Plumbing & hydronic heating supplies; metal ventilating equipment; ducts, sheet metal
PA: Imperial Manufacturing Group Inc
40 Industrial Park St
Richibucto NB E4W 4
506 523-9117

(G-560)
JADE SCREEN PRINTING
220 Main St (62002-1742)
PHONE.....................................618 463-2325
Ruth Ann Hellemeyer, *Owner*
EMP: 5
SALES (est): 357.9K **Privately Held**
SIC: 2752 Commercial printing, offset

(G-561)
JBL - ALTON
2345 State St (62002-4320)
PHONE.....................................618 466-0411
Rhonda Hausman, *Manager*
EMP: 3
SALES (est): 214.1K **Privately Held**
SIC: 1311 Crude petroleum & natural gas

(G-562)
KATHLEEN A BADASCH
31 E Broadway (62002-6203)
PHONE.....................................618 462-5881
Kathleen A Badasch, *Principal*
EMP: 3
SALES (est): 95.7K **Privately Held**
SIC: 2711 Newspapers, publishing & printing

(G-563)
LENHARDT TOOL AND DIE COMPANY
3400 Bloomer Dr (62002-1999)
PHONE.....................................618 462-1075
Jack E Lenhardt, *President*
Jean Webb, *Corp Secy*
Diana Lenhardt, *Shareholder*
EMP: 60 EST: 1960
SQ FT: 48,000
SALES (est): 11.5MM **Privately Held**
WEB: www.lenhardttool.com
SIC: 3544 3621 Special dies & tools; motors & generators

(G-564)
LYNNS PRINTING CO
3050 Homer M Adams Pkwy (62002-4859)
PHONE.....................................618 465-7701
Barbara Lynn, *Owner*
Rick Lynn, *Manager*
EMP: 6
SALES (est): 694.2K **Privately Held**
SIC: 2752 2791 2789 Commercial printing, offset; typesetting; bookbinding & related work

(G-565)
MARCAL ROPE & RIGGING INC (PA)
1862 E Broadway (62002-6664)
PHONE.....................................618 462-0172
Richard Miller, *CEO*
Thomas R Miller, *President*
Tom Horstman, *Opers Mgr*
Steve Sanders, *Branch Mgr*
Kenny Brackett, *Manager*
EMP: 26
SQ FT: 24,000
SALES (est): 7.4MM **Privately Held**
WEB: www.marcalrigging.com
SIC: 3496 Slings, lifting: made from purchased wire; chain, welded; cable, uninsulated wire: made from purchased wire

(G-566)
MATRIX SERVICE INC
3403 E Broadway (62002-2043)
PHONE.....................................618 466-4862
Brian Mans, *Manager*
EMP: 12
SALES (corp-wide): 1.4B **Publicly Held**
SIC: 1791 3443 7699 Storage tanks, metal: erection; tanks, standard or custom fabricated: metal plate; tank repair & cleaning services
HQ: Matrix Service Inc.
5100 E Skelly Dr Ste 100
Tulsa OK 74135

(G-567)
OLIVE OIL MARKETPLACE INC (PA)
108 W 3rd St (62002-6207)
PHONE.....................................618 304-3769
Timothy Meeks, *President*
EMP: 4
SQ FT: 1,600
SALES (est): 18.2MM **Privately Held**
WEB: www.oliveoilmarketplace.com
SIC: 2079 5411 Olive oil; grocery stores, independent

(G-568)
QUALITY DRILLING SERVICE LLP (PA)
1715 Liberty St (62002-4515)
PHONE.....................................937 663-4715
Mari-Lynn Slayton, *General Ptnr*
EMP: 1
SQ FT: 120
SALES: 1.4MM **Privately Held**
SIC: 1381 Drilling oil & gas wells

(G-569)
RIVERBEND KITCHEN & MLLWK LLC (PA)
215 Herbert St (62002-1924)
PHONE.....................................618 462-8955
Terry Hart,
EMP: 7
SALES (est): 1.1MM **Privately Held**
SIC: 5211 5713 2434 Counter tops; carpets; wood kitchen cabinets

(G-570)
RONEY MACHINE WORKS INC
412 Pearl St (62002-6675)
PHONE.....................................618 462-4113
Marianne Roney, *President*
Lee Roney, *Vice Pres*
Roger Roney, *Vice Pres*
EMP: 20 EST: 1950
SQ FT: 52,000
SALES (est): 4.1MM **Privately Held**
SIC: 3443 Heat exchangers: coolers (after, inter), condensers, etc.

(G-571)
SCHWARTZKOPF PRINTING INC
4121 Humbert Rd (62002-7116)
PHONE.....................................618 463-0747
James M Schwartzkopf, *President*
Teresa Dressel, *Corp Secy*
Donna Schwartzkopf, *Vice Pres*
EMP: 16
SQ FT: 15,000
SALES: 2.1MM **Privately Held**
SIC: 2752 Commercial printing, offset

(G-572)
SOFTHAUS LTD
Also Called: Vic Cook System
518 Beacon St (62002-6119)
PHONE.....................................618 463-1140
Victor Cook, *Partner*
EMP: 3
SALES (est): 230K **Privately Held**
SIC: 7372 7371 Prepackaged software; computer software systems analysis & design, custom

Alton - Madison County (G-573) GEOGRAPHIC SECTION

(G-573)
SURFACE MINING RECLAMATION OFF
501 Belle St Ste 216 (62002-6169)
PHONE..................................618 463-6460
Al Clayeborn, *Manager*
EMP: 29 **Publicly Held**
SIC: 1241 Coal mining services
HQ: Office Of Surface Mining Reclamation & Enforcement
1951 Constitution Ave N
Washington DC 20240

(G-574)
TODAYS ADVANTAGE INC
235 E Center Dr (62002-5931)
P.O. Box 867 (62002-0867)
PHONE..................................618 463-0612
James Seibold, *President*
Sharon McRoy, *Publisher*
Jim Seibold, *Publisher*
Angie Fulcham, *Prdtn Mgr*
Fred Pollard, *Manager*
EMP: 11
SALES (est): 705.3K **Privately Held**
SIC: 2711 Newspapers, publishing & printing

(G-575)
U WASH EQUIPMENT CO
116 Northport Dr (62002-5904)
P.O. Box 877 (62002-0877)
PHONE..................................618 466-9442
C Rick Meeks, *President*
Ruth Meeks, *Vice Pres*
EMP: 5
SQ FT: 7,300
SALES (est): 811.2K **Privately Held**
SIC: 3589 Car washing machinery

(G-576)
ZIEMER USA INC
620 E 3rd St (62002-6317)
PHONE..................................618 462-9301
David Bragg, *President*
Angela Braida, *Treasurer*
Beth Pratt, *Bookkeeper*
Pam Kaizer, *Marketing Staff*
EMP: 16
SQ FT: 24,000
SALES (est): 2.6MM
SALES (corp-wide): 23.1MM **Privately Held**
SIC: 3841 Surgical & medical instruments
HQ: Ziemer Group Ag
Allmendstrasse 11
Port BE 2562
323 327-070

Amboy
Lee County

(G-577)
ADDISON PRECISION PRODUCTS
200 E Kellen Dr (61310-1831)
P.O. Box 144 (61310-0144)
PHONE..................................815 857-4466
John T Smith, *President*
Steven Counihan, *Vice Pres*
EMP: 11
SQ FT: 17,000
SALES: 1.5MM **Privately Held**
SIC: 3599 Machine shop, jobbing & repair; machine & other job shop work

(G-578)
AMBOY NEWS
245 E Main St (61310-1439)
P.O. Box 162 (61310-0162)
PHONE..................................815 857-2311
Jhon Shank, *Principal*
Tonja Greenfeld, *Adv Dir*
EMP: 3
SALES (est): 161.5K **Privately Held**
SIC: 2711 2791 2752 Commercial printing & newspaper publishing combined; typesetting; commercial printing, lithographic

(G-579)
ARCHER-DANIELS-MIDLAND COMPANY
1193 Rock Rd (61310)
PHONE..................................815 857-2058
EMP: 4
SALES (corp-wide): 64.6B **Publicly Held**
SIC: 2041 Flour & other grain mill products
PA: Archer-Daniels-Midland Company
77 W Wacker Dr Ste 4600
Chicago IL 60601
312 634-8100

(G-580)
SENSIENT FLAVORS LLC
25 E Main St (61310-1668)
PHONE..................................815 857-3691
Lawrence Buckley, *Plant Supt*
Mark Allen, *Branch Mgr*
EMP: 12
SALES (corp-wide): 1.3B **Publicly Held**
WEB: www.sensient.com
SIC: 2087 Extracts, flavoring
HQ: Sensient Flavors Llc
2800 W Higgins Rd Ste 900
Hoffman Estates IL 60169
317 243-3521

Anna
Union County

(G-581)
ANNA QUARRIES INC
1000 Quarry Rd (62906)
P.O. Box 180 (62906-0180)
PHONE..................................618 833-5121
Edward T Simonds, *President*
William Pyatt, *Vice Pres*
Dale Usher, *Facilities Mgr*
EMP: 32
SQ FT: 1,800
SALES (est): 4.8MM **Privately Held**
WEB: www.annaquarries.com
SIC: 1411 1422 Limestone, dimension-quarrying; crushed & broken limestone

(G-582)
CUNNINGHAM ELECTRONICS CORP
120 N Main St (62906-1617)
PHONE..................................618 833-7775
Shirley Cunningham, *President*
William R Cunningham, *President*
A John Bigler, *Director*
EMP: 7
SQ FT: 2,500
SALES (est): 867.4K **Privately Held**
SIC: 7372 Application computer software

(G-583)
GAZETTE DEMOCRAT
Also Called: Repperts Warehouse Office Furn
108 Lafayette St 112 (62906-1544)
P.O. Box 529 (62906-0529)
PHONE..................................618 833-2150
Jerry L Reppert, *Owner*
EMP: 40
SQ FT: 6,300
SALES (est): 2.7MM **Privately Held**
WEB: www.annanews.com
SIC: 2711 5712 5943 Newspapers, publishing & printing; office furniture; office forms & supplies

(G-584)
GAZETTE-DEMOCRAT
Also Called: Mondays Pub
112 Lafayette St (62906-1544)
P.O. Box 529 (62906-0529)
PHONE..................................618 833-2158
Jerry Repert, *Owner*
Geof Skinner, *Advt Staff*
EMP: 25
SALES (est): 955.7K **Privately Held**
SIC: 2711 Newspapers, publishing & printing

(G-585)
ILLINI READY MIX INC
Also Called: Anna Plant
300 Mckinley St (62906-1830)
PHONE..................................618 833-7321
Perry Wright, *Manager*
EMP: 7
SALES (corp-wide): 2.8MM **Privately Held**
SIC: 3273 Ready-mixed concrete
PA: Illini Ready Mix, Inc
801 W Industrial Park Rd
Carbondale IL 62901
618 734-0287

(G-586)
J W REYNOLDS MONUMENT CO INC
517 E Vienna St Ste A (62906-2047)
PHONE..................................618 833-6014
Kurt Swinsford, *Principal*
Kurt Swinsford, *Principal*
EMP: 6
SALES (est): 296.6K
SALES (corp-wide): 2.1MM **Privately Held**
SIC: 5999 6553 3281 Monuments, finished to custom order; mausoleum operation; monuments, cut stone (not finishing or lettering only)
HQ: Rock Of Ages Corporation
560 Graniteville Rd
Graniteville VT 05654
802 476-3115

(G-587)
REHABILITATION AND VOCATIONAL
214 W Davie St (62906-1237)
PHONE..................................618 833-5344
Gary Griffith, *CEO*
EMP: 40
SALES (corp-wide): 2.3MM **Privately Held**
SIC: 5112 8331 2394 Office supplies; job training & vocational rehabilitation services; canvas & related products
PA: Rehabilitation And Vocational Education Program, Inc.
1390 State Route 127 S
Jonesboro IL 62952
618 833-5344

(G-588)
SHAWNEE STONE LLC
1275 Jonesboro Quarry Rd (62906-3842)
PHONE..................................618 833-2323
Rob Vogel, *President*
EMP: 7
SALES (est): 766.2K
SALES (corp-wide): 2MM **Privately Held**
SIC: 1422 Crushed & broken limestone
PA: Shawnee Stone, Llc
202 W Main St
Salem IL 62881
618 548-1585

(G-589)
TRAINOR AG PRODUCTS LLC (PA)
5380 State Route 146 E (62906-3859)
PHONE..................................618 614-5770
Paul Trainor,
Mary McDonald, *Admin Asst*
EMP: 8 **EST:** 2017
SQ FT: 16,000
SALES (est): 19.7MM **Privately Held**
SIC: 5153 2874 2879 Wheat; phosphatic fertilizers; agricultural chemicals

Annapolis
Crawford County

(G-590)
WERNZE FARMS INC
20563 N 400th St (62413-2205)
PHONE..................................618 569-4820
Scotty Davidson, *Owner*
EMP: 6
SALES (est): 241.8K **Privately Held**
SIC: 3523 Driers (farm): grain, hay & seed

Annawan
Henry County

(G-591)
PATRIOT FUELS BIODIESEL LLC
101 Patriot Way (61234-9753)
PHONE..................................309 935-5700
Cash Colbert, *Treasurer*
Gene A Griffith,
Richard Vondra,
▲ **EMP:** 10
SQ FT: 1,000
SALES (est): 1.6MM
SALES (corp-wide): 31.9B **Publicly Held**
SIC: 2911 Diesel fuels
PA: Chs Inc.
5500 Cenex Dr
Inver Grove Heights MN 55077
651 355-6000

(G-592)
PATRIOT RENEWABLE FUELS LLC
Also Called: CHS Annawan
101 Patriot Way (61234-9753)
P.O. Box 560 (61234-0560)
PHONE..................................309 935-5700
Gary Anderson, *President*
Tom Malecha, *Admin Sec*
EMP: 65
SALES (est): 19.7MM
SALES (corp-wide): 31.9B **Publicly Held**
SIC: 2869 Ethyl alcohol, ethanol
HQ: Patriot Holdings, Llc
101 Patriot Way
Annawan IL 61234
309 935-5700

Antioch
Lake County

(G-593)
A & S ARMS INC
847 Forest View Way (60002-6216)
PHONE..................................224 267-5670
Shaun Unell, *Principal*
EMP: 2
SALES (est): 203.8K **Privately Held**
SIC: 3482 3484 7389 Small arms ammunition; guns (firearms) or gun parts, 30 mm. & below;

(G-594)
ADVENT TOOL & MFG INC
710 Anita Ave (60002-1857)
PHONE..................................847 395-9707
James Hartford, *President*
Laszlo Frecska, *Principal*
Kathy Krieps, *Controller*
▲ **EMP:** 18 **EST:** 1974
SQ FT: 20,000
SALES (est): 4.1MM **Privately Held**
WEB: www.advent-threadmill.com
SIC: 3545 2284 Cutting tools for machine tools; thread mills

(G-595)
ADVENT TOOL AND MFG
712 Anita Ave (60002-1857)
PHONE..................................847 395-9707
Laszlo Frecska, *Principal*
EMP: 4
SALES (est): 372.6K **Privately Held**
WEB: www.advent-threadmill.com
SIC: 3545 Machine tool accessories

(G-596)
AJS PREMIER PRINTING INC
893 Main St (60002-1508)
PHONE..................................847 838-6350
EMP: 6
SALES (est): 560K **Privately Held**
SIC: 2759 2752 Commercial Printing Lithographic Commercial Printing

GEOGRAPHIC SECTION

Antioch - Lake County (G-625)

(G-597)
AKERUE INDUSTRIES LLC
Also Called: Kay Home Products
90 Mcmillen Rd (60002-1845)
PHONE..................847 395-3300
Murray John J, *Principal*
K M Borre, *Principal*
Michelle Olson, *Purch Mgr*
Gregory McNutt, *Controller*
Geraldine Ellis,
▲ **EMP:** 50
SQ FT: 355,000
SALES (est): 6.8MM **Privately Held**
SIC: 2599 Factory furniture & fixtures

(G-598)
ALL WEST PLASTICS INC
Also Called: Mgs Manufacturing Group
606 Drom Ct (60002-1825)
PHONE..................847 395-8830
Chris Navratil, *General Mgr*
◆ **EMP:** 60
SQ FT: 36,000
SALES (est): 9.9MM
SALES (corp-wide): 561.7MM **Privately Held**
SIC: 3089 Injection molding of plastics
HQ: Mgs Group North America, Inc.
W190n11701 Moldmakers Way
Germantown WI 53022
262 250-2950

(G-599)
ANTIOCH FINE ARTS FOUNDATION
41380 N Il Route 83 (60002-1907)
PHONE..................847 838-2274
Gayle Monde, *President*
Lisa Clark, *Vice Pres*
Roger Shule, *Vice Pres*
Richard A Ellinghusen, *Treasurer*
Kagie Diorio, *Admin Sec*
EMP: 7
SALES (est): 561.7K **Privately Held**
SIC: 3263 8412 Whiteware, fine type semivitreous table or kitchen articles; museums & art galleries

(G-600)
ART NEWVO INCORPORATED
25819 W Grail Lk Rd Ste 1 (60002)
PHONE..................847 838-0304
Tina Rengel, *President*
Lance Rengel, *Vice Pres*
EMP: 4
SQ FT: 1,500
SALES (est): 100K **Privately Held**
SIC: 2752 2396 Commercial printing, lithographic; automotive & apparel trimmings

(G-601)
ASH PALLET MANAGEMENT INC
61 Mcmillen Rd (60002-1844)
P.O. Box 8582, Gurnee (60031-7018)
PHONE..................847 473-5700
Anthony James Ash, *President*
EMP: 80 **EST:** 2012
SQ FT: 150,000
SALES (est): 10.4MM **Privately Held**
WEB: www.ashpallet.com
SIC: 2448 Pallets, wood; pallets, wood & wood with metal

(G-602)
ASSOCIATED PRINTERS INC
43215 N Grandview Ter (60002-8958)
PHONE..................847 548-8929
Melissa Hettlinger, *President*
EMP: 3
SALES (est): 295.7K **Privately Held**
SIC: 2752 Commercial printing, offset

(G-603)
BESCO AWARDS & EMBROIDERY
Also Called: Besco Marketing
43085 N Crawford Rd (60002-9573)
PHONE..................847 395-4862
Elgin Southgate, *Partner*
Barbara Southgate, *Partner*
EMP: 4
SALES (est): 386.5K **Privately Held**
SIC: 7699 3231 China firing & decorating to individual order; ornamental glass: cut, engraved or otherwise decorated; decorated glassware: chipped, engraved, etched, etc.

(G-604)
BILLER PRESS & MANUFACTURING
966 Victoria St (60002-1519)
PHONE..................847 395-4111
Raymond Nordling, *President*
David Plumb, *Corp Secy*
Norman E Biller, *Vice Pres*
EMP: 7 **EST:** 1956
SQ FT: 3,500
SALES (est): 690K **Privately Held**
WEB: www.billerpress.com
SIC: 2752 2791 2789 2759 Commercial printing, offset; lithographing on metal; typesetting; bookbinding & related work; commercial printing

(G-605)
BMI PRODUCTS NORTHERN ILL INC
Also Called: Maxit
28919 W Il Route 173 (60002-9115)
PHONE..................847 395-7110
Arnold Germann, *President*
Bernd Stern, *CFO*
Steven Gnorski, *Admin Sec*
▲ **EMP:** 20
SQ FT: 50,000
SALES (est): 3.8MM **Privately Held**
SIC: 3273 3255 2899 Ready-mixed concrete; clay refractories; chemical preparations

(G-606)
BRAESIDE HOLDINGS LLC
Also Called: Braeside Displays
945 Anita Ave (60002-1867)
PHONE..................847 395-8500
Nathan Kelly, *Branch Mgr*
EMP: 25
SQ FT: 38,000
SALES (corp-wide): 8MM **Privately Held**
SIC: 3993 Displays & cutouts, window & lobby
PA: Braeside Holdings, Llc
795 Bartlett Ave
Antioch IL 60002
847 395-8500

(G-607)
CABINETS DOORS AND MORE LLC
25819 W Grass Lake Rd (60002-8502)
PHONE..................847 395-6334
Justin Lauterbach,
EMP: 4
SQ FT: 2,800
SALES (est): 225K **Privately Held**
SIC: 2511 5712 2434 2431 Lawn furniture: wood; outdoor & garden furniture; wood kitchen cabinets; millwork

(G-608)
CHICAGO INK & RESEARCH CO INC
97 Ida Ave (60002-1887)
PHONE..................847 395-1078
Charles Doty, *President*
EMP: 5
SQ FT: 9,500
SALES (est): 614.2K **Privately Held**
WEB: www.ashdoty85.tripod.com
SIC: 2899 Ink or writing fluids

(G-609)
DIGITAL EDGE SIGNS INC
248 W Depot St A (60002-3200)
PHONE..................847 838-4760
Don Decks, *President*
EMP: 3
SALES (est): 262.5K **Privately Held**
WEB: www.digitaledgesigns.com
SIC: 3993 Signs & advertising specialties

(G-610)
DOMS INCORPORATED
940 Anita Ave (60002-1816)
PHONE..................847 838-6723
Mark Stevens, *President*
Matthew Wilhite, *Opers Staff*
EMP: 20 **EST:** 1960
SALES (est): 500K **Privately Held**
WEB: www.domsinc.com
SIC: 3569 Filter elements, fluid, hydraulic line

(G-611)
FISCHER PAPER PRODUCTS INC (PA)
179 Ida Ave (60002-1838)
PHONE..................847 395-6060
Joshua M Fischer, *CEO*
James Johnson, *Senior VP*
William C Fischer, *Vice Pres*
Robert Gatz, *Vice Pres*
Patty Decker, *Purch Mgr*
◆ **EMP:** 90
SQ FT: 65,000
SALES (est): 28.4MM **Privately Held**
SIC: 2674 2673 Paper bags: made from purchased materials; garment & wardrobe bags, (plastic film)

(G-612)
GFI INNOVATIONS LLC
861 Anita Ave (60002-1813)
PHONE..................847 263-9000
Justin Echterling, *Electrical Engi*
Jeff Baron, *Mng Member*
John Borkovec,
Robert Lerson,
Derek Pedreza,
EMP: 9
SALES (est): 1.6MM **Privately Held**
WEB: www.gfiis.com
SIC: 3586 Measuring & dispensing pumps

(G-613)
GILDAY SERVICES
Also Called: Gilday Service Company
25870 W Hermann Ave (60002-9639)
PHONE..................847 395-0853
Mark Gilday, *Owner*
EMP: 4
SQ FT: 1,500
SALES (est): 1MM **Privately Held**
SIC: 2299 7359 7699 Polishing felts; floor maintenance equipment rental; industrial machinery & equipment repair

(G-614)
GLK ENTERPRISES INC
Also Called: Alston Race Cars
248 E Depot St Unit 2 (60002)
PHONE..................847 395-7368
Larry Lichter, *President*
Mike Ruth, *Manager*
EMP: 6
SQ FT: 10,000
SALES (est): 600K **Privately Held**
SIC: 3714 Motor vehicle parts & accessories

(G-615)
HYPERAKTIVE PRFMCE SOLUTIONS
423 Joren Trl (60002-2526)
PHONE..................847 321-1982
Joe Oplawski, *Principal*
EMP: 2
SALES (est): 221.4K **Privately Held**
WEB: www.hyperaktiveps.com
SIC: 3714 Motor vehicle parts & accessories

(G-616)
IMPRESSIONS COUNT PRINTING
907 Main St (60002-1510)
PHONE..................847 395-2445
Randy Noland, *Owner*
EMP: 13
SQ FT: 3,800
SALES (est): 1MM **Privately Held**
SIC: 2752 Commercial printing, offset

(G-617)
JANIS PLASTICS INC
330 North Ave (60002-1858)
PHONE..................847 838-5500
Manu Graditor, *President*
Rick Lara, *Principal*
Marcy Penge, *Traffic Mgr*
Jonathan Graditor, *Cust Mgr*
Bob East, *Sales Staff*
▼ **EMP:** 100 **EST:** 1946
SQ FT: 180,000
SALES (est): 12.7MM **Privately Held**
WEB: www.janisplastics.com
SIC: 3993 Signs, not made in custom sign painting shops; displays & cutouts, window & lobby; advertising artwork

(G-618)
KITCHEN SUPPLY WHOLESALE
438 Birchwood Dr (60002-1604)
PHONE..................224 603-1208
Michael Maar, *Principal*
EMP: 4
SALES (est): 50.2K **Privately Held**
SIC: 5023 3089 5719 Kitchenware; plastic kitchenware, tableware & houseware; kitchenware, plastic; kitchenware

(G-619)
KTA TRUCKING SERVICES INC
346 North Ave (60002-1858)
PHONE..................224 788-8312
John Knowles, *CEO*
EMP: 6
SALES (est): 295.4K **Privately Held**
SIC: 3537 Trucks: freight, baggage, etc.; industrial, except mining

(G-620)
LAKES REG PRTG & GRAPHICS LLC
25325 W Hickory St (60002-8899)
PHONE..................847 838-5838
Balsanek Edward F, *Principal*
EMP: 2 **EST:** 2013
SALES (est): 205.7K **Privately Held**
SIC: 2752 Commercial printing, lithographic

(G-621)
LAKEVIEW METALS INC (PA)
905 Anita Ave (60002-1815)
PHONE..................847 838-9800
Kevin C Looby, *President*
▲ **EMP:** 75
SQ FT: 3,000
SALES (est): 14.1MM **Privately Held**
SIC: 3469 Metal stampings

(G-622)
LEGEND DYNAMIX INC
Also Called: Legend Engraving Company
77 Mcmillen Rd Ste 106 (60002-1820)
PHONE..................847 789-7007
Robert Linco, *President*
EMP: 4
SALES (est): 399.8K **Privately Held**
SIC: 3479 3231 Metal coating & allied service; products of purchased glass

(G-623)
M C STEEL INC
43160 N Crawford Rd (60002-9572)
PHONE..................847 350-9618
Thomas McClanahan, *President*
Marilyn Grace, *General Mgr*
EMP: 41 **EST:** 1974
SQ FT: 54,000
SALES (est): 6.6MM **Privately Held**
SIC: 3317 5051 Steel pipe & tubes; steel

(G-624)
MCARTHUR MACHINING INC
303 Main St Ste 100a (60002-3027)
PHONE..................847 838-6998
Rich McArthur, *President*
EMP: 2
SALES (est): 248.7K **Privately Held**
SIC: 3599 Machine shop, jobbing & repair

(G-625)
MEYER MACHINE & EQUIPMENT INC (PA)
351 Main St (60002-3012)
PHONE..................847 395-2977
James W Meyer, *President*
Dan Meyer, *Purchasing*
Louis Erenberg, *Sales Mgr*
▲ **EMP:** 28
SQ FT: 18,000
SALES (est): 6.2MM **Privately Held**
SIC: 7699 3589 Industrial equipment services; commercial cleaning equipment

Antioch - Lake County (G-626)

(G-626)
MIDWEST SCREENS LLC
Also Called: Chicago Retractable Awnings
303 Main St Ste 111 (60002-3027)
PHONE..................847 557-5015
Kyle Ketterhagen, *Sales Mgr*
EMP: 4
SALES (est): 283K **Privately Held**
SIC: 3442 Screen doors, metal

(G-627)
MODERN HOME PRODUCTS CORP (PA)
150 S Ram Rd (60002-1901)
PHONE..................847 395-6556
Thomas Koziol, *President*
Tom Nitz, *Vice Pres*
Dale Miller, *Business Anlyst*
George Koziol, *Admin Sec*
▲ EMP: 25
SQ FT: 50,000
SALES (est): 3.2MM **Privately Held**
SIC: 3648 Gas lighting fixtures

(G-628)
NETT INDUSTRIES
41736 N Lakeview Ter (60002-2108)
PHONE..................847 838-3300
EMP: 2
SALES (est): 208.5K **Privately Held**
SIC: 3599 Machine shop, jobbing & repair

(G-629)
PAULMAR INDUSTRIES INC
39804 N Stonebridge Ct (60002-2342)
PHONE..................847 395-2520
Robert Menary, *President*
Paula Menary, *Vice Pres*
EMP: 10
SALES (est): 720K **Privately Held**
SIC: 3861 7371 Photographic equipment & supplies; computer software development

(G-630)
PETER LEHMAN INC
40126 N Il Route 83 (60002-1903)
P.O. Box 298 (60002-0298)
PHONE..................847 395-7997
Peter Lehman, *President*
Jeanne Lehman, *Vice Pres*
EMP: 5
SQ FT: 2,600
SALES: 250K **Privately Held**
SIC: 3444 Sheet metal specialties, not stamped

(G-631)
PRO TOOLS & EQUIPMENT INC
Also Called: Technocure
23529 Eagles Nest Rd (60002-8725)
PHONE..................847 838-6666
James B Weinstein, *President*
EMP: 2
SALES (est): 1.5MM **Privately Held**
SIC: 3559 Automotive maintenance equipment

(G-632)
RAMS SHEET METAL EQUIPMENT INC
77 Mcmillen Rd Ste 100 (60002-1811)
PHONE..................224 788-9900
Ryan Kegg, *CEO*
Myllon Kegg, *Principal*
Aj Kegg, *Vice Pres*
EMP: 4
SQ FT: 1,750
SALES: 100K **Privately Held**
WEB: www.ramsequipment.com
SIC: 5084 5999 3542 Industrial machinery & equipment; electronic parts & equipment; sheet metalworking machines

(G-633)
RON & PATS PIZZA SHACK
40338 N Deep Lake Rd (60002-7201)
PHONE..................847 395-5005
Ron Ramig, *Owner*
EMP: 4
SALES (est): 160K **Privately Held**
SIC: 2041 5812 Flour & other grain mill products; eating places

(G-634)
SE STEEL INC (PA)
43160 N Crawford Rd (60002-9572)
PHONE..................847 350-9618
Thomas McClanahan, *President*
Marilyn Grace, *Admin Sec*
EMP: 3
SQ FT: 40,000
SALES (est): 1.4MM **Privately Held**
SIC: 3312 5051 Tubes, steel & iron; steel

(G-635)
SKACH MANUFACTURING CO INC
950 Anita Ave (60002-2447)
PHONE..................847 395-3560
Will H Shineflug, *President*
Robert Shineflug, *Vice Pres*
Connie Fisher, *Admin Sec*
EMP: 22 EST: 1953
SQ FT: 18,000
SALES (est): 4.4MM **Privately Held**
WEB: www.skachcoldform.com
SIC: 3452 3643 3316 Screws, metal; rivets, metal; current-carrying wiring devices; contacts, electrical; cold finishing of steel shapes

(G-636)
THELEN SAND & GRAVEL INC (PA)
Also Called: Westosha Airport
28955 W Il Route 173 # 1 (60002-9116)
PHONE..................847 838-8800
Steve Thelen, *President*
Tom Thelen, *Vice Pres*
Pam White, *Asst Controller*
Dan McMillan, *Manager*
Mary Varak, *Executive*
EMP: 70 EST: 1948
SQ FT: 10,000
SALES (est): 30.7MM **Privately Held**
WEB: www.thelensg.com
SIC: 1442 4581 3273 4212 Gravel mining; hangar operation; ready-mixed concrete; dump truck haulage; grading

(G-637)
THOMAS-ZIENTZ GROUP INC
925 Carney Ct (60002-2461)
PHONE..................847 395-2363
EMP: 5
SQ FT: 2,500
SALES (est): 510K **Privately Held**
SIC: 3545 Mfg Machine Tool Accessories

(G-638)
TRANSCEND CORP
90 Mcmillen Rd (60002-1845)
PHONE..................847 395-6630
EMP: 3 EST: 2010
SALES (est): 130K **Privately Held**
SIC: 3471 Plating/Polishing Service

(G-639)
TRI COUNTY LIFT TRUCKS INC
Also Called: Tricounty
1020 Anita Ave (60002-1818)
P.O. Box 967, Lake Villa (60046-0967)
PHONE..................847 838-0183
Joseph Gonzalez, *President*
John Norys, *Treasurer*
Tim Sheilds, *Admin Sec*
EMP: 5
SQ FT: 4,500
SALES: 500K **Privately Held**
SIC: 3537 Forklift trucks

(G-640)
TRIFAB INC
606 Longview Dr (60002-1843)
PHONE..................847 838-2083
William Crutchfield Jr, *Principal*
Al Ruck Jr, *Corp Secy*
Greg Crutchfield, *Vice Pres*
EMP: 4
SALES (est): 478.6K **Privately Held**
SIC: 3441 Building components, structural steel

(G-641)
UNITED CANVAS INC
Also Called: United Awning
25434 W Il Route 173 (60002-8356)
PHONE..................847 395-1470
John Hauser, *President*
Steven Gundelach, *Corp Secy*
EMP: 23
SQ FT: 8,000
SALES: 1.2MM **Privately Held**
SIC: 2394 7641 3444 Convertible tops, canvas or boat: from purchased materials; awnings, fabric: made from purchased materials; reupholstery & furniture repair; reupholstery; sheet metalwork

(G-642)
VEHICLE IMPROVEMENT PDTS INC
151 S Ram Rd (60002-1937)
PHONE..................847 395-7250
◆ EMP: 3
SQ FT: 50,000
SALES (est): 5.9MM
SALES (corp-wide): 277.8MM **Privately Held**
SIC: 3714 Motor vehicle parts & accessories
PA: Indiana Mills & Manufacturing Inc
18881 Immi Way
Westfield IN 46074
317 896-9531

(G-643)
WEX DISTRIBUTORS INC
40471 N Bluff Dr (60002-7921)
PHONE..................847 691-5823
David G Wechselberger, *President*
Marcia Wechselberger, *Vice Pres*
EMP: 4
SALES (est): 383.7K **Privately Held**
SIC: 2052 Cookies

(G-644)
WILLIAM DAVIS & CO
488 Donin Dr (60002-2510)
PHONE..................847 395-6860
William C Davis, *Owner*
Judith Davis, *Owner*
EMP: 2 EST: 1979
SALES: 2MM **Privately Held**
SIC: 3599 Machine shop, jobbing & repair

Arcola
Douglas County

(G-645)
ARCOLA RECORD HERALD
Also Called: Arcola Rcord Hrld-Rankin Publr
118 E Main St (61910-1435)
PHONE..................217 268-4950
Chris Slack, *Owner*
EMP: 5
SALES (est): 22.9K **Privately Held**
WEB: www.arcolarecordherald.com
SIC: 2711 Newspapers, publishing & printing

(G-646)
CENTRAL WOOD LLC
210 E County Road 200n (61910-3739)
PHONE..................217 543-2662
Willard A Miller,
Kathryn Miller,
Lorene Miller,
Noah Miller,
Omer A Miller,
EMP: 7
SQ FT: 19,352
SALES: 4MM **Privately Held**
SIC: 2431 2439 Moldings, wood: unfinished & prefinished; doors, wood; door frames, wood; window sashes, wood; structural wood members

(G-647)
DOUGLAS COUNTY MIL MOLDINGS
Also Called: Douglas County Molding
326 E County Road 100n (61910-3746)
PHONE..................217 268-4689
William Otto, *Owner*
EMP: 6 EST: 1998
SALES (est): 505.8K **Privately Held**
SIC: 2431 Moldings, wood: unfinished & prefinished

(G-648)
EFFINGHAM EQUITY
912 E County Road 600n (61910-3574)
PHONE..................217 268-5128
Greg Taylor, *Branch Mgr*
EMP: 15
SALES (corp-wide): 322.5MM **Privately Held**
SIC: 5191 5153 2048 5171 Feed; grain & field beans; prepared feeds; petroleum bulk stations & terminals; lumber & other building materials
PA: Effingham Equity
201 W Roadway Ave
Effingham IL 62401
217 342-4101

(G-649)
G L DOEMELT
Also Called: Cnc Machining
299 Egyptian Trl (61910-1904)
P.O. Box 157 (61910-0157)
PHONE..................217 268-4243
Gary L Doemelt, *President*
Clay Domelt, *Vice Pres*
EMP: 11
SQ FT: 20,000
SALES: 1.8MM **Privately Held**
SIC: 3599 Machine shop, jobbing & repair

(G-650)
GRABER BUILDING SUP & HDWR INC
111 W Springfield Rd (61910-1302)
PHONE..................217 268-3014
Vernon Kuhns, *President*
EMP: 8
SALES (est): 342.9K **Privately Held**
SIC: 3429 Builders' hardware

(G-651)
HERFF JONES LLC
Collegiate Cap & Gown
901 Bob King Dr (61910-1905)
PHONE..................217 268-4543
Terry Hayden, *Manager*
EMP: 180
SALES (corp-wide): 1.1B **Privately Held**
WEB: www.yearbookdiscoveries.com
SIC: 2389 Academic vestments (caps & gowns)
HQ: Herff Jones, Llc
4501 W 62nd St
Indianapolis IN 46268
800 419-5462

(G-652)
HUMBOLDT BROOM COMPANY
901 E County Road 300n (61910-3711)
P.O. Box 165 (61910-0165)
PHONE..................217 268-3718
Carol Turner, *Principal*
EMP: 5
SALES (est): 500K **Privately Held**
SIC: 3991 Brooms

(G-653)
KAUFMANS CUSTOM CABINETS
363 E County Road 200n (61910-3749)
PHONE..................217 268-4330
Reuben Kaufman, *Owner*
EMP: 16
SALES (est): 1.2MM **Privately Held**
SIC: 2511 5712 2499 2434 Wood household furniture; furniture stores; decorative wood & woodwork; vanities, bathroom: wood

(G-654)
LAVERNS WOOD ITEMS
421 E County Road 200n (61910-3750)
PHONE..................217 268-4544
Lavern Yoder, *Owner*
EMP: 6
SALES (est): 210K **Privately Held**
SIC: 2511 Wood household furniture

(G-655)
LIBMAN COMPANY (PA)
1 Libman Way (61910)
PHONE..................217 268-4200
Robert Libman, *President*
William Libman, *Corp Secy*
Megan Parsons, *Vice Pres*
Jon Willoughby, *Facilities Mgr*

GEOGRAPHIC SECTION   Arlington Heights - Cook County (G-681)

John Wheeler, *Maint Spvr*
◆ **EMP:** 250 **EST:** 1898
SQ FT: 800,000
SALES (est): 50.2MM **Privately Held**
WEB: www.libman.com
SIC: 3991 2392 Brooms & brushes; mops, floor & dust

(G-656)
MID-STATE INDUSTRIES OPER INC (PA)
908 Bob King Dr (61910-1906)
PHONE.................................217 268-3900
Kevin S Corely, *President*
EMP: 35
SQ FT: 70,000
SALES (est): 15.5MM **Privately Held**
SIC: 3316 5051 Cold finishing of steel shapes; metals service centers & offices

(G-657)
MONAHAN FILAMENTS LLC (HQ)
Also Called: Specialty Filaments
215 Egyptian Trl (61910-1904)
P.O. Box 250 (61910-0250)
PHONE.................................217 268-4957
Jon Monahan, *Sales Staff*
Chris Monahan, *Mng Member*
Jason Weber, *Manager*
Thomas F Monahan,
▲ **EMP:** 59
SQ FT: 82,000
SALES (est): 13.7MM
SALES (corp-wide): 15.3MM **Privately Held**
SIC: 3089 Molding primary plastic
PA: The Thomas Monahan Company
  202 N Oak St
  Arcola IL 61910
  217 268-5771

(G-658)
MONAHAN PARTNERS INC
200 N Oak St (61910-1425)
P.O. Box 248 (61910-0248)
PHONE.................................217 268-5758
Patrick Monahan, *President*
Kevin Monahan, *Vice Pres*
EMP: 13
SALES (est): 1.5MM **Privately Held**
SIC: 3751 Mopeds & parts

(G-659)
MORNINGSIDE WOODCRAFT
545 E County Road 200n (61910-3754)
PHONE.................................217 268-4313
Marcus L Mast, *Principal*
EMP: 3
SALES (est): 215.1K **Privately Held**
SIC: 2511 Wood household furniture

(G-660)
NORDCO INC
107 N Us Hwy 45 (61910)
P.O. Box 162 (61910-0162)
PHONE.................................414 766-2180
John York, *Purchasing*
Eric N Headrick, *Branch Mgr*
EMP: 44
SALES (corp-wide): 439.8MM **Privately Held**
SIC: 3743 Railroad equipment
HQ: Nordco Inc.
  245 W Forest Hill Ave
  Oak Creek WI 53154
  414 766-2180

(G-661)
OLD HERITAGE CREAMERY LLC
222 N County Road 575e (61910-3784)
PHONE.................................217 268-4355
Samuel L Gingerich, *Principal*
EMP: 4
SALES (est): 189.2K **Privately Held**
SIC: 2021 Creamery butter

(G-662)
PLANKS APPLE BUTTER
175 N County Road 525e (61910-3782)
PHONE.................................217 268-4933
Robert Hochstetler, *Owner*
EMP: 3

SALES (est): 186.6K **Privately Held**
SIC: 2033 Apple sauce: packaged in cans, jars, etc.

(G-663)
PRINTER CONNECTION
319 S Elm St (61910-1731)
P.O. Box 153 (61910-0153)
PHONE.................................217 268-3252
Derek Sitz, *Owner*
EMP: 4
SALES (est): 160K **Privately Held**
SIC: 2759 Commercial printing

(G-664)
RANKIN PUBLISHING INC
Also Called: Business Magazine
204 E Main St (61910-1416)
P.O. Box 130 (61910-0130)
PHONE.................................217 268-4959
Donald Rankin, *President*
Linda Rankin, *Admin Sec*
EMP: 12 **EST:** 1867
SQ FT: 1,625
SALES (est): 610K **Privately Held**
WEB: www.rankinpublishing.com
SIC: 2711 2721 Job printing & newspaper publishing combined; magazines: publishing & printing

(G-665)
SCHROCKS SAWMILL
59 N County Road 450e (61910-3757)
PHONE.................................217 268-3632
Allen Schrock, *Partner*
Jonas Schrock, *Partner*
EMP: 3
SALES (est): 332.2K **Privately Held**
SIC: 2421 Sawmills & planing mills, general

(G-666)
SLACK PUBLICATIONS
736 Dogwood Dr (61910-1604)
PHONE.................................217 268-4950
Chris Slack, *Owner*
Cindy Slack, *Co-Owner*
EMP: 5
SALES (est): 237K **Privately Held**
SIC: 2711 Newspapers, publishing & printing

(G-667)
THOMAS MONAHAN COMPANY (PA)
202 N Oak St (61910-1425)
P.O. Box 250 (61910-0250)
PHONE.................................217 268-5771
Thomas Monahan, *President*
Tom Monahan, *COO*
Paul Ridley, *Pastor*
James Monahan, *Vice Pres*
Jim Monahan, *Sales Mgr*
▲ **EMP:** 13 **EST:** 1922
SQ FT: 2,400
SALES (est): 15.3MM **Privately Held**
WEB: www.thomasmonahan.com
SIC: 2519 5159 Furniture, household: glass, fiberglass & plastic; broomcorn

(G-668)
TIMBER CREEK PALLETS
447 E County Road 200n (61910-3750)
PHONE.................................217 268-3062
Wayan M Gingerich, *Owner*
Mary J Gingerich, *Principal*
EMP: 4
SALES (est): 392.5K **Privately Held**
SIC: 2448 Pallets, wood

(G-669)
WALNUT GROVE PACKAGING
578 E County Road 200n (61910-3754)
PHONE.................................217 268-5112
Dennis L Yoder, *Owner*
EMP: 2 **EST:** 1999
SALES (est): 280.5K **Privately Held**
SIC: 2448 Pallets, wood

Arenzville
Cass County

(G-670)
COON RUN DRAINAGE & LEVEE DST
826 Arenzville Rd (62611-3007)
PHONE.................................217 248-5511
Thomas Burrus, *Principal*
Robert Fitzsimmons, *Principal*
EMP: 4
SALES (est): 121.4K **Privately Held**
SIC: 3259 Clay sewer & drainage pipe & tile

Argenta
Macon County

(G-671)
AUTUMN MILL
13014 Cemetery Rd (62501-8040)
PHONE.................................217 795-3399
Tammy Allen, *Owner*
EMP: 5
SALES (est): 360.8K **Privately Held**
SIC: 2421 5211 Sawmills & planing mills, general; lumber products

(G-672)
ROBERTS & DOWNEY CHAPEL EQP
101 S North St (62501-8234)
P.O. Box 198 (62501-0198)
PHONE.................................217 795-2391
Rick Roberts, *President*
Elizabeth Roberts, *Corp Secy*
EMP: 5
SALES (est): 500K **Privately Held**
SIC: 2531 Church furniture

Argo
Cook County

(G-673)
INGREDION INCORPORATED
6400 S Archer Rd Bldg 90 (60501-1935)
P.O. Box 345 (60501-0345)
PHONE.................................708 563-2400
Tom Siil, *Engineer*
EMP: 153
SALES (corp-wide): 6.2B **Publicly Held**
SIC: 2046 Corn starch
PA: Ingredion Incorporated
  5 Westbrook Corporate Ctr # 500
  Westchester IL 60154
  708 551-2600

(G-674)
OWENS CORNING SALES LLC
5824 S Archer Rd (60501-1410)
PHONE.................................708 594-6911
Jerry Moore, *Principal*
EMP: 350 **Publicly Held**
SIC: 3296 2952 Roofing mats, mineral wool; asphalt felts & coatings
HQ: Owens Corning Sales, Llc
  1 Owens Corning Pkwy
  Toledo OH 43659
  419 248-8000

(G-675)
OWENS CORNING SALES LLC
7800 W 59th St (60501-1434)
PHONE.................................708 594-6935
Russell K Snyder, *Exec VP*
Mark Schulte, *Manager*
EMP: 40 **Publicly Held**
SIC: 3996 2951 2952 2891 Asphalted-felt-base floor coverings: linoleum, carpet; asphalt paving mixtures & blocks; asphalt felts & coatings; adhesives & sealants; paints & allied products
HQ: Owens Corning Sales, Llc
  1 Owens Corning Pkwy
  Toledo OH 43659
  419 248-8000

(G-676)
OWENS-CORNING FIBERGLASS TECH
7734 W 59th St (60501-1428)
PHONE.................................708 563-9091
Dave Brown, *President*
Liz Reid, *Vice Pres*
EMP: 5
SALES (est): 708.1K **Publicly Held**
SIC: 3296 Fiberglass insulation
HQ: Owens Corning Sales, Llc
  1 Owens Corning Pkwy
  Toledo OH 43659
  419 248-8000

(G-677)
WELDBEND CORPORATION
6600 S Harlem Ave (60501-1930)
PHONE.................................708 594-1700
James J Coulas Jr, *President*
Irma Hammer, *Admin Asst*
▲ **EMP:** 200
SQ FT: 420,000
SALES (est): 78.1MM **Privately Held**
WEB: www.weldbend.com
SIC: 3462 Flange, valve & pipe fitting forgings, ferrous

(G-678)
WILLIMS-HYWARD INTL CTINGS INC
7400 W Archer Ave (60501-1218)
PHONE.................................708 458-0015
Ed Kurcz, *Manager*
EMP: 15
SALES (corp-wide): 9.7MM **Privately Held**
SIC: 8051 3743 2851 8731 Skilled nursing care facilities; railroad equipment; paints & allied products; commercial physical research
PA: Williams-Hayward International Coatings, Inc.
  7425 W 59th St
  Summit Argo IL 60501
  708 563-5182

Arlington Heights
Cook County

(G-679)
4EVER PRINTING INC
Also Called: 4ever Design Studio
3401b N Kennicott Ave (60004-1431)
PHONE.................................847 222-1525
Maksim Vaurysh, *President*
EMP: 3
SALES (est): 200.4K **Privately Held**
SIC: 7372 7389 Publishers' computer software; design services

(G-680)
A G MITCHELLS JEWELERS LTD
10 N Dunton Ave (60005-1426)
PHONE.................................847 394-0820
James Mitchell, *President*
Alfred Mitchell, *Principal*
Esther H Mitchell, *Exec VP*
Doug Mitchell, *Vice Pres*
EMP: 10
SQ FT: 6,500
SALES (est): 1.2MM **Privately Held**
WEB: www.mjltd.com
SIC: 3911 7631 5944 Jewelry apparel; watch repair; jewelry stores

(G-681)
AAA PRESS SPECIALISTS INC
Also Called: AAA Press International
3166 N Kennicott Ave (60004-1426)
PHONE.................................847 818-1100
Jack Ludwig, *President*
Pat Dacosta, *COO*
Sharon Ludwig, *Treasurer*
Mark Hahn, *Mktg Dir*
Aris Topacio, *Technology*
▲ **EMP:** 18
SALES (est): 3.6MM **Privately Held**
SIC: 3641 5084 7699 Ultraviolet lamps; printing trades machinery, equipment & supplies; industrial equipment services

Arlington Heights - Cook County (G-682)

(G-682)
ACCURATE TOOL INC
2460 E Oakton St (60005-4820)
PHONE..................847 437-8544
Anastasios Savvakis, *President*
Damianos Savvakis, *Vice Pres*
Eleni Savvakis, *Treasurer*
EMP: 3
SALES (est): 150K **Privately Held**
SIC: 3599 Machine shop, jobbing & repair

(G-683)
ADHES TAPE TECHNOLOGY INC
3339 N Ridge Ave (60004-1411)
PHONE..................847 496-7949
Jiliang Chen, *President*
Hong Qian, *Director*
EMP: 5
SQ FT: 2,400
SALES (est): 487.8K **Privately Held**
SIC: 2241 3069 5085 Fabric tapes; rubber tape; adhesives, tape & plasters

(G-684)
AFS INC
3232 Nordic Rd (60005-4729)
PHONE..................847 437-2345
Gary Murino, *President*
EMP: 12
SALES (est): 887.6K **Privately Held**
SIC: 2869 Fuels

(G-685)
AGILENT TECHNOLOGIES INC
720 W Algonquin Rd (60005-4416)
PHONE..................847 690-0431
EMP: 3275
SALES (corp-wide): 5.1B **Publicly Held**
SIC: 3825 Instruments to measure electricity
PA: Agilent Technologies, Inc.
    5301 Stevens Creek Blvd
    Santa Clara CA 95051
    408 345-8886

(G-686)
ALDEN & OTT PRINTING INKS CO (DH)
616 E Brook Dr (60005-4622)
PHONE..................847 956-6830
Thomas G Alden, *President*
Elaine Hecker, *Admin Sec*
▲ **EMP:** 70 **EST:** 1957
SQ FT: 30,000
SALES (est): 15.8MM
SALES (corp-wide): 355.8K **Privately Held**
WEB: www.aldenottink.com
SIC: 2893 Printing ink
HQ: Hubergroup Usa, Inc.
    1701 Golf Rd Ste 3-201
    Rolling Meadows IL 60008
    815 929-9293

(G-687)
ALPHA ACRYLIC DESIGN
3359 N Ridge Ave Ste A (60004-7812)
PHONE..................847 818-8178
Phillip Liu, *General Ptnr*
Jeffrey Rockenbach, *Manager*
EMP: 3
SALES (est): 290K **Privately Held**
SIC: 3089 5199 Plastic kitchenware, tableware & houseware; gifts & novelties

(G-688)
ALPS
2445 E Oakton St (60005-4819)
PHONE..................847 437-0665
EMP: 7
SALES (est): 1.1MM **Privately Held**
SIC: 3565 Packaging machinery

(G-689)
AMCOL INTERNATIONAL
1500 W Shure Dr Ste 500 (60004-1484)
PHONE..................847 392-4673
EMP: 6
SALES (est): 515.6K **Privately Held**
SIC: 2819 Industrial inorganic chemicals

(G-690)
AMERICAN COLLOID COMPANY
1500 W Shure Dr Fl 7 (60004-1477)
P.O. Box 95411, Hoffman Estates (60195-0411)
PHONE..................800 527-9948
Bruce J Birney, *Branch Mgr*
▼ **EMP:** 10 **Publicly Held**
SIC: 1459 Bentonite mining
HQ: American Colloid Company
    2870 Forbs Ave
    Hoffman Estates IL 60192

(G-691)
AMERICAN SOC PLASTIC SURGEONS (PA)
444 E Algonquin Rd # 100 (60005-4666)
PHONE..................847 228-9900
Lynn Jeffers, *President*
Michael Castello, *Exec VP*
Robert Micek, *CFO*
David Rigan, *Plastic Surgeon*
Alexandra Acevedo,
EMP: 80
SQ FT: 31,000
SALES (est): 23.9MM **Privately Held**
SIC: 8621 8322 2721 Medical field-related associations; individual & family services; periodicals

(G-692)
AMPEX SCREW MFG INC
2936 Malmo Dr (60005-4726)
PHONE..................847 228-1202
Herta Mueller, *President*
Charles Mueller, *Vice Pres*
EMP: 7
SQ FT: 10,000
SALES (est): 930K **Privately Held**
SIC: 3452 3451 Bolts, metal; rivets, metal; screw machine products

(G-693)
ANDERSON & VREELAND-ILLINOIS
525 W University Dr (60004-1815)
PHONE..................847 255-2110
▲ **EMP:** 10
SQ FT: 24,000
SALES (est): 2.9MM
SALES (corp-wide): 73.7MM **Privately Held**
SIC: 5084 3555 Whol Industrial Equipment Mfg Printing Trades Machinery
PA: Anderson & Vreeland, Inc.
    8 Evans St
    Fairfield NJ 07004
    973 227-2270

(G-694)
ARENS CONTROLS COMPANY LLC
3602 N Kennicott Ave (60004-1467)
PHONE..................847 844-4700
James Kauppila, *Opers Mgr*
Sean Naughton, *Engineer*
Mike Colombo, *Mng Member*
◆ **EMP:** 90
SQ FT: 97,000
SALES: 25MM
SALES (corp-wide): 2.4B **Publicly Held**
SIC: 3625 5199 Relays & industrial controls
PA: Curtiss-Wright Corporation
    130 Harbour Place Dr # 300
    Davidson NC 28036
    704 869-4600

(G-695)
ARLINGTON STRL STL CO INC
1727 E Davis St (60005-2811)
PHONE..................847 577-2200
Richard Clarbour, *President*
S Daniel Clarbour, *Vice Pres*
Ray Tomczak, *Opers Mgr*
Richard Shewczyk, *Purchasing*
Lee Clarbour, *Treasurer*
EMP: 28
SQ FT: 11,000
SALES (est): 10.6MM **Privately Held**
SIC: 3441 Fabricated structural metal

(G-696)
ARROWS UP INC
3 W College Dr Rear 1 (60004-1991)
PHONE..................847 305-2550
Fax: 847 305-2582
EMP: 5
SALES (est): 995.8K **Privately Held**
SIC: 3523 3412 2448 5039 Mfg Farm Machinery/Equip Mfg Metal Barrels/Pails Mfg Wood Pallets/Skids Whol Cnstn Materials Whol Industrial Supplies

(G-697)
ASCO LP
443 S Banbury Rd (60005-2001)
PHONE..................630 789-2082
Scott Manminato, *Manager*
EMP: 12
SALES (corp-wide): 18.3B **Publicly Held**
WEB: www.asco.com
SIC: 3443 Fabricated plate work (boiler shop)
HQ: Asco, L.P.
    160 Park Ave
    Florham Park NJ 07932
    800 972-2726

(G-698)
AURORA LINE
3407 N Ridge Ave Ste A (60004-1427)
PHONE..................847 670-1600
Tony Donik, *Principal*
EMP: 2
SALES (est): 225.8K **Privately Held**
SIC: 2434 Wood kitchen cabinets

(G-699)
AUTOMTIC LQUID PCKG SLTONS LLC
2445 E Oakton St (60005-4819)
PHONE..................847 372-3336
Arjun Ramrajhyani, *President*
Steve Karnatz, *Engineer*
EMP: 20
SQ FT: 100,000
SALES (est): 2.1MM **Privately Held**
SIC: 3565 Packaging machinery

(G-700)
AVANT TECNO USA INC
3020 Malmo Dr (60005-4728)
PHONE..................847 380-1308
John Losch, *CFO*
▲ **EMP:** 18
SQ FT: 27,250
SALES: 16.7MM **Privately Held**
SIC: 3523 3537 3531 7699 Loaders, farm type: manure, general utility; trucks, tractors, loaders, carriers & similar equipment; loaders, shovel: self-propelled; construction equipment repair; loaders (garden tractor equipment)

(G-701)
BACT PROCESS SYSTEMS INC
3345 N Arlington Hts B (60004-1591)
PHONE..................847 577-0950
N S Balakrishnan, *President*
Warren Wilke, *Opers Mgr*
Kevin Guynn, *Facilities Mgr*
EMP: 6
SQ FT: 2,000
SALES (est): 1.6MM **Privately Held**
WEB: www.bactprocess.com
SIC: 3564 Air cleaning systems

(G-702)
BALDWIN TECHNOLOGY COMPANY INC
Also Called: Web Printing Controls
3350 W Salt Creek Ln # 110 (60005-5023)
PHONE..................618 842-2664
EMP: 150 **Privately Held**
SIC: 3555 Printing trades machinery
HQ: Baldwin Technology Company, Inc.
    8040 Forsyth Blvd
    Saint Louis MO 63105
    314 726-2152

(G-703)
BAPTIST GENERAL CONFERENCE (PA)
Also Called: Harvest Publications Div
2002 S Arlington Hts Rd (60005-4193)
PHONE..................800 323-4215
Jerry Sheveland, *President*
Ray Swatkowski, *Exec VP*
Steve Schultz, *VP Finance*
EMP: 75
SQ FT: 28,500
SALES (est): 11.9MM **Privately Held**
SIC: 8661 8221 2731 2721 Non-church religious organizations; theological seminary; books: publishing only; periodicals: publishing only

(G-704)
BE MCGONAGLE INC
Also Called: Somebody's Pub & Grille
858 S Arthur Ave (60005-2828)
PHONE..................847 394-0413
Beth McGonagle, *President*
EMP: 4
SALES (est): 268K **Privately Held**
SIC: 2599 Bar, restaurant & cafeteria furniture

(G-705)
BIZSTARTERSCOM LLC
126 E Wing St Ste 321 (60004-6064)
PHONE..................847 305-4626
Jeff Williams, *Principal*
Jeffrey Williams, *Principal*
EMP: 3
SALES (est): 272.4K **Privately Held**
WEB: www.bizstarters.com
SIC: 3812 Defense systems & equipment

(G-706)
BLACK ROCK MILLING AND PAV CO
2400 Terminal Dr (60005)
PHONE..................847 952-0700
Danielle Peterson, *Owner*
EMP: 10
SALES (est): 710.3K **Privately Held**
SIC: 2952 Asphalt felts & coatings

(G-707)
BOX OF RAIN LTD
Also Called: Edr Electronics
1504 E Algonquin Rd (60005-4718)
PHONE..................847 640-6996
Donald Boe, *President*
EMP: 4
SQ FT: 1,750
SALES (est): 204.9K **Privately Held**
SIC: 3625 Electric controls & control accessories, industrial

(G-708)
BRAN-ZAN HOLDINGS LLC (PA)
Also Called: Chef M J Brando
1655 N Arlington Heights (60004-3958)
PHONE..................847 342-0000
Steven Marlowe, *Principal*
EMP: 15
SQ FT: 10,000
SALES (est): 50MM **Privately Held**
SIC: 2034 Potato products, dried & dehydrated

(G-709)
BRITE-O-MATIC MFG INC
527 W Algonquin Rd (60005-4411)
PHONE..................847 956-1100
Lynne Mohr, *President*
William J Gasser, *Chairman*
Jamie Reed, *Regional Mgr*
Paul Wojnicki, *Regional Mgr*
David Hamaker, *Plant Mgr*
EMP: 52
SQ FT: 25,000
SALES (est): 10.9MM **Privately Held**
SIC: 3589 Car washing machinery

(G-710)
BRITT INDUSTRIES INC
Also Called: Metal Finishers
3010 Malmo Dr (60005-4728)
PHONE..................847 640-1177
Caroline M Schroll, *President*
William R Schroll, *Vice Pres*
EMP: 20
SQ FT: 30,000
SALES: 2.4MM **Privately Held**
SIC: 3479 Coating of metals with plastic or resins; painting of metal products

(G-711)
BUHRKE INDUSTRIES LLC (HQ)
Also Called: IMS Buhrke-Olson
511 W Algonquin Rd (60005-4499)
PHONE..................847 981-7550
Mark Simanton, *CEO*

▲ = Import ▼ = Export
◆ = Import/Export

Keith Krutz, *President*
James Talarek, *COO*
▲ **EMP:** 450
SQ FT: 400,000
SALES (est): 41.9MM
SALES (corp-wide): 189.6MM **Privately Held**
SIC: 3469 Metal stampings
PA: Ims Companies, Llc
1 Innovation Dr
Des Plaines IL 60016
847 391-8100

(G-712)
BYD MOTORS INC
1500 W Shure Dr Ste 250 (60004-1465)
PHONE..................847 590-9002
EMP: 3
SALES (corp-wide): 2.4MM **Privately Held**
WEB: www.byd.com
SIC: 3714 Motor vehicle electrical equipment
HQ: Byd Motors Llc
1800 S Figueroa St
Los Angeles CA 90015

(G-713)
C L GREENSLADE SALES INC (PA)
505 E Golf Rd Ste H (60005-4000)
PHONE..................847 593-3450
John Brennan, *President*
EMP: 5
SQ FT: 2,000
SALES (est): 730.3K **Privately Held**
SIC: 3679 Electronic circuits

(G-714)
CHEF LMT FOODS LLC
1655 N Arlington Heights (60004-3958)
PHONE..................847 279-6490
Steven Marlowe, *CEO*
EMP: 20 **EST:** 2014
SALES (est): 671.8K **Privately Held**
SIC: 2034 Dehydrated fruits, vegetables, soups

(G-715)
CHICAGO
2045 S Arlington Heights (60005-4151)
PHONE..................847 437-7700
EMP: 4
SALES (est): 203.2K **Privately Held**
SIC: 2711 Newspapers, publishing & printing

(G-716)
COLOR SIGNS
3110 N Arlington Hts Rd (60004-1532)
PHONE..................847 368-0101
Jay Brown, *Owner*
EMP: 5
SALES (est): 352.3K **Privately Held**
SIC: 3993 Signs, not made in custom sign painting shops

(G-717)
COMMERCIAL DYNAMICS INC
2025 S Arlington Hts Rd (60005-4152)
PHONE..................847 439-5300
EMP: 4 **EST:** 2006
SALES (est): 260K **Privately Held**
SIC: 3599 Mfg Industrial Machinery

(G-718)
COMPUTER INDUSTRY ALMANAC INC
Also Called: Internet Industry Almanac
1013 S Belmont Ave (60005-3201)
PHONE..................847 758-1926
Karen Petska, *President*
Karen Tepska, *President*
EMP: 3
SALES (est): 125K **Privately Held**
SIC: 7379 2731 Computer related consulting services; books: publishing only

(G-719)
CONTOUR SCREW PRODUCTS INC
3014 Malmo Dr (60005-4728)
PHONE..................847 357-1190
Richard Tignino, *President*
Mary Tignino, *Corp Secy*

EMP: 35
SQ FT: 28,000
SALES (est): 2.5MM **Privately Held**
SIC: 3599 3451 Machine shop, jobbing & repair; screw machine products

(G-720)
CONVEYOR SYSTEMS & ENGINEERING
855 E Golf Rd (60005-5222)
PHONE..................847 593-2900
Peter Zuiko, *Principal*
EMP: 3
SALES (est): 177.3K **Privately Held**
SIC: 3535 Conveyors & conveying equipment

(G-721)
CRYSTAL CLEAR CNDLE DESIGN LLC
1313 N Rand Rd (60004-4307)
PHONE..................847 749-4782
Kim Moyal, *Principal*
EMP: 11
SALES (est): 1.1MM **Privately Held**
SIC: 3999 Candles

(G-722)
CUBIC GROUP INC
445 E Algonquin Rd Ste 2 (60005-4611)
PHONE..................859 494-5834
Yejunxiong Fang,
EMP: 3
SALES (est): 37.2K **Privately Held**
SIC: 7389 3821 Business services; chemical laboratory apparatus

(G-723)
CUSTOM RODS BY GRANDT LTD
Also Called: Grandt's Custom Fishing Rods
203 S Highland Ave (60005-1828)
PHONE..................847 577-0848
James A Grandt, *President*
EMP: 2
SALES (est): 297.6K **Privately Held**
SIC: 3949 5941 Rods & rod parts, fishing; sporting goods & bicycle shops

(G-724)
D&J ARLINGTON HEIGHTS INC
Also Called: Fastsigns
1814 N Arlington Hts Rd (60004-3910)
PHONE..................847 577-8200
Gerald A Becker, *President*
David Becker, *Admin Sec*
EMP: 3
SQ FT: 2,000
SALES (est): 455.3K **Privately Held**
SIC: 3993 Signs & advertising specialties

(G-725)
DANA PLASTIC CONTAINER CORP (HQ)
6 N Hickory Ave (60004-6205)
P.O. Box 545 (60006-0545)
PHONE..................847 670-0650
Daniel Hidding, *CEO*
David Hidding, *President*
Mike Haber, *CFO*
▲ **EMP:** 2
SQ FT: 45,000
SALES (est): 2.7MM
SALES (corp-wide): 15.6MM **Privately Held**
SIC: 3085 Plastics bottles
PA: Dana Molded Products, Inc.
810 Commerce Pkwy
Carpentersville IL 60110
847 783-1800

(G-726)
DAWES LLC (PA)
Also Called: Dawe's Laboratories
3355 N Arlington Hts Rd (60004-7706)
PHONE..................847 577-2020
Doug Foss, *QC Mgr*
Charles R Dawe,
Cameron Gillingham,
▼ **EMP:** 10 **EST:** 1926
SQ FT: 6,000
SALES (est): 4MM **Privately Held**
WEB: www.dawesnutrition.com
SIC: 2048 8731 2833 Prepared feeds; commercial physical research; medicinals & botanicals

(G-727)
DECAL SOLUTIONS UNLIMITED INC
3110 N Arlington Hts Rd (60004-1532)
PHONE..................847 590-5405
James Roman, *President*
EMP: 3
SALES (est): 1MM **Privately Held**
WEB: www.decalsolutionsinc.com
SIC: 2759 2399 3993 Screen printing; decals: printing; banners, pennants & flags; signs & advertising specialties

(G-728)
DIAMOND MACHINE WERKS INC
Also Called: Automtic Lquid Packg Solutions
2445 E Oakton St (60005-4879)
PHONE..................847 437-0665
Ted Geiselman, *President*
Siegfried Weiler, *Admin Sec*
▲ **EMP:** 50
SQ FT: 65,000
SALES (est): 12.5MM **Privately Held**
SIC: 3569 3565 Assembly machines, non-metalworking; bottling machinery: filling, capping, labeling

(G-729)
DJW ASSEMBLY INC
Also Called: Djw Machining & Assembly
2912 Malmo Dr (60005-4726)
PHONE..................847 956-5330
Tedd Wosny, *President*
EMP: 10
SALES (est): 1.4MM **Privately Held**
WEB: www.djwmachining.com
SIC: 3599 Machine shop, jobbing & repair

(G-730)
DURACLEAN INTERNATIONAL INC
220 W Campus Dr Ste A (60004-1498)
PHONE..................847 704-7100
Vincent Caffarello, *President*
Wilber Gage, *Exec VP*
Wilbur Gage, *Exec VP*
Bill Ondratschek, *Vice Pres*
EMP: 10 **EST:** 1930
SQ FT: 12,000
SALES (est): 3.2MM **Privately Held**
WEB: www.duraclean.com
SIC: 6794 7217 2842 Franchises, selling or licensing; carpet & upholstery cleaning; cleaning or polishing preparations

(G-731)
E J SELF FURNITURE (PA)
332 S Rammer Ave (60004-6871)
PHONE..................847 394-0899
Arthur H Self Sr, *President*
Barbara Bruhn, *Vice Pres*
Loretta Self, *Treasurer*
EMP: 7 **EST:** 1960
SALES (est): 750K **Privately Held**
WEB: www.ejselffurniture.com
SIC: 2391 2512 2511 Draperies, plastic & textile: from purchased materials; chairs: upholstered on wood frames; tables, household: wood

(G-732)
ELEKTRO-PHYSIK USA INC
778 W Algonquin Rd (60005-4416)
PHONE..................847 437-6616
Klaus Steingroever, *President*
Aivars Freidenfelds, *Exec VP*
Dennis Housecweart, *Manager*
EMP: 4
SQ FT: 3,000
SALES: 1MM
SALES (corp-wide): 6.6MM **Privately Held**
SIC: 3829 Measuring & controlling devices
PA: Elektrophysik Dr. Steingroever Gmbh & Co. Kg
Pasteurstr. 15
Koln 50735
221 752-040

(G-733)
EROWA TECHNOLOGY INC
2535 S Clearbrook Dr (60005-4623)
PHONE..................847 290-0295
Hans Hediger, *President*

Taras Vasilik, *Engineer*
Nils German, *Sales Mgr*
Mike Stevens, *Manager*
▲ **EMP:** 17
SQ FT: 10,000
SALES (est): 6.7MM
SALES (corp-wide): 1.3MM **Privately Held**
SIC: 5084 3544 7699 Machine tools & accessories; special dies, tools, jigs & fixtures; industrial equipment services
HQ: Erowa Ag
Winkelstrasse 8
Reinach AG 5734
627 650-707

(G-734)
FASPRO TECHNOLOGIES INC (PA)
500 W Campus Dr (60004-1408)
PHONE..................847 392-9500
Igor Shkarovsky, *CEO*
EMP: 155
SQ FT: 40,000
SALES (est): 30.7MM **Privately Held**
SIC: 3443 Plate work for the metalworking trade

(G-735)
FAUSTOS BAKERY
Also Called: Fausto's Bread Bakery
16 S Evergreen Ave (60005-1428)
PHONE..................847 255-9049
Fausto Bonica, *Owner*
EMP: 4
SALES (est): 199.9K **Privately Held**
SIC: 2051 Bread, cake & related products

(G-736)
FEDEX OFFICE & PRINT SVCS INC
205 W Rand Rd (60004-3144)
PHONE..................847 670-4100
EMP: 20
SALES (corp-wide): 69.6B **Publicly Held**
SIC: 7334 3993 2789 Photocopying & duplicating services; signs & advertising specialties; bookbinding & related work
HQ: Fedex Office And Print Services, Inc.
7900 Legacy Dr
Plano TX 75024
800 463-3339

(G-737)
FLUENCE AUTOMATION LLC
3323 N Kennicott Ave (60004-1429)
PHONE..................847 423-7400
Michael Swift, *President*
EMP: 161 **EST:** 2017
SQ FT: 100,000
SALES (est): 62.3MM **Privately Held**
SIC: 3579 Mailing machines

(G-738)
G & J ASSOCIATES INC
Also Called: Signs By Tomorrow
1315 E Davis St (60005-2132)
PHONE..................847 255-0123
Gerd K Loof, *President*
EMP: 4
SALES (est): 369.6K **Privately Held**
WEB: www.signsbytomorrow.com
SIC: 3993 Signs & advertising specialties

(G-739)
G AND D ENTERPRISES INC
Also Called: Shockwaves Promotional Apparel
1425 E Algonquin Rd (60005-4715)
PHONE..................847 981-8661
Doreen Gaardbo, *President*
Greg Gaardbo, *Vice Pres*
EMP: 30
SQ FT: 70,000
SALES (est): 4.7MM **Privately Held**
SIC: 2759 3993 2396 2395 Screen printing; signs & advertising specialties; automotive & apparel trimmings; pleating & stitching

(G-740)
G R LEONARD & CO INC (PA)
Also Called: Leonard's Guide
115 E University Dr (60004-1803)
PHONE..................847 797-8101
David Ercolani, *CEO*

Arlington Heights - Cook County (G-741)

Elizabeth Stern, *Corp Secy*
Ahmed Hawari, *Vice Pres*
Lyndsey Lebron, *Bookkeeper*
▲ **EMP:** 20
SQ FT: 30,000
SALES (est): 1.6MM **Privately Held**
WEB: www.leonardsguide.com
SIC: 2741 Directories: publishing only, not printed on site; guides: publishing only, not printed on site

(G-741)
GE HEALTHCARE HOLDINGS INC
3350 N Ridge Ave (60004-1412)
PHONE.................847 398-8400
Daniel Peters, *President*
William Clarke MD, *Exec VP*
J E Reller, *Vice Pres*
Sanghamitra Mukherjee, *Engineer*
Lori Sekera, *Engineer*
▲ **EMP:** 1498
SQ FT: 126,000
SALES (est): 161.1MM
SALES (corp-wide): 95.2B **Publicly Held**
SIC: 2833 5169 5122 2835 Medicinals & botanicals; chemicals & allied products; medicinals & botanicals; radioactive diagnostic substances
HQ: Ge Healthcare Limited
Pollards Wood
Chalfont St Giles BUCKS HP8 4
149 454-4000

(G-742)
GE HEALTHCARE INC
3350 N Ridge Ave (60004-1412)
PHONE.................774 249-6290
Cory W Romzo, *Branch Mgr*
EMP: 99
SALES (corp-wide): 95.2B **Publicly Held**
SIC: 2834 Pharmaceutical preparations
HQ: Ge Healthcare Inc.
251 Locke Dr
Marlborough MA 01752
800 526-3593

(G-743)
GRACELAND FERRAY PRODUCTS
736 W Algonquin Rd (60005-4416)
PHONE.................847 258-3828
Kaye Grand, *Owner*
EMP: 3
SALES (est): 289.5K **Privately Held**
SIC: 3812 Search & navigation equipment

(G-744)
GRAND FORMS & SYSTEMS INC
910 W Miner St (60005-1227)
P.O. Box 1128 (60006-1128)
PHONE.................847 259-4600
Gregory G Grana, *President*
Rita Grana, *Admin Sec*
EMP: 10
SALES (est): 1MM **Privately Held**
SIC: 2759 5112 2761 2752 Business forms: printing; business forms; manifold business forms; commercial printing, lithographic

(G-745)
H FIELD & SONS INC
2605 S Clearbrook Dr (60005-4625)
PHONE.................847 434-0970
Lew Field, *President*
Joe Field, *Chairman*
Charles Field, *Vice Pres*
Chuck Field, *Vice Pres*
Cindy Yokum, *CFO*
EMP: 10 **EST:** 1933
SQ FT: 48,000
SALES (est): 2.1MM **Privately Held**
WEB: www.fieldbox.com
SIC: 2653 5113 2657 Boxes, corrugated: made from purchased materials; boxes & containers; folding paperboard boxes

(G-746)
HAAKER MOLD CO INC
628 N Salem Ave (60004-5332)
PHONE.................847 253-8103
Ronald Haaker, *President*
Linda Steiner, *Office Mgr*
EMP: 3
SALES (est): 180K **Privately Held**
SIC: 3544 Industrial molds

(G-747)
HEARING SCREENING ASSOC LLC
Also Called: Hsa
3333 N Kennicott Ave (60004-1429)
PHONE.................855 550-9427
Thomas Larsen, *COO*
EMP: 9 **EST:** 2015
SALES (est): 615.1K
SALES (corp-wide): 1.2MM **Privately Held**
SIC: 3841 5047 Surgical & medical instruments; instruments, surgical & medical
HQ: Demant A/S
Kongebakken 9
SmOrum 2765
391 771-00

(G-748)
HEART PRINTING INC
Also Called: Heart Printing & Form Service
1624 W Northwest Hwy (60004-5254)
PHONE.................847 259-2100
Mark A Poe, *President*
Lyn Poe, *Vice Pres*
EMP: 4
SQ FT: 1,200
SALES (est): 390K **Privately Held**
SIC: 2752 2791 2789 2759 Commercial printing, offset; typesetting; bookbinding & related work; commercial printing

(G-749)
HIGH-5 PRINTWEAR INC
3311 N Ridge Ave (60004-1411)
PHONE.................847 818-0081
John Schram, *CEO*
Kristie Schram, *President*
EMP: 5
SALES (est): 495.9K **Privately Held**
SIC: 5699 2759 T-shirts, custom printed; screen printing

(G-750)
HOLLINGSWORTH & VOSE COMPANY
4256 N Arlington Hts Rd (60004-1300)
PHONE.................847 222-9228
Donna Kasper, *Manager*
EMP: 4
SALES (corp-wide): 681.4MM **Privately Held**
WEB: www.hollingsworth-vose.com
SIC: 2621 Paper mills
PA: Hollingsworth & Vose Company
112 Washington St
East Walpole MA 02032
508 850-2000

(G-751)
HOUSE OF DOOLITTLE LTD (PA)
3001 Malmo Dr (60004-4727)
PHONE.................847 228-9591
Bailey W Blethen, *President*
Ronald Stavoe, *Admin Sec*
▲ **EMP:** 40
SQ FT: 62,000
SALES (est): 9.1MM **Privately Held**
SIC: 2752 3993 2678 Calendars, lithographed; signs & advertising specialties; memorandum books, except printed: purchased materials; desk pads, paper: made from purchased materials

(G-752)
IBBOTSON HEATING CO
Also Called: Honeywell Authorized Dealer
514 S Arthur Ave (60005-2141)
PHONE.................847 253-0866
Ralph Ibbotson, *President*
John R Kelly, *President*
Marjorie Kelly, *Treasurer*
Mary Jane Ibbotson, *Admin Sec*
EMP: 29
SQ FT: 5,000
SALES (est): 4.9MM **Privately Held**
WEB: www.ibbotsonheating.com
SIC: 1711 3444 Warm air heating & air conditioning contractor; sheet metalwork

(G-753)
ID3 INC
768 W Algonquin Rd (60005-4416)
PHONE.................847 734-9781
Steven L Begor, *President*
EMP: 11 **EST:** 2001
SQ FT: 3,000
SALES (est): 1MM **Privately Held**
WEB: www.id3logos.com
SIC: 3089 Injection molding of plastics

(G-754)
IGAR BRIDAL INC
723 E Dundee Rd (60004-1542)
PHONE.................224 318-2337
Elzbieta Giezycka, *President*
EMP: 3 **EST:** 2015
SQ FT: 1,500
SALES (est): 200K **Privately Held**
SIC: 2335 7219 Wedding gowns & dresses; garment making, alteration & repair

(G-755)
IGT TESTING SYSTEMS INC
543 W Golf Rd (60005-3904)
PHONE.................847 952-2448
Fred Kooy, *President*
Thomas Klepper, *Technical Staff*
EMP: 4
SQ FT: 2,037
SALES: 500K
SALES (corp-wide): 4.2MM **Privately Held**
SIC: 3826 8748 Analytical instruments; systems analysis & engineering consulting services
PA: Reprotest Produktie B.V.
Randstad 22 22 2
Almere 1316
204 099-300

(G-756)
IMPREX INTERNATIONAL INC
2916 Malmo Dr (60005-4726)
PHONE.................847 364-4930
Jerry K Gantz, *President*
Erica Mason, *Corp Secy*
Lucas Mason, *Manager*
EMP: 3
SQ FT: 1,500
SALES (est): 986.6K **Privately Held**
SIC: 5085 3545 Industrial tools; machine tool accessories

(G-757)
IMPRO INTERNATIONAL INC
Also Called: Impro Graphics
3110 N Arlington Hts Rd (60004-1532)
PHONE.................847 398-3870
Richard Saetre, *President*
Mary Sannicandro, *Art Dir*
EMP: 4 **EST:** 1996
SQ FT: 2,500
SALES (est): 573.3K **Privately Held**
WEB: www.impro.com
SIC: 2759 Screen printing

(G-758)
INFINITE CNVRGNCE SLUTIONS INC (HQ)
3231 N Wilke Rd (60004-1437)
PHONE.................224 764-3400
Anurag Lal, *CEO*
EMP: 4
SQ FT: 15,000
SALES (est): 1.5MM **Privately Held**
WEB: www.icsmessaging.com
SIC: 7372 7373 8999 Prepackaged software; computer integrated systems design; communication services

(G-759)
J F SCHROEDER COMPANY INC
2616 S Clearbrook Dr (60005-4626)
PHONE.................847 357-8600
John R Schroeder, *President*
Elaine Schroeder, *Treasurer*
EMP: 20 **EST:** 1955
SQ FT: 15,000
SALES (est): 3.3MM **Privately Held**
WEB: www.jfschroederco.com
SIC: 3544 3469 3444 Die sets for metal stamping (presses); stamping metal for the trade; sheet metalwork

(G-760)
JAMTEC USA LLC
2622 N Stratford Rd (60004-2246)
PHONE.................224 392-1258
Dominic Vaglica, *Principal*
EMP: 3
SALES (est): 215.7K **Privately Held**
WEB: www.jamtec.com
SIC: 3999 Manufacturing industries

(G-761)
JET GRINDING & MANUFACTURING
2309 E Oakton St Ste A (60005-4809)
PHONE.................847 956-8646
Jerry Nosek, *President*
Ann Leenheer, *Info Tech Mgr*
EMP: 10 **EST:** 1966
SALES (est): 2MM **Privately Held**
WEB: www.jetgrinding.com
SIC: 3599 Machine shop, jobbing & repair

(G-762)
JOHNSON CONTROLS INC
3007 Malmo Dr (60004-4781)
PHONE.................847 364-1500
Mike Wolpert, *President*
Jim Ahern, *Manager*
EMP: 40 **Privately Held**
SIC: 2531 Seats, automobile
HQ: Johnson Controls, Inc.
5757 N Green Bay Ave
Milwaukee WI 53209
414 524-1200

(G-763)
JTEKT TOYODA AMERICAS CORP
316 W University Dr (60004-1812)
PHONE.................847 253-0340
Connie Vitale, *President*
Shelby Kohlmann, *Buyer*
Bill Wright, *Engineer*
Jeff Biedka, *Controller*
Michael Lucier, *Sales Mgr*
EMP: 4 **Privately Held**
SIC: 3541 Grinding machines, metalworking
HQ: Jtekt Toyoda Americas Corporation
316 W University Dr
Arlington Heights IL 60004
847 253-0340

(G-764)
JTEKT TOYODA AMERICAS CORP (DH)
Also Called: Toyoda Grinders For Industry
316 W University Dr (60004-1812)
P.O. Box 74053, Chicago (60690-8053)
PHONE.................847 253-0340
Kent Nakamura, *Ch of Bd*
Howard W Michael, *President*
Hiroyuki Kaijima, *Exec VP*
Casey Braheny, *Buyer*
Kunihiko Asada, *Admin Sec*
▲ **EMP:** 127 **EST:** 1977
SQ FT: 100,000
SALES (est): 57.4MM **Privately Held**
SIC: 5084 3625 3541 Machine tools & metalworking machinery; machine tools & accessories; controlling instruments & accessories; electric controls & control accessories, industrial; grinding machines, metalworking
HQ: Jtekt North America Corporation
7 Research Dr Ste A
Greenville SC 29607
440 835-1000

(G-765)
KEONIX CORPORATION
922 N Chicago Ave (60004-4425)
P.O. Box 87 (60006-0087)
PHONE.................847 259-9430
Michael McKee, *President*
EMP: 5
SQ FT: 1,000
SALES (est): 500K **Privately Held**
SIC: 3625 3545 Relays & industrial controls; machine tool accessories

(G-766)
KOZACZKA INC
3350 N Carriageway Dr (60004-1555)
PHONE.................224 435-6180

GEOGRAPHIC SECTION

Arlington Heights - Cook County (G-795)

Steven Kozaczka, *President*
EMP: 7
SALES (est): 225.7K **Privately Held**
SIC: 2519 Household furniture

(G-767)
LAWLOR MARKETING
2035 S Arlington Hts Rd (60005-4515)
PHONE 847 357-1080
Dan Lawlor, *Principal*
EMP: 4
SALES (est): 188.9K **Privately Held**
SIC: 2037 Frozen fruits & vegetables

(G-768)
LAWRENCE MADDOCK
Also Called: Morton Grove Auto Electric
500 S Arthur Ave (60005-2141)
PHONE 847 394-1698
Lawrence Maddock, *Owner*
EMP: 11
SQ FT: 2,600
SALES (est): 688.3K **Privately Held**
WEB: www.mgautoelectric.com
SIC: 7539 7694 Alternators & generators, rebuilding & repair; armature rewinding shops

(G-769)
LINE GROUP INC (PA)
Also Called: Line Tool & Stamping Co
539 W Algonquin Rd (60005-4411)
PHONE 847 593-6810
Al G Panico, *President*
Tom Mills, *Purchasing*
Joseph A Katalak, *Admin Sec*
EMP: 43
SQ FT: 40,000
SALES (est): 8.4MM **Privately Held**
WEB: www.thelinegroup.com
SIC: 3469 3544 3423 3824 Stamping metal for the trade; special dies & tools; hand & edge tools; electromechanical counters

(G-770)
LIVE WIRE & CABLE CO
409 W University Dr (60004-1813)
PHONE 847 577-5483
Perry Stein, *President*
Elisha M Prero, *Admin Sec*
EMP: 7
SQ FT: 20,000
SALES (est): 1.2MM **Privately Held**
SIC: 3357 Communication wire

(G-771)
LODAN ELECTRONICS INC
3311 N Kennicott Ave (60004-1429)
PHONE 847 398-5311
Raymond A Kedzior, *President*
Thomas Cornhoff, *President*
Brett Kedzior, *Vice Pres*
Patricia Bonner, *CFO*
Andrew Longhinl, *Director*
EMP: 200
SQ FT: 100,000
SALES (est): 37.2MM **Privately Held**
SIC: 3679 Harness assemblies for electronic use; wire or cable

(G-772)
LUCKY YUPPY PUPPY CO
Also Called: Gumball Machine Factory.com
533 W Golf Rd (60005-3904)
PHONE 847 437-7879
Terry Gold, *President*
Larry Glick, *Vice Pres*
◆ **EMP:** 6
SALES (est): 742.6K **Privately Held**
SIC: 3581 Automatic vending machines

(G-773)
LUXURY UPGRADE INC
987 W Happfield Dr (60004-7143)
PHONE 773 875-8018
Halyna Miska, *CEO*
EMP: 1
SALES: 225K **Privately Held**
SIC: 1389 Construction, repair & dismantling services

(G-774)
MANHATTAN EYELASH EXT SEW ON
8 S Dunton Ave (60005-1402)
PHONE 847 818-8774
Kyoung Jun, *Owner*
EMP: 3
SALES (est): 123.6K **Privately Held**
SIC: 3999 Eyelashes, artificial

(G-775)
MECHANICAL MUSIC CORP
Also Called: Advantage Worldwide Wholesale
3319 N Ridge Ave (60004-1411)
PHONE 847 398-5444
William A Walzak, *President*
EMP: 11
SQ FT: 5,000
SALES (est): 1.7MM **Privately Held**
SIC: 5099 3161 3931 3651 Musical instruments; musical instruments parts & accessories; musical instrument cases; musical instruments; household audio & video equipment

(G-776)
MINUTEMAN PRESS INC
1324 W Algonquin Rd (60005-3401)
PHONE 847 577-2411
Scott Clemetsen, *President*
EMP: 4
SQ FT: 1,500
SALES (est): 405.2K **Privately Held**
SIC: 2752 2789 2759 Commercial printing, lithographic; bookbinding & related work; commercial printing

(G-777)
MONTCLARE SCIENTIFIC GLASS
25 N Hickory Ave (60004-6204)
PHONE 847 255-6870
Peter Calandra, *President*
Kathleen Calandra, *Vice Pres*
EMP: 8
SQ FT: 3,000
SALES: 700K **Privately Held**
SIC: 3229 3231 Glassware, industrial; bulbs for electric lights; products of purchased glass

(G-778)
MORITEQ RUBBER CO
Also Called: Moriteq USA Contacts
710 W Algonquin Rd (60004-4416)
PHONE 847 734-0970
Hidenori Tanabe, *President*
Yoshihiro Mori, *Admin Sec*
EMP: 11 **EST:** 2000
SALES (est): 1.6MM **Privately Held**
WEB: www.moritequsa.com
SIC: 2822 Synthetic rubber

(G-779)
MOTOROLA SOLUTIONS INC
1155 W Dundee Rd (60004-1421)
PHONE 847 540-8815
Allen Dickson, *Principal*
EMP: 142
SALES (corp-wide): 7.8B **Publicly Held**
SIC: 3663 Radio & TV communications equipment
PA: Motorola Solutions, Inc.
500 W Monroe St Ste 4400
Chicago IL 60661
847 576-5000

(G-780)
NATIONAL COMPONENT SALES INC
Also Called: World Wide Broach
1229 E Algonquin Rd Jk (60005-4761)
PHONE 847 439-0333
Patricia L Reff, *Principal*
Peter Reff, *Vice Pres*
EMP: 10 **EST:** 1966
SQ FT: 5,000
SALES (est): 590K **Privately Held**
SIC: 3599 3544 Machine shop, jobbing & repair; special dies, tools, jigs & fixtures

(G-781)
NEUMANN CUSTOM WOODWORKING
2420 E Oakton St Ste Z (60005-4827)
PHONE 847 979-3199
Ron Neumann, *President*
EMP: 6 **EST:** 1999
SALES (est): 731.1K **Privately Held**
WEB: www.neumanncustomwoodworking.com
SIC: 2434 Wood kitchen cabinets

(G-782)
OBERWEIS DAIRY INC
Also Called: Oberweis Ice Cream and Dar Str
9 E Dundee Rd (60004-1539)
PHONE 847 368-9060
Elaine Oberweis, *Manager*
Sharon Ceranek, *Manager*
EMP: 12
SALES (corp-wide): 249.7MM **Privately Held**
WEB: www.oberweisdairy.com
SIC: 2026 5963 5451 Milk processing (pasteurizing, homogenizing, bottling); milk delivery; milk; ice cream (packaged)
PA: Oberweis Dairy, Inc.
951 Ice Cream Dr
North Aurora IL 60542
630 801-6100

(G-783)
OHARE PRECISION METALS LLC
2404 Hamilton Rd (60005-4812)
PHONE 847 640-6050
Ahmed Salem, *Owner*
Randall Brown, *Sales Mgr*
Tom Knowles,
EMP: 24
SQ FT: 12,000
SALES (est): 4.5MM **Privately Held**
SIC: 3599 Grinding castings for the trade

(G-784)
OLSON METAL PRODUCTS LLC (HQ)
Also Called: IMS Buhrke-Olson
511 W Algonquin Rd (60004-4411)
PHONE 847 981-7550
Mark Simanton, *CEO*
Abby Ahrens, *Human Res Mgr*
EMP: 17 **EST:** 2008
SALES: 45.5MM
SALES (corp-wide): 189.6MM **Privately Held**
WEB: www.metalstamper.com
SIC: 3469 Stamping metal for the trade
PA: Ims Companies, Llc
1 Innovation Dr
Des Plaines IL 60016
847 391-8100

(G-785)
OLYMPIC BINDERY INC
1105 N Chestnut Ave (60004-4615)
PHONE 847 577-8132
Dan Mooney, *President*
John A Welacha, *Vice Pres*
EMP: 97
SQ FT: 60,000
SALES (est): 8.9MM **Privately Held**
SIC: 2789 Paper cutting

(G-786)
PADDOCK PUBLICATIONS INC (PA)
Also Called: Daily Herald
95 W Algonquin Rd Ste 300 (60005-4451)
P.O. Box 280 (60006-0280)
PHONE 847 427-4300
Doug Ray, *President*
Caroline Linden, *Editor*
Brian Shamie, *Editor*
Susan Stark, *Editor*
Daniel E Baumann, *Chairman*
EMP: 450
SQ FT: 145,000
SALES (est): 79.9MM **Privately Held**
WEB: www.dailyheraldmediagroup.com
SIC: 2711 Commercial printing & newspaper publishing combined; newspapers, publishing & printing

(G-787)
PAN PAC INTERNATIONAL INC
3456 N Ridge Ave Ste 300 (60004-7817)
PHONE 847 222-9077
Fax: 847 222-9078
▲ **EMP:** 7
SQ FT: 12,000
SALES (est): 730K **Privately Held**
SIC: 3562 Mfg Ball & Roller Bearings & Casters

(G-788)
PLASTIC SERVICES GROUP
115 S Wilke Rd Ste 206e (60005-1519)
PHONE 847 368-1444
Dan Bendixon, *President*
EMP: 5
SALES (est): 448.7K **Privately Held**
WEB: www.plasticservicesgroup.com
SIC: 3089 8711 Extruded finished plastic products; engineering services

(G-789)
PRECISION-TEK MFG INC
Also Called: Precision-Tek Mfg
3206 Nordic Rd (60005-4729)
PHONE 847 364-7800
Keith Pflum, *President*
EMP: 36
SQ FT: 16,000
SALES (est): 7.4MM **Privately Held**
SIC: 3451 Screw machine products

(G-790)
PRIME TIME SPORTS LLC
216 W University Dr (60004-1810)
PHONE 847 637-3500
Debra Gurnack, *General Mgr*
Debra Bell, *Office Mgr*
Christy Commiso, *Office Mgr*
Freddie Lagroue, *Executive*
Mark Jiannechini,
EMP: 14
SQ FT: 1,500
SALES: 2.5MM **Privately Held**
SIC: 3663 Satellites, communications

(G-791)
PRINT TURNAROUND INC
3025 Malmo Dr (60005-4727)
PHONE 847 228-1762
Bruce Johnson, *President*
Pamela McKeown, *Opers Mgr*
Bob Lozano, *Director*
Dominick De Micco, *Shareholder*
EMP: 17
SQ FT: 3,600
SALES (est): 2.7MM **Privately Held**
SIC: 2752 2791 2789 Commercial printing, offset; typesetting; bookbinding & related work

(G-792)
PRINTING DIMENSIONS
1515 S Highland Ave (60005-3663)
PHONE 847 439-7521
Richard M Bilek, *Principal*
EMP: 3
SALES (est): 234.9K **Privately Held**
SIC: 2752 Commercial printing, offset

(G-793)
PROMO CORP
744 W Algonquin Rd (60005-4416)
PHONE 773 217-7666
EMP: 4
SALES (est): 442.3K **Privately Held**
SIC: 2752 Commercial printing, offset

(G-794)
QUICKSILVER MECHANICAL INC
3361 N Ridge Ave (60004-1411)
PHONE 847 577-1564
Michael Scanlan, *President*
EMP: 6
SALES (est): 993.9K **Privately Held**
SIC: 3444 Sheet metalwork

(G-795)
R L KOLBI COMPANY
Also Called: Kolbi Pipe Marker Co
416 W Campus Dr (60004-1406)
PHONE 847 506-1440
Rob Sietz, *President*
EMP: 18
SQ FT: 5,200

Arlington Heights - Cook County (G-796)

SALES (est): 4.7MM **Privately Held**
WEB: www.kolbipipemarkers.com
SIC: 3821 Pi tapes (metal periphery direct reading diameter tapes)

(G-796)
RARE BIRDS INC
321 E Rand Rd (60004-3103)
PHONE..................847 259-7286
Ron Zick, *President*
EMP: 4
SALES (est): 238.8K **Privately Held**
SIC: 2048 Bird food, prepared

(G-797)
REFLEJOS PUBLICATIONS LLC
155 E Algonquin Rd (60005-4617)
PHONE..................847 806-1111
Raul Ortiz, *Marketing Staff*
Linda Siete, *Manager*
Jerry Campagna,
EMP: 30
SQ FT: 2,000
SALES (est): 1.6MM **Privately Held**
WEB: www.reflejos.com
SIC: 2711 Newspapers, publishing & printing; newspapers: publishing only, not printed on site

(G-798)
REIGN PRINT SOLUTIONS INC
550 W Campus Dr (60004-1408)
PHONE..................847 590-7091
William Jourdan III, *President*
William G Jourdan III, *President*
Lynn Galizia, *Admin Sec*
EMP: 7
SQ FT: 3,000
SALES (est): 1.4MM **Privately Held**
SIC: 5112 7379 2752 5943 Business forms; office supplies; computer & photo-copying supplies; computer related consulting services; commercial printing, lithographic; office forms & supplies; business consulting

(G-799)
REILLY COMMUNICATION GROUP
3030 W Salt Creek Ln # 201 (60005-5002)
PHONE..................630 756-1225
EMP: 15
SALES (est): 992K **Privately Held**
SIC: 2721 Periodicals-Publishing/Printing

(G-800)
RELIANCE GRAPHICS INC
2035 S Arlington Hts Rd (60005-4515)
PHONE..................847 593-6688
Robert Napoleon, *President*
EMP: 5
SQ FT: 5,500
SALES (est): 797.7K **Privately Held**
SIC: 2752 Commercial printing, offset

(G-801)
RLS USA INC
3350 N Ridge Ave (60004-1412)
PHONE..................865 548-1449
Werner Gruner, *CEO*
EMP: 503
SALES (est): 81.8K **Privately Held**
SIC: 2834 Pharmaceutical preparations

(G-802)
RW WELDING INC (PA)
1511 S Princeton Ave (60005-3414)
PHONE..................847 541-5508
Robert O'Keith, *President*
EMP: 8
SALES (est): 216.4K **Privately Held**
SIC: 7692 Welding repair

(G-803)
S C C PUMPS INC
708 W Algonquin Rd (60005-4416)
PHONE..................847 593-8495
Kenneth Porter, *President*
Eric Porter, *Vice Pres*
Lucia A Porter, *Admin Sec*
▲ EMP: 7 EST: 1974
SQ FT: 4,000
SALES (est): 1.4MM **Privately Held**
SIC: 3561 Pumps & pumping equipment

(G-804)
SANTEC SYSTEMS INC
2924 Malmo Dr (60005-4726)
PHONE..................847 215-8884
Jaswinder Sandhu, *President*
Doug McLane, *Engineer*
EMP: 10
SQ FT: 2,025
SALES (est): 1.1MM **Privately Held**
SIC: 3829 Ultrasonic testing equipment; aircraft & motor vehicle measurement equipment

(G-805)
SCRANTON GLLTTE CMMNCTIONS INC (PA)
Also Called: S G C
3030 W Salt Creek Ln # 201 (60005-5025)
PHONE..................847 391-1000
Edward S Gillette, *President*
Ryan Hanson, *Publisher*
Jerome Butera, *Editor*
Stephen Schnurr, *Editor*
Nigel Maynard, *Chief*
◆ EMP: 62
SQ FT: 11,000
SALES (est): 15.4MM **Privately Held**
WEB: www.scrantongillette.com
SIC: 2721 Trade journals: publishing only, not printed on site

(G-806)
SEDECAL USA INC (HQ)
3190 N Kennicott Ave (60004-1426)
PHONE..................847 394-6960
Manuel Martinez, *Principal*
Daniel Moreta, *Admin Sec*
▲ EMP: 26
SQ FT: 5,000
SALES (est): 5.4MM
SALES (corp-wide): 142.1MM **Privately Held**
SIC: 3844 X-ray generators
PA: Sociedad Espalola De Electromedicina Y Calidad Sa
Calle De La Pelaya (Pg Industrial Rio De Janeiro) 9
Algete 28110
916 280-544

(G-807)
SEMPER FI PRINTING LLC
2420 E Oakton St Ste Q (60005-4827)
PHONE..................847 640-7737
Brett Schwartz, *Vice Pres*
Craig Brunk,
Cheryl Banas, *Graphic Designe*
EMP: 6 EST: 2008
SALES (est): 864.5K **Privately Held**
WEB: www.semperfiprinting.com
SIC: 2752 Commercial printing, offset

(G-808)
SGC HORIZON LLC
Also Called: S G C
3030 W Salt Creek Ln (60005-5001)
PHONE..................847 391-1000
Edward Gillette, *President*
EMP: 1
SALES (est): 337.4K
SALES (corp-wide): 15.4MM **Privately Held**
WEB: www.scrantongillette.com
SIC: 2721 Trade journals: publishing only, not printed on site
PA: Scranton Gillette Communications, Inc.
3030 W Salt Creek Ln # 201
Arlington Heights IL 60005
847 391-1000

(G-809)
SHEET METAL WERKS INC (PA)
455 E Algonquin Rd (60005-4620)
PHONE..................847 827-4700
Kevin Ryan, *President*
Patrick Ryan, *Vice Pres*
Jeremy Schwartz, *Purch Mgr*
Susan Ryan, *Admin Sec*
EMP: 51
SQ FT: 48,000
SALES (est): 10.4MM **Privately Held**
SIC: 3444 Sheet metalwork

(G-810)
SONOCO PROTECTIVE SOLUTIONS
Also Called: Thermal Safe Brands
3930 N Ventura Dr Ste 450 (60004-7432)
PHONE..................847 398-0110
EMP: 30
SALES (corp-wide): 5B **Publicly Held**
SIC: 3086 Mfg Expandable Polystyrene Foam
HQ: Sonoco Protective Solutions, Inc.
1 N 2nd St
Hartsville SC 29550
843 383-7000

(G-811)
SONOCO PRTECTIVE SOLUTIONS INC
Also Called: Sca Thermosafe
3930 N Ventura Dr Ste 450 (60004-7432)
PHONE..................847 398-0110
Dave Nicley, *Business Mgr*
Dave Arnold, *Engineer*
Alexander Poleshchuk, *Accountant*
Joy Butzke, *Credit Staff*
Richard Smith, *Manager*
EMP: 55
SALES (corp-wide): 5.3B **Publicly Held**
WEB: www.sonoco.com
SIC: 2631 Container, packaging & boxboard
HQ: Sonoco Protective Solutions, Inc.
1 N 2nd St
Hartsville SC 29550
843 383-7000

(G-812)
STELMONT INC
Also Called: Arlington Signs & Banners
1312 W Northwest Hwy (60004-5250)
PHONE..................847 870-0200
Monte Sellers, *President*
Stella Sellers, *Corp Secy*
EMP: 5 EST: 1998
SALES (est): 554.6K **Privately Held**
SIC: 3993 Signs, not made in custom sign painting shops

(G-813)
STONE FABRICATORS COMPANY
1604 N Clarence Ave (60004-4024)
PHONE..................847 788-8296
Kerry Kremer, *Partner*
EMP: 3
SALES (est): 208.6K **Privately Held**
SIC: 2541 Counter & sink tops

(G-814)
SU ENTERPRISE INC
403 N Reuter Dr (60005-1127)
PHONE..................847 394-1656
Neichung Su, *President*
Neiming Su, *Vice Pres*
EMP: 6 EST: 1993
SALES (est): 516.5K **Privately Held**
SIC: 7372 Business oriented computer software

(G-815)
SUMMIT SIGNWORKS INC
2265 E Ashbury Ct (60004-4363)
PHONE..................847 870-0937
EMP: 3
SALES (est): 200K **Privately Held**
SIC: 3993 Mfg Signs/Advertising Specialties

(G-816)
TAGORE TECHNOLOGY INC
5 E College Dr Ste 200 (60004-1963)
PHONE..................847 790-3799
Amitava Das, *President*
EMP: 15
SALES (est): 822K **Privately Held**
SIC: 3674 8731 Semiconductors & related devices; commercial physical research

(G-817)
TECHNIC INC
3265 N Ridge Ave (60004-1490)
PHONE..................773 262-2662
Jim Sincell, *Manager*
EMP: 8

SALES (corp-wide): 125.5MM **Privately Held**
WEB: www.technic.com
SIC: 2899 Metal treating compounds
PA: Technic, Inc.
47 Molter St
Cranston RI 02910
401 781-6100

(G-818)
TELEFLEX INCORPORATED
900 W University Dr (60004-1824)
PHONE..................847 259-7400
Evelyn Herron, *Human Res Mgr*
Kevin Rush, *Manager*
EMP: 100
SALES (corp-wide): 2.6B **Publicly Held**
SIC: 3842 3841 Surgical appliances & supplies; surgical & medical instruments
PA: Teleflex Incorporated
550 E Swedesford Rd # 400
Wayne PA 19087
610 225-6800

(G-819)
TERADYNE INC
715 W Algonquin Rd Ste A (60005-4438)
PHONE..................847 981-0400
Robert Weiss, *Sales/Mktg Mgr*
Kyle Morgensai, *Info Tech Dir*
EMP: 10
SALES (corp-wide): 2.3B **Publicly Held**
SIC: 3825 Semiconductor test equipment
PA: Teradyne, Inc.
600 Riverpark Dr
North Reading MA 01864
978 370-2700

(G-820)
TOWN SQUARE PUBLICATIONS LLC
155 E Arlington Hts Rd (60005)
PHONE..................847 427-4633
Dan Nugara, *President*
John Hubbard, *Sales Staff*
EMP: 1
SALES (est): 1.2MM
SALES (corp-wide): 79.9MM **Privately Held**
SIC: 2759 Publication printing
PA: Paddock Publications, Inc.
95 W Algonquin Rd Ste 300
Arlington Heights IL 60005
847 427-4300

(G-821)
TRIBEAM INC
1323 S Fernandez Ave (60005-3543)
PHONE..................847 409-9497
Michael Kazecki, *CEO*
▲ EMP: 9 EST: 2000
SQ FT: 1,000
SALES (est): 1.1MM **Privately Held**
SIC: 3663 Mobile communication equipment

(G-822)
TRICK PERCUSSION PRODUCTS INC
17 E University Dr (60004-1801)
PHONE..................847 342-2019
Michael R Dorfman, *President*
Bill Borenstein, *Admin Sec*
EMP: 3
SQ FT: 13,000
SALES: 1MM **Privately Held**
SIC: 3931 Percussion instruments & parts; drums, parts & accessories (musical instruments)

(G-823)
TRU GRIND INC
3803 N Ventura Dr (60004-7466)
PHONE..................847 749-3163
EMP: 12
SALES (est): 1.8MM **Privately Held**
SIC: 3599 Machine shop, jobbing & repair

(G-824)
UNIFIED SOLUTIONS CORP
Also Called: Unified Distributors
3456 N Ridge Ave Ste 200 (60004-7817)
PHONE..................847 478-9100
Yan Bolotin, *CEO*
Dmitry Shraybman, *COO*
EMP: 30

GEOGRAPHIC SECTION   Arthur - Douglas County (G-852)

SQ FT: 30,000
SALES: 12MM **Privately Held**
SIC: 7629 5999 3661 7389 Telecommunication equipment repair (except telephones); mobile telephones & equipment; telephone & telegraph apparatus; packaging & labeling services; testing laboratories; electronic parts & equipment

(G-825)
VANITIES INC
212 W University Dr (60004-1810)
PHONE...................847 483-0240
James Stubing, *President*
Barbara Stubing, *Corp Secy*
EMP: 6
SQ FT: 12,000
SALES: 600K **Privately Held**
SIC: 2434 Vanities, bathroom: wood

(G-826)
VIBGYOR OPTICAL SYSTEMS CORP
1140 N Phelps Ave (60004-5030)
PHONE...................847 818-0788
Bharat Verma, *President*
EMP: 45
SQ FT: 3,200
SALES (est): 5.1MM **Privately Held**
SIC: 3827 Optical instruments & lenses

(G-827)
VIBGYOR OPTICS INC
Also Called: Optical Systems
1140 N Phelps Ave (60004-5030)
PHONE...................847 818-0788
Bharat S Verma, *President*
Anuradha Verma, *Vice Pres*
Sonia Gill, *Admin Sec*
EMP: 40
SQ FT: 5,400
SALES (est): 2MM **Privately Held**
SIC: 5049 3827 Optical goods; optical instruments & lenses

(G-828)
VLAHOS ELECTRIC SERVICE DR
1707 N Dale Ave (60004-4328)
PHONE...................224 764-2335
Gus Vlahos, *Owner*
EMP: 3 EST: 2010
SALES (est): 196.4K **Privately Held**
SIC: 8011 3699 Offices & clinics of medical doctors; electrical equipment & supplies

(G-829)
VST AMERICA INC
85 W Algonquin Rd Ste 210 (60005-4423)
PHONE...................847 952-3800
Wakako Yamazaki, *Manager*
David Suhadolc, *Technical Staff*
◆ EMP: 3
SALES (est): 330K **Privately Held**
SIC: 3559 Optical lens machinery

(G-830)
W W BARTHEL & CO
220 W Campus Dr Ste C (60004-1479)
PHONE...................847 392-5643
EMP: 6 EST: 1974
SQ FT: 2,950
SALES (est): 420K **Privately Held**
SIC: 2759 2752 Commercial Printing Lithographic Commercial Printing

(G-831)
WEBER MARKING SYSTEMS INC (PA)
Also Called: Weber Packaging Solutions
711 W Algonquin Rd (60005-4455)
PHONE...................847 364-8500
Joseph A Weber Jr, *Ch of Bd*
Glenn C Gilly, *President*
Douglas A Weber, *Vice Pres*
Douglas Weber, *Vice Pres*
George Stieber, *VP Mfg*
◆ EMP: 425
SQ FT: 317,000
SALES (est): 159.1MM **Privately Held**
WEB: www.weberpackaging.com
SIC: 3555 2672 2675 Printing trades machinery; labels (unprinted), gummed: made from purchased materials; die-cut paper & board

(G-832)
WHERE 2 GET IT LLC
21 S Evergreen Ave 240a (60005-7800)
PHONE...................224 232-5550
Manish Patel, *Branch Mgr*
EMP: 15
SALES (corp-wide): 10.4MM **Privately Held**
SIC: 2741 Globe covers (maps): publishing & printing
PA: Where 2 Get It, Inc.
  222 S Harbor Blvd Ste 600
  Anaheim CA 92805
  714 660-4870

(G-833)
WILL HAMMS STAINED GLASS
628 N Highland Ave (60004-5514)
PHONE...................847 255-2230
William Hamm, *Owner*
William A Hamm, *Owner*
EMP: 10
SALES (est): 615.1K **Privately Held**
WEB: www.hammsglass.com
SIC: 3231 1793 Stained glass: made from purchased glass; glass & glazing work

(G-834)
WINDY CITY RC
220 W Rand Rd (60004-3145)
PHONE...................847 818-8354
EMP: 4
SALES (est): 352.6K **Privately Held**
SIC: 3644 Raceways

(G-835)
WITRON INTGRATED LOGISTICS INC
3721 N Ventura Dr (60004-7489)
PHONE...................847 398-6130
Karl Hoegen, *CEO*
Rick Jump, *Project Mgr*
Tim Verdoorn, *Site Mgr*
Thomas Heining, *Info Tech Mgr*
Agazzy Kan, *Software Dev*
▲ EMP: 180
SQ FT: 25,000
SALES (est): 64.8MM
SALES (corp-wide): 647.2MM **Privately Held**
SIC: 3535 Unit handling conveying systems
HQ: Witron Logistik + Informatik Gmbh
  Neustadter Str. 21
  Parkstein 92711
  960 260-00

(G-836)
WPC MACHINERY CORP
Also Called: Web Printing Control
3350 W Salt Creek Ln (60005-5023)
PHONE...................630 231-7721
Dean Fetherling, *President*
Patricia Fetherling, *Corp Secy*
Herman Gnuechtel, *Vice Pres*
EMP: 50 EST: 1976
SQ FT: 4,919
SALES (est): 3.3MM **Privately Held**
SIC: 7699 3555 Printing trades machinery & equipment repair; printing trades machinery

(G-837)
XPRESSIGNS INC
2470 E Oakton St (60005-4820)
PHONE...................888 303-0640
EMP: 3 EST: 2011
SQ FT: 3,000
SALES (est): 177.1K **Privately Held**
SIC: 3993 Signs & advertising specialties

(G-838)
YAMADA AMERICA INC
955 E Algonquin Rd (60005-4301)
PHONE...................847 228-9063
Shinji Kameyama, *Principal*
Karen Chambers, *Sales Staff*
Vaughn Mullet, *Manager*
Dayne Kono, *Admin Sec*
◆ EMP: 21
SQ FT: 30,000
SALES (est): 5.7MM **Privately Held**
SIC: 3561 5084 4813 Pumps & pumping equipment; pumps & pumping equipment;

PA: Yamada Corporation
  1-1-3, Minamimagome
  Ota-Ku TKY 143-0

Aroma Park
Kankakee County

(G-839)
ANCHOR WELDING & FABRICATION
2950 N Lowe Rd (60910-1069)
P.O. Box 26 (60910-0026)
PHONE...................815 937-1640
Janet Andreina, *President*
Nick Andreina, *Admin Sec*
EMP: 2
SQ FT: 5,200
SALES (est): 254.6K **Privately Held**
SIC: 3441 3442 7692 3446 Fabricated structural metal; window & door frames; welding repair; architectural metalwork; sheet metalwork; fabricated plate work (boiler shop)

(G-840)
NEW DIMENSION MODELS
Also Called: Fiberglass International
105 W Front St (60910-1058)
P.O. Box 28 (60910-0028)
PHONE...................815 935-1001
Fax: 815 935-1060
EMP: 6
SQ FT: 4,200
SALES (est): 460K **Privately Held**
SIC: 3469 Mfg Lawn/Garden Equipment Engineering Services Mfg Industrial Patterns

Arthur
Douglas County

(G-841)
ARTHUR CUSTOM TANK LLC
510 E Progress St (61911-1545)
PHONE...................217 543-4022
Patrick Hartman,
EMP: 5
SALES (est): 1.3MM **Privately Held**
SIC: 3443 Tanks for tank trucks, metal plate

(G-842)
ARTHUR GRAPHIC CLARION
113 E Illinois St (61911-1331)
P.O. Box 19 (61911-0019)
PHONE...................217 543-2151
Greg Hoskins, *President*
EMP: 4 EST: 1887
SQ FT: 3,000
SALES (est): 170K **Privately Held**
WEB: www.arthuril.us
SIC: 2711 2752 Job printing & newspaper publishing combined; commercial printing, lithographic

(G-843)
C B M PLASTICS INC
398 E St Rt 133 (61911-6232)
PHONE...................217 543-3870
Fred Helmuth, *President*
EMP: 10 EST: 1998
SALES (est): 1.8MM **Privately Held**
WEB: www.cbmplastics.com
SIC: 3442 Garage doors, overhead: metal

(G-844)
CARSTIN BRANDS INC
520 E 2nd St (61911-1129)
P.O. Box 285 (61911-0285)
PHONE...................217 543-3331
Sam S Petersheim Jr, *President*
EMP: 90
SQ FT: 37,000
SALES (est): 17MM **Privately Held**
SIC: 3088 Bathroom fixtures, plastic; sinks, plastic; tubs (bath, shower & laundry), plastic

(G-845)
CENTRAL ILLINOIS POULTRY PROC
119 N Cr 000 E (61911-6532)
PHONE...................217 543-2937
Andy Jess, *Owner*
EMP: 15
SALES (est): 1.4MM **Privately Held**
SIC: 2015 Poultry slaughtering & processing

(G-846)
CHI DOORS HOLDINGS INC (DH)
Also Called: CHI Overhead Doors
1485 Sunrise Dr (61911-1684)
PHONE...................217 543-2135
Jim Overholt, *President*
Pat Knoll, *CFO*
Jason Mills, *Technology*
◆ EMP: 2
SALES (est): 225.1MM **Publicly Held**
SIC: 3442 Metal doors, sash & trim
HQ: Kohlberg Kravis Roberts & Co. L.P.
  9 W 57th St Ste 4200
  New York NY 10019
  212 750-8300

(G-847)
COACH HOUSE INC
Also Called: Coach House Garages
700 E Mill St (61911-1689)
P.O. Box 320 (61911-0320)
PHONE...................217 543-3761
James Yoder, *President*
Larry Diener, *Prdtn Mgr*
Dave Binion, *Human Res Mgr*
EMP: 41
SQ FT: 68,000
SALES (est): 7.6MM **Privately Held**
SIC: 2452 Farm & agricultural buildings, prefabricated wood

(G-848)
CORNERSTONE BUILDING PRODUCTS
226 E Cr 600 N (61911-6223)
PHONE...................217 543-2829
Alan Dean Miller, *Owner*
EMP: 2
SQ FT: 940
SALES (est): 255.5K **Privately Held**
SIC: 2952 5211 Roofing materials; doors, storm: wood or metal

(G-849)
COUNTRY WORKSHOP
Also Called: Miller Ervin B
651 N Cr 125 E (61911-6220)
PHONE...................217 543-4094
Ervin D Miller, *Owner*
EMP: 5
SALES (est): 462.1K **Privately Held**
SIC: 2511 Wood household furniture

(G-850)
CUSTOM SCREEN PRINTING
111 N Vine St (61911-1116)
P.O. Box 144 (61911-0144)
PHONE...................217 543-3691
Alvie Jess, *Principal*
EMP: 4
SALES (est): 303K **Privately Held**
WEB: www.csparthur.com
SIC: 2759 Screen printing

(G-851)
DAVID L KAUFMAN
Also Called: Country Side Woodworking
550 N Cr 240 E (61911-6228)
PHONE...................217 543-4190
David L Kaufman, *Owner*
EMP: 16
SALES (est): 1.8MM **Privately Held**
SIC: 3533 Derricks, oil or gas field

(G-852)
DG WOOD PROCESSING
120 E Cr 200 N (61911-6515)
PHONE...................217 543-2128
David Gingerich, *Owner*
EMP: 16
SALES (est): 1.7MM **Privately Held**
SIC: 2448 5099 Pallets, wood; firewood

Arthur - Douglas County (G-853)

(G-853)
DOEROCK INC
Also Called: Tool World
901 E Columbia St (61911-9737)
P.O. Box 258 (61911-0258)
PHONE..................217 543-2101
Elmer A Schrock, *President*
Voleta Schrock, *Corp Secy*
EMP: 3
SQ FT: 2,500
SALES (est): 810.3K **Privately Held**
SIC: 5072 3423 5251 Hand tools; hand & edge tools; tools, hand

(G-854)
DOUGLAS COUNTY WOOD PRODUCTS
491 N Cr 100 E (61911-6501)
PHONE..................217 543-2888
Steve Kaufmann, *Owner*
EMP: 7
SALES (est): 1.2MM **Privately Held**
SIC: 2511 Wood bedroom furniture

(G-855)
E M C INDUSTRY
441 E Cr 400 N (61911-6243)
PHONE..................217 543-2894
Eldon Chutp, *Partner*
Eldon Chupp, *Partner*
EMP: 2
SALES: 200K **Privately Held**
SIC: 2512 Upholstered household furniture

(G-856)
E Z TRAIL INC (PA)
1050 E Columbia St (61911-9739)
P.O. Box 168 (61911-0168)
PHONE..................217 543-3471
Abe B Kuhns, *President*
Danny Kuhns, *Vice Pres*
Tim Kuhns, *Admin Sec*
▲ **EMP:** 30
SQ FT: 72,000
SALES (est): 6.7MM **Privately Held**
WEB: www.e-ztrail.com
SIC: 3523 Trailers & wagons, farm

(G-857)
F & B WOODWORKING INC
Also Called: F & B Distributors
1702 Cr 2300n (61911-6089)
PHONE..................217 543-2531
Freeman Beachy, *President*
Bertha Beachy, *Corp Secy*
EMP: 2
SQ FT: 45,000
SALES (est): 221.3K **Privately Held**
SIC: 6799 2434 Investors; wood kitchen cabinets

(G-858)
FOUR ACRE WOOD PRODUCTS
553 N Cr 240 E (61911-6227)
PHONE..................217 543-2971
David Kauffman, *Owner*
EMP: 13 **EST:** 1978
SQ FT: 50,000
SALES: 800K **Privately Held**
SIC: 2434 2431 Wood kitchen cabinets; door trim, wood

(G-859)
GDS ENTERPRISES
399 E Progress St (61911-1431)
PHONE..................217 543-3681
Glen Schlabach, *Owner*
EMP: 4
SQ FT: 250
SALES: 300K **Privately Held**
SIC: 5261 3511 Garden supplies & tools; turbines & turbine generator sets

(G-860)
GINGERICH CUSTOM WOODWORKING
750 N Cr 250 E (61911-6216)
PHONE..................217 578-3491
Ivan Gingerich, *Owner*
EMP: 15
SALES (est): 1MM **Privately Held**
WEB: www.dkkkitchens.com
SIC: 2431 Interior & ornamental woodwork & trim

(G-861)
HEARTLAND MACHINE AND SUP LLC
337 E Sr 133 (61911-6200)
PHONE..................217 543-2678
Joseph Mast, *Mng Member*
EMP: 18 **EST:** 1965
SQ FT: 4,000
SALES (est): 1.2MM **Privately Held**
SIC: 3599 Machine shop, jobbing & repair

(G-862)
HELMUTH CUSTOM KITCHENS LLC
Also Called: Family Health Foods
2004 Cr 1800e (61911-6062)
PHONE..................217 543-3588
Adlai L Helmuth, *Mng Member*
Edna Helmuth, *Mng Member*
Gladys Helmuth, *Mng Member*
Katie Helmuth, *Mng Member*
Paul Helmuth, *Mng Member*
EMP: 45
SQ FT: 20,000
SALES (est): 5.7MM **Privately Held**
SIC: 2434 5499 Wood kitchen cabinets; health foods

(G-863)
HERSCHBERGER WOOD WORKING
145 E Cr 300 N (61911-6541)
PHONE..................217 543-4075
Eli Herschberger, *Owner*
EMP: 3
SALES (est): 219.1K **Privately Held**
SIC: 2499 Decorative wood & woodwork

(G-864)
KAUFMAN WOODWORKING
29 E Cr 100 N (61911-6531)
PHONE..................217 543-3607
Lloyd Kaufman, *Owner*
EMP: 3
SALES (est): 209K **Privately Held**
SIC: 2499 Decorative wood & woodwork

(G-865)
LAMBRIGHT DISTRIBUTORS
35 E Cr 200 N (61911-6533)
PHONE..................217 543-2083
Vernon Lambright, *Owner*
Elsie Lambright, *Co-Owner*
EMP: 5
SALES (est): 656K **Privately Held**
SIC: 3632 5192 7623 Freezers, home & farm; books, periodicals & newspapers; refrigeration service & repair

(G-866)
LITTLE CREEK WOODWORKING
1473 Cr 1675e (61911-6043)
PHONE..................217 543-2815
Verna Herschberger, *Owner*
Mervin Herschberber, *Owner*
EMP: 1
SALES (est): 612K **Privately Held**
SIC: 3553 2499 Furniture makers' machinery, woodworking; decorative wood & woodwork

(G-867)
MASTERBRAND CABINETS INC
501 W Progress St (61911-1232)
PHONE..................217 543-3311
Paul Spivey, *Sales/Mktg Mgr*
EMP: 500
SQ FT: 325,000
SALES (corp-wide): 5.7B **Publicly Held**
WEB: www.masterbrand.com
SIC: 2434 Wood kitchen cabinets
HQ: Masterbrand Cabinets, Inc.
1 Masterbrand Cabinets Dr
Jasper IN 47546
812 482-2527

(G-868)
MASTERBRAND CABINETS INC
Also Called: Cabinet Factories Outlet
N Arthur Atwood Rd (61911)
PHONE..................217 543-3466
Dave Camp, *Manager*
EMP: 5
SALES (corp-wide): 5.7B **Publicly Held**
WEB: www.masterbrand.com
SIC: 2434 Wood kitchen cabinets
HQ: Masterbrand Cabinets, Inc.
1 Masterbrand Cabinets Dr
Jasper IN 47546
812 482-2527

(G-869)
MASTERBRAND CABINETS INC
Also Called: Diy Cabinet Warehouse
100 N Vine St (61911-1115)
PHONE..................503 241-4964
Jim Collins, *Branch Mgr*
EMP: 5
SALES (corp-wide): 5.7B **Publicly Held**
SIC: 2434 Wood kitchen cabinets
HQ: Masterbrand Cabinets, Inc.
1 Masterbrand Cabinets Dr
Jasper IN 47546
812 482-2527

(G-870)
MOULTRIE COUNTY HARDWOODS LLC
1618 Cr 2000n (61911-6077)
PHONE..................217 543-2643
Marion Miller, *Mng Member*
EMP: 5
SQ FT: 12,000
SALES (est): 676.5K **Privately Held**
SIC: 2426 5023 Hardwood dimension & flooring mills; wood flooring

(G-871)
NELSON DOOR CO
2245 Cr 1500e (61911-6024)
PHONE..................217 543-3489
Nelson Deener, *Owner*
Ruth Deener, *Co-Owner*
EMP: 5
SALES (est): 443.6K **Privately Held**
SIC: 2431 Doors, wood

(G-872)
O & I WOODWORKING
125 E County Rd 50 E (61911)
PHONE..................217 543-3155
Omer Otto, *Owner*
EMP: 4
SALES (est): 170K **Privately Held**
SIC: 2511 Wood household furniture

(G-873)
OKAW TRUSS INC
368 E Sr 133 (61911-6232)
PHONE..................217 543-3371
Fred Helmuth, *President*
Elvin Schrock, *General Mgr*
Darrick Yoder, *IT/INT Sup*
Floyd Yoder, *Admin Sec*
EMP: 425 **EST:** 1976
SALES (est): 79.1MM **Privately Held**
SIC: 2439 3441 Trusses, except roof: laminated lumber; fabricated structural metal

(G-874)
OKAW VALLEY WOODWORKING LLC
432 E Sr 133 (61911-6240)
PHONE..................217 543-5180
Merv Yoder, *Mng Member*
EMP: 10 **EST:** 2000
SQ FT: 9,000
SALES (est): 1.2MM **Privately Held**
WEB: www.okawvalleywoodworking.com
SIC: 2434 2511 Wood kitchen cabinets; wood household furniture

(G-875)
OTTOS CANVAS SHOP
1749b State Highway 133 (61911-6111)
PHONE..................217 543-3307
Melvin Otto, *Owner*
EMP: 5
SALES (est): 200K **Privately Held**
SIC: 2394 5499 5091 Canvas & related products; health & dietetic food stores; boat accessories & parts

(G-876)
PLANKS CABINET SHOP INC
1620 State Highway 133 (61911-6015)
PHONE..................217 543-2687
Mary Miller, *President*
Edward A Miller, *Vice Pres*
EMP: 8 **EST:** 1962
SQ FT: 1,000
SALES (est): 1MM **Privately Held**
SIC: 2434 2511 Wood kitchen cabinets; wood household furniture

(G-877)
PRAIRIE STATE MACHINE LLC
71 E Cr 100 N (61911-6531)
PHONE..................217 543-3768
Glen Herschberger, *Mng Member*
EMP: 9
SQ FT: 3,780
SALES (est): 800K **Privately Held**
SIC: 3553 Woodworking machinery

(G-878)
RICHARD SCHROCK
Also Called: Pineview Woodworking
41 E Cr 200 N (61911-6533)
PHONE..................217 543-3111
Richard Schrock, *Owner*
EMP: 6 **EST:** 1964
SALES (est): 850K **Privately Held**
SIC: 2434 Wood kitchen cabinets

(G-879)
SCHROCKS WOODWORKING
135 E Cr 800 N (61911-6211)
PHONE..................217 578-3259
Levi Schrock, *Owner*
EMP: 4
SALES (est): 319.7K **Privately Held**
SIC: 2434 Wood kitchen cabinets

(G-880)
TIMBERSIDE WOODWORKING
715 N Cr 125 E (61911-6209)
PHONE..................217 578-3201
Ray L Herschberger, *Owner*
EMP: 5
SALES (est): 363.4K **Privately Held**
SIC: 2517 Home entertainment unit cabinets, wood

(G-881)
TRI-CUNTY WLDG FABRICATION LLC
1031 E Columbia St (61911-9736)
P.O. Box 137 (61911-0137)
PHONE..................217 543-3304
Dennis L Plank,
EMP: 40
SQ FT: 86,000
SALES (est): 6.8MM **Privately Held**
SIC: 7692 1799 3441 Welding repair; welding on site; fabricated structural metal

(G-882)
WILLARD R SCHORCK
Also Called: Rocky Lane Woodworking
55 E Cr 300 N (61911-6551)
PHONE..................217 543-2160
Willard R Schorck, *Owner*
EMP: 12
SALES (est): 670K **Privately Held**
SIC: 2431 Millwork

Ashkum
Iroquois County

(G-883)
HEARTLAND CANDLE CO
2739 N 700 East Rd (60911-7153)
PHONE..................815 698-2200
A J Wilken, *Partner*
Pam Wilken, *Partner*
Lynn Wilken, *General Ptnr*
EMP: 4
SALES (est): 390.1K **Privately Held**
SIC: 3999 5947 Candles; gift, novelty & souvenir shop

GEOGRAPHIC SECTION

Ashland
Cass County

(G-884)
FULTON METAL WORKS INC
1763 Ashland Rd (62612-3456)
P.O. Box 242 (62612-0242)
PHONE.................................217 476-8223
Stan Fulton, *President*
Dustin Fulton, *Vice Pres*
Jeanne Fulton, *Treasurer*
EMP: 3
SQ FT: 9,000
SALES: 220K **Privately Held**
SIC: 3498 3444 Tube fabricating (contract bending & shaping); sheet metalwork

Ashley
Washington County

(G-885)
LICON INC
23297 County Highway 7 (62808-2723)
PHONE.................................618 485-2222
Lester Johannes, *President*
Rosemary Johannes, *Corp Secy*
Michael Johannes, *Vice Pres*
EMP: 3
SQ FT: 4,500
SALES (est): 330.9K **Privately Held**
SIC: 3599 3523 3444 Machine shop, jobbing & repair; farm machinery & equipment; sheet metalwork

Ashmore
Coles County

(G-886)
CHARLESTON STONE COMPANY
9709 N County Rd 2000 E (61912)
P.O. Box 260, Charleston (61920-0260)
PHONE.................................217 345-6292
Jerald Tarble, *President*
John Tarble, *Vice Pres*
EMP: 35 EST: 1937
SQ FT: 700
SALES: 4.6MM **Privately Held**
WEB: www.charlestonstoneco.com
SIC: 1422 Cement rock, crushed & broken-quarrying

Assumption
Christian County

(G-887)
A P LIVESTOCK DIVISION G S I
Also Called: G S I Group
1004 E Illinois St (62510-9529)
P.O. Box 20 (62510-0020)
PHONE.................................217 226-4449
Hans Luhman, *President*
Brian Johnson, *District Mgr*
◆ EMP: 2
SALES (est): 374.2K **Privately Held**
SIC: 3523 Farm machinery & equipment

(G-888)
B & B EQUIPMENT
401 S Business 5 (62510)
P.O. Box 53 (62510-0053)
PHONE.................................217 562-2511
Joe A Burton, *Partner*
Leota Burton, *Partner*
EMP: 11
SQ FT: 800
SALES (est): 484.8K **Privately Held**
SIC: 1389 Oil field services

(G-889)
GOLDEN PRAIRIE NEWS
301 S Chestnut St (62510-1299)
PHONE.................................217 226-3721
Fax: 217 226-3579
EMP: 4 EST: 1959
SQ FT: 2,400
SALES: 46K **Privately Held**
SIC: 2711 2759 2752 Newspapers-Publishing/Printing Commercial Printing Lithographic Commercial Printing

(G-890)
GRAIN SYSTEMS INC (DH)
Also Called: Gsi
1004 E Illinois St (62510-9529)
P.O. Box 20 (62510-0020)
PHONE.................................888 474-2467
Craig Sloan, *President*
EMP: 4
SALES (est): 33.6MM **Publicly Held**
SIC: 3523 Crop storage bins
HQ: The Gsi Group Llc
1004 E Illinois St
Assumption IL 62510
217 226-4421

(G-891)
GSI GROUP LLC
Gsi International
1004 E Illinois St (62510-9529)
P.O. Box 20 (62510-0020)
PHONE.................................217 226-4421
EMP: 5 **Publicly Held**
SIC: 3523 Crop storage bins
HQ: The Gsi Group Llc
1004 E Illinois St
Assumption IL 62510
217 226-4421

(G-892)
GSI HOLDINGS CORP (HQ)
1004 E Illinois St (62510-9529)
PHONE.................................217 226-4421
Scott Clawson, *CEO*
Wayne Jordan, *Credit Mgr*
David Nash, *Info Tech Mgr*
▼ EMP: 1
SALES (est): 118.2MM **Publicly Held**
SIC: 3523 Crop storage bins; driers (farm): grain, hay & seed; poultry brooders, feeders & waterers; hog feeding, handling & watering equipment

Astoria
Fulton County

(G-893)
KK STEVENS PUBLISHING CO
100 N Pearl St (61501-9545)
P.O. Box 590 (61501-0590)
PHONE.................................309 329-2151
Thomas Stevens, *President*
Devin Hickle, *President*
Judy Beaird, *Editor*
Timothy Stevens, *Treasurer*
Jodie Ragle, *Manager*
EMP: 48 EST: 1959
SQ FT: 30,000
SALES (est): 4.3MM **Privately Held**
WEB: www.kkspc.com
SIC: 2711 2791 2752 2732 Job printing & newspaper publishing combined; typesetting; commercial printing, lithographic; book printing

(G-894)
OIL FILTER RECYCLERS INC
Rr 1 (61501)
PHONE.................................309 329-2131
Donny Onken, *Owner*
EMP: 20 **Privately Held**
SIC: 3533 Oil & gas drilling rigs & equipment
PA: Oil Filter Recyclers, Inc.
320 E Main St
Easton IL 62633

(G-895)
PRAIRIELAND FS INC
2452 N Bader Rd (61501-8817)
P.O. Box 298 (61501-0298)
PHONE.................................309 329-2162
Tom Trone, *Branch Mgr*
EMP: 7 **Privately Held**
SIC: 2875 5191 Fertilizers, mixing only; fertilizers & agricultural chemicals
PA: Prairieland Fs, Inc.
1132 Veterans Dr
Jacksonville IL 62650

Athens
Menard County

(G-896)
DONNAS HOUSE OF TYPE INC
Also Called: Interactive Data Technologies
23267 Railsplitter Ln (62613-7613)
PHONE.................................217 522-5050
Donna Aschenbrenner, *President*
EMP: 4
SQ FT: 2,000
SALES (est): 476.5K **Privately Held**
SIC: 2791 7336 7374 Typesetting; graphic arts & related design; computer graphics service; service bureau, computer

(G-897)
MATERIAL SERVICE CORPORATION
25142 Quarry Ave (62613-7411)
PHONE.................................217 732-2117
Roger Brown, *Manager*
EMP: 20
SALES (corp-wide): 20.8B **Privately Held**
SIC: 1422 3281 Crushed & broken limestone; cut stone & stone products
HQ: Material Service Corporation
2235 Entp Dr Ste 3504
Westchester IL 60154
708 731-2600

(G-898)
METEER INC
16592 Kincaid St (62613-7575)
PHONE.................................217 636-7280
Wade E Meteer, *Principal*
EMP: 4
SALES (est): 438.6K **Privately Held**
SIC: 3523 Farm machinery & equipment

(G-899)
METEER MANUFACTURING CO
25904 Meteer Ln (62613-7578)
PHONE.................................217 636-8109
Patsy Meteer, *President*
Wade Meteer, *Vice Pres*
Chad Ishmael, *Buyer*
Jody Meteer, *Director*
William Meteer, *Director*
EMP: 7
SALES (est): 450K **Privately Held**
WEB: www.meteer.com
SIC: 3599 7692 Machine shop, jobbing & repair; welding repair

(G-900)
PRECISION TANK & EQUIPMENT CO
25203 Quarry Ave (62613-7410)
PHONE.................................217 636-7023
Harry Nichols, *Branch Mgr*
EMP: 10
SALES (est): 1.4MM
SALES (corp-wide): 25.4MM **Privately Held**
SIC: 3443 Tanks, standard or custom fabricated: metal plate
PA: Precision Tank & Equipment Co.
3503 Conover Rd
Virginia IL 62691
217 452-7228

Atkinson
Henry County

(G-901)
BROWN METAL PRODUCTS LTD
513 N Spring (61235-7755)
P.O. Box 386 (61235-0386)
PHONE.................................309 936-7384
Leonard Brown, *President*
Cheryl Brown, *Vice Pres*
EMP: 4
SQ FT: 6,000
SALES (est): 187K **Privately Held**
SIC: 3559 Metal finishing equipment for plating, etc.

(G-902)
MORTON BUILDINGS INC
605 E Henry St (61235-9555)
P.O. Box 602 (61235-0602)
PHONE.................................309 936-7282
Steve Hamm, *Manager*
EMP: 12
SQ FT: 5,000
SALES (corp-wide): 462.5MM **Privately Held**
SIC: 3448 1541 5039 1542 Buildings, portable: prefabricated metal; prefabricated building erection, industrial; prefabricated structures; agricultural building contractors
PA: Morton Buildings, Inc.
252 W Adams St
Morton IL 61550
800 447-7436

(G-903)
TRAEYNE CORPORATION
17982 E 2350th St (61235-9565)
PHONE.................................309 936-7878
Tom Enyeart, *Principal*
EMP: 6
SALES (est): 272.4K **Privately Held**
SIC: 3069 Tubes, hard rubber

Atlanta
Logan County

(G-904)
AMY WERTHEIM (PA)
Also Called: Rgw Candy Company
1865 2200th St Bldg 2 (61723-7629)
PHONE.................................309 830-4361
Amy Wertheim, *Owner*
EMP: 3
SQ FT: 1,215
SALES: 78K **Privately Held**
SIC: 2064 5145 Candy & other confectionery products; candy

Atwood
Douglas County

(G-905)
HARRIS COMPANIES INC
521 N Illinois St (61913-9750)
P.O. Box 1108, Arkansas City KS (67005-1108)
PHONE.................................217 578-2231
Roger Harris, *President*
Scott Harris, *Vice Pres*
Stan Harris, *Vice Pres*
EMP: 16
SQ FT: 25,000
SALES (est): 5MM **Privately Held**
SIC: 3534 Elevators & equipment

Auburn
Sangamon County

(G-906)
BRANDT CONSOLIDATED INC
300 W Jefferson St (62615-1424)
P.O. Box 77 (62615-0077)
PHONE.................................217 438-6158
Mark Powell, *Marketing Staff*
Josh Allen, *Branch Mgr*
EMP: 11
SALES (corp-wide): 159MM **Privately Held**
SIC: 5191 2875 Fertilizer & fertilizer materials; fertilizers, mixing only
PA: Brandt Consolidated, Inc.
2935 S Koke Mill Rd
Springfield IL 62711
217 547-5800

(G-907)
SOUTH COUNTY PUBLICATIONS (PA)
Also Called: Chatham Clarion
110 N 5th St (62615-1449)
P.O. Box 50 (62615-0050)
PHONE.................................217 438-6155

Auburn - Sangamon County (G-908) — GEOGRAPHIC SECTION

Joseph Michelich, *President*
EMP: 14
SQ FT: 2,200
SALES (est) 1.6MM **Privately Held**
WEB: www.southcountypublications.net
SIC: 2711 Newspapers: publishing only, not printed on site

(G-908)
SPRINGFIELD PLASTICS INC
7300 W State Route 104 (62615-9259)
PHONE..................................217 438-6167
Stephen W Baker, *President*
Doug Baker, *Engineer*
Fred Rice, *Treasurer*
Julie Loftis, *Human Resources*
Bradley Baker, *Marketing Staff*
EMP: 45 EST: 1978
SQ FT: 38,000
SALES (est) 9.6MM **Privately Held**
SIC: 3089 Injection molding of plastics

Augusta
Hancock County

(G-909)
AUGUSTA EAGLE
Also Called: Tri County Scribe
600 Main St (62311-1322)
P.O. Box 5 (62311-0005)
PHONE..................................217 392-2715
Stacey Nicholas, *Owner*
EMP: 3 EST: 1966
SQ FT: 252
SALES (est) 95K **Privately Held**
SIC: 2711 Job printing & newspaper publishing combined

Aurora
Dupage County

(G-910)
AERTRADE LLC (PA)
1585 Beverly Ct Ste 128 (60502-8767)
PHONE..................................630 428-4440
Mark Borows, *Mng Member*
▲ EMP: 8
SALES: 5MM **Privately Held**
SIC: 3724 Aircraft engines & engine parts; turbines, aircraft type; turbo-superchargers, aircraft

(G-911)
AMOS INDUSTRIES INC
1080 Corporate Blvd (60502-4703)
PHONE..................................630 393-0606
William Y Tein, *President*
Jack Chen, *Vice Pres*
▲ EMP: 12
SQ FT: 5,800
SALES (est): 2.9MM
SALES (corp-wide): 127.5MM **Privately Held**
SIC: 3429 Builders' hardware
PA: Shengrui Transmission Corporation Limited
No.518, Shengrui Street, East Of Weian Road, High-Tech Zone
Weifang 26120
536 560-5088

(G-912)
APEX ENGINEERING PRODUCTS CORP
1241 Shoreline Dr (60504-6768)
PHONE..................................630 820-8888
Eric Ostermeier, *CEO*
Mark Bickler, *President*
◆ EMP: 12 EST: 1942
SALES (est): 3.4MM **Privately Held**
WEB: www.apexengineeringproducts.com
SIC: 2842 2899 Cleaning or polishing preparations; chemical preparations

(G-913)
AR INET CORP
2336 Pagosa Springs Dr (60503-6463)
PHONE..................................603 380-3903
Anum Mirza, *President*
EMP: 3
SQ FT: 1,800

SALES (est): 102.7K **Privately Held**
SIC: 7375 7378 8748 7371 On-line data base information retrieval; computer & data processing equipment repair/maintenance; systems engineering consultant, ex. computer or professional; custom computer programming services; business oriented computer software

(G-914)
ARMARIUS SOFTWARE INC
2415 Wilson Creek Cir (60503-3603)
PHONE..................................630 639-6332
Brian Berglund, *President*
EMP: 1
SALES: 200K **Privately Held**
SIC: 7372 7389 Prepackaged software;

(G-915)
AURORA CIRCUITS INC
2250 White Oak Cir (60502-9675)
PHONE..................................630 978-3830
Christopher E Kalmus, *President*
Dave Zeno, *President*
John Holmquest, *Vice Pres*
Mike Szydlowski, *QC Mgr*
Craig Wilson, *CFO*
▲ EMP: 65 EST: 1937
SQ FT: 30,000
SALES (est): 9.7MM **Privately Held**
WEB: www.auroracircuits.com
SIC: 3672 Circuit boards, television & radio printed

(G-916)
AURORA CIRCUITS LLC
2250 White Oak Cir (60502-9675)
PHONE..................................630 978-3830
Christopher Kalmus,
David Zeno,
▼ EMP: 64
SQ FT: 38,000
SALES (est): 6.8MM **Privately Held**
SIC: 3672 Printed circuit boards

(G-917)
AVEC INC
Also Called: Goldy Metals Trading
762 Shoreline Dr Ste 100 (60504-6109)
PHONE..................................815 577-3122
Christopher Dandrow, *President*
EMP: 2
SALES (est): 269.6K **Privately Held**
SIC: 3291 Abrasive metal & steel products

(G-918)
AZTECH ENGINEERING INC
Also Called: Aztech Locknut Company
2675 White Oak Cir Ste 1 (60502-9611)
PHONE..................................630 236-3200
Mark Kaindl, *President*
Michael Kaindl, *Vice Pres*
Javier Villa, *Warehouse Mgr*
Carmen Sithammavong, *Opers Staff*
Mike Kaindl, *VP Engrg*
▲ EMP: 30 EST: 1978
SQ FT: 50,000
SALES (est): 10.8MM **Privately Held**
SIC: 3452 Nuts, metal

(G-919)
B A DIE MOLD INC
3685 Prairie Lake Ct (60504-3134)
PHONE..................................630 978-4747
Alan Petrucci, *President*
Francine Petrucci, *President*
Dale Malmer, *Engineer*
Patricia Petrucci, *Treasurer*
Wendy Cahill, *Admin Asst*
EMP: 18
SQ FT: 10,000
SALES (est): 3.4MM **Privately Held**
WEB: www.badiemold.com
SIC: 3544 Industrial molds; special dies & tools

(G-920)
B&B MACHINING INCORPORATED
24 Gastville St (60503-9302)
PHONE..................................630 898-3009
William Schmidt, *President*
EMP: 16 EST: 1981
SQ FT: 14,500

SALES (est): 2MM **Privately Held**
WEB: www.bbmachining.com
SIC: 3494 3599 Valves & pipe fittings; machine shop, jobbing & repair

(G-921)
B-O-F CORPORATION
2453 Prospect Dr Ste A (60502-7809)
PHONE..................................630 585-0020
James P Knorring, *President*
Laura Dooley, *CFO*
Karen Shaw, *Treasurer*
Joe Coretti, *Manager*
Kathleen Knorring, *Admin Sec*
EMP: 35
SQ FT: 66,000
SALES (est): 8.6MM **Privately Held**
SIC: 2542 Racks, merchandise display or storage: except wood; shelving angles or slotted bars: except wood

(G-922)
BALLCO MANUFACTURING CO INC (PA)
2375 Liberty St (60502-9442)
PHONE..................................630 898-1600
Ozzie Van Gelderen, *President*
Dennis Krachon, *Vice Pres*
Andrew Stritt, *Sales Staff*
Daniel Zauner, *Sales Staff*
Jose Cazares, *Maintence Staff*
▲ EMP: 57 EST: 1961
SQ FT: 42,000
SALES (est): 27MM **Privately Held**
WEB: www.ballcomfg.com
SIC: 3599 Machine shop, jobbing & repair

(G-923)
BERRY GLOBAL INC
999 Bilter Rd (60502-4719)
PHONE..................................630 375-0358
EMP: 5 **Publicly Held**
SIC: 3089 3081 Bottle caps, molded plastic; unsupported plastics film & sheet
HQ: Berry Global, Inc.
101 Oakley St
Evansville IN 47710

(G-924)
BOSE CORPORATION
Also Called: Bose Factory Store
1650 Premium Outlet Blvd # 1257 (60502-2911)
PHONE..................................630 585-6654
Jeff Anderson, *Branch Mgr*
EMP: 9
SALES (corp-wide): 2.1B **Privately Held**
SIC: 5731 3651 High fidelity stereo equipment; household audio equipment
PA: Bose Corporation
100 The Mountain Rd
Framingham MA 01701
508 879-7330

(G-925)
BOSTON WAREHOUSE TRADING CORP
2600 Beverly Dr (60502-8005)
PHONE..................................630 992-5604
James Wenz, *Branch Mgr*
EMP: 5
SALES (corp-wide): 17.2MM **Privately Held**
SIC: 3648 Decorative area lighting fixtures
PA: Boston Warehouse Trading Corp.
59 Davis Ave Ste 10
Norwood MA 02062
781 769-8550

(G-926)
BRAVILOR BONAMAT LLC
1204 Bilter Rd (60502-4729)
PHONE..................................630 423-9400
Maarten Ponne, *Sales Dir*
Eric Covelli, *Sales Mgr*
▲ EMP: 15
SALES (est): 2.6MM
SALES (corp-wide): 79.9MM **Privately Held**
SIC: 3589 Coffee brewing equipment
HQ: Bravilor Bonamat B.V.
Pascalstraat 20
Heerhugowaard 1704
725 751-751

(G-927)
BRK BRANDS INC (DH)
Also Called: First Alert
3901 Liberty St (60504-8122)
PHONE..................................630 851-7330
Thomas Russo, *President*
Mark Devine, *Vice Pres*
Mark Binter, *Engineer*
Adam Hervatin, *Engineer*
William B Brock, *CFO*
◆ EMP: 180
SQ FT: 60,000
SALES: 319.4MM
SALES (corp-wide): 9.7B **Publicly Held**
SIC: 3669 Fire detection systems, electric

(G-928)
BUCKEYE DIAMOND LOGISTICS INC
2453 Prospect Dr Ste A (60502-7809)
PHONE..................................630 236-1174
Mark Bates, *Principal*
EMP: 2
SALES (est): 255.3K **Privately Held**
SIC: 2448 Pallets, wood

(G-929)
CABLE MANAGEMENT PRODUCTS INC
1005 N Commons Dr (60504-4100)
PHONE..................................630 723-0470
Julian Good, *Vice Pres*
▲ EMP: 4 EST: 2008
SALES (est): 446.2K
SALES (corp-wide): 27.9B **Privately Held**
SIC: 3644 Electric conduits & fittings
HQ: Abb Installation Products Inc.
860 Ridge Lake Blvd
Memphis TN 38120
901 252-5000

(G-930)
CABOT MCRLECTRONICS GLOBL CORP (HQ)
870 N Commons Dr (60504-7963)
PHONE..................................630 375-6631
David H LI, *President*
EMP: 4
SALES (est): 16K
SALES (corp-wide): 1B **Publicly Held**
SIC: 2819 Industrial inorganic chemicals
PA: Cabot Microelectronics Corporation
870 N Commons Dr
Aurora IL 60504
630 375-6631

(G-931)
CABOT MICROELECTRONICS CORP (PA)
870 N Commons Dr (60504-7963)
PHONE..................................630 375-6631
David H LI, *President*
H Carol Bernstein, *Vice Pres*
Ananth Naman, *Vice Pres*
Brian O'Leary, *Vice Pres*
Dominic Banham, *Opers Staff*
◆ EMP: 61
SQ FT: 200,000
SALES: 1B **Publicly Held**
SIC: 2819 Industrial inorganic chemicals

(G-932)
CABOT MICROELECTRONICS CORP
845 Enterprise St (60504-7933)
PHONE..................................630 375-6631
Gary Lissy, *Branch Mgr*
EMP: 100
SALES (corp-wide): 1B **Publicly Held**
SIC: 3634 Heating pads, electric
PA: Cabot Microelectronics Corporation
870 N Commons Dr
Aurora IL 60504
630 375-6631

(G-933)
CABOT MICROELECTRONICS CORP
500 N Commons Dr (60504-4159)
P.O. Box 2026 (60507-2026)
PHONE..................................630 375-6631
Carlos Barros, *Engineer*
Dan Pike, *Manager*
EMP: 112

▲ = Import ▼ = Export
◆ = Import/Export

GEOGRAPHIC SECTION

Aurora - Dupage County (G-957)

SALES (corp-wide): 1B **Publicly Held**
SIC: 2819 8731 Industrial inorganic chemicals; commercial physical research
PA: Cabot Microelectronics Corporation
870 N Commons Dr
Aurora IL 60504
630 375-6631

(G-934)
CANO CONTAINER CORPORATION (PA)
3920 Enterprise Ct Ste A (60504-8154)
PHONE..................................630 585-7500
Juventino Cano, *President*
Amy Ferguson, *Admin Sec*
Lusila Mauricio, *Admin Asst*
EMP: 20
SQ FT: 60,000
SALES: 10.8MM **Privately Held**
SIC: 2653 Boxes, corrugated: made from purchased materials

(G-935)
CASCADES PLASTICS INC
Also Called: Cascades Enviropac Aurora
2300 Raddant Rd Ste B (60502-9108)
PHONE..................................450 469-3389
Randall C Mohler, *CEO*
Valerie Doyon, *Controller*
Ernie Carnegie, *Sales Associate*
Mark Weber, *Manager*
Alain Paradie, *Prgrmr*
EMP: 45 EST: 1969
SQ FT: 40,000
SALES (est): 10.2MM
SALES (corp-wide): 3.7B **Privately Held**
SIC: 2653 Boxes, corrugated: made from purchased materials; partitions, corrugated: made from purchased materials
HQ: Cascades Plastics Inc.
7501 S Spoede Ln
Warrenton MO 63380
636 456-9576

(G-936)
CENTOR NORTH AMERICA INC
966 Corporate Blvd # 130 (60502-9114)
PHONE..................................630 957-1000
James Thornton, *President*
Brent Johnson, *Regional Mgr*
Phil Wortman, *Regional Mgr*
Peter Ferguson, *Opers Mgr*
Curtis Pryor, *Warehouse Mgr*
◆ **EMP:** 30
SQ FT: 40,000
SALES (est): 6.6MM **Privately Held**
SIC: 3442 Window & door frames

(G-937)
CHICAGO ADHESIVE PRODUCTS
1105 S Frontenac St (60504-6451)
PHONE..................................630 978-7766
Raymond Kline, *Principal*
EMP: 4 EST: 2010
SALES (est): 455.1K **Privately Held**
WEB: www.chapco-adhesive.com
SIC: 2891 Adhesives

(G-938)
CHRONOS IMAGING LLC
555 N Commerce St (60504-8110)
PHONE..................................630 296-9220
Michele Mueller, *Human Resources*
Rudy Piskule,
EMP: 70
SALES: 1.9MM **Privately Held**
SIC: 3841 Diagnostic apparatus, medical

(G-939)
CITADEL SPECIALTY PRODUCTS INC
657 Wolverine Dr Ste 3 (60502-9403)
PHONE..................................630 820-4134
Ronald R Garrison, *Principal*
Stephen Saunders, *Technical Staff*
EMP: 3
SALES (est): 99.8K **Privately Held**
SIC: 2672 Adhesive papers, labels or tapes: from purchased material

(G-940)
CLARIOS
Also Called: Johnson Controls
3600 Thayer Ct Ste 300 (60504-6709)
PHONE..................................331 212-3800
EMP: 5 **Privately Held**
SIC: 2531 Seats, automobile
HQ: Johnson Controls, Inc.
5757 N Green Bay Ave
Milwaukee WI 53209
414 524-1200

(G-941)
CONTROL SOLUTIONS LLC
2520 Diehl Rd (60502-9497)
PHONE..................................630 806-7062
Karen Foster, *Vice Pres*
John Labahn, *Vice Pres*
Curt Motisi, *Mfg Spvr*
Todd Trowbridge, *Opers Staff*
Joe Ergun, *Engineer*
▲ **EMP:** 89
SQ FT: 96,000
SALES: 30MM **Privately Held**
SIC: 3613 3625 Time switches, electrical switchgear apparatus; relays & industrial controls; control equipment, electric; motor controls, electric; electric controls & control accessories, industrial
PA: Corinthian Capital Group, Llc
601 Lexington Ave Rm 5901
New York NY 10022

(G-942)
CRAFTSMAN TOOL & MOLD CO
2750 Church Rd (60502-9706)
PHONE..................................630 851-8700
Wayne Sikorcin, *President*
Justin Ball, *Data Proc Dir*
Anton D Sikorcin, *Shareholder*
EMP: 43 EST: 1965
SQ FT: 37,000
SALES (est): 29.3MM **Privately Held**
SIC: 5084 3544 Industrial machinery & equipment; industrial molds

(G-943)
CREATEASOFT INC
3909 75th St Ste 105 (60504-7934)
PHONE..................................630 851-9474
Brent Dillingham, *Sales Associate*
Hosni Adra, *Mng Member*
Caitlin Smith, *Planning*
EMP: 11
SQ FT: 6,000
SALES (est): 715.8K **Privately Held**
SIC: 5734 7379 8732 7372 Computer & software stores; computer related consulting services; business analysis; application computer software; computer software development & applications

(G-944)
CREATIVE CONTRACT PACKG LLC
3777 Exchange Ave (60504-8102)
PHONE..................................630 851-6226
Mike Van Hyfte, *Plant Mgr*
Gary Ray,
James Cavanaugh,
EMP: 80
SQ FT: 70,800
SALES (est): 11.5MM
SALES (corp-wide): 9.5B **Publicly Held**
SIC: 2099 Dessert mixes & fillings; gelatin dessert preparations; desserts, ready-to-mix
PA: Hormel Foods Corporation
1 Hormel Pl
Austin MN 55912
507 437-5611

(G-945)
CROCS INC
1650 Premium Outlet Blvd # 931 (60502-2923)
PHONE..................................630 820-3572
Karen Escobar, *Branch Mgr*
EMP: 14
SALES (corp-wide): 1.2B **Publicly Held**
WEB: www.crocs.com
SIC: 3021 5661 Shoes, rubber or rubber soled fabric uppers; shoe stores
PA: Crocs, Inc.
7477 Dry Creek Pkwy
Niwot CO 80503
303 848-7000

(G-946)
CROWN CORK & SEAL USA INC
3737 Exchange Ave (60504-8102)
PHONE..................................630 851-7774
Tom Gaffney, *Advt Staff*
David Sieroty, *Manager*
Thomas Gaffney, *Maintence Staff*
EMP: 50
SALES (corp-wide): 11.6B **Publicly Held**
SIC: 3411 Metal cans
HQ: Crown Cork & Seal Usa, Inc.
770 Township Line Rd # 100
Yardley PA 19067
215 698-5100

(G-947)
CUSTOM BLOW MOLDING
2560 White Oak Cir # 140 (60504-9683)
PHONE..................................630 820-9700
EMP: 9 EST: 2014
SALES (est): 1.3MM **Privately Held**
SIC: 3089 Molding primary plastic

(G-948)
CUSTOM FILTER LLC
2300 Raddant Rd Ste A (60502-9109)
PHONE..................................630 906-2100
John Copley, *President*
Bruce Plumb, *Vice Pres*
Patrick O Brien, *CFO*
Dave Fuller,
Bill Moreland,
▲ **EMP:** 60
SALES (est): 16.3MM **Privately Held**
SIC: 3569 Filters

(G-949)
CYNLAR INC
Also Called: AlphaGraphics
1585 Beverly Ct Ste 125 (60502-8764)
PHONE..................................630 820-2200
Larry Byers, *President*
EMP: 6
SQ FT: 2,200
SALES (est): 1MM **Privately Held**
SIC: 2752 Commercial printing, lithographic

(G-950)
CYRUS SHANK COMPANY
575 Exchange Ct (60504-8103)
PHONE..................................331 212-5488
Pat Woods, *Vice Pres*
Cyrus Shank, *Branch Mgr*
Angelo Turco, *Representative*
EMP: 12
SALES (corp-wide): 4.2MM **Privately Held**
WEB: www.cyrusshank.com
SIC: 3491 Industrial valves
HQ: Cyrus Shank Company
4645 W Roosevelt Rd
Cicero IL 60804
708 652-2700

(G-951)
DIAMOND ENVELOPE CORPORATION (PA)
2270 White Oak Cir (60502-9675)
PHONE..................................630 499-2800
Alan J Jania, *President*
Alan W Jania, *Vice Pres*
Michael Jania, *Vice Pres*
Susan A Jania, *Vice Pres*
EMP: 80
SQ FT: 100,000
SALES (est): 21MM **Privately Held**
SIC: 2677 2752 Envelopes; commercial printing, lithographic

(G-952)
DIRECT AEROSYSTEMS INC
2680 Diehl Rd (60502-9496)
PHONE..................................630 509-2141
Michael Wrobel, *President*
Herbert Das, *President*
EMP: 15

SALES (est): 684.5K **Privately Held**
SIC: 5088 3728 3364 Aeronautical equipment & supplies; aircraft parts & equipment; non-ferrous die-castings except aluminum

(G-953)
DU PAGE PRECISION PRODUCTS CO (PA)
3695 Darlene Ct Ste 101 (60504-6546)
PHONE..................................630 849-2940
Dennis Flynn, *President*
J Michael Schroeder, *Vice Pres*
John Blickem, *Analyst*
EMP: 10
SQ FT: 48,000
SALES (est): 16.8MM **Privately Held**
WEB: www.dupageprecision.com
SIC: 3599 Machine shop, jobbing & repair

(G-954)
DU PAGE PRECISION PRODUCTS CO
811 Shoreline Dr (60504-6195)
PHONE..................................630 849-2940
Dave Carlen, *Plant Mgr*
EMP: 75
SALES (corp-wide): 16.8MM **Privately Held**
WEB: www.dupageprecision.com
SIC: 3599 3369 5084 3365 Machine shop, jobbing & repair; nonferrous foundries; engines & parts, diesel; aluminum foundries; steel foundries; malleable iron foundries
PA: Du Page Precision Products Co.
3695 Darlene Ct Ste 101
Aurora IL 60504
630 849-2940

(G-955)
ECLI PRODUCTS LLC (HQ)
Also Called: Engineered Custom Lubricants
3851 Exchange Ave (60504-8106)
PHONE..................................630 449-5000
Ian Rowell, *President*
Chevy Mallhi, *Engineer*
Susan Bauernfeind, *Accountant*
Kevin Hu, *Sales Staff*
Xiaolan Huang, *Director*
EMP: 37
SALES: 28MM
SALES (corp-wide): 1.1B **Publicly Held**
WEB: www.eclube.com
SIC: 2992 Oils & greases, blending & compounding
PA: Quaker Chemical Corporation
901 E Hector St
Conshohocken PA 19428
610 832-4000

(G-956)
ELEMECH INC
2275 White Oak Cir Aurora (60502)
P.O. Box 1563 (60507-1563)
PHONE..................................630 417-2845
Robert Gorder, *President*
Shelly Gorder, *Production*
Sandra Claypool, *Purch Mgr*
Mike Nesnidal, *Project Engr*
Aaron Squires, *Project Engr*
EMP: 25
SQ FT: 22,500
SALES (est): 5.5MM **Privately Held**
SIC: 8711 3625 7371 Electrical or electronic engineering; relays & industrial controls; computer software systems analysis & design, custom

(G-957)
ENTAPPIA LLC
1052 Sundew Ct (60504-6876)
PHONE..................................630 546-4531
Padmanabhan Balamani,
Vijayalakshmi Kumar,
Anandtha Rajamani,
EMP: 5
SALES (est): 251.4K **Privately Held**
SIC: 7371 7379 7372 Computer software systems analysis & design, custom; software programming applications; computer related consulting services; prepackaged software; application computer software

Aurora - Dupage County (G-958)

(G-958)
ENZ (USA) INC
1585 Beverly Ct Ste 115 (60502-8731)
PHONE...................................630 692-7880
Albert Enz, *President*
Bryan Gardner, *Sales Staff*
EMP: 4
SQ FT: 3,300
SALES (est): 448.5K **Privately Held**
SIC: 3999 Pipe cleaners

(G-959)
FABRICATED PRODUCTS CO INC
1875 Plain Ave (60502-8568)
PHONE...................................630 898-6460
William W Witte, *CEO*
John Witte, *President*
Diann Witte, *Vice Pres*
EMP: 15
SQ FT: 15,000
SALES (est): 2.8MM **Privately Held**
SIC: 3443 Tanks, standard or custom fabricated: metal plate; vessels, process or storage (from boiler shops): metal plate; fuel tanks (oil, gas, etc.): metal plate; boilers: industrial, power, or marine

(G-960)
FGS-IL LLC (HQ)
Also Called: Freedom Graphic Systems
780 Mcclure Rd (60502-9509)
PHONE...................................630 375-8500
Tony Wang, *CEO*
Martin Liebert, *President*
William Greene, *Vice Pres*
Richard Wold, *Vice Pres*
Terry Brady, *CFO*
EMP: 250
SALES (est): 53.4MM
SALES (corp-wide): 88.7MM **Privately Held**
SIC: 7331 2752 Direct mail advertising services; commercial printing, lithographic
PA: Fgs-Wi, Llc
1101 S Janesville St
Milton WI 53563
608 373-6500

(G-961)
FHP-BERNER USA LP
2188a Diehl Rd (60502)
PHONE...................................630 270-1400
Sherry Dray, *Director*
▲ **EMP:** 40
SQ FT: 120,000
SALES: 14MM **Privately Held**
SIC: 2392 Mops, floor & dust

(G-962)
FIRST ALERT INC (DH)
3901 Liberty St (60504-8122)
PHONE...................................630 499-3295
Joseph Messner, *CEO*
Mark A Devine, *Vice Pres*
Edward J Tyranski, *Vice Pres*
Eber Enriquez, *Mfg Staff*
Nick Offerman, *Engineer*
◆ **EMP:** 140
SQ FT: 60,000
SALES (est): 631.9MM
SALES (corp-wide): 9.7B **Publicly Held**
SIC: 3669 3999 3446 3499 Smoke detectors; fire extinguishers, portable; stairs, fire escapes, balconies, railings & ladders; safes & vaults, metal; gas detectors; flashlights; lanterns: electric, gas, carbide, kerosene or gasoline
HQ: American Household, Inc.
2381 Nw Executive Ctr Dr
Boca Raton FL 33431
561 912-4100

(G-963)
FOX VALLEY WINDOWS LLC
2711 E New York St (60502-9443)
PHONE...................................630 210-6400
Stephen Jones, *Principal*
EMP: 3
SALES (est): 112.1K **Privately Held**
SIC: 3089 5031 Windows, plastic; doors & windows; windows

(G-964)
FREUDENBERG HOUSEHOLD PDTS LP
Also Called: Freudenberg & Co
2188 Diehl Rd (60502-8775)
PHONE...................................630 270-1400
Ron Tillery, *President*
Wolfram Freudenberg, *Chairman*
Werner Wenning, *Chairman*
Thomas Caruso, *Business Mgr*
Brian Barrett, *Sales Staff*
▲ **EMP:** 143
SALES (est): 45.2MM
SALES (corp-wide): 10.8B **Privately Held**
WEB: www.ocedar.com
SIC: 2392 3991 Mops, floor & dust; brooms & brushes
HQ: Freudenberg Home And Cleaning Solutions Gmbh
Im Technologiepark 19
Weinheim 69469
620 180-8710

(G-965)
FRONTIDA BIOPHARM INC
2500 Molitor Rd (60502-9441)
PHONE...................................215 620-3527
EMP: 5
SALES (corp-wide): 43.4MM **Privately Held**
SIC: 2833 Medicinal chemicals
PA: Frontida Biopharm, Inc.
1100 Orthodox St
Philadelphia PA 19124
610 232-0112

(G-966)
G-III APPAREL GROUP LTD
1650 Premium Outlet Blvd (60502-2901)
PHONE...................................630 236-8900
Donna Karan, *Branch Mgr*
EMP: 157 **Publicly Held**
SIC: 2335 Women's, juniors' & misses' dresses
PA: G-Iii Apparel Group, Ltd.
512 7th Ave Fl 35
New York NY 10018

(G-967)
GEORG-PCIFIC CORRUGATED IV LLC
Also Called: Excel Displays & Packaging
4390 Liberty St (60504-9502)
PHONE...................................630 896-3610
Gregg Hevey, *Vice Pres*
EMP: 119
SALES (corp-wide): 48.9B **Privately Held**
SIC: 2653 Boxes, corrugated: made from purchased materials
HQ: Georgia-Pacific Corrugated Iv Llc
133 Peachtree St Ne
Atlanta GA 30303
404 652-4000

(G-968)
GETEX CORPORATION
2158 Ogden Ave (60504-7215)
PHONE...................................630 993-1300
Afsar Ali Khan, *President*
EMP: 4
SALES (est): 488.7K **Privately Held**
SIC: 2841 2899 2842 Detergents, synthetic organic or inorganic alkaline; chemical preparations; specialty cleaning, polishes & sanitation goods

(G-969)
GLANBIA PERFORMANCE NTRTN INC
948 Meridian Lake Dr (60504-4901)
PHONE...................................630 256-7445
Juan Vega, *Manager*
Konrad Iwanski, *Technology*
EMP: 25 **Privately Held**
SIC: 2833 4225 Vitamins, natural or synthetic: bulk, uncompounded; general warehousing
HQ: Glanbia Performance Nutrition (Na), Inc.
3500 Lacey Rd
Downers Grove IL 60515

(G-970)
GLANBIA PERFORMANCE NTRTN INC
975 Medidian Lake Dr (60504)
PHONE...................................630 236-0097
Thomas Tench, *CEO*
Justin McCarthy, *Senior VP*
EMP: 12 **Privately Held**
SIC: 2833 5149 5122 Vitamins, natural or synthetic: bulk, uncompounded; health foods; vitamins & minerals
HQ: Glanbia Performance Nutrition (Na), Inc.
3500 Lacey Rd
Downers Grove IL 60515

(G-971)
GLANBIA PERFORMANCE NTRTN INC
600 N Commerce St (60504-8111)
PHONE...................................800 336-2183
Tom Stucker, *Branch Mgr*
Dan Devine, *Manager*
Adalberto Luna, *Supervisor*
EMP: 73 **Privately Held**
SIC: 2833 Vitamins, natural or synthetic: bulk, uncompounded
HQ: Glanbia Performance Nutrition (Na), Inc.
3500 Lacey Rd
Downers Grove IL 60515

(G-972)
GLOBALTECH INTERNATIONAL LLC (PA)
Also Called: Pro-Beam USA
3909 75th St Ste 105 (60504-7934)
PHONE...................................630 327-6909
Radwan Mourad, *Mng Member*
EMP: 6
SQ FT: 1,000
SALES: 626K **Privately Held**
WEB: www.pro-beam.com
SIC: 3548 7699 Electric welding equipment; welding equipment repair

(G-973)
GODIVA CHOCOLATIER INC
1650 Premium Outlet Blvd # 1213 (60502-2901)
PHONE...................................630 820-5842
EMP: 24 **Privately Held**
SIC: 2066 Mfg Chocolate/Cocoa Prdt
HQ: Godiva Chocolatier, Inc.
333 W 34th St Fl 6
New York NY 10001
212 984-5900

(G-974)
GONNELLA BAKING CO
2435 Church Rd (60502-9724)
PHONE...................................630 820-3433
William Smith, *Branch Mgr*
EMP: 90
SALES (corp-wide): 113.6MM **Privately Held**
SIC: 2051 Bread, cake & related products
PA: Gonnella Baking Co.
1117 Wiley Rd
Schaumburg IL 60173
312 733-2020

(G-975)
GRUNDFOS CBS INC
Also Called: Aurora Service Center
3905 Enterprise Ct (60504-8132)
PHONE...................................331 401-0057
Joseph Masterson, *Principal*
EMP: 10
SALES (corp-wide): 4B **Privately Held**
SIC: 3561 Pumps & pumping equipment
HQ: Grundfos Cbs Inc.
902 Koomey Rd
Brookshire TX 77423

(G-976)
GRUNDFOS WATER UTILITY INC
Also Called: Yeomans Pump
3905 Enterprise Ct (60504-8132)
PHONE...................................630 236-5500
Dieter Sauer, *President*
Michael Franzen, *President*
George Foster, *CFO*
Thomas Lund, *CTO*
Brian Bludgen, *Admin Sec*
▲ **EMP:** 100
SQ FT: 105,000
SALES (est): 50.9MM
SALES (corp-wide): 4B **Privately Held**
SIC: 3561 5084 Pump jacks & other pumping equipment; pumps & pumping equipment
HQ: Grundfos Holding A/S
Poul Due Jensens Vej 7
Bjerringbro 8850
875 014-00

(G-977)
HANGER PROSTHETICS &
Also Called: Hanger Clinic
4400 Mccoy Dr Ste 100 (60504-4591)
PHONE...................................630 820-5656
Sam Liang, *President*
Scott Scliski, *Branch Mgr*
EMP: 5
SALES (corp-wide): 1.1B **Publicly Held**
SIC: 5999 3842 Orthopedic & prosthesis applications; limbs, artificial
HQ: Hanger Prosthetics & Orthotics East, Inc.
33 North Ave Ste 101
Tallmadge OH 44278

(G-978)
HB FULLER CNSTR PDTS INC (HQ)
Also Called: H.B. Fuller Construction Pdts
1105 S Frontenac St (60504-6451)
PHONE...................................630 978-7766
Rose Mary Clyburn, *CEO*
◆ **EMP:** 125
SQ FT: 190,000
SALES (est): 89.3MM
SALES (corp-wide): 2.9B **Publicly Held**
SIC: 2891 Adhesives
PA: H.B. Fuller Company
1200 Willow Lake Blvd
Saint Paul MN 55110
651 236-5900

(G-979)
HIDROSTAL LLC
Also Called: Hidrostal Pumps
2225 White Oak Cir (60502-9604)
P.O. Box 3414, Oak Brook (60522-3414)
PHONE...................................630 240-6271
John Kelly, *General Mgr*
Brent Bailey, *Manager*
EMP: 12
SQ FT: 3,200
SALES: 10MM
SALES (corp-wide): 58.8MM **Privately Held**
SIC: 3561 Pumps & pumping equipment
PA: Hidrostal Holding Ag
Gigering 27
Neunkirch SH 8213
526 870-687

(G-980)
IDLR USA INC
2121 Ridge Ave Ste 103 (60504-7002)
PHONE...................................630 375-0101
Shrish Tomur, *President*
EMP: 4
SQ FT: 4,000
SALES: 50MM **Privately Held**
SIC: 1011 Iron ore preparation

(G-981)
INDUSTRIAL MSRMENT SYSTEMS INC
2760 Beverly Dr Ste 4 (60502-8604)
PHONE...................................630 236-5901
Donald E Yuhas, *President*
Jacek Remiasz, *Engineer*
Loretta Oleksak, *Info Tech Mgr*
EMP: 6
SQ FT: 6,400
SALES (est): 1.1MM **Privately Held**
SIC: 3829 Measuring & controlling devices

(G-982)
INEOS STYROLUTION AMERICA LLC (DH)
4245 Meridian Pkwy # 151 (60504-8018)
PHONE...................................630 820-9500
Kevin McQuade, *CEO*
Greg Fordyce, *Vice Pres*
William Gossett, *Vice Pres*

GEOGRAPHIC SECTION

Aurora - Dupage County (G-1007)

Tom Warren, *Vice Pres*
Cathy Culpepper, *VP Mfg*
◆ **EMP:** 125
SALES (est): 52MM
SALES (corp-wide): 1MM **Privately Held**
SIC: 2821 Plastics materials & resins
HQ: Ineos Styrolution Group Gmbh
   Mainzer Landstr. 50
   Frankfurt Am Main 60325
   695 095-5012

(G-983)
INNOVATIVE CUSTOM SOFTWARE INC
Also Called: Qt9 Software
2731 Beverly Dr (60502-8596)
PHONE.................................630 892-5022
Brant Engelhart, *President*
Heather Engelhart, *Admin Sec*
EMP: 2
SALES (est): 405.5K **Privately Held**
SIC: 7372 Business oriented computer software

(G-984)
INSIDE TRACK TRADING
2905 Lahinch Ct (60503-6271)
PHONE.................................630 585-9218
Eric Hadik, *Principal*
EMP: 3
SALES (est): 183.9K **Privately Held**
SIC: 2721 Periodicals

(G-985)
INTERNATIONAL PAPER COMPANY
2540 Prospect Ct (60502-9419)
PHONE.................................630 449-7200
Brian Chibudu, *Mfg Staff*
EMP: 11
SALES (corp-wide): 22.3B **Publicly Held**
SIC: 2621 Paper mills
PA: International Paper Company
   6400 Poplar Ave
   Memphis TN 38197
   901 419-9000

(G-986)
INTERNATIONAL PAPER COMPANY
4140 Campus Dr (60504-4172)
PHONE.................................630 585-3300
Ryan Carlton, *Plant Mgr*
Christina Reid, *Buyer*
Jason Kohler, *Branch Mgr*
Art Tyska, *Manager*
Rita Conway, *Executive Asst*
EMP: 120
SALES (corp-wide): 22.3B **Publicly Held**
SIC: 2653 Corrugated & solid fiber boxes
PA: International Paper Company
   6400 Poplar Ave
   Memphis TN 38197
   901 419-9000

(G-987)
INTERNATIONAL PAPER COMPANY
4160 Campus Dr (60504-4172)
PHONE.................................630 585-3400
Mark Hull, *General Mgr*
EMP: 130
SALES (corp-wide): 22.3B **Publicly Held**
SIC: 2621 Paper mills
PA: International Paper Company
   6400 Poplar Ave
   Memphis TN 38197
   901 419-9000

(G-988)
INTERNATIONAL WOOD PRODUCTS
2812 Stuart Kaplan Ct (60503-5774)
PHONE.................................630 530-6164
EMP: 6
SQ FT: 10,000
SALES: 500K **Privately Held**
SIC: 3949 Manufactures Wood Playground Equipment

(G-989)
ITERNA LLC
2600 Beverly Dr Ste 107 (60502-8004)
PHONE.................................630 585-7400
Omar Tabbara, *General Mgr*

Tamburrino Peter, *Mng Member*
▲ **EMP:** 20
SALES (est): 4.5MM **Privately Held**
WEB: www.iternacorp.com
SIC: 3691 Batteries, rechargeable; alkaline cell storage batteries

(G-990)
JCB INC
800 Bilter Rd Ste A (60502-4727)
PHONE.................................912 704-2995
Dustin Diplock, *Supervisor*
EMP: 4 **Privately Held**
SIC: 5082 5084 3531 3537 General construction machinery & equipment; materials handling machinery; backhoes; industrial trucks & tractors
HQ: Jcb, Inc.
   2000 Bamford Blvd
   Pooler GA 31322
   912 447-2000

(G-991)
KELVYN PRESS INC
Also Called: Demand One
880 Enterprise St Ste F (60504-4923)
PHONE.................................630 585-8160
James Galazin, *Technology*
EMP: 50 **Privately Held**
SIC: 2752 Commercial printing, offset
HQ: Kelvyn Press, Inc.
   2910 S 18th Ave
   Broadview IL 60155
   708 343-0448

(G-992)
KENDALL COUNTY CONCRETE INC
695 Route 34 (60503-9314)
PHONE.................................630 851-9197
Thomas Schnabel, *President*
Lorraine Schnabel, *Corp Secy*
EMP: 23
SQ FT: 9,000
SALES (est): 4.2MM **Privately Held**
SIC: 3273 Ready-mixed concrete

(G-993)
KESON INDUSTRIES INC
810 N Commerce St (60504-7931)
PHONE.................................630 820-4200
Aaron Nosek, *President*
Irvin Hemmerle, *CFO*
Cheryl Perez, *Marketing Mgr*
Ronald R Nosek, *Admin Sec*
▲ **EMP:** 50
SQ FT: 80,000
SALES (est): 10.4MM **Privately Held**
WEB: www.keson.com
SIC: 3953 3545 3829 Marking devices; precision measuring tools; measuring & controlling devices

(G-994)
KINDLON ENTERPRISES INC (PA)
2300 Raddant Rd Ste B (60502-9108)
PHONE.................................708 367-4000
Randall C Mohler, *President*
Margaret Dicaro, *Admin Sec*
EMP: 1
SQ FT: 160,000
SALES (est): 29.8MM **Privately Held**
SIC: 2653 Boxes, corrugated: made from purchased materials; pads, corrugated: made from purchased materials; partitions, corrugated: made from purchased materials

(G-995)
LABEL TEK INC
3505 Thayer Ct Ste 200 (60504-3141)
PHONE.................................630 820-8499
Dean Hummel, *President*
EMP: 10
SQ FT: 10,000
SALES (est): 1.6MM **Privately Held**
SIC: 2754 2759 2672 Labels: gravure printing; commercial printing; coated & laminated paper

(G-996)
LEGGETT & PLATT INCORPORATED
Also Called: Leggett & Platt 6003
969 Corporate Blvd (60502-9176)
PHONE.................................630 851-0101
Ray Teague, *Branch Mgr*
EMP: 14
SALES (corp-wide): 4.7B **Publicly Held**
WEB: www.leggett.com
SIC: 2515 Mattresses & bedsprings
PA: Leggett & Platt, Incorporated
   1 Leggett Rd
   Carthage MO 64836
   417 358-8131

(G-997)
LEHIGH CONSUMER PRODUCTS LLC (HQ)
3901 Liberty St (60504-8122)
PHONE.................................630 851-7330
Thomas Russo, *President*
◆ **EMP:** 205
SALES (est): 78MM
SALES (corp-wide): 9.7B **Publicly Held**
SIC: 3965 2298 3462 3452 Fasteners, buttons, needles & pins; ropes & fiber cables; iron & steel forgings; bolts, nuts, rivets & washers; financial consultant
PA: Newell Brands Inc.
   6655 Pachtree Dunwoody Rd
   Atlanta GA 30328
   770 418-7000

(G-998)
LETTER-RITE EXPRESS LLC
1660 Wind Song Ln (60504-5500)
PHONE.................................847 678-1100
Russell C Brewer Jr, *Mng Member*
Robert A Brewer,
EMP: 10 **EST:** 2007
SQ FT: 8,000
SALES (est): 1.1MM **Privately Held**
WEB: www.letter-rite.com
SIC: 3861 Graphic arts plates, sensitized

(G-999)
LULUS REAL FROYO
1147 N Eola Rd (60502-7003)
PHONE.................................630 299-3854
Julie Collins, *Principal*
EMP: 5
SALES (est): 261K **Privately Held**
SIC: 2026 Yogurt

(G-1000)
LUSE THERMAL TECHNOLOGIES LLC
3990 Enterprise Ct (60504-8132)
PHONE.................................630 862-2600
Bradford K Luse, *Principal*
EMP: 2
SALES (est): 378.4K **Privately Held**
SIC: 3823 Thermal conductivity instruments, industrial process type

(G-1001)
MAGNETROL INTERNATIONAL INC (PA)
705 Enterprise St (60504-8149)
PHONE.................................630 723-6600
Jeffrey K Swallow, *President*
John E Heiser, *COO*
Doug Ford, *Vice Pres*
Patrick Gainer, *Vice Pres*
Steve Meier, *Mfg Mgr*
▼ **EMP:** 250 **EST:** 1932
SQ FT: 85,000
SALES (est): 103.6MM **Privately Held**
SIC: 3823 3699 3643 3625 Level & bulk measuring instruments, industrial process; flow instruments, industrial process type; electrical equipment & supplies; current-carrying wiring devices; relays & industrial controls; machine tools, metal cutting type

(G-1002)
METTLER-TOLEDO LLC
Ci-Vision Division
2640 White Oak Cir Ste A (60502-4809)
PHONE.................................630 446-7700
Dwight Turner, *Regl Sales Mgr*
Tom Mc Lean, *Manager*
Fernando Flores, *Manager*

EMP: 41
SALES (corp-wide): 2.9B **Publicly Held**
SIC: 3596 5049 7699 3821 Industrial scales; weighing machines & apparatus; analytical instruments; professional instrument repair services; pipettes, hemocytometer; balances, laboratory; electrodes used in industrial process measurement; refractometers, except industrial process type; liquid chromatographic instruments; moisture analyzers; pH meters, except industrial process type
HQ: Mettler-Toledo, Llc
   1900 Polaris Pkwy Fl 6
   Columbus OH 43240
   614 438-4511

(G-1003)
NITREX INC
1900 Plain Ave (60502-8561)
PHONE.................................630 851-5880
Chris Morawski, *President*
Thomas Cooper, *General Mgr*
Dennis Wang, *General Mgr*
Joe Beal, *Facilities Mgr*
Walter Bill, *Production*
EMP: 28 **EST:** 1991
SQ FT: 25,000
SALES: 5MM
SALES (corp-wide): 419.3K **Privately Held**
SIC: 3398 Metal heat treating
HQ: Nitrex Inc.
   822 Kim Dr
   Mason MI 48854

(G-1004)
ORGANIZED NOISE INC
Also Called: Sole Unique
231 Raintree Ct (60504-2006)
PHONE.................................630 820-9855
Anthony James Foster, *President*
EMP: 3
SALES: 60K **Privately Held**
SIC: 3651 Audio electronic systems

(G-1005)
OSI INTERNATIONAL FOODS LTD
Also Called: Glen Oak Foods
1225 Corp Blvd Ste 300 (60504)
P.O. Box 2018 (60507-2018)
PHONE.................................630 851-6600
David G McDonald, *President*
Sheldon Lavin, *President*
George A Krzesinski, *Treasurer*
William S Lipsman, *Admin Sec*
▲ **EMP:** 100
SALES (est): 11.3MM **Privately Held**
SIC: 2013 Sausages & other prepared meats
PA: Osi International, Inc.
   1225 Corp Blvd Ste 300
   Aurora IL 60505

(G-1006)
PEERLESS INDUSTRIES INC (PA)
Also Called: Peerless-Av
2300 White Oak Cir (60502-9676)
PHONE.................................630 375-5100
John Potts, *President*
Walter Snodell, *Chairman*
Nick Belcore, *Exec VP*
Nicholas Belcore, *Vice Pres*
Ken Dillion, *Vice Pres*
◆ **EMP:** 218
SQ FT: 307,000
SALES (est): 45MM **Privately Held**
WEB: www.peerlessmounts.com
SIC: 3429 5099 Manufactured hardware (general); video & audio equipment

(G-1007)
PERFECT DESSERTS LLC
2605 White Oak Cir (60502-4810)
PHONE.................................630 579-6100
Robert Spadoni, *Counsel*
Rosa Parente, *Controller*
Mario J Demarco, *Mng Member*
EMP: 23
SALES (est): 754.9K **Privately Held**
SIC: 2051 Cakes, pies & pastries

Aurora - Dupage County (G-1008)

(G-1008)
PHILIPS NORTH AMERICA LLC
Dunlee Division
555 N Commerce St (60504-8110)
PHONE 630 585-2000
Pat Fitzgerald, *General Mgr*
Jim White, *Vice Pres*
Allison Hibbard, *Engineer*
Ken Schine, *Finance Mgr*
Sue Haggerty, *Human Res Mgr*
EMP: 250
SALES (corp-wide): 20.8B **Privately Held**
SIC: 3844 X-ray apparatus & tubes
HQ: Philips North America Llc
    222 Jacobs St Fl 3
    Cambridge MA 02141
    978 659-3000

(G-1009)
PINNAKLE TECHNOLOGIES INC
75 Executive Dr Ste 353 (60504-8121)
PHONE 630 352-0070
Ajay Kshatriya, *President*
Sunny Bamzai, *Recruiter*
EMP: 17
SALES (est): 3.3MM **Privately Held**
SIC: 5045 7371 7372 Computer software; computer software systems analysis & design, custom; prepackaged software

(G-1010)
PRISM ESOLUTIONS DV ANDY FRAIN
761 Shoreline Dr (60504-6194)
PHONE 630 820-3820
David Clayton, *President*
Laura Grund, *Vice Pres*
Dane Vontobel, *Vice Pres*
EMP: 10
SQ FT: 5,000
SALES: 980K
SALES (corp-wide): 274.4MM **Privately Held**
SIC: 7372 Prepackaged software
PA: Andy Frain Services, Inc.
    761 Shoreline Dr
    Aurora IL 60504
    630 820-3820

(G-1011)
QUADRANT MEDICAL CORPORATION
3500 Thayer Ct (60504-3108)
PHONE 312 800-1294
Joseph Fenoglio, *Principal*
Nicholas Diaz, *Principal*
Thomas Fenoglio, *Principal*
EMP: 5
SALES (est): 198.4K **Privately Held**
SIC: 3841 Surgical & medical instruments

(G-1012)
RAHN USA CORP
1005 N Commons Dr (60504-4100)
PHONE 630 851-4220
Marcel Gatti, *President*
Sean Desroches, *Manager*
▲ EMP: 28
SALES (est): 7.4MM
SALES (corp-wide): 20.5MM **Privately Held**
SIC: 2869 Industrial organic chemicals
PA: Rahn Ag
    Dorflistrasse 120
    ZUrich ZH 8050
    443 154-200

(G-1013)
REFLECTION SOFTWARE INC
900 S Frontenac St # 100 (60504-3247)
PHONE 630 270-1200
Timothy Schorr, *President*
Gabriella Spingola, *Info Tech Dir*
EMP: 35
SALES (est): 340.5K **Privately Held**
WEB: www.reflectionsoftware.com
SIC: 7372 Business oriented computer software

(G-1014)
ROANOKE COMPANIES GROUP INC (DH)
1105 S Frontenac St (60504-6451)
PHONE 630 375-0324
Richard Tripodi, *President*

▲ EMP: 90
SQ FT: 144,000
SALES: 14.4MM
SALES (corp-wide): 2.9B **Publicly Held**
SIC: 2891 Caulking compounds; adhesives

(G-1015)
RYANO RESINS INC
3808 Baybrook Dr (60504-6599)
P.O. Box 47, Willow Springs, (60480-0047)
PHONE 630 621-5677
Paul Mueller, *President*
Kimberlyu Mueller, *Admin Sec*
EMP: 2
SQ FT: 2,000
SALES (est): 330.8K **Privately Held**
SIC: 2861 Gum & wood chemicals

(G-1016)
SENOPLAST USA
75 Executive Dr Ste 129 (60504-8105)
PHONE 630 898-0731
Gunter Klepch, *Owner*
Jim Litkovitz, *Sales Dir*
Manuel Romero, *Sales Mgr*
Chris Trabert, *Sales Mgr*
Mark Sjoberg, *Sales Staff*
EMP: 6 EST: 2001
SQ FT: 1,000
SALES: 20MM **Privately Held**
WEB: www.senoplastusa.com
SIC: 3081 Unsupported plastics film & sheet

(G-1017)
SMC CORPORATION OF AMERICA
858 Meridian Lake Dr F (60504-4905)
PHONE 630 449-0600
Todd Umholtz, *Sales Mgr*
Sue Schlinger, *Sales Staff*
Randy Ayres, *Manager*
EMP: 40 **Privately Held**
WEB: www.smcusa.com
SIC: 5084 3492 3491 3559 Pneumatic tools & equipment; control valves, fluid power: hydraulic & pneumatic; pressure valves & regulators, industrial; automotive related machinery; fluid power actuators, hydraulic or pneumatic; pneumatic relays, air-conditioning type; switches, pneumatic positioning remote
HQ: Smc Corporation Of America
    10100 Smc Blvd
    Noblesville IN 46060
    317 899-4440

(G-1018)
SONOVA USA INC (DH)
750 N Commons Dr (60504-7940)
PHONE 763 744-3300
Sandra Brandmeir, *President*
Jason Mayer, *Vice Pres*
Nick Stephan, *Vice Pres*
Kevin Schulhof, *CFO*
EMP: 114
SQ FT: 90,000
SALES: 85MM
SALES (corp-wide): 2.7B **Privately Held**
SIC: 3842 Hearing aids

(G-1019)
SPECIALTY CNSTR BRANDS INC (HQ)
1105 S Frontenac St (60504-6451)
PHONE 630 851-0782
Luis Diego Rodriguez, *General Mgr*
◆ EMP: 15
SALES (est): 3.5MM
SALES (corp-wide): 3B **Publicly Held**
SIC: 2891 2899 Adhesives & sealants; chemical preparations
PA: H.B. Fuller Company
    1200 Willow Lake Blvd
    Saint Paul MN 55110
    651 236-5900

(G-1020)
SPRAYING SYSTEMS CO
Also Called: Fluid Air
2580 Diehl Rd Ste E (60502-5309)
PHONE 630 665-5001
Elizabeth Thomas, *Purchasing*
Joseph Szczap, *Engineer*
Brian Smith, *Project Engr*
Martin Bender, *Branch Mgr*

EMP: 18
SALES (corp-wide): 320.3MM **Privately Held**
SIC: 3499 5047 Nozzles, spray: aerosol, paint or insecticide; medical laboratory equipment
PA: Spraying Systems Co.
    200 W North Ave
    Glendale Heights IL 60139
    630 665-5000

(G-1021)
SUPERIOR TRUCK DOCK SERVICES
2431 Angela Ln (60502-9068)
PHONE 630 978-1697
William Meier, *President*
EMP: 5
SALES (est): 918.2K **Privately Held**
SIC: 3537 Truck trailers, used in plants, docks, terminals, etc.

(G-1022)
THERMAMAX INC
1207 Bilter Rd Ste 119 (60502-4723)
PHONE 630 340-5682
Dirk Balthasar, *President*
Bernd Petershans, *Admin Sec*
▲ EMP: 15
SQ FT: 2,000
SALES (est): 3.8MM **Privately Held**
WEB: www.thermamax.com
SIC: 3644 Insulators & insulation materials, electrical
HQ: Thermamax Hochtemperatur-
    dammungen Gmbh
    Olhafenstr. 20-28
    Mannheim
    621 322-350

(G-1023)
THOMAS PUMP COMPANY
Also Called: Liquid Lf Sprators Systems Div
2301 Liberty St (60502-9520)
PHONE 630 851-9393
Robert D Mc Cue Sr, *President*
Ron Mc Cue, *Corp Secy*
Robert A Mc Cue Jr, *Vice Pres*
EMP: 14
SQ FT: 12,000
SALES: 185K **Privately Held**
WEB: www.tpcoinc.com
SIC: 5084 3561 Pumps & pumping equipment; pumps & pumping equipment

(G-1024)
TIN TREE GIFTS
2720 Stuart Kaplan Dr (60503-5778)
PHONE 630 935-8086
EMP: 3
SALES (est): 274.1K **Privately Held**
WEB: www.tintreegifts.com
SIC: 3356 Tin

(G-1025)
TINSCAPE LLC
1050 Stockton Ct (60502-6966)
PHONE 630 236-7236
Thomas Doyle, *CEO*
Rick Larson, *Accounts Mgr*
▲ EMP: 5
SALES (est): 631K **Privately Held**
SIC: 3497 Metal foil & leaf

(G-1026)
TITAN US LLC
1585 Beverly Ct Ste 112 (60502-8725)
PHONE 331 212-5953
Johann Niederberger, *Mng Member*
Robert J Van Vorrst,
EMP: 4
SALES (est): 290K **Privately Held**
SIC: 8711 5085 3443 Mechanical engineering; packing, industrial; heat exchangers, condensers & components

(G-1027)
TRIGON INTERNATIONAL LLC
Also Called: Trigon International Corp
4000 Sussex Ave (60504-7948)
PHONE 630 978-9990
Chris Connor, *General Mgr*
John Manzi, *Vice Pres*
EMP: 90
SQ FT: 5,000

SALES: 8.8MM
SALES (corp-wide): 847.4MM **Publicly Held**
WEB: www.etrigon.com
SIC: 3842 Surgical appliances & supplies
PA: Nn, Inc.
    6210 Ardrey Kell Rd # 600
    Charlotte NC 28277
    980 264-4300

(G-1028)
TRINITY MACHINED PRODUCTS INC
2560 White Oak Cir (60502-9681)
PHONE 630 876-6992
EMP: 25
SALES (est): 14.9K
SALES (corp-wide): 135MM **Privately Held**
SIC: 3469 3449 3599 Mfg Metal Stampings Mfg Misc Structural Metalwork Machine Shop
PA: Wozniak Industries, Inc.
    2 Mid America Plz Ste 700
    Oakbrook Terrace IL 60195
    630 954-3400

(G-1029)
TT TECHNOLOGIES INC
2020 E New York St (60502-9515)
PHONE 630 851-8200
Chris J Brahler Jr, *President*
David Holcomb, *Vice Pres*
Kevin Nagle, *Safety Dir*
Craig Tholen, *Prdtn Mgr*
Eddie Ward, *Sales Dir*
◆ EMP: 55
SQ FT: 10,000
SALES: 11.7MM
SALES (corp-wide): 355.8K **Privately Held**
SIC: 3541 5084 Drilling & boring machines; drilling equipment, excluding bits
PA: Tt Schmidt Gmbh
    Paul-Schmidt-Str. 2
    Lennestadt
    272 380-80

(G-1030)
URL PHARMPRO LLC
2500 Molitor Rd (60502-9441)
PHONE 630 888-3820
Richard Roberts,
EMP: 7
SALES (est): 1.9MM
SALES (corp-wide): 1.3B **Privately Held**
SIC: 2834 Pharmaceutical preparations
PA: Sun Pharmaceutical Industries Limited
    Sun House, Plot No. 201 B/1, Western
    Express Highway,
    Mumbai MH 40006
    224 324-4324

(G-1031)
VICTAULIC COMPANY
1207 Bilter Rd Ste 103 (60502-4725)
PHONE 630 585-2919
Eric Carlson, *Sales Staff*
John Malloy, *Manager*
EMP: 260
SALES (corp-wide): 749.9MM **Privately Held**
WEB: www.victaulic.com
SIC: 3494 Couplings, except pressure & soil pipe
PA: Victaulic Company
    4901 Kesslersville Rd
    Easton PA 18040
    610 559-3300

(G-1032)
W L ENGLER DISTRIBUTING INC
Scott Wood & Metal
4 Gastville St (60503-9302)
PHONE 630 898-5400
Scott Miller, *Manager*
EMP: 8
SALES (corp-wide): 10.7MM **Privately Held**
SIC: 3444 5075 Furnace casings, sheet metal; warm air heating equipment & supplies

▲ = Import ▼ = Export
◆ = Import/Export

GEOGRAPHIC SECTION

Aurora - Kane County (G-1060)

PA: W. L. Engler Distributing, Inc.
1035 N Throop St
Chicago IL 60642
773 235-4924

(G-1033)
WEBSOLUTIONS TECHNOLOGY INC
Also Called: Wsol
3817 Mccoy Dr Ste 105 (60504-4220)
PHONE.................630 375-6833
Jeff Gahn, *President*
David Hansten, *CFO*
Gail Gahn, *Admin Sec*
EMP: 27
SALES: 3.9MM **Privately Held**
SIC: 7371 7372 4813 8731 Computer software development; prepackaged software; ; commercial physical research

(G-1034)
WESDAR TECHNOLOGIES INC
924 Vineyard Ln (60502-8502)
PHONE.................630 761-0965
Donald Wessendorf, *President*
EMP: 4
SQ FT: 3,200
SALES (est): 400K **Privately Held**
SIC: 7389 3089 Design services; injection molding of plastics

(G-1035)
WESTELL INC (HQ)
750 N Commons Dr (60504-7940)
PHONE.................630 898-2500
Timothy Duitsman, *CEO*
Charmaine Cartagena, *Accountant*
Chris Marshal, *CIO*
▲ **EMP:** 100
SQ FT: 173,000
SALES (est): 43.4MM **Publicly Held**
WEB: www.westell.com
SIC: 3661 Telephone & telegraph apparatus

(G-1036)
WESTELL TECHNOLOGIES INC (PA)
750 N Commons Dr (60504-7940)
PHONE.................630 898-2500
Kirk R Brannock, *Ch of Bd*
Timothy Duitsman, *President*
Jesse Swartwood, *Senior VP*
Jenny Jaynes, *Assoc VP*
Kit Donner, *Engineer*
EMP: 21
SQ FT: 83,000
SALES: 43.5MM **Publicly Held**
SIC: 3661 4813 7389 Telephones & telephone apparatus; telephone communication, except radio; ; telephone/video communications; teleconferencing services

(G-1037)
WIN TECHNOLOGIES INCORPORATED
Also Called: Scot Electrical Products
800 S Frontenac St Unit 1 (60504-3126)
PHONE.................630 236-1020
Albert Khant, *President*
Barbara Khant, *Vice Pres*
Gerald Khant, *Vice Pres*
Glen Khant, *Vice Pres*
Neil Khant, *Vice Pres*
EMP: 35
SALES: 3.5MM **Privately Held**
SIC: 3625 Control equipment, electric

(G-1038)
WM F MEYER CO (PA)
1855 E New York St (60502-8610)
P.O. Box 37 (60507-0037)
PHONE.................773 772-7272
William J Meyer, *President*
EMP: 30
SQ FT: 40,000
SALES (est): 45.2MM **Privately Held**
WEB: www.wmfmeyer.com
SIC: 5198 5074 5231 5211 Paints; plumbing & hydronic heating supplies; pipes & fittings, plastic; paint & painting supplies; lumber & other building materials; fixtures: display, office or store: except wood

(G-1039)
WORLD CLASS TAE KWON
627 S Route 59 (60504-8169)
PHONE.................630 870-9293
Travis Eskew, *President*
EMP: 2
SALES: 200K **Privately Held**
SIC: 7999 7372 Martial arts school; application computer software

(G-1040)
WOZNIAK INDUSTRIES INC
2560 White Oak Cir (60502-9681)
PHONE.................630 820-4052
EMP: 105
SALES (corp-wide): 150MM **Privately Held**
SIC: 3469 Mfg Metal Stampings
PA: Wozniak Industries, Inc.
2 Mid America Plz Ste 700
Oakbrook Terrace IL 60195
630 954-3400

Aurora
Kane County

(G-1041)
ACCURATE COLOR COMPOUNDING INC
1666 Dearborn Ave (60505-3171)
PHONE.................630 978-1227
Jay Wessels, *President*
Matt Babula, *Senior Buyer*
Judy Cain, *Controller*
Joe Kay, *Sales Mgr*
Jason Yelm, *Admin Sec*
▲ **EMP:** 45
SQ FT: 52,000
SALES (est): 13MM **Privately Held**
SIC: 2851 Paints & allied products

(G-1042)
ADVANTAGE MACHINING INC
601 W New York St Frnt (60506-3882)
PHONE.................630 897-1220
Steve Arbizzani, *CEO*
Anthony Seidelman, *President*
EMP: 42
SQ FT: 40,000
SALES (est): 5.6MM **Privately Held**
SIC: 3549 3599 Assembly machines, including robotic; machine & other job shop work

(G-1043)
ADVANTECH LIMITED
601 N Russell Ave (60506-2988)
PHONE.................815 289-7678
Dennis C Freeh, *President*
EMP: 2
SQ FT: 5,000
SALES (est): 277.6K **Privately Held**
SIC: 2899 Concrete curing & hardening compounds

(G-1044)
AIMEE M FORD
Also Called: Chad's Ford Snow Removal & Con
1005 Summerhill Dr (60506-8868)
PHONE.................630 308-9785
Aimee Ford, *Treasurer*
Chad Ford, *Mng Member*
EMP: 5
SALES: 300K **Privately Held**
SIC: 1771 3272 Blacktop (asphalt) work; concrete stuctural support & building material

(G-1045)
AIR-DUCT MANUFACTURING INC
319 E Benton St (60505-4355)
PHONE.................630 620-9866
Amir Sharify, *President*
Grace Pleticha, *Office Mgr*
EMP: 7
SQ FT: 21,000
SALES (est): 1MM **Privately Held**
SIC: 3444 Ducts, sheet metal

(G-1046)
ALL-PAK MANUFACTURING CORP
1221 Jackson St Ste A-B (60505-5691)
PHONE.................630 851-5859
Don Smith, *President*
Thomas E Binkowski, *Admin Sec*
EMP: 60
SQ FT: 40,000
SALES (est): 13.5MM **Privately Held**
SIC: 2653 5199 Boxes, corrugated: made from purchased materials; packaging materials

(G-1047)
ALLEGRA NETWORK LLC
Also Called: Allegra Print & Imaging
987 Oak Ave (60506-2422)
PHONE.................630 801-9335
EMP: 3
SALES (corp-wide): 34.2MM **Privately Held**
SIC: 2752 2789 Lithographic Commercial Printing Bookbinding/Related Work
PA: Allegra Network Llc
47585 Galleon Dr
Plymouth MI 48170
248 596-8600

(G-1048)
ALLOY ROD PRODUCTS INC
601 W New York St Ste 4 (60506-3888)
PHONE.................815 562-8200
EMP: 5
SALES (est): 433.4K **Privately Held**
SIC: 3356 Nonferrous Rolling/Drawing

(G-1049)
AMERICAN SPORTSWEAR INC
250 Heritage Dr (60506-4418)
PHONE.................630 859-8998
Jack Pasulka, *President*
Andy Pasulka, *Vice Pres*
Georgiana Pasulka, *Admin Sec*
▲ **EMP:** 7
SALES: 800K **Privately Held**
WEB: www.winnerwear.com
SIC: 2759 Screen printing

(G-1050)
AMERICHEM SYSTEMS INC
1740 Molitor Rd (60505-1346)
PHONE.................630 495-9300
Joseph A Garbarski, *President*
EMP: 24
SQ FT: 30,000
SALES: 9.6MM
SALES (corp-wide): 45.6MM **Privately Held**
SIC: 3559 Chemical machinery & equipment
PA: Enpro, Inc.
121 S Lombard Rd
Addison IL 60101
630 629-3504

(G-1051)
AMWELL
1740 Molitor Rd (60505-1398)
PHONE.................630 898-6900
Jim McNish, *Owner*
EMP: 11 **EST:** 2012
SALES (est): 109.5K **Privately Held**
WEB: www.amwell-inc.com
SIC: 2086 Water, pasteurized: packaged in cans, bottles, etc.

(G-1052)
ANDEL SERVICES INC
Also Called: Bristol Blacktop
1145 S Union St (60505-5741)
PHONE.................630 566-0210
Jill Calderon, *President*
Rhonda Rodriguez, *Vice Pres*
EMP: 3
SALES: 250K **Privately Held**
SIC: 7692 1611 1771 Welding repair; highway & street paving contractor; concrete work

(G-1053)
ARCH PRINTING INC
710 Morton Ave Ste N (60506-2817)
PHONE.................630 966-0235
Mary Arch, *President*
Anthony Arch, *Vice Pres*
Jessica Arch, *Officer*
EMP: 9
SQ FT: 15,000
SALES (est): 1.4MM **Privately Held**
SIC: 2752 2791 2789 Commercial printing, offset; typesetting; bookbinding & related work

(G-1054)
ASK PRODUCTS INC
Also Called: Ask Power
544 N Highland Ave (60506-2986)
PHONE.................630 896-4056
Vincent Roy, *President*
Dalila Vidaca, *Manager*
Steven J Kase, *Admin Sec*
◆ **EMP:** 70
SQ FT: 35,000
SALES (est): 14.2MM
SALES (corp-wide): 102.8MM **Privately Held**
SIC: 3469 Stamping metal for the trade
HQ: Sicame Group
1 Avenue Basile Lachaud
Arnac-Pompadour 19230
555 739-476

(G-1055)
ASTRAL POWER SYSTEMS INC
Also Called: Zhmin Power
31 W Downer Pl Ste 408 (60506-5187)
PHONE.................630 518-1741
Min Carroll, *Principal*
EMP: 3
SALES (est): 168.5K **Privately Held**
SIC: 1711 3646 3672 3645 Solar energy contractor; commercial indusl & institutional electric lighting fixtures; printed circuit boards; lamp & light shades

(G-1056)
ATMI DYNACORE LLC
960 Ridgeway Ave Ste 1 (60506-5473)
PHONE.................815 838-9492
John B Armbruster, *Mng Member*
James K Armbruster,
John Cordogan,
EMP: 60 **EST:** 1998
SALES (est): 3.4MM **Privately Held**
WEB: www.atmiprecast.com
SIC: 3272 Concrete products, precast

(G-1057)
ATMI PRECAST INC (PA)
960 Ridgeway Ave Fl 2 (60506-5473)
PHONE.................630 897-0577
John G Cordogan, *CEO*
Mike Pelz, *Principal*
Paul Carr, *COO*
Mike Walsh, *Vice Pres*
John Szostak, *Manager*
EMP: 25
SALES (est): 45.3MM **Privately Held**
SIC: 3272 Concrete products, precast

(G-1058)
ATMI PRECAST INC
Also Called: Atmi Plant
930 Ridgeway Ave (60506-5470)
PHONE.................630 897-0577
John Armbruster, *Manager*
EMP: 48
SALES (est): 4.9MM **Privately Held**
SIC: 3272 Concrete products, precast
PA: Atmi Precast, Inc.
960 Ridgeway Ave Fl 2
Aurora IL 60506

(G-1059)
AURORA FASTPRINT INC
54 E Galena Blvd (60505-3314)
PHONE.................630 896-5980
Kimberly A Granholm, *President*
Thomas M Bartlett, *Admin Sec*
Chad Jimenez, *Graphic Designe*
EMP: 5 **EST:** 1979
SQ FT: 3,500
SALES (est): 929.6K **Privately Held**
SIC: 2752 Commercial printing, offset

(G-1060)
AUTOMATION DESIGN & MFG INC
841 S River St (60506-5912)
PHONE.................630 896-4206

Aurora - Kane County (G-1061)

John M Masek, *President*
EMP: 5
SQ FT: 6,000
SALES (est): 655.4K **Privately Held**
SIC: 8711 3599 3312 3544 Designing: ship, boat, machine & product; machine shop, jobbing & repair; tool & die steel; special dies, tools, jigs & fixtures

(G-1061)
BARNABY INC
Also Called: Barnaby Complete Printing Svcs
1600 Mountain St (60505-2447)
PHONE..................................815 895-6555
Fax: 815 895-3617
EMP: 10 **EST:** 1915
SQ FT: 22,500
SALES (est): 1.7MM **Privately Held**
SIC: 2752 2791 2789 2759 Lithographic Coml Print Typesetting Services Bookbinding/Related Work Commercial Printing

(G-1062)
BAT BUSINESS SERVICES INC
Also Called: Allegra Marketing Print Web
987 Oak Ave (60506-2422)
PHONE..................................630 801-9335
Bart Troyer, *President*
EMP: 3
SALES (est): 500K **Privately Held**
SIC: 2752 Commercial printing, offset

(G-1063)
BENETECH INC (HQ)
2245 Sequoia Dr Ste 300 (60506-6220)
PHONE..................................630 844-1300
Ron Pircon, *President*
Mark Collett, *Principal*
Chris Stiles, *Area Mgr*
John Pircon, *Vice Pres*
Andrew Hunter, *Opers Staff*
EMP: 42
SQ FT: 24,000
SALES: 46MM
SALES (corp-wide): 70.3MM **Privately Held**
SIC: 5169 5084 3823 Chemicals, industrial & heavy; chemical process equipment; combustion control instruments
PA: Benetech Investments Corp.
2245 Sequoia Dr Ste 300
Aurora IL 60506
630 844-1300

(G-1064)
BENETECH (TAIWAN) LLC (DH)
2245 Sequoia Dr Ste 300 (60506-6220)
PHONE..................................630 844-1300
EMP: 4
SALES (est): 4MM
SALES (corp-wide): 70.3MM **Privately Held**
SIC: 5169 5084 3823 Chemicals, industrial & heavy; chemical process equipment; combustion control instruments
HQ: Benetech, Inc.
2245 Sequoia Dr Ste 300
Aurora IL 60506
630 844-1300

(G-1065)
BERRY GLOBAL INC
921 Industrial Dr (60506-1159)
PHONE..................................630 896-6200
Dale Ridenour, *Branch Mgr*
EMP: 20 **Publicly Held**
SIC: 3089 Bottle caps, molded plastic
HQ: Berry Global, Inc.
101 Oakley Ln
Evansville IN 47710

(G-1066)
BRICKS INC (PA)
723 S Lasalle St (60505-5126)
PHONE..................................630 897-6926
Kim Schmitt, *President*
EMP: 6
SALES (est): 6.9MM **Privately Held**
WEB: www.bricksinc.net
SIC: 5032 5211 5031 5074 Brick, except refractory; concrete & cinder block; brick; concrete & cinder block; door & window products; doors, garage; windows; doors; building materials, exterior; fireplaces, prefabricated; concrete products; concrete block & brick

(G-1067)
BUTTERFIELD COLOR INC (HQ)
625 W Illinois Ave (60506-2829)
PHONE..................................630 906-1980
Joseph G Garceau, *President*
Nick Wagner, *Purch Mgr*
◆ **EMP:** 30
SALES (est): 5.4MM
SALES (corp-wide): 8.1B **Privately Held**
SIC: 2899 Core wash or wax
PA: Sika Ag
Zugerstrasse 50
Baar ZG 6341
584 366-800

(G-1068)
C P O INC
Also Called: Century Pipe Organ Company
1500 Dearborn Ave Ofc (60505-3231)
PHONE..................................630 898-7733
John Hill, *President*
EMP: 3
SQ FT: 16,000
SALES (est): 128.6K **Privately Held**
SIC: 7699 3931 Organ tuning & repair; organs, all types: pipe, reed, hand, electronic, etc.

(G-1069)
CAPITAL PRTG & DIE CUTNG INC
Also Called: Capital Printing & Die-Cutting
303 S Highland Ave (60506-5519)
PHONE..................................630 896-5520
Jesus L Lozano, *President*
Leopoldo Lozano, *President*
Julia Lozano, *Vice Pres*
Lorena Herrera, *Office Mgr*
EMP: 8
SQ FT: 5,000
SALES (est): 1.4MM **Privately Held**
WEB: www.capitalprintinginc.com
SIC: 2675 2752 2759 Paper die-cutting; commercial printing, offset; embossing on paper

(G-1070)
CARROLL DISTRG & CNSTR SUP INC
1031 W Lake St (60506-5841)
PHONE..................................630 892-4855
Chuck Frazer, *Warehouse Mgr*
Alex Xula, *Manager*
EMP: 6
SALES (corp-wide): 128.2MM **Privately Held**
WEB: www.carrollsupply.com
SIC: 5032 3444 Concrete building products; concrete forms, sheet metal
PA: Carroll Distributing & Construction Supply, Inc.
207 W 2nd St Ste 3
Ottumwa IA 52501
641 683-1888

(G-1071)
CATERPILLAR INC
Rr 31 Box S (60507)
P.O. Box 348 (60507-0348)
PHONE..................................309 494-0858
Gary Alan Staupanto, *Branch Mgr*
EMP: 427
SALES (corp-wide): 53.8B **Publicly Held**
SIC: 1081 Metal mining exploration & development services
PA: Caterpillar Inc.
510 Lake Cook Rd Ste 100
Deerfield IL 60015
224 551-4000

(G-1072)
CHAMPION WOOD PALLETS INC
105 Hankes Ave Ste 100 (60505-6300)
PHONE..................................630 801-8036
Jeffrey Herzog, *President*
EMP: 9
SALES (est): 838.5K **Privately Held**
SIC: 2448 Pallets, wood & wood with metal

(G-1073)
CHI HOME IMPROVEMENT MAG INC
Also Called: Chicago Home Improvement Mag
2031 Bryn Mawr Dr (60506-5701)
P.O. Box 547, North Aurora (60542-0139)
PHONE..................................630 801-7788
Sherry W Schultz, *Mng Member*
EMP: 4
SALES (est): 170K **Privately Held**
SIC: 2721 7389 Magazines: publishing & printing;

(G-1074)
CHICAGO PANEL & TRUSS INC
875 Aurora Ave Ste 1 (60505-1751)
PHONE..................................630 870-1300
Michael Cummings, *President*
EMP: 50
SALES (est): 6.4MM **Privately Held**
SIC: 3448 Trusses & framing: prefabricated metal

(G-1075)
CHICAGOLAND CLOSETS LLC
Also Called: Closets By Design
850 Ridgeway Ave Ste A (60506-5498)
PHONE..................................630 906-0000
Paul Ridsdale, *Mng Member*
EMP: 20
SALES (est): 1.6MM **Privately Held**
SIC: 2511 Storage chests, household: wood

(G-1076)
CLEARLY KOSHER FOODS
8s696 Barnes Rd (60506-9249)
PHONE..................................630 546-2052
Daryl Feldott, *Principal*
Angela Frieders, *Principal*
EMP: 10
SALES (est): 434.8K **Privately Held**
SIC: 5149 2086 2033 Specialty food items; mineral water, carbonated: packaged in cans, bottles, etc.; maraschino cherries: packaged in cans, jars, etc.

(G-1077)
CLEVELAND HDWR & FORGING CO
Fox Valley Forge
138 Pierce St (60505-2116)
PHONE..................................630 896-9850
Jorge Cruz, *General Mgr*
Joseph Krantz, *Accounting Mgr*
EMP: 65
SQ FT: 60,000
SALES (corp-wide): 31.2MM **Privately Held**
SIC: 3462 Iron & steel forgings
PA: Cleveland Hardware And Forging Company
1341 State St
Green Bay WI 54304
216 641-5200

(G-1078)
CONNOR-WINFIELD CORP
Janus Remote Communications
2111 Comprehensive Dr (60505-1345)
PHONE..................................630 499-2121
Steve Overmyer, *Engineer*
Dave Jahr, *Sales Mgr*
David Jahr, *Manager*
Silvestre Liz, *Technician*
EMP: 91
SALES (corp-wide): 33.9MM **Privately Held**
WEB: www.janus-rc.com
SIC: 3661 Fiber optics communications equipment; modems
PA: Connor-Winfield Corp.
2111 Comprehensive Dr
Aurora IL 60505
630 851-4722

(G-1079)
CONNOR-WINFIELD CORP (PA)
2111 Comprehensive Dr (60505-1345)
PHONE..................................630 851-4722
Roberta A Olp, *President*
Dave Jahr, *General Mgr*
Cheryl Garcia, *Production*
Karen Hamby, *Senior Buyer*
Bill Beverley, *Engineer*
EMP: 120
SALES (est): 33.9MM **Privately Held**
WEB: www.conwin.com
SIC: 3625 3679 Timing devices, electronic; oscillators

(G-1080)
CORSICANA BEDDING LLC
970 S Lake St (60505-5901)
PHONE..................................708 331-9000
Jerry Fredette, *General Mgr*
Paul Lestzyski, *Branch Mgr*
EMP: 3
SALES (corp-wide): 473.8MM **Privately Held**
SIC: 2515 Mattresses & bedsprings
PA: Corsicana Bedding, Llc
1420 W Mockingbird Ln
Dallas TX 75247
800 323-4349

(G-1081)
CORYDON CONVERTING COMPANY INC (PA)
932 E Benton St (60505-3704)
P.O. Box 1688 (60507-1688)
PHONE..................................630 983-1900
William Dunbar, *President*
Robert McCaffrey, *Vice Pres*
Joanne Cooney, *Marketing Mgr*
◆ **EMP:** 25
SQ FT: 35,000
SALES (est): 5.2MM **Privately Held**
SIC: 2679 Paper products, converted

(G-1082)
D AND D PALLETS
725 S Broadway (60505-5101)
P.O. Box 7226 (60507-7226)
PHONE..................................630 800-1102
Damian Diaz, *Owner*
EMP: 10
SALES (est): 541.5K **Privately Held**
SIC: 2448 Pallets, wood

(G-1083)
D R SPERRY & CO
623 Rathbone Ave (60505-5940)
PHONE..................................630 892-4361
David Murray, *President*
▲ **EMP:** 55
SQ FT: 50,000
SALES (est): 11.5MM **Privately Held**
WEB: www.drsperry.com
SIC: 3589 3559 3542 3365 Water treatment equipment, industrial; chemical machinery & equipment; machine tools, metal forming type; aluminum foundries; secondary nonferrous metals; blast furnaces & steel mills

(G-1084)
DELTA PRODUCTS GROUP INC
1655 Eastwood Dr (60506-1121)
P.O. Box 6466 (60598-0466)
PHONE..................................630 357-5544
Mark Ostermeier, *President*
EMP: 10
SQ FT: 14,000
SALES: 10MM **Privately Held**
SIC: 2819 5169 5999 Chemicals, high purity: refined from technical grade; chemicals & allied products; cleaning equipment & supplies

(G-1085)
DIAZ PALLETS II CORPORATION
760 Prairie St (60506-5512)
PHONE..................................630 340-3736
Angelica Diaz, *President*
EMP: 3
SALES (est): 347.3K **Privately Held**
SIC: 2448 Pallets, wood

(G-1086)
ECOLOTECH ASL INC
611 Phoenix Ct (60505-2211)
PHONE..................................630 859-0485
EMP: 5
SQ FT: 3,900
SALES (est): 440K **Privately Held**
SIC: 3812 Mfg Detection Apparatus

▲ = Import ▼ = Export
◆ = Import/Export

GEOGRAPHIC SECTION

Aurora - Kane County (G-1114)

(G-1087)
EL VALLE FLORIDO
1028 Cypress Dr (60506-1638)
PHONE 630 898-0689
EMP: 3
SALES (est): 219.2K **Privately Held**
SIC: 2099 Tortillas, fresh or refrigerated

(G-1088)
ELC INDUSTRIES CORP
Also Called: Aurora Cord & Cable Company
401 Hankes Ave (60505-1716)
PHONE 630 851-1616
Augie Fabela, *President*
Mark Eckleberger, *Controller*
Joanne Houghtaylen, *Sales Mgr*
▲ EMP: 50
SQ FT: 65,000
SALES (est): 7.6MM **Privately Held**
SIC: 3647 3694 Vehicular lighting equipment; automotive electrical equipment

(G-1089)
EMV WELDING INC
544 S River St (60506-5550)
PHONE 630 264-0893
Eleazar Carbajal, *President*
EMP: 2
SALES (est): 258.3K **Privately Held**
SIC: 7692 Welding repair

(G-1090)
EPIX TUBE CO INC
500 N Broadway (60505-2644)
PHONE 630 844-0960
Paul Kasperski, *Branch Mgr*
EMP: 41
SALES (corp-wide): 6.6MM **Privately Held**
SIC: 3317 Steel pipe & tubes
PA: Epix Tube Co., Inc.
5800 Wolf Creek Pike
Dayton OH 45426
937 529-4858

(G-1091)
EQUIPTO ELECTRONICS CORP (PA)
351 Woodlawn Ave (60506-5575)
PHONE 630 897-4691
Praveen Pothapragada, *President*
Steven Golz, *Vice Pres*
Greg Young, *Vice Pres*
Dave Zielke, *Purch Mgr*
Gary Michelson, *CFO*
▼ EMP: 43 EST: 1960
SQ FT: 125,000
SALES (est): 10.6MM **Privately Held**
WEB: www.equiptoelec.com
SIC: 3469 Electronic enclosures, stamped or pressed metal

(G-1092)
EUPHORIA CATERING AND EVENTS
611 Pennsylvania Ave (60506-3029)
PHONE 630 301-4369
Rosalyn Spears, *Owner*
EMP: 4
SALES: 10K **Privately Held**
SIC: 2099 Food preparations

(G-1093)
EVANS TOOL & MANUFACTURING
6s252 Hankes Rd (60506-8987)
PHONE 630 897-8656
James Evans, *President*
EMP: 2
SQ FT: 900
SALES (est): 1MM **Privately Held**
SIC: 3089 Injection molding of plastics

(G-1094)
EXCEL FORMS INC
760 Donna Ave (60505-1010)
PHONE 630 801-1936
Karen Heriaud, *President*
Gene Heriaud, *Corp Secy*
EMP: 3
SALES (est): 442.2K **Privately Held**
SIC: 5112 2752 Business forms; color lithography

(G-1095)
FIBERBASIN INC
1500 Dearborn Ave Ste 13 (60505-3240)
P.O. Box 1870 (60507-1870)
PHONE 630 978-0705
Bradley Philo, *President*
Alex Navarro, *Co-Owner*
EMP: 14
SQ FT: 35,000
SALES (est): 3.4MM **Privately Held**
SIC: 3089 Plastic & fiberglass tanks

(G-1096)
FLORES PRECISION PRODUCTS
Also Called: A Flores
413 Cleveland Ave (60506-5516)
PHONE 630 264-2222
Angel Flores, *President*
Rose Flores, *Admin Sec*
EMP: 5
SQ FT: 4,000
SALES (est): 642.1K **Privately Held**
SIC: 3544 3599 Subpresses, metalworking; machine shop, jobbing & repair

(G-1097)
FM GRAPHIC IMPRESSIONS INC
84 S Lasalle St (60505-3332)
P.O. Box 4455 (60507-4455)
PHONE 630 897-8788
EMP: 50
SALES (est): 3.6MM
SALES (corp-wide): 5.4MM **Privately Held**
SIC: 2759 2752 3993 2791 Commercial Printing Lithographic Coml Print Mfg Signs/Ad Specialties Typesetting Services
PA: Professional Packaging Corp
208 E Benton St
Aurora IL
630 896-0574

(G-1098)
FOX VALLEY IRON & METAL CORP
1440 W Downer Pl (60506-4739)
PHONE 630 897-5907
Robert H Swickert Sr, *President*
Dolores A Swickert, *Corp Secy*
Robert H Swickert Jr, *Vice Pres*
▲ EMP: 10
SQ FT: 1,000
SALES (est): 2.4MM **Privately Held**
SIC: 5093 3341 3312 Ferrous metal scrap & waste; metal scrap & waste materials; secondary nonferrous metals; blast furnaces & steel mills

(G-1099)
FOX VALLEY LABOR NEWS INC
726 N Edgelawn Dr (60506-1866)
P.O. Box 4155 (60507-4155)
PHONE 630 897-4022
Ed Richardson, *President*
EMP: 5
SALES (est): 200K **Privately Held**
SIC: 2711 Newspapers: publishing only, not printed on site

(G-1100)
FOX VALLEY PARK DISTRICT
Also Called: Blackberry Historical Farm
100 S Barnes Rd (60506-8118)
PHONE 630 892-1550
Sandy Smith, *Branch Mgr*
EMP: 100
SALES (corp-wide): 37.7MM **Privately Held**
SIC: 7996 2711 8412 Theme park, amusement; newspapers; museums & art galleries
PA: Fox Valley Park District
101 W Illinois Ave
Aurora IL 60506
630 897-0516

(G-1101)
FRANKS DGTAL PRTG OFF SUPS INC
723 Aurora Ave (60505-2156)
P.O. Box 976 (60507-0976)
PHONE 630 892-2511
Frank Garcia, *President*
Maria Sanchez, *Office Mgr*
EMP: 4 EST: 2007
SALES (est): 413.5K **Privately Held**
WEB: www.franksdigitalprinting.com
SIC: 2752 Commercial printing, offset

(G-1102)
GARBE IRON WORKS INC
Also Called: G I W
456 N Broadway (60505-2672)
PHONE 630 897-5100
Terry Peshia, *Ch of Bd*
John Peshia, *Vice Pres*
Ted Peshia, *Vice Pres*
F James Garbe, *Admin Sec*
EMP: 25
SQ FT: 45,000
SALES: 12.2MM **Privately Held**
WEB: www.giwinc.com
SIC: 3441 Building components, structural steel

(G-1103)
GENGLER-LOWNEY LASER WORKS
899 Sullivan Rd (60506-1138)
PHONE 630 801-4840
John M Gengler, *President*
Marie Geltz, *Treasurer*
Susan Lowney, *Admin Sec*
EMP: 10 EST: 1946
SQ FT: 10,000
SALES (est): 1.5MM **Privately Held**
WEB: www.gengler-lowneylaserworks.com
SIC: 1761 1711 7692 3444 Sheet metalwork; warm air heating & air conditioning contractor; welding repair; sheet metalwork

(G-1104)
GOLD SEAL CABINETS COUNTERTOPS
1750 Eastwood Dr (60506-1153)
PHONE 630 906-0366
Lois A Farmer Balthazore, *President*
Thomas Balthazore, *Admin Sec*
EMP: 28
SQ FT: 10,000
SALES (est): 3.8MM **Privately Held**
SIC: 2434 5031 Wood kitchen cabinets; kitchen cabinets

(G-1105)
GREAT LAKES PRECISION TUBE INC
Also Called: GL Precision Tube
237 S Highland Ave (60506-5517)
PHONE 630 859-8940
Charles E Kuhn, *President*
Kuhn Matt, *Plant Mgr*
EMP: 30
SQ FT: 32,000
SALES (est): 8.1MM **Privately Held**
WEB: www.glptube.com
SIC: 3441 Fabricated structural metal

(G-1106)
GUSCO SILICONE RBR & SVCS LLC
1500 Dearborn Ave (60505-3231)
PHONE 773 770-5008
Gustavo Morales, *CFO*
EMP: 10 EST: 2010
SALES (est): 1.1MM **Privately Held**
WEB: www.guscosiliconerubber.com
SIC: 3052 3069 Rubber hose; molded rubber products; roll coverings, rubber; grommets, rubber

(G-1107)
HAN-WIN PRODUCTS INC
726 S Broadway (60505-5102)
P.O. Box 4515 (60507-4515)
PHONE 630 897-1591
S Richard Cherwin, *President*
Ginette M Cherwin, *Admin Sec*
EMP: 30
SQ FT: 18,000
SALES (est): 3.8MM **Privately Held**
WEB: www.han-win.com
SIC: 3089 Injection molding of plastics

(G-1108)
HENRY PRATT COMPANY LLC (DH)
401 S Highland Ave (60506-5580)
PHONE 630 844-4000
Dale B Smith, *President*
Susan Snowden, *Managing Dir*
Randy Berger, *Vice Pres*
Steve Sharp, *Vice Pres*
Jay Morse, *Facilities Mgr*
▲ EMP: 210
SQ FT: 133,000
SALES (est): 115.4MM
SALES (corp-wide): 968MM **Publicly Held**
SIC: 3491 Water works valves
HQ: Mueller Co. Llc
633 Chestnut St Ste 1200
Chattanooga TN 37450
423 209-4800

(G-1109)
HEVCO INDUSTRIES
1500 Dearborn Ave Ste 10 (60505-3239)
PHONE 708 344-1342
EMP: 4
SQ FT: 7,500
SALES (est): 457.7K **Privately Held**
SIC: 3524 Mfg Commercial Mowers & Parts

(G-1110)
HUBBELL INCORPORATED
1455 Sequoia Dr Ste 113 (60506-1171)
PHONE 972 756-1184
Peter G Sartori, *Branch Mgr*
EMP: 14
SQ FT: 81,200
SALES (corp-wide): 4.5B **Publicly Held**
SIC: 3643 Current-carrying wiring devices
PA: Hubbell Incorporated
40 Waterview Dr
Shelton CT 06484
475 882-4000

(G-1111)
INDUSTRIAL ENCLOSURE CORP
Also Called: I E C
619 N Loucks St Ste A (60505-2982)
P.O. Box 2817 (60507-2817)
PHONE 630 898-7499
John F Palmer, *President*
Rich Palmer, *Vice Pres*
Ron Sampson, *Prdtn Mgr*
Richard Palmer, *Admin Sec*
▼ EMP: 50
SQ FT: 85,000
SALES (est): 10.1MM **Privately Held**
SIC: 2542 3699 3469 Cabinets: show, display or storage: except wood; electrical equipment & supplies; metal stampings

(G-1112)
INDUSTRIAL SENSING AND SAFETY
1936 School House Ln (60506-4396)
PHONE 630 264-8249
Philip Brink, *Principal*
EMP: 3 EST: 2010
SALES (est): 291K **Privately Held**
SIC: 3625 Relays & industrial controls

(G-1113)
INTERGRTED THRMFORMING SYSTEMS
305 Hankes Ave (60506-1714)
PHONE 630 906-6895
Mike Curtis, *President*
Rina Srey, *Vice Pres*
EMP: 19
SQ FT: 12,000
SALES: 700K **Privately Held**
WEB: www.itspackaging.com
SIC: 3089 Injection molding of plastics

(G-1114)
J W TODD CO
709 Morton Ave (60506-2816)
P.O. Box 355, Batavia (60510-0355)
PHONE 630 406-5715
Steve Todd, *CEO*
David Todd, *Treasurer*
EMP: 5 EST: 1961
SQ FT: 2,400
SALES (est): 1MM **Privately Held**
SIC: 3535 3537 Belt conveyor systems, general industrial use; bucket type conveyor systems; industrial trucks & tractors

Aurora - Kane County (G-1115)

(G-1115)
J/B INDUSTRIES INC
601 N Farnsworth Ave (60505-3092)
P.O. Box 1180 (60507-1180)
PHONE.................................630 851-9444
Jeff Cherif, *President*
Ron Hill Jr, *Corp Secy*
Jeff Bodnar, *Site Mgr*
Steve Gaugel, *Purchasing*
Mike Lirot, *Controller*
▲ **EMP:** 60 **EST:** 1967
SQ FT: 210,000
SALES (est): 30.2MM **Privately Held**
WEB: www.jbind.com
SIC: 3494 3563 Plumbing & heating valves; steam fittings & specialties; vacuum pumps, except laboratory

(G-1116)
JAKES MCHNING RBILDING SVC INC
580 S Lake St (60506-5561)
PHONE.................................630 892-3291
Joseph Krippelz Sr, *President*
Jake Krippelz Jr, *Vice Pres*
Amanda Eggleston, *Purch Mgr*
EMP: 20
SQ FT: 60,000
SALES: 5.3MM **Privately Held**
SIC: 3599 3541 7692 Machine shop, jobbing & repair; machine tool replacement & repair parts, metal cutting types; welding repair

(G-1117)
JAMES L TRACEY CO
1480 Sequoia Dr Ste A2 (60506-1097)
PHONE.................................630 907-8999
James Tracey, *Principal*
EMP: 12
SALES (est): 2.4MM **Privately Held**
SIC: 3498 Fabricated pipe & fittings

(G-1118)
JEWEL OSCO INC
Also Called: Jewel-Osco 3252
1952 W Galena Blvd (60506-4306)
PHONE.................................630 859-1212
Cary Jiltey, *Manager*
EMP: 75
SALES (corp-wide): 60.5B **Privately Held**
SIC: 5411 2051 Supermarkets, chain; bread, cake & related products
HQ: Jewel Osco, Inc.
150 E Pierce Rd Ste 200
Itasca IL 60143
630 948-6000

(G-1119)
JOHNOS INC (PA)
Also Called: Main Surplus Store
1804 E New York St (60505-3262)
PHONE.................................630 897-6929
John Galles, *President*
Emilie Galles, *Vice Pres*
EMP: 6 **EST:** 1972
SQ FT: 4,000
SALES (est): 520K **Privately Held**
SIC: 5611 5699 5094 3479 Clothing, sportswear, men's & boys'; uniforms: trophies; engraving jewelry silverware, or metal; sporting goods & bicycle shops; pleating & stitching

(G-1120)
KACKERT ENTERPRISES INC
824 2nd Ave (60505-3792)
PHONE.................................630 898-9339
Charles Kackert, *President*
Edwin Kackert, *Corp Secy*
EMP: 4 **EST:** 1956
SALES: 250K **Privately Held**
SIC: 5063 5084 3714 3625 Generators; motors, electric; switchgear; engines & transportation equipment; motor vehicle parts & accessories; relays & industrial controls; motors & generators; refrigeration & heating equipment

(G-1121)
KRAFT HEINZ FOODS COMPANY
1700 N Edgelawn Dr (60506-1076)
PHONE.................................630 907-2590
Eileen Sussland, *Opers Staff*
James Pitts, *Contractor*
Amber Rivera, *Contractor*
EMP: 8
SALES (corp-wide): 24.9B **Publicly Held**
SIC: 2099 Food preparations
HQ: Kraft Heinz Foods Company
1 Ppg Pl Fl 34
Pittsburgh PA 15222
412 456-5700

(G-1122)
LABEL PRINTERS LP
1710 Landmark Rd (60506-1192)
PHONE.................................630 897-6970
Gerald Chouinard, *Partner*
Theodore Risch, *Partner*
Donald Tade, *Partner*
Dawn Tesch, *Purchasing*
William J Kane, *Mng Member*
EMP: 73
SQ FT: 54,000
SALES (est): 15.6MM **Privately Held**
WEB: www.thelabelprinters.com
SIC: 2759 Labels & seals: printing

(G-1123)
LEROYS PLASTIC CO INC
1650 Mountain St (60505-2497)
PHONE.................................630 898-7006
James Leroy Frieders, *President*
Brian Frieders, *Co-Owner*
EMP: 10
SQ FT: 8,500
SALES (est): 1.6MM **Privately Held**
WEB: www.leroysplastics.com
SIC: 3089 Injection molding of plastics

(G-1124)
LOUIS J HANSEN ENTERPRISES INC
Also Called: Indian Creek Development
1500 Dearborn Ave Ste 12a (60505-3240)
PHONE.................................630 956-3765
Louis J Hansen, *President*
Gary Hansen, *Vice Pres*
Alex Monroe, *Manager*
EMP: 10
SQ FT: 4,500
SALES (est): 900K **Privately Held**
SIC: 3061 Mechanical rubber goods

(G-1125)
MAGIC MOLD REMOVAL
689 Wood St (60505-2360)
PHONE.................................630 486-0912
Shane Knight, *Principal*
EMP: 2
SALES (est): 266.7K **Privately Held**
SIC: 3544 Industrial molds

(G-1126)
MAGICK WOODS INC
1600 Sequoia Dr (60506-1079)
PHONE.................................630 229-0121
Indrakumar Pathmanathan, *President*
Pathma Kumar Pathmanathan, *Director*
EMP: 5
SALES (est): 447.2K **Privately Held**
SIC: 2499 Woodenware, kitchen & household
PA: Magick Woods Exports Private Limited
A-8, Industrial Complex, Maraimalai Nagar,
Chengalpattu TN 60320

(G-1127)
MARTIN STEES LLC
2289 Copley St (60506-3248)
PHONE.................................630 664-6273
Martin Stees, *Principal*
EMP: 3
SALES (est): 186.4K **Privately Held**
SIC: 2759 Screen printing

(G-1128)
MCNISH CORPORATION (PA)
Also Called: Rbc Services
840 N Russell Ave (60506-2856)
PHONE.................................630 892-7921
James A McNish, *President*
Lloyd H Cates, *President*
Dan Harker, *COO*
Jim Barbel, *Vice Pres*
John Edwards, *Engineer*
▼ **EMP:** 100 **EST:** 1946
SQ FT: 93,000
SALES (est): 33.2MM **Privately Held**
SIC: 3589 Water treatment equipment, industrial

(G-1129)
MCS MIDWEST LLC
85 Hankes Ave (60505-1774)
PHONE.................................630 393-7402
EMP: 5
SALES (corp-wide): 4.3MM **Privately Held**
WEB: www.mcsmidwest.com
SIC: 3089 Plastic containers, except foam
PA: Mcs Midwest Llc
3876 Hendrickson Rd
Franklin OH 45005
513 217-0805

(G-1130)
MENASHA PACKAGING COMPANY LLC
1700 N Edgelawn Dr (60506-1076)
PHONE.................................630 236-4011
Yesica Aguilera, *Production*
EMP: 151
SALES (corp-wide): 2.2B **Privately Held**
SIC: 2653 Boxes, corrugated: made from purchased materials
HQ: Menasha Packaging Company, Llc
1645 Bergstrom Rd
Neenah WI 54956
920 751-1000

(G-1131)
MERIDIAN INDUSTRIES INC
Also Called: Aurora Textile Finishing Co
911 N Lake St (60506-2515)
P.O. Box 70 (60507-0070)
PHONE.................................630 892-7651
EMP: 76
SALES (corp-wide): 374.1MM **Privately Held**
SIC: 2261 7389 Cotton Finishing Plant Business Services
PA: Meridian Industries, Inc.
735 N Water St Ste 630
Milwaukee WI 53202
414 224-0610

(G-1132)
METAL ARTS FINISHING INC
1001 S Lake St (60506-5894)
PHONE.................................630 892-6744
Steve Mayotte, *President*
EMP: 28
SQ FT: 10,000
SALES (est): 1.5MM **Privately Held**
SIC: 3471 Electroplating of metals or formed products

(G-1133)
MFR MANUFACTURING CORP INC
1065 Sill Ave (60506-5837)
PHONE.................................815 552-3333
Gerhard Schiller, *President*
EMP: 3 **EST:** 2017
SQ FT: 20,000
SALES (est): 210.1K **Privately Held**
SIC: 3315 Fence gates posts & fittings: steel

(G-1134)
MID-AMERICA UNDERGROUND LLC
Also Called: Mgi Services
901 Ridgeway Ave (60506-5432)
PHONE.................................630 443-9999
Adam M Bosch, *President*
Benjamin J Engleson, *Mng Member*
Pablo E Guerra, *Mng Member*
EMP: 50
SALES (est): 9.9MM **Privately Held**
SIC: 1381 1799 1623 1794 Directional drilling oil & gas wells; boring for building construction; water, sewer & utility lines; telephone & communication line construction; pipeline construction; excavation work

(G-1135)
MILLPRO LLC
2245 Sequoia Dr Ste 300 (60506-6220)
PHONE.................................630 608-9241
EMP: 3
SALES (est): 197.2K **Privately Held**
SIC: 3823 Industrial instrmnts msrmnt display/control process variable

(G-1136)
MOBIS PARTS AMERICA LLC
1705 Sequoia Dr (60506-1033)
PHONE.................................630 907-4700
EMP: 270 **Privately Held**
SIC: 3714 Motor vehicle body components & frame
HQ: Mobis Parts America, Llc
10550 Talbert Ave Fl 4
Fountain Valley CA 92708
786 515-1101

(G-1137)
MY-LIN MANUFACTURING CO INC
820 N Russell Ave (60506-2823)
PHONE.................................630 897-4100
EMP: 20 **EST:** 1961
SQ FT: 13,000
SALES (est): 4MM **Privately Held**
SIC: 3469 Mfg Metal Stampings

(G-1138)
NANCO SALES CO INC
320 N Highland Ave (60506-3812)
P.O. Box 495 (60507-0495)
PHONE.................................630 892-9820
Nancy Mitchell, *President*
EMP: 3
SQ FT: 2,500
SALES (est): 304.7K **Privately Held**
SIC: 5113 5087 3492 Industrial & personal service paper; janitors' supplies; hose & tube fittings & assemblies, hydraulic/pneumatic

(G-1139)
NATIONAL METALWARES LP (HQ)
900 N Russell Ave (60506-2852)
PHONE.................................630 892-9000
Gary C Hill, *CEO*
Jerry Guthke, *COO*
Mark Strasser, *Materials Mgr*
Gary Harvala, *Traffic Mgr*
Ted Hendricks, *Foreman/Supr*
▲ **EMP:** 250 **EST:** 1946
SQ FT: 185,000
SALES (est): 50.3MM
SALES (corp-wide): 386.2MM **Privately Held**
SIC: 3317 3498 Steel pipe & tubes; fabricated pipe & fittings
PA: Upg Enterprises Llc
1400 16th St Ste 250
Oak Brook IL 60523
630 822-7000

(G-1140)
NUTRIVO LLC (PA)
Also Called: Rivalus
1785 N Edgelawn Dr (60506-1078)
PHONE.................................630 270-1700
Lon Messenger,
EMP: 20
SQ FT: 2,000
SALES (est): 4.7MM **Privately Held**
SIC: 2099 Food preparations

(G-1141)
NUYEN AWNING CO
850 Ridgeway Ave Ste C (60506-6450)
PHONE.................................630 892-3995
Fred T Nuyen, *President*
Richard Lawrence, *Vice Pres*
EMP: 8 **EST:** 1926
SALES (est): 580K **Privately Held**
SIC: 2394 1799 5999 Awnings, fabric: made from purchased materials; tarpaulins, fabric: made from purchased materials; liners & covers, fabric: made from purchased materials; awning installation; awnings

(G-1142)
ON-COR FROZEN FOODS LLC (HQ)
Also Called: Redi-Serve Foods
1225 Corp Blvd Ste 300 (60505)
PHONE.................................630 851-6600
Howard Friend, *Mng Member*

Susan Ribbens, *Manager*
Julie Yeary, *Recruiter*
▲ **EMP:** 20 **EST:** 1932
SALES (est): 14.2MM **Privately Held**
WEB: www.on-cor.com
SIC: 2038 2099 2013 Dinners, frozen & packaged; food preparations; sausages & other prepared meats

(G-1143)
OSI GROUP LLC (PA)
1225 Corp Blvd Ste 300 (60505)
PHONE 630 851-6600
Sheldon Lavin, *CEO*
David G McDonald, *President*
Jim Svajgl, *Division Mgr*
Jacob Olson, *Superintendent*
Mark Chaplin, *Vice Pres*
◆ **EMP:** 55
SALES (est): 2.6B **Privately Held**
SIC: 2099 Food preparations

(G-1144)
OSI INDUSTRIES LLC (HQ)
Also Called: Otto & Sons Div
1225 Corp Blvd Ste 105 (60505)
P.O. Box 2018 (60507-2018)
PHONE 630 851-6600
Sheldon Lavin, *CEO*
Gerald Kolschowsky, *Vice Pres*
Raj Salgia, *Manager*
Jerry Getka, *Director*
Joellen Beeden, *Personnel Assit*
◆ **EMP:** 90
SQ FT: 60,000
SALES (est): 1.9B **Privately Held**
WEB: www.osigroup.com
SIC: 2099 Ready-to-eat meals, salads & sandwiches

(G-1145)
PPG VPN
2570 Orchard Gateway Rd (60506-8895)
PHONE 630 907-8910
EMP: 4 **EST:** 2016
SALES (est): 422.9K **Privately Held**
SIC: 2851 Paints & allied products

(G-1146)
PROGRESSIVE TURNINGS INC
1680 Mountain St (60505-2439)
PHONE 630 898-3072
Lawrence S Niels, *President*
Clara Niels, *Corp Secy*
David Niels, *Vice Pres*
EMP: 15
SALES (est): 3.5MM **Privately Held**
SIC: 3451 Screw machine products

(G-1147)
RECO OF IL INC
1669 Dearborn Ave (60505-3134)
PHONE 630 898-2010
Fax: 630 898-7590
EMP: 5 **EST:** 1972
SQ FT: 42,000
SALES: 250K **Privately Held**
SIC: 7692 Welding Repair

(G-1148)
RIDGE ROAD DEFENSE
1850 Tall Oaks Dr # 2206 (60505-1276)
PHONE 630 820-8906
Jeff Mayr, *Principal*
EMP: 3
SALES (est): 150.8K **Privately Held**
SIC: 3812 Defense systems & equipment

(G-1149)
ROSKUSZKA & SONS INC
Also Called: Wally's Printing
969 N Farnsworth Ave (60505-2055)
PHONE 630 851-3400
William Roskuszka, *President*
EMP: 14
SQ FT: 3,000
SALES: 1.8MM **Privately Held**
SIC: 2752 Commercial printing, offset

(G-1150)
RWI HOLDINGS INC (PA)
600 S Lake St (60506-5582)
PHONE 630 897-6951
Manfred Haiderer, *President*
Scot Patrick, *Vice Pres*
Richard White, *Vice Pres*
EMP: 12
SALES: 30MM **Privately Held**
SIC: 2542 5046 Partitions & fixtures, except wood; shelving, commercial & industrial

(G-1151)
RWI MANUFACTURING INC
Also Called: Richards-Wilcox
600 S Lake St (60506-5582)
PHONE 800 277-1699
Manfred Haiderer, *Ch of Bd*
Roy Koch, *President*
Scott Patrick, *Vice Pres*
Richard White, *Vice Pres*
Michael Golevicz, *Opers Mgr*
◆ **EMP:** 150
SQ FT: 362,000
SALES (est): 31.4MM **Privately Held**
SIC: 2522 3535 Filing boxes, cabinets & cases: except wood; overhead conveyor systems
PA: Rwi Holdings, Inc.
600 S Lake St
Aurora IL 60506

(G-1152)
S & S METAL RECYCLERS INC
Also Called: Ecology Tech
336 E Sullivan Rd (60505-9740)
PHONE 630 844-3344
Quentin Podraza, *President*
Thomas Zacardi, *Treasurer*
EMP: 15
SQ FT: 12,500
SALES (est): 2.3MM **Privately Held**
SIC: 4953 3341 Recycling, waste materials; secondary nonferrous metals

(G-1153)
SAMECWEI INC
Also Called: Sir Speedy
205 N Lake St Ste 103 (60506-4072)
PHONE 630 897-7888
John WEI, *President*
Bill Samec, *Corp Secy*
EMP: 4 **EST:** 1971
SQ FT: 2,000
SALES (est): 360K **Privately Held**
SIC: 2752 7334 2791 2789 Commercial printing, lithographic; photocopying & duplicating services; typesetting; bookbinding & related work; commercial printing

(G-1154)
SBE VARVIT USA LLC
1455 Sequoia Dr Ste 101 (60506-1172)
PHONE 331 205-7000
Alessandro Vescovini,
Alberto Vescovini,
Federico Vescovini,
▲ **EMP:** 3
SALES (est): 694.3K **Privately Held**
WEB: www.varvit.com
SIC: 3559 Automotive related machinery
PA: Vescovini Group Spa
Via Enzo Lazzaretti 2/A
Reggio Emilia RE
011 470-4770

(G-1155)
SHANNON & SONS WELDING
Also Called: Shannon & Sons Welding Shop
1218 E New York St (60505-3922)
PHONE 630 898-7778
Ellis Shannon, *Owner*
EMP: 3
SQ FT: 2,450
SALES (est): 100K **Privately Held**
SIC: 1799 7692 3444 Welding on site; welding repair; sheet metalwork

(G-1156)
SHARE MACHINE INC
2175 Rochester Dr Ste C (60506-5674)
PHONE 630 906-1810
Zekir Share, *President*
Zejnep Share, *Admin Sec*
EMP: 10
SQ FT: 18,500
SALES (est): 2MM **Privately Held**
SIC: 3599 Machine shop, jobbing & repair

(G-1157)
STEVE JANIK CABINETRY LLC
314 N Lake St Ste 3 (60506-4086)
PHONE 630 553-8383
Janik Steven A, *Principal*
EMP: 3
SALES (est): 195.7K **Privately Held**
SIC: 2434 Wood kitchen cabinets

(G-1158)
SUPER TARGET SYSTEMS LLC
2055 Comprehensive Dr (60505-1374)
PHONE 800 556-3162
Daniel Dudici, *CEO*
EMP: 7
SALES (est): 481.9K **Privately Held**
SIC: 3448 Prefabricated metal buildings

(G-1159)
TAG DIAMOND & LABEL
100 Hankes Ave (60505-1747)
PHONE 630 844-9395
Tony Oliva, *President*
EMP: 20
SALES (est): 1.2MM **Privately Held**
SIC: 7389 2679 Printers' services: folding, collating; tags, paper (unprinted): made from purchased paper

(G-1160)
TANGENT TECHNOLOGIES LLC (PA)
1001 Sullivan Rd (60506-1065)
PHONE 630 264-1110
Guy De Feo, *CEO*
Francisco Morales,
Andrew Stephens,
▲ **EMP:** 106
SALES (est): 21.5MM **Privately Held**
SIC: 2821 Plastics materials & resins

(G-1161)
THALES VISIONIX INC
1444 N Farnsworth Ave # 604 (60505-1644)
PHONE 630 375-2008
Pete Roney, *CEO*
John Popoolapade, *Engineer*
David Spaven, *Director*
EMP: 61
SALES (est): 3.6MM **Privately Held**
SIC: 8731 3728 Electronic research; research & dev by manuf., aircraft parts & auxiliary equip

(G-1162)
TIN MAN HEATING & COOLING INC
Also Called: DCS Mechanical
419 Rathbone Ave (60506-5936)
PHONE 630 267-3232
Kenneth Smith, *President*
Nicholas Cellini, *Corp Secy*
EMP: 40
SQ FT: 1,300
SALES (est): 9.5MM **Privately Held**
WEB: www.dcsmechanical.com
SIC: 3356 Tin

(G-1163)
TOUGH ELECTRIC INC
717 Jackson St (60505-5210)
PHONE 630 236-8332
Rafael Fajardo, *President*
Evelyn Fajardo, *Admin Sec*
EMP: 6
SALES (est): 745.6K **Privately Held**
SIC: 3625 Relays, electric power

(G-1164)
UNILOCK
301 E Sullivan Rd (60505-9762)
PHONE 262 742-3890
Suede Remington, *Plant Mgr*
Chris Boster, *QC Mgr*
Jen Dodson, *Sales Staff*
John Russo, *Manager*
Tim Edick, *Manager*
▲ **SALES (est):** 407.3K **Privately Held**
SIC: 3281 Cut stone & stone products

(G-1165)
UNILOCK CHICAGO INC (PA)
301 E Sullivan Rd (60505-9762)
PHONE 630 892-9191
Edward J Bryant, *President*
Tony Hooper, *Vice Pres*
Joe Kerr, *Vice Pres*
James A Hooper, *Admin Sec*
▲ **EMP:** 100
SQ FT: 19,300
SALES (est): 17.2MM **Privately Held**
SIC: 3281 1741 Paving blocks, cut stone; retaining wall construction

(G-1166)
VIM RECYCLERS LP
920 Rathbone Ave (60506-5877)
PHONE 630 892-2559
Patrick McMahon, *Partner*
EMP: 160
SALES (est): 42MM **Privately Held**
SIC: 5093 7359 3999 Junk & scrap; equipment rental & leasing; pet supplies

(G-1167)
VOICE
314 N Lake St Ste 2 (60506-4086)
P.O. Box 123 (60507-0123)
PHONE 630 966-8642
Carter Crane, *President*
EMP: 7
SALES (est): 429.3K **Privately Held**
WEB: www.thevoice.us
SIC: 2711 Commercial printing & newspaper publishing combined; newspapers, publishing & printing

(G-1168)
WELDING COMPANY OF AMERICA
Also Called: Upshot Putter Company
335 E Sullivan Rd (60505-9762)
PHONE 630 806-2000
Hector Villarreal, *President*
Neal Patterson, *Engineer*
Shawn McDonough, *Controller*
Melissa Heard, *Marketing Mgr*
Gjelard Karrica, *Info Tech Mgr*
▼ **EMP:** 38
SQ FT: 17,900
SALES (est): 11.9MM **Privately Held**
WEB: www.weldcoa.com
SIC: 3499 7692 Welding tips, heat resistant: metal; welding repair

(G-1169)
WELDSTAR COMPANY (PA)
1750 Mitchell Rd (60505-9578)
P.O. Box 1150 (60507-1150)
PHONE 630 859-3100
John B Winkle, *CEO*
Matthew Winkle, *President*
Joseph Winkle, *Corp Secy*
Chet De King, *Vice Pres*
▼ **EMP:** 32 **EST:** 1948
SQ FT: 22,000
SALES (est): 24.6MM **Privately Held**
WEB: www.weldstar.com
SIC: 5084 2813 Welding machinery & equipment; industrial gases

(G-1170)
WESTROCK RKT LLC
1601 Mountain St (60505-2402)
PHONE 630 429-2400
Ed Curtis, *Manager*
EMP: 161
SALES (corp-wide): 18.2B **Publicly Held**
SIC: 2653 Boxes, corrugated: made from purchased materials
HQ: Westrock Rkt, Llc
1000 Abernathy Rd Ste 125
Atlanta GA 30328
770 448-2193

(G-1171)
WURST KITCHEN INC (PA)
638 2nd Ave (60505-4418)
PHONE 630 898-9242
Edward Schleining, *Principal*
EMP: 2
SQ FT: 1,740

Ava — Jackson County (G-1172)

SALES (est): 210.7K **Privately Held**
WEB: www.wurstkitchen.com
SIC: 2013 5421 Sausages from purchased meat; meat markets, including freezer provisioners

Ava
Jackson County

(G-1172)
HILL TOP PALLET
612 Bollman Rd (62907-2493)
PHONE..................618 426-9810
Howard Yoder, *Owner*
EMP: 6
SALES: 850K **Privately Held**
SIC: 2448 Pallets, wood

(G-1173)
KUNTRY KETTLE
178 Gordon Rd (62907-2402)
PHONE..................618 426-1600
James Yoder, *Owner*
EMP: 4
SQ FT: 5,000
SALES (est): 389.3K **Privately Held**
SIC: 2033 Jams, jellies & preserves: packaged in cans, jars, etc.

(G-1174)
LONEOAK TIMBER & VENEERE CO
45 Longhorn Trl (62907-2975)
PHONE..................618 426-3065
Mike Faults, *Owner*
EMP: 3
SALES (est): 254.1K **Privately Held**
SIC: 2411 Timber, cut at logging camp

(G-1175)
MILLERS COUNTRY CRAFTS INC
150 Millers Country Ln (62907-2094)
PHONE..................618 426-3108
Nevin Miller, *President*
Wilma Miller, *Vice Pres*
EMP: 2
SQ FT: 6,000
SALES: 700K **Privately Held**
SIC: 2033 5149 Jams, including imitation: packaged in cans, jars, etc.; jellies, edible, including imitation: in cans, jars, etc.; honey

(G-1176)
PAINTED QUARTER RIDGE
948 Possom Rd (62907-2955)
PHONE..................618 534-9734
EMP: 3
SALES (est): 203.3K **Privately Held**
SIC: 3131 Footwear cut stock

(G-1177)
RESEARCH MANNIKINS INC
143 Lupine Ln (62907-2101)
PHONE..................618 426-3456
Randy Hurst, *Branch Mgr*
EMP: 14
SALES (corp-wide): 7.5MM **Privately Held**
SIC: 3999 5087 Mannequins; taxidermist tools & equipment
PA: Research Mannikins, Inc.
315 W Sherman St
Lebanon OR 97355
541 451-1538

Aviston
Clinton County

(G-1178)
COBRAA INC
350 W 4th St (62216-3404)
P.O. Box 122 (62216-0122)
PHONE..................618 228-7380
Derek Sudholt, *President*
EMP: 3 EST: 2000
SALES (est): 373.8K **Privately Held**
WEB: www.sudholtsheetmetal.com
SIC: 3312 Coated or plated products

(G-1179)
HIDDEN LAKE WINERY LTD
10580 Wellen Rd (62216-1019)
PHONE..................618 228-9111
Dale E Holbrook, *President*
EMP: 50
SALES (est): 1.6MM **Privately Held**
SIC: 7299 2084 Banquet hall facilities; wines, brandy & brandy spirits

(G-1180)
JW WELDING
11 S Clement Dr (62216-3749)
PHONE..................618 228-7213
Jeff Woltering, *President*
EMP: 5
SALES (est): 118.1K **Privately Held**
SIC: 7692 Welding repair

(G-1181)
MARKUS CABINET MANUFACTURING (PA)
601 S Clinton St (62216-3418)
P.O. Box 95 (62216-0095)
PHONE..................618 228-7376
Keith Marcus, *President*
Randy Peek, *President*
Carl Marcus, *Vice Pres*
Larry Bair, *Treasurer*
EMP: 20
SALES (est): 2.2MM **Privately Held**
WEB: www.markuscabinet.com
SIC: 2434 Wood kitchen cabinets

(G-1182)
MHWP
Also Called: Recognitions
307 W Harrison St (62216-3547)
PHONE..................618 228-7600
Jeffrey Morgan, *Owner*
EMP: 4
SALES: 150K **Privately Held**
SIC: 2499 Wood products

(G-1183)
SUDHOLT SHEET METAL INC
350 W 4th St (62216-3404)
P.O. Box 122 (62216-0122)
PHONE..................618 228-7351
Derrik Sudholt, *President*
Amber Jansen, *Manager*
EMP: 9
SQ FT: 3,000
SALES (est): 1.6MM **Privately Held**
WEB: www.sudholtsheetmetal.com
SIC: 1711 3444 1796 Warm air heating & air conditioning contractor; ventilation & duct work contractor; sheet metalwork; installing building equipment

Baldwin
Randolph County

(G-1184)
FJCJ LLC
Also Called: Grangrit
11000 Baldwin Rd (62217-1500)
P.O. Box 25 (62217-0025)
PHONE..................618 785-2217
Steve Bremer, *Branch Mgr*
EMP: 13
SALES (corp-wide): 7.5MM **Privately Held**
SIC: 1446 1241 Abrasive sand mining; coal mining services
PA: Fjcj, Llc
2105 Northwinds Dr
Dyer IN

(G-1185)
HIGMAN LLC
Also Called: Tillock Steel Supply and Salv
609 W Myrtle St (62217-1211)
P.O. Box 144 (62217-0144)
PHONE..................618 785-2545
Joel Higman, *Owner*
EMP: 3
SQ FT: 22,000
SALES (est): 393.8K **Privately Held**
SIC: 3291 3569 Abrasive metal & steel products; baling machines, for scrap metal, paper or similar material

(G-1186)
NEXT LEVEL METAL
7525c State Route 154 (62217-1223)
PHONE..................636 627-9497
Kurt Stellhorn, *Principal*
EMP: 4
SALES (est): 505K **Privately Held**
SIC: 3441 Fabricated structural metal

(G-1187)
US MINERALS INC
11000 Baldwin Rd (62217-1500)
PHONE..................618 785-2217
Bill Hertfelder, *Manager*
EMP: 15
SALES (corp-wide): 34.3MM **Privately Held**
SIC: 3291 Abrasive products
PA: U.S. Minerals, Inc.
18635 West Creek Dr Ste 2
Tinley Park IL 60477
708 623-1935

Bannockburn
Lake County

(G-1188)
ABBOTT LABORATORIES
2355 Waukegan Rd Ste 300 (60015-5501)
PHONE..................312 944-0660
Cheryl Hess, *Sr Sys Analyst*
EMP: 18
SALES (corp-wide): 31.9B **Publicly Held**
SIC: 2834 Pharmaceutical preparations
PA: Abbott Laboratories
100 Abbott Park Rd
Abbott Park IL 60064
224 667-6100

(G-1189)
AVALIGN TECHNOLOGIES INC (PA)
2275 Half Day Rd Ste 126 (60015-1274)
PHONE..................855 282-5446
Forrest R Whittaker, *CEO*
Paul Rice, *Vice Pres*
David Dynako, *Opers Mgr*
Gary Fromm, *Opers Staff*
Rick Link, *Opers Staff*
EMP: 57
SALES (est): 56MM **Privately Held**
SIC: 3829 5047 3841 Thermometers, including digital: clinical; instruments, surgical & medical; surgical & medical instruments

(G-1190)
AVEXIS INC (HQ)
2275 Half Day Rd Ste 200 (60015-1274)
PHONE..................847 572-8280
Sean P Nolan, *President*
Page Bouchard, *Senior VP*
Andrew F Knudten, *Senior VP*
James J L'Italien, *Senior VP*
Lovena Chaput, *Vice Pres*
EMP: 147 EST: 2010
SQ FT: 4,795
SALES (est): 23.9MM
SALES (corp-wide): 47.5B **Privately Held**
SIC: 2836 Biological products, except diagnostic
PA: Novartis Ag
Lichtstrasse 35
Basel BS 4056
613 241-111

(G-1191)
B P I PRINTING & DUPLICATING
Also Called: University Printing
2801 Lakeside Dr Ste 110 (60015-1200)
PHONE..................773 822-0111
Lawrence Berland, *CEO*
EMP: 23
SALES (est): 2.4MM
SALES (corp-wide): 2.3MM **Privately Held**
SIC: 2752 Commercial printing, offset
PA: B P I Printing & Duplicating Inc
3223 N Lakewood Ave
Chicago IL 60657
773 327-7300

(G-1192)
BARCOR INC
1413 Aitken Dr (60015-1834)
P.O. Box 517, Northbrook (60065-0517)
PHONE..................847 940-0750
Ed Baria, *President*
Judy Baria, *President*
EMP: 10
SQ FT: 3,000
SALES (est): 1MM **Privately Held**
SIC: 3545 3829 3823 3229 Gauges (machine tool accessories); measuring & controlling devices; industrial instrmnts msrmnt display/control process variable; pressed & blown glass

(G-1193)
BAXALTA EXPORT CORPORATION
1200 Lakeside Dr (60015-1243)
PHONE..................224 948-2000
Ludwig N Hanton, *CEO*
▼ EMP: 237 EST: 2015
SALES (est): 435K
SALES (corp-wide): 15.1B **Privately Held**
SIC: 3841 2835 3842 2834 Surgical & medical instruments; catheters; medical instruments & equipment, blood & bone work; surgical instruments & apparatus; blood derivative diagnostic agents; surgical appliances & supplies; intravenous solutions
HQ: Baxalta Incorporated
1200 Lakeside Dr
Bannockburn IL 60015
224 940-2000

(G-1194)
BAXALTA INCORPORATED (DH)
1200 Lakeside Dr (60015-1243)
PHONE..................224 940-2000
Flemming Ornskov, *CEO*
Jacopo Leonardi, *President*
David D Meek, *President*
Dagmar Rosa-Bjorkeson, *President*
Patrice Zagame, *President*
EMP: 106
SQ FT: 260,000
SALES (est): 4B
SALES (corp-wide): 15.1B **Privately Held**
SIC: 2834 Intravenous solutions

(G-1195)
BAXALTA WORLD TRADE LLC (DH)
1200 Lakeside Dr (60015-1243)
PHONE..................224 940-2000
Ludwig N Hanton, *CEO*
EMP: 5
SALES (est): 29MM
SALES (corp-wide): 15.1B **Privately Held**
SIC: 3841 2835 3842 2834 Surgical & medical instruments; catheters; medical instruments & equipment, blood & bone work; surgical instruments & apparatus; blood derivative diagnostic agents; surgical appliances & supplies; intravenous solutions
HQ: Baxalta Incorporated
1200 Lakeside Dr
Bannockburn IL 60015
224 940-2000

(G-1196)
BERLAND PRINTING INC
Also Called: Berland Communications
2801 Lakeside Dr Ste 110 (60015-1200)
PHONE..................773 702-1999
Lawrence Berland, *President*
Bob Berland, *President*
EMP: 25 EST: 1933
SALES (est): 4MM **Privately Held**
WEB: www.berlandcommunications.com
SIC: 2752 Commercial printing, offset

(G-1197)
BIOLIFE PLASMA LLC
Also Called: Shire Biolife
1200 Lakeside Dr (60015-1243)
PHONE..................224 940-7611
David Bailey, *Manager*
EMP: 12
SALES (est): 924.7K **Privately Held**
SIC: 2834 Pharmaceutical preparations

GEOGRAPHIC SECTION

Barrington - Lake County (G-1225)

(G-1198)
CHAMPION LABORATORIES INC
2201 Waukegan Rd Ste 140 (60015-1560)
P.O. Box 147, Albion (62806-0147)
PHONE................................. 618 445-6011
EMP: 13
SALES (corp-wide): 553.7MM **Privately Held**
SIC: 3714 Filters: oil, fuel & air, motor vehicle
HQ: Champion Laboratories, Inc.
  200 S 4th St
  Albion IL 62806
  618 445-6011

(G-1199)
DIONEX CORPORATION
3000 Lakeside Dr Ste 116n (60015-1279)
PHONE................................. 847 295-7500
EMP: 6
SALES (est): 660K **Privately Held**
SIC: 3826 Chromatographic equipment, laboratory type

(G-1200)
ELEXA CONSUMER PRODUCTS INC
Also Called: Elexa Commercial Products
2275 Half Day Rd Ste 160 (60015-1221)
PHONE................................. 773 794-1300
Lawrence Beger, *President*
Julie Wright, *Opers Staff*
Matt Cwiokowski, *Director*
▲ **EMP:** 350
SQ FT: 40,000
SALES (est): 45.4MM **Privately Held**
WEB: www.elexausa.com
SIC: 3651 3661 Household audio & video equipment; telephones & telephone apparatus

(G-1201)
G & S MANUFACTURING INC
2345 Waukegan Rd Ste 155 (60015-1592)
PHONE................................. 847 674-7666
Aron Grunfeld, *President*
Rachel Grunfeld, *Admin Sec*
EMP: 10
SQ FT: 10,000
SALES (est): 1.6MM **Privately Held**
SIC: 3545 Tools & accessories for machine tools

(G-1202)
GCP APPLIED TECHNOLOGIES INC
2051 Waukegan Rd (60015-1828)
PHONE................................. 617 876-1400
Joe Bystron, *Branch Mgr*
EMP: 162
SALES (corp-wide): 1B **Publicly Held**
SIC: 2819 Industrial inorganic chemicals
PA: Gcp Applied Technologies Inc.
  62 Whittemore Ave
  Cambridge MA 02140
  617 876-1400

(G-1203)
MEXINOX USA INC
Also Called: Thyssenkrupp Stainless N Amer
2275 Half Day Rd Ste 300 (60015-1232)
PHONE................................. 224 533-6700
Stephan Lacor, *Vice Pres*
EMP: 55
SQ FT: 5,000
SALES (est): 9.6MM
SALES (corp-wide): 7B **Privately Held**
SIC: 3312 Plate, sheet & strip, except coated products
HQ: Outokumpu Mexinox, S.A. De C.V.
  Av. Industrias No. 4100
  San Luis Potosi S.L.P. 78395

(G-1204)
MUMFORD METAL CASTING LLC
Also Called: Callen Die Casting
2801 Lakeside Dr Ste 300 (60015-1275)
PHONE................................. 708 345-0400
Thomas Gibson, *Opers Staff*
EMP: 195
SALES (corp-wide): 17.1MM **Privately Held**
WEB: www.mumfordcompanies.com
SIC: 3364 Lead & zinc die-castings
PA: Mumford Metal Casting Llc
  2222 S Halsted St
  Chicago IL 60608
  312 733-2600

(G-1205)
NPN360
2801 Lakeside Dr Ste 100 (60015-1296)
PHONE................................. 847 215-7300
Arthur B Collins Jr, *Exec VP*
Ken Petrie, *Exec VP*
John Cunningham, *Vice Pres*
Karl Johnson, *Vice Pres*
Mark Marron, *Vice Pres*
EMP: 30
SALES (est): 8.5MM **Privately Held**
SIC: 2752 Commercial printing, offset

(G-1206)
PRINT & DESIGN SERVICES LLC
Also Called: AlphaGraphics
2561 Waukegan Rd (60015-1569)
PHONE................................. 847 317-9001
Ronald J Garsha, *Principal*
Uwe Trode, *Sales Staff*
EMP: 5
SQ FT: 2,400
SALES (est): 1MM **Privately Held**
SIC: 2752 7334 2791 2789 Commercial printing, lithographic; photocopying & duplicating services; typesetting; bookbinding & related work

(G-1207)
SHIRE PHARMACEUTICALS LLC
1200 Lakeside Dr (60015-1243)
PHONE................................. 224 940-2000
Amy Howard, *Traffic Mgr*
Janice Denton, *Credit Staff*
Gregory Block, *Manager*
Kurt Olsson, *Director*
David Poirier, *Director*
EMP: 32
SALES (corp-wide): 53.3MM **Privately Held**
SIC: 2834 Pharmaceutical preparations
HQ: Shire Pharmaceuticals Llc
  300 Shire Way
  Lexington MA 02421
  617 349-0200

(G-1208)
SOUTHLAND INDUSTRIES INC
2345 Waukegan Rd Ste 155 (60015-1592)
PHONE................................. 757 543-5701
Alex Granfield, *President*
Jim Jones, *President*
Theodore L Salter, *Vice Pres*
EMP: 25
SQ FT: 108,800
SALES (est): 2.9MM **Privately Held**
SIC: 3053 3069 Gaskets & sealing devices; molded rubber products

(G-1209)
TAKEDA PHARMACEUTICALS USA INC
2355 Waukegan Rd (60015-1586)
PHONE................................. 847 315-9228
Danielle Moyles, *Branch Mgr*
EMP: 5 **Privately Held**
SIC: 2834 Pharmaceutical preparations
HQ: Takeda Pharmaceuticals U.S.A., Inc.
  95 Hayden Ave
  Lexington MA 02421
  617 349-0200

(G-1210)
TAKEDA PHRMACEUTICALS INTL INC
1200 Lakeside Dr (60015-1243)
PHONE................................. 224 554-6500
Shinji Honda, *President*
EMP: 699
SALES (est): 221.2MM **Privately Held**
SIC: 2834 Pharmaceutical preparations
PA: Takeda Pharmaceutical Company Limited
  2-1-1, Nihombashihoncho
  Chuo-Ku TKY 103-0

(G-1211)
THERMO FISHER SCIENTIFIC INC
Also Called: Thermo Mattson
3000 Lakeside Dr Ste 116n (60015-1279)
PHONE................................. 847 295-7500
David Kage, *Sales Staff*
Susan Sage, *Sales Staff*
John Butler, *Branch Mgr*
Susan Cieslik, *Manager*
EMP: 8
SQ FT: 6,000
SALES (corp-wide): 25.5B **Publicly Held**
WEB: www.thermofisher.com
SIC: 3826 Analytical instruments
PA: Thermo Fisher Scientific Inc.
  168 3rd Ave
  Waltham MA 02451
  781 622-1000

(G-1212)
WRIGHT METALS INC
1405 Valley Rd (60015-1551)
PHONE................................. 847 267-1212
Kim A Wright, *President*
James Barkemeyer, *Corp Secy*
EMP: 3 **EST:** 1981
SALES (est): 493.7K **Privately Held**
SIC: 3444 Sheet metalwork

Barrington
Lake County

(G-1213)
BARRINGTON CARDINAL WHSE LLC
Also Called: Garfilds Bev Whse - Barrington
340 W Northwest Hwy (60010-3033)
PHONE................................. 847 387-3676
David Garfield, *Ch of Bd*
Adam Silvertein, *COO*
Bruce Garfield, *Mng Member*
EMP: 4
SQ FT: 10,000
SALES (est): 236.8K **Privately Held**
SIC: 2084 Wines

(G-1214)
BARRINGTON CLINICAL PARTNERS
25377 N Wagon Wheel Ct (60010-1430)
PHONE................................. 847 508-9737
Maelynn S McCrory, *Owner*
EMP: 4
SALES (est): 334K **Privately Held**
SIC: 3845 Electromedical equipment

(G-1215)
BARRINGTON PACKAGING SYSTEMS
Also Called: Barrington Packg Systems Group
835 Barrington Point Rd (60010-4625)
PHONE................................. 847 382-8063
George Burny, *President*
Larry Pence, *COO*
Lisa Pence, *Accounting Mgr*
Danny Lena, *Director*
▲ **EMP:** 8
SQ FT: 1,000
SALES (est): 2.3MM **Privately Held**
SIC: 3565 2631 Packaging machinery; packaging board

(G-1216)
CASTLEGATE PUBLISHERS INC
25597 W Drake Rd (60010-2417)
PHONE................................. 847 382-6420
Michael Mercer PHD, *President*
EMP: 3 **EST:** 1997
SALES (est): 169.4K **Privately Held**
WEB: www.positivelifeanswers.com
SIC: 2731 Book publishing

(G-1217)
CEM LLC
Also Called: Capital Engineering & Mfg Co
6000 Garlands Ln Ste 120 (60010-6029)
PHONE................................. 708 333-3761
John Herb, *President*
Michael Golevicz, *Vice Pres*
Tom Herb,
EMP: 60
SALES (est): 9MM **Privately Held**
SIC: 3441 Fabricated structural metal

(G-1218)
CONTINENTAL SALES INC
213 W Main St (60010-4205)
PHONE................................. 847 381-6530
Terry Wybel, *President*
▲ **EMP:** 5 **EST:** 1997
SALES (est): 380K **Privately Held**
WEB: www.continentalsalesinc.com
SIC: 2731 Book publishing

(G-1219)
FRESCO PLASTER FINISHES INC
Also Called: Nass Fresco Finishes
228 James St Ste 2 (60010-3328)
P.O. Box 281 (60011-0281)
PHONE................................. 847 277-1484
Dan Nass, *President*
EMP: 8
SQ FT: 5,000
SALES: 990K **Privately Held**
SIC: 2211 Upholstery, tapestry & wall coverings: cotton

(G-1220)
GNK TECHNOLOGIES INC
Also Called: Minuteman Press
200 James St (60010-3328)
PHONE................................. 847 382-1185
Gary Kreuz, *President*
Nancy Kreuz, *Admin Sec*
EMP: 7
SQ FT: 1,400
SALES: 100K **Privately Held**
SIC: 2752 Commercial printing, lithographic

(G-1221)
GRAPHIC ARTS STUDIO INC (PA)
28 W 111 Coml Ave Commercial (60010)
PHONE................................. 847 381-1105
Andrew J Macchia Jr, *President*
Don Wilson, *President*
Joseph Vitallo, *Production*
John Blackwell, *Sales Staff*
Mike Dillon, *Sales Staff*
EMP: 50
SQ FT: 17,000
SALES (est): 17.6MM **Privately Held**
SIC: 2796 2752 Color separations for printing; commercial printing, lithographic

(G-1222)
J AND J INTERNATIONAL
1016 S Summit St (60010-5059)
PHONE................................. 847 842-8628
John Zhu, *President*
EMP: 3
SALES (est): 270.5K **Privately Held**
SIC: 3999 Manufacturing industries

(G-1223)
LANCER MANUFACTURING INC (PA)
1021 Oakland Dr (60010-6309)
PHONE................................. 630 595-1150
EMP: 12 **EST:** 1965
SQ FT: 11,000
SALES (est): 1.8MM **Privately Held**
SIC: 3599 Machine Shop

(G-1224)
LINMORE PUBLISHING CO
409 South St (60010-4546)
PHONE................................. 847 382-7606
Linda Mrowicki, *President*
Dan Jackson, *Vice Pres*
EMP: 2
SALES: 200K **Privately Held**
SIC: 2731 Textbooks: publishing & printing

(G-1225)
LITTLE SHOP OF PAPERS LTD
740 W Northwest Hwy (60010-2640)
PHONE................................. 847 382-7733
Jean A Stahr, *President*
Scott Stahr, *Admin Sec*
EMP: 6
SQ FT: 500

Barrington - Lake County (G-1226)

SALES (est): 415.9K **Privately Held**
SIC: 5947 8999 2759 Gift shop; calligrapher; invitation & stationery printing & engraving

(G-1226)
MAC AMERICAN CORPORATION
530 Fox Glen Ct (60010-1833)
PHONE..................847 277-9450
Thomas D McAuley, *President*
▲ EMP: 6
SQ FT: 4,300
SALES (est): 12MM **Privately Held**
SIC: 2631 Paperboard mills

(G-1227)
MARSHALL PUBG & PROMOTIONS
123 S Hough St (60010-4376)
PHONE..................224 238-3530
Thomas Edinger, *Principal*
EMP: 1
SALES (est): 225K **Privately Held**
SIC: 2741 5961 Miscellaneous publishing; record &/or tape (music or video) club, mail order

(G-1228)
MIDWEST WHEEL COVERS INC
27175 W Flynn Creek Dr (60010-2306)
PHONE..................847 609-9980
Bob Palumbo, *President*
EMP: 1
SALES (est): 250K **Privately Held**
SIC: 3312 Wheels

(G-1229)
MINDFUL MDISPA MEDICLINIC PLLC
723 Division St (60010-4518)
PHONE..................847 922-4768
Lucie Bianchi, *President*
EMP: 3
SALES (est): 346.6K **Privately Held**
SIC: 3841 Diagnostic apparatus, medical

(G-1230)
MIYANOHITEC MACHINERY INC
Also Called: Amt Kikai
50 Dundee Ln (60010-5106)
PHONE..................847 382-2794
Thomas Miyano, *CEO*
Steven Miyano, *President*
EMP: 4
SALES (est): 362.8K **Privately Held**
SIC: 3545 Chucks: drill, lathe or magnetic (machine tool accessories)

(G-1231)
MURVIN & MEIER OIL CO
1531 S Grove Ave Unit 203 (60010-5251)
PHONE..................847 277-8380
M Meier, *Principal*
EMP: 4
SALES (est): 322.5K **Privately Held**
SIC: 1381 Drilling oil & gas wells

(G-1232)
NAUTILUS MEDICAL
1300 S Grove Ave Ste 200 (60010-5247)
PHONE..................847 323-1334
Timothy Kelley, *Principal*
Richard Rost, *Sales Staff*
EMP: 2
SQ FT: 8,000
SALES (est): 440.3K **Privately Held**
SIC: 7372 Application computer software

(G-1233)
PACE PRINT PLUS
1010 W Northwest Hwy (60010-2338)
PHONE..................847 381-1720
Flijah Fitzgerald, *Principal*
EMP: 4
SALES (est): 416.8K **Privately Held**
WEB: www.paceprintplus.com
SIC: 2752 Commercial printing, offset

(G-1234)
PEPSICO INC
617 W Main St (60010-4113)
PHONE..................847 767-2026
Al Bolles, *Vice Pres*
Sandy Mui, *Plant Mgr*
Todd Swedberg, *Opers Staff*
Scott Stella, *Sales Staff*
John Stofan, *Manager*
EMP: 265
SALES (corp-wide): 67.1B **Publicly Held**
SIC: 2086 Carbonated soft drinks, bottled & canned
PA: Pepsico, Inc.
700 Anderson Hill Rd
Purchase NY 10577
914 253-2000

(G-1235)
PINEAPPLE LED INC
395 Covington Dr (60010-6614)
PHONE..................847 255-3710
Sean Flahaven, *President*
Tushar Patel, *President*
EMP: 3 EST: 2017
SALES (est): 191.7K **Privately Held**
SIC: 3646 Commercial indusl & institutional electric lighting fixtures

(G-1236)
PJLA MUSIC
22n159 Pepper Rd (60010)
PHONE..................847 382-3212
Peter J Laplaca, *Owner*
▲ EMP: 1
SALES: 250K **Privately Held**
SIC: 3931 5099 Brass instruments & parts; musical instruments parts & accessories

(G-1237)
PRECIOUS METAL REF SVCS INC
Also Called: Progressive Environmental Svcs
1531 S Grove Ave Unit 104 (60010-5250)
PHONE..................847 756-2700
Sheldon B Goldner, *President*
Laurie Harrington, *Purchasing*
Jarret Niesse, *CFO*
David Caldwell, *Program Mgr*
Rob Mikel, *Manager*
EMP: 8
SALES (est): 970K **Privately Held**
SIC: 4953 3341 Hazardous waste collection & disposal; recovery & refining of nonferrous metals

(G-1238)
PRO REP SALE IL
25560 N Countryside Dr (60010-7028)
PHONE..................847 382-1592
Jay N Thompson, *Principal*
EMP: 3
SALES (est): 178.1K **Privately Held**
SIC: 2097 Manufactured ice

(G-1239)
R G CONTROLS INC
512 Rue Chamonix (60010-3710)
PHONE..................847 438-3981
Alena Guest, *CEO*
Raymond Gust, *President*
EMP: 2
SALES: 400K **Privately Held**
SIC: 3613 Control panels, electric

(G-1240)
RMB ENGINEERED PRODUCTS INC
18-1 E Dundee Rd Ste 220 (60010-5271)
PHONE..................847 382-0100
Margaret Blomquist, *President*
Scott Blomquist, *President*
EMP: 8
SALES (est): 423.5K **Privately Held**
SIC: 3443 Heat exchangers, condensers & components

(G-1241)
ROMAN SIGNS
819 W Northwest Hwy (60010-2641)
PHONE..................847 381-3425
Karen Roman, *Owner*
EMP: 9
SALES (est): 557.5K **Privately Held**
SIC: 7312 3993 Billboard advertising; neon signs

(G-1242)
ROOM DIVIDERS NOW LLC
38 Otis Rd (60010-5120)
PHONE..................847 224-7900
Lundmark Jackson, *Mng Member*
▲ EMP: 6
SALES (est): 169.6K **Privately Held**
SIC: 2542 Pallet racks; except wood

(G-1243)
SAN TELMO LTD
330 E Main St Fl 2 (60010-3203)
PHONE..................847 842-9115
Fred Weinert, *President*
Sylvia Weinert, *Vice Pres*
EMP: 5
SALES (est): 400K **Privately Held**
SIC: 2844 5122 Toilet preparations; cosmetics, perfumes & hair products

(G-1244)
SILVERLIGHT CNC INC
135 Park Ave (60010-4370)
PHONE..................847 450-1099
Jeffry Katzbeck, *Principal*
EMP: 2
SALES (est): 233K **Privately Held**
WEB: www.silverlightcnc.com
SIC: 3599 Machine shop, jobbing & repair

(G-1245)
STERLING TOOL & MANUFACTURING
28080 W Coml Ave Ste 8 (60010)
PHONE..................847 304-1800
Terry Wehrheim, *President*
Thomas Degroot, *Vice Pres*
Lee Manges, *Admin Sec*
EMP: 9
SQ FT: 3,000
SALES (est): 1MM **Privately Held**
SIC: 7389 3544 3599 7699 Grinding, precision; commercial or industrial; forms (molds), for foundry & plastics working machinery; grinding castings for the trade; industrial tool grinding

(G-1246)
SWISS AUTOMATION INC
1020 W Northwest Hwy (60010-2338)
PHONE..................847 381-4405
Kenneth Malo, *President*
Michael Merrill, *Foreman/Supr*
Chris Sitkowski, *Purch Agent*
Kyle Rogner, *Chief Engr*
Marc Moran, *Engineer*
EMP: 99
SQ FT: 28,000
SALES (est): 23MM **Privately Held**
WEB: www.swissautomation.com
SIC: 3451 Screw machine products

(G-1247)
TML INC
223 W Main St (60010-4205)
PHONE..................847 382-1550
Andrew Loughlin, *President*
▲ EMP: 2
SALES (est): 260.4K **Privately Held**
SIC: 3824 Mechanical & electromechanical counters & devices

Barry
Pike County

(G-1248)
CENTRAL STONE COMPANY
Hwy 36 (62312)
P.O. Box 101 (62312-0101)
PHONE..................217 335-2615
Darrell Quertermous, *Branch Mgr*
EMP: 7
SALES (corp-wide): 2.5B **Privately Held**
WEB: www.riverstonegrp.com
SIC: 1422 Crushed & broken limestone
HQ: Central Stone Company
4640 E 56th St
Davenport IA 52807
309 757-8250

(G-1249)
DEBBIE HARSHMAN
Also Called: Paper, The
725 Bainbridge St (62312-1205)
PHONE..................217 335-2112
Debbie Harshman, *Owner*
EMP: 3

SALES (est): 120K **Privately Held**
SIC: 2741 2752 2711 Business service newsletters; publishing & printing; commercial printing, lithographic; newspapers

(G-1250)
GATES INC
Also Called: Gates Repair & Machine
134 Smith St (62312-1046)
P.O. Box 134 (62312-0134)
PHONE..................217 335-2378
Rob Gates, *President*
Robert Gates, *President*
EMP: 4
SQ FT: 6,000
SALES (est): 399.3K **Privately Held**
SIC: 7537 3599 Automotive transmission repair shops; machine shop, jobbing & repair

(G-1251)
JIREH INC
1103 Highway 106 (62312)
P.O. Box 118 (62312-0118)
PHONE..................217 335-3276
Mark Patterson, *President*
EMP: 19
SQ FT: 20,000
SALES (est): 2.6MM **Privately Held**
WEB: www.jirehinc.com
SIC: 7534 3011 Tire retreading & repair shops; retreading materials, tire

Bartelso
Clinton County

(G-1252)
CHRISTIAN WOLF INC
12618 Pioneer Rd (62218-3003)
PHONE..................618 667-9522
Deanne Norrenberns, *President*
Tim Norrenberns, *Corp Secy*
EMP: 7
SALES: 175K **Privately Held**
SIC: 2052 8661 2099 Cookies; religious organizations; food preparations

Bartlett
Cook County

(G-1253)
AMERI LABEL COMPANY
2015 Pennsbury Ln (60133-6712)
PHONE..................847 895-8000
Ansar Saleem, *President*
Isaac Dean, *Vice Pres*
Syed K Rahimullah, *Vice Pres*
EMP: 19
SQ FT: 2,500
SALES: 1MM **Privately Held**
SIC: 2679 Labels, paper: made from purchased material

(G-1254)
CALPORT AVIATION COMPANY
4n220 84 Ct (60133-9200)
P.O. Box 793, Bloomingdale (60108-0793)
PHONE..................630 588-8091
Christopher Brown, *President*
EMP: 2 EST: 1998
SALES: 600K **Privately Held**
WEB: www.calportaviation.com
SIC: 3728 Aircraft parts & equipment

(G-1255)
INFORMATION RESOURCES INC
1201 Nashua Ln (60133-5524)
PHONE..................312 474-3154
Ramesh Wadhwani, *President*
EMP: 259
SALES (corp-wide): 356.4MM **Privately Held**
SIC: 7372 7374 Prepackaged software; data entry service
PA: Information Resources, Inc
150 N Clinton St
Chicago IL 60661
312 726-1221

Bartlett - Dupage County (G-1282)

(G-1256)
NOOR INTERNATIONAL INC
2015 Pennsbury Ln (60133-6712)
PHONE..................847 985-2300
Fazzu Saleem, *President*
Mohammed Saleem, *Vice Pres*
Syed Rash, *Admin Sec*
EMP: 7
SQ FT: 3,700
SALES (est): 685.1K **Privately Held**
SIC: 2759 5112 2672 2671 Business forms; printing; business forms; coated & laminated paper; packaging paper & plastics film, coated & laminated

(G-1257)
R & J SYSTEMS INC
1580 Birch Ave (60133-3704)
PHONE..................630 289-3010
Richard D Stephens, *President*
EMP: 5
SALES (est): 100K **Privately Held**
SIC: 7372 Prepackaged software

(G-1258)
UNI ELECTRIC ENTERPRISE INC
1889 Seneca Dr (60133-6751)
PHONE..................630 372-6312
EMP: 3
SALES (est): 189.4K **Privately Held**
SIC: 3694 Manufacturing Battery Cables

(G-1259)
VEGA TECHNOLOGY & SYSTEMS
Also Called: Vtsi
7980 Kingsbury Dr (60133-2348)
PHONE..................630 855-5068
Vincent Y Chow, *Principal*
EMP: 6
SALES: 300K **Privately Held**
SIC: 3827 8742 Optical instruments & lenses; management consulting services

(G-1260)
WESTROCK CP LLC
965 Muirfield Dr (60133-5458)
PHONE..................630 924-0104
Randy Haberman, *General Mgr*
EMP: 50
SALES (corp-wide): 18.2B **Publicly Held**
SIC: 2631 Paperboard mills
HQ: Westrock Cp, Llc
    1000 Abernathy Rd Ste 125
    Atlanta GA 30328

Bartlett
Dupage County

(G-1261)
A-B DIE MOLD INC
5n701 Meadowlark Dr (60103-2012)
PHONE..................847 658-1199
Alan Kaspar, *President*
Barbara Kaspar, *Treasurer*
EMP: 13
SQ FT: 10,000
SALES (est): 1MM **Privately Held**
SIC: 7389 3544 Grinding, precision: commercial or industrial; industrial molds

(G-1262)
ABRASIVE WEST LLC
1292 Humbracht Cir Ste F (60103-1688)
PHONE..................630 736-0818
Kenneth L Kummer, *CEO*
EMP: 8
SALES (est): 597.6K **Privately Held**
SIC: 7389 3841 Grinding, precision: commercial or industrial; surgical & medical instruments; holders, surgical needle

(G-1263)
ALICONA MANUFACTURING INC
1261 Humbracht Cir Ste A (60103-1632)
PHONE..................630 736-2718
Stefan Scherer, *President*
Mark Raleigh, *Principal*
EMP: 3
SQ FT: 10,000
SALES (est): 351.6K
SALES (corp-wide): 2B **Publicly Held**
SIC: 3599 3841 Electrical discharge machining (EDM); surgical & medical instruments
PA: Bruker Corporation
    40 Manning Rd
    Billerica MA 01821
    978 663-3660

(G-1264)
APACHE SUPPLY
647 Philip Dr (60103-1234)
PHONE..................708 409-1040
Douglas Macpherson, *Owner*
▲ EMP: 3
SALES: 100K **Privately Held**
SIC: 3631 Barbecues, grills & braziers (outdoor cooking)

(G-1265)
ASSURANCE TECHNOLOGIES INC
Also Called: Roentgen Industrial
1251 Humbracht Cir Ste A (60103-1693)
PHONE..................630 550-5000
Kenneth J Losacco, *President*
Kurt Stehlin, *Engineer*
Ryan Losacco, *Regl Sales Mgr*
Eric Baumler, *Sales Engr*
Scott Losacco, *Sales Engr*
EMP: 12
SQ FT: 6,500
SALES (est): 3.3MM **Privately Held**
WEB: www.atiquality.com
SIC: 3829 3844 3545 Gauging instruments, thickness ultrasonic; X-ray apparatus & tubes; machine tool accessories

(G-1266)
ATI OLDCO INC (DH)
Also Called: Auto Truck
1420 Brewster Creek Blvd (60103-1695)
PHONE..................630 860-5600
E James Dondlinger, *President*
Michael G McCotter, *Vice Pres*
▲ EMP: 115 EST: 1918
SQ FT: 103,000
SALES (est): 61.5MM
SALES (corp-wide): 1.5B **Privately Held**
SIC: 3713 Truck bodies & parts
HQ: Auto Truck Group, Llc
    1420 Brewster Creek Blvd
    Bartlett IL 60103
    630 860-5600

(G-1267)
AUTO TRUCK GROUP LLC (DH)
Also Called: Auto Truck Grp Wyn Flt Equipme
1420 Brewster Creek Blvd (60103-1695)
PHONE..................630 860-5600
James Dondlinger, *President*
Bryan Schieler, *General Mgr*
Brad Blanco, *Vice Pres*
Dennis Jones, *Vice Pres*
Joe Monteleone, *Plant Mgr*
◆ EMP: 200
SQ FT: 105,000
SALES (est): 242MM
SALES (corp-wide): 1.5B **Privately Held**
WEB: www.autotruck.com
SIC: 3713 1541 Truck bodies & parts; truck & automobile assembly plant construction
HQ: Automotive Rentals, Inc.
    4001 Leadenhall Rd
    Mount Laurel NJ 08054
    856 778-1500

(G-1268)
BBS AUTOMATION CHICAGO INC
Also Called: Ixmation North America
1580 Hecht Ct (60103-1691)
PHONE..................630 351-3000
Michael Macsek, *President*
Sean Richter, *Purchasing*
John Sever, *Engineer*
Michael Watkins, *Engineer*
Alex Bezborodko, *Design Engr*
▲ EMP: 150
SQ FT: 79,450
SALES (est): 43.1MM
SALES (corp-wide): 240.3K **Privately Held**
SIC: 3599 8711 Custom machinery; designing; ship, boat, machine & product
HQ: Bmt Swiss Ag
    Hagelstrasse 14
    HUttikon ZH 8115

(G-1269)
BEHR PROCESS CORPORATION
950 S Il Route 59 (60103-1668)
PHONE..................630 289-6247
Tim Fisher, *Principal*
EMP: 59
SALES (corp-wide): 6.7B **Publicly Held**
WEB: www.behr.com
SIC: 2851 Paints & paint additives
HQ: Behr Process Corporation
    1801 E Saint Andrew Pl
    Santa Ana CA 92705

(G-1270)
BROLITE PRODUCTS INCORPORATED
1335 Schiferl Rd (60103-1701)
PHONE..................630 830-0340
David Del Ghingaro, *President*
Virgil Del Ghingaro, *Principal*
Ken Skrzypiec, *Vice Pres*
EMP: 49
SQ FT: 30,000
SALES (est): 14MM **Privately Held**
SIC: 2045 Prepared flour mixes & doughs

(G-1271)
CATHAY INDUSTRIES (USA) INC (HQ)
Also Called: Cathay Pigments
2340 Kenyon Rd (60103-4700)
PHONE..................219 531-5359
Kevin Miles, *President*
Warren Prince, *Exec VP*
Julie Dwyer, *Cust Mgr*
Brett Fiorini, *Technical Staff*
Sam Prince, *Technical Staff*
▲ EMP: 8
SALES: 35MM **Privately Held**
SIC: 2816 Color pigments; iron oxide pigments (ochers, siennas, umbers)

(G-1272)
CHEESE MERCHANTS AMERICA LLC
1301 Schiferl Rd (60103-1701)
PHONE..................630 221-0580
Robert Greco, *President*
Jim Smart, *President*
Alan Bundy, *Regional Mgr*
Mark Basiliere, *Area Mgr*
Frank Cusumano, *Area Mgr*
▲ EMP: 315 EST: 1998
SQ FT: 277,000
SALES (est): 153.6MM **Privately Held**
WEB: www.cheesemerchants.com
SIC: 5143 2022 Cheese; cheese, natural & processed

(G-1273)
CREA AND CREA
1115 Struckman Blvd (60103-1724)
PHONE..................630 292-5625
Scott Crea, *Principal*
EMP: 2
SALES (est): 223.3K **Privately Held**
SIC: 2431 Millwork

(G-1274)
CREATIVE WERKS LLC
1350 Munger Rd (60103-1698)
PHONE..................630 860-2222
Brian Scott, *Branch Mgr*
EMP: 30
SALES (corp-wide): 54.6MM **Privately Held**
SIC: 3999 Novelties, bric-a-brac & hobby kits
PA: Creative Werks Llc
    1460 Brummel Ave
    Elk Grove Village IL 60007
    630 860-2222

(G-1275)
DYCO-TEC PRODUCTS LTD (PA)
29w600 Schick Rd (60103-2003)
PHONE..................630 837-6410
John Dyer Jr, *President*
Sandy Dyer, *Vice Pres*
EMP: 6
SQ FT: 2,000
SALES (est): 1.2MM **Privately Held**
SIC: 5085 2851 Ink, printers'; lacquers, varnishes, enamels & other coatings

(G-1276)
EDM DEPT INC
Also Called: EDM Department
1261 Humbracht Cir Ste A (60103-1632)
PHONE..................630 736-0531
Mark Raleigh, *CEO*
John Wank, *Vice Pres*
Susan Raleigh, *Administration*
EMP: 30
SQ FT: 3,000
SALES (est): 900K **Privately Held**
SIC: 3599 Machine shop, jobbing & repair

(G-1277)
ELITE WIREWORKS CORPORATION
Also Called: Active Wireworks
1239 Humbracht Cir (60103-1606)
PHONE..................630 837-9100
Eugene R Kudron, *President*
Ryan Kudron, *Opers Mgr*
EMP: 10
SQ FT: 25,000
SALES (est): 1.5MM **Privately Held**
SIC: 3496 Miscellaneous fabricated wire products

(G-1278)
ENBARR LLC
431 Ford Ln (60103-6612)
PHONE..................630 217-2101
Marvin Peplow, *Mng Member*
EMP: 2
SQ FT: 500
SALES: 1.2MM **Privately Held**
SIC: 3087 Custom compound purchased resins

(G-1279)
EXAMINER PUBLICATIONS INC
Also Called: Examiner, The
4n781 Gerber Rd (60103-2021)
P.O. Box 8287 (60103-8287)
PHONE..................630 830-4145
Randall Petrik, *President*
EMP: 5
SQ FT: 1,200
SALES (est): 364.9K **Privately Held**
SIC: 2711 Newspapers, publishing & printing

(G-1280)
FINE CIRCUITS INC
Also Called: Bu National
848 W Bartlett Rd Ste 9 (60103-4493)
PHONE..................630 213-8700
Bharati Upadhyay, *President*
Lynn Martin, *Business Mgr*
Yogenda Upadhyay, *Vice Pres*
Kathy Sammartino, *Sales Staff*
◆ EMP: 12
SQ FT: 2,000
SALES (est): 1.6MM **Privately Held**
SIC: 3672 Printed circuit boards

(G-1281)
FORNO PALESE BAKING COMPANY
1235 Humbracht Cir Ste 1 (60103-1683)
PHONE..................630 595-5502
EMP: 13 EST: 2013
SALES (est): 1.3MM **Privately Held**
SIC: 2053 Mfg Frozen Bakery Products

(G-1282)
GLENWOOD TOOL & MOLD INC
1251 Humbracht Cir Ste D (60103-1693)
PHONE..................630 289-3400
Glen Pari, *President*
Luke Turrilli, *Vice Pres*
Alicison Pari, *Admin Sec*
EMP: 17
SQ FT: 10,000

Bartlett - Dupage County (G-1283)   **GEOGRAPHIC SECTION**

SALES (est): 3.8MM **Privately Held**
SIC: 3544 Industrial molds

(G-1283)
GLOBAL TRACK PROPERTY USA INC
Also Called: Global Track Warehouse USA
31w300 W Bartlett Rd (60103-1253)
P.O. Box 8295 (60103-8295)
PHONE..................630 213-6863
Barry Min, *President*
Weixing Min, *Principal*
◆ EMP: 5
SALES (est): 1.9MM **Privately Held**
SIC: 5082 3531 General construction machinery & equipment; construction machinery attachments

(G-1284)
GMK FINISHING
1967 Southfield Dr (60103-1332)
P.O. Box 543, Streamwood (60107-0543)
PHONE..................630 837-0568
George Keith, *President*
EMP: 5
SQ FT: 4,000
SALES (est): 400.3K **Privately Held**
SIC: 7389 7641 2431 Finishing services; furniture repair & maintenance; millwork

(G-1285)
HERRMANN ULTRASONICS INC
1261 Hardt Cir (60103-1690)
PHONE..................630 626-1626
Thomas Herrmann, *President*
Walter Ochs, *Principal*
Eric Colley, *Engineer*
EMP: 35
SQ FT: 16,000
SALES (est): 5.3MM **Privately Held**
SIC: 5084 3699 Welding machinery & equipment; welding machines & equipment, ultrasonic

(G-1286)
HK AMERICA INC
1296 Humbracht Cir (60103-1631)
PHONE..................630 916-0200
Jay Kay, *CEO*
Robert Won, *Vice Pres*
▲ EMP: 8
SQ FT: 9,000
SALES (est): 1.7MM **Privately Held**
SIC: 3699 Laser welding, drilling & cutting equipment

(G-1287)
HK LASER AND SYSTEMS
1296 Humbracht Cir (60103-1631)
PHONE..................630 916-0200
Jay Kay, *CEO*
EMP: 4 EST: 2015
SALES (est): 543.9K **Privately Held**
SIC: 3699 Laser welding, drilling & cutting equipment

(G-1288)
ILLINOIS TOOL WORKS INC
Also Called: ITW Brands
1452 Brewster Creek Blvd (60103-1695)
PHONE..................630 372-2150
EMP: 104
SALES (corp-wide): 14.1B **Publicly Held**
WEB: www.itw.com
SIC: 3089 3965 3499 2891 Injection molded finished plastic products; fasteners; strapping, metal; adhesives & sealants; refrigeration & heating equipment
PA: Illinois Tool Works Inc.
155 Harlem Ave
Glenview IL 60025
847 724-7500

(G-1289)
INDUSTRIAL ELECTRIC SVC INC (PA)
1055 Martingale Dr (60103-5621)
PHONE..................708 997-2090
Raeesa Rahman, *President*
EMP: 1
SALES (est): 1.2MM **Privately Held**
SIC: 5063 3613 Panelboards; switchboards; panelboards & distribution boards, electric; switchboard apparatus, except instruments

(G-1290)
INDUSTRIAL PHRM RESOURCES INC (PA)
Also Called: I P R
1241 Hardt Cir (60103-1690)
PHONE..................630 823-4700
Joseph Dougherty, *President*
Jo Ann Garcia, *Controller*
Juanita Gallet, *Cust Svc Dir*
EMP: 12
SQ FT: 20,000
SALES (est): 5.1MM **Privately Held**
SIC: 8711 7372 5084 3559 Consulting engineer; prepackaged software; industrial machine parts; pharmaceutical machinery

(G-1291)
JW SEALANTS INC
1478 Beaumont Cir (60103-2972)
PHONE..................630 398-1010
Jacek Robak, *Principal*
EMP: 4
SALES (est): 425.1K **Privately Held**
SIC: 2891 Sealants

(G-1292)
KEEPER THERMAL BAG CO INC
1006 Poplar Ln (60103-5649)
PHONE..................630 213-0125
Eleanor Workman, *President*
Michael Leel, *Vice Pres*
EMP: 6
SQ FT: 2,500
SALES: 600K **Privately Held**
SIC: 2393 Bags & containers, except sleeping bags: textile

(G-1293)
KL WATCH SERVICE INC
191 Amherst Dr (60103-4671)
PHONE..................847 368-8780
Ken Kaczynski, *President*
EMP: 2
SALES (est): 212K **Privately Held**
SIC: 2754 3873 Circulars: gravure printing; watches & parts, except crystals & jewels

(G-1294)
M L RONGO INC
1281 Humbracht Cir Ste A (60103-1623)
PHONE..................630 540-1120
Michael L Rongo, *President*
Jeffrey D Rongo, *Vice Pres*
Mario Nunez, *Project Mgr*
Greb Straumann, *CFO*
Selena Rongo, *Treasurer*
EMP: 25 EST: 1956
SQ FT: 20,000
SALES (est): 3.8MM **Privately Held**
WEB: www.mlrongo.com
SIC: 2599 7389 Carts, restaurant equipment; personal service agents, brokers & bureaus; interior designer

(G-1295)
MARK YOUR SPACE INC
1235 Humbracht Cir Ste 9 (60103-1683)
PHONE..................630 289-7082
Michael P Sobel, *President*
EMP: 2 EST: 2009
SALES: 300K **Privately Held**
WEB: www.markyourspaceinc.com
SIC: 3993 Signs & advertising specialties

(G-1296)
MATRIX DESIGN LLC
Also Called: Matrix Legacy Holdings
1361 Schiferl Rd (60103-1701)
PHONE..................847 841-8260
Patrick Bertsche, *President*
Karl Dahlman, *Opers Mgr*
Alex Jucas, *Engineer*
Tom Looper, *Manager*
EMP: 100
SQ FT: 50,000
SALES (est): 32.2MM **Privately Held**
SIC: 3535 Robotic conveyors

(G-1297)
MEDICAL RADIATION CONCEPTS
857 Marina Ter W (60103-4741)
P.O. Box 123, Wood Dale (60191-0123)
PHONE..................630 289-1515
EMP: 4
SALES (est): 365.4K **Privately Held**
SIC: 3844 Mfg X-Ray Apparatus/Tubes

(G-1298)
MIDWEST MOLDING INC
1560 Hecht Ct (60103-1691)
PHONE..................224 208-1110
Pat Patel, *President*
Hitesh Patel, *Vice Pres*
Mayur Patel, *Admin Sec*
EMP: 60
SQ FT: 120,000
SALES (est): 25MM **Privately Held**
SIC: 3089 Injection molding of plastics

(G-1299)
NU AGAIN
494 E Thornwood Dr (60103)
PHONE..................630 564-5590
Nathan Rothlisberger, *Owner*
EMP: 10
SALES (est): 693.8K **Privately Held**
SIC: 2491 Wood preserving

(G-1300)
OEI PRODUCTS INC
1041 Georgian Pl (60103-7530)
P.O. Box 528, Saint Charles (60174-0528)
PHONE..................630 377-1121
Jim Geraghty, *President*
EMP: 2
SALES: 450K **Privately Held**
SIC: 5999 2679 Safety supplies & equipment; tags & labels, paper

(G-1301)
PROMARK INTERNATIONAL INC (PA)
Also Called: Smith-Victor
1268 Humbracht Cir (60103-1631)
PHONE..................630 830-2500
Kenneth M Orlando, *President*
▲ EMP: 70
SALES (est): 14.3MM **Privately Held**
SIC: 3861 Tripods, camera & projector; stands, camera & projector

(G-1302)
PSI SYSTEMS NORTH AMERICA INC
1243 Humbracht Cir (60103-1606)
PHONE..................630 830-9435
Matthew Wind, *President*
Elizabeth Yaksich, *Admin Sec*
▲ EMP: 5
SALES (est): 678.7K **Privately Held**
SIC: 3432 Faucets & spigots, metal & plastic

(G-1303)
RANA MEAL SOLUTIONS LLC
550 S Spitzer Rd (60103-6700)
P.O. Box 275 (60103)
PHONE..................630 581-4100
Angelo Iantosca, *President*
Salvatore Trupiano, *General Mgr*
Barbara Cola, *Vice Pres*
Kevin Poore, *Mfg Staff*
Valentina Sarracco, *QC Mgr*
EMP: 25
SALES (corp-wide): 485.8MM **Privately Held**
SIC: 2033 Spaghetti & other pasta sauce: packaged in cans, jars, etc.
HQ: Rana Meal Solutions, Llc
1400 16th St Ste 275
Oak Brook IL 60523
630 581-4100

(G-1304)
ROBERT BRYSIEWICZ INCORPORATED
Also Called: R B Engineering
956 S Bartlett Rd Ste 261 (60103-6500)
PHONE..................630 289-0903
Robert Brysiewicz, *President*
EMP: 2

SALES (est): 526.6K **Privately Held**
SIC: 5084 3549 Industrial machinery & equipment; metalworking machinery

(G-1305)
RODNEY J GIESEKE
342 Terrace Dr (60103-4462)
PHONE..................630 830-7063
Rodney J Gieseke, *Principal*
EMP: 3
SALES (est): 123.4K **Privately Held**
SIC: 2711 Newspapers, publishing & printing

(G-1306)
S & D PRODUCTS INC
1390 Schiferl Rd (60103-1701)
PHONE..................630 372-2325
David J Guanci, *President*
Joe Bianchini, *Sales Engr*
Kathleen Guanci, *Admin Sec*
EMP: 25 EST: 1957
SQ FT: 65,000
SALES (est): 5.6MM **Privately Held**
WEB: www.sdproducts.com
SIC: 3429 Manufactured hardware (general)

(G-1307)
S+S INSPECTION INC
1234 Hardt Cir (60103-1690)
PHONE..................770 493-9332
▲ EMP: 6
SALES (est): 577.5K
SALES (corp-wide): 562.8MM **Privately Held**
SIC: 3443 Mfg Fabricated Plate Work
HQ: Sesotec Gmbh
Regener Str. 130
Schonberg 94513
855 430-80

(G-1308)
SELECT TOOL & DIE INC
1261 Humbracht Cir Ste F (60103-1632)
PHONE..................630 372-0300
Robert Siemer, *President*
EMP: 5
SALES (est): 500.5K **Privately Held**
SIC: 3544 Special dies & tools

(G-1309)
SENIOR HOLDINGS INC (HQ)
Also Called: SEI
300 E Devon Ave (60103-4608)
PHONE..................630 837-1811
Michael W Sheppard, *CEO*
Gerry Blanchet, *Business Mgr*
Joseph Mockus, *Vice Pres*
Kevin R Williams, *Vice Pres*
Kevin Smith, *Plant Mgr*
◆ EMP: 95
SQ FT: 350,000
SALES (est): 420.8MM
SALES (corp-wide): 1.4B **Privately Held**
SIC: 3599 2821 Hose, flexible metallic; tubing, flexible metallic; bellows, industrial: metal; polytetrafluoroethylene resins (teflon)

(G-1310)
SENIOR OPERATIONS LLC
Senior Automotives
300 E Devon Ave (60103-4608)
PHONE..................630 837-1811
Mike Shepherd, *Manager*
EMP: 600
SALES (corp-wide): 1.4B **Privately Held**
SIC: 3599 Machine shop, jobbing & repair
HQ: Senior Operations Llc
300 E Devon Ave
Bartlett IL 60103
630 372-3500

(G-1311)
SENIOR OPERATIONS LLC (HQ)
300 E Devon Ave (60103-4608)
PHONE..................630 372-3500
David Squires, *CEO*
Amy Legenza, *Vice Pres*
Mark Davey, *Research*
Ryan Collins, *Engineer*
Jacob Pawelkiewicz, *Engineer*
◆ EMP: 400
SQ FT: 430,000

GEOGRAPHIC SECTION   Batavia - Kane County (G-1340)

SALES (est): 700.7MM
SALES (corp-wide): 1.4B **Privately Held**
SIC: 3599 3441 Hose, flexible metallic; tubing, flexible metallic; bellows, industrial: metal; fabricated structural metal

(G-1312)
SENIOR PLC
Also Called: Senior Automotive
300 E Devon Ave (60103-4608)
PHONE 630 372-3511
Scott Swich, *Manager*
Randy Gleason, *Technology*
EMP: 6
SALES (corp-wide): 1.4B **Privately Held**
SIC: 3599 8711 Amusement park equipment; engineering services
PA: Senior Plc
59-61 High Street
Rickmansworth HERTS WD3 1

(G-1313)
SIGNET SIGN COMPANY
608 White Oak Ln (60103-2123)
PHONE 630 830-8242
Gary W Zale, *President*
Gary Zale, *Sales Mgr*
EMP: 5
SALES (est): 490.4K **Privately Held**
SIC: 3993 5046 5099 1799 Electric signs; neon signs; signs, electrical; signs, except electric; sign installation & maintenance

(G-1314)
SPEEDOTRON CORPORATION
1268 Humbracht Cir (60103-1631)
PHONE 630 246-5001
Jerry B Schutt, *President*
Paul L Schutt, *Corp Secy*
▲ EMP: 4
SQ FT: 20,000
SALES (est): 1.5MM **Privately Held**
SIC: 3861 Photoflash equipment, except lamps
PA: Promark International, Inc.
1268 Humbracht Cir
Bartlett IL 60103

(G-1315)
SUFFOLK BUSINESS GROUP INC
132 N Prospect Ave (60103-4363)
PHONE 847 404-2486
Carroll McLeod, *President*
EMP: 3
SQ FT: 350
SALES: 800K **Privately Held**
SIC: 3825 Analog-digital converters, electronic instrumentation type

(G-1316)
THERMO FISHER SCIENTIFIC INC
Also Called: Barnant
1230 Hardt Cir (60103-1690)
PHONE 847 381-7050
Larry Jones, *Manager*
EMP: 89
SALES (corp-wide): 25.5B **Publicly Held**
SIC: 3826 Analytical instruments
PA: Thermo Fisher Scientific Inc.
168 3rd Ave
Waltham MA 02451
781 622-1000

(G-1317)
TRI-CITY CORRUGATED INC
1307 Schiferl Rd (60103-1701)
PHONE 630 372-6200
Steven M Callahan, *President*
Onofrio Lorusso, *Admin Sec*
EMP: 10
SQ FT: 50,000
SALES (est): 8MM **Privately Held**
SIC: 2653 Boxes, corrugated: made from purchased materials

(G-1318)
TROPHIES BY GEORGE
239 Cedarfield Dr (60103-1316)
PHONE 630 497-1212
Jamie George, *Owner*
EMP: 2

SALES: 300K **Privately Held**
SIC: 3914 5999 7389 Trophies; trophies, plated (all metals); trophies & plaques; engraving service

(G-1319)
UNIQUE BLISTER COMPANY
1296 Humbracht Cir (60103-1631)
PHONE 630 289-1232
Sue Young, *President*
EMP: 12
SALES (est): 1.2MM **Privately Held**
SIC: 3081 3565 Packing materials, plastic sheet; packaging machinery

(G-1320)
USL LOCK CORPORATION
Also Called: Ultra Seal Lock
241 Windsor Dr (60103-5175)
PHONE 815 739-4707
Daniel Blankenship, *President*
EMP: 4
SALES: 50K **Privately Held**
SIC: 3699 Security devices

(G-1321)
VISION SALES INCORPORATED (PA)
Also Called: Stewart S Pritikin Associates
1264 Appaloosa Way (60103-1872)
PHONE 630 483-1900
Stewart Pritikin, *President*
Jaca-Lynn Pritikin, *Admin Sec*
▲ EMP: 2
SALES (est): 498.8K **Privately Held**
SIC: 5039 3315 Wire fence, gates & accessories; wire & fabricated wire products

(G-1322)
VULCAN MATERIALS COMPANY
2000 Vulcan Pkwy (60103-1396)
PHONE 847 695-0057
Scotty Gerbes, *Manager*
Virginia Overton, *Administration*
EMP: 14 **Publicly Held**
SIC: 3273 Ready-mixed concrete
PA: Vulcan Materials Company
1200 Urban Center Dr
Vestavia AL 35242

(G-1323)
WESTROCK MWV LLC
Also Called: Westrock Healthcare
1534 Stockton Ct (60103-2938)
PHONE 630 289-8537
EMP: 234
SALES (corp-wide): 18.2B **Publicly Held**
SIC: 2631 Linerboard
HQ: Westrock Mwv, Llc
501 S 5th St
Richmond VA 23219
804 444-1000

(G-1324)
WINHERE BRAKE PARTS INC
1331 Schiferl Rd (60103-1701)
PHONE 630 307-0158
Jimmy Shum, *Principal*
Chuck Hise, *Director*
EMP: 8
SALES (est): 154.5K **Privately Held**
SIC: 3714 Brake drums, motor vehicle

(G-1325)
WITTENSTEIN INC
1249 Humbracht Cir (60103-1606)
PHONE 630 540-5300
Peter Riehle, *CEO*
Maria Jesionowski, *Controller*
Brian Dunkel, *Admin Sec*
▲ EMP: 30
SALES (est): 9.1MM
SALES (corp-wide): 291.4MM **Privately Held**
SIC: 3566 Speed changers, drives & gears
PA: Wittenstein Se
Walter-Wittenstein-Str. 1
Igersheim 97999
793 149-30

(G-1326)
WITTENSTEIN ARSPC SMLATION INC (PA)
1249 Humbracht Cir (60103-1606)
PHONE 630 540-5300

Manfred Wittenstein, *President*
Brian Dunkel, *CFO*
EMP: 1
SALES (est): 1MM **Privately Held**
WEB: www.wittenstein-us.com
SIC: 3699 3728 Flight simulators (training aids), electronic; electronic training devices; link trainers (aircraft training mechanisms)

Bartonville
Peoria County

(G-1327)
ALTER TRADING CORPORATION
Also Called: Alter Recycling
7000 S Adams St Ste 2 (61607-2856)
P.O. Box 4164, Peoria (61607-0164)
PHONE 309 697-6161
Chad Chatman, *Manager*
EMP: 18
SALES (corp-wide): 740.9MM **Privately Held**
SIC: 4953 3341 Recycling, waste materials; secondary nonferrous metals
HQ: Alter Trading Corporation
700 Office Pkwy
Saint Louis MO 63141
314 872-2400

(G-1328)
ALTORFER POWER SYSTEMS
Also Called: Caterpillar Authorized Dealer
6315 W Fauber Rd (61607-1001)
PHONE 309 697-1234
Bob Metzinger, *Principal*
▲ EMP: 2
SALES (est): 917.4K **Privately Held**
SIC: 3621 7353 5082 Motors & generators; heavy construction equipment rental; construction & mining machinery

(G-1329)
COCA-COLA REFRESHMENTS USA INC
5001 S Becker Dr (61607-2776)
PHONE 309 697-8600
Scott Tolan, *Sales/Mktg Mgr*
EMP: 65
SQ FT: 10,000
SALES (corp-wide): 37.2B **Publicly Held**
SIC: 2086 5149 Bottled & canned soft drinks; groceries & related products
HQ: Coca-Cola Refreshments Usa, Inc.
2500 Windy Ridge Pkwy Se
Atlanta GA 30339
770 989-3000

(G-1330)
CUSTOM GRAPHICS INC
4100 Ricketts Ave (61607-2347)
PHONE 309 633-0850
Doug Bartelmay, *President*
Doug Bartelmay, *President*
Mike Creed, *VP Sales*
Renee Lendman, *Admin Sec*
EMP: 22
SQ FT: 12,000
SALES (est): 3MM **Privately Held**
SIC: 2759 Flexographic printing

(G-1331)
CUSTOM PLASTICS OF PEORIA
4623 Enterprise Dr (61607-2760)
PHONE 309 697-2888
Kevin Flessner, *President*
Robert Scott, *Vice Pres*
EMP: 4
SQ FT: 4,000
SALES (est): 440K **Privately Held**
SIC: 3083 5051 3082 3081 Plastic finished products, laminated; sheets, metal; aluminum bars, rods, ingots, sheets, pipes, plates, etc.; tubing, metal; unsupported plastics profile shapes; unsupported plastics film & sheet

(G-1332)
HEARTLAND COCA-COLA BTLG LLC
5001 S Becker Dr (61607-2776)
PHONE 309 697-8600
EMP: 3090

SALES (corp-wide): 23.9B **Privately Held**
SIC: 5149 2086 Beverages, except coffee & tea; carbonated beverages, nonalcoholic: bottled & canned
PA: Heartland Coca-Cola Bottling Company Llc
9000 Marshall Dr
Lenexa KS

(G-1333)
J FRANCIS & ASSOC
4603 Carol Ct (61607-1508)
PHONE 309 697-5931
Suzanne Zircher, *President*
Jeff Zircher, *Corp Secy*
EMP: 3
SALES: 55K **Privately Held**
SIC: 3541 Electrical discharge erosion machines

(G-1334)
LOYALTY PUBLISHING INC
Also Called: Skyline Publishing
4414 Entec Dr (61607-2779)
PHONE 309 693-0840
Rodney Lindsay, *President*
EMP: 50
SALES (est): 3.8MM **Privately Held**
SIC: 2741 Miscellaneous publishing

(G-1335)
MIDWEST CNSTR SVCS INC PEORIA (PA)
4200 Ricketts Ave (61607-2314)
P.O. Box 4185, Peoria (61607-0185)
PHONE 309 697-1000
Sheila Shover, *President*
Donald D Shover, *Exec VP*
John Miller, *Vice Pres*
Daniel White II, *Vice Pres*
EMP: 18
SQ FT: 32,000
SALES (est): 3.5MM **Privately Held**
SIC: 3531 5085 7353 Construction machinery; industrial supplies; heavy construction equipment rental

(G-1336)
VERTICAL SOFTWARE INC
409 Keller St (61607-2556)
PHONE 309 633-0700
Pat Gilroy, *President*
Dave Markley, *Manager*
Marcus Butterfield, *Prgrmr*
EMP: 12
SALES (est): 1.5MM **Privately Held**
SIC: 7372 7379 Business oriented computer software; computer related consulting services

(G-1337)
XTREME DZIGNZ
4001 Constitution Dr (61607-2863)
PHONE 309 633-9311
Rhonda Condre, *Principal*
EMP: 3
SALES (est): 246.4K **Privately Held**
SIC: 2759 Screen printing

Batavia
Kane County

(G-1338)
360 CABINETRY INC
1417 Paramount Pkwy (60510-1462)
PHONE 630 879-0701
EMP: 2
SALES (est): 240K **Privately Held**
SIC: 2434 Wood kitchen cabinets

(G-1339)
ABZENCO WELDING INC
1183 Pierson Dr (60510-1528)
PHONE 630 234-8021
EMP: 5 EST: 2007
SALES (est): 312.9K **Privately Held**
SIC: 7692 Welding repair

(G-1340)
ACCEL CORPORATION
900 Douglas Rd (60510-2294)
PHONE 630 579-6961
Dwight Morgan, *CEO*

Batavia - Kane County (G-1341) GEOGRAPHIC SECTION

EMP: 50 **Privately Held**
SIC: 2816 Color pigments
HQ: Accel Corporation
38620 Chester Rd
Avon OH 44011

(G-1341)
AGCO CORPORATION
1500 N Raddant Rd (60510-1377)
PHONE..................630 406-3248
Scott Ward, *Opers Mgr*
Joseph Dipietro, *Opers Staff*
John Sloan, *Purchasing*
Teri Yackley, *Human Res Mgr*
Frank Amato, *Marketing Staff*
EMP: 50 **Publicly Held**
SIC: 3523 Farm machinery & equipment
PA: Agco Corporation
4205 River Green Pkwy
Duluth GA 30096

(G-1342)
AGGRESIVE MOTOR SPORTS
Also Called: Optek
201 Oswald Ave (60510-9320)
PHONE..................630 761-1550
Nicks Sotola, *President*
EMP: 7
SALES (est): 619.1K **Privately Held**
SIC: 3471 Polishing, metals or formed products

(G-1343)
AGGRESSIVE MOTORSPORTS INC
Also Called: Diamond Coat
227 Oswald Ave (60510-9320)
PHONE..................847 846-7488
Nicholas Sotola, *President*
EMP: 5
SALES (est): 750K **Privately Held**
SIC: 3479 Metal coating & allied service

(G-1344)
AGS TECHNOLOGY INC
951 Douglas Rd (60510-2295)
PHONE..................847 534-6600
Christopher Racelis, *President*
Aras George Staniulis, *Vice Pres*
Ramon Racelis, *Shareholder*
Ruta Staniulis, *Admin Sec*
▲ EMP: 40
SQ FT: 79,000
SALES (est): 8.5MM **Privately Held**
SIC: 3089 Injection molding of plastics

(G-1345)
ALTERNATIVE WASTEWATER SYSTEMS
1815 Phelps Dr (60510-1519)
P.O. Box 4375, Wheaton (60189-4375)
PHONE..................630 761-8720
Donald Savegnago, *President*
EMP: 3
SALES (corp-wide): 1.5MM **Privately Held**
SIC: 3589 1711 Sewage & water treatment equipment; septic system construction
PA: Alternative Wastewater Systems Inc
1111 Delles Rd
Wheaton IL 60189
630 668-8584

(G-1346)
AMAV ENTERPRISES LTD
Also Called: Diamant Toys Unlimited
1921 W Wilson St Ste A (60510-3195)
PHONE..................630 761-3077
Asher Diamant, *President*
Kovy Diamant, *Vice Pres*
Colleen Staniszewski, *Opers Mgr*
Michael Sochaccevski, *Treasurer*
▲ EMP: 1
SQ FT: 450
SALES (est): 7MM **Privately Held**
SIC: 3944 Games, toys & children's vehicles
PA: Diamant Toys Ltd.
29 Hacharoshet
Ashdod 77520

(G-1347)
AMCOR RIGID PLASTICS USA LLC
Also Called: Ball Plastic Container Div
1300 S River Rd (60510-9647)
PHONE..................630 406-3500
EMP: 14
SALES (corp-wide): 9.6B **Privately Held**
SIC: 3411 Mfg Metal Cans
HQ: Amcor Rigid Plastics Usa, Llc
10521 Mi State Road 52
Manchester MI 48170

(G-1348)
AMERICAN BOXBOARD LLC
1400 Paramount Pkwy (60510-1463)
PHONE..................708 924-9810
J Clayton Shaw, *Mng Member*
EMP: 40
SALES (est): 5.9MM **Privately Held**
SIC: 2653 Boxes, corrugated: made from purchased materials

(G-1349)
ANDERSON & MARTER CABINETS
Also Called: A & M Cabinets
845 E Wilson St (60510-2204)
PHONE..................630 406-9840
Brad Anderson, *President*
Joel Marter, *Treasurer*
EMP: 4
SQ FT: 1,200
SALES (est): 430K **Privately Held**
SIC: 2599 2541 2517 2434 Cabinets, factory; wood partitions & fixtures; wood television & radio cabinets; wood kitchen cabinets; cabinet & finish carpentry

(G-1350)
APPLE GRAPHICS INC
934 Paramount Pkwy (60510-1453)
PHONE..................630 389-2222
Kyle Hempel, *Sales Staff*
Roberto Ayala, *Manager*
EMP: 4
SQ FT: 4,000
SALES (est): 600K **Privately Held**
SIC: 2752 2791 2789 Commercial printing, offset; typesetting; bookbinding & related work

(G-1351)
AUBREY SIGN CO INC
1847 Suncast Ln (60510-1518)
PHONE..................630 482-9901
Michael Hoffer, *President*
Jeanne Hoffer, *Corp Secy*
EMP: 3
SQ FT: 1,800
SALES (est): 448.1K **Privately Held**
SIC: 3993 Electric signs

(G-1352)
AUTOMATED MATERIAL HDLG SVCS (PA)
725 Hunter Dr (60510-1425)
PHONE..................630 947-7605
Stephen J Arrigo, *President*
Frank Grill, *Manager*
Nancy M Arrigo, *Admin Sec*
EMP: 9
SQ FT: 2,800
SALES (est): 1.6MM **Privately Held**
SIC: 3535 Conveyors & conveying equipment

(G-1353)
BALAS INCORPORATED
1080 Kingsland Dr (60510-2287)
PHONE..................630 406-7971
Joseph Drag, *Vice Pres*
Alan Drag, *Vice Pres*
Gary Drag, *Vice Pres*
Mark Drag, *Vice Pres*
EMP: 12
SQ FT: 25,000
SALES (est): 1.6MM **Privately Held**
WEB: www.balas.com
SIC: 3599 Machine shop, jobbing & repair

(G-1354)
BATAVIA BIO PROCESSING LIMITED
Also Called: Keyleaf
970 Douglas Rd (60510-2294)
PHONE..................630 761-1180
Bruce E Garner,
EMP: 4
SALES (est): 56.8K **Privately Held**
SIC: 8734 8731 2819 Testing laboratories; commercial physical research; industrial inorganic chemicals

(G-1355)
BATAVIA CONTAINER INC
1400 Paramount Pkwy (60510-1463)
P.O. Box 550 (60510-0550)
PHONE..................630 879-2100
J Clayton Shaw, *President*
Manas Athanikar, *Exec VP*
Chuck Wasinger, *Vice Pres*
Victor Rivera, *Prdtn Mgr*
Dean Hernandez, *Maint Spvr*
EMP: 150 EST: 1961
SQ FT: 160,000
SALES (est): 50.9MM **Privately Held**
WEB: www.bataviacontainer.com
SIC: 2653 Boxes, corrugated: made from purchased materials

(G-1356)
BATAVIA FOUNDRY AND MACHINE CO
717 First St (60510-2409)
P.O. Box 6 (60510-0006)
PHONE..................630 879-1319
Scott Peterson, *President*
EMP: 5 EST: 1964
SALES (est): 1MM **Privately Held**
SIC: 3365 Aluminum foundries

(G-1357)
BEVSTREAM CORP
Also Called: 1 Engineering
600 Kingsland Dr (60510-2298)
PHONE..................630 761-0060
Robert Capua, *President*
◆ EMP: 8
SALES (est): 1.8MM **Privately Held**
SIC: 3312 3585 Pipes & tubes; refrigeration & heating equipment

(G-1358)
BFC FORMS SERVICE INC
1051 N Kirk Rd (60510-1438)
PHONE..................630 879-9240
Joseph Novak Jr, *President*
Matthew Novak, *Corp Secy*
Brad Novak, *Vice Pres*
Jeff Pogwizd, *Vice Pres*
Cedric Castillo, *Project Mgr*
EMP: 115 EST: 1975
SQ FT: 19,000
SALES (est): 33.9MM **Privately Held**
WEB: www.bfcprint.com
SIC: 2752 5112 Commercial printing, offset; business forms

(G-1359)
BFC PRINT
1051 N Kirk Rd (60510-1438)
PHONE..................630 879-9240
Dave Burdine, *Plant Mgr*
Kraig Hill, *Purchasing*
Laura Pogwizd, *Human Res Mgr*
Kim Johnsen, *Accounts Mgr*
Robin Urich, *Accounts Exec*
EMP: 8 EST: 2011
SALES (est): 1MM **Privately Held**
SIC: 2752 Commercial printing, offset

(G-1360)
BRASEL PRODUCTS INC
715 Hunter Dr (60510-1425)
P.O. Box 97 (60510-0097)
PHONE..................630 879-3759
Melody Brasel Davoust, *President*
Brian Davoust, *Prdtn Mgr*
Kerri Begovich, *Director*
Mark Davoust, *Executive*
EMP: 9 EST: 1947
SQ FT: 9,700
SALES (est): 1.6MM **Privately Held**
WEB: www.brasel.com
SIC: 3842 2672 2295 Gauze, surgical; bandages: plastic, muslin, plaster of paris, etc.; coated & laminated paper; coated fabrics, not rubberized

(G-1361)
BYUS STEEL INC
1750 Hubbard Ave (60510-1424)
PHONE..................630 879-2200
Bruno Gentile, *President*
Carol Gentile, *Admin Sec*
EMP: 20
SQ FT: 18,000
SALES (est): 5.9MM **Privately Held**
SIC: 3441 Fabricated structural metal

(G-1362)
CAST ALUMINUM SOLUTIONS LLC
1310 Kingsland Dr (60510-1327)
PHONE..................630 482-5325
Richard Ahern, *COO*
Rick Ahern, *COO*
John Bloch, *Engineer*
Jesse Mondigo, *Engineer*
Byron Anderson, *Electrical Engi*
▲ EMP: 90
SALES (est): 29.3MM **Privately Held**
SIC: 3363 Aluminum die-castings

(G-1363)
CCL LABEL (CHICAGO) INC
Also Called: Sertech
1862 Suncast Ln (60510-1516)
PHONE..................630 406-9991
Jeff Adeszko, *President*
Bill McDonough, *Vice Pres*
EMP: 50
SQ FT: 23,000
SALES (est): 15.4MM
SALES (corp-wide): 4B **Privately Held**
SIC: 2752 Commercial printing, offset
PA: Ccl Industries Inc
111 Gordon Baker Rd Suite 801
Toronto ON M2H 3
416 756-8500

(G-1364)
CFC WIRE FORMS INC
1000 Douglas Rd (60510-2278)
PHONE..................630 879-7575
Casimir Czekajlo, *President*
Beata Nowak, *Production*
Bernard Czekajlo, *Treasurer*
Mark Schultz, *Manager*
Frank Czekajlo, *Admin Sec*
▲ EMP: 26
SQ FT: 60,000
SALES (est): 6.7MM **Privately Held**
SIC: 3312 3496 3495 Wire products, steel or iron; miscellaneous fabricated wire products; wire springs

(G-1365)
CHALLENGER LIGHTING CO INC
1400 Kingsland Dr (60510-1375)
PHONE..................847 717-4700
Bonnie Proctor, *CEO*
Bruce Barna, *President*
Taras Hazek, *Engineer*
Pat Petrelli, *Cust Mgr*
Matt Proctor, *Sales Staff*
▲ EMP: 42
SQ FT: 28,000
SALES (est): 9MM **Privately Held**
SIC: 3646 Chandeliers, commercial

(G-1366)
CISKE & DRESCH
1125 Paramount Pkwy Ste F (60510-4417)
PHONE..................630 251-9200
Rudy Dresch, *President*
Agnes Dresch, *Corp Secy*
Victoria Dresch, *Vice Pres*
EMP: 3
SQ FT: 2,600
SALES (est): 188.6K **Privately Held**
SIC: 3471 Plating of metals or formed products; gold plating

▲ = Import ▼ = Export
◆ = Import/Export

GEOGRAPHIC SECTION

Batavia - Kane County (G-1395)

(G-1367)
CLEAN SWEEP ENVIRONMENTAL INC
1805 Phelps Dr (60510-1519)
PHONE..................630 879-8750
Bertram Hochsprung, *President*
Ryan Hochsprung, *Admin Sec*
EMP: 9
SQ FT: 10,000
SALES (est): 398.6K **Privately Held**
SIC: 7521 2951 Parking lots; composition blocks for paving

(G-1368)
COMPLETE MOLD POLISHING INC
1219 Paramount Pkwy (60510-1458)
PHONE..................630 406-7668
Roger A Delarche, *President*
Susan M Delarche, *Admin Sec*
EMP: 4
SQ FT: 2,000
SALES (est): 466.2K **Privately Held**
SIC: 3544 Industrial molds

(G-1369)
CU LAYER INC
214 Mill St (60510-9277)
PHONE..................630 802-7873
EMP: 4
SALES (est): 348.8K **Privately Held**
WEB: www.culayer.com
SIC: 3648 Lighting equipment

(G-1370)
CUSTOM CUTTINGEDGE TOOL INC
1217 Paramount Pkwy (60510-1458)
PHONE..................847 622-0457
John Sitarz, *Owner*
Robert Mesa, *Corp Secy*
EMP: 4
SALES: 400K **Privately Held**
SIC: 3544 Special dies & tools

(G-1371)
DAY INTERNATIONAL GROUP INC
1333 N Kirk Rd (60510-1444)
PHONE..................630 406-6501
EMP: 65
SALES (corp-wide): 53.9B **Publicly Held**
SIC: 3069 Printers' rolls & blankets: rubber or rubberized fabric
HQ: Day International, Inc.
  17177 N Laurel Park Dr # 30
  Livonia MI 48152

(G-1372)
DEAN DAIRY ICE CREAM LLC
1253 Kingsland Dr (60510-1324)
PHONE..................630 879-0800
Leonard Jackson, *Branch Mgr*
EMP: 29
SALES (corp-wide): 15.8B **Privately Held**
SIC: 2026 Milk processing (pasteurizing, homogenizing, bottling)
HQ: Dfa Dairy Brands Ice Cream, Llc
  1405 N 98th St
  Kansas City KS 66111
  816 801-6465

(G-1373)
DIMPLES DONUTS
328 E Wilson St (60510-2663)
PHONE..................630 406-0303
Henry Charles, *Owner*
EMP: 4
SALES (est): 153.2K **Privately Held**
SIC: 5461 2051 Doughnuts; doughnuts, except frozen

(G-1374)
DON JOHNS INC (PA)
701 N Raddant Rd (60510-4218)
PHONE..................630 454-4700
Brian Byrne, *President*
Logan Surles, *Vice Pres*
Raymond A Pouse, *Director*
EMP: 23 EST: 1950
SQ FT: 12,500
SALES (est): 11.9MM **Privately Held**
WEB: www.donjohns.com
SIC: 5087 5084 3613 3625 Liquor dispensing equipment & systems; pneumatic tools & equipment; control panels, electric; control equipment, electric

(G-1375)
DS CONTAINERS INC (PA)
1789 Hubbard Ave (60510-1423)
PHONE..................630 406-9600
Isamu Yamaguchi, *President*
James Fenhouse, *President*
Sarah Howard, *President*
John Duffy, *Vice Pres*
Matt Kuehn, *Vice Pres*
▲ EMP: 118
SALES (est): 36.2MM **Privately Held**
SIC: 3411 Metal cans

(G-1376)
ELITE CUSTOM WOODWORKING
219 S Water St (60510-2558)
PHONE..................630 888-4322
Jeff Schaaf, *Principal*
EMP: 3
SALES (est): 407.7K **Privately Held**
WEB: www.elitecw.net
SIC: 2431 Millwork

(G-1377)
FIDELITY TOOL & MOLD LTD (PA)
1885 Suncast Ln (60510-1510)
PHONE..................630 879-2300
James Vassar, *President*
▲ EMP: 18
SQ FT: 10,000
SALES (est): 5.8MM **Privately Held**
SIC: 3544 Special dies & tools; industrial molds

(G-1378)
FLINN SCIENTIFIC INC
770 N Raddant Rd (60510-4208)
P.O. Box 219 (60510-0219)
PHONE..................800 452-1261
Margaret Flinn, *Chairman*
Tony Leben, *VP Mfg*
Ed Machtemes, *Facilities Mgr*
Rebecca Greiner, *Purchasing*
Tom Lyons, *Purchasing*
◆ EMP: 228
SALES (est): 79.2MM **Privately Held**
SIC: 3821 5049 5961 Laboratory equipment: fume hoods, distillation racks, etc.; laboratory equipment, except medical or dental; educational supplies & equipment, mail order

(G-1379)
FLINT GROUP US LLC
1333 N Kirk Rd (60510-1444)
PHONE..................630 526-9903
Thomas Weiler, *Sales Staff*
Jack Ackerman, *Branch Mgr*
EMP: 25
SALES (corp-wide): 53.9B **Publicly Held**
SIC: 2893 Printing ink
HQ: Flint Group Us Llc
  17177 N Laurel Park Dr # 300
  Livonia MI 48152
  734 781-4600

(G-1380)
FONA INTERNATIONAL INC
1100 N Raddant Rd (60510)
PHONE..................630 578-8600
Joseph Slawek, *Branch Mgr*
EMP: 3
SALES (corp-wide): 67.8MM **Privately Held**
WEB: www.fona.com
SIC: 2087 Extracts, flavoring
PA: Fona International Inc.
  1900 Averill Rd
  Geneva IL 60134
  630 578-8600

(G-1381)
GORDON HANN
154 W Wilson St (60510-1945)
PHONE..................630 761-1835
Gordon Hann, *Owner*
EMP: 33

SALES (est): 2.2MM **Privately Held**
SIC: 2051 Bakery: wholesale or wholesale/retail combined

(G-1382)
GREEN LADDER TECHNOLOGIES LLC
1540 Louis Bork Dr (60510-1512)
PHONE..................630 457-1872
John Konieczka, *Mng Member*
Kenneth Kubitz, *President*
EMP: 25
SALES (est): 5.5MM **Privately Held**
SIC: 3822 Auto controls regulating residntl & coml environmt & applncs

(G-1383)
HEMPEL GROUP INC
934 Paramount Pkwy (60510-1453)
PHONE..................630 389-2222
Keith Hempel, *President*
Ken Hempel, *Vice Pres*
EMP: 9
SALES (est): 1MM **Privately Held**
SIC: 2752 Commercial printing, offset

(G-1384)
HENTZEN COATINGS INC
1500 Lathem St (60510-1449)
PHONE..................414 353-4200
Thomas Ellis, *Director*
EMP: 22
SALES (corp-wide): 82MM **Privately Held**
SIC: 2851 Lacquer: bases, dopes, thinner; enamels; polyurethane coatings; epoxy coatings
PA: Hentzen Coatings, Inc.
  6937 W Mill Rd
  Milwaukee WI 53218
  414 353-4200

(G-1385)
INCON PROCESSING LLC (DH)
970 Douglas Rd (60510-2294)
PHONE..................630 305-8556
John R Palmer III, *CEO*
EMP: 27
SQ FT: 30,000
SALES (est): 4.4MM
SALES (corp-wide): 268.6MM **Privately Held**
SIC: 8734 8731 2819 Testing laboratories; commercial physical research; industrial inorganic chemicals
HQ: Omega Protein Corporation
  610 Menhaden Rd
  Reedville VA 22539
  804 453-6262

(G-1386)
INNOVATIVE PLASTECH INC
1260 Kingsland Dr (60510-1325)
PHONE..................630 232-1808
Joanne Gustafson, *CEO*
James Gustafson, *President*
Edward Gustafson, *Exec VP*
Tracy Wolf, *Vice Pres*
Marianne Danielsen, *Sales Staff*
EMP: 67
SQ FT: 90,000
SALES (est): 13MM **Privately Held**
SIC: 3089 Thermoformed finished plastic products

(G-1387)
INTEGRATED GRAPHICS INC
1198 Nagel Blvd (60510-1564)
PHONE..................630 482-6100
Keith Murphy, *President*
Beth A Murphy, *Admin Sec*
EMP: 42
SALES (est): 9MM **Privately Held**
SIC: 2752 Commercial printing, offset

(G-1388)
J C SCHULTZ ENTERPRISES INC
Also Called: Flagsource
951 Swanson Dr (60510-4231)
PHONE..................800 323-9127
Janice M Christiansen, *Ch of Bd*
Jon Christiansen, *Vice Pres*
Ray Rankin, *Facilities Mgr*
Spencer Christiansen, *Admin Sec*
▲ EMP: 65 EST: 1920
SQ FT: 60,000

SALES (est): 8.4MM **Privately Held**
WEB: www.flagsource.com
SIC: 2399 5051 3446 Flags, fabric; banners, made from fabric; metals service centers & offices; architectural metalwork

(G-1389)
KOLORCURE CORPORATION
1180 Lyon Rd (60510-1365)
PHONE..................630 879-9050
Daniel Templeman, *President*
Brian Templeman, *President*
▼ EMP: 12
SQ FT: 20,000
SALES (est): 6MM **Privately Held**
SIC: 2893 Screen process ink

(G-1390)
KON PRINTING INC
316 E Wilson St (60510-2663)
PHONE..................630 879-2211
Nick Konsbruck, *President*
Mark Konsbruck, *Vice Pres*
EMP: 2
SQ FT: 4,000
SALES (est): 230K **Privately Held**
SIC: 2752 2759 Commercial printing, offset; letterpress printing; business forms; printing

(G-1391)
KWALYTI TLING MCHY RBLDING INC
1690 E Fabyan Pkwy (60510-1492)
PHONE..................630 761-8040
Gordon Erickson, *President*
▲ EMP: 18
SQ FT: 22,500
SALES: 5MM **Privately Held**
SIC: 5084 3542 Machine tools & accessories; rebuilt machine tools, metal forming types

(G-1392)
MASTERFEED CORPORATION
1326 Hollister Dr (60510-1391)
PHONE..................630 879-1133
Richard Rojic Jr, *President*
Cindy Rojic, *Admin Sec*
EMP: 3
SQ FT: 6,250
SALES: 380K **Privately Held**
SIC: 3559

(G-1393)
MATERIAL CONTROL INC
Also Called: Environmental Products Co Div
525 N River St Ste 100 (60510-2399)
P.O. Box 308, North Aurora (60542-0237)
PHONE..................630 892-4274
Keith Clayton, *Controller*
Kurt Pfoutz, *Marketing Staff*
EMP: 15
SQ FT: 16,000
SALES (corp-wide): 82.6MM **Privately Held**
SIC: 3844 3089 2394 5084 X-ray apparatus & tubes; plastic processing; canvas & related products; materials handling machinery
PA: Material Control Inc.
  130 Seltzer Rd
  Croswell MI 48422
  630 892-4274

(G-1394)
MAXON PLASTICS INC
1069 Kingsland Dr (60510-2290)
PHONE..................630 761-3667
Erika Meisen, *President*
Frank Dullnigg, *Vice Pres*
Sonja Bertone, *Admin Sec*
EMP: 8
SQ FT: 12,500
SALES (est): 1.4MM **Privately Held**
SIC: 3089 Injection molding of plastics

(G-1395)
MII INC
1380 Nagel Blvd (60510-1312)
PHONE..................630 879-3000
Joseph R Kelley, *President*
Linda Kelley, *CFO*
EMP: 14
SQ FT: 14,500

Batavia - Kane County (G-1396)

SALES (est): 4.3MM **Privately Held**
SIC: 2621 7336 3565 Printing paper; package design; labeling machines, industrial

(G-1396)
MUSCO SPORTS LIGHTING LLC
Also Called: Microlite
902 Paramount Pkwy Ste A (60510-4410)
PHONE..................................630 876-0500
Darrell Chelcun, *Vice Pres*
EMP: 40
SALES (corp-wide): 153.8MM **Privately Held**
SIC: 3648 Area & sports luminaries
HQ: Musco Sports Lighting, Llc.
100 1st Ave W
Oskaloosa IA 52577
800 825-6030

(G-1397)
NAPCO INC
Also Called: Napco Brands
1141 N Raddant Rd (60510-4214)
P.O. Box 849 (60510-0849)
PHONE..................................630 406-1100
Christopher Papanicholas, *President*
Vaughn Papanicholas, *Vice Pres*
Paul Goudreault, *CFO*
James Schlicher, *Admin Sec*
▲ EMP: 24
SQ FT: 20,000
SALES (est): 7.2MM **Privately Held**
SIC: 2095 5812 5149 Roasted coffee; eating places; coffee, green or roasted

(G-1398)
NBC MESHTEC AMERICAS INC
Also Called: Dynamesh Inc.
512 Kingsland Dr (60510-2299)
PHONE..................................630 293-5454
Shinya Yhamasaski, *President*
Hideaki Hayashi, *General Mgr*
Hiroyasu Takahashi, *Corp Secy*
Shane Waltmire, *Admin Sec*
▲ EMP: 25
SQ FT: 18,000
SALES (est): 4.2MM **Privately Held**
SIC: 2759 5131 5084 Screen printing; piece goods & other fabrics; industrial machinery & equipment
HQ: Nbc Meshtec Inc.
2-50-3, Toyoda
Hino TKY 191-0

(G-1399)
NEOMEK INCORPORATED
Also Called: Neomek Engineering
241 Oswald Ave (60510-9320)
PHONE..................................630 879-5400
Bradley Johnson, *President*
David Lajoie, *General Mgr*
James Clark, *Info Tech Mgr*
EMP: 12 EST: 1999
SQ FT: 20,000
SALES (est): 1.6MM **Privately Held**
SIC: 8711 3089 3444 Consulting engineer; plastic containers, except foam; sheet metalwork

(G-1400)
NEON PRISM ELECTRIC SIGN CO
1213 Paramount Pkwy (60510-1458)
PHONE..................................630 879-1010
Tim Phelps, *President*
Eric Smith, *Vice Pres*
EMP: 2
SQ FT: 1,650
SALES (est): 500K **Privately Held**
SIC: 3993 Neon signs

(G-1401)
ONTARIO DIE USA
950 Paramount Pkwy Ste 3 (60510-4412)
P.O. Box 69 (60510-0069)
PHONE..................................630 761-6562
Pat Kizziah, *General Mgr*
EMP: 10
SALES (est): 1.7MM **Privately Held**
SIC: 3544 Special dies & tools

(G-1402)
P & L MARK-IT INC (PA)
Also Called: Mark-It Company
291 Oswald Ave (60510-9394)
PHONE..................................630 879-7590
Lance Johnson, *President*
Philip Meere, *Chairman*
Mike Henson, *Info Tech Mgr*
▲ EMP: 29
SQ FT: 21,000
SALES (est): 2.4MM **Privately Held**
SIC: 2759 3993 Decals: printing; labels & seals: printing; signs & advertising specialties

(G-1403)
PAMARCO GLOBAL GRAPHICS INC
125 Flinn St (60510-2471)
PHONE..................................630 879-7300
John Clinton, *Opers-Prdtn-Mfg*
Robert Steffey, *Purch Agent*
Tracie Gilbert, *Office Mgr*
Natalie Meyer,
EMP: 25 **Privately Held**
WEB: www.pamarco.com
SIC: 3555 2796 Printing trades machinery; platemaking services
HQ: Pamarco Global Graphics, Inc.
235 E 11th Ave
Roselle NJ 07203
908 241-1200

(G-1404)
PMA FRICTION PRODUCTS INC
880 Kingsland Dr (60510-2296)
PHONE..................................630 406-9119
Philip Konrad, *President*
Tom Konrad, *Maint Spvr*
Joan Sweetman, *Controller*
Joan Konrad, *Human Res Mgr*
Paul Konrad, *Sales Mgr*
EMP: 60
SQ FT: 60,000
SALES (est): 11.8MM **Privately Held**
SIC: 3714 Motor vehicle parts & accessories

(G-1405)
PRIME LABEL GROUP LLC
1380 Nagel Blvd (60510-1312)
PHONE..................................773 630-8793
EMP: 4
SALES (est): 314.4K **Privately Held**
SIC: 2671 Mfg Packaging Paper/Film

(G-1406)
PRODUCERS ENVMTL PDTS LLC
Also Called: Environmental Solutions Intl
1261 N Raddant Rd (60510-4213)
PHONE..................................630 482-5995
Ken Arnswald, *Vice Pres*
Kenneth Arnswald, *VP Sales*
Kent Pullen,
Peter K Whinfrey,
EMP: 6 EST: 1996
SQ FT: 7,000
SALES (est): 1.1MM **Privately Held**
WEB: www.chompsolutions.com
SIC: 3589 Commercial cleaning equipment

(G-1407)
QUALITY CNC INCORPORATED
801 N Raddant Rd (60510-4217)
PHONE..................................630 406-0101
Greg Johnson, *President*
Peggy Johnson, *Admin Sec*
EMP: 11
SQ FT: 5,000
SALES (est): 800K **Privately Held**
SIC: 3599 Machine shop, jobbing & repair

(G-1408)
RADCO INDUSTRIES INC (PA)
700 Kingsland Dr (60510-2297)
P.O. Box 305, Lafox (60147-0305)
PHONE..................................630 232-7966
Michael Damiani, *CEO*
Lawrence Kendzior, *VP Finance*
Teresa Fiorenza, *Accounting Mgr*
Liz Allen, *Human Res Mgr*
John Campbell, *Sales Staff*
EMP: 21
SQ FT: 9,600

SALES (est): 4.5MM **Privately Held**
SIC: 2819 Industrial inorganic chemicals

(G-1409)
RANDAL WOOD DISPLAYS INC
Also Called: Randal Retail Group
507 N Raddant Rd (60510-4220)
PHONE..................................630 761-0400
Chris Randazzo, *President*
Chuck Bray, *Vice Pres*
Mike Kunert, *Vice Pres*
Thea R Sakelaris, *Vice Pres*
Chris Breedlove, *Project Mgr*
▲ EMP: 65 EST: 1981
SALES (est): 15.6MM **Privately Held**
WEB: www.randalretail.com
SIC: 2541 7389 4225 1796 Cabinets, except refrigerated: show, display, etc.: wood; counters or counter display cases, wood; shelving, office & store, wood; showcases, except refrigerated: wood; design services; general warehousing & storage; installing building equipment

(G-1410)
RENU ELECTRONICS PRIVATE LTD
336 Mckee St (60510-1920)
PHONE..................................630 879-8412
Ajay Bhagwat, *President*
Sanjay Madkar, *Prdtn Mgr*
Girish Ghate, *Sales Staff*
Shobha Bhagwat, *Admin Sec*
EMP: 2
SQ FT: 500
SALES (est): 347.1K **Privately Held**
SIC: 3559 Electronic component making machinery

(G-1411)
RMF PRODUCTS INC
1275 Paramount Pkwy (60510-1458)
P.O. Box 520 (60510-0520)
PHONE..................................630 879-0020
Richard M Frieders, *President*
EMP: 2 EST: 1969
SQ FT: 7,500
SALES (est): 300K **Privately Held**
SIC: 3861 Photographic equipment & supplies

(G-1412)
SALSA VERDE BATAVIA INC
107 N Batavia Ave (60510-1901)
PHONE..................................630 425-3521
EMP: 3
SALES (est): 223.9K **Privately Held**
SIC: 2099 Dips, except cheese & sour cream based

(G-1413)
SCHAEFER TECHNOLOGIES LLC
751 N Raddant Rd (60510-4218)
PHONE..................................630 406-9377
Wyatt George, *Vice Pres*
Karen Lopeman, *Manager*
EMP: 6
SQ FT: 2,500
SALES (est): 839.6K
SALES (corp-wide): 166.6K **Privately Held**
WEB: www.schaefer.biz
SIC: 3545 Machine tool accessories
HQ: Schafer Werkzeug- Und Sondermaschinenbau Gmbh
Dr.-Alfred-Weckesser-Str. 6
Bad Schonborn 76669
725 394-210

(G-1414)
SCIMATCO OFFICE
770 N Raddant Rd (60510-4208)
P.O. Box 305 (60510-0305)
PHONE..................................630 879-1306
Patrick Flinn, *President*
EMP: 50
SALES (est): 3.3MM **Privately Held**
SIC: 3999 Barber & beauty shop equipment

(G-1415)
SEALY MATTRESS COMPANY
1030 E Fabyan Pkwy (60510-1410)
PHONE..................................630 879-8011
Ray Pozecinski, *Manager*

EMP: 220
SQ FT: 101,000
SALES (corp-wide): 3.1B **Publicly Held**
SIC: 2515 Mattresses, containing felt, foam rubber, urethane, etc.; mattresses, innerspring or box spring
HQ: Sealy Mattress Company
1 Office Parkway Rd
Trinity NC 27370
336 861-3500

(G-1416)
SECOND CITY PRINTS
1521 Hubbard Ave (60510-1419)
PHONE..................................630 504-2423
EMP: 2 EST: 2017
SALES (est): 342K **Privately Held**
SIC: 2752 Commercial printing, lithographic

(G-1417)
SITECH INC
1101 N Raddant Rd (60510-4214)
P.O. Box 609, Geneva (60134-0609)
PHONE..................................630 761-3640
Ramesh D Sheth, *Ch of Bd*
Sandeep Sheth, *Vice Pres*
EMP: 12
SQ FT: 13,000
SALES (est): 2.5MM **Privately Held**
SIC: 3357 Fiber optic cable (insulated)

(G-1418)
SPECTRUM COS INTERNATIONAL
Also Called: Marsh Products
336 Mckee St (60510-1920)
PHONE..................................630 879-8008
Richard E Marsh, *CEO*
Doug Marsh, *President*
Ruth Marsh, *Corp Secy*
Kathlyn Marsh-Valentine, *Vice Pres*
Kathlyn Valentine, *VP Accounting*
▲ EMP: 7
SQ FT: 17,000
SALES (est): 935.6K **Privately Held**
SIC: 3625 3663 8731 7389 Control equipment, electric; radio & TV communications equipment; electronic research; design services

(G-1419)
STEVENSON PAPER CO INC
1775 Hubbard Ave (60510-1423)
PHONE..................................630 879-5000
Elizabeth Krohn, *President*
EMP: 6
SQ FT: 7,500
SALES (est): 1MM **Privately Held**
SIC: 2675 2631 Die-cut paper & board; paperboard mills

(G-1420)
STOKES SAND & GRAVEL INC
35w160 Butterfield Rd (60510-9338)
PHONE..................................815 489-0680
Danny Stokes, *President*
EMP: 3
SALES (est): 563.9K **Privately Held**
SIC: 1442 Construction sand & gravel

(G-1421)
SUMMIT METAL PRODUCTS INC
1351 Nagel Blvd (60510-1313)
PHONE..................................630 879-7008
Herbert Cozad, *President*
EMP: 9
SQ FT: 23,000
SALES (est): 1.1MM **Privately Held**
SIC: 3441 Fabricated structural metal

(G-1422)
SUNCAST CORPORATION (PA)
701 N Kirk Rd (60510-1433)
PHONE..................................630 879-2050
Thomas A Tisbo, *President*
Mike Hodges, *Superintendent*
Carl Smucker, *Principal*
Michael Hamilton, *Exec VP*
Bob Lehr, *Vice Pres*
◆ EMP: 750
SQ FT: 500,000

SALES (est): 294.1MM Privately Held
SIC: **2519** 3052 3432 Lawn furniture, except wood, metal, stone or concrete; garden furniture, except wood, metal, stone or concrete; rubber hose; lawn hose nozzles & sprinklers

(G-1423)
SUPERIOR HEALTH LINENS LLC
1160 Pierson Dr Ste 104 (60510-1527)
PHONE..................................630 593-5091
Scott Reppert, *CEO*
Steve Shabat, *General Mgr*
Greg Schermerhorn, *COO*
Bill Witowski, *CFO*
William Witowski,
EMP: 70
SALES (est): 10.1MM Privately Held
SIC: **2299** Linen fabrics

(G-1424)
TAYLOR & FRANCIS GROUP LLC
1292 Averill Dr (60510-3596)
PHONE..................................630 482-9886
EMP: 3
SALES (corp-wide): 3B Privately Held
SIC: **2731** Books: publishing & printing
HQ: Taylor & Francis Group, Llc
  6000 Broken Sound Pkwy Nw # 300
  Boca Raton FL 33487
  561 994-0555

(G-1425)
TEAM TECHNOLOGIES INC
1119 Lyon Rd (60510-1366)
PHONE..................................630 406-0678
Richard Wagner, *President*
Rebecca Edwards, *Human Resources*
Ashwin Patel, *Manager*
EMP: 10 Privately Held
WEB: www.teamtechinc.net
SIC: **3089** Molding primary plastic
HQ: Team Technologies, Inc.
  5949 Commerce Blvd
  Morristown TN 37814
  423 587-2199

(G-1426)
TEAM TECHNOLOGIES INC
1300 Nagel Blvd (60510-1312)
PHONE..................................630 937-0380
Ashwin Patel, *Manager*
EMP: 60 Privately Held
SIC: **3991** 3089 Brushes, except paint & varnish; plastic processing
HQ: Team Technologies, Inc.
  5949 Commerce Blvd
  Morristown TN 37814
  423 587-2199

(G-1427)
TECHMER PM LLC
900 Douglas Rd (60510-2294)
PHONE..................................630 579-6961
Mike Gross, *Exec VP*
EMP: 13 Privately Held
SIC: **2821** Plastics materials & resins
HQ: Techmer Pm, Llc
  1 Quality Cir
  Clinton TN 37716
  865 457-6700

(G-1428)
TEGRANT CORPORATION
Also Called: Clarke Div
1500 Paramount Pkwy (60510-1468)
PHONE..................................630 879-0121
William Kelly, *President*
EMP: 100
SALES (corp-wide): 5.3B Publicly Held
SIC: **2631** Paperboard mills
HQ: Tegrant Corporation
  1401 Pleasant St
  Dekalb IL 60115

(G-1429)
TEK PAK INC (PA)
1336 Paramount Pkwy (60510-1461)
PHONE..................................630 406-0560
Anthony Beyer, *President*
Chad Miller, *Director*
▲ EMP: 55
SQ FT: 20,000
SALES (est): 14.6MM Privately Held
SIC: **2672** 3086 5084 3559 Tape, pressure sensitive: made from purchased materials; plastics foam products; tapping attachments; plastics working machinery

(G-1430)
TIMEPILOT CORPORATION
340 Mckee St (60510-1920)
PHONE..................................630 879-6400
Douglas F Marsh, *President*
Michael C Hanlon, *Exec VP*
Sheree Womack, *Natl Sales Mgr*
Steven J Lemon, *Admin Sec*
◆ EMP: 7
SQ FT: 1,500
SALES (est): 815.5K Privately Held
SIC: **7372** Business oriented computer software

(G-1431)
TOOL RITE INDUSTRIES INC
570 S River St (60510-2675)
PHONE..................................630 406-6161
Tom Peck, *President*
EMP: 6
SQ FT: 7,500
SALES (est): 460K Privately Held
SIC: **3549** 3599 Assembly machines, including robotic; machine shop, jobbing & repair

(G-1432)
TREASURE KEEPER INC
Also Called: Treasure Keeper X
1355 Paramount Pkwy (60510-1460)
PHONE..................................630 761-1500
William Bradley, *President*
Brenda Bradley, *Corp Secy*
Debbie McIntyre,
EMP: 4
SALES (est): 426.4K Privately Held
WEB: www.sell4value.com
SIC: **3544** Special dies, tools, jigs & fixtures

(G-1433)
TREETOP MARKETING INC
Also Called: Park It Bike Racks Company
717 Main St (60510-2434)
PHONE..................................877 249-0479
Cyril W Matter, *President*
Robert H Runke, *Admin Sec*
EMP: 3
SALES (est): 299.5K Privately Held
SIC: **3429** Bicycle racks, automotive

(G-1434)
TRIANGLE DIES AND SUPPLIES INC (PA)
1436 Louis Bork Dr (60510-1511)
PHONE..................................630 454-3200
Joseph Marovich, *President*
Jeff Husom, *Plant Mgr*
Curt Almberg, *Manager*
Debra L Marovich, *Admin Sec*
▲ EMP: 60
SQ FT: 25,000
SALES (est): 10.5MM Privately Held
WEB: www.tridie.com
SIC: **3544** Dies, steel rule

(G-1435)
U S COLORS & COATINGS INC
1180 Lyon Rd (60510-1365)
PHONE..................................630 879-8898
Donald Templeman Sr, *President*
Brian Templeman, *Vice Pres*
EMP: 5
SQ FT: 10,000
SALES (est): 660K Privately Held
SIC: **2893** 2851 2865 Printing ink; enamels; cyclic crudes & intermediates

(G-1436)
UNIQUE MOLD & MACHINE INC
1485 Louis Bork Dr (60510-1530)
PHONE..................................630 406-8305
Dave Nutt, *Principal*
EMP: 5 EST: 2010
SALES (est): 486K Privately Held
SIC: **3599** Machine shop, jobbing & repair

(G-1437)
UR INC
859 Ravinia Ct (60510-3213)
PHONE..................................630 450-5279
Janice Carla Hastert, *CEO*
EMP: 3
SALES (est): 250.9K Privately Held
SIC: **2087** Powders, drink

(G-1438)
URBAN HOME FURNITURE & ACC INC
Also Called: Padma's Plantation
1375 Kingsland Dr (60510-1326)
PHONE..................................630 761-3200
Renee Maria Fanjon, *President*
Brenda J Sypolt, *General Mgr*
▲ EMP: 31
SQ FT: 48,000
SALES (est): 5.7MM Privately Held
SIC: **5021** 2511 Furniture; wood lawn & garden furniture

(G-1439)
VANDEVENTER MFG CO INC
Also Called: Vandee Mfg Co Div
812 Main St (60510-2437)
P.O. Box 249 (60510-0249)
PHONE..................................630 879-2511
Ronald J Link, *President*
Leland Weaver, *Vice Pres*
EMP: 44
SQ FT: 45,000
SALES (est): 7.7MM Privately Held
SIC: **3451** 3599 Screw machine products; machine shop, jobbing & repair

(G-1440)
VARN INTERNATIONAL INC
Also Called: Day International
1333 N Kirk Rd (60510-1444)
PHONE..................................630 406-6501
Grant Pieper, *VP Mfg*
EMP: 25
SALES (corp-wide): 53.9B Publicly Held
SIC: **5169** 2899 Chemicals & allied products; chemical preparations
HQ: Varn International Inc
  130 W 2nd St Ste 1700
  Dayton OH
  937 224-4000

(G-1441)
WEDI CORP
1160 Pierson Dr Ste 102 (60510-1526)
PHONE..................................847 357-9815
Stephan Wedi Hollefeldstr, *Principal*
Bastian Lohmann, *Principal*
Josh Stuart, *Regl Sales Mgr*
Maricela Huerta, *Sales Staff*
Jeff Theisen, *Sales Staff*
▲ EMP: 50
SALES (est): 14.7MM
SALES (corp-wide): 166.6K Privately Held
WEB: www.wedicorp.com
SIC: **3431** Shower stalls, metal
HQ: Wedi Gmbh
  Hollefeldtstr. 51
  Emsdetten 48282
  257 215-60

Batchtown
Calhoun County

(G-1442)
CALHOUN QUARRY INCORPORATED (PA)
25 Main St (62006)
P.O. Box 68 (62006-0068)
PHONE..................................618 396-2229
Jerome Sievers, *President*
Anthony Sievers, *Vice Pres*
Betty Sievers, *Admin Sec*
EMP: 11 EST: 1940
SALES (est): 1.2MM Privately Held
WEB: www.calhounquarry.com
SIC: **1422** Limestones, ground

Beach Park
Lake County

(G-1443)
LEPPALA MACHINING INC
12726d W Wadsworth Rd (60087)
PHONE..................................847 625-0270
John Kelley, *Principal*
EMP: 3
SALES (est): 309.4K Privately Held
SIC: **3599** Machine shop, jobbing & repair

(G-1444)
TILLER FARMS HOLDINGS LLC
37165 N Green Bay Rd (60087-3375)
PHONE..................................224 572-7814
David Matovhich, *Mng Member*
EMP: 3
SALES: 24K Privately Held
SIC: **2085** Grain alcohol for beverage purposes

Beardstown
Cass County

(G-1445)
BEARDSTOWN NEWSPAPERS INC
Also Called: CASS COUNTY STAR GAZZETTE
1210 Wall St (62618-2327)
P.O. Box 79 (62618-0079)
PHONE..................................217 323-1010
Murray Cohen, *President*
EMP: 7
SQ FT: 2,600
SALES: 516.8K Privately Held
SIC: **2711** 2741 Newspapers: publishing only, not printed on site; shopping news: publishing only, not printed on site

(G-1446)
CARAUSTAR INDUSTRIAL AND CON
Also Called: Beardstown Tube Plant
100 Forest Ln (62618-7881)
PHONE..................................217 323-5225
James E Cook, *Manager*
EMP: 58
SQ FT: 3,000
SALES (corp-wide): 4.6B Publicly Held
SIC: **2655** Tubes, fiber or paper: made from purchased material
HQ: Caraustar Industrial And Consumer Products Group Inc
  5000 Austell Powder Ste
  Austell GA 30106
  803 548-5100

(G-1447)
JBS USA FOOD COMPANY
8295 Arenzville Rd (62618-7859)
PHONE..................................217 323-6200
Meagan Zulauf, *Plant Engr*
Amy Sommers, *Controller*
Angela Thurman, *Human Res Mgr*
Glenn Karlinsey, *Branch Mgr*
EMP: 20 Privately Held
WEB: www.jbssa.com
SIC: **2011** 5147 Beef products from beef slaughtered on site; meats & meat products
HQ: Jbs Usa Food Company
  1770 Promontory Cir
  Greeley CO 80634
  970 506-8000

(G-1448)
KENT NUTRITION GROUP INC
8679 Kent Feed Rd (62618-8127)
P.O. Box 260 (62618-0260)
PHONE..................................217 323-1216
Mike Maberry, *Branch Mgr*
EMP: 10
SALES (corp-wide): 459.4MM Privately Held
SIC: **2048** Livestock feeds; poultry feeds

HQ: Kent Nutrition Group, Inc.
1600 Oregon St
Muscatine IA 52761
866 647-1212

(G-1449)
NEW LINE HARDWOODS INC
8727 Arenzville Rd (62618-7861)
P.O. Box 317 (62618-0317)
PHONE.................................309 657-7621
Derrick Newman, *President*
EMP: 65
SQ FT: 400,000
SALES (est): 4.3MM **Privately Held**
SIC: 2426 Furniture dimension stock, hardwood

(G-1450)
RIVERSIDE MEMORIAL CO
Also Called: Monument Company
216 W 2nd St (62618-1139)
PHONE.................................217 323-1280
Carl Hood, *Owner*
EMP: 3 **EST:** 1933
SQ FT: 2,800
SALES: 300K **Privately Held**
SIC: 5999 3999 Monuments, finished to custom order; monuments & tombstones; barber & beauty shop equipment

Bedford Park
Cook County

(G-1451)
1 HEAVY EQUIPMENT LOADING INC
6535 S Austin Ave (60638-6108)
PHONE.................................773 581-7374
Inga Kevliciene, *Principal*
EMP: 15
SALES (est): 842.6K **Privately Held**
SIC: 1389 Construction, repair & dismantling services

(G-1452)
A W ENTERPRISES INC
Also Called: Case Guys
6543 S Laramie Ave (60638-6413)
PHONE.................................708 458-8989
Edward Otrusina, *President*
Sergio Flores, *Accounts Mgr*
Rose Pavlik, *Office Mgr*
EMP: 42 **EST:** 1962
SQ FT: 28,400
SALES (est): 6.4MM **Privately Held**
WEB: www.awenterprises.com
SIC: 3172 3089 3161 Leather cases; cases, plastic; luggage

(G-1453)
A2 SALES LLC (PA)
Also Called: Alliance Steel
6499 W 65th St (60638-5118)
PHONE.................................708 924-1200
Andrew Gross, *President*
Liz Randolph, *QC Mgr*
William Vorderer, *Controller*
Jason Chio, *Sales Mgr*
Chuck Fritts, *Regl Sales Mgr*
EMP: 95
SQ FT: 80,000
SALES (est): 54MM **Privately Held**
WEB: www.alliancesteel.net
SIC: 3399 5051 Metal powders, pastes & flakes; steel

(G-1454)
AFTON CHEMICAL CORPORATION
7201 W 65th St (60638-4607)
PHONE.................................708 728-1546
EMP: 22
SALES (corp-wide): 2.1B **Publicly Held**
SIC: 2899 Mfg Chemical Preparations
HQ: Afton Chemical Corporation
500 Spring St
Richmond VA 23219
804 788-5086

(G-1455)
ALPHA PRODUCTS INC (PA)
5570 W 70th Pl (60638-6392)
PHONE.................................708 594-3883
George Derkach, *President*
Tod Jacobson, *Plant Supt*
Eric Marks, *Development*
Luci Rizzo, *Controller*
Travis Hansen, *Comptroller*
▲ **EMP:** 37 **EST:** 1946
SQ FT: 85,000
SALES (est): 7.3MM **Privately Held**
WEB: www.alphaproductsinc.com
SIC: 3469 Stamping metal for the trade

(G-1456)
ARCHER WIRE INTERNATIONAL CORP (PA)
7300 S Narragansett Ave (60638-6020)
PHONE.................................708 563-1700
Leonard J Svabek, *President*
Lenn Svabek, *Vice Pres*
Rick Svabek, *Vice Pres*
Don Vacco, *Vice Pres*
Len Svabek, *Opers Mgr*
▲ **EMP:** 120 **EST:** 1944
SALES (est): 35.3MM **Privately Held**
WEB: www.archerwire.com
SIC: 3496 Miscellaneous fabricated wire products

(G-1457)
ART WIRE WORKS INC
6711 S Leclaire Ave (60638-6417)
PHONE.................................708 458-3993
David Collignon, *Principal*
EMP: 19
SALES (est): 3.1MM **Privately Held**
SIC: 3496 3993 3498 3444 Woven wire products; lamp frames, wire; signs & advertising specialties; fabricated pipe & fittings; sheet metalwork; partitions & fixtures, except wood

(G-1458)
ASPEN GUARD LLC
Also Called: Folding Guard
5858 W 73rd St (60638-6216)
PHONE.................................708 325-0400
Matthew Johnson, *President*
EMP: 3
SALES (est): 131.1K **Privately Held**
SIC: 3315 Wire & fabricated wire products

(G-1459)
ASTORIA WIRE PRODUCTS INC
Also Called: Astoria Wire & Metal Products
5303 W 74th Pl (60638-6507)
PHONE.................................708 496-9950
Richard Zidek, *President*
Kevin Zidek, *Vice Pres*
Dan Candos, *Administration*
EMP: 75
SQ FT: 117,000
SALES (est): 14MM **Privately Held**
WEB: www.astoriawire.com
SIC: 2542 3496 3469 3444 Racks, merchandise display or storage: except wood; miscellaneous fabricated wire products; metal stampings; sheet metalwork

(G-1460)
BRUSIC-ROSE INC
7300 S Central Ave (60638-6514)
PHONE.................................708 458-9900
Edward A Brusic, *President*
Karen J Brusic, *Vice Pres*
EMP: 50
SALES (est): 5.5MM **Privately Held**
SIC: 2512 Upholstered household furniture

(G-1461)
CALMARK GROUP LLC (PA)
Also Called: Calmark Group, The
6755 S Sayre Ave (60638-4724)
PHONE.................................708 728-0101
Robert Doyle, *CEO*
Tom Vandermolen, *Purchasing*
Terry J Richardson, *Treasurer*
EMP: 31
SALES (est): 14.8MM **Privately Held**
SIC: 7331 2759 Mailing service; advertising literature: printing

(G-1462)
CENTRAL PRINTERS & GRAPHICS
6109 W 63rd St (60638-4301)
PHONE.................................773 586-3711
Edward J Osowiec, *President*
Kimberly A Osowiec, *Admin Sec*
EMP: 4
SQ FT: 1,500
SALES (est): 350K **Privately Held**
SIC: 2752 Commercial printing, offset

(G-1463)
CLEMENT INDUSTRIES INC DEL
Also Called: Clement Wheel
5939 W 66th St (60638-6205)
PHONE.................................708 458-9141
Richard Clement, *President*
Donald Wasil, *Principal*
EMP: 50
SQ FT: 175,000
SALES (est): 7.5MM **Privately Held**
SIC: 3714 Wheels, motor vehicle

(G-1464)
CONTRACT INDUSTRIES INC
6641 S Narragansett Ave (60638-5111)
PHONE.................................708 458-8150
Mark Weitzman, *President*
Rich Rusak, *Vice Pres*
Scott Weitzman, *Vice Pres*
Carol Luberda, *Admin Sec*
EMP: 23
SQ FT: 40,000
SALES (est): 4.2MM **Privately Held**
SIC: 2541 2599 2434 2431 Office fixtures, wood; cabinets, except refrigerated: show, display, etc.: wood; restaurant furniture, wood or metal; wood kitchen cabinets; millwork; carpentry work; nonresidential construction

(G-1465)
CORRUGATED SUPPLIES CO LLC (PA)
5043 W 67th St (60638-6409)
PHONE.................................708 458-5525
John Potocsnak, *COO*
Gregg Obodzinski, *Production*
Jessica Canales, *Accountant*
S Richard Van Horne Jr, *Mng Member*
Daniel Jensen, *Manager*
▲ **EMP:** 50 **EST:** 1964
SQ FT: 100,000
SALES (est): 52.5MM **Privately Held**
WEB: www.csclive.com
SIC: 2653 Sheets, solid fiber: made from purchased materials

(G-1466)
DAVIS ATHLETIC EQUIPMENT CO
5021 W 66th St (60638-6403)
PHONE.................................708 563-9006
Jerome Davis, *President*
Carol A Davis, *Corp Secy*
EMP: 11
SQ FT: 26,000
SALES: 1.2MM **Privately Held**
SIC: 3949 3069 Track & field athletic equipment; gymnasium equipment; football equipment & supplies, general; protective sporting equipment; pillows, sponge rubber

(G-1467)
FILTER TECHNOLOGY INC
7200 S Leamington Ave (60638-6620)
PHONE.................................773 523-7200
Herman Hertsberg, *President*
Raphael Hertsberg, *Sales Engr*
EMP: 48
SQ FT: 315,000
SALES (est): 10MM **Privately Held**
SIC: 2299 3399 Felts & felt products; laminating steel

(G-1468)
GOULDS PUMPS LLC
Also Called: ITT
6733 W 73rd St (60638-6006)
PHONE.................................708 563-1220
Bob Duffy, *Manager*
EMP: 14
SALES (corp-wide): 2.8B **Publicly Held**
SIC: 3561 Pumps & pumping equipment
HQ: Goulds Pumps Llc
240 Fall St
Seneca Falls NY 13148
315 568-2811

(G-1469)
HALLSTAR
5350 W 70th Pl (60638-6329)
PHONE.................................330 945-5292
EMP: 4
SALES (est): 292.9K **Privately Held**
SIC: 2869 Industrial organic chemicals

(G-1470)
HALLSTAR COMPANY
5851 W 73rd St (60638-6215)
P.O. Box 910 (60499-0910)
PHONE.................................708 594-5947
Jeff Jaworek, *Manager*
EMP: 55
SALES (corp-wide): 51.3MM **Privately Held**
SIC: 2869 2851 2822 Industrial organic chemicals; paints & allied products; synthetic rubber
PA: Hallstar Company
120 S Riverside Plz # 1620
Chicago IL 60606
312 554-7400

(G-1471)
HELIGEAR ACQUISITION CO (PA)
Also Called: Northstar Aerospace Chicago
6006 W 73rd St (60638-6106)
PHONE.................................708 728-2000
David McConnaughey, *CEO*
Brian Cheek, *Vice Pres*
Greg Harper, *Vice Pres*
Jason Young, *Vice Pres*
Ron Coley, *Foreman/Supr*
EMP: 241 **EST:** 2012
SQ FT: 8,000
SALES (est): 200MM **Privately Held**
SIC: 3724 7699 Aircraft engines & engine parts; aircraft flight instrument repair

(G-1472)
HEXION INC
8600 W 71st St (60501-1952)
PHONE.................................708 728-8834
Terry Rodeheaver, *Manager*
Larry Cardani, *Technician*
EMP: 47
SALES (corp-wide): 3B **Privately Held**
WEB: www.hexion.com
SIC: 2821 Plastics materials & resins
HQ: Hexion Inc.
180 E Broad St Fl 26
Columbus OH 43215
614 225-4000

(G-1473)
INTERNATIONAL PAPER COMPANY
7333 S Lockwood Ave (60638-6523)
PHONE.................................708 728-1000
Ed Morky, *Branch Mgr*
EMP: 30
SALES (corp-wide): 22.3B **Publicly Held**
SIC: 2652 Setup paperboard boxes
PA: International Paper Company
6400 Poplar Ave
Memphis TN 38197
901 419-9000

(G-1474)
ITALMATCH SC LLC
Also Called: Italmatch Chemicals Group
7201 W 65th St (60638-4607)
PHONE.................................708 929-9657
Robert A Lunoe,
EMP: 6
SALES (est): 701.5K **Privately Held**
SIC: 2992 5169 2821 Lubricating oils & greases; detergents; thermoplastic materials
HQ: Italmatch Chemicals Spa
Via Magazzini Del Cotone 17
Genova GE 16128

(G-1475)
J K MANUFACTURING CO
7301 W 66th St (60638-4709)
PHONE.................................708 563-2500
Jozef Koniecko, *CEO*
Mark Koniecko, *President*
Bob Mader, *VP Sales*
EMP: 58
SQ FT: 60,000

GEOGRAPHIC SECTION
Bedford Park - Cook County (G-1503)

SALES (est): 11MM **Privately Held**
SIC: 3599 3444 Machine shop, jobbing & repair; sheet metalwork

(G-1476)
KM4 MANUFACTURING
7420 S Meade Ave (60638-6125)
PHONE..................708 924-5150
EMP: 8
SALES (est): 616.7K **Privately Held**
SIC: 3999 Barber & beauty shop equipment

(G-1477)
L & P GUARDING LLC
Also Called: Folding Guard
5858 W 73rd St (60638-6216)
PHONE..................708 325-0400
David Flerlage, *Manager*
Doreen Clarke, *Assistant*
◆ EMP: 105
SALES (est): 20.6MM **Privately Held**
WEB: www.foldingguard.com
SIC: 3089 3496 Plastic hardware & building products; miscellaneous fabricated wire products

(G-1478)
L LAND HARDWOODS
6247 W 74th St (60638-6120)
PHONE..................708 496-9000
Rick Berryman, *Principal*
EMP: 4 EST: 2011
SALES (est): 688.4K **Privately Held**
WEB: www.landlhardwoods.com
SIC: 2435 Hardwood veneer & plywood

(G-1479)
LAPHAM-HICKEY STEEL CORP (PA)
5500 W 73rd St (60638-6587)
PHONE..................708 496-6111
William M Hickey Jr, *President*
Pat Domeier, *General Mgr*
Stephen Ford, *General Mgr*
Brian Hickey, *General Mgr*
Karen Kustich, *General Mgr*
▲ EMP: 150 EST: 1926
SQ FT: 200,000
SALES (est): 244.6MM **Privately Held**
WEB: www.lapham-hickey.com
SIC: 5051 3398 3355 3317 Bars, metal; strip, metal; tubing, metal; metal heat treating; aluminum rolling & drawing; steel pipe & tubes; cold finishing of steel shapes

(G-1480)
LEXINGTON STEEL CORPORATION
Also Called: Lexcentral Steel
5443 W 70th Pl (60638-6322)
PHONE..................708 594-9200
Robert S Douglass, *CEO*
Timothy M McFarland, *President*
Mr William Douglass, *General Mgr*
Mr Robert Blumenschein, *Vice Pres*
Mr William Huyser, *Vice Pres*
EMP: 85
SQ FT: 94,000
SALES (est): 74.8MM **Privately Held**
WEB: www.lexsteel.com
SIC: 5051 3312 Steel; blast furnaces & steel mills

(G-1481)
METAL-MATIC INC
7200 S Narragansett Ave (60638-6018)
PHONE..................708 594-7553
John Pak, *Department Mgr*
Dave Pratt, *Manager*
EMP: 145
SALES (est): 28.6MM
SALES (corp-wide): 164.2MM **Privately Held**
SIC: 3317 3312 Tubes, wrought: welded or lock joint; tubes, steel & iron
PA: Metal-Matic, Inc.
629 2nd St Se
Minneapolis MN 55414
612 378-0411

(G-1482)
MIDWAY DISPLAYS INC
6554 S Austin Ave (60638-6109)
PHONE..................708 563-2323
Wayne Lucht, *President*
Craig Gavrys, *Plant Mgr*
Tony Zartler, *Opers Staff*
Jim Judge, *Buyer*
Rodney Lucht, *Treasurer*
▲ EMP: 25
SALES (est): 4.5MM **Privately Held**
SIC: 3993 Signs & advertising specialties

(G-1483)
MIDWEST CONVERTING INC
6634 W 68th St (60638-4906)
PHONE..................708 924-1510
Robert Srebalus, *President*
Rose Ann Johnson, *Controller*
John Borkowski, *Admin Sec*
▲ EMP: 60
SQ FT: 256,000
SALES (est): 13MM **Privately Held**
SIC: 2621 Specialty papers

(G-1484)
MIDWEST REMANUFACTURING LLC
5836 W 66th St Fl 2 (60638-6204)
PHONE..................708 496-9100
Tim Mitchell, *Mng Member*
EMP: 7
SQ FT: 30,000
SALES (est): 804.6K **Privately Held**
SIC: 3711 Automobile bodies, passenger car, not including engine, etc.; truck & tractor truck assembly

(G-1485)
MODUSLINK CORPORATION
6112 W 73rd St (60638-6115)
PHONE..................708 496-7800
Bruce Beauchamp, *Branch Mgr*
EMP: 33
SALES (corp-wide): 819.8MM **Publicly Held**
SIC: 7372 Prepackaged software
HQ: Moduslink Corporation
1601 Trapelo Rd Ste 170
Waltham MA 02451
781 663-5000

(G-1486)
NORTHSTAR AEROSPACE (USA) INC
6006 W 73rd St (60638-6106)
PHONE..................708 728-2000
David McConnaughey, *President*
Alan Darmon, *Vice Pres*
Aaron Tam, *CFO*
Christine Desousa, *Controller*
Greg Harper, *VP Human Res*
EMP: 12
SALES (est): 245.5K **Privately Held**
SIC: 3728 Aircraft parts & equipment

(G-1487)
OLE MEXICAN FOODS INC
5140 W 73rd St Unit A (60638-6614)
PHONE..................708 458-3296
EMP: 20
SALES (corp-wide): 269.1MM **Privately Held**
SIC: 2032 Mfg Canned Specialties
PA: Ole' Mexican Foods, Inc.
6585 Crescent Dr
Norcross GA 30071
770 582-9200

(G-1488)
OMNIMAX INTERNATIONAL INC
Amerimax Home Products
6235 W 73rd St (60638-6116)
PHONE..................770 449-7066
Mitchell B Lewis, *CEO*
EMP: 25
SALES (corp-wide): 768.6MM **Privately Held**
SIC: 3444 Sheet metalwork
HQ: Omnimax International, Inc.
30 Technology Pkwy S # 400
Peachtree Corners GA 30092

(G-1489)
PACKAGING CORPORATION AMERICA
Also Called: Chicago Sheet Plant
5555 W 73rd St (60638-6505)
PHONE..................708 594-5260
EMP: 65
SALES (corp-wide): 6.9B **Publicly Held**
SIC: 2653 Boxes, corrugated: made from purchased materials
PA: Packaging Corporation Of America
1 N Field Ct
Lake Forest IL 60045
847 482-3000

(G-1490)
PACTIV LLC
7207 S Mason Ave (60638-6225)
PHONE..................708 496-2900
Brian Anderson, *Manager*
EMP: 207 **Publicly Held**
SIC: 3089 3421 Kitchenware, plastic; plates, plastic; table & food cutlery, including butchers'
HQ: Pactiv Llc
1900 W Field Ct
Lake Forest IL 60045
847 482-2000

(G-1491)
PERKINS PRODUCTS INC
7025 W 66th Pl (60638-4703)
PHONE..................708 458-2000
Richard Perkins, *President*
Ralph Prestidge, *Vice Pres*
Kathleen Flynn, *Human Res Dir*
James McLaughlin, *Sales Staff*
Gail Perkins, *Admin Sec*
EMP: 48
SQ FT: 45,000
SALES (est): 12.7MM **Privately Held**
SIC: 2992 Oils & greases, blending & compounding
PA: Dubois Chemicals, Inc.
3630 E Kemper Rd
Sharonville OH 45241

(G-1492)
POWER PLUS PRODUCTS INC
6410 W 74th St Ste A (60638-6037)
PHONE..................773 788-9794
James G Eaton, *President*
Sam Urso, *Vice Pres*
Linda Stefaniak, *Accounting Mgr*
Richard Petty, *Sales Mgr*
Ricardo Duran, *Regl Sales Mgr*
▲ EMP: 19
SQ FT: 20,000
SALES: 5MM **Privately Held**
SIC: 3714 Axle housings & shafts, motor vehicle

(G-1493)
PRAIRIE MATERIAL
7601 W 79th St Ste 1 (60455-1409)
P.O. Box 1888 (60499-1888)
PHONE..................708 458-0400
David Laymon, *Supervisor*
Keith Onchuck, *Technician*
EMP: 14
SALES (est): 2.9MM **Privately Held**
SIC: 3273 Ready-mixed concrete

(G-1494)
PRESSES INC
Also Called: Rousselle
5360 W 73rd St (60638)
PHONE..................708 496-7450
William Ramsey, *President*
Annie Heim, *CFO*
EMP: 45
SALES (est): 5.4MM **Privately Held**
SIC: 3542 Punching, shearing & bending machines

(G-1495)
PRO WOODWORKING
6554 S Menard Ave (60638-6208)
PHONE..................708 508-5948
Agnes Zabicki, *Owner*
Edmund Zabicki, *Owner*
EMP: 4
SALES: 220K **Privately Held**
SIC: 2431 Millwork

(G-1496)
RAANI CORPORATION
5202 W 70th Pl (60638-6320)
PHONE..................708 496-1035
Rashid A Chaudary, *CEO*
Samia Chaudary, *Vice Pres*
▼ EMP: 150
SQ FT: 275,000
SALES (est): 22.1MM **Privately Held**
SIC: 2844 Hair preparations, including shampoos

(G-1497)
RAYMUNDOS FOOD GROUP LLC
7424 S Lockwood Ave (60638-6526)
PHONE..................708 344-8400
Robert Levi, *CEO*
Jim Taylor, *COO*
Marilyn Pierson, *Manager*
EMP: 125 EST: 2015
SALES: 36MM **Privately Held**
SIC: 2099 Gelatin dessert preparations

(G-1498)
RELIABLE DIE SERVICE INC
6700 W 74th St (60638-6029)
PHONE..................708 458-5155
Robert D Shatkus, *President*
Robert A Shatkus, *Vice Pres*
Mary A Shatkus, *Admin Sec*
EMP: 10
SQ FT: 13,500
SALES (est): 1MM **Privately Held**
SIC: 3544 3469 Special dies & tools; boxes: tool, lunch, mail, etc.: stamped metal

(G-1499)
RINGWOOD COMPANY
Also Called: R.L. Ringwood
6715 W 73rd St (60638-6006)
PHONE..................708 458-6000
Charles J Nodus, *President*
Lisa Pratali, *Purch Mgr*
Jerry Schaaf, *Purchasing*
Steve Petrila, *Engineer*
Eric Sextonson, *Sales Mgr*
▲ EMP: 60
SALES (est): 19.5MM **Privately Held**
SIC: 3531 3554 Construction machinery; paper industries machinery

(G-1500)
RUSCORR LLC
5043 W 67th St (60638-6409)
PHONE..................708 458-5525
Jim Ryan, *Vice Pres*
Todd Price, *Opers Staff*
WEI Xu, *CIO*
Richard Vanhorne,
Robert Larusso, *Administration*
EMP: 2
SALES (est): 641.1K **Privately Held**
SIC: 2653 Sheets, solid fiber: made from purchased materials

(G-1501)
S 4 GLOBAL INC
7300 S Narragansett Ave (60638-6020)
PHONE..................708 325-1236
Lawrence J Svabek, *President*
EMP: 8 EST: 2006
SALES (est): 794.1K **Privately Held**
SIC: 3312 Wire products, steel or iron

(G-1502)
S A GEAR COMPANY INC
7252 W 66th St (60638-4702)
PHONE..................708 496-0395
Sal Abdallah, *President*
Riyad Abdallah, *Vice Pres*
Magdee Abdallah, *CFO*
Robert Abdallah, *Treasurer*
Georgene Cerniuk, *Cust Mgr*
▲ EMP: 25
SQ FT: 40,000
SALES (est): 7.3MM **Privately Held**
SIC: 3714 Gears, motor vehicle

(G-1503)
SCALETTA MOLONEY ARMORING (PA)
6755 S Belt Circle Dr (60638-4705)
PHONE..................708 924-0099
Suzanne C Scaletta, *President*
Joseph Scarletta, *COO*
Daniel Trainor, *Exec VP*
Scaletta Moloney, *Vice Pres*
Nathan Foster, *Prdtn Mgr*
▲ EMP: 135
SQ FT: 70,000

(PA)=Parent Co (HQ)=Headquarters (DH)= Div Headquarters
✪ = New Business established in last 2 years

Bedford Park - Cook County (G-1504)

SALES (est): 46.7MM **Privately Held**
SIC: 3799 Recreational vehicles

(G-1504)
SEBIS DIRECT INC (PA)
6516 W 74th St (60638-6011)
PHONE..................312 243-9300
Wes Sanders, *President*
Kathy Morrin, *Exec VP*
Jim Bardzinski, *Controller*
Wayne Kusy, *Web Dvlpr*
EMP: 41
SQ FT: 69,000
SALES (est): 7.5MM **Privately Held**
SIC: 2759 7374 Laser printing; data processing & preparation

(G-1505)
SPECIALIZED LIFTRUCK SVCS LLC
6650 S Narragansett Ave (60638-5112)
PHONE..................708 552-2705
Michael Swieter,
Martin J Flaska,
EMP: 12
SALES (est): 1.2MM **Privately Held**
SIC: 8711 8742 3537 Mechanical engineering; maintenance management consultant; forklift trucks

(G-1506)
STAR MOULDING & TRIM COMPANY
6606 W 74th St (60638-6013)
PHONE..................708 458-1040
David F O Keeffe, *President*
Patricia O Keeffe, *Admin Sec*
EMP: 25 **EST:** 1914
SQ FT: 30,000
SALES: 4MM **Privately Held**
WEB: www.starmoulding.com
SIC: 2431 Moldings, wood: unfinished & prefinished; trim, wood

(G-1507)
STERLING SPRING LLC
7171 W 65th St (60638-4605)
PHONE..................773 777-4647
John Shapiro, *Manager*
EMP: 43
SALES (corp-wide): 23.2MM **Privately Held**
SIC: 3495 Wire springs
PA: Sterling Spring, L.L.C.
5432 W 54th St
Chicago IL 60638
773 582-6464

(G-1508)
UNITED MAINT WLDG & MCHY C
5252 W 73rd St (60638-6616)
PHONE..................708 458-1705
Stanley Lukanus, *President*
Stanley Strama, *Treasurer*
EMP: 16
SQ FT: 34,000
SALES (est): 2.2MM **Privately Held**
SIC: 3599 7692 Machine shop, jobbing & repair; welding repair

(G-1509)
VEGETABLE JUICES INC
Also Called: V J I
7400 S Narragansett Ave (60638-6022)
PHONE..................708 924-9500
Elizabeth Doyle, *CEO*
Eugene J Garvy, *Chairman*
Samantha Firestone, *QA Dir*
Sandra Ferreyra, *Research*
Randy Decaire, *CFO*
▲ **EMP:** 90
SQ FT: 175,000
SALES (est): 18.6MM **Privately Held**
WEB: www.vegetablejuices.com
SIC: 7389 2033 Packaging & labeling services; vegetable juices: fresh
HQ: Naturex Inc.
375 Huyler St
South Hackensack NJ 07606
201 440-5000

(G-1510)
WARNER INDUSTRIES INC
Also Called: R & W Machine
6551 W 74th St (60638-6010)
P.O. Box 607 (60499-0607)
PHONE..................708 458-0627
Gerald G Warner, *President*
Herb Nelson, *QC Mgr*
Cynthia West, *Treasurer*
Craig Opacic, *Sales Staff*
Margie Brannigan, *Office Mgr*
▲ **EMP:** 57 **EST:** 1946
SQ FT: 30,000
SALES (est): 11.7MM **Privately Held**
WEB: www.rwmachine.com
SIC: 3599 Machine shop, jobbing & repair

(G-1511)
WASEET AMERICA
6000 W 79th St Ste 203 (60459-3124)
P.O. Box 278, Worth (60482-0278)
PHONE..................708 430-1950
Kaledra Ramaha, *Principal*
EMP: 5
SALES (est): 258.6K **Privately Held**
SIC: 2711 Newspapers, publishing & printing

(G-1512)
WELD-RITE SERVICE INC
6715 W 73rd St (60638-6006)
PHONE..................708 458-6000
Charles J Nodus, *President*
Lisa Pratali, *Purch Agent*
Carl W Nodus, *Admin Sec*
EMP: 40
SQ FT: 60,000
SALES (est): 15.9MM **Privately Held**
WEB: www.weldriteservices.com
SIC: 3441 7692 Fabricated structural metal; welding repair

(G-1513)
WESTROCK CP LLC
6131 W 74th St (60638-6118)
PHONE..................708 458-5288
Randy Haberman, *Manager*
EMP: 64
SALES (corp-wide): 18.2B **Publicly Held**
SIC: 2653 2631 Sheets, corrugated: made from purchased materials; paperboard mills
HQ: Westrock Cp, Llc
1000 Abernathy Rd Ste 125
Atlanta GA 30328

(G-1514)
WORKSHOP LTD INC
5900 W 51st St (60638-1443)
PHONE..................708 458-3222
Guilermo Brown, *President*
EMP: 2
SALES (est): 223.4K **Privately Held**
SIC: 2448 Pallets, wood

(G-1515)
WOZNIAK INDUSTRIES INC
Commercial Frged Pdts A Div Wz
5757 W 65th St (60638-5503)
PHONE..................708 458-1220
Herbert Little, *General Mgr*
Debbie Thiesse, *Materials Mgr*
Robert Trujillo, *Design Engr*
Ivan Chavez, *Cust Mgr*
Brian Bozek, *Sales Staff*
EMP: 120
SALES (corp-wide): 79.7MM **Privately Held**
SIC: 3462 3545 3429 Iron & steel forgings; machine tool accessories; manufactured hardware (general)
PA: Wozniak Industries, Inc.
1901 N Roselle Rd Ste 750
Schaumburg IL 60195
630 954-3400

Beecher
Will County

(G-1516)
ALUMINUM DRIVE LINE PRODUCTS
746 Penfield St (60401-6637)
P.O. Box 539 (60401-0539)
PHONE..................708 946-9777
Klaud Miller, *President*
EMP: 3
SQ FT: 4,000
SALES (est): 500K **Privately Held**
SIC: 3714 Drive shafts, motor vehicle

(G-1517)
JM CIRCLE ENTERPRISE INC
28255 S Cottage Grove Ave (60401-3757)
PHONE..................708 946-3333
Bethanie Lenting, *President*
Jacob Lenting, *Vice Pres*
Mark Wayne- Lenting, *Treasurer*
EMP: 3
SALES (est): 222.4K **Privately Held**
SIC: 3354 Aluminum pipe & tube

(G-1518)
LACHATA DESIGN LTD
3006 E Indiana Ave (60401-3168)
PHONE..................708 946-2757
Robert Lachata, *President*
EMP: 5
SQ FT: 9,000
SALES (est): 500K **Privately Held**
SIC: 3826 Analytical instruments

(G-1519)
OLDENDORF MACHINING & FABG
3041 E Offner Rd (60401-3242)
PHONE..................708 946-2498
Melvin Oldendorf, *Owner*
EMP: 8
SALES (est): 380K **Privately Held**
SIC: 3599 Machine shop, jobbing & repair

(G-1520)
PECSON DISTRIBUTORS LLC
27543 S Forest View Ln (60401-5021)
PHONE..................815 342-7977
Christina E Jackson, *President*
David Wolse, *Vice Pres*
▲ **EMP:** 8
SQ FT: 5,000
SALES: 1MM **Privately Held**
WEB: www.pecsondistributors.com
SIC: 3965 Fasteners

(G-1521)
SONOCO PRTECTIVE SOLUTIONS INC
Also Called: Thermosafe
30553 S Dixie Hwy (60401-3144)
PHONE..................708 946-3244
Stacy Grutzius, *Buyer*
Chris Kluge, *Manager*
Michael Lacheta, *Technician*
EMP: 49
SALES (corp-wide): 5.3B **Publicly Held**
SIC: 2676 Feminine hygiene paper products
HQ: Sonoco Protective Solutions, Inc.
1 N 2nd St
Hartsville SC 29550
843 383-7000

(G-1522)
TULIP TREE GARDENS CO
1236 E Eagle Lake Rd (60401-3421)
PHONE..................708 612-7094
Rachael Smedberg, *President*
EMP: 3
SALES: 500K **Privately Held**
SIC: 2834 Extracts of botanicals: powdered, pilular, solid or fluid

(G-1523)
VALLEY RACING INC
325 W 323rd St (60401-3518)
PHONE..................708 946-1440
Rollie Conley, *President*
Brian Conley, *Vice Pres*
Tina Conley, *Admin Sec*
EMP: 4 **EST:** 1984
SQ FT: 5,000
SALES (est): 372.5K **Privately Held**
SIC: 7699 3751 5571 7948 Motorcycle repair service; motorcycles, bicycles & parts; motorcycle dealers; motorcycle racing

(G-1524)
W L & J ENTERPRISES INC
Also Called: Fredette Racing Products
31745 S Dixie Hwy (60401-3148)
PHONE..................708 946-0999
Jeff Fredette, *President*
Wayne Fredette, *Vice Pres*
EMP: 3
SQ FT: 2,000
SALES (est): 495.1K **Privately Held**
SIC: 5571 3751 Motorcycle parts & accessories; motorcycles, bicycles & parts

Belle Rive
Jefferson County

(G-1525)
HOPKINS SAWS & KARTS INC
Also Called: Hopkins Saws & Cart
9398 N Markham Ln (62810-2003)
PHONE..................618 756-2778
Phillip Hopkins, *President*
Brad Hopkins, *Corp Secy*
Alta Jean Hopkins, *Vice Pres*
EMP: 2
SALES (est): 220K **Privately Held**
SIC: 3546 5599 Saws & sawing equipment; go-carts

Belleville
St. Clair County

(G-1526)
ABM MARKING LTD
Also Called: R M J Distributing
2799 S Belt W (62226-6777)
PHONE..................618 277-3773
Barbara Merchiori, *President*
Huston Liu, *Owner*
Roger Schaefer, *COO*
Alberto Merchiori, *Senior VP*
John Bock, *Admin Sec*
▲ **EMP:** 10
SQ FT: 6,000
SALES (est): 3.4MM **Privately Held**
SIC: 5085 2893 2899 Industrial supplies; printing ink; chemical preparations

(G-1527)
ABM MARKING SERVICES LTD
Also Called: Rmj Distributing
2799 S Belt W (62226-6777)
PHONE..................618 277-3773
Huston Liu, *Vice Pres*
John Bock, *Admin Sec*
EMP: 4
SQ FT: 4,500
SALES (est): 169.2K **Privately Held**
SIC: 3953 3825 Stencils, painting & marking; battery testers, electrical

(G-1528)
ADRENALINE PRINTS
126 E Main St (62220-1607)
PHONE..................618 277-9600
Ryan Malashack, *Owner*
EMP: 2
SALES (est): 212.6K **Privately Held**
SIC: 2752 Commercial printing, offset

(G-1529)
ALTERNATIVE TS
5300 N Belt W (62226-4609)
PHONE..................618 257-0230
Andy Kinsella, *Owner*
EMP: 8
SQ FT: 2,600
SALES (est): 350K **Privately Held**
SIC: 3955 2396 2395 Print cartridges for laser & other computer printers; automotive & apparel trimmings; tucking, for the trade

GEOGRAPHIC SECTION
Belleville - St. Clair County (G-1558)

(G-1530)
ARTWEAR
1916 Lebanon Ave (62221-2552)
PHONE..............................618 234-5522
Mary Rudman, *Owner*
EMP: 4
SALES (est): 252.6K **Privately Held**
SIC: 2759 Screen printing

(G-1531)
ATLAS TRADE SOLUTIONS LLC
18 Powder Valley Dr (62223-1925)
PHONE..............................618 954-6119
Andrew Raming, *Mng Member*
Christoph Gertzen,
Stephanie Pieper,
Osama Shiha,
EMP: 5
SALES (est): 158.8K **Privately Held**
SIC: 2062 0112 2063 3331 Granulated cane sugar from purchased raw sugar or syrup; rice; beet sugar; cathodes (primary), copper

(G-1532)
BACH & ASSOCIATES
120 N 36th St (62226-6232)
PHONE..............................618 277-1652
Gerry Bach, *Co-Owner*
Ann Bach, *Co-Owner*
EMP: 4
SQ FT: 7,000
SALES (est): 250K **Privately Held**
SIC: 7336 2752 Graphic arts & related design; commercial printing, lithographic

(G-1533)
BELLEVILLE NEWS DEMOCRAT
Also Called: Belleville News Democrat, The
120 S Illinois St (62220-2130)
PHONE..............................618 239-2552
Gary Berkely, *President*
Kiearra Jones, *Advt Staff*
EMP: 145
SALES (est): 9.7MM **Privately Held**
SIC: 2711 Newspapers, publishing & printing

(G-1534)
BENO J GUNDLACH COMPANY
211 N 21st St (62226-6658)
PHONE..............................618 233-1781
Gregory J Gundlach, *President*
Mike Timberland, *General Mgr*
Jeffrey B Gundlach, *Vice Pres*
Jeffrey Gundlach, *Vice Pres*
Stephen P Gundlach, *Vice Pres*
▲ **EMP:** 35 **EST:** 1923
SQ FT: 60,000
SALES (est): 8.1MM **Privately Held**
WEB: www.benojgundlachco.com
SIC: 3423 5072 Carpet layers' hand tools; builders' hardware

(G-1535)
BERTCO ENTERPRISES INC
108 N Jackson St (62220-1427)
PHONE..............................618 234-9283
EMP: 3
SQ FT: 11,250
SALES (est): 250K **Privately Held**
SIC: 5099 3479 7389 3953 Whol Durable Goods Coating/Engraving Svcs Business Services Mfg Marking Devices Mfg Prdt-Purchased Glass

(G-1536)
BUILDING PRODUCTS CORP (PA)
950 Freeburg Ave (62220-2623)
P.O. Box 566 (62222-0566)
PHONE..............................618 233-4427
Paul Mueth, *President*
Joan Mueth, *Vice Pres*
Aaron Rauls, *Sales Staff*
EMP: 25 **EST:** 1945
SQ FT: 1,000
SALES (est): 2.8MM **Privately Held**
WEB: www.buildingproductscorp.com
SIC: 3251 3271 Brick & structural clay tile; blocks, concrete or cinder: standard

(G-1537)
CALLISON DISTRIBUTING LLC
4 Premier Dr (62220-3421)
P.O. Box 463 (62222-0463)
PHONE..............................618 277-4300
Edwin H Callison Jr,
▲ **EMP:** 60 **EST:** 1933
SQ FT: 52,000
SALES (est): 6.2MM **Privately Held**
SIC: 5182 2085 Liquor; distilled & blended liquors

(G-1538)
CAROLINE COLE INC
711 S Illinois St (62220-2141)
PHONE..............................618 233-0600
Torre Tribout, *Vice Pres*
EMP: 12
SQ FT: 12,000
SALES (est): 500K **Privately Held**
SIC: 3069 5712 2392 Pillows, sponge rubber; furniture stores; household furnishings

(G-1539)
CHELAR TOOL & DIE INC
11 N Florida Ave (62221-5498)
PHONE..............................618 234-6550
Jared Katt, *President*
Malcolm Katt, *President*
Ray Klein, *Vice Pres*
Gary Doza, *Foreman/Supr*
Dick Wagner, *Purch Mgr*
EMP: 60
SQ FT: 38,000
SALES: 13.6MM **Privately Held**
WEB: www.chelar.com
SIC: 3544 Special dies & tools

(G-1540)
COMFORT COMPANIES LLC (DH)
100 N Florida Ave (62221-5429)
PHONE..............................406 522-8560
Rick Remitz, *President*
▲ **EMP:** 25
SALES (est): 21.5MM
SALES (corp-wide): 5.7B **Privately Held**
SIC: 3842 Orthopedic appliances; braces, elastic

(G-1541)
CURT SMITH SPORTING GOODS INC (PA)
213 E Main St (62220-1688)
PHONE..............................618 233-5177
Jeff Hall, *President*
John Vallero, *CFO*
Doris Smith, *Admin Sec*
EMP: 20 **EST:** 1946
SQ FT: 13,000
SALES (est): 4.9MM **Privately Held**
WEB: www.curtsmithsports.com
SIC: 2329 5091 Men's & boys' athletic uniforms; athletic goods

(G-1542)
CUSTOM CUT STENCIL COMPANY INC
132 Iowa Ave (62220-3940)
PHONE..............................618 277-5077
Carolyn Lewis, *President*
Steve Lewis, *Co-Owner*
EMP: 5
SALES (est): 609K **Privately Held**
SIC: 3953 Stencils, painting & marking

(G-1543)
DDK SCIENTIFIC CORPORATION
1 11th Fairway Ct (62220-4861)
P.O. Box 23952 (62223-0952)
PHONE..............................618 235-2849
Raul Duarte, *President*
EMP: 4
SALES (est): 518K **Privately Held**
SIC: 3641 Ultraviolet lamps

(G-1544)
DELI STAR VENTURES INC
Also Called: King's Food Products
3 Amann Ct (62220-3461)
PHONE..............................618 233-0400
Tom Siegel, *President*
Dan Siegel, *Vice Pres*
Stephanie Siegel, *Vice Pres*
Mike Weber, *Opers Staff*
Tom Wuller, *Opers Staff*
EMP: 15
SQ FT: 5,000
SALES (est): 7MM **Privately Held**
WEB: www.kingsfoodproducts.com
SIC: 2064 Fudge (candy)

(G-1545)
DELTA LABEL INC
920 Scheel St (62221-4830)
PHONE..............................618 233-8984
Mark Howell, *President*
Homer Howell, *Chairman*
Gwen Howell, *Exec VP*
EMP: 3
SQ FT: 3,500
SALES (est): 320.1K **Privately Held**
SIC: 2759 Labels & seals: printing

(G-1546)
DOVE INDUSTRIES INC
229 Taft St (62220-2868)
PHONE..............................618 234-4509
Eric Stephenson, *President*
Candy Stephenson, *Vice Pres*
EMP: 10
SQ FT: 24,000
SALES (est): 1.7MM **Privately Held**
SIC: 3496 Miscellaneous fabricated wire products

(G-1547)
DREXEL HOUSE OF DRAPES INC
Also Called: Drexel Vinisitian and Blind
3721 Lebanon Ave (62221-4490)
PHONE..............................618 624-5415
Deloris McAllister, *President*
Jack William Macallister, *Vice Pres*
Lynda Housick, *Treasurer*
EMP: 4 **EST:** 1954
SALES: 400K **Privately Held**
WEB: www.drexelwindowfashions.com
SIC: 5714 7349 5211 2391 Draperies; window blind cleaning; windows, storm: wood or metal; curtains & draperies

(G-1548)
E-LITE TOOL & MFG CO
122 Industrial Dr (62220-3432)
PHONE..............................618 236-1580
Scott Jones, *President*
Rick Baltz, *Vice Pres*
Debbie Baltz, *Treasurer*
EMP: 24 **EST:** 1957
SQ FT: 20,500
SALES (est): 4.5MM **Privately Held**
WEB: www.elitetoolmfgco.com
SIC: 3544 Special dies & tools

(G-1549)
ECKERT ORCHARDS INC (PA)
951 S Green Mount Rd (62220-4814)
PHONE..............................618 233-0513
James Eckert, *President*
Larry Eckert, *Corp Secy*
EMP: 250
SQ FT: 500
SALES (est): 33MM **Privately Held**
WEB: www.eckerts.com
SIC: 2099 0175 5431 0171 Cider, nonalcoholic; peach orchard; apple orchard; fruit & vegetable markets; berry crops

(G-1550)
ED BELL INVESTMENTS INC
34 Empire Dr Ste 1 (62220-3585)
PHONE..............................618 345-0799
Dan Feather, *Branch Mgr*
▼ **EMP:** 3
SALES (corp-wide): 89.5MM **Privately Held**
SIC: 3272 Concrete products, precast
PA: Ed Bell Investments, Inc.
10605 Harry Hines Blvd
Dallas TX 75220
214 358-3414

(G-1551)
EMPIRE COMFORT SYSTEMS INC
918 Freeburg Ave (62220-2623)
P.O. Box 529 (62222-0529)
PHONE..............................618 233-7420
Brian H Bauer, *Chairman*
Ken Belding, *Vice Pres*
Frank Kretchman, *Vice Pres*
Paul Potter, *Vice Pres*
Travis Knox, *Prdtn Mgr*
▲ **EMP:** 200 **EST:** 1932
SQ FT: 250,000
SALES (est): 42MM **Privately Held**
WEB: www.empirecomfort.com
SIC: 3949 3631 3433 Sporting & athletic goods; gas ranges, domestic; space heaters, except electric; room heaters, gas; wall heaters, except electric

(G-1552)
FIRE CAM
525 W Main St Ste 100 (62220-1534)
PHONE..............................618 416-8390
Jami L Schield, *CEO*
EMP: 5
SALES (est): 137.6K **Privately Held**
SIC: 3861 3651 Cameras & related equipment; video camera-audio recorders, household use

(G-1553)
FIRE CAM LLC
321 Clearwater Dr (62220-2969)
PHONE..............................618 416-8390
Robert Schield, *Mng Member*
EMP: 7
SALES (est): 270.4K **Privately Held**
SIC: 3651 Video camera-audio recorders, household use

(G-1554)
GUNDLACH EQUIPMENT CORPORATION
1 Freedom Dr (62226-5104)
P.O. Box 385 (62222-0385)
PHONE..............................618 233-7208
Mark Kohler, *President*
Alan Reuter, *Design Engr*
John R Zerkle, *Admin Sec*
▲ **EMP:** 80
SQ FT: 63,000
SALES (est): 7.3MM **Publicly Held**
SIC: 3532 Mining machinery
PA: Hillenbrand, Inc.
1 Batesville Blvd
Batesville IN 47006

(G-1555)
HEADBALL INC
Also Called: Mid America Web Solutions
41 Acorn Lake Dr (62221-4449)
PHONE..............................618 628-2656
Anthony Smallon, *President*
EMP: 3 **EST:** 1998
SALES (est): 252.7K **Privately Held**
WEB: www.headball.com
SIC: 3949 Soccer equipment & supplies

(G-1556)
I D TOGS
67 Cheshire Dr (62223-3413)
PHONE..............................618 235-1538
Tom Metzger, *President*
EMP: 3
SALES (est): 166.5K **Privately Held**
SIC: 2395 Embroidery products, except schiffli machine

(G-1557)
ILLINI CONCRETE INC (PA)
1300 E A St (62221-5400)
P.O. Box 684, Caseyville (62232-0684)
PHONE..............................618 235-4141
Amy Santen, *President*
Jeb Santen, *Vice Pres*
EMP: 15
SQ FT: 5,000
SALES (est): 2.7MM **Privately Held**
SIC: 3273 Ready-mixed concrete

(G-1558)
INTERNATIONAL PAPER COMPANY
3001 Otto St (62226-6711)
PHONE..............................618 233-5460
Ron Wise, *Principal*
Ken Dalton, *Manager*
Dwaine Hoffman, *Clerk*
EMP: 17
SALES (corp-wide): 22.3B **Publicly Held**
WEB: www.internationalpaper.com
SIC: 2621 Paper mills

Belleville - St. Clair County (G-1559)

PA: International Paper Company
6400 Poplar Ave
Memphis TN 38197
901 419-9000

(G-1559)
IV & RESPIRATORY CARE SERVICES
65 S 65th St Ste 1 (62223-2946)
PHONE..............................618 398-2720
Lori Weilmuenster, *Owner*
Chrystal Fisher,
EMP: 30
SALES (est): 3MM **Privately Held**
SIC: 8093 3845 Respiratory therapy clinic; respiratory analysis equipment, electromedical

(G-1560)
KEIL-FORNESS COMFORT SYSTEMS
301 N Illinois St (62220-1232)
PHONE..............................618 233-3039
David C Forness, *Owner*
EMP: 5 **EST:** 1899
SQ FT: 3,500
SALES (est): 410K **Privately Held**
WEB: www.weiscomfortsystems.com
SIC: 1711 3444 Warm air heating & air conditioning contractor; sheet metalwork

(G-1561)
KEMELL ENTERPRISES LLC
612 Ganim Dr (62221-2671)
PHONE..............................618 671-1513
Candice Kemp, *Principal*
EMP: 3
SALES (est): 117.8K **Privately Held**
SIC: 3728 Refueling equipment for use in flight, airplane

(G-1562)
KETTLER CASTING CO INC
2640 Old Freeburg Rd (62220-5204)
P.O. Box 852 (62222-0852)
PHONE..............................618 234-5303
Gregg W Kettler, *President*
Jeffrey R Lutz, *President*
John Bauer, *General Mgr*
Ruth Kettler, *Admin Sec*
EMP: 30
SQ FT: 15,000
SALES (est): 6.3MM **Privately Held**
WEB: www.kettlercasting.com
SIC: 3321 3369 Gray iron castings; nonferrous foundries

(G-1563)
KLM COMMERCIAL SWEEPING INC
320 Saint Sabre Dr (62226-1046)
PHONE..............................618 978-9276
Keith Kannewurf, *President*
Kevin Kannewurf, *Vice Pres*
EMP: 6
SALES: 500K **Privately Held**
SIC: 3991 Street sweeping brooms, hand or machine

(G-1564)
KM PRESS INCORPORATED
120 Iowa Ave (62220-3940)
P.O. Box 373 (62222-0373)
PHONE..............................618 277-1222
Kurt Matson, *President*
Carl Matson, *Treasurer*
Judy Matson, *Admin Sec*
EMP: 9
SALES: 1.3MM **Privately Held**
SIC: 2752 Commercial printing, offset

(G-1565)
KODERHANDT INC
Also Called: Quality Plating Works
1651 N Charles St (62221-4928)
PHONE..............................618 233-4808
Christy Koderhandt, *President*
James R Koderhandt, *Vice Pres*
EMP: 3 **EST:** 1927
SQ FT: 17,520
SALES (est): 310.4K **Privately Held**
SIC: 3471 Electrolizing steel; electroplating of metals or formed products

(G-1566)
KOSTELAC GREASE SERVICE INC
8105 Pecan Tree Ln (62223-7742)
PHONE..............................314 436-7166
John Kostelac III, *President*
James Kostelac, *Vice Pres*
EMP: 25
SQ FT: 3,000
SALES (est): 3.2MM **Privately Held**
SIC: 2077 4953 2992 Grease rendering, inedible; tallow rendering, inedible; refuse systems; lubricating oils & greases

(G-1567)
L M C AUTOMOTIVE INC
Also Called: Belleville Automotive
1200 W Main St (62220-1525)
PHONE..............................618 235-5242
Mark Schaefer, *President*
Linda Schaefer, *Admin Sec*
EMP: 3
SALES (est): 30K **Privately Held**
SIC: 3599 5013 Machine shop, jobbing & repair; automotive supplies & parts

(G-1568)
LIESE LUMBER CO INC
2215 S Belt W (62226-6797)
P.O. Box 306 (62222-0306)
PHONE..............................618 234-0105
Lennie Colbert, *Manager*
EMP: 7
SALES (est): 545.6K
SALES (corp-wide): 11.4MM **Privately Held**
SIC: 5211 2421 Lumber products; door & window products; resawing lumber into smaller dimensions; building & structural materials, wood
PA: Liese Lumber Co., Inc.
319 E Main St
Belleville IL 62220
314 421-3652

(G-1569)
MAC MEDICAL INC
325 W Main St (62220-1505)
PHONE..............................618 719-6757
Dennis Cooper, *President*
EMP: 10
SALES (est): 136.8K **Privately Held**
SIC: 5047 3999 Medical equipment & supplies; manufacturing industries

(G-1570)
MARBIL ENTERPRISES INC
Also Called: Advance Security Products
129 Wild Rose Dr (62221-3606)
PHONE..............................618 257-1810
William Douthitt, *CEO*
Mary Douthitt, *Vice Pres*
◆ **EMP:** 5
SQ FT: 2,000
SALES: 1.5MM **Privately Held**
SIC: 3699 Security control equipment & systems

(G-1571)
MARTIN GLASS COMPANY (PA)
25 Center Plz (62220-3400)
PHONE..............................618 277-1946
Martin S Kosydor, *President*
Martin J Kosydor, *Vice Pres*
Marla Wild, *Treasurer*
Marla K Wild, *Treasurer*
Dan Burton, *Sales Staff*
EMP: 18 **EST:** 1933
SQ FT: 9,000
SALES (est): 3.9MM **Privately Held**
WEB: www.martinglass.net
SIC: 7536 3231 5231 Automotive glass replacement shops; products of purchased glass; glass

(G-1572)
MAXS ONE STOP
1319 N 17th St (62226-6441)
PHONE..............................618 235-4005
Dennis Knoth, *Owner*
EMP: 4
SALES (est): 199.4K **Privately Held**
SIC: 2074 Cottonseed oil, cake or meal

(G-1573)
MCATEERS WHOLESALE
Also Called: McAteer's Landscape Lighting
3101 S Belt W (62226-5016)
PHONE..............................618 233-3400
EMP: 6
SALES (est): 571.5K **Privately Held**
SIC: 3645 Mfg Residential Lighting Fixtures

(G-1574)
MCCLATCHY NEWSPAPERS INC
Also Called: Belleville News Democrat
120 S Illinois St (62220-2130)
P.O. Box 427 (62222-0427)
PHONE..............................618 239-2624
Becky Pate, *Principal*
EMP: 275
SALES (corp-wide): 709.5MM **Publicly Held**
SIC: 2711 Newspapers, publishing & printing
HQ: Mcclatchy Newspapers, Inc.
2100 Q St
Sacramento CA 95816
916 321-1855

(G-1575)
MERSIGNS
1700 N Belt E (62221-5011)
PHONE..............................618 234-4450
Mike Rosciglione, *Owner*
EMP: 5
SALES (est): 383.5K **Privately Held**
SIC: 3993 Signs & advertising specialties

(G-1576)
MESSENGER
2620 Lebanon Ave Unit 2 (62221-3001)
PHONE..............................618 235-9601
Edward Braxton, *Owner*
EMP: 5
SALES (est): 180.5K **Privately Held**
SIC: 2711 Newspapers: publishing only, not printed on site

(G-1577)
METRO EAST FIBERGLASS REPAIR
1166 Heneral Ave (62220)
PHONE..............................618 235-9217
Randy G Heinlein, *President*
EMP: 5
SQ FT: 10,000
SALES: 1.7MM **Privately Held**
SIC: 3732 5551 Boats, fiberglass: building & repairing; boat dealers

(G-1578)
MILLSTADT RENDERING COMPANY
3151 Clover Leaf Schl Rd (62223-7748)
PHONE..............................618 538-5312
Robert Kostelac, *President*
Diane Rasp, *Office Mgr*
EMP: 25
SQ FT: 2,000
SALES (est): 7.2MM **Privately Held**
WEB: www.millstadtrendering.com
SIC: 5159 4953 2077 Farm animals; dead animal disposal; animal & marine fats & oils

(G-1579)
MINDSEYE
442 S Demazenod Dr (62223-1023)
PHONE..............................618 394-6444
Jason Fravier, *CEO*
EMP: 7
SALES (est): 124.2K **Privately Held**
SIC: 2741

(G-1580)
NPT AUTOMOTIVE MACHINE SHOP
308 N 44th St (62226-5226)
PHONE..............................618 233-1344
EMP: 2
SALES (est): 200K **Privately Held**
SIC: 3519 Mfg Internal Combustion Engines

(G-1581)
OBIES TACKLE CO INC
124 Cardinal Dr (62221-4311)
PHONE..............................618 234-5638
Pat Oberholtzer, *President*
EMP: 4
SALES: 50K **Privately Held**
SIC: 3949 5091 2298 Lures, fishing: artificial; sporting & recreation goods; cordage & twine

(G-1582)
P T L MANUFACTURING INC
101 Industrial Dr (62220-3412)
PHONE..............................618 277-6789
Joseph D Stock, *President*
Jane E Stock, *Corp Secy*
Brian Bert, *Engineer*
Bert Brian, *Engineer*
Jane Stock, *Human Res Mgr*
EMP: 44
SQ FT: 40,000
SALES (est): 8.6MM **Privately Held**
SIC: 3469 Stamping metal for the trade

(G-1583)
PAYNE CHAUNA
Also Called: Prima Donna Salon
333 Longview Dr (62223-4101)
PHONE..............................618 580-2584
Chauna Payne, *Owner*
EMP: 5 **EST:** 2012
SQ FT: 1,000
SALES (est): 38.5K **Privately Held**
SIC: 7231 7299 3842 Cosmetologist; hair weaving or replacement; prosthetic appliances; cosmetic restorations

(G-1584)
PEAK COMPUTER SYSTEMS INC
6400 W Main St Ste 1a (62223-3806)
PHONE..............................618 398-5612
Grant Wuller, *President*
Michele Wuller, *Vice Pres*
EMP: 11
SQ FT: 2,500
SALES (est): 1.1MM **Privately Held**
SIC: 7372 7371 Prepackaged software; computer software systems analysis & design, custom

(G-1585)
PEERLESS-PREMIER APPLIANCE CO (PA)
119 S 14th St (62220-1715)
P.O. Box 387 (62222-0387)
PHONE..............................618 233-0475
Alex Volansky, *President*
William T Sprague, *Chairman*
Judy Wagner, *VP Admin*
Gary Siburt, *Vice Pres*
Brian Volansky, *Opers Mgr*
◆ **EMP:** 160 **EST:** 1928
SQ FT: 250,000
SALES (est): 35.2MM **Privately Held**
WEB: www.peerless-premierappliance.com
SIC: 3631 Gas ranges, domestic; electric ranges, domestic

(G-1586)
PRUETT ENTERPRISES INC
Also Called: Marv's Scooters
10 E Cleveland Ave (62220-2108)
PHONE..............................618 235-6184
Marvin Pruett, *President*
EMP: 2
SALES (est): 215.4K **Privately Held**
SIC: 3751 Motor scooters & parts

(G-1587)
RAUCKMAN UTILITY PRODUCTS LLC
33 Empire Dr (62220-3451)
PHONE..............................618 234-0001
David Reinke, *Sales Staff*
Shirley Rauckman, *Mng Member*
James Rauckman,
▲ **EMP:** 11
SALES (est): 900.9K **Privately Held**
SIC: 3629 Electronic generation equipment

GEOGRAPHIC SECTION

Bellwood - Cook County (G-1614)

(G-1588)
REBEL INC
1 Rebel Pkwy (62226-6820)
P.O. Box 525 (62222-0525)
PHONE.................................618 235-0582
William Dahlmann, *President*
Paul Kroener, *Vice Pres*
Mary Kaye Graves, *Treasurer*
Tim Graves, *Sales Staff*
Gary Bruner, *Admin Sec*
EMP: 40
SQ FT: 7,500
SALES (est): 590.7K **Privately Held**
SIC: 1742 1761 3444 Insulation, buildings; gutter & downspout contractor; sheet metalwork

(G-1589)
ROC INDUSTRIES INC
101 Industrial Dr (62220-3412)
PHONE.................................618 277-6044
EMP: 8
SQ FT: 16,000
SALES (est): 1.5MM **Privately Held**
SIC: 3559 Mfg Misc Industry Machinery

(G-1590)
ROESCH ACQUISITIONS LLC
100 N 24th St (62226-6659)
PHONE.................................618 233-2760
Michael Koenigstein, *Mng Member*
EMP: 74
SQ FT: 100,000
SALES (est): 2.2MM **Privately Held**
SIC: 3469 Porcelain enameled products & utensils

(G-1591)
ROGER JOLLY SKATEBOARDS
28 S 14th St (62220-1714)
PHONE.................................618 277-7113
EMP: 2
SALES (est): 242K **Privately Held**
SIC: 3949 Skateboards

(G-1592)
ROHO INC (DH)
100 N Florida Ave (62221-5429)
PHONE.................................618 277-9173
Tom Boucherding, *President*
Larry Jackson, *Vice Pres*
Carl Bandhold, *CFO*
Jerry Lafferty, *Director*
Chris Javillonar, *Admin Sec*
EMP: 55 **EST:** 2006
SQ FT: 75,000
SALES: 50MM
SALES (corp-wide): 5.7B **Privately Held**
SIC: 3842 Orthopedic appliances
HQ: The Roho Group Inc
 100 N Florida Ave
 Belleville IL 62221
 618 277-9173

(G-1593)
ROHO INC
1501 S 74th St (62223-5900)
PHONE.................................618 234-4899
Tom Borcherding, *President*
Dan Wagner, *Regional Mgr*
Cynthia Cremeens, *Sales Mgr*
Elizabeth Cole, *Director*
Dan Hughes, *Director*
EMP: 150
SALES (corp-wide): 5.7B **Privately Held**
WEB: www.permobilus.com
SIC: 3069 Molded rubber products
HQ: Roho, Inc.
 100 N Florida Ave
 Belleville IL 62221
 618 277-9173

(G-1594)
RTS SENTRY INC
4401 N Belt W (62226-5215)
PHONE.................................618 257-7100
David Hollenbeck, *President*
Brent Boyles, *Vice Pres*
EMP: 13
SQ FT: 40,000
SALES: 2MM **Privately Held**
SIC: 3699 Security devices

(G-1595)
SAFE EFFECTIVE ALTERNATIVES
Also Called: Lice B Gone
6218 Old Saint Louis Rd (62223-4533)
P.O. Box 528 (62222-0528)
PHONE.................................618 236-2727
Jim Rompel, *President*
Steve Macaluso, *Partner*
EMP: 10
SQ FT: 12,000
SALES (est): 2MM **Privately Held**
SIC: 5122 2844 Hair preparations; hair preparations, including shampoos

(G-1596)
SNOW PRINTING LLC
6428 Old Saint Louis Rd (62223-4597)
PHONE.................................618 233-0712
Pam Hollenkamp, *Partner*
Barb O'Donnell, *Partner*
EMP: 5
SQ FT: 2,500
SALES (est): 912.7K **Privately Held**
WEB: www.snowprinting.net
SIC: 2752 Commercial printing, offset

(G-1597)
TERRASOURCE GLOBAL CORPORATION
1 Freedom Dr (62226-5104)
P.O. Box 385 (62222-0385)
PHONE.................................618 641-6985
Todd Ruff, *Plant Mgr*
Doug Saton, *Manager*
Mike Hamby, *Director*
Dwight Evitt, *Administration*
EMP: 80 **Publicly Held**
WEB: www.terrasource.com
SIC: 3532 Mining machinery
HQ: Terrasource Global Corporation
 100 N Broadway Ste 1600
 Saint Louis MO 63102
 618 641-6966

(G-1598)
TINNEY TOOL & MACHINE CO
815 N Church St (62220-4151)
PHONE.................................618 236-7273
Robin Tinney, *President*
Karl Tinney, *General Mgr*
EMP: 7
SQ FT: 10,000
SALES: 550K **Privately Held**
SIC: 3599 Machine shop, jobbing & repair

(G-1599)
TISCH MONUMENTS INC (PA)
Also Called: Tisch Granite & Marble
17 N 3rd St (62220-1101)
PHONE.................................618 233-3017
Donald Tisch, *President*
EMP: 3
SALES (est): 371.1K **Privately Held**
SIC: 5999 3281 Monuments, finished to custom order; rock & stone specimens; cut stone & stone products

(G-1600)
TOCO
825 W Main St (62220-1516)
PHONE.................................618 257-8626
Robyn Combs, *Manager*
Lea Compton, *Manager*
Kim Vrooman, *Director*
EMP: 7 **EST:** 2010
SALES: 50K **Privately Held**
WEB: www.tocofamily.org
SIC: 2211 Tapestry fabrics, cotton

(G-1601)
TOWN HALL SPORTS INC
Also Called: Town Hall Archery
5901 Cool Sports Rd (62223-6848)
PHONE.................................618 235-9881
Jack Hoffarth Sr, *President*
Diana Hoffarth, *Vice Pres*
J Monty Hoffarth Jr, *Manager*
EMP: 11 **EST:** 1969
SQ FT: 20,000
SALES: 1.5MM **Privately Held**
SIC: 5999 2395 5941 Trophies & plaques; embroidery & art needlework; archery supplies

(G-1602)
TRIPLE STICKS FOODS LLC
9200 W Main St (62223-1728)
PHONE.................................800 468-3354
Joseph Trover, *Mng Member*
Terry Nelson, *Manager*
John Sadlo, *Manager*
EMP: 68
SALES (est): 7.6MM **Privately Held**
SIC: 2099 Sandwiches, assembled & packaged: for wholesale market

(G-1603)
TROVERCO INC (PA)
9200 W Main St Ste 1 (62223-1728)
PHONE.................................800 468-3354
Joseph E Trover Jr, *CEO*
Dale J Musick, *President*
Jim Hicks, *Controller*
▲ **EMP:** 40
SQ FT: 15,000
SALES (est): 96.4MM **Privately Held**
SIC: 2099 5149 Sandwiches, assembled & packaged: for wholesale market; coffee, green or roasted

(G-1604)
U MARK INC
102 Iowa Ave (62220-3940)
P.O. Box 411 (62222-0411)
PHONE.................................618 235-7500
Marco Ziniti, *CEO*
▲ **EMP:** 28
SQ FT: 16,000
SALES: 2.4MM **Privately Held**
SIC: 3951 3953 Markers, soft tip (felt, fabric, plastic, etc.); stencils, painting & marking

(G-1605)
UPCHURCH READY MIX CONCRETE
950 West Blvd (62221-4073)
PHONE.................................618 235-6222
Greg Upchurch, *Manager*
EMP: 3
SALES (corp-wide): 1MM **Privately Held**
SIC: 3273 4212 Ready-mixed concrete; local trucking, without storage
PA: Upchurch Ready Mix Concrete Inc
 564 Mildred Ave
 East Saint Louis IL
 618 332-2954

(G-1606)
VI INC
1801 N Belt W Ste 4 (62226-8201)
PHONE.................................618 277-8703
John Massen, *President*
Joe Vassen, *Admin Sec*
EMP: 2 **EST:** 1999
SALES (est): 305.8K **Privately Held**
SIC: 3679 Electronic loads & power supplies

(G-1607)
VILLAGE TYPOGRAPHERS INC
1381 Rocky Creek Ct (62220-3082)
PHONE.................................618 235-6756
Daniel D Franklin, *President*
Terry Yokota, *Vice Pres*
EMP: 2
SALES (est): 247K **Privately Held**
SIC: 2791 Typographic composition, for the printing trade; typesetting, computer controlled

(G-1608)
VOGES INC (PA)
100 N 24th St (62226-6659)
P.O. Box 328 (62222-0328)
PHONE.................................618 233-2760
Pauline V Voges, *President*
Debra L Voges, *Exec VP*
Debra Voges-Schneider, *Exec VP*
Robert Voges, *Purch Mgr*
Chris Crowell, *QC Mgr*
▲ **EMP:** 60 **EST:** 1916
SQ FT: 140,000
SALES (est): 14.7MM **Privately Held**
WEB: www.roeschinc.com
SIC: 3469 3585 3479 3441 Appliance parts, porcelain enameled; air conditioning equipment, complete; aluminum coating of metal products; fabricated structural metal; porcelain electrical supplies; paints & allied products

(G-1609)
VOSS PATTERN WORKS INC
123 Iowa Ave (62220-3941)
PHONE.................................618 233-4242
Joseph Voss, *President*
Mina Voss, *Treasurer*
EMP: 7 **EST:** 1921
SQ FT: 5,000
SALES (est): 450K **Privately Held**
SIC: 3544 2796 5999 3499 Industrial molds; engraving on copper, steel, wood or rubber: printing plates; banners, flags, decals & posters; trophies, metal, except silver; industrial patterns

(G-1610)
WEINGARTEN LLC
1780 E State Route 15 (62221-8709)
PHONE.................................618 973-1879
Shannon Gastreich, *Principal*
EMP: 7
SALES (est): 529.1K **Privately Held**
WEB: www.theweingarten.com
SIC: 2084 Wines

(G-1611)
WEISS MONUMENT WORKS INC
Also Called: Philip W Weiss Monument Works
9904 W Main St (62223-1405)
PHONE.................................618 398-1811
Philip W Weiss, *President*
Cheryl Weiss, *Treasurer*
Joni Pascasio, *Sales Mgr*
▲ **EMP:** 3
SALES (est): 534.1K **Privately Held**
WEB: www.weissmonumentworks.com
SIC: 5999 3281 7389 Gravestones, finished; cut stone & stone products;

(G-1612)
WIEMAN FUELS LP GAS COMPANY
418 S Belt E (62220-2652)
PHONE.................................618 632-4015
David Young, *Manager*
EMP: 3 **EST:** 2010
SALES (est): 178.6K **Privately Held**
SIC: 2869 Fuels

Bellwood
Cook County

(G-1613)
ALDONEX INC
2917 Saint Charles Rd (60104-1543)
P.O. Box 148 (60104-0148)
PHONE.................................708 547-5663
Alan Miller, *President*
Wanda Miller, *Corp Secy*
EMP: 15
SQ FT: 27,000
SALES (est): 3.2MM **Privately Held**
WEB: www.aldonex.com
SIC: 3612 5063 Specialty transformers; rectifier transformers; power & distribution transformers; transformers & transmission equipment; transformers, electric; power transmission equipment, electric

(G-1614)
ASAP PALLETS INC
2711 Washington Blvd (60104-1941)
PHONE.................................630 917-0180
Maria Rodriguez, *Principal*
EMP: 6
SALES (corp-wide): 2.1MM **Privately Held**
WEB: www.asappalletsinc.com
SIC: 2448 Pallets, wood & wood with metal
PA: Asap Pallets Inc
 480 Podlin Dr
 Franklin Park IL 60131
 630 350-7689

Bellwood - Cook County (G-1615)

(G-1615)
BELLWOOD ELECTRIC MOTORS INC
200 25th Ave (60104-1203)
PHONE....................708 544-7223
Angelica Meza, *President*
Martha Meza, *Manager*
EMP: 7 **EST:** 1962
SQ FT: 5,000
SALES (est): 1.5MM **Privately Held**
WEB: www.bellwoodelectricmotors.com
SIC: 7694 5063 Electric motor repair; motors, electric

(G-1616)
BERGHAUS PIPE ORGAN BUILDERS
2151 Madison St Ste 1 (60104-1973)
PHONE....................708 544-4052
Leonard G Berghaus, *CEO*
Brian Berghaus, *President*
Collene Berghaus, *Treasurer*
Jean Obrien, *Office Mgr*
Judith Berghaus, *Shareholder*
EMP: 22
SQ FT: 30,000
SALES (est): 2.8MM **Privately Held**
SIC: 3931 7699 Organs, all types: pipe, reed, hand, electronic, etc.; organ tuning & repair

(G-1617)
BORGWARNER INC
700 25th Ave (60104-1908)
PHONE....................248 754-9200
Tom Hardies, *Business Mgr*
Jose Martinez, *Receiver*
Brad Bakall, *Senior Buyer*
Ron Kambach, *Buyer*
Sergio Gonzalez, *Engineer*
EMP: 30
SALES (corp-wide): 10.1B **Publicly Held**
SIC: 3714 Motor vehicle engines & parts
PA: Borgwarner Inc.
3850 Hamlin Rd
Auburn Hills MI 48326
248 754-9200

(G-1618)
BORGWARNER TRANSM SYSTEMS INC
Also Called: Borg Warner Automotive
700 25th Ave (60104-1908)
PHONE....................708 547-2600
Patrick Johnson, *Principal*
Nick Dalton, *Branch Mgr*
EMP: 820
SALES (corp-wide): 10.1B **Publicly Held**
SIC: 3714 3568 3469 3465 Transmissions, motor vehicle; power transmission equipment; metal stampings; automotive stampings
HQ: Borgwarner Transmission Systems Inc.
3800 Automation Ave # 500
Auburn Hills MI 48326
248 754-9200

(G-1619)
COMBINED METALS HOLDING INC
2401 Grant Ave (60104-1660)
PHONE....................708 547-8800
Cyrus Tang, *President*
EMP: 112
SALES (est): 7.6MM
SALES (corp-wide): 1.9B **Publicly Held**
SIC: 3312 3325 Blast furnaces & steel mills; steel foundries
HQ: Ak Steel Corporation
9227 Centre Pointe Dr
West Chester OH 45069

(G-1620)
D A MATOT INC
2501 Van Buren St (60104-2459)
PHONE....................708 547-1888
Anne Matot, *President*
Anne M Kolker, *Principal*
Steve Reynolds, *Engineer*
Kathryn Matot, *Admin Sec*
▼ **EMP:** 60 **EST:** 1888
SQ FT: 40,000
SALES (est): 15.8MM **Privately Held**
WEB: www.matot.com
SIC: 3534 Elevators & equipment; dumbwaiters

(G-1621)
DELTROL CORP
Also Called: Deltrol Fluid Products
3001 Grant Ave (60104-1289)
PHONE....................708 547-0500
Paul Goc, *Plant Mgr*
Dan Pruger, *Maint Mgr*
Ken Harner, *Purch Mgr*
Maria Flynn, *Purchasing*
Underwood Dan, *Engineer*
EMP: 125
SALES (corp-wide): 54.5MM **Privately Held**
WEB: www.deltrolcontrols.com
SIC: 3625 3594 3494 3492 Relays, for electronic use; fluid power pumps & motors; valves & pipe fittings; fluid power valves & hose fittings; industrial valves
PA: Deltrol Corp.
2740 S 20th St
Milwaukee WI 53215
414 671-6800

(G-1622)
DOUGLAS PRESS INC
2810 Madison St (60104-2295)
PHONE....................800 323-0705
Debra Fienberg, *President*
Sandra Fienberg, *Vice Pres*
Bill Thinnes, *Vice Pres*
Bill Thieness, *VP Opers*
Lamonte Walker, *Safety Dir*
EMP: 250
SQ FT: 17,500
SALES (est): 44.1MM **Privately Held**
WEB: www.douglaspress.com
SIC: 2752 Commercial printing, offset

(G-1623)
DRS ELECTROSTATIC PAINTING
4113 Butterfield Rd (60104-1743)
P.O. Box 352, Wood Dale (60191-0352)
PHONE....................708 681-5535
Daniel Slavik, *President*
Gary Slavik, *Treasurer*
EMP: 3 **EST:** 1960
SQ FT: 7,000
SALES: 500K **Privately Held**
SIC: 3479 Painting of metal products; coating of metals with silicon

(G-1624)
FERRARA CANDY COMPANY
3000 Washington Blvd (60104-1946)
PHONE....................708 432-4407
Eric Williams, *Project Engr*
Ron Montefusco, *Branch Mgr*
EMP: 15
SALES (corp-wide): 228MM **Privately Held**
SIC: 2064 Chewing candy, not chewing gum
HQ: Ferrara Candy Company
404 W Harrison St 650s
Chicago IL 60607
708 366-0500

(G-1625)
G J NIKOLAS & CO INC
2800 Washington Blvd (60104-1987)
PHONE....................708 544-0320
George J Nikolas Jr, *President*
Jacob Koch, *Exec VP*
James Koch, *Vice Pres*
▼ **EMP:** 20
SQ FT: 26,000
SALES (est): 5.3MM **Privately Held**
WEB: www.finish1.com
SIC: 2851 2891 Lacquer: bases, dopes, thinner; adhesives & sealants

(G-1626)
GRPHIC RICHARDS COMMUNICATIONS
2700 Van Buren St (60104-2409)
PHONE....................708 547-6000
Mary Lawrence, *President*
Kevin Richards, *Vice Pres*
Stephen H Richards, *Vice Pres*
Steve Mueller, *Engineer*
Jon Richards, *Executive*
EMP: 15 **EST:** 1925
SQ FT: 19,500
SALES: 3MM **Privately Held**
WEB: www.rgcnet.com
SIC: 2752 Commercial printing, offset

(G-1627)
H A FRAMBURG & COMPANY (PA)
941 Cernan Dr (60104-2294)
PHONE....................708 547-5757
Malcolm Tripp, *President*
Roberta Sikorsik, *Vice Pres*
David Jadrich, *Plant Supt*
Jeff Sokol, *Facilities Mgr*
▲ **EMP:** 36 **EST:** 1905
SQ FT: 75,000
SALES (est): 6.5MM **Privately Held**
WEB: www.framburg.com
SIC: 3645 3646 Residential lighting fixtures; commercial indusl & institutional electric lighting fixtures

(G-1628)
INTRA ACTION CORP
3719 Warren Ave (60104-2055)
PHONE....................708 547-6644
John A Lekavich, *President*
Jeanne Weiler, *Materials Mgr*
Mike Strijny, *Finance Dir*
Bernadette Panovich, *Admin Sec*
EMP: 32
SQ FT: 10,000
SALES (est): 6.7MM **Privately Held**
SIC: 3827 Optical instruments & apparatus

(G-1629)
JAMALI KOPY KAT PRINTING INC
2501 Saint Charles Rd (60104-1503)
PHONE....................708 544-6164
Dawood I Burhani, *President*
EMP: 3
SQ FT: 1,000
SALES: 200K **Privately Held**
SIC: 2752 7334 3993 7336 Commercial printing, offset; photocopying & duplicating services; signs & advertising specialties; graphic arts & related design

(G-1630)
JOHNSON STEEL RULE & DIE
2600 Washington Blvd A (60104-1953)
PHONE....................708 547-1726
William Drew, *Principal*
EMP: 6
SALES (est): 278.7K **Privately Held**
SIC: 3544 Dies, steel rule; special dies & tools

(G-1631)
LEZZA SPUMONI AND DESSERTS INC
4009 Saint Charles Rd (60104-1197)
PHONE....................708 547-5969
Edward S Lezza, *President*
Rosemarie Lezza, *Corp Secy*
Edward S Lezza Jr, *Vice Pres*
Victor E Lezza, *Vice Pres*
Louis Lezza, *VP Sales*
EMP: 22 **EST:** 1905
SQ FT: 10,000
SALES: 5MM **Privately Held**
WEB: www.lezza.com
SIC: 2024 2038 Ice cream & frozen desserts; frozen specialties

(G-1632)
MAJESTIC ARCHTCTURAL WDWRK INC
2150 Madison St (60104-1952)
PHONE....................708 240-8484
Mary V Dorio, *President*
EMP: 5 **EST:** 2011
SALES (est): 625.5K **Privately Held**
SIC: 2431 Millwork

(G-1633)
MARO CARTON INC
333 31st Ave (60104-1527)
PHONE....................708 649-9982
Joseph J Maro III, *President*
EMP: 2
SALES (est): 378.7K **Privately Held**
SIC: 2759 Commercial printing

(G-1634)
MOBILIA INC
1023 Cernan Dr (60104-2462)
PHONE....................708 865-0700
Melchiore Bonfiglio, *President*
Pat Smith, *Sales Staff*
EMP: 20
SQ FT: 35,000
SALES (est): 3MM **Privately Held**
SIC: 2521 2511 Wood office furniture; wood household furniture

(G-1635)
ORTMAN-MCCAIN CO
2715 Grant Ave (60104-1247)
PHONE....................312 666-2244
Nancy Newberger, *President*
David Allison, *Vice Pres*
EMP: 8 **EST:** 1947
SALES (est): 884.4K **Privately Held**
SIC: 3555 3563 Printing trades machinery; air & gas compressors

(G-1636)
R K J PALLETS INC
Also Called: Kitty Pallets
1003 Cernan Dr (60104-2462)
PHONE....................708 493-0701
Jesus Rodriguez, *President*
Nitza Anaya, *Principal*
Bill Galliger, *Principal*
Ray Rodriguez, *Vice Pres*
EMP: 10
SQ FT: 11,000
SALES: 608.7K **Privately Held**
SIC: 2448 Pallets, wood

(G-1637)
SB BORON CORPORATION
Also Called: Sb Boron
20 Davis Dr (60104-1047)
PHONE....................708 547-9002
Gary Resnick, *President*
Joel Stone, *Admin Sec*
▲ **EMP:** 9
SQ FT: 11,000
SALES (est): 1.6MM **Privately Held**
SIC: 2869 Industrial organic chemicals

(G-1638)
SHAMROCK SCIENTIFIC
Also Called: Shamrock Labels
34 Davis Dr (60104-1047)
PHONE....................800 323-0249
James Kornfeld, *President*
David Klonowski, *CFO*
EMP: 44 **EST:** 2016
SALES (est): 1MM
SALES (corp-wide): 95.6MM **Privately Held**
SIC: 2759 Labels & seals: printing; calendars; printing
PA: Pax Holdings, Llc
735 N Water St Ste 735 # 735
Milwaukee WI 53202
414 803-9983

(G-1639)
SKILL-DI INC
2655 Harrison St (60104-2463)
PHONE....................708 544-6080
Michael D Rosenquist, *President*
Richard Rosenquist, *Corp Secy*
EMP: 10 **EST:** 1951
SQ FT: 23,500
SALES (est): 1.7MM **Privately Held**
SIC: 3469 Stamping metal for the trade

(G-1640)
STEELE & LOEBER LUMBER (HQ)
801 Mannheim Rd (60104-2073)
PHONE....................708 544-8383
Richard Loeber, *President*
EMP: 6
SQ FT: 1,500
SALES: 843.4K
SALES (corp-wide): 3.6MM **Privately Held**
SIC: 3442 Metal doors
PA: Steele And Loeber Lumber Co.
801 Mannheim Rd
Bellwood IL 60104
708 636-5660

GEOGRAPHIC SECTION

Belvidere - Boone County (G-1667)

(G-1641)
TRU COAT PLATING AND FINISHING
130 Mannheim Rd (60104-1143)
PHONE..................................708 544-3940
Carmine N Mazzone Jr, *President*
Susan Ocwieja, *Corp Secy*
Rick Mazzone, *Vice Pres*
EMP: 12 **EST:** 1961
SQ FT: 14,000
SALES (est): 1MM **Privately Held**
SIC: 3471 Chromium plating of metals or formed products; plating of metals or formed products

(G-1642)
W-R INDUSTRIES INC
2715 Grant Ave (60104-1247)
PHONE..................................312 733-5200
Nancy Newberger, *President*
David Allison, *Vice Pres*
Anne Arnet, *Office Mgr*
▲ **EMP:** 7 **EST:** 1896
SALES (est): 1.5MM **Privately Held**
SIC: 2836 2844 Biological products, except diagnostic; toilet preparations

(G-1643)
WEST CHICAGO PLASTICS CORP
700 24th Ave (60104-1929)
PHONE..................................708 582-4014
Israel Torres, *Principal*
EMP: 3 **EST:** 2018
SALES (est): 159.5K **Privately Held**
SIC: 3089 Injection molding of plastics

Belvidere
Boone County

(G-1644)
ACME GRINDING & MANUFACTURING
6871 Belford Indus Dr (61008-8712)
P.O. Box 509 (61008-0509)
PHONE..................................815 323-1380
Jack Zaluckyj, *President*
Chuck Zaluckyj, *President*
Aaron Nicely, *Maintence Staff*
EMP: 110
SQ FT: 55,000
SALES (est): 2.3MM **Privately Held**
WEB: www.acmegrinding.com
SIC: 3599 Grinding castings for the trade

(G-1645)
AERO PLASTICS AND SUPPLY
754 Landmark Dr (61008-6715)
PHONE..................................815 975-9305
Britt Anderson, *President*
EMP: 2 **EST:** 2015
SALES (est): 214.2K **Privately Held**
WEB: www.aeroplasticsandsupply.com
SIC: 3599 Machine shop, jobbing & repair

(G-1646)
AERO PLASTICS AND SUPPLY CO
756 Landmark Dr (61008-6715)
PHONE..................................847 553-5578
Eric Kruger, *Principal*
EMP: 3
SALES (est): 445.6K **Privately Held**
WEB: www.aeroplasticsandsupply.com
SIC: 3599 Machine shop, jobbing & repair

(G-1647)
AIRO TOOL & MANUFACTURING INC
6823 Irene Rd (61008-8789)
PHONE..................................815 547-7588
Heidi Abramat, *President*
Roy Abramat, *Vice Pres*
Rachel Abramat, *Accounts Mgr*
Andrew Abramat, *Admin Sec*
▲ **EMP:** 15
SQ FT: 6,000
SALES (est): 2.8MM **Privately Held**
SIC: 3544 3599 Special dies & tools; machine shop, jobbing & repair

(G-1648)
AMERICAN COLLOID COMPANY
Also Called: Amcol
2786 Newburg Rd (61008-7997)
P.O. Box 37 (61008-0037)
PHONE..................................815 547-5369
Heather Bohn, *Manager*
EMP: 12 **Publicly Held**
SIC: 1459 Clays, except kaolin & ball
HQ: American Colloid Company
2870 Forbs Ave
Hoffman Estates IL 60192

(G-1649)
ANDROID INDSTRES- BLVIDERE LLC
1222 Crosslink Pkwy (61008-6310)
PHONE..................................815 547-3742
Dennis Donnay, *Plant Mgr*
Butch Elmer, *Engineer*
Gregory Nichols,
EMP: 220
SALES (est): 69.3MM
SALES (corp-wide): 584.1MM **Privately Held**
SIC: 3714 Motor vehicle parts & accessories
PA: Android Industries, L.L.C.
2155 Executive Hills Dr
Auburn Hills MI 48326
248 454-0500

(G-1650)
ARROWTECH PALLET & CRATING
860 E Jackson St (61008-2332)
PHONE..................................815 547-9300
John T Swenby, *President*
Ray Ridriguez, *Treasurer*
Larry W Johnson, *Admin Sec*
EMP: 60
SQ FT: 10,000
SALES (est): 3.7MM **Privately Held**
SIC: 2448 5031 2441 Pallets, wood; skids, wood; building materials, exterior; building materials, interior; nailed wood boxes & shook

(G-1651)
AWEGO ENTERPRISES INC
Also Called: Pet Loader
2967 Country Meadow Ln (61008-8511)
P.O. Box 27, Caledonia (61011-0027)
PHONE..................................815 765-1957
Evon Whalen, *President*
Robert Whalen, *Vice Pres*
▲ **EMP:** 5
SALES (est): 604.9K **Privately Held**
SIC: 3999 2399 Pet supplies; pet collars, leashes, etc.: non-leather

(G-1652)
BELROCK PRINTING INC
915 W Perry St (61008-3420)
PHONE..................................815 547-1096
Patrick Mattison, *President*
EMP: 4
SALES (est): 130.3K **Privately Held**
SIC: 2752 Commercial printing, offset

(G-1653)
BELVEDERE USA LLC (PA)
1 Belvedere Blvd (61008-8594)
PHONE..................................815 544-3131
Barry Sanders, *President*
Jerry Grossi, *General Mgr*
Horst Ackermann, *COO*
Chuck Jones, *Purch Dir*
Kevin McGraw, *Buyer*
▲ **EMP:** 180 **EST:** 1927
SALES (est): 69.6MM **Privately Held**
SIC: 3999 Barber & beauty shop equipment; chairs, hydraulic, barber & beauty shop; furniture, barber & beauty shop; massage machines, electric: barber & beauty shops

(G-1654)
BELVIDERE BROSE INC
725 Logistics Dr (61008-8507)
PHONE..................................779 552-7600
Michael Brosseau, *President*
Holly Swanson, *Admin Sec*
EMP: 14

SALES (est): 4.3MM **Privately Held**
SIC: 3714 Motor vehicle parts & accessories

(G-1655)
BELVIDERE DAILY REPUBLICAN CO
130 S State St Ste 101 (61008-3772)
PHONE..................................815 547-0084
Keith Cruger, *President*
EMP: 40
SQ FT: 13,000
SALES (est): 1.6MM **Privately Held**
WEB: www.bdrnews.com
SIC: 2711 Commercial printing & newspaper publishing combined

(G-1656)
BOONE COUNTY SHOPPER INC
112 Leonard Ct (61008-3694)
PHONE..................................815 544-2166
Ed Branom, *President*
Yvonne Branom, *President*
Joseph Bradaseric, *Director*
EMP: 17 **EST:** 1948
SQ FT: 8,000
SALES (est): 1.3MM **Privately Held**
WEB: www.boonecountyshopper.com
SIC: 2741 2711 Shopping news: publishing only, not printed on site; newspapers

(G-1657)
BT & E CO
6877 Belford Indus Dr (61008-8712)
P.O. Box 248 (61008-0248)
PHONE..................................815 544-6431
Robert A Buelte, *President*
Lavon Buelte, *Admin Sec*
EMP: 9 **EST:** 1945
SQ FT: 24,000
SALES: 1.1MM **Privately Held**
WEB: www.btetooling.com
SIC: 7389 3544 Grinding, precision: commercial or industrial; special dies & tools

(G-1658)
CAISSON INC (PA)
Also called: Interserve
720 Logistics Dr (61008-8507)
PHONE..................................815 547-5925
Dana T Richardson, *President*
Bill Ports, *Accounts Exec*
EMP: 21 **EST:** 1995
SQ FT: 35,000
SALES (est): 4.6MM **Privately Held**
SIC: 2449 2448 Rectangular boxes & crates, wood; skids, wood

(G-1659)
CAMCAR LLC
Also Called: Acument Tm Global Technologies
826 E Madison St (61008-2899)
PHONE..................................815 544-7574
Diana Tripp, *Regional Mgr*
Keith Holmes, *Manager*
EMP: 39 **Privately Held**
WEB: www.acument.com
SIC: 3452 Bolts, nuts, rivets & washers
HQ: Camcar Llc
6125 18 Mile Rd
Sterling Heights MI 48314
586 254-3900

(G-1660)
CAMRYN INDUSTRIES LLC
3458 Morreim Dr (61008-6308)
PHONE..................................815 544-1900
EMP: 150
SALES (corp-wide): 74K **Privately Held**
SIC: 2821 Mfg Plastic Materials/Resins
HQ: Camryn Industries, Llc
21624 Melrose Ave
Southfield MI 48075

(G-1661)
CENTRAL RUBBER COMPANY
844 E Jackson St (61008-2332)
PHONE..................................815 544-2191
J Michael Nauman, *President*
▲ **EMP:** 43
SQ FT: 36,000

SALES (est): 6.9MM
SALES (corp-wide): 48.9B **Privately Held**
WEB: www.centralrubbercompany.com
SIC: 3678 3679 3643 3357 Electronic connectors; electronic switches; electronic circuits; connectors & terminals for electrical devices; communication wire; fiber optic cable (insulated)
HQ: Woodhead Industries, Llc
333 Knightsbridge Pkwy # 200
Lincolnshire IL 60069
847 353-2500

(G-1662)
CHEMSCI TECHNOLOGIES INC
6574 Revlon Dr (61008-8532)
PHONE..................................815 608-9135
Kenn Blair, *President*
▲ **EMP:** 2 **EST:** 2008
SQ FT: 2,800
SALES (est): 211.8K **Privately Held**
WEB: www.chemscitech.com
SIC: 2833 Medicinal chemicals

(G-1663)
CORRUGATED METALS INC
6550 Revlon Dr (61008-8532)
PHONE..................................815 323-1310
Edward S Carlton Jr, *President*
Kenneth E Carlton, *Corp Secy*
Thomas J Carlton, *Vice Pres*
Manuela Martinez, *Traffic Mgr*
Jordan Hastings, *Sales Staff*
EMP: 18
SQ FT: 35,125
SALES (est): 9.8MM **Privately Held**
WEB: www.corrugated-metals.com
SIC: 3444 Roof deck, sheet metal; siding, sheet metal

(G-1664)
CURTIS WOODWORKING INC
4820 Newburg Rd (61008-7195)
PHONE..................................815 544-3543
Curtis Sherman, *CEO*
Courtney D Sherman, *Vice Pres*
EMP: 2
SALES: 200K **Privately Held**
SIC: 2499 2431 Decorative wood & woodwork; millwork

(G-1665)
DEAN DAIRY ICE CREAM LLC
630 Meadow St (61008-3328)
PHONE..................................815 544-2105
Dave Bell, *Plant Supt*
Dale Foltz, *Plant Mgr*
Greg Delzer, *QC Dir*
Al Szarzynski, *Engineer*
David Hilton, *Plant Engr*
EMP: 100
SALES (corp-wide): 15.8B **Privately Held**
WEB: www.deanfoods.com
SIC: 2026 Fluid milk
HQ: Dfa Dairy Brands Ice Cream, Llc
1405 N 98th St
Kansas City KS 66111
816 801-6455

(G-1666)
DODGE MACHINE TOOL
204 S Main St (61008-3320)
P.O. Box 589 (61008-0589)
PHONE..................................815 544-0967
Gary Dodge, *President*
Charlotte Dodge, *Managing Prtnr*
Kavin Dodge, *Treasurer*
EMP: 4 **EST:** 1979
SQ FT: 3,500
SALES (est): 454.9K **Privately Held**
SIC: 3599 Machine shop, jobbing & repair

(G-1667)
FAST LANE THREADS CUSTOM EMB
1467 Mckinley Ave Ste A (61008-1360)
P.O. Box 866 (61008-0866)
PHONE..................................815 544-9898
EMP: 5
SALES (est): 200K **Privately Held**
SIC: 2395 2396 5699 Emblems, embroidered; printing & embossing on plastics fabric articles; customized clothing & apparel

Belvidere - Boone County (G-1668)   GEOGRAPHIC SECTION

(G-1668)
FRANKLIN DISPLAY GROUP INC (PA)
910 E Lincoln Ave (61008-2928)
P.O. Box 127 (61008-0127)
PHONE..................815 544-6676
George Mutert, *President*
Donald Mutert Jr, *Admin Sec*
▲ **EMP:** 90 **EST:** 1978
SQ FT: 87,000
SALES (est): 25.9MM **Privately Held**
SIC: 3999 Advertising display products

(G-1669)
FRANKLIN DISPLAY GROUP INC
725 Landmark Dr (61008-6715)
PHONE..................815 544-5300
Sue Raupp, *Branch Mgr*
EMP: 5
SALES (corp-wide): 25.9MM **Privately Held**
SIC: 3496 Miscellaneous fabricated wire products
PA: Franklin Display Group, Inc.
910 E Lincoln Ave
Belvidere IL 61008
815 544-6676

(G-1670)
FRANKLIN WIRE WORKS INC
2519 Business Route 20 (61008-8717)
P.O. Box 127 (61008-0127)
PHONE..................815 544-6676
Fax: 815 547-9239
EMP: 2
SALES (est): 300.8K **Privately Held**
SIC: 3496 Mfg Misc Fabricated Wire Products

(G-1671)
GENERAL MILLS INC
915 E Pleasant St (61008-3350)
PHONE..................815 544-7399
Ronda Zimmerman-Turne, *Human Res Dir*
Ronda Zimmerman, *Human Resources*
Vince Castle, *Branch Mgr*
Don Beck, *Manager*
EMP: 50
SALES (corp-wide): 16.8B **Publicly Held**
SIC: 2033 2037 2038 Vegetables: packaged in cans, jars, etc.; vegetables, quick frozen & cold pack, excl. potato products; frozen specialties
PA: General Mills, Inc.
1 General Mills Blvd
Minneapolis MN 55426
763 764-7600

(G-1672)
GENERAL MILLS GREEN GIANT
725 Landmark Dr (61008-6715)
PHONE..................815 547-5311
Chris Masters, *Principal*
EMP: 3
SALES (est): 189.3K **Privately Held**
SIC: 2038 Frozen specialties

(G-1673)
GERDAU AMERISTEEL US INC
2595 Tripp Rd (61008-7206)
PHONE..................815 547-0400
Mike Hand, *Branch Mgr*
EMP: 50 **Privately Held**
SIC: 3444 3449 3441 Concrete forms, sheet metal; miscellaneous metalwork; fabricated structural metal
HQ: Gerdau Ameristeel Us Inc.
4221 W Boy Scout Blvd # 600
Tampa FL 33607
813 286-8383

(G-1674)
GRUPO ANTOLIN ILLINOIS INC
642 Crystal Pkwy (61008-4065)
PHONE..................815 544-8020
Russ Goemaere, *President*
Joseph Maximilan Rogers, *Principal*
Piotr Rowny, *Maint Spvr*
Kraig Hug, *Buyer*
Caitlin Larose, *Buyer*
EMP: 180
SALES (est): 24.9MM
SALES (corp-wide): 33.3MM **Privately Held**
SIC: 8741 3714 Management services; motor vehicle parts & accessories
HQ: Grupo Antolin-Irausa Sa
Carretera Madrid-Irun (Burgos) (- Km 244,8)
Burgos 09007
947 477-700

(G-1675)
GYMTEK INCORPORATED
6853 Indy Dr (61008-8769)
PHONE..................815 547-0771
Mary Yankus, *President*
EMP: 19
SQ FT: 20,000
SALES (est): 3.3MM **Privately Held**
SIC: 3599 Machine shop, jobbing & repair

(G-1676)
HALLEN BURIAL VAULT INC
3690 Newburg Rd (61008-8529)
P.O. Box 557 (61008-0557)
PHONE..................815 544-6138
Donald Freund, *President*
EMP: 6
SALES (est): 808.5K **Privately Held**
SIC: 3272 Burial vaults, concrete or precast terrazzo

(G-1677)
HOPPERSTAD CUSTOMS
6860 Imron Dr (61008-8587)
PHONE..................815 547-7534
Kerry Hopperstad, *Owner*
EMP: 2
SALES (est): 209.1K **Privately Held**
SIC: 3711 Motor vehicles & car bodies

(G-1678)
INFRASTRUCTURE DEF TECH LLC
6550 Revlon Dr (61008-8532)
PHONE..................800 379-1822
Ken Carlton, *Exec VP*
Joe Sheil, *VP Mktg*
Kenneth Carlton,
EMP: 2
SALES (est): 700K **Privately Held**
SIC: 3499 Barricades, metal

(G-1679)
INK ENTERPRISES INC
Also Called: I E Press & Graphics
9594 Ruth Ct (61008-8969)
PHONE..................815 547-5515
Donna K Bates, *President*
John W Bates, *Vice Pres*
EMP: 5
SALES (est): 591.9K **Privately Held**
SIC: 2752 Commercial printing, offset

(G-1680)
INTERNATIONAL AUTOMOTIVE COMPO
Also Called: IAC Belvidere
1236 Crosslink Pkwy (61008-6310)
PHONE..................815 544-2102
EMP: 273 **Privately Held**
SIC: 3089 Automotive parts, plastic
HQ: International Automotive Components Group North America, Inc.
28333 Telegraph Rd
Southfield MI 48034

(G-1681)
M & M PALTECH INC
Also Called: Paltech Enterprises Illinois
860 E Jackson St (61008-2332)
PHONE..................630 350-7890
John Swenby, *President*
Ray Rodriguez, *Treasurer*
Larry Johnson, *Admin Sec*
EMP: 60
SQ FT: 17,000
SALES (est): 11.1MM **Privately Held**
SIC: 2448 5031 5199 Pallets, wood; lumber, plywood & millwork; baling of wood shavings for mulch

(G-1682)
M & R CUSTOM MILLWORK INC
1979 Belford North Dr (61008-8582)
PHONE..................815 547-8549
Mark B Roden, *President*
Mark Roden, *President*
Renita L Roden, *Partner*
EMP: 5
SALES (est): 786.3K **Privately Held**
SIC: 2499 2541 2434 2431 Kitchen, bathroom & household ware: wood; wood partitions & fixtures; wood kitchen cabinets; millwork

(G-1683)
MAGNA EXTERIORS AMERICA INC
Magna Exteriors Belvidere
675 Corporate Pkwy (61008-4079)
PHONE..................779 552-7400
Josh Gasaway, *General Mgr*
EMP: 55
SALES (corp-wide): 39.4B **Privately Held**
SIC: 3089 Automotive parts, plastic
HQ: Magna Exteriors Of America, Inc.
750 Tower Dr
Troy MI 48098
248 631-1100

(G-1684)
MANITOU AMERICAS INC
Also Called: Gehl Company
888 Landmark Dr (61008-6715)
PHONE..................262 334-9461
Kevin Hogan, *President*
EMP: 7
SALES (corp-wide): 1.5B **Privately Held**
SIC: 3531 3523 Backhoes, tractors, cranes, plows & similar equipment; dozers, tractor mounted: material moving: cranes; excavators: cable, clamshell, crane, derrick, dragline, etc.; farm machinery & equipment; haying machines: mowers, rakes, stackers, etc.; balers, farm: hay, straw, cotton, etc.; harvesters, fruit, vegetable, tobacco, etc.
HQ: Manitou America Holding, Inc.
1 Gehl Way
West Bend WI 53095
262 334-9461

(G-1685)
MCDONNELL COMPONENTS INC
828 Landmark Dr (61008-6715)
P.O. Box 1678 (61008-1240)
PHONE..................815 547-9555
Tim McDonnell, *President*
Tim Schnoor, *Vice Pres*
EMP: 52
SQ FT: 10,000
SALES (est): 6MM **Privately Held**
SIC: 2452 5031 Panels & sections, prefabricated, wood; lumber, plywood & millwork

(G-1686)
MID-WEST FEEDER INC
Also Called: Midwest Feeder
601 E Pleasant St (61008-3300)
PHONE..................815 544-2994
Cindy Gustasson, *President*
Timothy Greenfield, *Vice Pres*
Cynthia Gustafson, *Treasurer*
EMP: 22
SQ FT: 11,000
SALES (est): 3.6MM **Privately Held**
SIC: 3545 Machine tool attachments & accessories; hopper feed devices

(G-1687)
MIDWEST ICE CREAM COMPANY LLC
630 Meadow St (61008-3328)
PHONE..................815 544-2105
Dale Foltz, *Mng Member*
EMP: 13
SALES (est): 3.1MM **Publicly Held**
SIC: 2026 Fluid milk
HQ: Dean East Ii, Llc
2515 Mckinney Ave # 1100
Dallas TX 75201

(G-1688)
NARITA MANUFACTURING INC
828 Landmark Dr (61008-6715)
PHONE..................248 345-1777
William Murakami, *Vice Pres*
EMP: 10 **EST:** 2012
SALES (est): 1.2MM **Privately Held**
SIC: 3743 3944 Train cars & equipment, freight or passenger; trains & equipment, toy: electric & mechanical

(G-1689)
NORTHERN ILLINOIS WILBERT VLT
Also Called: Northern Ill Wilbert Vlt Co
845 E Jackson St (61008-2341)
P.O. Box 252 (61008-0252)
PHONE..................815 544-3355
Michael Banks, *President*
Kathy Banks, *Corp Secy*
Sterling Wilbert, *Products*
EMP: 8
SQ FT: 15,000
SALES (est): 1MM **Privately Held**
SIC: 3272 7261 Burial vaults, concrete or precast terrazzo; funeral service & crematories

(G-1690)
NORTHERN PRECISION PLASTIC INC
Also Called: Northern Precision Plastics
6553 Revlon Dr (61008-7843)
PHONE..................815 544-8099
Robert Milnichuk, *President*
Jere Eyer, *Admin Sec*
▲ **EMP:** 35
SQ FT: 35,000
SALES (est): 6.7MM **Privately Held**
SIC: 3089 Injection molding of plastics; thermoformed finished plastic products

(G-1691)
NORTHWEST PALLET SERVICES LLC
3648 Morreim Dr (61008-6346)
PHONE..................815 544-6001
Jack Donnell, *CEO*
Brent Duelm, *COO*
Joseph Keenan, *General Counsel*
EMP: 716
SQ FT: 156,900
SALES (est): 91.1MM **Privately Held**
SIC: 4225 2448 General warehousing & storage; wood pallets & skids; pallets, wood

(G-1692)
OAKLEY INDUSTRIES SUB ASSEMBLY
2091 Tripp Rd (61008-7207)
PHONE..................815 544-6666
Tim Middleton, *Materials Mgr*
Michael McNulty, *Branch Mgr*
EMP: 17
SALES (corp-wide): 130.1MM **Privately Held**
SIC: 3714 Motor vehicle wheels & parts
PA: Oakley Industries Sub Assembly Division, Inc.
4333 Matthew
Flint MI 48507
810 720-4444

(G-1693)
OZINGA BROS INC
990 Ecs Way (61008-6805)
PHONE..................815 332-8198
EMP: 79
SALES (corp-wide): 434.5MM **Privately Held**
WEB: www.ozinga.com
SIC: 5211 5032 3273 Cement; concrete & cinder building products; ready-mixed concrete
PA: Ozinga Bros., Inc.
19001 Old Lagrange Rd # 30
Mokena IL 60448
708 326-4200

(G-1694)
PISTON AUTOMOTIVE LLC
3458 Morreim Dr (61008-6308)
PHONE..................313 541-8789
Robert Ajersch, *Finance Dir*
Jeff Williams, *Info Tech Mgr*
EMP: 120
SALES (corp-wide): 1.6B **Privately Held**
SIC: 3714 Motor vehicle parts & accessories
HQ: Piston Automotive, L.L.C.
12723 Telegraph Rd Ste 1
Redford MI 48239
313 541-8674

GEOGRAPHIC SECTION

Bensenville - Dupage County (G-1724)

(G-1695)
PREFORMANCE SIGNS
6593 Revlon Dr (61008-8553)
PHONE..................815 544-5044
Glen Tracy, *Principal*
EMP: 5
SALES (est): 512.2K **Privately Held**
SIC: 3993 Signs & advertising specialties

(G-1696)
PRINTWORLD
319 S State St (61008-3606)
P.O. Box 1106 (61008-1106)
PHONE..................815 544-1000
EMP: 3
SALES (est): 248.6K **Privately Held**
SIC: 2759 Commercial Printing

(G-1697)
RDC LINEAR ENTERPRISES LLC
6593 Revlon Dr Dr1 (61008-8553)
PHONE..................815 547-1106
Cheryl Riesselmann, *Engineer*
Dennis Schreier,
J Chris Arvidson,
Robert Bauchiero,
▲ **EMP:** 15
SQ FT: 21,000
SALES (est): 2.2MM **Privately Held**
SIC: 3593 Fluid power actuators, hydraulic or pneumatic

(G-1698)
REJUV-A-ROLLER LLC
2339 Newburg Rd (61008-7999)
PHONE..................815 975-9635
Collin Budron, *Principal*
EMP: 3
SALES (est): 141.3K **Privately Held**
WEB: www.paintrollercleaner.com
SIC: 3991 Brooms & brushes

(G-1699)
RING SCREW LLC
Also Called: Camcar
830 E Menomonie St (61008-2338)
PHONE..................815 544-7574
EMP: 9 **Privately Held**
SIC: 3452 Bolts, nuts, rivets & washers
HQ: Ring Screw Llc
6125 18 Mile Rd
Sterling Heights MI 48314

(G-1700)
ROCKFORD CHEMICAL CO
915 W Perry St (61008-3498)
PHONE..................815 544-3476
Vann Rossmiller, *President*
EMP: 3 **EST:** 1947
SQ FT: 20,000
SALES (est): 3MM **Privately Held**
SIC: 5074 2899 Boilers, steam; water treating compounds

(G-1701)
SPECIAL FASTENER OPERATIONS
1993 Belford North Dr # 102 (61008-7088)
PHONE..................815 544-6449
William E Truax, *President*
Donna Truax, *Admin Sec*
EMP: 4
SQ FT: 500
SALES (est): 500K **Privately Held**
SIC: 3451 3544 Screw machine products; special dies, tools, jigs & fixtures

(G-1702)
STANGER TOOL & MOLD INC
2713 Winfield Ln (61008-6436)
PHONE..................847 426-5826
Kevin Stanger, *Owner*
EMP: 3
SQ FT: 2,400
SALES: 350K **Privately Held**
SIC: 3089 Injection molded finished plastic products

(G-1703)
TAYLOR OFF ROAD RACING
6925 Imron Dr (61008-8590)
PHONE..................815 544-4500
Scott J Taylor, *President*
EMP: 2

SQ FT: 8,000
SALES (est): 279K **Privately Held**
SIC: 3441 3711 7692 Fabricated structural metal; chassis, motor vehicle; welding repair

(G-1704)
TLS WINDSLED INC
507 W 10th St (61008-5639)
PHONE..................815 262-5791
Terry Soltow, *CEO*
EMP: 3
SALES: 60K **Privately Held**
SIC: 3732 Boats, fiberglass: building & repairing

(G-1705)
TSM INC
6859 Belford Indus Dr (61008-8709)
PHONE..................815 544-5012
Ted Lindstorm, *President*
Linda Lindstorm, *Admin Sec*
EMP: 6
SALES (est): 1.2MM **Privately Held**
SIC: 3465 Automotive stampings

(G-1706)
TWIN TOWERS MARKETING
Also Called: Twin Towers Embroidery
1231 Logan Ave (61008-4001)
PHONE..................815 544-5554
Janet Paulsen, *Owner*
EMP: 5
SALES (est): 387.3K **Privately Held**
SIC: 2395 Embroidery products, except schiffli machine

(G-1707)
VALLEY CUSTOM WOODWORK INC
1626 Industrial Ct (61008-6345)
PHONE..................815 544-3939
Charles Siracusa, *President*
Sean Meinert, *Project Mgr*
Sharon Siracusa, *Treasurer*
EMP: 20
SQ FT: 23,000
SALES (est): 2.4MM **Privately Held**
WEB: www.vcwi.com
SIC: 2541 Table or counter tops, plastic laminated

(G-1708)
VHD INC
6833 Irene Rd (61008-8789)
PHONE..................815 544-2169
Michael Vore, *President*
Norland O Bolen, *President*
Kerrill Bolen, *Admin Sec*
▲ **EMP:** 29
SQ FT: 10,000
SALES (est): 4.9MM **Privately Held**
SIC: 3544 3545 Special dies & tools; reamers, machine tool

(G-1709)
WELCH BROS INC
1000 Town Hall Rd (61008-6300)
PHONE..................815 547-3000
Britt Lienau, *Sales Staff*
Scott Welch, *Branch Mgr*
EMP: 3
SALES (est): 723.9K
SALES (corp-wide): 20.1MM **Privately Held**
SIC: 3272 5211 Concrete products, precast; lumber & other building materials
PA: Welch Bros., Inc.
1050 Saint Charles St
Elgin IL 60120
847 741-6134

(G-1710)
WELCH PACKAGING GROUP INC
Also Called: Welch Paper
4133 Newburg Rd (61008-6700)
PHONE..................815 547-1505
EMP: 20
SALES (corp-wide): 353MM **Privately Held**
SIC: 5113 2653 Napkins, paper; towels, paper, containers, paper & disposable plastic; corrugated & solid fiber boxes; boxes, corrugated: made from purchased materials

PA: Welch Packaging Group, Inc.
1020 Herman St
Elkhart IN 46516
574 295-2460

(G-1711)
WILLIAM CHARLES CNSTR CO LLC
Also Called: Irene Quary
4525 Irene Rd (61008-8355)
PHONE..................815 654-4720
Charles Howard, *Owner*
Kyle Kubatzke, *Foreman/Supr*
EMP: 6
SALES (corp-wide): 1.4B **Publicly Held**
SIC: 5032 1422 Stone, crushed or broken; crushed & broken limestone
HQ: William Charles Construction Company, Llc
833 Featherstone Rd
Rockford IL 61107
815 877-0550

(G-1712)
YANFENG US AUTOMOTIVE
775 Logistics Dr (61008-8507)
PHONE..................779 552-7300
Todd Chase, *Branch Mgr*
EMP: 535 **Privately Held**
SIC: 2531 Seats, automobile
HQ: Yanfeng Us Automotive Interior Systems I Llc
41935 W 12 Mile Rd
Novi MI 48377
248 319-7333

(G-1713)
YOUNGBERG INDUSTRIES INC
6863 Indy Dr (61008-8769)
PHONE..................815 544-2177
Thomas Larson, *President*
Mike Carter, *COO*
Jeff Vincent, *Plant Mgr*
Jeff Kelly, *Purchasing*
Steven Kniep, *Engineer*
EMP: 65
SQ FT: 81,075
SALES: 13.9MM **Privately Held**
WEB: www.youngbergindustries.com
SIC: 3441 Fabricated structural metal

Bement
Piatt County

(G-1714)
PIATT COUNTY SERVICE CO
Also Called: Platt County Service
878 State Highway 105 (61813-3741)
PHONE..................217 678-5511
Mark Orr, *Manager*
EMP: 8
SALES (corp-wide): 4.2MM **Privately Held**
SIC: 5999 2875 5261 Feed & farm supply; fertilizers, mixing only; fertilizer
PA: Piatt County Service Co (Inc)
427 W Marion St Ste 1
Monticello IL 61856
217 762-2133

(G-1715)
RHYME OR REASON WOODWORKING
280 W Moultrie St (61813-1442)
PHONE..................217 678-8301
Gaila Roberts, *Principal*
EMP: 3
SALES (est): 266K **Privately Held**
SIC: 2431 Millwork

(G-1716)
WOOD SPECIALTIES INCORPORATED
964 E 1100 North Rd (61813-3517)
PHONE..................217 678-8420
Jeff Gallivan, *President*
John Gallivan, *Admin Sec*
EMP: 12
SALES (est): 1.2MM **Privately Held**
SIC: 2434 Wood kitchen cabinets

Benld
Macoupin County

(G-1717)
3-V INDUSTRIES INC
110 W Oak St (62009-1550)
PHONE..................217 835-4453
Ed La Roche, *President*
EMP: 7
SQ FT: 7,500
SALES: 800K **Privately Held**
SIC: 3599 Machine shop, jobbing & repair

(G-1718)
R & R MACHINING INC
125 Route 138 (62009-1453)
PHONE..................217 835-4579
Randy Ramseier, *President*
Cindy Rauker, *Vice Pres*
Leo Ramseier, *Treasurer*
EMP: 3 **EST:** 1979
SQ FT: 2,985
SALES: 450K **Privately Held**
SIC: 3544 7692 Jigs & fixtures; welding repair

Bensenville
Dupage County

(G-1719)
3D INDUSTRIES INC
500 Frontier Way (60106-1191)
PHONE..................630 616-8702
Frank Glavanovits, *President*
EMP: 20
SQ FT: 20,000
SALES (est): 3.2MM **Privately Held**
SIC: 3544 3599 Special dies & tools; machine shop, jobbing & repair.

(G-1720)
A & A CABINET CREATIONS INC
468 Country Club Dr (60106-1507)
PHONE..................630 350-1560
Steven Athanas, *President*
EMP: 15
SALES (est): 1.5MM **Privately Held**
SIC: 2434 Wood kitchen cabinets

(G-1721)
AAXIS ENGRAVERS INC
230 William St Ste A (60106-3308)
PHONE..................224 629-4045
Elizabeth Alcantar, *President*
EMP: 6
SALES (est): 630K **Privately Held**
SIC: 3555 Printing plates

(G-1722)
ABBCO INC
304 Meyer Rd (60106-1615)
PHONE..................630 595-7115
Joseph Abbate III, *President*
Rudy Sanchez, *Plant Mgr*
Phillip Cypcar, *Sales Engr*
Phil Cypcar, *Sales Executive*
EMP: 25 **EST:** 1960
SQ FT: 25,000
SALES (est): 4.5MM **Privately Held**
WEB: www.abbcoinc.net
SIC: 3545 3541 3451 Cutting tools for machine tools; machine tools, metal cutting type; screw machine products

(G-1723)
ABILITY WELDING SERVICE INC
500 Meyer Rd (60106-1604)
PHONE..................630 595-3737
Walter Kryczka, *President*
Aderine Spirick, *Office Mgr*
EMP: 6
SALES: 500K **Privately Held**
SIC: 7692 Welding repair

(G-1724)
ACCURATE PARTS MFG CO
220 Gateway Rd (60106-1953)
PHONE..................630 616-4125
Ozcan Yabukoglu, *President*
▲ **EMP:** 26

Bensenville - Dupage County (G-1725)

SALES (est): 3.8MM **Privately Held**
SIC: 3369 Castings, except die-castings, precision

(G-1725)
ACCUTECH MACHINING INC
381 Evergreen Ave (60106-2503)
PHONE..................................630 350-2066
Jeffrey Szwaya, *President*
Elizabeth Szwaya, *Corp Secy*
Michael James, *Vice Pres*
Natalie Stombock-Szwaya, *Human Resources*
EMP: 22 EST: 1999
SQ FT: 11,000
SALES (est): 3.7MM **Privately Held**
WEB: www.accutechmachining.com
SIC: 3599 Machine shop, jobbing & repair

(G-1726)
ACE METAL CRAFTS COMPANY
484 Thomas Dr (60106-1619)
PHONE..................................847 455-1010
Jean L Pitzo, *President*
Dale Ball, *President*
Mary Lichter, *VP Admin*
Kevin Bailey, *Vice Pres*
Keith Stout, *VP Opers*
EMP: 105
SQ FT: 82,000
SALES (est): 38.4MM **Privately Held**
WEB: www.acemetal.com
SIC: 3441 Fabricated structural metal

(G-1727)
ACROFAB
1100 Entry Dr Unit 1 (60106-3700)
PHONE..................................630 350-7941
Bhupen Patel, *Owner*
EMP: 5
SALES (est): 725.4K **Privately Held**
SIC: 3498 Tube fabricating (contract bending & shaping)

(G-1728)
ADVANCE MACHINING
405 Evergreen Ave (60106-2505)
PHONE..................................630 521-9392
Stefan Szefer, *President*
Stanley Pyrdol, *Vice Pres*
EMP: 4
SQ FT: 5,000
SALES (est): 302.5K **Privately Held**
SIC: 3599 Machine shop, jobbing & repair

(G-1729)
ADVANCED DIGITAL & MOLD INC
833 Eagle Dr (60106-1946)
PHONE..................................630 595-8242
J Alexandersson, *Principal*
EMP: 5
SALES (est): 571K **Privately Held**
SIC: 3544 Industrial molds

(G-1730)
ADVANCED GALVANICS
772 Foster Ave (60106-1509)
PHONE..................................630 422-5157
EMP: 3
SALES (est): 170.1K **Privately Held**
SIC: 3471 Plating of metals or formed products

(G-1731)
ADVANCED PRCSION MACHINING LTD
766 Birginal Dr (60106-1213)
PHONE..................................630 860-2549
Scott R Lamb, *President*
Andrzej Marchwiany, *Admin Sec*
EMP: 5 EST: 2007
SQ FT: 4,200
SALES (est): 302.5K **Privately Held**
WEB: www.pulleymfg.com
SIC: 3599 Machine shop, jobbing & repair

(G-1732)
ADVANCED THERMAL PROCESSING
501 Eastern Ave (60106-3811)
PHONE..................................630 595-9000
Mark A Bulaw, *President*
Christine Bulaw, *Admin Sec*
EMP: 2

SQ FT: 18,000
SALES (est): 344.7K **Privately Held**
SIC: 3398 Metal heat treating

(G-1733)
AGS MACHINE CO INC
872 Eagle Dr (60106-1947)
PHONE..................................630 766-7777
EMP: 6
SALES (est): 480K **Privately Held**
SIC: 3599 Machine Shop

(G-1734)
ALAGOR INDUSTRIES INCORPORATED (PA)
489 Thomas Dr (60106-1618)
PHONE..................................630 766-2910
Richard Rogala, *President*
Lynette Rogala, *Admin Sec*
▼ EMP: 60
SQ FT: 15,000
SALES: 3MM **Privately Held**
SIC: 3469 3496 Stamping metal for the trade; miscellaneous fabricated wire products

(G-1735)
ALLIANCE PLASTICS
830 Fairway Dr Ste 104 (60106-1348)
PHONE..................................888 643-1432
Ron Grubbs, *President*
EMP: 4
SALES (est): 327.9K **Privately Held**
WEB: www.allianceplastics.net
SIC: 3089 Injection molding of plastics

(G-1736)
ALLMETAL INC
636 Thomas Dr (60106-1623)
P.O. Box 850 (60106-0850)
PHONE..................................630 766-8500
Jeffrey Andresen, *Manager*
Jeff Andresen, *CTO*
Corinne Wiegand, *Director*
EMP: 46
SQ FT: 26,000
SALES (corp-wide): 78.4MM **Privately Held**
WEB: www.allmetalinc.com
SIC: 3442 Storm doors or windows, metal
PA: Allmetal, Inc.
   1 Pierce Pl Ste 295w
   Itasca IL 60143
   630 250-8090

(G-1737)
ALLMETAL INC
224-230 Foster Ave (60106)
PHONE..................................630 766-1407
Vincent Catalano, *General Mgr*
Nelson Martell, *Engineer*
EMP: 15
SALES (corp-wide): 78.4MM **Privately Held**
SIC: 3442 3089 Metal doors, sash & trim; injection molding of plastics
PA: Allmetal, Inc.
   1 Pierce Pl Ste 295w
   Itasca IL 60143
   630 250-8090

(G-1738)
ALLOYWELD INSPECTION CO INC
796 Maple Ln (60106-1585)
PHONE..................................630 595-2145
Edward Piecko, *President*
Edward J Piecko, *President*
Stanley W Piecko, *Chairman*
Jennifer Anaya, *Vice Pres*
Tamy Piecko, *Info Tech Mgr*
EMP: 30
SQ FT: 7,100
SALES (est): 3.4MM **Privately Held**
WEB: www.alloyweldinspection.com
SIC: 1799 7692 8071 8734 Welding on site; welding repair; brazing; testing laboratories; testing laboratories

(G-1739)
ALLSTAR TOOL & MOLDS INC
799 Eagle Dr Ste A (60106-1995)
PHONE..................................630 766-0162
Fred Kovacs, *President*
EMP: 10
SQ FT: 4,400

SALES: 680K **Privately Held**
SIC: 3544 Industrial molds

(G-1740)
ALU-BRA FOUNDRY INC
630 E Green St (60106-2548)
PHONE..................................630 766-3112
James E Torkelson, *President*
Joan Torkelson, *Corp Secy*
Amanda Krotz, *Vice Pres*
Tom Dore, *Engineer*
Amanda Dimaria, *Marketing Staff*
EMP: 80 EST: 1957
SQ FT: 17,000
SALES (est): 17.8MM **Privately Held**
WEB: www.alu-bra.com
SIC: 3366 Copper foundries

(G-1741)
AMCAST INC
350 Meyer Rd (60106-1615)
PHONE..................................630 766-7450
John C Kopp, *President*
Janet Kopp, *Corp Secy*
EMP: 17 EST: 1965
SQ FT: 12,000
SALES (est): 3.1MM **Privately Held**
SIC: 3364 3369 3366 3365 Copper & copper alloy die-castings; nonferrous foundries; copper foundries; aluminum foundries

(G-1742)
AMERICAN ENGRAVING INC
151 Wilson Ct (60106-1628)
PHONE..................................630 543-2525
Michael Gioia, *President*
Thomas Magarian, *Vice Pres*
▼ EMP: 6
SQ FT: 4,000
SALES (est): 929.5K **Privately Held**
SIC: 3599 3544 Machine shop, jobbing & repair; special dies, tools, jigs & fixtures

(G-1743)
AMERICAN RUBBER MFG INC
766 Foster Ave (60106-1509)
PHONE..................................331 551-9600
Vic Lakhani, *President*
Robert Langenfeld, *Vice Pres*
EMP: 6
SQ FT: 4,000
SALES: 1MM **Privately Held**
SIC: 3069 Molded rubber products

(G-1744)
AMGLO KEMLITE LABORATORIES INC (PA)
215 Gateway Rd (60106-1952)
PHONE..................................630 238-3031
James H Hyland, *Ch of Bd*
Hyland J Grant, *President*
Larry A Kerchenfaut, *Managing Dir*
Anna Czajkowski, *Vice Pres*
Ania Czajkowski, *VP Prdtn*
▲ EMP: 100
SQ FT: 20,000
SALES (est): 67.8MM **Privately Held**
SIC: 3641 Tubes, electric light

(G-1745)
AMSOIL INC
485 Thomas Dr (60106-1618)
PHONE..................................630 595-8385
Ray Gonzales, *Manager*
EMP: 8
SALES (corp-wide): 128.2MM **Privately Held**
SIC: 2992 3589 2873 3714 Lubricating oils & greases; water filters & softeners, household type; fertilizers: natural (organic), except compost; motor vehicle parts & accessories
PA: Amsoil Inc.
   925 Tower Ave
   Superior WI 54880
   715 392-7101

(G-1746)
AMTAB MANUFACTURING CORP
600 Eagle Dr (60106-1943)
PHONE..................................630 301-7600
Doss Samikkannu, *President*
Tadeusz Hanusiak, *President*
Jerry Rivera, *President*
Jason Samikkannu, *General Mgr*

Steve Samikkannu, *General Mgr*
▲ EMP: 54 EST: 2006
SALES (est): 13.1MM **Privately Held**
WEB: www.amtab.com
SIC: 2521 2522 2511 Tables, office: wood; tables, office: except wood; wood household furniture

(G-1747)
ART TECHNOLOGIES INC
Also Called: A Cnc Manufacturing Facility
450 Frontier Way Ste B (60106-1170)
PHONE..................................773 557-3896
Felipe Perez, *President*
EMP: 5 EST: 2016
SQ FT: 3,500
SALES: 320K **Privately Held**
SIC: 3549 3559 3728 3599 Assembly machines, including robotic; automotive related machinery; aircraft parts & equipment; machine & other job shop work; custom machinery

(G-1748)
ASPEN INDUSTRIES INC
480 Country Club Dr (60106-1507)
PHONE..................................630 238-0611
Ralph Iourio, *President*
John Barry, *President*
▲ EMP: 11 EST: 1999
SQ FT: 12,000
SALES (est): 1MM **Privately Held**
SIC: 3441 Fabricated structural metal

(G-1749)
B & M MACHINE INC
768 Industrial Dr (60106-1305)
PHONE..................................630 350-8950
Martin Nicpon, *President*
EMP: 4
SALES (est): 268.8K **Privately Held**
SIC: 3599 Machine shop, jobbing & repair

(G-1750)
B J PLASTIC MOLDING CO
778 County Line Rd (60106-3277)
PHONE..................................630 766-8750
Robert Jacobson, *Manager*
Jack Clark, *IT/INT Sup*
EMP: 20
SALES (est): 1.2MM
SALES (corp-wide): 10.8MM **Privately Held**
SIC: 3089 Injection molded finished plastic products; injection molding of plastics
PA: B. J. Plastic Molding Co., Inc
   435 S County Line Rd
   Franklin Park IL 60131
   630 766-3200

(G-1751)
BALA & ANULA FUELS INC
154 S York Rd (60106-2454)
PHONE..................................630 766-1807
EMP: 3
SALES (est): 240.6K **Privately Held**
SIC: 2869 Fuels

(G-1752)
BENSENVILLE SCREW PRODUCTS
796 County Line Rd (60106-3277)
PHONE..................................630 860-5222
Mark Tukiendorf, *President*
Tom Tukiendorf, *Manager*
Bonnie Tukiendorf, *Admin Sec*
EMP: 9
SQ FT: 10,000
SALES: 2MM **Privately Held**
WEB: www.bensenvillescrewproducts.com
SIC: 3451 Screw machine products

(G-1753)
BIBLE STUDENTS PUBLICATIONS
900 Brentwood Dr (60106-3211)
PHONE..................................630 595-0984
George Tabac, *President*
Florence Tabac, *Treasurer*
Thomas Ruggirello, *Admin Sec*
EMP: 3
SQ FT: 700
SALES: 50K **Privately Held**
SIC: 2732 7812 Books: printing only; video production

GEOGRAPHIC SECTION

Bensenville - Dupage County (G-1781)

(G-1754)
BLS ENTERPRISES INC
Also Called: Tuftads
1120 Thorndale Ave (60106-1144)
PHONE 630 766-1300
Barry Stoughton, *President*
◆ EMP: 13
SQ FT: 4,800
SALES (est): 1.1MM **Privately Held**
SIC: 3069 Liner strips, rubber

(G-1755)
BOBS BUSINESS INC
730 Thomas Dr (60106-1625)
PHONE 630 238-5790
Judd Smith, *Manager*
EMP: 6
SALES (corp-wide): 9.1MM **Privately Held**
WEB: www.bobsbusiness.com
SIC: 3949 Bowling equipment & supplies
PA: Bobs' Business, Inc.
1981 Old West Main St
Red Wing MN 55066
651 388-4742

(G-1756)
BRIERGATE TOOL & ENGRG CO
1007 Industrial Dr (60106-1298)
PHONE 630 766-7050
Robert L Sbertoli Jr, *President*
Terri Sbertoli, *Corp Secy*
EMP: 10
SQ FT: 20,000
SALES: 1MM **Privately Held**
WEB: www.briergatetool.net
SIC: 3469 3544 Stamping metal for the trade; special dies & tools

(G-1757)
BRINKMAN COMPANY INC
460 Evergreen Ave (60106-2506)
PHONE 630 595-3640
Howard A Brinkman, *President*
Johnnie Fernandez, *Partner*
EMP: 8 EST: 1944
SQ FT: 4,500
SALES (est): 929.8K **Privately Held**
WEB: www.brinkmancompany.com
SIC: 2821 Plastics materials & resins

(G-1758)
BRUNNER & LAY INC
300 Evergreen Ave (60106-2504)
P.O. Box 1329, Franklin Park (60131-8329)
PHONE 847 678-3232
EMP: 120
SALES (corp-wide): 51.9MM **Privately Held**
WEB: www.brunnerlay.com
SIC: 3545 3546 3531 Drills (machine tool accessories); hammers, portable: electric or pneumatic, chipping, etc.; construction machinery
PA: Brunner & Lay, Inc.
1510 N Old Missouri Rd
Springdale AR 72764
479 756-0880

(G-1759)
BSB INTERNATIONAL CORP
225 James St Ste 4 (60106-3367)
PHONE 847 791-9272
EMP: 4
SALES (est): 270K **Privately Held**
SIC: 3599 7699 Mfg & Repair Commercial Equipment

(G-1760)
C N C CENTRAL INC
177 Il Route 83 (60106-2011)
PHONE 630 595-1453
EMP: 8
SQ FT: 6,000
SALES: 2.5MM **Privately Held**
SIC: 3599 3565 Mfg Industrial Machinery Mfg Packaging Machinery

(G-1761)
CAPABLE CONTROLS INC (PA)
1062 Tower Ln (60106-1031)
PHONE 630 860-6514
Ted Singer, *President*
Paul Paluck, *Vice Pres*
EMP: 58
SQ FT: 7,000
SALES (est): 9.5MM **Privately Held**
SIC: 3625 Electric controls & control accessories, industrial

(G-1762)
CAPITAL RUBBER CORPORATION
1140 Tower Ln (60106-1028)
PHONE 630 595-6644
Barbara Feldman, *President*
Bryan Feldman, *Vice Pres*
▼ EMP: 11
SQ FT: 15,000
SALES (est): 4.9MM **Privately Held**
SIC: 5085 3429 Gaskets; clamps & couplings, hose

(G-1763)
CAVERO COATINGS COMPANY LLC
422 County Line Rd (60106-2536)
PHONE 630 616-2868
Jose Cavero, *Principal*
Elder Luna, *Production*
EMP: 5
SALES (est): 1MM **Privately Held**
WEB: www.caverocoatings.com
SIC: 3479 Coating of metals & formed products

(G-1764)
CENTRAL AUTMTC SCREW PDTS INC
372 Meyer Rd (60106-1615)
PHONE 630 766-7966
Daniel Flerlage, *President*
Dennis Flerlage, *Vice Pres*
EMP: 7
SQ FT: 11,000
SALES (est): 1.2MM **Privately Held**
WEB: www.centralautomatic.com
SIC: 3451 Screw machine products

(G-1765)
CENTURY METAL SPINNING CO INC
430 Meyer Rd (60106-1617)
PHONE 630 595-3900
Janet Kaiser, *President*
Danuta Skoczylas, *QC Mgr*
John Lipinski, *Manager*
Laura Carrillo,
EMP: 25 EST: 1933
SQ FT: 25,000
SALES (est): 4.5MM **Privately Held**
WEB: www.centurymetalspinning.com
SIC: 3469 Stamping metal for the trade

(G-1766)
CH MACHINING COMPANY
1044 Fairway Dr (60106-1317)
PHONE 630 595-1050
Andrzej Chomont, *President*
EMP: 3
SALES (est): 400.4K **Privately Held**
WEB: www.chmachiningco.com
SIC: 3599 Machine shop, jobbing & repair

(G-1767)
CHEMBLEND OF AMERICA LLC
240 Foster Ave (60106-1641)
PHONE 630 521-1600
John Godina, *President*
Joy Schmitt, *Purchasing*
Tom Hayward, *Director*
▲ EMP: 10
SALES (est): 2.2MM **Privately Held**
SIC: 2833 Medicinals & botanicals

(G-1768)
CHICAGO CABINET & FIXTURE CO
316 Meyer Rd (60106-1615)
PHONE 630 616-8071
Kurt Stushek, *President*
Dennis Horstman, *Vice Pres*
Maria Stushek, *Admin Sec*
EMP: 5
SQ FT: 10,000
SALES (est): 779.2K **Privately Held**
SIC: 2434 Wood kitchen cabinets

(G-1769)
CHICAGO WHITE METAL CAST INC
649 Il Route 83 (60106-1340)
PHONE 630 595-4424
Eric Treiber, *CEO*
Walter G Treiber, *Chairman*
William Baraglia, *VP Mfg*
Dan Oconnor, *Purchasing*
Ted Bystryk, *Manager*
◆ EMP: 200 EST: 1937
SQ FT: 136,000
SALES: 34.3MM **Privately Held**
WEB: www.cwmdiecast.com
SIC: 3363 3364 Aluminum die-castings; magnesium & magnesium-base alloy die-castings; zinc & zinc-base alloy die-castings

(G-1770)
CIRCOM INC
505 W Main St (60106-2137)
PHONE 630 595-4460
Lisa Esczuk, *President*
Marlene Rosenberg, *Vice Pres*
EMP: 28 EST: 1968
SQ FT: 12,000
SALES (est): 6.7MM **Privately Held**
WEB: www.circominc.com
SIC: 3679 3672 3357 8711 Electronic circuits; printed circuit boards; nonferrous wiredrawing & insulating; engineering services; commercial physical research

(G-1771)
CNC GRAPHICS
501 Frontier Way (60106-3801)
PHONE 630 766-6308
Sophie Skirucha, *Principal*
Mark Skirucha, *Agent*
EMP: 9
SALES (est): 946.6K **Privately Held**
SIC: 3993 Signs & advertising specialties

(G-1772)
CO-ORDINATED PACKAGING INC
Also Called: Coordinated Packaging
1001 Entry Dr (60106-3314)
PHONE 847 559-8877
Beverly Wolf, *President*
Greg Wolf, *Vice Pres*
Mark Lantz, *Treasurer*
▲ EMP: 10
SALES (est): 2.6MM **Privately Held**
SIC: 5113 3086 3081 Boxes, paperboard & disposable plastic; packaging & shipping materials, foamed plastic; unsupported plastics film & sheet

(G-1773)
COLLEY ELEVATOR COMPANY
226 William St (60106-3325)
PHONE 630 766-7230
Ray Zomchek, *President*
Craig Zomchek, *Business Mgr*
Pamela Zomchek, *Treasurer*
Alex Macias, *Accounts Mgr*
Dennis Jedd, *Sales Staff*
EMP: 20
SQ FT: 15,000
SALES (est): 3.1MM **Privately Held**
WEB: www.colleyelevator.com
SIC: 7699 1796 3534 Elevators: inspection, service & repair; elevator installation & conversion; elevators & moving stairways

(G-1774)
COLOREX CHEMICAL CO INC
834 Foster Ave (60106-1510)
PHONE 630 238-3124
Yvonne Matsoukas, *President*
EMP: 2
SQ FT: 5,000
SALES (est): 1.2MM **Privately Held**
WEB: www.colorexchemical.com
SIC: 2842 5169 Cleaning or polishing preparations; leather dressings & finishes; chemicals & allied products

(G-1775)
CONNOR SPORTS FLOORING LLC (DH)
595 Supreme Dr (60106-1123)
PHONE 847 290-9020
Ronald Cerny, *CEO*
Jon Isaacs, *Vice Pres*
Conrad Stromberg, *Plant Mgr*
Jay Perri, *Project Mgr*
Kenneth Bayne, *CFO*
◆ EMP: 87
SALES (est): 25.5MM
SALES (corp-wide): 533.7K **Privately Held**
SIC: 2426 5031 2439 Flooring, hardwood; lumber: rough, dressed & finished; structural wood members
HQ: Connor Sport Court International, Llc
5445 W Harold Gatty Dr
Salt Lake City UT 84116
801 972-0260

(G-1776)
CORE FINISHING INC
717 Thomas Dr (60106-1624)
PHONE 630 521-9635
Corey Coxe, *President*
EMP: 30
SQ FT: 24,000
SALES: 2.5MM **Privately Held**
SIC: 3479 Coating of metals & formed products

(G-1777)
CORRECT TOOL INC
869 Fairway Dr (60106-1312)
PHONE 630 595-6055
Janusz Szulinski, *President*
Barbara Szulinski, *President*
▲ EMP: 12
SQ FT: 9,000
SALES (est): 2.4MM **Privately Held**
SIC: 3544 5251 Special dies & tools; tools

(G-1778)
COSMOPOLITAN MACHINE REBUILDER
346 Evergreen Ave (60106-2504)
PHONE 630 595-8141
Wallace Szczekocki, *President*
Leona Szczekocki, *Admin Sec*
EMP: 5
SQ FT: 6,000
SALES (est): 544.4K **Privately Held**
SIC: 3599 Machine shop, jobbing & repair

(G-1779)
COYOTE TRANSPORTATION INC
600 Thomas Dr (60106-1623)
PHONE 630 204-5729
Anthony Varchetto, *President*
Jeff Gosmire, *CFO*
Edgar Arana, *Admin Sec*
EMP: 7 EST: 1996
SQ FT: 100,000
SALES: 900K
SALES (corp-wide): 29.3MM **Privately Held**
SIC: 4214 2611 3523 Local trucking with storage; pulp mills, mechanical & recycling processing; balers; farm: hay, straw, cotton, etc.
PA: Pri Group, Llc
600 Thomas Dr
Bensenville IL 60106
630 477-4040

(G-1780)
CP SCREW MACHINE PRODUCTS
211 Beeline Dr Ste 3 (60106-1640)
PHONE 630 766-2313
John M Woodward, *President*
EMP: 15
SQ FT: 9,000
SALES: 975K **Privately Held**
SIC: 3451 Screw machine products

(G-1781)
CRV INDUSTRIES INC
Also Called: Crv Lancaster Cams & Indexers
777 Maple Ln (60106-1513)
PHONE 630 595-3777
Michael Purner, *President*

Bensenville - Dupage County (G-1782)

Jacquelyn Purner, *Admin Sec*
EMP: 10
SQ FT: 10,000
SALES (est): 1MM **Privately Held**
WEB: www.crvlancasterinc.com
SIC: 3599 Machine shop, jobbing & repair

(G-1782)
CUSTOM BLADES & TOOLS INC
1084 Fairway Dr (60106-1317)
PHONE.................................630 860-7650
Henry Wszolek, *President*
EMP: 2
SQ FT: 1,800
SALES (est): 260K **Privately Held**
SIC: 3425 5084 Saw blades & handsaws; industrial machinery & equipment

(G-1783)
CUSTOM MACHINING COMPANY
401 Evergreen Ave (60106-2590)
PHONE.................................630 766-2600
William Carley, *President*
Diana Carley, *Corp Secy*
EMP: 7 **EST:** 1964
SQ FT: 3,000
SALES (est): 580K **Privately Held**
SIC: 3599 Machine shop, jobbing & repair

(G-1784)
CUTTING TOOL INNOVATIONS INC
759 Industrial Dr (60106-1304)
P.O. Box 50 (60106-0050)
PHONE.................................630 766-4839
Gohei George Osawa, *CEO*
Denny Denick, *President*
EMP: 4
SALES (est): 379.6K **Privately Held**
SIC: 3541 Screw & thread machines
HQ: Osg Usa, Inc.
1945 W Walnut Hill Ln
Irving TX 75038
800 837-2223

(G-1785)
DELTA SECONDARY INC
1000 Industrial Dr Ste 3d (60106-1259)
PHONE.................................630 766-1180
Alina Agresto, *President*
Dimitrios Vattis, *Vice Pres*
EMP: 40
SQ FT: 10,000
SALES (est): 3.5MM **Privately Held**
SIC: 3471 Finishing, metals or formed products

(G-1786)
DESIGNED PLASTICS INC
1133 Bryn Mawr Ave (60106-1242)
PHONE.................................630 694-7300
Mark Barnes, *President*
Kathy Barnes, *Corp Secy*
Joe Benka, *Opers Mgr*
Gerald Barnes, *CFO*
Dave Lawless, *Sales Staff*
EMP: 25
SQ FT: 20,000
SALES (est): 4.7MM **Privately Held**
WEB: www.designedplastics.com
SIC: 3089 3083 Injection molded finished plastic products; laminated plastics plate & sheet

(G-1787)
DISTINCTIVE FOODS LLC
Also Called: Pie Piper
450 Evergreen Ave (60106-2506)
PHONE.................................847 459-3600
Josh Harris, *Branch Mgr*
EMP: 40
SQ FT: 20,000
SALES (corp-wide): 25.1MM **Privately Held**
SIC: 2038 2051 Frozen specialties; bread, cake & related products
PA: Distinctive Foods Llc
654 Wheeling Rd
Wheeling IL 60090
847 459-3600

(G-1788)
DOUMAK INC (PA)
1004 Fairway Dr (60106-1317)
PHONE.................................800 323-0318
Mark G Schuessler, *President*
Gary G Conway, *Vice Pres*
Juan Morales, *Production*
Calvin Temple, *Production*
Lynn Roose, *QA Dir*
◆ **EMP:** 9
SQ FT: 225,000
SALES (est): 72.2MM **Privately Held**
SIC: 2064 Marshmallows

(G-1789)
DRIVER SERVICES
Also Called: Globe Telecom
120 George St Apt 517 (60106-3177)
PHONE.................................505 267-8686
Adrian Dorofte, *Principal*
EMP: 5
SALES (est): 150K **Privately Held**
SIC: 4812 3663 4111 8748 Cellular telephone services; radio & TV communications equipment; airport limousine, scheduled service; telecommunications consultant; domestic freight forwarding

(G-1790)
DRUMMOND INDUSTRIES INC
639 Thomas Dr (60106-1622)
PHONE.................................773 637-1264
Matthew Gieser, *President*
EMP: 30 **EST:** 1968
SQ FT: 28,000
SALES (est): 7MM **Privately Held**
WEB: www.drummondindustries.com
SIC: 3089 Injection molding of plastics

(G-1791)
DURABLE MANUFACTURING COMPANY
232 Evergreen Ave Unit B (60106-2578)
PHONE.................................630 766-0398
Edward Sowin, *Owner*
EMP: 12 **EST:** 1953
SQ FT: 11,000
SALES: 1MM **Privately Held**
WEB: www.durablefilters.com
SIC: 3589 3585 3564 Water filters & softeners, household type; parts for heating, cooling & refrigerating equipment; blowers & fans

(G-1792)
E M GLABUS CO INC
420 County Line Rd (60106-2536)
PHONE.................................630 766-3027
Dale F Glabus, *President*
Penny Glabus, *Corp Secy*
EMP: 10
SQ FT: 6,500
SALES (est): 1.5MM **Privately Held**
SIC: 3599 3462 Machine shop, jobbing & repair; iron & steel forgings

(G-1793)
ECOTURF MIDWEST INC
789 Golf Ln (60106-1563)
PHONE.................................630 350-9500
Susan Glatt, *President*
Ed Glatt, *Vice Pres*
Tom Miller, *Director*
EMP: 2
SQ FT: 16,000
SALES: 300K **Privately Held**
SIC: 3523 Turf & grounds equipment
PA: G.A.I.M. Plastics Incorporated.
789 Golf Ln
Bensenville IL 60106

(G-1794)
ELECTRONIC SYSTEM DESIGN INC
225 Foster Ave (60106-1631)
PHONE.................................847 358-8212
Harry Rueckel, *President*
Ruth C Rueckel, *Corp Secy*
EMP: 3
SQ FT: 3,700
SALES: 1.6MM **Privately Held**
SIC: 3823 3825 Analyzers, industrial process type; instruments to measure electricity

(G-1795)
EMC MACHINING INC
905 Fairway Dr (60106-1314)
PHONE.................................630 860-7076
Mila Pimentel, *President*
EMP: 10
SQ FT: 5,000
SALES (est): 1.4MM **Privately Held**
WEB: www.emcmachining.com
SIC: 3599 Machine shop, jobbing & repair

(G-1796)
EMLIN COSMETICS INC (PA)
290 Beeline Dr (60106-1600)
PHONE.................................630 860-5773
Lester Shapiro, *President*
Robert Shapiro, *Vice Pres*
David Weissman, *Vice Pres*
Sandra Geroulis, *Controller*
Nancy Lachus, *Technology*
EMP: 55 **EST:** 1964
SQ FT: 56,000
SALES (est): 9.6MM **Privately Held**
WEB: www.emlin.com
SIC: 2844 Cosmetic preparations; hair preparations, including shampoos

(G-1797)
ENERSTAR INC
838 Foster Ave (60106-1510)
PHONE.................................847 350-3400
Tim Carew, *President*
Ben Pomerantz, *Vice Pres*
Jean Carew, *Treasurer*
Pam Nordbrock, *Accountant*
EMP: 6
SQ FT: 2,500
SALES (est): 2.2MM **Privately Held**
SIC: 5084 3823 Industrial machinery & equipment; water quality monitoring & control systems

(G-1798)
EXCELLENT BINDERY INC
500 Eastern Ave (60106-3807)
PHONE.................................630 766-9050
Jozef Borzym, *President*
EMP: 20
SQ FT: 10,000
SALES (est): 2MM **Privately Held**
SIC: 2789 Binding only: books, pamphlets, magazines, etc.

(G-1799)
FEDERAL ENVELOPE COMPANY
608 Country Club Dr (60106-1303)
PHONE.................................630 595-2000
Howard L Shaw Sr, *Ch of Bd*
Michael Shaw, *President*
Howard Shaw Jr, *Vice Pres*
Don Hansen, *Purchasing*
Raymond Haffertepe, *Treasurer*
▲ **EMP:** 100
SQ FT: 106,000
SALES (est): 24.6MM **Privately Held**
WEB: www.federalenvelope.com
SIC: 2677 Envelopes

(G-1800)
FORM-ALL SPRING STAMPING INC
380 Meyer Rd (60106-1615)
PHONE.................................630 595-8833
Walter Bragiel, *President*
Mary Bragiel, *Vice Pres*
EMP: 20 **EST:** 1954
SQ FT: 20,000
SALES (est): 2.5MM **Privately Held**
WEB: www.excelspring.com
SIC: 3469 3495 Stamping metal for the trade; mechanical springs, precision

(G-1801)
FORMCO PLASTICS INC
Also Called: Litestage Lighting Systems
904 Fairway Dr (60106-1315)
PHONE.................................630 860-7998
Anthony J Tringali III, *CEO*
Joel Tringali, *Admin Sec*
EMP: 13
SQ FT: 18,000
SALES (est): 1.9MM **Privately Held**
WEB: www.formcoplastics.com
SIC: 3089 Injection molding of plastics

(G-1802)
FORSTER TOOL & MFG CO INC
1135 Industrial Dr (60106-1246)
PHONE.................................630 616-8177
Maureen Forster, *President*
Nick Bird, *Vice Pres*
Scott Forst, *Vice Pres*
EMP: 33
SQ FT: 15,000
SALES (est): 6MM **Privately Held**
WEB: www.forstertool.com
SIC: 3544 3451 3469 Special dies & tools; screw machine products; metal stampings

(G-1803)
FORTUNE ROPE & METAL CO INC
700 County Line Rd (60106-3276)
PHONE.................................630 787-9715
Ireta Enright, *Branch Mgr*
Dan Cunningham, *Manager*
EMP: 5 **Privately Held**
SIC: 3496 Miscellaneous fabricated wire products
PA: Fortune Rope & Metal Co. Inc.
67 Ballou Blvd
Bristol RI 02809

(G-1804)
FREEDOM FASTENER INC
1084 Industrial Dr Ste 6 (60106-1261)
PHONE.................................847 891-3686
Vicki Scharringhausen, *President*
EMP: 2
SALES (est): 334.9K **Privately Held**
SIC: 3452 Bolts, nuts, rivets & washers

(G-1805)
FRESENIUS KABI LLC
Also Called: Distribution Center
600 Supreme Dr (60106-1158)
PHONE.................................630 350-7150
Michael Bean, *General Mgr*
EMP: 40
SALES (corp-wide): 39.1B **Privately Held**
SIC: 2834 Pharmaceutical preparations
HQ: Fresenius Kabi, Llc
3 Corporate Dr
Lake Zurich IL 60047
847 550-2300

(G-1806)
GAIM PLASTICS INCORPORATED (PA)
Also Called: G A I M Engineering
789 Golf Ln (60106-1563)
PHONE.................................630 350-9500
Edward W Glatt Jr, *President*
Terry Pawula, *Materials Mgr*
Edward Glatt, *Branch Mgr*
EMP: 16
SQ FT: 13,700
SALES (est): 2.7MM **Privately Held**
SIC: 3089 Injection molding of plastics

(G-1807)
GAS COMPRESSION SYSTEMS INC
1035 Entry Dr (60106-3314)
PHONE.................................630 766-6049
Robert A Vogt, *President*
Chris Ashworth, *Engineer*
▲ **EMP:** 12
SALES (est): 398.6K **Privately Held**
SIC: 3561 Pumps, oil well & field

(G-1808)
GATEWAY CABLE INC
11 Gateway Rd (60106-1948)
PHONE.................................630 766-7969
Ronald Flerlage, *Partner*
EMP: 5
SALES (est): 350.8K
SALES (corp-wide): 1.9MM **Privately Held**
SIC: 3679 Harness assemblies for electronic use: wire or cable
PA: Gateway Cable, Inc.
1998 Ohio St Ste 100
Lisle IL 60532
630 766-7969

(G-1809)
GEIB INDUSTRIES INC
901 E Jefferson St (60106-3232)
PHONE.................................847 455-4550
Robert Geib, *President*
Christopher Geib, *President*
Thomas Geib, *Vice Pres*
Brian Hoaglin, *Sales Mgr*
Peter Tinsley, *Sales Mgr*

GEOGRAPHIC SECTION

Bensenville - Dupage County (G-1840)

EMP: 25
SQ FT: 15,000
SALES (est): 29.4MM Privately Held
WEB: www.geibind.com
SIC: 5084 3498 3429 3052 Hydraulic systems equipment & supplies; fabricated pipe & fittings; manufactured hardware (general); rubber & plastics hose & beltings

(G-1810)
GENERAL ELECTRO CORPORATION
Also Called: Bentronics
1069 Bryn Mawr Ave (60106-1244)
PHONE..................630 595-8989
J Patel, President
EMP: 10
SQ FT: 10,500
SALES: 2MM Privately Held
SIC: 3672 8711 Printed circuit boards; engineering services

(G-1811)
GIRARD CHEMICAL COMPANY
605 Country Club Dr Ste F (60106-1330)
PHONE..................630 293-5886
Jeff Girard, President
David Girard, Corp Secy
EMP: 8
SALES: 1MM Privately Held
SIC: 2899 Water treating compounds

(G-1812)
GMA INC
756 Birginal Dr (60106-1213)
PHONE..................630 595-1255
Osvaldo Grano, President
EMP: 5
SQ FT: 3,800
SALES (est): 605K Privately Held
SIC: 3444 7692 3441 Sheet metalwork; welding repair; fabricated structural metal

(G-1813)
GOGO LLC
814 Thorndale Ave (60106)
PHONE..................630 647-1400
EMP: 78
SALES (corp-wide): 699MM Publicly Held
SIC: 4812 4813 3663 Mfg Radio/Tv Comm Equip Radiotelephone Commun Telephone Communications
HQ: Gogo Llc
    111 N Canal St Fl 15
    Chicago IL 60606

(G-1814)
GOLD MEDAL PRODUCTS CO
450 N York Rd (60106-1606)
PHONE..................630 860-2525
Mike McKee, Branch Mgr
EMP: 8
SALES (corp-wide): 129.8MM Privately Held
SIC: 3556 Food products machinery
PA: Gold Medal Products Co.
    10700 Medallion Dr
    Cincinnati OH 45241
    513 769-7676

(G-1815)
GRACELAND CUSTOM PRODUCTS INC
1017 Graceland Ave (60106)
PHONE..................630 616-4143
Leah Abraham, President
EMP: 19
SQ FT: 5,000
SALES: 1.8MM Privately Held
WEB: www.gracelandferrayproducts.com
SIC: 3812 Detection apparatus: electronic/magnetic field, light/heat

(G-1816)
GRAPHIC ENGRAVERS INC
Also Called: Graphic Photo Engravers
691 Country Club Dr (60106-1324)
PHONE..................630 595-0400
Charles E Zidek, President
David Zidek, Plant Mgr
Dena Ptak, Production
James Zidek, Treasurer
EMP: 20 EST: 1946
SQ FT: 14,000
SALES (est): 3.2MM Privately Held
WEB: www.geigraphics.com
SIC: 2796 Photoengraving plates, linecuts or halftones

(G-1817)
HART PUZZLES INC
661 Frontier Way (60106-3802)
PHONE..................847 910-2290
Dan O'Malley, President
EMP: 6
SALES (est): 196.1K Privately Held
SIC: 3944 Puzzles

(G-1818)
HI PRCISION TL MAKERS MCHY INC
774 Foster Ave (60106-1509)
PHONE..................630 694-0200
Harold Irving, President
EMP: 5
SALES (est): 669.8K Privately Held
SIC: 3544 Special dies & tools

(G-1819)
HI-TECH WELDING SERVICES INC
233 William St (60106-3324)
PHONE..................630 595-8160
Julius Schwarzinger, President
Maggy Zols, Office Mgr
EMP: 7
SQ FT: 10,000
SALES (est): 630K Privately Held
SIC: 3451 Screw machine products

(G-1820)
I C UNIVERSAL INC
1040 Fairway Dr (60106-1317)
PHONE..................630 766-1169
Isaac Capistran, President
EMP: 2 EST: 1996
SQ FT: 1,200
SALES: 220K Privately Held
SIC: 3469 Machine parts, stamped or pressed metal

(G-1821)
IBERIA FOODS CORP
121 Foster Ave (60106-1629)
PHONE..................847 678-2200
Eric Miller, CEO
EMP: 5
SALES (corp-wide): 97.3MM Privately Held
SIC: 2086 Bottled & canned soft drinks
HQ: Iberia Foods Corp.
    1900 Linden Blvd
    Brooklyn NY 11207
    718 272-8900

(G-1822)
INNOVATIVE GRINGING INC
690 County Line Rd (60106-3260)
PHONE..................630 766-4567
Chris Kik, President
EMP: 4
SALES: 300K Privately Held
SIC: 3599 Machine shop, jobbing & repair

(G-1823)
INTERNATIONAL GOLDEN FOODS INC
819 Industrial Dr (60106-1306)
PHONE..................630 860-5552
Mansour C Amiran, President
Amiran Mansour, Administration
◆ EMP: 15
SQ FT: 40,000
SALES (est): 3.1MM Privately Held
SIC: 2044 5149 Rice milling; rice, polished

(G-1824)
INTERSOL INDUSTRIES INC
241 James St (60106-3318)
PHONE..................630 238-0385
Orest Hrynewycz, President
Maria Hrynewycz, Corp Secy
Roman Hrynewycz, Vice Pres
Henry Golde, Controller
EMP: 10
SQ FT: 3,000
SALES: 1MM Privately Held
SIC: 3625 3555 Solenoid switches (industrial controls); printing trades machinery

(G-1825)
IRMKO TOOL WORKS INC
205 Park St (60106-2556)
PHONE..................630 350-7550
Eric Fox, President
Charles Dwyer, Chairman
Charlie Dwyer, Admin Sec
EMP: 40 EST: 1970
SQ FT: 16,000
SALES (est): 6.4MM Privately Held
SIC: 3599 3471 Machine shop, jobbing & repair; plating & polishing

(G-1826)
ISENBERG BATH CORPORATION
1325 W Irving Park Rd (60106-1764)
PHONE..................972 510-5916
EMP: 6 EST: 2011
SALES (est): 366.5K Privately Held
SIC: 3432 Plumbing Fixture Fittings And Trim

(G-1827)
J C EMBROIDERY & SCREEN PRINT
406 Industrial Dr (60106-1323)
PHONE..................630 595-4670
Jeff Congine, President
EMP: 2
SQ FT: 2,800
SALES (est): 200K Privately Held
SIC: 2395 Embroidery products, except schiffli machine

(G-1828)
JB METALFAB MFG INC
Also Called: JB Metals
708 County Line Rd (60106-3276)
PHONE..................630 422-7420
Huy Nguyen, President
EMP: 2 EST: 2016
SALES (est): 283.4K Privately Held
SIC: 3444 Sheet metalwork

(G-1829)
JEM TOOL & MANUFACTURING CO
797 Industrial Dr (60106-1304)
PHONE..................630 595-1686
Wesley Cassidy, President
Jonathan Cassidy, Corp Secy
EMP: 13
SQ FT: 12,000
SALES (est): 1.9MM Privately Held
SIC: 3599 Machine shop, jobbing & repair

(G-1830)
JET X AEROSPACE LLC
400 N York Rd (60106-1606)
PHONE..................630 238-1920
Demetri Xydas, Partner
Brian Aranza, Vice Pres
Chris Spaid, Vice Pres
Spaid Chris, VP Opers
Jayson Carver, Mng Member
EMP: 30
SQ FT: 20,000
SALES (est): 5.8MM Privately Held
WEB: www.jetx.aero
SIC: 3728 Aircraft parts & equipment

(G-1831)
JM DIE TOOLING CO
466 Meyer Rd (60106-1617)
PHONE..................630 616-7776
John Norawa, President
EMP: 20
SQ FT: 12,000
SALES (est): 3.1MM Privately Held
SIC: 3599 Machine shop, jobbing & repair

(G-1832)
JM TOOL & DIE LLC
Also Called: Athena Precision Machining
299 Beeline Dr (60106-1612)
PHONE..................630 616-7776
Darren Sweeney, VP Bus Dvlpt
John Morawa,
EMP: 2 EST: 2010
SALES (est): 300K Privately Held
WEB: www.jmdie.com
SIC: 3544 Special dies & tools

(G-1833)
JOHNSON PRINTING
729 Il Route 83 Ste 323 (60106-1256)
P.O. Box 1045 (60106-8045)
PHONE..................630 595-8815
Russell Johnson, Owner
EMP: 4
SALES (est): 214K Privately Held
SIC: 2752 2759 Commercial printing, offset; commercial printing

(G-1834)
K & H TOOL CO
164 Devon Ave (60106-1148)
PHONE..................630 766-4588
Manuel Cervantes, President
EMP: 6
SQ FT: 1,900
SALES: 300K Privately Held
SIC: 3544 3599 Jigs & fixtures; machine shop, jobbing & repair

(G-1835)
K B TOOL INC
211 Beeline Dr Ste 7 (60106-1640)
PHONE..................630 595-4340
Kenneth Burg, President
EMP: 5 EST: 1994
SQ FT: 3,200
SALES (est): 511.4K Privately Held
SIC: 3089 3544 Injection molded finished plastic products; dies & die holders for metal cutting, forming, die casting

(G-1836)
K P ENTERPRISES INC
792 County Line Rd Ste A (60106-3204)
PHONE..................630 509-2174
Krystyna Pasek, President
Jan Pasek, Admin Sec
EMP: 3
SALES (est): 431.3K Privately Held
SIC: 3599 3544 Machine shop, jobbing & repair; special dies, tools, jigs & fixtures

(G-1837)
KDN SIGNS INC
890 Eagle Dr (60106-1947)
PHONE..................847 721-3848
Brendan Bailey, President
EMP: 12
SQ FT: 9,000
SALES (est): 55.7K Privately Held
SIC: 3993 Signs & advertising specialties

(G-1838)
L D REDMER SCREW PDTS INC (PA)
Also Called: Tanko Screw Products
515 Thomas Dr (60106-1620)
PHONE..................630 787-0504
Chris Grady, President
Ofelia Berrospe, Controller
Bill Landholt, Sales Dir
Ryan Mann, Accounts Mgr
David Gifford, Director
EMP: 52 EST: 1961
SQ FT: 15,000
SALES (est): 14.2MM Privately Held
WEB: www.ldredmer.com
SIC: 3451 Screw machine products

(G-1839)
L-V INDUSTRIES INC
508 Meyer Rd (60106-1604)
PHONE..................630 595-9251
Jennifer Vinyard, President
Jeffrey Vinyard, Corp Secy
EMP: 10
SQ FT: 4,500
SALES (est): 1.6MM Privately Held
SIC: 3599 3544 Machine shop, jobbing & repair; special dies, tools, jigs & fixtures

(G-1840)
LAKE CABLE LLC (PA)
529 Thomas Dr (60106-1620)
PHONE..................888 518-8086
William Runzel, CEO
Emile Tohme, President
Everett McCarty, Vice Pres
Somie Mossell, Vice Pres
Bill Vranek, Vice Pres
▲ EMP: 194
SQ FT: 62,000

(PA)=Parent Co (HQ)=Headquarters (DH)=Div Headquarters
✪ = New Business established in last 2 years

Bensenville - Dupage County (G-1841)

SALES (est): 66.4MM **Privately Held**
SIC: 3496 Miscellaneous fabricated wire products

(G-1841)
LAKE COPPER CONDUCTORS LLC
529 Thomas Dr (60106-1620)
PHONE..................................847 378-7006
EMP: 4
SALES (est): 404.9K **Privately Held**
SIC: 3357 Building wire & cable, nonferrous

(G-1842)
LECIP INC
881 Il Route 83 (60106-1219)
PHONE..................................312 626-2525
Masahiro Nagasawa, *CEO*
Akio Fujii, *President*
Seiji Hiramitsu, *CFO*
Toyoji Sugisawa, *Admin Sec*
▲ EMP: 10
SALES (est): 2MM **Privately Held**
SIC: 3647 3669 3699 Vehicular lighting equipment; transportation signaling devices; electrical equipment & supplies
PA: Lecip Holdings Corporation
1260-2, Kaminoho
Motosu GIF 501-0

(G-1843)
LESKER COMPANY INC
528 N York Rd (60106-1607)
PHONE..................................708 343-2277
Robert Lesker, *President*
EMP: 25
SQ FT: 15,000
SALES (est): 3.5MM **Privately Held**
WEB: www.leskerstrapping.com
SIC: 3441 Fabricated structural metal

(G-1844)
LEVITON MANUFACTURING CO INC
700 Golf Ln (60106-1511)
PHONE..................................630 350-2656
EMP: 319
SALES (corp-wide): 1.3B **Privately Held**
SIC: 3643 Plugs, electric; caps & plugs, electric: attachment; connectors, electric cord; sockets, electric
PA: Leviton Manufacturing Co., Inc.
201 N Service Rd
Melville NY 11747
631 812-6000

(G-1845)
LRE PRODUCTS INC
Also Called: Hpfs
733 Maple Ln (60106-1513)
PHONE..................................630 238-8321
Ronald L Yonkee, *President*
Edward P Kasprzycki, *Vice Pres*
Laura Z Stueve, *Treasurer*
▲ EMP: 30
SQ FT: 25,000
SALES (est): 4.6MM **Privately Held**
SIC: 3965 3452 Fasteners, buttons, needles & pins; bolts, nuts, rivets & washers

(G-1846)
M COR INC
227 James St Ste 6 (60106-3374)
P.O. Box 844, Wood Dale (60191-0844)
PHONE..................................630 860-1150
Raymond Mattera, *President*
EMP: 14
SQ FT: 2,500
SALES (est): 2MM **Privately Held**
SIC: 3053 5085 Gaskets, all materials; industrial supplies

(G-1847)
MARVEL MACHINING CO INC
231 Evergreen Ave (60106-2501)
PHONE..................................630 350-0075
John Obstalecki, *President*
EMP: 4
SQ FT: 5,000
SALES (est): 650K **Privately Held**
SIC: 3599 Machine shop, jobbing & repair

(G-1848)
MATTHEW WARREN INC
Also Called: Hi-Perfrmnce Fastening Systems
733 Maple Ln (60106-1513)
PHONE..................................630 860-7766
Jon Emrich, *Sales Mgr*
EMP: 5
SALES (corp-wide): 185.9MM **Privately Held**
SIC: 3965 3452 Fasteners, buttons, needles & pins; bolts, nuts, rivets & washers
HQ: Matthew Warren, Inc.
9501 Tech Blvd Ste 401
Rosemont IL 60018
847 349-5760

(G-1849)
MBA MANUFACTURING INC
1086 Industrial Dr Ste 3 (60106-1262)
PHONE..................................847 566-2555
Otto Wolters, *President*
Gertraud Wolters, *Corp Secy*
EMP: 8
SQ FT: 3,500
SALES (est): 1.1MM **Privately Held**
SIC: 3599 Machine shop, jobbing & repair

(G-1850)
MICRO WEST LTD
326 Evergreen Ave (60106-2504)
P.O. Box 18 (60106-0018)
PHONE..................................630 766-7160
Ivan Kucera, *President*
EMP: 6
SALES (est): 656.5K **Privately Held**
SIC: 3643 Current-carrying wiring devices

(G-1851)
MICROTHINCOM INC
661 Frontier Way (60106-3802)
PHONE..................................630 543-0501
Kenneth Reick, *President*
Daniel O Malley, *Admin Sec*
EMP: 10
SQ FT: 22,000
SALES (est): 1.6MM **Privately Held**
WEB: www.microthin.com
SIC: 3089 Plastic kitchenware, tableware & houseware

(G-1852)
MIDSTATES CUTTING TOOLS INC
Also Called: Mid States Tool & Cutter
304 Meyer Rd (60106-1615)
PHONE..................................630 595-0700
James B Surpless Jr, *President*
EMP: 30 EST: 2005
SALES (est): 6.1MM **Privately Held**
WEB: www.midstates-tool.com
SIC: 3545 Cutting tools for machine tools; reamers, machine tool; drills (machine tool accessories); tools & accessories for machine tools

(G-1853)
MIDWEST GRAPHIC INDUSTRIES
Also Called: Midwest Graphics
605 Country Club Dr Ste A (60106-1330)
PHONE..................................630 509-2972
James W Panter Jr, *President*
Jefferey Panter, *Treasurer*
Scott W Panter, *Admin Sec*
EMP: 16
SQ FT: 10,000
SALES (est): 1.8MM **Privately Held**
SIC: 2752 2761 Commercial printing, offset; manifold business forms

(G-1854)
MODERN GEAR & MACHINE INC
406 Evergreen Ave (60106-2506)
PHONE..................................630 350-9173
Kathy Naumowicz, *President*
Darick Naumowicz, *Vice Pres*
EMP: 10
SQ FT: 5,600
SALES (est): 1.7MM **Privately Held**
SIC: 3541 3462 Gear cutting & finishing machines; iron & steel forgings

(G-1855)
MW INDUSTRIES INC
Also Called: Automatic Spring Coiling
131 Foster Ave (60106-1629)
PHONE..................................773 539-5600
EMP: 100
SALES (corp-wide): 185.9MM **Privately Held**
SIC: 3493 3495 Mfg Steel Springs-Non-wire Mfg Wire Springs
HQ: Mw Industries, Inc.
9501 Tech Blvd Ste 401
Rosemont IL 60018
847 349-5760

(G-1856)
NATIONAL DATA-LABEL CORP
301 Arthur Ct (60106-3381)
PHONE..................................630 616-9595
William Iovino, *President*
Kent Dahlgren, *Vice Pres*
Mary Lynn Leland, *Controller*
Bill Iovino, *Sales Staff*
Suzanne Weingartner, *Marketing Staff*
EMP: 20 EST: 1976
SQ FT: 25,000
SALES (est): 2.9MM **Privately Held**
SIC: 2759 2672 Labels & seals: printing; coated & laminated paper

(G-1857)
NEW WAVE EXPRESS INC
842 Foster Ave (60106-1510)
PHONE..................................630 238-3129
Takayuki Hanai, *Owner*
▲ EMP: 4
SALES (est): 257.3K **Privately Held**
SIC: 2741 Miscellaneous publishing

(G-1858)
NORTH AMERICA O M C G INC
Also Called: Omcg North America
857 Industrial Dr Ste 1 (60106-1351)
PHONE..................................630 860-1016
Luigi Magg, *President*
Robert Sears, *Vice Pres*
EMP: 5
SQ FT: 16,000
SALES (est): 420K **Privately Held**
WEB: www.omcg.com
SIC: 3549 3544 Metalworking machinery; special dies, tools, jigs & fixtures

(G-1859)
NORTHWEST PRODUCTS
1090 Industrial Dr Ste 1 (60106-1263)
PHONE..................................630 860-2288
EMP: 4
SALES (est): 100.2K **Privately Held**
SIC: 5032 3281 Marble building stone; marble, building: cut & shaped

(G-1860)
NORTHWEST TOOL CO INC
342 Evergreen Ave (60106-2504)
PHONE..................................630 350-4770
Tomasz Dabkiewicz, *President*
EMP: 4
SQ FT: 1,000
SALES (est): 599.4K **Privately Held**
WEB: www.northwestool.com
SIC: 3599 Machine shop, jobbing & repair

(G-1861)
OMEGA PRINTING INC
201 William St (60106-3324)
PHONE..................................630 595-6344
Louis J Finger, *President*
Cynthia H Finger, *Vice Pres*
▼ EMP: 20
SQ FT: 16,000
SALES (est): 4.1MM **Privately Held**
SIC: 2752 Commercial printing, offset

(G-1862)
OPTI-VUE INC
224 James St (60106-3319)
PHONE..................................630 274-6121
Yordan Vulich, *President*
John Vulich, *Vice Pres*
Matthew Vulich, *Vice Pres*
Joseph Vulich, *CFO*
EMP: 4
SQ FT: 13,000
SALES: 500K **Privately Held**
SIC: 5049 3827 Optical goods; optical instruments & lenses

(G-1863)
OSG POWER TOOLS INC
759 Industrial Dr (60106-1304)
PHONE..................................630 561-4008
EMP: 200
SALES (est): 12.8MM **Privately Held**
SIC: 3541 Mfg Machine Tools-Cutting

(G-1864)
OSG USA INC
759 Industrial Dr (60106-1304)
PHONE..................................630 274-2100
David Bernstein, *Purch Mgr*
Gohei Osawa, *Branch Mgr*
EMP: 115
SQ FT: 25,000 **Privately Held**
SIC: 3545 Cutting tools for machine tools
HQ: Osg Usa, Inc.
1945 W Walnut Hill Ln
Irving TX 75038
800 837-2223

(G-1865)
P & A DRIVELINE & MACHINE INC
Also Called: Drivetrain Svc & Components
292 Devon Ave Ste 18 (60106-1145)
PHONE..................................630 860-7474
Paresh Patel, *President*
Steve Mankiewicz, *Opers Mgr*
Eugene Trojaniak, *Admin Sec*
EMP: 15 EST: 1980
SQ FT: 11,200
SALES (est): 6.3MM **Privately Held**
WEB: www.drivetrainservice.com
SIC: 5013 3599 5531 Truck parts & accessories; machine shop, jobbing & repair; truck equipment & parts

(G-1866)
PALLET SERVICES INC
13 Brookwood St (60106-1972)
P.O. Box 846 (60106-0846)
PHONE..................................630 860-9233
Robert Johnson, *President*
Russell Johnson, *Vice Pres*
EMP: 5
SQ FT: 10,000
SALES (est): 2.5MM **Privately Held**
SIC: 2448 Pallets, wood

(G-1867)
PATKO TOOL & MANUFACTURING
767 Larsen Ct (60106-1103)
PHONE..................................630 616-8802
Chris Pacocha, *President*
EMP: 5
SALES (est): 627.4K **Privately Held**
SIC: 3469 Machine parts, stamped or pressed metal

(G-1868)
PLASTECH INC
Also Called: Land-O-Tackle
873 Fairway Dr (60106-1312)
PHONE..................................630 595-7222
Bob Kenyon, *President*
John Haase, *Vice Pres*
Judy Mussillo, *Admin Sec*
EMP: 12
SQ FT: 12,000
SALES (est): 1.2MM **Privately Held**
SIC: 3089 3949 Injection molding of plastics; fishing tackle, general

(G-1869)
POLAR CONTAINER CORPORATION
1050 Entry Dr (60106-3315)
PHONE..................................847 299-5030
Robert OHM, *President*
Linda OHM, *Vice Pres*
EMP: 3 EST: 1958
SQ FT: 3,500
SALES (est): 550.9K **Privately Held**
SIC: 3714 Gears, motor vehicle

GEOGRAPHIC SECTION
Bensenville - Dupage County (G-1897)

(G-1870)
PONTIAC ENGRAVING
586 Meyer Rd (60106-1604)
PHONE.................................630 834-4424
Bruce Solyom, *Owner*
EMP: 3
SQ FT: 2,500
SALES: 120K **Privately Held**
SIC: 2796 3545 3544 3452 Engraving on copper, steel, wood or rubber; printing plates; machine tool accessories; special dies, tools, jigs & fixtures; bolts, nuts, rivets & washers; commercial printing

(G-1871)
PRECISE DIGITAL PRINTING INC
880 Industrial Dr (60106-1307)
PHONE.................................847 593-2645
Jugnu Shah, *President*
EMP: 40
SALES: 3.6MM **Privately Held**
SIC: 7336 5099 2399 Graphic arts & related design; signs, except electric; banners, made from fabric

(G-1872)
PRO-TECH MACHINING INC
301 Eastern Ave Ste B (60106-3813)
PHONE.................................773 406-9297
Borys B Jarymowycz, *President*
EMP: 4
SALES (est): 50K **Privately Held**
SIC: 3599 Machine shop, jobbing & repair

(G-1873)
PRODUCTIVE PORTABLE DISP INC
Also Called: Productive Displays
546 N York Rd (60106-1607)
PHONE.................................630 458-9100
Bruce Ulrich, *CEO*
Jay Volke, *Prdtn Mgr*
Kate Ulrich, *Admin Sec*
EMP: 7
SQ FT: 3,200
SALES (est): 628.3K **Privately Held**
SIC: 2759 Business forms: printing

(G-1874)
PROSPAN MANUFACTURING CO
540 Meyer Rd (60106-1604)
PHONE.................................630 860-1930
James Sullivan, *President*
Geralyn Sullivan, *Admin Sec*
EMP: 2
SALES (est): 500K **Privately Held**
SIC: 3599 Column clamps & shores

(G-1875)
PROSTAT CORPORATION
1072 Tower Ln (60106-1031)
PHONE.................................630 238-8883
Frank Coloccia, *President*
Alex Cardona, *Opers Spvr*
EMP: 11
SQ FT: 5,600
SALES: 2.4MM **Privately Held**
SIC: 3825 3829 3823 Test equipment for electronic & electric measurement; measuring & controlling devices; industrial instrmnts msrmnt display/control process variable

(G-1876)
PROTECTOSEAL COMPANY (PA)
225 Foster Ave (60106-1631)
P.O. Box 95588, Chicago (60694-5588)
PHONE.................................630 595-0800
James P Honan, *President*
James Evans, *Purch Agent*
Larry Petersen, *Purchasing*
Lori Cummings, *Credit Staff*
Deborah Hamilton, *Human Res Mgr*
◆ EMP: 115
SQ FT: 150,000
SALES (est): 6MM **Privately Held**
WEB: www.protectoseal.com
SIC: 3795 5999 Tanks & tank components; safety supplies & equipment

(G-1877)
PURELINE TREATMENT SYSTEMS LLC
Also Called: Sterline Bridge
1241 N Ellis St (60106-1118)
PHONE.................................847 963-8465
Tim Lathrop, *Vice Pres*
Kathy Damerjian, *Purchasing*
John Sokol, *Technical Mgr*
Anthony Divito, *CFO*
Bradford T Whitmore, *Mng Member*
▲ EMP: 116
SQ FT: 12,000
SALES (est): 23MM **Privately Held**
SIC: 3589 3443 Water treatment equipment, industrial; fumigating chambers, metal plate

(G-1878)
QUALITY IRON WORKS INC
449 Evergreen Ave (60106-2505)
PHONE.................................630 766-0885
Fax: 630 766-0887
EMP: 17
SQ FT: 5,500
SALES (est): 1.3MM **Privately Held**
SIC: 1799 3446 Trade Contractor Mfg Architectural Metalwork

(G-1879)
QUALITY PLASTIC PRODUCTS INC
Also Called: Noridge Die & Mold
830 Maple Ln (60106-1546)
PHONE.................................630 766-7593
Sten Olsen, *President*
Susan O'Shea, *Marketing Mgr*
EMP: 6
SQ FT: 8,000
SALES (est): 730.6K **Privately Held**
SIC: 3089 Injection molding of plastics

(G-1880)
QUALITY TECH TOOL INC
759 Industrial Dr (60106-1304)
PHONE.................................847 690-9643
Zoran Denic, *President*
William Rackow, *Vice Pres*
EMP: 42
SQ FT: 11,000
SALES (est): 6.6MM **Privately Held**
SIC: 3545 5251 Drill bits, metalworking; tools

(G-1881)
R N I INDUSTRIES INC
Also Called: Advantage Unlimited
236 William St (60106-3325)
PHONE.................................630 860-9147
Bradley Jordan, *President*
Manny Aguilar, *Prdtn Mgr*
EMP: 22
SQ FT: 22,000
SALES (est): 2.6MM **Privately Held**
SIC: 3089 Injection molding of plastics

(G-1882)
RACKOW POLYMERS CORPORATION
475 Thomas Dr (60106-1618)
PHONE.................................630 766-3982
Mario Rackow, *President*
Ed Matrowski, *Vice Pres*
EMP: 30
SQ FT: 60,000
SALES (est): 6.1MM **Privately Held**
SIC: 3089 Injection molding of plastics

(G-1883)
REX RADIATOR AND WELDING CO
Also Called: Rex Radiator Sales & Dist
367 Evergreen Ave (60106-2503)
PHONE.................................630 595-4664
Bill Rex, *Manager*
EMP: 7
SALES (corp-wide): 3.4MM **Privately Held**
SIC: 7539 7692 Radiator repair shop, automotive; automotive welding
PA: Rex Radiator And Welding Co Inc
1440 W 38th St
Chicago IL 60609
312 421-1531

(G-1884)
RICH INDUSTRIES INC
489 Thomas Dr (60106-2499)
PHONE.................................630 766-9150
Richard Rogala, *President*
Dan Osborn, *General Mgr*
▲ EMP: 20
SQ FT: 15,000
SALES (est): 1MM **Privately Held**
WEB: www.richindustries.com
SIC: 3469 Stamping metal for the trade
PA: Alagor Industries, Incorporated
489 Thomas Dr
Bensenville IL 60106

(G-1885)
RPK TECHNOLOGIES INC
272 Judson St (60106-2604)
PHONE.................................630 595-0911
Randal Krawiec, *President*
EMP: 2 EST: 2002
SALES (est): 237.7K **Privately Held**
SIC: 3563 Spraying & dusting equipment

(G-1886)
RPT TONER LLC
475 Supreme Dr (60106-1161)
PHONE.................................630 694-0400
Jayant Shah,
Eric Martin,
Krishna Patel,
▲ EMP: 50
SQ FT: 50,000
SALES: 3.5MM **Privately Held**
SIC: 3955 Print cartridges for laser & other computer printers

(G-1887)
RUBICON TECHNOLOGY INC (PA)
900 E Green St (60106-2553)
PHONE.................................847 295-7000
Timothy Brog, *President*
Inga A Slavutsky, *CFO*
Tom D'Arcy, *Sales Mgr*
▲ EMP: 20
SQ FT: 30,000
SALES: 3.5MM **Publicly Held**
SIC: 3679 Electronic crystals

(G-1888)
S & W MANUFACTURING CO INC
216 Evergreen Ave (60106-2502)
PHONE.................................630 595-5044
William Burr, *President*
Don E Secor, *Vice Pres*
Milka Ahlstrand, *Controller*
Don Secor, *VP Sales*
Ben Chantos, *Sales Staff*
▲ EMP: 45
SQ FT: 35,000
SALES (est): 11MM **Privately Held**
SIC: 3469 3451 3829 7692 Machine parts, stamped or pressed metal; screw machine products; surveying & drafting equipment; welding repair; machine tool accessories

(G-1889)
SATURN MANUFACTURING COMPANY
233 Park St (60106-2556)
PHONE.................................630 860-8474
William S Beckmeyer III, *President*
Larry Lumb, *Admin Sec*
EMP: 7
SQ FT: 8,870
SALES (est): 1MM **Privately Held**
SIC: 3451 Screw machine products

(G-1890)
SCHLESINGER MACHINERY INC
820 Maple Ln (60106-1546)
PHONE.................................630 766-4074
Michael Schlesinger, *President*
Cathy Schlesinger, *Admin Sec*
EMP: 4
SQ FT: 8,000
SALES (est): 343.6K **Privately Held**
SIC: 5084 3555 Printing trades machinery, equipment & supplies; printing presses

(G-1891)
SCHOLASTIC TESTING SERVICE
Also Called: Schools Processing Service
480 Meyer Rd (60106-1617)
PHONE.................................630 766-7150
Dennis Anderhalter, *Principal*
EMP: 13
SALES (corp-wide): 1.9MM **Privately Held**
SIC: 8748 2741 7371 Testing service, educational or personnel; miscellaneous publishing; computer software development & applications
PA: Scholastic Testing Service, Inc.
4320 Green Ash Dr
Earth City MO 63045
314 739-3650

(G-1892)
SERVICE PRO ELECTRIC MTR REPR
690 Industrial Dr (60106-1319)
PHONE.................................630 766-1215
Scott L Gibler, *President*
Ellen Keller, *CFO*
EMP: 5
SQ FT: 3,500
SALES (est): 470K **Privately Held**
SIC: 7694 5571 7999 Electric motor repair; motorcycle parts & accessories; bicycle & motorcycle rental services

(G-1893)
SINGER DATA PRODUCTS INC (PA)
Also Called: Scribe International Division
790 Maple Ln (60106-1560)
PHONE.................................630 860-6500
Theodore Singer, *President*
EMP: 8
SQ FT: 9,000
SALES (est): 4.1MM **Privately Held**
SIC: 3577 3581 3579 3578 Printers, computer; automatic vending machines; postage meters; change making machines; audiometers

(G-1894)
SINGER MEDICAL PRODUCTS INC
790 Maple Ln (60106-1513)
PHONE.................................630 860-6500
Theodore Singer, *President*
M Torres, *Director*
EMP: 6
SQ FT: 9,000
SALES (est): 612K
SALES (corp-wide): 4.1MM **Privately Held**
SIC: 3825 Audiometers
PA: Singer Data Products Inc
790 Maple Ln
Bensenville IL 60106
630 860-6500

(G-1895)
SNYDER INDUSTRIES INC
Also Called: Rmic
736 Birginal Dr (60106-1213)
PHONE.................................630 773-9510
Thomas O'Connell, *President*
EMP: 90 **Privately Held**
SIC: 3089 1446 2821 Plastic containers, except foam; molding sand mining; molding compounds, plastics
HQ: Snyder Industries, Llc
6940 O St Ste 100
Lincoln NE 68510
402 467-5221

(G-1896)
SOJUZ ENT
464 Country Club Dr (60106-1507)
PHONE.................................847 215-9400
Karolis Kaminskas, *Owner*
▲ EMP: 4
SALES: 700K **Privately Held**
SIC: 3556 Food products machinery

(G-1897)
SPIRAL-HELIX INC
500 Industrial Dr (60106-1321)
PHONE.................................224 659-7870
Tom Munro, *President*
▲ EMP: 12

Bensenville - Dupage County (G-1898)

SALES (est): 2.4MM **Privately Held**
SIC: 3444 Sheet metalwork
HQ: Lindab Ab
Jarnvagsgatan 41
Grevie 269 6
431 850-00

(G-1898)
SPYTEK AEROSPACE CORPORATION
Also Called: S A
450 Frontier Way Ste D (60106-1170)
PHONE.....................847 318-7515
Christopher J Spytek, *President*
Michael Spytek, *Engineer*
Elizabeth Spytek, *Treasurer*
EMP: 8
SALES (est): 430K **Privately Held**
SIC: 3599 3769 Machine shop, jobbing & repair; guided missile & space vehicle parts & auxiliary equipment

(G-1899)
STANDARD CAR TRUCK COMPANY
Also Called: Triangle Engineered Products
701 Maple Ln (60106-1513)
PHONE.....................630 860-5511
Fax: 630 860-5607
EMP: 75
SALES (corp-wide): 3.8B **Publicly Held**
SIC: 3743 3563 Mfg Railroad Equipment Mfg Air/Gas Compressors
HQ: Standard Car Truck Company Inc
6400 Shafer Ct Ste 450
Rosemont IL 60018
847 692-6050

(G-1900)
TAR-B PRECISION MACHINING CORP
605 Country Club Dr Ste D (60106-1330)
PHONE.....................630 521-9771
Maret Wieckowski, *President*
EMP: 5
SALES (est): 615.4K **Privately Held**
SIC: 3599 Machine shop, jobbing & repair

(G-1901)
THERMO-GRAPHIC LLC
301 Arthur Ct (60106-3381)
PHONE.....................630 350-2226
Alex Lopezalles, *Mng Member*
EMP: 35
SALES (est): 5.7MM **Privately Held**
SIC: 3993 3089 2759 Displays & cutouts, window & lobby; plastic processing; screen printing

(G-1902)
TJ ASSEMBLIES INC
511 E Pine Ave (60106-2527)
PHONE.....................847 671-0060
Dolores Jarosz, *President*
Bruce Jarosz, *Exec VP*
Brian Jarosz, *Vice Pres*
Don Jarosz, *Vice Pres*
Donald Jarosz, *Vice Pres*
EMP: 50
SQ FT: 22,000
SALES (est): 8.5MM **Privately Held**
SIC: 2655 Bobbins, textile spinning: made from purchased fiber

(G-1903)
TRANSPARENT CONTAINER CO INC
625 Thomas Dr (60106-1622)
PHONE.....................630 543-1818
Rich Orton, *Safety Mgr*
EMP: 53
SALES (corp-wide): 142.2MM **Privately Held**
SIC: 3089 Plastic containers, except foam; trays, plastic
HQ: Transparent Container Co., Inc.
325 S Lombard Rd
Addison IL 60101
708 449-8520

(G-1904)
TSA PROCESSING CHICAGO INC
520 Thomas Dr (60106-1621)
PHONE.....................630 860-5900
William Tresten, *President*
Marissa Vera, *Office Mgr*
Bobbie Medus, *Manager*
Bobby Medus, *Manager*
Monte Sneed, *Admin Sec*
▲ EMP: 8
SALES (est): 1.6MM **Privately Held**
WEB: www.tsaprocessing.com
SIC: 3312 Hot-rolled iron & steel products

(G-1905)
ULTRA PACKAGING INC
534 N York Rd (60106-1607)
PHONE.....................630 595-9820
Pamela Stockus, *President*
Pamlea Stockus, *President*
Robert Stockus, *Vice Pres*
EMP: 9
SALES (est): 1.9MM **Privately Held**
SIC: 3565 5084 3554 Packaging machinery; industrial machinery & equipment; paper industries machinery

(G-1906)
V & A MANUFACTURING
1054 Fairway Dr (60106-1317)
PHONE.....................630 595-1072
Ewa Lesko, *President*
Darek Lesko, *President*
EMP: 5
SQ FT: 1,800
SALES (est): 1.5MM **Privately Held**
SIC: 3599 Machine shop, jobbing & repair

(G-1907)
VAL CUSTOM CABINETS & FLRG INC
240 Evergreen Ave (60106-2502)
PHONE.....................708 790-8373
EMP: 8 EST: 2010
SALES (est): 56.5K **Privately Held**
SIC: 2434 Wood kitchen cabinets

(G-1908)
VICTOR ENVELOPE MFG CORP
301 Arthur Ct (60106-3381)
PHONE.....................630 616-2750
Kent Gundlach, *President*
Mary Lynn Leland, *Controller*
Kenneth Seroka, *Admin Sec*
EMP: 210
SQ FT: 250,000
SALES (est): 42.4MM **Privately Held**
SIC: 2759 Envelopes: printing

(G-1909)
VIKING PRTG GRAPHIC FORMS INC
530 E Green St (60106-2546)
PHONE.....................630 521-0150
William Karakosta, *CEO*
Jeff Schoner, *President*
Stephanie Shoner, *Treasurer*
Corrie D' Angelo, *Manager*
Stephanie Schoner, *Admin Sec*
EMP: 17
SQ FT: 11,000
SALES (est): 2.7MM **Privately Held**
SIC: 2752 Commercial printing, offset

(G-1910)
VISION ENGINEERING LABS (PA)
215 Gateway Rd (60106-1952)
PHONE.....................630 350-9470
Larry A Kerchenfaut, *Principal*
EMP: 6
SALES (est): 528K **Privately Held**
SIC: 3641 Electric lamps

(G-1911)
WENLYN SCREW COMPANY INC
810 Maple Ln (60106-1546)
PHONE.....................630 766-0050
Kenneth Hudziak, *President*
EMP: 4
SQ FT: 7,000
SALES (est): 436.9K **Privately Held**
WEB: www.wenlyn-screw.com
SIC: 3452 3451 Screws, metal; screw machine products

(G-1912)
WEST PRECISION TOOL INC
447 Evergreen Ave (60106-2592)
PHONE.....................630 766-8304
Bill Fielder, *President*
John Schweig, *Vice Pres*
Norma Fielder, *Admin Sec*
EMP: 14
SQ FT: 5,000
SALES (est): 2MM **Privately Held**
SIC: 3541 3545 Machine tools, metal cutting type; machine tool accessories

(G-1913)
WINDY CITY CUTTING DIE INC
104 Foster Ave (60106-1630)
PHONE.....................630 521-9410
John Rzeszot, *President*
William Wiard, *Vice Pres*
Rafal Strag, *Production*
John Iwanicki, *Treasurer*
EMP: 29
SQ FT: 29,000
SALES (est): 5.9MM **Privately Held**
SIC: 3544 Dies, steel rule; special dies & tools

(G-1914)
WORLD DRYER CORPORATION
340 County Line Rd Ste A (60106-2583)
PHONE.....................800 323-0701
Sean Martin, *Principal*
Susan Fan, *Vice Pres*
John Potts, *Vice Pres*
Dan Storto, *Vice Pres*
Joe Hernandez, *Opers Mgr*
▲ EMP: 30
SALES (est): 721.5K **Publicly Held**
SIC: 3634 Dryers, electric: hand & face
PA: Rexnord Corporation
511 W Freshwater Way
Milwaukee WI 53204

(G-1915)
WORLD WIDE ROTARY DIE
104 Foster Ave (60106-1630)
PHONE.....................630 521-9410
Janusz Iwanicki, *President*
William Wiard, *Vice Pres*
John Kathrein, *Treasurer*
Janusz Rzeszot, *Admin Sec*
EMP: 7
SQ FT: 10,000
SALES (est): 808.5K **Privately Held**
SIC: 3544 Special dies & tools

(G-1916)
XD INDUSTRIES INC
244 James St (60106-3319)
PHONE.....................630 766-2843
Sebastian Procek, *Owner*
EMP: 10
SALES (est): 819K **Privately Held**
SIC: 3471 7692 Cleaning, polishing & finishing; automotive welding

Benton
Franklin County

(G-1917)
AIRGAS USA LLC
12238 Petroff Rd (62812-6900)
PHONE.....................618 439-7207
Dan Davis, *Branch Mgr*
EMP: 8
SALES (corp-wide): 129.8MM **Privately Held**
SIC: 5084 5169 2813 Welding machinery & equipment; industrial gases; industrial gases
HQ: Airgas Usa, Llc
259 N Radnor Chester Rd
Radnor PA 19087
610 687-5253

(G-1918)
ALL STARS -N- STITCHES INC
418 E Main St (62812-2154)
P.O. Box 10 (62812-0010)
PHONE.....................618 435-5555
Dave Severin, *President*
Penny Severin, *Treasurer*
EMP: 7
SQ FT: 1,200
SALES (est): 590K **Privately Held**
SIC: 7389 5999 2759 2395 Cloth cutting, bolting or winding; sign painting & lettering shop; engraving service; banners; screen printing; embroidery products, except schiffli machine

(G-1919)
BENTON EVENING NEWS CO
111 E Church St (62812-2238)
P.O. Box 184, Du Quoin (62832-0184)
PHONE.....................618 438-5611
Danny Malkovich, *President*
EMP: 3
SQ FT: 3,500
SALES (est): 151.3K **Privately Held**
WEB: www.bentoneveningnews.com
SIC: 2711 2752 Commercial printing & newspaper publishing combined; commercial printing, lithographic

(G-1920)
BENTON GAZETTE
104 W Main St (62812-1346)
PHONE.....................618 438-6397
EMP: 3
SALES (est): 98.1K **Privately Held**
SIC: 2711 Newspapers, publishing & printing

(G-1921)
BIO FUELS BY AMERICAN FARMERS
Also Called: Bfafv
10163 Sugar Creek Rd (62812-4333)
PHONE.....................561 859-6251
Dennis Kinkade, *Mng Member*
John Carlyle,
EMP: 12
SALES (est): 1.1MM **Privately Held**
SIC: 2046 2041 2076 0723 Wet corn milling; flour & other grain mill products; vegetable oil mills; grain milling, custom services

(G-1922)
BRADEN ROCK BIT
14447 State Highway 34 (62812-6053)
PHONE.....................618 435-4519
William Braden, *Owner*
EMP: 6
SALES (est): 602.2K **Privately Held**
SIC: 3532 7699 Bits, except oil & gas field tools, rock; construction equipment repair

(G-1923)
CUSTOM ENTERPRISES
131 Industrial Park Rd (62812-4541)
PHONE.....................618 439-6626
Deanna Pyszka, *Owner*
Carey Pyszka, *Co-Owner*
EMP: 4
SQ FT: 3,500
SALES: 450K **Privately Held**
SIC: 2396 3993 2395 Screen printing on fabric articles; signs & advertising specialties; pleating & stitching

(G-1924)
CUSTOM STAINLESS STEEL INC (PA)
350 Industrial Park Dr (62812)
P.O. Box 1267 (62812-5267)
PHONE.....................618 435-2605
Joe Zsido, *President*
Mike Procaccini, *Vice Pres*
EMP: 15
SQ FT: 13,000
SALES (est): 1.8MM **Privately Held**
SIC: 3429 5091 Marine hardware; boat accessories & parts

(G-1925)
FOUR SEASONS ACE HARDWARE
11230 State Highway 37 (62812-4400)
PHONE.....................618 439-2101
Marino Presa, *Partner*
Terry Presa, *Partner*
EMP: 4
SQ FT: 4,000
SALES (est): 479.2K **Privately Held**
SIC: 5251 2097 Hardware; manufactured ice

GEOGRAPHIC SECTION

(G-1926)
HUTCHENS-BIT SERVICE INC
11898 Commerce Ln (62812-6532)
PHONE.................................618 439-9485
Kenneth Hutchens, *President*
Betty Hutchens, *Treasurer*
▼ **EMP:** 15
SALES (est): 2.9MM **Privately Held**
SIC: 3533 Bits, oil & gas field tools; rock

(G-1927)
ILLINOIS METER INC
Also Called: Imco
1500 W Webster St (62812)
P.O. Box 425 (62812-0425)
PHONE.................................618 438-6039
Dennis J Sheley, *President*
EMP: 5
SALES (corp-wide): 38.4MM **Privately Held**
WEB: www.stopsmartmeters.org
SIC: 3317 5051 Seamless pipes & tubes; pipe & tubing, steel
PA: Illinois Meter, Inc.
4390 Jeffory St
Springfield IL 62703
217 529-1672

(G-1928)
INFINITY TOOL MFG LLC
11648 Skylane Dr (62812-4357)
PHONE.................................618 439-4042
Loyd Shults, *Engineer*
Kenneth D Sentel, *Mng Member*
Bert Beatty, *Technical Staff*
Todd Taylor,
▲ **EMP:** 5 **EST:** 2008
SALES (est): 1MM **Privately Held**
WEB: www.infinitytoolmfg.com
SIC: 3545 Drills (machine tool accessories)

(G-1929)
JOE ZSIDO SALES & DESIGN INC
350 Industrial Park Rd (62812)
P.O. Box 1267 (62812-5267)
PHONE.................................618 435-2605
Joe Zsido, *President*
Elizabeth Zsido, *Corp Secy*
Mike Procaccini, *Vice Pres*
EMP: 40
SALES (est): 4.2MM **Privately Held**
SIC: 3312 Stainless steel

(G-1930)
KNIGHT BROS INC
Also Called: Heritage Custom Trailers
10764 Industrial Park Rd (62812-4537)
PHONE.................................618 439-9626
Mark Knight, *President*
Jason Knight, *Vice Pres*
EMP: 20
SQ FT: 35,000
SALES (est): 3.1MM **Privately Held**
SIC: 3799 5599 Boat trailers; utility trailers

(G-1931)
LAMPLEY OIL INC
720 W Main St Ste B (62812-1350)
PHONE.................................618 439-6288
Steve Lampley, *President*
EMP: 5
SQ FT: 600
SALES (est): 524.4K **Privately Held**
SIC: 1311 Crude petroleum production

(G-1932)
MINCON INC
Also Called: Mincon Rockdrills USA
107 Industrial Park Rd (62812-4541)
P.O. Box 189 (62812-0189)
PHONE.................................618 435-3404
Mike Jones, *President*
▲ **EMP:** 20
SQ FT: 10,000
SALES (est): 4.2MM **Privately Held**
SIC: 3545 Drill bits, metalworking
HQ: Mincon Group Public Limited Company
Smithstown Industrial Estate
Ballymote

(G-1933)
NATURAL RESOURCES ILL DEPT
Also Called: Office of Mines & Minerals
503 E Main St (62812-2522)
PHONE.................................618 439-4320
Don McBride, *Manager*
EMP: 30 **Privately Held**
SIC: 1481 9512 Test boring for nonmetallic minerals; land, mineral & wildlife conservation;
HQ: Illinois Department Of Natural Resources
1 Natural Resources Way # 100
Springfield IL 62702

(G-1934)
NEWMAN WELDING & MACHINE SHOP
400 W Bond St (62812-1003)
PHONE.................................618 435-5591
Lillian Newman, *Owner*
EMP: 3 **EST:** 1953
SQ FT: 5,440
SALES (est): 281.2K **Privately Held**
SIC: 7692 3443 3441 Welding repair; fabricated plate work (boiler shop); fabricated structural metal

(G-1935)
POSITIVE IMPRESSIONS
14190 State Highway 34 (62812-6041)
PHONE.................................618 438-7030
Allen Lampley, *Owner*
EMP: 4 **EST:** 1991
SALES (est): 396.3K **Privately Held**
SIC: 2759 Screen printing

(G-1936)
ROYAL BRASS INC
1202 Route 14 W (62812-1595)
P.O. Box 594 (62812-0594)
PHONE.................................618 439-6341
Gretchen Leonard, *Opers-Prdtn-Mfg*
EMP: 7
SALES (corp-wide): 54.3MM **Privately Held**
SIC: 3492 3533 3429 3052 Hose & tube fittings & assemblies, hydraulic/pneumatic; oil & gas field machinery; manufactured hardware (general); rubber & plastics hose & beltings
PA: Royal Brass, Inc.
1470 Amherst Rd Ste C
Knoxville TN 37909
865 558-0224

(G-1937)
THOMAS PRINTING & STY CO
301 S Du Quoin St (62812-1460)
PHONE.................................618 435-2801
William F Thomas, *President*
Michael Thomas, *Vice Pres*
EMP: 5
SQ FT: 2,000
SALES (est): 609.8K **Privately Held**
SIC: 2752 2759 2789 Commercial printing, offset; letterpress printing; bookbinding & related work

(G-1938)
TRI-CITY READY-MIX
302 E Bond St (62812-2004)
PHONE.................................618 439-2071
Robert Smith, *President*
Norma Smith, *Vice Pres*
Pamela Smith, *Admin Sec*
EMP: 6 **EST:** 1965
SQ FT: 1,000
SALES: 600K **Privately Held**
WEB: www.tri-citypaving.com
SIC: 3273 Ready-mixed concrete

Berkeley
Cook County

(G-1939)
BUHL PRESS
5656 Mcdermott Dr (60163-1101)
PHONE.................................708 449-8989
Fax: 708 449-8988
EMP: 24
SALES (est): 2.7MM **Privately Held**
SIC: 2752 Lithographic Commercial Printing

(G-1940)
DIGITAL HUB LLC
5656 Mcdermott Dr (60163-1101)
PHONE.................................312 943-6161
Charles J Anzilotti,
EMP: 29
SALES (est): 6.4MM **Privately Held**
SIC: 2759 Commercial printing

(G-1941)
KI INDUSTRIES INC
5540 Mcdermott Dr (60163-1203)
PHONE.................................708 449-1990
David Goltermann, *President*
Luis Moreno, *Business Mgr*
Elizabeth Goltermann, *Corp Secy*
Don Mitchell, *Safety Mgr*
Ruth Felske, *Opers Staff*
▲ **EMP:** 45
SQ FT: 25,000
SALES (est): 11.8MM **Privately Held**
WEB: www.kiindustries.com
SIC: 3089 3643 3446 3432 Injection molding of plastics; current-carrying wiring devices; architectural metalwork; plumbing fixture fittings & trim

(G-1942)
MITTERA ILLINOIS LLC
Also Called: Mittera Chicago
5656 Mcdermott Dr (60163-1101)
PHONE.................................708 449-8989
John Hamilton, *President*
EMP: 89
SALES (corp-wide): 320MM **Privately Held**
SIC: 2752 8742 Commercial printing, lithographic; marketing consulting services
HQ: Mittera Illinois, Llc
1312 Locust St Ste 202
Des Moines IA 50309
515 343-5359

(G-1943)
PETERSON ELC PANL MFG CO INC
5550 Mcdermott Dr (60163-1203)
PHONE.................................708 449-2270
Sue Todd, *CEO*
Richard M Todd Sr, *President*
Richard R Todd Jr, *Vice Pres*
EMP: 18 **EST:** 1917
SQ FT: 21,000
SALES (est): 7.1MM **Privately Held**
SIC: 3612 3613 Lighting transformers; street & airport; switchboards & parts, power

(G-1944)
PREFERRED PRINTING & GRAPHICS
5815 Saint Charles Rd (60163-1031)
PHONE.................................708 547-6880
Rosalie Joseph, *Owner*
EMP: 3
SQ FT: 1,500
SALES (est): 240.5K **Privately Held**
SIC: 2752 Commercial printing, offset

(G-1945)
VANEE FOODS COMPANY
5418 Mcdermott Dr (60163-1299)
PHONE.................................708 449-7300
Aloysius Van Eekeren, *President*
Brent Cristao, *Business Mgr*
Andrew Van Eekeren, *Vice Pres*
Alex Vaneekeren, *Vice Pres*
Chuck Vaneekeren, *Vice Pres*
▲ **EMP:** 100 **EST:** 1950
SQ FT: 500,000
SALES (est): 34.4MM **Privately Held**
WEB: www.vaneefoodservice.com
SIC: 2099 2034 2092 2032 Seasonings: dry mixes; sauces: gravy, dressing & dip mixes; dried & dehydrated soup mixes; fresh or frozen fish or seafood chowders, soups & stews; beef soup: packaged in cans, jars, etc.

(G-1946)
VORIS COMMUNICATION CO INC (PA)
Also Called: Kelmscott Communications
5656 Mcdermott Dr (60163-1101)
P.O. Box 875, Hillside (60162-0875)
PHONE.................................630 898-4268
Scott Voris, *President*
Jerry Heitschmidt, *Vice Pres*
Chuck Randazzo, *Vice Pres*
Jason Tews, *Vice Pres*
Deanna Heitschmidt, *Director*
EMP: 108 **EST:** 1938
SQ FT: 25,000
SALES (est): 25.9MM **Privately Held**
WEB: www.kelmscottedu.com
SIC: 2752 2791 2789 Commercial printing, lithographic; typesetting; bookbinding & related work

Berwyn
Cook County

(G-1947)
ABLE PRINTING SERVICE INC
6837 Stanley Ave (60402-3041)
PHONE.................................708 788-7115
Herman V Dernaald, *President*
Ryan Naald, *President*
Gary Vandernaald, *Admin Sec*
EMP: 7 **EST:** 1939
SQ FT: 1,800
SALES (est): 821.4K **Privately Held**
WEB: www.ableprintingchicago.com
SIC: 2752 Commercial printing, offset

(G-1948)
ALL DENTAL
6721 Cermak Rd (60402-2216)
PHONE.................................708 749-0277
Claudia Osorio, *Owner*
Laura Osorio, *Manager*
EMP: 5
SALES (est): 567.3K **Privately Held**
SIC: 8082 2844 Home health care services; cosmetic preparations

(G-1949)
C C P EXPRESS INC
2630 Highland Ave (60402-2716)
PHONE.................................773 315-0317
Castulo Cortes, *President*
Erica Aguero, *Admin Sec*
EMP: 4
SALES (est): 600.6K **Privately Held**
SIC: 3537 Trucks: freight, baggage, etc.: industrial, except mining

(G-1950)
DIAMOND GRAPHICS OF BERWYN
6625 26th St Ste 1 (60402-2585)
PHONE.................................708 749-2500
Paul Dimenna, *President*
EMP: 6
SALES: 2MM **Privately Held**
SIC: 2752 2791 2789 Commercial printing, offset; typesetting; bookbinding & related work

(G-1951)
EDGE COMMUNICATION
3825 Kenilworth Ave (60402-3911)
PHONE.................................708 749-7818
EMP: 9
SALES (est): 540K **Privately Held**
SIC: 7311 2741 Advertising Agency And Publishes Directories

(G-1952)
EL DIA NEWSPAPER
6331 26th St Apt 1 (60402-5658)
PHONE.................................708 956-7282
George Montesdeoca, *Owner*
EMP: 7
SALES (est): 308.9K **Privately Held**
SIC: 2711 Newspapers, publishing & printing

Berwyn - Cook County (G-1953)

(G-1953)
FATHER & DAUGHTERS PRINTING
6237 Roosevelt Rd (60402-1163)
PHONE..................708 749-8286
Carlos Zepea, *Owner*
EMP: 2
SALES (est): 210K **Privately Held**
SIC: 2759 Commercial printing

(G-1954)
FEDERAL-MOGUL MOTORPARTS LLC
Also Called: Federal Mogul Driveline Pdts
4929 S Mason (60402)
PHONE..................248 354-7700
Allen Gronner, *Manager*
EMP: 25
SALES (corp-wide): 17.4B **Publicly Held**
SIC: 3714 3053 Universal joints, motor vehicle; gaskets & sealing devices
HQ: Federal-Mogul Motorparts Llc
27300 W 11 Mile Rd
Southfield MI 48034
248 354-7700

(G-1955)
LITTLE VILLAGE PRINTING INC
3210 Grove Ave Apt 2w (60402-3494)
P.O. Box 243, Riverside (60546-0243)
PHONE..................708 749-4414
William Woznicki, *President*
Virginia Woznicki, *Corp Secy*
EMP: 3 **EST:** 1964
SQ FT: 900
SALES (est): 365K **Privately Held**
SIC: 2752 Lithographing on metal

(G-1956)
MASA UNO INC
6311 Cermak Rd Ste 2 (60402-5466)
PHONE..................708 749-4866
Yolanda Carreon, *President*
EMP: 7 **EST:** 2014
SALES (est): 714.1K **Privately Held**
SIC: 2096 Tortilla chips

(G-1957)
NORTHFIELD BLOCK COMPANY
Also Called: Chicago Block
5400 W Canal Bank Rd (60402)
PHONE..................708 458-8130
Rick Rasanelli, *Branch Mgr*
EMP: 7
SALES (corp-wide): 30.6B **Privately Held**
SIC: 5032 3271 3272 Masons' materials; blocks, concrete or cinder: standard; concrete products
HQ: Northfield Block Company
1 Hunt Ct
Mundelein IL 60060
847 816-9000

(G-1958)
OGDEN TOP & TRIM SHOP INC
6609 Ogden Ave (60402-3788)
PHONE..................708 484-5422
Carol Nesladek, *Owner*
EMP: 7
SQ FT: 3,800
SALES: 250K **Privately Held**
WEB: www.ogdentopandtrim.com
SIC: 7532 3714 2394 2221 Upholstery & trim shop, automotive; motor vehicle parts & accessories; canvas & related products; broadwoven fabric mills, manmade

(G-1959)
ORGANNICA INC
3437 Maple Ave (60402-3241)
P.O. Box 561 (60402-0561)
PHONE..................312 925-7272
Jennnifer Angone, *Principal*
EMP: 4
SALES: 3.4K **Privately Held**
SIC: 2833 7389 Organic medicinal chemicals: bulk, uncompounded;

(G-1960)
PHYSICIANS RECORD CO INC
3000 Ridgeland Ave (60402-0724)
PHONE..................800 323-9268
John C Voller, *President*
Marcy Voller, *Vice Pres*
Victoria Bocek, *Treasurer*
Roxane Hermosillo, *Cust Mgr*
Irma Voller, *Admin Sec*
▼ **EMP:** 56 **EST:** 1907
SQ FT: 60,000
SALES (est): 3MM **Privately Held**
WEB: www.physiciansrecord.com
SIC: 2752 2759 2761 Commercial printing, offset; letterpress printing; manifold business forms

(G-1961)
SWEETENER SUPPLY CORPORATION
2905 Ridgeland Ave (60402-2781)
PHONE..................708 484-3455
EMP: 10 **Privately Held**
SIC: 2099 Food preparations
PA: Sweetener Supply Corporation
9501 Southview Ave
Brookfield IL 60513

(G-1962)
VANGARD DISTRIBUTION INC
Also Called: Vangard Box & Packaging Group
2905 Ridgeland Ave (60402-2781)
PHONE..................708 484-9895
EMP: 3 **Privately Held**
SIC: 2653 3053 Corrugated & solid fiber boxes; packing materials
PA: Vangard Distribution, Inc.
9501 Southview Ave
Brookfield IL 60513

(G-1963)
ZEIGLER CHRYSLER DODGE
Also Called: Zeigler Preowned of Chicago
6539 Ogden Ave (60402-3700)
PHONE..................708 956-7700
Debbie Phillips,
EMP: 4
SALES (est): 710.5K **Privately Held**
WEB: www.zeiglerpreownedchicago.com
SIC: 5511 3714 Automobiles, new & used; motor vehicle parts & accessories

Bethalto
Madison County

(G-1964)
EAGLE EXPRESS MAIL LLC
Also Called: Mail Box Store, The
333 W Bethalto Dr Ste C (62010-1916)
PHONE..................618 377-6245
Eliot L Deters,
EMP: 6
SALES (est): 852.2K **Privately Held**
SIC: 7389 4783 2759 Packaging & labeling services; packing goods for shipping; commercial printing

(G-1965)
PART STOP INC
5120 State Route 140 (62010-2200)
PHONE..................618 377-5238
Ron Wolkinson, *President*
EMP: 9
SQ FT: 2,500
SALES (est): 1.3MM **Privately Held**
SIC: 5531 3599 Automotive parts; automotive accessories; machine shop, jobbing & repair

(G-1966)
PERFORMANCE AUTOMOTIVE
475 S Prairie St (62010-1815)
PHONE..................618 377-0020
Gordon Shifflett, *Owner*
EMP: 3
SALES (est): 325.5K **Privately Held**
SIC: 3599 Machine shop, jobbing & repair

Bethany
Moultrie County

(G-1967)
BETHANY PHARMACOL CO INC
131 Hwy 121 E (61914)
P.O. Box 248 (61914-0248)
PHONE..................217 665-3395
Jack J Scott, *CEO*
EMP: 9 **EST:** 1997
SALES (est): 657K
SALES (corp-wide): 2.4MM **Privately Held**
SIC: 2844 Face creams or lotions
PA: Bethany Sales Company, Inc.
131 W Main St
Bethany IL 61914
217 665-3395

(G-1968)
MONROE ASSOCIATES INC
1545 Cr 375e (61914-7048)
P.O. Box 233 (61914-0233)
PHONE..................217 665-3898
Rechele Monroe, *President*
Dennis Monroe, *Vice Pres*
EMP: 3
SALES (est): 346.6K **Privately Held**
WEB: www.monroeassociates.net
SIC: 7379 3571 Computer related consulting services; personal computers (microcomputers)

Big Rock
Kane County

(G-1969)
CAM CO INC
400 Rhodes Ave (60511-2034)
P.O. Box 94 (60511-0094)
PHONE..................630 556-3110
Gregory J Beels, *President*
Ronda Beels, *Admin Sec*
▲ **EMP:** 10
SQ FT: 4,000
SALES (est): 1.3MM **Privately Held**
SIC: 3599 3829 3812 Water leak detectors; measuring & controlling devices; search & navigation equipment

Blackstone
Livingston County

(G-1970)
ALLOY SPECIALTIES INC
32028 N 1500 East Rd (61313-9690)
P.O. Box 212, Ransom (60470-0212)
PHONE..................815 586-4728
James G Coonan, *President*
Richard A Brechlin, *Corp Secy*
Julia K Coonan, *Vice Pres*
EMP: 18 **EST:** 2000
SQ FT: 5,000
SALES (est): 5.9MM **Privately Held**
WEB: www.alloybuilt.com
SIC: 3441 Fabricated structural metal

(G-1971)
VERONA RUBBER WORKS INC
31577 N 1250 East Rd (61313-9504)
PHONE..................815 673-2929
Mike Othon, *President*
Catherine Othon, *Vice Pres*
EMP: 13
SQ FT: 18,000
SALES: 1.6MM **Privately Held**
SIC: 3069 Custom compounding of rubber materials

Blandinsville
Mcdonough County

(G-1972)
PEAK PRINTING
110 W Monroe St (61420-5187)
P.O. Box 404 (61420-0404)
PHONE..................309 652-3655
Linda Peak, *Owner*
EMP: 2
SQ FT: 1,200
SALES (est): 217.5K **Privately Held**
SIC: 2752 Commercial printing, offset

Bloomingdale
Dupage County

(G-1973)
ABRASIVE
454 Scott Dr (60108-3120)
PHONE..................630 893-7800
EMP: 9
SALES (est): 1.2MM **Privately Held**
SIC: 3291 Abrasive products

(G-1974)
ABRASIVE-FORM LLC (PA)
454 Scott Dr (60108-3120)
PHONE..................630 220-3437
Mike Sobieski, *CEO*
Rick Katanic, *Maint Spvr*
Trudy Herrera, *Purchasing*
Thomas Eckert, *Engineer*
Jon Stientjes, *Project Engr*
EMP: 127
SQ FT: 73,000
SALES (est): 50.7MM **Privately Held**
SIC: 3291 Abrasive products

(G-1975)
ALTAK INC
250 Covington Dr (60108-3106)
PHONE..................630 622-0300
Al Kabeshita, *President*
Miko Kabeshita, *Exec VP*
Minoru Kabeshita, *Vice Pres*
Yutaka Kabeshita, *Vice Pres*
Patrick Boivin, *Materials Mgr*
▲ **EMP:** 85
SQ FT: 42,000
SALES (est): 23MM **Privately Held**
WEB: www.altakinc.com
SIC: 3496 5084 Miscellaneous fabricated wire products; industrial machinery & equipment

(G-1976)
AMERILIGHTS INC
Also Called: A2z Green Lighting
146 Roundtree Ct (60108-3044)
PHONE..................847 219-1476
Manjula Vora, *CEO*
Gordhan Patel, *Admin Sec*
EMP: 4
SALES (est): 371.7K **Privately Held**
SIC: 3646 Commercial indusl & institutional electric lighting fixtures

(G-1977)
ARTISTRIES BY TOMMY MUSTO INC
Also Called: Tommy Rock
159 W Lake St Ste 1 (60108-1052)
PHONE..................630 674-8667
Thomas C Musto, *President*
Donna Musto, *Admin Sec*
EMP: 3
SQ FT: 3,000
SALES: 400K **Privately Held**
WEB: www.tommyrockusa.com
SIC: 3271 1721 Concrete block & brick; painting & paper hanging

(G-1978)
AURUBIS BUFFALO INC
129 Fairfield Way Ste 308 (60108-1557)
PHONE..................630 980-8400
Don Olson, *President*
Donald Howard, *Manager*
EMP: 6
SALES (corp-wide): 12B **Privately Held**
WEB: www.aurubis.com
SIC: 3351 Copper rolling & drawing
HQ: Aurubis Buffalo, Inc.
70 Sayre St
Buffalo NY 14207
716 879-6700

(G-1979)
BEE-JAY INDUSTRIES INC
148 Paxton Rd (60108-3048)
PHONE..................708 867-4431
Kenneth Feferman, *President*
Kenneth Feferman, *President*
EMP: 12
SQ FT: 5,000

Bloomingdale - Dupage County (G-2008)

SALES (est): 1MM **Privately Held**
SIC: 3993 3961 3911 Advertising novelties; costume jewelry; jewelry, precious metal

(G-1980)
BI-LINK METAL SPECIALTIES INC (PA)
125 Fairfield Way Ste 310 (60108-1599)
PHONE..................................630 858-5900
David Myers, *President*
Roy Spangler, *Senior VP*
Greg Bossingham, *CFO*
Joe Wagner, *Human Res Mgr*
Reuel Villanueva, *Sales Staff*
▲ EMP: 104
SALES (est): 28.6MM **Privately Held**
WEB: www.bi-link.com
SIC: 3469 3544 Stamping metal for the trade; special dies & tools

(G-1981)
BIG BOLT LLC
140 Covington Dr (60108-3105)
PHONE..................................630 539-9400
Patrick Partridge, *CEO*
Thomas J Partridge, *COO*
EMP: 110
SALES (est): 3MM **Privately Held**
SIC: 3452 Bolts, nuts, rivets & washers

(G-1982)
BRIGHT BRAIN
108 W Schick Rd Unit 6130 (60108-4045)
PHONE..................................844 272-4645
Abel Lopez, *CEO*
EMP: 10
SALES (est): 409.5K **Privately Held**
SIC: 2833 Vitamins, natural or synthetic: bulk, uncompounded

(G-1983)
C & F MACHINE CORP
176 Covington Dr (60108-3105)
PHONE..................................630 924-0300
Julian Kuta, *President*
EMP: 12
SQ FT: 32,000
SALES (est): 1.2MM **Privately Held**
WEB: www.cfmach.com
SIC: 3599 Machine shop, jobbing & repair

(G-1984)
CELLMARK INC
Also Called: Semper/Exeter Paper Company
1 Tiffany Pt Ste 300 (60108-2948)
PHONE..................................630 775-9500
Bill Kratohvil, *Branch Mgr*
EMP: 9
SALES (corp-wide): 3.1B **Privately Held**
SIC: 2621 Writing paper
HQ: Cellmark, Inc.
  88 Rowland Way Ste 300
  Novato CA 94945
  415 927-1700

(G-1985)
CHICAGO PASTRY INC
142 N Bloomingdale Rd (60108-1017)
PHONE..................................630 529-6161
Egidio Turano, *Purchasing*
Peter Turano, *Sales Staff*
Remo Turano, *Branch Mgr*
Jenna Turano, *Manager*
EMP: 100
SALES (corp-wide): 124.2MM **Privately Held**
SIC: 5149 5461 2052 2051 Bakery products; bread; cookies & crackers; bread, cake & related products
PA: Chicago Pastry, Inc.
  6501 Roosevelt Rd
  Berwyn IL 60402
  708 788-5320

(G-1986)
CLARIOS
Also Called: Johnson Controls
153 Stratford Square Mall (60108-2202)
PHONE..................................630 351-9407
EMP: 5 **Privately Held**
SIC: 2531 Seats, automobile
HQ: Johnson Controls, Inc.
  5757 N Green Bay Ave
  Milwaukee WI 53209
  414 524-1200

(G-1987)
DAUPHIN ENTERPRISE INC
Also Called: Cartridge World Bloomingdale
358 W Army Trail Rd # 150 (60108-5605)
PHONE..................................630 893-6300
Dominick Dauphin, *Owner*
Christopher Nowak, *Manager*
EMP: 3
SALES (est): 466.7K **Privately Held**
SIC: 5112 3955 Office filing supplies; carbon paper & inked ribbons; print cartridges for laser & other computer printers

(G-1988)
DIEQUA CORPORATION (PA)
180 Covington Dr (60108-3105)
PHONE..................................630 980-1133
Meikel Quaas, *President*
Tom Enochs, *Production*
Stefanie Howard, *Sales Staff*
Alex Malamos, *Marketing Staff*
Norman Quaas, *Officer*
▲ EMP: 29
SQ FT: 40,000
SALES (est): 10MM **Privately Held**
WEB: www.diequa.com
SIC: 3566 Speed changers (power transmission equipment), except auto

(G-1989)
DIVERSIFIED PRINT GROUP
358 W Army Trail Rd # 140 (60108-5605)
PHONE..................................630 893-8920
Bob Rusty, *Owner*
EMP: 4
SALES (est): 478K **Privately Held**
SIC: 2752 Commercial printing, offset

(G-1990)
ELBA TOOL CO INC
220 Covington Dr (60108-3105)
PHONE..................................847 895-4100
Horst Elendt, *President*
Erich Elendt, *Vice Pres*
Ursula Elendt, *Admin Sec*
EMP: 18 EST: 1962
SQ FT: 20,000
SALES (est): 3.2MM **Privately Held**
WEB: www.elbatool.com
SIC: 3544 Industrial molds; dies & die holders for metal cutting, forming, die casting

(G-1991)
ELITE MANUFACTURING TECH INC
Also Called: Emt
333 Munroe Dr (60108-2639)
PHONE..................................630 351-5757
James E Conlon Jr, *CEO*
James O'Keefe, *President*
Carlos Galicia, *Plant Mgr*
Judith Posada, *Purch Agent*
Sarah Anderson, *Purchasing*
▲ EMP: 175
SQ FT: 80,000
SALES: 32MM **Privately Held**
SIC: 3444 Sheet metalwork

(G-1992)
ENDURE HOLDINGS INC
Also Called: Polaris Technology Group
125 Fairfield Way Ste 108 (60108-1556)
PHONE..................................224 558-1828
Norman Moore, *President*
EMP: 4
SALES (est): 179.3K **Privately Held**
SIC: 7371 7372 Computer software development & applications; application computer software

(G-1993)
ENVISION GRAPHICS LLC
Also Called: Envision 3
225 Madsen Dr (60108-2638)
PHONE..................................630 825-1200
Kevin Franz, *CEO*
Jim Knapp, *Project Mgr*
Russell Tylka, *Project Mgr*
Michael Long, *Opers Mgr*
Shane Burke, *Opers Staff*
EMP: 65
SQ FT: 50,000
SALES (est): 17.2MM **Privately Held**
SIC: 2759 Commercial printing

(G-1994)
EPP COMPOSITES INC
129 Fairfield Way (60108-1560)
PHONE..................................847 612-3495
EMP: 3
SALES (est): 165.6K **Privately Held**
SIC: 3089 Plastics products

(G-1995)
FEDEX OFFICE & PRINT SVCS INC
369 W Army Trail Rd (60108-2358)
PHONE..................................630 894-1800
EMP: 13
SALES (corp-wide): 69.6B **Publicly Held**
SIC: 7334 2791 2789 2752 Photocopying & duplicating services; typesetting; bookbinding & related work; commercial printing, lithographic
HQ: Fedex Office And Print Services, Inc.
  7900 Legacy Dr
  Plano TX 75024
  800 463-3339

(G-1996)
GRABER CONCRETE PIPE COMPANY
24w121 Army Trail Rd (60108-1396)
PHONE..................................630 894-5950
Charles R Graber Jr, *President*
Charles S Graber, *Chairman*
Marilyn Graber, *Corp Secy*
EMP: 25 EST: 1966
SQ FT: 12,500
SALES (est): 3MM **Privately Held**
SIC: 3272 Pipe, concrete or lined with concrete

(G-1997)
LAVEZZI PRECISION INC
250 Madsen Dr (60108-2637)
PHONE..................................630 582-1230
Albert J La Vezzi, *President*
Douglas Kremer, *Exec VP*
Victor Guida, *Plant Mgr*
Andy Golak, *Buyer*
Stephanie La Vezzi, *Sales Executive*
EMP: 120
SQ FT: 90,000
SALES: 25MM
SALES (corp-wide): 185.9MM **Privately Held**
WEB: www.lavezzi.com
SIC: 3599 Machine shop, jobbing & repair
HQ: Mw Industries, Inc.
  9501 Tech Blvd Ste 401
  Rosemont IL 60018
  847 349-5760

(G-1998)
MADDEN COMMUNICATIONS INC
Also Called: Mbexpress
355 Longview Dr (60108-2640)
PHONE..................................630 784-4325
Bill Hendriksen, *Manager*
EMP: 46
SALES (corp-wide): 130.9MM **Privately Held**
SIC: 2752 Commercial printing, offset
PA: Madden Communications Inc.
  901 Mittel Dr
  Wood Dale IL 60191
  630 787-2200

(G-1999)
MARCUS PRESS
168 Constitution Dr (60108-1460)
PHONE..................................630 351-1857
Janet Marcus, *President*
EMP: 4
SQ FT: 3,800
SALES (est): 380K **Privately Held**
SIC: 2752 2796 2791 2789 Commercial printing, offset; platemaking services; typesetting; bookbinding & related work

(G-2000)
MCX PRESS
355 Longview Dr (60108-2640)
PHONE..................................630 784-4325
Bill Hendriksen, *Principal*
▲ EMP: 4
SALES (est): 210.8K **Privately Held**
SIC: 2741 Miscellaneous publishing

(G-2001)
MODERN TUBE LLC (PA)
193 Rosedale Ct (60108-1477)
PHONE..................................877 848-3300
Frank Perkins, *Vice Pres*
Michael Anton Jr III, *Mng Member*
Conrad Leupold, *Mng Member*
EMP: 3
SALES (est): 563.2K **Privately Held**
SIC: 3312 5051 Tubes, steel & iron; tubing, metal

(G-2002)
NINOS LLC
170 Covington Dr (60108-3105)
PHONE..................................708 932-5555
Carl Mazzone,
Cosmo Sansone,
EMP: 30
SALES (est): 931.3K **Privately Held**
SIC: 2099 Noodles, fried (Chinese); packaged combination products: pasta, rice & potato; pasta, uncooked: packaged with other ingredients

(G-2003)
NOLAN SEALANTS INC
1 Bloomingdale Pl Apt 104 (60108-1291)
P.O. Box 861 (60108-0861)
PHONE..................................630 774-5713
EMP: 3
SALES (est): 123.2K **Privately Held**
SIC: 2891 Sealants

(G-2004)
NOW HEALTH GROUP INC (PA)
Also Called: Now Foods
244 Knollwood Dr Ste 300 (60108-2288)
PHONE..................................888 669-3663
Elwood Richard, *Ch of Bd*
James P Emme, *President*
Albert Powers, *Principal*
Nathan Richard, *Opers Staff*
Lynn Stoppa, *Mfg Staff*
◆ EMP: 838
SQ FT: 203,000
SALES (est): 454.3MM **Privately Held**
SIC: 2834 Vitamin, nutrient & hematinic preparations for human use

(G-2005)
NOW HEALTH GROUP INC
Also Called: Now Foods
395 Glen Ellyn Rd (60108-2176)
PHONE..................................630 545-9098
Brynnen Lopez, *Human Resources*
Troy Taylor, *Sales Mgr*
Dennis Gutierrez, *Manager*
Hernan Esquivel, *Supervisor*
Timothy Krahulik, *Supervisor*
EMP: 838
SALES (corp-wide): 454.3MM **Privately Held**
SIC: 2834 Vitamin, nutrient & hematinic preparations for human use
PA: Now Health Group, Inc.
  244 Knollwood Dr Ste 300
  Bloomingdale IL 60108
  888 669-3663

(G-2006)
PARAGON PRINT & MAIL PROD INC
109 Fairfield Way Ste 202 (60108-1500)
PHONE..................................630 671-2222
Michael Schulkins, *President*
EMP: 2 EST: 2008
SALES (est): 298.7K **Privately Held**
WEB: www.paraprint.com
SIC: 2752 Commercial printing, offset

(G-2007)
PATRICK CABINETRY INC
192 Ring Neck Ln (60108-5414)
PHONE..................................630 307-9333
Mike Patrick, *President*
EMP: 3 EST: 1985
SALES (est): 280K **Privately Held**
SIC: 2512 Upholstered household furniture

(G-2008)
PC-TEL INC (PA)
471 Brighton Ct (60108-3102)
PHONE..................................630 372-6800
David A Neumann, *CEO*

Bloomingdale - Dupage County (G-2009)

Steven D Levy, *Ch of Bd*
Rishi Bharadwaj, *COO*
Arnt Arvik, *Vice Pres*
Kevin J McGowan, *CFO*
EMP: 199
SQ FT: 75,517
SALES: 90.6MM **Publicly Held**
SIC: 3663 Antennas, transmitting & communications

(G-2009)
PEARL DESIGN GROUP LLC
Also Called: Lakewood Countertop
154 S Bloomingdale Rd # 102 (60108-3400)
PHONE 630 295-8401
Christ Koumoundouros, *Sales Staff*
Jeff Rojek, *Sales Staff*
Jeff Stanley, *Sales Staff*
Bob Carlson,
Ron Brands,
EMP: 25
SQ FT: 29,000
SALES (est): 3.8MM **Privately Held**
SIC: 2499 Kitchen, bathroom & household ware: wood

(G-2010)
R D S CO
158 Covington Dr (60108-3105)
PHONE 630 893-2990
Scott Perreault, *President*
Dave Wille, *Treasurer*
Stanley Skowron, *Admin Sec*
EMP: 4
SALES (est): 637.6K **Privately Held**
SIC: 3599 Machine shop, jobbing & repair

(G-2011)
REALLY USEFUL BOXES INC
355 Longview Dr (60108-2640)
PHONE 847 238-0444
Michael Pickles, *President*
EMP: 12
SALES (est): 1.7MM
SALES (corp-wide): 67.3MM **Privately Held**
SIC: 3089 Boxes, plastic
HQ: Really Useful Products Ltd
Whistler Drive
Castleford WF10

(G-2012)
S & K LABEL CO
147 Covington Dr (60108-3107)
PHONE 630 307-2577
Kenneth J Harvanek, *President*
EMP: 4
SALES (est): 804.7K **Privately Held**
SIC: 2759 Labels & seals: printing

(G-2013)
S & S HINGE COMPANY
210 Covington Dr (60108-3105)
PHONE 630 582-9500
Christopher Stevenson, *President*
Al Sandoval, *Plant Mgr*
Rick Joseph, *Controller*
Richard St Joseph, *Controller*
Paul Shafar, *Sales Engr*
▼ **EMP:** 35
SQ FT: 50,000
SALES (est): 12.4MM **Privately Held**
WEB: www.sandshinge.com
SIC: 3429 Manufactured hardware (general)

(G-2014)
SAMEL BOTROS
1 Tiffany Pt Ste G1 (60108-2951)
PHONE 847 466-5905
Samuel F Botros, *Principal*
EMP: 5
SALES (est): 445.2K **Privately Held**
SIC: 8099 3845 8011 Blood related health services; laser systems & equipment, medical; gynecologist

(G-2015)
SPECTRON MANUFACTURING
328 Georgetown Ct Unit C (60108-2055)
PHONE 720 879-7605
Greg Askin, *Principal*
Danny Arnold, *Accounts Mgr*
Blair Gavan, *Accounts Mgr*
Penny Armstrong, *Office Mgr*
EMP: 7
SALES (est): 370K **Privately Held**
WEB: www.spectronmanufacturing.com
SIC: 1446 3543 3544 Industrial sand; industrial patterns; special dies, tools, jigs & fixtures

(G-2016)
TERCO INC
459 Camden Dr (60108-3128)
PHONE 630 894-8828
Dennis N Ahrens, *CEO*
Dan Ahrens, *President*
David Ahrens, *Corp Secy*
Dennis Brokke, *Vice Pres*
Scott Brill, *Purch Mgr*
EMP: 22 **EST:** 1964
SQ FT: 30,000
SALES (est): 6.5MM **Privately Held**
SIC: 3565 5084 Packaging machinery; industrial machinery & equipment

(G-2017)
TJ TOOL INC
224 Independence Ln (60108-1406)
PHONE 630 543-3595
EMP: 12
SQ FT: 5,000
SALES (est): 1.5MM **Privately Held**
SIC: 3312 Blast Furnace-Steel Works

(G-2018)
TOTAL PRINT SOLUTIONS INC
109 Fairfield Way (60108-1583)
PHONE 630 494-0160
EMP: 3 **EST:** 2014
SALES (est): 92.3K **Privately Held**
SIC: 2752 Commercial printing, lithographic

(G-2019)
ULTRATECH INC
251 Covington Dr (60108-3109)
PHONE 630 539-3578
Ken Dahm, *President*
Betty Dahm, *Admin Sec*
EMP: 25
SQ FT: 43,000
SALES: 18.2MM **Privately Held**
SIC: 3444 Sheet metalwork

(G-2020)
WEST SUBURBAN JOURNAL
229 Esprit Ct (60108-2542)
PHONE 708 344-5975
Nicole Trottie, *Owner*
EMP: 3
SALES (est): 141.3K **Privately Held**
SIC: 2711 Commercial printing & newspaper publishing combined

Bloomington
Mclean County

(G-2021)
ADOLPH KIEFER & ASSOCIATES LLC (PA)
Also Called: Kiefer Sports Group
903 Morrissey Dr (61701-6940)
PHONE 309 451-5858
Shelley Kiefer, *President*
William Fischer, *Vice Pres*
Adolph Kiefer, *Vice Pres*
Joyce Kiefer, *Treasurer*
◆ **EMP:** 73 **EST:** 1946
SQ FT: 85,000
SALES (est): 35.7MM **Privately Held**
SIC: 5091 2396 Swimming pools, equipment & supplies; fabric printing & stamping

(G-2022)
AKSHAR PLASTIC INC
1101 Bell St (61701-6979)
PHONE 815 635-3536
Bhavana Patel, *President*
Haksmuth Patel, *Vice Pres*
◆ **EMP:** 27
SQ FT: 155,000
SALES (est): 6MM **Privately Held**
SIC: 2821 Molding compounds, plastics

(G-2023)
ALTER TRADING CORPORATION
501 E Stewart St (61701-6863)
PHONE 309 828-6084
William J Bremner, *President*
EMP: 15
SALES (corp-wide): 740.9MM **Privately Held**
SIC: 5093 3312 Metal scrap & waste materials; structural shapes & pilings, steel
HQ: Alter Trading Corporation
700 Office Pkwy
Saint Louis MO 63141
314 872-2400

(G-2024)
AMRIC RESOURCES
2422 E Washington St # 102 (61704-1611)
PHONE 309 664-0391
Patricia Heimerdinger, *President*
EMP: 3
SALES (est): 199.6K **Privately Held**
SIC: 2752 Color lithography

(G-2025)
B AND B AMUSEMENT ILLINOIS LLC
1404 Mrtin Luther King Dr (61701-1454)
PHONE 309 585-2077
Gary Brewer, *Principal*
Germaine Walls, *Human Res Mgr*
Gary R Brewer,
EMP: 3
SALES (est): 444.6K **Privately Held**
SIC: 3999 Coin-operated amusement machines

(G-2026)
BLOOMINGTON OFFSET PROCESS INC
1705 S Veterans Pkwy (61701-7500)
P.O. Box 278 (61702-0278)
PHONE 309 662-3395
Thomas G Mercier, *President*
Jeff Fritzen, *Exec VP*
Paul S Macfarlane, *Vice Pres*
John L Pratt, *Admin Sec*
EMP: 79
SQ FT: 45,000
SALES (est): 15.2MM **Privately Held**
WEB: www.bopi.com
SIC: 2752 Commercial printing, offset

(G-2027)
BLOOMINGTON TENT & AWNING INC
226 E Market St (61701-4088)
PHONE 309 828-3411
Matthew Hagerty, *Owner*
EMP: 6 **EST:** 1957
SALES (est): 463.7K **Privately Held**
WEB: www.bloomingtontent-awning.com
SIC: 2394 5999 7359 Awnings, fabric: made from purchased materials; awnings; equipment rental & leasing

(G-2028)
BOPI
1705 S Veterans Pkwy (61701-7019)
PHONE 312 320-1109
David Hicks, *Principal*
Mary Demlow, *Accounts Exec*
Kristin Milashoski, *Sales Associate*
Todd Beecher, *Supervisor*
Gary Ploense, *Supervisor*
EMP: 5 **EST:** 2017
SALES (est): 561.8K **Privately Held**
SIC: 2752 Commercial printing, offset

(G-2029)
CAMTEK INC
Also Called: Circuit Assembly & Mfg
2402 E Empire St (61704-3630)
P.O. Box 5020 (61702-5020)
PHONE 309 661-0348
Christine Davis, *President*
Amy King, *Human Res Mgr*
Jerry Swartz, *Supervisor*
EMP: 70
SQ FT: 60,000
SALES: 13MM **Privately Held**
SIC: 3672 Printed circuit boards

(G-2030)
CAPITAL MERCHANT SOLUTIONS INC
3005 Gill St Ste 2 (61704-3428)
PHONE 309 452-5990
Christopher Nelson, *CEO*
Russ Link, *President*
Cory Nelson, *Vice Pres*
EMP: 15
SQ FT: 2,500
SALES (est): 1.9MM **Privately Held**
WEB: www.takecardstoday.com
SIC: 4813 7372 ; business oriented computer software

(G-2031)
CARGILL INCORPORATED
115 S Euclid Ave (61701-4785)
P.O. Box 1286 (61702-1286)
PHONE 309 827-7100
Ray Dostal, *Sales/Mktg Mgr*
EMP: 50
SALES (corp-wide): 113.4B **Privately Held**
SIC: 2075 Soybean oil mills
PA: Cargill, Incorporated
15407 Mcginty Rd W
Wayzata MN 55391
952 742-7575

(G-2032)
CLINTON JOURNAL
14 Kenfield Cir (61704-6295)
PHONE 309 242-3900
Katy Pyne, *Principal*
EMP: 3
SALES (est): 124K **Privately Held**
SIC: 2711 Newspapers, publishing & printing

(G-2033)
COPY MAT PRINTING
1103 Martin Luther King D (61701-1473)
PHONE 309 452-1392
Gary Rude, *Owner*
Virginia Rude, *Manager*
EMP: 5 **EST:** 1978
SQ FT: 3,000
SALES (est): 510K **Privately Held**
WEB: www.cpg-printing.com
SIC: 2752 7334 2791 2789 Commercial printing, offset; photocopying & duplicating services; typesetting; bookbinding & related work

(G-2034)
CPG PRINTING & GRAPHICS
1103 Martin Luther King D (61701-1473)
PHONE 309 820-1392
Gary Rude, *Executive*
EMP: 3
SALES (est): 308.6K **Privately Held**
SIC: 2752 Commercial printing, offset

(G-2035)
CROWN EQUIPMENT CORPORATION
Also Called: Crown Lift Trucks
1714 E Hamilton Rd (61704-9607)
PHONE 309 663-9200
Scott Furlow, *Branch Mgr*
EMP: 17
SALES (corp-wide): 6.3B **Privately Held**
SIC: 3537 Lift trucks, industrial: fork, platform, straddle, etc.
PA: Crown Equipment Corporation
44 S Washington St
New Bremen OH 45869
419 629-2311

(G-2036)
CURTIS 1000 INC
2 Hardman Dr (61701-6934)
PHONE 309 663-0325
EMP: 195
SALES (corp-wide): 2.5B **Privately Held**
SIC: 2752 Commercial printing, offset
HQ: Curtis 1000 Inc.
1725 Breckinridge Park
Duluth GA 30096
770 925-4500

GEOGRAPHIC SECTION
Bloomington - Mclean County (G-2063)

(G-2037)
D J PETERS ORTHOPEDICS LTD
908 N Hershey Rd Ste 1 (61704-3760)
PHONE.................309 664-6930
Donald S Peters, *President*
Janet L Peters, *Principal*
EMP: 7
SQ FT: 1,500
SALES: 1MM **Privately Held**
SIC: 3842 Limbs, artificial; prosthetic appliances

(G-2038)
DANCYN RECOVERY SYSTEMS
707 N East St (61701-3059)
PHONE.................309 829-5450
Daniel Kohlenberg, *President*
EMP: 4
SALES (est): 237.3K **Privately Held**
WEB: www.dancyn.com
SIC: 2711 Newspapers

(G-2039)
DARNALL PRINTING
801 W Chestnut St Ste B (61701-4500)
PHONE.................309 827-7212
Lorrane Darnall, *President*
David Darnall, *Treasurer*
EMP: 3
SALES (est): 320K **Privately Held**
SIC: 2752 3993 2791 2789 Commercial printing, offset; signs & advertising specialties; typesetting; bookbinding & related work; automotive & apparel trimmings

(G-2040)
DONALD J LEVENTHAL
Also Called: Heartland Printing
606 Iaa Dr (61701-2217)
PHONE.................309 662-8080
Donald J Leventhal, *Owner*
Don Leventhal, *Owner*
EMP: 8
SALES (est): 646.6K **Privately Held**
SIC: 2759 5932 Commercial printing; used merchandise stores

(G-2041)
FAMILY TIME COMPUTING INC
Also Called: FTC Family of Companies
4 Yount Dr (61704-3736)
P.O. Box 1361 (61702-1361)
PHONE.................309 664-1742
Michael Kessler, *President*
Susan Kessler, *Vice Pres*
EMP: 11
SALES (est): 902.8K **Privately Held**
WEB: www.ftcomp.com
SIC: 7372 Publishers' computer software

(G-2042)
FARM WEEK
Also Called: Illinois Agricultural Assn
1701 Towanda Ave (61701-2057)
P.O. Box 2901 (61702-2901)
PHONE.................309 557-3140
Philip Nelson, *President*
Ron Warfield, *President*
EMP: 20 EST: 1935
SALES: 2.5MM **Privately Held**
WEB: www.ilfb.org
SIC: 2711 2741 Newspapers, publishing & printing; miscellaneous publishing

(G-2043)
FIVE BROTHER INC
Also Called: Parrott and Assoc Formerly
2905 Gill St Ste B (61704-8591)
P.O. Box 790 (61702-0790)
PHONE.................309 663-6323
John Parrott, *CEO*
Sandra Parrott, *Treasurer*
EMP: 4
SALES: 1.3MM **Privately Held**
SIC: 5651 2253 Family clothing stores; cold weather knit outerwear, including ski wear

(G-2044)
FLEXITECH INC (DH)
1719 E Hamilton Rd (61704-9607)
PHONE.................309 665-0658
Randy Ross, *President*
▲ EMP: 180
SALES (est): 53.4MM
SALES (corp-wide): 177.9K **Privately Held**
SIC: 5013 3492 Automotive supplies & parts; fluid power valves & hose fittings; hose & tube fittings & assemblies, hydraulic/pneumatic
HQ: Flexitech Holding Sas
293 Rue Des Sagnes
St Andre Le Puy 42210
477 062-519

(G-2045)
FRANMAR CHEMICAL
11 Mary Ellen Way (61701-2014)
P.O. Box 5565 (61702-5565)
PHONE.................309 829-5952
Dan Brown, *Principal*
Chris Miller, *Opers Mgr*
EMP: 6
SALES (est): 473.8K **Privately Held**
SIC: 2869 Laboratory chemicals, organic

(G-2046)
FREESEN INC
1523 Cottage Ave (61701-1503)
P.O. Box 609 (61702-0609)
PHONE.................309 827-4554
Mike Goeken, *Manager*
EMP: 50
SALES (corp-wide): 117.9MM **Privately Held**
WEB: www.ucm.biz
SIC: 2951 1771 Asphalt paving mixtures & blocks; blacktop (asphalt) work
HQ: Freesen Inc.
3151 Robbins Rd Ste A
Springfield IL 62704
217 546-6192

(G-2047)
G D S PROFESSIONAL BUS DISPLAY
Also Called: Gds
1103 Martin Luther King D (61701-1486)
PHONE.................309 829-3298
Harvey Meister, *Owner*
Becky Berry, *Cust Mgr*
Dave Nelson, *Sales Associate*
John Woodall, *Info Tech Dir*
EMP: 25
SQ FT: 120,000
SALES (est): 7.2MM **Privately Held**
WEB: www.gdsdisplay.com
SIC: 5046 3993 Store fixtures & display equipment; signs & advertising specialties

(G-2048)
G3 MACHINING LLC
915 E Oakland Ave (61701-5456)
PHONE.................309 323-8310
Knecht Steven P, *Principal*
EMP: 1
SALES (est): 266.1K **Privately Held**
SIC: 3599 Machine shop, jobbing & repair

(G-2049)
GATEWAY INDUSTRIAL POWER INC
13958 Roberto Rd Ste 2 (61705-6360)
PHONE.................309 821-1035
Greg Jones, *Manager*
EMP: 5
SALES (corp-wide): 101.4MM **Privately Held**
SIC: 3585 7538 Refrigeration & heating equipment; diesel engine repair: automotive
PA: Gateway Industrial Power, Inc.
921 Fournie Ln
Collinsville IL 62234
618 345-0123

(G-2050)
GENERAL ELECTRIC COMPANY
1601 General Electric Rd (61704-2479)
PHONE.................309 664-1513
Mike Irwin, *Branch Mgr*
EMP: 250
SALES (corp-wide): 95.2B **Publicly Held**
WEB: www.ge.com
SIC: 3625 3613 3643 Starter, electric motor; electric controls & control accessories, industrial; panelboards & distribution boards, electric; current-carrying wiring devices
PA: General Electric Company
5 Necco St
Boston MA 02210
617 443-3000

(G-2051)
GENES ICE CREAM INC
2 Lake Pointe Ct (61704-1450)
PHONE.................309 846-5925
EMP: 4
SALES (est): 255K **Privately Held**
SIC: 2024 Ice cream & frozen desserts

(G-2052)
GREAT DISPLAY COMPANY LLC
704 S Mclean St (61701-5374)
PHONE.................309 821-1037
Jacob Duquenne, *Principal*
Tiffani Hambleton, *Art Dir*
Carina Beaty, *Executive Asst*
Aaron Hambleton,
EMP: 10 EST: 2010
SQ FT: 5,000
SALES (est): 1.2MM **Privately Held**
WEB: www.thegreatdisplaycompany.com
SIC: 2759 Decals: printing; posters, including billboards: printing

(G-2053)
GRIFOLS SHARED SVCS N AMER INC
511 W Washington St (61701-3809)
PHONE.................309 827-3031
Chris Crowell, *Manager*
EMP: 10
SALES (corp-wide): 2.1B **Privately Held**
SIC: 2836 Plasmas
HQ: Grifols Shared Services North America, Inc.
2410 Lillyvale Ave
Los Angeles CA 90032
323 225-2221

(G-2054)
GTI SPINDLE TECHNOLOGY INC
Also Called: G T I Spindle
14015 Carole Dr Ste 2 (61705-6202)
PHONE.................309 820-7887
Tom Hoenig, *Branch Mgr*
EMP: 10
SALES (corp-wide): 6.8MM **Privately Held**
WEB: www.gtispindle.com
SIC: 3599 7699 Machine & other job shop work; industrial equipment services
PA: Gti Spindle Technology, Inc.
33 Zachary Rd
Manchester NH 03109
603 669-5993

(G-2055)
H N C PRODUCTS INC (PA)
1619 Commerce Pkwy (61704-9608)
PHONE.................309 319-2151
Chrimpiramma Potini, *President*
Andrew Arndt, *QC Mgr*
Srilatha Potini, *Admin Sec*
EMP: 20
SALES: 50MM **Privately Held**
SIC: 2844 Toilet preparations

(G-2056)
HEARST COMMUNICATIONS INC
Also Called: The Pantagraph
301 W Washington St (61701-3827)
P.O. Box 2907 (61702-2907)
PHONE.................309 829-9000
Linda Lindus, *Publisher*
Jenny Kehl, *Accounts Exec*
Michael Plesha, *Supervisor*
Daniel McNeile, *Assistant*
EMP: 200
SALES (corp-wide): 8.2B **Privately Held**
SIC: 2711 Newspapers, publishing & printing
HQ: Hearst Communications, Inc.
300 W 57th St
New York NY 10019
212 649-2000

(G-2057)
HERON BAY INC
Also Called: Fastsigns
1605 General Elc Rd Ste 1 (61704)
PHONE.................309 661-1300
David Voigts, *President*
EMP: 5
SALES (est): 420K **Privately Held**
SIC: 3993 Signs & advertising specialties

(G-2058)
HOLDER PUBLISHING CORPORATION
25 Monarch Dr (61704-9092)
P.O. Box 186 (61702-0186)
PHONE.................309 828-7533
Dan Holder, *President*
Judy Holder, *Vice Pres*
EMP: 6
SALES (est): 530.9K **Privately Held**
SIC: 2731 2741 Books: publishing only; pamphlets: publishing only, not printed on site; miscellaneous publishing

(G-2059)
HOWMEDICA OSTEONICS CORP
7 Westport Ct (61704-3732)
PHONE.................309 663-6414
EMP: 9
SALES (corp-wide): 13.6B **Publicly Held**
SIC: 3842 Orthopedic appliances
HQ: Howmedica Osteonics Corp.
325 Corporate Dr
Mahwah NJ 07430
201 831-5000

(G-2060)
HP INC
303 N Hershey Rd (61704-3576)
PHONE.................309 664-4000
Dale Wittenberg, *Manager*
Virgil Hovar, *Manager*
EMP: 57
SALES (corp-wide): 58.7B **Publicly Held**
WEB: www.hp.com
SIC: 3571 Personal computers (microcomputers)
PA: Hp, Inc.
1501 Page Mill Rd
Palo Alto CA 94304
650 857-1501

(G-2061)
ILLINOIS STATE USBC WBA
402 W Hamilton Rd (61704-8610)
PHONE.................309 827-6355
Madeline Dotta, *Principal*
EMP: 2
SALES: 258.2K **Privately Held**
SIC: 3949 Bowling alleys & accessories

(G-2062)
INTEGRATED MEDICAL TECH INC (PA)
2422 E Washington St # 103 (61704-4478)
P.O. Box 5383 (61702-5383)
PHONE.................309 662-3614
William Smith, *President*
Norman Hester, *CFO*
EMP: 3 EST: 2008
SQ FT: 4,280
SALES (est): 2.3MM **Privately Held**
SIC: 3842 3843 3841 Sponges, surgical; sterilizers, hospital & surgical; sterilizers, dental; surgical & medical instruments

(G-2063)
JACK RUCH QUALITY HOMES INC
Also Called: Jack Ruch Archtctral Mouldings
2908 Gill St Ste 2 (61704-8104)
PHONE.................309 663-6595
Jack Ruch, *President*
EMP: 8
SALES (est): 890K **Privately Held**
SIC: 1521 3446 6552 2499 New construction, single-family houses; architectural metalwork; subdividers & developers; decorative wood & woodwork

Bloomington - Mclean County (G-2064)

(G-2064)
JULY 25TH CORPORATION
Also Called: Starnet Digital Publishing
1708 E Hamilton Rd Ste B (61704-9663)
P.O. Box 1145 (61702-1145)
PHONE................309 664-6444
Sandy Adams, *President*
David Mercier, *Chairman*
Karen Crusius, *Vice Pres*
Maryjo Adams, *Admin Sec*
EMP: 15
SQ FT: 5,000
SALES (est): 2MM **Privately Held**
SIC: 2752 2791 Commercial printing, offset; typesetting

(G-2065)
K & K TOOL & DIE INC
915 E Oakland Ave (61701-5456)
PHONE................309 829-4479
Gene A Kuppersmith, *President*
Frederick H Kuppersmith, *Admin Sec*
EMP: 10 **EST:** 1944
SALES (est): 950K **Privately Held**
WEB: www.kktooldie.com
SIC: 3599 7692 3444 Machine shop, jobbing & repair; welding repair; sheet metalwork

(G-2066)
KAHUNA LLC
Also Called: Kahuna Atm
807 Arcadia Dr Ste B (61704-6119)
PHONE................888 357-8472
Tammy Cook, *Exec VP*
Josh Hendon, *Vice Pres*
Pamela Philipps, *Vice Pres*
Becky Godbey, *Opers Mgr*
Scott Rathburn, *CFO*
EMP: 14
SALES (est): 2.1MM **Privately Held**
SIC: 3578 Automatic teller machines (ATM)

(G-2067)
KELLEY ORNAMENTAL IRON LLC
1206 Towanda Ave Ste 1 (61701-7416)
PHONE................309 820-7540
Brian Pinkston, *Manager*
EMP: 18
SALES (corp-wide): 3.2MM **Privately Held**
SIC: 3446 Fences or posts, ornamental iron or steel
PA: Kelley Ornamental Iron Llc
4303 N Main St
East Peoria IL 61611
309 697-9870

(G-2068)
KIRK WOOD PRODUCTS INC
10424 E 1400 North Rd (61705-6774)
PHONE................309 829-6661
Michael Kirk, *President*
EMP: 20
SQ FT: 60,000
SALES (est): 3.7MM **Privately Held**
SIC: 2448 Pallets, wood

(G-2069)
L & C IMAGING INC
908 White Oak Rd (61701-2670)
PHONE................309 829-1802
EMP: 9
SALES (est): 620K **Privately Held**
SIC: 3993 Mfg Signs/Advertising Specialties

(G-2070)
LEE ENTERPRISES INCORPORATED
301 W Washington St (61701-3827)
PHONE................309 829-9000
Chris Dietiker, *President*
EMP: 10
SALES (corp-wide): 509.8MM **Publicly Held**
SIC: 2711 Commercial printing & newspaper publishing combined
PA: Lee Enterprises, Incorporated
4600 E 53rd St
Davenport IA 52807
563 383-2100

(G-2071)
LIL BEAVER BREWERY LLC
16 Currency Dr Unit B (61704-9632)
PHONE................309 808-2590
Adam Bellas, *Mng Member*
Justin Bellas,
Chad Bevers,
EMP: 10
SALES (est): 1MM **Privately Held**
SIC: 2082 Ale (alcoholic beverage); beer (alcoholic beverage)

(G-2072)
MCLEAN COUNTY ASPHALT CO (PA)
Also Called: Mc Lean County Concrete Co
1100 W Market St (61701-2630)
P.O. Box 3547 (61702-3547)
PHONE................309 827-6115
Toll Free:................877 -
Forrest Kaufman, *President*
Randy Kaufman, *Vice Pres*
EMP: 95 **EST:** 1964
SQ FT: 2,000
SALES (est): 16.9MM **Privately Held**
WEB: www.mcleancountyasphalt.com
SIC: 1611 3273 Highway & street paving contractor; ready-mixed concrete

(G-2073)
MECHANICAL DEVICES COMPANY
2005 General Electric Rd (61704-1320)
PHONE................309 663-2843
Daniel R Sperry, *President*
Mark Sperry, *Vice Pres*
Robert Waller, *Plant Mgr*
Shane Daniels, *Prdtn Mgr*
Clint Wolfe, *QC Mgr*
▲ **EMP:** 3 **EST:** 1914
SALES (est): 1.4MM **Privately Held**
WEB: www.mechdev.com
SIC: 3599 Machine shop, jobbing & repair

(G-2074)
MELTDOWN CREATIVE WORKS INC
409 E Washington St (61701-4001)
PHONE................309 310-1978
Jeremy Plue, *President*
EMP: 5
SALES (est): 619.3K **Privately Held**
SIC: 7336 2759 3993 Graphic arts & related design; letterpress & screen printing; signs & advertising specialties

(G-2075)
MERRITT & EDWARDS CORPORATION
302 E Washington St (61701-4041)
PHONE................309 828-4741
Beverly Edwards, *President*
William Edwards, *Vice Pres*
EMP: 14
SQ FT: 3,500
SALES (est): 1.3MM **Privately Held**
SIC: 7334 5943 2789 2752 Blueprinting service; mimeographing; office forms & supplies; bookbinding & related work; commercial printing, lithographic

(G-2076)
MICKEY TRUCK BODIES INC
Also Called: Midwest Reconditioning Div
14661 Old Colonial Rd (61705-5947)
PHONE................309 827-8227
Mike Parker, *General Mgr*
David Perry, *Purch Mgr*
Craig Becker, *Engineer*
EMP: 17
SALES (corp-wide): 133.4MM **Privately Held**
SIC: 3713 7532 5531 3715 Beverage truck bodies; van bodies; truck bodies (motor vehicles); body shop, trucks; truck equipment & parts; truck trailers; motor vehicles & car bodies; general automotive repair shops
PA: Mickey Truck Bodies Inc.
1305 Trinity Ave
High Point NC 27260
336 882-6806

(G-2077)
MICROSOFT CORPORATION
2203 E Empire St Ste J (61704-3707)
PHONE................309 665-0113
Mark Rahn, *Accounts Exec*
Dave Youkers, *Branch Mgr*
EMP: 100
SALES (corp-wide): 125.8B **Publicly Held**
SIC: 7372 Application computer software
PA: Microsoft Corporation
1 Microsoft Way
Redmond WA 98052
425 882-8080

(G-2078)
MIDWEST MARKETING DISTRS INC
Sun Gard Window Fashions
904 S Eldorado Rd (61704-6073)
PHONE................309 663-6972
EMP: 4
SALES (corp-wide): 1.5MM **Privately Held**
SIC: 5719 3081 Ret Misc Homefurnishings Mfg Unsupported Plastic Film/Sheet
PA: Midwest Marketing Distributors, Inc.
2000 E War Memorial Dr # 2
Peoria IL 61614
309 688-8858

(G-2079)
MIDWEST MOLDING SOLUTIONS
3001 Gill St (61704-8508)
PHONE................309 663-7374
Joseph G Diemer, *President*
▲ **EMP:** 10
SQ FT: 3,000
SALES (est): 3MM **Privately Held**
SIC: 3089 Injection molding of plastics

(G-2080)
MINERVA SPORTSWEAR INC
608 Iaa Dr (61701-2217)
PHONE................309 661-2387
Tony Todaro, *President*
Louis Todaro, *Admin Sec*
Kersten Wilson, *Representative*
EMP: 12
SQ FT: 5,500
SALES (est): 1.7MM **Privately Held**
SIC: 5611 3993 2396 2395 Clothing, sportswear, men's & boys'; signs & advertising specialties; automotive & apparel trimmings; pleating & stitching; screen printing

(G-2081)
MORRIS PACKAGING LLC (PA)
211 N Williamsburg Dr A (61704-7735)
PHONE................309 663-9100
Steve Loethen, *Opers Mgr*
Mark Gentes, *Prdtn Mgr*
Dawn Gaddis, *Accountant*
Brian Steinwagner, *VP Sales*
Amy Adams, *Client Mgr*
EMP: 9
SQ FT: 2,000
SALES (est): 2.4MM **Privately Held**
SIC: 2674 2673 Flour bags: made from purchased materials; shipping bags or sacks, including multiwall & heavy duty; food storage & frozen food bags, plastic

(G-2082)
NEON NIGHTS DJ SVC
2902 Essington St (61705-6539)
PHONE................309 820-9000
EMP: 3
SALES (est): 140K **Privately Held**
SIC: 2813 Mfg Industrial Gases

(G-2083)
NESTLE USA INC
Also Called: Nestle Confections Factory
2501 Beich Rd (61705-6558)
PHONE................309 829-1031
Larry Popp, *Manager*
EMP: 139
SALES (corp-wide): 93.5B **Privately Held**
SIC: 2023 Evaporated milk
HQ: Nestle Usa, Inc.
1812 N Moore St Ste 118
Rosslyn VA 22209
440 264-7249

(G-2084)
PANTAGRAPH PRINTING AND STY CO (PA)
217 W Jefferson St (61703-3927)
PHONE................309 829-1071
Michael G Dolan, *President*
Larry Labounty, *Vice Pres*
EMP: 18 **EST:** 1860
SQ FT: 40,000
SALES (est): 8.1MM **Privately Held**
WEB: www.pantagraphprinting.com
SIC: 2752 2759 2732 Commercial printing, offset; commercial printing; book printing

(G-2085)
PANTAGRAPH PUBLISHING CO (PA)
Also Called: Farmercityjournal.com
301 W Washington St (61701-3827)
P.O. Box 2907 (61702-2907)
PHONE................309 829-9000
Linda Lindus, *President*
Henry Bird, *Publisher*
Caitlin Perry, *Editor*
Tyler Gillette, *IT/INT Sup*
Lorie Kletz, *Advisor*
EMP: 11
SALES (est): 1MM **Privately Held**
SIC: 2711 Newspapers, publishing & printing

(G-2086)
PRIDE PACKAGING LLC
211 N Williamsburg Dr A (61704-7735)
PHONE................309 663-9100
Amy Adams, *Manager*
Jim Morris,
Orlando Martinez,
Amy Vogel,
EMP: 3
SALES (est): 210K **Privately Held**
SIC: 2674 2673 Flour bags: made from purchased materials; plastic & pliofilm bags

(G-2087)
R G HANSON COMPANY INC (PA)
211 S Prospect Rd Ste 7 (61704-4907)
P.O. Box 1408 (61702-1408)
PHONE................309 661-9200
Thomas R Hanson, *President*
Mary Gerwig, *Finance Dir*
Elaine Mountjoy, *Accounting Mgr*
EMP: 10
SALES (est): 5.5MM **Privately Held**
WEB: www.rghanson.com
SIC: 5084 3599 Materials handling machinery; custom machinery

(G-2088)
RETTICK ENTERPRISES INC
Also Called: Right Angle Tool Division
13958 Roberto Rd Ste 1 (61705-6360)
PHONE................309 275-4967
James R Rettick, *President*
EMP: 4 **EST:** 1974
SALES (est): 280.4K **Privately Held**
SIC: 0116 3444 Soybeans; sheet metalwork

(G-2089)
ROAD READY SIGNS (PA)
Also Called: Traffic Sign Store, The
1231 N Mason St (61701-1648)
PHONE................309 828-1007
Randy Kull, *Partner*
Melvin Kull, *Partner*
EMP: 10
SQ FT: 1,400
SALES (est): 1.2MM **Privately Held**
SIC: 3993 Signs, not made in custom sign painting shops

(G-2090)
ROGERS MOTORCYCLE SHOP INC
2705 S Main St (61704-7384)
PHONE................309 828-3242
Roger Bachman, *President*
EMP: 1
SQ FT: 4,500

SALES (est): 201.4K **Privately Held**
SIC: 3714 5571 Motor vehicle parts & accessories; motorcycle parts & accessories

(G-2091)
ROUT A BOUT SHOP INC
Also Called: Rout-A-Bout
619 W Olive St (61701-4967)
PHONE 309 829-0674
William Smith, *President*
EMP: 4
SALES (est): 286.5K **Privately Held**
SIC: 3993 Neon signs

(G-2092)
SCOTTS EXTERIOR MAINTENANCE CO
14866 Craig Rd (61705-9018)
PHONE 309 660-3380
EMP: 8
SQ FT: 100,000
SALES (est): 141.2K **Privately Held**
SIC: 0781 1521 0782 3271 Garden planning services; patio & deck construction & repair; landscape contractors; blocks, concrete; landscape or retaining wall

(G-2093)
SELECT SCREEN PRINTS & EMB
112 Southgate Dr (61704-7683)
PHONE 309 829-6511
Charles Stevens, *President*
Barb Macke, *Marketing Staff*
Marlene M Crone, *Manager*
Molly Smith, *Assistant*
EMP: 12
SQ FT: 6,000
SALES (est): 1.1MM **Privately Held**
SIC: 5137 5136 5699 2395 Women's & children's sportswear & swimsuits; men's & boys' sportswear & work clothing; T-shirts, custom printed; embroidery & art needlework; automotive & apparel trimmings; screen printing

(G-2094)
SIEMENS INDUSTRY INC
14 Currency Dr (61704-9632)
PHONE 309 664-2460
Jeremy Hale, *Project Mgr*
Greg Wommac, *Manager*
EMP: 9
SALES (corp-wide): 96.9B **Privately Held**
SIC: 3822 1796 5084 Air conditioning & refrigeration controls; installing building equipment; conveyor systems
HQ: Siemens Industry, Inc.
1000 Deerfield Pkwy
Buffalo Grove IL 60089
847 215-1000

(G-2095)
SIGNS DIRECT INC
1703 S Veterans Pkwy (61701-7019)
PHONE 309 820-1070
Tom Dalton, *President*
◆ **EMP:** 14
SQ FT: 30,000
SALES (est): 728K **Privately Held**
SIC: 3993 Signs, not made in custom sign painting shops

(G-2096)
SOUTHFIELD CORPORATION
Also Called: Modahl & Scott
917 E Grove St (61704-4201)
PHONE 309 829-1087
John Drew, *Manager*
EMP: 22
SALES (corp-wide): 344.9MM **Privately Held**
SIC: 3273 4212 Ready-mixed concrete; local trucking, without storage
PA: Southfield Corporation
8995 W 95th St
Palos Hills IL 60465
708 344-1000

(G-2097)
STUDLEY PRODUCTS INC (PA)
903 Morrissey Dr (61701-6940)
PHONE 309 663-2313
Gary Wilder, *CEO*
Toni Jo Wilder, *Vice Pres*
▲ **EMP:** 137 **EST:** 1946
SQ FT: 145,000

SALES (est): 24.1MM **Privately Held**
SIC: 2674 Vacuum cleaner bags: made from purchased materials

(G-2098)
SUPER SIGN SERVICE
621 W Olive St (61701-4967)
P.O. Box 3336 (61702-3336)
PHONE 309 829-9241
William R Smith, *Partner*
George E Kletz Jr, *Partner*
EMP: 12 **EST:** 1973
SQ FT: 13,000
SALES (est): 1.6MM **Privately Held**
SIC: 3993 Electric signs

(G-2099)
TAURUS CYCLE
1 Lafayette Ct (61701-6883)
PHONE 309 454-1565
John D Earhart, *Owner*
EMP: 3
SALES (est): 227.9K **Privately Held**
SIC: 3751 Motorcycles & related parts

(G-2100)
TAYLOR COMMUNICATION
1 Hardman Dr (61701-6934)
PHONE 309 664-0444
EMP: 175
SALES (corp-wide): 2.5B **Privately Held**
SIC: 8742 2752 2759 Marketing consulting services; commercial printing, lithographic; commercial printing
HQ: Taylor Communications Secure & Customer Solutions, Inc.
1170 Grey Fox Rd
Arden Hills MN 55112
651 494-1740

(G-2101)
THOENNES & THOENNES INC
Also Called: Creative Kitchens & Baths
1102 Eastport Dr Ste B (61704-3735)
PHONE 309 663-4053
Mark Thoennes, *President*
Thelma Thoennes, *Corp Secy*
EMP: 7
SQ FT: 2,500
SALES (est): 999.9K **Privately Held**
SIC: 2434 Wood kitchen cabinets

(G-2102)
TIMPTE INDUSTRIES INC
2312 W Market St (61705-5147)
PHONE 309 820-1095
EMP: 78
SALES (corp-wide): 66.1MM **Privately Held**
WEB: www.timpte.com
SIC: 3715 Semitrailers for truck tractors; trailer bodies
PA: Timpte Industries, Inc.
700 N Broadway Ste 800
Denver CO 80203
303 839-1900

(G-2103)
TOYO USA MANUFACTURING INC
Also Called: Toyo Precision U S A
818 Avalon Way (61705-6609)
PHONE 309 827-8836
Atsushi Makino, *President*
Yuzuru Otsuka, *Admin Sec*
▲ **EMP:** 12
SALES (est): 491.4K **Privately Held**
SIC: 3714 Motor vehicle parts & accessories
PA: Toyo Seki Seisakusho, K.K.
3-10-6, Kamitsuchidananaka
Ayase KNG 252-1

(G-2104)
TRI PRO GRAPHICS LLC
2422 E Washington St # 102 (61704-1611)
PHONE 309 664-5875
John Heimerdinger,
EMP: 5
SALES (est): 524.4K **Privately Held**
SIC: 3086 5113 Packaging & shipping materials, foamed plastic; industrial & personal service paper
PA: Tri Pro Graphics, L.L.C.
3505 Tree Crt Indus Blvd
Saint Louis MO 63122

(G-2105)
TWIN CITY ELECTRIC INC
1701 Easy St Ste 5 (61701-6878)
PHONE 309 827-0636
Cheryl Mulcahey, *President*
Chloe Misch, *Vice Pres*
Larry Mulcahey, *Treasurer*
EMP: 20
SQ FT: 5,000
SALES (est): 2.5MM **Privately Held**
SIC: 1731 3643 General electrical contractor; current-carrying wiring devices

(G-2106)
TWIN CITY WOOD RECYCLING CORP
1606 W Oakland Ave (61701-4793)
PHONE 309 827-9663
John Wollrab, *President*
Phil McCrackin, *Treasurer*
EMP: 5
SALES (est): 622.9K **Privately Held**
SIC: 2421 2448 4953 Sawdust, shavings & wood chips; wood pallets & skids; recycling, waste materials

(G-2107)
WHERRY MACHINE & WELDING INC
11 Carri Dr (61705-5188)
PHONE 309 828-5423
Byron Young, *President*
Steve Young, *Vice Pres*
Connie Young, *Treasurer*
EMP: 9 **EST:** 1960
SALES (est): 1.1MM **Privately Held**
SIC: 7692 3599 3441 Welding repair; machine shop, jobbing & repair; fabricated structural metal

(G-2108)
WISH BONE RESCUE
1007 S Madison St (61701-6646)
PHONE 309 212-9210
EMP: 3 **EST:** 2011
SALES (est): 184.1K **Privately Held**
SIC: 3999 Pet supplies

Blue Island
Cook County

(G-2109)
AD DELUXE SIGN COMPANY INC
Also Called: Ad-Deluxe Sign Co
2747 York St (60406-1958)
PHONE 815 556-8469
Ahmed Demir Sr, *President*
EMP: 3
SQ FT: 30,000
SALES (est): 480K **Privately Held**
SIC: 3993 7629 1799 Neon signs; signs, not made in custom sign painting shops; electrical repair shops; sign installation & maintenance

(G-2110)
ADVANCED VALVE TECH LLC
Also Called: Avt Service Technologies
12601 Homan Ave (60406-1837)
PHONE 877 489-4909
Kevin Murphy, *Branch Mgr*
EMP: 40 **Privately Held**
SIC: 3491 Industrial valves
HQ: Advanced Valve Technologies, Llc
800 Busse Rd
Elk Grove Village IL 60007
847 364-3700

(G-2111)
BLUE ISLAND BEER CO
13357 Olde Western Ave (60406-5387)
PHONE 708 954-8085
EMP: 4
SALES (est): 266.4K **Privately Held**
WEB: www.blueislandbeerco.com
SIC: 2082 Beer (alcoholic beverage)

(G-2112)
BLUE ISLAND SUN
12607 Artesian Ave (60406-1705)
PHONE 708 388-9033

Joe Gatrell, *Owner*
EMP: 5
SALES (est): 180.2K **Privately Held**
SIC: 2711 Newspapers, publishing & printing

(G-2113)
C-V CSTOM CNTRTOPS CBINETS INC
12525 Irving Ave (60406-1669)
P.O. Box 87 (60406-0087)
PHONE 708 388-5066
Roger Christ, *President*
Robert C Volkart, *Vice Pres*
EMP: 10
SQ FT: 10,000
SALES (est): 1.5MM **Privately Held**
WEB: www.cvcustom.com
SIC: 2521 2522 2434 2542 Wood office filing cabinets & bookcases; office furniture, except wood; wood kitchen cabinets; partitions & fixtures, except wood; wood partitions & fixtures

(G-2114)
COLOR TONE PRINTING
Also Called: J N P
2619 Orchard St (60406-1535)
P.O. Box 183 (60406-0183)
PHONE 708 385-1442
Fax: 708 385-7329
EMP: 3
SQ FT: 4,000
SALES (est): 277.4K **Privately Held**
SIC: 2759 2752 2396 Commercial Printing Lithographic Coml Print Mfg Auto/Apparel Trim

(G-2115)
COLVIN PRINTING
12958 Ashland Ave (60406-2701)
PHONE 708 331-4580
Tanya Colvin, *Principal*
EMP: 4
SALES (est): 449.7K **Privately Held**
SIC: 2759 2752 Screen printing; commercial printing, lithographic

(G-2116)
CRYOGENIC SYSTEMS EQUIPMENT
2363 136th St (60406-3233)
PHONE 708 385-4216
Brian Sink, *President*
Gary Magdziarz, *Purch Mgr*
Todd Czernik, *Business Dir*
EMP: 27
SQ FT: 26,000
SALES (est): 6.8MM **Privately Held**
SIC: 3559 7699 Cryogenic machinery, industrial; industrial equipment services

(G-2117)
DARLING INGREDIENTS INC
Also Called: Darling Intl Grse Trp Pump Div
3000 Wireton Rd (60406-1861)
PHONE 708 388-3223
Jim Lucas, *Human Res Dir*
Jerome Levy, *Branch Mgr*
EMP: 47
SALES (corp-wide): 3.3B **Publicly Held**
WEB: www.darlingii.com
SIC: 4953 2048 Refuse collection & disposal services; prepared feeds
PA: Darling Ingredients Inc.
5601 N Macarthur Blvd
Irving TX 75038
972 717-0300

(G-2118)
DMARV DESIGN SPECIALTY PRTRS
13010 Western Ave (60406-2407)
PHONE 708 389-4420
Marvin Forbish, *President*
Delores Forbish, *CFO*
EMP: 5
SQ FT: 3,500
SALES (est): 732K **Privately Held**
WEB: www.dmarvdesigns.net
SIC: 2759 2752 2789 2396 Screen printing; offset & photolithographic printing; bookbinding & related work; automotive & apparel trimmings

Blue Island - Cook County (G-2119)

(G-2119)
E B BRONSON & CO INC
Also Called: Bronson Machine Shop
12826 Irving Ave (60406-2122)
P.O. Box 267 (60406-0267)
PHONE..................708 385-3600
James U Bronson Jr, *President*
Bruce S Bronson, *Vice Pres*
Bruce Bronson, *Vice Pres*
James U Bronson III, *Vice Pres*
Larry Schmudde, *Purchasing*
EMP: 25 **EST:** 1896
SQ FT: 18,000
SALES (est): 4.6MM **Privately Held**
WEB: www.ebbronson.com
SIC: 3599 Machine shop, jobbing & repair

(G-2120)
EISENHOWER HIGH SCHOOL - BLUE
12700 Sacramento Ave (60406-1899)
PHONE..................708 385-6815
Nicole Hite, *Principal*
Eric Schultz, *Director*
EMP: 6
SALES (est): 175.9K **Privately Held**
SIC: 2711 Newspapers

(G-2121)
ENTERPRISE SIGNS INC
2538 New St (60406-2322)
PHONE..................708 691-1273
Leo Milashoski, *Principal*
Phyllis Mahn, *Principal*
Steven Milashoski, *Principal*
EMP: 4 **EST:** 1951
SALES (est): 233.5K **Privately Held**
WEB: www.enterprisesigns.org
SIC: 3993 2396 7389 7532 Signs & advertising specialties; screen printing on fabric articles; sign painting & lettering shop; truck painting & lettering

(G-2122)
ERIN ROPE CORPORATION
2661 139th St (60406-2805)
PHONE..................708 377-1084
James J Doherty, *President*
Fran Doherty, *Vice Pres*
Joe Kairies, *Sales Staff*
Tom Leyden, *Marketing Staff*
▲ **EMP:** 15
SQ FT: 30,000
SALES (est): 2.9MM **Privately Held**
WEB: www.getrope.com
SIC: 2298 3357 Cordage & twine; nonferrous wiredrawing & insulating

(G-2123)
G & W ELECTRIC COMPANY
Manufacturers Brass Alum Fndry
3450 127th St (60406-1834)
PHONE..................708 388-6363
Erik Brandstaedter, *Business Mgr*
Milan Uzelac, *Chief Engr*
Sam Hipp, *Engineer*
Eeshwar Pitchiaya, *Engineer*
Kate Thompson, *Engineer*
EMP: 35
SALES (corp-wide): 176.7MM **Privately Held**
SIC: 3364 3363 3369 Brass & bronze die-castings; aluminum die-castings; nonferrous foundries
PA: G & W Electric Company
305 W Crossroads Pkwy
Bolingbrook IL 60440
708 388-5010

(G-2124)
GOLDEN HYDRAULIC & MACHINE
2966 Wireton Rd (60406-1869)
PHONE..................708 597-4265
John De Makas, *President*
EMP: 4
SALES (est): 527.4K **Privately Held**
WEB: www.goldenhydraulic.com
SIC: 7692 Welding repair

(G-2125)
HARVEY PALLETS INC
2200 138th St (60406-3209)
PHONE..................708 293-1831
Manuel Tavarez, *President*
Jose M Tavarez, *Principal*
Julia Tavarez, *Vice Pres*
Rodrigo Rojas, *Transportation*
Johana Lopez, *Accounts Mgr*
EMP: 120 **EST:** 1997
SQ FT: 225,000
SALES (est): 2.4MM **Privately Held**
SIC: 2448 Pallets, wood

(G-2126)
J & G FABRICATING INC
Also Called: Par Fabricating Co
12653 Irving Ave (60406-1652)
PHONE..................708 385-9147
Rafal Gliwiak, *Co-Owner*
Piotr Kajpust, *Co-Owner*
EMP: 8
SQ FT: 8,900
SALES (est): 750K **Privately Held**
WEB: www.parfabricating.com
SIC: 3444 3443 3441 Sheet metalwork; fabricated plate work (boiler shop); fabricated structural metal

(G-2127)
J E TOMES & ASSOCIATES INC
2513 140th Pl (60406-3588)
PHONE..................708 653-5100
Joe Tomes, *President*
Chris White, *Sales Staff*
EMP: 10
SQ FT: 1,000
SALES (est): 2.2MM **Privately Held**
SIC: 3272 5211 Concrete products, precast; lumber & other building materials

(G-2128)
KDK UPSET FORGING CO
2645 139th St (60406-3599)
P.O. Box 146 (60406-0146)
PHONE..................708 388-8770
Laxminarayan Mahisekar, *President*
Paul Knez, *Vice Pres*
EMP: 44 **EST:** 1947
SQ FT: 34,000
SALES (est): 8.4MM **Privately Held**
WEB: www.kdkforging.com
SIC: 3462 3841 3493 3452 Iron & steel forgings; surgical & medical instruments; steel springs, except wire; bolts, nuts, rivets & washers

(G-2129)
KOWAL CUSTOM CABINET & FURN
2900 Wireton Rd (60406)
PHONE..................708 597-3367
Jeff Kowalczyk, *President*
Ray Kowalczyk, *Vice Pres*
Judith Kowalczyk, *Admin Sec*
EMP: 6
SALES (est): 788.3K **Privately Held**
SIC: 2434 2511 Wood kitchen cabinets; wood household furniture

(G-2130)
M AND M PALLET INC
2810 Vermont St (60406-1870)
PHONE..................708 272-4447
Rodrigo Munoz, *President*
Elizabeth Munoz, *Sales Staff*
Hector Munoz, *Admin Sec*
EMP: 4 **EST:** 2006
SALES (est): 642.7K **Privately Held**
WEB: www.mandmpallet.com
SIC: 2448 Pallets, wood; pallets, wood & wood with metal

(G-2131)
MOLINO BAKING CO
13030 Western Ave (60406-2419)
PHONE..................708 385-6616
Lisa Gorajski, *Principal*
EMP: 3 **EST:** 2008
SALES (est): 157.4K **Privately Held**
WEB: www.molinobakery.com
SIC: 5149 2051 Bakery products; bakery: wholesale or wholesale/retail combined

(G-2132)
MONUMENTAL ART WORKS
2152 Vermont St Ste A2 (60406-2581)
PHONE..................708 389-3038
Ogal Bugayon, *President*
Victor Bugayon, *Co-Owner*
EMP: 4
SQ FT: 600
SALES (est): 400.3K **Privately Held**
WEB: www.monumentalartworks.com
SIC: 3272 3281 Monuments & grave markers, except terrazo; granite, cut & shaped

(G-2133)
NATIONAL INTERCHEM LLC
13750 Chatham St (60406-3218)
PHONE..................708 597-7777
Paul Killa, *Manager*
EMP: 4
SQ FT: 10,000
SALES (est): 1MM **Privately Held**
SIC: 2819 2869 Industrial inorganic chemicals; industrial organic chemicals
PA: Rna Corporation
13750 Chatham St
Blue Island IL 60406

(G-2134)
PRINTSOURCE PLUS INC
12128 Western Ave (60406-1328)
PHONE..................708 389-6252
EMP: 8
SQ FT: 2,500
SALES (est): 600K **Privately Held**
SIC: 2752 2791 2789 2759 Lithographic Coml Print Typesetting Services Bookbinding/Related Work Commercial Printing

(G-2135)
RED RIVER LUMBER INC
2200 Burr Oak Ave (60406-2107)
P.O. Box 43144, Chicago (60643-0144)
PHONE..................708 388-1818
Jeffrey B Currier, *President*
Taka De Hart, *CFO*
Celeste Burke, *Sales Staff*
▲ **EMP:** 65
SQ FT: 12,000
SALES (est): 1MM **Privately Held**
SIC: 2426 5211 2421 5031 Hardwood dimension & flooring mills; lumber products; sawmills & planing mills, general; lumber: rough, dressed & finished; hardwood veneer & plywood; wood preserving

(G-2136)
RIJON MANUFACTURING COMPANY
Also Called: Rijon Awning
13733 Chatham St (60406-3217)
P.O. Box 125 (60406-0125)
PHONE..................708 388-2295
Wayne Roman, *President*
EMP: 7
SALES (est): 1MM **Privately Held**
SIC: 3469 3444 3544 Stamping metal for the trade; awnings, sheet metal; dies & die holders for metal cutting, forming, die casting

(G-2137)
RNA CORPORATION (PA)
13750 Chatham St (60406-3218)
PHONE..................708 597-7777
Muhammad Akhtar, *President*
Archish Desai, *Director*
John Harms, *Director*
Rehana Akhtar, *Admin Sec*
Maria Ruiz, *Admin Asst*
◆ **EMP:** 85
SQ FT: 250,000
SALES (est): 24.9MM **Privately Held**
SIC: 2844 Cosmetic preparations

(G-2138)
SAVINO ENTERPRISES
12453 Gregory St (60406-1600)
PHONE..................708 385-5277
Anthony Savino, *President*
Pam Savino, *Vice Pres*
EMP: 3
SALES (est): 141.3K **Privately Held**
SIC: 7389 2752 1751 1521 Swimming pool & hot tub service & maintenance; commercial printing, offset; carpentry work; new construction, single-family houses

(G-2139)
SCHROEDERS PALLET SERVICE INC
3500 Burr Oak Ave (60406-1864)
PHONE..................708 371-9046
Dewain Schroeder, *President*
EMP: 19
SQ FT: 56,000
SALES (est): 1.5MM **Privately Held**
SIC: 2448 Pallets, wood

(G-2140)
SIGNODE INDUSTRIAL GROUP LLC
Also Called: Down River
14153 Western Ave (60406-3421)
P.O. Box 341, Posen (60469-0341)
PHONE..................708 371-9050
Wayne Dziadosz, *Manager*
EMP: 38
SALES (corp-wide): 11.6B **Publicly Held**
SIC: 2679 Paper products, converted
HQ: Signode Industrial Group Llc
3650 W Lake Ave
Glenview IL 60026
847 724-7500

(G-2141)
SOLVAY USA INC
14000 Seeley Ave (60406-3261)
PHONE..................708 371-2000
Brad Balint, *Plant Mgr*
EMP: 42
SALES (corp-wide): 13.8MM **Privately Held**
WEB: www.solvay.us
SIC: 2819 2869 2843 Inorganic acids, except nitric & phosphoric; industrial organic chemicals; surface active agents
HQ: Solvay Usa Inc.
504 Carnegie Ctr
Princeton NJ 08540
609 860-4000

Blue Mound
Macon County

(G-2142)
YODER JOHN
2580 N 1500 East Rd (62513-8626)
P.O. Box 111 (62513-0111)
PHONE..................217 676-3430
John Yoder, *Partner*
EMP: 3
SALES (est): 227.3K **Privately Held**
SIC: 3523 0291 Driers (farm): grain, hay & seed; livestock farm, general

Bolingbrook
Will County

(G-2143)
7000 INC
Also Called: Hmg
856 Fieldcrest Dr (60490-5444)
P.O. Box 9413, Naperville (60567-0413)
PHONE..................312 800-3612
Mary Gjondla, *CEO*
Fred K Gjondla, *CFO*
EMP: 10
SALES: 10MM **Privately Held**
SIC: 3829 7319 3845 3841 Thermometers & temperature sensors; media buying service; patient monitoring apparatus; diagnostic apparatus, medical; management consulting services; computer related maintenance services

(G-2144)
AAM MANUFACTURING
455 Gibraltar Dr (60440-3617)
PHONE..................708 606-9360
Nancy Hinsdale, *Principal*
EMP: 3
SALES (est): 223K **Privately Held**
SIC: 3999 Manufacturing industries

GEOGRAPHIC SECTION
Bolingbrook - Will County (G-2174)

(G-2145)
ABB INC
Also Called: Turbine Charging Unit
1 Territorial Ct Ste A (60440-3671)
PHONE.................630 759-7428
John Gustafson, *Sales Staff*
Rich Napul, *Branch Mgr*
Cathy Norton, *Executive Asst*
EMP: 11
SALES (corp-wide): 27.9B **Privately Held**
SIC: 1731 3511 Energy management controls; turbines & turbine generator sets
HQ: Abb, Inc.
  305 Gregson Dr
  Cary NC 27511

(G-2146)
ABB MOTORS AND MECHANICAL INC
1055 Remington Blvd Ste B (60440-4616)
PHONE.................630 296-1400
Ryan Fitts, *Director*
EMP: 157
SALES (corp-wide): 27.9B **Privately Held**
SIC: 3621 Motors & generators
HQ: Abb Motors And Mechanical Inc.
  5711 Rs Boreham Jr St
  Fort Smith AR 72901
  479 646-4711

(G-2147)
ADVANTAGE SEAL INC
694 Veterans Pkwy Ste A (60440-4618)
PHONE.................630 226-0200
Kelly Clark, *President*
Michael Compton, *Vice Pres*
Dennis Spears, *Vice Pres*
Nestor Solis, *Admin Sec*
▲ **EMP:** 14
SQ FT: 5,000
SALES: 1.3MM **Privately Held**
SIC: 3053 Oil seals, rubber

(G-2148)
AR IMPEX INC
106 Somerset Ln (60440-2912)
PHONE.................404 649-4581
Muhammad Aslam, *President*
EMP: 2
SALES: 500K **Privately Held**
SIC: 2259 Towels, washcloths & dishcloths: knit

(G-2149)
ARTISTIC DENTAL STUDIO INC
470 Woodcreek Dr (60440-4913)
PHONE.................630 679-8686
Jerry Ulaszek, *President*
Kathy Deady, *Accountant*
EMP: 47
SQ FT: 9,300
SALES (est): 5.4MM **Privately Held**
SIC: 8072 3843 3842 Crown & bridge production; dental equipment & supplies; surgical appliances & supplies

(G-2150)
ASTRO PLASTIC CONTAINERS INC
903 Carlow Dr (60490-3120)
PHONE.................708 458-7100
Magdalena Kolosa, *President*
Miroslaw Kolosa, *Shareholder*
EMP: 18
SALES (est): 3.9MM **Privately Held**
SIC: 3085 Plastics bottles

(G-2151)
ATHLLETE LLC
948 W Briarcliff Rd (60440-5216)
PHONE.................773 829-3752
Qaisar Imran, *President*
EMP: 10
SALES (est): 331.8K **Privately Held**
SIC: 2329 2339 5136 Men's & boys' sportswear & athletic clothing; women's & misses' athletic clothing & sportswear; men's & boys' sportswear & work clothing

(G-2152)
ATLANTIS PRODUCTS INC
586 Territorial Dr Ste H (60440-4885)
PHONE.................630 971-9680
Marie Murphy, *President*
◆ **EMP:** 5
SQ FT: 3,200
SALES (est): 715.8K **Privately Held**
SIC: 3446 3315 Railings, bannisters, guards, etc.: made from metal pipe; fence gates posts & fittings: steel

(G-2153)
AWARD EMBLEM MFG CO INC
179 E South Frontage Rd (60440-3512)
PHONE.................630 739-0800
R Jason Klein, *President*
EMP: 16 **EST:** 1946
SQ FT: 15,000
SALES (est): 2.9MM **Privately Held**
WEB: www.awardemblem.com
SIC: 5999 3911 3993 2395 Trophies & plaques; mountings, gold or silver: pens, leather goods, etc.; signs & advertising specialties; pleating & stitching

(G-2154)
C & S ELECTRIC SPECIALTIES
250 Gibraltar Dr (60440-3623)
PHONE.................630 406-6170
EMP: 4
SALES (est): 109.9K **Privately Held**
SIC: 3679 Harness assemblies for electronic use: wire or cable

(G-2155)
CASCO MANUFACTURING INC
600 Territorial Dr Ste C (60440-5128)
PHONE.................630 771-9555
Jackie K James, *President*
EMP: 30
SQ FT: 14,000
SALES (est): 7.9MM **Privately Held**
SIC: 3679 Harness assemblies for electronic use: wire or cable

(G-2156)
CHICAGO PASTRY INC
Knead Dough Bakery
556 Saint James Gate (60440-3635)
PHONE.................630 972-0404
John Kogelman, *Manager*
EMP: 150
SALES (corp-wide): 124.2MM **Privately Held**
SIC: 2051 Bakery: wholesale or wholesale/retail combined
PA: Chicago Pastry, Inc.
  6501 Roosevelt Rd
  Berwyn IL 60402
  708 788-5320

(G-2157)
COMTEC INDUSTRIES LTD
586 Territorial Dr Ste F (60440-4885)
PHONE.................630 759-9000
James Reilly, *President*
Dolores T Reilly, *Corp Secy*
Jim Reilly, *Officer*
Arthur J Reilly, *Shareholder*
EMP: 8 **EST:** 1964
SQ FT: 3,000
SALES (est): 1.4MM **Privately Held**
WEB: www.comtecindustriesltd.com
SIC: 3556 3544 Food products machinery; special dies, tools, jigs & fixtures

(G-2158)
CONTINENT CORP
227 Tiger St (60490-2054)
PHONE.................773 733-1584
Yuriy Makoviychuk, *General Mgr*
EMP: 4
SALES (est): 246.3K **Privately Held**
SIC: 2759 5137 Letterpress & screen printing; apparel belts, women's & children's

(G-2159)
CRANE COMPOSITES INC
594 Territorial Dr Ste D (60440-5143)
PHONE.................630 378-9580
Jeff Craney, *President*
EMP: 81
SALES (corp-wide): 3.2B **Publicly Held**
WEB: www.cranecomposites.com
SIC: 3089 Panels, building: plastic
HQ: Crane Composites, Inc.
  23525 W Eames St
  Channahon IL 60410
  815 467-8600

(G-2160)
CRANE NUCLEAR INC
Also Called: Crane Valve Services
860 Remington Blvd (60440-4910)
PHONE.................630 226-4900
Joann Conroy, *Manager*
EMP: 50
SALES (corp-wide): 3.2B **Publicly Held**
SIC: 3492 Electrohydraulic servo valves, metal
HQ: Crane Nuclear, Inc.
  2825 Cobb Intl Blvd Nw
  Kennesaw GA 30152

(G-2161)
CTG ADVANCED MATERIALS LLC
Also Called: Hc Materials
479 Quadrangle Dr Ste E (60440-3652)
PHONE.................630 226-9080
EMP: 21 **EST:** 2013
SALES (est): 1.8MM **Privately Held**
SIC: 3812 3845 Manufactures Piezoelectric Single Crystals For Acoustic Transduction Devices

(G-2162)
CUSTOM BOXES INC (PA)
681 W Briarcliff Rd (60440-6146)
PHONE.................630 364-3944
Amir Bashir, *President*
EMP: 14
SALES (est): 3.9MM **Privately Held**
SIC: 2653 Corrugated & solid fiber boxes

(G-2163)
D & D MANUFACTURING INC
500 Territorial Dr (60440-4814)
PHONE.................888 300-6869
Steve Capo, *Opers Staff*
Ed Titus, *Engineer*
Stanley Dybas, *Controller*
Yuri Steventon, *Cust Mgr*
Bill Diedrick, *Officer*
EMP: 7
SALES (est): 1.7MM **Privately Held**
SIC: 3544 Special dies & tools

(G-2164)
D & D TOOLING AND MFG INC (PA)
Also Called: D & D Manufacturing Entps
500 Territorial Dr (60440-4814)
PHONE.................888 300-6869
William Diedrick, *President*
Mike Shaven, *Plant Mgr*
Tim Hager, *Production*
Alberto Fry-Valladares, *Engineer*
Alberto Valladares, *Engineer*
EMP: 85
SALES (est): 24.1MM **Privately Held**
WEB: www.ddmfg.com
SIC: 3544 Special dies & tools

(G-2165)
D & D TOOLING INC
500 Territorial Dr (60440-4814)
PHONE.................630 759-0015
William Diedrick, *President*
Lawrence Diedrick, *Vice Pres*
EMP: 150
SQ FT: 10,000
SALES (est): 21.7MM **Privately Held**
SIC: 3544 Special dies & tools

(G-2166)
DANIEL M POWERS & ASSOC LTD
575 W Crossroads Pkwy B (60440-5096)
PHONE.................630 685-8400
Theresa Vanek, *CEO*
Pamela Newman, *Chairman*
Alan Vanichtheeranont, *COO*
▲ **EMP:** 60
SQ FT: 110,000
SALES (est): 24.3MM **Privately Held**
SIC: 5046 2541 2521 2434 Store fixtures; store fixtures, wood; wood office furniture; wood kitchen cabinets; millwork

(G-2167)
DE BOER & ASSOCIATES
736 Dorchester Dr (60440-1161)
PHONE.................630 972-1600
Douglas De Boer, *Owner*
EMP: 2
SALES (est): 250K **Privately Held**
SIC: 2711 Commercial printing & newspaper publishing combined

(G-2168)
DEJA INVESTMENTS INC (PA)
279 Marquette Dr (60440-3600)
P.O. Box 270, Hinsdale (60522-6004)
PHONE.................630 408-9222
Edward K Gignac, *President*
John Hartline, *Vice Pres*
Jim Gignac, *VP Sales*
James Gignac, *Admin Sec*
EMP: 95 **EST:** 1922
SQ FT: 43,000
SALES (est): 10.9MM **Privately Held**
SIC: 2023 2099 2026 2024 Ice cream mix, unfrozen: liquid or dry; yogurt mix; milkshake mix; whipped topping, dry mix; food preparations; fluid milk; ice cream & frozen desserts

(G-2169)
DRS NTWORK IMAGING SYSTEMS LLC
590 Territorial Dr Ste B (60440-4881)
PHONE.................214 215-5960
EMP: 3
SALES (est): 160.1K **Privately Held**
SIC: 3674 Infrared sensors, solid state

(G-2170)
DTRS ENTERPRISES INC
Also Called: Savile Rumtini
1317 Rosemary Dr (60490-4940)
PHONE.................630 296-6890
Didrielle D Tutt, *President*
Richard Smith, *Vice Pres*
EMP: 2
SALES (est): 242K **Privately Held**
SIC: 5182 7389 2085 Wine; ; distilled & blended liquors

(G-2171)
EFCO CORPORATION
595 Territorial Dr Ste A (60440-4631)
PHONE.................630 378-4720
Rob Jones, *Branch Mgr*
EMP: 27
SALES (corp-wide): 1.3B **Publicly Held**
SIC: 3442 3354 Window & door frames; aluminum extruded products
HQ: Efco Corporation
  1000 County Rd
  Monett MO 65708
  417 235-3193

(G-2172)
ELAN INDUSTRIES INC
650 S Schmidt Rd Ste A (60440-9404)
PHONE.................630 679-2000
Todd A Thomas, *President*
John Tomaras, *COO*
James M Ralson, *Vice Pres*
James Ralson, *VP Engrg*
Jim Dodis, *Engineer*
▲ **EMP:** 13
SQ FT: 35,000
SALES: 10.3MM **Privately Held**
SIC: 3679 Electronic circuits

(G-2173)
ELMHURST-CHICAGO STONE COMPANY
351 Royce Rd (60440-9053)
PHONE.................630 983-6410
Jim Wilson, *Manager*
EMP: 30
SALES (corp-wide): 127.2MM **Privately Held**
SIC: 1422 3273 3272 1442 Cement rock, crushed & broken-quarrying; ready-mixed concrete; concrete products; construction sand & gravel
PA: Elmhurst-Chicago Stone Company
  400 W 1st St
  Elmhurst IL 60126
  630 832-4000

(G-2174)
EPIR INC
586 Territorial Dr Ste A (60440-4886)
PHONE.................630 842-4486
Silviu Velicu, *President*
Paul Boieriu, *President*

Bolingbrook - Will County (G-2175)

EMP: 3
SALES (est): 390.5K Privately Held
SIC: 3674 Semiconductors & related devices

(G-2175)
EPIR TECHNOLOGIES INC
590 Territorial Dr Ste H (60440-4887)
PHONE.................................630 771-0203
Sivalingam Sivananthan, *CEO*
Kasivisvananthan Chelvakumar, *President*
Christoph H Grein, *Vice Pres*
Chelva Kumar, *CFO*
EMP: 43
SQ FT: 52,000
SALES (est): 7.8MM Privately Held
SIC: 3674 3812 8731 Infrared sensors, solid state; infrared object detection equipment; commercial physical research

(G-2176)
FEDEX OFFICE & PRINT SVCS INC
251 S Weber Rd (60490-1502)
PHONE.................................630 759-5784
EMP: 3
SALES (corp-wide): 69.6B Publicly Held
SIC: 2759 4822 5099 7334 Commercial printing; facsimile transmission services; signs, except electric; photocopying & duplicating services
HQ: Fedex Office And Print Services, Inc.
7900 Legacy Dr
Plano TX 75024
800 463-3339

(G-2177)
FERRARA CANDY COMPANY
910 Dalton Ln (60490-3128)
PHONE.................................630 378-4197
Jill Manchester, *Senior VP*
Heather Boggs, *Vice Pres*
EMP: 10
SALES (corp-wide): 228MM Privately Held
SIC: 2064 Chewing candy, not chewing gum
HQ: Ferrara Candy Company
404 W Harrison St 650s
Chicago IL 60607
708 366-0500

(G-2178)
FOREST ENVELOPE COMPANY
309 E Crossroads Pkwy (60440-3539)
PHONE.................................630 515-1200
Jack W Wagner, *President*
John F Wagner, *Vice Pres*
Brian Dietrich, *Manager*
Phyllis E Wagner, *Admin Sec*
EMP: 43 EST: 1976
SQ FT: 30,000
SALES (est): 12MM Privately Held
SIC: 2677 2759 Envelopes; envelopes: printing

(G-2179)
GENERAL CONVERTING INC
Also Called: GCI
250 W Crossroads Pkwy (60440-3546)
PHONE.................................630 378-9800
Robert W Ruebenson, *President*
Yvonne Wright, *Manager*
Shirley V Ruebenson, *Admin Sec*
EMP: 60
SQ FT: 125,000
SALES (est): 13MM Privately Held
SIC: 2752 Commercial printing, offset

(G-2180)
GRAPHIC SCIENCES INC
582 Territorial Dr Ste A (60440-4603)
PHONE.................................630 226-0994
Kent Wishart, *President*
EMP: 9 EST: 1989
SALES (est): 1.4MM Privately Held
SIC: 2899 Ink or writing fluids

(G-2181)
GRIMCO INC
575 W Crssrds Pkwy Ste B (60440)
PHONE.................................630 530-7756
Tina Bunag, *Sales Staff*
Allyson Dworak, *Sales Staff*
EMP: 10

SALES (corp-wide): 97.5MM Privately Held
WEB: www.grimco.com
SIC: 3993 Signs & advertising specialties
PA: Grimco, Inc.
11745 Sppngton Brracks Rd
Saint Louis MO 63127
636 305-0088

(G-2182)
H & H STONE LLC
1421 W 135th St (60490-4983)
PHONE.................................815 782-5700
David Hamman, *Mng Member*
Karen Kelly, *Mng Member*
EMP: 3
SALES (est): 277.6K Privately Held
SIC: 1442 Gravel & pebble mining

(G-2183)
HARMON INC
100 E Crssrads Pkwy Ste B (60440)
PHONE.................................630 759-8060
Thomas Niepokoj, *Branch Mgr*
EMP: 20
SALES (corp-wide): 1.3B Publicly Held
SIC: 3449 Curtain wall, metal; curtain walls for buildings, steel
HQ: Harmon, Inc.
7900 Xerxes Ave S # 1800
Bloomington MN 55431
952 944-5700

(G-2184)
HEARTHSIDE USA
1100 Remington Blvd (60440-3308)
PHONE.................................630 845-9400
David Byrne, *Branch Mgr*
EMP: 400 Privately Held
SIC: 3565 Packaging machinery
HQ: Hearthside Usa - Cpg Partners, Llc
1800 Averill Rd
Geneva IL 60134
630 845-9400

(G-2185)
HONEYWELL SAFETY PDTS USA INC
Also Called: W. H. Salisbury Elec Safety
101 E Crssrads Pkwy Ste A (60440)
PHONE.................................630 343-3731
Fred Mc Dowell, *Production*
Kenneth Mazurek, *Opers-Prdtn-Mfg*
EMP: 125
SALES (corp-wide): 36.7B Publicly Held
SIC: 3069 3429 3053 3842 Molded rubber products; manufactured hardware (general); gaskets, packing & sealing devices; surgical appliances & supplies; synthetic rubber
HQ: Honeywell Safety Products Usa, Inc.
300 S Tryon St Ste 500
Charlotte NC 28202
800 430-5490

(G-2186)
HOVI INDUSTRIES INCORPORATED (PA)
Also Called: Perkins Manfacturing
380 Veterans Pkwy Ste 110 (60440-4667)
PHONE.................................815 512-7500
Robert Hoppe Sr, *Ch of Bd*
◆ EMP: 38 EST: 1974
SALES (est): 13.2MM Privately Held
SIC: 5084 3444 7699 6719 Trucks, industrial; metal housings, enclosures, casings & other containers; sewer cleaning & rodding; investment holding companies, except banks

(G-2187)
HUSSAIN SHAHEEN
Also Called: Need
1900 Danube Way (60490-6500)
PHONE.................................630 405-8009
Shaheen Hussain, *Owner*
EMP: 3 EST: 2014
SALES (est): 146.9K Privately Held
SIC: 2819 Industrial inorganic chemicals

(G-2188)
IFCO
400 W Crssrads Pkwy Ste A (60440)
PHONE.................................630 226-0650
Jim Hillock, *General Mgr*
EMP: 6 EST: 2009

SALES (est): 988.9K Privately Held
SIC: 2448 Pallets, wood

(G-2189)
IL TOOL WORK
309 E Crossroads Pkwy (60440-3539)
PHONE.................................630 972-6400
Jim Turek, *Principal*
EMP: 3
SALES (est): 162.2K Privately Held
SIC: 3643 Current-carrying wiring devices

(G-2190)
IMI MANUFACTURING INC
694 Veterans Pkwy Ste B (60440-3599)
PHONE.................................630 771-0003
Theodore Hofmeister, *President*
Diane Hofmeister, *Admin Sec*
EMP: 6
SQ FT: 5,000
SALES (est): 689.9K Privately Held
SIC: 3599 Machine shop, jobbing & repair

(G-2191)
IMPRO INDUSTRIES USA INC
375 Sw Frontage Rd Ste D (60440)
PHONE.................................630 759-0280
Michelle Yuan, *Manager*
EMP: 5 Privately Held
SIC: 3369 Castings, except die-castings, precision
HQ: Impro Industries Usa, Inc.
21660 Copley Dr Ste 100
Diamond Bar CA 91765
909 396-6525

(G-2192)
INSTITUTIONAL EQUIPMENT INC (PA)
Also Called: Iei
704 Veterans Pkwy Ste B (60440-4612)
PHONE.................................630 771-0990
Franklin Fiene, *President*
EMP: 35
SQ FT: 21,000
SALES (est): 8MM Privately Held
SIC: 5046 3556 Restaurant equipment & supplies; food products machinery

(G-2193)
INTEGRATED LIGHTING TECH INC (PA)
Also Called: Integrating Green Technologies
1317 Rosemary Dr (60490-4940)
PHONE.................................630 750-3786
Carl Tutt, *President*
EMP: 1
SALES: 258K Privately Held
SIC: 3674 7389 Light emitting diodes;

(G-2194)
INTERSTATE CARGO INC
380 Internationale Dr A (60440-3638)
PHONE.................................630 701-7744
Ilhom Bobohonov, *President*
EMP: 24
SQ FT: 9,000
SALES (est): 4.4MM Privately Held
WEB: www.iscargoinc.com
SIC: 3537 Truck trailers, used in plants, docks, terminals, etc.

(G-2195)
ISHOT PRODUCTS INC
558 Payton Ln (60440-3520)
P.O. Box 1668 (60440-7368)
PHONE.................................312 497-4190
Christopher R Fliger, *President*
▲ EMP: 6
SQ FT: 900
SALES: 200K Privately Held
SIC: 3861 Tripods, camera & projector

(G-2196)
J DESIGN WORKS INC
210 Ironbark Way (60440-3076)
PHONE.................................847 812-0891
John Williams, *President*
▲ EMP: 2
SALES: 1MM Privately Held
SIC: 2393 Textile bags

(G-2197)
JERNBERG INDUSTRIES LLC
Also Called: Jernberg of Bolingbrook
455 Gibraltar Dr (60440-3617)
PHONE.................................630 972-7000
Larry Wolyniet, *Manager*
EMP: 130
SALES (corp-wide): 6.5B Publicly Held
SIC: 3462 Iron & steel forgings
HQ: Jernberg Industries, Llc
328 W 40th Pl
Chicago IL 60609

(G-2198)
JEWEL OSCO INC
Also Called: Jewel-Osco 3013
1200 W Boughton Rd (60440-6568)
PHONE.................................630 226-1892
Steven Ranch, *Manager*
EMP: 100
SALES (corp-wide): 60.5B Privately Held
WEB: www.jewelosco.mywebgrocer.com
SIC: 5411 5912 5421 2051 Supermarkets, chain; drug stores & proprietary stores; meat & fish markets; bread, cake & related products
HQ: Jewel Osco, Inc.
150 E Pierce Rd Ste 200
Itasca IL 60143
630 948-6000

(G-2199)
JOHN CRANE INC
175 E Crossroads Pkwy (60440-3639)
PHONE.................................630 410-4444
EMP: 3
SALES (corp-wide): 3.1B Privately Held
SIC: 3053 Gaskets & sealing devices; packing materials
HQ: John Crane Inc.
227 W Monroe St Ste 1800
Chicago IL 60606
312 605-7800

(G-2200)
KAM GROUP INC
486 W North Frontage Rd (60440-4904)
PHONE.................................630 679-9668
MEI Zheng, *Principal*
Dan Liberty, *Accounts Exec*
Joe Mugnolo, *Accounts Exec*
May Zheng, *VP Mktg*
▲ EMP: 13
SALES (est): 1.6MM Privately Held
SIC: 2673 Bags: plastic, laminated & coated

(G-2201)
KENT PRECISION FOODS GROUP INC
1000 Dalton Ln Ste A (60490-3258)
PHONE.................................630 226-0071
Mike Saniat, *Vice Pres*
EMP: 22
SALES (corp-wide): 459.4MM Privately Held
SIC: 2034 2024 Dehydrated fruits, vegetables, soups; ice cream & frozen desserts
HQ: Kent Precision Foods Group, Inc.
2905 N Highway 61
Muscatine IA 52761

(G-2202)
KENT PRECISION FOODS GROUP INC
850 Remington Blvd (60440-4910)
PHONE.................................630 226-0071
Chuck Pumberg, *Manager*
EMP: 17
SALES (corp-wide): 459.4MM Privately Held
SIC: 2034 2099 2035 Dehydrated fruits, vegetables, soups; food preparations; pickles, sauces & salad dressings
HQ: Kent Precision Foods Group, Inc.
2905 N Highway 61
Muscatine IA 52761

(G-2203)
KPS CAPITAL PARTNERS LP
Also Called: MST Div
455 Gibraltar Dr (60440-3617)
PHONE.................................630 972-7000
M E Wheeler, *CEO*
EMP: 260

GEOGRAPHIC SECTION

Bolingbrook - Will County (G-2231)

SALES (corp-wide): 2.4B **Privately Held**
SIC: 3559 Automotive related machinery
PA: Kps Capital Partners, Lp
   485 Lexington Ave Fl 31
   New York NY 10017
   212 338-5100

(G-2204)
LINCOLN ELECTRIC COMPANY
115 E Crlroads Pkwy Ste A (60440)
PHONE..................630 783-3600
Dave Thayer, *Principal*
EMP: 11
SALES (corp-wide): 3B **Publicly Held**
SIC: 5085 5169 2796 Welding supplies; gases, compressed & liquefied; electrotype plates
HQ: Lincoln Electric Company
   22801 Saint Clair Ave
   Cleveland OH 44117
   216 481-8100

(G-2205)
LITHOTYPE COMPANY INC
594 Territorial Dr Ste G (60440-5143)
PHONE..................630 771-1920
Bruce Weintraub, *Branch Mgr*
Elaine Zager, *Office Admin*
James McHugh, *Technician*
EMP: 12
SALES (corp-wide): 39MM **Privately Held**
SIC: 2752 Wrappers, lithographed
PA: Lithotype Company, Inc.
   333 Point San Bruno Blvd
   South San Francisco CA 94080
   650 871-1750

(G-2206)
LOCKER ROOM SCREEN PRINTING
253 S Schmidt Rd (60440-2746)
PHONE..................630 759-2533
Tom Pondel, *Owner*
EMP: 3
SQ FT: 1,700
SALES (est): 350K **Privately Held**
SIC: 2759 2396 Screen printing; automotive & apparel trimmings

(G-2207)
LURE GROUP LLC
5 Privett Ct (60490-2016)
PHONE..................630 222-6515
Marc A Eltoft,
EMP: 2
SALES (est): 215.5K **Privately Held**
SIC: 2752 8742 Commercial printing, lithographic; marketing consulting services

(G-2208)
LYNN ELECTRONICS CORP
Also Called: Keystone Wire & Cable
386 Internationale Dr H (60440-3601)
PHONE..................972 412-7240
EMP: 8
SALES (corp-wide): 19.1MM **Privately Held**
SIC: 3679 Harness assemblies for electronic use: wire or cable
PA: Lynn Electronics, Llc
   154 Railroad Dr
   Ivyland PA 18974
   215 355-8200

(G-2209)
MANDYS SOUL FOOD KITCHEN LLC
Also Called: A-Z Stepping Stones
431u N Bolingbrook Dr (60440-1954)
PHONE..................630 485-7291
Delicia Bowling, *Vice Pres*
EMP: 11
SALES (est): 1.3MM **Privately Held**
SIC: 2051 5812 Bakery: wholesale or wholesale/retail combined; family restaurants

(G-2210)
MENASHA CORP
465 W Crossroads Pkwy (60440-4937)
PHONE..................630 679-8000
Steve Vanlear, *Manager*
EMP: 3

SALES (est): 323.2K **Privately Held**
WEB: www.menasha.com
SIC: 2653 Boxes, corrugated: made from purchased materials

(G-2211)
MENASHA PACKAGING COMPANY LLC
800 S Weber Rd Ste A (60490-5612)
PHONE..................708 482-7619
EMP: 200
SALES (corp-wide): 2.2B **Privately Held**
SIC: 2653 Boxes, corrugated: made from purchased materials
HQ: Menasha Packaging Company, Llc
   1645 Bergstrom Rd
   Neenah WI 54956
   920 751-1000

(G-2212)
MENASHA PACKAGING COMPANY LLC
1251 115th St Ste B (60490-3309)
PHONE..................312 880-4631
Pam Horine, *Branch Mgr*
EMP: 105
SALES (corp-wide): 2.2B **Privately Held**
SIC: 2653 Sheets, corrugated: made from purchased materials
HQ: Menasha Packaging Company, Llc
   1645 Bergstrom Rd
   Neenah WI 54956
   920 751-1000

(G-2213)
METALS & METALS LLC
Also Called: Metalsupermarkets LLC
999 Remington Blvd Ste C (60440-4871)
PHONE..................630 866-4200
Shirin Lakdawala,
EMP: 5
SQ FT: 5,000
SALES (est): 500K **Privately Held**
SIC: 3441 Fabricated structural metal

(G-2214)
MIDWEST COATINGS INC
157 Oakwood Dr (60440-2828)
PHONE..................815 717-8914
Dennis Stemper, *Vice Pres*
EMP: 2 EST: 2013
SALES (est): 204.1K **Privately Held**
SIC: 3479 Coating of metals & formed products

(G-2215)
MOHAWK INDUSTRIES INC
969 Veterans Pkwy Ste B (60490-3520)
PHONE..................630 972-8000
Gary Bengtson, *Branch Mgr*
EMP: 70 **Publicly Held**
SIC: 2273 Wilton carpets; rugs, tufted
PA: Mohawk Industries, Inc.
   160 S Industrial Blvd
   Calhoun GA 30701

(G-2216)
MOLEX LLC
575 Veterans Pkwy Ste A (60440-4622)
PHONE..................630 527-4363
Jim Kicher, *Branch Mgr*
EMP: 8
SALES (corp-wide): 48.9B **Privately Held**
SIC: 3679 3643 3357 Antennas, receiving; electronic circuits; connectors & terminals for electrical devices; communication wire; fiber optic cable (insulated)
HQ: Molex, Llc
   2222 Wellington Ct
   Lisle IL 60532
   630 969-4550

(G-2217)
MPS CHICAGO INC
315 Eisenhower Ln S (60440)
PHONE..................630 932-5583
Fax: 630 691-2168
EMP: 50
SALES (corp-wide): 14.1B **Publicly Held**
SIC: 2759 Commercial Printing
HQ: Mps Chicago, Inc.
   1500 Centre Cir
   Downers Grove IL 60515
   630 932-9000

(G-2218)
MUSIC SOLUTIONS
490 Woodcreek Dr Ste D (60440-1394)
PHONE..................630 759-3033
Steve Dollinger, *Partner*
Ronald Lukowski, *Partner*
EMP: 10
SQ FT: 2,000
SALES: 320K **Privately Held**
SIC: 5735 3931 Record & prerecorded tape stores; guitars & parts, electric & nonelectric; musical instruments, electric & electronic

(G-2219)
NETRANIX ENTERPRISE
336 Pinto Dr (60440-1724)
PHONE..................630 312-8141
Carlos Johnson, *CEO*
Anitra Thomas, *COO*
EMP: 35
SALES (est): 1.5MM **Privately Held**
SIC: 2211 1521 5999 Apparel & outerwear fabrics, cotton; general remodeling, single-family houses; alarm & safety equipment stores

(G-2220)
NEVERIA MICHOACANA LLC
132 N Bolingbrook Dr (60440-2350)
PHONE..................630 783-3518
Dora Sanchez, *Owner*
EMP: 4
SALES (est): 178.9K **Privately Held**
SIC: 2024 Ice cream, bulk

(G-2221)
NEW YORK & COMPANY INC
639 E Boughton Rd Ste 135 (60440-3138)
PHONE..................630 783-2910
Heidi Velasquez, *Manager*
EMP: 17
SALES (corp-wide): 893.2MM **Publicly Held**
SIC: 5621 2389 5137 Women's specialty clothing stores; men's miscellaneous accessories; women's & children's clothing
PA: Rtw Retailwinds, Inc.
   330 W 34th St Fl 9
   New York NY 10001
   212 884-2000

(G-2222)
NEXUS SUPPLY CONSORTIUM INC
13g Fernwood Dr (60440-2926)
PHONE..................630 649-2868
Lavenia Tyler, *President*
Dorian Yamini, *Principal*
EMP: 7
SALES (est): 365.8K **Privately Held**
SIC: 7359 5045 2731 Office machine rental, except computers; computers, peripherals & software; books: publishing & printing

(G-2223)
ONE ACCORD UNITY NFP
1886 Marne Rd (60490-4596)
PHONE..................630 649-0793
Nathaniel Smith, *CEO*
EMP: 4
SALES (est): 225.8K **Privately Held**
SIC: 2721 Periodicals: publishing only

(G-2224)
PANCON ILLINOIS LLC
440 Quadrangle Dr Ste A (60440-3455)
PHONE..................630 972-6400
EMP: 7
SALES (est): 330K **Privately Held**
SIC: 3643 Mfg Conductive Wiring Devices

(G-2225)
PERFECTVISION MFG INC
1 Gateway Ct Ste Aa (60440-4669)
PHONE..................630 226-9890
Jay Siler, *Manager*
EMP: 11
SALES (est): 1.6MM **Privately Held**
SIC: 3679 Antennas, satellite: household use
PA: Perfectvision Manufacturing, Inc.
   16101 La Grande Dr
   Little Rock AR 72223

(G-2226)
PERKINS MANUFACTURING CO
380 Veterans Pkwy Ste 110 (60440-4667)
PHONE..................708 482-9500
Robert Hoppe, *President*
Cheryl Waite, *Admin Sec*
EMP: 28
SQ FT: 38,000
SALES (est): 4.5MM
SALES (corp-wide): 13.2MM **Privately Held**
SIC: 3423 Jacks: lifting, screw or ratchet (hand tools)
PA: Hovi Industries, Incorporated
   380 Veterans Pkwy Ste 110
   Bolingbrook IL 60440
   815 512-7500

(G-2227)
PHOENIX LEATHER GOODS LLC
Also Called: Beltoutlet.com
582 Territorial Dr Ste A (60440-4883)
PHONE..................815 676-6712
Kacey Bud, *Marketing Staff*
Gary Monds,
EMP: 8
SALES (est): 1.3MM **Privately Held**
SIC: 5948 2295 Leather goods, except luggage & shoes; leather, artificial or imitation

(G-2228)
PRATER INDUSTRIES INC (HQ)
Also Called: Prater-Sterling
2 Sammons Ct (60440-4995)
PHONE..................630 679-3200
Jeff Ehlers, *President*
Dirk Maroske, *Exec VP*
Pete Hinzy, *Vice Pres*
▲ EMP: 70 EST: 1925
SALES (est): 19.6MM
SALES (corp-wide): 28.1MM **Privately Held**
WEB: www.praterindustries.com
SIC: 3523 3559 3613 3541 Grading, cleaning, sorting machines, fruit, grain, vegetable; feed grinders, crushers & mixers; chemical machinery & equipment; control panels, electric; machine tools, metal cutting type; manufactured hardware (general); grinders, commercial, food
PA: Industrial Magnetics, Inc.
   1385 S M 75
   Boyne City MI 49712
   231 582-3100

(G-2229)
PRES-ON CORPORATION
Also Called: Pres-On Tape & Gasket
2600 E 107th St (60440-3196)
PHONE..................630 628-2255
Henry J Gianatasio, *President*
▲ EMP: 50 EST: 1949
SALES (est): 14.3MM **Privately Held**
WEB: www.pres-on.com
SIC: 3053 3842 3086 Gasket materials; surgical appliances & supplies; plastics foam products

(G-2230)
PRISMIER LLC
1049 Lily Cache Ln Unit B (60440-3298)
PHONE..................630 592-4515
John Petrusa, *Human Resources*
Justin Fuchs, *Sales Staff*
Alex Cosmas, *Marketing Mgr*
David Low, *Mng Member*
Lynn Low, *Info Tech Mgr*
▲ EMP: 40
SQ FT: 25,000
SALES (est): 12MM **Privately Held**
SIC: 3089 3444 3469 3363 Injection molding of plastics; housings for business machines, sheet metal; forming machine work, sheet metal; metal stampings; aluminum die-castings

(G-2231)
QUALITY BLUE & OFFSET PRINTING
7 Sunshine Ct (60490-5578)
PHONE..................630 759-8035
John Albarracin, *Owner*
EMP: 4 EST: 1990

Bolingbrook - Will County (G-2232)

SALES (est): 100K **Privately Held**
SIC: 2752 7334 2759 Commercial printing, offset; photocopying & duplicating services; commercial printing

(G-2232)
REGAL JOHNSON CO
229 Christine Way (60440-6138)
PHONE....................630 885-0688
Chunyu Tang, *President*
EMP: 3
SALES: 5MM **Privately Held**
SIC: 1081 Metal mining services

(G-2233)
RUSSELL STANLEY MIDWEST INC
1000 E 107th St (60440-3086)
PHONE....................630 739-7700
Kathy Loehman, *Principal*
EMP: 5
SALES (est): 408.1K **Privately Held**
SIC: 3089 Plastic containers, except foam

(G-2234)
SALISBURY ELEC SAFETY LLC
Also Called: Salisbury By Honeywell
101 E Crssroads Pkwy Ste A (60440)
PHONE....................877 406-4501
Mate Olds, *General Mgr*
Scott Clary,
◆ EMP: 420
SQ FT: 115,000
SALES (est): 101.1MM
SALES (corp-wide): 36.7B **Publicly Held**
SIC: 3842 Clothing, fire resistant & protective
PA: Honeywell International Inc.
300 S Tryon St
Charlotte NC 28202
704 627-6200

(G-2235)
SEGERDAHL CORP
Also Called: Data Service Solutions
401 E South Frontage Rd (60440-3063)
PHONE....................630 754-7104
West Biggs, *Vice Pres*
EMP: 53
SALES (corp-wide): 290.2MM **Privately Held**
SIC: 2752 Commercial printing, offset
PA: The Segerdahl Corp
1351 Wheeling Rd
Wheeling IL 60090
847 541-1080

(G-2236)
SEIDEL DIESEL GROUP
1 Seidel Ct (60490-3517)
PHONE....................877 373-6659
Bernd Seidel, *Owner*
EMP: 100
SALES (est): 2.8MM **Privately Held**
SIC: 3629 Electronic generation equipment

(G-2237)
SESAME SOLUTIONS LLC
279 Beaudin Blvd (60440-5520)
PHONE....................630 427-3400
Tj Harkins,
▲ EMP: 25
SALES (est): 3.1MM **Privately Held**
SIC: 2068 Seeds: dried, dehydrated, salted or roasted

(G-2238)
SHAKTHI SOLAR INC
590 Territorial Dr Ste B (60440-4881)
PHONE....................630 842-0893
Paul Boieriu, *Admin Sec*
EMP: 3
SALES (est): 180.8K **Privately Held**
SIC: 3674 Solar cells

(G-2239)
SIGN & BANNER EXPRESS
540 E Boughton Rd (60440-2181)
PHONE....................630 783-9700
Kevin Parker, *Owner*
EMP: 3
SQ FT: 2,500
SALES (est): 433.2K **Privately Held**
SIC: 3993 7336 Signs, not made in custom sign painting shops; graphic arts & related design

(G-2240)
SIGNS BY CUSTOM CUTTING INC
300 Dean Cir (60440-1827)
PHONE....................630 759-2734
Victor Drapal, *Principal*
EMP: 3
SALES (est): 295.4K **Privately Held**
SIC: 3993 Signs & advertising specialties

(G-2241)
SMART PIXEL INC
590 Territorial Dr Ste B (60440-4881)
PHONE....................630 771-0206
Sivalingam Sivananthan, *President*
EMP: 5
SALES (est): 1.2MM **Privately Held**
SIC: 3812 Detection apparatus: electronic/magnetic field, light/heat

(G-2242)
SMART SYSTEMS INC
554 Territorial Dr (60440-4814)
PHONE....................630 343-3333
Fred Halberg, *President*
▲ EMP: 47
SALES (est): 6.5MM **Privately Held**
SIC: 3625 5531 Relays & industrial controls; automotive & home supply stores

(G-2243)
SMITHFIELD PACKAGED MEATS CORP
Also Called: Saratoga Food Specialties
771 W Crssroads Pkwy Ste A (60490)
P.O. Box 39604
PHONE....................630 993-8763
Nathan Mestek, *Accounting Mgr*
Wade McGeorge, *Branch Mgr*
Gregg Blazina, *Manager*
EMP: 225
SQ FT: 95,000 **Privately Held**
WEB: www.johnmorrell.com
SIC: 2011 Meat packing plants
HQ: Smithfield Packaged Meats Corp.
805 E Kemper Rd
Cincinnati OH 45246
513 782-3800

(G-2244)
SONOCO DISPLAY & PACKAGING LLC
Also Called: Sonoco Corrflex
101 E Crossroads Pkwy (60440-3690)
PHONE....................630 972-1990
Rosa Martinez, *Branch Mgr*
EMP: 95
SALES (corp-wide): 5.3B **Publicly Held**
SIC: 3086 Packaging & shipping materials, foamed plastic
HQ: Sonoco Display & Packaging, Llc
555 Aureole St
Winston Salem NC 27107

(G-2245)
SONY/ATV MUSIC PUBLISHING LLC
351 Internationale Dr (60440-3628)
PHONE....................630 739-8129
EMP: 25 **Privately Held**
SIC: 2741 Music book & sheet music publishing
HQ: Sony/Atv Music Publishing Llc
25 Madison Ave Fl 24
New York NY 10010
212 833-7730

(G-2246)
SPEP ACQUISITION CORP
Also Called: Sierra Pacific Engrg & Pdts
1 Gateway Ct Ste E (60440-4671)
PHONE....................310 608-0693
Larry Mirick, *Branch Mgr*
EMP: 5
SALES (corp-wide): 18.4MM **Privately Held**
SIC: 3429 5072 8711 Manufactured hardware (general); hardware; engineering services
PA: S.P.E.P. Acquisition Corp.
4041 Via Oro Ave
Long Beach CA 90810
310 608-0693

(G-2247)
TDC FILTER
2 Territorial Ct (60440-3558)
PHONE....................503 521-9988
John Love, *Manager*
EMP: 19 EST: 2013
SALES (est): 4.5MM **Privately Held**
SIC: 3564 Air purification equipment

(G-2248)
TECHNICS INC
1000 W Crossroads Pkwy J (60490-3512)
PHONE....................630 938-4709
Thomas Edwards, *President*
◆ EMP: 11
SQ FT: 10,000
SALES (est): 2.5MM **Privately Held**
SIC: 3829 Testing equipment: abrasion, shearing strength, etc.

(G-2249)
TECHNROCK FABRICATION INC
1000 W Crossroads Pkwy (60490-3511)
PHONE....................630 938-4709
Thomas Edwards, *President*
Walter Nowacki, *Vice Pres*
EMP: 12
SALES (est): 118.1K **Privately Held**
SIC: 3569 Liquid automation machinery & equipment

(G-2250)
TIM WALLACE LDSCP SUP CO INC (PA)
1481 W Boughton Rd (60490-1552)
P.O. Box 277, Plainfield (60544-0277)
PHONE....................630 759-6813
Tim Wallace, *President*
EMP: 10
SQ FT: 3,200
SALES (est): 2.9MM **Privately Held**
SIC: 5261 3531 Nurseries & garden centers; snow plow attachments

(G-2251)
VISION INTGRTED GRPHICS GROUP
605 Territorial Dr Ste A (60440-4648)
PHONE....................331 318-7800
Angel Farmer, *Vice Pres*
Leticia Salgado, *Manager*
Douglas Powell,
EMP: 150 **Privately Held**
SIC: 2759 2752 2732 2741 Commercial printing; commercial printing, lithographic; book printing; miscellaneous publishing
PA: Vision Integrated Graphics Group Llc
208 S Jefferson St Fl 3
Chicago IL 60661

(G-2252)
WELSCH READY MIX INC
2000 W 135th St (60490-4901)
PHONE....................815 524-1850
EMP: 4
SALES (est): 272.9K **Privately Held**
SIC: 3273 Ready-mixed concrete

(G-2253)
WEST LIBERTY FOODS LLC
750 S Schmidt Rd (60440-4813)
PHONE....................603 679-2300
Peter Brown, *President*
Rachelle Bennett, *Transportation*
EMP: 351 **Privately Held**
SIC: 2015 Turkey processing & slaughtering
PA: West Liberty Foods, L.L.C.
228 W 2nd St
West Liberty IA 52776

(G-2254)
WESTROCK CONVERTING LLC
365 Crossing Rd (60440-3620)
PHONE....................630 783-6700
Greg Grasso, *Branch Mgr*
EMP: 20
SALES (corp-wide): 18.2B **Publicly Held**
SIC: 2631 Paperboard mills
HQ: Westrock Converting, Llc
1000 Abernathy Rd Ste 125
Atlanta GA 30328
770 448-2193

Bourbonnais
Kankakee County

(G-2255)
ALEXANDER SIGNS & DESIGNS INC
1511 Commerce Dr (60914-4644)
PHONE....................815 933-3100
Anna Alexander, *President*
EMP: 4 EST: 1991
SALES (est): 211.1K **Privately Held**
SIC: 3993 Signs & advertising specialties

(G-2256)
BELSON STEEL CENTER SCRAP INC
1685 N State Route 50 (60914-9303)
PHONE....................815 932-7416
Marc Pozan, *President*
Chase Pozan, *Vice Pres*
Kevin J Kennell, *CFO*
Dan Beasley, *Manager*
Eleanor Belson, *Director*
EMP: 25
SQ FT: 25,000
SALES (est): 18.2MM **Privately Held**
WEB: www.belsonsteel.com
SIC: 5093 3341 Ferrous metal scrap & waste; secondary nonferrous metals

(G-2257)
C & M ENGINEERING
110 Mooney Dr Ste 8 (60914-2172)
PHONE....................815 932-3388
Jim Mertin, *Partner*
Mike Chamness, *Partner*
Scott Chamness, *Manager*
EMP: 4
SQ FT: 1,800
SALES (est): 340K **Privately Held**
SIC: 3519 3714 Gas engine rebuilding; motor vehicle parts & accessories

(G-2258)
CB&I LLC
Also Called: CB & I Water
1035 E 5000n Rd (60914-4231)
P.O. Box 681508, Franklin TN (37068-1508)
PHONE....................815 936-5440
Gary Beaty, *Manager*
EMP: 7
SALES (corp-wide): 8.4B **Privately Held**
SIC: 3443 Tanks, standard or custom fabricated: metal plate
HQ: Cb&I Llc
3600 W Sam Houston Pkwy S
Houston TX 77042
281 870-5000

(G-2259)
DABRICO INC
1555 Commerce Dr (60914-4600)
PHONE....................815 939-0580
Efrain Davila, *President*
Jose E Davila, *Vice Pres*
Mario Trevino, *Purch Dir*
John McCummiskey, *Sales Staff*
Jose Pepe Davila, *Director*
▲ EMP: 21
SQ FT: 9,000
SALES: 4.7MM **Privately Held**
WEB: www.dabrico.com
SIC: 7389 3535 Industrial & commercial equipment inspection service; conveyors & conveying equipment

(G-2260)
ENTERPRISE PALLET INC
1166 E 6000n Rd (60914-4451)
PHONE....................815 928-8546
Thomas Edison, *President*
EMP: 10
SQ FT: 16,000
SALES (est): 1.2MM **Privately Held**
SIC: 2448 5031 2426 Pallets, wood; lumber: rough, dressed & finished; hardwood dimension & flooring mills

(G-2261)
GREG LAMBERT CONSTRUCTION
Also Called: Lambert Bridge & Iron
5485 N 5000e Rd (60914-4136)
P.O. Box 1111 (60914-7111)
PHONE..................815 468-7361
Greg Lambert, *Owner*
EMP: 27
SQ FT: 1,200
SALES (est): 4.7MM **Privately Held**
SIC: 3441 Fabricated structural metal

(G-2262)
HARRIS STEEL ULC
Also Called: Fisher & Ludlow
1115 E 5000n Rd (60914-4229)
PHONE..................815 932-1200
Bob Vangeertry, *Branch Mgr*
Robert Van Geertry, *Executive*
EMP: 60
SALES (corp-wide): 22.5B **Publicly Held**
SIC: 3446 Open flooring & grating for construction
HQ: Harris Steel Ulc
318 Arvin Ave
Stoney Creek ON L8E 2
905 662-0611

(G-2263)
JB & S MACHINING
1675 Enterprise Way (60914)
PHONE..................815 258-4007
Ricky Daniel, *Owner*
EMP: 4
SQ FT: 6,000
SALES (est): 396K **Privately Held**
SIC: 3441 Fabricated structural metal

(G-2264)
JOHN RIETVELD FARMS LLC
4067 E 4000n Rd (60914-4094)
PHONE..................815 936-9800
John Rietveld, *Mng Member*
▲ **EMP:** 30
SQ FT: 1,500
SALES: 1.5MM **Privately Held**
SIC: 0161 5083 3523 Onion farm; planting machinery & equipment; potato diggers, harvesters & planters

(G-2265)
LOADSYS CONSULTING INC
5645 Gatehouse Way (60914-4956)
PHONE..................708 873-1750
Donatas Kairys, *President*
Lee Forkenbrock, *Treasurer*
Rick Guyer, *Software Dev*
Omar Abhari, *Admin Sec*
EMP: 8
SALES (est): 640K **Privately Held**
SIC: 7372 Prepackaged software

(G-2266)
NUCOR STEEL KANKAKEE INC
1 Nucor Way (60914-3213)
PHONE..................815 937-3131
John J Fierrola, *CEO*
James Darsey, *President*
Alex Weisselberg, *President*
Matthew Brooks, *Principal*
Bill Vorderer, *Principal*
▲ **EMP:** 330
SALES (est): 109.2MM
SALES (corp-wide): 22.5B **Publicly Held**
SIC: 3312 3547 3449 Blast furnaces & steel mills; rolling mill machinery; miscellaneous metalwork
PA: Nucor Corporation
1915 Rexford Rd Ste 400
Charlotte NC 28211
704 366-7000

(G-2267)
O & P KINETIC
453 S Main St (60914-1918)
PHONE..................815 401-7260
Aaron Hays, *President*
Arron Hays, *President*
EMP: 3
SALES (est): 275.2K **Privately Held**
SIC: 5047 3842 Artificial limbs; braces, orthopedic

(G-2268)
SAWMILL CONSTRUCTION INC
5265 E 4000n Rd (60914-4447)
PHONE..................815 937-0037
Tim Jones, *President*
Donna Jones, *Admin Sec*
EMP: 3
SALES (est): 310K **Privately Held**
SIC: 2421 Sawmills & planing mills, general

(G-2269)
TEAM PRINT INC
1605 Commerce Dr (60914-4478)
PHONE..................815 933-5111
Albert Messier, *Owner*
EMP: 19 **EST:** 1971
SQ FT: 16,000
SALES (est): 2.7MM **Privately Held**
SIC: 7336 2284 Silk screen design; embroidery thread

(G-2270)
TMS INTERNATIONAL LLC
1 Nucor Way (60914-3213)
PHONE..................815 939-1178
EMP: 6 **Privately Held**
SIC: 3312 Blast furnaces & steel mills
HQ: Tms International, Llc
Southside Wrks Bldg 1 3f
Pittsburgh PA 15203
412 678-6141

(G-2271)
TMS INTERNATIONAL LLC
Also Called: IMS
1 Nucor Way (60914-3213)
PHONE..................815 939-9460
EMP: 8 **Privately Held**
SIC: 3295 3341 Minerals, Ground Or Treated, Nsk

(G-2272)
WW HENRY COMPANY LP
150 Mooney Dr (60914-2124)
PHONE..................815 933-8059
Jay Ashline, *Maint Spvr*
Mark Litton, *Manager*
EMP: 70
SALES (corp-wide): 1.7MM **Privately Held**
WEB: www.wwhenry.com
SIC: 2891 Adhesives
HQ: The W W Henry Company L P
400 Ardex Park Dr
Aliquippa PA 15001
704 203-5000

Bradford
Stark County

(G-2273)
GREEN GABLES COUNTRY STORE
201 Bonita Ave (61421-5305)
PHONE..................309 897-7160
Robert Rouse, *Principal*
EMP: 60 **EST:** 2012
SALES (est): 2.7MM **Privately Held**
SIC: 2511 Wood household furniture

(G-2274)
KEVINS SMALL ENGINE REPAIR
15080 Township Rd 1250 N (61421-7596)
P.O. Box 70 (61421-0070)
PHONE..................309 897-2026
Kevin Logsdon, *Principal*
EMP: 2
SALES (est): 215K **Privately Held**
SIC: 3546 Saws & sawing equipment

(G-2275)
MACON GC LLC
Also Called: Macon Construction
201 Bonita Ave (61421-5305)
PHONE..................309 897-8216
Benjamin Endress, *Manager*
Adam Endress, *Manager*
EMP: 90
SALES (est): 1.3MM **Privately Held**
SIC: 1389 1771 1796 Construction, repair & dismantling services; concrete work; millwright

Bradley
Kankakee County

(G-2276)
BARRINGTON COMPANY
195 N Euclid Ave (60915-1773)
PHONE..................815 933-3233
Mike Bysina, *President*
EMP: 3
SALES: 300K **Privately Held**
SIC: 2676 Feminine hygiene paper products

(G-2277)
BEAR MACHINE TOOL & DIE INC
928 E Broadway St (60915-1738)
PHONE..................815 932-4204
Jimm Moore, *President*
EMP: 6
SQ FT: 10,000
SALES (est): 600K **Privately Held**
SIC: 3599 7692 3549 3544 Machine shop, jobbing & repair; welding repair; metalworking machinery; special dies, tools, jigs & fixtures

(G-2278)
CROWN CORK & SEAL USA INC
1035 E North St (60915-1299)
PHONE..................815 933-9351
Ed House, *Plant Mgr*
Edward House, *Plant Mgr*
Rick Best, *Plant Engr*
EMP: 155
SALES (corp-wide): 11.6B **Publicly Held**
WEB: www.crowncork.com
SIC: 3411 3354 Metal cans; aluminum extruded products
HQ: Crown Cork & Seal Usa, Inc.
770 Township Line Rd # 100
Yardley PA 19067
215 698-5100

(G-2279)
CSL BEHRING LLC
1201 N Kinzie Ave (60915-1298)
P.O. Box 511, Kankakee (60901-0511)
PHONE..................815 932-6773
Marty Conroy, *Opers Staff*
Jonathan Signore, *Mfg Staff*
Danielle Bortoli, *Production*
Kellie Kwiecien, *Production*
Brandon Nordmeyer, *Production*
EMP: 400 **Privately Held**
SIC: 2836 3841 Blood derivatives; plasmas; surgical & medical instruments
HQ: Csl Behring L.L.C.
1020 1st Ave
King Of Prussia PA 19406

(G-2280)
DAWN FOOD PRODUCTS INC
785 N Kinzie Ave (60915-1228)
PHONE..................815 933-0600
Bernard Hinke, *Manager*
EMP: 240
SALES (corp-wide): 1.7B **Privately Held**
SIC: 2076 2013 2087 2079 Vegetable oil mills; sausages & other prepared meats; flavoring extracts & syrups; edible fats & oils; meat packing plants
HQ: Dawn Food Products, Inc.
3333 Sargent Rd
Jackson MI 49201

(G-2281)
FILTERS TO YOU
183 E North St (60915-1268)
PHONE..................815 939-0700
Kathy Landrey, *Principal*
EMP: 2 **EST:** 2010
SALES (est): 246.7K **Privately Held**
WEB: www.filters2youdirect.com
SIC: 3569 Filters

(G-2282)
G & G STUDIOS /BROADWAY PRTG
Also Called: G & G Printing
345 W Broadway St (60915-2237)
PHONE..................815 933-8181
Mark Gravlin, *President*
Karen Cross, *Treasurer*
EMP: 11
SQ FT: 7,500
SALES (est): 1.5MM **Privately Held**
SIC: 2752 7335 7336 Commercial printing, offset; commercial photography; graphic arts & related design

(G-2283)
GREIF INC
150 E North St (60915-1264)
PHONE..................815 935-7575
Jeffrey Lahey, *Plant Mgr*
Jeff Lahey, *Branch Mgr*
EMP: 30
SALES (corp-wide): 4.6B **Publicly Held**
SIC: 3089 3412 Pallets, plastic; metal barrels, drums & pails
PA: Greif, Inc.
425 Winter Rd
Delaware OH 43015
740 549-6000

(G-2284)
HANSENS MFRS WIN COVERINGS (PA)
235 N Kinzie Ave (60915-1743)
PHONE..................815 935-0010
Jeff F Hansen, *Partner*
F Harry Hansen, *Partner*
Jeff Lambert, *Partner*
EMP: 34
SALES (est): 3.1MM **Privately Held**
SIC: 5714 2591 Draperies; curtains; blinds vertical; window shades

(G-2285)
KANKAKEE INDUSTRIAL TECH
359 S Kinzie Ave (60915-2433)
PHONE..................815 933-6683
Trent Thompson, *President*
Philip Thompson, *Admin Sec*
EMP: 10
SALES (est): 4.2MM **Privately Held**
WEB: www.elect-mech.com
SIC: 5063 7694 Motors, electric; electric motor repair

(G-2286)
MAGNETEC INSPECTION INC (PA)
1159 E North St (60915-1210)
PHONE..................815 802-1363
Ethan Williams, *President*
EMP: 10
SALES (est): 1MM **Privately Held**
SIC: 3812 Magnetic field detection apparatus; aircraft control instruments

(G-2287)
MILLS MACHINING
295 Stebbings Ct Ste 4 (60915-1288)
PHONE..................815 933-9193
Scott Mills, *Owner*
EMP: 5
SALES: 500K **Privately Held**
SIC: 3599 Machine shop, jobbing & repair

(G-2288)
PEDDINGHAUS CORPORATION (PA)
300 N Washington Ave (60915-1600)
PHONE..................815 937-3800
Carl G Peddinghaus, *President*
Jose Cavazos, *Managing Dir*
Greg Kubick, *Corp Secy*
Terry Chinn, *Vice Pres*
Kenneth Coulter, *Vice Pres*
◆ **EMP:** 240 **EST:** 1977
SQ FT: 72,500
SALES (est): 119MM **Privately Held**
WEB: www.peddinghaus.com
SIC: 3541 Machine tools, metal cutting type

(G-2289)
Q SC DESIGN
230 E Broadway St (60915-2300)
PHONE..................815 933-6777
Steve Staniszeski, *Owner*
EMP: 4
SALES (est): 290.2K **Privately Held**
SIC: 3993 5099 Signs & advertising specialties; signs, except electric

Bradley - Kankakee County (G-2290)

(G-2290)
S & S HEATING & SHEET METAL
222 N Industrial Dr (60915-1279)
PHONE..................815 933-1993
Winnie Sippel, *President*
EMP: 5
SQ FT: 20,000
SALES (est): 911.2K **Privately Held**
SIC: 1711 1761 3444 Warm air heating & air conditioning contractor; sheet metalwork; sheet metalwork

(G-2291)
SECTIONAL SNOW PLOW
101 N Euclid Ave (60915-1754)
PHONE..................815 932-7569
Jeff Sexton, *General Mgr*
Blake L Strait, *Chief Engr*
Michelle Vaughn, *Office Mgr*
EMP: 50
SALES (est): 5.2MM **Privately Held**
WEB: www.arcticsnowandiceproducts.com
SIC: 2851 Removers & cleaners

(G-2292)
SECURITY METAL PRODUCTS INC
101 Lawn St (60915-1631)
PHONE..................815 933-3307
Edwin A Benson, *President*
EMP: 3
SALES (est): 210K **Privately Held**
SIC: 3353 Aluminum sheet & strip

(G-2293)
STRUCTURAL STEEL SYSTEMS LIMI
Also Called: Peddinghause
300 N Washington Ave (60915-1646)
PHONE..................815 937-3800
Carl G Peddinghause, *General Mgr*
Peddinghause Corporation, *General Ptnr*
Vern Gaus, *Purch Mgr*
Eric Carroll, *Purchasing*
Natalie Wellman, *Engineer*
▲ EMP: 18
SQ FT: 38,000
SALES: 3.6MM **Privately Held**
SIC: 3317 Steel pipe & tubes

(G-2294)
U S FILTERS
404 E Broadway St (60915-1702)
PHONE..................815 932-8154
EMP: 2 EST: 2010
SALES (est): 200K **Privately Held**
SIC: 3569 Mfg General Industrial Machinery

(G-2295)
UNIVERSAL PALLET INC
368 S Michigan Ave (60915-2271)
PHONE..................815 928-8546
Michael Krueger, *Principal*
EMP: 8
SALES (est): 738.3K **Privately Held**
SIC: 2448 Wood pallets & skids

Breese
Clinton County

(G-2296)
ARROW SHED LLC (DH)
Also Called: Arrow Group Industries
1101 N 4th St (62230-1755)
PHONE..................618 526-4546
Dale Wojtkowski, *Maint Spvr*
Curt Hemann, *Design Engr*
Judy Budroe, *Controller*
William Fischer, *Mktg Dir*
Robert Silinski, *Mng Member*
◆ EMP: 40 EST: 1945
SQ FT: 12,000
SALES (est): 58.6MM
SALES (corp-wide): 121.5MM **Privately Held**
SIC: 3448 Buildings, portable: prefabricated metal; farm & utility buildings
HQ: Shelterlogic Corp.
150 Callender Rd
Watertown CT 06795
860 945-6442

(G-2297)
BASS COMPANY LLC
8060 Old Us Highway 50 (62230-3924)
PHONE..................618 526-7211
Steven H Mahlandt, *Principal*
EMP: 4
SALES (est): 558.6K **Privately Held**
WEB: www.breesepub.com
SIC: 2752 Commercial printing, offset

(G-2298)
BEELMAN READY-MIX INC
8200 Old Us Highway 50 (62230-3921)
PHONE..................618 526-0260
Kurt Becker, *General Mgr*
EMP: 10 **Privately Held**
SIC: 5211 3273 Concrete & cinder block; ready-mixed concrete
PA: Beelman Ready-Mix, Inc.
1 Racehorse Dr
East Saint Louis IL 62205

(G-2299)
BREESE PUBLISHING CO INC (PA)
Also Called: Breese Journal
8060 Old Us Highway 50 (62230-3924)
P.O. Box 405 (62230-0405)
PHONE..................618 526-7211
Steven H Mahlandt, *President*
Steven Mahlandt, *President*
Dave Mahlandt, *Publisher*
David Mahlandt, *Vice Pres*
Quentin Glasscock, *Plant Mgr*
▼ EMP: 2 EST: 1920
SALES (est): 15.2MM **Privately Held**
WEB: www.breesepub.com
SIC: 2752 2711 Commercial printing, offset; newspapers, publishing & printing

(G-2300)
CANDLE ENTERPRISES INC
580 N 2nd St (62230-1650)
PHONE..................618 526-8070
Martha Ribbings, *Principal*
EMP: 3
SALES (est): 166.3K **Privately Held**
SIC: 3999 Candles

(G-2301)
COMPOUND BOW RIFLE SIGHT INC
Also Called: Peep Eliminator
1004 S Walnut St (62230-4118)
PHONE..................618 526-4427
Melvin Deien, *President*
Janet Deien, *Admin Sec*
EMP: 4
SALES: 150K **Privately Held**
SIC: 3949 Sporting & athletic goods

(G-2302)
EXCEL BOTTLING CO
488 S Broadway (62230-1805)
PHONE..................618 526-7159
Paul Meier, *President*
Joseph Meier, *Vice Pres*
Scott Holthaus, *Warehouse Mgr*
Ben Bruker, *Director*
William Meier, *Administration*
EMP: 30 EST: 1937
SQ FT: 4,000
SALES (est): 5MM **Privately Held**
WEB: www.excelbottling.com
SIC: 5149 2086 2082 Soft drinks; soft drinks: packaged in cans, bottles, etc.; beer (alcoholic beverage)

(G-2303)
FOODS & THINGS INC
604 N 1st St (62230-1626)
PHONE..................618 526-4478
Lois Garcia, *Partner*
Diane Hummert, *Partner*
EMP: 4
SALES (est): 281K **Privately Held**
SIC: 2035 Seasonings & sauces, except tomato & dry

(G-2304)
ILLINOIS EMBROIDERY SERVICE
Also Called: Logo's & More
580 N 2nd St (62230-1650)
PHONE..................618 526-8006
Martha Ribbing, *Owner*
Daniel Ribbing, *Co-Owner*
EMP: 4
SQ FT: 2,300
SALES (est): 222.9K **Privately Held**
SIC: 2395 Embroidery products, except schiffli machine

(G-2305)
JLG INNOVATIONS INC
Also Called: Vital
920 N 7th St (62230-1335)
PHONE..................618 363-2323
Jenna Gorlewicz, *President*
EMP: 5
SALES (est): 75.9K **Privately Held**
SIC: 7372 Prepackaged software

(G-2306)
QUAD-COUNTY READY MIX CORP
11 S Plum St (62230-1836)
P.O. Box 211 (62230-0211)
PHONE..................618 526-7130
Phillip Timmerman, *Manager*
EMP: 7
SALES (corp-wide): 16.1MM **Privately Held**
WEB: www.qcrm4.com
SIC: 3273 Ready-mixed concrete
PA: Quad-County Ready Mix Corp.
300 W 12th St
Okawville IL 62271
618 243-6430

(G-2307)
REHKEMPER & SONS INC (PA)
17817 Saint Rose Rd (62230-2503)
PHONE..................618 526-2269
Jerome Rehkemper, *President*
Mike Rehkemper, *Vice Pres*
Craig Becker, *Plant Mgr*
EMP: 45
SQ FT: 20,000
SALES (est): 22.6MM **Privately Held**
SIC: 2439 Trusses, except roof: laminated lumber; trusses, wooden roof

(G-2308)
STRAT-O-SPAN BUILDINGS INC (PA)
7980 Old Us Highway 50 (62230-3820)
PHONE..................618 526-4566
Mark Stratmann, *President*
Tom Stratmann, *Vice Pres*
Mary Moran, *Treasurer*
EMP: 4
SQ FT: 50,000
SALES (est): 1.2MM **Privately Held**
WEB: www.strat-o-span.com
SIC: 2452 3448 3441 2439 Farm buildings, prefabricated or portable: wood; buildings, portable: prefabricated metal; fabricated structural metal; structural wood members

Bridgeport
Lawrence County

(G-2309)
BINDERY MAINTENANCE SERVICES
777 E State St (62417-2105)
P.O. Box 63 (62417-0063)
PHONE..................618 945-7480
Gary Cornes, *Owner*
EMP: 3
SALES (est): 205.3K **Privately Held**
SIC: 2782 Blankbooks & looseleaf binders

(G-2310)
BRIDGEPORT AIR COMPRSR & TL CO
Also Called: B M S Tool & Equipment Co
745 Monroe St (62417-1119)
PHONE..................618 945-7163
Max R Schauf, *Owner*
EMP: 4
SQ FT: 10,000
SALES (est): 302K **Privately Held**
SIC: 5075 3563 5085 Compressors, air conditioning; air & gas compressors including vacuum pumps; tools

(G-2311)
CDG OPERATIONS LLC
8528 N Frontage Ln (62417-2510)
PHONE..................618 943-8700
John Quattrocchi, *Mng Member*
EMP: 4
SALES (est): 105.7K **Privately Held**
SIC: 1389 Pumping of oil & gas wells

(G-2312)
DARNELL WELDING
9210 Lanterman Rd (62417-2021)
P.O. Box 1 (62417-0001)
PHONE..................618 945-9538
David Darnell, *Owner*
Jeannie Darnell, *Office Mgr*
EMP: 4
SALES: 250K **Privately Held**
SIC: 7692 Welding repair

(G-2313)
FIVE P DRILLING INC
10585 Cabin Hill Dr (62417-4012)
PHONE..................618 943-9771
Carl Price, *President*
Jana Price, *Corp Secy*
Flossie Price, *Vice Pres*
EMP: 27
SALES: 900K **Privately Held**
SIC: 1381 Drilling oil & gas wells

(G-2314)
RUCKERS MKIN BATCH CANDIES INC
777 Rucker St (62417)
P.O. Box 27 (62417-0027)
PHONE..................618 945-7778
Ernest L Hoh, *President*
Richard R Rucker, *President*
Mike Mann, *District Mgr*
Chad Rucker, *Vice Pres*
Robert F Rucker, *Admin Sec*
▲ EMP: 25
SQ FT: 20,000
SALES (est): 3.4MM **Privately Held**
WEB: www.makinbatch.com
SIC: 2064 Candy & other confectionery products

(G-2315)
RUCKERS WHOLESALE & SERVICE CO
Also Called: Rucker's Candy
777 E State St (62417-2105)
P.O. Box 277 (62417-0277)
PHONE..................618 945-2411
Richard Rucker, *President*
Delbert Parrott, *Senior VP*
Dee Diggs, *Vice Pres*
Chad Rucker, *Vice Pres*
Robert Rucker, *Vice Pres*
EMP: 150
SQ FT: 128,500
SALES (est): 29.6MM **Privately Held**
SIC: 2064 Candy & other confectionery products

(G-2316)
TEAM ENERGY LLC (PA)
Also Called: Swager & Associates
Rr 1 Box 197 (62417-9739)
P.O. Box 3677, Evansville IN (47735-3677)
PHONE..................618 943-1010
Dennis Swager,
EMP: 15
SQ FT: 9,200
SALES (est): 855.7K **Privately Held**
SIC: 1389 1311 Oil consultants; crude petroleum production

Bridgeview
Cook County

(G-2317)
A R TECH & TOOL INC
8620 S Thomas Ave (60455-1880)
PHONE..................708 599-5745
Andrew Rytych, *President*

EMP: 4 EST: 1988
SQ FT: 2,400
SALES: 250K Privately Held
SIC: 3599 3545 3544 Machine shop, jobbing & repair; machine tool accessories; special dies, tools, jigs & fixtures

(G-2318)
A-SQUARED WOODWORKING INC
7900 W 75th St (60455-1237)
PHONE...................773 742-7234
Robert Navarro, President
EMP: 3
SALES (est): 171.4K Privately Held
SIC: 2431 Millwork

(G-2319)
ADEMCO INC
Also Called: ADI Global Distribution
9745 Industrial Dr Ste 2 (60455-2331)
PHONE...................708 599-1390
Kurt Hoover, Manager
EMP: 4
SALES (corp-wide): 4.9B Publicly Held
WEB: www.adi-dist.com
SIC: 5063 3669 3822 Electrical apparatus & equipment; emergency alarms; auto controls regulating residntl & coml environmt & applncs
HQ: Ademco Inc.
1985 Douglas Dr N
Golden Valley MN 55422
800 468-1502

(G-2320)
AIR-X REMANUFACTURING CORP
8909 Odell Ave (60455-1913)
PHONE...................708 598-0044
James R Dibiase, President
EMP: 3
SQ FT: 24,000
SALES (est): 285K Privately Held
SIC: 3714 Air brakes, motor vehicle

(G-2321)
ALWAN PRINTING INC
7825 S Roberts Rd (60455-1405)
PHONE...................708 598-9600
Berj M Khaleel, CEO
Yacoub Khaleel, Managing Prtnr
Edward McHugh, Graphic Designe
EMP: 10
SQ FT: 8,000
SALES (est): 2.1MM Privately Held
SIC: 2752 Commercial printing, offset

(G-2322)
AMERICA DISPLAY INC
10061 S 76th Ave (60455-2430)
PHONE...................708 430-7000
Amer Odeh, President
Monica Odeh, CFO
EMP: 11
SQ FT: 8,500
SALES: 4MM Privately Held
WEB: www.america-display.com
SIC: 3999 Advertising display products

(G-2323)
AMIS INC
Also Called: Alexi's One Stop Shop
7506 W 90th St (60455-2123)
PHONE...................708 598-9700
Alex Stevens, General Mgr
EMP: 3
SALES (est): 355.6K Privately Held
SIC: 3465 5065 7538 Body parts, automobile: stamped metal; radio parts & accessories; general automotive repair shops

(G-2324)
APCO ENTERPRISES INC
9901 S 76th Ave (60455-2402)
PHONE...................708 430-7333
Greg Hinton, President
EMP: 9
SQ FT: 15,000
SALES (est): 710K Privately Held
SIC: 2842 5169 Cleaning or polishing preparations; specialty cleaning & sanitation preparations

(G-2325)
ART CNC MACHINING LLC
Also Called: Accurate Reliable Technology
9824 Industrial Dr (60455-2327)
PHONE...................708 907-3090
Joseph Lis, Principal
Krzysztof Strychacz,
Stanislaw Slota,
EMP: 3
SALES (est): 157.9K Privately Held
SIC: 3575 8711 Keyboards, computer, office machine; engineering services

(G-2326)
ATI FLAT RLLED PDTS HLDNGS LLC
8687 S 77th Ave (60455-1800)
PHONE...................708 974-8801
Cory Hextall, Branch Mgr
EMP: 10 Publicly Held
SIC: 5051 3312 Steel; strip, metal, stainless steel
HQ: Ati Flat Rolled Products Holdings, Llc
1000 Six Ppg Pl
Pittsburgh PA 15222
412 394-3047

(G-2327)
BAK ELECTRIC
7951 S Oketo Ave (60455-1533)
PHONE...................708 458-3578
Gene Bak, President
EMP: 3 EST: 1979
SQ FT: 11,000
SALES (est): 210K Privately Held
SIC: 7694 5999 Electric motor repair; motors, electric

(G-2328)
BENKO LAMPS LTD
Also Called: Benko Manufacturing Co
7400 S Harlem Ave (60455-1315)
PHONE...................708 458-7965
Robert Kochman, President
Rose Marie Kochman, Admin Sec
EMP: 12
SQ FT: 1,000
SALES (est): 1MM Privately Held
WEB: www.benkolamp.com
SIC: 3645 5719 3641 Residential lighting fixtures; lamps & lamp shades; electric lamps

(G-2329)
BRIDGEVIEW CNC INC
9019 Odell Ave (60455-2127)
PHONE...................708 599-4641
Bogdan Suchecki, President
EMP: 2
SQ FT: 1,500
SALES: 400K Privately Held
SIC: 3599 Machine shop, jobbing & repair

(G-2330)
BRIDGEVIEW CUSTOM KIT CABINETS
8655 Beloit Ave (60455-1776)
PHONE...................708 598-1221
Tino Antonini, President
Brenda Sandidge, Admin Sec
EMP: 10
SQ FT: 5,000
SALES (est): 1.2MM Privately Held
SIC: 2434 Wood kitchen cabinets

(G-2331)
BRIDGEVIEW MACHINING INC
9009 S Thomas Ave (60455-2204)
PHONE...................708 599-4060
Edward Chorzepa, President
EMP: 5
SQ FT: 5,300
SALES (est): 793.3K Privately Held
SIC: 3599 Machine shop, jobbing & repair

(G-2332)
CAVANAUGH GOVERNMENT GROUP LLC
8432 Beloit Ave (60455-1774)
PHONE...................630 210-8668
Michael Cavanaugh, CEO
Dina Bedore, Purch Mgr
EMP: 10

SALES: 12MM Privately Held
SIC: 3714 Motor vehicle parts & accessories

(G-2333)
CHICAGO AEROSOL LLC
8407 S 77th Ave (60455-1738)
PHONE...................708 598-7100
EMP: 93 Privately Held
SIC: 2851 Paints & allied products
PA: Chicago Aerosol, Llc
1300 E North St
Coal City IL 60416

(G-2334)
CHICAGO CAN CONVEYOR CORP
8912 Moore Dr (60455-1920)
P.O. Box 2008 (60455-6008)
PHONE...................708 430-0988
Matthew M Bakosh, President
EMP: 4
SQ FT: 800
SALES (est): 480.5K Privately Held
SIC: 3535 Conveyors & conveying equipment

(G-2335)
CIMENTOS N VOTORANTIM AMER INC (PA)
Also Called: Prairie Material
7601 W 79th St (60455-1115)
PHONE...................708 458-0400
Jim Munro, President
EMP: 3
SALES (est): 40.4MM Privately Held
SIC: 3255 Cement, clay refractory

(G-2336)
CLOVER CUSTOM COUNTERS INC
9220 S Octavia Ave (60455-2108)
PHONE...................708 598-8912
Pam Baio, President
Jerry Baio, Vice Pres
EMP: 5
SQ FT: 2,400
SALES (est): 500K Privately Held
SIC: 2541 1799 Table or counter tops, plastic laminated; counter top installation

(G-2337)
COMMERCIAL FABRICATORS INC (PA)
7247 S 78th Ave Ste 1 (60455-1091)
PHONE...................708 594-1199
Francesco Scaglia, President
Evelyn Scaglia, Corp Secy
Frank Chmelir, Vice Pres
Greg Chmelir, Vice Pres
EMP: 9
SQ FT: 105,000
SALES (est): 10.4MM Privately Held
SIC: 3441 Expansion joints (structural shapes), iron or steel

(G-2338)
CREATIVE COVERS INC
7508 W 90th St (60455-2123)
PHONE...................708 233-6880
Brigit Calderon, President
EMP: 4
SALES (est): 292.1K Privately Held
SIC: 2394 Liners & covers, fabric: made from purchased materials

(G-2339)
D & M WELDING INC
8314 S 77th Ave (60455-1737)
PHONE...................708 233-6080
Dave Bakker, President
EMP: 5
SQ FT: 2,100
SALES (est): 572.4K Privately Held
SIC: 3441 7692 Fabricated structural metal; welding repair

(G-2340)
DIAMOND WHOLESALE GROUP INC
7325 W 87th St (60455-1823)
PHONE...................708 529-7495
Rami Zayed, President
EMP: 2 EST: 2011

SALES (est): 218.6K Privately Held
SIC: 2131 Chewing & smoking tobacco

(G-2341)
DUNAJEC BAKERY & DELI
8339 S Harlem Ave (60455-1718)
PHONE...................773 585-9611
EMP: 14 EST: 2000
SALES (est): 1.3MM Privately Held
SIC: 2051 Mfg Bread/Related Products

(G-2342)
E-INTRCTIVE MKTG SOLUTIONS INC
7551 W 99th St (60455-2403)
PHONE...................312 241-1692
Taha Ateyah, President
EMP: 5
SALES (est): 107K Privately Held
SIC: 7371 7374 8742 2752 Computer software development & applications; computer graphics service; marketing consulting services; commercial printing, offset

(G-2343)
ECONOPIN
8540 S Thomas Ave (60455-1701)
PHONE...................708 599-5002
Gerhard Haigis, Principal
EMP: 6
SALES (est): 710.8K Privately Held
SIC: 3565 Canning machinery, food

(G-2344)
EDDIE GAPASTIONE
Also Called: Bella Cabinet
8927 S Octavia Ave (60455-1911)
PHONE...................708 430-3881
Eddie Gapastione, Owner
EMP: 2 EST: 1994
SQ FT: 2,350
SALES (est): 200K Privately Held
WEB: www.bellacabinet.com
SIC: 1751 2541 2521 2517 Cabinet building & installation; wood partitions & fixtures; wood office furniture; wood television & radio cabinets; wood household furniture; wood kitchen cabinets

(G-2345)
EDUARDO ENTERPRISES INC
7461 W 93rd St Ste Unitf (60455-2134)
PHONE...................708 599-9700
EMP: 5
SQ FT: 2,500
SALES: 700K
SALES (corp-wide): 65MM Publicly Held
SIC: 3462 Iron And Steel Forgings, Nsk
HQ: Hy-Tech Machine, Inc.
25 Leonberg Rd
Cranberry Township PA 16066
724 776-6800

(G-2346)
FISHER PRINTING INC
8640 S Oketo Ave (60455-1827)
PHONE...................708 598-1500
Macy McKown, Sales Staff
Will Fisher, Manager
Michael Bradley, Manager
EMP: 150
SQ FT: 20,115
SALES (corp-wide): 60.1MM Privately Held
WEB: www.fisherprinting.com
SIC: 2752 2741 Commercial printing, offset; miscellaneous publishing
PA: Fisher Printing, Inc.
2257 N Pacific St
Orange CA 92865
714 998-9200

(G-2347)
FLEETPRIDE INC
7400 W 87th St (60455-1826)
PHONE...................708 430-2081
Peter E Pasdach, Branch Mgr
EMP: 200 Privately Held
SIC: 5013 3715 Truck parts & accessories; truck trailers
HQ: Fleetpride, Inc.
600 Las Colinas Blvd E # 400
Irving TX 75039
469 249-7500

Bridgeview - Cook County (G-2348) — GEOGRAPHIC SECTION

(G-2348)
FORMED FASTENER MFG INC
Also Called: Hardware Representatives
7247 S 78th Ave Ste 1 (60455-1091)
PHONE.................................708 496-1219
Francesco Scaglia, *President*
EMP: 46
SQ FT: 20,000
SALES (est): 7.5MM
SALES (corp-wide): 10.4MM **Privately Held**
SIC: 3452 Bolts, metal; nuts, metal; screws, metal
PA: Commercial Fabricators, Inc.
7247 S 78th Ave Ste 1
Bridgeview IL 60455
708 594-1199

(G-2349)
GERHARD DESIGNING & MFG INC
8540 S Thomas Ave Ste A (60455-1706)
PHONE.................................708 599-4664
Gerhard A Haigis, *President*
Nicolette Vlahaikis, *Admin Sec*
EMP: 26
SQ FT: 32,600
SALES (est): 4.6MM **Privately Held**
SIC: 3549 3544 Metalworking machinery; special dies & tools

(G-2350)
GLASS & WOOD WORK INC
10004 S 76th Ave Ste H (60455-2426)
PHONE.................................708 945-9558
EMP: 3
SALES (est): 78.3K **Privately Held**
SIC: 2431 Millwork

(G-2351)
GOLDEN GRAIN COMPANY
7700 W 71st St (60455-1051)
PHONE.................................708 458-7020
Stewart Seaton, *Principal*
EMP: 8
SALES (est): 3.5MM
SALES (corp-wide): 67.1B **Publicly Held**
SIC: 5149 2098 Pasta & rice; macaroni products (e.g. alphabets, rings & shells), dry
PA: Pepsico, Inc.
700 Anderson Hill Rd
Purchase NY 10577
914 253-2000

(G-2352)
GRANADINO FOOD SERVICES CORP
7506 W 85th Pl (60455-1799)
PHONE.................................708 717-2930
Arturo Orozco, *President*
EMP: 2
SQ FT: 3,000
SALES: 750K **Privately Held**
SIC: 2099 Seasonings & spices

(G-2353)
HANSEN PRINTING CO INC
9745 Industrial Dr Ste 10 (60455-2331)
PHONE.................................708 599-1500
Bruce Hansen, *President*
Dorothy Hansen, *Corp Secy*
Russ Hansen, *Vice Pres*
EMP: 43
SQ FT: 21,000
SALES (est): 5.9MM **Privately Held**
SIC: 2752 Business forms, lithographed; commercial printing, offset

(G-2354)
HAUS SIGN INCORPORATED
7325 W 90th St (60455-2148)
PHONE.................................708 598-8740
Marek Haus, *President*
EMP: 2
SALES (est): 238.9K **Privately Held**
WEB: www.haussigns.com
SIC: 3993 Signs & advertising specialties

(G-2355)
HOFFMAN BURIAL SUPPLIES INC
7501 W 99th Pl (60455-2404)
PHONE.................................708 233-1567
Philip Stermer, *Principal*
EMP: 7
SALES (corp-wide): 14.5MM **Privately Held**
WEB: www.hoffmanburial.com
SIC: 3995 5087 Burial caskets; caskets
PA: Hoffman Burial Supplies, Inc.
2315 W Altorfer Dr
Peoria IL 61615
309 693-1567

(G-2356)
ILLINOIS TOOL WORKS INC
Also Called: Signode
7201 S 78th Ave (60455-1061)
PHONE.................................708 325-2300
Jeff Hochleuter, *Opers-Prdtn-Mfg*
EMP: 160
SALES (corp-wide): 14.1B **Publicly Held**
WEB: www.itw.com
SIC: 3443 3053 Fabricated plate work (boiler shop); gaskets, packing & sealing devices
PA: Illinois Tool Works Inc.
155 Harlem Ave
Glenview IL 60025
847 724-7500

(G-2357)
ILLINOIS TOOL WORKS INC
7701 W 71st St (60455-1050)
PHONE.................................708 458-7320
Dennis Miller, *Vice Pres*
EMP: 180
SALES (corp-wide): 14.1B **Publicly Held**
SIC: 3499 Strapping, metal
PA: Illinois Tool Works Inc.
155 Harlem Ave
Glenview IL 60025
847 724-7500

(G-2358)
INDUSPAC RTP INC
8100 77th Ave (60455-1566)
P.O. Box 1582, Mebane NC (27302-1582)
PHONE.................................919 484-9484
Paul Gaulin, *President*
Gregory E Clifford, *Principal*
Dennis L Silver, *Principal*
EMP: 31
SALES (est): 2.8MM
SALES (corp-wide): 119.4MM **Privately Held**
SIC: 2449 Rectangular boxes & crates, wood
PA: Groupe Emballage Specialise S.E.C.
3300 Rte Transcanadienne
Pointe-Claire QC H9R 1
514 636-7951

(G-2359)
JJ WOOD WORKING
9016 Odell Ave (60455-2128)
PHONE.................................708 426-6854
EMP: 4
SALES (est): 225.9K **Privately Held**
SIC: 2431 Millwork

(G-2360)
KNIGHT PAPER BOX COMPANY (PA)
Also Called: Knight Packaging Group
8811 S 77th Ave (60455-1901)
PHONE.................................773 585-2035
Anderson Field, *President*
Thomas D Kemp, *Principal*
Robert Killelea, *CFO*
▲ EMP: 72 EST: 1950
SQ FT: 110,000
SALES (est): 16.1MM **Privately Held**
WEB: www.knightpack.com
SIC: 2657 Folding paperboard boxes

(G-2361)
MANITEX INTERNATIONAL INC (PA)
9725 Industrial Dr (60455-2304)
PHONE.................................708 430-7500
Steve Filipov, *CEO*
David Langevin, *Ch of Bd*
Steve Kiefer, *President*
Laura R Yu, *CFO*
Tyler Coburn, *Sales Staff*
▲ EMP: 50
SQ FT: 39,000
SALES: 224.7MM **Publicly Held**
SIC: 3536 3537 Hoists, cranes & monorails; forklift trucks

(G-2362)
MENASHA PACKAGING COMPANY LLC
7770 W 71st St (60455-1051)
PHONE.................................708 552-8946
EMP: 151
SALES (corp-wide): 2.2B **Privately Held**
SIC: 2653 Boxes, corrugated: made from purchased materials
HQ: Menasha Packaging Company, Llc
1645 Bergstrom Rd
Neenah WI 54956
920 751-1000

(G-2363)
MENASHA PACKAGING COMPANY LLC
7800 W 71st St (60455-1067)
PHONE.................................708 552-8946
Hannah Choi, *IT/INT Sup*
EMP: 4
SALES (corp-wide): 2.2B **Privately Held**
SIC: 2653 Boxes, corrugated: made from purchased materials
HQ: Menasha Packaging Company, Llc
1645 Bergstrom Rd
Neenah WI 54956
920 751-1000

(G-2364)
MICRON METAL FINISHING LLC
8585 S 77th Ave (60455-1779)
PHONE.................................708 599-0055
Ed Warda, *Director*
Watt Bradley,
Rauter Scott,
EMP: 2
SALES (est): 7.2MM **Privately Held**
SIC: 3479 Aluminum coating of metal products; coating of metals & formed products

(G-2365)
MIDWEST CONTROL CORP
9063 S Octavia Ave (60455-2185)
PHONE.................................708 599-1331
Ed J Tunstall, *President*
Mavis Wasil, *Treasurer*
Deborah Guerra, *Shareholder*
Linda Tunstall, *Shareholder*
Diane Wasil, *Admin Sec*
EMP: 15
SQ FT: 12,000
SALES (est): 3MM **Privately Held**
SIC: 3613 8711 Panel & distribution boards & other related apparatus; engineering services

(G-2366)
MIDWEST PRESS BRAKE DIES INC
7520 W 100th Pl (60455-2407)
PHONE.................................708 598-3860
Anton Berger, *President*
Karoline Berger, *Corp Secy*
Christine Gunther, *Vice Pres*
EMP: 19 EST: 1970
SQ FT: 11,000
SALES (est): 3.1MM **Privately Held**
SIC: 3544 Special dies & tools

(G-2367)
NABLUS SWEETS INC (PA)
8320 S Harlem Ave (60455-1719)
PHONE.................................708 529-3911
Mohommad Ahmad, *President*
◆ EMP: 38
SQ FT: 5,000
SALES (est): 2.8MM **Privately Held**
SIC: 2051 5461 Cakes, pies & pastries; pastries

(G-2368)
NORMAN FILTER COMPANY LLC (PA)
9850 Industrial Dr (60455-2324)
PHONE.................................708 233-5521
Phillip Netznik, *President*
Gary Uebel, *General Mgr*
Judy Harty, *Vice Pres*
David Ito, *Vice Pres*
Chris Koeppen, *Vice Pres*
▼ EMP: 71
SQ FT: 60,000
SALES (est): 17MM **Privately Held**
WEB: www.normanfilters.com
SIC: 3569 Filters

(G-2369)
NOSCO BRIDGEVIEW INC
8811 S 77th Ave (60455-1901)
PHONE.................................773 585-2035
Craig Curran, *President*
Greg Hamilton, *Corp Secy*
Joe Haas, *Vice Pres*
James Struhar, *CFO*
EMP: 72 EST: 2017
SALES (est): 3.3MM
SALES (corp-wide): 314MM **Privately Held**
SIC: 2752 Commercial printing, lithographic
HQ: Nosco, Inc
2199 N Delany Rd
Gurnee IL 60031
847 336-4200

(G-2370)
OREILLY AUTOMOTIVE STORES INC
Also Called: O'Reilly Auto Parts
7100 W 87th St (60455-2051)
PHONE.................................708 430-8155
Jeff Brown, *Manager*
EMP: 3 **Publicly Held**
SIC: 7699 7694 5531 Engine repair & replacement, non-automotive; rebuilding motors, except automotive; automotive parts
HQ: O'reilly Automotive Stores, Inc.
233 S Patterson Ave
Springfield MO 65802
417 862-2674

(G-2371)
PACO CORPORATION
9945 Industrial Dr (60455-2408)
PHONE.................................708 430-2424
Raymond P Paice, *President*
Esther Paice, *Admin Sec*
EMP: 14 EST: 1963
SQ FT: 20,000
SALES (est): 2.7MM **Privately Held**
WEB: www.pacograting.com
SIC: 3446 3441 Gratings, tread: fabricated metal; fabricated structural metal

(G-2372)
PACTIV LLC
7701 W 79th St (60455-1411)
PHONE.................................708 924-2402
EMP: 238 **Publicly Held**
SIC: 2673 Food storage & trash bags (plastic)
HQ: Pactiv Llc
1900 W Field Ct
Lake Forest IL 60045
847 482-2000

(G-2373)
PATTERSON PROMOTIONS & PRTG
9208 S Oketo Ave (60455-2100)
PHONE.................................708 430-0224
Dean Patterson, *Owner*
Lenore Stephens, *Managing Dir*
Allen Dabrwoski, *Exec Dir*
EMP: 2
SQ FT: 1,200
SALES (est): 215K **Privately Held**
SIC: 2752 Commercial printing, offset

(G-2374)
PESPICO
7700 W 71st St (60455-1051)
PHONE.................................708 625-3450
EMP: 6 EST: 2017
SALES (est): 623.9K **Privately Held**
SIC: 2086 Carbonated soft drinks, bottled & canned

(G-2375)
PRAIRIE GROUP MANAGEMENT LLC
7601 W 79th St Ste 1 (60455-1409)
PHONE.................................708 458-0400
Bobby Oremous,

EMP: 99
SALES (est): 9.9MM **Privately Held**
SIC: 3273 Ready-mixed concrete

(G-2376)
QUAKER OATS COMPANY
7700 W 71st St (60455-1051)
PHONE..................................708 458-7090
Jason Roggenbauer, *Branch Mgr*
Larry Czech, *Maintence Staff*
EMP: 185
SALES (corp-wide): 67.1B **Publicly Held**
SIC: 2086 Bottled & canned soft drinks
HQ: The Quaker Oats Company
555 W Monroe St Fl 1
Chicago IL 60661
312 821-1000

(G-2377)
R & L SIGNS INC
7430 W 90th St (60455-2122)
PHONE..................................708 233-0112
Rodolfo Cobos, *President*
EMP: 3
SALES (est): 180.9K **Privately Held**
SIC: 3993 Signs, not made in custom sign painting shops

(G-2378)
RAPID PALLETS INC (PA)
9700 S Harlem Ave (60455-2302)
PHONE..................................708 424-2306
Yolanda Martinez, *President*
EMP: 25
SALES (est): 2.7MM **Privately Held**
SIC: 2448 Pallets, wood

(G-2379)
REAG INC
9007 S Thomas Ave (60455-2204)
PHONE..................................708 344-0875
Michael Rasmussen, *President*
Paul Michaud, *Corp Secy*
Bill Herbert, *Exec VP*
EMP: 6
SQ FT: 5,500
SALES (est): 973.8K
SALES (corp-wide): 58.6MM **Publicly Held**
SIC: 3462 Gear & chain forgings
HQ: Hy-Tech Machine, Inc.
25 Leonberg Rd
Cranberry Township PA 16066
724 776-6800

(G-2380)
REBUILDERS ENTERPRISES INC
9004 S Octavia Ave (60455-2126)
PHONE..................................708 430-0030
Gerald C Roberts, *President*
EMP: 3
SQ FT: 2,400
SALES (est): 310K **Privately Held**
WEB: www.rebuildersenterprises.com
SIC: 3714 3563 3511 3491 Motor vehicle brake systems & parts; air & gas compressors; turbines & turbine generator sets; industrial valves

(G-2381)
REESHA PRINTING INC
Also Called: Reesha Printing & Signs
7236 W 90th Pl (60455-2150)
PHONE..................................708 233-6677
Bilal Shalan, *President*
EMP: 4
SALES (est): 478K **Privately Held**
SIC: 2752 Commercial printing, offset

(G-2382)
REX CARTON COMPANY INC
7400 Richards Rd (60455-2154)
PHONE..................................773 581-4115
Gildo Mazzolin, *Ch of Bd*
Ronald Lemar, *President*
Amy Mazzolin, *Vice Pres*
EMP: 30
SQ FT: 125,000
SALES (est): 11.5MM **Privately Held**
WEB: www.rexcarton.com
SIC: 2653 2657 Boxes, corrugated: made from purchased materials; folding paperboard boxes

(G-2383)
RITEWAY BRAKE DIES INC
7440 W 100th Pl (60455-2437)
PHONE..................................708 430-0795
Richard Bernecker, *President*
David Bernecker, *Corp Secy*
Bruno Bernecker, *Shareholder*
EMP: 19
SQ FT: 20,000
SALES (est): 4.2MM **Privately Held**
SIC: 3542 Press brakes; brakes, metal forming

(G-2384)
ROSE PALLET LLC
7647 W 100th Pl Ste D (60455-2434)
PHONE..................................708 333-3000
Brian Stephenson, *Principal*
Mia Allen, *Vice Pres*
David Burke, *Accounts Mgr*
Nick Scumaci, *Accounts Mgr*
Dori Fezzuoglio, *Manager*
EMP: 8
SALES (est): 1.5MM **Privately Held**
SIC: 2448 Pallets, wood

(G-2385)
RYANS GLASS & METAL INC (PA)
7549 W 99th Pl (60455-2404)
PHONE..................................708 430-7790
Dave Ryan, *President*
Michael W Ryan, *Vice Pres*
Mark Margolis, *Admin Sec*
EMP: 4
SALES (est): 626.5K **Privately Held**
SIC: 3442 Metal doors, sash & trim

(G-2386)
SIGNODE MIDWEST STEEL
7701 W 71st St (60455-1050)
PHONE..................................847 657-5385
W James Farrell, *CEO*
EMP: 4
SALES (est): 96.3K **Privately Held**
SIC: 3499 Fabricated metal products

(G-2387)
SIGNODE SUPPLY CORPORATION
7701 W 71st St (60455-1050)
PHONE..................................708 458-7320
Jeff Hochleutner, *Principal*
John Watson, *Supervisor*
EMP: 146
SALES (est): 28.2MM
SALES (corp-wide): 11.6B **Publicly Held**
SIC: 3565 Packaging machinery
HQ: Signode Industrial Group Llc
3650 W Lake Ave
Glenview IL 60026
847 724-7500

(G-2388)
SOUTHFIELD CORPORATION
Evanston Fuel & Mtl Co Div
7601 W 79th St (60455-1115)
PHONE..................................708 458-0400
Alan Oremus, *President*
EMP: 100
SALES (corp-wide): 344.9MM **Privately Held**
SIC: 3273 Ready-mixed concrete
PA: Southfield Corporation
8995 W 95th St
Palos Hills IL 60465
708 344-1000

(G-2389)
STAMPEDE MEAT INC (HQ)
7351 S 78th Ave (60455-1185)
PHONE..................................773 376-4300
Brock Furlong, *CEO*
Christina Hackney, *Principal*
Raymond McKiernan, *Senior VP*
John Cikowski, *Vice Pres*
Dennis Gruber, *Vice Pres*
▲ **EMP:** 656
SQ FT: 140,000
SALES (est): 234.1MM
SALES (corp-wide): 270.3MM **Privately Held**
SIC: 2013 Prepared beef products from purchased beef; prepared pork products from purchased pork

PA: Wynnchurch Capital, Llc
6250 N Rver Rd Ste 10-100
Rosemont IL 60018
847 604-6100

(G-2390)
SUPER-DRI CORP
9707 S 76th Ave (60455-2309)
P.O. Box 267, Coalville UT (84017-0267)
PHONE..................................708 599-8700
William R Battersby, *President*
Raymond Battersby, *Admin Sec*
EMP: 3
SALES (est): 330.4K **Privately Held**
SIC: 2899 Essential oils

(G-2391)
SUPERIOR CABINET COMPANY
8904 S Harlem Ave (60455-1915)
PHONE..................................708 658-6613
Anthony S Twohill, *President*
EMP: 3
SALES (est): 365.6K **Privately Held**
SIC: 2434 Wood kitchen cabinets

(G-2392)
SUPERIOR PILING INC
7247 S 78th Ave Ste 2 (60455-1091)
PHONE..................................708 496-1196
Francesco Scaglia, *President*
Frank Chmelir, *Vice Pres*
Gregg Chmelir, *Vice Pres*
EMP: 5
SQ FT: 42,000
SALES (est): 1.4MM **Privately Held**
SIC: 3312 Structural shapes & pilings, steel

(G-2393)
TIBOR MACHINE PRODUCTS INC (PA)
7400 W 100th Pl (60455-2406)
PHONE..................................708 499-0017
Mark A Lindemulder, *CEO*
Jerry L Stockton, *Exec VP*
Dennis Chervinko, *Opers Mgr*
Doug Clark, *Opers Staff*
Eric Overbey, *Purch Mgr*
EMP: 75
SQ FT: 75,000
SALES (est): 24.9MM **Privately Held**
WEB: www.tibormachine.com
SIC: 3599 Machine shop, jobbing & repair

(G-2394)
VCNA PRAIRIE LLC (PA)
7601 W 79th St Ste 1 (60455-1409)
PHONE..................................708 458-0400
Richard Olsen, *President*
David Plummer, *President*
Jeff Lesniak, *Opers Mgr*
Brian Kron, *Opers Staff*
Doris Curtis, *Credit Staff*
EMP: 2000
SALES (est): 228.8MM **Privately Held**
SIC: 3273 Ready-mixed concrete

(G-2395)
VCNA PRAIRIE ILLINOIS INC (PA)
7601 W 79th St Ste 1 (60455-1409)
PHONE..................................708 458-0400
Richard Stoker, *Manager*
EMP: 5
SALES (est): 1.2MM **Privately Held**
SIC: 3273 Ready-mixed concrete

(G-2396)
VCNA PRAIRIE INDIANA INC
Also Called: Prairie Material
7601 W 79th St Ste 1 (60455-1409)
PHONE..................................708 458-0400
Richard Olson, *President*
Jeff Lesniak, *Opers Mgr*
Jeffery Lesniak, *Opers Mgr*
Tim Huiner, *Sales Mgr*
Douglas Dalton, *Regl Sales Mgr*
EMP: 25
SALES: 950K **Privately Held**
SIC: 3272 Concrete products

(G-2397)
VPR UNLIMITED INC
10215 Camden Ln Apt E (60455-5500)
PHONE..................................708 830-6285

Nijole Astrauskiene, *President*
EMP: 5
SALES: 500K **Privately Held**
SIC: 3845 Medical cleaning equipment, ultrasonic

(G-2398)
WE ARE DONE LLC
8407 S 77th Ave (60455-1738)
PHONE..................................708 598-7100
Wally Bransen, *CEO*
Edward S Piszynski, *Principal*
Sarah Trumbull, *Vice Pres*
Michelle Valerio, *Purchasing*
Dante Ambrogi, *Engineer*
▲ **EMP:** 26 EST: 2011
SALES (est): 9.2MM **Privately Held**
WEB: www.chicagoaerosol.com
SIC: 2851 Paints & allied products

(G-2399)
WESTROCK CP LLC
7601 S 78th Ave (60455-1200)
PHONE..................................708 458-8100
Pat Feeny, *Branch Mgr*
EMP: 86
SALES (corp-wide): 18.2B **Publicly Held**
SIC: 2653 Boxes, corrugated: made from purchased materials
HQ: Westrock Cp, Llc
1000 Abernathy Rd Ste 125
Atlanta GA 30328

Brighton
Macoupin County

(G-2400)
H & B HAMS
202 W Plum St (62012-1242)
P.O. Box 172 (62012-0172)
PHONE..................................618 372-8690
EMP: 9
SQ FT: 2,500
SALES (est): 1.5MM **Privately Held**
SIC: 5147 2013 Whol Meats/Products Mfg Prepared Meats

(G-2401)
HISTORIC TIMBER & PLANK INC
16092 Lageman Ln (62012-3831)
PHONE..................................618 372-4546
Joe Adams, *President*
EMP: 20
SALES: 2.2MM **Privately Held**
WEB: www.historictimberandplank.com
SIC: 2426 2431 Flooring, hardwood; woodwork, interior & ornamental

(G-2402)
OLIN CORPORATION
15025 State Highway 111 (62012-1978)
PHONE..................................618 258-2245
Roger Jones, *Branch Mgr*
EMP: 8
SALES (corp-wide): 6.1B **Publicly Held**
SIC: 3351 Copper rolling & drawing
PA: Olin Corporation
190 Carondelet Plz # 1530
Saint Louis MO 63105
314 480-1400

(G-2403)
PIASA PLASTICS INC
Also Called: Clear Stand
615 N Main St (62012-1043)
P.O. Box 27 (62012-0027)
PHONE..................................618 372-7516
Steve Wilken, *President*
Roma Wilken, *Vice Pres*
EMP: 8
SQ FT: 5,700
SALES: 400K **Privately Held**
SIC: 3089 Injection molding of plastics

(G-2404)
TAMMY SMITH
14 Willow Way (62012-2403)
PHONE..................................618 372-8410
EMP: 3
SALES (est): 230.1K **Privately Held**
SIC: 3851 Mfg Ophthalmic Goods

Brighton - Macoupin County (G-2405) — GEOGRAPHIC SECTION

(G-2405)
WILMOUTH MACHINE WORKS INC
1723 Terpening Rd (62012-1529)
PHONE 618 372-3189
David Wilmouth, *President*
Karen Wilmouth, *Vice Pres*
EMP: 5
SALES (est): 605K **Privately Held**
SIC: 3599 3441 Machine shop, jobbing & repair; fabricated structural metal

Brimfield
Peoria County

(G-2406)
KRESS CORPORATION (PA)
227 W Illinois St (61517-8069)
PHONE 309 446-3395
Rita S Kress, *President*
Amy Munroe, *Warehouse Mgr*
Scott Wright, *Parts Mgr*
Nick Ripley, *Buyer*
Renee Staffeldt, *Buyer*
◆ EMP: 100
SQ FT: 200,000
SALES (est): 27.7MM **Privately Held**
WEB: www.kresscarrier.com
SIC: 3531 Trucks, off-highway

(G-2407)
OAK LEAF OUTDOORS INC
Also Called: Lone Wolf Portable Treestand
10216 W Civil Defense Rd (61517-9444)
P.O. Box 62, Edwards (61528-0062)
PHONE 309 691-9653
Jared Schlipf, *President*
Mike Walston, *COO*
Jeff Weaver, *Vice Pres*
EMP: 12
SALES (est): 1.5MM **Privately Held**
SIC: 3949 Hunting equipment

(G-2408)
WHITE RHINO LLC
10216 W Civil Defense Rd (61517-9444)
PHONE 309 691-9653
Frank Lovich,
Dennis Owens,
Rudy Rodich,
Jeff Weaver,
Rob Weletz,
EMP: 5
SALES: 700K **Privately Held**
SIC: 3949 Fishing equipment; hunting equipment

Bristol
Kendall County

(G-2409)
PRO GLASS CORPORATION
9318 Corneils Rd (60512-9772)
PHONE 630 553-3141
Bob Mayerle, *President*
Debra Mayerle, *Vice Pres*
EMP: 4
SQ FT: 390
SALES (est): 478.2K **Privately Held**
SIC: 3231 3083 Windshields, glass: made from purchased glass; laminated plastics plate & sheet

Broadlands
Champaign County

(G-2410)
SMITH AND SON MACHINE SHOP
454 County Road 2400 E (61816-9734)
PHONE 217 260-3257
Steven Smith, *Owner*
EMP: 3 EST: 2008
SALES: 100K **Privately Held**
SIC: 3599 Machine shop, jobbing & repair

Broadview
Cook County

(G-2411)
AABLE LICENSE CONSULTANTS
2600 S 25th Ave Ste B (60155-4514)
P.O. Box 7460, Westchester (60154-7460)
PHONE 708 836-1235
Gary F Leiss, *President*
Sharon Leiss, *Corp Secy*
EMP: 9
SALES (est): 1.2MM **Privately Held**
SIC: 3469 Automobile license tags, stamped metal

(G-2412)
AAM-RO CORPORATION
Also Called: Abrading Machinery Division
3110 S 26th Ave (60155-4524)
PHONE 708 343-5543
Richard J Carey, *President*
Bunny Carey, *Vice Pres*
Sarah Carey, *Executive*
EMP: 18
SQ FT: 31,000
SALES (est): 2.8MM **Privately Held**
WEB: www.aamroco.com
SIC: 3471 5084 Cleaning & descaling metal products; tumbling (cleaning & polishing) of machine parts; industrial machinery & equipment

(G-2413)
ACME WIRE PRODUCTS LLC
2915 S 18th Ave Fl 1 (60155-4735)
PHONE 708 345-4430
Maria Echeverria, *CFO*
Bernie Echeverria, *Mng Member*
▲ EMP: 30
SQ FT: 30,000
SALES (est): 6.4MM **Privately Held**
WEB: www.acmewirepro.com
SIC: 3496 Miscellaneous fabricated wire products

(G-2414)
ACTIVE GRINDING & MFG CO
Also Called: Agmaco
1796 Parkes Dr (60155-3959)
PHONE 708 344-0510
Richard A Pevitts, *CEO*
Carl Santucci, *President*
Virginia Pevitts, *Corp Secy*
Paula Limperis, *Asst Sec*
EMP: 15 EST: 1945
SQ FT: 15,000
SALES (est): 750K **Privately Held**
WEB: www.activegrinding.com
SIC: 3545 3599 3823 Gauges (machine tool accessories); machine shop, jobbing & repair; industrial instrmnts msrmnt display/control process variable

(G-2415)
ALL PRINTING & GRAPHICS INC (PA)
2250 S 14th Ave (60155-4002)
PHONE 708 450-1512
Hoyett Owens, *CEO*
Kim Popek, *President*
Betty Owens, *Vice Pres*
EMP: 17
SQ FT: 15,000
SALES (est): 1.9MM **Privately Held**
SIC: 2752 2789 Commercial printing, offset; bookbinding & related work

(G-2416)
ALLIANCE INDUSTRIES INC
Also Called: Thermal-Chem
2120 Roberts Dr Ste A (60155-4637)
PHONE 847 288-9090
Bert Neuland, *President*
EMP: 15
SQ FT: 27,000
SALES (est): 3.2MM **Privately Held**
SIC: 2891 2851 Adhesives; paints & allied products

(G-2417)
APH CUSTOM WOOD & METAL PDTS
2801 S 25th Ave (60155-4531)
PHONE 708 410-1274
Henry Kruski, *Owner*
▲ EMP: 5 EST: 2011
SALES (est): 369.2K **Privately Held**
SIC: 2499 Carved & turned wood

(G-2418)
ARROW PNEUMATICS INC
Also Called: AP
2111 W 21st St (60155-4627)
PHONE 708 343-6177
Jerry R Brown, *CEO*
Benny Kawa, *President*
Teena Smith, *Finance Mgr*
Tom Cichon, *Natl Sales Mgr*
Steven Fligel, *Executive*
▲ EMP: 55 EST: 1914
SQ FT: 60,000
SALES (est): 15.4MM **Privately Held**
SIC: 3569 Filters, general line: industrial; filters

(G-2419)
BELDEN MACHINE CORPORATION
2500 Braga Dr (60155-3943)
PHONE 708 344-4600
Len Sainati, *President*
Dave Carver, *Treasurer*
Al Wennerstrom, *Admin Sec*
EMP: 15
SQ FT: 20,000
SALES (est): 3MM **Privately Held**
SIC: 3541 5084 Machine tools, metal cutting type; industrial machinery & equipment

(G-2420)
BL DOWNEY COMPANY LLC
2125 Gardner Rd (60155-2826)
PHONE 708 345-8000
David C Wasz, *Mng Member*
Richard Metcalf, *Manager*
Michael Doan,
Isabel Gutierrez, *Representative*
EMP: 99
SQ FT: 325,000
SALES (est): 21.1MM **Privately Held**
SIC: 3479 Coating of metals & formed products

(G-2421)
BMC 1092 INC
Also Called: Solo Laboratories
2200 Parkes Dr (60155-3949)
PHONE 708 544-2200
Brian Corcoran, *President*
William Kokum, *Vice Pres*
Anibal Amezquita, *Plant Mgr*
Linnie Hughes, *Warehouse Mgr*
Helmut Schuster, *Engineer*
EMP: 20
SALES (est): 5.8MM **Privately Held**
SIC: 2834 Pharmaceutical preparations

(G-2422)
BOMEL TOOL MANUFACTURING CO
2111 Roberts Dr (60155-4630)
PHONE 708 343-3663
John E Gorman, *President*
Jim Bures, *Controller*
Sally Ganley, *Cust Mgr*
EMP: 110
SQ FT: 50,000
SALES (est): 14MM **Privately Held**
SIC: 3544 3469 Special dies & tools; metal stampings

(G-2423)
BRIGHT IMAGE CORPORATION
Also Called: Touch & Glow
2830 S 18th Ave (60155-4753)
PHONE 708 449-5656
Atiq Jilani, *President*
▲ EMP: 75
SQ FT: 60,000
SALES (est): 10.5MM **Privately Held**
SIC: 3643 Electric switches

(G-2424)
CENTRAL STEEL FABRICATORS
2100 Parkes Dr (60155-3951)
PHONE 708 652-2037
Gregory D Johnston, *President*
Mike Murzanski, *Vice Pres*
Bud Young, *Opers Staff*
Ana Lopez, *Sales Dir*
Greg Lawton, *Sales Mgr*
▼ EMP: 40 EST: 1904
SQ FT: 70,000
SALES (est): 10.5MM **Privately Held**
WEB: www.centralsteelfab.com
SIC: 3441 Fabricated structural metal

(G-2425)
CHASE PRODUCTS CO
2727 Gardner Rd (60155-4413)
P.O. Box 70, Maywood (60153-0070)
PHONE 708 865-1000
Donald R Virzi, *Vice Ch Bd*
Judith Albazi, *President*
Raul Marungo, *Plant Mgr*
Laura Radevski, *Technical Staff*
Ronald P Svendsen, *Admin Sec*
◆ EMP: 60 EST: 1949
SQ FT: 100,000
SALES (est): 34.5MM **Privately Held**
WEB: www.chaseproducts.com
SIC: 2813 3544 2879 2851 Aerosols; special dies, tools, jigs & fixtures; agricultural chemicals; paints & allied products

(G-2426)
CHICAGO CLAMP COMPANY
2350 S 27th Ave (60155-3855)
PHONE 708 343-8311
Sarah Holmgren, *Principal*
Kevin Barry, *Mng Member*
EMP: 5
SALES: 179.2K **Privately Held**
WEB: www.chicagoclampcompany.com
SIC: 3462 5251 Construction or mining equipment forgings, ferrous; hardware

(G-2427)
CLASSIC COLOR INC
2424 S 25th Ave (60155-3874)
PHONE 708 484-0000
Raymond E Bell, *President*
Jeff Hernandez, *Vice Pres*
Scott King, *Sales Dir*
Rick Helminiak, *Manager*
Marc J Bell, *Admin Sec*
EMP: 108
SALES (est): 29.1MM **Privately Held**
SIC: 2752 Commercial printing, offset

(G-2428)
CROOKED OAK LLC
1920 Beach St (60155-2861)
PHONE 708 344-6955
Joel Schellhase, *Mng Member*
Joe Daschbach,
EMP: 6
SQ FT: 10,000
SALES (est): 153.2K **Privately Held**
SIC: 2434 Wood kitchen cabinets

(G-2429)
DE ENTERPRISES INC
Also Called: Interntional Chem Formulations
1945 Gardner Rd (60155-3701)
PHONE 708 345-8088
Frank A De Santis, *President*
Laura De Santis, *Vice Pres*
▼ EMP: 10
SQ FT: 8,000
SALES (est): 1.6MM **Privately Held**
SIC: 2821 2899 Acrylic resins; chemical preparations

(G-2430)
DOMINIQUE GRAVES
Also Called: Nique Soul Catering
1929 S 14th Ave (60155-3135)
PHONE 773 368-5289
Dominique Graves, *Owner*
EMP: 6
SALES (est): 277.2K **Privately Held**
SIC: 2099 Ready-to-eat meals, salads & sandwiches

▲ = Import ▼ = Export
◆ = Import/Export

Broadview - Cook County

(G-2431)
DOWNEY INVESTMENTS INC
2125 Gardner Rd (60155-2826)
PHONE......................708 345-8000
David Wasz, *CEO*
Bernard L Downey, *President*
Robert Pokrywka, *Vice Pres*
D Smith, *Vice Pres*
Paul Wiesbach, *Plant Mgr*
▼ **EMP:** 260 **EST:** 1958
SQ FT: 320,000
SALES (est): 28.5MM **Privately Held**
WEB: www.bldowney.com
SIC: 3479 Coating of metals & formed products

(G-2432)
DURABILT DYVEX INC
2545 S 25th Ave (60155-3856)
PHONE......................708 397-4673
Thomas J Durbin, *President*
▲ **EMP:** 16
SQ FT: 30,000
SALES (est): 1MM **Privately Held**
SIC: 3317 3423 3496 3429 Steel pipe & tubes; wrenches, hand tools; chain, welded; tackle blocks, metal; stabilizing bars (cargo), metal

(G-2433)
ELEVATOR CABLE & SUPPLY CO
Also Called: E C S
2807 S 25th Ave (60155-4531)
PHONE......................708 338-9700
Raymond J Allen, *President*
Reid Goodrich, *CFO*
▲ **EMP:** 30
SQ FT: 21,000
SALES (est): 8.8MM **Privately Held**
SIC: 3534 2821 Elevators & equipment; plastics materials & resins

(G-2434)
ELKAY MANUFACTURING COMPANY
2700 S 17th Ave (60155-4778)
PHONE......................708 681-1880
Franco Savoni, *Vice Pres*
August R Campeotto, *Materials Mgr*
Mark Whittington, *Opers-Prdtn-Mfg*
Kim Jackson, *Purch Agent*
Bryan Carlson, *Engineer*
EMP: 500
SALES (corp-wide): 1B **Privately Held**
WEB: www.elkay.com
SIC: 3431 3585 3432 3261 Sinks: enameled iron, cast iron or pressed metal; refrigeration & heating equipment; plumbing fixture fittings & trim; vitreous plumbing fixtures
PA: Elkay Manufacturing Company Inc
1333 Butterfield Rd # 200
Downers Grove IL 60515
630 574-8484

(G-2435)
FIDELITY BINDERY COMPANY
2829 S 18th Ave (60155-4782)
PHONE......................708 343-6833
Earl Williams, *Owner*
EMP: 40 **EST:** 1964
SQ FT: 20,000
SALES (est): 3.1MM **Privately Held**
SIC: 2789 2752 Binding only: books, pamphlets, magazines, etc.; commercial printing, lithographic

(G-2436)
FIDELITY PRINT CMMNCATIONS LLC
2829 S 18th Ave 33 (60155-4725)
PHONE......................708 343-6833
Earl Williams, *Ch of Bd*
Nichole Williams, *President*
Bernard Williams, *Vice Pres*
EMP: 42
SQ FT: 20,000
SALES (est): 8.4MM **Privately Held**
SIC: 2752 Commercial printing, offset

(G-2437)
FINANCIAL GRAPHIC SERVICES INC (PA)
Also Called: Fgs - Fulfillment Services
2910 S 18th Ave (60155-4727)
PHONE......................708 343-0448
Richard Malacina Sr, *President*
Michael Campion, *Vice Pres*
Sharon Colarusso, *Vice Pres*
Mike Malacina, *Plant Mgr*
Brian Bielski, *Opers Mgr*
EMP: 100
SQ FT: 25,000
SALES (est): 53.9MM **Privately Held**
SIC: 2759 Financial note & certificate printing & engraving

(G-2438)
FRANKS IDEAL WELDING INC
2600 S 25th Ave Ste P (60155-4514)
PHONE......................708 344-4409
Frank Clavelli, *President*
EMP: 2
SALES (est): 440.2K **Privately Held**
WEB: www.franksidealwelding.com
SIC: 7692 Welding repair

(G-2439)
GRAYMILLS CORPORATION
2601 S 25th Ave (60155-4535)
PHONE......................773 477-4100
Craig Sheilds, *Ch of Bd*
Linda Shields, *VP Admin*
Anna Monterroso, *Sales Staff*
Rob Cotner, *Marketing Staff*
Vincent Aqulino, *Admin Sec*
▲ **EMP:** 72
SQ FT: 94,000
SALES (est): 21.9MM **Privately Held**
WEB: www.graymills.com
SIC: 3561 3559 Pumps & pumping equipment; degreasing machines, automotive & industrial

(G-2440)
HEADLY MANUFACTURING CO (PA)
2700 23rd St (60155-4512)
PHONE......................708 338-0800
Albert Giusfredi, *President*
Jim Oles, *General Mgr*
Stan Oles, *General Mgr*
Bill Steineke, *General Mgr*
John Santefort, *Plant Mgr*
EMP: 82 **EST:** 1921
SQ FT: 22,000
SALES (est): 23.9MM **Privately Held**
WEB: www.headlymfg.com
SIC: 3469 3544 Machine parts, stamped or pressed metal; special dies, tools, jigs & fixtures

(G-2441)
HEADLY MANUFACTURING CO
Also Called: Headly Mfg
2111 Roberts Dr (60155-4630)
PHONE......................708 338-0800
EMP: 51
SALES (corp-wide): 23.9MM **Privately Held**
SIC: 3544 3469 Special dies, tools, jigs & fixtures; automobile license tags, stamped metal
PA: Headly Manufacturing Co.
2700 23rd St
Broadview IL 60155
708 338-0800

(G-2442)
ILLINOIS TOOL WORKS INC
Also Called: ITW Shakeproof Group
2550 S 27th Ave (60155-3851)
PHONE......................708 681-3891
Jerry De Witz, *General Mgr*
Jason Martin, *Production*
Timothy Jacques, *Engineer*
Gerald Maas, *Engineer*
Tom Semrow, *Engineer*
EMP: 50
SALES (corp-wide): 14.1B **Publicly Held**
WEB: www.itw.com
SIC: 3429 Metal fasteners
PA: Illinois Tool Works Inc.
155 Harlem Ave
Glenview IL 60025
847 724-7500

(G-2443)
ILLINOIS TOOL WORKS INC
ITW Shakeproof Industrial Pdts
2550 S 27th Ave (60155-3851)
PHONE......................708 681-3891
Fax: 708 681-3690
EMP: 18
SALES (corp-wide): 14.3B **Publicly Held**
SIC: 3452 3469 Mfg Bolts/Screws/Rivets Mfg Metal Stampings
PA: Illinois Tool Works Inc.
155 Harlem Ave
Glenview IL 60025
847 724-7500

(G-2444)
INTEL PRINTING INC
1805 Beach St (60155-2862)
PHONE......................708 343-1144
EMP: 6
SQ FT: 8,000
SALES (est): 1.5MM **Privately Held**
SIC: 2752 Offset Printer

(G-2445)
JOHNSON POWER LTD (PA)
2530 Braga Dr (60155-3943)
P.O. Box 6399, Maywood (60155-6399)
PHONE......................708 345-4300
Lisa C Johnson Honig, *President*
Robert Honig, *Vice Pres*
Arlene Johnson, *Treasurer*
▲ **EMP:** 41
SQ FT: 22,000
SALES (est): 16.3MM **Privately Held**
SIC: 3714 Drive shafts, motor vehicle

(G-2446)
JOSEPHS FOOD PRODUCTS CO INC
2759 S 25th Ave (60155-4533)
PHONE......................708 338-4090
Reginald Van Eekeren, *President*
Aloysius Van Eekeren, *Admin Sec*
EMP: 240
SQ FT: 170,000
SALES (est): 29.8MM **Privately Held**
SIC: 2099 Spices, including grinding

(G-2447)
KARNAK MIDWEST LLC
2601 Gardner Rd (60155-4411)
PHONE......................708 338-3388
John McDermott, *Vice Pres*
EMP: 14
SALES (corp-wide): 18.5MM **Privately Held**
SIC: 2952 Roofing materials
HQ: Karnak Midwest, L.L.C.
330 Central Ave
Clark NJ 07066
732 388-0300

(G-2448)
KELVYN PRESS INC (HQ)
Also Called: Financial Graphic Service
2910 S 18th Ave (60155-4733)
PHONE......................708 343-0448
Richard J Malacina, *President*
Richard Malacina Jr, *Vice Pres*
Tony Malacina, *Plant Mgr*
Lynn Suchecki, *Safety Mgr*
Nancy Overholt, *CFO*
EMP: 100
SQ FT: 100,000
SALES (est): 34.9MM **Privately Held**
SIC: 2752 Commercial printing, offset

(G-2449)
LINDE GAS NORTH AMERICA LLC
2000 S 25th Ave Ste S (60155-2818)
PHONE......................630 857-6460
Kirk Phelps, *Area Mgr*
EMP: 15 **Privately Held**
SIC: 2813 Oxygen, compressed or liquefied; nitrogen; argon; hydrogen
HQ: Linde Gas North America Llc
10 Riverview Dr
Danbury CT 06810

(G-2450)
LITHOGRAPHIC INDUSTRIES INC
2445 Gardner Rd (60155-3798)
PHONE......................773 921-7955
Louis A Ebeqrt, *President*
John Kwiatkowski, *Opers Staff*
Roman A Ebert IV, *CFO*
Paula A Ebert, *Treasurer*
Roman Ebert, *Officer*
EMP: 45
SQ FT: 63,000
SALES: 12MM **Privately Held**
WEB: www.lithographic.com
SIC: 2752 Commercial printing, offset

(G-2451)
MIDWEST INK CO
2701 S 12th Ave (60155-4836)
PHONE......................708 345-7177
Frank Hannon, *President*
Joe Hannon, *Exec VP*
Joseph Hannon, *Admin Sec*
▲ **EMP:** 30
SQ FT: 20,000
SALES: 6.2MM **Privately Held**
SIC: 2893 Printing ink

(G-2452)
MIDWEST-DESIGN INC
2350 S 27th Ave (60155-3855)
PHONE......................708 615-1572
EMP: 2 **EST:** 1994
SQ FT: 6,700
SALES: 475K **Privately Held**
SIC: 3644 Mfg Nonconductive Wiring Devices

(G-2453)
MODERN PRINTING COLORS INC
1951 W 21st St (60155-4626)
PHONE......................708 681-5678
Suresh Mahajan, *President*
Neera Mahajan, *Vice Pres*
Neerah Mahajan, *Vice Pres*
Guy McCormick, *Sales Staff*
Gumaro Lopez, *Lab Dir*
▲ **EMP:** 15
SALES (est): 5.3MM **Privately Held**
SIC: 2899 7389 Ink or writing fluids; demonstration service

(G-2454)
MOREY INDUSTRIES INC
Also Called: Westmont Engineering Company
2000 Beach St (60155-2833)
PHONE......................708 343-3220
Douglas Morey, *President*
Scott Morey, *Admin Sec*
EMP: 110 **EST:** 1958
SQ FT: 40,000
SALES (est): 26.9MM **Privately Held**
WEB: www.westmontengineering.com
SIC: 3441 1796 1791 Fabricated structural metal; machinery installation; structural steel erection

(G-2455)
MULLINS FOOD PRODUCTS INC
2200 S 25th Ave (60155-4584)
PHONE......................708 344-3224
Jeanne Gannon, *President*
Ed Mullins, *General Mgr*
Michael Mullins, *COO*
Bob Frett, *Vice Pres*
Rich Vlach, *Safety Dir*
EMP: 405 **EST:** 1938
SQ FT: 325,000
SALES (est): 128.2MM **Privately Held**
WEB: www.mullinsfood.com
SIC: 2033 2035 Tomato products: packaged in cans, jars, etc.; barbecue sauce: packaged in cans, jars, etc.; catsup: packaged in cans, jars, etc.; dressings, salad: raw & cooked (except dry mixes)
PA: Newly Weds Foods, Inc.
4140 W Fullerton Ave
Chicago IL 60639
773 489-7000

(G-2456)
MULTI SWATCH CORPORATION
Also Called: M.S.i
2600 S 25th Ave Ste Y (60155-4514)
PHONE..................................708 344-9440
John M Mozis, *President*
▲ EMP: 87
SALES (est): 11.4MM **Privately Held**
SIC: 2782 Sample books

(G-2457)
PARKER-HANNIFIN CORPORATION
Refrigeration Specialties
2445 S 25th Ave (60155-3858)
PHONE..................................708 681-6300
Christopher Farage, *Vice Pres*
Dheepak Rajendran, *Engineer*
Jeff Teplan, *Engineer*
Patrick Melson, *Sales Staff*
Darryl Miller, *Branch Mgr*
EMP: 45
SALES (corp-wide): 14.3B **Publicly Held**
WEB: www.phtruck.com
SIC: 3491 5078 Industrial valves; refrigeration equipment & supplies
PA: Parker-Hannifin Corporation
6035 Parkland Blvd
Cleveland OH 44124
216 896-3000

(G-2458)
PRECISION CNNCTING ROD SVC INC
Also Called: Pcr Machining
2600 W Cermak Rd (60155-4505)
PHONE..................................708 345-3700
Richard Farrar, *President*
Edessa Farrar, *Vice Pres*
EMP: 12 EST: 1927
SQ FT: 20,000
SALES (est): 2.6MM **Privately Held**
WEB: www.connectingrod.com
SIC: 3599 Machine shop, jobbing & repair

(G-2459)
PRINCIPAL MANUFACTURING CORP
2800 S 19th Ave (60155-4754)
PHONE..................................708 865-7500
Paul A Barnett, *President*
Benjamin Barnett, *Vice Pres*
Richard Barnett, *Vice Pres*
Kevin Fox, *Vice Pres*
Stankus Robert, *Senior Buyer*
▲ EMP: 350 EST: 1957
SQ FT: 80,000
SALES (est): 124.2MM **Privately Held**
WEB: www.principalmfg.com
SIC: 3469 Stamping metal for the trade

(G-2460)
PRINTING ARTS CMMNICATIONS LLC
2001 W 21st St (60155-4632)
PHONE..................................708 938-1600
James Kosowski, *Vice Pres*
John Myszka, *Vice Pres*
John Earnest, *Project Mgr*
Dennis Figg, *Facilities Mgr*
Shawn Pack, *Sales Staff*
EMP: 50
SQ FT: 60,000
SALES (est): 17.4MM **Privately Held**
SIC: 2752 Commercial printing, offset

(G-2461)
PURES FOOD SPECIALTIES LLC
Also Called: Pures Food Specialties
2929 S 25th Ave (60155-4529)
PHONE..................................708 344-8884
Elliott Pure, *President*
Jonathan Pure, *Vice Pres*
Crystal Saporito, *Manager*
Ruth Pure, *Admin Sec*
EMP: 50 EST: 1989
SQ FT: 68,000
SALES (est): 11.2MM **Privately Held**
WEB: www.puresfood.com
SIC: 2052 Cookies

(G-2462)
R A KERLEY INK ENGINEERS INC (PA)
2700 S 12th Ave (60155-4837)
P.O. Box 6009, Maywood (60155-6009)
PHONE..................................708 344-1295
John J Whalen, *President*
Betty K Whalen, *Admin Sec*
◆ EMP: 24
SQ FT: 12,000
SALES (est): 6.4MM **Privately Held**
WEB: www.kerleyink.com
SIC: 2893 Printing ink

(G-2463)
RE-DO-IT CORP
1950 Beach St (60155-2861)
PHONE..................................708 343-7125
Virginia Donatell, *President*
Miss V Donatell, *Project Mgr*
John Donatell, *Opers Mgr*
EMP: 6 EST: 1990
SQ FT: 15,000
SALES (est): 700K **Privately Held**
SIC: 7699 3714 3593 Hydraulic equipment repair; motor vehicle parts & accessories; fluid power cylinders & actuators

(G-2464)
RIPA LLC
Also Called: Printing Arts
2001 W 21st St (60155-4632)
PHONE..................................708 938-1600
Dennis Figg, *Facilities Mgr*
James Kosowski, *Mng Member*
John Kosowski,
John Ropski,
EMP: 5
SALES (est): 1.4MM **Privately Held**
SIC: 8741 2759 2621 Management services; commercial printing; wrapping & packaging papers

(G-2465)
ROBERT BOSCH LLC
2800 S 25th Ave (60155-4532)
P.O. Box 4601, Carol Stream (60197-4601)
PHONE..................................708 865-5415
EMP: 14
SALES (corp-wide): 294.8MM **Privately Held**
WEB: www.bosch.us
SIC: 3714 Motor vehicle parts & accessories
HQ: Robert Bosch Llc
2800 S 25th Ave
Broadview IL 60155
917 421-7209

(G-2466)
ROBERT BOSCH LLC (DH)
Also Called: Bosch Engineering North Amer
2800 S 25th Ave (60155-4532)
P.O. Box 2609, Farmington Hills MI (48333-2609)
PHONE..................................917 421-7209
Marcus Heyn, *Ch of Bd*
Tim Frasier, *President*
Mike Mansuetti, *President*
Cara Reynolds, *Exec VP*
Jerry L Johnson, *Vice Pres*
◆ EMP: 300 EST: 1906
SALES (est): 2.4B
SALES (corp-wide): 294.8MM **Privately Held**
WEB: www.bosch.us
SIC: 3694 5013 5064 3565 Motors, starting: automotive & aircraft; distributors, motor vehicle engine; automotive supplies & parts; automotive engines & engine parts; automotive brakes; radios, motor vehicle; packaging machinery; deburring machines; motor vehicle brake systems & parts
HQ: Robert Bosch North America Corporation
2800 S 25th Ave
Broadview IL 60155
708 865-5200

(G-2467)
ROHBI ENTERPRISES INC
3020 S 25th Ave (60155-4503)
PHONE..................................708 343-2004
Ronald Gustafson, *President*
Helen Gustafson, *Corp Secy*
EMP: 7 EST: 1978
SQ FT: 14,500
SALES (est): 1.1MM **Privately Held**
SIC: 3599 Machine shop, jobbing & repair

(G-2468)
SG360 A SEGERDAHL COMPANY
1990 S 25th Ave (60155)
PHONE..................................847 465-3368
Richard D Joutras, *President*
EMP: 10 EST: 2014
SALES (est): 646.2K **Privately Held**
SIC: 2752 Commercial printing, offset

(G-2469)
STAR THERMOPLASTIC ALLOYS AND (PA)
Also Called: Star Thermoplastics
2121 W 21st St (60155-4634)
PHONE..................................708 343-1100
Thomas A Dieschbourg, *President*
EMP: 50
SQ FT: 30,000
SALES (est): 6.7MM **Privately Held**
SIC: 2821 Thermoplastic materials

(G-2470)
STAR THERMOPLASTIC ALLOYS AND
Also Called: Star Plastics
2121 W 21st St (60155-4634)
PHONE..................................708 343-1100
Tom Dieschburg, *Manager*
EMP: 14
SALES (corp-wide): 6.7MM **Privately Held**
SIC: 2821 2822 Thermoplastic materials; synthetic rubber
PA: Star Thermoplastic Alloys And Rubbers, Inc.
2121 W 21st St
Broadview IL 60155
708 343-1100

(G-2471)
SUBURBAN PLASTICS CO
3110 S 26th Ave (60155-4524)
P.O. Box 6249, Maywood (60155-6249)
PHONE..................................708 681-1475
EMP: 38
SALES (corp-wide): 86MM **Privately Held**
SIC: 3714 Motor vehicle parts & accessories
PA: Suburban Plastics Co.
509 Water St Sw
Bolivar OH 44612
847 741-4900

(G-2472)
TOTAL CONTROL SPORTS INC
2000 S 25th Ave Ste C (60155-2820)
PHONE..................................708 486-5800
Peter J Parenti, *President*
Amber Patton, *Sales Staff*
Diane M Parenti, *Admin Sec*
EMP: 3
SALES (est): 375.4K **Privately Held**
WEB: www.totalcontrolsports.com
SIC: 3949 Softball equipment & supplies

(G-2473)
TURBO TOOL & MOLD CO
3045 S 26th Ave (60155-4525)
PHONE..................................708 615-1730
Mike Turbonic, *President*
EMP: 4
SQ FT: 3,000
SALES (est): 533.2K **Privately Held**
SIC: 3599 3544 Machine shop, jobbing & repair; special dies, tools, jigs & fixtures

(G-2474)
WESTMONT METAL MFG LLC
2350 S 27th Ave (60155-3855)
PHONE..................................708 343-0214
Philip Solo, *General Mgr*
Douglas H Morey, *Mng Member*
EMP: 15
SQ FT: 26,000
SALES (est): 4.1MM **Privately Held**
WEB: www.westmontmetal.com
SIC: 3441 Fabricated structural metal

(G-2475)
WINCHESTER INTERCONNECT RUGGED (DH)
2150 Parkes Dr (60155-3951)
PHONE..................................708 594-5890
Reginald W Barrett, *CEO*
Sabit Inan, *Vice Pres*
Sharon Paradowski, *Purchasing*
Brandon Wall, *Engineer*
▲ EMP: 5
SQ FT: 50,000
SALES (est): 24.1MM
SALES (corp-wide): 14.4B **Privately Held**
SIC: 3542 3648 3643 3634 Machine tools, metal forming type; lighting equipment; electric connectors; fans, exhaust & ventilating, electric; household

Brookfield
Cook County

(G-2476)
10 4 IRP INC
8846 47th St (60513-2532)
PHONE..................................708 485-1040
Mara Lopez, *President*
Marcelino Bacerott, *Vice Pres*
EMP: 2
SALES: 300K **Privately Held**
SIC: 3469 Automobile license tags, stamped metal

(G-2477)
A TOUCH OF BEAUTY INC
Also Called: A Touch of Beauty Brass
9034 Brookfield Ave (60513-1635)
PHONE..................................708 387-0360
Roger Merenkov, *President*
EMP: 4
SQ FT: 4,200
SALES (est): 350K **Privately Held**
SIC: 3446 Architectural metalwork

(G-2478)
ALPHA PRODUCTS INC
Culen Tool & Manufacturing
9128 47th St (60513-2395)
PHONE..................................708 387-1580
EMP: 6
SALES (corp-wide): 7.3MM **Privately Held**
SIC: 3544 Special dies & tools
PA: Alpha Products, Inc.
5570 W 70th Pl
Bedford Park IL 60638
708 594-3883

(G-2479)
BOYLESTON 21ST CENTURY LLC
9118 47th St Ste 3 (60513-2768)
PHONE..................................708 387-2012
Robert Sandstone, *President*
EMP: 2
SALES (est): 369.7K **Privately Held**
SIC: 3822 Steam pressure controls, residential or commercial type

(G-2480)
CHICAGO NEON AND SIGN LLC
4140 Sunnyside Ave (60513-2011)
PHONE..................................708 255-5284
Hinton Patricia, *Principal*
EMP: 3
SALES (est): 123.2K **Privately Held**
SIC: 2813 Neon

(G-2481)
DADO LIGHTING LLC
9100 Plainfield Rd Ste 9 (60513-2458)
PHONE..................................708 243-9059
David Doubek, *Principal*
EMP: 4
SALES (est): 345.7K **Privately Held**
SIC: 3646 Commercial indusl & institutional electric lighting fixtures

(G-2482)
ENDOFIX LTD
9118 Ogden Ave Ste 1 (60513-1974)
PHONE..................................708 715-3472
Stephanie R McCollom, *CEO*

John McCollom, *President*
EMP: 5
SQ FT: 408
SALES (est): 1MM **Privately Held**
SIC: 3841 3541 Surgical instruments & apparatus; machine tool replacement & repair parts, metal cutting types

(G-2483)
FLEETWOOD PRESS INC
9321 Ogden Ave (60513-1817)
PHONE 708 485-6811
Bernard A Kowalski, *President*
Carmella Kowalski, *Admin Sec*
EMP: 3
SQ FT: 1,500
SALES (est): 441.4K **Privately Held**
SIC: 2752 7372 2791 2789 Commercial printing, offset; prepackaged software; typesetting; bookbinding & related work; commercial printing

(G-2484)
GARCOA INC
8838 Brookfield Ave (60513-2783)
PHONE 708 905-5118
EMP: 494
SALES (corp-wide): 123.9MM **Privately Held**
SIC: 5122 2844 Cosmetics; toilet preparations
PA: Garcoa, Inc.
26135 Mureau Rd Ste 100
Calabasas CA 91302
818 225-0375

(G-2485)
GEAR & REPAIR
9100 Plainfield Rd Ste 13 (60513-2458)
PHONE 708 387-0144
Gary Vimont, *Owner*
EMP: 2
SALES: 600K **Privately Held**
SIC: 5085 3462 Gears; iron & steel forgings

(G-2486)
IMPERIAL KITCHENS & BATH INC
8918 Ogden Ave (60513-2006)
PHONE 708 485-0020
Larry Rychlowski, *President*
Edward Pudalek, *Treasurer*
EMP: 10
SQ FT: 6,400
SALES: 1.9MM **Privately Held**
WEB: www.imperialkitchensandbaths.com
SIC: 1751 2511 2541 Cabinet building & installation; wood household furniture; cabinets, except refrigerated: show, display, etc.: wood

(G-2487)
JD PRO PRODUCTIONS INC
4123 Maple Ave (60513-1915)
PHONE 708 485-2126
Jerrold Dobes, *President*
Patricia Dobes, *Admin Sec*
EMP: 2
SALES (est): 239K **Privately Held**
SIC: 2791 Typographic composition, for the printing trade

(G-2488)
MD ORTHOTIC PROSTHETIC LAB INC (PA)
Also Called: MD Labs
8400 Brookfield Ave (60513-1989)
PHONE 708 387-9700
Amit Bhanti, *CEO*
Mark Devens, *President*
Corinne Devens, *General Mgr*
EMP: 23
SQ FT: 6,500
SALES (est): 3.8MM **Privately Held**
SIC: 3842 Braces, orthopedic; abdominal supporters, braces & trusses; cervical collars; limbs, artificial

(G-2489)
NICKS METAL FABG & SONS
9132 47th St (60513-2397)
PHONE 708 485-1170
Nick Tepavchevich Jr, *President*
Nick Tepavchevich Sr, *President*
Thomas Tepavchevich, *Treasurer*
Gloria Tepavchevich, *Admin Sec*
EMP: 18 **EST:** 1949
SQ FT: 11,000
SALES (est): 3.8MM **Privately Held**
WEB: www.nicksmetal.com
SIC: 3441 3446 Fabricated structural metal; architectural metalwork

(G-2490)
POWDER COATING SPECIALISTS
9436 47th St (60513-2830)
PHONE 708 387-8000
James R Dziewior, *Principal*
EMP: 2
SALES (est): 200.8K **Privately Held**
WEB: www.powdercoatingspecialists.com
SIC: 3479 Coating of metals & formed products

(G-2491)
PRIORITY PRINT
9433 Ogden Ave (60513-1896)
PHONE 708 485-7080
Will Knippenberg, *Owner*
EMP: 3
SQ FT: 3,500
SALES (est): 308.3K **Privately Held**
SIC: 2752 2759 2396 Commercial printing, offset; offset & photolithographic printing; commercial printing; automotive & apparel trimmings

(G-2492)
SMOKE RITE WOOD PRODUCTS
3801 Arthur Ave (60513-1555)
PHONE 708 485-8910
Gregg L Gorney, *Owner*
EMP: 3
SALES (est): 10.2K **Privately Held**
SIC: 2499 Wood products

(G-2493)
TAILORED INC
9520 47th St Ste 2 (60513-2833)
PHONE 708 387-9854
Kristine Vrhel, *President*
Marianne Spevacek, *COO*
Arlaina Tibensky, *Vice Pres*
EMP: 9 **EST:** 1946
SQ FT: 4,200
SALES (est): 270K **Privately Held**
WEB: www.tailoreddraperiesinc.com
SIC: 2391 2392 Draperies, plastic & textile: from purchased materials; bedspreads & bed sets: made from purchased materials

(G-2494)
TAYLOR COATING SALES INC
Also Called: Taylor Consultants
8520 Brookfield Ave (60513-1708)
PHONE 708 387-0305
Craig Taylor, *President*
Judy Hockemeyer, *Admin Sec*
EMP: 3
SALES (est): 352.5K **Privately Held**
SIC: 2851 Paints & allied products

(G-2495)
TAYLOR CONSULTANTS INC
Also Called: Taylor Coating Sales
8520 Brookfield Ave (60513-1708)
PHONE 708 387-0305
Craig Taylor, *President*
EMP: 4
SALES (est): 291.9K **Privately Held**
SIC: 2851 Paints & allied products

(G-2496)
TENCO HYDRO INC OF ILLINOIS
4620 Forest Ave (60513-2594)
PHONE 708 387-0700
Albert W Lee, *President*
Bill Schmidt, *Engineer*
EMP: 6 **EST:** 1980
SQ FT: 10,000
SALES (est): 1.2MM **Privately Held**
SIC: 3823 Industrial instmnts msrmnt display/control process variable

(G-2497)
VANGARD DISTRIBUTION INC (PA)
9501 Southview Ave (60513-1529)
PHONE 708 588-8400
Joseph P Gardella, *President*
Paul M Julien, *Admin Sec*
▲ **EMP:** 2
SQ FT: 30,000
SALES (est): 1MM **Privately Held**
SIC: 2653 3053 Corrugated & solid fiber boxes; packing materials

Brookport
Massac County

(G-2498)
HOYER OUTDOOR EQUIPMENT INC
7402 Unionville Rd (62910-2409)
PHONE 618 564-2080
Owen Hoyer, *President*
Cheryl Hoyer, *Admin Sec*
EMP: 10
SQ FT: 7,000
SALES (est): 1.3MM **Privately Held**
SIC: 5719 5261 3523 Wood burning stoves; fireplace equipment & accessories; lawnmowers & tractors; haying machines: mowers, rakes, stackers, etc.

Buckner
Franklin County

(G-2499)
CHRISTOPHER CONCRETE PRODUCTS
110 N Mine Rd (62819)
P.O. Box 60 (62819-0060)
PHONE 618 724-2951
Bert Bonner, *Owner*
EMP: 6 **EST:** 1965
SALES: 500K **Privately Held**
WEB: www.christopherconcrete.com
SIC: 3272 6513 3523 1771 Septic tanks, concrete; apartment building operators; farm machinery & equipment; concrete work

Buda
Bureau County

(G-2500)
VAN-PACKER CO
302 Mill St (61314-9539)
P.O. Box 307 (61314-0307)
PHONE 309 895-2311
Lauren Schulz, *President*
Lauren C Schulz, *President*
Joe Fernandez, *Sales Staff*
▲ **EMP:** 41
SQ FT: 82,000
SALES (est): 8.4MM **Privately Held**
SIC: 3272 Concrete products, precast

Buffalo
Sangamon County

(G-2501)
TROTTERS MANUFACTURING CO
101 S West St (62515-6228)
P.O. Box 176 (62515-0176)
PHONE 217 364-4540
Robert Turley, *President*
Dale Turley, *Vice Pres*
Linda Turley, *Admin Sec*
EMP: 8
SQ FT: 10,500
SALES (est): 1.1MM **Privately Held**
SIC: 5531 7699 7692 Automotive tires; farm machinery repair; welding repair

Buffalo Grove
Lake County

(G-2502)
4 U OPTICAL
125 E Lake Cook Rd # 110 (60089-4356)
PHONE 847 459-8598
EMP: 3
SALES (est): 172.8K **Privately Held**
WEB: www.isee4u.com
SIC: 3827 Optical instruments & lenses

(G-2503)
51 ELEMENTS
550 Cherbourg Ct S (60089-7711)
PHONE 847 712-5550
Eva Landesman, *Principal*
EMP: 3
SALES (est): 244.5K **Privately Held**
SIC: 2819 Industrial inorganic chemicals

(G-2504)
AD SPECIAL TZ INC
2456 Palazzo Ct (60089-4677)
PHONE 847 845-6767
Robyn Gomberg, *President*
Michael Gomberg, *Treasurer*
EMP: 4
SALES (est): 220K **Privately Held**
SIC: 3993 Signs & advertising specialties

(G-2505)
AEVERIE INC
129 Manchester Ct (60089-6706)
PHONE 844 238-3743
Rajesh Manghat, *President*
EMP: 8
SALES (est): 272.5K **Privately Held**
SIC: 7372 7371 Business oriented computer software; computer software development & applications

(G-2506)
AIM GRAPHIC MACHINERY LTD
Also Called: Aim Business Printers
1374 Abbott Ct (60089-2378)
P.O. Box 5407 (60089-5407)
PHONE 847 215-8000
Beverly Sussman, *Partner*
Howard Sussman, *Partner*
Richard Sussman, *Partner*
EMP: 15
SQ FT: 10,000
SALES (est): 2.3MM **Privately Held**
SIC: 3955 Print cartridges for laser & other computer printers

(G-2507)
ALL FOAM PRODUCTS
2546 Live Oak Ln (60089-4609)
PHONE 847 913-9341
Sue Kagebein, *General Mgr*
EMP: 3
SALES (est): 247.1K **Privately Held**
SIC: 3086 Plastics foam products

(G-2508)
ALLIED GRAPHICS INC
1398 Busch Pkwy (60089-4505)
PHONE 847 419-8830
Charles W Schmidt, *President*
Rebecca Schmidt, *Admin Sec*
▲ **EMP:** 2
SQ FT: 3,689
SALES (est): 378.1K **Privately Held**
SIC: 5112 7336 2759 2752 Stationery; graphic arts & related design; commercial printing; commercial printing, lithographic

(G-2509)
ALLSTAR EMBROIDERY
240 Blackthorn Dr (60089-6341)
PHONE 847 913-1133
Mike Spector, *Owner*
EMP: 3
SQ FT: 900
SALES (est): 234.8K **Privately Held**
SIC: 7389 2395 Textile & apparel services; embroidery products, except schiffli machine

Buffalo Grove - Lake County (G-2510)

(G-2510)
AMCOR FLEXIBLES LLC (DH)
2150 E Lake Cook Rd (60089-1862)
PHONE..................224 313-7000
Ron Delia, *CEO*
Tom Cochran, *President*
Aluisio Ragazzi Fonseca, *Vice Pres*
Curt Crogan, *Plant Mgr*
Robert Healy, *Plant Mgr*
◆ **EMP:** 250
SQ FT: 200,000
SALES (est): 259.8MM
SALES (corp-wide): 947.2K **Privately Held**
WEB: www.amcor.com
SIC: 2671 2621 2821 3081 Plastic film, coated or laminated for packaging; paper mills; plastics materials & resins; unsupported plastics film & sheet; crowns & closures

(G-2511)
AMERICAN NEEDLE INC (PA)
Also Called: Amer Needle & Novelty
1275 Busch Pkwy (60089-4536)
PHONE..................847 215-0011
Robert Kronenberger, *President*
Jeff Carey, *VP Opers*
Karen Garcia, *Credit Mgr*
Burke Kronenberger, *Sales Staff*
Darla Marabotti, *Office Mgr*
◆ **EMP:** 45 **EST:** 1918
SQ FT: 45,000
SALES (est): 5.5MM **Privately Held**
WEB: www.shop.americanneedle.com
SIC: 2353 Hats & caps

(G-2512)
AMIC GLOBAL INC
353 Hastings Dr (60089-6941)
PHONE..................847 600-3590
Baojun Liu, *President*
Robert Leptich, *Vice Pres*
Ashley Liu, *Opers Mgr*
Bob Liu, *Engineer*
▲ **EMP:** 7
SALES (est): 2.1MM **Privately Held**
SIC: 2621 5084 5113 Tissue paper; metal refining machinery & equipment; cups, disposable plastic & paper; dishes, disposable plastic & paper

(G-2513)
ARXIUM INC
1400 Busch Pkwy (60089-4541)
PHONE..................847 808-2600
Niels Erik Hansen, *CEO*
Ravee Navaretnam, *COO*
Joseph Persivale, *Project Mgr*
Keith Goodale, *Opers Mgr*
Tom Hege, *Opers Mgr*
EMP: 180 **EST:** 2004
SQ FT: 208,000
SALES (est): 37.9MM
SALES (corp-wide): 71.3MM **Privately Held**
SIC: 3845 7371 Electromedical equipment; custom computer programming services
PA: Arxium Inc
   96 Nature Park Way
   Winnipeg MB R3P 0
   204 943-0066

(G-2514)
BECHARA SIM
Also Called: MEI
121 Willow Pkwy (60089-4635)
PHONE..................847 913-9950
▲ **EMP:** 14
SALES (est): 1.6MM **Privately Held**
SIC: 5065 3699 Whol & Mfg Electronic Components

(G-2515)
BERRY GLOBAL INC
800 Corporate Grove Dr (60089-4512)
PHONE..................847 541-7900
Vin Raby, *President*
EMP: 125 **Publicly Held**
SIC: 3089 Bottle caps, molded plastic
HQ: Berry Global, Inc.
   101 Oakley St
   Evansville IN 47710

(G-2516)
BERTSCHE ENGINEERING CORP
711 Dartmouth Ln (60089-6902)
PHONE..................847 537-8757
Richard W Bertsche, *President*
Linda Bertsche, *Treasurer*
Shawn Conner, *Manager*
Linda Salkoff, *Agent*
▲ **EMP:** 16
SQ FT: 12,000
SALES (est): 3.8MM **Privately Held**
SIC: 3545 3541 Machine tool attachments & accessories; machine tool replacement & repair parts, metal cutting types

(G-2517)
BIAS POWER INC (PA)
975 Deerfield Pkwy (60089-4511)
PHONE..................847 419-9180
John Muntean, *President*
Robert T Geras, *President*
▲ **EMP:** 7
SALES (est): 1MM **Privately Held**
SIC: 3679 Static power supply converters for electronic applications

(G-2518)
BLACKJACK LIGHTING
1547 Barclay Blvd (60089-4518)
PHONE..................847 941-0588
Chad Bell, *Credit Mgr*
EMP: 3
SALES (est): 498.5K **Privately Held**
SIC: 3646 Commercial indusl & institutional electric lighting fixtures

(G-2519)
BPREX HEALTHCARE PACKAGING INC (DH)
Also Called: Rexam
600 Deerfield Pkwy (60089-7050)
PHONE..................800 537-0178
Frank C Brown, *CEO*
Ned Buddell, *Manager*
Peggy B Harrington, *Admin Sec*
◆ **EMP:** 72
SALES (est): 1.8B **Publicly Held**
SIC: 3565 Packaging machinery

(G-2520)
BRAINDOK LLC
2104 Birchwood Ln (60089-6683)
PHONE..................847 877-1586
Bishwajeet Kumar, *Principal*
Dhruv Kumar, *Principal*
Promila Kumar, *Principal*
EMP: 3
SALES (est): 211.7K **Privately Held**
SIC: 7373 7372 8243 8748 Systems engineering, computer related; prepackaged software; software training, computer; systems engineering consultant, ex. computer or professional

(G-2521)
BUILDING TECHNOLOGIES INC
1000 Deerfield Pkwy (60089-4547)
PHONE..................800 743-6367
EMP: 2
SALES (est): 331.1K **Privately Held**
SIC: 3822 Thermostats & other environmental sensors

(G-2522)
BURDEENS JEWELRY LTD
1151 W Lake Cook Rd (60089-1956)
PHONE..................847 459-8980
Matthew Burdeen, *President*
Rada Burdeen, *Vice Pres*
Sandra B Burdeen, *Vice Pres*
EMP: 7
SQ FT: 3,000
SALES (est): 1.2MM **Privately Held**
SIC: 5944 3911 Jewelry, precious stones & precious metals; jewelry, precious metal

(G-2523)
CAMA USA INC
Also Called: Cama Group
901 Corporate Grove Dr (60089-4508)
PHONE..................847 607-8797
Billy Goodman, *Managing Dir*
▲ **EMP:** 3
SALES: 515.9K **Privately Held**
SIC: 5084 3565 Packaging machinery & equipment; packaging machinery
HQ: Cama 1 Spa
   Via Como 9
   Garbagnate Monastero LC 23846
   031 879-811

(G-2524)
CHICAGO SHOW INC
1358 Busch Pkwy (60089-4505)
PHONE..................847 955-0200
James Snediker, *CEO*
Robert R Snediker Jr, *President*
Philip Marco, *Vice Pres*
Delia Snediker, *Accounts Exec*
▲ **EMP:** 20 **EST:** 1902
SALES (est): 3.3MM **Privately Held**
WEB: www.chicagoshow.com
SIC: 3993 Advertising artwork; displays & cutouts, window & lobby

(G-2525)
CITA TECHNOLOGIES LLC
975 Deerfield Pkwy (60089-4511)
PHONE..................847 419-9118
Harrison Yuan, *President*
Charles Liang, *Mng Member*
Kevin Hsueh,
▲ **EMP:** 8
SALES (est): 953.5K **Privately Held**
SIC: 3679 Electronic circuits

(G-2526)
COFFEE BREWMASTERS USA LLC
351 Hastings Dr (60089-6941)
PHONE..................773 294-9665
Sean Baumgartner,
EMP: 10
SALES (est): 342.9K **Privately Held**
SIC: 2095 Coffee extracts

(G-2527)
CONCEPTS AND CONTROLS INC
2530 Apple Hill Ct N (60089-4650)
PHONE..................847 478-9296
Anant Venkateswar, *President*
EMP: 10
SQ FT: 4,500
SALES: 250K **Privately Held**
SIC: 3599 8742 Custom machinery; automation & robotics consultant

(G-2528)
CONSOLIDATED FOAM INC
Also Called: Gardien
1670 Barclay Blvd (60089-4523)
PHONE..................847 850-5011
Michael Levitt, *CEO*
Daniel Levitt, *President*
◆ **EMP:** 10
SQ FT: 8,000
SALES (est): 2.1MM **Privately Held**
SIC: 3089 Planters, plastic

(G-2529)
CWH LLC
100 Lexington Dr Ste 201 (60089-6937)
PHONE..................847 489-7907
Jeffrey S Weisman,
EMP: 3
SALES (est): 138.9K **Privately Held**
SIC: 3537 Trucks, tractors, loaders, carriers & similar equipment

(G-2530)
DADUM INC
Also Called: Dadum Die & Design
950 Beechwood Rd (60089-3240)
PHONE..................847 541-7851
Gene Johnson, *President*
Diana Johnson, *Vice Pres*
EMP: 5
SALES (est): 150K **Privately Held**
SIC: 3544 7699 3469 Special dies, tools, jigs & fixtures; professional instrument repair services; metal stampings

(G-2531)
DELL SOFTWARE INC
975 Weiland Rd Unit 200 (60089-7051)
PHONE..................630 836-0503
Fax: 630 836-8431
EMP: 100
SALES (corp-wide): 45.6B **Privately Held**
SIC: 7372 Prepackaged Software Services
HQ: Dell Software, Inc.
   4 Polaris Way
   Aliso Viejo CA 92656
   949 754-8000

(G-2532)
DES PLAINES PRINTING LLC
Also Called: John S Swift of Des Plaines
999 Commerce Ct (60089-2375)
PHONE..................847 465-3300
Michael H Ford,
Deane M Fraser,
Kent T Lyons,
EMP: 15
SQ FT: 35,000
SALES (est): 1.9MM
SALES (corp-wide): 17.3MM **Privately Held**
SIC: 2752 Commercial printing, offset
PA: John S Swift Company Incorporated
   999 Commerce Ct
   Buffalo Grove IL 60089
   847 465-3300

(G-2533)
DISCOUNT COMPUTER SUPPLY INC
871 Shambliss Ln (60089-1242)
PHONE..................847 883-8743
Rick Rodriguez, *President*
EMP: 2
SALES (est): 400K **Privately Held**
SIC: 2678 2865 5045 Papeteries & writing paper sets; color lakes or toners; computers, peripherals & software

(G-2534)
ENGINEERED MATERIALS INC (PA)
89 Chestnut Ter (60089-6620)
PHONE..................847 821-8280
Keith Donaldson, *President*
Robert B Tweed, *Admin Sec*
▲ **EMP:** 2
SALES (est): 853.5K **Privately Held**
SIC: 2673 Plastic bags: made from purchased materials

(G-2535)
EPIX INC
381 Lexington Dr (60089-6934)
PHONE..................847 465-1818
Howard Dreizen, *President*
Alfred C Petersen, *Vice Pres*
Kevin Roos, *Engineer*
Erik A Peterson, *Accounts Exec*
Erik Petersen, *Webmaster*
EMP: 9
SQ FT: 15,000
SALES: 2.7MM **Privately Held**
SIC: 3577 Computer peripheral equipment

(G-2536)
FEDEX OFFICE & PRINT SVCS INC
76 W Dundee Rd (60089-3758)
PHONE..................847 459-8008
EMP: 9
SALES (corp-wide): 69.6B **Publicly Held**
SIC: 7334 2791 2789 Photocopying & duplicating services; typesetting; bookbinding & related work
HQ: Fedex Office And Print Services, Inc.
   7900 Legacy Dr
   Plano TX 75024
   800 463-3339

(G-2537)
FISHER CONTAINER HOLDINGS LLC (PA)
1111 Busch Pkwy (60089-4504)
PHONE..................847 541-0000
Kevin Keneally, *CEO*
Dan Donofrio, *COO*
EMP: 0
SALES (est): 84.5MM **Privately Held**
SIC: 6719 2673 5162 2671 Investment holding companies, except banks; plastic bags: made from purchased materials; plastics products; plastic film, coated or laminated for packaging; unsupported plastics film & sheet

GEOGRAPHIC SECTION
Buffalo Grove - Lake County (G-2563)

(G-2538)
FLEXTRONICS INTL USA INC
700 Corporate Grove Dr (60089-4554)
PHONE.................................847 383-1529
Carl Niedorowski, *Design Engr*
Mohit Chand, *Program Mgr*
Mike Marashli, *Manager*
Michael Humenik, *Director*
EMP: 54 **Privately Held**
SIC: 3089 Injection molding of plastics
HQ: Flextronics International Usa, Inc.
 6201 America Center Dr
 San Jose CA 95002

(G-2539)
FLUID LOGIC INC
1001 Commerce Ct (60089-2362)
PHONE.................................847 459-2202
Robert Popke, *President*
Andrew Huggins, *Vice Pres*
EMP: 4
SALES (est): 457K **Privately Held**
SIC: 3492 Control valves, fluid power: hydraulic & pneumatic

(G-2540)
FORD GUM & MACHINE COMPANY INC
1615 Barclay Blvd (60089-4544)
PHONE.................................847 955-0003
Steve Gold, *Senior VP*
Michael Crandell, *Regl Sales Mgr*
EMP: 18
SALES (corp-wide): 59.7MM **Privately Held**
SIC: 2067 5441 Chewing gum; candy
PA: Ford Gum & Machine Company, Inc.
 18 Newton Ave
 Akron NY 14001
 716 542-4561

(G-2541)
FUNK FAMILY HOLDINGS CORP (PA)
1081 Johnson Dr (60089-6917)
PHONE.................................847 276-2700
Craig Funk, *President*
Luis Morales, *Warehouse Mgr*
Duane Ratay, *Controller*
Edward Chavez, *Manager*
Daniel Minaghan, *Info Tech Dir*
▲ **EMP:** 8
SQ FT: 10,000
SALES (est): 1.8MM **Privately Held**
SIC: 3861 Toners, prepared photographic (not made in chemical plants)

(G-2542)
GLOBAL MATERIAL TECH INC (PA)
Also Called: G M T
750 W Lake Cook Rd # 480 (60089-2074)
PHONE.................................847 495-4700
Norman Soep, *President*
Steve Bouse, *Business Mgr*
Edwin Jones, *VP Admin*
Alex Krupnik, *Vice Pres*
Jason Krupnik, *Project Engr*
▲ **EMP:** 147 **EST:** 1977
SQ FT: 150,000
SALES (est): 64.9MM **Privately Held**
WEB: www.gmt-inc.com
SIC: 3291 Steel wool

(G-2543)
HAND TOOL AMERICA
45 Buckingham Ln (60089-6729)
PHONE.................................847 947-2866
Pingfeng Zhang, *Principal*
▲ **EMP:** 3
SALES (est): 160K **Privately Held**
SIC: 3423 Plumbers' hand tools

(G-2544)
HEART & SOUL MEMORIES INC
1938 Sheridan Rd (60089-8019)
PHONE.................................847 478-1931
Staci Kamp, *President*
Kim Raphaeli, *Vice Pres*
EMP: 2
SALES (est): 228.3K **Privately Held**
SIC: 2782 Scrapbooks

(G-2545)
HERITAGE PRODUCTS CORPORATION
1398 Busch Pkwy (60089-4505)
PHONE.................................847 419-8835
Charles W Schmidt, *President*
EMP: 3
SQ FT: 2,750
SALES (est): 273.5K **Privately Held**
SIC: 3089 2741 Plastic processing; miscellaneous publishing

(G-2546)
HEXACOMB CORPORATION (DH)
1296 Barclay Blvd (60089-4500)
PHONE.................................847 955-7984
Alexander Toeldte, *President*
Ken Berry, *Opers Staff*
Karen E Gowland, *Admin Sec*
EMP: 2
SQ FT: 10,000
SALES (est): 43MM
SALES (corp-wide): 6.9B **Publicly Held**
WEB: www.hexacomb.com
SIC: 2671 2499 Paper coated or laminated for packaging; decorative wood & woodwork
HQ: Boise Packaging Holdings Corp.
 1955 W Field Ct
 Lake Forest IL 60045
 847 482-3000

(G-2547)
HMC HOLDINGS LLC (PA)
720 Dartmouth Ln (60089-6902)
PHONE.................................800 874-6625
John Veleris, *Ch of Bd*
George Garis, *CFO*
▲ **EMP:** 19
SALES (est): 16.2MM **Privately Held**
SIC: 3469 2542 Boxes: tool, lunch, mail, etc.: stamped metal; cabinets: show, display or storage: except wood

(G-2548)
ILLINOIS TOOL WORKS INC
Also Called: Signode
180 Hastings Dr (60089-6989)
PHONE.................................847 215-8925
Dennis Gorman, *Controller*
EMP: 24
SALES (corp-wide): 14.1B **Publicly Held**
SIC: 3565 3499 5051 Packaging machinery; strapping, metal; metals service centers & offices
PA: Illinois Tool Works Inc.
 155 Harlem Ave
 Glenview IL 60025
 847 724-7500

(G-2549)
ILLINOIS TOOL WORKS INC
2550 Millbrook Dr (60089-4694)
P.O. Box 804358, Chicago (60680-4105)
PHONE.................................847 724-7500
Oguz Arif, *Branch Mgr*
EMP: 92
SALES (corp-wide): 14.1B **Publicly Held**
SIC: 3089 Injection molded finished plastic products
PA: Illinois Tool Works Inc.
 155 Harlem Ave
 Glenview IL 60025
 847 724-7500

(G-2550)
INK STOP INC
330 Foxford Dr (60089-6302)
PHONE.................................847 478-0631
Phillip Cole, *President*
EMP: 3
SALES (est): 250K **Privately Held**
SIC: 3955 Print cartridges for laser & other computer printers

(G-2551)
ISEWA LLC
2104 Birchwood Ln (60089-6683)
PHONE.................................847 877-1586
Vinod Jhajharia,
Bishwajeet Kumar,
Virendra Singh,
EMP: 3

SALES (est): 190K **Privately Held**
SIC: 7373 7372 Computer integrated systems design; application computer software

(G-2552)
JOHN S SWIFT COMPANY INC (PA)
999 Commerce Ct (60089-2375)
P.O. Box 5529 (60089-5529)
PHONE.................................847 465-3300
John S Swift III, *Ch of Bd*
Michael Ford, *President*
Deane M Fraser, *Senior VP*
Rick Frydrych, *Vice Pres*
Bill Zimmerman, *Vice Pres*
▲ **EMP:** 50 **EST:** 1912
SQ FT: 55,000
SALES (est): 17.3MM **Privately Held**
WEB: www.johnswiftprint.com
SIC: 2752 Commercial printing, offset

(G-2553)
KOBAC
1007 Commerce Ct (60089-2362)
PHONE.................................847 520-6000
EMP: 3
SALES (est): 168.9K **Privately Held**
WEB: www.kobac-us.com
SIC: 3479 Coating of metals & formed products

(G-2554)
KOBELCO ADVNCED CTING AMER INC
1007 Commerce Ct (60089-2362)
PHONE.................................847 520-6000
Kazuki Takahara, *President*
Yoshinobu Hosokawa, *Admin Sec*
EMP: 690
SALES (est): 44.7MM **Privately Held**
SIC: 3479 Coating of metals & formed products
HQ: Kobe Steel Usa Holdings Inc.
 535 Madison Ave Fl 5
 New York NY 10022

(G-2555)
KOGAN SELF DEFENSE
1549 Barclay Blvd (60089-4518)
PHONE.................................847 877-4711
EMP: 3
SALES (est): 210.6K **Privately Held**
SIC: 3812 Defense systems & equipment

(G-2556)
KOMAX CORPORATION (HQ)
1100 E Corp Grove Dr (60089)
PHONE.................................888 465-6629
Tim Macalpine, *President*
Chris V Ehrenkrook, *General Mgr*
Erich Moeri, *General Mgr*
Peter Everham, *Corp Secy*
Kevin Feil, *Warehouse Mgr*
▲ **EMP:** 61
SQ FT: 50,000
SALES (est): 17.7MM
SALES (corp-wide): 482.6MM **Privately Held**
SIC: 3599 Machine & other job shop work
PA: Komax Holding Ag
 Industriestrasse 6
 Dierikon LU
 414 550-455

(G-2557)
KOP-COAT INC
Valvtect Petroleum Products
1608 Barclay Blvd (60089-4523)
PHONE.................................847 272-2278
Gerald H Nessenson, *Principal*
EMP: 18
SQ FT: 1,200
SALES (corp-wide): 5.5B **Publicly Held**
SIC: 2899 Fuel tank or engine cleaning chemicals
HQ: Kop-Coat, Inc.
 3040 William Pitt Way
 Pittsburgh PA 15238
 412 227-2426

(G-2558)
KYOSEI INTERNATIONAL CORP
1000 Asbury Dr Ste 5 (60089-4551)
PHONE.................................847 821-0341
Satoshi Hiwatashi, *CEO*

Yukako Homma, *Admin Sec*
▲ **EMP:** 4
SALES (est): 552K **Privately Held**
SIC: 3751 Motorcycles & related parts

(G-2559)
LASER EXPRESSIONS LTD
165 N Arlington Hgts Rd (60089-1783)
PHONE.................................847 419-9600
Conni Rydz Karsten, *President*
Bob Karsten, *Admin Mgr*
EMP: 5
SQ FT: 1,340
SALES (est): 213.2K **Privately Held**
SIC: 7336 2791 Graphic arts & related design; typesetting

(G-2560)
LAW BULLETIN PUBLISHING CO
Sullivan Law
1360 Abbott Ct (60089-2378)
PHONE.................................847 883-9100
Debra Weatherford, *Manager*
EMP: 15
SQ FT: 1,000
SALES (corp-wide): 42.6MM **Privately Held**
SIC: 2741 Directories: publishing only, not printed on site
PA: Law Bulletin Publishing Co Inc
 415 N State St Ste 1
 Chicago IL 60654
 312 644-2763

(G-2561)
LEICA MCROSYSTEMS HOLDINGS INC
1700 Leider Ln (60089-6622)
PHONE.................................800 248-0123
Henry Smith, *President*
Dan Simkowski, *COO*
Deborah Rowells, *Vice Pres*
Robert Sykes, *Vice Pres*
Orlando Skeete, *Engineer*
EMP: 11 **EST:** 1999
SQ FT: 83,100
SALES (est): 2.8MM
SALES (corp-wide): 856.8K **Privately Held**
WEB: www.leica-microsystems.com
SIC: 5049 3827 Optical goods; optical instruments & lenses; optical instruments & apparatus
HQ: Leica Microsystems Gmbh
 Ernst-Leitz-Str. 17-37
 Wetzlar 35578
 644 129-0

(G-2562)
LEICA MICROSYSTEMS INC
1700 Leider Ln (60089-6622)
PHONE.................................847 405-0123
Sandra Ostrowski, *Branch Mgr*
EMP: 8
SALES (corp-wide): 17.9B **Publicly Held**
SIC: 3827 3841 Optical instruments & lenses; surgical & medical instruments
HQ: Leica Microsystems Inc.
 1700 Leider Ln
 Buffalo Grove IL 60089
 847 405-0123

(G-2563)
LEICA MICROSYSTEMS INC (HQ)
1700 Leider Ln (60089-6622)
PHONE.................................847 405-0123
Matthias Weber, *President*
Erik Velasquez, *Mfg Mgr*
Sherrie Erickson, *Opers Staff*
Ricarda Voss, *Opers Staff*
Karen Levin, *Finance Mgr*
▲ **EMP:** 150
SQ FT: 37,000
SALES (est): 88.5MM
SALES (corp-wide): 17.9B **Publicly Held**
SIC: 3821 3841 3827 Laboratory apparatus & furniture; diagnostic apparatus, medical; optical instruments & apparatus
PA: Danaher Corporation
 2200 Penn Ave Nw Ste 800w
 Washington DC 20037
 202 828-0850

Buffalo Grove - Lake County (G-2564)

(G-2564)
LLI ARCHITECTURAL LIGHTING LLC
1555 Barclay Blvd (60089-4518)
PHONE 847 412-4880
John Hossner, Asst Controller
William C Hood,
Gregory T Cesca,
EMP: 18
SALES (est): 2.9MM **Privately Held**
SIC: 3645 8711 Residential lighting fixtures; electrical or electronic engineering

(G-2565)
LONG GROVE CONFECTIONERY CO (PA)
Also Called: Mangel & Co
333 Lexington Dr (60089-6934)
PHONE 847 459-3100
John Mangel II, CEO
John Mangel III, Vice Pres
W David Mangel, Vice Pres
Dwayne Hallan, Purch Agent
Hilda B Mangel, Admin Sec
▲ **EMP:** 50
SQ FT: 65,000
SALES (est): 21.1MM **Privately Held**
SIC: 5441 2064 Confectionery; candy & other confectionery products

(G-2566)
MACLEAN FASTENER SERVICES LLC
Also Called: Tramac
355 W Dundee Rd Ste 105 (60089-3500)
PHONE 847 353-8402
Larry Owrutsky, Accounts Mgr
Larry Bryk,
▲ **EMP:** 5
SALES (est): 711.4K **Privately Held**
SIC: 3743 Railroad equipment

(G-2567)
MANGEL AND CO (PA)
333 Lexington Dr (60089-6542)
PHONE 847 459-3100
John Mangel II, President
Hilda Mangel, Vice Pres
William D Mangel, Vice Pres
EMP: 40
SQ FT: 1,200
SALES (est): 4.6MM **Privately Held**
SIC: 5992 5947 5921 2099 Flowers, fresh; gift shop; wine; cider, nonalcoholic

(G-2568)
MARKING SPECIALISTS/POLY
Also Called: Marking Specialists Group
1000 Asbury Dr Ste 2 (60089-4551)
PHONE 847 793-8100
Cliff Modlin, President
EMP: 10
SQ FT: 20,000
SALES (est): 3.3MM **Privately Held**
SIC: 3999 3993 2752 Identification badges & insignia; signs & advertising specialties; commercial printing, lithographic

(G-2569)
MARVEL INDUSTRIES INCORPORATED (PA)
700 Dartmouth Ln (60089-6902)
PHONE 847 325-2930
E Kurt Berg, Ch of Bd
EMP: 2 **EST:** 1947
SQ FT: 6,000
SALES (est): 1.4MM **Privately Held**
SIC: 3537 Industrial trucks & tractors

(G-2570)
MBH PROMOTIONS INC
1108 Gail Dr (60089-1138)
PHONE 847 634-2411
EMP: 1 **EST:** 1998
SALES (est): 200K **Privately Held**
SIC: 5199 2759 Whol Nondurable Goods Commercial Printing

(G-2571)
MEDICAL MEMORIES LLC
2274 Avalon Dr (60089-4682)
PHONE 847 478-0078
Craig Schnierow,
EMP: 5
SALES (est): 455.2K **Privately Held**
SIC: 2731 Textbooks: publishing & printing

(G-2572)
MERIDIAN LABORATORIES INC
1130 W Lake Cook Rd # 202 (60089-1986)
PHONE 847 808-0081
William Zhao, President
Jingou Liu, Vice Pres
EMP: 4
SALES (est): 247.8K **Privately Held**
SIC: 2834 Powders, pharmaceutical

(G-2573)
MID OAKS INVESTMENTS LLC (PA)
750 W Lake Cook Rd # 460 (60089-2090)
PHONE 847 215-3475
Wayne C Kocourek, CEO
Michael A Kocourek, President
David L Crouch, Managing Dir
David A Boyle, CFO
Donald F Piazza, Director
EMP: 5
SALES (est): 614.5MM **Privately Held**
SIC: 6726 3089 Investment offices; plastic kitchenware, tableware & houseware

(G-2574)
MIDMARK CORPORATION
Progeny
1001 Asbury Dr (60089-4528)
PHONE 800 643-6275
Edwin J McDonough, Branch Mgr
EMP: 69
SALES (corp-wide): 391.1MM **Privately Held**
SIC: 3844 X-ray apparatus & tubes
PA: Midmark Corporation
10170 Penny Ln Ste 300
Miamisburg OH 45342
937 526-8472

(G-2575)
MIDWEST SEALING PRODUCTS INC
1001 Commerce Ct (60089-2362)
PHONE 847 459-2202
Andrew Huggins, President
Robert Popke, Vice Pres
Jerry Lindgren, Sales Staff
Craig Silverman, Sales Staff
Antman Myra, Executive
EMP: 35
SQ FT: 18,000
SALES (est): 6.9MM **Privately Held**
WEB: www.midwestsealingproducts.com
SIC: 3053 3069 Gaskets, all materials; molded rubber products

(G-2576)
MONNEX INTERNATIONAL INC (PA)
330 Hastings Dr (60089-6940)
PHONE 847 850-5263
Moon S Yun, CEO
James Wallace, President
Andre Wallace, COO
Tony W Yun, Director
▲ **EMP:** 45
SQ FT: 4,000
SALES (est): 7.2MM **Privately Held**
SIC: 3363 3451 3679 4225 Aluminum die-castings; screw machine products; electronic circuits; general warehousing & storage

(G-2577)
MORSE AUTOMOTIVE CORPORATION (PA)
Also Called: Morse Heavy Duty
750 W Lake Cook Rd # 480 (60089-2069)
PHONE 773 843-9000
Peter Morse, CEO
Jay McCrory, Exec VP
Robert Kurasz, CFO
Norman Morse, Admin Sec
◆ **EMP:** 1500
SQ FT: 180,000
SALES (est): 226.8MM **Privately Held**
SIC: 3714 Motor vehicle brake systems & parts

(G-2578)
NAGANO INTERNATIONAL CORP
999 Deerfield Pkwy (60089-4511)
PHONE 847 537-0011
Yoshitaka Nagano, President
Hiromi Shiratori, Vice Pres
Yukio Nagano, Treasurer
Tadao Inui, Admin Sec
◆ **EMP:** 9
SQ FT: 34,000
SALES (est): 1.7MM **Privately Held**
SIC: 3492 Hose & tube fittings & assemblies, hydraulic/pneumatic

(G-2579)
NECTA SWEET INC
Also Called: Nsi
1554 Barclay Blvd (60089-4530)
P.O. Box 321, Lincolnshire (60069-0321)
PHONE 847 215-9955
Paul Przybyla, President
▲ **EMP:** 49
SQ FT: 3,000
SALES (est): 8.6MM **Privately Held**
SIC: 2869 2062 2099 2087 Sweeteners, synthetic; cane sugar refining; food preparations; flavoring extracts & syrups

(G-2580)
NEMERA BUFFALO GROVE LLC (DH)
600 Deerfield Pkwy (60089-7050)
PHONE 847 541-7900
Lauren Mudrak, Business Mgr
Elizabeth De Longeaux, Vice Pres
Denise Johnston, Vice Pres
Franck Demarest, Mfg Mgr
Brian Murray, Production
◆ **EMP:** 111
SALES (est): 82.7MM
SALES (corp-wide): 183.7K **Privately Held**
SIC: 3841 Surgical & medical instruments

(G-2581)
NEMERA BUFFALO GROVE LLC
800 Corporate Grove Dr (60089-4512)
PHONE 847 325-3629
EMP: 4
SALES (est): 537.4K **Privately Held**
SIC: 3841 Mfg Surgical/Medical Instruments

(G-2582)
NEMERA BUFFALO GROVE LLC
800 Corporate Grove Dr (60089-4512)
PHONE 847 325-3628
EMP: 5
SALES (corp-wide): 183.7K **Privately Held**
SIC: 3841 Surgical & medical instruments
HQ: Nemera Buffalo Grove Llc
600 Deerfield Pkwy
Buffalo Grove IL 60089
847 541-7900

(G-2583)
OUTDOOR ENVIRONMENTS LLC
288 S Buffalo Grove Rd (60089-2148)
PHONE 847 325-5000
Michael Pasternak, Owner
EMP: 2
SALES (est): 260.2K **Privately Held**
SIC: 3829 Weather tracking equipment

(G-2584)
PHATHOM PHARMACEUTICALS INC
2150 E Lake Cook Rd # 800 (60089-1862)
PHONE 650 325-5156
Terrie Curran, CEO
Tadataka Yamada, Ch of Bd
Azmi Nabulsi, COO
David Socks, CFO
Eckhard Leifke, Chief Mktg Ofcr
EMP: 16
SALES (est): 1MM **Privately Held**
SIC: 2834 Pharmaceutical preparations

(G-2585)
PHILOS TECHNOLOGIES INC
1011 Commerce Ct (60089-2362)
PHONE 630 945-2933
Samuel Ko, CEO
▲ **EMP:** 6
SQ FT: 4,500
SALES (est): 1MM **Privately Held**
SIC: 2899 Heat treating salts

(G-2586)
PILLSBURY COMPANY LLC
135 N Arlington Heghts (60089-8213)
PHONE 847 541-8888
Ron Krass, Branch Mgr
EMP: 6
SALES (corp-wide): 16.8B **Publicly Held**
SIC: 2041 Flour & other grain mill products
HQ: The Pillsbury Company Llc
1 General Mills Blvd
Minneapolis MN 55426

(G-2587)
PLEXUS CORP
Also Called: Plexus Manufacturing Solutions
2400 Millbrook Dr (60089-4698)
PHONE 847 793-4400
Steve Ver Keilen, Opers Staff
Joanne Straz, Branch Mgr
EMP: 323
SALES (corp-wide): 3.1B **Publicly Held**
SIC: 3672 Printed circuit boards
PA: Plexus Corp.
1 Plexus Way
Neenah WI 54956
920 969-6000

(G-2588)
PPC FLEXIBLE PACKAGING LLC (HQ)
1111 Busch Pkwy (60089-4504)
PHONE 847 541-0000
Kevin Keneally, CEO
Michael D Fisher, President
Marilyn Versten, Exec VP
Brian Ivey, VP Sales
Brandon Fisher, Accounts Mgr
▲ **EMP:** 215
SQ FT: 60,000
SALES (est): 202.9MM
SALES (corp-wide): 84.5MM **Privately Held**
SIC: 2673 5162 2671 3081 Plastic bags: made from purchased materials; plastics products; plastic film, coated or laminated for packaging; unsupported plastics film & sheet
PA: Fisher Container Holdings, Llc
1111 Busch Pkwy
Buffalo Grove IL 60089
847 541-0000

(G-2589)
PRECISE TECHNOLOGY
700 Corporate Grove Dr (60089-4554)
PHONE 847 459-1001
EMP: 4
SALES (est): 145.3K **Privately Held**
SIC: 3466 Mfg Crowns/Closures

(G-2590)
PROFILE PRODUCTS LLC (HQ)
750 W Lake Cook Rd # 440 (60089-2090)
PHONE 847 215-1144
Jim Tanner, President
Michael Robeson, Technical Mgr
John Banks, Engineer
Matt Labus, Controller
Michelle Lee, Human Resources
◆ **EMP:** 26
SQ FT: 10,000
SALES (est): 74.5MM
SALES (corp-wide): 84.8MM **Privately Held**
WEB: www.profileproducts.com
SIC: 2611 1459 Pulp manufactured from waste or recycled paper; pulp produced from wood base; fuller's earth mining
PA: Incline Management Corp
625 Liberty Ave Ste 2300
Pittsburgh PA 15222
412 762-9244

(G-2591)
PSA EQUITY LLC (PA)
485 E Half Day Rd Ste 500 (60089-8808)
PHONE 847 478-6000
Cyze James, Mng Member
Doherty Thomas B,
Duncan Joe,
Louzan Robert,

GEOGRAPHIC SECTION Buffalo Grove - Lake County (G-2619)

EMP: 139
SALES (est): 13.2MM Privately Held
SIC: 3089 7331 Identification cards, plastic; direct mail advertising services

(G-2592)
RF TECHNOLOGIES INC (PA)
330 Lexington Dr (60089-6933)
PHONE.................................618 377-2654
Babak Noorian, *President*
Steven Combs, *COO*
Mary Ann Trittschua, *VP Opers*
Fiona Noorian, *Opers Mgr*
Cherie Ingold, *Production*
▲ EMP: 50
SQ FT: 25,000
SALES (est): 10.2MM Privately Held
SIC: 3669 Burglar alarm apparatus, electric; emergency alarms; intercommunication systems, electric

(G-2593)
RICTER CORPORATION
Also Called: A & H Bindery, The
999 Commerce Ct (60089-2375)
PHONE.................................708 344-3300
Richard Bergman, *President*
Terence Murphy, *Vice Pres*
EMP: 12 EST: 1945
SALES (est): 1.4MM Privately Held
WEB: www.ahbindery.com
SIC: 2789 Binding only: books, pamphlets, magazines, etc.

(G-2594)
SAP ACQUISITION CO LLC
1200 Barclay Blvd (60089-4500)
PHONE.................................847 229-1600
Jerry Starr,
Michael Lewis,
Gene Wisenwoski,
◆ EMP: 27
SQ FT: 86,000
SALES (est): 2.3MM Privately Held
SIC: 3089 Floor coverings, plastic

(G-2595)
SBA WIRELESS INC
1287 Barclay Blvd Ste 200 (60089-4514)
PHONE.................................847 215-8720
Sam Agam, *President*
Mina Agam, *Admin Sec*
▲ EMP: 26
SALES (est): 4MM Privately Held
SIC: 3651 3579 Speaker systems; time clocks & time recording devices

(G-2596)
SCHULTES PRECISION MFG INC
Also Called: Rex Gauge Division
1250 Busch Pkwy (60089-4538)
PHONE.................................847 465-0300
Otto J Schultes, *President*
Joe Climaco, *QC Mgr*
Dale Little, *Engineer*
Judy Schultes, *Treasurer*
Josh Czarnik, *Human Res Dir*
EMP: 100 EST: 1946
SQ FT: 65,000
SALES (est): 20.3MM Privately Held
WEB: www.schultes.com
SIC: 3599 3829 Machine shop, jobbing & repair; testing equipment: abrasion, shearing strength, etc.

(G-2597)
SCOTTS COMPANY LLC
700 Eastwood Ln (60089-6905)
PHONE.................................847 777-0700
Frank Wilson, *Branch Mgr*
EMP: 40
SALES (corp-wide): 3.1B Publicly Held
SIC: 2873 Fertilizers: natural (organic), except compost
HQ: The Scotts Company Llc
  14111 Scottslawn Rd
  Marysville OH 43040
  937 644-0011

(G-2598)
SCT ALTERNATIVE INC
1655 Barclay Blvd (60089-4544)
PHONE.................................847 215-7488
Vadim Katsman, *CEO*
EMP: 10

SALES: 430K Privately Held
WEB: www.sctalt.com
SIC: 7372 Business oriented computer software

(G-2599)
SIEMENS INDUSTRY INC
740 Weidner Rd Apt 203 (60089-3386)
PHONE.................................847 520-9084
Tim Seitz, *District Mgr*
Aaron Fraser, *Business Mgr*
Cheyo Rogers, *Business Mgr*
Thomas Bolko, *Project Mgr*
Chris Lawrence, *Project Mgr*
EMP: 97
SALES (corp-wide): 96.9B Privately Held
SIC: 3822 Air conditioning & refrigeration controls; thermostats & other environmental sensors
HQ: Siemens Industry, Inc.
  1000 Deerfield Pkwy
  Buffalo Grove IL 60089
  847 215-1000

(G-2600)
SIEMENS INDUSTRY INC (HQ)
Also Called: Siemens Mobility
1000 Deerfield Pkwy (60089-4547)
PHONE.................................847 215-1000
Daryl D Dulaney, *CEO*
Kevin Lewis, *Business Mgr*
Joseph Gunn, *Counsel*
Juan Antonio Gutierrez, *Vice Pres*
Axel Meier, *Vice Pres*
◆ EMP: 1200
SALES (est): 4.9B
SALES (corp-wide): 96.9B Privately Held
WEB: www.new.siemens.com
SIC: 3625 5063 3669 1731 Relays & industrial controls; electric alarms & signaling equipment; emergency alarms; safety & security specialization; security systems services; air conditioning & refrigeration controls; thermostats & other environmental sensors
PA: Siemens Ag
  Werner-Von-Siemens-Str. 1
  Munchen 80333
  896 360-0

(G-2601)
SIEMENS INDUSTRY INC
Siemens Building Technologies
1000 Deerfield Pkwy (60089-4547)
PHONE.................................847 941-5050
Judy Marks, *CEO*
John Currie, *Engineer*
Pornsak Songkakul, *Engineer*
Steve Hoiberg, *Marketing Mgr*
Amy Rubio, *Marketing Staff*
EMP: 5
SALES (corp-wide): 96.9B Privately Held
SIC: 3822 Air conditioning & refrigeration controls
HQ: Siemens Industry, Inc.
  1000 Deerfield Pkwy
  Buffalo Grove IL 60089
  847 215-1000

(G-2602)
SIEMENS INDUSTRY INC
887 Deerfield Pkwy (60089-4511)
PHONE.................................847 215-1000
Shane Adams, *Opers Staff*
Jai Narayan, *Engineer*
Kenneth McQuillen, *Marketing Staff*
David Matula, *Branch Mgr*
Swaminathan Arunachalam, *Info Tech Mgr*
EMP: 87
SALES (corp-wide): 96.9B Privately Held
SIC: 3822 Air conditioning & refrigeration controls; thermostats & other environmental sensors
HQ: Siemens Industry, Inc.
  1000 Deerfield Pkwy
  Buffalo Grove IL 60089
  847 215-1000

(G-2603)
SIEMENS MED SOLUTIONS USA INC
Also Called: Ultrasound Div - Buffalo Grove
2500 Millbrook Dr Ste B (60089-4694)
PHONE.................................847 793-4429
Martin Klein, *CFO*
EMP: 15

SALES (corp-wide): 96.9B Privately Held
SIC: 2834 Pharmaceutical preparations
HQ: Siemens Medical Solutions Usa, Inc.
  40 Liberty Blvd
  Malvern PA 19355
  888 826-9702

(G-2604)
SIGN-A-RAMA OF BUFFALO GROVE
352 Lexington Dr (60089-6933)
PHONE.................................847 215-1535
Sherri Shodes, *President*
EMP: 7
SALES (est): 799.9K Privately Held
SIC: 3993 5199 Signs & advertising specialties; advertising specialties

(G-2605)
SIGNS FOR SUCCESS INC
1538 Madison Dr (60089-6830)
PHONE.................................847 800-4870
Susan Chesler, *President*
EMP: 12
SALES (est): 1.1MM Privately Held
SIC: 3993 Neon signs

(G-2606)
SIRIUS AUTOMATION GROUP INC
1558 Barclay Blvd (60089-4530)
PHONE.................................847 607-9378
Justin Lu, *President*
Tony Cox, *Vice Pres*
EMP: 10
SALES (est): 1.6MM Privately Held
SIC: 3821 Laboratory apparatus & furniture

(G-2607)
SMART-FAB INC
721 Armstrong Dr (60089-1885)
PHONE.................................855 276-2783
Rafi Levi, *Co-CEO*
ADI Ben ARI, *Co-CEO*
EMP: 8
SQ FT: 8,500
SALES (est): 318K Privately Held
SIC: 2297 Nonwoven fabrics

(G-2608)
SST FORMING ROLL INC
1318 Busch Pkwy (60089-4505)
PHONE.................................847 215-6812
Aki Washinushi, *President*
Shinsho American Corp, *Shareholder*
▲ EMP: 6
SQ FT: 2,000
SALES (est): 1.2MM Privately Held
SIC: 3599 Custom machinery

(G-2609)
STATELINE RENEWABLE FUELS LLC
6 Regent Ct W (60089-1941)
PHONE.................................608 931-4634
Jacob Ramsey, *Principal*
EMP: 3
SALES (est): 182.5K Privately Held
SIC: 2869 Fuels

(G-2610)
STATIONERY PRINT SHOP INC (PA)
925 Knollwood Dr (60089-1006)
PHONE.................................214 256-3583
Itamar David, *President*
Dana David, *Admin Sec*
EMP: 3
SALES (est): 607.3K Privately Held
SIC: 2752 Commercial printing, lithographic

(G-2611)
SUHNER MANUFACTURING INC
1360 Busch Pkwy (60089-4505)
PHONE.................................847 308-8900
Joe Agro, *Manager*
EMP: 3
SALES (corp-wide): 115.6MM Privately Held
SIC: 3546 Power-driven handtools
HQ: Suhner Manufacturing, Inc.
  43 Anderson Rd Se
  Rome GA 30161
  706 235-8046

(G-2612)
SYNAX INC
1374 Abbott Ct (60089-2378)
PHONE.................................224 352-2927
Yan Svidovsky, *President*
EMP: 12
SQ FT: 10,000
SALES (est): 1.2MM Privately Held
SIC: 3541 Machine tools, metal cutting type

(G-2613)
TOSHIBA AMERICA ELECTRONIC
2150 E Lake Cook Rd (60089-1862)
PHONE.................................847 484-2400
Laura Hubbard, *Manager*
EMP: 8 Privately Held
SIC: 3674 Semiconductors & related devices
HQ: Toshiba America Electronic Components Inc
  5231 California Ave
  Irvine CA 92617

(G-2614)
UNITED ADHESIVES INC (PA)
820 Port Clinton Ct E (60089-6675)
PHONE.................................224 436-0077
Xiarong Peng, *President*
EMP: 7
SALES (est): 660.1K Privately Held
SIC: 2891 Epoxy adhesives

(G-2615)
V-TEX INC
Also Called: Uncommon Threads
1027 Busch Pkwy (60089-4504)
PHONE.................................847 325-4140
Scott H Verson, *President*
Connie Taylor, *Accounting Mgr*
◆ EMP: 20
SQ FT: 1,500
SALES (est): 2.9MM Privately Held
SIC: 2326 5131 Service apparel (baker, barber, lab, etc.), washable: men's; textile converters

(G-2616)
VAPOR CORPORATION
Also Called: Vapor Bus International
1010 Johnson Dr (60089-6918)
PHONE.................................847 777-6400
William E Kassling, *Ch of Bd*
Clement R Arrison, *President*
Keith Nippes, *President*
John Condon, *Vice Pres*
Robert Gallant, *Vice Pres*
▲ EMP: 408
SQ FT: 330,000
SALES (est): 61.6MM Publicly Held
SIC: 3443 Boilers: industrial, power, or marine
PA: Westinghouse Air Brake Technologies Corporation
  30 Isabella St
  Pittsburgh PA 15212

(G-2617)
VERNON TOWNSHIP OFFICES
3050 N Main St (60089-2727)
PHONE.................................847 634-4600
Bill Peterson, *Manager*
Daniel Didech, *Supervisor*
Tracy Gastfield, *Admin Asst*
EMP: 21
SALES (est): 3.2MM Privately Held
SIC: 8111 2711 Taxation law; newspapers

(G-2618)
VISIPLEX INC
1287 Barclay Blvd Ste 100 (60089-4514)
PHONE.................................847 229-0250
Sam Agam, *President*
▼ EMP: 15
SQ FT: 8,000
SALES (est): 2.9MM Privately Held
SIC: 3663 5065 Pagers (one-way); paging & signaling equipment

(G-2619)
WELLINGTON DRIVE TECH US
1407 Barclay Blvd (60089-4537)
P.O. Box 4929 (60089-4929)
PHONE.................................847 922-5098

Buffalo Grove - Lake County (G-2620)

Greg Allen, *CEO*
Ronald Norman Jackson, *Admin Sec*
◆ **EMP:** 4 **EST:** 1994
SALES: 593K **Privately Held**
WEB: www.wdtl.com
SIC: 3621 Motors & generators
PA: Wellington Drive Technologies Limited
21 Arrenway Drive
Auckland 0632

(G-2620)
WES-TECH INC
720 Dartmouth Ln (60089-6999)
PHONE 847 541-5070
John Veleris, *President*
Keith McGovern, *Plant Mgr*
Michael Slaga, *Materials Mgr*
Tom Mallin, *Engineer*
Elliot Stelsel, *Engineer*
EMP: 8
SALES (est): 1.8MM **Privately Held**
SIC: 3594 Fluid power pumps & motors

(G-2621)
WES-TECH AUTOMTN SOLUTIONS LLC
720 Dartmouth Ln (60089-6999)
PHONE 847 541-5070
Jason Arends, *Engineer*
Michael Cohen, *Engineer*
Michael Gawel, *Engineer*
Don Gross, *VP Finance*
George Montgomery, *Human Res Mgr*
EMP: 65
SQ FT: 45,000
SALES (est): 18.9MM **Privately Held**
SIC: 3549 3535 Assembly machines, including robotic; conveyors & conveying equipment; belt conveyor systems, general industrial use; robotic conveyors

(G-2622)
WESTINGHOUSE A BRAKE TECH CORP
Also Called: Vapor Bus International
1010 Johnson Dr (60089-6918)
PHONE 847 777-6400
Bob Gallant, *Vice Pres*
Kenneth Krolak, *Controller*
EMP: 180 **Publicly Held**
SIC: 3442 Metal doors, sash & trim
PA: Westinghouse Air Brake Technologies Corporation
30 Isabella St
Pittsburgh PA 15212

(G-2623)
XELLIA PHARMACEUTICALS USA LLC (DH)
2150 E Lake Cook Rd # 101 (60089-1862)
PHONE 847 947-0254
Carl-Aake Carlsson, *CEO*
Gal Bernard, *Vice Pres*
James Bond, *Vice Pres*
Geelanie Briones, *Vice Pres*
Nora Elisabeth Hberg, *Vice Pres*
EMP: 120 **EST:** 2014
SQ FT: 15,000
SALES (est): 31.8MM
SALES (corp-wide): 21B **Privately Held**
SIC: 2834 Pharmaceutical preparations

(G-2624)
YANMAR (USA) INC
901 Corporate Grove Dr (60089-4508)
PHONE 847 541-1900
Fumihiro Kano, *President*
Ken Araki, *Treasurer*
Masaru Funai, *Admin Sec*
▼ **EMP:** 3
SQ FT: 72,000
SALES (est): 428.9K **Privately Held**
SIC: 3524 5084 Lawn & garden mowers & accessories; engines & parts, diesel
HQ: Yanmar Power Technology Co., Ltd.
1-32, Chayamachi, Kita-Ku
Osaka OSK 530-0

(G-2625)
ZEBRA TECHNOLOGIES CORPORATION
2550 Millbrook Dr (60089-4694)
PHONE 847 793-5911
Urszula Albrecht, *Vice Pres*
Drew Nathanson, *Research*
Michael Dobbelstein, *Engineer*
Kristavel Ortiz, *Engineer*
Kalinka Voukadinova, *Engineer*
EMP: 52
SALES (corp-wide): 4.4B **Publicly Held**
SIC: 3577 Computer peripheral equipment
PA: Zebra Technologies Corporation
3 Overlook Pt
Lincolnshire IL 60069
847 634-6700

Buffalo Prairie
Rock Island County

(G-2626)
REASONS INC
Also Called: Reason's Locker
18510 206th Sw (61237)
P.O. Box 183 (61237-0183)
PHONE 309 537-3424
Steve Reason, *President*
Amy Saddoris, *Business Mgr*
Bonnie Reason, *Treasurer*
EMP: 2
SQ FT: 1,500
SALES (est): 244.8K **Privately Held**
WEB: www.reasonsprairiepride.com
SIC: 5399 5722 5251 2011 Country general stores; electric household appliances; hardware; meat packing plants

Bull Valley
Mchenry County

(G-2627)
DEBOURG CORP
10004 Bull Valley Rd (60098-8185)
PHONE 815 338-7852
Bjorn Debourg, *President*
Leslie Schermerhorn, *Vice Pres*
EMP: 3
SALES (est): 260K **Privately Held**
SIC: 2899 Fuel treating compounds

Buncombe
Johnson County

(G-2628)
SOUTHERN ILLINOIS POWER COOP
Also Called: Southern Illinois Material
Rr 37 Box N (62912)
P.O. Box 5 (62912-0005)
PHONE 618 995-2371
Brian Cross, *Manager*
EMP: 3
SALES (corp-wide): 212.4MM **Privately Held**
SIC: 2911 Asphalt or asphaltic materials, made in refineries
PA: Southern Illinois Power Co-Operative
11543 Lake Of Egypt Rd
Marion IL 62959
618 964-1448

(G-2629)
SOUTHERN ILLINOIS STONE CO (DH)
4800 State Rte 37 N (62912)
P.O. Box 880, Cape Girardeau MO (63702-0880)
PHONE 573 334-5261
Richard C Neubert, *President*
Jim Weeks, *Chairman*
Del Elfrink, *Treasurer*
Stewart Fuhrmann, *Admin Sec*
EMP: 10 **EST:** 1950
SQ FT: 300
SALES (est): 36.1MM
SALES (corp-wide): 94MM **Privately Held**
WEB: www.deltacos.com
SIC: 1611 1422 3272 Highway & street construction; crushed & broken limestone; concrete products used to facilitate drainage

(G-2630)
SOUTHERN ILLINOIS STONE CO
4800 Hwy 37 N (62912)
PHONE 618 995-2392
Pearl Gibbons, *Manager*
EMP: 40
SALES (corp-wide): 94MM **Privately Held**
WEB: www.deltacos.com
SIC: 1422 5032 Limestones, ground; stone, crushed or broken
HQ: Southern Illinois Stone Co.
4800 State Rte 37 N
Buncombe IL 62912
573 334-5261

(G-2631)
WEAVER EQUIPMENT LLC
Also Called: Weaver Equitment Co
1240 Mount Pleasant Rd (62912-3327)
PHONE 618 833-5521
John Weaver, *Buyer*
Ruth Weaver, *Mng Member*
Ray Weaver,
EMP: 6 **EST:** 2011
SALES: 1.4MM **Privately Held**
SIC: 3523 Farm machinery & equipment

Bunker Hill
Macoupin County

(G-2632)
ALL TYPE HYDRAULICS CORP
149 S Washington St (62014-1315)
P.O. Box 11 (62014-0011)
PHONE 618 585-4844
John Chapman, *President*
EMP: 4
SQ FT: 6,000
SALES (est): 542.6K **Privately Held**
SIC: 3492 Hose & tube fittings & assemblies, hydraulic/pneumatic

(G-2633)
BUNKER HILL PUBLICATION
Also Called: Gazette News Office
150 N Washington St (62014)
PHONE 618 585-4411
John Galer, *President*
EMP: 8 **EST:** 1964
SALES: 250K **Privately Held**
SIC: 2711 Job printing & newspaper publishing combined; newspapers: publishing only, not printed on site

(G-2634)
JETS COMPUTING INC
200 S Brighton St (62014-1344)
PHONE 618 585-6676
James Dorrington, *President*
Ben Dorrington, *Vice Pres*
EMP: 4
SALES (est): 344.2K **Privately Held**
SIC: 3571 Electronic computers

Burbank
Cook County

(G-2635)
COPAR CORPORATION
Also Called: Copar International
5744 W 77th St (60459-1305)
PHONE 708 496-1859
Stephen R Schmidt, *President*
Gail Schmidt, *Vice Pres*
Jesse Hughes, *Prdtn Mgr*
John Casson, *Engineer*
EMP: 45 **EST:** 1953
SQ FT: 27,300
SALES (est): 9.6MM **Privately Held**
WEB: www.copar.com
SIC: 3625 3579 Control equipment, electric; mailing, letter handling & addressing machines; paper handling machines

(G-2636)
MARCA INDUSTRIES INC (PA)
5901 W 79th St 400 (60459-1272)
PHONE 773 884-4500
Annette Golden, *President*
Bruce Golden, *Principal*
Barry Dop, *Vice Pres*
Veronica Gandara, *Representative*
EMP: 6
SALES (est): 1.6MM **Privately Held**
SIC: 3999 Manufacturing industries

(G-2637)
PAT 24 INC
7107 W 79th St (60459-1005)
PHONE 708 336-8671
Patrycja Heldak, *Principal*
EMP: 3
SALES (est): 277.4K **Privately Held**
SIC: 3356 Tin

(G-2638)
TIFB MEDIA GROUP INC
Also Called: Massage Chair Deals
7608 Lockwood Ave (60459-1433)
PHONE 844 862-4391
Feras Ballout, *President*
EMP: 5
SALES: 500K **Privately Held**
SIC: 3634 Massage machines, electric, except for beauty/barber shops

Bureau
Bureau County

(G-2639)
TIMELESS REFLECTIONS
Also Called: Antique Mirror Glass Company
104 E Kansas St (61315-1005)
P.O. Box 185 (61315-0185)
PHONE 815 663-8148
Rob Schramm, *Owner*
EMP: 2 **EST:** 2010
SALES: 490K **Privately Held**
SIC: 3211 Antique glass

Burlington
Kane County

(G-2640)
D & M CUSTOM INJECTION M
Also Called: D & M Plastics
150 French Rd (60109-1112)
P.O. Box 158 (60109-0158)
PHONE 847 683-2054
Steve Motisi, *President*
Michael Teofilovich, *Chairman*
Diane Teofilovich, *Corp Secy*
Drew Christensen, *Mfg Mgr*
Mary Lake, *Materials Mgr*
EMP: 100
SQ FT: 10,000
SALES (est): 19.9MM **Privately Held**
SIC: 3089 Injection molding of plastics

(G-2641)
KUNVERJI ENTERPRISE CORP
Also Called: Veejay Plstic Injction Molding
395 S Main St (60109-1045)
P.O. Box 367 (60109-0367)
PHONE 847 683-2954
Shanti Satra, *President*
EMP: 15
SALES: 600K **Privately Held**
SIC: 3089 Injection molding of plastics

(G-2642)
OWEN PLASTICS LLC
Also Called: D&M Plastics
150 French Rd (60109-1112)
P.O. Box 158 (60109-0158)
PHONE 847 683-2054
Peyton H Owen Jr, *CEO*
Scott Hagen, *COO*
EMP: 45
SQ FT: 58,237
SALES (est): 5.4MM **Privately Held**
SIC: 3089 Injection molding of plastics

(G-2643)
VEEJAY PLASTICS INC
Also Called: Miniature Injection Molding
395 S Main St (60109-1045)
PHONE 847 683-2954
George Klebansky, *President*
EMP: 15 **EST:** 1965
SQ FT: 8,000

SALES (est): 990K **Privately Held**
WEB: www.veejayplastic.com
SIC: 3089 Injection molding of plastics

Burnham
Cook County

(G-2644)
CALUMET REFINING LLC
14000 S Mackinaw Ave (60633-1623)
PHONE..................................708 832-2463
John Newman, *Opers Spvr*
Henry Banach, *Opers-Prdtn-Mfg*
Dan Sajkowski,
EMP: 18
SQ FT: 4,000 **Publicly Held**
WEB: www.calumetspecialty.com
SIC: 2992 2842 Oils & greases, blending & compounding; specialty cleaning, polishes & sanitation goods
HQ: Calumet Refining, Llc
2780 Waterfront Pkwy
Indianapolis IN 46214

(G-2645)
DENNCO INC (PA)
14350 S Saginaw Ave (60633-2008)
PHONE..................................708 862-0070
Dennis I Slomski Jr, *President*
Tricia Yakas, *Vice Pres*
Beverly Slomski, *Treasurer*
EMP: 4
SQ FT: 20,000
SALES (est): 1.5MM **Privately Held**
SIC: 2087 2099 Extracts, flavoring; syrups, flavoring (except drink); dessert mixes & fillings

Burnside
Hancock County

(G-2646)
WESTERN ILL AGRI-SYSTEMS INC
1830 E County Road 2100 (62330-5107)
PHONE..................................217 746-2144
Landon Guymon, *President*
Kent Guymon, *Vice Pres*
EMP: 7
SQ FT: 10,000
SALES: 2MM **Privately Held**
WEB: www.wiasinc.com
SIC: 3523 5153 Farm machinery & equipment; grains

Burr Ridge
Dupage County

(G-2647)
A & M WOOD PRODUCTS INC
9900 S Madison St Unit A (60527-2704)
PHONE..................................630 323-2555
Melvin Marwitz, *President*
Sharon Marwitz, *Vice Pres*
EMP: 8
SQ FT: 30,000
SALES (est): 700K **Privately Held**
SIC: 2449 2431 Boxes, wood: wirebound; moldings & baseboards, ornamental & trim; moldings, wood: unfinished & prefinished; trim, wood

(G-2648)
ACCELERATED PHARMA INC (PA)
15w155 81st St (60527-7903)
PHONE..................................773 517-0789
Michael Fonstein, *CEO*
Daniel Perez, *Ch of Bd*
Ekaterina Nikolaevskaya, *COO*
Randy S Saluck, *CFO*
Randy Saluck, *CFO*
EMP: 5
SALES (est): 508.8K **Privately Held**
SIC: 2834 Pharmaceutical preparations

(G-2649)
ACCURATE PARTITIONS CORP
160 Tower Dr (60527-5720)
PHONE..................................708 442-6801
Michael F Rolla, *President*
Peter Rolla, *President*
John Stewack, *Purch Mgr*
Jay Orlando, *Info Tech Dir*
Linda Rhodes, *Technology*
▲ **EMP:** 7
SQ FT: 65,000
SALES (est): 2.1MM
SALES (corp-wide): 213MM **Privately Held**
SIC: 3446 2542 Partitions & supports/studs, including accousstical systems; partitions & fixtures, except wood; pallet racks: except wood
PA: Itr Industries, Inc
441 Saw Mill River Rd
Yonkers NY 10701
914 964-7063

(G-2650)
ADS LLC
Also Called: Hydra-Stop
144 Tower Dr (60527-6173)
PHONE..................................256 430-3366
Brett Hanes, *General Mgr*
EMP: 65
SALES (corp-wide): 2.4B **Publicly Held**
SIC: 3545 8742 3541 3498 Machine tool accessories; foreign trade consultant; machine tools, metal cutting type; fabricated pipe & fittings; valves & pipe fittings
HQ: Ads Llc
340 The Bridge St Ste 204
Huntsville AL 35806
256 430-3366

(G-2651)
ALBERT VIVO UPHOLSTERY CO INC
836 Lakeview Ln (60527-5629)
PHONE..................................312 226-7779
Albert Vivo, *President*
Anita Knitter, *Manager*
EMP: 8
SALES (est): 440K **Privately Held**
SIC: 7641 5712 2519 Reupholstery; furniture repair & maintenance; furniture stores; household furniture, except wood or metal: upholstered

(G-2652)
AMERIGUARD CORPORATION
Also Called: Colonade Interiors II
7701 S Grant St (60527-5999)
PHONE..................................630 986-1900
EMP: 7
SQ FT: 10,000
SALES: 750K **Privately Held**
SIC: 2392 2653 3496 3999 Mfg Household Furnishing Mfg Corrugated/Fiber Box Mfg Misc Fab Wire Prdts Mfg Misc Products Whol Appliances/Tv/Radio

(G-2653)
AUGUSTA LABEL CORP
7938 S Madison St (60527-5806)
PHONE..................................630 537-1961
Ryan Orniston, *President*
EMP: 6 **EST:** 2014
SALES (est): 275K **Privately Held**
WEB: www.augustalabel.com
SIC: 2759 Commercial printing

(G-2654)
BANNERVILLE USA INC
8168 S Madison St (60527-5854)
PHONE..................................630 455-0304
Patricia Sitkowski, *President*
Ken Sitkowski, *Vice Pres*
Mark Wangall, *Prdtn Mgr*
Tom Sitkowski, *VP Bus Dvlpt*
Pat Sitkowski, *Executive*
EMP: 12
SALES (est): 1.3MM **Privately Held**
SIC: 3993 Signs & advertising specialties

(G-2655)
BEST VENEER COMPANY LLC
Also Called: Bvc
16w273 83rd St Ste A (60527-7952)
PHONE..................................630 541-8312
McCracken James A, *Manager*
David McCracken,
EMP: 15 **EST:** 2014
SALES (est): 2MM **Privately Held**
SIC: 2435 2436 Hardwood veneer & plywood; softwood veneer & plywood

(G-2656)
BIOCONCEPTS INC (HQ)
100 Tower Dr Ste 101 (60527-8916)
PHONE..................................630 986-0007
Tom Gavin, *President*
EMP: 6
SALES (est): 890.1K
SALES (corp-wide): 1.1B **Publicly Held**
SIC: 3842 Prosthetic appliances; foot appliances, orthopedic
PA: Hanger, Inc.
10910 Domain Dr Ste 300
Austin TX 78758
512 777-3800

(G-2657)
BIROM CABINETRY LLC
7440 Forest Hill Rd (60527-7712)
PHONE..................................312 286-7132
Roman Birev, *Principal*
EMP: 4
SALES (est): 294.2K **Privately Held**
WEB: www.biromcabinetry.com
SIC: 2434 Wood kitchen cabinets

(G-2658)
BRONSON & BRATTON INC
220 Shore Dr (60527-5881)
PHONE..................................630 986-1815
Mark Bronson, *President*
Anne McClary, *Vice Pres*
Bob Cserep, *Plant Mgr*
Ginny Collins, *Mfg Staff*
Stephen Greene, *QC Mgr*
EMP: 110
SQ FT: 79,000
SALES (est): 21.5MM **Privately Held**
WEB: www.bronsonandbratton.com
SIC: 3544 5085 Dies & die holders for metal cutting, forming, die casting; forms (molds), for foundry & plastics working machinery; punches, forming & stamping; abrasives; bort; diamonds, industrial: natural, crude

(G-2659)
C HOFBAUER INC
11433 Ridgewood Ln (60527-5136)
PHONE..................................630 920-1222
Charles Hofbauer, *President*
Stephaine Hofbauer, *Admin Sec*
EMP: 8
SQ FT: 1,500
SALES: 17MM **Privately Held**
SIC: 3679 Electronic circuits

(G-2660)
CARL STAHL DECRCABL INNOVTNS I
Also Called: Carl Stahl Decorable LLC
8080 S Madison St (60527-5808)
PHONE..................................312 474-1100
Patrick S Kelly, *President*
Marc Alterman, *Admin Sec*
◆ **EMP:** 11
SQ FT: 10,000
SALES: 2.3MM
SALES (corp-wide): 324.1MM **Privately Held**
SIC: 2542 5039 Partitions & fixtures, except wood; architectural metalwork
HQ: Carl Stahl Sava Industries, Inc.
4 N Corporate Dr
Riverdale NJ 07457
973 835-0882

(G-2661)
CENTRAL DECAL COMPANY INC
6901 High Grove Blvd (60527-7583)
PHONE..................................630 325-9892
Robert Kaplan, *President*
Howard C Kaplan III, *President*
Howard Kaplan Jr, *Vice Pres*
Jennifer Loconte, *Admin Sec*
EMP: 70 **EST:** 1957
SQ FT: 30,000
SALES (est): 15.6MM **Privately Held**
WEB: www.centraldecal.com
SIC: 2759 Decals; printing

(G-2662)
CIRRUS PRODUCTS LLC
220 Shore Dr (60527-5820)
PHONE..................................630 501-1881
Ben Kirchhoff, *Owner*
EMP: 3 **EST:** 2013
SQ FT: 80,000
SALES (est): 351.9K **Privately Held**
SIC: 3599 Machine & other job shop work

(G-2663)
CMB PRINTING INC
15w700 79th St Unit 4 (60527-7964)
PHONE..................................630 323-1110
Thomas Banis, *President*
EMP: 18
SQ FT: 10,000
SALES (est): 2.5MM **Privately Held**
SIC: 2752 2791 2789 Commercial printing, offset; typesetting; bookbinding & related work

(G-2664)
CNH INDUSTRIAL AMERICA LLC
Also Called: Case New Holl Burr Ridge Opera
6900 Veterans Blvd (60527-5640)
PHONE..................................630 887-2233
Jeffrey Miller, *Branch Mgr*
EMP: 208
SALES (corp-wide): 28B **Privately Held**
SIC: 3523 Farm machinery & equipment
HQ: Cnh Industrial America Llc
700 State St
Racine WI 53404
262 636-6011

(G-2665)
CNH INDUSTRIAL CAPITL AMER LLC (PA)
Also Called: Geocap Financial Solutions
6900 Veterans Blvd (60527-5640)
PHONE..................................630 887-2233
Douglas Macleod, *Vice Pres*
Michael Wallm, *Vice Pres*
Benjamin Gallagher, *Purch Mgr*
Spenser King, *Engineer*
Andrea Paulis, *Treasurer*
EMP: 20
SALES (est): 5.5MM **Privately Held**
SIC: 3523 Farm machinery & equipment

(G-2666)
COMPUTER SVCS & CONSULTING INC
Also Called: CSC Learning
16w241 S Frontage Rd # 4 (60527-4400)
P.O. Box 456, Willow Springs (60480-0456)
PHONE..................................855 482-2267
Caroline Sanchez Crozier, *President*
Terry Crozier, *CFO*
EMP: 20
SQ FT: 2,000
SALES (est): 3MM **Privately Held**
SIC: 7372 7378 7373 Operating systems computer software; educational computer software; computer maintenance & repair; value-added resellers, computer systems; local area network (LAN) systems integrator

(G-2667)
DAUBERT INDUSTRIES INC (PA)
700 S Central Ave (60527)
PHONE..................................630 203-6800
Matthew Puz, *President*
Matt Puz, *Principal*
Tim Henderson, *CFO*
Casey Ravard, *Admin Sec*
Ann McVady, *Teacher*
◆ **EMP:** 10
SQ FT: 6,000
SALES (est): 65.8MM **Privately Held**
WEB: www.daubert.com
SIC: 2899 5169 2891 Rust resisting compounds; rustproofing chemicals; adhesives & sealants

(G-2668)
DAUBERT VCI INC (HQ)
1333 Burr Ridge Pkwy # 200 (60527-6423)
PHONE..................................630 203-6800
M Lawrence Garman, *President*
John R Cosbey, *Corp Secy*
Peter Miehl, *Vice Pres*
EMP: 10

Burr Ridge - Dupage County (G-2669)

SQ FT: 14,000
SALES (est): 4MM
SALES (corp-wide): 65.8MM **Privately Held**
SIC: 2672 Chemically treated papers: made from purchased materials
PA: Daubert Industries, Inc.
  700 S Central Ave
  Burr Ridge IL 60527
  630 203-6800

(G-2669)
DEARBORN TOOL & MFG INC
7749 S Grant St (60527-5944)
PHONE...................630 655-1260
Anthony J Hadley Jr, *President*
Cheryl Hadley, *Admin Sec*
EMP: 35 EST: 1950
SQ FT: 12,500
SALES (est): 7.4MM **Privately Held**
SIC: 3541 3544 Numerically controlled metal cutting machine tools; screw machines, automatic; special dies, tools, jigs & fixtures

(G-2670)
ENGINE EFFICIENCY SYSTEMS LLC
6125 S Madison St (60527-5165)
PHONE...................630 590-5241
EMP: 10
SQ FT: 10,000
SALES (est): 546.1K **Privately Held**
SIC: 3519 Mfg Internal Combustion Engines

(G-2671)
ET PRODUCTS LLC
8128 S Madison St (60527-5854)
PHONE...................800 325-5746
EMP: 3 EST: 2010
SALES (est): 322.9K **Privately Held**
SIC: 2911 Fuel additives

(G-2672)
ETCON CORP
Also Called: Electric Supply Direct
7750 S Grant St (60527-5945)
PHONE...................630 325-6100
Joseph Rocci, *President*
Joe Mulack, *Sales Mgr*
Elizabeth Rocci, *Admin Sec*
▲ EMP: 15
SQ FT: 35,000
SALES (est): 3.2MM **Privately Held**
WEB: www.etcon.com
SIC: 3825 3661 Demand meters, electric; volt meters; telephone & telegraph apparatus

(G-2673)
EVONIK CORPORATION
7420 S County Line Rd (60527-7947)
PHONE...................630 230-0176
Mark Lee, *Manager*
EMP: 3
SALES (corp-wide): 2.6B **Privately Held**
SIC: 2869 Industrial organic chemicals
HQ: Evonik Corporation
  299 Jefferson Rd
  Parsippany NJ 07054
  973 929-8000

(G-2674)
FLOWSERVE US INC
161 Tower Dr Ste D (60527-7818)
PHONE...................630 655-5700
David Vasil, *Manager*
EMP: 30
SALES (corp-wide): 3.9B **Publicly Held**
SIC: 3053 Gaskets, packing & sealing devices
HQ: Flowserve Us Inc.
  5215 N Oconnor Blvd Ste Connor
  Irving TX 75039
  972 443-6500

(G-2675)
FUSION SYSTEMS INCORPORATED
Also Called: Fusion OEM
6951 High Grove Blvd (60527-7583)
PHONE...................630 323-4115
Craig Zoberis, *President*
Ken Chess, *Sr Exec VP*
Phil Lullo, *Mfg Staff*
Dawn Moran, *Opers-Prdtn-Mfg*
Jack Quillin, *Project Engr*
▲ EMP: 45
SQ FT: 10,000
SALES (est): 11.1MM **Privately Held**
SIC: 3823 Industrial process measurement equipment; computer interface equipment for industrial process control

(G-2676)
GRAPHICS 2000 INC
161 Tower Dr Ste A (60527-7818)
PHONE...................630 920-0022
Kevin Muldowney, *Mktg Dir*
Dawn Hondros, *Manager*
EMP: 11
SALES (est): 1.4MM **Privately Held**
SIC: 2752 Commercial printing, offset

(G-2677)
GREAT LAKES WASHER COMPANY
Also Called: Prestige Threaded Products Co
127 Tower Dr (60527-5779)
PHONE...................630 887-7447
Suzanne Jasiak, *President*
Stanley Jasiak, *Vice Pres*
Robert H Strawbridge III, *Admin Sec*
▲ EMP: 10
SQ FT: 7,500
SALES (est): 1.8MM **Privately Held**
SIC: 3452 5085 Washers, metal; fasteners, industrial: nuts, bolts, screws, etc.

(G-2678)
GSIPC LLC
311 Shore Dr (60527-5859)
PHONE...................630 325-8181
David G Austin, *CEO*
Dominic Robert Zaccone II, *Vice Pres*
Suzanne M Zaccone, *Vice Pres*
Deirdre Sykes, *Finance*
Lisa Brace, *Business Anlyst*
▲ EMP: 60
SQ FT: 40,650
SALES (est): 17.9MM **Privately Held**
SIC: 2791 2759 Typesetting; letterpress & screen printing; screen printing; flexographic printing
PA: Nissha Si-Cal Technologies, Inc.
  311 Shore Dr
  Burr Ridge IL 60527
  508 898-1800

(G-2679)
H G ACQUISITION CORP (PA)
7020 High Grove Blvd (60527-7595)
PHONE...................630 382-1000
Mark S Holecek, *President*
Donald R Strummilo, *Admin Sec*
EMP: 5
SQ FT: 6,500
SALES (est): 2.8MM **Privately Held**
SIC: 2731 Books: publishing only

(G-2680)
HANGER PROSTHETICS &
100 Tower Dr Ste 101 (60527-5778)
PHONE...................630 986-0007
Vinit Asar, *Branch Mgr*
EMP: 4
SALES (est): 250.9K **Privately Held**
SIC: 3842 Surgical appliances & supplies

(G-2681)
HANGER PROSTHETICS &
100 Tower Dr Ste 101 (60527-5778)
PHONE...................630 986-0007
EMP: 4
SALES (est): 149.2K **Privately Held**
SIC: 3842 Surgical appliances & supplies

(G-2682)
HANSEN TECHNOLOGIES CORP (HQ)
681 Commerce St (60527-7599)
PHONE...................706 335-5551
Tony Ricci, *President*
Chris Knowles, *Vice Pres*
Param Kumar, *Vice Pres*
Mark Sebben, *Vice Pres*
Sabine Diehl, *Export Mgr*
◆ EMP: 94
SQ FT: 55,000
SALES (est): 15.1MM
SALES (corp-wide): 5.3B **Publicly Held**
WEB: www.hantech.com
SIC: 3822 5078 Air conditioning & refrigeration controls; refrigeration controls (pressure); refrigeration equipment & supplies
PA: Roper Technologies, Inc.
  6901 Prof Pkwy E Ste 200
  Sarasota FL 34240
  941 556-2601

(G-2683)
HOLLAND APPLIED TECHNOLOGIES (HQ)
7050 High Grove Blvd (60527-7595)
PHONE...................630 325-5130
David Chaney, *President*
Toby Hobick, *Vice Pres*
Jonathon Rhodes, *Vice Pres*
Robert Soukup, *Vice Pres*
Ron Bruno, *Warehouse Mgr*
◆ EMP: 47
SQ FT: 50,000
SALES (est): 38.1MM **Privately Held**
WEB: www.hollandapt.com
SIC: 5084 5169 3537 Industrial machinery & equipment; industrial chemicals; skids, metal
PA: Harry Holland & Son, Inc.
  7050 High Grove Blvd
  Burr Ridge IL 60527
  630 325-5130

(G-2684)
HYDRA-STOP LLC
144 Tower Dr Ste A (60527-5785)
PHONE...................708 389-5111
Amy Van Meter, *CFO*
Paulette Piecyk, *HR Admin*
EMP: 35
SALES (est): 1.2MM **Privately Held**
SIC: 3491 Industrial valves

(G-2685)
IMAGE FX CORP
16w109 83rd St (60527-5824)
PHONE...................630 655-2850
Matthew Gleitsman, *Admin Sec*
EMP: 5
SALES (est): 667.9K **Privately Held**
SIC: 3993 Signs & advertising specialties

(G-2686)
INNOVA SYSTEMS INC
8330 S Madison St Ste 60 (60527-6595)
PHONE...................630 920-8880
Cheryl Nordstrom, *President*
EMP: 5
SALES (est): 825.9K **Privately Held**
SIC: 3851 Ophthalmic goods

(G-2687)
INNOVA UEV LLC
16w235 83rd St Ste A (60527-5863)
PHONE...................630 568-5609
Roman Kuropas, *President*
EMP: 11
SQ FT: 10,000
SALES (est): 781.6K **Privately Held**
SIC: 3711 Automobile assembly, including specialty automobiles

(G-2688)
INTEGRAL AUTOMATION INC
Also Called: Premier Tool Works
16 W 171 Shore Ct (60527)
PHONE...................630 654-4300
Lucien J Wroblewski, *President*
▼ EMP: 15
SQ FT: 9,000
SALES (est): 1.2MM **Privately Held**
SIC: 3542 8711 3825 Spring winding & forming machines; engineering services; logic circuit testers

(G-2689)
INTELLIGENT INSTRUMENT SY
16w251 S Frontage Rd # 23 (60527-6163)
PHONE...................630 323-3911
Wang Zhao, *Owner*
▲ EMP: 2 EST: 2009
SALES (est): 261.3K **Privately Held**
SIC: 3931 Musical instruments

(G-2690)
INVEROM CORPORATION
16w235 83 St Ste A (60527-5863)
PHONE...................630 568-5609
Roman M Kuropas, *CEO*
EMP: 6
SALES (est): 3.1MM **Privately Held**
WEB: www.inverom.com
SIC: 5084 3571 Materials handling machinery; electronic computers

(G-2691)
JB MFG & SCREW MACHINE
16w154 Hillside Ln (60527-6296)
PHONE...................630 850-6978
Jerzy Roginski, *Principal*
EMP: 3
SALES (est): 153.4K **Privately Held**
SIC: 3451 Screw machine products

(G-2692)
JINDILLI BEVERAGES LLC
8100 S Madison St (60527-5854)
PHONE...................630 581-5697
Morgan Roy, *President*
Michael Schofield, *COO*
Blair Jackson, *Manager*
Jeremy Lovett, *Manager*
Jim Richards,
▲ EMP: 2 EST: 2012
SALES (est): 357.3K **Privately Held**
SIC: 2844 Face creams or lotions

(G-2693)
KOHLER CO
775 Village Center Dr (60527-4518)
PHONE...................630 323-7674
Frank Lynch, *Plant Mgr*
Miriam Huntley, *Branch Mgr*
Dave Zinn, *Executive*
EMP: 48
SALES (corp-wide): 8.3B **Privately Held**
SIC: 3431 Metal sanitary ware
PA: Kohler Co.
  444 Highland Dr
  Kohler WI 53044
  920 457-4441

(G-2694)
L & M HARDWARE LTD
145 Tower Dr Ste 5 (60527-7837)
PHONE...................630 493-1026
Michael Robinson, *President*
Willis L Collins, *President*
EMP: 2
SALES: 300K **Privately Held**
SIC: 5072 3429 Hardware; animal traps, iron or steel

(G-2695)
LABORATORY BUILDERS INC
166 Shore Dr (60527-5836)
PHONE...................630 598-0216
Trudy Chragal, *President*
Henry Grundin, *Sales Dir*
Michelle Smit, *Marketing Mgr*
Jennifer James, *Manager*
▲ EMP: 4
SQ FT: 3,000
SALES (est): 965.7K **Privately Held**
SIC: 3821 Laboratory apparatus & furniture

(G-2696)
LAYER SAVER LLC
9075 Turnberry Dr (60527-0315)
PHONE...................630 325-7287
EMP: 7
SALES (est): 1MM **Privately Held**
SIC: 3086 5113 Mfg Plastic Foam Products Whol Industrial/Service Paper

(G-2697)
M CA CHICAGO
7065 Veterans Blvd (60527-5624)
PHONE...................312 384-1220
Steve Lamb, *Principal*
EMP: 3
SALES (est): 355.7K **Privately Held**
WEB: www.mca.org
SIC: 3494 Valves & pipe fittings

GEOGRAPHIC SECTION — Burr Ridge - Dupage County (G-2725)

(G-2698)
MARQUARDT PRINTING COMPANY
161 Tower Dr Ste A (60527-7573)
PHONE.....................630 887-8500
Barton D J Marquardt Jr, *President*
Steve Marquardt, *Opers Mgr*
Lenny Pikowski, *Sales Staff*
Fredrick Marquardt, *Admin Sec*
EMP: 20
SQ FT: 15,000
SALES (est): 5MM Privately Held
SIC: 2752 2789 Commercial printing, offset; bookbinding & related work

(G-2699)
MARS CHOCOLATE NORTH AMER LLC
15w660 79th St (60527-5987)
PHONE.....................630 850-9898
Debi Roesel, *Purchasing*
Rose Verona, *Branch Mgr*
EMP: 220
SALES (corp-wide): 38.5B Privately Held
SIC: 2066 2064 Chocolate & cocoa products; candy & other confectionery products
HQ: Mars Chocolate North America, Llc
800 High St
Hackettstown NJ 07840
908 852-1000

(G-2700)
MEADEN PRECISION
16w210 83rd St (60527-5827)
PHONE.....................630 655-0888
Thomas F Meaden, *President*
EMP: 2
SALES (est): 204.7K Privately Held
SIC: 3451 Screw machine products

(G-2701)
MEADEN PRECISION MACHINED PDTS
Also Called: Meaden Screw Products Company
16w210 83rd St (60527-5827)
PHONE.....................630 655-0888
John A Meaden Jr, *Ch of Bd*
Thomas F Meaden, *President*
Robert Rackow, *VP Finance*
Maureen Meaden, *Admin Sec*
▲ EMP: 75 EST: 1939
SQ FT: 46,250
SALES (est): 17.7MM Privately Held
WEB: www.meadenprinting.com
SIC: 3451 Screw machine products

(G-2702)
MEDTEXT INC
Also Called: H D C
15w560 89th St (60527-6356)
PHONE.....................630 325-3277
Ona Daugirdas, *President*
John Thomas Daugirdas, *Vice Pres*
EMP: 6
SALES: 600K Privately Held
WEB: www.hdcn.com
SIC: 2721 Trade journals: publishing & printing

(G-2703)
MIDWEST ORTHOTIC & TECHNOLOGY
Also Called: Transcend Orthtics Prosthetics
7025 Veterans Blvd A (60527-5677)
PHONE.....................773 930-3770
EMP: 4
SALES (corp-wide): 14MM Privately Held
WEB: www.midwestorthotics.com
SIC: 3842 Braces, orthopedic
HQ: Midwest Orthotic & Technology Center Merrillville, Llc
112 E 90th Dr
Merrillville IN 46410
219 736-9960

(G-2704)
MIDWEST OUTDOORS LTD
Also Called: Fishing Facts
111 Shore Dr (60527-5885)
PHONE.....................630 887-7722
Eugene Laulunen, *President*
Gail E Laulunen, *President*
Mark Strand, *Editor*
Dena Gervasi, *Production*
Jeff Scharf, *Sales Mgr*
EMP: 20
SALES (est): 2.9MM Privately Held
WEB: www.midwestoutdoors.com
SIC: 2721 7812 2791 2752 Magazines: publishing & printing; television film production; typesetting; commercial printing, lithographic

(G-2705)
MIDWEST PROMOTIONAL GROUP CO
16w 211 S Frontage Rd (60527)
PHONE.....................708 563-0600
Casey Krajewski, *President*
David Lewandowski, *President*
Don Lewandowski, *Chairman*
Rick Daignault, *Exec VP*
Keith Vacey, *Vice Pres*
EMP: 44
SQ FT: 16,500
SALES (est): 8.8MM Privately Held
WEB: www.midwestgrp.com
SIC: 5199 7336 3993 Calendars; advertising specialties; silk screen design; advertising novelties

(G-2706)
NANOPHASE TECHNOLOGIES CORP
453 Commerce St (60527-7500)
PHONE.....................630 771-6747
Bob Roseland, *Branch Mgr*
EMP: 15 Publicly Held
WEB: www.nanophase.com
SIC: 3299 3399 Ceramic fiber; powder, metal
PA: Nanophase Technologies Corp
1319 Marquette Dr
Romeoville IL 60446

(G-2707)
NATIONAL CASEIN CO
6112 Woodcreek Ct (60527-5194)
PHONE.....................773 846-7300
Richard A Cook, *President*
Richard Cook, *Partner*
Charles Cook, *Partner*
Barbara Towery, *Principal*
Charles L Cook, *Vice Pres*
◆ EMP: 55
SALES: 6MM Privately Held
SIC: 2891 2821 Glue; plastics materials & resins

(G-2708)
NATIONAL CASEIN COMPANY (PA)
6112 Woodcreek Ct (60527-5194)
PHONE.....................773 846-7300
Hope T Cook, *President*
Charles Cook, *Vice Pres*
▲ EMP: 55 EST: 1921
SALES (est): 4.4MM Privately Held
WEB: www.nationalcasein.com
SIC: 2891 Glue; adhesives

(G-2709)
NATIONAL CASEIN NEW JERSEY INC
6112 Woodcreek Ct (60527-5194)
P.O. Box 20192, Chicago (60620-0192)
PHONE.....................773 846-7300
Charles L Cook, *President*
Hope T Cook, *Vice Pres*
Bob Gaida, *Executive*
Daniel Ferrarrio, *Admin Sec*
◆ EMP: 35 EST: 1951
SALES (est): 4.8MM Privately Held
WEB: www.nationalcasein.com
SIC: 2891 Adhesives

(G-2710)
NISSHA SI-CAL TECHNOLOGIES INC (PA)
311 Shore Dr (60527-5859)
PHONE.....................508 898-1800
Jaye Tyler, *President*
Richard Ponte, *President*
Dana Whitney, *Vice Pres*
Pamela Day, *Manager*
Paul Genest, *Technical Staff*
▲ EMP: 35

SALES (est): 17.9MM Privately Held
SIC: 2752 Commercial printing, lithographic

(G-2711)
OREMUS MATERIALS LLC
16w361 S Frontage Rd # 1 (60527-5830)
PHONE.....................520 820-2265
EMP: 8
SALES (est): 1.1MM Privately Held
SIC: 3273 Ready-mixed concrete

(G-2712)
PACKAGING DESIGN CORPORATION
101 Shore Dr (60527-5887)
PHONE.....................630 323-1354
Howard Jones, *President*
Scott H Jones, *President*
Randy Haberman, *COO*
George Budlovsky, *Design Engr*
Kyle Reuter, *Accounts Mgr*
EMP: 30
SQ FT: 35,000
SALES (est): 7.3MM Privately Held
WEB: www.pack-design.com
SIC: 2653 Boxes, corrugated: made from purchased materials

(G-2713)
PANATROL CORPORATION
161 Tower Dr Ste D (60527-7818)
PHONE.....................630 655-4700
Bruce Krebbers, *President*
Dean Chrones, *Admin Sec*
EMP: 20
SQ FT: 22,600
SALES: 3.5MM Privately Held
SIC: 3625 3629 Relays & industrial controls; electronic generation equipment

(G-2714)
PRECISION GAGE COMPANY
100 Shore Dr (60527-5819)
PHONE.....................630 655-2121
Barbara L Layland, *President*
Roger Layland, *Vice Pres*
H K Layland Jr, *Admin Sec*
◆ EMP: 10
SQ FT: 10,000
SALES (est): 1.7MM Privately Held
WEB: www.precisiongageco.com
SIC: 3545 Measuring tools & machines, machinists' metalworking type

(G-2715)
PYRAMID SCIENCES INC
9425 S Madison St (60527-6850)
PHONE.....................630 974-6110
Folim Halaka, *President*
EMP: 3
SALES: 100K Privately Held
SIC: 2835 In vitro & in vivo diagnostic substances

(G-2716)
RELCO LOCOMOTIVES INC (PA)
200 S Frontage Rd (60527-6915)
P.O. Box 217, Westmont (60559-0217)
PHONE.....................630 968-0670
Donald L Bachman, *CEO*
Howard W Clark III, *President*
Mark Bachman, *COO*
Eric C Bachman, *Vice Pres*
Daniel P Mc Gowan, *Vice Pres*
EMP: 80
SALES (est): 60.8MM Privately Held
WEB: www.relcolocomotives.com
SIC: 5088 3743 4741 Railroad equipment & supplies; locomotives & parts; railroad car cleaning, icing, ventilating & heating

(G-2717)
RICK STYFER
Also Called: Creative Menu's Plus
200 Lakewood Cir (60527-6340)
PHONE.....................630 734-3244
Rick Styfer, *Owner*
EMP: 3 EST: 1961
SQ FT: 5,000
SALES (est): 170K Privately Held
SIC: 2752 2759 Menus, lithographed; menus: printing

(G-2718)
SCRIBES INC
7725 S Grant St Ste 1 (60527-7274)
PHONE.....................630 654-3800
James J Finnegan, *President*
Joan K Finnegan, *Corp Secy*
EMP: 8
SALES (est): 1.2MM Privately Held
SIC: 2759 Commercial printing

(G-2719)
SEPIRE LLC
7600 S Grant St Ste 2 (60527-7260)
PHONE.....................312 965-2500
Michelle Steinberg, *CEO*
EMP: 40
SALES (est): 12MM Privately Held
SIC: 2759 Commercial printing

(G-2720)
SIGN CONTRACTORS
16w143 Hillside Ln (60527-6269)
PHONE.....................708 795-1761
Ken Cichon, *President*
EMP: 2
SQ FT: 1,500
SALES (est): 200K Privately Held
SIC: 3993 Signs & advertising specialties

(G-2721)
SPYCO INDUSTRIES INC
Also Called: Spyco Tool Co
7029 High Grove Blvd (60527-7593)
PHONE.....................630 655-5900
John Spytek, *President*
Christine Spytek, *Corp Secy*
Robert Spytek, *Vice Pres*
EMP: 40
SQ FT: 15,000
SALES (est): 7.6MM Privately Held
SIC: 3599 Machine shop, jobbing & repair

(G-2722)
STI HOLDINGS INC
Also Called: Midwest Utility
15w700 N Frontage Rd # 140 (60527-7544)
PHONE.....................630 789-2713
Ray O'Donnell, *President*
EMP: 12
SALES (corp-wide): 408.5MM Privately Held
SIC: 3715 3537 Semitrailers for truck tractors; industrial trucks & tractors
PA: Sti Holdings, Inc.
416 S Academy St
Stoughton WI 53589
608 873-2500

(G-2723)
TOWER PLASTICS MFG INC
181 Shore Ct Ste 2 (60527-5850)
PHONE.....................847 788-1700
David R Miller, *President*
EMP: 6 EST: 1970
SQ FT: 10,000
SALES (est): 942.8K Privately Held
SIC: 2782 Looseleaf binders & devices

(G-2724)
TRC ENVIRONMENTAL CORP
7521 Brush Hill Dr (60527-7575)
PHONE.....................630 953-9046
Scott Miller, *President*
EMP: 6 EST: 1996
SALES (est): 1.2MM Privately Held
SIC: 3829 Aircraft & motor vehicle measurement equipment
PA: Trc Companies, Inc.
21 Griffin Rd N
Windsor CT 06095

(G-2725)
TRINITY BRAND INDUSTRIES INC
280 Shore Dr (60527-5823)
P.O. Box 560, La Grange (60525-0560)
PHONE.....................708 482-4980
Ron Supeter, *President*
EMP: 10
SALES (est): 2MM Privately Held
SIC: 3829 Gauging instruments, thickness ultrasonic

Burr Ridge - Dupage County (G-2726)

(G-2726)
TUSCHALL ENGINEERING CO INC
15w700 79th St Unit 1 (60527-7958)
PHONE.....................................630 655-9100
James C Tuschall, *CEO*
James C Tuschall Sr, *President*
Hazel Tuschall, *Corp Secy*
Carolyn Dalby, *Vice Pres*
Dr John Tuschall Jr, *Vice Pres*
EMP: 25
SQ FT: 12,000
SALES (est): 4.3MM **Privately Held**
WEB: www.tuschalleng.com
SIC: **1791** 7389 3446 Structural steel erection; building inspection service; architectural metalwork

(G-2727)
TUTHILL CORPORATION (PA)
8500 S Madison St (60527-6284)
PHONE.....................................630 382-4900
Steven Westfall, *President*
Mark Hampshire, *President*
James G Tuthill Jr, *Principal*
Craig Cavanaugh, *Chief*
Anthony Belmonte, *Vice Pres*
◆ EMP: 35
SQ FT: 16,000
SALES (est): 165.5MM **Privately Held**
WEB: www.tuthill.com
SIC: **3561** 3586 3524 Pumps & pumping equipment; gasoline pumps, measuring or dispensing; blowers & vacuums, lawn

(G-2728)
UNIMODE INC
11s104 S Jackson St (60527-6885)
PHONE.....................................773 343-6754
Arunas Zabielskas, *Principal*
EMP: 2
SALES (est): 205.7K **Privately Held**
SIC: **2431** Millwork

(G-2729)
UNITED FOOD INGREDIENTS INC
15w700 S Frontage Rd (60527-7930)
PHONE.....................................630 655-9494
David Jacobson, *President*
Jim Audet, *Vice Pres*
▲ EMP: 5
SQ FT: 60,000
SALES (est): 684.9K **Privately Held**
SIC: **2099** Food preparations

(G-2730)
USA DRIVES INC
7900 S Madison St (60527-5806)
PHONE.....................................630 323-1282
Phillip E Reilly, *President*
Robert Carlson, *Treasurer*
Theodore P Woerner, *Admin Sec*
EMP: 32
SQ FT: 24,000
SALES (est): 5.9MM **Privately Held**
SIC: **3625** Timing devices, electronic

(G-2731)
WEGENER WELDING LLC
16w301 S Frontage Rd (60527-5804)
PHONE.....................................630 789-0990
Dagmar Ziegler, *Vice Pres*
Leah Dockter, *Marketing Staff*
Paul Karschkes, *Technical Staff*
Jeffrey Peterson,
▲ EMP: 10
SQ FT: 8,000
SALES (est): 1.9MM **Privately Held**
WEB: www.wegenerwelding.com
SIC: **7692** Welding repair

(G-2732)
WELLS-GARDNER TECHNOLOGIES INC
16w 281 S Frontage Rd (60527)
PHONE.....................................630 819-8219
Shihchieh Huang, *President*
Bob Urban, *Warehouse Mgr*
EMP: 3
SALES (est): 175K **Privately Held**
SIC: **3944** Electronic games & toys

(G-2733)
WESTROCK CP LLC
8170 S Madison St (60527-5854)
PHONE.....................................630 655-6951
Charles Timko, *Branch Mgr*
EMP: 9
SALES (corp-wide): 18.2B **Publicly Held**
SIC: **2421** Sawmills & planing mills, general
HQ: Westrock Cp, Llc
1000 Abernathy Rd Ste 125
Atlanta GA 30328

(G-2734)
WESTROCK RKT LLC
Athena Industries
51 Shore Dr Ste 1 (60527-5888)
PHONE.....................................630 325-9670
Dale Razee, *Branch Mgr*
EMP: 50
SALES (corp-wide): 18.2B **Publicly Held**
SIC: **2653** Hampers, solid fiber: made from purchased materials
HQ: Westrock Rkt, Llc
1000 Abernathy Rd Ste 125
Atlanta GA 30328
770 448-2193

(G-2735)
WHOLESALE POINT INC
260 Shore Ct (60527-5815)
PHONE.....................................630 986-1700
Lisa Haddad, *President*
Kamal J Haddad, *Senior VP*
EMP: 12
SQ FT: 18,000
SALES (est): 2MM **Privately Held**
SIC: **3841** 5047 Surgical & medical instruments; medical equipment & supplies

(G-2736)
WINLIND SKINCARE LLC
80 Burr Ridge Pkwy (60527-0832)
PHONE.....................................630 789-9408
▼ EMP: 6
SALES (est): 410K **Privately Held**
SIC: **5999** 2834 7389 Ret Misc Merchandise Mfg Pharmaceutical Preparations Business Services At Non-Commercial Site

Bushnell
Mcdonough County

(G-2737)
ARCHER-DANIELS-MIDLAND COMPANY
Also Called: ADM
160 E Main St (61422-1724)
P.O. Box 90 (61422-0090)
PHONE.....................................309 772-2141
Greg Shaw, *Branch Mgr*
EMP: 20
SALES (corp-wide): 64.6B **Publicly Held**
SIC: **2041** 2099 2032 Flour & other grain mill products; food preparations; canned specialties
PA: Archer-Daniels-Midland Company
77 W Wacker Dr Ste 4600
Chicago IL 60601
312 634-8100

(G-2738)
BUSHNELL ILLINOIS TANK CO
Also Called: Schuld-Bushnell
650 W Davis St (61422-1120)
P.O. Box 179 (61422-0179)
PHONE.....................................309 772-3106
Ernest R Schuld, *President*
Deana Nell, *Admin Sec*
▲ EMP: 60 EST: 1953
SQ FT: 50,000
SALES (est): 19.9MM **Privately Held**
WEB: www.schuldbushnell.com
SIC: **3523** Hog feeding, handling & watering equipment

(G-2739)
BUSHNELL LOCKER SERVICE
330 Green St (61422-1770)
PHONE.....................................309 772-2783
Larry Mason, *President*
Beth Mason, *Corp Secy*
EMP: 8
SQ FT: 2,000
SALES (est): 337.7K **Privately Held**
SIC: **0751** 2011 4222 1521 Slaughtering: custom livestock services; meat packing plants; warehousing, cold storage or refrigerated; storage, frozen or refrigerated goods; general remodeling, single-family houses

(G-2740)
BUSHNELL WELDING & RADIATOR
120 Charles St (61422-1740)
P.O. Box 141 (61422-0141)
PHONE.....................................309 772-9289
Kyle Pico, *Owner*
EMP: 3
SALES (est): 75K **Privately Held**
SIC: **7692** 7539 Automotive welding; radiator repair shop, automotive

(G-2741)
CORTELYOU EXCAVATING
494 W Davis St (61422-1116)
P.O. Box 148 (61422-0148)
PHONE.....................................309 772-2922
David Cortelyou, *Owner*
EMP: 2
SALES (est): 270K **Privately Held**
SIC: **1794** 3272 1711 Excavation work; concrete products; septic system construction

(G-2742)
DUNTEMAN AND CO
115 E Twyman St (61422-1320)
PHONE.....................................309 772-2166
Darrell Dunteman, *Owner*
EMP: 3
SALES (est): 296.8K **Privately Held**
SIC: **3599** Amusement park equipment

(G-2743)
MACOMB CONCRETE PRODUCTS INC
11 Hillcrest Dr (61422-9740)
PHONE.....................................309 772-3826
Dave Cadwalader, *President*
Rhonda Calwalader, *Treasurer*
EMP: 2
SQ FT: 2,400
SALES (est): 221.9K **Privately Held**
SIC: **5032** 3271 3272 Concrete building products; blocks, concrete or cinder: standard; concrete products

(G-2744)
MCDONOUGH DEMOCRAT INC
358 E Main St (61422-1338)
P.O. Box 269 (61422-0269)
PHONE.....................................309 772-2129
David S Norton, *President*
EMP: 16
SALES (est): 1.6MM **Privately Held**
SIC: **2711** Newspapers, publishing & printing

(G-2745)
MID STATE GRAPHICS (PA)
496 W Harris Ave (61422-1016)
PHONE.....................................309 772-3843
Dennis King, *Owner*
Linda King, *Co-Owner*
EMP: 4
SALES (est): 512.4K **Privately Held**
SIC: **2759** Screen printing

(G-2746)
S & P FARMS
19485 N 1700th Rd (61422-9453)
PHONE.....................................309 772-3936
Steven C Hess, *Owner*
EMP: 1
SALES: 750K **Privately Held**
SIC: **3523** Driers (farm): grain, hay & seed

(G-2747)
UTZ QUALITY FOODS LLC
Also Called: Kitchen Cooked
110 Industrial Park Rd (61422-1185)
P.O. Box 295 (61422-0295)
PHONE.....................................309 772-2798
Mary Starcevich, *President*
Corey Starcevich, *Finance*
EMP: 25
SALES (corp-wide): 660.5MM **Privately Held**
SIC: **2096** Potato chips & other potato-based snacks; popcorn, already popped (except candy covered)
PA: Utz Quality Foods, Llc
900 High St
Hanover PA 17331
800 367-7629

(G-2748)
VAUGHAN & BUSHNELL MFG CO
201 W Main St (61422-1350)
PHONE.....................................309 772-2131
W Parks, *Purchasing*
W H Mourning, *Engineer*
Laverne Parks, *Controller*
Elmer Heikes, *Personnel*
Lavoni Manning, *Sales Staff*
EMP: 250
SQ FT: 60,000
SALES (corp-wide): 48.4MM **Privately Held**
WEB: www.vaughanmfg.com
SIC: **3423** Hooks: bush, grass, baling, husking, etc.; axes & hatchets
PA: Vaughan & Bushnell Manufacturing Company
11414 Maple Ave
Hebron IL 60034
815 648-2446

Butler
Montgomery County

(G-2749)
R MACHINING INC
705 Elm St (62015-1020)
PHONE.....................................217 532-2174
Ron Reynolds, *President*
Diane Reynolds, *Admin Sec*
EMP: 8
SALES (est): 939.9K **Privately Held**
SIC: **3599** 7692 Machine shop, jobbing & repair; welding repair

Byron
Ogle County

(G-2750)
BRANATT ENTERPRISES LLC
400 N Walnut St (61010)
PHONE.....................................630 632-3532
Brandon Wolf, *Mng Member*
EMP: 4
SALES (est): 177.3K **Privately Held**
SIC: **3363** Aluminum die-castings

(G-2751)
BYRON BLACKTOP INC
Also Called: Rabine Paving
3499 E Tower Rd (61010-8824)
P.O. Box 250 (61010-0250)
PHONE.....................................815 234-2225
Kevin Herbig, *Branch Mgr*
EMP: 3 **Privately Held**
SIC: **2951** Paving mixtures
PA: Byron Blacktop Inc
1291 Kysor Dr
Byron IL 61010

(G-2752)
DANE INDUSTRIES LLC
Also Called: PQ Ovens
602 E Blackhawk Dr (61010-8940)
P.O. Box 921 (61010-0921)
PHONE.....................................815 234-2811
EMP: 99
SALES (est): 6.3MM **Privately Held**
SIC: **3567** Mfg Industrial Furnaces/Ovens

(G-2753)
INFRATROL LLC
602 E Blackhawk Dr (61010-8940)
PHONE.....................................779 475-3098
William Diemel, *President*
Steven Onsager, *Vice Pres*
EMP: 32
SQ FT: 80,000

SALES (est): 229K **Privately Held**
SIC: 3567 Industrial furnaces & ovens

(G-2754)
INTERNTIONAL METAL FINSHG SVCS
Also Called: Lights On Service
8692 Glacier Dr (61010-9766)
PHONE...............................815 234-5254
Alan Titterton, *President*
Pondelea Titterton, *Admin Sec*
EMP: 3
SALES (est): 224.8K **Privately Held**
SIC: 3471 Plating & polishing

(G-2755)
QUALITY METAL FINISHING CO
421 N Walnut St (61010)
P.O. Box 922 (61010-0922)
PHONE...............................815 234-2711
Mario Bortoli, *Ch of Bd*
Matthew Bortoli, *President*
Bill Wohrley, *CFO*
Chad Worman, *Manager*
William F Wohrley, *Admin Sec*
▲ EMP: 145 EST: 1947
SQ FT: 150,000
SALES (est): 34.2MM **Privately Held**
WEB: www.qmfco.com
SIC: 3364 Zinc & zinc-base alloy die-castings

(G-2756)
ROCK VALLEY PUBLISHING LLC
Also Called: Northern Orgle County Temple
418 W Blackhawk Dr (61010-8634)
P.O. Box 982 (61010-0982)
PHONE...............................815 234-4821
Randy Johnson, *Manager*
EMP: 3
SALES (corp-wide): 5.2MM **Privately Held**
SIC: 2711 Newspapers: publishing only, not printed on site
PA: Rock Valley Publishing Llc
7124 Windsor Lake Pkwy # 4
Loves Park IL 61111
815 467-6397

(G-2757)
ROGERS READY MIX & MTLS INC (PA)
8128 N Walnut St (61010)
P.O. Box 250 (61010-0250)
PHONE...............................815 234-8212
Toby Rogers, *President*
Robert Rogers, *Vice Pres*
EMP: 80
SQ FT: 7,000
SALES (est): 14.3MM **Privately Held**
WEB: www.rogersreadymix.net
SIC: 3273 5032 1442 Ready-mixed concrete; aggregate; construction sand & gravel

(G-2758)
SHERWIN INDUSTRIES INC
149 S Fox Run Ln (61010-9577)
PHONE...............................815 234-8007
EMP: 20
SALES (est): 1.6MM **Privately Held**
SIC: 2951 Mfg Asphalt Mixtures/Blocks

(G-2759)
SSN LLC
Also Called: Supply Solutions Network
4875 E Nordic Woods Dr (61010-9306)
PHONE...............................815 978-8729
Timm Devries, *COO*
Peter Devries, *Mng Member*
▲ EMP: 6
SALES: 100K **Privately Held**
WEB: www.supplysolutionsnetwork.com
SIC: 2759 7389 Screen printing; brokers, business: buying & selling business enterprises

Cahokia
St. Clair County

(G-2760)
A & S HELICOPTERS INC
4000 Vector Dr (62206-1466)
P.O. Box 5031 (62206-5031)
PHONE...............................618 337-2600
Steve Bortscheller, *President*
EMP: 3
SQ FT: 6,000
SALES (est): 27.2K **Privately Held**
SIC: 3721 Aircraft & heavy equipment repair services

(G-2761)
JET AVIATION ST LOUIS INC (DH)
6400 Curtiss Steinberg Dr (62206-1458)
PHONE...............................618 646-8000
Robert Smith, *President*
Kurt Sutterer, *President*
Patrick Kasate, *General Mgr*
Heinz Aebi, *Senior VP*
Stephan Bruhin, *Senior VP*
EMP: 99 EST: 1957
SQ FT: 160,000
SALES (est): 28.6MM
SALES (corp-wide): 39.3B **Publicly Held**
WEB: www.jetaviation.com
SIC: 4581 5172 3721 5088 Aircraft servicing & repairing; aircraft storage at airports; airport terminal services; aircraft fueling services; aircraft; aircraft & parts

(G-2762)
MEDICATE PHARMACY INC
Also Called: Medicate Pharmacy Dme
911 Water St (62206-1614)
PHONE...............................618 482-2002
EMP: 6
SALES (corp-wide): 4.7MM **Privately Held**
SIC: 2834 Pharmaceutical preparations
PA: Medicate Pharmacy, Inc
1833 Kingshighway
East Saint Louis IL 62204
618 874-3000

(G-2763)
PRAXAIR DISTRIBUTION INC
9 Judith Ln (62206-1352)
PHONE...............................314 664-7900
Ray Chapman, *Manager*
EMP: 28 **Privately Held**
WEB: www.praxair.com
SIC: 5084 5169 7359 2813 Welding machinery & equipment; gases, compressed & liquefied; equipment rental & leasing; industrial gases
HQ: Praxair Distribution, Inc.
10 Riverview Dr
Danbury CT 06810
203 837-2000

(G-2764)
STELLAR MANUFACTURING COMPANY
1647 Sauget Business Blvd (62206-1455)
PHONE...............................618 823-3761
Thomas V Connelly, *President*
Jerry Lewinski, *Vice Pres*
Tiffany Coney, *Human Res Mgr*
Mark Scott, *Manager*
Ben Wodicker, *Director*
EMP: 80
SQ FT: 130,000
SALES (est): 28.7MM **Privately Held**
SIC: 2819 3661 Industrial inorganic chemicals; telephone & telegraph apparatus

Cairo
Alexander County

(G-2765)
CAIRO DIAGNOSTIC CENTER
13289 Kessler Rd (62914-3101)
PHONE...............................618 734-1500
Susie Gies, *Administration*
EMP: 10
SALES (est): 237.2K **Privately Held**
SIC: 2835 In vitro & in vivo diagnostic substances

(G-2766)
CAIRO DRY KILNS INC
14372 State Highway 37 (62914-3180)
P.O. Box 547 (62914-0547)
PHONE...............................618 734-1039
Dennis Farrow, *President*
Linda Hanes, *General Mgr*
Terry Farrow, *Vice Pres*
EMP: 32
SQ FT: 12,000
SALES (est): 5.1MM **Privately Held**
SIC: 2421 Kiln drying of lumber

(G-2767)
FARROW LUMBER CO
Hwy 37 N (62914)
P.O. Box 547 (62914-0547)
PHONE...............................618 734-0255
Dennis Farrow, *President*
Linda Farrow, *Corp Secy*
EMP: 3
SQ FT: 12,000
SALES (est): 1.3MM **Privately Held**
SIC: 5031 2421 Lumber: rough, dressed & finished; custom sawmill

Caledonia
Boone County

(G-2768)
BACH TIMBER & PALLET INC
8858 Grove St (61011-9604)
PHONE...............................815 885-3774
Robert Bach, *President*
David Bach, *Corp Secy*
Rick Bach, *Vice Pres*
Douglas Bach, *Treasurer*
EMP: 5
SALES (est): 692.3K **Privately Held**
SIC: 2448 2421 Pallets, wood; sawmills & planing mills, general

(G-2769)
CHRISTIANSEN SAWMILL AND LOG
20080 Grade School Rd (61011-9527)
PHONE...............................815 315-7520
Dale Christiansen, *Owner*
Matthew Christiansen, *Co-Owner*
EMP: 3
SALES (est): 225K **Privately Held**
SIC: 2421 2426 2411 Sawmills & planing mills, general; hardwood dimension & flooring mills; logging

(G-2770)
MCCURDY TOOL & MACHINING CO
1912 Krupke Rd (61011-9567)
PHONE...............................815 765-2117
Floyd Laverne McCurdy, *President*
EMP: 60
SQ FT: 15,000
SALES (est): 9.5MM **Privately Held**
SIC: 3544 Special dies & tools

(G-2771)
SERAPH INDUSTRIES LLC
1175 Krupke Rd (61011-9567)
PHONE...............................815 222-9686
Vance Hirst Sr, *President*
Vance Hirst Jr, *Vice Pres*
EMP: 5
SQ FT: 150
SALES (est): 1MM **Privately Held**
SIC: 3312 Plate, steel; sheet or strip, steel, cold-rolled: own hot-rolled; sheet or strip, steel, hot-rolled

Calumet City
Cook County

(G-2772)
CAPLES-EL TRANSPORT INC
560 Buffalo Ave (60409-3415)
PHONE...............................708 300-2727
Yahco Caples, *President*
Ruby Caples, *Corp Secy*
EMP: 2 EST: 2013
SALES (est): 230.3K **Privately Held**
SIC: 3537 4213 7389 Trucks, tractors, loaders, carriers & similar equipment; contract haulers;

(G-2773)
CLARIOS
Also Called: Johnson Controls
1500 Huntington Dr (60409-5402)
PHONE...............................708 474-1717
Tom Hulett, *Manager*
EMP: 60
SQ FT: 3,200 **Privately Held**
SIC: 5085 5084 3822 1731 Valves & fittings; controlling instruments & accessories; temperature controls, automatic; general electrical contractor; electrical repair shops; plumbing & hydronic heating supplies
HQ: Johnson Controls, Inc.
5757 N Green Bay Ave
Milwaukee WI 53209
414 524-1200

(G-2774)
DATASOURCE
1931 Wilson Ave Apt 7 (60409-2928)
PHONE...............................312 405-9152
Sharon Williams, *Owner*
Richard Florence, *Principal*
EMP: 3
SALES: 250K **Privately Held**
SIC: 3677 3621 3661 5063 Transformers power supply, electronic type; storage battery chargers, motor & engine generator type; telephones, sound powered (no battery); flashlights; Christmas lights & decorations

(G-2775)
DOREENS PIZZA INC
Also Called: Doreen's Gourmet Frozen Pizza
130 State St (60409-2754)
PHONE...............................708 862-7499
Robert Wisz, *President*
Lisa Carroll, *Treasurer*
EMP: 10
SQ FT: 8,000
SALES: 2MM **Privately Held**
SIC: 2038 5142 5812 Pizza, frozen; packaged frozen goods; eating places

(G-2776)
GELITA USA CHICAGO
10 Wentworth Ave (60409-2744)
PHONE...............................708 891-8400
Paulo Reimann, *President*
Heinrich Schmidt, *Vice Pres*
Shirley Basta, *Opers Mgr*
Kevin Bachar, *Prdtn Mgr*
Thomas Ploog, *Purch Agent*
▲ EMP: 16
SALES (est): 5.7MM **Privately Held**
SIC: 2899 Gelatin

(G-2777)
GELITA USA INC
10 Wentworth Ave (60409-2744)
PHONE...............................708 891-8400
Jayna Beargeon, *Buyer*
Mayara Nosse, *Engineer*
Steve Chen, *Controller*
Teri Smith, *Human Res Mgr*
Melissa Simon, *Sales Staff*
EMP: 4
SALES (corp-wide): 797.3MM **Privately Held**
SIC: 2899 Chemical preparations
HQ: Gelita Usa Inc.
2445 Port Neal Indus Rd
Sergeant Bluff IA 51054
712 943-5516

(G-2778)
GENERAL MILLS INC
1600 Huntington Dr (60409-5404)
P.O. Box 368, West Chicago (60186-0368)
PHONE...............................630 231-1140
James Jackson, *Purch Mgr*
Mark Bednarz, *Buyer*
Dan Huebner, *Project Engr*
David Johnson, *Branch Mgr*
EMP: 500

Calumet City - Cook County (G-2779)

SALES (corp-wide): 16.8B **Publicly Held**
WEB: www.generalmills.com
SIC: **2043** 2099 2098 Cereal breakfast foods; food preparations; macaroni & spaghetti
PA: General Mills, Inc.
1 General Mills Blvd
Minneapolis MN 55426
763 764-7600

(G-2779)
HARBISONWALKER INTL INC
1400 Huntington Dr (60409-5464)
PHONE.................................708 474-5350
EMP: 8
SALES (corp-wide): 618.3MM **Privately Held**
SIC: **3255** Clay refractories
HQ: Harbisonwalker International, Inc.
1305 Cherrington Pkwy # 100
Moon Township PA 15108

(G-2780)
HEAVY HITTERS LLC
304 153rd Pl (60409-4106)
PHONE.................................630 258-2991
Thomas Pharris, *Mng Member*
EMP: 3
SALES (est): 117.3K **Privately Held**
SIC: **3993** Signs & advertising specialties

(G-2781)
HERMANITAS CUPCAKES
1067 Stewart Ave (60409-2007)
PHONE.................................708 620-9396
Gabriela Diaz, *Principal*
EMP: 3 EST: 2010
SALES (est): 74K **Privately Held**
SIC: **2051** Bread, cake & related products

(G-2782)
KAY MANUFACTURING COMPANY LLC
602 State St (60409-2041)
PHONE.................................708 862-6800
Brian Pelke, *President*
Scott Dekker, *Vice Pres*
Samarth Patel, *Engineer*
EMP: 180 EST: 1946
SQ FT: 96,000
SALES (est): 43.4MM **Privately Held**
WEB: www.kaymfg.com
SIC: **3089** 3469 Automotive parts, plastic; machine parts, stamped or pressed metal

(G-2783)
MEATS BY LINZ INC (PA)
414 State St (60409-2618)
P.O. Box 59 (60409-0059)
PHONE.................................708 862-0830
Robert Linz, *President*
John Majchrowicz, *COO*
Frederick Linz, *Vice Pres*
Frank Luna, *Vice Pres*
Becky Robbins, *Vice Pres*
▼ EMP: 44 EST: 1961
SQ FT: 10,000
SALES (est): 20.7MM **Privately Held**
WEB: www.meatsbylinz.com
SIC: **5147** 5812 2013 2011 Meats, cured or smoked; meats, fresh; eating places; sausages & other prepared meats; meat packing plants

(G-2784)
OSHKOSH SPECIALTY VEHICLES INC (DH)
2150 Dolton Rd (60409-1411)
P.O. Box 2017, Appleton WI (54912-2017)
PHONE.................................708 868-5071
Charles L Szews, *CEO*
James W Johnson, *President*
Dan Peters, *President*
Thtan L Blankfield, *Admin Sec*
♦ EMP: 110
SALES (est): 10MM
SALES (corp-wide): 8.3B **Publicly Held**
SIC: **3714** 3711 Motor vehicle parts & accessories; bus & other large specialty vehicle assembly

(G-2785)
PCC INC (HQ)
14201 Paxton Ave (60409-3235)
PHONE.................................708 868-3800
Gary E Kamins, *CEO*
Timothy Workman, *Ch of Bd*
Joe Byrne, *President*
T C Cheong, *CFO*
Sal Cuccio, *VP Finance*
EMP: 6
SQ FT: 40,000
SALES (est): 37.2MM
SALES (corp-wide): 53.3MM **Privately Held**
SIC: **2821** Plastics materials & resins
PA: Chroma Color Corporation
3900 W Dayton St
Mchenry IL 60050
877 385-8777

(G-2786)
PLASTICS COLOR & COMPOUNDING
14201 Paxton Ave (60409-3235)
PHONE.................................708 868-3800
Jim Christie, *President*
Lori M Johnson, *Exec VP*
EMP: 100
SQ FT: 4,000
SALES (est): 11.5MM
SALES (corp-wide): 53.3MM **Privately Held**
SIC: **2821** Plastics materials & resins
HQ: Pcc, Inc.
14201 Paxton Ave
Calumet City IL 60409
708 868-3800

(G-2787)
PLASTICS COLOR CORP ILLINOIS
14201 Paxton Ave (60409-3235)
P.O. Box 1474 (60409-7474)
PHONE.................................708 868-3800
▲ EMP: 75
SQ FT: 70,000
SALES (est): 14.4MM
SALES (corp-wide): 2.3B **Privately Held**
SIC: **2816** 2851 Inorganic pigments; paints & allied products
HQ: Pmc, Inc.
12243 Branford St
Sun Valley CA 91352
818 896-1101

(G-2788)
PMC INC
Also Called: Plastics Color-Chip
14201 Paxton Ave (60409-3235)
PHONE.................................708 868-3800
Ray Lachapelle, *Division Pres*
EMP: 70
SQ FT: 20,000
SALES (corp-wide): 2.3B **Privately Held**
WEB: www.pmcglobalinc.com
SIC: **2851** Paints & allied products
HQ: Pmc, Inc.
12243 Branford St
Sun Valley CA 91352
818 896-1101

(G-2789)
ROMAN HOLDINGS CORPORATION
824 State St (60409-2533)
PHONE.................................708 891-0770
Harry J Bruce, *Ch of Bd*
Richard P Bessette, *President*
Philip G Bessette, *Vice Pres*
Gerald M Russo, *CFO*
Jack Obiala, *Admin Sec*
EMP: 70
SQ FT: 120,000
SALES: 20MM **Privately Held**
SIC: **2891** Adhesives

(G-2790)
ROMAN PRODUCTS LLC
824 State St (60409-2533)
PHONE.................................708 891-0770
John W Penland, *President*
Dennis Skrabak, *Vice Pres*
Robin Patrick, *VP Sales*
♦ EMP: 50
SQ FT: 100,000
SALES: 15.3MM **Privately Held**
SIC: **2891** Adhesives

(G-2791)
SILVER LINE
1550 Huntington Dr (60409-5402)
PHONE.................................708 832-9100
Ken Silverman, *President*
EMP: 8
SALES (est): 478.4K **Privately Held**
SIC: **2499** Decorative wood & woodwork

(G-2792)
VICTORY PHARMACY DECATUR INC
Also Called: Victory Medical Equipment
1837 River Oaks Dr (60409-5071)
PHONE.................................708 801-9626
Wole Adeoye, *Principal*
Abiola Adeoye, *Admin Sec*
EMP: 3
SQ FT: 2,500
SALES (est): 2.9MM **Privately Held**
SIC: **3845** 5047 Ultrasonic medical equipment, except cleaning; medical equipment & supplies; electro-medical equipment

(G-2793)
WHITE DIAMONDS INC
96 River Oaks Ctr (60409-5503)
PHONE.................................708 868-4006
EMP: 4
SALES (est): 215.3K **Privately Held**
SIC: **3911** Jewelry, precious metal

Calumet Park
Cook County

(G-2794)
AMERICAN HOME ALUMINIUM CO
Also Called: American Home Aluminum Co
12127 S Paulina St (60827-5319)
PHONE.................................773 925-9442
Robert Roe, *President*
EMP: 1
SALES (est): 250K **Privately Held**
SIC: **3444** Gutters, sheet metal

(G-2795)
CHICAGO PRINT GROUP INC
12901 S Throop St (60827-6423)
PHONE.................................312 251-1962
Paul Denst, *President*
Ryan Walsh, *Corp Secy*
EMP: 5
SQ FT: 4,600
SALES (est): 1.1MM **Privately Held**
SIC: **2752** Commercial printing, offset

(G-2796)
CLARK TASHAUNDA
Also Called: Ddazzledistributors
12406 S Morgan St (60827-6225)
PHONE.................................708 247-8274
Tashaunda Clark, *Owner*
EMP: 3
SALES (est): 127.2K **Privately Held**
SIC: **3369** 3613 Machinery castings, non-ferrous: ex. alum., copper, die, etc.; power circuit breakers; circuit breakers, air; distribution boards, electric; generator control & metering panels

(G-2797)
CONTINENTAL MIDLAND
1340 W 127th St (60827-6129)
PHONE.................................708 441-1000
EMP: 3 EST: 2007
SALES (est): 160K **Privately Held**
SIC: **3451** 5072 5251 Mfg Screw Machine Products Whol Hardware Ret Hardware

(G-2798)
KAY & CEE
1204 W 127th St (60827-6107)
PHONE.................................773 425-9169
Kristine Knowles West, *Owner*
EMP: 6
SALES (est): 246.2K **Privately Held**
SIC: **3672** Printed circuit boards

(G-2799)
MOBILE MINI INC
12658 S Winchester Ave # 2 (60827-5608)
PHONE.................................708 297-2004
Joe Ruffo, *Branch Mgr*
EMP: 30
SALES (corp-wide): 612.6MM **Publicly Held**
SIC: **3448** 3441 3412 7359 Buildings, portable: prefabricated metal; fabricated structural metal; drums, shipping: metal; shipping container leasing
PA: Mobile Mini, Inc.
4646 E Van Buren St # 400
Phoenix AZ 85008
480 894-6311

(G-2800)
UNICORD CORPORATION
Also Called: Unicord Companies, The
12010 S Paulina St (60827-5318)
PHONE.................................708 385-7999
Arman Moseni, *President*
♦ EMP: 50
SQ FT: 30,000
SALES (est): 8MM **Privately Held**
SIC: **2298** Twine, cord & cordage

Camargo
Douglas County

(G-2801)
PRITCHARD ENTERPRISES INC
Also Called: Fisher Midwest
955 N State Route 130 (61919-3340)
PHONE.................................217 832-8588
Robert Pritchard, *President*
EMP: 3
SALES (corp-wide): 8.8MM **Privately Held**
SIC: **3949** Sporting & athletic goods
PA: Pritchard Enterprises Inc
2060 Cauble Rd
Salisbury NC 28144
704 636-5713

Cambridge
Henry County

(G-2802)
CAMBRIDGE CHRONICLE
119 W Exchange St (61238-1158)
P.O. Box 5 (61238-0005)
PHONE.................................309 937-3303
Sandy Hull, *Manager*
EMP: 4
SALES (est): 153.5K **Privately Held**
SIC: **2711** Newspapers, publishing & printing

(G-2803)
CAMBRIDGE PATTERN WORKS
105 E Railroad St (61238-1167)
PHONE.................................309 937-5370
David R Anderson, *Owner*
EMP: 4 EST: 1978
SQ FT: 1,600
SALES (est): 338K **Privately Held**
SIC: **3312** 3543 Blast furnaces & steel mills; industrial patterns

(G-2804)
CSI MANUFACTURING INC
Hwy 81 E (61238)
PHONE.................................309 937-2653
Gale Casteel, *Manager*
EMP: 50
SALES (corp-wide): 7.6MM **Privately Held**
SIC: **2452** Modular homes, prefabricated, wood
PA: Csi Manufacturing Inc
419 E Court St
Cambridge IL
309 937-5544

(G-2805)
LIBERTY GROUP PUBLISHING
Also Called: Geneseo Publication
119 W Exchange St (61238-1158)
P.O. Box 132 (61238-0132)
PHONE..................309 937-3303
Tim Evans, *Principal*
EMP: 3
SALES (corp-wide): 1.6MM Privately Held
WEB: www.geneseorepublic.com
SIC: 2759 2711 Commercial printing; newspapers
PA: Liberty Group Publishing
108 W 1st St
Geneseo IL 61254
309 944-1779

(G-2806)
RAILCRAFT NEXIM DESIGN
12165 N 850th Ave (61238-9293)
PHONE..................309 937-2360
Richard Nelson, *Owner*
▲ EMP: 3
SALES: 1MM Privately Held
SIC: 2599 5712 Factory furniture & fixtures; furniture stores

(G-2807)
SCHNOWSKE & SONS TRUCKING INC
10507 Illinois Highway 82 (61238-9480)
PHONE..................309 937-3323
Larry Schnowske, *President*
Troy Schnowski, *Principal*
EMP: 2
SALES (est): 258.4K Privately Held
SIC: 2077 Animal & marine fats & oils

Cameron
Warren County

(G-2808)
MIDWEST AWNINGS INC
2201 155th St (61423-9543)
P.O. Box 1382, Galesburg (61402-1382)
PHONE..................309 762-3339
Mike Haun, *President*
EMP: 8
SQ FT: 7,000
SALES (est): 902.6K Privately Held
SIC: 2394 3444 5999 5199 Awnings, fabric: made from purchased materials; sheet metalwork; awnings; tarpaulins

Camp Point
Adams County

(G-2809)
AUNTIE MMMMS
105 N Ohio St (62320-1365)
PHONE..................217 509-6012
Jeffrey Green, *Owner*
EMP: 4 EST: 2009
SALES (est): 201.2K Privately Held
SIC: 2051 Cakes, bakery: except frozen

(G-2810)
ELLIOTT PUBLISHING INC
202 E State St (62320-1114)
P.O. Box 200 (62320-0200)
PHONE..................217 593-6515
Jim Elliott, *President*
Marcia Elliott, *Vice Pres*
EMP: 6
SALES (est): 361.8K Privately Held
SIC: 2711 Newspapers, publishing & printing

(G-2811)
GOLDEN LOCKER INC (PA)
1880 E 2400th St (62320-2130)
PHONE..................217 696-4456
Bob Albers, *President*
EMP: 8 EST: 1943
SALES (est): 661.9K Privately Held
WEB: www.goldenlocker.com
SIC: 2011 2013 Meat packing plants; sausages & other prepared meats

(G-2812)
TRI-STATE TOOL & DESIGN INC
2537 N 2200th Ave (62320-2515)
P.O. Box 221, Golden (62339-0221)
PHONE..................217 696-2477
Bob Tangerose, *President*
EMP: 2
SQ FT: 3,000
SALES (est): 214.7K Privately Held
SIC: 3544 Special dies & tools

Campbell Hill
Jackson County

(G-2813)
APAC II LLC
39 Schatte Rd (62916-2509)
PHONE..................618 426-1338
Abraham J Beachy, *Mng Member*
EMP: 7
SALES (est): 671.9K Privately Held
SIC: 3089 Plastics products

(G-2814)
DAY STAR SYSTEMS LLC
Also Called: North Star Productions
14226 Highway 4 (62916-2340)
PHONE..................618 426-1868
Ken Schlabach, *Mng Member*
▲ EMP: 5
SALES (est): 765.6K Privately Held
SIC: 3211 Skylight glass

(G-2815)
DUSTY LANE WOOD PRODUCTS
295 Dusty Ln (62916-2421)
PHONE..................618 426-9045
Ruben Mast, *Owner*
Carolyn Mast, *Owner*
EMP: 2
SALES: 330K Privately Held
SIC: 2499 Decorative wood & woodwork

(G-2816)
MAST HARNESS SHOP
Also Called: Sunny Brook Farm
488 Post Oak Rd (62916-2009)
PHONE..................217 543-3463
Eli F Schlabach, *General Ptnr*
Kenneth S Schlabach, *Ltd Ptnr*
Merle S Schlabach, *Ltd Ptnr*
Rebecca S Schlabach, *Ltd Ptnr*
Rosemary S Schlabach, *Ltd Ptnr*
EMP: 25
SQ FT: 10,808
SALES (est): 2.2MM Privately Held
SIC: 3199 5191 Harness or harness parts; harness equipment

(G-2817)
MILLCRAFT
2116 Trico Rd (62916-2111)
PHONE..................618 426-9819
Gary Miller, *Owner*
Dorothea Miller, *Co-Owner*
EMP: 5
SALES (est): 200K Privately Held
SIC: 2434 Wood kitchen cabinets

(G-2818)
MISSELHORN WELDING & MACHINES
310 S Main St (62916-2525)
PHONE..................618 426-3714
David Misselhorn, *Owner*
EMP: 3
SALES: 200K Privately Held
SIC: 7692 Welding repair

(G-2819)
WK MACHINE
Also Called: Wk Drainage
98 Catalpa Ln (62916-2257)
PHONE..................618 426-3423
Edwin Beachy, *Owner*
EMP: 2
SALES (est): 235.6K Privately Held
SIC: 3599 Machine shop, jobbing & repair

Canton
Fulton County

(G-2820)
ABEL VAULT & MONUMENT CO INC
1001 E Linn St (61520-9401)
P.O. Box 452 (61520-0452)
PHONE..................309 647-0105
Bill Ayers, *Manager*
EMP: 5
SALES (corp-wide): 2.3MM Privately Held
SIC: 5999 3272 Monuments, finished to custom order; concrete products
PA: Abel Vault & Monument Co Inc
1917 N 8th St
Pekin IL
309 346-4186

(G-2821)
BASEMENT DEWATERING SYSTEMS
3100 N Main St (61520-1043)
P.O. Box 160 (61520-0160)
PHONE..................309 647-0331
Jerry Jarnagin, *President*
Edward L Ketcham, *Treasurer*
Dennis Dawson, *Admin Sec*
EMP: 16
SQ FT: 6,600
SALES (est): 2.1MM Privately Held
SIC: 1521 6531 3564 2851 General remodeling, single-family houses; real estate agents & managers; blowers & fans; paints & allied products

(G-2822)
CAMILLES OF CANTON INC
1400 S Avenue B (61520-3412)
PHONE..................309 647-7403
Ralph Plunk Jr, *President*
Todd Miller, *Vice Pres*
Camille Plunk, *Treasurer*
Marsha Miller, *Admin Sec*
EMP: 7
SQ FT: 6,000
SALES (est): 219.6K Privately Held
SIC: 5999 5699 2395 Trophies & plaques; T-shirts, custom printed; embroidery & art needlework

(G-2823)
CANTON REDI-MIX INC
Also Called: Lb Staley Elmwood
22381 N State Highway 78 (61520-8376)
PHONE..................309 668-2261
James M Curry, *President*
Jon Vrabel, *Vice Pres*
Adam Hoff, *Treasurer*
EMP: 12
SQ FT: 40,000
SALES (est): 1MM Privately Held
SIC: 3273 Ready-mixed concrete

(G-2824)
CANTON REDI-MIX INC
1130 W Locust St (61520-9681)
PHONE..................309 647-0019
Lydia E Davis, *President*
Patrick J Davis, *Vice Pres*
EMP: 25
SALES (est): 2.6MM Privately Held
SIC: 3273 Ready-mixed concrete

(G-2825)
COOK POLYMER TECHNOLOGY
225 S 3rd Ave (61520-2775)
PHONE..................309 740-2342
EMP: 3
SALES (est): 388.2K Privately Held
SIC: 3841 Surgical & medical instruments

(G-2826)
FULTON COUNTY REHABILITATION (PA)
500 N Main St (61520-1830)
PHONE..................309 647-6510
Rex Lewis, *Exec Dir*
EMP: 50
SQ FT: 14,000
SALES: 1.6MM Privately Held
SIC: 8361 8331 2448 Rehabilitation center, residential: health care incidental; job training & vocational rehabilitation services; wood pallets & skids

(G-2827)
JARVIS WELDING CO
124 E Pine St (61520-2799)
PHONE..................309 647-0033
Brad Jarvis, *Partner*
Randy Jarvis, *Partner*
EMP: 4
SQ FT: 4,800
SALES (est): 518.2K Privately Held
WEB: www.jarvisboiler.com
SIC: 7699 7692 3441 Boiler repair shop; aircraft & heavy equipment repair services; welding repair; fabricated structural metal

(G-2828)
MARTIN PUBLISHING CO
Also Called: Fulton County Democrat
31 S Main St (61520-2605)
P.O. Box 191, Lewistown (61542-0191)
PHONE..................309 647-9501
Robert Martin, *Manager*
EMP: 5
SALES (corp-wide): 2.5MM Privately Held
SIC: 2711 Newspapers: publishing only, not printed on site
PA: Martin Publishing Co.
217 W Market St
Havana IL 62644
309 543-2000

(G-2829)
MARTIN PUBLISHING CO
Also Called: Martin Publishing Company
31 S Main St (61520-2605)
PHONE..................309 647-9501
EMP: 15
SALES (corp-wide): 2.5MM Privately Held
SIC: 2711 Newspapers: publishing only, not printed on site
PA: Martin Publishing Co.
217 W Market St
Havana IL 62644
309 543-2000

(G-2830)
MCCLOSKEY EYMAN MLONE MFG SVCS
37 S 1st Ave (61520-2610)
PHONE..................309 647-4000
John Eyman, *President*
Becky Eyman, *Treasurer*
EMP: 7
SQ FT: 14,000
SALES: 400K Privately Held
SIC: 7699 7692 Industrial machinery & equipment repair; welding repair

(G-2831)
PRO GRAPHICS INK
322 N 15th Ave (61520-2331)
PHONE..................309 647-2526
Brenda Promen, *Principal*
EMP: 3
SALES (est): 186.4K Privately Held
SIC: 2752 Commercial printing, offset

Capron
Boone County

(G-2832)
CAPRON MFG CO (PA)
200 Burr Oak Rd (61012-9600)
PHONE..................815 569-2301
John Svabek, *President*
Pat Stanley, *Facilities Mgr*
Dan Lucas, *Opers Staff*
Lawrence Svabek, *Admin Sec*
▲ EMP: 60
SQ FT: 75,000
SALES (est): 9.5MM Privately Held
SIC: 3471 Chromium plating of metals or formed products; plating of metals or formed products

(G-2833)
K K O INC
100 E Grove St (61012-7710)
P.O. Box 187 (61012-0187)
PHONE..................................815 569-2324
Eliza Moravec, *Principal*
EMP: 2 **EST:** 2010
SALES (est): 206K **Privately Held**
SIC: 2599 Furniture & fixtures

(G-2834)
KEATING OF CHICAGO INC
100 E Grove St (61012-7710)
P.O. Box 187 (61012-0187)
PHONE..................................815 569-2324
Jack Lee, *Branch Mgr*
EMP: 25
SALES (corp-wide): 27.1MM **Privately Held**
SIC: 3589 3641 3634 3564 Commercial cooking & foodwarming equipment; electric lamps; electric housewares & fans; blowers & fans; food products machinery
PA: Keating Of Chicago, Inc.
 8901 W 50th St
 Mc Cook IL 60525
 708 246-3000

(G-2835)
LEROY E RITZERT
9092 Randall Rd (61012-9611)
PHONE..................................815 737-8210
Leroy E Ritzert, *Principal*
EMP: 3
SALES (est): 112K **Privately Held**
SIC: 2711 Newspapers, publishing & printing

(G-2836)
MELINDA I RHODES (PA)
15423 Capron Rd (61012-9519)
PHONE..................................815 569-2789
Melinda Rhodes, *Owner*
EMP: 2
SALES (est): 210.7K **Privately Held**
SIC: 2051 Bread, cake & related products

(G-2837)
SURFACE MANUFACTURING COMPANY
135 S 4th St (61012-8702)
P.O. Box 410 (61012-0410)
PHONE..................................815 569-2362
Patrick Bryan, *President*
Fred Bryan, *Vice Pres*
EMP: 18
SQ FT: 20,000
SALES (est): 1.6MM **Privately Held**
SIC: 3471 Chromium plating of metals or formed products; plating of metals or formed products

Carbondale
Jackson County

(G-2838)
ADAMS PRINTING CO
315 E College St (62901-3282)
PHONE..................................618 529-2396
Francis Ward Adams Jr, *Owner*
EMP: 5
SQ FT: 3,000
SALES (est): 300K **Privately Held**
SIC: 2752 2789 Lithographing on metal; bookbinding & related work

(G-2839)
CARBONDALE NIGHT LIFE
Also Called: Carbondale Times
2015 W Main St Ste 105 (62901-2073)
PHONE..................................618 549-2799
Jason Thomas, *Mng Member*
EMP: 12
SALES (est): 664.7K **Privately Held**
SIC: 2711 Newspapers: publishing only, not printed on site

(G-2840)
DAILY EGYPTIAN SIU NEWSPAPER
1100 Lincoln Dr Rm 1259 (62901-4306)
PHONE..................................618 536-3311
EMP: 75
SALES (est): 2.5MM **Privately Held**
SIC: 2711 5994 Newspapers, publishing & printing; newsstand

(G-2841)
EMAC INC
Also Called: EQUIPMENT MONITOR & CONTROL
2390 Emac Ln (62902-7293)
P.O. Box 2042 (62902-2042)
PHONE..................................618 529-4525
Eric Rossi, *President*
◆ **EMP:** 42
SQ FT: 8,000
SALES: 7MM **Privately Held**
SIC: 7371 3571 3823 8711 Computer software systems analysis & design, custom; computers, digital, analog or hybrid; computer interface equipment for industrial process control; engineering services; switchgear & switchboard apparatus; electronic research

(G-2842)
ET SIMONDS MATERIALS COMPANY
1500 N Oakland Ave (62901-5518)
P.O. Box 3928 (62902-3928)
PHONE..................................618 457-8191
Stephen B Simonds, *President*
Kathryn S Stevens, *Admin Sec*
EMP: 40
SALES (est): 2MM
SALES (corp-wide): 53.2MM **Privately Held**
SIC: 2951 Asphalt & asphaltic paving mixtures (not from refineries)
PA: The Simonds Group Ltd
 1500 N Oakland Ave
 Carbondale IL 62901
 618 457-8191

(G-2843)
H & H DRILLING CO
59 Pineview Rd (62901-5429)
PHONE..................................618 529-3697
Lester Holcomb, *President*
Timothy Holcomb, *Vice Pres*
EMP: 3 **EST:** 1999
SALES (est): 274.3K **Privately Held**
SIC: 3533 Drill rigs

(G-2844)
HAAKES AWNING
2525 Edgewood Ln (62901-6309)
PHONE..................................618 529-4808
Larry C Haake, *Owner*
EMP: 3
SALES (est): 100K **Privately Held**
SIC: 2211 2394 2221 5999 Awning stripes, cotton; canvas & related products; broadwoven fabric mills, manmade; awnings

(G-2845)
HENRY PRINTING INC
975 Charles Rd (62901-6300)
P.O. Box 2706 (62902-2706)
PHONE..................................618 529-3040
John M Henry, *President*
EMP: 9
SQ FT: 7,800
SALES (est): 1.6MM **Privately Held**
SIC: 2752 7334 Commercial printing, offset; photocopying & duplicating services

(G-2846)
ILLINI READY MIX INC (PA)
801 W Industrial Park Rd (62901-5515)
P.O. Box 2107 (62902-2107)
PHONE..................................618 734-0287
Edward Simonds, *President*
Katherine Stevens, *Vice Pres*
Michael McClay, *Treasurer*
EMP: 1
SALES (est): 2.8MM **Privately Held**
SIC: 3273 Ready-mixed concrete

(G-2847)
INTERTAPE POLYMER CORP
Also Called: Intertape Polymer Group
2200 N Mcroy Dr (62901-5628)
PHONE..................................618 549-2131
Craig Hoedel, *Manager*
Jarrod Knapp, *Maintence Staff*
EMP: 70
SALES (corp-wide): 1.1B **Privately Held**
SIC: 2672 Tape, pressure sensitive: made from purchased materials
HQ: Intertape Polymer Corp.
 100 Paramount Dr Ste 300
 Sarasota FL 34232
 888 898-7834

(G-2848)
KATY LYNN WINERY LLC
1801 Sneed Rd (62902-0434)
PHONE..................................618 964-1818
Debra Finch, *Principal*
EMP: 3
SALES (est): 222.9K **Privately Held**
SIC: 2084 Wines

(G-2849)
LEE ENTERPRISES INCORPORATED
Also Called: Southern Illinoisan
710 N Illinois Ave (62901-1283)
P.O. Box 2108 (62902-2108)
PHONE..................................618 529-5454
Dennis Derossett, *Publisher*
Marilyn Halstead, *Editor*
EMP: 200
SALES (corp-wide): 509.8MM **Publicly Held**
SIC: 2711 2752 7313 Newspapers: publishing only, not printed on site; commercial printing, lithographic; newspaper advertising representative
PA: Lee Enterprises, Incorporated
 4600 E 53rd St
 Davenport IA 52807
 563 383-2100

(G-2850)
MAC-WELD INC
Also Called: Mac-Weld Partnership
612 San Diego Rd (62901-0611)
PHONE..................................618 529-1828
Gerald Kaufmann, *President*
Clinton W Taylor, *Vice Pres*
Lynette Taylor, *Treasurer*
Debra Kaufmann, *Admin Sec*
EMP: 9
SALES (est): 450K **Privately Held**
SIC: 5013 7539 5084 3599 Automotive engines & engine parts; machine shop, automotive; welding machinery & equipment; machine shop, jobbing & repair

(G-2851)
NOTEWORTHY GROUP INC
Also Called: Beautiful Displays
2370 N Mcroy Dr (62901-5629)
PHONE..................................618 549-2505
Todd Freeman, *President*
Kevin Graham, *Vice Pres*
Brenda Henderson, *Admin Sec*
EMP: 8
SQ FT: 2,000
SALES: 1,000K **Privately Held**
SIC: 3993 Signs & advertising specialties

(G-2852)
OTIS ELEVATOR COMPANY
201 W Kennicott St (62901)
PHONE..................................618 529-3411
Charles Johnson, *Branch Mgr*
EMP: 12
SALES (corp-wide): 10B **Publicly Held**
SIC: 5084 7699 3534 Elevators; professional instrument repair services; dumbwaiters
HQ: Otis Elevator Company
 1 Carrier Pl
 Farmington CT 06032
 860 674-3000

(G-2853)
OVIS LOADER ATTACHMENTS INC
1555 S Wall St (62901-3732)
PHONE..................................618 203-2757
William Wright, *President*
Nathan Wright, *Vice Pres*
EMP: 3 **EST:** 2012
SALES (est): 342.3K **Privately Held**
SIC: 3531 Subsoiler attachments, tractor mounted

(G-2854)
PRAIRIE FARMS DAIRY INC
742 N Illinois Ave (62901-1283)
PHONE..................................618 457-4167
Ron Diuquid, *General Mgr*
Scott Judd, *Plant Supt*
EMP: 34
SALES (corp-wide): 1.7B **Privately Held**
WEB: www.prairiefarmsdairy.com
SIC: 2026 Milk processing (pasteurizing, homogenizing, bottling)
PA: Prairie Farms Dairy, Inc.
 3744 Staunton Rd
 Edwardsville IL 62025
 618 659-5700

(G-2855)
PRINTING PLANT
606 S Illinois Ave Ste 1 (62901-2852)
PHONE..................................618 529-3115
James Myers, *Partner*
Larry Fehmel, *Partner*
Sharon Fehmel, *Partner*
Cynthia Myers, *Partner*
EMP: 4 **EST:** 1975
SQ FT: 1,200
SALES (est): 370K **Privately Held**
SIC: 2752 Commercial printing, offset

(G-2856)
RJM MANUFACTURING INC
Also Called: Tara Tape
2200 N Mcroy Dr (62901-5628)
PHONE..................................215 736-3644
Thomas Dodd, *President*
John Leberatore, *Vice Pres*
Mikel T Dodd, *Treasurer*
Benson Goldberg, *Admin Sec*
▲ **EMP:** 54
SQ FT: 90,000
SALES (est): 17.1MM
SALES (corp-wide): 1.1B **Privately Held**
SIC: 2672 Tape, pressure sensitive: made from purchased materials
PA: Groupe Intertape Polymer Inc, Le
 9999 Boul Cavendish Bureau 200
 Saint-Laurent QC H4M 2

(G-2857)
RUDON ENTERPRISES INC
Also Called: Carbondale Trophy Co
118 N Illinois Ave (62901-1450)
PHONE..................................618 457-0441
Ruth Dalessio, *President*
EMP: 4
SQ FT: 5,000
SALES (est): 250K **Privately Held**
SIC: 3914 3999 Trophies, plated (all metals); plaques, picture, laminated

(G-2858)
SHUTTER BAG USA
193 Peachtree Ln (62902-8017)
PHONE..................................618 967-6247
EMP: 3 **EST:** 2018
SALES (est): 187.9K **Privately Held**
SIC: 3442 Shutters, door or window: metal

(G-2859)
SKELCHER CONCRETE PRODUCTS
490 San Diego Rd (62901-0811)
PHONE..................................618 457-2930
Cliff Skelcher, *Partner*
Paul M Skelcher, *Partner*
EMP: 5 **EST:** 1965
SQ FT: 5,000
SALES (est): 609.3K **Privately Held**
SIC: 3272 Manhole covers or frames, concrete; septic tanks, concrete; ties, railroad: concrete

(G-2860)
STEVE C GOUGH
Also Called: Little River Research & Design
550 N University Ave (62901-1375)
PHONE..................................618 529-7423
Steve Gough, *Owner*
EMP: 4
SALES (est): 333.6K **Privately Held**
SIC: 3999 8732 Education aids, devices & supplies; educational research

GEOGRAPHIC SECTION

Carlock - Mclean County (G-2888)

(G-2861)
SURE-RESPONSE INC
1075 N Reed Station Rd (62902-7339)
PHONE.................................888 530-5668
Curtis Baid, *President*
EMP: 2
SALES (est): 230.6K **Privately Held**
SIC: 3663 Transmitter-receivers, radio

(G-2862)
THOMAS PUBLISHING PRINTING DIV
701 W Main St (62901-2643)
PHONE.................................618 351-6655
Dan Sitarz, *Principal*
EMP: 2
SALES (est): 218.9K **Privately Held**
SIC: 2759 2741 Commercial printing; miscellaneous publishing

(G-2863)
WE INTERNATIONAL
54 Oakview Rd (62901-8125)
PHONE.................................618 549-1784
William W Liao, *Owner*
Elizabeth Liao, *Owner*
▲ **EMP:** 3
SALES (est): 283.4K **Privately Held**
SIC: 3629 Electronic generation equipment

(G-2864)
WEATHERFORD SIGNS
219 Weatherford Ln (62902-7780)
P.O. Box 2995 (62902-2995)
PHONE.................................618 529-2000
Larry Weatherford, *Owner*
EMP: 5
SQ FT: 1,800
SALES (est): 390.3K **Privately Held**
SIC: 3993 Electric signs

(G-2865)
WINN STAR INC
395 S Wolf Creek Rd Fl 1 (62902-0551)
P.O. Box 213, Marion (62959-0213)
PHONE.................................618 964-1811
Thomas J Throgmorton, *President*
Gwen Kelly, *Corp Secy*
Julia Throgmorton, *Vice Pres*
EMP: 5
SQ FT: 20,000
SALES (est): 250K **Privately Held**
SIC: 3812 2899 Search & navigation equipment; chemical preparations

(G-2866)
Z-PATCH INC
800 W Industrial Park Rd (62901-5514)
P.O. Box 2707 (62902-2707)
PHONE.................................618 529-2431
Greg Sprehe, *President*
Donald Wright, *Exec VP*
Amy Galloway, *Controller*
EMP: 20
SQ FT: 10,000
SALES (est): 1.4MM **Privately Held**
SIC: 3545 Machine tool accessories

Carlinville
Macoupin County

(G-2867)
AREA DIESEL SERVICE INC (PA)
Also Called: ADC
1300 University St (62626-9620)
PHONE.................................217 854-2641
Val Leefers, *President*
Laurie Despain, *Purch Mgr*
Von Leefers, *Treasurer*
Dave Cooonrod, *Sales Mgr*
Lynn Emery, *Sales Staff*
▲ **EMP:** 38
SQ FT: 10,000
SALES (est): 11.5MM **Privately Held**
SIC: 5531 5084 3724 3714 Truck equipment & parts; engines & parts, diesel; aircraft engines & engine parts; motor vehicle parts & accessories; turbines & turbine generator sets

(G-2868)
CARLINVILLE WASTE WATER PLANTS
1345 Mayo St (62626-1966)
PHONE.................................217 854-6506
Pat Bouillon, *Superintendent*
EMP: 4
SALES (est): 350K **Privately Held**
SIC: 3589 Sewage & water treatment equipment

(G-2869)
CENTRAL ILLINOIS STEEL COMPANY (PA)
Also Called: Cisco
21050 Route 4 (62626-3525)
P.O. Box 78 (62626-0078)
PHONE.................................217 854-3251
Daniel M Millard, *President*
Mark Millard, *Vice Pres*
Tim Millard, *Vice Pres*
Chris Millard, *Admin Sec*
EMP: 36 **EST:** 1967
SQ FT: 80,000
SALES: 45MM **Privately Held**
SIC: 5051 3441 Steel; fabricated structural metal

(G-2870)
CENTRAL MACHINING INC
502 W 1st North St (62626-1683)
PHONE.................................217 854-6646
Jon Theivagt, *Vice Pres*
EMP: 2
SALES (est): 391.5K **Privately Held**
SIC: 3599 Machine shop, jobbing & repair

(G-2871)
CHARLES K EICHEN
Also Called: Eichen's Saw Mill
20002 Claremont Rd (62626-4046)
PHONE.................................217 854-9751
Mike K Eichen, *President*
Steve Eichen, *Vice Pres*
EMP: 7
SALES (est): 339K **Privately Held**
SIC: 5211 2421 5031 Lumber & other building materials; sawmills & planing mills, general; lumber, plywood & millwork; lumber: rough, dressed & finished

(G-2872)
CUBBY HOLE OF CARLINVILLE INC (PA)
Also Called: Cubby Hole, The
12472 Route 108 (62626-3615)
PHONE.................................217 854-8511
Dale Tosh, *President*
Nancy Tosh, *Admin Sec*
EMP: 14
SQ FT: 6,000
SALES (est): 1MM **Privately Held**
SIC: 2396 2395 3993 Screen printing on fabric articles; embroidery & art needlework; signs & advertising specialties

(G-2873)
EAST SIDE JERSEY DAIRY INC (HQ)
1100 Broadway (62626-1183)
PHONE.................................217 854-2547
Jim Turner, *General Mgr*
Terry Carter, *Principal*
EMP: 30 **EST:** 1920
SQ FT: 10,000
SALES: 62MM
SALES (corp-wide): 1.7B **Privately Held**
WEB: www.prairiefarms.com
SIC: 2026 Milk processing (pasteurizing, homogenizing, bottling)
PA: Prairie Farms Dairy, Inc.
3744 Staunton Rd
Edwardsville IL 62025
618 659-5700

(G-2874)
EICHEN LUMBER CO INC
20002 Claremont Rd (62626-4046)
PHONE.................................217 854-9751
Michael Eichen, *President*
Charles K Eichen, *Owner*
Steve Eichen, *Admin Sec*
EMP: 7 **EST:** 1962

SALES: 500K **Privately Held**
SIC: 2421 2426 Sawmills & planing mills, general; hardwood dimension & flooring mills

(G-2875)
EXXON MOBIL CORPORATION
Monterey Coal
14491 Brushy Mound Rd (62626)
PHONE.................................217 854-3291
Howard Schultz, *Manager*
EMP: 300
SALES (corp-wide): 264.9B **Publicly Held**
SIC: 1241 1222 Coal mining services; bituminous coal-underground mining
PA: Exxon Mobil Corporation
5959 Las Colinas Blvd
Irving TX 75039
972 940-6000

(G-2876)
HUYEAR TRUCKING INC
708 Sumner St (62626-1169)
PHONE.................................217 854-3551
Robert H Huyear, *President*
Wilma Huyear, *Corp Secy*
EMP: 6
SALES (est): 370K **Privately Held**
SIC: 4212 1422 5191 6221 Local trucking, without storage; crushed & broken limestone; fertilizer & fertilizer materials; commodity brokers, contracts

(G-2877)
INTEGRATED MEDIA INC
Also Called: Illini Tech Services
21709 Route 4 (62626-3535)
PHONE.................................217 854-6260
Kevin Walker, *President*
Matthew Hupp, *Info Tech Mgr*
EMP: 10
SQ FT: 2,000
SALES (est): 953.3K **Privately Held**
SIC: 7374 7311 2754 Computer graphics service; advertising consultant; commercial printing, gravure

(G-2878)
KUCHAR COMBINE PERFORMANCE
Also Called: Kuchar High Perfomance Parts
18995 Route 4 (62626-3800)
PHONE.................................217 854-9838
George Kuchar, *President*
EMP: 4
SQ FT: 3,600
SALES (est): 311.3K **Privately Held**
SIC: 3523 4731 Combines (harvester-threshers); freight transportation arrangement

(G-2879)
MACOUPIN COUNTY ENQUIRER INC
125 E Main St (62626-1726)
P.O. Box 200 (62626-0200)
PHONE.................................217 854-2534
Christopher Schmitt, *President*
Susan Braham, *Vice Pres*
EMP: 20 **EST:** 1852
SQ FT: 30,000
SALES (est): 1.3MM **Privately Held**
WEB: www.enquirerdemocrat.com
SIC: 2711 2752 2791 2789 Newspapers, publishing & printing; commercial printing, offset; typesetting; bookbinding & related work; commercial printing

(G-2880)
MACOUPIN ENERGY LLC
14300 Brushy Mound Rd (62626-2385)
PHONE.................................217 854-3291
Todd Leverton, *Manager*
EMP: 13
SALES (est): 1MM **Privately Held**
SIC: 1241 Coal mining services

(G-2881)
MACOUPIN ENERGY LLC
Also Called: Shay Mine No. 1
14300 Brushy Mound Rd (62626-2385)
PHONE.................................217 854-3291
Todd Leverton, *Branch Mgr*
EMP: 115

SALES (corp-wide): 841.5MM **Publicly Held**
SIC: 1241 Coal mining services
HQ: Macoupin Energy Llc
211 N Broadway Ste 2600
Saint Louis MO 63102
314 932-6112

(G-2882)
MADISON FARMS BUTTER COMPANY (PA)
1100 Broadway (62626-1183)
PHONE.................................217 854-2547
Paul Benne, *Partner*
EMP: 21
SALES (est): 2.3MM **Privately Held**
SIC: 2021 Butter oil

(G-2883)
PM MACHINE SHOP
706 N Broad St (62626-1023)
PHONE.................................217 854-3504
Pete Maguire, *Owner*
EMP: 1 **EST:** 1966
SQ FT: 2,000
SALES (est): 250K **Privately Held**
SIC: 3599 Machine shop, jobbing & repair

(G-2884)
WILLS MILLING AND HARDWOOD INC
9674 Colt Rd (62626-2240)
PHONE.................................217 854-9056
Bryan Wills, *President*
Charles Wills, *President*
Brian Wills, *General Mgr*
Scott Wills, *Vice Pres*
Amy Wills, *Admin Sec*
EMP: 24
SQ FT: 30,000
SALES (est): 3.6MM **Privately Held**
WEB: www.willsmilling.com
SIC: 2434 Wood kitchen cabinets

Carlock
Mclean County

(G-2885)
COVINGTON SERVICE INSTALLATION
1907 County Road 275 N (61725-9014)
PHONE.................................309 376-4921
Wayne Covington, *Owner*
EMP: 3
SALES (est): 526.5K **Privately Held**
SIC: 3589 Garbage disposers & compactors, commercial

(G-2886)
DANIEL MFG INC
273 County Road 1850 E (61725-9013)
PHONE.................................309 963-4227
Tim Daniel, *President*
Lou Daniel, *Corp Secy*
Mark Jones, *Director*
Lori Geldes, *Admin Asst*
EMP: 12
SQ FT: 30,000
SALES (est): 2MM **Privately Held**
SIC: 7692 3444 Welding repair; sheet metalwork

(G-2887)
J AND J PRFMCE POWDR COATING
410 E Washington St (61725-9440)
PHONE.................................309 376-4340
James Dolan, *President*
EMP: 2
SALES (est): 320.7K **Privately Held**
SIC: 3479 Coating of metals & formed products

(G-2888)
WHITE OAK ENERGY LLC
11827 E 2100 North Rd (61725-9513)
PHONE.................................815 824-2182
Michael Polsky,
EMP: 2
SALES (est): 329.1K **Privately Held**
SIC: 3621 Windmills, electric generating

Carlyle
Clinton County

(G-2889)
CARLYLE SAND & GRAVEL LTD
11842 State Route 127 (62231-3314)
P.O. Box 106 (62231-0106)
PHONE.....................................618 594-8263
Brian Bailey, *Principal*
EMP: 3 **EST:** 2008
SALES (est): 279.5K **Privately Held**
SIC: 1442 Construction sand & gravel

(G-2890)
HUELS OIL COMPANY
16320 Old Us Highway 50 (62231-2408)
PHONE.....................................877 338-6277
Ronald Huels, *President*
Geralyn Huels, *Vice Pres*
EMP: 12
SQ FT: 8,000
SALES (est): 18.3MM **Privately Held**
SIC: 5172 2992 Fuel oil; lubricating oils

(G-2891)
JERRY BERRY CONTRACTING CO
1691 Kane St (62231-1128)
PHONE.....................................618 594-3339
EMP: 4 **EST:** 1969
SALES (est): 230K **Privately Held**
SIC: 1771 1794 3273 Concrete Contractor Excavation Contractor Mfg Ready-Mixed Concrete

(G-2892)
L&P PLASTICS
2510 Franklin St (62231-2402)
PHONE.....................................618 594-3692
Dan Piasecki, *Mfg Staff*
EMP: 4
SALES (est): 107.6K **Privately Held**
SIC: 3089 Injection molding of plastics

(G-2893)
LUEBBERS WELDING & MFG INC
2420 Old State Rd (62231-2412)
P.O. Box 248 (62231-0248)
PHONE.....................................618 594-2489
Ron Luebbers, *President*
Dana Luebbers, *Corp Secy*
Kevin Luebbers, *Vice Pres*
EMP: 15 **EST:** 1958
SQ FT: 20,000
SALES (est): 1.6MM **Privately Held**
WEB: www.luebberswelding.com
SIC: 3599 3444 3443 7692 Machine shop, jobbing & repair; concrete forms, sheet metal; tanks, standard or custom fabricated: metal plate; welding repair

(G-2894)
QUAD-COUNTY READY MIX CORP
2090 Washington St (62231-1624)
P.O. Box 24 (62231-0024)
PHONE.....................................618 594-2732
Charles Meyer, *Manager*
EMP: 10
SALES (corp-wide): 16.1MM **Privately Held**
SIC: 3273 Ready-mixed concrete
PA: Quad-County Ready Mix Corp.
300 W 12th St
Okawville IL 62271
618 243-6430

(G-2895)
SEIFFERTS LOCKER & MEAT PROC
Also Called: Seifferts Meat Proc & Lckr
1370 Fairfax St (62231-1705)
PHONE.....................................618 594-3921
Michael Seiffert, *Owner*
EMP: 18 **EST:** 1967
SQ FT: 2,400
SALES (est): 165K **Privately Held**
WEB: www.scottsprocessing.com
SIC: 2013 5421 5147 Sausages & other prepared meats; meat markets, including freezer provisioners; meats, fresh

(G-2896)
SIMONTON HARDWOOD LUMBER LLC
16515 Post Oak Rd (62231-3033)
PHONE.....................................618 594-2132
William C Simonton, *Mng Member*
Donna Simonton, *Mng Member*
EMP: 11 **EST:** 1961
SALES: 3.8MM **Privately Held**
WEB: www.simontonhardwoodlumber.com
SIC: 2421 2448 2426 3496 Sawmills & planing mills, general; wood pallets & skids; hardwood dimension & flooring mills; mats & matting

(G-2897)
UNION BANNER PUBLISHING LTD
17549 County Farm Rd (62231-6303)
PHONE.....................................618 594-3131
John Perrine, *President*
EMP: 7 **EST:** 1949
SALES (est): 365.1K **Privately Held**
SIC: 2711 Newspapers, publishing & printing

(G-2898)
WISE CO INC
3750 Industrial Dr (62231-6124)
PHONE.....................................618 594-4091
John Cooper, *Opers Mgr*
John Copper, *Manager*
EMP: 9
SALES (est): 1MM
SALES (corp-wide): 58.6MM **Privately Held**
SIC: 5013 2531 Seat covers; public building & related furniture
PA: The Wise Co Inc
79 S 2nd St
Memphis TN 38103
901 388-0155

Carmi
White County

(G-2899)
ARMSTRONG TOOL LLC
Also Called: Armstrong Hydraulic
1403 E Main St (62821-2109)
PHONE.....................................618 382-4184
Lois Duckworth, *Branch Mgr*
EMP: 7
SALES (est): 653.4K
SALES (corp-wide): 8.7MM **Privately Held**
SIC: 1389 Oil field services
PA: Armstrong Tool, Llc
24 Wooded Gate Dr
Dallas TX 75230
479 474-0181

(G-2900)
BROOKSTONE RESOURCES INC
1615 Oak St (62821-1371)
PHONE.....................................618 382-2893
Rich Kingston, *Partner*
EMP: 4 **EST:** 2001
SALES (est): 381.4K **Privately Held**
SIC: 1311 Crude petroleum production

(G-2901)
CAMPBELL ENERGY LLC
1238 County Road 1500 N (62821-4630)
PHONE.....................................618 382-3939
Matt Campbell,
Jack Campbell,
John Campbell,
EMP: 4
SALES (est): 992K **Privately Held**
SIC: 1389 Oil field services

(G-2902)
CARMI TIMES
323 E Main St (62821-1810)
P.O. Box 190 (62821-0190)
PHONE.....................................618 382-4176
Richard Beskow, *Editor*
Rhonda N Beason, *Prdtn Mgr*
Barry Cleveland, *Manager*
Cheryl Trout, *Manager*
EMP: 12
SALES (est): 398.6K **Privately Held**
WEB: www.carmitimes.com
SIC: 2711 Newspapers, publishing & printing

(G-2903)
CARTER ANNA BROOKS LLC
1238 County Road 1500 N (62821-4630)
PHONE.....................................618 382-3939
EMP: 3
SALES (est): 165.2K **Privately Held**
SIC: 1311 Crude Petroleum/Natural Gas Production

(G-2904)
ELASTEC INC (PA)
Also Called: Elastec / American Marine
1309 W Main St (62821-1389)
PHONE.....................................618 382-2525
Jeff Cantrell, *President*
Duane Bennish, *Division Mgr*
Stewart Ellis, *Vice Pres*
Tracy Nix, *Purch Agent*
Lee Beckel, *Research*
◆ **EMP:** 130
SQ FT: 57,000
SALES (est): 19.3MM **Privately Held**
SIC: 3599 3567 Custom machinery; incinerators, metal: domestic or commercial

(G-2905)
EVERGREEN ENERGY LLC
645 W Illinois Hwy 14 (62821)
PHONE.....................................618 384-9295
Edward Bruce,
Gary Evans,
Scott Pugsley,
EMP: 4
SALES (est): 458.1K **Privately Held**
SIC: 1381 Drilling oil & gas wells

(G-2906)
GHOLSON PUMP & REPAIRS CO
725 County Road 1450 N (62821-4814)
PHONE.....................................618 382-4730
EMP: 3
SALES (est): 255.7K **Privately Held**
SIC: 1389 Oil/Gas Field Services

(G-2907)
JIM HALEY OIL PRODUCTION CO
1415 W Main St (62821-1390)
P.O. Box 547 (62821-0547)
PHONE.....................................618 382-7338
Jim Haley, *President*
EMP: 10
SALES (est): 698.9K **Privately Held**
SIC: 1311 Crude petroleum production

(G-2908)
KEROGEN RESOURCES INC
645 Il Highway 14 (62821-4815)
PHONE.....................................618 382-3114
EMP: 2
SALES (est): 250K **Privately Held**
SIC: 1311 Crude Petroleum/Natural Gas Production

(G-2909)
LES WILSON INC
205 Industrial Ave (62821-2211)
P.O. Box 331 (62821-0331)
PHONE.....................................618 382-4667
Robert L Wilson, *President*
Stephanie L Wilson, *Treasurer*
EMP: 150 **EST:** 1942
SQ FT: 10,000
SALES (est): 26.7MM **Privately Held**
WEB: www.leswilsoninc.com
SIC: 1389 Oil field services

(G-2910)
MARSHALL ELECTRIC INC
1707 Oak St Ste B (62821-2367)
P.O. Box 455 (62821-0455)
PHONE.....................................618 382-3932
Wade Richard Marshall Jr, *President*
EMP: 10
SALES (est): 1.9MM **Privately Held**
SIC: 3613 1731 Panel & distribution boards & other related apparatus; control panels, electric; electrical work

(G-2911)
MITCHCO FARMS LLC
1239 County Road 1500 N (62821-4600)
P.O. Box 254 (62821-0254)
PHONE.....................................618 382-5032
George N Mitchell, *Owner*
EMP: 15
SQ FT: 4,000
SALES (est): 1.1MM **Privately Held**
SIC: 1311 1389 Crude petroleum production; servicing oil & gas wells

(G-2912)
ODANIEL TRUCKING CO
1249 County Road 1500 N (62821-4600)
PHONE.....................................618 382-5371
Ed O'Daniel Jr, *President*
William Edwards, *Vice Pres*
John E Mann, *Vice Pres*
EMP: 55
SQ FT: 15,000
SALES (est): 5.1MM **Privately Held**
SIC: 4212 3273 1611 1771 Coal haulage, local; ready-mixed concrete; general contractor, highway & street construction; driveway, parking lot & blacktop contractors

(G-2913)
R ENERGY LLC
1001 E Main St (62821)
P.O. Box 357 (62821-0357)
PHONE.....................................618 382-7313
Rebecca R Drone, *Principal*
EMP: 4
SALES (est): 229K **Privately Held**
SIC: 1389 Oil & gas field services

(G-2914)
ROARK OIL FIELD SERVICES INC
1036 County Road 1575 N (62821-4500)
P.O. Box 88 (62821-0088)
PHONE.....................................618 382-4703
Patt Morris, *President*
Herbert Roark, *President*
Judith Morris, *Admin Sec*
EMP: 3
SALES (est): 100K **Privately Held**
SIC: 1389 Oil field services

(G-2915)
SHAWNEE EXPLORATION PARTNERS
115 Smith St (62821-1426)
P.O. Box 338 (62821-0338)
PHONE.....................................618 382-3223
EMP: 3
SALES (est): 119.9K **Privately Held**
SIC: 1311 Crude petroleum production

(G-2916)
VIBRACOUSTIC USA INC
Also Called: Mixing Division
1500 E Main St (62821-2116)
PHONE.....................................618 382-5891
Trevor Combs, *Engineer*
Morris Warino, *Sales Engr*
Brad Olson, *Sales Staff*
Rick Estes, *Manager*
EMP: 50
SALES (corp-wide): 2.4B **Privately Held**
SIC: 3061 2891 2822 Mechanical rubber goods; adhesives & sealants; synthetic rubber
HQ: Vibracoustic Usa, Inc.
400 Aylworth Ave
South Haven MI 49090

(G-2917)
VIBRACOUSTIC USA INC
102 Industrial Ave (62821-2261)
PHONE.....................................618 382-2318
Dan Johnston, *Manager*
Dennis Jacobs, *Telecom Exec*
EMP: 115
SALES (corp-wide): 2.4B **Privately Held**
SIC: 3061 3714 3053 Mechanical rubber goods; motor vehicle parts & accessories; gaskets, packing & sealing devices
HQ: Vibracoustic Usa, Inc.
400 Aylworth Ave
South Haven MI 49090

GEOGRAPHIC SECTION

Carol Stream - Dupage County (G-2943)

(G-2918)
WARREN SERVICE COMPANY
1714 Oak St (62821-2368)
P.O. Box 372 (62821-0372)
PHONE 618 384-2117
Douglas S Warren, *Owner*
EMP: 6
SALES (est): 1.5MM **Privately Held**
SIC: 1389 Oil field services

(G-2919)
WHITE COUNTY COAL LLC (DH)
1525 County Rd 1300 N (62821)
PHONE 618 382-4651
Joseph W Craft III, *President*
Thomas Pearson,
Gary Rathburn,
▲ **EMP: 90 EST:** 1979
SQ FT: 1,000
SALES (est): 49.8MM **Publicly Held**
SIC: 1221 Bituminous coal & lignite-surface mining
HQ: Alliance Coal, Llc
　1717 S Boulder Ave # 400
　Tulsa OK 74119
　918 295-7600

(G-2920)
WILPRO
205 Industrial Ave (62821-2211)
PHONE 618 382-4667
Bob Wilson, *Owner*
Leslie W Wilson, *Co-Owner*
EMP: 3
SALES: 500K **Privately Held**
SIC: 1389 Pumping of oil & gas wells

Carol Stream
Dupage County

(G-2921)
360 DIGITAL PRINT INC
262 Tubeway Dr (60188-2214)
PHONE 630 682-3601
Lee Rady, *President*
Jim Boaha, *Opers Staff*
EMP: 4
SQ FT: 5,400
SALES: 1.2MM **Privately Held**
SIC: 2752 Commercial printing, lithographic

(G-2922)
A J ANTUNES & CO (PA)
Also Called: Roundup Food Equipment Div
180 Kehoe Blvd (60188-1814)
PHONE 630 784-1000
Virginia M Antunes, *Ch of Bd*
Glenn Bullock, *President*
Steve Deppe, *President*
John Han, *Managing Dir*
John Howard, *Business Mgr*
◆ **EMP:** 200
SQ FT: 115,000
SALES (est): 48.5MM **Privately Held**
WEB: www.ajantunes.com
SIC: 3589 Commercial cooking & food-warming equipment

(G-2923)
ABERDEEN TECHNOLOGIES INC
272 Commonwealth Dr (60188-2449)
PHONE 630 665-8590
John Michael, *President*
John M Schmitz, *President*
Susan M Vanmeter, *Admin Sec*
EMP: 15
SQ FT: 7,500
SALES (est): 2.7MM **Privately Held**
SIC: 3544 3089 Industrial molds; molding primary plastic

(G-2924)
ACCURATE WIRE STRIP FRMING INC
175 Tubeway Dr (60188-2249)
PHONE 630 260-1000
Richard Durante, *President*
Jack Domingo, *Vice Pres*
Jeff Durante, *Vice Pres*
EMP: 10
SQ FT: 11,000
SALES (est): 2.1MM **Privately Held**
SIC: 3496 3469 3315 Miscellaneous fabricated wire products; metal stampings; wire & fabricated wire products

(G-2925)
ADVANCED AUDIO TECHNOLOGY INC
Also Called: Aat
200 Easy St Ste E (60188-2399)
PHONE 630 665-3344
Robert Atkins, *President*
EMP: 4
SQ FT: 4,000
SALES (est): 1MM **Privately Held**
SIC: 3652 Magnetic tape (audio): prerecorded

(G-2926)
AEROFAST INC
360 Gundersen Dr (60188-2422)
PHONE 630 668-6575
Nadine Martens, *CEO*
Gary Miller, *President*
Gerardo Dominguez, *Prdtn Mgr*
Justin Fleming, *Sales Staff*
Sherrie Peluso, *Sales Staff*
EMP: 33 **EST:** 1958
SQ FT: 10,000
SALES (est): 5.3MM **Privately Held**
WEB: www.aerofastinc.com
SIC: 3965 Straight pins: steel or brass

(G-2927)
AFI INDUSTRIES INC
Also Called: A F I
475 Kehoe Blvd (60188-1879)
PHONE 630 462-0400
Robert Kleckner, *President*
Patricia Kleckner, *Admin Sec*
▲ **EMP:** 35
SQ FT: 130,000
SALES (est): 9.3MM **Privately Held**
SIC: 3451 3452 3965 Screw machine products; screws, metal; fasteners

(G-2928)
AGENA MANUFACTURING CO
360 Gundersen Dr (60188-2422)
PHONE 630 668-5086
Jack Martens, *President*
EMP: 30
SQ FT: 5,000
SALES (est): 1.8MM **Privately Held**
SIC: 3496 7699 3444 3429 Miscellaneous fabricated wire products; lock & key services; sheet metalwork; manufactured hardware (general)

(G-2929)
AJ OSTER LLC
180 Alexandra Way (60188-2048)
PHONE 630 260-1040
Robert James, *Manager*
EMP: 150
SALES (corp-wide): 4.8MM **Privately Held**
WEB: www.ajoster.com
SIC: 3366 Brass foundry
HQ: Wieland Metal Services, Llc
　301 Metro Center Blvd # 204
　Warwick RI 02886
　401 736-2600

(G-2930)
ALALI ENTERPRISES INC
Also Called: Coffee News of Dupage County
1228 Narragansett Dr (60188-6054)
P.O. Box 1018, Lombard (60148-8018)
PHONE 630 827-9231
Syed H Jaffery, *President*
Zakia Fatima, *Vice Pres*
EMP: 2
SALES (est): 230.1K **Privately Held**
SIC: 2721 Magazines: publishing & printing

(G-2931)
ALLEN ENTERTAINMENT MANAGEMENT
Also Called: Chicago Lifesttyle, The
471 Essex Pl (60188-9229)
PHONE 630 752-0903
Haven Allen, *Owner*
EMP: 25
SQ FT: 2,000
SALES: 150K **Privately Held**
SIC: 8742 2721 Business consultant; public utilities consultant; magazines: publishing & printing

(G-2932)
ALLURED PUBLISHING CORPORATION
Also Called: Global Cosmetics Industry
336 Gundersen Dr Ste A (60188-2403)
PHONE 630 653-2155
Janet Ludwig, *President*
Nancy Allured, *Principal*
Jeb Gleason, *Editor*
Stanley Allured, *Chairman*
Katie A Anderson, *Assoc Editor*
EMP: 50
SQ FT: 11,000
SALES (est): 7MM **Privately Held**
WEB: www.allured.com
SIC: 2741 2721 Miscellaneous publishing; trade journals: publishing only, not printed on site

(G-2933)
AMERICAN FLANGE & MFG CO INC (HQ)
Also Called: Trisure Closures Worldwide
290 Fullerton Ave (60188-1895)
PHONE 630 665-7900
David B Fischer, *President*
Michael C Patton, *Principal*
Joachem Van Der Schaaf, *Principal*
Steve Kipp, *Marketing Staff*
Rich Becker, *Director*
◆ **EMP:** 30 **EST:** 1950
SQ FT: 135,000
SALES (est): 5.5MM
SALES (corp-wide): 4.6B **Publicly Held**
WEB: www.tri-sure.com
SIC: 3089 Injection molding of plastics
PA: Greif, Inc.
　425 Winter Rd
　Delaware OH 43015
　740 549-6000

(G-2934)
AMERICAN LITHO INCORPORATED
175 Mercedes Dr (60188-9409)
PHONE 630 682-0600
EMP: 856
SALES (corp-wide): 313.7MM **Privately Held**
SIC: 2752 2759 2789 7331 Lithographic Coml Print Commercial Printing Bookbinding/Related Work Direct Mail Ad Svcs
PA: American Litho, Incorporated
　175 Mercedes Dr
　Carol Stream IL 60188
　630 462-1700

(G-2935)
AMERICAN LITHO INCORPORATED
175 Mercedes Dr (60188-9409)
PHONE 630 462-1700
Mike Fontana, *President*
Frank Arostegui, *Managing Dir*
Mike Gruper, *Business Mgr*
Cyndie Deiber, *Production*
Roy Pfaender, *Purch Dir*
▲ **EMP:** 350
SQ FT: 300,000
SALES (est): 187.9MM **Privately Held**
SIC: 2752 Commercial printing, offset

(G-2936)
AMERICAN PRECISION ELEC INC (PA)
Also Called: A.P.e
25w624 Saint Charles Rd (60188-2062)
PHONE 630 510-8080
Michael Hall, *President*
Jim Kopp, *Vice Pres*
Paul Miller, *QC Mgr*
James Kopp, *Sales Mgr*
James A Kopp, *Admin Sec*
◆ **EMP:** 87
SQ FT: 30,000
SALES (est): 25MM **Privately Held**
SIC: 3672 Printed circuit boards

(G-2937)
AMERICAN SLIDE-CHART CO (PA)
25w 550 Geneva Rd (60188)
P.O. Box 111, Wheaton (60187-0111)
PHONE 630 665-3333
David P Johnson, *President*
Mark Judy, *Natl Sales Mgr*
Kim Stime, *Regl Sales Mgr*
Karen Vidoni, *Regl Sales Mgr*
Marybeth Bittel, *Marketing Staff*
EMP: 80
SQ FT: 39,000
SALES (est): 7.6MM **Privately Held**
WEB: www.americanslidechart.com
SIC: 2752 Promotional printing, lithographic; calendars, lithographed

(G-2938)
AMERICO CHEMICAL PRODUCTS INC
551 Kimberly Dr (60188-1835)
PHONE 630 588-0830
Christopher Bozin, *President*
Shaun McGuire, *Vice Pres*
Mike Adams, *Sales Staff*
Lisa L Thiel, *Executive Asst*
Kristie Bozin, *Admin Sec*
EMP: 20
SQ FT: 28,000
SALES (est): 8.4MM **Privately Held**
SIC: 5169 2819 5199 Industrial chemicals; industrial inorganic chemicals; packaging materials

(G-2939)
ARCHITECTURAL MALL INC
323 Saint Paul Blvd (60188-1851)
PHONE 630 543-5253
Peter A Savenok, *President*
EMP: 3
SALES (est): 122.8K **Privately Held**
WEB: www.architecturalmall.com
SIC: 2431 Millwork

(G-2940)
ARMADA NUTRITION LLC
285 Fullerton Ave (60188-1886)
PHONE 931 451-7808
Donald K Thorp,
EMP: 4 **Privately Held**
SIC: 2023 Powdered whey
HQ: Armada Nutrition Llc
　4637 Port Royal Rd
　Spring Hill TN 37174
　931 451-7808

(G-2941)
ART JEWEL ENTERPRISES LTD
Also Called: Eagle Grips
460 Randy Rd (60188-2120)
PHONE 630 260-0400
Raj Singh, *President*
Indira Singh, *Admin Sec*
EMP: 10
SQ FT: 5,000
SALES (est): 1.5MM **Privately Held**
SIC: 3484 3421 5941 3161 Guns (firearms) or gun parts, 30 mm. & below; knives: butchers', hunting, pocket, etc.; sporting goods & bicycle shops; luggage; hardwood dimension & flooring mills

(G-2942)
ASSA ABLOY PRY
235 E Lies Rd (60188-9421)
PHONE 630 682-8800
EMP: 6
SALES (est): 897.7K **Privately Held**
SIC: 3442 Metal doors, sash & trim

(G-2943)
AUTUMN WOODS LTD (PA)
375 Gundersen Dr (60188-2421)
PHONE 630 668-2080
Garry Dedick, *President*
Yvonne Dedick, *Treasurer*
EMP: 30
SQ FT: 10,400
SALES (est): 4.7MM **Privately Held**
SIC: 2434 Vanities, bathroom: wood

Carol Stream - Dupage County (G-2944)

(G-2944)
BANNER SERVICE CORPORATION (HQ)
Also Called: Banner Medical
494 E Lies Rd (60188-9425)
PHONE..................630 653-7500
Mark Redding, *Ch of Bd*
Erik Hansen, *Vice Pres*
Justin Mautz, *Plant Mgr*
Tony Achim, *Mfg Staff*
Dave Hallin, *QC Mgr*
▲ **EMP:** 108 EST: 1961
SQ FT: 75,000
SALES (est): 69.1MM
SALES (corp-wide): 441.6MM Privately Held
WEB: www.bargrind.com
SIC: 3599 5051 Custom machinery; steel; aluminum bars, rods, ingots, sheets, pipes, plates, etc.
PA: Middleground Management, Lp
201 E Main St Ste 810
Lexington KY 40507
917 698-3754

(G-2945)
BARD BRACHYTHERAPY INC
295 E Lies Rd (60188-9421)
PHONE..................630 933-7610
Mark O Downey, *President*
Stephen J Long, *Admin Sec*
EMP: 22
SALES (est): 3.6MM
SALES (corp-wide): 17.2B Publicly Held
SIC: 3841 Surgical & medical instruments
HQ: C. R. Bard, Inc.
1 Becton Dr
Franklin Lakes NJ 07417
908 277-8000

(G-2946)
BELCAR PRODUCTS INC
500 Randy Rd Ste B (60188-2174)
PHONE..................630 462-1950
James R Bellandi, *President*
Carol A Bellandi, *Corp Secy*
Sharon Newton, *Manager*
EMP: 9
SQ FT: 2,000
SALES (est): 3.6MM Privately Held
SIC: 5085 5084 3545 3541 Tools; machine tools & metalworking machinery; machine tool accessories; machine tools, metal cutting type

(G-2947)
BKBG ENTERPRISES INC
Also Called: Devanco Foods
440 Mission St (60188-9414)
PHONE..................847 228-7070
Peter Bartzis, *CEO*
Michael D Burns, *CFO*
Randy Mahar, *Natl Sales Mgr*
Parker King, *Chief Mktg Ofcr*
▲ **EMP:** 70
SQ FT: 30,000
SALES (est): 57.3MM Privately Held
SIC: 5147 2013 Meats, fresh; cooked meats from purchased meat

(G-2948)
BLACKHAWK CORRUGATED LLC
700 Kimberly Dr (60188-9406)
PHONE..................844 270-2296
Jay Carman,
EMP: 48 EST: 2015
SALES (est): 194.5K Privately Held
SIC: 2653 Boxes, corrugated: made from purchased materials

(G-2949)
BLACKHAWK COURTYARDS LLC
700 Kimberly Dr (60188-9406)
PHONE..................416 298-8101
Jim Williamson, *Mng Member*
EMP: 6
SALES (est): 324.6K Privately Held
SIC: 2653 Corrugated boxes, partitions, display items, sheets & pad

(G-2950)
BLACKHAWK INDUSTRIAL DIST INC
245 E Lies Rd (60188-9421)
PHONE..................773 736-9600
Frank Bertucci, *General Mgr*
EMP: 10 Privately Held
SIC: 3541 3545 Grinding machines, metalworking; machine tool accessories
PA: Blackhawk Industrial Distribution, Inc.
1501 Sw Expressway Dr
Broken Arrow OK 74012

(G-2951)
BLASTLINE USA INC
Also Called: Blastline USA
226 S Westgate Dr Ste B (60188-2229)
PHONE..................630 871-0147
Charly Lonappan, *Admin Sec*
▼ **EMP:** 6
SQ FT: 13,500
SALES (est): 4.3MM Privately Held
SIC: 5084 5085 3589 Paint spray equipment, industrial; industrial supplies; sandblasting equipment

(G-2952)
CABINETS & GRANITE DIRECT LLC
1175 N Gary Ave (60188-9423)
PHONE..................630 588-8886
Fen Q Chen, *Principal*
Ivan Chen, *Sales Mgr*
Jasmine Ni,
▲ **EMP:** 10
SALES (est): 1.6MM Privately Held
SIC: 5031 2434 5211 Kitchen cabinets; wood kitchen cabinets; cabinets, kitchen

(G-2953)
CAC CORPORATION (PA)
Also Called: C A C
307 E Lies Rd (60188-9421)
PHONE..................630 221-5200
James J Coduti, *President*
Frances Geier, *Corp Secy*
Mike Jurgensen, *Plant Mgr*
Stan Spiewak, *IT/INT Sup*
EMP: 40
SQ FT: 40,000
SALES (est): 5.9MM Privately Held
SIC: 3469 3544 Stamping metal for the trade; special dies, tools, jigs & fixtures

(G-2954)
CAMBRDG PRINTING CORP
780 W Army Trail Rd (60188-9297)
PHONE..................630 510-2100
EMP: 3 EST: 2002
SALES (est): 300K Privately Held
SIC: 2752 Lithographic Commercial Printing

(G-2955)
CAPITAL ADVANCED TECHNOLOGIES
309 Village Dr (60188-1828)
PHONE..................630 690-1696
Robert Laschinski, *President*
Anna Laschinski, *Corp Secy*
EMP: 8
SQ FT: 6,000
SALES (est): 1.4MM Privately Held
SIC: 3679 Electronic circuits

(G-2956)
CARTPAC INC
Also Called: Frain Group
245 E North Ave (60188-2021)
PHONE..................630 283-8979
Richard E Frain Jr, *President*
John Frain, *Sales Mgr*
EMP: 40
SALES (est): 10.1MM Privately Held
SIC: 3565 7699 3556 Carton packing machines; industrial machinery & equipment repair; food products machinery

(G-2957)
CHICAGO ENVELOPE INC (PA)
Also Called: C.E. Printed Products
685 Kimberly Dr (60188-9403)
PHONE..................630 668-0400
Robert Ohr, *President*
Ryan Hamilton, *Production*
Stefanie Querry, *Purchasing*
Bob Ohr, *Marketing Mgr*
Kathy Syre, *Marketing Staff*
EMP: 50
SQ FT: 21,000
SALES (est): 19.3MM Privately Held
SIC: 2759 Commercial printing

(G-2958)
CHICAGO SIGN & LIGHT COMPANY
26w 535 St Charles Rd 8 26 W (60188)
P.O. Box 75, Wheaton (60187-0075)
PHONE..................630 407-0802
John Doyle, *President*
EMP: 8
SALES (est): 818.1K Privately Held
SIC: 3993 Signs & advertising specialties

(G-2959)
CHRISTIANITY TODAY INTL
465 Gundersen Dr (60188-2498)
PHONE..................630 260-6200
Harold B Smith, *CEO*
Mark J Galli, *Principal*
Carol Thompson, *Exec VP*
Theresa Hoffner, *Vice Pres*
Gary Johnson, *Accounting Mgr*
EMP: 168 EST: 1955
SQ FT: 25,000
SALES (est): 10.1MM Privately Held
WEB: www.christianitytoday.com
SIC: 2721 Magazines: publishing only, not printed on site

(G-2960)
CJT KOOLCARB INC (PA)
Also Called: C J T
494 Mission St (60188-9417)
P.O. Box 5941 (60197-5941)
PHONE..................630 690-5933
Andrew Piasecki, *President*
Don Egland, *General Mgr*
Michael Luedtke, *Vice Pres*
Thomas Trost, *Vice Pres*
Nicholas Havemann, *Mfg Spvr*
▲ **EMP:** 115 EST: 2005
SQ FT: 68,000
SALES (est): 34.3MM Privately Held
WEB: www.cjtkoolcarb.com
SIC: 3545 Drills (machine tool accessories); drill bits, metalworking; reamers, machine tool

(G-2961)
CLARIOS
Also Called: Johnson Controls
883 Carol Ct (60188-9408)
PHONE..................630 871-7700
Timothy Murphy, *Manager*
EMP: 14 Privately Held
SIC: 3585 1711 2531 3714 Refrigeration & heating equipment; heating & air conditioning contractors; seats, automobile; motor vehicle body components & frame; lead acid batteries (storage batteries); building services monitoring controls, automatic
HQ: Johnson Controls, Inc.
5757 N Green Bay Ave
Milwaukee WI 53209
414 524-1200

(G-2962)
CLARK GEAR WORKS INC
1218 Saratoga Dr (60188-4644)
PHONE..................630 561-2320
Jeffrey L Clark, *President*
Lori A Clark, *Treasurer*
EMP: 9
SALES (est): 50K Privately Held
SIC: 3462 Gears, forged steel

(G-2963)
COCA COLA
Also Called: Coca-Cola
775 East Dr (60188-9410)
PHONE..................630 588-8786
EMP: 3 EST: 2013
SALES (est): 362.6K Privately Held
SIC: 2086 Bottled & canned soft drinks

(G-2964)
COLLEENS CONFECTION
190 Easy St Ste I (60188-3515)
PHONE..................630 653-2231
Richard J Hamilton, *Owner*
▼ **EMP:** 4
SQ FT: 1,750
SALES (est): 227.1K Privately Held
SIC: 2064 Candy & other confectionery products

(G-2965)
COLONIAL BAG CORPORATION
205 Fullerton Ave (60188-1886)
PHONE..................630 690-3999
Howard F Anderson, *President*
Dean Anderson, *VP Mfg*
Mike Cowgill, *Regl Sales Mgr*
Mary Gee, *Marketing Staff*
William Kindorf, *Admin Sec*
▲ **EMP:** 98
SQ FT: 70,000
SALES (est): 23.5MM Privately Held
SIC: 2673 Trash bags (plastic film): made from purchased materials; plastic bags: made from purchased materials

(G-2966)
COPIES OVERNIGHT INC (PA)
Also Called: Copresco
262 Commonwealth Dr (60188-2449)
PHONE..................630 690-2000
Stephen Johnson, *President*
EMP: 32
SQ FT: 14,000
SALES (est): 5.3MM Privately Held
SIC: 2752 Commercial printing, offset

(G-2967)
CORE PIPE PRODUCTS INC
Also Called: Tube Line Stainless
170 Tubeway Dr (60188-2291)
PHONE..................630 690-7000
Steve Romanelli, *President*
Debbie Tsamoulos, *Human Res Dir*
David Romanelli, *Admin Sec*
▲ **EMP:** 120
SQ FT: 85,000
SALES (est): 26.2MM Privately Held
SIC: 3462 Flange, valve & pipe fitting forgings, ferrous

(G-2968)
CR BARD INC
295 E Lies Rd (60188-9421)
PHONE..................630 933-7653
Steve Fitch, *President*
Steven Goode, *President*
Bill Benson, *District Mgr*
Chris Drobnick, *Research*
Patrick McLean, *Manager*
EMP: 57
SALES (est): 6.7MM Privately Held
SIC: 3841 Surgical & medical instruments

(G-2969)
CTI/USA INC
Also Called: Globe Ticket
350 Randy Rd Ste 1 (60188-1831)
PHONE..................847 258-1000
Robert Dawson, *Principal*
Jacki Rutkowski, *Accountant*
Jason Shoats, *Sales Dir*
▲ **EMP:** 3
SALES (est): 338.4K Privately Held
WEB: www.globeticket.com
SIC: 2759 Screen printing

(G-2970)
DAINICHI MACHINERY INC
745 Kimberly Dr (60188-9407)
PHONE..................630 681-1572
Yutaka Koyama, *President*
Hidekazu Kawase, *Vice Pres*
Harris Kawase, *Engineer*
▲ **EMP:** 2 EST: 1973
SQ FT: 12,180
SALES (est): 369.2K Privately Held
SIC: 7699 3541 Industrial machinery & equipment repair; industrial tool grinding; lathes, metal cutting & polishing
PA: Dainichi Kinzoku Kogyo Co.,Ltd.
3-7-31, Chibune, Nishiyodogawa-Ku
Osaka OSK 555-0

(G-2971)
DALCO MARKETING SERVICES
Also Called: Connections Company
362 Sherwood Dr (60188-2207)
PHONE..................630 961-3366

David A Lindblade, *Owner*
EMP: 5
SALES (est): 475.7K **Privately Held**
SIC: 5063 3679 Electrical apparatus & equipment; electronic circuits

(G-2972)
DANCO CONVERTING
455 E North Ave (60188-2123)
PHONE..................................630 949-8112
Daniel J Mulvey, *President*
Diana Hollerbach, *Cust Mgr*
▲ **EMP:** 3
SALES (est): 652K **Privately Held**
SIC: 2621 Paper mills

(G-2973)
DAVES AUTO REPIAR
211 E Saint Charles Rd (60188-2308)
PHONE..................................630 682-4411
Dave Deiszke, *Owner*
EMP: 4
SALES (est): 188.1K **Privately Held**
WEB: www.davesautoradiatorrepair.com
SIC: 3599 Air intake filters, internal combustion engine, except auto

(G-2974)
DAVIES MOLDING LLC
350 Kehoe Blvd (60188-1818)
PHONE..................................630 510-8188
Daniel Horneck, *Business Mgr*
Rick Friel, *VP Opers*
Shu Shah, *Purch Mgr*
Bob Reisel, *VP Engrg*
Justin Thomas, *QC Mgr*
▲ **EMP:** 125 **EST:** 1933
SQ FT: 99,000
SALES (est): 29.3MM
SALES (corp-wide): 1.2B **Privately Held**
WEB: www.daviesmolding.com
SIC: 3089 3825 Extruded finished plastic products; instruments to measure electricity
HQ: Pettibone L.L.C.
27501 Bella Vista Pkwy
Warrenville IL 60555
630 353-5000

(G-2975)
DECORE TOOL & MFG INC
159 Easy St (60188-2314)
PHONE..................................630 681-9760
Scott Decore, *President*
EMP: 16
SALES (est): 2.9MM **Privately Held**
SIC: 3544 Special dies & tools

(G-2976)
DESIGN METALS FABRICATION INC
361 Randy Rd Ste 106 (60188-1869)
PHONE..................................630 752-9060
Thang Nguyen, *President*
Toan Nguyen, *Vice Pres*
EMP: 8 **EST:** 2008
SALES (est): 1.4MM **Privately Held**
WEB: www.dmetalsfab.com
SIC: 3599 Machine shop, jobbing & repair

(G-2977)
DONKEY BRANDS LLC
Also Called: Donkey Chips
281 Carlton Dr (60188-2405)
PHONE..................................630 251-2007
Amanda Gallo,
Dominic Gallo,
Lauren Pisljar,
Robert Pisljar,
EMP: 13
SQ FT: 6,600
SALES (est): 2.4MM **Privately Held**
SIC: 2096 Tortilla chips

(G-2978)
DYNACUT INDUSTRIES INC
Also Called: Dyna Cut Industries
500 Randy Rd Ste A (60188-2175)
PHONE..................................630 462-1900
James R Bellandi, *President*
Carol Bellandi, *Corp Secy*
James Bellandi, *Executive*
EMP: 20
SQ FT: 4,000
SALES (est): 3.6MM **Privately Held**
SIC: 3545 Cutting tools for machine tools

(G-2979)
EQUI-CHEM INTERNATIONAL INC
510 Tower Blvd (60188-9426)
P.O. Box 10249, Chicago (60610-0249)
PHONE..................................630 784-0432
Luis C Lovis, *President*
◆ **EMP:** 10
SQ FT: 20,000
SALES (est): 1.6MM **Privately Held**
WEB: www.equichem.com
SIC: 2099 2087 Food preparations; flavoring extracts & syrups

(G-2980)
ERGOSEAL INC
Also Called: Sieber Tooling Solutions
344 Commerce Dr (60188-1809)
PHONE..................................630 462-9370
Tom Hilaris, *President*
EMP: 7 **Privately Held**
SIC: 3312 Tool & die steel & alloys
PA: Ergoseal, Inc.
346 Commerce Dr
Carol Stream IL 60188

(G-2981)
ERGOSEAL INC (PA)
Also Called: Norman Technology
346 Commerce Dr (60188-1809)
PHONE..................................630 462-9600
Athanasios Hilaris, *CEO*
John Hilaris, *Ch of Bd*
Thomaie Hilaris, *Officer*
Toula Hilaris, *Admin Sec*
▲ **EMP:** 27
SQ FT: 17,000
SALES (est): 5.6MM **Privately Held**
SIC: 3561 Industrial pumps & parts

(G-2982)
EUROPEAN WOOD WORKS INC
1151 Woodlake Dr (60188-6028)
PHONE..................................773 662-6607
Krzysztof Lukaszek, *President*
EMP: 4 **EST:** 2010
SQ FT: 7,000
SALES (est): 45.5K **Privately Held**
SIC: 2431 Millwork

(G-2983)
FERN MANUFACTURING COMPANY
333 Kimberly Dr (60188-1836)
PHONE..................................630 260-9350
William R Fern, *President*
Laurel Fern, *Admin Sec*
EMP: 6 **EST:** 1977
SQ FT: 17,220
SALES (est): 979.6K **Privately Held**
SIC: 3599 Machine shop, jobbing & repair

(G-2984)
FIC AMERICA CORP (HQ)
485 E Lies Rd (60188-9422)
PHONE..................................630 871-7609
Kenzo Yanase, *President*
William T Murakami, *Vice Pres*
Jeff Sharin, *Safety Mgr*
Vidal Rios, *Production*
Joseph Dimaano, *Project Engr*
▲ **EMP:** 670
SQ FT: 700,000
SALES (est): 215.3MM **Privately Held**
SIC: 3469 Stamping metal for the trade

(G-2985)
FLAVOR SAVOR INC
285 Fullerton Ave (60188-1886)
PHONE..................................630 868-0350
Don Thorp, *President*
Damon Dabels, *Credit Staff*
EMP: 19
SALES (est): 643.7K **Privately Held**
SIC: 2087 Flavoring extracts & syrups

(G-2986)
FLEXOGRAFIX INC
27 W 136 St Charles (60188)
PHONE..................................630 350-0100
Ken Pavett, *President*
EMP: 10
SQ FT: 5,000
SALES (est): 1.6MM **Privately Held**
SIC: 2759 Flexographic printing

(G-2987)
FORTUNA BAKING COMPANY
149 Easy St (60188-2314)
PHONE..................................630 681-3000
Pete Fourtounis, *President*
George Fourtounis, *President*
EMP: 3
SALES (est): 400.5K **Privately Held**
SIC: 2051 Bakery: wholesale or wholesale/retail combined

(G-2988)
FRESH FACTORY
Also Called: 87p, LLC
238 Tubeway Dr (60188-2214)
PHONE..................................630 580-9038
Randy Krahmer, *Info Tech Mgr*
Jeff Singleton, *Director*
Micheal Weglarz,
William Besenhoser,
EMP: 40 **EST:** 2014
SQ FT: 36,000
SALES (est): 7MM **Privately Held**
WEB: www.87p.me
SIC: 2099 2037 2033 Sauces: gravy, dressing & dip mixes; fruit juices; vegetable juices: fresh
PA: Here Holdings, Llc
238 Tubeway Dr
Carol Stream IL 60188
563 723-1008

(G-2989)
GALAXY CIRCUITS INC
383 Randy Rd (60188-1802)
PHONE..................................630 462-1010
Anil Patel, *President*
Kanti Patel, *Vice Pres*
Shankar Patel, *Shareholder*
Pankaj Patel, *Admin Sec*
▲ **EMP:** 20
SQ FT: 15,000
SALES (est): 4MM **Privately Held**
SIC: 3672 Printed circuit boards

(G-2990)
GENERAL ELECTRIC COMPANY
775 East Dr (60188-9410)
PHONE..................................630 588-8853
EMP: 226
SALES (corp-wide): 95.2B **Publicly Held**
WEB: www.ge.com
SIC: 3844 Radiographic X-ray apparatus & tubes
PA: General Electric Company
5 Necco St
Boston MA 02210
617 443-3000

(G-2991)
GERLIN INC
Also Called: Core Pipe
170 Tubeway Dr (60188-2250)
PHONE..................................630 653-5232
Steve Romanelli, *President*
Tim Warren, *Vice Pres*
Steve Hall, *Plant Mgr*
Jerry Livorsi, *Purch Agent*
Bill Burn, *CFO*
▲ **EMP:** 2 **EST:** 1984
SALES (est): 466.5K **Privately Held**
SIC: 3498 3317 Fabricated pipe & fittings; pipes, seamless steel

(G-2992)
GIVAUDAN FLAVORS CORPORATION
Also Called: Spicetec Flavors & Seasonings
195 Alexandra Way (60188-2047)
PHONE..................................630 682-5600
Mauricio Graber, *President*
EMP: 188
SALES (corp-wide): 6.2B **Privately Held**
SIC: 2038 2013 2099 Frozen specialties; dinners, frozen & packaged; lunches, frozen & packaged; sausages & other prepared meats; dessert mixes & fillings
HQ: Givaudan Flavors Corporation
1199 Edison Dr
Cincinnati OH 45216

(G-2993)
GRAPHIC PACKAGING INTL LLC
Also Called: Altivity Packaging
400 E North Ave (60188-2130)
PHONE..................................630 260-6500
Mike Egan, *General Mgr*
Angie Vandenheuvel, *Purch Mgr*
Robert Wolfe, *Technical Staff*
Brittany Howard, *Administration*
Helen Hawkins, *Analyst*
EMP: 400 **Publicly Held**
WEB: www.graphicpkg.com
SIC: 2631 2657 2653 Folding boxboard; folding paperboard boxes; corrugated & solid fiber boxes
HQ: Graphic Packaging International, Llc
1500 Riveredge Pkwy # 100
Atlanta GA 30328

(G-2994)
GRAPHIC PACKAGING INTL LLC
Also Called: Altivity Packaging
400 E North Ave (60188-2130)
P.O. Box 105, Cantonment FL (32533-0105)
PHONE..................................630 260-6500
Jack Forbes, *Principal*
EMP: 228 **Publicly Held**
SIC: 2674 Bags: uncoated paper & multiwall; folding boxboard
HQ: Graphic Packaging International, Llc
1500 Riveredge Pkwy # 100
Atlanta GA 30328

(G-2995)
GREEN ORGANICS INC
290 S Main Pl Ste 103 (60188-2476)
PHONE..................................630 871-0108
Joe Mazza, *President*
EMP: 10
SALES (est): 1.2MM **Privately Held**
SIC: 2875 Compost

(G-2996)
HART & COOLEY INC
Commercial Products Group
815 Kimberly Dr (60188-1801)
PHONE..................................630 665-5549
Bernard Roy, *Principal*
EMP: 250 **Privately Held**
SIC: 3446 Registers (air), metal
HQ: Hart & Cooley, Inc.
5030 Corp Exch Blvd Se
Grand Rapids MI 49512
616 656-8200

(G-2997)
HERE HOLDINGS LLC (PA)
238 Tubeway Dr (60188-2214)
PHONE..................................563 723-1008
Jeff Olshesky, *Mng Member*
EMP: 6
SALES (est): 7MM **Privately Held**
SIC: 2099 2037 2033 Sauces: gravy, dressing & dip mixes; fruit juices; vegetable juices: fresh

(G-2998)
HILL ENGINEERING INC
373 Randy Rd (60188-1802)
PHONE..................................630 315-5070
Bruce Dewey, *President*
EMP: 50
SQ FT: 30,000
SALES (est): 7.2MM
SALES (corp-wide): 629.1MM **Privately Held**
SIC: 3544 Special dies & tools
HQ: Formtek Inc
711 Ogden Ave
Lisle IL 60532
630 285-1500

(G-2999)
HOPE PUBLISHING COMPANY
Also Called: Providence Press
380 S Main Pl (60188-2475)
PHONE..................................630 665-3200
John Shorney, *President*
June Bollweg, *Managing Prtnr*
Jane Holstein, *Editor*
Joel Raney, *Editor*
Scott Shorney, *Vice Pres*
EMP: 16 **EST:** 1892
SQ FT: 10,000
SALES (est): 2MM **Privately Held**
WEB: www.hopepublishing.com
SIC: 2731 2741 Book music: publishing only, not printed on site; miscellaneous publishing

Carol Stream - Dupage County (G-3000)

(G-3000)
HOUSE OF GRAPHICS
370 Randy Rd (60188-1880)
PHONE..................................630 682-0810
Phillis Herbold, *President*
C Robert Herbold, *Manager*
EMP: 25 **EST:** 1969
SQ FT: 34,500
SALES (est): 4.1MM **Privately Held**
SIC: 2752 2791 2789 Commercial printing, offset; typesetting; bookbinding & related work

(G-3001)
ILLINOIS TAG CO
287 Commonwealth Dr (60188-2450)
P.O. Box 4082, Wheaton (60189-4082)
PHONE..................................773 626-0542
Robert A Oliva, *President*
EMP: 20
SQ FT: 1,300
SALES (est): 2.1MM **Privately Held**
SIC: 2679 2759 2671 Labels, paper: made from purchased material; commercial printing; packaging paper & plastics film, coated & laminated

(G-3002)
ILLINOIS TOOL WORKS INC
ITW Trans Tech
475 N Gary Ave (60188-1820)
PHONE..................................630 752-4000
Justin Cooper, *Division Mgr*
Kris Bender, *Production*
Paul Konrath, *Engineer*
Eva Tomszak, *Accounting Mgr*
Cheryl Elliott, *Accountant*
EMP: 65
SQ FT: 130,000
SALES (corp-wide): 14.1B **Publicly Held**
WEB: www.itw.com
SIC: 2754 Commercial printing, gravure
PA: Illinois Tool Works Inc.
155 Harlem Ave
Glenview IL 60025
847 724-7500

(G-3003)
ILLINOIS TOOL WORKS INC
ITW Linx
425 N Gary Ave (60188-1823)
PHONE..................................630 315-2150
EMP: 104
SALES (corp-wide): 14.1B **Publicly Held**
SIC: 3089 Injection molded finished plastic products
PA: Illinois Tool Works Inc.
155 Harlem Ave
Glenview IL 60025
847 724-7500

(G-3004)
IMTRAN INDUSTRIES INC
475 N Gary Ave (60188-1820)
PHONE..................................630 752-4000
Joe Olson, *President*
Douglas Parker, *Vice Pres*
EMP: 75
SALES (est): 2.4MM **Privately Held**
SIC: 2759 3555 Commercial printing; printing trades machinery

(G-3005)
INTERNATIONAL PAPER COMPANY
139 Fullerton Ave (60188-1825)
PHONE..................................630 653-3500
John Janda, *Safety Mgr*
Pat Leggett, *Branch Mgr*
EMP: 12
SALES (corp-wide): 22.3B **Publicly Held**
SIC: 2621 Paper mills
PA: International Paper Company
6400 Poplar Ave
Memphis TN 38197
901 419-9000

(G-3006)
INTERSTATE POWER SYSTEMS INC
Also Called: Interstate Power Systemd
210 Alexandra Way (60188-2068)
PHONE..................................630 871-1111
Myron Birschbach, *Manager*
EMP: 11
SQ FT: 50,000
SALES (corp-wide): 228MM **Privately Held**
SIC: 3714 5084 Motor vehicle parts & accessories; industrial machinery & equipment
HQ: Interstate Power Systems, Inc.
2901 E 78th St
Minneapolis MN 55425
952 854-2044

(G-3007)
ISA CHICAGO
470 Mission St Unit 7 (60188-9424)
PHONE..................................630 317-7169
Mohammed Inayat, *Principal*
EMP: 4 **EST:** 2010
SALES (est): 610.7K **Privately Held**
SIC: 3911 Cigar & cigarette accessories

(G-3008)
ITW FLUIDS NORTH AMERICA
475 N Gary Ave (60188-1820)
PHONE..................................630 384-0146
EMP: 8 **EST:** 2014
SALES (est): 1MM **Privately Held**
SIC: 2899 Chemical preparations

(G-3009)
KGBAL MANUFACTURING LLC
Also Called: Wholesale For Industrial Beari
493 Mission St (60188-9431)
PHONE..................................312 841-3545
Xiao Zheng, *Principal*
▲ **EMP:** 5
SALES (est): 82K **Privately Held**
SIC: 3568 Power transmission equipment

(G-3010)
KIK INTERNATIONAL INC
780 W Army Trail Rd 209 (60188-9297)
PHONE..................................905 660-0444
Kathleen Lucia, *Principal*
EMP: 18
SALES (est): 2.8MM **Privately Held**
SIC: 2842 Cleaning or polishing preparations

(G-3011)
KLIMP INDUSTRIES INC
175 Tubeway Dr (60188-2249)
PHONE..................................630 682-0752
James R Bonde, *President*
Katherine Porter, *Principal*
EMP: 5
SALES (est): 477.1K **Privately Held**
SIC: 3496 Wire fasteners

(G-3012)
KLIMP INDUSTRIES INC
175 Tubeway Dr (60188-2249)
P.O. Box 709, Warrenville (60555-0709)
PHONE..................................630 790-0600
James R Bonde, *President*
Richard Durante, *Vice Pres*
EMP: 4
SALES (est): 1MM **Privately Held**
SIC: 3496 Wire fasteners

(G-3013)
KNS COMPANIES INC
475 Randy Rd (60188-2119)
P.O. Box 88762 (60188-0762)
PHONE..................................630 665-9010
Raymond Bellino, *President*
Maria Evangelista, *Technical Mgr*
Jean Maloney, *Office Mgr*
Joseph Chess, *Technical Staff*
John Schulz, *Technician*
EMP: 23
SQ FT: 15,000
SALES (est): 12MM **Privately Held**
WEB: www.knscompanies.com
SIC: 2821 2851 3081 Epoxy resins; paints & allied products; unsupported plastics film & sheet

(G-3014)
KOWALSKI MEMORIALS INC
195 Kehoe Blvd Ste 1 (60188-5202)
PHONE..................................630 462-7226
Peter Kowalski, *President*
Holly Klemz, *Manager*
EMP: 5
SQ FT: 3,200

SALES (est): 715.2K **Privately Held**
SIC: 3272 5087 Monuments & grave markers, except terrazo; cemetary supplies & equipment

(G-3015)
LAMP WORKS INC
332 Commerce Dr (60188-1809)
PHONE..................................630 871-7663
EMP: 11
SQ FT: 1,400
SALES (est): 1.5MM **Privately Held**
SIC: 3641 3645 Mfg Electric Lamps Mfg Residential Lighting Fixtures

(G-3016)
LAVA WORLD INTERNATIONAL INC
430 Kimberly Dr (60188-1804)
PHONE..................................630 315-3300
James Winchell, *Manager*
EMP: 3
SALES (est): 169.9K **Privately Held**
SIC: 3646 Commercial indusl & institutional electric lighting fixtures

(G-3017)
LEW ELECTRIC FITTINGS CO
371 Randy Rd (60188-1802)
P.O. Box 470, Saint Charles (60174-0470)
PHONE..................................630 665-2075
John E Romer, *CEO*
Graham Romer, *President*
Susan Cozzi, *CFO*
Keith Romer, *VP Sales*
▲ **EMP:** 18 **EST:** 1901
SQ FT: 17,000
SALES: 6MM **Privately Held**
WEB: www.lewelectric.com
SIC: 3644 Outlet boxes (electric wiring devices)

(G-3018)
LEWIS PROCESS SYSTEMS INC
294 Commonwealth Dr (60188-2449)
PHONE..................................630 510-8200
Alfred E Gudenkauf, *President*
Bernice Gudenkauf, *Corp Secy*
EMP: 10 **EST:** 1972
SQ FT: 10,000
SALES (est): 956.7K **Privately Held**
WEB: www.lewisprocess.com
SIC: 3444 5085 7692 3494 Sheet metalwork; valves & fittings; welding repair; valves & pipe fittings; fabricated plate work (boiler shop)

(G-3019)
MAAC MACHINERY CO INC
590 Tower Blvd (60188-9426)
PHONE..................................630 665-1700
Paul V Alongi, *Founder*
James Alongi, *Admin Sec*
EMP: 40
SQ FT: 46,000
SALES (est): 11.2MM **Privately Held**
SIC: 3559 5084 Plastics working machinery; industrial machinery & equipment

(G-3020)
MALLOF ABRUZINO NASH MKTG INC
Also Called: Man Marketing
765 Kimberly Dr (60188-9407)
PHONE..................................630 929-5200
Edward G Mallof, *President*
Erika Costello, *Marketing Staff*
EMP: 26
SQ FT: 10,900
SALES (est): 5.6MM **Privately Held**
SIC: 7311 2752 Advertising consultant; commercial printing, offset

(G-3021)
MASTER MARKETING INTL INC (PA)
Also Called: Magnetstreet
280 Gerzevske Ln (60188-2049)
PHONE..................................630 653-5525
Neville B Baird, *Ch of Bd*
Mark Syswerda, *Vice Pres*
▲ **EMP:** 35
SQ FT: 10,000

SALES (est): 21.5MM **Privately Held**
SIC: 2759 Promotional printing; invitation & stationery printing & engraving

(G-3022)
MEDIA ASSOCIATES INTL INC
Also Called: M A I
351 S Main Pl Ste 230 (60188-2455)
PHONE..................................630 260-9063
Mark Carpenter, *Ch of Bd*
John D Maust, *President*
Daniel Elliott, *Admin Sec*
Bonnie McCullough, *Admin Asst*
EMP: 16
SQ FT: 802
SALES (est): 867K **Privately Held**
SIC: 8742 8331 2731 Business consultant; sheltered workshop; pamphlets: publishing only, not printed on site

(G-3023)
MEGADYNE AMERICA LLC
Also Called: Jason Industrial
221 S Westgate Dr Ste N2 (60188-2053)
P.O. Box 87288 (60188-7288)
PHONE..................................630 752-0600
Philip Cohenca, *President*
Emmy Cohenca, *Corp Secy*
Michael Kurtzner, *Sales Staff*
Mike Andersen, *Manager*
▲ **EMP:** 21
SQ FT: 25,000
SALES: 5MM **Privately Held**
WEB: www.jasonindustrial.com
SIC: 3052 3492 5085 Rubber & plastics hose & beltings; hose & tube fittings & assemblies, hydraulic/pneumatic; industrial supplies

(G-3024)
MESSER LLC
640 Kimberly Dr (60188-9402)
PHONE..................................630 690-3010
Mike Totteleer, *Manager*
EMP: 10
SALES (corp-wide): 1.1B **Privately Held**
SIC: 5169 2813 Industrial gases; industrial gases
HQ: Messer Llc
200 Somerset Corp Blvd # 7000
Bridgewater NJ 08807
908 464-8100

(G-3025)
METALS TECHNOLOGY CORPORATION
120 N Schmale Rd (60188-2151)
PHONE..................................630 221-2500
John B Bell, *President*
Thomas J Bell, *President*
Jerome Bell Jr, *Vice Pres*
Jerry Bell, *Vice Pres*
Ed Hanrahan, *Plant Mgr*
EMP: 115
SQ FT: 70,000
SALES (est): 29.3MM **Privately Held**
WEB: www.metalstechnology.com
SIC: 3398 Metal heat treating

(G-3026)
MEYERCORD REVENUE INC
475 Village Dr (60188-1830)
PHONE..................................630 682-6200
Jim E Bonhivert, *President*
Jeff Van Domelen, *Prdtn Mgr*
Jeff Domelen, *Plant Engr*
Steve Bednar, *Manager*
▲ **EMP:** 50
SALES (est): 9.1MM
SALES (corp-wide): 355.8K **Privately Held**
SIC: 2752 Commercial printing, lithographic
HQ: Sicpa Securink, Corp.
8000 Research Way
Springfield VA 22153
703 455-8050

(G-3027)
MGN TOOL & MFG CO INC
373 Randy Rd (60188-1802)
PHONE..................................630 849-3575
Michael Nawroth, *Owner*
EMP: 3 **EST:** 2011

GEOGRAPHIC SECTION
Carol Stream - Dupage County (G-3054)

SALES (est): 261.8K **Privately Held**
SIC: 3999 Barber & beauty shop equipment

(G-3028)
MICRON MOLD & MFG INC
1085 Idaho St (60188-1348)
PHONE................................630 871-9531
Josekutty Parackal, *President*
Benny Parackal, *Vice Pres*
EMP: 4
SQ FT: 2,000
SALES (est): 135K **Privately Held**
SIC: 3089 Injection molding of plastics

(G-3029)
MICROWAVE RES & APPLICATIONS
190 Easy St Ste A (60188-3500)
PHONE................................630 480-7456
Wayne G Love, *President*
James C Stratton, *Vice Pres*
EMP: 3
SQ FT: 3,200
SALES (est): 420.2K **Privately Held**
SIC: 3631 8733 Microwave ovens, including portable: household; safety research, noncommercial

(G-3030)
MIDWEST COACH BUILDERS INC
Also Called: Mobility Masters
200 Easy St Ste I (60188-2399)
PHONE................................630 690-1420
William Karris, *President*
David Edwards, *Vice Pres*
EMP: 4
SQ FT: 2,000
SALES (est): 350K **Privately Held**
SIC: 3711 Automobile assembly, including specialty automobiles

(G-3031)
MIDWEST WOODCRAFTERS INC
26w415 Saint Charles Rd (60188-1942)
PHONE................................630 665-0901
Michael Allessi, *President*
Russell Krella, *Admin Sec*
EMP: 6
SALES (est): 930.1K **Privately Held**
SIC: 2431 2517 2434 Millwork; wood television & radio cabinets; wood kitchen cabinets

(G-3032)
MILLER PHARMACAL GROUP INC
350 Randy Rd Ste 2 (60188-1831)
PHONE................................800 323-2935
Steve Wonsil, *President*
Sigrid Wonsil, *Shareholder*
EMP: 4
SQ FT: 3,150
SALES (est): 1.2MM **Privately Held**
SIC: 2834 Pharmaceutical preparations

(G-3033)
MOUNTAIN GRAPHIX LLC
226 S Westgate Dr Ste A (60188-2229)
PHONE................................630 681-8300
Joe Galloni, *Mng Member*
▲ EMP: 14
SALES (est): 2.3MM **Privately Held**
SIC: 2752 Commercial printing, lithographic

(G-3034)
MULTITECH COLD FORMING LLC
250 Kehoe Blvd (60188-1816)
PHONE................................630 949-8200
Rahul Parikh, *Mng Member*
▲ EMP: 25
SALES (est): 4.4MM **Privately Held**
SIC: 3451 3452 3965 Screw machine products; rivets, metal; fasteners
PA: Multitech Industries, Inc.
250 Kehoe Blvd
Carol Stream IL 60188

(G-3035)
MULTITECH INDUSTRIES INC (PA)
250 Kehoe Blvd (60188-1816)
PHONE................................630 784-9200
Rahul Parikh, *President*
Bob Prochnow, *Opers Mgr*
Bonnie Arndt, *Purch Agent*
Anthony Falcone, *Sales Staff*
Casie Browning, *Office Admin*
▲ EMP: 25
SQ FT: 46,000
SALES (est): 53.5MM **Privately Held**
SIC: 3559 Automotive related machinery

(G-3036)
MULTITECH MCHNED CMPONENTS LLC
250 Kehoe Blvd (60188-1816)
PHONE................................630 949-8200
Thomas Falcone, *Mng Member*
Lee Divito, *Manager*
Rahul Parikh,
▲ EMP: 30
SALES (est): 6.4MM **Privately Held**
SIC: 3559 Automotive related machinery
PA: Multitech Industries, Inc.
250 Kehoe Blvd
Carol Stream IL 60188

(G-3037)
MULTITECH SWISS MACHINING LLC
350 Village Dr (60188-1828)
PHONE................................260 894-4180
Rahul Parikh, *President*
Charles Wetherford, *Manager*
Joel Brown, *Director*
Thomas Falcone, *Admin Sec*
EMP: 9
SALES (est): 366.7K **Privately Held**
SIC: 3451 Screw machine products
PA: Multitech Industries, Inc.
250 Kehoe Blvd
Carol Stream IL 60188

(G-3038)
NATIONAL DATA SVCS CHICAGO INC (DH)
Also Called: Diamond Marketing Solutions
900 Kimberly Dr (60188-1859)
PHONE................................630 597-9100
Bruce D'Angello, *CEO*
Michael Nevolo, *President*
Mark Peterson, *President*
John Puffer, *President*
Moore David, *Vice Pres*
EMP: 114
SALES (est): 37.6MM
SALES (corp-wide): 53.3MM **Privately Held**
SIC: 7371 7331 2759 Custom computer programming services; direct mail advertising services; commercial printing

(G-3039)
NEW WORLD PRODUCTS INC
494 Mission St (60188-9417)
PHONE................................630 690-5625
Chuck Trose, *President*
Eugene Lurye, *Vice Pres*
◆ EMP: 7
SALES (est): 652.2K **Privately Held**
SIC: 3545 Cutting tools for machine tools

(G-3040)
NOVA METALS INC
279 Commonwealth Dr (60188-2450)
PHONE................................630 690-4300
Scott Lorenz, *President*
Steve Maniaci, *Treasurer*
▼ EMP: 12
SQ FT: 15,000
SALES (est): 1.7MM **Privately Held**
SIC: 3444 Sheet metal specialties, not stamped

(G-3041)
NTA PRECISION AXLE CORPORATION
795 Kimberly Dr (60188-9407)
PHONE................................630 690-6300
Jason Cotte, *Engineer*
Yukihiro Yoshida, *Admin Sec*
Steve Summers, *Assistant*
▲ EMP: 260
SALES (est): 108MM **Privately Held**
SIC: 3714 Bearings, motor vehicle
PA: Ntn Corporation
1-3-17, Kyomachibori, Nishi-Ku
Osaka OSK 550-0

(G-3042)
OASIS AUDIO LLC
289 S Main Pl (60188-2425)
PHONE................................630 668-5367
Ken Lorenz, *Marketing Staff*
Ed Elliott,
EMP: 8
SALES (est): 793.9K **Privately Held**
SIC: 2731 Books: publishing only

(G-3043)
ON TIME ENVELOPES & PRINTING
615 Kimberly Dr (60188-9403)
PHONE................................630 682-0466
Syed Zaidi, *Owner*
EMP: 5 EST: 2008
SALES (est): 500K **Privately Held**
WEB: www.oteprinting.com
SIC: 2752 Commercial printing, offset

(G-3044)
P-S BUSINESS ACQUISITION INC
Also Called: Packaging Personified
246 Kehoe Blvd (60188-1816)
PHONE................................616 887-8837
EMP: 7
SALES (corp-wide): 97MM **Privately Held**
WEB: www.packagingpersonified.com
SIC: 2673 Plastic bags: made from purchased materials
HQ: P-S Business Acquisition, Inc.
122 S Aspen St
Sparta MI 49345
616 887-8837

(G-3045)
PARVIN-CLAUSS SIGN CO INC
165 Tubeway Dr (60188-2249)
PHONE................................866 490-2877
Robert A Clauss, *President*
Al Paprocki, *Production*
Steve Galasso, *Purch Mgr*
Kishore Mahadev, *Sales Mgr*
Matt Sopchyk, *Sales Mgr*
EMP: 42
SQ FT: 10,000
SALES (est): 7.3MM **Privately Held**
WEB: www.parvinclauss.com
SIC: 7389 3993 Sign painting & lettering shop; signs & advertising specialties

(G-3046)
PHOTO TECHNIQUES CORP (PA)
Also Called: Nameplate & Panel Technology
387 Gundersen Dr (60188-2421)
PHONE................................630 690-9360
Lisa Savegnago, *President*
Randy Johnson, *Vice Pres*
Dave Savegnago, *Vice Pres*
Jeff Friedman, *QC Mgr*
Daniel Brame, *Manager*
EMP: 45
SQ FT: 20,000
SALES (est): 5.8MM **Privately Held**
WEB: www.nptec.com
SIC: 3479 3083 2759 3993 Name plates: engraved, etched, etc.; laminated plastics plate & sheet; screen printing; signs & advertising specialties; packaging paper & plastics film, coated & laminated

(G-3047)
PIERCE & STEVENS CHEMICAL
245 Kehoe Blvd (60188-1815)
PHONE................................630 653-3800
Fax: 630 510-0927
EMP: 4 EST: 2010
SALES (est): 320K **Privately Held**
SIC: 2891 Mfg Adhesives/Sealants

(G-3048)
PREFERRED FASTENERS INC
250 S Westgate Dr (60188-2243)
PHONE................................630 510-0200
John Waichulis, *President*

Tony Waichulis, *Plant Mgr*
EMP: 5
SQ FT: 5,500
SALES (est): 843.3K **Privately Held**
WEB: www.prefastinc.com
SIC: 3451 5072 Screw machine products; bolts, nuts & screws

(G-3049)
PRIME SYSTEMS INC
Also Called: Prime Uv
416 Mission St (60188-9414)
PHONE................................630 681-2100
Elinor Midlik, *President*
Erich Rassow, *Vice Pres*
Erich Midlik, *Treasurer*
Elias Baer, *Manager*
Barbara Reggio, *Admin Sec*
▲ EMP: 45
SQ FT: 80,000
SALES (est): 8.9MM **Privately Held**
SIC: 3826 Ultraviolet analytical instruments

(G-3050)
PRINCE CASTLE LLC (DH)
355 Kehoe Blvd (60188-1833)
PHONE................................630 462-8800
Randy Garvin, *President*
N L Terry, *President*
Loren Veltrop, *President*
Michael Valentino, *Principal*
Lance Cermainn, *CFO*
◆ EMP: 135
SQ FT: 187,500
SALES (est): 105.6MM
SALES (corp-wide): 327.2B **Publicly Held**
WEB: www.princecastle.com
SIC: 3589 Commercial cooking & food-warming equipment
HQ: Marmon Industrial Llc
181 W Madison St Fl 26
Chicago IL 60602
312 372-9500

(G-3051)
PRINCE FABRICATORS INC
Also Called: Prince Fabricators Division
745 N Gary Ave (60188-1812)
PHONE................................630 588-0088
Nancy Miller, *President*
Edward K Miller, *Vice Pres*
Mark S Miller, *Admin Sec*
EMP: 22
SALES (est): 3.5MM **Privately Held**
SIC: 3444 Sheet metal specialties, not stamped

(G-3052)
PRINCE INDUSTRIES INC (PA)
Also Called: Prince Industries Shanghai
745 N Gary Ave (60188-1812)
PHONE................................630 588-0088
Mark S Miller, *CEO*
Gregory W Roskuszka, *President*
Kevin Koehler, *Vice Pres*
Mark Paluch, *Vice Pres*
Mark Wooten, *Vice Pres*
▲ EMP: 275 EST: 1956
SQ FT: 65,000
SALES (est): 63.2MM **Privately Held**
WEB: www.princeind.com
SIC: 3599 Machine shop, jobbing & repair

(G-3053)
PRINOVA SOLUTIONS LLC (HQ)
285 Fullerton Ave (60188-1886)
PHONE................................630 868-0300
Donald K Thorp, *President*
Michael Petrushka, *General Mgr*
Ronald E Juergens, *Vice Pres*
◆ EMP: 42
SQ FT: 25,000
SALES (est): 11.3MM **Privately Held**
SIC: 2869 2099 Flavors or flavoring materials, synthetic; food preparations

(G-3054)
PROFESSNAL MLING PRTG SVCS INC
269 Commonwealth Dr (60188-2450)
PHONE................................630 510-1000
Jennifer Rawls, *CEO*
Samuel Bonafede, *President*
EMP: 10
SQ FT: 12,000

Carol Stream - Dupage County (G-3055)   GEOGRAPHIC SECTION

SALES (est): 1MM **Privately Held**
SIC: 2752 7331 Commercial printing, lithographic; mailing service

(G-3055)
PUBLISHERS GRAPHICS LLC (PA)
140 Della Ct (60188-2200)
PHONE..................630 221-1850
Nick A Lewis, *Mng Member*
Kathleen M Lewis,
EMP: 49
SQ FT: 10,000
SALES (est): 13.8MM **Privately Held**
SIC: 2759 Commercial printing

(G-3056)
PURE PROCESSING LLC
130 E Saint Charles Rd C (60188-2059)
PHONE..................877 718-6868
Dan Gusanders,
EMP: 6
SALES: 150K **Privately Held**
SIC: 3088 Plastics plumbing fixtures

(G-3057)
R D NIVEN & ASSOCIATES LTD
955 Kimberly Dr (60188-1806)
PHONE..................630 580-6000
Don Hubbard, *President*
Fred Musnicki, *Senior VP*
Stefanie Hajer, *Vice Pres*
Bev Sampson, *Vice Pres*
Ronald Zromkoski, *Vice Pres*
▲ **EMP:** 50
SQ FT: 154,000
SALES (est): 9.6MM **Privately Held**
SIC: 3993 Signs & advertising specialties

(G-3058)
R T M PRECISION MACHINING INC
739 Kimberly Dr (60188-9407)
PHONE..................630 595-0946
Stanislaw Tokarz, *President*
Henry Kuprinski, *Vice Pres*
Chris Tokarz, *Opers Mgr*
EMP: 4
SQ FT: 3,200
SALES: 500K **Privately Held**
WEB: www.rtmpm.com
SIC: 3599 Machine shop, jobbing & repair

(G-3059)
RELIANCE SPECIALTY PDTS INC
154 Easy St (60188-2314)
PHONE..................847 640-8923
Marc Skiersch, *President*
Cindy Marciniak, *Controller*
Laurie Lamantia, *Sales Staff*
▲ **EMP:** 10
SALES (est): 2.5MM **Privately Held**
SIC: 2819 Charcoal (carbon), activated

(G-3060)
ROYAL DIE & STAMPING CO INC (HQ)
Also Called: Royal Power Solutions
125 Mercedes Dr (60188-9409)
PHONE..................630 766-2685
Henrik Freitag, *CEO*
Erik Freitag, *President*
Chris Pepoy, *Vice Pres*
Martha Rojas, *Mfg Staff*
Neal Devine, *Engineer*
▲ **EMP:** 150
SQ FT: 78,000
SALES (est): 36.1MM
SALES (corp-wide): 59.5MM **Privately Held**
WEB: www.royaldie.com
SIC: 3544 3469 Dies & die holders for metal cutting, forming, die casting; industrial molds; metal stampings
PA: Igp Industries, Llc
101 Mission St Ste 1500
San Francisco CA 94105
415 882-4550

(G-3061)
RYESON CORPORATION (HQ)
Also Called: Sturtevant Richmont
555 Kimberly Dr (60188-1835)
PHONE..................847 455-8677
Raymond Reynertson, *President*

Edward J Lehner, *Exec VP*
Robert C J Klein, *CFO*
Don Reynertson, *Admin Sec*
▲ **EMP:** 55
SQ FT: 30,000
SALES (est): 9.2MM
SALES (corp-wide): 3.7B **Publicly Held**
SIC: 3545 3423 3829 Measuring tools & machines, machinists' metalworking type; hand & edge tools; measuring & controlling devices
PA: Snap-On Incorporated
2801 80th St
Kenosha WI 53143
262 656-5200

(G-3062)
SAINT-GOBAIN ABRASIVES INC
Also Called: Superabrasives
200 Fullerton Ave (60188-1826)
PHONE..................630 238-3300
Barbara CHI, *Regl Sales Mgr*
Mike Kornaus, *Manager*
EMP: 125
SALES (corp-wide): 328.4MM **Privately Held**
SIC: 3291 Abrasive products
HQ: Saint-Gobain Abrasives, Inc.
1 New Bond St
Worcester MA 01606
508 795-5000

(G-3063)
SAINT-GOBAIN ABRASIVES INC
Also Called: Super-Cut Abrasives
200 Fullerton Ave (60188-1826)
PHONE..................630 868-8060
Urban Kurczek, *Marketing Staff*
Samuel H Odeh, *Branch Mgr*
Nancy Kromrey, *Supervisor*
EMP: 169
SALES (corp-wide): 328.4MM **Privately Held**
SIC: 3291 3559 3545 Wheels, abrasive; coated abrasive products; sandpaper; concrete products machinery; diamond cutting tools for turning, boring, burnishing, etc.; dressers, abrasive wheel: diamond point or other
HQ: Saint-Gobain Abrasives, Inc.
1 New Bond St
Worcester MA 01606
508 795-5000

(G-3064)
SAVEX MANUFACTURING COMPANY
170 Easy St (60188-2314)
PHONE..................630 668-7219
George Wimpffen, *President*
Eva Wimpffen, *Corp Secy*
EMP: 5
SQ FT: 12,000
SALES (est): 858.5K **Privately Held**
SIC: 3599 Machine shop, jobbing & repair

(G-3065)
SCALE RAILROAD EQUIPMENT
Also Called: All Nation Line Division
23w546 Saint Charles Rd (60188-2868)
PHONE..................630 682-9170
William Pope, *President*
Danny Pope, *Vice Pres*
EMP: 2
SQ FT: 1,900
SALES (est): 217K **Privately Held**
SIC: 3944 Railroad models: toy & hobby

(G-3066)
SEACO DATA SYSTEMS INC
1360 Rolling Oaks Dr (60188-4606)
PHONE..................630 876-2169
Michael Wade, *President*
EMP: 70 **EST:** 1990
SALES (est): 4MM **Privately Held**
SIC: 3679 Electronic components

(G-3067)
SENSIO AMERICA LLC
270 Tubeway Dr (60188-2214)
PHONE..................877 501-5337
Gary Rutherford, *CTO*
EMP: 3 **EST:** 2010

SALES (est): 99.8K **Privately Held**
SIC: 3646 3648 Ornamental lighting fixtures, commercial; decorative area lighting fixtures

(G-3068)
SERAC INC (DH)
160 E Elk Trl (60188-9300)
PHONE..................630 510-9343
Acyr Borges, *CEO*
Marc Binet, *President*
Andre Jj Graffin, *President*
John Ryzka, *Project Mgr*
Jean Hostachy, *Technical Mgr*
▲ **EMP:** 40 **EST:** 1981
SQ FT: 40,000
SALES (est): 9.3MM
SALES (corp-wide): 355.8K **Privately Held**
WEB: www.serac-inc.com
SIC: 3565 Packaging machinery
HQ: Serac Group
12 Route De Mamers
La Ferte Bernard 72400
243 602-828

(G-3069)
SIEBER TOOLING SOLUTIONS INC
344 Commerce Dr (60188-1809)
PHONE..................630 462-9370
Tom Hilaris, *President*
Chris Blum, *Manager*
EMP: 7 **EST:** 1979
SQ FT: 20,000
SALES: 1MM **Privately Held**
SIC: 3544 Special dies & tools
PA: Ergoseal, Inc.
346 Commerce Dr
Carol Stream IL 60188

(G-3070)
SOLID IMPRESSIONS INC
26w455 Saint Charles Rd (60188-1942)
PHONE..................630 543-7300
John Mantia, *President*
Beth Gear, *Graphic Designe*
EMP: 5
SQ FT: 1,500
SALES (est): 864.6K **Privately Held**
SIC: 2752 2791 Commercial printing, offset; typesetting

(G-3071)
SONY ELECTRONICS INC
1064 Idaho St (60188-1310)
PHONE..................630 773-7500
EMP: 227 **Privately Held**
WEB: www.sony.com
SIC: 3651 Household audio & video equipment
HQ: Sony Electronics Inc.
16535 Via Esprillo Bldg 1
San Diego CA 92127
858 942-2400

(G-3072)
SPECIALTY PUBLISHING COMPANY
Also Called: Start Magazine
135 E Saint Charles Rd D (60188-2078)
PHONE..................630 933-0844
Peggy Smedley, *President*
David Smedley, *Vice Pres*
Lynne Flakus, *Marketing Staff*
Tim Henderson, *Graphic Designe*
EMP: 25
SQ FT: 8,000
SALES (est): 3.7MM **Privately Held**
SIC: 2721 Magazines: publishing only, not printed on site

(G-3073)
SQUEEGEE BROTHERS INC (PA)
398 E Saint Charles Rd (60188-2115)
PHONE..................630 510-9152
Jim Fruzyna, *President*
Joe Fruzyna, *Partner*
EMP: 10
SALES (est): 1.1MM **Privately Held**
SIC: 2759 Screen printing

(G-3074)
STABILOC LLC
Also Called: Swiveloc
545 Kimberly Dr (60188-1805)
PHONE..................586 412-1147
Thomas McClanaghan,
David Stadler,
EMP: 3
SQ FT: 2,000
SALES (est): 609.8K **Privately Held**
SIC: 3699 Security devices

(G-3075)
STAND FAST GROUP LLC
Also Called: Ipr Group
710 Kimberly Dr (60188-9406)
PHONE..................630 600-0900
John Pulido, *Production*
Jim Cunningham, *CFO*
Jay Carman, *Mng Member*
Dana Remus, *IT/INT Sup*
Keith Carman, *Admin Sec*
EMP: 90 **EST:** 2013
SQ FT: 17,000
SALES: 46MM **Privately Held**
SIC: 2653 Boxes, corrugated: made from purchased materials
PA: Stand Fast Packaging Products Incorporated
710 Kimberly Dr
Carol Stream IL 60188
630 600-0900

(G-3076)
STANDEX INTERNATIONAL CORP
Also Called: Mold-Tech Midwest
279 E Lies Rd (60188-9421)
PHONE..................630 588-0400
Matt Crost, *Branch Mgr*
EMP: 25
SALES (corp-wide): 791.5MM **Publicly Held**
SIC: 7389 3544 Engraving service; special dies, tools, jigs & fixtures
PA: Standex International Corporation
11 Keewaydin Dr Ste 300
Salem NH 03079
603 893-9701

(G-3077)
STEWARTS PRVATE BLEND FODS INC (PA)
301 Carlton Dr (60188-2405)
PHONE..................773 489-2500
Donald Stwewart Jr, *President*
Robert Stewart, *Vice Pres*
Dawn Stewart, *Sales Dir*
Steve Blair, *Director*
EMP: 43 **EST:** 1913
SQ FT: 48,000
SALES (est): 5.2MM **Privately Held**
WEB: www.stewarts.com
SIC: 2095 2099 Coffee roasting (except by wholesale grocers); tea blending

(G-3078)
STORAGE BATTERY SYSTEMS LLC
179 Easy St (60188-2314)
PHONE..................630 221-1700
Bill Rubenzer, *CEO*
Dan Curtin, *Sales Staff*
Joseph Wuenstel, *Marketing Staff*
Brian Marsalli, *Branch Mgr*
Frank Collingwood, *Supervisor*
EMP: 8
SALES (corp-wide): 18.9MM **Privately Held**
SIC: 3691 3612 5063 Storage batteries; transformers, except electric; batteries
PA: Storage Battery Systems, Llc
N56w16665 Ridgewood Dr
Menomonee Falls WI 53051
262 703-5800

(G-3079)
TEAM CNCEPT PRTG THRMGRPHY INC
540 Tower Blvd (60188-9426)
PHONE..................630 653-8326
Anthony E Rouse, *President*
Jeff Howicz, *Vice Pres*
Vince Manini, *Vice Pres*
Vincent Minini, *Vice Pres*

GEOGRAPHIC SECTION
Carpentersville - Kane County (G-3107)

Armando Cantarero, *Manager*
EMP: 50
SQ FT: 25,000
SALES (est): 12.3MM **Privately Held**
WEB: www.teamconceptprinting.com
SIC: 2759 2752 Commercial printing; commercial printing, lithographic

(G-3080)
TECHNOLOGY ONE WELDING INC
210 Easy St Ste D (60188-3544)
PHONE 630 871-1296
John Kotvan, *President*
▲ **EMP:** 4
SQ FT: 2,250
SALES: 500K **Privately Held**
SIC: 7692 Welding repair

(G-3081)
TITAN TOOL WORKS LLC
615 Kimberly Dr (60188-9403)
P.O. Box 1130, Libertyville (60048-4130)
PHONE 630 221-1080
David Bogetz, *Mng Member*
EMP: 11
SALES (est): 794.2K **Privately Held**
SIC: 7692 3599 Welding repair; machine shop, jobbing & repair

(G-3082)
UNIFAB MFG INC
450 Saint Paul Blvd (60188-4917)
PHONE 630 682-8970
Tam Nguyen, *President*
EMP: 25
SQ FT: 1,000
SALES (est): 5.2MM **Privately Held**
SIC: 3444 Sheet metalwork

(G-3083)
VALBRUNA STAINLESS INC
370 Village Dr (60188-1828)
PHONE 630 871-5524
Craig Hockings, *Branch Mgr*
EMP: 10
SALES (corp-wide): 723.6MM **Privately Held**
SIC: 3312 Stainless steel
HQ: Valbruna Stainless, Inc.
2400 Taylor St
Fort Wayne IN 46802

(G-3084)
VAXCEL INTERNATIONAL CO LTD
121 E North Ave (60188-1400)
PHONE 630 260-0067
C Chen, *President*
Ann Chen, *Technology*
▲ **EMP:** 47
SALES (est): 9.7MM **Privately Held**
SIC: 3645 5063 Residential lighting fixtures; lighting fixtures

(G-3085)
W B MASON CO INC
810 Kimberly Dr (60188-1875)
PHONE 888 926-2766
EMP: 42
SALES (corp-wide): 1B **Privately Held**
SIC: 5943 5712 2752 Office forms & supplies; office furniture; commercial printing, lithographic
PA: W. B. Mason Co., Inc.
59 Center St
Brockton MA 02301
508 586-3434

(G-3086)
WALEGA PRECISION COMPANY INC
205 Kehoe Blvd Ste 3 (60188-1897)
PHONE 630 682-5000
Adam Walega, *President*
Jennifer Walega, *Admin Sec*
EMP: 6
SQ FT: 5,000
SALES (est): 958.4K **Privately Held**
SIC: 3541 Machine tool replacement & repair parts, metal cutting types

(G-3087)
WESTROCK CP LLC
450 E North Ave (60188-2130)
PHONE 630 384-5200
Michael Streny, *Manager*
EMP: 100
SALES (corp-wide): 18.2B **Publicly Held**
SIC: 2653 Boxes, corrugated: made from purchased materials
HQ: Westrock Cp, Llc
1000 Abernathy Rd Ste 125
Atlanta GA 30328

(G-3088)
WHEATON RESOURCE CORP
Also Called: Wheaton Brace
380 S Schmale Rd Ste 121 (60188-2790)
PHONE 630 690-5795
Catherine Chong, *President*
Dean Schoeller, *Sales Staff*
Andrew Chong, *Executive*
EMP: 5
SALES (est): 460K **Privately Held**
WEB: www.wheatonbrace.com
SIC: 5999 3842 Orthopedic & prosthesis applications; surgical appliances & supplies

(G-3089)
WOODWORKING UNLIMITED INC
23w450 Burdette Ave (60188-2144)
PHONE 630 469-7023
Sally Kennard, *President*
EMP: 12
SQ FT: 5,000
SALES (est): 1.2MM **Privately Held**
SIC: 2541 1799 Cabinets, lockers & shelving; home/office interiors finishing, furnishing & remodeling; counter top installation

Carpentersville
Kane County

(G-3090)
ACME INDUSTRIAL COMPANY (HQ)
441 Maple Ave (60110-1939)
PHONE 847 428-3911
John W Evans, *President*
Megan Evans, *General Mgr*
George Margelos, *General Mgr*
Esther A Schron, *Chairman*
Gary Woytko, *Prdtn Mgr*
▼ **EMP:** 110 **EST:** 1914
SQ FT: 30,000
SALES (est): 21.6MM
SALES (corp-wide): 62.1MM **Privately Held**
WEB: www.acmeindustrial.com
SIC: 3545 Drill bushings (drilling jig); precision measuring tools
PA: Jergens, Inc.
15700 S Waterloo Rd
Cleveland OH 44110
216 486-5540

(G-3091)
ADVANCED POLYMER ALLOYS LLC
400 Maple Ave Ste A (60110-1978)
PHONE 847 836-8119
E David Santoleri,
EMP: 5 **EST:** 1997
SALES (est): 829.6K **Privately Held**
WEB: www.apainfo.com
SIC: 2821 Plastics materials & resins

(G-3092)
AMK AUTOMATION CORP
256 S Washington St 1 (60110-2627)
PHONE 804 348-2125
Eberhard Mueller, *President*
Jurgen Steuer, *Exec VP*
EMP: 6
SALES (est): 1MM
SALES (corp-wide): 1.7B **Privately Held**
SIC: 3566 Speed changers, drives & gears
HQ: Amk Holding Gmbh & Co. Kg
GauBstr. 37-39
Kirchheim Unter Teck 73230
702 150-050

(G-3093)
AMLING DONUTS INC
Also Called: Country Donuts
98 N Kennedy Dr (60110-1671)
PHONE 847 426-5327
EMP: 24
SALES (corp-wide): 29MM **Privately Held**
SIC: 2051 Bread, Cake, And Related Products
PA: Amling Donuts, Inc.
181 Virginia St
Crystal Lake IL 60014
815 455-2028

(G-3094)
AUTONETICS INC
425 Maple Ave (60110-1939)
PHONE 847 426-8525
Robert Trzaska, *President*
Stanley Trzaska, *Vice Pres*
Christine Trzaska, *Treasurer*
Mark Trzaska, *Director*
Barbara Colletier, *Admin Sec*
EMP: 10
SQ FT: 10,000
SALES (est): 1MM **Privately Held**
SIC: 3451 Screw machine products

(G-3095)
BLI LEGACY INC (PA)
Also Called: Bulk Lift International
1013 Tamarac Dr (60110-1967)
PHONE 847 428-6059
Brian M Kelly, *President*
Andrew Dun, *Exec VP*
Ron Lanier, *Vice Pres*
David Nattrass, *Vice Pres*
Gary Nattrass, *Vice Pres*
▲ **EMP:** 25
SQ FT: 20,000
SALES (est): 34.3MM **Privately Held**
SIC: 7389 3089 Packaging & labeling services; plastic containers, except foam

(G-3096)
CARPENTERSVILLE QUARRY INC
800 Bolz Rd (60110-1179)
PHONE 847 836-1550
EMP: 14 **EST:** 2000
SALES (est): 2.4MM **Privately Held**
SIC: 1459 Clay/Related Mineral Mining

(G-3097)
CASTER WAREHOUSE INC
1011 Tamarac Dr (60110-1967)
PHONE 847 836-5712
Peter Im, *Branch Mgr*
EMP: 13
SALES (corp-wide): 9.3MM **Privately Held**
SIC: 3562 3312 Casters; wheels
PA: Caster Warehouse, Inc.
4405 Business Park Ct Sw
Lilburn GA 30047
800 522-5998

(G-3098)
COATING METHODS INCORPORATED
853 Commerce Pkwy (60110-1721)
PHONE 847 428-8800
Chuck Rowe, *President*
EMP: 13
SQ FT: 15,000
SALES (est): 2.2MM **Privately Held**
SIC: 3479 Coating of metals & formed products

(G-3099)
CROSS CONTAINER CORPORATION
400 Maple Ave Ste B (60110-1978)
PHONE 847 844-3200
Gerald Matlock, *President*
EMP: 50
SQ FT: 260,000
SALES: 10.5MM **Privately Held**
SIC: 2653 Boxes, corrugated: made from purchased materials

(G-3100)
DIES PLUS INC
2 E Main St (60110-2624)
PHONE 630 285-1065
Gerald Dohe, *President*
Craig Dohe, *Vice Pres*
Neil Dohe, *Vice Pres*
Candice Dohe, *Systems Mgr*
EMP: 10
SALES (est): 1.4MM **Privately Held**
SIC: 3544 Special dies & tools

(G-3101)
DONALD KRANZ
Also Called: Cabcraft
10 W Main St Fl 1 (60110-1720)
PHONE 847 428-1616
Donald Kranz, *Owner*
EMP: 4
SALES (est): 183.8K **Privately Held**
SIC: 2434 2521 Wood kitchen cabinets; wood office furniture

(G-3102)
GRAYHILL INC
459 Maple Ave (60110-3004)
PHONE 847 428-6990
Adam Tesch, *Production*
Jeff Goodmanson, *Branch Mgr*
EMP: 120
SALES (corp-wide): 155.3MM **Privately Held**
SIC: 3679 3643 Electronic switches; current-carrying wiring devices
PA: Grayhill, Inc
561 W Hillgrove Ave
La Grange IL 60525
708 354-1040

(G-3103)
GROTH MANUFACTURING
845 Commerce Pkwy (60110-1721)
PHONE 847 428-5950
John Groth, *President*
EMP: 25
SALES (est): 5.6MM **Privately Held**
SIC: 3599 Machine shop, jobbing & repair

(G-3104)
I PULLOMA PAINTS
1 Day Ln (60110-1846)
PHONE 847 426-4140
Pulloma Kamdar, *President*
EMP: 10
SALES (est): 2MM **Privately Held**
SIC: 2851 Lacquers, varnishes, enamels & other coatings

(G-3105)
ILLINOIS WOOD FIBER PRODUCTS
99 Day Ln (60110-1846)
PHONE 847 836-6176
Stephen Johansen, *President*
EMP: 4
SQ FT: 200
SALES (est): 330K **Privately Held**
SIC: 2499 Mulch, wood & bark

(G-3106)
KDM ENTERPRISES LLC
820 Commerce Pkwy (60110-1721)
PHONE 877 591-9768
Craig Campagna, *Traffic Mgr*
Joseph Marzullo, *CFO*
Newman Larry,
▲ **EMP:** 43 **EST:** 2000
SQ FT: 52,000
SALES (est): 26.3MM **Privately Held**
WEB: www.gokdm.com
SIC: 2621 4731 Paper mills; freight transportation arrangement

(G-3107)
LYONDLLBSELL ADVNCED PLYMERS I
400 Maple Ave Ste A (60110-1978)
PHONE 847 426-3350
Raza Naseri, *Plant Mgr*
Henry Addante, *Manager*
June Swanson, *Executive*
EMP: 40
SALES (corp-wide): 39.1B **Privately Held**
SIC: 2821 Molding compounds, plastics

Carpentersville - Kane County (G-3108)

HQ: Lyondellbasell Advanced Polymers Inc.
1221 Mckinney St Ste 300
Houston TX 77010
713 309-7200

(G-3108)
M & M EXPOSED AGGREGATE CO
Also Called: M & M Patio Stone Company
155 S Washington St (60110-2625)
PHONE..................847 551-1818
Norman Mitchell Sr, *President*
Lester Mitchell, *Treasurer*
▲ **EMP:** 6 **EST:** 1976
SALES: 380K **Privately Held**
SIC: 3272 3271 Furniture, garden: concrete; concrete products, precast; concrete block & brick; blocks, concrete: landscape or retaining wall

(G-3109)
NATION INC
400 Maple Ave Ste B (60110-1978)
PHONE..................847 844-7300
Jerry Matlock, *President*
▲ **EMP:** 50
SQ FT: 60,000
SALES (est): 5MM **Privately Held**
SIC: 2653 2671 Boxes, corrugated: made from purchased materials; paper coated or laminated for packaging

(G-3110)
OXYTECH SYSTEMS INC
852 Commerce Pkwy (60110-1721)
PHONE..................847 888-8611
Doug Hammer, *Partner*
John Dziedzic, *Partner*
Jack Karas, *Partner*
Martin Belovicz, *Engineer*
Richard Slosarski, *Sales Mgr*
EMP: 10
SALES (est): 292.8K **Privately Held**
SIC: 3823 Industrial instrmnts msrmnt display/control process variable

(G-3111)
PERFORMANCE INDUSTRIES INC
Also Called: Metal Substrates
20 Lake Marian Rd (60110-1929)
PHONE..................972 393-6881
Mike Van Patten, *President*
EMP: 40
SQ FT: 75,000
SALES (est): 6.7MM **Privately Held**
SIC: 3441 Fabricated structural metal

(G-3112)
PERFORMANCE STAMPING CO INC
20 Lake Marian Rd (60110-1929)
PHONE..................847 426-2233
David B Maxwell, *President*
W Jean Spencer, *Vice Pres*
James Maratea, *CFO*
Scott V Spencer, *Admin Sec*
▲ **EMP:** 50 **EST:** 1971
SQ FT: 75,000
SALES (est): 16MM **Privately Held**
WEB: www.performancestamping.com
SIC: 3469 3544 Stamping metal for the trade; special dies & tools

(G-3113)
POLYNT COMPOSITES II LLC (PA)
99 E Cottage Ave (60110-1803)
PHONE..................847 428-2657
Chuck Doebler, *Plant Mgr*
Robert Page, *Purch Mgr*
Mike Knight, *Technical Mgr*
Debbie Hudson, *Human Res Mgr*
Karen Johnson, *Marketing Staff*
EMP: 6 **EST:** 2014
SALES (est): 753.7K **Privately Held**
SIC: 2655 Cans, composite: foil-fiber & other: from purchased fiber

(G-3114)
POLYNT COMPOSITES USA INC (DH)
99 E Cottage Ave (60110-1803)
PHONE..................847 428-2657
Rosario Valido, *CEO*

Sergio Conni, *Exec VP*
Chuck Doebler, *Plant Mgr*
Robert Page, *Purch Mgr*
Christi Cragg, *Buyer*
▲ **EMP:** 120
SALES (est): 255.6MM
SALES (corp-wide): 2.4B **Privately Held**
SIC: 2821 Polyurethane resins; polyethylene resins
HQ: Polynt Spa
Via Enrico Fermi 51
Scanzorosciate BG 24020
035 652-111

(G-3115)
PRESS PROOF PRINTING
180 S Western Ave (60110-1738)
PHONE..................847 466-7156
Sante Furio, *President*
EMP: 2
SALES (est): 234.4K **Privately Held**
WEB: www.pressprooflabels.com
SIC: 2752 Commercial printing, lithographic

(G-3116)
QUARTERS CONCESSIONS INC
4064 Stratford Ln (60110-3414)
PHONE..................847 343-4864
Tom Thebault, *Principal*
EMP: 3 **EST:** 2010
SALES (est): 215.4K **Privately Held**
SIC: 3131 Footwear cut stock

(G-3117)
QUILTMASTER INC
1 S Wisconsin St (60110-2697)
PHONE..................847 426-6741
Raymond A Weishaar, *President*
Robert C Weishaar, *Vice Pres*
EMP: 35 **EST:** 1967
SQ FT: 20,000
SALES (est): 2.2MM **Privately Held**
WEB: www.quiltmasterinc.com
SIC: 2395 2392 Quilting & quilting supplies; quilted fabrics or cloth; quilting, for the trade; comforters & quilts: made from purchased materials; bedspreads & bed sets: made from purchased materials

(G-3118)
REICHHOLD INDUSTRIES INC (PA)
100 E Cottage Ave (60110-1884)
PHONE..................919 990-7500
John S Gaither, *Ch of Bd*
Jeff Reynolds, *Business Mgr*
Mitzi Vanleeuwen, *Vice Pres*
Robert Eftang, *Plant Mgr*
Curtis Symmes, *Plant Mgr*
EMP: 48
SALES (est): 79.6MM **Privately Held**
SIC: 2821 Plastics materials & resins

(G-3119)
REVCOR INC (PA)
251 Edwards Ave (60110-1941)
PHONE..................847 428-4411
John Reichwein Jr, *CEO*
Lee Frick, *Vice Pres*
Craig Hall, *Vice Pres*
Paul Vogel, *Vice Pres*
Jose Davila, *VP Mfg*
▲ **EMP:** 300
SQ FT: 30,000
SALES (est): 94.1MM **Privately Held**
WEB: www.revcor.com
SIC: 3564 3089 Air purification equipment; blowers & fans; injection molded finished plastic products

(G-3120)
STANLEY MACHINING & TOOL CORP (PA)
425 Maple Ave (60110-1939)
PHONE..................847 426-4560
Stanley Trzaska, *CEO*
Krysyna Trzaska, *President*
Walter Cwik, *General Mgr*
Barbara Colletier, *Vice Pres*
Christopher Mikucki, *Plant Mgr*
▲ **EMP:** 95
SQ FT: 110,000
SALES (est): 29.7MM **Privately Held**
WEB: www.stanleymachining.com
SIC: 3599 Machine shop, jobbing & repair

(G-3121)
TRIM-RITE FOOD CORPORATION
801 Commerce Pkwy (60110-1721)
PHONE..................847 649-3400
James Jendruczek, *President*
Michael Lookingland, *Vice Pres*
Dave Piotrowski, *CFO*
David Piotrowski, *CFO*
Julie Kidd, *Accountant*
▼ **EMP:** 200
SQ FT: 76,000
SALES (est): 79.2MM **Privately Held**
SIC: 2013 Prepared pork products from purchased pork; ham, boiled: from purchased meat; ham, boneless: from purchased meat; pork, cured: from purchased meat

(G-3122)
VIDEO REFURBISHING SVCS INC
Also Called: Inflight Entertainment Pdts
850 Commerce Pkwy (60110-1721)
PHONE..................847 844-7366
James Shipley, *COO*
Dan Olstinske, *Sales Staff*
Teressa Marquardt, *Office Admin*
Robert Hickey, *Officer*
◆ **EMP:** 20 **EST:** 2002
SQ FT: 7,510
SALES: 3.4MM **Privately Held**
SIC: 3728 Aircraft parts & equipment

Carrier Mills
Saline County

(G-3123)
AMY SCHUTT
Also Called: Girls In The Garage
420 N Thompson St (62917-1141)
PHONE..................618 994-7405
Amy Schutt, *Principal*
EMP: 3
SALES (est): 249.4K **Privately Held**
SIC: 7539 2759 Automotive repair shops; screen printing

(G-3124)
CATERPILLAR GLOBL MIN AMER LLC
Also Called: Caterpilar
9580 Highway 13 W (62917-2013)
PHONE..................618 982-9000
Pat Higgins, *Manager*
EMP: 75
SALES (corp-wide): 53.8B **Publicly Held**
SIC: 3532 7629 Mining machinery; electrical repair shops
HQ: Caterpillar Global Mining America, Llc
2045 W Pike St
Houston PA 15342
724 743-1200

(G-3125)
WILLARD MILLER
Also Called: Millers Wood Shop
265 Battleford Rd (62917-2356)
PHONE..................618 252-4407
Willard Miller, *Owner*
EMP: 3
SQ FT: 6,000
SALES: 796K **Privately Held**
SIC: 2491 Millwork, treated wood

Carrollton
Greene County

(G-3126)
GREENE JERSEY SHOPPERS (PA)
428 N Main St (62016-1178)
PHONE..................217 942-3626
Albert Scott III, *Owner*
EMP: 9 **EST:** 1846
SQ FT: 2,000
SALES (est): 799.8K **Privately Held**
SIC: 2711 Newspapers: publishing only, not printed on site

(G-3127)
MARY MCHELLE WINERY VINYRD LLC
54 Ponderosa Ln (62016-1175)
PHONE..................217 942-6250
David C Nelson,
▲ **EMP:** 11
SALES (est): 1MM **Privately Held**
SIC: 2084 Wines

Carterville
Williamson County

(G-3128)
ADVANCED ENRGY SOLUTIONS GROUP
Also Called: AES Solar
1804 Supply Rd (62918-3395)
PHONE..................618 988-0888
Aur J Beck, *President*
EMP: 10 **EST:** 2000
SQ FT: 5,200
SALES: 1.2MM **Privately Held**
WEB: www.aessolar.com
SIC: 1711 1731 3621 3629 Solar energy contractor; general electrical contractor; generators for gas-electric or oil-electric vehicles; inverters, nonrotating: electrical

(G-3129)
BEST DESIGNS INC
11521 Kevin Ln (62918-3384)
P.O. Box 456, Herrin (62948-0456)
PHONE..................618 985-4445
Mark Shasteen, *CEO*
Rona Shasteen, *President*
Lyndon Forby, *COO*
Joan Shasteen, *Vice Pres*
EMP: 18
SQ FT: 1,000
SALES (est): 3MM **Privately Held**
SIC: 3011 Tires & inner tubes

(G-3130)
CARTERVILLE COURIER
122 S Division St (62918-1478)
PHONE..................618 985-6187
Devin Miller, *Principal*
Maryjane Fuller, *Clerk*
EMP: 5
SALES (est): 194.4K **Privately Held**
SIC: 2711 Newspapers: publishing only, not printed on site

(G-3131)
CELLAR LLC (PA)
Also Called: Walker's Bluff
326 Vermont Rd (62918-3105)
PHONE..................618 956-9900
EMP: 4
SALES (est): 607.3K **Privately Held**
SIC: 2084 Wines

(G-3132)
JON CAGLE
Also Called: Handy Filler Systems
1611 Lindbergh Rd (62918-1946)
PHONE..................618 559-3578
Jon Cagle, *Principal*
EMP: 4 **EST:** 2010
SALES (est): 319.8K **Privately Held**
WEB: www.handyfiller.com
SIC: 3565 Packaging machinery

(G-3133)
MASON ELECTRIC
1300 Pin Oak Dr (62918-1665)
PHONE..................618 457-8900
EMP: 2
SALES (est): 213.9K **Privately Held**
SIC: 3699 Mfg Electrical Equipment/Supplies

Carthage
Hancock County

(G-3134)
COKEL WELDING SHOP
117 S Madison St (62321-1332)
PHONE..................217 357-3312

Lawrence Cokel, *Owner*
Richard Cokel, *Co-Owner*
EMP: 7
SALES: 100K **Privately Held**
SIC: 7692 1799 Welding repair; welding on site

(G-3135)
DEMOCRAT COMPANY CORP
Also Called: Hancock County Journal-Pilot
31 N Washington St (62321-1450)
P.O. Box 478 (62321-0478)
PHONE.................................217 357-2149
Mark Smidt, *Manager*
EMP: 6
SALES (corp-wide): 184MM **Privately Held**
SIC: 2711 Newspapers, publishing & printing
HQ: The Democrat Company Corp
1226 Avenue H
Fort Madison IA 52627

(G-3136)
GARY GRIMM & ASSOCIATES INC
1204 Buchanan St (62321-1510)
P.O. Box 378 (62321-0378)
PHONE.................................217 357-3401
Gary Grimm, *President*
Phoebe Wear, *Vice Pres*
▲ **EMP:** 9
SALES (est): 600K **Privately Held**
SIC: 2731 2721 Book publishing; magazines: publishing only, not printed on site

(G-3137)
LAKE HILL WINERY INC
1822 E County Road 1540 N (62321-3415)
P.O. Box 305 (62321-0305)
PHONE.................................217 357-2675
Ryan Jacquot, *Officer*
EMP: 5 **EST:** 2011
SALES (est): 398.4K **Privately Held**
SIC: 2084 Wines

(G-3138)
MERRITT FARM EQUIPMENT INC
Also Called: Merritt Rv
1875 E County Road 2000 N (62321-3023)
PHONE.................................217 746-5331
Richard Merritt, *President*
Marlena Siverly, *Corp Secy*
EMP: 6
SQ FT: 6,100
SALES: 1.3MM **Privately Held**
SIC: 5561 7538 7692 Campers (pickup coaches) for mounting on trucks; recreational vehicle parts & accessories; recreational vehicle repairs; welding repair

(G-3139)
METHODE ELECTRONICS INC
Automotive Electronic Controls
111 W Buchanan St (62321-1250)
P.O. Box 130 (62321-0130)
PHONE.................................217 357-3941
John Lee, *Purch Agent*
Drew Beeler, *Engineer*
James Kendrick, *Manager*
EMP: 1500
SQ FT: 30,000
SALES (corp-wide): 1B **Publicly Held**
SIC: 3678 3714 3643 3625 Electronic connectors; motor vehicle parts & accessories; current-carrying wiring devices; relays & industrial controls; switchgear & switchboard apparatus
PA: Methode Electronics, Inc
8750 W Bryn Mawr Ave # 1000
Chicago IL 60631
708 867-6777

(G-3140)
MORTON BUILDINGS INC
1825 E Us Highway 136 (62321-3540)
P.O. Box 318 (62321-0318)
PHONE.................................217 357-3713
Jim Hills, *Manager*
Paul Bradshaw, *Manager*
EMP: 9
SALES (corp-wide): 462.5MM **Privately Held**
WEB: www.mortonbuildings.com
SIC: 3448 5039 Prefabricated metal buildings; prefabricated structures

PA: Morton Buildings, Inc.
252 W Adams St
Morton IL 61550
800 447-7436

(G-3141)
NORTHERN ILLINOIS GAS COMPANY
Also Called: Nicor Gas
1375 Buchanan St (62321-1574)
PHONE.................................217 357-3105
David Schoff, *Branch Mgr*
EMP: 12
SALES (corp-wide): 21.4B **Publicly Held**
SIC: 4924 1382 4923 Natural gas distribution; oil & gas exploration services; gas transmission & distribution
HQ: Northern Illinois Gas Company
1844 W Ferry Rd
Naperville IL 60563
630 983-8676

Cary
Mchenry County

(G-3142)
A B KELLY INC
212 W Main St Ste 5 (60013-2769)
PHONE.................................847 639-1022
William Braun, *President*
Patrice Beck, *Admin Sec*
EMP: 5
SALES (est): 198K **Privately Held**
SIC: 2391 3081 7641 2394 Curtains & draperies; vinyl film & sheet; reupholstery & furniture repair; upholstery work; reupholstery; canvas & related products

(G-3143)
ACCURATE RADIATION SHIELDING
206 Cleveland St (60013-2971)
PHONE.................................847 639-5533
Blake Denker, *President*
Joseph Pesce, *Vice Pres*
EMP: 7
SQ FT: 22,000
SALES (est): 1MM **Privately Held**
SIC: 3842 5047 Radiation shielding aprons, gloves, sheeting, etc.; hospital equipment & supplies

(G-3144)
ACTION PUMP CO
170 Chicago St (60013-2948)
PHONE.................................847 516-3636
Robert M Barrett, *President*
Marty Barrett, *Vice Pres*
▲ **EMP:** 15
SQ FT: 17,000
SALES (est): 4.4MM **Privately Held**
SIC: 3561 Pumps & pumping equipment

(G-3145)
AEROSTARS INC
6413 Kingsbridge Dr (60013-1485)
P.O. Box 962 (60013-0962)
PHONE.................................847 736-8171
David Monroe, *Treasurer*
EMP: 3
SALES: 90K **Privately Held**
SIC: 3721 Aircraft

(G-3146)
AIRGUN DESIGNS USA INC
401 Florine Ct (60013-1501)
PHONE.................................847 520-7507
David Zupan, *President*
EMP: 5
SQ FT: 2,000
SALES (est): 494.5K **Privately Held**
SIC: 3944 5941 5091 Air rifles, toy; sporting goods & bicycle shops; firearms, sporting

(G-3147)
AMPAC FLEXICON LLC (DH)
Also Called: Ampac Flexibles
165 Chicago St (60013-2948)
PHONE.................................847 639-3530
Cathy Lebron, *Principal*
Brian Scampini, *Director*
▲ **EMP:** 72 **EST:** 2004

SQ FT: 58,000
SALES (est): 13.5MM
SALES (corp-wide): 1.2B **Privately Held**
SIC: 2671 Plastic film, coated or laminated for packaging; paper coated or laminated for packaging
HQ: Ampac Holdings, Llc
12025 Tricon Rd
Cincinnati OH 45246
513 671-1777

(G-3148)
APTARGROUP INC
Aptar Cary
1160 Silver Lake Rd (60013-1658)
PHONE.................................847 639-2124
Daphane Robinson-Winfre, *Safety Mgr*
Deana Nordengren, *Foreman/Supr*
Steve Paul, *Chief Engr*
Esser Tom, *Engineer*
Jennifer Wood, *Finance*
EMP: 400 **Publicly Held**
SIC: 3499 3561 3491 Aerosol valves, metal; pumps & pumping equipment; industrial valves
PA: Aptargroup, Inc.
265 Exchange Dr Ste 100
Crystal Lake IL 60014

(G-3149)
BASE 2 MARKETING AND SUPPLY
720 Industrial Dr Ste 103 (60013-1900)
PHONE.................................847 516-0012
Vincent J Barzano, *President*
Mary A Barzano, *Admin Sec*
EMP: 5
SQ FT: 2,000
SALES (est): 909.1K **Privately Held**
SIC: 3565 Packaging machinery

(G-3150)
BFW COATING
740 Industrial Dr Ste G (60013-3373)
PHONE.................................847 639-2155
Bill Wilson, *Owner*
EMP: 2
SALES (est): 272.4K **Privately Held**
SIC: 3479 Coating of metals & formed products

(G-3151)
C & B SERVICES
6305 Lake Shore Dr (60013-1267)
PHONE.................................847 462-8484
Cassandra Booker, *Owner*
EMP: 4
SALES (est): 214K **Privately Held**
SIC: 3679 7389 Electronic components;

(G-3152)
D M C MOLD & TOOL CORP
740 Industrial Dr Ste H (60013-3373)
PHONE.................................847 639-3098
Dustin Carlson, *President*
Virginia Carlson, *Vice Pres*
Leo Rivas, *Engineer*
Brandon Tsuji, *Engineer*
EMP: 8
SQ FT: 4,500
SALES (est): 989K **Privately Held**
SIC: 3544 Special dies & tools

(G-3153)
D O D TECHNOLOGIES INC
675 Industrial Dr (60013-1944)
PHONE.................................815 788-5200
Daniel O'Donnell, *President*
▲ **EMP:** 30
SQ FT: 4,500
SALES: 3MM **Privately Held**
SIC: 3829 Gas detectors

(G-3154)
DEBORAH MORRIS GULBRANDSON PT
Also Called: Cary Physcl Therapy Spt Rehab
2615 3 Oaks Rd Ste 1a (60013-6123)
PHONE.................................847 639-4140
Deborah Gulbrandson, *President*
EMP: 12
SALES (est): 1MM **Privately Held**
SIC: 8049 3842 Physical therapist; surgical appliances & supplies

(G-3155)
DECORE-ATIVE SPECIALTIES
387 Oakmont Dr (60013-1179)
PHONE.................................630 947-6294
Matthew Landvick, *Principal*
EMP: 314
SALES (corp-wide): 184.2MM **Privately Held**
WEB: www.decorehome.com
SIC: 2431 Doors, wood
PA: Decore-Ative Specialties Nc Llc
2772 Peck Rd
Monrovia CA 91016
626 254-9191

(G-3156)
DURAFLEX INC
765 Industrial Dr (60013-1918)
PHONE.................................847 462-1007
Dean Dellacecca, *President*
Mark Saban, *Production*
Kim Mack, *Purchasing*
Jenn Jones-Reynolds, *Data Proc Staff*
▲ **EMP:** 50
SQ FT: 48,000
SALES (est): 10.9MM **Privately Held**
SIC: 3498 3599 3769 Pipe fittings, fabricated from purchased pipe; flexible metal hose, tubing & bellows; bellows, industrial: metal; bellows assemblies, missiles: metal

(G-3157)
DUREX INTERNATIONAL CORP
Also Called: Durex Industries
190 Detroit St (60013-2979)
PHONE.................................847 639-5600
Edward Hinz, *President*
Kathleen Robinson, *Accountant*
Ed Vickers, *Regl Sales Mgr*
Joe Meckl, *Supervisor*
Randy Nelson, *Admin Sec*
▲ **EMP:** 370
SQ FT: 120,000
SALES (est): 97.8MM **Privately Held**
WEB: www.durexindustries.com
SIC: 3567 3823 3829 Electrical furnaces, ovens & heating devices, exc. induction; temperature measurement instruments, industrial; thermometers & temperature sensors

(G-3158)
EXPERIMENTAL AIRCRAFT EXAMINER
69 Mohawk St (60013-1877)
PHONE.................................847 226-0777
Edward Finnegan, *Principal*
EMP: 3
SALES (est): 123.6K **Privately Held**
WEB: www.finneganaviationservices.com
SIC: 2711 Newspapers, publishing & printing

(G-3159)
FLOCON INC (PA)
339 Cary Point Dr (60013-2974)
P.O. Box 609 (60013-0609)
PHONE.................................815 444-1500
Richard W Ballot, *CEO*
Patricia Ballot, *Vice Pres*
Bob Forschler, *Exec Dir*
▲ **EMP:** 47
SQ FT: 35,000
SALES (est): 5.1MM **Privately Held**
SIC: 3491 Industrial valves

(G-3160)
FUGIEL RAILROAD SUPPLY CORP
700 Industrial Dr Ste E (60013-1950)
P.O. Box 158 (60013-0158)
PHONE.................................847 516-6862
Kathleen Fugiel, *President*
Robert Fugiel, *Vice Pres*
EMP: 5
SALES (est): 953.8K **Privately Held**
SIC: 3743 5088 Railroad equipment; railroad equipment & supplies

(G-3161)
GAGE GRINDING COMPANY INC (PA)
40 Detroit St Unit D (60013-6605)
PHONE.................................847 639-3888

Cary - Mchenry County (G-3162)

Gary Fischer, *President*
EMP: 17 **EST:** 1961
SQ FT: 9,000
SALES (est): 3.2MM **Privately Held**
WEB: www.gagegrinding.com
SIC: 3544 Special dies & tools

(G-3162)
GALAXY INDUSTRIES INC
231 Jandus Rd (60013-2861)
PHONE 847 639-8580
Joseph M Lebar, *Ch of Bd*
Kenneth Lebar, *Vice Pres*
Steve J Lebar, *Treasurer*
Martin J Lebar, *Admin Sec*
▲ **EMP:** 100 **EST:** 1971
SQ FT: 55,000
SALES (est): 9.8MM **Privately Held**
SIC: 5084 5082 3423 3545 Drilling equipment, excluding bits; drilling bits; tapping attachments; metalworking tools (such as drills, taps, dies, files); masonry equipment & supplies; masons' hand tools; drill bits, metalworking

(G-3163)
GENERAL ASSEMBLY & MFG CORP
750 Industrial Dr Ste B (60013-1988)
PHONE 847 516-6462
Paul A Tomaszek, *President*
Mike Hamby, *Corp Secy*
EMP: 45
SQ FT: 30,000
SALES (est): 6.2MM **Privately Held**
SIC: 7389 3491 Packaging & labeling services; industrial valves

(G-3164)
GENERAL LAMINATING COMPANY
179 Northwest Hwy Ste 3 (60013-6601)
PHONE 847 639-8770
Don Cooper, *Owner*
EMP: 3
SQ FT: 5,000
SALES: 250K **Privately Held**
SIC: 2679 2672 Paperboard products, converted; cardboard: pasted, laminated, lined, or surface coated; coated & laminated paper

(G-3165)
GLAMOX AQUA SIGNAL CORPORATION (DH)
1125 Alexander Ct (60013-1892)
PHONE 847 639-6412
Jan Berner, *Ch of Bd*
Alena Heede, *President*
Jorg Koch-Losekamm, *Principal*
Greg Gibson, *Purch Mgr*
Kathy Jordan, *Personnel*
◆ **EMP:** 16
SQ FT: 20,300
SALES (est): 2.1MM
SALES (corp-wide): 177.9K **Privately Held**
SIC: 3646 3647 Commercial indusl & institutional electric lighting fixtures; boat & ship lighting fixtures
HQ: Glamox Marine And Offshore Gmbh
Linzer Str. 9a
Bremen 28359
421 369-3520

(G-3166)
HARTLAND CUTTING TOOLS INC
240 Jandus Rd (60013-2862)
PHONE 847 639-9400
Mike Polizzi, *President*
Oscar Gomez, *Mfg Staff*
EMP: 14
SQ FT: 14,000
SALES (est): 2.5MM **Privately Held**
WEB: www.hartlandtool.com
SIC: 3541 5084 3545 Machine tools, metal cutting type; industrial machinery & equipment; machine tool accessories

(G-3167)
HORIZON STEEL TREATING INC
Also Called: Trucut
231 Jandus Rd (60013-2861)
PHONE 847 639-4030

Joseph R Lebar, *President*
Steven J Lebar, *Admin Sec*
▲ **EMP:** 100
SQ FT: 10,000
SALES (est): 9.9MM **Privately Held**
SIC: 3398 Metal heat treating

(G-3168)
ILLINOIS BLOWER INC
Also Called: Ibi
750 Industrial Dr Ste E (60013-1988)
PHONE 847 639-5500
Tyler S Barth, *President*
William Howarth, *Vice Pres*
Jeff Sauck, *Opers Staff*
Joel Rivera, *Project Engr*
Gregory Furtek, *Director*
▲ **EMP:** 85
SQ FT: 75,000
SALES (est): 25MM **Privately Held**
SIC: 3564 Blowing fans: industrial or commercial; exhaust fans: industrial or commercial; ventilating fans: industrial or commercial

(G-3169)
ILLINOIS LIFT EQUIPMENT INC
640 Industrial Dr (60013-1944)
PHONE 888 745-0577
Michael Lopez, *President*
Matt Reif, *Sales Mgr*
Mario Labalestra, *Sales Staff*
Dave Yelaska, *Sales Associate*
Paul Dee, *Web Dvlpr*
◆ **EMP:** 24 **EST:** 2010
SALES (est): 17.2MM **Privately Held**
WEB: www.illinoislift.com
SIC: 5084 3537 Materials handling machinery; industrial trucks & tractors

(G-3170)
ILLINOIS PRO-TURN INC
309 Cary Point Dr Ste F (60013-2901)
PHONE 847 462-1870
Daniel Lamz, *President*
EMP: 8
SALES (est): 1.3MM **Privately Held**
SIC: 3599 Machine shop, jobbing & repair

(G-3171)
INSERTECH LLC (PA)
711 Indl Dr (60013)
PHONE 847 516-6184
David Butt, *Mng Member*
Robert Harney,
◆ **EMP:** 55
SQ FT: 30,000
SALES (est): 30.1MM **Privately Held**
SIC: 3089 Injection molding of plastics; plastic processing

(G-3172)
INSERTECH INTERNATIONAL INC
711 Industrial Dr (60013-1962)
PHONE 847 416-6184
David C Butt, *CEO*
Cory Cramer, *Program Mgr*
EMP: 40
SALES (est): 4.9MM **Privately Held**
SIC: 3089 Injection molded finished plastic products

(G-3173)
JHB GROUP INC
766 Industrial Dr Ste G (60013-1903)
PHONE 657 888-3473
Christopher Gantz, *Principal*
Heather Gantz, *Principal*
EMP: 3
SALES (est): 208.5K **Privately Held**
SIC: 3715 Truck trailers

(G-3174)
KOFLO CORPORATION
309 Cary Point Dr Ste A (60013-2901)
PHONE 847 516-3700
James Federighi, *President*
Anthony Federighi, *Exec VP*
EMP: 10
SQ FT: 12,000
SALES (est): 2.3MM **Privately Held**
SIC: 3559 3531 Refinery, chemical processing & similar machinery; construction machinery

(G-3175)
LGB INDUSTRIES
91 Fairfield Ln (60013-1945)
P.O. Box 99 (60013-0099)
PHONE 847 639-1691
Larry G Bachner, *Owner*
EMP: 7
SQ FT: 2,000
SALES (est): 371.2K **Privately Held**
SIC: 3714 7515 Motor vehicle parts & accessories; passenger car leasing

(G-3176)
LUXO CORPORATION
1125 Alexander Ct (60013-1892)
PHONE 914 345-0067
Sam Gumins, *President*
▲ **EMP:** 19 **EST:** 1953
SALES: 7.5MM
SALES (corp-wide): 177.9K **Privately Held**
WEB: www.luxogroupinc.com
SIC: 3646 Commercial indusl & institutional electric lighting fixtures
HQ: Glamox As
Birger Hatlebakks Veg 15
Molde 6415
712 460-00

(G-3177)
LUXURY LIVING INC
5 Tamarack Ct (60013-2469)
P.O. Box 3622, Barrington (60011-3622)
PHONE 847 845-3863
Diane Pawelko, *President*
Edmund Pawelko, *CFO*
▲ **EMP:** 6
SALES (est): 600K **Privately Held**
SIC: 3999 Pet supplies

(G-3178)
MASTER CABINETS
209 Cleveland St Ste D (60013-2978)
PHONE 847 639-1323
Johann Merkhofer, *Owner*
EMP: 3
SALES (est): 90K **Privately Held**
SIC: 2431 2511 2434 Millwork; wood household furniture; wood kitchen cabinets

(G-3179)
MITCHELL AIRCRAFT SPARES INC
1160 Alexander Ct (60013-1892)
PHONE 847 516-3773
Richard C Sebion, *Chairman*
Peter Davis, *Exec VP*
Jim Glockner, *Exec VP*
Greg Fletcher, *Vice Pres*
Craig Cero, *CFO*
▲ **EMP:** 45
SQ FT: 30,000
SALES (est): 22.1MM **Privately Held**
SIC: 3728 Aircraft parts & equipment

(G-3180)
MITCHELL ARCFT EXPENDABLES LLC
1160 Alexander Ct (60013-1892)
PHONE 847 516-3773
Craig Cero, *VP Finance*
Terri Wood, *Accounting Mgr*
Vecchio Pam, *Sales Staff*
EMP: 47 **EST:** 1996
SALES (est): 10.8MM **Privately Held**
SIC: 3721 Aircraft

(G-3181)
MULTIMAIL SOLUTIONS
700 Industrial Dr (60013-1957)
PHONE 847 516-9977
Douglas Conte, *Principal*
EMP: 3
SALES (est): 221.7K **Privately Held**
SIC: 3579 Mailing machines

(G-3182)
PFIZER INC
2323 Grove Ln (60013-2830)
PHONE 847 639-3020
Liz Boem, *Branch Mgr*
EMP: 52
SALES (corp-wide): 51.7B **Publicly Held**
SIC: 2879 Fungicides, herbicides

PA: Pfizer Inc.
235 E 42nd St Rm 107
New York NY 10017
212 733-2323

(G-3183)
PLASPROS INC
511 Cove Dr (60013-6307)
PHONE 847 639-6492
Sherry L Hull, *Principal*
EMP: 3
SALES (est): 285.5K **Privately Held**
SIC: 3089 Plastics products

(G-3184)
RAMCO TOOL & MANUFACTURING INC
760 Industrial Dr Ste I (60013-1989)
PHONE 847 639-9899
Don M Beene Jr, *President*
Don M Beene Sr, *Treasurer*
Shirley Beene, *Admin Sec*
EMP: 10 **EST:** 1964
SQ FT: 6,000
SALES (est): 1.4MM **Privately Held**
SIC: 3599 Machine shop, jobbing & repair

(G-3185)
RENNER & CO
160 Chicago St (60013-2948)
P.O. Box 50, Des Plaines (60016-0001)
PHONE 847 639-4900
James W Renner, *President*
Robert A Renner, *Corp Secy*
Robert Renner, *Treasurer*
EMP: 10 **EST:** 1933
SQ FT: 13,500
SALES (est): 1.4MM **Privately Held**
SIC: 3499 Novelties & specialties, metal

(G-3186)
RESTORATIONS UNLIMITED II INC
304 Jandus Rd (60013-3002)
PHONE 847 639-5818
Ralph Morey, *President*
EMP: 4
SQ FT: 4,000
SALES (est): 200K **Privately Held**
SIC: 7532 3711 Antique & classic automobile restoration; automobile assembly, including specialty automobiles

(G-3187)
ROSS AND WHITE COMPANY
1090 Alexander Ct (60013-1890)
P.O. Box 970 (60013-0970)
PHONE 847 516-3900
Jeffrey A Ross, *President*
Roy A Schuetz, *Vice Pres*
EMP: 15 **EST:** 1933
SQ FT: 20,000
SALES (est): 3.4MM **Privately Held**
WEB: www.rossandwhite.com
SIC: 3589 3582 3443 High pressure cleaning equipment; commercial laundry equipment; fabricated plate work (boiler shop)

(G-3188)
SAGE PRODUCTS LLC (HQ)
Also Called: Stryker Corporation
3909 Three Oaks Rd (60013-1804)
PHONE 815 455-4700
Kevin Lobo, *CEO*
Kyle Palmer, *Design Engr*
Nancy Engels, *VP Finance*
Chip Bartel, *Sales Staff*
Scott Brown, *Sales Staff*
◆ **EMP:** 224 **EST:** 1971
SQ FT: 620,000
SALES: 150.9MM
SALES (corp-wide): 14.8B **Publicly Held**
SIC: 3842 5047 Surgical appliances & supplies; medical & hospital equipment
PA: Stryker Corporation
2825 Airview Blvd
Portage MI 49002
269 385-2600

(G-3189)
SAGE PRODUCTS HOLDINGS II LLC
3909 Three Oaks Rd (60013-1804)
PHONE 800 323-2220

▲ = Import ▼ = Export
◆ = Import/Export

GEOGRAPHIC SECTION

Caseyville - St. Clair County (G-3217)

Scott Brown, *President*
EMP: 4
SALES (est): 115.3K
SALES (corp-wide): 14.8B **Publicly Held**
SIC: 3842 5047 Surgical appliances & supplies; medical & hospital equipment
PA: Stryker Corporation
2825 Airview Blvd
Portage MI 49002
269 385-2600

(G-3190)
SIGNX CO INC
508 Cary Algonquin Rd (60013-6712)
PHONE.................................847 639-7917
Edward D Synek, *President*
EMP: 6
SALES (est): 440K **Privately Held**
SIC: 3993 Signs & advertising specialties

(G-3191)
SPEED TECH TECHNOLOGY INC
314 Cary Point Dr (60013-2975)
PHONE.................................847 516-2001
John Mykytiuk, *President*
William Mykytiuk, *Vice Pres*
Lilian Mykytiuk, *Admin Sec*
EMP: 9
SQ FT: 8,000
SALES (est): 790K **Privately Held**
SIC: 3519 5013 Gasoline engines; automotive engines & engine parts

(G-3192)
STRYKER CORPORATION
3909 3 Oaks Rd (60013-1804)
PHONE.................................847 829-5238
EMP: 3
SALES (corp-wide): 14.8B **Publicly Held**
SIC: 3841 Surgical instruments & apparatus
PA: Stryker Corporation
2825 Airview Blvd
Portage MI 49002
269 385-2600

(G-3193)
T D J GROUP INC
760 Industrial Dr Ste A (60013-1989)
PHONE.................................847 639-1113
Redmond R Clark PHD, *President*
Bob Bruton, *COO*
Robert Burton, *Vice Pres*
Mary Harvey, *Manager*
EMP: 9
SQ FT: 20,000
SALES: 1MM **Privately Held**
SIC: 2899 5169 8732 Chemical supplies for foundries; chemicals, industrial & heavy; research services, except laboratory

(G-3194)
TADD LLC
Also Called: Light Efficient Design
188 Northwest Hwy (60013-2998)
PHONE.................................847 380-3540
Michael Benz, *Vice Pres*
Chuck EBY, *Finance*
Jean Cullen, *Regl Sales Mgr*
Michael Cristante, *Marketing Staff*
Jon Fredrikson, *Marketing Staff*
▲ EMP: 12 EST: 2008
SALES (est): 6.5MM **Privately Held**
WEB: www.led-llc.com
SIC: 3229 Bulbs for electric lights

(G-3195)
TRU-CUT INC
231 Jandus Rd (60013-2861)
PHONE.................................847 639-2090
Kenneth W Lebar, *President*
Steve J Lebar, *Vice Pres*
Martin Lebar, *Purchasing*
Joseph A Lebar, *Treasurer*
Marty Lebar, *VP Human Res*
▲ EMP: 60
SQ FT: 55,000
SALES (est): 9.6MM **Privately Held**
WEB: www.trucutmfg.com
SIC: 3545 3546 Drill bits, metalworking; power-driven handtools

(G-3196)
TRUE VALUE COMPANY LLC
201 Jandus Rd (60013-2861)
PHONE.................................847 639-5383
Allen Mangrum, *Safety Mgr*
Bud Marlewski, *Production*
Rich White, *Sales Dir*
John Vanderpool, *Manager*
James Wallace, *Technology*
EMP: 36 **Privately Held**
WEB: www.truevaluecompany.com
SIC: 5072 2851 3991 Hardware; paints & paint additives; paint & varnish brushes
HQ: True Value Company, L.L.C.
8600 W Bryn Mawr Ave 100s
Chicago IL 60631
773 695-5000

(G-3197)
XACT WIRE EDM CORP
720 Industrial Dr Ste 126 (60013-1992)
PHONE.................................847 516-0903
Jason Mueller, *Plant Mgr*
Jason Mueler, *Manager*
EMP: 11
SALES (corp-wide): 7.3MM **Privately Held**
SIC: 3599 Electrical discharge machining (EDM)
PA: Xact Wire E.D.M., Corp.
N8w22399 Johnson Dr
Waukesha WI 53186
262 549-9005

Casey
Clark County

(G-3198)
ASHLEY OIL CO
508 Deere Run Ln (62420-1936)
P.O. Box 486 (62420-0486)
PHONE.................................217 932-2112
Wilford Ashley, *President*
EMP: 3
SALES (est): 346.7K **Privately Held**
SIC: 1311 Crude petroleum production

(G-3199)
CHARLES INDUSTRIES LLC
Charles Marine Products
400 Se 8th St (62420-2054)
P.O. Box 68 (62420-0068)
PHONE.................................217 932-2068
Ted Weber, *Manager*
Nancy Spurgeon, *Manager*
EMP: 55
SALES (corp-wide): 8.2B **Publicly Held**
SIC: 3661 3629 Telephones & telephone apparatus; battery chargers, rectifying or nonrotating
HQ: Charles Industries, Llc
1450 American Ln Fl 20
Schaumburg IL 60173
847 806-6300

(G-3200)
CHARLES INDUSTRIES LLC
503 Ne 15th St (62420-2174)
PHONE.................................217 932-5292
Trent Wallace, *Engineer*
Mike Henderson, *Manager*
EMP: 57
SALES (corp-wide): 8.2B **Publicly Held**
SIC: 3661 5065 3575 Telephones & telephone apparatus; telephone equipment; computer terminals, monitors & components
HQ: Charles Industries, Llc
1450 American Ln Fl 20
Schaumburg IL 60173
847 806-6300

(G-3201)
GARVER INC
10234 N 230th St (62420-3249)
PHONE.................................217 932-2441
Jason Garver, *President*
Lelia Roubal, *Manager*
EMP: 6
SALES (est): 927K **Privately Held**
SIC: 0721 2434 Crop spraying services; wood kitchen cabinets

(G-3202)
GOBLE MANUFACTURING INC
704 W Main St (62420-1256)
PHONE.................................217 932-5615
James Goble, *CEO*
EMP: 5
SALES (est): 569.7K **Privately Held**
WEB: www.goblemanufacturing.com
SIC: 3999 Manufacturing industries

(G-3203)
HUTTON WELDING SERVICE INC
11995 N 180th St (62420-3100)
PHONE.................................217 932-5585
David S Hutton, *President*
Debby Hutton, *Admin Sec*
EMP: 2
SQ FT: 5,000
SALES (est): 441.9K **Privately Held**
SIC: 7692 Welding repair

(G-3204)
L & J PRODUCERS INC
3795 E 700th Rd (62420-3603)
PHONE.................................217 932-5639
Terry Montgomery, *President*
Denice Whaley, *Admin Sec*
EMP: 2
SALES (est): 233.1K **Privately Held**
SIC: 1311 Crude petroleum production

(G-3205)
LEGACY VULCAN LLC
Midwest Division
9129 N 230th St (62420)
P.O. Box 128 (62420-0128)
PHONE.................................217 932-2611
Ron Sparks, *Manager*
Brian Hartke, *Manager*
Ron Shields, *Manager*
EMP: 12 **Publicly Held**
SIC: 3273 Ready-mixed concrete
HQ: Legacy Vulcan, Llc
1200 Urban Center Dr
Vestavia AL 35242
205 298-3000

(G-3206)
MID ILLINOIS QUARRY COMPANY
9129 N 230th St (62420)
P.O. Box 128 (62420-0128)
PHONE.................................217 932-2611
Jeff Light, *Principal*
EMP: 3
SALES (est): 317.8K **Privately Held**
SIC: 1429 Slate, crushed & broken-quarrying

(G-3207)
MILLER FERTILIZER INC (PA)
601 W Main St (62420-1257)
PHONE.................................217 382-4241
Kim Fritts, *President*
Greg Keller, *Admin Sec*
EMP: 9
SQ FT: 600
SALES (est): 2.5MM **Privately Held**
SIC: 5191 2875 Fertilizer & fertilizer materials; fertilizers, mixing only

(G-3208)
REPORTER INC (PA)
216 S Central Ave (62420-1775)
P.O. Box 158 (62420-0158)
PHONE.................................217 932-5211
Rickie Williams, *President*
Ken Wilmering, *President*
EMP: 21
SALES (est): 1.6MM **Privately Held**
SIC: 2711 Newspapers, publishing & printing

(G-3209)
WESCOM PRODUCTS
503 Ne 15th St (62420-2174)
PHONE.................................217 932-5292
Mike Henderson, *Plant Mgr*
EMP: 5
SALES (est): 471K **Privately Held**
SIC: 3661 5065 Telephones & telephone apparatus; telephone & telegraphic equipment

Caseyville
St. Clair County

(G-3210)
BELZONA GATEWAY INC
8124 Bunkum Rd (62232-2104)
P.O. Box 304 (62232-0304)
PHONE.................................888 774-2984
Brian Portera, *Owner*
EMP: 2 EST: 2012
SALES (est): 254K **Privately Held**
WEB: www.belzonagateway.com
SIC: 2851 Shellac (protective coating)

(G-3211)
BRECKENRIDGE MATERIAL COMPANY
10 Tucker Dr (62232-2328)
PHONE.................................618 398-4141
Jeb Santan, *Principal*
EMP: 28
SALES (corp-wide): 80.2MM **Privately Held**
WEB: www.breckenridgematerial.com
SIC: 3273 Ready-mixed concrete
HQ: Breckenridge Material Company
2833 Breckenridge Ind Ct
Saint Louis MO 63144
314 962-1234

(G-3212)
EAST SIDE TOOL & DIE CO INC
2762 N 89th St (62232-2315)
PHONE.................................618 397-1633
James Quinn, *President*
Joan Quinn, *Corp Secy*
Anthony T Quinn, *Vice Pres*
EMP: 10
SQ FT: 15,000
SALES (est): 1.3MM **Privately Held**
WEB: www.ebeindustrial.com
SIC: 3544 Special dies & tools

(G-3213)
H & R TOOL & MACHINE CO
19 W Scates St (62232-1549)
P.O. Box 450 (62232-0450)
PHONE.................................618 344-7683
Fax: 618 344-7689
EMP: 4 EST: 1961
SQ FT: 4,800
SALES: 289K **Privately Held**
SIC: 3599 3544 Mfg Industrial Machinery Mfg Dies/Tools/Jigs/Fixtures

(G-3214)
ILLINI CONCRETE INC
10 Tucker Dr (62232-2328)
PHONE.................................618 398-4141
Jeb Santan, *Manager*
EMP: 5 **Privately Held**
SIC: 3273 Ready-mixed concrete
PA: Illini Concrete, Inc
1300 E A St
Belleville IL 62221

(G-3215)
JESSIS HIDEOUT
421 S Main St (62232-1819)
PHONE.................................618 343-4346
EMP: 6
SALES (est): 438.6K **Privately Held**
SIC: 2064 5812 Candy bars, including chocolate covered bars; barbecue restaurant

(G-3216)
JOSEPH D SMITHIES
Also Called: Signs N Such
7409 N Illinois St (62232-2067)
PHONE.................................618 632-6141
Joseph Smithies, *Owner*
Joseph D Smithies, *Owner*
EMP: 3
SALES: 165K **Privately Held**
SIC: 3993 Signs & advertising specialties

(G-3217)
KEVIN ROBINSON
Also Called: T & K Trucking
8898 Bunkum Rd (62232)
PHONE.................................618 410-3083
Kevin Robinson, *Owner*

EMP: 4
SQ FT: 6,000
SALES: 230K **Privately Held**
SIC: 3743 Freight cars & equipment

(G-3218)
PURE 111
923 Far Oaks Dr (62232-2814)
PHONE..................618 558-7888
Amy L Katsikas, *Principal*
EMP: 3
SALES (est): 158.9K **Privately Held**
WEB: www.pure111.com
SIC: 3231 Medical & laboratory glassware: made from purchased glass

Cave In Rock
Hardin County

(G-3219)
HASTIE MIN & TRCKG LTD PARTNR (PA)
Hwy 146 (62919)
Rural Route 1 Box 55 (62919-9711)
PHONE..................618 289-4536
Donald Hastie, *Partner*
Robert Hastie, *Partner*
EMP: 35
SQ FT: 2,240
SALES (est): 19.2MM **Privately Held**
SIC: 1442 1479 4212 1422 Gravel mining; fluorspar mining; local trucking, without storage; crushed & broken limestone

(G-3220)
MID-AMERICA CARBONATES LLC
Il 146 (62919)
PHONE..................618 944-6171
EMP: 69
SALES (est): 3.1MM **Publicly Held**
SIC: 1222 Bituminous coal-underground mining
HQ: Alliance Resource Partners Lp
1717 S Boulder Ave # 400
Tulsa OK 74119
918 295-7600

Centralia
Marion County

(G-3221)
AMERICAN EQUIPMENT & MCH INC
2400 S Wabash Ave (62801-6188)
PHONE..................618 533-3857
Robert D Moore, *President*
Michael O McKown, *Admin Sec*
▲ EMP: 80
SQ FT: 460,000
SALES (est): 17.3MM
SALES (corp-wide): 3.7B **Privately Held**
SIC: 3532 Stamping mill machinery (mining machinery)
HQ: Murray Energy Corporation
46226 National Rd
Saint Clairsville OH 43950
740 338-3100

(G-3222)
BIG 3 PRECISION PRODUCTS INC (HQ)
2923 S Wabash Ave (62801-6284)
P.O. Box A (62801-9199)
PHONE..................618 533-3251
Todd Riley, *President*
Clinton Hyde, *Vice Pres*
Clifford Rowcliff, *Production*
Susan Niepoetter, *CFO*
▲ EMP: 182
SQ FT: 142,205
SALES: 54.5MM
SALES (corp-wide): 251.7MM **Publicly Held**
WEB: www.big3precision.com
SIC: 3544 3599 3469 Special dies & tools; custom machinery; metal stampings
PA: The Eastern Company
112 Bridge St
Naugatuck CT 06770
203 729-2255

(G-3223)
CENTRALIA MACHINE & FAB INC
306 S Chestnut St (62801-3822)
P.O. Box 1686 (62801-9124)
PHONE..................618 533-9010
Robert P Gilbert, *President*
EMP: 1
SALES (est): 280K **Privately Held**
SIC: 3537 Industrial trucks & tractors

(G-3224)
CENTRALIA MORNING SENTINEL
232 E Broadway (62801-3251)
PHONE..................618 532-5601
Dan Nickels, *Executive*
EMP: 100
SALES (est): 3.9MM **Privately Held**
SIC: 2711 Newspapers: publishing only, not printed on site

(G-3225)
CENTRALIA PRESS LTD (PA)
Also Called: Centralia Sentinel
232 E Broadway (62801-3251)
PHONE..................618 532-5604
John A Perrine, *President*
William Perrine, *Admin Sec*
Michael Beal, *Administration*
EMP: 81
SQ FT: 9,000
SALES (est): 9.9MM **Privately Held**
SIC: 2711 Newspapers: publishing only, not printed on site

(G-3226)
CLINTON COUNTY MATERIALS CORP
Also Called: Quad-County Rdymx Centralia
100 Rhodes St (62801-2359)
PHONE..................618 533-4252
Mike Johnson, *Manager*
EMP: 10
SALES (est): 699.4K
SALES (corp-wide): 2.4MM **Privately Held**
WEB: www.qcrm4.com
SIC: 3273 Ready-mixed concrete
PA: Clinton County Materials Corp
300 W 12th St
Okawville IL 62271
618 243-6430

(G-3227)
CORRUGATED CONVERTING EQP
306 S Chestnut St (62801-3822)
P.O. Box 1686 (62801-9124)
PHONE..................618 532-2138
Steve Gilbert, *President*
EMP: 10
SQ FT: 20,000
SALES (est): 1.2MM **Privately Held**
SIC: 5084 3443 7692 3544 Industrial machinery & equipment; fabricated plate work (boiler shop); welding repair; special dies, tools, jigs & fixtures

(G-3228)
DIE CUTTERS INC
306 S Chestnut St (62801-3822)
P.O. Box 1686 (62801-9124)
PHONE..................618 532-3448
Robert P Gilbert, *President*
EMP: 12
SALES (est): 1.3MM **Privately Held**
SIC: 3599 Machine shop, jobbing & repair

(G-3229)
DURATECH CORPORATION
2520 S Wabash Ave (62801)
P.O. Box 1720 (62801-9124)
PHONE..................618 533-8891
Joe Fulton, *President*
Shelia Kapes, *Corp Secy*
EMP: 5
SQ FT: 18,500
SALES (est): 859.2K **Privately Held**
SIC: 3089 Plastic & fiberglass tanks

(G-3230)
ENGINEERED FLUID INC (PA)
Also Called: E F I
1308 N Maple St (62801-2417)
PHONE..................618 533-1351
Bill Goodspeed, *President*
Michael English, *Vice Pres*
George Wootten, *Vice Pres*
Jason Holle, *Project Mgr*
Mike Neudecker, *Prdtn Mgr*
EMP: 107
SQ FT: 9,000
SALES (est): 29.9MM **Privately Held**
WEB: www.engineeredfluid.com
SIC: 3561 3613 3491 Pumps & pumping equipment; control panels, electric; industrial valves

(G-3231)
ENGINEERED FLUID INC
1308 N Maple St (62801-2417)
PHONE..................618 533-1351
Deppto Goodbe, *Manager*
EMP: 100
SALES (corp-wide): 29.9MM **Privately Held**
WEB: www.engineeredfluid.com
SIC: 3561 Pumps & pumping equipment
PA: Engineered Fluid, Inc.
1308 N Maple St
Centralia IL 62801
618 533-1351

(G-3232)
G-M SERVICES
309 Country Club Rd (62801-3741)
PHONE..................618 532-2324
Gregory Marcum, *Owner*
EMP: 4
SALES: 250K **Privately Held**
SIC: 3823 1711 Water quality monitoring & control systems; plumbing, heating, air-conditioning contractors

(G-3233)
GRAPHIC PACKAGING INTL LLC
2333 S Wabash Ave (62801-6187)
P.O. Box 787 (62801-9113)
PHONE..................618 533-2721
Paul Delong, *Prdtn Mgr*
Carol Maxey, *Persnl Dir*
Arthur Rideout, *Manager*
David Buckmore, *Supervisor*
Amanda Thomas, *Maintence Staff*
EMP: 97 **Publicly Held**
SIC: 2657 Folding paperboard boxes
HQ: Graphic Packaging International, Llc
1500 Riveredge Pkwy # 100
Atlanta GA 30328

(G-3234)
GREENS MACHINE SHOP
315 E Kell St (62801-2335)
PHONE..................618 532-4631
David Stover, *Owner*
EMP: 3
SQ FT: 1,600
SALES (est): 230K **Privately Held**
WEB: www.greens-machine.com
SIC: 3599 7692 Machine shop, jobbing & repair; welding repair

(G-3235)
INTERMOUNTAIN ELECTRONICS INC
400 Swan Ave (62801-6220)
PHONE..................618 339-6743
Rick Benedict, *Branch Mgr*
William Acord, *Manager*
EMP: 9
SALES (corp-wide): 75.4MM **Privately Held**
SIC: 3699 Household electrical equipment
PA: Intermountain Electronics, Inc. Of Price, Utah
1511 S Highway 6
Price UT 84501
435 637-7160

(G-3236)
JAMES RAY MONROE CORPORATION (PA)
Also Called: Mitchell Printing
308 W Noleman St (62801-3129)
P.O. Box 950 (62801-9115)
PHONE..................618 532-4575
David J Mitchell, *President*
Bruce Jones, *Treasurer*
EMP: 10 EST: 1976
SQ FT: 4,000
SALES: 1MM **Privately Held**
SIC: 2752 5943 5712 3069 Commercial printing, offset; office forms & supplies; office furniture; stationers' rubber sundries; typewriters & business machines; typesetting

(G-3237)
LEE GILSTER-MARY CORPORATION
100 W Calumet St (62801-4130)
PHONE..................618 533-4808
Wayne Malzhon, *Manager*
EMP: 180
SALES (corp-wide): 1B **Privately Held**
SIC: 5149 2074 Groceries & related products; cottonseed oil mills
HQ: Gilster-Mary Lee Corporation
1037 State St
Chester IL 62233
618 826-2361

(G-3238)
MICHAEL REGGIS CLARK
Also Called: Kaco Signs
1308 N Elm St (62801-2307)
PHONE..................618 533-3841
Reggis M Clark, *Owner*
Kay Clark, *Owner*
Reggie Clark, *Owner*
EMP: 3
SQ FT: 2,800
SALES (est): 130K **Privately Held**
SIC: 3993 Signs & advertising specialties

(G-3239)
MONSANTO COMPANY
3421 Us Highway 51 (62801-6691)
P.O. Box 1837 (62801-9125)
PHONE..................618 249-6150
Duane Scott, *Branch Mgr*
Kimberly Farthing, *Admin Asst*
EMP: 62
SALES (corp-wide): 48.1B **Privately Held**
WEB: www.monsanto.com
SIC: 2879 Agricultural chemicals
HQ: Monsanto Company
800 N Lindbergh Blvd
Saint Louis MO 63167
314 694-1000

(G-3240)
NATURAL GAS PIPELINE AMER LLC
7501 Huey Rd (62801-7115)
PHONE..................618 495-2211
Larry Ullrick, *Branch Mgr*
EMP: 25 **Publicly Held**
WEB: www.kindermorgan.com
SIC: 4922 1311 Natural gas transmission; crude petroleum & natural gas
HQ: Natural Gas Pipeline Company Of America Llc
1001 Louisiana St
Houston TX 77002
713 369-9000

(G-3241)
NEW METAL FABRICATION CORP
931 S Brookside St (62801-5451)
P.O. Box 473 (62801-9107)
PHONE..................618 532-9000
Jon Bain, *CEO*
EMP: 22
SALES (est): 4.7MM **Privately Held**
SIC: 3441 Fabricated structural metal

(G-3242)
NU-ART PRINTING
614 W Broadway (62801-5302)
PHONE..................618 533-9971
Art Borum, *Owner*
EMP: 6

GEOGRAPHIC SECTION

Champaign - Champaign County (G-3269)

SALES (est): 290K **Privately Held**
SIC: 2752 2759 3993 2791 Commercial printing, offset; commercial printing; signs & advertising specialties; typesetting; bookbinding & related work; automotive & apparel trimmings

(G-3243)
NVENT ELECTRIC PUBLIC LTD CO
Also Called: Wbt
115 Harting Dr (62801-5903)
PHONE...............................618 918-3821
Richard G Winn, *Branch Mgr*
EMP: 7 **Privately Held**
SIC: 3496 Miscellaneous fabricated wire products
HQ: Nvent Electric Public Limited Company
8th Floor
Brentford MIDDX TW8 9

(G-3244)
PINNACLE FOODS GROUP LLC
100 W Calumet St (62801-4130)
PHONE...............................731 343-4995
Michael D French, *Manager*
EMP: 159
SALES (corp-wide): 9.5B **Publicly Held**
SIC: 2038 Frozen specialties
HQ: Pinnacle Foods Group Llc
399 Jefferson Rd
Parsippany NJ 07054

(G-3245)
PIONEER CONTAINER MCHY INC
1674 Woods Ln (62801-6774)
PHONE...............................618 533-7833
James Michael McMillan, *President*
EMP: 2
SQ FT: 13,500
SALES (est): 350K **Privately Held**
SIC: 3565 Packaging machinery

(G-3246)
PROMIZ LLC
2228 Green Street Rd (62801-8404)
PHONE...............................618 533-3950
Valery Tokar, *Mng Member*
EMP: 4
SALES (est): 405.2K **Privately Held**
SIC: 3241 Masonry cement

(G-3247)
QUALITY SPORT NETS INC
2330 E Calumet St (62801-6578)
P.O. Box 962 (62801-9115)
PHONE...............................618 533-0700
Daniel Koller, *President*
Daniel N Koller, *President*
Mary Lynn Koller, *Admin Sec*
▲ EMP: 7
SQ FT: 8,000
SALES (est): 757K **Privately Held**
SIC: 3949 Nets: badminton, volleyball, tennis, etc.

(G-3248)
ROSE BUSINESS FORMS & PRINTING
125 N Walnut St (62801-3134)
PHONE...............................618 533-3032
Phillip McDaniel, *President*
EMP: 5
SQ FT: 8,000
SALES (est): 627.6K **Privately Held**
SIC: 2752 5112 2791 2789 Commercial printing, offset; business forms; typesetting; bookbinding & related work; commercial printing

(G-3249)
SAY CHEESE CAKE
421 W Noleman St (62801-3130)
PHONE...............................618 532-6001
Rick Wooters, *Owner*
EMP: 4
SALES (est): 281.8K **Privately Held**
SIC: 2051 Cakes, bakery: except frozen

(G-3250)
SEIP SERVICE & SUPPLY INC
221 E Broadway Ste 101 (62801-3250)
PHONE...............................618 532-1923
Kris Kourdouvelis, *President*
Elizabeth B Kourdouvelis, *Vice Pres*
Luann Pugh, *Admin Sec*
EMP: 18 EST: 1956
SQ FT: 1,000
SALES (est): 769.7K **Privately Held**
WEB: www.seipusa.com
SIC: 1389 5084 Oil field services; oil well machinery, equipment & supplies

(G-3251)
SHOPPERS WEEKLY INC
Also Called: Shopper Weekly Publishings
301 E Broadway (62801-3252)
P.O. Box 1223 (62801-9118)
PHONE...............................618 533-7283
Cathy Stuehmeier, *President*
John Stuehmeier, *Corp Secy*
EMP: 10
SALES (est): 820K **Privately Held**
SIC: 2741 Shopping news: publishing only, not printed on site

(G-3252)
SWAN SURFACES LLC
200 Swan Ave (62801-6124)
PHONE...............................618 532-5673
Eric Fagan, *Publications*
Mike Vincent, *Manager*
EMP: 130
SALES (corp-wide): 433.4MM **Privately Held**
SIC: 3088 3431 3261 2541 Shower stalls, fiberglass & plastic; metal sanitary ware; vitreous plumbing fixtures; wood partitions & fixtures
HQ: Swan Surfaces, Llc
515 Olive St Ste 900
Saint Louis MO 63101
800 325-7008

(G-3253)
TONYS WELDING SERVICE INC
624 N Elm St (62801-2320)
PHONE...............................618 532-9353
Tony Sloat Sr, *President*
Tony R Sloat Jr, *Vice Pres*
Marilyn Sloat, *Admin Sec*
EMP: 3
SQ FT: 6,000
SALES (est): 795.3K **Privately Held**
SIC: 7692 7699 Welding repair; industrial machinery & equipment repair

(G-3254)
WB TRAY LLC
115 Harting Dr (62801-5903)
PHONE...............................618 918-3821
Gary Turner, *Mng Member*
EMP: 2
SALES (est): 278.1K **Privately Held**
SIC: 3443 Cable trays, metal plate

Centreville
St. Clair County

(G-3255)
STEEL REBAR MANUFACTURING LLC
Also Called: Srm
4926 Church Rd (62207-1392)
PHONE...............................618 920-2748
Donald J Johnson, *Mng Member*
EMP: 8
SQ FT: 25,000
SALES (est): 597.6K **Privately Held**
SIC: 1761 3449 5051 Architectural sheet metal work; bars, concrete reinforcing: fabricated steel; steel

Cerro Gordo
Piatt County

(G-3256)
CLARKSON SOY PRODUCTS LLC
320 E South St (61818-4035)
P.O. Box 80 (61818-0080)
PHONE...............................217 763-9511
Curtis Bennett, *President*
Lynn E Clarkson,
▲ EMP: 7
SALES: 796K **Privately Held**
SIC: 2075 Soybean oil, deodorized

Chadwick
Carroll County

(G-3257)
CHADWICK MANUFACTURING LTD
Also Called: US Ignition
224 N Main St (61014)
P.O. Box 85 (61014-0085)
PHONE...............................815 684-5152
Allen L Smith, *Partner*
Dwight Smith, *Partner*
Kay Smith, *Partner*
EMP: 6 EST: 1946
SQ FT: 16,600
SALES (est): 300K **Privately Held**
WEB: www.chadwickmfg.com
SIC: 3599 3631 3499 3443 Machine shop, jobbing & repair; barbecues, grills & braziers (outdoor cooking); furniture parts, metal; fabricated plate work (boiler shop)

(G-3258)
JOHNSONS PROCESSING PLANT
201 Il Route 40 E (61014-9368)
PHONE...............................815 684-5183
Greg Adolph, *Owner*
EMP: 7 EST: 1960
SALES (est): 600.5K **Privately Held**
WEB: www.johnsonsprocessingplant.com
SIC: 2011 2013 Meat packing plants; sausages & other prepared meats

Chambersburg
Pike County

(G-3259)
CENTRAL STONE COMPANY
38084 County Highway 21 (62323-2116)
PHONE...............................217 327-4300
Bruce Mowen, *Branch Mgr*
EMP: 4
SALES (corp-wide): 2.5B **Privately Held**
WEB: www.riverstonegrp.com
SIC: 1422 Crushed & broken limestone
HQ: Central Stone Company
4640 E 56th St
Davenport IA 52807
309 757-8250

Champaign
Champaign County

(G-3260)
ADVANCED FILTRATION SYSTEMS INC (HQ)
3206 Farber Dr (61822-1084)
PHONE...............................217 351-3073
Nickolas Priadka, *President*
◆ EMP: 121
SQ FT: 228,000
SALES: 45.1MM
SALES (corp-wide): 2.8B **Publicly Held**
SIC: 3599 Oil filters, internal combustion engine, except automotive; gasoline filters, internal combustion engine, except auto
PA: Donaldson Company, Inc.
1400 W 94th St
Minneapolis MN 55431
952 887-3131

(G-3261)
ALLERTON CHARTER COACH
714 S 6th St (61820-5708)
P.O. Box 4048, Lisle (60532-9048)
PHONE...............................217 344-2600
EMP: 4
SALES (est): 404.2K **Privately Held**
SIC: 2295 Coated Fabrics, Not Rubberized

(G-3262)
AM KO ORIENTAL FOODS
Also Called: Am-Ko Oriental Grocery
101 E Springfield Ave (61820-5309)
PHONE...............................217 398-2922
Soon K Chung, *Partner*
Michael Pulliam, *Partner*
▲ EMP: 2
SALES (est): 257K **Privately Held**
SIC: 5411 3993 5499 5947 Grocery stores, independent; signs, not made in custom sign painting shops; health & dietetic food stores; gift, novelty & souvenir shop

(G-3263)
AM-DON PARTNERSHIP
Also Called: SBC
1819 S Neil St Ste A (61820-7271)
PHONE...............................217 355-7750
Bob Donahoe, *Manager*
EMP: 7 **Privately Held**
SIC: 8742 2741 Sales (including sales management) consultant; miscellaneous publishing
PA: Am-Don Partnership
200 E Randolph St # 7000
Chicago IL 60601

(G-3264)
AMERICAN BOTTLING COMPANY
815 Pioneer St (61820-2512)
PHONE...............................217 356-0577
Dale McElhanew, *Manager*
EMP: 27 **Publicly Held**
WEB: www.drpeppersnapplegroup.com
SIC: 2086 Bottled & canned soft drinks
HQ: The American Bottling Company
5301 Legacy Dr
Plano TX 75024

(G-3265)
ANDY DALLAS & CO
Also Called: Dallas & Co Costumes & Magic
101 E University Ave (61820-4110)
PHONE...............................217 351-5974
Andrew Dallas, *President*
Barb Dallas, *Treasurer*
EMP: 10
SQ FT: 12,000
SALES (est): 851K **Privately Held**
SIC: 5947 5699 7299 2389 Novelties; party favors; costumes, masquerade or theatrical; costume rental; costumes

(G-3266)
AQUEOUS SOLUTIONS LLC
301 N Neil St Ste 400 (61820-3169)
PHONE...............................217 531-1206
Carla Barcus, *Sales Staff*
Craig Bethke, *Mng Member*
Dan Saalfeld, *Prgrmr*
EMP: 10 EST: 2011
SALES (est): 282.6K **Privately Held**
SIC: 7372 Application computer software

(G-3267)
ARCHER-DANIELS-MIDLAND COMPANY
2021 S 1st St (61820-7484)
PHONE...............................217 419-5100
Carlos Dassori, *Branch Mgr*
EMP: 3
SALES (corp-wide): 64.6B **Publicly Held**
SIC: 2041 Flour & other grain mill products
PA: Archer-Daniels-Midland Company
77 W Wacker Dr Ste 4600
Chicago IL 60601
312 634-8100

(G-3268)
AT HOME MAGAZINE
15 E Main St (61820-3625)
PHONE...............................217 351-5282
Deanne Johnson, *Manager*
EMP: 3
SALES (est): 130.8K **Privately Held**
SIC: 2721 Magazines: publishing only, not printed on site

(G-3269)
ATSP INNOVATIONS INC
60 Hazelwood Dr Ste 145 (61820-7460)
PHONE...............................217 778-4400

Champaign - Champaign County (G-3270)

Gaetan Bonhomme, *CEO*
James Economy, *President*
David Carroll, *COO*
EMP: 8
SQ FT: 24,000
SALES: 379.9K **Privately Held**
SIC: 8731 2821 Commercial physical research; commercial research laboratory; plastics materials & resins

(G-3270)
AUTONOMIC MATERIALS INC
495 County Road 1300 N (61820-9746)
PHONE.................................217 863-2023
Joe Giuliani, *CEO*
Gerald Wilson, *Office Mgr*
EMP: 11
SALES: 1.8MM **Privately Held**
SIC: 2851 Paints & paint additives

(G-3271)
BELL RACING USA LLC
Also Called: Bell Racing Co
301 Mercury Dr Ste 8 (61822-9654)
P.O. Box 877, Rantoul (61866-0877)
PHONE.................................217 239-5355
Kyle Kietzmann, *President*
Allison Hunt, *Manager*
Graham Sellers, *Manager*
▲ **EMP:** 8 **EST:** 2010
SALES (est): 965.8K **Privately Held**
SIC: 3949 Helmets, athletic

(G-3272)
BOW BROTHERS CO INC
3108 W Springfield Ave (61822-2865)
PHONE.................................217 359-0555
Jeffery Wandell, *President*
EMP: 5
SALES (est): 209.8K **Privately Held**
SIC: 2396 Automotive & apparel trimmings

(G-3273)
BUZARD PIPE ORGAN BUILDERS LLC
Also Called: Buzard Pipe Organ Craftsmen
112 W Hill St (61820-8643)
PHONE.................................217 352-1955
Jef Player, *Office Mgr*
John P Buzard, *Mng Member*
John Paul, *Director*
Linda Buzard,
Philip Campbell,
▲ **EMP:** 17 **EST:** 1980
SQ FT: 20,000
SALES: 1.2MM **Privately Held**
WEB: www.buzardorgans.com
SIC: 3931 7699 Pipes, organ; organ tuning & repair

(G-3274)
CAMPUS SPORTSWEAR INCORPORATED
710 S 6th St Ste B (61820-9200)
P.O. Box 2482 (61825-2482)
PHONE.................................217 344-0944
Tom Coleman, *President*
Jedd Swisher, *Vice Pres*
EMP: 10 **EST:** 1948
SQ FT: 2,700
SALES: 800K **Privately Held**
WEB: www.campussportswearinc.com
SIC: 2759 Screen printing

(G-3275)
CARDTHARTIC LLC
30102 Research Rd (61822)
PHONE.................................217 239-5895
Joanna Steven,
EMP: 12
SQ FT: 5,000
SALES (est): 1.3MM **Privately Held**
SIC: 2771 Greeting cards

(G-3276)
CATERPILLAR INC
1901 S 1st St Ste C1 (61820-7475)
PHONE.................................217 255-8500
Christopher Ha, *Engineer*
EMP: 355
SALES (corp-wide): 53.8B **Publicly Held**
SIC: 3531 Construction machinery
PA: Caterpillar Inc.
510 Lake Cook Rd Ste 100
Deerfield IL 60015
224 551-4000

(G-3277)
CBANA LABS INC (PA)
2021 S 1st St Ste 206 (61820-7484)
PHONE.................................217 819-5201
Tim Hoerr, *President*
Curtis Ray, *Vice Pres*
Qingmei Chen, *Research*
Junghoon Yeom, *Research*
EMP: 7
SQ FT: 7,500
SALES (est): 300K **Privately Held**
SIC: 3826 5049 Analytical instruments; analytical instruments

(G-3278)
CDS OFFICE SYSTEMS INC
3108 Farber Dr Ofc (61822-1074)
PHONE.................................217 351-5046
Jay Watson, *Owner*
Rob Reckers, *Branch Mgr*
EMP: 15
SALES (corp-wide): 43.8MM **Privately Held**
SIC: 5044 2759 5999 Office equipment; commercial printing; photocopy machines
PA: C.D.S. Office Systems Incorporated
612 S Dirksen Pkwy
Springfield IL 62703
800 367-1508

(G-3279)
CENTRAL IL BUSINESS MAGAZINE
15 E Main St (61820-3625)
PHONE.................................217 351-5281
Greta Hale, *Principal*
EMP: 5
SALES (est): 232.5K **Privately Held**
SIC: 2759 Magazines: printing

(G-3280)
CLARK PRINTING & MARKETING
501 Mercury Dr (61822-9649)
PHONE.................................217 363-5300
David Clark, *Owner*
EMP: 3
SALES (est): 216.8K **Privately Held**
SIC: 2752 Commercial printing, lithographic

(G-3281)
COMMON GROUND PUBLISHING LLC
2001 S 1st St Ste 202 (61820-7478)
PHONE.................................217 721-6839
William Cope,
EMP: 25
SALES: 50K **Privately Held**
SIC: 2741 Miscellaneous publishing

(G-3282)
COMPUTING INTEGRITY INC
3102 Valleybrook Dr (61822-6112)
PHONE.................................217 355-4469
EMP: 1
SQ FT: 1,200
SALES: 400K **Privately Held**
SIC: 7372 Software Development

(G-3283)
COUNTY MATERIALS CORP
702 N Edwin St (61821-2537)
PHONE.................................217 352-4181
Scott Boma, *Branch Mgr*
EMP: 33
SALES (corp-wide): 338.2MM **Privately Held**
SIC: 3271 5211 3273 3272 Blocks, concrete or cinder: standard; lumber & other building materials; masonry materials & supplies; ready-mixed concrete; concrete products; construction sand & gravel
PA: County Materials Corp.
205 North St
Marathon WI 54448
715 443-2434

(G-3284)
DABEL INCORPORATED
Also Called: A & A Graphx
602 E Green St (61820-5770)
P.O. Box 373, Savoy (61874-0373)
PHONE.................................217 398-3389
EMP: 9
SQ FT: 1,800
SALES (est): 794.4K **Privately Held**
SIC: 2396 2395 Automotive And Apparel Trimmings

(G-3285)
DIXON GRAPHICS INCORPORATED
105 W John St (61820-5215)
PHONE.................................217 351-6100
Lance Dixon, *President*
EMP: 6
SQ FT: 8,000
SALES (est): 828.9K **Privately Held**
WEB: www.dixon-graphics.com
SIC: 7336 2752 7752 Graphic arts & related design; commercial printing, offset; advertising literature: printing; screen printing

(G-3286)
DOTS UT INC
2716 W Clark Rd Ste E (61822-2842)
PHONE.................................217 390-3286
Yuri T Didenko, *President*
EMP: 5
SQ FT: 1,800
SALES (est): 50K **Privately Held**
SIC: 2893 Printing ink

(G-3287)
EDEN PARK ILLUMINATION INC
903 N Country Fair Dr (61821-3259)
PHONE.................................217 403-1866
Bill Thalheimer, *CEO*
Sung-Jin Park, *Vice Pres*
Ted Scott, *Engineer*
EMP: 9
SALES (est): 1.5MM **Privately Held**
SIC: 3641 Electric lamps

(G-3288)
EFFIMAX SOLAR
60 Hazelwood Dr (61820-7460)
PHONE.................................217 550-2422
Rui Cai, *CEO*
EMP: 4
SALES (est): 284.4K **Privately Held**
SIC: 3674 Semiconductors & related devices

(G-3289)
EMBEDOR TECHNOLOGIES INC
60 Hazelwood Dr (61820-7460)
PHONE.................................202 681-0359
Bill Spencer, *President*
Kirill Mechitov, *Treasurer*
EMP: 3 **EST:** 2014
SQ FT: 43,000
SALES (est): 201K **Privately Held**
SIC: 3823 Data loggers, industrial process type; telemetering instruments, industrial process type

(G-3290)
EP TECHNOLOGY CORPORATION USA
Also Called: E P Computer
1401 Interstate Dr (61822-1172)
PHONE.................................217 351-7888
Kevin Wan, *President*
Pan Bruce, *Manager*
Helena Lin, *Manager*
▲ **EMP:** 70
SALES (est): 11.9MM **Privately Held**
SIC: 5734 7382 7372 Personal computers; protective devices, security; application computer software

(G-3291)
EPIWORKS INC
1606 Rion Dr (61822-9598)
PHONE.................................217 373-1590
Quesnell J Hartmann, *President*
Ronald L Chez, *Chairman*
David A Ahmari, *Exec VP*
Robert Hasken, *Prdtn Mgr*
Curt Dickinson, *Materials Mgr*
▲ **EMP:** 55 **EST:** 1997
SQ FT: 25,000
SALES (est): 283.5K
SALES: 1.3B **Publicly Held**
WEB: www.epiworks.com
SIC: 3674 Semiconductors & related devices

PA: Ii-Vi Incorporated
375 Saxonburg Blvd
Saxonburg PA 16056
724 352-4455

(G-3292)
FEDEX OFFICE & PRINT SVCS INC
505 S Mattis Ave (61821-4276)
PHONE.................................217 355-3400
EMP: 30
SALES (corp-wide): 69.6B **Publicly Held**
SIC: 7334 2789 2759 7221 Photocopying & duplicating services; bookbinding & related work; commercial printing; photographic studios, portrait
HQ: Fedex Office And Print Services, Inc.
7900 Legacy Dr
Plano TX 75024
800 463-3339

(G-3293)
FROSTDEFENSE ENVIROTECH INC
509 S Garfield Ave (61821-3831)
PHONE.................................217 979-3052
Manfredo Seufferheld, *Principal*
EMP: 6
SALES (est): 282.4K **Privately Held**
SIC: 3812 Defense systems & equipment

(G-3294)
GILL ATHLETICS
2808 Gemini Ct (61822-9648)
PHONE.................................217 367-8438
Gill Athletics, *CEO*
▼ **EMP:** 2
SALES (est): 245.5K **Privately Held**
SIC: 3949 Sporting & athletic goods

(G-3295)
GLASS FX
202 S 1st St (61820-4120)
PHONE.................................217 359-0048
Richard Taylor, *Owner*
EMP: 7
SQ FT: 1,400
SALES (est): 534.8K **Privately Held**
SIC: 3231 7699 3471 Stained glass: made from purchased glass; china & glass repair; plating & polishing

(G-3296)
GLD INDUSTRIES INC
4411 Southford Trace Dr (61822-8565)
PHONE.................................217 390-9594
Brad Giffel, *President*
Brian Downing, *COO*
EMP: 3
SALES (est): 161.6K **Privately Held**
SIC: 7379 3825 3571 7389 Computer related consulting services; test equipment for electronic & electric measurement; electronic computers;

(G-3297)
GLUCOSENTIENT INC
2100 S Oak St Ste 101 (61820-0910)
PHONE.................................217 487-4087
Tian Lan, *Principal*
EMP: 5 **EST:** 2011
SALES (est): 438.7K **Privately Held**
SIC: 2835 In vitro diagnostics

(G-3298)
GOOD VIBES SOUND INC (PA)
2010 Round Barn Rd (61821-3623)
PHONE.................................217 351-0909
Steven Suderman, *President*
Gary Burson, *Vice Pres*
Patrick Coyne, *Treasurer*
EMP: 15
SALES: 1.7MM **Privately Held**
SIC: 5731 3861 5099 5063 High fidelity stereo equipment; projectors, still or motion picture, silent or sound; video & audio equipment; antennas, receiving, satellite dishes

(G-3299)
HARAN VENTURES LLC
Also Called: Haran Technologies
1804 Vale St (61822-3563)
PHONE.................................217 239-1628
Kiruba Haran, *CEO*

GEOGRAPHIC SECTION

Champaign - Champaign County (G-3326)

EMP: 3
SALES (est): 103.7K **Privately Held**
SIC: 8748 3621 Systems analysis & engineering consulting services; motors, electric

(G-3300)
HERFF JONES LLC
Herff Jones Cap & Gowns
1000 N Market St (61821-3009)
PHONE...................217 351-9500
Tom Tanton, *General Mgr*
EMP: 10
SALES (corp-wide): 1.1B **Privately Held**
SIC: 3911 Rings, finger: precious metal
HQ: Herff Jones, Llc
4501 W 62nd St
Indianapolis IN 46268
800 419-5462

(G-3301)
HINETICS LLC
1804 Vale St (61822-3563)
PHONE...................217 239-1628
Kiruba Haran,
EMP: 3
SALES (est): 121.3K **Privately Held**
SIC: 3621 Motors, electric

(G-3302)
HL PRECISION MANUFACTURING LLC
2110 Round Barn Rd (61821-3621)
PHONE...................217 398-6881
Steven Hillard, *Mng Member*
Jeff Hodgson,
Jeremy Holmes,
Richard King,
Xavier Palacios,
EMP: 61
SALES (est): 1.8MM **Privately Held**
SIC: 3599 Machine shop, jobbing & repair

(G-3303)
HOTTINGER BLDWIN MSREMENTS INC
Also Called: Hbm Somat
1806 Fox Dr Ste A (61820-7278)
PHONE...................217 328-5359
James Cirk, *Branch Mgr*
EMP: 20
SALES (corp-wide): 2B **Privately Held**
SIC: 3541 Machine tools, metal cutting type
HQ: Hottinger Baldwin Measurements, Inc.
19 Bartlett St
Marlborough MA 01752
508 624-4500

(G-3304)
HUDSON TECHNOLOGIES INC
3402 N Mattis Ave (61822-1082)
P.O. Box 1541, Pearl River NY (10965)
PHONE...................217 373-1414
Kevin Zugibe, *Principal*
Nat Krishnamurti, *CFO*
Jeff Spencer, *Manager*
EMP: 30 **Publicly Held**
SIC: 1711 2869 Refrigeration contractor; fluorinated hydrocarbon gases
PA: Hudson Technologies, Inc.
1 Blue Hill Plz Ste 1541
Pearl River NY 10965

(G-3305)
IEP QUALITY INC
2705 N Salisbury Ct (61821-6900)
PHONE...................217 840-0570
Gdavid Frye, *Principal*
Susan Carty, *Principal*
James Shriner, *Principal*
Stephen Zahos, *Principal*
EMP: 4
SALES: 25K **Privately Held**
SIC: 7372 8299 Educational computer software; educational services

(G-3306)
ILLINI MEDIA CO (PA)
Also Called: WPGU-FM
1001 S Wright St (61820-6225)
PHONE...................217 337-8300
Mary Cory, *Publisher*
Blake Landa, *Prdtn Dir*
Nikhil Mehta, *Engrg Dir*
Lucas Mohs, *Engrg Dir*
Ben Foutch, *Sales Dir*
EMP: 414 EST: 1911
SQ FT: 10,000
SALES: 837K **Privately Held**
WEB: www.wpgu.com
SIC: 2711 4832 2741 2721 Newspapers: publishing only, not printed on site; radio broadcasting stations; yearbooks: publishing & printing; periodicals

(G-3307)
ILLINOIS NI CAST LLC
Also Called: Alloy Engineering & Casting Co
1700 W Washington St (61821-2412)
PHONE...................217 398-3200
Rich Grimm,
EMP: 1
SALES (est): 255K
SALES (corp-wide): 42.5MM **Privately Held**
SIC: 3317 3325 Steel pipe & tubes; steel foundries
PA: Wirco, Inc.
105 Progress Way
Avilla IN 46710
260 897-3768

(G-3308)
INPRENTUS INC
Also Called: Inprentus Precision Optics
51 E Kenyon Rd (61820-2216)
PHONE...................217 239-9862
Ron Van Os, *CEO*
Jonathan Manton, *President*
Cody Jensen, *Research*
Lingyun Jiang, *Engineer*
Charles Strehlow, *Sales Engr*
EMP: 19
SQ FT: 11,000
SALES: 365K **Privately Held**
SIC: 3827 Optical instruments & apparatus

(G-3309)
IRIA PHARMA INC
60 Hazelwood Dr Ste 245 (61820-7460)
PHONE...................217 979-1417
Jianjun Cheng, *President*
Kaimin Cai, *Principal*
EMP: 3
SALES (est): 184.1K **Privately Held**
SIC: 2834 Pharmaceutical preparations

(G-3310)
ISS (USA) INC
Also Called: ISS
1602 Newton Dr (61822-1061)
P.O. Box 6930 (61826-6930)
PHONE...................217 359-8681
Beniamino Barbieri, *President*
Annie Ruth Abbott, *Admin Sec*
EMP: 32
SQ FT: 20,000
SALES (est): 6.9MM **Privately Held**
SIC: 3826 Analytical instruments

(G-3311)
ISS MEDICAL INC
1602 Newton Dr (61822-1061)
PHONE...................217 359-8681
Beniamino Barbieri, *President*
EMP: 4
SQ FT: 22,000
SALES (est): 174.7K **Privately Held**
SIC: 3841 Diagnostic apparatus, medical

(G-3312)
KAELCO ENTRMT HOLDINGS INC
3 Henson Pl Ste 1 (61820-7858)
PHONE...................217 600-7815
EMP: 3 EST: 2013
SQ FT: 1,000
SALES (est): 80.2K **Privately Held**
SIC: 7819 2741 7929 Motion Picture Services Misc Publishing Entertainment

(G-3313)
KELLEY VAULT CO INC
Also Called: Kelley Crematory
1901 W Springer Dr (61821-2468)
PHONE...................217 355-5551
Bonnie B Kelley, *President*
Roland W Kelley, *Corp Secy*
Richard Herr, *Vice Pres*
Jeff Brouse, *Marketing Staff*
EMP: 13 EST: 1928
SQ FT: 1,400
SALES (est): 2MM **Privately Held**
SIC: 3272 Burial vaults, concrete or precast terrazzo

(G-3314)
KITCHEN & BATH CABINET COMPANY
1806 Camp Dr (61821-2464)
PHONE...................217 352-1900
Daniel J Webber, *Owner*
EMP: 3
SQ FT: 5,000
SALES (est): 292.3K **Privately Held**
SIC: 2434 Wood kitchen cabinets

(G-3315)
KRAFT HEINZ FOODS COMPANY
Also Called: Kraft Foods
1701 W Bradley Ave (61821-2201)
PHONE...................217 378-1900
Bart Huchel, *Engineer*
Randy Klongland, *Manager*
EMP: 75
SALES (corp-wide): 24.9B **Publicly Held**
SIC: 2099 2098 2035 2026 Food preparations; macaroni & spaghetti; pickles, sauces & salad dressings; fluid milk; cheese, natural & processed; local trucking with storage
HQ: Kraft Heinz Foods Company
1 Ppg Pl Fl 34
Pittsburgh PA 15222
412 456-5700

(G-3316)
KWS CEREALS USA LLC
4101 Colleen Dr (61822-3501)
PHONE...................815 200-2666
Ken Davis, *Mng Member*
Stefan Bruns,
Juergen Leitzke,
Eric Ricard,
EMP: 5 EST: 2010
SALES (est): 96.7K
SALES (corp-wide): 1.2B **Privately Held**
SIC: 2041 2043 Grain mills (except rice); coffee substitutes, made from grain
PA: Kws Saat Se & Co. Kgaa
Grimsehlstr. 31
Einbeck 37574
556 131-10

(G-3317)
LITANIA SPORTS GROUP INC
Also Called: Gill Athletics
601 Mercury Dr (61822-9675)
P.O. Box 1790 (61824-1790)
PHONE...................217 367-8438
C David Hodge, *President*
Steve Vogelsang, *Vice Pres*
Ken Hursey, *Production*
Jason Norton, *CFO*
Brenda Delaurier, *Manager*
◆ EMP: 135
SQ FT: 225,000
SALES (est): 27.8MM **Privately Held**
WEB: www.gillathletics.com
SIC: 3949 Track & field athletic equipment

(G-3318)
MBM BUSINESS ASSISTANCE INC
Also Called: Fastsigns
313 N Mattis Ave Ste 114 (61821-7901)
PHONE...................217 398-6600
James Murphy, *President*
Linda Murphy, *Corp Secy*
EMP: 3
SQ FT: 3,700
SALES (est): 385.7K **Privately Held**
SIC: 3993 8243 5999 Signs & advertising specialties; operator training, computer; banners, flags, decals & posters

(G-3319)
MEALPLOT INC
60 Hazelwood Dr (61820-7460)
PHONE...................217 419-2681
Jeanette Andrade, *CEO*
Manabu Nakamura, *Vice Pres*
EMP: 3 EST: 2014
SALES (est): 113.3K **Privately Held**
SIC: 7372 Prepackaged software

(G-3320)
MENASHA PACKAGING COMPANY LLC
710 N Mattis Ave (61821-2450)
PHONE...................630 263-4547
EMP: 6
SALES (corp-wide): 2.2B **Privately Held**
SIC: 2653 Boxes, corrugated: made from purchased materials
HQ: Menasha Packaging Company, Llc
1645 Bergstrom Rd
Neenah WI 54956
920 751-1000

(G-3321)
MICROPLASMA OZONE TECH INC
2105 W Park Ct (61821-2986)
PHONE...................217 693-7950
Cassie Leigh, *President*
JD Brookhart, *Bd of Directors*
Carl Johnson, *Bd of Directors*
EMP: 11
SQ FT: 7,500
SALES: 300K **Privately Held**
SIC: 3589 Water treatment equipment, industrial

(G-3322)
MILLER ROGER WESTON
Also Called: Miller Enterprises
2611 W Cardinal Rd (61822)
PHONE...................217 352-0476
Roger Weston Miller, *Owner*
EMP: 5
SQ FT: 36,000
SALES (est): 1MM **Privately Held**
SIC: 1794 3599 1711 Excavation & grading, building construction; machine shop, jobbing & repair; mechanical contractor

(G-3323)
MIMOSA ACOUSTICS INC
335 N Fremont St (61820-3612)
PHONE...................217 359-9740
Patricia Jeng, *President*
Mike Katzenbach, *Engineer*
Don Wallace, *Software Engr*
Kyle Rust, *Director*
EMP: 9
SQ FT: 1,100
SALES: 300K **Privately Held**
SIC: 3842 8099 Hearing aids; hearing testing service

(G-3324)
MMPCU LIMITED
Also Called: Minuteman Press
905 S Neil St Ste B (61820-6567)
PHONE...................217 355-0500
Paul Conforti, *Principal*
Nani Baker, *Principal*
Dick Carlson, *Principal*
Corrine Conforti, *Principal*
EMP: 5
SQ FT: 1,250
SALES (est): 647.3K **Privately Held**
WEB: www.champaignprinting.com
SIC: 2752 3555 Commercial printing, lithographic; printing presses

(G-3325)
NEWS-GAZETTE INC
Also Called: Direct Impressions
2006 Round Barn Rd (61821-3623)
PHONE...................217 373-7450
William Klingman, *Branch Mgr*
EMP: 5 **Privately Held**
WEB: www.news-gazette.com
SIC: 2711 Newspapers, publishing & printing
PA: The News-Gazette Inc
15 E Main St
Champaign IL 61820

(G-3326)
NEWS-GAZETTE INC
Also Called: W D W S
2301 S Neil St (61820-7507)
P.O. Box 3939 (61826-3939)
PHONE...................217 351-5300
Jim Lewis, *Opers Mgr*
Steve Khachaturian, *Branch Mgr*
Mike Haile, *Manager*
Jim Turpin, *Producer*

Champaign - Champaign County (G-3327)

Lawrence Fredrickson, *Executive*
EMP: 24 **Privately Held**
SIC: 2711 Newspapers, publishing & printing
PA: The News-Gazette Inc
   15 E Main St
   Champaign IL 61820

(G-3327)
NEWS-GAZETTE INC
810 Hamilton Dr (61820-6814)
PHONE.....................217 351-8128
John Foreman, *Branch Mgr*
EMP: 4 **Privately Held**
SIC: 2711 Newspapers, publishing & printing
PA: The News-Gazette Inc
   15 E Main St
   Champaign IL 61820

(G-3328)
NEWS-GAZETTE INC
3202 Apollo Dr (61822-9668)
PHONE.....................217 384-2302
EMP: 5 **Privately Held**
SIC: 2711 Newspapers, publishing & printing
PA: The News-Gazette Inc
   15 E Main St
   Champaign IL 61820

(G-3329)
NEWS-GAZETTE INC (PA)
Also Called: News Gazette
15 E Main St (61820-3641)
P.O. Box 423, Ballwin MO (63022-0423)
PHONE.....................217 351-5252
John Foreman, *President*
Dave Burleson, *Editor*
Jeff D'Alessio, *Editor*
Jim Dey, *Editor*
Niko Dugan, *Editor*
EMP: 300
SQ FT: 15,000
SALES (est): 53.8MM **Privately Held**
SIC: 2711 Commercial printing & newspaper publishing combined; newspapers, publishing & printing

(G-3330)
PEPSI-COLA CHMPIGN URBANA BTLR
Also Called: Pepsico
1306 W Anthony Dr (61821-1199)
PHONE.....................217 352-4126
Michael Comet, *President*
John P Trebellas, *Principal*
Glenn Landl, *Engineer*
Eric Benson, *Sales Staff*
John T Comet, *Admin Sec*
EMP: 75
SQ FT: 50,000
SALES (est): 13.2MM **Privately Held**
WEB: www.pepsicolacu.com
SIC: 2086 Carbonated soft drinks, bottled & canned

(G-3331)
PETRONICS INC (PA)
60 Hazelwood Dr Rm 216 (61820-7460)
PHONE.....................608 630-6527
David Cohen, *Principal*
Erin Yerges, *Principal*
EMP: 3
SQ FT: 200
SALES (est): 474.6K **Privately Held**
SIC: 3944 Electronic toys

(G-3332)
PHI OPTICS INC
1800 S Oak St Ste 106 (61820-6974)
PHONE.....................217 819-1570
Gabriel Popescu, *President*
Mikhail Kandel, *Software Dev*
EMP: 2
SALES (est): 350.5K **Privately Held**
SIC: 3827 Interferometers

(G-3333)
PHOTONICARE INC
1902 Fox Dr Ste F (61820-7378)
PHONE.....................866 411-3277
Ryan Shelton, *CEO*
Ryan Nolan, *Vice Pres*
Andrew Zhang, *Senior Engr*
Stephen Boppart, *Chief Mktg Ofcr*
EMP: 4
SALES (est): 372.5K **Privately Held**
SIC: 3841 Surgical & medical instruments

(G-3334)
PLASTIPAK PACKAGING INC
3310 W Springfield Ave (61822-2869)
PHONE.....................217 398-1832
Dennis Nuesmeyer, *Plant Mgr*
Aaron Freeze, *Engineer*
Dennis Nesnuyer, *Manager*
Jeff Willard, *Maintence Staff*
EMP: 300
SALES (corp-wide): 1.3B **Privately Held**
SIC: 3089 3085 Pallets, plastic; plastics bottles
HQ: Plastipak Packaging, Inc.
   41605 Ann Arbor Rd E
   Plymouth MI 48170
   734 455-3600

(G-3335)
POLYCONVERSIONS INC
3202 Apollo Dr (61822-9668)
PHONE.....................217 893-3330
Ronald Smith, *President*
Dennis B Smith, *Principal*
William B Smith, *Corp Secy*
Robert Smith, *Vice Pres*
Tracy McDade, *Planning*
EMP: 50
SQ FT: 50,000
SALES (est): 12.3MM **Privately Held**
SIC: 2821 2385 3021 Plastics materials & resins; gowns, plastic: made from purchased materials; rubber & plastics footwear

(G-3336)
POLYVINYL RECORD CO
717 S Neil St (61820-5203)
PHONE.....................217 403-1752
Matt Lunsford, *President*
Darcie Lunsford, *Owner*
Patrick Wood, *Manager*
Andy Desantis, *Director*
Pilar Broggi, *Assistant*
EMP: 4
SALES (est): 300K **Privately Held**
SIC: 5735 5961 2782 Records; record &/or tape (music or video) club, mail order; record albums

(G-3337)
PORTER ATHLETIC EQUIPMENT CO
601 Mercury Dr (61822-9675)
PHONE.....................888 277-7778
Gregory Hege, *President*
Dalton Shasteen, *Natl Sales Mgr*
Ivan Davis Jr, *Admin Sec*
◆ **EMP:** 200 **EST:** 1867
SQ FT: 170,000
SALES (est): 31K **Privately Held**
WEB: www.porterathletic.com
SIC: 3949 Gymnasium equipment

(G-3338)
PRE PACK MACHINERY INC
520 S Country Fair Dr (61821-3668)
P.O. Box 3875 (61826-3875)
PHONE.....................217 352-1010
Rick Martin, *President*
Steve Bray, *Vice Pres*
EMP: 4
SQ FT: 5,000
SALES (est): 721.5K **Privately Held**
WEB: www.prepackmachinery.com
SIC: 3565 7359 3556 3535 Packaging machinery; rental store, general; food products machinery; conveyors & conveying equipment

(G-3339)
PREMIER PRINTING ILLINOIS INC
Also Called: Premier Print Group
3104 Farber Dr (61822-1074)
PHONE.....................217 359-2219
Dan Paulson, *CEO*
Bob Spence, *Prdtn Mgr*
Terry Wadley, *Marketing Staff*
Bill Williams, *Manager*
Wanda Brake, *Consultant*
EMP: 96
SALES (est): 20.7MM **Privately Held**
SIC: 2752 2759 Commercial printing, offset; commercial printing

(G-3340)
PSYONIC INC
60 Hazelwood Dr (61820-7460)
PHONE.....................888 779-6642
Aadeel Akhtar, *CEO*
EMP: 8
SQ FT: 400
SALES (est): 218.5K **Privately Held**
SIC: 3842 Limbs, artificial

(G-3341)
RESEARCH PRESS COMPANY INC
2612 N Mattis Ave (61822-1053)
P.O. Box 7886 (61826-7886)
PHONE.....................217 352-3273
David R Parkinson, *Ch of Bd*
Judy Parkinson, *President*
Russell Pence, *President*
Cythia Martin, *Principal*
Ann O Parkinson, *Principal*
EMP: 14
SQ FT: 10,500
SALES (est): 2.5MM **Privately Held**
SIC: 2731 5192 Books: publishing only; pamphlets: publishing only, not printed on site; books

(G-3342)
RICHARDSON IRONWORKS LLC
313 N Mattis Ave Ste 208 (61821-2461)
PHONE.....................217 359-3333
EMP: 5
SALES (est): 440K **Privately Held**
SIC: 2514 Mfg Metal Household Furniture

(G-3343)
RIVERBED TECHNOLOGY INC
2100 S Oak St (61820-0909)
PHONE.....................217 344-8091
Braden Ehrat, *Principal*
Xiaoyu Jin, *Technical Staff*
EMP: 4
SALES (est): 264.8K **Privately Held**
SIC: 3577 Computer peripheral equipment

(G-3344)
ROCKWELL AUTOMATION INC
2802 W Bloomington Rd (61822-9548)
PHONE.....................901 367-4220
Bill Beiter, *Manager*
EMP: 13 **Publicly Held**
SIC: 3625 Relays & industrial controls
PA: Rockwell Automation, Inc.
   1201 S 2nd St
   Milwaukee WI 53204

(G-3345)
SAGAMORE PUBLISHING LLC
3611 N Staley Rd Ste B (61822-8950)
P.O. Box 647 (61824-0647)
PHONE.....................217 359-5940
Joseph Bannon, *Ch of Bd*
Peter Bannon, *President*
Amy Dagit, *Production*
Misti Gilles, *Sales Staff*
EMP: 12
SALES (est): 1.2MM **Privately Held**
SIC: 2731 2721 Books: publishing only; trade journals: publishing only, not printed on site

(G-3346)
SHO TECHNOLOGIES INC
Also Called: Smart Home Office
4410 Stonebridge Dr (61822-9343)
PHONE.....................217 954-0020
Hua Lin, *President*
Qin Wang, *Vice Pres*
EMP: 2
SALES (est): 200K **Privately Held**
SIC: 3651 7389 Electronic kits for home assembly: radio, TV, phonograph;

(G-3347)
SILGAN WHITE CAP LLC
Also Called: Silgan Closures
3209 Farber Dr (61822-1456)
PHONE.....................217 398-1600
Dennis Turman, *Branch Mgr*
EMP: 109 **Publicly Held**
SIC: 3411 Metal cans
HQ: Silgan White Cap Llc
   1140 31st St
   Downers Grove IL 60515
   630 515-8383

(G-3348)
SILVER MACHINE SHOP INC
713 N Market St (61820-3004)
PHONE.....................217 359-5717
Scott Silver, *President*
John Silver, *Principal*
Margaret Silver, *Treasurer*
EMP: 8 **EST:** 1969
SALES (est): 867.3K **Privately Held**
SIC: 7692 3599 3444 3441 Welding repair; machine shop, jobbing & repair; sheet metalwork; fabricated structural metal

(G-3349)
SOMAT CORPORATION (PA)
2202 Fox Dr Ste A (61820-7595)
PHONE.....................800 578-4260
Jim Kirk, *CEO*
Steve Fleet, *Corp Secy*
Scott Burner, *CFO*
EMP: 27
SQ FT: 10,000
SALES (est): 1.7MM **Privately Held**
SIC: 3829 Measuring & controlling devices

(G-3350)
SONISTIC
60 Hazelwood Dr Ste 230g (61820-7460)
PHONE.....................217 377-9698
Aaron Jones, *Principal*
EMP: 3
SALES (est): 168.2K **Privately Held**
SIC: 3651 Household audio & video equipment

(G-3351)
SPECTROCLICK INC
904 Mayfair Rd (61821-4437)
PHONE.....................217 356-4829
Dr Alexander Scheeline, *President*
EMP: 2
SALES (est): 288.5K **Privately Held**
SIC: 3826 Analytical instruments

(G-3352)
SPORT REDI-MIX LLC (PA)
401 Wilbur Ave (61822-1319)
P.O. Box 292 (61824-0292)
PHONE.....................217 355-4222
Christopher Q Knipfer, *Mng Member*
Kevin Wilhelm, *Manager*
Janet Boerngen,
Michael F Ducey,
EMP: 25 **EST:** 2001
SALES (est): 4.8MM **Privately Held**
WEB: www.sportredimix.com
SIC: 3241 5251 Cement, hydraulic; tools

(G-3353)
STALEY CONCRETE CO
4106 Kearns Dr (61822-8531)
PHONE.....................217 356-9533
Ron Kenny, *President*
EMP: 22
SALES (est): 3.6MM **Privately Held**
SIC: 3273 Ready-mixed concrete

(G-3354)
STANDARD ELECTRIC SUPPLY INC
1904 W Springer Dr (61821-2469)
PHONE.....................217 239-0800
Larry Stern, *President*
EMP: 3
SALES (est): 150.5K **Privately Held**
SIC: 5065 5063 3699 Electronic parts & equipment; electrical apparatus & equipment; electrical equipment & supplies

(G-3355)
STANS SPORTSWORLD INC
47 E Green St (61820-5311)
PHONE.....................217 359-8474
Cameron S Wallace, *President*
EMP: 4
SQ FT: 3,000

GEOGRAPHIC SECTION

Channahon - Will County (G-3381)

SALES: 600K **Privately Held**
SIC: 5199 2396 2395 3993 Advertising specialties; screen printing on fabric articles; embroidery & art needlework; signs & advertising specialties

(G-3356)
STARFIRE INDUSTRIES LLC
2109 S Oak St Ste 100 (61820-0914)
PHONE..................217 721-4165
Brian Jurczyk, *Co-Venturer*
Brian E Jurczyk,
Robert A Stubbers,
EMP: 33
SQ FT: 12,000
SALES (est): 820K **Privately Held**
SIC: 3844 3671 8731 3677 Nuclear irradiation equipment; transmittal, industrial & special purpose electron tubes; commercial physical research; commercial research laboratory; transformers power supply, electronic type; electrostatic particle accelerators; particle accelerators, high voltage; high vacuum coaters, metal plate

(G-3357)
TE SHURT SHOP INC
Also Called: Teshurt
711 S Wright St (61820-5710)
PHONE..................217 344-1226
Robert Sammons, *President*
EMP: 17
SQ FT: 3,500
SALES: 950K **Privately Held**
SIC: 5611 2759 Clothing, sportswear, men's & boys'; letterpress & screen printing

(G-3358)
TEKMILL INC
210 Hazelwood Dr Ste 103 (61822-7488)
P.O. Box 17128, Urbana (61803-7128)
PHONE..................217 353-5111
Gary Durack, *President*
Angela McFarland, *CFO*
EMP: 21
SALES (est): 3.3MM **Privately Held**
SIC: 3599 Machine & other job shop work

(G-3359)
TROPHYTIME INC
223 S Locust St (61820-4125)
PHONE..................217 351-7958
Keith Bowman, *President*
EMP: 7 EST: 1977
SQ FT: 3,600
SALES (est): 1MM **Privately Held**
SIC: 5999 3993 Trophies & plaques; signs & advertising specialties

(G-3360)
UNDERWOOD DENTAL LABORATORIES
301 S 1st St (61820-4121)
P.O. Box 1158, Mattoon (61938-1158)
PHONE..................217 398-0090
Richard Kepp, *President*
Ron Hatfield, *Vice Pres*
Harold Turner, *Treasurer*
James Hone, *Admin Sec*
EMP: 10
SQ FT: 4,000
SALES (est): 810K **Privately Held**
SIC: 8072 3843 Dental laboratories; dental equipment & supplies

(G-3361)
UNIVERSITY OF ILLINOIS
Also Called: Document Services
54 E Gregory Dr (61820-6607)
PHONE..................217 333-9350
Barbara Childers, *Director*
EMP: 50
SALES (corp-wide): 3.9B **Privately Held**
SIC: 2752 Commercial printing, lithographic
PA: University Of Illinois
 364 Henry Adm Bldg
 Urbana IL 61801
 217 333-1000

(G-3362)
VARSITY STRIPING & CNSTR CO
2601 W Cardinal Rd (61822)
P.O. Box 3055 (61826-3055)
PHONE..................217 352-2203
Bonnie B Kemper, *President*
Kristen S Kemper, *Corp Secy*
EMP: 30 EST: 1981
SQ FT: 3,000
SALES (est): 2.4MM **Privately Held**
SIC: 1721 3993 Pavement marking contractor; signs & advertising specialties

(G-3363)
VCNA PRAIRIE ILLINOIS INC
3208 W Springfield Ave (61822-2867)
PHONE..................217 398-4346
EMP: 15 **Privately Held**
SIC: 3273 Ready-mixed concrete
PA: Vcna Prairie Illinois, Inc.
 7601 W 79th St Ste 1
 Bridgeview IL 60455

(G-3364)
VERTICAL TOWER PARTNER
2626 Midwest Ct (61822-8929)
PHONE..................217 819-3040
Darrin Peters, *Principal*
Kyle Fulton, *Director*
EMP: 4
SALES (est): 438.3K **Privately Held**
SIC: 2591 Blinds vertical

(G-3365)
VESUVIUS CRUCIBLE COMPANY (DH)
1404 Newton Dr (61822-1069)
P.O. Box 4014 (61824-4014)
PHONE..................217 351-5000
Jerry Taylor, *General Mgr*
Charles L Turner, *Vice Pres*
Tony Midea, *Technical Mgr*
Jean P Malherbe, *CFO*
Parker Hathaway, *Credit Mgr*
▲ EMP: 4 EST: 1916
SQ FT: 85,000
SALES (est): 589.5MM
SALES (corp-wide): 2.3B **Privately Held**
WEB: www.vesuvius.com
SIC: 3297 5051 Nonclay refractories; foundry products

(G-3366)
VESUVIUS U S A CORPORATION (DH)
Also Called: Foseco
1404 Newton Dr (61822-1069)
P.O. Box 4080 (61824-4080)
PHONE..................217 351-5000
Glenn Cowie, *President*
Dale Bower, *District Mgr*
Brett Ferrara, *District Mgr*
Pascal Dubois, *Vice Pres*
Claudine Essique, *Vice Pres*
◆ EMP: 180 EST: 1966
SALES (est): 545.1MM
SALES (corp-wide): 2.3B **Privately Held**
WEB: www.vesuvius.com
SIC: 5085 3297 Refractory material; nonclay refractories; graphite refractories: carbon bond or ceramic bond
HQ: Vesuvius Crucible Company
 1404 Newton Dr
 Champaign IL 61822
 217 351-5000

(G-3367)
VISUAL INFORMATION TECH INC
60 Hazelwood Dr (61820-7460)
PHONE..................217 841-2155
Randall J Sandone, *CEO*
EMP: 4
SALES (est): 179.7K **Privately Held**
SIC: 7372 Prepackaged software

(G-3368)
WANT ADS OF CHAMPAIGN INC (PA)
Also Called: Thrifty Nckel Amrcn Clssifieds
505 E University Ave C (61820-3847)
PHONE..................217 356-4804
Denny Merrifield, *President*
EMP: 8

SALES (est): 1.2MM **Privately Held**
SIC: 2711 2741 Newspapers: publishing only, not printed on site; miscellaneous publishing

(G-3369)
WARBLER OF ILLINOIS COMPANY
3127 Village Office Pl (61822-7673)
P.O. Box 5131, Springfield (62705-5131)
PHONE..................301 520-0438
Linda K May, *President*
Mark Cullen, *Counsel*
EMP: 6
SALES: 950K **Privately Held**
SIC: 3826 Environmental testing equipment

(G-3370)
WEISKAMP SCREEN PRINTING
312 S Neil St (61820-4914)
PHONE..................217 398-8428
Edward Weiskamp, *Owner*
EMP: 9
SALES (est): 722K **Privately Held**
SIC: 2759 3993 2396 Screen printing; signs & advertising specialties; automotive & apparel trimmings

(G-3371)
WIRCO INC
1700 W Washington St (61821-2412)
PHONE..................217 398-3200
Chad Wright, *President*
EMP: 76
SALES (corp-wide): 42.5MM **Privately Held**
WEB: www.wirco.com
SIC: 3544 3496 3322 3599 Industrial molds; woven wire products; malleable iron foundries; machine shop, jobbing & repair
PA: Wirco, Inc.
 105 Progress Way
 Avilla IN 46710
 260 897-3768

(G-3372)
WOLFRAM RESEARCH INC (PA)
100 Trade Centre Dr 6th (61820-6858)
P.O. Box 6059 (61826-6059)
PHONE..................217 398-0700
Stephen Wolfram, *President*
Robin Augsburg, *Editor*
William Young, *Editor*
Alex Upellini, *Area Mgr*
Igor Antonio, *Project Dir*
EMP: 148
SQ FT: 60,000
SALES (est): 94.5MM **Privately Held**
SIC: 7372 Prepackaged software

Channahon
Will County

(G-3373)
AIR PRODUCTS AND CHEMICALS INC
25915 S Frontage Rd (60410-8723)
PHONE..................815 423-5032
Mark Steinman, *Branch Mgr*
EMP: 23
SALES (corp-wide): 8.9B **Publicly Held**
SIC: 2813 Industrial gases
PA: Air Products And Chemicals, Inc.
 7201 Hamilton Blvd
 Allentown PA 18195
 610 481-4911

(G-3374)
AMERICAS STYRENICS LLC
26332 S Frontage Rd (60410-5288)
PHONE..................815 418-6403
Jon Timbers, *Mng Member*
EMP: 92
SALES (corp-wide): 8.3B **Privately Held**
SIC: 2821 Plastics materials & resins
HQ: Americas Styrenics Llc
 24 Waterway Ave Ste 1200
 The Woodlands TX 77380

(G-3375)
AMSTY
26332 S Frontage Rd (60410-5288)
PHONE..................815 418-6430
EMP: 5
SALES (est): 509.6K **Privately Held**
WEB: www.amsty.com
SIC: 2821 Plastics materials & resins

(G-3376)
CRANE COMPOSITES INC (DH)
23525 W Eames St (60410-3220)
PHONE..................815 467-8600
Jeff Craney, *President*
Rob Hancock, *Vice Pres*
Bill Beckwith, *Manager*
Darell Jones, *Manager*
Robert Flores, *Technology*
◆ EMP: 253 EST: 1954
SQ FT: 145,000
SALES (est): 88.7MM
SALES (corp-wide): 3.2B **Publicly Held**
WEB: www.cranecomposites.com
SIC: 3089 Panels, building: plastic

(G-3377)
CRANE COMPOSITES INC
Also Called: Kemlite Sequentia Products
23525 W Eames St (60410-3220)
PHONE..................815 467-1437
Michael Sheron, *Opers-Prdtn-Mfg*
EMP: 173
SALES (corp-wide): 3.2B **Publicly Held**
SIC: 3089 Panels, building: plastic
HQ: Crane Composites, Inc.
 23525 W Eames St
 Channahon IL 60410
 815 467-8600

(G-3378)
DEDICATED TCS LLC
23330 S Frontage Rd W (60410-8648)
PHONE..................815 467-9560
Jim Coleman, *Manager*
EMP: 12 **Privately Held**
WEB: www.dedicatedtcs.com
SIC: 3792 Travel trailers & campers
PA: Dedicated Tcs, Llc
 2700 175th St
 Lansing IL 60438

(G-3379)
DIAMOND QUALITY MANUFACTURING
24109 S Northern Ill Dr (60410-5358)
PHONE..................815 521-4184
Joseph Majewski, *Owner*
EMP: 8
SALES (est): 1.2MM **Privately Held**
SIC: 3999 Manufacturing industries

(G-3380)
DIVERSIFIED CPC INTL INC (DH)
24338 W Durkee Rd (60410-9719)
PHONE..................815 424-2000
Bill Auriemma, *CEO*
John P Dowd II, *Vice Pres*
William A Frauenheim III, *Vice Pres*
William Frauenheim, *Vice Pres*
Bill Madigan, *Vice Pres*
◆ EMP: 25
SQ FT: 9,600
SALES (est): 145MM **Privately Held**
WEB: www.diversifiedcpc.com
SIC: 2813 5169 Industrial gases; aerosols
HQ: Sumitomo Corporation Of Americas
 300 Madison Ave Frnt 3
 New York NY 10017
 212 207-0700

(G-3381)
DOW CHEMICAL COMPANY
26332 S Frontage Rd (60410-5592)
PHONE..................815 423-5921
Greg Kuhn, *Manager*
EMP: 158
SALES (corp-wide): 42.9B **Publicly Held**
WEB: www.dow.com
SIC: 2821 3086 Plastics materials & resins; plastics foam products
HQ: The Dow Chemical Company
 2211 H H Dow Way
 Midland MI 48642
 989 636-1000

Channahon - Will County (G-3382)

(G-3382)
EMC FIRE INC
22824 W Winchester Dr (60410-3308)
PHONE............................480 225-5498
Kevin Sears, *Principal*
EMP: 5 **EST:** 2012
SALES (est): 425.3K **Privately Held**
SIC: 3572 Computer storage devices

(G-3383)
EXCEL MACHINE & TOOL
24050 S Northern Ill Dr (60410-5183)
PHONE............................815 467-1177
Richard Sorg, *President*
EMP: 6
SQ FT: 5,000
SALES (est): 969.2K **Privately Held**
SIC: 3599 Custom machinery

(G-3384)
INEOS JOLIET LLC (DH)
23425 Amoco Rd (60410)
PHONE............................815 467-3200
Michele West, *Vice Pres*
Holger Muller, *Mng Member*
David Barnes, *Manager*
EMP: 250
SALES (est): 53.7MM
SALES (corp-wide): 1MM **Privately Held**
SIC: 2869 Laboratory chemicals, organic
HQ: Ineos Group Ag
Avenue Des Uttins 3
Rolle VD
216 277-040

(G-3385)
INEOS STYROLUTION AMERICA LLC
25846 S Frontage Rd (60410-5222)
PHONE............................815 423-5541
EMP: 4
SALES (corp-wide): 1MM **Privately Held**
SIC: 2821 Plastics materials & resins
HQ: Ineos Styrolution America Llc
4245 Meridian Pkwy # 151
Aurora IL 60504

(G-3386)
LODERS CROKLAAN BV
24708 W Durkee Rd (60410-5249)
PHONE............................815 730-5200
Don Grubba, *General Mgr*
EMP: 154
SALES (corp-wide): 2.3B **Privately Held**
SIC: 2079 2045 Edible oil products, except corn oil; doughs, frozen or refrigerated; flour from purchased flour
HQ: Bunge Loders Croklaan B.V.
Hogeweg 1
Wormerveer 1521
756 292-911

(G-3387)
LODERS CROKLAAN USA LLC
Also Called: Bunge Loders Croklaan
24708 W Durkee Rd (60410-5249)
PHONE............................815 730-5200
Lori King, *Sales Mgr*
David Corp, *Accounts Mgr*
Sherry Shugart, *Manager*
Cory Cummens, *Supervisor*
Brian Hudson, *Director*
▲ **EMP:** 180
SQ FT: 100
SALES (est): 356.4MM
SALES (corp-wide): 2.4B **Privately Held**
SIC: 2079 Edible oil products, except corn oil
HQ: Bunge Loders Croklaan Usa B.V.
Hogeweg 1
Wormerveer 1521
756 292-911

(G-3388)
MCNDT PIPELINE LTD (PA)
24154 S Northern Ill Dr (60410-5391)
P.O. Box 545 (60410-0545)
PHONE............................815 467-5200
Cindy McCain, *President*
Jim McCain, *Vice Pres*
EMP: 12
SALES: 1MM **Privately Held**
SIC: 1389 8734 Pipe testing, oil field service; construction, repair & dismantling services; testing laboratories

(G-3389)
MECHANICAL INDUS STL SVCS INC (PA)
24226 S Northern Ill Dr (60410-5111)
PHONE............................815 521-1725
Michael Hannon, *President*
Bob McCauliffe, *Foreman/Supr*
Karen Hannon, *Controller*
Michelle Linc, *Admin Sec*
Anthony Davis, *Assistant*
EMP: 37
SQ FT: 14,000
SALES (est): 8.3MM **Privately Held**
SIC: 1791 3446 3441 Structural steel erection; architectural metalwork; fabricated structural metal

(G-3390)
MIDWEST EDM SPECIALTIES INC
24108 S Northern Ill Dr (60410-5391)
PHONE............................815 521-2130
Richard Thompson, *President*
EMP: 6
SQ FT: 2,000
SALES (est): 742.9K **Privately Held**
SIC: 3599 Machine shop, jobbing & repair

(G-3391)
NEKG HOLDINGS INC
26709 S Kimberly Ln (60410-5408)
PHONE............................815 383-1379
Erik Harrington, *President*
Neil Harrington, *Principal*
EMP: 3
SALES: 500K **Privately Held**
SIC: 3452 Bolts, nuts, rivets & washers

(G-3392)
ROMAR CABINET & TOP CO INC
23949 S Northern Ill Dr (60410-5181)
PHONE............................815 467-4452
Anthony De Angelis, *President*
Bob Hill, *President*
Robert Hill, *Vice Pres*
Laurie Pillion, *Human Resources*
John Horn, *Manager*
EMP: 100
SQ FT: 40,000
SALES (est): 14.1MM **Privately Held**
SIC: 2434 5712 Wood kitchen cabinets; furniture stores

(G-3393)
SCOTTS COMPANY LLC
23580 W Bluff Rd (60410-8614)
PHONE............................815 467-1605
Anita Wood, *Branch Mgr*
EMP: 40
SALES (corp-wide): 3.1B **Publicly Held**
SIC: 2873 Fertilizers: natural (organic), except compost
HQ: The Scotts Company Llc
14111 Scottslawn Rd
Marysville OH 43040
937 644-0011

(G-3394)
SMID HEATING & AIR
23864 W Sussex Dr (60410-3064)
P.O. Box 828, Plainfield (60544-0828)
PHONE............................815 467-0362
EMP: 1
SALES: 500K **Privately Held**
SIC: 1711 3444 Plumbing/Heating/Air Cond Contractor Mfg Sheet Metalwork

(G-3395)
TESTA STEEL CONSTRUCTORS INC
22449 Thomas Dilon Dr (60410)
P.O. Box 51 (60410-0051)
PHONE............................815 729-4777
Michael J Testa, *President*
EMP: 11
SALES (est): 2.4MM **Privately Held**
SIC: 3441 Fabricated structural metal

Chapin
Morgan County

(G-3396)
TRAILERS INC
Also Called: Trailers Machine & Welding
1839 Saint Pauls Ch Rd (62628-4008)
PHONE............................217 472-6000
Marsha Schoth, *President*
EMP: 3
SQ FT: 5,000
SALES (est): 356.2K **Privately Held**
SIC: 7692 7539 3599 Welding repair; machine shop, automotive; machine shop, jobbing & repair

Charleston
Coles County

(G-3397)
CCAR INDUSTRIES
200 W Locust Ave (61920-1044)
PHONE............................217 345-3300
Christine Puckle, *Exec Dir*
EMP: 30
SALES (corp-wide): 6.8MM **Privately Held**
SIC: 3999 Barber & beauty shop equipment
PA: Ccar Industries
1530 Lincoln Ave
Charleston IL 61920
217 345-7058

(G-3398)
CHARLESTON CONCRETE SUPPLY CO
Also Called: Charleston Farrier Contruction
2417 18th St (61920-4344)
P.O. Box 373 (61920-0373)
PHONE............................217 345-6404
Jerry Tarble, *President*
John Tarble, *Vice Pres*
Ronald Murphy, *Treasurer*
EMP: 10
SALES (est): 1.1MM **Privately Held**
SIC: 3273 Ready-mixed concrete

(G-3399)
CHARLESTON COUNTY MARKET
Also Called: Walker's Supersaver Foods
551 W Lincoln Ave (61920-2443)
PHONE............................217 345-7031
Robert L Walker, *President*
Wilbur D Walker, *Corp Secy*
EMP: 80
SALES (est): 5.4MM **Privately Held**
SIC: 5411 2052 2051 Grocery stores, independent; cookies & crackers; bread, cake & related products

(G-3400)
COCA-COLA REFRESHMENTS USA INC
1321 Loxa Rd (61920-7690)
PHONE............................217 348-1001
EMP: 8
SALES (corp-wide): 37.2B **Publicly Held**
WEB: www.us.coca-cola.com
SIC: 2086 5499 Bottled & canned soft drinks; carbonated beverages, nonalcoholic; bottled & canned; beverage stores
HQ: Coca-Cola Refreshments Usa, Inc.
2500 Windy Ridge Pkwy Se
Atlanta GA 30339
770 989-3000

(G-3401)
DIETZGEN CORPORATION
1555 N 5th St (61920-1181)
PHONE............................217 348-8111
Darren A Letang, *President*
EMP: 12 **Privately Held**
SIC: 2679 Paper products, converted
PA: Dietzgen Corporation
121 Kelsey Ln Ste G
Tampa FL 33619

(G-3402)
GANO WELDING SUPPLIES INC
320 Railroad Ave (61920-1416)
P.O. Box 295 (61920-0295)
PHONE............................217 345-3777
Patrick Slaughter, *President*
T K Slaughter, *Vice Pres*
EMP: 12
SQ FT: 2,400
SALES (est): 4.4MM **Privately Held**
WEB: www.ganowelding.com
SIC: 5084 2813 5169 Welding machinery & equipment; acetylene; chemicals & allied products

(G-3403)
HEARTLAND COCA-COLA BTLG LLC
1321 Loxa Rd (61920-7690)
PHONE............................217 348-1001
EMP: 3090
SALES (corp-wide): 23.9B **Privately Held**
SIC: 5149 2086 Beverages, except coffee & tea; carbonated beverages, nonalcoholic; bottled & canned
PA: Heartland Coca-Cola Bottling Company Llc
9000 Marshall Dr
Lenexa KS

(G-3404)
ILLINOIS TOOL WORKS INC
Also Called: ITW Hi-Cone
155 5th St (61920)
PHONE............................217 345-2166
John Ballard, *Branch Mgr*
EMP: 53
SALES (corp-wide): 14.1B **Publicly Held**
SIC: 3089 Plastic containers, except foam
PA: Illinois Tool Works Inc.
155 Harlem Ave
Glenview IL 60025
847 724-7500

(G-3405)
J J COLLINS SONS INC
Also Called: Jj Collins Printers
2351 Madison Ave (61920-9382)
PHONE............................217 345-7606
Jim Collins Jr, *Manager*
EMP: 100
SALES (corp-wide): 50MM **Privately Held**
SIC: 2752 Business forms, lithographed
PA: J. J. Collins' Sons, Inc.
2300 Warrenville Rd # 190
Downers Grove IL 60515
630 960-2525

(G-3406)
LESTER BUILDING SYSTEMS LLC
750 W State St (61920-1000)
PHONE............................217 364-8664
Ed Janowski, *Branch Mgr*
EMP: 35
SALES (corp-wide): 71MM **Privately Held**
SIC: 2452 Prefabricated wood buildings
PA: Lester Building Systems, Llc
1111 2nd Ave S
Lester Prairie MN 55354
320 395-5212

(G-3407)
MID-ILLINOIS CONCRETE INC
Also Called: Charleston Ready Mix
2417 18th St (61920-4344)
PHONE............................217 345-6404
Robert Kepley, *Manager*
EMP: 3
SALES (corp-wide): 17.2MM **Privately Held**
SIC: 3273 Ready-mixed concrete
PA: Mid-Illinois Concrete, Inc.
1805 S 4th St
Effingham IL
217 342-2498

(G-3408)
OCE-VAN DER GRINTEN NV
Also Called: Oce Bruning
815 Reasor Dr (61920-9462)
PHONE............................217 348-8111
Noreen Connolly, *Branch Mgr*

GEOGRAPHIC SECTION

Chenoa - Mclean County (G-3435)

EMP: 47 **Privately Held**
SIC: 2679 Pressed fiber & molded pulp products except food products
HQ: Canon Production Printing Holding B.V.
Van Der Grintenstraat 10
Venlo 5914
773 592-222

(G-3409)
PAAP PRINTING
507 Jackson Ave (61920-2031)
PHONE.....................217 345-6878
Cathy Paap, *Partner*
Terry Paap, *Partner*
EMP: 5
SQ FT: 1,600
SALES (est): 589.2K **Privately Held**
SIC: 2752 Commercial printing, offset

(G-3410)
PRO-TRAN INC
1671 Olive Ave (61920-1207)
PHONE.....................217 348-9353
Pierre Chouinard, *President*
Darla Chouinard, *Treasurer*
EMP: 3
SQ FT: 7,500
SALES (est): 453.7K **Privately Held**
SIC: 3441 3443 3444 7699 Fabricated structural metal; tanks for tank trucks, metal plate; sheet metalwork; tank repair & cleaning services; welding on site

(G-3411)
RKM ENTERPRISES
Also Called: Sign Appeal
1003 Madison Ave (61920-1667)
PHONE.....................217 348-5437
Robert Murphy, *Owner*
EMP: 2
SALES: 300K **Privately Held**
SIC: 3993 Signs & advertising specialties

(G-3412)
SAFETY STORAGE INC
855 N 5th St (61920-1153)
PHONE.....................217 345-4422
Lynn R Dufek, *CEO*
Michael Ames, *President*
Brian Keown, *COO*
Emmy Dowden, *Engineer*
Jim Stone, *Marketing Staff*
▼ **EMP:** 70
SQ FT: 70,000
SALES (est): 17.7MM **Privately Held**
SIC: 3448 Prefabricated metal buildings
PA: Lone Star Investment Advisors Llc
4455 Lyndon B Johnson Fwy # 300
Dallas TX 75244

(G-3413)
SPENCE MONUMENTS CO
525 W State St (61920-1366)
PHONE.....................217 348-5992
Daniel Spence, *Owner*
EMP: 6
SQ FT: 1,900
SALES: 500K **Privately Held**
SIC: 3272 3281 Grave markers, concrete; monuments, concrete; cut stone & stone products

(G-3414)
STEARNS PRINTING OF CHARLESTON
Also Called: Printco Printing
304 8th St (61920-1504)
PHONE.....................217 345-7518
Kevin Jenkins, *President*
EMP: 4
SQ FT: 3,300
SALES (est): 322.9K **Privately Held**
SIC: 2789 2791 Bookbinding & related work; typesetting

(G-3415)
VESUVIUS U S A CORPORATION
955 N 5th St (61920-1160)
P.O. Box 290 (61920-0290)
PHONE.....................217 345-7044
Carl Corbin, *Project Mgr*
Steve Slaminko, *Manager*
EMP: 150

SALES (corp-wide): 2.3B **Privately Held**
SIC: 3297 5085 Graphite refractories: carbon bond or ceramic bond; refractory material
HQ: Vesuvius U S A Corporation
1404 Newton Dr
Champaign IL 61822
217 351-5000

(G-3416)
WENDELL ADAMS (PA)
Also Called: Adams Memorials
1286 W State St (61920-8602)
PHONE.....................217 345-9587
Wendell Adams, *Owner*
▲ **EMP:** 30
SQ FT: 15,000
SALES (est): 8.3MM **Privately Held**
SIC: 5999 3281 1411 Monuments, finished to custom order; cut stone & stone products; dimension stone

(G-3417)
WINNING STITCH
725 Windsor Rd (61920-7474)
PHONE.....................217 348-8279
Doris Hill, *Owner*
EMP: 6
SALES (est): 379.9K **Privately Held**
SIC: 2395 2396 5699 5621 Emblems, embroidered; automotive & apparel trimmings; formal wear; bridal shops

Chatham
Sangamon County

(G-3418)
CENTRAL STATES PALLETS
26 Highland Ln (62629-1015)
PHONE.....................217 494-2710
Gary Bowsher, *Principal*
EMP: 4 **EST:** 2007
SALES (est): 333.1K **Privately Held**
SIC: 2448 Pallets, wood

(G-3419)
CHATHAM PLASTICS INC
7 Kemp Dr (62629-9769)
PHONE.....................217 483-1481
Scott Moore, *President*
▲ **EMP:** 4
SALES (est): 687.9K **Privately Held**
SIC: 3089 Injection molding of plastics

(G-3420)
EVANS HEATING AND AIR INC
6172 Lick Rd (62629)
P.O. Box 46 (62629-0046)
PHONE.....................217 483-8440
Fax: 217 483-8441
EMP: 7
SQ FT: 10,500
SALES: 800K **Privately Held**
SIC: 3444 7623 Mfg Sheet Metalwork Refrigeration Service/Repair

(G-3421)
HENRY TECHNOLOGIES INC (HQ)
Also Called: Henry Tech Inc Intl Sls Co
701 S Main St (62629-1655)
PHONE.....................217 483-2406
Michael Giordano, *President*
Tony Grissom, *Opers Mgr*
John Murray, *Opers Staff*
Keila Jackson, *Purch Mgr*
Andrew Williams, *Finance Dir*
▲ **EMP:** 4 **EST:** 1914
SQ FT: 101,000
SALES (est): 85.9MM **Privately Held**
WEB: www.henrytech.com
SIC: 3491 3585 3567 3564 Gas valves & parts, industrial; automatic regulating & control valves; regulators (steam fittings); refrigeration equipment, complete; evaporative condensers, heat transfer equipment; industrial furnaces & ovens; blowers & fans; machine tool accessories; valves & pipe fittings

(G-3422)
HENRY TECHNOLOGIES INC
701 S Main St (62629-1655)
PHONE.....................217 483-2406
Scott Rahmel, *Branch Mgr*
EMP: 78
SQ FT: 65,000 **Privately Held**
SIC: 3585 Refrigeration equipment, complete
HQ: Henry Technologies, Inc.
701 S Main St
Chatham IL 62629
217 483-2406

(G-3423)
KOKES KID ZONE
1033 Jason Pl (62629-2018)
P.O. Box 514 (62629-0514)
PHONE.....................217 483-4615
EMP: 4 **EST:** 2008
SALES (est): 240K **Privately Held**
SIC: 3663 Mfg Radio/Tv Communication Equipment

(G-3424)
SPRINGFIELD WOODWORKS
6651 Wesley Chapel Rd (62629-8717)
PHONE.....................217 483-7234
Moore Springfield, *Owner*
EMP: 3
SALES (est): 96K **Privately Held**
SIC: 2499 Chair cane, rattan or reed

Chatsworth
Livingston County

(G-3425)
ACE PLASTIC INC
7942 N 3350 East Rd (60921-8117)
PHONE.....................815 635-3737
Sachin Suresh Patel, *President*
▼ **EMP:** 10
SQ FT: 13,000
SALES (est): 1.7MM **Privately Held**
SIC: 4953 4785 3089 Recycling, waste materials; toll operations; plastic processing

(G-3426)
PRINSCO INC
111 E Pine St (60921-9368)
P.O. Box 727 (60921-0727)
PHONE.....................815 635-3131
Doug Berg, *Sales Staff*
Chad Farnworth, *Sales Staff*
Nick Nissen, *Branch Mgr*
EMP: 30
SALES (corp-wide): 90.9MM **Privately Held**
WEB: www.prinsco.com
SIC: 3559 Plastics working machinery
PA: Prinsco, Inc.
1717 16th St Ne Fl 3
Willmar MN 56201
320 978-4116

(G-3427)
QUANEX HOMESHIELD LLC
32140 E 830 North Rd (60921-8184)
PHONE.....................815 635-3171
Teresa Freehill, *Financial Analy*
EMP: 80 **Publicly Held**
WEB: www.quanex.com
SIC: 3444 Sheet metalwork
HQ: Quanex Homeshield, Llc
311 W Coleman St
Rice Lake WI 54868
715 234-9061

(G-3428)
QUANEX HOMESHIELD LLC
32140 E 830 North Rd (60921-8184)
PHONE.....................815 635-3171
Kevin Delaney, *Principal*
EMP: 10
SALES (est): 3.3MM **Publicly Held**
SIC: 3353 Aluminum sheet, plate & foil
PA: Quanex Building Products Corporation
1800 West Loop S Ste 1500
Houston TX 77027

Chebanse
Iroquois County

(G-3429)
CLIFTON CHEMICAL COMPANY (PA)
160 S Locust St (60922-2057)
P.O. Box 25 (60922-0025)
PHONE.....................815 697-2343
Rick Kuntz, *President*
Todd Kuntz, *Manager*
EMP: 11
SQ FT: 7,200
SALES (est): 2.1MM **Privately Held**
SIC: 2842 7389 Specialty cleaning preparations; window cleaning preparations; packaging & labeling services

(G-3430)
NORDMEYER GRAPHICS
100 Dieter Rd (60922-2104)
P.O. Box 238 (60922-0238)
PHONE.....................815 697-2634
Kevin Nordmeyer, *Owner*
EMP: 3
SALES (est): 245.9K **Privately Held**
WEB: www.ngsigns.com
SIC: 3993 Signs & advertising specialties

(G-3431)
WOLFE BURIAL VAULT CO INC
310 N Oak St (60922-2016)
PHONE.....................815 697-2012
Rodney Wolfe, *President*
Rod Wolfe, *Principal*
EMP: 4
SQ FT: 7,800
SALES (est): 415.7K **Privately Held**
SIC: 3272 Burial vaults, concrete or precast terrazzo

Chenoa
Mclean County

(G-3432)
CHENOA LOCKER INC
113 N Veto St (61726-1067)
P.O. Box 31 (61726-0031)
PHONE.....................815 945-7323
Terry Bittner, *President*
Dana Muir, *Manager*
EMP: 8
SALES (est): 1.2MM **Privately Held**
SIC: 2011 7299 Meat packing plants; butcher service, processing only

(G-3433)
MELTERS AND MORE
512 N Division St (61726-1052)
PHONE.....................815 419-2043
EMP: 6 **EST:** 2015
SALES (est): 602.7K **Privately Held**
SIC: 3443 Mfg Fabricated Plate Wrk

(G-3434)
RELIABLE AUTOTECH USA LLC
600 N Division St (61726-9322)
PHONE.....................815 945-7838
Debasish Chakravarty, *Principal*
Sutapa Chakravarty, *Principal*
Kishor Ashokrao Salunkhe, *Principal*
EMP: 8 **EST:** 1976
SQ FT: 16,000 **Privately Held**
WEB: www.reliableautotech.com
SIC: 3444 3479 Sheet metalwork; painting of metal products

(G-3435)
WEBER METAL PRODUCTS INC
10702 E 1400 North Rd (61726-9082)
PHONE.....................815 844-3169
Stanley R Weber, *President*
Marsha Weber, *Treasurer*
EMP: 12 **EST:** 1948
SQ FT: 14,500
SALES (est): 1.8MM **Privately Held**
WEB: www.webermetalproducts.com
SIC: 3599 3451 Machine shop, jobbing & repair; custom machinery; screw machine products

Cherry Valley
Winnebago County

(G-3436)
ACME SCREW CO
125 E State St (61016-7707)
P.O. Box 906, Wheaton (60187-0906)
PHONE.................................815 332-7548
Rl Litten, *Manager*
EMP: 10
SQ FT: 1,500
SALES (corp-wide): 22.9MM **Privately Held**
SIC: 3463 3451 Nonferrous forgings; screw machine products
PA: Acme Screw Co.
1201 W Union Ave
Wheaton IL 60187
630 665-2200

(G-3437)
ATLAS COMPONENTS INC
4055 S Perryville Rd (61016-9729)
P.O. Box 5423, Rockford (61125-0423)
PHONE.................................815 332-4904
Michael Karceski, *President*
EMP: 50 **EST:** 1980
SQ FT: 15,500
SALES (est): 11.3MM **Privately Held**
SIC: 2439 Trusses, wooden roof

(G-3438)
BAR CODE DR INC
4337 S Perryville Rd (61016-9100)
PHONE.................................815 547-1001
Lynn Godina, *President*
EMP: 4
SALES (est): 190K **Privately Held**
SIC: 2711 Commercial printing & newspaper publishing combined

(G-3439)
EVAC NORTH AMERICA INC
Also Called: Evac Environmental Solutions
1445 Huntwood Dr (61016-9560)
PHONE.................................815 654-8300
Kenneth Postle, *President*
◆ **EMP:** 30
SALES (est): 9.5MM **Privately Held**
SIC: 3561 3589 Pumps & pumping equipment; sewage & water treatment equipment
HQ: Zodiac Pool Solutions
Parc Des Chenes
Bron 69500
800 842-340

(G-3440)
F P M LLC
Fpm Ipsen
648 Bypass Us Hwy 20 (61016)
PHONE.................................815 332-4961
Bryan Ames, *Branch Mgr*
Rudolf Vedo, *Med Doctor*
EMP: 60
SALES (corp-wide): 41.4MM **Privately Held**
SIC: 3398 Metal heat treating
PA: F P M, L.L.C.
1501 Lively Blvd
Elk Grove Village IL 60007
847 228-2525

(G-3441)
FPM HEAT TREATING
648 Us Highway 20 (61016-9545)
PHONE.................................815 332-4961
Fax: 815 332-3022
EMP: 14
SALES (est): 2.8MM **Privately Held**
SIC: 3398 Metal Heat Treating

(G-3442)
IPSEN INC (HQ)
984 Ipsen Rd (61016-3800)
PHONE.................................815 332-4941
Geoffrey Somary, *President*
John Kehoe, *Vice Pres*
Mitch Goodall, *Purch Mgr*
Vikki Demus, *Buyer*
Jennifer Knight, *Purchasing*
◆ **EMP:** 150
SQ FT: 110,000
SALES: 90MM
SALES (corp-wide): 240MM **Privately Held**
SIC: 3567 Heating units & devices, industrial: electric
PA: Ipsen International Holding Gmbh
Flutstr. 78
Kleve 47533
282 180-40

(G-3443)
L & S LABEL PRINTING INC
Also Called: Photo Copy Service
4337 S Perryville Rd # 102 (61016-9100)
PHONE.................................815 964-6753
Dave Roliardi, *President*
EMP: 4
SQ FT: 14,000
SALES (est): 848K **Privately Held**
SIC: 2672 2752 7334 Labels (unprinted), gummed: made from purchased materials; commercial printing, offset; photocopying & duplicating services

(G-3444)
NORTHWEST GRAPHICS INC
4337 S Perryville Rd (61016-9100)
P.O. Box 5167, Rockford (61125-0167)
PHONE.................................815 544-3676
Lynn B Godina, *President*
Terry Godina, *Sales Mgr*
EMP: 5
SALES (est): 907.2K **Privately Held**
SIC: 2752 Commercial printing, lithographic

(G-3445)
RAWSON CUSTOM WOODWORKS LLC
601 E State St (61016-9295)
P.O. Box 110 (61016-0110)
PHONE.................................815 332-9222
Rachel Rawson, *Mng Member*
Brian Rawson,
EMP: 2
SALES (est): 275.3K **Privately Held**
WEB: www.rawsoncustomwoodworks.com
SIC: 2434 Wood kitchen cabinets

(G-3446)
SHELVING AND BATH UNLIMITED
Also Called: Closet Concpts By Shlvng Unlim
4337 S Perryville Rd # 103 (61016-9100)
PHONE.................................815 378-3328
Joseph Weller, *President*
EMP: 6
SALES (est): 550K **Privately Held**
SIC: 2541 Cabinets, lockers & shelving

(G-3447)
TOP NOTCH TOOL & SUPPLY INC
3175 Tuggle Dr (61016-9283)
PHONE.................................815 633-6295
Lyle Zellner, *President*
Shana Fuller, *Admin Sec*
EMP: 5
SQ FT: 3,450
SALES (est): 725.1K **Privately Held**
SIC: 3599 5085 3545 3544 Machine shop, jobbing & repair; industrial tools; machine tool accessories; special dies, tools, jigs & fixtures

(G-3448)
WEILAND WELDING INC
4727 Lindbloom Ln (61016-9111)
PHONE.................................815 580-8079
Anita Weiland, *Principal*
EMP: 2
SALES (est): 268.5K **Privately Held**
SIC: 7692 Welding repair

Chester
Randolph County

(G-3449)
ARDENT MILLS LLC
Also Called: Conagra
101 Water St (62233-1843)
PHONE.................................618 826-2371
Alan Bindel, *Branch Mgr*
EMP: 31
SALES (corp-wide): 476.9MM **Privately Held**
SIC: 2041 2048 5149 Flour & other grain mill products; prepared feeds; flour
PA: Ardent Mills, Llc
1875 Lawrence St Ste 1400
Denver CO 80202
800 851-9618

(G-3450)
BLAZING COLOR INC
1007 State St (62233-1657)
P.O. Box 567 (62233-0567)
PHONE.................................618 826-3001
Kenneth Wagner, *President*
Norma Woods, *CIO*
EMP: 3
SQ FT: 5,000
SALES (est): 950K **Privately Held**
SIC: 2759 2791 Commercial printing; typesetting

(G-3451)
CHESTER BRASS AND ALUMINUM
Also Called: Chester Foundry
600 Barron St (62233-1548)
P.O. Box 30 (62233-0030)
PHONE.................................618 826-2391
Jeffrey Lutz, *President*
EMP: 11 **EST:** 1955
SQ FT: 6,000
SALES (est): 420K **Privately Held**
WEB: www.chesterill.com
SIC: 3365 3366 Aluminum & aluminum-based alloy castings; castings (except die): bronze

(G-3452)
CHESTER DAIRY COMPANY INC (PA)
Also Called: Farm Fresh Str D&M Dar Stores
1915 State St (62233-1115)
P.O. Box 605 (62233-0605)
PHONE.................................618 826-2394
Jason Ohlau, *President*
Elizabeth Ohlau, *Admin Sec*
EMP: 17 **EST:** 1931
SQ FT: 10,000
SALES (est): 13.7MM **Privately Held**
WEB: www.chesterillinois.com
SIC: 2026 Fermented & cultured milk products

(G-3453)
CHESTER DAIRY COMPANY INC
1912 Swanwick St (62233-1127)
P.O. Box 605 (62233-0605)
PHONE.................................618 826-2395
Barbara Johnson, *Manager*
EMP: 4
SALES (corp-wide): 13.7MM **Privately Held**
SIC: 2026 Fermented & cultured milk products
PA: Chester Dairy Company, Inc.
1915 State St
Chester IL 62233
618 826-2394

(G-3454)
EBERS DRILLING CO
4318 State Route 150 (62233-3218)
PHONE.................................618 826-5398
Lonny Ebers, *Owner*
EMP: 5
SALES (est): 325K **Privately Held**
SIC: 1031 1381 Lead ores mining; drilling oil & gas wells

(G-3455)
GILSTER-MARY LEE CORPORATION
111 Industrial Dr (62233-2555)
PHONE.................................618 826-3102
Shane Rock, *Manager*
EMP: 6
SALES (corp-wide): 1B **Privately Held**
WEB: www.gilstermarylee.com
SIC: 3999 Barber & beauty shop equipment
HQ: Gilster-Mary Lee Corporation
1037 State St
Chester IL 62233
618 826-2361

(G-3456)
GILSTER-MARY LEE CORPORATION (HQ)
1037 State St (62233-1657)
P.O. Box 227 (62233-0227)
PHONE.................................618 826-2361
Donald E Welge, *President*
Michael W Welge, *Exec VP*
Delbert Dethrow, *Vice Pres*
Ron Tretter, *Vice Pres*
Tom Welge, *Vice Pres*
◆ **EMP:** 600
SQ FT: 145,000
SALES: 942.4MM
SALES (corp-wide): 1B **Privately Held**
SIC: 2043 2098 2099 2045 Cereal breakfast foods; macaroni products (e.g. alphabets, rings & shells), dry; popcorn, packaged: except already popped; blended flour: from purchased flour; plastic containers, except foam
PA: Mary Lee Packaging Corporation
1037 State St
Chester IL 62233
618 826-2361

(G-3457)
LEE GILSTER-MARY CORPORATION
981 State St (62233-1654)
P.O. Box 227 (62233-0227)
PHONE.................................618 826-2361
Donald Wegle, *President*
EMP: 5
SALES (corp-wide): 1B **Privately Held**
WEB: www.gilstermarylee.com
SIC: 2098 2043 2099 2045 Macaroni products (e.g. alphabets, rings & shells), dry; cereal breakfast foods; popcorn, packaged: except already popped; blended flour: from purchased flour; plastic containers, except foam
HQ: Gilster-Mary Lee Corporation
1037 State St
Chester IL 62233
618 826-2361

(G-3458)
MARY LEE PACKAGING CORPORATION (PA)
Also Called: Gilster-Mary Lee
1037 State St (62233-1657)
P.O. Box 227 (62233-0227)
PHONE.................................618 826-2361
Donald E Welge, *President*
Michael W Welge, *Treasurer*
◆ **EMP:** 40 **EST:** 1969
SALES (est): 1B **Privately Held**
SIC: 2043 2099 3089 2098 Corn flakes: prepared as cereal breakfast food; syrups; plastic containers, except foam; macaroni & spaghetti

(G-3459)
MCCLOUD MTLWRKS INDUS SVCS INC
114 John Dr (62233-2102)
PHONE.................................618 713-2318
Chris Congiardo, *CFO*
EMP: 5
SALES (est): 500K **Privately Held**
SIC: 3441 Fabricated structural metal

(G-3460)
RANDOLPH COUNTY HERALD TRIBUNE
1205 Swanwick St (62233-1667)
P.O. Box 184, Du Quoin (62832-0184)
PHONE.................................618 826-2385
Mike Reed, *President*
EMP: 11 **EST:** 1861
SQ FT: 3,000
SALES (est): 502.2K **Privately Held**
WEB: www.randolphcountyheraldtribune.com
SIC: 2711 Newspapers, publishing & printing

GEOGRAPHIC SECTION

Chicago
Cook County

(G-3461)
10TH MAGNITUDE LLC (PA)
20 N Wacker Dr Ste 3250 (60606-2102)
PHONE..................................224 628-9047
Alex Brown, *CEO*
Sarah Winchester, *Manager*
Ira Bell, *CTO*
EMP: 24
SALES (est): 4.9MM **Privately Held**
SIC: 8748 3572 Business consulting; computer storage devices

(G-3462)
2 M TOOL COMPANY INC
Also Called: Mince Master
6530 W Dakin St (60634-2412)
PHONE..................................773 282-0722
Milivoje Mihailovic, *President*
Vesna Doyle, *Vice Pres*
Ruzica Mihailovic, *Treasurer*
Vladan Mihailovic, *Admin Sec*
EMP: 12
SQ FT: 12,000
SALES (est): 1.2MM **Privately Held**
SIC: 3599 Machine shop, jobbing & repair

(G-3463)
2000PLUS GROUPS INC (PA)
Also Called: Crescent Foods
4343 W 44th Pl (60632-4303)
PHONE..................................800 939-6268
Ahmad A Adam, *President*
Ibrahim Abed, *Vice Pres*
Maan Kudaimi, *Purchasing*
EMP: 130
SQ FT: 26,000
SALES: 43.3MM **Privately Held**
SIC: 2015 Chicken, processed

(G-3464)
21ST CENTURY US-SINO SERVICES
Also Called: Sea Horse Blinds
500 W 18th St Fl 1 (60616-1254)
PHONE..................................312 808-9328
Jimmy Lee, *President*
▲ EMP: 5
SALES: 800K **Privately Held**
SIC: 2591 Window blinds

(G-3465)
2L TECHNOLOGIES LLC
445 N Franklin St (60654-4901)
PHONE..................................312 526-3900
Luca Lanzetta, *Principal*
▲ EMP: 5
SALES (est): 527.8K **Privately Held**
WEB: www.2ltechnologies.com
SIC: 3545 Tools & accessories for machine tools

(G-3466)
3-SWITCH LLC
Also Called: Swoon Living
2940 N Albany Ave (60618-7607)
PHONE..................................217 721-4546
EMP: 3 EST: 2013
SALES: 250K **Privately Held**
SIC: 7336 2599 Art design services; factory furniture & fixtures

(G-3467)
3B MEDIA INC
401 N Michigan Ave # 1200 (60611-4255)
PHONE..................................312 563-9363
Ops Dir, *Branch Mgr*
EMP: 14
SALES (est): 386.8K
SALES (corp-wide): 3.2MM **Privately Held**
SIC: 2731 5735 5736 6794 Book music: publishing only, not printed on site; record & prerecorded tape stores; musical instrument stores; patent owners & lessors; advertising agencies
PA: 3b Media, Inc.
401 N Michigan Ave # 1200
Chicago IL 60611
312 563-9363

(G-3468)
3D PRINTER EXPERIENCE LLC
350 N Clark St Ste 400 (60654-4980)
PHONE..................................312 896-3399
Julie Steele, *Mng Member*
Julie Friedman Steele, *Manager*
EMP: 6
SALES (est): 264.3K **Privately Held**
WEB: www.the3dprinterexperience.com
SIC: 2851 2752 Paints & paint additives; commercial printing, lithographic

(G-3469)
3PRIMEDX INC
191 N Wacker Dr Ste 1500 (60606-1899)
PHONE..................................312 621-0643
Charles Polsky, *CEO*
Samuel Dudley, *Director*
EMP: 5
SQ FT: 500
SALES (est): 479.3K **Privately Held**
SIC: 2835 In vitro & in vivo diagnostic substances

(G-3470)
3RD COAST IMAGING INC
228 S Wabash Ave Ste 350 (60604-2310)
PHONE..................................312 322-3111
George Chrisopulos, *President*
Joshua Cole, *Production*
EMP: 5
SQ FT: 1,500
SALES (est): 601K **Privately Held**
SIC: 7389 2759 Design services; post cards, picture: printing; visiting cards (including business): printing; promotional printing; advertising literature: printing

(G-3471)
4C INSIGHTS INC
1 E Wacker Dr Ste 700 (60601-2007)
PHONE..................................602 881-9127
Lance Neuhauser, *CEO*
Alok Choudhary, *Chairman*
Mark Kappelman, *Opers Staff*
Anthony Freeman, *Engineer*
Abigail Adler, *Manager*
EMP: 12
SALES (est): 183.8K **Privately Held**
SIC: 7372 Prepackaged software

(G-3472)
4DEGREES AV INC
5254 S Dorchester Ave # 205 (60615-4125)
PHONE..................................903 253-7398
Ablorde Ashigbi, *CEO*
David Vandegrift, *Officer*
EMP: 5
SALES (est): 213.4K **Privately Held**
SIC: 7372 Business oriented computer software

(G-3473)
555 DESIGN FABRICATION MGT INC
Also Called: 555 Design Fabrication MGT
4501 S Western Blvd (60609-3026)
PHONE..................................773 869-0555
Paul Ohadi, *President*
Eileen Rodriguez, *Accounting Mgr*
EMP: 2
SALES (est): 237K **Privately Held**
SIC: 3441 Fabricated structural metal

(G-3474)
555 INTERNATIONAL INC
New Star Lighting Company
2225 W Pershing Rd (60609-2210)
PHONE..................................773 847-1400
John Pena, *Branch Mgr*
EMP: 25
SALES (corp-wide): 20MM **Privately Held**
WEB: www.555.com
SIC: 3446 3646 3442 3444 Architectural metalwork; commercial indusl & institutional electric lighting fixtures; metal doors, sash & trim; sheet metalwork
PA: 555 International, Inc.
4501 S Western Blvd
Chicago IL 60609
773 869-0555

(G-3475)
555 INTERNATIONAL INC
New Star Custom Lighting Co
4000 S Bell Ave (60609-2208)
PHONE..................................773 869-0555
James Geier, *Manager*
EMP: 25
SALES (corp-wide): 20MM **Privately Held**
WEB: www.555.com
SIC: 3646 Commercial indusl & institutional electric lighting fixtures
PA: 555 International, Inc.
4501 S Western Blvd
Chicago IL 60609
773 869-0555

(G-3476)
555 INTERNATIONAL INC (PA)
Also Called: New Star Lighting Company
4501 S Western Blvd (60609-3026)
PHONE..................................773 869-0555
Paul Ohadi, *CEO*
James Geier, *President*
John Pena, *General Mgr*
Richard Marohn, *Vice Pres*
Thomas Wabik, *CFO*
◆ EMP: 60
SQ FT: 140,000
SALES (est): 20MM **Privately Held**
SIC: 2542 Fixtures: display, office or store: except wood

(G-3477)
773 LLC (PA)
Also Called: Ch Distillery
1629 S Clinton St (60616-1109)
P.O. Box 617785 (60661-7785)
PHONE..................................312 707-8780
Tanya Kregul, *CFO*
Katie Cote, *Director*
Tremaine Atkinson,
Beth Boyle,
▲ EMP: 4 EST: 2012
SALES (est): 577.5K **Privately Held**
SIC: 2085 Vodka (alcoholic beverage)

(G-3478)
773 LLC
564 W Randolph St (60661-2218)
PHONE..................................312 707-8780
Tremaine Atkinson, *Mng Member*
EMP: 4
SALES (corp-wide): 577.5K **Privately Held**
SIC: 2085 Vodka (alcoholic beverage)
PA: 773 Llc
1629 S Clinton St
Chicago IL 60616
312 707-8780

(G-3479)
78 BRAND CO
Also Called: 78 Red Ketchup
1655 S Blue Island Ave (60608-2133)
PHONE..................................312 344-1602
Patrick Pilewski, *Managing Prtnr*
Bernard Utrata, *Exec Dir*
▲ EMP: 6
SALES (est): 330K **Privately Held**
SIC: 2033 8742 Tomato products: packaged in cans, jars, etc.; food & beverage consultant

(G-3480)
A & B METAL POLISHING INC
1900 S Washtenaw Ave (60608-2428)
PHONE..................................773 847-1077
Joseph Norvilas, *President*
Maria Norvilas, *Admin Sec*
EMP: 11
SQ FT: 3,500
SALES (est): 1.4MM **Privately Held**
SIC: 3471 3441 Finishing, metals or formed products; fabricated structural metal

(G-3481)
A & E RUBBER STAMP CORP
215 N Desplaines St 2n (60661-1243)
PHONE..................................312 575-1416
Phillip T De Francisco, *President*
William De Francisco, *Vice Pres*
Bill Defrancisco, *Vice Pres*
Leona Martinez, *Admin Sec*
EMP: 3 EST: 1950
SQ FT: 2,200
SALES (est): 444.8K **Privately Held**
WEB: www.aerubberstamp.com
SIC: 3953 5943 3993 Embossing seals & hand stamps; writing supplies; signs & advertising specialties

(G-3482)
A & F PALLET SERVICE INC
4333 S Knox Ave (60632-4347)
PHONE..................................773 767-9500
Jose Muniz, *President*
EMP: 12
SQ FT: 50,000
SALES (est): 1MM **Privately Held**
SIC: 2448 Pallets, wood

(G-3483)
A - SQUARE MANUFACTURING INC (PA)
1100 S Kostner Ave (60624-3835)
PHONE..................................800 628-6720
Andrez J Komar, *President*
EMP: 30
SALES: 4.1MM **Privately Held**
SIC: 3499 Fire- or burglary-resistive products

(G-3484)
A AND R CUSTOM CHROME
6528 S Lavergne Ave (60638-5807)
PHONE..................................708 728-1005
James Faxon, *Director*
EMP: 3
SALES (est): 156.9K **Privately Held**
SIC: 3471 Electroplating of metals or formed products

(G-3485)
A ASHLAND LOCK COMPANY (PA)
Also Called: Ashland Lock & SEC Solutions
2510 N Ashland Ave (60614-2004)
PHONE..................................773 348-5106
Anne M Gruber, *President*
James E Gruber, *Vice Pres*
Elaine Rivkin, *Office Mgr*
Joe Gruber, *Manager*
EMP: 12
SQ FT: 3,000
SALES (est): 1.6MM **Privately Held**
WEB: www.ashlandlock.com
SIC: 3429 7699 5251 1751 Locks or lock sets; locksmith shop; builders' hardware; door locks & lock sets; window & door installation & erection

(G-3486)
A CLOSET WHOLESALER
1155 N Howe St (60610-2473)
PHONE..................................312 654-1400
Allen Brown, *Owner*
EMP: 15
SALES (est): 1.3MM **Privately Held**
SIC: 2511 China closets

(G-3487)
A DIVISION OF A&A STUDIOS INC
350 N Ogden Ave Ste 10 (60607-1117)
PHONE..................................312 278-1144
Anthony Vizzari, *President*
Andrea Vizzari, *Vice Pres*
EMP: 10
SALES: 610K **Privately Held**
WEB: www.aastudiosinc.com
SIC: 3861 Photographic equipment & supplies

(G-3488)
A FINKL & SONS CO (HQ)
Also Called: Finkl Steel - Chicago
412 S Wells St Ste 500 (60607-3921)
P.O. Box 92576 (60675-2576)
PHONE..................................773 975-2510
Bruce C Liimatainen, *CEO*
Joseph E Curci, *President*
David Erhardt, *Superintendent*
Sami Liimatainen, *Superintendent*
Bryan Brown, *Vice Pres*
◆ EMP: 351 EST: 1974
SQ FT: 462,240

Chicago - Cook County (G-3489)

SALES (est): 109MM
SALES (corp-wide): 3.7B **Privately Held**
WEB: www.finkl.com
SIC: 3312 Ingots, steel; forgings, iron & steel
PA: Schmolz+Bickenbach Ag
Landenbergstrasse 11
Luzern LU
415 814-000

(G-3489)
A NEW DAIRY COMPANY
Also Called: Randolph Dairy
1234 W Randolph St (60607-1604)
PHONE.................................312 421-1234
George R Schuster, *President*
Steven Schuster, *Vice Pres*
EMP: 38
SQ FT: 19,000
SALES (est): 23.4MM **Privately Held**
SIC: 5143 2013 2038 Cheese; milk & cream, fluid; butter; yogurt; smoked meats from purchased meat; frozen specialties; dinners, frozen & packaged

(G-3490)
A P L PLASTICS
3501 W Fillmore St (60624-4312)
P.O. Box 23273 (60623-0273)
PHONE.................................773 265-1370
Jeff Dennis, *Owner*
EMP: 5
SALES (est): 225.9K **Privately Held**
SIC: 3089 Injection molding of plastics

(G-3491)
A TO Z TYPE & GRAPHIC INC
Also Called: Digital Publishing Group
1703 N Vine St (60614-5119)
PHONE.................................312 587-1887
Paul Hanover, *President*
Maynard Kabak, *Treasurer*
EMP: 8
SQ FT: 3,200
SALES (est): 580K **Privately Held**
SIC: 7336 2791 Graphic arts & related design; typesetting

(G-3492)
A TRUSTWORTHY SUP SOURCE INC
6047 N Central Park Ave (60659-3204)
PHONE.................................773 480-0255
Marcella Davis, *President*
EMP: 2
SALES (est): 317.6K **Privately Held**
SIC: 2653 2731 5112 3993 Corrugated & solid fiber boxes; textbooks: publishing only, not printed on site; stationery & office supplies; letters for signs, metal; business oriented computer software

(G-3493)
A&J PAVING INC
1911 N Sayre Ave (60707-3839)
PHONE.................................773 889-9133
Anthony Cocco, *President*
Joseph Cocco Jr, *Admin Sec*
EMP: 2
SALES (est): 280.1K **Privately Held**
SIC: 3272 1611 Concrete products; surfacing & paving

(G-3494)
A-KORN ROLLER INC (PA)
3545 S Morgan St (60609-1590)
PHONE.................................773 254-5700
Michael E Koren, *President*
Charles G Koren, *Principal*
Robert Owensby, *Purchasing*
Mike O'Connor, *Controller*
Lisa Rodriguez, *Accountant*
▲ **EMP:** 60
SQ FT: 20,000
SALES (est): 18MM **Privately Held**
SIC: 3555 Printing presses

(G-3495)
A-Z SALES INC
Also Called: AZ Foods
3717 N Cicero Ave (60641-3617)
PHONE.................................630 334-2869
Asya Zingerman, *CEO*
EMP: 3
SQ FT: 2,800

SALES (est): 285.8K **Privately Held**
SIC: 2099 Salads, fresh or refrigerated

(G-3496)
AA PALLET INC
900 W 49th Pl (60609-5153)
PHONE.................................773 536-3699
Donald Somerville, *President*
Don Huske, *Principal*
EMP: 20
SQ FT: 33,000
SALES (est): 3.3MM **Privately Held**
SIC: 2448 Pallets, wood

(G-3497)
AA SUPERB FOOD CORPORATION
2455 S Damen Ave (60608-5231)
PHONE.................................773 927-3233
Sandy Tsai, *President*
EMP: 44 **EST:** 1998
SALES (est): 5.3MM **Privately Held**
SIC: 2032 Chinese foods: packaged in cans, jars, etc.

(G-3498)
AAA MOLD FINISHERS INC
7208 W Pratt Ave (60631-1159)
PHONE.................................773 775-3977
Brian Miller, *President*
Judith Miller, *Admin Sec*
EMP: 6 **EST:** 1963
SQ FT: 6,000
SALES (est): 210K **Privately Held**
SIC: 3471 Polishing, metals or formed products

(G-3499)
AABBITT ADHESIVES INC (PA)
Also Called: Advance Adhesives
2403 N Oakley Ave (60647-2093)
PHONE.................................773 227-2700
Benjamin B Sarmas, *President*
Louise Sarmas, *Corp Secy*
David Sarmas, *Sr Corp Ofcr*
Daniel Sarmas, *Vice Pres*
Gregory Sarmas, *Vice Pres*
EMP: 60
SQ FT: 67,500
SALES (est): 16.9MM **Privately Held**
SIC: 2891 3087 2821 Adhesives; custom compound purchased resins; plastics materials & resins

(G-3500)
AABBITT ADHESIVES INC
Also Called: Advance Adhesives
601 W 81st St (60620)
PHONE.................................773 723-6780
Daniel Sarmas, *Manager*
EMP: 35
SALES (corp-wide): 16.9MM **Privately Held**
SIC: 2891 Adhesives
PA: Aabbitt Adhesives, Inc.
2403 N Oakley Ave
Chicago IL 60647
773 227-2700

(G-3501)
ABB POWER PROTECTION LLC
Also Called: Thomas & Betts Power Solutions
29029 Network Pl (60673-1290)
PHONE.................................804 236-3300
Christian M Tecca, *VP*
EMP: 16
SALES (corp-wide): 27.9B **Privately Held**
SIC: 3643 Current-carrying wiring devices
HQ: Abb Power Protection Llc
5900 Eastport Blvd Ste V
Richmond VA 23231
804 236-3300

(G-3502)
ABBEY METAL SERVICES INC
820 W 120th St (60643-5532)
PHONE.................................773 568-0330
Mark W Okonski, *President*
Alfred G Bialkowski, *Treasurer*
EMP: 12 **EST:** 1954
SQ FT: 32,000
SALES (est): 2.7MM **Privately Held**
WEB: www.abbeymetal.net
SIC: 3443 Fabricated plate work (boiler shop)

(G-3503)
ABBOTT LABORATORIES
6235 N Newark Ave (60631-2109)
P.O. Box 319022 (60631-9022)
PHONE.................................847 937-2210
Lynn Pavlis Jenkins, *Principal*
Jennifer Peterson, *Counsel*
Kathleen Riggens, *Opers Staff*
Matthew Ishu, *Research*
Larry Cohen, *Engineer*
EMP: 764
SALES (corp-wide): 31.9B **Publicly Held**
WEB: www.abbott.com
SIC: 2834 Pharmaceutical preparations
PA: Abbott Laboratories
100 Abbott Park Rd
Abbott Park IL 60064
224 667-6100

(G-3504)
ABBOTT LABORATORIES
Also Called: Abbott Nutrition
75 Remittance Dr (60675-1001)
PHONE.................................800 551-5838
Doris Xie, *Finance*
Kevin Callear, *Technical Staff*
EMP: 46
SALES (corp-wide): 31.9B **Publicly Held**
SIC: 2023 Baby formulas; dietary supplements, dairy & non-dairy based
PA: Abbott Laboratories
100 Abbott Park Rd
Abbott Park IL 60064
224 667-6100

(G-3505)
ABBOTT SCOTT MANUFACTURING CO
4215 W Grand Ave (60651-1857)
PHONE.................................773 342-7200
Joel Michaels, *President*
Lawrence Roseman, *Corp Secy*
▲ **EMP:** 40
SQ FT: 40,000
SALES (est): 10.7MM **Privately Held**
SIC: 3469 3599 3451 3444 Metal stampings; machine shop, jobbing & repair; screw machine products; sheet metalwork

(G-3506)
ABC INC
190 N State St Fl 7 (60601-3310)
PHONE.................................312 980-1000
Kim Pastor, *Manager*
EMP: 30
SALES (corp-wide): 69.5B **Publicly Held**
SIC: 4832 2721 Radio broadcasting stations; periodicals
HQ: Abc, Inc.
77 W 66th St Rm 100
New York NY 10023
212 456-7777

(G-3507)
ABC BUSINESS FORMS INC
Also Called: ABC Printing
5654 N Elston Ave (60646-6599)
PHONE.................................773 774-8282
Robert J Strauss, *President*
Steven C Strauss, *Vice Pres*
Chad Sohl, *Prdtn Mgr*
Steve Straussvice, *Treasurer*
Joe Lucarelli, *Controller*
▲ **EMP:** 13 **EST:** 1963
SQ FT: 12,000
SALES (est): 3.5MM **Privately Held**
SIC: 2752 Commercial printing, offset

(G-3508)
ABC IMAGING OF WASHINGTON
161 W Harrison St C-101 (60605-1043)
PHONE.................................312 253-0040
Mehdi Falsafi, *President*
EMP: 41
SALES (corp-wide): 218.9MM **Privately Held**
SIC: 2759 Commercial printing
PA: Abc Imaging Of Washington, Inc
5290 Shawnee Rd Ste 300
Alexandria VA 22312
202 429-8870

(G-3509)
ABCO METALS CORPORATIONS
1020 W 94th St (60620-3664)
PHONE.................................773 881-1504

Ray L Ebinger, *President*
Allen Ebinger, *Vice Pres*
EMP: 13
SQ FT: 20,000
SALES (est): 2.1MM **Privately Held**
SIC: 5093 4953 3341 Metal scrap & waste materials; refuse systems; secondary nonferrous metals

(G-3510)
ABLE ELECTROPOLISHING CO INC
2001 S Kilbourn Ave (60623-2390)
PHONE.................................773 277-1600
Don Esser, *President*
Scott Potter, *Vice Pres*
EMP: 59 **EST:** 2011
SALES (est): 10.3MM **Privately Held**
SIC: 3471 Polishing, metals or formed products

(G-3511)
ABUNDANCE HOUSE TREASURE NFP
1309 S Kedzie Ave (60623-1840)
PHONE.................................312 788-4316
Ernest Jones, *Vice Pres*
Farrah Brown, *Asst Sec*
EMP: 3 **EST:** 2015
SQ FT: 1,500
SALES (est): 159.9K **Privately Held**
SIC: 1389 Construction, repair & dismantling services

(G-3512)
ABYSS SALON INC
67 E 16th St Ste 5 (60616-1275)
PHONE.................................312 880-0263
Sharon E Miles-Gilty, *President*
David Gilty, *Vice Pres*
EMP: 4
SQ FT: 950
SALES (est): 85K **Privately Held**
SIC: 2844 7241 Manicure preparations; hair stylist, men

(G-3513)
AC AMERICOS
633 S Plymouth Ct Apt 201 (60605-1858)
PHONE.................................312 366-2943
Amy L Kleckner, *President*
EMP: 10 **EST:** 2016
SALES (est): 924.7K **Privately Held**
SIC: 3312 Forgings, iron & steel

(G-3514)
ACCESS INTERNATIONAL INC
Also Called: A I 2
180 N Stetson Ave # 3660 (60601-6706)
PHONE.................................312 920-9366
Douglas Katich, *President*
David Contreras, *Vice Pres*
Derek Morgan, *Vice Pres*
Dorothy Zwierz, *Vice Pres*
John E Katich, *CFO*
EMP: 25
SQ FT: 6,000
SALES (est): 2.6MM **Privately Held**
SIC: 7371 7372 Computer software development; business oriented computer software

(G-3515)
ACCIONA WINDPOWER N AMER LLC
333 W Wacker Dr Ste 1500 (60606-1226)
PHONE.................................319 643-9463
Donald Points, *CFO*
EMP: 8
SALES (corp-wide): 3.6B **Privately Held**
SIC: 3511 Turbines & turbine generator sets
HQ: Acciona Windpower North America, Llc
155 Fawcett Dr
West Branch IA 52358

(G-3516)
ACCRO PRECISION GRINDING INC
6648 S Narragansett Ave (60638-5112)
PHONE.................................708 681-0520
Marshall Klenske, *President*
Kristin Klenske, *Vice Pres*
EMP: 8

GEOGRAPHIC SECTION
Chicago - Cook County (G-3543)

SALES (est): 1MM **Privately Held**
WEB: www.accroprecision.com
SIC: **3599** Machine shop, jobbing & repair

(G-3517)
ACCURATE ENGINE & MACHINE INC
5053 W Diversey Ave (60639-1609)
PHONE..................................773 237-4942
Rey Villareal, *President*
EMP: 2
SALES (est): 247.5K **Privately Held**
SIC: **7539** 3714 Machine shop, automotive; motor vehicle parts & accessories

(G-3518)
ACCURATE METAL FABRICATING LLC
1657 N Kostner Ave (60639-4704)
PHONE..................................773 235-0400
Raymond J Meinsen Jr, *President*
Raymond Scott Meinsen, *Vice Pres*
Joan C Meinsen, *Admin Sec*
EMP: 70 EST: 1939
SQ FT: 53,000
SALES (est): 11MM **Privately Held**
WEB: www.accuratemetalfab.com
SIC: **3993** 3599 3441 Displays & cutouts, window & lobby; machine shop, jobbing & repair; fabricated structural metal

(G-3519)
ACCURATE PERFORATING CO INC
Also Called: Standard Perforating & Mfg
3636 S Kedzie Ave (60632-2786)
PHONE..................................773 254-3232
Aaron J Kamins, *President*
Larry H Cohen, *Owner*
Alan J Cohen, *Admin Sec*
EMP: 90 EST: 1946
SQ FT: 175,000
SALES (est): 34.2MM **Privately Held**
WEB: www.accuratepeforating.com
SIC: **3469** Perforated metal, stamped

(G-3520)
ACCURATE PRODUCTS INCORPORATED
4645 N Ravenswood Ave (60640-4573)
PHONE..................................773 878-2200
Graham Satherlie, *President*
Tim Satherlie, *COO*
Shawn Satherlie, *QC Mgr*
Karina Navarro, *Cust Mgr*
Johnny Khuc, *IT Specialist*
▲ EMP: 28
SQ FT: 20,000
SALES: 15MM **Privately Held**
SIC: **3069** 5085 Molded rubber products; rubber goods, mechanical

(G-3521)
ACE BAKERIES
3241 S Halsted St (60608-6605)
PHONE..................................312 225-4973
Lisa Pack, *Owner*
Bonnie Bisignano, *Regl Sales Mgr*
EMP: 10
SALES (est): 440K **Privately Held**
SIC: **2051** 5461 Bread, cake & related products; bakeries

(G-3522)
ACE PLATING COMPANY
Also Called: Ace Industries
3433 W 48th Pl (60632-3026)
PHONE..................................773 927-2711
Michael Holewinski, *President*
David Flores, *Vice Pres*
EMP: 35 EST: 1962
SQ FT: 40,000
SALES (est): 4.7MM **Privately Held**
SIC: **3471** 3544 3469 Plating of metals or formed products; special dies, tools, jigs & fixtures; metal stampings

(G-3523)
ACE SANDBLAST COMPANY
Also Called: Ace Sand Blast
4601 W Roscoe St (60641-4484)
PHONE..................................773 777-6654
Robert Largay, *President*
Julianne Largay, *Vice Pres*
EMP: 13 EST: 1942

SQ FT: 35,000
SALES (est): 1.4MM **Privately Held**
SIC: **1799** 3398 1721 Sandblasting of building exteriors; shot peening (treating steel to reduce fatigue); commercial painting; industrial painting; interior commercial painting contractor

(G-3524)
ACJ PARTNERS LLC
11552 S Bell Ave (60643-4714)
PHONE..................................630 745-1335
Astor Rogers, *President*
EMP: 3 EST: 2008
SQ FT: 3,000
SALES (est): 220K **Privately Held**
WEB: www.acjpartners.com
SIC: **2759** Commercial printing

(G-3525)
ACL INC
840 W 49th Pl (60609-5151)
PHONE..................................773 285-0295
Frank Ungari, *President*
Tony Banks, *Vice Pres*
Dan Cooke, *Purchasing*
Marykay Botkins, *Technical Mgr*
Mary K Botkins, *Sales Staff*
▲ EMP: 16
SQ FT: 18,000
SALES (est): 6.2MM **Privately Held**
SIC: **2819** 3825 3812 2842 Industrial inorganic chemicals; instruments to measure electricity; search & navigation equipment; specialty cleaning, polishes & sanitation goods

(G-3526)
ACME BUTTON & BUTTONHOLE CO
Also Called: Acme Sales
4638 N Ravenswood Ave # 2 (60640-4510)
PHONE..................................773 907-8400
EMP: 3 EST: 1937
SALES (est): 26.5K **Privately Held**
SIC: **3965** 2395 3961 Mfg Fastener/Button/Pins Pleating/Stitching Svcs Mfg Costume Jewelry

(G-3527)
ACME CONTROL SERVICE INC
6140 W Higgins Ave (60630-1845)
PHONE..................................773 774-9191
Robert Huening, *President*
Shirley M Huening, *Corp Secy*
Mark Huening, *Vice Pres*
Steven Huening, *Vice Pres*
Chris Molinaro, *Sales Dir*
EMP: 25
SQ FT: 5,000
SALES (est): 4.1MM **Privately Held**
WEB: www.acmecontrols.com
SIC: **7699** 7694 Thermostat repair; armature rewinding shops

(G-3528)
ACME SPINNING COMPANY INC
Also Called: Ace Industries
3433 W 48th Pl Fl 1 (60632-3026)
PHONE..................................773 927-2711
Michael Holewinski, *President*
Mary Holewinski, *Admin Sec*
▲ EMP: 14 EST: 1954
SQ FT: 35,000
SALES (est): 1.9MM **Privately Held**
WEB: www.acmespinningcompany.com
SIC: **3469** Stamping metal for the trade; spinning metal for the trade

(G-3529)
ACO INC
Also Called: Aeronautical Electric Company
5656 N Northwest Hwy (60646-6136)
PHONE..................................773 774-5200
William Nordlof, *President*
Virginia Nordlof, *Admin Sec*
EMP: 26
SQ FT: 10,500
SALES: 1.2MM **Privately Held**
WEB: www.aeronauticalelectric.com
SIC: **3651** 3644 3643 3641 Household audio & video equipment; noncurrent-carrying wiring services; current-carrying wiring devices; electric lamps; manufactured hardware (general)

(G-3530)
ACORN WIRE AND IRON WORKS LLC
2415 W 21st St (60608-2412)
PHONE..................................312 243-6414
Dan Patel, *General Mgr*
Dean Wynne,
▼ EMP: 20 EST: 1913
SQ FT: 30,000
SALES (est): 3.5MM **Privately Held**
WEB: www.acornwire.com
SIC: **3496** Miscellaneous fabricated wire products

(G-3531)
ACP TOWER HOLDINGS LLC
311 S Wacker Dr Ste 4300 (60606-6655)
PHONE..................................800 835-8527
EMP: 155
SALES (est): 9.1MM **Privately Held**
SIC: **3663** 7372 Cellular radio telephone; prepackaged software

(G-3532)
ACRYLIC DESIGN WORKS INC
5023 W 66th St (60638-6403)
PHONE..................................773 843-1300
Mike Palka, *President*
Robert Palka, *Vice Pres*
Cole Thomas, *Engineer*
EMP: 10
SALES (est): 1.2MM **Privately Held**
SIC: **2824** Acrylic fibers

(G-3533)
ACTA PUBLICATIONS
4848 N Clark St (60640-4839)
PHONE..................................773 989-3036
Gregory Pierce, *President*
EMP: 5
SQ FT: 5,000
SALES (est): 713K **Privately Held**
SIC: **2731** 3652 3695 Books: publishing only; pamphlets: publishing only, not printed on site; magnetic tape (audio): prerecorded; magnetic tape; video recording tape, blank

(G-3534)
ACTION ADVERTISING INC
2420 S Michigan Ave (60616-2302)
PHONE..................................312 791-0660
Merilyn Rutsky, *President*
EMP: 3
SQ FT: 8,000
SALES: 240K **Privately Held**
SIC: **2399** 1799 8742 Banners, made from fabric; flags, fabric; sign installation & maintenance; merchandising consultant

(G-3535)
ACTION ELECTRIC SALES CO INC (PA)
Also Called: Basic Wire & Cable Co
3900 N Rockwell St (60618-3719)
PHONE..................................773 539-1800
Philip Garoon, *President*
Tom Maksud, *General Mgr*
Howard Garoon, *Vice Pres*
Lisa Garoon, *CFO*
Dennis McCabe, *Sales Staff*
EMP: 65 EST: 1952
SQ FT: 520,000
SALES: 20.7MM **Privately Held**
WEB: www.basicwire.com
SIC: **3496** Miscellaneous fabricated wire products

(G-3536)
ACTIVE OFFICE SOLUTIONS
Also Called: Active Copier
3839 W Devon Ave (60659-1024)
PHONE..................................773 539-3333
Charlie Jung, *Principal*
EMP: 10
SALES (est): 1MM **Privately Held**
SIC: **3955** Print cartridges for laser & other computer printers

(G-3537)
ADA HOLDING COMPANY INC (HQ)
211 E Chicago Ave B29 (60611-2678)
PHONE..................................312 440-2897
Wiiliam Zimmerman, *CEO*

EMP: 15
SQ FT: 7,000
SALES (est): 9.6MM
SALES (corp-wide): 123.4MM **Privately Held**
SIC: **8748** 2721 2711 Business consulting; magazines: publishing & printing; commercial printing & newspaper publishing combined
PA: American Dental Association
211 E Chicago Ave
Chicago IL 60611
312 440-2500

(G-3538)
ADAMS ELEVATOR EQUIPMENT CO (DH)
Also Called: Schindler Logistics Center
100 S Wacker Dr Ste 1250 (60606-6004)
PHONE..................................847 581-2900
Robert Schreck, *CEO*
Rick Stumpf, *General Mgr*
Marie McIntosh, *Sales Staff*
EMP: 34 EST: 1930
SQ FT: 135,000
SALES (est): 10.3MM
SALES (corp-wide): 11.3B **Privately Held**
WEB: www.adamselevator.com
SIC: **7389** 3534 3825 3312 Field warehousing; elevators & equipment; signal generators & averagers; locomotive wheels, rolled
HQ: Schindler Enterprises Inc.
20 Whippany Rd
Morristown NJ 07960
973 397-6500

(G-3539)
ADAPTIVE TESTING TECH INC
217 N Jefferson St # 601 (60661-1103)
PHONE..................................312 878-6490
Yehuda Cohen, *CEO*
EMP: 12
SALES (est): 189.4K **Privately Held**
SIC: **7372** 8748 Business oriented computer software; testing services

(G-3540)
ADDISON PRECISION TECH LLC
4343 S Oakley Ave (60609-2610)
PHONE..................................773 626-4747
Ryan Cunningham,
EMP: 3
SALES (est): 99.9K **Privately Held**
SIC: **3317** Steel pipe & tubes

(G-3541)
ADE INC (PA)
Also Called: Lewibelle Company, The
1430 E 130th St (60633-2399)
PHONE..................................773 646-3400
Lewis C Lofgren, *CEO*
Jason C Lofgren, *President*
Nancy Christien Zidek, *Controller*
▲ EMP: 20
SQ FT: 92,000
SALES (est): 5.9MM **Privately Held**
SIC: **3086** 2821 2675 Insulation or cushioning material, foamed plastic; plastics materials & resins; die-cut paper & board

(G-3542)
ADELLO BIOLOGICS LLC
3440 S Dearborn St # 300 (60616-5074)
PHONE..................................312 620-1500
Leann Pruitt, *Senior Mgr*
EMP: 7
SALES (est): 646K **Privately Held**
SIC: **2834** Pharmaceutical preparations

(G-3543)
ADEPTIA INC
343 W Erie St Ste 430 (60654-5735)
PHONE..................................312 229-1727
Lou Ennuso, *CEO*
Deepak Singh, *President*
Gaurav Gautam, *Engineer*
David Paras, *Engineer*
Jim Wisch, *Accounts Exec*
EMP: 50
SALES (est): 8.3MM **Privately Held**
SIC: **7372** Prepackaged software
PA: Adeptia India Private Limited
Flat No 194,Pocket 7, Sector-23
New Delhi DL 11008

Chicago - Cook County (G-3544)

(G-3544)
ADFLOW NETWORKS
203 N Lasalle St Ste 2100 (60601)
PHONE..................866 423-3569
EMP: 4
SALES (corp-wide): 569.7MM **Publicly Held**
SIC: 7372 Prepackaged software
HQ: Adflow Networks Inc
3425 Harvester Rd Suite 105
Burlington ON L7N 3
905 333-0200

(G-3545)
ADHEREON CORPORATION
222 Mdse Mart Plz # 1230 (60654-1103)
PHONE..................312 997-5002
Kelley Folino, *CEO*
EMP: 4
SALES (est): 164.1K **Privately Held**
SIC: 3841 Surgical & medical instruments

(G-3546)
ADJUSTABLE CLAMP COMPANY (PA)
Also Called: Pony Tools
404 N Armour St (60642-6323)
P.O. Box 1899, Oak Park (60304-0605)
PHONE..................312 666-0640
Daniel V Holman, *Ch of Bd*
Joseph Krueger, *President*
Linda Willford, *Treasurer*
◆ EMP: 150 EST: 1893
SQ FT: 10,000
SALES (est): 15.5MM **Privately Held**
WEB: www.adjustableclamp.com
SIC: 3429 3423 3545 Clamps, metal; hand & edge tools; vises, machine (machine tool accessories)

(G-3547)
ADM CUSTOME CABINET CHICAGO
1900 N Austin Ave (60639-5010)
PHONE..................773 688-5379
EMP: 4 EST: 2015
SALES (est): 476.6K **Privately Held**
WEB: www.admccc.com
SIC: 2434 Wood kitchen cabinets

(G-3548)
ADM HOLDINGS LLC
191 N Wacker Dr Ste 1500 (60606-1899)
PHONE..................312 634-8100
Marc D Bassewitz, *President*
EMP: 3
SALES (corp-wide): 64.6B **Publicly Held**
SIC: 2046 Wet corn milling
HQ: Adm Holdings, Llc
4666 E Faries Pkwy
Decatur IL 62526

(G-3549)
ADNAMA INC
1513 S State St (60605-2804)
PHONE..................312 922-0509
Aleda Goodwin, *President*
EMP: 2
SALES: 330K **Privately Held**
SIC: 3993 Signs & advertising specialties

(G-3550)
ADORA BELLA MEDSPA LLC
3035 W Wilson Ave (60625-4331)
PHONE..................779 206-8331
Kulsum Vally,
EMP: 7
SALES: 150K **Privately Held**
SIC: 3061 Medical & surgical rubber tubing (extruded & lathe-cut)

(G-3551)
ADP PALLET INC
7300 S Kostner Ave (60629-5821)
PHONE..................773 638-3800
Edgardo Saldana, *President*
Everardo Saldana, *President*
EMP: 10
SALES (est): 1MM **Privately Held**
SIC: 2448 Pallets, wood

(G-3552)
ADSENSA CORPORATION
404 S Wells St Fl 5 (60607-3964)
PHONE..................312 559-2881
Martin Anderson, *President*
EMP: 3 EST: 2011
SALES (est): 210K **Privately Held**
SIC: 3695 Computer software tape & disks: blank, rigid & floppy

(G-3553)
ADVANCE AUTOMATION COMPANY
3526 N Elston Ave (60618-5692)
PHONE..................773 539-7633
Joseph Hanley Jr, *President*
Annette Stollenwerk, *Treasurer*
Michael Hanley, *Admin Sec*
EMP: 12 EST: 1958
SQ FT: 15,000
SALES (est): 2.6MM **Privately Held**
WEB: www.advanceautomationco.com
SIC: 3593 Fluid power cylinders, hydraulic or pneumatic

(G-3554)
ADVANCE ENAMELING CO
5849 S Bishop St (60636-1712)
PHONE..................773 737-7356
Jerry Grunert, *President*
Kurt Grunert, *Vice Pres*
EMP: 50
SQ FT: 72,000
SALES (est): 5.3MM **Privately Held**
SIC: 3479 Coating of metals & formed products

(G-3555)
ADVANCE EQUIPMENT MFG CO
4615 W Chicago Ave (60651-3386)
PHONE..................773 287-8220
John Wedakind, *President*
Mildred Wedakind, *Vice Pres*
Richard Bodenstab, *Admin Sec*
Deanne Shallcross, *Admin Sec*
▲ EMP: 14 EST: 1919
SQ FT: 20,000
SALES (est): 3.1MM **Privately Held**
WEB: www.advance-equipment.com
SIC: 3423 5072 Hand & edge tools; hand tools

(G-3556)
ADVANCE PLASTIC CORP
4866 W Cortland St (60639-4632)
PHONE..................773 637-5922
William Mason III, *President*
Lisa A Mason, *Treasurer*
EMP: 12
SQ FT: 3,500
SALES (est): 1.8MM **Privately Held**
SIC: 3089 Injection molding of plastics

(G-3557)
ADVANCE PRINTERS MACHINE SHOP
4271 N Elston Ave (60618-1899)
PHONE..................773 588-3169
Edwin H Dolatowski, *President*
Cindy Lehmen, *Corp Secy*
Susan Axelrood, *Manager*
EMP: 6 EST: 1919
SQ FT: 6,200
SALES: 500K **Privately Held**
WEB: www.advanceprintersmachine.com
SIC: 3599 Machine shop, jobbing & repair

(G-3558)
ADVANCE STEEL SERVICES INC
4722 W Harrison St (60644-5122)
PHONE..................773 619-2977
Ninos Oshana, *President*
Patricia Daugherty, *Accounts Mgr*
▼ EMP: 2
SQ FT: 7,500
SALES (est): 256.1K **Privately Held**
SIC: 5051 3312 1791 Steel decking; structural shapes & pilings, steel; bars & bar shapes, steel, cold-finished: own hot-rolled; bars, iron: made in steel mills; structural steel erection

(G-3559)
ADVANCE UNIFORM COMPANY
33 E 13th St Ste 1 (60605-2381)
PHONE..................312 922-1797
Joan Bovit, *President*
Mark Bovit, *Corp Secy*
EMP: 10
SQ FT: 12,000
SALES: 1.5MM **Privately Held**
SIC: 5699 2326 2337 Uniforms; work uniforms; uniforms, except athletic: women's, misses' & juniors'

(G-3560)
ADVANCE WHEEL CORPORATION
5335 S Western Blvd Ste H (60609-5450)
PHONE..................773 471-5734
William L Dods, *President*
Grace Rivas, *Persnl Mgr*
John Korpak, *Admin Sec*
▲ EMP: 70
SQ FT: 100,000
SALES (est): 14.6MM **Privately Held**
SIC: 3714 Wheel rims, motor vehicle

(G-3561)
ADVANCE WORLD TRADE INC (PA)
Also Called: A.W.T. World Trade
4321 N Knox Ave (60641-1906)
PHONE..................773 777-7100
Michael Green, *President*
Jorge Fuentes, *Plant Mgr*
Bryan Green, *Sales Staff*
Julie Kerkhoven, *Info Tech Mgr*
▲ EMP: 68
SQ FT: 85,000
SALES (est): 43.1MM **Privately Held**
SIC: 5084 3555 Printing trades machinery, equipment & supplies; printing trades machinery

(G-3562)
ADVANCED COOLING THERAPY INC
Also Called: Attune Medical
3440 S Dearborn St 215-S (60616-5074)
PHONE..................888 534-4873
Keith Warner, *CEO*
Erik Kulstad, *Chief Mktg Ofcr*
Melissa Naiman, *Marketing Staff*
EMP: 25
SALES (est): 1MM **Privately Held**
SIC: 3841 Surgical & medical instruments

(G-3563)
ADVANCED CSTM ENRGY SLTONS INC
Also Called: Aces
2545 W Diversey Ave (60647-7172)
PHONE..................312 428-9540
Lucas Payne, *Ch of Bd*
▲ EMP: 86 EST: 2012
SQ FT: 6,000
SALES (est): 15MM **Privately Held**
SIC: 3564 7389 Public lighting fixtures;

(G-3564)
ADVANCED FLEXIBLE MTLS LLC
Also Called: Afm Heatsheets
150 N Wacker Dr Ste 2160 (60606-1608)
PHONE..................312 961-9231
Michelle Christensen, *Vice Pres*
Lacie Whyte, *VP Sales*
Chris Falk,
Clay Hunter,
EMP: 10
SALES (est): 709.6K **Privately Held**
SIC: 2395 Quilted fabrics or cloth

(G-3565)
ADVANCED MACHINE CO INC
4450 W Belmont Ave (60641-4529)
PHONE..................773 545-9790
Beniamin Grama, *President*
EMP: 2
SALES (est): 220K **Privately Held**
SIC: 3545 Precision tools, machinists'

(G-3566)
ADVANCED ON-SITE CONCRETE INC
5308 W Grand Ave (60639-3010)
PHONE..................773 622-7836
James Viola, *President*
Natalia Viola, *Admin Sec*
EMP: 20
SALES (est): 5.6MM **Privately Held**
SIC: 5032 3273 Concrete mixtures; ready-mixed concrete

(G-3567)
ADVANCED STROBE PRODUCTS INC
7227 W Wilson Ave (60706-4705)
PHONE..................708 867-3100
Jaro Bijak, *CEO*
Katherine Beres, *Vice Pres*
Andrzej Bujnowski, *Engineer*
▲ EMP: 62
SQ FT: 28,000
SALES (est): 16.4MM **Privately Held**
SIC: 3641 3679 Electric lamps; electronic loads & power supplies

(G-3568)
ADVANCED WINDOW CORP
4935 W Le Moyne St (60651-1519)
PHONE..................773 379-3500
Robert Gibes, *President*
Jack Gibes, *Vice Pres*
Janucz Gibes, *Vice Pres*
▲ EMP: 50
SQ FT: 85,000
SALES (est): 9.6MM **Privately Held**
SIC: 3089 5211 Window frames & sash, plastic; lumber & other building materials

(G-3569)
ADVANTAGE MANUFACTURING INC
1458 N Lamon Ave (60651-1512)
PHONE..................773 626-2200
Andrew Radziwonski, *President*
Chris Halat, *CFO*
▲ EMP: 15
SALES (est): 3.2MM **Privately Held**
SIC: 3442 Window & door frames

(G-3570)
ADVANTAGE STRUCTURES LLC
10554 S Muskegon Ave (60617-5708)
PHONE..................773 734-9305
Joe Vaccaro,
EMP: 1
SALES (est): 287.7K **Privately Held**
SIC: 2655 Fiber shipping & mailing containers
PA: J M Vaccaro Trucking Inc
10554 S Muskegon Ave
Chicago IL 60617

(G-3571)
AERIAL INTELLIGENCE INC
100 S State St (60603-5504)
PHONE..................312 914-1259
Matthew Derolf, *CEO*
EMP: 10
SALES (est): 101.8K **Privately Held**
SIC: 7372 Prepackaged software

(G-3572)
AERODYNE INCORPORATED
Also Called: Aeromotive
2612 W Barry Ave (60618-7145)
PHONE..................773 588-2905
Carl Dumele, *Principal*
EMP: 5
SALES: 750K **Privately Held**
SIC: 3694 Engine electrical equipment

(G-3573)
AEROGENAEROGEN
410 N Michigan Ave (60611-4213)
PHONE..................312 624-9598
EMP: 3
SALES (est): 224.2K **Privately Held**
WEB: www.aerogen.com
SIC: 3841 Surgical & medical instruments

(G-3574)
AEROSOLS DANVILLE INC
340 E 138th St (60827-1828)
PHONE..................773 816-5132
Yolanda Velasquez, *Principal*
Jerry Murphy, *Manager*
EMP: 9
SALES (corp-wide): 3.2MM **Privately Held**
SIC: 2841 2844 Soap & other detergents; toilet preparations

▲ = Import ▼ = Export
◆ = Import/Export

GEOGRAPHIC SECTION

Chicago - Cook County (G-3602)

HQ: Aerosols Danville Inc.
1 W Hegeler Ln
Danville IL 61832

(G-3575)
AEROTRONIC CONTROLS CO (PA)
1512 N Fremont St Ste 103 (60642-2567)
PHONE.................................847 228-6504
Chris L Seth, *President*
Barry Seth, *Vice Pres*
Irene Seth, *Treasurer*
▲ EMP: 11 EST: 1958
SALES (est): 2.8MM **Privately Held**
SIC: 3672 3679 Printed circuit boards; power supplies, all types: static

(G-3576)
AEROVISION ENGINE SERVICES LLC
500 W Madison St Ste 2800 (60661-2506)
PHONE.................................231 799-9000
Greg Venboxel, *President*
Rick Cramblet, *Exec VP*
Jeff Bardal, *Vice Pres*
Pete Gibson, *Vice Pres*
EMP: 46 EST: 2004
SALES: 5MM
SALES (corp-wide): 12.5B **Publicly Held**
SIC: 3721 3724 Aircraft; aircraft engines & engine parts; air scoops, aircraft
PA: Lkq Corporation
500 W Madison St Ste 2800
Chicago IL 60661
312 621-1950

(G-3577)
AETNA ENGINEERING WORKS INC
12001 S Calumet Ave (60628-6798)
PHONE.................................773 785-0489
Richard J Zajeski, *President*
EMP: 23
SQ FT: 34,000
SALES (est): 2.7MM **Privately Held**
WEB: www.aetna.com
SIC: 1791 3441 3446 3444 Structural steel erection; fabricated structural metal; ornamental metalwork; sheet metalwork; studs & joists, sheet metal

(G-3578)
AFAM CONCEPT INC
Also Called: Jf Labs
7401 S Pulaski Rd Ste A (60629-5843)
PHONE.................................773 838-1336
Akhtar Ali, *CEO*
Korkor Owusu Akoto, *Admin Sec*
◆ EMP: 150
SQ FT: 200,000
SALES (est): 21.7MM **Privately Held**
WEB: www.vitaleproducts.com
SIC: 3999 Hair & hair-based products

(G-3579)
AFFORDABLE WELDING US INC
Also Called: Affordable Welding Ironworks
3100 E 87th St (60617-3301)
PHONE.................................773 374-2000
EMP: 5
SALES (est): 169.2K **Privately Held**
SIC: 7692 Welding repair

(G-3580)
AG INDUSTRIES LLC
28782 Network Pl (60673-1287)
PHONE.................................636 349-4466
EMP: 27
SALES (corp-wide): 16.9MM **Privately Held**
SIC: 3841 Surgical & medical instruments
PA: Ag Industries Llc
1031 Executive Parkway Dr # 101
Saint Louis MO 63141
636 349-4466

(G-3581)
AGGREGATE INDUSTRIES MGT INC (DH)
8700 W Bryn Mawr Ave # 300 (60631-3512)
PHONE.................................773 372-1000
Guy Edwards, *President*
Michael Hayes, *President*

Al Stone, *Vice Pres*
Renee Davis, *Plant Mgr*
▲ EMP: 4
SALES (est): 852MM
SALES (corp-wide): 4.5B **Privately Held**
SIC: 3273 Ready-mixed concrete
HQ: Holcim Participations (Us) Inc.
8700 W Bryn Mawr Ave
Chicago IL 60631
773 372-1000

(G-3582)
AGILENT TECHNOLOGIES INC
4187 Collection Center Dr (60693-0041)
PHONE.................................800 227-9770
EMP: 38
SALES (corp-wide): 5.1B **Publicly Held**
WEB: www.agilent.com
SIC: 3825 Instruments to measure electricity
PA: Agilent Technologies, Inc.
5301 Stevens Creek Blvd
Santa Clara CA 95051
408 345-8886

(G-3583)
AGROFRESH INC (DH)
222 N Lasalle St (60601)
P.O. Box 904, Spring House PA (19477-0904)
PHONE.................................267 317-9135
Stanton J Howell, *President*
EMP: 207
SALES (est): 185.6K
SALES (corp-wide): 2.9MM **Publicly Held**
SIC: 2879 Agricultural chemicals
HQ: Agrofresh Solutions, Inc.
510-530 Wlnut St Ste 1350
Philadelphia PA 19106
267 317-9139

(G-3584)
AHEAD INC (HQ)
Also Called: Thinkahead
401 N Michigan Ave # 3400 (60611-4249)
PHONE.................................312 924-4492
Daniel Adamany, *CEO*
Stephen Ayoub, *President*
Scott Reder, *Chief*
Maggie Brown, *Opers Staff*
Andrew Szafran, *CFO*
EMP: 100
SQ FT: 3,500
SALES (est): 68.5MM
SALES (corp-wide): 6.1MM **Privately Held**
SIC: 7372 5734 Business oriented computer software; computer peripheral equipment
PA: Ahead Data Blue, Llc
401 N Michigan Ave # 3400
Chicago IL 60611
866 577-2902

(G-3585)
AHEAD DATA BLUE LLC (PA)
401 N Michigan Ave # 3400 (60611-4249)
PHONE.................................866 577-2902
Daniel Adamany, *CEO*
Stephen Ayoub, *President*
EMP: 3
SALES (est): 6.1MM **Privately Held**
SIC: 7372 5734 Business oriented computer software; computer peripheral equipment

(G-3586)
AI IND
Also Called: Ai Industries
4015 W Carroll Ave (60624-1802)
PHONE.................................773 265-6640
EMP: 30
SALES (est): 950K **Privately Held**
SIC: 2326 Mfg Men's/Boy's Work Clothing

(G-3587)
AIDAR EXPRESS INC
2814 W Arthur Ave Apt 1 (60645-5292)
PHONE.................................773 757-3447
Marat Tolonov, *Owner*
EMP: 2
SALES: 250K **Privately Held**
SIC: 3537 Trucks: freight, baggage, etc.: industrial, except mining

(G-3588)
AIRGAS INC
12722 S Wentworth Ave (60628-7251)
PHONE.................................773 785-3000
Kevin Spellman, *Branch Mgr*
EMP: 17
SALES (corp-wide): 129.8MM **Privately Held**
SIC: 5169 5084 3548 2911 Industrial gases; industrial machinery & equipment; welding apparatus; petroleum refining; industrial gases
HQ: Airgas, Inc.
259 N Radnor Chester Rd # 100
Radnor PA 19087
610 687-5253

(G-3589)
AIRPORT AVIATION PROFESSIONALS
5757 S Cicero Ave (60638-3817)
PHONE.................................773 948-6631
Jeff Crosby, *Exec Dir*
EMP: 4
SALES (est): 387.6K **Privately Held**
SIC: 3728 Refueling equipment for use in flight, airplane

(G-3590)
AIRPORT PARK AND FLY LLC
4901 4925 W 47th (60638)
PHONE.................................708 310-2442
Jorge Torres, *Mng Member*
EMP: 5
SALES (est): 50.4K **Privately Held**
SIC: 7521 7372 7389 Automobile parking; application computer software;

(G-3591)
AIWA CORPORATION (PA)
965 W Chicago Ave (60642-5413)
PHONE.................................305 394-4119
Joseph Born, *CEO*
▲ EMP: 5 EST: 2011
SQ FT: 60,000
SALES: 1.4MM **Privately Held**
SIC: 3678 Electronic connectors

(G-3592)
AJ WELDING SERVICES
3640 S Kedzie Ave (60632-2727)
PHONE.................................708 843-2701
Alejandro Jaimes, *Owner*
EMP: 3
SALES: 10K **Privately Held**
SIC: 3446 Architectural metalwork

(G-3593)
AKAMAI TECHNOLOGIES INC
444 N Michigan Ave (60611-3903)
PHONE.................................312 893-7900
Joseph Gebauer, *Technical Staff*
Ellen Starmann, *Executive*
Anna King, *Executive Asst*
EMP: 20
SALES (corp-wide): 2.8B **Publicly Held**
WEB: www.akamai.com
SIC: 7372 Prepackaged software
PA: Akamai Technologies, Inc.
145 Broadway
Cambridge MA 02142
617 444-3000

(G-3594)
AKERS PACKAGING SERVICE INC
1037 E 87th St (60619-6398)
PHONE.................................773 731-2900
Scott Larsen, *General Mgr*
Ron Danczyk, *Plant Mgr*
Ralph Bateman, *Safety Mgr*
Kevin Matthews, *Sales Staff*
Phyllis McClory, *Admin Mgr*
EMP: 95
SALES (est): 21.8MM
SALES (corp-wide): 90.2MM **Privately Held**
SIC: 2653 Boxes, corrugated: made from purchased materials
PA: Akers Packaging Service, Inc.
2820 Lefferson Rd
Middletown OH 45044
513 422-6312

(G-3595)
AKZO NOBEL COATINGS INC
131 S Dearborn St # 1000 (60603-5566)
PHONE.................................312 544-7057
Ton Buchner, *CEO*
Jerry Leonard, *Manager*
EMP: 12
SALES (corp-wide): 10.2B **Privately Held**
SIC: 2851 Paints & allied products
HQ: Akzo Nobel Coatings Inc.
8220 Mohawk Dr
Strongsville OH 44136
440 297-5100

(G-3596)
ALANSON MANUFACTURING LLC
4408 W Cermak Rd (60623-2905)
PHONE.................................773 762-2530
Jerry Tamburrino,
EMP: 15
SQ FT: 13,000
SALES (est): 4.1MM **Privately Held**
WEB: www.alansonmfg.com
SIC: 3599 Machine shop, jobbing & repair

(G-3597)
ALBERTO DAZA
Also Called: Technoweld
4243 W Arthington St (60624-3507)
PHONE.................................773 638-9880
Alberto Daza, *Owner*
EMP: 10
SALES (est): 432.3K **Privately Held**
SIC: 7692 Welding repair

(G-3598)
ALCON TOOL & MFG CO INC
5266 N Elston Ave (60630-1673)
P.O. Box 480421, Niles (60714-0421)
PHONE.................................773 545-8742
EMP: 10 EST: 1946
SQ FT: 8,000
SALES (est): 93.3K **Privately Held**
SIC: 3545 3544 3469 3643 Mfg Machine Tool Access Mfg Dies/Tools/Jigs/Fixt Mfg Metal Stampings Mfg Conductive Wire Dvcs Mfg Crowns/Closures

(G-3599)
ALCON VISION LLC
400 W Superior St (60654-3409)
PHONE.................................312 751-6200
Kevin Ryan, *CFO*
EMP: 50
SALES (corp-wide): 14.8B **Privately Held**
SIC: 3851 Contact lenses
HQ: Alcon Vision, Llc
6201 South Fwy
Fort Worth TX 76134
817 293-0450

(G-3600)
ALE SYNDICATE BREWERS LLC
2601 W Diversey Ave (60647-1817)
PHONE.................................773 340-2337
Jesse Evans,
Samuel Evans,
EMP: 7
SALES: 1.1MM **Privately Held**
WEB: www.alesyndicate.com
SIC: 5181 2082 Ale; ale (alcoholic beverage)

(G-3601)
ALEGRIA COMPANY
2952 N Kilbourn Ave (60641-5360)
PHONE.................................608 726-2336
EMP: 200
SALES (est): 13.5MM **Privately Held**
SIC: 3571 Computer Manufactur

(G-3602)
ALESSCO INC (PA)
Also Called: Flip Flop Puzzle Mats
2237 N Janssen Ave (60614-3017)
PHONE.................................773 327-7919
Jeffrey A D'Alessio, *President*
Alex Chellberg, *Sales Associate*
Gary A D'Alessio, *Admin Sec*
◆ EMP: 15
SQ FT: 3,500

Chicago - Cook County (G-3603)

SALES (est): 13MM **Privately Held**
SIC: **3961** 3069 2542 Earrings, except precious metal; necklaces, except precious metal; bracelets, except precious metal; ornaments, costume, except precious metal & gems; floor coverings, rubber; partitions & fixtures, except wood

(G-3603)
ALEX DISPLAYS & CO
401 N Leavitt St (60612-1617)
PHONE..................................312 829-2948
Charles Felder, *CEO*
Steven Felder, *President*
Steve Felder, *President*
Reva Felder, *Admin Sec*
EMP: 12 **EST:** 1959
SQ FT: 38,000
SALES: 2MM **Privately Held**
WEB: www.alexdisplays.com
SIC: 3993 Signs & advertising specialties

(G-3604)
ALEX SMART INC
1800 W Grace St Apt 322 (60613-6086)
PHONE..................................773 244-9275
EMP: 4
SQ FT: 3,500
SALES (est): 450K **Privately Held**
SIC: 2771 Mfg And Designs Greeting Cards

(G-3605)
ALEXIA FOODS
222 Merchandise Mart Plz (60654-1103)
PHONE..................................312 374-3449
EMP: 3
SALES (est): 90.7K **Privately Held**
SIC: 2099 Food preparations

(G-3606)
ALI VS KITCHEN LLC
Also Called: Skinny Souping
110 W Kinzie St Fl 3 (60654-6266)
PHONE..................................312 852-5090
Alison Velasquez,
EMP: 3
SQ FT: 800
SALES: 300K **Privately Held**
SIC: 2034 Dehydrated fruits, vegetables, soups

(G-3607)
ALL CELL TECHNOLOGIES LLC
Also Called: Allcell Technologies
2321 W 41st St (60609-2215)
PHONE..................................872 281-7606
Azeezat Tijjani, *Purchasing*
Sebastian Maes, *Engineer*
Said Al-Hallaj, *Mng Member*
Hamdi Mohamed, *Manager*
Nazar Al-Khayat,
▲ **EMP:** 44 **EST:** 2001
SQ FT: 10,000
SALES (est): 6.4MM **Privately Held**
SIC: 3691 Batteries, rechargeable

(G-3608)
ALL CITY BRICK STAINING LLC
3635 W Dickens Ave Apt 1b (60647-3668)
PHONE..................................312 459-8937
Christopher Balke, *Principal*
EMP: 3
SALES (est): 175.6K **Privately Held**
SIC: 1771 1721 3479 Concrete work; painting & paper hanging; exterior residential painting contractor; exterior commercial painting contractor; painting, coating & hot dipping

(G-3609)
ALL ELECTRIC MTR REPR SVC INC (PA)
6726 S Ashland Ave (60636-3431)
PHONE..................................773 925-2404
Patrick Macias, *President*
Mark Stabosz, *Vice Pres*
EMP: 12
SQ FT: 5,000
SALES (est): 2MM **Privately Held**
SIC: 7699 7694 5084 5999 Pumps & pumping equipment repair; electric motor repair; pumps & pumping equipment; motors, electric

(G-3610)
ALL METAL SOLUTIONS INC (PA)
2044 N Whipple St (60647-3809)
PHONE..................................312 483-4178
Jonathan Egan, *President*
▲ **EMP:** 1
SQ FT: 50,000
SALES: 4MM **Privately Held**
SIC: 3441 Fabricated structural metal

(G-3611)
ALL PRINTING & GRAPHICS INC
125 S Clark St Fl 3 (60603-5200)
PHONE..................................773 553-3049
Ralph Folks, *Manager*
EMP: 5
SALES (est): 227.1K
SALES (corp-wide): 1.9MM **Privately Held**
SIC: 2752 Commercial printing, offset
PA: All Printing & Graphics, Inc.
2250 S 14th Ave
Broadview IL 60155
708 450-1512

(G-3612)
ALL SHE WROTE
825 W Armitage Ave (60614-4307)
PHONE..................................773 529-0100
Wendy Beard, *Owner*
EMP: 17
SALES (est): 2.6MM **Privately Held**
SIC: 2759 Invitation & stationery printing & engraving

(G-3613)
ALLEGRO PUBLISHING INC
2421 N Artesian Ave (60647-1902)
PHONE..................................847 565-9083
Robert Mueller, *CEO*
Nathan Wysocki, *Director*
▼ **EMP:** 2
SQ FT: 2,000
SALES (est): 200K **Privately Held**
SIC: 2731 Books: publishing only

(G-3614)
ALLEN LARSON
Also Called: Galactic Clothing
1914 N Washtenaw Ave (60647-4222)
PHONE..................................773 454-2210
EMP: 3
SALES (est): 76K **Privately Held**
SIC: 2389 Mfg Apparel/Accessories

(G-3615)
ALLEN PAPER COMPANY
641 W Lake St Ste L101 (60661-1058)
PHONE..................................312 454-4500
Charles Walther, *President*
Alice Johnson, *Corp Secy*
EMP: 7
SQ FT: 10,000
SALES (est): 860K **Privately Held**
SIC: 3955 5112 Ribbons, inked: typewriter, adding machine, register, etc.; stationery; computer paper; business forms

(G-3616)
ALLIANCE FOR ILLINOIS MFG
8420 W Bryn Mawr Ave (60631-3479)
PHONE..................................773 594-9292
EMP: 1
SALES (est): 283.6K **Privately Held**
SIC: 3999 Mfg Misc Products

(G-3617)
ALLIANCE GRAPHICS
1652 W Ogden Ave Apt 4 (60612-3491)
PHONE..................................312 280-8000
Richard Haft, *Owner*
EMP: 3
SQ FT: 1,000
SALES (est): 250K **Privately Held**
SIC: 2752 7331 Commercial printing, offset; mailing service

(G-3618)
ALLIED METAL CO (PA)
1300 N Kostner Ave (60651-1605)
PHONE..................................312 225-2800
Joel Fink, *President*
Michael Gilford, *CFO*
▲ **EMP:** 30 **EST:** 1955
SQ FT: 60,000
SALES (est): 38.3MM **Privately Held**
WEB: www.alliedmetalcompany.com
SIC: 3341 Aluminum smelting & refining (secondary); zinc smelting & refining (secondary)

(G-3619)
ALLIED PRINTING INC
Also Called: Allied Print & Copy
5640 N Broadway St (60660-4414)
PHONE..................................773 334-5200
Khoushab Alam, *President*
EMP: 3
SALES (est): 383.9K **Privately Held**
SIC: 2752 Commercial printing, offset

(G-3620)
ALLIGATOR REC & ARTIST MGT INC
Also Called: Eyeball Music
1441 W Devon Ave (60660-1311)
PHONE..................................773 973-7736
Bruce Iglauer, *President*
Kerry Peace, *Sales Staff*
Bob De Pugh, *Director*
Tim Kolleth, *Director*
Chris Levick, *Director*
▼ **EMP:** 15
SQ FT: 8,600
SALES: 2.8MM **Privately Held**
SIC: 3652 8742 Phonograph record blanks; business consultant

(G-3621)
ALLSCRIPTS HEALTHCARE LLC
222 Merchandise Mart Plz (60654-1103)
PHONE..................................312 506-1200
Chip Bustle, *President*
Lisa Khorey, *Exec VP*
John Gomez, *Vice Pres*
Gabrielle Rivera, *Senior Buyer*
Mark Barr, *Senior Engr*
EMP: 5
SALES (corp-wide): 1.7B **Publicly Held**
SIC: 7372 Prepackaged software
HQ: Allscripts Healthcare, Llc
305 Church At N Hills St
Raleigh NC 27609
919 847-8102

(G-3622)
ALLSCRIPTS HOLDINGS LLC
222 Merchandise Mart Plz # 2024 (60654-1010)
PHONE..................................800 334-8534
EMP: 3 **EST:** 2017
SALES (est): 81.3K
SALES (corp-wide): 1.7B **Publicly Held**
SIC: 7372 Prepackaged software
PA: Allscripts Healthcare Solutions, Inc.
222 Merchandise Mart Plz
Chicago IL 60654
800 334-8534

(G-3623)
ALLSCRPTS HLTHCARE SLTIONS INC (PA)
222 Merchandise Mart Plz (60654-1103)
PHONE..................................800 334-8534
Paul M Black, *CEO*
Richard Poulton, *President*
Lisa Khorey, *Exec VP*
Dan Evans, *Vice Pres*
Michelle Souferian, *Vice Pres*
EMP: 130
SALES: 1.7B **Publicly Held**
SIC: 7372 Prepackaged software

(G-3624)
ALLTECH ASSOCIATES INC (HQ)
Also Called: Grace Dvson Discovery Sciences
415 S Kilpatrick Ave (60644-4923)
PHONE..................................773 261-2252
Lafred E Festa, *President*
Bonnie Przybylski, *Principal*
Sharon McKinley, *Vice Pres*
Thomas W Rendl, *Vice Pres*
John A McFarland, *Admin Sec*
EMP: 100 **EST:** 1970
SQ FT: 60,000
SALES (est): 38.9MM
SALES (corp-wide): 1.9B **Publicly Held**
SIC: 2819 Industrial inorganic chemicals
PA: W. R. Grace & Co.
7500 Grace Dr
Columbia MD 21044
410 531-4000

(G-3625)
ALLY GLOBAL CORPORATION
Also Called: Ally International Trading
6033 N Sheridan Rd 23d (60660-3003)
PHONE..................................773 822-3373
Tony Liu, *President*
EMP: 7
SALES (est): 785.7K **Privately Held**
SIC: 3546 3572 5045 5065 Power-driven handtools; computer storage devices; computers, peripherals & software; electronic parts & equipment

(G-3626)
ALOHA DOCUMENT SERVICES INC
Also Called: Aloha Print Group
141 W Jackson Blvd A10a (60604-3040)
PHONE..................................312 542-1300
Virginia Peak, *President*
John Mrochen, *Manager*
EMP: 29
SALES (est): 3.5MM **Privately Held**
SIC: 7336 2759 Commercial art & graphic design; laser printing

(G-3627)
ALOMAR INC
5 S Wabash Ave Ste 316 (60603-3518)
PHONE..................................312 855-0714
Omar Alvarez, *President*
Onelio Alvarez, *Vice Pres*
Maria G Alvarez, *Treasurer*
▲ **EMP:** 3
SQ FT: 1,400
SALES: 1.1MM **Privately Held**
SIC: 3911 5094 Jewelry, precious metal; jewelry

(G-3628)
ALPHA CONSULTINGS
2240 N Leavitt St (60647-0560)
PHONE..................................773 251-0053
David Ash, *President*
EMP: 3 **EST:** 2016
SALES (est): 90.5K **Privately Held**
SIC: 1099 Metal ores

(G-3629)
ALPHA INDUSTRIES MGT INC
Also Called: Isoflex Packaging
1650 E 95th St (60617-4706)
PHONE..................................773 359-8000
Mark Teo, *Branch Mgr*
EMP: 75 **Privately Held**
SIC: 3081 Plastic film & sheet; polyethylene film
PA: Alpha Industries Management, Inc.
800 Page Ave
Lyndhurst NJ 07071

(G-3630)
ALPHA PACKAGING MINNESOTA INC
Also Called: Technigraph
6824 Paysphere Cir (60674-0068)
PHONE..................................507 454-3830
Beth Hoven, *Branch Mgr*
EMP: 3 **Privately Held**
SIC: 3085 Plastics bottles
HQ: Alpha Packaging (Minnesota) Inc.
850 W 3rd St
Winona MN 55987
507 454-3830

(G-3631)
ALPHA PCB DESIGNS INC
6815 W Higgins Ave (60656-2009)
PHONE..................................773 631-5543
Dean Bassias, *President*
▲ **EMP:** 4
SQ FT: 3,000
SALES (est): 621.8K **Privately Held**
SIC: 3672 Printed circuit boards

GEOGRAPHIC SECTION

Chicago - Cook County (G-3657)

(G-3632)
ALPS GROUP INC
55 E Monroe St Ste 3800 (60603-6030)
PHONE...................................815 469-3800
EMP: 3
SALES (corp-wide): 825.8K Privately Held
SIC: 3421 Cutlery
PA: Alps Group, Inc.
8779 W Laraway Rd
Frankfort IL 60423
815 469-3800

(G-3633)
ALSTER MACHINING CORP
4243 W Diversey Ave (60639-2002)
PHONE...................................773 384-2370
Adam Widula, President
EMP: 10
SQ FT: 16,000
SALES (est): 1.5MM Privately Held
SIC: 3599 Machine shop, jobbing & repair

(G-3634)
ALTA VISTA SOLUTIONS INC
2035 W Grand Ave (60612-1501)
PHONE...................................312 473-3050
Ernesto Pedroza, President
EMP: 15
SQ FT: 25,000
SALES (est): 568.1K Privately Held
SIC: 2759 Commercial printing

(G-3635)
ALTATHERA PHARMACEUTICALS LLC
311 S Wacker Dr Ste 2275a (60606-6675)
PHONE...................................312 445-8900
Merrill Barden, Vice Pres
Mahlaqa Patel, Vice Pres
Michelle Wilkes, Finance
Stephen Osullivan, Director
Omar Sinno, Associate Dir
EMP: 10 EST: 2014
SALES (est): 1.2MM Privately Held
SIC: 2834 Pharmaceutical preparations

(G-3636)
ALTMAN & KOEHLER FOUNDRY
505 W Root St (60609-2733)
PHONE...................................773 373-7737
Fax: 773 373-7737
EMP: 5
SQ FT: 9,300
SALES: 110K Privately Held
SIC: 3365 3369 Aluminum Foundry Non-ferrous Metal Foundry

(G-3637)
ALTMAN PATTERN AND FOUNDRY CO
6820 W 63rd St (60638-4026)
PHONE...................................773 586-9100
Ronald Altman, President
Mary Altman, Treasurer
EMP: 15
SQ FT: 12,000
SALES: 800K Privately Held
SIC: 3365 3366 Aluminum & aluminum-based alloy castings; brass foundry

(G-3638)
ALTURDYNE POWER SYSTEMS LLC
5023 N Clark St (60640-2823)
PHONE...................................619 440-5531
EMP: 3
SALES (est): 130.5K Privately Held
SIC: 3511 Turbines & turbine generator sets

(G-3639)
ALVAREZ & MARSAL INC
540 W Madison St Fl 18 (60661-7698)
PHONE...................................312 601-4220
Tom Hill, Branch Mgr
Alyssa Davis, Director
John Goodman, Director
Kurt Knipp, Director
Nancy Lee, Director
EMP: 50
SALES (corp-wide): 209.5MM Privately Held
SIC: 8742 3523 3448 Financial consultant; farm machinery & equipment; prefabricated metal buildings
HQ: Alvarez & Marsal, Inc.
600 Madison Ave Fl 8
New York NY 10022
212 759-4433

(G-3640)
AM HARPER PRODUCTS INC
Also Called: A.M.H. Products
2300 W Jarvis Ave Apt 3 (60645-1777)
PHONE...................................312 767-8283
Andre Harper, CEO
Dejaney Hinds, President
Jermaine Moodie, General Mgr
Damion Beckford, Business Mgr
Melissa Harper, COO
EMP: 10
SALES (est): 335.7K Privately Held
SIC: 5699 2841 5999 Customized clothing & apparel; designers, apparel; textile soap; toiletries, cosmetics & perfumes

(G-3641)
AM2PAT INC (PA)
Also Called: Salient Hct
3034 W Devon Ave (60659-1455)
PHONE...................................847 726-9443
Dushyant Patel, President
▲ EMP: 7
SQ FT: 4,400
SALES (est): 2.4MM Privately Held
SIC: 2834 Pills, pharmaceutical

(G-3642)
AMAG MANUFACTURING INC
4940 S East End Ave 11c (60615-3159)
PHONE...................................773 667-5184
Michael Ahasay, President
Bruce Strong, Corp Secy
Dana Norwick, Vice Pres
EMP: 6 EST: 2000
SQ FT: 800
SALES (est): 399.3K Privately Held
SIC: 3443 3496 Metal parts; miscellaneous fabricated wire products

(G-3643)
AMAZING MASCOTS
4913 W Montrose Ave 3 (60641-1525)
PHONE...................................727 475-0255
Kelly Frank, Principal
EMP: 3
SALES (est): 163.6K Privately Held
SIC: 2323 Men's & boys' neckwear

(G-3644)
AMBERLEAF CABINETRY INC
1400 W 37th St (60609-2109)
PHONE...................................773 247-8282
Jim Wong, Manager
Nelson Carlo, Representative
EMP: 10
SALES: 1.2MM Privately Held
SIC: 2434 Wood kitchen cabinets

(G-3645)
AMENITIES HOME DESIGN
Also Called: Cynthia Espy
1529 W Glenlake Ave (60660-1825)
PHONE...................................312 421-2450
Cynthia E Espy, Owner
EMP: 2
SQ FT: 500
SALES (est): 200K Privately Held
SIC: 2353 Hats, caps & millinery

(G-3646)
AMER SPORTS COMPANY (DH)
8750 W Bryn Mawr Ave (60631-3655)
PHONE...................................773 714-6400
Hekey Takala, Ch of Bd
Gary Diehl, President
Juha Vaisanen, President
Mike O'Connell, Vice Pres
Ronald Ostrowski, Vice Pres
◆ EMP: 350
SQ FT: 100,000
SALES (est): 559.6MM Privately Held
SIC: 3949 Golf equipment
HQ: Amer Sports Oy
Konepajankuja 6
Helsinki 00510
207 122-500

(G-3647)
AMERICAN AIR FILTER CO INC
Also Called: AAF International
24828 Network Pl (60673-1248)
P.O. Box 35690 (60654)
PHONE...................................502 637-0011
Michelle Ecken, Marketing Staff
EMP: 86 Privately Held
SIC: 3564 Filters, air: furnaces, air conditioning equipment, etc.
HQ: American Air Filter Company, Inc.
9920 Corp Cmpus Dr Ste 22
Louisville KY 40223
502 637-0011

(G-3648)
AMERICAN ASSN ENDODONTISTS
180 N Stetson Ave # 1500 (60601-6811)
PHONE...................................312 266-7255
Jerry McDonald, CFO
Rebecca Perry, CFO
Paul Young, Human Res Mgr
Donna Verga, Marketing Mgr
Andrea Bass-Allen, Business Anlyst
EMP: 24
SALES: 9.9MM Privately Held
WEB: www.aae.org
SIC: 8621 2721 Medical field-related associations; comic books: publishing only, not printed on site

(G-3649)
AMERICAN ASSOCIATION OF INDIVI (PA)
Also Called: Aaii
625 N Michigan Ave # 1900 (60611-3110)
PHONE...................................312 280-0170
James B Cloonan, Ch of Bd
John Bajkowski, President
Harry L Madorin, Corp Secy
EMP: 28
SQ FT: 7,000
SALES: 8MM Privately Held
SIC: 6282 7331 2731 8621 Investment advisory service; mailing list management; mailing list brokers; books: publishing only; professional membership organizations

(G-3650)
AMERICAN BAR ASSOCIATION (PA)
321 N Clark St Ste Ll2 (60654-7598)
PHONE...................................312 988-5000
Michael E Burke, Ch of Bd
Linda Klein, President
Reginald Turner Jr, President
Mary McNulty, Publisher
Donna Mosher, Managing Dir
EMP: 700 EST: 1878
SQ FT: 160,000
SALES (est): 136.5MM Privately Held
WEB: www.americanbar.org
SIC: 8621 2721 2731 Bar association; magazines: publishing only, not printed on site; books: publishing only

(G-3651)
AMERICAN CITY BUS JOURNALS INC
Also Called: City Business Journals Network
141 W Jackson Blvd # 1795 (60604-3064)
PHONE...................................312 873-2200
Megan Omeara, Branch Mgr
Joepsh Di Pietro, Manager
EMP: 3
SALES (corp-wide): 5.6B Privately Held
SIC: 2721 Trade journals: publishing only, not printed on site
HQ: American City Business Journals, Inc.
120 W Morehead St Ste 400
Charlotte NC 28202
704 973-1000

(G-3652)
AMERICAN ENLIGHTENMENT LLC
Also Called: Luckyprints
2023 W Carroll Ave # 303 (60612-1691)
PHONE...................................773 687-8996
Adam Smith, Mng Member
EMP: 7
SALES: 900K Privately Held
SIC: 2396 5699 Screen printing on fabric articles; customized clothing & apparel

(G-3653)
AMERICAN GRINDING & MACHINE CO (PA)
2000 N Mango Ave (60639-2899)
PHONE...................................773 889-4343
Greg Leonard, President
Scott Collins, Vice Pres
David Potts, Opers Mgr
Paul Becker, Sales Staff
Debby Kehoe, Sales Staff
EMP: 66
SQ FT: 11,000
SALES (est): 12.1MM Privately Held
WEB: www.americangrinding.com
SIC: 3599 5051 7692 Machine shop, jobbing & repair; steel; welding repair

(G-3654)
AMERICAN HOSP ASSN SVCS DEL (HQ)
155 N Wacker Dr Ste 400 (60606-1719)
PHONE...................................312 422-2000
Jonathan Lord, COO
Fredric J Entin, Admin Sec
James Henderson, Asst Sec
EMP: 25
SALES (est): 4.6MM
SALES (corp-wide): 79.3MM Privately Held
SIC: 2721 2731 8721 Periodicals; book publishing; billing & bookkeeping service
PA: American Hospital Association
155 N Wacker Dr Ste 400
Chicago IL 60606
312 422-3000

(G-3655)
AMERICAN INQUIRY LLC
3238 N Wolcott Ave Fl 2 (60657-2053)
PHONE...................................312 922-1910
Susan Barsy, Principal
EMP: 3 EST: 2010
SALES (est): 227.7K Privately Held
WEB: www.americaninquiry.com
SIC: 2721 Magazines: publishing only, not printed on site

(G-3656)
AMERICAN LABELMARK COMPANY (PA)
Also Called: Labelmaster Division
5724 N Pulaski Rd (60646-6797)
PHONE...................................773 478-0900
Gary S Mostow, Ch of Bd
Dwight Curtis, President
Clay Moore, Principal
Bob Richard, Vice Pres
Jeanne Zmich, Vice Pres
◆ EMP: 120
SQ FT: 90,000
SALES (est): 71.6MM Privately Held
SIC: 2752 2731 2754 5192 Commercial printing, offset; advertising posters, lithographed; poster & decal printing, lithographic; book publishing; labels: gravure printing; posters: gravure printing; books, periodicals & newspapers; safety equipment; publishers' computer software

(G-3657)
AMERICAN LIBRARY ASSOCIATION
Also Called: Booklist
50 E Huron St (60611-2788)
PHONE...................................312 280-5718
EMP: 25
SALES (corp-wide): 49MM Privately Held
SIC: 2721 Magazines: publishing only, not printed on site

Chicago - Cook County (G-3658)

PA: American Library Association
50 E Huron St
Chicago IL 60611
800 545-2433

(G-3658)
AMERICAN MACHINE TOOLS INC
5864 N Northwest Hwy (60631-2641)
PHONE.................................773 775-6285
Michael Desjardins, *President*
▼ EMP: 7
SQ FT: 1,000
SALES: 5MM **Privately Held**
SIC: 3541 3542 3545 Machine tools, metal cutting type; machine tools, metal forming type; machine tool accessories

(G-3659)
AMERICAN MACHINING & WLDG INC
6009 S New England Ave (60638-4005)
PHONE.................................773 586-2585
Stanley Sieczka, *President*
Joe Sieczka, *Vice Pres*
Andy Sieczka, *Treasurer*
▲ EMP: 25
SQ FT: 11,000
SALES (est): 6.1MM **Privately Held**
SIC: 3599 7692 Machine shop, jobbing & repair; welding repair

(G-3660)
AMERICAN MEDICAL ASSOCIATION (PA)
Also Called: A M A
330 N Wabash Ave # 39300 (60611-5885)
PHONE.................................312 464-5000
James Madera, *CEO*
Gerald E Harmon, *Ch of Bd*
Patrice Harris, *President*
Elaine Williams, *General Mgr*
Sarah Sanders, *Principal*
EMP: 800 EST: 1847
SQ FT: 360,000
SALES: 284.3MM **Privately Held**
WEB: www.apps.ama-assn.org
SIC: 8621 2721 6321 6282 Medical field-related associations; trade journals: publishing only, not printed on site; reinsurance carriers, accident & health; investment advice

(G-3661)
AMERICAN METAL CHEMICAL CORP (PA)
Also Called: Amcor
3546 S Morgan St (60609-1524)
PHONE.................................773 254-1818
Erin Fauber, *President*
Margaret Fauber, *Exec VP*
Ted Fauber, *Treasurer*
◆ EMP: 37
SQ FT: 60,000
SALES (est): 14.9MM **Privately Held**
SIC: 2899 Fluxes: brazing, soldering, galvanizing & welding

(G-3662)
AMERICAN METAL MFG INC
6323 N Avondale Ave # 125 (60631-1958)
PHONE.................................847 651-6097
Tim Blanks, *President*
EMP: 2
SQ FT: 15,000
SALES (est): 242K **Privately Held**
WEB: www.americanmetalmanufacturing.com
SIC: 3499 5051 Aerosol valves, metal; sheets, metal

(G-3663)
AMERICAN NAME PLATE & METAL DE
4501 S Kildare Ave (60632-4477)
PHONE.................................773 376-1400
Michael Stevens, *President*
Mark Hofmeister, *Vice Pres*
Jim Meitz, *Prdtn Mgr*
Bob Desbles, *Sales Mgr*
Alan Stevens, *Administration*
EMP: 25 EST: 1934
SQ FT: 45,000
SALES (est): 3.6MM **Privately Held**
WEB: www.american-nameplate.com
SIC: 3993 3083 2672 2671 Name plates: except engraved, etched, etc.: metal; plastic finished products, laminated; coated & laminated paper; packaging paper & plastics film, coated & laminated; automotive & apparel trimmings

(G-3664)
AMERICAN PLATING & MFG CO
Also Called: Amplate
3941 S Keeler Ave (60632-3815)
PHONE.................................773 890-4907
Karl Urban, *President*
▲ EMP: 16 EST: 1903
SQ FT: 14,000
SALES (est): 2.1MM **Privately Held**
WEB: www.apmchicago.com
SIC: 3931 3471 Musical instruments; plating & polishing

(G-3665)
AMERICAN SCIENCE & SURPLUS INC
5316w N Milwaukee Ave (60630-1223)
PHONE.................................773 763-0313
Joey Walker, *Manager*
EMP: 15
SALES (corp-wide): 9.8MM **Privately Held**
SIC: 3944 Science kits: microscopes, chemistry sets, etc.; dishes, toy
PA: American Science & Surplus, Inc.
7410 N Lehigh Ave
Niles IL 60714
847 647-0011

(G-3666)
AMERICAN SCIENCE AND TECH CORP (PA)
1367 W Chicago Ave (60642-5761)
PHONE.................................312 433-3800
Ali Manesh, *President*
EMP: 2
SALES (est): 536.2K **Privately Held**
SIC: 3728 Aircraft parts & equipment

(G-3667)
AMERICAN SIGN & LIGHTING CO
350 N La Salle Dr # 1100 (60654-5126)
PHONE.................................847 258-8151
Todd Jackson, *CEO*
Jordan Uditsky, *President*
▲ EMP: 22
SQ FT: 10,000
SALES (est): 2.3MM **Privately Held**
SIC: 3993 1799 Electric signs; sign installation & maintenance

(G-3668)
AMERICAN SODA FTN EXCH INC
455 N Oakley Blvd (60612-1452)
PHONE.................................312 733-5000
Ray Schy, *President*
Phil Schy, *Vice Pres*
Terry Schy, *Treasurer*
EMP: 14
SQ FT: 15,000
SALES (est): 3.9MM **Privately Held**
WEB: www.americansodafountain.com
SIC: 5046 7699 3585 Restaurant equipment & supplies; soda fountain fixtures, except refrigerated; restaurant equipment repair; soda fountains, parts & accessories

(G-3669)
AMERICAN SPECIALTY TOY
432 N Clark St Ste 305 (60654-4536)
PHONE.................................312 222-0984
Kathleen J Mc Hugh, *President*
Dee Marsden, *Marketing Staff*
Dina Velasquez, *Director*
Ahren Hoffman, *Business Dir*
Cora McCarron, *Administration*
EMP: 3
SQ FT: 850
SALES: 2.2MM **Privately Held**
SIC: 3944 5084 Games, toys & children's vehicles; industrial machinery & equipment

(G-3670)
AMERICAN TAPE MEASURES
6717 W Foster Ave (60656-2137)
PHONE.................................312 208-0282
Kurt Pusczan, *President*
Anne Pusczan, *Admin Sec*
EMP: 3 EST: 1962
SQ FT: 2,000
SALES: 97K **Privately Held**
SIC: 3999 7311 Tape measures; advertising agencies

(G-3671)
AMERICAN TRADE MAGAZINES LLC
650 W Lake St Ste 320 (60661-1036)
PHONE.................................312 497-7707
Bruce Beggs, *Director*
Nathan Frerichs, *Director*
Charles R Thompson,
EMP: 4
SALES (est): 326.8K **Privately Held**
SIC: 2721 Magazines: publishing & printing

(G-3672)
AMERICAN TROPHY & AWARD CO INC
Also Called: American Dragway Trophy Co
1006 S Michigan Ave # 503 (60605-2216)
PHONE.................................312 939-3252
Ben Goldberg, *President*
EMP: 3 EST: 1962
SQ FT: 5,000
SALES: 500K **Privately Held**
SIC: 3499 Trophies, metal, except silver

(G-3673)
AMERICAN WHEEL CORP
5939 W 66th St (60638-6205)
PHONE.................................708 458-9141
Bill Dods, *President*
Richard Clements, *Director*
EMP: 20
SALES (est): 4.6MM **Privately Held**
SIC: 3714 Wheels, motor vehicle

(G-3674)
AMERICAN WILBERT VAULT CORP
11118 S Rockwell St (60655-1900)
PHONE.................................773 238-2746
EMP: 18
SALES (corp-wide): 6.4MM **Privately Held**
SIC: 3272 Mfg Concrete Products
PA: American Wilbert Vault Corp.
7525 W 99th Pl
Bridgeview IL 60162
708 366-3210

(G-3675)
AMERICAS COMMUNITY BANKERS
Also Called: P & D Center
363 W Erie St Fl 4 (60654-6903)
PHONE.................................312 644-3100
Bob Clifford, *Branch Mgr*
EMP: 22
SQ FT: 4,500
SALES (corp-wide): 7.8MM **Privately Held**
SIC: 4225 2759 2782 General warehousing & storage; envelopes: printing; stationery: printing; looseleaf binders & devices
PA: Americas Community Bankers
900 19th St Nw Ste 400
Washington DC

(G-3676)
AMERICN FOREIGN LANG NEWSPAPER
55 E Jackson Blvd Ste 920 (60604-4249)
PHONE.................................312 368-4815
Rich Bourjaily, *Owner*
EMP: 25
SALES (est): 724.7K **Privately Held**
SIC: 2711 Newspapers: publishing only, not printed on site

(G-3677)
AMERISCAN DESIGNS INC
4147 W Ogden Ave (60623-2877)
PHONE.................................773 542-1291
William W Mac Williams, *President*
Bill Mac Williams, *President*
Janet Harrell, *Vice Pres*
Mirek Mastela, *Supervisor*
▲ EMP: 55
SQ FT: 65,000
SALES (est): 16.4MM **Privately Held**
SIC: 5712 2434 2431 3083 Cabinet work, custom; wood kitchen cabinets; millwork; laminated plastics plate & sheet

(G-3678)
AMEROPAN OIL CORP
3301 S California Ave (60608-5113)
PHONE.................................773 847-4400
Jeff Guzman, *Manager*
EMP: 10
SALES (est): 1.8MM **Privately Held**
SIC: 3443 Fuel tanks (oil, gas, etc.): metal plate

(G-3679)
AMIBERICA INC
3701 S Ashland Ave (60609-2130)
PHONE.................................773 247-3600
William Diaz, *President*
Chris Vargas, *Project Mgr*
Marty Kosiek, *Sales Executive*
Joseph Sidebotham, *Manager*
Grace Vargas, *Admin Sec*
▼ EMP: 20
SQ FT: 56,000
SALES (est): 5.3MM **Privately Held**
SIC: 3559 3567 Metal finishing equipment for plating, etc.; industrial furnaces & ovens

(G-3680)
AMITY PACKING COMPANY INC (PA)
4220 S Kildare Ave (60632-3930)
PHONE.................................312 942-0270
Brian Tyler, *President*
Bruce Degonia, *Vice Pres*
Roger A Pfiel, *Vice Pres*
Joseph Pirelli, *Plant Mgr*
Bob Yanz, *VP Sales*
▼ EMP: 150 EST: 1966
SQ FT: 100,000
SALES: 60MM **Privately Held**
WEB: www.amitypacking.com
SIC: 5147 5812 2011 Meats, fresh; eating places; meat packing plants

(G-3681)
AMK ENTERPRISES CHICAGO INC
3605 S Calumet Ave (60653-1103)
PHONE.................................312 523-7212
Allyson Kennon, *CEO*
EMP: 5
SALES: 350K **Privately Held**
SIC: 3999 5023 7389 Manufacturing industries; home furnishings; interior design services

(G-3682)
AMOCO TECHNOLOGY COMPANY (DH)
Also Called: Amoco Technology Company Del
200 E Randolph St # 3500 (60601-6436)
PHONE.................................312 861-6000
Robert C Carr, *President*
F J Sroka, *Admin Sec*
EMP: 200
SALES (est): 63.5MM
SALES (corp-wide): 278.4B **Privately Held**
SIC: 2835 3821 7374 7372 In vitro & in vivo diagnostic substances; laser beam alignment devices; computer time-sharing; application computer software; solar cells; silicon wafers, chemically doped; laser scientific & engineering instruments
HQ: Bp Corporation North America Inc.
501 Westlake Park Blvd
Houston TX 77079
281 366-2000

(G-3683)
AMP AMERICAS LLC (PA)
Also Called: AMP CNG
811 W Evergreen Ave # 201 (60642-3435)
PHONE.................................312 300-6700
Nate Laurell, *CEO*

Chicago - Cook County (G-3712)

Donna Rolf, *President*
Sam Bramfeld, *Vice Pres*
Saad Qais, *CFO*
Chad Schlaepfer, *Sales Staff*
EMP: 28
SALES (est): 5.1MM **Privately Held**
SIC: 2869 5171 Fuels; petroleum bulk stations

(G-3684)
AMPHIX BIO INC
57 E Del Pl Apt 2802 (60611)
PHONE 720 840-7327
Samuel Stupp, *President*
Nicholas Sather, *Principal*
Devora Grynspan, *Admin Sec*
EMP: 3
SALES (est): 127.2K **Privately Held**
SIC: 2834 2836 Solutions, pharmaceutical; culture media

(G-3685)
AMSTED INDUSTRIES INCORPORATED (PA)
180 N Stetson Ave # 1800 (60601-6808)
PHONE 312 645-1700
Donna Grover, *CEO*
Steven R Smith, *Ch of Bd*
Edward Brosius, *Counsel*
Michael Krautner, *Counsel*
Thomas Petermann, *Counsel*
◆ **EMP:** 277 **EST:** 1902
SQ FT: 18,000
SALES (est): 2.3B **Privately Held**
WEB: www.amsted.com
SIC: 3443 3325 3585 3321 Cooling towers, metal plate; railroad car wheels, cast steel; refrigeration & heating equipment; gray & ductile iron foundries; freight cars & equipment

(G-3686)
AMSTED INDUSTRIES INCORPORATED
2 Prudential Plaza 180 (60601)
PHONE 312 645-1700
Laura Sleeman, *Manager*
David Brower, *Director*
Wing Wong, *Administration*
EMP: 11
SALES (corp-wide): 2.3B **Privately Held**
SIC: 3443 Cooling towers, metal plate
PA: Amsted Industries Incorporated
180 N Stetson Ave # 1800
Chicago IL 60601
312 645-1700

(G-3687)
AMSTED INDUSTRIES INCORPORATED
205 N Michigan Ave (60601-5927)
PHONE 312 819-1181
Shirley J Whitesell, *Branch Mgr*
EMP: 9
SALES (corp-wide): 2.3B **Privately Held**
SIC: 3325 Steel foundries
PA: Amsted Industries Incorporated
180 N Stetson Ave # 1800
Chicago IL 60601
312 645-1700

(G-3688)
AMSTED RAIL COMPANY INC
Asf-Keystone
10 S Riverside Plz Fl 10 # 10 (60606-3728)
PHONE 312 258-8000
Ronald Barker, *President*
John Trankar, *General Mgr*
EMP: 65
SALES (corp-wide): 2.3B **Privately Held**
SIC: 3743 Railroad equipment
HQ: Amsted Rail Company, Inc.
311 S Wacker Dr Ste 5300
Chicago IL 60606

(G-3689)
AMYLU FOODS LLC (PA)
Also Called: Atk Foods
1400 W 44th St (60609-3332)
PHONE 312 829-2250
Gary McNelly, *Exec VP*
Steve Voll, *Mng Member*
EMP: 24

SALES (est): 10.6MM **Privately Held**
SIC: 2013 Sausages & other prepared meats

(G-3690)
ANASH EDUCATIONAL INSTITUTE
2929 W Greenleaf Ave (60645-2915)
PHONE 773 338-7704
Moshe Miller, *Director*
Yochanan Nathan, *Director*
EMP: 8
SALES (est): 421.6K **Privately Held**
SIC: 2741 Miscellaneous publishing

(G-3691)
ANCHOR MECHANICAL INC (PA)
255 N California Ave (60612-1903)
PHONE 312 492-6994
Michael Rosner, *President*
Brian Weir, *Superintendent*
Rick Connell, *Principal*
Frank Manna, *Exec VP*
Dan Galovich, *Vice Pres*
EMP: 4
SALES (est): 1.1MM **Privately Held**
SIC: 3531 1542 1711 7389 Finishers, concrete & bituminous; powered; commercial & office building contractors; mechanical contractor;

(G-3692)
ANCILLARY GENOMIC SYSTEMS LLC
1524 E 59th St Apt B1 (60637-2009)
PHONE 765 714-3799
Timothy Herr, *Principal*
EMP: 3
SALES (est): 138.1K **Privately Held**
SIC: 2835 Microbiology & virology diagnostic products

(G-3693)
ANDREWS AUTOMOTIVE COMPANY
10055 S Torrence Ave (60617-5337)
PHONE 773 768-1122
David C Andrews, *President*
EMP: 18
SQ FT: 22,000
SALES (est): 3.5MM **Privately Held**
SIC: 5013 3061 3089 Automotive supplies & parts; automotive rubber goods (mechanical); corrugated panels, plastic

(G-3694)
ANDYS DELI AND MIKOLAJCZYK (PA)
4021 W Kinzie St (60624-1807)
PHONE 773 722-1000
Andrzej Kolasa, *President*
Simon Kolasa, *Sales Executive*
Halina Kolasa, *Admin Sec*
▲ **EMP:** 20
SQ FT: 1,000
SALES (est): 4.6MM **Privately Held**
WEB: www.andysdeli.com
SIC: 5411 2013 Delicatessens; sausages from purchased meat

(G-3695)
ANEES UPHOLSTERY
1500 S Western Ave Ste 3 (60608-1828)
PHONE 312 243-2919
Anees Jaber, *Owner*
Marika Jaber, *Sales Executive*
EMP: 1
SALES (est): 258.7K **Privately Held**
SIC: 7641 2211 Upholstery work; furniture denim

(G-3696)
ANGELS HEAVENLY FUNERAL HOME
10634 S Wallace St (60628-2445)
PHONE 773 239-8700
Jimmie Higgins, *Mng Member*
EMP: 5 **EST:** 2015
SALES (est): 208.5K **Privately Held**
SIC: 2396 5087 Veils & veiling: bridal, funeral, etc.; cemetery & funeral directors' equipment & supplies

(G-3697)
ANGELS SHARE BRANDS LLC
Also Called: Angel's Envy
119 W Hubbard St Fl 5 (60654-7579)
PHONE 312 494-1100
Cassie Mendoza, *Owner*
EMP: 4
SALES (est): 263.7K **Privately Held**
SIC: 2085 Distilled & blended liquors

(G-3698)
ANIMATED ADVG TECHNIQUES INC
Also Called: Central Die Cutting
210 S Desplaines St (60661-5500)
PHONE 312 372-4694
Jim March, *President*
EMP: 5 **EST:** 1943
SQ FT: 10,000
SALES (est): 800K **Privately Held**
SIC: 7319 2675 Display advertising service; die-cut paper & board

(G-3699)
ANNAS DRAPERIES & ASSOCIATES
5908 W Montrose Ave (60634-1625)
PHONE 773 282-1365
Dodd Otic, *President*
EMP: 3
SALES (est): 276.5K **Privately Held**
SIC: 5714 2211 Curtains; draperies & drapery fabrics, cotton

(G-3700)
ANNS BAKERY INC
2158 W Chicago Ave (60622-5257)
PHONE 773 384-5562
Walter Siryj, *President*
EMP: 7
SQ FT: 3,000
SALES: 800K **Privately Held**
SIC: 5461 2051 Bread; cakes; pastries; bread, all types (white, wheat, rye, etc): fresh or frozen; crullers, except frozen; pastries, e.g. danish: except frozen

(G-3701)
ANONYMOUS PRESS INC
1658 N Milwaukee Ave (60647-6905)
PHONE 509 779-4094
John Gillen, *President*
Kim Gillen, *Administration*
EMP: 1
SALES (est): 230.6K **Privately Held**
SIC: 2731 Book publishing

(G-3702)
ANOTHER CHANCE COMMUNITY DEV
1641 W 79th St (60620-4212)
PHONE 773 998-1641
Kenyatta Smith, *CEO*
EMP: 30
SALES (est): 2.5MM **Privately Held**
SIC: 2013 Sausages & other prepared meats

(G-3703)
ANSWER CALL
10633 S Green St (60643-3017)
PHONE 773 573-6369
EMP: 3 **EST:** 2018
SALES (est): 186.3K **Privately Held**
SIC: 3672 Printed circuit boards

(G-3704)
ANTARES COMPUTER SYSTEMS INC
Also Called: ACS
8114 S Maryland Ave # 12 (60619-5191)
PHONE 773 783-8855
Maurice Johnson, *President*
EMP: 5
SALES: 300K **Privately Held**
SIC: 3571 3577 Personal computers (microcomputers); computer peripheral equipment

(G-3705)
ANTEK MADISON PLASTICS USA LTD
8822 S Dobson Ave (60619-6952)
PHONE 773 933-0900

John Ioannou, *President*
Jorge Farr-Aguilar, *General Mgr*
Jim Angelopoulos, *Vice Pres*
Victor Tay, *Admin Sec*
EMP: 17
SQ FT: 185,000
SALES (est): 4MM **Privately Held**
SIC: 3087 Custom compound purchased resins

(G-3706)
ANTLIA DISPLAYS LLC
1720 W Division St 2 (60622-3212)
PHONE 773 353-2223
Michael George,
EMP: 2
SALES (est): 206.9K **Privately Held**
SIC: 3993 Signs & advertising specialties

(G-3707)
ANTOLAK MANAGEMENT CO INC
Also Called: Fastsigns
447 E Ohio St (60611-3626)
PHONE 312 464-1800
Dan Antolak, *President*
EMP: 6
SALES (est): 990.6K **Privately Held**
SIC: 3993 Signs & advertising specialties

(G-3708)
ANVIL INTERNATIONAL INC
24023 Network Pl (60673-1240)
PHONE 603 418-2800
Sammy Colon, *President*
EMP: 34
SALES (est): 4.5MM **Privately Held**
SIC: 3498 Fabricated pipe & fittings

(G-3709)
ANYTIME WINDOW CLEANING INC
2517 N Monticello Ave (60647-1113)
PHONE 773 235-5677
David Bernstein, *Owner*
EMP: 4
SALES (est): 264.5K **Privately Held**
SIC: 2842 Window cleaning preparations

(G-3710)
APEX COLORS
1031 W Bryn Mawr Ave 1a (60660-4658)
P.O. Box 3966, Barrington (60011-3966)
PHONE 219 764-3301
Paul Bykowski, *President*
Siddhartha Zalani, *President*
EMP: 3
SALES (est): 253.3K **Privately Held**
SIC: 2865 Color pigments, organic

(G-3711)
API PUBLISHING SERVICES LLC
Also Called: Smith Bucklin & Associates
330 N Wabash Ave Ste 2000 (60611-7621)
PHONE 312 644-6610
Thomas Morgan, *CEO*
EMP: 20
SQ FT: 12,000
SALES: 4.4MM
SALES (corp-wide): 120.8MM **Privately Held**
SIC: 2721 Periodicals: publishing & printing
PA: Smithbucklin Corporation
330 N Wabash Ave
Chicago IL 60611
312 644-6610

(G-3712)
APOLLO PLASTICS CORPORATION
5333 N Elston Ave (60630-1610)
PHONE 773 282-9222
John Lucas, *CEO*
Alberto Silva, *President*
Donald Lucas, *Corp Secy*
Stanley Skrbis, *Administration*
Neal Brandenburg, *Maintence Staff*
▲ **EMP:** 60 **EST:** 2000
SALES (est): 10.8MM
SALES (corp-wide): 17.2MM **Privately Held**
SIC: 3089 Injection molding of plastics

Chicago - Cook County (G-3713)

PA: Specialty Manufacturers, Inc.
2410 Executive Dr Ste 201
Indianapolis IN
317 241-1111

(G-3713)
APOSTROPHE BRANDS
225 W Hubbard St Ste 600 (60654-4916)
PHONE.................................312 832-0300
Mark Boyle, COO
Brad Treysar,
▲ EMP: 15
SALES (est): 2.2MM **Privately Held**
SIC: 2085 Rum (alcoholic beverage)

(G-3714)
APPLUS TECHNOLOGIES INC (DH)
120 S La Salle St # 1450 (60603-3449)
PHONE.................................312 661-1100
Darrin Greene, CEO
Celia Forsythe, CFO
Chris Engel, Accountant
Rob Enright, Accountant
Angela Noguer, Admin Sec
EMP: 33
SALES: 48.9MM
SALES (corp-wide): 72.5MM **Privately Held**
SIC: 7373 3577 7379 7371 Computer integrated systems design; optical scanning devices; computer related maintenance services; computer software development & applications

(G-3715)
APRIMO US LLC
Also Called: Aprimo Marketing Operations Uk
230 W Monroe St Ste 1200 (60606-4704)
PHONE.................................877 794-8556
Michael Nelson, CFO
Jordan Garretson, Manager
EMP: 90
SALES: 1.8MM **Privately Held**
SIC: 7372 Application computer software

(G-3716)
APTEAN INC
2000 N Racine Ave (60614-4045)
PHONE.................................773 975-3100
Gene Climer, Manager
EMP: 15
SALES (corp-wide): 411.1MM **Privately Held**
SIC: 7372 Prepackaged software
PA: Aptean, Inc.
4325 Alexander Dr Ste 100
Alpharetta GA 30022
770 351-9600

(G-3717)
ARACON DRPERY VNTIAN BLIND LTD
Also Called: Aracon Venetian Blind-Drapery
3015 N Kedzie Ave (60618-6906)
PHONE.................................773 252-1281
Gregory Struhar, CEO
EMP: 7
SQ FT: 4,500
SALES (est): 1.1MM **Privately Held**
WEB: www.araconblinds.com
SIC: 2591 2391 Venetian blinds; draperies, plastic & textile: from purchased materials

(G-3718)
ARBOR PRIVATE INV CO LLC (PA)
Also Called: Arbor Investments
676 N Michigan Ave # 3400 (60611-2883)
PHONE.................................312 981-3770
Gregory J Purcell, CEO
Joseph P Campolo, President
Roberta R McQuade, Senior VP
Alan A Weed, Vice Pres
J David Foster, CFO
EMP: 9 EST: 1999
SQ FT: 1,500
SALES (est): 992.2MM **Privately Held**
SIC: 2086 2671 2752 2657 Bottled & canned soft drinks; packaging paper & plastics film, coated & laminated; commercial printing, lithographic; folding paperboard boxes

(G-3719)
ARCELORMITTAL INTL AMER LLC (DH)
1 S Dearborn St Ste 1800 (60603-2308)
PHONE.................................312 899-3400
Paul Ciesielski, Office Mgr
Brian Elgart, Office Mgr
Bruno Lesor, Mng Member
Taylor Groth, Executive
David Trachtenberg, Analyst
◆ EMP: 75 EST: 1995
SQ FT: 20,000
SALES (est): 66.1MM **Privately Held**
WEB: www.arcelormittal.com
SIC: 3312 Blast furnaces & steel mills

(G-3720)
ARCELORMITTAL SOUTH CHICAGO
1 S Dearborn St Ste 2100 (60603-2307)
PHONE.................................312 899-3300
Fax: 773 768-6407
EMP: 2
SALES (est): 224.3K **Privately Held**
SIC: 3315 Mfg Steel Wire/Related Products

(G-3721)
ARCELORMITTAL USA INC
1 S Dearborn St Ste 1800 (60603-2308)
PHONE.................................312 899-3500
Lou Schorch, Principal
Chandan Roy, Engineer
Kathy Erickson, Human Resources
EMP: 8
SALES (est): 1.3MM **Privately Held**
SIC: 3312 Blast furnaces & steel mills

(G-3722)
ARCELORMITTAL USA LLC
Also Called: Arcelormittal USA of Chicago
1 S Dearborn St Ste 2100 (60603-2307)
PHONE.................................312 899-3400
Ronnie Masliansky, General Mgr
Ryan Robinson, Opers Mgr
Marcia Altobell, Engineer
Kenneth Blazek, Engineer
Matthew Domsic, Engineer
EMP: 225 **Privately Held**
WEB: www.arcelormittal.com
SIC: 3325 Rolling mill rolls, cast steel; alloy steel castings, except investment; railroad car wheels, cast steel
HQ: Arcelormittal Usa Llc
1 S Dearborn St Ste 1800
Chicago IL 60603
312 346-0300

(G-3723)
ARCELORMITTAL USA LLC (HQ)
Also Called: Arcelormittal North America
1 S Dearborn St Ste 1800 (60603-2308)
PHONE.................................312 346-0300
Bradley Davey, CEO
William Bond, Division Mgr
Lyle Bufogle, Division Mgr
Larry Frey, Division Mgr
John G Sakelaris, Division Mgr
◆ EMP: 277
SQ FT: 53,484
SALES (est): 4.6B **Privately Held**
SIC: 3312 3325 3356 3316 Blast furnaces & steel mills; rolling mill rolls, cast steel; tin; cold finishing of steel shapes
PA: Arcelormittal
Boulevard D'avranches 24-26
Luxembourg
479 21 -

(G-3724)
ARCELRMTTAL N AMER HLDINGS LLC (DH)
1 S Dearborn St Ste 1900 (60603-2307)
PHONE.................................312 899-3400
Paul M Liebenson, President
Daniel Wallden, Treasurer
Christine F Fleps, Asst Treas
Therese Vande Hey, Asst Treas
Richard Lenehan, Asst Treas
EMP: 3031
SALES (est): 253.4MM **Privately Held**
SIC: 3317 Tubes, seamless steel; tubes, wrought: welded or lock joint

HQ: Arcelormittal Holdings Llc
3210 Watling St
East Chicago IN 46312
219 399-1200

(G-3725)
ARCHER MANUFACTURING CORP
4439 S Knox Ave (60632-4343)
PHONE.................................773 585-7181
Stan Sekula, President
Margrate Sekula, Vice Pres
EMP: 25 EST: 1948
SQ FT: 28,000
SALES (est): 4.9MM **Privately Held**
WEB: www.archermfg.com
SIC: 3469 3599 Stamping metal for the trade; machine shop, jobbing & repair

(G-3726)
ARCHER METAL & PAPER CO
Also Called: C & R Scrap Metal
4619 S Knox Ave (60632-4805)
PHONE.................................773 585-3030
Ron Nisson, Owner
Ronald Nisson, Principal
EMP: 10
SQ FT: 10,000
SALES (est): 1.8MM **Privately Held**
SIC: 5093 4953 3341 3312 Metal scrap & waste materials; refuse systems; secondary nonferrous metals; blast furnaces & steel mills

(G-3727)
ARCHER TINNING & RE-TINNING CO (PA)
1019 W 47th St (60609-3325)
PHONE.................................773 927-7240
Arjen Byvoets, President
EMP: 12 EST: 1931
SQ FT: 10,000
SALES (est): 928.8K **Privately Held**
WEB: www.archertinning.com
SIC: 3471 Plating of metals or formed products

(G-3728)
ARCHER-DANIELS-MIDLAND COMPANY (PA)
Also Called: ADM
77 W Wacker Dr Ste 4600 (60601-1667)
P.O. Box 1470, Decatur (62525-1820)
PHONE.................................312 634-8100
Juan R Luciano, Ch of Bd
Donald Chen, President
Pierre Duprat, President
Tedd Kruse, President
Domingo Lastra, President
◆ EMP: 600 EST: 1902
SALES: 64.6B **Publicly Held**
WEB: www.adm.com
SIC: 2046 2041 2075 2074 Wet corn milling; high fructose corn syrup (HFCS); corn starch; corn oil products; wheat flour; soybean oil mills; cottonseed oil, cake or meal; grain elevators; malt; malt byproducts

(G-3729)
ARCHITECTURAL FAN COIL INC
3900 W Palmer St (60647-2216)
PHONE.................................312 399-1203
Harvey Dessler, President
EMP: 3
SALES (est): 424.9K **Privately Held**
SIC: 3564 Air purification equipment

(G-3730)
ARMBRUST PAPER TUBES INC
6255 S Harlem Ave (60638-3906)
PHONE.................................773 586-3232
Michael Johnstone, President
Bernerd Armbrust, President
Marc Armbrust, Marketing Staff
EMP: 22 EST: 1938
SQ FT: 85,000

SALES (est): 4.2MM **Privately Held**
WEB: www.tubesrus.com
SIC: 2655 2542 2653 3089 Tubes, fiber or paper: made from purchased material; cans, fiber: made from purchased material; cores, fiber: made from purchased material; partitions & fixtures, except wood; corrugated & solid fiber boxes; plastic containers, except foam; setup paperboard boxes; paperboard mills

(G-3731)
ARMITAGE WELDING
3212 W Armitage Ave (60647-3716)
PHONE.................................773 772-1442
Manuel Vasquez, Owner
EMP: 4
SALES (est): 441.3K **Privately Held**
SIC: 1799 7692 Athletic & recreation facilities construction; welding repair

(G-3732)
ARPWAVE USA LLC
1354 W Taylor St (60607-4754)
PHONE.................................773 835-0122
Randy A Sanders, Principal
EMP: 5
SALES (est): 265K **Privately Held**
SIC: 3841 Surgical & medical instruments

(G-3733)
ARRO CORPORATION
Also Called: Arro Packing
10459 S Muskegon Ave (60617-5727)
PHONE.................................773 978-1251
Patrick Gaughan, Branch Mgr
EMP: 8
SALES (corp-wide): 133.3MM **Privately Held**
SIC: 5141 2045 4225 Groceries, general line; pancake mixes, prepared: from purchased flour; general warehousing & storage
PA: Arro Corporation
7440 Santa Fe Dr
Hodgkins IL 60525
708 352-8200

(G-3734)
ART BOOKBINDERS OF AMERICA
451 N Claremont Ave (60612-1440)
PHONE.................................312 226-4100
Mario Poulet, President
Greg Poulet, Vice Pres
Louis B Poulet, Vice Pres
EMP: 28
SQ FT: 24,000
SALES (est): 4.4MM **Privately Held**
SIC: 7334 2789 Photocopying & duplicating services; bookbinding & related work; bookbinding & repairing: trade, edition, library, etc.

(G-3735)
ART IN PRINT REVIEW
3500 N Lake Shore Dr (60657-1815)
PHONE.................................773 697-9478
Susan Tallman, President
EMP: 3
SALES: 155.1K **Privately Held**
SIC: 2721 2741 Periodicals: publishing only; miscellaneous publishing

(G-3736)
ART MEDIA RESOURCES INC
1965 W Pershing Rd Ste 4 (60609-2319)
PHONE.................................312 663-5351
Shane Suvikapakornkul, President
▲ EMP: 3
SALES: 250K **Privately Held**
SIC: 2731 5192 Books: publishing only; books

(G-3737)
ART OF SHAVING - FL LLC
520 N Michigan Ave # 122 (60611-6985)
PHONE.................................312 527-1604
Alex Davidson, Branch Mgr
EMP: 6
SALES (corp-wide): 67.6B **Publicly Held**
WEB: www.theartofshaving.com
SIC: 5999 2844 3421 5122 Hair care products; toilet preparations; razor blades & razors; razor blades

GEOGRAPHIC SECTION

Chicago - Cook County (G-3765)

HQ: The Art Of Shaving - Fl Llc
6100 Blue Lagoon Dr # 150
Miami FL 33126

(G-3738)
ART-FLO SHIRT & LETTERING CO
Also Called: AF
6939 W 59th St (60638-3205)
PHONE..................708 656-5422
Michael Dastice, *President*
Margaret Stewart, *President*
Joanne Zendol, *President*
James Dastice, *Vice Pres*
Bill Hanna, *Info Tech Mgr*
EMP: 23
SQ FT: 13,000
SALES (est): 10.8MM **Privately Held**
SIC: 5136 5137 2396 2759 Sportswear, men's & boys'; sportswear, women's & children's; screen printing on fabric articles; commercial printing; pleating & stitching

(G-3739)
ARTHUR COYLE PRESS
2730 W Coyle Ave (60645-3018)
PHONE..................773 465-8418
Jerome Yanoff, *Owner*
EMP: 1
SALES: 700K **Privately Held**
SIC: 2741 2731 Business service newsletters: publishing & printing; book publishing

(G-3740)
ARTISAN HANDPRINTS INC
4234 N Pulaski Rd (60641-2398)
PHONE..................773 725-1799
Murray Plotkin, *President*
▼ **EMP:** 8
SQ FT: 8,500
SALES (est): 908.6K **Privately Held**
SIC: 2759 Screen printing

(G-3741)
ARTISTRY ENGRAVING & EMBOSSING
6000 N Northwest Hwy (60631-2518)
PHONE..................773 775-4888
Tammy Gattuso, *President*
Michael Gattuso, *Vice Pres*
EMP: 9 **EST:** 1956
SQ FT: 12,000
SALES: 750K **Privately Held**
SIC: 2759 2791 Invitation & stationery printing & engraving; typesetting

(G-3742)
ARTPOL PRINTING INC
7011 W Higgins Ave (60656-1901)
PHONE..................773 622-0498
Wojzak Zalog, *President*
Jolata Kowlik, *Vice Pres*
EMP: 3
SQ FT: 1,800
SALES (est): 480K **Privately Held**
SIC: 2752 Commercial printing, offset

(G-3743)
ARTS & LETTERS MARSHALL SIGNS
Also Called: Marshall Sign Co
3610 S Albany Ave (60632-2309)
PHONE..................773 927-4442
Luis Cazares, *President*
EMP: 5
SQ FT: 12,000
SALES (est): 460K **Privately Held**
SIC: 3993 Electric signs; neon signs

(G-3744)
ARX NIMBUS LLC
323 E Wacker Dr Ste 300 (60601-5282)
PHONE..................888 422-6584
EMP: 5
SALES (est): 599.7K **Privately Held**
SIC: 3861 Photographic equipment & supplies

(G-3745)
ARYZTA LLC
350 N Orleans St 7500s (60654-1608)
PHONE..................312 836-2300
Alejandra Gallardo, *Branch Mgr*
Sarah Warren, *Manager*
Pam Fiore, *Info Tech Dir*
Kurt Fryzek, *Technology*
Carmelita Smith, *Technician*
EMP: 96
SALES (corp-wide): 3.4B **Privately Held**
SIC: 2052 Cookies
HQ: Aryzta Llc
6080 Center Dr Ste 900
Los Angeles CA 90045
310 417-4700

(G-3746)
AS 1902 LLC
Also Called: Anderson Shumaker Company
824 S Central Ave (60644-5501)
PHONE..................773 287-0874
William Klaczynski, *President*
Robert Pollman, *Corp Secy*
Mark Mendyk, *Sales Staff*
Bruce Liimatainen, *Mng Member*
Ginny Morgan, *Manager*
EMP: 55
SQ FT: 88,000
SALES: 15MM **Privately Held**
SIC: 3462 Iron & steel forgings

(G-3747)
ASCENT TRANZ GROUP LLC (PA)
Also Called: A-Line
5620 W 51st St (60638-1525)
PHONE..................844 424-7347
John Kelvin, *Mng Member*
Jessica Badali
Patricia Kelvin,
◆ **EMP:** 6 **EST:** 2015
SQ FT: 750
SALES (est): 1MM **Privately Held**
SIC: 3714 Brake drums, motor vehicle; air brakes, motor vehicle

(G-3748)
ASHLAND ABC CHOICE INC
7903 S Ashland Ave (60620-4336)
PHONE..................773 488-7800
Samed Yusuf, *President*
EMP: 3
SALES (est): 227.6K **Privately Held**
SIC: 2834 Pills, pharmaceutical

(G-3749)
ASSEMBLERS INC (PA)
2850 W Columbus Ave (60652-1620)
PHONE..................773 378-3000
Joel Rosenbacher, *President*
Gigi Salcedo, *Vice Pres*
John Yesko, *Web Proj Mgr*
Cindy Martinez, *Director*
Jed Swartz, *Executive*
◆ **EMP:** 122
SQ FT: 480,000
SALES (est): 11MM **Privately Held**
WEB: www.assemblers.com
SIC: 3999 7389 Advertising display products; packaging & labeling services

(G-3750)
ASSOCIATED ATTRACTIONS ENTPS
4834 S Halsted St 14 (60609)
PHONE..................773 376-1900
Steve Johnson, *President*
Chuck Huser, *General Mgr*
EMP: 12 **EST:** 1973
SQ FT: 50,000
SALES (est): 725K **Privately Held**
SIC: 7359 3993 Party supplies rental services; signs & advertising specialties

(G-3751)
ASSOCIATED GROUP HOLDINGS LLC (PA)
156 N Jefferson St # 300 (60661-1436)
PHONE..................312 662-5488
Tim Ritchie, *CEO*
Jim Hanson, *CFO*
EMP: 1 **EST:** 2012
SALES (est): 267.5MM **Privately Held**
SIC: 3448 Prefabricated metal buildings

(G-3752)
ASSOCIATED PUBLICATIONS INC
Also Called: Complete Woman
875 N Michigan Ave # 3100 (60611-1981)
PHONE..................312 266-8680
Jim L Spurlock, *President*
Rachelle Brooks, *Advt Staff*
Bonnie L Krueger, *Admin Sec*
Linda Rolle, *Associate*
▲ **EMP:** 13 **EST:** 1978
SALES (est): 2.1MM **Privately Held**
WEB: www.associatedpub.com
SIC: 2721 Magazines: publishing only, not printed on site

(G-3753)
ASSOCIATION MANAGEMENT CENTER
8735 W Higgins Rd Ste 300 (60631-2738)
P.O. Box 3781, Oak Brook (60522-3781)
PHONE..................847 375-4700
Dagny M Engle, *President*
Scott Engle, *Principal*
Jeff Engle, *Principal*
Mark Engle, *Principal*
Barbara Hofmaier, *Editor*
EMP: 100
SALES (est): 19.4MM **Privately Held**
SIC: 8742 2721 Administrative services consultant; trade journals: publishing & printing

(G-3754)
ASTRO PRINTING INC
6550 S Kedzie Ave Fl 1 (60629-3440)
PHONE..................773 436-0500
Kathy Khatib, *President*
EMP: 2
SALES (est): 226.3K **Privately Held**
SIC: 2752 Commercial printing, lithographic

(G-3755)
AT&T CORP
1 S Wacker Dr Ste 3900 (60606-4635)
PHONE..................312 602-4108
Bob Allen, *Branch Mgr*
EMP: 12
SALES (corp-wide): 181.1B **Publicly Held**
SIC: 3661 3677 Autotransformers for telephone switchboards; electronic coils, transformers & other inductors
HQ: At&T Corp.
1 At&T Way
Bedminster NJ 07921
800 403-3302

(G-3756)
AT&T TELEHOLDINGS INC (HQ)
Also Called: AT&T Midwest
30 S Wacker Dr Fl 34 (60606-7413)
PHONE..................800 288-2020
Edward Whitacre Jr, *Ch of Bd*
Andrew M Geisse, *President*
Paul M Wilson, *Admin Sec*
EMP: 10
SQ FT: 146,000
SALES (est): 10.9B
SALES (corp-wide): 181.1B **Publicly Held**
SIC: 4812 2741 5065 6159 Cellular telephone services; paging services; directories, telephone: publishing only, not printed on site; telephone equipment; machinery & equipment finance leasing; security systems services; local telephone communications
PA: At&T Inc.
208 S Akard St
Dallas TX 75202
210 821-4105

(G-3757)
ATELIER JVNCE STNCARVING TILES
Also Called: Atelier Juvence Cstm Stonework
1601 S Ind Ave Ste 209 (60616)
PHONE..................312 492-7922
Sonia Dumont, *President*
Olivier Dumont, *Vice Pres*
▲ **EMP:** 5
SALES: 500K **Privately Held**
SIC: 3281 Cut stone & stone products

(G-3758)
ATHENA DESIGN GROUP INC
3500 S Morgan St 1 (60609-1524)
PHONE..................312 733-2828
Christopher Huang, *President*
▲ **EMP:** 27
SALES (est): 4.4MM **Privately Held**
SIC: 2752 7311 7336 3993 Commercial printing, lithographic; advertising agencies; advertising consultant; commercial art & graphic design; signs & advertising specialties; direct mail advertising services

(G-3759)
ATHLETIC SEWING MFG CO (PA)
7449 W Irving Park Rd # 1 (60634-2142)
PHONE..................773 589-0361
Liz Quilici, *President*
Sylvia Helms, *Corp Secy*
EMP: 30
SQ FT: 5,000
SALES (est): 2.5MM **Privately Held**
SIC: 2329 Men's & boys' athletic uniforms; hockey uniforms: men's, youths' & boys'

(G-3760)
ATKS INC
2946 N Clybourn Ave # 101 (60618-8369)
PHONE..................715 914-0395
EMP: 3
SALES (est): 94.6K **Privately Held**
SIC: 3764 Propulsion units for guided missiles & space vehicles

(G-3761)
ATLANTIS ENTP INVESTMENTS INC
Also Called: Global Signs & Printing
3432 W Diversey Ave Fl 2 (60647-1221)
PHONE..................432 237-0404
Jacqueline Espinoza, *President*
Luis Espinoza, *CFO*
EMP: 7
SQ FT: 6,000
SALES (est): 40.5K **Privately Held**
SIC: 3993 2752 7335 Signs & advertising specialties; commercial printing, lithographic; commercial photography

(G-3762)
ATLAS COPCO COMPRESSORS LLC
75 Remittance Dr # 3009 (60675-3009)
PHONE..................281 590-7500
EMP: 19
SALES (corp-wide): 10.5B **Privately Held**
SIC: 3563 3621 Air & gas compressors; motors & generators
HQ: Atlas Copco Compressors Llc
300 Technology Center Way # 5
Rock Hill SC 29730
866 472-1015

(G-3763)
ATLAS HOLDING INC (HQ)
1855 E 122nd St (60633-2401)
PHONE..................773 646-4500
Barry Zekelman, *CEO*
Dave Seeger, *President*
Andrew Klaus, *Vice Pres*
Michael McNamara, *Vice Pres*
John Feenan, *CFO*
◆ **EMP:** 10
SALES (est): 61MM **Privately Held**
SIC: 3317 Tubes, seamless steel

(G-3764)
ATLAS MAINTENANCE SERVICE INC
2055 N Kedzie Ave (60647-3703)
PHONE..................773 486-3386
Piotr Fadrowski, *President*
EMP: 3
SALES (est): 203.1K **Privately Held**
SIC: 3559 Automotive maintenance equipment

(G-3765)
ATLAS MANUFACTURING
4114 N Ravenswood Ave (60613-1786)
PHONE..................773 327-3005
▲ **EMP:** 3
SALES (est): 233.5K **Privately Held**
SIC: 3999 Mfg Misc Products

Chicago - Cook County (G-3766)

(G-3766)
ATLAS MATERIAL TSTG TECH LLC
Also Called: Dset Laboratories
1800 W Belle Plaine Ave (60613-1827)
P.O. Box 71016 (60694-1016)
PHONE..................................773 327-4520
Carmen Zimmer, *Engineer*
Tom Lyon, *Sales Staff*
Scott Zimmerman, *Technical Staff*
EMP: 4
SALES (corp-wide): 5.1B **Publicly Held**
WEB: www.atlas-mts.com
SIC: 3599 Amusement park equipment
HQ: Atlas Material Testing Technology Llc
 1500 Bishop Ct
 Mount Prospect IL 60056
 773 327-4520

(G-3767)
ATLAS MATERIAL TSTG TECH LLC
Kaan Engineering
1800 W Belle Plaine Ave F (60613-1827)
PHONE..................................773 327-4520
Joel Goldberg, *President*
EMP: 30
SALES (corp-wide): 5.1B **Publicly Held**
SIC: 3569 3599 8734 Testing chambers for altitude, temperature, ordnance, power; machine shop, jobbing & repair; product testing laboratory, safety or performance
HQ: Atlas Material Testing Technology Llc
 1500 Bishop Ct
 Mount Prospect IL 60056
 773 327-4520

(G-3768)
ATLAS TUBE (CHICAGO) LLC
1855 E 122nd St (60633-2401)
PHONE..................................312 275-1672
Michael Graham, *Principal*
Michael McNamara, *Principal*
Bill Barnes, *Vice Pres*
Linda Thomson, *Hum Res Coord*
Ketul Patel, *Info Tech Dir*
▲ EMP: 100
SALES (est): 43.7MM **Privately Held**
SIC: 3317 Tubes, seamless steel
HQ: Atlas Holding Inc.
 1855 E 122nd St
 Chicago IL 60633

(G-3769)
ATLAS UNIFORM COMPANY
1412 W Wa Blvd Fl 2 (60607-1844)
PHONE..................................312 492-8527
Steve Grys, *President*
EMP: 7 EST: 1946
SALES (est): 513.7K **Privately Held**
WEB: www.atlas.com
SIC: 5699 2326 2337 Uniforms; work uniforms; uniforms, except athletic: women's, misses' & juniors'

(G-3770)
ATM AMERICA CORP
1900 N Austin Ste 69 (60639-5042)
PHONE..................................800 298-0030
Manzar T Zuberi, *President*
MO Akindtu, *Purchasing*
Ted Zuberi, *Sales Staff*
Trent Raaf, *Manager*
Zeba Zuberi, *Admin Sec*
◆ EMP: 50 EST: 1976
SQ FT: 50,000
SALES (est): 8MM **Privately Held**
SIC: 2842 2992 2844 3545 Specialty cleaning preparations; lubricating oils; shampoos, rinses, conditioners: hair; machine tool accessories; soap & other detergents

(G-3771)
ATMARK TRADING INC
1965 W Pershing Rd (60609-2315)
PHONE..................................312 933-7907
Mark Glover, *President*
EMP: 50
SQ FT: 2,000
SALES (est): 5.1MM **Privately Held**
SIC: 3571 3572 5045 Computers, digital, analog or hybrid; personal computers (microcomputers); computer storage devices; computers, peripherals & software

(G-3772)
ATMOSPHERE GLOBAL LLC
55 W Goethe St Unit 1241 (60610-7401)
PHONE..................................630 660-2833
Shane Ormsby, *President*
Rebecca Jones, *Admin Sec*
▼ EMP: 6
SQ FT: 1,000
SALES: 1.5MM **Privately Held**
SIC: 2869 Industrial organic chemicals

(G-3773)
AUREL CONSTRUCTION LLC ○
9209 S Peoria St (60620-2726)
PHONE..................................312 998-5000
Alix Aurel, *CEO*
EMP: 5 EST: 2019
SALES (est): 182.1K **Privately Held**
SIC: 1389 Construction, repair & dismantling services

(G-3774)
AURORA NARINDER
Also Called: Number One
4549 N Clark St (60640-5406)
PHONE..................................773 275-2100
EMP: 2
SQ FT: 2,500
SALES (est): 211.8K **Privately Held**
SIC: 2341 5122 5999 Mfg Women's/Youth Underwear Whol Drugs/Sundries Ret Misc Merchandise

(G-3775)
AUTO INJURY SOLUTIONS INC (DH)
222 Merchandise Mart Plz # 900 (60654-1105)
PHONE..................................312 229-2704
Matthew K Elges, *President*
David D Merritt, *Admin Sec*
EMP: 37 EST: 2008
SALES (est): 6.4MM **Privately Held**
SIC: 7372 Prepackaged software
HQ: Ccc Information Services Inc.
 222 Mchds Mart Plz 900
 Chicago IL 60654
 312 222-4636

(G-3776)
AUTOMATED INSIGHTS INC
203 N La Salle St # 2200 (60601-1267)
PHONE..................................919 442-8865
Robbie Allen, *CEO*
Kaleb Jessee, *Business Mgr*
Scott Frederick, *COO*
Pam Heline, *Vice Pres*
Adam Long, *Vice Pres*
EMP: 150
SALES: 8.9MM
SALES (corp-wide): 5.6B **Privately Held**
WEB: www.automatedinsights.com
SIC: 7372 7373 Word processing computer software; systems software development services
HQ: Stats Llc
 203 N Lasalle St Ste 2200
 Chicago IL 60601

(G-3777)
AUTOMATIC ANODIZING CORP
3340 W Newport Ave (60618-5594)
PHONE..................................773 478-3304
Howard Penner, *President*
Scott Penner, *Vice Pres*
Ted Penner, *Admin Sec*
EMP: 25
SQ FT: 20,000
SALES (est): 3.4MM **Privately Held**
SIC: 3471 2851 Anodizing (plating) of metals or formed products; paints & allied products

(G-3778)
AUTOMATIC PRECISION INC
4609 N Ronald St (60706-4718)
PHONE..................................708 867-1116
Peter Bulat, *President*
Chris Bulat, *Vice Pres*
Tony Jurkowski, *Engineer*
John Bulat, *Treasurer*
Maureen Geraghty, *Manager*
▲ EMP: 30
SQ FT: 20,000
SALES (est): 5.5MM **Privately Held**
SIC: 3451 3545 Screw machine products; precision tools, machinists'

(G-3779)
AUTOSPEC INC
Also Called: F1r Wheels
1464 W 37th St (60609-2128)
PHONE..................................773 254-2288
LI Q Feng, *President*
▲ EMP: 2
SALES (est): 365.9K **Privately Held**
SIC: 3714 Motor vehicle wheels & parts

(G-3780)
AUTOTECH TECH LTD PARTNR
28617 Network Pl (60673-1286)
PHONE..................................563 359-7501
Hyder Han, *General Mgr*
EMP: 25 **Privately Held**
SIC: 3625 Industrial electrical relays & switches
PA: Autotech Technologies Limited Partnership
 4140 Utica Ridge Rd
 Bettendorf IA 52722

(G-3781)
AVAILABLE BUSINESS GROUP INC
Also Called: Source 4-Integrated Business
3944 S Morgan St (60609-2511)
PHONE..................................773 247-4141
Patrick Fitzgerald, *President*
Kathy Shine, *Vice Pres*
EMP: 75
SQ FT: 39,000
SALES (est): 10.3MM
SALES (corp-wide): 74.1MM **Privately Held**
SIC: 2759 2752 Business forms: printing; commercial printing, offset
PA: Dominion Holdings, Inc.
 3473 Brandon Ave Sw
 Roanoke VA 24018
 540 989-6848

(G-3782)
AVAN TOOL & DIE CO INC
4612 W Maypole Ave (60644-2726)
PHONE..................................773 287-1670
John J Brownfield, *President*
EMP: 15 EST: 1957
SQ FT: 12,000
SALES: 1MM **Privately Held**
SIC: 3599 3544 3451 3369 Machine shop, jobbing & repair; special dies, tools, jigs & fixtures; screw machine products; nonferrous foundries

(G-3783)
AVANT DIAGNOSTICS INC (PA)
40 E 9th St Apt 804 (60605-2143)
PHONE..................................732 410-9810
Philippe Goix, *CEO*
EMP: 1
SALES (est): 255.9K **Publicly Held**
SIC: 3841 Diagnostic apparatus, medical

(G-3784)
AVENIR PUBLISHING INC
Also Called: Ddc Journal
1 N State St Ste 1500 (60602-3206)
PHONE..................................872 228-2830
Jim Potter, *President*
Natalie Bartolozzi, *Vice Pres*
Adam Wynn, *Vice Pres*
Ryan Nolen, *Accounts Exec*
Jake Breunig, *Marketing Staff*
▲ EMP: 25
SALES (est): 1.9MM **Privately Held**
SIC: 2741 Miscellaneous publishing

(G-3785)
AVENUE METAL MANUFACTURING CO
1640 W Ogden Ave (60612-3288)
PHONE..................................312 243-3483
James N Brunetti, *President*
Basil N Brunetti, *Treasurer*
Mark Brunetti, *Manager*
EMP: 14 EST: 1953
SQ FT: 14,200
SALES (est): 2MM **Privately Held**
WEB: www.avenuemetal.com
SIC: 3444 1796 Restaurant sheet metalwork; ducts, sheet metal; ventilators, sheet metal; installing building equipment

(G-3786)
AVERY DENNISON RFID COMPANY
13424 Collection Ctr Dr (60693-0001)
PHONE..................................626 304-2000
Starla Parrish, *Director*
EMP: 11
SALES (est): 1.1MM **Privately Held**
SIC: 2672 Coated & laminated paper

(G-3787)
AVERY DNNSON RET INFO SVCS LLC
15178 Collection Ctr Dr (60693-0151)
PHONE..................................626 304-2000
EMP: 6
SALES (corp-wide): 7B **Publicly Held**
SIC: 2671 Packaging paper & plastics film, coated & laminated
HQ: Avery Dennison Retail Information Services, Llc
 207 N Goode Ave Fl 6
 Glendale CA 91203

(G-3788)
AVOCET POLYMER TECH INC
4047 W 40th St (60632-3901)
PHONE..................................773 523-2872
Raphael Lee, *President*
James Helke, *Administration*
EMP: 4
SALES (est): 736.9K **Privately Held**
SIC: 5122 2834 Pharmaceuticals; pharmaceutical preparations

(G-3789)
AVONDALE ADVENTURES
Also Called: Holey Cards
3817 N Pulaski Rd (60641-3141)
PHONE..................................773 588-5761
William Rankin, *Partner*
Vivian Rankin, *Partner*
EMP: 4
SQ FT: 4,500
SALES: 210K **Privately Held**
SIC: 2741 3999 3499 Miscellaneous publishing; forms: display, dress & show; book ends, metal

(G-3790)
AVONDALE CUSTOMS INC
Also Called: Avondale Cstm Bldg Fabrication
3241 N Lawndale Ave (60618-5323)
PHONE..................................773 680-4631
Ryan Ruiz-Gibson, *President*
EMP: 2
SALES (est): 210.2K **Privately Held**
SIC: 3499 Fabricated metal products

(G-3791)
AWARD/VISIONPS INC
208 S Jefferson St # 203 (60661-5809)
PHONE..................................331 318-7800
Steven Smits, *CEO*
Douglas Powell, *President*
EMP: 2
SQ FT: 80,000
SALES (est): 494.2K **Privately Held**
SIC: 2759 2752 2732 2741 Commercial printing; commercial printing, lithographic; book printing; miscellaneous publishing

(G-3792)
AWARDS AND MORE INC
8544 S Pulaski Rd (60652-3631)
PHONE..................................773 581-7771
Gerald Skizas, *President*
EMP: 5
SQ FT: 1,200
SALES (est): 631K **Privately Held**
SIC: 3499 5999 Trophies, metal, except silver; trophies & plaques

(G-3793)
AWNINGS EXPRESS
2415 W 24th Pl (60608-5310)
PHONE..................................773 579-1437
Javier Ortega, *Owner*

▲ = Import ▼ =Export
◆ =Import/Export

GEOGRAPHIC SECTION

Chicago - Cook County (G-3822)

EMP: 3
SALES (est): 173.5K **Privately Held**
SIC: 3993 Signs & advertising specialties

(G-3794)
AXIOMATICS INC
525 W Monroe St Ste 2310 (60661-3796)
PHONE..................312 374-3443
Niklas Jakobsson, *CEO*
Marty Leamy, *President*
Aj Harring, *VP Sales*
Lauren Negaard, *Marketing Staff*
Kelly Shelton, *Marketing Staff*
EMP: 11
SQ FT: 1,000
SALES: 10MM **Privately Held**
SIC: 7372 Application computer software

(G-3795)
AXLETECH INTERNATIONAL
Also Called: Heat Treat
1120 W 119th St (60643-5106)
PHONE..................773 264-1234
Mark Garfien, *President*
Donald Garfield, *Vice Pres*
Andy Blysniuk, *Engineer*
Antonio Davis, *Engineer*
Chet Lempicki, *Controller*
▲ **EMP:** 63
SQ FT: 70,000
SALES (est): 14.8MM **Privately Held**
SIC: 3398 Shot peening (treating steel to reduce fatigue); annealing of metal; brazing (hardening) of metal

(G-3796)
AXODE CORP
35 E Wacker Dr Ste 670 (60601-2114)
PHONE..................312 578-9897
Nicolas Vendryes, *CEO*
EMP: 2
SALES (est): 211.9K **Privately Held**
SIC: 3823 Industrial instrmnts msrmnt display/control process variable

(G-3797)
AXXENT ENERGY INC
W 1016 Ste 502 (60601)
PHONE..................312 288-8640
Felix Umanah, *President*
EMP: 25
SALES (est): 607.8K **Privately Held**
SIC: 3999 Manufacturing industries

(G-3798)
AZ PLASTICS INC (PA)
5300 W Roscoe St (60641-4140)
PHONE..................773 679-0988
Mariusz Zymon, *President*
Aleksandra Zymon, *Vice Pres*
EMP: 2
SQ FT: 30,000
SALES (est): 3MM **Privately Held**
SIC: 2671 Plastic film, coated or laminated for packaging

(G-3799)
AZ PLASTICS INC
1232 Mckinley Ave (60641)
PHONE..................773 679-0988
Mariusz Zymon, *President*
EMP: 20
SALES (corp-wide): 3MM **Privately Held**
SIC: 2671 Plastic film, coated or laminated for packaging
PA: Az Plastics, Inc
    5300 W Roscoe St
    Chicago IL 60641
    773 679-0988

(G-3800)
AZTEC MATERIAL SERVICE CORP (PA)
3624 W 26th St Fl 2 (60623-3936)
PHONE..................773 521-0909
Joel Arce, *President*
EMP: 59
SQ FT: 2,000
SALES (est): 6.8MM **Privately Held**
SIC: 3273 Ready-mixed concrete

(G-3801)
AZTEC PLASTIC COMPANY
1747 W Carroll Ave (60612-2503)
PHONE..................312 733-0900
Martin S Wielgus, *President*
Deanna Brend, *Office Mgr*
Suzanne Wielgus, *Office Admin*
EMP: 20
SQ FT: 10,000
SALES (est): 4.4MM **Privately Held**
SIC: 3089 Injection molded finished plastic products; injection molding of plastics

(G-3802)
AZTECA FOODS INC (PA)
5005 S Nagle Ave (60638-1318)
P.O. Box 427, Summit Argo (60501-0427)
PHONE..................708 563-6600
Arthur R Velasquez, *CEO*
Renee Velasquez Togher, *President*
Christian Fauser, *Vice Pres*
Julie Forbes, *Vice Pres*
Nannette Zander, *Vice Pres*
▲ **EMP:** 140
SQ FT: 120,000
SALES (est): 30.4MM **Privately Held**
SIC: 2096 2099 Tortilla chips; tortillas, fresh or refrigerated

(G-3803)
AZTECA JEWELRY (PA)
3334 N Lincoln Ave (60657-1108)
PHONE..................773 929-0796
Juan Romero, *President*
EMP: 6
SQ FT: 2,100
SALES (est): 642.9K **Privately Held**
SIC: 5944 3911 5094 Jewelry, precious stones & precious metals; jewelry, precious metal; jewelry

(G-3804)
B & B FORMICA APPLIERS INC
5617 W Grand Ave (60639-2910)
PHONE..................773 804-1015
Alex Polazkowyj, *President*
Jerry Wereszczak, *Vice Pres*
EMP: 15
SQ FT: 18,000
SALES (est): 1.1MM **Privately Held**
WEB: www.bbformica.com
SIC: 3083 2521 5722 5712 Plastic finished products, laminated; wood office furniture; kitchens, complete (sinks, cabinets, etc.); furniture stores; wood partitions & fixtures; wood kitchen cabinets

(G-3805)
B & J WIRE INC
1919 S Fairfield Ave # 1 (60608-2498)
PHONE..................877 787-9473
Veronica Ronnie Soltysiak, *President*
Xavier Garcia, *Vice Pres*
Josephine Soltysiak, *Admin Sec*
EMP: 45
SQ FT: 80,000
SALES (est): 10.1MM **Privately Held**
WEB: www.bjwire.com
SIC: 3444 3496 Sheet metalwork; shelving, made from purchased wire

(G-3806)
B & T POLISHING CO
2433 W Fulton St (60612)
PHONE..................847 658-6415
Allen Svejcar, *President*
John Svejcar, *Corp Secy*
Ellen Svejcar, *Vice Pres*
EMP: 30
SQ FT: 43,000
SALES (est): 2.2MM **Privately Held**
SIC: 3471 Polishing, metals or formed products; plating of metals or formed products

(G-3807)
B B M PACKING CO INC
874 N Milwaukee Ave (60642-4107)
PHONE..................312 243-1061
Dimitra Baziotes, *President*
Costa Michalopoulos, *Admin Sec*
EMP: 7
SQ FT: 1,200
SALES (est): 6MM **Privately Held**
SIC: 5147 5142 2013 Meats, fresh; meat, frozen: packaged; poultry, frozen: packaged; sausages & other prepared meats

(G-3808)
B P I PRINTING & DUPLICATING (PA)
3223 N Lakewood Ave (60657-3215)
PHONE..................773 327-7300
Lawrence Berland, *President*
EMP: 15
SALES (est): 2.3MM **Privately Held**
SIC: 2752 Commercial printing, lithographic

(G-3809)
B-CLEAN LAUNDROMAT INC
5419 S Halsted St (60609-6168)
PHONE..................678 983-5492
Ronald Martinez II, *President*
Maria S Hernandez, *Vice Pres*
EMP: 5
SALES (est): 289.9K **Privately Held**
SIC: 3582 Washing machines, laundry: commercial, incl. coin-operated; dryers, laundry: commercial, including coin-operated

(G-3810)
BA LE MEAT PROCESSING & WHL CO
2405 W Ardmore Ave (60659-5007)
PHONE..................773 506-2499
Son Tran, *President*
EMP: 12
SQ FT: 5,000
SALES (est): 795K **Privately Held**
SIC: 2013 5147 Sausages & other prepared meats; meats & meat products

(G-3811)
BABBLETEES
3322 W Washington Blvd (60624-2453)
PHONE..................815 780-1953
EMP: 3 **EST:** 2017
SALES (est): 121.7K **Privately Held**
SIC: 2759 Screen printing

(G-3812)
BACK OF YARDS COFFEE LLC
2059 W 47th St Fl 1 (60609-4009)
PHONE..................773 475-6381
Mayra Hernandez,
EMP: 6
SALES (est): 505.4K **Privately Held**
SIC: 2095 Roasted coffee

(G-3813)
BACKYARD BUCKET CO
1726 S Halsted St (60608-2330)
PHONE..................773 771-0743
Alfonso Castillo, *Owner*
EMP: 3
SALES (est): 156.1K **Privately Held**
WEB: www.backyardbucket.co
SIC: 2323 Men's & boys' neckwear

(G-3814)
BAGCRAFTPAPERCON I LLC (DH)
Also Called: Packaging Dynamics
3900 W 43rd St (60632-3421)
PHONE..................620 856-2800
Stanley B Bikulege, *CEO*
Patrick T Chambliss, *Exec VP*
Dan Vice, *Opers Staff*
Chris Brady, *Purch Dir*
Paul Palmisano, *CFO*
◆ **EMP:** 215
SQ FT: 150,000
SALES: 181.6MM
SALES (corp-wide): 2.5B **Privately Held**
WEB: www.bagcraft.com
SIC: 2671 2674 2673 3497 Packaging paper & plastics film, coated & laminated; paper bags: made from purchased materials; bags: plastic, laminated & coated; metal foil & leaf; commercial printing

(G-3815)
BAGCRAFTPAPERCON II LLC (DH)
3900 W 43rd St (60632-3421)
PHONE..................773 843-8000
Roger Prevot, *CEO*
Patrick Chamdliss, *CFO*
Patrick Dunne, *Controller*
EMP: 620 **EST:** 2006
SALES (est): 39.9MM
SALES (corp-wide): 2.5B **Privately Held**
SIC: 2671 Packaging paper & plastics film, coated & laminated

(G-3816)
BAILY INTERNATIONAL INC
3823 S Halsted St 27 (60609-1612)
PHONE..................773 927-3233
Sandy Tsai, *President*
EMP: 69 **Privately Held**
SIC: 2098 Macaroni & spaghetti
PA: Baily International, Inc.
    2501 W 20th St
    Granite City IL 62040

(G-3817)
BAKA VITALIY
Also Called: Interntonal Creative RES Group
2224 W Chicago Ave (60622-4827)
PHONE..................773 370-5522
Vitaliy Baka, *Owner*
EMP: 5
SALES (est): 142.9K **Privately Held**
SIC: 7379 2741 7311 ; miscellaneous publishing; advertising agencies

(G-3818)
BALDI CANDY CO (PA)
Also Called: Arway Confections
3425 N Kimball Ave (60618-5505)
PHONE..................773 267-5770
Craig Leva, *President*
EMP: 50 **EST:** 1950
SQ FT: 80,000
SALES (est): 35MM **Privately Held**
WEB: www.arwayconfections.com
SIC: 2064 5145 Candy & other confectionery products; chewing candy, not chewing gum; confectionery

(G-3819)
BALDI CANDY CO
Also Called: Arway Confections
3323 W Newport Ave (60618-5509)
PHONE..................773 267-5770
Craig Leva, *President*
EMP: 60
SALES (corp-wide): 35MM **Privately Held**
SIC: 2064 Candy & other confectionery products
PA: Baldi Candy Co.
    3425 N Kimball Ave
    Chicago IL 60618
    773 267-5770

(G-3820)
BALLOTREADY INC
1626 N Honore St (60622-1308)
PHONE..................301 706-0708
Alexandra C Niemczewski, *President*
Aviva Rosman, *COO*
EMP: 3 **EST:** 2015
SALES (est): 148.2K **Privately Held**
SIC: 2741 Miscellaneous publishing

(G-3821)
BALON INTERNATIONAL CORP
Also Called: R T Beverage
5410 W Roosevelt Rd 133a (60644-1478)
PHONE..................773 379-7779
Ramon Travieso, *President*
Patrick Travieso, *CFO*
Kim Kanakes, *Admin Sec*
▲ **EMP:** 32
SQ FT: 26,000
SALES (est): 5.3MM **Privately Held**
SIC: 2086 5499 Carbonated beverages, nonalcoholic: bottled & canned; beverage stores

(G-3822)
BALTON CORPORATION
1001 E 99th St (60628-1538)
PHONE..................773 933-7927
Shari Wilson, *President*
William Malone, *Shareholder*
EMP: 10
SQ FT: 120,000

Chicago - Cook County (G-3823)

SALES (est): 3.2MM **Privately Held**
SIC: **5046** 2041 8322 5812 Restaurant equipment & supplies; pizza dough, prepared; meal delivery program; pizza restaurants; food products manufacturing or packing plant construction; pizza, frozen

(G-3823)
BAMENDA COFFEE COMPANY INC
924 E High Park Blvd (60615)
PHONE.....................214 566-8175
Felix Leshey, *Officer*
EMP: 4
SALES (est): 116.1K **Privately Held**
SIC: **2095** 5149 Roasted coffee; coffee & tea

(G-3824)
BAND OF SHOPPERS INC
Also Called: Whittl
2669 N Greenview Ave F (60614-1180)
PHONE.....................312 857-4250
Michael Zivin, *CEO*
Hemant Kashyap, *COO*
EMP: 5
SQ FT: 1,000
SALES (est): 415K **Privately Held**
SIC: **2741**

(G-3825)
BANDGRIP INC
311 S Wacker Dr Ste 650 (60606-6728)
PHONE.....................844 968-6322
Fred Smith, *CEO*
Keith Hoglund, *COO*
EMP: 5 EST: 2015
SALES (est): 218.2K **Privately Held**
SIC: **3841** Surgical & medical instruments

(G-3826)
BANYAN TECHNOLOGIES INC
1452 E 53rd St Fl 2 (60615-4512)
PHONE.....................312 967-9885
Sanchit Mulmuley, *CEO*
Rishi Bhat, *Chief Engr*
EMP: 3
SALES (est): 86K **Privately Held**
SIC: **7372** Prepackaged software

(G-3827)
BAR CODE GRAPHICS INC
65 E Wacker Pl Ste 1800 (60601-7247)
PHONE.....................312 664-0700
Robert Verb, *CEO*
Andrew Verb, *President*
Jonathan Verb, *COO*
Lois Verb, *Vice Pres*
Brien Fennell, *Program Mgr*
EMP: 19
SQ FT: 5,500
SALES (est): 1.8MM **Privately Held**
SIC: **7336** 2759 Package design; labels & seals; printing

(G-3828)
BAR CODES INC
200 W Monroe St Ste 2300 (60606-5088)
PHONE.....................800 351-9962
Dan Nettesheim, *CEO*
Andrew Learned, *Finance*
Adam Kroos, *Sales Mgr*
Brian Denham, *Accounts Mgr*
Sean Foley, *Accounts Mgr*
▲ EMP: 80
SALES (est): 2.5MM **Privately Held**
WEB: www.barcodesinc.com
SIC: **5112** 3577 Office supplies; bar code (magnetic ink) printers

(G-3829)
BAR-B-QUE INDUSTRIES INC
Also Called: Henry J'S Famous Foods
4460 W Armitage Ave (60639-3574)
PHONE.....................773 227-5400
Forest Krisco, *President*
Cindy Krisco, *Corp Secy*
EMP: 12
SQ FT: 15,000
SALES (est): 2.5MM **Privately Held**
SIC: **2013** 2011 Corned beef from purchased meat; canned meats (except baby food), meat slaughtered on site

(G-3830)
BARBECUE SELECT INC
1421 W 47th St (60609-3233)
P.O. Box 9273 (60609-0273)
PHONE.....................773 847-0230
Paul Buehler, *President*
Nathan Anderson, *Vice Pres*
EMP: 15
SQ FT: 20,000
SALES (est): 1.5MM **Privately Held**
SIC: **2013** Sausages & other prepared meats

(G-3831)
BARDASH & BUKOWSKI INC
Also Called: National Printing Resources
329 W 18th St Ste 908 (60616-1772)
PHONE.....................312 829-2080
EMP: 4
SQ FT: 2,000
SALES (est): 399.4K **Privately Held**
SIC: **2752** Lithographic Commercial Printing

(G-3832)
BARE METALS INC
3065 N Rockwell St (60618-7934)
PHONE.....................773 583-1100
EMP: 3
SALES (est): 145.6K **Privately Held**
SIC: **3451** Screw machine products

(G-3833)
BARKER METALCRAFT INC
2955 N California Ave (60618-7702)
PHONE.....................773 588-9300
Ronald Kedzorski, *President*
Barbara Kedzorski, *Treasurer*
EMP: 5 EST: 1967
SQ FT: 7,500
SALES: 790K **Privately Held**
SIC: **3444** 3446 3443 Sheet metalwork; architectural metalwork; fabricated plate work (boiler shop)

(G-3834)
BARKS PUBLICATIONS INC
Also Called: Electrmchnical Bench Reference
17 N State St Ste 1650 (60602-3570)
PHONE.....................312 321-9440
Horace B Barks, *President*
Elsie Dickson, *Principal*
Elizabeth Van Ness, *COO*
Kevin Jones, *Senior Editor*
EMP: 10 EST: 1969
SQ FT: 2,500
SALES (est): 1.3MM **Privately Held**
WEB: www.barks.com
SIC: **2721** 2731 Magazines: publishing only, not printed on site; books: publishing only

(G-3835)
BAROQUE SILVERSMITH INC (PA)
55 E Washington St # 302 (60602-2103)
PHONE.....................312 357-2813
Hagop Dirilen, *Exec VP*
EMP: 2
SALES (est): 384.7K **Privately Held**
SIC: **3914** 3471 Silversmithing; plating & polishing

(G-3836)
BARREL
2015 S Damen Ave Ste A (60608-4773)
PHONE.....................312 754-0156
EMP: 4 EST: 2013
SALES (est): 239.8K **Privately Held**
SIC: **2085** Distilled & blended liquors

(G-3837)
BARREL MAKER PRINTING
3065 N Rockwell St Ste 8 (60618-7925)
PHONE.....................773 490-3065
Justin Moore, *Principal*
EMP: 7
SALES (est): 667K **Privately Held**
SIC: **2752** Commercial printing, lithographic

(G-3838)
BARRETT NJIDE YVONNE
Also Called: Oui Wee Designs
1011 W 18th St (60608-2306)
PHONE.....................312 701-3962
N'Jide Yvonne Barrett, *Owner*
EMP: 10
SQ FT: 2,000
SALES (est): 40K **Privately Held**
SIC: **3911** 2211 3143 Pearl jewelry, natural or cultured; apparel & outerwear fabrics, cotton; dress shoes, men's

(G-3839)
BARRY CALLEBAUT USA LLC
2144 Paysphere Cir (60610)
PHONE.....................312 496-7300
EMP: 4
SALES (corp-wide): 45.7MM **Privately Held**
SIC: **2066** 8741 Chocolate; management services
HQ: Barry Callebaut U.S.A. Llc
    600 W Chicago Ave Ste 860
    Chicago IL 60654

(G-3840)
BARRY CALLEBAUT USA LLC (DH)
600 W Chicago Ave Ste 860 (60654-2530)
PHONE.....................312 496-7300
Peter Boone, *President*
Ashley Vargas, *Opers Staff*
Stuartredfiel Redfield, *QC Mgr*
Gall Isabelle, *Research*
Julie Mates, *Research*
◆ EMP: 277
SQ FT: 10,000
SALES (est): 710.7MM
SALES (corp-wide): 45.7MM **Privately Held**
SIC: **2066** 8741 Chocolate; administrative management
HQ: Barry Callebaut Ag
    Westpark
    ZUrich ZH
    432 040-404

(G-3841)
BARRY SIGNS INC
6950 W Imlay St (60631-1771)
PHONE.....................773 327-1183
Robert Szymanski, *President*
Janice Szymanski, *Corp Secy*
EMP: 3
SQ FT: 1,200
SALES (est): 200K **Privately Held**
SIC: **3993** Signs, not made in custom sign painting shops

(G-3842)
BARSANTI WOODWORK CORPORATION
3838 W 51st St (60632-3614)
PHONE.....................773 284-6888
Eugene Barsanti, *President*
Constance Barsanti, *Corp Secy*
EMP: 50 EST: 1978
SQ FT: 58,000
SALES (est): 5.2MM **Privately Held**
WEB: www.barsantiwoodwork.com
SIC: **2499** Decorative wood & woodwork

(G-3843)
BARTEC ORB INC
4724 S Christiana Ave (60632-3016)
PHONE.....................773 927-8600
Doug Korslund, *President*
EMP: 20
SALES (est): 4.5MM **Privately Held**
SIC: **3444** 8711 3672 3533 Sheet metalwork; designing: ship, boat, machine & product; printed circuit boards; oil & gas field machinery

(G-3844)
BARTESIAN CORP
303 W Erie St Ste 320 (60654-3973)
PHONE.....................847 302-4467
Henry Cowie, *CFO*
EMP: 6
SALES (est): 745.2K **Privately Held**
SIC: **2085** Cocktails, alcoholic

(G-3845)
BASSWOOD ASSOCIATES INC (PA)
Also Called: AlphaGraphics
1017 W Washington Blvd (60607-2119)
PHONE.....................312 240-9400
Sheila Moran, *President*
Richard Moran, *Vice Pres*
EMP: 15
SQ FT: 4,800
SALES (est): 6MM **Privately Held**
SIC: **2752** 2672 Commercial printing, lithographic; coated & laminated paper

(G-3846)
BAXALTA US INC
135 S Lasalle St Ste 3425 (60603)
PHONE.....................312 648-2244
EMP: 10
SALES (corp-wide): 15.1B **Privately Held**
SIC: **2835** Blood derivative diagnostic agents
HQ: Baxalta Us Inc.
    1200 Lakeside Dr
    Bannockburn IL 60015
    224 948-2000

(G-3847)
BAY VALLEY FOODS LLC
Also Called: Schwartz Pickle
4401 W 44th Pl (60632-4305)
PHONE.....................773 927-7700
Gary Newman, *General Mgr*
Maria Gomez, *Materials Mgr*
EMP: 100
SALES (corp-wide): 4.2B **Publicly Held**
SIC: **2099** Food preparations
HQ: Bay Valley Foods, Llc
    3200 Riverside Dr Ste A
    Green Bay WI 54301
    800 558-4700

(G-3848)
BE GROUP INC
Also Called: Contractor Advisors
4850 S Lake Park Ave # 1906 (60615-2130)
PHONE.....................312 436-0301
Suzanne Stantley, *President*
EMP: 4
SALES (est): 173.6K **Privately Held**
SIC: **2721** 7374 7389 8611 Magazines: publishing only, not printed on site; service bureau, computer; convention & show services; contractors' association; training & development consultant

(G-3849)
BE PRODUCTS INC
180 W Washington St Fl 10 (60602-2315)
PHONE.....................312 201-9669
EMP: 6
SALES (est): 682.1K **Privately Held**
SIC: **2844** Mfg Toilet Preparations

(G-3850)
BEACON SOLUTIONS INC
111 E Wacker Dr Ste 3000 (60601-4803)
PHONE.....................303 513-0469
Gabe Vehosky, *CEO*
EMP: 15
SQ FT: 2,500
SALES (est): 396.6K **Privately Held**
SIC: **2711** Newspapers

(G-3851)
BEAM GLOBAL SPIRITS & WINE LLC (DH)
Also Called: Beam Suntory
222 Merchandise Mart Plz # 1600 (60654-4262)
PHONE.....................847 948-8888
Matthew Shattock, *President*
Alonzo Johnson, *President*
Tom V Wilen, *COO*
Jeffrey J Buresh, *Senior VP*
Lauren Marks, *Project Mgr*
◆ EMP: 140
SQ FT: 50,000
SALES (est): 382.1MM **Privately Held**
WEB: www.beamsuntory.com
SIC: **2085** Distilled & blended liquors

GEOGRAPHIC SECTION
Chicago - Cook County (G-3877)

HQ: Beam Suntory Inc.
222 Merchandise Mart Plz # 1600
Chicago IL 60654
312 964-6999

(G-3852)
BEAM SUNTORY INC (DH)
222 Merchandise Mart Plz # 1600
(60654-4262)
PHONE.....................312 964-6999
Yasuhiro Fukuyama, *CEO*
Matthew J Shattock, *President*
Albert Baladi, *President*
Nicholas Fink, *President*
Pryce Greenow, *President*
◆ **EMP:** 130
SALES (est): 1B **Privately Held**
WEB: www.beamsuntory.com
SIC: 2085 Bourbon whiskey

(G-3853)
BEAN PRODUCTS INC
1500 S Western Ave Ste 40 (60608-1819)
PHONE.....................312 666-3600
Chuck Blumenthal, *President*
▲ **EMP:** 21
SQ FT: 14,000
SALES (est): 2.4MM **Privately Held**
SIC: 2392 2833 Cushions & pillows; medicinals & botanicals

(G-3854)
BEAR-STEWART CORPORATION (PA)
1025 N Damen Ave (60622-3637)
PHONE.....................773 276-0400
Clifford Brooks, *President*
Michael Hossman, *Corp Secy*
EMP: 20
SQ FT: 45,000
SALES (est): 9.6MM **Privately Held**
WEB: www.bearstewart.com
SIC: 2033 5149 2045 2051 Jams, including imitation: packaged in cans, jars, etc.; jellies, edible, including imitation: in cans, jars, etc.; baking supplies; prepared flour mixes & doughs; bread, cake & related products; food preparations; frozen bakery products, except bread

(G-3855)
BEARING SALES CORPORATION
4153 N Kostner Ave (60641-1928)
PHONE.....................773 282-8686
John Hilton, *Ch of Bd*
James B White, *President*
Jim White, *President*
Terry Robertson, *Regional Mgr*
Carrie Grundas, *Manager*
▲ **EMP:** 35
SQ FT: 30,000
SALES (est): 8.8MM **Privately Held**
SIC: 5085 3399 3568 3366 Bearings; metal powders, pastes & flakes; power transmission equipment; copper foundries

(G-3856)
BEARINGS MANUFACTURING COMPANY
Also Called: BMC
1033 N Kolmar Ave (60651-3337)
PHONE.....................773 583-6703
Steven Sivo, *President*
EMP: 12
SQ FT: 12,200
SALES (corp-wide): 12.1MM **Privately Held**
WEB: www.bmcbearing.com
SIC: 3568 3562 Bearings, bushings & blocks; ball & roller bearings
PA: Bearings Manufacturing Company
15157 Foltz Pkwy
Strongsville OH 44149
440 846-5517

(G-3857)
BEARSE MANUFACTURING CO
Also Called: Bearse USA
3815 W Cortland St (60647-4691)
PHONE.....................773 235-8710
Thomas F Auer, *President*
William Ackerley, *COO*
Joseph E Auer, *Vice Pres*
Christina Ciesla, *CFO*
Joe Auer, *Director*
▲ **EMP:** 100 **EST:** 1921
SQ FT: 50,000
SALES (est): 37.8MM **Privately Held**
WEB: www.bearsusa.com
SIC: 5099 5949 2393 Cases, carrying; patterns: sewing, knitting & needlework; bags & containers, except sleeping bags: textile

(G-3858)
BEECKEN PETTY OKEEFE & CO LLC (PA)
131 S Dearborn St Ste 122 (60603-5581)
PHONE.....................312 435-0300
Adam Hentze, *Vice Pres*
Ryan Ilacqua, *Vice Pres*
Peter Magas, *Vice Pres*
Greg Trento, *Vice Pres*
Ann Koerner, *Controller*
EMP: 561
SALES (est): 347MM **Privately Held**
SIC: 6799 3841 Venture capital companies; surgical & medical instruments

(G-3859)
BEL AMERICAS INC
30 S Wacker Dr Ste 3000 (60606-7459)
PHONE.....................646 454-8220
Eric Deponcis, *President*
EMP: 5
SALES (est): 213.8K
SALES (corp-wide): 174.8MM **Privately Held**
SIC: 2022 Natural cheese
PA: Bel Brands Usa, Inc.
30 S Wacker Dr Ste 3000
Chicago IL 60606
312 462-1500

(G-3860)
BEL BRANDS USA INC (PA)
30 S Wacker Dr Ste 3000 (60606-7459)
PHONE.....................312 462-1500
Lance Chambers, *President*
Vonda Degner, *Production*
Jean-Michel Dos Remedios, *Purch Dir*
John Bryerton, *Engineer*
Patrick Lennon, *Project Engr*
◆ **EMP:** 40
SQ FT: 130,000
SALES (est): 174.8MM **Privately Held**
SIC: 2022 Natural cheese; processed cheese

(G-3861)
BEL MAR WIRE PRODUCTS INC
2343 N Damen Ave (60647-3352)
PHONE.....................773 342-3800
Anastase Marinos, *President*
George Marinos, *Treasurer*
EMP: 15
SQ FT: 28,000
SALES (est): 2.4MM **Privately Held**
WEB: www.belmarwire.net
SIC: 3496 2542 Miscellaneous fabricated wire products; partitions & fixtures, except wood

(G-3862)
BEL-AIR MANUFACTURING INC
3525 W Potomac Ave (60651-2231)
PHONE.....................773 276-7550
Frank Defrank, *President*
Mustafa Macit, *QC Dir*
Mary Frank, *Finance Mgr*
Jason Ziomek, *Sales Staff*
EMP: 16
SQ FT: 40,000
SALES (est): 1.3MM **Privately Held**
WEB: www.belairmfg.com
SIC: 3544 3469 Special dies & tools; stamping metal for the trade

(G-3863)
BELAIR HD STUDIOS LLC
2233 S Throop St (60608-5002)
PHONE.....................312 254-5188
Clyde Scott, *CEO*
EMP: 30
SQ FT: 35,000
SALES: 180MM **Privately Held**
SIC: 7335 2711 Commercial photography; commercial printing & newspaper publishing combined

(G-3864)
BELLWOOD INDUSTRIES INC (PA)
4351 W Roosevelt Rd (60624-3839)
PHONE.....................773 522-1002
Gerald Cychosz, *Owner*
Joesph Palik, *General Mgr*
EMP: 8 **EST:** 1970
SQ FT: 2,800
SALES (est): 900K **Privately Held**
SIC: 3471 Electroplating of metals or formed products

(G-3865)
BELVIN J & F SHEET METAL CO
675 N Milwaukee Ave (60642-5920)
PHONE.....................312 666-5222
Javier Tellez, *President*
Ben Belvin, *Chairman*
Fidel Tellez, *Vice Pres*
Carrie Clayton, *Admin Sec*
EMP: 5
SALES (est): 400K **Privately Held**
SIC: 3444 Sheet metal specialties, not stamped

(G-3866)
BENDINGER BRUCE CRTVE COMM IN
Also Called: Copy Workshop, The
2144 N Hudson Ave Ste 1 (60614-4572)
PHONE.....................773 871-1179
Lorelei Bendinger, *President*
Bruce Bendinger, *Exec VP*
EMP: 6
SALES (est): 721.4K **Privately Held**
SIC: 2731 8742 2741 Book publishing; marketing consulting services; miscellaneous publishing

(G-3867)
BENEFICIAL REUSE MGT LLC (PA)
372 W Ontario St Ste 501 (60654-5779)
PHONE.....................312 784-0300
Robert C Spoerri,
David Schuurman,
EMP: 15
SALES (est): 5.5MM **Privately Held**
SIC: 3822 Auto controls regulating residntl & coml environmt & applncs

(G-3868)
BENESTAR BRANDS LLC (PA)
4118 S Halsted St (60609-2612)
PHONE.....................773 254-7400
Carl E Lee Jr, *President*
EMP: 2
SALES (est): 95.3MM **Privately Held**
SIC: 2096 Pork rinds

(G-3869)
BENTLEYS PET STUFF LLC
3657 N Suthport Ave Ste 1 (60613)
PHONE.....................773 857-7600
Giovanni Senafe, *Manager*
EMP: 3
SALES (corp-wide): 1.1MM **Privately Held**
SIC: 3999 Pet supplies
HQ: Bentley's Pet Stuff, Llc
4192 Ill Rte 83 Ste C
Long Grove IL 60047
224 567-4700

(G-3870)
BEST CHICAGO MEAT COMPANY LLC
Also Called: Glenmark Burgers
4649 W Armitage Ave (60639-3405)
PHONE.....................773 523-8161
Peter Garcia, *Plant Mgr*
Brandon T Beavers,
Cathy Spanow, *Executive Asst*
Dominick Pinto,
EMP: 15
SALES (est): 4.6MM **Privately Held**
SIC: 2011 Meat by-products from meat slaughtered on site
PA: Beavers Holdings, Llc
3550 Hobson Rd Fl 3
Woodridge IL 60517

(G-3871)
BEST DIAMOND PLASTICS LLC
1401 E 98th St (60628-1701)
PHONE.....................773 336-3485
Karla Tolliver, *Vice Pres*
Mark Tolliver,
Brandon Beavers,
Robert Beavers III,
▲ **EMP:** 10
SALES (est): 3.3MM **Privately Held**
WEB: www.bestdiamondplastics.com
SIC: 2656 Straws, drinking: made from purchased material

(G-3872)
BEST NEON SIGN CO
6025 S New England Ave (60638-4005)
PHONE.....................773 586-2700
Marvin Goldzweig, *President*
Michael Goldzweig, *Treasurer*
Steve Goldzweig, *Admin Sec*
EMP: 8
SQ FT: 12,000
SALES (est): 2.3MM **Privately Held**
SIC: 3993 1799 Neon signs; signs, not made in custom sign painting shops; sign installation & maintenance

(G-3873)
BEST PALLET COMPANY LLC (PA)
Also Called: Great Lakes Pallet
166 W Washington St # 300 (60602-2311)
PHONE.....................312 242-4009
Andrew Urnezis, *Sales Staff*
Joseph S Messer,
EMP: 18
SQ FT: 3,000
SALES (est): 2.7MM **Privately Held**
SIC: 2448 Pallets, wood; pallets, wood & wood with metal

(G-3874)
BETTER EARTH LLC (PA)
2444 W 16th St Ste 4r (60608-1731)
PHONE.....................844 243-6333
John Hamilton, *Mng Member*
EMP: 3
SALES (est): 939K **Privately Held**
SIC: 2611 Pulp manufactured from waste or recycled paper

(G-3875)
BEVERAGE ART INC
Also Called: Bev Art HM Brewing Winemaking
9030 S Hermitage Ave (60620-5561)
PHONE.....................773 881-9463
Greg Fischer, *President*
EMP: 5
SQ FT: 2,000
SALES (est): 689.5K **Privately Held**
SIC: 2084 Wines

(G-3876)
BEVERAGE FLAVORS INTL LLC
Also Called: B F I
3150 N Campbell Ave (60618-7921)
PHONE.....................773 248-3860
Gregg Goga, *Vice Pres*
Dennis Reid, *Vice Pres*
Rich Baughman, *Opers Mgr*
Daniel T Manoogian,
Jenna Satterthwaite, *Relations*
▼ **EMP:** 10
SALES (est): 2.1MM **Privately Held**
SIC: 2087 Beverage bases

(G-3877)
BEVERLY SHEAR MFG CORPORATION
3004 W 111th St Ste 1a (60655-2292)
PHONE.....................773 233-2063
Joseph A Nebel, *President*
Rose Christensen, *Vice Pres*
Bob Christensen, *Purch Mgr*
EMP: 6 **EST:** 1931
SQ FT: 2,000
SALES (est): 735.9K **Privately Held**
SIC: 3444 3549 3541 Sheet metalwork; metalworking machinery; machine tools, metal cutting type

Chicago - Cook County (G-3878) GEOGRAPHIC SECTION

(G-3878)
BEYOND LIMITS MEDIA GROUP LLC
9930 S Bensley Ave (60617-5345)
PHONE..................773 948-9296
Brandon Cook,
EMP: 3
SALES: 80K **Privately Held**
SIC: 2741 7929 ; entertainment service

(G-3879)
BHS MEDIA LLC
Also Called: Bh Sports
29 E Madison St Ste 809 (60602-3571)
PHONE..................312 701-0000
Kevin Harrington, *Mng Member*
Michael Velazquez, *Director*
EMP: 30 **EST:** 2012
SALES (est): 2.2MM **Privately Held**
SIC: 2721 Magazines: publishing only, not printed on site

(G-3880)
BIAGIOS GOURMET FOODS INC
Also Called: Suparossa Pizza
7319 W Lawrence Ave (60706-3503)
PHONE..................708 867-4641
Salvatore Cirrincione, *President*
Peter Lesniak, *Accountant*
Rose Cirrincione, *Admin Sec*
▲ **EMP:** 20
SQ FT: 30,000
SALES (est): 798K **Privately Held**
SIC: 5812 2038 Caterers; pizza, frozen

(G-3881)
BIG CITY SETS INC
4318 W Carroll Ave (60624-1705)
PHONE..................312 421-3210
Charles P Grundy, *President*
Christopher Gapinski, *Vice Pres*
EMP: 8
SQ FT: 6,250
SALES (est): 740K **Privately Held**
SIC: 3999 Theatrical scenery

(G-3882)
BIG SHOULDERS COFFEE WORKS (PA)
2415 W 19th St Ste 1c (60608-4489)
PHONE..................312 888-3042
Patricia Coonan, *Bd of Directors*
EMP: 2 **EST:** 2012
SALES (est): 472.9K **Privately Held**
SIC: 5499 2095 Coffee; roasted coffee

(G-3883)
BIG TEN NETWORK SERVICES LLC
Also Called: Btn
600 W Chicago Ave Ste 875 (60654-2531)
PHONE..................312 329-3666
Mark Silverman, *President*
Joe Haning, *Opers Staff*
Brett Hartle, *Opers Staff*
Alana Judd, *Opers Staff*
Cortney Rush, *Finance*
EMP: 68
SALES (est): 28.1MM **Privately Held**
SIC: 3663 Television broadcasting & communications equipment

(G-3884)
BIGHAND INC (DH)
125 S Wacker Dr Ste 300 (60606-4421)
PHONE..................312 893-5906
Jon Ardron, *CEO*
Carla Murphy, *Opers Mgr*
Sam Toulson, *CFO*
James Davis, *Controller*
Earl Konietzko, *Accounts Mgr*
EMP: 13
SALES (est): 3.7MM
SALES (corp-wide): 42.9MM **Privately Held**
WEB: www.bighand.com
SIC: 7372 Business oriented computer software
HQ: Bighand Limited
27-29 Union Street
London SE1 1
207 940-5900

(G-3885)
BIGTIME SOFTWARE INC
311 S Wacker Dr Ste 2300 (60606-6675)
PHONE..................312 346-4646
Brian Saunders, *CEO*
E Jeffrey Lyons, *President*
Jake Matyas, *COO*
Sherry Cross, *Accountant*
Samuel Muniz, *Consultant*
EMP: 20
SALES (est): 2.4MM **Privately Held**
SIC: 7372 Prepackaged software

(G-3886)
BILL WELDING & FABRICATION LLC
939 W North Ave Ste 750 (60642-7142)
PHONE..................312 871-2623
Cassandra Harris, *CEO*
EMP: 5
SALES (est): 49.5K **Privately Held**
SIC: 7692 Welding repair

(G-3887)
BILLINIUM RECORDS LLC
Also Called: Billinium Films
200 W Madison St Ste 2100 (60606-3521)
PHONE..................800 651-8059
Emiel Loyd,
John Morton,
EMP: 3
SALES (est): 10K **Privately Held**
SIC: 3651 Music distribution apparatus

(G-3888)
BILLS SHADE & BLIND SERVICE (PA)
6029 1/2 S Harper Ave (60637-2926)
PHONE..................773 493-5000
Leon Jackson, *President*
EMP: 8 **EST:** 1932
SQ FT: 26,250
SALES: 900K **Privately Held**
SIC: 2591 Venetian blinds; window shades

(G-3889)
BIMBO BAKEHOUSE LLC (DH)
8550 W Bryn Mawr Ave (60631-3222)
PHONE..................800 550-6810
Joseph McCarthy, *President*
Zachary Selskey, *Regl Sales Mgr*
Emily Liang, *Mktg Dir*
Robert Hale, *Exec Dir*
Jassen Whiteman, *Director*
▼ **EMP:** 50
SALES (est): 658.6MM **Privately Held**
SIC: 2051 Bagels, fresh or frozen

(G-3890)
BIMBO BAKERIES USA INC
2503 S Blue Island Ave (60608-4903)
PHONE..................773 254-3578
EMP: 21
SALES (corp-wide): 13.7B **Privately Held**
SIC: 2051 Mfg Bread/Related Products
HQ: Bimbo Bakeries Usa, Inc
255 Business Center Dr # 200
Horsham PA 19044
215 347-5500

(G-3891)
BIMBO QSR CHICAGO LLC
Also Called: East Balt Bakeries
1801 W 31st Pl (60608-6144)
PHONE..................773 376-4444
Mark Bendix, *CEO*
David Dvorak, *Exec VP*
David Watkins, *CFO*
EMP: 12
SALES (est): 161.8K **Privately Held**
SIC: 2051 Bakery: wholesale or wholesale/retail combined
HQ: Bbu, Inc.
255 Business Center Dr # 200
Horsham PA 19044

(G-3892)
BIMBO QSR US LLC (HQ)
Also Called: East Balt Bakery
1801 W 31st Pl (60608-6144)
PHONE..................740 450-3869
John Kent, *Senior VP*
Donna Rodriguez, *Vice Pres*
Nelia Wolan, *Production*
Emiliano Santoro, *QC Mgr*

Dave Watkins, *CFO*
◆ **EMP:** 106
SQ FT: 100,000
SALES (est): 297.5MM **Privately Held**
WEB: www.eastbalt.com
SIC: 2051 Bakery: wholesale or wholesale/retail combined

(G-3893)
BIO ASCEND LLC
980 N Michigan Ave # 1400 (60611-4501)
PHONE..................888 476-9129
Kraig Steubing, *Director*
EMP: 4
SALES (est): 90K **Privately Held**
SIC: 2834 Solutions, pharmaceutical

(G-3894)
BIO STAR FILMS LLC
4848 S Hoyne Ave (60609-4028)
PHONE..................773 254-5959
Mitch Atamian, *Executive*
Jerome Starr,
Alfred Teo,
Gene Wisniewski,
EMP: 9
SALES (est): 1.5MM **Privately Held**
SIC: 3081 Unsupported plastics film & sheet

(G-3895)
BIOELEMENTS INC
4619 N Ravenswood Ave 202a (60640-4579)
PHONE..................773 525-3509
Callie Lushina, *Branch Mgr*
EMP: 15
SALES (corp-wide): 5.6MM **Privately Held**
SIC: 2844 Depilatories (cosmetic); face creams or lotions
PA: Bioelements, Inc.
3502 E Boulder St
Colorado Springs CO 80909
719 260-0297

(G-3896)
BION DILLOS BAKING CO
4900 W Division St (60651-3158)
PHONE..................773 921-8282
John Lasorella, *President*
EMP: 20 **EST:** 2001
SALES (est): 2.1MM **Privately Held**
SIC: 2051 Bakery: wholesale or wholesale/retail combined

(G-3897)
BIONIC CHICAGO
4315 N Lincoln Ave (60618-1711)
PHONE..................773 698-6269
EMP: 3
SALES (est): 163.3K **Privately Held**
WEB: www.bionicpo.com
SIC: 3842 Surgical appliances & supplies

(G-3898)
BIOVIE INC (PA)
25 W 15th St Apt B (60605-2796)
PHONE..................978 998-4756
Jonathan Adams, *CEO*
Amrit Shahzad, *President*
Richard Wieland II, *CFO*
EMP: 6
SALES (est): 559K **Privately Held**
SIC: 2034 Dehydrated fruits, vegetables, soups

(G-3899)
BIRD DOG BAY INC
2010 W Fulton St F280b (60612-2361)
PHONE..................312 631-3108
Steve Mayer, *President*
Preston Lees, *Mktg Coord*
Eric Stefenson, *Business Dir*
EMP: 1
SALES (est): 379.3K **Privately Held**
SIC: 5136 2253 3961 Men's & boys' clothing; collar & cuff sets, knit; cuff-links & studs, except precious metal & gems

(G-3900)
BISHOP IMAGE GROUP INC
5244 N Elston Ave (60630-1609)
P.O. Box 18134 (60618-0134)
PHONE..................312 735-8153
Joshua Cravens, *Business Mgr*

Chris Bishop, *Manager*
Kristin Swanson,
Chad Taylor,
EMP: 5
SALES (est): 894K **Privately Held**
SIC: 3577 Graphic displays, except graphic terminals

(G-3901)
BISHOPS ENGRV & TROPHY SVC INC
Also Called: Bets
6708 W Belmont Ave (60634-4848)
PHONE..................773 777-5014
Linda Bishop, *President*
Kendal Bishop, *General Mgr*
Laurence Bishop, *Vice Pres*
EMP: 7
SQ FT: 8,000
SALES (est): 199.6K **Privately Held**
SIC: 3479 5094 Etching & engraving; trophies

(G-3902)
BITTER END YACHT CLUB INTL
875 N Michigan Ave # 3707 (60611-1803)
PHONE..................312 506-6205
Dana Hokin, *President*
Joseph Durham, *Finance*
Delores Creque, *Human Res Dir*
Eva Shillingford, *Sales Staff*
Robert Gorman, *Director*
▼ **EMP:** 10
SALES (est): 956.4K
SALES (corp-wide): 25MM **Privately Held**
SIC: 7389 2452 Hotel & motel reservation service; purchasing service; marinas, prefabricated, wood
PA: Century America Llc
1 Thorndal Cir Ste 2
Darien CT 06820
203 655-8735

(G-3903)
BIZ 3 PUBLICITY
1321 N Milwaukee Ave (60622-9151)
PHONE..................773 342-3331
Kathryn Frazier, *Owner*
EMP: 7 **EST:** 2008
SALES (est): 284.9K **Privately Held**
WEB: www.biz3.net
SIC: 2741 Miscellaneous publishing

(G-3904)
BIZBASH MEDIA INC
5437 N Ashland Ave (60640-1153)
PHONE..................312 436-2525
Robert Fitzgerald, *Branch Mgr*
EMP: 5
SALES (corp-wide): 11.9MM **Privately Held**
WEB: www.bizbash.com
SIC: 2759 Advertising literature: printing
PA: Bizbash Media, Inc.
115 W 27th St Fl 8
New York NY 10001
646 638-3602

(G-3905)
BJS WELDING SERVICES ETC CO
1521 E 83rd St (60619-4645)
PHONE..................773 964-5836
Brandon Shearer,
EMP: 7
SALES (est): 410.1K **Privately Held**
SIC: 3441 7389 Dam gates, metal plate;

(G-3906)
BLACK BEAR DEFENSE LLC
1350 E 75th St (60619-1447)
PHONE..................708 357-7233
EMP: 3
SALES (est): 180.3K **Privately Held**
SIC: 3812 Defense systems & equipment

(G-3907)
BLACK BISON WATER SERVICES LLC (PA)
953 W Fulton St U 2 2 U (60607)
PHONE..................630 272-5935
Richard C Kreul, *CEO*
Matt Kruger, *Managing Prtnr*
Joe Solari, *Managing Prtnr*

GEOGRAPHIC SECTION
Chicago - Cook County (G-3934)

Justin Haigler, *Partner*
EMP: 20
SALES (est): 1.2MM Privately Held
SIC: 1381 Drilling oil & gas wells

(G-3908)
BLACK SWAN MANUFACTURING CO
4540 W Thomas St (60651-3387)
PHONE.................................773 227-3700
Jeffrey Lichten, *President*
Francine Mills Lichten, *Vice Pres*
Francine Lichten, *Vice Pres*
Luz Galvan, *Admin Sec*
▲ EMP: 17 EST: 1928
SQ FT: 15,000
SALES (est): 5.4MM Privately Held
WEB: www.blackswanmfg.com
SIC: 2851 2891 3432 3053 Putty; sealing compounds for pipe threads or joints; cement, except linoleum & tile; plumbing fixture fittings & trim; gaskets, packing & sealing devices; chemical preparations; soap & other detergents

(G-3909)
BLAIGE
980 N Michigan Ave # 1080 (60611-4521)
PHONE.................................312 337-5200
Bernie Washington, *Principal*
Terry Brown, *CFO*
EMP: 7 EST: 2011
SALES (est): 606.8K Privately Held
SIC: 3083 Plastic finished products, laminated

(G-3910)
BLAXTAIR INC
330 N Wabash Ave Fl 23 (60611-7619)
PHONE.................................312 299-5590
Franck Gayraud, *CEO*
EMP: 6
SALES (est): 236.5K Privately Held
SIC: 3812 Search & detection systems & instruments

(G-3911)
BLOMMER CHOCOLATE COMPANY
600 W Kinzie St (60654-5585)
PHONE.................................800 621-1606
Jeffrey Rasinski, *President*
David Meggs, *Vice Pres*
Michael Krieger, *Opers Mgr*
Ch-Owen Silva, *Opers Mgr*
Henry Porada, *Maint Spvr*
EMP: 10 Privately Held
WEB: www.blommer.com
SIC: 2066 Cocoa butter; powdered cocoa; chocolate coatings & syrup
HQ: The Blommer Chocolate Company
    1101 Blommer Dr
    East Greenville PA 18041
    800 825-8181

(G-3912)
BLU PRIME INC
Also Called: Bluprime Playing Cards
1030 W North Ave Ste 104 (60642-2500)
PHONE.................................800 709-5413
Adams S Levy, *President*
▲ EMP: 5
SALES (est): 34.2K Privately Held
SIC: 3993 Advertising artwork

(G-3913)
BLUE COMET TRANSPORT INC
4919 W Parker Ave (60639-1713)
PHONE.................................773 617-9512
EMP: 3
SALES (est): 189.1K Privately Held
SIC: 2448 4491 4789 Mfg Wood Pallets/Skids Marine Cargo Handler Transportation Services

(G-3914)
BLUE SOFTWARE LLC
Also Called: Schwak
8430 W Bryn Mawr Ave # 1100 (60631-3473)
PHONE.................................773 957-1600
Ali Moosani, *CEO*
Doug Inda, *Exec VP*
John Bohrer, *Vice Pres*
Stewart Day, *CFO*
Eric Pufahl, *Accountant*

EMP: 87
SALES (est): 8.9MM
SALES (corp-wide): 61.6K Privately Held
SIC: 7372 7311 Business oriented computer software; advertising agencies
HQ: Esko-Graphics
    Kortrijksesteenweg 1095
    Gent 9051
    921 692-11

(G-3915)
BLUEAIR INC
100 N La Salle St # 1900 (60602-3523)
PHONE.................................888 258-3247
Bengt Rittri, *President*
Bob McDonald, *Exec VP*
Margaret Keane, *Accountant*
Nicholas Nowak, *Sales Staff*
Erik Carlson, *Marketing Mgr*
▲ EMP: 13
SALES (est): 2.8MM
SALES (corp-wide): 9.6B Privately Held
SIC: 3634 Air purifiers, portable
HQ: Blueair Ab
    Karlavagen 108
    Stockholm 115 2
    867 945-00

(G-3916)
BLUEMASTIFF GROUP LLC
903 W 35th St Ste 562 (60609-1539)
PHONE.................................708 704-3529
Samuel Winters, *Manager*
EMP: 4
SALES (est): 180K Privately Held
SIC: 1442 Construction sand & gravel

(G-3917)
BLUENRGY LLC
Also Called: Draker
410 S Michigan Ave # 933 (60605-1308)
PHONE.................................802 865-3866
Emmanuel Cotrel,
EMP: 61 Privately Held
SIC: 3825 Energy measuring equipment, electrical
HQ: Bluenrgy, Llc
    110 E Broward Blvd Fl 19
    Fort Lauderdale FL
    954 892-6658

(G-3918)
BLUETOWN SKATEBOARD CO LLC
1344 N Oakley Blvd Ste 2 (60622-3048)
PHONE.................................312 718-4786
Jeshua Neuhaus, *Principal*
EMP: 3
SALES (est): 183.2K Privately Held
SIC: 3949 Skateboards

(G-3919)
BLUSTOR PMC INC
401 N Michigan Ave # 1200 (60611-4255)
PHONE.................................312 265-3058
Finis Conner, *CEO*
Mark Bennett, *COO*
EMP: 8
SALES (est): 490.5K Privately Held
SIC: 3699 Security control equipment & systems

(G-3920)
BMT PRNTING CRTGRAPH ESPCLISTS
12941 S Exchange Ave (60633-1225)
PHONE.................................773 646-4700
Brian Twardosz, *Owner*
EMP: 5
SALES (est): 279.6K Privately Held
SIC: 2752 Commercial printing, lithographic

(G-3921)
BMW SPORTSWEAR INC
Also Called: Better Mens Wear
3967 W Madison St (60624-2337)
PHONE.................................773 265-0110
Yousuf Tabani, *President*
Shawn Molnar, *Assoc Editor*
Andrew Murphy, *Assoc Editor*
EMP: 3
SQ FT: 2,400

SALES: 1.6MM Privately Held
SIC: 5661 2329 5611 Men's shoes; men's & boys' sportswear & athletic clothing; clothing, sportswear, men's & boys'

(G-3922)
BOBAK SAUSAGE COMPANY
4551 W Adams St (60624-2502)
PHONE.................................773 735-5334
Jose Delatorre, *Production*
Stanley Bobak, *Branch Mgr*
EMP: 41
SALES (corp-wide): 47.5MM Privately Held
SIC: 2013 Sausages & other prepared meats
PA: Bobak Sausage Company
    4550 W Jackson Blvd
    Chicago IL 60624
    773 735-5334

(G-3923)
BOBBI SCREEN PRINTING
4573 S Archer Ave (60632-2961)
PHONE.................................773 847-8200
Bobbi Moore, *President*
EMP: 6
SALES (est): 250K Privately Held
SIC: 2396 Screen printing on fabric articles

(G-3924)
BOE INTERMEDIATE HOLDING CORP
3200 S Kilbourn Ave (60623-4829)
PHONE.................................773 890-3300
Kenneth M Roessler, *CEO*
EMP: 500
SALES (corp-wide): 25.1MM Privately Held
SIC: 3089 3411 Plastic containers, except foam; tubs, plastic (containers); can lids & ends, metal
PA: Boe Intermediate Holding Corporation
    8607 Roberts Dr Ste 250
    Atlanta GA 30350
    770 645-4800

(G-3925)
BOEING COMPANY (PA)
100 N Riverside Plz (60606-2016)
P.O. Box 3707, Seattle WA (98124-2207)
PHONE.................................312 544-2000
Lawrence W Kellner, *Ch of Bd*
David L Calhoun, *President*
Bertrand-Marc Allen, *President*
Michael A Arthur, *President*
Leanne G Caret, *President*
EMP: 231 EST: 1916
SALES: 76.5B Publicly Held
WEB: www.boeing.com
SIC: 3721 3663 3761 3764 Airplanes, fixed or rotary wing; helicopters; research & development on aircraft by the manufacturer; airborne radio communications equipment; guided missiles, complete; guided missiles & space vehicles, research & development; propulsion units for guided missiles & space vehicles; guided missile & space vehicle engines, research & devel.; search & navigation equipment; defense systems & equipment; aircraft control systems, electronic; navigational systems & instruments; aircraft body & wing assemblies & parts

(G-3926)
BOEING GLOBAL HOLDINGS CORP (HQ)
100 N Riverside Plz (60606-2016)
PHONE.................................312 544-2000
EMP: 2
SALES (est): 1.4MM
SALES (corp-wide): 76.5B Publicly Held
SIC: 3721 Airplanes, fixed or rotary wing
PA: The Boeing Company
    100 N Riverside Plz
    Chicago IL 60606
    312 544-2000

(G-3927)
BOEING INTERNATIONAL CORP (HQ)
100 N Riverside Plz (60606-2016)
PHONE.................................312 544-2000
Thomas J Downey, *President*

Lianne Stein, *Vice Pres*
EMP: 24
SALES (est): 65.2MM
SALES (corp-wide): 76.5B Publicly Held
SIC: 3721 Aircraft
PA: The Boeing Company
    100 N Riverside Plz
    Chicago IL 60606
    312 544-2000

(G-3928)
BOEING IRVING COMPANY
100 N Riverside Plz Fl 35 (60606-2016)
PHONE.................................312 544-2000
James A Bell, *President*
Larry Hensley, *Engineer*
Blair Jadwin, *Engineer*
Andrew Matthews, *Engineer*
Matthew Cowles, *Manager*
EMP: 1001
SALES: 123MM
SALES (corp-wide): 76.5B Publicly Held
SIC: 3663 Airborne radio communications equipment
PA: The Boeing Company
    100 N Riverside Plz
    Chicago IL 60606
    312 544-2000

(G-3929)
BOEING LTS INC
100 N Riverside Plz (60606-2016)
PHONE.................................312 544-2000
Jim McNerney, *President*
Mitchell Quejado, *Agent*
EMP: 286
SALES (est): 42.9MM
SALES (corp-wide): 76.5B Publicly Held
SIC: 3721 Airplanes, fixed or rotary wing
PA: The Boeing Company
    100 N Riverside Plz
    Chicago IL 60606
    312 544-2000

(G-3930)
BOLD DIAGNOSTICS LLC
222 Merchandise Mart Plz (60654-1103)
PHONE.................................806 543-5743
Kyle Miller, *Manager*
Sean Connell, *Manager*
Jay Pandit, *Manager*
EMP: 4
SALES (est): 239K Privately Held
SIC: 3841 7389 Blood pressure apparatus;

(G-3931)
BOLD RENEWABLES HOLDINGS LLC (PA)
222 N Lasalle Ste 705 (60601)
PHONE.................................541 312-3832
Erik Nara,
EMP: 2
SALES (est): 31.9MM Privately Held
SIC: 3674 Photovoltaic devices, solid state

(G-3932)
BOLT & HIDE CO
321 N Clark St Ste 2300 (60654-4746)
PHONE.................................773 231-2002
Frank Voznak, *President*
EMP: 4
SALES (est): 326.6K Privately Held
SIC: 3452 Bolts, nuts, rivets & washers

(G-3933)
BONANNO VINTNERS LLC
2614 N Paulina St (60614-1018)
PHONE.................................773 477-8351
Bonanno Matthew, *Principal*
Matthew Bonanno, *Webmaster*
EMP: 4
SALES (est): 236.1K Privately Held
SIC: 2084 Wines, brandy & brandy spirits

(G-3934)
BOOKENDS PUBLISHING
2001 N Halsted St Ste 201 (60614-4365)
PHONE.................................312 988-1500
Thomas Kuczmarski, *Partner*
Susan Kuczmarski, *Partner*
EMP: 3
SALES (est): 173.9K Privately Held
SIC: 2731 Books: publishing & printing

Chicago - Cook County (G-3935)

(G-3935)
BOREE UNLIMITED LLC
3014 W 63rd St (60629-2796)
PHONE...........................773 498-6591
Anthea McSwain, *Mng Member*
EMP: 4
SALES (est): 366.2K **Privately Held**
SIC: 2759 Commercial printing

(G-3936)
BORGWARNER TRANSM SYSTEMS INC
10807 S Fairfield Ave (60655-1722)
PHONE...........................815 469-7819
Vladimir Slivka, *Production*
Ravi Narayanaswamy, *Program Mgr*
Michael Oswald, *Manager*
EMP: 438
SALES (corp-wide): 10.1B **Publicly Held**
SIC: 3714 Transmission housings or parts, motor vehicle
HQ: Borgwarner Transmission Systems Inc.
3800 Automation Ave # 500
Auburn Hills MI 48326
248 754-9200

(G-3937)
BOSTIC PUBLISHING COMPANY
3236 N Sacramento Ave (60618-5826)
PHONE...........................773 551-7065
James Bostic, *President*
EMP: 2
SALES (est): 254.9K **Privately Held**
SIC: 2732 Book printing

(G-3938)
BOX FORM INC
1334 W 43rd St (60609-3308)
PHONE...........................773 927-8808
Amanda Choi, *Officer*
EMP: 25
SQ FT: 55,000
SALES (est): 5MM **Privately Held**
SIC: 2656 2657 Paper cups, plates, dishes & utensils; folding paperboard boxes

(G-3939)
BP PRODUCTS NORTH AMERICA INC
BP Oil Supply, Company
30 S Wacker Dr Ste 900 (60606-7403)
PHONE...........................312 594-7689
EMP: 99
SALES (corp-wide): 222.8B **Privately Held**
SIC: 2911 5172 Petroleum Refiner Whol Petroleum Products
HQ: Bp Products North America Inc.
501 Westlake Park Blvd
Houston TX 77079
281 366-2000

(G-3940)
BPN CHICAGO
875 N Michigan Ave # 1850 (60611-2975)
PHONE...........................312 799-4100
Mauricio Sabogal, *CEO*
Elizabeth Ross, *President*
Donald Morrison, *COO*
Neil Smith, *Senior VP*
Meghan Pisano, *Associate Dir*
EMP: 20
SALES (est): 2.7MM **Privately Held**
SIC: 7311 3695 Advertising consultant; magnetic & optical recording media

(G-3941)
BRADLEY TERRACE INC
Also Called: Bradley Terrace Outdoor Furn
8770 W Bryn Mawr Ave # 1300
(60631-3515)
PHONE...........................773 775-6579
Susanah Gill, *President*
Zannah Bradley, *Sales Staff*
EMP: 2
SQ FT: 400
SALES: 500K **Privately Held**
SIC: 2519 Lawn & garden furniture, except wood & metal; lawn furniture, except wood, metal, stone or concrete

(G-3942)
BRAHMAN SPIRIT TRIBE
Also Called: Brahman Spirit Tribe, The
5841 S Peoria St (60621-2167)
PHONE...........................773 957-2828
Clinton Montgomery, *CEO*
El Haq Malak Bey, *CEO*
Janika Montgomery, *Vice Pres*
EMP: 10
SALES (est): 54.1K **Privately Held**
SIC: 7389 8748 2621 3555 Business services; ; telecommunications consultant; printing paper; printing plates; printing equipment, photographic

(G-3943)
BRAINWARE COMPANY
4802 N Broadway St 201a (60640-3622)
PHONE...........................773 250-6465
Roger Stark, *CEO*
EMP: 4
SQ FT: 1,700
SALES (est): 310.9K **Privately Held**
SIC: 7372 Educational computer software

(G-3944)
BRAINWORX STUDIO
6531 N Albany Ave (60645-4103)
PHONE...........................773 743-8200
Mercedes Santos, *President*
Theresa Volpe, *Vice Pres*
Sandy Petroshius, *Director*
EMP: 15
SQ FT: 5,000
SALES: 1.1MM **Privately Held**
SIC: 2731 Book publishing

(G-3945)
BRANCH
500 E 33rd St Apt 801 (60616-4239)
PHONE...........................312 213-0138
Denise Schaffer, *Owner*
EMP: 3
SALES (est): 147.7K **Privately Held**
SIC: 3652 Pre-recorded records & tapes

(G-3946)
BRANDMUSCLE INC
4141 S Peoria St (60609-2522)
PHONE...........................866 236-8481
EMP: 3
SALES (est): 238.8K **Privately Held**
SIC: 3695 Magnetic & optical recording media

(G-3947)
BRD DEVELOPMENT GROUP LLC
Also Called: Real Estate Developer
253 E Delaware Pl Apt 21c (60611-5749)
PHONE...........................312 912-7110
Christopher McGruder, *CEO*
EMP: 10
SQ FT: 500
SALES (est): 557.6K **Privately Held**
SIC: 1542 2491 8711 1794 Nonresidential construction; commercial & office building, new construction; piles, foundation & marine construction; treated wood; building construction consultant; excavation & grading, building construction

(G-3948)
BREAKER PRESS CO INC
Also Called: Commercial Printers
2421 S Western Ave (60608-4704)
PHONE...........................773 927-1666
Richard J Lewandowski, *President*
Michael J Lewandowski, *Vice Pres*
EMP: 6
SQ FT: 2,500
SALES: 1.1MM **Privately Held**
SIC: 2752 2791 Commercial printing, offset; typesetting, computer controlled

(G-3949)
BREAKROOM BREWERY
2925 W Montrose Ave (60618-1403)
PHONE...........................773 564-9534
Eric Padilla, *Principal*
EMP: 8
SALES (est): 905K **Privately Held**
SIC: 2082 Malt beverages

(G-3950)
BRENNER TANK SERVICES LLC
803 E 120th St (60628-5743)
PHONE...........................773 468-6390
Robert Agnew, *Branch Mgr*
EMP: 7
SALES (corp-wide): 2.3B **Publicly Held**
WEB: www.brennertank.com
SIC: 3443 Tanks for tank trucks, metal plate
HQ: Brenner Tank Services Llc
N3760 Hwys 12 & 16 E
Mauston WI 53948
608 847-4131

(G-3951)
BREVITY LLC
3838 N Kenneth Ave (60641-2814)
PHONE...........................949 250-0701
Leonard Wanger,
EMP: 12 **EST:** 2017
SALES (est): 340.8K **Privately Held**
SIC: 7372 Business oriented computer software

(G-3952)
BREWERS BOTTLERS & BEV CORP
7233 N Sheridan Rd Ste 5 (60626-5495)
PHONE...........................773 262-9711
Jim Krejicie, *President*
EMP: 5
SALES (est): 553.7K **Privately Held**
SIC: 2086 Bottled & canned soft drinks

(G-3953)
BRICKS INC
3425 S Kedzie Ave Ste 1 (60623-5181)
PHONE...........................773 523-5718
Kim Schmitt, *Owner*
EMP: 14
SALES (est): 1.7MM
SALES (corp-wide): 6.9MM **Privately Held**
SIC: 3271 Concrete block & brick
PA: Bricks Inc
723 S Lasalle St
Aurora IL 60505
630 897-6926

(G-3954)
BRIDGE PRINTING & PROMOTIONAL
70 W Madison St (60602-4252)
PHONE...........................312 929-1456
Mike Douglas, *Manager*
EMP: 18
SQ FT: 2,700
SALES (corp-wide): 1.5MM **Privately Held**
SIC: 2752 Commercial printing, lithographic
PA: Bridge Printing And Promotional Inc
52 Congress Cir W
Roselle IL 60172
847 776-0200

(G-3955)
BRIDGELINE DIGITAL INC
30 N La Salle St Ste 2000 (60602-4346)
PHONE...........................312 784-5720
EMP: 6
SALES (corp-wide): 9.9MM **Publicly Held**
WEB: www.bridgelinedigital.com
SIC: 7372 Prepackaged software
PA: Bridgeline Digital, Inc.
100 Sylan Rd Ste G700
Woburn MA 01801
781 376-5555

(G-3956)
BRIDGEPORT PHARMACY INC
3201 S Wallace St (60616-3501)
PHONE...........................312 791-9000
Snehal Bhavsar, *President*
EMP: 5
SALES (est): 853.5K **Privately Held**
SIC: 2834 5912 Adrenal pharmaceutical preparations; drug stores

(G-3957)
BRIDGEPORT STEEL SALES INC
2730 S Hillock Ave (60608-5712)
PHONE...........................312 326-4800
Willie Conrad, *President*
Bernice Jordan, *Admin Sec*
EMP: 10
SQ FT: 5,000
SALES (est): 2.2MM **Privately Held**
WEB: www.bridgeportsteelsales.com
SIC: 3441 Fabricated structural metal

(G-3958)
BRIDGFORD FOODS CORPORATION
Also Called: Bridgford Marketing
170 N Green St (60607-2313)
PHONE...........................312 733-0300
Allan L Bridgford Sr, *CEO*
H W Bridgford, *Ch of Bd*
John V Simmons, *President*
William L Bridgford, *Chairman*
Barren Bridgford, *COO*
▲ **EMP:** 375
SQ FT: 225,000
SALES (est): 62.1MM
SALES (corp-wide): 188.7MM **Publicly Held**
SIC: 2013 Prepared pork products from purchased pork; prepared beef products from purchased beef; sausages from purchased meat; sausages & related products, from purchased meat
HQ: Bridgford Foods Corporation
1308 N Patt St
Anaheim CA 92801
714 526-5533

(G-3959)
BRITE SITE SUPPLY INC
4616 W Fullerton Ave (60639-1816)
PHONE...........................773 772-7300
Andreas Vassilos, *President*
EMP: 5
SQ FT: 18,000
SALES (est): 868.9K **Privately Held**
SIC: 2842 5087 2899 Specialty cleaning preparations; janitors' supplies; chemical preparations

(G-3960)
BRITESEED LLC
4660 N Ravenswood Ave (60640-4510)
PHONE...........................206 384-0311
Paul Fehrenbacher,
Jonathan Gunn,
Mayank Vijayvergia,
EMP: 5
SALES (est): 440.6K **Privately Held**
SIC: 3841 Surgical & medical instruments

(G-3961)
BROC LLC
Also Called: Queen Pin
5100 W Grand Ave # 390645 (60639-5400)
PHONE...........................773 709-9931
Lamonica Henderson, *Mng Member*
EMP: 10
SALES (est): 250K **Privately Held**
SIC: 3999

(G-3962)
BROCKWAY STANDARD INC
1440 S Kilbourn Ave (60623-1033)
PHONE...........................773 893-2100
William Eichlin, *Principal*
EMP: 4
SALES (est): 271.1K **Privately Held**
SIC: 3411 Metal cans

(G-3963)
BRONZE MEMORIAL INC
Also Called: Wagner Brass Foundry
1842 N Elston Ave (60642-1216)
PHONE...........................773 276-7972
Richard Wagner, *President*
EMP: 7
SQ FT: 5,000
SALES (est): 480K **Privately Held**
SIC: 3499 Tablets, bronze or other metal

(G-3964)
BROOME & GREENE ONLINE LLC ◆
222 Merchandise Mart Plz (60654-1103)
PHONE...........................312 584-1580
EMP: 4 **EST:** 2019
SALES (est): 446.9K **Privately Held**
SIC: 2511 Wood household furniture

GEOGRAPHIC SECTION

Chicago - Cook County (G-3994)

(G-3965)
BROS LITHOGRAPHING COMPANY
1326 W Washington Blvd (60607-1984)
PHONE.................................312 666-0919
Fax: 312 666-0441
EMP: 9 **EST:** 1945
SQ FT: 38,000
SALES: 900K **Privately Held**
SIC: 2752 Lithographic Commercial Printing

(G-3966)
BROTHERS PALLETS CO
7711 S Claremont Ave (60620-5810)
PHONE.................................773 306-2695
EMP: 4
SALES (est): 335.4K **Privately Held**
SIC: 2448 Pallets, wood

(G-3967)
BROWN & MILLER LITERARY ASSOC
410 S Michigan Ave # 460 (60605-1390)
PHONE.................................312 922-3063
Danielle Egan-Miller, *President*
Danielle Egan Miller, *President*
EMP: 3
SALES (est): 241K **Privately Held**
SIC: 2731 Book publishing

(G-3968)
BROWN LINE METAL WORKS LLC
4001 N Ravenswood Ave 303a (60613-6126)
PHONE.................................312 884-7644
James Werner,
▲ **EMP:** 6
SALES (est): 660.4K **Privately Held**
SIC: 3621 Torque motors, electric

(G-3969)
BRUSS COMPANY (DH)
Also Called: Golden Trophy Steaks
3548 N Kostner Ave (60641-3898)
PHONE.................................773 282-2900
Donnie Smith, *President*
Anthony Cericola, *General Mgr*
Anthony Cericoa, *Principal*
Dan Bernkopf, *Vice Pres*
Maryellen Mulligan, *Engineer*
▲ **EMP:** 36 **EST:** 1937
SQ FT: 52,000
SALES (est): 53.5M
SALES (corp-wide): 42.4B **Publicly Held**
WEB: www.bruss.com
SIC: 5147 5142 2013 2011 Meats, fresh; meat, frozen: packaged; sausages & other prepared meats; meat packing plants
HQ: Tyson Fresh Meats, Inc.
800 Stevens Port Dr
Dakota Dunes SD 57049
479 290-6397

(G-3970)
BSC IMPORTS INCORPORATED
Also Called: Purple Clay Pottery
213 N Morgan St Unit 2c (60607-1721)
PHONE.................................773 844-4788
▲ **EMP:** 3
SQ FT: 2,000
SALES (est): 120K **Privately Held**
SIC: 3269 Mfg Pottery Products

(G-3971)
BUCKTOWN POLYMERS
1658 N Milwaukee Ave # 421 (60647-6905)
PHONE.................................312 436-1460
EMP: 2
SALES (est): 335.8K **Privately Held**
SIC: 5162 2671 Plastics products; packaging paper & plastics film, coated & laminated

(G-3972)
BUFF & GO INC
4345 S Langley Ave Apt 1n (60653-3510)
P.O. Box 8558 (60680-8558)
PHONE.................................773 719-4436
Leatrice Woody, *President*
EMP: 10

SALES (est): 304.6K **Privately Held**
SIC: 3999 5999 Furniture, barber & beauty shop; business machines & equipment

(G-3973)
BULLEN MIDWEST INC (PA)
Also Called: Nuance Solutions
900 E 103rd St Ste D (60628-3091)
PHONE.................................773 785-2300
Jim Flanagan, *President*
Bob Warda, *Regional Mgr*
Cornelius J Houtsma, *Exec VP*
Matt Aherns, *Vice Pres*
Matt Ahrens, *Vice Pres*
EMP: 20
SQ FT: 64,000
SALES (est): 26.2MM **Privately Held**
SIC: 2841 2842 2819 2869 Soap: granulated, liquid, cake, flaked or chip; detergents, synthetic organic or inorganic alkaline; scouring compounds; floor waxes; disinfectants, household or industrial; industrial inorganic chemicals; industrial organic chemicals

(G-3974)
BUNDLAR LLC
222 Merchandise Mart Plz (60654-1103)
PHONE.................................773 839-3976
John Martin,
Gareth Davies,
Matthew Wren,
EMP: 3
SALES (est): 100K **Privately Held**
SIC: 7372 8099 Business oriented computer software; health & allied services

(G-3975)
BUREAU OF NATIONAL AFFAIRS INC
Also Called: Bloomberg Bna
6692 N Sioux Ave (60646-2845)
PHONE.................................773 775-8801
Michaei Bologna, *President*
EMP: 4
SALES (corp-wide): 1.6B **Privately Held**
SIC: 2741 Miscellaneous publishing
HQ: The Bureau Of National Affairs Inc
1801 S Bell St Ste Cn110
Arlington VA 22202
703 341-3000

(G-3976)
BURGOPAK LIMITED
213 W Institute Pl # 301 (60610-3121)
PHONE.................................312 255-0827
Tracy Young, *Finance Mgr*
Jeremy Light, *Branch Mgr*
EMP: 20
SALES (corp-wide): 3.4MM **Privately Held**
SIC: 2671 7336 Packaging paper & plastics film, coated & laminated; commercial art & graphic design
HQ: Burgopak Limited
Unit A-D
London SE1 1
207 089-1950

(G-3977)
BURRELL BEVERAGE CO
22 W Washington St # 1500 (60602-1605)
PHONE.................................708 581-6953
Charles Campbell, *CEO*
EMP: 20
SALES (est): 350K **Privately Held**
SIC: 2082 Malt beverages

(G-3978)
BURRITO BEACH LLC
233 N Michigan Ave C023 (60601-5502)
PHONE.................................312 861-1986
Greg Chusble, *Owner*
EMP: 13 **Privately Held**
WEB: www.burritobeach.com
SIC: 3421 Table & food cutlery, including butchers'
PA: Burrito Beach L.L.C.
414 N Orleans St Ste 402
Chicago IL 60654

(G-3979)
BUSINESS FORMS FINISHING SVC
5410 S Sayre Ave (60638-2218)
PHONE.................................773 229-0230
Raymond Wojcik, *President*
Joe Martin, *Vice Pres*
Len Hauskey, *Asst Treas*
EMP: 6 **EST:** 1956
SQ FT: 6,000
SALES: 350K **Privately Held**
SIC: 2789 2675 Binding only: books, pamphlets, magazines, etc.; die-cut paper & board

(G-3980)
BUSINESS INSURANCE (PA)
150 N Michigan Ave # 1800 (60601-7553)
PHONE.................................877 812-1587
Keith Crain, *CEO*
Arielle Bassett, *Opers Staff*
Jen Jonasson, *Marketing Staff*
EMP: 18
SALES (est): 1.6MM **Privately Held**
SIC: 2721 Periodicals

(G-3981)
BUSINESS SYSTEMS CONSULTANTS
333 N Michigan Ave # 912 (60601-3965)
P.O. Box 5381, Skokie (60076-5381)
PHONE.................................312 553-1253
Jon R Guenther, *President*
EMP: 12
SQ FT: 3,000
SALES (est): 1MM **Privately Held**
SIC: 7372 Business oriented computer software

(G-3982)
BUSINESS VALUATION GROUP INC
400 N La Salle Dr # 3905 (60654-8539)
PHONE.................................312 595-1900
Thomas E Holl, *President*
EMP: 3
SALES (est): 356.4K **Privately Held**
SIC: 3578 7389 Calculating & accounting equipment; financial services

(G-3983)
BUSTER SERVICES INC
Also Called: Fiber Options Div
3301 W 47th Pl (60632-3012)
PHONE.................................773 247-2070
Michael J Finn, *President*
David Levinson, *Vice Pres*
EMP: 50
SQ FT: 40,000
SALES (est): 15.1MM **Privately Held**
SIC: 5093 2611 Waste paper & cloth materials; pulp mills

(G-3984)
BUSWAYS LLC
445 W Barry Ave Apt 329 (60657-5594)
PHONE.................................617 697-2009
Pedro De Almeida, *Mng Member*
EMP: 5
SALES (est): 30K **Privately Held**
SIC: 7382 7372 Security systems services; application computer software

(G-3985)
BUSY BEAVER BUTTON COMPANY
3407 W Armitage Ave (60647-3719)
PHONE.................................773 645-3359
Christen Carter, *President*
Joel Carter, *Opers Staff*
Denise Gibson, *Marketing Staff*
Ben Billington, *Manager*
EMP: 6
SALES (est): 675K **Privately Held**
SIC: 3999 Buttons: Red Cross, union, identification

(G-3986)
BUTCHER BLOCK FURN BY ONEILL
Also Called: O'Neill Products
555 W 16th St (60616-1146)
PHONE.................................312 666-9144
Larry Grossmann, *President*

Don Marubio, *General Mgr*
EMP: 6
SALES (est): 518.5K **Privately Held**
SIC: 2511 Wood household furniture

(G-3987)
BWAY CORPORATION
3200 S Kilbourn Ave (60623-4829)
PHONE.................................773 254-8700
Terry Kline, *CEO*
Scot Evans, *Opers Mgr*
John Tucker, *Opers Staff*
Byron Bubloni, *Production*
Rita Senese,
EMP: 117
SALES (corp-wide): 1.2B **Privately Held**
SIC: 3411 3089 Metal cans; plastic containers, except foam
HQ: Bway Corporation
375 Northridge Rd Ste 600
Atlanta GA 30350

(G-3988)
BYCAP INC
5505 N Wolcott Ave (60640-1019)
PHONE.................................773 561-4976
Peter C Berry, *President*
Joanne P Tecic, *Admin Sec*
EMP: 20 **EST:** 1971
SALES (est): 3MM **Privately Held**
SIC: 3675 3577 Electronic capacitors; computer peripheral equipment

(G-3989)
BYTEBIN LLC
516 N Ogden Ave 55 (60642-6421)
PHONE.................................312 286-0740
Michael Smith,
Jason Pearl,
Quinn M Stephens,
EMP: 3
SALES (est): 138.6K **Privately Held**
SIC: 7371 7372 Computer software development; application computer software

(G-3990)
C & B WELDERS INC
2645 W Monroe St (60612-2820)
PHONE.................................773 722-0097
Arlan Burton, *President*
Julie Burton, *Admin Sec*
EMP: 8
SQ FT: 10,000
SALES: 300K **Privately Held**
WEB: www.cbweldersinc.com
SIC: 7692 Welding repair

(G-3991)
C & C BAKERY INC
2655 W Huron St (60612-1142)
PHONE.................................773 276-4233
John M Bottigliero, *President*
Carl Phillips, *Admin Sec*
EMP: 3 **EST:** 1953
SQ FT: 2,500
SALES: 150K **Privately Held**
SIC: 2051 Bakery: wholesale or wholesale/retail combined

(G-3992)
C & C CAN CO INC
1838 W Grand Ave (60622-6230)
PHONE.................................312 421-2372
William Choporis, *President*
Antonia Choporis, *Admin Sec*
EMP: 3 **EST:** 1939
SQ FT: 2,500
SALES: 124K **Privately Held**
SIC: 3469 Stamping metal for the trade

(G-3993)
C & L PRINTING COMPANY
228 S Wabash Ave Ste 260 (60604-2398)
PHONE.................................312 235-0380
Stephen Chan, *Partner*
Jack Lee, *Partner*
EMP: 10
SALES (est): 1.4MM **Privately Held**
SIC: 2752 Commercial printing, offset

(G-3994)
C & S STEEL RULE DIE CO INC
4305 S Homan Ave (60632-3523)
PHONE.................................773 254-4027
Charles Spicuzza, *President*
EMP: 4

Chicago - Cook County (G-3995)

SQ FT: 3,500
SALES (est): 250K Privately Held
SIC: 3544 Dies, steel rule

(G-3995)
C STREETER ENTERPRISE
28 E Jackson Blvd Fl 10 (60604-2263)
PHONE...................................773 858-4388
Cynthia Streeter, *President*
EMP: 4
SALES: 45K Privately Held
SIC: 3633 Household laundry equipment

(G-3996)
C2 IMAGING LLC
600 W Van Buren St # 604 (60607-3708)
PHONE...................................312 238-3800
Glen Hoffmann, *Manager*
EMP: 20
SALES (corp-wide): 108.4MM Privately Held
SIC: 2754 2759 Commercial printing, gravure; commercial printing
HQ: C2 Imaging, Llc
   201 Plaza Two
   Jersey City NJ 07311

(G-3997)
C6 AGILITY LLC
1415 W Winona St (60640-2820)
PHONE...................................734 548-0008
Larry A Mercier, *Principal*
EMP: 4
SALES (est): 296.8K Privately Held
SIC: 3949 Sporting & athletic goods

(G-3998)
CA INC
123 N Wacker Dr Ste 2125 (60606-1766)
PHONE...................................312 201-8557
EMP: 7
SALES (corp-wide): 4.2B Publicly Held
SIC: 7372 Prepackaged Software Services
PA: Ca, Inc.
   520 Madison Ave Fl 22
   New York NY 10022
   800 225-5224

(G-3999)
CABANAS MANUFACTURING JEWELERS
9 N Wabash Ave Ste 555 (60602-4729)
PHONE...................................312 726-0333
Edward Guini, *President*
EMP: 4
SQ FT: 900
SALES (est): 500K Privately Held
SIC: 3911 Jewelry, precious metal

(G-4000)
CADE COMMUNICATIONS INC
3018 N Sheridan Rd Apt 2s (60657-5525)
PHONE...................................773 477-7184
Michel K Cade, *President*
Ann H Cade, *Vice Pres*
EMP: 2
SALES: 220K Privately Held
SIC: 2741 8748 Miscellaneous publishing; publishing consultant

(G-4001)
CADUCEUS COMMUNICATIONS INC
Also Called: Craft Beer Institute
4043 N Ravenswood Ave # 309
(60613-1155)
PHONE...................................773 549-4800
Ray Daniels, *President*
EMP: 6
SQ FT: 1,200
SALES (est): 727.9K Privately Held
SIC: 8743 2721 Public relations & publicity; periodicals

(G-4002)
CAL-ILL GASKET CO
4716 W Rice St (60651-3329)
PHONE...................................773 287-9605
Brian Burkross, *President*
EMP: 13
SQ FT: 9,500
SALES (est): 1.7MM Privately Held
SIC: 3496 3089 3053 Miscellaneous fabricated wire products; extruded finished plastic products; gaskets, all materials

(G-4003)
CALDWELL & MOTEN LLC
910 S Michigan Ave # 1010 (60605-2356)
PHONE...................................773 619-2584
Erik Caldwell,
Danielle Moten,
EMP: 6
SALES (est): 244.7K Privately Held
SIC: 3714 3537 Motor vehicle parts & accessories; industrial trucks & tractors

(G-4004)
CALIFORNIA MUFFLER AND BRAKES
5059 S California Ave (60632-2006)
PHONE...................................773 776-8990
Magnolia Zepeda, *Principal*
EMP: 5
SALES (est): 98.5K Privately Held
SIC: 3714 7538 Mufflers (exhaust), motor vehicle; general automotive repair shops

(G-4005)
CALIFORNIA TECHNICAL PLTG CORP
3758 W Belmont Ave (60618-5246)
PHONE...................................818 365-8205
David Anzures Sr, *President*
Brett Lpio, *General Mgr*
Sandra Anzures, *Corp Secy*
EMP: 45
SALES (est): 5.1MM Privately Held
SIC: 3471 Electroplating of metals or formed products; cleaning & descaling metal products; chromium plating of metals or formed products

(G-4006)
CALLAHAN MINING CORPORATION
104 S Michigan Ave # 900 (60603-5902)
PHONE...................................312 489-5800
James A Sabala, *Treasurer*
William Boyd, *Admin Sec*
▼EMP: 74
SQ FT: 10,000
SALES (est): 27MM Privately Held
SIC: 1044 Silver ores

(G-4007)
CALLPOD INC (PA)
850 W Jackson Blvd # 500 (60607-3025)
PHONE...................................312 829-2680
Darren S Guccione, *President*
Lauren Word, *Sales Staff*
Craig Lurey, *CTO*
▲EMP: 13
SALES (est): 1.6MM Privately Held
SIC: 3663 Microwave communication equipment

(G-4008)
CALUMET RUBBER CORP
3545 S Normal Ave Ste A (60609-1799)
PHONE...................................773 536-6350
Edward T Woike, *President*
EMP: 5
SQ FT: 18,000
SALES (est): 992.6K Privately Held
SIC: 3061 Appliance rubber goods (mechanical)

(G-4009)
CAM SYSTEMS
Also Called: Nienhouse Media
30 S Wacker Dr Ste 2200 (60606-7452)
PHONE...................................800 208-3244
Robert Nienhouse, *CEO*
Amy Ceisel, *Vice Pres*
EMP: 4
SALES (est): 340K Privately Held
WEB: www.cam-sys.net
SIC: 7389 2721 ; periodicals

(G-4010)
CAMBRIDGE BRANDS MFG INC (DH)
7401 S Cicero Ave (60629-5818)
PHONE...................................773 838-3400
Ellen R Gordon, *President*
G Howard Ember Jr, *Vice Pres*
Barry Bowen, *Treasurer*
EMP: 4
SALES (est): 31.8MM
SALES (corp-wide): 527.1MM Publicly Held
SIC: 2064 Candy & other confectionery products

(G-4011)
CAMEO CONTAINER CORPORATION
1415 W 44th St (60609-3333)
PHONE...................................773 254-1030
Patrick Moore, *President*
EMP: 239
SQ FT: 165,000
SALES (est): 31.9MM Privately Held
SIC: 2653 2542 Boxes, corrugated: made from purchased materials; partitions & fixtures, except wood

(G-4012)
CAMERON ELECTRIC MOTOR CORP
551 W Lexington St (60607-4308)
PHONE...................................312 939-5770
John Nomikos, *President*
Soter Nomikos, *Corp Secy*
Mary Nomikos, *Vice Pres*
EMP: 10
SQ FT: 4,500
SALES (est): 1.1MM Privately Held
WEB: www.cameronelectricmotor.com
SIC: 7694 Electric motor repair; rebuilding motors, except automotive

(G-4013)
CAMMUN LLC
345 N Canal St Apt 1408 (60606-1366)
PHONE...................................312 628-1201
EMP: 5
SALES (est): 130.5K Privately Held
SIC: 2741 Internet Publishing And Broadcasting

(G-4014)
CANDRIENE LOGISTICS LLC
1016 W Jackson Blvd (60607-2914)
PHONE...................................312 260-0740
Muriel Butcher,
EMP: 5
SALES (est): 334.8K Privately Held
SIC: 3537 Truck trailers, used in plants, docks, terminals, etc.

(G-4015)
CANRIGHT & PAULE INC
Also Called: Canright Communications
333 S Wabash Ave Ste 2700 (60604-4129)
PHONE...................................888 202-3894
Christina Paule Canright, *Corp Secy*
Katy Myers, *Marketing Staff*
Collin Canright, *Mng Member*
EMP: 5
SQ FT: 4,000
SALES (est): 313.6K Privately Held
SIC: 8999 8742 8743 2741 Writing for publication; marketing consulting services; banking & finance consultant; public relations services; technical manual & paper publishing

(G-4016)
CANYON FOODS INC
1150 W 40th St (60609-2505)
PHONE...................................773 890-9888
EMP: 5
SALES (est): 249K Privately Held
SIC: 2099 Food preparations

(G-4017)
CAPITOL CARTON COMPANY (PA)
Also Called: Capitol Containers
346 N Justine St Ste 406 (60607-1014)
PHONE...................................312 563-9690
Neil R Gurevitz, *President*
Jeffery Gurebitz, *Corp Secy*
EMP: 24 EST: 1933
SQ FT: 70,000
SALES (est): 3.1MM Privately Held
WEB: www.capitolcarton.com
SIC: 2653 2657 2655 2631 Boxes, corrugated: made from purchased materials; folding paperboard boxes; fiber cans, drums & similar products; paperboard mills; partitions & fixtures, except wood; office furniture, except wood

(G-4018)
CAPITOL CARTON COMPANY
1917 W Walnut St (60612-2405)
PHONE...................................312 491-2220
James Wodarczyk, *Branch Mgr*
EMP: 25
SALES (corp-wide): 3.1MM Privately Held
SIC: 2653 Boxes, corrugated: made from purchased materials
PA: Capitol Carton Company
   346 N Justine St Ste 406
   Chicago IL 60607
   312 563-9690

(G-4019)
CAPSIM MGT SIMULATIONS INC
55 E Monroe St Ste 3210 (60603-5824)
PHONE...................................312 477-7200
Craig Watters, *CEO*
Daniel Smith, *President*
EMP: 36
SQ FT: 2,000
SALES (est): 4.6MM Privately Held
SIC: 7372 Educational computer software

(G-4020)
CAPSONIC AUTOMOTIVE INC
4219 Solutions Ctr (60677-4002)
PHONE...................................915 872-3585
EMP: 400 Privately Held
SIC: 3625 Motor controls & accessories; switches, electric power
PA: Capsonic Automotive, Inc.
   460 2nd St
   Elgin IL 60123

(G-4021)
CAPTAINS EMPORIUM INC
1200 W 35th St (60609-1305)
PHONE...................................773 972-7609
Don Glasell, *President*
EMP: 2
SALES (est): 202.6K Privately Held
SIC: 3914 8748 Trophies; business consulting

(G-4022)
CARAUSTAR INDUSTRIES INC
Also Called: Chicago Carton Plant
555 N Tripp Ave (60624-1066)
PHONE...................................773 308-7622
Brian Coffe, *Branch Mgr*
Timothy Nebel, *Admin Mgr*
EMP: 50
SALES (corp-wide): 4.6B Publicly Held
SIC: 2631 Paperboard mills
HQ: Caraustar Industries, Inc.
   5000 Austell Powder Sprin
   Austell GA 30106
   770 948-3101

(G-4023)
CARBIT CORPORATION (PA)
Also Called: Carbit Paint Co
927 W Blackhawk St (60642-2519)
PHONE...................................312 280-2300
James S Westerman, *President*
David Westerman Sr, *Vice Pres*
Chip Bevan, *Project Mgr*
Bob Lyons, *Project Mgr*
Reynaldo Marchan, *Opers Staff*
EMP: 52 EST: 1925
SQ FT: 84,000
SALES (est): 13MM Privately Held
WEB: www.carbit.com
SIC: 2851 Paints & paint additives; enamels; lacquers, varnishes, enamels & other coatings

(G-4024)
CARBON CLEAN SOLUTIONS USA INC
1712 N Wood St Apt 3w (60622-1424)
PHONE...................................872 206-0197
John Lee, *CFO*
EMP: 2 EST: 2012

GEOGRAPHIC SECTION

Chicago - Cook County (G-4051)

SQ FT: 1,000
SALES: 1MM
SALES (corp-wide): 1.3MM **Privately Held**
SIC: 2899 Carbon removing solvent
PA: Carbon Clean Solutions Limited
  4th Floor
  Reading BERKS RG1 2
  203 865-0639

(G-4025)
CARBON SOLUTIONS GROUP LLC
1130 W Monroe St Ste 1 (60607-2500)
PHONE..................312 638-9077
Justin Brewer, *Sales Staff*
Peter Jenkins, *Manager*
Scott Maloney, *Director*
Kory Trapp, *Business Dir*
Rory Mahesh Gopaul,
EMP: 15
SALES (est): 2.6MM **Privately Held**
SIC: 3624 Carbon & graphite products

(G-4026)
CARDINAL PALLET CO
505 W 43rd St (60609-2718)
PHONE..................773 725-5387
Thomas J Murrihy Jr, *President*
EMP: 25
SQ FT: 50,000
SALES (est): 4.8MM **Privately Held**
SIC: 2448 7699 Pallets, wood; skids, wood; pallet repair

(G-4027)
CARDWELL WESTINGHOUSE COMPANY
Also Called: Wabtec
8400 S Stewart Ave (60620-1754)
PHONE..................773 483-7575
Raymond T Betler, *CEO*
David J Meyer, *Vice Pres*
▲ EMP: 62
SALES (est): 30.2MM **Publicly Held**
SIC: 3743 Freight cars & equipment
HQ: Wabtec Corporation
  30 Isabella St
  Pittsburgh PA 15212

(G-4028)
CAREMATIX INC
Also Called: Wellness Monitoring
209 W Jackson Blvd # 401 (60606-6966)
PHONE..................312 627-9300
Sukhwant Khanuja, *CEO*
Preety Singh, *Cust Mgr*
Kathy Boedeker, *Sales Staff*
Deepak Pandey, *Director*
EMP: 20
SQ FT: 5,500
SALES: 400K **Privately Held**
WEB: www.carematix.com
SIC: 3841 5047 5999 Diagnostic apparatus, medical; diagnostic equipment, medical; medical apparatus & supplies

(G-4029)
CARGILL INCORPORATED
12201 S Torrence Ave (60617-7214)
PHONE..................773 374-3808
Peter Hynes, *General Mgr*
Adam Waehner, *Assistant VP*
Julian Crunkleton, *Plant Mgr*
Ben Bobell, *Sales Staff*
Eric Cepek, *Branch Mgr*
EMP: 11
SQ FT: 13,500
SALES (corp-wide): 113.4B **Privately Held**
WEB: www.cargill.com
SIC: 2992 Lubricating oils & greases
PA: Cargill, Incorporated
  15407 Mcginty Rd W
  Wayzata MN 55391
  952 742-7575

(G-4030)
CARGILL INCORPORATED
12200 S Torrence Ave (60617-7200)
PHONE..................773 375-7255
Jill Bayer, *Manager*
EMP: 12

SALES (corp-wide): 113.4B **Privately Held**
SIC: 2079 2992 Edible fats & oils; lubricating oils & greases
PA: Cargill, Incorporated
  15407 Mcginty Rd W
  Wayzata MN 55391
  952 742-7575

(G-4031)
CARGILL INCORPORATED
954 W Wa Blvd Ste 225 (60607-2224)
PHONE..................630 505-7788
Pete Richter, *Manager*
Monica Babbington, *Executive Asst*
EMP: 25
SALES (corp-wide): 113.4B **Privately Held**
SIC: 0723 2046 Grain milling, custom services; corn milling by-products
PA: Cargill, Incorporated
  15407 Mcginty Rd W
  Wayzata MN 55391
  952 742-7575

(G-4032)
CARSTENS INCORPORATED
7310 W Wilson Ave (60706-4787)
PHONE..................708 669-1500
Barbara Vanderkloot, *President*
Barbara Block Vanderkloot, *President*
Janvier Hammonds, *Purchasing*
John Visk, *Engineer*
Donna Dzieciol, *Finance Mgr*
▲ EMP: 100 EST: 1886
SQ FT: 100,000
SALES (est): 15.3MM **Privately Held**
WEB: www.carstens.com
SIC: 3841 Surgical & medical instruments

(G-4033)
CARUS PUBLISHING COMPANY (HQ)
Also Called: Cricket Magazine Group
70 E Lake St Ste 800 (60601-5913)
PHONE..................603 924-7209
Jason Patenaude, *President*
Edmund Fish, *President*
Aric Holsinger, *Admin Sec*
▲ EMP: 1
SQ FT: 12,000
SALES (est): 1.7MM **Privately Held**
SIC: 2731 Book music: publishing & printing; textbooks: publishing only, not printed on site

(G-4034)
CARUS PUBLISHING COMPANY
Also Called: Cricket Publishing
70 E Lake St Ste 800 (60601-5913)
PHONE..................312 701-1720
Andre Carus, *President*
EMP: 14 **Privately Held**
SIC: 2731 Book publishing
HQ: Carus Publishing Company
  70 E Lake St Ste 800
  Chicago IL 60601

(G-4035)
CASSETICA SOFTWARE INC
22 W Washington St # 1500 (60602-1607)
PHONE..................312 546-3668
EMP: 3
SALES: 800K **Privately Held**
SIC: 7372 Prepackaged Software Services

(G-4036)
CAST21 INC
965 W Chicago Ave (60642-5413)
PHONE..................847 772-8547
Ashley Moy, *CEO*
EMP: 8
SQ FT: 53,000
SALES (est): 300K **Privately Held**
SIC: 3842 Surgical appliances & supplies

(G-4037)
CASTING HOUSE INC
5 S Wabash Ave Ste 614 (60603-3291)
PHONE..................312 782-7160
Jason W Borgstahl, *President*
Anyeli Murillo, *Mfg Mgr*
Jamie Paun, *Production*
Justin Shelby, *Treasurer*
Adam Stern, *Sales Staff*
EMP: 15

SQ FT: 2,000
SALES (est): 2.7MM **Privately Held**
SIC: 3911 Jewelry, precious metal

(G-4038)
CASTRO FOODS WHOLESALE INC
1365 W 37th St (60609-2108)
PHONE..................773 869-0641
EMP: 28
SQ FT: 17,000
SALES: 5MM **Privately Held**
SIC: 2099 2032 Mfg Food Preparations Mfg Canned Specialties

(G-4039)
CATALINA GRAPHICS INC
2325 W Farwell Ave Apt 3s (60645-4759)
P.O. Box 598112 (60659-8112)
PHONE..................773 973-7780
Richard Bordwell, *President*
Carmen Ignacio, *Controller*
EMP: 2
SQ FT: 1,400
SALES (est): 289.8K **Privately Held**
WEB: www.catalinagraphicsinc.com
SIC: 2752 Lithographing on metal

(G-4040)
CATALYST CHICAGO
332 S Michigan Ave Ste 37 (60604-4434)
PHONE..................312 427-4830
Veronica Anderson, *Principal*
Carlos Azcoitia, *Principal*
Tim King, *Principal*
EMP: 8
SALES (est): 510.2K **Privately Held**
SIC: 2731 Books: publishing only

(G-4041)
CATALYTIC INC
954 W Wa Blvd Ste 700 (60607-2211)
PHONE..................844 787-4268
Sean Chou, *CEO*
Tom Coughlin, *Software Engr*
EMP: 42 EST: 2001
SQ FT: 700
SALES (est): 351.1K **Privately Held**
SIC: 7372 Business oriented computer software

(G-4042)
CATAPULT INTEGRATED SVCS LLC
104 S Michigan Ave # 1500 (60603-5902)
PHONE..................312 216-4460
Paul Kramer, *Branch Mgr*
EMP: 3
SALES (est): 184.3K
SALES (corp-wide): 13.7MM **Privately Held**
WEB: www.catapultmarketing.com
SIC: 3599 Catapults
PA: Catapult Integrated Services, Llc
  55 Post Rd W Ste 1
  Westport CT 06880
  203 682-4000

(G-4043)
CATHOLIC PRESS ASSN OF THE US
205 W Monroe St (60606-5013)
PHONE..................312 380-6789
Terry Wessels, *Manager*
Timothy M Walter, *Director*
EMP: 3
SALES: 803.6K **Privately Held**
SIC: 2711 Newspapers, publishing & printing

(G-4044)
CAXTON CLUB
Also Called: Caxton Club Chicago, The
60 W Walton St (60610-3305)
PHONE..................312 266-8825
Don Chatham, *President*
EMP: 4
SQ FT: 1,000
SALES: 148K **Privately Held**
SIC: 5961 2731 Book club, mail order; book clubs: publishing only, not printed on site

(G-4045)
CAYENNE COUTURE ATELIER
1665 E 79th St (60649-4901)
PHONE..................773 408-4664
Khalilah Howard, *Owner*
EMP: 4
SALES (est): 120K **Privately Held**
SIC: 2389 Apparel & accessories

(G-4046)
CBC RESTAURANT CORP
Also Called: Corner Bakery Cafe
2711 W George St (60618-7810)
PHONE..................773 463-0665
Anthony Machias, *Manager*
EMP: 80
SALES (corp-wide): 4.8B **Privately Held**
SIC: 2051 Bakery: wholesale or wholesale/retail combined
HQ: Cbc Restaurant Corp.
  12700 Park Central Dr # 1300
  Dallas TX 75251

(G-4047)
CD LLC
363 W Erie St Ste 400w (60654-6906)
PHONE..................312 275-5747
Scott Emalfarb, *Manager*
Brad Emalfarb, *Manager*
Hal Emalfarb,
EMP: 10
SALES (est): 500K **Privately Held**
SIC: 3829 Measuring & controlling devices

(G-4048)
CDI COMPUTERS US CORPORATION
Also Called: CDI Computer Dealers
500 N Michigan Ave # 600 (60611-3777)
P.O. Box 95096 (60694-5096)
PHONE..................888 226-5727
Saar Pikar, *CEO*
Erez Pikar, *President*
Fred Hastings, *Vice Pres*
Frank Leone, *Vice Pres*
Ed Moore, *Warehouse Mgr*
EMP: 4 EST: 2010
SALES (est): 1.6MM
SALES (corp-wide): 1.4MM **Privately Held**
SIC: 7373 3577 5734 Value-added resellers, computer systems; computer peripheral equipment; computer software & accessories
PA: Cdi Computer Dealers Inc
  130 South Town Centre Blvd
  Markham ON L6G 1
  905 946-1119

(G-4049)
CDI CORP
3440 N Knox Ave (60641-3744)
PHONE..................773 205-2960
Robert Tucker, *CEO*
Joe Nardi, *General Mgr*
Joe Karsznia, *Opers Staff*
Megan Sweeney, *Natl Sales Mgr*
▲ EMP: 40
SQ FT: 5,700
SALES: 647K **Privately Held**
SIC: 2752 Decals, lithographed

(G-4050)
CEDAR CONCEPTS CORPORATION
4100 S Packers Ave (60609-2425)
PHONE..................773 890-5790
Linda McGill Boasmond, *President*
▲ EMP: 31
SQ FT: 60,000
SALES (est): 15MM **Privately Held**
SIC: 2869 5169 2841 2843 Industrial organic chemicals; chemicals & allied products; soap & other detergents; surface active agents; toilet preparations

(G-4051)
CEDAR ELEC HOLDINGS CORP (PA)
6500 W Cortland St (60707-4013)
PHONE..................630 862-7282
Christopher Cowger, *CEO*
Mark Karnes, *Vice Pres*
Jonas Forsberg, *Ch Credit Ofcr*
Joy Hong, *Sales Staff*

Chicago - Cook County (G-4052)   GEOGRAPHIC SECTION

Antonio Martinez, *Marketing Staff*
EMP: 2
SALES (est): 125.3MM **Privately Held**
SIC: 3812 5088 Navigational systems & instruments; navigation equipment & supplies

(G-4052)
CEDILLE CHICAGO NFP
Also Called: CEDILLE RECORDS
1205 W Balmoral Ave (60640-1308)
PHONE..................773 989-2515
James Ginsburg, *President*
Bill Flowers, *Business Mgr*
Madeleine Richter, *Mktg Coord*
Julia Corry, *Manager*
Julie Polanski, *Director*
EMP: 4 **EST:** 1989
SQ FT: 1,750
SALES: 1.3MM **Privately Held**
WEB: www.cedillerecords.org
SIC: 3652 Compact laser discs, prerecorded

(G-4053)
CELLAS CONFECTIONS INC (HQ)
7401 S Cicero Ave (60629-5818)
PHONE..................773 838-3400
Ellen Gordon, *President*
Melvin J Gordon, *Vice Pres*
EMP: 65
SALES (est): 8.3MM
SALES (corp-wide): 527.1MM **Publicly Held**
SIC: 2064 Candy & other confectionery products
PA: Tootsie Roll Industries, Inc.
7401 S Cicero Ave
Chicago IL 60629
773 838-3400

(G-4054)
CEMEX CEMENT INC
12101 S Doty Ave (60633-2322)
PHONE..................773 995-5100
Larry Woodward, *Branch Mgr*
EMP: 5 **Privately Held**
SIC: 3273 Ready-mixed concrete
HQ: Cemex Cement, Inc.
10100 Katy Fwy Ste 300
Houston TX 77043
713 650-6200

(G-4055)
CENTER-111 W BURNHAM WASH LLC
111 W Washington St # 1017 (60602-2703)
PHONE..................312 368-5320
Fax: 312 807-4948
EMP: 22
SQ FT: 600,000
SALES (est): 3.9MM **Privately Held**
SIC: 2531 Mfg Public Building Furniture

(G-4056)
CENTRAL CAN COMPANY INC
3200 S Kilbourn Ave (60623-4829)
PHONE..................773 254-8700
Kenneth Roessler, *President*
▲ **EMP:** 180 **EST:** 1925
SQ FT: 300,000
SALES (est): 20.1MM
SALES (corp-wide): 1.2B **Privately Held**
WEB: www.centralcancompany.com
SIC: 3411 3412 Metal cans; metal barrels, drums & pails
HQ: Bway Corporation
375 Northridge Rd Ste 600
Atlanta GA 30350

(G-4057)
CENTRAL MOLDED PRODUCTS LLC
1978 N Lockwood Ave (60639-3020)
P.O. Box 1437, Deerfield (60015-6007)
PHONE..................773 622-4000
Robert G Garritano,
Thomas Garritano,
EMP: 17
SQ FT: 15,000
SALES (est): 2.4MM **Privately Held**
SIC: 3089 Injection molded finished plastic products; injection molding of plastics

(G-4058)
CENTRIC MFG SOLUTIONS INC
875 N Michigan Ave # 3614 (60611-1803)
PHONE..................815 315-9258
Mario Perez, *President*
Rebecca Perez, *Vice Pres*
EMP: 7
SALES (est): 810.8K **Privately Held**
SIC: 3542 Machine tools, metal forming type

(G-4059)
CENTURY ALUMINUM COMPANY (PA)
1 S Wacker Dr Ste 1000 (60606-4616)
PHONE..................312 696-3101
Michael A Bless, *President*
Jesse E Gary, *COO*
John E Hoerner, *Vice Pres*
Rick T Dillon, *CFO*
Michelle M Harrison, *Treasurer*
▲ **EMP:** 122
SALES: 1.8B **Publicly Held**
SIC: 3354 Aluminum extruded products

(G-4060)
CENTURY FILTER PRODUCTS INC
2939 N Oakley Ave (60618-8029)
PHONE..................773 477-1790
Victor La Porta, *President*
George Koltse, *Vice Pres*
EMP: 5
SQ FT: 5,000
SALES (est): 853.2K **Privately Held**
SIC: 3569 5084 Filters, general line: industrial; industrial machinery & equipment

(G-4061)
CENTURY MALLET INSTR SVC LLC
1770 W Berteau Ave # 204 (60613-1849)
PHONE..................773 248-7733
Andres Bautista, *Mng Member*
EMP: 3
SQ FT: 5,000
SALES (est): 220K **Privately Held**
SIC: 7699 3931 Piano tuning & repair; bells (musical instruments); chimes & parts (musical instruments)

(G-4062)
CENTURY SPRING CORPORATION
4045 W Thorndale Ave (60646-6011)
PHONE..................800 237-5225
James Frelka, *Principal*
EMP: 2 **EST:** 2008
SALES (est): 247.6K **Privately Held**
WEB: www.centuryspring.com
SIC: 5051 3495 Metals service centers & offices; wire springs

(G-4063)
CENVEO WORLDWIDE LIMITED
3001 N Rockwell St (60618-7917)
PHONE..................636 240-5817
Craig Condry, *Vice Pres*
Gene Hanyzewski, *Controller*
Deval Shah, *Accountant*
Frank Ball, *Branch Mgr*
Shanna Zakson, *Manager*
EMP: 81
SALES (corp-wide): 2.9B **Privately Held**
WEB: www.cenveo.com
SIC: 2752 Commercial printing, offset
HQ: Cenveo Worldwide Limited
200 First Stamford Pl # 2
Stamford CT 06902
203 595-3000

(G-4064)
CERAGEM 26TH ST
3948 W 26th St Ste 207 (60623-3741)
PHONE..................773 277-0672
Esusim Heonseoung, *President*
EMP: 3
SALES (est): 150K **Privately Held**
SIC: 7299 2515 Massage parlor & steam bath services; sleep furniture

(G-4065)
CERTIFIED BUSINESS FORMS INC
5732 W Patterson Ave (60634-2620)
PHONE..................773 286-8194
Charles J Schneider, *President*
Charles J Scheider, *Treasurer*
EMP: 3
SQ FT: 600
SALES (est): 300K **Privately Held**
SIC: 5112 2761 Business forms; manifold business forms

(G-4066)
CGC CORPORATION
7401 S Cicero Ave (60629-5818)
PHONE..................773 838-3400
EMP: 65 **EST:** 2014
SALES (est): 200.5K
SALES (corp-wide): 527.1MM **Publicly Held**
SIC: 2064 Breakfast bars
HQ: Cella's Confections Inc
7401 S Cicero Ave
Chicago IL 60629
773 838-3400

(G-4067)
CHALLENGE PRINTERS
4354 W Armitage Ave (60639-3507)
PHONE..................773 252-0212
Taide Villasenor, *Owner*
EMP: 5
SALES (est): 300K **Privately Held**
SIC: 2752 2791 2789 2759 Commercial printing, offset; typesetting; bookbinding & related work; commercial printing

(G-4068)
CHAMBERS GASKET & MFG CO
4701 W Rice St (60651-3377)
PHONE..................773 626-8800
Heide Kenny, *President*
Alicia Avitia, *Purch Agent*
Peter Madler, *Sales Mgr*
Ronald Owens, *Sales Staff*
Mack Calcote, *Manager*
EMP: 40
SQ FT: 65,000
SALES (est): 10.1MM **Privately Held**
WEB: www.chambersgasket.com
SIC: 3053 Gaskets, all materials

(G-4069)
CHANNELED RESOURCES INC (PA)
Also Called: C. R. G.
240 N Ashland Ave Ste 130 (60607-1423)
PHONE..................312 733-4200
Calvin S Frost Jr, *Ch of Bd*
Cynthia White, *President*
Paula Russell, *Vice Pres*
Teresa Bafia, *Accountant*
Sandy Briolat, *Accounts Mgr*
◆ **EMP:** 20
SQ FT: 5,000
SALES: 28MM **Privately Held**
SIC: 2672 Chemically treated papers: made from purchased materials; coated paper, except photographic, carbon or abrasive

(G-4070)
CHAOS AI ART LLC
410 N Paulina St (60622-6317)
PHONE..................847 274-9158
Mike Mages,
EMP: 4
SALES (est): 116.1K **Privately Held**
SIC: 2077 Rendering

(G-4071)
CHAR CRUST CO INC
3017 N Lincoln Ave (60657-4242)
PHONE..................773 528-0600
Bernard Silver, *President*
Susan Eriksen, *Vice Pres*
EMP: 3
SQ FT: 5,000
SALES (est): 414.4K **Privately Held**
WEB: www.charcrust.com
SIC: 2099 Seasonings: dry mixes

(G-4072)
CHARLES AUTIN LIMITED
Also Called: Kwok's Food Service
1801 S Canal St (60616-1522)
PHONE..................312 432-0888
Charlie Chun, *President*
EMP: 80
SQ FT: 16,500
SALES (est): 38MM **Privately Held**
SIC: 2013 5147 2015 Prepared beef products from purchased beef; prepared pork products from purchased pork; meats & meat products; chicken slaughtering & processing

(G-4073)
CHARLES CICERO FINGERHUT (PA)
Also Called: Charles Fingerhut Bakeries
5537 W Cermak Rd (60804-2218)
PHONE..................708 652-3643
Herbert Fingerhut Sr, *President*
Francis Fingerhut, *Treasurer*
EMP: 14
SQ FT: 7,500
SALES (est): 1.3MM **Privately Held**
SIC: 2051 Bread, all types (white, wheat, rye, etc): fresh or frozen

(G-4074)
CHARLES HORBERG JEWELERS INC
5 S Wabash Ave Ste 706 (60603-3197)
PHONE..................312 263-4924
Charles Horberg, *President*
Sandra Horberg, *Treasurer*
EMP: 3
SQ FT: 800
SALES (est): 560.6K **Privately Held**
WEB: www.charleshorbergjewelers.com
SIC: 5094 5944 3911 Jewelry; jewelry, precious stones & precious metals; jewelry, precious metal

(G-4075)
CHARLES N BENNER INC
Also Called: Bcs Industries
401 N Western Ave Ste 4 (60612-1418)
PHONE..................312 829-4300
Brian Benner, *President*
Gail Benner, *Corp Secy*
▲ **EMP:** 25
SQ FT: 40,000
SALES (est): 2.3MM **Privately Held**
SIC: 2434 Wood kitchen cabinets

(G-4076)
CHARLOTTE LOUISE TATE
Also Called: Mickhali Local Distributors
1304 E 87th St (60619-7025)
PHONE..................773 849-3236
Charlotte Tate, *Owner*
Michael Harris, *Administration*
EMP: 3
SALES (est): 115.2K **Privately Held**
SIC: 3694 Ignition apparatus & distributors

(G-4077)
CHARTWELL STUDIO INC
320 W Ohio St Ste 3w (60654-7887)
PHONE..................847 868-8674
Jeanette McCallum, *President*
EMP: 2
SALES: 8MM **Privately Held**
SIC: 2621 2782 5092 Wallpaper (hanging paper); scrapbooks; arts & crafts equipment & supplies

(G-4078)
CHASE SECURITY SYSTEMS INC
5947 N Milwaukee Ave (60646-5419)
P.O. Box 30179 (60630-0179)
PHONE..................773 594-1919
Charles Villanueva, *CEO*
EMP: 5
SALES (est): 550K **Privately Held**
WEB: www.chasesec.com
SIC: 3699 8742 3446 3357 Security control equipment & systems; marketing consulting services; architectural metalwork; nonferrous wiredrawing & insulating

GEOGRAPHIC SECTION

Chicago - Cook County (G-4108)

(G-4079)
CHATEAU FOOD PRODUCTS INC
6137 W Cermak Rd (60804-2024)
PHONE.................................708 863-4207
Donald L Shotola, *President*
M Anita Shotola, *Corp Secy*
EMP: 10 **EST:** 1927
SQ FT: 4,000
SALES (est): 944.6K **Privately Held**
WEB: www.chateaufoods.com
SIC: 2051 2099 2038 Bread, cake & related products; food preparations; frozen specialties

(G-4080)
CHEAP DUMPSTER FOR RENT
1210 W Granville Ave # 200 (60660-1900)
PHONE.................................773 770-4334
EMP: 3
SALES (est): 148.6K **Privately Held**
SIC: 3443 Dumpsters, garbage

(G-4081)
CHEETAH DIGITAL INC (HQ)
72 W Adams St Fl 8 (60603-5107)
PHONE.................................312 858-8200
Sameer Kazi, *CEO*
Sharon Forder, *Vice Pres*
Ryan Hooper, *Vice Pres*
Fenton Johnson, *Manager*
Rick Gallagher, *Director*
EMP: 98
SALES (est): 40MM
SALES (corp-wide): 488.3MM **Privately Held**
SIC: 8742 7372 Marketing consulting services; application computer software
PA: Vector Capital Management, L.P.
1 Market St Ste 2300
San Francisco CA 94105
415 293-5000

(G-4082)
CHEMTRADE LOGISTICS (US) INC
2250 E 130th St (60633-2306)
PHONE.................................704 369-2496
Mark Davis, *President*
EMP: 4
SALES (corp-wide): 1.1B **Privately Held**
SIC: 2819 Industrial inorganic chemicals
HQ: Chemtrade Logistics (Us), Inc.
814 Tyvola Rd Ste 126
Charlotte NC 28217
704 369-2496

(G-4083)
CHERRY MEAT PACKERS INC
Also Called: Chicago Meat, The
4750 S California Ave (60632-2016)
PHONE.................................773 927-1200
Robert Vicino, *Vice Pres*
Keith Pozulp, *Vice Pres*
EMP: 48 **EST:** 1912
SQ FT: 47,000
SALES (est): 6.9MM **Privately Held**
SIC: 2013 2011 Sausages from purchased meat; cured meats from purchased meat; luncheon meat from purchased meat; meat packing plants

(G-4084)
CHEWY SOFTWARE LLC
507 W Aldine Ave Apt 1b (60657-3758)
PHONE.................................773 935-2627
Sherri A Wandler, *Principal*
EMP: 2
SALES (est): 212.1K **Privately Held**
SIC: 7372 Application computer software

(G-4085)
CHI-TOWN PRINTING INC
6025 N Cicero Ave (60646-4301)
PHONE.................................773 577-2500
Thomas P Stapka, *Principal*
EMP: 5
SALES (est): 290.2K **Privately Held**
SIC: 2752 Commercial printing, offset

(G-4086)
CHICAGO AGENT MAGAZINE
2000 N Racine Ave (60614-4045)
PHONE.................................773 296-6001
Marry Sepulveda, *CEO*
Michael Dennis, *Marketing Staff*
EMP: 7
SALES (est): 876.9K **Privately Held**
SIC: 2721 Magazines: publishing only, not printed on site

(G-4087)
CHICAGO ALUM CASTINGS CO INC
205 W Wacker Dr Ste 1818 (60606-1429)
PHONE.................................773 762-3009
Richard A Wagner, *President*
Richard Gurrieri, *Vice Pres*
Derek Horton, *Vice Pres*
EMP: 4 **EST:** 1910
SQ FT: 14,000
SALES (est): 479.4K **Privately Held**
SIC: 3366 Copper foundries

(G-4088)
CHICAGO AMERICAN MFG LLC
4500 W 47th St (60632-4450)
PHONE.................................773 376-0100
Terry Morgan, *Design Engr*
Mark A Herman, *Mng Member*
▲ **EMP:** 200
SQ FT: 27,500
SALES (est): 49.9MM **Privately Held**
SIC: 2514 2542 2531 Metal household furniture; partitions & fixtures, except wood; public building & related furniture

(G-4089)
CHICAGO AND SUBURBS
3325 N Nottingham Ave (60634-3612)
PHONE.................................773 306-3787
EMP: 3 **EST:** 2016
SALES (est): 99.1K **Privately Held**
SIC: 2721 Magazines: publishing only, not printed on site

(G-4090)
CHICAGO ANODIZING COMPANY
4112 W Lake St (60624-1792)
PHONE.................................773 533-3737
Norman Americus, *President*
Victor Orihuelav, *Plant Mgr*
Bill Petrow, *Purchasing*
Fanny Calderon, *Office Mgr*
Olga Calderon, *Program Mgr*
EMP: 65 **EST:** 1948
SQ FT: 30,000
SALES (est): 9.9MM **Privately Held**
WEB: www.chicagoanodizing.com
SIC: 3471 Electroplating of metals or formed products

(G-4091)
CHICAGO ART CENTER CO
6540 N Washtenaw Ave (60645-5308)
PHONE.................................773 817-2725
Plamen Iordanov, *President*
EMP: 4
SALES (est): 193.6K **Privately Held**
SIC: 3999 Manufacturing industries

(G-4092)
CHICAGO BOATING PUBLICATIONS
Also Called: Great Lakes Boating Magazine
851 N La Salle Dr (60610-3276)
PHONE.................................312 266-8400
Ned Dikman, *President*
Tom Janus, *Treasurer*
Karen Malonis, *Admin Sec*
EMP: 9
SQ FT: 1,000
SALES (est): 1.2MM **Privately Held**
SIC: 2721 Magazines: publishing only, not printed on site

(G-4093)
CHICAGO BOOTH MFG INC
5000 W Roosevelt Rd # 202 (60644-1474)
PHONE.................................773 378-8400
David Bochniak, *President*
Ed Salutric, *Engineer*
Joe Wilkinson, *Manager*
Intan Chen, *Director*
Alex Decamp, *Associate Dir*
EMP: 10 **EST:** 1981
SQ FT: 25,000
SALES (est): 1.8MM **Privately Held**
SIC: 2599 2541 2531 2511 Restaurant furniture, wood or metal; bar furniture; stools, factory; wood partitions & fixtures; public building & related furniture; wood household furniture

(G-4094)
CHICAGO CANDLE COMPANY
Also Called: Holy Hill Gourmet
2701 N Sayre Ave (60707-1712)
PHONE.................................773 637-5279
Rose Marrie, *Principal*
EMP: 3
SALES (est): 192.9K **Privately Held**
SIC: 5199 3999 Candles; candles

(G-4095)
CHICAGO CAR SEAL COMPANY
594 Brookside Rd (60612)
PHONE.................................773 278-9400
Dorothea Nyman, *Corp Secy*
▲ **EMP:** 7 **EST:** 1892
SQ FT: 12,000
SALES (est): 1MM **Privately Held**
SIC: 3469 3496 3429 3357 Metal stampings; miscellaneous fabricated wire products; manufactured hardware (general); nonferrous wiredrawing & insulating

(G-4096)
CHICAGO CITIZEN NEWSPPR GROUP (PA)
Also Called: Chicago Weekend
806 E 78th St (60619-2937)
PHONE.................................773 783-1251
William Garth, *CEO*
EMP: 12
SQ FT: 2,000
SALES (est): 3MM **Privately Held**
SIC: 2711 2791 Newspapers, publishing & printing; typesetting

(G-4097)
CHICAGO COML & CONSMR BRANDS
501 W 82nd St (60620-1743)
PHONE.................................773 484-5771
EMP: 3
SALES (est): 175.8K **Privately Held**
SIC: 2099 Food preparations

(G-4098)
CHICAGO COML CONSMR BRANDS LLC
Also Called: CCC Brands
7437 S Vincennes Ave (60621-3437)
PHONE.................................773 488-2639
Thomas A Traficano, *Mng Member*
EMP: 2
SQ FT: 2,100
SALES (est): 297.7K **Privately Held**
SIC: 2099 Spices, including grinding; desserts, ready-to-mix; seasonings: dry mixes

(G-4099)
CHICAGO CRUSADER NEWS GROUP (PA)
6429 S King Dr (60637-3116)
PHONE.................................773 752-2500
Dorothy R Leavell, *President*
John Smith, *Vice Pres*
EMP: 5
SQ FT: 1,500
SALES (est): 350K **Privately Held**
WEB: www.chicagocrusader.com
SIC: 2711 Newspapers: publishing only, not printed on site

(G-4100)
CHICAGO DROPCLOTH TARPAULIN CO
3719 W Lawrence Ave (60625-5712)
PHONE.................................773 588-3123
Cheryl Warren, *President*
Karen Mangurten, *Vice Pres*
EMP: 20 **EST:** 1948
SQ FT: 12,750
SALES (est): 3.2MM **Privately Held**
WEB: www.chicagodropcloth.com
SIC: 2394 Cloth, drop (fabric): made from purchased materials; tarpaulins, fabric: made from purchased materials

(G-4101)
CHICAGO DRYER COMPANY
2200 N Pulaski Rd (60639-3737)
PHONE.................................773 235-4430
Bruce W Johnson, *President*
Diane Dickow, *Publisher*
Bob Keller, *Opers Staff*
Casey Faust, *Human Resources*
Tom Egebrecht, *Sales Staff*
◆ **EMP:** 125 **EST:** 1896
SQ FT: 55,000
SALES (est): 31.7MM **Privately Held**
WEB: www.chidry.com
SIC: 3582 5087 Commercial laundry equipment; laundry equipment & supplies

(G-4102)
CHICAGO EXPORT PACKING CO
1501 W 38th St (60609-2117)
P.O. Box 1349, Deerfield (60015-6005)
PHONE.................................773 247-8911
James Nashan, *President*
Mike Costantini, *General Mgr*
Ruben Meraz, *Engineer*
Lindsey Nashan, *Mktg Coord*
EMP: 40
SQ FT: 78,000
SALES (est): 5.4MM **Privately Held**
SIC: 4225 4783 2441 General warehousing; packing goods for shipping; crating goods for shipping; nailed wood boxes & shook

(G-4103)
CHICAGO FILM ARCHIVE NFP
5746 N Drake Ave (60659-4402)
PHONE.................................773 478-3799
Nancy Watrous, *President*
EMP: 3
SALES: 225.6K **Privately Held**
SIC: 3861 Motion picture film

(G-4104)
CHICAGO FLYHOUSE INCORPORATED
2925 W Carroll Ave (60612-1719)
PHONE.................................773 533-1590
Mark Witteveen, *President*
Brendan Bernacki, *Project Mgr*
Matthew Braddock, *Project Mgr*
David Millard, *Project Mgr*
Brent Miller, *Project Mgr*
▲ **EMP:** 10
SALES (est): 3.6MM **Privately Held**
WEB: www.flyhouse.com
SIC: 1796 3731 Machine moving & rigging; marine rigging

(G-4105)
CHICAGO GROUP ACQUISITION LLC
350 N Orleans St Fl 10-S (60654-1975)
PHONE.................................312 755-0720
EMP: 3
SALES (est): 135.7K **Privately Held**
SIC: 2711 Newspapers-Publishing/Printing

(G-4106)
CHICAGO HONEYMOONERS LLC
3341 W Sunnyside Ave # 2 (60625-5425)
PHONE.................................312 399-5699
Harlan Wayne Fails,
Rebekah Fails,
EMP: 2
SALES: 500K **Privately Held**
SIC: 2511 Wood household furniture

(G-4107)
CHICAGO I AND D SERVICES INC
5600 S Melvina Ave (60638-3506)
PHONE.................................312 623-8071
Frieda Steffens, *Principal*
EMP: 3
SALES (est): 209.2K **Privately Held**
SIC: 3993 Signs & advertising specialties

(G-4108)
CHICAGO IRON WORKS CORPORATION (PA)
439 N Western Ave (60612-1419)
PHONE.................................312 829-1062
Frank Galasso, *President*

Chicago - Cook County (G-4109)

EMP: 14
SQ FT: 8,000
SALES (est): 770K Privately Held
WEB: www.chicagoironworksinc.com
SIC: 3446 3442 Stairs, staircases, stair treads: prefabricated metal; fire escapes, metal; balconies, metal; fences, gates, posts & flagpoles; metal doors, sash & trim

(G-4109)
CHICAGO LAB PRODUCTS
660 N Union Ave (60654-5526)
PHONE..................................312 942-0730
Bob Carjos, *Principal*
EMP: 4
SALES (est): 327.1K Privately Held
SIC: 3821 Laboratory equipment: fume hoods, distillation racks, etc.

(G-4110)
CHICAGO LIGHTHOUSE INDUSTRIES
1850 W Roosevelt Rd Ste 1 (60608-1247)
PHONE..................................312 666-1331
Janet Szlyk, *CEO*
Michael Meehan, *Ch of Bd*
Marvin Lader, *Vice Chairman*
Mary Lynne Januszewski, *CFO*
Ted Mazola, *Treasurer*
EMP: 65
SALES: 2MM Privately Held
SIC: 3873 Watches, clocks, watchcases & parts

(G-4111)
CHICAGO LOCAL FOODS LLC
1427 W Willow St (60642-1525)
PHONE..................................312 432-6575
Andrew Lutsey, *CEO*
Dave Rand, *COO*
Murphy Jim, *Manager*
Lutsey Andrew, *Manager*
Julie Martin,
EMP: 37
SALES (est): 6.5MM Privately Held
SIC: 5141 2013 Food brokers; boneless meat, from purchased meat

(G-4112)
CHICAGO MAILING TUBE COMPANY
400 N Leavitt St (60612-1618)
PHONE..................................312 243-6050
Kenneth R Barmore, *President*
Keith Shimon, *President*
Jose Macias, *Sales Staff*
▲ EMP: 40
SQ FT: 90,000
SALES (est): 11.2MM Privately Held
WEB: www.mailing-tube.com
SIC: 2655 Tubes, fiber or paper: made from purchased material; cores, fiber: made from purchased material; fiber cans, drums & containers

(G-4113)
CHICAGO MEAT AUTHORITY INC
1120 W 47th Pl (60609-4302)
PHONE..................................773 254-3811
Jordan Dorfman, *President*
Patricia Almanza, *Human Res Mgr*
Bartek Woroniecki, *Marketing Staff*
Dennis Myrda, *Manager*
Wayne Bartosiak, *Info Tech Mgr*
EMP: 330
SQ FT: 50,000
SALES (est): 118MM Privately Held
SIC: 2011 Meat packing plants

(G-4114)
CHICAGO METAL FABRICATORS INC
3724 S Rockwell St Ste 1 (60632-1051)
PHONE..................................773 523-5755
Randy Hauser, *President*
John Nalbach, *President*
Randal Hauser, *General Mgr*
Alice Cook, *Vice Pres*
Kevin Condon, *Opers Mgr*
EMP: 80 EST: 1923
SQ FT: 200,000
SALES (est): 26.5MM Privately Held
WEB: www.chicagometal.com
SIC: 3469 5084 3498 3441 Metal stampings; industrial machinery & equipment; fabricated pipe & fittings; fabricated structural metal; blast furnaces & steel mills

(G-4115)
CHICAGO METAL ROLLED PDTS CO (PA)
3715 S Rockwell St (60632-1030)
PHONE..................................773 523-5757
Joseph Wendt, *President*
George F Wendt, *President*
Elise Spadavecchio, *Opers Staff*
Ken Pecho, *Project Engr*
Raymond Reitz, *Treasurer*
◆ EMP: 66
SQ FT: 100,000
SALES (est): 22MM Privately Held
SIC: 3444 3446 3498 3449 Sheet metalwork; architectural metalwork; fabricated pipe & fittings; miscellaneous metalwork; fabricated structural metal

(G-4116)
CHICAGO METAL SUPPLY INC
4930 W Grand Ave (60639-4413)
PHONE..................................773 417-7439
Ski Wysocki, *President*
▲ EMP: 3
SALES (est): 552.9K Privately Held
WEB: www.chicagometalsupply.com
SIC: 3444 Sheet metalwork

(G-4117)
CHICAGO MIDWAY AIRPORT
5700 S Cicero Ave Ste 57 (60638-3843)
PHONE..................................773 838-0600
Erin Odonnell, *Manager*
EMP: 3
SALES (est): 194.5K Privately Held
SIC: 3728 7832 Aircraft landing assemblies & brakes; exhibitors for airlines, motion picture

(G-4118)
CHICAGO MOLDING OUTLET
5858 S Kedzie Ave Ste 1 (60629-3242)
PHONE..................................773 471-6870
Nivene Judeh, *President*
EMP: 4
SALES (est): 431.5K Privately Held
SIC: 3089 Molding primary plastic

(G-4119)
CHICAGO MTAL SUP FBRCATION INC
4940 W Grand Ave (60639-4413)
PHONE..................................773 227-6200
Bogdan Bosak, *President*
Rossi Clark, *Manager*
EMP: 14
SALES (est): 3MM Privately Held
SIC: 3444 Downspouts, sheet metal

(G-4120)
CHICAGO ORIENTAL CNSTR INC
Also Called: Chicago Oriental Wholesale Mkt
1835 S Canal St 2f (60616-1522)
PHONE..................................312 733-9633
Anna Fang, *Principal*
EMP: 4
SALES (est): 238.9K Privately Held
SIC: 2099 Sandwiches, assembled & packaged: for wholesale market

(G-4121)
CHICAGO ORNAMENTAL IRON INC
Also Called: Coi Company
1237 51 W 47th St (60609)
PHONE..................................773 321-9635
Jonathan Samek, *President*
Munish Mehta, *COO*
EMP: 46
SQ FT: 30,000
SALES (est): 13.8MM Privately Held
SIC: 3446 1791 3449 Architectural metalwork; stairs, fire escapes, balconies, railings & ladders; balconies, metal; bannisters, made from metal pipe; structural steel erection; iron work, structural; curtain wall, metal

(G-4122)
CHICAGO PIPE BENDING & COIL CO
4535 W Lake St (60624-1685)
PHONE..................................773 379-1918
Phillis E Melton, *Ch of Bd*
Michael Melton, *President*
Michael M Melton, *Manager*
Robert Melton, *Admin Sec*
EMP: 12
SQ FT: 13,000
SALES (est): 5MM Privately Held
SIC: 5051 3498 3494 3312 Pipe & tubing, steel; pipe fittings, fabricated from purchased pipe; valves & pipe fittings; blast furnaces & steel mills

(G-4123)
CHICAGO PIXELS SRC
3600 W Sunnyside Ave 1 (60625-5924)
PHONE..................................312 513-7949
Gregory Tarczynski, *CEO*
EMP: 3
SALES (est): 158.8K Privately Held
SIC: 3674 Semiconductors & related devices

(G-4124)
CHICAGO PREMIER MEATS INC
822 W Exchange Ave (60609-2507)
P.O. Box 9083 (60609-0601)
PHONE..................................773 847-5400
James J Broad, *President*
John S Bubuca, *Admin Sec*
EMP: 4
SALES (est): 320.2K Privately Held
SIC: 2011 Meat packing plants

(G-4125)
CHICAGO PRINTERS GUILD
1009 N Mozart St 2 (60622-2758)
P.O. Box 221282 (60622-0029)
PHONE..................................303 819-6197
Alexandra Blom, *President*
Robert Sims, *Vice Pres*
Rachelle Hill, *Treasurer*
EMP: 4
SALES (est): 216.2K Privately Held
SIC: 2752 Commercial printing, lithographic

(G-4126)
CHICAGO REVIEW PRESS INC (PA)
Also Called: Independent Publishers Group
814 N Franklin St Ste 100 (60610-3813)
PHONE..................................312 337-0747
Curtis Matthews Jr, *CEO*
Mark Suchomel, *President*
Cynthia Sherry, *Publisher*
Devon Freeny, *Editor*
Michelle Williams, *Editor*
▲ EMP: 43
SQ FT: 6,000
SALES (est): 70.3MM Privately Held
SIC: 5192 2731 Books; books: publishing only

(G-4127)
CHICAGO SCENIC STUDIOS INC
955 W Cermak Rd (60608-4518)
PHONE..................................312 274-9900
Blasko Ristic, *President*
Brian Morgan, *Project Mgr*
Scott Sondergaard, *Marketing Staff*
Dan Clodfelter, *Sr Project Mgr*
Ross Hamilton, *Sr Project Mgr*
EMP: 75
SQ FT: 140,000
SALES (est): 10.4MM Privately Held
SIC: 3999 3993 Theatrical scenery; signs & advertising specialties

(G-4128)
CHICAGO SCHOOL WOODWORKING LLC
5680 N Northwest Hwy (60646-6136)
PHONE..................................773 275-1170
Shaun Devine, *Principal*
EMP: 4
SALES (est): 402.6K Privately Held
SIC: 2431 Millwork

(G-4129)
CHICAGO SILK SCREEN SUP CO INC
882 N Milwaukee Ave (60642-4195)
PHONE..................................312 666-1213
Frank Zigmond, *President*
EMP: 20 EST: 1956
SQ FT: 14,000
SALES (est): 3.1MM Privately Held
WEB: www.chicagosilkscreen.net
SIC: 3953 5085 Stencils, painting & marking; textile printers' supplies

(G-4130)
CHICAGO STEEL INC
875 N Michigan Ave Fl 31 (60611-1962)
PHONE..................................800 344-3032
Brian Steigerwald, *President*
EMP: 34
SALES: 3.2MM Privately Held
SIC: 1542 3448 1791 1751 Design & erection, combined: non-residential; prefabricated metal buildings; structural steel erection; carpentry work; operative builders; bridge, tunnel & elevated highway

(G-4131)
CHICAGO SUN-TIMES FEATURES INC (DH)
350 N Orleans St Fl 10 (60654-1975)
PHONE..................................312 321-3000
Tim Knight, *CEO*
David Radler, *President*
EMP: 1300
SQ FT: 500,000
SALES (est): 54.6MM
SALES (corp-wide): 4.3MM Privately Held
SIC: 2711 2752 Newspapers, publishing & printing; commercial printing, lithographic
HQ: Cnlc-Stc, Inc.
    350 N Orleans St
    Chicago IL 60654
    312 321-3000

(G-4132)
CHICAGO TEMPERED GLASS INC
2945 N Mozart St (60618-7701)
PHONE..................................773 583-2300
Adam Kaczynski, *President*
Kathy Rizzo, *Vice Pres*
Slaw Weobel, *Sales Staff*
▲ EMP: 13
SALES (est): 1.7MM Privately Held
SIC: 3211 Building glass, flat

(G-4133)
CHICAGO TRIBUNE COMPANY
Also Called: Tribune Freedom Center
777 W Chicago Ave (60654-2850)
PHONE..................................312 222-3232
Dick Malone, *General Mgr*
EMP: 3
SALES (corp-wide): 983.1MM Publicly Held
SIC: 2711 Newspapers, publishing & printing
HQ: Chicago Tribune Company, Llc
    160 N Stetson Ave
    Chicago IL 60601
    312 222-3232

(G-4134)
CHICAGO TRIBUNE COMPANY LLC (HQ)
160 N Stetson Ave (60601-6725)
PHONE..................................312 222-3232
David Hiller, *President*
Brian Gilligan, *President*
Kyle Betts, *Editor*
Jeff Cercone, *Editor*
Jordan Dziura, *Editor*
▲ EMP: 2700
SALES (est): 721.7MM
SALES (corp-wide): 983.1MM Publicly Held
WEB: www.chicagotribune.com
SIC: 2711 7383 7389 7331 Newspapers, publishing & printing; news feature syndicate; switchboard operation, private branch exchanges; mailing service

GEOGRAPHIC SECTION

Chicago - Cook County (G-4162)

PA: Tribune Publishing Company
160 N Stetson Ave
Chicago IL 60601
312 222-9100

(G-4135)
CHICAGO TURNRITE CO INC
4459 W Lake St (60624-1636)
PHONE 773 626-8404
Ray Carlson, *CEO*
Raymond F Carlson, *Treasurer*
Laura George, *Office Mgr*
▼ **EMP:** 43 **EST:** 1948
SQ FT: 80,000
SALES (est): 9.4MM **Privately Held**
WEB: www.turnrite.com
SIC: 3599 Machine shop, jobbing & repair

(G-4136)
CHICAGO WEEKLY
1131 E 57th St (60637-1503)
PHONE 773 702-7718
EMP: 3
SALES (est): 132.4K **Privately Held**
SIC: 2711 Newspapers

(G-4137)
CHICAGONE DEVELOPERS INC
1350 E 75th St (60619-1447)
PHONE 773 783-2105
Darryl A Hicks, *President*
Conway Bennett, *Vice Pres*
EMP: 20
SALES (est): 2.5MM **Privately Held**
SIC: 3442 Shutters, door or window: metal; garage doors, overhead: metal

(G-4138)
CHICAGOS FINEST IRON WORKS
3319 W Washington Blvd (60624)
PHONE 773 646-4484
John Macon, *Owner*
EMP: 10
SALES (est): 386.9K **Privately Held**
SIC: 3446 Ornamental metalwork

(G-4139)
CHII CLOTHING COMPANY
Also Called: Culture Studio
1151 W 40th St (60609-2506)
PHONE 312 243-8304
Carlo Oviedo, *Vice Pres*
Joey Santo, *VP Prdtn*
Nick Santo, *Opers Staff*
Anthony Gentile, *Production*
Sridip Mukhopadhyaya, *VP Finance*
EMP: 20 **EST:** 2005
SALES (est): 1.9MM **Privately Held**
WEB: www.culturestudio.net
SIC: 2759 Screen printing

(G-4140)
CHINA JOURNAL INC
2146a S Archer Ave (60616-1514)
PHONE 312 326-3228
May Zheng, *President*
▲ **EMP:** 5
SALES (est): 398.7K **Privately Held**
SIC: 2711 Newspapers, publishing & printing

(G-4141)
CHINESE AMERICAN NEWS
610 W 31st St (60616-3023)
PHONE 312 225-5600
James Chang, *President*
EMP: 6
SQ FT: 2,000
SALES (est): 350K **Privately Held**
SIC: 2711 Newspapers, publishing & printing

(G-4142)
CHOI BRANDS INC
3401 W Division St (60651-2356)
PHONE 773 489-2800
Tony Choi, *President*
Sue Kang, *Vice Pres*
▲ **EMP:** 120
SQ FT: 90,000
SALES (est): 11.5MM **Privately Held**
SIC: 2326 2337 2329 2339 Work uniforms; work garments, except raincoats: waterproof; industrial garments, men's & boys'; uniforms, except athletic: women's, misses' & juniors'; men's & boys' sportswear & athletic clothing; uniforms, athletic: women's, misses' & juniors'; sewing contractor

(G-4143)
CHRIS DJ MIX LLC
1408 W Fillmore St (60607-4689)
PHONE 312 725-3838
Christopher Calip, *Principal*
EMP: 6 **EST:** 2012
SALES (est): 349.9K **Privately Held**
WEB: www.djchrismix.com
SIC: 3273 Ready-mixed concrete

(G-4144)
CHRISTIAN CENTURY
104 S Michigan Ave # 1100 (60603-5919)
PHONE 312 263-7510
Rev John M Buchanan, *President*
▲ **EMP:** 16
SALES (est): 2.7MM **Privately Held**
SIC: 2721 Magazines: publishing only, not printed on site

(G-4145)
CHROMIUM INDUSTRIES INC
4645 W Chicago Ave (60651-3385)
PHONE 773 287-3716
Peter J Heidengren, *President*
Keith Summers, *Manager*
▲ **EMP:** 40
SQ FT: 47,000
SALES (est): 5.4MM **Privately Held**
WEB: www.chromiumindustries.com
SIC: 3471 3312 2891 2851 Chromium plating of metals or formed products; blast furnaces & steel mills; adhesives & sealants; paints & allied products; inorganic pigments; platemaking services

(G-4146)
CHROMIUM INDUSTRIES LLC
4645 W Chicago Ave (60651-3385)
PHONE 773 287-3716
Michael Tannura, *Owner*
EMP: 20
SQ FT: 50,000
SALES (est): 549.2K **Privately Held**
SIC: 3471 Chromium plating of metals or formed products

(G-4147)
CHURCHILL WILMSLOW CORPORATION
Also Called: Signs Now
162 N Franklin St Ste 200 (60606-1861)
PHONE 312 759-8911
Linda George, *President*
EMP: 5
SQ FT: 40,000
SALES (est): 520K **Privately Held**
SIC: 3993 2759 Signs & advertising specialties; commercial printing

(G-4148)
CHURNY COMPANY INC
200 E Randolph St (60601-6436)
PHONE 847 646-5500
Georges El-Zoghbi, *President*
Kim K W Rucker, *Admin Sec*
▲ **EMP:** 473 **EST:** 1941
SQ FT: 7,500
SALES (est): 1MM
SALES (corp-wide): 24.9B **Publicly Held**
WEB: www.churnyfoodservice.com
SIC: 2022 Natural cheese; processed cheese
PA: The Kraft Heinz Company
1 Ppg Pl Fl 34
Pittsburgh PA 15222
412 456-5700

(G-4149)
CHWEY SOFTWARE LLC
4809 N Ravenswood Ave # 422 (60640-4495)
PHONE 773 525-6445
Pete Hallenberg, *Owner*
EMP: 20
SALES (est): 1.4MM **Privately Held**
WEB: www.chewysoft.com
SIC: 7372 Application computer software

(G-4150)
CICERONE CERTIFICATION PROGRAM
4043 N Ravenswood Ave # 306 (60613-1155)
PHONE 773 549-4800
Shana Solarte, *Editor*
Virginia Thomas, *Business Mgr*
Caleb Kim, *Business Mgr*
Pat Fahey, *Manager*
EMP: 6
SALES (est): 283.3K **Privately Held**
SIC: 2082 Beer (alcoholic beverage)

(G-4151)
CINTAS CORPORATION
Also Called: Pride Manufacturing
5600 W 73rd St (60638-6273)
PHONE 708 563-2626
Donnie Hicks, *General Mgr*
Christine Duffy, *Principal*
Robert Lugo, *Vice Pres*
Dorman Carney, *Project Mgr*
Shawn Jackson, *Project Mgr*
EMP: 70
SALES (corp-wide): 6.8B **Publicly Held**
WEB: www.cintas.com
SIC: 2337 2326 2339 Uniforms, except athletic: women's, misses' & juniors'; medical & hospital uniforms, men's; women's & misses' outerwear
PA: Cintas Corporation
6800 Cintas Blvd
Cincinnati OH 45262
513 459-1200

(G-4152)
CIRCLE STUDIO STAINED GLASS
3928 N Elston Ave (60618-4228)
PHONE 773 588-4848
Joseph Badalpour, *President*
George Badalpour, *Vice Pres*
Susan Wiltshire, *Manager*
EMP: 2
SQ FT: 3,000
SALES: 200K **Privately Held**
SIC: 8999 3471 3231 Artist; stained glass art; plating & polishing; products of purchased glass

(G-4153)
CISION LTD (HQ)
130 E Randolph St Fl 7 (60601-6164)
PHONE 866 639-5087
Kevin Akeroyd, *President*
EMP: 24
SQ FT: 46,000
SALES: 730.3MM **Privately Held**
SIC: 7372 8743 Prepackaged software; public relations services

(G-4154)
CISION US INC (DH)
130 E Randolph St Fl 7 (60601-6164)
PHONE 312 922-2400
Kevin Akeroyd, *CEO*
Jason Edelboim, *President*
Matt Henehan, *Business Mgr*
Max Jansons, *Business Mgr*
Andrea Mandarino, *Business Mgr*
EMP: 133 **EST:** 1892
SQ FT: 50,000
SALES (est): 255.5MM **Privately Held**
WEB: www.cision.com
SIC: 7389 2741 7331 Press clipping service; miscellaneous publishing; mailing service
HQ: Cision Ltd.
130 E Randolph St Fl 7
Chicago IL 60601
866 639-5087

(G-4155)
CITY FOODS INC
Also Called: Bea's Best
4230 S Racine Ave (60609-2526)
P.O. Box 9190 (60609-0190)
PHONE 773 523-1566
Kenneth Kohn, *President*
John Campbell, *Purch Mgr*
Jerry Kohn, *CFO*
Chris Humberg, *Info Tech Mgr*
▼ **EMP:** 110
SQ FT: 30,000
SALES: 38MM **Privately Held**
WEB: www.beasbest.com
SIC: 2011 Meat packing plants

(G-4156)
CITY LIVING DESIGN INC
401 E Ontario St Apt 1302 (60611-7169)
PHONE 312 335-0711
Hollis Favin, *President*
EMP: 3
SALES (est): 471K **Privately Held**
SIC: 7299 2211 2511 Banquet hall facilities; furniture denim; wood household furniture

(G-4157)
CITY OF CHICAGO
Also Called: Department Streets Sanitation
6441 N Ravenswood Ave # 49 (60626-3927)
PHONE 312 744-0940
William Nortkett, *Manager*
EMP: 20 **Privately Held**
SIC: 2842 9111 4953 Sanitation preparations; ; garbage: collecting, destroying & processing
PA: City Of Chicago
121 N La Salle St Rm 700
Chicago IL 60602
312 744-6558

(G-4158)
CITY OF CHICAGO
Also Called: 13th Ward Office
6500 S Pulaski Rd Ste 2 (60629-5150)
PHONE 773 581-8000
Frank Olivo, *Director*
EMP: 8 **Privately Held**
SIC: 9199 2731 General government administration; ; book publishing
PA: City Of Chicago
121 N La Salle St Rm 700
Chicago IL 60602
312 744-6558

(G-4159)
CITY OF CHICAGO
Also Called: Streets and Sanitation, Dept
4211 W Ferdinand St (60624)
PHONE 312 746-6583
Excell Brown, *Administration*
EMP: 20 **Privately Held**
SIC: 2842 Sanitation preparations, disinfectants & deodorants; sanitation preparations
PA: City Of Chicago
121 N La Salle St Rm 700
Chicago IL 60602
312 744-6558

(G-4160)
CITY PRESS JUICE & BOTTLE
2931 N Broadway St (60657-5301)
PHONE 773 360-7226
Angela Maicki, *Principal*
EMP: 3
SALES (est): 55K **Privately Held**
WEB: www.citypressjuice.com
SIC: 2741 Miscellaneous publishing

(G-4161)
CITY SCREEN INC (PA)
Also Called: Pengo Products Company
5540 N Kedzie Ave (60625-3924)
PHONE 773 588-5642
Gary Langwell, *President*
Diana Langwell, *Corp Secy*
EMP: 8 **EST:** 1941
SQ FT: 1,800
SALES (est): 1.2MM **Privately Held**
WEB: www.cityscreeninc.com
SIC: 3496 5063 3446 3444 Screening, woven wire: made from purchased wire; electrical apparatus & equipment; architectural metalwork; sheet metalwork; metal doors, sash & trim; millwork

(G-4162)
CITY SUBN AUTO SVC GOODYEAR
5674 N Northwest Hwy (60646-6136)
PHONE 773 355-5550
Soneal Asija, *President*

Chicago - Cook County (G-4163)

EMP: 4
SQ FT: 10,000
SALES: 360K **Privately Held**
SIC: 5531 5511 7549 3714 Automotive tires; automobiles, new & used; towing service, automotive; motor vehicle parts & accessories; truck rental & leasing, no drivers

(G-4163)
CITY WIDE PALLET
4045 S Wallace St (60609-2704)
PHONE 773 891-2561
EMP: 4
SALES (est): 260.6K **Privately Held**
SIC: 2448 Pallets, wood

(G-4164)
CITYZENITH LLC
Also Called: City Zenith
2506 N Clark St Ste 235 (60614-1848)
PHONE 312 883-5554
Michael Jansen, *Mng Member*
EMP: 12 **EST:** 2013
SQ FT: 200
SALES: 500K **Privately Held**
SIC: 7372 Application computer software

(G-4165)
CIVIQ SMARTSCAPES LLC
Also Called: Elevate Digital
200 S Michigan Ave # 1305 (60604-2402)
PHONE 312 300-4776
George Burciaga, *General Mgr*
Tony Filko, *CFO*
EMP: 8
SALES (corp-wide): 25MM **Privately Held**
SIC: 3429 7371 Manufactured hardware (general); software programming applications
PA: Civiq Smartscapes, Llc
430 Fortune Blvd
Milford MA 01757
508 381-2900

(G-4166)
CLARIANCE INC
4809 N Ravenswood Ave # 119 (60640-4417)
PHONE 773 868-7041
Sylvain Chambat, *CEO*
Alain Tornier, *President*
Pascal Rokegem, *Principal*
EMP: 10 **EST:** 2013
SALES (est): 1.5MM **Privately Held**
WEB: www.clariance-spine.com
SIC: 3841 Surgical & medical instruments

(G-4167)
CLARK FILTER INC
13000 Collections Ctr Dr (60693-0001)
PHONE 216 896-3000
EMP: 20
SALES (corp-wide): 14.3B **Publicly Held**
SIC: 3564 3714 Filters, air: furnaces, air conditioning equipment, etc.; motor vehicle parts & accessories
HQ: Clark Filter, Inc.
3649 Hempland Rd
Lancaster PA 17601
717 285-5941

(G-4168)
CLASSIC EMBROIDERY INC
6939 W 59th St (60638-3205)
PHONE 708 485-7034
Anna Chraca, *President*
EMP: 15
SALES (est): 1.1MM **Privately Held**
SIC: 2395 Embroidery products, except schiffli machine; embroidery & art needlework

(G-4169)
CLASSIC MIDWEST DIE MOLD INC
1140 N Kostner Ave (60651-3499)
PHONE 773 227-8000
Luigi Scala Sr, *President*
EMP: 10
SQ FT: 40,000
SALES (est): 2MM **Privately Held**
SIC: 3089 3993 Injection molded finished plastic products; signs & advertising specialties

(G-4170)
CLASSIC REMIX
116 W Illinois St Fl 6w-B (60654-2758)
PHONE 312 915-0521
EMP: 4
SALES (est): 240K **Privately Held**
SIC: 2599 Mfg Furniture/Fixtures

(G-4171)
CLASSIC VENDING INC
Also Called: Classic Group, The
2155 S Carpenter St (60608-4502)
PHONE 773 252-7000
Michael Klong, *President*
Jim Carbone, *COO*
EMP: 30
SALES (est): 12.8MM **Privately Held**
SIC: 5046 3581 Coffee brewing equipment & supplies; automatic vending machines

(G-4172)
CLAY VOLLMAR PRODUCTS CO (PA)
5835 W Touhy Ave (60646-1264)
PHONE 773 774-1234
Eric W Schulenburg, *President*
H J Schulenberg, *President*
Eric Schulenberg, *Vice Pres*
Marilyn Schulenberg, *Admin Sec*
EMP: 10
SQ FT: 2,000
SALES (est): 2.9MM **Privately Held**
WEB: www.vollmarclayproducts.com
SIC: 3272 5032 Septic tanks, concrete; sewer pipe, clay

(G-4173)
CLEAN MOTION INC
4444 W Chicago Ave (60651-3424)
PHONE 607 323-1778
Dionysis Alissandratos, *President*
EMP: 10 **EST:** 2014
SALES (est): 637.2K **Privately Held**
SIC: 2869 Industrial organic chemicals

(G-4174)
CLEARTRIAL LLC
233 S Wacker Dr Ste 4500 (60606-6376)
PHONE 877 206-4846
Mike Soenen, *President*
EMP: 14 **EST:** 2009
SALES: 1.3MM
SALES (corp-wide): 39.5B **Publicly Held**
SIC: 7372 Educational computer software
PA: Oracle Corporation
500 Oracle Pkwy
Redwood City CA 94065
650 506-7000

(G-4175)
CLEATS MFG INC (PA)
Also Called: Cleats Manufacturing Company
1855 S Kilbourn Ave (60623-2307)
PHONE 773 521-0300
Stephen Passannante Jr, *President*
Ernest De Lord, *Treasurer*
Grace Albano, *Sales Staff*
Marty Kackys, *Sales Staff*
Gary Fisk, *Sales Executive*
EMP: 18 **EST:** 1961
SQ FT: 25,000
SALES (est): 4.3MM **Privately Held**
WEB: www.cleatsmfg.com
SIC: 3444 3429 1761 Ducts, sheet metal; metal fasteners; sheet metalwork

(G-4176)
CLEATS MFG INC
1701 S Kostner Ave (60623-2338)
PHONE 773 542-0453
Jim Wagner, *Manager*
EMP: 15
SALES (corp-wide): 4.3MM **Privately Held**
SIC: 3999 Barber & beauty shop equipment
PA: Cleats Mfg., Inc.
1855 S Kilbourn Ave
Chicago IL 60623
773 521-0300

(G-4177)
CLEMENTI PRINTING INC
2832 N Narragansett Ave (60634-4911)
PHONE 773 622-0795
Anthony Clementi, *President*
Christine Clementi, *Admin Sec*
EMP: 3
SQ FT: 600
SALES (est): 306.6K **Privately Held**
SIC: 2752 2791 Commercial printing, offset; typesetting

(G-4178)
CLIMATE GUARD DESIGN
Also Called: Climateguard
155 W 84th St (60620-1204)
PHONE 773 873-0000
Joey Tapper, *Mng Member*
EMP: 2
SALES (est): 290K **Privately Held**
SIC: 3442 5031 Screens, window, metal; windows

(G-4179)
CLINTEX LABORATORIES INC
140 W 62nd St (60621-3809)
PHONE 773 493-9777
Stephen G Luster, *President*
Josie Luster, *Vice Pres*
Nancy Rachell, *Purch Mgr*
Brandon Waiters, *Sales Executive*
Helen Hall, *Admin Asst*
EMP: 29
SQ FT: 50,000
SALES (est): 7.1MM **Privately Held**
WEB: www.essations.com
SIC: 2844 Cosmetic preparations

(G-4180)
CLOVER CLUB BOTTLING CO INC
356 N Kilbourn Ave (60624-1623)
PHONE 773 261-7100
Joseph Troy, *President*
Edward Kennelly, *Vice Pres*
▲ **EMP:** 12 **EST:** 1934
SQ FT: 65,000
SALES (est): 3.2MM **Privately Held**
SIC: 5149 2086 Soft drinks; carbonated beverages, nonalcoholic: bottled & canned

(G-4181)
CLOVER SIGNS
2944 W Montrose Ave Apt 1 (60618-1485)
PHONE 773 588-2828
Kwang Yi, *Owner*
EMP: 4
SQ FT: 2,000
SALES (est): 273.1K **Privately Held**
SIC: 3993 Neon signs

(G-4182)
CLYBOURN 1200
1249 N Clybourn Ave # 300 (60610-6693)
PHONE 312 477-7442
EMP: 3
SALES (est): 174.1K **Privately Held**
SIC: 3471 Plating & polishing

(G-4183)
CLYBOURN METAL FINISHING CO
2240 N Clybourn Ave (60614-3087)
PHONE 773 525-8162
Tim Collins, *President*
William G Romaniuk, *Corp Secy*
William Romaniuck, *Executive*
EMP: 50
SQ FT: 11,250
SALES: 2MM **Privately Held**
WEB: www.clybournmetal.com
SIC: 3471 5084 Polishing, metals or formed products; industrial machinery & equipment

(G-4184)
CLYDE PRINTING COMPANY
3520 S Morgan St Fl 2a (60609-1582)
PHONE 773 847-5900
Collen Woulfe, *President*
John V Woulfe Jr, *Vice Pres*
Nancy Woulfe, *Admin Sec*
EMP: 10
SQ FT: 28,000
SALES (est): 1.4MM **Privately Held**
WEB: www.clydeprinting.com
SIC: 2752 2791 2759 Commercial printing, offset; typesetting; commercial printing

(G-4185)
CMV SHARPER FINISH INC
4500 W Augusta Blvd (60651-3301)
PHONE 773 276-4800
Mark J Camelotto, *President*
Craig Roberts, *Vice Pres*
Venkat Tripurenani, *Vice Pres*
▼ **EMP:** 25
SALES (est): 5.3MM **Privately Held**
WEB: www.cmvsharperfinish.com
SIC: 3582 Ironers, commercial laundry & drycleaning

(G-4186)
CNLC-STC INC (DH)
350 N Orleans St (60654-1975)
PHONE 312 321-3000
John O'Neill, *Publisher*
Jeff Britt, *Editor*
John Cruickshank, *COO*
Carol Fowler, *Vice Pres*
Frederic R Lebolt, *Vice Pres*
EMP: 1350
SQ FT: 500,000
SALES (est): 120.8MM
SALES (corp-wide): 4.3MM **Privately Held**
SIC: 2711 Commercial printing & newspaper publishing combined; newspapers, publishing & printing
HQ: Sun-Times Media Group, Inc.
30 N Racine Ave Ste 300
Chicago IL 60607
312 321-3000

(G-4187)
COALESSE
222 Merchds Mrt Plz 1032 (60654)
PHONE 312 622-6269
Michelle Riley, *Principal*
Lisa Clark, *Vice Pres*
Mark Groenheide, *Project Mgr*
Natasha Sides, *Project Mgr*
Brian Scholten, *Opers Staff*
EMP: 17 **EST:** 2011
SALES (est): 1.9MM **Privately Held**
WEB: www.coalesse.com
SIC: 3553 Furniture makers' machinery, woodworking

(G-4188)
COCA-COLA REFRESHMENTS USA INC
12200 S Laramie Ave (60803-3194)
PHONE 708 597-4700
Thomas Pawelczyk, *Manager*
EMP: 100
SALES (corp-wide): 37.2B **Publicly Held**
SIC: 2086 5149 Bottled & canned soft drinks; carbonated beverages, nonalcoholic: bottled & canned; groceries & related products
HQ: Coca-Cola Refreshments Usa, Inc.
2500 Windy Ridge Pkwy Se
Atlanta GA 30339
770 989-3000

(G-4189)
CODA RESOURCES LTD
Also Called: Cambridge Resources
600 N Kilbourn Ave (60624-1041)
PHONE 718 649-1666
Chrisy Issac, *Project Mgr*
EMP: 16
SALES (corp-wide): 24.7MM **Privately Held**
SIC: 3317 Steel pipe & tubes
PA: Coda Resources Ltd.
100 Matawan Rd Ste 300
Matawan NJ 07747
718 649-1666

(G-4190)
CODA RESOURCES LTD
Also Called: Cambridge Resources
4444 W Ferdinand St (60624-1019)
PHONE 718 649-1666
EMP: 16
SALES (corp-wide): 24.7MM **Privately Held**
SIC: 3469 2821 Metal stampings; molding compounds, plastics
PA: Coda Resources Ltd.
100 Matawan Rd Ste 300
Matawan NJ 07747
718 649-1666

GEOGRAPHIC SECTION
Chicago - Cook County (G-4217)

(G-4191)
CODE BLACK LLC
Also Called: Code B Magazine
9 W Washington St (60602-1603)
PHONE.................................773 493-4500
Regina Washington, *CEO*
EMP: 3
SALES (est): 148.8K **Privately Held**
SIC: 2721 5192 Magazines: publishing & printing; magazines

(G-4192)
CODY METAL FINISHING INC
1620 N Throop St (60642-1515)
PHONE.................................773 252-2026
Stephen Obert, *President*
David Yaris, *Vice Pres*
Margret Obert, *Treasurer*
EMP: 15
SQ FT: 25,000
SALES (est): 1.1MM **Privately Held**
WEB: www.codyzincplating.com
SIC: 3471 Electroplating of metals or formed products

(G-4193)
COEUR CAPITAL INC
104 S Michigan Ave (60603-5902)
PHONE.................................312 489-5800
Mitchell J Krebs, *President*
Casey M Nault, *Vice Pres*
Luis Chavez, *Manager*
Jeffrey Melody, *Senior Mgr*
EMP: 8
SALES (est): 469.9K
SALES (corp-wide): 711.5MM **Publicly Held**
SIC: 1081 Metal mining exploration & development services
PA: Coeur Mining, Inc.
    104 S Michigan Ave # 800
    Chicago IL 60603
    312 489-5800

(G-4194)
COEUR MINING INC (PA)
104 S Michigan Ave # 800 (60603-5925)
PHONE.................................312 489-5800
Robert E Mellor, *Ch of Bd*
Mitchell J Krebs, *President*
Frank L Hanagarne Jr, *COO*
Michael Routledge, *COO*
Casey M Nault, *Senior VP*
EMP: 74
SALES: 711.5MM **Publicly Held**
WEB: www.coeur.com
SIC: 1041 1044 Gold ores mining; gold ores processing; silver ores mining; silver ores processing

(G-4195)
COEUR ROCHESTER INC
104 S Michigan Ave (60603-5902)
PHONE.................................312 661-2436
Rochester Green, *Principal*
Matthew Zietlow, *Manager*
EMP: 8 **EST:** 2013
SALES (est): 826K
SALES (corp-wide): 711.5MM **Publicly Held**
WEB: www.coeur.com
SIC: 1044 Silver ores
PA: Coeur Mining, Inc.
    104 S Michigan Ave # 800
    Chicago IL 60603
    312 489-5800

(G-4196)
COHERA MEDICAL INC
10 S La Salle St Ste 3300 (60603-1026)
PHONE.................................602 418-8788
EMP: 3
SALES (est): 123.2K **Privately Held**
SIC: 2891 Adhesives & sealants

(G-4197)
COLD HEADERS INC (PA)
5514 N Elston Ave 14 (60630-1380)
PHONE.................................773 775-7900
Bruce Duncan, *President*
Richard Duncan, *Vice Pres*
Dave Effert, *Vice Pres*
Michelle Silk, *Office Mgr*
▲ **EMP:** 18 **EST:** 1962
SQ FT: 40,000
SALES (est): 4.8MM **Privately Held**
WEB: www.coldheaders.com
SIC: 5072 3599 Screws; machine shop, jobbing & repair

(G-4198)
COLEMAN COMPANY INC (DH)
180 N Lasalle St Ste 700 (60601)
P.O. Box 2931, Wichita KS (67201-2931)
PHONE.................................316 832-2653
Robert Marcovitch, *CEO*
Bruno Cercley, *President*
Dan Hogan, *CFO*
Riika Jorgensen, *Info Tech Mgr*
Rick Looslie, *Director*
◆ **EMP:** 200
SALES (est): 1.1B
SALES (corp-wide): 9.7B **Publicly Held**
SIC: 3949 Camping equipment & supplies

(G-4199)
COLES APPLIANCE & FURN CO
4026 N Lincoln Ave (60618-3010)
PHONE.................................773 525-1797
Barry Krasney, *President*
Mari Krasney, *Admin Sec*
EMP: 5 **EST:** 1957
SQ FT: 10,000
SALES (est): 3.6MM **Privately Held**
WEB: www.shopcoles.com
SIC: 5722 5712 5731 2512 Electric household appliances, small; furniture stores; consumer electronic equipment; television sets; high fidelity stereo equipment; video cameras, recorders & accessories; upholstered household furniture

(G-4200)
COLLAGEN USA INC
3048 N Milwaukee Ave (60618-6624)
PHONE.................................708 716-0251
EMP: 2
SALES (est): 220K **Privately Held**
SIC: 2844 Mfg Toilet Preparations/Skin Care Products

(G-4201)
COLLEGE BOUND PUBLICATIONS
7658 N Rogers Ave (60626-7290)
P.O. Box 6526, Evanston (60204-6526)
PHONE.................................773 262-5810
R Craig Sautter, *President*
EMP: 2
SALES (est): 229.9K **Privately Held**
SIC: 2721 8748 Magazines: publishing & printing; publishing consultant

(G-4202)
COLNAGO AMERICA INC
1528 W Adams St Ste 4b (60607-2450)
PHONE.................................312 239-6666
Alessandro Colnago, *President*
Soren Krebs Siekierski, *Admin Sec*
▲ **EMP:** 3
SQ FT: 2,500
SALES (est): 390.7K **Privately Held**
SIC: 3751 Frames, motorcycle & bicycle

(G-4203)
COLOR COMMUNICATIONS LLC
4000 W Fillmore St (60624-3905)
PHONE.................................773 638-1400
Greg O'Brien, *Vice Pres*
Cynthia Cornell, *Project Dir*
Brian Pawlicki, *Purch Mgr*
Tom Patzler, *CFO*
Angie Grant, *Sales Staff*
EMP: 3
SALES (est): 80.6K **Privately Held**
SIC: 2759 Promotional printing

(G-4204)
COLOR COMMUNICATIONS LLC (PA)
230 W Monroe St Ste 2000 (60606-4913)
PHONE.................................312 223-0204
Michael S Felvey,
EMP: 3
SALES (est): 231.8K **Privately Held**
SIC: 2752 3993 Cards, lithographed; advertising artwork

(G-4205)
COLT TECHNOLOGY SERVICES LLC
141 W Jackson Blvd # 2808 (60604-3307)
PHONE.................................312 465-2484
Michelle Lockwood, *Accounts Mgr*
Juan Montoya, *Accounts Exec*
Derek Sprunk, *Manager*
Alex Lewis, *Manager*
John Baldwin, *Senior Mgr*
EMP: 12 **EST:** 2015
SALES (est): 527.1K
SALES (corp-wide): 533.7K **Privately Held**
SIC: 3663 Radio & TV communications equipment
HQ: Colt Technology Services Group Limited
    Colt House
    London EC2A
    207 390-3900

(G-4206)
COLUMBIA METAL SPINNING CO
4351 N Normandy Ave (60634-1395)
PHONE.................................773 685-2800
Fred Haberkamp, *President*
Dawn Koleman, *Vice Pres*
Don Konieczny, *Vice Pres*
EMP: 55 **EST:** 1952
SQ FT: 45,000
SALES (est): 10.3MM **Privately Held**
WEB: www.cmspinning.com
SIC: 3469 Spinning metal for the trade

(G-4207)
COLUMBUS MEATS INC
906 W Randolph St Fl 1 (60607)
PHONE.................................312 829-2480
George Dervenis, *President*
EMP: 9
SQ FT: 1,900
SALES (est): 722K **Privately Held**
SIC: 5421 5147 2013 Meat markets, including freezer provisioners; meats, fresh; sausages & other prepared meats

(G-4208)
COM-GRAPHICS INC
329 W 18th St Fl 10 (60616-1120)
PHONE.................................312 226-0900
Denise Kretzer, *President*
Lydia Erickson, *CFO*
Susan Askew, *Manager*
Connie Priess, *Senior Mgr*
Greg Pfirman, *CIO*
EMP: 70
SQ FT: 50,000
SALES (est): 8.8MM **Privately Held**
WEB: www.cgichicago.com
SIC: 7389 2759 7331 Microfilm recording & developing service; commercial printing; mailing service

(G-4209)
COMMERCIAL PALLET INC
2029 W Hubbard St (60612-1609)
PHONE.................................312 226-6699
Lester Hagan, *President*
Doris Hagan, *Corp Secy*
Tim Hagan, *Vice Pres*
EMP: 30 **EST:** 1978
SQ FT: 3,500
SALES (est): 2.7MM **Privately Held**
SIC: 7699 2448 Pallet repair; wood pallets & skids

(G-4210)
COMMUNITY MAGAZINE GROUP
1550 S Indiana Ave (60605-2857)
PHONE.................................312 880-0370
Jim Distasio, *Principal*
EMP: 4
SALES (est): 284K **Privately Held**
SIC: 2721 Magazines: publishing only, not printed on site

(G-4211)
CON-TROL-CURE INC
Also Called: Uv Process Supply
1229 W Cortland St (60614-4805)
PHONE.................................773 248-0099
Stephen B Siegel, *President*
EMP: 11
SALES (est): 1.6MM
SALES (corp-wide): 3.8MM **Privately Held**
SIC: 3625 3621 Control equipment, electric; motors & generators
PA: U. V. Process Supply, Inc.
    1229 W Cortland St
    Chicago IL 60614
    773 248-0099

(G-4212)
CONAGRA BRANDS INC (PA)
222 Mdse Mart Plz (60654-1103)
PHONE.................................312 549-5000
Richard L Lenny, *Ch of Bd*
Sean M Connolly, *President*
Rebecca Bortolotti, *Counsel*
Colleen R Batcheler, *Exec VP*
David B Biegger, *Exec VP*
EMP: 250 **EST:** 1919
SALES: 9.5B **Publicly Held**
WEB: www.conagrabrands.com
SIC: 2038 2013 2099 Frozen specialties; dinners, frozen & packaged; lunches, frozen & packaged; sausages & other prepared meats; dessert mixes & fillings

(G-4213)
CONAGRA DAIRY FOODS COMPANY (HQ)
222 Merchandise Mart Plz # 1300 (60654-1010)
PHONE.................................630 848-0975
Richard G Scalise, *President*
Greg Lambier, *Director*
Wes Wasson, *Director*
Linda Westerhold, *Administration*
◆ **EMP:** 484
SALES (est): 139.7MM
SALES (corp-wide): 9.5B **Publicly Held**
SIC: 2022 Natural cheese; processed cheese
PA: Conagra Brands, Inc.
    222 Mdse Mart Plz
    Chicago IL 60654
    312 549-5000

(G-4214)
CONCEPT LABORATORIES INC
Also Called: Pure Valley
1400 W Wabansia Ave (60642-1522)
PHONE.................................773 395-7300
Joel Heifitz, *CEO*
Adam Lustbader, *President*
John M Zomchek, *VP Opers*
Henry Hong, *CFO*
Stephen Sands, *CFO*
▲ **EMP:** 72
SQ FT: 30,000
SALES: 10.5MM **Privately Held**
SIC: 2844 2842 Cosmetic preparations; specialty cleaning, polishes & sanitation goods

(G-4215)
CONCIERGE PREFERRED
101 W Grand Ave Ste 404 (60654-7129)
PHONE.................................312 360-1770
Tim O'Malley, *Principal*
Samantha Krause, *Vice Pres*
Trisha Carey, *Mktg Dir*
EMP: 2
SQ FT: 9,300
SALES (est): 237.9K **Privately Held**
SIC: 2721 Magazines: publishing only, not printed on site

(G-4216)
CONCORDE PRTG DGTAL IMGING INC
180 N Michigan Ave # 1700 (60601-7401)
PHONE.................................312 552-3006
Dominic Abbadi, *President*
Craig Murphy, *Prdtn Mgr*
Rob York, *Production*
Dom Abbadi, *Sales Staff*
Robb Douglas, *Sales Staff*
EMP: 8
SQ FT: 2,000
SALES (est): 1.6MM **Privately Held**
SIC: 2752 Commercial printing, offset

(G-4217)
CONDOR MACHINE TOOL
5315 W 63rd St (60638-5641)
PHONE.................................773 767-5985

Chicago - Cook County (G-4218)

Gerry Wozniak, *Owner*
EMP: 4 **EST:** 1983
SALES (est): 364.2K **Privately Held**
SIC: 3541 Machine tool replacement & repair parts, metal cutting types

(G-4218)
CONNECTERIORS LLC
3100 N Clybourn Ave (60618-6425)
PHONE..................................773 549-3333
Brian Miller,
EMP: 9
SQ FT: 3,000
SALES (est): 1MM **Privately Held**
SIC: 3651 Household audio equipment

(G-4219)
CONNELLY-GPM INC
3154 S California Ave (60608-5176)
Stephen M Klein, *President*
PHONE..................................773 247-7231
▼ **EMP:** 28
SQ FT: 17,000
SALES (est): 7.5MM **Privately Held**
WEB: www.connellygpm.com
SIC: 3399 3272 3312 Iron, powdered; precast terrazo or concrete products; sponge iron

(G-4220)
CONOPCO INC
Unilever Bestfoods North Amer
2816 S Kilbourn Ave (60623-4212)
PHONE..................................773 916-4400
Renee Plaza, *Manager*
EMP: 126
SQ FT: 12,800
SALES (corp-wide): 9.6B **Privately Held**
SIC: 2844 Toilet preparations
HQ: Conopco, Inc.
700 Sylvan Ave
Englewood Cliffs NJ 07632
201 894-7760

(G-4221)
CONOR SPORTS LLC
444 N Michigan Ave # 3600 (60611-3903)
PHONE..................................847 903-6639
M Prentice, *Principal*
EMP: 3 **EST:** 2013
SALES (est): 102.5K **Privately Held**
SIC: 7372 Prepackaged software

(G-4222)
CONSOLIDATED CHEM WORKS LTD
Also Called: Conchemco
400 N Ashland Ave Ste 2 (60622-7304)
PHONE..................................312 226-6150
Warren Weisberg, *President*
Henry A Waller, *Vice Pres*
EMP: 36 **EST:** 1932
SQ FT: 37,000
SALES (est): 9.5MM **Privately Held**
WEB: www.consolidatedchemicalworks.com
SIC: 2841 2842 Detergents, synthetic organic or inorganic alkaline; specialty cleaning, polishes & sanitation goods

(G-4223)
CONSULATE GENERAL LITHUANIA
455 N Ctyfrnt Plz Dr # 800 (60611-5504)
PHONE..................................312 397-0382
Giedrius Apuokas, *Manager*
EMP: 6
SALES (est): 450K **Privately Held**
SIC: 2752 Commercial printing, lithographic

(G-4224)
CONSUMERBASE LLC
Also Called: Exact Data
33 N Dearborn St Ste 200 (60602-3100)
PHONE..................................312 600-8000
Larry Organ, *CEO*
Kevin Dwyer, *Vice Pres*
Johanna Kotyuk, *Vice Pres*
Amir Patel, *Vice Pres*
Hannah Rivera, *Vice Pres*
EMP: 125
SQ FT: 18,269
SALES (est): 11.7MM **Privately Held**
SIC: 7331 2741 Mailing service; telephone & other directory publishing

PA: Alesco Data Group, Llc
5276 Smmrlin Cmmons Way S
Fort Myers FL 33907

(G-4225)
CONTEMPO MARBLE & GRANITE INC
411 N Paulina St (60622-6318)
PHONE..................................312 455-0022
Mike Losurlello, *President*
Gilbert R Truillo, *Treasurer*
EMP: 8
SQ FT: 7,500
SALES: 600K **Privately Held**
SIC: 3281 1743 2541 Marble, building: cut & shaped; tile installation, ceramic; wood partitions & fixtures

(G-4226)
CONTINENTAL ASSEMBLY INC
4317 N Ravenswood Ave (60613-1111)
PHONE..................................773 472-8004
Mike Hwang, *President*
▲ **EMP:** 11 **EST:** 1974
SQ FT: 10,000
SALES: 350K **Privately Held**
SIC: 3679 Electronic circuits

(G-4227)
CONTINENTAL MARKETING INC
Also Called: CMI Display
5696 N Milwaukee Ave (60646-6222)
PHONE..................................773 467-8300
Marion Fadrowski, *President*
Annette Fadrowski, *Sales Staff*
▲ **EMP:** 12
SQ FT: 1,500
SALES (est): 1MM **Privately Held**
SIC: 2541 Store & office display cases & fixtures

(G-4228)
CONTINENTAL MATERIALS CORP (HQ)
440 S La Salle St # 3100 (60605-5020)
PHONE..................................312 541-7200
James G Gidwitz, *Ch of Bd*
Ryan Sullivan, *President*
EMP: 12
SALES: 113.2MM
SALES (corp-wide): 20.2MM **Privately Held**
WEB: www.continental-materials.com
SIC: 3585 3273 5031 Refrigeration & heating equipment; ready-mixed concrete; building materials, exterior; doors
PA: Bee Street Holdings Llc
13337 Bee St
Dallas TX 75234
972 394-0881

(G-4229)
CONTINENTAL MILLS INC
600 W Chicago Ave Ste 670 (60654-2517)
PHONE..................................800 426-0955
EMP: 12
SALES (corp-wide): 223.6MM **Privately Held**
WEB: www.continentalmills.com
SIC: 2045 Flours & flour mixes, from purchased flour
PA: Continental Mills, Inc.
18100 Andover Park W
Tukwila WA 98188
206 816-7000

(G-4230)
CONTINENTAL STUDIOS INC
1300 S Kostner Ave (60623-4970)
PHONE..................................773 542-0309
Joseph Motroni, *President*
Randy Motroni, *Corp Secy*
Lois Motroni, *Vice Pres*
Mary Motroni, *Vice Pres*
EMP: 38 **EST:** 1986
SQ FT: 18,000
SALES: 4MM **Privately Held**
WEB: www.continentalstudiosinc.com
SIC: 3299 3275 Ornamental & architectural plaster work; gypsum products

(G-4231)
CONTINENTAL WINDOW AND GL CORP
4311 W Belmont Ave (60641-4525)
PHONE..................................773 794-1600
Greg Sztejkowski, *President*
▼ **EMP:** 50
SQ FT: 380,000
SALES (est): 9.3MM **Privately Held**
SIC: 3089 Windows, plastic; doors, folding: plastic or plastic coated fabric

(G-4232)
CONTINENTAL WINDOW SOUTH INC
4600 S Kolmar Ave (60632-4302)
PHONE..................................773 767-1300
Jessie Gorski, *President*
EMP: 16
SALES (est): 2MM **Privately Held**
SIC: 3442 Window & door frames

(G-4233)
COORENS COMMUNICATIONS INC
2134 W Pierce Ave (60622-1821)
PHONE..................................773 235-8688
Elaine Coorens, *President*
Larry Clary, *Vice Pres*
EMP: 12
SALES (est): 257.4K **Privately Held**
WEB: www.ccisite.com
SIC: 7372 Business oriented computer software

(G-4234)
CORBETT ACCEL HEALTHCARE GRP C
Also Called: Potentia
225 N Michigan Ave (60601-7757)
PHONE..................................312 475-2505
Scott D Cotherman, *CEO*
EMP: 180
SQ FT: 42,705
SALES (est): 27.7MM
SALES (corp-wide): 14.9B **Publicly Held**
SIC: 7311 2721 Advertising consultant; periodicals
PA: Omnicom Group Inc.
437 Madison Ave
New York NY 10022
212 415-3600

(G-4235)
CORNELL FORGE COMPANY
6666 W 66th St (60638-4994)
PHONE..................................708 458-1582
Bill Brewer, *CEO*
William H Brewer, *President*
Ken Mathas, *President*
Don James, *Safety Dir*
Robin Adelman, *Opers Staff*
EMP: 60 **EST:** 1930
SQ FT: 126,000
SALES (est): 29.6MM **Privately Held**
WEB: www.cornellforge.com
SIC: 3462 Iron & steel forgings

(G-4236)
CORNERSTONE COMMUNICATIONS
Also Called: Corner Stone
920 W Wilson Ave (60640-6447)
PHONE..................................773 989-2087
Dawn Mortimer, *President*
Janet Cameron, *Treasurer*
Pat Peterson, *Admin Sec*
EMP: 35
SALES: 33.4K **Privately Held**
SIC: 7336 5812 2721 Package design; eating places; periodicals

(G-4237)
CORNERSTONE COMMUNITY OUTREACH
Also Called: LELAND HOUSE
4615 N Clifton Ave (60640-5013)
PHONE..................................773 506-4904
Curtiss Mortimer, *President*
Andrew Winter, *Principal*
Chuck Escue, *Purch Agent*
Rick Mills, *Webmaster*
Sandra Ramsey, *Exec Dir*
EMP: 12

SALES: 3.6MM **Privately Held**
SIC: 8322 2731 Outreach program; book publishing

(G-4238)
CORONADO CONSERVATION INC
5807 S Woodlawn Ave (60637-1610)
PHONE..................................301 512-4671
Shane Durkin, *CEO*
EMP: 3 **EST:** 2016
SALES (est): 109.7K **Privately Held**
SIC: 3261 Bathroom accessories/fittings, vitreous china or earthenware

(G-4239)
CORPORATE GRAPHICS AMERICA INC
5312 N Elston Ave (60630-1611)
PHONE..................................773 481-2100
William Goers, *President*
Mary R Goers, *Vice Pres*
John Kawula, *Prdtn Mgr*
EMP: 16
SQ FT: 11,800
SALES (est): 3.6MM **Privately Held**
WEB: www.corporategraphicsinc.com
SIC: 2752 Commercial printing, offset

(G-4240)
CORPORATE IDENTIFICATION SOLUT
5563 N Elston Ave (60630-1314)
PHONE..................................773 763-9600
Ben Dehayes, *President*
Timothy Sulda, *Sales Staff*
EMP: 27
SQ FT: 21,000
SALES: 8.1MM **Privately Held**
SIC: 3993 Electric signs

(G-4241)
CORPORATION SUPPLY CO INC (PA)
205 W Randolph St Ste 610 (60606-1814)
PHONE..................................312 726-3375
David Brenner, *President*
EMP: 20
SQ FT: 8,000
SALES (est): 1.9MM **Privately Held**
SIC: 7389 2759 5199 5943 Design, commercial & industrial; stock certificates: printing; general merchandise, nondurable; office forms & supplies; notary & corporate seals; stationery & office supplies; commercial printing, lithographic

(G-4242)
CORPS LEVL VENTURES INC
Also Called: Chicago Speedpro Imaging
2028 S Michigan Ave # 101 (60616-1707)
PHONE..................................312 846-1441
Eric Lazar, *President*
Rebecca Considine, *Principal*
EMP: 12
SQ FT: 3,468
SALES (est): 1.8MM **Privately Held**
SIC: 2752 Commercial printing, lithographic

(G-4243)
COSAS INC
2170 S Canalport Ave (60608)
PHONE..................................312 492-6100
Sean Brodie, *Principal*
EMP: 4
SALES (est): 357.4K **Privately Held**
WEB: www.cosaslighting.com
SIC: 3645 Garden, patio, walkway & yard lighting fixtures: electric

(G-4244)
COSITAS CUPCAKES & MORE
4138 W 57th St (60629-4822)
PHONE..................................773 992-7088
Perla Hernandez, *Principal*
EMP: 3
SALES (est): 79.9K **Privately Held**
SIC: 2051 Bread, cake & related products

(G-4245)
COSMEDENT INC
401 N Michigan Ave # 2500 (60611-4243)
PHONE..................................312 644-9388
Michael O'Malley, *President*

GEOGRAPHIC SECTION — Chicago - Cook County (G-4272)

Robert Mopper, *VP Sales*
K William Mopper, *Admin Sec*
EMP: 21
SQ FT: 2,000
SALES (est): 3.8MM **Privately Held**
SIC: 3842 Cosmetic restorations

(G-4246)
COSMOPOLITAN FOOT CARE
1 S Wacker Dr Fl 11 (60606-4614)
PHONE.....................312 984-5111
Alisa French, *Manager*
EMP: 5
SALES (corp-wide): 540.4K **Privately Held**
SIC: 2721 Periodicals
PA: Charles Kaplan Dpm
220 W 98th St Apt 1k
New York NY 10025
212 663-3668

(G-4247)
COTTON GOODS MANUFACTURING CO
259 N California Ave (60612-1903)
PHONE.....................773 265-0088
Edward J Lewis, *President*
Anne Lewis, *Corp Secy*
▼ **EMP:** 18 **EST:** 1923
SQ FT: 11,000
SALES (est): 900K **Privately Held**
WEB: www.cottongoodsmfg.com
SIC: 2392 Blankets: made from purchased materials; slip covers & pads; shower curtains: made from purchased materials; tablecloths: made from purchased materials

(G-4248)
COUDAL PARTNERS INC
Also Called: Field Notes
401 N Racine Ave (60642-5839)
PHONE.....................312 243-1107
Jim Coudal, *President*
Michele Seiler, *Manager*
EMP: 8
SQ FT: 1,000
SALES (est): 1.8MM **Privately Held**
SIC: 2678 Memorandum books, notebooks & looseleaf filler paper

(G-4249)
COUNTER
666 W Diversey Pkwy (60614-1511)
PHONE.....................312 666-5335
Edward Mark Casey, *Partner*
EMP: 3 **EST:** 2008
SALES (est): 298.6K **Privately Held**
SIC: 3131 Counters

(G-4250)
COVEY MACHINE INC
3604 S Morgan St (60609-1526)
PHONE.....................773 650-1530
Michael Koren, *President*
Gary Koren, *General Mgr*
EMP: 14
SQ FT: 20,000
SALES (est): 2.5MM **Privately Held**
SIC: 3441 3366 3312 Fabricated structural metal; copper foundries; blast furnaces & steel mills

(G-4251)
COWTAN AND TOUT INC
222 Merchds Mart Plz 638 (60654)
PHONE.....................312 644-0717
Nancy Cordin, *Manager*
EMP: 10
SALES (corp-wide): 113.8MM **Privately Held**
SIC: 2297 2621 Nonwoven fabrics; wallpaper (hanging paper)
HQ: Cowtan And Tout, Inc.
205 Hudson St Fl 6
New York NY 10013
212 334-5128

(G-4252)
CPG INTERNATIONAL LLC (DH)
Also Called: Azek Company, The
1330 W Fulton St Ste 350 (60607-1153)
PHONE.....................570 558-8000
Jesse Singh, *CEO*
Joe Ochoa, *President*
Ken Buck, *Senior VP*
Christopher Eppel, *Vice Pres*
Jim Gross, *Vice Pres*
EMP: 80
SALES (est): 630MM
SALES (corp-wide): 1.7B **Publicly Held**
SIC: 3089 3272 6722 Plastic hardware & building products; prefabricated plastic buildings; building materials, except block or brick: concrete; management investment, open-end
HQ: Ares Management Llc
2000 Avenue Of The Stars # 12
Los Angeles CA 90067
310 201-4100

(G-4253)
CPG NEWCO LLC
1330 W Fulton St Ste 350 (60607-1153)
PHONE.....................877 275-2935
Gary Hendrickson, *Ch of Bd*
Jesse Singh, *President*
Jose Ochoa, *President*
Scott Van Winter, *President*
Bobby Gentile, *Senior VP*
EMP: 1540
SALES: 794.2MM **Privately Held**
SIC: 3089 Kits, plastic

(G-4254)
CRAFT DIE CASTING CORPORATION
1831 N Lorel Ave (60639-4390)
PHONE.....................773 237-9710
James Sanabria, *President*
Susan Sanabria, *Vice Pres*
EMP: 20 **EST:** 1953
SQ FT: 7,200
SALES (est): 2.6MM **Privately Held**
WEB: www.craftdiecasting.com
SIC: 3363 Aluminum die-castings

(G-4255)
CRAFT METAL SPINNING CO
Also Called: Columbia Metal Spinning Co
4351 N Normandy Ave (60634-1395)
PHONE.....................773 685-4700
Fred Haberkamp, *President*
Elenore Haberkamp, *Vice Pres*
EMP: 15 **EST:** 1947
SQ FT: 75,000
SALES (est): 935K **Privately Held**
WEB: www.cmspinning.com
SIC: 3469 Stamping metal for the trade

(G-4256)
CRAFTMASTER MANUFACTURING INC
Also Called: CMI
500 W Monroe St Ste 2010 (60661-3762)
P.O. Box 311, Towanda PA (18848-0311)
PHONE.....................800 405-2233
Robert E Merrill, *President*
EMP: 900 **EST:** 2001
SQ FT: 1,000,000
SALES (est): 82.9MM **Publicly Held**
SIC: 2493 Hardboard, tempered
HQ: Jeld-Wen, Inc.
1162 Keystone Blvd
Charlotte NC 17901
800 535-3936

(G-4257)
CRAFTSMAN PLTG & TINNING CORP (PA)
1250 W Melrose St (60657-3295)
PHONE.....................773 477-1040
James B Blacklidge, *President*
Anthony J Merges, *Vice Pres*
Cyndy Blacklidge, *Purch Agent*
Ted Kodama, *Plant Engr*
Tim Blacklidge, *Manager*
EMP: 37 **EST:** 1945
SQ FT: 31,000
SALES (est): 5.3MM **Privately Held**
WEB: www.craftsmanplating.com
SIC: 3471 Plating of metals or formed products

(G-4258)
CRAIN COMMUNICATIONS INC (PA)
Also Called: Workforce On Line
150 N Michigan Ave # 1800 (60601-7553)
PHONE.....................312 649-5200
Rance Crane, *CEO*
Kieth Crane, *CEO*
Clark Bell, *Publisher*
Jim Kirk, *Publisher*
Erin Beaven, *Editor*
▲ **EMP:** 22
SALES (est): 3.8MM **Privately Held**
WEB: www.crain.com
SIC: 2721 Magazines: publishing only, not printed on site

(G-4259)
CRAIN COMMUNICATIONS INC
Also Called: Advertising Age
150 E Michigan Ave (60601)
PHONE.....................312 649-5200
Barry Burr, *Owner*
Gloria Scoby, *Principal*
Mary Kay Crain, *Treasurer*
EMP: 190
SALES (corp-wide): 225MM **Privately Held**
SIC: 2721 2711 Magazines: publishing only, not printed on site; newspapers, publishing & printing
PA: Crain Communications, Inc.
1155 Gratiot Ave
Detroit MI 48207
313 446-6000

(G-4260)
CRAWFORD SAUSAGE CO INC
2310 S Pulaski Rd (60623-3098)
PHONE.....................773 277-3095
John Zicha, *President*
Gregg Zicha, *Manager*
EMP: 25
SQ FT: 19,500
SALES (est): 3.2MM **Privately Held**
WEB: www.crawfordsausage.com
SIC: 2013 Luncheon meat from purchased meat; smoked meats from purchased meat; sausages from purchased meat; frankfurters from purchased meat

(G-4261)
CREATIVE DESIGNS KITC
Also Called: Creative Design Builders
4355 N Ravenswood Ave (60613-1151)
PHONE.....................773 327-8400
Ibrahim Shihadeh, *President*
Yaser Shihadeh, *Vice Pres*
Natasa Taseva, *Financial Analy*
Dora Arana, *Officer*
▲ **EMP:** 50
SQ FT: 30,000
SALES (est): 6.2MM **Privately Held**
SIC: 1799 6552 2434 1542 Kitchen & bathroom remodeling; subdividers & developers; wood kitchen cabinets; nonresidential construction

(G-4262)
CREATIVE DIRECTORY INC
Also Called: Chicago Creative Directory
5219 W Belle Plaine Ave (60641-1460)
PHONE.....................773 427-7777
Kurt Hanson, *President*
EMP: 4
SQ FT: 600
SALES (est): 395.5K **Privately Held**
SIC: 2741 Directories: publishing only, not printed on site

(G-4263)
CREATIVE INDS TERRAZZO PDTS
1753 N Spaulding Ave (60647-4920)
P.O. Box 47649 (60647-7212)
PHONE.....................773 235-9088
Carlo Banducci, *President*
EMP: 8
SQ FT: 11,000
SALES (est): 1.1MM **Privately Held**
SIC: 3272 3281 Terrazzo products, precast; cut stone & stone products

(G-4264)
CREATIVE METAL PRODUCTS
Also Called: Kagan Industries
1101 S Kilbourn Ave (60624-3822)
PHONE.....................773 638-3200
Stuart Kagan, *President*
Dale Kagan, *Vice Pres*
EMP: 15 **EST:** 1947
SQ FT: 80,000
SALES: 1MM **Privately Held**
WEB: www.kaganind.com
SIC: 2542 3469 2842 3411 Partitions & fixtures, except wood; ash trays, stamped metal; specialty cleaning preparations; metal cans

(G-4265)
CREATIVE PRTG & SMART IDEAS
3406 N Cicero Ave (60641-3718)
PHONE.....................773 481-6522
Nikolos Parnassos, *President*
May Parnassos, *Co-Owner*
EMP: 3
SALES (est): 185.2K **Privately Held**
SIC: 2752 Commercial printing, offset

(G-4266)
CREATIVE RLCAR MKTG SVCS II LL
1700 W Irving Park Rd # 3 (60613-2559)
PHONE.....................773 396-1114
EMP: 3
SALES (est): 209.5K **Privately Held**
SIC: 3743 Railway maintenance cars

(G-4267)
CREATIVE RLCAR MKTG SVCS II LL
Also Called: Crms
1700 W Irving Park Rd # 310 (60613-2559)
PHONE.....................773 396-1114
Craig Bargowski, *Mng Member*
EMP: 3
SALES (est): 530.1K **Privately Held**
SIC: 3743 Railway maintenance cars

(G-4268)
CREATIVE WOOD CONCEPTS INC
1680 N Ada St (60642-1504)
PHONE.....................773 384-9960
Eric Krause, *President*
Marc Shannon, *General Mgr*
EMP: 8
SQ FT: 7,000
SALES (est): 740K **Privately Held**
SIC: 2511 2517 Wood household furniture; wood television & radio cabinets

(G-4269)
CREST GREETINGS INC
444 W 31st St (60616-3136)
PHONE.....................708 210-0800
Steven J Colen, *President*
EMP: 10
SALES (est): 1.1MM **Privately Held**
SIC: 5961 5112 2771 2759 Cards, mail order; greeting cards; greeting cards; commercial printing

(G-4270)
CREST METAL CRAFT INC
2900 E 95th St (60617-5001)
PHONE.....................773 978-0950
Nicklais Horvath, *President*
Maria Horvath, *Admin Sec*
EMP: 6
SQ FT: 18,500
SALES (est): 956.3K **Privately Held**
SIC: 3441 Fabricated structural metal

(G-4271)
CRJ CABINETS
1925 W 51st St (60609-4843)
PHONE.....................331 303-0326
Maria Bedia, *Principal*
EMP: 4 **EST:** 2015
SALES (est): 218.6K **Privately Held**
SIC: 2434 Wood kitchen cabinets

(G-4272)
CRONUS CHEMICALS LLC
150 N Michigan Ave # 2800 (60601-7553)
PHONE.....................312 863-8638
Erzin Atac, *CEO*
EMP: 4 **EST:** 2012
SALES (est): 156.7K **Privately Held**
SIC: 2873 Anhydrous ammonia

(PA)=Parent Co (HQ)=Headquarters (DH)=Div Headquarters
✪ = New Business established in last 2 years

Chicago - Cook County (G-4273)

(G-4273)
CROSSTECH COMMUNICATIONS INC
111 N Jefferson St (60661-2306)
PHONE.................................312 382-0111
Andrew McPherson, *President*
Jeffrey Larson, *Principal*
Andy McPherson, *Exec VP*
Jeff Larson, *Vice Pres*
Bob Westland, *Sales Mgr*
EMP: 20
SQ FT: 12,000
SALES (est): 3.5MM **Privately Held**
SIC: 2791 2796 7336 Typographic composition, for the printing trade; platemaking services; graphic arts & related design

(G-4274)
CROSSTREE INC
1906 N Milwaukee Ave (60647-4321)
PHONE.................................773 227-1234
Travis Nam, *President*
EMP: 4
SQ FT: 2,500
SALES (est): 483.5K **Privately Held**
SIC: 3446 Ornamental metalwork

(G-4275)
CROWDMATRIX FX LLC
333 W Hubbard St Apt 901 (60654-4928)
PHONE.................................312 329-1170
Gregory Pine, *Principal*
Jordan Mulloy,
Elijah Wood,
EMP: 3
SALES (est): 114.8K **Privately Held**
SIC: 7372 Application computer software

(G-4276)
CROWLEYS YACHT YARD LAKESIDE
3434 E 95th St (60617-5101)
PHONE.................................773 221-9990
John Crowley, *Principal*
Carole Boulais,
EMP: 13
SALES (est): 2.1MM **Privately Held**
WEB: www.crowleys.com
SIC: 3732 Boats, fiberglass: building & repairing

(G-4277)
CROWN CORNED BEEF AND FOODS
351 N Justine St (60607-1017)
PHONE.................................312 738-0099
Demetra T Lagios, *President*
Ted Lagios, *Vice Pres*
EMP: 7
SQ FT: 4,800
SALES (est): 92.2K **Privately Held**
SIC: 2013 Sausages & other prepared meats; corned beef from purchased meat

(G-4278)
CRYONIZE
2716 N Ashland Ave Ste 1 (60614-7471)
PHONE.................................773 935-8803
EMP: 3 EST: 2013
SALES (est): 214.3K **Privately Held**
WEB: www.cryonize.com
SIC: 3841 Surgical & medical instruments

(G-4279)
CS ELEMENTS LLC
2619 W Agatite Ave Apt 1b (60625-3090)
PHONE.................................219 508-9270
Colin Stiscak,
EMP: 4 EST: 2017
SALES (est): 207.8K **Privately Held**
SIC: 2819 Industrial inorganic chemicals

(G-4280)
CSI CHICAGO INC
2216 W Winnemac Ave (60625-1816)
PHONE.................................773 665-2226
Gary Wing, *President*
EMP: 6
SALES (est): 425.5K **Privately Held**
SIC: 2253 T-shirts & tops, knit

(G-4281)
CST SIGN & MANUFACTURING LLC
4108 W Division St (60651-1835)
PHONE.................................312 222-0020
Chris Bambulas, *President*
EMP: 3 EST: 2014
SALES (est): 292.5K **Privately Held**
WEB: www.cstsigns.com
SIC: 3993 Signs & advertising specialties

(G-4282)
CUBIC TRNSP SYSTEMS INC
221 N La Salle St Ste 500 (60601-1208)
PHONE.................................312 257-3242
EMP: 9
SALES (corp-wide): 1.5B **Publicly Held**
SIC: 3829 Fare registers for street cars, buses, etc.
HQ: Cubic Transportation Systems, Inc.
5650 Kearny Mesa Rd
San Diego CA 92111
858 268-3100

(G-4283)
CUDNER & OCONNOR CO
Also Called: Candoc
4035 W Kinzie St (60624-1895)
PHONE.................................773 826-0200
David Knoll, *President*
Mary Miller, *Vice Pres*
EMP: 12 EST: 1935
SQ FT: 15,000
SALES (est): 3.1MM **Privately Held**
WEB: www.candocinks.com
SIC: 2893 Lithographic ink

(G-4284)
CUP O JOE COFFEE LLC
Also Called: Veteran Roasters
2032 W Iowa St (60622-4957)
PHONE.................................877 828-7656
Kip Doyle,
EMP: 5 EST: 2017
SALES (est): 244.7K **Privately Held**
SIC: 2095 Coffee roasting (except by wholesale grocers)

(G-4285)
CURBSIDE SPLENDOR
2816 N Kedzie Ave (60618-7602)
PHONE.................................224 515-6512
Naomi Huffman, *Chief*
Ben Tanzer, *Director*
EMP: 3
SALES (est): 204.3K **Privately Held**
WEB: www.curbsidesplendor.com
SIC: 2731 Books: publishing only

(G-4286)
CURLMIX INC
Also Called: Curl Mix Popup Party
325 N Hoyne Ave Ste C318 (60612-1628)
PHONE.................................773 234-6891
Kimberly Lewis, *President*
EMP: 4
SQ FT: 8,000
SALES (est): 200.4K **Privately Held**
WEB: www.curlmix.com
SIC: 2844 Hair preparations, including shampoos

(G-4287)
CUSHING AND COMPANY (PA)
213 W Institute Pl # 200 (60610-3196)
PHONE.................................312 266-8228
Cathleen Cushing Duff, *President*
Joe Cushing, *Exec VP*
Joseph X Cushing, *Vice Pres*
Matt Hausler, *Production*
Julia Kaufman, *Production*
EMP: 46
SQ FT: 28,000
SALES (est): 11.7MM **Privately Held**
WEB: www.cushingco.com
SIC: 7334 5049 3861 3952 Blueprinting service; scientific & engineering equipment & supplies; drafting supplies; blueprint cloth or paper, sensitized; lead pencils & art goods; coated & laminated paper

(G-4288)
CUSTOM & HARD TO FIND WIGS
4065 N Milwaukee Ave (60641-1834)
PHONE.................................773 777-0222
Fax: 773 777-4228
EMP: 10
SALES (est): 500.8K **Privately Held**
SIC: 2389 5699 Mfg Apparel/Accessories Ret Misc Apparel/Accessories

(G-4289)
CUSTOM CASE CO INC
6045 S Knox Ave (60629-5421)
PHONE.................................773 585-1164
Brian Reid, *President*
Darin Reid, *Vice Pres*
EMP: 20
SQ FT: 12,000
SALES (est): 1.6MM **Privately Held**
SIC: 3161 Cases, carrying

(G-4290)
CUSTOM MENU INSIGHTS LLC
73 W Monroe St 215 (60603-4955)
PHONE.................................312 237-3860
Thomas M Fitzpatrick,
Rick Garcia,
◆ **EMP:** 5
SALES (est): 419.6K **Privately Held**
SIC: 2099 Ready-to-eat meals, salads & sandwiches

(G-4291)
CUSTOM RAILZ & STAIRZ INC
6740 S Belt Circle Dr (60638-4706)
PHONE.................................773 592-7210
EMP: 2
SALES (est): 294.1K **Privately Held**
WEB: www.customrailzandstairz.com
SIC: 2431 Staircases & stairs, wood

(G-4292)
CUSTOM SIGN CONSULTANTS INC
1928 W Fulton St Ste 5 (60612-2410)
PHONE.................................312 533-2302
Al Frapolli, *President*
Erik Woolsey, *Vice Pres*
Angel Agosto, *Production*
EMP: 7
SQ FT: 3,500
SALES: 2MM **Privately Held**
SIC: 3993 Signs, not made in custom sign painting shops

(G-4293)
CYBORG SYSTEMS INC (DH)
233 S Wacker Dr Lob -001 (60606-7147)
PHONE.................................312 279-7000
Michael D Blair, *CEO*
Sean Blair, *President*
Paul Martin, *President*
Steven J Weinberg, *President*
EMP: 220 EST: 1974
SQ FT: 72,000
SALES: 19MM
SALES (corp-wide): 23.4B **Privately Held**
SIC: 7372 7371 Business oriented computer software; custom computer programming services

(G-4294)
CYGNUS CORPORATION
Also Called: Cygnus Corp Packaging Div
340 E 138th St (60827-1828)
PHONE.................................773 785-2845
Andrew Friedl, *President*
▲ **EMP:** 85
SQ FT: 74,400
SALES (est): 36.7MM **Privately Held**
SIC: 2841 Detergents, synthetic organic or inorganic alkaline

(G-4295)
CYN INDUSTRIES INC
Also Called: Boaters World
1661 N Elston Ave (60642-1545)
PHONE.................................773 895-4324
David Ritz, *President*
EMP: 12
SQ FT: 15,000
SALES (est): 1.4MM **Privately Held**
SIC: 5551 3728 5088 Marine supplies; aircraft assemblies, subassemblies & parts; marine supplies

(G-4296)
D & G PALLET SERVICE INC
4445 W 5th Ave (60624-3404)
P.O. Box 12329 (60612-0329)
PHONE.................................773 265-8470
Demetrio Delgado, *President*
EMP: 13
SQ FT: 3,500
SALES (est): 1.7MM **Privately Held**
SIC: 2448 Pallets, wood

(G-4297)
D & H GRANITE AND MARBLE SUP
1520 W Pershing Rd (60609-2408)
PHONE.................................773 869-9988
Rendee Du, *Owner*
Johnny Du, *Co-Owner*
EMP: 20
SALES (est): 1.2MM **Privately Held**
SIC: 3281 Granite, cut & shaped

(G-4298)
D & J METALCRAFT COMPANY INC
4451 N Ravenswood Ave (60640-5802)
PHONE.................................773 878-6446
Ivan Panayotov, *President*
Nicola Aglikin, *Treasurer*
Kostadin Pachof, *Treasurer*
Jeffrey Panayotov, *Accounting Mgr*
EMP: 15
SQ FT: 16,000
SALES (est): 2.6MM **Privately Held**
SIC: 3444 Sheet metal specialties, not stamped

(G-4299)
D & P CONSTRUCTION CO INC (PA)
5521 N Cmderland Ste 1106 (60656)
PHONE.................................773 714-9330
Josephine Di Fronzo, *President*
John Kaleta, *Sales Associate*
Kathleen S Clementi, *Admin Sec*
EMP: 29 EST: 1974
SQ FT: 1,200
SALES (est): 3.7MM **Privately Held**
SIC: 3443 4953 Dumpsters, garbage; recycling, waste materials

(G-4300)
D & W MFG CO INC
3237 W Lake St (60624-2004)
PHONE.................................773 533-1542
Michael Leavitt, *President*
▲ **EMP:** 45 EST: 1963
SQ FT: 40,000
SALES (est): 23.5MM **Privately Held**
WEB: www.dwmfg.com
SIC: 5051 3498 Tubing, metal; tube fabricating (contract bending & shaping)

(G-4301)
D L V PRINTING SERVICE INC
5825 W Corcoran Pl (60644-1854)
PHONE.................................773 626-1661
Bonito Johnson, *President*
Vernita Johnson, *Vice Pres*
Kesha Forrest, *Graphic Designe*
EMP: 12
SALES (est): 1.4MM **Privately Held**
SIC: 2759 2791 2789 2752 Screen printing; typesetting; bookbinding & related work; commercial printing, lithographic

(G-4302)
D-ORUM CORPORATION
325 W 103rd St (60628-2503)
PHONE.................................773 567-2064
Ernest Daurham, *President*
Claudia Daurham, *Vice Pres*
EMP: 10
SQ FT: 8,000
SALES (est): 2MM **Privately Held**
SIC: 2844 7231 Shampoos, rinses, conditioners: hair; beauty shops

(G-4303)
D5 DESIGN MET FABRICATION LLC
2439 N Pulaski Rd (60639-2113)
PHONE.................................773 770-4705
Jonathan Becker, *Partner*
Jon Becker, *Partner*

GEOGRAPHIC SECTION

Chicago - Cook County (G-4331)

EMP: 8
SALES (est): 1.4MM **Privately Held**
WEB: www.d5metals.com
SIC: 3441 7389 3446 Fabricated structural metal; design services; ornamental metalwork

(G-4304)
DABECCA NATURAL FOODS INC
700 E 107th St (60628-3806)
P.O. Box 15, Clifton TX (76634-0015)
PHONE..................773 291-1428
David A Pederson, *President*
Bill Vree, *CFO*
EMP: 150
SQ FT: 130,000
SALES: 56MM **Privately Held**
WEB: www.dabeccafoods.com
SIC: 2013 Cured meats from purchased meat

(G-4305)
DAILY GENERAL LLC
2757 W Le Moyne St Apt 2 (60622-2339)
PHONE..................217 273-0719
Elizabeth Daily, *Principal*
EMP: 4
SALES (est): 174.7K **Privately Held**
SIC: 2711 Newspapers, publishing & printing

(G-4306)
DAILY NEWS CONDOMINIUM ASSN
222 S Racine Ave (60607-2894)
PHONE..................312 492-8526
Agata Lipinsky, *President*
Juan Consuegra, *Admin Sec*
EMP: 22 EST: 2001
SALES (est): 1.4MM **Privately Held**
SIC: 2711 Newspapers, publishing & printing

(G-4307)
DAILY WHALE
222 W Ontario St (60654-3652)
PHONE..................312 787-5204
Tom Butala, *Principal*
EMP: 3
SALES (est): 124K **Privately Held**
WEB: www.dailywhale.com
SIC: 2711 Newspapers, publishing & printing

(G-4308)
DAKKOTA INTEGRATED SYSTEMS LLC
12525 S Carondolet Ave (60633-1157)
PHONE..................517 694-6500
Don Canada, *Manager*
EMP: 98
SALES (corp-wide): 242.2MM **Privately Held**
SIC: 3711 Automobile assembly, including specialty automobiles
PA: Dakkota Integrated Systems, Llc
123 Brighton Lake Rd # 202
Brighton MI 48116
517 694-6500

(G-4309)
DAMATOS BAKERY INC
1332 W Grand Ave (60642-6443)
PHONE..................312 733-6219
Mateo D'Amato, *President*
Nicola D'Amato, *Treasurer*
EMP: 6
SQ FT: 1,400
SALES (est): 350K **Privately Held**
SIC: 2051 2052 5461 Bakery: wholesale or wholesale/retail combined; breads, rolls & buns; cookies & crackers; bakeries

(G-4310)
DAMRON CORPORATION
Also Called: Damron Tea
4433 W Ohio St (60624-1054)
PHONE..................773 265-2724
Ronald Damper, *President*
John Danan, *Facilities Mgr*
Selena Pitman, *Controller*
Charlotte Calloway, *Prgrmr*
Dianne Damper, *Admin Sec*
▲ EMP: 25

SQ FT: 50,000
SALES (est): 5.6MM **Privately Held**
SIC: 3089 2099 Food casings, plastic; tea blending

(G-4311)
DANGIOS FINE ART INC
3050 W Taylor St (60612-3919)
PHONE..................773 533-3000
EMP: 2
SALES (est): 226.1K **Privately Held**
SIC: 3544 Industrial molds

(G-4312)
DANIEL J NICKEL & ASSOCS PC
3052 N Haussen Ct (60618-6519)
PHONE..................312 345-1850
Daniel Nickel, *Principal*
EMP: 4
SALES (est): 277.8K **Privately Held**
WEB: www.nickellawoffice.com
SIC: 3356 Nickel

(G-4313)
DANIELS SHARPSMART INC (DH)
Also Called: Daniels Health
111 W Jackson Blvd # 1900 (60604-3585)
P.O. Box 7697, Carol Stream (60197-7697)
PHONE..................312 546-8900
Dan Daniels, *President*
Grayson Wickard, *Plant Supt*
Darla Carney, *Plant Mgr*
Evan August, *Opers Staff*
James Vanhofwegen, *Accountant*
▲ EMP: 42
SALES (est): 278.2MM **Privately Held**
SIC: 4953 2834 7371 Medical waste disposal; pharmaceutical preparations; computer software development & applications

(G-4314)
DANIELSON FOOD PRODUCTS INC
215 W Root St (60609-2899)
PHONE..................773 285-2111
Thomas R Danielson, *President*
Linda J Danielson, *Corp Secy*
EMP: 20 EST: 1939
SQ FT: 23,000
SALES (est): 3.1MM **Privately Held**
WEB: www.danielsonfoodproducts.net
SIC: 2013 5147 Sausages & other prepared meats; meats, fresh

(G-4315)
DANISH MAID BUTTER COMPANY
8512 S Commercial Ave (60617-2533)
PHONE..................773 731-8787
Susan E Wagner, *President*
EMP: 10 EST: 1959
SQ FT: 18,000
SALES (est): 1.3MM **Privately Held**
WEB: www.danishmaid.com
SIC: 2021 Creamery butter

(G-4316)
DANZIGER KOSHER CATERING INC
Also Called: Classic Foods
3931 S Leavitt St (60609-2203)
PHONE..................847 982-1818
Stuart Morginstin, *President*
Merry Jean, *Sales Staff*
Merry Nano-Lee, *Sales Staff*
Kathy Ramos, *Sales Staff*
Lisa Correa, *Office Mgr*
▲ EMP: 30 EST: 1948
SQ FT: 30,000
SALES (est): 1.6MM **Privately Held**
WEB: www.danzigerkosher.com
SIC: 5812 2038 Caterers; frozen specialties

(G-4317)
DAPRATO RIGALI STUDIOS INC
6030 N Northwest Hwy (60631-2518)
PHONE..................773 763-5511
John Rigali, *President*
Elizabeth Rigali-Galvin, *Corp Secy*
Michael Rigali, *Vice Pres*
Robert J Rigali Jr, *Vice Pres*
EMP: 40 EST: 1860

SALES (est): 396.6K **Privately Held**
WEB: www.dapratorigali.com
SIC: 3299 3281 Statuary: gypsum, clay, papier mache, metal, etc.; art goods: plaster of paris, papier mache & scagliola; plaques: clay, plaster or papier mache cut stone & stone products

(G-4318)
DARIOS PALLETS CORP
339 N California Ave (60612)
P.O. Box 12617 (60612-0617)
PHONE..................312 421-3413
Jorge Aguilar, *President*
Pedro Perez, *Admin Sec*
◆ EMP: 35
SQ FT: 80,000
SALES (est): 4.2MM **Privately Held**
WEB: www.dariospallets.com
SIC: 2448 Pallets, wood

(G-4319)
DARLING INGREDIENTS INC
3443 S Lawndale Ave (60623-5009)
PHONE..................773 376-5550
Vince Gryb, *CEO*
EMP: 45
SALES (corp-wide): 3.3B **Publicly Held**
WEB: www.darlingii.com
SIC: 2077 Grease rendering, inedible
PA: Darling Ingredients Inc.
5601 N Macarthur Blvd
Irving TX 75038
972 717-0300

(G-4320)
DAS FOODS LLC
2041 W Carroll Ave C222 (60612-1635)
PHONE..................224 715-9289
Katie Das,
Dhruba Das,
▲ EMP: 3
SALES (est): 268.9K **Privately Held**
SIC: 2064 Candy & other confectionery products

(G-4321)
DATASITE GLOBAL CORPORATION
311 S Wacker Dr Ste 2450 (60606-6640)
PHONE..................312 263-3524
Mark Rossi, *Branch Mgr*
EMP: 200
SALES (corp-wide): 566.6MM **Privately Held**
SIC: 2759 Commercial printing
PA: Datasite Global Corporation
733 Marquette Ave Ste 600
Minneapolis MN 55402
651 646-4501

(G-4322)
DATIX (USA) INC
311 S Wacker Dr Ste 4900 (60606-6627)
PHONE..................312 724-7776
Jonathan Hazan, *Director*
EMP: 2 EST: 2011
SALES (est): 280.5K **Privately Held**
SIC: 7372 Prepackaged software

(G-4323)
DAVID ARCHITECTURAL METALS INC
3100 S Kilbourn Ave (60623-4894)
PHONE..................773 376-3200
Richard Schneider, *President*
Alan Schneider, *Chairman*
Jeffrey N Schnider, *Vice Pres*
Bernadette Ciciora, *Bookkeeper*
Albert Cacini, *Admin Sec*
EMP: 30
SQ FT: 48,000
SALES (est): 7.8MM **Privately Held**
WEB: www.davidarchitecturalmetals.com
SIC: 3441 Fabricated structural metal

(G-4324)
DAVID CORPORATION (PA)
227 W Monroe St Ste 650 (60606-5123)
PHONE..................781 587-3008
Mark Dorn, *President*
Kyle G Caswell, *Senior VP*
EMP: 50

SALES (est): 6.4MM **Privately Held**
SIC: 7372 5734 7373 Prepackaged software; software, business & non-game; value-added resellers, computer systems

(G-4325)
DAVID HORTON
1530 S State St Apt 17g (60605-2978)
PHONE..................312 917-8610
David Horton, *Principal*
EMP: 4
SALES (est): 237.8K **Privately Held**
SIC: 3714 Motor vehicle parts & accessories

(G-4326)
DE VINE DISTRIBUTORS LLC
3034 W Devon Ave Ste 104 (60659-1400)
PHONE..................773 248-7005
Alpana Hansoty, *Mng Member*
▲ EMP: 5
SALES (est): 305.6K **Privately Held**
WEB: www.devinedistributors.com
SIC: 2084 5182 Wines; wine

(G-4327)
DE VRIES INTERNATIONAL INC
3139 N Lincoln Ave (60657-3114)
PHONE..................773 248-6695
EMP: 25
SALES (corp-wide): 22.8MM **Privately Held**
SIC: 1389 Lease tanks, oil field: erecting, cleaning & repairing
PA: De Vries International, Inc.
17671 Armstrong Ave
Irvine CA 92614
949 252-1212

(G-4328)
DEBORAH ZEITLER ASSOCIATES INC
222 Merchandise Mart Plz (60654-1103)
PHONE..................312 527-3733
Deborah R Radek, *President*
Joseph Laporte, *Sales Staff*
EMP: 3 EST: 1997
SALES (est): 248.3K **Privately Held**
WEB: www.deborah-zeitler.com
SIC: 2421 5712 Outdoor wood structural products; mattresses

(G-4329)
DECORATIVE INDUSTRIES INC
6935 W 62nd St (60638-3901)
PHONE..................773 229-0015
Bartley Bryerton Sr, *President*
Bartley Bryerton Jr, *Vice Pres*
EMP: 25
SQ FT: 60,000
SALES (est): 8.9MM **Privately Held**
SIC: 5085 2759 Plastic bottles; screen printing

(G-4330)
DECORATORS SUPPLY CORPORATION
3610 S Morgan St Ste 2 (60609-1587)
PHONE..................773 847-6300
Steve Grage, *President*
Jack Meingast, *Vice Pres*
John Meingast, *Treasurer*
William Denis, *Admin Sec*
EMP: 40
SQ FT: 35,000
SALES (est): 5.5MM **Privately Held**
WEB: www.decoratorssupply.com
SIC: 2431 3299 Millwork; ornamental & architectural plaster work

(G-4331)
DEKS NORTH AMERICA INC
2700 W Roosevelt Rd (60608-1048)
PHONE..................312 219-2110
Jim Sharp, *President*
Anthony R Taglia, *Principal*
▲ EMP: 3
SALES (est): 527.2K **Privately Held**
WEB: www.deks.com.au
SIC: 3432 2952 Plumbing fixture fittings & trim; roofing materials
HQ: Deks Industries Pty Ltd
5/841 Mountain Hwy
Bayswater VIC 3153

Chicago - Cook County (G-4332)

GEOGRAPHIC SECTION

(G-4332)
DELANTE GROUP INC
401 N Michigan Ave (60611-4255)
PHONE.................................312 493-4371
David Skerke, *President*
EMP: 3 **EST:** 2012
SALES (est): 191.7K **Privately Held**
SIC: 7372 Application computer software

(G-4333)
DELL COVE SPICE CO
4900 N Hermitage Ave 3 (60640-3404)
PHONE.................................312 339-8389
David Beets, *Principal*
EMP: 3
SALES (est): 231.5K **Privately Held**
WEB: www.dellcovespices.com
SIC: 2099 5149 5499 Seasonings & spices; condiments; spices & herbs

(G-4334)
DELMARK RECORDS LLC
4121 N Rockwell St (60618-2822)
PHONE.................................773 539-5001
Julia Miller, *President*
Elbio Barilari, *Vice Pres*
Steve Wagner, *Manager*
EMP: 4
SQ FT: 6,000
SALES (est): 485.6K **Privately Held**
WEB: www.delmark.com
SIC: 3652 5735 Compact laser discs, prerecorded; phonograph records, prerecorded; magnetic tape (audio): prerecorded; compact discs; records; audio tapes, prerecorded

(G-4335)
DELOBIAN FOODS
7424 N Western Ave (60645-1707)
PHONE.................................773 564-0913
Olubambo O Opanuga, *Owner*
EMP: 6
SALES (est): 413.5K **Privately Held**
SIC: 2099 Food preparations

(G-4336)
DELTA METAL PRODUCTS CO
Also Called: Pinter Sheet Metal Work
1953 N Latrobe Ave (60639-3011)
PHONE.................................773 745-9220
Albert E Pinter, *Owner*
EMP: 7
SQ FT: 9,600
SALES (est): 695.4K **Privately Held**
SIC: 3469 Metal stampings

(G-4337)
DELUXE PRINTING
2816 S Wentworth Ave # 1 (60616-2762)
PHONE.................................312 225-0061
Pong Pong Wong, *President*
Michelle Chau, *Admin Sec*
EMP: 3
SALES (est): 289.2K **Privately Held**
SIC: 2759 2752 Commercial printing; commercial printing, lithographic

(G-4338)
DEMETER MILLWORK LLC
135 W Carroll Ave (60612)
PHONE.................................312 224-4440
Hans Fedderke, *Mng Member*
EMP: 17 **EST:** 2010
SQ FT: 27,000
SALES (est): 1.6MM **Privately Held**
SIC: 2431 Millwork

(G-4339)
DENNIS KELLOGG OFC
4104 N Elston Ave (60618-2108)
PHONE.................................773 588-3421
Dennis E Kellogg, *Owner*
EMP: 3
SALES (est): 95.7K **Privately Held**
SIC: 2711 Newspapers

(G-4340)
DENOVX LLC (PA)
3440 S Dearborn St Ste 20 (60616-5148)
PHONE.................................910 333-6689
Kevin M Schaab, *Manager*
EMP: 6
SALES (est): 1.1MM **Privately Held**
SIC: 2834 Pharmaceutical preparations

(G-4341)
DENTALEZ ALABAMA INC
Also Called: Nevin Labs
5000 S Halsted St (60609-5130)
PHONE.................................773 624-4330
Jason Hodkowski, *Sales Staff*
Ed Holland, *Branch Mgr*
EMP: 200
SIC: 3843 Dental equipment & supplies
PA: Dentalez Alabama, Inc.
  2500 S Us Highway 31
  Bay Minette AL 36507

(G-4342)
DEPUTANTE INC
4113 W Newport Ave (60641-4009)
P.O. Box 412298 (60641-7898)
PHONE.................................773 545-9531
EMP: 5 **EST:** 2004
SALES (est): 360K **Privately Held**
SIC: 2844 Mfg Toilet Preparations

(G-4343)
DESFORTE LLC
Also Called: Des4ta
5634 N Kenmore Ave # 106 (60660-4615)
P.O. Box 408977 (60640-0023)
PHONE.................................224 301-5364
Schivon Braswell, *Mng Member*
Blajia Braswell,
Maureen Braswell,
EMP: 3
SALES: 55K **Privately Held**
SIC: 2844 7389 Toilet preparations;

(G-4344)
DESHAMUSIC INC
Also Called: Sge Group, The
1645 W Ogden Ave Unit 713 (60612-4390)
PHONE.................................818 257-2716
Omar D Harris, *CEO*
EMP: 5
SALES (est): 486K **Privately Held**
SIC: 8741 7922 7389 2741 Management services; entertainment promotion; music distribution systems; music book & sheet music publishing; popular music groups or artists

(G-4345)
DESI TALK LLC
Also Called: Desi Talk Chicago
2652 W Devon Ave Ste B (60659-1811)
PHONE.................................212 675-7515
Sudhir Parikh, *Chairman*
EMP: 4 **Privately Held**
SIC: 2711 Newspapers, publishing & printing
PA: Desi Talk, Llc
  35 Journal Sq Ste 204
  Jersey City NJ 07306

(G-4346)
DEV BASE LLC
111 W Wacker Dr Apt 4607 (60601-1691)
PHONE.................................319 321-3014
Noah Berkson,
EMP: 50
SALES (est): 531.1K **Privately Held**
SIC: 7361 7372 Employment agencies; operating systems computer software

(G-4347)
DEVCO CASTING
5 S Wabash Ave Ste 407 (60603-3503)
PHONE.................................312 456-0076
Deveci Sali, *President*
EMP: 3
SALES (est): 242.9K **Privately Held**
SIC: 3325 Alloy steel castings, except investment

(G-4348)
DEVILS DUE PUBLISHING
3021 W Diversey Ave Apt 2 (60647-0021)
PHONE.................................773 412-6427
Josh Blaylock, *President*
▲ **EMP:** 6
SALES (est): 601.5K **Privately Held**
SIC: 2741 Miscellaneous publishing

(G-4349)
DEZIGN SEWING INC
4001 N Rvnswd Ave 505 (60613)
PHONE.................................773 549-4336
Barbara Vincent, *President*
EMP: 8
SQ FT: 5,000
SALES (est): 924.2K **Privately Held**
WEB: www.dezignsewing.com
SIC: 2591 2391 Drapery hardware & blinds & shades; curtains & draperies

(G-4350)
DGS IMPORT LLC
5513 N Cumberland Ave # 707 (60656-1563)
PHONE.................................800 211-9646
Thomas Vogt, *CEO*
Jennifer Zaroogian, *Business Mgr*
Joe Skinner, *Controller*
Randy Methling, *Sr Project Mgr*
Joseph Roth, *Admin Sec*
◆ **EMP:** 30
SALES (est): 5.5MM
SALES (corp-wide): 189.3MM **Privately Held**
SIC: 3993 Neon signs
PA: Dgs Retail, Llc
  5513 N Cumberland Ave # 707
  Chicago IL 60656
  800 211-9646

(G-4351)
DIAGNOSTIC PHOTONICS INC
222 Merchandise Mart Plz # 1230 (60654-4342)
PHONE.................................312 320-5478
Andrew Cittatine, *President*
Kathryn Hyer, *VP Business*
Stephen Boppart, *Officer*
Scott Carney, *Officer*
EMP: 4
SALES (est): 322K **Privately Held**
SIC: 3841 Diagnostic apparatus, medical

(G-4352)
DIAMOND INDUSTRIES LLC
3041 S Shields Ave (60616-4867)
PHONE.................................612 859-1210
Justin Diamond,
EMP: 4
SALES (est): 266.4K **Privately Held**
SIC: 3999 Manufacturing industries

(G-4353)
DIANAS BANANAS INC
2733 W Harrison St (60612-3422)
PHONE.................................773 638-6800
Robert Carmody, *President*
EMP: 11
SQ FT: 33,000
SALES (est): 2.1MM **Privately Held**
SIC: 2024 Ice cream & frozen desserts

(G-4354)
DIAZ PRINTING
4725 W Grand Ave (60639-4602)
PHONE.................................773 887-3366
Ruben Diaz, *CEO*
EMP: 2
SALES (est): 207.4K **Privately Held**
SIC: 2752 Commercial printing, offset

(G-4355)
DICOM TRANSPORTATION GROUP LP (PA)
676 N Michigan Ave # 3700 (60611-2883)
PHONE.................................312 255-4800
Scott Dobak, *Manager*
EMP: 7 **EST:** 2014
SALES (est): 21MM **Privately Held**
SIC: 3537 Trucks: freight, baggage, etc.: industrial, except mining

(G-4356)
DIEBOLDS CABINET SHOP
1938 N Springfield Ave (60647-3489)
PHONE.................................773 772-3076
Richard A Diebold Jr, *Partner*
John P Diebold, *Partner*
Richard G Diebold III, *Partner*
EMP: 5 **EST:** 1937
SQ FT: 6,000
SALES (est): 729.1K **Privately Held**
WEB: www.dieboldscabinetshop.com
SIC: 2521 2511 Wood office furniture; wood household furniture

(G-4357)
DIGISTITCH EMBROIDERY & DESIGN
6535 W Archer Ave (60638-2438)
PHONE.................................773 229-8630
Patricia Vainisi, *President*
Gina Viviano, *Owner*
EMP: 4
SALES (est): 302.5K **Privately Held**
SIC: 2395 Embroidery products, except schiffli machine

(G-4358)
DIGITAL FACTORY TECH INC
801 S Financial Pl # 2310 (60605-1795)
PHONE.................................513 560-4074
Lawrence Griffith, *CEO*
Allan Tsao, *Exec VP*
Caroline Murphy, *Financial Analy*
Enrique Rivero, *Analyst*
EMP: 33
SALES (est): 1.4MM **Privately Held**
SIC: 3993 Signs & advertising specialties

(G-4359)
DIGITAL GREENSIGNS INC
1606 W Grace St (60613-2710)
PHONE.................................312 624-8550
Christopher Bissonnette, *Principal*
EMP: 3
SALES (est): 254.9K **Privately Held**
WEB: www.greensignschicago.com
SIC: 3993 Signs & advertising specialties

(G-4360)
DIGITAL H2O INC
18 S Michigan Ave Fl 12 (60603-3200)
PHONE.................................847 456-8424
EMP: 11
SALES (est): 415.4K **Privately Held**
SIC: 7371 1382 Custom Computer Programming Oil/Gas Exploration Services
HQ: Genscape, Inc.
  195 Broad St
  Perth Amboy NJ 40203
  502 583-3435

(G-4361)
DIKE-O-SEAL INCORPORATED
3965 S Keeler Ave (60632-3879)
PHONE.................................773 254-3224
Thomas Slepski, *President*
James P Doyle, *Vice Pres*
John M Palka, *Treasurer*
Catherine M Palka, *Admin Sec*
EMP: 14
SQ FT: 16,500
SALES (est): 1.1MM **Privately Held**
WEB: www.dike-o-seal.com
SIC: 3089 3053 8711 3544 Plastic hardware & building products; gaskets, packing & sealing devices; consulting engineer; special dies, tools, jigs & fixtures

(G-4362)
DINKELS BAKERY INC
3329 N Lincoln Ave (60657-1107)
PHONE.................................773 281-7300
Norman Dinkel, *President*
Luke Karl, *General Mgr*
Eric Dinkel, *Vice Pres*
Holly Dinkel, *Manager*
Jill Glascott, *Manager*
EMP: 25
SQ FT: 15,000
SALES (est): 1.4MM **Privately Held**
WEB: www.dinkels.com
SIC: 5461 5961 5149 2052 Bread; cakes; cookies; mail order house; bakery products; cookies & crackers; bread, cake & related products

(G-4363)
DINO PUBLISHING LLC
350 W Hubbard St Ste 400 (60654-6900)
PHONE.................................312 822-9266
Jennifer Chesak, *Editor*
Kraig Devenport, *Prdtn Dir*
Annie Brown, *Accounts Mgr*
Annie Ethridge, *Accounts Exec*
Douglas A Leik, *Manager*
EMP: 4
SALES (est): 395.7K **Privately Held**
WEB: www.dinopublishing.com
SIC: 2741 Miscellaneous publishing

GEOGRAPHIC SECTION

(G-4364)
DIRTT ENVMTL SOLUTIONS INC
325 N Wells St Ste 1000 (60654-7023)
PHONE..................................312 245-2870
Mogens Smed, *CEO*
▲ **EMP:** 145
SQ FT: 81,000
SALES (est): 19.4MM **Privately Held**
SIC: 2522 2521 Office furniture, except wood; wood office furniture

(G-4365)
DISCUSS MUSIC EDUCATION CO
2720 W Winnemac Ave Apt 1 (60625-2778)
PHONE..................................773 561-2796
Les Dean, *Owner*
EMP: 4
SALES: 34K **Privately Held**
SIC: 3999 Education aids, devices & supplies

(G-4366)
DISPLAY PLAN LPDG
Also Called: Displayplan US
1901 N Clybourn Ave # 400 (60614-5090)
PHONE..................................773 525-3787
EMP: 21 **EST:** 2008
SALES (est): 1.5MM **Privately Held**
SIC: 2599 Mfg Furniture/Fixtures

(G-4367)
DISPLAY SIGNS & DESIGN
5578 N Northwest Hwy (60630-1116)
PHONE..................................800 782-1558
Ken Monroe, *President*
EMP: 2
SALES (est): 232.7K **Privately Held**
SIC: 3993 Signs & advertising specialties

(G-4368)
DISTILLERY GEEKS INC
2020 N California Ave (60647-6319)
PHONE..................................630 240-7259
EMP: 6 **EST:** 2011
SALES (est): 535.5K **Privately Held**
SIC: 2085 Distilled & blended liquors

(G-4369)
DIVERSFIED ILL GREEN WORKS LLC
2419 W Byron St (60618-3709)
PHONE..................................773 544-7777
EMP: 75
SALES (est): 1.3MM **Privately Held**
SIC: 0111 2045 Wheat

(G-4370)
DIXON PALLET SERVICE
10340 S Lowe Ave (60628-2326)
PHONE..................................773 238-9569
James E Dixon, *Principal*
EMP: 8
SALES (est): 653.7K **Privately Held**
SIC: 2448 Pallets, wood

(G-4371)
DJ TITANIUM
4016 S California Ave (60632-1815)
PHONE..................................312 823-2963
EMP: 3
SALES (est): 99.9K **Privately Held**
SIC: 3356 Titanium

(G-4372)
DJR INC
Also Called: Meilahn Manufacturing Company
5900 W 65th St (60638-5406)
PHONE..................................773 581-5204
Gary R Clarin, *President*
David Sawyer, *Admin Sec*
EMP: 16
SQ FT: 23,000
SALES: 1.9MM **Privately Held**
WEB: www.meilahnmfg.com
SIC: 2521 5046 Bookcases, office: wood; cabinets, office: wood; shelving, commercial & industrial

(G-4373)
DMI INFORMATION PROCESS CENTER
5090 W Harrison St (60644-5141)
PHONE..................................773 378-2644
Mary Denson, *Exec Dir*
EMP: 25
SQ FT: 7,000
SALES: 76.7K **Privately Held**
SIC: 8243 2711 Data processing schools; newspapers

(G-4374)
DNEPR TECHOLOGIES INC
3304 N Broadway St # 163 (60657-3517)
PHONE..................................773 603-3360
Marian Cotor, *President*
▼ **EMP:** 11
SQ FT: 1,600
SALES: 398.6K **Privately Held**
SIC: 2329 Shirt & slack suits: men's, youths' & boys'

(G-4375)
DO YOU SEE WHAT I SEE ENTERTAI
Also Called: Do You See Entertainment
2544 W North Ave Apt 3d (60647-5225)
PHONE..................................773 612-1269
Jeff Ramsey, *CEO*
Robert Jones, *President*
Christopher Snyder, *Vice Pres*
Joseph Carver, *CFO*
EMP: 5
SALES (est): 314.5K **Privately Held**
SIC: 2731 Book music: publishing & printing

(G-4376)
DOBINSKI MARKETING
3843 N Fremont St (60613-3001)
PHONE..................................773 248-5880
Richard S Dobinski, *Principal*
EMP: 3
SALES (est): 189K **Privately Held**
WEB: www.dobinski.com
SIC: 2721 Magazines: publishing & printing

(G-4377)
DOCKET TECHNOLOGIES INC
211 W Wacker Dr Ste 1703 (60606-1217)
PHONE..................................415 489-0127
Shreyas Gosalia, *CEO*
Eric Harrison, *CTO*
EMP: 3
SALES (est): 134.5K **Privately Held**
SIC: 7372 Prepackaged software

(G-4378)
DOCTORS CHOICE INC
Also Called: Nuway Distributors
600 W Cermak Rd Ste 1a (60616-4880)
PHONE..................................312 666-1111
Daniel L Gray, *President*
EMP: 9 **EST:** 2002
SALES (est): 1.4MM **Privately Held**
WEB: www.nuway-distributors.com
SIC: 5722 5047 3841 Electric household appliances; medical equipment & supplies; surgical & medical instruments

(G-4379)
DOMINO FOODS INC
Also Called: Domino Sugar
2905 S Western Ave (60608-5221)
PHONE..................................773 254-8282
Ray Francis, *Opers Staff*
Ed Furgat, *Branch Mgr*
EMP: 30
SQ FT: 55,000
SALES (corp-wide): 2B **Privately Held**
SIC: 2062 Granulated cane sugar from purchased raw sugar or syrup
HQ: Domino Foods Inc.
    99 Wood Ave S Ste 901
    Iselin NJ 08830
    732 590-1173

(G-4380)
DOMINO FOODS INC
Also Called: Domino Sugar
2400 E 130th St (60633-1725)
PHONE..................................773 646-2203
Lou Delich, *Opers-Prdtn-Mfg*
EMP: 19
SALES (corp-wide): 2B **Privately Held**
SIC: 2099 Sugar
HQ: Domino Foods Inc.
    99 Wood Ave S Ste 901
    Iselin NJ 08830
    732 590-1173

(G-4381)
DONCHEF INC
1408 W Diversey Pkwy (60614-1112)
PHONE..................................224 619-2223
Eleonora I Nikolova, *President*
EMP: 8
SALES (est): 506.4K **Privately Held**
SIC: 2051 Bread, cake & related products

(G-4382)
DONERMEN LLC
2849 W Belmont Ave A (60618-5897)
PHONE..................................773 430-2828
Floyd Nicholas G, *Managing Prtnr*
Philip Naumann, *Mng Member*
EMP: 6
SQ FT: 1,800
SALES: 520K **Privately Held**
WEB: www.donermen.com
SIC: 3713 Truck bodies (motor vehicles)

(G-4383)
DONGHIA SHOWROOMS INC
631 Merchandise Mart 63 (60654)
PHONE..................................312 822-0766
Linda Stevens, *Manager*
EMP: 7
SALES (corp-wide): 5.9MM **Privately Held**
SIC: 2395 5231 Quilted fabrics or cloth; paint, glass & wallpaper
PA: Donghia Showrooms Inc
    500 Bic Dr Ste 200
    Milford CT 06461
    203 701-2940

(G-4384)
DONNELLEY FINANCIAL LLC (HQ)
Also Called: Bowne Enterprise Solutions
35 W Wacker Dr (60601-1723)
PHONE..................................844 866-4337
Thomas J Quinlan III, *CEO*
William P Penders, *President*
Mark Haley, *Managing Dir*
Scott L Spitzer, *Senior VP*
Leeanne Sexton, *Vice Pres*
▲ **EMP:** 420
SQ FT: 143,000
SALES (est): 720.3MM
SALES (corp-wide): 874.7MM **Publicly Held**
WEB: www.rrdonnelley.com
SIC: 2752 Commercial printing, lithographic; business forms, lithographed
PA: Donnelley Financial Solutions, Inc.
    35 W Wacker Dr
    Chicago IL 60601
    844 866-4337

(G-4385)
DORENFEST GROUP LTD
444 N Michigan Ave # 1200 (60611-3903)
PHONE..................................312 464-3000
Sheldon I Dorenfest, *President*
Mitch Work, *Vice Pres*
EMP: 80
SQ FT: 15,000
SALES (est): 4MM **Privately Held**
SIC: 8742 2721 Hospital & health services consultant; trade journals: publishing only, not printed on site

(G-4386)
DOS BRO CORP
Also Called: Quicker Printers
1208 W Glenlake Ave (60660-2504)
PHONE..................................773 334-1919
Matthew Gilliana, *President*
Sargon Gilliana, *Treasurer*
EMP: 6
SALES (est): 810.9K **Privately Held**
WEB: www.quickerprinters.com
SIC: 2752 Commercial printing, offset

(G-4387)
DOTTIKON ES AMERICA INC
3559 N Cumberland Ave # 106 (60634-2865)
PHONE..................................215 295-2295
Stephan Kirschbaum, *CEO*
Sean Bradley, *Manager*
Andreas Becker, *Info Tech Dir*
Benno Liechtsteiner, *Admin Sec*
EMP: 5
SALES: 157MM **Privately Held**
SIC: 2833 Organic medicinal chemicals: bulk, uncompounded

(G-4388)
DOUBLE K TOWERS INC
5114 N Western Ave (60625-2586)
PHONE..................................773 964-3104
Daniel Zajchowski, *Principal*
EMP: 2
SALES (est): 211.8K **Privately Held**
SIC: 3829 Measuring & controlling devices

(G-4389)
DOUGHMAN DON & ASSOC
222 Merchandise Mart Plz # 947 (60654-1311)
PHONE..................................312 321-1011
Carol Curry, *Owner*
EMP: 3
SALES (est): 201.4K **Privately Held**
SIC: 2339 Women's & misses' accessories

(G-4390)
DOVE FOUNDATION
Also Called: Magnify Peace
5056 N Marine Dr Apt C4 (60640-6324)
PHONE..................................312 217-3683
Barbara Mc Donald, *CEO*
Wanda Mc Donald, *Treasurer*
EMP: 4 **EST:** 2007
SALES (est): 349.6K **Privately Held**
SIC: 2678 Writing paper & envelopes: made from purchased materials

(G-4391)
DOVER INDUSTRIAL CHROME INC
Also Called: Tvj Electroforming Division
2929 N Campbell Ave (60618-7903)
PHONE..................................773 478-2022
Fax: 773 478-0008
EMP: 5
SQ FT: 16,000
SALES: 500K **Privately Held**
SIC: 3471 3479 Electroplating And Electroforming Of Metals Or Formed Products

(G-4392)
DOVETAIL BREWERY INC
1800 W Belle Plaine Ave (60613-1827)
PHONE..................................773 683-1414
Hagen Dost, *President*
EMP: 23
SALES (est): 3.7MM **Privately Held**
WEB: www.dovetailbrewery.com
SIC: 2082 Beer (alcoholic beverage)

(G-4393)
DOW JONES & COMPANY INC
1 S Wacker Dr Ste 1700 (60606-4653)
PHONE..................................312 580-1023
EMP: 90
SALES (corp-wide): 10B **Publicly Held**
SIC: 2711 2721 Newspapers: publishing only, not printed on site; magazines: publishing only, not printed on site; periodicals: publishing only
HQ: Dow Jones & Company, Inc.
    1211 Avenue Of The Americ
    New York NY 10036
    609 627-2999

(G-4394)
DPE INCORPORATED
7647 S Kedzie Ave (60652-1507)
PHONE..................................773 306-0105
Jose Marquez, *General Mgr*
EMP: 6 **EST:** 2013
SALES (est): 900K **Privately Held**
WEB: www.dpechicago.com
SIC: 2211 2395 2759 Apparel & outerwear fabrics, cotton; embroidery & art needlework; screen printing

(G-4395)
DR EARLES LLC
2930 S Michigan Ave # 100 (60616-3270)
PHONE..................................312 225-7200
Robert Earles,
Andrea Earles,
Brian Johnson,
EMP: 5
SQ FT: 2,000
SALES: 70K **Privately Held**
SIC: 2834 Pharmaceutical preparations

Chicago - Cook County (G-4396)

(G-4396)
DRAG CITY
2921 N Cicero Ave (60641-5131)
P.O. Box 476867 (60647-0980)
PHONE.................................312 455-1015
Daniel Koretzky, *Owner*
Dan Osborn, *Co-Owner*
Grant Engstrom, *Warehouse Mgr*
Rian Murphy, *Sales Staff*
▲ **EMP:** 8
SALES (est): 770K **Privately Held**
SIC: 3652 7389 Pre-recorded records & tapes; music recording producer

(G-4397)
DRAWN LLC
35 E Wacker Dr Fl 14 (60601-2314)
PHONE.................................312 982-0040
Shanon Marks, *CEO*
Shanon R Marks, *CEO*
Patrick J Bickett, *COO*
Kristen Kligis, *Program Mgr*
Patrick Dimichele, *Officer*
EMP: 30
SQ FT: 10,000
SALES: 3MM **Privately Held**
SIC: 7372 7336 7373 7371 Prepackaged software; commercial art & graphic design; art design services; computer integrated systems design; custom computer programming services

(G-4398)
DS AIR & HEATING INC (PA)
549 N Monticello Ave (60624-1259)
PHONE.................................773 826-7411
Darryl Q Joyner Sr, *CEO*
Karon Y Hill Joyner, *Manager*
EMP: 4
SALES (est): 20K **Privately Held**
WEB: www.dsairheating.com
SIC: 1711 7389 7699 3433 Heating systems repair & maintenance; warm air heating & air conditioning contractor; ; boiler repair shop; boilers, low-pressure heating: steam or hot water

(G-4399)
DS SERVICES OF AMERICA INC
Also Called: Hinckley Springs
6055 S Harlem Ave (60638-3984)
PHONE.................................773 586-8600
Tom Houlihan, *Branch Mgr*
EMP: 250
SQ FT: 76,000
SALES (corp-wide): 2.3B **Publicly Held**
SIC: 2086 5149 7359 Water, pasteurized: packaged in cans, bottles, etc.; water, distilled; mineral or spring water bottling; equipment rental & leasing
HQ: Ds Services Of America, Inc.
2300 Windy Ridge Pkwy Se
Atlanta GA 30339
770 933-1400

(G-4400)
DUBOIS CHEMICALS GROUP INC
7025 W 66th Pl (60638-4703)
PHONE.................................708 458-2000
EMP: 9
SALES (est): 313.5K **Privately Held**
SIC: 2869 Industrial organic chemicals
PA: Dubois Chemicals, Inc.
3630 E Kemper Rd
Sharonville OH 45241

(G-4401)
DUDE PRODUCTS INC
3501 N Southport Ave 476c (60657-1475)
PHONE.................................800 898-7304
Sean Riley, *President*
Ryan Meegan, *Principal*
Brian Wilkin, *Principal*
Jeffrey Klimkowski, *Admin Sec*
EMP: 6
SALES (est): 545.1K **Privately Held**
SIC: 2621 2676 Sanitary tissue paper; sanitary paper products

(G-4402)
DUDEK & BOCK SPRING MFG CO (PA)
5100 W Roosevelt Rd (60644-1437)
PHONE.................................773 379-4100
John Dudek, *President*
Roman Krzanowski, *Vice Pres*
Jim Zhao, *Vice Pres*
Ron Bojik, *VP Opers*
Jerzy Siwek, *Plant Mgr*
▲ **EMP:** 227
SQ FT: 250,000
SALES (est): 57.1MM **Privately Held**
WEB: www.dudek-bock.com
SIC: 3493 3496 3469 Steel springs, except wire; miscellaneous fabricated wire products; metal stampings

(G-4403)
DUMORE SUPPLIES INC
Also Called: Do It Best
2525 S Wabash Ave (60616-2308)
P.O. Box 16200 (60616-0121)
PHONE.................................312 949-6260
Howard Rosenstein, *President*
Arlene Leshner, *Treasurer*
Lindsey Rosenstein, *Director*
Howie Rosenstein, *Executive*
Deena Rosenstein, *Admin Sec*
EMP: 14
SQ FT: 17,300
SALES (est): 2.1MM **Privately Held**
SIC: 5251 3429 5063 5074 Hardware; manufactured hardware (general); electrical apparatus & equipment; light bulbs & related supplies; plumbing & hydronic heating supplies; chemicals & allied products; industrial equipment services

(G-4404)
DUN-WEL LITHOGRAPH CO INC
3338 N Ravenswood Ave (60657-2047)
PHONE.................................773 327-8811
Guy Grundhoefer, *President*
Julie Grundhoefer, *Admin Sec*
EMP: 4 **EST:** 1948
SQ FT: 5,600
SALES (est): 570.8K **Privately Held**
WEB: www.dun-wel.com
SIC: 2752 Lithographing on metal; commercial printing, offset

(G-4405)
DUNAMIS INTERNATIONAL
1239 W Madison St (60607-2172)
PHONE.................................773 504-5733
EMP: 4 **EST:** 2009
SALES (est): 300K **Privately Held**
SIC: 2851 Paints And Allied Products, Nec

(G-4406)
DUO NORTH AMERICA
329 W 18th St Ste 607 (60616-1120)
PHONE.................................312 421-7755
Francois Frezzouls, *President*
▲ **EMP:** 3 **EST:** 1998
SALES (est): 900K **Privately Held**
SIC: 7319 2399 Display advertising service; banners, pennants & flags

(G-4407)
DUO USA INCORPORATED
Also Called: Duo Display
332 S Michigan Ave # 900 (60604-4393)
PHONE.................................312 421-7755
Philippe Beille, *President*
Francois Frezouls, *Principal*
Nicolas Crestin, *Marketing Staff*
▲ **EMP:** 4
SALES (est): 515.4K **Privately Held**
SIC: 2541 5046 Display fixtures, wood; store fixtures & display equipment

(G-4408)
DUPLI GROUP INC
3628 N Lincoln Ave (60613-3516)
PHONE.................................773 549-5285
Walter E Mc Cormack Jr, *President*
Rich Roth, *Accounts Exec*
Gilda Francisco, *Office Mgr*
Robert Dombrowski, *Manager*
EMP: 10 **EST:** 1948
SQ FT: 14,000
SALES (est): 1.8MM **Privately Held**
WEB: www.dupli.com
SIC: 2796 2752 2791 Lithographic plates, positives or negatives; commercial printing, lithographic; typesetting

(G-4409)
DURACARE SEATING COMPANY INC
4800 W Roosevelt Rd # 201 (60644-1481)
PHONE.................................888 592-1102
Abraham Prawer, *President*
▲ **EMP:** 18
SALES (est): 2.4MM **Privately Held**
SIC: 2514 Chairs, household: metal

(G-4410)
DURACELL COMPANY
181 W Madison St Fl 44 (60602-4510)
PHONE.................................203 796-4000
EMP: 9
SALES (corp-wide): 327.2B **Publicly Held**
SIC: 3691 Alkaline cell storage batteries
HQ: The Duracell Company
14 Research Dr
Bethel CT 06801
203 796-4000

(G-4411)
DURACELL DISTRIBUTING LLC
181 W Madison St Ste 4400 (60602-4521)
PHONE.................................203 796-4000
Mark Leckie, *President*
EMP: 1
SALES (est): 308.4K
SALES (corp-wide): 327.2B **Publicly Held**
SIC: 3691 Storage batteries
HQ: The Duracell Company
14 Research Dr
Bethel CT 06801
203 796-4000

(G-4412)
DURACELL US OPERATIONS INC ◆
135 S La Salle St (60603-4177)
PHONE.................................312 469-5266
Thom Lachman, *President*
EMP: 3 **EST:** 2019
SALES (est): 255.1K **Privately Held**
SIC: 3691 Batteries, rechargeable

(G-4413)
DURITE SCREW CORPORATION
1815 N Long Ave 35 (60639-4326)
PHONE.................................773 622-3410
Edmund Nowak Jr, *President*
Patricia Nowak, *Treasurer*
EMP: 23 **EST:** 1945
SQ FT: 15,000
SALES (est): 4.1MM **Privately Held**
WEB: www.duritescrew.com
SIC: 3599 Machine shop, jobbing & repair

(G-4414)
DUSTCATCHERS INC
8801 S South Chicago Ave (60617-2445)
PHONE.................................773 768-1440
Grant Denormandie, *President*
EMP: 6 **EST:** 2015
SALES (est): 168.2K **Privately Held**
SIC: 3564 Dust or fume collecting equipment, industrial

(G-4415)
DUVAS USA LIMITED
676 N Michigan Ave # 2800 (60611-2883)
PHONE.................................312 266-1420
EMP: 4
SALES (est): 195K **Privately Held**
SIC: 3699 Mfg Electrical Equipment/Supplies

(G-4416)
DYSON INC (DH)
1330 W Fulton St Fl 5 (60607-1137)
PHONE.................................312 469-5950
Ed Culley, *President*
Jane Farley, *Partner*
Andrea Fry, *Partner*
Tammy Potter, *Partner*
Jennifer Waldrip, *Partner*
▲ **EMP:** 100
SQ FT: 10,000
SALES (est): 52.8MM **Privately Held**
SIC: 3635 Household vacuum cleaners

(G-4417)
DYSON B2B INC
1330 W Fulton St Ste 500 (60607-1152)
PHONE.................................312 469-5950
James Dyson, *President*
Jacinta Tan, *Human Res Mgr*
Kent Woo, *Sales Staff*
Helen Boardman, *Corp Comm Staff*
Jamie Ettwein, *Manager*
▲ **EMP:** 25
SALES (est): 2.7MM **Privately Held**
SIC: 3635 Household vacuum cleaners
HQ: Dyson, Inc.
1330 W Fulton St Fl 5
Chicago IL 60607
312 469-5950

(G-4418)
DYSON DIRECT INC (DH)
1330 W Fulton St Ste 500 (60607-1152)
PHONE.................................312 469-5950
James Dyson, *President*
EMP: 4
SALES (est): 663.8K **Privately Held**
SIC: 3635 Household vacuum cleaners
HQ: Dyson, Inc.
1330 W Fulton St Fl 5
Chicago IL 60607
312 469-5950

(G-4419)
E & H TUBING INC (PA)
Also Called: Indiana Steel & Tube
4401 W Roosevelt Rd (60624-3841)
PHONE.................................773 522-3100
EMP: 13
SALES (est): 8.2MM **Privately Held**
SIC: 3317 Mfg Steel Pipe/Tubes

(G-4420)
E & L COMMUNICATION
2644 W 47th St (60632-1350)
PHONE.................................773 890-1656
Fax: 773 890-2467
EMP: 8
SALES (est): 349.7K **Privately Held**
SIC: 2711 Newspapers-Publishing/Printing

(G-4421)
E & R POWDER COATINGS INC
3729 W 49th St (60632-3601)
PHONE.................................773 523-9510
Mark Clausius, *President*
Paulette Clausius, *Vice Pres*
EMP: 45
SQ FT: 38,000
SALES (est): 6.2MM **Privately Held**
SIC: 3479 Coating of metals & formed products

(G-4422)
E AND J POLISHING AND BUFFING
4729 S Kostner Ave (60632-4435)
PHONE.................................773 569-0661
EMP: 3
SALES (est): 252.7K **Privately Held**
SIC: 3471 Polishing, metals or formed products

(G-4423)
E GORNELL & SONS INC
2241 N Knox Ave (60639-3486)
PHONE.................................773 489-2330
Gus H Treslo, *President*
Ericka Swaim, *General Mgr*
Marjorie Gornell, *Vice Pres*
▲ **EMP:** 36 **EST:** 1892
SQ FT: 30,000
SALES (est): 5.8MM **Privately Held**
WEB: www.gornellbrush.com
SIC: 3991 7389 Brushes, household or industrial; design, commercial & industrial

(G-4424)
E J KUPJACK & ASSOCIATES INC
2233 S Throop St Apt 319 (60608-5011)
PHONE.................................847 823-6661
Henry Kupjack, *President*
Jay Kupjack, *Admin Sec*
EMP: 4 **EST:** 1938
SQ FT: 3,500

GEOGRAPHIC SECTION

Chicago - Cook County (G-4454)

SALES: 275K **Privately Held**
SIC: 3999 3944 Models, general, except toy; games, toys & children's vehicles

(G-4425)
E N M COMPANY
Also Called: E N M Digital Counters
5617 N Northwest Hwy (60646-6177)
PHONE..................................773 775-8400
Nicholas G Polydoris, *President*
Fran Klein, *Vice Pres*
Joyce Picur, *Purch Mgr*
Albert Coney, *QC Mgr*
Stan Kocol, *Chief Engr*
▲ **EMP:** 100 EST: 1957
SQ FT: 80,000
SALES (est): 17.7MM **Privately Held**
WEB: www.enmco.com
SIC: 3824 3625 3568 3699 Counters, revolution; electronic totalizing counters; mechanical counters; timing devices, electronic; sprockets (power transmission equipment); pulleys, power transmission; electrical equipment & supplies; switchgear & switchboard apparatus; computer storage devices

(G-4426)
E&B EXERCISE LLC
Also Called: Eb Brands
55 W Monroe St Ste 2350 (60603-5114)
PHONE..................................844 425-5025
EMP: 2 EST: 2004
SALES (est): 287.6K **Privately Held**
SIC: 5091 3842 Whol Sporting/Recreational Goods Mfg Surgical Appliances/Supplies

(G-4427)
E-J INDUSTRIES INC
1275 S Campbell Ave (60608-1013)
PHONE..................................312 226-5023
Keith Weitzman, *President*
EMP: 55
SQ FT: 170,000
SALES (est): 10.8MM **Privately Held**
WEB: www.ejindus.com
SIC: 2599 Restaurant furniture, wood or metal; hotel furniture

(G-4428)
E-Z TREE RECYCLING INC
7050 S Dorchester Ave (60637-4704)
PHONE..................................773 493-8600
Michael Q Fowler, *President*
Yolanda E Fowler, *Admin Sec*
EMP: 6
SALES (est): 1MM **Privately Held**
SIC: 5099 2499 5989 5211 Firewood; mulch, wood & bark; wood (fuel); lumber & other building materials; lumber, plywood & millwork; sawmills & planing mills, general

(G-4429)
EAGLE MACHINE COMPANY
1725 W Walnut St (60612-2523)
PHONE..................................312 243-7407
Sigmund Kamionka, *President*
EMP: 5
SQ FT: 10,000
SALES (est): 609.9K **Privately Held**
SIC: 3599 7692 Machine shop, jobbing & repair; welding repair

(G-4430)
EAGLE PLASTICS & SUPPLY INC
814 W 120th St (60643-5532)
PHONE..................................708 331-6232
Jack Panek, *President*
EMP: 7
SALES: 400K **Privately Held**
SIC: 3089 Plastic & fiberglass tanks

(G-4431)
EARL AD INC
2201 S Union Ave Ste 2 (60616-2159)
PHONE..................................312 666-7106
Michael Hoffman, *President*
Roberta Hoffman, *Vice Pres*
EMP: 4
SALES (est): 394.5K **Privately Held**
SIC: 2759 2396 Screen printing; advertising literature: printing; automotive & apparel trimmings

(G-4432)
EARL G GRAVES PUBG CO INC
625 N Michigan Ave # 401 (60611-3110)
PHONE..................................312 274-0682
EMP: 4
SALES (corp-wide): 20.7MM **Privately Held**
SIC: 2721 Magazine Publisher
HQ: Earl G. Graves Publishing Co., Inc.
260 Madison Ave Ste 11
New York NY 10169
212 242-8000

(G-4433)
EARSHOT INC
560 W Washington Blvd # 240 (60661-2695)
PHONE..................................773 383-1798
David Rush, *CEO*
EMP: 12
SQ FT: 1,100
SALES (est): 842.3K **Privately Held**
SIC: 7372 Application computer software

(G-4434)
EAST WEST MARTIAL ARTS SUPS
5544 N Western Ave (60625-2217)
PHONE..................................773 878-7711
Kyung Sun Shin, *President*
EMP: 5
SQ FT: 30,000
SALES (est): 787K **Privately Held**
WEB: www.bearbrandinc.com
SIC: 5091 5941 3842 3699 Athletic goods; martial arts equipment & supplies; surgical appliances & supplies; electrical equipment & supplies; special dies, tools, jigs & fixtures; carpets & rugs

(G-4435)
EASTERN ACCENTS INC
Also Called: Feathersound
4201 W Belmont Ave (60641-4621)
PHONE..................................773 604-7300
Ridvan Tatargil, *President*
Siw Tatargil, *Principal*
Ron Jericho, *CFO*
EMP: 220
SQ FT: 88,000
SALES (est): 18.7MM
SALES (corp-wide): 87.6MM **Privately Held**
SIC: 2392 5719 7389 Cushions & pillows; beddings & linens; interior designer
PA: Ezine Incorporated
4201 W Belmont Ave
Chicago IL 60641
773 866-1212

(G-4436)
EASY TRAC GPS INC
233 S Wacker Dr Fl 8 (60606-6415)
PHONE..................................630 359-5804
Luis R Vera, *President*
Daniel Villalobos, *Sales Staff*
EMP: 3
SALES (est): 368.5K **Privately Held**
SIC: 3663 Radio & TV communications equipment

(G-4437)
EASY WARE CORP
2052 N Lincoln Park W (60614-4753)
PHONE..................................773 755-7732
Charlie Frankel, *President*
Ryan Brewster, *Cust Mgr*
EMP: 4
SALES (est): 351.9K **Privately Held**
SIC: 7372 Prepackaged software

(G-4438)
EATSEE INC
1132 S Wabash Ave Ste 606 (60605-2326)
PHONE..................................312 846-1492
Xu Liang, *CTO*
EMP: 3
SALES (est): 50K **Privately Held**
SIC: 7372 Prepackaged software

(G-4439)
EAZYPOWER CORPORATION
2321 N Keystone Ave (60639-3709)
PHONE..................................773 278-5000
Burton Kozak, *President*

EMP: 35
SALES (corp-wide): 1.3MM **Privately Held**
SIC: 3699 5063 5999 Household electrical equipment; electrical apparatus & equipment; electronic parts & equipment
PA: Eazypower Corporation
60639 W Belden St Ste 10
Chicago IL 60639
773 278-5000

(G-4440)
EAZYPOWER CORPORATION (PA)
60639 W Belden St Ste 10 (60639)
PHONE..................................773 278-5000
Burton Kozak, *President*
Joan Kozak, *Vice Pres*
◆ **EMP:** 9
SQ FT: 40,000
SALES (est): 1.3MM **Privately Held**
SIC: 3699 5072 Household electrical equipment; power tools & accessories

(G-4441)
EBLING ELECTRIC COMPANY
2222 W Hubbard St (60612-1614)
PHONE..................................312 455-1885
Charles Salemi, *President*
EMP: 12 EST: 1937
SQ FT: 12,000
SALES (est): 1.6MM **Privately Held**
SIC: 7694 Electric motor repair

(G-4442)
EBONYENERGY PUBLISHING INC NFP
Also Called: The Gem Group
10960 S Prospect Ave (60643-3442)
PHONE..................................773 851-5159
Cheryl Katherine Wash, *President*
EMP: 3
SALES: 10K **Privately Held**
SIC: 2731 Book publishing

(G-4443)
EBRO FOODS INC
Also Called: Ebro Packing Company
1330 W 43rd St (60609-3308)
PHONE..................................773 696-0150
Zenaida E Abreu, *President*
Silvio G Vega Jr, *Treasurer*
Andrew Vega, *Finance*
Pedro Morales, *Sales Dir*
Keith Kehl, *Regl Sales Mgr*
▼ **EMP:** 80
SQ FT: 112,000
SALES (est): 27.2MM **Privately Held**
WEB: www.ebrofoods.com
SIC: 2099 Food preparations

(G-4444)
ECD-NETWORK LLC
320 W Ohio St Ste 3w (60654-7887)
PHONE..................................917 670-0821
Kyoko Crawford, *CEO*
Jean Christophe Lapiere,
EMP: 5
SQ FT: 500
SALES (est): 176.8K **Privately Held**
WEB: www.ecd-network.com
SIC: 7372 Business oriented computer software

(G-4445)
ECHELON CAPITAL LLC (PA)
121 W Wacker Dr (60601-1781)
PHONE..................................312 263-0263
Chelsea Berg, *Director*
Louis E Berg,
EMP: 3
SALES (est): 114.1MM **Privately Held**
WEB: www.echeloncapital.com
SIC: 2542 Shelving, office & store: except wood

(G-4446)
ECO-PUR SOLUTIONS LLC
694 Veterans Pkwy Ste F (60606)
PHONE..................................630 917-8789
David Frank, *Mng Member*
▲ **EMP:** 4
SALES (est): 250K **Privately Held**
SIC: 2891 Adhesives & sealants

(G-4447)
ECO-SMART FLOORING COMPANY
550 W Wshnton Blvd Ste 20 (60661)
P.O. Box 377, Wayne NJ (07470)
PHONE..................................847 404-5032
Sue Hua Tao, *President*
Valerie Short, *Vice Pres*
EMP: 7
SALES (est): 85.1K **Privately Held**
SIC: 3069 Flooring, rubber: tile or sheet

(G-4448)
ECOCO INC
1830 N Lamon Ave (60639-4512)
PHONE..................................773 745-7700
Aaron Tiram, *President*
Hulya Akbulut, *Manager*
◆ **EMP:** 40
SQ FT: 85,000
SALES (est): 12.2MM **Privately Held**
SIC: 2844 7231 Hair preparations, including shampoos; shampoos, rinses, conditioners: hair; beauty shops

(G-4449)
ED STAN FABRICATING CO
Also Called: Stan-Ed Metal Mfg Co
4859 W Ogden Ave (60804-3662)
PHONE..................................708 863-7668
Edward A Wadas, *President*
Melanie Wadas, *Admin Sec*
EMP: 6 EST: 1952
SQ FT: 2,475
SALES (est): 290K **Privately Held**
SIC: 3469 3446 3444 3443 Stamping metal for the trade; perforated metal, stamped; architectural metalwork; sheet metalwork; fabricated plate work (boiler shop); fabricated structural metal

(G-4450)
EDGAR PALLETS
4122 W Ogden Ave (60623-2821)
PHONE..................................773 454-8919
Edgar J Mendez, *Owner*
EMP: 4 EST: 2009
SALES (est): 282.2K **Privately Held**
SIC: 2448 Pallets, wood

(G-4451)
EDGE CAPITAL GROUP INC
Also Called: Edge Carrier
55 E Monroe St Ste 3800 (60603-6030)
PHONE..................................773 295-4774
Jonathan Caballero, *President*
EMP: 15
SALES (est): 1MM **Privately Held**
SIC: 1442 Construction sand & gravel

(G-4452)
EDMARK VISUAL IDENTIFICATION
4552 N Kilbourn Ave (60630-4120)
PHONE..................................800 923-8333
Ed Yerke, *Owner*
EMP: 2
SALES (est): 250K **Privately Held**
SIC: 3999 Identification tags, except paper

(G-4453)
EDMUND D SCHMELZIE & SONS
29 E Madison St Ste 1214 (60602-4472)
PHONE..................................312 782-7230
Carl Schmelzie, *President*
Paul Schmelzie, *Vice Pres*
EMP: 3
SQ FT: 1,000
SALES (est): 500K **Privately Held**
SIC: 3915 Jewel cutting, drilling, polishing, recutting or setting

(G-4454)
EDSAL MANUFACTURING CO LLC (PA)
4400 S Packers Ave (60609-3388)
PHONE..................................773 475-3000
Bruce Saltzberg, *CEO*
Joseph Zaplatosch, *Materials Mgr*
Ken Heiman, *Purch Mgr*
Mark Robb, *Purch Mgr*
Diane Korach, *Human Res Dir*
◆ **EMP:** 1200 EST: 1957
SQ FT: 700,000

Chicago - Cook County (G-4455)

SALES (est): 383.6MM **Privately Held**
WEB: www.edsal.com
SIC: 2599 2542 2522 Factory furniture & fixtures; shelving, office & store: except wood; cabinets: show, display or storage: except wood; office furniture, except wood

(G-4455)
EDSAL MANUFACTURING CO LLC
4000 S Racine Ave (60609-2524)
PHONE.................................773 475-3165
Bruce Saltzberg, *Branch Mgr*
EMP: 111
SALES (corp-wide): 383.6MM **Privately Held**
WEB: www.edsal.com
SIC: 2599 2542 2522 Factory furniture & fixtures; shelving, office & store: except wood; office furniture, except wood
PA: Edsal Manufacturing Company, Llc
4400 S Packers Ave
Chicago IL 60609
773 475-3000

(G-4456)
EDSAL MANUFACTURING CO LLC
1555 W 44th St (60609-3335)
PHONE.................................773 475-3013
Denise White, *Principal*
Chris Kruger, *Vice Pres*
Bob Blassick, *CFO*
Julie Lonergan, *Admin Asst*
EMP: 189
SALES (corp-wide): 383.6MM **Privately Held**
SIC: 2599 2542 2522 Factory furniture & fixtures; shelving, office & store: except wood; office furniture, except wood
PA: Edsal Manufacturing Company, Llc
4400 S Packers Ave
Chicago IL 60609
773 475-3000

(G-4457)
EDUCATION EQUITY INC
30 W Webster Ave Unit A (60614)
PHONE.................................800 339-7985
EMP: 500
SALES (est): 4.8MM **Privately Held**
SIC: 7372 Educational computer software

(G-4458)
EDUCATION PARTNERS PROJECT LTD
4800 S Chicago Beach Dr 1901s (60615-7032)
PHONE.................................773 675-6643
Vernon McCallum, *Director*
Malika Diamond, *Director*
Gloria McCallum, *Director*
EMP: 4
SALES (est): 241.1K **Privately Held**
SIC: 8111 8742 8732 3953 Legal services; business consultant; educational research; seal presses, notary & hand

(G-4459)
EDV DSTRICT 7 CLRINGHOUSE VINE (PA)
8034 S Ellis Ave Apt 1w (60619-4328)
PHONE.................................312 380-1349
Vine Evette Dorthea, *Owner*
EMP: 2
SALES (est): 280.3K **Privately Held**
SIC: 2759 Currency: engraved

(G-4460)
EDVENTURE PROMOTIONS INC
1953 N Clybourn Ave Ste R (60614-4992)
PHONE.................................312 440-1800
Edward Levy, *President*
EMP: 2
SALES (est): 308.7K **Privately Held**
SIC: 3993 5199 Signs & advertising specialties; advertising specialties

(G-4461)
EDWARD FIELDS INCORPORATED
222 Merchandise Mart Plz # 635 (60654-1026)
PHONE.................................312 644-0400
Monica Reily, *Branch Mgr*
EMP: 4
SALES (corp-wide): 16.3MM **Privately Held**
SIC: 2273 Carpets & rugs
PA: Edward Fields, Incorporated
150 E 58th St Ste 1101
New York NY 10155
212 310-0400

(G-4462)
EECO SERVICES INC
Also Called: Ecker-Erhardt
2347 W 18th St (60608-1808)
PHONE.................................312 226-6030
Gerson S Ecker, *President*
Frank Padalak, *President*
EMP: 16 **EST:** 1923
SQ FT: 15,000
SALES (est): 2.4MM **Privately Held**
WEB: www.eckererhardt.com
SIC: 3599 Machine shop, jobbing & repair

(G-4463)
EIGHTY NINE ROBOTICS LLC
Also Called: 89robotics
965 W Chicago Ave (60642-5413)
PHONE.................................512 573-9091
Yue Wu, *CEO*
EMP: 3
SALES (est): 63.5K **Privately Held**
SIC: 7371 7372 8711 8731 Computer software development & applications; business oriented computer software; mechanical engineering; computer (hardware) development; automation & robotics consultant

(G-4464)
EL ENCANTO PRODUCTS INC
4041 W Ogden Ave Ste 12 (60623-2806)
PHONE.................................773 940-1807
Horacio Rodriguez, *President*
EMP: 15
SQ FT: 10,000
SALES (est): 7MM **Privately Held**
SIC: 2022 Cheese, natural & processed

(G-4465)
EL MORO DE LETRAN CHURROS & BA
Also Called: Don Churro
1626 S Blue Island Ave (60608-2134)
PHONE.................................312 733-3173
Deletran Moro, *Principal*
EMP: 12
SALES (est): 385.8K
SALES (corp-wide): 1MM **Privately Held**
SIC: 2051 5812 Bread, cake & related products; ethnic food restaurants
PA: Molina Enterprises Llc
1626 S Blue Island Ave
Chicago IL 60608
312 733-3173

(G-4466)
EL POPOCATAPETL INDUSTRIES INC
4246 W 47th St (60632-4402)
PHONE.................................773 843-0888
Elizabeth A Avina, *President*
EMP: 96
SALES (corp-wide): 13.1MM **Privately Held**
WEB: www.elpopotortillas.com
SIC: 2096 Corn chips & other corn-based snacks
PA: El Popocatapetl Industries, Inc.
1854 W 21st St
Chicago IL 60608
312 421-6143

(G-4467)
EL POPOCATAPETL INDUSTRIES INC (PA)
Also Called: Tortilleria Industries
1854 W 21st St (60608-2715)
PHONE.................................312 421-6143
Ernesto Avina, *President*
Margaret Avina, *Admin Sec*
EMP: 34 **EST:** 1971
SQ FT: 7,200
SALES (est): 13.1MM **Privately Held**
SIC: 2099 Tortillas, fresh or refrigerated

(G-4468)
EL SOL DECHICAGO NEWSPAPER
4217 W Fullerton Ave (60639-2069)
PHONE.................................773 235-7655
Fernando Moreno, *Principal*
EMP: 5
SALES (est): 243.1K **Privately Held**
SIC: 2711 Newspapers, publishing & printing

(G-4469)
EL TRADICIONAL
7647 S Kedzie Ave (60652-1507)
PHONE.................................773 925-0335
EMP: 3 **EST:** 2007
SALES (est): 90K **Privately Held**
SIC: 2099 Mfg Food Preparations

(G-4470)
EL-MILAGRO INC (PA)
3050 W 26th St (60623-4130)
PHONE.................................773 579-6120
Raphael Lopez, *President*
Manuela Loyola, *General Mgr*
Jerry Slowik, *Vice Pres*
Manuel Lopez, *Research*
Alex Arevalo, *Human Resources*
▲ **EMP:** 300
SQ FT: 3,000
SALES (est): 127.5MM **Privately Held**
SIC: 2099 5812 Tortillas, fresh or refrigerated; Mexican restaurant

(G-4471)
EL-MILAGRO INC
2919 S Western Ave Fl 1 (60608-5221)
PHONE.................................773 650-1614
Monro Lopez, *Branch Mgr*
Jessica Reyes, *Manager*
Tony Rojas, *Supervisor*
Freddy Dongo, *Technology*
Susana Gordillo, *Technology*
EMP: 200
SALES (corp-wide): 127.5MM **Privately Held**
SIC: 2099 5812 Tortillas, fresh or refrigerated; Mexican restaurant
PA: El-Milagro, Inc.
3050 W 26th St
Chicago IL 60623
773 579-6120

(G-4472)
EL-MILAGRO INC
2759 S Kedzie Ave (60623-4735)
PHONE.................................773 299-1216
Jose Apolinar, *Manager*
EMP: 40
SALES (corp-wide): 127.5MM **Privately Held**
SIC: 2099 Tortillas, fresh or refrigerated
PA: El-Milagro, Inc.
3050 W 26th St
Chicago IL 60623
773 579-6120

(G-4473)
EL-RANCHERO FOOD PRODUCTS
4457 S Kildare Ave (60632-4316)
PHONE.................................773 843-0430
Salvadore Hernandez, *Owner*
EMP: 15
SALES (corp-wide): 5.2MM **Privately Held**
WEB: www.rancherofood.com
SIC: 2096 Tortilla chips
PA: El-Ranchero Food Products
4545 S Tripp Ave
Chicago IL 60632
773 847-9167

(G-4474)
EL-RANCHERO FOOD PRODUCTS (PA)
4545 S Tripp Ave (60632-4416)
PHONE.................................773 847-9167
Salvador Hernandez, *Owner*
▲ **EMP:** 50 **EST:** 1971
SALES (est): 5.2MM **Privately Held**
SIC: 2096 2099 Tortilla chips; food preparations

(G-4475)
ELANZA TECHNOLOGIES INC
500 N Michigan Ave # 600 (60611-3777)
PHONE.................................312 396-4187
Tanvir Bukht, *CEO*
David Nancrede, *Chairman*
EMP: 40 **EST:** 2001
SQ FT: 2,000
SALES (est): 3.3MM **Privately Held**
SIC: 3661 Telephones & telephone apparatus

(G-4476)
ELDEST DAUGHTER LLC
1305 N Damen Ave (60622-1936)
PHONE.................................949 677-7385
Griffin Caprio, *Chief Engr*
Matt Kowalec, *CFO*
Brett Moody,
EMP: 3
SALES (est): 183K **Privately Held**
SIC: 3841 Surgical instruments & apparatus

(G-4477)
ELECTRO-MATIC PRODUCTS CO
2235 N Knox Ave (60639-3487)
PHONE.................................773 235-4010
Eric A Littwin, *President*
Kenneth M Littwin, *Admin Sec*
Kenneth Littwin, *Admin Sec*
EMP: 10 **EST:** 1946
SQ FT: 20,000
SALES (est): 3.7MM **Privately Held**
WEB: www.em-chicago.com
SIC: 3625 3545 3629 3823 Electric controls & control accessories, industrial; chucks: drill, lathe or magnetic (machine tool accessories); rectifiers (electrical apparatus); industrial instrmnts msrmnt display/control process variable

(G-4478)
ELECTRO-TECHNIC PRODUCTS INC
4642 N Ravenswood Ave (60640-4592)
PHONE.................................773 561-2349
Gerald T Cuzelis, *President*
EMP: 17 **EST:** 1942
SQ FT: 10,000
SALES (est): 1.2MM **Privately Held**
WEB: www.electrotechnic.com
SIC: 3812 3699 Search & detection systems & instruments; electrical equipment & supplies

(G-4479)
ELECTRONICA AVIATION LLC
150 S Wacker Dr Ste 2403 (60606-4103)
PHONE.................................407 498-1092
Simon Agassian,
EMP: 5
SQ FT: 500
SALES (est): 206.2K **Privately Held**
SIC: 3728 Research & dev by manuf., aircraft parts & auxiliary equip

(G-4480)
ELEMENT BARS INC
Also Called: Elementbars.com
1140 S Washtenaw Ave (60612-4016)
PHONE.................................888 411-3536
Jonathan Miller, *President*
Tom Kane, *General Mgr*
▲ **EMP:** 27
SALES: 1.5MM **Privately Held**
SIC: 2064 Granola & muesli, bars & clusters

(G-4481)
ELEMENTAL ART JEWELRY
5917 N Broadway St (60660-3526)
PHONE.................................773 844-4812
EMP: 3 **EST:** 2011
SALES (est): 199.6K **Privately Held**
SIC: 2819 Mfg Industrial Inorganic Chemicals

(G-4482)
ELEMENTS GROUP
2033 N Larrabee St (60614-4418)
PHONE.................................312 664-2252
EMP: 5

GEOGRAPHIC SECTION

Chicago - Cook County (G-4509)

SALES (est): 602.5K **Privately Held**
SIC: 2819 Mfg Industrial Inorganic Chemicals

(G-4483)
ELFI LLC
Also Called: Elfi Wall Systems
6001 S Knox Ave (60629)
PHONE..................................815 439-1833
George Modrovic, *Mng Member*
▼ **EMP:** 25
SQ FT: 50,000
SALES (est): 4.8MM **Privately Held**
SIC: 3449 8711 3448 Miscellaneous metalwork; energy conservation engineering; building construction consultant; prefabricated metal buildings

(G-4484)
ELG METALS INC
103rd St The Calumet Riv (60617)
PHONE..................................773 374-1500
Rich Jones, *General Mgr*
Kevin Nealis, *Mktg Dir*
EMP: 42
SALES (corp-wide): 5.3B **Privately Held**
SIC: 3312 3341 Stainless steel; secondary nonferrous metals
HQ: Elg Metals, Inc.
369 River Rd
Mckeesport PA 15132
412 672-9200

(G-4485)
ELIS CHEESECAKE COMPANY
6701 W Forest Preserve Dr (60634-1470)
PHONE..................................773 205-3800
Marc S Schulman, *President*
Walter Babian, *Vice Pres*
Patti Carroll, *Vice Pres*
Steve Dahl, *Vice Pres*
Peter A Filippelli, *Vice Pres*
▼ **EMP:** 220
SQ FT: 65,000
SALES (est): 47.1MM **Privately Held**
WEB: www.elicheesecake.com
SIC: 2053 5812 Cakes, bakery: frozen; pies, bakery: frozen; pastries (danish): frozen; eating places

(G-4486)
ELITE FABRICATION INC
1524 W Jarvis Ave (60626-2188)
PHONE..................................773 274-4474
Sean Kelley, *President*
EMP: 7
SQ FT: 15,000
SALES (est): 700K **Privately Held**
SIC: 3443 Fabricated plate work (boiler shop)

(G-4487)
ELLISON EYEWEAR INC
314 W Institute Pl Ste 2e (60610-3043)
PHONE..................................312 880-7609
EMP: 3
SALES (est): 257.5K **Privately Held**
SIC: 3851 Glasses, sun or glare

(G-4488)
ELMOS TOMBSTONE SERVICE
6023 S State St (60621-3930)
PHONE..................................773 643-0200
Hosea Knox, *Owner*
Bobbie Knox, *Co-Owner*
EMP: 3
SALES (est): 263.2K **Privately Held**
SIC: 3272 Tombstones, precast terrazzo or concrete

(G-4489)
ELMOT INC
4923 W Fullerton Ave (60639-2505)
PHONE..................................773 791-7039
Eugene Ballarin, *President*
EMP: 4
SQ FT: 800
SALES (est): 339.1K **Privately Held**
SIC: 7694 7699 Electric motor repair; industrial equipment services

(G-4490)
ELSTON MATERIALS LLC
1420 N Elston Ave (60642-2418)
PHONE..................................773 235-3100
Alex Puig,
Leonard Puig,
Luis Puig,
EMP: 9 **EST:** 2008
SQ FT: 43,000
SALES (est): 2.5MM **Privately Held**
WEB: www.elstonmaterials.com
SIC: 3271 5082 5211 Blocks, concrete or cinder: standard; general construction machinery & equipment; lumber & other building materials

(G-4491)
EMC CORPORATION
4246 Collection Center Dr (60693-0042)
PHONE..................................312 577-0026
EMP: 27 **Publicly Held**
WEB: www.emc.com
SIC: 3572 Computer storage devices
HQ: Emc Corporation
176 South St
Hopkinton MA 01748
508 435-1000

(G-4492)
EMC CORPORATION
353 N Clark St 19th (60654-4704)
PHONE..................................312 577-0026
Gene Maxwell, *Technical Staff*
Jim Ramberg, *Executive*
EMP: 6 **Publicly Held**
SIC: 3572 Computer storage devices
HQ: Emc Corporation
176 South St
Hopkinton MA 01748
508 435-1000

(G-4493)
EMEELYS SOCKS AND MORE
2415 1/2 W 63rd St (60629-1203)
PHONE..................................847 529-3026
EMP: 3
SALES (est): 88.8K **Privately Held**
SIC: 2252 Mfg Hosiery

(G-4494)
EMERALD BIOFUELS LLC (PA)
300 N La Salle Dr # 4925 (60654-3406)
P.O. Box 318, Sardinia OH (45171-0318)
PHONE..................................847 420-0898
Howard Jensen,
James Baclawski,
David Drew,
Robert Fleming,
EMP: 3
SALES (est): 363.9K **Privately Held**
SIC: 2869 Industrial organic chemicals

(G-4495)
EMERALD MACHINE INC
4641 S Halsted St (60609-4415)
P.O. Box 9269 (60609-0269)
PHONE..................................773 924-3659
Robert Matz, *President*
Dianne Krawczyk, *Vice Pres*
EMP: 6
SQ FT: 5,500
SALES: 350K **Privately Held**
SIC: 3599 7692 3444 Machine shop, jobbing & repair; welding repair; sheet metalwork

(G-4496)
EMERALD ONE LLC
300 N La Salle Dr # 4925 (60654-3406)
P.O. Box 318, Sardinia OH (45171-0318)
PHONE..................................601 529-6793
David Drew,
James Baclawski,
Robert Fleming,
Howard Jensen,
EMP: 3
SQ FT: 10,000
SALES (est): 167.2K **Privately Held**
SIC: 2869 Industrial organic chemicals
PA: Emerald Biofuels Llc
300 N La Salle Dr # 4925
Chicago IL 60654

(G-4497)
EMERSON ELECTRIC CO
Also Called: Blending and Transfer Systems
222 W Adams St Ste 400 (60606-5308)
PHONE..................................312 803-4321
EMP: 29

SALES (corp-wide): 18.3B **Publicly Held**
SIC: 3823 Industrial instrmnts msrmnt display/control process variable
PA: Emerson Electric Co.
8000 West Florissant Ave
Saint Louis MO 63136
314 553-2000

(G-4498)
EMHART TEKNOLOGIES LLC
12337 Collections Ctr Dr (60693-0001)
P.O. Box 73141 (60673-7141)
PHONE..................................877 364-2781
EMP: 17
SALES (corp-wide): 14.4B **Publicly Held**
SIC: 3541 Machine tools, metal cutting type
HQ: Emhart Teknologies Llc
480 Myrtle St
New Britain CT 06053
800 783-6427

(G-4499)
EMMERT JOHN
Also Called: Coca-Cola
1401 N Cicero Ave (60651-1600)
PHONE..................................773 292-6580
John Emmert, *Principal*
▼ **EMP:** 13 **EST:** 2007
SALES (est): 2.7MM **Privately Held**
WEB: www.coca-cola.com
SIC: 2086 Bottled & canned soft drinks

(G-4500)
EMPIRE HARD CHROME INC (PA)
1615 S Kostner Ave (60623-2336)
PHONE..................................773 762-3156
William G Horne Jr, *CEO*
Steven J Wallin, *President*
Mark Zetterquist, *General Mgr*
Thomas Boland, *Vice Pres*
Dolores Horne, *Vice Pres*
EMP: 258
SQ FT: 40,000
SALES (est): 26.3MM **Privately Held**
WEB: www.empirehardchrome.com
SIC: 3471 3599 Electroplating of metals or formed products; polishing, metals or formed products; grinding castings for the trade

(G-4501)
EMPIRE HARD CHROME INC
1537 S Wood St (60608-1919)
PHONE..................................312 226-7548
Thomas Boland, *Vice Pres*
EMP: 150
SALES (est): 5.3MM
SALES (corp-wide): 26.3MM **Privately Held**
SIC: 3471 Electroplating of metals or formed products
PA: Empire Hard Chrome, Inc.
1615 S Kostner Ave
Chicago IL 60623
773 762-3156

(G-4502)
EMS ACRYLICS & SILK SCREENER (PA)
4840 W Diversey Ave (60639-1704)
PHONE..................................773 777-5656
Eileen M Macey, *President*
EMP: 10
SQ FT: 6,000
SALES (est): 1.5MM **Privately Held**
SIC: 7336 3089 2821 Silk screen design; plastic processing; plastics materials & resins

(G-4503)
EMX DIGITAL LLC
Also Called: Breal Time
222 N Lasalle St (60601)
PHONE..................................212 792-6810
EMP: 4
SALES (corp-wide): 5.5MM **Privately Held**
SIC: 7372 Prepackaged software
PA: Emx Digital, Llc
261 Madison Ave Fl 4
New York NY 10016
212 633-4567

(G-4504)
ENAMELED STEEL AND SIGN CO
4568 W Addison St (60641-3886)
PHONE..................................773 481-2270
George Davies, *President*
Garth Davies, *General Mgr*
Jean Davies, *Vice Pres*
Jesse Hernandez, *Manager*
EMP: 23 **EST:** 1902
SQ FT: 56,000
SALES (est): 3.3MM **Privately Held**
WEB: www.enameledsteel.com
SIC: 3479 3471 3231 Coating of metals & formed products; finishing, metals or formed products; industrial glassware: made from purchased glass

(G-4505)
ENCYCLOPAEDIA BRITANNICA INC (HQ)
325 N Lasalle St Ste 200 (60654)
PHONE..................................312 347-7000
Jorge Cauz, *President*
Jacob Safra, *Chairman*
Leah Mansoor, *Senior VP*
Michael Ross, *Senior VP*
Letricia Dixon, *Production*
▲ **EMP:** 129 **EST:** 1768
SQ FT: 88,000
SALES (est): 123.1MM
SALES (corp-wide): 2.6MM **Privately Held**
WEB: www.britannica.com
SIC: 2731 Books: publishing only

(G-4506)
ENERGY ABSORPTION SYSTEMS INC (DH)
70 W Madison St Ste 2350 (60602-4295)
PHONE..................................312 467-6750
Tim Wallace, *CEO*
Gregory B Mitchell, *President*
Bruce Reimer, *Principal*
Daniel P Gorey, *Treasurer*
Jim D Crowley, *VP Sales*
◆ **EMP:** 39
SQ FT: 18,000
SALES (est): 16.1MM
SALES (corp-wide): 3B **Publicly Held**
SIC: 3499 3089 Barricades, metal; injection molded finished plastic products
HQ: Quixote Corporation
70 W Madison St Ste 2350
Chicago IL 60602
312 705-8400

(G-4507)
ENGINEERED GLASS PRODUCTS LLC
Also Called: ENGINEERED GLASS PRODUCTS, L.L.C.
929 W Exchange Ave (60609-2530)
PHONE..................................773 843-1964
Chris Hobbs, *Vice Pres*
Juan Rodriquez, *Branch Mgr*
EMP: 35 **Privately Held**
SIC: 3211 3231 Flat glass; products of purchased glass
HQ: Marsco Glass Products, L.L.C.
2857 S Halsted St
Chicago IL 60608
312 326-4710

(G-4508)
ENGINEERED GLASS PRODUCTS LLC (PA)
Also Called: Egp
2857 S Halsted St (60608-5902)
PHONE..................................312 326-4710
Mike Hobbs, *CEO*
EMP: 125
SQ FT: 20,000
SALES (est): 37.6MM **Privately Held**
SIC: 3231 Products of purchased glass

(G-4509)
ENGINEERED IRON WORKS INC
1071 Waveland Ave (60639)
PHONE..................................773 887-5701
Frankie Guzman, *CEO*
Jennifer Guzman, *President*
EMP: 14
SALES (est): 3.1MM **Privately Held**
SIC: 3441 Fabricated structural metal

Chicago - Cook County (G-4510)

(G-4510)
ENGLEWOOD CO OP
900 W 63rd Pkwy (60621-2000)
PHONE..................773 873-1201
Laura Dennis, *Manager*
EMP: 3
SALES (est): 207.1K **Privately Held**
SIC: 3272 Housing components, prefabricated concrete

(G-4511)
ENJOY LIFE NATURAL BRANDS LLC (HQ)
Also Called: Enjoy Life Foods
8770 W Bryn Mawr Ave (60631-3515)
PHONE..................773 632-2163
Scott Mandell, *CEO*
Philip D Gregorcy, *President*
Tom Lipon, *Vice Pres*
Damon Jackson, *Opers Staff*
Nick Alex, *CFO*
EMP: 50
SALES (est): 18.3MM **Publicly Held**
SIC: 2046 2051 Wheat gluten; bread, cake & related products

(G-4512)
ENR GENERAL MACHINING CO
3725 W 49th St (60632-3601)
P.O. Box 32168 (60632-0168)
PHONE..................773 523-2944
Eugene Szydlo, *President*
Andrea Portilloo, *Manager*
Richard Szydlo, *Admin Sec*
EMP: 20
SQ FT: 23,000
SALES (est): 4.4MM **Privately Held**
WEB: www.enrmachine.com
SIC: 3599 Machine shop, jobbing & repair

(G-4513)
ENSOURCE INC
2826 S Union Ave (60616-2539)
PHONE..................312 912-1048
Rongsong MEI, *President*
EMP: 3 **EST:** 2014
SALES (est): 166.1K **Privately Held**
SIC: 1311 Crude petroleum & natural gas

(G-4514)
ENTERPRISE OIL CO
3200 S Western Ave (60608-6003)
PHONE..................312 487-2025
Richard H Kruke, *President*
Dawn Mackie, *Admin Sec*
EMP: 23
SALES (est): 8.2MM **Privately Held**
SIC: 2899 2992 Chemical preparations; lubricating oils & greases

(G-4515)
ENTERPRISES ONE STOP
48 E Garfield Blvd (60615-4789)
PHONE..................773 924-5506
Eddy Baker, *Manager*
EMP: 4
SALES (est): 407.1K **Privately Held**
SIC: 3589 Car washing machinery

(G-4516)
ENTREPRENEUR MEDIA INC
205 W Wacker Dr Ste 1820 (60606-1428)
PHONE..................312 923-0818
Steve Meisner, *Manager*
EMP: 3 **Privately Held**
SIC: 2721 Magazines: publishing only, not printed on site
PA: Entrepreneur Media, Inc.
 18061 Fitch
 Irvine CA 92614

(G-4517)
ENVESTNET INC
Also Called: Envestnet PMC Prtflio MGT Cons
35 E Wacker Dr Ste 2400 (60601-2310)
PHONE..................866 924-8912
Aaron Bauer, *Vice Pres*
Eric Fowler, *Vice Pres*
Tony Leparco, *Vice Pres*
Dale Seier, *Vice Pres*
Robert Lane, *Sales Staff*
EMP: 3
SALES (corp-wide): 900.1MM **Publicly Held**
SIC: 7389 7372 6282 Financial services; prepackaged software; business oriented computer software; investment advice
PA: Envestnet, Inc.
 35 E Wacker Dr Ste 2400
 Chicago IL 60601
 312 827-2800

(G-4518)
ENVESTNET INC (PA)
35 E Wacker Dr Ste 2400 (60601-2310)
PHONE..................312 827-2800
Judson Bergman, *Ch of Bd*
Anil Arora, *Vice Ch Bd*
Bob Auclair, *President*
Robert Auclair, *President*
Christen Brown, *President*
EMP: 185
SQ FT: 43,000
SALES: 900.1MM **Publicly Held**
SIC: 7389 6282 7372 Financial services; investment advice; prepackaged software; business oriented computer software

(G-4519)
ENVESTNET RTRMENT SLUTIONS LLC (HQ)
35 E Wacker Dr (60601-2314)
PHONE..................312 827-7957
Babu Slvadasan, *President*
Kelly Michel, *Officer*
EMP: 5
SALES (est): 1.6MM
SALES (corp-wide): 900.1MM **Publicly Held**
SIC: 6411 7372 7389 Pension & retirement plan consultants; business oriented computer software; financial services
PA: Envestnet, Inc.
 35 E Wacker Dr Ste 2400
 Chicago IL 60601
 312 827-2800

(G-4520)
ENVIRONMENTAL SYSTEMS RES INST
Also Called: Esri
221 N La Salle St Ste 863 (60601-1314)
PHONE..................312 609-0966
Michael Johnson, *Manager*
Crystal Dorn, *Technical Staff*
EMP: 3
SALES (est): 1.1B **Privately Held**
SIC: 7372 Prepackaged software
PA: Environmental Systems Research Institute, Inc.
 380 New York St
 Redlands CA 92373
 909 793-2853

(G-4521)
ENVISION UNLIMITED
Also Called: Halas Vocational Center
8562 S Vincennes Ave (60620-1942)
PHONE..................773 651-1100
Stanley F Watson, *Manager*
EMP: 250
SALES (corp-wide): 23.2MM **Privately Held**
SIC: 8322 2392 8331 Social services for the handicapped; household furnishings; job training & vocational rehabilitation services
PA: Envision Unlimited
 8 S Michigan Ave Ste 1700
 Chicago IL 60603
 312 346-6230

(G-4522)
EPUBLISHING INC
720 N Franklin St (60654-7214)
PHONE..................312 768-6800
Connell Trey, *Principal*
Gloria Grafals, *Business Mgr*
Andy Kowl, *Senior VP*
EMP: 5
SALES (est): 545K **Privately Held**
SIC: 7372 Publishers' computer software

(G-4523)
EQUILON ENTERPRISES LLC
Also Called: Shell Oil Products U S
1001 W Jackson Blvd (60607-2913)
PHONE..................312 733-1849
Bob Stambolic, *Branch Mgr*
EMP: 15
SALES (corp-wide): 344.8B **Privately Held**
SIC: 5541 2911 Filling stations, gasoline; petroleum refining
HQ: Equilon Enterprises Llc
 910 Louisiana St Ste 2
 Houston TX 77002
 713 767-5337

(G-4524)
EQUINOX GROUP INC
329 W 18th St Ste 1000 (60616-1122)
PHONE..................312 226-7002
Joe Jeschawitz, *President*
EMP: 17
SQ FT: 18,000
SALES: 2MM **Privately Held**
SIC: 3469 Metal stampings

(G-4525)
ERASERMITT INCORPORATED
2001 S Michigan Ave 18q (60616-1735)
PHONE..................312 842-2855
Duane Lewis, *President*
Artis Lewis, *Treasurer*
Diane Lewis, *Admin Sec*
EMP: 3
SALES (est): 240K **Privately Held**
SIC: 3952 7389 Eraser guides & shields;

(G-4526)
ERIE VEHICLE COMPANY
60 E 51st St (60615-2192)
PHONE..................773 536-6300
Edward F Kean, *President*
Michael L Kean, *Corp Secy*
EMP: 13
SQ FT: 27,500
SALES (est): 2MM **Privately Held**
WEB: www.erievehicle.com
SIC: 3713 5084 Truck bodies (motor vehicles); hydraulic systems equipment & supplies

(G-4527)
ERQ SYSTEMS INC
10439 S Maplewood Ave (60655-1024)
PHONE..................815 469-1072
James J Broad, *President*
EMP: 22
SALES (est): 1.5MM **Privately Held**
SIC: 3443 Industrial vessels, tanks & containers

(G-4528)
ERVA TOOL & DIE COMPANY
3100 W Grand Ave (60622-4324)
PHONE..................773 533-7806
Erwin J Heyek, *President*
Theresia Heyek, *Corp Secy*
▲ **EMP:** 4
SQ FT: 17,000
SALES (est): 450K **Privately Held**
WEB: www.naturehouseinc.com
SIC: 3544 3469 7692 Die sets for metal stamping (presses); stamping metal for the trade; welding repair

(G-4529)
ESAFETY LIGHTS LLC
Also Called: Eco Safety Lights
7144 N Harlem Ave Ste 113 (60631-1017)
PHONE..................800 236-8621
Robert Chowaniec, *President*
EMP: 11
SALES: 800K **Privately Held**
SIC: 3648 3647 Strobe lighting systems; locomotive & railroad car lights

(G-4530)
ESCO LIGHTING INC
3254 N Kilbourn Ave (60641-4505)
PHONE..................773 427-7000
Donna Franklin, *President*
David Michalski, *COO*
Dave Klotz, *Opers Spvr*
Thomas Franklin, *Admin Sec*
Jessica Valenzuela,
◆ **EMP:** 30 **EST:** 1975
SQ FT: 25,000
SALES (est): 7.4MM **Privately Held**
SIC: 3646 Commercial indusl & institutional electric lighting fixtures

(G-4531)
ESP PROPERTIES LLC
Also Called: Ieg Sponsorship Conference
123 N Wacker Dr Ste 880 (60606-1775)
PHONE..................312 725-5100
Laren Ukman, *CEO*
Lesa Ukman, *CEO*
Dan Kowitz, *COO*
Jim Andrews, *Senior VP*
Larry Albus, *Vice Pres*
EMP: 50
SALES (est): 5.5MM **Privately Held**
SIC: 8748 2721 Business consulting; magazines: publishing only, not printed on site

(G-4532)
ESSANNAY SHOW IT INC
451 W Grand Ave (60642)
PHONE..................312 733-5511
Christopher Chambers, *President*
▲ **EMP:** 5 **EST:** 1964
SQ FT: 3,000
SALES (est): 877.4K **Privately Held**
WEB: www.essannay.com
SIC: 3861 7359 7377 7389 Motion picture apparatus & equipment; equipment rental & leasing; computer rental & leasing;

(G-4533)
ESSENTIAL CREAT CHICAGO INC
2112 W 95th St (60643-1118)
PHONE..................773 238-1700
Sandtricia Strickland, *President*
EMP: 5
SQ FT: 1,600
SALES: 180K **Privately Held**
SIC: 2395 7336 Embroidery products, except schiffli machine; silk screen design

(G-4534)
ESTRUCTURAS INC
2232 S Pulaski Rd (60623-3051)
P.O. Box 83, Glenview (60025-0083)
PHONE..................773 522-2200
Valentine Isasi, *Principal*
EMP: 15
SALES (est): 1.4MM **Privately Held**
SIC: 7692 Welding repair

(G-4535)
EVANG LTHN CH DR MRTN LUTH KG
Also Called: Lutheran Magazine
8765 W Higgins Rd Ste 600 (60631-4100)
PHONE..................773 380-2540
Bette Bruce, *Manager*
EMP: 10
SALES (corp-wide): 590.1K **Privately Held**
SIC: 2721 8661 Magazines: publishing only, not printed on site; religious organizations
PA: Evangelical Lutheran Church Of Dr Martin Luther
 5344 S Francisco Ave
 Chicago IL 60632
 773 776-8104

(G-4536)
EVANS FOOD GROUP LTD (HQ)
4118 S Halsted St (60609-2693)
PHONE..................773 254-7400
Carl E Lee Jr, *President*
Mauricio Olloqui, *Plant Mgr*
Salvador Perez, *Plant Mgr*
Franklin Jackson, *Info Tech Mgr*
EMP: 74
SQ FT: 100,000
SALES (est): 104.9MM
SALES (corp-wide): 95.3MM **Privately Held**
SIC: 2096 Pork rinds
PA: Benestar Brands Llc
 4118 S Halsted St
 Chicago IL 60609
 773 254-7400

▲ = Import ▼ = Export
◆ = Import/Export

GEOGRAPHIC SECTION

Chicago - Cook County (G-4564)

(G-4537)
EVANS FOODS INC (DH)
Also Called: Mac's Snacks
4118 S Halsted St (60609-2693)
PHONE.................................773 254-7400
Alex Silva, *CEO*
Jim Speakes, *President*
◆ **EMP:** 65
SQ FT: 100,000
SALES (est): 23.6MM
SALES (corp-wide): 95.3MM **Privately Held**
WEB: www.evansfood.com
SIC: 2096 Pork rinds
HQ: Evans Food Group Ltd.
 4118 S Halsted St
 Chicago IL 60609
 773 254-7400

(G-4538)
EVAPCO INC
62140 Collection Ctr (60693-0621)
PHONE.................................410 756-2600
EMP: 33
SALES (corp-wide): 378.8MM **Privately Held**
SIC: 3443 Cooling towers, metal plate
PA: Evapco, Inc.
 5151 Allendale Ln
 Taneytown MD 21787
 410 756-2600

(G-4539)
EVENTION LLC
121 W Wacker Dr Ste 3200 (60601-1781)
PHONE.................................773 733-4256
Marie Davis, *Project Dir*
Marie Rossignol, *Project Dir*
Elizabeth Kenney, *Mktg Coord*
Brian Roth, *Mng Member*
Erik Nejman, *Mng Member*
EMP: 25 **EST:** 2004
SQ FT: 4,500
SALES: 28MM **Privately Held**
WEB: www.eventionllc.com
SIC: 7372 7373 Business oriented computer software; systems software development services

(G-4540)
EVOYS CORP
Also Called: Yoos Imports
4142 W Lawrence Ave (60630-2823)
PHONE.................................773 736-4200
SE Lee, *President*
EMP: 2
SQ FT: 3,000
SALES: 8MM **Privately Held**
SIC: 3678 Electronic connectors

(G-4541)
EVRAZ INC NA (HQ)
Also Called: Evraz Oregon Steel
71 S Wacker Dr Ste 1700 (60606-4637)
PHONE.................................312 533-3555
Skip Herald, *President*
Will Baker, *General Mgr*
Jerry Reed, *Exec VP*
Pat Christie, *Vice Pres*
Dave Coffin, *Vice Pres*
◆ **EMP:** 100 **EST:** 1986
SQ FT: 12,300
SALES: 1B
SALES (corp-wide): 177.9K **Privately Held**
WEB: www.evrazna.com
SIC: 3312 3317 3325 Plate, steel; bar, rod & wire products; rails, steel or iron; steel pipe & tubes; tubes, seamless steel; railroad car wheels, cast steel

(G-4542)
EW BREDEMEIER AND CO
6625 W Diversey Ave (60707-2218)
PHONE.................................773 237-1600
Roland Leupolt, *President*
Denise Adkins, *Admin Sec*
EMP: 14 **EST:** 2002
SALES (est): 1.9MM **Privately Held**
SIC: 2231 Upholstery fabrics, wool

(G-4543)
EXCEL MACHINING INC
5654 W 65th St (60638-5502)
PHONE.................................773 585-6666
Bob Ciszek, *President*
Chris Ciszek, *Vice Pres*
EMP: 7
SQ FT: 6,400
SALES (est): 934.6K **Privately Held**
SIC: 3599 Machine shop, jobbing & repair

(G-4544)
EXPANDED METAL PRODUCTS CORP
Also Called: Empcor
4633 S Knox Ave (60632-4805)
P.O. Box 2272, Leavenworth WA (98826-2272)
PHONE.................................773 735-4500
Mark J Polan, *President*
Mark Polan, *President*
Ann Polan, *Corp Secy*
Jon Soehren, *Admin Sec*
EMP: 14 **EST:** 1958
SQ FT: 20,000
SALES (est): 1.9MM **Privately Held**
SIC: 3444 3449 Studs & joists, sheet metal; lath, expanded metal

(G-4545)
EXPRESS PUBLISHING INC
Also Called: Pole Express Publishing
6121 W Belmont Ave (60634-4004)
PHONE.................................773 725-6218
Janusz Wasewicz, *President*
Yanush Wasewicz, *President*
EMP: 8 **EST:** 1991
SALES (est): 250K **Privately Held**
SIC: 2721 Periodicals

(G-4546)
EXPRI PUBLISHING & PRINTING
6220 N Hermitage Ave (60660-1117)
PHONE.................................773 274-5955
Joseph Mihailidis, *President*
Theodora Kyrtsos, *Admin Sec*
EMP: 2
SQ FT: 2,700
SALES (est): 267.2K **Privately Held**
SIC: 2752 Commercial printing, offset

(G-4547)
F AND L PALLETS INC
3018 S Spaulding Ave Fl 1 (60623-4747)
PHONE.................................773 364-0798
Faustino Juarez, *President*
EMP: 5
SALES: 1MM **Privately Held**
SIC: 2448 5031 Pallets, wood; pallets, wood

(G-4548)
F H LEINWEBER CO INC
346 W 107th Pl (60628-3336)
PHONE.................................773 568-7722
F H Leinweber, *President*
EMP: 20
SALES (est): 1.7MM
SALES (corp-wide): 1.4MM **Privately Held**
WEB: www.leinwebercompany.com
SIC: 2891 1752 3272 2851 Sealants; floor laying & floor work; concrete products; paints & allied products
PA: F. H. Leinweber Co., Inc.
 9812 S Cicero Ave
 Oak Lawn IL 60453
 708 424-7000

(G-4549)
F HYMAN & CO
1329 N Clybourn Ave Fl 1 (60610-1797)
PHONE.................................312 664-3810
Ravindra Kobawala, *President*
Pallavi Kobawala, *Vice Pres*
Ashwin Shah, *Admin Sec*
▲ **EMP:** 7
SQ FT: 5,000
SALES (est): 658.5K **Privately Held**
WEB: www.importgenius.com
SIC: 2241 Cotton narrow fabrics

(G-4550)
F KREUTZER & CO
2646 W Madison St (60612-2064)
PHONE.................................773 826-5767
Stephen J Kreutzer, *President*
Frank M Kreutzer, *Treasurer*
Anna M Kreutzer, *Admin Sec*
EMP: 4
SQ FT: 10,000

(G-4551)
F M AQUISITION CORP
Also Called: Content That Works
3750 N Lake Shore Dr 8d (60613-4238)
PHONE.................................773 728-8351
Paul A Camp, *President*
Matthew Miller, *Editor*
Jen Champion-Gobel, *Vice Pres*
Mary Connor, *Director*
EMP: 9
SQ FT: 1,500
SALES (est): 1MM **Privately Held**
SIC: 2741 Directories: publishing & printing

(G-4552)
F T I INC
416 W Erie St (60654-5705)
PHONE.................................312 943-4015
EMP: 20
SALES (est): 1.7MM **Privately Held**
SIC: 3825 Designs/Mfg Fiber Optics

(G-4553)
F&A SPECIALTY FOODS INC
2nd Fl E 53rd St Fl Flr (60615)
PHONE.................................312 887-1344
Gerardo Fernandez Arche, *Vice Pres*
EMP: 7 **Privately Held**
SIC: 2091 Fish, smoked; salmon, smoked
HQ: F&A Specialty Foods, Inc
 40 Sw 13th St Ste 802
 Miami FL 33130
 312 887-1344

(G-4554)
FABBRI SAUSAGE MANUFACTURING
166 N Aberdeen St (60607-1606)
PHONE.................................312 829-6363
Ray Fabbri, *President*
Larry Fabbri, *Marketing Mgr*
Lawrence Fabbri, *Admin Sec*
EMP: 38
SQ FT: 30,000
SALES (est): 6.2MM **Privately Held**
WEB: www.fabbrisausage.com
SIC: 2013 5147 5142 2011 Sausages from purchased meat; roast beef from purchased meat; meats, fresh; meat, frozen: packaged; meat packing plants

(G-4555)
FABRICATING & WELDING CORP
12246 S Halsted St (60628-6400)
PHONE.................................773 928-2050
Pasquale Del Cotto, *President*
Gregory D Cotto, *Vice Pres*
Gregory Del Cotto, *Vice Pres*
Liset Ontiverous, *Admin Sec*
EMP: 21 **EST:** 1945
SQ FT: 30,000
SALES (est): 5.9MM **Privately Held**
WEB: www.fabricatingandwelding.com
SIC: 3441 7692 Fabricated structural metal; welding repair

(G-4556)
FALSE HOPE BRAND CO
1211 S Wstn Ave Ste 205 (60608)
PHONE.................................312 265-1364
Timothy Dupree II, *CEO*
Quesean Dupree, *COO*
Rashawn Dupree, *CFO*
EMP: 6
SALES (est): 233.9K **Privately Held**
SIC: 7389 5699 2326 6719 Textile & apparel services; customized clothing & apparel; service apparel (baker, barber, lab, etc.), washable: men's; investment holding companies, except banks

(G-4557)
FAMOUS LUBRICANTS INC
124 W 47th St (60609-4696)
PHONE.................................773 268-2555
Vaughn Hapeman II, *President*
James Goodale, *Treasurer*
Mary Thompson, *Admin Sec*
EMP: 8 **EST:** 1907

SQ FT: 18,000
SALES: 2.5MM **Privately Held**
SIC: 2992 5172 Lubricating oils & greases; lubricating oils & greases

(G-4558)
FANNIE MAY CNFCTONS BRANDS INC (DH)
Also Called: Fannie May Fine Chocolate
9 W Washington St (60602-1603)
PHONE.................................330 494-0833
David Taiclet, *CEO*
Terry Mitchell, *President*
Alan Petrik, *COO*
Tina Johnson, *Opers Mgr*
Jennifer Peterson, *Marketing Staff*
EMP: 15
SALES (est): 180.1MM
SALES (corp-wide): 228MM **Privately Held**
SIC: 2064 5441 Candy & other confectionery products; candy, nut & confectionery stores
HQ: Ferrero U.S.A., Inc.
 7 Sylvan Way Fl 4
 Parsippany NJ 07054
 732 764-9300

(G-4559)
FANTASTIC LETTERING INC
5644 W Lawrence Ave (60630-3220)
PHONE.................................773 685-7650
Tony Didlik, *President*
EMP: 6
SALES: 500K **Privately Held**
SIC: 2759 2396 Screen printing; automotive & apparel trimmings

(G-4560)
FAR EAST FOOD INC
Also Called: Far East Trading Co
1836 S Canal St (60616-1502)
PHONE.................................312 733-1688
Lydia Chen, *President*
▲ **EMP:** 5
SQ FT: 185,000
SALES (est): 1MM **Privately Held**
SIC: 5141 2099 Food brokers; food preparations

(G-4561)
FASHAHNN CORPORATION
8016 S Cottage Grove Ave (60619-4004)
PHONE.................................773 994-3132
Fax: 773 994-0839
EMP: 3
SALES (est): 240K **Privately Held**
SIC: 2337 5621 5611 2339 Mfg Women/Miss Suit/Coat Ret Women's Clothing Ret Men's/Boy's Clothing Mfg Women/Miss Outerwear

(G-4562)
FAST FORWARD ENERGY INC
Also Called: Bean and Body
2023 W Carroll Ave (60612-1691)
PHONE.................................312 860-0978
Ben Heins, *President*
EMP: 4
SALES: 400K **Privately Held**
SIC: 2086 Bottled & canned soft drinks

(G-4563)
FAST RADIUS INC (PA)
113 N May St (60607-2015)
PHONE.................................866 222-5458
Lou Rassey, *CEO*
Patrick McCusker, *COO*
Scott Schpero, *Finance*
Chad Jennings, *Sales Staff*
John Nanry,
EMP: 24 **EST:** 2014
SALES (est): 2.2MM **Privately Held**
SIC: 3559 Plastics working machinery

(G-4564)
FAST SIGNS
Also Called: Fastsigns
1101 W Belmont Ave (60657-3312)
PHONE.................................773 698-8115
Todd Fisher, *Owner*
EMP: 5 **EST:** 2014
SALES (est): 178.4K **Privately Held**
WEB: www.fastsigns.com
SIC: 3993 Signs & advertising specialties

(PA)=Parent Co (HQ)=Headquarters (DH)=Div Headquarters
✪ = New Business established in last 2 years

2020 Harris Illinois Industrial Directory

Chicago - Cook County (G-4565)

(G-4565)
FASTSIGNS
118 N Halsted St (60661-1042)
PHONE.................................312 344-1765
Walt Thoms, *President*
EMP: 4
SALES (est): 179.5K **Privately Held**
WEB: www.fastsigns.com
SIC: 3993 Signs & advertising specialties

(G-4566)
FATHER AND SON COMMERCIAL
4940 S Kilbourn Ave (60632-4523)
PHONE.................................773 424-3301
Angel Ocampo, *Manager*
EMP: 3 EST: 2013
SALES (est): 247.7K **Privately Held**
SIC: 2099 Food preparations

(G-4567)
FATHER MARCELLOS & SON
645 W North Ave (60610)
PHONE.................................312 654-2565
Bill Bauer, *Owner*
EMP: 130
SALES (est): 2.1MM **Privately Held**
SIC: 5812 5813 2051 Italian restaurant; drinking places; bread, cake & related products

(G-4568)
FATTAH TRADING COMPANY INC (PA)
4545 W Armitage Ave (60639-3403)
PHONE.................................773 227-2525
Abraham Fattah, *President*
Wally Fattah, *Sales Mgr*
EMP: 5
SALES (est): 5MM **Privately Held**
SIC: 2064 Candy & other confectionery products

(G-4569)
FBS GROUP INC
6513 W 64th St (60638-4913)
PHONE.................................773 229-8675
Maryann Hutson, *President*
Mat Hutson Jr, *Admin Sec*
EMP: 10
SQ FT: 10,000
SALES (est): 1.1MM **Privately Held**
SIC: 1791 3496 3446 3444 Structural steel erection; miscellaneous fabricated wire products; architectural metalwork; sheet metalwork; fabricated structural metal

(G-4570)
FBSA LLC
4545 W Augusta Blvd (60651-3315)
PHONE.................................773 524-2440
Craig Freedman, *Managing Prtnr*
EMP: 6 EST: 2011
SALES (est): 7.5MM
SALES (corp-wide): 128.6MM **Privately Held**
SIC: 2531 Seats, miscellaneous public conveyances
PA: Freedman Seating Company
4545 W Augusta Blvd
Chicago IL 60651
773 524-3255

(G-4571)
FEDERAL-MOGUL MOTORPARTS LLC
3440 N Kedzie Ave (60618)
PHONE.................................773 478-0404
Jim Borys, *General Mgr*
Rick Sotelo, *Inv Control Mgr*
John Horton, *Engineer*
EMP: 203
SALES (corp-wide): 17.4B **Publicly Held**
SIC: 3714 3568 Universal joints, motor vehicle; power transmission equipment
HQ: Federal-Mogul Motorparts Llc
27300 W 11 Mile Rd
Southfield MI 48034
248 354-7700

(G-4572)
FEDERATED PAINT MFG CO (PA)
5812 S Homan Ave (60629-3637)
PHONE.................................708 345-4848
John Bauchwitz, *CEO*
Norman Wechter, *President*
Marshall Wechter, *Corp Secy*
▲ EMP: 15 EST: 1948
SQ FT: 100,000
SALES (est): 1.9MM **Privately Held**
SIC: 2851 Varnishes

(G-4573)
FEDEX OFFICE & PRINT SVCS INC
71 E Jackson Blvd (60604-4101)
PHONE.................................312 341-9644
EMP: 11
SALES (corp-wide): 69.6B **Publicly Held**
WEB: www.fedex.com
SIC: 7389 7334 5099 2752 Packaging & labeling services; photocopying & duplicating services; signs, except electric; commercial printing, lithographic
HQ: Fedex Office And Print Services, Inc.
7900 Legacy Dr
Plano TX 75024
800 463-3339

(G-4574)
FEDEX OFFICE & PRINT SVCS INC
540 N Michigan Ave (60611-3890)
PHONE.................................312 755-0325
EMP: 10
SALES (corp-wide): 47.4B **Publicly Held**
SIC: 7389 7334 5099 2752 Business Services Photocopying Service Whol Durable Goods Lithographic Coml Print
HQ: Fedex Office And Print Services, Inc.
7900 Legacy Dr
Dallas TX 75024
214 550-7000

(G-4575)
FEDEX OFFICE & PRINT SVCS INC
505 N Michigan Ave (60611-3827)
PHONE.................................312 595-0768
EMP: 11
SALES (corp-wide): 69.6B **Publicly Held**
SIC: 7389 7334 5099 2752 Packaging & labeling services; photocopying & duplicating services; signs, except electric; commercial printing, lithographic
HQ: Fedex Office And Print Services, Inc.
7900 Legacy Dr
Plano TX 75024
800 463-3339

(G-4576)
FEDEX OFFICE & PRINT SVCS INC
720 S Michigan Ave (60605-2116)
PHONE.................................312 663-1149
EMP: 11
SALES (corp-wide): 69.6B **Publicly Held**
SIC: 7389 7334 5099 2752 Packaging & labeling services; photocopying & duplicating services; signs, except electric; commercial printing, lithographic
HQ: Fedex Office And Print Services, Inc.
7900 Legacy Dr
Plano TX 75024
800 463-3339

(G-4577)
FEDEX OFFICE & PRINT SVCS INC
444 N Wells St Fl 1 (60654-4522)
PHONE.................................312 670-4460
EMP: 18
SALES (corp-wide): 69.6B **Publicly Held**
SIC: 7334 2791 2789 2759 Photocopying & duplicating services; typesetting; bookbinding & related work; commercial printing
HQ: Fedex Office And Print Services, Inc.
7900 Legacy Dr
Plano TX 75024
800 463-3339

(G-4578)
FELICE HOSIERY CO INC (PA)
632 W Roosevelt Rd (60607-4912)
PHONE.................................312 922-3710
Felice Nelson, *President*
Irving Weinberg, *Vice Pres*
EMP: 1
SQ FT: 3,500
SALES (est): 1.3MM **Privately Held**
SIC: 2252 2251 Men's, boys' & girls' hosiery; dyeing & finishing women's full- & knee-length hosiery

(G-4579)
FELICE HOSIERY COMPANY INC
632 W Roosevelt Rd (60607-4912)
PHONE.................................312 922-3710
Felice Nelson, *President*
EMP: 23
SQ FT: 9,500
SALES (est): 1.3MM **Privately Held**
SIC: 2252 Anklets & socks

(G-4580)
FERALLOY CORPORATION (HQ)
8755 W Higgins Rd Ste 970 (60631-2735)
PHONE.................................503 286-8869
Carlos Rodriguez Borjas, *President*
Lori Dorie, *Partner*
John A Hirt, *Vice Pres*
Jack D Love, *Vice Pres*
Alan Webster, *Manager*
▲ EMP: 20
SQ FT: 10,000
SALES (est): 251.9MM
SALES (corp-wide): 10.9B **Publicly Held**
WEB: www.feralloy.com
SIC: 5051 3471 3444 3312 Iron or steel flat products; plating & polishing; sheet metalwork; blast furnaces & steel mills
PA: Reliance Steel & Aluminum Co.
350 S Grand Ave Ste 5100
Los Angeles CA 90071
213 687-7700

(G-4581)
FERNANDEZ WINDOWS CORP
2535 S Ridgeway Ave (60623-3831)
PHONE.................................773 762-2365
Juan Fernandez, *Principal*
EMP: 3
SALES (est): 263.6K **Privately Held**
SIC: 3952 Chalk: carpenters', blackboard, marking, tailors', etc.

(G-4582)
FERRARA CANDY COMPANY (HQ)
404 W Harrison St 650s (60607-0406)
PHONE.................................708 366-0500
Todd Siwak, *CEO*
Jim Nicketta, *President*
Thomas P Polke, *President*
Cynthia Hiskes, *Chairman*
Megan Oconnor, *Business Mgr*
◆ EMP: 450 EST: 1908
SQ FT: 300,000
SALES (est): 778.1MM
SALES (corp-wide): 228MM **Privately Held**
WEB: www.ferrarausa.com
SIC: 2064 Chewing candy, not chewing gum
PA: Ferrero International
R. De Treves 1
Sandweiler
349 711-1

(G-4583)
FERRARA CANDY COMPANY
404 W Harrison St 650s (60607-0406)
PHONE.................................507 452-3433
Rande Clerk, *Branch Mgr*
EMP: 223
SALES (corp-wide): 228MM **Privately Held**
SIC: 2064 Candy & other confectionery products
HQ: Ferrara Candy Company
404 W Harrison St 650s
Chicago IL 60607
708 366-0500

(G-4584)
FGS INC
815 W Van Buren St # 302 (60607-3593)
PHONE.................................312 421-3060
Thomas R Schaefer, *President*
Ryan Garth, *Exec VP*
Chuck Libman, *Exec VP*
Kevin Vertone, *Exec VP*
Ryan Doyle, *Vice Pres*
▲ EMP: 10
SALES (est): 2.6MM **Privately Held**
SIC: 2752 2759 Commercial printing, offset; commercial printing

(G-4585)
FIBERLINK LLC
230 E Ohio St Ste 212 (60611-3267)
PHONE.................................312 951-8500
Kenneth Anderson,
EMP: 5
SALES (est): 364K
SALES (corp-wide): 2.5B **Privately Held**
SIC: 3366 Copper foundries
HQ: Zayo Group, Llc
1805 29th St Unit 2050
Boulder CO 80301

(G-4586)
FIBROBLAST INC
222 Merchandise Mart Plz # 1230 (60654-4342)
PHONE.................................800 396-6463
Scott Vold, *CEO*
EMP: 12
SQ FT: 2,000
SALES (est): 256K **Privately Held**
SIC: 7372 Business oriented computer software

(G-4587)
FINAL CALL INC
Also Called: Final Call Newspaper, The
734 W 79th St (60620-2424)
PHONE.................................773 602-1230
James G Muhammad, *Editor*
EMP: 100 EST: 1985
SALES (est): 6MM **Privately Held**
SIC: 2711 2731 Newspapers, publishing & printing; books: publishing & printing; pamphlets: publishing & printing

(G-4588)
FINCHS BEER COMPANY LLC
1800 W Walnut St (60612-2526)
PHONE.................................312 929-4773
Sean Dowd, *Sales Staff*
Ben Finch, *Mng Member*
Paul Finch,
EMP: 5 EST: 2009
SALES: 500K **Privately Held**
WEB: www.finchbeer.com
SIC: 2082 5181 Beer (alcoholic beverage); beer & other fermented malt liquors

(G-4589)
FINE ARTS ENGRAVING CO
311 S Wacker Dr Ste 300 (60606-6699)
PHONE.................................800 688-4400
Joseph L Fontana Sr, *President*
EMP: 5
SALES (est): 436.7K **Privately Held**
SIC: 2759 Commercial printing

(G-4590)
FINE LINE PRINTING
5181 S Archer Ave (60632-4758)
PHONE.................................773 582-9709
Mark Stone, *Owner*
EMP: 4
SALES (est): 281.3K **Privately Held**
SIC: 2752 2791 2759 Commercial printing, offset; typesetting; commercial printing

(G-4591)
FINISHED METALS INCORPORATED
6146 S New England Ave (60638-4008)
PHONE.................................773 229-1600
Ronald Fisher, *President*
Mary Francis Johnstone, *Admin Sec*
EMP: 10 EST: 1961
SQ FT: 30,000
SALES (est): 1.6MM **Privately Held**
WEB: www.finishedmetals.com
SIC: 3471 Finishing, metals or formed products

(G-4592)
FINISHING TOUCH INC
5580 N Northwest Hwy (60630-1116)
PHONE.................................773 774-7349
Mark A Silich, *President*
Suzanne L Silich, *Admin Sec*
EMP: 14
SQ FT: 6,000

GEOGRAPHIC SECTION
Chicago - Cook County (G-4620)

SALES (est): 800K Privately Held
SIC: 3471 Polishing, metals or formed products

(G-4593)
FINKL STEEL - HOUSTON LLC (DH)
412 S Wells St Ste 500 (60607-3921)
PHONE..................................773 975-2540
Jason Wilkerson, *Controller*
Jack Miller, *Manager*
EMP: 15
SALES: 4MM
SALES (corp-wide): 3.7B Privately Held
SIC: 3312 3462 Tool & die steel & alloys; iron & steel forgings
HQ: A. Finkl & Sons Co.
412 S Wells St Ste 500
Chicago IL 60607
773 975-2510

(G-4594)
FIRST IMPRESSION OF CHICAGO
218 E 79th St (60619-2802)
PHONE..................................773 224-3434
Hayes A Bynum, *Owner*
EMP: 6
SQ FT: 8,000
SALES (est): 546.6K Privately Held
SIC: 2791 2759 2789 7336 Typesetting; commercial printing; business forms; printing; bookbinding & related work; graphic arts & related design

(G-4595)
FISH KING INC
5228 W Giddings St (60630-3602)
PHONE..................................773 736-4974
Frank Suerth, *President*
Eileen Bond, *Admin Sec*
EMP: 6
SALES (est): 701.2K Privately Held
SIC: 2048 Fish food; frozen pet food (except dog & cat); dry pet food (except dog & cat)

(G-4596)
FISHER CONTROLS INTL LLC
1124 Tower Rd (60673-0001)
P.O. Box 73735 (60673-7735)
PHONE..................................847 956-8020
EMP: 82
SALES (corp-wide): 18.3B Publicly Held
SIC: 3823 Industrial instrmnts msrmnt display/control process variable
HQ: Fisher Controls International Llc
205 S Center St
Marshalltown IA 50158
641 754-3011

(G-4597)
FISHER SCIENTIFIC COMPANY LLC
Also Called: Fisher Diagnostics
13795 Collections Ctr Dr (60693-0001)
PHONE..................................800 528-0494
EMP: 3
SALES (corp-wide): 25.5B Publicly Held
SIC: 2835 8071 3841 In vitro diagnostics; testing laboratories; diagnostic apparatus, medical
HQ: Fisher Scientific Company Llc
300 Industry Dr
Pittsburgh PA 15275
724 517-1500

(G-4598)
FISHEYE SERVICES INCORPORATED
Also Called: Fisheye Graphics
5443 N Broadway St (60640-1703)
PHONE..................................773 942-6314
Lee Nagen, *President*
EMP: 2
SQ FT: 1,000
SALES (est): 210K Privately Held
SIC: 2759 2791 2789 2752 Commercial printing; typesetting; bookbinding & related work; commercial printing, lithographic

(G-4599)
FIVE STAR DESSERTS AND FOODS
8559 S Constance Ave (60617-2220)
PHONE..................................773 375-5100
Gwendolyn Meeks, *Owner*
EMP: 5
SALES (est): 281.9K Privately Held
WEB: www.realbreadpudding.com
SIC: 2024 Ice cream & frozen desserts

(G-4600)
FIXTURE COMPANY
8770 W Bryn Mawr Ave (60631-3515)
PHONE..................................847 214-3100
James Buster, *General Mgr*
EMP: 7
SQ FT: 37,000
SALES (est): 871.6K Privately Held
SIC: 3534 3613 1796 Elevators & moving stairways; switchgear & switchboard apparatus; installing building equipment

(G-4601)
FLEETWOOD FIXTURES
848 W Eastman St (60642-2652)
PHONE..................................773 271-3390
Nellie Quintana, *COO*
Bill Goddu, *Vice Pres*
Michael Boyer, *Vice Pres*
Todd Miller, *Engineer*
EMP: 2
SALES (est): 222K Privately Held
WEB: www.fleetwoodfixtures.com
SIC: 2542 Partitions & fixtures, except wood

(G-4602)
FLEISCHMANNS VINEGAR CO INC
4801 S Oakley Ave (60609-4035)
PHONE..................................773 523-2817
Kurt Avery, *Branch Mgr*
EMP: 15 Privately Held
SIC: 2099 Vinegar
HQ: Fleischmann's Vinegar Company, Inc.
12604 Hiddencreek Way A
Cerritos CA 90703
562 483-4619

(G-4603)
FLEX LIGHTING II LLC
Also Called: Flex Lighting,
11 W Illinois St Fl 3 (60654-8173)
PHONE..................................312 929-3488
Mike Casper, *President*
Eric Blair, *Research*
Areli Aguilar, *Accounting Mgr*
Andy Gray, *Manager*
Nathan Byram, *Director*
EMP: 5
SALES (est): 1.1MM Privately Held
SIC: 3648 Lighting equipment

(G-4604)
FLEX-N-GATE LLC
Also Called: Flex N Gate
2924 E 126th St (60633-1133)
PHONE..................................773 437-5686
EMP: 3
SALES (corp-wide): 3.3B Privately Held
SIC: 3714 Motor vehicle parts & accessories
PA: Flex-N-Gate Llc
1306 E University Ave
Urbana IL 61802
217 384-6600

(G-4605)
FLEX-O-GLASS INC (PA)
Also Called: Warp Bros
4647 W Augusta Blvd Ste 1 (60651-3310)
PHONE..................................773 261-5200
Harold G Warp, *President*
Euphelia De Pasquale, *Admin Sec*
EMP: 175 EST: 1924
SQ FT: 300,000
SALES (est): 51.6MM Privately Held
WEB: www.flexoglass.com
SIC: 3081 3082 2673 2394 Plastic film & sheet; unsupported plastics profile shapes; bags: plastic, laminated & coated; canvas & related products

(G-4606)
FLEX-O-GLASS INC
Also Called: Industrial Packaging Division
1100 N Cicero Ave Ste 1 (60651-3214)
PHONE..................................773 379-7878
Harold Warp, *Branch Mgr*
EMP: 8
SALES (est): 759.7K
SALES (corp-wide): 51.6MM Privately Held
WEB: www.flexoglass.com
SIC: 3081 3082 Plastic film & sheet; unsupported plastics profile shapes
PA: Flex-O-Glass, Inc.
4647 W Augusta Blvd Ste 1
Chicago IL 60651
773 261-5200

(G-4607)
FLEXAN LLC
Also Called: Flexan Chicago
6626 W Dakin St (60634-2879)
PHONE..................................773 685-6446
Pravin Mistry, *QC Mgr*
Amy Shepley, *VP Human Res*
Ned Milic, *Manager*
EMP: 17
SALES (corp-wide): 208.3MM Privately Held
SIC: 3089 Injection molding of plastics
HQ: Flexan, Llc
500 Bond St
Lincolnshire IL 60069
224 543-0003

(G-4608)
FLEXICRAFT INDUSTRIES INC
Stayflow
2323 N Hubbard St (60612-1403)
PHONE..................................312 428-4750
Paul Berg, *President*
EMP: 15 Privately Held
SIC: 3491 3494 3499 3498 Valves, automatic control; line strainers, for use in piping systems; fire- or burglary-resistive products; fabricated pipe & fittings
PA: Flexicraft Industries, Inc.
2315 W Hubbard St
Chicago IL 60612

(G-4609)
FLEXICRAFT INDUSTRIES INC
Hosecraft USA
2315 W Hubbard St (60612-1403)
PHONE..................................312 229-7550
Paul Berg, *President*
EMP: 15 Privately Held
SIC: 3052 3494 5085 3499 Rubber & plastics hose & beltings; steam fittings & specialties; industrial supplies; chests, fire or burglary resistive: metal
PA: Flexicraft Industries, Inc.
2315 W Hubbard St
Chicago IL 60612

(G-4610)
FLEXICRAFT INDUSTRIES INC (PA)
Also Called: Headquarters
2315 W Hubbard St (60612-1403)
PHONE..................................312 738-3588
Paul Berg, *President*
Stephanie Hatfield, *Director*
Douglas S Limberg, *Admin Sec*
▲ EMP: 20
SALES (est): 11.1MM Privately Held
SIC: 3498 3494 3491 3052 Fabricated pipe & fittings; valves & pipe fittings; industrial valves; air line or air brake hose, rubber or rubberized fabric; chests, fire or burglary resistive: metal; screw machine products

(G-4611)
FLORIDA FRUIT JUICES INC
Also Called: California Pure Delite Juice &
7001 W 62nd St (60638-3924)
PHONE..................................773 586-6200
Donald Franko Sr, *President*
Don Franko Jr, *Vice Pres*
EMP: 25 EST: 1959
SQ FT: 50,000
SALES (est): 6.5MM Privately Held
WEB: www.puredelitebev.com
SIC: 2033 2086 Fruit juices: fresh; bottled & canned soft drinks

(G-4612)
FMC TECHNOLOGIES INC
Also Called: Blending and Transfer Systems
222 W Adams St Ste 400 (60606-5308)
PHONE..................................312 803-4321
EMP: 9
SALES (est): 611.8K Privately Held
SIC: 1321 Natural gas liquids

(G-4613)
FOCAL POINT LIGHTING INC
4201 S Pulaski Rd (60632-3415)
PHONE..................................773 247-9494
Peter Thornton, *President*
EMP: 200
SALES (est): 457.8K Privately Held
SIC: 3646 Commercial indusl & institutional electric lighting fixtures

(G-4614)
FOCAL POINT LLC (DH)
Also Called: Focal Point Lighting
4141 S Pulaski Rd (60632-3414)
PHONE..................................773 247-9494
Andrew Offenbacher, *President*
Tasha Ramos, *Materials Mgr*
Jesus Lebron, *Facilities Mgr*
John Sternisha, *Production*
Cathy Santiago, *Senior Buyer*
▲ EMP: 35
SQ FT: 102,000
SALES (est): 35MM
SALES (corp-wide): 27.3MM Privately Held
SIC: 3646 Commercial indusl & institutional electric lighting fixtures
HQ: Legrand Holding, Inc.
60 Woodlawn St
West Hartford CT 06110
860 233-6251

(G-4615)
FOLA COMMUNITY ACTION SERVICES
8014 S Ashland Ave (60620-4317)
PHONE..................................773 487-4310
Fload Floaoadinde, *Owner*
EMP: 10
SALES: 1MM Privately Held
SIC: 2842 Specialty cleaning preparations

(G-4616)
FONTERRA (USA) INC (HQ)
8700 W Bryn Mawr Ave 500s (60631-3681)
PHONE..................................847 928-1600
Mark Piper, *Principal*
◆ EMP: 63 EST: 1971
SALES (est): 34.4MM Privately Held
SIC: 2023 Dried milk; powdered whey

(G-4617)
FOODSERVICE DATABASE CO INC
5724 W Diversey Ave (60639-1203)
PHONE..................................773 745-9400
Ray Mitchell, *President*
EMP: 10
SALES (est): 670K Privately Held
SIC: 2741 Atlas, map & guide publishing

(G-4618)
FOREST LEE LLC
440 N Wells St Ste 530 (60654-4566)
PHONE..................................312 379-0032
John Cunningham,
Thomas Engel,
EMP: 2
SALES (est): 5MM Privately Held
SIC: 3552 Knot tying machines, textile

(G-4619)
FOREVER FLY LLC
934 N Waller Ave (60651-2649)
PHONE..................................312 981-9161
EMP: 3
SALES (est): 190K Privately Held
SIC: 2329 2331 Mfg Men's/Boy's Clothing Mfg Women's/Misses' Blouses

(G-4620)
FORMCRAFT TOOL COMPANY
6453 S Bell Ave (60636-2598)
PHONE..................................773 476-8727
William Matevich, *President*
EMP: 12 EST: 1948

Chicago - Cook County (G-4621)

SQ FT: 15,000
SALES (est): 2MM **Privately Held**
SIC: 3679 Microwave components

(G-4621)
FORTE PRINT CORPORATION
3139 W Chicago Ave (60622-4364)
PHONE.................................773 391-0105
Francisco Forte, *President*
EMP: 3
SQ FT: 600
SALES (est): 162.2K **Privately Held**
SIC: 2759 Commercial printing

(G-4622)
FORTELLA COMPANY INC
Also Called: Fortella Forture Cookies
214 W 26th St (60616-2204)
PHONE.................................312 567-9000
▲ EMP: 7
SQ FT: 6,250
SALES: 1MM **Privately Held**
SIC: 2052 Mfg Fortune Cookies

(G-4623)
FOTOFAB LLC
Also Called: Fotofabrication
3758 W Belmont Ave (60618-5246)
PHONE.................................773 463-6211
Dan Brumlik, *CEO*
Charles Cohen, *President*
Scott Bekemeyer, *Chairman*
Charlie Cohen, *Vice Pres*
Richard Sobon, *Opers Mgr*
EMP: 50
SALES (est): 9.5MM **Privately Held**
SIC: 3499 Fire- or burglary-resistive products

(G-4624)
FOUND INC
3401 N Kedzie Ave (60618-5619)
PHONE.................................773 279-3000
James York, *President*
EMP: 6 EST: 2017
SALES (est): 658.3K **Privately Held**
SIC: 2679 5112 Gift wrap & novelties, paper; greeting cards

(G-4625)
FOUNDRY PRINTERS ROW CROSSFIT
730 S Clark St (60605-1743)
PHONE.................................312 566-7201
Justin Quandt, *Principal*
EMP: 2
SALES (est): 207.3K **Privately Held**
WEB: www.thefoundrychicago.com
SIC: 2752 Commercial printing, lithographic

(G-4626)
FOUR STAR DENIM AND AP LLC
Also Called: Dearborn Denim & Apparel
3333 W Harrison St (60624-3703)
PHONE.................................847 707-6365
Robert McMillan, *Mng Member*
EMP: 15
SALES: 800K **Privately Held**
SIC: 2389 5961 5621 5699 Men's miscellaneous accessories; ; ready-to-wear apparel, women's; uniforms & work clothing

(G-4627)
FOX INTERNATIONAL CORP
Also Called: Bremner-Davis Eductl Systems
7366 N Greenview Ave (60626-1924)
PHONE.................................773 465-3634
Kathleen S Fox, *President*
EMP: 10
SALES (est): 1MM **Privately Held**
SIC: 3532 5049 Sedimentation machinery, mineral; scientific instruments

(G-4628)
FRAGRANCE ISLAND INC
641 E 79th St (60619-3036)
PHONE.................................773 488-2700
Mohammad Babul, *President*
▲ EMP: 4 EST: 2007
SALES (est): 404.3K **Privately Held**
WEB: www.fragranceislandinc.com
SIC: 2899 5199 Oils & essential oils; gifts & novelties

(G-4629)
FRANK A EDMUNDS & CO INC (PA)
6111 S Sayre Ave (60638-3911)
PHONE.................................773 586-2772
Dennis J Clegg, *President*
Paul Stepuszek, *General Mgr*
Jim Mann, *Vice Pres*
Paul Stepuzick, *Vice Pres*
▲ EMP: 14
SQ FT: 35,000
SALES (est): 1.4MM **Privately Held**
WEB: www.wooddowels.frankedmunds.com
SIC: 2499 Picture & mirror frames, wood

(G-4630)
FRANK O CARLSON & CO INC
3622 S Morgan St Ste 2r (60609-1576)
PHONE.................................773 847-6900
Rose Carlson, *President*
Matt Pendowski, *Vice Pres*
David Carlson, *Treasurer*
Kathy Camarillo, *Manager*
Scott Steckenrider, *Manager*
▲ EMP: 11
SQ FT: 28,000
SALES (est): 1.5MM **Privately Held**
SIC: 3993 Signs & advertising specialties

(G-4631)
FRANKLIN FUELING SYSTEMS INC
21054 Network Pl (60673-1210)
PHONE.................................207 283-0156
Don Kenny, *President*
EMP: 15
SALES (corp-wide): 1.3B **Publicly Held**
SIC: 3586 Gasoline pumps, measuring or dispensing
HQ: Franklin Fueling Systems, Llc
3760 Marsh Rd
Madison WI 53718
608 838-8786

(G-4632)
FREDERICS FRAME STUDIO INC
680 N Lk Shr Dr Apt 903 (60611-4477)
PHONE.................................312 243-2950
Frederick S Baker, *President*
Amy Baker, *Admin Sec*
Lisa Baker, *Admin Sec*
EMP: 12 EST: 1952
SALES (est): 470K **Privately Held**
WEB: www.fredericsframestudio.com
SIC: 2499 3499 3089 Picture & mirror frames, wood; picture frames, metal; plastic kitchenware, tableware & houseware

(G-4633)
FREEDMAN SEATING COMPANY (PA)
4545 W Augusta Blvd (60651-3338)
PHONE.................................773 524-3255
Craig Freedman, *CEO*
Gerald Freedman, *CEO*
Dan Cohen, *Vice Pres*
Dave Cohen, *Vice Pres*
Marc Caruso, *Purch Mgr*
▲ EMP: 246
SQ FT: 233,000
SALES (est): 128.6MM **Privately Held**
WEB: www.freedmanseating.com
SIC: 2531 Seats, automobile

(G-4634)
FREEDOM FUEL & FOOD INC
8950 S Ashland Ave (60620-4952)
PHONE.................................773 233-5350
EMP: 3
SALES (est): 256.7K **Privately Held**
SIC: 2869 Fuels

(G-4635)
FREIGHTCAR AMERICA INC (PA)
125 S Wacker Dr Ste 1500 (60606-4477)
PHONE.................................800 458-2235
William D Gehl, *Ch of Bd*
James R Meyer, *President*
Scott Finney, *Area Mgr*
Steve Cianci, *Senior VP*
Mike Kelly, *Vice Pres*
◆ EMP: 78
SQ FT: 15,540

SALES: 229.9MM **Publicly Held**
SIC: 3743 Train cars & equipment, freight or passenger

(G-4636)
FRIEDRICH KLATT AND ASSOCIATES
5240 S Hyde Park Blvd (60615-4213)
PHONE.................................773 753-1806
Dan Friedrich, *Partner*
Marcia Klatt, *Partner*
EMP: 5
SQ FT: 3,900
SALES (est): 672.9K **Privately Held**
SIC: 7379 8243 5734 7372 Computer related consulting services; operator training, computer; computer & software stores; business oriented computer software

(G-4637)
FRIENDS FUEL
8200 S Kedzie Ave (60652-3329)
PHONE.................................773 434-9387
George Dinker, *Manager*
EMP: 4
SALES (est): 328.7K **Privately Held**
SIC: 2869 Fuels

(G-4638)
FRUIT FANCY
1116 W 110th St (60643-3744)
PHONE.................................708 724-2613
Yashicka Johnsom, *CEO*
EMP: 30
SALES (est): 942.1K **Privately Held**
SIC: 2099 Food preparations

(G-4639)
FULL COURT PRESS INC
9146 S Pleasant Ave (60643-6011)
PHONE.................................773 779-1135
Michael Ryan, *President*
EMP: 2
SALES: 500K **Privately Held**
SIC: 2752 Commercial printing, offset

(G-4640)
FULL LINE PRINTING INC
361 W Chicago Ave (60654-5125)
PHONE.................................312 642-8080
Jeff Juhasz, *President*
Stephen Juhasz, *Vice Pres*
Patrick Kasch,
EMP: 5
SQ FT: 4,500
SALES (est): 1.5MM **Privately Held**
WEB: www.fulllineprinting.com
SIC: 2752 5947 Commercial printing, offset; greeting cards

(G-4641)
FULLY EQUIPPED INC
1751d W Howard St 103 (60626-1626)
PHONE.................................312 978-9936
Artjoms Kalinicenko, *President*
EMP: 2
SALES: 300K **Privately Held**
SIC: 2741

(G-4642)
FULTONWORKS LLC
1165 N Clark St (60610-2702)
PHONE.................................312 544-9639
EMP: 3
SALES (est): 167.1K **Privately Held**
WEB: www.fultonworks.co
SIC: 3652 Pre-recorded records & tapes

(G-4643)
FUNNY VALENTINE PRESS INC
4923 N Oakley Ave (60625-1925)
P.O. Box 25734 (60625-8614)
PHONE.................................773 769-6552
EMP: 3 EST: 2008
SALES (est): 145.1K **Privately Held**
WEB: www.nostalgiadigest.com
SIC: 2741 Miscellaneous publishing

(G-4644)
FURDGE TRUCKING INC ◉
7704 S Loomis Blvd (60620-3750)
PHONE.................................773 800-5431
Juan A Furdge, *President*
EMP: 1 EST: 2020

SALES: 300K **Privately Held**
SIC: 3537 Trucks, tractors, loaders, carriers & similar equipment

(G-4645)
FUTURE BRANDS LLC (DH)
222 Merchandise Mart Plz # 1600 (60654-4262)
PHONE.................................847 444-1880
Steve Bellini, *Mng Member*
▲ EMP: 250
SQ FT: 30,000
SALES (est): 39.7MM **Privately Held**
SIC: 2085 Distilled & blended liquors
HQ: Beam Suntory Inc.
222 Merchandise Mart Plz # 1600
Chicago IL 60654
312 964-6999

(G-4646)
FUTURES MAGAZINE INC
107 W Van Buren St # 203 (60605-1054)
PHONE.................................312 846-4600
Steve Zwick, *Principal*
EMP: 2
SALES (est): 749.3K
SALES (corp-wide): 1MM **Privately Held**
SIC: 2721 Magazines: publishing & printing
PA: The Alpha Pages Llc
107 W Van Buren St # 203
Chicago IL 60605
847 733-1740

(G-4647)
G & H BALANCER SERVICE
2919 W Irving Park Rd (60618-3511)
PHONE.................................773 509-1988
Gary Hildreth, *Owner*
EMP: 3
SALES (est): 190.7K **Privately Held**
SIC: 3596 Industrial scales

(G-4648)
G B HOLDINGS INC
600 N Kilbourn Ave (60624-1041)
PHONE.................................773 265-3000
Dennis Greenspon, *President*
Steve Greenspon, *Vice Pres*
Lawrence Greenspon, *Treasurer*
David Pollens, *VP Finance*
EMP: 117
SQ FT: 150,000
SALES (est): 10MM **Privately Held**
SIC: 3432 Plumbing fixture fittings & trim

(G-4649)
G E MATHIS COMPANY
6100 S Oak Park Ave (60638-4014)
PHONE.................................773 586-3800
Lael Mathis, *President*
Craig Mathis, *Vice Pres*
Paul Mathis, *Vice Pres*
Robert Brown, *Project Mgr*
Patricia Kaishas, *Traffic Mgr*
▲ EMP: 96 EST: 1905
SQ FT: 125,000
SALES (est): 37MM **Privately Held**
WEB: www.gemathis.com
SIC: 3443 Tanks, standard or custom fabricated: metal plate

(G-4650)
G I A PUBLICATIONS INC (PA)
7404 S Mason Ave (60638-6230)
PHONE.................................708 496-3800
Edward J Harris, *CEO*
Alexander Harris, *President*
Gladys Guerrero, *General Mgr*
Maria Peccia, *General Mgr*
Rett Richards, *Editor*
▲ EMP: 50
SQ FT: 50,000
SALES (est): 10.4MM **Privately Held**
SIC: 2741 Music books: publishing & printing; music, sheet: publishing & printing

(G-4651)
G Y INDUSTRIES LLC
70 W Madison St Ste 2300 (60602-4250)
PHONE.................................708 210-0800
Bill Dustin,
EMP: 12
SQ FT: 28,000
SALES (est): 1.7MM **Privately Held**
SIC: 2759 Letterpress & screen printing

GEOGRAPHIC SECTION
Chicago - Cook County (G-4677)

(G-4652)
G2 CROWD INC (PA)
Also Called: G2 Labs
20 N Wacker Dr Ste 1800 (60606-2905)
PHONE.....................847 748-7559
Godard Abel, *CEO*
Adam Goyette, *Vice Pres*
Heather Reed, *Vice Pres*
Andrew Stapleton, *Vice Pres*
Jake Rudnik, *Research*
EMP: 51
SQ FT: 1,600
SALES (est): 26.6MM **Privately Held**
SIC: 7372 7371 5045 Business oriented computer software; computer software development & applications; computer software

(G-4653)
GABEL & SCHUBERT BRONZE
4500 N Ravenswood Ave (60640-5202)
PHONE......................773 878-6800
Thomas A Hillis, *President*
EMP: 12 **EST:** 1973
SQ FT: 11,000
SALES (est): 1.1MM **Privately Held**
SIC: 3993 3999 Name plates: except engraved, etched, etc.: metal; plaques, picture, laminated

(G-4654)
GABRIEL ENTERPRISES
1734 W North Ave (60622-2147)
PHONE......................773 342-8705
Poothakallil M Gabriel, *President*
Saramma Gabriel, *Corp Secy*
EMP: 4 **EST:** 1974
SQ FT: 6,000
SALES (est): 280K **Privately Held**
SIC: 5099 2396 5136 Cases, carrying; automotive & apparel trimmings; hats, men's & boys'

(G-4655)
GADGETWORLD ENTERPRISES INC
10956 S Western Ave (60643-3234)
PHONE......................773 703-0796
James Grider, *CEO*
Sheila Edwards, *Vice Pres*
Erica Edwards, *Director*
EMP: 5
SQ FT: 10,000
SALES (est): 200K **Privately Held**
SIC: 2051 Bakery: wholesale or wholesale/retail combined

(G-4656)
GALLAS LABEL & DECAL
Also Called: Andrews Decal & Label Company
6559 N Avondale Ave (60631-1521)
PHONE......................773 775-1000
Gary Gallas, *President*
EMP: 10
SQ FT: 16,000
SALES (est): 1.8MM **Privately Held**
WEB: www.gallaslabel.com
SIC: 2752 2759 2672 Commercial printing, offset; transfers, decalcomania or dry: lithographed; letterpress printing; flexographic printing; screen printing; coated & laminated paper

(G-4657)
GALLOY AND VAN ETTEN INC (PA)
11756 S Halsted St (60628-5823)
P.O. Box 288145 (60628-8145)
PHONE......................773 928-4800
Bernard Vanetten Jr, *President*
John Vanetten, *Corp Secy*
EMP: 27 **EST:** 1899
SQ FT: 20,000
SALES (est): 7.9MM **Privately Held**
WEB: www.galloyvanetten.com
SIC: 5032 1741 3281 Stone, crushed or broken; marble building stone; marble masonry, exterior construction; cut stone & stone products

(G-4658)
GAMESTOP INC
800 N Kedzie Ave (60651-4100)
PHONE......................773 568-0457
Bryan McMillen, *District Mgr*
Robert Alan Lloyd, *Vice Pres*
EMP: 7 **Publicly Held**
WEB: www.gamestop.com
SIC: 5945 5092 3944 Hobby, toy & game shops; video games; video game machines, except coin-operated
HQ: Gamestop, Inc.
625 Westport Pkwy
Grapevine TX 76051

(G-4659)
GARDNER ASPHALT CORPORATION
Also Called: Gardner-Gibson
4718 W Roosevelt Rd (60644-1431)
PHONE......................800 237-1155
Al Bolado, *Branch Mgr*
EMP: 40
SQ FT: 25,000
SALES (corp-wide): 270.5MM **Privately Held**
WEB: www.gardner-gibson.com
SIC: 2952 3297 2951 2891 Asphalt felts & coatings; nonclay refractories; asphalt paving mixtures & blocks; adhesives & sealants
HQ: Gardner Asphalt Corporation
4161 E 7th Ave
Tampa FL 33605
813 248-2101

(G-4660)
GAST MONUMENTS INC (PA)
1900 W Peterson Ave (60660-3111)
PHONE......................773 262-2400
Michelle Geverola, *Sales Staff*
Tom Gast, *Manager*
James Gast, *Director*
John Gast, *Director*
EMP: 7
SQ FT: 5,000
SALES (est): 1MM **Privately Held**
WEB: www.gastmonuments.com
SIC: 5999 3281 Monuments, finished to custom order; cut stone & stone products

(G-4661)
GATHER VOICES INC
4021 N Broadway St (60613-2110)
PHONE......................312 476-9465
Michael Hoffman,
EMP: 7
SQ FT: 5,000
SALES (est): 39.6K **Privately Held**
SIC: 7372 Business oriented computer software

(G-4662)
GATORADE COMPANY (DH)
555 W Monroe St Fl 1 (60661-3700)
PHONE......................312 821-1000
Charles I Maniscalco, *President*
Mary Doherty, *Comms Dir*
Charles Williamson, *Clerk*
▼ **EMP:** 1200
SQ FT: 300,000
SALES (est): 197.5MM
SALES (corp-wide): 67.1B **Publicly Held**
SIC: 2086 5149 Soft drinks: packaged in cans, bottles, etc.; beverages, except coffee & tea
HQ: The Quaker Oats Company
555 W Monroe St Fl 1
Chicago IL 60661
312 821-1000

(G-4663)
GATTO INDUSTRIAL PLATERS INC
4620 W Roosevelt Rd (60644-1430)
PHONE......................773 287-0100
George Gatto, *President*
Robert N Swanson, *Vice Pres*
Andy Gruda, *QC Mgr*
Dominick Gatto, *Treasurer*
Deanna Jackson, *Controller*
EMP: 185
SQ FT: 211,000
SALES (est): 26.8MM **Privately Held**
SIC: 3471 Plating of metals or formed products

(G-4664)
GAW-OHARA ENVELOPE CO (PA)
500 N Sacramento Blvd (60612-1024)
P.O. Box 325, Western Springs (60558-0325)
PHONE......................773 638-1200
EMP: 40 **EST:** 1913
SQ FT: 70,000
SALES (est): 28.4MM **Privately Held**
SIC: 2677 Mfg Envelopes

(G-4665)
GCP APPLIED TECHNOLOGIES
6051 W 65th St (60638-5301)
PHONE......................708 728-2420
EMP: 13
SALES (est): 2.8MM **Privately Held**
SIC: 2819 Industrial inorganic chemicals

(G-4666)
GE TRANSPORTATION PARTS LLC (HQ)
500 W Monroe St (60661-3671)
PHONE......................814 875-2755
Rafael Santana, *President*
Greg Sbrocco, *Vice Pres*
▲ **EMP:** 35
SALES (est): 108.9MM **Publicly Held**
SIC: 4731 3743 7373 Freight forwarding; locomotives & parts; systems integration services

(G-4667)
GEM ACQUISITION COMPANY INC
Also Called: Gem Business Forms
5942 S Central Ave (60638-3711)
PHONE......................773 735-3300
Katharine Owens, *President*
Christopher J Owens, *Vice Pres*
EMP: 15 **EST:** 1940
SQ FT: 13,000
SALES (est): 1.4MM **Privately Held**
SIC: 2761 Manifold business forms

(G-4668)
GEMA INC (PA)
Also Called: Ballert Orthopedic of Chicago
2434 W Peterson Ave (60659-4113)
PHONE......................773 508-6690
Gene P Bernardoni, *President*
EMP: 11
SALES (est): 5MM **Privately Held**
SIC: 3842 5047 3841 Limbs, artificial; artificial limbs; surgical & medical instruments

(G-4669)
GENERAL DESIGN JEWELERS INC
5 S Wabash Ave Ste 217 (60603-3522)
PHONE......................312 201-9047
Jose Tobias, *President*
Arturo Tobias, *Principal*
EMP: 7
SQ FT: 3,200
SALES (est): 1.1MM **Privately Held**
SIC: 3911 Jewelry, precious metal

(G-4670)
GENERAL DYNMICS MSSION SYSTEMS
50 S La Salle St (60603-1008)
PHONE......................703 876-3000
EMP: 151
SALES (corp-wide): 39.3B **Publicly Held**
SIC: 3571 Electronic computers
HQ: General Dynamics Mission Systems, Inc.
12450 Fair Lakes Cir
Fairfax VA 22033
877 449-0600

(G-4671)
GENERAL LATTICE INC
2415 W 19th St (60608-3054)
PHONE......................312 374-3158
Nick Florek,
Marek Moffett,
Alex Rhoades,
EMP: 3
SALES (est): 252.7K **Privately Held**
SIC: 3674 Semiconductors & related devices

(G-4672)
GENERAL LOOSE LEAF BINDERY INC
350 N La Salle Dr # 1100 (60654-5131)
PHONE......................847 244-9700
Glenn Nickow, *President*
Meghan Mercier, *Principal*
Ed Nickow, *Chairman*
Ross Nickow, *Vice Pres*
Todd Nickow, *Vice Pres*
EMP: 35 **EST:** 1923
SQ FT: 50,000
SALES (est): 4.9MM **Privately Held**
WEB: www.looseleaf.com
SIC: 2782 Looseleaf binders & devices

(G-4673)
GENERAL MACHINE & TL WORKS INC
990 N Lk Shr Dr Apt 20e (60611-1378)
PHONE......................312 337-2177
Julius G Howard Jr, *President*
William J Howard, *Vice Pres*
EMP: 10
SALES (est): 1.6MM **Privately Held**
SIC: 3599 Machine shop, jobbing & repair

(G-4674)
GENERAL MACHINERY & MFG CO
Also Called: Gmmco
2634 N Keeler Ave (60639-2169)
PHONE......................773 235-3700
Eric Junkunc, *President*
Noel Junkunc, *Treasurer*
Kevin Curth, *Admin Sec*
EMP: 15 **EST:** 1918
SQ FT: 20,000
SALES (est): 12MM **Privately Held**
WEB: www.gmmco.com
SIC: 3724 3429 3544 3469 Aircraft engines & engine parts; casket hardware; special dies, tools, jigs & fixtures; metal stampings; sheet metalwork

(G-4675)
GENERAL PACKAGING PRODUCTS INC (DH)
1700 S Canal St (60616-1108)
PHONE......................312 226-5611
Mark Mehring, *Controller*
John Strubulis, *Sales Mgr*
Jose Rodriguez, *Manager*
Debbie Sands, *Manager*
Linda Romano, *Executive*
▲ **EMP:** 52 **EST:** 1932
SQ FT: 51,000
SALES (est): 15.1MM
SALES (corp-wide): 2.5B **Privately Held**
WEB: www.generalpk.com
SIC: 2754 2671 2759 Rotogravure printing; packaging paper & plastics film, coated & laminated; paper coated or laminated for packaging; flexographic printing

(G-4676)
GENERAL PALLET
13513 S Calumet Ave (60827-1834)
PHONE......................773 660-8550
Hermen Delgado, *Owner*
EMP: 3
SALES (est): 427.7K **Privately Held**
SIC: 2448 Pallets, wood; pallets, wood & wood with metal

(G-4677)
GENERAL PRESS COLORS LTD
53 W Jackson Blvd # 1115 (60604-3566)
PHONE......................630 543-7878
Casimir J Grabacki, *CEO*
Richard J Kuebel, *President*
Andrew S Grabacki, *Vice Pres*
Gregory C Grabacki, *Vice Pres*
▲ **EMP:** 50
SQ FT: 40,000
SALES (est): 11.8MM **Privately Held**
SIC: 2865 Color pigments, organic

Chicago - Cook County (G-4678)

(G-4678)
GENERAL PRODUCTS
Also Called: G P Albums
4045 N Rockwell St (60618-3797)
PHONE...................................773 463-2424
Anne Henning, *Marketing Mgr*
Ronald Kalwajtys, *Mng Member*
Ray Kalwajtys, *Officer*
Arlene Newburn, *Officer*
▲ **EMP:** 28 **EST:** 1934
SQ FT: 70,000
SALES (est): 3.9MM **Privately Held**
SIC: 2782 Scrapbooks, albums & diaries; albums

(G-4679)
GENERAL SURFACE HARDENING INC (PA)
2108 W Fulton St (60612-2314)
PHONE...................................312 226-5472
Stanley Peebles, *President*
EMP: 50
SQ FT: 12,500
SALES (est): 8.6MM **Privately Held**
SIC: 3398 Metal heat treating

(G-4680)
GENESIS COMICS GROUP
2631 S Ind Ave Apt 1410 (60616)
PHONE...................................312 544-7473
Samuel L Gilbert, *Owner*
EMP: 4
SALES (est): 237.4K **Privately Held**
SIC: 2721 Comic books: publishing & printing

(G-4681)
GENUINE PARTS COMPANY
Also Called: NAPA Auto Parts
1225 W Roosevelt Rd (60608)
PHONE...................................630 293-1300
Cliff Watts, *Manager*
EMP: 13
SALES (corp-wide): 19.3B **Publicly Held**
SIC: 5531 3714 5013 Automobile & truck equipment & parts; motor vehicle parts & accessories; automotive supplies & parts
PA: Genuine Parts Company
2999 Wildwood Pkwy
Atlanta GA 30339
678 934-5000

(G-4682)
GEORGE LAUTERER CORPORATION
Also Called: Geo Lauterer
310 S Racine Ave (60607-2841)
PHONE...................................312 913-1881
Earl Joyce, *CEO*
John Joyce, *Vice Pres*
Patrick Joyce, *Vice Pres*
EMP: 30 **EST:** 1881
SQ FT: 10,000
SALES (est): 3MM **Privately Held**
WEB: www.lauterer.com
SIC: 2399 5199 7389 3993 Flags, fabric; banners, made from fabric; pennants; emblems, badges & insignia: from purchased materials; gifts & novelties; engraving service; signs & advertising specialties; automotive & apparel trimmings

(G-4683)
GEORGE NOTTOLI & SONS INC
Also Called: Original Notolli & Sons
7652 W Belmont Ave (60634-3110)
PHONE...................................773 589-1010
George A Nottoli, *President*
Loretta Nottoli, *Treasurer*
EMP: 5
SQ FT: 2,000
SALES (est): 640K **Privately Held**
SIC: 2013 5411 Sausages & other prepared meats; grocery stores, independent

(G-4684)
GEORGE S MUSIC ROOM
600 E Grand Ave (60611-3419)
PHONE...................................773 767-4676
EMP: 5
SALES (est): 384.4K **Privately Held**
SIC: 2782 Mfg Blankbooks/Binders

(G-4685)
GEORGIES GREEK TASTY FOOD INC
2527 W Carmen Ave (60625-2607)
PHONE...................................773 987-1298
Georgia Orr, *Principal*
EMP: 3
SALES (est): 142.8K **Privately Held**
SIC: 2099 Food preparations

(G-4686)
GERARDO AND QUINTANA AUTO ELC
4034 W 63rd St (60629-4639)
PHONE...................................773 424-0634
Rosa Quintana, *President*
EMP: 4
SALES (est): 232K **Privately Held**
SIC: 3699 7538 7539 Electrical equipment & supplies; general automotive repair shops; automotive repair shops

(G-4687)
GERDAU AMERISTEEL US INC
Also Called: Gerdau Long Steel
13535 S Torrence Ave # 5 (60633-2166)
PHONE...................................800 237-0230
EMP: 4 **Privately Held**
SIC: 3312 3449 3315 Blast furnace & related products; miscellaneous metalwork; steel wire & related products
HQ: Gerdau Ameristeel Us Inc.
4221 W Boy Scout Blvd # 600
Tampa FL 33607
813 286-8383

(G-4688)
GERMAN AMERICAN NAT CONGRESS (PA)
4740 N Western Ave Fl 2 (60625-2013)
PHONE...................................773 561-9181
Beverly Pochatko, *President*
EMP: 15
SQ FT: 500
SALES: 842.1K **Privately Held**
SIC: 8641 2711 Social club, membership; newspapers: publishing only, not printed on site

(G-4689)
GIANT GLOBES INC
4433 W Montana St (60639-1915)
PHONE...................................773 772-2917
Eugene Protas, *Principal*
EMP: 2
SALES (est): 231.9K **Privately Held**
WEB: www.mattbinns.com
SIC: 3542 Bending machines

(G-4690)
GIBA ELECTRIC
4054 W Warwick Ave (60641-3142)
PHONE...................................773 685-4420
EMP: 2 **EST:** 2008
SALES (est): 200K **Privately Held**
SIC: 3699 Mfg Electrical Equipment/Supplies

(G-4691)
GILBERT SPRING CORPORATION
2301 N Knox Ave (60639-3415)
PHONE...................................773 486-6030
Anthony E Indihar Jr, *President*
Patricia Indihar, *Vice Pres*
▲ **EMP:** 30 **EST:** 1960
SQ FT: 23,000
SALES (est): 5.5MM **Privately Held**
WEB: www.gilbertspring.com
SIC: 3469 3493 Stamping metal for the trade; torsion bar springs

(G-4692)
GINAS JAMS
1941 N Newcastle Ave (60707-3331)
PHONE...................................773 622-1051
Gina Koeller, *Principal*
EMP: 3
SALES (est): 116.3K **Privately Held**
SIC: 2033 Jams, jellies & preserves: packaged in cans, jars, etc.

(G-4693)
GLASS MANAGEMENT SERVICES INC
Also Called: U.S. Architectural Glass & Met
1002 E 87th St (60619)
PHONE...................................312 462-3257
Calvin Toone, *Business Mgr*
Sam Tailor, *CFO*
EMP: 4 **EST:** 2015
SALES (est): 75.1K **Privately Held**
SIC: 3449 Miscellaneous metalwork

(G-4694)
GLENMARK INDUSTRIES LTD
4545 S Racine Ave Ste 1 (60609-3384)
PHONE...................................773 927-4800
Dave Van Kampen, *President*
George Krzesinski, *Treasurer*
Robert Martin, *VP Finance*
EMP: 250
SQ FT: 50,000
SALES (est): 58.5MM **Privately Held**
SIC: 2013 Sausages & other prepared meats

(G-4695)
GLOBAL CONTRACT MFG INC
Also Called: Gcm
156 N Jefferson St # 300 (60661-1411)
PHONE...................................312 432-6200
Robert Wolters Jr, *President*
Danielle Wolters, *Corp Secy*
▲ **EMP:** 2 **EST:** 1994
SALES (est): 235.9K **Privately Held**
SIC: 3089 3631 Plastic kitchenware, tableware & houseware; household cooking equipment

(G-4696)
GLOBAL MATERIAL TECH INC
Also Called: Rhodes/American
2825 W 31st St (60623-5102)
PHONE...................................773 247-6000
Alex Krupnik, *Principal*
Arnette Gary, *Human Res Mgr*
EMP: 120
SALES (corp-wide): 64.9MM **Privately Held**
WEB: www.gmt-inc.com
SIC: 3291 5198 Aluminum oxide (fused) abrasives; paints, varnishes & supplies
PA: Global Material Technologies, Incorporated
750 W Lake Cook Rd # 480
Buffalo Grove IL 60089
847 495-4700

(G-4697)
GLOBAL PACKAGING DEV LLC
540 N State St Apt 2504 (60654-7235)
PHONE...................................847 209-3270
Mark Faber, *Mng Member*
EMP: 10
SALES (est): 362.1K **Privately Held**
SIC: 3089 Injection molded finished plastic products

(G-4698)
GLOBAL PHARMA DEVICE SOLUTIONS
6454 W 74th St (60638-6009)
PHONE...................................708 212-5801
Mathew Azuh, *President*
EMP: 3
SALES (est): 181.1K **Privately Held**
SIC: 2834 Pharmaceutical preparations

(G-4699)
GLOBAL TECHNOLOGIES I LLC (PA)
Also Called: Strateg Telekom
980 N Michigan Ave # 1400 (60611-7500)
PHONE...................................312 255-8350
Joseph Machulla, *President*
EMP: 56
SQ FT: 14,000
SALES (est): 9.1MM **Privately Held**
SIC: 1731 1041 4813 4789 Energy management controls; underground gold mining; telephone communication, except radio; cargo loading & unloading services; underground iron ore mining; electronic media advertising representatives

(G-4700)
GLOBAL TELEPHONY MAGAZINE
330 N Wabash Ave Ste 2300 (60611-7619)
PHONE...................................312 840-8405
CAM Bishop, *President*
EMP: 45
SALES (est): 1.8MM **Privately Held**
SIC: 2721 Magazines: publishing only, not printed on site
PA: Global Epoint, Inc.
339 Cheryl Ln
City Of Industry CA 91789

(G-4701)
GLOOKO
303 E Wacker Dr Ste 339 (60601-5218)
PHONE...................................513 307-0903
Tara Leveline, *Principal*
EMP: 3 **EST:** 2018
SALES (est): 237.3K **Privately Held**
SIC: 3841 Surgical & medical instruments

(G-4702)
GLUE INC
5701 N Sheridan Rd Apt 4m (60660-4793)
PHONE...................................312 451-4018
Craig Easly, *Principal*
EMP: 3
SALES (est): 149.1K **Privately Held**
SIC: 2891 Adhesives & sealants

(G-4703)
GMB PARTNERS LLC (PA)
Also Called: Half Acre Beer Company
4257 N Lincoln Ave (60618-2953)
PHONE...................................773 248-4038
Eric Kapraun, *Vice Pres*
Matt Young, *Opers Staff*
David Bowers, *Controller*
Phil McFarland, *Sales Staff*
Gabriel Magliaro, *Mng Member*
EMP: 33
SALES (est): 5.2MM **Privately Held**
WEB: www.halfacrebeer.com
SIC: 8748 2082 Business consulting; malt beverages

(G-4704)
GMD MOBILE PRESSURE WSHG SVCS
539 N Saint Louis Ave (60624-1648)
PHONE...................................773 826-1903
Dwain Williamson, *Principal*
EMP: 3
SALES (est): 119.2K **Privately Held**
SIC: 2711 Newspapers, publishing & printing

(G-4705)
GMI PACKAGING CO
1600 E 122nd St (60633-2359)
PHONE...................................734 972-7389
Joyce Mueller, *President*
EMP: 30
SALES (corp-wide): 1.5MM **Privately Held**
SIC: 3535 Bulk handling conveyor systems
PA: Gmi Packaging Co.
1371 Centennial Ln
Ann Arbor MI 48103
734 972-7389

(G-4706)
GMM HOLDINGS LLC
175 E Delaware Pl Unit 6 (60611-1756)
PHONE...................................312 255-9830
Ravin Gandhi, *Mng Member*
EMP: 10 **EST:** 2007
SALES: 10MM **Privately Held**
SIC: 2819 Catalysts, chemical

(G-4707)
GNOME BREW LLC
2026 W Montrose Ave (60618-1908)
PHONE...................................773 961-7750
David W Odefey, *Principal*
EMP: 8
SALES (est): 707.9K **Privately Held**
SIC: 2082 Beer (alcoholic beverage)

(G-4708)
GOAT WOLF & CABBAGE LLC
1917 N Elston Ave (60642-1219)
PHONE...................................563 580-0617

GEOGRAPHIC SECTION

Michael Boxleiter, *President*
EMP: 4
SALES (est): 217.7K **Privately Held**
SIC: 3944 Board games, puzzles & models, except electronic

(G-4709)
GOEDUCATION LLC
Also Called: Conferences I/O
222 Merchandise Mart Plz # 1225 (60654-4357)
PHONE..............................312 800-1838
John Pytel, *General Mgr*
Megan Lehrman, *Vice Pres*
Kristin Snow, *Sales Executive*
David Mulder,
EMP: 5
SQ FT: 200
SALES (est): 345.5K **Privately Held**
WEB: www.conferences.io
SIC: 7372 Educational computer software

(G-4710)
GOGO INTERMEDIATE HOLDINGS LLC (HQ)
111 N Canal St Fl 15 (60606-7205)
PHONE..............................630 647-1400
EMP: 6 **EST:** 2012
SALES (est): 288.3MM
SALES (corp-wide): 835.7MM **Publicly Held**
SIC: 3663 Radio & TV communications equipment
PA: Gogo Inc.
   111 N Canal St Ste 1500
   Chicago IL 60606
   312 517-5000

(G-4711)
GOGO LLC (DH)
111 N Canal St Fl 15 (60606-7205)
PHONE..............................630 647-1400
Michael J Small, *President*
Tim Twohig, *Partner*
Margee Elias, *Exec VP*
Anand K Chari, *Exec VP*
Jonathan Cobin, *Exec VP*
EMP: 448
SQ FT: 55,000
SALES (est): 268.2MM
SALES (corp-wide): 835.7MM **Publicly Held**
SIC: 4812 4813 4899 3663 Cellular telephone services; telephone communications, except radio; data communication services; cellular radio telephone
HQ: Gogo Intermediate Holdings Llc
   111 N Canal St Fl 15
   Chicago IL 60606
   630 647-1400

(G-4712)
GOLD STANDARD BAKING INC (PA)
3700 S Kedzie Ave (60632-2768)
PHONE..............................773 523-2333
Yianny Caparos, *President*
Christian Funduianu, *President*
Constantin Caparos, *General Mgr*
Sean Kowalski, *Prdtn Mgr*
Segundo Salas, *Prdtn Mgr*
EMP: 152
SQ FT: 150,000
SALES (est): 67.9MM **Privately Held**
SIC: 2051 Bakery: wholesale or wholesale/retail combined

(G-4713)
GOLDA HOUSE
3128 W 41st St (60632-2428)
PHONE..............................773 927-0140
EMP: 4 **EST:** 2001
SALES (est): 160K **Privately Held**
SIC: 2711 Newspapers-Publishing/Printing

(G-4714)
GOLFCO INC
Also Called: Delta Golf
4727 W Montrose Ave (60641-1504)
P.O. Box 21, Golf (60029-0021)
PHONE..............................773 777-7877
Joseph R Morisco, *President*
▲ **EMP:** 20 **EST:** 1983
SQ FT: 35,000

SALES (est): 2.1MM **Privately Held**
WEB: www.foundationtavern.com
SIC: 3949 Shafts, golf club

(G-4715)
GOOD FOODS INC
700 E 107th St (60628-3806)
PHONE..............................773 260-9110
Charles Zandstra, *CFO*
EMP: 11 **EST:** 1990
SALES (est): 1.5MM **Privately Held**
SIC: 2099 Food preparations

(G-4716)
GOOD WORLD NOODLE INC
2522 S Halsted St (60608-5931)
PHONE..............................312 326-0441
Miu Ching Lam, *President*
Yuk Lem, *Admin Sec*
EMP: 4
SALES (est): 300.9K **Privately Held**
SIC: 2099 Noodles, uncooked: packaged with other ingredients

(G-4717)
GOODALE CORPORATION
Also Called: Goodwood Country Firewood
1619-1635 S Canal St 1 (60616)
PHONE..............................312 421-9663
John Goodale, *President*
EMP: 6 **EST:** 2012
SALES (est): 609.7K **Privately Held**
SIC: 2421 Sawmills & planing mills, general

(G-4718)
GOOSE HOLDINGS INC
Also Called: Goose Island Brewer
1800 W Fulton St (60612-2512)
PHONE..............................312 226-1119
John R Hall, *President*
Rich Heller, *Representative*
EMP: 45
SALES (est): 7.5MM
SALES (corp-wide): 1.5B **Privately Held**
WEB: www.gooseisland.com
SIC: 2082 5813 Beer (alcoholic beverage); drinking places
HQ: Anheuser-Busch Companies, Llc
   1 Busch Pl
   Saint Louis MO 63118
   314 632-6777

(G-4719)
GOTHAM GREENS PULLMAN LLC
720 E 11th St (60628)
PHONE..............................779 379-0307
EMP: 22
SALES (corp-wide): 2.5MM **Privately Held**
SIC: 2099 Salads, fresh or refrigerated
PA: Gotham Greens Pullman, Llc
   810 Humboldt St Ste 3
   Brooklyn NY 11222
   718 935-0600

(G-4720)
GOURMET GORILLA INC (PA)
1200 W Cermak Rd (60608-4779)
PHONE..............................877 219-3663
Jason Weedon, *CEO*
Danielle Hrzic, *President*
▲ **EMP:** 61 **EST:** 2014
SQ FT: 24,000
SALES (est): 4.4MM **Privately Held**
SIC: 5812 2099 Caterers; ready-to-eat meals, salads & sandwiches

(G-4721)
GRACE ENTERPRISES INC (PA)
Also Called: Eco Print Mail Consultants
2050 W Devon Ave Ste 2 (60659-2231)
PHONE..............................847 423-2100
K M Eapen, *President*
Ajith Eapen, *Vice Pres*
James Younan, *Manager*
Leo Douglas, *Executive*
Tim Lofgren, *Executive*
EMP: 4
SQ FT: 3,500
SALES (est): 3.8MM **Privately Held**
SIC: 2752 Commercial printing, offset

Chicago - Cook County (G-4737)

(G-4722)
GRAND PRINTING & GRAPHICS INC
105 W Madison St Ste 1100 (60602-4600)
PHONE..............................312 218-6780
James Marshall, *President*
Bruce Frentz, *Vice Pres*
James Kellas, *Treasurer*
EMP: 12
SQ FT: 7,000
SALES (est): 1.8MM **Privately Held**
SIC: 2752 Commercial printing, offset

(G-4723)
GRANDMA MAUDS INC
1525 E 55th St Ste 304 (60615-5570)
PHONE..............................773 493-5353
Paul D Fregia, *President*
EMP: 2
SALES (est): 241.5K **Privately Held**
SIC: 2044 2034 Rice milling; dried & dehydrated soup mixes

(G-4724)
GRANJA & SONS PRINTING
2707 S Pulaski Rd (60623-4412)
PHONE..............................773 762-3840
Ignacio Granja Sr, *Partner*
Agustin Granja, *Partner*
Ignacio Granja Jr, *Partner*
Nathan Ward, *COO*
EMP: 10
SQ FT: 5,000
SALES (est): 605K **Privately Held**
SIC: 2759 2752 Letterpress printing; commercial printing, lithographic

(G-4725)
GRANT TECHNOLOGIES LLC
111 E Wacker Dr (60601-3713)
PHONE..............................847 370-9306
Pat Woodward,
EMP: 5
SALES (est): 194.3K **Privately Held**
SIC: 2241 Trimmings, textile

(G-4726)
GRAPHIC PARTS INTL INC
4321 N Knox Ave (60641-1906)
PHONE..............................773 725-4900
Michael Green, *President*
EMP: 15
SQ FT: 15,000
SALES (est): 3.4MM **Privately Held**
SIC: 3469 Machine parts, stamped or pressed metal

(G-4727)
GRAPHIC PRESS
545 N Dearborn St # 3002 (60654-2658)
PHONE..............................312 909-6100
John Semora, *CEO*
EMP: 3
SALES (est): 170K **Privately Held**
SIC: 2741 Miscellaneous publishing

(G-4728)
GRAPHICS 255 LLC (PA)
Also Called: AlphaGraphics
811 W Evergreen Ave 101a (60642-2682)
PHONE..............................312 266-9266
Rob Halverson, *Mng Member*
EMP: 14
SALES: 2MM **Privately Held**
SIC: 2752 Commercial printing, lithographic

(G-4729)
GRAPHICS GROUP LLC
4600 N Olcott Ave (60706-4604)
PHONE..............................708 867-5500
Bill Stout, *President*
EMP: 65 **EST:** 1936
SQ FT: 50,000
SALES (est): 429.6K **Privately Held**
SIC: 2752 2791 2789 2759 Commercial printing, offset; typesetting; bookbinding & related work; commercial printing

(G-4730)
GRAYMON GRAPHICS INC
4934 S Rockwell St (60632-1431)
PHONE..............................773 737-0176
Martin Moncaba, *President*
EMP: 4

SALES: 250K **Privately Held**
SIC: 3993 Signs, not made in custom sign painting shops

(G-4731)
GRAYMONT PROF PDTS IP LLC
Also Called: Lake Effect Medical Ip
1621 W Carroll Ave (60612-2501)
PHONE..............................312 374-4376
Nathan Gray,
EMP: 15
SALES (est): 528.8K **Privately Held**
SIC: 3841 Medical instruments & equipment, blood & bone work

(G-4732)
GREAT BOOKS FOUNDATION
233 N Michigan Ave # 420 (60601-2298)
PHONE..............................312 332-5870
Valentina Texera-Parissi, *CEO*
Mary Williams, *Editor*
Denise Ahlquist, *Vice Pres*
Steve Craig, *Vice Pres*
Donald Whitfield, *Vice Pres*
▲ **EMP:** 31
SQ FT: 12,500
SALES: 3.7MM **Privately Held**
WEB: www.greatbooks.org
SIC: 2731 8299 Books: publishing only; educational services

(G-4733)
GREAT DANE LLC (HQ)
Also Called: Great Dane Trailers
222 N Lasalle St Ste 920 (60601)
PHONE..............................773 254-5533
William H Crown, *President*
Andy Klink, *Opers Staff*
Mandy Wells, *Accounting Mgr*
Sandra Borto, *Manager*
Todd M Capozza, *Manager*
◆ **EMP:** 100
SALES (est): 682.5MM
SALES (corp-wide): 1.5B **Privately Held**
SIC: 3715 Truck trailers; demountable cargo containers
PA: Henry Crown And Company
   222 N La Salle St # 2000
   Chicago IL 60601
   312 236-6300

(G-4734)
GREAT LAKES ENVMTL MAR DEL
39 S La Salle St Ste 308 (60603-1603)
PHONE..............................312 332-3377
Paul A Kakuris, *President*
John Swenson, *Admin Sec*
EMP: 3
SQ FT: 600
SALES (est): 274.8K **Privately Held**
SIC: 3272 8711 Concrete products; marine engineering

(G-4735)
GREAT LAKES FORGE COMPANY
Also Called: Lock & Roll Trailer Hitch
2141 S Spaulding Ave (60623-3321)
PHONE..............................773 277-2800
Gregory Russell, *President*
Ralph Russell III, *Admin Sec*
EMP: 7
SQ FT: 20,000
SALES: 500K **Privately Held**
SIC: 3799 3714 3462 Trailer hitches; trailer hitches, motor vehicle; ornamental metal forgings, ferrous

(G-4736)
GREAT LAKES LBR & PALLET INC
3333 W 47th Pl (60632-3041)
PHONE..............................773 243-6839
David Radzieta, *President*
EMP: 6 **EST:** 2011
SALES (est): 56.8K **Privately Held**
SIC: 2448 Pallets, wood

(G-4737)
GREAT LAKES PACKING CO INTL
1535 W 43rd St (60609-3329)
PHONE..............................773 927-6660
Robert Oates, *President*

Chicago - Cook County (G-4738)

▼ EMP: 6 EST: 1959
SQ FT: 22,000
SALES (est): 670K Privately Held
SIC: 2011 Meat packing plants

(G-4738)
GREAT SOFTWARE LABORATORY INC
60 E Monroe St Unit 4301 (60603-2765)
PHONE..................630 655-8905
Sunil Gaitonde, *Principal*
Nikhil Joshi, *Business Dir*
EMP: 8
SALES (est): 582.6K Privately Held
WEB: www.gslab.com
SIC: 7372 Prepackaged software
PA: Great Software Laboratory Private Limited
 6th Floor Amar Arma Genesis, Baner Road
 Pune MH 41104

(G-4739)
GREATLKES ARCHTCTRAL MLLWRKS L
2135 W Fulton St (60612-2313)
PHONE..................312 829-7110
Odonnell Winchester, *Mng Member*
EMP: 24
SQ FT: 3,000
SALES: 6MM Privately Held
SIC: 2426 2431 Carvings, furniture: wood; interior & ornamental woodwork & trim

(G-4740)
GREEN THUMB INDUSTRIES INC (PA)
Also Called: Gti
325 W Huron St Ste 412 (60654-5848)
PHONE..................312 471-6720
Benjamin Kovler, *Ch of Bd*
Armen Yemenidjian, *President*
Anthony Georgiadis, *CFO*
Beth Burk, *General Counsel*
Jennifer Dooley, *Security Dir*
EMP: 15
SALES: 216.4MM Publicly Held
SIC: 5999 2833 5122 ; medicinals & botanicals; medicinals & botanicals

(G-4741)
GREGORY LAMAR & ASSOC INC
Also Called: Fingers
345 N La Salle Dr # 2103 (60654-6101)
PHONE..................312 595-1545
Alfred D Gregory, *President*
Edward Lamar, *Vice Pres*
EMP: 2
SQ FT: 1,800
SALES (est): 400K Privately Held
SIC: 3842 Splints, pneumatic & wood

(G-4742)
GRIFFIN PLATING CO INC
1636 W Armitage Ave (60622-1203)
PHONE..................773 342-5181
Dan Griffin, *President*
Tom Griffin, *Vice Pres*
EMP: 9
SALES (est): 332.7K Privately Held
SIC: 3471 Plating of metals or formed products; polishing, metals or formed products

(G-4743)
GRIFFITH FOODS INC
Innova Flavors
1437 W 37th St (60609-2110)
PHONE..................773 523-7509
Michael Snodgrass, *Vice Pres*
Matt Vieceli, *Vice Pres*
Keith Toomey, *Plant Mgr*
Colleen Gagnon, *Mktg Dir*
Kelly Akel, *Manager*
EMP: 40
SALES (corp-wide): 1B Privately Held
SIC: 2099 Food preparations
HQ: Griffith Foods Inc.
 1 Griffith Ctr
 Alsip IL 60803
 708 371-0900

(G-4744)
GROOVJOINT LLC (PA)
155 N Wacker Dr Ste 4250 (60606-1750)
PHONE..................312 803-2627
Ian McNeill, *Manager*
Gerald C Condon,
EMP: 7
SALES (est): 518.5K Privately Held
SIC: 3494 Pipe fittings

(G-4745)
GROUPE LACASSE LLC
222 Merchandise Mart Plz # 1042 (60654-1129)
PHONE..................312 670-9100
Sylvain Garneau, *President*
Kevin Glynn, *Exec VP*
Michael Moon, *Vice Pres*
Joshua Benton, *Sales Staff*
Jeff Lewis, *Sales Staff*
◆ EMP: 232 EST: 1981
SALES (est): 24.3MM
SALES (corp-wide): 2B Privately Held
WEB: www.groupelacasse.com
SIC: 2522 2521 2512 Desks, office: except wood; chairs, office: padded or plain, except wood; cabinets, office: except wood; bookcases, office: except wood; desks, office: wood; chairs, office: padded, upholstered or plain: wood; cabinets, office: wood; panel systems & partitions (free-standing), office: wood; upholstered household furniture
HQ: Haworth, Inc.
 1 Haworth Ctr
 Holland MI 49423
 616 393-3000

(G-4746)
GTI ROCK ISLAND LLC (PA)
Also Called: Green Thumb Industries
325 W Huron St Ste 412 (60654-5848)
PHONE..................312 664-5050
Benjamin Kovler,
Wes Moore,
Glen T Senk,
EMP: 10
SALES (est): 1.2MM Privately Held
SIC: 2833 Drugs & herbs: grading, grinding & milling

(G-4747)
GUARDIAN EQUIPMENT INC
Also Called: Chicago Laboratory Pdts Inc
1140 N North Branch St (60642-4201)
PHONE..................312 447-8100
Steven Kersten, *President*
Carsten Birch, *Vice Pres*
Donald Schoen, *Vice Pres*
Kevin Helin, *Prdtn Mgr*
Lindsey Spiwak, *Engineer*
▲ EMP: 30
SQ FT: 17,000
SALES (est): 6.8MM Privately Held
WEB: www.gesafety.com
SIC: 3842 5084 3432 Personal safety equipment; safety equipment; plumbing fixture fittings & trim

(G-4748)
GUEROS PALLETS INC
355 N Lavergne Ave (60644-2538)
PHONE..................312 523-5561
Agustin Razo, *President*
EMP: 8
SALES (est): 1MM Privately Held
WEB: www.gueropallets.com
SIC: 2448 Pallets, wood

(G-4749)
GUESS INC
605 N Michigan Ave # 200 (60611-3115)
PHONE..................312 440-9592
EMP: 25
SALES (corp-wide): 2.2B Publicly Held
SIC: 2325 Mfg Men's/Boy's Trousers
PA: Guess , Inc.
 1444 S Alameda St
 Los Angeles CA 90021
 213 765-3100

(G-4750)
GUESS WHACKIT & HOPE INC
Also Called: Gard, Ron
1883 N Milwaukee Ave (60647-4464)
PHONE..................773 342-4273
Ronald J Gard, *President*
EMP: 1
SQ FT: 7,000
SALES (est): 350K Privately Held
SIC: 7922 2511 Scenery design, theatrical; wood household furniture

(G-4751)
GUIDANCE SOFTWARE INC
300 S Wacker Dr Ste 1100 (60606-6760)
PHONE..................847 994-7324
EMP: 5
SALES (corp-wide): 2.8B Privately Held
SIC: 7372 3572 Business oriented computer software; computer storage devices
HQ: Guidance Software, Inc.
 1055 E Colo Blvd Ste 400
 Pasadena CA 91106
 626 229-9191

(G-4752)
GUS BERTHOLD ELECTRIC COMPANY (PA)
1900 W Carroll Ave (60612-2402)
PHONE..................312 243-5767
Roderick Berthold, *President*
Charles Berthold, *Chairman*
Scott Sremaniak, *Engineer*
Rob Karolczak, *Project Engr*
▲ EMP: 57 EST: 1925
SQ FT: 30,000
SALES (est): 14.7MM Privately Held
WEB: www.bertholdelectric.com
SIC: 3613 3822 3643 Switchboards & parts, power; switchboard apparatus, except instruments; auto controls regulating residntl & coml environmt & applncs; current-carrying wiring devices

(G-4753)
GV WELDING INC
4849 W Grand Ave (60639-4507)
PHONE..................312 863-0071
Gerardo Vega, *President*
Maria Dubon Vega, *Admin Sec*
EMP: 5
SALES (est): 259.9K Privately Held
SIC: 7692 1799 Welding repair; fence construction

(G-4754)
GYOOD
2048 W Belmont Ave (60618-6412)
PHONE..................773 360-8810
Sushil H Narsinghani, *Principal*
EMP: 4
SALES (est): 212.6K Privately Held
WEB: www.gyoodsoftserve.com
SIC: 2024 Ice cream, bulk

(G-4755)
GYRO PROCESSING INC
3338 N Ashland Ave (60657-2109)
PHONE..................800 491-0733
Jose Parra, *President*
Ramon Iniguez, *Vice Pres*
EMP: 45
SQ FT: 39,000
SALES (est): 3.7MM Privately Held
SIC: 3471 Finishing, metals or formed products

(G-4756)
H & B MACHINE CORPORATION
1943 W Walnut St (60612-2405)
PHONE..................312 829-4850
Philip J Bracht, *President*
Evelyn Bracht, *Corp Secy*
George Bracht, *Vice Pres*
EMP: 4
SQ FT: 5,000
SALES (est): 489.4K Privately Held
WEB: www.hbmachine.com
SIC: 3599 3537 3536 Machine shop, jobbing & repair; industrial trucks & tractors; hoists, cranes & monorails

(G-4757)
H & H FABRIC CUTTERS
4431 W Rice St (60651-3457)
PHONE..................773 772-1904
Alexandro Herdia, *Owner*
EMP: 4
SALES (est): 190K Privately Held
SIC: 7389 2329 Sewing contractor; riding clothes:, men's, youths' & boys'

(G-4758)
H B TAYLOR CO
4830 S Christiana Ave (60632-3092)
PHONE..................773 254-4805
Saul Juskaitis, *President*
Martin Ives, *Vice Pres*
Tracey Powell, *Purchasing*
Vanja Pistalo, *QC Mgr*
Stacy Potter, *Manager*
EMP: 37 EST: 1953
SQ FT: 25,000
SALES (est): 8MM Privately Held
WEB: www.hbtaylor.com
SIC: 2087 Extracts, flavoring; food colorings

(G-4759)
H KRAMER & CO
1345 W 21st St (60608-3111)
PHONE..................312 226-6600
Howard K Chapman Jr, *President*
Adam Chapman, *Exec VP*
Ryan Heller, *Exec VP*
Pat Boyle, *Vice Pres*
Tom Mavronicles, *Safety Dir*
▼ EMP: 150 EST: 1888
SQ FT: 125,000
SALES (est): 43.5MM Privately Held
WEB: www.hkramer.com
SIC: 3341 Brass smelting & refining (secondary)

(G-4760)
H R SLATER CO INC
2050 W 18th St (60608-1816)
PHONE..................312 666-1855
Robert Kurzka, *President*
Daniel Moore, *Sales Mgr*
Bill St Hilaire, *Admin Sec*
EMP: 11 EST: 1920
SQ FT: 10,000
SALES (est): 2.1MM Privately Held
WEB: www.hrslater.com
SIC: 3545 3555 3537 3423 Machine tool attachments & accessories; printing trades machinery; industrial trucks & tractors; hand & edge tools

(G-4761)
H WATSON JEWELRY CO
29 E Madison St Ste 1007 (60602-4407)
PHONE..................312 236-1104
James Watson, *Owner*
EMP: 4
SQ FT: 1,100
SALES: 780K Privately Held
WEB: www.watsonjewelry.com
SIC: 3911 5944 Jewelry, precious metal; jewelry, precious stones & precious metals

(G-4762)
H&K PERFORATING LLC (PA)
5470 W Roosevelt Rd (60644-1467)
PHONE..................773 626-1800
Greg McCallister, *CEO*
Bryce Fisher, *Ch of Bd*
Andrew Strang, *COO*
EMP: 45
SALES (est): 19MM Privately Held
SIC: 3469 3089 Perforated metal, stamped; plastic processing

(G-4763)
HACH COMPANY
2207 Collection Center Dr (60693-0022)
PHONE..................800 227-4224
Miguel Molina, *Manager*
EMP: 143
SALES (corp-wide): 17.9B Publicly Held
SIC: 3826 Analytical instruments
HQ: Hach Company
 5600 Lindbergh Dr
 Loveland CO 80538
 800 227-4224

(G-4764)
HACKETT PRECISION COMPANY INC
Also Called: Hpc Automation
70 W Madison St Ste 2300 (60602-4250)
PHONE..................615 227-3136
Joel Pepper, *President*
Eric Hender, *Chairman*
Alton Miles, *Vice Pres*
David Schleicher, *Vice Pres*

GEOGRAPHIC SECTION

Chicago - Cook County (G-4791)

Rick Barksdale, *Treasurer*
▲ **EMP:** 42
SQ FT: 40,000
SALES (est): 5.4MM
SALES (corp-wide): 12.3MM **Privately Held**
SIC: 3559 Automotive related machinery
PA: Aavin Llc
   1245 1st Ave Se
   Cedar Rapids IA 52402
   319 247-1072

(G-4765)
HADLEY GEAR MANUFACTURING CO
4444 W Roosevelt Rd (60624-3840)
PHONE 773 722-1030
John Davey, *President*
Dennis Kempski, *Vice Pres*
EMP: 17 **EST:** 1950
SQ FT: 24,000
SALES (est): 3.6MM **Privately Held**
SIC: 3566 3452 3568 3462 Gears, power transmission, except automotive; screws, metal; sprockets (power transmission equipment); iron & steel forgings; nonferrous rolling & drawing

(G-4766)
HAFNER DUPLICATING COMPANY
601 S La Salle St (60605-1725)
PHONE 312 362-0120
Michael Shallberg, *Principal*
EMP: 3
SALES (est): 265.8K **Privately Held**
SIC: 3577 Printers & plotters

(G-4767)
HAFNER PRINTING CO INC
111 N Jefferson St (60661-2306)
PHONE 312 362-0120
Michael Shallberg, *President*
EMP: 10 **EST:** 1987
SQ FT: 6,000
SALES (est): 1.2MM **Privately Held**
WEB: www.hafnerprint.com
SIC: 2752 7334 2759 Commercial printing, offset; photocopying & duplicating services; commercial printing

(G-4768)
HAIR PLUS STUDIOS LLC
Also Called: 4urhair
2860 N Broadway St Ste 12 (60657-6017)
PHONE 530 487-4247
Aishia Nunez, *Principal*
Amari Herron, *Principal*
EMP: 3
SALES (est): 91.3K **Privately Held**
SIC: 3999 Barber & beauty shop equipment

(G-4769)
HAIRLINE CREATIONS INC (PA)
5850 W Montrose Ave 54 (60634-1748)
PHONE 773 282-5454
Paul Finamore, *President*
Karen Finamore, *Exec VP*
Sandy Tatkus, *Manager*
EMP: 15 **EST:** 1963
SQ FT: 5,400
SALES (est): 7.2MM **Privately Held**
WEB: www.hairlinecreations.com
SIC: 3999 5699 7389 Hair & hair-based products; wigs, toupees & wiglets; styling, wigs

(G-4770)
HAKIMIAN GEM CO
Also Called: Ace of Diamonds
5 S Wabash Ave Ste 1212 (60603-3136)
PHONE 312 236-6969
Fred Hakimian, *President*
EMP: 6
SQ FT: 800
SALES (est): 1.1MM **Privately Held**
SIC: 5094 3911 5944 Precious stones (gems); diamonds (gems); jewelry; jewelry, precious metal; jewelry stores

(G-4771)
HALLSTAR COMPANY
120 S Riverside Plz # 1620 (60606-3911)
PHONE 901 948-8663
Kim Buchholz, *Branch Mgr*

Jeff Beckman, *Director*
EMP: 32
SALES (corp-wide): 51.3MM **Privately Held**
WEB: www.hallstar.com
SIC: 2869 2819 4225 2899 Industrial organic chemicals; industrial inorganic chemicals; general warehousing; chemical preparations
PA: Hallstar Company
   120 S Riverside Plz # 1620
   Chicago IL 60606
   312 554-7400

(G-4772)
HALLSTAR COMPANY (PA)
120 S Riverside Plz # 1620 (60606-3911)
PHONE 312 554-7400
John J Paro, *CEO*
Keith Carlson, *Vice Pres*
Germano S Coelho, *Vice Pres*
Gail A Gerono, *Vice Pres*
Jeff Jaworek, *Vice Pres*
◆ **EMP:** 142
SQ FT: 20,000
SALES (est): 51.3MM **Privately Held**
SIC: 2869 5169 Plasticizers, organic: cyclic & acyclic; industrial chemicals

(G-4773)
HALLSTAR SERVICES CORP
120 S Riverside Plz # 1620 (60606-3911)
PHONE 312 554-7400
Richard M Trojan, *President*
William J Holbrook, *Admin Sec*
EMP: 6 **EST:** 2004
SALES (est): 108.9K **Privately Held**
SIC: 2869 5169 Plasticizers, organic: cyclic & acyclic; industrial chemicals

(G-4774)
HALSTED PACKING HOUSE CO
445 N Halsted St (60642-6518)
PHONE 312 421-5147
William Davos, *Owner*
EMP: 6 **EST:** 1937
SQ FT: 2,000
SALES (est): 400.7K **Privately Held**
SIC: 2011 2013 Lamb products from lamb slaughtered on site; sausages & other prepared meats

(G-4775)
HAMPDEN CORPORATION
1550 W Carroll Ave # 207 (60607-1035)
PHONE 312 583-3000
Joseph Wein, *Chairman*
Roger Hohl, *Vice Pres*
▲ **EMP:** 26 **EST:** 1922
SQ FT: 22,000
SALES (est): 4.7MM **Privately Held**
SIC: 3873 Watches & parts, except crystals & jewels

(G-4776)
HANDCUT FOODS LLC
1441 W Willow St (60642)
PHONE 312 239-0381
Andrew Morgan, *General Mgr*
Andrew Osterman,
EMP: 85
SALES (est): 9.1MM **Privately Held**
SIC: 2034 2022 2015 Dried & dehydrated fruits; cheese spreads, dips, pastes & other cheese products; variety meats (fresh edible organs), poultry

(G-4777)
HANGOUT LIGHTING LLC
2100 W Grand Ave Ste 2 (60612-1796)
PHONE 224 817-4101
EMP: 3
SALES (est): 291.6K **Privately Held**
SIC: 3648 Lighting equipment

(G-4778)
HANLON GROUP LTD
1872 N Clybourn Ave # 604 (60614-4964)
PHONE 773 525-3666
John T Hanlon, *President*
Catherine Sheridan, *Admin Sec*
EMP: 3

SALES (est): 4MM **Privately Held**
SIC: 2671 5162 2821 Packaging paper & plastics film, coated & laminated; plastics materials & basic shapes; plastics materials & resins

(G-4779)
HARBOR VILLAGE LLC
2241 W Howard St (60645-1908)
PHONE 773 338-2222
Don Schein,
EMP: 5 **EST:** 2012
SALES (est): 264.2K **Privately Held**
SIC: 2241 Narrow fabric mills

(G-4780)
HARDWOOD LINE MANUFACTURING CO
4045 N Elston Ave (60618-2193)
PHONE 773 463-2600
Anton Lazaro Sr, *CEO*
Anton E Lazaro Jr, *President*
Frank Pusateri, *General Mgr*
Bill Matusiak, *Chief Engr*
Cesar Fuentes, *Design Engr*
EMP: 20
SQ FT: 15,000
SALES (est): 5MM **Privately Held**
WEB: www.hardwoodline.com
SIC: 3559 3089 Electroplating machinery & equipment; plastic containers, except foam

(G-4781)
HARRINGTON KING PRFORATING INC
5655 W Fillmore St (60644-5504)
P.O. Box 22, Berwyn (60402-0022)
PHONE 773 626-1800
EMP: 110
SALES (corp-wide): 42.2MM **Privately Held**
SIC: 3469 Mfg Perforating Metal
PA: The Harrington & King Perforating Co Inc
   5655 W Fillmore St
   Chicago IL 60644
   773 626-1800

(G-4782)
HARRIS WILLIAM & COMPANY INC (PA)
Also Called: William Harris Investors
191 N Wacker Dr Ste 1500 (60606-1899)
PHONE 312 621-0590
Jack R Polsky, *CEO*
Adam Langsam, *COO*
Carolyn Watson, *Accountant*
Duane Dibble, *Info Tech Dir*
Mary Freeburg, *Director*
EMP: 50
SALES (est): 79.8MM **Privately Held**
SIC: 6799 3317 Investment clubs; steel pipe & tubes

(G-4783)
HARRISON HARMONICAS LLC
4541 N Ravenswood Ave # 203 (60640-5296)
PHONE 312 379-9427
Michael Peloquin, *Mng Member*
Bradley Harrison,
John Noel,
EMP: 7
SQ FT: 1,100
SALES (est): 547.9K **Privately Held**
SIC: 3931 Harmonicas

(G-4784)
HATCHER ASSOCIATES INC
1612 N Throop St (60642-1515)
PHONE 773 252-2171
John Cecchini, *President*
Franco Cecchini, *Vice Pres*
Joseph Bertucci, *Prgrmr*
Greg Kiesow, *Software Dev*
Larry Cecchini, *Shareholder*
EMP: 14
SQ FT: 10,000
SALES (est): 2.3MM **Privately Held**
WEB: www.hatchermodels.com
SIC: 3544 Forms (molds), for foundry & plastics working machinery

(G-4785)
HATS FOR YOU
7509 W Belmont Ave (60634-3317)
PHONE 773 481-1611
Margaret Foltyn, *Owner*
EMP: 4
SALES (est): 446.7K **Privately Held**
SIC: 2353 Hats & caps

(G-4786)
HAUTE DIGGITY DAWGS
3043 W 5th Ave (60612-2757)
PHONE 773 801-0195
Antae Manierre,
EMP: 4 **EST:** 2017
SALES (est): 155.8K **Privately Held**
SIC: 2599 Food wagons, restaurant

(G-4787)
HAUTE NOIR MEDIA GROUP INC
Also Called: Haute Noir Magzine
220 N Green St (60607-1702)
PHONE 312 869-4526
Gina Vaughn, *CEO*
Mark Topps, *Sales Mgr*
Deborah Martin, *Exec Sec*
EMP: 3
SALES (est): 83.9K **Privately Held**
SIC: 2741 7941 7221 7336 ; sports field or stadium operator, promoting sports events; photographer, still or video; commercial art & graphic design; booking agency, theatrical

(G-4788)
HAVAS BARN
36 E Grand Ave (60611-3506)
PHONE 312 640-6800
Mike Kowalczyk, *Production*
Will Ryan, *Production*
Liz Bera, *Finance*
Melissa Gildner, *Accounts Exec*
Judy Fox, *Branch Mgr*
EMP: 9
SALES (corp-wide): 81.3MM **Privately Held**
SIC: 2741 Telephone & other directory publishing
HQ: Havas
   29 30
   Puteaux 92800
   158 478-000

(G-4789)
HAYMARKET BREWING COMPANY LLC
Also Called: Haymarket Pub & Brewery
737 W Randolph St (60661-2103)
PHONE 312 638-0700
Janna Mestan, *General Mgr*
Kris Nielsen, *Human Resources*
Steven Forbes, *Mng Member*
Pete Crowley,
EMP: 7 **EST:** 2010
SALES (est): 220K **Privately Held**
WEB: www.haymarketbrewing.com
SIC: 5813 2082 Bars & lounges; beer (alcoholic beverage)

(G-4790)
HEALTH ADMINISTRATION PRESS
1 N Franklin St Ste 1600 (60606-3421)
PHONE 312 424-2800
Thomas Dolan, *Owner*
EMP: 90
SALES (est): 4.9MM **Privately Held**
WEB: www.ache.org
SIC: 2741 Miscellaneous publishing

(G-4791)
HEALTH KING ENTERPRISE INC
Also Called: Balanceuticals Group
238 W 31st St Ste 1 (60616-3600)
PHONE 312 567-9978
Xingwu Liu, *President*
◆ **EMP:** 4
SALES (est): 1.4MM **Privately Held**
SIC: 2023 5149 5499 Dietary supplements, dairy & non-dairy based; diet foods; dietetic foods

Chicago - Cook County (G-4792)   **GEOGRAPHIC SECTION**

(G-4792)
HEALTHCARE RESEARCH LLC
744 N Wells St Fl 3 (60654-3521)
PHONE.................................773 592-3508
Brandi Kurtyka, *CEO*
EMP: 10
SALES (est): 492.2K **Privately Held**
SIC: 7372 Application computer software

(G-4793)
HEALTHLEADERS INC
1404 N Cleveland Ave (60610-1108)
PHONE.................................312 932-0848
Alexandra Rose, *Marketing Staff*
Chris Cote, *Manager*
Erika Randall, *Manager*
EMP: 40
SALES (est): 2.4MM **Privately Held**
SIC: 2721 Magazines: publishing only, not printed on site

(G-4794)
HEALTHY-TXT LLC
950 W Monroe St Unit 813 (60607-2987)
PHONE.................................630 945-1787
Sharon Schreiber, *Partner*
Vishal Mehta, *Partner*
EMP: 8 **EST:** 2011
SALES (est): 308.2K **Privately Held**
SIC: 7372 7389 Application computer software;

(G-4795)
HEARST CORPORATION
Also Called: Elle Magazine
333 W Wacker Dr Ste 950 (60606-1250)
PHONE.................................312 984-5100
Kelly Mair, *Manager*
EMP: 50
SALES (corp-wide): 8.2B **Privately Held**
SIC: 2721 Magazines: publishing only, not printed on site
PA: The Hearst Corporation
    300 W 57th St Fl 42
    New York NY 10019
    212 649-2000

(G-4796)
HEAVEN HILL DISTILLERY INC
4418 N Wolcott Ave (60640-5833)
PHONE.................................773 564-9791
EMP: 3
SALES (est): 129.9K **Privately Held**
SIC: 2085 Distilled & blended liquors

(G-4797)
HEAVY QUIP INCORPORATED
55 W Wacker Dr Ste 1120 (60601-1796)
PHONE.................................312 368-7997
Howard Gossage, *President*
Kenny Soraghan, *Buyer*
Randy Seilig, *Admin Sec*
Dave Gwizdalski, *Sr Consultant*
◆ **EMP:** 17
SALES (est): 3.7MM **Privately Held**
WEB: www.heavyquipsales.com
SIC: 3519 Engines, diesel & semi-diesel or dual-fuel

(G-4798)
HEICO COMPANIES LLC (PA)
70 W Madison St Ste 5600 (60602-4211)
PHONE.................................312 419-8220
E A Roskovensky, *President*
Emily Heisley Stoeckel, *Chairman*
L G Wolski, *CFO*
Costa Yasmine, *Train & Dev Mgr*
Meredith Shepard, *Payroll Mgr*
◆ **EMP:** 15
SQ FT: 40,000
SALES (est): 1.7B **Privately Held**
SIC: 3315 3589 3448 3531 Wire, ferrous/iron; wire products, ferrous/iron: made in wiredrawing plants; sewage & water treatment equipment; sewer cleaning equipment, power; shredders, industrial & commercial; prefabricated metal buildings; prefabricated metal buildings; construction machinery; cranes; logging equipment; cranes, locomotive; electrical work; radio & television switching equipment

(G-4799)
HELIX RE INC
515 N State St Fl 15 (60654-2782)
PHONE.................................415 254-2724
EMP: 72
SALES (corp-wide): 9.6MM **Privately Held**
SIC: 2899 Fluxes: brazing, soldering, galvanizing & welding
PA: Helix Re, Inc.
    1911 4th St Ste 200
    Berkeley CA 94710
    415 254-2724

(G-4800)
HENDERSON CO INC
6020 N Keating Ave (60646-4902)
PHONE.................................773 628-7216
Jack Henderson, *President*
EMP: 10
SQ FT: 5,500
SALES (est): 1.3MM **Privately Held**
SIC: 2791 7336 2796 Typographic composition, for the printing trade; commercial art & graphic design; color separations for printing

(G-4801)
HENKEL CONSUMER GOODS INC
1122 N Clark St Apt 2007 (60610-7882)
PHONE.................................847 426-4552
Rachel Blakeney, *Branch Mgr*
EMP: 100
SALES (corp-wide): 22.2B **Privately Held**
SIC: 2841 Soap & other detergents
HQ: Henkel Consumer Goods Inc.
    200 Elm St
    Stamford CT 06902

(G-4802)
HENKEL TECHNOLOGY CORPORATION (PA)
6050 W 51st St (60638-1405)
PHONE.................................708 924-9582
EMP: 4
SALES (est): 1.3MM **Privately Held**
SIC: 2899 Chemical preparations

(G-4803)
HENNIG GASKET & SEALS INC
2350 W Cullerton St (60608-2515)
PHONE.................................312 243-8270
James E Hennig, *President*
EMP: 7
SQ FT: 9,000
SALES (est): 2.7MM **Privately Held**
SIC: 5085 3053 Gaskets & seals; gaskets; seals, industrial; gaskets & sealing devices

(G-4804)
HENSAAL MANAGEMENT GROUP INC
4632 W Monroe St (60644-4605)
PHONE.................................312 624-8133
Kenneth M Hennings, *President*
Rick Humphries, *Vice Pres*
Bonnie Hennings, *Admin Sec*
EMP: 7
SQ FT: 1,100
SALES: 5.5MM **Privately Held**
SIC: 5141 2099 5145 Food brokers; seasonings & spices; snack foods

(G-4805)
HEPALINK USA INC (PA)
233 S Wacker Dr Ste 9300 (60606-6319)
PHONE.................................630 206-1788
Shawn Lu, *CFO*
EMP: 7
SALES (est): 28.2MM **Privately Held**
SIC: 2834 Pharmaceutical preparations

(G-4806)
HERALD NEWSPAPERS INC
Also Called: Hyde Park Herald
1525 E 53rd St Ste 920 (60615-3096)
PHONE.................................773 643-8533
Bruce Sagan, *President*
EMP: 20
SQ FT: 5,000
SALES (est): 1.3MM **Privately Held**
SIC: 2711 Commercial printing & newspaper publishing combined

(G-4807)
HERFF JONES LLC
Also Called: Nystrom
3333 N Elston Ave (60618-6098)
PHONE.................................773 463-1144
Patrick McKeon, *Branch Mgr*
James Cerza, *Administration*
EMP: 75
SALES (corp-wide): 1.1B **Privately Held**
SIC: 3911 Rings, finger: precious metal
HQ: Herff Jones, Llc
    4501 W 62nd St
    Indianapolis IN 46268
    800 419-5462

(G-4808)
HERMITAGE GROUP INC
5151 N Ravenswood Ave (60640-2722)
P.O. Box 2499, Anderson IN (46018-2499)
PHONE.................................773 561-3773
Robert A Brenner, *President*
Sara Brenner, *CFO*
EMP: 25
SQ FT: 10,000
SALES (est): 2.1MM **Privately Held**
WEB: www.hermitageart.com
SIC: 2741 2759 2752 Miscellaneous publishing; commercial printing; commercial printing, lithographic

(G-4809)
HERNER-GEISSLER WDWKG CORP
400 N Hermitage Ave (60622-6206)
PHONE.................................312 226-3400
Anthony Herner Sr, *President*
Becky Dittmer, *Treasurer*
Jeffrey J Herner, *Admin Sec*
EMP: 55 **EST:** 1965
SQ FT: 25,000
SALES (est): 8MM **Privately Held**
WEB: www.hernergeisslerwoodworking.com
SIC: 2431 Millwork

(G-4810)
HERTZBERG ERNST & SONS
Also Called: Monastery Hill Bindery
1751 W Belmont Ave (60657-3019)
PHONE.................................773 525-3518
Blair Clark, *President*
Rhoda H Clark, *Chairman*
◆ **EMP:** 40 **EST:** 1868
SQ FT: 13,000
SALES (est): 6MM **Privately Held**
WEB: www.monasteryhill.com
SIC: 2752 3172 3199 Menus, lithographed; leather cases; embossed leather goods

(G-4811)
HEXAGON METROLOGY INC
Also Called: Hexagon Marketing
455 N Ctyfrnt Plz Dr # 3030 (60611-5503)
PHONE.................................312 624-8786
EMP: 3
SALES (corp-wide): 4.3B **Privately Held**
SIC: 3823 Industrial instrmnts msrmnt display/control process variable
HQ: Hexagon Metrology, Inc.
    250 Circuit Dr
    North Kingstown RI 02852
    401 886-2000

(G-4812)
HH BACKER ASSOCIATES INC
Also Called: Pet Age Magazine
18 S Michigan Ave # 1100 (60603-3233)
PHONE.................................312 578-1818
Patty Backer, *Ch of Bd*
Mark Mitera, *Vice Pres*
Karen Pedroni, *Admin Sec*
EMP: 17 **EST:** 1966
SALES (est): 1.9MM **Privately Held**
SIC: 2721 7389 Trade journals: publishing only, not printed on site; trade show arrangement

(G-4813)
HI INDIA ✪
2544 W Devon Ave (60659-1810)
PHONE.................................773 552-6083
EMP: 3 **EST:** 2019
SALES (est): 136.7K **Privately Held**
SIC: 2711 Newspapers, publishing & printing

(G-4814)
HIG CHEMICALS HOLDINGS
4650 S Racine Ave (60609-3321)
PHONE.................................773 376-9000
Anthony Tamer, *President*
EMP: 240
SALES (est): 15MM **Privately Held**
SIC: 2899 Chemical preparations

(G-4815)
HIGGINS BROS INC
1428 W 37th St (60609-2109)
PHONE.................................773 523-0124
Thomas Higgins, *President*
Ron Gentile, *Vice Pres*
EMP: 10
SQ FT: 5,000
SALES: 600K **Privately Held**
SIC: 5085 3412 2823 Drums, new or re-conditioned; metal barrels, drums & pails; cellulosic manmade fibers

(G-4816)
HIGH PERFORMANCE ENTP INC
Also Called: High Performance Uniforms
3500 N Kostner Ave (60641-3807)
PHONE.................................773 283-1778
Sabrina Gershkovich, *President*
▲ **EMP:** 20
SQ FT: 8,000
SALES (est): 11.6MM **Privately Held**
WEB: www.highperformanceuniforms.com
SIC: 2326 5136 Work uniforms; uniforms, men's & boys'

(G-4817)
HIGH POWER INC
8457 S Pulaski Rd (60652-3135)
PHONE.................................773 581-7650
Ahmad Ansari, *President*
EMP: 10
SALES (est): 970K **Privately Held**
SIC: 3571 8748 Electronic computers; business consulting

(G-4818)
HIGHLIGHT OF CHICAGO BRESS
Also Called: Bernard C Turner
912 W Sunnyside Ave 1e (60640-6018)
P.O. Box 408874 (60640-0021)
PHONE.................................773 944-0085
EMP: 3
SALES (est): 225.9K **Privately Held**
SIC: 2731 Books-Publishing/Printing

(G-4819)
HILL-ROM HOLDINGS INC (PA)
130 E Randolph St # 1000 (60601-6214)
PHONE.................................312 819-7200
Rolf A Classon, *Ch of Bd*
John J Greisch, *President*
Alton Shader, *President*
Francisco Canal Vega, *President*
Bill Jones, *Vice Pres*
EMP: 300 **EST:** 1969
SALES: 2.9B **Publicly Held**
SIC: 3841 7352 Surgical & medical instruments; medical equipment rental

(G-4820)
HILLSHIRE BRANDS COMPANY (HQ)
Also Called: Sara Lee Food & Beverage
400 S Jefferson St Fl 1 (60607-3812)
PHONE.................................312 614-6000
Sean M Connolly, *President*
Scott Graham, *Business Mgr*
Carlos Hurtado, *Business Mgr*
Barry Jacobs, *Business Mgr*
David McMillan, *Business Mgr*
▼ **EMP:** 277 **EST:** 1942
SQ FT: 230,000
SALES (est): 2.8B
SALES (corp-wide): 42.4B **Publicly Held**
WEB: www.hillshirebrands.com
SIC: 2013 2051 2053 Sausages & other prepared meats; breads, rolls & buns; frozen bakery products, except bread
PA: Tyson Foods, Inc.
    2200 W Don Tyson Pkwy
    Springdale AR 72762
    479 290-4000

GEOGRAPHIC SECTION
Chicago - Cook County (G-4846)

(G-4821)
HILLSHIRE BRANDS COMPANY
400 S Jefferson St Fl 1 (60607-3812)
PHONE.................................312 614-6000
Robert S Kopriva, *Branch Mgr*
EMP: 517
SQ FT: 1,800
SALES (corp-wide): 42.4B **Publicly Held**
WEB: www.sterlingbay.com
SIC: 2013 Sausages & other prepared meats
HQ: The Hillshire Brands Company
400 S Jefferson St Fl 1
Chicago IL 60607
312 614-6000

(G-4822)
HILLSHIRE BRANDS COMPANY
Hillshire Brnds Consmr Affairs
400 S Jefferson St Fl 1 (60607-3812)
P.O. Box 3901, Peoria (61612-3901)
PHONE.................................888 317-5867
Randy Forton, *Opers Mgr*
Elizabeth Tennis, *Branch Mgr*
Jennifer Floyd, *Manager*
EMP: 3
SALES (corp-wide): 42.4B **Publicly Held**
SIC: 2013 Sausages & other prepared meats
HQ: The Hillshire Brands Company
400 S Jefferson St Fl 1
Chicago IL 60607
312 614-6000

(G-4823)
HINCKLEY & SCHMITT INC
Also Called: Hinckley Springs
6055 S Harlem Ave (60638-3985)
PHONE.................................773 586-8600
David A Krishcok, *President*
▲ **EMP:** 2190
SQ FT: 55,000
SALES (est): 147.2MM **Privately Held**
SIC: 2086 5149 7359 Water, pasteurized: packaged in cans, bottles, etc.; water, distilled; mineral or spring water bottling; equipment rental & leasing
HQ: Suntory International Corp.
4141 Parklake Ave Ste 600
Raleigh NC 27612
917 756-2747

(G-4824)
HM WITT & CO
3313 W Newport Ave (60618-5509)
PHONE.................................773 250-5000
H Matthew Witt IV, *President*
Robert Haddon, *Partner*
Nora Tormey, *Project Mgr*
▼ **EMP:** 20
SQ FT: 26,500
SALES (est): 3.2MM **Privately Held**
SIC: 3993 Electric signs

(G-4825)
HML ELEVATORS INC
70 W Madison St Ste 5750 (60602-4292)
PHONE.................................757 822-8285
Emile Van Der Starre, *President*
Jennifer Faulkenberry, *Principal*
Jeroen Van Der Starre, *Principal*
EMP: 3
SALES (est): 138.9K **Privately Held**
SIC: 3534 Elevators & moving stairways

(G-4826)
HO BROTHERS LLC
5 S Wabash Ave Ste 1503 (60603-3088)
PHONE.................................312 854-3008
Allan Ho, *Mng Member*
Henry Ho,
Tommy Ho,
EMP: 3
SALES (est): 258.2K **Privately Held**
SIC: 5944 3911 Jewelry, precious stones & precious metals; jewelry, precious metal

(G-4827)
HOLCIM (US) INC (DH)
Also Called: Holcim USA
8700 W Bryn Mawr Ave (60631-3512)
P.O. Box 122, Dundee MI (48131-0122)
PHONE.................................773 372-1000
Filiberto Ruiz, *President*
GA Tan Jacques, *Senior VP*
Norman L Jagger, *Senior VP*
Alyse Martinelli, *Senior VP*
Jeff Ouhl, *Senior VP*
◆ **EMP:** 75
SALES (est): 726.5MM
SALES (corp-wide): 4.5B **Privately Held**
SIC: 3241 3272 Portland cement; concrete products
HQ: Holcim Participations (Us) Inc.
8700 W Bryn Mawr Ave
Chicago IL 60631
773 372-1000

(G-4828)
HOLCIM PARTICIPATIONS US INC (HQ)
8700 W Bryn Mawr Ave (60631-3512)
P.O. Box 122, Dundee MI (48131-0122)
PHONE.................................773 372-1000
Guy Edwards, *CEO*
Eric Ervin, *Plant Mgr*
Jerry McCarty, *Controller*
Ruslan Aghabayli, *Human Res Dir*
Remo Bernasconi, *Manager*
EMP: 4
SALES (est): 1.5B
SALES (corp-wide): 4.5B **Privately Held**
SIC: 3241 3272 Portland cement; concrete products
PA: Lafargeholcim Ltd
Zurcherstrasse 156
Jona SG 8645
588 585-858

(G-4829)
HOLDEN AMERICA IL LLC
6235 S Oak Park Ave (60638-4015)
PHONE.................................708 552-4070
Gregory R Winsor, *Mng Member*
▲ **EMP:** 6
SALES (est): 588.5K **Privately Held**
SIC: 3743 Railroad equipment

(G-4830)
HOLIDAY BRIGHT LIGHTS INC (PA)
Also Called: Holidynamics
954 W Wa Blvd Ste 705 (60607-2224)
PHONE.................................312 226-8281
Rich Martini, *CEO*
Greg Dondelinger, *CFO*
Steve Harrison, *Director*
Aric Kulm,
▲ **EMP:** 8
SQ FT: 8,000
SALES (est): 4MM **Privately Held**
SIC: 5063 3646 Lighting fixtures, commercial & industrial; commercial indusl & institutional electric lighting fixtures

(G-4831)
HOLOGRAM INC (PA)
1 N Lasalle St Ste 850 (60602)
PHONE.................................716 771-8308
Benjamin Forgan, *President*
Pat Wilbur, *CTO*
EMP: 9
SALES (est): 2MM **Privately Held**
SIC: 5065 3674 7371 Modems, computer; integrated circuits, semiconductor networks, etc.; computer software development & applications

(G-4832)
HOMAN BINDERY
1112 N Homan Ave (60651-4007)
PHONE.................................773 276-1500
Mitchell Harrison, *Partner*
J S Harrison Trust, *Partner*
Mitchell H Harrison, *Principal*
Jerome Harrison, *Trustee*
EMP: 25 **EST:** 1927
SQ FT: 20,000
SALES (est): 2.7MM **Privately Held**
SIC: 2789 Binding only: books, pamphlets, magazines, etc.

(G-4833)
HOME CITY ICE (PA)
Also Called: Jefferson Ice
2248 N Natchez Ave (60707-3424)
PHONE.................................773 622-9400
Robert H Rustman, *President*
EMP: 15
SQ FT: 31,000
SALES (est): 1.6MM **Privately Held**
SIC: 2097 Manufactured ice

(G-4834)
HOME PDTS INTL - N AMER INC (HQ)
Also Called: Homz
4501 W 47th St (60632-4407)
PHONE.................................773 890-1010
George Hamilton, *CEO*
Kathy Evans, *Senior VP*
Grant Fagan, *Senior VP*
John Pugh, *Vice Pres*
Dennis Doheny, *CFO*
◆ **EMP:** 300 **EST:** 1952
SQ FT: 300,000
SALES (est): 182MM
SALES (corp-wide): 551.5MM **Privately Held**
WEB: www.homzproducts.com
SIC: 3089 3499 Boxes, plastic; organizers for closets, drawers, etc.: plastic; ironing boards, metal
PA: Home Products International, Inc.
4501 W 47th St
Chicago IL 60632
773 890-1010

(G-4835)
HOMETOWN FOOD COMPANY (PA)
Also Called: Hometown Foods
500 W Madison St (60661-4544)
PHONE.................................312 500-7710
Tom Polke, *President*
Anthony P Raucci, *President*
Daniel Anglemyer, *COO*
David Meltzer, *Exec VP*
Scott Baird, *Senior VP*
EMP: 13
SQ FT: 640,000
SALES (est): 335MM **Privately Held**
SIC: 2052 Bakery products, dry

(G-4836)
HOMNAY MAGAZINE
1114 W Argyle St (60640-3610)
PHONE.................................773 334-6655
Khanh Tran, *Owner*
EMP: 3
SALES (est): 144.1K **Privately Held**
SIC: 2721 Magazines: publishing only, not printed on site

(G-4837)
HONEYWELL INTERNATIONAL INC
1 Bank One Plz (60670-0001)
PHONE.................................480 353-3020
EMP: 718
SALES (corp-wide): 36.7B **Publicly Held**
SIC: 3724 Research & development on aircraft engines & parts
PA: Honeywell International Inc.
300 S Tryon St
Charlotte NC 28202
704 627-6200

(G-4838)
HONEYWELL INTERNATIONAL INC
24004 Network Pl (60673-1240)
PHONE.................................973 455-2000
EMP: 657
SALES (corp-wide): 40.5B **Publicly Held**
SIC: 3724 Mfg Aircraft Engines/Parts
PA: Honeywell International Inc.
115 Tabor Rd
Morris Plains NJ 28202
973 455-2000

(G-4839)
HOP KEE INCORPORATED (PA)
Also Called: Hong Kong Market
2425 S Wallace St (60616-1855)
PHONE.................................312 791-9111
Thomas Lam, *President*
Gloria F Lam, *Treasurer*
▲ **EMP:** 31
SQ FT: 42,500
SALES (est): 19.9MM **Privately Held**
SIC: 5148 5141 2032 2099 Banana ripening; food brokers; beans & bean sprouts, canned, jarred, etc.; food preparations; cookies & crackers; pickles, sauces & salad dressings

(G-4840)
HOPKINS MACHINE CORPORATION
4243 W Diversey Ave (60639-2002)
PHONE.................................773 772-2800
Adam Widula, *President*
Alicia Widula, *Vice Pres*
EMP: 7 **EST:** 1915
SQ FT: 16,000
SALES: 1MM **Privately Held**
WEB: www.hopkinsmachine.com
SIC: 3599 Machine shop, jobbing & repair

(G-4841)
HORIZON FUEL CELL AMERICAS
18 S Michigan Ave # 1200 (60603-3200)
PHONE.................................312 316-8050
EMP: 5 **EST:** 2014
SALES (est): 578.8K **Privately Held**
SIC: 2869 Fuels

(G-4842)
HORIZON THERAPEUTICS USA INC
150 S Wacker Dr (60606-4103)
PHONE.................................312 332-1401
Shao-Lee Lin, *Exec VP*
Paul Peloso, *Vice Pres*
James Inglis, *Mktg Dir*
Lynn Kator, *Marketing Staff*
Denelle Robinson, *Marketing Staff*
EMP: 15 **Privately Held**
SIC: 2834 Pharmaceutical preparations
HQ: Horizon Therapeutics Usa, Inc.
150 Saunders Rd Ste 150 # 150
Lake Forest IL 60045

(G-4843)
HORWEEN LEATHER COMPANY
2015 N Elston Ave Ste 1 (60614-3943)
PHONE.................................773 772-2026
Arnold Horween Jr, *President*
Thomas Culliton, *Plant Secy*
John Culliton, *Vice Pres*
Christopher Koelblinger, *VP Prdtn*
Dan Cordova, *Prdtn Mgr*
▲ **EMP:** 175 **EST:** 1905
SQ FT: 260,000
SALES (est): 29MM **Privately Held**
WEB: www.horween.com
SIC: 3111 Hides: tanning, currying & finishing

(G-4844)
HOSTESS BRANDS LLC
2035 N Narragansett Ave (60639-3842)
PHONE.................................773 745-9800
EMP: 55
SALES (corp-wide): 907.6MM **Publicly Held**
SIC: 2053 2051 Frozen bakery products, except bread; cakes, pies & pastries
HQ: Hostess Brands, Llc
7905 Quivira Rd
Lenexa KS 66215
816 701-4600

(G-4845)
HOSTFORWEB INCORPORATED
7061 N Kedzie Ave Ste 302 (60645-2857)
PHONE.................................312 343-4678
Alex Korneyev, *President*
EMP: 2
SALES (est): 274.4K **Privately Held**
SIC: 7372 Operating systems computer software

(G-4846)
HOT FOOD BOXES INC
4109 W Lake St (60624-1719)
P.O. Box 1089, Mooresville IN (46158-5089)
PHONE.................................773 533-5912
EMP: 25 **EST:** 1948
SQ FT: 32,000
SALES: 2.5MM
SALES (corp-wide): 8.9MM **Privately Held**
SIC: 3556 3444 Mfg Food Products Machinery Mfg Sheet Metalwork
PA: Gm Specialties Inc
4107 W Lake St
Chicago IL
773 533-5912

Chicago - Cook County (G-4847)   GEOGRAPHIC SECTION

(G-4847)
HOT MEXICAN PEPPERS INC
2215 W 47th St (60609-4013)
PHONE.................................773 843-9774
Alejandro L Correa, *President*
◆ EMP: 2
SALES (est): 294.2K **Privately Held**
SIC: 2034 Dried & dehydrated fruits

(G-4848)
HOTEL AMERIKA
434 W Briar Pl Apt 4 (60657-4776)
PHONE.................................219 508-9418
David Lazar, *Exec Dir*
EMP: 3
SALES (est): 136.6K **Privately Held**
SIC: 2721 Magazines: publishing & printing

(G-4849)
HOUGHTON INTERNATIONAL INC
6600 S Nashville Ave (60638)
PHONE.................................610 666-4000
Craig Patterson, *Regl Sales Mgr*
John V Livaich, *Branch Mgr*
EMP: 18
SALES (corp-wide): 1.1B **Publicly Held**
WEB: www.houghtonintl.com
SIC: 2869 2992 2899 2842 Hydraulic fluids, synthetic base; re-refining lubricating oils & greases; rust arresting compounds, animal or vegetable oil base; cutting oils, blending: made from purchased materials; heat treating salts; cleaning or polishing preparations; processing assistants
HQ: Houghton International Inc.
945 Madison Ave
Norristown PA 19403
888 459-9844

(G-4850)
HOWARD MEDICAL COMPANY
3450 N Kostner Ave (60641-3805)
PHONE.................................773 278-1440
Mark Litton, *Owner*
Ross Litton, *Principal*
Bill Chilcutt, *Executive*
▲ EMP: 9
SALES (est): 2.8MM **Privately Held**
SIC: 5047 2782 Medical equipment & supplies; ledgers & ledger sheets

(G-4851)
HOWE CORPORATION
1650 N Elston Ave (60642-1585)
PHONE.................................773 235-0200
Mary C Howe, *President*
Avinash Ahuja, *Exec VP*
Jean Spiegelhalter, *Senior VP*
John Myrda, *VP Mfg*
Arnie Chaidez, *Purch Mgr*
▲ EMP: 37 EST: 1912
SQ FT: 60,000
SALES (est): 10.5MM **Privately Held**
WEB: www.howecorp.com
SIC: 3585 3563 3498 3443 Refrigeration equipment, complete; ice making machinery; compressors for refrigeration & air conditioning equipment; air & gas compressors; fabricated pipe & fittings; fabricated plate work (boiler shop)

(G-4852)
HOWMET AEROSPACE INC
5414 S Archer Ave (60638-3002)
PHONE.................................773 581-7200
Anthony Salton, *Branch Mgr*
EMP: 135
SALES (corp-wide): 14.1B **Publicly Held**
SIC: 3353 Aluminum sheet & strip
PA: Howmet Aerospace Inc.
201 Isabella St Ste 200
Pittsburgh PA 15212
412 553-1950

(G-4853)
HP INC
303 E Wacker Dr Ste 2700 (60601-7804)
PHONE.................................650 857-1501
Jonathan Wu, *Branch Mgr*
Lauren Grady, *Manager*
EMP: 350
SALES (corp-wide): 58.7B **Publicly Held**
WEB: www.hp.com
SIC: 3571 Personal computers (microcomputers)
PA: Hp, Inc.
1501 Page Mill Rd
Palo Alto CA 94304
650 857-1501

(G-4854)
HP INC
100 N Riverside Plz # 152 (60606-1501)
PHONE.................................650 857-1501
Kyle Nielsen, *Partner*
Steven Stubitz, *VP Sales*
Bob Stevenson, *Branch Mgr*
EMP: 36
SALES (corp-wide): 58.7B **Publicly Held**
SIC: 3571 Personal computers (microcomputers)
PA: Hp, Inc.
1501 Page Mill Rd
Palo Alto CA 94304
650 857-1501

(G-4855)
HP INTERACTIVE INC
2461 W Balmoral Ave (60625-2301)
PHONE.................................773 681-4440
Boulos Mikhail, *President*
EMP: 5
SALES (est): 368.4K **Privately Held**
SIC: 2741

(G-4856)
HPI NORTH AMERICA INC
4501 W 47th St (60632-4407)
PHONE.................................773 890-8927
George Haminton, *President*
EMP: 1
SALES (est): 207K **Privately Held**
SIC: 3089 Injection molding of plastics

(G-4857)
HQ PRINTERS INC
200 N La Salle St Lbby 2 (60601-1046)
PHONE.................................312 782-2020
Prakash Patel, *President*
EMP: 2
SQ FT: 2,000
SALES (est): 650K **Privately Held**
SIC: 7334 2752 2791 2789 Photocopying & duplicating services; business forms, lithographed; typesetting; bookbinding & related work

(G-4858)
HU-FRIEDY MFG CO LLC (HQ)
3232 N Rockwell St (60618-5935)
PHONE.................................773 975-3975
Ron Saslow, *Ch of Bd*
Ken Serota, *President*
Mark Wawrzyniak, *General Mgr*
Charley Zhai, *General Mgr*
Jim Ahlborn, *Vice Pres*
▲ EMP: 245 EST: 1908
SQ FT: 80,000
SALES (est): 120.9MM
SALES (corp-wide): 918.1MM **Publicly Held**
WEB: www.hu-friedy.com
SIC: 3843 Dental hand instruments
PA: Cantel Medical Corp.
150 Clove Rd Ste 36
Little Falls NJ 07424
973 890-7220

(G-4859)
HUB MANUFACTURING COMPANY INC
Also Called: Hub Stamping & Mfg Co
1212 N Central Park Ave (60651-2299)
PHONE.................................773 252-1373
Gerald F Benda, *President*
EMP: 28
SQ FT: 36,000
SALES (est): 2.2MM **Privately Held**
SIC: 3469 3364 3498 Stamping metal for the trade; zinc & zinc-base alloy die-castings; fabricated pipe & fittings

(G-4860)
HUCUAI LLC
222 Merchandise Mart Plz (60654-1103)
PHONE.................................312 608-6101
Asif Khan, *CEO*
EMP: 6
SALES (est): 135.3K **Privately Held**
SIC: 7372 Application computer software

(G-4861)
HYBRIS (US) CORPORATION (DH)
20 N Wacker Dr Ste 2900 (60606-3101)
PHONE.................................312 265-5010
Ariel Ludi, *CEO*
Carsten Thoma, *President*
Michael Zips, *COO*
Steven Kramer, *Exec VP*
Katrin Gunter, *Senior VP*
EMP: 30
SQ FT: 14,000
SALES (est): 8.4MM
SALES (corp-wide): 30.4B **Privately Held**
SIC: 7371 7372 Software programming applications; computer software systems analysis & design, custom; business oriented computer software
HQ: Hybris Gmbh
Nymphenburger Str. 86
Munchen 80636
898 906-50

(G-4862)
HYDROLOGY INC
435 N La Salle Dr Ste 100 (60654-4589)
P.O. Box 31877 (60631-0877)
PHONE.................................312 832-9000
David Kotowsky, *Principal*
Paige Yohay, *Sales Staff*
Jenna Kendall, *Manager*
▲ EMP: 2
SALES (est): 215.6K **Privately Held**
WEB: www.hydrologychicago.com
SIC: 3432 Plumbing fixture fittings & trim

(G-4863)
HYLAN DESIGN LTD
329 W 18th St Ste 700 (60616-1122)
PHONE.................................312 243-7341
Theodore H Schultz, *President*
Noemi Pita, *Office Mgr*
Elizabeth Schultz, *Admin Sec*
EMP: 4
SQ FT: 7,500
SALES (est): 750K **Privately Held**
SIC: 2599 5712 2541 2511 Cabinets, factory; furniture stores; wood partitions & fixtures; wood household furniture; wood kitchen cabinets; millwork

(G-4864)
HYMANS AUTO SUPPLY CO (PA)
Also Called: E-Z Mix
8600-8614 S Coml Ave (60617)
PHONE.................................773 978-8221
Richard E Hyman, *President*
Dennis E Hyman, *Vice Pres*
Martyn Hyman, *Treasurer*
Dave Hyman, *Sales Staff*
◆ EMP: 50
SQ FT: 50,000
SALES (est): 39.7MM **Privately Held**
WEB: www.ezmix.com
SIC: 5531 5251 5198 3429 Automotive parts; hardware; paints; motor vehicle hardware

(G-4865)
HYPERERA INC
Also Called: (A DEVELOPMENT STAGE ENTERPRISE)
2316 S Wentworth Ave Fl 1 (60616-2014)
PHONE.................................312 842-2288
Zhi Yong LI, *Ch of Bd*
WEI Wu, *President*
Hong Tao Bai, *Vice Pres*
Simon Bai, *CFO*
Nan Su, *CTO*
EMP: 17
SQ FT: 350
SALES (est): 162.8K **Privately Held**
SIC: 7372 Prepackaged software

(G-4866)
I M M INC
Also Called: International Marketing & Mfg
5262 S Kolmar Ave (60632-4711)
PHONE.................................773 767-3700
Anne K Stewart, *President*
EMP: 10 EST: 1979
SQ FT: 39,000
SALES (est): 1.6MM **Privately Held**
SIC: 2679 Paper products, converted

(G-4867)
I P G WAREHOUSE LTD
Also Called: Independent Publishers Group
600 N Pulaski Rd (60624-1059)
PHONE.................................773 722-5527
Kurt Matthews, *CEO*
Mark Suchonel, *President*
Berianne Bramman, *Publisher*
Teresa Gamboa, *CFO*
▲ EMP: 24 EST: 2002
SALES (est): 2.2MM **Privately Held**
WEB: www.ipgbook.com
SIC: 1541 2741 Industrial buildings & warehouses; miscellaneous publishing

(G-4868)
I Q INFINITY LLC
7624 S Wood St (60620-4448)
PHONE.................................773 651-2556
Fred Sampson, *President*
▲ EMP: 3
SALES (est): 173.5K **Privately Held**
SIC: 2893 Printing ink

(G-4869)
IB SOURCE INC
Also Called: Cie Source
516 N Ogden Ave Ste 111 (60642-6421)
PHONE.................................312 698-7062
Andrew T Culley, *President*
John J Cummins, *Admin Sec*
EMP: 7
SALES (est): 865.7K **Privately Held**
SIC: 2731 Book publishing

(G-4870)
IBARRA GROUP LLC
3100 S Homan Ave (60623-5018)
PHONE.................................773 650-0503
Rosa Ibarra, *Principal*
Roberts Ibarra, *Mng Member*
EMP: 2
SQ FT: 6,000
SALES (est): 200K **Privately Held**
SIC: 3446 Ornamental metalwork

(G-4871)
ICANDEE LLC
Also Called: Icandee Marketing
954 W Carmen Ave (60640-3225)
PHONE.................................773 754-0493
William H Stevenson, *Principal*
John Lashmett, *Officer*
EMP: 3
SALES (est): 144.7K **Privately Held**
WEB: www.icandeemarketing.com
SIC: 5651 3951 5199 5112 Unisex clothing stores; fountain pens & fountain pen desk sets; gifts & novelties; stationery & office supplies; banners, flags, decals & posters

(G-4872)
ICON ACQUISITION HOLDINGS LP (PA)
680 N Lake Shore Dr (60611-4546)
PHONE.................................312 751-8000
EMP: 3
SALES (est): 56.5MM **Privately Held**
SIC: 7812 4841 2721 Motion Pict/Video Prodtn Cable/Pay Tv Services Periodical-Publish/Print

(G-4873)
ICREAM GROUP LLC
1537 N Milwaukee Ave # 1 (60622-2209)
PHONE.................................773 342-2834
EMP: 2
SALES (est): 210K **Privately Held**
SIC: 2024 Mfg Ice Cream/Frozen Desert

(G-4874)
IDEA TOOL & MANUFACTURING CO
5615 S Claremont Ave (60636-1011)
P.O. Box 520, La Grange (60525-0520)
PHONE.................................312 476-1080
Eric Sund, *Director*
EMP: 51
SALES (est): 2.9MM **Privately Held**
SIC: 3544 Special dies & tools

GEOGRAPHIC SECTION

Chicago - Cook County (G-4903)

(G-4875)
IDEAL BOX CO (PA)
4800 S Austin Ave (60638-1484)
PHONE.................................708 594-3100
Scott Eisen, *President*
Stephen Eisen, *Chairman*
Yale Eisen, *COO*
Jeff Craig, *Vice Pres*
Mike Sebring, *VP Opers*
▲ **EMP**: 178 **EST**: 1924
SQ FT: 310,000
SALES (est): 80MM **Privately Held**
WEB: www.idealpop.com
SIC: 2653 3993 Boxes, corrugated: made from purchased materials; display items, corrugated: made from purchased materials; signs & advertising specialties

(G-4876)
IDEAL MEDIA LLC (PA)
200 E Randolph St # 7000 (60601-6436)
PHONE.................................312 456-2822
Brian Reshefsky,
Tim Cramer,
◆ **EMP**: 56
SALES (est): 3.3MM **Privately Held**
SIC: 2721 Magazines: publishing only, not printed on site

(G-4877)
IDEVCONCEPTS INC
100 E 14th St Apt 904 (60605-3666)
PHONE.................................312 351-1615
Mario Mamalis, *President*
Derek Demas, *Director*
EMP: 5
SALES (est): 177.3K **Privately Held**
SIC: 7371 7372 7389 Computer software development; custom computer programming services; application computer software;

(G-4878)
IEMCO CORPORATION
Also Called: Illinois Engraving & Mfg Co
4530 N Ravenswood Ave (60640-5202)
PHONE.................................773 728-4400
Wayne Tumminello, *President*
Nathan Tumminello, *Engineer*
EMP: 6
SQ FT: 5,600
SALES (est): 500K **Privately Held**
WEB: www.illinoisengraving.com
SIC: 3544 3479 3953 2796 Special dies & tools; etching & engraving; marking devices; platemaking services; commercial printing

(G-4879)
IG US HOLDINGS INC
200 W Jackson Blvd # 1450 (60606-6993)
PHONE.................................312 884-0179
EMP: 3
SALES (est): 153.9K **Privately Held**
SIC: 3577 Computer peripheral equipment

(G-4880)
IGNITE USA LLC
Also Called: Contigo
180 N La Salle St Ste 700 (60601-2503)
PHONE.................................312 432-6223
Mark W Johnson,
Sami El-Saden,
Bradford R Turner,
Karen Wolters,
Robert Wolters Sr,
▲ **EMP**: 45
SQ FT: 15,000
SALES (est): 14.4MM
SALES (corp-wide): 9.7B **Publicly Held**
SIC: 3411 Food & beverage containers
PA: Newell Brands Inc.
6655 Pachtree Dunwoody Rd
Atlanta GA 30328
770 418-7000

(G-4881)
IGUANAMED LLC
363 W Erie St Ste 200e (60654-7061)
PHONE.................................312 546-4182
Ryan Hertz, *Sales Staff*
Gregory Lilien, *Mng Member*
Ryan Saunders,
▲ **EMP**: 6
SALES (est): 6MM **Privately Held**
SIC: 2337 2326 Uniforms, except athletic: women's, misses' & juniors'; medical & hospital uniforms, men's

(G-4882)
IHEARTCOMMUNICATIONS INC
Also Called: 1035 Kiss
875 N Michigan Ave # 4000 (60611-1803)
PHONE.................................312 255-5100
Cathy Steinehour, *General Mgr*
EMP: 30 **Publicly Held**
SIC: 3663 Radio receiver networks
HQ: Iheartcommunications, Inc.
20880 Stone Oak Pkwy
San Antonio TX 78258
210 822-2828

(G-4883)
IHI TERRASUN SOLUTIONS INC
100 N Riverside Plz # 220 (60606-1501)
PHONE.................................312 878-8532
Toshiaki Nishio, *President*
EMP: 3
SALES (est): 125.3K **Privately Held**
SIC: 3812 Search & navigation equipment

(G-4884)
IKAN CREATIONS LLC
2010 S Wabash Ave Ste H (60616-1775)
PHONE.................................312 204-7333
Jason Frazier, *President*
EMP: 5 **EST**: 2016
SQ FT: 700
SALES (est): 172.3K **Privately Held**
SIC: 2396 7812 7819 7929 Screen printing on fabric articles; music video production; sound (effects & music production); motion picture; entertainers & entertainment groups; entertainers

(G-4885)
IKO MIDWEST INC
6600 S Central Ave (60638-6306)
PHONE.................................815 936-9600
David Koschitzky, *President*
Randy Dalton, *Plant Supt*
Ronald Healey, *Treasurer*
Carol Perkins, *Marketing Staff*
Eileen Kane, *Admin Asst*
◆ **EMP**: 50
SALES (est): 18.1MM
SALES (corp-wide): 53.6MM **Privately Held**
SIC: 2429 Shingle & shingle mills
PA: Goldis Enterprises, Inc.
120 Hay Rd
Wilmington DE 19809
302 764-3100

(G-4886)
IL INTERNATIONAL LLC (PA)
1720 N Elston Ave (60642-1532)
PHONE.................................773 276-0070
Marion Cameron, *Principal*
Robert Glidden, *Vice Pres*
EMP: 6
SALES (est): 7.4MM **Privately Held**
SIC: 3356 Precious metals

(G-4887)
ILIGHT TECHNOLOGIES INC (PA)
Also Called: Optiva Signs
118 S Clinton St Ste 370 (60661-3661)
PHONE.................................312 876-8630
Sean Callahan, *CEO*
Mark Cleaver, *President*
James Adolfino, *Engineer*
Tim Newbold, *CFO*
Timothy Newbold, *CFO*
▲ **EMP**: 12
SQ FT: 4,000
SALES (est): 4MM **Privately Held**
SIC: 3993 Signs & advertising specialties

(G-4888)
ILLINOIS BAKING
10839 S Langley Ave (60628-3814)
PHONE.................................773 995-7200
Fax: 773 995-6982
EMP: 4 **EST**: 2010
SALES (est): 170K **Privately Held**
SIC: 2051 Mfg Bread/Related Products

(G-4889)
ILLINOIS ENGINEERED PDTS INC
2415 W 21st St (60608-2412)
PHONE.................................312 850-3710
Dean Wynne, *President*
Carina Diaz, *Vice Pres*
Laura Marzullo, *Accounting Mgr*
Brad Chainey, *Sales Mgr*
▲ **EMP**: 20
SQ FT: 150,000
SALES (est): 6.2MM **Privately Held**
SIC: 3312 3315 Rails, steel or iron; fence gates posts & fittings: steel

(G-4890)
ILLINOIS FIBRE SPECIALTY CO (PA)
Also Called: I F S C O Industries
4301 S Western Blvd (60609-3089)
PHONE.................................773 376-1122
Casimir W Kasper, *President*
Victoria Kasper, *Admin Sec*
EMP: 25
SQ FT: 72,000
SALES (est): 3.5MM **Privately Held**
WEB: www.ifscoind.com
SIC: 3429 5032 5131 Furniture hardware; drywall materials; piece goods & other fabrics

(G-4891)
ILLINOIS GREEN CNSTR INC
3651 N Nora Ave (60634-2375)
PHONE.................................847 975-2312
Marcin Proszek, *Principal*
EMP: 15
SALES (est): 480.1K **Privately Held**
SIC: 1522 1521 1751 1761 Hotel/motel & multi-family home renovation & remodeling; single-family home remodeling, additions & repairs; window & door installation & erection; roofing, siding & sheet metal work; roofing & gutter work; roofing contractor; sunrooms, prefabricated metal

(G-4892)
ILLUMIVATION STUDIOS LLC
4425 S Western Blvd Ste 1 (60609-3033)
PHONE.................................312 261-5561
Michael Dunbar, *Mng Member*
EMP: 4 **EST**: 2011
SALES (est): 381.9K **Privately Held**
WEB: www.illumivation.com
SIC: 3999 Theatrical scenery

(G-4893)
ILOILO CUSTOM FRAMING
850 W Argyle St Apt 506 (60640-7855)
PHONE.................................773 334-2844
EMP: 3
SALES (est): 232.4K **Privately Held**
SIC: 2499 Picture frame molding, finished

(G-4894)
IMAGINATION PUBLISHING LLC
Also Called: Baumer Financial Publishing
600 W Fulton St Ste 600 # 600 (60661-1256)
PHONE.................................312 887-1000
Sahar Dika, *Editor*
Becky Maughan, *Editor*
Kristen Menke, *Editor*
Chuck Ulie, *Editor*
Jackson Van Meter, *Editor*
EMP: 50
SQ FT: 17,500
SALES (est): 10MM **Privately Held**
SIC: 2721 2741 Magazines: publishing only, not printed on site; newsletter publishing

(G-4895)
IMANAGE LLC (PA)
540 W Madison St Ste 300 (60661-2513)
PHONE.................................312 667-7000
Neil Araujo, *CEO*
Rafiq Mohammadi, *Vice Pres*
Saud Ahmad, *Engineer*
Linda Zhou, *Engineer*
Andy Huber, *Accounts Exec*
EMP: 160 **EST**: 1998
SQ FT: 26,000
SALES (est): 76MM **Privately Held**
SIC: 7372 Business oriented computer software

(G-4896)
IMEDIA NETWORK INC
2532 W Irving Park Rd 1e (60618-3742)
PHONE.................................847 331-1774
Horatiu Boeriu, *President*
EMP: 1 **EST**: 2009
SALES: 300K **Privately Held**
SIC: 2741 Miscellaneous publishing

(G-4897)
IMPERIAL GROUP MFG INC
640 N La Salle Dr Ste 670 (60654-3763)
PHONE.................................615 325-9224
EMP: 383
SALES (corp-wide): 529.1MM **Privately Held**
SIC: 3715 Trailer bodies
PA: Imperial Group Manufacturing, Inc.
4545 Airport Rd
Denton TX 76207
940 565-8505

(G-4898)
IMPERIAL OIL INC
4346 N Western Ave (60618-1647)
PHONE.................................773 866-1235
Mahboob Abbas, *President*
EMP: 2
SALES (est): 237.1K **Privately Held**
SIC: 3713 Automobile wrecker truck bodies

(G-4899)
IMPERIAL PLATING COMPANY ILL
7030 W 60th St (60638-3102)
PHONE.................................773 586-3500
Walter Kuziel Jr, *President*
Monica Kuziel, *Business Mgr*
Charles Brass, *Vice Pres*
Anthony Kuziel, *VP Prdtn*
Rey Reyes, *Office Mgr*
EMP: 44
SQ FT: 40,000
SALES (est): 3.2MM **Privately Held**
WEB: www.imperialplating.com
SIC: 3471 Electroplating of metals or formed products; buffing for the trade; polishing, metals or formed products

(G-4900)
IMPERIAL STEEL TANK
10439 S Maplewood Ave (60655-1024)
PHONE.................................773 779-4284
James Broad, *CEO*
EMP: 3
SALES (est): 254.3K **Privately Held**
SIC: 3443 Fabricated plate work (boiler shop)

(G-4901)
IMPERIAL STORE FIXTURES INC
3768 N Clark St (60613-3810)
PHONE.................................773 348-1137
Rose T Stranc, *President*
Edward L Stranc Jr, *Admin Sec*
EMP: 8
SQ FT: 3,000
SALES (est): 1.2MM **Privately Held**
WEB: www.imperialmidwest.com
SIC: 2542 2431 Shelving, office & store: except wood; millwork

(G-4902)
IMPRESSIVE IMPRESSIONS
329 W 18th St Ste 306 (60616-1772)
PHONE.................................312 432-0501
EMP: 4
SALES: 395K **Privately Held**
SIC: 2759 Commercial Printing

(G-4903)
IN SIGHT SIGN COMPANY INC
3910 W Grand Ave (60651-2009)
PHONE.................................773 267-4002
Christopher Zwirn, *President*
EMP: 4
SALES: 775.6K **Privately Held**
SIC: 3993 Signs, not made in custom sign painting shops

Chicago - Cook County (G-4904)

(G-4904)
IN3GREDIENTS INC
Also Called: Gelnex
30 N Michigan Ave Ste 505 (60602-3836)
PHONE...................................312 577-4275
Luiz Perondi, *President*
▲ **EMP:** 6
SQ FT: 1,250
SALES (est): 601.9K **Privately Held**
WEB: www.gelnex.com
SIC: 2899 Gelatin

(G-4905)
INDIA TRIBUNE LTD CORPORATION (PA)
3304 W Peterson Ave (60659-3510)
PHONE...................................773 588-5077
Prashant Shah, *President*
Eric Shah, *Publisher*
Ravi Ponangi, *Chief*
Rinku Patel, *Prdtn Mgr*
EMP: 11 **EST:** 1977
SQ FT: 5,000
SALES (est): 800K **Privately Held**
WEB: www.indiatribune.com
SIC: 2721 2711 Periodicals: publishing only; newspapers

(G-4906)
INDUSTRIAL FENCE INC
1300 S Kilbourn Ave (60623-1045)
PHONE...................................773 521-9900
Mike Saltijeral, *CEO*
Miguel A Saltijeral, *President*
Alan Tutje, *CFO*
Maria E Saltijeral, *Admin Sec*
EMP: 75 **EST:** 1999
SQ FT: 80,000
SALES: 23.4MM **Privately Held**
SIC: 3446 1799 1611 Fences or posts, ornamental iron or steel; fence construction; highway signs & guardrails

(G-4907)
INDUSTRIAL INSTRUMENT SVC CORP
5643 W 63rd Pl (60638-5515)
PHONE...................................773 581-3355
Armon Schmidt, *President*
Majorie Schmidt, *Vice Pres*
EMP: 6 **EST:** 1959
SQ FT: 1,700
SALES (est): 830K **Privately Held**
WEB: www.industrialinstrument.net
SIC: 5084 7699 3546 3545 Metalworking machinery; industrial machinery & equipment repair; power-driven handtools; machine tool accessories

(G-4908)
INDUSTRIAL MINT WLDG MACHINING
1431 W Pershing Rd (60609-2407)
P.O. Box 385, Kingsbury IN (46345-0385)
PHONE...................................773 376-6526
Jacek Pater, *Purch Agent*
Stephen Sularski, *Manager*
EMP: 85
SQ FT: 69,500
SALES (corp-wide): 22.2MM **Privately Held**
SIC: 7699 7692 3441 Industrial equipment services; welding repair; fabricated structural metal
PA: Industrial Maintenance Welding & Machining Co Inc
2nd & Hupp Rd
Kingsbury IN 46345
219 393-5531

(G-4909)
INDUSTRIAL PIPE AND SUPPLY CO
5100 W 16th St (60804-1926)
PHONE...................................708 652-7511
Stuart J Feinberg, *President*
William J Bero, *Vice Pres*
EMP: 45
SQ FT: 51,000
SALES (est): 16.6MM **Privately Held**
WEB: www.indpipeco.com
SIC: 5085 3569 3498 3312 Valves & fittings; sprinkler systems, fire: automatic; fabricated pipe & fittings; blast furnaces & steel mills

(G-4910)
INDUSTRIAL SERVICE SOLUTIONS (PA)
875 N Michigan Ave (60611-1803)
PHONE...................................917 609-6979
Jim Rogers, *CEO*
Angie Holbert, *Office Mgr*
EMP: 157
SALES (est): 27.1MM **Privately Held**
SIC: 7694 3625 5063 6719 Electric motor repair; motor controls, electric; motors, electric; investment holding companies, except banks

(G-4911)
INDUSTRIAL TECH CENTL LLC
333 S Wabash Ave Ste 2700 (60604-4129)
PHONE...................................312 785-2520
Lee Hedrick,
EMP: 1
SALES: 250K **Privately Held**
SIC: 3999 Manufacturing industries

(G-4912)
INFINISCENE INC
25 W Hubbard St Fl 5 (60654-5644)
PHONE...................................630 567-0452
Stuart Grubbs, *CEO*
Aaron Hassell, *COO*
EMP: 7
SALES (est): 270.6K **Privately Held**
SIC: 7372 Application computer software

(G-4913)
INFINITY METAL SPINNING INC
10247 S Avenue O (60617-5904)
PHONE...................................773 731-4467
EMP: 9
SALES: 200K **Privately Held**
SIC: 3542 Mfg Machine Tools-Forming

(G-4914)
INFOR (US) INC
Also Called: Ssa Global
8725 W Higgins Rd (60631-2716)
PHONE...................................312 279-1245
Teshome Kassa, *Branch Mgr*
Joseph Stalzer, *Consultant*
EMP: 65
SALES (corp-wide): 48.9B **Privately Held**
WEB: www.infor.com
SIC: 7372 Business oriented computer software
HQ: Infor (Us), Inc.
13560 Morris Rd Ste 4100
Alpharetta GA 30004
678 319-8000

(G-4915)
INFORMA BUSINESS MEDIA INC
200 W Madison St Ste 2610 (60606-3407)
PHONE...................................312 595-1080
Kurt Nelson, *Manager*
EMP: 75
SALES (corp-wide): 3B **Privately Held**
WEB: www.penton.com
SIC: 2721 Magazines: publishing only, not printed on site
HQ: Informa Business Media, Inc.
605 3rd Ave Fl 22
New York NY 10158
212 204-4200

(G-4916)
INFORMA MEDIA INC
Also Called: Penton Media - Aviation Week
24652 Network Pl (60673-1246)
PHONE...................................212 204-4200
EMP: 11
SALES (corp-wide): 3B **Privately Held**
SIC: 2721 7389 7313 7375 Magazines: publishing only, not printed on site; advertising, promotional & trade show services; printed media advertising representatives; on-line data base information retrieval
HQ: Informa Media, Inc.
605 3rd Ave Fl 22
New York NY 10158
212 204-4200

(G-4917)
INFORMATION RESOURCES INC
150 N Clinton St (60661-1402)
PHONE...................................312 474-3380
Janet Kruse, *Exec VP*
Ellen Schmitz, *Senior VP*
David Ackert, *Vice Pres*
Kimberly Kaplan, *Vice Pres*
David Kulbok, *Vice Pres*
EMP: 5
SALES (corp-wide): 356.4MM **Privately Held**
SIC: 7372 8732 Prepackaged software; business research service
PA: Information Resources, Inc
150 N Clinton St
Chicago IL 60661
312 726-1221

(G-4918)
INFORMATION RESOURCES INC
550 W Washington Blvd # 6 (60661-2595)
PHONE...................................312 474-8900
Joseph Durret, *Manager*
EMP: 900
SALES (corp-wide): 356.4MM **Privately Held**
SIC: 7372 8732 Business oriented computer software; market analysis or research
PA: Information Resources, Inc
150 N Clinton St
Chicago IL 60661
312 726-1221

(G-4919)
INFORMATION USA INC
Also Called: Hirise Promotions & Marketing
1555 N Dearborn Pkwy Ofc (60610-7426)
PHONE...................................312 943-6288
Kim Mc Coy, *Mktg Dir*
EMP: 3
SALES (corp-wide): 871.9K **Privately Held**
SIC: 2731 Books: publishing only
PA: Information Usa, Inc.
1851 Columbia Rd Nw # 402
Washington DC 20009
301 929-8400

(G-4920)
ING BANK FSB
21 E Chestnut St (60611-2050)
PHONE...................................312 981-1236
James Cummings, *Principal*
EMP: 4 **Publicly Held**
SIC: 3944 Banks, toy
HQ: Ing Bank Fsb
802 Delaware Ave
Wilmington DE 19801

(G-4921)
INGLOT ELECTRONICS CORP
Also Called: Inelco
4878 N Elston Ave (60630-2578)
PHONE...................................773 286-5881
Christopher Inglot, *CEO*
Andrew Platowski, *President*
Andy Platowski, *General Mgr*
Kerry Kaczmare, *Purchasing*
Diane Inglot, *Admin Sec*
▲ **EMP:** 58 **EST:** 1964
SQ FT: 28,000
SALES (est): 9.5MM **Privately Held**
WEB: www.inglotelec.com
SIC: 3677 5065 3643 3621 Electronic transformers; coil windings, electronic; inductors, electronic; electronic parts & equipment; current-carrying wiring devices; motors & generators; transformers, except electric

(G-4922)
INGREDIENTS GOLDEN HILL
2020 N California Ave (60647-6319)
PHONE...................................773 852-5112
EMP: 3
SALES (est): 129.2K **Privately Held**
SIC: 2099 Food preparations

(G-4923)
INGREDION INCORPORATED
Also Called: Corn Products International
141 W Jackson Blvd # 340 (60604-2992)
PHONE...................................708 551-2600
Cesar Alvarez, *Auditor*
A J Didominicis, *Manager*
Vicky Melcher, *Admin Asst*
EMP: 8
SALES (corp-wide): 6.2B **Publicly Held**
SIC: 2046 Wet corn milling
PA: Ingredion Incorporated
5 Westbrook Corporate Ctr # 500
Westchester IL 60154
708 551-2600

(G-4924)
INHERIS BIOPHARMA INC
Also Called: Inheris Pharmaceuticals, Inc.
150 N Riverside Plz # 1840 (60606-1598)
PHONE...................................415 482-5652
Howard Robin, *President*
Kris Ford, *Vice Pres*
Gil Labrucherie, *CFO*
Mark Wilson, *Admin Sec*
EMP: 100
SALES (est): 3.5MM **Publicly Held**
SIC: 2834 Pharmaceutical preparations
PA: Nektar Therapeutics
455 Mssion Bay Blvd S Ste
San Francisco CA 94158

(G-4925)
INJURY SCIENCES LLC
222 Merchandise Mart Plz # 900 (60654-1105)
PHONE...................................210 691-0674
Scott Palmer, *President*
Jim Bumiller, *Vice Pres*
Scott Kidd, *Vice Pres*
Maria Guerra, *Controller*
EMP: 19
SQ FT: 3,400
SALES (est): 1.8MM **Privately Held**
SIC: 7372 Prepackaged software

(G-4926)
INK SPOT PRINTING
2 N Riverside Plz Ste 365 (60606-2620)
PHONE...................................773 528-0288
Stuart Fisher, *Owner*
Sura Fisher, *Co-Owner*
Todd Fisher, *Co-Owner*
EMP: 6
SQ FT: 5,000
SALES (est): 604.9K **Privately Held**
SIC: 2752 2791 Commercial printing, offset; typesetting

(G-4927)
INNERWORKINGS INC (PA)
203 N Lasalle St Ste 1800 (60601)
PHONE...................................312 642-3700
Richard S Stoddart, *President*
Oren B Azar, *Exec VP*
Ronald C Provenzano, *Exec VP*
Renae D Chorzempa, *Officer*
EMP: 100
SALES: 1.1B **Publicly Held**
SIC: 7389 2752 7374 7372 Advertising, promotional & trade show services; commercial printing, lithographic; data processing & preparation; publishers' computer software

(G-4928)
INNOLITICA LABS LLC
1620 S Michigan Ave # 910 (60616-1281)
PHONE...................................224 434-1238
Sanjay Kumar, *Director*
EMP: 3 **EST:** 2015
SALES (est): 86.5K **Privately Held**
SIC: 7371 7372 Computer software development; application computer software; business oriented computer software

(G-4929)
INNOPHOS INC
512 E 138th St (60803)
PHONE...................................773 468-2300
Eric Haaijer, *Branch Mgr*
EMP: 5
SALES (corp-wide): 801.8MM **Privately Held**
SIC: 2874 2819 Phosphates; industrial inorganic chemicals
HQ: Innophos, Inc.
259 Prospect Plains Rd A
Cranbury NJ 08512
609 495-2495

(G-4930)
INNOVANT INC
222 Merchandise Mart Plz (60654-1103)
PHONE...................................646 368-6254

GEOGRAPHIC SECTION
Chicago - Cook County (G-4960)

Charles Braham, *Branch Mgr*
EMP: 100
SALES (corp-wide): 49.2MM **Privately Held**
SIC: 2521 Wood office furniture
PA: Innovant, Inc.
   37 W 20th St Frnt 2
   New York NY 10011
   212 929-4883

(G-4931)
INNOVATIVE MAG DRIVE LLC
6911 W 59th St (60638-3205)
PHONE...................................630 543-4240
EMP: 3
SALES (est): 142.6K **Privately Held**
SIC: 3568 Mfg Power Transmission Equipment

(G-4932)
INNOVATIVE SPORTS TRAINING INC
3711 N Ravenswood Ave # 150 (60613-5944)
PHONE...................................773 244-6470
Lee Johnson, *President*
EMP: 1
SQ FT: 2,000
SALES (est): 285.8K **Privately Held**
SIC: 3825 Measuring instruments & meters, electric

(G-4933)
INRULE TECHNOLOGY INC
651 W Washington Blvd # 500 (60661-2125)
PHONE...................................312 648-1800
Paul Hessinger, *CEO*
David Labe, *CFO*
EMP: 24
SQ FT: 3,000
SALES (est): 3.2MM **Privately Held**
SIC: 7372 Business oriented computer software

(G-4934)
INSERVIO3 LLC
17 N State St Ste 1520 (60602-3295)
PHONE...................................310 343-3486
Joe Bernal, *Manager*
EMP: 7
SALES (corp-wide): 4.1MM **Privately Held**
SIC: 2621 Book, bond & printing papers
PA: Inservio3 Llc
   624 S Austin Ave Ste 230
   Georgetown TX 78626
   213 439-9656

(G-4935)
INSIDE COUNCIL
222 S Riverside Plz # 620 (60606-5808)
PHONE...................................312 654-3500
Charles H Carman, *President*
Nat Flavin, *Principal*
Mike Walker, *Regional*
EMP: 14
SQ FT: 6,800
SALES (est): 1.1MM **Privately Held**
SIC: 2721 8111 Trade journals: publishing only, not printed on site; legal services

(G-4936)
INSTANA INC (PA)
222 S Riverside Plz # 1500 (60606-6000)
PHONE...................................415 340-2777
Pete Abrams, *COO*
Jason J Heine, *CFO*
EMP: 7
SALES (est): 4.6MM **Privately Held**
SIC: 7372 Prepackaged software

(G-4937)
INSTANT COLLATING SERVICE INC
2443 W 16th St (60608-1780)
PHONE...................................312 243-4703
Cecelia Calandrino, *President*
Harvey Honig, *Treasurer*
EMP: 12
SQ FT: 25,000
SALES: 750K **Privately Held**
SIC: 2789 Trade binding services

(G-4938)
INSTITUTE FOR PUBLIC AFFAIRS
Also Called: In These Times
2040 N Milwaukee Ave Fl 2 (60647-4002)
PHONE...................................773 772-0100
Joel Blifus, *Director*
Jamie Hendry, *Assistant*
EMP: 12
SQ FT: 8,000
SALES: 2MM **Privately Held**
SIC: 2721 Magazines: publishing only, not printed on site

(G-4939)
INSTRUMENT & VALVE SERVICES CO
Also Called: Emerson
4320 W 166 St (60673-0001)
PHONE...................................281 998-6673
EMP: 16
SALES (corp-wide): 18.3B **Publicly Held**
SIC: 3823 Industrial instrmnts msrmnt display/control process variable
HQ: Instrument & Valve Services Company
   205 S Center St
   Marshalltown IA 50158

(G-4940)
INTEGRATED INDUSTRIES INC
4201 W 36th St Ste 1 (60632-3826)
PHONE...................................773 299-1970
Maureen Godino, *Principal*
EMP: 5 **Privately Held**
SIC: 3999 Atomizers, toiletry
PA: Integrated Industries, Inc.
   1 Penville Rd
   Woodbridge NJ 07095

(G-4941)
INTEL CORPORATION
21003 Network Pl (60673-1210)
PHONE...................................408 765-8080
Sam Habbal, *Branch Mgr*
John Dunkin, *Manager*
EMP: 57
SALES (corp-wide): 71.9B **Publicly Held**
SIC: 3674 7372 Microprocessors; prepackaged software
PA: Intel Corporation
   2200 Mission College Blvd
   Santa Clara CA 95054
   408 765-8080

(G-4942)
INTER SOLUTIONS CO
6134 N Milwaukee Ave C (60646-3831)
PHONE...................................773 657-4437
EMP: 3 **EST:** 2015
SALES (est): 205K **Privately Held**
SIC: 2752 Commercial printing, offset

(G-4943)
INTER SWISS LTD
5410 W Roosevelt Rd # 242 (60644-1478)
PHONE...................................773 379-0400
Debbie Seidel, *Principal*
EMP: 14
SALES (est): 2MM **Privately Held**
SIC: 2531 Seats, railroad

(G-4944)
INTERESTING PRODUCTS INC
Also Called: Design Lab
328 N Albany Ave (60612-1718)
PHONE...................................773 265-1100
Larry Schoeneman, *President*
EMP: 3
SQ FT: 30,000
SALES (est): 321.9K **Privately Held**
SIC: 3999 Theatrical scenery

(G-4945)
INTERFACEFLOR LLC
440 N Wells St Ste 200 (60654-4550)
PHONE...................................312 836-3389
EMP: 20
SALES (corp-wide): 1B **Publicly Held**
SIC: 2273 Mfg Carpets/Rugs
HQ: Interfaceflor, Llc
   1503 Orchard Hill Rd
   Lagrange GA 30240
   706 882-1891

(G-4946)
INTERFACEFLOR LLC
222 Merchandise Mart Plz # 130 (60654-1103)
PHONE...................................312 822-9640
Greg Colando, *Branch Mgr*
EMP: 16
SALES (corp-wide): 1.3B **Publicly Held**
SIC: 2273 Carpets & rugs
HQ: Interfaceflor, Llc
   1503 Orchard Hill Rd
   Lagrange GA 30240

(G-4947)
INTERIOR TECTONICS LLC
1716 N Cleveland Ave (60614-5603)
PHONE...................................312 515-7779
Pamela De Varela,
EMP: 5
SQ FT: 1,100
SALES: 700K **Privately Held**
SIC: 5712 3699 Furniture stores; security devices

(G-4948)
INTERMEDIX HOLDINGS INC (DH)
401 N Michigan Ave # 2700 (60611-4217)
PHONE...................................312 324-7820
Joseph Flanagan, *President*
EMP: 2
SALES (est): 328.6MM
SALES (corp-wide): 1.1B **Publicly Held**
SIC: 7372 Business oriented computer software
HQ: Project Links Parent, Inc.
   401 N Michigan Ave # 2700
   Chicago IL 60611
   312 324-7820

(G-4949)
INTERMERICAN CLINICAL SVCS INC
2651 W Division St (60622-2851)
PHONE...................................773 252-1147
Ana E Castellanos, *President*
EMP: 10
SALES (est): 1MM **Privately Held**
SIC: 3821 Clinical laboratory instruments, except medical & dental

(G-4950)
INTERMINAL SERVICES
2040 E 106th St (60617-6455)
PHONE...................................773 978-8129
▲ **EMP:** 20
SALES (est): 954.9K **Privately Held**
SIC: 1221 Bituminous Coal/Lignite Surface Mining

(G-4951)
INTERNATIONAL BUS MCHS CORP
Also Called: IBM
222 S Riverside Plz # 1 (60606-6828)
PHONE...................................312 423-6640
EMP: 200
SALES (corp-wide): 79.1B **Publicly Held**
SIC: 3572 Manufacturing Of Computer Software Storage Devices
PA: International Business Machines Corporation
   1 New Orchard Rd Ste 1 # 1
   Armonk NY 10504
   914 499-1900

(G-4952)
INTERNATIONAL COLLEGE SURGEONS (PA)
Also Called: INTERNATIONAL MUSEUM OF SURGIC
1516 N Lake Shore Dr Fl 3 (60610-6652)
PHONE...................................312 642-6502
Fidel Ruiz-Healy, *President*
Jennifer Tran, *Controller*
Michelle Rinard, *Manager*
Catherine White, *Asst Mgr*
Max C Downham, *Exec Dir*
EMP: 8
SQ FT: 20,000
SALES: 1MM **Privately Held**
SIC: 8621 2721 8412 Medical field-related associations; periodicals: publishing only; museum

(G-4953)
INTERNATIONAL NEWS
4917 N Milwaukee Ave 14 (60630-2105)
PHONE...................................773 283-8323
EMP: 4 **EST:** 2013
SALES (est): 216.3K **Privately Held**
SIC: 2711 Newspapers-Publishing/Printing

(G-4954)
INTERNATIONAL PAPER COMPANY
5300 W 73rd St (60638-6502)
PHONE...................................708 728-8200
Brian Totzke, *Safety Mgr*
Anna Pille, *Mfg Staff*
Gary Randolph, *Manager*
Jose Nieves, *Supervisor*
David Pearce, *Supervisor*
EMP: 130
SQ FT: 150,000
SALES (corp-wide): 22.3B **Publicly Held**
WEB: www.internationalpaper.com
SIC: 2653 Boxes, corrugated: made from purchased materials
PA: International Paper Company
   6400 Poplar Ave
   Memphis TN 38197
   901 419-9000

(G-4955)
INTERNATIONAL REVERE CO
2333 W Nelson St (60618-8015)
PHONE...................................773 248-1841
George Belitz, *President*
Renaldo Borges, *Plant Mgr*
EMP: 3 **EST:** 1953
SQ FT: 3,125
SALES (est): 220K **Privately Held**
SIC: 3599 Machine shop, jobbing & repair

(G-4956)
INTERNATIONAL WOOD DESIGN INC
941 N California Ave (60622-4478)
PHONE...................................773 227-9270
Julian Pyjor, *President*
EMP: 2
SALES (est): 218.6K **Privately Held**
SIC: 2511 Wood household furniture

(G-4957)
INTERSPORTS SCREEN PRINTING
2407 N Central Park Ave (60647-2326)
PHONE...................................773 489-7383
Mario Saduirre, *Principal*
EMP: 2
SALES (est): 210.7K **Privately Held**
SIC: 2752 Commercial printing, lithographic

(G-4958)
INTERSTATE MECHANICAL INC
1882 S Normal Ave Ste 1 (60616-1016)
PHONE...................................312 961-9291
Henry Tam, *President*
EMP: 1
SALES (est): 250K **Privately Held**
SIC: 3531 Construction machinery

(G-4959)
INTERSTUHL USA INC
625 W Adams St (60661-3603)
PHONE...................................312 385-0240
Helmut Link, *Director*
EMP: 3
SALES (est): 419.8K **Privately Held**
WEB: www.interstuhl.com
SIC: 2521 Chairs, office: padded, upholstered or plain: wood

(G-4960)
INTRA-CUT DIE CUTTING INC
5559 N Northwest Hwy (60630-1130)
PHONE...................................773 775-6228
Angie Wilson, *President*
Joe Bellisario, *Vice Pres*
EMP: 10
SQ FT: 10,000
SALES (est): 2.1MM **Privately Held**
SIC: 2675 Paper die-cutting

Chicago - Cook County (G-4961)

(G-4961)
INVEKTEK LLC
2039 N Lincoln Ave Unit P (60614-4531)
PHONE 312 343-0600
EMP: 3 EST: 2015
SALES (est): 146.7K **Privately Held**
SIC: 3625 Mfg Relays/Industrial Controls

(G-4962)
INVENERGY INVESTMENT COMPANY L
1 S Wacker Dr Ste 1800 (60606-4630)
PHONE 312 224-1400
EMP: 5
SALES (est): 431.2K **Privately Held**
SIC: 1389 Construction, repair & dismantling services

(G-4963)
INVENERGY WIND FIN CO III LLC
1 S Wacker Dr Ste 1900 (60606-4644)
PHONE 312 224-1400
Michael Polsky, *Mng Member*
EMP: 3
SALES (est): 28.6K **Privately Held**
SIC: 3612 Power & distribution transformers

(G-4964)
INVISIBLE INSTITUTE
6100 S Blackstone Ave (60637-2912)
PHONE 415 669-4691
Rajiv Clair, *Treasurer*
Jamie Kalven, *Exec Dir*
EMP: 6
SALES: 849.1K **Privately Held**
SIC: 7372 Publishers' computer software

(G-4965)
INVISIO COMMUNICATIONS INC
150 N Michigan Ave # 1950 (60601-7553)
PHONE 412 327-6578
Lars Hojgard Hansen, *CEO*
Thomas Larson, *CFO*
Raymond Clarke, *Director*
EMP: 8
SALES (est): 319.7K **Privately Held**
SIC: 3663 7389 Carrier equipment, radio communications;

(G-4966)
INX INTERNATIONAL INK CO
5001 S Mason Ave (60638)
PHONE 708 496-3600
James Kochanny, *General Mgr*
Edward Westfall, *Research*
Christopher Rodgers, *Manager*
EMP: 20
SQ FT: 25,000 **Privately Held**
SIC: 2893 Printing ink
HQ: Inx International Ink Co.
    150 N Martingale Rd # 700
    Schaumburg IL 60173
    630 382-1800

(G-4967)
INX INTERNATIONAL INK CO
1419 W Carroll Ave (60607-1148)
PHONE 630 382-1800
Scott Strachota, *Manager*
EMP: 22 **Privately Held**
SIC: 2893 Printing ink
HQ: Inx International Ink Co.
    150 N Martingale Rd # 700
    Schaumburg IL 60173
    630 382-1800

(G-4968)
IRON & WIRE LLC
3600 W Potomac Ave (60651-2232)
PHONE 773 255-2672
David K Greene,
EMP: 3
SALES: 150K **Privately Held**
SIC: 3446 Architectural metalwork

(G-4969)
IRON CASTLE INC
3847 S Kedzie Ave (60632-2730)
PHONE 773 890-0575
Hamidreza Alaviharisi, *CEO*
EMP: 15
SALES (est): 1.3MM **Privately Held**
SIC: 3446 2499 Fences or posts, ornamental iron or steel; snow fence, wood

(G-4970)
IRONFORM HOLDINGS CO (PA)
640 N La Salle Dr Ste 670 (60654-3763)
PHONE 312 374-4810
Terence Wogan, *CEO*
Bob Gossage, *Mfg Staff*
Bharath Sivakumar, *Engineer*
Edward White, *Regl Sales Mgr*
Mike Lacey, *CIO*
EMP: 289
SALES (est): 111.9MM **Privately Held**
WEB: www.ironform.com
SIC: 3469 3444 Metal stampings; sheet metalwork

(G-4971)
ISACHS SONS INC
4500 S Kolin Ave Ste 1a (60632-4460)
PHONE 312 733-2815
Steve Sachs, *President*
▲ EMP: 10
SALES (est): 1.1MM **Privately Held**
SIC: 2843 Leather finishing agents

(G-4972)
ISKY NORTH AMERICA INC (PA)
47 W Polk St Ste 208 (60605-2157)
PHONE 937 641-1368
Delin Hu, *President*
Fan LI, *Admin Sec*
▲ EMP: 2
SALES (est): 229.3K **Privately Held**
SIC: 2879 Agricultural chemicals

(G-4973)
ISOSTATIC INDUSTRIES INC
Also Called: Bearning Sales
4153 N Kostner Ave Fl 1 (60641-1928)
PHONE 773 286-3444
Jim White, *President*
EMP: 42
SQ FT: 30,000
SALES (est): 6.1MM **Privately Held**
SIC: 5085 3568 Bearings; bearings, bushings & blocks

(G-4974)
ISRAEL LEVY DIAMND CUTTERS INC
29 E Madison St Ste 700 (60602-4543)
PHONE 312 368-8540
Israel Levy, *President*
Albert Levy, *Admin Sec*
Noah Levy, *Admin Sec*
EMP: 50
SQ FT: 13,000
SALES (est): 6.8MM **Privately Held**
SIC: 3915 Jewelers' materials & lapidary work

(G-4975)
IT TRANSPORTATION COMPANY
5156 W Winnemac Ave (60630-2330)
PHONE 773 383-5073
Aleksandar Pavicevic, *President*
EMP: 17
SALES: 950K **Privately Held**
SIC: 3537 Industrial trucks & tractors

(G-4976)
ITERATIVE THERAPEUTICS INC
2201 W Campbell Park Dr (60612-4092)
PHONE 773 455-7203
Barry Arnason, *President*
David White, *Treasurer*
Cindy Bayley, *Director*
Mark Jensen, *Admin Sec*
EMP: 4
SALES (est): 344.6K **Privately Held**
SIC: 2834 Pharmaceutical preparations

(G-4977)
ITERUM THERAPEUTICS US LIMITED
200 S Wacker Dr Ste 650 (60606-5915)
PHONE 312 763-3975
Judith Matthews, *President*
EMP: 8
SALES (est): 430.7K **Privately Held**
SIC: 2834 Pharmaceutical preparations

(G-4978)
ITTA CORPORATION
2449 W Coyle Ave (60645-4609)
P.O. Box 59833 (60659-0833)
PHONE 872 221-4882
Lawrence Lujan, *Publisher*
Aaron Cunningham, *Chairman*
Andrew Fayal, *Vice Pres*
Mark Stephenson, *Vice Pres*
Sung Joo Lee, *CFO*
EMP: 5 EST: 2012
SALES (est): 267K **Privately Held**
SIC: 3691 Storage batteries

(G-4979)
IVAN CARLSON ASSOCIATES INC
2224 W Fulton St (60612-2206)
PHONE 312 829-4616
Jeff Mueller, *General Mgr*
Tina Marie Carson, *Chairman*
Scott T Carson, *Vice Pres*
Tim Amlung, *Controller*
Earl Huntley, *Controller*
EMP: 26 EST: 1973
SALES: 4MM **Privately Held**
WEB: www.ivancarlson.com
SIC: 7922 3993 2542 Scenery design, theatrical; signs & advertising specialties; partitions & fixtures, except wood

(G-4980)
IXTAPA FOODS
6135 S Nottingham Ave (60638-3909)
PHONE 773 788-9701
Humberto Cano, *Principal*
Bernard Rose, *Vice Pres*
▲ EMP: 3
SALES (est): 476.2K **Privately Held**
SIC: 5141 2099 5149 Groceries, general line; food preparations; groceries & related products

(G-4981)
J & A SHEET METAL SHOP INC
1800 N Campbell Ave (60647-4303)
PHONE 773 276-3739
Andy Favilla, *President*
Joe Favilla, *Vice Pres*
EMP: 20
SQ FT: 13,000
SALES (est): 3.5MM **Privately Held**
SIC: 3599 3644 3613 Machine shop, jobbing & repair; electric outlet, switch & fuse boxes; cubicles (electric switchboard equipment)

(G-4982)
J & B SIGNS INC
105 W Chicago Ave (60654-3209)
PHONE 312 640-8181
Robert E Hoelterhoff, *President*
Sandy Hoelterhoff, *Treasurer*
EMP: 5
SQ FT: 1,000
SALES (est): 505.6K **Privately Held**
SIC: 3993 Signs & advertising specialties

(G-4983)
J & I RESOURCES LLC
5301 S Western Blvd Ste 1 (60609-5425)
PHONE 773 436-4028
John Cantalupo,
Tom Dawson,
Terry Jannotta,
EMP: 45
SQ FT: 65,000
SALES (est): 9.5MM **Privately Held**
SIC: 2611 Pulp manufactured from waste or recycled paper

(G-4984)
J & J MR QUICK PRINT INC
Also Called: J & J Printing
5740 S Archer Ave Ste 1 (60638-1674)
PHONE 773 767-7776
Sally Rodzak, *President*
James Rodzak, *Treasurer*
John Rodzak, *Admin Sec*
EMP: 5
SQ FT: 3,000
SALES (est): 350K **Privately Held**
SIC: 2752 2791 2789 Commercial printing, offset; typesetting; bookbinding & related work

(G-4985)
J & J SILK SCREENING
5316 S Monitor Ave (60638-2716)
PHONE 773 838-9000
Monserrate Wright, *Principal*
EMP: 3
SALES (est): 185.5K **Privately Held**
SIC: 2759 Screen printing

(G-4986)
J B BURLING GROUP LTD
540 W Aldine Ave Ste 6 (60657-3889)
PHONE 773 327-5362
Jerry J Field, *Exec VP*
EMP: 3
SALES (est): 148.9K **Privately Held**
SIC: 3999 Manufacturing industries

(G-4987)
J B WATTS COMPANY INC
Also Called: Impac Products
6224 S Vernon Ave (60637-2320)
PHONE 773 643-1855
James B Watts Sr, *President*
James B Watts Jr, *Vice Pres*
Barbara Hunt, *Admin Sec*
EMP: 4
SALES (est): 277.6K **Privately Held**
SIC: 2819 5169 5085 Industrial inorganic chemicals; chemicals & allied products; fasteners & fastening equipment

(G-4988)
J C COMMUNICATIONS COMPANY
318 W Adams St Ste 1406 (60606-5173)
P.O. Box 6563 (60606-0563)
PHONE 312 236-5122
Fax: 312 236-3297
EMP: 4
SALES (est): 345.7K **Privately Held**
SIC: 2741 Misc Publishing

(G-4989)
J C DECAUX NEW YORK INC
3959 S Morgan St (60609-2512)
PHONE 312 456-2999
Nicholas Clochard-Bossue, *COO*
Daniel Egan, *Vice Pres*
Raul Arana, *Maint Spvr*
Anita Dierker, *Accounts Exec*
Angie Paniello, *Sales Staff*
EMP: 50
SALES (corp-wide): 108.7MM **Privately Held**
SIC: 2531 Benches for public buildings
HQ: J C Decaux New York Inc
    350 5th Ave Fl 73
    New York NY 10118

(G-4990)
J G UNIFORMS INC
Also Called: J G B Uniforms & Career AP
5949 W Irving Park Rd (60634-2618)
PHONE 773 545-4644
Halina Gala, *President*
Joseph Gala, *Admin Sec*
EMP: 8
SQ FT: 1,900
SALES (est): 1MM **Privately Held**
SIC: 2311 Policemen's uniforms: made from purchased materials; military uniforms, men's & youths': purchased materials; firemen's uniforms: made from purchased materials

(G-4991)
J J MATA INC
2524 W Devon Ave (60659-1904)
PHONE 773 750-0643
Zeena Patel, *President*
Anand Patel, *Owner*
EMP: 3
SALES (est): 192.7K **Privately Held**
SIC: 2037 Fruit juices

(G-4992)
J OSHANA & SON PRINTING
4021 W Irving Park Rd (60641-2926)
PHONE 773 283-8311
Ron Oshana, *Principal*
EMP: 3 EST: 1968
SQ FT: 3,100

SALES (est): 333.6K **Privately Held**
SIC: **2752** 2791 Commercial printing, offset; typesetting

(G-4993)
J P PRINTING INC
5639 W Division St (60651-1141)
PHONE.................................773 626-5222
Veronica Polk, *President*
EMP: 4
SQ FT: 1,200
SALES (est): 530K **Privately Held**
SIC: **5111** 2791 Printing & writing paper; typesetting

(G-4994)
J R HUSAR INC
Also Called: Husar Picture Frame
1631 W Carroll Ave (60612-2501)
PHONE.................................312 243-7888
Jeffery R Husar, *President*
Jeffrey R Husar, *President*
Thomas Lynch, *Vice Pres*
EMP: 18
SQ FT: 25,000
SALES (est): 2.8MM **Privately Held**
WEB: www.husarpictureframe.com
SIC: **2431** Millwork

(G-4995)
J T C INC
Also Called: Ncc
4710 W North Ave (60639-4613)
PHONE.................................773 292-9262
Al Cantar, *President*
Juan Berez, *Superintendent*
Robert Mann, *Manager*
EMP: 17
SALES (est): 2.6MM **Privately Held**
SIC: **3568** Power transmission equipment

(G-4996)
JA-T & ASSOCIATES INC
37 N Long Ave (60644-3224)
PHONE.................................773 744-2094
Aubrey Earls Jr, *President*
Aubrey Earls Jr, *President*
EMP: 10
SALES (est): 821.3K **Privately Held**
SIC: **5046** 1711 1389 Commercial cooking & food service equipment; heating & air conditioning contractors; construction, repair & dismantling services

(G-4997)
JACKHAMMER
6406 N Clark St (60626-4913)
PHONE.................................773 743-5772
Rudolph Johnson, *Principal*
EMP: 2 EST: 2007
SALES (est): 261.2K **Privately Held**
SIC: **2599** Bar, restaurant & cafeteria furniture

(G-4998)
JACOBS BOILER & MECH INDS INC
6632 W Diversey Ave (60707-2217)
PHONE.................................773 385-9900
Matthew D Jacobs, *President*
Victoria Ottenfeld, *Office Mgr*
Thomas G Jacobs, *Shareholder*
Joseph J Jacobs, *Admin Sec*
EMP: 25
SQ FT: 15,000
SALES (est): 4.1MM **Privately Held**
WEB: www.jacobsboiler.com
SIC: **7699** 7692 7629 3564 Boiler repair shop; welding repair; electrical repair shops; blowers & fans; blast furnaces & steel mills; plumbing & hydronic heating supplies

(G-4999)
JAFFEE INVESTMENT PARTNR LP
410 N Michigan Ave # 400 (60611-4213)
PHONE.................................312 321-1515
Richard M Jaffee, *General Ptnr*
Karen Jaffee Cofsky, *General Ptnr*
Susan Jaffee Hardin, *General Ptnr*
Daniel S Jaffee, *General Ptnr*
Nancy E Jaffee, *General Ptnr*
EMP: 125

SALES (est): 3.2MM **Privately Held**
SIC: **6733** 2842 3295 Personal investment trust management; sweeping compounds, oil or water absorbent, clay or sawdust; cat box litter

(G-5000)
JAIX LEASING COMPANY
2 N Riverside Plz (60606-2600)
PHONE.................................312 928-0850
Ted Baun, *Principal*
EMP: 4
SALES (est): 484.4K
SALES (corp-wide): 229.9MM **Publicly Held**
SIC: **3743** Railroad car rebuilding
PA: Freightcar America, Inc.
    125 S Wacker Dr Ste 1500
    Chicago IL 60606
    800 458-2235

(G-5001)
JAMES D AHERN COMPANY (PA)
3257 S Harding Ave (60623-4912)
PHONE.................................773 254-0717
Carol Sheehan, *President*
EMP: 10 EST: 1901
SQ FT: 10,000
SALES (est): 1.2MM **Privately Held**
WEB: www.ahernsigns.com
SIC: **3993** Signs & advertising specialties

(G-5002)
JAMES INSTRUMENTS INC (PA)
Also Called: Windsor Systems
3727 N Kedzie Ave (60618-4503)
PHONE.................................773 463-6565
Michael W Hoag, *President*
William Hogg, *Chairman*
Anthony Gale, *COO*
Nestor Chonillo, *Vice Pres*
Cary Kafely, *Vice Pres*
EMP: 10
SQ FT: 10,000
SALES (est): 2.5MM **Privately Held**
SIC: **3829** Measuring & controlling devices

(G-5003)
JAMES PRECIOUS METALS PLATING
5700 N Northwest Hwy (60646-6138)
PHONE.................................773 774-8700
Ken Jacobsen, *President*
EMP: 10 EST: 1950
SQ FT: 6,000
SALES (est): 750K **Privately Held**
WEB: www.jamesplating.com
SIC: **3471** Electroplating of metals or formed products

(G-5004)
JANITOR LTD
218 N Jefferson St # 202 (60661-1121)
PHONE.................................773 936-3389
Cory Hohs,
Noah Levens,
EMP: 3
SALES (est): 168.8K **Privately Held**
SIC: **7372** Application computer software

(G-5005)
JANLER CORPORATION
6545 N Avondale Ave (60631-1583)
PHONE.................................773 774-0166
Carol K Ebel, *President*
Carol K Ebell, *President*
Alan Klingler, *Exec VP*
Joe Montalbano, *Project Mgr*
Kurt Mohrbacher, *Opers Mgr*
▼ EMP: 40
SQ FT: 14,500
SALES (est): 9.5MM **Privately Held**
WEB: www.janler.com
SIC: **3544** 3089 Forms (molds), for foundry & plastics working machinery; industrial molds; injection molding of plastics

(G-5006)
JANS GRAPHICS INC
Also Called: Ink Well
2 N Riverside Plz Ste 365 (60606-2620)
PHONE.................................312 644-4700
Alvin Holtzman, *President*
Judith Holtzman, *Treasurer*
EMP: 12

SQ FT: 2,600
SALES: 1.6MM **Privately Held**
SIC: **2752** 7336 Commercial printing, offset; graphic arts & related design

(G-5007)
JANSSEN PHARMACEUTICALS INC
20 N Wacker Dr Ste 1442 (60606-2906)
PHONE.................................312 750-0507
Paula Costa, *Owner*
EMP: 14
SALES (corp-wide): 82B **Publicly Held**
SIC: **2833** Anesthetics, in bulk form
HQ: Janssen Pharmaceuticals, Inc.
    1125 Trnton Harbourton Rd
    Titusville NJ 08560
    609 730-2000

(G-5008)
JARRIES SHOE BAGS
107 S Parkside Ave (60644-3944)
PHONE.................................773 379-4044
Jarrie Brown, *Principal*
EMP: 3
SALES (est): 169.9K **Privately Held**
SIC: **2393** Textile bags

(G-5009)
JAS DAHERN SIGNS
3257 S Harding Ave (60623-4912)
PHONE.................................773 254-0717
Patty Bowermaster, *Principal*
EMP: 3 EST: 2007
SALES (est): 170K **Privately Held**
SIC: **3993** Signs & advertising specialties

(G-5010)
JASON LAU JEWELRY
29 E Madison St Ste 1107 (60602-4492)
PHONE.................................312 750-1028
Jason W Lau, *Owner*
EMP: 4
SALES (est): 409.5K **Privately Held**
SIC: **3911** 5094 Jewelry, precious metal; jewelry

(G-5011)
JAV MACHINE CRAFT INC
4624 N Oketo Ave (60706-4601)
PHONE.................................708 867-8608
Kenneth Valin, *President*
EMP: 7 EST: 1950
SQ FT: 9,000
SALES (est): 1.2MM **Privately Held**
SIC: **3599** 7692 Machine shop, jobbing & repair; welding repair

(G-5012)
JAY CEE PLASTIC FABRICATORS
2133 W Mclean Ave (60647-4524)
PHONE.................................773 276-1920
Jerome J Boruch, *President*
EMP: 10
SQ FT: 11,000
SALES (est): 780K **Privately Held**
SIC: **3089** Plastic hardware & building products; washers, plastic; bearings, plastic

(G-5013)
JCDECAUX CHICAGO LLC
3959 S Morgan St (60609-2512)
PHONE.................................312 456-2999
Bernard Parisot, *President*
EMP: 30
SALES: 4.2MM
SALES (corp-wide): 108.7MM **Privately Held**
SIC: **2531** Public building & related furniture
HQ: Jcdecaux North America, Inc.
    350 5th Ave Fl 73
    New York NY 10118
    646 834-1200

(G-5014)
JELD-WEN INC
500 W Monroe St Ste 2010 (60661-3762)
PHONE.................................312 544-5041
EMP: 159 **Publicly Held**
SIC: **2493** Reconstituted wood products

HQ: Jeld-Wen, Inc.
    1162 Keystone Blvd
    Pottsville PA 17901
    800 535-3936

(G-5015)
JELLYVISION INC
848 W Eastman St Ste 104 (60642-2635)
PHONE.................................312 266-0606
Amanda Lannert, *President*
Harry N Gottlieb, *Chairman*
Travis Mandrell, *Vice Pres*
Collin Eggertz, *Opers Staff*
Elizabeth Baxter, *Production*
EMP: 100
SALES (est): 12.8MM **Privately Held**
SIC: **7372** Business oriented computer software

(G-5016)
JEM ASSOCIATES LTD (PA)
5206 N Meade Ave (60630-1041)
PHONE.................................847 808-8377
Joseph E Murrow, *Partner*
Geraldine Murrow, *Partner*
EMP: 1
SALES (est): 305.8K **Privately Held**
SIC: **2752** Commercial printing, lithographic

(G-5017)
JEN-SKO-VEC MACHINING & ENGRG
5335 S Western Blvd (60609-5450)
PHONE.................................773 776-7400
Phil Jenskovec, *Partner*
Paul Jenskovec, *Partner*
Rene Jenskovec, *Accountant*
EMP: 5
SQ FT: 8,000
SALES: 350K **Privately Held**
SIC: **3599** Machine shop, jobbing & repair

(G-5018)
JENNY CAPP CO
6605 S Harvard Ave (60621-3125)
PHONE.................................773 217-0057
Jennipher Adkins, *Vice Pres*
EMP: 10
SQ FT: 4,500
SALES (est): 331.8K **Privately Held**
SIC: **2353** 7389 2339 Silk hats; textile & apparel services; women's & misses' accessories

(G-5019)
JENSEN PLATING WORKS INC (PA)
183844 N Western Ave (60647)
PHONE.................................773 252-7733
Thomas Jensen, *President*
▼ EMP: 20
SQ FT: 3,000
SALES (est): 2.9MM **Privately Held**
SIC: **3471** Electroplating of metals or formed products

(G-5020)
JERJERB LLC
6715 N Ionia Ave (60646-2836)
PHONE.................................917 415-3319
Leeann Witt, *Principal*
EMP: 4
SALES (est): 269.1K **Privately Held**
SIC: **2323** Men's & boys' neckwear

(G-5021)
JERNBERG INDUSTRIES LLC (DH)
328 W 40th Pl (60609-2815)
PHONE.................................773 268-3004
George Thanopoulos, *CEO*
EMP: 135
SQ FT: 400,000
SALES (est): 119.8MM
SALES (corp-wide): 6.5B **Publicly Held**
SIC: **3462** 3463 Iron & steel forgings; non-ferrous forgings
HQ: Jernberg Holdings, Llc
    1 Dauch Dr
    Detroit MI 48211
    313 758-2000

Chicago - Cook County (G-5022)

(G-5022)
JERO MEDICAL EQP & SUPS INC
4444 W Chicago Ave (60651-3424)
PHONE..................................773 305-4193
Obie C Wordlaw, *Ch of Bd*
Dr Julia A Bowen, *President*
Shirley Wordlaw, *Admin Sec*
▲ EMP: 27
SQ FT: 17,000
SALES (est): 5.1MM **Privately Held**
SIC: 5047 7699 8742 2389 Medical equipment & supplies; professional instrument repair services; hospital & health services consultant; disposable garments & accessories

(G-5023)
JESUS PEOPLE USA FULL GOS
Also Called: Lakefront Supply
5242 N Elston Ave (60630-1609)
PHONE..................................773 989-2083
Terry Gaffron, *Manager*
EMP: 7
SALES (corp-wide): 18MM **Privately Held**
SIC: 2952 Roofing materials
PA: Jesus People, U.S.A., Full Gospel Ministries
2950 N Western Ave
Chicago IL 60618
773 252-1812

(G-5024)
JET INDUSTRIES INC
6025 S Oak Park Ave (60638-4011)
PHONE..................................773 586-8900
Elizabeth Twardowski, *President*
John Twardowski, *Vice Pres*
EMP: 35
SQ FT: 18,000
SALES (est): 7.9MM **Privately Held**
SIC: 3441 3599 7692 Fabricated structural metal; machine shop, jobbing & repair; welding repair

(G-5025)
JET RACK CORP
6200 S New England Ave (60638-4083)
PHONE..................................773 586-2150
George Samiotakis, *President*
Andrew Kittridge, *Vice Pres*
EMP: 20
SQ FT: 19,600
SALES (est): 2.8MM **Privately Held**
SIC: 2542 7699 3479 3443 Racks, merchandise display or storage: except wood; metal reshaping & replating services; coating of metals with plastic or resins; fabricated plate work (boiler shop); paints & allied products

(G-5026)
JEWEL OSCO INC
Also Called: Jewel-Osco 3407
5516 N Clark St (60640-1214)
PHONE..................................773 728-7730
Dennis Corsco, *Branch Mgr*
EMP: 145
SALES (corp-wide): 60.5B **Privately Held**
SIC: 5411 2051 Supermarkets, chain; bread, cake & related products
HQ: Jewel Osco, Inc.
150 E Pierce Rd Ste 200
Itasca IL 60143
630 948-6000

(G-5027)
JEWEL OSCO INC
Also Called: Jewel-Osco 3443
5343 N Broadway St (60640-2311)
PHONE..................................773 784-1922
Paul Scyscka, *Manager*
EMP: 150
SALES (corp-wide): 60.5B **Privately Held**
SIC: 5411 2051 5461 Supermarkets, chain; bread, cake & related products; bakeries
HQ: Jewel Osco, Inc.
150 E Pierce Rd Ste 200
Itasca IL 60143
630 948-6000

(G-5028)
JF INDUSTRIES INC
7751 W Rosedale Ave (60631-2201)
PHONE..................................773 775-8840
Joe Fragola, *President*
EMP: 3
SALES: 400K **Privately Held**
SIC: 1731 3629 3999 General electrical contractor; electronic generation equipment; barber & beauty shop equipment

(G-5029)
JHELSA METAL POLSG FABRICATION
1900 N Austin Ave Ste 71 (60639-5017)
PHONE..................................773 385-6628
Jorge Henaine, *President*
EMP: 7
SALES (est): 977.8K **Privately Held**
SIC: 3441 Fabricated structural metal

(G-5030)
JIFFY METAL PRODUCTS INC
5025 W Lake St (60644-2599)
PHONE..................................773 626-8090
Jim Mueller, *President*
Teresa Muller, *Vice Pres*
EMP: 8 EST: 1939
SQ FT: 25,000
SALES (est): 1.2MM **Privately Held**
WEB: www.jiffymetalproducts.com
SIC: 3469 3443 Stamping metal for the trade; fabricated plate work (boiler shop)

(G-5031)
JINNY CORP
3505 N Kimball Ave (60618-5507)
PHONE..................................773 588-7200
EMP: 3
SALES (est): 350K **Privately Held**
SIC: 2721 Magazine Publication

(G-5032)
JLO METAL PRODUCTS CO A CORP
5841 W Dickens Ave (60639-4095)
PHONE..................................773 889-6242
John L Oberrieder Jr, *President*
Richard Phillips, *Engineer*
Corinne Vargas, *Human Res Mgr*
EMP: 80
SQ FT: 100,000
SALES (est): 16.5MM **Privately Held**
SIC: 3469 3411 Stamping metal for the trade; metal cans

(G-5033)
JO SNOW INC
4536 W Altgeld St (60639-1904)
PHONE..................................773 732-3045
Melissa Dawn Yen, *President*
Melissa Yen, *Officer*
EMP: 3
SALES (est): 249.5K **Privately Held**
SIC: 2087 2063 Cocktail mixes, nonalcoholic; sugar syrup from sugar beets

(G-5034)
JOES PRINTING
6025 N Cicero Ave (60646-4301)
PHONE..................................773 545-6063
Joe Solaka, *Owner*
EMP: 3
SQ FT: 1,200
SALES: 300K **Privately Held**
SIC: 2752 3953 2789 2759 Commercial printing, offset; marking devices; bookbinding & related work; commercial printing

(G-5035)
JOHN BEAN TECHNOLOGIES CORP
2707 Solutions Ctr (60677-0001)
PHONE..................................845 340-9727
EMP: 6 **Publicly Held**
SIC: 3556 Food products machinery
PA: John Bean Technologies Corporation
70 W Madison St Ste 4400
Chicago IL 60602

(G-5036)
JOHN BEAN TECHNOLOGIES CORP (PA)
Also Called: JBT
70 W Madison St Ste 4400 (60602-4546)
PHONE..................................312 861-5900
Thomas W Giacomini, *Ch of Bd*
Jason T Clayton, *Exec VP*
James L Marvin, *Exec VP*
Megan J Rattigan, *Vice Pres*
John Collins, *Site Mgr*
EMP: 55
SQ FT: 24,000
SALES: 1.9B **Publicly Held**
SIC: 3556 3585 3537 Food products machinery; refrigeration & heating equipment; containers (metal), air cargo

(G-5037)
JOHN BEYER RACE CARS
10718 S Homan Ave (60655-2610)
PHONE..................................773 779-5313
Olive Beyer, *Principal*
EMP: 3
SALES (est): 278.5K **Privately Held**
SIC: 3711 Motor vehicle assembly, including specialty automobiles

(G-5038)
JOHN BUECHNER INC
8 S Michigan Ave Ste 607 (60603-3467)
PHONE..................................312 263-2226
John Buechner, *President*
Margaret Krizmanic, *Corp Secy*
Clifford Wallace, *Vice Pres*
EMP: 5
SQ FT: 1,700
SALES (est): 2MM **Privately Held**
SIC: 3911 5094 Jewelry, precious metal; precious stones & metals

(G-5039)
JOHN CRANE INC (HQ)
227 W Monroe St Ste 1800 (60606-5053)
PHONE..................................312 605-7800
Duncan Gillis, *President*
Jacob Tillson, *Business Mgr*
Olivier Lacquemanne, *Exec VP*
Patrick Thompson, *Exec VP*
John F Donatiello, *Vice Pres*
◆ EMP: 650 EST: 1917
SQ FT: 450,000
SALES (est): 1.2B
SALES (corp-wide): 3.1B **Privately Held**
WEB: www.johncrane.com
SIC: 3053 Gaskets & sealing devices; packing materials
PA: Smiths Group Plc
4th Floor
London SW1Y
207 004-1600

(G-5040)
JOHN GALT DEVELOPMENT INC
17 N State St Ste 1890 (60602-3291)
PHONE..................................312 701-9026
Anne Ormod, *President*
Chris Noorian, *Manager*
EMP: 8
SALES (corp-wide): 8MM **Privately Held**
SIC: 7372 Publishers' computer software
PA: Galt John Development Inc
1919 Mckinney Ave
Dallas TX 75201
312 701-9026

(G-5041)
JOHN HOFMEISTER & SON INC
Also Called: Hofhaus
2386 S Blue Island Ave (60608-4228)
PHONE..................................773 847-0700
Matt Hofmeister, *President*
Robert Bukala, *Vice Pres*
Mark J Rataj, *Vice Pres*
Joel Dia, *Production*
Justo Sanchez, *Plant Engr*
▼ EMP: 60
SQ FT: 60,000
SALES (est): 15.9MM **Privately Held**
WEB: www.hofhaus.com
SIC: 2011 Hams & picnics from meat slaughtered on site

(G-5042)
JOHN J MOESLE WHL MEATS INC
Also Called: Moesle Meat Company
4725 S Talman Ave (60632-1406)
PHONE..................................773 847-4900
Joel Janecek, *President*
Barbara Moesle, *Corp Secy*
Michael Moesle, *Vice Pres*
EMP: 11
SQ FT: 26,000
SALES: 1.8MM **Privately Held**
SIC: 2013 5147 Prepared pork products from purchased pork; meats & meat products

(G-5043)
JOHN MANEELY COMPANY
Also Called: Wheatland Tube Company
4435 S Western Blvd (60609-3024)
PHONE..................................773 254-0617
Shawn Londrie, *Principal*
Kevin Kelly, *Vice Pres*
Kelly Saling, *Plant Mgr*
Camille Grayson, *Marketing Mgr*
Christine Walczak, *Manager*
EMP: 150
SQ FT: 115,000 **Privately Held**
SIC: 3317 3498 3312 3083 Pipes, seamless steel; fabricated pipe & fittings; blast furnaces & steel mills; laminated plastics plate & sheet; electric conduits & fittings
HQ: Wheatland Tube, Llc
700 S Dock St
Sharon PA 16146
800 257-8182

(G-5044)
JOHNNY RCKETS FIREWRKS DISPLAY
4410 N Hamilton Ave (60625-1789)
PHONE..................................847 501-1270
John G Panchisin, *President*
▲ EMP: 2
SALES (est): 201.9K **Privately Held**
SIC: 2899 Flares, fireworks & similar preparations

(G-5045)
JOHNNY VANS SMOKEHOUSE
924 W Gordon Ter Apt 3 (60613-2079)
PHONE..................................773 750-1589
Brandi K Landreth, *Partner*
Bk Landreth, *Business Mgr*
EMP: 3 EST: 2012
SALES (est): 182.5K **Privately Held**
SIC: 2099 Sauces: dry mixes

(G-5046)
JOHNSON STEEL RULE DIE CO
5410 W Roosevelt Rd # 228 (60644-1480)
PHONE..................................773 921-4334
EMP: 12 EST: 1951
SQ FT: 10,000
SALES (est): 1.6MM **Privately Held**
SIC: 3544 Mfg Steel Rule Dies

(G-5047)
JONES SOFTWARE CORP
Also Called: J-Soft Tech
531 S Plymouth Ct Ste 104 (60605-1510)
PHONE..................................312 952-0011
Kevin Jones, *CEO*
Kenya Brooks, *President*
EMP: 5
SALES (est): 141.8K **Privately Held**
SIC: 7372 7371 3991 Educational computer software; computer software development & applications; push brooms

(G-5048)
JORDAN PAPER BOX COMPANY
5045 W Lake St (60644-2596)
PHONE..................................773 287-5362
John M Jordan, *President*
Corinne F Jordan, *Vice Pres*
EMP: 12 EST: 1921
SQ FT: 32,000
SALES (est): 1.1MM **Privately Held**
WEB: www.jordanpaperboxcompany.com
SIC: 2652 2653 2657 2441 Setup paperboard boxes; corrugated & solid fiber boxes; folding paperboard boxes; nailed wood boxes & shook

Chicago - Cook County (G-5080)

(G-5049)
JORGE A CRUZ
240 N Harding Ave (60624-1836)
PHONE..................................773 722-2828
Jorge Cruz, *Principal*
EMP: 4 **EST:** 2008
SALES (est): 256K **Privately Held**
SIC: 7532 3711 Paint shop, automotive; automobile bodies, passenger car, not including engine, etc.

(G-5050)
JORIKI LLC
1220 W Wrightwood Ave (60614-1224)
PHONE..................................312 848-1136
James Langer,
EMP: 3 **EST:** 2013
SALES (est): 190.2K **Privately Held**
SIC: 2331 Women's & misses' blouses & shirts

(G-5051)
JOSCO INC
Also Called: American Speedy Printing
4830 N Harlem Ave (60706-3506)
PHONE..................................708 867-7189
Josephine Harrison, *President*
Joseph Harrison Jr, *Shareholder*
Joseph Harrison Sr, *Admin Sec*
EMP: 5
SQ FT: 1,500
SALES (est): 717.3K **Privately Held**
SIC: 2752 2791 2789 Commercial printing, offset; typesetting; bookbinding & related work

(G-5052)
JOSE PALLETS
4506 S Mcdowell Ave (60609-3261)
PHONE..................................773 376-8320
EMP: 4
SALES (est): 25.5K **Privately Held**
SIC: 2448 Pallets, wood

(G-5053)
JOSEPH C WOLF
5 S Wabash Ave Ste 1018 (60603-3156)
PHONE..................................312 332-3135
Gerald Wolf, *Owner*
EMP: 4
SALES (est): 750K **Privately Held**
SIC: 3911 Jewelry, precious metal

(G-5054)
JOSEPH COPPOLINO
Also Called: Coppolinos Itln BF Grill & Bar
4455 W 55th St (60632-4736)
PHONE..................................773 735-8647
Joseph Coppolino, *Owner*
EMP: 4
SALES (est): 259.6K **Privately Held**
SIC: 3011 Tires & inner tubes

(G-5055)
JR BAKERY
Also Called: Cheese Cake
2841 W Howard St (60645-1228)
PHONE..................................773 465-6733
Janet Rosing, *President*
EMP: 32
SQ FT: 3,600
SALES (est): 5.2MM **Privately Held**
SIC: 2051 2052 Cakes, bakery: except frozen; cookies & crackers

(G-5056)
JR INDUSTRIES LLC
4218 N California Ave (60618-1513)
PHONE..................................773 908-5317
Jesse Richardson, *Mng Member*
EMP: 15
SALES (est): 1.8MM **Privately Held**
SIC: 3999 Atomizers, toiletry

(G-5057)
JS POOLE INC
3553 W Peterson Ave # 101 (60659-3217)
PHONE..................................847 241-8441
Kevin L Johnson, *President*
Rodney P Allen, *CFO*
EMP: 12
SALES (est): 2.7MM **Privately Held**
SIC: 3571 Electronic computers

(G-5058)
JUICE TYME INC (HQ)
Also Called: Bevolution Group
4401 S Oakley Ave (60609-3020)
PHONE..................................773 579-1291
Sam Lteif, *CEO*
Matt Marten, *COO*
Matt Martens, *COO*
Jerry Desmond, *Exec VP*
Mike Carter, *Vice Pres*
◆ **EMP:** 18
SQ FT: 30,000
SALES (est): 45MM
SALES (corp-wide): 2MM **Privately Held**
SIC: 2033 2037 Fruit juices: packaged in cans, jars, etc.; frozen fruits & vegetables
PA: Lx/Jt Intermediate Holdings Inc
4401 S Oakley Ave
Chicago IL 60609
773 369-2652

(G-5059)
JUNIORS CUSTOM CABINETS
2539 W Moffat St (60647-4312)
PHONE..................................773 495-6962
EMP: 3
SALES (est): 289.2K **Privately Held**
SIC: 2434 Wood kitchen cabinets

(G-5060)
JUNIPER NETWORKS INC
8755 W Higgins Rd Ste 960 (60631-2746)
PHONE..................................773 632-1200
Lynn Gates, *Engrg Dir*
Joe Vranicar, *Manager*
EMP: 30 **Publicly Held**
SIC: 7373 7372 Computer integrated systems design; prepackaged software
PA: Juniper Networks, Inc.
1133 Innovation Way
Sunnyvale CA 94089

(G-5061)
JURY VERDICT REPORTER
415 N State St Ste 1 (60654-4607)
PHONE..................................312 644-7800
Sandy Macfarland, *CEO*
EMP: 5
SALES (est): 260.4K **Privately Held**
WEB: www.juryverdictreporters.com
SIC: 2711 Commercial printing & newspaper publishing combined

(G-5062)
JUST ICE INC
1400 W 46th St (60609-3225)
PHONE..................................773 301-7323
Rosanna Lloyd, *President*
EMP: 5
SQ FT: 900
SALES (est): 374K **Privately Held**
WEB: www.icecoldjustice.com
SIC: 2097 Block ice

(G-5063)
K & K ABRASIVES & SUPPLIES
5161 S Millard Ave (60632-3797)
PHONE..................................773 582-9500
Carl Kaplan, *President*
Edward Kaplan, *Treasurer*
EMP: 20
SQ FT: 20,000
SALES (est): 5MM **Privately Held**
SIC: 5085 3291 Abrasives; abrasive products

(G-5064)
K & K IRON WORKS LLC
2340 S Springfield Ave (60623-3046)
PHONE..................................773 619-6899
Luke Koollarik, *Branch Mgr*
EMP: 2
SALES (est): 243.5K
SALES (corp-wide): 37MM **Privately Held**
SIC: 3441 Fabricated structural metal
PA: K & K Iron Works, Llc
5100 S Lawndale Ave Ste 7
Mc Cook IL 60525
708 924-0000

(G-5065)
K & S PRECISION METALS CO
6911 W 59th St (60638-3205)
PHONE..................................773 586-8503
Antoinette L Kuberski, *President*
EMP: 3
SALES (est): 401.9K **Privately Held**
SIC: 3542 Presses: forming, stamping, punching, sizing (machine tools)

(G-5066)
K FLEYE DESIGNS
532 N Long Ave (60644-1952)
PHONE..................................773 531-0716
Kelley D Moseley, *Owner*
EMP: 4
SALES (est): 212.9K **Privately Held**
SIC: 3961 Costume novelties

(G-5067)
K THREE WELDING SERVICE INC
814 W 120th St (60643-5532)
PHONE..................................708 563-2911
Michael T Kuper, *President*
EMP: 7
SQ FT: 9,800
SALES (est): 1.4MM **Privately Held**
SIC: 3441 3446 7692 3444 Fabricated structural metal; railings, prefabricated metal; welding repair; sheet metalwork

(G-5068)
K&I LIGHT KANDI LED INC
2600 N Cicero Ave (60639-1767)
PHONE..................................773 745-1533
Ihsan B Paterson, *President*
▲ **EMP:** 4
SALES (est): 426.1K **Privately Held**
WEB: www.kandiled.com
SIC: 3645 Residential lighting fixtures

(G-5069)
K+S MONTANA HOLDINGS LLC (DH)
123 N Wacker Dr (60606-1743)
PHONE..................................312 807-2000
EMP: 9
SALES (est): 997.6MM
SALES (corp-wide): 4.5B **Privately Held**
SIC: 2899 Salt
HQ: K+S Finance Belgium
Culliganlaan 2, Internal Postal Box G
Machelen (Bt.)
240 311-80

(G-5070)
K+S SALT LLC (DH)
444 W Lake St Ste 3000 (60606-0090)
PHONE..................................844 789-3991
Norbert Steiner, *Chairman*
Michael Resetar, *Facilities Dir*
Maria Belmonte, *Human Resources*
Leigh Denny, *Analyst*
EMP: 1
SALES (est): 914.4MM
SALES (corp-wide): 4.5B **Privately Held**
SIC: 2899 5149 5169 Salt; salt, edible; salts, industrial

(G-5071)
K-DISPLAY CORP
6150 S Oak Park Ave (60638-4014)
PHONE..................................773 586-2042
Michael Kubacki, *President*
Karen Kubacki, *Vice Pres*
Len Kubacki, *Treasurer*
EMP: 14
SQ FT: 30,000
SALES (est): 2.1MM **Privately Held**
SIC: 3993 Displays & cutouts, window & lobby

(G-5072)
K-TECHNOLOGY INC
6200 W 51st St Ste 6 (60638-1349)
PHONE..................................708 458-4890
Chris Kambesis, *CEO*
EMP: 2
SALES (est): 505.6K **Privately Held**
SIC: 2842 Specialty cleaning, polishes & sanitation goods

(G-5073)
KAAGES NEWS SERVICE
6700 N Northwest Hwy (60631-1320)
PHONE..................................847 529-7199
Michael Kaage, *Owner*
EMP: 3 **EST:** 2015
SALES (est): 76.2K **Privately Held**
SIC: 2711 Newspapers

(G-5074)
KAE DJ PUBLISHING
12003 S Pulaski Rd # 202 (60803-1221)
PHONE..................................773 233-2609
Kathy Jones, *Principal*
EMP: 3 **EST:** 2007
SALES (est): 166K **Privately Held**
WEB: www.kaedj.com
SIC: 2741 Miscellaneous publishing

(G-5075)
KAI LEE COUTURE INC
5612 S King Dr (60637-1266)
PHONE..................................773 426-1668
EMP: 4
SALES (est): 30K **Privately Held**
SIC: 2341 Mfg Handmade Women's Lingerie

(G-5076)
KAISER MFG CO
4700 W Le Moyne St (60651-1627)
PHONE..................................773 235-4705
Thomas Kaiser, *President*
Mary Lee Geesbreght, *Corp Secy*
Phillip Kaiser Jr, *Vice Pres*
EMP: 134 **EST:** 1967
SQ FT: 40,000
SALES (est): 9.5MM **Privately Held**
WEB: www.kaisermfg.com
SIC: 3469 Stamping metal for the trade

(G-5077)
KALAMAZOO OUTDOOR GOURMET LLC (HQ)
810 W Washington Blvd (60607-2302)
PHONE..................................312 423-8770
Scott Kohler, *Vice Pres*
Lisa Rodriguez, *Vice Pres*
Andrew Manning, *Engineer*
Alexis Hiller, *Marketing Staff*
Jennifer Rounds, *Manager*
▼ **EMP:** 2
SQ FT: 7,500
SALES (est): 2.2MM
SALES (corp-wide): 6.8MM **Privately Held**
SIC: 3631 Barbecues, grills & braziers (outdoor cooking)
PA: Synetro Group, Llc
810 W Washington Blvd
Chicago IL 60607
312 372-2600

(G-5078)
KALENA LLC
1937 N Mohawk St (60614-5219)
PHONE..................................773 598-0033
Tarik Tahini,
David Venouziou,
EMP: 4
SALES (est): 900K **Privately Held**
SIC: 2086 Bottled & canned soft drinks

(G-5079)
KANA SOFTWARE INC
30 S Wacker Dr Ste 1300 (60606-7466)
PHONE..................................312 447-5600
Erin Kana, *Branch Mgr*
EMP: 3 **Publicly Held**
SIC: 7372 Prepackaged software
HQ: Kana Software, Inc.
2550 Walsh Ave Ste 120
Santa Clara CA 95051
650 614-8300

(G-5080)
KANE GRAPHICAL CORPORATION
2255 W Logan Blvd (60647-2114)
PHONE..................................773 384-1200
Michael N Kane, *President*
Jonathan Kane, *Treasurer*
Daniel Chenoweth, *Sales Staff*
Brian Pollard, *Director*
Vivian Zook, *Director*
EMP: 30
SQ FT: 40,000
SALES (est): 4MM **Privately Held**
WEB: www.kanegraphical.com
SIC: 7336 3993 Silk screen design; signs & advertising specialties

Chicago - Cook County (G-5081)

(G-5081)
KAREN YOUNG
Also Called: Loose Petals
10 W Elm St Apt 900 (60610-5015)
PHONE...................312 202-0142
Karen Young, *Owner*
EMP: 10
SALES (est): 774.7K **Privately Held**
SIC: 2771 5947 Greeting cards; gift, novelty & souvenir shop

(G-5082)
KARL LAMBRECHT CORP
4204 N Lincoln Ave (60618-2902)
PHONE...................773 472-5442
Alvin Lambrecht, *President*
Frances Lambrecht, *Principal*
Raymond Lambrecht, *Treasurer*
Anita Banas, *Marketing Mgr*
EMP: 22 EST: 1933
SQ FT: 22,000
SALES: 4.4MM **Privately Held**
WEB: www.klccgo.com
SIC: 3827 Lenses, optical: all types except ophthalmic; prisms, optical; polarizers

(G-5083)
KARMA YACHT SALES LLC (PA)
3434 E 95th St (60617-5101)
PHONE...................773 254-0200
Louis Sandoval, *Mng Member*
EMP: 6
SALES (est): 1.2MM **Privately Held**
SIC: 5551 7699 3732 Motor boat dealers; boat repair; boats, fiberglass: building & repairing

(G-5084)
KASHIV BIOSCIENCES LLC
3440 S Dearborn St # 300 (60616-5074)
PHONE...................908 895-1576
Richard Phillips, *Purch Mgr*
Tushar Patel, *Branch Mgr*
EMP: 3
SALES (corp-wide): 3.3MM **Privately Held**
SIC: 2834 Pharmaceutical preparations
PA: Kashiv Biosciences, Llc
  995 Us Highway 202/206
  Bridgewater NJ 08807
  908 895-1520

(G-5085)
KASTLE THERAPEUTICS LLC
181 W Madison St Ste 3745 (60602-4640)
PHONE...................312 883-5695
Tony Smolcich,
EMP: 6
SALES (est): 391.6K **Privately Held**
SIC: 2834 Pharmaceutical preparations

(G-5086)
KAYE LEE & COMPANY INC
5 S Wabash Ave Ste 200 (60603-3520)
PHONE...................312 236-9686
Anthony Liacone, *President*
Mark Engle, *Vice Pres*
EMP: 6
SQ FT: 1,750
SALES: 1.9MM **Privately Held**
SIC: 5944 3911 7631 Jewelry, precious stones & precious metals; jewel settings & mountings, precious metal; jewelry repair services

(G-5087)
KAZMIER TOOLING INC
6001 S Oak Park Ave (60638-4011)
PHONE...................773 586-0300
Shawn J Ofarrell, *President*
Brian O Farrell, *Admin Sec*
EMP: 8
SQ FT: 12,500
SALES: 1.1MM **Privately Held**
SIC: 3544 Special dies & tools

(G-5088)
KCP METAL FABRICATIONS INC
Also Called: Associated Metal Mfg
5475 N Northwest Hwy (60630-1133)
PHONE...................773 775-0318
Conrad Pioli, *President*
Karin Pioli, *Admin Sec*
EMP: 43 EST: 1982
SQ FT: 11,187
SALES (est): 10.7MM **Privately Held**
SIC: 3444 Sheet metalwork

(G-5089)
KELCO CONSTRUCTION INC
5572 N Lynch Ave (60630-1453)
PHONE...................773 853-2974
Kelly Gallagher, *President*
EMP: 8 EST: 2011
SQ FT: 6,000
SALES: 324K **Privately Held**
SIC: 3441 Fabricated structural metal

(G-5090)
KELLOGG COMPANY
2945 W 31st St (60623-5104)
PHONE...................773 254-0900
James Jenness, *CEO*
Mary Rodriguez, *Financial Analy*
Brett Henderson, *Finance*
Amber Jefferson, *Human Res Dir*
Miguel Guerrero, *Program Mgr*
EMP: 500
SALES (corp-wide): 13.5B **Publicly Held**
WEB: www.kelloggcompany.com
SIC: 2043 Cereal breakfast foods
PA: Kellogg Company
  1 Kellogg Sq
  Battle Creek MI 49017
  269 961-2000

(G-5091)
KELLOGG COMPANY
750 E 110th St (60628-3826)
PHONE...................773 995-7200
Matt Lenart, *Controller*
Bob Green, *Manager*
EMP: 703
SALES (corp-wide): 13.5B **Publicly Held**
SIC: 2043 Corn flakes: prepared as cereal breakfast food
PA: Kellogg Company
  1 Kellogg Sq
  Battle Creek MI 49017
  269 961-2000

(G-5092)
KELLY CORNED BEEF CO CHICAGO
Also Called: Kelly Eisenberg
3531 N Elston Ave (60618-5631)
PHONE...................773 588-2882
Howard Eisenberg, *President*
Carol Ayres, *Controller*
Calvin Eisenberg, *Admin Sec*
▼ EMP: 45
SQ FT: 1,200
SALES (est): 38.9MM **Privately Held**
SIC: 5147 2011 Meats, fresh; meats, cured or smoked; meat packing plants

(G-5093)
KELLY SYSTEMS INC (PA)
422 N Western Ave (60612-1491)
PHONE...................312 733-3224
Walter M Kelly Jr, *President*
Michael J Kelly, *Vice Pres*
Phil McGeever, *Materials Mgr*
Connie Saliba, *Safety Mgr*
Walter Kelly, *Branch Mgr*
EMP: 28 EST: 1904
SQ FT: 20,000
SALES (est): 7.9MM **Privately Held**
SIC: 3535 1796 7699 Pneumatic tube conveyor systems; installing building equipment; industrial equipment services

(G-5094)
KEMIS KOLLECTIONS
240 E 115th St Chicago (60628)
PHONE...................773 431-2307
Kemi Ijaola, *Principal*
EMP: 3
SALES: 25K **Privately Held**
SIC: 3999 Candles

(G-5095)
KEMPNER COMPANY INC
629 W Cermak Rd Ste 201 (60616-2260)
PHONE...................312 733-1606
James Kempner, *President*
◆ EMP: 10
SQ FT: 15,000
SALES (est): 1.4MM **Privately Held**
SIC: 2431 2434 Interior & ornamental woodwork & trim; wood kitchen cabinets

(G-5096)
KERALA EXPRESS NEWSPAPER
2050 W Devon Ave Apt 1w (60659-2152)
PHONE...................773 465-5359
K M Eathen, *President*
EMP: 5 EST: 1992
SALES: 500K **Privately Held**
WEB: www.keralaexpress.com
SIC: 2711 Newspapers, publishing & printing

(G-5097)
KESHER STAM
2817 W Touhy Ave (60645-2901)
PHONE...................773 973-7826
Stam Kesher, *Owner*
EMP: 4
SALES (est): 356.5K **Privately Held**
SIC: 3911 Rosaries or other small religious articles, precious metal

(G-5098)
KESTLER DIGITAL PRINTING INC
2845 W 48th Pl (60632-2012)
PHONE...................773 581-5918
Mario R Kestler, *President*
EMP: 17
SALES (est): 2.4MM **Privately Held**
SIC: 2752 Commercial printing, offset

(G-5099)
KEYSTONE PRINTING SERVICES
2451 N Harlem Ave (60707-2047)
PHONE...................773 622-7210
John Iozzo, *President*
EMP: 2
SQ FT: 1,500
SALES (est): 270K **Privately Held**
SIC: 2752 Commercial printing, offset

(G-5100)
KIBAR AMERICAS INC
1 N Wacker Dr Ste 1900 (60606-2809)
PHONE...................312 285-2553
Scott Croft, *President*
EMP: 6
SALES (est): 639.5K
SALES (corp-wide): 658.2MM **Privately Held**
SIC: 3353 Flat rolled shapes, aluminum
PA: Kibar Holding Anonim Sirketi
  Ofisler Bol K:t4 Zorlu Cen, No:2 Levazim Mahallesi
  Istanbul (Europe) 34340
  212 924-7327

(G-5101)
KIDSBOOKS LLC (PA)
3535 W Peterson Ave (60659-3212)
PHONE...................773 509-0707
Greg Sizelove,
Wief Wikkerink,
◆ EMP: 14
SQ FT: 3,400
SALES (est): 8.5MM **Privately Held**
SIC: 2731 Books: publishing only

(G-5102)
KIMBALL OFFICE INC
325 N Wells St Ste 100 (60654-7023)
PHONE...................800 349-9827
Brent Johnson, *Business Mgr*
Phyllis M Goetz, *Branch Mgr*
EMP: 10
SALES (corp-wide): 768MM **Publicly Held**
WEB: www.kimballoffice.com
SIC: 2522 Office desks & tables: except wood
HQ: Kimball Office Inc.
  1600 Royal St
  Jasper IN 47546

(G-5103)
KIMBERLY-CLARK CORPORATION
20 N Wacker Dr Ste 4200 (60606-3191)
PHONE...................847 885-1050
Mike Frey, *Branch Mgr*
EMP: 5
SALES (corp-wide): 18.4B **Publicly Held**
SIC: 2621 2676 Sanitary tissue paper; infant & baby paper products
PA: Kimberly-Clark Corporation
  351 Phelps Dr
  Irving TX 75038
  972 281-1200

(G-5104)
KIMMYKAKES CO
2616 W 85th Pl (60652-3930)
PHONE...................312 927-3933
Kimberly Lenore Mesa, *President*
EMP: 4
SALES (est): 146.9K **Privately Held**
SIC: 2053 Cakes, bakery: frozen

(G-5105)
KINAXIS CORP
40 E Chicago Ave (60611-2026)
PHONE...................613 592-5780
Doug Colbeth, *Branch Mgr*
EMP: 13
SALES (corp-wide): 191.5MM **Privately Held**
SIC: 7372 Prepackaged software
PA: Kinaxis Inc
  700 Silver Seven Rd Suite 500
  Kanata ON K2V 1
  613 592-5780

(G-5106)
KIRBY SHEET METAL WORKS INC
Also Called: Mark Radtke Co Division
4209 S Western Blvd (60609-2280)
PHONE...................773 247-6477
Jack Young, *President*
Phil Kirk, *Vice Pres*
Robert Novick, *Vice Pres*
EMP: 20 EST: 1924
SQ FT: 12,000
SALES (est): 3.9MM **Privately Held**
WEB: www.kirbysheetmetalworks.com
SIC: 1761 3444 Sheet metalwork; sheet metalwork

(G-5107)
KISS ME COMIX
9654 S Forest Ave (60628-1408)
PHONE...................773 982-8334
Rod Jenkins, *Owner*
Robert Boyd, *Co-Owner*
Barbara Coni-Jenkins, *Co-Owner*
EMP: 3
SALES (est): 174.5K **Privately Held**
SIC: 2721 Comic books: publishing & printing

(G-5108)
KLEIN PRINTING INC
Also Called: I AM A Print Shoppe
3035 W Fullerton Ave (60647-2807)
PHONE...................773 235-2121
Ralph Klein, *President*
Jesus Cruz, *Manager*
EMP: 7 EST: 1957
SQ FT: 6,800
SALES (est): 750K **Privately Held**
SIC: 2752 2759 7334 2791 Commercial printing, offset; thermography; photocopying & duplicating services; typesetting; bookbinding & related work

(G-5109)
KLIUX ENERGIES INTL INC
300 N La Salle Dr # 4925 (60654-3406)
PHONE...................312 985-7717
Inaki Eguizabal, *President*
EMP: 20
SALES (est): 500K **Privately Held**
SIC: 3511 Turbines & turbine generator set units, complete

(G-5110)
KNIGHTHOUSE MEDIA INC
Also Called: Knighthouse Publishing
150 N Michigan Ave # 900 (60601-7524)
PHONE...................312 676-1100
Christopher Schofield, *President*
Lunice Weeden, *Admin Sec*
EMP: 150 EST: 2011
SALES (est): 9.6MM **Privately Held**
WEB: www.knighthousemedia.com
SIC: 2741 Business service newsletters: publishing & printing

GEOGRAPHIC SECTION   Chicago - Cook County (G-5137)

(G-5111)
KNOCK ON METAL INC (PA)
221 N La Salle St # 3315 (60601-1206)
PHONE 312 372-4569
Van A Schwab, President
EMP: 2
SALES (est): 450.1K Privately Held
WEB: www.schwabfamilylaw.com
SIC: 3369 Lead castings, except die-castings

(G-5112)
KNOLL INC
Also Called: Knoll Textiles
811 W Fulton Market (60607-1326)
PHONE 312 454-6920
Edward Godwin, Vice Pres
Jody Fitzgibbons, Sales Staff
Matt McCormick, Branch Mgr
Rick Guerin, Director
Chris Kennedy, Bd of Directors
EMP: 30 Publicly Held
WEB: www.knoll.com
SIC: 2521 Wood office furniture
PA: Knoll, Inc.
    1235 Water St
    East Greenville PA 18041

(G-5113)
KOCH MEAT CO INC
Also Called: Aspen Foods
4404 W Berteau Ave (60641-1907)
PHONE 847 384-5940
Tyler Davis, Plant Mgr
Jose Hernandez, Purch Mgr
Hank Paasman, Engineer
Isabel Martinez, Human Res Mgr
Peter Owens, Sales Staff
EMP: 375
SALES (corp-wide): 2.2B Privately Held
WEB: www.kochfoods.com
SIC: 5142 2015 Packaged frozen goods; poultry slaughtering & processing
HQ: Koch Meat Co., Inc.
    1300 Higgins Rd Ste 100
    Park Ridge IL 60068
    847 384-8018

(G-5114)
KOCOUR CO
4800 S Saint Louis Ave (60632-3091)
PHONE 773 847-1111
Leslie Kocour Jr, Ch of Bd
Dan Johnson, President
Dennis Masarik, President
Iris A Poltrock, Admin Sec
EMP: 20 EST: 1923
SQ FT: 40,000
SALES: 4.8MM Privately Held
WEB: www.kocour.net
SIC: 3829 5085 2842 Testing equipment: abrasion, shearing strength, etc.; industrial supplies; specialty cleaning, polishes & sanitation goods

(G-5115)
KODIAK LLC
4320 S Knox Ave (60632-4342)
PHONE 248 545-7520
Laura McQiugg, Manager
Shaeyanne Mooter,
EMP: 20
SALES (est): 2MM Privately Held
SIC: 2653 Corrugated & solid fiber boxes

(G-5116)
KODIAK LLC
Also Called: Packpors
4320 S Knox Ave (60632-4342)
PHONE 773 284-9975
Kathy Dunn, Sales Staff
Anthony J Mooter, Mng Member
Leonard Horton, Mng Member
John Madigan, Mng Member
EMP: 20
SQ FT: 85,000
SALES (est): 3.8MM Privately Held
SIC: 2653 Display items, corrugated: made from purchased materials

(G-5117)
KOEBERS PROSTHETIC ORTHPD LAB (PA)
3834 W Irving Park Rd # 1 (60618-3122)
PHONE 309 676-2276
Amit Bhanti, CEO

Donald Smerko, President
Loretta Smerko, Vice Pres
EMP: 8
SQ FT: 5,000
SALES: 850K Privately Held
SIC: 3842 Limbs, artificial; braces, orthopedic

(G-5118)
KOHLER CO
91283 Collections Ctr Dr (60693-0001)
PHONE 920 457-4441
EMP: 3
SALES (corp-wide): 8.3B Privately Held
SIC: 3431 Plumbing fixtures: enameled iron cast iron or pressed metal
PA: Kohler Co.
    444 Highland Dr
    Kohler WI 53044
    920 457-4441

(G-5119)
KOLCRAFT ENTERPRISES INC (PA)
1100 W Monroe St Ste 1 (60607-2496)
PHONE 312 361-6315
Sanfred Koltun, Ch of Bd
Thomas N Koltun, President
Sharon M Danko, Corp Secy
Edward Bretschger, Senior VP
Andrew Newmark, Senior VP
◆ EMP: 75
SQ FT: 75,000
SALES (est): 51.1MM Privately Held
SIC: 2515 Mattresses, containing felt, foam rubber, urethane, etc.

(G-5120)
KOMATSU AMERICA CORP (HQ)
8770 W Bryn Mawr Ave (60631-3515)
PHONE 847 437-5800
Rod Schrader, Ch of Bd
Max Masayuki Moriyama, President
Toru Niina, General Mgr
Dave Grzelak, Principal
Hisashi Shinozuka, COO
◆ EMP: 300
SQ FT: 102,000
SALES (est): 4.5B Privately Held
SIC: 5082 3532 3531 Mining machinery & equipment, except petroleum; mining machinery; construction machinery

(G-5121)
KOMODO BRANDS LLC
150 S Wacker Dr Ste 2400 (60606-4211)
PHONE 312 788-2730
Francois Lubin,
EMP: 5
SALES (est): 139.9K Privately Held
SIC: 2086 Carbonated soft drinks, bottled & canned; fruit drinks (less than 100% juice): packaged in cans, etc.

(G-5122)
KONVEAU INC
805 E Drexel Sq (60615-3781)
PHONE 312 476-9385
Jason Johnson, CEO
Jason Triche, Co-Owner
EMP: 4
SALES (est): 98.3K Privately Held
SIC: 7372 Application computer software

(G-5123)
KOOMBEA INC
3409 N Paulina St (60657-1220)
PHONE 408 786-5290
Jonathan Tarud, CEO
Oscar Rodriguez, Enginr/R&D Asst
Tony Meazell, Director
EMP: 3 EST: 2010
SALES (est): 154.6K Privately Held
SIC: 7371 7372 7379 Computer software writing services; business oriented computer software; computer related consulting services

(G-5124)
KOREX CHICAGO LLC
6200 W 51st St Ste 7 (60638-1349)
PHONE 708 458-4890
James Barca, General Mgr
Cheryl Livner, Controller
Ivan Doyadzhiev, Director
EMP: 26

SQ FT: 125,000
SALES (est): 7.7MM Privately Held
SIC: 2841 2842 Soap & other detergents; bleaches, household: dry or liquid
HQ: Korex Corporation
    50000 Pontiac Trl
    Wixom MI 48393
    248 624-0000

(G-5125)
KOTHE DISTILLING TECH INC
5121 N Ravenswood Ave (60640-5386)
PHONE 312 878-7766
Sonat Birnecker Hart, President
◆ EMP: 3
SALES (est): 147.1K Privately Held
SIC: 2085 Distilled & blended liquors

(G-5126)
KOVAL INC
5121 N Ravenswood Ave Grw (60640-5386)
PHONE 312 878-7988
Sonat Hart, Principal
Rene Cousineau, Corp Comm Staff
▲ EMP: 19 Privately Held
WEB: www.koval-distillery.com
SIC: 2085 Distilled & blended liquors
PA: Koval Inc.
    4241 N Ravenswood Ave # 2
    Chicago IL 60613

(G-5127)
KOVAL INC (PA)
Also Called: Koval Distillery
4241 N Ravenswood Ave # 2 (60613-1199)
PHONE 773 944-0089
Robert Birnecker, CEO
Sonat Birnecker, President
Mark Desimone, COO
Rene Cousineau, Corp Comm Staff
▲ EMP: 16
SALES (est): 3MM Privately Held
SIC: 2085 Distilled & blended liquors

(G-5128)
KOZA
13548 S Burley Ave (60633-1842)
PHONE 773 646-0958
EMP: 6
SALES (est): 372K Privately Held
SIC: 2731 Books-Publishing/Printing

(G-5129)
KRAFT HEINZ COMPANY
200 E Randolph St # 7300 (60601-7012)
PHONE 847 646-2000
Joe Dugan, Business Mgr
Devin Graham, Business Mgr
Troy Lafollette, Business Mgr
Raul Lozano, Business Mgr
Lisa McCarthy, Business Mgr
EMP: 120
SALES (corp-wide): 24.9B Publicly Held
SIC: 2022 3411 2095 2043 Natural cheese; processed cheese; spreads, cheese; dips, cheese-based; food & beverage containers; coffee roasting (except by wholesale grocers); freeze-dried coffee; instant coffee; cereal breakfast foods; dressings, salad: raw & cooked (except dry mixes); powders, drink
PA: The Kraft Heinz Company
    1 Ppg Pl Fl 34
    Pittsburgh PA 15222
    412 456-5700

(G-5130)
KRAFT HEINZ FOODS COMPANY
Aon Center 200 E St Aon Cent (60601)
PHONE 412 456-5700
Lark Larkins, Business Mgr
Chris Skinger, Vice Pres
Gregory Andol, Research
Samy Darwan, Engineer
Ricardo Oliva, Finance
EMP: 4
SALES (corp-wide): 24.9B Publicly Held
SIC: 2022 2032 Cheese spreads, dips, pastes & other cheese products; baby foods, including meats: packaged in cans, jars, etc.
HQ: Kraft Heinz Foods Company
    1 Ppg Pl Fl 34
    Pittsburgh PA 15222
    412 456-5700

(G-5131)
KRAFT HEINZ RECEIVABLES LLC
200 E Randolph St # 7600 (60601-6436)
PHONE 847 646-2000
Cherie Jones, Manager
EMP: 6
SALES (est): 91.3K
SALES (corp-wide): 24.9B Publicly Held
SIC: 2033 Tomato sauce: packaged in cans, jars, etc.
PA: The Kraft Heinz Company
    1 Ppg Pl Fl 34
    Pittsburgh PA 15222
    412 456-5700

(G-5132)
KREL LABORATORIES INC
388 N Avers Ave (60624-1892)
PHONE 773 826-4487
Michael D Mitchell, President
Michael Ratliff, Vice Pres
Dalaura Throns, Office Mgr
Sansi Mitchell, Shareholder
EMP: 14
SQ FT: 15,000
SALES (est): 1.6MM Privately Held
WEB: www.krellabs.com
SIC: 3471 Electroplating of metals or formed products; buffing for the trade; polishing, metals or formed products

(G-5133)
KROH-WAGNER INC
2331 N Pulaski Rd (60639-3798)
PHONE 773 252-2031
Robert C Wagner, President
Robert Wagner, COO
Margaret Wagner, Vice Pres
Cathy Wagner, Marketing Mgr
EMP: 20 EST: 1924
SQ FT: 20,000
SALES (est): 3.7MM Privately Held
WEB: www.krohwagner.com
SIC: 3317 3442 3449 3444 Tubing, mechanical or hypodermic sizes: cold drawn stainless; moldings & trim, except automobile; metal; miscellaneous metalwork; sheet metalwork; fabricated structural metal; copper rolling & drawing

(G-5134)
KRUEGER INTERNATIONAL INC
Also Called: Ki
1181 Merchandise Mart (60654)
PHONE 312 467-6850
Dave Fairburn, Manager
EMP: 15
SALES (corp-wide): 649.9MM Privately Held
SIC: 2752 Commercial printing, lithographic
PA: Krueger International, Inc.
    1330 Bellevue St
    Green Bay WI 54302
    920 468-8100

(G-5135)
KUHN SPECIAL STEEL N AMER INC
55 W Monroe St Ste 2900 (60603-5058)
PHONE 262 788-9358
EMP: 4
SALES (est): 251.9K Privately Held
SIC: 3317 3592 Steel pipe & tubes; carburetors, pistons, rings, valves

(G-5136)
KUNZ GLOVE CO INC
1532 W Fulton St (60607-1004)
PHONE 312 733-8780
Kevin G Deady, President
Kelly Deady, Opers Staff
▲ EMP: 39 EST: 1900
SQ FT: 20,000
SALES (est): 6.3MM Privately Held
WEB: www.kunzglove.com
SIC: 3151 2381 Gloves, leather: work; fabric dress & work gloves

(G-5137)
KW FABRICATION
4724 S Christiana Ave (60632-3016)
PHONE 773 523-2420
EMP: 3 EST: 2017

Chicago - Cook County (G-5138)

SALES (est): 290.8K **Privately Held**
SIC: 3599 Machine shop, jobbing & repair

(G-5138)
KW PLASTICS
Also Called: Kw Container
270 S State St (60604)
PHONE....................708 757-5140
Steven Lux, *General Mgr*
EMP: 15
SALES (corp-wide): 70.7MM **Privately Held**
SIC: 3081 Polypropylene film & sheet
PA: Kw Plastics
  279 Pike County Lake Rd
  Troy AL 36079
  334 566-1563

(G-5139)
KYLON MIDWEST
238 E 108th St Apt 2w (60628-3676)
PHONE....................773 699-3640
Karolyn Wright, *Principal*
EMP: 4
SALES: 400K **Privately Held**
SIC: 3678 Electronic connectors

(G-5140)
L & L FLOORING INC
Also Called: Carpet One
3071 N Lincoln Ave (60657-4207)
PHONE....................773 935-9314
Joel Schreiner, *Manager*
EMP: 30
SALES (corp-wide): 16.9MM **Privately Held**
SIC: 5713 2273 Floor covering stores; carpets & rugs
PA: L. & L. Flooring, Inc.
  3071 N Lincoln Ave
  Chicago IL
  773 935-9314

(G-5141)
L A BEDDING CORP
3421 W 48th Pl (60632-3026)
PHONE....................773 715-9641
Luis Martines Sr, *President*
EMP: 6
SALES (est): 640.7K **Privately Held**
SIC: 2515 Mattresses & bedsprings

(G-5142)
L A MOTORS INCORPORATED
4034 N Tripp Ave (60641-1942)
PHONE....................773 736-7305
Art Ambriz, *President*
EMP: 3 EST: 2008
SALES: 57K **Privately Held**
WEB: www.lamotorschicago.com
SIC: 7694 7539 7538 5531 Rebuilding motors, except automotive; automotive repair shops; engine repair; automotive parts

(G-5143)
L STREET COLLABORATIVE LLC (PA)
Also Called: 3p Works
20 N Upper Wacker (60606)
P.O. Box 678, Downers Grove (60515-0678)
PHONE....................630 243-5783
Jeremy Sebben, *President*
Carolyn Eckert, *Finance Dir*
Alisa Creaney, *Software Engr*
EMP: 19 EST: 2013
SALES (est): 5.3MM **Privately Held**
SIC: 7372 Business oriented computer software

(G-5144)
L-DATA CORPORATION
203 N La Salle St # 2169 (60601-1267)
PHONE....................312 552-7855
Florin Dragomir, *President*
Ann E Harris, *Officer*
EMP: 32
SQ FT: 2,200
SALES: 9.2MM **Privately Held**
WEB: www.ldatacorporation.com
SIC: 7372 5045 Educational computer software; anti-static equipment & devices; computer software; computers; terminals, computer

(G-5145)
L2 SUPPLY DBA ICA CAB SUPPLY
4250 N Milwaukee Ave (60641-1643)
PHONE....................773 382-8037
Siu Lan Linda Tan, *President*
EMP: 2
SALES (est): 207.2K **Privately Held**
WEB: www.icacabinet.com
SIC: 2434 Wood kitchen cabinets

(G-5146)
LA ESPAÑOLA FOOD DIST CORP
Also Called: La Mexicana Food Prducts
401 N Oakley Blvd (60612-2587)
PHONE....................312 733-0775
Carlos Martinez, *President*
EMP: 11
SQ FT: 9,000
SALES (est): 1MM **Privately Held**
SIC: 2099 Seasonings & spices

(G-5147)
LA HISPAMEX FOOD PRODUCTS INC
6955 S Harlem Ave (60638-4712)
PHONE....................708 780-1808
Jose A Galvez, *President*
EMP: 5
SALES (est): 812.1K **Privately Held**
SIC: 2022 Processed cheese

(G-5148)
LA MEXICANA TORTILLERIA INC
Also Called: Tortilleria La Mexicana
2703 S Kedzie Ave (60623-4735)
PHONE....................773 247-5443
Rudolph Guerrero, *President*
EMP: 7
SQ FT: 27,500
SALES (est): 6.6MM **Privately Held**
SIC: 2099 Tortillas, fresh or refrigerated

(G-5149)
LA RAZA CHICAGO INC
Also Called: La Raza Newspaper
605 N Michigan Ave # 400 (60611-3145)
PHONE....................312 870-7000
Robert Armband, *President*
EMP: 46
SALES (est): 2.6MM **Privately Held**
SIC: 2711 Newspapers, publishing & printing

(G-5150)
LA TROPICANA INC
5646 S Kedzie Ave (60629-3471)
PHONE....................773 476-1107
Felix Magana, *Owner*
Paul Carr, *Plant Mgr*
Valerie Knoll, *Technology*
EMP: 4
SALES (est): 233.3K **Privately Held**
WEB: www.tropicana.com
SIC: 2033 Canned fruits & specialties

(G-5151)
LABAQUETTE KEDZIE INC
5859 S Kedzie Ave (60629-3212)
PHONE....................773 925-0455
Julie Urebe, *Owner*
EMP: 4
SALES (est): 283.3K **Privately Held**
SIC: 2051 Bakery: wholesale or wholesale/retail combined

(G-5152)
LABELS UNLIMITED INCORPORATED
Also Called: Hospital Labels Co Div
3400 W 48th Pl (60632-3075)
PHONE....................773 523-7500
Michael Shiel, *President*
Bill Woolf, *Corp Secy*
Steve Van Dort, *Graphic Designe*
Martha Campos,
EMP: 45 EST: 1968
SQ FT: 60,000
SALES (est): 7.1MM **Privately Held**
SIC: 2759 2752 2672 2671 Flexographic printing; screen printing; letterpress printing; commercial printing, offset; tape, pressure sensitive: made from purchased materials; packaging paper & plastics film, coated & laminated

(G-5153)
LACAVA
1100 W Cermak Rd B-403 (60608-4500)
PHONE....................773 637-9600
Carmine Lacava, *Principal*
EMP: 2 EST: 2010
SALES (est): 344.8K **Privately Held**
WEB: www.lacava.com
SIC: 2599 Furniture & fixtures

(G-5154)
LACAVA LLC
Also Called: Lacava Design
6630 W Wrightwood Ave (60707-2228)
PHONE....................773 637-9600
Carmine Lacava, *COO*
Sachin Sharma, *Opers Staff*
Justin Kusserow, *Accounts Mgr*
Jeremy Sterling, *Accounts Mgr*
▲ EMP: 50
SQ FT: 100,000
SALES (est): 9.8MM **Privately Held**
SIC: 3432 3261 2434 2521 Plumbing fixture fittings & trim; vitreous plumbing fixtures; bathroom accessories/fittings, vitreous china or earthenware; vanities, bathroom: wood; wood office furniture

(G-5155)
LAFARGE BUILDING MATERIALS INC (DH)
8700 W Bryn Mawr Ave 300n (60631-3512)
PHONE....................678 746-2000
Jean M Lechene, *CEO*
Peter L Keeley, *CEO*
Robert Fiolek, *CFO*
Stacey Ruby, *Manager*
▲ EMP: 100
SQ FT: 30,000
SALES: 847.7MM
SALES (corp-wide): 4.5B **Privately Held**
SIC: 3241 3274 3273 3271 Masonry cement; natural cement; portland cement; lime; ready-mixed concrete; blocks, concrete or cinder: standard
HQ: Lafarge North America Inc.
  8700 W Bryn Mawr Ave
  Chicago IL 60631
  773 372-1000

(G-5156)
LAFARGE NORTH AMERICA INC (DH)
8700 W Bryn Mawr Ave (60631-3512)
PHONE....................773 372-1000
Bernard L Kasriel, *CEO*
Isaac Preston, *CEO*
John Stull, *President*
Jose A Primo, *General Mgr*
Sonia Cattoi, *Principal*
◆ EMP: 120
SALES (est): 3.2B
SALES (corp-wide): 4.5B **Privately Held**
SIC: 3273 3272 3271 1442 Ready-mixed concrete; concrete products; precast terrazo or concrete products; prestressed concrete products; cylinder pipe, prestressed or pretensioned concrete; blocks, concrete or cinder: standard; construction sand & gravel; construction sand mining; gravel mining; asphalt paving mixtures & blocks; paving mixtures; asphalt & asphaltic paving mixtures (not from refineries); portland cement
HQ: Lafarge
  2 Avenue Du General De Gaulle
  Clamart 92140
  158 006-000

(G-5157)
LAFARGE NORTH AMERICA INC
8700 W Bryn Mawr Ave (60631-3512)
PHONE....................773 372-1000
Steve Lawler, *Manager*
EMP: 27
SALES (corp-wide): 4.5B **Privately Held**
SIC: 3241 Cement, hydraulic
HQ: Lafarge North America Inc.
  8700 W Bryn Mawr Ave
  Chicago IL 60631
  773 372-1000

(G-5158)
LAFARGE NORTH AMERICA INC
2150 E 130th St (60633-2300)
PHONE....................773 646-5228
Anthony Gianakis, *Plant Mgr*
Frank Lavarowicv, *Manager*
EMP: 4
SALES (corp-wide): 4.5B **Privately Held**
SIC: 3241 Cement, hydraulic
HQ: Lafarge North America Inc.
  8700 W Bryn Mawr Ave
  Chicago IL 60631
  773 372-1000

(G-5159)
LAGUNITAS BREWING COMPANY
2607 W 17th St (60608-1823)
PHONE....................773 522-1308
Brandon Greenwood, *Branch Mgr*
EMP: 180
SALES (corp-wide): 12.5MM **Privately Held**
SIC: 2082 Beer (alcoholic beverage)
HQ: The Lagunitas Brewing Company
  1280 N Mcdowell Blvd
  Petaluma CA 94954

(G-5160)
LAKE IRON INC
Also Called: Troy Iron Works
5520 W Lake St (60644-1913)
PHONE....................708 870-0546
Bronislaw Lanowski, *President*
EMP: 2
SALES (est): 263.5K **Privately Held**
SIC: 3444 3499 Sheet metalwork; ironing boards, metal

(G-5161)
LAKE PACIFIC PARTNERS LLC
120 S La Salle St # 1510 (60603-3574)
PHONE....................312 578-1110
Emma Sorenson, *Partner*
Wayne Carpenter, *Managing Dir*
Dara Griffith, *Finance Dir*
William R Voss,
EMP: 500
SALES (est): 34.5MM **Privately Held**
WEB: www.lakepacific.com
SIC: 6211 3089 2013 2011 Investment firm, general brokerage; food casings, plastic; sausages & other prepared meats; meat packing plants

(G-5162)
LAKE STREET PALLETS
4600 W Armitage Ave (60639-3406)
PHONE....................773 889-2266
Florence Rogers, *President*
Patricia Cuevas, *Vice Pres*
Chuck Rogers, *Treasurer*
Carlos Cuevas, *Admin Sec*
Emily Hartnell, *Administration*
EMP: 8
SALES: 100K **Privately Held**
SIC: 7699 2448 Pallet repair; wood pallets & skids

(G-5163)
LAKEFRONT ROOFING SUPPLY (HQ)
Also Called: Jesus People USA Full Gospel M
2950 N Western Ave (60618-8021)
PHONE....................773 509-0400
Tim Bock, *General Mgr*
Rick J Mills, *CFO*
Kathy Anderson, *Human Resources*
Fernando Amaro, *Sales Associate*
Bill Baldauf, *Mktg Dir*
EMP: 27
SALES (est): 12.6MM
SALES (corp-wide): 18MM **Privately Held**
SIC: 2952 3444 Roofing materials; siding, sheet metal
PA: Jesus People, U.S.A., Full Gospel Ministries
  2950 N Western Ave
  Chicago IL 60618
  773 252-1812

GEOGRAPHIC SECTION

Chicago - Cook County (G-5190)

(G-5164)
LAKEFRONT SCULPTURE EXHIBIT
1807 N Orleans St Ste 1s (60614-7377)
PHONE..................................312 719-0207
Vi Jaley, *Owner*
EMP: 4
SALES: 139.3K *Privately Held*
SIC: 3299 Architectural sculptures: gypsum, clay, papier mache, etc.

(G-5165)
LAKESHORE OPERATING LLC
2637 N Sawyer Ave (60647-1611)
PHONE..................................844 557-4763
Leslie Ketecham, *President*
EMP: 20
SALES: 10MM *Privately Held*
SIC: 1311 5172 Crude petroleum production; crude oil

(G-5166)
LAKESIDE LITHOGRAPHY LLC
1600 S Laflin St (60608-2123)
PHONE..................................312 243-3001
Noe Lopez, *Plant Mgr*
Dee York, *Purchasing*
Louie Vandermeer, *Manager*
Lee Nadler,
▼ EMP: 25
SQ FT: 60,000
SALES (est): 4.4MM *Privately Held*
SIC: 2752 Lithographing on metal
PA: Lakeside Metals, Inc.
7000 S Adams St Ste 210
Willowbrook IL 60527

(G-5167)
LAKEVIEW ENERGY LLC (PA)
300 W Adams St Ste 830 (60606-5109)
PHONE..................................312 386-5897
Tim Cowhig, *Chairman*
Earmonn Byrne, *COO*
Charles Stremick, *Vice Pres*
Jim Galvin, *CFO*
Steve Meyer, *CFO*
EMP: 28 EST: 2010
SALES (est): 18MM *Privately Held*
SIC: 2869 3621 3523 Fuels; windmills, electric generating; windmills for pumping water, agricultural

(G-5168)
LAKEVIEW SIGN CO
1101 W Belmont Ave (60657-3312)
PHONE..................................773 698-8104
EMP: 2 EST: 2012
SALES (est): 232.4K *Privately Held*
SIC: 3993 Signs & advertising specialties

(G-5169)
LAMBDA PUBLICATIONS INC
Also Called: Windy City Times
5443 N Broadway St # 101 (60640-1703)
PHONE..................................773 871-7610
Tracy Baim, *President*
EMP: 10
SALES (est): 1.1MM *Privately Held*
SIC: 2721 2711 Magazines: publishing only, not printed on site; newspapers

(G-5170)
LAMINATION SPECIALTIES LLC
4444 S Kildare Ave (60632-4345)
PHONE..................................773 254-7500
Robert E Stewart, *CEO*
EMP: 5
SALES (corp-wide): 386.2MM *Privately Held*
SIC: 3399 Laminating steel
HQ: Lamination Specialties Llc
1400 16th St
Oak Brook IL 60523
312 243-2181

(G-5171)
LAMINET COVER COMPANY
Also Called: Lamco Advertising Specialties
4900 W Bloomingdale Ave (60639-4562)
PHONE..................................773 622-6700
Frank Lieber, *CEO*
Michael Lieber, *President*
Leigh Deyoung, *Vice Pres*
Michael Briney, *CIO*
Lynne G Lieber, *Admin Sec*
▲ EMP: 25
SQ FT: 25,000
SALES (est): 5.3MM *Privately Held*
WEB: www.laminet.com
SIC: 2673 Plastic bags: made from purchased materials; garment & wardrobe bags, (plastic film)

(G-5172)
LAMONICA ORNAMENTAL IRON WORKS
3311 W Chicago Ave (60651-4107)
PHONE..................................773 638-6633
Rob Lamonica, *President*
Dominic Lamonaca, *Vice Pres*
EMP: 5 EST: 1965
SQ FT: 1,600
SALES (est): 300K *Privately Held*
SIC: 3446 1791 Architectural metalwork; iron work, structural

(G-5173)
LAMPHOLDERS ASSEMBLIES INC
4106 N Nashville Ave (60634-1429)
PHONE..................................773 205-0005
Mae Valentino, *President*
▲ EMP: 9
SQ FT: 3,500
SALES (est): 500K *Privately Held*
SIC: 3648 3641 Lighting equipment; electric lamps

(G-5174)
LAMPSHADE INC
4041 W Ogden Ave Ste 1 (60623-2857)
P.O. Box 23199 (60623-0199)
PHONE..................................773 522-2300
Michael A Lawlor, *President*
▲ EMP: 17
SQ FT: 19,000
SALES (est): 2.8MM *Privately Held*
SIC: 3645 Lamp shades, metal

(G-5175)
LANG EXTERIOR INC (PA)
Also Called: Lang Exterior Mfg Co
2323 W 59th St (60636-1518)
PHONE..................................773 737-4500
Darb Lang, *President*
Doreen Lang, *Marketing Mgr*
Eugene Lang, *Admin Sec*
EMP: 61 EST: 1953
SQ FT: 180,000
SALES (est): 21.2MM *Privately Held*
WEB: www.langwindowsinc.com
SIC: 3442 3211 3229 Storm doors or windows, metal; insulating glass, sealed units; blocks & bricks, glass

(G-5176)
LAQUEUS INC
Also Called: Andria Lieu
7435 N Western Ave (60645-1735)
PHONE..................................773 508-1993
Andria Lieu, *President*
▲ EMP: 15
SQ FT: 3,500
SALES (est): 4MM *Privately Held*
SIC: 2339 Sportswear, women's

(G-5177)
LAREDO FOODS INC
Also Called: Laredo Spices & Herbs
3401 W Cermak Rd (60623-3240)
PHONE..................................773 762-1500
Art Jimenez, *President*
Mary B Jimenez, *Treasurer*
EMP: 20
SQ FT: 22,000
SALES (est): 2.9MM *Privately Held*
SIC: 5149 5145 2099 Spices & seasonings; sauces; snack foods; food preparations

(G-5178)
LASNER BROS INC
Also Called: Lasner Beauty Supply
3649 N Ashland Ave (60613-3617)
PHONE..................................773 935-7383
Daniel Lasner, *Vice Pres*
EMP: 5 EST: 1940
SQ FT: 3,000
SALES: 600K *Privately Held*
SIC: 5087 2844 Beauty parlor equipment & supplies; toilet preparations

(G-5179)
LASONS LABEL CO
5666 N Northwest Hwy (60646-6161)
PHONE..................................773 775-2606
William A Lasiewicz, *President*
Bernard M Lasiewicz, *Treasurer*
Kathleen Lasiewicz, *Asst Sec*
EMP: 2 EST: 1960
SQ FT: 5,000
SALES (est): 279.9K *Privately Held*
WEB: www.lasonslabel.com
SIC: 2759 2796 2789 2672 Letterpress printing; labels & seals: printing, platemaking services; bookbinding & related work; coated & laminated paper; packaging paper & plastics film, coated & laminated

(G-5180)
LATINO ARTS & COMMUNICATIONS
3514 W Diversey Ave 212 (60647-1233)
PHONE..................................773 501-0029
Ruben Calderon, *CEO*
EMP: 4
SALES (est): 316.8K *Privately Held*
SIC: 3663 Radio & TV communications equipment

(G-5181)
LAVELL GENERAL HANDYMAN SVCS
8150 S Anthony Ave (60617-1727)
PHONE..................................773 691-3101
Lavell Bolden, *Principal*
EMP: 5
SALES (est): 243.4K *Privately Held*
SIC: 3432 Plumbing fixture fittings & trim

(G-5182)
LAW BULLETIN PUBLISHING CO (PA)
Also Called: Real Estate Communications
415 N State St Ste 1 (60654-4674)
PHONE..................................312 644-2763
L Macfarland Jr, *Ch of Bd*
B Macfarland, *President*
Brewster McFarland, *President*
Mark Menzies, *Publisher*
John Corcoran, *Editor*
EMP: 150 EST: 1854
SQ FT: 60,000
SALES (est): 42.6MM *Privately Held*
WEB: www.lawbulletin.com
SIC: 2741 Guides: publishing & printing; directories: publishing & printing; business service newsletters: publishing & printing

(G-5183)
LAWNDALE FORGING & TOOL WORKS
2141 S Spaulding Ave (60623-3321)
PHONE..................................773 277-2800
Ralph Russell, *President*
Greg Rusell, *Vice Pres*
Gregory Russell, *Train & Dev Mgr*
EMP: 7 EST: 1916
SQ FT: 12,500
SALES (est): 575K *Privately Held*
WEB: www.lawndaleforge.com
SIC: 3462 3452 3446 3443 Iron & steel forgings; bolts, nuts, rivets & washers; architectural metalwork; fabricated plate work (boiler shop); hand & edge tools; blast furnaces & steel mills

(G-5184)
LAWRENCE RGAN CMMNICATIONS INC
10 S La Salle St Ste 310 (60603-1094)
PHONE..................................312 960-4100
Mark Ragan, *CEO*
Marc Thiessen, *President*
Ralph Gaillard, *Publisher*
Scott Lester, *Editor*
Cheryl Byrne, *Vice Pres*
EMP: 43 EST: 1970
SALES: 11.7MM *Privately Held*
WEB: www.ragan.com
SIC: 2721 Periodicals

(G-5185)
LAWTER INC (DH)
200 N La Salle St # 2600 (60601-1060)
PHONE..................................312 662-5700
Ichiro Taninaka, *President*
Yoshihiro Hasegawa, *Chairman*
Peter Biesheuvel, *Vice Pres*
Tony Carter, *Production*
Michael Anzeljc, *Controller*
▲ EMP: 24
SALES (est): 141.5MM
SALES (corp-wide): 484.2K *Privately Held*
SIC: 2899 2851 Chemical preparations; paints & allied products
HQ: Lawter Capital B.V.
Ankerkade 81
Maastricht
433 525-354

(G-5186)
LAYSTROM MANUFACTURING CO
3900 W Palmer St (60647-2216)
PHONE..................................773 342-4800
Robert A Laystrom, *President*
Jeff Dec, *Plant Mgr*
Cindy Weglarz, *Opers Staff*
Barbara Hartwig, *Purchasing*
Ed Suerth, *Purchasing*
EMP: 55
SQ FT: 75,000
SALES (est): 9MM *Privately Held*
WEB: www.laystrom.com
SIC: 3441 3444 3469 3465 Fabricated structural metal; sheet metalwork; electronic enclosures, stamped or pressed metal; machine parts, stamped or pressed metal; stamping metal for the trade; automotive stampings; special dies, tools, jigs & fixtures; welding repair

(G-5187)
LAZARE PRINTING CO INC
709 W Wrightwood Ave # 1 (60614-2599)
PHONE..................................773 871-2500
David Bullard, *President*
Omar Guzman, *Prdtn Mgr*
EMP: 8
SQ FT: 8,000
SALES (est): 1MM *Privately Held*
WEB: www.lazareprinting.com
SIC: 2752 2759 Commercial printing, offset; letterpress printing

(G-5188)
LCG SALES INC
5410 W Roosevelt Rd # 231 (60644-1439)
PHONE..................................773 378-7455
Laura Gordon, *President*
Edward Clamage, *Vice Pres*
▲ EMP: 100
SQ FT: 89,000
SALES (est): 11.4MM *Privately Held*
SIC: 3999 Artificial trees & flowers

(G-5189)
LE PETIT PAIN HOLDINGS LLC (PA)
676 N Michigan Ave (60611-2883)
PHONE..................................312 981-3770
David Foster, *CFO*
Mike Schultz, *Manager*
EMP: 8 EST: 2013
SALES (est): 137.3MM *Privately Held*
SIC: 2051 Bakery: wholesale or wholesale/retail combined

(G-5190)
LEADERS BEV CONSULTING INC
4038 N Nshvlle Ave Chcago Chicago (60634)
PHONE..................................312 497-5602
Drew Larson, *President*
Kevin Busch, *CFO*
Rich Zerbian, *Office Mgr*
EMP: 12 EST: 2012
SQ FT: 4,600
SALES (est): 461.3K *Privately Held*
SIC: 3585 7699 Beer dispensing equipment; beer pump coil cleaning & repair service

Chicago - Cook County (G-5191)

(G-5191)
LEAN PROTEIN TEAM LLC
235 W Van Buren St (60607-3918)
PHONE..................440 525-1532
Christopher Arlinghaus, *Mng Member*
Dave Gooch,
Alan Knuckman,
EMP: 3 **EST:** 2017
SQ FT: 5,900
SALES: 20K **Privately Held**
SIC: 2015 Chicken, processed: frozen

(G-5192)
LEAPFROG PRODUCT DEV LLC
159 N Racine Ave Ste 3e (60607-1651)
PHONE..................312 229-0089
Derek Leatzow, *Engineer*
Steve Pinelli, *Engineer*
Lisa Wirth, *Manager*
Ellison Richard E,
Richard E Ellison,
▲ **EMP:** 19 **EST:** 2009
SALES (est): 1.5MM **Privately Held**
WEB: www.lfipd.com
SIC: 3089 Plastic containers, except foam

(G-5193)
LEARNING SEED LLC
208 S Jefferson St # 205 (60661-5759)
P.O. Box 617880 (60661-7880)
PHONE..................847 540-8855
Joseph Lombardo, *Mng Member*
Christine Schrank,
EMP: 5
SALES (est): 516.9K **Privately Held**
SIC: 3999 7812 Education aids, devices & supplies; educational motion picture production

(G-5194)
LEE ARMAND & CO LTD
840 N Milwaukee Ave (60642-4103)
PHONE..................312 455-1200
Norman P Olson, *President*
M J Forbes, *Admin Sec*
EMP: 26 **EST:** 1941
SQ FT: 20,000
SALES (est): 3MM **Privately Held**
WEB: www.armandlee.com
SIC: 2499 7641 Picture & mirror frames, wood; antique furniture repair & restoration

(G-5195)
LEE QUIGLEY COMPANY
5301 W 65th St Ste D (60638-5640)
PHONE..................708 563-1600
Anita Kasper, *Branch Mgr*
EMP: 5
SALES (corp-wide): 5MM **Privately Held**
SIC: 3471 5169 Finishing, metals or formed products; chemicals & allied products
PA: The Lee Quigley Company
21013 Old Sorters Rd A
Porter TX 77365
281 358-9608

(G-5196)
LEG UP LLC
639 W Diversey Pkwy # 205 (60614-1535)
PHONE..................312 282-2725
Shelby Mason, *CEO*
EMP: 5 **EST:** 2010
SALES (est): 526.4K **Privately Held**
SIC: 2339 4215 Leotards: women's, misses' & juniors'; package delivery, vehicular

(G-5197)
LEGACY VULCAN LLC
Also Called: Pershing Road Recycle
3910 S Racine Ave (60609-2537)
PHONE..................773 890-2360
Cosme Velasquez, *Manager*
EMP: 6 **Publicly Held**
SIC: 3272 Concrete products
HQ: Legacy Vulcan, Llc
1200 Urban Center Dr
Vestavia AL 35242
205 298-3000

(G-5198)
LEGGETT & PLATT INCORPORATED
13535 S Torrence Ave (60633-2164)
PHONE..................773 907-0261
Susan Terry, *Accountant*
Marlien Samaan, *Manager*
Maxime Samain, *Director*
Brian Isaacson, *Business Dir*
Dominique Ghess, *Assistant*
EMP: 92
SALES (corp-wide): 4.7B **Publicly Held**
WEB: www.leggett.com
SIC: 2515 Box springs, assembled
PA: Leggett & Platt, Incorporated
1 Leggett Rd
Carthage MO 64836
417 358-8131

(G-5199)
LEGGETT & PLATT INCORPORATED
Also Called: Leggett & Platt 0338
205 W Wacker Dr Ste 1020 (60606-1452)
PHONE..................312 529-2053
Tj Banks, *Design Engr*
Marali Oregel, *Human Resources*
John Wainwright, *Branch Mgr*
EMP: 30
SALES (corp-wide): 4.7B **Publicly Held**
WEB: www.leggett.com
SIC: 2515 Mattresses & bedsprings
PA: Leggett & Platt, Incorporated
1 Leggett Rd
Carthage MO 64836
417 358-8131

(G-5200)
LEGGETT & PLATT INCORPORATED
Also Called: Atlanta Warehouse 1023
6755 W 65th St (60638-4801)
PHONE..................800 699-0607
Steve Nelson, *Vice Pres*
Gary Franzen, *Manager*
EMP: 4
SALES (corp-wide): 4.7B **Publicly Held**
SIC: 2515 Mattresses & bedsprings
PA: Leggett & Platt, Incorporated
1 Leggett Rd
Carthage MO 64836
417 358-8131

(G-5201)
LEGISTEK CORPORATION
211 W Wacker Dr Ste 201 (60606-1217)
PHONE..................312 399-4891
Peter Moore, *CEO*
William Williford, *COO*
EMP: 3 **EST:** 2015
SALES (est): 211.3K **Privately Held**
SIC: 7372 7389 Business oriented computer software;

(G-5202)
LEGO SYSTEMS INC
835 N Michigan Ave # 3000 (60611-2203)
PHONE..................312 202-0946
Jake Martinez, *Manager*
EMP: 6 **Privately Held**
SIC: 3944 Games, toys & children's vehicles
HQ: Lego Systems, Inc.
555 Taylor Rd
Enfield CT 06082
860 749-2291

(G-5203)
LEGRAND AV INC
15457 Collection Ctr Dr (60693-0001)
PHONE..................719 661-8134
Scott Gill, *President*
Kris Barone, *Sales Staff*
EMP: 6
SALES (corp-wide): 27.3MM **Privately Held**
WEB: www.legrandav.com
SIC: 3669 Intercommunication systems, electric
HQ: Legrand Av Inc.
6436 City West Pkwy
Eden Prairie MN 55344
866 977-3901

(G-5204)
LEO A BACHRACH JEWELERS INC
Also Called: Leo Bachrach and Son
55 E Washington St # 801 (60602-2103)
PHONE..................312 263-3111
Leo A Bachrach, *President*
Mark Bachrach, *Treasurer*
Audrey Bachrach, *Admin Sec*
EMP: 4
SQ FT: 1,000
SALES (est): 436.5K **Privately Held**
WEB: www.leobachrachjewelers.com
SIC: 3911 5944 Jewelry, precious metal; jewelry, precious stones & precious metals

(G-5205)
LEO BURNETT COMPANY INC (DH)
Also Called: Farmhouse Lb
35 W Wacker Dr Fl 21 (60601-1755)
PHONE..................312 220-5959
Thomas L Bernardin, *CEO*
Leo Burnett Milan, *CEO*
Bob Raidt, *President*
Joe Chemali, *General Mgr*
Andy St Heli, *Managing Dir*
EMP: 108 **EST:** 1999
SQ FT: 615,000
SALES (est): 152.4MM
SALES (corp-wide): 29.8MM **Privately Held**
WEB: www.leoburnett.com
SIC: 7311 3993 Advertising agencies; signs & advertising specialties

(G-5206)
LEOS SIGN
1334 N Kostner Ave (60651-1604)
PHONE..................773 227-2460
Leonina Rodriguez, *Owner*
EMP: 3
SALES (est): 173.3K **Privately Held**
SIC: 3993 Signs & advertising specialties

(G-5207)
LEOS SWEET SENSATIONS INC
1900 N Austin Ave (60639-5010)
PHONE..................773 237-1200
Patrick Oden, *President*
EMP: 57
SALES: 8.5MM **Privately Held**
SIC: 2051 5149 Cakes, pies & pastries; bakery products

(G-5208)
LESTER LAMPERT INC
Also Called: Lester Lampert Jewelers
7 E Huron St (60611-2290)
PHONE..................312 944-6888
Lester Lampert, *CEO*
David Lampert, *President*
Maureen Lampert, *Vice Pres*
David Fozailoff, *Buyer*
Sue Skarren, *CFO*
EMP: 26
SQ FT: 8,000
SALES (est): 4.9MM **Privately Held**
WEB: www.lesterlampert.com
SIC: 3911 5944 Jewelry, precious metal; jewelry, precious stones & precious metals

(G-5209)
LET THERE BE DISTILLERS LLC
1815 W Berteau Ave (60613-1321)
PHONE..................217 741-0392
Eric Brenton, *Exec Dir*
EMP: 5
SALES (est): 313.1K **Privately Held**
SIC: 2085 Distilled & blended liquors

(G-5210)
LEVEL DEVELOPMENTS LTD
1016 W Jackson Blvd 251 (60607-2914)
PHONE..................312 465-1082
EMP: 3
SALES (est): 149.2K **Privately Held**
SIC: 3823 Level & bulk measuring instruments, industrial process

(G-5211)
LEVI STRAUSS & CO
1552 N Milwaukee Ave (60622-2284)
PHONE..................773 486-3900
Elaine Deveney, *Manager*
EMP: 15
SALES (corp-wide): 5.7B **Publicly Held**
SIC: 2325 2339 Jeans: men's, youths' & boys'; jeans: women's, misses' & juniors'
PA: Levi Strauss & Co.
1155 Battery St
San Francisco CA 94111
415 501-6000

(G-5212)
LEW-EL TOOL & MANUFACTURING CO
1935 N Leclaire Ave (60639-4422)
PHONE..................773 804-1133
Richard J Milburn, *President*
Maureen Milburn, *Corp Secy*
EMP: 15
SQ FT: 10,000
SALES (est): 2.9MM **Privately Held**
WEB: www.leweltool.com
SIC: 3493 3544 3496 3469 Cold formed springs; special dies & tools; miscellaneous fabricated wire products; metal stampings; wire springs

(G-5213)
LEXINGTON LEATHER GOODS CO
5414 W Roosevelt Rd (60644-1467)
PHONE..................773 287-5500
Camerina Torres, *Principal*
▲ **EMP:** 13
SALES (est): 3MM **Privately Held**
SIC: 2674 Bags: uncoated paper & multiwall

(G-5214)
LEYBOLD USA INC
25968 Network Pl (60673-1259)
PHONE..................724 327-5700
Lori Arola, *President*
EMP: 25
SALES (corp-wide): 10.5B **Privately Held**
SIC: 3821 Vacuum pumps, laboratory
HQ: Leybold Usa Inc.
5700 Mellon Rd
Export PA 15632
724 327-5700

(G-5215)
LI CHOU METALS INC
2150b S Archer Ave (60616-1514)
PHONE..................312 451-4834
David Liang, *President*
Ruiqiu Liang, *Manager*
EMP: 2
SALES (est): 364.1K **Privately Held**
SIC: 3569 Baling machines, for scrap metal, paper or similar material

(G-5216)
LIBAERTY LLC
1343 W Irving Park Rd (60613-8328)
PHONE..................312 330-2767
Tobias Pagel, *Manager*
EMP: 1
SALES: 450K **Privately Held**
SIC: 2339 Women's & misses' athletic clothing & sportswear

(G-5217)
LIBATION CONTAINER INC
4519 N Mozart St (60625-3816)
PHONE..................312 636-7206
Lawrence Brown, *President*
Cynthia Hing, *Vice Pres*
Cynthia Hing Brown, *Admin Sec*
EMP: 9 **EST:** 2010
SALES (est): 1.1MM **Privately Held**
SIC: 3221 3229 5085 Bottles for packing, bottling & canning: glass; glassware, art or decorative; glass bottles

(G-5218)
LIBERTY TIRE RECYCLING LLC
2044 N Dominick St (60614-3006)
PHONE..................773 871-6360
Ken Lakin, *Principal*
Mario Aguirre, *Info Tech Mgr*
EMP: 8 **Privately Held**

SIC: **3011** 5014 4953 Tires & inner tubes; tires & tubes; recycling, waste materials
HQ: Liberty Tire Services, Llc
600 River Ave Ste 3
Pittsburgh PA 15212
412 562-1700

(G-5219)
LIDERS LLC
Also Called: Celectiv
155 N Wacker Dr Ste 4250 (60606-1750)
P.O. Box B, Princeton (61356-9833)
PHONE..................................312 873-1112
Gregory Carrott, *CEO*
Lou Walker, *Vice Pres*
Thomas Fitzpatrick, *Director*
Sheena Iyengar, *Director*
Mark Schulz, *Director*
EMP: 7
SQ FT: 3,000
SALES: 1MM **Privately Held**
SIC: 7372 Business oriented computer software

(G-5220)
LIGHT OF MINE LLC
Also Called: Lom
401 N Michigan Ave # 1200 (60611-4255)
PHONE..................................312 840-8570
Suzette E Webb,
EMP: 3
SALES (est): 303.8K **Privately Held**
SIC: 3671 3711 3672 3625 Cathode ray tubes, including rebuilt; ambulances (motor vehicles), assembly of; circuit boards, television & radio printed; industrial electrical relays & switches

(G-5221)
LIGHTHOUSE MARKETING INC (PA)
343 W Erie St Ste 320 (60654-5735)
PHONE..................................949 542-4558
Jon Horowitz, *CEO*
Bob McGeeney, *President*
Fred Bucher, *Vice Pres*
Steve Embree, *Vice Pres*
Lou Gervolino, *Vice Pres*
EMP: 5
SALES (est): 2MM **Privately Held**
SIC: 3634 Electric household cooking appliances

(G-5222)
LIGHTITECH LLC
200 W Superior St Ste 400 (60654-3556)
PHONE..................................847 910-4177
Patricia N Harada,
EMP: 1
SALES (est): 225K **Privately Held**
SIC: 1731 3648 Energy management controls; lighting equipment

(G-5223)
LIMITLESS COFFEE LLC
Also Called: Limitless Sparkling
676 N Kingsbury St # 402 (60654-8100)
PHONE..................................630 779-3778
Matthew Matros, *CEO*
EMP: 40 EST: 2016
SALES (est): 2.7MM **Publicly Held**
SIC: 2095 Coffee extracts
PA: Keurig Dr Pepper Inc.
53 South Ave
Burlington MA 01803

(G-5224)
LINCOLN BARK LLC
858 W Armitage Ave 240 (60614-4383)
PHONE..................................800 428-4027
Bobbye Cochran,
EMP: 3
SALES (est): 196.6K **Privately Held**
SIC: 2047 Dog food

(G-5225)
LINCOLN SQUARE PRINTING
4607 N Western Ave Fl 1 (60625-2022)
PHONE..................................773 334-9030
Hazem Beia, *Partner*
EMP: 3
SALES (est): 371.6K **Privately Held**
SIC: 2752 Commercial printing, offset

(G-5226)
LINDA LEVINSON DESIGNS INC
111 E Oak St 3 (60611-1202)
PHONE..................................312 951-6943
Linda Levinson, *President*
EMP: 4
SQ FT: 2,500
SALES (est): 369.4K **Privately Held**
SIC: 3965 2396 Buckles & buckle parts; automotive & apparel trimmings

(G-5227)
LINE OF ADVANCE NFP
2126 W Armitage Ave Apt 3 (60647-4594)
PHONE..................................312 768-0043
Matt Marcus, *Admin Sec*
EMP: 3
SALES: 0 **Privately Held**
SIC: 2741 Miscellaneous publishing

(G-5228)
LINEAR SOLUTIONS INC
1727 S Ind Ave Apt 211 (60616)
PHONE..................................724 426-6384
Patrick Fay, *President*
EMP: 3
SQ FT: 2,400
SALES (est): 326K **Privately Held**
SIC: 3644 Electric conduits & fittings

(G-5229)
LINK TOOLS INTL (USA) INC
2440 N Lakeview Ave (60614-2872)
PHONE..................................773 549-3000
▲ **EMP:** 5
SALES (est): 596.6K **Privately Held**
SIC: 3423 3546 Mfg Hand Tools

(G-5230)
LINKEDHEALTH SOLUTIONS
700 N Green St (60642-5996)
PHONE..................................312 600-6684
Lawrence Miller, *CEO*
EMP: 15
SALES (est): 681.5K **Privately Held**
SIC: 7372 Prepackaged software

(G-5231)
LINN WEST PAPER COMPANY
4649 N Magnolia Ave (60640-4940)
PHONE..................................773 561-3839
Doug Scott, *Chairman*
EMP: 2 EST: 2008
SALES (est): 219.1K **Privately Held**
SIC: 2679 Paperboard products, converted

(G-5232)
LINX ENTERPRISES LLC
5051 S Forrestville Ave (60615-2428)
P.O. Box 437404 (60643-7311)
PHONE..................................224 409-2206
Asia Taylor,
EMP: 3
SALES (est): 73.4K **Privately Held**
SIC: 7389 7812 7929 7336 Music recording producer; motion picture & video production; music video production; motion picture production & distribution; television; entertainers & entertainment groups; commercial art & graphic design; cakes, bakery: except frozen; music distribution apparatus

(G-5233)
LINX GLOBAL MFG LLC
4809 N Ravenswood Ave (60640-4495)
PHONE..................................847 910-5303
Alan Rosenfield, *Mng Member*
Lindsey Rosenfield,
EMP: 8
SQ FT: 2,600
SALES (est): 1.1MM **Privately Held**
SIC: 5063 3599 Electrical supplies; machine & other job shop work

(G-5234)
LIQUIDFIRE
8554 W Rascher Ave Apt 2n (60656-1321)
PHONE..................................312 376-7448
Kim Sykes, *Owner*
EMP: 8
SALES (est): 433.5K **Privately Held**
SIC: 7372 Prepackaged software

(G-5235)
LITETRONICS TECHNOLOGIES INC
Also Called: Life Tronics International
6969 W 73rd St (60638-6025)
PHONE..................................708 333-6707
Robert C Sorensen, *President*
Thomas Hendrickson, *Vice Pres*
EMP: 6
SQ FT: 30,000
SALES (est): 897.6K **Privately Held**
SIC: 3648 Lighting equipment

(G-5236)
LITHUANIAN CATHOLIC PRESS
Also Called: DRAUGAS PUBLISHING
4545 W 63rd St (60629-5532)
PHONE..................................773 585-9500
Marian Remys, *President*
Valentine Krumplis, *Vice Pres*
EMP: 20
SQ FT: 2,000
SALES (est): 647.1K **Privately Held**
SIC: 2711 2791 2759 2752 Newspapers: publishing only, not printed on site; typesetting; commercial printing; commercial printing, lithographic; periodicals

(G-5237)
LITHUANIAN PRESS INC
2711 W 71st St (60629-2005)
PHONE..................................773 776-3399
Domas Adomaitis, *President*
Edmund Jasiunas, *President*
Vyt Radcius, *Principal*
EMP: 3
SALES (est): 55.3K **Privately Held**
SIC: 2721 Magazines: publishing only, not printed on site; periodicals: publishing only

(G-5238)
LITTELFUSE INC (PA)
8755 W Higgins Rd Ste 500 (60631-2701)
PHONE..................................773 628-1000
Gordon Hunter, *Ch of Bd*
David W Heinzmann, *President*
G Lesperance, *Managing Dir*
Tim Micun, *Business Mgr*
Matthew J Cole, *Senior VP*
▲ **EMP:** 700
SALES: 1.5B **Publicly Held**
WEB: www.littelfuse.com
SIC: 3613 3679 Fuses & fuse equipment; electronic circuits

(G-5239)
LITTELFUSE INC
8755 W Higgins Rd Ste 300 (60631-4016)
PHONE..................................773 628-1000
Howard B Witt, *President*
EMP: 20
SALES (corp-wide): 1.5B **Publicly Held**
SIC: 3625 Control circuit relays, industrial; electric controls & control accessories, industrial; relays, for electronic use
PA: Littelfuse, Inc.
8755 W Higgins Rd Ste 500
Chicago IL 60631
773 628-1000

(G-5240)
LIV LABS INC
5516 S Everett Ave 2nd (60637-5400)
PHONE..................................630 373-1471
Melody A Roberts, *CEO*
Carly Price, *Ch of Bd*
Tad Simons, *Ch of Bd*
EMP: 4
SALES (est): 168.5K **Privately Held**
SIC: 3999 Manufacturing industries

(G-5241)
LIVE DAILY LLC
2627 W Lunt Ave (60645-3216)
PHONE..................................312 286-6706
EMP: 4
SALES (est): 201.6K **Privately Held**
SIC: 2711 Newspapers-Publishing/Printing

(G-5242)
LIVEONE INC
333 N Michigan Ave # 2800 (60601-3901)
PHONE..................................312 282-2320
Jimmy Chamberlin, *CEO*
Timothy C Ganschow, *President*
EMP: 8
SALES (est): 916.8K **Privately Held**
SIC: 3823 Digital displays of process variables

(G-5243)
LKQ CORPORATION (PA)
500 W Madison St Ste 2800 (60661-2506)
PHONE..................................312 621-1950
Joseph M Holsten, *Ch of Bd*
Dominick P Zarcone, *President*
Charles Black, *General Mgr*
Daryl Masters, *District Mgr*
Ashley T Brooks, *Senior VP*
EMP: 114
SALES: 12.5B **Publicly Held**
WEB: www.lkqcorp.com
SIC: 5093 5015 3714 Automotive wrecking for scrap; motor vehicle parts, used; automotive parts & supplies, used; motor vehicle parts & accessories

(G-5244)
LL DISPLAY GROUP LTD
5414 W Roosevelt Rd B (60644-1467)
PHONE..................................847 982-0231
Scott Durham, *Vice Pres*
EMP: 35
SALES (est): 7.2MM **Privately Held**
SIC: 2542 Partitions & fixtures, except wood

(G-5245)
LLOYD M HUGHES ENTERPRISES INC
Also Called: Laundryworld
6331 S Martin L King Dr (60637-3114)
PHONE..................................773 363-6331
Lloyd M Hughes, *President*
EMP: 6
SQ FT: 6,250
SALES (est): 492.2K **Privately Held**
SIC: 7215 7389 2329 Laundry, coin-operated; interior decorating; athletic (warmup, sweat & jogging) suits: men's & boys'

(G-5246)
LMNO TECHNOLOGIES LLC
1720 S Michigan Ave # 25 (60616-1465)
PHONE..................................773 418-2875
Joshua Horvath, *Principal*
EMP: 3
SALES (est): 145.9K **Privately Held**
WEB: www.lmnotech.com
SIC: 3652 Pre-recorded records & tapes

(G-5247)
LMS INNOVATIONS INC
Also Called: Work Song Productions
2734 W Leland Ave Apt 3 (60625-3792)
PHONE..................................312 613-2345
Laura St John, *President*
Marlon St John, *Vice Pres*
EMP: 3 EST: 2016
SALES (est): 89.2K **Privately Held**
SIC: 2731 2741 8299 8748 Textbooks: publishing only, not printed on site; music books: publishing only, not printed on site; educational services; educational consultant; educational aids & electronic training materials

(G-5248)
LOCUSVIEW SOLUTIONS INC
626 W Randolph St (60661-2207)
PHONE..................................312 548-3848
Alicia Farag, *President*
Larissa Gonzales, *Accountant*
Justin Beynon, *Manager*
EMP: 30 EST: 2014
SALES (est): 3.8MM **Privately Held**
SIC: 3663 8713 7389 7371 ; surveying services; industrial & commercial equipment inspection service; computer software development & applications
PA: Nortecview Ltd
2 Hatidhar
Raanana 43665

Chicago - Cook County (G-5249)

(G-5249)
LOGAN SQUARE ALUMINUM SUP INC
Also Called: Remodeler's Supply Center
2622 N Pulaski Rd (60639-2118)
PHONE..................773 278-3600
Chuck Liszka, *Branch Mgr*
EMP: 170
SALES (corp-wide): 113MM **Privately Held**
SIC: 3442 Window & door frames; screen & storm doors & windows; metal doors
PA: Logan Square Aluminum Supply, Inc.
2500 N Pulaski Rd
Chicago IL 60639
773 235-2500

(G-5250)
LOGICGATE INC
320 W Ohio St Ste 5e (60654-7816)
PHONE..................312 279-2775
Matthew Kunkel, *CEO*
Jonathan Siegler, *COO*
Kaitlyn Martin, *Accounts Exec*
Andrew Rice, *Accounts Exec*
Daniel Hartman, *Executive*
EMP: 102
SALES (est): 1.1MM **Privately Held**
SIC: 7371 7372 7379 8748 Computer software development; business oriented computer software; computer related consulting services; business consulting

(G-5251)
LOGOSKIRT CORPORATION
4500 W 46th St (60632-4359)
PHONE..................773 584-7300
Janice A Murphy, *President*
Todd Peterson, *Vice Pres*
EMP: 15
SALES (est): 113.1K **Privately Held**
SIC: 2391 2591 2392 Curtains & draperies; drapery hardware & blinds & shades; household furnishings

(G-5252)
LOKMAN ENTERPRISES INC
7240 N Ridge Blvd Apt 102 (60645-2039)
PHONE..................773 654-0525
Lokman Hossain, *CEO*
R Khan, *Treasurer*
B Khan, *Admin Sec*
EMP: 4 **EST:** 2014
SALES (est): 50K **Privately Held**
SIC: 2048 7389 Poultry feeds;

(G-5253)
LOMBARD ARCHTCTRAL PRCAST PDTS
4245 W 123rd St (60803-1805)
PHONE..................708 389-1060
George E Lombard, *President*
Floyd Page, *Exec VP*
John Lombard, *Vice Pres*
EMP: 40
SQ FT: 50,000
SALES (est): 313.9K
SALES (corp-wide): 784.8K **Privately Held**
SIC: 3272 1791 Concrete products, precast; precast concrete structural framing or panels, placing of
PA: The Lombard Investment Company
4245 W 123rd St
Alsip IL 60803
708 389-1060

(G-5254)
LONELYBRAND LLC (PA)
118 N Kinzie St (60654-4508)
PHONE..................312 880-7506
Nicholas Kinports, *Founder*
EMP: 4
SALES (est): 1.8MM **Privately Held**
SIC: 7372 Business oriented computer software

(G-5255)
LONG VIEW PUBLISHING CO INC
Also Called: People's Weekly World
3339 S Halsted St Ste 4 (60608-6883)
PHONE..................773 446-9920
Barb Russum, *Branch Mgr*
EMP: 18
SALES (corp-wide): 3.9MM **Privately Held**
SIC: 2711 Newspapers, publishing & printing
PA: Long View Publishing Co Inc
235 W 23rd St Fl 4
New York NY
212 924-2523

(G-5256)
LOOP ATTACHMENT CO
1509 N Hudson Ave Apt 3 (60610-5833)
PHONE..................847 922-0642
Evan J Derman, *COO*
Evan Derman, *COO*
Christopher Peterson, *Ch Credit Ofcr*
Daniel Selden, *CTO*
▲ **EMP:** 3
SALES (est): 245.9K **Privately Held**
WEB: www.loopattachment.com
SIC: 3069 Molded rubber products

(G-5257)
LOOP AUTOMOTIVE LLC
303 W Ohio St Apt 2609 (60654-7971)
PHONE..................847 912-9090
Konstantin Selikhov,
EMP: 30
SALES (est): 1.1MM **Privately Held**
SIC: 3089 5013 Automotive parts, plastic; automotive supplies & parts

(G-5258)
LOPEZ PLUMBING SYSTEMS INC
5816 S Claremont Ave (60636)
PHONE..................773 424-8225
Josue Lopez, *President*
EMP: 5 **EST:** 2010
SALES (est): 700K **Privately Held**
WEB: www.lopezplumbingsystems.com
SIC: 3822 Water heater controls

(G-5259)
LORAINES LOGISTICS LLC
Also Called: Www.loraineslogisticsllc.com
1014 N Mason Ave 2 (60651-2554)
PHONE..................800 839-6943
Deangelo Woods, *Owner*
EMP: 4
SALES: 120K **Privately Held**
SIC: 3799 Transportation equipment

(G-5260)
LOS ANGLES TMES CMMNCTIONS LLC
Also Called: Los Angeles Times
435 N Michigan Ave Fl 2 (60611-4067)
PHONE..................312 467-4670
EMP: 3
SALES (corp-wide): 769.2MM **Privately Held**
SIC: 2711 Newspaper
PA: Los Angeles Times Communications, Llc
2300 E Imperial Hwy
El Segundo CA 90245
213 237-5000

(G-5261)
LOS GAMAS INC
3333 W Armitage Ave (60647-3717)
PHONE..................872 829-3514
Alejandro Gama, *President*
EMP: 6
SALES: 580K **Privately Held**
SIC: 2099 Tortillas, fresh or refrigerated

(G-5262)
LOS MANGOS
Also Called: Los Mangos I
3058 S Avers Ave (60623-4542)
PHONE..................773 542-1522
EMP: 7
SALES (est): 368.1K **Privately Held**
SIC: 2024 Ice cream, bulk

(G-5263)
LOS PRIMOS PALLETS INC
2013 W Ferdinand St (60612-1549)
PHONE..................773 418-3584
Juan Rodriguez, *President*
EMP: 5 **EST:** 2009
SALES (est): 334.5K **Privately Held**
SIC: 2448 Pallets, wood

(G-5264)
LOSO TRUCKING INC
55 E Monroe St Ste 3800 (60603-6030)
PHONE..................312 601-2231
Ronald Harris, *President*
EMP: 3
SALES (est): 138.9K **Privately Held**
SIC: 3537 Trucks, tractors, loaders, carriers & similar equipment

(G-5265)
LOTTOBOT LLC
1116 W Hubbard St Apt 4e (60642-5879)
PHONE..................773 909-6656
Aleksandar Videnovic, *Mng Member*
EMP: 5
SALES: 250K **Privately Held**
SIC: 7372 4215 Application computer software; courier services, except by air

(G-5266)
LOUIS MESKAN ALUMINUM & BRASS
2000 N Parkside Ave (60639-2925)
PHONE..................773 637-8236
Dave Meskan, *President*
EMP: 3
SALES (est): 150K **Privately Held**
SIC: 3366 Copper foundries

(G-5267)
LOUIS MESKAN BRASS FOUNDRY INC
Also Called: Meskan Foundry
2007 N Major Ave (60639-2951)
PHONE..................773 237-7662
David Meskan, *President*
Don Meskan, *General Mgr*
Allen Meskan, *Exec VP*
Joe Schrepfer, *Plant Mgr*
Paul Kuldanek, *Manager*
EMP: 102 **EST:** 1907
SQ FT: 90,000
SALES: 17.7MM **Privately Held**
WEB: www.meskan.com
SIC: 3366 3365 Castings (except die); brass; aluminum & aluminum-based alloy castings

(G-5268)
LOVE JOURNEY INC
8121 S Colfax Ave (60617-1379)
PHONE..................773 447-5591
Janine Ingram, *CEO*
EMP: 3 **EST:** 2016
SALES (est): 83.9K **Privately Held**
SIC: 3999 7389 Education aids, devices & supplies;

(G-5269)
LOYOLA PRESS
3441 N Ashland Ave (60657-1397)
PHONE..................800 621-1008
Teresa Locke, *President*
Paul Campbell, *Publisher*
Cathy Joyce, *Editor*
Mark Knapke, *Editor*
Peggy Kulling, *Editor*
EMP: 31
SALES: 16.9MM **Privately Held**
SIC: 2741 Miscellaneous publishing

(G-5270)
LPI WORLDWIDE INC
4821 S Aberdeen St (60609-4312)
PHONE..................773 826-8600
Norman H Wexler, *President*
EMP: 5
SALES (est): 521.2K **Privately Held**
SIC: 3441 Fabricated structural metal

(G-5271)
LPZ INC
2919 S Western Ave (60608-5221)
PHONE..................773 579-6120
Rafael Lopez, *President*
Jesus Lopez, *Admin Sec*
EMP: 3
SALES (est): 208.8K **Privately Held**
SIC: 2032 Tortillas: packaged in cans, jars etc.

(G-5272)
LSC COMMUNICATIONS INC (PA)
191 N Wacker Dr Ste 1400 (60606-1921)
PHONE..................773 272-9200
Thomas J Quinlan III, *Ch of Bd*
Ernesto Manzon, *Regional Mgr*
Ridge Clyde, *District Mgr*
John Branstad, *Vice Pres*
Peter Conway, *Vice Pres*
EMP: 189
SALES: 3.3B **Publicly Held**
SIC: 2732 2721 2621 Book printing; magazines: publishing & printing; catalog, magazine & newsprint papers

(G-5273)
LSC COMMUNICATIONS MM LLC
191 N Wacker Dr Ste 1400 (60606-1921)
PHONE..................815 844-1819
Rick Stone,
EMP: 14 **EST:** 2016
SALES (est): 2.1MM
SALES (corp-wide): 3.3B **Publicly Held**
SIC: 2732 2721 2621 Book printing; magazines: publishing & printing; catalog, magazine & newsprint papers
PA: Lsc Communications, Inc.
191 N Wacker Dr Ste 1400
Chicago IL 60606
773 272-9200

(G-5274)
LSC COMMUNICATIONS US LLC (HQ)
191 N Wacker Dr Ste 1400 (60606-1921)
PHONE..................844 572-5720
Christopher Berardelli, *Vice Pres*
Debra Lang, *Vice Pres*
Kehinde Noah, *Vice Pres*
Thomas J Quinlan III,
EMP: 263
SALES (est): 1.1B
SALES (corp-wide): 3.3B **Publicly Held**
SIC: 2732 2721 2621 Book printing; magazines: publishing & printing; catalog, magazine & newsprint papers
PA: Lsc Communications, Inc.
191 N Wacker Dr Ste 1400
Chicago IL 60606
773 272-9200

(G-5275)
LSK IMPORT
100 S Wacker Dr Ste 700 (60606-4028)
PHONE..................847 342-8447
Steve Kaplan, *Principal*
▲ **EMP:** 2
SALES (est): 240.3K **Privately Held**
SIC: 2752 Commercial printing, lithographic

(G-5276)
LUBY PUBLISHING INC
Also Called: Billiards Digest
55 E Jackson Blvd Ste 401 (60604-4307)
PHONE..................312 341-1110
Keith Hamilton, *President*
Barb Peltz, *Publisher*
Gianmarc Manzione, *Chief*
Laura Vinci, *Prdtn Mgr*
Kim Levandowski, *Manager*
EMP: 17 **EST:** 1913
SQ FT: 8,000
SALES (est): 3MM **Privately Held**
SIC: 2721 2741 Trade journals: publishing only, not printed on site; directories: publishing only, not printed on site

(G-5277)
LUCKSFOOD
1109 W Argyle St (60640-3609)
PHONE..................773 878-7778
EMP: 4
SALES (est): 197.2K **Privately Held**
SIC: 2051 Mfg Bread/Related Products

(G-5278)
LUDIS FOODS ADAMS INC
23 E Adams St (60603-5603)
PHONE..................312 939-2877
EMP: 3
SALES (est): 81K **Privately Held**
SIC: 2099 Mfg Food Preparations

GEOGRAPHIC SECTION

Chicago - Cook County (G-5307)

(G-5279)
LUKE GRAPHICS INC
6000 N Northwest Hwy (60631-2518)
P.O. Box 31816 (60631-0816)
PHONE.................................773 775-6733
Frances Lukasik, *President*
Kim Irving, *Assistant VP*
▲ **EMP:** 11
SQ FT: 3,000
SALES (est): 1.2MM **Privately Held**
SIC: 2752 Commercial printing, offset

(G-5280)
LULUS
2401 S Ridgeway Ave (60623-3833)
PHONE.................................773 865-8978
Erika Lechuga, *Owner*
EMP: 4
SALES (est): 309.9K **Privately Held**
SIC: 3421 Table & food cutlery, including butchers'

(G-5281)
LUMENART LTD
Also Called: Lumenart Lighting Solutions
3333 W 47th St (60632-2940)
PHONE.................................773 254-0744
Derrick Gurski, *President*
▲ **EMP:** 5
SALES (est): 1.3MM **Privately Held**
WEB: www.lumenartltd.com
SIC: 5063 3645 Lighting fixtures; residential lighting fixtures

(G-5282)
LUMENTUM OPERATIONS LLC
33186 Collection Ctr Dr (60693-0001)
PHONE.................................408 546-5483
EMP: 3
SALES (corp-wide): 1.5B **Publicly Held**
SIC: 3669 8748 3999 Emergency alarms; telecommunications consultant; atomizers, toiletry
HQ: Lumentum Operations Llc
1001 Ridder Park Dr
San Jose CA 95131
408 546-5483

(G-5283)
LUMINA INC
512 N Racine Ave (60642-5842)
P.O. Box 47146 (60647-0003)
PHONE.................................312 829-8970
Rocco Saliano, *President*
EMP: 2
SQ FT: 200
SALES (est): 276.6K **Privately Held**
SIC: 2899 Fireworks

(G-5284)
LUMINAID LAB LLC
211 W Wacker Dr (60606-1217)
PHONE.................................312 600-8997
Andrea Sreshta,
▲ **EMP:** 5
SALES (est): 845.7K **Privately Held**
SIC: 3674 Light emitting diodes

(G-5285)
LUMINESCENCE MEDIA GROUP NFP
3740 N Lake Shore Dr (60613-4237)
PHONE.................................312 602-3302
Mitchell Lieber, *Exec Dir*
EMP: 4
SALES: 120K **Privately Held**
SIC: 3999 Education aids, devices & supplies

(G-5286)
LUNA MEDICAL INC
1057 W Grand Ave Ste 1 (60642-6600)
PHONE.................................800 380-4379
Marianne Luh, *CEO*
Curtis Bumgarner, *COO*
EMP: 12
SALES (est): 1.2MM **Privately Held**
SIC: 2389 Disposable garments & accessories

(G-5287)
LUSTER PRODUCTS INC (PA)
1104 W 43rd St (60609-3342)
PHONE.................................773 579-1800
Blondell Luster, *Ch of Bd*
Jory Luster, *President*
Fred Luster II, *Vice Pres*
Sonia Luster, *Vice Pres*
Sonja Luster, *Admin Sec*
◆ **EMP:** 401 **EST:** 1955
SQ FT: 200,000
SALES (est): 82.8K **Privately Held**
WEB: www.lusterproducts.com
SIC: 2844 Hair preparations, including shampoos; shampoos, rinses, conditioners: hair

(G-5288)
LUXURY MBL & GRAN DESIGN INC
3206 N Kilpatrick Ave (60641-4421)
PHONE.................................773 656-2125
Beatriz Trigueros, *President*
EMP: 5
SQ FT: 5,000
SALES (est): 610.3K **Privately Held**
WEB: www.luxurymarblegranitedesign.com
SIC: 3281 Cut stone & stone products

(G-5289)
LV VENTURES INC (PA)
440 S La Salle St (60605-1028)
PHONE.................................312 993-1800
William Farley, *President*
Martin Pajor, *Vice Pres*
Todd Sluzas, *CFO*
EMP: 5 **EST:** 1982
SALES (est): 31.5MM **Privately Held**
SIC: 3544 3568 3519 Special dies, tools, jigs & fixtures; railroad car journal bearings; diesel, semi-diesel or duel-fuel engines, including marine

(G-5290)
LV VENTURES INC
Farley Indstries/ Frt Ogf Loom
440 S La Salle St (60605-1028)
PHONE.................................312 993-1758
Patty McDonald, *Manager*
EMP: 30
SALES (corp-wide): 31.5MM **Privately Held**
SIC: 3544 6799 3567 Special dies, tools, jigs & fixtures; investors; electrical furnaces, ovens & heating devices, exc. induction
PA: Lv Ventures, Inc.
440 S La Salle St
Chicago IL 60605
312 993-1800

(G-5291)
LX/JT INTERMEDIATE HOLDINGS (PA)
Also Called: Bevolution Group
4401 S Oakley Ave (60609-3020)
PHONE.................................773 369-2652
Samir Lteif, *CEO*
Alex Guiva, *Chairman*
David Prill, *CFO*
EMP: 0
SALES: 2MM **Privately Held**
SIC: 6719 2037 Investment holding companies, except banks; fruit juice concentrates, frozen

(G-5292)
LYKO WOODWORKING & CNSTR
4157 N Elston Ave (60618-2107)
PHONE.................................773 583-4561
Ireneusz Lyko, *President*
EMP: 6
SQ FT: 2,844
SALES (est): 744.7K **Privately Held**
SIC: 2434 1751 2431 Wood kitchen cabinets; carpentry work; millwork

(G-5293)
LYON & HEALY HARPS INC
168 N Ogden Ave (60607-1465)
PHONE.................................312 786-1881
Victor Salvi, *President*
▲ **EMP:** 3
SALES (est): 552.5K **Privately Held**
SIC: 3931 Harps & parts

(G-5294)
LYON & HEALY HOLDING CORP (HQ)
168 N Ogden Ave (60607-1412)
PHONE.................................312 786-1881
Antonio Forero, *Ch of Bd*
Ronald Koltz, *CFO*
Natalie Bilik, *Sales Mgr*
▲ **EMP:** 21
SQ FT: 65,000
SALES (est): 12.8MM
SALES (corp-wide): 392.5K **Privately Held**
WEB: www.lyonhealy.com
SIC: 3931 5736 Harps & parts; string instruments
PA: L.A.M. - Les Arts Mecaniques Sa
Rue De La Sagne 17
Ste-Croix VD
223 204-242

(G-5295)
M & G GRAPHICS INC
3500 W 38th St (60632-3306)
PHONE.................................773 247-1596
Josephine Meyer, *President*
Bob Meyer Jr, *Vice Pres*
John Weiss, *Prdtn Mgr*
Donna Calandriello, *Purch Mgr*
Brian Parshall, *Accounts Mgr*
EMP: 22
SQ FT: 40,000
SALES (est): 4.1MM **Privately Held**
SIC: 2759 2796 2789 2741 Commercial printing; color separations for printing; bookbinding & related work; miscellaneous publishing

(G-5296)
M & I HEATING AND COOLING INC
6405 N Campbell Ave (60645-5313)
PHONE.................................773 743-7073
Musan Imamovic, *Owner*
Bahrija Imamovic, *Office Mgr*
Elzana Imamovic, *Admin Sec*
EMP: 4
SALES (est): 530.2K **Privately Held**
SIC: 3585 Parts for heating, cooling & refrigerating equipment

(G-5297)
M & S INDUSTRIAL CO INC
4334 W Division St (60651-1713)
PHONE.................................773 252-1616
Andrew Metelski, *President*
Stanley Nowak, *Vice Pres*
Andrew Sniezynski, *Vice Pres*
John Biernat, *Treasurer*
Alexandra Spalek, *Admin Sec*
EMP: 25
SQ FT: 16,000
SALES (est): 1.5MM **Privately Held**
SIC: 3599 Machine shop, jobbing & repair

(G-5298)
M AND M BOX PARTITION CO
4141 W Grand Ave (60651-1804)
PHONE.................................773 276-8400
Joseph A Mariella, *CEO*
Catherine Mariella, *President*
EMP: 35
SQ FT: 50,000
SALES: 5MM **Privately Held**
WEB: www.mmboxpartitions.com
SIC: 2653 Boxes, corrugated: made from purchased materials

(G-5299)
M B JEWELERS INC
Also Called: Royal Casting
29 E Madison St Ste 1835 (60602-4865)
PHONE.................................312 853-3490
Yacoub Boyrazian, *President*
Michael Boyrazian, *Corp Secy*
EMP: 2
SALES (est): 275K **Privately Held**
SIC: 3915 3911 Jewelers' castings; jewel cutting, drilling, polishing, recutting or setting; jewelry, precious metal

(G-5300)
M G M DISPLAYS INC
4956 S Monitor Ave (60638-1544)
PHONE.................................708 594-3699
Mark Perrone, *President*
Milt Plude, *Vice Pres*
EMP: 3
SQ FT: 25,000
SALES (est): 1MM **Privately Held**
SIC: 3993 7319 Advertising artwork; displays & cutouts, window & lobby; display advertising service

(G-5301)
M INC
Also Called: Mattaliano Furniture
205 W Wacker Dr Ste 307 (60606-1487)
PHONE.................................312 853-0512
Darcy Bonner, *President*
EMP: 7 **EST:** 1938
SALES (est): 941.3K **Privately Held**
WEB: www.mattaliano.com
SIC: 2511 Wood household furniture

(G-5302)
M K ADVANTAGE INC
1055 W Bryn Mawr Ave F216 (60660-4691)
PHONE.................................773 902-5272
Christopher Schaf, *President*
EMP: 12
SALES (est): 871.1K **Privately Held**
SIC: 7379 3695 Computer related consulting services; computer software tape & disks: blank, rigid & floppy

(G-5303)
M MAURITZON & COMPANY INC
3939 W Belden Ave (60647-2207)
PHONE.................................773 235-6000
Steven Karlin, *President*
Charles Karlin, *Principal*
▲ **EMP:** 50
SQ FT: 110,000
SALES (est): 9.6MM **Privately Held**
SIC: 2394 Tarpaulins, fabric: made from purchased materials

(G-5304)
M PUTTERMAN & CO LLC (HQ)
815 W Van Buren St # 550 (60607-3566)
PHONE.................................773 927-4120
Doug Roth, *Regl Sales Mgr*
Zack Jarrell, *Marketing Staff*
Alan Berman,
Joan Koza,
Edward Reicin,
◆ **EMP:** 63
SQ FT: 52,000
SALES (est): 13.3MM **Privately Held**
WEB: www.puttermanathletics.com
SIC: 3089 2394 Plastic processing; canvas & related products

(G-5305)
M WELLS PRINTING CO
329 W 18th St Ste 502 (60616-1121)
PHONE.................................312 455-0400
Michael E Wells, *Owner*
EMP: 6
SQ FT: 3,500
SALES (est): 890K **Privately Held**
SIC: 2759 8742 2761 2752 Promotional printing; marketing consulting services; manifold business forms; commercial printing, lithographic; die-cut paper & board; automotive & apparel trimmings

(G-5306)
M&J HAULING INC
2048 W Hubbard St (60612-1610)
PHONE.................................312 342-6596
Marian Flasch, *President*
Micheal Stevens, *Vice Pres*
John Flasch, *Treasurer*
EMP: 4
SALES: 340K **Privately Held**
SIC: 3537 Industrial trucks & tractors

(G-5307)
M&M RESTAURANT GROUP LLC
1463 W Leland Ave (60640-4627)
PHONE.................................773 253-5326
Matthew Keslar, *Mng Member*
EMP: 15
SALES: 480K **Privately Held**
SIC: 5812 7372 Caterers; application computer software

Chicago - Cook County (G-5308)

(G-5308)
MAB PHARMACY INC
2724 W Division St Ste A (60622-2841)
PHONE...................................773 342-5878
Mahendra T Amin, *President*
EMP: 4
SALES (est): 504.7K **Privately Held**
SIC: 2834 Pharmaceutical preparations

(G-5309)
MACHINE TOOL ACC & MFG CO
1915 W Fullerton Ave (60614-1915)
PHONE...................................773 489-0903
Tibor Halasz, *President*
EMP: 2 EST: 1967
SQ FT: 3,000
SALES (est): 302.9K **Privately Held**
WEB: www.mtachicago.com
SIC: 3545 3599 3498 3462 Boring machine attachments (machine tool accessories); machine shop, jobbing & repair; fabricated pipe & fittings; iron & steel forgings; bolts, nuts, rivets & washers; thread mills

(G-5310)
MADE BY HANDS INC
3501 N Southport Ave # 352 (60657-1475)
PHONE...................................773 761-4200
Ava Berry, *Co-President*
Dena Hirschberg, *Co-President*
EMP: 2
SALES (est): 226.4K **Privately Held**
SIC: 3944 5945 Craft & hobby kits & sets; hobby & craft supplies

(G-5311)
MADEMOISELLE INC
4200 W Schubert Ave (60639-2017)
P.O. Box 1708, Deerfield (60015-6011)
PHONE...................................773 394-4555
Scott Goldstein, *CEO*
EMP: 10 EST: 1930
SQ FT: 8,000
SALES: 1.3MM **Privately Held**
WEB: www.mademoiselleinc.com
SIC: 2353 2337 2339 Hats, trimmed: women's, misses' & children's; capes, except fur or rubber: women's, misses' & juniors'; collar & cuff sets: women's, misses' & juniors'; scarves, hoods, headbands, etc.: women's

(G-5312)
MADISON CAPITAL PARTNERS CORP (PA)
500 W Madison St Ste 3890 (60661-4593)
PHONE...................................312 277-0323
Larry W Gies, *President*
Aaron J Vangetson, *Vice Pres*
John E Udelhofen, *CFO*
George Nolen, *Director*
Kimberly Martiny, *Associate*
▲ EMP: 6
SQ FT: 6,000
SALES (est): 191.3MM **Privately Held**
SIC: 3542 8741 Machine tools, metal forming type; management services

(G-5313)
MADISON INDS HOLDINGS LLC (PA)
500 W Madison St Ste 3890 (60661-4593)
PHONE...................................312 277-0156
Larry W Gies, *President*
Daniel F Fitzgibbons, *Vice Pres*
John E Udelhofen, *Treasurer*
EMP: 0
SALES (est): 201.2MM **Privately Held**
SIC: 6719 5051 3443 3316 Investment holding companies, except banks; steel; fabricated plate work (boiler shop); cold finishing of steel shapes

(G-5314)
MAGAZINE PLUS
2445 N Clark St (60614-7777)
PHONE...................................773 281-4106
Mohammed Sultan, *Principal*
EMP: 5
SALES (est): 401.8K **Privately Held**
SIC: 2721 5993 Magazines: publishing & printing; tobacco stores & stands

(G-5315)
MAGIC SOLUTIONS INC
5455 N Sheridan Rd # 3809 (60640-1958)
PHONE...................................312 647-8688
Maksym Kolodii, *President*
EMP: 3
SALES (est): 103.6K **Privately Held**
SIC: 3965 Fasteners, buttons, needles & pins

(G-5316)
MAGID GLOVE SAFETY MFG CO LLC
1805 N Hamlin Ave (60647-4651)
PHONE...................................773 384-2070
EMP: 485
SALES (corp-wide): 162.5MM **Privately Held**
SIC: 3151 2381 Mfg & Whol Leather & Woven Work Gloves
PA: Magid Glove & Safety Manufacturing Co Llc
1300 Naperville Dr
Romeoville IL 60446
773 384-2070

(G-5317)
MAGNETIC SIGNS
4922 S Western Ave (60609-4742)
PHONE...................................773 476-6551
James Sommer, *Owner*
EMP: 6 EST: 2007
SALES (est): 508.6K **Privately Held**
SIC: 3993 Signs & advertising specialties

(G-5318)
MAGNUS SCREW PRODUCTS CO
1818 N Latrobe Ave (60639-4351)
PHONE...................................773 889-2344
Edward A Magnuski Jr, *President*
Terry Magnus, *Opers Mgr*
Terrence Magnuski, *Admin Sec*
EMP: 20
SQ FT: 9,000
SALES (est): 4.3MM **Privately Held**
WEB: www.magnusmachine.com
SIC: 3451 Screw machine products

(G-5319)
MAID O MIST LLC
3217 N Pulaski Rd (60641-4795)
PHONE...................................773 685-7300
Warren Alm,
◆ EMP: 50
SALES: 5MM **Privately Held**
SIC: 3585 Refrigeration & heating equipment

(G-5320)
MAKERS MARK DISTILLERY INC
222 Merchandise Mart Plz # 1600 (60654-4262)
PHONE...................................312 964-6999
EMP: 3
SALES (est): 113.2K **Privately Held**
SIC: 2085 Distilled & blended liquors

(G-5321)
MAKOWSKIS REAL SAUSAGE CO
2710 S Poplar Ave (60608-5909)
PHONE...................................312 842-5330
Nicole Makowski, *President*
EMP: 40 EST: 1919
SQ FT: 30,000
SALES (est): 6.4MM **Privately Held**
WEB: www.realsausage.com
SIC: 2013 Sausages from purchased meat; luncheon meat from purchased meat

(G-5322)
MALCA-AMIT NORTH AMERICA INC
5 S Wabash Ave Ste 1414 (60603-3093)
PHONE...................................312 346-1507
Suzanne Clark, *Manager*
EMP: 3
SALES (corp-wide): 46.9MM **Privately Held**
SIC: 3462 Armor plate, forged iron or steel
PA: Malca-Amit North America, Inc.
580 5th Ave Lbby 1
New York NY 10036
212 840-8330

(G-5323)
MALTHANDLINGCOM LLC
800 N Winthrop Ave S 2 (60660)
PHONE...................................773 888-7718
Marc Marashi, *Sales Staff*
Richard Riley, *Mng Member*
▲ EMP: 3 EST: 2012
SQ FT: 6,000
SALES (est): 778.9K **Privately Held**
SIC: 3523 Cleaning machines for fruits, grains & vegetables

(G-5324)
MALVAES SOLUTIONS INCORPORATED
4243 W Ogden Ave (60623-2931)
PHONE...................................773 823-1034
Jesse Malvaes, *Director*
EMP: 6
SALES (est): 276.9K **Privately Held**
SIC: 4953 2448 Recycling, waste materials; pallets, wood

(G-5325)
MAMAGREEN LLC (PA)
Also Called: Mamagreen Sstnble Otdoor Lxury
222 Merchandise Mart Plz 1519a (60654-1103)
PHONE...................................312 953-3557
Jon Bray, *Vice Pres*
Michael Hasenfang, *Manager*
Kristen Somerville, *Manager*
William Kruzel,
Justin Riegler,
EMP: 9
SALES (est): 2MM **Privately Held**
WEB: www.mamagreen.com
SIC: 2511 Wood household furniture

(G-5326)
MANHATTAN ISLAND
209 S Lasalle Ste 1200 (60604)
PHONE...................................312 762-5152
Dan Sullivan,
EMP: 3
SALES (corp-wide): 100K **Privately Held**
SIC: 2095 Roasted coffee
PA: Manhattan Island Coffee Roasters, Llc
64 Buckeye Rd
Glen Cove NY 11542
516 375-5821

(G-5327)
MANUFCTRERS CLRING HSE ILL INC (PA)
4875 N Elston Ave (60630-2551)
PHONE...................................773 545-6300
W Paul Nagel, *President*
William W Nagel, *Corp Secy*
EMP: 8
SQ FT: 4,000
SALES (est): 1MM **Privately Held**
SIC: 7322 7323 2731 Collection agency, except real estate; credit clearinghouse; books: publishing only

(G-5328)
MARANTHA WRLD RVVAL MINISTRIES (PA)
Also Called: Maranatha Christian Revival Ch
4301 W Diversey Ave (60639-2027)
PHONE...................................773 384-7717
Nahum Rosario, *Pastor*
Cynthia Rosario, *Exec Dir*
EMP: 1
SQ FT: 37,000
SALES (est): 901.3K **Privately Held**
SIC: 8661 2731 Christian Reformed Church; textbooks: publishing only, not printed on site

(G-5329)
MARCELLS PALLET INC (PA)
4221 W Ferdinand St (60624-1016)
PHONE...................................773 265-1200
Scott Lowell, *President*
EMP: 6
SALES (est): 912.4K **Privately Held**
SIC: 3537 Pallets, metal

(G-5330)
MARCO LIGHTING COMPONENTS INC (PA)
457 N Leavitt St (60612-1597)
PHONE...................................312 829-6900
Mario Salamone, *President*
Janet Salamone, *Corp Secy*
Vicki Vitez, *Asst Sec*
EMP: 14
SQ FT: 40,000
SALES (est): 1.8MM **Privately Held**
SIC: 3441 Fabricated structural metal

(G-5331)
MARENA MARENA TWO INC
665 W Sheridan Rd (60613-3877)
PHONE...................................773 327-0619
Marjorie M Noland, *President*
EMP: 6
SQ FT: 200
SALES (est): 810K **Privately Held**
SIC: 2339 Women's & misses' outerwear

(G-5332)
MARGIES BRANDS INC
6122 S Dorchester Ave (60637-2811)
PHONE...................................773 643-1417
Wilbur Reneau, *President*
Georgia Arnolds, *President*
Margie Reneau, *Chairman*
EMP: 27
SALES (est): 3.7MM **Privately Held**
SIC: 2033 2099 Jams, jellies & preserves: packaged in cans, jars, etc.; syrups

(G-5333)
MARIACHI MONUMENTAL DE MEXICO
4550 W 57th St (60629-5343)
PHONE...................................520 878-8688
EMP: 3
SALES (est): 118.1K **Privately Held**
SIC: 3272 Monuments & grave markers, except terrazo

(G-5334)
MARIAH MEDIA INC
444 N Michigan Ave # 3350 (60611-3903)
PHONE...................................312 222-1100
Lisa Glass, *Manager*
EMP: 8
SALES (corp-wide): 14.4MM **Privately Held**
SIC: 2721 Magazines: publishing only, not printed on site
PA: Mariah Media, Inc.
400 Market St
Santa Fe NM 87501
505 989-7100

(G-5335)
MARIEGOLD BAKE SHOPPE
5752 N California Ave (60659-4726)
PHONE...................................773 561-1978
Carmelita Bagtus, *Owner*
EMP: 5
SALES (est): 166.1K **Privately Held**
SIC: 5812 2051 Eating places; bakery: wholesale or wholesale/retail combined

(G-5336)
MARIES CUSTOM MADE CHOIR ROBES
3838 W Madison St (60624-2334)
PHONE...................................773 826-1214
Marie Pickett, *Owner*
EMP: 3
SQ FT: 5,000
SALES (est): 256.7K **Privately Held**
SIC: 2384 Robes & dressing gowns

(G-5337)
MARIETTA CORPORATION
Also Called: Cygnus D/B/A Marietta Chicago
340 E 138th St (60827-1828)
PHONE...................................773 816-5137
Rey Salvadore, *Manager*
EMP: 200 **Privately Held**
SIC: 2841 5122 5131 5139 Soap: granulated, liquid, cake, flaked or chip; toiletries; sewing accessories; shoe accessories; display equipment, except refrigerated; packaging & labeling services

GEOGRAPHIC SECTION

Chicago - Cook County (G-5361)

HQ: Marietta Corporation
37 Huntington St
Cortland NY 13045
607 753-6746

(G-5338)
MARIN SOFTWARE INCORPORATED
140 S Dearborn St 300a (60603-5204)
PHONE.................312 267-2083
Tal Nathan, *Senior VP*
Efrat Aharonovich, *Marketing Staff*
Chris Jetton, *Marketing Staff*
Adam Scott, *Director*
Anne Schoberth, *Account Dir*
EMP: 3 **Publicly Held**
SIC: 7372 Prepackaged software
PA: Marin Software Incorporated
123 Mission St Fl 27
San Francisco CA 94105

(G-5339)
MARK ANTHONY BREWING INC (DH)
Also Called: Mike's Hard Beverage Company
300 W Hubbard St Ste 301 (60654-8725)
PHONE.................312 202-3700
John Sacksteder, *President*
Anthony Von Mandl, *Admin Sec*
EMP: 7
SALES (est): 2.4MM
SALES (corp-wide): 73MM **Privately Held**
SIC: 2084 Wines
HQ: Mark Anthony Group Inc
887 Great Northern Way Suite 500
Vancouver BC V5T 4
888 394-1122

(G-5340)
MARKETING & TECHNOLOGY GROUP
Also Called: Mmt
1415 N Dayton St Ste 115 (60642-7033)
PHONE.................312 266-3311
Jim Franklin, *Ch of Bd*
Mark Lefens, *President*
▲ **EMP:** 21
SALES (est): 3.4MM **Privately Held**
SIC: 2721 Magazines: publishing only, not printed on site

(G-5341)
MARMON ENGINEERED COMPONENTS (DH)
181 W Madison St Fl 26 (60602-4510)
PHONE.................312 372-9500
Elwood Petchel, *President*
EMP: 6
SALES (est): 28MM
SALES (corp-wide): 327.2B **Publicly Held**
SIC: 3699 Electrical equipment & supplies

(G-5342)
MARMON GROUP LLC (DH)
Also Called: Pan American Screw Div
181 W Madison St Ste 2600 (60602-4504)
PHONE.................312 372-9500
Frank Ptak, *CEO*
▲ **EMP:** 3 **EST:** 1973
SQ FT: 1,000
SALES (est): 389MM
SALES (corp-wide): 327.2B **Publicly Held**
WEB: www.marmon.com
SIC: 3452 5072 Bolts, nuts, rivets & washers; bolts, nuts & screws
HQ: Union Tank Car Company
175 W Jackson Blvd # 2100
Chicago IL 60604
312 431-3111

(G-5343)
MARMON HOLDINGS INC (HQ)
181 W Madison St Ste 2600 (60602-4504)
PHONE.................312 372-9500
John Nichols, *Vice Ch Bd*
Frank Ptak, *President*
Thomas J Pritzker, *Chairman*
Robert W Webb, *Senior VP*
Robert K Lorch, *CFO*
◆ **EMP:** 75 **EST:** 1987
SQ FT: 33,000
SALES (est): 5.5B
SALES (corp-wide): 327.2B **Publicly Held**
SIC: 5051 3351 3743 4741 Metals service centers & offices; copper pipe; tubing, copper & copper alloy; wire, copper & copper alloy; railway motor cars; rental of railroad cars; caulking tools, hand; can openers, not electric; water treatment equipment, industrial; water purification equipment, household type
PA: Berkshire Hathaway Inc.
3555 Farnam St Ste 1140
Omaha NE 68131
402 346-1400

(G-5344)
MARMON INDUSTRIAL LLC (DH)
181 W Madison St Fl 26 (60602-4510)
PHONE.................312 372-9500
John Nichols, *President*
Robert W Webb, *Senior VP*
Bob Lorch, *CFO*
Annmarie Bach, *Manager*
◆ **EMP:** 6
SQ FT: 33,000
SALES (est): 625.4MM
SALES (corp-wide): 327.2B **Publicly Held**
WEB: www.marmon.com
SIC: 3743 4741 3589 6159 Railway motor cars; rental of railroad cars; water treatment equipment, industrial; machinery & equipment finance leasing; fasteners; control valves, fluid power: hydraulic & pneumatic
HQ: Marmon Holdings, Inc.
181 W Madison St Ste 2600
Chicago IL 60602
312 372-9500

(G-5345)
MARMON INDUSTRIES LLC (DH)
181 W Madison St Ste 2600 (60602-4504)
PHONE.................312 372-9500
Robert A Pritzker, *President*
Robert C Gluth, *Vice Pres*
Robert W Webb, *Vice Pres*
◆ **EMP:** 4 **EST:** 1969
SQ FT: 33,000
SALES (est): 57.6MM **Publicly Held**
WEB: www.marmon.com
SIC: 3465 3621 3714 Hub caps, automobile: stamped metal; rotors, for motors; wheels, motor vehicle; brake drums, motor vehicle

(G-5346)
MARMON RETAIL TECHNOLOGIES CO (DH)
181 W Madison St (60602-4510)
PHONE.................312 332-0317
Richard Winted,
EMP: 12
SQ FT: 33,000
SALES (est): 345.8MM
SALES (corp-wide): 327.2B **Publicly Held**
SIC: 2541 2542 Store fixtures, wood; fixtures, store: except wood
HQ: Marmon Holdings, Inc.
181 W Madison St Ste 2600
Chicago IL 60602
312 372-9500

(G-5347)
MARS CHOCOLATE NORTH AMER LLC
Also Called: M&M Mars
2019 N Oak Park Ave (60707-3360)
PHONE.................662 335-8000
Cahrles Painter, *Principal*
EMP: 590
SALES (corp-wide): 38.5B **Privately Held**
SIC: 2064 2066 Candy & other confectionery products; chocolate & cocoa products
HQ: Mars Chocolate North America, Llc
800 High St
Hackettstown NJ 07840
908 852-1000

(G-5348)
MARS SNACKFOOD US
2019 N Oak Park Ave (60707-3360)
PHONE.................773 637-0659
Guillaume Labat, *Opers Staff*
Erika Polacek, *Sales Staff*
Timothy Scheel, *Marketing Staff*
Nicole Kouzoukas, *Manager*
EMP: 12
SALES (est): 1.7MM **Privately Held**
WEB: www.effem.com
SIC: 2064 Candy & other confectionery products

(G-5349)
MARSCO GLASS PRODUCTS LLC (HQ)
2857 S Halsted St (60608-5907)
PHONE.................312 326-4710
Mike Hobbs, *CEO*
Michael E Hobbs Sr,
EMP: 64 **EST:** 1945
SQ FT: 30,000
SALES (est): 19.7MM **Privately Held**
WEB: www.egpglass.com
SIC: 3211 3231 Sheet glass; products of purchased glass

(G-5350)
MARTINEZ PRINTING LLC
2714 N Mulligan Ave (60639-1028)
PHONE.................773 732-8108
Martinez Ricardo, *Principal*
Hector Martinez,
Ricardo Martinez,
EMP: 2 **EST:** 2013
SALES (est): 269.2K **Privately Held**
SIC: 2752 Commercial printing, lithographic

(G-5351)
MARUICHI LEAVITT PIPE TUBE LLC
3655 Solutions Ctr (60677-3006)
PHONE.................800 532-8488
Mark Desforges, *Prdtn Mgr*
Kyle Maloney, *Sales Staff*
David Klima, *Branch Mgr*
EMP: 4 **Privately Held**
SIC: 3317 Seamless pipes & tubes
HQ: Maruichi Leavitt Pipe & Tube, Llc
1717 W 115th St
Chicago IL 60643

(G-5352)
MARUICHI LEAVITT PIPE TUBE LLC (HQ)
1717 W 115th St (60643-4398)
PHONE.................773 239-7700
T Konishi, *President*
Joe Fattori, *Vice Pres*
S Honda, *Vice Pres*
Bill Goodrich, *Plant Mgr*
David J Klima, *CFO*
◆ **EMP:** 125
SQ FT: 1,000,000
SALES (est): 23.3MM **Privately Held**
SIC: 3317 Seamless pipes & tubes

(G-5353)
MARV-O-LUS MANUFACTURING CO (PA)
Also Called: Sign Holders Supply
220 N Washtenaw Ave (60612-2014)
PHONE.................773 826-1717
Michael Glassenberg, *President*
Paul Bryant, *Sales Staff*
Shimmy Atlas, *Manager*
◆ **EMP:** 12
SQ FT: 24,500
SALES (est): 3MM **Privately Held**
WEB: www.marvolus.com
SIC: 2542 2541 Fixtures: display, office or store: except wood; display fixtures, wood

(G-5354)
MARVEL GROUP INC
3800 W 44th St (60632-3520)
PHONE.................773 523-4804
John Dellamore, *President*
EMP: 245
SQ FT: 44,300
SALES (corp-wide): 106.7MM **Privately Held**
SIC: 2522 2521 Office furniture, except wood; wood office furniture

PA: The Marvel Group Inc
3843 W 43rd St
Chicago IL 60632
773 523-4804

(G-5355)
MARVEL GROUP INC (PA)
3843 W 43rd St (60632-3409)
PHONE.................773 523-4804
John J Dellamore, *President*
Chris Bone, *Vice Pres*
Joe Fortin, *Vice Pres*
Michael Glab, *Vice Pres*
Ken Wolfanger, *Vice Pres*
▲ **EMP:** 180
SQ FT: 120,000
SALES (est): 106.7MM **Privately Held**
WEB: www.marvelgroup.com
SIC: 2522 Office furniture, except wood

(G-5356)
MARVEL GROUP INC
4417 S Springfield Ave (60632)
PHONE.................773 523-4804
John Dellamore, *Branch Mgr*
EMP: 15
SALES (corp-wide): 106.7MM **Privately Held**
SIC: 2522 Office furniture, except wood
PA: The Marvel Group Inc
3843 W 43rd St
Chicago IL 60632
773 523-4804

(G-5357)
MARZEYA BAKERY INC
8908 S Commercial Ave (60617-3201)
PHONE.................773 374-7855
Jose Luis Padilla, *President*
Irma Padilla, *Corp Secy*
EMP: 5
SQ FT: 1,300
SALES (est): 437.9K **Privately Held**
SIC: 2051 5461 Bread, cake & related products; bakeries

(G-5358)
MASTER PAPER BOX COMPANY INC
3641 S Iron St (60609-1322)
PHONE.................773 927-0252
Bill Farago Sr, *President*
Lauren Farago, *Manager*
EMP: 103
SQ FT: 103,000
SALES (est): 22MM **Privately Held**
WEB: www.masterpaperbox.com
SIC: 2657 2652 Folding paperboard boxes; setup paperboard boxes

(G-5359)
MASTER POLISHING & BUFFING
10247 S Avenue O (60617-5904)
PHONE.................773 731-3883
Roberto Ramirez, *Owner*
EMP: 5
SALES (est): 443.6K **Privately Held**
SIC: 3471 Buffing for the trade

(G-5360)
MASTER TAPE PRINTERS INC
4517 N Elston Ave (60630-4420)
PHONE.................773 283-8273
Robert Grant, *President*
Caryne Casey, *Corp Secy*
Andy Casey, *Vice Pres*
Terese Grant, *Vice Pres*
Lisa Vernon, *Prdtn Mgr*
EMP: 20 **EST:** 1954
SQ FT: 6,200
SALES (est): 3.2MM **Privately Held**
SIC: 2759 Labels & seals: printing

(G-5361)
MASTERCRAFT FURN RFNISHING INC
3140 W Chicago Ave (60622-4320)
PHONE.................773 722-5730
James Antoni, *President*
Marina Antoni, *Admin Sec*
EMP: 19 **EST:** 1939
SQ FT: 16,000

Chicago - Cook County (G-5362)

SALES (est): 1.2MM **Privately Held**
WEB: www.mastercraftfurniture.net
SIC: 7641 2511 2521 Furniture refinishing; reupholstery; wood household furniture; wood office furniture

(G-5362)
MASTERS HAND ENTERPRISES LLC
4021 W Harrison St (60624-3548)
PHONE.................................312 933-7674
Lisa Burnett,
EMP: 2
SALES: 500K **Privately Held**
SIC: 3589 Car washing machinery

(G-5363)
MASUD JEWELERS INC
Also Called: Superior Findings
17 N Wabash Ave Ste 430 (60602-4871)
PHONE.................................312 236-0547
Jose Masud, *President*
EMP: 5 EST: 1976
SQ FT: 1,000
SALES (est): 590K **Privately Held**
SIC: 5094 3911 7631 Precious stones & metals; jewelry, precious metal; jewelry repair services

(G-5364)
MATCHLESS PARISIAN NOVELTY INC (PA)
840 W 49th Pl (60609-5151)
PHONE.................................773 924-1515
Frank Ungari, *President*
Rose Sherlock, *Accountant*
EMP: 2
SALES (est): 1MM **Privately Held**
SIC: 3965 Button backs & parts

(G-5365)
MATHEU TOOL WORKS INC
2426 N Clybourn Ave Fl 1 (60614-1918)
PHONE.................................773 327-9274
Ellis Matheu, *President*
Cornella Matheu, *Admin Sec*
EMP: 3 EST: 1945
SQ FT: 4,000
SALES (est): 270K **Privately Held**
SIC: 3545 Machine tool attachments & accessories

(G-5366)
MATRIX NORTH AMERCN CNSTR INC (HQ)
Also Called: Matrix Nac
1 E Wacker Dr Ste 1110 (60601-1474)
PHONE.................................312 754-6605
Jason W Turner, *President*
Thomas Brian, *Superintendent*
Harry Short, *Superintendent*
J Steven Harker, *Senior VP*
Troy Blair, *Vice Pres*
EMP: 1
SALES (est): 1.2MM
SALES (corp-wide): 1.4B **Publicly Held**
SIC: 5063 1389 8711 Electrical construction materials; construction, repair & dismantling services; building construction consultant
PA: Matrix Service Company
   5100 E Skelly Dr Ste 700
   Tulsa OK 74135
   918 838-8822

(G-5367)
MAUSER USA LLC
903 N Kilpatrick Ave (60651-3326)
PHONE.................................773 261-2332
Mark Zymon, *Branch Mgr*
EMP: 11
SALES (corp-wide): 1.2B **Privately Held**
SIC: 3412 Barrels, shipping: metal
HQ: Mauser Usa, Llc
   35 Cotters Ln Ste C
   East Brunswick NJ 08816

(G-5368)
MAVERICK ALES & LAGERS LLC
Also Called: Midwest Coast Brewing Company
2137 W Walnut St (60612-2323)
PHONE.................................408 605-1508
Cameron Compton, *Mng Member*
EMP: 4
SALES (est): 192.3K **Privately Held**
SIC: 2082 Beer (alcoholic beverage)

(G-5369)
MAX-BLOCK DEVELOPMENT LLC
10500 S Hamilton Ave (60643-2514)
PHONE.................................773 220-6214
Mark Weber, *Mng Member*
EMP: 3
SALES (est): 128.1K **Privately Held**
SIC: 3271 Blocks, concrete: drystack interlocking

(G-5370)
MAXS SCREEN MACHINE INC (PA)
Also Called: Msm Promotions
6125 N Nrthwst Hwy Frnt 1 (60631-2175)
PHONE.................................773 878-4949
Jeff Maksud, *President*
Walter Abraham, *Vice Pres*
Venessa Martinez, *Admin Sec*
EMP: 9
SQ FT: 6,000
SALES (est): 1.2MM **Privately Held**
SIC: 2396 3993 Screen printing on fabric articles; signs & advertising specialties

(G-5371)
MAYNARD INC
1421 S Plymouth Ct (60605-2862)
PHONE.................................773 235-5225
Maynard Kier, *President*
Jeffrey Kier, *Vice Pres*
EMP: 5 EST: 1930
SQ FT: 4,000
SALES (est): 200K **Privately Held**
WEB: www.maynardinc.com
SIC: 2844 Cosmetic preparations

(G-5372)
MAZEL & CO INC (PA)
4300 W Ferdinand St (60624-1095)
PHONE.................................773 533-1600
Joel Handelman, *President*
Nancy Beckley, *CFO*
Ralph Handelman, *Treasurer*
▲ EMP: 17
SQ FT: 80,000
SALES (est): 18.5MM **Privately Held**
SIC: 5032 3496 Concrete building products; concrete reinforcing mesh & wire

(G-5373)
MCCLENDON HOLDINGS LLC
Also Called: McClendon Holdings Affiliates
7200 S Exchange Ave Ste A (60649-2526)
P.O. Box 490050 (60649-0012)
PHONE.................................773 251-2314
John McClendon, *President*
EMP: 4
SALES (est): 101.8K **Privately Held**
SIC: 8742 5169 5047 2819 Management consulting services; chemicals & allied products; medical & hospital equipment; charcoal (carbon), activated

(G-5374)
MCCONNELL CHASE SOFTWARE WORKS
360 E Randolph St # 3202 (60601-5069)
PHONE.................................312 540-1508
Joseph K McConnell, *Owner*
EMP: 3
SQ FT: 1,600
SALES (est): 148.5K **Privately Held**
SIC: 7372 Prepackaged software

(G-5375)
MCCRACKEN LABEL CO
5303 S Keeler Ave (60632-4209)
P.O. Box 32256 (60632-0256)
PHONE.................................773 581-8860
John F Coaker III, *President*
Mike Polizvi, *General Mgr*
Michael Polizzi, *General Mgr*
Christopher Buday, *Opers Staff*
Luke Vassiliades, *Opers Staff*
◆ EMP: 40
SQ FT: 69,900
SALES (est): 7.6MM **Privately Held**
WEB: www.mccrackenlabel.com
SIC: 2759 5023 Letterpress printing; flexographic printing; glassware

(G-5376)
MCGILL ASPHALT CONSTRUCTION CO
4956 S Monitor Ave (60638-1544)
PHONE.................................708 924-1755
Dwayne McGill, *President*
EMP: 6
SALES (est): 401.5K **Privately Held**
SIC: 3295 Minerals, ground or treated

(G-5377)
MCKENZIE & KEIM LLC
2850 N Pulaski Rd Ste 1r (60641-5456)
PHONE.................................317 443-6663
Taylor McKenzie Veal, *Principal*
EMP: 3
SALES (est): 235.7K **Privately Held**
SIC: 3645 Residential lighting fixtures

(G-5378)
MCKLEIN COMPANY LLC
Also Called: McKlein USA
4447 W Cortland St Ste A (60639-5115)
PHONE.................................773 235-0600
Parinda Saetia,
▲ EMP: 17
SQ FT: 29,042
SALES: 7.4MM **Privately Held**
SIC: 3161 Attache cases

(G-5379)
MEAD JOHNSON NUTRITION COMPANY (HQ)
225 N Canal St Fl 25 (60606-1791)
PHONE.................................312 466-5800
Peter Kasper Jakobsen, *President*
April Dugger, *Business Mgr*
Vrushank Pandya, *Business Mgr*
Gina Wheeler, *Business Mgr*
Ian E Ormesher, *Senior VP*
EMP: 150
SALES: 3.7B
SALES (corp-wide): 16.5B **Privately Held**
SIC: 2023 2834 Baby formulas; vitamin preparations
PA: Reckitt Benckiser Group Plc
   Turner House
   Slough BERKS SL1 3
   175 321-7800

(G-5380)
MECHANICAL ENGINEERING PDTS
1319 W Lake St (60607-1511)
PHONE.................................312 421-3375
Jon Knudsen, *President*
Anne-Judine Knudsen, *Admin Sec*
EMP: 3
SQ FT: 36,000
SALES (est): 396.9K **Privately Held**
WEB: www.mepco.net
SIC: 3494 3594 3561 Pipe fittings; fluid power pumps & motors; pumps & pumping equipment

(G-5381)
MEDBOT INC
856 W Nelson St Apt 1006 (60657-5103)
PHONE.................................213 200-6658
Mohammed Zubair, *President*
EMP: 4
SALES (est): 161K **Privately Held**
SIC: 3842 8011 Surgical appliances & supplies; offices & clinics of medical doctors

(G-5382)
MEDEXUS PHARMA INC
29 N Wacker Dr Ste 704 (60606-9590)
PHONE.................................312 854-0500
Terri Shoemaker, *President*
Bill Poncy Sr, *Opers Staff*
Luyan LI, *Treasurer*
Brandon Tiller, *Accountant*
Pat Pheffer, *Human Resources*
EMP: 5
SALES (est): 1.1MM
SALES (corp-wide): 25.6MM **Privately Held**
SIC: 2834 5122 8731 Pharmaceutical preparations; drugs & drug proprietaries; medical research, commercial
PA: Medexus Pharmaceuticals Inc
   1 Place Du Commerce Bureau 225
   Verdun QC H3E 1
   514 762-2626

(G-5383)
MEDFORD AERO ARMS LLC
4541 N Ravenswood Ave (60640-5296)
PHONE.................................773 961-7686
Stuart Urkov, *Mng Member*
Kurt Wilhelm,
Luke Wojtasik,
EMP: 5
SALES (est): 242.3K **Privately Held**
SIC: 3549 Metalworking machinery

(G-5384)
MEDIAFLY INC (PA)
150 N Michigan Ave # 2000 (60601-7569)
PHONE.................................312 281-5175
Carson V Conant, *CEO*
EMP: 32
SQ FT: 18,000
SALES: 5.9MM **Privately Held**
SIC: 7372 Business oriented computer software

(G-5385)
MEDIAOCEAN
120 S Riverside Plz # 1900 (60606-3937)
PHONE.................................312 676-4646
Katie Stadius, *Manager*
EMP: 14
SALES (est): 1.4MM **Privately Held**
SIC: 7372 Prepackaged software

(G-5386)
MEDIATEC PUBLISHING INC (PA)
111 E Wacker Dr Ste 1200 (60601-4203)
PHONE.................................312 676-9900
Norman B Kamikow, *President*
John R Taggart, *Exec VP*
Gwen Connelly, *Senior VP*
EMP: 22 EST: 1999
SALES: 10MM **Privately Held**
SIC: 2721 2741 7389 Magazines: publishing only, not printed on site; catalogs: publishing & printing; decoration service for special events

(G-5387)
MEDIATEC PUBLISHING INC
150 N Michigan Ave # 550 (60601-7567)
PHONE.................................510 834-0100
John Taggart, *Branch Mgr*
EMP: 4
SALES (est): 298.8K
SALES (corp-wide): 10MM **Privately Held**
SIC: 2721 Periodicals: publishing only
PA: Mediatec Publishing, Inc
   111 E Wacker Dr Ste 1200
   Chicago IL 60601
   312 676-9900

(G-5388)
MEINHARDT DIAMOND TOOL CO
3800 W Belmont Ave (60618-5206)
PHONE.................................773 267-3260
Roy F Scholz, *President*
La Scholz, *Corp Secy*
EMP: 8 EST: 1941
SQ FT: 3,500
SALES (est): 680K **Privately Held**
WEB: www.meinhardtdiamond.com
SIC: 3545 3291 Diamond cutting tools for turning, boring, burnishing, etc.; abrasive products

(G-5389)
MEITHEAL PHARMACEUTICALS INC
8700 W Bryn Mawr Ave 600s (60631-3529)
PHONE.................................773 951-6542
Tom Shea, *CEO*
EMP: 6 EST: 2016

GEOGRAPHIC SECTION

Chicago - Cook County (G-5413)

SALES (est): 521.2K
SALES (corp-wide): 244.9MM **Privately Held**
SIC: 2834 Pharmaceutical preparations
HQ: Hong Kong King-Friend Industrial Company Limited
 Rm 2702 27/F Omega Plz
 Mongkok KLN

(G-5390)
MEKANISM INC
950 W Washington Blvd (60607-2217)
PHONE.....................................415 908-4000
Jason Harris, *CEO*
Matt Fischvogt, *Creative Dir*
EMP: 15
SALES (corp-wide): 13.2MM **Privately Held**
SIC: 3993 Advertising artwork
PA: Mekanism, Inc.
 640 2nd St Fl 3
 San Francisco CA 94107
 415 908-4000

(G-5391)
MENASHA PACKAGING COMPANY LLC
4545 W Palmer St (60639-3421)
PHONE.....................................773 227-6000
Michelle Staton, *Project Mgr*
Mark Britcliffe, *Maint Spvr*
Dennis Graf, *Opers Staff*
David Drewry, *Info Tech Dir*
EMP: 127
SALES (corp-wide): 2.2B **Privately Held**
SIC: 2653 Boxes, corrugated: made from purchased materials
HQ: Menasha Packaging Company, Llc
 1645 Bergstrom Rd
 Neenah WI 54956
 920 751-1000

(G-5392)
MENASHA PACKAGING COMPANY LLC
350 N Clark St Ste 300 (60654-4980)
PHONE.....................................312 880-4620
Chad Louderman, *QC Mgr*
Adil Sadikovic, *Manager*
Barbara Tomczak, *Manager*
EMP: 500
SALES (corp-wide): 2.2B **Privately Held**
SIC: 2653 Boxes, corrugated: made from purchased materials
HQ: Menasha Packaging Company, Llc
 1645 Bergstrom Rd
 Neenah WI 54956
 920 751-1000

(G-5393)
MER-PLA INC
Also Called: T-G Ad Service
4535 W Fullerton Ave (60639-1933)
PHONE.....................................847 530-9798
John Goldman, *President*
Joseph Rosey, *Vice Pres*
EMP: 12 EST: 1961
SQ FT: 16,000
SALES: 800K **Privately Held**
SIC: 3993 2396 Displays & cutouts, window & lobby; automotive & apparel trimmings

(G-5394)
MERCURY PLASTICS INC
Also Called: Felpak
4535 W Fullerton Ave (60639-1933)
PHONE.....................................888 884-1864
Richard J Goldman, *President*
Kim Gilbert, *Human Res Mgr*
Steven Pighini, *Accounts Mgr*
Jonathan Hurd, *Accounts Exec*
Kevin Kinane, *Accounts Exec*
▲ EMP: 40 EST: 1955
SQ FT: 145,000
SALES (est): 11MM **Privately Held**
WEB: www.mercuryplasticsinc.com
SIC: 3993 3089 Displays & cutouts, window & lobby; thermoformed finished plastic products

(G-5395)
MEREDITH CORP
Also Called: Country Home Magazine
130 E Randolph St # 1700 (60601-6221)
PHONE.....................................312 580-1623
Cortland Lamee, *President*
Ted Meredith, *Principal*
Nina Elder, *Editor*
Sherry Huang, *Editor*
Ryan Mays, *Editor*
EMP: 100
SALES (est): 4MM
SALES (corp-wide): 3.1B **Publicly Held**
SIC: 2721 Periodicals
PA: Meredith Corporation
 1716 Locust St
 Des Moines IA 50309
 515 284-3000

(G-5396)
MERISANT COMPANY (DH)
125 S Wacker Dr Ste 3150 (60606-4414)
PHONE.....................................312 840-6000
Paul Block, *President*
Brian Alsvig, *Vice Pres*
Jonathan W Cole, *Vice Pres*
Angelo Di Benedetto, *Vice Pres*
Yann Kervoern, *Vice Pres*
◆ EMP: 17
SQ FT: 26,300
SALES (est): 130.5MM **Publicly Held**
SIC: 2869 Industrial organic chemicals
HQ: Flavors Holdings Inc.
 35 E 62nd St
 New York NY 10065
 212 572-8677

(G-5397)
MERISANT FOREIGN HOLDINGS I (DH)
33 N Dearborn St Ste 200 (60602-3100)
PHONE.....................................312 840-6000
Paul Block, *Ch of Bd*
▲ EMP: 13
SALES (est): 9.8MM **Publicly Held**
SIC: 2869 Sweeteners, synthetic
HQ: Merisant Us, Inc.
 125 S Wacker Dr Ste 3150
 Chicago IL 60606
 312 840-6000

(G-5398)
MERISANT US INC (DH)
125 S Wacker Dr Ste 3150 (60606-4414)
PHONE.....................................312 840-6000
Albert Manzone, *CEO*
Brian Alsvig, *Vice Pres*
Olivier Bouret, *Vice Pres*
Trisha Rosado, *CFO*
◆ EMP: 258
SQ FT: 10,000
SALES (est): 117.7MM **Publicly Held**
SIC: 2869 Sweeteners, synthetic

(G-5399)
MERISANT US INC
125 S Wacker Dr Ste 3150 (60606-4414)
PHONE.....................................815 929-2700
EMP: 200 **Privately Held**
SIC: 2869 2063 Mfg Industrial Organic Chemicals Mfg Beet Sugar
HQ: Merisant Us, Inc.
 125 S Wacker Dr Ste 3150
 Chicago IL 60606
 312 840-6000

(G-5400)
MERRILL CORPORATION
200 W Jackson Blvd Fl 11 (60606-6910)
PHONE.....................................312 386-2200
Fax: 312 930-5985
EMP: 150
SALES (corp-wide): 579.3MM **Privately Held**
SIC: 2759 7334 Commercial Printing Photocopying Services
PA: Merrill Corporation
 1 Merrill Cir
 Saint Paul MN 55402
 651 646-4501

(G-5401)
MERRILL FINE ARTS ENGRV INC (HQ)
311 S Wacker Dr Ste 300 (60606-6699)
PHONE.....................................312 786-6300
▲ EMP: 100
SQ FT: 38,000
SALES (est): 9.4MM
SALES (corp-wide): 579.3MM **Privately Held**
SIC: 2759 2752 Commercial Printing Lithographic Commercial Printing
PA: Merrill Corporation
 1 Merrill Cir
 Saint Paul MN 55402
 651 646-4501

(G-5402)
MESHPLUSPLUS INC
935 W Chestnut St Ste 505 (60642-5444)
PHONE.....................................847 494-6325
Daniel Gardner, *CEO*
EMP: 4
SQ FT: 400
SALES (est): 186.5K **Privately Held**
SIC: 3663 4813 Telemetering equipment, electronic;

(G-5403)
MESSAGE MEDIUMS LLC
Also Called: Signal
222 Merchandise Mart Plz # 1818 (60654-1103)
PHONE.....................................312 566-4300
James Blacher, *Engineer*
Maria Power, *Engineer*
Jessica Graeser, *Marketing Staff*
Jeffrey Judge, *Mng Member*
Eric Lunt, *Officer*
EMP: 14
SALES (est): 1.6MM **Privately Held**
SIC: 7372 Prepackaged software

(G-5404)
METAL FINISHING RESEARCH CORP
Also Called: Dubois Chemicals
4025 S Princeton Ave (60609-2825)
PHONE.....................................773 373-0800
Ernest Walen, *President*
James Casey, *Admin Sec*
EMP: 14
SQ FT: 20,000
SALES (est): 1.9MM **Privately Held**
SIC: 2819 2899 Industrial inorganic chemicals; chemical preparations
HQ: Heatbath Corporation
 107 Front St
 Indian Orchard MA 01151
 413 452-2000

(G-5405)
METAL MANAGEMENT INC
9331 S Ewing Ave (60617-4641)
PHONE.....................................773 721-1100
Miguel Milaro, *Manager*
EMP: 25
SQ FT: 1,200 **Privately Held**
SIC: 5093 3341 Ferrous metal scrap & waste; secondary nonferrous metals
HQ: Metal Management, Inc.
 200 W Madison St Ste 3600
 Chicago IL 60606
 312 645-0700

(G-5406)
METAL MANAGEMENT INC
1509 W Cortland St (60642-1215)
PHONE.....................................773 489-1800
Mary Cook, *Manager*
EMP: 20
SQ FT: 9,300 **Privately Held**
SIC: 5093 3341 Ferrous metal scrap & waste; secondary nonferrous metals
HQ: Metal Management, Inc.
 200 W Madison St Ste 3600
 Chicago IL 60606
 312 645-0700

(G-5407)
METCO TREATING AND DEV CO
Also Called: Able Electropolishing
2001 S Kilbourn Ave (60623-2311)
PHONE.....................................773 277-1600
John Glass, *President*
Matt Van Acker, *Accounts Mgr*
EMP: 100 EST: 1954
SQ FT: 40,000
SALES (est): 11.7MM **Privately Held**
WEB: www.ableelectropolishing.com
SIC: 3471 Polishing, metals or formed products

(G-5408)
METHODE DEVELOPMENT CO
7401 W Wilson Ave (60706-4548)
PHONE.....................................708 867-6777
Albert C Chiappetta, *Principal*
EMP: 75 EST: 1967
SQ FT: 15,000
SALES (est): 15MM
SALES (corp-wide): 1B **Publicly Held**
SIC: 3678 3672 3644 3643 Electronic connectors; printed circuit boards; non-current-carrying wiring services; current-carrying wiring devices; transformers, except electric; nonferrous wiredrawing & insulating
PA: Methode Electronics, Inc
 8750 W Bryn Mawr Ave # 1000
 Chicago IL 60631
 708 867-6777

(G-5409)
METHODE ELECTRONICS INC (PA)
8750 W Bryn Mawr Ave # 1000 (60631-3554)
PHONE.....................................708 867-6777
Cyndi Burns, *CEO*
Walter J Aspatore, *Ch of Bd*
Christopher J Hornung, *Vice Ch Bd*
Donald W Duda, *President*
Joseph Khoury, *COO*
◆ EMP: 300 EST: 1946
SQ FT: 118,000
SALES: 1B **Publicly Held**
WEB: www.methode.com
SIC: 3678 3674 3676 3672 Electronic connectors; semiconductor circuit networks; microcircuits, integrated (semiconductor); resistor networks; printed circuit boards; wiring boards; test equipment for electronic & electrical circuits; current-carrying wiring devices; bus bars (electrical conductors); connectors & terminals for electrical devices

(G-5410)
METOMIC CORPORATION
Also Called: Gearon Company, The
2944 W 26th St (60623-4194)
PHONE.....................................773 247-4716
Sam Palumbo Jr, *President*
Paul Bernstein, *Vice Pres*
Peter Palumbo, *Vice Pres*
▲ EMP: 20 EST: 1945
SQ FT: 11,000
SALES (est): 4.2MM **Privately Held**
WEB: www.metomic.com
SIC: 3451 3645 Screw machine products; residential lighting fixtures

(G-5411)
METRAFLEX COMPANY
2323 W Hubbard St (60612-1403)
PHONE.....................................312 738-3800
S G Nudel, *CEO*
James Richter, *President*
Dan Holbach, *Engineer*
Marty Rogin, *Engineer*
D R Limberg, *CFO*
▲ EMP: 60 EST: 1958
SQ FT: 59,000
SALES (est): 14.5MM **Privately Held**
WEB: www.metraflex.com
SIC: 3494 3824 3441 3411 Valves & pipe fittings; fluid meters & counting devices; expansion joints (structural shapes), iron or steel; metal cans

(G-5412)
METRONET INTEGRATION INC
811 W Oakdale Ave Apt G (60657-5181)
PHONE.....................................312 781-0045
Jack Schultz, *Vice Pres*
EMP: 7
SALES: 600K **Privately Held**
SIC: 3651 Household audio & video equipment

(G-5413)
METROPOLITAN BREWING LLC
3057 N Rockwell St (60618-7917)
PHONE.....................................773 474-6893
Douglas E Hurst, *CEO*
Tracy Hurst, *Production*
EMP: 7

Chicago - Cook County (G-5414)

SALES (est): 617.7K **Privately Held**
WEB: www.metrobrewing.com
SIC: 2082 Near beer

(G-5414)
MEXICANDY DISTRIBUTOR INC
2332 S Blue Island Ave (60608-4314)
PHONE..................................773 847-0024
Erick Hauser, *President*
EMP: 7
SALES (est): 819.9K **Privately Held**
SIC: 2064 Candy bars, including chocolate covered bars

(G-5415)
MEXICO ENTERPRISE CORPORATION
6859 W 64th Pl (60638-4898)
PHONE..................................920 568-8900
Olga Ramirez, *Owner*
EMP: 5
SALES (est): 352.4K **Privately Held**
SIC: 2032 Mexican foods: packaged in cans, jars, etc.

(G-5416)
MEYER STEEL DRUM INC
2000 S Kilbourn Ave (60623-2310)
PHONE..................................773 522-3030
Brian T Meyer Jr, *Branch Mgr*
EMP: 23
SALES (corp-wide): 70MM **Privately Held**
SIC: 3412 5085 Drums, shipping: metal; drums, new or reconditioned
PA: Meyer Steel Drum, Inc.
   3201 S Millard Ave
   Chicago IL 60623
   773 376-8376

(G-5417)
MEYER STEEL DRUM INC (PA)
Also Called: Ideal Gerit Drum Ring Mfg
3201 S Millard Ave (60623-5078)
PHONE..................................773 376-8376
William Meyer, *President*
Edward Meyer, *Corp Secy*
John Brazis, *Controller*
Bob Conway, *Branch Mgr*
▲ EMP: 180
SQ FT: 85,000
SALES (corp-wide): 70MM **Privately Held**
SIC: 3412 5085 Drums, shipping: metal; drums, new or reconditioned

(G-5418)
MFP HOLDING CO (DH)
1414 S Western Ave (60608-1802)
PHONE..................................312 666-3366
Wyman C Harris, *Ch of Bd*
Doss Samikkannu, *President*
EMP: 8
SQ FT: 145,000
SALES (est): 12.4MM
SALES (corp-wide): 2.2B **Publicly Held**
SIC: 2531 5021 6512 5064 Public building & related furniture; public building furniture; shopping center, property operation only; electric household appliances
HQ: Sagus International, Inc.
   1302 Industrial Blvd
   Temple TX 76504
   630 413-5540

(G-5419)
MHS LTD
Also Called: Wear-Flex Slings
6616 W Irving Park Rd (60634-2435)
PHONE..................................773 736-3333
Barry Young, *Branch Mgr*
EMP: 10
SALES (est): 915.4K
SALES (corp-wide): 2.2MM **Privately Held**
WEB: www.wear-flex.com
SIC: 2298 3537 3496 3429 Nets, seines, slings & insulator pads; industrial trucks & tractors; miscellaneous fabricated wire products; manufactured hardware (general); broadwoven fabric mills, manmade
PA: Mhs Ltd.
   4959 Home Rd
   Winston Salem NC 27106
   336 767-2641

(G-5420)
MHUB
Also Called: Catalyze
965 W Chicago Ave (60642-5413)
PHONE..................................773 580-1485
Haven Allen, *President*
William Fienup, *Vice Pres*
Manas Mehandru, *Admin Sec*
EMP: 3
SALES (est): 323K **Privately Held**
WEB: www.catalyzechicago.org
SIC: 3842 Infant incubators

(G-5421)
MI-TE FAST PRINTERS INC (PA)
Also Called: Mi-Te Printing & Graphics
180 W Washington St Fl 2 (60602-4450)
PHONE..................................312 236-8352
Thomas Sackley, *President*
Sandra Sackley, *Admin Sec*
EMP: 27
SALES (est): 4MM **Privately Held**
SIC: 2752 Commercial printing, offset

(G-5422)
MIC QUALITY SERVICE INC
3500 S Morgan St (60609-1524)
PHONE..................................847 778-5676
Genj Genj Guo, *President*
Wenxiu Zhao, *CFO*
◆ EMP: 25
SQ FT: 20,000
SALES (est): 2.1MM **Privately Held**
SIC: 3639 Major kitchen appliances, except refrigerators & stoves

(G-5423)
MICHELANGELO & DONATA BURDI
6411 W Addison St (60634-3809)
PHONE..................................773 427-1437
Michelangelo Burdi, *Owner*
EMP: 12
SALES (est): 767.4K **Privately Held**
SIC: 3714 Transmissions, motor vehicle

(G-5424)
MICROLUTION INC
6635 W Irving Park Rd (60634-2410)
PHONE..................................773 282-6495
Andrew Phillip, *President*
Brendon Divincenzo, *Engineer*
Attila Farkas, *Engineer*
Kyle Stacy, *Engineer*
Jeremy Von Hatten, *Engineer*
EMP: 25
SQ FT: 4,000
SALES (est): 5.8MM
SALES (corp-wide): 3.7B **Privately Held**
SIC: 3599 Bellows, industrial: metal; machine shop, jobbing & repair
PA: Georg Fischer Ag
   Amsler-Laffon-Strasse 9
   Schaffhausen SH 8200
   526 311-111

(G-5425)
MICRON TECHNOLOGY INC
Also Called: Micron Semiconductor
12829 Collections Ctr Dr (60693-0001)
PHONE..................................208 368-4000
EMP: 9
SALES (corp-wide): 23.4B **Publicly Held**
SIC: 3674 Semiconductors & related devices
PA: Micron Technology, Inc.
   8000 S Federal Way
   Boise ID 83716
   208 368-4000

(G-5426)
MID CITY PRINTING SERVICE
5566 N Northwest Hwy (60630-1116)
PHONE..................................773 777-5400
Stanley Jasiuwienas, *President*
Janina Przybylowska, *Treasurer*
EMP: 7
SQ FT: 4,000
SALES (est): 1MM **Privately Held**
SIC: 2752 2791 2789 2759 Commercial printing, offset; typesetting; bookbinding & related work; commercial printing

(G-5427)
MID PACK
4610 W West End Ave (60644-2759)
PHONE..................................773 626-3500
Mark Scott, *Manager*
EMP: 2
SALES (est): 235.2K **Privately Held**
SIC: 2067 Chewing gum

(G-5428)
MID-AMERICAN ELEVATOR CO INC (PA)
Also Called: USA Hoist Company
820 N Wolcott Ave (60622-4937)
PHONE..................................773 486-6900
Robert R Bailey Jr, *Ch of Bd*
Brian Selke, *President*
Robert R Bailey III, *President*
Cullen Bailey, *Corp Secy*
Greg Selke, *Vice Pres*
▲ EMP: 130
SQ FT: 24,000
SALES (est): 51MM **Privately Held**
SIC: 1796 7699 3823 3535 Elevator installation & conversion; elevators: inspection, service & repair; controllers for process variables, all types; conveyors & conveying equipment; elevators & moving stairways

(G-5429)
MID-AMERICAN ELEVATOR EQP CO
820 N Wolcott Ave (60622-4937)
PHONE..................................773 486-6900
Robert R Bailey Jr, *Chairman*
Litschewski Jacka, *Vice Pres*
Andreananna Triliegi, *Admin Sec*
EMP: 35
SALES (est): 2MM **Privately Held**
SIC: 3823 Industrial instrmnts msrmnt display/control process variable

(G-5430)
MID-CITY DIE & MOLD CORP
1743 N Keating Ave (60639-4688)
PHONE..................................773 278-4844
Timothy Sterrett, *President*
Robin Sterrett, *Vice Pres*
EMP: 2
SQ FT: 2,300
SALES (est): 250K **Privately Held**
SIC: 3544 8711 Dies, steel rule; forms (molds), for foundry & plastics working machinery; consulting engineer

(G-5431)
MID-STATES WIRE PROC CORP
4642 W Maypole Ave (60644-2787)
P.O. Box 440550 (60644-0560)
PHONE..................................773 379-3775
Scott Richer, *President*
EMP: 10 EST: 1955
SQ FT: 13,500
SALES (est): 1MM **Privately Held**
SIC: 3496 Miscellaneous fabricated wire products

(G-5432)
MID-WEST SCREW PRODUCTS INC (PA)
3523 N Kenton Ave (60641-3819)
PHONE..................................773 283-6032
Walter E Lisowski, *President*
Kenneth Lisowski, *Vice Pres*
Jeff Wolford, *Foreman/Supr*
Virginia Lisowski, *Treasurer*
Emily Doyle, *Office Mgr*
EMP: 38 EST: 1946
SQ FT: 15,000
SALES (est): 7.3MM **Privately Held**
WEB: www.m-wsp.com
SIC: 3599 Machine shop, jobbing & repair

(G-5433)
MIDCO INTERNATIONAL INC
Also Called: Emberglo Div of Midco Intl
4140 W Victoria St (60646-6790)
PHONE..................................773 604-8700
Keith Malek, *CEO*
Teryl A Stanger, *President*
Hal F Beyer III, *Chairman*
Stan Beinarauskas, *COO*
Frank Tibuzio, *Purch Mgr*
▲ EMP: 50 EST: 1941

SQ FT: 82,000
SALES (est): 13.7MM **Privately Held**
WEB: www.midcointernational.com
SIC: 3433 3567 3589 Gas burners, domestic; gas burners, industrial; incinerators, metal: domestic or commercial; cooking equipment, commercial

(G-5434)
MIDLAND INDUSTRIES INC
1424 N Halsted St (60642-2618)
PHONE..................................312 664-7300
Laurence S Spector, *President*
Tim Mohs, *Vice Pres*
Peter Russell, *Vice Pres*
Susan Spector, *Admin Sec*
Helen Weinger, *Admin Sec*
◆ EMP: 42
SQ FT: 35,000
SALES (est): 16.4MM **Privately Held**
WEB: www.zincbig.com
SIC: 3356 5093 Zinc & zinc alloy bars, plates, sheets, etc.; nonferrous metals scrap

(G-5435)
MIDPOINT TRADE BOOKS INC (PA)
814 N Franklin St Ste 100 (60610-3813)
PHONE..................................212 727-0190
Eric M Kampmann, *President*
Chris Bell, *Vice Pres*
Alison Kampmann, *Marketing Mgr*
Bill Huhn, *Manager*
Antonio Lorenzo, *Manager*
◆ EMP: 12
SALES (est): 1MM **Privately Held**
SIC: 2731 Books: publishing only

(G-5436)
MIDWAY CAP COMPANY
1239 W Madison St Fl 3 (60607)
PHONE..................................773 384-0911
Merle Spertoli, *President*
Dave Lajb, *Vice Pres*
EMP: 20 EST: 1958
SQ FT: 17,000
SALES (est): 2.5MM **Privately Held**
WEB: www.midwaycapcompany.com
SIC: 2353 Police hats & caps

(G-5437)
MIDWAY CAP COMPANY
4513 W Armitage Ave (60639-3403)
PHONE..................................773 384-0911
Merle Stertoli, *President*
EMP: 20
SALES (est): 1.8MM **Privately Held**
WEB: www.midwaycapcompany.com
SIC: 2353 Uniform hats & caps

(G-5438)
MIDWAY INDUSTRIES INC
Also Called: Midway Windows and Doors
6750 S Belt Circle Dr (60638-4706)
PHONE..................................708 594-2600
Arthur J Strauss Jr, *CEO*
Jerome E Joseph, *President*
Jerry Joseph, *Vice Pres*
Marianne Hayes, *Admin Sec*
EMP: 150
SQ FT: 91,000
SALES (est): 36.1MM **Privately Held**
WEB: www.midwaywindows.com
SIC: 3442 Metal doors; window & door frames; screen & storm doors & windows

(G-5439)
MIDWEST AIR PRO INC
2054 N New England Ave (60707-3328)
PHONE..................................773 622-4566
Rosette Viola, *President*
Michael Viola, *Admin Sec*
EMP: 4
SALES (est): 674.6K **Privately Held**
SIC: 3564 Air cleaning systems

(G-5440)
MIDWEST CANVAS CORP (PA)
4635 W Lake St (60644-2798)
PHONE..................................773 287-4400
Barry A Handwerker, *President*
Paul Wynn, *Vice Pres*
Scott Kramer, *Plant Mgr*
Barry Handwerker, *Opers Staff*
Donnie Lytton, *Engineer*

◆ **EMP:** 137 **EST:** 1947
SQ FT: 200,000
SALES (est): 101.7MM **Privately Held**
WEB: www.midwestcanvas.com
SIC: 3949 3081 3089 Swimming pools, plastic; plastic film & sheet; laminating of plastic

(G-5441)
MIDWEST GALVANIZING INC
7400 S Damen Ave (60636-3722)
P.O. Box 528140 (60652-8140)
PHONE...................................773 434-2682
James Kucia, *President*
Ed Finnegan, *President*
EMP: 15
SQ FT: 60,000
SALES (est): 814K **Privately Held**
SIC: 3479 3471 Galvanizing of iron, steel or end-formed products; hot dip coating of metals or formed products; plating & polishing

(G-5442)
MIDWEST GOLD STAMPERS INC
5707 N Northwest Hwy (60646-6137)
PHONE...................................773 775-5253
Terrence Strauch, *President*
EMP: 15
SQ FT: 17,500
SALES (est): 161.7K **Privately Held**
SIC: 2789 3554 2759 Gold stamping on books; die cutting & stamping machinery; paper converting; embossing on paper

(G-5443)
MIDWEST MANUFACTURING & DISTRG
6025 N Keystone Ave (60646-5209)
PHONE...................................773 866-1010
Erno Bakondi, *President*
Klara Bakondi, *Admin Sec*
EMP: 15
SQ FT: 12,500
SALES (est): 3.8MM **Privately Held**
SIC: 3444 Sheet metal specialties, not stamped

(G-5444)
MIDWEST METAL CASTINGS INC
Also Called: Chicago Aluminum Castings
1838 N Elston Ave 42 (60642-1216)
PHONE...................................773 762-3009
Richard Wagner, *Principal*
Harold Horton, *Principal*
EMP: 3
SALES (est): 166.4K **Privately Held**
SIC: 3599 Machine shop, jobbing & repair

(G-5445)
MIDWEST METAL FINISHING INC
2215 S Christiana Ave (60623-3215)
PHONE...................................773 521-0700
Robert Alley, *President*
Paul Mallo, *Manager*
EMP: 8
SQ FT: 40,000
SALES (est): 650K **Privately Held**
SIC: 3471 Plating of metals or formed products

(G-5446)
MIDWEST MODEL AIRCRAFT CO
Also Called: K & S Engineering
6917 W 59th St (60638-3205)
PHONE...................................773 229-0740
Wallace M Simmers, *President*
Wally Findysz, *Vice Pres*
Evelyn Simmers, *Admin Sec*
▲ **EMP:** 19
SQ FT: 13,000
SALES (est): 4.2MM **Privately Held**
WEB: www.ksmetals.com
SIC: 3351 3354 Tubing, copper & copper alloy; aluminum pipe & tube

(G-5447)
MIDWEST SOCKS LLC
4120 N Leamington Ave (60641-1432)
PHONE...................................773 283-3952
Zelek Rosalena, *Principal*
EMP: 4
SALES (est): 107.4K **Privately Held**
SIC: 2252 Socks

(G-5448)
MIDWEST SWISS EMBROIDERIES CO
5590 N Northwest Hwy (60630-1178)
PHONE...................................773 631-7120
Marvin Mazzucchelli, *President*
John Mazzucchelli, *Exec VP*
Dorothy Mazzucchelli, *Admin Sec*
EMP: 20 **EST:** 1935
SQ FT: 15,000
SALES (est): 935K **Privately Held**
WEB: www.midwestswiss.com
SIC: 2395 2397 Emblems, embroidered; schiffli machine embroideries

(G-5449)
MIDWEST TOOL INC
4055 W Peterson Ave # 205 (60646-6183)
PHONE...................................773 588-1313
Mitchell Zamost, *President*
EMP: 4
SALES (est): 448.3K **Privately Held**
SIC: 3699 Electrical equipment & supplies

(G-5450)
MIDWEST UNCUTS INC
Also Called: Midwest Labs
5585 N Lynch Ave (60630-1417)
PHONE...................................312 664-3131
Robert Pretzie, *Manager*
EMP: 11
SALES (corp-wide): 1.7B **Publicly Held**
SIC: 3851 Eyeglasses, lenses & frames
HQ: Midwest Uncuts Inc
310 Seven Springs Way
Brentwood TN 37027
515 961-6593

(G-5451)
MIDWESTERN RUST PROOF INC
3636 N Kilbourn Ave (60641-3643)
PHONE...................................773 725-6636
Garth Davies, *President*
Phyllis Rozmus, *Sales Staff*
Saigo Fujii, *Manager*
▲ **EMP:** 100
SALES (est): 12.3MM **Privately Held**
SIC: 3471 Electroplating of metals or formed products

(G-5452)
MIFAB INC (PA)
1321 W 119th St (60643-5109)
PHONE...................................773 341-3030
Michael J Whiteside, *President*
Mike Bellavance, *COO*
Biswarup Bhattacharjee, *Vice Pres*
Paul Lacourciere, *Vice Pres*
Courtlen Hagemeyer, *CFO*
▲ **EMP:** 35
SALES (est): 8.4MM **Privately Held**
SIC: 3432 Plumbing fixture fittings & trim

(G-5453)
MIGHTY HOOK INC
1017 N Cicero Ave (60651-3202)
PHONE...................................773 378-1909
Scott Rempala, *President*
Leigh Baird, *Cust Mgr*
Edward Rolison, *Admin Sec*
▲ **EMP:** 30
SQ FT: 51,000
SALES (est): 5MM **Privately Held**
SIC: 2298 3452 Wire rope centers; bolts, nuts, rivets & washers

(G-5454)
MIGLIO DI MARIO UOMO INC
Also Called: Fly Ball
436 E 47th St Unit 302 (60653-4106)
PHONE...................................312 391-0831
Bruce Gage, *President*
James Gage, *Admin Sec*
EMP: 2
SQ FT: 1,000
SALES (est): 275K **Privately Held**
SIC: 5136 2353 2329 Men's & boys' clothing; hats & caps; sweaters & sweater jackets: men's & boys'

(G-5455)
MIHALIS MARINE
1224 W 91st St (60620-3505)
PHONE...................................773 445-6220
Tracy Howard, *Owner*
EMP: 5
SALES (est): 380.3K **Privately Held**
SIC: 7692 Welding repair

(G-5456)
MIKES ANODIZING CO
859 N Spaulding Ave (60651-4134)
PHONE...................................773 722-5778
Michael S Balice, *President*
Michelle Balice Jr, *Corp Secy*
EMP: 48 **EST:** 1946
SQ FT: 50,000
SALES (est): 4.2MM **Privately Held**
WEB: www.mikesanodizing.com
SIC: 3471 Electroplating of metals or formed products

(G-5457)
MILITARY MEDICAL NEWS
11 E Adams St Ste 906 (60603-6306)
PHONE...................................312 368-4860
Paul Stevens, *President*
EMP: 21
SALES (est): 681.1K **Privately Held**
WEB: www.militarymedical.com
SIC: 2711 Newspapers, publishing & printing

(G-5458)
MILLER FABRICATION LLC
303 E Wacker Dr Ste 1040 (60601-5216)
PHONE...................................307 358-4777
Eric Jessen, *President*
EMP: 100
SALES (est): 10MM **Privately Held**
SIC: 3441 Fabricated structural metal
PA: High Plains Gas, Inc.
1200 E Lincoln St
Gillette WY 82716

(G-5459)
MILLERS EUREKA INC
2121 W Hubbard St (60612-1611)
PHONE...................................312 666-9383
Carol Miller, *President*
Betty J Miller, *Admin Sec*
EMP: 10
SQ FT: 16,000
SALES (est): 3.6MM **Privately Held**
SIC: 5051 3446 7692 Steel; railings, bannisters, guards, etc.: made from metal pipe; welding repair

(G-5460)
MILLIKEN & COMPANY
222 Merchandise Mart Plz # 1149 (60654-1167)
PHONE...................................800 241-4826
Robert Dillon, *Branch Mgr*
EMP: 14
SALES (corp-wide): 2.9B **Privately Held**
SIC: 5023 2273 Carpets; carpets & rugs
PA: Milliken & Company
920 Milliken Rd
Spartanburg SC 29303
864 503-2020

(G-5461)
MILLIKEN & COMPANY
Also Called: Keystone Aniline
2501 W Fulton St (60612-2103)
PHONE...................................864 473-1601
EMP: 65
SALES (corp-wide): 2.9B **Privately Held**
SIC: 2819 Industrial inorganic chemicals
PA: Milliken & Company
920 Milliken Rd
Spartanburg SC 29303
864 503-2020

(G-5462)
MILLS PALLET
4500 W Roosevelt Rd (60624-3842)
PHONE...................................773 533-6458
Robert Zirves, *President*
EMP: 12 **EST:** 1973
SALES (est): 1.7MM **Privately Held**
SIC: 2448 7699 Pallets, wood; pallet repair

(G-5463)
MILVIA
222 Merchandise Mart Plz 1427a (60654-1419)
PHONE...................................312 527-3403

EMP: 3 **EST:** 2011
SALES (est): 238.3K **Privately Held**
SIC: 3842 Mfg Surgical Appliances/Supplies

(G-5464)
MING TRADING LLC
2845 W 48th Pl (60632-2012)
PHONE...................................773 442-2221
Peter Ming,
▲ **EMP:** 3 **EST:** 2014
SQ FT: 3,000
SALES (est): 500K **Privately Held**
SIC: 3999 Pet supplies

(G-5465)
MINIMILL TECHNOLOGIES INC
505 N Lake Shore Dr # 5407 (60611-6446)
PHONE...................................315 857-7107
EMP: 2
SALES (est): 212.3K **Privately Held**
SIC: 2431 Mfg Millwork

(G-5466)
MIO MED ORTHOPEDICS INC
2502 N Clark St 212 (60614-1850)
PHONE...................................773 477-8991
Mark Sorensen, *President*
EMP: 3
SALES (est): 386.3K **Privately Held**
SIC: 3842 Surgical appliances & supplies

(G-5467)
MIRACLE PRESS COMPANY
2951 W Carroll Ave (60612-1788)
PHONE...................................773 722-6176
John G Novak, *President*
Bruce Novak, *Vice Pres*
Bruce N Novak, *Vice Pres*
Nancy Novak, *Vice Pres*
Wayne Bradstreet, *Project Mgr*
EMP: 15 **EST:** 1933
SQ FT: 24,000
SALES (est): 2.7MM **Privately Held**
WEB: www.miraclepress.net
SIC: 2752 2671 Commercial printing, offset; packaging paper & plastics film, coated & laminated

(G-5468)
MISTER INC OF CHICAGO
4215 W Grand Ave (60651-1857)
PHONE...................................773 342-7200
Lawrence Roseman, *President*
Dale Schmoldt, *Vice Pres*
Loren Roseman, *Information Mgr*
Joel Michaels, *Admin Sec*
EMP: 3
SQ FT: 2,000
SALES (est): 369.7K **Privately Held**
WEB: www.misterinc.com
SIC: 3599 Machine shop, jobbing & repair

(G-5469)
MITCHEL HOME
3652 N Tripp Ave (60641-3037)
PHONE...................................773 205-9902
John Mitchel, *Partner*
Kathy Mitchel, *Partner*
EMP: 4
SALES (est): 272.1K **Privately Held**
SIC: 2519 Household furniture

(G-5470)
MITCHELL BLACK LLC
1922 N Damen Ave (60647-4504)
PHONE...................................312 667-4477
Lynai Jones,
Carlton Jones,
EMP: 11 **EST:** 2012
SQ FT: 3,400
SALES (est): 1.2MM **Privately Held**
SIC: 5023 5231 2679 Decorative home furnishings & supplies; paint, glass & wallpaper; wallpaper; wallpaper: made from purchased paper

(G-5471)
MITEL NETWORKS INC
70 W Madison St Ste 1600 (60602-4262)
PHONE...................................312 479-9000
John Uehling, *Vice Pres*
EMP: 13
SALES (corp-wide): 1B **Privately Held**
SIC: 3661 Telephones & telephone apparatus

Chicago - Cook County (G-5472)

HQ: Mitel Networks, Inc.
1146 N Alma School Rd
Mesa AZ 85201

(G-5472)
MITTAL STEEL USA INC
1 S Dearborn St Ste 1800 (60603-2308)
PHONE................................312 899-3440
Andy Harshaw, *President*
▲ EMP: 11
SALES (est): 1MM **Privately Held**
SIC: 3312 Plate, steel

(G-5473)
MK SIGNS INC
4900 N Elston Ave Ste M (60630-2573)
PHONE................................773 545-4444
Ralph Cilia, *President*
Anthony Cilia Jr, *Treasurer*
▲ EMP: 46 EST: 1957
SQ FT: 18,000
SALES (est): 5.5MM **Privately Held**
SIC: 3993 1799 7336 Neon signs; signs, not made in custom sign painting shops; sign installation & maintenance; art design services

(G-5474)
MK TILE INK
5851 S Neenah Ave (60638-3314)
PHONE................................773 964-8905
Marcin Krol, *Principal*
EMP: 1
SALES: 522K **Privately Held**
SIC: 1743 5211 5032 3272 Tile installation, ceramic; tile, ceramic; ceramic wall & floor tile; tile, precast terrazzo or concrete; floor tile

(G-5475)
MOBILE HEALTH & WELLNESS INC
1820 W Webster Ave # 206 (60614-2927)
PHONE................................773 697-9892
Jennifer Evola, *Owner*
EMP: 2
SALES (est): 200K **Privately Held**
WEB: www.mobilehealthandwellness.com
SIC: 7299 3841 8299 Massage parlor; suction therapy apparatus; meditation therapy

(G-5476)
MOBILEHOP TECHNOLOGY LLC
838 W 31st St Unit 3g (60608-5874)
PHONE................................312 504-3773
EMP: 3 EST: 2011
SALES (est): 180K **Privately Held**
SIC: 7372 Prepackaged Software Services

(G-5477)
MODERN GRAPHIC SYSTEMS INC
4922 S Western Ave (60609-4742)
PHONE................................773 476-6898
James Sommer, *CEO*
Lucille G Sommer, *Vice Pres*
EMP: 6
SQ FT: 6,250
SALES (est): 726K **Privately Held**
SIC: 3552 Silk screens for textile industry

(G-5478)
MODERN LIGHTING TECH LLC
1751 W Grand Ave (60622-6050)
PHONE................................312 624-9267
EMP: 5 EST: 2012
SQ FT: 8,500
SALES (est): 380K **Privately Held**
SIC: 3641 Mfg Electric Lamps

(G-5479)
MODERN LUXURY MEDIA LLC
Also Called: Cs Magazine Front Desk Chicago
33 W Monroe St Ste 2100 (60603-5410)
PHONE................................312 274-2500
Becca West, *Publisher*
Kamil Galimski, *Editor*
Kelly Ryan, *Accounts Exec*
Denise Borkowski, *Sales Executive*
Sher Dionisio, *Marketing Staff*
EMP: 30
SALES (corp-wide): 41MM **Privately Held**
WEB: www.modernluxury.com
SIC: 2721 Magazines: publishing only, not printed on site
HQ: Modern Luxury Media, Llc
243 Vallejo St
San Francisco CA 94111
404 443-0004

(G-5480)
MODERN PROCESS EQUIPMENT INC
3125 S Kolin Ave (60623-4890)
PHONE................................773 254-3929
D Ephraim, *President*
Stephen Chu, *Project Mgr*
Peter Rios, *Project Mgr*
Jim Martin, *Prdtn Mgr*
Michael Baker, *Opers Staff*
EMP: 50 EST: 1957
SQ FT: 50,000
SALES (est): 13.5MM **Privately Held**
WEB: www.mpechicago.com
SIC: 8711 3556 Engineering services; grinders, commercial, food

(G-5481)
MODERN SPECIALTIES COMPANY
661 W Lake St Ste 1s (60661-1052)
PHONE................................312 648-5800
Gerissa French, *President*
Keith Carlson, *Manager*
▲ EMP: 2 EST: 1929
SQ FT: 6,000
SALES (est): 1.1MM **Privately Held**
WEB: www.themodernspecialtiescompany.com
SIC: 3421 3999 3541 3423 Knives: butchers', hunting, pocket, etc.; knife blades & blanks; dusters, feather; machine tools, metal cutting type; hand & edge tools; broadwoven fabric mills, wool

(G-5482)
MODERN SPROUT LLC
1451 N Ashland Ave (60622-8087)
PHONE................................312 342-2114
Nicholas J Behr, *Mng Member*
Sarah D Burrows, *Mng Member*
EMP: 2 EST: 2013
SALES (est): 228.3K **Privately Held**
WEB: www.modernsproutplanter.com
SIC: 3999 Hydroponic equipment

(G-5483)
MODINEER P-K TOOL LLC
4700 W Le Moyne St (60651-1627)
PHONE................................773 235-4700
Edward Hamilton, *CEO*
EMP: 50
SALES (est): 2.2MM
SALES (corp-wide): 156.4MM **Privately Held**
SIC: 3469 3545 3549 Stamping metal for the trade; precision tools, machinists'; machine tool attachments & accessories; assembly machines, including robotic
PA: Modineer Co. Llc
2190 Industrial Dr
Niles MI 49120
269 683-2550

(G-5484)
MOES RIVER NORTH LLC
155 W Kinzie St (60654-4514)
PHONE................................312 245-2000
EMP: 3
SALES (est): 137.3K **Privately Held**
SIC: 3421 Table & food cutlery, including butchers'

(G-5485)
MOHICAN PETROLEUM INC
21 S Clark St Ste 3980 (60603-2017)
PHONE................................312 782-6385
F M Bransfield, *President*
Charles Bransfield, *Vice Pres*
Dorothy Huntoon, *Treasurer*
James Murphy, *Admin Sec*
EMP: 4
SALES: 1MM **Privately Held**
SIC: 1382 Oil & gas exploration services

(G-5486)
MOLD EXPRESS INC
8142 W Frest Preserve Ave (60634-2908)
PHONE................................773 766-0874
EMP: 2 EST: 2013
SALES (est): 214.8K **Privately Held**
SIC: 3544 Industrial molds

(G-5487)
MOLD-RITE PLASTICS LLC (HQ)
30 N La Salle St Ste 2425 (60602-3361)
P.O. Box 160, Plattsburgh NY (12901-0160)
PHONE................................518 561-1812
Tom Recny, *CFO*
Dawnya Lamantia, *Sales Staff*
Brian Bauerbach,
◆ EMP: 118
SQ FT: 335,000
SALES (est): 126.1MM **Privately Held**
SIC: 3089 Closures, plastic; injection molding of plastics

(G-5488)
MOLSON COORS BEV CO USA LLC (HQ)
250 S Wacker Dr Ste 800 (60606-5888)
P.O. Box 5293, Parsippany NJ (07054-6293)
PHONE................................312 496-2700
Vicky Cookson, *Principal*
Kelly Grebe, *Principal*
David Kroll, *Principal*
Pete Marino, *Principal*
Fernando Palacios, *Principal*
◆ EMP: 800 EST: 1855
SQ FT: 225,000
SALES (est): 1.7B
SALES (corp-wide): 10.5B **Publicly Held**
WEB: www.millercoors.com
SIC: 2082 Beer (alcoholic beverage)
PA: Molson Coors Beverage Company
1801 Calif St Ste 4600
Denver CO 80202
303 927-2337

(G-5489)
MONDA WINDOW & DOOR CORP
4101 W 42nd Pl (60632-3938)
PHONE................................773 254-8888
Elias Abubeker, *President*
Min Ouyang, *Admin Sec*
▲ EMP: 25
SQ FT: 50,000
SALES (est): 7.4MM **Privately Held**
SIC: 3354 2431 3089 3353 Aluminum extruded products; windows, wood; washers, plastic; aluminum sheet, plate & foil

(G-5490)
MONDELEZ INTERNATIONAL INC (PA)
905 W Fulton Market # 200 (60607-1308)
PHONE................................847 943-4000
Dirk Van De Put, *Ch of Bd*
Sandra Macquillan, *Exec VP*
Gerhard W Pleuhs, *Exec VP*
◆ EMP: 2000
SALES: 25.8B **Publicly Held**
SIC: 2022 2013 2095 2043 Processed cheese; natural cheese; spreads, cheese; dips, cheese-based; sausages & other prepared meats; bacon, side & sliced: from purchased meat; frankfurters from purchased meat; luncheon meat from purchased meat; coffee roasting (except by wholesale grocers); freeze-dried coffee; instant coffee; cereal breakfast foods; dressings, salad: raw & cooked (except dry mixes); powders, drink

(G-5491)
MONITOR PUBLISHING INC
6304 N Nagle Ave Ste B (60646-3619)
PHONE................................773 205-0303
Jack Zaworski, *President*
EMP: 6
SALES (est): 381.2K **Privately Held**
SIC: 2731 2721 Book publishing; periodicals

(G-5492)
MONOGEN INC
140 S Dearborn St Ste 420 (60603-5233)
PHONE................................847 573-6700
Norman J Pressman, *President*
EMP: 40 EST: 1996
SALES (est): 5.1MM **Privately Held**
SIC: 3841 Medical instruments & equipment, blood & bone work; diagnostic apparatus, medical

(G-5493)
MONTAUK CHICAGO INC
401 N Wells St Ste 108a (60654-7026)
PHONE................................312 951-5688
Tim Zyto, *President*
EMP: 3
SALES (est): 197.5K **Privately Held**
SIC: 5712 2599 Mattresses; furniture & fixtures

(G-5494)
MONTROSE GLASS & MIRROR CORP
3916 W Montrose Ave Fl 1 (60618-1019)
PHONE................................773 478-6433
Paul Sikar, *President*
Galina Sikar, *Vice Pres*
EMP: 3
SQ FT: 3,500
SALES (est): 371.9K **Privately Held**
SIC: 5231 5719 3231 3211 Glass; mirrors; products of purchased glass; flat glass

(G-5495)
MOODY BIBLE INST OF CHICAGO (PA)
Also Called: Moody Global Ministries
820 N La Salle Dr (60610-3263)
PHONE................................312 329-4000
Jerry Jenkins, *Ch of Bd*
Paul Nyquist, *President*
Bill Bielawski, *Division Mgr*
William Thrasher, *Division Mgr*
Diana Childers, *Principal*
◆ EMP: 575 EST: 1886
SQ FT: 100,000
SALES: 111.9MM **Privately Held**
WEB: www.moody.edu
SIC: 8661 8299 8221 4832 Religious organizations; bible school; professional schools; radio broadcasting stations; books: publishing only

(G-5496)
MOODY BIBLE INST OF CHICAGO
Also Called: Moody Press A Division of MBI
210 W Chestnut St (60610-3112)
PHONE................................312 329-2102
Gregory Thornton, *Branch Mgr*
EMP: 50
SALES (corp-wide): 111.9MM **Privately Held**
SIC: 8741 2721 2731 Administrative management; periodicals; book publishing
PA: The Moody Bible Institute Of Chicago
820 N La Salle Dr
Chicago IL 60610
312 329-4000

(G-5497)
MORAN GRAPHICS INC
Also Called: AlphaGraphics
1017 W Wa Blvd Unit 101 (60607-2108)
PHONE................................312 226-3900
Sheila D Moran, *President*
Richard F Moran, *Vice Pres*
Nathan Wakefield, *Manager*
EMP: 26
SQ FT: 1,500
SALES (est): 4.2MM **Privately Held**
WEB: www.alphagboutique.com
SIC: 2752 Commercial printing, lithographic

(G-5498)
MORAN PROPERTIES INC
1407 N Dearborn St (60610-1505)
PHONE................................312 440-1962
Susan J Moran, *President*
John McDonough, *Treasurer*
EMP: 2

GEOGRAPHIC SECTION

Chicago - Cook County (G-5526)

SALES (est): 264.6K **Privately Held**
SIC: **1382** Oil & gas exploration services

(G-5499)
MORE CUPCAKES LLC
1 E Delaware Pl Ste 4 (60611-1452)
PHONE..................................312 951-0001
Mira Horoszowski, *Principal*
Edward P Langefeld, *Principal*
Patricia C Rothman, *Manager*
EMP: 4
SALES (est): 134.3K **Privately Held**
WEB: www.morecupcakes.com
SIC: **5461** 2051 Cakes; cakes, pies & pastries

(G-5500)
MORRIS KURTZON INCORPORATED
Also Called: Kurtzon Lighting
1420 S Talman Ave (60608-1693)
PHONE..................................773 277-2121
Daniel Koch, *CEO*
Victor Morales, *General Mgr*
Mario Castrejon, *Engineer*
Kamla Koch, *Human Res Mgr*
Henry Bradford, *Marketing Staff*
EMP: 22 EST: 1946
SQ FT: 75,000
SALES (est): 8.9MM **Privately Held**
WEB: www.kurtzon.com
SIC: **3646** Fluorescent lighting fixtures, commercial

(G-5501)
MORTON SALT INC (DH)
Also Called: Chicago Salt Service
444 W Lake St Ste 3000 (60606-0090)
PHONE..................................312 807-2000
Christian Herrmann, *CEO*
Jeanette Googe, *QC Mgr*
John Kroha, *Engineer*
Jason McGrath, *Controller*
Sue Brose, *Manager*
◆ EMP: 250
SQ FT: 95,838
SALES (est): 914.4MM
SALES (corp-wide): 4.5B **Privately Held**
SIC: **2891** 2851 2822 1479 Adhesives & sealants; paints & allied products; synthetic rubber; salt & sulfur mining; chemical preparations

(G-5502)
MOSAICOS INC
4948 N Pulaski Rd (60630-2813)
PHONE..................................773 777-8453
Lisa M Bannelos, *President*
George A Bannelos, *Admin Sec*
EMP: 5
SALES (est): 708.3K **Privately Held**
SIC: **3253** Ceramic wall & floor tile

(G-5503)
MOSS INC
222 N Maplewood Ave (60612-2144)
PHONE..................................800 341-1557
Victoria Weidner, *Plant Mgr*
EMP: 85
SALES (corp-wide): 12.4MM **Privately Held**
SIC: **2759** Commercial printing
PA: Moss Inc.
2600 Elmhurst Rd
Elk Grove Village IL 60007
800 341-1557

(G-5504)
MOST ENTERPRISE INC
1007 W Fulton Market Fl 2 (60607-1222)
PHONE..................................800 792-4669
Thomas William McGrath, *CEO*
EMP: 93
SALES (est): 3.1MM **Privately Held**
SIC: **1541** 2326 2085 4731 Pharmaceutical manufacturing plant construction; medical & hospital uniforms, men's; distilled & blended liquors; freight forwarding; consulting engineer

(G-5505)
MOTAMED MEDICAL PUBLISHING CO
7141 N Kedzie Ave # 1504 (60645-2847)
PHONE..................................773 761-6667
Dr Hosein A Motamed, *President*
EMP: 3
SALES (est): 206.9K **Privately Held**
SIC: **2731** Textbooks: publishing only, not printed on site

(G-5506)
MOTIVEQUEST LLC (HQ)
Also Called: Lrwmotivequest
200 S Wacker Dr Ste 625 (60606-5802)
PHONE..................................847 905-6100
Andy Moens, *Marketing Staff*
Brook Miller, *CTO*
David Rabjohns,
EMP: 15
SQ FT: 5,000
SALES (est): 4.8MM
SALES (corp-wide): 43MM **Privately Held**
SIC: **8748** 7372 Business consulting; business oriented computer software
PA: Lieberman Research Worldwide, Llc
1900 Avenue Of The Stars
Los Angeles CA 90067
310 553-0550

(G-5507)
MOTOR ROW DEVELOPMENT CORP
2303 S Mich Ave Ste Assoc (60616)
PHONE..................................773 525-3311
Paul Zucker, *President*
EMP: 1
SALES (est): 276.8K **Privately Held**
SIC: **3714** Motor vehicle parts & accessories

(G-5508)
MOTOROLA MOBILITY HOLDINGS LLC (HQ)
222 Merchandise Mart Plz # 1800 (60654-4203)
PHONE..................................800 668-6765
Dennis Woodside, *CEO*
Rick Osterloh, *President*
Gary Cunningham, *Counsel*
Iqbal Arshad, *Senior VP*
Kouji Kodera, *Senior VP*
▲ EMP: 13
SALES: 3.5B **Privately Held**
SIC: **3663** Mobile communication equipment

(G-5509)
MOTOROLA MOBILITY LLC
222 Merchandise Mart Plz # 1800 (60654-4203)
PHONE..................................847 576-5000
Anthony Wade, *Opers Staff*
Ted Kozlowski, *VP Engrg*
Girish Chandraiah, *Engineer*
Samarth Inamdar, *Engineer*
Luiz Salgado, *Finance Mgr*
EMP: 13 **Privately Held**
SIC: **3663** Radio & TV communications equipment
HQ: Motorola Mobility Llc
222 Mdse Mart Plz # 1800
Chicago IL 60654

(G-5510)
MOTOROLA MOBILITY LLC (DH)
222 Mdse Mart Plz # 1800 (60654-4203)
P.O. Box 391597, Mountain View CA (94039-1597)
PHONE..................................847 523-5000
Lisa Turner, *Principal*
Sergio Buniac, *Senior VP*
Jeff Millery, *Vice Pres*
Patrick Cox, *Engineer*
Ngee Lee, *Engineer*
▲ EMP: 346
SALES (est): 343.8MM **Privately Held**
SIC: **3663** 4812 Mobile communication equipment; cellular telephone services

(G-5511)
MOTOROLA SOLUTIONS INC (PA)
500 W Monroe St Ste 4400 (60661-3781)
PHONE..................................847 576-5000
Gregory Q Brown, *Ch of Bd*
Mark S Hacker, *Exec VP*
Kelly S Mark, *Exec VP*
Kelly Mark, *Exec VP*
John P Molloy, *Exec VP*
EMP: 225 EST: 1928
SALES (est): 7.8B **Publicly Held**
WEB: www.motorolasolutions.com
SIC: **3663** 3661 Radio broadcasting & communications equipment; mobile communication equipment; pagers (one-way); cellular radio telephone; modems; multiplex equipment, telephone & telegraph

(G-5512)
MOXIE APPAREL LLC
222 S Morgan St Ste 3c (60607-3728)
PHONE..................................312 243-9040
EMP: 3
SALES (corp-wide): 1.6MM **Privately Held**
SIC: **2329** Mfg Men's/Boy's Clothing
PA: Moxie Apparel Llc
145 E 27th St Apt 11g
New York NY 10016
212 779-0195

(G-5513)
MOZAICS LLC
Also Called: Mozaics Snacks
5960 N Broadway St (60660-3524)
PHONE..................................614 306-1881
Todd Bamberg,
EMP: 5
SALES (est): 234.3K **Privately Held**
WEB: www.deliciousness.com
SIC: **2096** Potato chips & similar snacks

(G-5514)
MP STEEL CHICAGO LLC
5757 W Ogden Ave Ste 4 (60804-3881)
PHONE..................................773 242-0853
Jack Desai, *General Mgr*
EMP: 50
SALES (est): 5.1MM **Privately Held**
SIC: **3398** Metal heat treating

(G-5515)
MPC CONTAINMENT SYSTEMS LLC (HQ)
815 W Van Buren St # 520 (60607-3506)
PHONE..................................773 927-4121
Tony Bonilla, *Purchasing*
Benjamin Beiler, *Mng Member*
Alan Berman,
Edward E Reicin,
EMP: 65
SQ FT: 52,000
SALES (est): 20.7MM **Privately Held**
WEB: www.mpccontainment.com
SIC: **2394** Canvas & related products

(G-5516)
MPC CONTAINMENT SYSTEMS LLC
3820 W 74th St (60629)
PHONE..................................773 927-4120
EMP: 4
SALES (est): 257.5K **Privately Held**
SIC: **3443** Fabricated plate work (boiler shop)
HQ: Mpc Containment Systems Llc
815 W Van Buren St # 520
Chicago IL 60607
773 927-4121

(G-5517)
MPC GROUP LLC (PA)
815 W Van Buren St # 520 (60607-3506)
PHONE..................................773 927-4120
Benjamin Beiler, *CEO*
Alan Berman,
Edward Reicin,
EMP: 112
SALES (est): 13.5MM **Privately Held**
SIC: **2394** 3089 Canvas & related products; plastic processing

(G-5518)
MRC POLYMERS INC (PA)
3307 S Lawndale Ave (60623-5007)
PHONE..................................773 890-9000
Paul Binks, *President*
Brett Miller, *General Mgr*
Sergio Cabrales, *Plant Mgr*
Hernan Masso, *Plant Mgr*
Brendon Parrish, *Safety Mgr*
◆ EMP: 95
SQ FT: 75,000
SALES (est): 16.9MM **Privately Held**
WEB: www.mrcpolymers.com
SIC: **2821** Polycarbonate resins; polypropylene resins; polyesters

(G-5519)
MSI GREEN INC
1958 W Grand Ave (60622-6232)
PHONE..................................312 421-6550
Irene Weiss, *President*
Marc Weiss, *Vice Pres*
EMP: 4 EST: 2012
SALES (est): 563.6K **Privately Held**
SIC: **2023** 2033 2064 Dry, condensed, evaporated dairy products; fruits & fruit products in cans, jars, etc.; candy & other confectionery products

(G-5520)
MT CONTAINERS INC
6410 W 74th St Ste B (60638-6037)
P.O. Box 126, Bedford Park (60499-0126)
PHONE..................................708 458-9420
Kevin E Tyrrell, *President*
Marilyn Tyrrell, *Treasurer*
EMP: 2
SQ FT: 12,000
SALES (est): 1MM **Privately Held**
SIC: **3411** Metal cans

(G-5521)
MT GREENWOOD EMBROIDERY
3136 W 111th St (60655-2206)
PHONE..................................773 779-5798
Sam Costas, *President*
EMP: 1
SQ FT: 2,400
SALES (est): 200K **Privately Held**
SIC: **7336** 2395 Silk screen design; embroidery & art needlework

(G-5522)
MULLEN FOODS LLC
6740 N Edgebrook Ter (60646-2703)
PHONE..................................773 716-9001
James Mullen,
EMP: 6
SALES (est): 507K **Privately Held**
SIC: **2033** 7389 Canned fruits & specialties;

(G-5523)
MULTI PACKAGING SOLUTIONS INC
Also Called: Chicago Paper Tub & Can
4221 N Normandy Ave (60634-1402)
PHONE..................................773 283-9500
Marc Shore, *CEO*
EMP: 5
SALES (corp-wide): 18.2B **Publicly Held**
SIC: **2731** 2761 3089 5092 Books: publishing & printing; continuous forms, office & business; identification cards, plastic; arts & crafts equipment & supplies; packaging paper & plastics film, coated & laminated; screen printing
HQ: Multi Packaging Solutions, Inc.
885 3rd Ave Fl 28
New York NY 10022

(G-5524)
MUMFORD METAL CASTING LLC (PA)
2222 S Halsted St (60608-4531)
PHONE..................................312 733-2600
Phil Mumford Sr,
EMP: 4
SALES (est): 17.1MM **Privately Held**
SIC: **3369** White metal castings (lead, tin, antimony), except die

(G-5525)
MUNOZ FLOUR TORTILLERIA INC
1707 W 47th St (60609-3823)
PHONE..................................773 523-1837
Oscar Munoz, *President*
EMP: 10
SALES (est): 720.1K **Privately Held**
SIC: **2099** Tortillas, fresh or refrigerated

(G-5526)
MURFF ENTERPRISES LLC
9331 S Clyde Ave (60617-3745)
PHONE..................................203 685-5556

Chicago - Cook County (G-5527)

Daniel Murff,
EMP: 4
SALES (est): 151.4K **Privately Held**
SIC: 3999 Manufacturing industries

(G-5527)
MURO PALLETS CORP
5208 S Mozart St (60632-2248)
PHONE...................................773 640-8606
Javier Muro, *Principal*
EMP: 3
SALES (est): 153.9K **Privately Held**
SIC: 2448 Pallets, wood & wood with metal

(G-5528)
MURRIHY PALLET CO
1919 W 74th St (60636-3747)
P.O. Box 9054 (60609-0054)
PHONE...................................615 370-7000
John Murrihy Sr, *President*
John Murrihy Jr, *Vice Pres*
EMP: 20
SALES (est): 3.1MM **Privately Held**
SIC: 2448 7699 Pallets, wood; skids, wood; pallet repair

(G-5529)
MY LOCAL BEACON LLC
73 W Monroe St Ste 323 (60603-4955)
PHONE...................................888 482-6691
Shijo Mathew, *Vice Pres*
EMP: 5
SALES (est): 219.8K **Privately Held**
SIC: 7372 Business oriented computer software

(G-5530)
MY OWN MEALS INC
Also Called: J&M Food Products Company
5410 W Roosevelt Rd # 301 (60644-1490)
PHONE...................................773 378-6505
Mary Anne Jackson, *President*
Maria Duarte, *Branch Mgr*
EMP: 5
SALES (corp-wide): 15.2MM **Privately Held**
WEB: www.myownmeals.com
SIC: 2099 Food preparations
PA: My Own Meals, Inc.
400 Lake Cook Rd Ste 107
Deerfield IL 60015
847 948-1118

(G-5531)
MYERSON LLC
Also Called: Pinnacle
5106 N Ravenswood Ave (60640-2713)
PHONE...................................312 432-8200
Jim Swartout, *COO*
Janine Pierre, *Human Res Mgr*
Scott McMillen, *Sales Staff*
James Swartout,
Allan Filek,
EMP: 2
SALES: 527.2K **Privately Held**
SIC: 3843 Teeth, artificial (not made in dental laboratories)

(G-5532)
MYHOMEEQ LLC
1741 N Western Ave (60647-6513)
PHONE...................................773 328-7034
John Blaser, *Manager*
Robert Weissbourd,
EMP: 3
SALES (est): 113K **Privately Held**
SIC: 7372 Prepackaged software

(G-5533)
N E S TRAFFIC SAFETY
8770 W Bryn Mawr Ave (60631-3515)
PHONE...................................312 603-7444
Garry Culver, *Principal*
EMP: 10
SALES (est): 1MM **Privately Held**
SIC: 3669 Traffic signals, electric

(G-5534)
NABLUS SWEETS INC
4800 N Kedzie Ave (60625)
PHONE...................................708 205-6354
EMP: 30
SALES (corp-wide): 1.7MM **Privately Held**
SIC: 2061 5461 Mfg Raw Cane Sugar Retail Bakery
PA: Nablus Sweets Inc.
8320 S Harlem Ave
Bridgeview IL 60455
708 529-3911

(G-5535)
NACME STEEL PROCESSING LLC
Also Called: National Processing Co-Plant 1
429 W 127th St (60628-7109)
PHONE...................................847 806-7200
John Dubrock,
EMP: 60
SALES (est): 12.8MM **Privately Held**
SIC: 3312 Blast furnaces & steel mills

(G-5536)
NADER WHOLESALE GROCERS INC
3636 W 83rd Pl (60652-3204)
PHONE...................................773 582-1000
Equab Ali, *President*
Mohammed Hinnawi, *Vice Pres*
Mohammed Ali, *Admin Sec*
EMP: 14
SALES (est): 5.2MM **Privately Held**
SIC: 5141 5145 5149 5194 Groceries, general line; candy; soft drinks; tobacco & tobacco products; cigarettes; soap & other detergents

(G-5537)
NADIG NEWSPAPERS INC
Also Called: Northwest Side Press
4937 N Milwaukee Ave (60630-2114)
PHONE...................................773 286-6100
Glenn Nadig, *President*
EMP: 16
SQ FT: 5,500
SALES (est): 1.1MM **Privately Held**
SIC: 2711 Commercial printing & newspaper publishing combined; newspapers, publishing & printing

(G-5538)
NAK WON KOREAN BAKERY
3746 W Lawrence Ave (60625-5726)
PHONE...................................773 588-8769
To Mon Cha, *Owner*
EMP: 3
SALES (est): 126.3K **Privately Held**
SIC: 2051 5963 Cakes, bakery: except frozen; direct selling establishments

(G-5539)
NAMASTE LABORATORIES LLC (HQ)
310 S Racine Ave Fl 8 (60607-2841)
PHONE...................................708 824-1393
Clarisa Wilson, *CEO*
Vikram Bali, *Sales Staff*
◆ **EMP:** 80
SQ FT: 100,000
SALES (est): 64.3MM **Privately Held**
SIC: 2844 Hair preparations, including shampoos

(G-5540)
NARDA INC
Also Called: North Amercn Ret Dealers Assn
222 S Riverside Plz (60606-5808)
P.O. Box 676, Downers Grove (60515-0676)
PHONE...................................312 648-2300
Tom Drake, *Exec Dir*
Deal - Robert Goldberg, *General Counsel*
EMP: 11 **EST:** 1943
SQ FT: 6,500
SALES: 149.9K **Privately Held**
SIC: 8611 2721 5961 Merchants' association; trade journals: publishing & printing; catalog & mail-order houses

(G-5541)
NARRATIVE HEALTH NETWORK INC
1201 S Prrie Ave Apt 4103 (60605)
PHONE...................................312 600-9154
EMP: 7 **EST:** 2015
SALES (est): 275.6K **Privately Held**
SIC: 7372 Prepackaged Software Services

(G-5542)
NATAZ SPECIALTY COATINGS INC
3300 W 31st St (60623-5016)
PHONE...................................773 247-7030
John J Francis, *President*
Michael K Francis, *Vice Pres*
▼ **EMP:** 12 **EST:** 1927
SQ FT: 25,000
SALES (est): 1.5MM **Privately Held**
WEB: www.pureasphalt.com
SIC: 2952 2899 2891 2851 Asphalt felts & coatings; chemical preparations; adhesives & sealants; paints & allied products; soap & other detergents

(G-5543)
NATIONAL ASSOCIATION REALTORS (PA)
Also Called: Realtor Magazine
430 N Michigan Ave Lowr 2 (60611-4088)
PHONE...................................800 874-6500
Dale Stinton, *CEO*
Steve Brown, *President*
John Smaby, *President*
Maurice Veissi, *President*
John Pierpoint, *Principal*
EMP: 250
SQ FT: 180,000
SALES (est): 242.1MM **Privately Held**
WEB: www.realtor.org
SIC: 8611 2721 8299 Trade associations; periodicals: publishing & printing; educational service, nondegree granting: continuing educ.

(G-5544)
NATIONAL BEEF PACKING CO LLC
Also Called: National Beef Packing Intl
30 N Michigan Ave # 1702 (60602-3643)
PHONE...................................312 332-6166
Mark Domanski, *President*
EMP: 3 **Privately Held**
SIC: 2011 Meat packing plants
HQ: National Beef Packing Company, L.L.C.
12200 N Ambassador Dr # 101
Kansas City MO 64163
800 449-2333

(G-5545)
NATIONAL BISCUIT COMPANY
7300 S Kedzie Ave (60629-3595)
PHONE...................................773 925-0654
EMP: 4
SALES (est): 258.4K **Privately Held**
SIC: 2051 Mfg Bread/Related Products

(G-5546)
NATIONAL MATERIAL COMPANY LLC
429 W 127th St (60628-7108)
PHONE...................................773 468-2800
Brenda Streight, *Branch Mgr*
John Marino, *Programmer Anys*
David Susler, *General Counsel*
EMP: 3
SALES (corp-wide): 824.7MM **Privately Held**
SIC: 3341 Aluminum smelting & refining (secondary)
HQ: National Material Company, L.L.C.
1965 Pratt Blvd
Elk Grove Village IL 60007

(G-5547)
NATIONAL MATERIAL LP
Also Called: Cox Metal Processing
12100 S Stony Island Ave (60633-2430)
PHONE...................................773 646-6300
David Ziegelski, *Vice Pres*
Charles Sudwischer, *VP Opers*
Quentin Morlier, *Sales Engr*
Eddie Mendoza, *Manager*
EMP: 28
SALES (corp-wide): 824.7MM **Privately Held**
SIC: 3312 Sheet or strip, steel, hot-rolled
PA: National Material L.P.
1965 Pratt Blvd
Elk Grove Village IL 60007
847 806-7200

(G-5548)
NATIONAL MATERIAL PROCESSING
12100 S Stony Island Ave # 1 (60633-2430)
PHONE...................................773 646-6300
EMP: 2
SALES (est): 327.2K **Privately Held**
SIC: 3312 Blast furnaces & steel mills

(G-5549)
NATIONAL MICRO SYSTEMS INC
2 E 8th St Ste 100 (60605-2122)
PHONE...................................312 566-0414
Terry R Peters, *President*
Bernard Linzmeier, *Vice Pres*
Richard Peters, *Treasurer*
Barbara Peters, *Admin Sec*
EMP: 5
SALES (est): 75K **Privately Held**
SIC: 3571 7378 3823 Electronic computers; computer maintenance & repair; industrial instrmnts msrmnt display/control process variable

(G-5550)
NATIONAL PORGES RADIATOR CORP
320 W 83rd St (60620-1704)
PHONE...................................773 224-3000
James Porges, *President*
EMP: 18 **EST:** 1982
SQ FT: 23,000
SALES (est): 3.5MM **Privately Held**
SIC: 3714 Radiators & radiator shells & cores, motor vehicle

(G-5551)
NATIONAL POWER LLC
4330 W Belmont Ave (60641-4524)
PHONE...................................773 685-2662
Ira Alport, *President*
Thomas Vrablik, *President*
Joe Chatman, *Natl Sales Mgr*
▲ **EMP:** 50 **EST:** 1980
SQ FT: 23,000
SALES (est): 13.5MM **Privately Held**
SIC: 5999 3691 Batteries, non-automotive; batteries, rechargeable

(G-5552)
NATIONAL RUBBER STAMP CO INC
5320 N Lowell Ave Apt 311 (60630-1780)
PHONE...................................773 281-6522
Donna Heintz, *President*
Wayne Heintz, *Vice Pres*
EMP: 2 **EST:** 1933
SQ FT: 3,000
SALES: 280K **Privately Held**
SIC: 3479 7389 3953 Name plates: engraved, etched, etc.; engraving service; cancelling stamps, hand: rubber or metal

(G-5553)
NATURES AMERICAN CO
3105 N Ashland Ave (60657-3013)
PHONE...................................630 246-4274
Kevin Hannan, *CEO*
Jay Sebben, *Admin Sec*
EMP: 8 **EST:** 1972
SALES: 700K **Privately Held**
SIC: 2041 Grain cereals, cracked

(G-5554)
NATURES HEALING REMEDIES INC
7742 W Addison St (60634-3018)
PHONE...................................773 589-9996
Leon Kolodziej, *President*
June Demma, *Manager*
EMP: 12
SALES (est): 1.4MM **Privately Held**
SIC: 2833 Drugs & herbs: grading, grinding & milling

(G-5555)
NAUTIC GLOBAL GROUP LLC
333 W Wacker Dr Ste 600 (60606-1284)
PHONE...................................574 457-5731
Steven L Smilay,
▼ **EMP:** 4
SALES (est): 838.8K **Privately Held**
SIC: 3732 Boat building & repairing

GEOGRAPHIC SECTION
Chicago - Cook County (G-5584)

(G-5556)
NAVILLUS WOODWORKS LLC
2100 N Major Ave (60639-2901)
PHONE..................312 375-2680
Daniel F Sullivan, *Mng Member*
EMP: 6
SALES: 1MM Privately Held
WEB: www.navilluswoodworks.com
SIC: 2431 3549 Woodwork, interior & ornamental; cutting & slitting machinery

(G-5557)
NAVISTARSINFOSOFT INC
4323 S Emerald Ave (60609-3445)
PHONE..................877 270-3543
Hitesh Joshi, *CEO*
Jorge Carson, *President*
EMP: 20
SALES: 70K Privately Held
SIC: 7372 7389 Prepackaged software;

(G-5558)
NAYLOR AUTOMOTIVE ENGRG CO INC
4645 S Knox Ave (60632-4805)
PHONE..................773 582-6900
Paul Januska, *President*
EMP: 18 EST: 1950
SQ FT: 17,000
SALES (est): 2.7MM Privately Held
WEB: www.naylorautomotive.com
SIC: 7539 3714 3568 Automotive repair shops; motor vehicle parts & accessories; power transmission equipment

(G-5559)
NDUJA ARTISANS CO
2817 N Harlem Ave (60707-1638)
PHONE..................312 550-6991
Agostino Fiasche, *President*
Tony Fiasche, *President*
EMP: 2
SALES: 500K Privately Held
SIC: 2015 Poultry sausage, luncheon meats & other poultry products

(G-5560)
NEA AGORA PACKING CO
1056 W Taylor St (60607-4223)
PHONE..................312 421-5130
Rose Musollami, *Owner*
EMP: 3
SQ FT: 2,500
SALES (est): 360.2K Privately Held
SIC: 5147 5421 2013 2011 Meats, fresh; meat markets, including freezer provisioners; sausages & other prepared meats; meat packing plants

(G-5561)
NECKBONE SKUNKS LOGISTICS & TE
6835 S Dorchester Ave # 1 (60637-4714)
PHONE..................312 218-0281
Elester Drake, *CEO*
Gladys Billups, *Vice Pres*
Kyndal Buchanan, *Vice Pres*
Ronnye Buchanan, *Vice Pres*
Sade Drake, *Vice Pres*
EMP: 10
SALES (est): 352.6K Privately Held
SIC: 3151 6799 7389 3711 Mittens, leather; investment clubs; real estate investors, except property operators; ; wreckers (tow truck), assembly of; unisex hair salons; personal care home, with health care

(G-5562)
NEFAB INC
3105 N Ashland Ave 394 (60657-3013)
PHONE..................705 748-4888
▲ EMP: 7
SQ FT: 1,000
SALES (est): 1.6MM
SALES (corp-wide): 470.8MM Privately Held
SIC: 2631 Paperboard Mills, Nsk
HQ: Nefab Ab
    Lantmatargrand 5
    Jonkoping 553 2
    771 590-000

(G-5563)
NEGS & LITHO INC
Also Called: Business Express R & A Prtg
6501 N Avondale Ave (60631-1521)
PHONE..................847 647-7770
Arthur Milbrandt, *President*
Allen Milbrandt, *Vice Pres*
EMP: 4
SQ FT: 3,500
SALES: 300K Privately Held
SIC: 2752 7331 7374 7338 Commercial printing, offset; mailing service; data processing service; word processing service; typesetting

(G-5564)
NEIMAN BROS CO INC
Also Called: Neiman Brothers Co
3322 W Newport Ave (60618-5595)
PHONE..................773 463-3000
Laura Neiman, *President*
Bill Juckett, *Sales Staff*
Phyllis Neiman, *Admin Sec*
▲ EMP: 26 EST: 1920
SQ FT: 35,000
SALES (est): 14.3MM Privately Held
WEB: www.neimanbrothers.com
SIC: 5149 2099 2087 Flour; honey; baking supplies; food preparations; flavoring extracts & syrups

(G-5565)
NELSON & LAVOLD MANUFACTURING
1530 N Halsted St 34 (60642-2528)
PHONE..................312 943-6300
Thor Sveinsvoll, *President*
EMP: 6 EST: 1946
SQ FT: 9,700
SALES (est): 831.7K Privately Held
SIC: 3451 Screw machine products

(G-5566)
NEON ART
4752 N Avers Ave (60625-6201)
PHONE..................773 588-5883
Hochul Shin, *Owner*
EMP: 3
SALES (est): 140K Privately Held
SIC: 3993 Electric signs; neon signs

(G-5567)
NEON EXPRESS SIGNS
5026 N Broadway St (60640-3006)
PHONE..................773 463-7335
EMP: 4
SALES (est): 334.4K Privately Held
SIC: 3993 Mfg Signs/Advertising Specialties

(G-5568)
NEON ONE LLC
Also Called: Neon Crm
4545 N Ravenswood Ave 2ndf (60640-5201)
PHONE..................888 860-6366
Jeff Gordy, *President*
Brendan Noone, *COO*
Kyle Curry, *Sales Mgr*
Sula Hitzeman, *Client Mgr*
Michael Evert, *Sales Staff*
EMP: 43
SALES: 4.5MM Privately Held
WEB: www.neoncrm.com
SIC: 7372 Business oriented computer software

(G-5569)
NEON SHOP INC
2247 N Western Ave (60647-3142)
PHONE..................773 227-0303
Tom Brickler, *President*
EMP: 4
SQ FT: 1,000
SALES (est): 433.8K Privately Held
SIC: 3993 Neon signs

(G-5570)
NEOPENDA PBC
965 W Chicago Ave (60642-5413)
PHONE..................919 622-2487
Sona Shah, *CEO*
EMP: 4
SALES (est): 66.8K Privately Held
SIC: 8731 3845 Commercial physical research; patient monitoring apparatus

(G-5571)
NEPALEY LLC
1900 N Austin Ave (60639-5010)
PHONE..................224 420-2310
Vivek Kunwar,
EMP: 5
SALES (est): 139.9K Privately Held
SIC: 2099 Food preparations

(G-5572)
NETSUITE INC
200 N La Salle St # 2000 (60601-1014)
PHONE..................312 273-4100
EMP: 14 EST: 2018
SALES (est): 1.2MM Privately Held
SIC: 7372 Prepackaged software

(G-5573)
NEUROTHERAPEUTICS PHARMA INC
8750 W Bryn Mawr Ave # 440 (60631-3655)
PHONE..................773 444-4180
Stephen D Collins, *President*
EMP: 7
SALES (est): 700K Privately Held
WEB: www.ntprx.com
SIC: 2834 Pharmaceutical preparations

(G-5574)
NEW C F & I INC
Also Called: Rockey Mountain Steel Mills
200 E Randolph St # 7800 (60601-6436)
PHONE..................312 533-3555
William Swindels, *Chairman*
Rob Simon, *Vice Pres*
Jennifer Murray, *Vice Pres*
Bruce Barrett, *Senior Engr*
▲ EMP: 750
SQ FT: 10,000
SALES (est): 86.9MM
SALES (corp-wide): 177.9K Privately Held
SIC: 3312 Blast furnaces & steel mills
HQ: Evraz Inc. Na
    71 S Wacker Dr Ste 1700
    Chicago IL 60606
    312 533-3555

(G-5575)
NEW CENTURY PICTURE CORP (PA)
2737 W Fulton St (60612-2068)
P.O. Box 1349, Deerfield (60015-6005)
PHONE..................773 638-8888
Gerald Sharlin, *Chairman*
Martin Shames, *Treasurer*
▲ EMP: 35
SQ FT: 28,000
SALES (est): 4.3MM Privately Held
SIC: 2499 3231 Picture & mirror frames, wood; art glass: made from purchased glass

(G-5576)
NEW CITY COMMUNICATIONS
Also Called: New City News
770 N Halsted St Ste 183 (60642-5999)
PHONE..................312 243-8786
Brian Hieggelke, *President*
David Aniol, *CFO*
Todd Hieggelke, *Marketing Mgr*
Jan Hieggelke, *Admin Sec*
EMP: 29
SQ FT: 6,638
SALES (est): 3.5MM Privately Held
SIC: 2752 2791 2711 Newspapers, lithographed only; typesetting; newspapers

(G-5577)
NEW ERA CAP CO INC
106 N Aberdeen St Ste 200 (60607-2162)
PHONE..................504 581-2445
Christopher H Koch, *Branch Mgr*
EMP: 283
SALES (corp-wide): 666.8MM Privately Held
SIC: 2353 Uniform hats & caps
PA: New Era Cap Co., Inc.
    160 Delaware Ave
    Buffalo NY 14202
    716 604-9000

(G-5578)
NEW SBL INC
1001 W 45th St Ste B (60609-3327)
PHONE..................773 376-8280
Yuk C Chan, *President*
Yu HEI Tung, *Manager*
EMP: 34
SQ FT: 12,000
SALES (est): 17MM Privately Held
SIC: 5147 2011 Meats & meat products; meat packing plants

(G-5579)
NEW SPECIALTY PRODUCTS INC
Also Called: Barbeque Select
1421 W 47th St (60609-3233)
P.O. Box 9273 (60609-0273)
PHONE..................773 847-0230
Paul H Buehler, *President*
EMP: 23
SALES (est): 3.9MM Privately Held
SIC: 2035 2013 2015 Pickles, sauces & salad dressings; prepared beef products from purchased beef; prepared pork products from purchased pork; chicken, processed: fresh

(G-5580)
NEW SPIN CYCLE
1400 E 47th St Ste A (60653-4520)
PHONE..................773 952-7490
Kirk Bargle, *Owner*
EMP: 7 EST: 2012
SALES (est): 488.2K Privately Held
WEB: www.cityspincycle.com
SIC: 3582 Commercial laundry equipment

(G-5581)
NEW STYLE CABINETS INC
1840 N Major Ave (60639-4118)
PHONE..................773 622-3114
Michal Tracz, *President*
EMP: 4
SALES (est): 225.5K Privately Held
SIC: 2434 Wood kitchen cabinets

(G-5582)
NEW TASTE GOOD NOODLE INC
2559 S Archer Ave (60608-5935)
PHONE..................312 842-8980
WEI Min Xu, *Admin Sec*
EMP: 5
SALES (est): 501.1K Privately Held
SIC: 2099 Noodles, uncooked: packaged with other ingredients

(G-5583)
NEW WORLD TRNSP SYSTEMS
5895 N Rogers Ave (60646-5953)
PHONE..................773 509-5931
David W Marx, *President*
Abby Jones, *CFO*
Edward M Marx Jr, *Admin Sec*
EMP: 133
SQ FT: 76,800
SALES (est): 290.1K
SALES (corp-wide): 96.9MM Privately Held
SIC: 3799 Trailers & trailer equipment
PA: New World Van Lines, Inc.
    5875 N Rogers Ave
    Chicago IL 60646
    773 685-3399

(G-5584)
NEWLY WEDS FOODS INC (PA)
4140 W Fullerton Ave (60639-2198)
PHONE..................773 489-7000
Charles T Angell, *President*
John J Seely, *Senior VP*
Sharon Angell, *Vice Pres*
Leo Culligan, *Vice Pres*
Lynn Theiss, *Vice Pres*
◆ EMP: 600 EST: 1932
SQ FT: 375,000
SALES (est): 128.2MM Privately Held
WEB: www.newlywedsfoods.com
SIC: 2099 Bread crumbs, not made in bakeries; sugar powdered from purchased ingredients; seasonings & spices

Chicago - Cook County (G-5585)

(G-5585)
NEWLY WEDS FOODS INC
4849 N Milwaukee Ave # 700 (60630-2394)
PHONE..................773 628-6900
Angel Calvillo, *Engineer*
Brian Johnson, *Branch Mgr*
Jason Feinberg, *Manager*
Julian Torres, *Administration*
Joseph Cavataio, *Technician*
EMP: 67
SALES (corp-wide): 128.2MM **Privately Held**
SIC: 2099 Food preparations
PA: Newly Weds Foods, Inc.
4140 W Fullerton Ave
Chicago IL 60639
773 489-7000

(G-5586)
NEWLY WEDS FOODS INC
Also Called: Accounting Department
2501 N Keeler Ave (60639-2131)
PHONE..................773 489-7000
Sharon Angell, *Vice Pres*
Stan Herrera, *Opers Mgr*
Dave Bautz, *Traffic Mgr*
Carlos Gravis, *Purch Mgr*
Carolyn Davis, *Purchasing*
EMP: 340
SALES (corp-wide): 128.2MM **Privately Held**
SIC: 2099 Food preparations
PA: Newly Weds Foods, Inc.
4140 W Fullerton Ave
Chicago IL 60639
773 489-7000

(G-5587)
NEWS & LETTERS
59 E Van Buren St (60605-1230)
PHONE..................312 663-0839
Al Walchirk, *Principal*
EMP: 3
SALES (est): 111.3K **Privately Held**
SIC: 2711 Newspapers: publishing only, not printed on site

(G-5588)
NEWSER LLC
222 N Columbus Dr Lbby 1 (60601-7831)
PHONE..................312 284-2300
Michael Harthorne, *Editor*
Kate Seamons, *Chief*
Gary Burtka, *Marketing Staff*
Patrick Spain, *Mng Member*
Patrick J Spain, *Mng Member*
EMP: 11
SALES (est): 602.4K **Privately Held**
WEB: www.newser.com
SIC: 2711 Newspapers, publishing & printing

(G-5589)
NEWSPAPER NATIONAL NETWORK
500 N Michigan Ave # 2210 (60611-3776)
PHONE..................312 644-1142
EMP: 4
SALES (est): 190.9K **Privately Held**
SIC: 2711 Newspapers-Publishing/Printing

(G-5590)
NEWSPAPER SOLUTIONS INC
4968 N Milwaukee Ave 1n (60630-2385)
PHONE..................773 930-3404
Daniel Harris, *Principal*
EMP: 10
SALES (est): 607.1K **Privately Held**
SIC: 2711 Newspapers, publishing & printing

(G-5591)
NEWSWEB CORPORATION (PA)
2401 N Halsted St (60614-2451)
PHONE..................773 975-5727
Fred J Eychaner, *President*
Charles Gross, *President*
Camille Dziewiontka, *Executive Asst*
Jon Barry, *Admin Sec*
EMP: 47 EST: 1971
SALES (est): 8.2MM **Privately Held**
SIC: 2752 Newspapers, lithographed only

(G-5592)
NEXLP INC
318 W Adams St Ste 1100a (60606-5139)
PHONE..................773 383-4114
Leib Jason, *Principal*
EMP: 12
SALES (est): 1.2MM **Privately Held**
WEB: www.nexlp.com
SIC: 7372 Prepackaged software

(G-5593)
NEXTPOINT INC
4043 N Ravenswood Ave (60613-1155)
PHONE..................773 929-4000
Rakesh Madhava, *CEO*
Tricia Boguslawski, *Vice Pres*
Dakota Dux, *Senior Engr*
Jodi Hrbek, *Bus Dvlpt Dir*
Lauren Chingo, *Finance Mgr*
EMP: 20
SALES (est): 2.4MM **Privately Held**
SIC: 7372 Application computer software

(G-5594)
NFC COMPANY INC
Also Called: NFC Suburban
2944 N Leavitt St (60618-8115)
PHONE..................773 472-6468
Norbert Francis, *President*
EMP: 5
SQ FT: 3,000
SALES (est): 1.1MM **Privately Held**
SIC: 5046 8742 2087 Restaurant equipment & supplies; soda fountain fixtures, except refrigerated; management consulting services; flavoring extracts & syrups

(G-5595)
NICADO PUBLISHING COMPANY INC
Also Called: Negocios Now
1522 W Fuller St Apt 2s (60608)
PHONE..................312 593-2557
Clemente Nicado, *President*
Kelly Yelmene, *Admin Sec*
EMP: 4
SALES (est): 160K **Privately Held**
SIC: 2711 Newspapers; newspapers, publishing & printing

(G-5596)
NICHE INTERACTIVE MEDIA INC
Also Called: Shoppinggives
212 W Van Buren St 2s (60607-3909)
PHONE..................312 498-7933
Ronny Sage, *President*
EMP: 12
SALES (est): 256K **Privately Held**
SIC: 7372 Business oriented computer software

(G-5597)
NICKEL COMPOSITE COATINGS INC
6454 W 74th St (60638-6009)
PHONE..................708 563-2780
Philip Fabiyi, *President*
Wilbur Passley, *Plant Engr*
EMP: 20
SALES (est): 1.6MM **Privately Held**
SIC: 3479 Varnishing of metal products

(G-5598)
NICKEL PUTTER
1229 N North Branch St (60642-2473)
PHONE..................312 337-7888
EMP: 5
SALES (est): 22.4K **Privately Held**
SIC: 3356 Nonferrous Rolling/Drawing

(G-5599)
NIEDERMAIER INC (PA)
Also Called: Niedermaier Furniture
55 E Erie St Apt 3306 (60611-2257)
PHONE..................312 492-9400
Judith Niedermaier, *President*
Jeffrey Niedermaier, *Vice Pres*
EMP: 60 EST: 1965
SQ FT: 110,000
SALES (est): 8.6MM **Privately Held**
SIC: 2522 5021 Office furniture, except wood; office & public building furniture

(G-5600)
NIEMAN & CONSIDINE INC
Also Called: Uk Sailmakers
2323 S Michigan Ave (60616-2104)
PHONE..................312 326-1053
James Considine, *President*
Patrick Considine, *Vice Pres*
EMP: 10
SQ FT: 10,000
SALES (est): 1.5MM **Privately Held**
SIC: 2394 5551 Sails: made from purchased materials; boat dealers

(G-5601)
NIJHUIS WATER TECHNOLOGY INC
770 N Halsted St Ste 301 (60642-6010)
PHONE..................312 466-9900
Ronald Ruijtenberg, *President*
Thomas Thorelli, *Admin Sec*
EMP: 6 EST: 2011
SALES (est): 779.8K **Privately Held**
WEB: www.nijhuisindustries.com
SIC: 3589 Water treatment equipment, industrial

(G-5602)
NIKE INC
8510 S Cottage Grove Ave (60619-6116)
PHONE..................773 846-5460
Vanessa Wallace, *Marketing Staff*
Henderson Foster, *Manager*
EMP: 50
SALES (corp-wide): 39.1B **Publicly Held**
SIC: 3021 Rubber & plastics footwear
PA: Nike, Inc.
1 Sw Bowerman Dr
Beaverton OR 97005
503 671-6453

(G-5603)
NIMBL WORLDWIDE INC
Also Called: Nimbl, LLC
444 N Michigan Ave # 2550 (60611-3903)
PHONE..................303 800-0245
Yosh Eisbart, *CEO*
Domenico Restuccia, *Principal*
Casey Winterbower, *Principal*
Shannon Baldwin, *Vice Pres*
Lisa Gonzales, *Vice Pres*
EMP: 34
SALES (est): 5.7MM **Privately Held**
SIC: 7379 7372 ; prepackaged software; business oriented computer software
PA: Techedge Spa
Via Caldera 21
Milano MI 20153

(G-5604)
NISSHIN HOLDING INC
Also Called: Nisshin Steel USA
900 N Michigan Ave # 1820 (60611-6537)
PHONE..................847 290-5100
Y Fukami, *Exec Dir*
EMP: 4 **Privately Held**
SIC: 3325 Steel foundries
HQ: Nisshin Holding, Inc.
900 N Michigan Ave # 1820
Chicago IL 60611

(G-5605)
NITROGEN LABS INC
201 W Lake St Ste 155 (60606-0239)
PHONE..................312 504-8134
Giraldo Rosales, *President*
EMP: 3
SALES (est): 255.3K **Privately Held**
SIC: 2813 Nitrogen

(G-5606)
NO DENIAL FOODS
1137 W Monroe St Unit 20 (60607-2582)
PHONE..................312 890-5267
EMP: 3
SALES (est): 169.1K **Privately Held**
SIC: 2099 Food preparations

(G-5607)
NO SURRENDER INC
Also Called: Something Old, Something New
1056 W Belmont Ave (60657-3326)
PHONE..................773 929-7920
Jack Mages, *President*
EMP: 13
SQ FT: 13,000
SALES (est): 2.2MM **Privately Held**
SIC: 5065 5651 2671 Security control equipment & systems; unisex clothing stores; packaging paper & plastics film, coated & laminated

(G-5608)
NOBERT PLATING CO (PA)
340 N Ashland Ave (60607-1015)
PHONE..................312 421-4040
Diann Sickles, *President*
Rob Sickles, *Vice Pres*
Yolanda Amaro, *Purch Mgr*
Jamie Sickles, *QC Mgr*
Sherri Goforth, *Human Res Dir*
EMP: 5 EST: 1903
SQ FT: 45,000
SALES (est): 823.5K **Privately Held**
WEB: www.nobertplating.com
SIC: 3471 Electroplating of metals or formed products

(G-5609)
NONIPRINT
6150 N Milwaukee Ave (60646-3821)
PHONE..................773 366-2846
Michael Nierman, *Principal*
EMP: 4
SALES (est): 193.1K **Privately Held**
SIC: 2752 Commercial printing, offset

(G-5610)
NOODLE PARTY
4205 W Lawrence Ave (60630-2728)
PHONE..................773 205-0505
Nisanart Konkrasung, *President*
EMP: 8 EST: 2008
SALES (est): 525.6K **Privately Held**
WEB: www.noodlesparty.com
SIC: 2098 Noodles (e.g. egg, plain & water), dry

(G-5611)
NOODLES FACTORY LLC
610 W 26th St (60616-1806)
PHONE..................312 842-6500
Yongjian Ouyang, *Mng Member*
EMP: 5
SALES: 300K **Privately Held**
SIC: 2099 Noodles, fried (Chinese)

(G-5612)
NOON HOUR FOOD PRODUCTS INC (PA)
Also Called: Swedish Food Products
215 N Desplaines St Fl 1 (60661-1072)
PHONE..................312 382-1177
Paul A Buhl, *President*
Peter S Buhl, *Exec VP*
Larry Buhl, *Vice Pres*
William L Buhl, *Vice Pres*
Doris Buhl, *Director*
EMP: 35 EST: 1876
SALES (est): 13.6MM **Privately Held**
WEB: www.noonhourfoods.com
SIC: 5149 2034 Groceries & related products; potato products, dried & dehydrated

(G-5613)
NOOR JEWELS LLC
865 N Marshfield Ave # 3 (60622-5132)
PHONE..................847 505-9849
Joseph Zaki, *Mng Member*
EMP: 1
SALES: 1MM **Privately Held**
SIC: 3961 Costume jewelry

(G-5614)
NORDEX USA INC (HQ)
300 S Wacker Dr Ste 1400 (60606-6762)
PHONE..................312 386-4100
Jrgen Zeschky, *CEO*
Ralf Sigrist, *President*
Christoph Burkhard, *CFO*
Bernard Schferbarthold, *CFO*
Patxi Landa, *Officer*
◆ EMP: 85
SALES (est): 119.4MM
SALES (corp-wide): 3.6B **Privately Held**
SIC: 3511 7389 Turbines & turbine generator sets; industrial & commercial equipment inspection service
PA: Nordex Se
Langenhorner Chaussee 600
Hamburg 22419
403 003-0100

GEOGRAPHIC SECTION
Chicago - Cook County (G-5642)

(G-5615)
NORDSON ASYMTEK INC
25033 Network Pl (60673-1250)
PHONE.....................760 431-1919
EMP: 101
SALES (corp-wide): 2.1B **Publicly Held**
SIC: 3823 Industrial flow & liquid measuring instruments
HQ: Nordson Asymtek, Inc.
2747 Loker Ave W
Carlsbad CA 92010
760 431-1919

(G-5616)
NORKIN JEWELRY CO INC
55 E Washington St # 203 (60602-2103)
PHONE.....................312 782-7311
Galina Norkin, *President*
EMP: 20
SQ FT: 1,900
SALES (est): 1.9MM **Privately Held**
SIC: 3911 7631 5094 Jewelry, precious metal; jewelry repair services; diamonds (gems); precious stones (gems)

(G-5617)
NORRIDGE JEWELRY
29 E Madison St Ste 1202 (60602-4485)
PHONE.....................312 984-1036
Richard J Kohler, *President*
David Kohler, *Co-Owner*
EMP: 4
SALES (est): 238.8K **Privately Held**
SIC: 3911 Jewelry, precious metal

(G-5618)
NORTH AMERICAN BEAR CO INC (PA)
1200 W 35th St (60609-1305)
PHONE.....................773 376-3457
Paul Levy, *CEO*
Raymond Miller, *COO*
Steven Isenberg, *Vice Pres*
Barbara Isenberg, *Creative Dir*
▲ EMP: 28 EST: 1979
SQ FT: 2,000
SALES (est): 3.5MM **Privately Held**
WEB: www.nabear.com
SIC: 3942 Stuffed toys, including animals

(G-5619)
NORTH AMERICAN FUND III LP (PA)
135 S La Salle St # 3225 (60603-4177)
PHONE.....................312 332-4950
Charles L Palmer, *Managing Prtnr*
▲ EMP: 3
SQ FT: 3,000
SALES (est): 73.3MM **Privately Held**
SIC: 3089 5162 Injection molding of plastics; plastics resins

(G-5620)
NORTH POINT INVESTMENTS INC (PA)
70 W Madison St Ste 3500 (60602-4224)
PHONE.....................312 977-4386
William A Bryant, *President*
Dale G Marcus, *Treasurer*
EMP: 2
SALES (est): 10.5MM **Privately Held**
SIC: 3531 5063 3677 3621 Construction machinery; electrical apparatus & equipment; electronic coils, transformers & other inductors; motors & generators

(G-5621)
NORTH SAILS GROUP LLC
1665 N Elston Ave (60642-1545)
PHONE.....................773 489-1308
Perry Lewis, *Manager*
EMP: 4 **Privately Held**
SIC: 2394 7641 Sails: made from purchased materials; reupholstery & furniture repair
HQ: North Sails Group, Llc
125 Old Gate Ln Ste 7
Milford CT 06460
203 874-7548

(G-5622)
NORTH-WEST DRAPERY SERVICE
4507 N Milwaukee Ave (60630-3711)
PHONE.....................773 282-7117
Brian C Lydon, *President*
EMP: 8
SQ FT: 2,380
SALES (est): 923.1K **Privately Held**
SIC: 2391 Draperies, plastic & textile: from purchased materials

(G-5623)
NORTHWEST PREMIER PRINTING
5421 W Addison St (60641-3203)
PHONE.....................773 736-1882
Lee Stroh, *President*
James Henaghan, *Vice Pres*
Jeanne Henaghan, *Treasurer*
EMP: 5
SQ FT: 8,000
SALES: 850K **Privately Held**
SIC: 2752 2791 2789 2759 Commercial printing, offset; typesetting; bookbinding & related work; commercial printing

(G-5624)
NORTHWEST PUBLISHING LLC
Also Called: Chicago Collection Magazine
500 N Dearborn St # 1014 (60654-3363)
PHONE.....................312 329-0600
Louis Weiss, *Mng Member*
EMP: 5
SALES (est): 972K **Privately Held**
SIC: 2721 Magazines: publishing only, not printed on site

(G-5625)
NORTHWESTERN CUP & LOGO INC
41 W 84th St Fl 1 (60620-1251)
PHONE.....................773 874-8000
EMP: 8
SQ FT: 500
SALES (est): 920.7K **Privately Held**
SIC: 3089 Mfg Cups With Logos For Bottles

(G-5626)
NORTHWSTERN GLOBL HLTH FNDTION
2707 N Lincoln Ave Apt B (60614-1363)
P.O. Box 1969, Evanston (60204-1969)
PHONE.....................214 207-9485
Kara Palamountain, *President*
EMP: 3
SALES (est): 1.1MM **Privately Held**
SIC: 3999 Manufacturing industries

(G-5627)
NORWAY PRESS INC
400 W 76th St Ste 1105 (60620-1641)
PHONE.....................773 846-9422
Samuel Hill, *President*
EMP: 5
SALES (est): 350K **Privately Held**
WEB: www.norwaypresscorp.com
SIC: 2759 Commercial printing

(G-5628)
NORWOOD HOUSE PRESS INC
6150 N Milwaukee Ave # 2 (60646-3821)
P.O. Box 316598 (60631-6598)
PHONE.....................866 565-2900
Patti Hall, *President*
Zoe Del Mar, *Marketing Staff*
▲ EMP: 2
SALES (est): 218.5K **Privately Held**
SIC: 2741 Miscellaneous publishing

(G-5629)
NORWOOD INDUSTRIES INC
Also Called: Norwood Paper
7001 W 60th St Ste 1 (60638-3100)
PHONE.....................773 788-1508
Kathleen A Zeman, *CEO*
Laura Z Martin, *President*
Robert I Zeman III, *Vice Pres*
Darin Rakowsky, *Sales Mgr*
Tracy Alvarez, *Manager*
EMP: 13
SQ FT: 130,000
SALES (est): 4MM **Privately Held**
SIC: 2679 Paper products, converted

(G-5630)
NOURYON CHEMICALS LLC
Also Called: Specialty Chemicals
131 S Dearborn St # 1000 (60603-5566)
PHONE.....................312 544-7000
Larry Ryan, *President*
EMP: 242
SALES (est): 5.8MM
SALES (corp-wide): 5.6B **Privately Held**
SIC: 2819 Industrial inorganic chemicals
HQ: Nouryon Industrial Chemicals B.V.
Velperweg 76
Arnhem 6824
263 664-433

(G-5631)
NOURYON FUNCTIONAL CHEM LLC (HQ)
Also Called: Akzonobel
131 S Dearborn St # 1000 (60603-5517)
PHONE.....................312 544-7000
Larry Ryan, *President*
Carina Brink, *Business Mgr*
Anne-Cathrine Samuelsson, *Business Mgr*
Ernst Westendorp, *Business Mgr*
Pat Ealy, *Plant Mgr*
▲ EMP: 53
SALES: 653.4MM
SALES (corp-wide): 5.6B **Privately Held**
SIC: 2869 Industrial organic chemicals
PA: Nouryon Cooperatief U.A.
Christian Neefestraat 2
Amsterdam
889 697-809

(G-5632)
NOURYON SURFACE CHEMISTRY LLC (HQ)
131 S Dearborn St # 1000 (60603-5517)
PHONE.....................312 544-7000
Larry Ryan, *President*
Han Bevinakatti, *Research*
Will Bryant, *Controller*
Michael Puthoff, *Business Anlyst*
Simon Parker, *Director*
▼ EMP: 45
SALES: 511MM
SALES (corp-wide): 5.6B **Privately Held**
SIC: 2899 Chemical preparations
PA: Nouryon Cooperatief U.A.
Christian Neefestraat 2
Amsterdam
889 697-809

(G-5633)
NOURYON USA LLC
525 W Van Buren St (60607-3823)
PHONE.....................312 544-7000
EMP: 16
SALES (est): 5.7MM **Privately Held**
SIC: 2819 Industrial inorganic chemicals

(G-5634)
NOVUM PHARMA LLC
200 S Wacker Dr Ste 3100 (60606-5877)
PHONE.....................877 404-4724
Michael Cutler, *Sales Mgr*
Anne Powell, *Sales Mgr*
Eric Russell, *Sales Mgr*
Todd Smith, *Mng Member*
Jordyn Hughes, *Manager*
EMP: 10 EST: 2015
SQ FT: 3,372
SALES (est): 1.4MM **Privately Held**
SIC: 2834 Pharmaceutical preparations

(G-5635)
NRTX LLC
1454 W Melrose St Ste 2 (60657-2116)
PHONE.....................224 717-0465
Matthieu Chardon, *
EMP: 3
SALES (est): 210.2K **Privately Held**
SIC: 3841 Diagnostic apparatus, medical

(G-5636)
NU VISION MEDIA INC
1327 W Wa Blvd Ste 102b (60607-2193)
PHONE.....................773 495-5254
Roland S Martin, *President*
EMP: 2
SALES (est): 204.7K **Privately Held**
SIC: 3825 Multimeters

(G-5637)
NU-DELL MANUFACTURING CO INC (PA)
Also Called: Nu-Dell Plastics
400 E Randolph St (60601-7329)
PHONE.....................847 803-4500
David M Block, *CEO*
Beverly Berg, *Treasurer*
◆ EMP: 10 EST: 1926
SQ FT: 3,200
SALES (est): 4.9MM **Privately Held**
SIC: 3993 3089 2499 3281 Signs & advertising specialties; plastic hardware & building products; picture frame molding, finished; cut stone & stone products; public building & related furniture

(G-5638)
NUANCE INCORPORATED
2702 W Chicago Ave Apt 2 (60622-8504)
PHONE.....................207 449-6398
Christopher Blodgett, *President*
Daniel Luby, *Principal*
Gracelyn Newhouse, *Treasurer*
Charles Miller, *Admin Sec*
EMP: 4
SALES (est): 298.5K **Privately Held**
SIC: 3823 Industrial instrmnts msrmnt display/control process variable

(G-5639)
NUCOR TUBULAR PRODUCTS INC (HQ)
Also Called: Independence Tube Corporation
6226 W 74th St (60638-6121)
PHONE.....................708 496-0380
Dave Grohne, *CEO*
Phillip Alonzo, *Division Mgr*
Christopher Ambrosini, *Vice Pres*
John Koschwanez, *Vice Pres*
Tom Reynolds, *Traffic Mgr*
◆ EMP: 90
SQ FT: 220,000
SALES (est): 41.6MM
SALES (corp-wide): 22.5B **Publicly Held**
SIC: 3317 Tubes, wrought: welded or lock joint
PA: Nucor Corporation
1915 Rexford Rd Ste 400
Charlotte NC 28211
704 366-7000

(G-5640)
NUCURRENT INC
641 W Lake St Ste 304 (60661-1308)
PHONE.....................312 575-0388
Jacob Babcock, *CEO*
Jay Knobloch, *Exec VP*
Jim Crnkovic, *Vice Pres*
Michael Gotlieb, *Vice Pres*
Tim Tumilty, *Vice Pres*
EMP: 14
SALES (est): 887.3K **Privately Held**
SIC: 3663 Antennas, transmitting & communications

(G-5641)
NUESTRO QUESO LLC (PA)
100 S Wacker Dr Ste 1950 (60606-4051)
PHONE.....................224 366-4320
Arturo Nava, *Mktg Dir*
Anthony Andrate, *Mng Member*
Mark Braun, *Mng Member*
EMP: 25
SQ FT: 33,000
SALES (est): 48.3MM **Privately Held**
SIC: 2022 5143 Cheese, natural & processed; cheese

(G-5642)
NURTURE LIFE INC (PA)
358 W Ontario St (60654-7586)
PHONE.....................312 517-1888
Steven Minisini, *CEO*
Brent Berger, *Vice Pres*
Rachael Janas, *Production*
Christina Kline, *Chief Mktg Ofcr*
Leah Valenti, *Marketing Staff*
EMP: 26 EST: 2016
SALES (est): 8.6MM **Privately Held**
WEB: www.nurturelife.com
SIC: 2032 Baby foods, including meats: packaged in cans, jars, etc.

Chicago - Cook County (G-5643)   GEOGRAPHIC SECTION

(G-5643)
NUTRASWEET COMPANY (DH)
222 Merchandise Mart Plz # 936
(60654-1103)
PHONE..................312 873-5000
Craig Petray, *CEO*
Larry Benjamin, *President*
Marsha Lusignan, *Senior Buyer*
William Schumacher, *CFO*
▲ **EMP:** 9 **EST:** 1965
SALES (est): 1.6MM **Privately Held**
SIC: 2869 Industrial organic chemicals
HQ: Nutrasweet Property Holdings, Inc.
222 Merchandise Mart Plz
Chicago IL 60654
312 873-5000

(G-5644)
O & K AMERICAN CORP (HQ)
4630 W 55th St (60632-4908)
PHONE..................773 767-2500
Kazuta Oku, *President*
Takao Oku, *Chairman*
Michal Pasek, *Mfg Mgr*
William M Getzoff, *Admin Sec*
▲ **EMP:** 90
SQ FT: 150,000
SALES (est): 34.9MM **Privately Held**
SIC: 3312 Blast furnace & related products

(G-5645)
O & W WIRE CO INC
7816 S Oakley Ave (60620-5814)
PHONE..................773 776-5919
Wenceslao Ramirez, *President*
EMP: 10
SQ FT: 13,900
SALES (est): 1.3MM **Privately Held**
SIC: 3312 Wire products, steel or iron

(G-5646)
O SIGNS INC
325 N Hoyne Ave (60612-1636)
PHONE..................312 888-3386
Patrick M Oleary, *President*
EMP: 3
SALES (est): 249.1K **Privately Held**
SIC: 3993 Signs, not made in custom sign painting shops

(G-5647)
O2COOL LLC
Also Called: Bobble
300 S Riverside Plz (60606-6613)
PHONE..................312 951-6700
Linda Usher, *CEO*
Michael Ksiazek, *Exec VP*
Spencer Malcolm, *Vice Pres*
Peggy Moloney, *Vice Pres*
Drew Lissuzzo, *Production*
▲ **EMP:** 20
SQ FT: 7,500
SALES (est): 5MM
SALES (corp-wide): 55.1MM **Privately Held**
SIC: 3634 Fans, electric: desk
PA: Middleton Partners, Llc
400 Skokie Blvd Ste 405
Northbrook IL

(G-5648)
O2M TECHNOLOGIES LLC
2242 W Harrison St Ste 20 (60612-3719)
PHONE..................773 910-8533
Mrignayani Kotecha,
Boris Epel,
Howard Halpern,
EMP: 3
SALES (est): 128K **Privately Held**
SIC: 3826 Magnetic resonance imaging apparatus

(G-5649)
OBAN COMPOSITES LLC
1300 W Belmont Ave # 311 (60657-3200)
PHONE..................866 607-0284
Ralph Reichert, *VP Sales*
EMP: 7 **EST:** 2009
SQ FT: 2,000
SALES (est): 552.8K **Privately Held**
WEB: www.obanshafts.com
SIC: 5941 3949 Golf goods & equipment; sporting & athletic goods

(G-5650)
OBRIEN ARCHITECTURAL MTLS INC
858 W Armitage Ave # 205 (60614-4383)
PHONE..................773 868-1065
John O'Brien, *President*
EMP: 10 **EST:** 2007
SALES (est): 2.2MM **Privately Held**
SIC: 3441 Fabricated structural metal

(G-5651)
OCCIDENTAL CHEMICAL CORP
4201 W 69th St (60629-5718)
PHONE..................773 284-0079
James Hughes, *Plant Supt*
Donna Fiscus,
EMP: 19
SQ FT: 2,700
SALES (corp-wide): 21.2B **Publicly Held**
SIC: 2874 Phosphatic fertilizers
HQ: Occidental Chemical Corporation
14555 Dallas Pkwy Ste 400
Dallas TX 75254
972 404-3800

(G-5652)
OCCLY LLC
2835 N Sheffield Ave (60657-5081)
PHONE..................773 969-5080
Marc Harris, *Mng Member*
EMP: 3
SQ FT: 2,000
SALES (est): 161.4K **Privately Held**
SIC: 3699 Electrical equipment & supplies

(G-5653)
OCEANCOMM INCORPORATED
1431 W Hubbard St Ste 205 (60642-6308)
PHONE..................800 757-3266
Andrew Singer, *Principal*
EMP: 6
SALES (est): 347.9K **Privately Held**
SIC: 3577 3812 Input/output equipment, computer; search & navigation equipment

(G-5654)
OCHEM INC
2201 W Campbell Park Dr # 34 (60612-4160)
PHONE..................847 403-7044
EMP: 18
SALES (corp-wide): 2MM **Privately Held**
SIC: 2899 Chemical preparations
PA: Ochem, Inc.
9044 Buckingham Park Dr
Des Plaines IL 60016
847 403-7044

(G-5655)
ODIN TECHNOLOGIES LLC
4660 N Ravenswood Ave (60640-4510)
PHONE..................408 309-1925
Steven Hansen,
EMP: 5
SALES (est): 412.3K **Privately Held**
SIC: 3845 3841 Electromedical equipment; diagnostic apparatus, medical

(G-5656)
ODWALLA INC
2837 N Cambridge Ave (60657-7553)
PHONE..................773 687-8667
EMP: 39
SALES (corp-wide): 37.2B **Publicly Held**
WEB: www.odwalla.com
SIC: 2033 Fruit juices: packaged in cans, jars, etc.
HQ: Odwalla, Inc.
1 Coca Cola Plz Nw
Atlanta GA 30313
479 721-6260

(G-5657)
OETEE LLC
1814 N Lincoln Park W # 1 (60614-5362)
PHONE..................630 373-4671
Robert Tivadar, *Principal*
EMP: 5
SALES (est): 595.7K **Privately Held**
SIC: 2431 Millwork

(G-5658)
OFFICE OF EXPERIENCE LLC
125 S Wacker Dr Ste 3000 (60606-4310)
PHONE..................872 228-5126
Stratton Cherouny, *Mng Member*
Maritza Eru, *Manager*
Kim Brannigan, *Director*
Amit Patel, *Director*
Matthew Quinn, *Director*
EMP: 4
SALES (est): 173.5K **Privately Held**
SIC: 7372 Business oriented computer software

(G-5659)
OFFSPRINGS INC
Also Called: Vertical Blinds Factory
1451 W Webster Ave (60614-3049)
PHONE..................773 525-1800
Jay Pinsky, *President*
EMP: 6
SALES (est): 480K **Privately Held**
SIC: 2591 5719 Drapery hardware & blinds & shades; window furnishings

(G-5660)
OGDEN FOODS LLC (PA)
4320 W Ogden Ave (60623-2924)
PHONE..................773 277-8207
Barsh Janusz,
Janusz Barsh,
Eva Jakubowski,
▼ **EMP:** 22
SQ FT: 27,000
SALES (est): 1MM **Privately Held**
SIC: 2013 Boneless meat, from purchased meat

(G-5661)
OGDEN FOODS LLC
4325 W Ogden Ave (60623-2925)
PHONE..................773 801-0125
Dorota Mietus, *Branch Mgr*
EMP: 8
SALES (corp-wide): 1MM **Privately Held**
SIC: 2013 Boneless meat, from purchased meat
PA: Ogden Foods Llc
4320 W Ogden Ave
Chicago IL 60623
773 277-8207

(G-5662)
OGDEN MINUTEMAN INC
3939 W Ogden Ave (60623-2486)
PHONE..................773 542-6917
Musa Tadros, *Owner*
EMP: 4
SALES (est): 319.5K **Privately Held**
SIC: 2752 Commercial printing, offset

(G-5663)
OGDEN OFFSET PRINTERS INC
6150 S Archer Ave (60638-2641)
PHONE..................773 284-7797
Sandra H William, *President*
John Williams, *Vice Pres*
EMP: 4
SQ FT: 4,800
SALES (est): 500K **Privately Held**
SIC: 2752 3993 2789 Commercial printing, offset; signs & advertising specialties; bookbinding & related work

(G-5664)
OGWURU UZOAKU
Also Called: Farmstead Business Solutions
7022 S 5th Shr Dr Apt 305 (60649-2260)
PHONE..................312 286-5593
Uzoaku Ogwuru, *Owner*
EMP: 5
SALES (est): 311.5K **Privately Held**
SIC: 5063 5045 3571 Electrical apparatus & equipment; computers, peripherals & software; electronic computers

(G-5665)
OHIO PULP MILLS INC (PA)
737 N Michigan Ave # 1450 (60611-2615)
PHONE..................312 337-7822
Robert Mendelson, *President*
Thomas Imming, *President*
David Mendelson, *Exec VP*
David Berkenstein, *Treasurer*
Matt Burskey, *Sales Staff*
EMP: 13
SQ FT: 5,088
SALES (est): 3.1MM **Privately Held**
SIC: 2611 Pulp manufactured from waste or recycled paper

(G-5666)
OIL-DRI CORPORATION AMERICA (PA)
410 N Michigan Ave # 400 (60611-4293)
PHONE..................312 321-1515
Richard M Jaffee, *Ch of Bd*
Joseph C Miller, *Vice Ch Bd*
Daniel S Jaffee, *President*
Molly D Vandenheuvel, *COO*
Michael A McPherson, *Vice Pres*
EMP: 90
SALES: 277MM **Publicly Held**
WEB: www.oildri.com
SIC: 2842 2833 3295 Sweeping compounds, oil or water absorbent, clay or sawdust; medicinals & botanicals; earths, ground or otherwise treated; cat box litter; filtering clays, treated

(G-5667)
OIL-DRI CORPORATION AMERICA
410 N Michigan Aveste 400 (60611)
PHONE..................312 321-1516
Carol Groom, *Manager*
EMP: 500
SALES (corp-wide): 277MM **Publicly Held**
SIC: 1459 3295 Clays (common) quarrying; cat box litter
PA: Oil-Dri Corporation Of America
410 N Michigan Ave # 400
Chicago IL 60611
312 321-1515

(G-5668)
OLD FASHIONED MEAT CO INC
920 W Fulton Market (60607-1309)
PHONE..................312 421-4555
Roberto Casmilo, *President*
Thomas G Stapleton, *President*
Veronica Castillo, *Controller*
EMP: 6
SQ FT: 2,000
SALES (est): 2.4MM **Privately Held**
SIC: 5147 2013 Meats, fresh; sausages & other prepared meats

(G-5669)
OLD GARY INC (DH)
Also Called: Post-Tribune
350 N Orleans St Fl 10 (60654-1975)
PHONE..................219 648-3000
Boni L Fine, *Publisher*
EMP: 13 **EST:** 1909
SQ FT: 30,000
SALES (est): 21.4MM
SALES (corp-wide): 4.3MM **Privately Held**
SIC: 2711 Newspapers, publishing & printing
HQ: Sun-Times Media Group, Inc.
30 N Racine Ave Ste 300
Chicago IL 60607
312 321-3000

(G-5670)
OLD STYLE IRON WORKS INC
7843 S Claremont Ave (60620-5812)
PHONE..................773 265-5787
Fax: 773 476-4431
EMP: 7
SQ FT: 10,000
SALES (est): 840K **Privately Held**
SIC: 3441 1791 3446 Structural Metal Fabrication Structural Steel Erection Mfg Architectural Metalwork

(G-5671)
OLDCASTLE BUILDINGENVELOPE INC
4161 S Morgan St (60609-2516)
PHONE..................773 523-8400
Philip F Albrecht, *Manager*
EMP: 6
SALES (corp-wide): 30.6B **Privately Held**
WEB: www.obe.com
SIC: 3231 5231 Tempered glass: made from purchased glass; insulating glass: made from purchased glass; glass
HQ: Oldcastle Buildingenvelope, Inc.
5005 Lyndon B Johnson Fwy # 1050
Dallas TX 75244
214 273-3400

GEOGRAPHIC SECTION
Chicago - Cook County (G-5700)

(G-5672)
OLYMPIC TROPHY AND AWARDS CO
5860 N Northwest Hwy (60631-2641)
PHONE...............773 631-9500
Susan McMahon, *President*
Lawrence McCann, *CTO*
EMP: 13
SALES (est): 1.5MM **Privately Held**
SIC: **3499** 2759 3993 2396 Novelties & giftware, including trophies; trophies, metal, except silver; novelties & specialties, metal; screen printing; signs & advertising specialties; automotive & apparel trimmings

(G-5673)
OMAR MEDICAL SUPPLIES INC (PA)
Also Called: Omar Supplies
345 E Wacker Dr Unit 4601 (60601-5275)
PHONE...............708 922-4276
Willie Wilson, *President*
Dale Wilson, *Vice Pres*
Contreras Jaime, *Office Mgr*
Angela Bender, *Receptionist*
Patricia Watkins, *Representative*
◆ EMP: 14 EST: 1997
SQ FT: 75,000
SALES (est): 58.8MM **Privately Held**
WEB: www.omarinc.com
SIC: **5085** 5047 2259 Industrial supplies; dental equipment & supplies; dyeing & finishing knit gloves & mittens

(G-5674)
OMEGACOM INC
5331 N Lincoln Ave (60625-8407)
PHONE...............773 750-4621
James Baar, *Principal*
EMP: 3 EST: 2011
SALES (est): 120.1K **Privately Held**
WEB: www.qwickguide.com
SIC: **2741** Miscellaneous publishing

(G-5675)
OMG HANDBAGS LLC
2045 W Grand Ave Ste 202 (60612-1577)
PHONE...............847 337-9499
Ann Narter,
▲ EMP: 4
SALES (est): 340K **Privately Held**
SIC: **2393** Textile bags

(G-5676)
OMNILIGHT INC
6501 N Avondale Ave (60631-1521)
PHONE...............773 696-1602
David Meyer Jr, *President*
Dominic Dibiaso, *Principal*
EMP: 6
SALES: 2.5MM **Privately Held**
SIC: **5063** 3646 Light bulbs & related supplies; commercial indusl & institutional electric lighting fixtures

(G-5677)
OMOBONO INC
325 W Huron St Ste 215 (60654-3642)
PHONE...............312 523-2179
Ben Dansie, *Principal*
EMP: 4
SALES (est): 114.4K
SALES (corp-wide): 15.3MM **Privately Held**
SIC: **3572** Computer storage devices
PA: Omobono Limited
St Giles Hall
Cambridge CAMBS
122 330-7000

(G-5678)
ONEILL PRODUCTS INC
Also Called: Midwest Marine Div
555 W 16th St (60616-1146)
PHONE...............312 243-3413
Larry Grossman, *President*
Mary Grossman, *Treasurer*
EMP: 2
SQ FT: 2,500
SALES: 500K **Privately Held**
SIC: **5085** 2511 Rubber goods, mechanical; wood household furniture

(G-5679)
OPALEK FRONTIER INC
1117 W Grand Ave (60642-5803)
PHONE...............312 733-2700
Terence M Opalek, *President*
Silvester Padilla, *Sales Staff*
EMP: 3
SALES (est): 328.1K **Privately Held**
SIC: **2064** 5441 Candy bars, including chocolate covered bars; candy

(G-5680)
OPEN KITCHENS INC (PA)
2121 S Racine Ave (60608-3397)
PHONE...............312 666-5334
Terese M Fiore, *President*
Tim Lacey, *General Mgr*
Anthony Fiore, *Opers Staff*
Pankaj Patel, *Purch Mgr*
Linda Padilla, *Research*
EMP: 250
SQ FT: 65,000
SALES: 30.5MM **Privately Held**
WEB: www.openkitchens.com
SIC: **2099** Food preparations

(G-5681)
OPEN KITCHENS INC
2141 S Racine Ave (60608-3222)
PHONE...............312 666-5334
Terese Fiore, *Branch Mgr*
EMP: 25
SALES (est): 352.5K
SALES (corp-wide): 30.5MM **Privately Held**
SIC: **5812** 2099 2038 4215 Caterers; food preparations; frozen specialties; courier services, except by air
PA: Open Kitchens, Inc.
2121 S Racine Ave
Chicago IL 60608
312 666-5334

(G-5682)
OPEX ANALYTICS LLC
350 N Orleans St 8500n (60654-1601)
PHONE...............847 733-7439
Tiffany Robertson, *Accounting Mgr*
Michael S Watson,
Diego Klabjan,
Ganesh Ramakrishna,
EMP: 33
SALES (est): 566.1K **Privately Held**
SIC: **7372** Business oriented computer software
PA: Llamasoft, Inc.
201 S Division St Ste 200
Ann Arbor MI 48104

(G-5683)
OPS 3 LLC
Also Called: Screen Works, The
2201 W Fulton St (60612-2205)
PHONE...............312 243-8265
Ellen Parker, *Principal*
David Hull, *Sales Executive*
EMP: 1
SALES (est): 209.3K **Privately Held**
SIC: **3861** Screens, projection

(G-5684)
OPSDIRT LLC
948 N Winchester Ave # 3 (60622-4963)
PHONE...............773 412-1179
Jeffrey Waugh,
Brian Garriotte,
Jason Garriotte,
Mike Kostorowski,
Jay Walley,
EMP: 6
SALES (est): 542.4K **Privately Held**
SIC: **2899** 7389 Fusees: highway, marine or railroad;

(G-5685)
OPTIMUS ADVANTAGE LLC
10 S Lasalle (60606)
PHONE...............847 905-1000
Michael Harris, *Principal*
EMP: 3
SALES (est): 66.9K **Privately Held**
SIC: **7371** 7372 Computer software systems analysis & design, custom; application computer software

(G-5686)
OPTIONSCITY SOFTWARE INC
150 S Wacker Dr Ste 2300 (60606-4212)
PHONE...............312 605-4500
Hazem Dawani, *CEO*
Victor Glava, *Principal*
Steve Kosanovich, *Principal*
Douglas Tucker, *Principal*
EMP: 5
SALES (est): 504.8K **Privately Held**
SIC: **7372** Prepackaged software

(G-5687)
OQ 168 NM PROPCO LLC
168 N Michigan Ave (60601-7937)
PHONE...............312 542-6116
EMP: 4
SALES (est): 431.6K **Privately Held**
SIC: **1311** Gas & hydrocarbon liquefaction from coal

(G-5688)
ORACLE CORPORATION
980 N Michigan Ave # 1400 (60611-4501)
PHONE...............773 404-9300
Diane Cleary, *Branch Mgr*
EMP: 310
SALES (corp-wide): 39.5B **Publicly Held**
SIC: **7372** Business oriented computer software
PA: Oracle Corporation
500 Oracle Pkwy
Redwood City CA 94065
650 506-7000

(G-5689)
ORACLE CORPORATION
330 N Wabash Ave Ste 2400 (60611-7619)
PHONE...............312 692-5270
Greg Hilbrich, *Vice Pres*
Alex Kallend, *Manager*
Daniel Diga, *Consultant*
Dave Miglieri, *Technology*
Dave Farr, *Software Engr*
EMP: 191
SALES (corp-wide): 39.5B **Publicly Held**
SIC: **7372** Business oriented computer software
PA: Oracle Corporation
500 Oracle Pkwy
Redwood City CA 94065
650 506-7000

(G-5690)
ORACLE CORPORATION
233 S Wacker Dr Ste 4500 (60606-6406)
PHONE...............262 957-3000
Paul Disborough, *Partner*
Dave Oliva, *General Mgr*
John Sawa, *Principal*
Avery J Lerner, *Vice Pres*
Jonathan Lamarre, *Sales Staff*
EMP: 302
SALES (corp-wide): 39.5B **Publicly Held**
SIC: **7372** Business oriented computer software
PA: Oracle Corporation
500 Oracle Pkwy
Redwood City CA 94065
650 506-7000

(G-5691)
ORACLE HCM USER GROUP INC
330 N Wabash Ave Ste 2000 (60611-7621)
PHONE...............312 222-9350
EMP: 2
SALES: 1.1MM **Privately Held**
SIC: **7372** Prepackaged Software Services

(G-5692)
ORACLE SYSTEMS CORPORATION
3122 Paysphere Circle (60674-0001)
PHONE...............312 673-5863
Mike Cavanagh, *Regional Mgr*
Bijo Thomas, *Sales Staff*
EMP: 3
SALES (corp-wide): 39.5B **Publicly Held**
SIC: **7372** Prepackaged software
HQ: Oracle Systems Corporation
500 Oracle Pkwy
Redwood City CA 94065

(G-5693)
ORBIS RPM LLC
4400 W 45th St Ste C (60632-4304)
PHONE...............312 343-4902
Angel Barreto, *Branch Mgr*
EMP: 10
SALES (corp-wide): 2.2B **Privately Held**
SIC: **3081** Unsupported plastics film & sheet
HQ: Orbis Rpm, Llc
1055 Corporate Center Dr
Oconomowoc WI 53066
262 560-5000

(G-5694)
ORBIT ROOM
2959 N California Ave (60618-7702)
PHONE...............773 588-8540
Dirk Nebbeling, *Principal*
EMP: 7
SALES (est): 560.8K **Privately Held**
SIC: **2064** Candy bars, including chocolate covered bars

(G-5695)
ORCHARD HILL CABINETRY INC (PA)
Also Called: Builders Cabinet Supply
401 N Western Ave Ste 3 (60612-1418)
PHONE...............312 829-4300
Brian Benner, *President*
EMP: 43
SALES (est): 6.9MM **Privately Held**
SIC: **2434** Wood kitchen cabinets

(G-5696)
ORECX
1 N La Salle St Ste 1375 (60602-4351)
PHONE...............312 895-5292
Bruce Kaskey, *CEO*
Steve Kaiser, *Co-Founder*
Bruce D Kaskey, *CFO*
Sean Nelen, *Sales Mgr*
Tim Kunkel, *Sales Staff*
EMP: 15
SALES (est): 1MM **Privately Held**
SIC: **7372** Prepackaged software

(G-5697)
ORGANIC LOOMS INC (PA)
401 N Wells St Ste 3 (60654-7025)
PHONE...............312 832-0900
Christopher Frederick, *President*
Patricia A Frederick, *Admin Sec*
▲ EMP: 5
SALES (est): 651.5K **Privately Held**
SIC: **2273** Rugs, hand & machine made

(G-5698)
ORIENTAL KITCHEN CORPORATION
Also Called: R R Sausage Factory
223 N Justine St (60607-1403)
PHONE...............312 738-2850
Roman P Badiola, *President*
Rosario Manio, *Vice Pres*
Cleo S Badiola, *Admin Sec*
EMP: 14
SALES (est): 1.8MM **Privately Held**
SIC: **2013** 2011 Sausages from purchased meat; pork, cured: from purchased meat; meat packing plants

(G-5699)
ORIGAMI RISK LLC (PA)
222 N Lasalle St Ste 2125 (60601)
PHONE...............312 546-6515
Wesley P Foster, *Vice Pres*
Glen Carey, *Sales Staff*
Shannon Falvey, *Marketing Staff*
Adam Buhot, *Executive*
Elizabeth Dykas, *Executive*
EMP: 35
SALES (est): 613.7K **Privately Held**
SIC: **7372** Business oriented computer software

(G-5700)
ORIGINAL FERRARA INC
Also Called: Original Ferrara Bakery
2210 W Taylor St (60612-4234)
PHONE...............312 666-2200
Nello V Ferrara, *Ch of Bd*
William J Davy, *President*
Nella Davy, *Vice Pres*

Chicago - Cook County (G-5701) GEOGRAPHIC SECTION

EMP: 16 **EST:** 1908
SQ FT: 14,000
SALES (est): 750K **Privately Held**
WEB: www.ferrarabakery.com
SIC: 5149 5461 2051 Bakery products; bakeries; bread; cakes; cookies; bread, cake & related products

(G-5701)
ORIGINAL SHUTTER MAN
1231 W 74th Pl (60636-4143)
PHONE.................................773 966-7160
James Johnson, *Founder*
EMP: 4
SALES (est): 407K **Privately Held**
WEB: www.originalshutterman.com
SIC: 2431 Door shutters, wood

(G-5702)
ORIOLE ENTERPRISES INC
7354 W Addison St (60634-3428)
PHONE.................................773 589-9696
Raymond Demo, *President*
Jackie Demo, *Corp Secy*
Joseph C Demo, *Vice Pres*
EMP: 6
SQ FT: 2,200
SALES (est): 1.2MM **Privately Held**
SIC: 2752 Commercial printing, lithographic

(G-5703)
ORLAND SPORTS LTD
Also Called: Club House Designs
5610 W Bloomingdale Ave G (60639-4113)
PHONE.................................773 685-3711
Jon Sollberger, *Principal*
EMP: 5
SALES (est): 409.2K **Privately Held**
WEB: www.clubhousedesigns.com
SIC: 2759 Screen printing

(G-5704)
ORLANDI STATUARY COMPANY
1801 N Central Park Ave (60647-4703)
PHONE.................................773 489-0303
Fabio Orlandi, *President*
Dani Orlandi, *Vice Pres*
Bianca Orlandi, *Sales Dir*
▲ **EMP:** 54 **EST:** 1911
SQ FT: 70,000
SALES (est): 6.5MM **Privately Held**
SIC: 3999 3299 3272 Mannequins; art goods: plaster of paris, papier mache & scagliola; concrete products

(G-5705)
ORSOLINIS WELDING & FABG
3040 W Carroll Ave (60612-1722)
PHONE.................................773 722-9855
Theresa Orsolini, *President*
Robert O Orsolini, *COO*
Joseph Orsolini, *Vice Pres*
Robert Orsolini, *Vice Pres*
Debbie Auggello, *Admin Sec*
▲ **EMP:** 15
SQ FT: 30,000
SALES: 1.4MM **Privately Held**
WEB: www.orsoweld.com
SIC: 7692 3446 3441 Welding repair; architectural metalwork; fabricated structural metal

(G-5706)
ORTHO SEATING LLC
4444 W Ohio St (60624-1053)
PHONE.................................773 276-3539
▲ **EMP:** 12
SQ FT: 28,000
SALES (est): 1.7MM **Privately Held**
SIC: 2522 5021 Mfg Office Furniture-Nonwood Whol Furniture

(G-5707)
ORVIS COMPANY INC
142 E Ontario St Ste 1 (60611-5424)
PHONE.................................312 440-0662
Tj Roy, *General Mgr*
EMP: 10
SALES (corp-wide): 322.1MM **Privately Held**
SIC: 5961 5941 3949 Catalog sales; fitness & sporting goods, mail order; sporting goods & bicycle shops; fishing tackle, general
PA: The Orvis Company Inc
178 Conservation Way
Sunderland VT 05250
802 362-3622

(G-5708)
OSCARS FOODS INC (PA)
6125 W Belmont Ave (60634-4004)
PHONE.................................773 622-6822
Oscar Gramata, *President*
Lolita Gramata, *Admin Sec*
EMP: 8
SQ FT: 4,000
SALES (est): 750K **Privately Held**
SIC: 2013 Sausages from purchased meat; smoked meats from purchased meat; bacon, side & sliced: from purchased meat

(G-5709)
OSI INDUSTRIES LLC
4201 S Ashland Ave (60609-2305)
PHONE.................................773 650-4000
Steven Gray, *Manager*
Michael Wayne, *Supervisor*
Todd Stahl, *Technical Staff*
EMP: 5 **Privately Held**
SIC: 2099 Ready-to-eat meals, salads & sandwiches
HQ: Osi Industries, Llc
1225 Corp Blvd Ste 105
Aurora IL 60505
630 851-6600

(G-5710)
OSI INDUSTRIES LLC
Auto & Sons Stockyards
4545 S Racine Ave (60609-3371)
PHONE.................................773 847-2000
Brent Afman, *Vice Pres*
Phil Pierchala, *Vice Pres*
Bill Moody, *Maint Spvr*
John Dobias, *Opers-Prdtn-Mfg*
Ken Knezevich, *Purch Mgr*
EMP: 340
SQ FT: 20,000 **Privately Held**
SIC: 5147 2013 Meats, fresh; sausages & other prepared meats
HQ: Osi Industries, Llc
1225 Corp Blvd Ste 105
Aurora IL 60505
630 851-6600

(G-5711)
OSO900 NFP
6447 N Sacramento Ave (60645-4286)
PHONE.................................312 206-4219
Ameir Finney, *CEO*
Bryant C Hogan, *Principal*
Azeez Alimi, *Director*
Terrance Bramlett, *Director*
Chris Hogan, *Director*
EMP: 5
SALES (est): 104.7K **Privately Held**
SIC: 7389 5091 8711 3949 ; sporting & recreation goods; engineering services; sporting & athletic goods; picture & mirror frames, wood; manufactured hardware (general)

(G-5712)
OTIS ELEVATOR COMPANY
651 W Washington Blvd 1n (60661-2140)
PHONE.................................312 454-1616
Daniel McCutchan, *Superintendent*
Bryan Sanders, *Production*
Sherry Kim, *Engineer*
Marva Rayman, *Accountant*
Whitney Hollinger, *Sales Mgr*
EMP: 60
SALES (corp-wide): 10B **Publicly Held**
WEB: www.otis.com
SIC: 3446 3534 Elevator guide rails; elevators & equipment
HQ: Otis Elevator Company
1 Carrier Pl
Farmington CT 06032
860 674-3000

(G-5713)
OTTOS DRAPERY SERVICE INC
5219 W Cullom Ave (60641-1402)
PHONE.................................773 777-7755
Otto Perez, *President*
EMP: 5
SALES: 200K **Privately Held**
SIC: 2591 Drapery hardware & blinds & shades

(G-5714)
OTUS LLC
900 N Michigan Ave # 1600 (60611-1542)
PHONE.................................312 229-7648
David Tooby, *CTO*
Andrew Bluhm,
EMP: 32
SALES (est): 135.6K **Privately Held**
SIC: 7372 Educational computer software

(G-5715)
OUTDOOR SPACE LLC
Also Called: Synlawn of Chicago
3120 N Sheffield Ave # 1 (60657-9314)
PHONE.................................773 857-5296
Fax: 773 857-5297
EMP: 30
SQ FT: 10,000
SALES (est): 2.7MM **Privately Held**
SIC: 3523 Mfg Turf

(G-5716)
OUTPUT MEDICAL INC
4660 N Ravenswood Ave (60640-4510)
PHONE.................................630 430-8024
Jay Joshi, *CEO*
EMP: 3
SQ FT: 100
SALES (est): 108.2K **Privately Held**
SIC: 3845 Automated blood & body fluid analyzers, except laboratory

(G-5717)
OVERGRAD INC
11 E Adams St Ste 200 (60603-6337)
PHONE.................................312 324-4952
Ryan Hoch, *CEO*
Kevin Hoffman, *Co-Owner*
EMP: 4
SQ FT: 373
SALES (est): 130.9K **Privately Held**
SIC: 7372 Educational computer software

(G-5718)
OVERT PRESS INC
4625 W 53rd St (60632-4903)
PHONE.................................773 284-0909
Eileen Turcich, *President*
George W Turcich, *Corp Secy*
EMP: 35
SQ FT: 15,000
SALES (est): 4.2MM **Privately Held**
SIC: 2759 7374 2752 2677 Letterpress printing; data processing service; commercial printing, lithographic; envelopes

(G-5719)
OVERTON CHICAGO GEAR CORP
2823 W Fulton St (60612-1705)
PHONE.................................773 638-0508
Donald Brown, *CEO*
Chris Wellman, *Vice Pres*
Chris Boudreau, *Production*
Adam Arters, *Finance*
Ramze Dahleh, *Human Resources*
▲ **EMP:** 62 **EST:** 1913
SQ FT: 46,000
SALES (est): 18.9MM **Privately Held**
WEB: www.oc-gear.com
SIC: 3566 Reduction gears & gear units for turbines, except automotive; drives, high speed industrial, except hydrostatic; gears, power transmission, except automotive

(G-5720)
OVS LLC
5419 N Sheridan Rd # 103 (60640-1964)
PHONE.................................312 428-3548
Richard Melman, *Principal*
EMP: 4
SALES (est): 198.5K **Privately Held**
SIC: 3421 Table & food cutlery, including butchers'

(G-5721)
OWN THE NIGHT APP
1735 N Paulina St Apt 305 (60622-1461)
PHONE.................................773 216-0245
Kevin Yu, *Principal*
John Sun, *Principal*
Paul Zhang, *Principal*
EMP: 3
SALES (est): 122.1K **Privately Held**
SIC: 7372 Application computer software

(G-5722)
OXALO THERAPEUTICS INC
1452 E 53rd St Fl 2 (60615-4512)
PHONE.................................530 848-3499
Yang Zheng, *Principal*
Hatim Hassan, *Principal*
EMP: 2
SALES (est): 223.7K **Privately Held**
SIC: 2834 Pharmaceutical preparations

(G-5723)
OXXFORD CLOTHES XX INC (HQ)
5635 S Archer Ave Unit 2 (60638-1673)
PHONE.................................312 829-3600
Spencer Hayes, *Ch of Bd*
Sergio Casalena, *President*
Chris Brueckner, *VP Sales*
Lindsay Grundy, *Mktg Coord*
Maria Acosta, *Manager*
EMP: 119
SQ FT: 105,000
SALES (est): 25.5MM
SALES (corp-wide): 522.3MM **Privately Held**
SIC: 2325 2311 Men's & boys' trousers & slacks; suits, men's & boys': made from purchased materials; jackets, tailored suit-type: men's & boys'; tailored dress & sport coats: men's & boys'
PA: Tom James Company
263 Seaboard Ln
Franklin TN 37067
615 771-1122

(G-5724)
OZINGA CHICAGO READY MIX CON
1818 E 103rd St (60617-5641)
PHONE.................................312 432-5700
EMP: 43
SALES (corp-wide): 434.5MM **Privately Held**
SIC: 3273 Ready-mixed concrete
HQ: Ozinga Chicago Ready Mix Concrete, Inc
2255 S Lumber St
Chicago IL 60616

(G-5725)
OZINGA CHICAGO READY MIX CON
2001 N Mendell St (60614-3033)
PHONE.................................773 862-2817
Rick Schicitano, *Manager*
EMP: 40
SQ FT: 53,700
SALES (corp-wide): 434.5MM **Privately Held**
SIC: 3273 Ready-mixed concrete
HQ: Ozinga Chicago Ready Mix Concrete, Inc
2255 S Lumber St
Chicago IL 60616

(G-5726)
OZINGA CHICAGO READY MIX CON (HQ)
2255 S Lumber St (60616-2198)
PHONE.................................847 447-0353
Justin Ozinga, *President*
Mattew Huisman, *Treasurer*
Barry N Voorn, *Admin Sec*
EMP: 40
SQ FT: 17,000
SALES (est): 18.2MM
SALES (corp-wide): 434.5MM **Privately Held**
SIC: 3273 Ready-mixed concrete
PA: Ozinga Bros., Inc.
19001 Old Lagrange Rd # 30
Mokena IL 60448
708 326-4200

(G-5727)
OZINGA READY MIX CONCRETE INC
11701 S Torrence Ave (60617-7212)
PHONE.................................800 786-6382
EMP: 43 **Privately Held**

GEOGRAPHIC SECTION Chicago - Cook County (G-5756)

SIC: 3273 Ready-mixed concrete
PA: Ozinga Ready Mix Concrete, Inc.
19001 Old Lagrange Rd # 300
Mokena IL 60448

(G-5728)
P B A CORP
Also Called: Avis Commercial Anodizing
522 N Western Ave (60612)
PHONE.................312 666-7370
EMP: 13 **EST:** 1963
SQ FT: 12,000
SALES (est): 97.2K **Privately Held**
SIC: 3471 3312 Plating/Polishing Service Blast Furnace-Steel Works

(G-5729)
P S GREETINGS INC (PA)
Also Called: Fantus Paper Products
5730 N Tripp Ave (60646-6741)
PHONE.................708 831-5340
Mark McCracken, *President*
Randy Zagorski, *Plant Mgr*
Jennifer Dodson, *Sales Staff*
Linda Augustine, *Info Tech Mgr*
Ryan Cozzo, *Info Tech Mgr*
▲ **EMP:** 150
SQ FT: 125,000
SALES (est): 48.2MM **Privately Held**
SIC: 2771 2657 Greeting cards; folding paperboard boxes

(G-5730)
P&L GROUP LTD OF ILLINOIS
24 E 107th St (60628-3502)
PHONE.................833 362-2100
Pamela McElvane, *CEO*
EMP: 10
SALES (est): 1MM **Privately Held**
SIC: 2721 Magazines: publishing & printing

(G-5731)
P-AMERICAS LLC
Also Called: Pepsico
1400 W 35th St (60609-1311)
PHONE.................773 893-2300
Lucy Hanik, *Accountant*
Sara Dorn, *Human Resources*
Neha Patel, *Human Resources*
Jim Doyle, *Sales Staff*
Adam Hissong, *Sales Staff*
EMP: 500
SALES (corp-wide): 67.1B **Publicly Held**
SIC: 2086 Carbonated soft drinks, bottled & canned
HQ: P-Americas Llc
1 Pepsi Way
Somers NY 10589
336 896-5740

(G-5732)
P-AMERICAS LLC
Also Called: Pepsico
555 W Monroe St Fl 1 (60661-3700)
PHONE.................312 821-2266
Robert Scharringhausen, *Principal*
Dan Rehard, *Finance Spvr*
Katie Newberger, *Marketing Staff*
Mike Roche, *Senior Mgr*
EMP: 75
SALES (corp-wide): 67.1B **Publicly Held**
SIC: 2086 5149 Carbonated soft drinks, bottled & canned; soft drinks
HQ: P-Americas Llc
1 Pepsi Way
Somers NY 10589
336 896-5740

(G-5733)
P-AMERICAS LLC
Also Called: Pepsico
650 W 51st St (60609-5221)
PHONE.................773 624-8013
Rich Schutzenhofer, *President*
Charles Paulinski, *Purch Agent*
Michal Barej, *Research*
Andy Ramirez, *Branch Mgr*
Laura Vandyke, *Manager*
EMP: 150
SALES (corp-wide): 67.1B **Publicly Held**
SIC: 2086 Carbonated soft drinks, bottled & canned
HQ: P-Americas Llc
1 Pepsi Way
Somers NY 10589
336 896-5740

(G-5734)
PAANI FOODS INC
6167 N Broadway St # 300 (60660-2501)
PHONE.................312 420-4624
◆ **EMP:** 10
SALES: 500K **Privately Held**
SIC: 2038 5142 Mfg & Whol Frozen Foods

(G-5735)
PAC PARTNERS LLC
1815 W Berteau Ave (60613-1321)
PHONE.................773 315-0828
Jason L Klein, *Principal*
EMP: 8 **EST:** 2012
SALES (est): 772.8K **Privately Held**
WEB: www.spitefulbrewing.com
SIC: 2082 Malt beverages

(G-5736)
PAC TEAM US PRODUCTIONS LLC
4447 W Armitage Ave (60639-3573)
PHONE.................773 360-8960
John Gedeon, *Mng Member*
EMP: 8 **EST:** 2015
SALES (est): 751.1K **Privately Held**
SIC: 2541 Display fixtures, wood
PA: Pac Team America Inc
205 Robin Rd Ste 200
Paramus NJ 07652

(G-5737)
PACE INDUSTRIES INC (PA)
2545 W Polk St (60612-4127)
P.O. Box 8393, Bartlett (60103-8393)
PHONE.................312 226-5500
James Palka, *President*
Richard Bontkowski, *Vice Pres*
◆ **EMP:** 240
SQ FT: 100,000
SALES (est): 43.7MM **Privately Held**
SIC: 2434 2514 3645 Vanities, bathroom: wood; medicine cabinets & vanities: metal; residential lighting fixtures

(G-5738)
PACIFIC GRANITES INC
17 N State St Ste 1585 (60602-3295)
P.O. Box 1162, Elk Grove Village (60009-1162)
PHONE.................312 835-7777
Mihir Karia, *Principal*
Shweta Mundhra, *Principal*
EMP: 9
SALES: 8.1MM **Privately Held**
SIC: 1423 Crushed & broken granite

(G-5739)
PACKAGING CORPORATION AMERICA
Also Called: PCA Chicago Container
5445 W 73rd St (60638-6500)
PHONE.................708 821-1600
Paul Dueringer, *General Mgr*
Arturo Arroyo, *Plant Supt*
Dave Kuffel, *Facilities Mgr*
Steven Possler, *Branch Mgr*
Alaina Murray, *Associate*
EMP: 86
SALES (corp-wide): 6.9B **Publicly Held**
SIC: 2653 Boxes, corrugated: made from purchased materials
PA: Packaging Corporation Of America
1 N Field Ct
Lake Forest IL 60045
847 482-3000

(G-5740)
PACKAGING CORPORATION AMERICA
Also Called: PCA
5230 W Roosevelt Rd (60644-1438)
PHONE.................773 378-8700
Scott Slager, *Regl Sales Mgr*
Joe Gibson, *Sales Staff*
Nate McFadyen, *Representative*
EMP: 6
SALES (corp-wide): 6.9B **Publicly Held**
SIC: 2653 Boxes, corrugated: made from purchased materials
PA: Packaging Corporation Of America
1 N Field Ct
Lake Forest IL 60045
847 482-3000

(G-5741)
PACKAGING WORLD
330 N Wabash Ave Ste 2401 (60611-3586)
PHONE.................305 448-6875
Gretchen Edelbrock, *Editor*
Anne Marie Mohan, *Senior Editor*
EMP: 5 **EST:** 2016
SALES (est): 319.6K **Privately Held**
SIC: 2721 Magazines: publishing only, not printed on site

(G-5742)
PACTIV LLC
7200 S Mason Ave (60638-6226)
PHONE.................708 496-2900
Lauren Grant, *Sales Staff*
Scarlett Stone, *Supervisor*
Bruce Chesney, *Administration*
EMP: 11 **Publicly Held**
SIC: 3089 3421 Kitchenware, plastic; plates, plastic; table & food cutlery, including butchers'
HQ: Pactiv Llc
1900 W Field Ct
Lake Forest IL 60045
847 482-2000

(G-5743)
PAKET CORPORATION
Also Called: Packet
9165 S Lake Shore Dr (60617-4407)
PHONE.................773 221-7300
Mark O'Malley, *President*
David Alvarez, *Vice Pres*
Stella Diaz, *Vice Pres*
Juan R Mateu, *Vice Pres*
Brian O'Malley, *Vice Pres*
EMP: 50
SQ FT: 105,000
SALES (est): 7.3MM **Privately Held**
WEB: www.paketcorp.com
SIC: 7389 2844 Packaging & labeling services; face creams or lotions

(G-5744)
PAKISTAN NEWS
6033 N Sheridan Rd (60660-3003)
PHONE.................773 271-6400
Ifti Nasim, *Manager*
EMP: 4
SALES (est): 180K **Privately Held**
SIC: 2711 Newspapers, publishing & printing

(G-5745)
PALEO PRIME LLC
2425 W Gnnison St Chicago (60625)
PHONE.................312 659-6596
Casey M McMillin, *Mng Member*
EMP: 1
SALES: 200K **Privately Held**
SIC: 2052 Cookies

(G-5746)
PALETERIA AZTECA INC
Also Called: Paleteria Azteca 2
3119 W Cermak Rd (60623-3451)
PHONE.................773 277-1423
Sabas Guzman, *President*
▲ **EMP:** 4
SALES (est): 368.7K **Privately Held**
SIC: 2024 Ice cream, bulk

(G-5747)
PALETERIA CARRUCEL
6317 W Grand Ave (60639-2615)
PHONE.................773 310-5749
Jose Ocampo, *Owner*
EMP: 5
SALES (est): 211.8K **Privately Held**
SIC: 2024 Ice cream & frozen desserts

(G-5748)
PALETERIA EL SABOR
1639 W 18th St (60608-2835)
PHONE.................312 243-2308
Jose C Fierro, *President*
EMP: 4 **EST:** 2011
SALES (est): 300.2K **Privately Held**
SIC: 2024 Ice cream & frozen desserts

(G-5749)
PALETERIA EL SABOR DE MICHOACN
2456 W 47th St (60632-1336)
PHONE.................773 376-3880
Angelica Barajas, *President*
EMP: 3
SALES (est): 251.2K **Privately Held**
SIC: 2024 Ice cream, bulk

(G-5750)
PANDA MARKETING GROUP INC
451 N Racine Ave (60642-5841)
PHONE.................847 383-5270
Algirdas J Juozaitis, *President*
Gary Johnson, *Vice Pres*
EMP: 20
SQ FT: 11,000
SALES (est): 2MM **Privately Held**
SIC: 2796 Color separations for printing

(G-5751)
PAOLI INC
222 Merchandise Mart Plz # 380 (60654-1245)
PHONE.................312 644-5509
▲ **EMP:** 4
SALES (est): 440K **Privately Held**
SIC: 2522 Mfg Office Furniture-Nonwood

(G-5752)
PAPA CHARLIES INC
1800 S Kostner Ave (60623-2339)
PHONE.................773 522-7900
Joe Hall, *President*
Chris Hall, *Vice Pres*
Paul Sapata, *Vice Pres*
Melissa Elmore, *Manager*
EMP: 25
SQ FT: 20,000
SALES (est): 10.6MM **Privately Held**
SIC: 2013 Sausages from purchased meat

(G-5753)
PAPIROS GRAPHICS
4557 W 59th St (60629-5437)
PHONE.................773 581-3000
Rodolfo A Alvarado, *Partner*
EMP: 4
SALES (est): 427K **Privately Held**
SIC: 2752 Commercial printing, offset

(G-5754)
PAPPONE INC
Also Called: Pasta Pappone
2041 W Carroll Ave C214 (60612-1692)
PHONE.................630 234-4738
Jonathan P Mulholland, *CEO*
EMP: 5 **EST:** 2013
SQ FT: 1,200
SALES (est): 350.5K **Privately Held**
SIC: 5499 2033 Gourmet food stores; spaghetti & other pasta sauce: packaged in cans, jars, etc.

(G-5755)
PAPYRUS PRESS INC
3441 W Grand Ave (60651-4001)
PHONE.................773 342-0700
Gus Lymperopoulos, *President*
Constantine Lymperopoulos, *President*
Nick Lymperopoulos, *Vice Pres*
Angelos Sidereas, *Treasurer*
EMP: 10
SQ FT: 25,000
SALES (est): 1.1MM **Privately Held**
SIC: 2759 2752 2791 2396 Screen printing; commercial printing, offset; typesetting; automotive & apparel trimmings

(G-5756)
PARADE PUBLICATIONS INC
Also Called: Parade Magazine
500 N Michigan Ave # 910 (60611-3777)
PHONE.................312 661-1620
Heather Faust, *Sales/Mktg Mgr*
Beverly Vacval, *Manager*
EMP: 12
SQ FT: 3,000
SALES (corp-wide): 5.6B **Privately Held**
SIC: 2721 Magazines: publishing only, not printed on site

Chicago - Cook County (G-5757) GEOGRAPHIC SECTION

HQ: Parade Publications, Inc.
711 3rd Ave
New York NY 10017
212 450-7000

(G-5757)
PARADISE GROUP LLC
67 E Madison St Ste 1603a (60603-3062)
PHONE 779 207-9077
Andy Dimnych, *Mng Member*
EMP: 5
SALES: 350K **Privately Held**
SIC: 3577 Computer peripheral equipment

(G-5758)
PARAGON PACKAGING INC (PA)
1201 S Prrie Ave Apt 2801 (60605)
PHONE 707 786-4004
Ron Cohn, *President*
▲ **EMP:** 4 **EST:** 1921
SQ FT: 3,000
SALES (est): 346K **Privately Held**
WEB: www.paragonpackaging.com
SIC: 7389 3944 Brokers, business: buying & selling business enterprises; board games, children's & adults'

(G-5759)
PARAGON SPRING COMPANY
4435 W Rice St Ste 45 (60651-3457)
PHONE 773 489-6300
Marilyn L Whittle, *CEO*
Amy L Whittle, *President*
Amy Whittle, *General Mgr*
EMP: 20 **EST:** 1945
SQ FT: 32,000
SALES (est): 4.4MM **Privately Held**
WEB: www.paragonspring.com
SIC: 3493 3312 3469 3496 Flat springs, sheet or strip stock; wire products, steel or iron; stamping metal for the trade; miscellaneous fabricated wire products; wire springs

(G-5760)
PARAMOUNT PLASTICS INC
140 S Dearborn St Ste 420 (60603-5233)
PHONE 815 834-4100
Doug Mulay, *President*
Larry Scales, *Principal*
Peggy Scales, *Corp Secy*
EMP: 80
SQ FT: 120,000
SALES (est): 17.4MM **Privately Held**
SIC: 3089 Injection molding of plastics

(G-5761)
PARAMOUNT PLASTICS LLC
140 S Dearborn St Ste 420 (60603-5233)
PHONE 815 834-4100
Doug Mulay,
Matt Simpson,
Ken Swanick,
EMP: 100
SQ FT: 140,000
SALES (est): 14.4MM **Privately Held**
SIC: 2131 Chewing tobacco

(G-5762)
PARAMOUNT TRUCK BODY CO INC
4929 S Mason Ave (60638-1442)
PHONE 312 666-6441
Joseph Smolucha, *President*
Greg Smolucha, *Corp Secy*
EMP: 20
SALES (est): 4.1MM **Privately Held**
SIC: 3713 3715 Truck bodies (motor vehicles); trailer bodies

(G-5763)
PARISO INC
Also Called: Vp Finish
1836 N Lockwood Ave (60639-4353)
PHONE 773 889-4383
Victor Pariso, *President*
John Pariso, *Vice Pres*
Sandra Pariso, *Director*
EMP: 10 **EST:** 1919
SQ FT: 10,000
SALES (est): 1.3MM **Privately Held**
WEB: www.vpfinish.com
SIC: 3471 Electroplating of metals or formed products; anodizing (plating) of metals or formed products; plating of metals or formed products; coloring & finishing of aluminum or formed products

(G-5764)
PARK PACKING COMPANY INC
4107 S Ashland Ave (60609-2331)
PHONE 773 254-0100
Athanasios Bairaktaris, *President*
Emily Bairaktaris, *Admin Sec*
EMP: 28
SQ FT: 10,000
SALES (est): 11.8MM **Privately Held**
WEB: www.parkpacking.com
SIC: 5147 2011 5421 2013 Meats, fresh; meat packing plants; meat & fish markets; sausages & other prepared meats; slaughtering: custom livestock services

(G-5765)
PARK-HIO FRGED MCHNED PDTS LLC
Also Called: Kropp Forge
5301 W Roosevelt Rd (60804-1224)
PHONE 708 652-6691
Thomas Pollard, *President*
▲ **EMP:** 85
SQ FT: 450,000
SALES (est): 32.2MM
SALES (corp-wide): 1.6B **Publicly Held**
SIC: 3462 Iron & steel forgings
HQ: Park-Ohio Industries, Inc.
6065 Parkland Blvd Ste 1
Cleveland OH 44124
440 947-2000

(G-5766)
PARK-OHIO INDUSTRIES INC
Park Ohio Forged Machined Pdts
5301 W Roosevelt Rd (60804-1224)
PHONE 708 652-6691
John Chrzanowski, *Senior VP*
Vickey Weber, *QC Mgr*
Rochelle Kosmos, *Branch Mgr*
David Hill,
EMP: 85
SALES (corp-wide): 1.6B **Publicly Held**
SIC: 3911 Medals, precious or semi-precious metal
HQ: Park-Ohio Industries, Inc.
6065 Parkland Blvd Ste 1
Cleveland OH 44124
440 947-2000

(G-5767)
PARKER-HANNIFIN CORPORATION
Also Called: Aircraft Wheel & Brake Div
7939 Collection Center Dr (60693-0079)
PHONE 216 896-3000
EMP: 32
SALES (corp-wide): 14.3B **Publicly Held**
WEB: www.phtruck.com
SIC: 3594 Fluid power pumps & motors
PA: Parker-Hannifin Corporation
6035 Parkland Blvd
Cleveland OH 44124
216 896-3000

(G-5768)
PARROT PRESS
4484 S Archer Ave (60632-2846)
PHONE 773 376-6333
David Hines, *Owner*
EMP: 3
SQ FT: 1,800
SALES (est): 170K **Privately Held**
SIC: 2752 2789 Commercial printing, offset; bookbinding & related work

(G-5769)
PASTAFRESH CO
Also Called: Pastafresh Homemade Pasta
3418 N Harlem Ave (60634-3605)
PHONE 773 745-5888
Anthony Bartucci, *President*
Gino Bartucci, *Admin Sec*
▲ **EMP:** 4
SQ FT: 1,200

SALES (est): 347.1K **Privately Held**
SIC: 2099 2098 2035 Packaged combination products: pasta, rice & potato; pasta, uncooked: packaged with other ingredients; macaroni & spaghetti; pickles, sauces & salad dressings

(G-5770)
PASTORELLI FOOD PRODUCTS INC
901 W Lake St (60607)
PHONE 312 455-1006
Noe Lara, *Manager*
EMP: 3
SQ FT: 61,000
SALES (corp-wide): 2.4MM **Privately Held**
SIC: 2032 2033 2099 2079 Italian foods: packaged in cans, jars, etc.; spaghetti: packaged in cans, jars, etc.; pizza sauce: packaged in cans, jars, etc.; vinegar; cooking oils, except corn: vegetable refined; vegetable shortenings (except corn oil)
PA: Pastorelli Food Products, Inc.
162 N Sangamon St
Chicago IL 60607
312 666-2041

(G-5771)
PAUL D METAL PRODUCTS INC
2225 W Pershing Rd (60609-2210)
PHONE 773 847-1400
Farshid Paul Ohadi, *President*
David Nohava, *Vice Pres*
Ruth Ravve, *Producer*
EMP: 55
SQ FT: 180,000
SALES (est): 6.9MM **Privately Held**
SIC: 3646 3446 Commercial indusl & institutional electric lighting fixtures; architectural metalwork

(G-5772)
PAUL SISTI
Also Called: Paul Sisti Studio
3520 N Lake Shore Dr (60657-1860)
PHONE 773 472-5615
Paul Sisti, *Owner*
EMP: 3
SALES (est): 60K **Privately Held**
SIC: 7219 2339 Dressmaking service, material owned by customer; women's & misses' outerwear

(G-5773)
PCJ II INC (HQ)
Also Called: Sausages By Amy
1143 W Lake St (60607-1618)
PHONE 312 829-2250
Richard Kurzawski, *CEO*
Amylu T Kurzawski, *President*
Mike McGuire, *Sales Executive*
EMP: 40 **EST:** 1926
SQ FT: 27,000
SALES (est): 7.9MM
SALES (corp-wide): 10.6MM **Privately Held**
WEB: www.atkfoods.com
SIC: 2013 Sausages from purchased meat; luncheon meat from purchased meat
PA: Amylu Foods, Llc
1400 W 44th St
Chicago IL 60609
312 829-2250

(G-5774)
PDOC LLC (DH)
3900 W 43rd St (60632-3421)
PHONE 773 843-8000
Phillip D Harris, *Principal*
EMP: 121
SALES (est): 142.3K
SALES (corp-wide): 2.5B **Privately Held**
SIC: 2671 Paper coated or laminated for packaging

(G-5775)
PEAK HEALTHCARE ADVISORS LLC
Also Called: Battle Balls Bubble Soccer
4043 N Ravenswood Ave # 225 (60613-1155)
PHONE 646 479-0005
Randy Carlson, *CEO*

EMP: 4
SALES (est): 152.5K **Privately Held**
WEB: www.battle-balls.com
SIC: 3949 Team sports equipment

(G-5776)
PEAPOD DIGITAL LABS LLC
300 S Riverside Plz (60606-6613)
PHONE 800 573-2763
Jj Fleeman, *Mng Member*
EMP: 3
SALES: 85.3K
SALES (corp-wide): 71.8B **Privately Held**
SIC: 7372 Business oriented computer software
PA: Koninklijke Ahold Delhaize N.V.
Provincialeweg 11
Zaandam
886 599-111

(G-5777)
PEARL BATH BOMBS INC
2850 N Pulaski Rd Unit 10 (60641-5456)
PHONE 312 661-2881
Pavel Melnichuk, *Director*
EMP: 10 **EST:** 2015
SALES (est): 2.5MM **Privately Held**
SIC: 5094 5122 7372 2844 Pearls; toiletries; application computer software; toilet preparations

(G-5778)
PECHINEY CAST PLATE
8770 W Bryn Mawr Ave Fl 9 (60631-3780)
P.O. Box 58447, Los Angeles CA (90058-0447)
PHONE 847 299-0220
Tom Reynolds, *General Mgr*
EMP: 120 **EST:** 1940
SQ FT: 611,000
SALES (est): 14.7MM **Privately Held**
SIC: 3353 Plates, aluminum

(G-5779)
PECO PALLET
9355 S Damen Ave (60643-6336)
PHONE 773 646-0976
EMP: 3
SALES (est): 150.7K **Privately Held**
SIC: 2448 Pallets, wood & wood with metal

(G-5780)
PEDRAZA INC
Also Called: Andee Boiler & Welding Co
7649 S State St (60619-2316)
PHONE 773 874-9020
Edgar Pedraza, *President*
EMP: 15
SQ FT: 8,000
SALES (est): 1.4MM **Privately Held**
WEB: www.andeeboiler.com
SIC: 7699 7692 Boiler repair shop; welding repair

(G-5781)
PEER FOODS INC (HQ)
1200 W 35th St Fl 3 (60609-1305)
PHONE 773 927-1440
Larry O'Connell, *President*
Ramon Barba, *Plant Mgr*
David Wells, *Prdtn Mgr*
Tom Grantner, *Research*
Donna Recupido, *Treasurer*
EMP: 13
SQ FT: 10,000
SALES (est): 2.2MM
SALES (corp-wide): 38.9MM **Privately Held**
SIC: 2011 Meat packing plants
PA: Peer Foods Group, Inc.
1200 W 35th St Fl 3
Chicago IL 60609
773 927-1440

(G-5782)
PEERLESS
4855 S Racine Ave (60609-4320)
PHONE 773 294-2667
Bill A Dowell, *Principal*
EMP: 3
SALES (est): 438.8K **Privately Held**
WEB: www.emb1925.com
SIC: 3552 Embroidery machines

GEOGRAPHIC SECTION

Chicago - Cook County (G-5809)

(G-5783)
PEGAI LLC
3550 W Montrose Ave # 4 (60618-1187)
PHONE...................312 799-0417
Volkan Yilmaz, *Principal*
EMP: 3
SALES (est): 359.5K **Privately Held**
SIC: 3199 Leather goods

(G-5784)
PEKAY MACHINE & ENGRG CO INC
2520 W Lake St (60612-2108)
PHONE...................312 829-5530
Jules T Parisi Jr, *President*
Charles J Parisi, *Vice Pres*
Jean Parisi, *Asst Sec*
EMP: 13 **EST:** 1945
SQ FT: 25,000
SALES (est): 2.4MM **Privately Held**
WEB: www.pekay.com
SIC: 3559 3498 Foundry machinery & equipment; tube fabricating (contract bending & shaping)

(G-5785)
PEOPLE AGAINST DIRTY MFG PBC
720 E 111th St (60628-4669)
PHONE...................415 568-4600
Drew Fraser, *COO*
EMP: 66
SALES (est): 13.8MM **Privately Held**
SIC: 2841 Soap & other detergents
HQ: Ecover Co-Ordination Center
Steenovenstraat 1, Internal Postal Box A
Malle 2390
468 189-222

(G-5786)
PEOPLEADMIN INC
4611 N Ravenswood Ave # 201 (60640-7564)
PHONE...................877 637-5800
Kermit S Randa, *Manager*
EMP: 50
SALES (corp-wide): 5.6B **Privately Held**
SIC: 7372 8299 Educational computer software; educational services
HQ: Peopleadmin, Inc.
805 Las Cimas Pkwy # 400
Austin TX 78746
877 637-5800

(G-5787)
PEORIA PACKING LTD (PA)
1307 W Lake St (60607-1511)
PHONE...................312 226-2600
Harry Katsiavelos, *President*
Georgia Katsiavelos, *Partner*
Louis Manis, *Vice Pres*
EMP: 15
SQ FT: 18,000
SALES (est): 11MM **Privately Held**
SIC: 2011 5147 5421 Meat packing plants; meats & meat products; meat markets, including freezer provisioners

(G-5788)
PEPSI-COLA METRO BTLG CO INC
555 W Monroe St Fl 1 (60661-3700)
PHONE...................847 598-3000
Eric Mann, *Counsel*
Brad Braun, *Vice Pres*
Keith Melaragno, *Vice Pres*
Dustin Benway, *Safety Mgr*
Chris Maertens, *Controller*
EMP: 100
SALES (corp-wide): 67.1B **Publicly Held**
SIC: 2086 5085 Carbonated soft drinks, bottled & canned; bottler supplies
HQ: Pepsi-Cola Metropolitan Bottling Company, Inc.
1111 Westchester Ave
White Plains NY 10604
914 767-6000

(G-5789)
PEPSICO INC
555 W Monroe St Fl 1 (60661-3700)
PHONE...................312 821-1000
Janice Hilldale, *Buyer*
Shannon Rice, *Engineer*
Jeffery Swearingen, *Treasurer*
Jim Spalding, *Mktg Dir*
Kelli Bentley, *Marketing Mgr*
EMP: 56
SALES (corp-wide): 67.1B **Publicly Held**
SIC: 2086 2087 2096 Carbonated soft drinks, bottled & canned; flavoring extracts & syrups; potato chips & similar snacks
PA: Pepsico, Inc.
700 Anderson Hill Rd
Purchase NY 10577
914 253-2000

(G-5790)
PERFICIENT INC
Also Called: Truth Labs
212 W Superior St Ste 505 (60654-2608)
PHONE...................312 291-9035
EMP: 10
SALES (corp-wide): 565.5MM **Publicly Held**
SIC: 7371 7372 Software programming applications; application computer software
PA: Perficient, Inc.
555 Mryvlle Univ Dr Ste 6
Saint Louis MO 63141
314 930-2900

(G-5791)
PERFORMITIV LLC
220 N Green St Ste 6015 (60607-1702)
PHONE...................312 307-5716
Kent Barnett, *CEO*
Jeb Metric, *Principal*
Jeffrey Berk, *COO*
EMP: 3 **EST:** 2016
SALES (est): 138.6K **Privately Held**
SIC: 7372 Application computer software

(G-5792)
PERSONIFY INC
212 W Superior St Ste 202 (60654-5812)
PHONE...................855 747-9940
Sanjay J Patel, *CEO*
Paul Gavura, *Chief*
Jim Kosmach, *Engineer*
EMP: 10 **Privately Held**
WEB: www.personify.com
SIC: 7372 7819 Application computer software; services allied to motion pictures
PA: Personify, Inc.
208a W Main St
Urbana IL 61801

(G-5793)
PERVASIVE HEALTH INC
1 N La Salle St Ste 1825 (60602-3933)
PHONE...................312 257-2967
Paul Magelli, *CEO*
Geoff Phillips, *CFO*
EMP: 5
SALES (est): 481.1K **Privately Held**
SIC: 7372 7373 Business oriented computer software; computer integrated systems design

(G-5794)
PETERS CONSTRUCTION
3441 W Grand Ave (60651-4001)
PHONE...................773 489-5555
Aracela Perez, *Owner*
EMP: 9
SALES (est): 1.1MM **Privately Held**
WEB: www.peterswoodrefinishing.com
SIC: 2431 1751 1521 Millwork; carpentry work; new construction, single-family houses

(G-5795)
PETERSON BROTHERS PLASTICS
2929 N Pulaski Rd (60641-5421)
PHONE...................773 286-5666
Kenneth Peterson, *President*
Keith Peterson, *Vice Pres*
Kevin Peterson, *Admin Sec*
EMP: 12 **EST:** 1943
SQ FT: 16,000
SALES (est): 2MM **Privately Held**
WEB: www.petersenplastics.com
SIC: 5162 3993 Plastics materials; signs, not made in custom sign painting shops

(G-5796)
PETOTE LLC
2444 W 16th St Ste 4 (60608-1731)
PHONE...................312 455-0873
Janet Lee,
▲ **EMP:** 7
SALES (est): 821.9K **Privately Held**
SIC: 3999 Pet supplies

(G-5797)
PETRA MANUFACTURING CO
6600 W Armitage Ave (60707-3908)
PHONE...................773 622-1475
Norman C Hoffberg, *President*
Cheryl Visockis, *Vice Pres*
Pat Walczewski, *Sales Staff*
▲ **EMP:** 70
SQ FT: 68,000
SALES (est): 8.9MM **Privately Held**
WEB: www.petramanufacturing.com
SIC: 2396 2385 2671 Printing & embossing on plastics fabric articles; screen printing on fabric articles; aprons, waterproof: made from purchased materials; gowns, plastic: made from purchased materials; plastic film, coated or laminated for packaging

(G-5798)
PETRO CHEM ECHER ERHARDT LLC
Also Called: Petro-Chem Industries Div
2628 S Sacramento Ave (60623-5118)
PHONE...................773 847-7535
Charles Schroeder, *Manager*
EMP: 8 **EST:** 1951
SQ FT: 15,000
SALES (est): 1.4MM **Privately Held**
WEB: www.petrochemind.com
SIC: 7699 3443 Boiler & heating repair services; fabricated plate work (boiler shop)

(G-5799)
PETROCHEM CORP (DH)
8600 W Bryn Mawr Ave 800n (60631-3579)
PHONE...................431 205-8122
Garry Masse, *CEO*
Charlie Dawson, *Vice Pres*
David Ramos, *Vice Pres*
Mike Alger, *CFO*
Duane Owens, *Treasurer*
◆ **EMP:** 4
SQ FT: 9,500
SALES (est): 10.3MM
SALES (corp-wide): 2.2B **Privately Held**
SIC: 3089 Plastic containers, except foam

(G-5800)
PFIZER INC
1101 S State St Apt 1903 (60605-3205)
PHONE...................847 778-9237
Julie Ronin, *Mktg Dir*
Maria Alaniz, *Business Anlyst*
EMP: 3
SALES (corp-wide): 51.7B **Publicly Held**
SIC: 2834 Drugs acting on the cardiovascular system, except diagnostic
PA: Pfizer Inc.
235 E 42nd St Rm 107
New York NY 10017
212 733-2323

(G-5801)
PHILS AUTO BODY
833 W 35th St (60609-1511)
PHONE...................773 847-7156
Phil Winstead, *Principal*
EMP: 7 **EST:** 2008
SALES (est): 342.1K **Privately Held**
SIC: 7532 3713 3711 Body shop, automotive; truck & bus bodies; automobile bodies, passenger car, not including engine, etc.

(G-5802)
PHOENIX ELECTRIC MFG CO
3625 N Halsted St (60613-4394)
PHONE...................773 477-8855
Sanford Bank, *Ch of Bd*
Norberto Anselmi, *President*
Saul Perez, *Vice Pres*
▲ **EMP:** 44 **EST:** 1936
SQ FT: 15,000
SALES (est): 7.4MM **Privately Held**
WEB: www.phoenixelectric.com
SIC: 3089 Handles, brush or tool: plastic

(G-5803)
PHOENIX INTL PUBLICATIONS INC
Also Called: Pikids
8501 W Higgins Rd Ste 300 (60631-2812)
PHONE...................877 277-9441
Vincent Douglas, *CEO*
Cory Moyars, *General Mgr*
Michael Murphy, *Exec VP*
Liang Qian, *Senior VP*
Jim Harbison, *Vice Pres*
▲ **EMP:** 300
SALES (est): 100MM
SALES (corp-wide): 1.7B **Privately Held**
SIC: 5942 2731 Children's books; books: publishing & printing
PA: Jiangsu Phoenix Publishing And Media Corporation Limited
27/F, Block B, Phoenix Plaza, No.1 Hunan Road
Nanjing 21000
255 188-3338

(G-5804)
PHOENIX TREE PUBLISHING INC
5660 N Jersey Ave (60659-3626)
PHONE...................773 251-0309
Shijia Sheng, *Business Mgr*
Chao Shi, *Sales Mgr*
Bohua LI, *Marketing Staff*
▲ **EMP:** 4
SALES (est): 271.7K **Privately Held**
WEB: www.phoenixtree.com
SIC: 2741 Miscellaneous publishing

(G-5805)
PHOTON PARTNERS LLC
3435 N Avers Ave (60618-5213)
PHONE...................773 991-9788
Catherine E Hanby, *Manager*
EMP: 2
SALES (est): 267.8K **Privately Held**
SIC: 3661 Fiber optics communications equipment

(G-5806)
PICKLES SORREL INC
Also Called: Puckered Pickle
5610 W Taylor St (60644-5507)
PHONE...................773 379-4748
Steven Nathan, *President*
Wayne Newman, *Vice Pres*
EMP: 15
SQ FT: 12,000
SALES (est): 2.8MM **Privately Held**
SIC: 2099 Food preparations

(G-5807)
PILLA EXEC INC
2447 W 80th St (60652-2863)
PHONE...................312 882-8263
James Perkins, *CEO*
EMP: 3
SQ FT: 700
SALES (est): 180K **Privately Held**
SIC: 6798 3253 5511 Real estate investment trusts; ceramic wall & floor tile; automobiles, new & used

(G-5808)
PILZ AUTOMTN SAFETY LTD PARTNR
7021 Solutions Ctr (60677-7000)
PHONE...................734 354-0272
EMP: 4
SALES (corp-wide): 299.8MM **Privately Held**
SIC: 3625 Relays & industrial controls
HQ: Pilz Automation Safety, Limited Partnership
7150 Commerce Blvd
Canton MI 48187

(G-5809)
PIONEER NEWSPAPERS INC (DH)
Also Called: Pioneer Press
350 N Orleans St Fl 10 (60654-1975)
PHONE...................847 486-0600
Mark Cohen, *COO*

Chicago - Cook County (G-5810) GEOGRAPHIC SECTION

Greg Powell, *Vice Pres*
Michael Sperling, *Vice Pres*
EMP: 230
SQ FT: 38,500
SALES (est): 31.6MM
SALES (corp-wide): 4.3MM **Privately Held**
SIC: 2711 Commercial printing & newspaper publishing combined; newspapers, publishing & printing
HQ: Sun-Times Media Group, Inc.
  30 N Racine Ave Ste 300
  Chicago IL 60607
  312 321-3000

(G-5810)
PIONEER PRINTING SERVICE INC
1340 N Astor St (60610-2171)
PHONE.................312 337-4283
Deborah Schnitzius, *President*
Frances Schnitzius, *Treasurer*
EMP: 3
SQ FT: 5,000
SALES (est): 361.6K **Privately Held**
SIC: 2752 2759 Commercial printing, offset; commercial printing

(G-5811)
PIPELINE TRADING SYSTEMS LLC
1 S Dearborn St Ste 2100 (60603-2307)
PHONE.................312 212-4288
Marilou Giustini, *Director*
EMP: 3
SALES (est): 252K **Privately Held**
SIC: 3699 Electronic training devices
HQ: Pipeline Trading Systems Llc
  60 E 42nd St Ste 624
  New York NY 10165

(G-5812)
PITCHFORK MEDIA INC
3317 W Fullerton Ave (60647-2513)
PHONE.................773 395-5937
Fax: 773 395-5992
EMP: 40
SALES (est): 5.5MM **Privately Held**
SIC: 2721 Periodicals-Publishing/Printing

(G-5813)
PITNEY BOWES INC
3640 N Bosworth Ave 3s (60613-5371)
PHONE.................773 755-5808
Alan Montague, *Principal*
Dave Crawford, *Engineer*
Mark Malec, *Consultant*
EMP: 35
SALES (corp-wide): 3.2B **Publicly Held**
SIC: 3579 Mailing machines
PA: Pitney Bowes Inc.
  3001 Summer St Ste 3
  Stamford CT 06905
  203 356-5000

(G-5814)
PIVOT POINT USA INC (PA)
Also Called: Pivot Point Beauty School
8725 W Higgins Rd Ste 700 (60631-2700)
PHONE.................800 886-4247
Robert Passage, *CEO*
Rachel Marano, *Managing Prtnr*
Lisa Hemming, *Business Mgr*
Robert Sieh, *Senior VP*
Kevin Cameron, *Vice Pres*
▲ **EMP:** 117
SQ FT: 42,000
SALES (est): 16.5MM **Privately Held**
WEB: www.pivot-point.com
SIC: 2731 5087 8299 Books: publishing only; beauty parlor equipment & supplies; finishing school, charm & modeling; educational services

(G-5815)
PIVOTAL PRODUCTION LLC
356 E Sutherland St (60619)
P.O. Box 198545 (60619-8545)
PHONE.................773 726-7706
Letitia Jenkins, *CEO*
EMP: 3 **EST:** 2008
SQ FT: 1,000
SALES (est): 2K **Privately Held**
WEB: www.pivotalchicago.com
SIC: 2844 Toilet preparations

(G-5816)
PKND LLC
480 N Mcclurg Ct (60611-4326)
PHONE.................773 491-0070
Piter Kostopoulos, *Mng Member*
EMR: 2
SALES: 200K **Privately Held**
SIC: 2034 Dehydrated fruits, vegetables, soups

(G-5817)
PLANTER INC
Also Called: Victory Division of Planter
1820 N Major Ave (60639-4118)
PHONE.................773 637-7777
Steven Kite, *President*
Eric Priceman, *Vice Pres*
Stan Rosenberg, *Vice Pres*
Alan Starks, *Vice Pres*
▲ **EMP:** 75 **EST:** 1948
SQ FT: 45,000
SALES (est): 13.4MM **Privately Held**
WEB: www.buyvictory.com
SIC: 3499 3599 Trophies, metal, except silver; machine shop, jobbing & repair

(G-5818)
PLASTICREST PRODUCTS INC
4519 W Harrison St (60624-3099)
PHONE.................773 826-2163
Robert W Pauley, *President*
▲ **EMP:** 10 **EST:** 1942
SQ FT: 17,000
SALES (est): 1.4MM **Privately Held**
WEB: www.signaturejewelrypackaging.com
SIC: 3469 3089 3172 2657 Boxes, stamped metal; boxes, plastic; personal leather goods; folding paperboard boxes

(G-5819)
PLASTICS D-E-F
3065 W Armitage Ave (60647-5911)
P.O. Box 50, Skokie (60076-0050)
PHONE.................312 226-4337
Jack H Beck, *Partner*
Robert Klovstad, *Partner*
EMP: 4
SQ FT: 2,500
SALES (est): 200K **Privately Held**
SIC: 2673 Bags: plastic, laminated & coated

(G-5820)
PLASTICS PRINTING GROUP INC
5414 W Roosevelt Rd (60644-1467)
PHONE.................773 473-4481
Lee Masover, *President*
EMP: 11
SQ FT: 13,500
SALES (est): 1.9MM **Privately Held**
SIC: 2759 2675 2396 Screen printing; die-cut paper & board; automotive & apparel trimmings

(G-5821)
PLATT LUGGAGE INC
Also Called: Platt Cases
4051 W 51st St (60632-4294)
PHONE.................773 838-2000
Daniel Platt, *CEO*
▲ **EMP:** 75 **EST:** 1921
SQ FT: 70,000
SALES (est): 14.3MM **Privately Held**
WEB: www.plattcases.com
SIC: 3161 3089 Attache cases; cases, plastic

(G-5822)
PLAYER SPORTS LTD
2956 W Peterson Ave (60659-3810)
PHONE.................773 764-4111
Anthony Chronis, *Partner*
James Chronis, *Partner*
EMP: 3 **EST:** 1976
SQ FT: 4,600
SALES (est): 513.8K **Privately Held**
SIC: 5091 2261 Sporting & recreation goods; screen printing of cotton broadwoven fabrics

(G-5823)
PLUMROSE USA INC
651 W Washington Blvd # 304 (60661-2137)
PHONE.................732 253-5257
EMP: 3 **Privately Held**
SIC: 2011 Hams & picnics from meat slaughtered on site
HQ: Plumrose Usa, Inc.
  1901 Butterfield Rd # 305
  Downers Grove IL 60515

(G-5824)
PLYMOUTH TUBE COMPANY
4555 W Armitage Ave (60639-3403)
PHONE.................773 489-0226
Edward Blessman, *Technical Mgr*
John Zeilman, *Asst Controller*
Diane Augustine, *Human Res Mgr*
Diane Frederick, *Accounts Exec*
Steve Koch, *Branch Mgr*
EMP: 98
SALES (corp-wide): 221.4MM **Privately Held**
SIC: 3317 3354 Tubes, seamless steel; tubes, wrought: welded or lock joint; shapes, extruded aluminum; tube, extruded or drawn, aluminum
PA: Plymouth Tube Company
  29w 150 Warrenville Rd
  Warrenville IL 60555
  630 393-3550

(G-5825)
PMC CONVERTING CORP
5080 N Kimberly Ave # 107 (60630-1770)
PHONE.................773 481-2269
Rocio Medina, *President*
Lorena Medina, *Vice Pres*
EMP: 7
SALES (est): 714K **Privately Held**
SIC: 2675 Paper die-cutting

(G-5826)
PNE USA INC
150 N Michigan Ave # 1500 (60601-7570)
PHONE.................773 329-3705
Roland Stanze, *President*
EMP: 3
SALES (est): 424K **Privately Held**
SIC: 3511 Turbines & turbine generator sets

(G-5827)
PNG TRANSPORT LLC
3543 S Parnell Ave Apt B (60609-1796)
PHONE.................312 218-8116
Peter Ng, *President*
EMP: 2
SALES: 230K **Privately Held**
SIC: 2421 Building & structural materials, wood

(G-5828)
POERSCH METAL MANUFACTURING CO
4027 W Kinzie St (60624-1807)
PHONE.................773 722-0890
Robert C Kruse Sr, *President*
EMP: 14
SQ FT: 6,000
SALES (est): 2.2MM **Privately Held**
WEB: www.poerschmetal.com
SIC: 3844 3861 X-ray apparatus & tubes; photographic equipment & supplies

(G-5829)
POETRY CENTER
Also Called: Chicago Poetry Center
641 W Lake St Ste 200 (60661-1308)
PHONE.................312 899-1229
Franchesco Levato, *Director*
EMP: 4
SALES: 65.4K **Privately Held**
SIC: 8641 2731 Educator's association; book publishing

(G-5830)
POETRY FOUNDATION
Also Called: POETRY MAGAZINE
61 W Superior St (60654-5457)
PHONE.................312 787-7070
Ydalmi Noriega, *President*
Robert Polito, *President*
Fred Sasaki, *Publisher*
Beyza Ozer, *Editor*
Michael Slosek, *Editor*
EMP: 25
SQ FT: 22,000
SALES (est): 11.2MM **Privately Held**
SIC: 2721 Magazines: publishing only, not printed on site

(G-5831)
POETS STUDY INC
4366 N Elston Ave (60641-2146)
PHONE.................773 286-1355
Alfred Schuch, *President*
EMP: 7 **EST:** 1939
SQ FT: 2,700
SALES (est): 700K **Privately Held**
WEB: www.poetsstudy.com
SIC: 2759 2791 2752 Card printing & engraving, except greeting; typesetting; commercial printing, lithographic

(G-5832)
POLAMER INC
Also Called: Polamer & Parcel Travel Svc
6401 N Milwaukee Ave (60646)
PHONE.................773 774-3600
Ledia Janowski, *Manager*
EMP: 5
SALES (corp-wide): 18.1MM **Privately Held**
SIC: 2449 Shipping cases & drums, wood: wirebound & plywood
PA: Polamer, Inc
  3094 N Milwaukee Ave
  Chicago IL 60618
  773 685-8222

(G-5833)
POLLACK SERVICE
3701 N Ravenswood Ave (60613-3553)
PHONE.................773 528-8096
Gerald Pollack, *Principal*
EMP: 65
SALES (est): 1.9MM **Privately Held**
SIC: 2389 Regalia

(G-5834)
POLLARD BROS MFG CO
5504 N Northwest Hwy (60630-1116)
PHONE.................773 763-6868
Jason Hein, *President*
Steve F Hein, *Admin Sec*
EMP: 11 **EST:** 1921
SQ FT: 20,000
SALES (est): 1.6MM **Privately Held**
WEB: www.pollardbros.com
SIC: 2599 Factory furniture & fixtures

(G-5835)
POLONIA BOOK STORE INC
4738 N Milwaukee Ave (60630-3614)
PHONE.................773 481-6968
Mira Puacz, *President*
EMP: 3
SQ FT: 8,200
SALES (est): 193.6K **Privately Held**
WEB: www.polonia.com
SIC: 5942 2731 Books, religious; books: publishing only

(G-5836)
POLPRESS INC
Also Called: Polpress Priniting
5566 N Northwest Hwy (60630-1116)
PHONE.................773 792-1200
Roman Majewski, *President*
EMP: 6
SQ FT: 2,000
SALES (est): 1.1MM **Privately Held**
SIC: 2752 Commercial printing, offset

(G-5837)
POLYAIR CORPORATION
808 E 113th St (60628-5150)
PHONE.................773 253-1220
Donald Engel, *Principal*
Tyrone Jeffcoat, *COO*
Steve Dwyer, *Plant Mgr*
Keith Cameron, *Manager*
Marc Owens, *Manager*
EMP: 3 **EST:** 1996
SALES (est): 156K
SALES (corp-wide): 1.1B **Privately Held**
SIC: 5999 3089 Foam & foam products; blister or bubble formed packaging, plastic

Chicago - Cook County (G-5865)

PA: Groupe Intertape Polymer Inc, Le
9999 Boul Cavendish Bureau 200
Saint-Laurent QC H4M 2

(G-5838)
POLYAIR INTER PACK INC
808 E 113th St (60628-5150)
PHONE..................................773 995-1818
Ben Drew, *Sales Staff*
Mike Glynn, *VP Mktg*
Joe Miller, *Branch Mgr*
EMP: 70
SALES (est): 15.1MM **Privately Held**
WEB: www.polyair.com
SIC: 3433 2394 3949 3086 Solar heaters & collectors; liners & covers, fabric: made from purchased materials; water sports equipment; packaging & shipping materials, foamed plastic; plastic film, coated or laminated for packaging; unsupported plastics film & sheet

(G-5839)
POLYSYSTEMS INC (PA)
225 W Washington St # 2300 (60606-3560)
PHONE..................................312 332-2114
Roger W Smith, *President*
Robert Arendt, *COO*
R Thomas Herget, *Exec VP*
John Adduci, *Vice Pres*
Matt Covalle, *Vice Pres*
EMP: 80
SALES (est): 8.3MM **Privately Held**
SIC: 7374 7372 7373 Computer time-sharing; application computer software; computer systems analysis & design

(G-5840)
POLYTECH INC (PA)
315 W 23rd St (60616-1905)
PHONE..................................806 338-2008
Chan Dan Trinh, *Principal*
EMP: 5
SALES (est): 401.6K **Privately Held**
SIC: 2673 Plastic bags: made from purchased materials

(G-5841)
POP BOX LLC
1700 W Irving Park Rd # 302 (60613-2559)
PHONE..................................630 509-2281
Joy Kitt, *Mng Member*
Catherine Berthault,
Francois Berthault,
EMP: 10
SQ FT: 7,000
SALES (est): 530.4K **Privately Held**
SIC: 2099 Food preparations

(G-5842)
POP BRANDS LLC
635 N Dearborn St Apt 906 (60654-6742)
PHONE..................................630 205-7146
Foram Soni Sheth, *Principal*
EMP: 3
SALES (est): 119.2K **Privately Held**
SIC: 2099 Food preparations

(G-5843)
POPSUGAR INC
1 E Wacker Dr Ste 225 (60601-2010)
PHONE..................................312 595-0533
Michelle Blam, *Project Mgr*
Brian Sugar, *Branch Mgr*
EMP: 4 **Privately Held**
SIC: 2741 Miscellaneous publishing
PA: Popsugar Inc.
111 Sutter St Fl 16
San Francisco CA 94104

(G-5844)
POPULAR PAYS INC
130 S Jefferson St # 400 (60661-5763)
PHONE..................................435 767-7297
Corbett Drummey, *CEO*
EMP: 3
SALES (est): 179.3K **Privately Held**
SIC: 7311 7372 Advertising agencies; business oriented computer software

(G-5845)
PORCELAIN ENAMEL FINISHERS
1530 S State St Apt 1018 (60605-2987)
PHONE..................................312 808-1560
EMP: 6 **EST:** 1945
SQ FT: 3,600
SALES: 300K **Privately Held**
SIC: 3469 3479 3545 3264 Mfg Metal Stampings Coating/Engraving Svcs Mfg Machine Tool Access Mfg Porcelain Elc Supply Mfg Adhesives/Sealants

(G-5846)
POSH LASH INC
1652 E 53rd St (60615-4210)
PHONE..................................630 388-6828
Ingrid Cheatham, *CEO*
EMP: 4
SALES (est): 31.6K **Privately Held**
SIC: 7231 3999 Beauty shops; eyelashes, artificial

(G-5847)
POWER PARTNERS LLC
Also Called: Devon Discount Pharmacy
1542 W Devon Ave (60660-1344)
PHONE..................................773 465-8688
Karen Wheet, *Regl Sales Mgr*
Andreas Iskos, *Mng Member*
Jiten Patel,
Andy Politis,
EMP: 6
SQ FT: 400
SALES (est): 1.4MM **Privately Held**
SIC: 2834 Pharmaceutical preparations

(G-5848)
POWERCOCO LLC
1658 N Milwaukee Ave # 546 (60647-6905)
PHONE..................................614 323-5890
Christopher Henneforth,
Tyler Beuerlein,
Jaisen Freeman,
Christopher Hunter,
Steve Vasquez,
EMP: 6
SALES (est): 627.5K **Privately Held**
SIC: 2086 7389 Bottled & canned soft drinks;

(G-5849)
POWERHOUSE ENT INC
2218 W Granville Ave (60659-2191)
PHONE..................................312 877-4303
Julia L Gham, *President*
EMP: 3
SALES: 450K **Privately Held**
WEB: www.juliagham360.net
SIC: 7929 7313 2599 Entertainment service; radio, television, publisher representatives; food wagons, restaurant

(G-5850)
POWERSCHOOL GROUP LLC
Also Called: Sungard
2290 Collection Center Dr (60693-0022)
PHONE..................................610 867-9200
EMP: 17
SALES (corp-wide): 5.6B **Privately Held**
SIC: 7372 Prepackaged software
HQ: Powerschool Group Llc
150 Parkshore Dr
Folsom CA 95630
916 288-1636

(G-5851)
PPG INDUSTRIES INC
Also Called: PPG 5527
345 N Morgan St (60607-1322)
PHONE..................................312 666-2277
Dave Bartozi, *Manager*
EMP: 24
SALES (corp-wide): 15.1B **Publicly Held**
SIC: 2851 Paints & allied products
PA: Ppg Industries, Inc.
1 Ppg Pl
Pittsburgh PA 15272
412 434-3131

(G-5852)
PRAIRIE WI-FI SYSTEMS
935 W Chestnut St Ste 530 (60642-5491)
P.O. Box 12994 (60612-5076)
PHONE..................................515 988-3260
Andrew Tomka, *Principal*
EMP: 3

SALES (est): 137.9K **Privately Held**
SIC: 8748 7372 7371 7359 Systems engineering consultant, ex. computer or professional; educational computer software; business oriented computer software; computer software development; electronic equipment rental, except computers

(G-5853)
PRAXAIR INC
Also Called: Unknown
7400 S Central Ave (60638-6516)
PHONE..................................708 728-9353
EMP: 3 **Privately Held**
SIC: 2813 Industrial gases
HQ: Praxair, Inc.
10 Riverview Dr
Danbury CT 06810
203 837-2000

(G-5854)
PRECISION DIALOGUE INC
5501 W Grand Ave (60639-2909)
PHONE..................................773 237-2264
Tim Thies, *Business Mgr*
Greg Rentsch, *Vice Pres*
Tom Orgler, *VP Opers*
Suzanne Maicke, *Mktg Dir*
Virginia Emmerich, *Program Mgr*
EMP: 225
SALES (est): 88.5K
SALES (corp-wide): 6.2B **Publicly Held**
SIC: 2754 Catalogs: gravure printing, not published on site
PA: R. R. Donnelley & Sons Company
35 W Wacker Dr
Chicago IL 60601
312 326-8000

(G-5855)
PRECISION DIALOGUE DIRECT INC (HQ)
5501 W Grand Ave (60639-2909)
PHONE..................................773 237-2264
Thomas Rogers, *President*
David Joss, *President*
Ross Priester, *Business Mgr*
Michael Joss, *Vice Pres*
Jill Friedman, *Controller*
EMP: 100 **EST:** 1953
SQ FT: 86,000
SALES (est): 29.2MM
SALES (corp-wide): 6.2B **Publicly Held**
WEB: www.nwmail.com
SIC: 7331 2752 Mailing service; commercial printing, offset
PA: R. R. Donnelley & Sons Company
35 W Wacker Dr
Chicago IL 60601
312 326-8000

(G-5856)
PRECISION DIE CUTTING & FINISH
4027 W Le Moyne St (60651-1930)
P.O. Box 51574 (60651-0574)
PHONE..................................773 252-5625
William Bardeleben, *President*
EMP: 8 **EST:** 1974
SQ FT: 7,000
SALES (est): 1.5MM **Privately Held**
SIC: 2653 2796 2789 2675 Display items, corrugated: made from purchased materials; display items, solid fiber: made from purchased materials; platemaking services; bookbinding & related work; die-cut paper & board

(G-5857)
PRECISION FORMING STAMPING CO
2419 W George St (60618-7930)
PHONE..................................773 489-6868
Kathy Hill, *President*
EMP: 30
SQ FT: 16,000
SALES (est): 3.7MM **Privately Held**
SIC: 3469 3496 Stamping metal for the trade; miscellaneous fabricated wire products

(G-5858)
PRECISION REMANUFACTURING INC
4520 W Fullerton Ave (60639-1934)
PHONE..................................773 489-7225
John Kaufman Beidler Jr, *President*
Jerald Joseph Mudryj, *Admin Sec*
EMP: 12
SQ FT: 10,000
SALES (est): 1.9MM **Privately Held**
SIC: 3714 Steering mechanisms, motor vehicle

(G-5859)
PRECISION SCREW MACHINING CO
3511 N Kenton Ave (60641-3819)
PHONE..................................773 205-4280
Sandra Greene, *President*
Hilliard Franklin Greene, *President*
Hilliard Greene, *Vice Pres*
EMP: 10 **EST:** 1946
SALES (est): 975.2K **Privately Held**
SIC: 3743 3451 Railroad locomotives & parts, electric or nonelectric; screw machine products

(G-5860)
PREFERRED FREEZER SERVICES OF
4500 W 42nd Pl (60632-0001)
PHONE..................................773 254-9500
Kosta Aneziris, *Sales Mgr*
▲ **EMP:** 10 **EST:** 2012
SALES (est): 1.3MM **Privately Held**
SIC: 3821 Freezers, laboratory

(G-5861)
PREFERRED PRINTING SERVICE
2343 W Roosevelt Rd (60608-1193)
PHONE..................................312 421-2343
EMP: 3
SALES: 100K **Privately Held**
SIC: 2759 2752 2791 2789 Commercial Printing Lithographic Coml Print Typesetting Services Bookbinding/Related Work Mfg Coat/Laminated Paper

(G-5862)
PREMIER INTL ENTPS INC
221 N La Salle St Ste 900 (60601-1300)
PHONE..................................312 857-2200
Craig M Wood, *CEO*
Mikel L Naples, *President*
Jim Hempleman, *Software Engr*
EMP: 20
SALES: 50.5K **Privately Held**
SIC: 7371 7379 7372 Computer software development; computer related consulting services; prepackaged software

(G-5863)
PREMIER METAL WORKS INC
1616 S Clinton St (60616-1110)
PHONE..................................312 226-7414
Andrew Michyeta III, *President*
Michyet IV Andrew, *Vice Pres*
Andrew Michyeta IV, *Vice Pres*
EMP: 8 **EST:** 1928
SQ FT: 18,000
SALES (est): 690K **Privately Held**
WEB: www.premiermetalworks.com
SIC: 3469 Stamping metal for the trade

(G-5864)
PREMIUM CONVERTING LLC
2743 W 36th Pl Unit C (60632-1687)
PHONE..................................708 510-1842
Echevarria Frank,
EMP: 2
SALES (est): 238K **Privately Held**
WEB: www.premiumconverting.com
SIC: 3555 Printing plates

(G-5865)
PRENOSIS INC
3440 S Dearborn St (60616-5074)
PHONE..................................949 246-3113
Bobby Reddy Jr, *CEO*
EMP: 9
SALES (est): 623.4K **Privately Held**
SIC: 2835 In vitro diagnostics

Chicago - Cook County (G-5866)

(G-5866)
PREREO LLC
819 S Wabash Ave Ste 606 (60605-2153)
PHONE..................................800 555-1055
Jorge Newbery,
EMP: 3
SALES (est): 86.5K Privately Held
SIC: 2741

(G-5867)
PRESS SYNDICATION GROUP LLC
4141 N Sacramento Ave (60618-2619)
PHONE..................................646 325-3221
Niels Warren Winter, *Mng Member*
EMP: 5
SALES (est): 290.4K Privately Held
SIC: 2731 Book publishing

(G-5868)
PRESSD APPAREL LLC
1200 W 35th St 192 (60609-1305)
PHONE..................................312 767-1877
Bryan Neubauer, *Mng Member*
EMP: 4
SQ FT: 1,200
SALES: 90K Privately Held
SIC: 2396 Fabric printing & stamping

(G-5869)
PRESSPAGE INC
350 N Orleans St (60654-1975)
PHONE..................................312 256-9985
Lambertus Verhulst, *President*
Tom Gubbins, *Sales Staff*
Michael Patrick King, *Director*
Mike King, *Director*
EMP: 6
SQ FT: 500
SALES: 1MM
SALES (corp-wide): 1.1MM Privately Held
SIC: 7372 Application computer software; business oriented computer software
PA: Presspage B.V.
    Hoogoorddreef 54 D
    Amsterdam 1101
    202 610-056

(G-5870)
PREVUE PET PRODUCTS INC (PA)
Also Called: Prevue Hendyrx
224 N Maplewood Ave (60612-2110)
PHONE..................................773 722-1052
Richard C Savitt, *CEO*
Jason Savitt, *President*
Mike Fradimiko, *Vice Pres*
Paul Tang, *Vice Pres*
Felipe Mendoza, *Warehouse Mgr*
▲ EMP: 40
SQ FT: 50,000
SALES (est): 6.2MM Privately Held
WEB: www.prevuepet.com
SIC: 3999 5199 Pet supplies; pet supplies

(G-5871)
PRICE FX INC
150 S Riverside Plz # 422 (60606)
PHONE..................................312 763-3121
Aaron D Werner, *CEO*
EMP: 6
SALES (est): 624.5K
SALES (corp-wide): 3.7MM Privately Held
SIC: 7372 Prepackaged software
PA: Price F(X) Ag
    Lautenring 16
    Pfaffenhofen A.D.Glonn 85235
    613 169-3495

(G-5872)
PRIDE IN GRAPHICS INC (PA)
739 S Clark St Fl 2 (60605-1760)
PHONE..................................312 427-2000
John Ekizian, *Ch of Bd*
Mike Ekizian, *President*
EMP: 11 EST: 1953
SQ FT: 10,000
SALES (est): 782.3K Privately Held
WEB: www.prideingraphics.com
SIC: 2752 Commercial printing, offset; lithographing on metal

(G-5873)
PRIME DENTAL MANUFACTURING
4555 W Addison St (60641-3816)
PHONE..................................773 283-2914
Pedro Segura, *President*
Adres Segura, *Chairman*
▲ EMP: 30
SQ FT: 16,000
SALES (est): 5.3MM Privately Held
SIC: 3843 Denture materials

(G-5874)
PRIME GROUP INC
Also Called: Prime Group Realty Trust
122 S Michigan Ave # 2040 (60603-6191)
PHONE..................................312 922-3883
Valerie Chavez, *Manager*
EMP: 7
SALES (corp-wide): 23.1MM Privately Held
WEB: www.primegroupinc.com
SIC: 3531 Marine related equipment
PA: The Prime Group Inc
    120 N Lasalle St Fl 32 Flr 32
    Chicago IL 60602
    312 917-1500

(G-5875)
PRIMROSE CANDY CO
4111 W Parker Ave (60639-2176)
PHONE..................................800 268-9522
Mark Puch, *President*
Carrie Lin, *General Mgr*
Jeffrey Puch, *Vice Pres*
David Zimmermann, *Warehouse Mgr*
Jackie Gredell, *Production*
▲ EMP: 103 EST: 1928
SQ FT: 130,000
SALES (est): 46.7MM Privately Held
WEB: www.primrosecandy.com
SIC: 2064 Lollipops & other hard candy

(G-5876)
PRINT AND MKTG SOLUTIONS GROUP
180 N Stetson Ave # 3500 (60601-6769)
PHONE..................................847 498-9640
Mark Sterne, *President*
EMP: 50
SALES (est): 243.2K Privately Held
WEB: www.printmsg.com
SIC: 8742 2752 Marketing consulting services; commercial printing, lithographic

(G-5877)
PRINT SERVICE & DIST ASSN PSDA
401 N Michigan Ave (60611-4255)
PHONE..................................312 321-5120
Tressa McLaughlin, *President*
Emily Marxer, *Sales Staff*
Alexa Schlosser, *Department Mgr*
Anita O Boyle, *Director*
EMP: 3
SALES (est): 211.4K Privately Held
SIC: 2752 Commercial printing, lithographic

(G-5878)
PRINTERS ROW LOFT
732 S Fincl Pl Ste Mgmt (60605)
PHONE..................................312 431-1019
EMP: 2 EST: 2010
SALES (est): 213.8K Privately Held
SIC: 2752 Commercial printing, offset

(G-5879)
PRINTERS ROW PRESS INC
739 S Clark St Fl 1 (60605-1760)
PHONE..................................312 427-7150
Ciro A Rossini, *Ch of Bd*
Edmund Rossini, *President*
Douglas Doolittle, *Sales Mgr*
John Burke, *Manager*
EMP: 38 EST: 1935
SQ FT: 15,000
SALES: 8MM Privately Held
WEB: www.palmer-printing.com
SIC: 2752 2732 Commercial printing, offset; book printing

(G-5880)
PRINTERS SQUARE CONDO ASSN
680 S Federal St (60605-1844)
PHONE..................................312 765-8794
Michael Pfammatter, *Principal*
EMP: 2 EST: 2012
SALES (est): 244.4K Privately Held
SIC: 2752 Commercial printing, lithographic

(G-5881)
PRINTING INC (DH)
Also Called: P I X
35 W Wacker Dr Ste 3600 (60601-1839)
PHONE..................................316 265-1201
Brad Haralson, *President*
Mark Mosher, *Foreman/Supr*
Stephanie Brown, *Sales Staff*
EMP: 60 EST: 1958
SALES (est): 15.1MM
SALES (corp-wide): 6.2B Publicly Held
WEB: www.printinginc.com
SIC: 2796 2791 2752 2789 Lithographic plates, positives or negatives; typesetting; commercial printing, lithographic; bookbinding & related work
HQ: Consolidated Graphics, Inc.
    5858 Westheimer Rd # 200
    Houston TX 77057
    713 787-0977

(G-5882)
PRINTING GALLERY INC
201 W Lake St (60606-0239)
PHONE..................................773 525-7102
Mark E Hicks, *Manager*
EMP: 4 Privately Held
SIC: 2759 Commercial printing
PA: The Printing Gallery Inc
    1255 Eastland Dr
    Lexington KY 40505

(G-5883)
PRINTING ON ASHLAND INC
8227 S Ashland Ave Ste 1 (60620-4682)
PHONE..................................773 488-4707
Onesa Aton, *President*
Rodney Payton, *Vice Pres*
EMP: 4
SQ FT: 1,750
SALES (est): 455.3K Privately Held
SIC: 2752 Commercial printing, offset

(G-5884)
PRIORITY PRINTING
6942 W Diversey Ave (60707-1725)
PHONE..................................773 889-6021
Fred Edwards, *Owner*
EMP: 4
SQ FT: 5,000
SALES (est): 333.5K Privately Held
SIC: 2752 2796 Commercial printing, offset; platemaking services

(G-5885)
PRISM COMMERCIAL PRINTING CTRS
6130 S Pulaski Rd (60629-4628)
PHONE..................................773 735-5400
Frank Lazarz, *Branch Mgr*
EMP: 5
SALES (corp-wide): 2.3MM Privately Held
SIC: 2752 Commercial printing, offset
PA: Prism Corp Commercial Printing Centers
    6957 W Archer Ave
    Chicago IL

(G-5886)
PRIVACY ONE LLC
70 W Burton Pl Apt 1205 (60610-1467)
PHONE..................................312 872-3757
Alexander Cato, *CEO*
EMP: 6
SALES (est): 437.5K Privately Held
SIC: 7372 Application computer software

(G-5887)
PRO ENERGY TRADE INC
3180 N Lake Shore Dr # 16 (60657-4831)
PHONE..................................312 961-6404
Obi Nwora, *Director*
EMP: 49
SALES (est): 2MM Privately Held
SIC: 3533 Oil field machinery & equipment

(G-5888)
PRO TEC METAL FINISHING CORP
1428 N Kilpatrick Ave (60651-1624)
PHONE..................................773 384-7853
Dale Weincouff, *President*
EMP: 8
SQ FT: 10,000
SALES: 750K Privately Held
SIC: 2899 3471 Chemical preparations; plating & polishing

(G-5889)
PRO-PARTS
4727 S Ingleside Ave # 1 (60615-1851)
PHONE..................................773 595-5966
Anthony Henderson, *Manager*
EMP: 3
SALES (est): 121.3K Privately Held
SIC: 3571 Electronic computers

(G-5890)
PROCESS SUPPLY COMPANY INC (DH)
Also Called: Nar-Dar/Kc St Louis
1087 N North Branch St (60642-4234)
PHONE..................................312 943-8338
J Jeffery Thrall, *Ch of Bd*
Michael P Fox, *President*
James F Walsh, *Exec VP*
Stanley D Christianson, *Vice Pres*
Robin Killion, *Supervisor*
▲ EMP: 3
SQ FT: 50,000
SALES (est): 6.7MM
SALES (corp-wide): 200.3MM Privately Held
SIC: 2893 Printing ink
HQ: Nazdar Company
    8501 Hedge Lane Ter
    Shawnee KS 66227
    913 422-1888

(G-5891)
PROCON GENERAL SERVICES INC
1035 N Damen Ave (60622-7454)
PHONE..................................773 227-8258
Christine Siutryk, *President*
Derrick Siutryk, *Vice Pres*
▲ EMP: 2
SQ FT: 800
SALES (est): 260K Privately Held
SIC: 3993 Signs, not made in custom sign painting shops

(G-5892)
PROCTER & GAMBLE COMPANY
10275 W Higgins Rd (60605)
PHONE..................................847 375-5400
Jim Busch, *Technology*
EMP: 6
SALES (corp-wide): 67.6B Publicly Held
SIC: 2844 2676 3421 2842 Deodorants, personal; towels, napkins & tissue paper products; razor blades & razors; specialty cleaning preparations; soap: granulated, liquid, cake, flaked or chip
PA: The Procter & Gamble Company
    1 Procter And Gamble Plz
    Cincinnati OH 45202
    513 983-1100

(G-5893)
PRODUCTIGEAR INC
1900 W 34th St (60608-6894)
PHONE..................................773 847-4505
Richard Wieker, *President*
Dorothy Stevens, *Vice Pres*
EMP: 35 EST: 1946
SQ FT: 9,000
SALES (est): 8.5MM Privately Held
WEB: www.productigear.com
SIC: 3566 3568 3462 Speed changers (power transmission equipment), except auto; power transmission equipment; iron & steel forgings

GEOGRAPHIC SECTION
Chicago - Cook County (G-5921)

(G-5894)
PRODUCTION TOOL CORPORATION (PA)
1229 E 74th St (60619-2098)
PHONE.................................773 288-4400
Joe Dangelo, *Vice Pres*
▲ **EMP:** 45
SQ FT: 125,000
SALES (est): 7.5MM **Privately Held**
SIC: 3599 Machine shop, jobbing & repair

(G-5895)
PRODUCTIVE EDGE LLC (PA)
Also Called: Open Point Solutions
11 E Illinois St Ste 200 (60611-5654)
PHONE.................................312 561-9000
Max Artyukhov, *Regional Mgr*
David Pellissier, *Exec VP*
Bill McCall, *Senior VP*
Dave Pellissier, *Vice Pres*
Dustin Kennedy, *Engineer*
EMP: 100
SQ FT: 500
SALES (est): 11.2MM **Privately Held**
WEB: www.productiveedge.com
SIC: 7371 7372 Computer software development; prepackaged software

(G-5896)
PROFESSIONAL FREEZING SVCS LLC
7035 W 65th St (60638-4603)
PHONE.................................773 847-7500
Karen Grzywacz, *CEO*
Edward Grzywacz, *President*
EMP: 6
SALES (est): 1.6MM **Privately Held**
WEB: www.professionalfreezing.com
SIC: 5064 5421 3822 Refrigerators & freezers; freezer provisioners, meat; temperature controls, automatic

(G-5897)
PROFESSIONAL GEM SCIENCES INC
5 S Wabash Ave Ste 315 (60603-3517)
PHONE.................................312 920-1541
Myriam Tashtey, *President*
EMP: 7
SALES (est): 663.2K **Privately Held**
SIC: 1499 8734 Gem stones (natural) mining; testing laboratories

(G-5898)
PROGRESS PRINTING CORPORATION
3324 S Halsted St Ste 1 (60608-6969)
PHONE.................................773 927-0123
Martin Gapshis, *President*
Marilyn Gapshis, *Treasurer*
EMP: 23
SQ FT: 20,000
SALES (est): 3.2MM **Privately Held**
WEB: www.progressprintcorp.com
SIC: 2759 2752 2791 2789 Letterpress printing; commercial printing, offset; typesetting; bookbinding & related work

(G-5899)
PROGRESSIVE BRONZE WORKS INC
3550 N Spaulding Ave (60618-5523)
PHONE.................................773 463-5500
Joseph E Rossi, *President*
Bobbi Rossi, *Admin Sec*
EMP: 25
SQ FT: 33,000
SALES (est): 3.1MM **Privately Held**
WEB: www.pbronze.com
SIC: 3499 Novelties & specialties, metal

(G-5900)
PROGRESSIVE COATING CORP
900 S Cicero Ave (60644-5213)
PHONE.................................773 261-8900
Joseph Tompa, *President*
Diana Tompa, *Treasurer*
Edgar Rosales, *Manager*
EMP: 15
SQ FT: 30,000
SALES (est): 1.1MM **Privately Held**
SIC: 3479 Coating of metals & formed products

(G-5901)
PROGRESSIVE SHEET METAL INC
2850 S Tripp Ave (60623-4336)
PHONE.................................773 376-1155
Juan Gallegos, *President*
Julio Gallegos, *Vice Pres*
EMP: 9 **EST:** 1960
SQ FT: 2,200
SALES (est): 1.1MM **Privately Held**
SIC: 3444 Sheet metalwork

(G-5902)
PROGRESSIVE SYSTEMS NETWRK INC
1500 S Western Ave Ste 19 (60608-1828)
PHONE.................................312 382-8383
Jeff Stangel, *President*
Jerry Piaskowy, *Vice Pres*
EMP: 4
SQ FT: 5,000
SALES (est): 1MM **Privately Held**
SIC: 5111 2752 7373 8743 Printing & writing paper; commercial printing, offset; office computer automation systems integration; promotion service

(G-5903)
PROMUS EQUITY PARTNERS LLC (PA)
156 N Jefferson St # 300 (60661-1436)
PHONE.................................312 784-3990
Julian Cheng, *Vice Pres*
Zach Musso, *Mng Member*
Steven Brown, *Mng Member*
EMP: 11
SALES (est): 30.4MM
SALES (corp-wide): 30.7MM **Privately Held**
WEB: www.promusequity.com
SIC: 3499 5999 Doors, safe & vault: metal; vaults & safes

(G-5904)
PROSHIP INC
29 N Wacker Dr Ste 700 (60606-3228)
PHONE.................................312 332-7447
EMP: 3
SALES (corp-wide): 23.6MM **Privately Held**
SIC: 7371 7372 5734 Custom Computer Programing Prepackaged Software Services
HQ: Proship, Inc.
400 N Executive Dr # 210
Brookfield WI 53005
414 302-2929

(G-5905)
PROTE USA LLC
7145 N Ionia Ave (60646-1231)
PHONE.................................773 576-9079
Roberto Maso,
EMP: 3
SALES (est): 83.9K **Privately Held**
SIC: 3999 Manufacturing industries

(G-5906)
PROTEX PRODUCTS LLC
3104 W Touhy Ave (60645-2956)
PHONE.................................312 292-1310
Brad Wells, *Opers Staff*
Ben Brener,
Trent Dehel,
EMP: 5
SALES (est): 112.6K **Privately Held**
SIC: 2672 2679 Coated & laminated paper; pressed fiber & molded pulp products except food products

(G-5907)
PROTUS CONSTRUCTION
1429 N Oakley Blvd (60622-1848)
PHONE.................................773 405-9999
Stanislaw Swierczyk, *Owner*
EMP: 5
SALES (est): 303.4K **Privately Held**
SIC: 1389 Construction, repair & dismantling services

(G-5908)
PROVISUR TECHNOLOGIES
222 N La Salle St (60601-1003)
PHONE.................................312 284-4698
Brian Perkins, *Exec VP*
Brian Ernat, *Opers Staff*
Jennifer Ash, *Senior Buyer*
Brad Deblecourt, *Engineer*
John Chonarzewski, *Electrical Engi*
EMP: 3
SALES (est): 472.1K **Privately Held**
SIC: 8731 3621 Commercial physical research; motors & generators

(G-5909)
PROXIMITY CAPITAL PARTNERS LLC
Also Called: Asutra
4159 W Montrose Ave (60641-2160)
PHONE.................................773 628-7751
Stephanie Morimoto, *President*
Matthew King,
EMP: 16
SQ FT: 7,500
SALES (est): 5.5MM **Privately Held**
SIC: 2844 5999 Toilet preparations; toiletries, cosmetics & perfumes

(G-5910)
PTC/USER INC
330 N Wabash Ave Ste 2000 (60611-7621)
PHONE.................................619 417-2050
Chris Moretti, *Treasurer*
Daniel Glenn, *Director*
EMP: 6
SALES (est): 150K **Privately Held**
SIC: 7372 Application computer software

(G-5911)
PTM BIOLABS INC
2201 W Campbell Park Dr (60612-4092)
PHONE.................................312 802-6843
Zhongyi Cheng, *President*
Ying Ming Zhao, *Treasurer*
Peter Lee, *Accounts Mgr*
Hsiao Lai, *Associate*
Hsiao-Lei Lai, *Associate*
EMP: 4
SALES: 300K **Privately Held**
SIC: 2836 Biological products, except diagnostic

(G-5912)
PUBLISHING PROPERTIES LLC (DH)
350 N Orleans St Fl 10 (60654-1975)
PHONE.................................312 321-2299
Michael Mackey, *Principal*
EMP: 3
SALES (est): 579K
SALES (corp-wide): 4.3MM **Privately Held**
SIC: 2711 7313 Newspapers; electronic media advertising representatives; printed media advertising representatives

(G-5913)
PULLMAN SUGAR LLC
Also Called: Pullman Logistics
700 E 107th St (60628-3806)
PHONE.................................773 260-9180
Brian Boomsma, *President*
Matt Dyer, *COO*
Brandon Boomsma, *Vice Pres*
▲ **EMP:** 42
SQ FT: 100,000
SALES (est): 51.5MM
SALES (corp-wide): 348.5MM **Privately Held**
SIC: 2062 Cane sugar refining
PA: Dutch Farms, Inc.
700 E 107th St
Chicago IL 60628
773 660-0900

(G-5914)
PUMPKIN PATCH VENTURES INC
1343 W Grace St Apt 2 (60613-2859)
PHONE.................................708 699-4396
Anthony Chuinard, *CEO*
Troy Chuinard, *CFO*
EMP: 3
SALES: 10K **Privately Held**
SIC: 7372 7389 Application computer software;

(G-5915)
PUNCH PRODUCTS MANUFACTURING
Also Called: A-Punch Products Mfg Co
500 S Kolmar Ave (60624-3095)
PHONE.................................773 533-2800
Moin Shaikh, *President*
Shaukat Kazi, *Admin Sec*
EMP: 35
SQ FT: 24,000
SALES (est): 2MM **Privately Held**
SIC: 3053 3086 2672 3842 Gaskets & sealing devices; insulation or cushioning material, foamed plastic; adhesive papers, labels or tapes: from purchased material; surgical appliances & supplies; machine tools, metal forming type; pressed & blown glass

(G-5916)
PURE ASPHALT COMPANY
Also Called: Pure Alphalt
3455 W 31st Pl (60623-5082)
PHONE.................................773 247-7030
Alan Brooker, *Info Tech Mgr*
Michael K Francis, *Admin Sec*
EMP: 15
SALES (est): 4.8MM **Privately Held**
SIC: 2952 Asphalt felts & coatings

(G-5917)
PURE LIGHTING LLC
1718 W Fullerton Ave (60614-1922)
PHONE.................................773 770-1130
Gregory L Kay,
Mike Donovan,
▲ **EMP:** 13
SALES (est): 1.5MM **Privately Held**
SIC: 3646 Commercial indusl & institutional electric lighting fixtures

(G-5918)
PUZZLES BUS OFF SOLUTIONS INC
47 W Polk St (60605-2000)
PHONE.................................773 891-7688
John Sullen, *President*
Michele Sullen, *Admin Sec*
EMP: 2 **EST:** 2012
SALES (est): 235.7K **Privately Held**
WEB: www.puzzlesbusinesslogos.com
SIC: 3944 Puzzles

(G-5919)
PVS CHEMICAL SOLUTIONS INC
12260 S Carondolet Ave (60633-1197)
PHONE.................................773 933-8800
Scott Ribo, *Manager*
EMP: 36
SALES (corp-wide): 649.9MM **Privately Held**
WEB: www.pvschemicals.com
SIC: 2819 2899 2869 Sulfur chloride; chemical preparations; industrial organic chemicals
HQ: Pvs Chemical Solutions, Inc.
10900 Harper Ave
Detroit MI 48213

(G-5920)
PYAR & CO LLC
807 W Dickens Ave (60614-4303)
P.O. Box 14814 (60614-8532)
PHONE.................................312 451-5073
Paula Queen, *Mng Member*
Shalini Gupta, *Mng Member*
EMP: 5
SALES: 300K **Privately Held**
WEB: www.pyarandco.com
SIC: 2392 3651 5023 Cushions & pillows; blanket bags, plastic: made from purchased materials; blankets, comforters & beddings; pillows, stereo; linens, table

(G-5921)
Q LOTUS HOLDINGS INC
520 N Kingsbury St # 1810 (60654-8772)
PHONE.................................312 379-1800
Gary A Rosenberg, *Ch of Bd*
Jorge Gonzalez, *CFO*
Ingrid Diaz, *Admin Sec*
EMP: 3

Chicago - Cook County (G-5922)

SALES (est): 326.6K **Privately Held**
SIC: **1011** 7389 Iron ores; financial services

(G-5922)
QABOSS PARTNERS
27 N Wacker Dr Ste 155 (60606-2800)
PHONE.................................312 203-4290
Kvi El, *Partner*
EMP: 300
SALES (est): 12.3MM **Privately Held**
WEB: www.qabosspartners.net
SIC: **3663** Mobile communication equipment

(G-5923)
QST INDUSTRIES INC (PA)
Also Called: Q S T
550 W Adams St Ste 200 (60661-3665)
PHONE.................................312 930-9400
Lacramioara Curcan, *General Mgr*
John Schellenbach, *General Mgr*
Paul N Wilson, *Counsel*
Alex Danch, *Vice Pres*
Michael Danch, *Vice Pres*
◆ EMP: 50
SQ FT: 20,000
SALES (est): 170.6MM **Privately Held**
WEB: www.qst.com
SIC: **2396** 2392 2752 Automotive & apparel trimmings; household furnishings; commercial printing, lithographic

(G-5924)
QST INDUSTRIES INC
Samuel Haber Son Division
550 W Adams St Ste 200 (60661-3665)
PHONE.................................312 930-9400
Jeff Carlevato, *Manager*
EMP: 55
SALES (corp-wide): 170.6MM **Privately Held**
SIC: **2396** Automotive & apparel trimmings
PA: Qst Industries, Inc.
    550 W Adams St Ste 200
    Chicago IL 60661
    312 930-9400

(G-5925)
QT INFO SYSTEMS INC
141 W Jackson Blvd # 125 (60604-2992)
PHONE.................................800 240-8761
Terrence Linn, *Principal*
Terry Linn, *Vice Pres*
EMP: 15
SQ FT: 500
SALES (est): 1.2MM **Privately Held**
SIC: **2741** 7371 ; software programming applications

(G-5926)
QUADRAMED CORPORATION
440 N Wells St Ste 505 (60654-4584)
PHONE.................................312 396-0700
Joanne August, *Branch Mgr*
EMP: 23
SALES (corp-wide): 3B **Privately Held**
SIC: **8742** 7322 7373 7372 Hospital & health services consultant; collection agency, except real estate; computer integrated systems design; prepackaged software; custom computer programming services
HQ: Quadramed Corporation
    2300 Corp Park Dr Ste 400
    Herndon VA 20171
    703 709-2300

(G-5927)
QUAKER OATS COMPANY (HQ)
555 W Monroe St Fl 1 (60661-3716)
PHONE.................................312 821-1000
Jose Luis Prado, *President*
Kim Cox, *Counsel*
Adriana Reyes-Villanuev, *Counsel*
Melissa Diaz, *Vice Pres*
Mary Dillon, *Vice Pres*
◆ EMP: 1000 EST: 1901
SQ FT: 300,000
SALES (est): 3.6B
SALES (corp-wide): 67.1B **Publicly Held**
WEB: www.quakeroats.com
SIC: **2086** 2043 2045 2052 Bottled & canned soft drinks; cereal breakfast foods; flours & flour mixes, from purchased flour; rice cakes; granola & muesli, bars & clusters; rice, uncooked: packaged with other ingredients; pasta, uncooked: packaged with other ingredients; maple syrup
PA: Pepsico, Inc.
    700 Anderson Hill Rd
    Purchase NY 10577
    914 253-2000

(G-5928)
QUAKER OATS EUROPE INC (HQ)
555 W Monroe St Fl 1 (60661-3716)
PHONE.................................312 821-1000
Gary Rodkin, *President*
EMP: 6
SALES (est): 723.2K
SALES (corp-wide): 67.1B **Publicly Held**
SIC: **2043** 2045 Cereal breakfast foods; flours & flour mixes, from purchased flour
PA: Pepsico, Inc.
    700 Anderson Hill Rd
    Purchase NY 10577
    914 253-2000

(G-5929)
QUALITY ARMATURE INC
5259 W Grand Ave (60639-3043)
PHONE.................................773 622-3951
Michele Rubino, *President*
Michele Filomeno, *President*
Filomena Rubino, *Corp Secy*
Rocco Rubino, *Manager*
EMP: 7 EST: 1973
SQ FT: 6,000
SALES (est): 1.3MM **Privately Held**
SIC: **7694** Electric motor repair

(G-5930)
QUALITY OPTICAL INC
4610 N Lincoln Ave (60625-2008)
PHONE.................................773 561-0870
Ted Carillo, *President*
EMP: 1
SQ FT: 3,200
SALES (est): 234.5K **Privately Held**
SIC: **5995** 3851 3827 Eyeglasses, prescription; ophthalmic goods; optical instruments & lenses

(G-5931)
QUALITY TOOL & MACHINE INC
8050 S Constance Ave (60617-1027)
PHONE.................................773 721-8655
Anthony Martincic Jr, *President*
Anton Martincic Jr, *President*
EMP: 6 EST: 1940
SQ FT: 7,000
SALES (est): 500K **Privately Held**
WEB: www.qualitytoolandmachine.com
SIC: **3544** 7692 Special dies & tools; welding repair

(G-5932)
QUAM-NICHOLS COMPANY
234 E Marquette Rd Ste 1 (60637-4090)
PHONE.................................773 488-5800
Randy Moore, *Principal*
Denise Toliver, *Purch Agent*
Bruce Arndt, *CFO*
Joda Boykin, *Sales Staff*
Jon Heuer, *Sales Staff*
▲ EMP: 108 EST: 1930
SQ FT: 120,000
SALES (est): 21.3MM **Privately Held**
WEB: www.quamspeakers.com
SIC: **3651** Loudspeakers, electrodynamic or magnetic

(G-5933)
QUANTUM CORPORATION
1 S Wacker Dr (60606-4614)
PHONE.................................312 372-2857
Kevin Marston, *Manager*
EMP: 90
SALES (corp-wide): 402.6MM **Publicly Held**
SIC: **3572** Computer storage devices

PA: Quantum Corporation
    224 Airport Pkwy Ste 550
    San Jose CA 95110
    408 944-4000

(G-5934)
QUARTIX INC
875 N Michigan Ave # 3100 (60611-1962)
PHONE.................................855 913-6663
Andrew Walters, *President*
Daniel Mendis, *CFO*
EMP: 14
SALES (est): 264.5K **Privately Held**
SIC: **3812** Navigational systems & instruments

(G-5935)
QUESTILY LLC (PA)
3619 N Claremont Ave (60618-4817)
PHONE.................................312 636-6657
John Miniati, *CEO*
EMP: 7
SALES (est): 15K **Privately Held**
SIC: **7372** 7389 Educational computer software;

(G-5936)
QUESTILY LLC
2 N La Salle St Fl 14 (60602-3702)
PHONE.................................312 636-6657
John Miniati, *CEO*
EMP: 4
SALES (est): 15K **Privately Held**
SIC: **7372** Educational computer software
PA: Questily Llc
    3619 N Claremont Ave
    Chicago IL 60618
    312 636-6657

(G-5937)
QUIDDITY SOLUTIONS LLC
6316 N Magnolia Ave (60660-1406)
PHONE.................................773 844-2058
Robert Gerovski, *Mng Member*
EMP: 3
SQ FT: 100
SALES (est): 74.7K **Privately Held**
SIC: **7372** Business oriented computer software

(G-5938)
QUINCY LAB INC
1928 N Leamington Ave (60639-4421)
PHONE.................................773 622-2428
Anthony Guanci Jr, *President*
Cheri McKown, *Principal*
EMP: 35
SQ FT: 38,000
SALES (est): 2MM **Privately Held**
SIC: **3821** 3842 3567 Ovens, laboratory; incubators, laboratory; surgical appliances & supplies; industrial furnaces & ovens

(G-5939)
QUIXOTE CORPORATION (HQ)
70 W Madison St Ste 2350 (60602-4295)
PHONE.................................312 705-8400
Bruce Reimer, *President*
Joan R Riley, *Vice Pres*
Daniel P Gorey, *CFO*
◆ EMP: 25
SQ FT: 21,000
SALES (est): 44MM
SALES (corp-wide): 3B **Publicly Held**
SIC: **3089** 4899 Plastic hardware & building products; communication signal enhancement network system; radar station operation
PA: Trinity Industries, Inc.
    2525 N Stemmons Fwy
    Dallas TX 75207
    214 631-4420

(G-5940)
QUIXOTE TRANSPORTATION SAFETY
70 W Madison St Ste 2350 (60602-4295)
PHONE.................................312 467-6750
Leslie Jezuit, *President*
Daniel Gorey, *CFO*
Joan Riley, *Admin Sec*
EMP: 90
SQ FT: 19,000

SALES (est): 8.1MM
SALES (corp-wide): 3B **Publicly Held**
SIC: **3499** 3089 Barricades, metal; injection molded finished plastic products
HQ: Quixote Corporation
    70 W Madison St Ste 2350
    Chicago IL 60602
    312 705-8400

(G-5941)
R & B POWDER COATINGS INC
4000 S Bell Ave (60609-2208)
PHONE.................................773 247-8300
Tony Cash, *President*
Lois Thompson, *Vice Pres*
EMP: 30
SQ FT: 40,000
SALES (est): 4.2MM **Privately Held**
SIC: **3479** Coating of metals & formed products

(G-5942)
R & E QUALITY MFG CO
7005 W School St (60634-3647)
PHONE.................................773 286-6846
Edward Gray, *Owner*
EMP: 3
SALES (est): 200K **Privately Held**
SIC: **3312** Tool & die steel

(G-5943)
R & J TRUCKING AND RECYCL INC
6650 S Oak Park Ave (60638-4812)
PHONE.................................708 563-2600
Balbina Alvear, *President*
Julian Catalan, *Warehouse Mgr*
EMP: 12
SALES: 3.4MM **Privately Held**
SIC: **2611** 4212 Pulp manufactured from waste or recycled paper; local trucking, without storage

(G-5944)
R C INDUSTRIES INC
1420 N Lamon Ave (60651-1512)
PHONE.................................773 378-1118
Robert A Calabrese, *President*
Mildred J Calabrese, *Corp Secy*
Stuart Schwartz, *Exec VP*
EMP: 12
SQ FT: 16,500
SALES (est): 1.1MM **Privately Held**
SIC: **3471** 2851 Finishing, metals or formed products; paints & allied products

(G-5945)
R E Z PACKAGING INC
3735 S Racine Ave (60609-2137)
PHONE.................................773 247-0800
Debra Zarazee, *President*
Richard Zarazee, *Treasurer*
EMP: 4
SQ FT: 20,000
SALES: 500K **Privately Held**
SIC: **2842** Cleaning or polishing preparations; deodorants, nonpersonal

(G-5946)
R L D COMMUNICATIONS INC (PA)
Also Called: Box Office Magazine
725 S Wells St Fl 4 (60607-4521)
PHONE.................................312 338-7007
EMP: 10
SALES (est): 661.5K **Privately Held**
SIC: **2721** Periodicals-Publishing/Printing

(G-5947)
R MADERITE INC
1616 N Washtenaw Ave (60647-5231)
PHONE.................................773 235-1515
Fax: 773 235-1527
EMP: 2 EST: 2006
SALES (est): 230K **Privately Held**
SIC: **5211** 2499 Ret Lumber/Building Materials Mfg Wood Products

(G-5948)
R P SOLUTIONS LLC
3920 W 68th St (60629-4106)
PHONE.................................773 971-1363
Rosa Rojas, *Principal*
Olga Rojas, *Manager*
EMP: 3

GEOGRAPHIC SECTION

Chicago - Cook County (G-5973)

SALES (est): 197.5K **Privately Held**
SIC: **3444** 5021 Guard rails, highway; sheet metal; racks

(G-5949)
R POPERNIK CO INC
2313 W 59th St (60636-1518)
PHONE...................................773 434-4300
Ronald J Popernik, *CEO*
Michelle Kibler, *Corp Secy*
EMP: 15
SQ FT: 22,800
SALES (est): 2.5MM **Privately Held**
SIC: **2759** 2673 Flexographic printing; food storage & frozen food bags, plastic

(G-5950)
R R DONNELLEY & SONS COMPANY (PA)
Also Called: RR Donnelley
35 W Wacker Dr (60601-1723)
PHONE...................................312 326-8000
John C Pope, *Ch of Bd*
Daniel L Knotts, *President*
John Pecaric, *President*
Lisa Pruett, *President*
Doug Ryan, *President*
EMP: 231 EST: 1864
SALES: 6.2B **Publicly Held**
WEB: www.rrdonnelley.com
SIC: **2759** 2752 2732 7331 Commercial printing; letterpress printing; commercial printing, offset; books: printing & binding; direct mail advertising services; graphic arts & related design; catalogs: gravure printing, not published on site

(G-5951)
R R STREET & CO INC
4600 S Tripp Ave (60632-4419)
PHONE...................................773 247-1190
L Ross Beard, *President*
EMP: 50
SQ FT: 19,500
SALES (corp-wide): 34MM **Privately Held**
WEB: www.4streets.com
SIC: **2842** Cleaning or polishing preparations
PA: R. R. Street & Co., Inc.
 184 Shuman Blvd Ste 150
 Naperville IL 60563
 630 416-4244

(G-5952)
R R STREET & CO INC
2353 S Blue Island Ave (60608-4227)
PHONE...................................773 254-1277
Clarence Overby, *Manager*
EMP: 13
SALES (corp-wide): 34MM **Privately Held**
SIC: **2842** Drycleaning preparations
PA: R. R. Street & Co., Inc.
 184 Shuman Blvd Ste 150
 Naperville IL 60563
 630 416-4244

(G-5953)
R S OWENS & CO INC
Also Called: Elegance In Awards & Gifts
5535 N Lynch Ave (60630-1417)
PHONE...................................773 282-6000
Scott Siegel, *President*
Shirlie L Siegel, *Corp Secy*
Mark Avenson, *Vice Pres*
Mark Psaros, *Vice Pres*
Jorge Marroquin, *Project Mgr*
▲ EMP: 251
SQ FT: 82,000
SALES (est): 47.6MM **Privately Held**
WEB: www.rsowens.com
SIC: **3499** 3999 3911 3961 Trophies, metal, except silver; plaques, picture, laminated; medals, precious or semi-precious metal; pins (jewelry), precious metal; pins (jewelry), except precious metal

(G-5954)
R T P INC
Also Called: Minuteman Press
1249 N Clybourn Ave (60610-6693)
PHONE...................................312 664-6150
Gary Allison, *President*
Sarah Allison, *Treasurer*

Joe Hernandez, *Marketing Staff*
EMP: 4
SALES (est): 702.4K **Privately Held**
SIC: **2752** Commercial printing, lithographic

(G-5955)
R-K PRESS BRAKE DIES INC
12512 S Springfield Ave (60803-1409)
PHONE...................................708 371-1756
Tom Bosinski, *President*
Dan Orseske, *Sales Staff*
EMP: 18
SQ FT: 20,000
SALES (est): 3.2MM **Privately Held**
SIC: **3542** 3544 Press brakes; special dies, tools, jigs & fixtures

(G-5956)
RA ENERGY DRINK INC
6816 S Paxton Ave (60649-1603)
PHONE...................................773 503-8574
Lisa Diggs, *President*
EMP: 4
SALES (est): 116.1K **Privately Held**
SIC: **2087** Concentrates, drink

(G-5957)
RACHEL SWITALL MAG GROUP NFP
1441b W Wrightwood Ave (60614-1121)
PHONE...................................773 344-7123
Rachel Switall, *CEO*
EMP: 4
SALES (est): 152.7K **Privately Held**
SIC: **2711** Newspapers: publishing only, not printed on site

(G-5958)
RACINE PAPER BOX MANUFACTURING
3522 W Potomac Ave (60651-2230)
PHONE...................................773 227-3900
Navnit Patel, *President*
Atul Patel, *Vice Pres*
Savita Patel, *Admin Sec*
EMP: 20
SQ FT: 29,000
SALES (est): 450K **Privately Held**
SIC: **2652** 3944 2675 2657 Setup paperboard boxes; games, toys & children's vehicles; die-cut paper & board; folding paperboard boxes

(G-5959)
RADIO FLYER INC
6515 W Grand Ave Ste 1 (60707-3436)
PHONE...................................773 637-7100
Robert Pasin, *President*
Alex Hiltgen, *Opers Staff*
Eric Selner, *Opers Staff*
Dan Greenberg, *Engineer*
Kelsey Knox, *Engineer*
◆ EMP: 50 EST: 1930
SALES (est): 16.9MM **Privately Held**
WEB: www.radioflyer.com
SIC: **3944** Wagons: coaster, express & play: children's

(G-5960)
RADIONIC HI-TECH INC
6625 W Diversey Ave (60707-2218)
PHONE...................................773 804-0100
Jeffrey Winton, *President*
EMP: 52
SQ FT: 85,000
SALES (est): 7MM **Privately Held**
SIC: **3629** 3641 3648 3643 Battery chargers, rectifying or nonrotating; lamps, incandescent filament, electric; lamps, fluorescent, electric; lighting equipment; starting switches, fluorescent

(G-5961)
RADIONIC INDUSTRIES INC
6625 W Diversey Ave (60707-2218)
PHONE...................................773 804-0100
Jeff Winton, *President*
Joseph Nowik, *Opers Staff*
Joyce Elliott, *Sales Staff*
Alan Scott, *Manager*
Jerry Vida, *Director*
▲ EMP: 110
SQ FT: 85,000

SALES (est): 19.8MM **Privately Held**
WEB: www.radionic.net
SIC: **3612** Fluorescent ballasts; lighting transformers, fluorescent

(G-5962)
RADIUS SOLUTIONS INCORPORATED
150 N Michigan Ave # 300 (60601-7553)
PHONE...................................312 648-0800
David Taylor, *President*
EMP: 11
SALES (est): 1MM **Privately Held**
WEB: www.radiussolutions.com
SIC: **7372** Business oriented computer software

(G-5963)
RAHMANIMS IMPORTS INC (PA)
Also Called: RI Diamonds
5 S Wabash Ave Ste 1211 (60603-3135)
PHONE...................................312 236-2200
Naser Rahmanim, *President*
Vahideh Rahmanim, *Vice Pres*
EMP: 8
SQ FT: 2,100
SALES (est): 656.9K **Privately Held**
SIC: **3911** 5094 Jewelry, precious metal; jewelry

(G-5964)
RAILWAY PROGRAM SERVICES INC
Also Called: Rpsi
6235 S Oak Park Ave (60638-4015)
PHONE...................................708 552-4000
Gregory R Winsor, *President*
EMP: 8 EST: 1993
SQ FT: 2,000
SALES (est): 879.6K
SALES (corp-wide): 14.2MM **Privately Held**
SIC: **3743** Railroad car rebuilding
PA: Steelhead Corporation
 6235 S Oak Park Ave
 Chicago IL 60638
 708 552-4000

(G-5965)
RAINBOW ART INC
2224 W Grand Ave (60612-1512)
PHONE...................................312 421-5600
Norman Korenthal, *President*
Jack Korenthal, *President*
Susan Korenthal, *Vice Pres*
EMP: 15 EST: 1941
SQ FT: 9,600
SALES (est): 1.8MM **Privately Held**
WEB: www.rainbowartinc.com
SIC: **3479** 2759 3471 2396 Coating of metals & formed products; imprinting; plating & polishing; automotive & apparel trimmings

(G-5966)
RAMPTECH INC ○
6235 S Oak Park Ave (60638-4015)
PHONE...................................303 936-3641
EMP: 4 EST: 2019
SALES (est): 251.1K **Privately Held**
SIC: **3743** Railroad equipment

(G-5967)
RAMPTECH INC
6900 S Central Ave (60638-6304)
PHONE...................................708 594-2179
Gregory R Winsor, *President*
James Schmidt, *Opers Dir*
▲ EMP: 22
SQ FT: 13,500
SALES (est): 3.1MM **Privately Held**
SIC: **3743** Railroad equipment

(G-5968)
RAND MCNALLY & COMPANY (HQ)
8770 W Bryn Mawr Ave # 1400 (60631-3584)
PHONE...................................847 329-8100
Peter Nolan, *Ch of Bd*
Robert S Apatoff, *President*
▲ EMP: 262 EST: 1856

SALES (est): 21MM
SALES (corp-wide): 4.1B **Privately Held**
SIC: **2741** 5045 Maps: publishing only, not printed on site; atlases: publishing only, not printed on site; globe covers (maps): publishing only, not printed on site; computer software
PA: Patriarch Partners, Llc
 1 Liberty Plz Rm 3500
 New York NY 10006
 212 825-0550

(G-5969)
RAND MCNALLY INTERNATIONAL CO
8770 W Bryn Mawr Ave # 1400 (60631-3584)
PHONE...................................847 329-8100
Andrzej Wrobel, *President*
EMP: 200
SALES (est): 7MM **Privately Held**
SIC: **2741** Maps: publishing only, not printed on site; atlases: publishing only, not printed on site; globe covers (maps): publishing only, not printed on site

(G-5970)
RAPID CIRCULAR PRESS INC
526 N Western Ave (60612-1422)
PHONE...................................312 421-5611
George Korecky, *President*
Barry Korecky, *Vice Pres*
Audry Korecky, *Treasurer*
Sherry Gabrielatos, *MIS Mgr*
EMP: 15 EST: 1955
SQ FT: 12,500
SALES: 1.2MM **Privately Held**
WEB: www.rapidcircularpress.com
SIC: **2752** 2791 2759 2741 Commercial printing, offset; circulars, lithographed; typesetting; commercial printing; miscellaneous publishing

(G-5971)
RAPID DISPLAYS INC (HQ)
Also Called: Cadaco Division
4300 W 47th St (60632-4404)
PHONE...................................773 927-5000
David P Abramson, *CEO*
Scott Weiler, *General Mgr*
Ralph Weil, *Managing Dir*
Earl Abramson, *Chairman*
Mark Abramson, *Vice Pres*
▲ EMP: 250 EST: 1938
SQ FT: 350,000
SALES: 108.8MM
SALES (corp-wide): 506.3MM **Privately Held**
WEB: www.rapiddisplays.com
SIC: **2675** 3944 Die-cut paper & board; board games, children's & adults'
PA: Gemspring Capital, Llc
 54 Wilton Rd
 Westport CT 06880
 203 842-8886

(G-5972)
RAPID DISPLAYS INC
4100 W 76th St Unit F (60652-5600)
PHONE...................................773 884-0900
Mark Abramson, *General Mgr*
EMP: 6
SALES (corp-wide): 506.3MM **Privately Held**
WEB: www.rapiddisplays.com
SIC: **2084** Wines, brandy & brandy spirits
HQ: Rapid Displays, Inc.
 4300 W 47th St
 Chicago IL 60632
 773 927-5000

(G-5973)
RAPID DISPLAYS INC
4300 W 47th St (60632-4404)
PHONE...................................773 927-1500
Mark Abramson, *General Mgr*
EMP: 100
SALES (corp-wide): 506.3MM **Privately Held**
SIC: **2084** Wines
HQ: Rapid Displays, Inc.
 4300 W 47th St
 Chicago IL 60632
 773 927-5000

Chicago - Cook County (G-5974)

(G-5974)
RAPID PALLETS INC
4631 S Saint Louis Ave (60632-2935)
PHONE......................708 259-4016
Yolanda Martinez, *Branch Mgr*
EMP: 14 **Privately Held**
SIC: 2448 Pallets, wood
PA: Rapid Pallets Inc.
9700 S Harlem Ave
Bridgeview IL 60455

(G-5975)
RAPID WIRE FORMS INC
6932 W 62nd St (60638-3934)
PHONE......................773 586-6600
Mary Iuliano, *President*
Anthony Iuliano, *Vice Pres*
EMP: 5
SALES (est): 586.7K **Privately Held**
SIC: 3496 Miscellaneous fabricated wire products

(G-5976)
RAVENS WOOD PHARMACY
4211 N Cicero Ave (60641-1651)
PHONE......................708 667-0525
EMP: 4
SALES (est): 187K **Privately Held**
SIC: 5912 5122 2834 Drug stores & proprietary stores; pharmaceuticals; pharmaceutical preparations

(G-5977)
RAWNATURE5 LLC
3026 W Carroll Ave (60612-1722)
P.O. Box 10914 (60610-0914)
PHONE......................312 800-3239
Dustin Baker, *President*
Chris Fanucchi, *Vice Pres*
EMP: 13
SALES (est): 1.4MM **Privately Held**
SIC: 2099 5141 Food preparations; food brokers

(G-5978)
RAYCO PRINTING SERVICES INC
6025 N Cicero Ave (60646-4301)
PHONE......................773 545-4545
Joseph R Khasho, *President*
EMP: 2 **EST:** 1993
SALES (est): 257.5K **Privately Held**
SIC: 2752 Commercial printing, offset

(G-5979)
RCP PUBLICATIONS INC
3449 N Sheffield Ave (60657-1613)
P.O. Box 3486 (60654-0486)
PHONE......................773 227-4066
Robert Avakian, *President*
William Klingel, *Vice Pres*
Christopher Menchine, *Treasurer*
EMP: 8
SQ FT: 2,500
SALES (est): 560.7K **Privately Held**
SIC: 2711 2721 Newspapers; periodicals

(G-5980)
RDL MARKETING INC
2600 W 19th St (60608-3898)
PHONE......................773 254-7600
Robert Lebovitz, *President*
EMP: 6
SQ FT: 2,000
SALES: 1MM **Privately Held**
SIC: 2851 2879 Paints & allied products; stains: varnish, oil or wax; insecticides & pesticides

(G-5981)
RE MET CORP
Also Called: United American Metals
2246 W Hubbard St (60612-1614)
PHONE......................312 733-6700
William Renotti, *President*
Alan Renotti, *Vice Pres*
EMP: 6 **EST:** 1915
SQ FT: 20,000
SALES: 1.3MM **Privately Held**
SIC: 3339 Tin refining (primary); lead smelting & refining (primary); zinc refining (primary), including slabs & dust

(G-5982)
READ WORLDWIDE LLC
116 W Jckson Blvd Ste 106 (60604)
P.O. Box 1109 (60690-1109)
PHONE......................312 301-6276
Ebony Andrews-Hill,
EMP: 6
SALES (est): 663K **Privately Held**
SIC: 8211 8231 2741 Elementary & secondary schools; libraries; miscellaneous publishing

(G-5983)
REAL ESTATE NEWS CORP
Also Called: Chicago Going Out Guide
3525 W Peterson Ave T10 (60659-3312)
PHONE......................773 866-9900
Steven N Polydoris, *President*
EMP: 7
SQ FT: 2,900
SALES (est): 888.7K **Privately Held**
SIC: 2721 Magazines: publishing only, not printed on site

(G-5984)
REAL TASTE NOODLES MFG INC
1838 S Canal St (60616-1502)
PHONE......................312 738-1893
Charlie Len, *President*
EMP: 3 **EST:** 2000
SQ FT: 5,000
SALES (est): 200K **Privately Held**
SIC: 2099 Noodles, fried (Chinese)

(G-5985)
REAL TIMES II LLC (PA)
Also Called: Chicago Defender Newspaper
4445 S Dr Mrtn Lther King Martin Luther King (60653)
PHONE......................312 225-2400
Michael House, *President*
Kurt Cherry, *CFO*
EMP: 2
SALES (est): 7.2MM **Privately Held**
SIC: 2711 Newspapers: publishing only, not printed on site

(G-5986)
REALCLEARPOLITICS (PA)
6160 N Cicero Ave Ste 410 (60646-4337)
PHONE......................773 255-5846
David Desrosiers, *Principal*
EMP: 15
SALES (est): 958.5K **Privately Held**
WEB: www.realclearpolitics.com
SIC: 2711 Newspapers, publishing & printing

(G-5987)
REB STEEL EQUIPMENT CORP (PA)
Also Called: REB Storage Systems Intl
4556 W Grand Ave (60639-4734)
PHONE......................773 252-0400
Thomas E Lesko, *CEO*
Lori Palmer, *Exec VP*
William Welton, *Senior VP*
Mike Baily, *Vice Pres*
Joseph Budz, *Vice Pres*
◆ **EMP:** 50
SQ FT: 100,000
SALES (est): 34.5MM **Privately Held**
WEB: www.rebsteel.com
SIC: 5084 5021 2542 5046 Materials handling machinery; lockers; shelving, office & store: except wood; racks, merchandise display or storage: except wood; lockers (not refrigerated): except wood; shelving, commercial & industrial

(G-5988)
REBEL SCREENERS INC
820 W Jackson Blvd # 400 (60607-3026)
PHONE......................312 525-2670
Edward Wormser, *President*
▲ **EMP:** 70 **EST:** 1957
SQ FT: 10,000
SALES (est): 4.4MM **Privately Held**
SIC: 2396 Screen printing on fabric articles

(G-5989)
RECORD INC
207 E Ohio St Ste 164 (60611-4092)
PHONE......................312 985-7270
Brian Timpone, *Publisher*
EMP: 9 **EST:** 2013
SQ FT: 727
SALES (est): 268.9K **Privately Held**
SIC: 2711 Newspapers: publishing only, not printed on site

(G-5990)
RECSOLU INC
Also Called: Yello
55 E Monroe St Ste 3600 (60603-6032)
P.O. Box 1235 (60690-1235)
PHONE......................312 517-3200
Jason Weingarden, *CEO*
Dan Bartfield, *President*
David Stiefel, *Senior VP*
Kelley Clark, *Vice Pres*
Gabriela Davidson, *Opers Staff*
EMP: 32
SQ FT: 3,700
SALES (est): 7MM **Privately Held**
WEB: www.yello.co
SIC: 7371 7372 7373 Computer software writing services; computer software development; business oriented computer software; application computer software; systems software development services

(G-5991)
RECYCLED PAPER GREETINGS INC
111 N Canal St Ste 700 (60606-7210)
PHONE......................773 348-6410
Leonard Levine, *COO*
Julie Erickson, *Vice Pres*
Philip Friedmann, *Vice Pres*
Michael Keiser, *Treasurer*
Olivia Bacon, *Marketing Staff*
▲ **EMP:** 25 **EST:** 1972
SQ FT: 75,000
SALES (est): 4.4MM
SALES (corp-wide): 4.3B **Privately Held**
SIC: 2771 5199 Greeting cards; gifts & novelties
HQ: American Greetings Corporation
1 American Way
Cleveland OH 44145
216 252-7300

(G-5992)
RECYCLING SOLUTIONS INC
6348 N Milwaukee Chicago (60646)
PHONE......................773 617-6955
Daniel Helfenbein, *President*
▲ **EMP:** 22
SALES (est): 3.9MM **Privately Held**
SIC: 2673 2674 2821 Bags: plastic, laminated & coated; shipping & shopping bags or sacks; shipping bags or sacks, including multiwall & heavy duty; thermoplastic materials

(G-5993)
REDBOX WORKSHOP LTD
3121 N Rockwell St (60618-7919)
PHONE......................773 478-7077
Pamela L Parker, *President*
Pamela Parker, *President*
Tony Labrosse, *Partner*
Anthony Labrosse, *Vice Pres*
Teresa Gegare, *Finance*
EMP: 22
SQ FT: 17,000
SALES (est): 4.4MM **Privately Held**
SIC: 2541 2531 2426 Showcases, except refrigerated: wood; public building & related furniture; frames for upholstered furniture, wood

(G-5994)
REDSHELF INC
Also Called: Redshelf/Virdocs
500 N Dearborn St # 1200 (60654-3347)
PHONE......................312 878-8586
Tom Scotty, *COO*
Tim Haitaian, *CFO*
Christian Conley, *Accounting Mgr*
Megan Hejmej, *Accountant*
Lauren Johnson, *Human Res Dir*
EMP: 11
SALES (est): 163.6K **Privately Held**
SIC: 2741 Miscellaneous publishing

(G-5995)
REDWOOD LANDINGS LLC
1 E Wacker Dr Ste 1100 (60601-1803)
PHONE......................312 508-4953
Isaacson Mark A, *Principal*
EMP: 3
SALES (est): 280.3K **Privately Held**
SIC: 2711 Newspapers, publishing & printing

(G-5996)
REED-UNION CORPORATION (PA)
875 N Michigan Ave # 3718 (60611-1946)
PHONE......................312 644-3200
Peter D Goldman, *President*
Jeff Goldman, *Vice Pres*
Carol Goldman, *Admin Sec*
EMP: 10 **EST:** 1929
SQ FT: 3,500
SALES: 2.2MM **Privately Held**
WEB: www.nufinish.com
SIC: 2842 Automobile polish

(G-5997)
REELCHICAGOCOM ENTERPRISES INC
5000 N Marine Dr 4d (60640-3226)
P.O. Box 46376 (60646-0376)
PHONE......................312 274-9980
Barbara Roche, *President*
EMP: 3
SALES (est): 218.9K **Privately Held**
SIC: 2721 Magazines: publishing only, not printed on site

(G-5998)
REFINED HAYSTACK INC
1959 N Sheffield Ave (60614-5018)
PHONE......................773 627-3534
Sabrina Vodnik, *President*
Alison Clark, *Marketing Staff*
EMP: 3
SQ FT: 200
SALES (est): 150.4K **Privately Held**
SIC: 2711 Newspapers: publishing only, not printed on site

(G-5999)
REGAL CUT STONE LLC
4213 W Chicago Ave (60651-3518)
PHONE......................773 826-8796
Gary Gofron,
EMP: 13
SALES (est): 1.2MM **Privately Held**
SIC: 3281 Cut stone & stone products

(G-6000)
REGAL HEALTH FOODS INTL INC
2701 N Normandy Ave (60707-2227)
PHONE......................773 252-1044
Gregory Piatigorsky, *President*
◆ **EMP:** 50
SALES (est): 7.6MM **Privately Held**
SIC: 2099 Food preparations

(G-6001)
REGENCY HAND LAUNDRY
2739 N Racine Ave (60614-1205)
PHONE......................773 871-3950
Michael Park, *Owner*
EMP: 6
SALES (est): 253.8K **Privately Held**
SIC: 7216 3589 Cleaning & dyeing, except rugs; servicing machines, except dry cleaning, laundry: coin-oper.

(G-6002)
REGENT AUTOMOTIVE ENGINEERING
2107 N Cicero Ave (60639-3309)
PHONE......................773 889-5744
EMP: 3 **EST:** 1954
SQ FT: 2,000
SALES (est): 274K **Privately Held**
SIC: 3593 3599 Mfg Fluid Power Cylinders Mfg Industrial Machinery

GEOGRAPHIC SECTION

Chicago - Cook County (G-6028)

(G-6003)
REGENT WINDOW FASHIONS LLC
Also Called: JP O'Callaghan
917 W Irving Park Rd (60613-4585)
PHONE.................................773 871-6400
John Ellis, *Owner*
EMP: 3 **EST:** 1946
SQ FT: 2,400
SALES (est): 220K **Privately Held**
WEB: www.regentwindowfashions.com
SIC: 2591 5719 1799 Blinds vertical; window furnishings; venetian blinds; vertical blinds; window shades; window treatment installation

(G-6004)
REGGIOS PIZZA INC (PA)
1001 E 99th St (60628-1538)
PHONE.................................773 933-7927
Shari Wilson, *President*
Sydney Ward, *CFO*
EMP: 70
SALES (est): 8.2MM **Privately Held**
SIC: 5812 2038 Pizzeria, independent; pizza, frozen

(G-6005)
REINO TOOL & MANUFACTURING CO
Also Called: Chicago Wire
3668 N Elston Ave (60618-4316)
PHONE.................................773 588-5800
Donald R Michonski, *President*
Martin Michonski, *Vice Pres*
EMP: 16 **EST:** 1962
SQ FT: 5,000
SALES: 810K **Privately Held**
SIC: 3545 3443 3496 3452 Precision tools, machinists'; cylinders, pressure: metal plate; miscellaneous fabricated wire products; bolts, nuts, rivets & washers; screw machine products; steel wire & related products

(G-6006)
REKTRIX
4545 S Ashland Ave (60609-3250)
PHONE.................................773 475-7926
Fabiola Flores, *President*
EMP: 4
SALES (est): 244.5K **Privately Held**
SIC: 2752 Commercial printing, lithographic

(G-6007)
RELATIVITY ODA LLC (HQ)
231 S Lasalle St Fl 8 Flr 8 (60604)
PHONE.................................312 263-1177
Mike Gamson, *CEO*
Andrew Sieja, *Chairman*
Mateen Khadir, *Vice Pres*
Perry Marchant, *Vice Pres*
George Orr, *Vice Pres*
EMP: 200
SALES (est): 51.5MM
SALES (corp-wide): 53.4MM **Privately Held**
SIC: 7372 5045 Business oriented computer software; computer software
PA: Green Couch Corp.
  231 S La Salle St Fl 8
  Chicago IL 60604
  312 263-1177

(G-6008)
RELAY SERVICES MFG CORP
1300 N Pulaski Rd Ste 12 (60651-1932)
PHONE.................................773 252-2700
Hugo Francisco, *President*
EMP: 11
SQ FT: 8,200
SALES (est): 1.3MM **Privately Held**
WEB: www.relayserviceco.com
SIC: 3625 3679 3612 Relays, for electronic use; electronic switches; specialty transformers

(G-6009)
RELIABLE ASPHALT CORPORATION (PA)
3741 S Pulaski Rd (60623-4927)
PHONE.................................773 254-1121
Michael Vondra, *President*
Donna Elischer, *Corp Secy*
Sam Aprile, *Vice Pres*
Bill Howorth, *Vice Pres*
Mary Kissel, *IT/INT Sup*
EMP: 20
SQ FT: 3,000
SALES (est): 2.3MM **Privately Held**
SIC: 2951 Asphalt & asphaltic paving mixtures (not from refineries)

(G-6010)
RELIABLE PLATING CORPORATION
1538 W Lake St (60607-1468)
PHONE.................................312 421-4747
James R Greenwell, *President*
James Greenwell, *Plant Mgr*
Juan Ruiz, *Engineer*
Judy Welsh, *Controller*
Coult Greenwell, *VP Sales*
EMP: 75 **EST:** 1919
SQ FT: 50,000
SALES (est): 11MM **Privately Held**
WEB: www.reliableplating.com
SIC: 3471 Finishing, metals or formed products; chromium plating of metals or formed products

(G-6011)
RELIEFWATCH INC
1425 E 53rd St Fl 2 Flr 2 (60615)
PHONE.................................646 678-2336
Daniel Yu, *CEO*
EMP: 7
SALES (est): 390K **Privately Held**
SIC: 7372 7371 8243 Application computer software; business oriented computer software; custom computer programming services; software training, computer

(G-6012)
RELISH LABS LLC (HQ)
Also Called: Home Chef
433 W Van Buren St 750n (60607-0433)
PHONE.................................872 225-2433
Pat Vihtelic, *CEO*
Nathan Baldwin, *COO*
Shane Mulrooney, *Vice Pres*
Patrick Vihtelic, *Manager*
Matt Pulley, *CTO*
EMP: 7 **EST:** 2013
SALES (est): 3.1MM
SALES (corp-wide): 122.2B **Publicly Held**
SIC: 5499 8322 2099 Health foods; meal delivery program; ready-to-eat meals, salads & sandwiches
PA: The Kroger Co
  1014 Vine St Ste 1000
  Cincinnati OH 45202
  513 762-4000

(G-6013)
RELX INC
Also Called: Lexisnexis
28544 Network Pl (60673-1285)
PHONE.................................937 247-3469
Mark Kelsey, *CEO*
EMP: 16
SALES (corp-wide): 9.6B **Privately Held**
SIC: 2721 Periodicals
HQ: Relx Inc.
  230 Park Ave Ste 700
  New York NY 10169
  212 309-8100

(G-6014)
RENEW PACKAGING LLC
2444 W 16th St Ste 4r (60608-1731)
PHONE.................................312 421-6699
John Hamilton,
◆ **EMP:** 7
SQ FT: 18,000
SALES (est): 1.1MM **Privately Held**
SIC: 5113 2673 Bags, paper & disposable plastic; bags: plastic, laminated & coated

(G-6015)
RENSEL-CHICAGO INC (PA)
2300 N Kilbourn Ave (60639-3402)
PHONE.................................773 235-2100
Brian H Johnson, *President*
EMP: 50
SQ FT: 35,000
SALES (est): 6.1MM **Privately Held**
WEB: www.singersafety.com
SIC: 3861 3625 3089 Screens, projection; noise control equipment; injection molding of plastics

(G-6016)
REPUBLIC SYSTEMS INC (HQ)
9160 S Green St (60620-2797)
PHONE.................................773 233-6530
Charles R Wood, *President*
Rosweith Wood, *Corp Secy*
EMP: 2
SQ FT: 45,000
SALES (est): 319.3K
SALES (corp-wide): 7.9MM **Privately Held**
SIC: 3086 Insulation or cushioning material, foamed plastic
PA: Republic Packaging Corp.
  9160 S Green St
  Chicago IL 60620
  773 233-6530

(G-6017)
RESONANCE MEDICAL LLC
222 Merchandise Mart Plz # 1230 (60654-4342)
PHONE.................................229 292-2094
Christopher Heddon, *CEO*
EMP: 5
SALES (est): 461.1K **Privately Held**
SIC: 3841 Surgical & medical instruments

(G-6018)
REUM CORPORATION
140 S Dearborn St Ste 420 (60603-5233)
PHONE.................................847 625-7386
▲ **EMP:** 120
SALES (est): 13MM
SALES (corp-wide): 57MM **Privately Held**
SIC: 3089 Mfg Plastic Products
PA: Rm Trust Gmbh
  Heidelberger Str. 64
  Hopfingen 74746
  628 357-0

(G-6019)
REVOLUTION COMPANIES INC
Also Called: Mission Popcorn
332 S Michigan Ave # 1032 (60604-4434)
PHONE.................................800 826-4083
Malik Thomas, *CEO*
EMP: 30
SQ FT: 3,500
SALES (est): 2.5MM **Privately Held**
SIC: 2096 Potato chips & other potato-based snacks

(G-6020)
REX RADIATOR AND WELDING CO (PA)
1440 W 38th St (60609-2114)
PHONE.................................312 421-1531
William H Rex, *President*
Stephen C Rex, *Treasurer*
Robert A Rex, *Admin Sec*
EMP: 7
SQ FT: 4,000
SALES (est): 3.4MM **Privately Held**
WEB: www.rexradiator.com
SIC: 7539 7692 Radiator repair shop, automotive; welding repair; automotive welding

(G-6021)
RGB LIGHTS INC
6045 N Keystone Ave (60646-5209)
PHONE.................................312 421-6080
Brett Gardner, *CEO*
Jameson Green, *President*
Julie Green, *COO*
Brian Rothschild, *Production*
Lyndee Hallahan, *Sales Staff*
▲ **EMP:** 12
SQ FT: 10,000
SALES (est): 3MM **Privately Held**
SIC: 3646 5063 3645 Commercial indusl & institutional electric lighting fixtures; lighting fittings & accessories; residential lighting fixtures

(G-6022)
RH PREYDA COMPANY (PA)
Also Called: Hall Shrpning Stnes A Rh Pryda
333 N Michigan Ave # 3000 (60601-4048)
PHONE.................................212 880-1477
Oscar Cozzini, *President*
Monika Cozzini, *Vice Pres*
Melissa Davis, *Office Mgr*
Alexis Cozzini, *Director*
▲ **EMP:** 14 **EST:** 2013
SQ FT: 2,000
SALES (est): 1.8MM **Privately Held**
SIC: 3291 Abrasive products

(G-6023)
RHINE HALL
2010 W Fulton St F104f (60612-2359)
PHONE.................................312 243-4313
EMP: 5 **EST:** 2014
SALES (est): 241.7K **Privately Held**
WEB: www.rhinehall.com
SIC: 2084 Wines, brandy & brandy spirits

(G-6024)
RI-DEL MFG INC (PA)
Also Called: Power Parts Sign Co
1754 W Walnut St (60612-2524)
PHONE.................................312 829-8720
Stephen Hrajnoha, *President*
Virginia Strahan, *Technology*
James Hrajnoha, *Admin Sec*
▲ **EMP:** 56
SQ FT: 40,000
SALES (est): 13.1MM **Privately Held**
WEB: www.ridelmfg.com
SIC: 3599 7692 3441 3469 Machine shop, jobbing & repair; welding repair; fabricated structural metal; stamping metal for the trade

(G-6025)
RICHARDS FABULOUS FINDS
2545 W North Ave (60647-5296)
PHONE.................................773 943-0710
Richard Biasi, *Principal*
EMP: 3
SALES (est): 150.1K **Privately Held**
SIC: 3961 Cuff-links & studs, except precious metal & gems

(G-6026)
RICHARDS SPER PRMIUM ICE CREAM
Also Called: Richards Sper Prmium Ice Cream
11033 S Langley Ave (60628-3818)
PHONE.................................773 614-8999
Jason Johnson, *Manager*
Rickey Singleton,
EMP: 10
SALES: 1MM **Privately Held**
SIC: 2024 Ice cream & frozen desserts

(G-6027)
RICHARDSON SEATING CORPORATION
2545 W Arthington St (60612-4107)
PHONE.................................312 829-4040
Earl Lichtenstein, *President*
Sharon Lichtenstien, *Admin Sec*
▲ **EMP:** 40 **EST:** 1975
SQ FT: 75,000
SALES (est): 7.5MM **Privately Held**
SIC: 2522 Office chairs, benches & stools, except wood

(G-6028)
RICKARD CIRCULAR FOLDING CO
Also Called: Rickard Bindery
325 N Ashland Ave (60607-1077)
PHONE.................................312 243-6300
Jack Rickard, *Ch of Bd*
Kevin Rickard, *President*
Bonnie Rickard, *Admin Sec*
EMP: 85 **EST:** 1900
SQ FT: 80,000
SALES: 4MM **Privately Held**
WEB: www.rickardbindery.com
SIC: 2789 Binding only: books, pamphlets, magazines, etc.; pamphlets, binding

---

(PA)=Parent Co (HQ)=Headquarters (DH)=Div Headquarters
✪ = New Business established in last 2 years

Chicago - Cook County (G-6029) GEOGRAPHIC SECTION

(G-6029)
RICO COMPUTERS ENTERPRISES INC
7022 W 73rd Pl (60638-5921)
PHONE.................................708 594-7426
John Rico, *President*
Antonio Rico, *Vice Pres*
Guadalupe Rico, *Treasurer*
EMP: 13
SQ FT: 500
SALES (est): 1.1MM **Privately Held**
SIC: 7378 3571 7371 Computer maintenance & repair; electronic computers; computer software development & applications

(G-6030)
RIDDLE MCINTYRE INC
175 N Franklin St Frnt 1 (60606-1835)
PHONE.................................312 782-3317
Hee Kang, *President*
Wha Kang, *Admin Sec*
EMP: 6 **EST:** 1916
SQ FT: 2,300
SALES: 440K **Privately Held**
SIC: 5699 2321 Custom tailor; men's & boys' furnishings

(G-6031)
RIGHT LANE INDUSTRIES LLC (PA)
222 N La Salle St Ste 705 (60601-1009)
PHONE.................................857 869-4132
Eric Mara, *Mng Member*
Dan Drexler,
EMP: 6
SALES (est): 28.1MM **Privately Held**
SIC: 3081 3053 3089 3069 Plastic film & sheet; gaskets, packing & sealing devices; plastic hardware & building products; pillows, sponge rubber; press brakes; presses: forming, stamping, punching, sizing (machine tools); shearing machines, power; rebuilt machine tools, metal forming types

(G-6032)
RIGHT WAY SIGNS LLC
1134 N Homan Ave (60651-4007)
PHONE.................................773 930-4361
Alexander H Perry, *President*
Vanessa Collazo, *Office Mgr*
Sam McMorris, *Graphic Designe*
EMP: 2
SALES (est): 279.7K **Privately Held**
WEB: www.rightwaysigns.com
SIC: 3993 Electric signs

(G-6033)
RIGHTHAND TECHNOLOGIES INC
7450 W Wilson Ave (60706-4549)
PHONE.................................773 774-7600
Mark Loffredo, *President*
Bruce Neely, *Mfg Staff*
Yvonne Marcial, *Purchasing*
Jerry Deren, *Engineer*
Ryan Lane, *Engineer*
▲ **EMP:** 50
SQ FT: 25,000
SALES (est): 15.7MM **Privately Held**
SIC: 3825 7373 8711 Digital test equipment, electronic & electrical circuits; computer integrated systems design; electrical or electronic engineering

(G-6034)
RINKER BOAT COMPANY
333 W Wacker Dr Ste 600 (60606-1284)
PHONE.................................574 457-5731
Robert Moran, *CEO*
EMP: 26
SALES (est): 5.9MM **Privately Held**
WEB: www.rinkerboats.com
SIC: 3731 Offshore supply boats, building & repairing

(G-6035)
RISK NEVER DIE INC
1001 W 15th St Unit 222 (60608-2765)
PHONE.................................708 240-4194
EMP: 5
SALES (est): 310K **Privately Held**
SIC: 3544 Mfg Dies/Tools/Jigs/Fixtures

(G-6036)
RIVALFLY NATIONAL NETWORK LLC
320 W Ohio St (60654-6566)
PHONE.................................847 867-8660
Allen Marrinson, *Mng Member*
Rich Babich,
Albert Goodman,
EMP: 6
SQ FT: 1,500
SALES (est): 249.2K **Privately Held**
SIC: 7372 Business oriented computer software

(G-6037)
RIVERSIDE GRAPHICS CORPORATION
2 N Riverside Plz Ste 365 (60606-2620)
PHONE.................................312 372-3766
Patrick Monahan, *President*
John Denoyer, *President*
Dan Moss, *General Mgr*
Terry Vigor, *Sales Staff*
Christie Renfroe, *Marketing Staff*
EMP: 9
SQ FT: 3,000
SALES (est): 1.8MM **Privately Held**
WEB: www.riversidegx.com
SIC: 2752 Commercial printing, offset

(G-6038)
RKF ENTERPRISES
7331 S Michigan Ave Ste 1 (60619-1618)
PHONE.................................773 723-7038
Khan Franklin, *Owner*
Robert Franklin, *Owner*
EMP: 3 **EST:** 1988
SALES (est): 165.3K **Privately Held**
SIC: 2789 Bookbinding & repairing: trade, edition, library, etc.

(G-6039)
RM ACQUISITION LLC (PA)
Also Called: Rand McNally
8770 W Bryn Mawr Ave # 1400 (60631-3515)
PHONE.................................847 329-8100
Bob Delaney, *Vice Pres*
Samuel Palmer, *Manager*
Venky RAO, *Director*
Dave Muscatel,
◆ **EMP:** 140 **EST:** 2006
SALES (est): 54.8MM **Privately Held**
WEB: www.randmcnally.com
SIC: 2741 Miscellaneous publishing

(G-6040)
RM LUCAS CO
3211 S Wood St (60608-6118)
PHONE.................................773 523-4300
EMP: 35
SALES (corp-wide): 11.9MM **Privately Held**
SIC: 2891 1761 Adhesives & sealants; roofing contractor
PA: R.M. Lucas Co.
   12400 S Laramie Ave
   Alsip IL 60803
   773 523-4300

(G-6041)
RNFL ACQUISITION LLC
Also Called: Michigan Renewable Carbon
10 S La Salle St Ste 3300 (60603-1026)
PHONE.................................651 442-6011
Jim Mennell, *CEO*
Rico Biasetti, *President*
Todd Smreker, *Vice Pres*
EMP: 50
SALES (est): 6.3MM
SALES (corp-wide): 8.8MM **Privately Held**
SIC: 3624 Carbon specialties for electrical use
PA: Biogenic Reagents, Llc
   133 1st Ave N
   Minneapolis MN 55401
   651 442-6011

(G-6042)
ROBERT B SCOTT OCULARISTS LTD (PA)
111 N Wabash Ave Ste 1620 (60602-3453)
PHONE.................................312 782-3558
Roland B Scott, *President*
Bonny Scott, *Treasurer*
Vivian Scott, *Admin Sec*
EMP: 45 **EST:** 1953
SQ FT: 1,600
SALES (est): 5.2MM **Privately Held**
WEB: www.ocularistsupplies.com
SIC: 5169 3851 3842 Chemicals & allied products; eyes, glass & plastic; surgical appliances & supplies

(G-6043)
ROBERT-LESLIE PUBLISHING LLC
4147 N Ravenswood Ave # 301 (60613-2472)
P.O. Box 1514, Jonesboro AR (72403-1514)
PHONE.................................773 935-8358
Judith Coffey, *CEO*
Beth Wise, *Editor*
EMP: 3
SALES (est): 226.6K **Privately Held**
SIC: 2741 Miscellaneous publishing

(G-6044)
ROBERTS ELECTRIC COMPANY
Also Called: Arbee Sales
311 N Morgan St (60607-1310)
PHONE.................................773 725-7323
Jeff Boos, *Owner*
Evelyn Boos, *Vice Pres*
Greg Boss, *Office Mgr*
EMP: 3 **EST:** 1949
SQ FT: 40,000
SALES (est): 588.7K **Privately Held**
SIC: 3621 5063 3594 Motors, electric; motors, electric; fluid power pumps & motors

(G-6045)
ROBIN HOOD MAT & QUILTING CORP (PA)
4800 S Richmond St (60632-2007)
PHONE.................................312 953-2960
Robin Hood, *Principal*
EMP: 5
SALES (est): 474.5K **Privately Held**
SIC: 2515 Mattresses & bedsprings

(G-6046)
ROBIT INC (HQ)
639 W Diversey Pkwy # 217 (60614-1535)
PHONE.................................708 667-7892
Jussi Rautiainen, *President*
David Delorne, *Vice Pres*
EMP: 1
SQ FT: 200,000
SALES: 2MM
SALES (corp-wide): 95.6MM **Privately Held**
WEB: www.robitgroup.com
SIC: 3533 Drilling tools for gas, oil or water wells
PA: Robit Oyj
   Vikkiniityntie 9
   Lempaala 33880
   331 403-400

(G-6047)
ROCA INC
Also Called: El Superior Mexican Foods
5275 S Archer Ave (60632-4731)
PHONE.................................312 421-2345
Robert Casimiro, *President*
EMP: 14 **EST:** 2001
SQ FT: 15,000
SALES (est): 1.3MM **Privately Held**
SIC: 2013 Sausages & other prepared meats

(G-6048)
ROCKWELL METAL PRODUCTS INC
3232 W Cermak Rd (60623-3312)
PHONE.................................773 762-7030
Rudy Lung, *President*
Jane Taccola, *Admin Sec*
▲ **EMP:** 8 **EST:** 1949
SQ FT: 12,000
SALES (est): 1MM **Privately Held**
SIC: 3469 Machine parts, stamped or pressed metal

(G-6049)
RODGER HOWARD
Also Called: Shop Espresso Mchs Svcs & Sls
5951 W Lawrence Ave (60630-3129)
PHONE.................................773 481-6990
Roger Howard, *Owner*
EMP: 7
SQ FT: 1,400
SALES: 900K **Privately Held**
SIC: 3556 Beverage machinery

(G-6050)
ROESERS BAKERY
3216 W North Ave (60647-4985)
PHONE.................................773 489-6900
John Roeser III, *Owner*
EMP: 25
SQ FT: 7,500
SALES (est): 2.6MM **Privately Held**
WEB: www.roeserscakes.com
SIC: 2051 2024 Bakery: wholesale or wholesale/retail combined; ice cream & ice milk

(G-6051)
ROHNER ENGRAVING INC
5410 W Roosevelt Rd # 202 (60644-1875)
PHONE.................................773 244-8343
David Rohner, *President*
EMP: 2
SQ FT: 3,000
SALES (est): 265K **Privately Held**
SIC: 2759 Stationery: printing

(G-6052)
ROHNER LETTERPRESS INC
Also Called: Rohner Press
5410 W Roosevelt Rd # 202 (60644-1478)
PHONE.................................773 248-0800
Bruno Rohner, *President*
Hannah King, *Production*
EMP: 11 **EST:** 1997
SQ FT: 5,000
SALES (est): 1.7MM **Privately Held**
WEB: www.rohnerletterpress.com
SIC: 2752 Commercial printing, offset

(G-6053)
ROLL ROLL MET FABRICATORS INC
2310 W 58th St (60636-1516)
PHONE.................................773 434-1315
Antonio Alvarez, *President*
Marina Alvarez, *Admin Sec*
EMP: 24
SQ FT: 87,000
SALES (est): 2.5MM **Privately Held**
SIC: 3499 Machine bases, metal

(G-6054)
ROLLED EDGE INC
Also Called: Chicago Paper Tube & Can Co.
4221 N Normandy Ave (60634-1402)
PHONE.................................773 283-9500
John Dudlak, *President*
Molly Dudlak, *Exec VP*
Daniel Dudlak, *Plant Mgr*
Dan Dudlak, *Prdtn Mgr*
▲ **EMP:** 25
SQ FT: 65,000
SALES (est): 7.3MM **Privately Held**
WEB: www.chicagopapertube.com
SIC: 2655 Tubes, fiber or paper: made from purchased material

(G-6055)
ROMA PACKING CO
2354 S Leavitt St (60608-4030)
PHONE.................................773 927-7371
Steve Lombardi, *President*
Marsha Caputo, *Corp Secy*
Marcia Caputo, *Vice Pres*
EMP: 7 **EST:** 1945
SQ FT: 3,125
SALES (est): 750K **Privately Held**
WEB: www.lombardisausageco.com
SIC: 5147 2013 Meats, fresh; sausages from purchased meat

(G-6056)
ROMAINE EMPIRE INC
Also Called: Farmer's Fridge
2000 W Fulton St Ste F310 (60612-2363)
PHONE.................................312 229-0099
Luke Saunders, *CEO*

Shayna Harris, *Vice Pres*
Kevin Price, *Treasurer*
Tanvee Agrawal, *Manager*
Sarah Affholter, *Director*
EMP: 68
SALES (est): 18.7MM **Privately Held**
SIC: 2099 5812 Ready-to-eat meals, salads & sandwiches; carry-out only (except pizza) restaurant

(G-6057)
ROME METAL MFG INC
4612 W Ohio St (60644-1794)
PHONE.................................773 287-1755
Omelia Garcia, *President*
EMP: 6 **EST:** 1904
SQ FT: 12,000
SALES: 400K **Privately Held**
SIC: 3444 3443 2542 2522 Sheet metal specialties, not stamped; fabricated plate work (boiler shop); partitions & fixtures, except wood; office furniture, except wood; household furnishings

(G-6058)
ROOMS REDUX CHICAGO INC
6033 N Sheridan Rd 25d (60660-3003)
PHONE.................................312 835-1192
Philip George Popowici, *Principal*
EMP: 10
SALES (est): 915.8K **Privately Held**
SIC: 2511 Bed frames, except water bed frames: wood

(G-6059)
ROQ INNOVATION LLC
1616 E 56th St Unit 604 (60637-2706)
PHONE.................................917 770-2403
Raquel Graham, *President*
EMP: 4
SALES: 80K **Privately Held**
SIC: 2389 7389 Apparel for handicapped;

(G-6060)
RORKE & RILEY SPECIALTY B
3712 N Broadway St # 252 (60613-4235)
PHONE.................................773 929-2522
Peter Page, *President*
EMP: 6
SALES: 270.3K **Privately Held**
SIC: 2086 Soft drinks: packaged in cans, bottles, etc.

(G-6061)
ROSE PACKING CO INC
4900 S Major Ave (60638-1589)
PHONE.................................708 458-9300
Peter Rose, *President*
Maria Maris, *COO*
Luis Villasenor, *Prdtn Mgr*
Calvin Beaton, *Warehouse Mgr*
Terry Harris, *Traffic Mgr*
EMP: 3
SALES: 205.2K **Privately Held**
SIC: 2011 Meat packing plants

(G-6062)
ROSE PACKING COMPANY INC
4900 S Major Ave (60638-1589)
PHONE.................................708 458-9300
Peter Rose, *Branch Mgr*
EMP: 530
SQ FT: 135,000 **Privately Held**
SIC: 2011 2013 Pork products from pork slaughtered on site; sausages & other prepared meats
HQ: Rose Packing Company, Inc.
65 S Barrington Rd
South Barrington IL 60010
847 381-5700

(G-6063)
ROSE PACKING COMPANY INC
5656 W 51st St (60638-1525)
PHONE.................................708 458-9300
EMP: 12 **Privately Held**
SIC: 2011 Meat packing plants
HQ: Rose Packing Company, Inc.
65 S Barrington Rd
South Barrington IL 60010
847 381-5700

(G-6064)
ROSHAN AG INC
Also Called: Rosen Printing Services
3525 W Peterson Ave # 120 (60659-3313)
PHONE.................................773 267-1635
Asnan Ghaziani, *CEO*
Roshan A Ghaziani, *President*
EMP: 4
SALES (est): 284.3K **Privately Held**
WEB: www.rosenmanagement.com
SIC: 2759 Commercial printing

(G-6065)
ROTATION DYNAMICS CORPORATION
Also Called: Rotadyne Precision Mch Roller
6120 S New England Ave (60638-4008)
PHONE.................................630 769-9700
Timu Gallies, *Manager*
EMP: 20
SQ FT: 18,400
SALES (corp-wide): 145.7MM **Privately Held**
SIC: 3861 3354 2796 Graphic arts plates, sensitized; aluminum extruded products; platemaking services
PA: Rotation Dynamics Corporation
1101 Windham Pkwy
Romeoville IL 60446
630 769-9255

(G-6066)
ROTATION DYNAMICS CORPORATION
Also Called: Ideal Roller
2512 W 24th St (60608-3709)
PHONE.................................773 247-5600
Len Kruizenga, *Manager*
EMP: 77
SALES (corp-wide): 145.7MM **Privately Held**
SIC: 3555 3061 2796 Printing trades machinery; mechanical rubber goods; platemaking services
PA: Rotation Dynamics Corporation
1101 Windham Pkwy
Romeoville IL 60446
630 769-9255

(G-6067)
ROWBOAT CREATIVE LLC
2649 N Kildare Ave # 1 (60639-2051)
PHONE.................................773 675-2628
Lucas Guariglia,
Joseph Zangrilli,
EMP: 14 **EST:** 2010
SALES (est): 1.7MM **Privately Held**
WEB: www.rowboatcreative.com
SIC: 2759 Commercial printing

(G-6068)
ROXUL USA INC
Also Called: Rockfon
4849 S Austin Ave (60638-1400)
PHONE.................................800 323-7164
Rick Diantonio, *Plant Mgr*
Dan Aiken, *Sales Staff*
Chris King, *Manager*
Christian Kofod, *Manager*
Christine Uhlir, *Manager*
EMP: 1112
SALES (corp-wide): 3B **Privately Held**
SIC: 5033 3446 Roofing, asphalt & sheet metal; acoustical suspension systems, metal
HQ: Roxul Usa Inc.
4594 Cayce Rd
Byhalia MS 38611
662 851-4755

(G-6069)
ROYAL ENVELOPE CORPORATION
4114 S Peoria St (60609-2521)
PHONE.................................773 376-1212
Michael Pusatera, *President*
Anthony Pusatera, *President*
Mike Pusatera, *President*
Eileen Pusatera, *Vice Pres*
EMP: 80 **EST:** 1978
SQ FT: 55,000
SALES (est): 16.6MM **Privately Held**
SIC: 2759 Commercial printing

(G-6070)
RPI BUSINESS CO INC
2501 S Rockwell St (60608-4806)
P.O. Box 166753 (60616-6753)
PHONE.................................773 254-7095
Hugo Portales, *Principal*
EMP: 2
SALES (est): 304.3K **Privately Held**
SIC: 2448 Pallets, wood

(G-6071)
RR DONNELLEY & SONS COMPANY
111 S Wacker Dr Fl 36 (60606-4300)
PHONE.................................312 236-8000
EMP: 109
SALES (corp-wide): 11.2B **Publicly Held**
SIC: 2754 2759 0752 2732 Gravure Commercial Printing
PA: R.R. Donnelley & Sons Company
35 W Wacker Dr Ste 3650
Chicago IL 60601
312 326-8000

(G-6072)
RR DONNELLEY PRINTING CO LP (PA)
Also Called: R R Donnelley
35 W Wacker Dr Ste 3650 (60601-1840)
PHONE.................................312 326-8000
Ronald Daly, *President*
Douglas Johnson, *Managing Prtnr*
Glynn Perry, *Exec VP*
Elif Sagsen-Ercel, *Exec VP*
Eric A Eisenstein, *Vice Pres*
▲ **EMP:** 3 **EST:** 1864
SQ FT: 220,000
SALES (est): 548.5MM **Privately Held**
SIC: 2754 2752 5085 Rotogravure printing; commercial printing, offset; industrial supplies

(G-6073)
RS FUELS INC
4650 W Lawrence Ave (60630-2533)
PHONE.................................773 205-9833
Robert Stambolic, *Branch Mgr*
EMP: 10
SALES (corp-wide): 1.4MM **Privately Held**
SIC: 2869 Fuels
PA: Rs Fuels Inc
200 W Higgins Rd Ste 326
Schaumburg IL

(G-6074)
RSM INTERNATIONAL
1 S Wacker Dr Ste 800 (60606-4650)
PHONE.................................312 634-3400
Jamie Lidel, *Partner*
David Fiszer, *Consultant*
EMP: 5 **EST:** 2015
SALES (est): 131.5K **Privately Held**
SIC: 2721 Periodicals

(G-6075)
RTC INDUSTRIES INC
3101 S Kedzie Ave Apt S (60623)
PHONE.................................847 640-2400
Larry O'Neill, *COO*
Jenny Tanquary, *Accounting Mgr*
Beth Weber, *Human Res Mgr*
Iqbal Khan, *Manager*
EMP: 100
SALES (corp-wide): 636MM **Privately Held**
SIC: 3993 2671 2542 Displays & cutouts, window & lobby; packaging paper & plastics film, coated & laminated; partitions & fixtures, except wood
PA: Rtc Industries, Inc.
2800 Golf Rd
Rolling Meadows IL 60008
847 640-2400

(G-6076)
RTD HALLSTAR INC
120 S Riverside Plz # 1620 (60606-3911)
PHONE.................................908 852-6128
James Savavastano, *President*
▲ **EMP:** 120
SALES (est): 9.3MM
SALES (corp-wide): 51.3MM **Privately Held**
SIC: 2869 Industrial organic chemicals

PA: Hallstar Company
120 S Riverside Plz # 1620
Chicago IL 60606
312 554-7400

(G-6077)
RUBIN MANUFACTURING INC
2241 S Halsted St (60608-4521)
PHONE.................................312 942-1111
David Rubin, *President*
▲ **EMP:** 285
SQ FT: 85,000
SALES (est): 39.5MM **Privately Held**
SIC: 2211 Apparel & outerwear fabrics, cotton

(G-6078)
RUBIN NSA BROS LLC
Also Called: Rubin Brothers, Inc.
2241 S Halsted St (60608-4521)
PHONE.................................312 942-1111
David A Rubin, *President*
Miguel Garcia, *Vice Pres*
EMP: 2
SQ FT: 85,000
SALES (est): 19.7MM **Privately Held**
WEB: www.unionmadeclothing.com
SIC: 2326 2331 Industrial garments, men's & boys'; women's & misses' blouses & shirts
PA: National Safety Apparel, Inc.
15825 Industrial Pkwy
Cleveland OH 44135

(G-6079)
RUDD CONTAINER CORPORATION
4600 S Kolin Ave (60632-4497)
PHONE.................................773 847-7600
Darrell Rudd, *Ch of Bd*
Ted Bihun, *Vice Pres*
EMP: 60 **EST:** 1920
SQ FT: 93,000
SALES (est): 16.4MM **Privately Held**
WEB: www.ruddcontainer.com
SIC: 2653 5113 Boxes, corrugated: made from purchased materials; corrugated & solid fiber boxes

(G-6080)
RYAN PARTNERSHIP LLC
Also Called: Chicago Catalog
343 W Erie St Ste 600 (60654-5789)
PHONE.................................312 343-2611
Charlene Gervais, *Branch Mgr*
EMP: 15
SALES (corp-wide): 8.3MM **Privately Held**
SIC: 2741 Catalogs: publishing & printing
PA: Ryan Partnership, Llc
100 Montgomery St # 1500
San Francisco CA 94104
415 289-1110

(G-6081)
RYCOLINE PRODUCTS LLC
5540 N Northwest Hwy (60630-1134)
P.O. Box 97043 (60690-7043)
PHONE.................................773 775-6755
Charles L Palmer,
Gary Anderson,
Norman J Nichol,
◆ **EMP:** 143 **EST:** 1957
SQ FT: 40,000
SALES (est): 20.9MM **Privately Held**
SIC: 2842 3555 2899 Cleaning or polishing preparations; printing trades machinery; chemical preparations
HQ: Sun Chemical Corporation
35 Waterview Blvd Ste 100
Parsippany NJ 07054
973 404-6000

(G-6082)
S & B FINISHING CO INC
3005 W Franklin Blvd (60612-1007)
PHONE.................................773 533-0033
Kenneth Spielman, *President*
Marcy Roth, *Admin Sec*
EMP: 55
SQ FT: 35,000
SALES (est): 9.1MM **Privately Held**
SIC: 3479 Coating of metals & formed products

Chicago - Cook County (G-6083)   GEOGRAPHIC SECTION

(G-6083)
S & C ELECTRIC COMPANY (PA)
6601 N Ridge Blvd (60626-3997)
P.O. Box 71704 (60694-1704)
PHONE..................................773 338-1000
Kyle Seymour, *President*
Eric Welty, *General Mgr*
Bob Ternand, *Superintendent*
John E Johann, *Corp Secy*
Randy Gucwa, *Vice Pres*
◆ **EMP:** 1900 **EST:** 1911
SQ FT: 1,200,000
SALES (est): 577MM **Privately Held**
WEB: www.sandc.com
SIC: 3613 3643 3625 8711 Fuses, electric; switches, electric power except snap, push button, etc.; switchgear & switchgear accessories; current-carrying wiring devices; relays & industrial controls; engineering services

(G-6084)
S & G STEP TOOL INC
5203 N Rose St (60656-1014)
PHONE..................................773 992-0808
Sabin Torlo, *President*
Gregory Matiasek, *Vice Pres*
EMP: 5
SQ FT: 4,000
SALES (est): 470.4K **Privately Held**
SIC: 3423 Hand & edge tools

(G-6085)
S C JOHNSON & SON INC
550 W Washington Blvd # 1400
(60661-2698)
PHONE..................................312 702-3100
Tony Thomas, *Manager*
EMP: 170
SALES (corp-wide): 4.1B **Privately Held**
SIC: 2842 2844 2879 2865 Floor waxes; furniture polish or wax; stain removers; disinfectants, household or industrial plant; shampoos, rinses, conditioners: hair; shaving preparations; face creams or lotions; insecticides, agricultural or household; exterminating products, for household or industrial use; cyclic crudes & intermediates; exhaust hood or fan cleaning; air duct cleaning; building maintenance, except repairs
PA: S. C. Johnson & Son, Inc.
1525 Howe St
Racine WI 53403
262 260-2000

(G-6086)
S V C PRINTING CO
3008 N Laramie Ave (60641-5010)
PHONE..................................773 286-2219
Frank Canino, *Owner*
Dominica Canino, *Co-Owner*
EMP: 3 **EST:** 1939
SQ FT: 3,000
SALES (est): 60K **Privately Held**
SIC: 2759 Letterpress printing

(G-6087)
SABINAS FOOD PRODUCTS INC
1509 W 18th St (60608-2803)
PHONE..................................312 738-2412
Antonio Avina, *President*
Alex Reynoso, *Vice Pres*
EMP: 25 **EST:** 1961
SQ FT: 9,000
SALES (est): 1MM **Privately Held**
WEB: www.sabinasfoodproducts.com
SIC: 2099 Tortillas, fresh or refrigerated

(G-6088)
SAFE FAIR FOOD COMPANY LLC
1 N La Salle St Ste 2850 (60602-4062)
PHONE..................................904 930-4277
Will Holsworth, *CEO*
Tati Rezende, *CFO*
Ashley Maynard, *Finance*
EMP: 10
SALES: 2.5MM **Privately Held**
SIC: 2096 Potato chips & similar snacks

(G-6089)
SAFE-T-QUIP CORPORATION
2300 N Kilbourn Ave (60639-3402)
PHONE..................................773 235-2100
Brian Johnson, *President*
EMP: 12
SALES (est): 1.1MM
SALES (corp-wide): 6.1MM **Privately Held**
SIC: 3089 3296 Injection molding of plastics; mineral wool
PA: Rensel-Chicago, Inc.
2300 N Kilbourn Ave
Chicago IL 60639
773 235-2100

(G-6090)
SAINT MARY FUEL COMPANY
6700 S Ashland Ave (60636-3414)
PHONE..................................773 918-1681
Simon Abraham, *Owner*
EMP: 4
SALES (est): 605.9K **Privately Held**
SIC: 2869 Fuels

(G-6091)
SAINTS VOLO & OLHA UK CATH PAR
2245 W Superior St (60612-1327)
PHONE..................................312 829-5209
Izan Krotec, *Pastor*
EMP: 4 **EST:** 1968
SALES (est): 233.4K **Privately Held**
WEB: www.stsvo.org
SIC: 8661 2752 Catholic Church; lithographing on metal

(G-6092)
SALAMANDER STUDIOS CHICAGO INC
Also Called: Stockwell Greetings
5410 W Roosevelt Rd # 306 (60644-1875)
PHONE..................................773 379-2211
Judith R Gillman, *President*
John Fenwick, *Vice Pres*
▲ **EMP:** 15
SQ FT: 30,000
SALES: 1.3MM **Privately Held**
SIC: 2771 Greeting cards

(G-6093)
SALESFORCECOM INC
205 W Wacker Dr Fl 22 (60606-1216)
PHONE..................................312 361-3555
EMP: 8
SALES (corp-wide): 17.1B **Publicly Held**
SIC: 7372 Business oriented computer software
PA: Salesforce.Com, Inc.
415 Mission St Fl 3
San Francisco CA 94105
415 901-7000

(G-6094)
SALESFORCECOM INC
111 W Illinois St (60654-4505)
PHONE..................................312 288-3600
Brian Cline, *Engineer*
Bryan Boncosky, *Accounts Exec*
Tim Schirack, *Accounts Exec*
George Hu, *Director*
Jack Eberle, *Executive*
EMP: 12
SALES (corp-wide): 17.1B **Publicly Held**
SIC: 7372 Business oriented computer software
PA: Salesforce.Com, Inc.
415 Mission St Fl 3
San Francisco CA 94105
415 901-7000

(G-6095)
SALMONS AND BROWN
44 E Superior St 1 (60611-2506)
PHONE..................................312 929-6756
EMP: 8 **EST:** 2010
SALES (est): 320K **Privately Held**
SIC: 2321 2335 Mfg Men's/Boy's Furnishings Mfg Women's/Misses' Dresses

(G-6096)
SALSEDO PRESS INC
3139 W Chicago Ave (60622-4364)
PHONE..................................773 533-9900
Victor Cortes, *President*
Pat Gleason, *Corp Secy*
Maria Arroyo, *Shareholder*
Chris Burke, *Shareholder*
Juan Carlos Martinez, *Shareholder*
EMP: 12
SQ FT: 12,500
SALES (est): 1.2MM **Privately Held**
SIC: 2752 Commercial printing, offset

(G-6097)
SAME DAY SIGNS
2416 W Barry Ave (60618-7914)
P.O. Box 11856, Chandler AZ (85248-0015)
PHONE..................................773 697-4896
Ryan Stan, *President*
EMP: 2 **EST:** 2012
SALES (est): 207.9K **Privately Held**
SIC: 3993 Signs & advertising specialties

(G-6098)
SANCHEM INC
1600 S Canal St (60616-1199)
PHONE..................................312 733-6100
Estelle Flicher, *President*
Jonathan J Flicher, *Admin Sec*
▼ **EMP:** 22
SALES (est): 5.6MM **Privately Held**
SIC: 2899 Rust resisting compounds; corrosion preventive lubricant

(G-6099)
SANDERSON AND ASSOCIATES
400 N Racine Ave Apt 211 (60642-6096)
PHONE..................................312 829-4350
Rhonda Sanderson, *Owner*
Heather Klee, *Accounts Exec*
EMP: 10
SALES (est): 1.1MM **Privately Held**
SIC: 8743 2721 Public relations & publicity; periodicals

(G-6100)
SANGO EMBROIDERY
5220 S Pulaski Rd (60632-4222)
PHONE..................................773 582-4354
Julio Santiagio, *Owner*
EMP: 6
SALES (est): 232.1K **Privately Held**
SIC: 2395 Embroidery products, except schiffli machine

(G-6101)
SANSABELT
101 N Wacker Dr (60606-1784)
PHONE..................................312 357-5119
Warwick Jones, *Principal*
EMP: 3
SALES (est): 172.6K **Privately Held**
SIC: 2329 Men's & boys' clothing

(G-6102)
SANTUCCI ENTERPRISES
6345 W Warwick Ave (60634-2432)
PHONE..................................773 286-5629
Carmen Santucci, *Owner*
EMP: 4
SALES (est): 333.5K **Privately Held**
SIC: 3677 3621 Electronic coils, transformers & other inductors; motors & generators

(G-6103)
SAPORITO FINISHING CO
Also Called: Accurate Anodizing Division
3130 S Austin Blvd (60804-3729)
PHONE..................................708 222-5300
Frank Voltarel, *Branch Mgr*
EMP: 50
SALES (corp-wide): 22.8MM **Privately Held**
SIC: 3471 Anodizing (plating) of metals or formed products
PA: Saporito Finishing Co.
3119 S Austin Blvd
Cicero IL 60804
708 222-5300

(G-6104)
SARCO PUTTY COMPANY
5959 S Knox Ave (60629-5498)
PHONE..................................773 735-5577
Myrtle Sarsfield, *President*
James Sarsfield, *Vice Pres*
Denise Sarsfield, *Treasurer*
Edward Sarsfield III, *Admin Sec*
EMP: 4
SQ FT: 16,000
SALES (est): 800K **Privately Held**
WEB: www.sarcoputty.com
SIC: 2851 2891 Putty; caulking compounds; sealing compounds for pipe threads or joints; sealing compounds, synthetic rubber or plastic

(G-6105)
SARCOL
3050 W Taylor St (60612-3998)
PHONE..................................773 533-3000
Sergio Rodriguez, *President*
EMP: 4 **EST:** 2010
SALES (est): 310K **Privately Held**
WEB: www.mae-sarieng.com
SIC: 3369 Nonferrous foundries

(G-6106)
SASHE LUX LLC
835 N Michigan Ave # 6000 (60611-2203)
PHONE..................................312 593-1379
Sabrina Davis,
EMP: 4
SALES (est): 125.1K **Privately Held**
SIC: 3999 Candles

(G-6107)
SAVANNAH INDUSTRIES INC
Also Called: Eager Polymers
3350 W 48th Pl (60632-3000)
PHONE..................................773 927-3484
Mark Villegas, *President*
▼ **EMP:** 3
SQ FT: 18,000
SALES (est): 102.1K **Privately Held**
SIC: 2821 Plastics materials & resins

(G-6108)
SAZERAC NORTH AMERICA INC (HQ)
75 Remittance Dr # 3312 (60675-3312)
PHONE..................................502 423-5225
Mark Brown, *President*
▲ **EMP:** 25
SALES (est): 57.7MM
SALES (corp-wide): 306.3MM **Privately Held**
SIC: 2085 Distilled & blended liquors
PA: Sazerac Company, Inc.
3850 N Causeway Blvd # 1695
Metairie LA 70002
504 831-9450

(G-6109)
SC INDUSTRIES LLC
Also Called: Mdhearingaid
150 N Michigan Ave # 400 (60601-7524)
PHONE..................................407 484-2081
Raymond Douglas Stroud, *President*
Eric Woolard, *Corp Secy*
David Bartok, *Vice Pres*
EMP: 12
SQ FT: 12,000
SALES (est): 87.6K **Privately Held**
SIC: 3842 Hearing aids

(G-6110)
SCHAUMBURG REVIEW
Also Called: Pioneer Press
350 N Orleans St Fl 10 (60654-1700)
PHONE..................................847 998-3400
Fax: 847 486-7450
EMP: 14
SALES (est): 1MM **Privately Held**
SIC: 2711 7313 Newspapers-Publishing/Printing Advertising Representative

(G-6111)
SCHECK SIRESS PROSTHETICS INC
1304 E 47th St 204 (60653-4508)
PHONE..................................312 757-5270
Michael H Oros, *Branch Mgr*
EMP: 3
SALES (corp-wide): 11.4MM **Privately Held**
SIC: 3842 Surgical appliances & supplies
PA: Scheck & Siress Prosthetics, Inc
1 S 376 Summit Ave Ct E
Oakbrook Terrace IL
708 383-2257

GEOGRAPHIC SECTION
Chicago - Cook County (G-6140)

(G-6112)
SCHNEIDER ELECTRIC USA INC
311 S Wacker Dr Ste 4550 (60606-6622)
PHONE...................312 697-4770
Paul Havlik, *Marketing Staff*
EMP: 9
SALES (corp-wide): 177.9K **Privately Held**
SIC: 3613 Circuit breakers, air
HQ: Schneider Electric Usa, Inc.
201 Wshington St Ste 2700
Boston MA 02108
978 975-9600

(G-6113)
SCHOLARSHIP SOLUTIONS LLC
Also Called: Awardspring
200 W Jackson Blvd # 2700 (60606-6943)
PHONE...................847 859-5629
Kurt H Reilly, *CEO*
Valerie Henderson, *Project Mgr*
Christopher Jerles, *Business Anlyst*
EMP: 14 **EST:** 2012
SQ FT: 13,868
SALES (est): 1.2MM **Privately Held**
SIC: 7372 Application computer software

(G-6114)
SCHOLD HOLDINGS INC
7201 W 64th Pl (60638-4639)
PHONE...................708 458-3788
Jerome P Tippett, *Ch of Bd*
Mike Barr, *Engineer*
Karen Varnes, *Admin Sec*
EMP: 20
SQ FT: 35,000
SALES (est): 5.3MM **Privately Held**
WEB: www.schold.com
SIC: 3599 Machine shop, jobbing & repair

(G-6115)
SCHULZE AND BURCH BISCUIT CO (PA)
1133 W 35th St (60609-1485)
PHONE...................773 927-6622
Kevin M Boyle, *President*
Fabian Guerra, *Vice Pres*
David Hensler, *Vice Pres*
James McBride, *Vice Pres*
Steve Podracky, *Vice Pres*
▲ **EMP:** 277
SQ FT: 400,000
SALES (est): 111.6MM **Privately Held**
WEB: www.schulzeburch.com
SIC: 2051 2052 2099 Bread, cake & related products; cookies & crackers; food preparations

(G-6116)
SCIAKY INC
4915 W 67th St (60638-6408)
PHONE...................708 594-3841
Scott Phillips, *CEO*
William S Phillips, *President*
Alex Sopko, *Purchasing*
Ken Lachenberg, *Engineer*
Antone Long, *Engineer*
EMP: 50
SQ FT: 155,000
SALES (est): 12.8MM
SALES (corp-wide): 67.8MM **Privately Held**
SIC: 3699 Electron beam metal cutting, forming or welding machines; laser welding, drilling & cutting equipment
PA: Phillips Service Industries, Inc.
14492 N Sheldon Rd # 300
Plymouth MI 48170
734 853-5000

(G-6117)
SCIBOR UPHOLSTERING & GALLERY
12210 S Harlem Ave (60643)
PHONE...................708 671-9700
Yvonne Scibor, *President*
EMP: 3
SQ FT: 3,700
SALES (est): 309.5K **Privately Held**
SIC: 5712 7641 2512 Custom made furniture, except cabinets; reupholstery; upholstered household furniture

(G-6118)
SCIENCE SOLUTIONS LLC (PA)
5000 W Roosevelt Rd Dock29 (60644-1789)
PHONE...................773 261-1197
Manjit Singh, *Mng Member*
Greg Rubin,
EMP: 4
SALES (est): 628K **Privately Held**
SIC: 2842 Cleaning or polishing preparations

(G-6119)
SCORPION GRAPHICS INC
3221 W 36th St (60632-2701)
PHONE...................773 927-3203
Maria Collins, *President*
Richard Collins, *Vice Pres*
EMP: 14 **EST:** 1995
SQ FT: 4,000
SALES (est): 1.7MM **Privately Held**
WEB: www.tshirtexperts.com
SIC: 2759 Screen printing

(G-6120)
SCOTT JANCZAK
Also Called: Blaz Cartage
6285 N Knox Ave (60646-5032)
PHONE...................773 545-7233
Scott Janczak, *Owner*
EMP: 8 **EST:** 1999
SALES (est): 667.6K **Privately Held**
SIC: 3537 Trucks, tractors, loaders, carriers & similar equipment

(G-6121)
SCOTTS POPCORN LLC
Also Called: Scott's Popcorn & Company
7129 S Euclid Ave Apt 2 (60649-2438)
PHONE...................773 608-9625
Scott Chapman,
EMP: 1
SALES: 300K **Privately Held**
SIC: 2096 7389 Popcorn, already popped (except candy covered);

(G-6122)
SCREW MACHINE ENGRG CO INC
6425 N Avondale Ave (60631-1998)
PHONE...................773 631-7600
Richard C Baumgart, *President*
EMP: 45 **EST:** 1937
SQ FT: 22,000
SALES (est): 9MM **Privately Held**
WEB: www.smeco-inc.com
SIC: 3451 Screw machine products

(G-6123)
SDR CORP
Also Called: Stuart Hale Company
4350 W Ohio St (60624-1051)
PHONE...................773 638-1800
Dave Schulman, *President*
Stuart Schulman, *Treasurer*
Rochelle Schulman, *Admin Sec*
▲ **EMP:** 4
SQ FT: 9,375
SALES (est): 798.5K **Privately Held**
WEB: www.stuarthale.com
SIC: 2099 2077 Food preparations; animal & marine fats & oils

(G-6124)
SEA-RICH CORP
Also Called: American Cotton Products Div
5000 W Roosevelt Rd # 104 (60644-1474)
PHONE...................773 261-6633
Fax: 773 533-0226
EMP: 8
SQ FT: 17,000
SALES: 750K **Privately Held**
SIC: 5199 2211 5113 2221 Whol Nondurable Goods Brdwv Fabric Mill Whol Indstl/Svc Paper Manmad Brdwv Fabric Mill

(G-6125)
SEADOG
1500 W Division St (60642-3344)
PHONE...................773 235-8100
Sompol Chaosaowapa, *President*
EMP: 4 **EST:** 2010
SALES (est): 395.5K **Privately Held**
SIC: 3421 Table & food cutlery, including butchers'

(G-6126)
SEAMCRAFT INTERNATIONAL LLC
5610 W Bloomingdale Ave # 4 (60639-4113)
PHONE...................773 281-5150
Ed Kuhr, *Exec VP*
Iriss Blaine, *Office Mgr*
Edward Kuhr, *Mng Member*
Richard Lefauve Jr,
Darek Mecinski,
▼ **EMP:** 22
SALES (est): 1.2MM **Privately Held**
SIC: 2399 3161 2394 Emblems, badges & insignia; sample cases; liners & covers, fabric: made from purchased materials

(G-6127)
SECOND CITY FLOORING LLC
365 N Jefferson St # 2911 (60661-1226)
PHONE...................973 262-3272
Thomas Maloney,
EMP: 6
SALES (est): 538.4K **Privately Held**
SIC: 2426 Flooring, hardwood

(G-6128)
SECURESLICE INC
6300 N Rockwell St (60659-1838)
PHONE...................800 984-0494
Ismail Mohammed, *Exec Dir*
EMP: 50 **EST:** 2012
SALES (est): 1.7MM **Privately Held**
SIC: 7379 7372 Computer data escrow service; ; business oriented computer software

(G-6129)
SEDIA SYSTEMS INC (PA)
1820 W Hubbard St Ste 300 (60622-6290)
PHONE...................312 212-8010
Wilson Troup III, *President*
Ken Avery, *Sales Mgr*
▲ **EMP:** 9
SQ FT: 3,500
SALES (est): 3.3MM **Privately Held**
SIC: 2531 Public building & related furniture

(G-6130)
SEE ALL INDUSTRIES INC (PA)
3623 S Laflin Pl (60609-1397)
PHONE...................773 927-3232
Carmela Celenza, *President*
Jer Cel, *General Mgr*
Gerald Celenza, *Treasurer*
Joseph Celenza Jr, *Admin Sec*
▲ **EMP:** 16
SQ FT: 30,000
SALES: 4MM **Privately Held**
SIC: 3231 Mirrored glass

(G-6131)
SEE WHAT YOU SEND INC
727 S Dearborn St Apt 912 (60605-3828)
PHONE...................781 780-1483
Chris Stacey, *President*
Salvatore Migliaccio, *Treasurer*
EMP: 3
SALES (est): 131.4K **Privately Held**
SIC: 7372 7389 Application computer software;

(G-6132)
SEEC TRASPORTATION CORP
190 S Lasalle Ste 2100 (60603)
PHONE...................800 215-4003
Sabrina Chambers, *President*
EMP: 4
SQ FT: 965
SALES (est): 164.7K **Privately Held**
SIC: 3743 Train cars & equipment, freight or passenger

(G-6133)
SELECT SNACKS COMPANY INC
825 E 99th St (60628-1526)
PHONE...................773 933-2167
EMP: 75
SALES (est): 4MM **Privately Held**
SIC: 2096 5145 Mfg Potato Chips/Snacks Whol Confectionery

(G-6134)
SELF PRO MOTIONS LLC
448 E 134th St (60827-1870)
PHONE...................847 749-6077
Earle Chisolm-El, *Mng Member*
EMP: 3
SQ FT: 1,000
SALES: 78K **Privately Held**
WEB: www.spm.life
SIC: 2759 7311 Screen printing; advertising agencies

(G-6135)
SENSIBLE PRODUCTS INC
7290 W Devon Ave (60631-1620)
P.O. Box 31695 (60631-0695)
PHONE...................773 774-7400
Michael G Rubino, *President*
▲ **EMP:** 5
SQ FT: 2,000
SALES (est): 600K **Privately Held**
SIC: 3545 Machine tool accessories

(G-6136)
SENSUS LLC
Also Called: Sensus Wine
1435 W Arthur Ave Ste B (60626-5909)
PHONE...................312 379-9463
Lee Shaffer, *Manager*
EMP: 4
SALES (est): 190.9K **Privately Held**
SIC: 2084 Wines

(G-6137)
SERIOUS ENERGY INC
1333 N Hickory Ave (60642-2433)
PHONE...................312 515-4606
EMP: 48
SALES (corp-wide): 12.6MM **Privately Held**
SIC: 2531 Public building & related furniture
PA: Serious Energy, Inc.
1250 Elko Dr
Sunnyvale CA 94089
408 541-8000

(G-6138)
SERLIN IRON & METAL CO INC
1810 N Kilbourn Ave (60639-5107)
PHONE...................773 227-3826
Mark Kalter, *President*
Mitch Kalter, *Vice Pres*
Evelyn Kalter, *Admin Sec*
EMP: 15 **EST:** 1892
SQ FT: 32,500
SALES (est): 3.8MM **Privately Held**
WEB: www.serlinironmetals.com
SIC: 5093 3341 Ferrous metal scrap & waste; secondary nonferrous metals

(G-6139)
SERRALA SOLUTIONS US CORP (PA)
Also Called: Dolphin
205 N Michigan Ave # 4110 (60601-5925)
PHONE...................650 655-3939
Werner Hopf, *President*
Stefan Freyer, *COO*
Jaime Ryan, *Senior VP*
Dirk Schilling, *CFO*
Stephan Benkendorf, *Officer*
EMP: 4
SALES (est): 12.3MM **Privately Held**
WEB: www.dolphin-corp.com
SIC: 7372 5045 Application computer software; computers, peripherals & software

(G-6140)
SERVI-SURE CORPORATION
2020 W Rascher Ave (60625-1004)
PHONE...................773 271-5900
Jon Rosner, *President*
Ronald Mann, *Vice Pres*
Jose Santacruz, *Research*
Mike Wolfer, *Engineer*
EMP: 24 **EST:** 1959
SALES (est): 3.7MM **Privately Held**
SIC: 2796 Platemaking services

Chicago - Cook County (G-6141)   GEOGRAPHIC SECTION

(G-6141)
SERVICE & MANUFACTURING CORP
5414c W Roosevelt Rd C (60644-1467)
PHONE..................773 287-5500
Camerina Torres, *President*
EMP: 26
SALES: 1,000K **Privately Held**
SIC: 3161 Sample cases

(G-6142)
SERVICE CUTTING & WELDING
2911 N Moody Ave (60634-5027)
PHONE..................773 622-8366
Peter Harris, *Owner*
EMP: 3
SALES (est): 60K **Privately Held**
SIC: 7692 7699 Welding repair; industrial machinery & equipment repair

(G-6143)
SERVICE SHEET METAL WORKS INC
5000 W 73rd St (60638-6612)
PHONE..................773 229-0031
Todd Carmichael, *President*
Roger Wolf, *Vice Pres*
EMP: 14 EST: 1945
SQ FT: 15,000
SALES (est): 2.1MM **Privately Held**
WEB: www.servicemetalworks.com
SIC: 3444 3312 7692 3993 Sheet metalwork; pipes & tubes; welding repair; signs & advertising specialties; fabricated pipe & fittings; metal stampings

(G-6144)
SFC CHEMICALS LTD
1031 W Bryn Mawr Ave 1a (60660-4658)
P.O. Box 3966, Barrington (60011-3966)
PHONE..................847 221-2152
Shyam R Zalani,
EMP: 3
SALES: 15MM **Privately Held**
SIC: 2834 Druggists' preparations (pharmaceuticals)

(G-6145)
SHADE BROOKLINE CO
Also Called: Aberdeen Window Shade Service
6246 N Broadway St (60660-1903)
PHONE..................773 274-5513
John Licthfess, *President*
Ronald J Silverman, *Vice Pres*
Jerry Lichtfuss, *Treasurer*
EMP: 13 EST: 1924
SQ FT: 2,000
SALES (est): 1MM **Privately Held**
WEB: www.brooklineshade.com
SIC: 2591 2391 7699 Window shades; venetian blinds; draperies, plastic & textile: from purchased materials; window blind repair services

(G-6146)
SHADEMAKER PRODUCTS CORP
7300 S Kimbark Ave (60619-1430)
P.O. Box 5271, Buffalo Grove (60089-5271)
PHONE..................773 955-0998
Sidney M Levin, *CEO*
EMP: 7
SQ FT: 25,000
SALES: 100K **Privately Held**
SIC: 3444 Awnings, sheet metal

(G-6147)
SHARLEN ELECTRIC CO (PA)
9101 S Baltimore Ave (60617-4417)
P.O. Box 17597 (60617-0597)
PHONE..................773 721-0700
William Cullen, *President*
Jim Cullen, *Vice Pres*
Ken Genovese, *Sales Staff*
Tom Denton, *Telecomm Mgr*
EMP: 50
SQ FT: 75,000
SALES (est): 17.5MM **Privately Held**
SIC: 1731 3498 General electrical contractor; tube fabricating (contract bending & shaping)

(G-6148)
SHARPRINT SLKSCRN & GRPHCS
Also Called: Sharprint Promotional Apparel
4200 W Wrightwood Ave (60639-2023)
PHONE..................877 649-2554
George Kilian, *President*
Maureen Alfonso, *CFO*
Jordan Frank, *Sales Staff*
Stephanie Larios, *Sales Staff*
Jeff Driskill, *Art Dir*
EMP: 65
SQ FT: 40,000
SALES (est): 10MM **Privately Held**
SIC: 2759 Screen printing

(G-6149)
SHAW INDUSTRIES GROUP INC
Also Called: Shaw Contract Group
222 Merchandise Mart Plz (60654-1103)
PHONE..................312 467-1331
Greg Klaus, *Principal*
EMP: 7
SALES (corp-wide): 327.2B **Publicly Held**
SIC: 2273 Carpets & rugs
HQ: Shaw Industries Group, Inc.
    616 E Walnut Ave
    Dalton GA 30721
    800 446-9332

(G-6150)
SHAWNIMALS LLC
2825 W Wellington Ave 1 (60618-7013)
PHONE..................312 235-2625
Shawn Smith, *Manager*
EMP: 4
SQ FT: 1,400
SALES (est): 288.1K **Privately Held**
SIC: 3942 Stuffed toys, including animals

(G-6151)
SHELTER SYSTEMS
3729 N Ravenswood Ave (60613-3590)
PHONE..................773 281-9270
John Jameson, *Owner*
EMP: 3
SQ FT: 1,500
SALES: 225K **Privately Held**
SIC: 2394 Canopies, fabric: made from purchased materials

(G-6152)
SHERWIN-WILLIAMS COMPANY
11700 S Cottage Grove Ave (60628-5724)
PHONE..................773 821-3027
Dennis Stevens, *Opers-Prdtn-Mfg*
EMP: 86
SALES (corp-wide): 17.9B **Publicly Held**
SIC: 5231 5198 2851 Paint; paints, varnishes & supplies; paints & paint additives
PA: The Sherwin-Williams Company
    101 W Prospect Ave # 1020
    Cleveland OH 44115
    216 566-2000

(G-6153)
SHIIR LLC
Also Called: Shiir Rugs
208 W Kinzie St Ste 5 (60654-4911)
PHONE..................312 828-0400
Oscar Tatosian,
Shea Soucie,
EMP: 10
SALES (est): 120.8K **Privately Held**
SIC: 2273 2392 Carpets & rugs; linings, carpet: textile, except felt

(G-6154)
SHIPBOB INC
1260 W Madison St (60607-1933)
PHONE..................217 819-8539
Disha Sekhri, *Principal*
Jon Jobb, *Business Mgr*
Divey Gulati, *COO*
Todd Bills, *Vice Pres*
Jivko Bojinov, *Vice Pres*
EMP: 301
SALES (corp-wide): 3.8MM **Privately Held**
SIC: 7372 Prepackaged software
PA: Shipbob, Inc.
    120 N Racine Ave Ste 100
    Chicago IL 60607
    844 474-4726

(G-6155)
SHIPBOB INC (PA)
120 N Racine Ave Ste 100 (60607-2082)
PHONE..................844 474-4726
Dhruv Saxena, *CEO*
Connell O'Brien, *Business Mgr*
Ariana Chen, *Opers Staff*
Conor Callanan, *Accounts Exec*
Pete Cashen, *Accounts Exec*
EMP: 10
SALES (est): 3.8MM **Privately Held**
SIC: 7372 Prepackaged software

(G-6156)
SHOPPERTRAK RCT CORPORATION (DH)
233 S Wacker Dr Fl 41 (60606-7147)
PHONE..................312 529-5300
Christopher Ainsley, *President*
Bill Martin, *Exec VP*
Kurt Phillips, *CFO*
EMP: 17
SQ FT: 40,000
SALES (est): 45.8MM **Privately Held**
SIC: 7371 3824 Computer software development & applications; mechanical & electromechanical counters & devices
HQ: Sensormatic Electronics, Llc
    6600 Congress Ave
    Boca Raton FL 33487
    561 912-6000

(G-6157)
SHORE CAPITAL PARTNERS LLC (PA)
1 E Wacker Dr Ste 2900 (60601-2026)
PHONE..................312 348-7580
Justin Ishbia, *Partner*
John Hennegan, *Partner*
Cameron Perkins, *Partner*
Jeff Williams, *COO*
Sarah Hirsch, *Vice Pres*
EMP: 21
SALES (est): 56.1MM **Privately Held**
WEB: www.shorecp.com
SIC: 6799 3069 Investors; medical & laboratory rubber sundries & related products

(G-6158)
SHOWCASE CORPORATION (PA)
233 S Wacker Dr Ste 5150 (60606-6371)
PHONE..................312 651-3000
EMP: 160
SQ FT: 9,000
SALES (est): 20.4MM **Privately Held**
SIC: 7372 7371 Prepackaged Software Services Custom Computer Programing

(G-6159)
SHREE MAHAVIR INC
Also Called: Print Express
311 S Wacker Dr Ste 4550 (60606-6622)
PHONE..................312 408-1080
Kishore Kuvadia, *President*
Tina Kuvadia, *Admin Sec*
▼ EMP: 5
SQ FT: 1,500
SALES (est): 615.7K **Privately Held**
SIC: 2752 2791 2789 2759 Commercial printing, offset; typesetting; bookbinding & related work; commercial printing; automotive & apparel trimmings

(G-6160)
SHREE PRINTING CORP
3011 W Irving Park Rd (60618-3513)
PHONE..................773 267-9500
Jagdish Suthar, *President*
Manju J Suthar, *Vice Pres*
Manish Suthar, *Manager*
Himan Suther, *Manager*
EMP: 2
SQ FT: 4,000
SALES (est): 307.9K **Privately Held**
SIC: 2752 7334 7336 2791 Commercial printing, offset; photocopying & duplicating services; commercial art & graphic design; typesetting; bookbinding & related work

(G-6161)
SHUFFLE TECH INTERNATIONAL LLC
1440 N Kingsbury St # 218 (60642-2690)
PHONE..................312 787-7780
Rick Schultz, *CEO*
Richard J Schultz, *Mng Member*
EMP: 3
SQ FT: 2,000
SALES: 1MM **Privately Held**
SIC: 3949 Shuffleboards & shuffleboard equipment

(G-6162)
SHURE PRODUCTS INC
Also Called: T.S. Shure
4529 N Ravenswood Ave (60640-5201)
PHONE..................773 227-1001
Thomas Shure, *President*
Doug Sissom, *Vice Pres*
Maggie Morgan, *Mktg Dir*
◆ EMP: 13
SALES (est): 3.3MM **Privately Held**
SIC: 3944 2731 Games, toys & children's vehicles; book publishing

(G-6163)
SIEDEN STICKER USA LTD
1506 W Grand Ave Apt 3e (60642-7525)
PHONE..................312 280-7711
Alice Heredia, *Vice Pres*
EMP: 5
SALES (est): 310K **Privately Held**
SIC: 2389 Men's miscellaneous accessories

(G-6164)
SIGENICS INC (PA)
3440 S Dearborn St 126s (60616-5074)
PHONE..................312 448-8000
Philip R Troyk, *President*
Douglas A Kerns, *Principal*
Glenn A Demichele, *Admin Sec*
EMP: 10
SQ FT: 3,441
SALES: 2.2MM **Privately Held**
SIC: 3674 8711 8731 Wafers (semiconductor devices); engineering services; biotechnical research, commercial

(G-6165)
SIGN AMERICA INC
Also Called: America International Dist
2748 W Devon Ave (60659-1711)
PHONE..................773 262-7800
Muhammed Rameez, *President*
Salim Shariff, *Owner*
Loretta Miller, *Sales Staff*
EMP: 4
SALES (est): 402.8K **Privately Held**
WEB: www.signamerica.co
SIC: 3993 Signs, not made in custom sign painting shops

(G-6166)
SIGN-A-RAMA
1513 S State St (60605-2804)
PHONE..................312 922-0509
Aleda Goodwin, *President*
Cornelius Goodwin, *Admin Sec*
Cornelius A Goodwin, *Admin Sec*
EMP: 3
SALES (est): 327.6K **Privately Held**
SIC: 3993 Signs & advertising specialties

(G-6167)
SIGNAL DIGITAL INC (PA)
222 N La Salle St # 1600 (60601-1112)
PHONE..................312 685-1911
Michael Sands, *President*
Patrick Venetucci, *COO*
Cassi Barron, *Counsel*
Ana Milicevic, *Senior VP*
Blane Sims, *Senior VP*
EMP: 42
SALES (est): 27.5MM **Privately Held**
WEB: www.signal.co
SIC: 7372 Application computer software

(G-6168)
SIGNATURE DESIGN & TAILORING
8027 S Stony Island Ave (60617-1747)
PHONE..................773 375-4915
Valencio Hinton, *Owner*
EMP: 15 EST: 1997
SALES: 420K **Privately Held**
SIC: 2311 5611 5621 Jackets, tailored suit-type: men's & boys'; men's & boys' clothing stores; women's clothing stores

▲ = Import ▼=Export
◆ =Import/Export

GEOGRAPHIC SECTION
Chicago - Cook County (G-6198)

(G-6169)
SIGNATURE SCREEN PRINTING CORP
Also Called: Autograph
3508 N Elston Ave (60618-5618)
PHONE.................................773 866-0070
Dana Kessler, *President*
Dina Kessler, *President*
EMP: 7
SQ FT: 7,900
SALES (est): 596.2K **Privately Held**
SIC: 7336 7389 3993 2396 Silk screen design; film strip, slide & still film production; lettering service; signs & advertising specialties; automotive & apparel trimmings

(G-6170)
SIGNS NOW
2525 N Hutchinson St (60618-1503)
PHONE.................................800 356-3373
Michele Kunze, *Owner*
EMP: 4
SQ FT: 1,200
SALES (est): 286.5K **Privately Held**
SIC: 3993 Signs & advertising specialties

(G-6171)
SILVER BELL CNSTR & FURN INC
1500 S Western Ave (60608-1828)
PHONE.................................773 578-9450
Yura Hrudzevych, *President*
Paul P Matwyshyn, *Principal*
EMP: 2
SALES (est): 227.9K **Privately Held**
SIC: 2434 2511 2517 Wood kitchen cabinets; wood household furniture; wood television & radio cabinets

(G-6172)
SIM PARTNERS (HQ)
141 W Jackson Blvd # 1850 (60604-3379)
PHONE.................................800 260-3380
Jon Schepke, *CEO*
Adam Dorfman, *Vice Pres*
Emily Helander, *Marketing Staff*
Xucheng Miao, *Software Dev*
Krishna Patibanda, *Software Dev*
EMP: 35
SQ FT: 5,000
SALES: 5MM **Privately Held**
SIC: 2741

(G-6173)
SIMON GLOBAL SERVICES LLC
5655 N Clark St Ste 5 (60660-4038)
PHONE.................................773 334-7794
Gabriel Bedoya, *Principal*
EMP: 4
SALES (est): 290K **Privately Held**
SIC: 2741 Miscellaneous publishing

(G-6174)
SIMPLE MILLS INC
435 N Lasalle St Fl 2 Flr 2 (60654)
PHONE.................................312 600-6196
Katlin Smith, *CEO*
Nicole Eltzroth, *Vice Pres*
Emily Lafferty, *Manager*
EMP: 45
SQ FT: 10,000
SALES (est): 20.4MM **Privately Held**
SIC: 2099 Food preparations

(G-6175)
SINGER SAFETY COMPANY
Also Called: UNI-Glide
2300 N Kilbourn Ave (60639-3402)
PHONE.................................773 235-2100
Brian Johnson, *President*
Anna Marie Johnson, *Vice Pres*
Tom Kiolbassa, *Controller*
John Scara, *Sales Staff*
James Dicicco, *Manager*
EMP: 17 **EST:** 1950
SQ FT: 36,000
SALES (est): 5MM
SALES (corp-wide): 6.1MM **Privately Held**
WEB: www.singersafety.com
SIC: 3448 Screen enclosures

PA: Rensel-Chicago, Inc.
2300 N Kilbourn Ave
Chicago IL 60639
773 235-2100

(G-6176)
SIPI METALS CORP (PA)
1720 N Elston Ave (60642-1532)
PHONE.................................773 276-0070
Marion A Cameron, *President*
Len Stack, *Exec VP*
Robert S Glidden, *Senior VP*
Joris Coopmans, *Vice Pres*
Kelly M Coyle, *Vice Pres*
▲ **EMP:** 120 **EST:** 1905
SQ FT: 200,000
SALES (est): 28.5MM **Privately Held**
WEB: www.sipimetals.com
SIC: 3339 3341 Gold refining (primary); platinum group metal refining (primary); silver refining (primary); brass smelting & refining (secondary); copper smelting & refining (secondary); zinc smelting & refining (secondary)

(G-6177)
SIR SPEEDY PRINTING
1711 N Clybourn Ave (60614-5519)
PHONE.................................312 337-0774
George Lesniak, *President*
Brian Erickson, *Vice Pres*
EMP: 4
SALES (est): 506K **Privately Held**
SIC: 2752 2791 2789 Commercial printing, lithographic; typesetting; bookbinding & related work

(G-6178)
SIX OAKS COMPANY
2033 W 108th Pl (60643-3304)
PHONE.................................312 343-4037
Michael P Walsh, *President*
EMP: 3
SALES: 500K **Privately Held**
SIC: 3559 Special industry machinery

(G-6179)
SKENDER CONSTRUCTION LLC
1330 W Fulton St Ste 200 (60607-1137)
PHONE.................................312 781-0265
Tony Fontanetta, *Superintendent*
Tom Herman, *Superintendent*
Mike Hester, *Superintendent*
John Kozielek, *Superintendent*
Jamie Stewart, *Superintendent*
EMP: 100
SQ FT: 17,000
SALES (est): 12.7MM **Privately Held**
SIC: 1542 2451 Commercial & office building, new construction; commercial & office buildings, renovation & repair; mobile homes, industrial or commercial use

(G-6180)
SKILLED PLATING CORP
151618 N Kilpatrick Ave (60651)
PHONE.................................773 227-0262
Gary Weincouff, *President*
Dawna Maggard, *Vice Pres*
EMP: 6 **EST:** 1965
SQ FT: 8,300
SALES (est): 500K **Privately Held**
WEB: www.skildplatingcorp.com
SIC: 3471 Electroplating of metals or formed products; finishing, metals or formed products

(G-6181)
SKOL MFG CO
4444 N Ravenswood Ave (60640-5803)
PHONE.................................773 878-5959
Raymond Skolorzynski, *President*
Junanita Skolorzynski, *CFO*
Juanita Figueroa, *Payroll Mgr*
EMP: 20 **EST:** 1943
SQ FT: 20,000
SALES (est): 5.1MM **Privately Held**
WEB: www.skolmfg.com
SIC: 3444 Sheet metalwork

(G-6182)
SKW INDUSTRIES LLC
Also Called: Progressive Coating
900 S Cicero Ave (60644-5213)
PHONE.................................773 261-8900
Stephen K Walters,
EMP: 15
SALES (est): 1.2MM **Privately Held**
SIC: 3479 Coating of metals & formed products

(G-6183)
SKYBITZ TANK MONITORING CORP
Also Called: Tanklink Corporation
200 S Wacker Dr Ste 1800 (60606-5911)
PHONE.................................312 379-8397
John Crump, *President*
EMP: 20
SQ FT: 7,017
SALES (est): 2.5MM
SALES (corp-wide): 5.1B **Publicly Held**
SIC: 3663 Cellular radio telephone
HQ: Telular Corporation
200 S Wacker Dr Ste 1800
Chicago IL 60606

(G-6184)
SKYLINE DESIGN INC
1240 N Homan Ave Ste 1 (60651-4202)
PHONE.................................773 278-4660
Charles Rizzo, *President*
Nick Corriero, *Vice Pres*
◆ **EMP:** 85 **EST:** 1982
SQ FT: 120,000
SALES (est): 16.3MM **Privately Held**
SIC: 3231 Novelties, glass: fruit, foliage, flowers, animals, etc.; furniture tops, glass: cut, beveled or polished; art glass: made from purchased glass

(G-6185)
SKYWAY CEMENT COMPANY LLC (PA)
3020 E 103rd St (60617-5809)
PHONE.................................800 643-1808
Wayne Emmer, *Principal*
Andrew Hixson, *Plant Mgr*
EMP: 28
SALES (est): 6MM **Privately Held**
SIC: 3241 Masonry cement

(G-6186)
SLEEP6 LLC
1332 N Halsted St (60642-2624)
PHONE.................................844 375-3376
Robert Taglianetti,
EMP: 4
SALES (est): 140.1K **Privately Held**
SIC: 2394 Air cushions & mattresses, canvas

(G-6187)
SLEEPECK PRINTING COMPANY
70 W Madison St Ste 2300 (60602-4250)
PHONE.................................708 544-8900
EMP: 200 **EST:** 1904
SQ FT: 100,000
SALES (est): 26MM **Privately Held**
SIC: 2752 Lithographic Commercial Printing

(G-6188)
SLEEPY WOODWORKS
10644 S Drake Ave (60655-2506)
PHONE.................................773 779-2990
William Morrin, *Principal*
EMP: 3
SALES (est): 197.8K **Privately Held**
SIC: 2431 Millwork

(G-6189)
SLIDEMATIC PRODUCTS CO
4520 W Addison St (60641-3814)
PHONE.................................773 545-4213
Mark Magnuson, *President*
Maia Dyke, *Engineer*
Mike Kalajian, *Engineer*
Marino Petropoulos, *CFO*
David L Magnuson, *Admin Sec*
EMP: 27 **EST:** 2006
SALES (est): 7.5MM **Privately Held**
WEB: www.slidematicproducts.com
SIC: 3469 Stamping metal for the trade

(G-6190)
SMART OFFICE SERVICES INC
3720 W Chicago Ave (60651-3820)
P.O. Box 97 (60690-0097)
PHONE.................................773 227-1121
EMP: 5

SALES (est): 490K **Privately Held**
SIC: 2752 7334 Lithographic Commercial Printing Photocopying Services

(G-6191)
SMH2 MANUFACTURING LLC
2021 W Fulton St K-215 (60612-2367)
PHONE.................................773 793-6643
Stephen A Martin, *Mng Member*
Herbert Henderson,
John Meyer,
EMP: 7 **EST:** 2015
SALES (est): 90.9K **Privately Held**
SIC: 2038 Ethnic foods, frozen

(G-6192)
SMILE LEE FACES
4197 S Archer Ave (60632-1849)
PHONE.................................773 376-9999
Andrea Lacayo, *Principal*
EMP: 4
SALES (est): 404.1K **Privately Held**
SIC: 3843 Enamels, dentists'

(G-6193)
SMITH POWER TRANSMISSION CO
5335 S Western Blvd Ste C (60609-5450)
PHONE.................................773 526-5512
Robert Smith, *President*
EMP: 3
SQ FT: 2,000
SALES (est): 652.2K **Privately Held**
SIC: 3569 5085 Filters; gears

(G-6194)
SNAIDERO USA
222 Mrchnds Mrt Pl 140 (60654)
PHONE.................................312 644-6662
Erika Klimenko, *Branch Mgr*
EMP: 3
SALES (corp-wide): 8.5MM **Privately Held**
SIC: 2434 Wood kitchen cabinets
PA: Snaidero U.S.A.
19700 S Vt Ave Ste 100
Torrance CA 90502
310 516-8499

(G-6195)
SNOWBALL INDUSTRIES
3404 N Harding Ave (60618-5136)
PHONE.................................773 316-0051
EMP: 3
SALES (est): 97.7K **Privately Held**
SIC: 3999 Mfg Misc Products

(G-6196)
SOCK OBSESSED
345 E Ohio St Apt 403 (60611-3970)
PHONE.................................847 920-4834
Christian Ricci, *Principal*
EMP: 5
SALES (est): 107.4K **Privately Held**
SIC: 2252 Socks

(G-6197)
SOLO CUP OPERATING CORPORATION
7575 S Kostner Ave Ste 3 (60652-1151)
PHONE.................................773 767-3300
Jim Shine, *Facilities Mgr*
Robert Dusich, *QA Dir*
Glen Ohlerking, *Engineer*
Vernon Scholl, *Engineer*
Greg Baugh, *Sales Staff*
EMP: 150
SALES (corp-wide): 965.8MM **Privately Held**
SIC: 3089 3421 Cups, plastic, except foam; cutlery
HQ: Solo Cup Operating Corporation
500 Hogsback Rd
Mason MI 48854
800 248-5960

(G-6198)
SOLOINSIGHT INC
Also Called: R&D Lab
1260 W Madison St (60607-1933)
PHONE.................................312 846-6729
EMP: 18
SALES (corp-wide): 2.7MM **Privately Held**
SIC: 7372 Application computer software

Chicago - Cook County (G-6199)

PA: Soloinsight Inc.
29 N Wacker Dr Ste 1000
Chicago IL 60606
773 354-6776

(G-6199)
SOLUTION 3 GRAPHICS INC
10547 S Western Ave (60643-2592)
PHONE.................................773 233-3600
George Herzog, *President*
Charles Bennett, *Foreman/Supr*
Art Hoover, *Sales Staff*
Charlene Herzog, *Admin Sec*
EMP: 14 **EST:** 1966
SQ FT: 10,000
SALES (est): 2.2MM **Privately Held**
WEB: www.solution3graphics.com
SIC: 2752 Commercial printing, offset

(G-6200)
SOLVAY FINANCE (AMERICA) LLC
23424 Network Pl (60673-1234)
PHONE.................................713 525-6000
EMP: 16
SALES (est): 2MM **Privately Held**
SIC: 2819 Industrial inorganic chemicals

(G-6201)
SOMMERS & FAHRENBACH INC
3301 W Belmont Ave (60618-5578)
PHONE.................................773 478-3033
Thomas M Sommers, *President*
Robert Walsh, *Treasurer*
Joseph Prieboy, *Office Mgr*
Dan Sommers, *Technology*
EMP: 11 **EST:** 1919
SQ FT: 8,000
SALES: 2MM **Privately Held**
WEB: www.sfprinting.net
SIC: 2752 2791 2789 7336 Commercial printing, offset; typesetting; bookbinding & related work; graphic arts & related design; printing presses

(G-6202)
SONOCO PRTECTIVE SOLUTIONS INC
91218 Collection Ctr Dr (60693-0912)
PHONE.................................717 757-2683
EMP: 16
SALES (corp-wide): 5.3B **Publicly Held**
SIC: 3086 Packaging & shipping materials, foamed plastic
HQ: Sonoco Protective Solutions, Inc.
1 N 2nd St
Hartsville SC 29550
843 383-7000

(G-6203)
SORINI MANUFACTURING CORP
Also Called: Sorini Ring
2524 S Blue Island Ave (60608-4934)
PHONE.................................773 247-5858
Peter M May, *President*
Peter May Jr, *Vice Pres*
Pauline May, *Admin Sec*
▲ **EMP:** 27 **EST:** 1963
SQ FT: 40,000
SALES (est): 8MM **Privately Held**
WEB: www.soriniring.com
SIC: 3466 Closures, stamped metal

(G-6204)
SOUDAN METALS COMPANY INC (PA)
Also Called: Steel Fab & Finish
319 W 40th Pl (60609-2816)
P.O. Box 9044 (60609-0044)
PHONE.................................773 548-7600
Thomas A Soudan Sr, *CEO*
Thomas L Soudan Jr, *President*
Marion Cameron, *CFO*
Elie Aravelo, *Human Res Dir*
Brian Aubin, *Sales Staff*
EMP: 115
SQ FT: 105,000
SALES (est): 31.7MM **Privately Held**
SIC: 5051 3316 Steel; cold finishing of steel shapes

(G-6205)
SOUL TRAINING PROGRAM INC
903 S Ashland Ave # 1108 (60607-4002)
PHONE.................................312 725-9768
Andrea McNeil, *President*
EMP: 1
SALES: 500K **Privately Held**
SIC: 2835 Microbiology & virology diagnostic products

(G-6206)
SOUTH CHICAGO PACKING LLC
945 W 38th St (60609)
PHONE.................................708 589-2400
David J Miniat, *President*
EMP: 100
SALES (corp-wide): 397.8MM **Privately Held**
SIC: 2079 2077 Compound shortenings; rendering
HQ: South Chicago Packing Llc
16250 Vincennes Ave
South Holland IL 60473
708 589-2400

(G-6207)
SOUTHWEST SIGNS INC
5641 W 63rd St (60638-5513)
PHONE.................................773 585-3530
Charles Wilmarth, *President*
Daniel Kamba, *Vice Pres*
EMP: 3
SQ FT: 2,300
SALES (est): 317.5K **Privately Held**
SIC: 3993 Signs & advertising specialties

(G-6208)
SPARRER SAUSAGE COMPANY INC
Also Called: El Campeon Food Products
4325 W Ogden Ave (60623-2925)
PHONE.................................773 762-3334
Brian Graves, *President*
EMP: 120
SQ FT: 49,800
SALES (est): 16.9MM **Privately Held**
WEB: www.sparrers.com
SIC: 2013 Smoked meats from purchased meat; sausages from purchased meat

(G-6209)
SPARROW SOUND DESIGN
Also Called: Southport Records
3501 N Southport Ave (60657-1475)
PHONE.................................773 281-8510
Bradley Parker, *Partner*
Joanie Pallatto, *Partner*
EMP: 5
SQ FT: 2,300
SALES: 7.8K **Privately Held**
SIC: 3652 Pre-recorded records & tapes

(G-6210)
SPARTAN SHEET METAL INC
3006 W Bryn Mawr Ave (60659-3725)
PHONE.................................773 895-7266
George Sinodinos, *President*
EMP: 2
SALES (est): 306.3K **Privately Held**
SIC: 3444 Sheet metalwork

(G-6211)
SPD PRESS PRTG SOLUTIONS LLC
1444 W 37th Ave (60609-2112)
PHONE.................................773 299-1700
Zabala Daniel Ceasar, *Principal*
EMP: 3
SALES (est): 101.5K **Privately Held**
SIC: 2752 Commercial printing, offset

(G-6212)
SPECIAL TOOL ENGINEERING CO
4539 S Knox Ave (60632-4892)
PHONE.................................773 767-6690
John Kristmann, *President*
Judi Orsi, *Admin Sec*
EMP: 10
SQ FT: 14,000
SALES (est): 1MM **Privately Held**
SIC: 3555 7692 3535 Printing trades machinery; welding repair; conveyors & conveying equipment

(G-6213)
SPECIALTY FOODS GROUP LLC
Also Called: Scott Petersen Co
4550 W Jackson Blvd (60624-2503)
PHONE.................................773 378-1300
Ken Schissler, *Principal*
EMP: 120 **Privately Held**
SIC: 2011 2013 Meat packing plants; sausages & other prepared meats
HQ: Specialty Foods Group, Llc
6 Dublin Ln
Owensboro KY 42301

(G-6214)
SPINNER MEDICAL PRODUCTS INC
900 N Lake Shore Dr Ste 1 (60611-1544)
PHONE.................................312 944-8700
EMP: 326
SQ FT: 375,000
SALES (est): 18.5MM **Privately Held**
SIC: 3089 Mfg Molded Plastic Products

(G-6215)
SPL-USA LLC
123 N Wacker Dr (60606-1743)
PHONE.................................312 807-2000
Daniel Nott, *Principal*
EMP: 4
SALES (est): 276.1K
SALES (corp-wide): 4.5B **Privately Held**
SIC: 2891 Adhesives & sealants
HQ: Morton Salt, Inc.
444 W Lake St Ste 3000
Chicago IL 60606

(G-6216)
SPLAT CREATIVE INC
2150 S Canalport Ave (60608-4559)
PHONE.................................708 567-8412
Nicholas Florek, *President*
Alex Rhoads, *Treasurer*
EMP: 2
SQ FT: 850
SALES: 250K **Privately Held**
SIC: 2752 7389 Commercial printing, lithographic; design services

(G-6217)
SPLIT NUTRITION LLC
2405 N Shffeld Ave 1446 # 14466 (60614)
P.O. Box 14466 (60614-8507)
PHONE.................................855 775-4801
Patti Hudson, *Mng Member*
Jeffrey Mahin,
Christopher Meers,
EMP: 3
SALES: 100K **Privately Held**
SIC: 2033 7389 Jams, jellies & preserves: packaged in cans, jars, etc.;

(G-6218)
SPOOKY COOL LABS LLC
5515 N Cumberland Ave # 803 (60656-4737)
PHONE.................................773 577-5555
Joe Kaminkow,
EMP: 40 **EST:** 2011
SALES (est): 2.3MM
SALES (corp-wide): 1.3B **Publicly Held**
WEB: www.spookycool.com
SIC: 7372 Application computer software
PA: Zynga Inc.
699 8th St
San Francisco CA 94103
855 449-9642

(G-6219)
SPORTS ILLUSTRATED FOR KIDS
303 E Ohio St Ste D (60611-3373)
PHONE.................................312 321-7828
Dave Morris, *President*
EMP: 8
SALES (est): 434.3K **Privately Held**
SIC: 2721 Magazines: publishing only, not printed on site

(G-6220)
SPRINGCOIN INC (PA)
20 W Kinzie St Ste 1700 (60654-6398)
PHONE.................................323 577-9322
EMP: 4
SALES (est): 610.3K **Privately Held**
SIC: 7372 Prepackaged software

(G-6221)
SPROUT SOCIAL INC (PA)
131 S Dearborn St Ste 700 (60603-5569)
PHONE.................................866 878-3231
Justyn Howard, *President*
Buck Flather, *Partner*
Jennifer Beese, *Editor*
Ryan Barretto, *Senior VP*
Alan Boyce, *Vice Pres*
EMP: 71
SQ FT: 128,000
SALES: 102.7MM **Publicly Held**
WEB: www.sproutsocial.com
SIC: 7372 7375 Prepackaged software; information retrieval services

(G-6222)
SPUDNIK PRESS COOPERATIVE
1821 W Hubbard St Ste 302 (60622-6273)
PHONE.................................312 563-0302
Angela Lennard, *Principal*
Alison Kleiman, *Vice Pres*
Tom Wilder, *Treasurer*
Ruby Figueroa, *Manager*
Angee Lennard, *Director*
EMP: 10
SALES: 304.8K **Privately Held**
WEB: www.spudnikpress.org
SIC: 2741 8699 Miscellaneous publishing; charitable organization

(G-6223)
SRAM LLC (PA)
1000 W Fulton Market Fl 4 (60607-1299)
PHONE.................................312 664-8800
Ken Lousberg, *CEO*
Stanley R Day Jr, *President*
Fk Day, *Exec VP*
April Hall, *Vice Pres*
Michael D Mercuri, *Vice Pres*
◆ **EMP:** 80
SQ FT: 30,000
SALES (est): 598.2MM **Privately Held**
SIC: 3751 Gears, motorcycle & bicycle

(G-6224)
ST MARYS CEMENT
12101 S Doty Ave (60633-2322)
PHONE.................................773 995-5100
Dave White, *Principal*
Larry Woodward, *Manager*
EMP: 8
SALES (est): 584.3K **Privately Held**
SIC: 1422 Cement rock, crushed & broken-quarrying

(G-6225)
STABLE FOODS INC
Also Called: Soul Vegan
7130 S Yates Blvd Apt 3 (60649-2559)
P.O. Box 208818 (60620-8818)
PHONE.................................773 793-2547
Ronald King, *President*
Tenasae Kidane-Maria, *President*
John Cotton, *Principal*
EMP: 14
SALES: 920K **Privately Held**
SIC: 5148 2033 Fresh fruits & vegetables; vegetables: packaged in cans, jars, etc.

(G-6226)
STADIUM
1901 W Madison St 5 (60612-2459)
PHONE.................................312 455-2582
Lauren Johnson, *Principal*
EMP: 5
SALES (est): 332K **Privately Held**
SIC: 2711 Newspapers, publishing & printing

(G-6227)
STAGNITO PARTNERS LLC (HQ)
Also Called: Stagnito Media
8550 W Bryn Mawr Ave # 200 (60631-3731)
PHONE.................................224 632-8200
Kollin Stagnito, *CEO*
Katrina Lopez, *Accounts Exec*
Greg Cole, *Sales Staff*
Gina Acosta, *Manager*
Jonathan Obar, *Manager*
EMP: 47

GEOGRAPHIC SECTION

Chicago - Cook County (G-6254)

SALES (est): 24.1MM
SALES (corp-wide): 28.6MM **Privately Held**
WEB: www.stagnitomedia.com
SIC: **2721** 8742 7389 Magazines: publishing only, not printed on site; marketing consulting services; convention & show services
PA: Ensembleiq, Inc.
8550 W Bryn Mawr Ave # 200
Chicago IL 60631
773 992-4450

(G-6228)
STANDARD HEAT TREATING CO INC
5757 W Ogden Ave (60804-3877)
PHONE.................................708 447-7504
Wendell Matthews, *President*
James Matthews, *Vice Pres*
Wayne Matthews Jr, *Vice Pres*
EMP: 55
SQ FT: 35,000
SALES (est): 6.5MM **Privately Held**
WEB: www.standardht.com
SIC: **3398** Brazing (hardening) of metal; tempering of metal

(G-6229)
STANDARD MARBLE & GRANITE
4551 W 5th Ave (60624-3410)
PHONE.................................773 533-0450
Jeanjacques Porret, *President*
Jean Porret, *President*
Vija Reinfelds, *Corp Secy*
▲ EMP: 10
SQ FT: 12,000
SALES (est): 973.3K **Privately Held**
WEB: www.standardmarble.com
SIC: **1743** 1741 3281 Tile installation, ceramic; marble installation, interior; marble masonry, exterior construction; marble, building: cut & shaped; granite, cut & shaped

(G-6230)
STANLEY SPRING & STAMPING CORP
5050 W Foster Ave (60630-1614)
PHONE.................................773 777-2600
Ronald J Banas, *CEO*
Tom Lusinski, *General Mgr*
▲ EMP: 80 EST: 1944
SQ FT: 85,000
SALES (est): 25.8MM **Privately Held**
WEB: www.stanleyspring.com
SIC: **3469** 3495 3493 Stamping metal for the trade; wire springs; steel springs, except wire

(G-6231)
STANRON CORPORATION (PA)
Also Called: Stanron Steel Specialties Div
5050 W Foster Ave (60630-1614)
PHONE.................................773 777-2600
Ronald J Banas, *President*
EMP: 60
SQ FT: 2,500
SALES (est): 18MM **Privately Held**
SIC: **3469** Stamping metal for the trade

(G-6232)
STANTON WIND ENERGY LLC
1 S Wacker Dr Ste 1900 (60606-4644)
PHONE.................................312 224-1400
Invenergy Wind North America L, *Mng Member*
Michael Polsky, *President*
EMP: 10
SALES (est): 811.6K **Privately Held**
SIC: **3621** Windmills, electric generating

(G-6233)
STAR CABINETRY
4440 W Belmont Ave (60641-4529)
PHONE.................................773 725-4651
Francisco Launas, *President*
EMP: 2
SALES (est): 203.1K **Privately Held**
SIC: **2499** Decorative wood & woodwork

(G-6234)
STARLINE DESIGNS
750 E 43rd St (60653-2947)
PHONE.................................773 683-7506
EMP: 4 EST: 2010
SALES: 100K **Privately Held**
SIC: **2262** Manmade Fiber & Silk Finishing Plant

(G-6235)
STATE OF ILLINOIS
Also Called: Office of Spcial Dputy Rceiver
222 Merchandise Mart Plz # 1450 (60654-1103)
PHONE.................................312 836-9500
Asha Puri, *President*
EMP: 137 **Privately Held**
SIC: **3663** 9651 8742 8111 Radio receiver networks; insurance commission, government; ; management consulting services; legal services; real estate agents & managers
HQ: Illinois Department Of Financial And Professional Regulation
320 W Washington St Fl 3
Springfield IL 62701
217 785-0820

(G-6236)
STAY STRAIGHT MANUFACTURING
4145 W Kinzie St (60624-1715)
PHONE.................................312 226-2137
Louis Brandt, *President*
EMP: 4 EST: 1999
SQ FT: 5,000
SALES (est): 544.5K **Privately Held**
SIC: **2521** Cabinets, office: wood

(G-6237)
STEELCASE INC
222 Merchandise Mart Plz # 300 (60654-1175)
P.O. Box 99315 (60693-9315)
PHONE.................................312 321-3720
Ingrid Ferguson, *Manager*
Lauren Bearden, *Technology*
EMP: 14
SALES (corp-wide): 3.7B **Publicly Held**
SIC: **2522** 2521 Office furniture, except wood; wood office furniture
PA: Steelcase Inc.
901 44th St Se
Grand Rapids MI 49508
616 247-2710

(G-6238)
STEINBACH PROVISION COMPANY
741 W 47th St (60609-4409)
PHONE.................................773 538-1511
Tom Steinbach, *President*
EMP: 7 EST: 1945
SQ FT: 7,000
SALES (est): 5MM **Privately Held**
WEB: www.dev.steinbachpro.com
SIC: **2011** 2013 Meat packing plants; sausages & other prepared meats

(G-6239)
STEINER ELECTRIC COMPANY
Steiner/Excell Motor Repair
2225 W Hubbard St (60612-1613)
PHONE.................................312 421-7220
Bob Hanson, *Manager*
EMP: 50
SALES (corp-wide): 325MM **Privately Held**
SIC: **7694** 5063 Electric motor repair; electrical supplies
PA: Steiner Electric Company
1250 Touhy Ave
Elk Grove Village IL 60007
847 228-0400

(G-6240)
STEINER INDUSTRIES INC
5801 N Tripp Ave (60646-6013)
PHONE.................................773 588-3444
Robert J Steiner, *President*
Robert H Gerstein, *Corp Secy*
Judi Steiner, *Vice Pres*
Cindy Flores, *Purch Agent*
Darren Garbutt, *Natl Sales Mgr*
▲ EMP: 60

SQ FT: 45,000
SALES (est): 1.1MM **Privately Held**
WEB: www.steinerindustries.com
SIC: **3842** Personal safety equipment

(G-6241)
STEINMETZ R (US) LTD
Also Called: Orli Diamonds
67 E Madison St Ste 1606 (60603-3062)
PHONE.................................312 332-0990
EMP: 4
SALES (est): 775.3K **Privately Held**
SIC: **5094** 3915 Whol Jewelry/Precs Stone Mfg Jewelers' Materials

(G-6242)
STELLAR PERFORMANCE MFG LLC
640 N La Salle Dr Ste 540 (60654-3749)
PHONE.................................312 951-2311
Jake Trigo, *Finance Dir*
Kevin Berg, *Mng Member*
▲ EMP: 30
SALES (est): 5.3MM **Privately Held**
SIC: **2821** Plastics materials & resins

(G-6243)
STELLAR RECOGNITION INC
Also Called: Sports Awards
5544 W Armstrong Ave (60646-6514)
PHONE.................................773 282-8060
Roy T Newton, *President*
Eileen M Newton, *Admin Sec*
▲ EMP: 80 EST: 1933
SQ FT: 23,000
SALES (est): 13.5MM **Privately Held**
WEB: www.sportsawards.biz
SIC: **3914** 3999 2396 3993 Trophies, plated (all metals); plaques, picture, laminated; ribbons & bows, cut & sewed; advertising novelties; commercial printing

(G-6244)
STEREO OPTICAL COMPANY INC
8600 W Catalpa Ave (60656-1656)
PHONE.................................773 867-0380
Christophe Condat, *President*
David Milan, *Admin Sec*
EMP: 15
SQ FT: 10,000
SALES (est): 4.9MM
SALES (corp-wide): 1.7MM **Privately Held**
SIC: **3841** Ophthalmic instruments & apparatus; retinoscopes
HQ: Essilor Of America, Inc.
13555 N Stemmons Fwy
Dallas TX 75234

(G-6245)
STERLING SPRING LLC (PA)
Also Called: Wesco
5432 W 54th St (60638-2998)
PHONE.................................773 582-6464
John Shapiro, *General Mgr*
Stanley Graczyk, *Plant Mgr*
Eric Dickinson, *Accounts Mgr*
Mike Malesky, *Accounts Mgr*
Robert D Dickinson, *Mng Member*
EMP: 60 EST: 1997
SQ FT: 50,000
SALES: 23.2MM **Privately Held**
WEB: www.sterlingspring.com
SIC: **3495** Wire springs

(G-6246)
STEVENS EXHIBITS & DISPLAYS
3900 S Union Ave (60609-2623)
PHONE.................................773 523-3900
Thomas Mc Kernin, *President*
Charles Mc Kernin, *Treasurer*
Sharon Mc Kernin, *Admin Sec*
EMP: 35 EST: 1966
SQ FT: 94,000
SALES: 2MM **Privately Held**
WEB: www.stevensexhibits.com
SIC: **7389** 3993 Trade show arrangement; displays & cutouts, window & lobby

(G-6247)
STEVENSON OIL INC
3200 N Harlem Ave (60634-4501)
PHONE.................................773 237-6185
EMP: 3 EST: 2017

SALES (est): 241.5K **Privately Held**
SIC: **1382** Oil & gas exploration services

(G-6248)
STEWART INGRDIENTS SYSTEMS INC
1843 W Fulton St (60612-2511)
PHONE.................................312 254-3539
Keith F Stewart, *President*
Bill Braun, *Vice Pres*
Constantine Nicholas, *Treasurer*
Stephanie Lazzeroni, *Admin Sec*
Stephanie Wilz, *Admin Sec*
EMP: 18
SQ FT: 15,000
SALES (est): 3.7MM **Privately Held**
WEB: www.stewartis.com
SIC: **2033** Jellies, edible, including imitation: in cans, jars, etc.; fruits: packaged in cans, jars, etc.

(G-6249)
STM READER LLC
Also Called: Chicago Reader
350 N Orleans St (60654-1975)
PHONE.................................312 222-6920
Alison Draper, *Principal*
EMP: 7
SALES (est): 345.2K **Privately Held**
SIC: **2711** Newspapers, publishing & printing

(G-6250)
STORIANT INC
70 W Madison St Ste 2300 (60602-4250)
P.O. Box 182, Marblehead MA (01945-0182)
PHONE.................................617 431-8000
Jeffry Flowers, *President*
John Hogan, *Vice Pres*
Amy Berenson, *Director*
Susan Pravda, *Admin Sec*
David Friend, *Admin Sec*
EMP: 34
SQ FT: 6,500
SALES (est): 2.1MM **Privately Held**
SIC: **7372** Business oriented computer software

(G-6251)
STORMS INDUSTRIES INC
1500 S Western Ave Ste 5 (60608-1828)
PHONE.................................312 243-7480
William A Ross, *President*
Dave Murphy, *Principal*
David Gilliam, *Manager*
▲ EMP: 35
SQ FT: 16,000
SALES (est): 8.8MM **Privately Held**
WEB: www.stormsindustries.com
SIC: **5087** 3564 Laundry equipment & supplies; filters, air: furnaces, air conditioning equipment, etc.

(G-6252)
STREETWISE
4554 N Broadway St # 350 (60640-7962)
PHONE.................................773 334-6600
George Mavrogenes, *Treasurer*
James Lobianco, *Exec Dir*
Patrick Edwards, *Admin Asst*
EMP: 16
SQ FT: 3,500
SALES: 706.4K **Privately Held**
SIC: **2711** Newspapers, publishing & printing

(G-6253)
STRETCH CHI
4765 N Lincoln Ave # 207 (60625-2077)
PHONE.................................773 420-9355
Carrie L Collins, *Owner*
EMP: 3 EST: 2011
SALES (est): 211.6K **Privately Held**
WEB: www.stretchchi.com
SIC: **3841** Muscle exercise apparatus, ophthalmic

(G-6254)
STRIVE CONVERTING CORPORATION
4545 W Palmer St (60639-3421)
PHONE.................................773 227-6000
Michael K Waite, *President*
Jeffrey T Sharfstein, *Manager*
Douglas R Sharfstein, *Manager*

Chicago - Cook County (G-6255)

Jeffrey T McReynolds, *Systems Mgr*
▲ **EMP:** 160 **EST:** 1982
SQ FT: 235,000
SALES (est): 17.5MM **Privately Held**
SIC: 2653 Boxes, corrugated: made from purchased materials; display items, corrugated: made from purchased materials

(G-6255)
STRYDE TECHNOLOGIES INC
Also Called: Mypowr
300 N Canal St Apt 1505 (60606-1278)
PHONE.................510 786-8890
Tejas Shastry, *CEO*
Michael Geier, *Co-Owner*
Alexander Smith, *Co-Owner*
EMP: 5
SALES (est): 548.5K **Privately Held**
SIC: 3677 Electronic coils, transformers & other inductors

(G-6256)
STRYKER CORPORATION
Stryker Performance Solutions
350 N Orleans St Ste 650 (60654-1575)
PHONE.................312 386-9780
Ken Agrella, *Project Mgr*
Anthony Furio, *Opers Staff*
Cassius Hartl, *Engineer*
James Myers, *Engineer*
Brandon Naber, *Engineer*
EMP: 412
SALES (corp-wide): 14.8B **Publicly Held**
SIC: 3841 Surgical instruments & apparatus
PA: Stryker Corporation
2825 Airview Blvd
Portage MI 49002
269 385-2600

(G-6257)
STUDIO 88 CREATIVE DESIGN LLC
55 E Monroe St Ste 3800 (60603-6030)
PHONE.................312 288-3955
Terran Watson,
EMP: 7
SQ FT: 5,000
SALES (est): 317.6K **Privately Held**
SIC: 2752 Commercial printing, lithographic

(G-6258)
STUMPFOLL TOOL & MFG
1713 W Hubbard St (60622-6213)
PHONE.................312 733-2632
Joseph Stumpfoll, *Owner*
EMP: 7
SQ FT: 7,500
SALES (est): 300K **Privately Held**
SIC: 3469 3544 Stamping metal for the trade; special dies, tools, jigs & fixtures

(G-6259)
STUTZ COMPANY
4450 W Carroll Ave (60624-1696)
PHONE.................773 287-1068
James Stutz, *President*
Paul David Stutz, *Corp Secy*
▲ **EMP:** 16 **EST:** 1921
SQ FT: 30,000
SALES (est): 9MM **Privately Held**
WEB: www.stutzcompany.com
SIC: 5084 5169 3559 2899 Industrial machinery & equipment; industrial chemicals; metal finishing equipment for plating, etc.; plating compounds

(G-6260)
STYLISH KIT BATH CABINETS CORP
3535 N Lincoln Ave (60657-7582)
PHONE.................773 525-8667
Aneta Lupinska, *President*
EMP: 7
SALES (est): 942.7K **Privately Held**
SIC: 2434 Wood kitchen cabinets

(G-6261)
STZ INDUSTRIES LLC
600 N Kilbourn Ave (60624-1041)
PHONE.................773 265-3000
Hillel Tropper, *CEO*
Moshe Tropper, *President*
David Pollans, *Vice Pres*
Baruch Travitsky, *CFO*

Christopher Kostecka, *Manager*
▲ **EMP:** 45
SALES (est): 17.1MM
SALES (corp-wide): 24.7MM **Privately Held**
SIC: 3432 5074 5999 Plumbing fixture fittings & trim; plumbing fittings & supplies; plumbing & heating supplies
PA: Coda Resources Ltd.
100 Matawan Rd Ste 300
Matawan NJ 07747
718 649-1666

(G-6262)
SUCCESS PUBLISHING GROUP INC
Also Called: Comptons Encyclopedia
310 S Michigan Ave Fl 9 (60604-4202)
PHONE.................708 565-2681
Fred Bruno, *CEO*
Mike Capetanakis, *President*
EMP: 14
SALES (est): 3MM **Privately Held**
SIC: 2731 Textbooks: publishing & printing

(G-6263)
SUCCESS VENDING MFG CO LLC
Also Called: International Services
5128 W Irving Park Rd (60641-2624)
PHONE.................773 262-1685
Chris Pentell, *Partner*
Steve Zatz, *Partner*
EMP: 22
SQ FT: 22,000
SALES (est): 14.2MM **Privately Held**
SIC: 3581 Automatic vending machines

(G-6264)
SULTRY SATCHELS INC
8159 S Troy St (60652-2616)
PHONE.................312 810-1081
Charessa Maiden-Mcneal, *Principal*
EMP: 3
SALES (est): 193.1K **Privately Held**
SIC: 3161 Satchels

(G-6265)
SUMMIT ARCHITECTURAL MTLS LLC
Also Called: Div. 5
455 N Campbell Ave (60612-1146)
PHONE.................815 934-3484
Vince Cambell, *President*
EMP: 10
SALES (est): 104.6K **Privately Held**
SIC: 3446 Architectural metalwork

(G-6266)
SUMMIT POLYMERS INC
12359 S Burley Ave (60633-1460)
PHONE.................269 532-1900
EMP: 3
SALES (est): 171.6K **Privately Held**
SIC: 3089 Injection molding of plastics

(G-6267)
SUN BEAM LOGISTICS INC
630 N Franklin St Apt 618 (60654-8351)
PHONE.................847 454-5884
Ivo Ppanayotov, *Principal*
EMP: 3
SALES (est): 113.2K **Privately Held**
SIC: 2085 Distilled & blended liquors

(G-6268)
SUN DOME INC
3641 S Washtenaw Ave (60632-1645)
PHONE.................773 890-5350
Ashley Ross, *President*
EMP: 12
SALES (est): 1.6MM **Privately Held**
SIC: 3089 Closures, plastic

(G-6269)
SUN GRAPHIC INC
5540 N Northwest Hwy (60630-1116)
PHONE.................773 775-6755
Charles L Palmer, *Ch of Bd*
◆ **EMP:** 75
SQ FT: 25,000
SALES (est): 6.1MM **Privately Held**
SIC: 2893 Printing ink

HQ: Sun Chemical Corporation
35 Waterview Blvd Ste 100
Parsippany NJ 07054
973 404-6000

(G-6270)
SUN-TIMES MEDIA LLC
Also Called: Chicago Reader
350 N Orleans St 1000b-1 (60654-1975)
PHONE.................312 222-6920
Jeremy L Halbreich,
EMP: 10
SALES (est): 821.1K
SALES (corp-wide): 4.3MM **Privately Held**
SIC: 2711 7313 Newspapers; electronic media advertising representatives; printed media advertising representatives
PA: St Acquisition Holdings, Llc
350 N Orleans St Ste 10s
Chicago IL

(G-6271)
SUN-TIMES MEDIA GROUP INC (DH)
30 N Racine Ave Ste 300 (60607-2184)
PHONE.................312 321-3000
Tim Knight, *CEO*
Jeremy Deedes, *CEO*
Jerry J Strader, *President*
Blair Richard Surkamer, *President*
David C Martin, *Senior VP*
EMP: 51
SQ FT: 320,000
SALES (est): 292.6MM
SALES (corp-wide): 4.3MM **Privately Held**
SIC: 2711 Newspapers, publishing & printing

(G-6272)
SUN-TIMES MEDIA HOLDINGS LLC (DH)
350 N Orleans St 1000b-1 (60654-1975)
PHONE.................312 321-2299
Timothy P Knight, *CEO*
Rodney O'Neal, *CEO*
Bradley Phillip Bell, *President*
John A Canning, *Chairman*
Michael W Ferro, *Chairman*
EMP: 21
SALES (est): 305MM
SALES (corp-wide): 4.3MM **Privately Held**
SIC: 2711 Commercial printing & newspaper publishing combined; newspapers, publishing & printing
HQ: Wrapports, Llc
350 N Orleans St Fl 10
Chicago IL 60654
312 321-3000

(G-6273)
SUNDSTROM PRESSED STEEL CO
8030 S South Chicago Ave (60617-1029)
PHONE.................773 721-2237
Richard F Sundstrom, *President*
Herbert D Rentschler, *Vice Pres*
Calvin Thomas, *Executive*
Robert J Barnes, *Admin Sec*
▲ **EMP:** 25
SQ FT: 53,000
SALES (est): 5.1MM **Privately Held**
WEB: www.sundstrompressedsteel.com
SIC: 3441 Fabricated structural metal

(G-6274)
SUNNY ENTERPRISES INC
Also Called: Subway 25858
2811 S Kedzie Ave (60623-4712)
PHONE.................847 219-1045
Pratik Patel, *President*
Shakuben D Patel, *Vice Pres*
Dilip Patel, *Admin Sec*
EMP: 10
SQ FT: 2,500
SALES: 750K **Privately Held**
SIC: 2099 Ready-to-eat meals, salads & sandwiches

(G-6275)
SUNRISE FUTURES LLC
30 S Wacker Dr Ste 1706 (60606-7414)
PHONE.................312 612-1041

Allan San, *Principal*
Alysha Tardiff, *Vice Pres*
Charley Chen, *CTO*
Michael Sisson, *Director*
EMP: 5
SALES (est): 772K **Privately Held**
SIC: 7372 Prepackaged software

(G-6276)
SUNRISE HITEK GROUP LLC
5915 N Northwest Hwy (60631-2644)
PHONE.................773 792-8880
Jimmy Sun, *Mng Member*
▲ **EMP:** 25
SALES (est): 2.7MM **Privately Held**
SIC: 2752 Commercial printing, offset

(G-6277)
SUNRISE HITEK SERVICE INC
Also Called: Sunrise Digital
5915 N Northwest Hwy (60631-2644)
PHONE.................773 792-8880
Libo Sun, *President*
Katie Kelly, *Manager*
Thomas Callahan, *Exec Dir*
Chengrong Xie, *Admin Sec*
▲ **EMP:** 20
SQ FT: 14,000
SALES (est): 3.6MM **Privately Held**
SIC: 2759 7389 2752 Commercial printing; design services; platemaking services; commercial printing, lithographic; miscellaneous publishing

(G-6278)
SUNSET HALTHCARE SOLUTIONS INC (PA)
180 N Michigan Ave # 2000 (60601-7401)
PHONE.................877 578-6738
Christopher Slosar, *President*
Liz Fuertges, *Area Mgr*
Greg Wood, *Vice Pres*
Tierney Obrien, *Sales Staff*
Pj Ruflin, *Sales Staff*
▲ **EMP:** 40
SALES (est): 7.9MM **Privately Held**
SIC: 3841 Cannulae

(G-6279)
SUPALICIOUS SOUPS INC
7251 S Luella Ave (60649-2513)
PHONE.................708 491-9738
EMP: 4
SALES: 75K **Privately Held**
SIC: 2032 5149 5499 Mfg Canned Specialties Whol Groceries Ret Misc Foods

(G-6280)
SUPERIOR GRAPHITE CO (PA)
10 S Riverside Plz # 1470 (60606-3838)
PHONE.................312 559-2999
Edward O Carney, *President*
Peter R Carney, *Chairman*
Jorge Ayala, *Business Mgr*
Jeff Hopkins, *Exec VP*
Jeffrey M Hopkins, *Exec VP*
◆ **EMP:** 35
SALES (est): 80.9MM **Privately Held**
WEB: www.superiorgraphite.com
SIC: 3295 Graphite, natural: ground, pulverized, refined or blended

(G-6281)
SUPERIOR GRAPHITE CO
6540 S Laramie Ave (60638-6499)
PHONE.................708 458-0006
Kathleen Brennan, *Bookkeeper*
Denis Murphy, *Branch Mgr*
Gerardo Mora, *Manager*
Sandy T Fonta, *Executive*
Aldo Lopez, *Maintece Staff*
EMP: 50
SQ FT: 30,000
SALES (corp-wide): 80.9MM **Privately Held**
WEB: www.superiorgraphite.com
SIC: 3295 3823 3624 2992 Graphite, natural: ground, pulverized, refined or blended; industrial instrmnts msrmnt display/control process variable; carbon & graphite products; lubricating oils & greases
PA: Superior Graphite Co.
10 S Riverside Plz # 1470
Chicago IL 60606
312 559-2999

GEOGRAPHIC SECTION

Chicago - Cook County (G-6310)

(G-6282)
SUPERIOR GRAPHITE CO
4201 W 36th St Bldg Rear (60632-3825)
PHONE..................773 890-4100
Denis Murphy, *Manager*
EMP: 20
SALES (corp-wide): 80.9MM **Privately Held**
SIC: 3295 Graphite, natural; ground, pulverized, refined or blended
PA: Superior Graphite Co.
10 S Riverside Plz # 1470
Chicago IL 60606
312 559-2999

(G-6283)
SUPERIOR MFG GROUP - EUROPE (PA)
5655 W 73rd St Bestle Par (60638)
PHONE..................708 458-4600
John V Wood, *CEO*
Vincent De Phillips, *President*
Charles F Wood, *Vice Pres*
▲ **EMP:** 8
SALES (est): 2.1MM **Privately Held**
SIC: 3069 5085 Door mats, rubber; industrial supplies

(G-6284)
SUPERIOR TABLE PAD CO
3010 N Oakley Ave (60618-8000)
PHONE..................773 248-7232
Steven Antler, *President*
Geoffrey Garland, *Vice Pres*
EMP: 9
SQ FT: 10,000
SALES (est): 1.2MM **Privately Held**
WEB: www.superiortablepad.com
SIC: 2392 3949 Pads & padding, table: except asbestos, felt or rattan; sporting & athletic goods

(G-6285)
SUPPLY VISION INC
171 N Aberdeen St Ste 400 (60607-1670)
PHONE..................847 388-0064
Mike Powell, *CEO*
Cris Arens, *Principal*
EMP: 2
SALES (est): 203.2K **Privately Held**
WEB: www.supply-vision.com
SIC: 7372 Business oriented computer software

(G-6286)
SUPREME FRAME & MOULDING CO
652 W Randolph St (60661-2114)
PHONE..................312 930-9056
Barry Fript, *President*
Leonard Fript, *Corp Secy*
EMP: 10 **EST:** 1935
SQ FT: 25,000
SALES (est): 1MM **Privately Held**
WEB: www.supremeframe.com
SIC: 2499 7699 5719 3499 Picture frame molding, finished; picture framing, custom; pictures, wall; picture frames, metal; metal doors, sash & trim

(G-6287)
SURCOM INDUSTRIES INC
1017 N Cicero Ave (60651-3202)
PHONE..................773 378-0736
Scott Rempala, *President*
EMP: 6
SALES (est): 451.1K **Privately Held**
SIC: 3471 Plating & polishing

(G-6288)
SURFACE SOLUTIONS GROUP LLC
5492 N Northwest Hwy (60630-1114)
PHONE..................773 427-2084
Amy Jordan, *President*
Mike Osterhout, *Sales Mgr*
Bruce Nesbitt,
George Osterhout,
EMP: 60
SQ FT: 6,800
SALES (est): 5.7MM
SALES (corp-wide): 24.5MM **Privately Held**
WEB: www.surfacesolutionsgroup.com
SIC: 3479 Painting, coating & hot dipping

PA: Orion Industries, Ltd.
5492 N Northwest Hwy
Chicago IL 60630
773 282-9100

(G-6289)
SURGICAL INNOVATION ASSOC INC (PA)
Also Called: Sia
800 Liberty Dr (60601)
PHONE..................626 372-4884
Alexei Mlodinow, *Principal*
Todd Cruikshank, *COO*
EMP: 2
SALES (est): 935.1K **Privately Held**
SIC: 3841 7389 Surgical & medical instruments;

(G-6290)
SURPLUS RECORD LLC
20 N Wacker Dr Ste 2400 (60606-3004)
PHONE..................312 372-9077
Thomas C Scanlan, *President*
Jon Stephenson, *Senior VP*
Kathryn McNeil, *Controller*
Liz Ranes, *Adv Dir*
Tom Dean, *Manager*
EMP: 12
SQ FT: 3,000
SALES (est): 36.3K **Privately Held**
WEB: www.surplusrecord.com
SIC: 2721 Periodicals

(G-6291)
SUSTANBLE SLTIONS AMER LED LLC
Also Called: Sustainable Solutions Amer Led
910 W Van Buren St Ste 6a (60607-7900)
PHONE..................866 323-3494
William Ryan, *CEO*
Dale Bianco, *CFO*
EMP: 15
SQ FT: 30,000
SALES (est): 2.8MM **Privately Held**
WEB: www.sustainablesolutionsled.com
SIC: 3646 Commercial indusl & institutional electric lighting fixtures

(G-6292)
SWABY MANUFACTURING COMPANY (PA)
5420 W Roosevelt Rd 300b (60644-1439)
PHONE..................773 626-1400
Mohammad Khalil, *President*
Rick Hunt, *VP Sales*
Kuzida Khalil, *Admin Sec*
▲ **EMP:** 8 **EST:** 1893
SQ FT: 2,500
SALES (est): 4.3MM **Privately Held**
WEB: www.swabypump.com
SIC: 3561 Pumps, domestic: water or sump; industrial pumps & parts

(G-6293)
SWAPP TECHNOLOGIES INC
505 N Mcclurg Ct Apt 1505 (60611-5381)
PHONE..................312 912-1515
Tural Bayev, *CEO*
Kevin Hong, *Officer*
EMP: 4
SALES (est): 62.1K **Privately Held**
SIC: 7372 Application computer software

(G-6294)
SWEET MANUFACTURING CORP
111 E Chestnut St Apt 36k (60611-6013)
PHONE..................847 546-5575
Richard K Sweet, *President*
Helen R Sweet, *Admin Sec*
▲ **EMP:** 30
SQ FT: 5,000
SALES (est): 375.3K **Privately Held**
SIC: 3429 3469 Cabinet hardware; metal stampings

(G-6295)
SWIFT EDUCATION SYSTEMS INC
332 S Michigan Ave # 1032 (60604-4734)
PHONE..................312 257-3751
Louie Huang, *CEO*
Zachary Schneirov, *President*
William Nelson, *Admin Sec*
EMP: 3

SALES (est): 217.7K **Privately Held**
SIC: 7372 Educational computer software

(G-6296)
SWIFT IMPRESSIONS INC
Also Called: Cut Rate Printers
70 E Lake St Ste 1010 (60601-7627)
PHONE..................312 372-0002
Anthony Musto, *President*
EMP: 4
SQ FT: 1,500
SALES (est): 616.9K **Privately Held**
SIC: 2752 Commercial printing, offset

(G-6297)
SWISS PRODUCTS LP
4333 W Division St (60651-1792)
PHONE..................773 394-6480
Senya R Kalpake, *Partner*
Paul Kalpake, *General Ptnr*
EMP: 39 **EST:** 1941
SQ FT: 50,000
SALES (est): 7.4MM **Privately Held**
WEB: www.swissfoodproducts.com
SIC: 2034 2099 Dehydrated fruits, vegetables, soups; gravy mixes, dry; seasonings: dry mixes; spices, including grinding

(G-6298)
SWISSPORT FUELING INCORPO
5000 W 63rd St (60638-5719)
PHONE..................773 203-5419
EMP: 5
SALES (est): 695K **Privately Held**
SIC: 2869 Fuels

(G-6299)
SWITCHCRAFT INC (HQ)
5555 N Elston Ave (60630-1386)
PHONE..................773 792-2700
Keith A Bandolik, *President*
Cheryl Book, *President*
Jerry Zahara, *Transptn Dir*
Ken Trendel, *Purch Mgr*
Art Aguilar, *QC Mgr*
▲ **EMP:** 365 **EST:** 1946
SQ FT: 220,000
SALES (est): 89.7MM **Publicly Held**
WEB: www.switchcraft.com
SIC: 3613 3679 3663 3661 Switchgear & switchboard apparatus; electronic switches; radio & TV communications equipment; telephone cords, jacks, adapters, etc.; electronic connectors; current-carrying wiring devices

(G-6300)
SWITCHCRAFT HOLDCO INC (HQ)
5555 N Elston Ave (60630-1386)
PHONE..................773 792-2700
Keith A Bandolik, *President*
▲ **EMP:** 6
SALES (est): 25.6MM **Publicly Held**
SIC: 3613 3679 3663 3661 Switchgear & switchboard apparatus; electronic switches; radio & TV communications equipment; telephone cords, jacks, adapters, etc.; electronic connectors; current-carrying wiring devices

(G-6301)
SYMFACT INC
55 W Monroe St Ste 2900 (60603-5058)
PHONE..................847 380-4174
Andreas Kyriakakis, *President*
Chris Kraddock, *COO*
Harry Angel, *Vice Pres*
EMP: 35
SALES (est): 2.7MM
SALES (corp-wide): 1.8MM **Privately Held**
SIC: 7372 Prepackaged software
PA: Symfact Ag
Bankstrasse 4
Uster ZH 8610
449 051-995

(G-6302)
SYNERGY ADVNCED PHRMCTCALS INC
300 N La Salle Dr # 4925 (60654-3406)
PHONE..................212 297-0020
Gary G Gemignani, *Vice Pres*
EMP: 269

SALES (est): 69.1K **Privately Held**
SIC: 2834 Pharmaceutical preparations
PA: Synergy Pharmaceuticals, Llc
620 Lee Rd Ste 200
Chesterbrook PA 19087

(G-6303)
SYNERGY TECHNOLOGY GROUP INC
Also Called: Shartega Systems
1250 W Augusta Blvd # 201 (60642-4277)
PHONE..................773 305-3500
Jake Kunda, *President*
Nic Connor, *Vice Pres*
Ricky Garza, *Finance Mgr*
Jose Flores, *Technician*
EMP: 15 **EST:** 2003
SALES (est): 1MM **Privately Held**
SIC: 7371 7372 7379 Computer software development & applications; prepackaged software; business oriented computer software; computer related consulting services

(G-6304)
SYSTEM SCIENCE CORPORATION
1408 W Taylor St Apt 301 (60607-4687)
PHONE..................708 214-2264
Andreas Linninger, *President*
EMP: 5
SALES (est): 508.4K **Privately Held**
SIC: 3845 Electromedical equipment

(G-6305)
T & T COMPLETE CONSTRUCTION
205 S Peoria St Apt 1306 (60607-3135)
PHONE..................312 929-5352
Tamika Underwood, *Mng Member*
EMP: 10
SALES (est): 375K **Privately Held**
SIC: 1389 Construction, repair & dismantling services

(G-6306)
T 26 INC
Also Called: 5inch
1110 N Milwaukee Ave (60642-4017)
PHONE..................773 862-1201
EMP: 5
SALES (est): 540K **Privately Held**
SIC: 3575 Mfg Computer Terminals

(G-6307)
T R COMMUNICATIONS INC
Also Called: Beverly Review
10546 S Western Ave (60643-2528)
PHONE..................773 238-3366
Robert Olzewski Jr, *President*
Toby Olszewski, *Vice Pres*
EMP: 12
SQ FT: 2,000
SALES (est): 969.5K **Privately Held**
SIC: 2741 2791 2711 Business service newsletters: publishing & printing; typesetting; newspapers

(G-6308)
T2 CABINETS INC
1400 W 37th St (60609-2109)
PHONE..................312 593-1507
Mao MEI, *Principal*
▲ **EMP:** 13 **EST:** 2008
SALES (est): 1.8MM **Privately Held**
WEB: www.t2cabinet.com
SIC: 2434 Wood kitchen cabinets

(G-6309)
TA DELAWARE INC
Also Called: Tower Automotive Chicago
12350 S Avenue O (60633-1171)
PHONE..................773 646-6550
Doug Barger, *Branch Mgr*
EMP: 31 **Privately Held**
SIC: 3469 Metal stampings
PA: Ta Delaware, Inc.
17672 N Lrel Pk Dr Ste 40
Novi MI 48377

(G-6310)
TAHINI EMPIRE INC
4938 N Elston Ave (60630-1730)
PHONE..................773 742-2382
EMP: 4

Chicago - Cook County (G-6311)

SALES: 80K **Privately Held**
SIC: 2051 Bakery: wholesale or wholesale/retail combined

(G-6311)
TAILS INC
Also Called: Chicagoland Tails
4410 N Ravenswood Ave # 1 (60640-5999)
PHONE 773 564-9300
Janice Brown, *President*
Charlene Underly, *Accounts Exec*
EMP: 12
SALES (est): 1.3MM **Privately Held**
SIC: 2721 Magazines: publishing & printing

(G-6312)
TAITT BURIAL GARMENTS
6649 S Wabash Ave (60637-3034)
PHONE 773 483-7424
Ernestine Taitt, *Owner*
EMP: 15
SALES (est): 937.2K **Privately Held**
SIC: 2389 Disposable garments & accessories

(G-6313)
TALCOTT COMMUNICATIONS CORP (PA)
Also Called: Giftware News
704 N Wells St Fl 2 (60654-3569)
PHONE 312 849-2220
Daniel Von Rabenau, *President*
▲ **EMP:** 28
SQ FT: 2,700
SALES (est): 4.2MM **Privately Held**
WEB: www.giftwarenews.com
SIC: 2721 Magazines: publishing only, not printed on site

(G-6314)
TALIS BIOMEDICAL CORPORATION (PA)
125 S Clark St Fl 17 (60603-4054)
PHONE 312 589-5000
Brian Coe, *CEO*
EMP: 3
SALES (est): 6.6MM **Privately Held**
SIC: 3826 Spectroscopic & other optical properties measuring equipment

(G-6315)
TALLY METALS HOLDINGS LLC
1031 E 103rd St (60628-3007)
PHONE 773 264-5900
Jay Sandler,
Deborah Farina,
David Kozin,
EMP: 4 **Privately Held**
SIC: 6719 2819 Personal holding companies, except banks; zinc chloride

(G-6316)
TAM TAV BAKERY INC
Also Called: Tel Aviv Kosher Bakery
2944 W Devon Ave (60659-1556)
PHONE 773 764-8877
David Ackerman, *President*
Esther Sabo, *Vice Pres*
Naftula Basman, *Shareholder*
Diane Ackerman, *Admin Sec*
Judy Glock, *Admin Sec*
EMP: 20
SQ FT: 3,900
SALES (est): 1.2MM **Privately Held**
SIC: 5461 5149 2051 Bakeries; bakery products; bread, cake & related products

(G-6317)
TAMMY BANKS
Also Called: Fotowatch
500 N Michigan Ave # 600 (60611-3777)
PHONE 312 280-1388
Tammy Banks, *Owner*
EMP: 5
SALES (est): 557.7K **Privately Held**
SIC: 5944 3873 Watches; watches, clocks, watchcases & parts

(G-6318)
TAMPICO BEVERAGES INC
2425 W Barry Ave (60618-7913)
PHONE 773 296-0190
EMP: 12 **Privately Held**
SIC: 2087 Flavoring extracts & syrups
HQ: Tampico Beverages Inc.
3106 N Campbell Ave
Chicago IL 60618
773 296-0190

(G-6319)
TAMPICO BEVERAGES INC (DH)
3106 N Campbell Ave (60618-7994)
PHONE 773 296-0190
Scott Miller, *CEO*
Terry Boden, *President*
Mark Kent, *Exec VP*
Pedro Dejesus Jr, *Senior VP*
Dawn Stanislaw, *CFO*
◆ **EMP:** 50
SQ FT: 70,000
SALES (est): 18.3MM **Privately Held**
SIC: 2087 Concentrates, drink; fruit juices: concentrated for fountain use
HQ: Houchens Food Group, Inc.
700 Church St
Bowling Green KY 42101
270 843-3252

(G-6320)
TAMPICO PRESS
1919 S Blue Island Ave (60608-3014)
PHONE 312 243-5448
Marcos Urbano, *Owner*
Marcos Urbana, *Partner*
EMP: 3
SQ FT: 2,500
SALES (est): 288.5K **Privately Held**
SIC: 2759 2752 Letterpress printing; commercial printing, offset

(G-6321)
TAMPOPRINT MID-WEST CORP
525 W Monroe St Ste 2360 (60661-3720)
PHONE 312 971-7715
Klaus U Thiedmann, *Principal*
EMP: 4
SALES (est): 284.4K **Privately Held**
SIC: 2752 Commercial printing, offset

(G-6322)
TANK IN A BOX LLC
333 S Wabash Ave Ste 2700 (60604-4129)
PHONE 847 624-1234
Michael Agins,
EMP: 5
SALES (est): 172.8K **Privately Held**
SIC: 3999 Manufacturing industries

(G-6323)
TANK NOODLE INC
4953 N Broadway St (60640-3001)
PHONE 773 878-2253
Huc Huynh, *President*
EMP: 8
SALES (est): 649.8K **Privately Held**
WEB: www.tank-noodle.com
SIC: 2098 Noodles (e.g. egg, plain & water), dry

(G-6324)
TANNERY ROW LLC
1515 W Carroll Ave (60607-1003)
PHONE 847 840-7647
Eric Frank, *Principal*
EMP: 2 **EST:** 2011
SALES (est): 206K **Privately Held**
SIC: 3111 Tanneries, leather

(G-6325)
TANVAS INC
600 W Van Buren St # 710 (60607-3758)
PHONE 773 295-6220
Phillip Lopresti, *CEO*
Michael Peshkin, *CTO*
EMP: 6
SALES (est): 798.7K **Privately Held**
SIC: 3679 Electronic circuits

(G-6326)
TAO TRADING CORPORATION
1420 W Howard St Apt 201 (60626-1433)
PHONE 773 764-6542
Mona K Buechler, *President*
▲ **EMP:** 7
SALES (est): 874.2K **Privately Held**
SIC: 2531 Chairs, table & arm

(G-6327)
TARNEY INC
4520 W North Ave (60639-4723)
PHONE 773 235-0331
Raymond Peterson, *President*
EMP: 20 **EST:** 1970
SALES: 600K **Privately Held**
SIC: 3599 3469 Machine shop, jobbing & repair; metal stampings

(G-6328)
TARRERIAS-BONJEAN USA INC
541 N Fairbanks Ct # 2200 (60611-3319)
PHONE 216 217-1726
Eric Tarrerias, *CEO*
EMP: 1
SQ FT: 100
SALES: 300K **Privately Held**
SIC: 3421 Cutlery
HQ: Ets Tarrerias Bonjean Sas
Lieu Dit Le Moulin Neuf
Celles-Sur-Durolle 63250
473 515-164

(G-6329)
TATINE
4200 W Diversey Ave (60639-2047)
PHONE 312 733-0173
Kaytlin Costus, *Manager*
EMP: 5 **EST:** 2015
SALES (est): 377.2K **Privately Held**
SIC: 3999 Candles

(G-6330)
TAUBER BROTHERS TOOL & DIE CO
4701 N Olcott Ave (60706-4692)
PHONE 708 867-9100
Joseph P Tauber Jr, *President*
Cynthia Tauber, *Vice Pres*
EMP: 20
SQ FT: 30,000
SALES (est): 3.5MM **Privately Held**
WEB: www.tauberinc.com
SIC: 3469 3544 3541 Stamping metal for the trade; die sets for metal stamping (presses); machine tools, metal cutting: exotic (explosive, etc.)

(G-6331)
TAYLOR FARMS ILLINOIS INC
Also Called: Last Minute Gourmet
200 N Artesian Ave (60612-2149)
PHONE 312 432-6800
Bruce Taylor, *CEO*
Kate Brooks, *Executive*
EMP: 300
SALES (est): 44.7MM **Privately Held**
SIC: 2099 Vegetables, peeled for the trade
PA: Taylor Fresh Foods, Inc.
150 Main St Ste 400
Salinas CA 93901

(G-6332)
TDR EXPRESS INC
5231 N Oakview St Apt 3e (60656-3077)
P.O. Box 302, Des Plaines (60016-0005)
PHONE 224 805-0070
Dan Balbaie, *President*
Tony S Ardelean, *Admin Sec*
EMP: 4 **EST:** 2010
SALES (est): 503.5K **Privately Held**
SIC: 3537 Trucks: freight, baggage, etc.: industrial, except mining

(G-6333)
TEC FOODS INC
4300 W Ohio St (60624-1051)
PHONE 800 315-8002
Anastasios E Costianis, *President*
Ted Cossanis, *Director*
TAS Cospianis, *Executive*
Moscha Costianis, *Admin Sec*
EMP: 42
SQ FT: 37,000
SALES (est): 694.7K **Privately Held**
SIC: 2034 2041 5149 Soup mixes; flour; fruits, dried

(G-6334)
TECHNOLOGY ASSISTANCE USA LLC
5117 Ne River Rd Unit 1j (60656-2629)
PHONE 773 671-6712
Juan Arias, *Mng Member*
EMP: 4
SALES (est): 150.3K **Privately Held**
SIC: 3563 Air & gas compressors including vacuum pumps

(G-6335)
TECHNOX MACHINE & MFG INC
2619 N Normandy Ave (60707-2225)
PHONE 773 745-6800
Shamkant S Shirsat, *President*
Sham Shirsat, *Technology*
Amit Shirsat, *Admin Sec*
EMP: 25
SQ FT: 35,000
SALES (est): 5.9MM **Privately Held**
SIC: 3599 Machine shop, jobbing & repair

(G-6336)
TED MULLER
Also Called: Muller Roofing & Construction
910 S Michigan Ave # 1612 (60605-2356)
PHONE 312 435-0978
Ted Muller, *Owner*
EMP: 9 **EST:** 1981
SALES (est): 524K **Privately Held**
SIC: 2952 2899 1799 2621 Mastic roofing composition; waterproofing compounds; waterproofing; building & roofing paper, felts & insulation siding

(G-6337)
TEES AND THINGS
537 W 111th St (60628-4045)
PHONE 708 351-8584
Toyja Brister, *Principal*
EMP: 3 **EST:** 2017
SALES (est): 166K **Privately Held**
SIC: 2759 Screen printing

(G-6338)
TELCO MACHINE & MANUFACTURING (PA)
3957 N Normandy Ave (60634-2422)
PHONE 773 725-4441
Neil David, *President*
EMP: 31
SQ FT: 7,000
SALES (est): 3.8MM **Privately Held**
SIC: 3599 Machine shop, jobbing & repair

(G-6339)
TELCO MACHINE & MANUFACTURING
6610 W Dakin St (60634-2413)
PHONE 773 725-4441
Anil David, *Branch Mgr*
EMP: 6
SALES (corp-wide): 3.8MM **Privately Held**
SIC: 3599 Machine shop, jobbing & repair
PA: Telco Machine & Manufacturing Inc
3957 N Normandy Ave
Chicago IL 60634
773 725-4441

(G-6340)
TELEDYNE MONITOR LABS INC
12497 Collection Ctr Dr (60693-0001)
PHONE 303 792-3300
EMP: 11
SALES (corp-wide): 3.1B **Publicly Held**
SIC: 3829 Measuring & controlling devices
HQ: Teledyne Monitor Labs, Inc.
35 Inverness Dr E
Englewood CO 80112
303 792-3300

(G-6341)
TELULAR CORPORATION (HQ)
Also Called: Telguard
200 S Wacker Dr Ste 1800 (60606-5911)
PHONE 800 835-8527
Doug Milner, *CEO*
Henry Popplewell, *Vice Pres*
Jerry Deutsch, *Opers Staff*
Alicia Milner, *Purch Agent*
Maxwell Chen, *Engineer*
▲ **EMP:** 99
SQ FT: 11,700
SALES: 165MM
SALES (corp-wide): 5.1B **Publicly Held**
SIC: 3663 3669 ; burglar alarm apparatus, electric

GEOGRAPHIC SECTION

Chicago - Cook County (G-6368)

PA: Ametek, Inc.
1100 Cassatt Rd
Berwyn PA 19312
610 647-2121

(G-6342)
TELZA WELDING INC
Also Called: Telza Welding Co
1624 N Kilbourn Ave (60639-4716)
PHONE 773 777-4467
Jesse Kolekosky, *President*
EMP: 5
SQ FT: 3,000
SALES (est): 497.3K Privately Held
SIC: 7692 Welding repair

(G-6343)
TEMPEL HOLDINGS INC (PA)
Also Called: Tempel Farms
5500 N Wolcott Ave (60640-1020)
PHONE 773 250-8000
Clifford Nastas, *CEO*
Jon Mellin, *President*
Larens Leffingwell, *Admin Sec*
Nykia Carter, *Administration*
◆ EMP: 554 EST: 1947
SQ FT: 5,000
SALES (est): 389MM Privately Held
WEB: www.tempel.com
SIC: 3469 3313 3316 3398 Stamping metal for the trade; electrometallurgical products; cold finishing of steel shapes; metal heat treating; metals service centers & offices

(G-6344)
TEMPEL HOLDINGS INC
5454 N Wolcott Ave (60640-1018)
PHONE 773 250-8000
Mark Buckner, *Manager*
EMP: 800
SQ FT: 46,100
SALES (corp-wide): 389MM Privately Held
WEB: www.tempel.com
SIC: 3469 Stamping metal for the trade
PA: Tempel Holdings, Inc.
5500 N Wolcott Ave
Chicago IL 60640
773 250-8000

(G-6345)
TEMPEL STEEL COMPANY (HQ)
5500 N Wolcott Ave (60640-1020)
PHONE 773 250-8000
Timothy N Taylor, *CEO*
EMP: 7
SALES (est): 2.1MM
SALES (corp-wide): 389MM Privately Held
SIC: 3469 Stamping metal for the trade
PA: Tempel Holdings, Inc.
5500 N Wolcott Ave
Chicago IL 60640
773 250-8000

(G-6346)
TEMPRIAN THERAPEUTICS INC
222 Merchandise Mart Plz (60654-1103)
PHONE 513 374-1180
Kettil Cedercreutz, *CEO*
EMP: 4
SALES (est): 156.7K Privately Held
SIC: 2834 Pharmaceutical preparations

(G-6347)
TEMPUS LABS INC
600 W Chicago Ave Ste 510 (60654-2282)
PHONE 312 784-4400
Eric Lefkofsky, *CEO*
Ezequiel Renzulli, *District Mgr*
Erik Phelps, *Exec VP*
Una Pipic, *Opers Staff*
Kevin Torres, *Manager*
EMP: 25
SALES (est): 286.4K Privately Held
SIC: 7374 7371 7372 Data processing & preparation; computer software systems analysis & design, custom; business oriented computer software

(G-6348)
TENEX CORPORATION
230 W Superior St Ste 200 (60654-3581)
PHONE 847 504-0400
James Rabinowitz, *President*
Penny Burg, *Accounting Mgr*
▲ EMP: 35
SALES (est): 9.3MM Privately Held
WEB: www.tenex.com
SIC: 3089 Plastic kitchenware, tableware & houseware; plastic hardware & building products

(G-6349)
TENGGREN-MEHL CO INC
7019 W Higgins Ave (60656-1901)
PHONE 773 763-3290
James C Weilandt, *President*
Susan Weilandt, *Vice Pres*
EMP: 7 EST: 1927
SQ FT: 1,400
SALES (est): 800K Privately Held
SIC: 2391 Curtains & draperies

(G-6350)
TENNANT COMPANY
Also Called: Florock
1120 W Exchange Ave (60609-2510)
PHONE 773 376-7132
Byron Beamer, *Business Mgr*
Sharon Payne, *Marketing Staff*
Michael Thill, *Manager*
Cliff Ganza, *Technician*
Ashley Shew,
EMP: 38
SALES (corp-wide): 1.1B Publicly Held
SIC: 2851 Paints & allied products
PA: Tennant Company
701 Lilac Dr N
Minneapolis MN 55422
763 540-1200

(G-6351)
TENTH AND BLAKE BEER COMPANY (DH)
250 S Wacker Dr Ste 800 (60606-5888)
PHONE 312 496-2759
Tom Cardella, *President*
Gavin Hattersley, *CFO*
EMP: 8 EST: 2010
SALES (est): 9MM
SALES (corp-wide): 10.5B Publicly Held
SIC: 2082 Beer (alcoholic beverage)
HQ: Molson Coors Beverage Company Usa Llc
250 S Wacker Dr Ste 800
Chicago IL 60606
312 496-2700

(G-6352)
TEPROMARK INTERNATIONAL INC
140 S Dearborn St Ste 420 (60603-5233)
PHONE 847 329-7881
Robert J Morris, *President*
Harold Klein, *Vice Pres*
EMP: 8
SQ FT: 15,000
SALES (est): 1MM Privately Held
SIC: 2499 Decorative wood & woodwork

(G-6353)
TERCOR INC (PA)
Also Called: Wallpaperwiz.com
4343 N Claredon (60613)
PHONE 773 549-8303
Steven Terkel, *President*
▲ EMP: 7
SQ FT: 45,000
SALES (est): 1.3MM Privately Held
SIC: 2679 5231 Wallpaper; paint & painting supplies

(G-6354)
TESLA INC
1053 W Grand Ave (60642-6556)
PHONE 312 733-9780
Veronica Szklarzewski, *Engineer*
Krystal Petrovskis, *Sales Staff*
Timothy Andrews, *Manager*
Justin Jansen, *Advisor*
EMP: 12
SALES (corp-wide): 24.5B Publicly Held
WEB: www.tesla.com
SIC: 3714 3711 Motor vehicle parts & accessories; cars, electric, assembly of
PA: Tesla, Inc.
3500 Deer Creek Rd
Palo Alto CA 94304
650 681-5000

(G-6355)
TEX TANA INC (PA)
2243 W Belmont Ave Ste 1 (60618-7289)
PHONE 773 561-9270
Hans J Weil, *Ch of Bd*
Anat Unruh, *President*
Michael Cook, *Vice Pres*
Daniel Spohn, *Sales Staff*
Tony Tedesco, *Sales Staff*
◆ EMP: 5 EST: 1949
SQ FT: 8,000
SALES (est): 8.1MM Privately Held
WEB: www.tana-tex.com
SIC: 2299 Jute & flax textile products

(G-6356)
TEYS (USA) INC (HQ)
770 N Halsted St Ste 202 (60642-6930)
PHONE 312 492-7163
Brad Teys, *CEO*
Allan Teys, *Ch of Bd*
Michael Forrest, *President*
Thomas James Gallagher, *Admin Sec*
Jessica Monge, *Admin Sec*
◆ EMP: 9 EST: 2000
SQ FT: 2,300
SALES (est): 350.3MM Privately Held
SIC: 2011 Beef products from beef slaughtered on site

(G-6357)
TFA SIGNS
5500 N Kedzie Ave (60625-3924)
PHONE 773 267-6007
Abel Dejene, *General Mgr*
EMP: 4
SALES (est): 253.1K Privately Held
WEB: www.tfasigns.com
SIC: 3993 Electric signs

(G-6358)
TFO GROUP LLC
Also Called: Field Outfitting Co., The
2140 W Fulton St Ste F (60612-2338)
P.O. Box 671, Skokie (60076-0671)
PHONE 608 469-7519
Ross Paladin, *Owner*
Dan Winders, *COO*
EMP: 6
SQ FT: 3,000
SALES: 8MM Privately Held
SIC: 2329 2337 Men's & boys' sportswear & athletic clothing; women's & misses' suits & coats

(G-6359)
THANASI FOODS LLC
222 Merchandise Mart Plz # 1300 (60654-1010)
P.O. Box 3534 (60654-0534)
PHONE 720 570-1065
Justin Havlick,
▲ EMP: 35
SALES (est): 12.1MM
SALES (corp-wide): 9.5B Publicly Held
SIC: 2096 5145 Potato chips & similar snacks; confectionery
PA: Conagra Brands, Inc.
222 Mdse Mart Plz
Chicago IL 60654
312 549-5000

(G-6360)
THE SYNTEK GROUP INC
3415 N Pulaski Rd 23 (60641-4025)
PHONE 773 279-0131
Wan S Shin, *President*
Joon Shin, *Vice Pres*
Michael Shin, *Shareholder*
▲ EMP: 5
SQ FT: 7,000
SALES (est): 824.4K Privately Held
WEB: www.syntekinc.com
SIC: 3672 Printed circuit boards

(G-6361)
THERMATOME CORPORATION
2242 W Harrison St 201-22 (60612-3738)
PHONE 312 772-2201
Tom Ryan, *CEO*
Kambiz Dowlatshahi, *President*
Thomas Ryan, *General Mgr*
Christopher Valadez, *COO*
Fay Stanley, *Admin Sec*
EMP: 4
SALES (est): 260K Privately Held
SIC: 3841 3845 Surgical & medical instruments; electromedical equipment

(G-6362)
THERMOELECTRIC COOLG AMER CORP
Also Called: T E C A
4048 W Schubert Ave (60639-2122)
PHONE 773 342-4900
Mike Mikalauskis, *President*
Vasilakopoulo George, *Finance*
EMP: 2
SALES (est): 543.3K Privately Held
SIC: 3585 Refrigeration & heating equipment

(G-6363)
THG INTERNATIONAL PUBLISHING
Also Called: Interntnal Cmmnctons For MGT G
303 E Wacker Dr (60601-5212)
PHONE 312 540-3000
Marcus Evans, *President*
Paul Northover, *General Mgr*
Karen Anderson, *Mktg Dir*
Claudio A Cortes, *Director*
EMP: 20
SALES (est): 106K Privately Held
SIC: 2721 2731 Magazines: publishing only, not printed on site; book publishing

(G-6364)
THINK JERKY LLC
500 N Michigan Ave # 600 (60611-3777)
PHONE 917 623-1989
Ricchard Hirsch, *Mng Member*
EMP: 4
SALES (est): 383K Privately Held
SIC: 2013 5499 Snack sticks, including jerky: from purchased meat; dried fruit

(G-6365)
THINKCERCACOM INC
440 N Wells St Ste 720 (60654-4548)
PHONE 224 412-3722
Eileen M Buckley, *CEO*
Abby Ross, *COO*
Josh Tolman, *COO*
Brian Bar, *Vice Pres*
Ryan Dupuis, *VP Sales*
EMP: 13
SALES (est): 1.3MM Privately Held
SIC: 8299 7372 Educational services; application computer software

(G-6366)
THIRD WRLD PRESS FUNDATION INC
7822 S Dobson Ave (60619-3204)
P.O. Box 19730 (60619-0730)
PHONE 773 651-0700
Donald L Lee, *President*
Bennett Johnson, *Vice Pres*
EMP: 10
SQ FT: 7,100
SALES: 48.4K Privately Held
SIC: 2731 Books: publishing only

(G-6367)
THIS WEEK IN CHICAGO INC
Also Called: Key Magazine
222 W Ontario St Ste 420 (60654-3654)
PHONE 312 943-0838
Walter L West Jr, *President*
Walter L West III, *Publisher*
EMP: 7 EST: 1920
SQ FT: 3,000
SALES (est): 1.2MM Privately Held
WEB: www.keymagazine.com
SIC: 2721 Magazines: publishing only, not printed on site

(G-6368)
THOMSON QUANTITATIVE ANALYTICS
230 S La Salle St Ste 688 (60604-1433)
PHONE 847 610-0574
William Aronin, *President*
EMP: 20

Chicago - Cook County (G-6369)

SALES (est): 2.3MM
SALES (corp-wide): 10.6B **Publicly Held**
SIC: 5045 7372 7371 Computer software; prepackaged software; custom computer programming services
HQ: Thomson Reuters Corporation
333 Bay St
Toronto ON M5H 2
416 687-7500

(G-6369)
THOMSON REUTERS CORPORATION
1 N Dearborn St Ste 1400 (60602-4336)
PHONE 312 288-4654
EMP: 89
SALES (corp-wide): 10.6B **Publicly Held**
WEB: www.thomsonreuters.com
SIC: 2731 Books: publishing only
HQ: Thomson Reuters Corporation
333 Bay St
Toronto ON M5H 2
416 687-7500

(G-6370)
THOMSON STEEL POLISHING CORP
6150 S New England Ave (60638-4008)
PHONE 773 586-2345
Ronald Fisher, *President*
EMP: 7 EST: 1955
SQ FT: 30,000
SALES (est): 490K **Privately Held**
WEB: www.polishedstainless.com
SIC: 3471 3479 Polishing, metals or formed products; coating of metals & formed products

(G-6371)
THOUGHTLY CORP
750 N Rush St Apt 1906 (60611-2581)
PHONE 772 559-2008
Chase Perkins, *CEO*
EMP: 3
SALES (est): 182.6K **Privately Held**
SIC: 7372 Application computer software

(G-6372)
THRALL ENTERPRISES INC (PA)
180 N Stetson Ave # 4330 (60601-6794)
PHONE 312 621-8200
Jeffrey J Thrall, *Ch of Bd*
James R Thrall, *Vice Pres*
Marilynn Thrall, *Vice Pres*
◆ EMP: 11
SQ FT: 5,000
SALES (est): 200.3MM **Privately Held**
SIC: 2893 Printing ink

(G-6373)
THRILLED LLC
Also Called: Pulpulp
555 W Jackson Blvd # 400 (60661-5700)
PHONE 312 404-1929
Jacob Dehart, *Principal*
EMP: 4 EST: 2015
SALES (est): 90.8K **Privately Held**
SIC: 5651 3999 Family clothing stores; framed artwork

(G-6374)
THYNG LLC
351 W Hubbard St Ste 510 (60654-4498)
PHONE 312 262-5703
Edward Lahood,
Howard Tullman,
EMP: 9
SQ FT: 2,500
SALES (est): 451.2K **Privately Held**
SIC: 7372 Application computer software

(G-6375)
THYSSENKRUPP NORTH AMERICA INC (HQ)
111 W Jackson Blvd # 2400 (60604-4154)
PHONE 312 525-2800
Torsten Gessner, *CEO*
Mark Nettles, *Superintendent*
Derrick Richter, *Principal*
Jonathan Evans, *Vice Pres*
John Murnane, *Vice Pres*
◆ EMP: 35
SQ FT: 90,000

SALES (est): 11.8B
SALES (corp-wide): 46.8B **Privately Held**
SIC: 6719 3714 Investment holding companies, except banks; axles, motor vehicle
PA: Thyssenkrupp Ag
Thyssenkrupp Allee 1
Essen 45143
201 844-0

(G-6376)
TI GOTHAM INC
Also Called: In Style Magazine
303 E Ohio St Fl 22 (60611-3373)
PHONE 312 321-7833
Julie Trotter, *Advt Staff*
George Calzada, *Technology*
Tim Hanley, *Director*
EMP: 4
SALES (corp-wide): 3.1B **Publicly Held**
SIC: 2721 Magazines: publishing only, not printed on site
HQ: Ti Gotham Inc.
225 Liberty St
New York NY 10281
212 522-1212

(G-6377)
TIEGE HANLEY LLC
2023 W Carroll Ave C212 (60612-1690)
PHONE 312 953-4131
Kelley Thorton, *Mng Member*
Robert Hoxie,
EMP: 4 EST: 2015
SALES (est): 300K **Privately Held**
SIC: 5961 2844 Catalog & mail-order houses; toilet preparations

(G-6378)
TIGHE PUBLISHING SERVICES INC
1700 W Irvng Park Rd # 210 (60613-2599)
PHONE 773 281-9100
Suzanne H Tighe, *President*
Austin Tighe, *Vice Pres*
Susan Deming, *Manager*
Michael Anderson, *Director*
Sue Evans, *Director*
EMP: 19
SALES (est): 1.8MM **Privately Held**
SIC: 2741 8748 Miscellaneous publishing; business consulting

(G-6379)
TIME OUT CHICAGO PARTNERS LLLP
247 S State St Fl 17 (60604-2053)
PHONE 312 924-9555
Alison Tocci, *President*
EMP: 19
SALES (est): 2.6MM
SALES (corp-wide): 62.6MM **Privately Held**
SIC: 2759 Magazines: printing
HQ: Time Out Digital Limited
77 Wicklow Street
London WC1X
207 813-3000

(G-6380)
TIMKEN DRIVES LLC
875 N Michigan Ave (60611-1803)
P.O. Box 71523 (60694-1523)
PHONE 312 274-9710
Mark Millmore, *Branch Mgr*
EMP: 5
SALES (corp-wide): 3.7B **Publicly Held**
SIC: 3462 Chains, forged steel
HQ: Timken Drives, Llc
901 19th Ave
Fulton IL 61252
815 589-2211

(G-6381)
TINI MARTINI
2169 N Milwaukee Ave (60647-4058)
PHONE 773 269-2900
EMP: 3 EST: 2005
SALES (est): 150K **Privately Held**
SIC: 2711 5813 Newspapers-Publishing/Printing Drinking Place

(G-6382)
TMB INDUSTRIES INC
Also Called: Begel Industries
980 N Michigan Ave # 11400 (60611-4501)
PHONE 312 280-2565
Tom Begel, *Chairman*
Tim Masek, *Director*
EMP: 580
SQ FT: 3,000
SALES (est): 33.4MM **Privately Held**
SIC: 6799 3321 Real estate investors, except property operators; gray & ductile iron foundries

(G-6383)
TODAYS TEMPTATIONS INC
1900 N Austin Ave Ste 72 (60639-5078)
PHONE 773 385-5355
Al Filin, *President*
▲ EMP: 14
SALES (est): 1.2MM **Privately Held**
SIC: 2051 Bakery: wholesale or wholesale/retail combined

(G-6384)
TOGGLE INC (PA)
2004 Wattles Dr (60614)
PHONE 323 882-6339
Adam Johnson, *CEO*
John Cho, *COO*
EMP: 9
SALES (est): 1.1MM **Privately Held**
SIC: 3571 Computers, digital, analog or hybrid

(G-6385)
TOHO TECHNOLOGY INC
4809 N Ravenswood Ave (60640-4495)
PHONE 773 583-7183
John B Coomes, *President*
EMP: 9
SALES (est): 1.4MM **Privately Held**
SIC: 3699 Electrical equipment & supplies

(G-6386)
TOM CROWN MUTE CO
4110 N Nashville Ave (60634-1429)
PHONE 773 930-4979
Tom Crown, *President*
William Camp, *Vice Pres*
EMP: 4
SALES (est): 225.9K **Privately Held**
SIC: 3931 Musical instruments

(G-6387)
TOM TOM TAMALES MFG CO INC
Also Called: Tom Tom Tamales & Baking Co
4750 S Washtenaw Ave (60632-2096)
PHONE 773 523-5675
Nick C Petros, *President*
George Anos, *Director*
Chris Lito, *Director*
Joan Pratt, *Admin Sec*
EMP: 10
SQ FT: 16,000
SALES (est): 995.5K **Privately Held**
SIC: 2032 5149 Tamales: packaged in cans, jars, etc.; bakery products

(G-6388)
TOMAHAWK DEFENSE
1230 W Altgeld St (60614-2105)
PHONE 773 871-7268
Nick Pontikes, *Principal*
EMP: 3
SALES (est): 187.5K **Privately Held**
SIC: 3812 Defense systems & equipment

(G-6389)
TOMCYNDI INC
Also Called: Chicago Steaks
822 W Exchange Ave (60609-2507)
P.O. Box 9083 (60609-0601)
PHONE 773 847-5400
Thomas Summers, *President*
EMP: 25
SQ FT: 26,500
SALES (est): 4.4MM **Privately Held**
SIC: 5147 2013 2011 Meats & meat products; sausages & other prepared meats; meat packing plants

(G-6390)
TONY PATTERSON
Also Called: Street Comedy Records
623 E 89th St (60619-6829)
PHONE 773 487-4000
Tony Patterson, *Principal*
EMP: 3 EST: 2000
SALES (est): 130K **Privately Held**
SIC: 3652 Compact laser discs, prerecorded

(G-6391)
TOOTSIE ROLL COMPANY INC
7401 S Cicero Ave (60629-5885)
PHONE 773 838-3400
Ellen R Gordon, *President*
Barry Bowen, *Treasurer*
G Howard Ember Jr, *VP Finance*
EMP: 1000
SQ FT: 1,500,000
SALES (est): 119.4MM
SALES (corp-wide): 527.1MM **Publicly Held**
SIC: 2064 Candy & other confectionery products
HQ: Tootsie Roll Industries, Llc
7401 S Cicero Ave
Chicago IL 60629

(G-6392)
TOOTSIE ROLL INDUSTRIES INC (PA)
7401 S Cicero Ave (60629-5885)
PHONE 773 838-3400
Ellen R Gordon, *Ch of Bd*
Peter Lebron, *Vice Pres*
John P Majors, *Vice Pres*
John Majors, *Vice Pres*
Stephen P Green, *VP Mfg*
▲ EMP: 850 EST: 1896
SQ FT: 2,354,000
SALES: 527.1MM **Publicly Held**
WEB: www.tootsie.com
SIC: 2064 Candy & other confectionery products

(G-6393)
TOOTSIE ROLL INDUSTRIES LLC (HQ)
7401 S Cicero Ave (60629-5885)
PHONE 773 245-4202
Ellen Gordon, *President*
G Howard Ember, *CFO*
Barry Bowen, *Treasurer*
EMP: 4
SALES (est): 168MM
SALES (corp-wide): 527.1MM **Publicly Held**
SIC: 2064 Candy & other confectionery products
PA: Tootsie Roll Industries, Inc.
7401 S Cicero Ave
Chicago IL 60629
773 838-3400

(G-6394)
TOOTSIE ROLL WORLDWIDE LTD (DH)
7401 S Cicero Ave (60629-5885)
PHONE 773 838-3400
Ellen Gordon, *President*
G Howard Ember Jr, *Admin Sec*
◆ EMP: 2
SALES (est): 210.7K
SALES (corp-wide): 527.1MM **Publicly Held**
SIC: 2064 Candy & other confectionery products

(G-6395)
TOP NOTCH SILK SCREENING
3382 S Archer Ave (60608-6810)
PHONE 773 847-6335
Sam Vainisi, *President*
Tony Slezak, *Treasurer*
Maggie Slezak, *Sales Staff*
EMP: 7
SQ FT: 7,500
SALES (est): 986.3K **Privately Held**
SIC: 2261 2396 Screen printing of cotton broadwoven fabrics; automotive & apparel trimmings

GEOGRAPHIC SECTION   Chicago - Cook County (G-6421)

(G-6396)
TOPWEB LLC
5450 N Northwest Hwy (60630-1114)
PHONE.................................773 975-0400
Charles Gross, *President*
EMP: 41
SQ FT: 55,000
SALES (est): 5.3MM
SALES (corp-wide): 8.2MM **Privately Held**
WEB: www.topweb.net
SIC: 2752 Commercial printing, offset
PA: Newsweb Corporation
2401 N Halsted St
Chicago IL 60614
773 975-5727

(G-6397)
TORSTENSON GLASS CO
3233 N Sheffield Ave (60657-2210)
PHONE.................................773 525-0435
Douglas Studt, *President*
Brad Studt, *Vice Pres*
Kevin Byczek, *Manager*
▲ EMP: 25 EST: 1889
SQ FT: 50,000
SALES (est): 4.1MM **Privately Held**
WEB: www.tglass.com
SIC: 3231 5039 Products of purchased glass; exterior flat glass: plate or window; interior flat glass: plate or window

(G-6398)
TORTILLERIA ATOTONILCO INC
1850 W 47th St (60609-3845)
PHONE.................................773 523-0800
Oscar Munoz, *President*
EMP: 20
SQ FT: 25,200
SALES (corp-wide): 14.2MM **Privately Held**
WEB: www.tortilleriaatotonilco.com
SIC: 5149 5461 2051 Crackers, cookies & bakery products; bakeries; bread, cake & related products
PA: Tortilleria Atotonilco, Inc.
1707 W 47th St
Chicago IL 60609
773 523-0800

(G-6399)
TOTALWORKS INC
420 W Huron St (60654-8475)
PHONE.................................773 489-4313
Gail Ludeven, *President*
Bruce Jensen, *Corp Secy*
EMP: 35
SQ FT: 15,000
SALES (est): 2.9MM **Privately Held**
WEB: www.totalworks.net
SIC: 2741 Catalogs: publishing only, not printed on site

(G-6400)
TOWER ATMTIVE OPRTONS USA I LL
12350 S Avenue O (60633-1171)
PHONE.................................773 646-6550
Matt Pollick, *Branch Mgr*
EMP: 358
SALES (corp-wide): 2.2B **Privately Held**
SIC: 3465 Automotive stampings
HQ: Tower Automotive Operations Usa I, Llc
17672 N Laurel Park Dr 400e
Livonia MI 48152

(G-6401)
TOWER OIL & TECHNOLOGY CO
Also Called: Industrial Technology
4300 S Tripp Ave (60632-4319)
PHONE.................................773 927-6161
Ron Bielech, *Branch Mgr*
EMP: 35
SALES (corp-wide): 5.3MM **Privately Held**
SIC: 5172 2992 2899 Petroleum products; lubricating oils & greases; chemical preparations
PA: Tower Oil & Technology Co.
4300 S Tripp Ave
Chicago IL 60632
773 927-6161

(G-6402)
TRADE PRINT INC
7748 W Addison St (60634-3018)
PHONE.................................773 625-0792
John Pratola, *President*
EMP: 1
SQ FT: 3,000
SALES (est): 600K **Privately Held**
SIC: 2731 2752 Book publishing; commercial printing, lithographic

(G-6403)
TRAENA INC (PA)
2158 Pine St 2 (60602)
PHONE.................................630 605-3087
Christopher Wade, *President*
Aram Taghavi, *Co-President*
EMP: 3
SALES (est): 323.3K **Privately Held**
SIC: 7371 7372 Computer software development & applications; business oriented computer software

(G-6404)
TRAFFCO PRODUCTS LLC
7731 S South Chicago Ave (60619-2721)
PHONE.................................773 374-6645
Alex Degutis, *Vice Pres*
Paul Leitelt, *Mng Member*
Andrew Leitelt,
EMP: 9
SQ FT: 25,000
SALES (est): 500K **Privately Held**
SIC: 3669 Traffic signals, electric

(G-6405)
TRAFFICCOM (DH)
425 W Randolph St (60606-1530)
PHONE.................................773 997-8351
Judson Green, *President*
EMP: 7
SALES (est): 636.2K
SALES (corp-wide): 1.6B **Privately Held**
SIC: 2752 Maps, lithographed
HQ: Here Holding Corporation
425 W Randolph St
Chicago IL 60606
312 894-7000

(G-6406)
TRANE TECHNOLOGIES COMPANY LLC
Also Called: Ingersoll-Rand
15768 Collection Ctr Dr (60693-0001)
PHONE.................................704 655-4000
EMP: 34 **Privately Held**
SIC: 3561 3563 2899 Pumps & pumping equipment; air & gas compressors including vacuum pumps; corrosion preventive lubricant
HQ: Trane Technologies Company Llc
800 Beaty St
Davidson NC 28036
704 655-4000

(G-6407)
TRANSAGRA INTERNATIONAL INC (PA)
155 N Michigan Ave # 720 (60601-7707)
PHONE.................................312 856-1010
Henry A Sakai, *President*
Lisa Sakai, *Vice Pres*
Jane Caldwell, *Research*
Megan Alexander, *Marketing Staff*
EMP: 2
SQ FT: 450
SALES (est): 1.1MM **Privately Held**
WEB: www.transagra.com
SIC: 2048 Feed supplements

(G-6408)
TRANSCO INC
Also Called: Transco Railway Products
200 N La Salle St Lbby 5 (60601-1088)
PHONE.................................419 562-1031
EMP: 143
SALES (corp-wide): 96.7MM **Privately Held**
SIC: 3441 Fabricated structural metal
PA: Transco Inc.
200 N La Salle St # 1550
Chicago IL 60601
312 896-8527

(G-6409)
TRANSCO RAILWAY PRODUCTS INC (DH)
200 N La Salle St Lbby 5 (60601-1088)
PHONE.................................312 427-2818
Bob Nelson, *President*
▲ EMP: 6
SALES (est): 74.1MM
SALES (corp-wide): 327.2B **Publicly Held**
SIC: 3743 4789 Railroad equipment; railroad car repair
HQ: Marmon Holdings, Inc.
181 W Madison St Ste 2600
Chicago IL 60602
312 372-9500

(G-6410)
TRANSCONTINENTAL HOLDING CORP (DH)
8600 W Bryn Mawr Ave (60631-3579)
P.O. Box 5687, Spartanburg SC (29304-5687)
PHONE.................................773 877-3300
Dimitri Panayotopoulos, *CEO*
Steve Mullins, *COO*
Michael Alger, *CFO*
Duane Owens, *Treasurer*
Gary Masse, *Director*
◆ EMP: 0
SALES (est): 878.2MM
SALES (corp-wide): 2.2B **Privately Held**
SIC: 6719 2673 2631 Investment holding companies, except banks; bags: plastic, laminated & coated; container, packaging & boxboard

(G-6411)
TRANSCONTINENTAL TECH LLC
Also Called: Exopack
8600 W Bryn Mawr Ave (60631-3579)
PHONE.................................877 447-3539
Gary Masse, *CEO*
EMP: 2
SALES (est): 15.2MM
SALES (corp-wide): 2.2B **Privately Held**
SIC: 2673 Bags: plastic, laminated & coated
HQ: Transcontinental Holding Corp.
8600 W Bryn Mawr Ave
Chicago IL 60631

(G-6412)
TRANSFER LOGISTICS INC
11600 S Burley Ave (60617-7203)
PHONE.................................773 646-0529
EMP: 2
SALES (est): 290K **Privately Held**
SIC: 3537 Mfg Industrial Trucks/Tractors

(G-6413)
TRANSLUCENT PUBLISHING CORP
222 W Ontario St Ste 410 (60654-3654)
PHONE.................................312 447-5450
Richard Rueckheim, *Director*
EMP: 15 EST: 2013
SALES (est): 1.1MM **Privately Held**
SIC: 2741 Miscellaneous publishing

(G-6414)
TREATMENT PRODUCTS LTD
4701 W Augusta Blvd (60651-3307)
PHONE.................................773 626-8888
Jeff Victor, *President*
Jeff A Victor, *Vice Pres*
Ken Victor, *Vice Pres*
Luis Vasquez, *Representative*
◆ EMP: 40
SQ FT: 60,000
SALES (est): 11MM **Privately Held**
SIC: 2842 7389 Automobile polish; waxes for wood, leather & other materials; packaging & labeling services

(G-6415)
TREND PUBLISHING INC
Also Called: Modern Metal Products
625 N Michigan Ave # 1050 (60611-3112)
PHONE.................................312 654-2300
William J D'Alexander, *President*
Jim Dalexander, *COO*
Carlotta Lacy, *VP Prdtn*
Traci Fonville, *Sales Staff*
Tracy Fonville, *Manager*
EMP: 24
SQ FT: 8,000
SALES (est): 3.2MM **Privately Held**
SIC: 2741 Miscellaneous publishing

(G-6416)
TRENDLER INC
4540 W 51st St (60632-4554)
PHONE.................................773 284-6600
Andreas R Gfesser, *President*
Martin F Gfesser, *President*
Anton Gfesser, *Chairman*
Steven A Gfesser, *Corp Secy*
Tom Byers, *CFO*
▲ EMP: 45 EST: 1933
SQ FT: 120,000
SALES (est): 12.1MM **Privately Held**
WEB: www.trendler.com
SIC: 3499 2511 Furniture parts, metal; unassembled or unfinished furniture, household: wood; rockers, except upholstered: wood

(G-6417)
TRI INTERNATIONAL CO
Also Called: Tootsie Roll Industries
7401 S Cicero Ave (60629-5818)
PHONE.................................773 838-3400
Howard Denver, *CEO*
Ellen R Gordon, *President*
Thomas Corr, *Vice Pres*
John Major, *Vice Pres*
Howard Ember, *CFO*
EMP: 650
SALES (est): 37.7MM
SALES (corp-wide): 527.1MM **Publicly Held**
SIC: 2064 Chocolate candy, except solid chocolate
PA: Tootsie Roll Industries, Inc.
7401 S Cicero Ave
Chicago IL 60629
773 838-3400

(G-6418)
TRI SALES CO
Charms Division
7401 S Cicero Ave (60629-5818)
PHONE.................................773 838-3400
EMP: 16
SALES (corp-wide): 527.1MM **Publicly Held**
SIC: 2064 Candy & other confectionery products
HQ: Tri Sales Co.
7401 S Cicero Ave
Chicago IL 60629

(G-6419)
TRI SALES CO
Tootsie Roll Division
7401 S Cicero Ave (60629-5818)
PHONE.................................773 838-3400
EMP: 16
SALES (corp-wide): 527.1MM **Publicly Held**
SIC: 2064 Candy & other confectionery products
HQ: Tri Sales Co.
7401 S Cicero Ave
Chicago IL 60629

(G-6420)
TRI SALES CO
Concord Division
7401 S Cicero Ave (60629-5818)
PHONE.................................773 838-3400
EMP: 16
SALES (corp-wide): 527.1MM **Publicly Held**
SIC: 2064 Candy & other confectionery products
HQ: Tri Sales Co.
7401 S Cicero Ave
Chicago IL 60629

(G-6421)
TRI SALES CO (DH)
7401 S Cicero Ave (60629-5818)
PHONE.................................773 838-3400
Ellen R Gordon, *President*
▼ EMP: 1

Chicago - Cook County (G-6422)

SALES (est): 6.6MM
SALES (corp-wide): 527.1MM **Publicly Held**
SIC: 2064 Candy & other confectionery products

(G-6422)
TRI-LITE INC
1642 N Besly Ct (60642-1526)
PHONE 773 384-7765
Robert Hearling, *President*
Barry Seid, *Chairman*
Mike Mackin, *Engineer*
Kathy Mann, *Rector*
▲ EMP: 22
SQ FT: 20,000
SALES (est): 5.2MM **Privately Held**
SIC: 3647 3648 3646 3669 Automotive lighting fixtures; lighting fixtures, except electric: residential; stage lighting equipment; commercial indusl & institutional electric lighting fixtures; emergency alarms; sirens, electric: vehicle, marine, industrial & air raid; intercommunication systems, electric; electric household fans, heaters & humidifiers

(G-6423)
TRIBUNE PUBLISHING COMPANY (PA)
160 N Stetson Ave (60601-6725)
PHONE 312 222-9100
Terry Jimenez, *President*
EMP: 101
SALES: 983.1MM **Publicly Held**
SIC: 2711 Newspapers, publishing & printing

(G-6424)
TRIBUNE PUBLISHING COMPANY LLC (HQ)
435 N Michigan Ave Fl 2 (60611-4067)
PHONE 312 222-9100
Jack Fuller, *President*
Dean Magnavite, *Editor*
John Bode, *Exec VP*
Robert Gremillion, *Exec VP*
Julie Xanders, *Exec VP*
EMP: 20
SALES (est): 1B
SALES (corp-wide): 983.1MM **Publicly Held**
SIC: 2711 Newspapers, publishing & printing
PA: Tribune Publishing Company
160 N Stetson Ave
Chicago IL 60601
312 222-9100

(G-6425)
TRIBUNE PUBLISHING COMPANY LLC
Also Called: Chicago Magazine
435 N Michigan Ave Fl 2 (60611-4067)
PHONE 312 832-6711
Christine Cossette, *Accounts Exec*
Carlas Gilbert, *Branch Mgr*
Jessica Sedgwick, *Art Dir*
Tal Rosenberg, *Senior Editor*
EMP: 55
SALES (corp-wide): 983.1MM **Publicly Held**
SIC: 2711 2721 Newspapers, publishing & printing; periodicals
HQ: Tribune Publishing Company, Llc
435 N Michigan Ave Fl 2
Chicago IL 60611

(G-6426)
TRIBUS AEROSPACE CORP
10 S Wacker Dr Ste 3300 (60606-7429)
PHONE 312 876-2683
C Scott Shedd, *Co-COB*
Simon Farhi, *Co-COB*
Douglas Knoch, *Vice Pres*
David Hawkins, *Treasurer*
Mary-Elizabeth Hadley, *Associate*
EMP: 5 EST: 2017
SALES (est): 287.3K **Privately Held**
SIC: 3721 Aircraft

(G-6427)
TRIBUS AEROSPACE LLC (PA)
10 S Wacker Dr Ste 3300 (60606-7429)
PHONE 312 876-7267
C Scott Shedd, *Co-COB*
Simon Farhi, *Co-COB*
Douglas Knoch, *Vice Pres*
David Hawkins, *Treasurer*
EMP: 5
SALES (est): 56.9MM **Privately Held**
SIC: 3599 Machine shop, jobbing & repair

(G-6428)
TRINKET STUDIOS
3701 N Ravenswood Ave # 206 (60613-3553)
PHONE 773 888-3454
Benjamin Perez, *Treasurer*
Ben Perez, *Prgrmr*
EMP: 3 EST: 2012
SALES (est): 166.7K **Privately Held**
SIC: 7372 Application computer software

(G-6429)
TRIPPE MANUFACTURING COMPANY
Also Called: Tripp Lite
1111 W 35th St Fl 12 (60609-1404)
PHONE 773 869-1111
Elbert Howell, *CEO*
Glen Haeflinger, *President*
Caroline Perigny, *Business Mgr*
Ed Komoski, *COO*
Tony Locker, *Vice Pres*
◆ EMP: 500 EST: 1930
SQ FT: 950,000
SALES (est): 342MM **Privately Held**
WEB: www.tripplite.com
SIC: 3577 Computer peripheral equipment

(G-6430)
TRITON INDUSTRIES INC (PA)
1020 N Kolmar Ave (60651-3343)
PHONE 773 384-3700
Marvin R Wortell, *Ch of Bd*
Brenton R Wortell, *President*
Thomas Fuss, *CFO*
Cindy Churak, *Executive*
EMP: 149 EST: 1961
SQ FT: 100,000
SALES (est): 19.6MM **Privately Held**
WEB: www.tritonindustries.com
SIC: 3469 3441 Stamping metal for the trade; electronic enclosures, stamped or pressed metal; kitchen fixtures & equipment: metal, except cast aluminum; fabricated structural metal

(G-6431)
TRIUMPH BOOKS LLC
814 N Franklin St (60610-3813)
PHONE 800 888-4741
Mitch Rogatz, *President*
EMP: 3
SALES (est): 107.9K **Privately Held**
SIC: 2731 Book publishing

(G-6432)
TRIUMPH BOOKS CORP
814 N Franklin St Fl 3 (60610-3813)
PHONE 312 337-0747
Mitchell Rogatz, *President*
Noah Amstadter, *Editor*
Bill Ames, *Manager*
Adam Motin, *Manager*
Michael Michalak, *Administration*
◆ EMP: 22
SQ FT: 4,100
SALES (est): 4.4MM **Privately Held**
SIC: 2731 Books: publishing only

(G-6433)
TROTTA ENTERPRISES INC
Also Called: Marko International, Inc
1050 W Hubbard St (60642-8383)
PHONE 312 829-7084
Carmen Trotta, *President*
EMP: 75 EST: 1979
SALES: 10MM
SALES (corp-wide): 326.5MM **Privately Held**
SIC: 2392 Tablecloths: made from purchased materials; napkins, fabric & nonwoven: made from purchased materials; tablecloths & table settings; shower curtains: made from purchased materials
HQ: Cfs Brands, Llc
4711 E Hefner Rd
Oklahoma City OK 73131
405 475-5600

(G-6434)
TROY DESIGN & MANUFACTURING CO
3400 E 126th St (60633-1293)
PHONE 312 692-9706
John Lowery, *President*
EMP: 8
SALES (corp-wide): 155.9B **Publicly Held**
SIC: 3465 Automotive stampings
HQ: Troy Design & Manufacturing Co
14425 N Sheldon Rd
Plymouth MI 48170
734 738-2300

(G-6435)
TRU SERV CORP
8600 W Bryn Mawr Ave (60631-3579)
P.O. Box 31850 (60631-0850)
PHONE 773 695-5674
Fax: 773 695-6566
EMP: 18 EST: 2008
SALES (est): 2.4MM **Privately Held**
SIC: 2851 Mfg Paints/Allied Products

(G-6436)
TRUCKERS OIL PROS INC
2756 W 35th St (60632-1604)
PHONE 773 523-8990
Michael Marden, *President*
Ponch Acosta, *Admin Sec*
EMP: 11
SQ FT: 20,000
SALES (est): 1.4MM **Privately Held**
SIC: 2992 7542 Oils & greases, blending & compounding; carwashes

(G-6437)
TRUE VALUE COMPANY LLC (HQ)
8600 W Bryn Mawr Ave 100s (60631-3505)
PHONE 773 695-5000
Brent Burger, *Ch of Bd*
John Hartmann, *President*
John Klinge, *Superintendent*
Jeffrey Brewer, *Regional Mgr*
Erin Stimmell-Clark, *Regional Mgr*
◆ EMP: 500
SQ FT: 175,000
SALES (est): 651.2MM **Privately Held**
WEB: www.truevaluecompany.com
SIC: 7359 2851 3991 Equipment rental & leasing; paints & paint additives; paint & varnish brushes

(G-6438)
TRUEPAD LLC
180 N Wabash Ave Ste 730 (60601-3600)
P.O. Box 3364 (60654-0341)
PHONE 847 274-6898
Paul Lazarre,
Scott Hammack,
EMP: 18
SALES (est): 1.2MM **Privately Held**
SIC: 7372 7389 Business oriented computer software;

(G-6439)
TRUSTED MEDIA BRANDS INC
Also Called: Reader's Digest
233 N Michigan Ave # 1740 (60601-5519)
PHONE 312 540-0035
Kelly Maier, *Branch Mgr*
Bonnie Hutchinson, *Director*
EMP: 20 **Privately Held**
SIC: 2721 Magazines: publishing only, not printed on site
HQ: Trusted Media Brands, Inc.
750 3rd Ave Fl 3
New York NY 10017
914 238-1000

(G-6440)
TRUSTWAVE HOLDINGS INC (DH)
70 W Madison St Ste 600 (60602-4210)
PHONE 312 750-0950
Arthur Wong, *CEO*
Julie Nagle, *Senior VP*
George Tomic, *Senior VP*
Mark Domzal, *Vice Pres*
Al Hannagan, *Vice Pres*
EMP: 1
SALES (est): 102.4MM **Privately Held**
SIC: 7373 7372 Systems integration services; prepackaged software
HQ: Singtel Enterprise Security (Us), Inc.
901 Marshall St Ste 125
Redwood City CA 94063
650 508-6800

(G-6441)
TRUVANITY BEAUTY LLC (PA)
55 E Monroe St Ste 3800 (60603-6030)
PHONE 312 778-6499
Tiffany Myers, *Mng Member*
EMP: 4
SALES (est): 327K **Privately Held**
SIC: 7231 3999 5999 Hairdressers; hair & hair-based products; hair care products

(G-6442)
TRX PUBCO LLC (HQ)
435 N Michigan Ave (60611-4066)
PHONE 312 222-9100
EMP: 4
SALES (est): 331.9MM
SALES (corp-wide): 983.1MM **Publicly Held**
SIC: 2711 6719 Commercial printing & newspaper publishing combined; investment holding companies, except banks
PA: Tribune Publishing Company
160 N Stetson Ave
Chicago IL 60601
312 222-9100

(G-6443)
TURFMAPP INC
3550 N Lake Shore Dr (60657-1944)
PHONE 703 473-5678
Triratana Sanguanbun, *President*
Trisikh Sanguanbun, *Vice Pres*
EMP: 6
SALES (est): 238.9K **Privately Held**
SIC: 7372 7389 Prepackaged software;

(G-6444)
TURNER AGWARD
Also Called: Intelliginix Consulting Svcs
5642 W Div St Ste 212 (60651)
PHONE 773 669-8559
Agward Turner, *Owner*
EMP: 5
SALES (est): 240K **Privately Held**
SIC: 1731 7372 7373 8748 Voice, data & video wiring contractor; operating systems computer software; systems engineering, computer related; systems engineering consultant, ex. computer or professional;

(G-6445)
TWEETEN FIBRE CO
Also Called: Masters Billiard Chalk
1756 W Hubbard St (60622-6214)
PHONE 312 733-7878
Robert R Knight, *President*
Irvin Nemecek, *Vice Pres*
▲ EMP: 20
SQ FT: 18,000
SALES (est): 2.3MM **Privately Held**
WEB: www.tweeten.us
SIC: 3949 Billiard & pool equipment & supplies, general

(G-6446)
TWO J S SHEET METAL WORKS INC
5828 S Oakley Ave (60636-1525)
PHONE 773 436-9424
Juan Macias, *President*
Jesus Macias, *Vice Pres*
EMP: 4
SQ FT: 5,600
SALES (est): 619.1K **Privately Held**
WEB: www.twojssheetmetalworks.com
SIC: 3444 Sheet metalwork

(G-6447)
TWO JS COPIES NOW INC
Also Called: Sir Speedy
6725 N Northwest Hwy (60631-1319)
PHONE 847 292-2679
John Crocello, *President*
Jeanne Crocello, *Vice Pres*
EMP: 6
SQ FT: 1,200

GEOGRAPHIC SECTION

Chicago - Cook County (G-6474)

SALES (est): 832K **Privately Held**
SIC: 2752 Commercial printing, lithographic

(G-6448)
TWO TOWER FRAMES INC
Also Called: Safigel
3501 N Sthport Ave Chcago Chicago (60657)
PHONE.................................773 517-0394
EMP: 4
SALES (est): 464.7K **Privately Held**
SIC: 3827 5048 Optical instruments & lenses; ophthalmic goods; contact lenses; frames, ophthalmic

(G-6449)
TWT MARKETING INC
Also Called: Wecaretoo
2719 W Lunt Ave (60645-3005)
PHONE.................................773 274-4470
Shelby Miller, *President*
Richard Scheafer, *Vice Pres*
EMP: 2 EST: 1992
SALES (est): 200K **Privately Held**
WEB: www.wecaretoo.com
SIC: 4813 2741 ; telephone & other directory publishing

(G-6450)
TYLU WIRELESS TECHNOLOGY LLC
3424 S State St (60616-5374)
P.O. Box 436900 (60643-6900)
PHONE.................................312 260-7934
Michael E Aldridge, *CEO*
Roger Hutchings, *President*
Tom Freeburg, *Vice Pres*
Paul Schaafsma, *Vice Pres*
EMP: 8
SQ FT: 2,000
SALES (est): 625.5K **Privately Held**
SIC: 3699 4812 7373 Security control equipment & systems; cellular telephone services; systems software development services

(G-6451)
TYSON
3548 N Kostner Ave (60641-3807)
PHONE.................................773 282-2900
Donnie Smith, *President*
Jonathan Perez-Rodriguez, *Persnl Mgr*
Anthony Cericoa, *Maintence Staff*
EMP: 12
SALES (est): 1.1MM
SALES (corp-wide): 42.4B **Publicly Held**
WEB: www.tyson.com
SIC: 2011 Meat packing plants
PA: Tyson Foods, Inc.
2200 W Don Tyson Pkwy
Springdale AR 72762
479 290-4000

(G-6452)
TYSON FOODS (DH)
400 S Jefferson St (60607-3822)
PHONE.................................312 614-6000
Steve McMilliam, *CEO*
Berna Barnes, *CEO*
Eric Schulze, *Counsel*
Mary Bedell, *Vice Pres*
John Reicks, *Vice Pres*
EMP: 112
SALES (est): 52.6MM
SALES (corp-wide): 42.4B **Publicly Held**
SIC: 2013 Sausages & other prepared meats
HQ: The Hillshire Brands Company
400 S Jefferson St Fl 1
Chicago IL 60607
312 614-6000

(G-6453)
TYSON FOODS INC
4201 S Ashland Ave (60609-2305)
P.O. Box 96080 (60693-6080)
PHONE.................................773 650-4000
Alex Dyadenko, *Maintence Staff*
EMP: 10
SALES (corp-wide): 42.4B **Publicly Held**
SIC: 2015 Poultry slaughtering & processing
PA: Tyson Foods, Inc.
2200 W Don Tyson Pkwy
Springdale AR 72762
479 290-4000

(G-6454)
UBER TECHNOLOGIES INC
111 N Canal St Ste 900 (60606-7204)
PHONE.................................612 600-4737
EMP: 133
SALES (corp-wide): 750.5MM **Privately Held**
SIC: 7372 Prepackaged Software Services
PA: Uber Technologies, Inc.
1455 Market St Fl 4
San Francisco CA 94103

(G-6455)
UHLIR MANUFACTURING CORP
2642 W Cullerton St (60608-2422)
PHONE.................................773 376-5289
Jim Uhlir, *President*
Jana Uhlir, *Corp Secy*
EMP: 6
SQ FT: 5,000
SALES: 420.1K **Privately Held**
SIC: 3599 Machine shop, jobbing & repair

(G-6456)
UIC
1747 W Roosevelt Rd 145 (60608-1264)
PHONE.................................312 413-7697
Octavia Kincaid, *Principal*
Charles Hoch, *Vice Chairman*
Anna Sandoval, *Research*
Anne Fink, *Med Doctor*
Rebecca Mischak, *Med Doctor*
EMP: 17 EST: 2009
SALES (est): 1.8MM **Privately Held**
WEB: www.uicflames.com
SIC: 3999 Stage hardware & equipment, except lighting

(G-6457)
ULLA OF FINLAND
6221 N Leona Ave (60646-4829)
PHONE.................................773 763-0700
Ulla Marzolf, *Managing Prtnr*
Serge Marzolf, *Partner*
EMP: 2
SALES (est): 200K **Privately Held**
SIC: 3911 Jewelry, precious metal

(G-6458)
ULTIMATE SIGN CO
5511 W Pensacola Ave (60641-1335)
PHONE.................................773 282-4595
Jack Fraizer, *President*
EMP: 6
SALES (est): 200K **Privately Held**
SIC: 3993 Signs, not made in custom sign painting shops

(G-6459)
ULTRA-METRIC TOOL CO
2952 N Leavitt St (60618-8197)
PHONE.................................773 281-4200
Steven Huy, *President*
Frank Gieger, *Vice Pres*
EMP: 17
SQ. FT: 17,000
SALES (est): 1.7MM **Privately Held**
SIC: 3599 3544 Machine shop, jobbing & repair; special dies, tools, jigs & fixtures

(G-6460)
UMPHREYS MCGEE INC
1530 W Oakdale Ave (60657-4011)
PHONE.................................773 880-0024
Vince Iwinski, *Manager*
EMP: 3
SALES (est): 263.8K **Privately Held**
SIC: 3931 Musical instruments

(G-6461)
UNCOMMON RADIANT
2826 W Fitch Ave (60645-2906)
PHONE.................................773 640-1674
Hildi Dvora, *President*
Yakov Dvora, *Vice Pres*
▲ EMP: 3
SALES (est): 285.3K **Privately Held**
SIC: 3645 Residential lighting fixtures

(G-6462)
UNI-GLIDE CORP
2300 N Kilbourn Ave (60639-3402)
PHONE.................................773 235-2100
Brian H Johnson, *President*
EMP: 7
SALES (est): 296.3K
SALES (corp-wide): 6.1MM **Privately Held**
SIC: 2591 5072 Curtain & drapery rods, poles & fixtures; hardware
PA: Rensel-Chicago, Inc.
2300 N Kilbourn Ave
Chicago IL 60639
773 235-2100

(G-6463)
UNICHEM CORPORATION
1201 W 37th St (60609-2122)
PHONE.................................773 376-8872
Eugene O Korey, *President*
Nowell Korey, *President*
Irv O Korey, *Vice Pres*
EMP: 12
SQ FT: 25,000
SALES (est): 2.8MM **Privately Held**
WEB: www.unichemco.com
SIC: 2841 Soap: granulated, liquid, cake, flaked or chip; detergents, synthetic organic or inorganic alkaline

(G-6464)
UNICUT CORPORATION
Also Called: Super Life
1770 W Berteau Ave # 401 (60613-1849)
PHONE.................................773 525-4210
Marcel Bolchis, *President*
EMP: 6
SQ FT: 10,000
SALES (est): 560K **Privately Held**
WEB: www.unicut.com
SIC: 3425 3546 Saw blades, chain type; saw blades for hand or power saws; power-driven handtools

(G-6465)
UNION FOODS INC
Also Called: Dunkin' Donuts
233 N Michigan Ave (60601-5519)
PHONE.................................201 327-2828
Sirajuddin Virani, *President*
EMP: 3 EST: 1990
SALES (est): 96.1K **Privately Held**
SIC: 5461 2024 5812 Doughnuts; ice cream & frozen desserts; eating places

(G-6466)
UNION TANK CAR COMPANY (DH)
175 W Jackson Blvd # 2100 (60604-2683)
PHONE.................................312 431-3111
Kenneth Fischl, *President*
Robert Lorch, *Vice Pres*
Mark Garrette, *CFO*
Robert Webb, *Admin Secy*
◆ EMP: 200 EST: 1980
SQ FT: 16,000
SALES (est): 2.3B
SALES (corp-wide): 327.2B **Publicly Held**
WEB: www.utlx.com
SIC: 3743 4741 4789 5051 Train cars & equipment, freight or passenger; railroad car rebuilding; rental of railroad cars; railroad car repair; metals service centers & offices
HQ: Marmon Holdings, Inc.
181 W Madison St Ste 2600
Chicago IL 60602
312 372-9500

(G-6467)
UNION TANK CAR COMPANY
175 W Jackson Blvd # 2100 (60604-2683)
PHONE.................................312 431-3111
Cynthia Rein, *Principal*
EMP: 136
SALES (corp-wide): 327.2B **Publicly Held**
SIC: 3743 Train cars & equipment, freight or passenger
HQ: Union Tank Car Company
175 W Jackson Blvd # 2100
Chicago IL 60604
312 431-3111

(G-6468)
UNIQUE ENVELOPE CORPORATION
5958 S Oak Park Ave (60638-3202)
PHONE.................................773 586-0330
Melvin Kozbiel, *President*
Darrell Kozbiel, *Vice Pres*
Colette Kozbiel, *Admin Sec*
EMP: 25 EST: 1966
SQ FT: 40,000
SALES (est): 3.9MM **Privately Held**
SIC: 2754 2759 2677 Envelopes: gravure printing; commercial printing; envelopes

(G-6469)
UNITED AMERCN HEALTHCARE CORP (PA)
303 E Wacker Dr Ste 1040 (60601-5216)
PHONE.................................313 393-4571
John M Fife, *Ch of Bd*
Cathy Chen, *Project Mgr*
Donna Killian, *Project Mgr*
Robert T Sullivan, *CFO*
Connie Dyas, *Accounts Mgr*
▲ EMP: 45
SQ FT: 1,000
SALES: 8.4MM **Publicly Held**
SIC: 3841 3699 Surgical & medical instruments; laser welding, drilling & cutting equipment; laser systems & equipment

(G-6470)
UNITED BINDERY SERVICE
1845 W Carroll Ave (60612-2589)
PHONE.................................312 243-0240
Bruce Kosaka, *President*
Jim Yoshimoto, *Vice Pres*
▲ EMP: 24
SQ FT: 70,000
SALES (est): 5MM **Privately Held**
SIC: 2789 Bookbinding & repairing: trade, edition, library, etc.

(G-6471)
UNITED CONTAINER CORPORATION
1350 N Elston Ave (60642-2440)
PHONE.................................773 342-2200
Bill Heymann, *President*
Michael Heymann, *Corp Secy*
Cindy Heymann, *Shareholder*
Karen Heymann, *Shareholder*
EMP: 27
SQ FT: 30,000
SALES (est): 6.3MM **Privately Held**
WEB: www.uccpkg.com
SIC: 2653 Boxes, corrugated: made from purchased materials; display items, solid fiber: made from purchased materials

(G-6472)
UNITED FENCE CO INC
3617 W 83rd St (60652-2409)
PHONE.................................773 924-0773
Robert H Hill, *President*
Mildred Hill, *Admin Sec*
EMP: 5
SALES (est): 601.1K **Privately Held**
SIC: 1799 5039 3446 Fence construction; wire fence, gates & accessories; architectural metalwork

(G-6473)
UNITED PRINTERS INC
1540 W 44th St (60609-3334)
PHONE.................................773 376-1955
Christina Hernandez, *President*
EMP: 3 EST: 2010
SALES (est): 197.9K **Privately Held**
SIC: 2752 Commercial printing, offset

(G-6474)
UNITED SKYS LLC
71 S Wacker Dr Ste 1600 (60606-4637)
PHONE.................................847 546-7776
Charles McCartney, *President*
EMP: 15
SALES (est): 5.4MM **Privately Held**
SIC: 1761 3444 Skylight installation; skylights, sheet metal

Chicago - Cook County (G-6475)

(G-6475)
UNITED SPRING & MANUFACTURING
830 N Pulaski Rd (60651-3608)
PHONE..................773 384-8464
Mitchell Celarek, *CEO*
Helen Celarek, *Treasurer*
Barbara Celarek, *Admin Sec*
EMP: 20
SQ FT: 35,000
SALES (est): 3.1MM **Privately Held**
SIC: 3493 3495 Steel springs, except wire; wire springs

(G-6476)
UNITED STATES AUDIO CORP
Also Called: Kowalik Brothers
1658 W 35th St (60609-1310)
PHONE..................312 316-2929
John Kowalik, *President*
EMP: 4 **Privately Held**
SIC: 3651 Household audio & video equipment
PA: United States Audio Corporation
411 Crabtree Ln
Glenview IL 60025

(G-6477)
UNITED STATES GEAR CORPORATION
Also Called: North American Gear and Axel
1020 W 119th St (60643-5216)
PHONE..................773 821-5450
Pete Hamby, *Director*
EMP: 7 **Publicly Held**
WEB: www.usgear.com
SIC: 3714 Gears, motor vehicle
HQ: United States Gear Corporation
9420 S Stony Island Ave
Chicago IL 60617
773 375-4900

(G-6478)
UNITED STATES GYPSUM COMPANY (DH)
550 W Adams St Ste 1300 (60661-3692)
PHONE..................312 606-4000
James S Metcalf, *President*
Timothy V Bixler, *Senior VP*
Dominic A Danessa, *Senior VP*
Robert B Waterhouse, *Senior VP*
Bill St Leger, *Plant Mgr*
◆ EMP: 385
SALES (est): 1.5B
SALES (corp-wide): 8.2B **Privately Held**
WEB: www.usg.com
SIC: 3275 Gypsum board
HQ: Usg Corporation
550 W Adams St
Chicago IL 60661
312 436-4000

(G-6479)
UNITY HARDWOODS LLC
5950 W 66th St Unit C (60638-5461)
PHONE..................708 701-2943
Michael Dittmer,
Rick Berryman,
Gina Guare,
EMP: 14 EST: 2015
SQ FT: 38,000
SALES (est): 1.6MM **Privately Held**
SIC: 2426 Flooring, hardwood

(G-6480)
UNIVERSAL ELECTRIC FOUNDRY INC
1523 W Hubbard St (60642-6387)
PHONE..................312 421-7233
Rodney Norwell, *President*
James H Hartman, *Vice Pres*
EMP: 33 EST: 1912
SQ FT: 22,000
SALES (est): 8MM **Privately Held**
WEB: www.universalfoundry.com
SIC: 3325 3351 3365 3369 Alloy steel castings, except investment; bronze rolling & drawing; brass rolling & drawing; aluminum & aluminum-based alloy castings; nonferrous foundries; copper foundries

(G-6481)
UNIVERSAL LIGHTING CORPORATION
Also Called: Universal Lighting & Clg Sup
3084 S Lock St (60608-5517)
P.O. Box 166013 (60616-6011)
PHONE..................773 927-2000
Joseph Difazio, *President*
EMP: 6
SALES (est): 701.4K **Privately Held**
SIC: 3641 Electric lamps

(G-6482)
UNIVERSAL OVERALL COMPANY
1060 W Van Buren St (60607-2988)
PHONE..................312 226-3336
Sara Eckerling Greenberg, *President*
Heather Eckerling, *Vice Pres*
Amy Dunada, *Executive*
Jason Greenberg, *Admin Sec*
◆ EMP: 50 EST: 1924
SQ FT: 112,000
SALES (est): 7.2MM **Privately Held**
WEB: www.universaloverall.com
SIC: 2326 Men's & boys' work clothing

(G-6483)
UNIVERSAL SCIENTIFIC ILL INC
1512 N Fremont St Ste 103 (60642-2567)
PHONE..................847 228-6464
Chris L Seth, *President*
Barry Seth, *Vice Pres*
EMP: 24 EST: 1930
SALES (est): 2.8MM **Privately Held**
WEB: www.usipcb.com
SIC: 3672 Printed circuit boards
PA: Aerotronic Controls Co.
1512 N Fremont St Ste 103
Chicago IL 60642
847 228-6504

(G-6484)
UNIVERSAL TRNSPT SYSTEMS LLC
474 N Lake Shore Dr # 5805 (60611-3400)
PHONE..................312 994-2349
Mike Malloy, *Engineer*
David L Summers,
EMP: 10
SALES (est): 650K **Privately Held**
SIC: 3724 7389 Aircraft engines & engine parts;

(G-6485)
UNIVERSITY OF CHICAGO
University of Chicago Press
1427 E 60th St (60637-2902)
PHONE..................773 702-1722
Albert Madansky, *Chief*
Kelli Morrison, *Opers Staff*
Christine Schwab, *Production*
Sandra Curry, *Human Res Mgr*
Robert Shirrell, *Branch Mgr*
EMP: 300
SALES (corp-wide): 2B **Privately Held**
SIC: 2721 2731 Periodicals: publishing only; books: publishing only
PA: The University Of Chicago
5801 S Ellis Ave Ste 1
Chicago IL 60637
773 702-1234

(G-6486)
UNIVERSITY OF CHICAGO
Also Called: University of Chicago Press
11030 S Langley Ave (60628-3830)
PHONE..................773 702-7000
Paula Duffy, *President*
Karen M Darling, *Editor*
Timothy Mennel, *Editor*
Yvonne Zipter, *Editor*
Lexyne Jackson, *Research*
EMP: 32
SALES (corp-wide): 2B **Privately Held**
SIC: 2732 8221 Book printing; university
PA: The University Of Chicago
5801 S Ellis Ave Ste 1
Chicago IL 60637
773 702-1234

(G-6487)
UNIVERSITY OF CHICAGO
Also Called: Steam Plant
6101 S Blackstone Ave (60637-2911)
PHONE..................773 702-9780
Dan Carey, *Manager*
EMP: 19
SALES (corp-wide): 2B **Privately Held**
SIC: 3511 8221 Steam turbines; university
PA: The University Of Chicago
5801 S Ellis Ave Ste 1
Chicago IL 60637
773 702-1234

(G-6488)
UOP LLC
2820 N Southport Ave (60657-4111)
PHONE..................708 442-3681
Alice Driscoll, *Principal*
James Hagen, *Project Mgr*
Jeffrey Tyska, *Engineer*
Mark Little, *Info Tech Mgr*
EMP: 133
SALES (corp-wide): 36.7B **Publicly Held**
WEB: www.uop.com
SIC: 2819 Catalysts, chemical
HQ: Uop Llc
25 E Algonquin Rd
Des Plaines IL 60016
847 391-2000

(G-6489)
UPPER URBAN GREEN PRPRTY MAINT
3135 S Throop St (60608-6344)
PHONE..................312 218-5903
Marianne Marrero, *President*
EMP: 3
SALES (est): 201.5K **Privately Held**
SIC: 6512 3131 Nonresidential building operators; uppers

(G-6490)
UPS POWER MANAGEMENT INC
4940 S Kilbourn Ave (60632-4523)
P.O. Box 3871, Barrington (60011-3871)
PHONE..................844 877-2288
Jin Zheng, *Director*
EMP: 10
SQ FT: 20,000
SALES (est): 557.8K **Privately Held**
SIC: 3621 Storage battery chargers, motor & engine generator type

(G-6491)
UPS STORE
27 N Wacker Dr (60606-2814)
PHONE..................312 372-2727
Robert Yee, *President*
EMP: 4
SALES: 500K **Privately Held**
WEB: www.theupsstore.com
SIC: 7389 4731 2631 7334 Mailbox rental & related service; agents, shipping; container, packaging & boxboard; blueprinting service

(G-6492)
URANTIA CORP
533 W Diversey Pkwy (60614-1643)
PHONE..................773 248-6616
Richard Keeler, *President*
EMP: 10
SALES (est): 435.1K
SALES (corp-wide): 2MM **Privately Held**
SIC: 2731 8661 Book publishing; religious organizations
PA: Urantia Foundation
533 W Diversey Pkwy
Chicago IL 60614
773 525-3319

(G-6493)
URANTIA FOUNDATION (PA)
533 W Diversey Pkwy (60614-1698)
PHONE..................773 525-3319
Paula Thompson, *Managing Dir*
J Peregrine, *Exec Dir*
Jay Peregrine, *Exec Dir*
Joanne Strobel, *Executive Asst*
EMP: 20 EST: 1950
SQ FT: 4,500
SALES: 2MM **Privately Held**
SIC: 2731 8661 Books: publishing only; religious organizations

(G-6494)
URBAN ACCENTS INCORPORATED
4043 N Ravenswood Ave # 216 (60613-5685)
PHONE..................773 528-9515
Thomas Knibbs, *President*
Jim Dygas, *Vice Pres*
▲ EMP: 6
SQ FT: 1,000
SALES (est): 1.1MM **Privately Held**
SIC: 2099 Food preparations

(G-6495)
URBAN IMAGING GROUP INC
3246 N Elston Ave (60618-5828)
PHONE..................773 961-7500
Richard Chavez Jr, *President*
EMP: 8
SALES (est): 1MM **Privately Held**
WEB: www.urbanimaging.com
SIC: 2752 Advertising posters, lithographed

(G-6496)
URDU TIMES
7061 N Kedzie Ave # 1102 (60645-2846)
PHONE..................773 274-3100
Tariq Hawaja, *Owner*
Nasim Farooqa, *Owner*
EMP: 4
SALES: 190K **Privately Held**
SIC: 2711 Commercial printing & newspaper publishing combined

(G-6497)
US ADHESIVES
1735 W Carroll Ave (60612-2590)
PHONE..................312 829-7438
Brian Creevy, *President*
Pamela Creevy, *Corp Secy*
EMP: 7
SALES: 994.5K **Privately Held**
SIC: 2891 Adhesives

(G-6498)
US ALUMINIUM IL
Also Called: Cr Laurence
5501 W Ogden Ave (60804-3507)
PHONE..................708 458-9070
Michael Kalisiak, *Principal*
Harry Kuffel, *Manager*
EMP: 2 EST: 2011
SALES (est): 224.2K **Privately Held**
SIC: 3448 Prefabricated metal buildings

(G-6499)
US BORAX INC (DH)
200 E Randolph St # 7100 (60601-7011)
PHONE..................773 270-6500
Dean Gehring, *CEO*
Chris J Robinson, *COO*
Frank Wawrzos, *Research*
Jeffery R Olsen, *CFO*
Garth Sandsness, *Controller*
◆ EMP: 150 EST: 1872
SALES (est): 1.4B
SALES (corp-wide): 43.1B **Privately Held**
SIC: 1474 2819 Borate compounds (natural) mining; industrial inorganic chemicals
HQ: Rio Tinto London Limited
6 St. James's Square
London SW1Y
207 781-2000

(G-6500)
US CATHOLIC MAGAZINE
205 W Monroe St Fl 9 (60606-5060)
PHONE..................312 236-7782
John Molyneux, *Principal*
EMP: 3 EST: 2008
SALES (est): 165.4K **Privately Held**
WEB: www.uscatholic.org
SIC: 2721 Magazines: publishing only, not printed on site

(G-6501)
US INTERNATIONAL INC
Also Called: US International Supply
1950 W Armitage Ave # 1 (60622-1024)
PHONE..................312 671-9207
Urvashi Bhushan, *President*
▼ EMP: 3

GEOGRAPHIC SECTION
Chicago - Cook County (G-6528)

SALES: 50K Privately Held
SIC: 3999 Manufacturing industries

(G-6502)
US PLATING CO INC
2136 S Sawyer Ave (60623-3337)
PHONE..................773 522-7300
Robert Alley, *President*
EMP: 11 **EST:** 1959
SQ FT: 26,000
SALES (est): 1.3MM Privately Held
WEB: www.usplating.net
SIC: 3471 Plating of metals or formed products; finishing, metals or formed products

(G-6503)
US SILICA HOLDINGS INC
200 N La Salle St # 2100 (60601-1026)
PHONE..................312 589-7539
Bryan Shinn, *President*
Ronnie Pierce, *Prdtn Mgr*
Janice Casey, *Transportation*
Alden Patterson, *Planning*
EMP: 104
SALES (corp-wide): 1.4B Publicly Held
WEB: www.ussilica.com
SIC: 2819 Industrial inorganic chemicals
PA: U.S. Silica Holdings, Inc.
 24275 Katy Fwy Ste 600
 Katy TX 77494
 281 258-2170

(G-6504)
US SILICA HOLDINGS INC
200 N Lasalle St Ste 2100 (60601)
PHONE..................312 291-4400
Bryan Shinn, *Branch Mgr*
EMP: 10
SALES (corp-wide): 1.4B Publicly Held
SIC: 2819 Industrial inorganic chemicals
PA: U.S. Silica Holdings, Inc.
 24275 Katy Fwy Ste 600
 Katy TX 77494
 281 258-2170

(G-6505)
USA STAR GROUP OF COMPANY
4403 N Broadway St (60640-5682)
PHONE..................773 456-6677
Mohammad Faisal, *Vice Pres*
EMP: 3
SALES (est): 168.1K Privately Held
SIC: 3531 Bucket or scarifier teeth

(G-6506)
USG CORPORATION (HQ)
550 W Adams St (60661-3665)
PHONE..................312 436-4000
Christopher R Griffin, *President*
Christopher Macey, *President*
Jennifer Adams, *Counsel*
Matthew Craig, *Plant Mgr*
Matthew Huss, *Plant Mgr*
EMP: 277
SALES: 3.3B
SALES (corp-wide): 8.2B Privately Held
SIC: 3296 3275 Mineral wool insulation products; acoustical board & tile, mineral wool; gypsum board
PA: Gebr. Knauf Kg
 Am Bahnhof 7
 Iphofen 97346
 932 331-0

(G-6507)
USSPICE MILL INC
4537 W Fulton St (60624-1609)
PHONE..................773 378-6800
Naren M Patel, *President*
Hansa N Patel, *Admin Sec*
▲ **EMP:** 10
SQ FT: 40,000
SALES (est): 1.5MM Privately Held
SIC: 2099 5149 Spices, including grinding; spices & seasonings

(G-6508)
UTC RAILCAR REPAIR SVCS LLC
161 N Clark St (60601-3206)
PHONE..................312 431-5053
Kenneth P Fischl, *President*
Robert K Lorch, *Vice Pres*
Mark J Garrette, *CFO*
Robert W Webb, *Admin Sec*
EMP: 937
SQ FT: 56,000
SALES: 66.1MM
SALES (corp-wide): 327.2B Publicly Held
SIC: 4789 3743 5088 4741 Railroad car repair; railroad car rebuilding; transportation equipment & supplies; rental of railroad cars
HQ: Union Tank Car Company
 175 W Jackson Blvd # 2100
 Chicago IL 60604
 312 431-3111

(G-6509)
UTLX MANUFACTURING INC
175 W Jackson Blvd (60604-2615)
PHONE..................312 431-3111
Anthony Zepeda, *Engineer*
Gregory Cieslak, *Manager*
Jeff Prunty, *Manager*
EMP: 8 **EST:** 2010
SALES (est): 811.9K Privately Held
SIC: 3999 Manufacturing industries

(G-6510)
V & O STYLE JEWELRY MFG CO
Also Called: V & O Style Jewelers
5 S Wabash Ave Ste 415 (60603-3508)
PHONE..................312 372-2454
Diruhi Dory Arakelian, *President*
John Arakelian, *President*
EMP: 4
SALES (est): 555.5K Privately Held
SIC: 3911 Jewelry, precious metal

(G-6511)
V & V SUPREMO FOODS INC (PA)
2141 S Throop St (60608-4410)
PHONE..................312 733-5652
Gilberto Villasenor, *President*
Philip Villasenor, *General Mgr*
Conrad Flores, *Business Mgr*
Manuel Carrasco, *Warehouse Mgr*
Antonio Carmona, *Production*
EMP: 250
SQ FT: 75,000
SALES (est): 56.9MM Privately Held
WEB: www.vvsupremo.com
SIC: 2022 5149 Natural cheese; specialty food items

(G-6512)
V A M D INC
7035 W Higgins Ave (60656-1976)
PHONE..................773 631-8400
Vidan Lazic, *President*
Aleks Lazic, *Senior VP*
Dusica Lazic, *Admin Sec*
EMP: 6
SQ FT: 4,800
SALES: 1MM Privately Held
SIC: 5147 5421 2013 Meats & meat products; meat & fish markets; sausages & other prepared meats

(G-6513)
V A ROBINSON LTD
2850 N Pulaski Rd Ste 4r (60641-5456)
PHONE..................773 205-4364
Virgil Robinson III, *President*
EMP: 5
SALES (est): 440K Privately Held
WEB: www.varobinson.com
SIC: 3441 Fabricated structural metal

(G-6514)
V J DOLAN & COMPANY INC
1830 N Laramie Ave (60639-4486)
PHONE..................773 237-0100
David D Dolan, *President*
Roberta Mizera, *Office Mgr*
Stephen J Dolan, *Admin Sec*
EMP: 25
SQ FT: 35,000
SALES (est): 6.2MM Privately Held
WEB: www.vjdolan.com
SIC: 2851 Lacquer: bases, dopes, thinner; stains: varnish, oil or wax

(G-6515)
V P ANODIZING INC
1819 N Lorel Ave (60639-4330)
PHONE..................773 622-9100
Victor V Pariso, *President*
EMP: 6
SQ FT: 10,000
SALES (est): 722.4K Privately Held
SIC: 3471 Electroplating of metals or formed products

(G-6516)
V W BROACHING SERVICE INC
3250 W Lake St (60624-2003)
PHONE..................773 533-9000
Russell W Roschman, *President*
Georgiann Dytrych, *Vice Pres*
Russell Roschman, *Executive*
EMP: 19
SQ FT: 54,000
SALES (est): 3.8MM Privately Held
WEB: www.vwbroaching.com
SIC: 3599 Machine shop, jobbing & repair; electrical discharge machining (EDM)

(G-6517)
VAIMO INC
20 N Wade Dr Ste 1200 (60606)
PHONE..................502 767-9550
David Holender, *CEO*
Martin Hjalm, *Manager*
Christian Dreisbach, *Manager*
EMP: 3
SALES (est): 33.8K Privately Held
SIC: 7372 7373 Business oriented computer software; systems software development services
PA: Vaimo Ab
 Katarinavagen 15
 Stockholm 116 4

(G-6518)
VAL P ENTERPRISES
12045 S Emerald Ave (60628-6364)
PHONE..................708 982-6561
Valarie Ponder, *Owner*
EMP: 3
SALES (est): 89.8K Privately Held
SIC: 5999 7389 7374 7373 Miscellaneous retail stores; advertising, promotional & trade show services; data processing & preparation; computer integrated systems design; prepackaged software; custom computer programming services

(G-6519)
VAN HESSEN USA INC (DH)
Also Called: Interntional Casings Group Inc
4420 S Wolcott Ave (60609-3159)
PHONE..................773 376-9200
Thijs Lingsama, *President*
Jimmy Wilt, *Opers Mgr*
Bob Strange, *Engineer*
Israel Saldivar, *Sales Staff*
Bob Zickus, *Manager*
▼ **EMP:** 30
SQ FT: 52,000
SALES (est): 31MM
SALES (corp-wide): 8.2MM Privately Held
SIC: 2013 Sausage casings, natural; frozen meats from purchased meat
HQ: Van Hessen B.V.
 Hoogeveenenweg 115
 Nieuwerkerk A.D. Ijssel 2913
 180 330-100

(G-6520)
VANGUARD CHEMICAL CORPORATION
429 W Ohio St (60654-4506)
PHONE..................312 751-0717
Mark Rotblatt, *President*
Maureen Rotblatt, *Vice Pres*
EMP: 15
SALES (est): 1MM Privately Held
SIC: 2842 5169 Specialty cleaning, polishes & sanitation goods; chemicals & allied products

(G-6521)
VANS INC
113 N Elizabeth St (60607-1621)
PHONE..................718 349-2311
EMP: 10
SALES (corp-wide): 10.4B Publicly Held
WEB: www.vans.com
SIC: 3021 Canvas shoes, rubber soled
HQ: Vans, Inc.
 1588 S Coast Dr
 Costa Mesa CA 92626
 855 909-8267

(G-6522)
VANTAGE OLEOCHEMICALS INC
4650 S Racine Ave (60609-3321)
PHONE..................773 376-9000
Julian Steinberg, *CEO*
Robert Drennan, *Ch of Bd*
Anthony Tamer, *President*
Noel Beavis, *COO*
Don Ciancio, *Exec VP*
▲ **EMP:** 103
SALES (est): 26.4MM
SALES (corp-wide): 247.2MM Privately Held
SIC: 2869 2841 5169 Fatty acid esters, aminos, etc.; glycerin, crude or refined: from fats; industrial chemicals
HQ: Vantage Specialty Chemicals, Inc.
 4650 S Racine Ave
 Chicago IL 60609
 773 376-9000

(G-6523)
VANTAGE SPECIALTIES INC
4650 S Racine Ave (60609-3321)
PHONE..................847 244-3410
Andy Harris, *Branch Mgr*
EMP: 9
SALES (corp-wide): 247.2MM Privately Held
SIC: 2843 5199 5169 8999 Surface active agents; oils, animal or vegetable; industrial chemicals; chemical consultant
HQ: Vantage Specialties, Inc
 3938 Porett Dr
 Gurnee IL 60031
 773 376-9000

(G-6524)
VAS DESIGN INC
3356 N Milwaukee Ave (60641-4004)
PHONE..................773 794-1368
Vas Gabrov, *President*
EMP: 3
SQ FT: 2,900
SALES (est): 209.1K Privately Held
SIC: 2431 Millwork

(G-6525)
VAULT FURNITURE INC
1965 W Pershing Rd Ste 1 (60609-2319)
PHONE..................734 323-4166
Andrew Gooding, *Principal*
EMP: 3 **EST:** 2015
SALES: 170K Privately Held
SIC: 5712 5961 2599 5021 Customized furniture & cabinets; furniture & furnishings, mail order; factory furniture & fixtures; furniture

(G-6526)
VCNA PRAIRE YARD 1033
3300 S California Ave (60608-5114)
PHONE..................708 458-0400
James Munro, *President*
EMP: 4
SALES (est): 270.2K Privately Held
SIC: 3273 Ready-mixed concrete

(G-6527)
VCNA PRAIRIE INC
865 N Peoria St (60642-5429)
PHONE..................312 733-0094
EMP: 1942 Privately Held
SIC: 3272 Building materials, except block or brick: concrete
PA: Vcna Prairie, Llc
 7601 W 79th St Ste 1
 Bridgeview IL 60455

(G-6528)
VECTOR CUSTOM FABRICATING INC
2128 W Fulton St (60612-2314)
PHONE..................312 421-5161
Stephen Mueller, *President*
Michael Wilkie, *Treasurer*
Erik Lowe, *Manager*
Barry Hehemann, *Admin Sec*
▲ **EMP:** 10
SQ FT: 6,000

Chicago - Cook County (G-6529)

(G-6529)
VECTORBUILDER INC (PA)
1010 W 35th St (60609-1401)
PHONE...................510 552-3632
Bruce Lahn, *Owner*
EMP: 13 **EST:** 2017
SALES (est): 2.8MM **Privately Held**
WEB: www.vectorbuilder.com
SIC: 2836 Biological products, except diagnostic

(G-6530)
VELTEX CORPORATION (PA)
123 W Madison St Ste 1500 (60602-4612)
PHONE...................312 235-4014
▲ **EMP:** 35
SQ FT: 25,000
SALES: 70MM **Privately Held**
SIC: 2211 5199 Holding Company Whol & Mfg Promotional Products

(G-6531)
VENETIAN MONUMENT COMPANY
Also Called: Mary Hill Memorials
527 N Western Ave (60612-1421)
PHONE...................312 829-9622
Frank P Troost, *President*
Robert F Troost, *Corp Secy*
EMP: 11
SQ FT: 5,600
SALES (est): 3MM
SALES (corp-wide): 14MM **Privately Held**
SIC: 5999 3281 Tombstones; cut stone & stone products
PA: Peter Troost Monument Co.
4300 Roosevelt Rd
Hillside IL
708 544-0916

(G-6532)
VENT PRODUCTS CO INC
1901 S Kilbourn Ave (60623-2309)
PHONE...................773 521-1900
Diana Ehrenfried, *President*
Felix Cantu, *Purch Agent*
Dennis Dwyer, *Controller*
Justin Navarro, *VP Sales*
Robert Colon, *Sales Staff*
EMP: 45 **EST:** 1962
SQ FT: 60,000
SALES (est): 10MM **Privately Held**
WEB: www.ventprod.com
SIC: 3444 3564 3442 3441 Sheet metal specialties, not stamped; blowers & fans; metal doors, sash & trim; fabricated structural metal

(G-6533)
VENT URE AIR
1855 S 54th Ave (60804-1815)
PHONE...................708 652-7200
Michael Friedman, *Owner*
EMP: 2
SALES (est): 271.2K **Privately Held**
SIC: 3822 Auto controls regulating residntl & coml environmt & applncs

(G-6534)
VENTFABRICS INC
Also Called: Vent Fabrics
5520 N Lynch Ave (60630-1418)
PHONE...................773 775-4477
David Mac Arthur, *President*
Jason Barone, *Regl Sales Mgr*
Deanna Pieczko, *Admin Sec*
EMP: 17 **EST:** 1951
SQ FT: 13,000
SALES (est): 3.7MM **Privately Held**
SIC: 3585 Air conditioning units, complete: domestic or industrial

(G-6535)
VENTUREDYNE LTD
Also Called: Chisholm, Boyd & White Company
4101 W 126th St (60803-1901)
PHONE...................708 597-7550
Michael T Gerardi, *General Mgr*
EMP: 26
SALES (corp-wide): 146.4MM **Privately Held**
WEB: www.venturedyne.com
SIC: 3542 3613 3452 3429 Pressing machines; switchgear & switchboard apparatus; bolts, nuts, rivets & washers; manufactured hardware (general)
PA: Venturedyne, Ltd.
600 College Ave
Pewaukee WI 53072
262 691-9900

(G-6536)
VERENA SOLUTIONS LLC
965 W Chicago Ave (60642-5413)
PHONE...................314 651-1908
Michael M Infanger, *Principal*
EMP: 3
SALES (est): 208K **Privately Held**
SIC: 3845 Ultrasonic scanning devices, medical

(G-6537)
VERONE PUBLISHING INC
Also Called: Via Times News Organization
5421 Ne Rver Rd Apt 1605 (60656)
PHONE...................773 866-0811
Veronica Leighton, *President*
Joe Maurizio, *Vice Pres*
EMP: 7
SALES (est): 250K **Privately Held**
SIC: 2721 Magazines: publishing only, not printed on site

(G-6538)
VERSATILE MATERIALS INC
600 W 52nd St (60609-5203)
PHONE...................773 924-3700
Tansukh Chadia, *President*
Carl Albee, *Principal*
William G Lerch, *Admin Sec*
EMP: 5
SALES (est): 738.3K **Privately Held**
SIC: 2891 2816 Adhesives & sealants; inorganic pigments

(G-6539)
VERTICAL WEB MEDIA LLC
Also Called: Internet Retailer
125 S Wacker Dr Ste 1900 (60606-4419)
PHONE...................312 362-0076
Jack Love, *Ch of Bd*
Molly Rogers, *President*
Nancy Bernardini,
Thomas Chambers,
John Love,
EMP: 21
SQ FT: 3,400
SALES (est): 4.1MM **Privately Held**
WEB: www.verticalwebmedia.com
SIC: 2721 Trade journals: publishing only, not printed on site

(G-6540)
VETERAN GREENS LLC
7552 S Union Ave (60620-2401)
PHONE...................773 599-9689
Melvin Ward,
William Jones,
Domonicque Tatum,
Lawrence Van Meter,
EMP: 4
SALES (est): 202.9K **Privately Held**
SIC: 5431 2875 5148 0182 Fruit & vegetable markets; compost; fresh fruits & vegetables; food crops grown under cover;

(G-6541)
VHRK FOOD INC
Also Called: Dharti Food
810 Bonnie Ln (60656)
PHONE...................630 640-6525
Mohammedsiddik Khatri, *President*
EMP: 3
SALES (est): 172.4K **Privately Held**
SIC: 2013 Frozen meats from purchased meat

(G-6542)
VIA GALANTE CEMENT CON IN
3641 N Pittsburgh Ave (60634-1955)
PHONE...................773 589-9893
Carmela Bonafede, *Principal*
EMP: 8
SALES (est): 969.1K **Privately Held**
SIC: 3273 Ready-mixed concrete

(G-6543)
VICLARITY INC
300 N Lasalle St (60654)
PHONE...................201 214-5405
Ogie Sheehy, *Principal*
Richard Butti, *Vice Pres*
EMP: 9 **EST:** 2015
SQ FT: 2,400
SALES (est): 247K **Privately Held**
SIC: 7372 Application computer software

(G-6544)
VICTOR FOOD PRODUCTS
Also Called: Victor's Food
4194 N Elston Ave (60618-1829)
PHONE...................773 478-9529
Zenida Brosas, *President*
EMP: 4
SALES (est): 270K **Privately Held**
SIC: 2011 Meat packing plants

(G-6545)
VICTOR LEVY JEWELRY CO INC
Also Called: National Jewelers Co.
29 E Madison St Ste 1640 (60602-4427)
PHONE...................312 782-5297
Victor Levy, *President*
EMP: 2
SQ FT: 350
SALES (est): 376.6K **Privately Held**
SIC: 7631 3911 Jewelry repair services; diamond setter; rings, finger: precious metal

(G-6546)
VICTORIA METAL PROCESSOR INC
4836 W Division St (60651-3208)
PHONE...................773 633-7497
EMP: 5 **EST:** 2018
SALES (est): 400.6K **Privately Held**
SIC: 3471 Electroplating of metals or formed products

(G-6547)
VICTORIAS SECRET STORES LLC
1138 S Delano Ct W (60605-3733)
PHONE...................312 583-0488
EMP: 3
SALES (corp-wide): 12.9B **Publicly Held**
SIC: 5632 2341 Lingerie (outerwear); women's & children's underwear
HQ: Victoria's Secret Stores, Llc
4 Limited Pkwy E
Reynoldsburg OH 43068
614 577-7111

(G-6548)
VIENNA BEEF LTD (PA)
2501 N Damen Ave (60647-2101)
PHONE...................773 278-7800
John P Bodman, *President*
Howard Eirinberg, *President*
James Bodman, *Chairman*
Jack P Bodman, *Senior VP*
Rick Ewert, *Senior VP*
▼ **EMP:** 39 **EST:** 1893
SQ FT: 100,000
SALES (est): 76.1MM **Privately Held**
WEB: www.viennabeef.com
SIC: 2013 2035 2053 5411 Prepared beef products from purchased beef; prepared pork products from purchased pork; sausages & related products, from purchased meat; cucumbers, pickles & pickle salting; relishes, fruit & vegetable; cakes, bakery: frozen; delicatessens; groceries & related products; meats & meat products

(G-6549)
VIENNA BEEF LTD
1000 W Pershing Rd (60609-1426)
PHONE...................800 366-3647
EMP: 12
SALES (corp-wide): 76.1MM **Privately Held**
SIC: 2013 Sausages & other prepared meats
PA: Vienna Beef Ltd.
2501 N Damen Ave
Chicago IL 60647
773 278-7800

(G-6550)
VIGIL PRINTING INC
4415 W Lawrence Ave (60630-2510)
P.O. Box 70, Carpentersville (60110-0070)
PHONE...................773 794-8808
Michael Pearson, *President*
Rose Pearson, *Admin Sec*
EMP: 9
SQ FT: 5,000
SALES (est): 968K **Privately Held**
SIC: 2752 7331 Commercial printing, offset; direct mail advertising services

(G-6551)
VIKING PRINTING & COPYING INC
53 W Jackson Blvd Lbby (60604-3606)
PHONE...................312 341-0985
Bill Anderson, *President*
David Anderson, *Vice Pres*
EMP: 3
SQ FT: 1,200
SALES (est): 300K **Privately Held**
SIC: 2752 7334 2791 2789 Commercial printing, offset; photocopying & duplicating services; typesetting; bookbinding & related work

(G-6552)
VILLAGE OF BURNHAM
Also Called: Burnham Village Pump Station
14450 S Manistee Ave (60633-2081)
PHONE...................708 868-0661
Jerry Hunter, *Branch Mgr*
EMP: 3 **Privately Held**
SIC: 5084 3931 Water pumps (industrial); violins & parts
PA: Village Of Burnham
14450 S Manistee Ave
Burnham IL 60633
708 891-2122

(G-6553)
VINCIT OMNIA LLC
7312 N Oriole Ave (60631-4254)
PHONE...................773 631-4020
R Cary Capparelli, *Principal*
EMP: 3
SALES (est): 117.4K **Privately Held**
SIC: 2085 Distilled & blended liquors

(G-6554)
VINTAGE MODERN COLLECTION INC
Also Called: Vintage Roxx
1401 E 55th St Apt 606n (60615-5472)
PHONE...................312 774-8424
Roxanne Brown, *President*
EMP: 2
SALES (est): 206.3K **Privately Held**
SIC: 5712 2512 7389 Furniture stores; upholstered household furniture; interior design services

(G-6555)
VIRTU
2034 N Damen Ave (60647-4547)
PHONE...................773 235-3790
Julie Horowitz, *Principal*
EMP: 4 **EST:** 2007
SALES (est): 182.4K **Privately Held**
WEB: www.virtuchicago.com
SIC: 5947 5092 3944 Gift shop; arts & crafts equipment & supplies; craft & hobby kits & sets

(G-6556)
VISION I SYSTEMS
2416 S Canal St (60616-2224)
PHONE...................312 326-9188
John Lee, *Owner*
EMP: 5
SALES (est): 647.3K **Privately Held**
SIC: 7372 4813 Prepackaged software;

(G-6557)
VISION INTGRTED GRPHICS GROUP (PA)
208 S Jefferson St Fl 3 (60661-5758)
PHONE...................312 373-6300
Brad Moore, *CEO*
James Capstick, *Exec VP*
Mike Herbert, *Vice Pres*
Mario Christopher, *CFO*
Barbara Sherman, *Accounting Mgr*

GEOGRAPHIC SECTION

Chicago - Cook County (G-6585)

EMP: 30
SQ FT: 125,000
SALES (est): 72MM Privately Held
SIC: 2752 Commercial printing, lithographic

(G-6558)
VISION WHOLESALE CORP
5620 W 51st St (60638-1525)
PHONE..................708 496-6015
Mohammad Ali, *President*
◆ EMP: 8
SQ FT: 40,000
SALES (est): 3.3MM Privately Held
SIC: 5169 5145 2086 3089 Detergents & soaps, except specialty cleaning; candy; carbonated beverages, nonalcoholic; bottled & canned; holders: paper towel, grocery bag, etc.: plastic

(G-6559)
VISUAL MARKETING INC
154 W Erie St (60654-3987)
PHONE..................312 664-9177
Lawrence J Zock, *CEO*
Keith Rojc, *President*
Jack Michaelis, *Vice Pres*
Dean Stahnke, *Vice Pres*
Tim Zock, *Vice Pres*
▲ EMP: 20
SQ FT: 16,000
SALES (est): 3.5MM Privately Held
SIC: 3993 Displays & cutouts, window & lobby

(G-6560)
VITA FOOD PRODUCTS INC (PA)
2222 W Lake St (60612-2281)
PHONE..................312 738-4500
Clifford K Bolen, *President*
Howard E Bedford, *Chairman*
R Anthony Nelson, *CFO*
Gregg Cox, *Retailers*
◆ EMP: 100 EST: 1898
SQ FT: 82,200
SALES (est): 48.2MM Privately Held
WEB: www.vitafoodproducts.com
SIC: 2091 Fish, canned & cured; spices & seasonings

(G-6561)
VITAL PROTEINS LLC (PA)
939 W Fulton Market (60607-1324)
PHONE..................224 544-9110
Caryn Johnson, *Vice Pres*
Scott Springer, *Vice Pres*
John Schroeder, *Opers Dir*
Susanne Michalek, *Project Mgr*
Corey Friese, *Opers Mgr*
EMP: 150 EST: 2017
SALES: 120MM Privately Held
WEB: www.vitalproteins.com
SIC: 2834 5122 Proprietary drug products; vitamins & minerals

(G-6562)
VITAL PROTEINS LLC
1201 W Washington Blvd (60607-1915)
PHONE..................224 544-9110
Kurt Seidensticker, *CEO*
EMP: 25
SALES (corp-wide): 120MM Privately Held
SIC: 2023 5499 Dietary supplements, dairy & non-dairy based; vitamin food stores
PA: Vital Proteins, Llc
    939 W Fulton Market
    Chicago IL 60607
    224 544-9110

(G-6563)
VIVOTRONIX INC
965 W Chicago Ave (60642-5413)
PHONE..................312 536-3130
Mohamed Ali, *President*
Luigi Zevola, *Principal*
Fausto Annicchiarico Petruzzel, *Director*
EMP: 3
SALES (est): 246.6K Privately Held
SIC: 3845 Electromedical apparatus

(G-6564)
VIZR TECH LLC
400 N Mcclurg Ct Apt 2906 (60611-4346)
PHONE..................312 420-4466

Richard Buchler, *CEO*
EMP: 5
SALES (est): 156K Privately Held
SIC: 7372 Application computer software

(G-6565)
VM ELECTRONICS LLC
5080 N Kimberly Ave # 110 (60630-1770)
PHONE..................847 663-9310
Ned Pavlovic, *Engineer*
Wayne Pavlovic,
Vukasin Pavlovic,
EMP: 4
SALES (est): 786.8K Privately Held
SIC: 3555 Electrotyping machines

(G-6566)
VODORI INC
171 W Aberdeen St Ste 400 (60607-1670)
PHONE..................312 324-3992
Scott Rovegno, *President*
Staci McNelis, *Engineer*
Jessy Horrell, *Manager*
Sarah Steensen, *Manager*
Jessy Wetzler, *Manager*
EMP: 60
SALES: 7MM Privately Held
SIC: 7372 Business oriented computer software

(G-6567)
VOGEL/HILL CORPORATION
Also Called: Decardy Diecasting
3935 W Shakespeare Ave (60647-3430)
PHONE..................773 235-6916
William Vogel, *President*
Victoria Vogel, *Vice Pres*
EMP: 24 EST: 1907
SQ FT: 17,000
SALES (est): 4.7MM Privately Held
WEB: www.decardy.com
SIC: 3364 Zinc & zinc-base alloy die-castings; lead die-castings

(G-6568)
VOLTRONICS INC
7746 W Addison St (60634-3095)
PHONE..................773 625-1779
Edwin E Hedeen, *President*
Claudia Panos, *Vice Pres*
EMP: 14
SQ FT: 3,500
SALES (est): 2.1MM Privately Held
SIC: 3676 Electronic resistors

(G-6569)
VOODOO RIDE LLC
1341 W Fullerton Ave # 255 (60614-2362)
PHONE..................312 944-0465
Christopher Ferraro, *President*
EMP: 3
SQ FT: 2,000
SALES: 4MM
SALES (corp-wide): 24.8MM Privately Held
SIC: 2842 Automobile polish
PA: Pilot Inc.
    13000 Temple Ave
    City Of Industry CA 91746
    626 937-6988

(G-6570)
VOSGES LTD (PA)
Also Called: Vosges Haut Chocolate
2950 N Oakley Ave (60618-8010)
PHONE..................773 388-5560
Katrina Markoff, *President*
▲ EMP: 73 EST: 1997
SALES (est): 65.7MM Privately Held
SIC: 5441 2066 Candy; chocolate candy, solid

(G-6571)
VOYANT DIAGNOSTICS INC
1600 S Ind Ave Apt 1101 (60616)
PHONE..................630 456-6340
Michael Tu, *President*
Burhan Adhami, *Vice Pres*
EMP: 5
SALES (est): 229.7K Privately Held
SIC: 2835 In vitro diagnostics

(G-6572)
VPI HOLDING COMPANY LLC (PA)
676 N Michigan Ave (60611-2883)
PHONE..................312 255-4800
Scott Almquist, *CEO*
EMP: 0
SALES (est): 27.4MM Privately Held
SIC: 6719 2844 Investment holding companies, except banks; hair preparations, including shampoos

(G-6573)
W G N FLAG & DECORATING CO
798488 S Chicago Ave (60617)
PHONE..................773 768-8076
Carl Porter Jr, *President*
Carl Porter III, *Vice Pres*
Pamela S Porter, *Admin Sec*
EMP: 15 EST: 1915
SALES (est): 1.4MM Privately Held
WEB: www.nifda.net
SIC: 2399 5999 3993 3446 Flags, fabric; pennants; flags; signs & advertising specialties; architectural metalwork

(G-6574)
W G N RADIO MASS CALLING
435 N Michigan Ave Ste 1 (60611-4096)
PHONE..................312 591-7200
EMP: 3
SALES (est): 34.5K Privately Held
SIC: 4832 2711 Radio broadcasting stations; newspapers

(G-6575)
W R GRACE & CO
Also Called: W R Grace Davison Chemical Div
4099 W 71st St (60629-5839)
PHONE..................773 838-3200
Henry Saternus, *Engineer*
Paul Zarembski, *Engineer*
Al Jordon, *Branch Mgr*
Ben Craft, *Manager*
EMP: 125
SALES (corp-wide): 1.9B Publicly Held
WEB: www.grace.com
SIC: 3081 2819 Film base, cellulose acetate or nitrocellulose plastic; catalysts, chemical
PA: W. R. Grace & Co.
    7500 Grace Dr
    Columbia MD 21044
    410 531-4000

(G-6576)
W R GRACE & CO
W R Grace Construction Pdts
6051 W 65th St (60638-5396)
PHONE..................708 458-9700
Lorin Lewis, *Mfg Staff*
Ernesto Magana, *Manager*
EMP: 11
SALES (corp-wide): 1.9B Publicly Held
SIC: 2899 Concrete curing & hardening compounds
PA: W. R. Grace & Co.
    7500 Grace Dr
    Columbia MD 21044
    410 531-4000

(G-6577)
W R GRACE & CO-CONN
Also Called: W R Grace Construction Pdts
6051 W 65th St (60638-5396)
PHONE..................708 458-9700
James Hansen, *General Mgr*
EMP: 16
SALES (corp-wide): 1.9B Publicly Held
WEB: www.grace.com
SIC: 3086 2891 2819 3531 Plastics foam products; adhesives & sealants; industrial inorganic chemicals; construction machinery; chemical preparations
HQ: W. R. Grace & Co.-Conn.
    7500 Grace Dr
    Columbia MD 21044

(G-6578)
W R PABICH MFG CO INC
Also Called: Ideal Stitcher & Manufacturing
2323 N Knox Ave (60639-3484)
PHONE..................773 486-4141
Clifford Mistretta, *General Mgr*
EMP: 14 EST: 1933

SQ FT: 14,500
SALES (est): 2.6MM Privately Held
WEB: www.idealstitcher.com
SIC: 3315 Wire & fabricated wire products

(G-6579)
W S C INC
70 W Madison St Ste 2300 (60602-4250)
PHONE..................312 372-1121
EMP: 3
SALES (corp-wide): 83.2MM Privately Held
SIC: 3571 5045 Electronic computers; computers, peripherals & software
HQ: W S C Inc
    8938 Ridgeland Ave
    Oak Lawn IL 60453
    708 430-6675

(G-6580)
W-D TOOL ENGINEERING COMPANY
3128 W Grand Ave (60622-4387)
PHONE..................773 638-2688
Walter Dychie, *President*
John Zwarycz, *Vice Pres*
EMP: 10
SQ FT: 5,000
SALES (est): 1.3MM Privately Held
SIC: 3599 Machine shop, jobbing & repair

(G-6581)
WABASH PUBLISHING CO INC (PA)
Also Called: Illinois Sports News
906 S Wabash Ave (60605-2205)
PHONE..................312 939-5900
Thomas F Kelly III, *President*
EMP: 6 EST: 1927
SQ FT: 10,000
SALES (est): 1.4MM Privately Held
SIC: 2741 Racing forms & programs: publishing & printing

(G-6582)
WACO MANUFACTURING CO INC
2233 W Ferdinand St (60612-1584)
P.O. Box 888, Addison (60101-0888)
PHONE..................312 733-0054
Mike Troccoli, *President*
Frank Troccoli, *Vice Pres*
Ron Sarno, *Admin Sec*
◆ EMP: 15
SQ FT: 25,000
SALES (est): 2.1MM Privately Held
WEB: www.wacoseating.com
SIC: 2599 7641 2531 2522 Stools with casters (not household or office), metal; reupholstery; public building & related furniture; office furniture, except wood; wood household furniture

(G-6583)
WAGNER BRASS FOUNDRY INC
1838 N Elston Ave (60642-1284)
PHONE..................773 276-7907
Richard A Wagner, *President*
EMP: 9
SQ FT: 10,000
SALES (est): 1.4MM Privately Held
WEB: www.wagnerfoundry.com
SIC: 3365 3369 3366 Aluminum & aluminum-based alloy castings; nonferrous foundries; copper foundries

(G-6584)
WAH KING NOODLE CO INC (PA)
5770 S Perry Ave (60621-4057)
PHONE..................323 268-0222
Lawrence Tan, *Vice Pres*
▲ EMP: 10
SQ FT: 5,000
SALES (est): 1.5MM Privately Held
SIC: 2099 5149 Pasta, uncooked: packaged with other ingredients; pasta & rice

(G-6585)
WALACH MANUFACTURING CO INC
5049 W Diversey Ave (60639-1609)
PHONE..................773 836-2060
David Walach, *President*
EMP: 10
SQ FT: 10,000

Chicago - Cook County (G-6586)

SALES: 3.1MM **Privately Held**
SIC: **3569** 3599 3593 Jacks, hydraulic; machine shop, jobbing & repair; fluid power cylinders & actuators

(G-6586)
WAPRO INC
150 N Michigan Ave (60601-7553)
PHONE..................888 927-8677
Magnus Munkahusagan, *President*
Magnus Larsson Munkahusagan, *President*
Monica Magnusson, *CFO*
Richard Neal, *Regl Sales Mgr*
Gabe Lederman, *Sales Staff*
EMP: 3 EST: 2010
SALES (est): 249.9K **Privately Held**
SIC: **3544** Industrial molds

(G-6587)
WARGAMING (USA) INC (PA)
Also Called: Wargaming West
651 W Washington Blvd # 600 (60661-2122)
PHONE..................312 258-0500
Jeremy Monroe, *President*
EMP: 20 EST: 2013
SALES (est): 23.8MM **Privately Held**
SIC: **7372** Application computer software

(G-6588)
WATER SAVER FAUCET CO (PA)
701 W Erie St (60654-5503)
PHONE..................312 666-5500
Steven A Kersten, *President*
Priscilla Kersten, *Corp Secy*
▲ EMP: 125
SQ FT: 80,000
SALES (est): 18.9MM **Privately Held**
WEB: www.wsflab.com
SIC: **3432** Faucets & spigots, metal & plastic; plumbers' brass goods: drain cocks, faucets, spigots, etc.

(G-6589)
WATERS TECHNOLOGIES CORP
4559 Paysphere Cir (60674-0045)
PHONE..................508 482-8365
EMP: 10 **Publicly Held**
SIC: **3826** Chromatographic equipment, laboratory type
HQ: Waters Technologies Corporation,
34 Maple St
Milford MA 01757
508 478-2000

(G-6590)
WATERWAY RV LLC MFG HOME
2 N Riverside Plz Ste 800 (60606-2682)
PHONE..................312 207-1835
EMP: 2
SALES (est): 226.2K **Privately Held**
SIC: **3999** Manufacturing industries

(G-6591)
WAVE MECHANICS NEON
450 N Leavitt St (60612-1544)
PHONE..................312 829-9283
EMP: 3
SALES (est): 180K **Privately Held**
SIC: **3993** Mfg Signs/Advertising Specialties

(G-6592)
WAVSYS LLC
2333 N Seeley Ave (60647-3326)
PHONE..................773 442-0888
EMP: 15
SALES (est): 1.4MM **Privately Held**
SIC: **7372** Prepackaged software

(G-6593)
WAXMAN CANDLES INC
3044 N Lincoln Ave (60657-4208)
PHONE..................773 929-3000
Anne Olson, *Branch Mgr*
EMP: 4
SALES (corp-wide): 1.2MM **Privately Held**
SIC: **3999** 5961 5999 Candles; mail order house; candle shops
PA: Waxman Candles Inc
609 Massachusetts St
Lawrence KS 66044
785 843-8593

(G-6594)
WEARY & BAITY INC
Also Called: UPS Stores 2872, The
333 W North Ave Ste F (60610-2587)
PHONE..................312 943-6197
Barbara Weary, *President*
Ray Vaity, *Admin Sec*
EMP: 4
SQ FT: 1,208
SALES (est): 500K **Privately Held**
SIC: **5999** 5084 5113 2752 Packaging materials: boxes, padding, etc.; razors, electric; packaging machinery & equipment; processing & packaging equipment; shipping supplies; commercial printing, lithographic

(G-6595)
WEB PRODUCTION & FABG INC
448 N Artesian Ave (60612-1446)
PHONE..................312 733-6800
Maureen Kendziera, *President*
David Kendziera, *Project Mgr*
Sharon Broms,
EMP: 14 EST: 1993
SQ FT: 10,000
SALES (est): 1.9MM **Privately Held**
WEB: www.webproductionandfabricating.com
SIC: **7692** 3446 1791 3441 Welding repair; gratings, open steel flooring; lintels light gauge steel; structural steel erection; building components, structural steel; joists, open web steel: long-span series

(G-6596)
WEBER PRESS INC
5746 N Western Ave (60659-5114)
PHONE..................773 561-9815
Harry Weber, *President*
Peter Weber, *Vice Pres*
EMP: 5 EST: 1925
SQ FT: 5,000
SALES (est): 600K **Privately Held**
WEB: www.weberpresschicago.com
SIC: **2752** 2759 2791 Commercial printing, offset; letterpress printing; typesetting

(G-6597)
WEDNESDAY JOURNAL INC
Also Called: Chicago Parent News Magazine
332 S Michigan Ave # 900 (60604-4434)
PHONE..................708 386-5555
Dan Haley, *Publisher*
Katina Beniaris, *Editor*
Timothy Inklebarger, *Editor*
Tamara Oshaughnessy, *Editor*
Karen Skinner, *Area Mgr*
EMP: 80
SALES (est): 6.4MM **Privately Held**
SIC: **2711** Newspapers, publishing & printing

(G-6598)
WEILER RUBBER TECHNOLOGIES LLC
4223 W Lake St (60624-1723)
PHONE..................773 826-8900
Sean Duffy, *Mng Member*
▲ EMP: 2
SQ FT: 1,000
SALES (est): 300K **Privately Held**
SIC: **2822** Synthetic rubber

(G-6599)
WELDING SHOP
Also Called: Andersen Welding
109 W 103rd St (60628-2607)
PHONE..................773 785-1305
Dave Andersen, *Owner*
EMP: 2
SQ FT: 1,800
SALES (est): 221.6K **Privately Held**
SIC: **7692** Welding repair

(G-6600)
WELLS JANITORIAL SERVICE INC
11006 S Michigan Ave # 4 (60628-4352)
PHONE..................872 226-9983
Jamaine J Wells, *President*
EMP: 3
SQ FT: 850

SALES (est): 94.7K **Privately Held**
SIC: **7349** 7389 2676 Janitorial service, contract basis; ; sanitary paper products; towels, napkins & tissue paper products

(G-6601)
WELLS SINKWARE CORP
916 W 21st St (60608-4542)
P.O. Box 166137 (60616-6137)
PHONE..................312 850-3466
Honghai Wang, *President*
Eric Chang, *Director*
▲ EMP: 2
SQ FT: 35,000
SALES (est): 2MM **Privately Held**
SIC: **3261** Sinks, vitreous china

(G-6602)
WELLSPRING INVESTMENTS LLC
Also Called: All Seasons Screen Prtg & EMB
5470 N Elston Ave (60630-1454)
PHONE..................773 736-1213
Judy Reneau,
Randy Reneau,
EMP: 5
SQ FT: 5,500
SALES (est): 750K **Privately Held**
SIC: **2395** 2396 Embroidery & art needlework; screen printing on fabric articles

(G-6603)
WESLING PRODUCTS INC
2912 W Lake St (60612-1924)
PHONE..................773 533-2850
S Scott Spirakes, *President*
EMP: 6 EST: 1923
SQ FT: 10,000
SALES (est): 900K **Privately Held**
SIC: **2441** 2449 3861 Cases, wood; wood containers; photographic equipment & supplies

(G-6604)
WEST LOOP SALUMI CO
200 N Jefferson St # 704 (60661-1199)
PHONE..................312 255-7004
Gregory Laketek, *President*
EMP: 2
SQ FT: 1,500
SALES (est): 215K **Privately Held**
SIC: **2013** Cured meats from purchased meat

(G-6605)
WEST PUBLISHING CORPORATION
Also Called: Bar/Bri Group
111 W Jackson Blvd # 1700 (60604-3597)
PHONE..................312 894-1690
Patrick Kraska, *Branch Mgr*
EMP: 61
SALES (corp-wide): 10.6B **Publicly Held**
SIC: **2731** Book publishing
HQ: West Publishing Corporation
610 Opperman Dr
Eagan MN 55123
651 687-7000

(G-6606)
WEST WATER INC
463 W 24th St Ste 1 (60616-4947)
PHONE..................312 326-7480
Chaolian Chen, *President*
▲ EMP: 3
SALES (est): 299.9K **Privately Held**
SIC: **2086** Pasteurized & mineral waters, bottled & canned; mineral water, carbonated: packaged in cans, bottles, etc.

(G-6607)
WESTERN ARCHITECTURAL IRON CO
3455 N Elston Ave (60618-5697)
PHONE..................773 463-1500
John F Rundgren, *President*
Edward M Rundgren Jr, *Vice Pres*
Edward Rundgren, *Vice Pres*
Camille Anderson, *Office Mgr*
John Rundgren, *Technology*
EMP: 35 EST: 1925
SQ FT: 39,000
SALES (est): 8.6MM **Privately Held**
WEB: www.waico.com
SIC: **3446** Architectural metalwork

(G-6608)
WESTERN DIGITAL TECH INC
15535 Collection Ctr Dr (60693-0001)
PHONE..................949 672-7000
EMP: 6
SALES (corp-wide): 16.5B **Publicly Held**
SIC: **3572** Computer storage devices
HQ: Western Digital Technologies, Inc.
5601 Great Oaks Pkwy
San Jose CA 95119

(G-6609)
WESTERN-CULLEN-HAYES INC (PA)
2700 W 36th Pl (60632-1617)
PHONE..................773 254-9600
Ronald L Mc Daniel, *President*
Barbara Gulick, *Vice Pres*
Jeff Hein, *Foreman/Supr*
Donna Adamus, *Purch Agent*
Jerry Kranczyk, *Engineer*
EMP: 70
SQ FT: 81,000
SALES (est): 17MM **Privately Held**
SIC: **3643** 3743 3669 Current-carrying wiring devices; railroad equipment; railroad signaling devices, electric

(G-6610)
WESTROCK CP LLC
1415 W 44th St (60609-3333)
PHONE..................773 254-1030
Diane Anderson, *Branch Mgr*
EMP: 8
SALES (corp-wide): 18.2B **Publicly Held**
WEB: www.westrock.com
SIC: **2631** Linerboard; container, packaging & boxboard
HQ: Westrock Cp, Llc
1000 Abernathy Rd Ste 125
Atlanta GA 30328

(G-6611)
WESTROCK CP LLC
Stone Southwest
150 N Michigan Ave (60601-7553)
PHONE..................312 346-6600
Roger W Stone, *Ch of Bd*
EMP: 86
SALES (corp-wide): 18.2B **Publicly Held**
SIC: **2631** 2611 2621 2435 Linerboard; container, packaging & boxboard; pulp produced from wood base; newsprint paper; plywood, hardwood or hardwood faced; panels, softwood plywood; veneer stock, softwood; lumber: rough, sawed or planed
HQ: Westrock Cp, Llc
1000 Abernathy Rd Ste 125
Atlanta GA 30328

(G-6612)
WESTROCK CP LLC
626 E 111th St (60628-4632)
PHONE..................773 264-3516
EMP: 9
SALES (corp-wide): 14.1B **Publicly Held**
SIC: **2631** Paperboard Mill
HQ: Westrock Cp, Llc
504 Thrasher St
Norcross GA 30328

(G-6613)
WESTROCK MWV LLC
9540 S Dorchester Ave (60628-1721)
PHONE..................773 221-9015
Brian Porrett, *Branch Mgr*
EMP: 200
SQ FT: 100,000
SALES (corp-wide): 18.2B **Publicly Held**
SIC: **2631** Linerboard
HQ: Westrock Mwv, Llc
501 S 5th St
Richmond VA 23219
804 444-1000

(G-6614)
WESTROCK RKT LLC
222 N La Salle St (60601-1003)
PHONE..................312 346-6600
Cooper Gordon, *Vice Pres*
EMP: 6561

GEOGRAPHIC SECTION

Chicago - Cook County (G-6639)

SALES (corp-wide): 18.2B **Publicly Held**
SIC: **2631** 2653 2621 2674 Container board; corrugated boxes, partitions, display items, sheets & pad; kraft paper; shipping & shopping bags or sacks
HQ: Westrock Rkt, Llc
1000 Abernathy Rd Ste 125
Atlanta GA 30328
770 448-2193

(G-6615)
WHI CAPITAL PARTNERS (HQ)
191 N Wacker Dr Ste 1500 (60606-1899)
PHONE..................312 621-0590
Adam Schecter, *Partner*
Eric Cohen, *Partner*
EMP: 6
SALES (est): 79.8MM **Privately Held**
SIC: **6799** 3317 Investment clubs; steel pipe & tubes
PA: Harris William & Company Inc
191 N Wacker Dr Ste 1500
Chicago IL 60606
312 621-0590

(G-6616)
WHINER BREWERY LLC
Also Called: Whiner Beer Company
1400 W 46th St 104 (60609-3225)
PHONE..................312 810-2271
EMP: 3
SALES (est): 116.6K **Privately Held**
SIC: **3556** Brewers' & maltsters' machinery

(G-6617)
WHITE DIAMOND BUBBLES HAND
4532 W Madison St (60624-2229)
PHONE..................773 417-3237
Jermaine Jordan, *President*
EMP: 5
SALES (est): 210.9K **Privately Held**
SIC: **3589** Car washing machinery

(G-6618)
WHITE EAGLE SPRING &
1637 N Lowell Ave (60639-4888)
PHONE..................773 384-4455
Robert Ambroziak, *President*
John Ambroziak, *Treasurer*
EMP: 12
SQ FT: 22,500
SALES (est): 2.5MM **Privately Held**
SIC: **3495** 3496 Mechanical springs, precision; miscellaneous fabricated wire products

(G-6619)
WHITE WAY SIGN & MAINT CO
2722 N Racine Ave (60614-6775)
PHONE..................847 391-0200
Robert B Flannery Jr, *President*
James G Flannery, *Chairman*
Robert B Flannery Sr, *Vice Pres*
Willard Martens, *CFO*
EMP: 200
SQ FT: 36,000
SALES (est): 28.2MM **Privately Held**
SIC: **3993** 7629 Electric signs; scoreboards, electric; electrical repair shops

(G-6620)
WHITING PARTNERS LLC
8614 S Commercial Ave (60617-2535)
PHONE..................773 978-8221
Richard Hyman, *Mng Member*
EMP: 3
SALES (est): 287.9K
SALES (corp-wide): 39.7MM **Privately Held**
SIC: **5198** 5531 5251 3429 Paints; automotive parts; hardware; motor vehicle hardware
PA: Hyman's Auto Supply Co.
8600-8614 S Coml Ave
Chicago IL 60617
773 978-8221

(G-6621)
WHOSPOPPIN ENTERPRISES INC
5618 S Indiana Ave (60637-1204)
PHONE..................312 912-8480
Reg Ramey, *President*
Cheryl Cammon, *Admin Sec*
EMP: 3

SALES (est): 73.7K **Privately Held**
SIC: **7372** 7371 7373 Business oriented computer software; computer software systems analysis & design, custom; computer software development & applications; systems software development services

(G-6622)
WICHITA PACKING CO
340 N Oakley Blvd (60612-2216)
PHONE..................312 421-0606
Robert Golant, *President*
Jerry Guon, *Vice Pres*
Andrew Bloom, *Sales Staff*
Mark Guon, *Marketing Mgr*
Casandra Powell, *Manager*
EMP: 45
SQ FT: 13,500
SALES (est): 1.4MM **Privately Held**
WEB: www.wichitapacking.com
SIC: **2011** Meat packing plants

(G-6623)
WIELAND ROLLED PDTS N AMER LLC
Olin Brass
3832 Collection Center Dr (60693-0038)
PHONE..................630 260-0802
Luis Nunez, *Finance*
EMP: 3
SALES (corp-wide): 4.8MM **Privately Held**
SIC: **3351** Copper rolling & drawing
HQ: Wieland Rolled Products North America, Llc
4801 Olympia Park Plz # 3
Louisville KY 40241

(G-6624)
WIELGUS PRODUCT MODELS INC
1435 W Fulton St (60607-1109)
PHONE..................312 432-1950
J Andrew Metelnick, *President*
Gertrude Metelnick, *Treasurer*
Louis Soucek, *Manager*
John H Metelnick, *Admin Sec*
EMP: 25 EST: 1950
SQ FT: 12,000
SALES (est): 3.1MM **Privately Held**
WEB: www.wielgus.com
SIC: **3999** Models, general, except toy

(G-6625)
WILIAMS INTERACTIVE LLC
2718 W Roscoe St (60618)
PHONE..................773 961-1920
EMP: 200
SALES (est): 13.4MM
SALES (corp-wide): 2.8B **Publicly Held**
SIC: **3944** Mfg Games/Toys
HQ: Wms Industries Inc
3401 N California Ave
Chicago IL 60654
847 785-3000

(G-6626)
WILKENS-ANDERSON COMPANY (PA)
Also Called: Waco
4525 W Division St (60651-1674)
PHONE..................773 384-4433
Bruce Wilkens, *President*
Eric Jensen, *Purchasing*
John Wilkens, *Engineer*
Tad Rock, *CFO*
Nancy Jensen, *Treasurer*
EMP: 23
SQ FT: 55,000
SALES (est): 12.8MM **Privately Held**
WEB: www.wacolab.com
SIC: **5049** 3829 Scientific instruments; analytical instruments; measuring & controlling devices

(G-6627)
WILL DON CORP
Also Called: O & G Spring & Wire
7171 W 65th St (60638-1200)
PHONE..................773 276-7081
Richard Greg, *President*
EMP: 85 EST: 1965

SALES (est): 9.9MM **Privately Held**
WEB: www.ogspring.com
SIC: **3496** Miscellaneous fabricated wire products

(G-6628)
WILLDON CORP
Also Called: Oandg Spring and Wire
7171 W 65th St (60638-4605)
PHONE..................773 276-7080
EMP: 50
SALES (est): 4.7MM **Privately Held**
SIC: **3495** 3993 3496 Mfg Wire Springs Mfg Signs/Advertising Specialties Mfg Misc Fabricated Wire Products

(G-6629)
WILLIAM DUDEK MANUFACTURING CO
4901 W Armitage Ave (60639-3214)
PHONE..................773 622-2727
William Dudek, *President*
Victoria Macy, *Treasurer*
Ingred Peavy, *Human Res Mgr*
Theresa Barcal, *Admin Sec*
Michael Dudek, *Admin Sec*
◆ EMP: 28
SQ FT: 23,000
SALES (est): 5MM **Privately Held**
WEB: www.dudekmfg.com
SIC: **3496** 3469 3493 3444 Miscellaneous fabricated wire products; metal stampings; steel springs, except wire; sheet metalwork; manufactured hardware (general)

(G-6630)
WILLIAMS ELECTRONIC GAMES DE (DH)
350 N Orleans St (60654-1975)
PHONE..................773 961-1000
Orrin Edidin, *CEO*
K Fedesna, *Vice Pres*
D Hassler, *Vice Pres*
W Smolucha, *Vice Pres*
J Dillon, *VP Sales*
EMP: 420
SALES (est): 27.4MM
SALES (corp-wide): 3.4B **Publicly Held**
SIC: **3999** Coin-operated amusement machines

(G-6631)
WILLIAMS ELECTRONIC GAMES DE
Also Called: WMS Gaming
350 N Orleans St (60654-1975)
PHONE..................773 961-1000
Tom Byczek, *Manager*
EMP: 8
SALES (corp-wide): 3.4B **Publicly Held**
SIC: **3999** Coin-operated amusement machines
HQ: Williams Electronic Games, Inc De
350 N Orleans St
Chicago IL 60654
773 961-1000

(G-6632)
WILLIS STEIN & PARTNERS MANAGE (PA)
444 W Lake St Ste 4700 (60606-0096)
PHONE..................312 422-2400
John R Willis,
Avy H Stein,
EMP: 19
SQ FT: 22,180
SALES (est): 16.8MM **Privately Held**
SIC: **6799** 3479 2721 8721 Investors; painting of metal products; painting, coating & hot dipping; magazines: publishing & printing; payroll accounting service

(G-6633)
WILLOW CREEK ENERGY LLC (PA)
1 S Wacker Dr Ste 1900 (60606-4644)
PHONE..................312 224-1400
Michael Polsky, *President*
EMP: 1
SQ FT: 5,000
SALES (est): 792.6K **Privately Held**
SIC: **3621** Windmills, electric generating

(G-6634)
WILMETTE SCREW PRODUCTS
4432 N Elston Ave (60630-4475)
PHONE..................773 725-2626
Charles Raia, *President*
Louis Raia, *President*
EMP: 2 EST: 1955
SALES: 350K **Privately Held**
SIC: **3451** Screw machine products

(G-6635)
WILSON SPORTING GOODS CO (DH)
1 Prudntial Pl 130 E Rndl (60601)
PHONE..................773 714-6400
Mike Dowse, *President*
Chris Considine, *Principal*
Dave Scholz, *District Mgr*
Joe Dudy, *Vice Pres*
Bill Kirchner, *Vice Pres*
◆ EMP: 280
SQ FT: 100,000
SALES (est): 500.9MM **Privately Held**
WEB: www.wilson.com
SIC: **5091** 3949 Sporting & recreation goods; sporting & athletic goods; golf equipment; baseball equipment & supplies, general; tennis equipment & supplies

(G-6636)
WILSON SPORTING GOODS CO
Also Called: Wilson Racket Division
8700 W Bryn Mawr Ave (60631-3512)
PHONE..................773 714-6500
Eloisa Compostizo, *Project Engr*
Preston Lemon, *Sales Staff*
Alan Davenport, *Marketing Staff*
Chris Considine, *Manager*
Kendra Bochner, *Manager*
EMP: 200 **Privately Held**
SIC: **3949** Sporting & athletic goods
HQ: Wilson Sporting Goods Co.
1 Prudntial Pl 130 E Rndl
Chicago IL 60601
773 714-6400

(G-6637)
WIND POINT PARTNERS LP (PA)
676 N Michigan Ave # 3700 (60611-2838)
PHONE..................312 255-4800
Nathan Brown, *Partner*
Joe Lawler, *Vice Pres*
Matt Moran, *Vice Pres*
Dan Williams, *Vice Pres*
Daniel Williams, *Vice Pres*
◆ EMP: 11
SQ FT: 4,909
SALES (est): 1.8B **Privately Held**
SIC: **6799** 7363 3089 Venture capital companies; help supply services; blister or bubble formed packaging, plastic

(G-6638)
WIND POINT PARTNERS VI LP (HQ)
676 N Michigan Ave # 3700 (60611-2838)
PHONE..................312 255-4800
Bob Cummings, *Partner*
James E Forrest, *Partner*
Michael Solot, *Partner*
James Tenbroek, *Partner*
Joe Lawler, *Principal*
EMP: 9
SALES (est): 298.4MM
SALES (corp-wide): 1.8B **Privately Held**
SIC: **6799** 2542 2541 3429 Investors; partitions & fixtures, except wood; wood partitions & fixtures; manufactured hardware (general)
PA: Wind Point Partners, L.P.
676 N Michigan Ave # 3700
Chicago IL 60611
312 255-4800

(G-6639)
WINDWRAP LLC
6943 N Minnetonka Ave (60646-1517)
PHONE..................773 594-1724
Peter Carbonaro, *Manager*
EMP: 4
SALES (est): 145.5K **Privately Held**
SIC: **5211** 2297 5039 Lumber & other building materials; nonwoven fabrics; construction materials

Chicago - Cook County (G-6640)

(G-6640)
WINDY CITY ENGINEERING INC
3244 W 30th St (60623-4728)
PHONE..................773 254-8113
Darryl Wagner, *President*
Diane Wagner, *Corp Secy*
Dale Wagner, *Vice Pres*
Maria Ramirez, *Manager*
EMP: 11
SQ FT: 10,000
SALES (est): 2.1MM **Privately Held**
SIC: 3714 Rebuilding engines & transmissions, factory basis

(G-6641)
WINDY CITY FINE FRAMING LLC
840 N Milwaukee Ave (60642-4103)
PHONE..................312 455-1213
Joseph Liss,
EMP: 40
SALES (est): 1.1MM **Privately Held**
SIC: 2499 Picture & mirror frames, wood

(G-6642)
WINDY CITY LASER SERVICE INC
820 W 120th St (60643-5532)
PHONE..................773 995-0188
Jose Briones, *President*
EMP: 3
SALES (est): 611.3K **Privately Held**
SIC: 3699 7699 Laser systems & equipment; industrial equipment services

(G-6643)
WINDY CITY PLASTICS INC
263 N California Ave (60612-1903)
PHONE..................773 533-1099
Matthias Wanezek, *President*
Keith Bosker, *Admin Sec*
EMP: 5
SQ FT: 7,000
SALES (est): 665.6K **Privately Held**
SIC: 3993 Signs & advertising specialties

(G-6644)
WINDY CITY SILKSCREENING INC
2715 S Archer Ave (60608-5926)
PHONE..................312 842-0030
Ronald Szczesniak, *President*
Jim Szczesniak, *COO*
Marybeth Szczesniak, *Vice Pres*
Jeanine Kurpeikis, *Sales Staff*
Paul Macchione, *Sales Staff*
EMP: 40
SQ FT: 15,000
SALES (est): 4.6MM **Privately Held**
SIC: 2396 5699 Screen printing on fabric articles; sports apparel

(G-6645)
WINSCRIBE USA INC (DH)
10 S Lasalle St (60603)
PHONE..................773 399-1608
Matthew Weavers, *President*
EMP: 11
SQ FT: 5,000
SALES (est): 2.3MM **Privately Held**
SIC: 7372 Prepackaged software

(G-6646)
WINSIGHT LLC (HQ)
300 S Riverside Plz # 1600 (60606-6756)
PHONE..................312 876-0004
Kurt Reisenberg, *President*
Tom Cindric, *President*
Alanna Young, *President*
Patricia Cobe, *Publisher*
Jeff Friedman, *Exec VP*
EMP: 173
SALES (est): 24.6MM
SALES (corp-wide): 15.9MM **Privately Held**
SIC: 2721 Magazines: publishing only, not printed on site
PA: Redwood Acquisitions, Llc
1101 30th St Nw
Washington DC 20007
202 625-8340

(G-6647)
WINSTON PRIVACY INC
311 W Monroe St (60606-4659)
PHONE..................312 282-0162
Richard Stokes, *CEO*
EMP: 8
SALES (est): 420.4K **Privately Held**
SIC: 3663 Encryption devices

(G-6648)
WINTERS WELDING INC
7122 S Seeley Ave (60636-3728)
P.O. Box 201026 (60620-0927)
PHONE..................773 860-7735
Deborah D Miller, *President*
EMP: 3
SALES (est): 164.8K **Privately Held**
SIC: 1799 3446 Fence construction; ornamental metal work; fences or posts, ornamental iron or steel

(G-6649)
WIREMASTERS INCORPORATED
Also Called: W/M Display Group
1040 W 40th St 1050 (60609-2503)
PHONE..................773 254-3700
Paul Scriba, *President*
Drew Heinemann, *Vice Pres*
Kevin Meyers, *Vice Pres*
James Street, *Design Engr*
Kristie Marie Scriba, *Admin Sec*
▲ **EMP:** 50 **EST:** 1947
SQ FT: 76,300
SALES (est): 10.6MM **Privately Held**
WEB: www.wmdisplay.com
SIC: 2542 3499 3496 3993 Office & store showcases & display fixtures; novelties & specialties, metal; miscellaneous fabricated wire products; signs & advertising specialties

(G-6650)
WISEPAK FOODS LLC
Also Called: Mr. Pak's
4225 N Pulaski Rd (60641-2331)
PHONE..................773 772-0072
Greg Wiseman,
Jung Pak,
EMP: 35
SQ FT: 6,000
SALES (est): 2MM **Privately Held**
WEB: www.wisepakfoods.com
SIC: 2092 Fresh or frozen packaged fish

(G-6651)
WISNIWSKI RCHARD STL RULE DIES
4422 N Elston Ave (60630-4419)
PHONE..................773 282-1144
Richard A Wisniewski, *President*
Linda Groselak, *Treasurer*
EMP: 4
SQ FT: 3,000
SALES (est): 690.7K **Privately Held**
SIC: 3544 Dies & die holders for metal cutting, forming, die casting; dies, steel rule

(G-6652)
WITHOUT A TRACE WEAVER INC (PA)
3344 W Bryn Mawr Ave (60659-4511)
PHONE..................773 588-4922
Michael Ehrlich, *President*
Linda Lee Mrkvicka, *Admin Sec*
EMP: 12
SALES: 980K **Privately Held**
SIC: 2231 Weaving mill, broadwoven fabrics: wool or similar fabric

(G-6653)
WM HUBER CABINET WORKS
2400 N Campbell Ave (60647-1913)
PHONE..................773 235-7660
Michael Huber, *President*
Daniel Huber, *Corp Secy*
Ervin E Huber, *Vice Pres*
Gary Huber, *Vice Pres*
William Huber, *Project Mgr*
EMP: 50 **EST:** 1941
SQ FT: 34,000
SALES (est): 8MM **Privately Held**
WEB: www.hubercabinet.com
SIC: 2431 2521 Interior & ornamental woodwork & trim; wood office furniture

(G-6654)
WM WRIGLEY JR COMPANY (HQ)
930 W Evergreen Ave (60642-2437)
PHONE..................312 280-4710
Martin Radvan, *President*
Dushan Petrovich, *President*
ADI-Micu, *Area Mgr*
Weili LI, *Business Mgr*
Howard Malovany, *Senior VP*
▼ **EMP:** 345 **EST:** 1891
SQ FT: 453,400
SALES (est): 664.8MM
SALES (corp-wide): 38.5B **Privately Held**
SIC: 2064 2087 2899 2067 Candy & other confectionery products; chewing candy, not chewing gum; lollipops & other hard candy; flavoring extracts & syrups; peppermint oil; spearmint oil; chewing gum base
PA: Mars, Incorporated
6885 Elm St Ste 1
Mc Lean VA 22101
703 821-4900

(G-6655)
WM WRIGLEY JR COMPANY
Also Called: Wrigley's
1300 N North Branch St (60642-2731)
PHONE..................312 205-2300
Sunny Ishikawa, *Manager*
EMP: 35
SALES (corp-wide): 38.5B **Privately Held**
SIC: 2067 Chewing gum
HQ: Wm. Wrigley Jr. Company
930 W Evergreen Ave
Chicago IL 60642
312 280-4710

(G-6656)
WM WRIGLEY JR COMPANY
600 W Chicago Ave Ste 500 (60654-2282)
PHONE..................312 644-2121
Howard Malovany, *Vice Pres*
EMP: 800
SALES (corp-wide): 38.5B **Privately Held**
SIC: 2064 2087 2899 2067 Candy & other confectionery products; extracts, flavoring; peppermint oil; spearmint oil; chewing gum base
HQ: Wm. Wrigley Jr. Company
930 W Evergreen Ave
Chicago IL 60642
312 280-4710

(G-6657)
WMS GAMES INC (DH)
350 N Orleans St 2000s (60654-1510)
PHONE..................773 728-2300
Brian R Gamache, *CEO*
Louis Nicastro, *Ch of Bd*
EMP: 15
SALES (est): 44.2MM
SALES (corp-wide): 3.4B **Publicly Held**
SIC: 3999 Coin-operated amusement machines
HQ: Wms Industries Inc
350 N Orleans St 2000s
Chicago IL 60654
847 785-3000

(G-6658)
WMS GAMING INC
350 N Orleans St 2000s (60654-1510)
PHONE..................773 961-1747
Brian Pierce, *Branch Mgr*
EMP: 125
SALES (corp-wide): 3.4B **Publicly Held**
SIC: 3999 Slot machines
HQ: Wms Gaming Inc.
350 N Orleans St 2000s
Chicago IL 60654

(G-6659)
WMS GAMING INC (DH)
350 N Orleans St 2000s (60654-1510)
PHONE..................773 961-1000
Brian R Gamache, *CEO*
Scott Schweinfurth, *CFO*
Jeorge Pena, *Supervisor*
Kathleen J McJohn, *Admin Sec*
◆ **EMP:** 621
SALES (est): 125.7MM
SALES (corp-wide): 3.4B **Publicly Held**
SIC: 3999 Slot machines
HQ: Wms Industries Inc
350 N Orleans St 2000s
Chicago IL 60654
847 785-3000

(G-6660)
WMS INDUSTRIES INC (HQ)
350 N Orleans St 2000s (60654-1510)
PHONE..................847 785-3000
Brian R Gamache, *Ch of Bd*
Orrin J Edidin, *President*
Robert J Bahash, *Principal*
Patricia M Nazemetz, *Principal*
Kenneth Lochiatto, *COO*
EMP: 44
SALES: 697.3MM
SALES (corp-wide): 3.4B **Publicly Held**
WEB: www.wms.com
SIC: 3999 7999 Coin-operated amusement machines; lottery operation
PA: Scientific Games Corporation
6601 Bermuda Rd
Las Vegas NV 89119
702 897-7150

(G-6661)
WODACK ELECTRIC TOOL CORP
4627 W Huron St (60644-1309)
PHONE..................773 287-9866
EMP: 10
SQ FT: 6,000
SALES: 200K **Privately Held**
SIC: 3546 3621 3635 Mfg Motors/Generators Mfg Power-Driven Handtools Mfg Home Vacuum Cleaners

(G-6662)
WOLFAM HOLDINGS CORPORATION
Also Called: Kwik Kopy Printing
120 W Madison St Ste 510 (60602-4418)
PHONE..................312 407-0100
Darryl Wolf, *President*
EMP: 8
SQ FT: 2,500
SALES: 500K **Privately Held**
SIC: 2759 Thermography

(G-6663)
WOLFART MACIEJ
Also Called: Black Fodder Coffee
6150 N Hamilton Ave Apt 3 (60659-4217)
PHONE..................312 248-3575
EMP: 5
SALES (est): 70.7K **Privately Held**
SIC: 5812 2095 7389 5149 Coffee shop; coffee roasting (except by wholesale grocers); coffee service; coffee & tea; coffee tables: wood; coffee

(G-6664)
WOLFSWORD PRESS
7144 N Harlem Ave 325 (60631-1017)
PHONE..................773 403-1144
Valya Lupescu, *President*
Mark P Lupescu, *Admin Sec*
EMP: 3
SALES (est): 167.4K **Privately Held**
SIC: 2741 Miscellaneous publishing

(G-6665)
WOOD CREATIONS INCORPORATED (PA)
Also Called: WCI
3918 W Shakespeare Ave (60647-3431)
PHONE..................773 772-1375
George Malishewsky, *President*
Ted Pyciak, *Vice Pres*
▲ **EMP:** 5
SQ FT: 25,000
SALES (est): 1.2MM **Privately Held**
SIC: 2431 Millwork

(G-6666)
WOOD CREATIONS INCORPORATED
4627 W Fullerton Ave (60639-1876)
PHONE..................773 772-1375
John Ocnei, *Manager*
EMP: 8
SQ FT: 14,000

GEOGRAPHIC SECTION — Chicago - Cook County (G-6692)

SALES (corp-wide): 1.2MM **Privately Held**
WEB: www.wearewci.org
SIC: 2431 Millwork
PA: Wood Creations Incorporated
3918 W Shakespeare Ave
Chicago IL 60647
773 772-1375

(G-6667)
WOOD SHOP
Also Called: Woodshop, The
441 E 75th St (60619-2228)
PHONE..................773 994-6666
Lawrance Dantignac, *Owner*
Marbita Dantignac, *Co-Owner*
EMP: 4
SQ FT: 3,000
SALES (est): 300K **Privately Held**
SIC: 2499 2434 5999 Picture & mirror frames, wood; wood kitchen cabinets; art dealers

(G-6668)
WOODWAYS INDUSTRIES LLC
850 S Wabash Ave Ste 300 (60605-3642)
PHONE..................616 956-3070
EMP: 44 **Privately Held**
SIC: 2434 Wood kitchen cabinets
PA: Woodways Industries, Llc
4265 28th St Se Ste A
Grand Rapids MI 49512

(G-6669)
WORDSPACE PRESS LIMITED
2259 N Kedzie Blvd (60647-2561)
PHONE..................773 292-0292
Dave Glowacz, *President*
EMP: 3
SALES: 100K **Privately Held**
SIC: 2741 Miscellaneous publishing

(G-6670)
WORLD BOOK ENCYCLOPEDIA DEL (DH)
Also Called: World Book Direct Marketing
180 N La Salle St Ste 900 (60601-2500)
PHONE..................312 729-5800
Donald Keller, *President*
EMP: 150
SALES (est): 8.7MM
SALES (corp-wide): 327.2B **Publicly Held**
SIC: 2741 Miscellaneous publishing
HQ: The Scott Fetzer Company
28800 Clemens Rd
Westlake OH 44145
440 892-3000

(G-6671)
WORLD BOOK INC (DH)
Also Called: World Book Direct Marketing
180 N La Salle St Ste 900 (60601-2500)
PHONE..................312 729-5800
Robert D McBride, *President*
Kenneth Semelsberger, *Principal*
Donald Keller, *Vice Pres*
William W Stephans, *Treasurer*
▲ EMP: 50 EST: 1957
SALES (est): 48.8MM
SALES (corp-wide): 327.2B **Publicly Held**
WEB: www.worldbook.com
SIC: 2731 2741 5961 Textbooks: publishing only, not printed on site; atlases: publishing only, not printed on site; books, mail order (except book clubs)
HQ: The Scott Fetzer Company
28800 Clemens Rd
Westlake OH 44145
440 892-3000

(G-6672)
WORLD CLASS TECHNOLOGIES INC
Also Called: Lmsys
70 E Lake St Ste 600 (60601-7642)
PHONE..................312 758-3114
Steve Williams, *President*
Marion Williams, *Vice Pres*
EMP: 6
SQ FT: 5,000
SALES (est): 450K **Privately Held**
SIC: 3842 3949 Orthopedic appliances; braces, orthopedic; sporting & athletic goods

(G-6673)
WORLD FUEL SERVICES INC
2458 Paysphere Cir (60674-0024)
PHONE..................305 428-8000
Michael J Kasbar, *CEO*
Michael Crosby, *Exec VP*
John P Rau, *Exec VP*
Ira M Birns, *CFO*
Alexander Lake, *Admin Sec*
EMP: 11
SALES (est): 772.8K **Privately Held**
SIC: 1731 8741 2869 Energy management controls; management services; fuels

(G-6674)
WORLD JOURNAL LLC
2116 S Archer Ave (60616-1514)
PHONE..................312 842-8005
Tom Lai, *Manager*
EMP: 10
SQ FT: 19,000 **Privately Held**
SIC: 2711 2791 Newspapers: publishing only, not printed on site; typesetting
HQ: World Journal Llc
14107 20th Ave Fl 2
Whitestone NY 11357
718 746-8889

(G-6675)
WORLD JOURNAL LLC
Also Called: World Journal Chinese Daily
2471 S Archer Ave Ste 1 (60616-1847)
PHONE..................312 842-8080
W J Hwang, *Owner*
Huey Tzy Chang, *Manager*
EMP: 12 **Privately Held**
SIC: 2711 Commercial printing & newspaper publishing combined
HQ: World Journal Llc
14107 20th Ave Fl 2
Whitestone NY 11357
718 746-8889

(G-6676)
WORLD OF SOUL INC
9131 S La Salle St (60620-1410)
P.O. Box 288656 (60628-8543)
PHONE..................773 840-4839
Terry Hardy, *President*
EMP: 3 EST: 2013
SALES (est): 191.8K **Privately Held**
SIC: 3751 7389 Motorcycles & related parts;

(G-6677)
WORLDS FINEST CHOCOLATE INC (PA)
Also Called: Cook Chocolate Company
4801 S Lawndale Ave (60632-3065)
PHONE..................773 847-4600
Edmond F Opler, *Ch of Bd*
Howard Zodikoff, *President*
Mike Morris, *COO*
Bill Erickson, *Purch Mgr*
Al Gomez, *Controller*
▲ EMP: 350
SQ FT: 500,000
SALES (est): 196.9MM **Privately Held**
WEB: www.worldsfinestchocolate.com
SIC: 2066 5947 Chocolate & cocoa products; gift, novelty & souvenir shop

(G-6678)
WORLDS PRINTING & SPC CO LTD
233 N Michigan Ave (60601-5519)
PHONE..................312 565-1401
William Walden, *President*
Anne Fritzinger, *President*
Jake Bumgardner, *Editor*
Nicholas Kilzer, *Editor*
Dawn Krajcik, *Editor*
EMP: 5
SQ FT: 1,000
SALES (est): 97.4K **Privately Held**
WEB: www.worldsprinting.espwebsite.com
SIC: 2741 Miscellaneous publishing

(G-6679)
WORLDWIDE TRANS AND DIFF CORP
5663 N Mason Ave (60646-6211)
P.O. Box 480714, Niles (60714-0714)
PHONE..................773 930-3447
James Raymond Skawski, *President*
EMP: 2
SALES (est): 215.4K **Privately Held**
SIC: 3568 Power transmission equipment

(G-6680)
WOW BAO LLC
230 W Huron St Ste 430 (60654-3952)
PHONE..................888 496-9226
Geoff Alexander, *President*
EMP: 52
SALES: 6MM **Privately Held**
SIC: 5812 7372 Chinese restaurant; application computer software
PA: Hot Asian Buns Llc
875 N Michigan Ave # 3214
Chicago IL
773 433-5322

(G-6681)
WPG US HOLDCO LLC (DH)
330 N Wabash Ave Ste 3750 (60611-5697)
PHONE..................312 517-3750
Philip Brown, *President*
EMP: 419
SALES (corp-wide): 242.1K **Privately Held**
SIC: 6719 3714 3568 5083 Investment holding companies, except banks; motor vehicle transmissions, drive assemblies & parts; clutches, motor vehicle; drive shafts, motor vehicle; universal joints, motor vehicle; power transmission equipment; agricultural machinery & equipment
HQ: Wpg Holdco B.V.
Herengracht 466
Amsterdam
204 203-000

(G-6682)
WRAPPING INC
3600 N Lake Shore Dr (60613-4684)
PHONE..................773 871-2898
Leszek Mirecki, *President*
John Badie, *Vice Pres*
EMP: 1
SALES: 1MM **Privately Held**
SIC: 3086 Packaging & shipping materials, foamed plastic

(G-6683)
WRAPPORTS LLC (HQ)
350 N Orleans St Fl 10 (60654-1975)
PHONE..................312 321-3000
Timothy P Knight, *CEO*
Bradley Phillip Bell, *President*
Elaine Taussig, *Counsel*
EMP: 17
SALES (est): 314.8MM
SALES (corp-wide): 4.3MM **Privately Held**
SIC: 7379 2711 ; newspapers, publishing & printing

(G-6684)
WRENCH
Also Called: Food Bikes
1208 W Hubbard St (60642)
PHONE..................773 609-1698
George Olec,
Oliver Kavanaugh,
EMP: 6
SALES (est): 320K **Privately Held**
SIC: 5941 3751 3568 Bicycle & bicycle parts; motorcycles, bicycles & parts; handle bars, motorcycle & bicycle; drive chains, bicycle or motorcycle

(G-6685)
WRIGHTWOOD TECHNOLOGIES INC
Also Called: Cherry Instruments
3440 S Dearborn St Ste 39 (60616-5148)
PHONE..................312 238-9512
Samuel M Pro, *President*
Laura Velazquez, *Property Mgr*
Warren R Freidl, *Bd of Directors*
▲ EMP: 3
SQ FT: 500
SALES: 1.3MM **Privately Held**
SIC: 3821 Laboratory apparatus & furniture

(G-6686)
WRIGLEY MANUFACTURING CO LLC (DH)
Also Called: Wrigley's
410 N Michigan Ave (60611-4213)
P.O. Box 3900, Peoria (61612-3900)
PHONE..................312 644-2121
Martin Radvan, *President*
Andy Pharoah, *Vice Pres*
Anthony Gedeller, *Treasurer*
▲ EMP: 600
SALES (est): 122.4MM
SALES (corp-wide): 38.5B **Privately Held**
SIC: 2067 Chewing gum
HQ: Wm. Wrigley Jr. Company
930 W Evergreen Ave
Chicago IL 60642
312 280-4710

(G-6687)
WRIGLEY MANUFACTURING CO LLC
Also Called: Wrigley's
1452 N Cherry Ave (60642-7559)
PHONE..................312 644-2121
EMP: 567
SALES (corp-wide): 38.5B **Privately Held**
SIC: 2067 Chewing gum
HQ: Wrigley Manufacturing Company Llc
410 N Michigan Ave
Chicago IL 60611
312 644-2121

(G-6688)
WRIGLEY SALES COMPANY LLC
410 N Michigan Ave C-1 (60611-4211)
PHONE..................312 644-2121
Ralph P Scozzafoua, *Principal*
▼ EMP: 12
SALES (est): 3.2MM
SALES (corp-wide): 38.5B **Privately Held**
SIC: 2067 Chewing gum
HQ: Wm. Wrigley Jr. Company
930 W Evergreen Ave
Chicago IL 60642
312 280-4710

(G-6689)
WSW INDUSTRIAL MAINTENANCE
2701 E 105th St (60617-5713)
PHONE..................773 721-0675
Walter S Stuczynski, *President*
Lorina Stuczynski, *Admin Sec*
EMP: 15
SQ FT: 20,000
SALES (est): 3.1MM **Privately Held**
SIC: 3441 Fabricated structural metal

(G-6690)
WW ENGINEERING COMPANY LLC
4321 W 32nd St (60623-4814)
PHONE..................773 376-9494
Claude Giudice, *Executive*
Al Giudice,
Thomas F Baldacci,
EMP: 15 EST: 1971
SQ FT: 20,000
SALES (est): 3.9MM **Privately Held**
SIC: 3443 3536 7699 Tanks, standard or custom fabricated: metal plate; hoppers, metal plate; hoists, cranes & monorails; industrial machinery & equipment repair

(G-6691)
XAPTUM INC
541 N Fairbanks Ct # 2200 (60611-3710)
PHONE..................312 852-1595
Rohit Pasam, *CEO*
Brian Gratch, *Exec VP*
Helena Stelnicki, *CFO*
EMP: 7
SQ FT: 500
SALES (est): 203.3K **Privately Held**
SIC: 7372 Application computer software

(G-6692)
XELERATED INC (PA)
150 N Michigan Ave # 1950 (60601-7553)
PHONE..................408 222-2500
Thomas Axelsson, *President*
Johan Borje, *Co-President*

Chicago - Cook County (G-6693)

Mats L Fling, *VP Engrg*
Per-Olov Stberg, *CFO*
Johan Hellqvist, *Treasurer*
EMP: 7
SALES (est): 626.5K **Privately Held**
SIC: 3674 Semiconductors & related devices

(G-6693)
XERIS PHARMACEUTICALS INC (PA)
180 N Lasalle St Ste 1600 (60601)
PHONE..................844 445-5704
Paul Edick, *Ch of Bd*
Beth Hecht, *Senior VP*
Ken Johnson, *Senior VP*
Krista Johnson, *Finance*
Pamela Kelley, *Associate Dir*
EMP: 48
SQ FT: 40,850
SALES: 2.7MM **Publicly Held**
SIC: 2834 Pharmaceutical preparations

(G-6694)
XFORM POWER AND EQP SUPS LLC
3023 N Clark St (60657-5200)
PHONE..................773 260-0209
Nelda Connors, *CEO*
EMP: 4
SQ FT: 2,000
SALES (est): 354.9K **Privately Held**
SIC: 5063 3621 Generators; motors & generators

(G-6695)
XL MANUFACTURE
2717 W Lawrence Ave (60625-3490)
PHONE..................773 271-8900
Hristos Lalopoulos, *Principal*
EMP: 3
SALES (est): 271.1K **Privately Held**
SIC: 3999 Manufacturing industries

(G-6696)
XMT SOLUTIONS LLC
Also Called: Mobell Muscle
1749 N Wells St Apt 2010 (60614-5829)
PHONE..................703 338-9422
Michael Humenansky, *Mng Member*
EMP: 4
SALES (est): 180K **Privately Held**
SIC: 3949 Exercise equipment

(G-6697)
YANA HOUSE
7120 S Normal Blvd (60621-3025)
PHONE..................773 874-7120
Charlie Powell, *Exec Dir*
EMP: 3
SALES (est): 174.8K **Privately Held**
SIC: 3545 Machine tool accessories

(G-6698)
YES PRINT MANAGEMENT INC
Also Called: Yes Packaging
3636 S Iron St (60609-1321)
PHONE..................312 226-4444
Gerald A Cox Jr, *President*
EMP: 7 **EST:** 1999
SQ FT: 1,000
SALES (est): 1.2MM **Privately Held**
WEB: www.yesprintmgt.com
SIC: 2752 Commercial printing, lithographic

(G-6699)
YFY JUPITER INC
445 N Wells St Ste 401 (60654-4534)
PHONE..................312 419-8565
Sean Murphy, *Principal*
Scott Wang, *Accounts Mgr*
Joel Wang, *Director*
Nancy Schachtner, *Officer*
EMP: 22
SALES (corp-wide): 45MM **Privately Held**
WEB: www.elementcode.com
SIC: 3577 Printers & plotters
PA: Jupiter Prestige Group North America Inc.
4100 W Royal Ln
Irving TX 75063
972 573-6800

(G-6700)
YHLSOFT INC
Also Called: Advyzon
935 W Chestnut St (60642-5441)
PHONE..................844 829-0039
EMP: 10 **EST:** 2012
SALES (est): 770.5K **Privately Held**
SIC: 7372 Business oriented computer software

(G-6701)
YIELD MANAGEMENT SYSTEMS LLC
2626 N Lakeview Ave # 708 (60614-1810)
PHONE..................312 665-1595
Steven Gelb, *Manager*
EMP: 2
SALES (est): 510K **Privately Held**
SIC: 7372 Prepackaged software

(G-6702)
YMC CORP
Also Called: Canton Noodle Company
481 W 26th St (60616-2235)
PHONE..................312 842-4900
Harry Moy, *President*
Tom Moy, *Treasurer*
Kris Ryan, *Business Anlyst*
James Moy, *Admin Sec*
▲ **EMP:** 17
SQ FT: 5,000
SALES (est): 1.5MM **Privately Held**
SIC: 2099 Noodles, fried (Chinese)

(G-6703)
YOLANDA LORENTE LTD (PA)
4424 N Ravenswood Ave 1 (60640-5803)
PHONE..................773 334-4536
Yolanda Lorente, *President*
Arthur Szefer, *Vice Pres*
▲ **EMP:** 20
SQ FT: 25,000
SALES (est): 1.2MM **Privately Held**
SIC: 2331 2335 2337 2339 Women's & misses' blouses & shirts; women's, juniors' & misses' dresses; women's & misses' suits & coats; women's & misses' outerwear

(G-6704)
Z PRINT INC
5257 N Central Ave (60630-4656)
PHONE..................773 685-4878
Dariusz Gorecki, *President*
EMP: 6
SALES (est): 647.6K **Privately Held**
SIC: 2752 Commercial printing, offset

(G-6705)
Z-MODULAR LLC
227 W Monroe St Ste 2600 (60606-5082)
PHONE..................312 275-1600
Mickey McNamara, *President*
Lewis Lockwood, *VP Opers*
EMP: 50
SQ FT: 106,000
SALES: 1MM **Privately Held**
SIC: 2452 Modular homes, prefabricated, wood
PA: Zekelman Industries, Inc.
227 W Monroe St Ste 2600
Chicago IL 60606

(G-6706)
ZAIBAK BROS (PA)
207 E Ohio St Ste 374 (60611-4092)
PHONE..................312 564-5800
Khaled Elzeibak, *President*
Manuel Perez, *Admin Sec*
▲ **EMP:** 46
SQ FT: 22,000
SALES (est): 3.8MM **Privately Held**
SIC: 2099 5141 Food preparations; food brokers

(G-6707)
ZAKROSE INC
2100 N Major Ave (60639-2901)
PHONE..................847 372-7309
Zachary M Rose, *Principal*
EMP: 5
SALES (est): 498.3K **Privately Held**
SIC: 2511 Wood household furniture

(G-6708)
ZAXIS FACTORY INC
2150 S Canalport Ave (60608-4559)
PHONE..................888 299-5516
EMP: 2
SALES (est): 235.6K **Privately Held**
SIC: 3599 Machine shop, jobbing & repair

(G-6709)
ZB IMPORTING INC
5400 W 35th St (60804-4431)
PHONE..................708 222-8330
Abraham Ziyad, *President*
EMP: 45
SALES (corp-wide): 60.3MM **Privately Held**
SIC: 5149 2051 2064 Specialty food items; bread, all types (white, wheat, rye, etc): fresh or frozen; candy & other confectionery products
PA: Zb Importing, Inc.
5400 W 35th St
Cicero IL 60804
708 222-8330

(G-6710)
ZEBRA OUTLET
5750 W Bloomingdale Ave # 1 (60639-4139)
PHONE..................312 416-1518
Arman Yavuz, *President*
EMP: 12
SQ FT: 20,000
SALES: 1MM **Privately Held**
WEB: www.zebraoutlet.com
SIC: 3555 Copy holders, printers'

(G-6711)
ZEBRA TECHNOLOGIES CORPORATION
6048 Eagle Way (60678-1060)
PHONE..................847 634-6700
Tatsiana Kopilevich, *Human Resources*
Denise Snep, *Director*
EMP: 400
SALES (corp-wide): 4.4B **Publicly Held**
SIC: 3577 Bar code (magnetic ink) printers
PA: Zebra Technologies Corporation
3 Overlook Pt
Lincolnshire IL 60069
847 634-6700

(G-6712)
ZEKELMAN INDUSTRIES INC
Also Called: Jmc Steel Group
1855 E 122nd St (60633-2401)
PHONE..................773 646-4500
EMP: 5 **Privately Held**
SIC: 3317 Steel pipe & tubes
PA: Zekelman Industries, Inc.
227 W Monroe St Ste 2600
Chicago IL 60606

(G-6713)
ZEKELMAN INDUSTRIES INC (PA)
227 W Monroe St Ste 2600 (60606-5082)
PHONE..................312 275-1600
Barry M Zekelman, *Ch of Bd*
Michael P McNamara, *Exec VP*
Michael E Mechley, *Exec VP*
▲ **EMP:** 50
SALES: 2.1B **Privately Held**
SIC: 3317 Pipes, seamless steel

(G-6714)
ZELL CO
329 W 18th St Ste 507 (60616-1121)
PHONE..................312 226-9191
Eugene Zell, *President*
Meredith Zell, *Admin Sec*
EMP: 6 **EST:** 1982
SQ FT: 12,000
SALES (est): 829.1K **Privately Held**
SIC: 7331 2759 Mailing service; commercial printing

(G-6715)
ZENB US INC
950 W Fulton Market (60607-1323)
PHONE..................312 581-6574
EMP: 6
SALES (est): 416.9K **Privately Held**
SIC: 2099 Food preparations

(G-6716)
ZENDER ENTERPRISES LTD
Also Called: Zender Molding Solutions
3692 N Milwaukee Ave (60641-3032)
PHONE..................773 282-2293
Joyce Zender, *President*
Joe Zender, *Vice Pres*
George Avila, *Dir Ops-Prd-Mfg*
EMP: 8
SQ FT: 10,000
SALES: 511.9K **Privately Held**
SIC: 3544 3089 Industrial molds; injection molding of plastics

(G-6717)
ZENITH FABRICATING COMPANY
Also Called: Zenfab
1928 N Leamington Ave (60639-4490)
PHONE..................773 622-2601
Cheri McKown, *President*
Cheri McKwon, *Vice Pres*
Patti Kalal, *Admin Sec*
EMP: 37 **EST:** 1965
SQ FT: 33,000
SALES (est): 6.9MM **Privately Held**
SIC: 3499 Boxes for packing & shipping, metal

(G-6718)
ZF CHASSIS COMPONENTS LLC
Also Called: ZF Chassis Systems Tuscaloosa
3400 E 126th St (60633-1293)
PHONE..................773 371-4550
Brad Neuman, *Plant Mgr*
Steve Schoenborn, *Materials Mgr*
EMP: 330
SALES (corp-wide): 216.2K **Privately Held**
SIC: 3714 5013 Motor vehicle engines & parts; automotive supplies & parts
HQ: Zf Chassis Components, Llc
3300 John Conley Dr
Lapeer MI 48446
810 245-2000

(G-6719)
ZIMMERMAN BRUSH CO
Also Called: Zimco
6320 N Whipple St (60659-1420)
PHONE..................773 761-6331
Yale Zimmerman, *President*
EMP: 100 **EST:** 1960
SALES (est): 6.9MM **Privately Held**
SIC: 3991 Brushes, household or industrial

(G-6720)
ZIRLIN INTERIORS INC
5540 N Broadway St (60640-1406)
PHONE..................773 334-5530
Irving Zirlin, *President*
Paul Zirlin, *Vice Pres*
Shelly Bland, *Treasurer*
Shelly Peterson, *Executive*
Glenn Zirlin, *Admin Sec*
EMP: 24
SQ FT: 9,000
SALES (est): 3.1MM **Privately Held**
WEB: www.zirlininteriorsinc.com
SIC: 2391 7641 3429 2591 Curtains & draperies; reupholstery; manufactured hardware (general); drapery hardware & blinds & shades

(G-6721)
ZIRMED INC
Also Called: Waystar
1330 W Fulton Market # 300 (60607)
PHONE..................312 207-0889
EMP: 21
SALES (corp-wide): 60.7MM **Privately Held**
SIC: 7372 Utility computer software
HQ: Zirmed Inc.
888 W Market St Ste 400
Louisville KY 40202
502 473-7709

(G-6722)
ZOES MFGCO LLC
Also Called: C.A. Zoes Mfg Co
168 N Sangamon St (60607-2210)
PHONE..................312 666-4018
Phillip Collias Jr, *Mng Member*

GEOGRAPHIC SECTION

Chicago Heights - Cook County (G-6747)

EMP: 13
SALES (corp-wide): 2.2MM **Privately Held**
SIC: 2842 3111 Polishing preparations & related products; shoe polish or cleaner; shoe leather
PA: Zoes Mfgco Llc
166 N Sangamon St 172
Chicago IL
312 666-4018

(G-6723)
ZORCH INTERNATIONAL INC
223 W Erie St Ste 5nw (60654-3995)
PHONE....................312 751-8010
Mike Wolfe, *CEO*
Mike Callahan, *Accounts Mgr*
McKenzie Sharpe, *Marketing Staff*
Susan King, *Manager*
Debbie Yuen, *Manager*
EMP: 43
SQ FT: 10,000
SALES (est): 11.2MM
SALES (corp-wide): 11.7MM **Privately Held**
SIC: 2759 Promotional printing
PA: Satori Capital, L.L.C.
2501 N Harwood St # 2001
Dallas TX 75201
214 390-6270

(G-6724)
ZORIN MATERIAL HANDLING CO (PA)
1937 W Wolfram St (60657-4031)
PHONE....................773 342-3818
Jeffrey Farlander, *President*
▼ EMP: 1
SALES (est): 378.1K **Privately Held**
SIC: 5984 3412 7389 Liquefied petroleum gas dealers; drums, shipping: metal;

(G-6725)
ZSI-FOSTER INC
6571 Solutions Ctr (60677-6005)
PHONE....................800 323-7053
EMP: 8
SALES (corp-wide): 221.2MM **Privately Held**
SIC: 3429 Clamps, metal
HQ: Zsi-Foster, Inc.
45065 Michigan Ave
Canton MI 48188

(G-6726)
ZUCHEM INC
2242 W Harrison St 201-3 (60612-3719)
PHONE....................312 997-2150
David Demirjian PHD, *President*
Rajni Aneja, *Vice Pres*
EMP: 7
SALES (est): 1MM **Privately Held**
SIC: 2099 Sugar

(G-6727)
ZWEIBEL WORLDWIDE PRODUCTIONS
212 W Superior St Ste 200 (60654-3562)
PHONE....................312 751-0503
EMP: 14
SALES (est): 111K
SALES (corp-wide): 15.4MM **Privately Held**
SIC: 2711 Newspapers-Publishing/Printing
PA: Onion Inc.
730 N Franklin St Ste 701
Chicago IL 60654
312 751-0503

Chicago Heights
Cook County

(G-6728)
AEN INDUSTRIES INC
Also Called: Clean Shop Division
1522 Union Ave (60411-3511)
PHONE....................708 758-3000
Mike Schreiber, *President*
EMP: 15
SALES (est): 3.6MM **Privately Held**
WEB: www.aenindustries.com
SIC: 3564 5075 Air purification equipment; air conditioning & ventilation equipment & supplies

(G-6729)
AEP NVH OPCO LLC
Also Called: Applied Acoustic International
1001 State St (60411-2907)
PHONE....................708 758-0211
John Jacinto, *President*
Faye Pan, *Purch Mgr*
Erik Greene, *Controller*
Kamita Terrell, *Accountant*
Maria Owens, *Human Resources*
EMP: 10
SALES (est): 52.4MM
SALES (corp-wide): 55.8MM **Privately Held**
SIC: 3711 Motor vehicles & car bodies
HQ: Vistech Manufacturing Solutions, Llc
1156 Scenic Dr Ste 120
Modesto CA 95350
209 544-9333

(G-6730)
ALCO SPRING INDUSTRIES INC
2300 Euclid Ave (60411-4085)
PHONE....................708 755-0438
William Kiefer, *President*
Karen Thoma, *Vice Pres*
Jennifer Thoma-Romines, *Asst Controller*
Mary Apking, *Sales Staff*
Brian Livingston, *Sales Staff*
▲ EMP: 70
SQ FT: 150,000
SALES (est): 17.7MM **Privately Held**
WEB: www.alcospring.com
SIC: 3493 Hot wound springs, except wire

(G-6731)
ARYZTA LLC
401 E Joe Orr Rd (60411-1202)
PHONE....................708 757-4671
Chris Woo,
Dave Johnson,
John Malone,
EMP: 3
SALES (est): 367.7K **Privately Held**
SIC: 2051 Bakery: wholesale or wholesale/retail combined

(G-6732)
ASHLAND SCREENING CORPORATION
475 E Joe Orr Rd (60411-1286)
PHONE....................708 758-8800
Robert K Starmann, *President*
EMP: 30
SQ FT: 50,000
SALES (est): 2.5MM **Privately Held**
SIC: 2759 2396 Screen printing; automotive & apparel trimmings

(G-6733)
BAR PROCESSING CORPORATION
1601 Wentworth Ave Ste 33 (60411-3711)
PHONE....................708 757-4570
Nick Vaandrager, *Engineer*
Jeff Kolbus, *Manager*
EMP: 40
SALES (corp-wide): 39.9MM **Privately Held**
SIC: 3471 3312 Finishing, metals or formed products; polishing, metals or formed products; blast furnaces & steel mills
HQ: Bar Processing Corporation
26601 W Huron River Dr
Flat Rock MI 48134
734 782-4454

(G-6734)
BEHR PROCESS CORPORATION
21701 Mark Collins Dr # 200 (60411-5197)
PHONE....................708 753-0136
Jimmy Taylor, *Branch Mgr*
EMP: 59
SALES (corp-wide): 6.7B **Publicly Held**
SIC: 2851 Paints & paint additives; stains; varnish, oil or wax; varnishes
HQ: Behr Process Corporation
1801 E Saint Andrew Pl
Santa Ana CA 92705

(G-6735)
BEHR PROCESS CORPORATION
270 State St Ste 1 (60411-1287)
PHONE....................708 757-6350
Jeffrey D Filley, *Branch Mgr*
EMP: 104
SALES (corp-wide): 6.7B **Publicly Held**
SIC: 2851 Paints & paint additives; stains; varnish, oil or wax; varnishes
HQ: Behr Process Corporation
1801 E Saint Andrew Pl
Santa Ana CA 92705

(G-6736)
BULL MOOSE TUBE COMPANY
555 E 16th St (60411-3731)
PHONE....................708 757-7700
Rick Thyem, *Manager*
EMP: 100
SQ FT: 95,000
SALES (corp-wide): 197.9MM **Privately Held**
SIC: 3317 Steel pipe & tubes
PA: Bull Moose Tube Company
1819 Clarkson Rd Ste 100
Chesterfield MO 63017
636 537-1249

(G-6737)
C F C INTERNATIONAL
385 E Joe Orr Rd (60411-1237)
PHONE....................708 753-0679
Greg Jehlik, *President*
EMP: 2 EST: 1891
SQ FT: 28,000
SALES (est): 246.4K **Privately Held**
WEB: www.cfcintl.com
SIC: 7389 2752 2796 2759 Engraving service; commercial printing, offset; platemaking services; commercial printing

(G-6738)
CERAMIC DESIGNS UNLIMITED
475 E Joe Orr Rd (60411-1202)
PHONE....................708 758-0690
Robert K Starmann, *President*
Dana I Romito, *Corp Secy*
EMP: 4
SQ FT: 10,000
SALES (est): 510K **Privately Held**
SIC: 3231 Products of purchased glass

(G-6739)
CFC INTERNATIONAL INC
500 State St (60411-1293)
PHONE....................708 891-3456
Philip M Gresh, *President*
Dan Szumski, *Technical Mgr*
Roger Strasemeier, *Research*
Beth Prigge, *Accountant*
Walter Floyd, *Sales Staff*
EMP: 9
SALES (est): 150.9K **Privately Held**
SIC: 3083 3081 Laminated plastics plate & sheet; unsupported plastics film & sheet

(G-6740)
CFC INTERNATIONAL CORPORATION (HQ)
Also Called: CFC Applied Holographics
500 State St (60411-1293)
PHONE....................708 323-4131
Nicolas Martino, *President*
William A Herring, *Senior VP*
Dennis W Lakomy, *CFO*
Maryann Spiegel, *Admin Sec*
▲ EMP: 240
SQ FT: 150,000
SALES (est): 71.8MM
SALES (corp-wide): 14.1B **Publicly Held**
SIC: 3053 3081 Packing materials; unsupported plastics film & sheet
PA: Illinois Tool Works Inc.
155 Harlem Ave
Glenview IL 60025
847 724-7500

(G-6741)
CHICAGO HEIGHTS PALLETS CO
1200 State St (60411-2968)
P.O. Box 506 (60412-0506)
PHONE....................708 757-7641
EMP: 10
SALES (est): 1.1MM **Privately Held**
SIC: 2448 Mfg Wood Pallets/Skids

(G-6742)
CHICAGO HEIGHTS STAR TOOL AND
640 217th St (60411-4327)
PHONE....................708 758-2525
John Montella, *President*
Don Krause, *Engineer*
Thomas Montella, *Treasurer*
Eric Almquist, *Sales Engr*
Al James, *Sales Staff*
▲ EMP: 13 EST: 1925
SQ FT: 8,500
SALES (est): 2.8MM **Privately Held**
WEB: www.startoolanddie.com
SIC: 3544 5084 Dies & die holders for metal cutting, forming, die casting; dies, plastics forming; extrusion dies; jigs & fixtures; industrial machinery & equipment

(G-6743)
CHS ACQUISITION CORP
Also Called: Chicago Heights Steel
211 E Main St (60411-4270)
P.O. Box 1249, Calumet City (60409-1249)
PHONE....................708 756-5648
Bradley R Corral, *President*
Richard R Gollner, *Corp Secy*
Kevin Groner, *Technician*
▼ EMP: 250
SQ FT: 250,000
SALES (est): 87.4MM **Privately Held**
SIC: 3312 Fence posts, iron & steel; structural shapes & pilings, steel

(G-6744)
CONCEPT PRINTERS (PA)
209 Glenwood Rd (60411-8217)
PHONE....................708 481-2430
Terrance Murphy, *Owner*
Pamela Murphy, *Owner*
EMP: 2
SQ FT: 1,200
SALES (est): 401.6K **Privately Held**
SIC: 2752 Commercial printing, offset

(G-6745)
CROSSMARK PRINTING INC
Olympic Printing
410 Ashland Ave Ste 300 (60411-1679)
PHONE....................708 754-4000
Robert Carstensen, *Branch Mgr*
EMP: 6
SALES (corp-wide): 1.9MM **Privately Held**
SIC: 2759 Letterpress printing; screen printing
PA: Crossmark Printing, Inc.
18400 76th Ave Ste A
Tinley Park IL 60477
708 532-8263

(G-6746)
FH AYER MANUFACTURING CO
2015 S Halsted St (60411-4283)
P.O. Box 247 (60412-0247)
PHONE....................708 755-0550
Robert C Debolt, *President*
George Kowalsky, *Project Mgr*
Frank Smith, *Purchasing*
Ron Bakhaus, *Sales Mgr*
John Dennison, *Sales Staff*
EMP: 45
SQ FT: 30,000
SALES (est): 8.4MM **Privately Held**
WEB: www.fhayer.com
SIC: 3599 3561 8734 7629 Machine shop, jobbing & repair; pumps & pumping equipment; testing laboratories; electrical repair shops

(G-6747)
GERRESHEIMER GLASS INC
1131 Arnold St (60411-2904)
PHONE....................708 843-4246
Mike McCartney, *Plt & Fclts Mgr*
Anna Diaz, *Human Res Dir*
EMP: 200
SALES (corp-wide): 1.5B **Privately Held**
SIC: 3231 3221 Products of purchased glass; glass containers
HQ: Gerresheimer Glass Inc.
537 Crystal Ave
Vineland NJ 08360

Chicago Heights - Cook County (G-6748)

(G-6748)
GOODER-HENRICHSEN COMPANY INC
2900 State St (60411-4843)
PHONE.....................708 757-5030
Tom Ryan, *President*
Gregg Baldwin, *Vice Pres*
Paul Oconnor, *Vice Pres*
Eric Siew, *Vice Pres*
Greg Huck, *Executive*
EMP: 53 **EST:** 1927
SQ FT: 115,000
SALES (est): 629.6K **Privately Held**
WEB: www.gooderjoist.com
SIC: 3441 Joists, open web steel: long-span series

(G-6749)
HMM PALLETS INC
20500 Stoney Island Ave (60411-8661)
PHONE.....................773 927-3448
Hector M Munoz, *President*
EMP: 2
SALES (est): 302.5K **Privately Held**
SIC: 2448 Pallets, wood; pallets, wood & wood with metal

(G-6750)
INNOPHOS INC
1101 Arnold St (60411-2904)
PHONE.....................708 757-6111
Susan Turner, *Plant Mgr*
Kurt Hudspeth, *Safety Mgr*
Jeffery Stevens, *Opers Staff*
Lawrence Benson, *Engineer*
Robert Petrella, *Engineer*
EMP: 168
SALES (corp-wide): 801.8MM **Privately Held**
SIC: 2819 2874 Phosphates, except fertilizers: defluorinated & ammoniated; phosphates
HQ: Innophos, Inc.
  259 Prospect Plains Rd A
  Cranbury NJ 08512
  609 495-2495

(G-6751)
J&A PALLETS SERVICE INC
1225 Arnold St (60411-2905)
PHONE.....................708 333-6601
Antonio Munice, *President*
EMP: 10
SALES (est): 1.5MM **Privately Held**
SIC: 2448 Pallets, wood

(G-6752)
JM INDUSTRIES LLC
330 E Joe Orr Rd (60411-1290)
PHONE.....................708 758-2600
EMP: 3
SALES (est): 116.8K **Privately Held**
SIC: 3999 Manufacturing industries

(G-6753)
JN PUMP HOLDINGS INC (PA)
Also Called: Nagle Pumps
1249 Center Ave (60411-2805)
PHONE.....................708 754-2940
James Nagle, *President*
Kay Sue Nagle, *Vice Pres*
EMP: 19 **EST:** 1946
SQ FT: 30,000
SALES (est): 2.6MM **Privately Held**
WEB: www.naglepumps.com
SIC: 3561 5084 Industrial pumps & parts; industrial machinery & equipment

(G-6754)
JOHNSTON & JENNINGS INC
1200 State St Ste 1 (60411-2968)
PHONE.....................708 757-5375
Craig Yort, *President*
Julie Yort, *Admin Sec*
EMP: 7
SQ FT: 65,000
SALES (est): 1.2MM **Privately Held**
SIC: 3321 Gray iron castings

(G-6755)
KEMPCO WINDOW TREATMENTS INC
74 E 23rd St (60411-4285)
PHONE.....................708 754-4484
Thomas Kemp, *President*
Serge Sokol, *Corp Secy*
Frank Casto, *Vice Pres*
James Kemp, *Shareholder*
EMP: 30
SQ FT: 13,000
SALES (est): 4.5MM **Privately Held**
SIC: 5023 2211 5131 Draperies; draperies & drapery fabrics, cotton; drapery material, woven

(G-6756)
KEYSTONE BAR PRODUCTS INC
317 E 11th St (60411-2852)
P.O. Box 726 (60412-0726)
PHONE.....................708 753-1200
Robert J Beecham Below, *President*
Mark Brachdill, *Vice Pres*
EMP: 40
SQ FT: 50,000
SALES (corp-wide): 633.2K **Privately Held**
SIC: 3441 Fabricated structural metal
HQ: Keystone Consolidated Industries, Inc.
  5430 Lyndon B Johnson Fwy
  Dallas TX 75240
  800 441-0308

(G-6757)
KEYSTONE CONSOLIDATED INDS INC
Keystone Calumetals
317 E 11th St (60411-2852)
PHONE.....................708 753-1200
Michael Goich, *Branch Mgr*
EMP: 33
SALES (corp-wide): 633.2K **Privately Held**
SIC: 3312 Bar, rod & wire products
HQ: Keystone Consolidated Industries, Inc.
  5430 Lyndon B Johnson Fwy
  Dallas TX 75240
  800 441-0308

(G-6758)
MIDSTATES RAIL LLC
901 State St (60411-2263)
PHONE.....................708 758-7245
Eric Ruzkowski, *Principal*
EMP: 19
SALES (est): 4.9MM **Privately Held**
SIC: 3535 Conveyors & conveying equipment

(G-6759)
MINORITY AUTO HDLG SPECIALISTS (HQ)
22401 Sauk Pointe Dr (60411-4833)
PHONE.....................708 757-8758
Theodore Vance, *President*
Dave Howard, *Manager*
George Klien, *Admin Sec*
EMP: 16
SALES (est): 12.4MM
SALES (corp-wide): 46.6MM **Privately Held**
SIC: 4731 3448 Freight forwarding; prefabricated metal buildings
PA: T.V. Minority Company, Inc.
  9400 Pelham Rd
  Taylor MI 48180
  313 386-1048

(G-6760)
MOBILE 7 GROUP INC
642 Hickory St (60411-3925)
PHONE.....................312 600-8952
Leslie Labranche, *CEO*
EMP: 2
SALES: 3.5MM **Privately Held**
SIC: 7372 Publishers' computer software

(G-6761)
MORGAN LI LLC (PA)
383 E 16th St (60411-3701)
PHONE.....................708 758-5300
Debra Knoll, *Vice Pres*
Antonio Lopez, *Opers Staff*
Dalia Elizondo, *Controller*
Jeremy Delgado, *Manager*
Tery R Young, *Officer*
▲ **EMP:** 40
SQ FT: 230,000
SALES: 47.7MM **Privately Held**
SIC: 2541 Store & office display cases & fixtures

(G-6762)
NUFARM AMERICAS INC
220 E 17th St Fl 2 (60411-3602)
PHONE.....................708 756-2010
Melissa Keil, *Purch Mgr*
Laura Williams, *Human Res Mgr*
Steve Clements, *Branch Mgr*
EMP: 60
SQ FT: 75,000 **Privately Held**
SIC: 2879 Insecticides, agricultural or household
HQ: Nufarm Americas Inc.
  11901 S Austin Ave
  Alsip IL 60803
  708 377-1330

(G-6763)
OZINGA BROS INC
1750 State St (60411-3710)
PHONE.....................708 326-4200
Bill Clark, *President*
EMP: 80
SQ FT: 6,400
SALES (corp-wide): 434.5MM **Privately Held**
SIC: 3273 Ready-mixed concrete
PA: Ozinga Bros., Inc.
  19001 Old Lagrange Rd # 30
  Mokena IL 60448
  708 326-4200

(G-6764)
POLL ENTERPRISES INC
Also Called: Core Integrated Marketing
209 Glenwood Rd (60411-8217)
PHONE.....................708 756-1120
Howard L Budrow, *President*
Greg Budrow, *VP Sales*
Judith L Budrow, *Admin Sec*
EMP: 18 **EST:** 1983
SQ FT: 6,500
SALES (est): 3.7MM **Privately Held**
SIC: 7334 2752 Photocopying & duplicating services; commercial printing, offset

(G-6765)
PRINTCRAZY LLC
209 Glenwood Rd (60411-8217)
PHONE.....................630 573-1020
Howard Budrow, *President*
EMP: 4
SALES (est): 418.4K **Privately Held**
SIC: 2752 Commercial printing, lithographic

(G-6766)
PTC GROUP HOLDINGS CORP
Also Called: Dixmor Division
475 E 16th St (60411-3702)
PHONE.....................708 757-4747
Marty Strutz, *Branch Mgr*
EMP: 51 **Privately Held**
SIC: 3312 3317 3316 Well casings, iron & steel: made in steel mills; steel pipe & tubes; cold finishing of steel shapes
PA: Ptc Group Holdings Corp.
  6051 Wallace Road Ext # 2
  Wexford PA 15090

(G-6767)
RAIL EXCHANGE INC
1150 State St (60411-3700)
P.O. Box 340 (60412-0340)
PHONE.....................708 757-3317
Dean M Bartolini, *CEO*
Michael Bartolini, *President*
Cheryl Pohrte, *CFO*
Jason Farver, *Manager*
Dianne Andel, *Admin Asst*
EMP: 50
SQ FT: 36,000
SALES (est): 13.3MM **Privately Held**
SIC: 3469 3743 3462 3441 Machine parts, stamped or pressed metal; railroad locomotives & parts, electric or nonelectric; iron & steel forgings; fabricated structural metal

(G-6768)
REAL ALLOY RECYCLING LLC
400 E Lincoln Hwy (60411-2973)
P.O. Box 751 (60412-0751)
PHONE.....................708 757-8900
Larry Lipa, *Plant Mgr*
Carie Elliott, *Controller*
EMP: 60
SALES (corp-wide): 114.3MM **Privately Held**
WEB: www.realalloy.com
SIC: 3341 Secondary nonferrous metals
HQ: Real Alloy Recycling, Llc
  3700 Park East Dr Ste 300
  Beachwood OH 44122
  216 755-8900

(G-6769)
RHONE-POULENC BASIC CHEM CO
1101 Arnold St (60411-2995)
PHONE.....................708 757-6111
Paul Pruett, *Principal*
EMP: 3
SALES (est): 283.8K **Privately Held**
SIC: 2819 Industrial inorganic chemicals

(G-6770)
RMI INC
211 E Main St (60411-4270)
PHONE.....................708 756-5640
Brad Corral, *President*
Scott Long, *Vice Pres*
Richard Gollner, *CFO*
Dave Fuss, *Manager*
▲ **EMP:** 10
SALES (est): 3.3MM **Privately Held**
SIC: 3312 Structural & rail mill products

(G-6771)
ROBEY PACKAGING EQP & SVC
3236 Rennie Smith Dr (60411-5564)
PHONE.....................708 758-8250
Rich Robey, *President*
Patricia Robey, *Corp Secy*
Heather Henle, *Admin Sec*
EMP: 4
SALES (est): 440K **Privately Held**
SIC: 3565 7699 Bag opening, filling & closing machines; industrial machinery & equipment repair

(G-6772)
ROEDA SIGNS INC
Also Called: Screentech
20530 Stoney Island Ave (60411-8661)
PHONE.....................708 333-3021
Randy Roeda, *President*
Robert Roeda, *Corp Secy*
Brent Guynes, *Production*
Robert J Roeda, *Treasurer*
▲ **EMP:** 27
SALES (est): 4.6MM **Privately Held**
WEB: www.roeda.com
SIC: 3993 2759 Signs, not made in custom sign painting shops; screen printing

(G-6773)
RUTHMAN PUMP AND ENGINEERING
Also Called: Nagle Pumps
1249 Center Ave (60411-2805)
PHONE.....................708 754-2940
William Hein, *Manager*
EMP: 5
SALES (corp-wide): 36.7MM **Privately Held**
SIC: 3561 Industrial pumps & parts
PA: Ruthman Pump And Engineering, Inc
  7236 Tylers Corner Dr
  West Chester OH 45069
  513 559-1901

(G-6774)
SOLID METAL GROUP INC
1633 5th Ave (60411-3726)
PHONE.....................708 757-7421
Xochitl Valenzuela, *President*
Steven Goff, *General Mgr*
Timothy Waters, *COO*
EMP: 5
SQ FT: 3,000

GEOGRAPHIC SECTION

Chicago Ridge - Cook County (G-6801)

SALES (est): 400K **Privately Held**
WEB: www.solidmg.com
SIC: 3498 3441 3499 1799 Tube fabricating (contract bending & shaping); fabricated structural metal for ships; fabricated structural metal for bridges; fire- or burglary-resistive products; sign installation & maintenance; highway signs & guardrails

(G-6775)
SOLVAY USA INC
1020 State St (60411-2908)
PHONE 708 441-6041
Sam Agle, *Branch Mgr*
EMP: 31
SALES (corp-wide): 13.8MM **Privately Held**
WEB: www.solvay.us
SIC: 2819 Industrial inorganic chemicals
HQ: Solvay Usa Inc.
   504 Carnegie Ctr
   Princeton NJ 08540
   609 860-4000

(G-6776)
STARMONT MANUFACTURING INC
640 217th St (60411-4327)
PHONE 708 758-2525
John Montella, *President*
Carey Hendrix, *Sales Staff*
Thomas Montella, *Admin Sec*
EMP: 10
SQ FT: 5,000
SALES: 800K **Privately Held**
SIC: 3469 Metal stampings

(G-6777)
SURE PLUS MANUFACTURING CO
185 E 12th St (60411-2780)
PHONE 708 756-3100
Gordon P Henschel, *President*
Paul Henschel, *Vice Pres*
EMP: 64 **EST:** 1965
SQ FT: 200,000
SALES (est): 8.4MM **Privately Held**
WEB: www.sureplus.com
SIC: 3231 3714 Mirrors, truck & automobile: made from purchased glass; motor vehicle parts & accessories

(G-6778)
T & J MEATPACKING INC
635 Glenwood Dyer Rd (60411-8625)
P.O. Box 215, Glenwood (60425-0215)
PHONE 708 758-6748
Tony Lilovich, *President*
John Lilovich, *Vice Pres*
EMP: 55 **EST:** 1935
SQ FT: 1,100
SALES (est): 8MM **Privately Held**
WEB: www.tandjmeatpacking.com
SIC: 2011 5147 5421 0751 Meat by-products from meat slaughtered on site; meats & meat products; meat & fish markets; slaughtering: custom livestock services; sausages & other prepared meats

(G-6779)
TANKO SCRW PRD CORP
19830 Stoney Island Ave (60411-8671)
PHONE 708 418-0300
William Landholt, *Principal*
EMP: 3
SALES (est): 263.9K **Privately Held**
SIC: 3451 Screw machine products

(G-6780)
TGM FABRICATING INC
57 E 24th St (60411-4177)
PHONE 708 533-0857
Rosaoia Turner, *President*
EMP: 2 **EST:** 2010
SALES (est): 345.9K **Privately Held**
SIC: 3441 Fabricated structural metal

(G-6781)
TRIALCO INC (PA)
900 E Lincoln Hwy Ste 1 (60411-2992)
PHONE 708 757-4200
Jay Armstrong, *President*
Jun Dee, *Treasurer*
Russell Renaud, *Asst Controller*
Rick Milnes, *Sales Staff*
Mike Bailey, *Manager*
EMP: 50
SQ FT: 175,000
SALES (est): 10.2MM **Privately Held**
SIC: 3341 Aluminum smelting & refining (secondary)

(G-6782)
TURNCO INC
Also Called: Turnco Products
2200 S Halsted St (60411-4284)
PHONE 708 756-6565
Jerry Hindel Jr, *President*
EMP: 5 **EST:** 1961
SQ FT: 7,200
SALES (est): 884.4K **Privately Held**
SIC: 3451 Screw machine products

(G-6783)
VACUDYNE INCORPORATED (DH)
375 E Joe Orr Rd (60411-1292)
PHONE 708 757-5200
Gary Tracy, *President*
Jon Lane, *General Mgr*
George Collins, *Vice Pres*
Phillip Casarez, *Mfg Mgr*
Mike Strawn, *Purchasing*
EMP: 40 **EST:** 1957
SQ FT: 34,000
SALES (est): 7.9MM
SALES (corp-wide): 52.4MM **Privately Held**
WEB: www.vacudyne.com
SIC: 3559 Tobacco products machinery
HQ: Altair Corporation
   350 Barclay Blvd
   Lincolnshire IL 60069
   847 634-9540

(G-6784)
VESUVIUS U S A CORPORATION
333 State St (60411-1203)
PHONE 708 757-7880
Shawn Buckley, *Engineer*
Jack Lee, *Engineer*
Troy Devault, *Manager*
Adam Eggleston, *Manager*
Eric Jaworsky, *Manager*
EMP: 75
SALES (corp-wide): 2.3B **Privately Held**
SIC: 3297 Graphite refractories: carbon bond or ceramic bond
HQ: Vesuvius U S A Corporation
   1404 Newton Dr
   Champaign IL 61822
   217 351-5000

(G-6785)
VITELLI CONCRETE PRODUCTS INC
2410 S Halsted St (60411-4131)
PHONE 708 754-5846
Jason Hering, *President*
EMP: 4 **EST:** 1900
SQ FT: 3,000
SALES (est): 585.8K **Privately Held**
SIC: 3272 Concrete products, precast

(G-6786)
VOESTALPINE NORTRAK INC
2705 State St (60411-4841)
PHONE 708 753-2125
Robert Fixter, *Plant Engr*
Dave Kallgren, *Branch Mgr*
EMP: 100
SALES (corp-wide): 15.3B **Privately Held**
SIC: 5088 3312 3743 Transportation equipment & supplies; blast furnaces & steel mills; railroad equipment
HQ: Voestalpine Railway Systems Nortrak Inc.
   1740 Pacific Ave
   Cheyenne WY 82007
   307 778-8700

(G-6787)
ZOETIS LLC
Also Called: Animal Health Div
400 State St (60411-1242)
PHONE 708 757-2592
Bryan Hunt, *Opers-Prdtn-Mfg*
EMP: 70
SALES (corp-wide): 6.2B **Publicly Held**
SIC: 2833 2834 2048 4225 Antibiotics; pharmaceutical preparations; prepared feeds; general warehousing
HQ: Zoetis Llc
   10 Sylvan Way Ste 105
   Parsippany NJ 07054
   973 822-7000

Chicago Ridge
Cook County

(G-6788)
AVIATION SERVICES GROUP INC
Also Called: Aviation Services Group of IL
10524 Major Ave (60415-2033)
PHONE 708 425-4700
EMP: 4
SALES (corp-wide): 1.4MM **Privately Held**
SIC: 3721 Mfg Aircraft
PA: Aviation Services Group Inc
   4243 E Lake Blvd
   Birmingham AL 35217
   205 849-3848

(G-6789)
CELTIC ENVIRONMENTAL
6640 99th Pl (60415-1211)
PHONE 708 442-5823
Joseph Smrz, *Owner*
EMP: 6
SALES (est): 918K **Privately Held**
SIC: 3292 Asbestos products

(G-6790)
CHICAGO FLORAL PLANTERS INC
10139 S Harlem Ave (60415-1366)
PHONE 708 423-2754
James Wrobel, *President*
Janet Wrobel, *Admin Sec*
EMP: 3
SALES (est): 230K **Privately Held**
SIC: 2449 Containers, plywood & veneer wood

(G-6791)
CLOPAY BUILDING PDTS CO INC
10047 Virginia Ave Ste A (60415-3716)
PHONE 708 346-0901
John Elgin, *Manager*
EMP: 5
SALES (corp-wide): 2.2B **Publicly Held**
SIC: 2431 Garage doors, overhead: wood
HQ: Clopay Building Products Company, Inc.
   8585 Duke Blvd
   Mason OH 45040

(G-6792)
CMD CONVEYOR INC
10008 Anderson Ave (60415-1257)
PHONE 708 237-0996
Casey Czochara, *President*
EMP: 34
SQ FT: 13,000
SALES (est): 9.2MM **Privately Held**
SIC: 3535 Conveyors & conveying equipment

(G-6793)
CROWLEY-SHEPPARD ASPHALT INC
6525 99th Pl (60415-1233)
P.O. Box 157 (60415-0157)
PHONE 708 499-2900
Richard A Sheppard, *President*
Michael J Sheppard, *Vice Pres*
EMP: 10 **EST:** 1943
SQ FT: 3,000
SALES (est): 10MM **Privately Held**
WEB: www.csasphaltinc.com
SIC: 2951 1771 Asphalt & asphaltic paving mixtures (not from refineries); blacktop (asphalt) work

(G-6794)
ENTERPRISE AC & HTG CO
6112 111th St (60415-2105)
PHONE 708 430-2212
John Coleman, *Manager*
EMP: 6
SALES (corp-wide): 883.1K **Privately Held**
SIC: 3444 1711 Sheet metalwork; plumbing, heating, air-conditioning contractors
PA: Enterprise Air Conditioning & Heating Co
   6100 W 82nd Pl
   Oak Lawn IL 60459
   708 430-2212

(G-6795)
G & M EMBROIDERY
Also Called: Stitch N Print
260 Chicago Ridge Mall (60415-2636)
PHONE 708 636-7005
Gokhan Yegen, *CEO*
EMP: 6
SALES (est): 87.4K **Privately Held**
SIC: 2395 Embroidery products, except schiffli machine

(G-6796)
GREAT LAKES STAIR & STEEL INC
10130 Virginia Ave (60415-1378)
PHONE 708 430-2323
Don Ziblis, *President*
Tony Ziblis, *Prdtn Mgr*
Samantha Ziblis, *Web Dvlpr*
EMP: 9
SQ FT: 3,000
SALES (est): 3.1MM **Privately Held**
SIC: 3441 Fabricated structural metal

(G-6797)
HARRIS PRECISION TOOLS INC
10081 Anderson Ave (60415-1200)
PHONE 708 422-5808
Robert Harris, *President*
Donna Harris, *Admin Sec*
EMP: 6
SQ FT: 6,000
SALES (est): 300K **Privately Held**
SIC: 3541 3625 3546 3545 Cutoff machines (metalworking machinery); relays & industrial controls; power-driven handtools; machine tool accessories; cutlery

(G-6798)
HOHMANN & BARNARD ILLINOIS LLC
9999 Virginia Ave (60415-1368)
P.O. Box 5270, Hauppauge NY (11788-0270)
PHONE 773 586-6700
Ronald Hohmann,
Christopher Hohmann,
Robert Hohmann,
EMP: 34
SQ FT: 34,000
SALES (est): 5.7MM **Privately Held**
WEB: www.h-b.com
SIC: 3496 3315 Concrete reinforcing mesh & wire; steel wire & related products

(G-6799)
HOHMANN & BARNARD INC
9999 Virginia Ave (60415-1368)
PHONE 773 586-6700
Ronald P Hohmann Jr, *President*
Janet C Crusing, *Manager*
Joseph Carr Jr, *Admin Sec*
EMP: 5
SALES (est): 450.5K **Privately Held**
SIC: 3496 Miscellaneous fabricated wire products

(G-6800)
JMJOCS LLC
6119 103rd St (60415-1642)
PHONE 708 769-7981
Odeh Alfarah,
EMP: 3
SALES (est): 94.1K **Privately Held**
SIC: 3295 Silicon, ultra high purity: treated

(G-6801)
LHO ENTERPRISES INC (PA)
Also Called: Tivor Machine Products
6350 Birmingham St (60415-1504)
PHONE 708 499-0017
Mark Lindemulder, *President*
David Greco, *Engineer*
EMP: 1
SQ FT: 36,000

Chicago Ridge - Cook County (G-6802)

SALES (est): 294.7K **Privately Held**
SIC: 3599 Machine shop, jobbing & repair

(G-6802)
MATIS INC
10235 Southwest Hwy (60415-1350)
P.O. Box 1437, Bridgeview (60455-0437)
PHONE 708 425-7100
Dorothy Matis, *Ch of Bd*
Daniel J Matis, *President*
Sandra Matis, *Admin Sec*
EMP: 10 EST: 1955
SQ FT: 10,000
SALES: 3.2MM **Privately Held**
WEB: www.matis.com
SIC: 3599 Machine shop, jobbing & repair

(G-6803)
MIDWEST MIXING INC
5630 Pleasant Blvd (60415-2306)
PHONE 708 422-8100
Robert R Smith, *President*
Gary Grenier, *Corp Secy*
Louis Fandrey, *Manager*
EMP: 6
SQ FT: 7,000
SALES (est): 800K **Privately Held**
WEB: www.midwestmixing.com
SIC: 3559 3531 Refinery, chemical processing & similar machinery; chemical machinery & equipment; construction machinery

(G-6804)
MOORE MEMORIALS
5960 111th St (60415-2275)
PHONE 708 636-6532
Maurice Moore Jr, *President*
Patricia Moore, *Vice Pres*
Maurice Moore Sr, *Admin Sec*
EMP: 11
SQ FT: 4,200
SALES (est): 1.4MM **Privately Held**
WEB: www.mauricemoorememorials.com
SIC: 5999 5039 3281 Gravestones, finished; glass construction materials; cut stone & stone products

(G-6805)
MWM EXPRESS INC
6730 107th St Apt 1d (60415-3702)
PHONE 630 401-0528
Mohamed Mejri, *President*
EMP: 4 EST: 2016
SALES (est): 435.7K **Privately Held**
SIC: 3829 Measuring & controlling devices

(G-6806)
PETRO ENTERPRISES INC
10242 Ridgeland Ave (60415-1328)
PHONE 708 425-1551
Ken Petropolus, *President*
EMP: 5
SALES (est): 582.5K **Privately Held**
SIC: 2519 5021 5712 Household furniture, except wood or metal: upholstered; furniture; furniture stores

(G-6807)
PLUG ELECTRIC LLC
10538 Ridgeland Ave Apt 3 (60415-1853)
PHONE 630 788-1018
Stephanie Alvarez, *Principal*
EMP: 3 EST: 2018
SALES (est): 220.5K **Privately Held**
SIC: 3643 Plugs, electric

(G-6808)
PRECISION PRISMATIC INC
10247 Ridgeland Ave Ste 1 (60415-2807)
PHONE 708 424-0905
Joseph Pristo, *President*
EMP: 6
SQ FT: 5,000
SALES: 500K **Privately Held**
SIC: 3599 Machine shop, jobbing & repair

(G-6809)
PRODUCT FEEDING SOLUTIONS INC
5632 Pleasant Blvd (60415-2306)
PHONE 630 709-9546
Noel Parlour, *CEO*
Barbara Parlour, *President*
EMP: 5
SQ FT: 2,000

SALES (est): 698.3K **Privately Held**
SIC: 3829 Measuring & controlling devices

(G-6810)
SELCO INDUSTRIES
6655 Kitty Ave (60415-1286)
PHONE 708 499-1060
Joseph Heneghan, *President*
Robert Scellato, *Opers Mgr*
EMP: 8
SQ FT: 18,000
SALES (est): 1.6MM **Privately Held**
SIC: 3446 5039 Railings, bannisters, guards, etc.: made from metal pipe; stairs, staircases, stair treads: prefabricated metal; joists; structural assemblies, prefabricated: non-wood

(G-6811)
WW TIMBERS INC (PA)
10150 Virginia Ave Ste K (60415-3715)
PHONE 708 423-9112
Philip Weibel, *President*
Leonard Schultz III, *Admin Sec*
EMP: 1
SQ FT: 20,000
SALES (est): 1.9MM **Privately Held**
SIC: 2439 Timbers, structural: laminated lumber

Chillicothe
Peoria County

(G-6812)
A C GENTROL INC
100 S 4th St (61523-2245)
P.O. Box 452 (61523-0452)
PHONE 309 274-5486
Angelito M Capati, *President*
EMP: 35
SQ FT: 14,000
SALES (est): 7MM **Privately Held**
SIC: 3613 Generator control & metering panels; control panels, electric

(G-6813)
ALLIED WELDING INC
1820 N Santa Fe Ave (61523-1042)
P.O. Box 410 (61523-0410)
PHONE 309 274-6227
Terry Nelson, *President*
David Roahrig, *Purch Agent*
Matt Nelson, *Sales Executive*
Samantha Rudd, *Manager*
Michael Roberts, *Info Tech Dir*
EMP: 50 EST: 1962
SQ FT: 35,700
SALES (est): 11.1MM **Privately Held**
WEB: www.alliedwelding.net
SIC: 7692 Welding repair

(G-6814)
BLUE RIDGE FORGE INC
316 W Cedar St (61523-1642)
P.O. Box 43 (61523-0043)
PHONE 309 274-5377
John Morris, *Vice Pres*
EMP: 6
SALES (est): 1.1MM **Privately Held**
SIC: 3315 Welded steel wire fabric

(G-6815)
C J HOLDINGS INC
Also Called: J & J Manufacturing
110 W Walnut St (61523-1833)
PHONE 309 274-3141
Caryn Knop, *President*
Carl A Gross, *Shareholder*
Jackie Gross, *Admin Sec*
EMP: 6 EST: 2004
SQ FT: 15,000
SALES: 500K **Privately Held**
SIC: 3469 7692 3444 3443 Machine parts, stamped or pressed metal; welding repair; sheet metalwork; fabricated plate work (boiler shop)

(G-6816)
EAGLE COMPANIES INC
4214 E Rome Rd (61523-9384)
PHONE 309 686-9054
Timothy J Tobin, *President*
EMP: 10

SQ FT: 24,000
SALES (est): 1.7MM **Privately Held**
SIC: 3448 Prefabricated metal buildings

(G-6817)
GALENA ROAD GRAVEL INC
5129 E Truitt Rd (61523-9340)
P.O. Box 50 (61523-0050)
PHONE 309 274-6388
Rich Lucas, *President*
Peter Powell, *Vice Pres*
Judy Samayao, *Treasurer*
EMP: 35
SQ FT: 500
SALES (est): 8.8MM
SALES (corp-wide): 5MM **Privately Held**
SIC: 1442 Construction sand & gravel
HQ: B.S.C. Holding, Inc.
10955 Lowell Ave Ste 500
Overland Park KS 66210
913 262-7263

(G-6818)
IMAGINATION PRODUCTS CORP
Also Called: Flexisnake
227 W Cedar St (61523-1638)
PHONE 309 274-6223
Scott Turner, *President*
Stephen Turner, *Vice Pres*
▼ EMP: 25
SQ FT: 17,000
SALES (est): 100K **Privately Held**
SIC: 2842 3999 5087 Drain pipe solvents or cleaners; pipe cleaners; cleaning & maintenance equipment & supplies

(G-6819)
J T FENNELL CO INC (PA)
1104 N Front St (61523-1650)
P.O. Box 337 (61523-0337)
PHONE 309 274-2145
James T Fennell, *President*
Jerry P Fennell, *Vice Pres*
Danny Colwell, *Prdtn Mgr*
Scott Meints, *IT/INT Sup*
John Merdian, *Admin Sec*
EMP: 95 EST: 1946
SQ FT: 90,000
SALES (est): 18.6MM **Privately Held**
WEB: www.jtfennell.com
SIC: 3599 Machine shop, jobbing & repair

(G-6820)
NOVEL ELECTRONIC DESIGNS INC
143 N 3rd St (61523-2156)
PHONE 309 224-9945
Durwin D Nigus, *President*
Pamela Nigus, *President*
EMP: 4
SALES (est): 385K **Privately Held**
SIC: 3679 Electronic circuits

(G-6821)
POWER ENCLOSURES INC (PA)
100 S 4th St (61523-2245)
P.O. Box 452 (61523-0452)
PHONE 309 274-9000
Angelito Capati, *President*
Teresita Capati, *Treasurer*
EMP: 13
SQ FT: 14,000
SALES (est): 1.8MM **Privately Held**
SIC: 3621 Motor housings

(G-6822)
TER-SON CORPORATION
Also Called: Allied Welding
1801 N Logan St (61523-1102)
P.O. Box 410 (61523-0410)
PHONE 309 274-6227
Terry Nelson, *President*
Susan Nelson, *Vice Pres*
EMP: 75
SALES (est): 5.6MM **Privately Held**
SIC: 3599 Machine shop, jobbing & repair

(G-6823)
WESTERN YEAST COMPANY INC
305 W Ash St (61523-1603)
P.O. Box 257 (61523-0257)
PHONE 309 274-3160
Keith Turner, *President*
La Von Turner, *Corp Secy*
Michael Turner Dvm, *Vice Pres*

EMP: 20 EST: 1932
SQ FT: 20,000
SALES (est): 2.3MM **Privately Held**
WEB: www.westernyeast.com
SIC: 2048 Livestock feeds

Christopher
Franklin County

(G-6824)
DIVA DREAM SIGNS
807 E Main St (62822-1915)
PHONE 618 201-4348
Mindy Vansosan, *Owner*
EMP: 3
SALES (est): 203.9K **Privately Held**
SIC: 3993 Signs & advertising specialties

(G-6825)
HOP BREWERY LLC
203 W Market St (62822-1223)
PHONE 866 724-4677
Adam Porter,
Jennifer Porter,
EMP: 6
SALES (est): 542.9K **Privately Held**
SIC: 2082 Beer (alcoholic beverage)

(G-6826)
SIMION FABRICATION INC
901 W Egyptian Ave (62822)
P.O. Box 33 (62822-0033)
PHONE 618 724-7331
Darrell Simion, *President*
Rosalee Simion, *Corp Secy*
EMP: 8
SQ FT: 8,400
SALES (est): 1.5MM **Privately Held**
SIC: 3441 Fabricated structural metal

Cicero
Cook County

(G-6827)
ACTIVE GRAPHICS INC
5500 W 31st St (60804-3957)
PHONE 708 656-8900
George Hayes, *President*
Tim Koenig, *Exec VP*
Rich Milne, *Vice Pres*
Mike Egan, *Production*
James Radermacher, *CFO*
EMP: 45
SQ FT: 23,000
SALES (est): 12.1MM **Privately Held**
SIC: 2752 7336 2759 Commercial printing, offset; commercial art & graphic design; commercial printing

(G-6828)
ALANG PATTERN INC
3635 S 61st Ave (60804-4147)
PHONE 773 722-9481
EMP: 4
SALES (est): 355.1K **Privately Held**
SIC: 3543 Industrial patterns

(G-6829)
AMERICAN/JEBCO CORPORATION
Also Called: Jebco" Screw" and Speciality
3250 S Central Ave (60804-3939)
PHONE 847 455-3150
Matthew O'Connor, *President*
▲ EMP: 130 EST: 1956
SQ FT: 40,000
SALES (est): 24.9MM **Privately Held**
WEB: www.americanjebco.com
SIC: 3451 3452 3356 Screw machine products; screws, metal; bolts, metal; rivets, metal; nonferrous rolling & drawing

(G-6830)
ASPHALT MTLS DBA HRITG ASP LLC
4950 W 41st St (60804-4506)
PHONE 773 735-2233
David Blackburn, *Principal*
EMP: 3 EST: 2010

GEOGRAPHIC SECTION

Cicero - Cook County (G-6857)

SALES (est): 545.6K **Privately Held**
WEB: www.asphalt-materials.com
SIC: 2951 Asphalt paving mixtures & blocks

(G-6831)
BROADWIND ENERGY INC (PA)
3240 S Central Ave (60804-3939)
PHONE..................708 780-4800
David P Reiland, *Ch of Bd*
Eric B Blashford, *President*
Gilbert M Mayo Jr, *President*
Daniel E Schueller, *President*
Erik W Jensen, *Vice Pres*
EMP: 37
SQ FT: 301,000
SALES: 178.2MM **Publicly Held**
SIC: 3511 Turbines & turbine generator sets & parts

(G-6832)
CHARLES HORN LUMBER COMPANY
4700 W 19th St (60804-2503)
PHONE..................773 847-7397
Bruce Scott Horn, *President*
Norman B Horn, *Corp Secy*
Steven Horn, *Vice Pres*
EMP: 15
SQ FT: 38,000
SALES (est): 2.8MM **Privately Held**
WEB: www.hornlumber.com
SIC: 2421 Sawmills & planing mills, general

(G-6833)
CHURCHILL CABINET COMPANY
4616 W 19th St (60804-2502)
PHONE..................708 780-0070
Roger E Duba, *President*
Douglas Duba, *Vice Pres*
Marion Loboz, *Admin Sec*
▲ EMP: 50
SQ FT: 94,000
SALES (est): 9.1MM **Privately Held**
SIC: 2541 2511 Cabinets, except refrigerated: show, display, etc.: wood; unassembled or unfinished furniture, household: wood

(G-6834)
CICERO IRON METAL & PAPER INC
5901 W Ogden Ave Ste 7 (60804-3811)
PHONE..................708 863-8601
Bob Hernandez, *President*
EMP: 6
SQ FT: 10,000
SALES (est): 806.2K **Privately Held**
SIC: 5093 3341 2611 Ferrous metal scrap & waste; secondary nonferrous metals; pulp mills

(G-6835)
CIRCLE GEAR & MACHINE CO INC
1501 S 55th Ct (60804-1842)
PHONE..................708 652-1000
Albert J Knez, *CEO*
Edward Kaske, *President*
Michael McKernin, *President*
Scott Reid, *Vice Pres*
Charlotte Schmidt, *Vice Pres*
▲ EMP: 49
SQ FT: 125,000
SALES (est): 13.3MM **Privately Held**
SIC: 3599 Machine shop, jobbing & repair

(G-6836)
CLEAN HRBORS ES INDUS SVCS INC
6001 W Pershing Rd (60804-4112)
PHONE..................708 652-0575
Steve Waters, *Branch Mgr*
EMP: 16
SALES (corp-wide): 3.4B **Publicly Held**
SIC: 2873 Nitrogenous fertilizers
HQ: Clean Harbors Es Industrial Services, Inc.
4760 World Houston Pkwy # 100
Houston TX 77032
713 672-8004

(G-6837)
COREY STEEL COMPANY
2800 S 61st Ct (60804-3091)
P.O. Box 5137, Chicago (60680-5137)
PHONE..................708 735-8000
Michael Laughlin, *General Mgr*
Michael A Solamon, *COO*
Robert Drab, *QC Mgr*
Bill Popper, *Plant Engr Mgr*
Anthony Verkruyse, *CFO*
▲ EMP: 175 EST: 1924
SQ FT: 600,000
SALES (est): 127MM
SALES (corp-wide): 506MM **Privately Held**
WEB: www.coreysteel.com
SIC: 3316 5051 Bars, steel, cold finished, from purchased hot-rolled; aluminum bars, rods, ingots, sheets, pipes, plates, etc.
PA: Specialty Steel Works Incorporated
1412 150th St
Hammond IN 46327
877 289-2277

(G-6838)
CYRUS SHANK COMPANY (HQ)
Also Called: Shank Precision Machine Co
4645 W Roosevelt Rd (60804-1522)
PHONE..................708 652-2700
Frank Kruppe Jr, *President*
Robert T Kruppe Jr, *Vice Pres*
EMP: 29
SQ FT: 14,000
SALES (est): 3.4MM
SALES (corp-wide): 4.2MM **Privately Held**
SIC: 3491 Industrial valves
PA: Shank Manufacturing
575 Exchange Ct
Aurora IL
331 212-5488

(G-6839)
DEFENDER STEEL DOOR & WINDOW (PA)
6119 W 35th St (60804-4108)
PHONE..................708 780-7320
Robert Bianco, *President*
Robert Smith, *Corp Secy*
EMP: 27
SQ FT: 500
SALES (est): 4.1MM **Privately Held**
WEB: www.defenderdoor.com
SIC: 5211 3442 Doors, storm: wood or metal; metal doors, sash & trim

(G-6840)
DI-CARR PRINTING COMPANY
1630 S Cicero Ave (60804-1519)
PHONE..................708 863-0069
Larry Jaskunas, *Owner*
Cindy Jaskunas, *Owner*
EMP: 3 EST: 1946
SQ FT: 1,500
SALES (est): 250K **Privately Held**
SIC: 2752 Commercial printing, offset

(G-6841)
DIECRAFTERS INC
1349 S 55th Ct (60804-1211)
PHONE..................708 656-3336
Robert J Windler, *President*
David Windler, *Vice Pres*
Norman Engelberg, *Sales Dir*
Erik Windler, *Accounts Exec*
Gloria Windler, *Admin Sec*
EMP: 30 EST: 1946
SALES (est): 7.5MM **Privately Held**
WEB: www.diecrafters.com
SIC: 2675 Paperboard die-cutting; cards: die-cut & unprinted: made from purchased materials

(G-6842)
DORBIN METAL STRIP MFG CO
2404 S Cicero Ave (60804-3442)
PHONE..................708 656-2333
Chris Duda, *President*
Carol Dorosz, *Treasurer*
EMP: 12 EST: 1938
SQ FT: 12,000
SALES: 1MM **Privately Held**
WEB: www.dorbinws.com
SIC: 3442 Weather strip, metal

(G-6843)
DUNDICK CORPORATION
4616 W 20th St (60804-2593)
PHONE..................708 656-6363
Len Pernecky, *President*
Mike Bran, *Vice Pres*
EMP: 40 EST: 1944
SQ FT: 20,000
SALES (est): 6.1MM **Privately Held**
WEB: www.dundick.com
SIC: 3545 3599 Gauges (machine tool accessories); machine shop, jobbing & repair

(G-6844)
ELECTRONIC PLATING CO
1821 S 54th Ave (60804-1815)
P.O. Box 50469 (60804-0469)
PHONE..................708 652-8100
Robert Porcelli, *President*
Carl Porcelli, *Vice Pres*
EMP: 30
SQ FT: 8,000
SALES (est): 4.5MM **Privately Held**
WEB: www.electronicplating.net
SIC: 3471 Electroplating of metals or formed products; finishing, metals or formed products

(G-6845)
ELEGANT ACQUISITION LLC
Also Called: Elegant Packaging
5253 W Roosevelt Rd (60804-1222)
PHONE..................708 652-3400
Robert Waltz, *COO*
Bob Walz, *COO*
Sheldon Gottlieb, *Vice Pres*
Frank Ambrose, *VP Opers*
Anicia Fye, *Project Mgr*
▲ EMP: 80
SQ FT: 96,000
SALES (est): 23.6MM **Privately Held**
SIC: 2652 3172 Setup paperboard boxes; sewing cases

(G-6846)
EMCO METALS LLC
1505 S Laramie Ave (60804-1939)
PHONE..................312 925-1553
Brent Campbell, *Mng Member*
EMP: 15
SALES (est): 3.5MM **Privately Held**
SIC: 3441 Fabricated structural metal

(G-6847)
EXPO ENGINEERED INC
1824 S Cicero Ave (60804-2543)
PHONE..................708 780-7155
Ruben Rivera, *President*
EMP: 1
SQ FT: 5,000
SALES (est): 203K **Privately Held**
WEB: www.expoengineered.com
SIC: 3634 Immersion heaters, electric: household; wall heaters, electric: household

(G-6848)
GENERAL ELECTRIC COMPANY
1543 S 54th Ave (60804-1813)
PHONE..................708 780-2600
Laura Whieeis, *Manager*
EMP: 11
SALES (corp-wide): 95.2B **Publicly Held**
WEB: www.ge.com
SIC: 3634 Heating units, for electric appliances
PA: General Electric Company
5 Necco St
Boston MA 02210
617 443-3000

(G-6849)
GIANNI INCORPORATED
4615 W Roosevelt Rd (60804-1522)
PHONE..................708 863-6696
Marcello Gianni, *President*
Gianni Angelo, *Treasurer*
EMP: 58
SQ FT: 56,000
SALES (est): 9.3MM **Privately Held**
SIC: 2521 Desks, office: wood

(G-6850)
H & H MOTOR SERVICE INC
5130 W 16th St (60804-1927)
PHONE..................708 652-6100
Thomas W Green, *President*
Larry Fulgenzi, *Admin Sec*
EMP: 7
SQ FT: 10,000
SALES (est): 1.6MM **Privately Held**
SIC: 7694 Electric motor repair

(G-6851)
HARRIS STEEL COMPANY (PA)
1223 S 55th Ct (60804-1297)
PHONE..................708 656-5500
Thomas Eliasek, *President*
Jack Harris Jr, *Chairman*
Scott Decker, *Plant Mgr*
Frankie Malone, *Prdtn Mgr*
Donald Eliasek, *Purchasing*
EMP: 69 EST: 1950
SQ FT: 150,000
SALES (est): 29MM **Privately Held**
WEB: www.harrissteelco.com
SIC: 5051 3316 Steel; cold finishing of steel shapes

(G-6852)
HAWTHORNE PRESS
5615 W Roosevelt Rd (60804-1229)
PHONE..................708 652-9000
Anthony Sarno, *President*
EMP: 2
SQ FT: 1,800
SALES (est): 234.6K **Privately Held**
SIC: 2759 2789 2752 Commercial printing; bookbinding & related work; commercial printing, lithographic

(G-6853)
ICC INTRNTONAL CELSIUS CONCEPT
2385 S 59th Ct (60804)
PHONE..................773 993-4405
Luis Saquimux, *Vice Pres*
EMP: 7
SALES (est): 331.4K **Privately Held**
SIC: 3569 3585 3571 Robots, assembly line: industrial & commercial; refrigeration & heating equipment; electronic computers

(G-6854)
ILF TECHNOLOGIES LLC
1215 S Laramie Ave (60804-1354)
PHONE..................630 759-1776
Robert Allison,
Milan Pecharich,
EMP: 16
SALES (est): 3.1MM **Privately Held**
SIC: 3555 Printing trades machinery

(G-6855)
INDUSTRIAL FILTER PUMP MFG CO
5900 W Ogden Ave (60804-3873)
PHONE..................708 656-7800
Paul Eggerstedt, *Principal*
EMP: 2 EST: 2009
SALES (est): 294.8K **Privately Held**
WEB: www.industrialfilter.com
SIC: 3569 Filters, general line: industrial; filters

(G-6856)
INTEGRATED DISPLAY SYSTEMS INC (PA)
Also Called: IDS Lift-Net
5130 W 16th St (60804-1927)
PHONE..................708 298-9661
Winslow D Soule, *President*
Frank Holmes, *Engineer*
Ricky Williams, *VP Bus Dvlpt*
EMP: 12
SQ FT: 4,000
SALES (est): 2.8MM **Privately Held**
SIC: 3534 Elevators & equipment

(G-6857)
ITRON CORPORATION DEL (PA)
3131 S Austin Blvd (60804-3730)
PHONE..................708 222-5320
Charles J Saporito Jr, *President*
John Saporito III, *President*
James Mirabile, *Vice Pres*

(PA)=Parent Co (HQ)=Headquarters (DH)=Div Headquarters
✪ = New Business established in last 2 years

2020 Harris Illinois Industrial Directory

Cicero - Cook County (G-6858)

EMP: 13 EST: 1982
SQ FT: 17,000
SALES (est): 2.2MM Privately Held
SIC: 3643 Connectors & terminals for electrical devices

(G-6858)
KAMAN TOOL CORPORATION
3147 S Austin Blvd (60804-3730)
PHONE.................................708 652-9023
Ronald W Roderweiss, President
EMP: 5 EST: 1974
SQ FT: 8,000
SALES (est): 900K Privately Held
SIC: 3599 3469 Machine shop, jobbing & repair; stamping metal for the trade

(G-6859)
KOPPERS INDUSTRIES INC
Koppers Carbon Mtls & Chem Div
3900 S Laramie Ave (60804-4523)
PHONE.................................708 656-5900
Joe Lynch, Superintendent
Greg Bambule, Safety Mgr
George Trent, Branch Mgr
Stephen Tucker, Supervisor
EMP: 45 Publicly Held
SIC: 2865 2911 2869 Cyclic crudes, coal tar; petroleum refining; industrial organic chemicals
HQ: Koppers Industries Of Delaware Inc.
436 7th Ave Ste 2026
Pittsburgh PA 15219

(G-6860)
KORINEK & CO INC
4828 W 25th St (60804-3489)
PHONE.................................708 652-2870
George F Korinek, President
Scott Korineck, Vice Pres
EMP: 7
SQ FT: 6,000
SALES (est): 1MM Privately Held
WEB: www.frankkorinek.com
SIC: 5149 2033 2051 Bakery products; preserves, including imitation: in cans, jars, etc.; jams, including imitation: packaged in cans, jars, etc.; jellies, edible, including imitation: in cans, jars, etc.; bread, cake & related products

(G-6861)
KRALY TIRE REPAIR MATERIALS
5936 W 35th St (60804-4167)
PHONE.................................708 863-5981
Kenneth Kraly, Owner
EMP: 3
SQ FT: 2,100
SALES (est): 250K Privately Held
SIC: 3011 Tire sundries or tire repair materials, rubber

(G-6862)
LAWNDALE PRESS INC (PA)
Also Called: Lawndale News
5533 W 25th St (60804-3319)
P.O. Box 50599 (60804-0593)
PHONE.................................708 656-6900
Linda Nardini, CEO
Robert Nardini, President
Ashmar Mandou, Editor
James Nardini, Senior VP
EMP: 16
SQ FT: 6,000
SALES (est): 958.8K Privately Held
SIC: 2711 Newspapers: publishing only, not printed on site

(G-6863)
LBP MANUFACTURING LLC (PA)
1325 S Cicero Ave (60804-1404)
PHONE.................................800 545-6200
Matthew Cook, CEO
Mary Medina, General Mgr
Lauren Mikos, General Mgr
Earl Jewett, COO
Ken Eme, Vice Pres
▲ EMP: 375
SQ FT: 200,000
SALES (est): 110.7MM Privately Held
WEB: www.lbpmfg.com
SIC: 2657 Folding paperboard boxes

(G-6864)
MAH MACHINE COMPANY
3301 S Central Ave (60804-3986)
PHONE.................................708 656-1826
Martin Hozjan, CEO
Robert Hozjan, President
Anna Hozjan, Principal
Christopher Hozjan, Vice Pres
Martina Hozjan Ruda, Vice Pres
▲ EMP: 105
SQ FT: 100,000
SALES (est): 33.7MM Privately Held
SIC: 3599 7699 Machine shop, jobbing & repair; printing trades machinery & equipment repair

(G-6865)
MARES SERVICE INC
4611 W 34th St (60804-4590)
P.O. Box 50028 (60804-0028)
PHONE.................................708 656-1660
Frank Mares Sr, President
Marylou Mares, Vice Pres
EMP: 8 EST: 1956
SALES (est): 1.1MM Privately Held
SIC: 3711 Wreckers (tow truck), assembly of

(G-6866)
METAL-RITE INC
3140 S 61st Ave (60804-3793)
PHONE.................................708 656-3832
Mark W Kuchan, President
Kurt Kuchan, Treasurer
Nancy Kuchan, Admin Sec
EMP: 15
SQ FT: 11,600
SALES (est): 3.2MM Privately Held
WEB: www.metalriteinc.com
SIC: 3444 Sheet metal specialties, not stamped

(G-6867)
MILANS MACHINING & MFG CO INC
1301 S Laramie Ave (60804-1355)
PHONE.................................708 780-6600
Milan Pecharich, President
Martha Pecharich, Corp Secy
Marrko Pecharich, Vice Pres
EMP: 55 EST: 1969
SQ FT: 65,000
SALES (est): 11.1MM Privately Held
SIC: 3599 7692 3555 3544 Machine shop, jobbing & repair; welding repair; printing trades machinery; special dies, tools, jigs & fixtures; metal stampings

(G-6868)
OLYMPIC PETROLEUM CORPORATION (HQ)
5000 W 41st St (60804-4524)
PHONE.................................708 876-7900
Yasar Samarah, President
Amit Shukla, CFO
Dean Mettler, Manager
◆ EMP: 75
SQ FT: 120,000
SALES (est): 52.7MM
SALES (corp-wide): 4.6B Publicly Held
SIC: 2992 Lubricating oils
PA: Greif, Inc.
425 Winter Rd
Delaware OH 43015
740 549-6000

(G-6869)
ON TIME DECORATIONS INC
1411 S Laramie Ave (60804-1328)
PHONE.................................708 357-6072
Victor Loggins, Owner
EMP: 14
SALES (est): 500K Privately Held
WEB: www.ontimedecorationsinc.com
SIC: 3552 Silk screens for textile industry

(G-6870)
POLISH YOUR LF NAIL SALON LLC
5017 W 14th St Apt 208 (60804-1301)
PHONE.................................312 838-1018
Vicki T Brown,
EMP: 3
SALES (est): 83.9K Privately Held
SIC: 3999 Fingernails, artificial

(G-6871)
ROYAL BOX GROUP LLC (HQ)
Also Called: Royal Continental Box Company
1301 S 47th Ave (60804-1598)
PHONE.................................708 656-2020
Robert L Mc Ilvaine, President
Tim Tootle, General Mgr
David Rodenhouser, Principal
J Jordan Nerenberg, Chairman
Tony Chervinko, Vice Pres
EMP: 249
SQ FT: 350,000
SALES (est): 244.6MM
SALES (corp-wide): 369.4MM Privately Held
WEB: www.teamtrg.com
SIC: 2653 Boxes, corrugated: made from purchased materials
PA: Schwarz Partners, L.P.
3600 Woodview Trce # 300
Indianapolis IN 46268
317 290-1140

(G-6872)
ROYAL BOX GROUP LLC
Also Called: Continental Concepts
4600 W 12th Pl (60804-1501)
PHONE.................................708 222-4650
Wayne Provus, Manager
EMP: 10
SALES (corp-wide): 369.4MM Privately Held
SIC: 2653 Boxes, corrugated: made from purchased materials
HQ: Royal Box Group, Llc
1301 S 47th Ave
Cicero IL 60804
708 656-2020

(G-6873)
SAFE-AIR OF ILLINOIS INC
1855 S 54th Ave (60804-1896)
PHONE.................................708 652-9100
Frank Ruiz, CEO
Michael Friedman, President
EMP: 45
SQ FT: 67,000
SALES (est): 12.7MM Privately Held
SIC: 3444 Ducts, sheet metal

(G-6874)
SAPORITO FINISHING CO (PA)
Also Called: Accurate Anodizing Div
3119 S Austin Blvd (60804-3730)
PHONE.................................708 222-5300
Charles Saporito Jr, President
Charles Saporito Sr, Chairman
Josephine Saporito, Corp Secy
James Mirabile, Vice Pres
EMP: 92
SQ FT: 94,000
SALES (est): 22.8MM Privately Held
WEB: www.saporitofinishing.com
SIC: 3471 Anodizing (plating) of metals or formed products; electroplating of metals or formed products; finishing, metals or formed products

(G-6875)
STANDARD HEAT TREATING LLC
5757 W Ogden Ave (60804-3877)
PHONE.................................773 242-0853
Greg Loredo, Persnl Mgr
Jack Christ, Mng Member
Santoyo Walter, Info Tech Mgr
EMP: 41
SALES (est): 8.9MM Privately Held
SIC: 3398 Metal heat treating

(G-6876)
STEEL FABRICATION AND WELDING
3200 S 61st Ave (60804-3718)
PHONE.................................773 343-0731
Ignacio Servin, Owner
EMP: 6
SALES (est): 170K Privately Held
WEB: www.steelfabricationandwelding.com
SIC: 3312 1791 Wire products, steel or iron; concrete reinforcement, placing of

(G-6877)
SUNTIMEZ ENTERTAINMENT
5811 W Roosevelt Rd (60804-1136)
PHONE.................................630 747-0712
EMP: 3 EST: 2008
SALES (est): 120K Privately Held
SIC: 3931 Mfg Musical Instruments

(G-6878)
SUPREME FELT & ABRASIVES INC
1633 S 55th Ave (60804-1817)
PHONE.................................708 344-0134
David McNeilly, President
David Neiman, Vice Pres
EMP: 25
SQ FT: 20,000
SALES (est): 4.5MM Privately Held
SIC: 3053 5199 Gasket materials; felt

(G-6879)
TELE GUIA SPANISH TV GUIDE
Also Called: CHI Montes
3116 S Austin Blvd (60804)
PHONE.................................708 656-9800
Rose Montes, Vice Pres
Patricia Scolera, Treasurer
EMP: 22
SALES (est): 971.8K Privately Held
SIC: 2741 Miscellaneous publishing

(G-6880)
TELEGUIA INC
Also Called: Elimparcial Newspaper
3116 S Austin Blvd (60804)
PHONE.................................708 656-6675
Ezequiel Montes, President
Rose Montes, Vice Pres
EMP: 20
SALES (est): 700K Privately Held
SIC: 2711 Newspapers, publishing & printing

(G-6881)
TERRACE HOLDING COMPANY
1325 S Cicero Ave (60804-1404)
PHONE.................................708 652-5600
Barry Silver, President
EMP: 930
SQ FT: 150,000
SALES (est): 78.5MM Privately Held
SIC: 3556 Food products machinery

(G-6882)
TVO ACQUISITION CORPORATION (PA)
Also Called: John Gillen Company
2540 S 50th Ave (60804-3416)
PHONE.................................708 656-4240
Thomas V O'Neill, President
Veronica S O'Neill, Vice Pres
EMP: 37 EST: 1918
SQ FT: 55,000
SALES (est): 11.9MM Privately Held
WEB: www.johngillenco.com
SIC: 3541 Screw & thread machines

(G-6883)
UNIQUE PRTRS LITHOGRAPHERS INC
5500 W 31st St (60804-3957)
PHONE.................................708 656-8900
John Collins, President
Charles Deets, Chairman
Steve Deets, Vice Pres
EMP: 65
SQ FT: 26,000
SALES (est): 13.8MM Privately Held
SIC: 2752 Commercial printing, offset

(G-6884)
UNIQUE/ACTIVE LLC
5500 W 31st St (60804-3957)
PHONE.................................708 656-8900
Bill Thompson, Vice Pres
Tom Howard, Production
Anthony Sipiora, Production
Pat Calcagno, Accounts Exec
John Ohalloran, Accounts Exec
EMP: 27
SALES (est): 6.2MM Privately Held
SIC: 2752 Commercial printing, offset

GEOGRAPHIC SECTION

Clayton - Adams County (G-6910)

(G-6885)
UNITED GASKET CORPORATION
1633 S 55th Ave (60804-1889)
PHONE..................708 656-3700
Mark Pahios, *President*
Doug Valley, *COO*
Mitchell Kiesler, *Plant Mgr*
Failon Cindy, *CFO*
Cynthia Phelan, *Accounting Mgr*
▲ **EMP:** 70 **EST:** 1940
SQ FT: 35,000
SALES (est): 24.8MM **Privately Held**
WEB: www.unitedgasket.com
SIC: 3554 3714 5013 3053 Die cutting & stamping machinery, paper converting; motor vehicle parts & accessories; motor vehicle supplies & new parts; gaskets, packing & sealing devices

(G-6886)
V BROTHERS MACHINE CO
4900 W 16th St (60804-1531)
PHONE..................708 652-0062
Damjan Vujanovic, *President*
Dragen Vujanovic, *Vice Pres*
Michelle Gurak, *Receptionist*
EMP: 20 **EST:** 1981
SQ FT: 23,000
SALES (est): 3.2MM **Privately Held**
SIC: 3599 7692 Machine shop, jobbing & repair; welding repair

(G-6887)
WEST TOWN PLATING INC
5243 W 25th Pl (60804-3391)
PHONE..................708 652-1600
Gerald Glab, *Ch of Bd*
Keith Glab, *Vice Pres*
Russell Glab, *Vice Pres*
EMP: 20 **EST:** 1953
SQ FT: 10,000
SALES (est): 2.1MM **Privately Held**
WEB: www.westtownplating.com
SIC: 3471 Plating of metals or formed products

(G-6888)
WIRTZ BEVERAGE ILLINOIS LLC (PA)
Also Called: Wirtz Bev Ill Metro-Chicago
3333 S Laramie Ave (60804-4520)
PHONE..................847 228-9000
Alex Gonzalez, *Human Resources*
Daniel R Wirtz, *Mng Member*
Felix Martinez, *Director*
Arthur M Wirtz III,
Rockwell W Wirtz,
▲ **EMP:** 120
SALES (est): 42MM **Privately Held**
SIC: 2082 5169 Ale (alcoholic beverage); alcohols

(G-6889)
WRIGHT QUICK SIGNS INC
Also Called: Wright Advertising
1347 S Laramie Ave (60804-1355)
PHONE..................708 652-6020
Ralph Pontrelli, *President*
EMP: 7 **EST:** 1967
SQ FT: 2,500
SALES (est): 851.2K **Privately Held**
SIC: 7312 7311 3993 Billboard advertising; advertising agencies; signs & advertising specialties

(G-6890)
ZB IMPORTING INC (PA)
Also Called: Ziyad Brothers Importing
5400 W 35th St (60804-4431)
PHONE..................708 222-8330
Ibrahim Ziad, *President*
Mohammad Atwi, *Business Mgr*
Terry Samara, *Business Mgr*
Gene Hamilton, *Vice Pres*
Nemer Ziyad, *VP Opers*
◆ **EMP:** 85
SQ FT: 150,000
SALES (est): 60.3MM **Privately Held**
SIC: 5149 2064 2051 Specialty food items; candy & other confectionery products; bread, all types (white, wheat, rye, etc): fresh or frozen

Cisco
Piatt County

(G-6891)
BOYD SPOTTING INC
1310 N 300 East Rd (61830-6534)
PHONE..................217 669-2418
Jacquelyn Boyd, *President*
EMP: 5
SALES (est): 647.9K **Privately Held**
SIC: 3792 Travel trailers & campers

Cisne
Wayne County

(G-6892)
DAVE WHITE
1269 Conty Rod 970 E (62823)
PHONE..................618 898-1130
Dave White, *Owner*
EMP: 5
SALES (est): 330K **Privately Held**
SIC: 2452 Farm & agricultural buildings, prefabricated wood

(G-6893)
HAROLD L RAY TRUCK & TRCTR SVC
Hwy 45 N (62823)
P.O. Box 130 (62823-0130)
PHONE..................618 673-2701
Harold L Ray, *President*
Billye Ray, *Admin Sec*
EMP: 12
SALES (est): 800.2K **Privately Held**
SIC: 4212 1389 Heavy machinery transport, local; gas field services

Cissna Park
Iroquois County

(G-6894)
BAIER HOME CENTER
120 S 2nd St (60924-6131)
P.O. Box 120 (60924-0120)
PHONE..................815 457-2300
David L Baier, *Owner*
EMP: 5
SALES (est): 525.7K **Privately Held**
SIC: 3634 Housewares, excluding cooking appliances & utensils

(G-6895)
BAIER PUBLISHING COMPANY
Also Called: Cissna Park News
119 W Garfield Ave (60924-6125)
P.O. Box 8 (60924-0008)
PHONE..................815 457-2245
Rick Baier, *President*
EMP: 5 **EST:** 1948
SQ FT: 8,000
SALES (est): 146.4K **Privately Held**
WEB: www.beyondmedianetworks.com
SIC: 2711 Newspapers

(G-6896)
CP DIESEL INC
289 N 1700 East Rd (60924-8807)
PHONE..................815 979-9600
Bre Schmid, *Administration*
EMP: 3 **EST:** 2017
SALES (est): 109.8K **Privately Held**
SIC: 2911 Diesel fuels

(G-6897)
KSI CONVEYOR INC
454 N State Route 49 (60924-8876)
P.O. Box 69 (60924-0069)
PHONE..................815 457-2403
Adam Renyer, *Prdtn Mgr*
Ronnie Edelman, *Mfg Mgr*
Amy Walder, *Purch Agent*
Kevin Broxterman, *Engineer*
Neal Kellenberger, *CFO*
EMP: 63
SALES (corp-wide): 34MM **Privately Held**
SIC: 3523 Farm machinery & equipment
PA: Ksi Conveyor, Inc.
2345 U Rd
Sabetha KS 66534
785 284-0600

Claremont
Richland County

(G-6898)
HERSHEYS METAL MEISTER LLC
Also Called: Hersheys Metal Meister
7405 E Mount Pleasant Ln (62421-2727)
PHONE..................217 234-4700
Nelson Hershberger, *Mng Member*
Miriam Hershberger,
▲ **EMP:** 20
SQ FT: 50,000
SALES (est): 10.8MM **Privately Held**
SIC: 5072 5033 3542 Builders' hardware; insulation materials; presses: forming, stamping, punching, sizing (machine tools)

Clarendon Hills
Dupage County

(G-6899)
AMARIKO INC
123 Ogden Ave (60514-1045)
PHONE..................630 734-1000
Tom Marik, *President*
EMP: 7
SALES (est): 378.5K **Privately Held**
SIC: 7372 Prepackaged software

(G-6900)
MEDTEX HEALTH SERVICES INC
554 Willowcreek Ct (60514-3602)
PHONE..................630 789-0330
John Maras, *President*
EMP: 2
SALES (est): 250K **Privately Held**
SIC: 3845 3841 5047 Electromedical equipment; surgical & medical instruments; medical & hospital equipment

(G-6901)
THOLEO DESIGN INC
418 Ridge Ave (60514-2706)
PHONE..................630 325-3792
Blake Thoele, *President*
Karin Thoele, *Vice Pres*
EMP: 3 **EST:** 2000
SALES (est): 253.5K **Privately Held**
SIC: 3069 Rubber floor coverings, mats & wallcoverings

Clay City
Clay County

(G-6902)
ABNER TRUCKING CO INC
207 S 1st St Se (62824-1055)
P.O. Box 375 (62824-0375)
PHONE..................618 676-1301
Arthur Thomas Abner, *President*
EMP: 9
SQ FT: 1,800
SALES (est): 753.1K **Privately Held**
SIC: 4212 1389 Local trucking, without storage; servicing oil & gas wells

(G-6903)
BANGERT CASING PULLING CORP
1 Industrial Park Rd (62824-7400)
P.O. Box 441 (62824-0441)
PHONE..................618 676-1411
Ronald G Bangert, *President*
Andrew Bangert, *Vice Pres*
Naomi Bangert, *Treasurer*
Ronald Bangert II, *Admin Sec*
Ronald Bangert, *Admin Sec*
EMP: 9
SQ FT: 4,800
SALES (est): 1.4MM **Privately Held**
SIC: 1389 5084 Oil field services; oil well machinery, equipment & supplies

(G-6904)
CITATION OIL & GAS CORP
3943 Big Four Rd (62824-2357)
PHONE..................618 676-1044
Jay Decker, *Principal*
David Carter, *Foreman/Supr*
EMP: 4
SALES (corp-wide): 283.5MM **Privately Held**
WEB: www.cogc.com
SIC: 1311 Crude petroleum production
PA: Citation Oil & Gas Corp.
14077 Cutten Rd
Houston TX 77069
281 891-1000

(G-6905)
FRANCIS L MORRIS
1377 Angling Rd (62824-2353)
PHONE..................618 676-1724
Francis L Morris, *Owner*
EMP: 3
SALES (est): 152.9K **Privately Held**
SIC: 2421 Sawmills & planing mills, general

(G-6906)
J W RUDY CO INC
506 S 1st St Se (61208-1208)
P.O. Box 485 (62824-0485)
PHONE..................618 676-1616
Kay Rudy, *President*
Steve Rudy, *Manager*
Crystal Rudy, *Admin Sec*
EMP: 18 **EST:** 1948
SQ FT: 1,500
SALES (est): 1.1MM **Privately Held**
SIC: 1311 4212 Crude petroleum production; local trucking, without storage

(G-6907)
M & I ACID COMPANY INC
1107 S Main St (62824-1165)
P.O. Box 443 (62824-0443)
PHONE..................618 676-1638
Ivan Brikker, *Vice Pres*
Mick Mason, *Administration*
EMP: 4 **EST:** 1993
SALES (est): 324.7K **Privately Held**
SIC: 1389 Oil field services

(G-6908)
TRI STATE ACID CO INC
110 Industrial Park (62824)
P.O. Box 343 (62824-0343)
PHONE..................618 676-1111
Ivan Bricker, *Owner*
EMP: 5
SALES (est): 200.8K **Privately Held**
SIC: 1389 Acidizing wells

Clayton
Adams County

(G-6909)
CONCORD CABINETS INC (PA)
1276 E 2575th St (62324-2716)
PHONE..................217 894-6507
Gene Daggett, *CEO*
Greg Daggett, *President*
Steven Spilker, *Vice Pres*
Sharron Daggett, *Admin Sec*
EMP: 10
SQ FT: 25,000
SALES: 1MM **Privately Held**
SIC: 2599 1751 Cabinets, factory; cabinet & finish carpentry

(G-6910)
MOTOROLA SOLUTIONS INC
1699 E 2950th St (62324-2606)
PHONE..................217 894-6451
Mark Barllow, *Owner*
EMP: 4
SALES (corp-wide): 7.8B **Publicly Held**
WEB: www.motorolasolutions.com
SIC: 3663 Radio & TV communications equipment

Clayton - Adams County (G-6911)

PA: Motorola Solutions, Inc.
500 W Monroe St Ste 4400
Chicago IL 60661
847 576-5000

(G-6911)
WEATHERGUARD BUILDINGS
1654 E 2950th St (62324-2622)
PHONE 217 894-6213
Melvin Schrock, *Owner*
EMP: 3
SALES (est): 230.9K **Privately Held**
SIC: 2421 Building & structural materials, wood

Cleveland
Henry County

(G-6912)
RIVERSTONE GROUP INC
Also Called: Cleveland Quarry
1001 N Broadway St (61241-8547)
PHONE 309 933-1123
John Swan, *Branch Mgr*
EMP: 18
SALES (corp-wide): 2.5B **Privately Held**
SIC: 1422 5032 Limestones, ground; limestone
PA: Riverstone Group, Inc.
4640 E 56th St
Davenport IA 52807
309 757-8250

Clifton
Iroquois County

(G-6913)
ADVOCATE
Also Called: Advocate Printing
330 N 4th St (60927-7232)
P.O. Box 548 (60927-0548)
PHONE 815 694-2122
Theresa M Simoneau, *Owner*
EMP: 4
SALES: 100K **Privately Held**
SIC: 2711 2752 Newspapers, publishing & printing; commercial printing, lithographic

(G-6914)
CRANE QUALITY EQUIPMENT LLC
188 E 3100 North Rd (60927-7205)
PHONE 815 258-5375
Brian Crane, *Mng Member*
Mike Brooks,
Brent Crane,
EMP: 3
SQ FT: 10,000
SALES (est): 414.3K **Privately Held**
SIC: 3523 Farm machinery & equipment

(G-6915)
JDL GRAPHICS INC
3043 N 1600 East Rd (60927-7044)
PHONE 815 694-2979
EMP: 3 EST: 1987
SALES: 100K **Privately Held**
SIC: 2262 Manmade Fiber & Silk Finishing Plant

(G-6916)
SYSTEMS BY LAR INC
841 E 3000 North Rd (60927-7188)
PHONE 815 694-3141
Lynn A Rosenbaum, *President*
Sally Rosenbaum, *Vice Pres*
EMP: 5 EST: 2002
SALES (est): 1MM **Privately Held**
SIC: 3061 Mechanical rubber goods

Clinton
De Witt County

(G-6917)
AAK MECHANICAL INC
10962 Riddle Rd (61727-9373)
PHONE 217 935-8501
Steven R Coppenbarger, *President*
Jennifer Coppenbarger, *Admin Sec*
EMP: 52
SALES: 11.8MM **Privately Held**
SIC: 1796 3441 Machinery installation; fabricated structural metal

(G-6918)
ARCOSA WIND TOWERS INC
10000 Tabor Rd (61727-9645)
PHONE 217 935-7900
EMP: 16
SALES (corp-wide): 1.7B **Publicly Held**
SIC: 3441 3621 Fabricated structural metal; windmills, electric generating
HQ: Arcosa Wind Towers, Inc.
500 N Akard St
Dallas TX 75201
972 942-6500

(G-6919)
AREA DISPOSAL SERVICE INC
9550 Heritage Rd (61727-2819)
PHONE 217 935-1300
Ken Heuerman, *Branch Mgr*
EMP: 10 **Privately Held**
SIC: 3589 Garbage disposers & compactors, commercial
HQ: Area Disposal Service, Inc.
4700 N Sterling Ave
Peoria IL 61615
309 686-8033

(G-6920)
CENTRAL ILLINOIS NEWSPAPERS
Also Called: Clinton Daily Journal
111 S Monroe St (61727-2057)
P.O. Box 615 (61727-0615)
PHONE 217 935-3171
John Tompkins, *President*
Mike Tompkins, *Vice Pres*
Susan Munoz, *Sales Staff*
EMP: 4
SQ FT: 7,000
SALES (est): 411.4K **Privately Held**
SIC: 2711 2752 Newspapers: publishing only, not printed on site; commercial printing, lithographic
HQ: Rochelle Newspapers, Inc.
211 E Illinois Rte 38
Rochelle IL 61068
815 562-4171

(G-6921)
H N C PRODUCTS INC
8631 Sunset Rd (61727-8987)
PHONE 217 935-9100
Dan Toohill, *Vice Pres*
EMP: 30
SALES (corp-wide): 50MM **Privately Held**
SIC: 3579 Mailing, letter handling & addressing machines
PA: H N C Products Inc.
1619 Commerce Pkwy
Bloomington IL 61704
309 319-2151

(G-6922)
HARBACH GILLAN & NIXON INC (PA)
Also Called: H G & N Fertilizer
618 W Van Buren St (61727-2183)
P.O. Box 457 (61727-0457)
PHONE 217 935-8378
Curtis Harbach, *President*
Bob Anderson, *Corp Secy*
Robert C Anderson, *Admin Sec*
EMP: 10
SQ FT: 2,000
SALES (est): 13.7MM **Privately Held**
SIC: 2873 5191 2875 Nitrogenous fertilizers; fertilizer & fertilizer materials; fertilizers, mixing only

(G-6923)
HARBACH NIXON & WILLSON INC (HQ)
618 W Van Buren St (61727-2183)
P.O. Box 457 (61727-0457)
PHONE 217 935-8378
Virgil T Harbach, *President*
John Buerk, *Treasurer*
Richard Graves, *Admin Sec*

EMP: 3
SALES (est): 343.2K
SALES (corp-wide): 13.7MM **Privately Held**
SIC: 2879 Agricultural chemicals
PA: Harbach, Gillan & Nixon, Inc.
618 W Van Buren St
Clinton IL 61727
217 935-8378

(G-6924)
ILLINOIS OIL MARKETING EQP INC
601 E Leander St (61727-2511)
PHONE 217 935-5107
Dan Ballenger, *Manager*
EMP: 15
SALES (corp-wide): 22.5MM **Privately Held**
SIC: 3443 Tanks, standard or custom fabricated: metal plate
PA: Illinois Oil Marketing Equipment, Inc.
850 Brenkman Dr
Pekin IL 61554
309 347-1819

(G-6925)
LIBERTY DIVERSIFIED INTL INC
10670 State Highway 10 (61727-9277)
P.O. Box 443 (61727-0443)
PHONE 217 935-8361
Thomas Sivil, *Manager*
EMP: 50
SALES (corp-wide): 390.1MM **Privately Held**
SIC: 2653 3412 Boxes, corrugated: made from purchased materials; metal barrels, drums & pails
PA: Liberty Diversified International, Inc.
5600 Highway 169 N
New Hope MN 55428
763 536-6600

(G-6926)
M & M PUMP CO
404 S Portland Pl Apt 2 (61727-2388)
PHONE 217 935-2517
Carol McClur, *President*
Rod Wortz, *Vice Pres*
EMP: 4
SALES (est): 310K **Privately Held**
SIC: 3589 5084 High pressure cleaning equipment; cleaning equipment, high pressure, sand or steam

(G-6927)
MCELROY METAL MILL INC
10940 State Hwy 10 (61727)
PHONE 217 935-9421
John Hinthorne, *Branch Mgr*
EMP: 48
SQ FT: 70,000
SALES (corp-wide): 373.4MM **Privately Held**
WEB: www.mcelroymetal.com
SIC: 3448 Prefabricated metal buildings
PA: Mcelroy Metal Mill, Inc.
1500 Hamilton Rd
Bossier City LA 71111
318 747-8000

(G-6928)
R R DONNELLEY & SONS COMPANY
Also Called: Colorforms
900 S Cain St (61727-2537)
P.O. Box 379 (61727-0379)
PHONE 217 935-2113
Jeff Massey, *Engineer*
Gayle Waddle, *Personnel*
Keith Gonnerman, *Prgrmr*
Marty Morris, *Director*
Kirk Fornella, *Executive*
EMP: 230
SQ FT: 160,000
SALES (corp-wide): 6.2B **Publicly Held**
SIC: 2752 2761 Commercial printing, lithographic; manifold business forms
PA: R. R. Donnelley & Sons Company
35 W Wacker Dr
Chicago IL 60601
312 326-8000

(G-6929)
TEKNI-PLEX INC
Action Technology
10610 State Highway 10 (61727-9277)
P.O. Box 111 (61727-0111)
PHONE 217 935-8311
Bryan Foster, *Plant Mgr*
Dan Leevey, *Plant Mgr*
Julie Tedrick, *Controller*
Gary Seitzer, *Maintence Staff*
EMP: 29
SALES (corp-wide): 1.3B **Privately Held**
SIC: 3089 Air mattresses, plastic
PA: Tekni-Plex, Inc.
460 E Swedesford Rd # 3000
Wayne PA 19087
484 690-1520

Coal City
Grundy County

(G-6930)
COAL CITY COURANT
Also Called: Free Press Newspapers
271 S Broadway St (60416-1534)
P.O. Box 215 (60416-0215)
PHONE 815 634-0315
Eric Fisher, *President*
EMP: 3
SALES (est): 150.6K **Privately Held**
SIC: 2711 Newspapers, publishing & printing

(G-6931)
COAL CITY REDI-MIX CO INC
640 S Mazon St (60416)
P.O. Box 116 (60416-0116)
PHONE 815 634-4455
Steven W Dearth, *President*
Timothy Bradley, *Trustee*
Michael Dearth, *Vice Pres*
Bonnie Wieczorek, *Admin Asst*
EMP: 13 EST: 1952
SQ FT: 2,000
SALES (est): 1.6MM **Privately Held**
WEB: www.coalcityredimix.com
SIC: 3273 3241 Ready-mixed concrete; cement, hydraulic

(G-6932)
ELCO LABORATORIES INC (PA)
Also Called: Fresh Solutions For Your Home
1300 E North St (60416-1254)
PHONE 708 534-3000
Norman L Elliott, *President*
Robert Hettinger, *President*
William G Elliott, *Vice Pres*
Debra Adomaitis, *Purch Mgr*
Anthony Rogganbuck, *Supervisor*
▲ **EMP:** 55
SALES (est): 4.9MM **Privately Held**
SIC: 2842 Rug, upholstery, or dry cleaning detergents or spotters; specialty cleaning preparations

(G-6933)
HESTER CABINETS & MILLWORK
655 S Marguerite St (60416-1486)
PHONE 815 634-4555
Steven R Hester, *President*
EMP: 6 EST: 1933
SQ FT: 5,000
SALES (est): 850.2K **Privately Held**
WEB: www.hestercabinets.com
SIC: 2434 Wood kitchen cabinets

Coal Valley
Rock Island County

(G-6934)
COMPLETE CUSTOM WOODWORKS
3 Crestview Dr (61240-9409)
PHONE 309 644-1911
James Jermigan, *Owner*
EMP: 1
SQ FT: 1,000
SALES: 750K **Privately Held**
SIC: 2521 Cabinets, office: wood

GEOGRAPHIC SECTION

Collinsville - Madison County (G-6961)

(G-6935)
DEER PROCESSING
11928 Niabi Zoo Rd (61240-9530)
PHONE................309 799-5994
Teri Dean, *Owner*
EMP: 12
SALES (est): 596.3K **Privately Held**
SIC: 2011 Meat packing plants

(G-6936)
FCA LLC
2212 Us Highway 6 (61240-9602)
PHONE................309 949-3999
Jim Eddy, *Branch Mgr*
EMP: 43 **Privately Held**
WEB: www.fcapackaging.com
SIC: 5085 2653 2441 Industrial supplies; corrugated & solid fiber boxes; nailed wood boxes & shook
PA: Fca, Llc
7601 John Deere Pkwy
Moline IL 61265

(G-6937)
KONE INC
Also Called: Kone Escalator Div
2266 Us Highway 6 (61240-9602)
PHONE................309 945-4961
Godfrey Allen, *Vice Pres*
EMP: 200
SALES (corp-wide): 11B **Privately Held**
SIC: 7699 3534 Elevators: inspection, service & repair; elevators & moving stairways
HQ: Kone Inc.
4225 Naperville Rd # 400
Lisle IL 60532
630 577-1650

(G-6938)
PRAIRIE AREA LIBRARY SYSTEM (PA)
220 W 23rd Ave (61240-9624)
PHONE................309 799-3155
Barry Levine, *President*
Penny O'Rouke, *Vice Pres*
Robert McKay, *Exec Dir*
EMP: 20
SALES (est): 3.1MM **Privately Held**
WEB: www.railslibraries.info
SIC: 7372 8741 8231 Operating systems computer software; management services; libraries

(G-6939)
VALLEY MEATS LLC
2302 1st St Sr (61240-9408)
P.O. Box 69 (61240-0069)
PHONE................309 799-7341
Jeff Joeb, *President*
Randy Ehrlich, *Vice Pres*
Richard Koehler, *Vice Pres*
EMP: 49
SALES (est): 6.8MM **Privately Held**
SIC: 8741 2011 Business management; boxed beef from meat slaughtered on site

Coatsburg
Adams County

(G-6940)
AREA FABRICATORS
1735 Highway 24 (62325-2202)
PHONE................217 455-3426
Ronald Conover, *Partner*
Jeffery A Conover, *Partner*
Steve M Conover, *Partner*
EMP: 3
SALES (est): 441.2K **Privately Held**
SIC: 3441 Fabricated structural metal

Cobden
Union County

(G-6941)
COOK SALES INC (PA)
Also Called: Cook Portable Warehouses
3455 Old Highway 51 N (62920-3666)
P.O. Box 687, Anna (62906-0687)
PHONE................618 893-2114
Greg Cook, *President*
William Mugno, *Division Mgr*
Tim Yearack, *Engineer*
Megan Skaggs, *Sales Staff*
Jacob Lyon, *Manager*
EMP: 50
SQ FT: 46,500
SALES (est): 19.2MM **Privately Held**
SIC: 2452 Prefabricated wood buildings

(G-6942)
LINCOLN HERITAGE WINERY LLC
772 Kaolin Rd (62920-3783)
PHONE................618 833-3783
Homer L Cissell,
Bonnie Cissell,
EMP: 2
SALES (est): 239.1K **Privately Held**
WEB: www.lincolnheritagewinery.com
SIC: 5182 2084 Wine; wines

(G-6943)
SHAWNEE GRAPEVINES LLC
Also Called: Starview Vineyard
5100 Wing Hill Rd (62920-3211)
PHONE................618 893-9463
Regina Morrison, *Director*
Ron Dalius,
EMP: 4
SALES (est): 263.2K **Privately Held**
WEB: www.starviewvineyards.com
SIC: 0762 2084 Vineyard management & maintenance services; wines

(G-6944)
SPHINX PANEL AND DOOR INC
317 Locust St (62920-2104)
PHONE................618 351-9266
Terry A Bovee, *President*
EMP: 8
SQ FT: 3,200
SALES (est): 1MM **Privately Held**
SIC: 3632 Refrigerators, mechanical & absorption: household

Coffeen
Montgomery County

(G-6945)
US MINERALS INC
796 Cips Trl (62017-2137)
PHONE................217 534-2370
Eric White, *Plant Mgr*
EMP: 15
SALES (corp-wide): 34.3MM **Privately Held**
SIC: 3291 Abrasive products
PA: U.S. Minerals, Inc.
18635 West Creek Dr Ste 2
Tinley Park IL 60477
708 623-1935

Colchester
Mcdonough County

(G-6946)
CENTRAL STONE COMPANY
5533 E 400th St (62326-1887)
PHONE................309 776-3900
Harvey Fueling, *Manager*
EMP: 12
SALES (corp-wide): 2.5B **Privately Held**
WEB: www.riverstonegrp.com
SIC: 1422 5032 Agricultural limestone, ground; stone, crushed or broken
HQ: Central Stone Company
4640 E 56th St
Davenport IA 52807
309 757-8250

(G-6947)
YETTER M CO INC EMP B TR
109 S Mcdonough St (62326-1303)
P.O. Box 358 (62326-0358)
PHONE................309 776-4111
Bernard Lelan, *President*
EMP: 1
SALES: 1.5MM **Privately Held**
SIC: 3999 Manufacturing industries

(G-6948)
YETTER MANUFACTURING COMPANY (PA)
Also Called: Yetter Farm Equipment
109 S Mcdonough St (62326-1303)
P.O. Box 358 (62326-0358)
PHONE................309 776-3222
Bernard F Whalen, *President*
Patrick T Whalen, *Vice Pres*
Ron Arteaga, *Purchasing*
Garry Hopping, *QC Mgr*
Ryan Dougherty, *Research*
▲ EMP: 80 EST: 1930
SQ FT: 46,500
SALES (est): 26.8MM **Privately Held**
WEB: www.yetterco.com
SIC: 2542 3523 Racks, merchandise display or storage: except wood; cutters & blowers, ensilage

Coleta
Whiteside County

(G-6949)
GIBBS MACHINE CORP
411 S Main (61081-5117)
PHONE................815 336-9000
Jerry A Gibbs, *President*
Pam Beyer, *Purchasing*
Bobbie L Gibbs, *Admin Sec*
EMP: 20
SALES (est): 3.4MM **Privately Held**
WEB: www.gibbsmachinecorp.com
SIC: 3599 Machine shop, jobbing & repair

Colfax
Mclean County

(G-6950)
MUSIC PLUG LLC
33275 E 1700 North Rd (61728-9437)
PHONE................309 826-5238
David Crego,
Johnathan Crego,
Lincoln Marti,
EMP: 4
SALES (est): 75.2K **Privately Held**
SIC: 7372 7389 Application computer software;

(G-6951)
TFT INC
31784 E 1400 North Rd (61728-7523)
PHONE................309 531-2012
Gerald Thompson, *President*
EMP: 1
SALES: 1MM **Privately Held**
SIC: 3523 Driers (farm): grain, hay & seed

Collinsville
Madison County

(G-6952)
ADVANCED PATTERN WORKS LLC
305 Railroad Ave (62234-2831)
PHONE................618 346-9039
John Harris, *Mng Member*
EMP: 5
SALES (est): 900K **Privately Held**
SIC: 3322 3543 Malleable iron foundries; industrial patterns

(G-6953)
ALAO TEMITOPE
Also Called: Topilonio
29 Brookhill Ct (62234-6044)
PHONE................331 454-3333
Temitope Ajayi, *Owner*
EMP: 15
SALES (est): 550K **Privately Held**
SIC: 2082 7389 Malt syrups;

(G-6954)
ALEXANDER BREWSTER LLC
1401 N Bluff Rd (62234-7303)
PHONE................618 346-8580
John W Thomas Jr,
Zachary A Kaesberg,
Jerod B Thomas,
Jerod Thomas,
Nancy L Thomas,
EMP: 7
SQ FT: 4,800
SALES (est): 1.2MM **Privately Held**
SIC: 3651 Video camera-audio recorders, household use

(G-6955)
COLLINSVILLE ICE & FUEL CO
800 N Bluff Rd (62234-5818)
PHONE................618 344-3272
John J O'Donnell, *President*
Maureen O'Donnell, *Vice Pres*
EMP: 15
SQ FT: 5,000
SALES (est): 1.6MM **Privately Held**
WEB: www.cifcoinc.com
SIC: 1741 2097 Stone masonry; block ice

(G-6956)
CUSTOM WOOD CREATIONS
776 Timberlane Dr (62234-4132)
PHONE................618 346-2208
Martin E Plute Jr, *Principal*
EMP: 2
SALES (est): 232.7K **Privately Held**
SIC: 2431 Millwork

(G-6957)
D L AUSTIN STEEL SUPPLY CORP (PA)
500 Camelot Dr (62234-4717)
P.O. Box 166 (62234-0166)
PHONE................618 345-7200
David Austin Sr, *President*
David L Austin II, *President*
Kathleen Austin, *Corp Secy*
EMP: 2
SQ FT: 4,200
SALES (est): 1MM **Privately Held**
SIC: 3441 5051 Fabricated structural metal; metals service centers & offices

(G-6958)
EAST BANK NEON INC
8146 Gass Ln (62234-7009)
PHONE................618 345-9517
Dennis Wick, *President*
Sam Glasser, *Manager*
EMP: 8
SALES (corp-wide): 1.1MM **Privately Held**
SIC: 3993 Signs & advertising specialties
PA: East Bank Neon Inc
1511 Washington Ave
Saint Louis MO

(G-6959)
ESI FUEL & ENERGY GROUP LLC
1997 Lemontree Ln (62234-5252)
PHONE................716 465-4289
Valerie Durley, *Partner*
Richard Eilering, *Partner*
Brad Frank, *Partner*
Montie Miner, *Partner*
Kelly Planzo, *Partner*
EMP: 4
SALES (est): 183.5K **Privately Held**
SIC: 2911 4911 Jet fuels; diesel fuels; gases & liquefied petroleum gases; ;

(G-6960)
FEDDER OIL CO INC
417 Short St (62234-2616)
P.O. Box 141 (62234-0141)
PHONE................618 344-0050
Daniuel L Fedder, *President*
Donald J Fedder, *Director*
EMP: 2
SQ FT: 1,800
SALES (est): 280.1K **Privately Held**
SIC: 1389 5983 Oil field services; fuel oil dealers

(G-6961)
FOURNIE FARMS INC
925 Mcdonough Lake Rd (62234-7401)
PHONE................618 344-8527
Robert L Fournie, *President*
Dorothy Fournie, *Corp Secy*
EMP: 26

Collinsville - Madison County (G-6962)

SALES (est): 252.8K **Privately Held**
SIC: 0161 2035 Vegetables & melons; horseradish, prepared

(G-6962)
G & M INDUSTRIES INC
208 Yorktown Dr (62234-4352)
P.O. Box 561 (62234-0561)
PHONE.................................618 344-6655
William Graebe, *President*
Annette Graebe, *Vice Pres*
EMP: 4
SQ FT: 2,000
SALES (est): 304.3K **Privately Held**
SIC: 3842 3999 Wheelchairs; desk pads, except paper

(G-6963)
J D REFRIGERATION
Also Called: Darlington Climate Control
6849 Fedder Ln (62234-6507)
PHONE.................................618 345-0041
Dan Darlington, *President*
Jim Kerner, *Corp Secy*
Greg Darlington, *Admin Sec*
EMP: 2 EST: 1980
SQ FT: 1,000
SALES (est): 241.2K **Privately Held**
SIC: 1711 3585 Warm air heating & air conditioning contractor; refrigeration & heating equipment

(G-6964)
JDS LABS INC
909 N Bluff Rd (62234-5803)
PHONE.................................618 550-9359
John Seaber, *President*
Nick Amizich, *Design Engr*
EMP: 5 EST: 2010
SALES (est): 784.4K **Privately Held**
SIC: 3679 7389 Headphones, radio;

(G-6965)
LESS COST COPY CENTER INC
2103 Vandalia St (62234-4891)
PHONE.................................618 345-3121
Jim Fraker, *President*
EMP: 4
SALES (est): 256.3K **Privately Held**
SIC: 2752 Commercial printing, offset

(G-6966)
LONDON SHOE SHOP & WESTERN WR
125 W Main St (62234-3001)
PHONE.................................618 345-9570
Mark Allard, *Owner*
EMP: 4
SQ FT: 3,000
SALES (est): 320.3K **Privately Held**
SIC: 5661 3143 Custom & orthopedic shoes; shoes, orthopedic; men's footwear, except athletic

(G-6967)
M O W PRINTING INC
526 Vandalia St (62234-4041)
PHONE.................................618 345-5525
John Meehan Jr, *President*
Kelly Jean Ossola, *Vice Pres*
Darrell Walling, *Vice Pres*
EMP: 11
SQ FT: 8,000
SALES (est): 1.8MM **Privately Held**
SIC: 2752 2791 2789 Commercial printing, offset; typesetting; bookbinding & related work

(G-6968)
MANDIS DENTAL LABORATORY
607 Vandalia St Ste 300 (62234-4081)
PHONE.................................618 345-3777
Nicholas C Mandis, *President*
EMP: 4
SQ FT: 1,500
SALES (est): 403.5K **Privately Held**
SIC: 8072 3843 3842 Crown & bridge production; dental equipment & supplies; surgical appliances & supplies

(G-6969)
MARSH SHIPPING SUPPLY CO LLC (PA)
Also Called: Mssc
926 Mcdonough Lake Rd E (62234-7437)
PHONE.................................618 343-1006
Craig Eversmann, *President*
John Burnett, *General Mgr*
Lee Wehmeyer, *Mfg Staff*
Michael Strope, *Sales Mgr*
Susan Engler, *Teacher*
▼ EMP: 12 EST: 2000
SQ FT: 15,000
SALES (est): 9.5MM **Privately Held**
WEB: www.msscllc.com
SIC: 3565 3542 Packaging machinery; marking machines

(G-6970)
MIDLAND WOOD PRODUCTS
105 Greer Ct (62234-1490)
PHONE.................................618 344-5640
Michael Krisher, *Principal*
EMP: 3
SALES (est): 435K **Privately Held**
SIC: 2448 Pallets, wood

(G-6971)
MSSC LLC
926 Mcdonough Lake Rd E (62234-7437)
PHONE.................................618 343-1006
Craig Eversmann, *Mng Member*
EMP: 1 EST: 2007
SALES (est): 358.4K
SALES (corp-wide): 9.5MM **Privately Held**
SIC: 3565 Packaging machinery
PA: Marsh Shipping Supply Co Llc
926 Mcdonough Lake Rd E
Collinsville IL 62234
618 343-1006

(G-6972)
PRECISION SERVICE
Also Called: Herbs License Service
407 W Main St (62234-3004)
PHONE.................................618 345-2047
Larry Hrabusicky, *Owner*
EMP: 5
SQ FT: 4,000
SALES (est): 639K **Privately Held**
SIC: 3556 7699 2599 Bakery machinery; restaurant equipment repair; carts, restaurant equipment

(G-6973)
QUALITY SAND COMPANY INC
1327 N Bluff Rd (62234-7301)
PHONE.................................618 346-1070
Tony O'Donnell, *President*
Tony O Donnell, *President*
Bob Zoelizer, *Treasurer*
EMP: 7 EST: 1963
SQ FT: 500
SALES (est): 621.4K
SALES (corp-wide): 404.4MM **Privately Held**
SIC: 1442 Construction sand mining; gravel mining
PA: Fred Weber, Inc.
2320 Creve Coeur Mill Rd
Maryland Heights MO 63043
314 344-0070

(G-6974)
RSN MAILING
1985 Raintree Trl (62234-4930)
PHONE.................................314 724-3364
John Hess, *Principal*
EMP: 2
SALES (est): 216.3K **Privately Held**
WEB: www.rsnmailing.com
SIC: 7331 2732 2759 Mailing service; textbooks: printing & binding, not publishing; commercial printing; advertising literature: printing

Colona
Henry County

(G-6975)
LAVENDER CREST WINERY
5401 Us Highway 6 (61241-8617)
PHONE.................................309 949-2565
Martha Rittmueller, *President*
Greg Backes, *Vice Pres*
Wilbert Rittemuller, *Treasurer*
Gina Backes, *Admin Sec*
EMP: 20
SALES (est): 500K **Privately Held**
SIC: 2084 Wines

(G-6976)
LEONARDS UNIT STEP OF MOLINE
Also Called: Unit Step Company
24415 Ridge Rd (61241-9064)
PHONE.................................309 792-9641
EMP: 2
SQ FT: 17,000
SALES (est): 302.4K **Privately Held**
SIC: 3272 3446 Precast Concrete Products & Ornamental Ironwork

(G-6977)
QUALITY TRUCKING INC
5715 Us Highway 6 (61241-8614)
PHONE.................................309 949-2021
Leah Garrison, *President*
Leah M Garrison, *President*
Randal W Garrison, *Admin Sec*
EMP: 2
SALES (est): 225.4K **Privately Held**
SIC: 3523 Farm machinery & equipment

(G-6978)
REXROAT SOUND
4531 W High St (61241-8721)
PHONE.................................309 764-1663
Scott Rexroat, *Owner*
Brandon Gustafson, *Administration*
Eric Kranz, *Technician*
EMP: 3 EST: 1999
SQ FT: 7,500
SALES (est): 405.5K **Privately Held**
SIC: 3651 5065 1731 7359 Sound reproducing equipment; sound equipment, electronic; sound equipment specialization; sound & lighting equipment rental

(G-6979)
ROCK RIVER ARMS INC
1042 Cleveland Rd (61241-8974)
PHONE.................................309 792-5780
Lester C Larson Jr, *President*
Sarah Larson, *General Mgr*
Chuck Larson, *Vice Pres*
Gay Larson, *Treasurer*
Tom Carbone, *Sales Staff*
▼ EMP: 60
SQ FT: 15,000
SALES (est): 13.9MM **Privately Held**
WEB: www.rockriverarms.com
SIC: 3484 5941 Guns (firearms) or gun parts, 30 mm. & below; sporting goods & bicycle shops

(G-6980)
SOUTHWICK MACHINE & DESIGN CO
21300 Briar Bluff Rd (61241)
P.O. Box 578 (61241-0578)
PHONE.................................309 949-2868
Robert Southwick, *President*
Peggy Southwick, *Admin Sec*
EMP: 3
SQ FT: 2,500
SALES: 270K **Privately Held**
SIC: 3444 3599 7692 1799 Sheet metalwork; machine & other job shop work; welding repair; welding on site

(G-6981)
T&J TURNING INC
4 Goembel Dr (61241-9081)
PHONE.................................309 738-8762
Anthony Lieving, *President*
Joanne Lieving, *Vice Pres*
EMP: 3

SALES (est): 236.3K **Privately Held**
SIC: 3541 Lathes

Columbia
Monroe County

(G-6982)
AAC MICROTEC NORTH AMERICA INC
5 Berry Patch Ln (62236-4325)
PHONE.................................602 284-7997
Mikael Andersson, *Ch of Bd*
Michael Carey, *President*
Mats Thideman, *Director*
EMP: 25
SALES (est): 1.6MM **Privately Held**
SIC: 3699 3769 Electrical equipment & supplies; guided missile & space vehicle parts & auxiliary equipment

(G-6983)
ACTION GRAPHICS AND SIGNS INC
8802 Summer Rd (62236-3502)
PHONE.................................618 939-5755
Jane Kolmer, *President*
EMP: 4
SQ FT: 3,000
SALES: 500K **Privately Held**
SIC: 3993 Signs & advertising specialties

(G-6984)
B&H MACHINE INC
251 Southwoods Ctr Ste 1 (62236-2493)
P.O. Box 626 (62236-0626)
PHONE.................................618 281-3737
Robert D Wooters, *President*
Len Shields, *General Mgr*
Eric Wooters, *Vice Pres*
Christine Wooters, *Treasurer*
EMP: 10
SQ FT: 3,600
SALES (est): 1.4MM **Privately Held**
SIC: 3953 3544 Printing dies, rubber or plastic, for marking machines; special dies, tools, jigs & fixtures

(G-6985)
BESTWORDS ORG CORP
8934 Trolley Rd (62236-3422)
P.O. Box 202 (62236-0202)
PHONE.................................618 939-4324
EMP: 2 EST: 2000
SALES: 200K **Privately Held**
SIC: 2731 Books-Publishing/Printing

(G-6986)
BUDNICK CONVERTING INC
Also Called: Budnick Supply
340 Parkway Dr (62236-2791)
P.O. Box 197 (62236-0197)
PHONE.................................618 281-8090
Ann Wegmann, *President*
Chris Kenner, *General Mgr*
Chris Schoentag, *Plant Mgr*
Eric White, *Opers Mgr*
Tom Belcher, *Engineer*
▲ EMP: 110
SQ FT: 48,000
SALES (est): 46.8MM **Privately Held**
WEB: www.budnick.com
SIC: 2672 Masking tape: made from purchased materials

(G-6987)
COLUMBIA QUARRY COMPANY (PA)
210 State Route 158 (62236-3241)
P.O. Box 18 (62236-0018)
PHONE.................................618 281-7631
Charles H Krause Jr, *Ch of Bd*
Klyde Trexler, *President*
R L Trexler, *President*
Bill Groh, *Superintendent*
John Schmidt, *Treasurer*
EMP: 20 EST: 1906
SQ FT: 7,000
SALES (est): 6.5MM **Privately Held**
WEB: www.columbiaquarry.com
SIC: 1411 Dimension stone

GEOGRAPHIC SECTION

(G-6988)
COMPUTER PWR SOLUTIONS ILL LTD
Also Called: CPSI
235 Southwoods Ctr (62236-2466)
P.O. Box 108 (62236-0108)
PHONE..................................618 281-8898
Michelle Elia, *President*
Justin Elia, *Sales Staff*
Gay Sherman, *Sales Staff*
Aziz Elia, *Technology*
Joe Dobronski, *Director*
▼ **EMP:** 26
SQ FT: 10,000
SALES (est): 3.8MM **Privately Held**
SIC: 7371 7379 7372 7373 Computer software development; computer related consulting services; prepackaged software; publishers' computer software; application computer software; systems software development services

(G-6989)
CONTEMPORARY MARBLE INC
Also Called: McCarty's Contemporary Marble
8533 Hanover Indus Dr (62236-4635)
PHONE..................................618 281-6200
Harold McCarty, *President*
Donna McCarty, *President*
EMP: 4
SQ FT: 12,000
SALES (est): 501K **Privately Held**
SIC: 3281 Bathroom fixtures, cut stone

(G-6990)
KELLYJO MAKES SCENTS
3050 Steppig Rd (62236-4106)
PHONE..................................618 281-4241
EMP: 3 **EST:** 2015
SALES (est): 150.1K **Privately Held**
SIC: 2844 Mfg Toilet Preparations

(G-6991)
NOOTER/ERIKSEN INC
3014 Croatia Dr (62236-4175)
PHONE..................................636 651-1028
Kevin McGill, *Principal*
EMP: 3
SALES (est): 118.7K **Privately Held**
SIC: 3511 Turbines & turbine generator sets

(G-6992)
ORNAMENTAL IRON SHOP
148 Hill Castle Dr (62236-4542)
PHONE..................................618 281-6072
Chris Shaw, *Owner*
EMP: 3 **EST:** 2008
SALES (est): 202.6K **Privately Held**
WEB: www.ornairon.com
SIC: 7299 5211 3446 1799 Home improvement & renovation contractor agency; railings, railings, bannisters, guards, etc.: made from metal pipe; ornamental metal work

(G-6993)
ORTHO-CLINICAL DIAGNOSTICS INC
8 Briarhill Ln (62236-1004)
PHONE..................................618 281-3882
Kathy Bursak, *President*
EMP: 200
SALES (corp-wide): 556.7MM **Privately Held**
WEB: www.orthoclinical.com
SIC: 2835 Blood derivative diagnostic agents
PA: Ortho-Clinical Diagnostics, Inc.
1001 Route 202
Raritan NJ 08869
908 218-8000

(G-6994)
TOWER ROCK STONE COMPANY (PA)
250 W Sand Bank Rd (62236-1044)
P.O. Box 50 (62236-0050)
PHONE..................................618 281-4106
Jay Luhr, *President*
Rodney Linker, *Vice Pres*
Michael Luhr, *Vice Pres*
Sheryl Metzger, *Treasurer*
Tammy Duffy, *Info Tech Dir*
EMP: 10
SQ FT: 25,000
SALES: 41MM **Privately Held**
SIC: 1422 Crushed & broken limestone

(G-6995)
TRUSS COMPONENTS INC (PA)
607 N Main St Ste 100 (62236-1462)
PHONE..................................800 678-7877
Mary P Keller, *President*
EMP: 12
SQ FT: 26,000
SALES (est): 2.8MM **Privately Held**
SIC: 2439 Trusses, wooden roof

Compton
Lee County

(G-6996)
JAMES HOWARD CO
623 W Chestnut St (61318-9504)
P.O. Box 200 (61318-0200)
PHONE..................................815 497-2831
James Mc Innis, *Owner*
Howard Mc Innis, *Co-Owner*
Jim McInnis, *Sales Staff*
Karen Hamilton, *Manager*
EMP: 5
SQ FT: 6,000
SALES (est): 567.6K **Privately Held**
WEB: www.jameshowardco.com
SIC: 5199 2531 3952 Artists' materials; school furniture; lead pencils & art goods

(G-6997)
LOTUS CREATIVE INNOVATIONS LLC
970 Melugins Grove Rd (61318-9727)
PHONE..................................815 440-8999
Ashish Gavali, *President*
Delsie Gavili, *President*
EMP: 4
SALES (est): 250K **Privately Held**
SIC: 3542 Machine tools, metal forming type

Concord
Morgan County

(G-6998)
M & F FABRICATION & WELDING
2243 Mud Creek Rd (62631-5026)
PHONE..................................217 457-2221
EMP: 3
SALES (est): 140K **Privately Held**
SIC: 7692 Welding Repair

Congerville
Woodford County

(G-6999)
HEARTLAND FABRICATION LLC
210 W Lantz St (61729-9539)
P.O. Box 9 (61729-0009)
PHONE..................................309 448-2644
Rodney L Wiegand,
EMP: 5
SALES (est): 711.1K **Privately Held**
SIC: 3441 3444 Fabricated structural metal; boat & barge sections, prefabricated metal; booths, spray: prefabricated sheet metal

(G-7000)
PREMIER FABRICATION LLC
303 County Highway 8 (61729-9511)
P.O. Box 36 (61729-0036)
PHONE..................................309 448-2338
Scott Aberle, *President*
Dale Eastman, *Opers Staff*
Steve Grimes, *Director*
▲ **EMP:** 120
SQ FT: 75,000
SALES: 19MM **Privately Held**
SIC: 3441 Fabricated structural metal

(G-7001)
R & S STEEL CORPORATION
301 W Washington St (61729-9745)
P.O. Box 8 (61729-0008)
PHONE..................................309 448-2645
Randy Phelps, *President*
Susan Phelps, *Treasurer*
EMP: 2
SQ FT: 9,000
SALES: 350K **Privately Held**
SIC: 3599 Machine shop, jobbing & repair

(G-7002)
RESIDENTIAL STEEL SERVICES
315 County Highway 8 (61729-9511)
PHONE..................................309 448-2900
Daniel J Bauman, *President*
EMP: 2
SQ FT: 6,500
SALES: 800K **Privately Held**
SIC: 3312 Structural shapes & pilings, steel

(G-7003)
RIVER VIEW MOTOR SPORTS INC
1792 Hillside Rd (61729-9552)
PHONE..................................309 467-4569
James Ely, *Owner*
EMP: 3 **EST:** 2001
SALES (est): 332.1K **Privately Held**
SIC: 3647 7011 Motorcycle lamps; motor inn

Cooksville
Mclean County

(G-7004)
WISSMILLER & EVANS ROAD EQP
Also Called: Wissmiller Welding
102 S Jeffrey St (61730-7534)
P.O. Box 81 (61730-0081)
PHONE..................................309 725-3598
Joseph Wissmiller, *President*
Lori Wissmiller, *Admin Sec*
EMP: 3
SALES: 600K **Privately Held**
SIC: 5251 7692 5082 1799 Snowblowers; welding repair; road construction equipment; welding on site

Cordova
Rock Island County

(G-7005)
3M COMPANY
22614 Route 84 N (61242-9799)
PHONE..................................309 654-2291
Jean Sweeney, *Vice Pres*
Kipp Troutman, *Buyer*
Andy Isenhour, *QC Dir*
Greg Carpenter, *Engineer*
Daniel Johnson, *Regl Sales Mgr*
EMP: 332
SALES (corp-wide): 32.1B **Publicly Held**
SIC: 3841 Surgical instruments & apparatus
PA: 3m Company
3m Center
Saint Paul MN 55144
651 733-1110

(G-7006)
FRYER TO FUEL INC
26700 171st Ave N (61242-9666)
PHONE..................................309 654-2875
Harold A Coers, *President*
▲ **EMP:** 5
SALES (est): 710.5K **Privately Held**
SIC: 3569 Filters

(G-7007)
GOLDEN VALLEY HARDSCAPES LLC
18715 Route 84 N (61242-9757)
PHONE..................................309 654-2261
Thomas Messer, *Principal*
EMP: 2

SALES (est): 218.3K **Privately Held**
SIC: 2499 5154 Mulch or sawdust products, wood; livestock

(G-7008)
MATCON MANUFACTURING INC
15509 Route 84 N (61242-9002)
P.O. Box 437, Port Byron (61275-0437)
PHONE..................................309 755-1020
Donn Larson, *President*
EMP: 40
SALES (est): 4MM **Privately Held**
SIC: 3312 Structural shapes & pilings, steel

(G-7009)
MATERIAL CONTROL SYSTEMS INC
Also Called: Matcon 2
15509 Route 84 N (61242-9002)
PHONE..................................309 654-9031
Judy Scott, *Branch Mgr*
EMP: 7
SALES (corp-wide): 28.7MM **Privately Held**
SIC: 5099 2542 Containers: glass, metal or plastic; racks, merchandise display or storage: except wood
PA: Material Control Systems, Inc.
375 36th St
East Moline IL 61244
309 523-3774

(G-7010)
MELYX INC (PA)
Also Called: Xylem
18715 Route 84 N (61242-9757)
PHONE..................................309 654-2551
Charles Dornfeld, *President*
▲ **EMP:** 10
SQ FT: 1,200
SALES (est): 4.7MM **Privately Held**
SIC: 2499 Mulch, wood & bark

(G-7011)
WESTWAY FEED PRODUCTS LLC
Also Called: Westway Trading
22220 Route 84 N (61242-9664)
PHONE..................................309 654-2211
Steve Pohlmaier, *Manager*
EMP: 15
SALES (corp-wide): 8.1B **Privately Held**
SIC: 2048 2061 Feed supplements; raw cane sugar
HQ: Westway Feed Products Llc
365 Canal St Ste 2929
New Orleans LA 70130
504 934-1850

Cornell
Livingston County

(G-7012)
DICKS CUSTOM CABINET SHOP
202 W Main St (61319)
P.O. Box 148 (61319-0148)
PHONE..................................815 358-2663
Richard Leonard, *Owner*
EMP: 5
SQ FT: 5,600
SALES (est): 540.2K **Privately Held**
SIC: 5712 2511 2434 Cabinet work, custom; wood household furniture; wood kitchen cabinets

(G-7013)
LAFEBER DISTRIBUTION LLC
24981 N 1400 East Rd (61319-9770)
PHONE..................................630 524-4845
Christine Davis, *Managing Dir*
EMP: 3
SALES: 1.1MM **Privately Held**
SIC: 2048 5149 5199 Feed supplements; pet foods; pets & pet supplies; pet supplies

(G-7014)
VALLEY VIEW INDUSTRIES INC (PA)
7551e 2500 N Rd (61319)
PHONE..................................815 358-2236
Richard Hatzer, *President*

Cortland - Dekalb County (G-7015)

Bonnie Oneill, *Exec VP*
Bill Kenney, *Vice Pres*
Joan Mullen, *Vice Pres*
William Kenney, *Treasurer*
EMP: 30 **EST:** 1951
SALES (est): 3.8MM **Privately Held**
WEB: www.valleyviewindustries.com
SIC: 4213 4212 1422 Trucking, except local; local trucking, without storage; lime rock, ground

Cortland
Dekalb County

(G-7015)
ACE MACHINE & TOOL INC
Also Called: Cnc / Machine Shop
300 W Lincoln Hwy Ste 6 (60112-7918)
PHONE.................................815 793-5077
Elissa Jarke, *Owner*
Ronald Jarke, *Co-Owner*
EMP: 5
SALES (est): 192.5K **Privately Held**
WEB: www.acemachinetoolinc.com
SIC: 3559 7389 Automotive related machinery;

(G-7016)
ALEXANDER LUMBER CO
Also Called: Coutland Components
160 S Loves Rd (60112-4038)
PHONE.................................815 754-1000
Robert Fitz Gerarld, *Manager*
EMP: 5 **Privately Held**
WEB: www.alexlbr.com
SIC: 2439 5211 Trusses, except roof: laminated lumber; lumber products
HQ: Alexander Lumber Co.
515 Redwood Dr
Aurora IL 60506
630 844-5123

(G-7017)
ALFREDOS IRON WORKS INC
280 W Lincoln Hwy (60112-8420)
PHONE.................................815 748-1177
Luis A De La Cruz, *President*
EMP: 23
SQ FT: 4,037
SALES: 325K **Privately Held**
SIC: 3446 1791 1799 3441 Architectural metalwork; structural steel erection; iron work, structural; fence construction; ornamental metal work; fabricated structural metal

(G-7018)
CUSTOM STONE WORKS INC
165 W Stephenie Dr (60112-4081)
PHONE.................................815 748-2109
Betty Lindgren, *President*
EMP: 32
SQ FT: 17,500
SALES (est): 5.2MM **Privately Held**
WEB: www.customstoneworks.net
SIC: 3272 Concrete products

(G-7019)
CUSTOM STONE WRKS ACQSTION INC
165 W Stephenie Dr (60112-4081)
PHONE.................................630 669-1119
Jamie Bastone, *Principal*
EMP: 5
SALES (est): 570.4K **Privately Held**
SIC: 3281 Cut stone & stone products

(G-7020)
DUN-RITE TOOL & MACHINE CO
Also Called: Dun-Rite Tooling
55 W Lincoln Hwy (60112-4078)
PHONE.................................815 758-5464
Jack Cress, *CEO*
John Connor, *President*
Ryan Butzman, *General Mgr*
Ron Weihofen, *Materials Mgr*
Mark Anderson, *Engineer*
EMP: 30 **EST:** 1964
SQ FT: 30,000
SALES (est): 10MM **Privately Held**
WEB: www.dun-rite.com
SIC: 3531 3589 5072 Crushers, grinders & similar equipment; shredders, industrial & commercial; power tools & accessories

(G-7021)
JOHNSON SEAT & CANVAS SHOP
25 S Somonauk Rd (60112-4147)
P.O. Box 548 (60112-0548)
PHONE.................................815 756-2037
Fred Johnson, *President*
Fred F Johnson, *Vice Pres*
EMP: 8 **EST:** 1947
SQ FT: 5,000
SALES: 490K **Privately Held**
WEB: www.johnsoncanvas.com
SIC: 2394 Awnings, fabric: made from purchased materials

(G-7022)
JUST PARTS INC (PA)
121 W Elm Ave (60112-4023)
PHONE.................................815 756-2184
David N Waters, *President*
▲ **EMP:** 7
SQ FT: 15,000
SALES (est): 1.1MM **Privately Held**
SIC: 3714 5013 Motor vehicle electrical equipment; automotive supplies & parts

(G-7023)
KRIESE MFG
231 N Juniper St (60112-4132)
PHONE.................................815 748-2683
Patrick Kriese, *President*
Wendy Kriese, *Vice Pres*
EMP: 2
SALES (est): 271.9K **Privately Held**
SIC: 3548 3999 Welding & cutting apparatus & accessories; manufacturing industries

(G-7024)
MICHAEL BURZA
Also Called: AM PM Printers
122 E Meadow Dr (60112-4136)
P.O. Box 267 (60112-0267)
PHONE.................................815 909-0233
Michael Burza, *Principal*
EMP: 2
SALES (est): 215.6K **Privately Held**
SIC: 2752 Commercial printing, lithographic

(G-7025)
NATURAL POLYMERS LLC
14438 E North Ave (60112)
PHONE.................................888 563-3111
Benjamin Brown, *President*
EMP: 5
SALES (est): 1.9MM **Privately Held**
SIC: 2821 Polyurethane resins

(G-7026)
POWER EQUIPMENT COMPANY
211 W Stephenie Dr (60112-4082)
PHONE.................................815 754-4090
David E Olson, *President*
David H Olson, *President*
Richard Olson, *Vice Pres*
Mary McKnight, *Marketing Staff*
Jon Brennan, *Manager*
EMP: 22
SQ FT: 28,000
SALES (est): 21.8MM **Privately Held**
WEB: www.peco1948.com
SIC: 5083 3679 Lawn & garden machinery & equipment; electronic loads & power supplies

(G-7027)
SUNNY DAY DISTRIBUTING INC
76 E Meadow Dr (60112-4137)
PHONE.................................630 779-8466
Jim Cunningham, *President*
EMP: 1 **EST:** 2015
SALES (est): 500K **Privately Held**
SIC: 2099 Tortillas, fresh or refrigerated

Cottage Hills
Madison County

(G-7028)
GM SCRAP METALS
220 Franklin Ave (62018-1273)
PHONE.................................618 259-8570
Margaret Ivanuck, *Owner*
Paul Ivanuck, *Manager*
EMP: 5
SALES (est): 462.5K **Privately Held**
SIC: 5093 4953 3341 Ferrous metal scrap & waste; recycling, waste materials; secondary nonferrous metals

Coulterville
Randolph County

(G-7029)
BRIAN HOBBS
Also Called: Handy Helper Fencing
207 E Mill St (62237-1741)
PHONE.................................618 758-1303
Brian Hobbs, *Owner*
EMP: 1
SALES (est): 230K **Privately Held**
SIC: 3446 Fences, gates, posts & flagpoles

(G-7030)
CORRPAK INC
Also Called: Fabcorr
1231 State Route 13 (62237-3326)
PHONE.................................618 758-2755
Tom Talbert, *Manager*
EMP: 3
SALES (corp-wide): 3.4MM **Privately Held**
SIC: 3444 Sheet metalwork
PA: Corrpak, Inc.
719 Spirit 40 Park Dr
Chesterfield MO 63005
636 537-2885

(G-7031)
GATEWAY NORTH MINE
12968 State Route 13 (62237-1112)
PHONE.................................618 758-1515
EMP: 6
SALES (est): 371.5K **Privately Held**
WEB: www.peabodyenergy.com
SIC: 1222 Bituminous coal-underground mining

(G-7032)
HNRC DISSOLUTION CO
12626 Sarah Rd (62237-1916)
PHONE.................................618 758-4501
EMP: 250
SALES (corp-wide): 405.9MM **Privately Held**
SIC: 1221 Bituminous Coal/Lignite Surface Mining
PA: Hnrc Dissolution Co
201 E Main St 100
Lexington KY 40507
606 327-5450

(G-7033)
PEABODY COAL COMPANY
Also Called: Gateway Mine
13101 Zeigler 11 Rd (62237-2046)
PHONE.................................618 758-2395
Greg Boyce, *Branch Mgr*
EMP: 197
SALES (corp-wide): 4.6B **Publicly Held**
WEB: www.peabodyenergy.com
SIC: 1221 Bituminous coal & lignite-surface mining
HQ: Peabody Coal Company
701 Market St
Saint Louis MO 63101
314 342-3400

(G-7034)
PEABODY COULTERVILLE MIN LLC
13101 Zeigler 11 Rd (62237-2046)
PHONE.................................618 758-3597
K L Wagner, *Mng Member*

Wagner Kl, *Mng Member*
Tichenor J A,
Hathhorn ME,
Quinn Jf,
EMP: 3
SALES (est): 172.5K **Privately Held**
SIC: 1221 Bituminous coal & lignite-surface mining

Country Club Hills
Cook County

(G-7035)
AMITY HOSPITAL SERVICES INC
4921 173rd St Ste 2 (60478-2026)
PHONE.................................708 206-3970
Edward Button, *President*
EMP: 4
SQ FT: 2,500
SALES: 400K **Privately Held**
SIC: 3821 7699 5999 Sterilizers; hospital equipment repair services; hospital equipment & supplies

(G-7036)
COACHING FOR EXCELLENCE LLC
Also Called: Coaching For Excelence
4131 191st Pl (60478-5803)
PHONE.................................708 957-6047
Nicolette Bautista, *Vice Pres*
Michele Vesely, *Opers Staff*
Susan Gnesa, *Controller*
Greg Cadger, *Accountant*
Craig Jones, *Marketing Staff*
EMP: 10
SALES (est): 602.6K **Privately Held**
SIC: 8748 8742 8322 2731 Safety training service; training & development consultant; family counseling services; family (marriage) counseling; general counseling services; book publishing;

(G-7037)
COOK JV PRINTING
4061 183rd St (60478-5306)
PHONE.................................708 799-0007
J Cook, *Principal*
EMP: 10
SALES (est): 1.2MM **Privately Held**
SIC: 2752 Commercial printing, offset

(G-7038)
DA CLOSET
4139 167th St (60478-2035)
PHONE.................................708 206-1414
Dorron Neely, *Principal*
EMP: 5 **EST:** 2009
SALES (est): 615K **Privately Held**
SIC: 2329 Knickers, dress (separate): men's & boys'

(G-7039)
GREAT LAKES LIFTING
4910 Wilshire Blvd (60478-3153)
PHONE.................................815 931-4825
Don Brooks, *Owner*
Mitch Valenti, *Manager*
John Hensley, *Consultant*
Kevin Obrien, *Consultant*
EMP: 5
SALES (est): 631.5K **Privately Held**
WEB: www.greatlakeslifting.com
SIC: 3272 Building materials, except block or brick: concrete

(G-7040)
HARTS TOP AND CABINET SHOP
Also Called: Harts Top Shop
4941 173rd St Ste 1 (60478-2030)
PHONE.................................708 957-4666
Kenneth Hartsfield, *Owner*
EMP: 5
SQ FT: 8,000
SALES (est): 675K **Privately Held**
SIC: 2541 5211 Table or counter tops, plastic laminated; cabinets, kitchen

GEOGRAPHIC SECTION

Countryside - Cook County (G-7068)

(G-7041)
IODON INC
18610 John Ave (60478-5298)
P.O. Box 21, Dolton (60419-0021)
PHONE..................................708 799-4062
Iona J Boersma, *President*
EMP: 3
SALES (est): 365.3K **Privately Held**
SIC: 3432 Plumbing fixture fittings & trim

(G-7042)
MIDWEST SIGN & LIGHTING INC
4910 Wilshire Blvd (60478-3153)
PHONE..................................708 365-5555
Billy Don Brooks, *President*
Frank Nielson, *Vice Pres*
EMP: 7
SQ FT: 3,000
SALES (est): 1MM **Privately Held**
SIC: 3993 3648 2752 Signs & advertising specialties; lighting equipment; commercial printing, lithographic

Countryside
Cook County

(G-7043)
AIRGAS USA LLC
5235 9th Ave (60525-3629)
PHONE..................................708 354-0813
Veronica Caljkusic, *Branch Mgr*
EMP: 23
SALES (corp-wide): 129.8MM **Privately Held**
WEB: www.airgas.com
SIC: 5169 5047 2813 Industrial gases; medical & hospital equipment; industrial gases
HQ: Airgas Usa, Llc
  259 N Radnor Chester Rd
  Radnor PA 19087
  610 687-5253

(G-7044)
BARE DEVELOPMENT INC
Also Called: Golf Trucks
5425 9th Ave (60525-3604)
PHONE..................................708 352-2273
William Moldenhauer, *President*
Theresa Demetry, *Vice Pres*
Jefferey Mielkey, *Treasurer*
EMP: 10
SALES (est): 3MM **Privately Held**
WEB: www.baredevelopment.com
SIC: 3674 Light emitting diodes

(G-7045)
BO INC
10725 Forestview Rd (60525-4701)
PHONE..................................312 459-0013
Bojan Grubjesic, *Principal*
EMP: 10
SALES (est): 411.2K **Privately Held**
SIC: 3537 Trucks: freight, baggage, etc.: industrial, except mining

(G-7046)
CHICAGO CHAIN AND TRANSM CO (PA)
650 E Plainfield Rd (60525-6914)
P.O. Box 705, La Grange (60525-0705)
PHONE..................................630 482-9000
James D Schwarz, *President*
Ron Triska, *Vice Pres*
Scott Walis, *Vice Pres*
Carrie Guinta, *Controller*
Keith Clayton, *Sales Staff*
EMP: 20
SQ FT: 17,500
SALES (est): 11.6MM **Privately Held**
WEB: www.chicagochain.com
SIC: 5085 5084 5063 3535 Power transmission equipment & apparatus; bearings, bushings, wheels & gears; industrial machinery & equipment; electrical apparatus & equipment; conveyors & conveying equipment

(G-7047)
CONTAINER HDLG SYSTEMS CORP
621 E Plainfield Rd (60525-6913)
PHONE..................................708 482-9900
John C Nalbach, *President*
Jerry E Norbut, *Vice Pres*
Jerry Norbut, *VP Sales*
David Haskell, *Manager*
EMP: 46
SQ FT: 22,000
SALES (est): 13.7MM **Privately Held**
SIC: 3535 Conveyors & conveying equipment

(G-7048)
COOPERS HAWK INTRMDATE HLDG LL
430 E Plainfield Rd (60525-6910)
PHONE..................................708 215-5674
EMP: 13
SALES (corp-wide): 246.9MM **Privately Held**
SIC: 8741 2084 5182 5812 Restaurant management; wines; wine; eating places
PA: Cooper's Hawk Intermediate Holding, Llc
  3500 Lacey Rd Ste 1000
  Downers Grove IL 60515
  708 839-2920

(G-7049)
COOPERS HAWK PRODUCTION LLC
430 E Plainfield Rd (60525-6910)
PHONE..................................708 839-2920
Dee Sortino, *CFO*
▲ EMP: 6
SALES (est): 835.5K **Privately Held**
SALES (corp-wide): 246.9MM **Privately Held**
SIC: 2084 Wines
PA: Cooper's Hawk Intermediate Holding, Llc
  3500 Lacey Rd Ste 1000
  Downers Grove IL 60515
  708 839-2920

(G-7050)
DADO LIGHTING LLC
5446 Dansher Rd (60525-3126)
PHONE..................................877 323-6584
David Doubek, *President*
EMP: 5 EST: 2017
SALES (est): 649K **Privately Held**
SIC: 3646 Commercial indusl & institutional electric lighting fixtures

(G-7051)
EAGLE SCREEN PRINT INDS INC
5326 East Ave (60525-3134)
PHONE..................................708 579-0454
Mahendra Patel, *President*
EMP: 15
SQ FT: 9,300
SALES (est): 1.5MM **Privately Held**
SIC: 2759 Screen printing

(G-7052)
FGFI LLC
411 E Plainfield Rd (60525-6909)
PHONE..................................708 598-0909
Kathy Formella, *Mng Member*
EMP: 38
SALES (est): 2.2MM **Privately Held**
SIC: 2079 2035 Cooking oils, except corn: vegetable refined; seasonings & sauces, except tomato & dry

(G-7053)
G BLANDO JEWELERS INC
Also Called: Blando's Marry ME Jewelry
3 Countryside Plz (60525-3980)
PHONE..................................630 627-7963
Gino Blando, *President*
EMP: 4
SQ FT: 3,000
SALES (est): 865K **Privately Held**
SIC: 5944 3911 Jewelry, precious stones & precious metals; jewelry, precious metal

(G-7054)
GALL MACHINE CO
9640 Joliet Rd (60525-4138)
PHONE..................................708 352-2800
John G Harper, *President*
John A Harper, *Vice Pres*
Tiffiney K Harper, *Treasurer*
Mary C Harper, *Admin Sec*
EMP: 10
SQ FT: 15,000
SALES (est): 2MM **Privately Held**
SIC: 3496 Miscellaneous fabricated wire products

(G-7055)
GOODCO PRODUCTS LLC
6688 Joliet Rd Ste 185 (60525-4575)
PHONE..................................630 258-6384
Jonathan Bradley, *Sales Dir*
Jon Bradley,
EMP: 4
SQ FT: 1,000
SALES (est): 533.9K **Privately Held**
SIC: 3421 3089 5199 Table cutlery, except with handles of metal; clothespins, plastic; matches

(G-7056)
HOGAN WOODWORK INC
5328 East Ave (60525-3134)
PHONE..................................708 354-4525
Martin Hogan, *President*
Joyce Hogan, *Admin Sec*
EMP: 6
SQ FT: 6,200
SALES: 800K **Privately Held**
SIC: 2431 Doors & door parts & trim, wood

(G-7057)
HOLLYMATIC CORPORATION
600 E Plainfield Rd (60525-6900)
PHONE..................................708 579-3700
James D Azzar, *President*
Marilyn Krische, *General Mgr*
Bruce Buchholtz, *Sales Staff*
▲ EMP: 55
SQ FT: 55,000
SALES (est): 29MM **Privately Held**
WEB: www.hollymatic.com
SIC: 5113 3556 2672 Industrial & personal service paper; meat processing machinery; mixers, commercial, food; grinders, commercial, food; sausage stuffers; coated & laminated paper

(G-7058)
HONEY FLUFF DOUGHNUTS
6566 Joliet Rd (60525-4649)
PHONE..................................708 579-1826
Vimala Gupta, *President*
EMP: 3
SQ FT: 1,000
SALES (est): 147.5K **Privately Held**
SIC: 5461 2051 Doughnuts; doughnuts, except frozen

(G-7059)
HOUSE OF COLOR
9912 W 55th St (60525-3612)
PHONE..................................708 352-3222
Donald Musillami, *Owner*
EMP: 10
SALES (est): 841K **Privately Held**
SIC: 2499 5039 Picture & mirror frames, wood; glass construction materials

(G-7060)
INFINITY COMMUNICATIONS GROUP
Also Called: Infinity Signs
5350 East Ave (60525-3134)
PHONE..................................708 352-1086
Brian Lappin, *President*
Russell Nicoletti, *Vice Pres*
EMP: 10
SQ FT: 10,000
SALES (est): 1.4MM **Privately Held**
SIC: 3993 Signs & advertising specialties

(G-7061)
JEWEL OSCO INC
Also Called: Jewel-Osco 3154
5545 S Brainard Ave (60525-3542)
PHONE..................................708 352-0120
Mary Pruzs, *President*
EMP: 225
SALES (corp-wide): 60.5B **Privately Held**
SIC: 5411 2051 Supermarkets, chain; bread, cake & related products
HQ: Jewel Osco, Inc.
  150 E Pierce Rd Ste 200
  Itasca IL 60143
  630 948-6000

(G-7062)
JOHN R NALBACH ENGRG CO INC
621 E Plainfield Rd (60525-6913)
PHONE..................................708 579-9100
John C Nalbach, *President*
Phil Testa, *VP Mfg*
Tony Anton, *Purchasing*
Kevin Loeb, *Engineer*
David Nowaczyk, *Project Engr*
EMP: 23 EST: 1945
SQ FT: 74,000
SALES (est): 7.3MM **Privately Held**
WEB: www.nalbach.com
SIC: 3565 Packing & wrapping machinery

(G-7063)
MAK DESIGN GROUP INCORPORATED
1023 W 55th St Ste A (60525-6544)
PHONE..................................847 682-4504
Robert Byrne, *President*
▲ EMP: 3
SALES (est): 299.4K **Privately Held**
WEB: www.makdesigngroup.net
SIC: 3083 Laminated plastic sheets

(G-7064)
MINUTEMAN PRESS OF COUNTRYSIDE
6566 Joliet Rd (60525-4649)
PHONE..................................708 354-2190
Christopher Zurowski, *President*
Julie Zurowski, *Vice Pres*
Veronica Zurowski, *Treasurer*
George Zurowski, *Shareholder*
EMP: 4
SQ FT: 1,000
SALES (est): 480K **Privately Held**
SIC: 2752 Commercial printing, lithographic

(G-7065)
MITSUBISHI ELECTRIC US INC
Also Called: Mitsubshi Elevators Escalators
5218 Dansher Rd (60525-3122)
PHONE..................................708 354-2900
Kirk R Maier, *Sales Staff*
Jared Elfvin, *Manager*
EMP: 30 **Privately Held**
WEB: www.mitsubishielectric-usa.com
SIC: 3534 Elevators & equipment; escalators, passenger & freight
HQ: Mitsubishi Electric Us, Inc.
  5900 Katella Ave Ste A
  Cypress CA 90630
  714 220-2500

(G-7066)
NAZDAR SOURCEONE
5444 East Ave Ste B (60525-3671)
PHONE..................................800 677-4657
Jay Thrall, *CEO*
EMP: 3 EST: 2015
SALES (est): 215.4K **Privately Held**
SIC: 3571 Electronic computers

(G-7067)
PELSTAR LLC
Also Called: Health O Meter Professional
9500 W 55th St Ste C (60525-7110)
PHONE..................................708 377-0600
Ken Harris, *Vice Pres*
Lindsay Carroll, *Opers Staff*
Julie Ivanoff, *Marketing Mgr*
Dan J Maeir,
◆ EMP: 20
SQ FT: 160,000
SALES (est): 5.6MM **Privately Held**
WEB: www.homscales.com
SIC: 3596 Scales & balances, except laboratory

(G-7068)
ROLLSTOCK INC
600 E Plainfield Rd (60525-6914)
PHONE..................................708 579-3700
James D Azzar, *President*
EMP: 6
SALES (est): 830.7K **Privately Held**
SIC: 3565 Packaging machinery

Countryside - Cook County (G-7069)

(G-7069)
SHIRT PRINTING 4U INC
5410 S La Grange Rd Ste 1 (60525-3146)
PHONE..................................708 588-8272
Michael McHenry, *President*
EMP: 2
SALES (est): 220.8K **Privately Held**
SIC: 2759 Screen printing

(G-7070)
SKI SEAL COATING INC
7100 Pleasantdale Dr (60525-5071)
PHONE..................................708 246-5656
Richard Zwolinski, *President*
EMP: 6
SALES (est): 1MM **Privately Held**
SIC: 2891 Adhesives & sealants

(G-7071)
SOKOL AND COMPANY
5315 Dansher Rd (60525-3192)
PHONE..................................708 482-8250
John S Novak Jr, *President*
Desiree Mendoza, *Buyer*
Michael Novak, *Engineer*
Mathew McNulty, *CFO*
John Decarlo, *Sales Mgr*
◆ EMP: 100 EST: 1907
SQ FT: 110,000
SALES (est): 44.5MM **Privately Held**
WEB: www.solofoods.com
SIC: 2099 2033 5149 2091 Cake fillings, except fruit; peanut butter; spaghetti & other pasta sauce: packaged in cans, jars, etc.; jams, jellies & preserves: packaged in cans, jars, etc.; sauces; canned & cured fish & seafoods

(G-7072)
SOLO FOODS
5315 Dansher Rd (60525-3101)
PHONE..................................800 328-7656
John A Sokol, *Principal*
Courtney Kowalski, *Buyer*
Michael Morris, *CFO*
Shannon Pimmel, *Manager*
Antonio Marungo, *Technical Staff*
EMP: 3 EST: 2012
SALES (est): 246K **Privately Held**
SIC: 2099 Desserts, ready-to-mix

(G-7073)
SUPREME SCREW PRODUCTS
5227 Dansher Rd (60525-3123)
PHONE..................................708 579-3500
EMP: 3 EST: 2013
SALES (est): 192.4K **Privately Held**
SIC: 3451 Screw machine products

(G-7074)
T & H LEMONT INC
5118 Dansher Rd (60525-6906)
PHONE..................................708 482-1800
Michael Strand, *President*
Gary Seebert, *Treasurer*
Walter Heller Sr, *VP Sales*
Lawrence A Krupnik, *Admin Sec*
▲ EMP: 80
SQ FT: 68,000
SALES (est): 17.2MM
SALES (corp-wide): 713.4MM **Privately Held**
SIC: 3544 3325 Special dies & tools; steel foundries
PA: Rowan Technologies, Inc.
    10 Indel Ave
    Rancocas NJ 08073
    609 267-9000

(G-7075)
TRU VUE INC (HQ)
9400 W 55th St (60525-3636)
PHONE..................................708 485-5080
Jane Boyce, *President*
Kevin Thornton, *COO*
Tim Culhane, *Vice Pres*
Joe Maxwell, *Vice Pres*
Erik Wilson, *Prdtn Mgr*
◆ EMP: 110
SQ FT: 300,000
SALES (est): 61.4MM
SALES (corp-wide): 1.3B **Publicly Held**
WEB: www.tru-vue.com
SIC: 3211 3496 Picture glass; mats & matting

PA: Apogee Enterprises, Inc.
    4400 W 78th St Ste 520
    Minneapolis MN 55435
    952 835-1874

(G-7076)
VEE PAK LLC
5321 Dansher Rd (60525-3125)
PHONE..................................708 482-8881
Scott Almquist, *CEO*
EMP: 20
SALES (corp-wide): 27.4MM **Privately Held**
SIC: 2844 Cosmetic preparations
HQ: Vee Pak, Llc
    6710 River Rd
    Hodgkins IL 60525
    708 482-8881

(G-7077)
VINYL GRAPHICS INC
Also Called: Sign-A-Rama
35 E Plainfield Rd Ste 2 (60525-3086)
PHONE..................................708 579-1234
Shibu Kurian, *President*
EMP: 3
SQ FT: 1,100
SALES (est): 331.2K **Privately Held**
SIC: 3993 Signs & advertising specialties

(G-7078)
WEXFORD HOME CORP
430 E Plainfield Rd (60525-6910)
PHONE..................................331 225-0979
Feng Xu, *CEO*
EMP: 4
SALES (est): 549.2K **Privately Held**
SIC: 3999 5199 Framed artwork; art goods

Cowden
Shelby County

(G-7079)
MILLERS FERTILIZER & FEED
300 E Cedar St (62422)
P.O. Box 91 (62422-0091)
PHONE..................................217 783-6321
Steve Miller, *Owner*
EMP: 12
SQ FT: 750
SALES (est): 1.7MM **Privately Held**
WEB: www.milleragsupply.net
SIC: 5191 2875 Fertilizer & fertilizer materials; feed; limestone, agricultural; fertilizers, mixing only

Creal Springs
Williamson County

(G-7080)
BELLA TERRA WINERY LLC
Also Called: Bella T Winery
755 Parker City Rd (62922-1013)
PHONE..................................618 658-8882
Edward Russell,
EMP: 12
SQ FT: 150
SALES (est): 720K **Privately Held**
SIC: 2084 0172 5921 5182 Wines; grapes; wine; wine; recreational vehicle rental

Crescent City
Iroquois County

(G-7081)
AILEYS 3 WELDING
Rr 24 Box West (60928)
PHONE..................................815 683-2181
Norman Ailey, *Managing Prtnr*
Randy Strom, *Partner*
Bill Weakley, *Partner*
EMP: 3
SALES (est): 216.2K **Privately Held**
SIC: 7692 Welding repair

(G-7082)
SCHEIWES PRINT SHOP
Also Called: Scheiwes Print and Christn Sup
407 Main St (60928-8082)
P.O. Box 57 (60928-0057)
PHONE..................................815 683-2398
Glenn Scheiwe, *Partner*
Irma Scheiwe, *Partner*
EMP: 3 EST: 1972
SQ FT: 1,875
SALES (est): 433.7K **Privately Held**
SIC: 2752 2759 5999 2789 Commercial printing, offset; screen printing; letterpress printing; religious goods; bookbinding & related work; automotive & apparel trimmings

Crest Hill
Will County

(G-7083)
AMERICAN MARBLE & GRANITE INC
1930 Donmaur Dr (60403-1905)
PHONE..................................815 741-1710
Phillip Varsek, *President*
EMP: 2
SALES (est): 615.6K **Privately Held**
SIC: 5032 3281 Marble building stone; cut stone & stone products

(G-7084)
BRING YOUR OWN AUTO PARTS INC
2123 Plainfield Rd (60403-1843)
PHONE..................................815 730-6900
William Haney, *CEO*
EMP: 11
SALES (est): 1.3MM **Privately Held**
SIC: 1711 3812 7533 7538 Heating & air conditioning contractors; light or heat emission operating apparatus; auto exhaust system repair shops; general automotive repair shops

(G-7085)
CREATIVE POWDER COATING INC
920 Brian Dr (60403-2484)
PHONE..................................815 260-3124
EMP: 4
SALES (est): 470.3K **Privately Held**
SIC: 3479 Coating of metals & formed products

(G-7086)
FAB WERKS INC
911 Brian Dr (60403-2484)
PHONE..................................815 724-0317
Kenneth Charles Krier, *President*
Karen Lombardo, *Purchasing*
Rebecca Lyn Krier, *Admin Sec*
EMP: 25 EST: 1998
SQ FT: 3,000
SALES (est): 5.5MM **Privately Held**
SIC: 3444 Sheet metal specialties, not stamped

(G-7087)
J M PRINTERS INC (PA)
Also Called: J M Office Products
510 Pasadena Ave (60403-2406)
PHONE..................................815 727-1579
Glen Conklin, *President*
Mark Conklin, *Treasurer*
EMP: 17 EST: 1965
SQ FT: 7,500
SALES (est): 2.9MM **Privately Held**
WEB: www.jmprinters.net
SIC: 2752 5112 Commercial printing, offset; office supplies

(G-7088)
JOLIET PATTERN WORKS INC
508 Pasadena Ave (60403-2406)
PHONE..................................815 726-5373
Andrew D Wood, *President*
Robert Benbow, *Vice Pres*
EMP: 53 EST: 1946
SQ FT: 67,000
SALES (est): 14MM **Privately Held**
WEB: www.jolietpattern.com
SIC: 2759 3993 Screen printing; displays & cutouts, window & lobby

(G-7089)
JOLIET TECHNOLOGIES LLC
1724 Tomich Ct (60403-0940)
PHONE..................................815 725-9696
Greg Thornton, *Prdtn Mgr*
John Gierich, *QA Dir*
Clay Johnson,
Gregory Hill,
EMP: 8
SQ FT: 3,000
SALES (est): 1.6MM **Privately Held**
SIC: 3625 Control equipment, electric

(G-7090)
LEGACY 3D LLC
2020 N Raynor Ave (60403-2700)
PHONE..................................815 727-5454
Paul Ciesiun,
Walter Lee Mauney,
Richard K Rudie,
EMP: 10
SALES (est): 1MM **Privately Held**
SIC: 3993 7389 Signs & advertising specialties; design services

(G-7091)
LOS MANGOS
1701 N Larkin Ave (60403-1970)
PHONE..................................815 630-2611
EMP: 8
SALES (est): 105.4K **Privately Held**
WEB: www.los-mangos.com
SIC: 5812 2024 Mexican restaurant; ice cream & frozen desserts

(G-7092)
MORENO AND SONS INC
2366 Plainfield Rd (60403-1847)
P.O. Box 1307, Plainfield (60544-1307)
PHONE..................................815 725-8600
Mario Moreno, *President*
EMP: 8
SALES (est): 1MM **Privately Held**
SIC: 3949 Gymnasium equipment

(G-7093)
R&M PALLETS
950 Brian Dr (60403-2400)
PHONE..................................773 317-0574
EMP: 3
SALES (est): 143.1K **Privately Held**
SIC: 2448 Pallets, wood & wood with metal

(G-7094)
RAILWAY & INDUSTRIAL SVCS INC
Also Called: Railway & Industrial Spc
2201 N Center St (60403-2521)
PHONE..................................815 726-4224
Richard Vetter, *President*
Daniel T Schwarz, *Vice Pres*
Don Kroesch, *Opers Mgr*
Glenn Dian, *Finance*
Donald Kroesch, *Manager*
EMP: 125 EST: 1933
SQ FT: 10,000
SALES (est): 34.2MM **Privately Held**
WEB: www.risxinc.com
SIC: 5088 3743 Railroad equipment & supplies; railroad car rebuilding

(G-7095)
RAPID LANDSCAPING INC
2031 N Raynor Ave (60403-2487)
PHONE..................................815 740-1000
EMP: 9
SALES (est): 52K **Privately Held**
SIC: 0781 3251 Landscape services; paving brick, clay

(G-7096)
RICH PRODUCTS CORPORATION
21511 Division St (60403-2020)
PHONE..................................815 729-4509
Javier Reinoso, *Plant Mgr*
Justin Thompson, *Manager*
EMP: 750

GEOGRAPHIC SECTION

Crestwood - Will County (G-7123)

SALES (corp-wide): 5B Privately Held
WEB: www.richs.com
SIC: 2053 Frozen bakery products, except bread
PA: Rich Products Corporation
1 Robert Rich Way
Buffalo NY 14213
716 878-8000

(G-7097)
STELLATO PRINTING INC (PA)
1801 Jared Dr (60403-0922)
PHONE..................815 280-5664
Anthony Stellato, *President*
EMP: 2
SALES (est): 452.9K Privately Held
SIC: 2752 Commercial printing, offset

(G-7098)
TEMPER ENTERPRISES INC
Also Called: Precision Printing
2218 Plainfield Rd Ste B (60403-1880)
PHONE..................815 553-0374
Tony Temper, *President*
EMP: 1
SQ FT: 2,800
SALES: 200K Privately Held
SIC: 2752 2759 Commercial printing, offset; commercial printing

(G-7099)
TRX EXPRESS INC
820 Brian Dr (60403-2482)
PHONE..................815 582-3792
Naumce Alexsoff, *President*
EMP: 2
SALES (est): 287.8K Privately Held
SIC: 3537 Trucks: freight, baggage, etc.: industrial, except mining

(G-7100)
USA HOIST COMPANY INC (HQ)
1000 Sak Dr Unit A (60403-2562)
PHONE..................815 740-1890
Robert Bailey III, *President*
Robby Bailey, *Vice Pres*
Robert Bailey IV, *Vice Pres*
Justin Messer, *CFO*
Lori Marquardt, *Office Mgr*
▲ EMP: 35
SQ FT: 20,000
SALES (est): 12.2MM
SALES (corp-wide): 51MM Privately Held
WEB: www.usahoist.com
SIC: 7353 3531 5082 Heavy construction equipment rental; aerial work platforms; hydraulic/elec. truck/carrier mounted; general construction machinery & equipment
PA: Mid-American Elevator Company, Inc.
820 N Wolcott Ave
Chicago IL 60622
773 486-6900

Creston
Ogle County

(G-7101)
DAVIDSON GRAIN INCORPORATED
Also Called: Davidson Farms of Creston
5960 S Woodlawn Rd (60113)
P.O. Box 95 (60113-0095)
PHONE..................815 384-3208
Ronald W Davidson, *President*
John Davidson, *Vice Pres*
Hadley Forbes, *Treasurer*
Carol Davidson, *Admin Sec*
EMP: 45
SQ FT: 800
SALES (est): 2.5MM Privately Held
SIC: 4212 3523 Local trucking, without storage; elevators, farm

(G-7102)
HUEBER LLC (PA)
110 S Main St (60113)
P.O. Box 85 (60113-0085)
PHONE..................815 393-4879
Jon Hueber, *President*
Jan Hueber, *Vice Pres*
EMP: 12

SQ FT: 4,800
SALES (est): 9.9MM Privately Held
WEB: www.hueberfeed.com
SIC: 5191 5153 2048 Feed; seeds: field, garden & flower; grain elevators; prepared feeds

Crestwood
Will County

(G-7103)
A & R SCREENING LLC
4611 136th St (60418-1980)
PHONE..................708 598-2480
Jo-Ellen Doranzo, *President*
Joe Doran, *Principal*
Jamie Guerrero, *Cust Mgr*
Brian Hitz, *Manager*
Joe Ramirez, *Graphic Designe*
EMP: 12
SQ FT: 3,500
SALES: 400K Privately Held
SIC: 2759 2396 Screen printing; automotive & apparel trimmings

(G-7104)
AAA CNC MANUFACTURING CORP
Also Called: Cnc Milling & Turning
14005 Kostner Ave (60418-2207)
PHONE..................708 288-2678
Stephen Fudala, *President*
EMP: 2
SALES (est): 212.3K Privately Held
SIC: 3544 Special dies, tools, jigs & fixtures

(G-7105)
ALL AMERICAN TROPHY KING INC
13811 Cicero Ave (60418-1826)
PHONE..................708 597-2121
James Seidel, *President*
Geraldine Seidel, *Corp Secy*
Chuck Tate, *CTO*
EMP: 10
SQ FT: 14,000
SALES: 1.2MM Privately Held
SIC: 3914 5094 5999 Trophies; trophies; trophies & plaques

(G-7106)
ALLIED MACHINE TOOL & DYE
13430 Kolmar Ave (60418-1443)
PHONE..................708 388-7676
Christopher Galik, *President*
Frances Galik, *Vice Pres*
EMP: 3
SALES (est): 394.8K Privately Held
SIC: 3599 Machine shop, jobbing & repair

(G-7107)
BEST BRAKE DIE INC
13434 Kolmar Ave (60418-1443)
PHONE..................708 388-1896
Dennis Malloy, *President*
John Hughes, *Treasurer*
EMP: 7
SQ FT: 10,000
SALES: 750K Privately Held
SIC: 3542 Machine tools, metal forming type

(G-7108)
CAMCO MANUFACTURING INC
Also Called: Camco Screw Machine Products
13933 Kildare Ave (60418-2356)
PHONE..................708 597-4288
Jack Rochon, *President*
EMP: 10
SQ FT: 7,500
SALES (est): 1MM Privately Held
SIC: 3599 3451 Machine shop, jobbing & repair; screw machine products

(G-7109)
CAMSHOP INDUSTRIAL LLC
Also Called: Camco Manufacturing
13933 Kildare Ave (60418-2356)
PHONE..................708 597-4288
Emmanuel Arevalo-Nowell, *Vice Pres*
Mario Arevalo, *Mng Member*
EMP: 8 EST: 2013

SALES (est): 634.4K Privately Held
SIC: 3599 Machine shop, jobbing & repair

(G-7110)
CC DISTRIBUTING SERVICES INC
Also Called: Smith Brothers Converters
13655 Kenton Ave (60418-1938)
P.O. Box 221047, Chicago (60622-0008)
PHONE..................800 931-2668
EMP: 2
SQ FT: 4,000
SALES: 1MM Privately Held
SIC: 5013 5531 3714 Whol Auto Parts/Supplies Ret Auto/Home Supplies Mfg Motor Vehicle Parts/Accessories

(G-7111)
CERTIWELD INC
13953 Kostner Ave (60418-2205)
PHONE..................708 389-0148
John Flynn, *President*
EMP: 3
SQ FT: 1,800
SALES (est): 201.5K Privately Held
SIC: 7692 Welding repair

(G-7112)
CLASSIC AUTOMATION & TOOL
4329 136th Ct (60418-1904)
PHONE..................708 388-6311
Ron Hadar, *President*
EMP: 4
SQ FT: 6,000
SALES (est): 100K Privately Held
SIC: 3599 Machine shop, jobbing & repair

(G-7113)
CONTEMPO AUTOGRAPHIC & SIGNS
Also Called: Signs By Design
13866 Cicero Ave (60418-1883)
PHONE..................708 371-5499
Dan Gorecki, *Partner*
Chris Gorecki, *Partner*
John Gorecki, *Partner*
EMP: 3
SQ FT: 1,400
SALES (est): 295K Privately Held
SIC: 3993 Signs, not made in custom sign painting shops

(G-7114)
COUNTY PACKAGING INC
Also Called: Doosan
13600 Kildare Ave (60418-2326)
PHONE..................708 597-1100
Jack Kent, *President*
Jacob Kent, *COO*
Michael Cerva, *Vice Pres*
Michael Ceva, *Opers Spvr*
Kandice Banker, *Technology*
▲ EMP: 70
SQ FT: 60,000
SALES (est): 6.9MM Privately Held
WEB: www.countypkg.com
SIC: 7389 3694 Packaging & labeling services; automotive electrical equipment

(G-7115)
CRESTWOOD CUSTOM CABINETS
13960 Kildare Ave (60418-2357)
PHONE..................708 385-3167
Dennis Kersten, *Partner*
Frank Kersten, *Partner*
EMP: 4 EST: 1961
SQ FT: 4,000
SALES: 250K Privately Held
WEB: www.crestwoodcustomcabinets.com
SIC: 2434 2521 2517 Vanities, bathroom: wood; wood office furniture; wood television & radio cabinets

(G-7116)
CUSTOM WOOD DESIGNS INC
14237 Kilbourne Ave (60418-2674)
PHONE..................708 799-3439
Louis Mascitti Jr, *President*
EMP: 3
SQ FT: 4,800
SALES (est): 159.5K Privately Held
SIC: 7641 2511 2434 Reupholstery & furniture repair; wood household furniture; wood kitchen cabinets

(G-7117)
FAMAR FLAVOR LLC
4711 137th St (60418-1928)
PHONE..................708 926-2951
Justine Kos,
Martin Pawlus,
EMP: 5
SALES (est): 439K Privately Held
WEB: www.famarflavors.com
SIC: 2099 Seasonings & spices; spices, including grinding

(G-7118)
FANNING COMMUNICATIONS INC
Also Called: Advertising Designs
4701 Midlothian Tpke # 4 (60418-1976)
PHONE..................708 293-1430
John J Fanning, *President*
Karl Paloucek, *Chief*
Mariah Beavers, *Graphic Designe*
Deanna Clark, *Graphic Designe*
Alex Boerner, *Representative*
EMP: 8 EST: 2001
SALES (est): 1.7MM Privately Held
WEB: www.fanningcommunications.com
SIC: 7311 8999 2721 7374 Advertising consultant; technical writing; magazines: publishing & printing; computer graphics service; administrative management

(G-7119)
INNOVTIVE PRCESS APPLCTONS LLC
14011 Kostner Ave (60418-2207)
PHONE..................708 844-6100
Gerald A Cain, *President*
Mike Stachowicz, *Engineer*
John Stoch, *Manager*
◆ EMP: 8 EST: 2016
SQ FT: 6,000
SALES: 2.3MM Privately Held
SIC: 3559 3821 Chemical machinery & equipment; particle size reduction apparatus, laboratory

(G-7120)
INTEGRA GRAPHICS AND FORMS INC
4749 136th St (60418-1968)
PHONE..................708 385-0950
Rick Richter, *President*
Gene Egan, *Vice Pres*
Eugene Egan, *Admin Sec*
EMP: 10
SQ FT: 5,500
SALES (est): 1.6MM Privately Held
SIC: 2759 7389 2789 2752 Commercial printing; brokers' services; bookbinding & related work; commercial printing, lithographic

(G-7121)
KEY WEST METAL INDUSTRIES INC
13831 Kostner Ave (60418-1912)
PHONE..................708 371-1470
William A Slabich Jr, *President*
EMP: 120
SQ FT: 13,000
SALES: 19MM Privately Held
SIC: 1711 3444 3494 3498 Plumbing contractors; process piping contractor; sheet metal specialties, not stamped; line strainers, for use in piping systems; piping systems for pulp paper & chemical industries; millwright

(G-7122)
MACHINING SYSTEMS CORPORATION
14003 Kostner Ave (60418-2207)
PHONE..................708 385-7903
Lucy Fudala, *President*
Stanley Fudala, *Vice Pres*
EMP: 6
SQ FT: 3,600
SALES (est): 1MM Privately Held
SIC: 3599 Machine shop, jobbing & repair

(G-7123)
OMEGA PLATING INC
4704 137th St (60418-1929)
PHONE..................708 389-5410

Crestwood - Will County (G-7124)

Mithabhai Patel, *President*
Jayanpibhai K Patel, *Treasurer*
Shirish Shah, *Admin Sec*
EMP: 15
SQ FT: 15,000
SALES: 2.5MM **Privately Held**
SIC: 3471 3479 Plating of metals or formed products; coating of metals & formed products

(G-7124)
PALLETMAXX INC
4818 137th St Ste 1 (60418-1977)
PHONE 708 385-9595
Kenneth Conway, *President*
Todd Conway, *Vice Pres*
Claudia Hurst, *Sales Staff*
EMP: 7
SALES (est): 1.5MM **Privately Held**
SIC: 2448 Pallets, wood

(G-7125)
PRECISION IBC INC
13612 Lawler Ave (60418-1714)
PHONE 708 396-0750
Anthony Beard, *Branch Mgr*
EMP: 10 **Privately Held**
SIC: 3443 Water tanks, metal plate
PA: Precision Ibc, Inc.
 8054 Mcgowin Dr
 Fairhope AL 36532

(G-7126)
SCS COMPANY
13633 Crestview Ct (60418-1830)
PHONE 708 269-2094
Jeff Nemeh, *President*
Diala Nemeh, *Corp Secy*
EMP: 22
SQ FT: 10,500
SALES: 950K **Privately Held**
SIC: 2842 4959 Specialty cleaning preparations; sweeping service: road, airport, parking lot, etc.

(G-7127)
SENECA PETROLEUM CO INC (PA)
13301 Cicero Ave (60418-1427)
PHONE 708 396-1100
Owen E Hulse Jr, *CEO*
Owen E Hulse III, *President*
Catherine Grcevic, *Admin Sec*
EMP: 20 **EST:** 1921
SQ FT: 8,000
SALES (est): 17.9MM **Privately Held**
SIC: 2911 1611 Asphalt or asphaltic materials, made in refineries; highway & street construction

(G-7128)
SPIRIT CONCEPTS INC
4365 136th Ct (60418-1904)
PHONE 708 388-4500
Michael Kupchek III, *President*
Karen Kupchek, *Admin Sec*
EMP: 9
SQ FT: 3,500
SALES (est): 750K **Privately Held**
SIC: 2511 2517 Wood household furniture; wood television & radio cabinets

(G-7129)
STARLIGHT EXPRESS COACHES INC
13720 Kostner Ave (60418-1911)
PHONE 708 388-3365
William Ferry, *Branch Mgr*
EMP: 6
SALES (est): 521.3K
SALES (corp-wide): 855K **Privately Held**
SIC: 2741 Miscellaneous publishing
PA: Starlight Express Coaches Inc
 8945 S 87th Ave
 Oak Lawn IL 60457
 708 388-3365

(G-7130)
STRICTLY NEON INC
Also Called: Strictly Signs
4608 137th St Ste D (60418-4305)
PHONE 708 597-1616
Wally Wysocki, *President*
Walter Wysocki, *President*
Jim Givens, *Vice Pres*
EMP: 8
SQ FT: 1,400
SALES: 950K **Privately Held**
SIC: 3993 1799 Electric signs; neon signs; sign installation & maintenance

(G-7131)
TAL-MAR CSTM MET FBRCTORS CORP
4632 138th St (60418-1931)
PHONE 708 371-0333
James A Cesak, *President*
Ronald Dibasilio, *Treasurer*
Robert Talerico, *Director*
Michael A Martin, *Admin Sec*
EMP: 77
SQ FT: 25,000
SALES: 15MM **Privately Held**
SIC: 3599 Machine shop, jobbing & repair

(G-7132)
TRIEZENBERG MILLWORK CO
4737 138th St Ste 202 (60418-4301)
PHONE 708 489-9062
Clarence Triezenberg, *President*
David Noort, *Admin Sec*
EMP: 4 **EST:** 1946
SQ FT: 10,000
SALES: 590K **Privately Held**
WEB: www.triezenbergmillwork.net
SIC: 5031 5211 2431 2421 Millwork; millwork & lumber; millwork; sawmills & planing mills, general

(G-7133)
VALLEY VIEW INDUSTRIES HC INC
Also Called: Valley View Specialties
13834 Kostner Ave (60418-1913)
PHONE 800 323-9369
Howard J Rynberk, *President*
Bonnie Oneill, *Exec VP*
Nancy Schoeneman, *Accounting Mgr*
Dominick Bertucci, *Natl Sales Mgr*
Gina Delgiudice, *Manager*
EMP: 50 **EST:** 1963
SQ FT: 75,000
SALES (est): 9.4MM **Privately Held**
WEB: www.valleyviewind.com
SIC: 3271 3524 Blocks, concrete: landscape or retaining wall; lawn & garden equipment

Crete
Will County

(G-7134)
AFRICAN-AMERICAN IMAGES INC
24906 S Wllow Broke Trl (60417)
PHONE 708 672-4909
Jawanza Kunjufu, *President*
Rita Kunjufu, *Manager*
Dr Aliza Kunzufu, *Manager*
EMP: 12
SQ FT: 27,000
SALES (est): 1MM **Privately Held**
SIC: 2731 8748 5942 Books: publishing only; educational consultant; book stores

(G-7135)
BUILDERS IRONWORKS INC (PA)
399 Greenbriar Dr (60417-1110)
PHONE 708 672-1047
Rick Wories, *President*
Richard Wories, *President*
Joel Worries, *Vice Pres*
Julie Wories, *Admin Sec*
EMP: 9
SALES (est): 680.6K **Privately Held**
SIC: 3446 Fences or posts, ornamental iron or steel

(G-7136)
COMPONENT TOOL & MFG CO
25416 S Dixie Hwy Ste 1 (60417-3952)
P.O. Box 373 (60417-0373)
PHONE 708 672-5505
Timothy G Piepenbrink, *President*
Chrissy Santana, *Admin Sec*
EMP: 13
SQ FT: 7,000
SALES (est): 2.4MM **Privately Held**
SIC: 3544 3599 8711 7692 Special dies & tools; machine shop, jobbing & repair; consulting engineer; welding repair; metal stampings

(G-7137)
COOPER EQUIPMENT COMPANY INC
763 W Old Monee Rd (60417-3947)
PHONE 708 367-1291
Scott Cooper, *President*
EMP: 2
SALES (est): 240.8K **Privately Held**
SIC: 2835 7629 In vitro & in vivo diagnostic substances; electrical repair shops

(G-7138)
CRETE TWP
26730 S Stoney Island Ave (60417-4746)
PHONE 708 672-3111
Mark Rosandich, *Trustee*
Jeff Pangea, *Manager*
EMP: 3
SALES (est): 531.9K **Privately Held**
WEB: www.ctfpdwebsite.wix.com
SIC: 3711 Fire department vehicles (motor vehicles), assembly of

(G-7139)
DUTCH AMERICAN FOODS
25393 S Dixie Hwy (60417-3901)
PHONE 708 304-2648
Jake Andringa, *Controller*
Nancy Smith, *Manager*
EMP: 3
SALES (est): 243.2K **Privately Held**
SIC: 2099 Food preparations

(G-7140)
HOLLAND LP (HQ)
Also Called: Holland Company
1000 Holland Dr (60417-2120)
PHONE 708 672-2300
Jordan Wolf, *President*
Felix Krupczynski, *General Mgr*
Lawrence Brewer, *Business Mgr*
Mike Hakenjos, *Business Mgr*
Andrew Smith, *Business Mgr*
◆ **EMP:** 150
SQ FT: 60,000
SALES (est): 318.9MM
SALES (corp-wide): 585.3MM **Privately Held**
WEB: www.hollandco.com
SIC: 2899 3743 Fluxes: brazing, soldering, galvanizing & welding; railroad equipment
PA: Curran Group, Inc.
 286 Memorial Ct
 Crystal Lake IL 60014
 815 455-5100

(G-7141)
LOTTON ART GLASS CO
24760 S Country Ln (60417-2658)
PHONE 708 672-1400
Charles Lotton, *Owner*
EMP: 4
SALES (est): 436.7K **Privately Held**
SIC: 3231 3229 Art glass: made from purchased glass; pressed & blown glass

(G-7142)
NATIONAL MACHINE REPAIR INC
115 W Burville Rd (60417-3324)
PHONE 708 672-7711
Lou Novelli, *President*
Angelo Novelli, *Vice Pres*
EMP: 18
SQ FT: 33,000
SALES (est): 2.5MM **Privately Held**
SIC: 3599 7629 3441 Machine shop, jobbing & repair; custom machinery; electrical repair shops; fabricated structural metal

(G-7143)
ON SITE MECHANICAL SVCS INC
25250 S State St (60417-4027)
PHONE 708 367-0470
Ashley McGinley, *CEO*
EMP: 12
SALES (est): 117.2K **Privately Held**
SIC: 7699 7692 Repair services; welding repair

(G-7144)
ROCK TOPS INC
295 W Burville Rd (60417-3340)
P.O. Box 397 (60417-0397)
PHONE 708 672-1450
Robert Kasper, *President*
EMP: 5
SALES (est): 402.2K **Privately Held**
SIC: 2395 2399 Quilted fabrics or cloth; aprons, breast (harness)

(G-7145)
SOUTHLAND VOICE
1712 S Dixie Hwy Trlr 133 (60417-3948)
PHONE 708 214-8582
EMP: 25
SALES (est): 517.5K **Privately Held**
SIC: 2711 7389 Newspapers

(G-7146)
SUPERIOR MOBILE HOME SERVICE
3421 E Reichert Dr (60417-4875)
PHONE 708 672-7799
Kevin Clomp, *President*
Henriette Clomp, *Corp Secy*
EMP: 4
SALES (est): 477K **Privately Held**
SIC: 2451 Mobile homes

(G-7147)
ZETA MANUFACTURING COMPANY
3549 E Reichert Dr (60417-4876)
PHONE 708 301-3766
Joyce Horvath, *President*
EMP: 3
SALES: 250K **Privately Held**
SIC: 3999 Manufacturing industries

Creve Coeur
Tazewell County

(G-7148)
ARCHER-DANIELS-MIDLAND COMPANY
910 Wesley Rd (61610-3828)
PHONE 309 699-9581
Jeff Hoffman, *Branch Mgr*
EMP: 25
SALES (corp-wide): 64.6B **Publicly Held**
SIC: 2041 Wheat flour
PA: Archer-Daniels-Midland Company
 77 W Wacker Dr Ste 4600
 Chicago IL 60601
 312 634-8100

Crossville
White County

(G-7149)
BAKER PETROLITE LLC
315 S State St (62827-1119)
PHONE 618 966-3688
Ken Hake, *Manager*
EMP: 14 **Privately Held**
SIC: 1389 Oil field services
HQ: Baker Petrolite Llc
 12645 W Airport Blvd
 Sugar Land TX 77478
 281 276-5400

(G-7150)
CITATION OIL & GAS CORP
Hwy 14 E (62827)
P.O. Box 310 (62827-0310)
PHONE 618 966-2101
Jim Schreifels, *Manager*
EMP: 28
SALES (corp-wide): 283.5MM **Privately Held**
SIC: 1311 2911 Crude petroleum production; petroleum refining

PA: Citation Oil & Gas Corp.
14077 Cutten Rd
Houston TX 77069
281 891-1000

(G-7151)
ROYAL DRILLING & PRODUCING
Also Called: Royal Drilling & Production
Hwy 14 (62827)
P.O. Box 329 (62827-0329)
PHONE................................618 966-2221
James Cantrell, *President*
Chris Cantrell, *Vice Pres*
EMP: 3 **EST:** 1973
SALES (est): 1.2MM **Privately Held**
SIC: 1381 Drilling oil & gas wells

Crystal Lake
Mchenry County

(G-7152)
20 20 MEDICAL SYSTEMS INC
Also Called: K2 Tables
111 Erick St Ste 125 (60014-1314)
PHONE................................815 455-7161
Gary Chianakas, *Principal*
Michelle Larkin, *Vice Pres*
Karen Chianakas, *Treasurer*
▲ **EMP:** 7
SALES (est): 999.1K **Privately Held**
SIC: 3842 Surgical appliances & supplies

(G-7153)
ABA CUSTOM WOODWORKING
765 Duffy Dr Ste B (60014-1716)
PHONE................................815 356-9663
Roger Schultz, *Principal*
EMP: 3
SQ FT: 6,000
SALES: 350K **Privately Held**
SIC: 2499 1751 2521 2511 Decorative wood & woodwork; cabinet & finish carpentry; wood office furniture; wood household furniture; wood kitchen cabinets

(G-7154)
ACCUMATION INC
6211 Factory Rd (60014-7914)
P.O. Box 387 (60039-0387)
PHONE................................815 455-6250
Roland Gigon, *President*
EMP: 17
SQ FT: 10,000
SALES (est): 3MM **Privately Held**
SIC: 3451 Screw machine products

(G-7155)
ALL AMERICAN WOOD REGISTER CO
7103 Sands Rd (60014-6526)
PHONE................................815 356-1000
Patti Stasiak, *President*
Tom Stasiak, *Vice Pres*
EMP: 12
SALES (est): 1.5MM **Privately Held**
SIC: 2499 3433 2431 Decorative wood & woodwork; heating equipment, except electric; millwork

(G-7156)
ALPHA STAR TOOL AND MOLD INC
11 Burdent Dr (60014-4233)
PHONE................................815 455-2802
John Thurow, *President*
Audrey Thurow, *Corp Secy*
EMP: 18
SQ FT: 12,000
SALES (est): 2.9MM **Privately Held**
SIC: 3544 3089 Dies & die holders for metal cutting, forming, die casting; injection molding of plastics

(G-7157)
ALPHA SWISS INDUSTRIES INC
Also Called: Asi
700 Tek Dr (60014-8100)
PHONE................................815 455-3031
Jeff Koepke, *President*
Joe Rusciano, *Vice Pres*
Sandra Lamberg, *Admin Asst*
EMP: 8
SQ FT: 4,500
SALES (est): 1.4MM **Privately Held**
SIC: 3545 3451 Measuring tools & machines, machinists' metalworking type; precision tools, machinists'; screw machine products

(G-7158)
ALTRAN CORP
365 E Terra Cotta Ave (60014-3608)
PHONE................................815 455-5650
David Peterson, *President*
Peggy J Peterson, *Corp Secy*
Mike Lenio, *Engineer*
Jim Tadvick, *Sales Staff*
Steve Smith, *Manager*
▲ **EMP:** 28
SQ FT: 9,000
SALES (est): 5.3MM **Privately Held**
WEB: www.altrancorp.com
SIC: 3677 Coil windings, electronic

(G-7159)
AMBROTOS INC
4219 Belson Ln (60014-6589)
PHONE................................815 355-8217
James Kondrat, *President*
EMP: 3
SALES: 75K **Privately Held**
SIC: 3479 Metal coating & allied service

(G-7160)
APTARGROUP INC (PA)
265 Exchange Dr Ste 100 (60014-6230)
PHONE................................815 477-0424
Stephan B Tanda, *President*
Eldon Schaffer, *Exec VP*
Shiela Vinczeller, *Officer*
◆ **EMP:** 171
SALES: 2.8B **Publicly Held**
SIC: 3089 3499 Closures, plastic; aerosol valves, metal

(G-7161)
APTARGROUP INTERNATIONAL LLC
475 W Terra Cotta Ave E (60014-3407)
PHONE................................815 477-0424
Stephen J Hagge, *CEO*
James Meyer, *Vice Pres*
Gary Mente, *Maint Spvr*
Robert Kuhn, *Admin Sec*
EMP: 9
SALES (est): 971.8K **Publicly Held**
SIC: 3089 Boxes, plastic
PA: Aptargroup, Inc.
265 Exchange Dr Ste 100
Crystal Lake IL 60014

(G-7162)
ARCHER-DANIELS-MIDLAND COMPANY
Also Called: ADM
8550 Ridgefield Rd (60012-2800)
P.O. Box 69 (60039-0069)
PHONE................................815 459-1600
Robert Seegers Jr, *Branch Mgr*
EMP: 12
SALES (corp-wide): 64.6B **Publicly Held**
SIC: 2041 Flour & other grain mill products
PA: Archer-Daniels-Midland Company
77 W Wacker Dr Ste 4600
Chicago IL 60601
312 634-8100

(G-7163)
ARQUILLA INC
Also Called: X-Cel X-Ray
4220 Waller St Ste 1 (60012-2816)
PHONE................................815 455-2470
Guido Arquilla, *President*
Shannon Haney, *Engineer*
Dolores Morris, *Admin Sec*
EMP: 14
SQ FT: 16,000
SALES (est): 1.9MM **Privately Held**
SIC: 3844 5047 X-ray apparatus & tubes; X-ray machines & tubes

(G-7164)
ARROW SHEET METAL COMPANY
1032 Ascot Dr (60014-8831)
PHONE................................815 455-2019
EMP: 35 **EST:** 1937
SQ FT: 2,000
SALES (est): 3MM **Privately Held**
SIC: 1761 3444 Roofing/Siding Contractor Mfg Sheet Metalwork

(G-7165)
AUTOMATED MFG SOLUTIONS INC
6096 Commercial Rd (60014-7909)
P.O. Box 1616 (60039-1616)
PHONE................................815 477-2428
Steven A Gauger, *President*
EMP: 10
SALES (est): 2MM **Privately Held**
SIC: 3599 Custom machinery

(G-7166)
AUTROL CORPORATION OF AME
796 Tek Dr (60014-8133)
PHONE................................847 874-7545
EMP: 8 **EST:** 2010
SALES (est): 1.1MM **Privately Held**
SIC: 3823 Transmitters of process variables, stand. signal conversion

(G-7167)
BAESSLER CARL DGN MFG REP
360 Memorial Dr (60014-6291)
PHONE................................779 994-4103
EMP: 3
SALES (est): 145.1K **Privately Held**
SIC: 3999 Manufacturing industries

(G-7168)
BBC INNOVATION CORPORATION
Also Called: BIO BIDET
7900 S Illinois Rte 31 (60014)
PHONE................................847 458-2334
Dong Sok Han, *President*
▲ **EMP:** 25
SQ FT: 60,000
SALES: 21.6MM **Privately Held**
SIC: 3261 Bidets, vitreous china

(G-7169)
BIG BEAM EMERGENCY SYSTEMS INC
290 E Prairie St (60014-4415)
P.O. Box 518 (60039-0518)
PHONE................................815 459-6100
Nikunj H Shah, *President*
Steven J Loria, *Corp Secy*
Thomas Smonskey, *Vice Pres*
Vijay Shah, *Manager*
Sam Goldberg, *Supervisor*
▲ **EMP:** 25
SQ FT: 44,000
SALES: 10MM **Privately Held**
SIC: 3648 Lanterns: electric, gas, carbide, kerosene or gasoline

(G-7170)
BOLTSWITCH INC
6208 Commercial Rd (60014-7991)
PHONE................................815 459-6900
John Erickson Sr, *Ch of Bd*
James Erickson, *President*
Tom Kozicki, *Foreman/Supr*
Douglas Nickels, *Purch Agent*
Eric Maier, *QC Mgr*
◆ **EMP:** 45
SQ FT: 53,000
SALES: 10.2MM **Privately Held**
WEB: www.boltswitch.com
SIC: 3613 Power circuit breakers

(G-7171)
BRENCO MACHINE AND TOOL INC
6117 Factory Rd (60014-7953)
PHONE................................815 356-5100
Dietrich Bronst, *President*
Birgit Bronst, *Corp Secy*
Debbie Golladay, *Office Mgr*
EMP: 12
SQ FT: 8,700
SALES (est): 1.5MM **Privately Held**
WEB: www.brencomachine.com
SIC: 3599 Machine shop, jobbing & repair

(G-7172)
BROWN WOODWORKING
1804 Blue Island Dr (60012-2204)
PHONE................................815 477-8333
David Brown, *Owner*
EMP: 3
SALES (est): 227.8K **Privately Held**
SIC: 2499 2434 2431 Decorative wood & woodwork; wood kitchen cabinets; millwork

(G-7173)
BUBBLE BUBBLE INC
35 Berkshire Dr Ste 3 (60014-7700)
PHONE................................815 455-2366
Judy Delaware, *Owner*
EMP: 4
SALES (est): 428.6K **Privately Held**
SIC: 3421 Table & food cutlery, including butchers'

(G-7174)
BULL VALLEY HARDWOOD
820 E Terra Cotta Ave # 244 (60014-3655)
P.O. Box 2029, Woodstock (60098-2029)
PHONE................................815 701-9400
Daniel Deserto, *Branch Mgr*
EMP: 3
SALES (est): 239.5K
SALES (corp-wide): 1MM **Privately Held**
SIC: 2421 5031 5211 Sawmills & planing mills, general; lumber, plywood & millwork; millwork & lumber
PA: Bull Valley Hardwood & Portable Sawmill Services, Inc.
18014 Collins Rd
Woodstock IL 60098
815 701-9400

(G-7175)
BUZZ SALES COMPANY INC
6110 Official Rd (60014-7921)
P.O. Box 463 (60039-0463)
PHONE................................815 459-1170
Peter N Anderson, *President*
Roger G Angelkorte, *Vice Pres*
Jeffrey Kohnke, *Vice Pres*
Margaret R Anderson, *Admin Sec*
EMP: 8
SALES (est): 1.6MM **Privately Held**
WEB: www.buzzsales.com
SIC: 2893 2899 Gravure ink; chemical preparations

(G-7176)
CALCO CONTROLS INC
Also Called: Calco Cutaways
439 S Dartmoor Dr (60014-8726)
PHONE................................847 639-3858
Neil Sivertson, *President*
Lisa Richter, *Purch Agent*
Dan Fierla, *Executive*
EMP: 10
SQ FT: 5,000
SALES (est): 1MM **Privately Held**
SIC: 3599 3567 Machine shop, jobbing & repair; heating units & devices, industrial: electric

(G-7177)
CAMFIL USA INC
Also Called: Os Farr
500 S Main St (60014-6205)
PHONE................................815 459-6600
Peggy Rubeck, *Hum Res Coord*
Patricia Lambert, *Branch Mgr*
Patrica Lamberg, *Manager*
Brad Spletter, *Clerk*
EMP: 95
SQ FT: 128,000
SALES (corp-wide): 921.6MM **Privately Held**
WEB: www.camfil.com
SIC: 3569 3564 Filters; blowers & fans
HQ: Camfil Usa, Inc.
1 N Corporate Dr
Riverdale NJ 07457
973 616-7300

(G-7178)
CERTUS INDUSTRIES N AMER LLC
301 E Congress Pkwy (60039-3516)
PHONE................................847 217-2537
Safwen Hijazi,
Brad Toman,
EMP: 4
SALES (est): 172.1K **Privately Held**
SIC: 3555 Printing plates

Crystal Lake - Mchenry County (G-7179)

(G-7179)
CHEMTOOL INC
8200 Ridgefield Rd (60012-2912)
PHONE...............815 459-1250
David Klesmith, *President*
David Kincaid, *Plant Mgr*
Patrick Bernard, *Controller*
Andrew Rust, *Sales Engr*
Klaus Boelk, *Manager*
▲ EMP: 13
SALES (est): 3.6MM **Privately Held**
SIC: 2992 Lubricating oils & greases

(G-7180)
CHEMTOOL INCORPORATED
8200 Ridgefield Rd (60012-2912)
PHONE...............815 459-1250
Dean Athens, *General Mgr*
EMP: 75
SALES (corp-wide): 327.2B **Publicly Held**
WEB: www.chemtool.com
SIC: 2899 3471 2842 2841 Rust resisting compounds; water treating compounds; plating & polishing; specialty cleaning, polishes & sanitation goods; soap & other detergents; cutting oils, blending: made from purchased materials
HQ: Chemtool Incorporated
   801 W Rockton Rd
   Rockton IL 61072
   815 957-4140

(G-7181)
CHICAGO PLASTIC SYSTEMS INC
161 Virginia Rd (60014-7903)
P.O. Box 304 (60039-0304)
PHONE...............815 455-4599
Leif R Heggem, *President*
Dirk F Howell, *Admin Sec*
Dirk Howell, *Admin Sec*
EMP: 28
SALES (est): 8.5MM **Privately Held**
SIC: 3564 3089 Air purification equipment; plastic & fiberglass tanks

(G-7182)
CLASSIC WOODWORK INC
6704 Pingree Rd Ste 2 (60014-6227)
P.O. Box 158, Algonquin (60102-0158)
PHONE...............815 356-9000
Kristine Spillar, *President*
Bruce A Spillar, *Admin Sec*
▲ EMP: 4
SQ FT: 5,100
SALES (est): 523.3K **Privately Held**
SIC: 2431 Millwork

(G-7183)
CLINTON OIL CORP
250 N Il Route 31 176 (60014-4517)
PHONE...............815 356-1124
Dipdi Kapadia, *Business Mgr*
EMP: 5 EST: 2012
SALES (est): 460.3K **Privately Held**
SIC: 1389 Oil field services

(G-7184)
COMPONENT PARTS COMPANY
7301 Foxfire Dr (60012-1603)
PHONE...............815 477-2323
John Vlk, *President*
▲ EMP: 7
SALES (est): 665.5K **Privately Held**
SIC: 3443 Metal parts

(G-7185)
CONSOLIDATED MATERIALS INC
1320 S Virginia Rd (60014-8730)
PHONE...............847 658-4342
EMP: 19
SALES (corp-wide): 3.4MM **Privately Held**
SIC: 1442 Construction sand & gravel
PA: Consolidated Materials, Inc.
   8920 S Rt 23
   Marengo IL 60152
   815 568-1538

(G-7186)
CRAIGER INC
Also Called: Craiger Custom Design
2510 Rte 176 Unit D (60014)
PHONE...............815 479-9660
Craig Harthan, *President*
EMP: 5
SQ FT: 3,400
SALES (est): 701.1K **Privately Held**
SIC: 2431 1751 Interior & ornamental woodwork & trim; exterior & ornamental woodwork & trim; carpentry work

(G-7187)
CRYSTAL LAKE BEER COMPANY
Also Called: Crystal Lake Brewing
150 N Main St (60014-4433)
PHONE...............779 220-9288
John O'Fallon, *President*
Charles Ross, *Admin Sec*
EMP: 10
SQ FT: 13,200
SALES (est): 250K **Privately Held**
SIC: 2082 Beer (alcoholic beverage)

(G-7188)
CRYSTAL LAKE PALLETS
650 W Terra Cotta Ave (60014-3441)
PHONE...............815 526-3637
EMP: 3
SALES (est): 143.1K **Privately Held**
SIC: 2448 Pallets, wood

(G-7189)
CURRAN CONTRACTING COMPANY (HQ)
286 Memorial Ct (60014-6277)
PHONE...............815 455-5100
Rick Noe, *President*
Tim Curran, *Exec VP*
Dan Curran, *Vice Pres*
Mike Curran, *Vice Pres*
Catherine Curran, *Admin Sec*
EMP: 25
SQ FT: 4,000
SALES (est): 8.2MM
SALES (corp-wide): 585.3MM **Privately Held**
SIC: 2951 1611 Asphalt & asphaltic paving mixtures (not from refineries); highway & street construction
PA: Curran Group, Inc.
   286 Memorial Ct
   Crystal Lake IL 60014
   815 455-5100

(G-7190)
CURRAN GROUP INC (PA)
286 Memorial Ct (60014-6277)
PHONE...............815 455-5100
Timothy Curran, *President*
Mike Curran, *President*
Todd Gierke, *CFO*
Jordan Wolf, *Treasurer*
Catherine C Curran, *Admin Sec*
◆ EMP: 69
SQ FT: 4,000
SALES (est): 585.3MM **Privately Held**
WEB: www.currangroup.com
SIC: 7231 3253 1611 Unisex hair salons; wall tile, ceramic; highway & street paving contractor

(G-7191)
CUTTING EDGE COMMUNICATIONS
764 Grandview Dr (60014-7319)
PHONE...............815 788-9419
Myron Hillers, *President*
EMP: 2
SALES (est): 217.8K **Privately Held**
SIC: 4813 3661 Telephone communication, except radio; fiber optics communications equipment

(G-7192)
DEAL MOLD POLISHING INC
1242 Manchester Dr (60014-1814)
PHONE...............815 363-8200
EMP: 6
SALES (est): 506.2K **Privately Held**
SIC: 3471 Polishing, metals or formed products

(G-7193)
DELTA-THERM CORPORATION
6711 Sands Rd Ste A (60014-6594)
PHONE...............847 526-2407
Tom Slagis, *President*
EMP: 18 EST: 1968
SQ FT: 10,000
SALES (est): 3.9MM **Privately Held**
WEB: www.delta-therm.com
SIC: 3699 3567 Heat emission operating apparatus; heating units & devices, industrial: electric

(G-7194)
DEMARCO INDUSTRIAL VACUUM CORP
1030 Lutter Dr (60014-8189)
P.O. Box 1138 (60039-1138)
PHONE...............815 344-2222
Thomas Demarco, *President*
Christine Demarco, *Vice Pres*
EMP: 3
SALES (est): 983.3K **Privately Held**
SIC: 3563 Vacuum (air extraction) systems, industrial

(G-7195)
EAST WEST INTERGRATED THERAPYS
2719 Red Barn Rd (60012-1015)
PHONE...............815 788-0574
EMP: 4
SALES (est): 130K **Privately Held**
SIC: 2834 Mfg Pharmaceutical Preparations

(G-7196)
ELEC EASEL
2600 Behan Rd (60014-2224)
PHONE...............815 444-9700
EMP: 2 EST: 2007
SALES (est): 203K **Privately Held**
SIC: 3699 Mfg Electrical Equipment/Supplies

(G-7197)
FALCON PRESS INC
341 E Crystal Lake Ave (60014-6211)
PHONE...............815 455-9099
Rod Russell, *President*
EMP: 4
SQ FT: 4,000
SALES (est): 529.6K **Privately Held**
SIC: 2752 2759 Commercial printing, offset; letterpress printing

(G-7198)
FAYE JEWELLERY CHEZ
6314 Tilgee Rd (60012)
PHONE...............815 477-1818
Jeff Faye, *Owner*
EMP: 3
SQ FT: 2,000
SALES (est): 218.5K **Privately Held**
SIC: 5944 5094 3911 Jewelry, precious stones & precious metals; jewelry; jewelry, precious metal

(G-7199)
FISHSTONE STUDIO INC
110 East St (60014-4407)
PHONE...............815 276-0299
Thomas Fischer, *President*
Carrie Fischer, *Vice Pres*
EMP: 5
SQ FT: 87,000
SALES (est): 355.7K **Privately Held**
SIC: 3273 Ready-mixed concrete

(G-7200)
FORMS PRESS INC
1006 Bennington Dr (60014-8876)
PHONE...............815 455-4466
Richard G Skibbe, *President*
EMP: 2
SQ FT: 2,500
SALES (est): 700K **Privately Held**
SIC: 2752 Commercial printing, offset

(G-7201)
G & M MANUFACTURING CORP
111 S Main St (60014-6249)
PHONE...............815 455-1900
Marcia Goerner, *President*
John Goerner, *Vice Pres*
Kristen Carey, *Manager*
EMP: 43
SQ FT: 52,000
SALES (est): 10.1MM **Privately Held**
WEB: www.gandm.com
SIC: 3469 3465 Electronic enclosures, stamped or pressed metal; automotive stampings

(G-7202)
GESKE AND SONS INC (PA)
400 E Terra Cotta Ave (60014-3611)
PHONE...............815 459-2407
Leroy Geske, *President*
Larry G Geske, *Vice Pres*
EMP: 12
SQ FT: 8,600
SALES (est): 2.7MM **Privately Held**
WEB: www.geskeandsonsinc.com
SIC: 1611 2951 4212 4959 Surfacing & paving; asphalt & asphaltic paving mixtures (not from refineries); local trucking, without storage; snowplowing

(G-7203)
GESKE AND SONS INC
Also Called: Geske & Sons
400 E Terra Cotta Ave (60014-3611)
PHONE...............815 459-2407
Lori Geske, *Manager*
EMP: 3
SALES (corp-wide): 2.7MM **Privately Held**
SIC: 2951 Asphalt & asphaltic paving mixtures (not from refineries)
PA: Geske And Sons Inc
   400 E Terra Cotta Ave
   Crystal Lake IL 60014
   815 459-2407

(G-7204)
H R LARKE CORP
999 Saddle Creek Ln (60014-1934)
PHONE...............847 204-2776
Harold Larke, *President*
EMP: 5
SALES (est): 330.2K **Privately Held**
SIC: 3714 Motor vehicle engines & parts

(G-7205)
HARRISON MARTHA PRINT STUDIO
3222 Carrington Dr (60014-4760)
PHONE...............949 290-8630
Martha Harrison, *Principal*
EMP: 4
SALES (est): 370.2K **Privately Held**
SIC: 2752 Commercial printing, lithographic

(G-7206)
HUGHES & SON INC
Also Called: Hughes Sign Co
305 Dearborn Ct (60014-3468)
P.O. Box 367 (60039-0367)
PHONE...............815 459-1887
Dennis Hughes, *President*
Kathryn Hughes, *Corp Secy*
Howard Hughes, *Vice Pres*
EMP: 6 EST: 1955
SQ FT: 4,800
SALES (est): 494K **Privately Held**
SIC: 1799 7389 3993 Sign installation & maintenance; sign painting & lettering shop; signs & advertising specialties

(G-7207)
HUYGEN CORPORATION (PA)
1025 Lutter Dr (60014-8190)
P.O. Box 2424 (60039-2424)
PHONE...............815 455-2200
Garrett Wade, *President*
Richard A Wade, *CFO*
Sharon Wade, *Admin Sec*
EMP: 10
SQ FT: 10,000
SALES (est): 1.9MM **Privately Held**
WEB: www.huygen.com
SIC: 3825 5065 7629 3826 Test equipment for electronic & electrical circuits; measuring instruments & meters, electric; electronic parts; electrical equipment repair services; analytical instruments

GEOGRAPHIC SECTION

(G-7208)
IDENTATRONICS INC
Also Called: ID Direct
2510 Il Route 176 Ste E (60014-2217)
PHONE..................................847 437-2654
William L Bangston, *President*
Alex Smoler, *Info Tech Dir*
EMP: 30
SQ FT: 17,000
SALES (est): 2.7MM **Privately Held**
SIC: 7389 3089 5084 3651 Laminating service; identification cards, plastic; printing trades machinery, equipment & supplies; household audio & video equipment

(G-7209)
INAV LLC
300 Exchange Dr Ste C (60014-6290)
PHONE..................................847 847-3600
Craig Hackendal, *President*
EMP: 11
SALES (est): 3MM **Privately Held**
SIC: 3721 Aircraft

(G-7210)
INDUCTION HEAT TREATING CORP
Also Called: Iht
775 Tek Dr (60014-8172)
PHONE..................................815 477-7788
David Haimbaugh, *President*
Gary Tudor, *Vice Pres*
EMP: 50
SQ FT: 35,000
SALES (est): 13.3MM **Privately Held**
SIC: 3398 Metal heat treating

(G-7211)
JAMETHER INCORPORATED
Also Called: AlphaGraphics US 590
6294 Northwest Hwy (60014-7933)
PHONE..................................815 444-9971
James Davis, *President*
Therese Davis, *Vice Pres*
EMP: 5
SQ FT: 4,000
SALES: 600K **Privately Held**
SIC: 2752 Commercial printing, lithographic

(G-7212)
JEANNIE WAGNER
Also Called: Minuteman Press
835 Virginia Rd Ste G (60014-8732)
PHONE..................................815 477-2700
Jeannie Wagner, *Owner*
Brad Wagner, *Opers Mgr*
Samantha Wagner, *Relations*
EMP: 4
SQ FT: 4,400
SALES (est): 362.8K **Privately Held**
SIC: 2752 2791 2789 Commercial printing, lithographic; typesetting; bookbinding & related work

(G-7213)
JME TECHNOLOGIES INC
2520 Rt 176 Bldg 3 Unit 3 (60014)
PHONE..................................815 477-8800
Jerald Ewert, *CEO*
Karen Ewert, *Business Mgr*
EMP: 24
SALES (est): 1.3MM **Privately Held**
SIC: 5065 4581 3827 Electronic parts; aircraft maintenance & repair services; optical test & inspection equipment

(G-7214)
JOHN CRANE INC
Also Called: Smith, John Crane
29-31 Burdent Dr (60014)
PHONE..................................815 459-0420
Dan Schoenveck, *General Mgr*
EMP: 23
SALES (corp-wide): 3.1B **Privately Held**
SIC: 3295 3541 Minerals, ground or treated; lapping machines
HQ: John Crane Inc.
227 W Monroe St Ste 1800
Chicago IL 60606
312 605-7800

(G-7215)
KARLY IRON WORKS INC
4014 Northwest Hwy Ste 4c (60014-8211)
PHONE..................................815 477-3430
Daryl Kendrick, *President*
EMP: 5
SALES (est): 293.5K **Privately Held**
SIC: 7692 Welding repair

(G-7216)
KELLY & SON FORESTRY & LOG LLC
1783 Ashford Ln (60014-2013)
PHONE..................................815 275-6877
Kelly David C, *Principal*
EMP: 3
SALES (est): 272.7K **Privately Held**
WEB: www.kellyforestry.com
SIC: 2411 Logging camps & contractors

(G-7217)
KNAACK LLC
Also Called: Knaack Manufacturing
420 E Terra Cotta Ave (60014-3611)
PHONE..................................815 459-6020
Chad Severson, *President*
Chuck Sawyers, *Maintence Staff*
Brian Conn,
Jim Pahno,
Bill Zbylut,
◆ **EMP:** 100 **EST:** 1960
SQ FT: 450,000
SALES (est): 48.3MM **Privately Held**
WEB: www.knaack.com
SIC: 3499 Chests, fire or burglary resistive: metal
HQ: Werner Co.
93 Werner Rd
Greenville PA 16125

(G-7218)
KONICA MINOLTA HEALTHCARE
Also Called: 20/20 Imaging
829 Virginia Rd Ste A (60014-8714)
PHONE..................................815 893-0691
EMP: 3 **Privately Held**
SIC: 3841 Surgical & medical instruments
HQ: Konica Minolta Healthcare Americas, Inc.
411 Newark Pompton Tpke
Wayne NJ 07470
973 633-1500

(G-7219)
LAC ENTERPRISES INC
Also Called: Eagle Press
2530 Il Route 176 Ste 9 (60014-2226)
PHONE..................................815 455-5044
Michael Lacomb, *President*
Debra Lacomb, *Corp Secy*
EMP: 5
SQ FT: 2,500
SALES (est): 832.3K **Privately Held**
SIC: 5112 2791 2789 5699 Stationery & office supplies; typesetting; bookbinding & related work; uniforms & work clothing

(G-7220)
LEE JENSEN SALES CO INC (PA)
101 W Terra Cotta Ave (60014-3507)
PHONE..................................815 459-0929
James Jensen, *President*
Rick Metropulos, *Vice Pres*
EMP: 30
SQ FT: 5,000
SALES (est): 13.6MM **Privately Held**
SIC: 5082 7353 3496 General construction machinery & equipment; heavy construction equipment rental; slings, lifting: made from purchased wire

(G-7221)
MACHINE TECHNOLOGY INC
221 Erick St (60014-4594)
PHONE..................................815 444-4837
Kurt W Schraut, *President*
James Schraut, *Principal*
Courtney Gutierrez, *Purchasing*
Jacob Shaffer, *Manager*
◆ **EMP:** 4
SQ FT: 6,000
SALES (est): 483.5K **Privately Held**
WEB: www.sequoiaweb.com
SIC: 3599 Machine shop, jobbing & repair

(G-7222)
MAGNETIC DEVICES INC
150 Virginia Rd Ste 5 (60014-7940)
PHONE..................................815 459-0077
EMP: 6
SQ FT: 4,400
SALES (est): 500K **Privately Held**
SIC: 3677 3621 3612 Mfg Electronic Coils/Transformers Mfg Motors/Generators Mfg Transformers

(G-7223)
MATHEWS COMPANY
Also Called: Mathew Equipment Company
500 Industrial Rd (60012-3684)
PHONE..................................815 459-2210
David L Mathews, *Ch of Bd*
Joseph Shulfer, *President*
Jeff Sedlack, *Vice Pres*
Stoyan Kovatchev, *Engineer*
Michael Wilke, *Engineer*
EMP: 85
SQ FT: 25,000
SALES (est): 23.3MM **Privately Held**
WEB: www.mathewscompany.com
SIC: 3523 Haying machines: mowers, rakes, stackers, etc.; cutters & blowers, ensilage; driers (farm): grain, hay & seed; grounds mowing equipment

(G-7224)
MCGRATH PRESS INC
Also Called: McGrath Printing Custom Ap
740 Duffy Dr (60014-8199)
PHONE..................................815 356-5246
Kevin McGrath, *President*
Kevin Mc Grath, *President*
Dixie Church, *Manager*
EMP: 20
SQ FT: 11,700
SALES (est): 4.2MM **Privately Held**
SIC: 2752 7336 2789 2791 Commercial printing, offset; commercial art & graphic design; bookbinding & related work; typesetting; die-cut paper & board; letterpress & screen printing

(G-7225)
MEDTRONIC INC
815 Tek Dr (60014-8172)
PHONE..................................815 444-2500
Chad Rasmussen, *Safety Mgr*
EMP: 10 **Privately Held**
SIC: 3841 Surgical & medical instruments
HQ: Medtronic, Inc.
710 Medtronic Pkwy
Minneapolis MN 55432
763 514-4000

(G-7226)
METO-GRAFICS INC
111 Erick St Ste 116 (60014-1312)
PHONE..................................847 639-0044
Michael V Emrich, *President*
Julie Tomaso, *Purch Agent*
Chris Craig, *Manager*
EMP: 14
SQ FT: 30,000
SALES (est): 3.6MM **Privately Held**
WEB: www.meto-grafics.com
SIC: 2759 3471 3479 3625 Screen printing; anodizing (plating) of metals or formed products; etching & engraving; etching on metals; relays & industrial controls; switchgear & switchboard apparatus; scales & balances, except laboratory

(G-7227)
METROM RAIL LLC
1125 Mitchell Ct (60014-1723)
PHONE..................................855 943-8726
Juliane Huynh, *Director*
James Marchi,
EMP: 40
SALES (est): 2MM **Privately Held**
SIC: 3531 Railway track equipment

(G-7228)
MICRON ENGINEERING CO
2125 E Dean Woodstock (60039)
P.O. Box 2412 (60039-2412)
PHONE..................................815 455-2888
John Karr, *Owner*
EMP: 3

SALES: 375K **Privately Held**
SIC: 3544 3612 Special dies & tools; transformers, except electric

(G-7229)
MIDWEST MOBILE CANNING LLC
1228 Westport Rdg (60014-8989)
PHONE..................................815 861-4515
Terry McGinnis, *Mng Member*
EMP: 2 **EST:** 2013
SALES (est): 700K **Privately Held**
SIC: 3565 7389 Bottling & canning machinery;

(G-7230)
MIDWEST WATER GROUP INC
Also Called: RMS Utility Services
72 East St Ste 1 (60014-4457)
P.O. Box 909, Lake Geneva WI (53147-0909)
PHONE..................................866 526-6558
Michelle Harrod, *President*
Irene Harrod, *Manager*
EMP: 25 **EST:** 2007
SALES (est): 741.7K **Privately Held**
SIC: 3491 3842 7389 5084 Water works valves; personal safety equipment; sewer inspection service; safety equipment; water treatment equipment, industrial; sewer & manhole block, concrete

(G-7231)
MILLENNIUM ELECTRONICS INC
300 Millennium Dr (60012-3740)
PHONE..................................815 479-9755
Duane R Benn, *President*
Marc Damman, *Vice Pres*
▲ **EMP:** 97
SQ FT: 60,000
SALES (est): 10.2MM
SALES (corp-wide): 24.2MM **Privately Held**
SIC: 3679 Harness assemblies for electronic use: wire or cable
PA: Adco Circuits, Inc.
2868 Bond St
Rochester Hills MI 48309
248 853-6620

(G-7232)
MODERN FLUID TECHNOLOGY INC
93 Berkshire Dr Ste F (60014-2809)
PHONE..................................815 356-0001
Louis Licastro Jr, *President*
EMP: 5
SQ FT: 2,300
SALES (est): 1.1MM **Privately Held**
SIC: 7699 3823 8742 Industrial machinery & equipment repair; industrial process control instruments; industry specialist consultants

(G-7233)
MOLD REPAIR AND MANUFACTURING
2520 Il Route 176 Ste 5 (60014-2227)
PHONE..................................815 477-1332
John Demmikus, *Owner*
EMP: 3 **EST:** 2008
SALES (est): 76.5K **Privately Held**
SIC: 7699 3999 Repair services; manufacturing industries

(G-7234)
MOULDTEC INC
8015 Pyott Rd (60014)
PHONE..................................815 893-0908
EMP: 2
SALES (est): 253.8K **Privately Held**
SIC: 3714 Motor vehicle parts & accessories

(G-7235)
MURPHY USA INC
985 Central Park Dr (60014-8217)
PHONE..................................815 356-7633
EMP: 9 **Publicly Held**
SIC: 5531 2911 Automotive & home supply stores; petroleum refining
PA: Murphy Usa Inc.
200 E Peach St
El Dorado AR 71730

Crystal Lake - Mchenry County (G-7236)

(G-7236)
NATIONAL GIFT CARD CORP (PA)
300 Millennium Dr (60012-3740)
PHONE....................815 477-4288
Adam Van Witzenburg, *CEO*
Andrew Johnson, *CEO*
Dj Asad, *President*
Rick Rubin, *Exec VP*
Bill St Clair, *Senior VP*
EMP: 45
SALES (est): 11MM **Privately Held**
SIC: 2754 7334 Business form & card printing, gravure; photocopying & duplicating services

(G-7237)
NELSON-WHITTAKER LTD
Also Called: Central Specialties
8550 Ridgefield Rd Ste C (60012-2800)
PHONE....................815 459-6000
Jay A Maher, *President*
Barbara Kwiatkowsky, *President*
Susan Maher, *Vice Pres*
Joe Mancuso, *Plant Mgr*
Rus Budde, *Sales Executive*
▲ **EMP:** 26 **EST:** 1992
SQ FT: 27,300
SALES (est): 5.5MM **Privately Held**
WEB: www.csltd.com
SIC: 3914 3944 3484 Stainless steel ware; strollers, baby (vehicle); guns (firearms) or gun parts, 30 mm. & below

(G-7238)
NIDEC MOTOR CORPORATION
4218 East Dr (60012-3009)
PHONE....................815 444-1229
Brian Wolek, *Manager*
EMP: 4 **Privately Held**
SIC: 3621 Motors & generators
HQ: Nidec Motor Corporation
8050 West Florissant Ave
Saint Louis MO 63136

(G-7239)
NIMCO CORPORATION
1000 Nimco Dr (60014-1704)
P.O. Box 320 (60039-0320)
PHONE....................815 459-4200
Larry G Bachner, *CEO*
Jerry G Bachner, *President*
Laverne E Bachner, *Vice Pres*
▲ **EMP:** 55 **EST:** 1972
SQ FT: 40,000
SALES (est): 13.8MM **Privately Held**
SIC: 3556 Food products machinery

(G-7240)
NORTHERN ILLINOIS GAS COMPANY
Also Called: Nicor Gas
300 W Terra Cotta Ave (60014-3512)
PHONE....................630 983-8676
Cathy Chivari, *Branch Mgr*
EMP: 129
SALES (corp-wide): 21.4B **Publicly Held**
SIC: 4924 1382 4923 Natural gas distribution; oil & gas exploration services; gas transmission & distribution
HQ: Northern Illinois Gas Company
1844 W Ferry Rd
Naperville IL 60563
630 983-8676

(G-7241)
NU-METAL PRODUCTS INC
260 E Prairie St (60014-4413)
PHONE....................815 459-2075
Francene Weyland, *President*
Cyntheea White, *Corp Secy*
EMP: 18
SQ FT: 15,000
SALES (est): 3MM **Privately Held**
SIC: 3451 Screw machine products

(G-7242)
P F PETTIBONE & CO
Also Called: P.F.
2220 Il Route 176 (60014-2218)
PHONE....................815 344-7811
William J Poggensee III, *President*
Deborah Cherney, *Vice Pres*
Stella M Poggensee, *Admin Sec*
EMP: 5 **EST:** 1895

SALES (est): 783.4K **Privately Held**
WEB: www.pfpettibone.com
SIC: 5199 2752 5192 Badges; commercial printing, offset; books

(G-7243)
PARAGON MILL & CASEWORK INC
2819 Jenny Jae Ln (60012-1352)
PHONE....................815 388-7453
Jennifer C Degenova, *Principal*
EMP: 12
SALES (est): 1.6MM **Privately Held**
SIC: 2431 Millwork

(G-7244)
PIN UP TATTOO
424 W Virginia St (60014-5936)
PHONE....................815 477-7515
EMP: 3
SALES (est): 182.8K **Privately Held**
SIC: 3452 Pins

(G-7245)
PRECISION WATERJET INC
684 Tek Dr (60014-8100)
PHONE....................847 462-9381
Richard Edwards, *CEO*
Bill Kirkelie, *Sales Mgr*
Alexander Stark, *Sales Staff*
EMP: 5
SALES (est): 1.1MM **Privately Held**
SIC: 3599 Machine shop, jobbing & repair

(G-7246)
PRESSURE SPECIALIST INC
186 Virginia Rd (60014-7904)
PHONE....................815 477-0007
John R Ripkey, *President*
Ray Trimble, *Sales Mgr*
▲ **EMP:** 40
SQ FT: 20,000
SALES (est): 8.8MM **Privately Held**
SIC: 3491 Regulators (steam fittings)

(G-7247)
PRO INTERCOM LLC (PA)
4500 Us Highway 14 # 400 (60014-7334)
P.O. Box 7035, Algonquin (60102-7035)
PHONE....................815 680-5205
Diana Mullis, *Software Dev*
▲ **EMP:** 5
SQ FT: 2,000
SALES (est): 1MM **Privately Held**
SIC: 3357 Communication wire

(G-7248)
PRO TECHMATION INC
370 E Prairie St Ste 5 (60014-4475)
P.O. Box 1769 (60039-1769)
PHONE....................815 459-5909
Don Meyer, *President*
EMP: 5
SALES: 600K **Privately Held**
SIC: 3569 Assembly machines, non-metalworking

(G-7249)
PRO TUFF DECAL INC
7505 Eastgate Aly (60014-7945)
P.O. Box 1800 (60039-1800)
PHONE....................815 356-9160
Ross J Teresi, *President*
▲ **EMP:** 40
SQ FT: 10,000
SALES (est): 7.6MM **Privately Held**
SIC: 2759 Screen printing

(G-7250)
PROCESS ENGINEERING CORP (PA)
7426 Virginia Rd (60014-7906)
P.O. Box 279 (60039-0279)
PHONE....................815 459-1734
Maridelle McKesson, *President*
James McKesson, *Vice Pres*
Ted McKesson, *Vice Pres*
Carl Schaden, *Plant Mgr*
Tim Boyd, *Sales Mgr*
EMP: 17 **EST:** 1942
SQ FT: 18,000
SALES (est): 2.5MM **Privately Held**
WEB: www.pecfrictionfighters.com
SIC: 3624 Carbon & graphite products

(G-7251)
PROCESSED STEEL COMPANY
3703 S Il Route 31 (60012-1412)
PHONE....................815 459-2400
George A Berry IV, *President*
Kathleen M Martinez, *Admin Sec*
▲ **EMP:** 363
SALES (est): 1.9MM
SALES (corp-wide): 131.1MM **Privately Held**
SIC: 3312 Tool & die steel & alloys
HQ: Tc Industries, Inc.
3703 S Il Route 31
Crystal Lake IL 60012
815 459-2401

(G-7252)
RAMCO GROUP LLC
Also Called: Ramco Tool
764 Tek Dr (60014-8100)
PHONE....................847 639-9899
Curtis Kenney, *President*
EMP: 12
SALES (est): 1.3MM **Privately Held**
SIC: 3541 8711 Machine tools, metal cutting type; machine tool design

(G-7253)
RAVEN TREE PRESS LLC
6213 Factory Rd Ste B (60014-7908)
PHONE....................800 323-8270
Dawn Jeffers,
Steve Stiles,
Rob Straebel,
EMP: 5
SALES (est): 313.7K **Privately Held**
SIC: 2731 Book publishing

(G-7254)
REPROGRAPHICS (PA)
26 Crystal Lake Plz (60014-7929)
P.O. Box 1157 (60039-1157)
PHONE....................815 477-1018
Herman C Braun, *Owner*
EMP: 4
SQ FT: 5,600
SALES (est): 641.5K **Privately Held**
SIC: 7334 7374 2791 2789 Blueprinting service; data processing & preparation; typesetting; bookbinding & related work

(G-7255)
RESEARCH IN MOTION RF INC
500 Coventry Ln Ste 260 (60014-7592)
PHONE....................815 444-1095
Anthon Thomas, *Branch Mgr*
EMP: 8
SALES (corp-wide): 1B **Privately Held**
SIC: 3812 3663 Search & navigation equipment; antennas, transmitting & communications
HQ: Research In Motion Rf, Inc.
22 Technology Way Fl 5
Nashua NH 03060
603 598-8880

(G-7256)
RIDGEFIELD INDUSTRIES CO LLC
Also Called: Tall Trees Farm
8420 Railroad St (60012-2806)
PHONE....................800 569-0316
Michael V Mitchell, *Principal*
▲ **EMP:** 39
SQ FT: 25,000
SALES (est): 15.1MM **Privately Held**
SIC: 5023 2426 5713 Wood flooring; flooring, hardwood; floor covering stores

(G-7257)
RITA CORPORATION (PA)
850 S Rte 31 (60014)
P.O. Box 457 (60039-0457)
PHONE....................815 337-2500
Stephen T Goode Jr, *Ch of Bd*
Brian J Goode, *President*
Ron Corbick, *Vice Pres*
Gayle Johnson, *Production*
Mike Valentino, *Purch Mgr*
◆ **EMP:** 50
SQ FT: 120,000

SALES (est): 31.6MM **Privately Held**
WEB: www.rita.com
SIC: 2833 2844 2824 5169 Animal oils, medicinal grade: refined or concentrated; face creams or lotions; protein fibers; chemicals & allied products

(G-7258)
RITE-TEC COMMUNICATIONS
5812 Marietta Dr (60014-4508)
PHONE....................815 459-7712
John Riska, *Owner*
EMP: 6
SALES (est): 132.3K **Privately Held**
SIC: 8999 7336 2791 2731 Writing for publication; commercial art & graphic design; typesetting; book publishing

(G-7259)
RW TECHNOLOGIES US LLC
387 E Congress Pkwy A1 (60014-6287)
PHONE....................815 444-6887
Troy Richert, *Managing Prtnr*
Micheal Walker, *Purchasing*
EMP: 10
SQ FT: 10,000
SALES: 1.2MM **Privately Held**
SIC: 3672 Printed circuit boards

(G-7260)
SAGE PRODUCTS LLC
815 Tek Dr (60014-8172)
PHONE....................815 455-4700
Paul Hanifi, *President*
Pam Allen, *Branch Mgr*
EMP: 9
SALES (corp-wide): 14.8B **Publicly Held**
WEB: www.sageproducts.com
SIC: 3061 Mechanical rubber goods
HQ: Sage Products, Llc
3909 Three Oaks Rd
Cary IL 60013
815 455-4700

(G-7261)
SEAN MATTHEW INNOVATIONS INC
314 Lorraine Dr (60012-3611)
PHONE....................815 455-4525
Michael Lohmeyer, *President*
EMP: 4
SALES (est): 249.8K **Privately Held**
SIC: 3999 Manufacturing industries

(G-7262)
SEAQUIST CLOSURES LLC
265 Exchange Dr Ste 30 (60014-6230)
PHONE....................262 363-7191
EMP: 4
SALES (est): 434.1K **Privately Held**
SIC: 3089 Plastics products

(G-7263)
SERV-ALL DIE & TOOL COMPANY
110 Erick St (60014-4534)
PHONE....................815 459-2900
Dan Johnson, *President*
Phillip Moreton, *Vice Pres*
Richard Sample, *Treasurer*
Rande Knabusch, *Manager*
Sheila Groden, *Shareholder*
EMP: 52 **EST:** 1944
SQ FT: 60,000
SALES (est): 11.1MM **Privately Held**
WEB: www.serv-all.com
SIC: 3364 3544 Zinc & zinc-base alloy die-castings; special dies & tools

(G-7264)
SHAW SUBURBAN MEDIA GROUP INC
Also Called: Kane County Chronicle
7717 S Il Route 31 (60014-8132)
P.O. Box 250 (60039-0250)
PHONE....................815 459-4040
Laura Shaw, *Publisher*
Steve Vanisko, *Publisher*
Thomas Shaw, *Vice Pres*
Stephanie Barrons, *Accounts Exec*
Brett Carr, *Marketing Staff*
EMP: 225

SALES (est): 12.7MM
SALES (corp-wide): 73.4MM **Privately Held**
SIC: 2711 Newspapers, publishing & printing
PA: 'b. F. Shaw Printing Company, The'
3200 E Lincolnway
Sterling IL
815 284-4000

(G-7265)
SHOELACE INC (PA)
Also Called: Ms. Bossy Boots
23 N Williams St (60014-4403)
P.O. Box 1696, Palatine (60078-1696)
PHONE..................847 854-2500
Robert J Guss, *President*
EMP: 7
SALES (est): 470.1K **Privately Held**
SIC: 2241 Shoe laces, except leather

(G-7266)
SIGGS RIGS
3810 S Oak Knoll Rd (60012-2043)
PHONE..................847 456-4012
Karen Siggeman, *Principal*
EMP: 4
SALES (est): 256.7K **Privately Held**
WEB: www.siggsrigs.com
SIC: 3949 Hooks, fishing

(G-7267)
SPARTAN FLAME RETARDANTS INC
345 E Terra Cotta Ave (60014-3608)
P.O. Box 395 (60039-0395)
PHONE..................815 459-8500
John Kuetemeyer, *President*
EMP: 10
SALES (est): 1.1MM **Privately Held**
SIC: 2819 Industrial inorganic chemicals

(G-7268)
SPARTAN PRODUCTS INC
345 E Terra Cotta Ave (60014-3608)
PHONE..................815 459-8500
James Athans, *President*
Dean Athans, *Vice Pres*
David Klesmith, *Admin Sec*
▲ EMP: 11 EST: 1969
SQ FT: 25,000
SALES (est): 2.6MM **Privately Held**
WEB: www.spartancompany.com
SIC: 2891 Adhesives

(G-7269)
STOP & GO INTERNATIONAL INC
3610 Thunderbird Ln (60012-2089)
PHONE..................815 455-9080
William G Merriman, *CEO*
Bonnie F Merriman, *Vice Pres*
▲ EMP: 6
SQ FT: 3,500
SALES (est): 532.4K **Privately Held**
WEB: www.stopngo.com
SIC: 3011 5531 Tires & inner tubes; automotive & home supply stores

(G-7270)
SUB-SEM INC
473 S Dartmoor Dr (60014-8700)
P.O. Box 161 (60039-0161)
PHONE..................815 459-4139
Ronald Miller, *President*
Mike Lyons, *Vice Pres*
Marty Viets, *QC Mgr*
Thomas Mull, *Engineer*
Jackie Farr, *Sales Staff*
▲ EMP: 37
SQ FT: 18,600
SALES (est): 10.5MM **Privately Held**
SIC: 3679 Electronic circuits

(G-7271)
SUN CENTRE USA INC
930 Pyott Rd Ste 100 (60014-8721)
PHONE..................224 699-9058
James Pease, *President*
▼ EMP: 12
SQ FT: 8,900
SALES (est): 5.7MM **Privately Held**
SIC: 3565 3599 5084 7699 Packaging machinery; machine shop, jobbing & repair; packaging machinery & equipment; industrial machinery & equipment repair

(G-7272)
SUR-FIT CORPORATION
110 Erick St (60014-4534)
PHONE..................815 301-5815
Kevin Belousek, *President*
▲ EMP: 20
SQ FT: 20,000
SALES (est): 4MM **Privately Held**
SIC: 3511 Hydraulic turbines

(G-7273)
SYSTEMS LIVE LTD
6917 Red Barn Rd (60012-1053)
PHONE..................815 455-3383
J Kennedy Nicholson, *President*
EMP: 4
SQ FT: 2,000
SALES (est): 231.8K **Privately Held**
SIC: 7372 7371 Application computer software; custom computer programming services

(G-7274)
T & C METAL CO
378 E Prairie St (60014-4415)
PHONE..................815 459-4445
Thomas E Lindley Jr, *President*
Cynthia Lindley, *Corp Secy*
EMP: 4
SQ FT: 5,000
SALES (est): 624.9K **Privately Held**
SIC: 5093 4953 3341 Nonferrous metals scrap; refuse systems; secondary nonferrous metals

(G-7275)
TAKASAGO INTL CORP USA
Also Called: TAKASAGO INTERNATIONAL CORPORATION (U.S.A.)
300 Memorial Dr Ste 100 (60014-6273)
PHONE..................815 479-5030
Carolyn Chen, *Marketing Mgr*
Antony Montenario, *Manager*
Teresa Pendergast, *Manager*
Amira Shahid, *Manager*
Anthony Montanaro, *Director*
EMP: 6 **Privately Held**
SIC: 2844 Perfumes & colognes
HQ: Takasago International Corporation (U.S.A)
4 Volvo Dr
Rockleigh NJ 07647
201 767-9001

(G-7276)
TC INDUSTRIES INC (HQ)
Also Called: Mill Products Division
3703 S Il Route 31 (60012-1412)
PHONE..................815 459-2401
Thomas Z Hayward Jr, *Ch of Bd*
George A Berry IV, *President*
Ben Davidson, *General Mgr*
James Davidson, *General Mgr*
Kathleen Martinez, *General Mgr*
▼ EMP: 151 EST: 1881
SQ FT: 500,000
SALES (est): 76.6MM
SALES (corp-wide): 131.1MM **Privately Held**
WEB: www.tcindustries.com
SIC: 3499 3398 Machine bases, metal; metal heat treating
PA: Terra Cotta Holdings Co.
3703 S Il Route 31
Crystal Lake IL 60012
815 459-2400

(G-7277)
TECHNIPAQ INC
975 Lutter Dr (60014-8190)
PHONE..................815 477-1800
Philip Rosenburg, *President*
Janice Rosenburg, *Vice Pres*
Jay Virgil, *Vice Pres*
Kory Beckman, *Opers Staff*
Kent Groves, *Sales Staff*
◆ EMP: 160
SQ FT: 60,000
SALES (est): 25.3MM **Privately Held**
SIC: 3089 Laminating of plastic

(G-7278)
TECHNOLOGIES DVLPMNT
3517 Braberry Ln (60012-2079)
PHONE..................815 943-9922
David Levitan, *Owner*
EMP: 5
SALES (est): 2MM **Privately Held**
SIC: 3083 Laminated plastic sheets

(G-7279)
TEKTROL LLC
796 Tek Dr Ste 300 (60014-8133)
PHONE..................847 857-6076
Hemant Narayan, *Principal*
EMP: 12
SALES (est): 753.9K **Privately Held**
SIC: 3829 Measuring & controlling devices

(G-7280)
TELLENAR INC
727 Tek Dr (60014-8172)
PHONE..................815 356-8044
Richard J Schmidt, *President*
Lawrence Schmidt, *Admin Sec*
EMP: 15
SQ FT: 35,000
SALES (est): 3.3MM **Privately Held**
SIC: 3469 3549 Electronic enclosures, stamped or pressed metal; assembly machines, including robotic

(G-7281)
TERRA COTTA HOLDINGS CO (PA)
3703 S Il Route 31 (60012-1412)
PHONE..................815 459-2400
Thomas Hayward Jr, *Ch of Bd*
George Berry III, *Vice Ch Bd*
Robert Berry, *President*
George Berry IV, *Exec VP*
Frank Celmer, *CFO*
EMP: 25
SQ FT: 20,000
SALES (est): 131.1MM **Privately Held**
WEB: www.tcindustries.com
SIC: 3499 3398 6531 Machine bases, metal; metal heat treating; real estate agents & managers

(G-7282)
THINK INK INC
890 Cog Cir (60014-7311)
PHONE..................815 459-4565
Fred Kaiser Sr, *CEO*
Fred Kaiser Jr, *President*
Klara Kaiser, *Treasurer*
EMP: 8
SQ FT: 5,100
SALES (est): 1.1MM **Privately Held**
SIC: 2759 2396 Screen printing; automotive & apparel trimmings

(G-7283)
TMJ ARCHITECTURAL LLC
Also Called: T M J
430 Everett Ave (60014-7129)
PHONE..................815 388-7820
Terry Mercer Jr, *President*
EMP: 1
SALES (est): 272K **Privately Held**
WEB: www.tmjarchitectural.com
SIC: 5033 2952 Roofing & siding materials; roofing materials

(G-7284)
TORQEEDO INC
171 Erick St Ste A1 (60014-4539)
PHONE..................815 444-8806
Christoph Ballin, *CEO*
Sven Kirchhoff, *QC Mgr*
Yvonne Princk, *Finance Mgr*
Mary Reinhart, *Sales Staff*
Mike Shafar, *Sales Staff*
▲ EMP: 5
SQ FT: 13,000
SALES (est): 1.2MM
SALES (corp-wide): 2B **Privately Held**
SIC: 3621 Electric motor & generator auxillary parts
HQ: Torqeedo Gmbh
Friedrichshafener Str. 4a
Gilching 82205
815 392-1510

(G-7285)
TRICAST/PRESFORE CORPORATION
169 Virginia Rd (60014-7903)
PHONE..................815 459-1820
Truman E Moore, *Owner*
EMP: 6
SQ FT: 9,000
SALES (est): 864.5K **Privately Held**
WEB: www.tricastcorp.com
SIC: 3365 3369 3366 Aluminum foundries; nonferrous foundries; brass foundry

(G-7286)
TRIUMPH TWIST DRILL CO INC
Also Called: Northern Division
301 Industrial Rd (60012-3602)
PHONE..................815 459-6250
James H Beck, *Ch of Bd*
Arthur R Beck, *President*
Robert Maxey, *Vice Pres*
Mark M Harwell, *VP Opers*
Norman E Margolin, *CFO*
EMP: 500
SQ FT: 57,000
SALES: 59.5MM
SALES (corp-wide): 11.1B **Privately Held**
SIC: 3545 5084 3546 3544 Cutting tools for machine tools; drill bits, metalworking; industrial machinery & equipment; power-driven handtools; special dies, tools, jigs & fixtures
HQ: Precision Twist Drill Co.
301 Industrial Rd
Crystal Lake IL 60012
815 459-2040

(G-7287)
UTILITY BUSINESS MEDIA INC
Also Called: UTILITY SAFETY & OPS LEADERSHI
360 Memorial Dr Ste 10 (60014-6291)
PHONE..................815 459-1796
Carla Housh, *President*
Rich Kunkel, *Business Mgr*
EMP: 15
SALES: 343.8K **Privately Held**
SIC: 2721 8748 Magazines: publishing only, not printed on site; safety training service

(G-7288)
VARIABLE OPERATIONS TECH INC
Also Called: Vo-Tech
1145 Paltronics Ct (60014-1729)
PHONE..................815 479-8528
Wojciech Furman, *President*
EMP: 21 EST: 1996
SQ FT: 14,000
SALES (est): 5.9MM **Privately Held**
WEB: www.vo-tech.net
SIC: 3549 3541 3499 3599 Metalworking machinery; machine tools, metal cutting type; linings, safe & vault: metal; machine shop, jobbing & repair

(G-7289)
VERLO MATTRESS OF LAKE GENEVA
5150 Northwest Hwy Ste 1 (60014-8058)
PHONE..................815 455-2570
Tom Wisniewski, *Manager*
EMP: 3
SALES (corp-wide): 1.2MM **Privately Held**
SIC: 5712 2515 2511 Mattresses; mattresses & bedsprings; wood household furniture
PA: Verlo Mattress of Lake Geneva, Inc
2462 State Road 120
Lake Geneva WI
262 249-0420

(G-7290)
VINYLWORKS INC
8550 Ridgefield Rd Ste E (60012-2800)
PHONE..................815 477-9680
Joel Berkland, *President*
Craig Steagall, *Admin Sec*
EMP: 5
SALES (est): 659.7K **Privately Held**
SIC: 2824 Vinyl fibers

(G-7291)
VIPAR HEAVY DUTY INC (PA)
760 Mcardle Dr Ste D (60014-8149)
PHONE..................815 788-1700
Steve Crowley, *CEO*
Chris A Baer, *President*
Larry Griffin, *Vice Pres*
Beth Sanfilippo, *Accounting Mgr*

Kristin Friesen, *Accountant*
EMP: 13
SQ FT: 4,500
SALES (est): 2.9MM **Privately Held**
SIC: 3714 Motor vehicle parts & accessories

(G-7292)
VULCAN LADDER USA LLC
Also Called: G P International
675 Seybrooke Ln (60012-3775)
P.O. Box 864, Island Lake (60042-0864)
PHONE...............................847 526-6321
Candy Powers, *Sales Staff*
David Briggs, *Mng Member*
Michael Lee,
▲ **EMP:** 5
SALES (est): 214.3K **Privately Held**
WEB: www.vulcanladderusa.com
SIC: 3499 7389 Metal ladders;

(G-7293)
WEEKLY JOURNALS
7717 S Il Route 31 (60014-8132)
P.O. Box 250 (60039-0250)
PHONE...............................815 459-4040
John Rung, *Publisher*
EMP: 3
SALES (est): 168.1K **Privately Held**
SIC: 2711 Newspapers, publishing & printing

(G-7294)
WERNER CO
Also Called: Knack
420 E Terra Cotta Ave (60014-3611)
PHONE...............................815 459-6020
EMP: 26 **Privately Held**
SIC: 3499 3355 3089 3446 Ladders, portable: metal; extrusion ingot, aluminum: made in rolling mills; synthetic resin finished products; scaffolds, mobile or stationary: metal; stepladders, wood
HQ: Werner Co.
93 Werner Rd
Greenville PA 16125

(G-7295)
WEVAULTCOM LLC
190 Liberty Rd Unit 3 (60014-8067)
PHONE...............................877 938-2858
Eric Peterson,
EMP: 3
SALES (est): 1.1MM **Privately Held**
WEB: www.wevault.com
SIC: 3572 Computer storage devices
PA: Converged Technology Professionals, Inc.
820 E Terra Cotta Ave # 244
Crystal Lake IL 60014

(G-7296)
X-RAY CASSETTE REPAIR CO INC
Also Called: Reina Imaging
6107 Lou St (60014-7916)
PHONE...............................815 356-8181
Leo J Reina, *President*
Reina Tony, *General Mgr*
Dawm Farrar, *CFO*
Jody Dessent, *Manager*
▲ **EMP:** 25
SQ FT: 25,000
SALES (est): 4.6MM **Privately Held**
SIC: 3844 7699 X-ray apparatus & tubes; X-ray equipment repair

Cuba
Fulton County

(G-7297)
BANNER PUBLICATIONS
Also Called: Banner Sale Management Service
350 N 1st St (61427-5117)
P.O. Box 500 (61427-0500)
PHONE...............................309 338-3294
Greg Deakin, *Owner*
EMP: 5

SALES: 750K **Privately Held**
WEB: www.bannersheepmagazine.com
SIC: 2721 5154 2791 Trade journals: publishing only, not printed on site; auctioning livestock; typesetting

Cullom
Livingston County

(G-7298)
EVERGREEN FS INC
19484 N 3000 East Rd (60929-7093)
PHONE...............................815 934-5422
Paul Sutter, *Manager*
EMP: 3
SALES (corp-wide): 69.7MM **Privately Held**
SIC: 2875 Fertilizers, mixing only
PA: Evergreen Fs, Inc
402 N Hershey Rd
Bloomington IL 61704
877 963-2392

(G-7299)
HAHN INDUSTRIES
300 S Walnut St (60929-7201)
P.O. Box 355 (60929-0355)
PHONE...............................815 689-2133
Marjorie Hahn, *Owner*
Robert Hahn, *Owner*
EMP: 5
SQ FT: 600
SALES (est): 414.6K **Privately Held**
WEB: www.hahnindustries.com
SIC: 3272 Concrete products, precast

(G-7300)
REGENCY CUSTOM WOODWORKING
215 E Van Alstyne St (60929-7157)
P.O. Box 337 (60929-0337)
PHONE...............................815 689-2117
James Alling, *President*
Joan Alling, *Admin Sec*
EMP: 15
SQ FT: 25,000
SALES (est): 1MM **Privately Held**
SIC: 2541 2521 5211 2434 Wood partitions & fixtures; wood office furniture; cabinets, kitchen; vanities, bathroom: wood

(G-7301)
REMMERS WELDING AND MACHINE
17809 N 3500 East Rd (60929-9757)
PHONE...............................815 689-2765
Jim Remmers, *Owner*
EMP: 2 **EST:** 1939
SALES (est): 400K **Privately Held**
SIC: 3599 Machine shop, jobbing & repair

(G-7302)
SUN AG INC
236 S Cherry St (60929-7207)
PHONE...............................815 689-2144
Andrew Biskie, *President*
EMP: 8
SALES (corp-wide): 29.1MM **Privately Held**
SIC: 2843 Surface active agents
PA: Sun Ag, Inc.
2702 County Road 800 N
El Paso IL 61738
309 527-6500

Custer Park
Will County

(G-7303)
WILDERNESS WOODWORKS LLC
36931 Irish Ln (60481-8420)
PHONE...............................815 210-3751
Jacen P James, *Principal*
EMP: 2
SALES (est): 214.6K **Privately Held**
SIC: 2431 Millwork

Cutler
Perry County

(G-7304)
KNIGHT HAWK COAL LLC
7290 County Line Rd (62238-1309)
PHONE...............................618 497-2768
Steve Carter, *Branch Mgr*
EMP: 203
SALES (corp-wide): 544.3MM **Privately Held**
SIC: 1241 Coal mining services
PA: Knight Hawk Coal, L.L.C.
500 Cutler Trico Rd
Percy IL 62272
618 426-3662

Dahinda
Knox County

(G-7305)
KING SYSTEMS INC (PA)
1130 Lakeview Rd S (61428-9790)
PHONE...............................309 879-2668
Brent King, *President*
EMP: 3
SQ FT: 800
SALES (est): 397.5K **Privately Held**
SIC: 3523 Barn, silo, poultry, dairy & livestock machinery; hog feeding, handling & watering equipment; incubators & brooders, farm

Dahlgren
Hamilton County

(G-7306)
COUNTERTOP CREATIONS
6th St And Hwy 142 (62828)
P.O. Box 8 (62828-0008)
PHONE...............................618 736-2700
Steven Dodson, *Owner*
Alberta Dodson, *Co-Owner*
EMP: 13
SALES (est): 1.2MM **Privately Held**
SIC: 2541 Counter & sink tops

(G-7307)
HAMILTON COUNTY COAL LLC
18033 County Road 500 E (62828-4294)
PHONE...............................618 648-2603
Joseph W Craft III, *CEO*
EMP: 310 **EST:** 2012
SALES: 123.7MM **Publicly Held**
SIC: 1241 Coal mining services
HQ: Alliance Coal, Llc
1717 S Boulder Ave # 400
Tulsa OK 74119
918 295-7600

(G-7308)
JACOB CHAMBLISS
Also Called: Chambliss Welding
127 County Road 600 E (62828-9003)
PHONE...............................618 731-6632
Jacob Chambliss, *Owner*
EMP: 3
SQ FT: 4,500
SALES (est): 114K **Privately Held**
SIC: 7692 Welding repair

(G-7309)
RAPP CABINETS & WOODWORKS INC
501 E Illinois Hwy 142 (62828)
P.O. Box 88 (62828-0088)
PHONE...............................618 736-2955
Jim Rapp, *President*
James Rapp, *Owner*
Cletus Rapp, *Vice Pres*
EMP: 12
SALES (est): 1.4MM **Privately Held**
SIC: 2541 2434 Cabinets, lockers & shelving; wood kitchen cabinets

(G-7310)
WHITE OAK RESOURCES LLC
18033 County Road 500 E (62828-4294)
PHONE...............................618 643-5500
B Scott Spears, *Mng Member*
Jeffery D Brock,
Shyla Hendrickson,
Chris James,
A Wellford Tabor,
▲ **EMP:** 2280
SALES (est): 57.6MM **Publicly Held**
WEB: www.whiteoakresources.com
SIC: 1241 Coal mining services
HQ: Alliance Resource Partners Lp
1717 S Boulder Ave # 400
Tulsa OK 74119
918 295-7600

Dakota
Stephenson County

(G-7311)
BERNER FOOD & BEVERAGE LLC (PA)
Also Called: Berner Foods
2034 E Factory Rd (61018-9736)
PHONE...............................815 563-4222
Stephen A Kneubuehl, *CEO*
Bill Marchido, *President*
Tyler Kneubuehl, *Business Mgr*
Edward Kneubuehl, *COO*
Tim Lethcoe, *COO*
EMP: 290
SALES (est): 128.2MM **Privately Held**
WEB: www.bernerfoods.com
SIC: 2022 2026 2095 2086 Cheese spreads, dips, pastes & other cheese products; dips, cheese-based; dips, sour cream based; instant coffee; soft drinks: packaged in cans, bottles, etc.; spaghetti & other pasta sauce: packaged in cans, jars, etc.;

Dallas City
Hancock County

(G-7312)
D & D CONSTRUCTION CO LLC
220 Cherry St (62330)
P.O. Box 508 (62330-0508)
PHONE...............................217 852-6631
David Greenig, *Mng Member*
EMP: 3
SALES (est): 900K **Privately Held**
SIC: 3448 Prefabricated metal buildings

(G-7313)
DADANT & SONS INC
Hwy 9 S (62330)
P.O. Box 237 (62330-0237)
PHONE...............................217 852-3324
Kent Robertson, *Manager*
EMP: 10
SALES (corp-wide): 27.4MM **Privately Held**
SIC: 3823 3444 Industrial process measurement equipment; sheet metalwork
PA: Dadant & Sons, Inc.
51 S 2nd St Ste 2
Hamilton IL 62341
217 847-3324

(G-7314)
JACK BARTLETT
Also Called: Bartlett Farms
2745 N County Road 2150 (62330-2300)
PHONE...............................217 659-3575
Jack Bartlett, *Owner*
EMP: 2
SALES (est): 220K **Privately Held**
SIC: 2452 Farm & agricultural buildings, prefabricated wood

Dalton City
Moultrie County

(G-7315)
WISHZING
320 S East St (61925-1031)
P.O. Box 191 (61925-0191)
PHONE....................217 413-8469
Tonya Walker, *Owner*
EMP: 20
SALES: 20K **Privately Held**
SIC: 3369 Nonferrous foundries

Damiansville
Clinton County

(G-7316)
WIEGMANN WOODWORKING
105 Sugar Creek Ln (62215-1353)
PHONE....................618 248-1300
Bobby Wiegmann, *Principal*
EMP: 10
SALES (est): 1.2MM **Privately Held**
SIC: 2431 Millwork

Danvers
Mclean County

(G-7317)
PROGRESS RAIL SERVICES CORP
5704 E 1700 North Rd (61732-9251)
PHONE....................309 963-4425
Rich Harris, *Branch Mgr*
EMP: 46
SALES (corp-wide): 53.8B **Publicly Held**
SIC: 4789 7389 3312 Railroad maintenance & repair services; railroad car repair; metal cutting services; structural & rail mill products
HQ: Progress Rail Services Corporation
  1600 Progress Dr
  Albertville AL 35950
  256 505-6421

Danville
Vermilion County

(G-7318)
AEROSOLS DANVILLE INC (HQ)
Also Called: Kik Custom Products, Inc.
1 W Hegeler Ln (61832-8341)
PHONE....................217 442-1400
William Smith, *President*
Michael Beckett, *General Mgr*
Manny Perea, *Opers Mgr*
Juvelle Johnson, *Manager*
Reid Page, *Manager*
▲ **EMP:** 450
SQ FT: 315,000
SALES (est): 925.6MM
SALES (corp-wide): 3.2MM **Privately Held**
SIC: 2841 2842 2843 2844 Soap & other detergents; specialty cleaning, polishes & sanitation goods; surface active agents; toilet preparations
PA: Kik Custom Products Inc
  101 Macintosh Blvd
  Concord ON L4K 4
  905 660-0444

(G-7319)
AMERICAN EVENT SERVICES LLC
1706 Warrington Ave (61832-5361)
PHONE....................217 709-1811
Anthony Tauer, *Mng Member*
Thomas M Strader,
EMP: 4
SALES (est): 1.9MM **Privately Held**
SIC: 3585 Air conditioning condensers & condensing units

(G-7320)
APF US INC
2204 Kickapoo Dr (61832-5379)
PHONE....................217 304-0027
Martin Schwarzenberger, *CEO*
EMP: 1
SALES: 200K **Privately Held**
SIC: 3569 Assembly machines, non-metalworking

(G-7321)
ARCONIC CORPORATION
1 Customer Pl (61834-9481)
PHONE....................217 431-3800
Valerie Andrade, *Engineer*
Julie Peelman, *Human Res Mgr*
Lee Leathers, *Manager*
Jason Pickett, *Manager*
EMP: 53
SALES (corp-wide): 2.9B **Publicly Held**
WEB: www.arconic.com
SIC: 3353 Aluminum sheet & strip; coils, sheet aluminum; plates, aluminum; foil, aluminum
PA: Arconic Corporation
  201 Isabella St Ste 400
  Pittsburgh PA 15212
  412 992-2500

(G-7322)
AUTOMATION INTERNATIONAL INC
Also Called: A I I
1020 Bahls St (61832-3367)
PHONE....................217 446-9500
Larry E Moss, *President*
Maurice M Taylor Jr, *President*
Dennis Howard, *Buyer*
Gary Ingold, *Engineer*
Keith Rancuret, *Engineer*
◆ **EMP:** 55 **EST:** 1955
SQ FT: 80,000
SALES (est): 19MM **Privately Held**
WEB: www.automation-intl.com
SIC: 3548 Resistance welders, electric; arc welders, transformer-rectifier

(G-7323)
BES DESIGNS & ASSOCIATES INC (PA)
2412 Georgetown Rd (61832-8425)
PHONE....................217 443-4619
Robert Jackson, *President*
Ted Hollen, *Corp Secy*
EMP: 4
SQ FT: 4,000
SALES (est): 742.6K **Privately Held**
SIC: 2759 Screen printing

(G-7324)
BOBS MARKET & GREENHOUSE
1118 E Voorhees St (61832-2130)
PHONE....................217 442-8155
Robert Wiese, *Owner*
Sharon Wiese, *Partner*
EMP: 1
SQ FT: 3,000
SALES: 300K **Privately Held**
SIC: 5431 3272 Fruit stands or markets; vegetable stands or markets; monuments, concrete

(G-7325)
BRAINERD CHEMICAL MIDWEST LLC
209 Brewer Rd (61834-6707)
P.O. Box 521150, Tulsa OK (74152-1150)
PHONE....................918 622-1214
Bruce Schofield, *Manager*
EMP: 3
SALES (corp-wide): 78.9MM **Privately Held**
SIC: 2819 Hydrochloric acid
HQ: Brainerd Chemical Midwest Llc
  427 S Boston Ave
  Tulsa OK 74103
  918 622-1214

(G-7326)
CHEM-CAST LTD
1009 Lynch Rd (61834-5804)
PHONE....................217 443-5532
Kenneth A Craig, *Partner*
EMP: 138
SQ FT: 140,000
SALES (est): 30.2MM **Privately Held**
SIC: 3544 3543 Special dies, tools, jigs & fixtures; industrial patterns

(G-7327)
CREATIVE CABINETS COUNTERTOPS
3817 N Vermilion St (61832-1159)
PHONE....................217 446-6406
Chris White, *President*
Allen Norris, *General Mgr*
Linda White, *Vice Pres*
EMP: 14
SQ FT: 17,000
SALES: 1.3MM **Privately Held**
SIC: 5031 2434 Kitchen cabinets; vanities, bathroom: wood

(G-7328)
DANVILLE METAL STAMPING CO INC (PA)
20 Oakwood Ave (61832-5452)
PHONE....................217 446-0647
Judd Peck, *President*
Judd C Peck, *Principal*
Brian Barnes, *Engineer*
Sue Beck, *Admin Sec*
EMP: 12 **EST:** 1946
SQ FT: 175,000
SALES (est): 78.7MM **Privately Held**
WEB: www.danvillemetalstamping.com
SIC: 3724 Engine mount parts, aircraft

(G-7329)
DANVILLE METAL STAMPING CO INC
17 Oakwood Ave (61832-5598)
PHONE....................217 446-0647
Judd Peck, *President*
EMP: 12
SALES (corp-wide): 78.7MM **Privately Held**
WEB: www.danvillemetalstamping.com
SIC: 3724 Engine mount parts, aircraft
PA: Danville Metal Stamping Co., Inc.
  20 Oakwood Ave
  Danville IL 61832
  217 446-0647

(G-7330)
DEL STORM PRODUCTS INC
2003 E Voorhees St (61834-6242)
P.O. Box 893 (61834-0893)
PHONE....................217 446-3377
John Ives, *President*
EMP: 12 **EST:** 1955
SQ FT: 30,000
SALES: 1.8MM **Privately Held**
SIC: 3429 3442 Manufactured hardware (general); screen & storm doors & windows

(G-7331)
ESTAD STAMPING & MFG CO
Also Called: Brennan Engineering
1005 Griggs St (61832-4116)
P.O. Box 825 (61834-0825)
PHONE....................217 442-4600
Robert B Rew, *President*
Bill Barglaw, *Vice Pres*
Greg Rew, *Vice Pres*
Eva Cotton, *Treasurer*
EMP: 24
SQ FT: 35,000
SALES: 5.3MM **Privately Held**
SIC: 3315 3429 3469 3695 Nails, steel; wire or cut; casket hardware; stamping metal for the trade; drums, magnetic
PA: Gemco
  1019 Griggs St
  Danville IL 61832
  217 446-7900

(G-7332)
FAULSTICH PRINTING COMPANY INC
2001 E Voorhees St (61834-6242)
P.O. Box 732 (61834-0732)
PHONE....................217 442-4994
Fred J Faulstich, *President*
Con Bateman, *Corp Secy*
William Faulstich, *Vice Pres*
EMP: 9
SQ FT: 11,000
SALES: 821.8K **Privately Held**
WEB: www.faulstichprinting.com
SIC: 2752 2759 Commercial printing, offset; letterpress printing

(G-7333)
FIBERTEQ LLC
3650 Southgate Dr (61834-9400)
PHONE....................217 431-2111
▲ **EMP:** 80
SQ FT: 150,000
SALES (est): 16.2MM **Privately Held**
SIC: 2221 Fiberglass fabrics

(G-7334)
FLEX-N-GATE CORPORATION
Also Called: Bumper Works
3403 Lynch Creek Dr (61834-9388)
PHONE....................217 442-4018
Karen McGinnis, *Purchasing*
Kevin Lee, *Engineer*
Bill Lang, *Manager*
Brandon Edwards, *Maintence Staff*
EMP: 100
SALES (corp-wide): 3.3B **Privately Held**
WEB: www.flex-n-gate.com
SIC: 3714 Bumpers & bumperettes, motor vehicle
PA: Flex-N-Gate Llc
  1306 E University Ave
  Urbana IL 61802
  217 384-6600

(G-7335)
FLEX-N-GATE CORPORATION
Also Called: Flex N Gate Plastics
3403 Lynch Creek Dr (61834-9388)
PHONE....................217 442-4018
Kevin Lee, *Branch Mgr*
EMP: 4
SALES (corp-wide): 3.3B **Privately Held**
SIC: 3089 Injection molding of plastics
PA: Flex-N-Gate Llc
  1306 E University Ave
  Urbana IL 61802
  217 384-6600

(G-7336)
FREIGHT CAR SERVICES INC
2313 Cannon St Ste 2 (61832-4200)
PHONE....................217 443-4106
John E Carroll Jr, *President*
Glenn Caren, *Vice Pres*
Ken Bridges, *VP Opers*
▲ **EMP:** 480
SALES (est): 27.1MM
SALES (corp-wide): 229.9MM **Publicly Held**
SIC: 4789 3743 3537 Railroad car repair; railroad car rebuilding; train cars & equipment, freight or passenger; industrial trucks & tractors
PA: Freightcar America, Inc.
  125 S Wacker Dr Ste 1500
  Chicago IL 60606
  800 458-2235

(G-7337)
FURRY INC
2005 E Voorhees St (61834-6242)
P.O. Box 453 (61834-0453)
PHONE....................217 446-0084
Dann E Furry, *President*
EMP: 13
SQ FT: 20,000
SALES (est): 2.8MM **Privately Held**
WEB: www.furryinc.net
SIC: 3599 Machine shop, jobbing & repair

(G-7338)
G P COLE INC
Also Called: Dines Machine & Manufacturing
1120 Industrial St (61832-3351)
PHONE....................217 431-3029
Gary C Parks, *President*
EMP: 15
SQ FT: 9,545
SALES: 1.5MM **Privately Held**
SIC: 3599 Machine shop, jobbing & repair

(G-7339)
GEMCO (PA)
1019 Griggs St (61832-4116)
P.O. Box 846 (61834-0846)
PHONE....................217 446-7900
Robert B Rew, *CEO*

Danville - Vermilion County (G-7340)

Greg Rew, *President*
EMP: 38 **EST:** 1941
SQ FT: 27,350
SALES (est): 5.3MM **Privately Held**
WEB: www.gemcoinsulation.com
SIC: 3399 Metal fasteners

(G-7340)
GRACE AND TRUTH
210 Chestnut St (61832-2633)
PHONE..................217 442-1120
Paul Alberts, *President*
Paul Van Ryn, *Vice Pres*
◆ **EMP:** 6 **EST:** 1948
SQ FT: 7,200
SALES: 361.5K **Privately Held**
SIC: 2731 Books: publishing & printing

(G-7341)
GREENWOOD INC (PA)
Also Called: Greenwood Plastics
1126 N Kimball St (61832-3124)
PHONE..................800 798-4900
Donna Darby-Walthall, *President*
Richard Darby, *Treasurer*
Beth Vadebonceour, *Controller*
Ethan Darby, *Mktg Dir*
Linda Sempsrott, *Admin Sec*
▲ **EMP:** 15
SQ FT: 2,000
SALES (est): 18MM **Privately Held**
SIC: 3995 3089 7261 Burial vaults, fiberglass; thermoformed finished plastic products; funeral home

(G-7342)
GREENWOOD INC
Also Called: Greenwood Plastics Industries
1126 N Kimball St (61832-3124)
PHONE..................217 431-6034
Jim Darby, *President*
Tom Edwards, *Branch Mgr*
EMP: 25
SALES (corp-wide): 18MM **Privately Held**
SIC: 3089 Thermoformed finished plastic products
PA: Greenwood, Inc.
　　1126 N Kimball St
　　Danville IL 61832
　　800 798-4900

(G-7343)
HEARING AID WAREHOUSE INC
1005 N Gilbert St (61832-3848)
PHONE..................217 431-4700
Jeff Elkin, *President*
EMP: 3
SALES (est): 201.8K **Privately Held**
SIC: 3842 5999 Hearing aids; miscellaneous retail stores

(G-7344)
HEATCRAFT RFRGN PDTS LLC
Also Called: Heatcraft Refrigeration Pdts
1001 E Voorhees St Ste B (61832-2145)
PHONE..................217 446-3710
Larry Golen, *President*
James Lavery, *Director*
EMP: 325
SALES (corp-wide): 3.8B **Publicly Held**
SIC: 3585 Parts for heating, cooling & refrigerating equipment; condensers, refrigeration
HQ: Heatcraft Refrigeration Products Llc
　　2175 W Park Place Blvd
　　Stone Mountain GA 30087
　　770 465-5600

(G-7345)
HOLMES BROS INC
510 Junction St (61832-4800)
PHONE..................217 442-1430
Robert Muirhead, *President*
Barbara Muirhead, *Vice Pres*
Matthew Muirhead, *Vice Pres*
EMP: 30 **EST:** 1872
SQ FT: 100,000
SALES (est): 2.9MM **Privately Held**
SIC: 3829 3599 Physical property testing equipment; machine shop, jobbing & repair

(G-7346)
HONEYWELL INTERNATIONAL INC
3401 Lynch Creek Dr (61834-9388)
PHONE..................217 431-3710
EMP: 3
SALES (corp-wide): 39.3B **Publicly Held**
SIC: 3724 Mfg Aircraft Engines/Parts
PA: Honeywell International Inc.
　　115 Tabor Rd
　　Morris Plains NJ 28202
　　973 455-2000

(G-7347)
HYSTER CO
1010 E Fairchild St (61832-3393)
PHONE..................217 443-7000
John Bartho, *Vice Pres*
EMP: 9
SALES (est): 1.8MM **Privately Held**
SIC: 3536 Hoists, cranes & monorails

(G-7348)
HYSTER-YALE GROUP INC
1010 E Fairchild St (61832-3393)
PHONE..................217 443-7416
Tom Hedenberg, *Opers Staff*
Gary Miller, *Opers Staff*
Brian Barr, *Manager*
Michael Souza, *Technical Staff*
Cindi Will, *Prgrmr*
EMP: 30 **Publicly Held**
SIC: 4225 5084 3537 General warehousing & storage; industrial machinery & equipment; industrial trucks & tractors
HQ: Hyster-Yale Group, Inc.
　　1400 Sullivan Dr
　　Greenville NC 27834
　　252 931-5100

(G-7349)
ILLINI CASTINGS LLC
1940 E Fairchild St (61832-3515)
P.O. Box 827 (61834-0827)
PHONE..................217 446-6365
John Widmer, *President*
▲ **EMP:** 16 **EST:** 2009
SALES (est): 4.1MM
SALES (corp-wide): 161.2MM **Privately Held**
SIC: 5093 3743 Ferrous metal scrap & waste; plastics scrap; waste paper; railroad equipment
PA: Mervis Industries, Inc.
　　3295 E Main St Ste C
　　Danville IL 61834
　　217 442-5300

(G-7350)
INDEPENDENT NEWS
Also Called: Independent News, The
2202 Kickapoo Dr (61832-5379)
PHONE..................217 662-6001
Doyne Lenhart, *Owner*
EMP: 5
SQ FT: 1,000
SALES (est): 239.7K **Privately Held**
SIC: 2711 Newspapers: publishing only, not printed on site; newspapers, publishing & printing

(G-7351)
INDIANA PRECISION INC
130 N Jackson St (61832-4728)
PHONE..................765 361-0247
EMP: 15
SALES (est): 1.9MM
SALES (corp-wide): 9.2B **Privately Held**
SIC: 3089 3599 3544 Mfg Plastic Products Mfg Industrial Machinery Mfg Dies/Tools/Jigs/Fixtures
HQ: Kaydon Corporation
　　2723 S State St Ste 300
　　Ann Arbor MI 48104
　　734 747-7025

(G-7352)
INTERNTIONAL GRNHSE CONTRS INC (PA)
70 Eastgate Dr (61834-9361)
PHONE..................217 443-0600
David George Jr, *President*
Ben George, *Vice Pres*
Benjamin George, *Vice Pres*
Jeff Bridgewater, *Project Mgr*
Travis Talbot, *Mktg Dir*
◆ **EMP:** 43
SQ FT: 89,000
SALES (corp-wide): 31MM **Privately Held**
WEB: www.greenhousemegastore.com
SIC: 5191 5211 3448 8742 Greenhouse equipment & supplies; greenhouse kits, prefabricated; greenhouses: prefabricated metal; construction project management consultant

(G-7353)
JAMES R CHITTICK
32 N Jackson St (61832-5837)
PHONE..................217 446-0925
James R Chittick, *Owner*
EMP: 3
SALES (est): 195.9K **Privately Held**
SIC: 3651 Household audio & video equipment

(G-7354)
KAYDON ACQUISITION XII INC
Also Called: Tridan International
130 N Jackson St (61832-4728)
PHONE..................217 443-3592
Michael Purchase, *CEO*
Bill Benner, *Plant Mgr*
Bob Cromwell, *Safety Mgr*
Phillip Stumph, *Engineer*
Todd Sowers, *Controller*
EMP: 30
SALES (est): 6.6MM
SALES (corp-wide): 8.9B **Privately Held**
WEB: www.tridan.com
SIC: 3545 Machine tool accessories
HQ: Kaydon Corporation
　　2723 S State St Ste 300
　　Ann Arbor MI 48104
　　734 747-7025

(G-7355)
KELLY PRINTING CO INC
205 Oregon Ave (61832-4237)
PHONE..................217 443-1792
Thomas Kelly, *President*
Tom Kelly, *Office Mgr*
EMP: 20 **EST:** 1968
SQ FT: 5,000
SALES: 900K **Privately Held**
SIC: 2752 2791 2789 2759 Commercial printing, offset; typesetting; bookbinding & related work; commercial printing

(G-7356)
KELLYS SIGN SHOP
1004 N Vermilion St (61832-3057)
PHONE..................217 477-0167
Art Tabels, *Principal*
EMP: 3
SALES (est): 250.6K **Privately Held**
SIC: 3993 Signs & advertising specialties

(G-7357)
KILE MACHINE & TOOL INC
3231 Illini Rd (61834-6278)
PHONE..................217 446-8616
Albert J Kile, *President*
Anna C Kile, *Corp Secy*
Albet L Kile, *Vice Pres*
Russell W Kile, *Vice Pres*
Russell Kile, *Vice Pres*
EMP: 5 **EST:** 1967
SQ FT: 8,500
SALES (est): 400K **Privately Held**
SIC: 3466 3545 3452 Crowns & closures; machine tool accessories; bolts, nuts, rivets & washers

(G-7358)
LEBANON SEABOARD CORPORATION
Also Called: Lebanon Chemical
508 W Ross Ln (61834-5137)
P.O. Box 686 (61834-0686)
PHONE..................217 446-0983
Vernon Bishop, *President*
Jerri Cooper, *QC Mgr*
Bill Kelso, *VP Sales*
Bill Stafford, *Regl Sales Mgr*
Theresa Ford, *Corp Comm Staff*
EMP: 40
SALES (corp-wide): 147.6MM **Privately Held**
SIC: 2875 5191 2048 Fertilizers, mixing only; pesticides; insecticides; chemicals, agricultural; prepared feeds; bird food, prepared
PA: Lebanon Seaboard Corporation
　　1600 E Cumberland St
　　Lebanon PA 17042
　　717 273-1685

(G-7359)
LINNE MACHINE COMPANY INC
209 Avenue C (61832-5498)
PHONE..................217 446-5746
Kim Linne, *President*
Pam Linne, *Vice Pres*
EMP: 3 **EST:** 1975
SQ FT: 3,200
SALES (est): 387.4K **Privately Held**
SIC: 3599 7692 Machine shop, jobbing & repair; welding repair

(G-7360)
LONG CONSTRUCTION SERVICES
617 1/2 E Voorhees St (61832-2144)
PHONE..................217 443-2876
John N Long, *President*
Jackie Long, *Vice Pres*
EMP: 5
SALES (est): 270K **Privately Held**
SIC: 3479 Painting, coating & hot dipping

(G-7361)
MARBLE MACHINE INC (PA)
21204 Rileysburg Rd (61834-5892)
PHONE..................217 431-3014
Jeff Marble, *President*
EMP: 23
SQ FT: 25,000
SALES (est): 3.9MM **Privately Held**
SIC: 3599 Machine shop, jobbing & repair

(G-7362)
MARBLE MACHINE INC
Also Called: Danville Brass and Aluminum
205 Oakwood Ave (61832-5426)
PHONE..................217 442-0746
Mike Hoskins, *Manager*
EMP: 3
SALES (corp-wide): 3.9MM **Privately Held**
SIC: 3365 3369 Aluminum foundries; non-ferrous foundries
PA: Marble Machine Inc
　　21204 Rileysburg Rd
　　Danville IL 61834
　　217 431-3014

(G-7363)
MCENGLEVAN INDUS FRNC MFG INC
Also Called: Mifco
708 Griggs St (61832-4011)
P.O. Box 31 (61834-0031)
PHONE..................217 446-0941
William Walter, *President*
William Walter Jr, *Vice Pres*
Nancy Harmon, *Admin Sec*
▼ **EMP:** 3
SQ FT: 31,000
SALES: 997K **Privately Held**
WEB: www.mifco.com
SIC: 3567 Heating units & devices, industrial: electric

(G-7364)
MEL PRICE COMPANY INC (PA)
Also Called: Mel Price Containers
16395 Lewis Rd (61834-7704)
P.O. Box 1637 (61834-1637)
PHONE..................217 442-9092
Melvin L Price, *President*
Jill Price, *Vice Pres*
EMP: 10
SALES: 289K **Privately Held**
SIC: 4212 1794 1442 Delivery service, vehicular; excavation & grading, building construction; sand mining; gravel & pebble mining

GEOGRAPHIC SECTION
Danville - Vermilion County (G-7391)

(G-7365)
MERVIS INDUSTRIES INC (PA)
Also Called: Mervis Iron & Metal Div
3295 E Main St Ste C (61834-9302)
P.O. Box 827 (61834-0827)
PHONE..........................217 442-5300
Louis L Mervis, *Ch of Bd*
Adam Mervis, *President*
David Hicks, *General Mgr*
George Matherly, *General Mgr*
Michael A Smith, *Vice Pres*
EMP: 145
SQ FT: 60,000
SALES (est): 161.2MM **Privately Held**
WEB: www.mervis.com
SIC: 5093 3087 Ferrous metal scrap & waste; plastics scrap; waste paper; custom compound purchased resins

(G-7366)
MH EQUIPMENT COMPANY
1010 E Fairchild St (61832-3393)
P.O. Box 847 (61834-0847)
PHONE..........................217 443-7210
Ray Seguin, *Branch Mgr*
Brad Langford, *Technical Staff*
EMP: 100
SALES (corp-wide): 256.5MM **Privately Held**
WEB: www.mhequipment.com
SIC: 3537 3634 Forklift trucks; electric household cooking appliances; toasters, electric: household; irons, electric: household; coffee makers, electric: household
HQ: Mh Equipment Company
8901 N Industrial Rd
Peoria IL 61615
309 579-8020

(G-7367)
MIDWEST ELC MTR INC DANVILLE
819 N Bowman Ave (61832-4031)
P.O. Box 1516 (61834-1516)
PHONE..........................217 442-5656
Walter Burress, *President*
Zeke Yoho, *Vice Pres*
EMP: 4
SQ FT: 30,000
SALES (est): 585.8K **Privately Held**
SIC: 7694 5999 5063 Electric motor repair; motors, electric; motor controls, starters & relays: electric; motors, electric

(G-7368)
NEON STREET PRODUCTIONS
409 S Buchanan St Apt 4 (61832-6862)
PHONE..........................217 304-4514
Scott Murphy, *Principal*
EMP: 3
SALES (est): 123.2K **Privately Held**
SIC: 2813 Neon

(G-7369)
NEWS-GAZETTE INC
2202 Kickapoo Dr (61832-5379)
PHONE..........................217 443-8484
John Foreman, *Branch Mgr*
EMP: 10 **Privately Held**
SIC: 2711 Newspapers, publishing & printing
PA: The News-Gazette Inc
15 E Main St
Champaign IL 61820

(G-7370)
NEWSPAPER HOLDING INC
17 W North St (61832-5765)
P.O. Box 787 (61834-0787)
PHONE..........................217 446-1000
Amy Winter, *Branch Mgr*
Carolyn Van Pelt, *Manager*
EMP: 38 **Privately Held**
SIC: 2711 Newspapers: publishing only, not printed on site
HQ: Newspaper Holding, Inc.
425 Locust St
Johnstown PA 15901
814 532-5102

(G-7371)
P-AMERICAS LLC
Also Called: Pepsico
211 S Bowman Ave (61832-6424)
PHONE..........................217 446-0123
Mike Pilkington, *Manager*
EMP: 40
SQ FT: 33,000
SALES (corp-wide): 67.1B **Publicly Held**
SIC: 2086 5149 Carbonated soft drinks, bottled & canned; groceries & related products
HQ: P-Americas Llc
1 Pepsi Way
Somers NY 10589
336 896-5740

(G-7372)
PARK ELECTRIC MOTOR SERVICE
1204 N Collett St (61832-3111)
PHONE..........................217 442-1977
Laura Park, *President*
Steven Park, *Principal*
Timothy Park, *Principal*
Gerald Park, *Treasurer*
EMP: 5 **EST:** 1978
SQ FT: 4,000
SALES (est): 350K **Privately Held**
SIC: 7694 5063 Electric motor repair; motors, electric

(G-7373)
PEPSICO
1703 E Voorhees St (61834-6256)
PHONE..........................217 443-8607
Michaeld Gregory, *Principal*
Tamara Lambert, *Technology*
EMP: 11
SALES (est): 1.5MM **Privately Held**
WEB: www.pepsico.com
SIC: 2086 Carbonated soft drinks, bottled & canned

(G-7374)
PIX NORTH AMERICA INC
1222 E Voorhees St (61834-6249)
PHONE..........................855 800-0720
Scott Eppinga, *Principal*
EMP: 19
SALES (est): 3.3MM **Privately Held**
SIC: 3052 Rubber & plastics hose & beltings

(G-7375)
QUAKER OATS COMPANY
1703 E Voorhees St (61834-6262)
PHONE..........................217 443-4995
Chris Powers, *Plant Engr*
Mike Sacre, *Project Engr*
Dave Bechtold, *Senior Engr*
Vince Crudele, *Finance*
Pat Burke, *Manager*
EMP: 600
SALES (corp-wide): 67.1B **Publicly Held**
SIC: 2099 2043 2041 Food preparations; cereal breakfast foods; flour & other grain mill products
HQ: The Quaker Oats Company
555 W Monroe St Fl 1
Chicago IL 60661
312 821-1000

(G-7376)
RAHN EQUIPMENT COMPANY
2400 Georgetown Rd (61832-8425)
PHONE..........................217 431-1232
Chris Rahn, *President*
Joyce Rahn, *Corp Secy*
Richard Helton, *Manager*
EMP: 9
SQ FT: 10,000
SALES (est): 3.6MM **Privately Held**
WEB: www.rahnequipmentcompany.com
SIC: 5082 5083 3711 General construction machinery & equipment; mowers, power; truck & tractor truck assembly; snow plows (motor vehicles), assembly of

(G-7377)
RATHJE ENTERPRISES INC
Also Called: Bodine Electric of Decatur
19 Withner St (61834-5326)
P.O. Box 701 (61834-0701)
PHONE..........................217 443-0022
Mike Dell, *Principal*
EMP: 12
SALES (corp-wide): 69.3MM **Privately Held**
SIC: 1731 3621 General electrical contractor; motors & generators
PA: Rathje Enterprises, Inc.
1845 N 22nd St
Decatur IL 62526
217 423-2593

(G-7378)
RED WING
2418 Georgetown Rd (61832-8425)
PHONE..........................217 655-2772
Chuck Haga, *President*
EMP: 3
SALES (est): 94.8K **Privately Held**
SIC: 5661 5087 3131 Shoe stores; caskets; boot & shoe accessories

(G-7379)
ROWDY STAR CUSTOM CREATIONS
1936 Delong St (61832-2622)
PHONE..........................217 497-1789
Kathy A Pichon, *Owner*
Kathy Pichon, *Owner*
EMP: 3
SALES (est): 75K **Privately Held**
SIC: 3993 Signs & advertising specialties

(G-7380)
SAND VALLEY SAND & GRAVEL INC
16395 Lewis Rd (61834)
PHONE..........................217 446-4210
Melvin Price, *Principal*
EMP: 15
SALES (est): 861.9K **Privately Held**
SIC: 1442 Construction sand & gravel

(G-7381)
SPEEDYS QUICK PRINT
44 N Vermilion St (61832-5802)
PHONE..........................217 431-0510
Ivan Solgard, *Owner*
Lynda Solgard, *Co-Owner*
EMP: 4 **EST:** 1977
SQ FT: 3,600
SALES (est): 558K **Privately Held**
SIC: 7334 2752 2791 2789 Photocopying & duplicating services; commercial printing, offset; typesetting; bookbinding & related work

(G-7382)
TEEPAK USA LLC
915 N Michigan Ave (61834-3500)
PHONE..........................217 446-6460
Cliff Harper, *Principal*
EMP: 2
SALES (est): 371K **Privately Held**
SIC: 3089 Food casings, plastic

(G-7383)
THYSSENKRUPP CRANKSHAFT CO LLC (DH)
1000 Lynch Rd (61834-5811)
PHONE..........................217 431-0060
Joseph A Pycz III, *CEO*
Richard W Clark,
◆ **EMP:** 200
SQ FT: 175,000
SALES (est): 119.7MM
SALES (corp-wide): 46.8B **Privately Held**
SIC: 3462 3714 Automotive & internal combustion engine forgings; universal joints, motor vehicle

(G-7384)
THYSSENKRUPP CRANKSHAFT CO LLC
1200 International Pl (61834-6291)
PHONE..........................217 444-5400
Joseph Pycz III, *President*
EMP: 130
SALES (corp-wide): 46.8B **Privately Held**
SIC: 3462 Iron & steel forgings
HQ: Thyssenkrupp Crankshaft Company Llc
1000 Lynch Rd
Danville IL 61834

(G-7385)
THYSSENKRUPP CRANKSHAFT CO LLC
75 Walz Crk (61834-9373)
P.O. Box 1997 (61834-1997)
PHONE..........................217 444-5500
Adolf Pfeiffer, *Branch Mgr*
EMP: 210
SALES (corp-wide): 46.8B **Privately Held**
SIC: 3714 3462 Universal joints, motor vehicle; iron & steel forgings
HQ: Thyssenkrupp Crankshaft Company Llc
1000 Lynch Rd
Danville IL 61834

(G-7386)
THYSSENKRUPP PRESTA COLD FORGI
69 Walz Crk (61834-9373)
PHONE..........................217 431-4212
Peter Allaart, *Mng Member*
EMP: 40
SALES (est): 5.7MM
SALES (corp-wide): 46.8B **Privately Held**
SIC: 3714 Steering mechanisms, motor vehicle
HQ: Thyssenkrupp Automotive Sales & Technical Center, Inc.
3155 W Big Beaver Rd # 260
Troy MI 48084

(G-7387)
THYSSNKRUPP PRSTA DANVILLE LLC
75 Walz Crk (61834-9373)
PHONE..........................217 444-5500
Thomas Warner, *President*
Ryan Garrison, *Engineer*
Paul Meisel, *Treasurer*
Eric Harris, *Manager*
Kevin C Backus, *Admin Sec*
◆ **EMP:** 300
SALES (est): 78.4MM
SALES (corp-wide): 46.8B **Privately Held**
SIC: 3714 Camshafts, motor vehicle
PA: Thyssenkrupp Ag
Thyssenkrupp Allee 1
Essen 45143
201 844-0

(G-7388)
TILTON PATTERN WORKS INC
21204 Rileysburg Rd (61834-5892)
PHONE..........................217 442-1502
Jeff Marble, *President*
EMP: 12 **EST:** 1947
SQ FT: 4,000
SALES (est): 1.4MM **Privately Held**
SIC: 3543 3366 Industrial patterns; castings (except die): brass; castings (except die): bronze

(G-7389)
TOWNE MACHINE TOOL COMPANY
1009 Lynch Rd (61834-5804)
P.O. Box 685 (61834-0685)
PHONE..........................217 442-4910
Clinton S Towne, *CEO*
Scott Towne, *Vice Pres*
Randy Williamson, *Sales Staff*
Charlett Towne, *Shareholder*
Curt Towne, *Shareholder*
EMP: 17 **EST:** 1950
SQ FT: 15,000
SALES (est): 4.4MM **Privately Held**
WEB: www.townemachinetool.com
SIC: 3599 Machine shop, jobbing & repair

(G-7390)
VERMILION MILLWORKS LLC
Also Called: Th Snyder Company
611 Oak St (61832-3943)
PHONE..........................217 446-8443
Scott Degenova, *Vice Pres*
Paul Kass, *Vice Pres*
Roger Irle,
Dan Nobbe,
EMP: 19
SALES (est): 2.7MM **Privately Held**
SIC: 2431 Millwork

(G-7391)
VERMILION STEEL FABRICATION
Also Called: Electronic Equipment Exchange
3295 E Main St Ste A (61834-9302)
PHONE..........................217 442-5300
Adam Mervis, *President*
Micheal Smith, *CFO*
Jennifer Klein, *Treasurer*

Danville - Vermilion County

Darrin Jolas, *Director*
▲ **EMP:** 8
SALES (est): 925.5K **Privately Held**
WEB: www.mervis.com
SIC: 3449 5399 Bars, concrete reinforcing; fabricated steel; warehouse club stores

(G-7392)
VISCOFAN USA INC
915 Michigan St (61834)
PHONE..................................217 444-8000
James Blackford, *Engineer*
Todd Goodner, *Electrical Engi*
Doug Dunningham, *Branch Mgr*
Cliff Harper, *Manager*
EMP: 73
SALES (corp-wide): 207.4MM **Privately Held**
WEB: www.viscofan.com
SIC: 3089 2013 Food casings, plastic; sausage casings, natural
HQ: Viscofan Usa, Inc.
50 County Ct
Montgomery AL 36105
334 396-0092

(G-7393)
WATCHFIRE ENTERPRISES INC (DH)
1015 Maple St (61832-3200)
PHONE..................................217 442-0611
Steve Harriott, *CEO*
Adam Grimes, *CFO*
▲ **EMP:** 20
SALES (est): 130.6MM **Privately Held**
WEB: www.watchfiresigns.com
SIC: 3993 Electric signs
HQ: Watchfire Technologies Holdings Ii, Inc.
1015 Maple St
Danville IL 61832
217 442-0611

(G-7394)
WATCHFIRE SIGNS LLC (DH)
Also Called: Time-O-Matic Inc.
1015 Maple St (61832-3200)
PHONE..................................217 442-0611
Steve Harriott, *President*
Kim Weninger, *COO*
Kyle Dines, *Vice Pres*
Barry Pearman, *Engineer*
Adam Grimes, *CFO*
◆ **EMP:** 276 EST: 1971
SALES (est): 87.6MM
SALES (corp-wide): 130.6MM **Privately Held**
WEB: www.watchfiresigns.com
SIC: 3993 Electric signs
HQ: Watchfire Enterprises, Inc.
1015 Maple St
Danville IL 61832
217 442-0611

(G-7395)
WATCHFIRE TECH HOLDINGS I INC (PA)
1015 Maple St (61832-3200)
PHONE..................................217 442-6971
Steve Harriott, *CEO*
Kim Weninger, *COO*
EMP: 9
SALES (est): 130.6MM **Privately Held**
SIC: 3993 Electric signs

(G-7396)
WATCHFIRE TECH HOLDINGS II INC (HQ)
1015 Maple St (61832-3200)
PHONE..................................217 442-0611
Steve Harriott, *CEO*
EMP: 6 EST: 2013
SALES (est): 130.6MM **Privately Held**
WEB: www.watchfiresigns.com
SIC: 3993 Electric signs
PA: Watchfire Technologies Holdings I, Inc.
1015 Maple St
Danville IL 61832
217 442-6971

(G-7397)
WESTROCK MWV LLC
Also Called: Envelope Division
202 Eastgate Dr (61834-9472)
PHONE..................................217 442-2247
Linda Cribes, *Manager*
EMP: 25
SALES (corp-wide): 18.2B **Publicly Held**
SIC: 2631 2791 2752 Linerboard; typesetting; commercial printing, lithographic
HQ: Westrock Mwv, Llc
501 S 5th St
Richmond VA 23219
804 444-1000

(G-7398)
WILLIAM INGRAM
Also Called: Quick Lube
216 S Gilbert St (61832-6232)
PHONE..................................217 442-5075
Kevin Davis, *Owner*
EMP: 4
SALES (corp-wide): 224K **Privately Held**
SIC: 2992 7549 Lubricating oils; automotive maintenance services
PA: William Ingram

Danville IL 61832
217 446-6887

Darien
Dupage County

(G-7399)
ACME MARBLE CO INC
1103 Belair Dr (60561-4013)
PHONE..................................630 964-7162
George Binder, *President*
Thomas Satler, *Vice Pres*
Delores Satler, *Admin Sec*
EMP: 6
SQ FT: 4,000
SALES: 300K **Privately Held**
SIC: 1743 3281 Marble installation, interior; cut stone & stone products

(G-7400)
ALL CUT INC
8195 S Lemont Rd (60561-1755)
PHONE..................................630 910-6505
Andrew Widlacki, *President*
Stan Widlacki, *Vice Pres*
EMP: 3
SALES: 400K **Privately Held**
SIC: 3599 Custom machinery

(G-7401)
ANGELA YANG CHINGJUI
Also Called: Bridge Wave Electronics
1026 Sean Cir (60561-3877)
PHONE..................................630 724-0596
Angela C Yang, *Owner*
EMP: 3
SALES (est): 235.7K **Privately Held**
SIC: 3674 Semiconductors & related devices

(G-7402)
ARCHER ENGINEERING COMPANY
2015 S Frontage Rd (60561-1779)
PHONE..................................773 247-3501
Ronald Lanie, *President*
Virginia Lanie, *Admin Sec*
EMP: 7 EST: 1951
SALES: 1.3MM **Privately Held**
WEB: www.archerengineeringco.com
SIC: 3451 Screw machine products

(G-7403)
CHEM FREE SOLUTIONS (PA)
Also Called: Naturally Clean
8420 Evergreen Ln (60561-8400)
PHONE..................................630 541-7931
Michael Wallrich, *President*
Dennis Voss, *Principal*
EMP: 2
SQ FT: 6,500
SALES (est): 466.8K **Privately Held**
SIC: 2869 Enzymes

(G-7404)
CHICAGO BAKING COMPANY (HQ)
Also Called: Butternut Bread
6818 Rte 83 (60561-3973)
PHONE..................................630 684-2335
Jack Lewis, *President*
Richard Wilson, *Manager*
EMP: 750
SQ FT: 250,000
SALES (est): 60.4MM
SALES (corp-wide): 456.5MM **Privately Held**
SIC: 2951 5461 2051 Asphalt paving mixtures & blocks; bakeries; bread, cake & related products
PA: Lewis Brothers Bakeries Inc
500 N Fulton Ave
Evansville IN 47710
812 425-4642

(G-7405)
DAVES WELDING SERVICE INC
7201 Leonard Dr (60561-4147)
PHONE..................................630 655-3224
Dave Norlag, *President*
EMP: 4
SALES (est): 450K **Privately Held**
SIC: 1799 7692 3446 3444 Welding on site; welding repair; architectural metalwork; sheet metalwork;

(G-7406)
EDK CONSTRUCTION INC
1325 Chapman Dr (60561-5388)
PHONE..................................630 853-3484
Elaine Kindt, *CEO*
EMP: 2
SALES (est): 209.8K **Privately Held**
SIC: 1442 Gravel mining

(G-7407)
HONEYWELL INTERNATIONAL INC
7714 Baker Ct (60561-4549)
PHONE..................................630 960-5282
EMP: 699
SALES (corp-wide): 40.5B **Publicly Held**
SIC: 3724 Mfg Aircraft Engines/Parts
PA: Honeywell International Inc.
115 Tabor Rd
Morris Plains NJ 28202
973 455-2000

(G-7408)
KERINS INDUSTRIES INC
8408 Wilmette Ave Ste A (60561-6446)
PHONE..................................630 515-9111
James Kerins, *President*
Sue Kerins, *Corp Secy*
Dave Van Vreede Sales, *Manager*
▲ **EMP:** 2
SQ FT: 6,000
SALES (est): 315.7K **Privately Held**
SIC: 3799 Trailer hitches

(G-7409)
MIDWEST ULTRASONICS INC
2000 Harper Rd (60561-6701)
PHONE..................................630 434-9458
Stephen B Highland, *Principal*
EMP: 4
SALES (est): 485.3K **Privately Held**
SIC: 3829 Ultrasonic testing equipment

(G-7410)
MULTI PRINT AND DIGITAL LLC
Also Called: Multi Business Forms
8113 S Lemont Rd (60561-1755)
PHONE..................................630 985-2600
Patrice E Price, *CEO*
EMP: 5
SQ FT: 6,000
SALES: 653.6K **Privately Held**
SIC: 2741 8742 Patterns, paper: publishing & printing; marketing consulting services

(G-7411)
PLAIN & POSH LLC
1016 Oakfern Ln (60561-3891)
PHONE..................................630 960-0048
Stephanie Frees, *Administration*
EMP: 4 EST: 2014

SALES (est): 332.6K **Privately Held**
WEB: www.plainandposh.com
SIC: 2434 Wood kitchen cabinets

(G-7412)
TAGITSOLD INC
Also Called: Fire Place By Ignite
1136 Lacebark Ct (60561-3886)
PHONE..................................630 724-1800
Randall Schorle, *President*
EMP: 2
SALES: 400K **Privately Held**
SIC: 3272 Fireplace & chimney material: concrete

(G-7413)
TDS MACHINING INC
8402 Wilmette Ave Ste B (60561-5433)
PHONE..................................630 964-0004
Ted Jablonski, *President*
EMP: 10
SQ FT: 3,000
SALES (est): 1.3MM **Privately Held**
SIC: 3599 Machine shop, jobbing & repair

(G-7414)
WILLOW FARM PRODUCT INC
Also Called: Wf Machining Product
8193 S Lemont Rd (60561-1755)
PHONE..................................630 395-9246
Richard Polivka, *Owner*
EMP: 6 EST: 2014
SALES (est): 545.9K **Privately Held**
SIC: 3411 Metal cans

(G-7415)
YESIMPACT
8202 Ripple Rdg (60561-6424)
P.O. Box 11126, Chicago (60611-0121)
PHONE..................................765 413-9667
Jean Kedler Abelard, *Exec Dir*
EMP: 6 EST: 2017
SALES: 50K **Privately Held**
SIC: 8299 8699 7372 Educational services; charitable organization; application computer software

Davis
Stephenson County

(G-7416)
CUSTOM KARTS AND MORE LLC
1570 Chadbourne Dr (61019-9643)
PHONE..................................815 703-6438
Steven Carlson, *Principal*
EMP: 3 EST: 2016
SALES (est): 202.5K **Privately Held**
SIC: 3999 Manufacturing industries

(G-7417)
EFFECTIVE ENERGY ASSOC LLC
1979 Sunline Dr (61019-9455)
P.O. Box 57 (61019-0057)
PHONE..................................815 248-9280
Bob Abele, *Mng Member*
Jacob Scheid, *Manager*
▼ **EMP:** 5
SALES: 250K **Privately Held**
SIC: 3559 7389 Refinery, chemical processing & similar machinery;

(G-7418)
HAZEN DISPLAY CORPORATION (PA)
537 Baintree Rd (61019-9440)
PHONE..................................815 248-2925
Gerald E Osowski, *President*
Marvin O Conrad, *Vice Pres*
EMP: 20 EST: 1946
SQ FT: 33,000
SALES (est): 1.5MM **Privately Held**
SIC: 3993 2759 3089 2396 Displays & cutouts, window & lobby; screen printing; plastic processing; automotive & apparel trimmings

(G-7419)
T R MACHINE INC
103 Il Route 75 E Ste 100 (61019-9584)
PHONE..................................815 865-5711

GEOGRAPHIC SECTION

Decatur - Macon County (G-7444)

Jana Olsen, *President*
Thomas R Olsen, *Vice Pres*
EMP: 36
SQ FT: 20,000
SALES (est): 8.9MM **Privately Held**
SIC: 3599 Machine shop, jobbing & repair

(G-7420)
WENGERS SPRINGBROOK CHEESE INC
12805 N Spring Brook Rd (61019-9719)
PHONE.................................815 865-5855
Fred Winger, *President*
John H Wenger, *Vice Pres*
EMP: 15
SALES (est): 2.5MM **Privately Held**
SIC: 2022 Natural cheese

Davis Junction
Ogle County

(G-7421)
DJ LIQUORS INC
5657 N Junction Way (61020-9433)
PHONE.................................815 645-1145
Mark Fritzen, *President*
EMP: 4
SQ FT: 500
SALES: 150K **Privately Held**
SIC: 2082 Malt liquors

(G-7422)
FOREST CITY SATELLITE
432 Heartland Dr (61020-9741)
PHONE.................................815 639-0500
EMP: 4
SALES (est): 250.8K **Privately Held**
SIC: 3663 Cameras, television

(G-7423)
FORM RELIEF TOOL CO INC
14499 E Il Route 72 (61020-9775)
PHONE.................................815 393-4263
James Marx, *President*
Jim Marx, *Marketing Mgr*
Judy Marx, *Admin Sec*
EMP: 16
SQ FT: 5,600
SALES (est): 2.7MM **Privately Held**
SIC: 3541 4225 5251 Machine tools, metal cutting type; miniwarehouse, warehousing; tools

(G-7424)
GENSLER GARDENS INC (PA)
8631 11th St (61020-9604)
PHONE.................................815 874-9634
William Gensler, *President*
Scott Gensler, *Vice Pres*
Eleanor Gensler, *Admin Sec*
EMP: 12
SALES (est): 1.5MM **Privately Held**
SIC: 2519 0161 0171 Garden furniture, except wood, metal, stone or concrete; vegetables & melons; berry crops

(G-7425)
KRESSER PRECISION INDS INC
700 Golden Prairie Dr (61020-9442)
PHONE.................................815 899-2202
John Kresser, *President*
Lisa Kresser, *Admin Sec*
EMP: 5
SALES: 250K **Privately Held**
SIC: 3599 Machine shop, jobbing & repair

(G-7426)
ROLL RITE INC
6549 N Junction Rd (61020-9780)
P.O. Box 153 (61020-0153)
PHONE.................................815 645-8600
Jerry Hanna, *President*
Patricia Hanna, *Vice Pres*
EMP: 6
SQ FT: 7,800
SALES (est): 1.1MM **Privately Held**
SIC: 3542 3599 3545 3541 Knurling machines; grinding castings for the trade; machine tool accessories; machine tools, metal cutting type

(G-7427)
SKANDIA INC
5000 Il 251 (61020)
PHONE.................................800 945-7135
Gary Palmer, *President*
Laurie Pink, *Admin Sec*
EMP: 70
SQ FT: 80,000
SALES: 26MM
SALES (corp-wide): 5.2B **Publicly Held**
SIC: 4581 8734 2273 3728 Aircraft maintenance & repair services; aircraft upholstery repair; product testing laboratories; aircraft floor coverings, except rubber or plastic; aircraft parts & equipment
PA: Transdigm Group Incorporated
1301 E 9th St Ste 3000
Cleveland OH 44114
216 706-2960

Dawson
Sangamon County

(G-7428)
ALL WEATHER COURTS INC
Rr Box 276 (62520)
PHONE.................................217 364-4546
Fax: 217 364-4436
EMP: 4 **EST:** 1962
SQ FT: 5,200
SALES: 400K **Privately Held**
SIC: 1629 1611 2891 Tennis Courts Resurfacing Contractor & Mfg Sealer

De Kalb
Dekalb County

(G-7429)
E B INC
Also Called: Hiatt Brothers
116 E State St (60115)
P.O. Box 607, Dekalb (60115-0607)
PHONE.................................815 758-6646
Edward J Bosic, *President*
Eileen S Bosic, *Corp Secy*
Bill Gibbons, *Vice Pres*
Ann Bosic, *Office Mgr*
◆ **EMP:** 10
SQ FT: 12,000
SALES (est): 1.7MM **Privately Held**
SIC: 3441 Fabricated structural metal

De Soto
Jackson County

(G-7430)
ANDREW MCDONALD
Also Called: Flatland Forge & Design
100 N Ash St (62924-1115)
PHONE.................................618 867-2323
Andrew McDonald, *Owner*
EMP: 3
SALES: 50K **Privately Held**
SIC: 3462 Iron & steel forgings

Decatur
Macon County

(G-7431)
300 BELOW INC
2999 E Parkway Dr (62526-5296)
PHONE.................................217 423-3070
Pete Paulin, *President*
John Koucky, *Vice Pres*
Susan Brown, *Opers Staff*
Stephen Kamykowski, *Research*
James Reed, *Research*
▲ **EMP:** 6
SQ FT: 10,000
SALES: 1.7MM **Privately Held**
SIC: 3398 8731 2899 2842 Metal heat treating; energy research; electronic research; rifle bore cleaning compounds; specialty cleaning preparations

(G-7432)
ADM GRAIN COMPANY
4666 E Faries Pkwy (62526-5678)
PHONE.................................217 424-5200
Doug Gooden, *Manager*
EMP: 35
SALES (est): 20.1MM
SALES (corp-wide): 64.6B **Publicly Held**
WEB: www.adm.com
SIC: 5153 2041 Grain elevators; flour & other grain mill products
PA: Archer-Daniels-Midland Company
77 W Wacker Dr Ste 4600
Chicago IL 60601
312 634-8100

(G-7433)
ADM HOLDINGS LLC
350 N Water St (62523-1106)
PHONE.................................217 422-7281
EMP: 3
SALES (corp-wide): 64.6B **Publicly Held**
WEB: www.adm.com
SIC: 2046 Wet corn milling
HQ: Adm Holdings, Llc
4666 E Faries Pkwy
Decatur IL 62526

(G-7434)
ADM HOLDINGS LLC (HQ)
4666 E Faries Pkwy (62526-5678)
P.O. Box 1470 (62525-1820)
PHONE.................................217 424-5200
Juan R Luciano, *President*
◆ **EMP:** 5
SALES (est): 1.4MM
SALES (corp-wide): 64.6B **Publicly Held**
SIC: 2046 High fructose corn syrup (HFCS)
PA: Archer-Daniels-Midland Company
77 W Wacker Dr Ste 4600
Chicago IL 60601
312 634-8100

(G-7435)
AGRI-FAB INC
3490 L & A Industrial Dr (62521)
PHONE.................................217 875-7051
Joe Cohan, *Branch Mgr*
EMP: 10
SALES (corp-wide): 29.3MM **Privately Held**
SIC: 3523 Farm machinery & equipment
HQ: Agri-Fab, Inc.
809 S Hamilton St
Sullivan IL 61951
217 728-8388

(G-7436)
AIR CASTER LLC
2887 N Woodford St (62526-4713)
PHONE.................................217 877-1237
Filip Van Der Borght,
Mike Skaff,
EMP: 25 **EST:** 2016
SQ FT: 25,000
SALES (est): 1.7MM **Privately Held**
SIC: 3599 Custom machinery

(G-7437)
AKORN INC
150 S Wyckles Rd (62522-1038)
PHONE.................................217 428-1100
Andrew Micali, *QC Mgr*
Krystal Topps, *Finance*
Janet Foster, *Human Res Dir*
Russ Gall, *Branch Mgr*
Kevin Kessler, *Manager*
EMP: 200
SALES (corp-wide): 682.4MM **Privately Held**
SIC: 2834 Pharmaceutical preparations
PA: Akorn, Inc.
1925 W Field Ct Ste 300
Lake Forest IL 60045
847 279-6100

(G-7438)
AKORN INC
Also Called: Akorn Pharmaceuticals
1222 W Grand Ave (62522-1412)
PHONE.................................217 423-9715
Karen Logan, *Human Resources*
Kim Wasserkrug, *Branch Mgr*
Jamie McClellan, *Manager*
EMP: 125

SALES (corp-wide): 682.4MM **Privately Held**
SIC: 2834 Pharmaceutical preparations
PA: Akorn, Inc.
1925 W Field Ct Ste 300
Lake Forest IL 60045
847 279-6100

(G-7439)
ALIGN PRODUCTION SYSTEMS LLC
2230 N Brush College Rd (62526-5522)
PHONE.................................217 423-6001
Jason Stoecker, *CEO*
Shane Metzger, *COO*
Lane Fredrickson, *Plant Mgr*
Jose Intharaphet, *Engineer*
Josh McKenna, *Engineer*
EMP: 41
SALES (est): 13.4MM **Privately Held**
SIC: 3537 3535 Industrial trucks & tractors; bulk handling conveyor systems

(G-7440)
ALL SEASONS HEATING & AC
Also Called: All Seasons Co
167 S Excelsior St (62521-8763)
PHONE.................................217 429-2022
Clarence Pickering, *Owner*
EMP: 6
SALES (est): 352.6K **Privately Held**
SIC: 1711 7699 3444 1799 Ventilation & duct work contractor; refrigeration contractor; filter cleaning; hoods, range: sheet metal; steam cleaning of building exteriors

(G-7441)
ARCHER-DANIELS-MIDLAND COMPANY
Also Called: ADM
3665 E Division (62525)
PHONE.................................217 424-5882
Rob Jacobson, *Branch Mgr*
EMP: 100
SALES (corp-wide): 64.6B **Publicly Held**
WEB: www.adm.com
SIC: 2041 4212 Flour & other grain mill products; local trucking, without storage
PA: Archer-Daniels-Midland Company
77 W Wacker Dr Ste 4600
Chicago IL 60601
312 634-8100

(G-7442)
ARCHER-DANIELS-MIDLAND COMPANY
Also Called: ADM
3095 E Parkway Dr (62526-5260)
PHONE.................................217 451-8909
EMP: 5
SALES (corp-wide): 64.6B **Publicly Held**
WEB: www.adm.com
SIC: 2041 Flour & other grain mill products
PA: Archer-Daniels-Midland Company
77 W Wacker Dr Ste 4600
Chicago IL 60601
312 634-8100

(G-7443)
ARCHER-DANIELS-MIDLAND COMPANY
Also Called: ADM
466 Ferrys Pkwy (62525)
P.O. Box 1470 (62525-1820)
PHONE.................................217 424-5236
Jerome Pala, *Principal*
EMP: 4
SALES (corp-wide): 64.6B **Publicly Held**
WEB: www.adm.com
SIC: 2041 Flour & other grain mill products
PA: Archer-Daniels-Midland Company
77 W Wacker Dr Ste 4600
Chicago IL 60601
312 634-8100

(G-7444)
ARCHER-DANIELS-MIDLAND COMPANY
Also Called: ADM Milling
4666 E Faries Pkwy Ste 1 (62526-5632)
P.O. Box 2576 (62525-2576)
PHONE.................................800 257-5743
Glenn Ginalick, *General Mgr*
Chad West, *General Mgr*

Decatur - Macon County (G-7445)

James Burt, *Superintendent*
Jerry Garduno, *Area Mgr*
Vincent Cambruzzi, *Business Mgr*
EMP: 277
SALES (corp-wide): 64.6B **Publicly Held**
SIC: 2041 Flour & other grain mill products
PA: Archer-Daniels-Midland Company
77 W Wacker Dr Ste 4600
Chicago IL 60601
312 634-8100

(G-7445)
ARCHER-DANIELS-MIDLAND COMPANY
Also Called: ADM
3605 E Division St (62526)
PHONE..............................217 424-5806
John Wilhour, *Branch Mgr*
EMP: 4
SALES (corp-wide): 64.6B **Publicly Held**
SIC: 2041 Flour & other grain mill products
PA: Archer-Daniels-Midland Company
77 W Wacker Dr Ste 4600
Chicago IL 60601
312 634-8100

(G-7446)
ARCHER-DANIELS-MIDLAND COMPANY
Also Called: ADM
3350 N 27th St (62526-2190)
PHONE..............................217 451-4460
EMP: 17
SALES (corp-wide): 64.6B **Publicly Held**
SIC: 2041 Flour & other grain mill products
PA: Archer-Daniels-Midland Company
77 W Wacker Dr Ste 4600
Chicago IL 60601
312 634-8100

(G-7447)
ARCHER-DANIELS-MIDLAND COMPANY
Also Called: ADM
350 N Water St (62523-1106)
P.O. Box 2576 (62525-2576)
PHONE..............................217 424-5413
Juan R Luciano, *Ch of Bd*
EMP: 28
SALES (corp-wide): 64.6B **Publicly Held**
SIC: 2041 Flour & other grain mill products
PA: Archer-Daniels-Midland Company
77 W Wacker Dr Ste 4600
Chicago IL 60601
312 634-8100

(G-7448)
ARCHER-DANIELS-MIDLAND COMPANY
Also Called: ADM
2235 N Brush College Rd (62526-5521)
PHONE..............................217 424-5200
Bill Manley, *Manager*
EMP: 58
SALES (corp-wide): 64.6B **Publicly Held**
SIC: 2041 2083 Flour & other grain mill products; malt
PA: Archer-Daniels-Midland Company
77 W Wacker Dr Ste 4600
Chicago IL 60601
312 634-8100

(G-7449)
ARCHER-DANIELS-MIDLAND COMPANY
Also Called: ADM
4666 E Faries Pkwy Ste 1 (62526-5632)
PHONE..............................217 424-5200
EMP: 112
SALES (corp-wide): 64.6B **Publicly Held**
SIC: 2041 Flour & other grain mill products
PA: Archer-Daniels-Midland Company
77 W Wacker Dr Ste 4600
Chicago IL 60601
312 634-8100

(G-7450)
ARCHER-DANIELS-MIDLAND COMPANY
Also Called: ADM
4083 E Faries Pkwy (62526-5654)
PHONE..............................217 424-5830
Lonnie Ferguson, *Manager*
EMP: 25
SALES (corp-wide): 64.6B **Publicly Held**
SIC: 2041 Flour & other grain mill products
PA: Archer-Daniels-Midland Company
77 W Wacker Dr Ste 4600
Chicago IL 60601
312 634-8100

(G-7451)
ARCHER-DANIELS-MIDLAND COMPANY
Also Called: ADM
2311 N 22nd St (62525)
PHONE..............................217 451-8169
Shaun Brewer, *Branch Mgr*
EMP: 70
SALES (corp-wide): 64.6B **Publicly Held**
SIC: 2041 Flour & other grain mill products
PA: Archer-Daniels-Midland Company
77 W Wacker Dr Ste 4600
Chicago IL 60601
312 634-8100

(G-7452)
ARCHER-DANIELS-MIDLAND COMPANY
Also Called: ADM
3601 E Division St (62526-5638)
P.O. Box 1470 (62525-1820)
PHONE..............................217 424-5660
Pat Laegeler, *Principal*
EMP: 30
SALES (corp-wide): 64.6B **Publicly Held**
SIC: 2041 Flour & other grain mill products
PA: Archer-Daniels-Midland Company
77 W Wacker Dr Ste 4600
Chicago IL 60601
312 634-8100

(G-7453)
ARCHER-DANIELS-MIDLAND COMPANY
ADM
3883 E Faries Pkwy (62526-5656)
P.O. Box 1470 (62525-1820)
PHONE..............................217 424-5858
Brad Birkholtz, *Manager*
EMP: 49
SALES (corp-wide): 64.6B **Publicly Held**
SIC: 2041 2075 Flour & other grain mill products; soybean oil mills
PA: Archer-Daniels-Midland Company
77 W Wacker Dr Ste 4600
Chicago IL 60601
312 634-8100

(G-7454)
ARCHER-DANIELS-MIDLAND COMPANY
2254 N 40th St (62526-5519)
PHONE..............................217 429-3054
▼ **EMP:** 3
SALES (corp-wide): 64.6B **Publicly Held**
SIC: 2041 Wheat flour
PA: Archer-Daniels-Midland Company
77 W Wacker Dr Ste 4600
Chicago IL 60601
312 634-8100

(G-7455)
ARCHER-DANIELS-MIDLAND COMPANY
ADM
3615 E Faries Pkwy (62526-5658)
P.O. Box 1470 (62525-1820)
PHONE..............................217 424-5785
Gary Bingham, *Manager*
EMP: 75
SALES (corp-wide): 64.6B **Publicly Held**
SIC: 2041 Flour & other grain mill products
PA: Archer-Daniels-Midland Company
77 W Wacker Dr Ste 4600
Chicago IL 60601
312 634-8100

(G-7456)
ARCHER-DANIELS-MIDLAND COMPANY
Also Called: ADM
3210 E Parkway Dr (62526-5261)
PHONE..............................217 451-4481
Todd Werpy, *Branch Mgr*
EMP: 14
SALES (corp-wide): 64.6B **Publicly Held**
SIC: 2041 Flour & other grain mill products
PA: Archer-Daniels-Midland Company
77 W Wacker Dr Ste 4600
Chicago IL 60601
312 634-8100

(G-7457)
ARCHER-DANIELS-MIDLAND COMPANY
Also Called: ADM Research
1001 N Brush College Rd (62521-1656)
PHONE..............................217 451-6528
Tom Bind, *Branch Mgr*
EMP: 400
SALES (corp-wide): 64.6B **Publicly Held**
SIC: 2041 Flour & other grain mill products
PA: Archer-Daniels-Midland Company
77 W Wacker Dr Ste 4600
Chicago IL 60601
312 634-8100

(G-7458)
ARCHER-DANIELS-MIDLAND COMPANY
Also Called: ADM
2120 N 40th St (62526-5517)
PHONE..............................217 423-2788
EMP: 9
SALES (corp-wide): 64.6B **Publicly Held**
SIC: 2041 Flour & other grain mill products
PA: Archer-Daniels-Midland Company
77 W Wacker Dr Ste 4600
Chicago IL 60601
312 634-8100

(G-7459)
ARCHER-DANIELS-MIDLAND COMPANY
Also Called: ADM
3700 E Division St (62526-5669)
PHONE..............................217 424-5200
Steve Obrien, *General Mgr*
EMP: 58
SALES (corp-wide): 64.6B **Publicly Held**
SIC: 2041 2834 Flour & other grain mill products; pharmaceutical preparations
PA: Archer-Daniels-Midland Company
77 W Wacker Dr Ste 4600
Chicago IL 60601
312 634-8100

(G-7460)
ARCHER-DANIELS-MIDLAND COMPANY
Also Called: ADM
2505 N Jasper St (62526-4881)
PHONE..............................217 424-5669
Mark Bemis, *Vice Pres*
Gary Towne, *Vice Pres*
EMP: 10
SALES (corp-wide): 64.6B **Publicly Held**
SIC: 2041 Flour & other grain mill products
PA: Archer-Daniels-Midland Company
77 W Wacker Dr Ste 4600
Chicago IL 60601
312 634-8100

(G-7461)
AURA SYSTEMS INC
2345 E Garfield Ave (62526-5125)
PHONE..............................217 423-4100
Mark L Sadorus, *President*
Joyce Sadorus, *Corp Secy*
Lowell Sadorus, *Vice Pres*
EMP: 22
SQ FT: 11,500
SALES: 2.4MM **Privately Held**
SIC: 3599 Custom machinery

(G-7462)
BARTON MANUFACTURING LLC (HQ)
1395 S Taylorville Rd (62521-4034)
PHONE..............................217 428-0711
Greg Mason, *President*
▲ **EMP:** 44
SQ FT: 65,000
SALES (est): 12.1MM
SALES (corp-wide): 12.8MM **Privately Held**
SIC: 3599 Machine shop, jobbing & repair
PA: Tag-Barton Llc
1395 S Taylorville Rd
Decatur IL 62521
217 428-0711

(G-7463)
BARTON MANUFACTURING LLC
600 E Wabash Ave (62523-1012)
PHONE..............................217 428-0726
Tony Leffler, *Manager*
EMP: 10
SALES (corp-wide): 12.8MM **Privately Held**
SIC: 7699 7692 Welding equipment repair; tank & boiler cleaning service; welding repair
HQ: Barton Manufacturing Llc
1395 S Taylorville Rd
Decatur IL 62521
217 428-0711

(G-7464)
BENDSEN SIGNS & GRAPHICS INC
1506 E Mcbride Ave (62526-5082)
PHONE..............................217 877-2345
Tom Pistorius, *President*
EMP: 10 **EST:** 2001
SQ FT: 5,000
SALES (est): 1.8MM **Privately Held**
WEB: www.bsg1946.com
SIC: 1799 7353 3993 3953 Sign installation & maintenance; cranes & aerial lift equipment, rental or leasing; signs & advertising specialties; marking devices

(G-7465)
BODINES BAKING COMPANY
2136 N Dennis Ave (62526-3523)
PHONE..............................217 853-7707
Amanda Bodine, *Principal*
EMP: 4
SALES (est): 91.3K **Privately Held**
SIC: 2051 Bakery: wholesale or wholesale/retail combined

(G-7466)
BOLD MACHINE WORKS INC
1677 S Taylorville Rd (62521-3950)
PHONE..............................217 428-6644
Donald Williams, *President*
Jennifer Latshaw, *Vice Pres*
Nancy Williams, *Vice Pres*
EMP: 10 **EST:** 1880
SQ FT: 6,000
SALES (est): 1.5MM **Privately Held**
WEB: www.boldmachineworks.com
SIC: 3599 Machine shop, jobbing & repair

(G-7467)
BONE A FIDE PET GROOMING
1220 E Pershing Rd Ste 1 (62526-4795)
PHONE..............................217 872-0907
James Woodrum, *Partner*
EMP: 3
SALES (est): 79K **Privately Held**
SIC: 0752 3999 Grooming services, pet & animal specialties; pet supplies

(G-7468)
CACHERA AND KLEMM INC
Also Called: C & K Custom Signs
2271 W Packard St (62522-1378)
PHONE..............................217 876-7446
Marie Klemm, *President*
Otto Klemm, *Vice Pres*
EMP: 4
SALES (est): 444.3K **Privately Held**
SIC: 3993 Electric signs

(G-7469)
CARGILL INCORPORATED
765 E Pythian Ave (62526-2412)
PHONE..............................217 872-7653
Jim Miller, *Branch Mgr*
EMP: 12
SALES (corp-wide): 113.4B **Privately Held**
SIC: 3552 Yarn texturizing machines
PA: Cargill, Incorporated
15407 Mcginty Rd W
Wayzata MN 55391
952 742-7575

(G-7470)
CARTRIDGE WORLD DECATUR
215 E Ash Ave Ste D (62526-6159)
PHONE..............................217 875-0465
EMP: 5

SALES (est): 462K **Privately Held**
SIC: 3955 Carbon Paper And Inked Ribbons

(G-7471)
CATERPILLAR INC
3000 N 27th St (62525)
P.O. Box 1430 (62525-1809)
PHONE..................................217 475-4000
Ashley Offermann, *Accountant*
Rob Bussell, *Branch Mgr*
Shane Meis, *Manager*
Patrick Robinson, *Info Tech Mgr*
EMP: 650
SQ FT: 3,000,000
SALES (corp-wide): 53.8B **Publicly Held**
WEB: www.caterpillar.com
SIC: 3713 3531 Truck & bus bodies; tractors, construction
PA: Caterpillar Inc.
510 Lake Cook Rd Ste 100
Deerfield IL 60015
224 551-4000

(G-7472)
CATERPILLAR INC
3125 N 22nd St (62526-2105)
PHONE..................................217 475-4355
Michael Flexenher, *Manager*
EMP: 355
SALES (corp-wide): 53.8B **Publicly Held**
WEB: www.caterpillar.com
SIC: 3531 Tractors, construction
PA: Caterpillar Inc.
510 Lake Cook Rd Ste 100
Deerfield IL 60015
224 551-4000

(G-7473)
CATERPILLAR INC
2701 Pershing Rd (62526)
PHONE..................................217 424-1809
James Owens, *Branch Mgr*
EMP: 355
SALES (corp-wide): 53.8B **Publicly Held**
SIC: 3531 Tractors, construction
PA: Caterpillar Inc.
510 Lake Cook Rd Ste 100
Deerfield IL 60015
224 551-4000

(G-7474)
CATERPILLAR INC
2500 N 22nd St (62526-4744)
PHONE..................................217 475-4322
EMP: 3
SALES (corp-wide): 53.8B **Publicly Held**
SIC: 3531 Construction machinery
PA: Caterpillar Inc.
510 Lake Cook Rd Ste 100
Deerfield IL 60015
224 551-4000

(G-7475)
CLASSIC PRINTING CO INC
529 N Martin Luther King (62523-1114)
P.O. Box 497 (62525-0497)
PHONE..................................217 428-1733
Melvin D Mills, *President*
Debra J Mills, *Admin Sec*
EMP: 6 EST: 1954
SALES (est): 800.9K **Privately Held**
SIC: 2752 Commercial printing, offset

(G-7476)
CONTINENTAL CARBONIC PDTS INC (DH)
3985 E Harrison Ave (62526-5534)
PHONE..................................217 428-2068
John W Funk, *President*
Tom Desanty, *General Mgr*
Nathan Carl, *Area Mgr*
Mark D Hatton, *Vice Pres*
Mark Hatton, *Vice Pres*
EMP: 50
SQ FT: 12,000
SALES (est): 288.4MM **Privately Held**
SIC: 2813 Carbon dioxide; dry ice, carbon dioxide (solid)
HQ: Matheson Tri-Gas, Inc.
150 Allen Rd Ste 302
Basking Ridge NJ 07920
908 991-9200

(G-7477)
COUNTRY JOURNAL PUBLISHING CO
Also Called: Grain Journal
3065 Pershing Ct (62526-1564)
PHONE..................................217 877-9660
Mark Avery, *President*
Jerry Perkins, *Editor*
Mary Matiya, *Human Res Dir*
EMP: 16
SQ FT: 5,000
SALES (est): 2.3MM **Privately Held**
SIC: 2721 Magazines: publishing only, not printed on site

(G-7478)
CROWN CORK & SEAL USA INC
255 W Pershing Rd (62526-3200)
PHONE..................................217 872-6100
Cecil Tuyl, *Vice Pres*
EMP: 118
SALES (corp-wide): 11.6B **Publicly Held**
SIC: 3411 Metal cans
HQ: Crown Cork & Seal Usa, Inc.
770 Township Line Rd # 100
Yardley PA 19067
215 698-5100

(G-7479)
CURRY READY-MIX OF DECATUR
Also Called: The Curry Companies
2200 N Woodford St (62526-5017)
PHONE..................................217 428-7177
Lou Marcy, *President*
EMP: 15
SQ FT: 625
SALES (est): 1.3MM
SALES (corp-wide): 2.9MM **Privately Held**
SIC: 3273 Ready-mixed concrete
PA: Capitol Ready-Mix, Inc
1900 E Mason St
Springfield IL 62702
217 528-1100

(G-7480)
CUSTOM TROPHIES
947 N Water St (62523-1020)
PHONE..................................217 422-3353
Diane Doty, *Owner*
EMP: 3
SQ FT: 1,600
SALES (est): 200K **Privately Held**
SIC: 5999 7336 3993 2396 Trophies & plaques; silk screen design; signs & advertising specialties; automotive & apparel trimmings

(G-7481)
D C T/PRECISION LLC
Also Called: Dct
1260 E North St (62521-2001)
P.O. Box 500 (62525-0500)
PHONE..................................217 475-0141
John D Lambrick,
James Gahwiler,
Julia Leurck,
EMP: 12
SQ FT: 4,800
SALES (est): 1.5MM **Privately Held**
SIC: 3544 Special dies & tools

(G-7482)
DARK MATTER PRINTING
7 Ridge Dr (62521-5421)
PHONE..................................217 791-4059
Chris Morrison, *Principal*
EMP: 3 EST: 2015
SALES (est): 171K **Privately Held**
SIC: 2752 Commercial printing, lithographic

(G-7483)
DEAN DAIRY FLUID LLC
965 S Wyckles Rd (62522-1082)
PHONE..................................217 428-6726
Carl Johnson, *Branch Mgr*
EMP: 7
SALES (corp-wide): 15.8B **Privately Held**
SIC: 2026 Milk processing (pasteurizing, homogenizing, bottling)
HQ: Dfa Dairy Brands Fluid, Llc
1405 N 98th St
Kansas City KS 66111
816 801-6455

(G-7484)
DECATUR BLUE PRINT COMPANY
230 W Wood St (62523-1277)
PHONE..................................217 423-7589
Dann W Nelson, *President*
Margaret Hickman, *CFO*
Suzanne Snyder, *Office Mgr*
Matthew Swarthout, *MIS Mgr*
EMP: 9
SQ FT: 6,000
SALES (est): 1.2MM **Privately Held**
WEB: www.decaturblue.com
SIC: 7334 2752 5049 Blueprinting service; offset & photolithographic printing; engineers' equipment & supplies; drafting supplies

(G-7485)
DECATUR BOTTLING CO
Also Called: Pepsico
2112 N Brush College Rd (62526-5555)
PHONE..................................217 429-5415
Michael L Vitale, *President*
G Louis Vitale, *Corp Secy*
Guy L Vitale Jr, *Vice Pres*
EMP: 73 EST: 1914
SQ FT: 45,000
SALES (est): 6.3MM **Privately Held**
SIC: 2086 Carbonated soft drinks, bottled & canned

(G-7486)
DECATUR FOUNDRY INC
1745 N Illinois St (62526-4932)
PHONE..................................217 429-5261
Terry R Young, *President*
Tommy L Young, *Vice Pres*
Larry Stevens, *Purch Mgr*
Todd Ray, *Human Res Mgr*
Tommy Young, *Sales Executive*
EMP: 80 EST: 1918
SQ FT: 205,000
SALES (est): 19.5MM **Privately Held**
WEB: www.decaturfoundry.com
SIC: 3321 Gray iron castings; ductile iron castings

(G-7487)
DECATUR INDUSTRIAL ELC INC (PA)
Also Called: Kankakee Industrial Technology
1650 E Garfield Ave (62526-5108)
P.O. Box 1188 (62525-1188)
PHONE..................................217 428-6621
Philip Thompson Sr, *Ch of Bd*
Trent Thompson, *President*
Cole Namken, *Plant Mgr*
Dean Ortianu, *Controller*
Vinny Thomas, *Accounts Mgr*
EMP: 35 EST: 1971
SQ FT: 20,000
SALES (est): 47.4MM **Privately Held**
WEB: www.decaturindustrial.com
SIC: 5063 7694 Electrical supplies; electric motor repair

(G-7488)
DECATUR PLATING & MFG CO
1147 E Garfield Ave (62526-4825)
PHONE..................................217 422-8514
William J Stuckey, *President*
Lona Stuckey, *Vice Pres*
David Stuckey, *Manager*
EMP: 10 EST: 1948
SQ FT: 12,000
SALES: 1.4MM **Privately Held**
SIC: 3471 Electroplating of metals or formed products

(G-7489)
DECATUR RAS LLC
2121 S Imboden Ct (62521-5286)
PHONE..................................217 433-2794
Phillip L Pugsley, *Principal*
EMP: 3
SALES: 400K **Privately Held**
WEB: www.pugsleycontainerdecaturil.com
SIC: 4953 2952 Refuse collection & disposal services; roofing materials

(G-7490)
DIXIE CARBONIC INC
3985 E Harrison Ave (62526-5534)
PHONE..................................217 428-2068
Robert Wiesemann II, *President*
Randy Spitz, *CFO*
EMP: 61
SALES (est): 12MM **Privately Held**
SIC: 2813 Dry ice, carbon dioxide (solid)
HQ: Continental Carbonic Products, Inc.
3985 E Harrison Ave
Decatur IL 62526
217 428-2068

(G-7491)
DONNELLY AUTOMOTIVE MACHINE
Also Called: Carquest Auto Parts
1298 E Eldorado St (62521-2032)
PHONE..................................217 428-7414
Patrick E Donnelly, *President*
Cecilia M Donnelly, *Corp Secy*
Robert H Donnelly, *Vice Pres*
EMP: 14 EST: 1950
SQ FT: 5,000
SALES (est): 2.1MM **Privately Held**
WEB: www.donnellyautoparts.com
SIC: 5531 3599 Automotive parts; machine shop, jobbing & repair

(G-7492)
DYNAGRAPHICS INCORPORATED
Also Called: Fast Impressions
3220 N Woodford St (62526-2836)
P.O. Box 2730 (62524-2730)
PHONE..................................217 876-9950
David Bowers, *President*
Scott Bowers, *Vice Pres*
Cindy Staudenmaier, *CFO*
Jim Ashby, *Marketing Staff*
Rusty Spellman, *Supervisor*
EMP: 34
SQ FT: 22,000
SALES (est): 9.9MM **Privately Held**
SIC: 2752 Commercial printing, offset

(G-7493)
ENSIGN EMBLEM LTD
2435 E Federal Dr (62526-2160)
PHONE..................................217 877-8224
Thomas Chambers, *Principal*
Kristine Shreve, *Mktg Dir*
Sylvester Zreliak, *Manager*
EMP: 65
SALES (corp-wide): 13.4MM **Privately Held**
WEB: www.ensignemblem.com
SIC: 2395 Embroidery products, except schiffli machine
PA: Ensign Emblem Ltd.
1746 Keane Dr
Traverse City MI 49696
231 946-7703

(G-7494)
FIRE HOUSE PRESS
5070 E Firehouse Rd (62521-9755)
PHONE..................................217 864-2864
Gary Woolington, *Principal*
EMP: 3
SALES (est): 150.3K **Privately Held**
SIC: 2741 Miscellaneous publishing

(G-7495)
FUYAO GLASS ILLINOIS INC
Also Called: PPG Industries
2768 E Elwin Rd (62521-7848)
PHONE..................................217 864-2392
Gauthier John, *President*
David Burkett,
Shushe Ng WA Ng, *Principal*
EMP: 175
SALES (est): 43.8MM **Privately Held**
SIC: 3211 5231 3999 Flat glass; glass; atomizers, toiletry
HQ: Fuyao Glass America Inc.
2801 W Stroop Rd
Dayton OH 45439
937 496-5777

(G-7496)
GARVER FEEDS (PA)
222 E Wabash Ave (62523-1007)
PHONE..................................217 422-2201

Decatur - Macon County (G-7497)

Edward Larry Garver Jr, *Partner*
Gene Garver, *Partner*
EMP: 20
SQ FT: 5,400
SALES (est): 6.2MM **Privately Held**
SIC: 5999 5149 2048 Pet food; feed & farm supply; pet foods; prepared feeds

(G-7497)
GRAHAM WELDING INC
813 E North St (62521-1932)
PHONE.................................217 422-1423
Charles Graham, *President*
EMP: 8
SQ FT: 50,000
SALES (est): 926.6K **Privately Held**
SIC: 7692 Welding repair

(G-7498)
GROHNE CONCRETE PRODUCTS CO
2594 N Water St (62526-4229)
P.O. Box 828 (62525-0828)
PHONE.................................217 877-4197
Hal Shintzler, *President*
Tom Grohne, *Vice Pres*
EMP: 2 **EST:** 1922
SALES (est): 398.9K
SALES (corp-wide): 31.8MM **Privately Held**
WEB: www.grohneconcreteproducts.com
SIC: 3273 Ready-mixed concrete
PA: Christy-Foltz, Inc.
  740 S Main St
  Decatur IL 62521
  217 428-8601

(G-7499)
HANGER PROSTHETICS &
Also Called: Hanger Clinic
1910 S Mount Zion Rd D (62521-8419)
PHONE.................................217 429-6656
Sam Liang, *President*
Gunther Konigsmann, *Branch Mgr*
EMP: 7
SALES (corp-wide): 1.1B **Publicly Held**
WEB: www.hanger.com
SIC: 3842 Surgical appliances & supplies
HQ: Hanger Prosthetics & Orthotics East, Inc.
  33 North Ave Ste 101
  Tallmadge OH 44278

(G-7500)
HANGER PRSTHETCS & ORTHO INC
1910 S Mount Zion Rd D (62521-8419)
PHONE.................................217 429-6656
Shanie Scott, *Branch Mgr*
EMP: 4
SALES (corp-wide): 1.1B **Publicly Held**
SIC: 3842 Surgical appliances & supplies
HQ: Hanger Prosthetics & Orthotics, Inc.
  10910 Domain Dr Ste 300
  Austin TX 78758
  512 777-3800

(G-7501)
HEINKELS PACKING COMPANY INC
2005 N 22nd St (62526-4734)
P.O. Box 2134 (62524-2134)
PHONE.................................217 428-4401
Miles Wright, *President*
Robert Neal Wright, *Corp Secy*
Dennis Heinkel, *Vice Pres*
EMP: 22 **EST:** 1912
SALES (est): 3.1MM **Privately Held**
WEB: www.heinkelspacking.com
SIC: 2011 Sausages from meat slaughtered on site; luncheon meat from meat slaughtered on site; beef products from beef slaughtered on site; pork products from pork slaughtered on site

(G-7502)
HENRY PRATT COMPANY LLC
500 W Eldorado St (62522-2165)
PHONE.................................620 208-8100
EMP: 9
SALES (est): 2MM **Privately Held**
SIC: 3491 Industrial valves

(G-7503)
HUSTON-PATTERSON CORPORATION (PA)
Also Called: Huston Patterson Printers
123 W North St Fl 4 (62522-3396)
P.O. Box 260 (62525-0260)
PHONE.................................217 429-5161
Thomas W Kowa, *President*
Stephen E Frantz, *COO*
Donald Ellis, *Vice Pres*
Tonya Kowa Morelli, *Vice Pres*
Zachary Kowa, *Opers Staff*
EMP: 65 **EST:** 1895
SQ FT: 133,000
SALES (est): 23MM **Privately Held**
WEB: www.hustonpatterson.com
SIC: 2752 2791 Commercial printing, offset; typesetting

(G-7504)
ILLINI PRECISION MACHINING INC
750 E Prairie Ave (62523-1149)
PHONE.................................217 425-5780
Robert Hauskins, *President*
Rose Hauskins, *Vice Pres*
EMP: 9
SQ FT: 8,000
SALES (est): 740K **Privately Held**
SIC: 3599 Machine shop, jobbing & repair

(G-7505)
ILLMO R/X SERVICE
Also Called: Illmo R/X Services
3373 N Woodford St (62526-2837)
P.O. Box 2138 (62524-2138)
PHONE.................................217 877-1192
Fax: 217 875-7333
EMP: 15
SALES (corp-wide): 2.2MM **Privately Held**
SIC: 5048 3851 Whol Ophthalmic Goods Mfg Ophthalmic Goods
PA: Illmo R/X Service
  52 Progress Pkwy
  Maryland Heights MO
  314 434-6858

(G-7506)
INDUSTRIAL CSTM PWDR CTING INC
Also Called: Industrial Cstm Powdr Coating
661 E Wood St (62523-1152)
PHONE.................................217 423-4272
Nancy Platzbecker, *President*
Bill Platzbecker, *Vice Pres*
EMP: 10
SQ FT: 3,500
SALES (est): 1.1MM **Privately Held**
SIC: 3479 Coating of metals & formed products

(G-7507)
INDUSTRIAL RUBBER & SUP ENTP
2670 E Garfield Ave (62526-5325)
PHONE.................................217 429-3747
William H Veteto, *President*
Clarence D Golden, *Admin Sec*
EMP: 4
SQ FT: 2,500
SALES (est): 620K **Privately Held**
SIC: 5085 3429 3052 Rubber goods, mechanical; manufactured hardware (general); rubber & plastics hose & beltings

(G-7508)
INTERNATIONAL CONTROL SVCS INC
Also Called: I C S
606 W Imboden Dr (62521-9067)
PHONE.................................217 422-6700
Dennis M Espinoza, *President*
Christopher Expinoza, *CFO*
Robert Johnston, *CFO*
▲ **EMP:** 110
SQ FT: 50,000
SALES (est): 47MM **Privately Held**
SIC: 3672 Printed circuit boards

(G-7509)
J A K ENTERPRISES INC
Also Called: Bard Optical
288 N Park St (62523-1306)
PHONE.................................217 422-3881
Angie Oyer, *Manager*
EMP: 6
SALES (corp-wide): 11MM **Privately Held**
SIC: 5995 5084 3827 Opticians; industrial machinery & equipment; optical instruments & lenses
PA: J A K Enterprises, Inc
  8309 N Knoxville Ave # 1
  Peoria IL 61615
  309 693-9540

(G-7510)
JAMIEL INC
Also Called: A-1 Food & Liquor
151 N Jasper St (62521-2801)
PHONE.................................217 423-1000
Amanda Asad, *President*
EMP: 3 **EST:** 2010
SALES (est): 547.2K **Privately Held**
SIC: 5182 3411 Liquor; food & beverage containers

(G-7511)
JARVIS DRILLING CO
132 S Water St Ste 331 (62523-2376)
P.O. Box 1631 (62525-1631)
PHONE.................................217 422-3120
T Stephen Ballance, *President*
EMP: 9
SALES: 1.2MM **Privately Held**
SIC: 1311 Crude petroleum production

(G-7512)
JUSTICE MANUFACTURING INC
Also Called: B & R Alarm Co
291 Michael Ave (62526-1160)
P.O. Box 291 (62525-0291)
PHONE.................................217 877-2250
Richard V Colbeck, *President*
EMP: 7
SALES (est): 440K **Privately Held**
SIC: 3625 Electric controls & control accessories, industrial

(G-7513)
KELLEY CONSTRUCTION INC
2454 N 27th St (62526-5262)
P.O. Box 2440 (62524-2440)
PHONE.................................217 422-1800
I Dean Benson, *President*
Gary Cooper, *Vice Pres*
Steve Morse, *Safety Mgr*
Virginia A Foster, *Treasurer*
Ben Short, *Manager*
EMP: 300
SQ FT: 4,000
SALES (est): 42.7MM **Privately Held**
SIC: 1541 3444 Industrial buildings, new construction; sheet metalwork

(G-7514)
KLAMAN HARDWOOD
4351 N Macarthur Rd (62526-9332)
PHONE.................................217 972-7888
Timothy Klaman, *Principal*
EMP: 4
SALES (est): 248.8K **Privately Held**
SIC: 2435 Panels, hardwood plywood

(G-7515)
LEE ENTERPRISES INCORPORATED
Also Called: Herald & Review
601 E William St (62523-1142)
P.O. Box 311 (62525)
PHONE.................................217 421-6920
Tim Cain, *Editor*
Jeana Matherly, *Editor*
Mark Tupper, *Editor*
Joel Fletcher, *Director*
Justin Conn, *Relations*
EMP: 140
SALES (corp-wide): 509.8MM **Publicly Held**
SIC: 2711 Newspapers, publishing & printing
PA: Lee Enterprises, Incorporated
  4600 E 53rd St
  Davenport IA 52807
  563 383-2100

(G-7516)
LEGACY VULCAN LLC
Also Called: Macon Sand & Gravel
2855 S Lincoln Memorial P (62522-8812)
PHONE.................................217 963-2196
Tom Heft, *Superintendent*
EMP: 8 **Publicly Held**
SIC: 1422 Crushed & broken limestone
HQ: Legacy Vulcan, Llc
  1200 Urban Center Dr
  Vestavia AL 35242
  205 298-3000

(G-7517)
LIAISON HOME AUTOMATION LLC
288 N Park St (62523-1306)
PHONE.................................888 279-1235
Steven Weber, *President*
Joe Laurin, *Director*
Matt Saxhaug, *Director*
Penny Powell, *Executive Asst*
EMP: 9
SALES (est): 972.7K **Privately Held**
SIC: 7372 Home entertainment computer software

(G-7518)
M E BARBER CO INC
1660 S Taylorville Rd (62521-3951)
PHONE.................................217 428-4591
D J Hynds, *President*
Steve Hynds, *General Mgr*
EMP: 6
SQ FT: 2,000
SALES: 600K **Privately Held**
SIC: 3423 3643 Wrenches, hand tools; current-carrying wiring devices

(G-7519)
MACHINE WORKS OF DECATUR INC
2035 E Garfield Ave (62526-5094)
PHONE.................................217 428-3896
Jeff Conour, *President*
Jemremy Conour, *Principal*
Lynette Conour, *Admin Sec*
EMP: 4
SALES: 390K **Privately Held**
SIC: 3599 Machine shop, jobbing & repair

(G-7520)
MACON RESOURCES INC
2121 Hubbard Ave (62526-2876)
P.O. Box 2760 (62524-2760)
PHONE.................................217 875-1910
Brad Auten, *Production*
Stanley Rives, *CFO*
Rachel Barter, *Manager*
Dreux Lewandoski, *Exec Dir*
Blaine Smith, *Director*
EMP: 200 **EST:** 1970
SQ FT: 105,000
SALES: 11.3MM **Privately Held**
SIC: 8093 3469 7349 0782 Rehabilitation center, outpatient treatment; automobile license tags, stamped metal; janitorial service, contract basis; lawn services; adult day care center

(G-7521)
MCLEAN SUBSURFACE UTILITY
2150 N Main St (62526-4338)
PHONE.................................336 988-2520
Stacey E Slaw, *Principal*
EMP: 5
SALES (est): 210.4K **Privately Held**
SIC: 1623 8711 1389 8713 Underground utilities contractor; engineering services; testing, measuring, surveying & analysis services; surveying services

(G-7522)
MICROTEK PATTERN INC
2035 N Jasper St (62526-4847)
PHONE.................................217 428-0433
Nelson Mosley, *President*
Robin Shively, *Treasurer*
EMP: 7 **EST:** 1996
SQ FT: 3,500
SALES (est): 1.1MM **Privately Held**
WEB: www.microtekpattern.com
SIC: 3543 Industrial patterns

GEOGRAPHIC SECTION
Decatur - Macon County (G-7550)

(G-7523)
MIDSTATE CORE CO
777 E William St (62521-1950)
P.O. Box 25318 (62525-5318)
PHONE.................................217 429-2673
John R Phillips, *President*
Barbara Phillips, *Corp Secy*
EMP: 25
SQ FT: 14,000
SALES (est): 1.2MM Privately Held
SIC: 3543 Foundry cores

(G-7524)
MIDWEST FIBER INC DECATUR
1781 Hubbard Ave (62526-2819)
PHONE.................................217 424-9460
Ron Shumaker, *President*
Mike Shumaker, *General Mgr*
Jacob Welker, *Opers Staff*
Todd Shumaker, *Sales Dir*
Patrick Freeman, *Sales Staff*
▼ **EMP:** 40
SALES (est): 11MM Privately Held
SIC: 5093 4953 3341 Waste paper; refuse systems; secondary nonferrous metals

(G-7525)
MIDWEST PROCESSING COMPANY
4666 E Faries Pkwy (62526-5630)
PHONE.................................217 424-5200
Charles Bayless, *Vice Pres*
EMP: 60
SALES (est): 7MM
SALES (corp-wide): 64.6B Publicly Held
SIC: 2079 Edible fats & oils
PA: Archer-Daniels-Midland Company
   77 W Wacker Dr Ste 4600
   Chicago IL 60601
   312 634-8100

(G-7526)
MILLIKEN VALVE CO INC
500 W Eldorado St (62522-2165)
PHONE.................................217 425-7410
EMP: 3 **EST:** 2011
SALES (est): 254.9K Privately Held
SIC: 3592 Valves

(G-7527)
MOTOR PARTS & EQUIPMENT CORP
Also Called: Napa-Decatur Auto Supply
3110 N Woodford St (62526-2834)
PHONE.................................217 877-7456
Joe Stanberry, *Principal*
EMP: 36
SALES (corp-wide): 53.3MM Privately Held
SIC: 5531 5013 3714 Automobile & truck equipment & parts; automotive supplies & parts; motor vehicle parts & accessories
PA: Motor Parts & Equipment Corporation
   1670 Northrock Ct
   Rockford IL 61103
   779 500-6100

(G-7528)
MUELLER CO LLC
Gas Products Division
500 W Eldorado St (62522-2165)
P.O. Box 671 (62525-1808)
PHONE.................................217 423-4471
James Clark, *Plant Mgr*
Tracy Douglass, *Opers Staff*
Steve Crawford, *Engineer*
Mark Dillow, *Engineer*
Derek Holley, *Sales Staff*
EMP: 20
SALES (corp-wide): 968MM Publicly Held
SIC: 3533 3592 Gas field machinery & equipment; valves
HQ: Mueller Co. Llc
   633 Chestnut St Ste 1200
   Chattanooga TN 37450
   423 209-4800

(G-7529)
MUELLER COMPANY PLANT 4
1226 E Garfield Ave (62526-4923)
PHONE.................................217 425-7424
EMP: 4
SALES (est): 284.1K Privately Held
WEB: www.muellermuseum.org
SIC: 3399 Iron ore recovery from open hearth slag

(G-7530)
MUELLER SERVICE CO LLC (DH)
500 W Eldorado St (62522-2165)
P.O. Box 671 (62525-1808)
PHONE.................................217 423-4471
Dale Smith, *President*
EMP: 33
SQ FT: 50,000
SALES (est): 6.4MM
SALES (corp-wide): 968MM Publicly Held
SIC: 3491 Industrial valves
HQ: Mueller Co. Llc
   633 Chestnut St Ste 1200
   Chattanooga TN 37450
   423 209-4800

(G-7531)
MULTI-STATE INDUS CONTRS INC
2345 E Garfield Ave (62526-5125)
PHONE.................................217 423-4100
Jeff Locher, *President*
Joyce Sadorus, *Principal*
Mark Sadorus, *Principal*
EMP: 4
SALES (est): 319.8K Privately Held
SIC: 3531 Construction machinery

(G-7532)
MYLAN INC
Also Called: Meda Pharmaceuticals
705 E Eldorado St (62523-1118)
PHONE.................................217 424-8400
EMP: 3 Privately Held
SIC: 2834 Mfg Pharmaceutical Preparations
HQ: Mylan Inc
   1000 Mylan Blvd
   Canonsburg PA 15317
   724 514-1800

(G-7533)
ORBIS RPM LLC
1781 Hubbard Ave (62526-2819)
PHONE.................................217 876-8655
EMP: 16
SALES (corp-wide): 2.2B Privately Held
SIC: 3081 Unsupported plastics film & sheet
HQ: Orbis Rpm, Llc
   1055 Corporate Center Dr
   Oconomowoc WI 53066
   262 560-5000

(G-7534)
OSBORNE PUBLICATIONS INC
Also Called: Decatur Tribune
132 S Water St Ste 424 (62523-2306)
P.O. Box 1490 (62525-1490)
PHONE.................................217 422-9702
Paul V Osborne, *President*
Janet Osborne, *Vice Pres*
EMP: 4 **EST:** 1964
SQ FT: 3,500
SALES (est): 349.1K Privately Held
WEB: www.decaturtribune.com
SIC: 2711 2791 2759 Newspapers, publishing & printing; typesetting; newspapers: printing

(G-7535)
PARKE & SON INC
Parke Toll Processing
3523 Rupp Pkwy (62526-2170)
PHONE.................................217 875-0572
Paul Doolen, *Manager*
EMP: 3
SALES (corp-wide): 9.5MM Privately Held
SIC: 2045 Prepared flour mixes & doughs
PA: Parke & Son, Inc.
   1800 E Garfield Ave
   Decatur IL 62526
   217 429-5255

(G-7536)
PIONEER PUMP AND PACKING INC
1501 N 22nd St (62526-5107)
PHONE.................................217 791-5293
EMP: 11
SALES (corp-wide): 33MM Privately Held
SIC: 3491 Industrial valves
PA: Pioneer Pump And Packing, Inc.
   400 Russell Blvd
   Saint Louis MO 63104
   314 771-0700

(G-7537)
PRAIRIE CENTRAL READY MIX
800 E Mckinley Ave (62526-2409)
PHONE.................................217 877-5210
Richard Goken, *Manager*
EMP: 4
SALES (est): 318.3K Privately Held
SIC: 3273 Ready-mixed concrete

(G-7538)
R & R SERVICES ILLINOIS INC
800 E Garfield Ave (62526-4500)
P.O. Box 319, Argenta (62501-0319)
PHONE.................................217 424-2602
Jeffery S Rose, *President*
Steve Richards, *Vice Pres*
EMP: 8
SALES (est): 830.8K Privately Held
SIC: 2448 Wood pallets & skids

(G-7539)
RANDYS EXPER-CLEAN
4925 W Main St (62522-1062)
PHONE.................................217 423-1975
Randy Goodrich, *Owner*
EMP: 4
SALES (est): 185.7K Privately Held
SIC: 7217 3524 Carpet & upholstery cleaning; snowblowers & throwers, residential

(G-7540)
RATHJE ENTERPRISES INC (PA)
Also Called: Bodine Electric of Decatur
1845 N 22nd St (62526-5113)
P.O. Box 976 (62526-1810)
PHONE.................................217 423-2593
David W Rathje, *President*
Harry B Rakers, *President*
Jeanne Jones, *Exec VP*
Warren Elder, *Manager*
EMP: 265
SQ FT: 57,000
SALES (est): 69.3MM Privately Held
SIC: 1731 7694 5063 General electrical contractor; armature rewinding shops; electrical supplies

(G-7541)
REFRESHMENT SERVICES INC
Also Called: Pepsico
2112 N Brush College Rd (62526-5555)
PHONE.................................217 429-5415
Dave Moran, *Branch Mgr*
EMP: 40
SALES (corp-wide): 88.8MM Privately Held
SIC: 2086 Carbonated soft drinks, bottled & canned
PA: Refreshment Services, Inc.
   1121 Locust St
   Quincy IL 62301
   217 223-8600

(G-7542)
RING CONTAINER TECH LLC
Also Called: Ringwood
2454 E Hubbard Ave (62526-2148)
PHONE.................................217 875-5084
Ken Landreth, *Executive*
EMP: 50
SALES (corp-wide): 284.7MM Privately Held
SIC: 3085 3089 Plastics bottles; blow molded finished plastic products
PA: Ring Container Technologies, Llc.
   1 Industrial Park
   Oakland TN 38060
   800 280-7464

(G-7543)
ROSEMOUNT INC
2241 E Hubbard Ave (62526-2149)
PHONE.................................217 877-5278
Teresa Edwards, *Manager*
EMP: 4
SALES (corp-wide): 18.3B Publicly Held
SIC: 3823 Manometers, industrial process type
HQ: Rosemount Inc.
   8200 Market Blvd
   Chanhassen MN 55317
   952 906-8888

(G-7544)
ROTARY DRYER PARTS INC
2590 E Federal Dr Ste 508 (62526-2181)
PHONE.................................217 877-2787
Charles Brown, *President*
EMP: 2
SALES (est): 334.9K Privately Held
SIC: 3621 Motors & generators

(G-7545)
S L FIXTURES INC
2222 E Logan St (62526-5133)
PHONE.................................217 423-9907
Matthew Long, *President*
EMP: 5 **EST:** 1986
SQ FT: 3,000
SALES (est): 716.2K Privately Held
SIC: 2599 3429 Cabinets, factory; cabinet hardware

(G-7546)
SHUR CO OF ILLINOIS
3993 E Mueller Ave (62526-5548)
PHONE.................................217 877-8277
Bill Shorna, *Owner*
EMP: 9
SALES (est): 797.6K Privately Held
SIC: 2451 5199 Mobile home frames; tarpaulins

(G-7547)
SOIL CHEMICAL CORPORATION
3150 N Woodford St (62526-2834)
PHONE.................................714 761-3292
Kevin Willet, *District Mgr*
John Sansone, *Branch Mgr*
EMP: 8
SALES (corp-wide): 3.5MM Privately Held
WEB: www.cardinalproducts.com
SIC: 2879 Insecticides & pesticides
PA: Soil Chemical Corporation
   8770 Hwy 25
   Hollister CA 95023
   831 637-1992

(G-7548)
SOUTHFIELD CORPORATION
Also Called: Prairie Central
705 E Mckinley Ave (62526-2407)
PHONE.................................217 875-5455
Sally O'Brien, *Manager*
EMP: 15
SALES (corp-wide): 344.9MM Privately Held
WEB: www.illinoisbrick.com
SIC: 5211 3272 3271 Brick; concrete products; concrete block & brick
PA: Southfield Corporation
   8995 W 95th St
   Palos Hills IL 60465
   708 344-1000

(G-7549)
SOUTHFIELD CORPORATION
800 E Mckinley Ave (62526-2409)
PHONE.................................217 877-5210
Dean Bush, *Manager*
EMP: 15
SALES (corp-wide): 344.9MM Privately Held
SIC: 3273 Ready-mixed concrete
PA: Southfield Corporation
   8995 W 95th St
   Palos Hills IL 60465
   708 344-1000

(G-7550)
STAR SILKSCREEN DESIGN INC
2281 E Hubbard Ave (62526-2149)
PHONE.................................217 877-0804
Jon Kozeliski, *President*

Decatur - Macon County (G-7551)

Karen Ragee, *Vice Pres*
EMP: 5
SQ FT: 2,700
SALES (est): 600K **Privately Held**
SIC: 2396 2395 Screen printing on fabric articles; embroidery & art needlework

(G-7551)
STEWART BROTHERS PACKING CO
1004 N Country Club Rd (62521-1812)
PHONE..............................217 422-7741
Jeffrey J Stewart, *Partner*
John J Stewart, *Partner*
EMP: 8 **EST:** 1935
SQ FT: 1,200
SALES (est): 1.1MM **Privately Held**
SIC: 2011 Meat by-products from meat slaughtered on site

(G-7552)
STRATAS FOODS LLC
3601 E Division St (62526-5638)
PHONE..............................217 424-5660
Rod Logan, *Branch Mgr*
EMP: 22 **Privately Held**
SIC: 2079 Edible fats & oils
PA: Stratas Foods Llc
7130 Goodlett Frm Pkwy # 200
Cordova TN 38016

(G-7553)
STRIPMASTERS SERVICES INC
2500 N 22nd St (62526-4744)
PHONE..............................217 429-0904
EMP: 6 **EST:** 2013
SALES (est): 634.5K **Privately Held**
SIC: 3471 Sand blasting of metal parts

(G-7554)
SURE SHINE POLISHING
1455 N Main St (62526-4418)
PHONE..............................217 853-4888
Jason Eddinger, *Principal*
EMP: 3
SALES (est): 145.1K **Privately Held**
SIC: 3471 Polishing, metals or formed products

(G-7555)
T/CCI MANUFACTURING LLC (PA)
2120 N 22nd St (62526-4737)
PHONE..............................217 423-0066
Richard J Demirjian, *Mfg Staff*
Marilyn Corley, *Human Res Mgr*
Charles Demirjian, *Mng Member*
Eric Droit, *Executive*
Amy Nash, *Executive*
▲ **EMP:** 100
SALES: 55MM **Privately Held**
SIC: 3714 Air conditioner parts, motor vehicle

(G-7556)
TAG-BARTON LLC (PA)
1395 S Taylorville Rd (62521-4034)
PHONE..............................217 428-0711
EMP: 3
SALES (est): 12.8MM **Privately Held**
SIC: 3599 6719 Machine & other job shop work; machine shop, jobbing & repair; investment holding companies, except banks

(G-7557)
TATE & LYLE AMERICAS LLC
2200 E Eldorado St (62521-1578)
PHONE..............................217 421-3268
John Schnake, *CEO*
Suzanne Anderson, *Counsel*
Gayle Albert, *Controller*
Debbie Norman, *Analyst*
◆ **EMP:** 140
SQ FT: 5,000
SALES (est): 46.5MM
SALES (corp-wide): 3.5B **Privately Held**
WEB: www.tateandlyle.com
SIC: 2046 Corn & other vegetable starches
PA: Tate & Lyle Public Limited Company
1 Kingsway
London WC2B
207 257-2100

(G-7558)
TATE LYLE INGRDNTS AMRICAS LLC (HQ)
Also Called: Tate & Lyle Citric Acid
2200 E Eldorado St (62521-1578)
P.O. Box 151 (62525-1801)
PHONE..............................217 423-4411
John Schnake, *CEO*
Javed Ahmed, *CEO*
Dustin Martin, *Area Mgr*
Andrew Bailey, *Business Mgr*
Robert Gibber, *Exec VP*
◆ **EMP:** 1145
SQ FT: 500,000
SALES: 844.6MM
SALES (corp-wide): 3.5B **Privately Held**
SIC: 2046 Wet corn milling
PA: Tate & Lyle Public Limited Company
1 Kingsway
London WC2B
207 257-2100

(G-7559)
TAYLOR PHARMACAL CO
1222 W Grand Ave (62522-1412)
PHONE..............................217 423-9715
Les Sabo, *Principal*
EMP: 3
SALES (est): 199.4K **Privately Held**
SIC: 2834 Pharmaceutical preparations

(G-7560)
TCR SYSTEMS LLC
4900 N Brush College Rd (62526-9766)
P.O. Box 3398 (62524-3398)
PHONE..............................217 877-5622
Terry Randles, *President*
John Ellis,
Dan Wrigley,
EMP: 100
SQ FT: 280,000
SALES (est): 24.8MM **Privately Held**
SIC: 3444 Sheet metalwork

(G-7561)
TIN MAUNG
1770 E Lake Shore Dr (62521-3832)
PHONE..............................217 233-1405
Maung Tin, *Principal*
EMP: 3
SALES (est): 202.5K **Privately Held**
SIC: 3356 Tin

(G-7562)
TRANSFRMTIONAL ENRGY SOLUTIONS
1418 W King St (62522-1445)
PHONE..............................828 226-7821
George Coulthard, *Owner*
EMP: 3
SALES (est): 114.4K **Privately Held**
SIC: 3621 7389 Motors & generators;

(G-7563)
TRUMP PRINTING INC
Also Called: Trump Direct
1591 N Water St (62526-4441)
P.O. Box 17 (62525-0017)
PHONE..............................217 429-9001
Dennis Trump, *CEO*
EMP: 12 **EST:** 1979
SQ FT: 9,000
SALES (est): 2.1MM **Privately Held**
SIC: 2752 2791 2789 Commercial printing, offset; typesetting; bookbinding & related work

(G-7564)
UNION IRON INC (HQ)
3550 E Mound Rd (62521-8514)
P.O. Box 1038 (62525-1038)
PHONE..............................217 429-5148
Gary Anderson, *President*
Ralph Hansen, *Production*
Donald Deal, *Engineer*
Judith Curry, *Treasurer*
Tom Duffy, *Sales Mgr*
▼ **EMP:** 27
SQ FT: 20,000
SALES: 8.6MM
SALES (corp-wide): 747.8MM **Privately Held**
SIC: 3523 3511 Elevators, farm; steam engines

PA: Ag Growth International Inc
198 Commerce Dr
Winnipeg MB R3P 0
204 489-1855

(G-7565)
UP-N-RUNNIN LLC
3388 E Boyd Rd (62526-9618)
PHONE..............................217 413-6293
Tim Duncan, *President*
Stacey Brohard,
EMP: 3
SALES (est): 442.7K **Privately Held**
SIC: 3524 0782 Lawn & garden mowers & accessories; lawnmowers, residential: hand or power; hedge trimmers, electric; mowing services, lawn

(G-7566)
VANTAGE CORN PROCESSORS LLC (HQ)
4666 E Faries Pkwy (62526-5630)
PHONE..............................217 424-5200
Chris Cuddy, *President*
Ron Bandler, *Vice Pres*
Ray Bradbury, *Vice Pres*
Cynthia Ervin, *Vice Pres*
D Cameron Findlay, *Vice Pres*
EMP: 350
SALES (est): 10.1MM
SALES (corp-wide): 64.6B **Publicly Held**
SIC: 2869 Industrial organic chemicals
PA: Archer-Daniels-Midland Company
77 W Wacker Dr Ste 4600
Chicago IL 60601
312 634-8100

(G-7567)
VOESTALPINE NORTRAK INC
690 E Kenwood Ave (62526-4584)
PHONE..............................217 876-9160
Sean Betty, *Manager*
EMP: 100
SALES (corp-wide): 15.3B **Privately Held**
SIC: 3743 Railroad equipment
HQ: Voestalpine Railway Systems Nortrak Inc.
1740 Pacific Ave
Cheyenne WY 82007
307 778-8700

(G-7568)
WABEL TOOL COMPANY
1020 E Eldorado St (62521-1916)
PHONE..............................217 429-3656
Virginia M Hornback, *President*
Jenny Hornback, *Principal*
Rudy Hubner, *Vice Pres*
Dennis Elam, *Engineer*
William R Friend, *Treasurer*
EMP: 30 **EST:** 1971
SQ FT: 22,000
SALES (est): 5.5MM **Privately Held**
SIC: 3599 Machine shop, jobbing & repair

(G-7569)
WHEELS & DEALS
170 N Oakdale Blvd (62522-1918)
PHONE..............................217 423-6333
Rick Reynolds, *Owner*
EMP: 7
SALES (est): 365.3K **Privately Held**
SIC: 2711 Newspapers

(G-7570)
WOODWIND SPECIALISTS
890 W William St (62522-2330)
P.O. Box 1024 (62525-1024)
PHONE..............................217 423-4122
Sande Hackel, *Owner*
EMP: 3 **EST:** 1973
SQ FT: 6,000
SALES (est): 24K **Privately Held**
SIC: 2499 Decorative wood & woodwork

Deer Creek
Tazewell County

(G-7571)
AUNT EMS GOURMET POPCORN INC
405 E 1st Ave (61733-9539)
PHONE..............................309 447-6612

Marianne Strawn, *President*
EMP: 12
SQ FT: 15,000
SALES (est): 2MM **Privately Held**
SIC: 2096 Popcorn, already popped (except candy covered)

(G-7572)
CENTRAL ILLINOIS TRUSS (PA)
105 Prospect Dr (61733-1001)
PHONE..............................309 447-6644
Todd Erwin, *Principal*
Corey Crawford, *Sales Staff*
EMP: 10
SALES (est): 300.9K **Privately Held**
SIC: 2439 Trusses, wooden roof

(G-7573)
COOK FABRICATION SIGNS GRAPHIC
325 N Deer Crk (61733)
PHONE..............................309 360-3805
Gary Cook, *Owner*
EMP: 6
SALES (est): 219.8K **Privately Held**
SIC: 3993 Signs & advertising specialties

(G-7574)
DEER CREEK FLANGE PIPE CO INC
300 N Logan St (61733-9314)
P.O. Box 50 (61733-0050)
PHONE..............................309 447-6981
Gerald A Rich Jr, *President*
Tammy Rich, *Corp Secy*
Brian Rich, *Vice Pres*
EMP: 3
SQ FT: 5,000
SALES (est): 353.9K **Privately Held**
SIC: 3462 Flange, valve & pipe fitting forgings, ferrous

(G-7575)
HOMEWAY HOMES INC
100 Homeway Ct (61733-9018)
PHONE..............................309 965-2312
Brian R Schieler, *President*
Rich Schieler, *Plant Mgr*
Adam Armstrong, *Purch Mgr*
Jim Stoller, *QC Mgr*
John Rassi, *CFO*
EMP: 60
SALES (est): 11.8MM **Privately Held**
SIC: 2452 Modular homes, prefabricated, wood

(G-7576)
TITAN INDUSTRIES INC
100 Prspect Dr Deer Crk Deer Creek (61733)
P.O. Box 226 (61733-0226)
PHONE..............................309 440-1010
Angela Rich, *President*
Suzanne M McQueary, *Admin Sec*
EMP: 6
SALES (est): 1.2MM **Privately Held**
SIC: 3441 Fabricated structural metal

Deer Grove
Whiteside County

(G-7577)
H W HOSTETLER & SONS
Also Called: Prairie View Farms
27445 Hurd Rd (61243-9722)
PHONE..............................815 438-7816
H W Hostetler, *Owner*
EMP: 3 **EST:** 1944
SALES (est): 140K **Privately Held**
SIC: 0191 3523 General farms, primarily crop; farm machinery & equipment

(G-7578)
STERLING GEAR INC
Also Called: Stainless Steel Prod
1582 Hoover Rd (61243-9739)
P.O. Box 68 (61243-0068)
PHONE..............................815 438-4327
Robert Elfline, *President*
▲ **EMP:** 10 **EST:** 2000
SALES (est): 797.2K **Privately Held**
SIC: 3541 Gear cutting & finishing machines

▲ = Import ▼ = Export
◆ = Import/Export

Deer Park
Lake County

(G-7579)
CONTINENTAL AUTO SYSTEMS INC
21440 W Lake Cook Rd (60010-3609)
PHONE...................................847 862-5000
EMP: 1 **EST:** 1998
SALES (est): 1.8MM **Privately Held**
SIC: 7549 3625 Automotive Services Mfg Relays/Industrial Controls

(G-7580)
CONTINENTAL AUTO SYSTEMS INC
21440 W Lake Cook Rd (60010-3609)
PHONE...................................847 862-6300
Scott Beutler, *Vice Pres*
Thorsten Behrens, *Engineer*
Thomas Gill, *Engineer*
Keith Meny, *Engineer*
Steve Nordhougen, *Engineer*
EMP: 400
SALES (corp-wide): 49.2B **Privately Held**
SIC: 3714 Motor vehicle brake systems & parts
HQ: Continental Automotive Systems, Inc.
1 Continental Dr
Auburn Hills MI 48326
248 393-5300

(G-7581)
ETON PHARMACEUTICALS INC (PA)
21925 W Feld Pkwy Ste 235 (60010)
PHONE...................................847 787-7361
Norbert G Riedel, *Ch of Bd*
Sean E Brynjelsen, *President*
W Wilson Troutman, *CFO*
EMP: 15
SQ FT: 5,507
SALES: 959K **Publicly Held**
SIC: 2834 Pharmaceutical preparations

(G-7582)
NEOVISION USA INC
21720 W Long Grove Rd C33 (60010-3732)
PHONE...................................847 533-0541
Howard Leventhal, *President*
EMP: 10
SALES: 950K **Privately Held**
SIC: 3669 Communications equipment

(G-7583)
VITESCO TECHNOLOGIES USA LLC
21440 W Lake Cook Rd (60010-3609)
PHONE...................................847 862-5000
Daniel Peistrup, *Electrical Engi*
EMP: 4
SALES (corp-wide): 23.9MM **Privately Held**
SIC: 3714 Motor vehicle parts & accessories
HQ: Vitesco Technologies Usa, Llc
2400 Executive Hills Dr
Auburn Hills MI 48326
248 209-4000

Deerfield
Lake County

(G-7584)
ALPHA INDUSTRIES INC
1720 Christopher Dr (60015-3912)
PHONE...................................847 945-1740
Jerry Becker, *Principal*
EMP: 3
SALES (corp-wide): 63MM **Privately Held**
WEB: www.alphaindustries.com
SIC: 3999 Barber & beauty shop equipment
PA: Alpha Industries, Inc.
14200 Pk Madow Dr Ste 110
Chantilly VA 20151
703 378-1420

(G-7585)
AMERICAN CHEMET CORPORATION (PA)
Also Called: American Chemet Export
740 Waukegan Rd Ste 202 (60015-4400)
P.O. Box 437 (60015-0437)
PHONE...................................847 948-0800
W H Shropshire, *President*
Daniel B Brimhall, *Vice Pres*
Kim A Klatt, *Vice Pres*
Brad Smith, *Treasurer*
Kim Klatt, *VP Sales*
◆ **EMP:** 11
SQ FT: 3,300
SALES: 218.2MM **Privately Held**
WEB: www.chemet.com
SIC: 2819 2816 Copper compounds or salts, inorganic; zinc pigments: zinc oxide, zinc sulfide

(G-7586)
ARLA GRAPHICS INC
875 Mountain Dr (60015-1801)
P.O. Box 1204 (60015-6003)
PHONE...................................847 470-0005
Lee Bendersky, *President*
Armand Bendersky, *Benefits Mgr*
EMP: 4
SQ FT: 2,000
SALES (est): 602.2K **Privately Held**
SIC: 2752 Commercial printing, offset

(G-7587)
ASTELLAS US LLC
3 Parkway North Blvd (60015-2537)
PHONE...................................800 888-7704
Yoshihiko Hatanaka, *Principal*
David Musselman, *Sales Dir*
Doug Noland, *VP Mktg*
Edwin Molina, *IT/INT Sup*
Chris Abboushi, *Director*
EMP: 163
SQ FT: 140,000
SALES: 858.8K **Privately Held**
HQ: Astellas Us Holding, Inc.
1 Astellas Way
Northbrook IL 60062

(G-7588)
ASTELLAS US TECHNOLOGIES INC
3 Parkway North Blvd # 300 (60015-2537)
PHONE...................................847 317-8800
Makoto Nishimura, *CEO*
Hadir Sesi, *Technology*
EMP: 400
SALES (est): 37.4MM **Privately Held**
SIC: 2834 Pharmaceutical preparations
HQ: Astellas Pharma Us, Inc.
1 Astellas Way
Northbrook IL 60062

(G-7589)
AVEXIS
3 Parkway North Blvd (60015-2537)
PHONE...................................847 964-9948
EMP: 5
SALES (est): 1MM **Privately Held**
SIC: 2834 Pharmaceutical preparations

(G-7590)
BAXALTA WORLDWIDE LLC
1 Baxter Pkwy (60015-4625)
PHONE...................................224 948-2000
Ludwig N Hanton, *CEO*
EMP: 223
SALES: 259K
SALES (corp-wide): 15.1B **Privately Held**
SIC: 2834 3841 2835 3842 Pharmaceutical preparations; intravenous solutions; solutions, pharmaceutical; surgical & medical instruments; catheters; medical instruments & equipment, blood & bone work; surgical instruments & apparatus; blood derivative diagnostic agents; surgical appliances & supplies
HQ: Baxalta Incorporated
1200 Lakeside Dr
Bannockburn IL 60015
224 940-2000

(G-7591)
BAXTER GLOBAL HOLDINGS II INC (HQ)
1 Baxter Pkwy (60015-4625)
PHONE...................................224 948-1812
Robert L Parkinson Jr, *CEO*
Jean-Luc Butel, *President*
Selene Mojica, *Principal*
Molly Chacko, *Research*
Ryan Marchetta, *Engineer*
▼ **EMP:** 33
SALES (est): 21.1MM
SALES (corp-wide): 11.3B **Publicly Held**
SIC: 2834 Surgical & medical instruments; pharmaceutical preparations
PA: Baxter International Inc.
1 Baxter Pkwy Df2-1w
Deerfield IL 60015
224 948-2000

(G-7592)
BAXTER HEALTHCARE CORPORATION
1 Baxter Pkwy (60015-4625)
PHONE...................................800 422-9837
Peter S Hellman, *Branch Mgr*
EMP: 200
SALES (corp-wide): 11.3B **Publicly Held**
WEB: www.baxter.com
SIC: 2836 Plasmas
HQ: Baxter Healthcare Corporation
1 Baxter Pkwy
Deerfield IL 60015
224 948-2000

(G-7593)
BAXTER HEALTHCARE CORPORATION
1435 Lake Cook Rd (60015-5213)
PHONE...................................847 948-2000
Jim Stoner, *Branch Mgr*
EMP: 300
SALES (corp-wide): 11.3B **Publicly Held**
SIC: 3841 Surgical & medical instruments
HQ: Baxter Healthcare Corporation
1 Baxter Pkwy
Deerfield IL 60015
224 948-2000

(G-7594)
BAXTER HEALTHCARE CORPORATION
Baxter Pharmaceutical Solution
1 Baxter Pkwy (60015-4625)
PHONE...................................847 948-2000
Thomas F Chen, *Branch Mgr*
EMP: 401
SALES (corp-wide): 11.3B **Publicly Held**
SIC: 3841 Surgical & medical instruments
HQ: Baxter Healthcare Corporation
1 Baxter Pkwy
Deerfield IL 60015
224 948-2000

(G-7595)
BAXTER INTERNATIONAL INC (PA)
1 Baxter Pkwy Df2-1w (60015-4634)
PHONE...................................224 948-2000
Jose E Almeida, *Ch of Bd*
Giuseppe Accogli, *President*
Cristiano Franzi, *President*
Andrew Frye, *President*
Jacqueline Kunzler, *Senior VP*
EMP: 1500
SALES: 11.3B **Publicly Held**
WEB: www.baxter.com
SIC: 3841 2835 3842 2834 Surgical & medical instruments; catheters; medical instruments & equipment, blood & bone work; surgical instruments & apparatus; blood derivative diagnostic agents; surgical appliances & supplies; intravenous solutions

(G-7596)
BAXTER WORLD TRADE CORPORATION (HQ)
1 Baxter Pkwy (60015-4625)
PHONE...................................224 948-2000
Robert Parkinson, *President*
EMP: 10
SQ FT: 17,915
SALES (est): 98.5MM
SALES (corp-wide): 11.3B **Publicly Held**
SIC: 2834 3841 Intravenous solutions; blood transfusion equipment; hemodialysis apparatus; diagnostic apparatus, medical; needles, suture
PA: Baxter International Inc.
1 Baxter Pkwy Df2-1w
Deerfield IL 60015
224 948-2000

(G-7597)
BIRNBERG MACHINERY INC
1450 Northwoods Rd (60015-2224)
PHONE...................................847 673-5242
Robert W Birnberg, *President*
Cynthia Haskins, *Treasurer*
Robert Birnberg, *Human Res Mgr*
Birnberg Robert, *Manager*
▼ **EMP:** 4
SALES (est): 1.2MM **Privately Held**
SIC: 5084 3565 3554 3552 Packaging machinery & equipment; packaging machinery; paper industries machinery; textile machinery; conveyors & conveying equipment

(G-7598)
BNP MEDIA INC
155 N Pfingsten Rd (60015-5293)
PHONE...................................847 205-5660
Erin Murphy, *Marketing Staff*
Gisele Manelli, *Manager*
Jeff Bagwell, *Manager*
Karen Close, *Manager*
Brent Miller, *Art Dir*
EMP: 149
SALES (corp-wide): 156.9MM **Privately Held**
WEB: www.bnpmedia.com
SIC: 2721 Magazines: publishing only, not printed on site
PA: Bnp Media, Inc.
2401 W Big Beaver Rd # 700
Troy MI 48084
248 362-3700

(G-7599)
CAPOL LLC
707 Lake Cook Rd Ste 320 (60015-5276)
PHONE...................................224 545-5095
Dr Matthias Seemann, *CEO*
Cahterine Clark, *President*
Bernd Strack, *CFO*
▲ **EMP:** 8
SALES (est): 1.1MM
SALES (corp-wide): 10.8B **Privately Held**
SIC: 2064 2087 Candy & other confectionery products; glace, for glazing food
HQ: Capol Gmbh
Otto-Hahn-Str. 10
Elmshorn 25337
412 147-740

(G-7600)
CATERPILLAR INC (PA)
510 Lake Cook Rd Ste 100 (60015-5031)
PHONE...................................224 551-4000
Donald James Umpleby III, *Ch of Bd*
William P Ainsworth, *President*
Bob De Lange, *President*
Denise C Johnson, *President*
Ramin Younessi, *President*
▲ **EMP:** 1176
SALES: 53.8B **Publicly Held**
WEB: www.caterpillar.com
SIC: 3531 3519 3511 6531 Construction machinery; engines, diesel & semi-diesel or dual-fuel; gasoline engines; gas turbine generator set units, complete; hydraulic turbine generator set units, complete; fiduciary, real estate; accident insurance carriers; fire, marine & casualty insurance: stock

(G-7601)
CF INDUSTRIES INC (HQ)
4 Parkway North Blvd # 400 (60015-2590)
PHONE...................................847 405-2400
Tony Will, *CEO*
Steve Wilson, *President*
Bert Frost, *Senior VP*
Dennis Kelleher, *Senior VP*
Doug Barnard, *Vice Pres*
◆ **EMP:** 277
SQ FT: 88,000

Deerfield - Lake County (G-7602)

SALES (est): 4.4B **Publicly Held**
WEB: www.cfindustries.com
SIC: 2873 2874 Anhydrous ammonia; urea; phosphoric acid; superphosphates, ammoniated or not ammoniated; diammonium phosphate; calcium meta-phosphate

(G-7602)
CF INDUSTRIES HOLDINGS INC (PA)
4 Parkway North Blvd # 400 (60015-2590)
PHONE 847 405-2400
Stephen A Furbacher, *Ch of Bd*
W Anthony Will, *President*
Duane Lee, *Superintendent*
Tim Dewitte, *Regional Mgr*
Michael Heavener, *Regional Mgr*
EMP: 83
SALES: 4.5B **Publicly Held**
SIC: 2874 2873 Phosphatic fertilizers; fertilizers: natural (organic), except compost

(G-7603)
CF INDUSTRIES NITROGEN LLC (HQ)
4 Parkway North Blvd # 400 (60015-2590)
PHONE 847 405-2400
Anthony Will, *CEO*
◆ **EMP:** 300
SQ FT: 100,000
SALES (est): 4.4B **Publicly Held**
SIC: 2874 2873 Phosphatic fertilizers; nitrogenous fertilizers

(G-7604)
CM WOODWORDS INC
20968 Deerrun Dr (60015-2506)
PHONE 847 945-7689
Chris Mazurk, *Principal*
EMP: 2
SALES (est): 200.4K **Privately Held**
SIC: 2431 Millwork

(G-7605)
CRL INDUSTRIES INC
500 Lake Cook Rd Ste 430 (60015-5268)
PHONE 847 940-3550
D H Carroll, *Ch of Bd*
Gary J Minta, *Vice Pres*
Kathryn V Heller, *Manager*
Thomas Z Hayward Jr, *Admin Sec*
▲ **EMP:** 1
SALES (est): 16.2MM
SALES (corp-wide): 16.5MM **Privately Held**
SIC: 3553 3549 Sanding machines, except portable floor sanders: woodworking; metalworking machinery
PA: Lc Holdings Of Delaware, Inc
500 Lake Cook Rd Ste 430
Deerfield IL 60015
847 940-3550

(G-7606)
CRLI ACCEPTANCE CORP
500 Lake Cook Rd Ste 400 (60015-5269)
PHONE 847 940-1500
Joseph S Haas, *President*
David W Danielski, *Treasurer*
Joe Walsh, *Info Tech Dir*
Gregory R Hamilton, *Admin Sec*
EMP: 4
SALES: 122.7K
SALES (corp-wide): 314MM **Privately Held**
SIC: 2752 Commercial printing, lithographic
PA: Holden Industries, Inc.
500 Lake Cook Rd Ste 400
Deerfield IL 60015
847 940-1500

(G-7607)
EASTWOOD ENTERPRISES INC
1020 Chapel Ct (60015-2211)
P.O. Box 219, Highland Park (60035-0219)
PHONE 847 940-4008
Paul D Levi, *President*
Sue E Clements, *Admin Sec*
EMP: 51
SQ FT: 16,000
SALES (est): 6.5MM **Privately Held**
SIC: 3599 Machine & other job shop work

(G-7608)
ECO GREEN ANALYTICS LLC
735 Castlewood Ln (60015-3972)
PHONE 847 691-1148
Diego Klabjan, *Principal*
EMP: 6
SALES (est): 558.1K **Privately Held**
WEB: www.ecogreenanalytics.com
SIC: 3621 Generators for gas-electric or oil-electric vehicles

(G-7609)
FOR OUR GENERATION INC
944 Woodward Ave (60015-2867)
PHONE 312 282-1257
Andrew Levin, *President*
▲ **EMP:** 4
SALES (est): 900K **Privately Held**
SIC: 3229 Art, decorative & novelty glassware

(G-7610)
FORTUNE BRANDS HOME & SEC INC (PA)
520 Lake Cook Rd (60015-5611)
PHONE 847 484-4400
Christopher J Klein, *CEO*
Brett E Finley, *President*
Nicholas I Fink, *President*
David M Randich, *President*
Tracey L Belcourt, *Senior VP*
▲ **EMP:** 79
SALES: 5.7B **Publicly Held**
SIC: 2531 2599 3429 3469 Public building & related furniture; cabinets, factory; keys, locks & related hardware; boxes: tool, lunch, mail, etc.: stamped metal

(G-7611)
FREE-FLOW PACKAGING INTL INC (DH)
Also Called: FP International
1650 Lake Cook Rd Ste 400 (60015-4747)
PHONE 650 261-5300
Arthur Graham Emeritus, *CEO*
Joseph Nezwek, *President*
James Taylor, *COO*
Ken Willingham, *Plant Mgr*
Alex Van Vuren, *Engineer*
▲ **EMP:** 25
SALES (est): 93.2MM **Privately Held**
WEB: www.fpintl.com
SIC: 3086 Insulation or cushioning material, foamed plastic

(G-7612)
FUJI IMPULSE AMERICAN CORP
1735 Lisa Marie Ct (60015-3921)
PHONE 847 236-9190
Jun Sota, *Principal*
Angela Davis, *Marketing Staff*
▲ **EMP:** 6 **EST:** 2007
SALES (est): 784.7K **Privately Held**
WEB: www.fuji-sotex.com
SIC: 3565 Packaging machinery

(G-7613)
HEALTHY LIFE NUTRACEUTICS INC
500 Lake Cook Rd Ste 350 (60015-5268)
P.O. Box 1492 (60015-6008)
PHONE 201 253-9053
Ravi Patel, *President*
Swapnil Shah, *Vice Pres*
EMP: 5
SALES (est): 581K **Privately Held**
SIC: 5122 2834 Vitamins & minerals; vitamin, nutrient & hematinic preparations for human use

(G-7614)
HERSHEY COMPANY
1751 Lake Cook Rd (60015-5615)
PHONE 800 468-1714
EMP: 3
SALES (corp-wide): 7.9B **Publicly Held**
WEB: www.thehersheycompany.com
SIC: 2066 Chocolate & cocoa products
PA: Hershey Company
19 E Chocolate Ave
Hershey PA 17033
717 534-4200

(G-7615)
HIGH TECH RESEARCH INC (PA)
Also Called: Expert Manufacturing Systems
1020 Milwaukee Ave # 330 (60015-3562)
PHONE 847 215-9797
Steven Birman, *President*
Alex Liberov, *Vice Pres*
EMP: 10
SALES (est): 1.8MM **Privately Held**
SIC: 7371 7372 Computer software development; software programming applications; prepackaged software

(G-7616)
HOLDEN INDUSTRIES INC (PA)
500 Lake Cook Rd Ste 400 (60015-5269)
PHONE 847 940-1500
Joseph S Haas, *Ch of Bd*
Daryl Hively, *Purch Mgr*
Greg Hamilton, *CFO*
Gregory R Hamilton, *CFO*
David W Danielski, *Controller*
◆ **EMP:** 13
SALES (est): 314MM **Privately Held**
SIC: 2752 2672 3545 3589 Commercial printing, lithographic; adhesive papers, labels or tapes: from purchased material; machine tool accessories; sewage & water treatment equipment; sewer cleaning equipment, power; machine tools, metal cutting type; fabricated structural metal

(G-7617)
HORIZON THERAPEUTICS USA INC
1 Takeda Pkwy (60015-5713)
PHONE 224 383-3000
Timothy P Walbert, *Ch of Bd*
EMP: 31
SALES (est): 9.8MM **Privately Held**
WEB: www.horizonpharma.com
SIC: 2834 Pharmaceutical preparations
HQ: Horizon Therapeutics Usa, Inc.
150 Saunders Rd Ste 150 # 150
Lake Forest IL 60045

(G-7618)
JAMES R WILBAT GLASS STUDIO
924 Woodward Ave (60015-2867)
PHONE 847 940-0015
James R Wilbat, *President*
Cara Wilbat, *Treasurer*
EMP: 3
SQ FT: 500
SALES: 20K **Privately Held**
SIC: 3229 Pressed & blown glass

(G-7619)
JDP THERAPEUTICS LLC
520 Lake Cook Rd Ste 500 (60015-5633)
PHONE 847 739-0490
Ed Fiorentino, *Mng Member*
EMP: 6
SQ FT: 500
SALES (est): 761.6K **Privately Held**
SIC: 2834 Pharmaceutical preparations

(G-7620)
JIM BEAM BRANDS CO (DH)
Also Called: James B Beam Import
510 Lake Cook Rd Ste 200 (60015-5031)
PHONE 847 948-8903
Matthew J Shattock, *CEO*
Richard B Reese, *President*
Craig M Smith, *Exec VP*
Joseph J Winkler, *Exec VP*
Bob Probst, *Senior VP*
◆ **EMP:** 325 **EST:** 1923
SQ FT: 50,000
SALES (est): 301MM **Privately Held**
WEB: www.jimbeam.com
SIC: 2085 Bourbon whiskey
HQ: Beam Suntory Inc.
222 Merchandise Mart Plz # 1600
Chicago IL 60654
312 964-6999

(G-7621)
JORDAN INDUSTRIES INC (PA)
1751 Lake Cook Rd Ste 550 (60015-5658)
PHONE 847 945-5591
John W Jordan II, *Ch of Bd*
Thomas H Quinn, *President*
Lisa M Ondrula, *CFO*
Gordon L Nelson, *Treasurer*
Christina Murray, *Controller*
◆ **EMP:** 15
SQ FT: 13,411
SALES (est): 579.2MM **Privately Held**
SIC: 3621 3625 3714 3089 Motors, electric; electric motor & generator auxillary parts; motor starters & controllers, electric; motor vehicle engines & parts; rebuilding engines & transmissions, factory basis; gears, motor vehicle; thermoformed finished plastic products; labels & seals: printing; art, picture frames & decorations; picture frames, ready made

(G-7622)
JORDAN SPECIALTY PLASTICS INC (HQ)
1751 Lake Cook Rd Ste 550 (60015-5624)
PHONE 847 945-5591
Lisa Ondrula, *Principal*
EMP: 7
SALES (est): 179.3MM
SALES (corp-wide): 579.2MM **Privately Held**
SIC: 3089 3081 Plastic containers, except foam; unsupported plastics film & sheet
PA: Jordan Industries, Inc.
1751 Lake Cook Rd Ste 550
Deerfield IL 60015
847 945-5591

(G-7623)
JP LEATHERWORKS INC
1038 Somerset Ave (60015-2942)
PHONE 847 317-9804
P Grace Blumenthal, *President*
Pamela Grace Blumenthal, *President*
EMP: 6
SALES: 1MM **Privately Held**
SIC: 3961 Watchbands, base metal

(G-7624)
JSOLO CORP
Also Called: Minuteman Press
607 Carriage Way (60015-4536)
PHONE 847 964-9188
James S Solotke, *President*
EMP: 4
SALES (est): 381.4K **Privately Held**
SIC: 2752 Commercial printing, lithographic

(G-7625)
JUSTRITE MANUFACTURING CO LLC
Also Called: Justrite Mfg
1751 Lake Cook Rd Ste 370 (60015-5639)
PHONE 800 798-9250
Kathy Awalt, *Purch Agent*
Dan Carr, *CFO*
Allyn Buric, *Sales Mgr*
John Norman, *Manager*
Marilyn Allison, *Manager*
EMP: 150
SQ FT: 150,000
SALES (corp-wide): 104.6MM **Privately Held**
SIC: 3411 Metal cans
PA: Justrite Manufacturing Company, L.L.C.
3921 Dewitt Ave
Mattoon IL 61938
217 234-7486

(G-7626)
KIMBERLY-CLARK CORPORATION
2275 Half Day Rd Ste 350 (60015-1277)
PHONE 312 371-5166
Wayne R Sanders, *Chairman*
EMP: 66
SALES (corp-wide): 18.4B **Publicly Held**
SIC: 2621 2676 Sanitary tissue paper; infant & baby paper products
PA: Kimberly-Clark Corporation
351 Phelps Dr
Irving TX 75038
972 281-1200

(G-7627)
KRAFT FOODS ASIA PCF SVCS LLC (HQ)
3 Parkway North Blvd # 300 (60015-2537)
PHONE 847 943-4000

GEOGRAPHIC SECTION

Deerfield - Lake County (G-7652)

Irene B Rosenfeld, *CEO*
Jamie Miller, *Finance*
EMP: 7
SALES (est): 1.2MM **Publicly Held**
SIC: 2022 2013 2095 2043 Processed cheese; natural cheese; spreads, cheese; dips, cheese-based; sausages & other prepared meats; bacon, side & sliced: from purchased meat; frankfurters from purchased meat; luncheon meat from purchased meat; coffee roasting (except by wholesale grocers); freeze-dried coffee; instant coffee; cereal breakfast foods; dressings, salad: raw & cooked (except dry mixes); powders, drink

(G-7628)
LABJACKSCOM INC
151 S Pfingsten Rd Ste N (60015-4934)
  PHONE 847 537-2099
Stephen Litcher, *President*
EMP: 3
SQ FT: 3,000
SALES (est): 20.9K **Privately Held**
SIC: 3821 Laboratory apparatus, except heating & measuring

(G-7629)
LC HOLDINGS OF DELAWARE INC (PA)
500 Lake Cook Rd Ste 430 (60015-5268)
  PHONE 847 940-3550
D H Carroll, *President*
Gary J Minta, *Vice Pres*
Thomas Z Hayward Jr, *Admin Sec*
▲ **EMP:** 1
SALES (est): 16.5MM **Privately Held**
SIC: 3553 3549 5084 3541 Sanding machines, except portable floor sanders: woodworking; metalworking machinery; industrial machinery & equipment; grinding, polishing, buffing, lapping & honing machines; grinding machines, metalworking

(G-7630)
LUNA AZUL COMMUNICATIONS INC
1340 Hackberry Rd (60015-4020)
  PHONE 773 616-0007
Stefan Nikolov, *President*
EMP: 20
SALES (est): 736.9K **Privately Held**
SIC: 2741 Miscellaneous publishing

(G-7631)
LUNDBECK LLC (DH)
6 Parkway North Blvd # 400 (60015-2522)
  PHONE 847 282-1000
Sean Nolan, *CEO*
Catherine Courtin, *Vice Pres*
Curtis Rhine, *CFO*
Maria T Greene, *Finance Mgr*
Vibe Hansen, *Personnel*
▲ **EMP:** 113 **EST:** 2000
SQ FT: 34,000
SALES (est): 239.2MM
SALES (corp-wide): 5B **Privately Held**
WEB: www.lundbeck.com
SIC: 2834 5122 Pharmaceutical preparations; pharmaceuticals
HQ: H. Lundbeck A/S
  Ottiliavej 9
  Valby 2500
  363 013-11

(G-7632)
LUNDBECK PHARMACEUTICALS LLC
6 Parkway North Blvd # 400 (60015-2522)
  PHONE 847 282-1000
Peter Anastasiou, *President*
EMP: 1000
SALES (est): 73.5MM
SALES (corp-wide): 5B **Privately Held**
WEB: www.lundbeckincgrants.com
SIC: 2834 Pharmaceutical preparations
HQ: Lundbeck Llc
  6 Parkway North Blvd # 400
  Deerfield IL 60015
  847 282-1000

(G-7633)
M L S PRINTING CO INC
537 Hermitage Dr (60015-4444)
  PHONE 847 948-8902
John Mc Loughlin, *President*
Elizabeth Mc Loughlin, *Corp Secy*
EMP: 3 **EST:** 1957
SQ FT: 6,000
SALES (est): 240K **Privately Held**
SIC: 2752 2796 2761 2759 Commercial printing, offset; platemaking services; manifold business forms; commercial printing

(G-7634)
MALCOLITE CORPORATION (PA)
1161 Lake Cook Rd Ste I (60015-5277)
  PHONE 847 562-1350
Jason B Howard, *President*
Cindy Reese, *General Mgr*
EMP: 70
SQ FT: 36,000
SALES (est): 10.4MM **Privately Held**
WEB: www.malcolite.com
SIC: 3641 Electric lamps & parts for generalized applications

(G-7635)
MAPLE HILL CREAMERY LLC (PA)
540 Lake Cook Rd Ste 120 (60015-5657)
P.O. Box 323, Kinderhook NY (12106-0323)
  PHONE 518 758-7777
Peter Meck, *Vice Pres*
Pete Meck, *Opers Staff*
Anne Trost, *Opers Staff*
Charles Zentay, *CFO*
Chris O'Grady, *Controller*
EMP: 20
SQ FT: 6,000
SALES: 8MM **Privately Held**
WEB: www.maplehillcreamery.com
SIC: 2026 Yogurt

(G-7636)
MEDICAL ID FASHIONS COMPANY
Also Called: Webzonepro.com
408 Swan Blvd (60015-3673)
  PHONE 847 404-6789
Olaf Moetus, *President*
Abbe Sennett, *Principal*
EMP: 4
SALES (est): 249.7K **Privately Held**
WEB: www.medicalidfashions.com
SIC: 3961 Bracelets, except precious metal

(G-7637)
MONDELEZ GLOBAL LLC (HQ)
3 N Pkwy Ste 300 (60015)
  PHONE 847 943-4000
Christine Hayatian, *Manager*
David A Brearton,
Pluehs W Gerhard,
May J Karen,
Irene B Rosenfeld,
▲ **EMP:** 132
SALES (est): 4.3B **Publicly Held**
SIC: 2052 2066 3999 2067 Crackers, dry; biscuits, dry; chocolate; candies; chewing gum; cheese, natural & processed; beverage bases

(G-7638)
MONDELEZ INTL HOLDINGS LLC (HQ)
3 Parkway North Blvd # 300 (60015-2565)
  PHONE 800 572-3847
Matthew Sims, *Plant Mgr*
Jody Wright, *Controller*
Charles McDonough, *VP Finance*
Daniel Roe, *Finance Dir*
Dean Spanos, *Finance Mgr*
EMP: 17
SALES (est): 30.6MM **Publicly Held**
SIC: 2038 Snacks, including onion rings, cheese sticks, etc.

(G-7639)
MY OWN MEALS INC (PA)
400 Lake Cook Rd Ste 107 (60015-4929)
P.O. Box 334 (60015-0334)
  PHONE 847 948-1118
Mary A Jackson, *President*
Elizabeth M Doyle, *Vice Pres*
Joseph D'Onofrio, *CFO*
▼ **EMP:** 4
SQ FT: 1,500
SALES: 15.2MM **Privately Held**
SIC: 2099 Food preparations

(G-7640)
NANO GAS TECHNOLOGIES INC
506 Cambridge Cir (60015-4209)
  PHONE 847 317-0656
Leonard Bland, *CEO*
EMP: 5
SALES (est): 576.7K **Privately Held**
SIC: 3589 Water treatment equipment, industrial

(G-7641)
ORACLE BIGMACHINES LLC (HQ)
Also Called: Bigmachines A G
1405 Lake Cook Rd (60015-5213)
  PHONE 847 572-0300
David Bonnette, *CEO*
Sean Fallon, *COO*
Thomas P Padgett, *Senior VP*
Marlene Williamson, *Chief Mktg Ofcr*
EMP: 100
SQ FT: 5,000
SALES (est): 13.3MM
SALES (corp-wide): 39.5B **Publicly Held**
SIC: 7372 Prepackaged software
PA: Oracle Corporation
  500 Oracle Pkwy
  Redwood City CA 94065
  650 506-7000

(G-7642)
PELICAN HOLDCO LLC (PA)
1650 Lake Cook Rd Ste 400 (60015-4747)
  PHONE 847 597-2200
Glenn M Fischer, *President*
Michael T McDonnell, *President*
EMP: 13
SALES (est): 237.2MM **Privately Held**
SIC: 2671 5199 7336 Packaging paper & plastics film, coated & laminated; packaging materials; package design

(G-7643)
PREGIS INNOVATIVE PACKG LLC
1650 Lake Cook Rd Ste 400 (60015-4747)
  PHONE 847 597-2200
Kevin Baudhuin, *President*
Keith Lavanway, *CFO*
EMP: 41
SALES (est): 14.2MM **Privately Held**
SIC: 2671 5199 Packaging paper & plastics film, coated & laminated; packaging materials
HQ: Pregis Llc
  1650 Lake Cook Rd Ste 400
  Deerfield IL 60015

(G-7644)
PREGIS LLC (HQ)
1650 Lake Cook Rd Ste 400 (60015-4747)
P.O. Box 309 (60015-0309)
  PHONE 847 597-2200
Kevin Baudhuin, *CEO*
Tom Pienkowski, *President*
Thomas Condrea, *Principal*
Jeffrey Mueller, *Vice Pres*
Daniel Schoen, *Technical Mgr*
◆ **EMP:** 70
SALES (est): 571.2MM **Privately Held**
SIC: 2441 Packing cases, wood: nailed or lock corner

(G-7645)
PREGIS LLC
1650 Lake Cook Rd Ste 400 (60015-4747)
  PHONE 847 597-2200
Kevin J Baudhuin, *President*
D Keith Lavanway, *CFO*
EMP: 4000
SALES (est): 216.2MM **Privately Held**
SIC: 2671 2673 3086 Packaging paper & plastics film, coated & laminated; bags: plastic, laminated & coated; insulation or cushioning material, foamed plastic; packaging & shipping materials, foamed plastic
PA: Pelican Holdco Llc
  1650 Lake Cook Rd Ste 400
  Deerfield IL 60015

(G-7646)
PRINTING YOU CAN TRUST
707 Mallard Ln (60015-3680)
  PHONE 224 676-0482
Aaron Marsh, *Owner*
EMP: 3 **EST:** 2009
SALES (est): 350.7K **Privately Held**
WEB: www.printingyoucantrust.com
SIC: 2752 Commercial printing, offset

(G-7647)
RTI SURGICAL HOLDINGS INC (PA)
520 Lake Cook Rd Ste 315 (60015-4926)
  PHONE 386 418-8888
Curtis M Selquist, *Ch of Bd*
Camille I Farhat, *President*
Terry M Rich, *President*
Olivier M Visa, *President*
Jonathon M Singer, *COO*
EMP: 10
SALES (est): 308.3MM **Publicly Held**
SIC: 3842 3841 Surgical appliances & supplies; surgical & medical instruments

(G-7648)
SIEMENS HLTHCARE DGNOSTICS INC
1717 Deerfield Rd Ste 1 (60015-3909)
  PHONE 847 267-5300
Greg Sorsenson, *CEO*
Vikas Saxena, *General Mgr*
Eric Miles, *Regional Mgr*
Adam Bender, *Business Mgr*
Erin Camp, *Counsel*
▲ **EMP:** 106
SALES (est): 12.5MM
SALES (corp-wide): 96.9B **Privately Held**
SIC: 3841 Surgical & medical instruments
HQ: Siemens Healthcare Gmbh
  Henkestr. 127
  Erlangen 91052
  913 184-0

(G-7649)
SILICON CONTROL INC (PA)
155 N Pfingsten Rd # 360 (60015-5293)
  PHONE 847 215-7947
Paul Schur, *President*
EMP: 4
SQ FT: 2,000
SALES (est): 902.6K **Privately Held**
SIC: 8711 8731 3825 3823 Consulting engineer; commercial physical research; instruments to measure electricity; industrial instrmnts mesrmnt display/control process variable

(G-7650)
SURGICAL SOLUTIONS LLC
1751 Lake Cook Rd Ste 230 (60015-5641)
  PHONE 847 607-6098
Alyssa Rapp, *CEO*
Anthony Dawson, *COO*
Amy Davalle, *Senior VP*
Vladan Jovanovic, *Vice Pres*
Logan Derck, *Finance*
EMP: 170
SALES: 26MM **Privately Held**
SIC: 8099 3841 Medical services organization; surgical & medical instruments

(G-7651)
SYSTEMS PIPING
1625 Half Day Rd (60015-1233)
  PHONE 847 948-1373
Karen Vanderbilt, *Owner*
EMP: 7
SALES (est): 688.1K **Privately Held**
SIC: 3569 Sprinkler systems, fire: automatic

(G-7652)
TERRA NITROGEN COMPANY LP (DH)
4 Parkway North Blvd # 400 (60015-2502)
  PHONE 847 405-2400
W Anthony Will, *President*
Dennis P Kelleher, *CFO*
▲ **EMP:** 2

Deerfield - Lake County (G-7653)

SALES: 397.2MM **Publicly Held**
SIC: 2873 Nitrogen solutions (fertilizer)
HQ: Terra Nitrogen Gp Inc.
4 Parkway North Blvd # 400
Deerfield IL 60015
847 405-2400

(G-7653)
TERRA NITROGEN GP INC (HQ)
Also Called: Tngp
4 Parkway North Blvd # 400 (60015-2502)
PHONE.....................847 405-2400
Douglas C Barnard, *Ch of Bd*
W Anthony Will, *President*
Christopher D Bohn, *Senior VP*
Bert A Frost, *Senior VP*
Susan L Menzel, *Senior VP*
EMP: 3
SALES (est): 397.2MM **Publicly Held**
SIC: 2873 Nitrogen solutions (fertilizer)

(G-7654)
TEXTURA CORPORATION (HQ)
1405 Lake Cook Rd (60015-5213)
PHONE.....................866 839-8872
Patrick Allin, *President*
Michael Antis, *Exec VP*
Linda Debruin, *Exec VP*
David Kelly, *Exec VP*
Jeff Adams, *Sales Dir*
EMP: 250
SQ FT: 63,000
SALES: 86.6MM
SALES (corp-wide): 39.5B **Publicly Held**
SIC: 7372 Prepackaged software
PA: Oracle Corporation
500 Oracle Pkwy
Redwood City CA 94065
650 506-7000

(G-7655)
UNOFFICIAL CARDBOARD INC
1115 Walden Ln (60015)
PHONE.....................224 565-5391
David Nachbar, *COO*
EMP: 4
SALES (est): 445.3K **Privately Held**
SIC: 2631 Cardboard

(G-7656)
VAN STOCKUM KRISTINE
Also Called: Kristine Van Stockum's Hand PA
827 Woodward Ave (60015-2864)
PHONE.....................847 914-0015
Kristine Van Stockum, *Owner*
EMP: 4
SALES (est): 50K **Privately Held**
SIC: 2392 Tablecloths & table settings

(G-7657)
VICRON OPTICAL INC
1020 Milwaukee Ave # 235 (60015-3555)
PHONE.....................847 412-5530
EMP: 10
SQ FT: 2,000
SALES: 1MM **Privately Held**
SIC: 3851 5047 Manufactures And Wholsales Opthalmic Supplies

(G-7658)
VMM USA UNIQUE MASTER MOD
1042 Inverrary Ln (60015-3610)
PHONE.....................847 537-0867
John Vojtech, *Owner*
EMP: 3
SALES (est): 296K **Privately Held**
SIC: 3944 Games, toys & children's vehicles

(G-7659)
W-F PROFESSIONAL ASSOC INC
400 Lake Cook Rd Ste 207 (60015-4930)
P.O. Box 1634 (60015-6010)
PHONE.....................847 945-8050
William Feinberg, *President*
EMP: 3
SALES (est): 266.7K **Privately Held**
SIC: 2741 8748 Miscellaneous publishing; business consulting

(G-7660)
WOODHEAD INDUSTRIES INC
3 Parkway North Blvd (60015-2537)
PHONE.....................847 236-9300
Jesus James, *Manager*

Russell Young, *Manager*
EMP: 3
SALES (est): 67.2K **Privately Held**
SIC: 3678 Electronic connectors

(G-7661)
WORTH-PFAFF INNOVATIONS INC (PA)
Also Called: Flashcut Cnc
444 Lake Cook Rd Ste 17 (60015-4931)
PHONE.....................847 940-9305
Ronald K Worth, *President*
Eric Pfaff, *Admin Sec*
▲ EMP: 6
SQ FT: 5,000
SALES (est): 3.4MM **Privately Held**
SIC: 5084 3829 Instruments & control equipment; measuring & controlling devices

(G-7662)
WOW SIGNS INC
150 Augusta Dr (60015-5069)
PHONE.....................847 910-4405
Larry Feld, *President*
EMP: 6
SALES (est): 393.1K **Privately Held**
SIC: 3993 Neon signs

(G-7663)
ZOOKBINDERS INC
151 S Pfingsten Rd Ste K (60015-4934)
PHONE.....................847 272-5745
Mark Zucker, *President*
Carrie Rooney, *Human Resources*
EMP: 70
SALES (est): 11.6MM **Privately Held**
SIC: 2782 Albums

Dekalb
Dekalb County

(G-7664)
3M DEKALB DISTRIBUTION
12101 Barber Greene Rd (60115-7901)
PHONE.....................815 756-5087
Robert Hughes, *Principal*
◆ EMP: 23
SALES (est): 2.6MM **Privately Held**
SIC: 5199 3999 Anatomical specimens & research material; atomizers, toiletry

(G-7665)
ALGUS PACKAGING INC
200 N Peace Rd (60115-9500)
PHONE.....................815 756-1881
Arthur Gustafson, *President*
Larry Aska, *Vice Pres*
Pat Stoner, *Vice Pres*
Karen Gustafson, *Admin Sec*
EMP: 100
SQ FT: 200,000
SALES (est): 33.9MM **Privately Held**
SIC: 3089 3565 Blister or bubble formed packaging, plastic; packaging machinery

(G-7666)
ARMOLOY OF ILLINOIS INC
Also Called: Bi Protec
114 Simonds Ave (60115-3969)
PHONE.....................815 758-6657
Michael Bejbl, *President*
EMP: 45
SQ FT: 22,750
SALES (est): 3.9MM **Privately Held**
SIC: 3479 Coating of metals & formed products
PA: Investment Holdings Inc
114 Simons Ave
De Kalb IL

(G-7667)
CASTLE-PRINTECH INC
121 Industrial Dr (60115-3931)
PHONE.....................815 758-5484
John M Gavelda, *President*
Vern Sisson, *Vice Pres*
Bruce Johnson, *Purch Agent*
Chris Neal, *Manager*
John Whitaker, *Info Tech Mgr*
EMP: 1 EST: 1990
SALES: 220.5K **Privately Held**
SIC: 2759 Commercial printing

(G-7668)
COLE PALLET SERVICES CORP
1600 S 7th St (60115-4742)
PHONE.....................815 758-3226
Brett Cole, *President*
John Cole, *Vice Pres*
John A Cole, *Vice Pres*
Jerry Hyde, *Plant Mgr*
Collin Bredeson, *Production*
EMP: 35
SALES (est): 4.7MM **Privately Held**
WEB: www.colepallet.com
SIC: 2448 2449 Pallets, wood; skids, wood; wood containers

(G-7669)
CONEX CABLE LLC
1007 E Locust St (60115-3967)
P.O. Box 822 (60115-0822)
PHONE.....................800 877-8089
Brian Starr, *Prdtn Mgr*
Raymond Charles Hott,
Renee Kozin,
Melissa Spellman,
▲ EMP: 35
SQ FT: 64,000
SALES (est): 11.5MM **Privately Held**
SIC: 3355 Aluminum wire & cable

(G-7670)
COPY SERVICE INC
1005 W Lincoln Hwy (60115-3019)
PHONE.....................815 758-1151
David Baker, *President*
EMP: 5 EST: 1976
SQ FT: 7,000
SALES (est): 631.4K **Privately Held**
WEB: www.dekalbcountyselfstorage.com
SIC: 7334 5943 2791 2789 Photocopying & duplicating services; office forms & supplies; typesetting; bookbinding & related work

(G-7671)
CURRAN CONTRACTING COMPANY
2220 County Farm Rd (60115-9429)
PHONE.....................815 758-8113
Rick Noe, *Principal*
EMP: 8
SALES (corp-wide): 585.3MM **Privately Held**
WEB: www.currancontracting.com
SIC: 1611 2951 5032 Highway & street paving contractor; asphalt paving mixtures & blocks; paving materials
HQ: Curran Contracting Company
286 Memorial Ct
Crystal Lake IL 60014

(G-7672)
CURT HERRMANN CONSTRUCTION INC
512 Maplewood Ave (60115-4214)
PHONE.....................815 748-0531
Curt Herrmann, *President*
EMP: 4
SALES (est): 375K **Privately Held**
SIC: 3131 Counters

(G-7673)
CUSHIONEER INC
1651 Pleasant St (60115-2604)
PHONE.....................815 748-5505
Andrew Swift, *President*
Warren B Swift, *Shareholder*
EMP: 53
SQ FT: 80,000
SALES (est): 9.2MM **Privately Held**
SIC: 3086 Packaging & shipping materials, foamed plastic

(G-7674)
CY-TEC INC
221 Industrial Dr (60115-3933)
P.O. Box 46 (60115-0046)
PHONE.....................815 756-8416
Dan Pritchard, *President*
Patrice Pritchard, *Shareholder*
EMP: 5 EST: 1979
SQ FT: 14,000
SALES: 600K **Privately Held**
SIC: 3555 Printing presses; presses, gravure; printing trade parts & attachments

(G-7675)
DE KALB PLATING CO INC
221 Grove St (60115-3701)
PHONE.....................815 756-6112
Bruce Miller, *President*
EMP: 7 EST: 1962
SQ FT: 7,700
SALES (est): 994.7K **Privately Held**
SIC: 3471 Electroplating of metals or formed products

(G-7676)
DEKALB CONFECTIONARY INC (PA)
149 N 2nd St (60115-3203)
PHONE.....................815 758-5990
Thomas Smith, *President*
Sharon Smith, *Vice Pres*
EMP: 21
SQ FT: 3,300
SALES (est): 1.9MM **Privately Held**
SIC: 5441 2066 Candy; chocolate & cocoa products

(G-7677)
FASTRACK STAIRS & RAILS LTD
303 N 11th St (60115-3503)
PHONE.....................847 531-6252
EMP: 6
SALES (est): 348.1K **Privately Held**
SIC: 3446 Mfg Architectural Metalwork

(G-7678)
FORGE GROUP DEKALB LLC (PA)
Also Called: Forge Resources Group
1801 Pleasant St (60115-2608)
P.O. Box 369 (60115-0369)
PHONE.....................815 756-3538
Donald G Jones, *President*
Jeffrey Jones, *Vice Pres*
Brian Urfer, *Project Mgr*
Scott Holdiman, *Purch Mgr*
Lance Robinson, *QC Dir*
EMP: 75 EST: 1946
SQ FT: 102,000
SALES (est): 13.4MM **Privately Held**
WEB: www.forgeresourcesgroup.com
SIC: 3462 Iron & steel forgings

(G-7679)
FORGE RESOURCES GROUP LLC
1832 Pleasant St (60115-2609)
P.O. Box 369 (60115-0369)
PHONE.....................815 758-6400
EMP: 200
SALES (est): 6.9MM **Privately Held**
SIC: 3399 Mfg Primary Metal Products

(G-7680)
FORGE RESOURCES GROUP LLC
1801 Pleasant St (60115-2608)
PHONE.....................815 758-6400
EMP: 189 **Privately Held**
SIC: 3399 Iron ore recovery from open hearth slag
PA: Forge Resources Group Llc
1832 Pleasant St
Dekalb IL 60115

(G-7681)
FORGE RESOURCES GROUP LLC (PA)
1832 Pleasant St (60115-2609)
P.O. Box 369 (60115-0369)
PHONE.....................815 758-6400
Donald G Jones, *President*
Jeffrey Jones, *Vice Pres*
Eric Loomis, *Design Engr*
Kent Paul, *CFO*
Kate Marach, *Accounts Mgr*
EMP: 11
SALES (est): 19.6MM **Privately Held**
SIC: 3462 3399 Iron & steel forgings; iron ore recovery from open hearth slag

(G-7682)
GEM ELECTRIC MOTOR REPAIR
1400 E Lincoln Hwy (60115-3971)
PHONE.....................815 756-5317
Hirlande Erker, *President*

GEOGRAPHIC SECTION

Dekalb - Dekalb County (G-7709)

John Erker, *Corp Secy*
Paul Erker, *Vice Pres*
EMP: 2
SQ FT: 2,500
SALES (est): 250K **Privately Held**
SIC: 5063 7694 Motors, electric; electric motor repair

(G-7683)
H A PHILLIPS & CO (PA)
770 Enterprise Ave (60115-7904)
PHONE.................................630 377-0050
Michael.Ryan, *CEO*
Janet Jones, *Vice Pres*
Steve L Yagla, *Vice Pres*
Brian J Youssi, *Vice Pres*
Michelle L Polly, *Treasurer*
▼ **EMP:** 30 **EST:** 1928
SQ FT: 22,000
SALES (est): 8.7MM **Privately Held**
WEB: www.haphillips.com
SIC: 3585 3491 3443 3822 Refrigeration & heating equipment; industrial valves; fabricated plate work (boiler shop); refrigeration controls (pressure); household refrigerators & freezers

(G-7684)
HERFF JONES LLC
901 N 1st St Ste 7 (60115-2395)
PHONE.................................815 756-4743
Bernard W Elsner, *Manager*
EMP: 6
SALES (corp-wide): 1.1B **Privately Held**
SIC: 3911 Rings, finger; precious metal
HQ: Herff Jones, Llc
4501 W 62nd St
Indianapolis IN 46268
800 419-5462

(G-7685)
HORIZON DOWNING LLC
1115 E Locust St (60115-3964)
P.O. Box 827 (60115-0827)
PHONE.................................815 758-6867
Michael J Scherer,
EMP: 27 **EST:** 1979
SQ FT: 52,500
SALES (est): 3.2MM
SALES (corp-wide): 13.6MM **Privately Held**
SIC: 7389 4225 3993 Promoters of shows & exhibitions; advertising, promotional & trade show services; general warehousing; advertising artwork
PA: Downing Displays, Inc.
550 Techne Center Dr
Milford OH 45150
513 248-9800

(G-7686)
JANELLE PUBLICATIONS INC
116 Twombly Rd (60115)
P.O. Box 811 (60115-0811)
PHONE.................................815 756-2300
Janet Dawson, *President*
Sten Kresatck, *Vice Pres*
EMP: 2
SQ FT: 1,350
SALES: 350K **Privately Held**
SIC: 2741 8049 Miscellaneous publishing; speech therapist

(G-7687)
L M C INC
Also Called: APM Process Center
1142 Glidden Ave (60115-4377)
PHONE.................................815 758-3514
Lennart Lindell, *Ch of Bd*
Gordon D Goranson, *President*
▲ **EMP:** 1
SQ FT: 40,000
SALES (est): 210.9K **Privately Held**
SIC: 3542 3535 Pressing machines; conveyors & conveying equipment

(G-7688)
LOTHSON GUITARS
10580 Keslinger Rd (60115-8829)
PHONE.................................815 756-2031
Larry Lothson, *Owner*
EMP: 3
SALES: 150K **Privately Held**
SIC: 5736 3931 String instruments; musical instruments

(G-7689)
LUXIS INTERNATIONAL INC
1292 S 7th St (60115-4746)
PHONE.................................800 240-1473
Laura Steubbing, *Principal*
EMP: 3
SALES (est): 226.6K **Privately Held**
SIC: 2844 Toilet preparations

(G-7690)
MANITOWOC LIFTS AND MFG LLC
155 Harvestore Dr (60115-8675)
PHONE.................................815 748-9500
Doug Climenhaga,
EMP: 6 **EST:** 2010
SQ FT: 75,000
SALES (est): 847.1K **Privately Held**
WEB: www.mlmliftsandmfg.com
SIC: 5084 3593 Lift trucks & parts; fluid power cylinders, hydraulic or pneumatic

(G-7691)
NANCY J PERKINS
Also Called: Le Print Express
1950 Dekalb Ave Ste D (60115)
PHONE.................................815 748-7121
Nancy J Perkins, *Owner*
Jim Perkins, *Co-Owner*
EMP: 5
SQ FT: 2,500
SALES: 550K **Privately Held**
SIC: 2752 Commercial printing, offset

(G-7692)
NATHAN WINSTON SERVICE INC
132 N 3rd St (60115-3302)
PHONE.................................815 758-4545
Barry Nathan Haber, *CEO*
Carolyn Haber, *President*
EMP: 4
SQ FT: 1,700
SALES (est): 240K **Privately Held**
SIC: 7389 3993 3953 Engraving service; signs & advertising specialties; marking devices

(G-7693)
NEHRING ELECTRICAL WORKS CO
1005 E Locust St (60115-3967)
P.O. Box 965 (60115-0965)
PHONE.................................815 756-2741
Raymond C Hott, *President*
David Kozin, *Principal*
Russ Sineni, *Production*
Matt Bush, *Purchasing*
Neftali Bautista, *Engineer*
▲ **EMP:** 130 **EST:** 1912
SQ FT: 200,000
SALES (est): 54.9MM **Privately Held**
WEB: www.nehringwire.com
SIC: 3351 3355 7692 Wire, copper & copper alloy; aluminum wire & cable; welding repair

(G-7694)
NESTLE USA INC
Also Called: Nestle Distribution Center
800 Nestle Ct (60115-8676)
PHONE.................................815 754-2550
Steve Papke, *Manager*
EMP: 139
SALES (corp-wide): 93.5B **Privately Held**
SIC: 2023 Evaporated milk
HQ: Nestle Usa, Inc.
1812 N Moore St Ste 118
Rosslyn VA 22209
440 264-7249

(G-7695)
NORTHERN ILLINOIS UNIVERSITY
310 N 5th St (60115-3311)
PHONE.................................815 753-1826
J Schwartz, *Branch Mgr*
EMP: 19
SALES (corp-wide): 491.7MM **Privately Held**
WEB: www.niu.edu
SIC: 2741 Miscellaneous publishing
PA: The Northern Illinois University
1425 W Lincoln Hwy
Dekalb IL 60115
815 753-9500

(G-7696)
OFFICEMAX NORTH AMERICA INC
2350 Sycamore Rd Ste E (60115-2000)
PHONE.................................815 748-3007
Dave Schwaller, *Manager*
EMP: 25
SALES (corp-wide): 10.6B **Privately Held**
SIC: 5712 5943 2759 Office furniture; office forms & supplies; business forms; printing
HQ: Officemax North America, Inc.
263 Shuman Blvd
Naperville IL 60563

(G-7697)
ON PAINT IT COMPANY
140 Tygert Ln (60115-8259)
P.O. Box 439, Crown Point IN (46308-0439)
PHONE.................................219 765-5639
Steven Becker, *Owner*
EMP: 3 **EST:** 1980
SALES (est): 154.5K **Privately Held**
SIC: 3952 Lettering instruments, artists'

(G-7698)
PREMIUM WOOD PRODUCTS INC
436 E Locust St (60115-3327)
PHONE.................................815 787-3669
Michael A Wood, *President*
EMP: 30
SQ FT: 40,000
SALES (est): 3MM **Privately Held**
SIC: 2499 Decorative wood & woodwork

(G-7699)
PSYTEC INC
520 Linden Pl (60115-3130)
P.O. Box 564 (60115-0564)
PHONE.................................815 758-1415
Renanne Brock, *Manager*
EMP: 3
SALES (est): 224.6K **Privately Held**
SIC: 2731 5192 Books: publishing only; books

(G-7700)
RIGHT/POINTE LLC (PA)
234 Harvestore Dr (60115-8769)
P.O. Box 467 (60115-0467)
PHONE.................................815 754-5700
S Patrick Giersch, *Mng Member*
George F Connell,
EMP: 55 **EST:** 1996
SQ FT: 16,200
SALES (est): 14.7MM **Privately Held**
WEB: www.rightpointe.com
SIC: 2899 2891 Concrete curing & hardening compounds; adhesives & sealants

(G-7701)
SISLERS ICE INC
274 Harvestore Dr (60115-8769)
PHONE.................................815 756-6903
Scott Sisler, *President*
Brian Sisler, *Sales Staff*
EMP: 20
SQ FT: 7,000
SALES (est): 2.7MM **Privately Held**
SIC: 2097 5999 5078 Manufactured ice; ice; ice making machines

(G-7702)
SK EXPRESS INC
310 Dietz Ave (60115-2671)
P.O. Box 1139 (60115-7139)
PHONE.................................815 748-4388
Saeed Saffaei, *President*
Anna Gomez, *Engineer*
Jim Luebke, *Manager*
EMP: 190
SQ FT: 22,000
SALES (est): 42.5MM **Privately Held**
WEB: www.sk-expressinc.com
SIC: 3694 Battery cable wiring sets for internal combustion engines

(G-7703)
SONOCO PRTECTIVE SOLUTIONS INC
1401 Pleasant St (60115-2663)
PHONE.................................815 787-5244
Dean Kalmerton, *Mfg Staff*

Linda Jensen, *Accounting Mgr*
EMP: 40
SQ FT: 50,000
SALES (corp-wide): 5.3B **Publicly Held**
SIC: 3365 3544 Machinery castings, aluminum; special dies, tools, jigs & fixtures
HQ: Sonoco Protective Solutions, Inc.
1 N 2nd St
Hartsville SC 29550
843 383-7000

(G-7704)
SOTA SERVICE CTR BY BODINETS
Also Called: Sota Turntable
436 E Locust St (60115-3327)
PHONE.................................608 538-3500
Mona Lisa Hook, *President*
Kirk Bodinet, *President*
EMP: 5 **EST:** 1997
SQ FT: 1,200
SALES (est): 240.8K **Privately Held**
WEB: www.sotaturntables.com
SIC: 7622 3679 Home entertainment repair services; recording & playback apparatus, including phonograph

(G-7705)
SOUTHMOOR ESTATES INC
Also Called: Mikari
1032 S 7th St (60115-4526)
PHONE.................................815 756-1299
Patrick C Lasco, *President*
Kari Lasco, *Corp Secy*
EMP: 7
SALES (est): 839.9K **Privately Held**
SIC: 5271 6515 2451 Mobile homes; mobile home site operators; mobile homes

(G-7706)
SPORTS ALL SORTS AP & DESIGN
147 N 2nd St Ste 2 (60115-3276)
PHONE.................................815 756-9910
John Launer, *Owner*
EMP: 6
SQ FT: 6,000
SALES (est): 350K **Privately Held**
SIC: 2759 Screen printing

(G-7707)
TANK WIND-DOWN CORP
Also Called: Engineered Storage Products Co
345 Harvestore Dr (60115-9646)
PHONE.................................815 756-1551
Chris Forbes, *Sales Dir*
Richard Jones, *Branch Mgr*
EMP: 60 **Privately Held**
SIC: 3448 3523 3443 Farm & utility buildings; farm machinery & equipment; fabricated plate work (boiler shop)
PA: Tank Wind-Down Corp.
903 E 104th St Ste 900
Kansas City MO 64131

(G-7708)
TEGRANT ALLOYD BRANDS INC (DH)
Also Called: Sonoco Alloyd
1401 Pleasant St (60115-2663)
P.O. Box 627 (60115-0627)
PHONE.................................815 756-8451
Ron Leach, *President*
James L Price, *Senior VP*
EMP: 325 **EST:** 1961
SQ FT: 300,000
SALES (est): 77.4MM
SALES (corp-wide): 5.3B **Publicly Held**
WEB: www.alloyd.com
SIC: 3089 3565 Blister or bubble formed packaging, plastic; trays, plastic; packaging machinery

(G-7709)
TIM DETWILER ENTERPRISES INC
Also Called: Wholesale Gate Co
1140 S 7th St (60115-4528)
PHONE.................................815 758-9950
Tim Detwiler, *President*
Rae Detwiler, *Vice Pres*
▲ **EMP:** 8
SQ FT: 9,000

Dekalb - Dekalb County (G-7710)

SALES: 500K **Privately Held**
WEB: www.wholesalegate.com
SIC: 3446 Gates, ornamental metal; ornamental metalwork

(G-7710)
UNIFIED WIRE AND CABLE COMPANY
338 Wurlitzer Dr (60115-2675)
P.O. Box 452 (60115-0452)
PHONE..................................815 748-4876
Brian Foley, *President*
Dorothy Klecan, *Office Mgr*
Rob Graham, *Director*
Judith Sid, *Admin Sec*
EMP: 20
SQ FT: 25,000
SALES (est): 10.2MM **Privately Held**
SIC: 3357 Nonferrous wiredrawing & insulating

(G-7711)
WEHRLI CUSTOM FABRICATION
300 Harvestore Dr (60115-8680)
PHONE..................................630 277-8239
Jason Wehrli, *Owner*
EMP: 17
SALES (est): 3.7MM **Privately Held**
WEB: www.wcfab.com
SIC: 3441 Fabricated structural metal

(G-7712)
WELSH INDUSTRIES LTD
6 Evergreen Cir (60115-2214)
P.O. Box 783 (60115-0783)
PHONE..................................815 756-1111
Michael Welsh, *CEO*
Rosemarie Welsh, *President*
EMP: 50
SQ FT: 14,000
SALES (est): 5.1MM **Privately Held**
SIC: 2395 Emblems, embroidered

(G-7713)
WESTROCK RKT LLC
Also Called: Alliance Display
800 Nestle Ct (60115-8676)
PHONE..................................815 756-8913
David Rose, *Manager*
EMP: 37
SALES (corp-wide): 18.2B **Publicly Held**
WEB: www.rocktenn.com
SIC: 2653 Corrugated & solid fiber boxes
HQ: Westrock Rkt, Llc
1000 Abernathy Rd Ste 125
Atlanta GA 30328
770 448-2193

(G-7714)
WHISKEY ACRES DISTILLING CO
11504 Keslinger Rd (60115-8810)
PHONE..................................815 739-8711
James Walter, *President*
EMP: 10 **EST:** 2015
SALES: 200K **Privately Held**
SIC: 2085 Distilled & blended liquors

Delavan
Tazewell County

(G-7715)
DELAVAN TIMES
314 S Locust St (61734-7528)
P.O. Box 199 (61734-0199)
PHONE..................................309 244-7111
Sandra Larimore Denman, *Owner*
EMP: 3
SALES (est): 145.3K **Privately Held**
SIC: 2711 Newspapers: publishing only, not printed on site

Depue
Bureau County

(G-7716)
DEPUE MECHANICAL INC (PA)
216 W 4th S (61322)
P.O. Box 80 (61322-0080)
PHONE..................................815 447-2267

Jim Jacobsen Sr, *CEO*
James Jacobsen Jr, *President*
Tom Herrigan, *Treasurer*
EMP: 25
SQ FT: 3,000
SALES (est): 13MM **Privately Held**
WEB: www.depuemechanical.com
SIC: 1711 3444 Boiler maintenance contractor; sheet metalwork

Des Plaines
Cook County

(G-7717)
A WHEELS INC
666 Garland Pl (60016-4788)
PHONE..................................847 699-7000
EMP: 3 **EST:** 2015
SALES (est): 68.8K **Privately Held**
SIC: 3291 Wheels, grinding: artificial

(G-7718)
ABBOTT LABORATORIES
215 E Washington St (60016-2925)
P.O. Box 64, North Chicago (60064-0064)
PHONE..................................847 937-6100
Stafford O'Kelly, *Division Pres*
EMP: 1000
SALES (corp-wide): 31.9B **Publicly Held**
SIC: 2834 Druggists' preparations (pharmaceuticals)
PA: Abbott Laboratories
100 Abbott Park Rd
Abbott Park IL 60064
224 667-6100

(G-7719)
ABBOTT MOLECULAR INC
1300 E Touhy Ave (60018-3315)
PHONE..................................224 361-7800
EMP: 3
SALES (corp-wide): 31.9B **Publicly Held**
SIC: 2835 3826 In vitro & in vivo diagnostic substances; analytical instruments
HQ: Abbott Molecular Inc.
1300 E Touhy Ave
Des Plaines IL 60018

(G-7720)
ABBOTT MOLECULAR INC (HQ)
1300 E Touhy Ave (60018-3315)
PHONE..................................224 361-7800
Edward L Michael, *President*
Shyrl Hoover, *Manager*
▲ **EMP:** 100
SQ FT: 56,551
SALES (est): 74.4MM
SALES (corp-wide): 31.9B **Publicly Held**
SIC: 2835 3826 In vitro & in vivo diagnostic substances; analytical instruments
PA: Abbott Laboratories
100 Abbott Park Rd
Abbott Park IL 60064
224 667-6100

(G-7721)
ABKI TECH SERVICE INC
Also Called: Abkitech
764 Meadow Dr (60016-1146)
P.O. Box 1362 (60017-1362)
PHONE..................................847 818-8403
Kitty Thomas, *President*
EMP: 10
SALES (est): 263.2K **Privately Held**
SIC: 7372 7373 7374 7389 Application computer software; systems engineering, computer related; service bureau, computer; ; custom computer programming services

(G-7722)
ACUITY BRANDS LIGHTING INC
Also Called: Juno Lighting
1300 S Wolf Rd (60018-1300)
P.O. Box 5065 (60017-5065)
PHONE..................................847 827-9880
Chris Walsh, *President*
Eric Westphal, *President*
Larry Alfrey, *Safety Mgr*
Doug Jennings, *Buyer*
Eileen Curtin, *Purchasing*
EMP: 12
SALES (corp-wide): 3.6B **Publicly Held**
SIC: 3648 Lighting equipment

HQ: Acuity Brands Lighting, Inc.
1 Acuity Way
Conyers GA 30012

(G-7723)
ADVANCED CUSTOM METALS INC
1024 North Ave (60016-3331)
PHONE..................................847 803-2090
John Schaefer, *President*
EMP: 8
SALES (corp-wide): 2.9MM **Privately Held**
SIC: 3444 3469 3441 3429 Sheet metalwork; metal stampings; fabricated structural metal; manufactured hardware (general)
PA: Advanced Custom Metals, Inc.
1028 North Ave Ste A
Des Plaines IL 60016
847 391-0970

(G-7724)
ADVANCED FIBER PRODUCTS LLC
200 Howard Ave Ste 244 (60018-5909)
PHONE..................................847 768-9001
Saladeen Muhammad, *Opers Mgr*
Richard Durrant, *Mng Member*
Greg Ristau, *Manager*
Julie Durrant,
EMP: 6
SQ FT: 2,000
SALES (est): 764.3K
SALES (corp-wide): 13.9B **Privately Held**
SIC: 3229 Fiber optics strands
HQ: Advanced Fiber Products Limited
Hollands Road Industrial Estate
Haverhill

(G-7725)
ALL SAINTS MONUMENT CO INC
20 S River Rd (60016-3457)
PHONE..................................847 824-1248
Frank Troost, *President*
EMP: 2
SALES (est): 546.6K
SALES (corp-wide): 14MM **Privately Held**
SIC: 3281 5999 Monument or burial stone, cut & shaped; monuments & tombstones
PA: Peter Troost Monument Co.
4300 Roosevelt Rd
Hillside IL
708 544-0916

(G-7726)
AMCOR PHRM PACKG USA LLC
1731 S Mount Prospect Rd (60018-1803)
PHONE..................................847 298-5626
EMP: 110
SQ FT: 80,000
SALES (corp-wide): 9.1B **Privately Held**
SIC: 3089 3221 Mfg Plastic Products Mfg Glass Containers
HQ: Amcor Pharmaceutical Packaging Usa, Llc
625 Sharp St N
Millville NJ 08332
856 327-1540

(G-7727)
AMERICAN LOUVER COMPANY
100 Howard Ave (60018-1958)
PHONE..................................800 772-0355
EMP: 8
SALES (est): 1MM **Privately Held**
SIC: 3444 Sheet metalwork

(G-7728)
AMERICAN SOC HM INSPECTORS INC (PA)
Also Called: ASHI
932 Lee St Ste 101 (60016-6594)
PHONE..................................847 759-2820
Randy Sipe, *President*
Frank Lesh, *Exec Dir*
EMP: 12
SALES: 3.4MM **Privately Held**
SIC: 2721 8621 Trade journals: publishing only, not printed on site; professional membership organizations

(G-7729)
AMERICAN WILBERT VAULT CORP
165 S River Rd (60016-3415)
PHONE..................................847 824-4415
Brian Doyle, *Branch Mgr*
EMP: 9
SALES (est): 736.6K
SALES (corp-wide): 8.2MM **Privately Held**
SIC: 3272 Burial vaults, concrete or precast terrazzo
PA: American Wilbert Vault Corp
4415 Harrison St Ste 246
Hillside IL 60162
708 366-3210

(G-7730)
AMNETIC LLC
1645 S River Rd Ste 8 (60018-2206)
PHONE..................................877 877-3678
Fred Kortmann,
EMP: 6
SALES (est): 267.4K **Privately Held**
SIC: 2819 Alkali metals: lithium, cesium, francium, rubidium

(G-7731)
AMPHENOL EEC INC
1701 Birchwood Ave (60018-3005)
PHONE..................................773 463-8343
R Adam Norwitt, *President*
◆ **EMP:** 30
SALES (est): 4.6MM
SALES (corp-wide): 8.2B **Publicly Held**
SIC: 3643 Electric connectors
PA: Amphenol Corporation
358 Hall Ave
Wallingford CT 06492
203 265-8900

(G-7732)
ANDERSON SAFFORD MKG GRAPHICS
Also Called: Rubber Stamp Man
570 E Northwest Hwy Ste 7 (60016-2269)
PHONE..................................847 827-8968
Ralph Kipnis, *President*
Gayle Kipnis, *President*
Madeline Scrima, *Exec VP*
EMP: 14
SQ FT: 17,000
SALES (est): 2MM **Privately Held**
SIC: 3953 7336 Embossing seals & hand stamps; graphic arts & related design; silk screen design

(G-7733)
ARGYLE CUT STONE CO
1046 Woodlawn Ave (60016-3337)
PHONE..................................847 456-6210
Daniel Peterson, *President*
Alfred Peterson, *President*
B James Larson, *Corp Secy*
EMP: 30 **EST:** 1929
SQ FT: 8,125
SALES: 900K **Privately Held**
WEB: www.argylecutstone.com
SIC: 3281 1422 Limestone, cut & shaped; crushed & broken limestone

(G-7734)
ASPEN API INC (DH)
Also Called: Organon API
2136 S Wolf Rd (60018-1932)
PHONE..................................847 635-0985
Andrea Keith Vasel, *President*
Gene Godawa, *Corp Secy*
Pat Nikowitz, *Opers Staff*
Mark Crosley, *Associate Dir*
▲ **EMP:** 10
SQ FT: 6,600
SALES (est): 4.4MM
SALES (corp-wide): 2.8B **Privately Held**
WEB: www.aspenoss.com
SIC: 2836 2869 2834 2812 Coagulation products; industrial organic chemicals; pharmaceutical preparations; alkalies & chlorine
HQ: Aspen Oss B.V.
Kloosterstraat 6
Oss
882 779-000

GEOGRAPHIC SECTION

Des Plaines - Cook County (G-7760)

(G-7735)
AXIS INTERNATIONAL MARKETING
1800 S Wolf Rd Ste 2 (60018-1905)
PHONE 847 297-0744
Linda Chen-Berger, *President*
Andy Berger, *Vice Pres*
Heidi Bassie, *Sales Staff*
Kathy Rogoz, *Relations*
▲ **EMP:** 170 **EST:** 1998
SQ FT: 3,000
SALES (est): 16.7MM **Privately Held**
SIC: 5023 3631 Aluminumware; household cooking equipment

(G-7736)
BASS BROTHER INCORPORATED (PA)
Also Called: Bradley Systems
2720 S River Rd Ste 146 (60018-4110)
PHONE 800 252-1114
Mark N Bass, *President*
EMP: 9
SQ FT: 1,000
SALES: 3MM **Privately Held**
SIC: 2842 Sanitation preparations

(G-7737)
BAY PLASTICS
1245 E Forest Ave Ste 8 (60018-1564)
PHONE 847 299-2045
Norman Knurek, *Principal*
Ruth Michael, *Administration*
▲ **EMP:** 11
SALES (est): 1.5MM **Privately Held**
SIC: 3089 Injection molding of plastics

(G-7738)
BEASTGRIP CO
1269 Rand Rd (60016-3402)
PHONE 312 283-5283
Vadym Chalenko, *CEO*
EMP: 2
SQ FT: 4,000
SALES (est): 372.4K **Privately Held**
SIC: 5043 3827 Photographic equipment & supplies; lenses, optical: all types except ophthalmic

(G-7739)
BIO-RAD LABORATORIES INC
1400 E Touhy Ave (60018-3305)
PHONE 847 699-2217
David G Dutton, *Division Mgr*
Andrew Stapleton, *Business Mgr*
Susan Stewart, *Materials Mgr*
Diane Dahowski, *Opers Staff*
Matthew Nill, *Manager*
EMP: 473
SALES (corp-wide): 2.2B **Publicly Held**
WEB: www.bio-rad.com
SIC: 3826 Analytical instruments
PA: Bio-Rad Laboratories, Inc.
1000 Alfred Nobel Dr
Hercules CA 94547
510 724-7000

(G-7740)
BION ENTERPRISES LTD
Also Called: MBL Bion
455 State St Ste 100 (60016-2280)
PHONE 847 544-5044
Jun Sasaki, *CEO*
Melinda Ascher, *COO*
Judy Rasmussen, *Safety Mgr*
Kathy Joiner, *Human Res Dir*
Marc Delcommenne, *Manager*
EMP: 30 **EST:** 1978
SQ FT: 17,000
SALES: 4MM **Privately Held**
WEB: www.bionenterprises.com
SIC: 2835 In vitro & in vivo diagnostic substances
HQ: Mbl International Corporation
15a Constitution Way
Woburn MA 01801

(G-7741)
BRG SPORTS INC (HQ)
1700 E Higgins Rd Ste 500 (60018-3800)
PHONE 224 585-5200
Dan Arment, *CEO*
Timothy P Mayhew, *President*
Chris Zimmerman, *President*
Thomas T Merrigan, *Exec VP*
Jackelyn E Werblo, *Senior VP*
▲ **EMP:** 92
SQ FT: 56,647
SALES (est): 645.2MM **Privately Held**
SIC: 3751 3949 Bicycles & related parts; helmets, athletic; pads: football, basketball, soccer, lacrosse, etc.; protective sporting equipment

(G-7742)
CF GEAR HOLDINGS LLC (PA)
Also Called: Process Gear
2064 Mannheim Rd (60018-2909)
PHONE 847 376-8322
Rishi Chandra,
Salisha Chandra,
EMP: 40
SALES (est): 3.3MM **Privately Held**
SIC: 3599 Machine shop, jobbing & repair

(G-7743)
CFC INC (PA)
Also Called: Columbus Foods Company
30 E Oakton St (60018-1945)
PHONE 847 257-8920
Paulette Gagliardo, *President*
John Healy, *General Mgr*
Joe Feely, *Prdtn Mgr*
Ricardo Aguinaga, *Purchasing*
Rick Cummisford, *QC Dir*
▼ **EMP:** 100
SQ FT: 330,000
SALES (est): 79.6MM **Privately Held**
WEB: www.columbusfoods.com
SIC: 2079 2099 Olive oil; sauces: gravy, dressing & dip mixes

(G-7744)
CHICAGO DIAL INDICATOR COMPANY
1372 Redeker Rd (60016-3421)
PHONE 847 827-7186
Jerry R Iverson, *CEO*
Erick Iverson, *President*
Mark Dams, *Design Engr*
Terry Iverson, *Admin Sec*
▲ **EMP:** 35
SQ FT: 14,700
SALES (est): 7.3MM **Privately Held**
WEB: www.dialindicator.com
SIC: 3829 Measuring & controlling devices

(G-7745)
CHICAGO QUADRILL CO
1840 Busse Hwy (60016-6727)
PHONE 847 824-4196
Carl Grunschel Sr, *President*
Gladys Grunschel, *Corp Secy*
Carl Grunschel Jr, *Exec VP*
EMP: 9
SQ FT: 13,000
SALES (est): 1MM **Privately Held**
SIC: 3545 3544 3546 Drilling machine attachments & accessories; dies & die holders for metal cutting, forming, die casting; drill attachments, portable

(G-7746)
CHROMATECH PRINTING INC
16 Mary St (60016-3407)
PHONE 847 699-0333
Barbara Vanslambrouck, *President*
Michael Vanslambrouck, *Corp Secy*
EMP: 10
SQ FT: 18,000
SALES (est): 1.8MM **Privately Held**
SIC: 2752 Commercial printing, offset

(G-7747)
CISCO SYSTEMS INC
9501 Tech Blvd Ste 100 (60018)
PHONE 847 678-6600
Eva Beko-Rogers, *Partner*
Chris Danca, *Partner*
Scott Foringer, *Partner*
Rajji Chander, *Vice Pres*
Jim Bennett, *Engineer*
EMP: 350
SALES (corp-wide): 51.9B **Publicly Held**
WEB: www.cisco.com
SIC: 3577 5065 Data conversion equipment, media-to-media: computer; electronic parts & equipment
PA: Cisco Systems, Inc.
170 W Tasman Dr
San Jose CA 95134
408 526-4000

(G-7748)
COMMUNITY ADVANTAGE NETWORK (PA)
1163 Lee St (60016-6516)
PHONE 847 376-8943
EMP: 4
SALES (est): 507.8K **Privately Held**
SIC: 3663 Cellular radio telephone

(G-7749)
CONTOUR SAWS INC (PA)
900 Graceland Ave (60016)
PHONE 800 259-6834
Michael L Wilkie, *Ch of Bd*
Jon Henricks, *Vice Ch Bd*
Chuck B Davis, *Senior VP*
Carol Shannon, *Manager*
Timothy P Moran, *Admin Sec*
◆ **EMP:** 35
SQ FT: 125,000
SALES (est): 16.6MM **Privately Held**
WEB: www.contoursawsinc.com
SIC: 3425 Saw blades for hand or power saws

(G-7750)
CONTOUR SAWS INC
1217 E Thacker St (60016-6412)
PHONE 800 259-6834
Steve Lund, *Vice Pres*
Cheri Ferrari, *Manager*
EMP: 85
SALES (corp-wide): 16.6MM **Privately Held**
SIC: 3425 Saw blades & handsaws
PA: Contour Saws, Inc.
900 Graceland Ave
Des Plaines IL 60016
800 259-6834

(G-7751)
COPYSET SHOP INC
1801 E Oakton St (60018-2111)
PHONE 847 768-2679
Daniel Davidson, *President*
Ed Davidson, *Vice Pres*
EMP: 9
SQ FT: 7,000
SALES (est): 1.2MM **Privately Held**
SIC: 7334 2791 Photocopying & duplicating services; typesetting

(G-7752)
CRYSTATECH INC
1700 S Mount Prospect Rd (60018-1804)
PHONE 847 768-0500
Eric Klasson, *President*
David Seeger, *Vice Pres*
Bryan Petrinec, *Admin Sec*
▲ **EMP:** 10 **EST:** 2000
SQ FT: 10,000
SALES (est): 590K **Privately Held**
WEB: www.gastechnology.org
SIC: 1389 Construction, repair & dismantling services

(G-7753)
DELUXE CORPORATION
Also Called: Deluxe Check Printers
1600 E Touhy Ave (60018-3607)
PHONE 847 635-7200
Craig Lederman, *Manager*
EMP: 246
SALES (corp-wide): 2B **Publicly Held**
WEB: www.sitekreator.com
SIC: 2782 2759 Checkbooks; commercial printing
PA: Deluxe Corporation
3680 Victoria St N
Shoreview MN 55126
651 483-7111

(G-7754)
DELUXE JOHNSON
Also Called: Johnson Group
1600 E Touhy Ave (60018-3607)
P.O. Box 5566, Rockford (61125-0566)
PHONE 847 635-7200
Dennis W Johnson, *Principal*
Dale H Johnson, *Principal*
▲ **EMP:** 160 **EST:** 1957
SQ FT: 20,000
SALES (est): 12.5MM
SALES (corp-wide): 2B **Publicly Held**
SIC: 2752 2791 2789 Commercial printing, lithographic; typesetting; bookbinding & related work
PA: Deluxe Corporation
3680 Victoria St N
Shoreview MN 55126
651 483-7111

(G-7755)
DES PLAINES JOURNAL INC
Also Called: Journal & Topics Newspapers
622 Graceland Ave (60016-4519)
PHONE 847 299-5511
Todd C Wessell, *President*
Todd Wessell, *Publisher*
Todd C Wessell, *Purchasing*
Melody Walker, *VP Sales*
EMP: 70 **EST:** 1931
SQ FT: 12,500
SALES: 3MM **Privately Held**
WEB: www.journal-topics.com
SIC: 2711 7331 2791 2752 Newspapers: publishing only, not printed on site; mailing service; typesetting; commercial printing, lithographic

(G-7756)
DESIGN GROUP SIGNAGE CORP
2135 Frontage Rd (60018-3009)
PHONE 847 390-0350
Bridget Gilmore, *President*
Bridgit Gilmore, *President*
James Gilmore, *Admin Sec*
EMP: 12
SQ FT: 30,000
SALES (est): 1.9MM **Privately Held**
SIC: 3993 Electric signs

(G-7757)
DT METRONIC INC
1253 Rand Rd (60016-3402)
PHONE 224 567-8414
Rolf Klausmann, *CEO*
◆ **EMP:** 4
SQ FT: 2,000
SALES: 869K **Privately Held**
SIC: 3479 Chasing on metals; coating of metals & formed products; engraving jewelry silverware, or metal

(G-7758)
ENTERPRISE SERVICE CORPORATION
5400 Milton Pkwy (60018)
P.O. Box 855, Rosemont (60018-0855)
PHONE 773 589-2727
John Schwab, *Branch Mgr*
EMP: 3
SALES (est): 160.5K
SALES (corp-wide): 663.7K **Privately Held**
SIC: 1731 3711 Electric power systems contractors; snow plows (motor vehicles), assembly of
PA: Enterprise Service Corporation
2648 Paula Ln
Des Plaines IL 60018
847 299-2727

(G-7759)
EPIC METALS CORPORATION
2400 E Devon Ave Ste 205 (60018-4617)
PHONE 847 803-6411
Don Landis, *Branch Mgr*
EMP: 9
SALES (corp-wide): 21MM **Privately Held**
SIC: 3444 Roof deck, sheet metal
PA: Epic Metals Corporation
11 Talbot Ave
Rankin PA 15104
412 351-3913

(G-7760)
ERMAK USA INC
2860 S River Rd Ste 145 (60018-6008)
PHONE 847 640-7765
Emre Varisli, *Principal*
▲ **EMP:** 18

Des Plaines - Cook County (G-7761)

SALES (est): 3.1MM
SALES (corp-wide): 79.6MM **Privately Held**
SIC: 3441 Fabricated structural metal
PA: Ermaksan Makina Sanayi Ve Ticaret Anonim Sirketi
No.6 Isiktepeosb Mahallesi
Bursa 16140
224 294-7500

(G-7761)
EVERGREEN SCALE MODELS INC
65 Bradrock Dr (60018-1937)
PHONE..................224 567-8099
Brian Ellerby, *President*
Mary Ellerby, *Vice Pres*
EMP: 12
SALES (est): 1.4MM **Privately Held**
SIC: 3999 2821 Models, general, except toy; plastics materials & resins

(G-7762)
EXSEL EXHIBITS INC
Also Called: Nimlok-Chicago
111 Rawls Rd (60018-1328)
PHONE..................847 647-1012
Peter Crouch, *President*
Deb Venable, *Managing Dir*
Larry E Slad, *Admin Sec*
▲ **EMP:** 17
SQ FT: 6,000
SALES (est): 381.6K **Privately Held**
SIC: 3993 Signs & advertising specialties

(G-7763)
EXTON CORP
Also Called: Exton Corporation
1 Innovation Dr (60016-3161)
PHONE..................847 391-8100
Mark Simanton, *President*
EMP: 107
SQ FT: 90,000
SALES (est): 9MM
SALES (corp-wide): 189.6MM **Privately Held**
SIC: 3444 3469 Sheet metal specialties, not stamped; stamping metal for the trade
PA: Ims Companies, Llc
1 Innovation Dr
Des Plaines IL 60016
847 391-8100

(G-7764)
FASTENERS FOR RETAIL INC
Also Called: Ffr Merchandising
1600 Birchwood Ave (60018-3004)
PHONE..................847 296-5511
Scott Luedke, *Plant Mgr*
EMP: 153 **Privately Held**
WEB: www.fastenersforretail.com
SIC: 3089 Extruded finished plastic products
HQ: Fasteners For Retail, Inc.
8181 Darrow Rd
Twinsburg OH 44087
330 998-7800

(G-7765)
FILTER FRIEND Z INC
2280 Magnolia St (60018-3127)
PHONE..................847 824-4049
Mildred Phillips, *President*
EMP: 4
SALES (est): 276.8K **Privately Held**
SIC: 3564 Blower filter units (furnace blowers)

(G-7766)
FILTRAN HOLDINGS LLC (PA)
875 Seegers Rd (60016-3045)
PHONE..................847 635-6670
Larry W Gies Jr, *President*
John E Udelhofen, *Vice Pres*
Brett Wall, *Vice Pres*
Bruce Lussow, *Production*
Ryan Booth, *Engineer*
EMP: 1
SALES (est): 149MM **Privately Held**
SIC: 3433 Heating equipment, except electric

(G-7767)
FILTRAN LLC (HQ)
875 Seegers Rd (60016-3045)
PHONE..................847 635-6670
Brett Wall, *President*
Dennis Barn, *Vice Pres*
John Eleftherakis, *Vice Pres*
John E Udelhofen, *Vice Pres*
Steve Cammarata, *Senior Buyer*
◆ **EMP:** 240
SALES (est): 145.6MM **Privately Held**
SIC: 3433 Heating equipment, except electric

(G-7768)
FINZER HOLDING LLC (PA)
Also Called: Finzer Roller Pennsylvania
129 Rawls Rd (60018-1328)
PHONE..................847 390-6200
Randy Apperson, *Sales Staff*
John O Finzer III,
David M Finzer,
EMP: 4
SQ FT: 36,000
SALES (est): 12.7MM **Privately Held**
SIC: 3069 Rubber hardware

(G-7769)
FINZER ROLLER INC
Also Called: Finzer Roller Maryland
129 Rawls Rd (60018-1328)
PHONE..................410 939-1850
John O Finzer III, *CEO*
David M Finzer, *President*
Martin B Finzer, *Vice Pres*
EMP: 21
SQ FT: 23,000
SALES (est): 3.2MM
SALES (corp-wide): 28.1MM **Privately Held**
WEB: www.finzerroller.com
SIC: 3069 3061 Roll coverings, rubber; mechanical rubber goods
PA: Finzer Roller, Inc.
129 Rawls Rd
Des Plaines IL 60018
847 390-6200

(G-7770)
FINZER ROLLER INC (PA)
129 Rawls Rd (60018-1328)
PHONE..................847 390-6200
John Finzer, *CEO*
David M Finzer, *President*
Joe Sheridan, *General Mgr*
Ron Bradley, *Plant Mgr*
Ron Pynos, *Plant Mgr*
◆ **EMP:** 35
SQ FT: 28,000
SALES (est): 28.1MM **Privately Held**
WEB: www.finzerroller.com
SIC: 3069 Rubber rolls & roll coverings; roll coverings, rubber

(G-7771)
FINZER ROLLER INC
Also Called: Finzer Roller Indiana
129 Rawls Rd (60018-1328)
PHONE..................812 829-1455
David M Finzer, *President*
Martin Finzer, *Vice Pres*
EMP: 24
SALES (est): 3.7MM
SALES (corp-wide): 28.1MM **Privately Held**
SIC: 3069 3061 Roll coverings, rubber; mechanical rubber goods
PA: Finzer Roller, Inc.
129 Rawls Rd
Des Plaines IL 60018
847 390-6200

(G-7772)
FOOD SERVICE PUBLISHING CO
Also Called: Food Industry News
3166 S River Rd Ste 40 (60018)
PHONE..................847 699-3300
James S Contis, *President*
Mark Braun, *Publisher*
Valerie Miller, *Editor*
Terry Minich, *Editor*
Cary Miller, *Vice Pres*
EMP: 10
SQ FT: 2,200
SALES (est): 550K **Privately Held**
SIC: 2711 2741 2721 Newspapers: publishing only, not printed on site; directories: publishing only, not printed on site; periodicals

(G-7773)
GEPCO INTERNATIONAL INC (DH)
1770 Birchwood Ave (60018-3006)
PHONE..................847 795-9555
Gary Geppert, *Ch of Bd*
▲ **EMP:** 45
SQ FT: 60,000
SALES (est): 4.1MM **Privately Held**
SIC: 3357 5065 Communication wire; electronic parts & equipment

(G-7774)
GILCO REAL ESTATE COMPANY
515 Jarvis Ave (60018-1957)
PHONE..................847 298-1717
Hunter J Gilbertson, *President*
Gus Gilbertson, *Vice Pres*
EMP: 50 **EST:** 1938
SQ FT: 50,000
SALES (est): 2.8MM **Privately Held**
WEB: www.gilcoscaffolding.com
SIC: 1799 7359 5082 3446 Scaffolding construction; equipment rental & leasing; scaffolding; architectural metalwork

(G-7775)
GTX INC
300 E Touhy Ave (60018-2611)
PHONE..................847 699-7421
Bom Lee Hee, *Principal*
EMP: 3
SALES (est): 426.6K **Privately Held**
WEB: www.gtxchi.com
SIC: 2992 Lubricating oils

(G-7776)
HIGGINS QUICK PRINT
Also Called: Higgins Forms & Systems
2410 S River Rd (60018-3201)
PHONE..................847 635-7700
Murray Burns, *Owner*
EMP: 4
SALES (est): 397.5K **Privately Held**
SIC: 2752 Commercial printing, offset

(G-7777)
HOMWAREHOUSE
1683 S Mount Prospect Rd (60018-1814)
PHONE..................224 500-3367
Adnan Salim, *Owner*
EMP: 2
SALES (est): 257.1K **Privately Held**
SIC: 2515 Sofa beds (convertible sofas)

(G-7778)
HONEYWELL INTERNATIONAL INC
95 E Algonquin Rd Bldg D (60016-6101)
PHONE..................847 797-4000
Bill Lagrotta, *Area Mgr*
Louise Quilter-Wood, *Vice Pres*
Camille Medina, *Buyer*
Stephen C Houdek, *Research*
Shelly Kelly, *Research*
EMP: 60
SALES (corp-wide): 36.7B **Publicly Held**
SIC: 8711 3585 8731 7382 Heating & ventilation engineering; air conditioning units, complete: domestic or industrial; heating equipment, complete; commercial physical research; security systems services
PA: Honeywell International Inc.
300 S Tryon St
Charlotte NC 28202
704 627-6200

(G-7779)
HONEYWELL INTERNATIONAL INC
200 E Algonquin Rd (60016-6104)
PHONE..................847 797-4612
EMP: 22
SALES (corp-wide): 36.7B **Publicly Held**
SIC: 3724 Aircraft engines & engine parts
PA: Honeywell International Inc.
300 S Tryon St
Charlotte NC 28202
704 627-6200

(G-7780)
HONEYWELL INTERNATIONAL INC
25 E Algonquin Rd (60016-6101)
P.O. Box 5017 (60017-5017)
PHONE..................847 391-2000
Carlos A Cabrera, *CEO*
Mark Featherstone, *Engineer*
EMP: 3000
SQ FT: 800
SALES (corp-wide): 36.7B **Publicly Held**
SIC: 5013 3519 Automotive supplies & parts; diesel engine rebuilding
PA: Honeywell International Inc.
300 S Tryon St
Charlotte NC 28202
704 627-6200

(G-7781)
HU-FRIEDY MFG CO LLC
1666 E Touhy Ave (60018-3607)
PHONE..................847 257-4500
Ron Saslow, *Branch Mgr*
EMP: 18
SALES (corp-wide): 918.1MM **Publicly Held**
WEB: www.hu-friedy.com
SIC: 3999 Barber & beauty shop equipment
HQ: Hu-Friedy Mfg. Co., Llc
3232 N Rockwell St
Chicago IL 60618
773 975-3975

(G-7782)
ICEBERG ENTERPRISES LLC (PA)
2700 S River Rd Ste 303 (60018-4107)
PHONE..................847 685-9500
Howard Green, *CEO*
Richard Gilbert, *President*
Richard Fox, *Vice Pres*
David Parzynski Sr, *Vice Pres*
Shawn Reniker, *Vice Pres*
▲ **EMP:** 15
SQ FT: 3,700
SALES: 35MM **Privately Held**
SIC: 2522 Office furniture, except wood

(G-7783)
ILLINOIS CAPACITOR INC
2400 E Devon Ave Ste 292 (60018-4613)
PHONE..................847 675-1760
Basil Jacobson, *President*
Michael Shade, *Vice Pres*
Mary McKirchy, *Manager*
EMP: 272
SALES: 69.1K
SALES (corp-wide): 115.5MM **Privately Held**
SIC: 2819 3675 Aluminum compounds; electronic capacitors
HQ: Cornell-Dubilier Marketing, Inc.
140 Technology Pl
Liberty SC 29657

(G-7784)
ILLINOIS TOOL WORKS INC
Also Called: ITW Switches
195 E Algonquin Rd (60016-6197)
PHONE..................847 724-7500
Brian Truesdale, *Manager*
Candy Banks, *Manager*
EMP: 180
SALES (corp-wide): 14.1B **Publicly Held**
WEB: www.itw.com
SIC: 3679 3643 3621 3613 Electronic switches; current-carrying wiring devices; motors & generators; switchgear & switchboard apparatus; computer peripheral equipment
PA: Illinois Tool Works Inc.
155 Harlem Ave
Glenview IL 60025
847 724-7500

(G-7785)
ILLINOIS TOOL WORKS INC
ITW Nexus
195 E Algonquin Rd (60016-6197)
P.O. Box 2444 (60017-2444)
PHONE..................847 299-2222
Mark Udelhofen, *General Mgr*
Rob Proksa, *Mfg Mgr*
Chris Danz, *Materials Mgr*

GEOGRAPHIC SECTION
Des Plaines - Cook County (G-7810)

Trung Ngo, *Engineer*
EMP: 170
SALES (corp-wide): 14.1B **Publicly Held**
SIC: 3089 5085 3469 3965 Injection molding of plastics; industrial supplies; metal stampings; fasteners, buttons, needles & pins
PA: Illinois Tool Works Inc.
155 Harlem Ave
Glenview IL 60025
847 724-7500

(G-7786)
IMS COMPANIES LLC (PA)
1 Innovation Dr (60016-3161)
PHONE..............................847 391-8100
Mark Simanton, *CEO*
Steve Tokarz, *President*
James Talarek, *COO*
Steve Szczech, *Vice Pres*
Bert A Getz Jr, *Director*
▼ **EMP:** 55
SQ FT: 245,000
SALES: 189.6MM **Privately Held**
SIC: 3469 8711 3679 3714 Metal stampings; engineering services; harness assemblies for electronic use: wire or cable; gears, motor vehicle; sheet metal specialties, not stamped

(G-7787)
IMS ENGINEERED PRODUCTS LLC
1 Innovation Dr (60016-3161)
PHONE..............................847 391-8100
Joe Urbauer, *Business Mgr*
Jacob Dybala, *Vice Pres*
Ken Wesseln, *Vice Pres*
Ben Maggio, *Maint Spvr*
Rex Giesler, *Purch Mgr*
▲ **EMP:** 163 **EST:** 2005
SALES: 41.6MM
SALES (corp-wide): 189.6MM **Privately Held**
WEB: www.imsepcustom.com
SIC: 3444 2522 3699 3469 Housings for business machines, sheet metal; office cabinets & filing drawers: except wood; filing boxes, cabinets & cases: except wood; office desks & tables: except wood; electrical equipment & supplies; metal stampings; partitions & fixtures, except wood
PA: Ims Companies, Llc
1 Innovation Dr
Des Plaines IL 60016
847 391-8100

(G-7788)
INTERNATIONAL PAPER COMPANY
100 E Oakton St (60018-1956)
PHONE..............................847 390-1300
EMP: 26
SALES (corp-wide): 22.3B **Publicly Held**
SIC: 2621 Paper mills
PA: International Paper Company
6400 Poplar Ave
Memphis TN 38197
901 419-9000

(G-7789)
INTRAVATION INC (PA)
1113 Hewitt Dr (60016-6040)
PHONE..............................847 299-6423
Anthony Salah, *President*
Michael Ruddick, *Treasurer*
EMP: 1
SALES: 800K **Privately Held**
SIC: 7372 Application computer software

(G-7790)
J B METAL WORKS INC
1325 Lee St (60018-1514)
PHONE..............................847 824-4253
Steven Burval, *President*
Carole Burval, *Corp Secy*
EMP: 5 **EST:** 1938
SQ FT: 11,000
SALES (est): 600K **Privately Held**
WEB: www.jbmetalworks.com
SIC: 3446 3443 3441 7692 Architectural metalwork; fabricated plate work (boiler shop); fabricated structural metal; welding repair

(G-7791)
JEWEL OSCO INC
Also Called: Jewel-Osco 3425
1500 Lee St (60018-1544)
PHONE..............................847 296-7786
Tom Hong, *Manager*
EMP: 200
SALES (corp-wide): 60.5B **Privately Held**
SIC: 5411 5912 5421 2051 Supermarkets, chain; drug stores & proprietary stores; meat & fish markets; bread, cake & related products
HQ: Jewel Osco, Inc.
150 E Pierce Rd Ste 200
Itasca IL 60143
630 948-6000

(G-7792)
JPH ENTERPRISES INC
Also Called: Citywide Printing
420 Lee St (60016-4610)
PHONE..............................847 390-0900
James Hess, *President*
EMP: 7
SQ FT: 5,000
SALES (est): 117.5K **Privately Held**
WEB: www.citywide.ws
SIC: 2752 7334 2796 2791 Commercial printing, offset; photocopying & duplicating services; platemaking services; typesetting; bookbinding & related work; commercial printing

(G-7793)
KING OF SOFTWARE INC
1232 Willow Ave (60016-4234)
PHONE..............................847 354-8745
EMP: 4
SALES (est): 200.4K **Privately Held**
SIC: 7372 Prepackaged software

(G-7794)
KRAUS & NAIMER INC
200 Howard Ave Ste 270 (60018-5910)
PHONE..............................847 298-2450
Ray Ploski, *Manager*
EMP: 7
SALES (corp-wide): 15.8MM **Privately Held**
WEB: www.krausnaimer.us
SIC: 3679 Electronic switches
PA: Kraus & Naimer, Inc.
760 New Brunswick Rd
Somerset NJ 08873
732 560-1240

(G-7795)
LA MARCHE MFG CO (PA)
106 Bradrock Dr (60018-1967)
PHONE..............................847 299-1188
Judith La Marche, *Ch of Bd*
Richard Rutkowski, *President*
Julio Vargas, *COO*
Rajesh Dhiman, *Exec VP*
Michael Britton, *Vice Pres*
◆ **EMP:** 120
SQ FT: 66,000
SALES: 13.7MM **Privately Held**
WEB: www.lamarchemfg.com
SIC: 3629 Battery chargers, rectifying or nonrotating; inverters, nonrotating: electrical

(G-7796)
LEA & SACHS INC (PA)
1267 Rand Rd (60016-3402)
P.O. Box 1667 (60017-1667)
PHONE..............................847 296-8000
George B Martin, *President*
Robert Martin, *Vice Pres*
Bill Magill, *Sales Staff*
Beth Keane, *Technology*
George Martin, *Executive*
EMP: 13 **EST:** 1937
SQ FT: 4,000
SALES (est): 1.5MM **Privately Held**
WEB: www.leasachs.com
SIC: 2241 Elastic narrow fabrics, woven or braided; elastic webbing

(G-7797)
LEARJET INC
Also Called: Bombardier Learjet
251 Wille Rd Ste A (60018-1861)
PHONE..............................847 553-0172
Dave Hanna, *Branch Mgr*
EMP: 450
SALES (corp-wide): 15.7B **Privately Held**
SIC: 3721 3812 Aircraft; search & navigation equipment
HQ: Learjet Inc.
1 Learjet Way
Wichita KS 67209
316 946-2000

(G-7798)
LEGGETT & PLATT INCORPORATED
Also Called: Vertex Fasteners
1798 Sherwin Ave (60018-3015)
PHONE..............................847 768-6139
Mike Devito, *Safety Dir*
Scott Bridges, *Branch Mgr*
EMP: 53
SALES (corp-wide): 4.7B **Publicly Held**
SIC: 3549 3965 Metalworking machinery; fasteners, buttons, needles & pins
PA: Leggett & Platt, Incorporated
1 Leggett Rd
Carthage MO 64836
417 358-8131

(G-7799)
MAK-SYSTEM CORP
2720 S River Rd Ste 225 (60018-4111)
PHONE..............................847 803-4863
Simon Kiskovski, *President*
EMP: 15
SALES (est): 2MM **Privately Held**
SIC: 3695 Computer software tape & disks: blank, rigid & floppy
PA: Mak-System France
10 Avenue De La Grande Armee
Paris 75017

(G-7800)
MARTIN SPROCKET & GEAR INC
1505 Birchwood Ave (60018-3001)
PHONE..............................847 298-8844
Mylan Tyrrell, *Manager*
EMP: 13
SALES (corp-wide): 539MM **Privately Held**
WEB: www.martinsprocket.com
SIC: 3566 3568 Gears, power transmission, except automotive; power transmission equipment
PA: Martin Sprocket & Gear, Inc.
3100 Sprocket Dr
Arlington TX 76015
817 258-3000

(G-7801)
MEDERER GROUP
733 Lee St Ste 206 (60016-6580)
PHONE..............................630 860-4587
Herbert Mederer, *Owner*
▲ **EMP:** 3
SALES (est): 241.3K **Privately Held**
SIC: 2064 Candy & other confectionery products

(G-7802)
MIGHTY MITES AWARDS AND SONS
1297 Rand Rd (60016-3402)
PHONE..............................847 297-0035
Sam A Donatucci, *President*
Mike Donatucci, *Manager*
Virginia Donatucci, *Admin Sec*
EMP: 9
SQ FT: 7,800
SALES (est): 1.4MM **Privately Held**
SIC: 3499 2396 2326 Trophies, metal, except silver; automotive & apparel trimmings; men's & boys' work clothing

(G-7803)
MONTANA METAL PRODUCTS LLC (HQ)
Also Called: Mmp
25 Howard Ave (60018-1901)
PHONE..............................847 803-6600
Charles Kelley, *VP Opers*
Michael Faten, *CFO*
Tom Purvin, *Sales Staff*
Anthony Sobel,
Kenneth Peandro,
EMP: 115 **EST:** 1957
SQ FT: 98,500
SALES (est): 21.1MM
SALES (corp-wide): 37.3MM **Privately Held**
WEB: www.mmpllc.com
SIC: 3444 Sheet metalwork
PA: The Mifsud Group Llc
140 Blaze Industrial Pkwy
Berea OH 44017
216 325-7280

(G-7804)
MOTOR COACH INDS INTL INC (HQ)
Also Called: Mcli
200 E Oakton St (60018-1948)
PHONE..............................847 285-2000
Paul Soubry, *President*
Michael Apple, *Vice Pres*
Steve Batho, *Vice Pres*
Timothy J Nalepka, *Vice Pres*
Scott Robertson, *Vice Pres*
EMP: 125
SALES (est): 535.8MM
SALES (corp-wide): 2.8B **Privately Held**
SIC: 3713 3711 3714 Bus bodies (motor vehicles); buses, all types, assembly of; motor vehicle parts & accessories
PA: Nfi Group Inc
711 Kernaghan Ave
Winnipeg MB R2C 3
204 224-1251

(G-7805)
MOTOR COACH INDUSTRIES
200 E Oakton St (60018-1948)
PHONE..............................847 285-2000
EMP: 5
SALES (est): 610.6K **Privately Held**
SIC: 5063 5012 3711 Whol Electrical Equipment Whol Autos/Motor Vehicles Mfg Motor Vehicle/Car Bodies

(G-7806)
MOTUS DIGITAL LLC
131 Cornell Ave (60018-2128)
PHONE..............................972 943-0008
Kieth Brock,
Howard Blietz,
EMP: 25
SALES (est): 2.5MM **Privately Held**
WEB: www.motusdigital.com
SIC: 3861 Motion picture film

(G-7807)
MOVIE FACTS INC (PA)
1870 Busse Hwy Ste 200 (60016-6773)
PHONE..............................847 299-9700
Glen T Wilmes, *President*
Lawrence Fils, *Treasurer*
Jill Wilmes Ovnik, *Admin Sec*
EMP: 40
SQ FT: 9,000
SALES (est): 8.2MM **Privately Held**
SIC: 2731 7313 Pamphlets: publishing only, not printed on site; radio, television, publisher representatives

(G-7808)
MSF GRAPHICS INC
959 Lee St (60016-6545)
P.O. Box 8164, Northfield (60093-8164)
PHONE..............................847 446-6900
Michael S French, *President*
EMP: 6
SALES (est): 480K **Privately Held**
SIC: 2752 2759 2789 Commercial printing, offset; screen printing; bookbinding & related work

(G-7809)
MYECCHO LLC
550 Graceland Ave Apt 11 (60016-4451)
PHONE..............................224 639-3068
Srujesh Shah, *Principal*
Suj Shah, *Professor*
EMP: 5
SALES (est): 159.8K **Privately Held**
SIC: 8249 7372 Business training services; business oriented computer software

(G-7810)
NIDEC MOTOR CORPORATION
Merkle-Korff
1905 S Mount Prospect Rd (60018-1856)
PHONE..............................847 439-3760

Des Plaines - Cook County (G-7811)

John Brown, *General Mgr*
EMP: 100 **Privately Held**
SIC: 3694 Ignition apparatus & distributors
HQ: Nidec Motor Corporation
   8050 West Florissant Ave
   Saint Louis MO 63136

(G-7811)
NIESE WALTER MACHINE MFG CO
172 Touhy Ct (60018-1852)
PHONE 773 774-7337
Walter Niese Jr, *President*
Karen Niese, *Corp Secy*
Steve Niese, *Vice Pres*
EMP: 7
SALES: 1MM **Privately Held**
SIC: 3599 7629 Machine shop, jobbing & repair; electrical repair shops

(G-7812)
NU-WAY INDUSTRIES INC
555 Howard Ave (60018-1981)
PHONE 847 298-7710
Steven Southwell, *President*
Mary Howard, *Exec VP*
Tracy Corso, *Vice Pres*
John Herbst, *Project Mgr*
Jack Calka, *Purch Mgr*
▲ **EMP:** 250
SQ FT: 293,000
SALES (est): 32MM **Privately Held**
WEB: www.nuwayindustries.com
SIC: 3469 3599 3444 Stamping metal for the trade; machine shop, jobbing & repair; sheet metal specialties, not stamped

(G-7813)
OAKLEY SIGNS & GRAPHICS INC
471 N 3rd Ave (60016-1160)
PHONE 224 612-5045
Kenneth D Levitt, *Branch Mgr*
EMP: 10
SALES (est): 1.1MM
SALES (corp-wide): 9.4MM **Privately Held**
SIC: 3993 Signs & advertising specialties
PA: Oakley Signs & Graphics, Inc.
   2701 Maitland Center Pkwy # 110
   Maitland FL 32751
   407 262-8200

(G-7814)
OCHEM INC (PA)
9044 Buckingham Park Dr (60016-5102)
PHONE 847 403-7044
Weizhong Liu, *President*
EMP: 2
SQ FT: 10,000
SALES: 2MM **Privately Held**
WEB: www.ocheminc.com
SIC: 2899 Chemical preparations

(G-7815)
OHARE SPRING COMPANY INC
2190 Oxford Rd (60018-1920)
PHONE 847 298-1360
Kathy Schneider, *Treasurer*
EMP: 9
SALES (est): 1.1MM **Privately Held**
WEB: www.oharespring.com
SIC: 3495 Wire springs

(G-7816)
OZINGA BROS INC
200 Jarvis Ave (60018-1952)
PHONE 847 768-1697
Lisa Goyette, *Principal*
EMP: 76
SALES (corp-wide): 434.5MM **Privately Held**
SIC: 3273 Ready-mixed concrete
PA: Ozinga Bros., Inc.
   19001 Old Lagrange Rd # 30
   Mokena IL 60448
   708 326-4200

(G-7817)
PAMCO PRINTED TAPE LABEL INC (HQ)
2200 S Wolf Rd (60018-1934)
PHONE 847 803-2200
Robert Simko, *CEO*
William E Burch, *President*
Treina Blair, *CFO*
EMP: 150 **EST:** 1990
SQ FT: 54,000
SALES (est): 35.6MM **Privately Held**
WEB: www.pamcolabel.com
SIC: 2759 2752 Screen printing; commercial printing, lithographic

(G-7818)
PARKWAY METAL PRODUCTS INC
130 Rawls Rd (60018-1329)
PHONE 847 789-4000
Ted Martin, *President*
Swionder-Mart Barbara, *Exec VP*
Daniel Brown, *Senior VP*
Tom Raczka, *Office Mgr*
EMP: 90 **EST:** 1966
SQ FT: 71,000
SALES (est): 23.6MM **Privately Held**
WEB: www.parkwaymetal.com
SIC: 3441 3469 Fabricated structural metal; stamping metal for the trade

(G-7819)
PETNET SOLUTIONS INC
200 Howard Ave Ste 240 (60018-5909)
PHONE 847 297-3721
Tim Huston, *Manager*
EMP: 4
SALES (corp-wide): 96.9B **Privately Held**
SIC: 2835 Radioactive diagnostic substances
HQ: Petnet Solutions, Inc.
   810 Innovation Dr
   Knoxville TN 37932
   865 218-2000

(G-7820)
PEXCO LLC (DH)
1600 Birchwood Ave (60018-3004)
PHONE 847 296-5511
Steve Spear, *Director*
Paula Christian, *Admin Sec*
▲ **EMP:** 160 **EST:** 1960
SQ FT: 96,600
SALES (est): 28MM
SALES (corp-wide): 344.8MM **Privately Held**
SIC: 3089 Plastic hardware & building products
HQ: Porex Technologies Corp.
   1625 Ashton Park Dr Ste A
   South Chesterfield VA 23834
   804 524-4983

(G-7821)
PH TOOL MANUFACTURING
1200 Andrea Ln (60018-5501)
PHONE 847 952-9441
Halil Tuskar, *Owner*
EMP: 4
SALES (est): 244.8K **Privately Held**
SIC: 3599 Machine shop, jobbing & repair

(G-7822)
PHARMA NATURE
537 Radcliffe Ave (60016-2034)
PHONE 224 659-0906
EMP: 3
SALES (est): 224.2K **Privately Held**
SIC: 2834 Pharmaceutical preparations

(G-7823)
PHOENIX GRAPHICS INC
2375 Magnolia St (60018-3128)
PHONE 847 699-9520
Bruce H Holmberg, *President*
EMP: 3 **EST:** 1920
SQ FT: 2,000
SALES (est): 342.6K **Privately Held**
SIC: 2759 7311 Screen printing; advertising consultant

(G-7824)
PLASTRUCT INC
65 Bradrock Dr (60018-1937)
PHONE 626 912-7017
John J Wanderman, *President*
EMP: 57
SALES (est): 6.9MM
SALES (corp-wide): 11.2MM **Privately Held**
SIC: 3089 5945 3952 Plastic processing; hobby, toy & game shops; lead pencils & art goods
PA: Engineering Model Associates, Inc.
   1020 Wallace Way
   City Of Industry CA 91748
   626 912-7011

(G-7825)
PLATFORM TECHNOLOGIES
2200 S Mount Prospect Rd (60018-1858)
PHONE 847 357-0435
▲ **EMP:** 3
SALES (est): 262.1K **Privately Held**
SIC: 2759 Commercial printing

(G-7826)
PLATINUM TOUCH INDUSTRIES LLC
471 N 3rd Ave (60016-1160)
PHONE 773 775-9988
Vincent Gendusa, *Principal*
EMP: 8
SALES (est): 1.3MM **Privately Held**
WEB: www.pti-llc.net
SIC: 3999 Manufacturing industries

(G-7827)
PLITEK LLC
69 Rawls Rd (60018-1326)
PHONE 847 827-6680
Karl K Hoffman, *President*
Joseph Weber, *General Mgr*
David Huffman, *Purchasing*
Michael Starr, *Engineer*
Patrick Tuggle, *Engineer*
▲ **EMP:** 62
SQ FT: 54,000
SALES (est): 18.3MM **Privately Held**
SIC: 2672 3089 3053 Coated & laminated paper; plastic processing; gaskets, packing & sealing devices

(G-7828)
POWERPATH MICROPRODUCTS INC
200 Howard Ave Ste 238 (60018-5909)
PHONE 847 827-6330
Kerry Dulin, *President*
Joe L Lekostaj, *Admin Sec*
EMP: 3
SQ FT: 4,500
SALES (est): 375K **Privately Held**
SIC: 3089 Injection molding of plastics

(G-7829)
PRAIRIE GLEN IMAGING CTR LLC
9680 Golf Rd (60016-1522)
PHONE 847 296-5366
P Shirazi,
EMP: 4
SALES (est): 480K **Privately Held**
SIC: 3826 Magnetic resonance imaging apparatus

(G-7830)
PRECISION INSTRUMENTS INC
1846 Miner St (60016-4712)
P.O. Box 1306 (60017-1306)
PHONE 847 824-4194
John K Larson, *President*
Andrew Larson, *Vice Pres*
John A Larson, *Vice Pres*
R Glenn Meier, *Vice Pres*
Lundgren Ron, *Plant Mgr*
EMP: 56 **EST:** 1938
SQ FT: 48,000
SALES (est): 5.5MM **Privately Held**
WEB: www.torqwrench.com
SIC: 3423 Wrenches, hand tools

(G-7831)
PRECISION PRODUCTS MFG INTL
1400 E Touhy Ave Ste 402 (60018-3341)
PHONE 847 299-8500
EMP: 23
SQ FT: 3,000
SALES (est): 1.5MM **Privately Held**
SIC: 3841 8742 Mfg Surgical/Medical Instruments Management Consulting Services

(G-7832)
PRESS TECH INC
959 Lee St (60016-6545)
PHONE 847 824-4485
Robert Soske, *President*
Edward Soske, *Vice Pres*
Joan Soske, *CFO*
Chris Kunesh, *Accounts Exec*
Carlos Collazo, *Manager*
EMP: 14
SQ FT: 4,400
SALES (est): 3.6MM **Privately Held**
WEB: www.presstechus.com
SIC: 2752 Commercial printing, offset

(G-7833)
PRINT MANAGEMENT PARTNERS INC (PA)
Also Called: Go2 Partners
701 Lee St Ste 1050 (60016-4572)
PHONE 847 699-2999
James O'Brien, *President*
Tim Bagsby, *Accounts Exec*
Tim Doyle, *Accounts Exec*
Dana Kaczmarski, *Administration*
Robert Singraber, *Graphic Designe*
EMP: 22
SQ FT: 5,500
SALES (est): 45.5MM **Privately Held**
SIC: 8742 2759 7379 Marketing consulting services; commercial printing; computer related consulting services

(G-7834)
QUALITY NEON SERVICE
1350 Oakwood Ave Ste A (60016-6577)
PHONE 847 299-2969
EMP: 3 **EST:** 2014
SALES (est): 264.2K **Privately Held**
SIC: 2813 Neon

(G-7835)
RAHCO RUBBER INC
1633 Birchwood Ave (60018-3003)
PHONE 847 298-4200
William R Anton, *President*
John M Anton, *Vice Pres*
John Anton, *Vice Pres*
Stephen Anton, *Vice Pres*
Kevin Magner, *Plant Mgr*
EMP: 90
SQ FT: 57,000
SALES (est): 18.1MM **Privately Held**
SIC: 3069 Grommets, rubber; washers, rubber; hard rubber products; molded rubber products

(G-7836)
RAPID WASH GROUP LTD
622 E Northwest Hwy (60016-3059)
PHONE 847 376-8442
Patricia L Smith, *President*
Shirlee Smith, *Vice Pres*
EMP: 5
SQ FT: 33,000
SALES (est): 411.6K **Privately Held**
SIC: 3469 Garbage cans, stamped & pressed metal

(G-7837)
RIDDELL INC (DH)
Also Called: Riddell Sports
1700 E Higgins Rd Ste 500 (60018-3800)
PHONE 847 292-1472
William Sherman, *President*
Paul E Harrigton, *President*
Robert Brasser, *Senior VP*
Mike Devel, *Vice Pres*
Thad Ide, *Vice Pres*
▲ **EMP:** 140 **EST:** 1929
SQ FT: 95,000
SALES (est): 136.8MM **Privately Held**
WEB: www.riddell.com
SIC: 5091 3949 Athletic goods; helmets, athletic
HQ: Brg Sports, Inc.
   1700 E Higgins Rd Ste 500
   Des Plaines IL 60018
   224 585-5200

(G-7838)
ROGUS TOOL INC
354 N East River Rd (60016-1224)
PHONE 847 824-5939
Dennis Rogus, *President*
Bera Rogus, *Admin Sec*
EMP: 3
SALES (est): 186.2K **Privately Held**
SIC: 3599 3544 Machine shop, jobbing & repair; special dies, tools, jigs & fixtures

GEOGRAPHIC SECTION
Des Plaines - Cook County (G-7868)

(G-7839)
SCIENTIFIC DEVICE LAB INC
411 Jarvis Ave (60018-1911)
P.O. Box 1006 (60017-1006)
PHONE..................847 803-9495
Dr Stewart Lipton, *CEO*
Jose Eguiguren, *COO*
Francine Lasky, *Vice Pres*
Lauren Mayeroff, *Mfg Staff*
Dale Patton, *Purchasing*
▲ **EMP:** 26
SQ FT: 22,000
SALES (est): 10.1MM **Privately Held**
SIC: 5047 2835 Medical laboratory equipment; in vitro diagnostics

(G-7840)
SEEDBURO EQUIPMENT COMPANY
2293 S Mount Prospect Rd (60018-1810)
PHONE..................312 738-3700
Thomas E Runyon, *President*
Katherine Reading, *Vice Pres*
Kathy Reading, *Vice Pres*
Michael Coffey, *Mfg Mgr*
Cali Cepa, *Purch Agent*
▼ **EMP:** 19 **EST:** 1912
SQ FT: 14,000
SALES (est): 9.8MM **Privately Held**
WEB: www.seedburo.com
SIC: 5083 3523 Agricultural machinery; farm machinery & equipment

(G-7841)
SEJASMI CORP
30 N River Rd Ste 102 (60016-1283)
PHONE..................586 725-5300
Avani Patel, *Accountant*
EMP: 5
SALES (est): 659K **Privately Held**
SIC: 2821 Molding compounds, plastics

(G-7842)
SEOCLARITY
2800 S River Rd Ste 290 (60018-6091)
PHONE..................773 831-4500
Mitul Gandhi, *Owner*
Orrin Wolf, *COO*
Chris Sachs, *Human Res Mgr*
Rick Behrman, *Accounts Exec*
Jt Thrall, *Sales Staff*
EMP: 10
SALES (est): 876K **Privately Held**
SIC: 7372 Prepackaged software

(G-7843)
SHERMAR INDUSTRIES LLC
1245 S Leslie Ln (60018-5563)
PHONE..................847 378-8073
Ronald B Cooper, *Principal*
EMP: 3 **EST:** 2012
SALES (est): 192K **Privately Held**
SIC: 3999 Manufacturing industries

(G-7844)
SIGNS PLUS
Also Called: Bill's Auto & Truck Repair
1216 Rand Rd (60016-3403)
PHONE..................847 489-9009
Rob Zimmerman, *Owner*
EMP: 4
SALES (est): 260K **Privately Held**
SIC: 3993 Signs & advertising specialties

(G-7845)
SIMPLE CANVAS PRINTS LLC
471 N 3rd Ave (60016-1160)
PHONE..................800 900-4244
EMP: 3
SALES (est): 189.7K **Privately Held**
SIC: 2752 Commercial printing, lithographic

(G-7846)
SKYFLY NETWORKS INC
1210 E Washington St # 203 (60016-4396)
PHONE..................312 429-4580
Jorge Castillo, *President*
EMP: 3
SALES (est): 108.9K **Privately Held**
SIC: 3679 Electronic switches; antennas, receiving

(G-7847)
SMILE AROMATICS INC
2454 E Dempster St # 422 (60016-5320)
PHONE..................847 759-0350
EMP: 20
SQ FT: 2,000
SALES: 3MM **Privately Held**
SIC: 2844 Mfg Air Freshner

(G-7848)
SONI MOHNISH
Also Called: Chikki Bars
1700 Pratt Ave (60018-3812)
PHONE..................312 473-7669
Tk Soni, *Owner*
Juhi Soni, *Owner*
Mohnish Soni, *Owner*
EMP: 7
SQ FT: 1,000
SALES: 5K **Privately Held**
SIC: 2599 Bar, restaurant & cafeteria furniture

(G-7849)
SPECTACLE ZOOM LLC
8671 Josephine St Apt A (60016-1876)
PHONE..................504 352-7237
Joshua Seib, *Principal*
EMP: 3
SALES (est): 190K **Privately Held**
SIC: 3851 Spectacles

(G-7850)
SPLASH DOG THERAPY INC
42 N Broadway St (60016-2348)
PHONE..................847 296-4007
Traci Szwed, *Principal*
EMP: 3 **EST:** 2008
SALES (est): 306.5K **Privately Held**
WEB: www.swimatsplashdog.com
SIC: 2836 Veterinary biological products

(G-7851)
SPOUTS OF WATER INC (PA)
9416 Margail Ave (60016-3811)
PHONE..................303 570-5104
John Kye, *Principal*
Seul Ku, *Principal*
William Raseman, *Director*
EMP: 5 **EST:** 2013
SALES (est): 134.7K **Privately Held**
SIC: 3269 Filtering media, pottery

(G-7852)
STEPHEN FOSSLER COMPANY
1600 E Touhy Ave (60018-3607)
PHONE..................847 635-7200
Robert Murray, *CEO*
Steven Fosler, *President*
EMP: 60
SQ FT: 16,000
SALES (est): 8.1MM
SALES (corp-wide): 2B **Publicly Held**
SIC: 2759 2672 2671 Labels & seals: printing; coated & laminated paper; packaging paper & plastics film, coated & laminated
HQ: New England Business Service, Inc.
500 Main St
Groton MA 01471
978 448-6111

(G-7853)
SUKGYUNG AT INC
2400 E Devon Ave Ste 283 (60018-4631)
PHONE..................847 298-6570
Hyung Sup Lim, *President*
Eun Hee Ahn, *Director*
◆ **EMP:** 8
SALES (est): 3MM **Privately Held**
SIC: 2834 Powders, pharmaceutical

(G-7854)
SUPREME MANUFACTURING COMPANY
Also Called: C & L Supreme Mfg Co
1755 Birchwood Ave (60018-3005)
PHONE..................847 297-8212
Louis Spizziri, *President*
Peter Spizziri, *Vice Pres*
Chris Spizziri, *Plant Mgr*
John Osborne, *Materials Mgr*
Michael Sronkoski, *Site Mgr*
EMP: 35 **EST:** 1956
SQ FT: 21,000
SALES (est): 9.1MM **Privately Held**
WEB: www.clsupreme.com
SIC: 3599 3451 Machine shop, jobbing & repair; screw machine products

(G-7855)
TECHPOL AUTOMATION INC
2083 Maple St (60018-3018)
PHONE..................847 347-4765
Janusz M Piotrowski, *Principal*
EMP: 4
SQ FT: 2,200
SALES: 400K **Privately Held**
SIC: 3651 Household audio & video equipment

(G-7856)
TIMOTHY DARREY
Also Called: Universal Display Products
1153 Lee St Bldg 223 (60016-6516)
PHONE..................847 231-2277
Timothy Darrey, *Owner*
EMP: 2
SALES: 250K **Privately Held**
SIC: 3993 Signs & advertising specialties

(G-7857)
TORNOS TECHNOLOGIES US CORP (PA)
200 Howard Ave Ste 220 (60018-5908)
PHONE..................630 812-2040
Jon Dobosenski, *Vice Pres*
Naiane Nunes, *Sales Staff*
Jennifer Bryk, *Manager*
▲ **EMP:** 8 **EST:** 2010
SALES (est): 1.6MM **Privately Held**
WEB: www.tornos.com
SIC: 3545 Machine tool attachments & accessories

(G-7858)
TOUHY DIAGNOSTIC AT HOME LLC
1293 Rand Rd (60016-3402)
PHONE..................847 803-1111
Noreen Khan, *President*
Mohammad Akbar Zahid, *Principal*
EMP: 15
SQ FT: 1,000
SALES (est): 1.2MM **Privately Held**
SIC: 3829 Medical diagnostic systems, nuclear

(G-7859)
TRANSOMATIC DES PLAINES LLC
1500 Rand Rd (60016-3444)
PHONE..................847 625-1500
Jerry Smith,
EMP: 6 **EST:** 2016
SQ FT: 10,000
SALES (est): 269.2K **Privately Held**
SIC: 3714 Rebuilding engines & transmissions, factory basis

(G-7860)
U O P EQUITEC SERVICES INC
25 E Algonquin Rd (60016-6100)
PHONE..................847 391-2000
Carlos Guimaraes, *President*
Graeme Donald, *President*
George Davidson, *Treasurer*
EMP: 2000
SALES (est): 138.7MM
SALES (corp-wide): 36.7B **Publicly Held**
SIC: 3533 Oil & gas field machinery
HQ: Universal Oil Products Company
2466 E 22nd St
Tulsa OK

(G-7861)
UNITED LITHOGRAPH INC
1670 S River Rd (60018-2290)
PHONE..................847 803-1700
Michael Adams, *President*
EMP: 4
SALES (est): 482.2K **Privately Held**
SIC: 2752 7334 2791 2789 Commercial printing, offset; photocopying & duplicating services; typesetting; bookbinding & related work

(G-7862)
UOP LLC
201 W Oakton St Ste 2 (60018-1855)
PHONE..................847 391-2540
EMP: 164
SALES (corp-wide): 36.7B **Publicly Held**
SIC: 2819 Catalysts, chemical
HQ: Uop Llc
25 E Algonquin Rd
Des Plaines IL 60016
847 391-2000

(G-7863)
V FORMUSA CO
Also Called: Marconi
2150 Oxford Rd (60018-1920)
PHONE..................224 938-9360
Robert Johnson, *President*
Joey Schramm, *General Mgr*
Pasquale Giampietro, *Mktg Dir*
Suzanne Johnson, *Admin Sec*
▲ **EMP:** 10 **EST:** 1898
SQ FT: 25,000
SALES (est): 1.7MM **Privately Held**
WEB: www.marconi-foods.com
SIC: 0723 5141 2079 2035 Vegetable packing services; groceries, general line; edible fats & oils; pickles, sauces & salad dressings; canned fruits & specialties; cheese, natural & processed

(G-7864)
VETTER CM USA LLC
10 W Algonquin Rd (60016-6000)
PHONE..................847 813-5895
EMP: 4
SALES (est): 295K **Privately Held**
SIC: 2834 Pharmaceutical preparations

(G-7865)
VISIONARY SOLUTIONS INC
129 Rawls Rd (60018-1328)
PHONE..................847 296-9615
Marty Finzer, *Mng Member*
EMP: 1
SALES (est): 250K **Privately Held**
SIC: 5084 3999 Conveyor systems; manufacturing industries

(G-7866)
W DIAMOND GROUP CORPORATION (PA)
Also Called: Hart Schaffner & Marx
901 W Oakton St (60018-1843)
PHONE..................646 647-2790
Douglas L Williams, *CEO*
Kenneth Ragland, *COO*
Robert Ton, *Manager*
Ken Ragland, *Officer*
▲ **EMP:** 600
SQ FT: 240,000
SALES (est): 78MM **Privately Held**
SIC: 2311 Men's & boys' suits & coats

(G-7867)
WAREHOUSE DIRECT INC (PA)
Also Called: Warehuse Drect Wrkplace Sltons
2001 S Mount Prospect Rd (60018-1808)
PHONE..................847 952-1925
Ken Johnson, *Chairman*
Robert D Swanson, *Exec VP*
Josephine Gnutek, *VP Opers*
Von Miller, *Warehouse Mgr*
Marie Hayslette, *Purchasing*
EMP: 153 **EST:** 1979
SQ FT: 66,000
SALES (est): 255.5MM **Privately Held**
SIC: 5112 2759 2752 7389 Office supplies; promotional printing; promotional printing, lithographic; advertising, promotional & trade show services; cleaning & maintenance equipment & supplies; carpet & rug cleaning equipment & supplies, commercial

(G-7868)
WESLEY-JESSEN CORPORATION DEL
333 Howard Ave (60018-1907)
PHONE..................847 294-3000
Glen Bradley, *President*
George McCrary, *Vice Pres*
EMP: 1000
SQ FT: 340,000

Des Plaines - Cook County (G-7869)

SALES (est): 103.7MM **Privately Held**
SIC: 3851 Contact lenses

(G-7869)
YASKAWA AMERICA INC
1297 E Walnut Ave (60016-6506)
PHONE..................847 887-7909
Terry Willett, *Principal*
EMP: 250 **Privately Held**
SIC: 3621 5063 Motors, electric; motors, electric
HQ: Yaskawa America, Inc.
2121 Norman Dr
Waukegan IL 60085
847 887-7000

(G-7870)
ZIM MANUFACTURING CO
2275 Sprucewood Ave (60018-2641)
PHONE..................773 622-2500
Kenneth Kukla, *President*
EMP: 50
SQ FT: 34,000
SALES (est): 7.2MM **Privately Held**
WEB: www.zimmfgco.com
SIC: 3423 Mechanics' hand tools

(G-7871)
ZIMMERMAN ENTERPRISES INC (PA)
Also Called: Best Bus Sales
1216 Rand Rd (60016-3403)
PHONE..................847 297-3177
Robert L Zimmerman, *President*
EMP: 12
SQ FT: 43,000
SALES (est): 2.2MM **Privately Held**
SIC: 3993 4111 7538 Signs & advertising specialties; bus transportation; general automotive repair shops

Detroit
Pike County

(G-7872)
DYNO NOBEL INC
1353 W Washington St (62363-9549)
P.O. Box 349, Pittsfield (62363-0349)
PHONE..................217 285-5531
Brian Jockisch, *Branch Mgr*
EMP: 28 **Privately Held**
SIC: 2892 Explosives
HQ: Dyno Nobel Inc.
2795 E Cottonwood Pkwy # 500
Salt Lake City UT 84121
801 364-4800

Dewey
Champaign County

(G-7873)
DATA COMM FOR BUSINESS INC (PA)
2949 County Road 1000 E (61840-9639)
P.O. Box 6329, Champaign (61826-6329)
PHONE..................217 897-1741
Russell Straayer, *President*
Michael Gadel, *Vice Pres*
Randy Peterson, *VP Sales*
Dan Smith, *Manager*
Jack H De Atley, *Shareholder*
EMP: 18
SQ FT: 80,000
SALES (est): 4.2MM **Privately Held**
SIC: 3669 5065 Intercommunication systems, electric; communication equipment

(G-7874)
PRICE MACHINE INC
1021 County Road 2850 N (61840-9637)
PHONE..................217 892-8958
Kenny Price, *President*
EMP: 3
SQ FT: 2,400
SALES (est): 411K **Privately Held**
SIC: 3599 Machine shop, jobbing & repair

Dieterich
Effingham County

(G-7875)
CANDLEART CANDLE COMPANY INC
10084 N 1950th St (62424-2131)
PHONE..................217 925-5905
Phil Niemerg, *President*
EMP: 5
SALES (est): 137.5K **Privately Held**
SIC: 3999 Candles

(G-7876)
HIGGS WELDING LLC
101 Zumbahlen Ave (62424-1053)
P.O. Box 212 (62424-0212)
PHONE..................217 925-5999
Troy Higgs, *Partner*
Brett Higgs, *Partner*
EMP: 8
SALES (est): 1MM **Privately Held**
SIC: 7692 Automotive welding

(G-7877)
IDEAL MACHINE INC
400 Amy St (62424-1066)
PHONE..................217 925-5109
Neil Breer, *President*
EMP: 3
SALES (est): 385.4K **Privately Held**
SIC: 3599 Machine shop, jobbing & repair

(G-7878)
SEPTIC SOLUTIONS INC
314 W Center St (62424-1048)
PHONE..................217 925-5992
Jesse James, *President*
James Backhoe, *Vice Pres*
Casey James, *Sales Staff*
Jodi Mulvey, *Marketing Staff*
Jodi James, *Manager*
◆ EMP: 9
SALES (est): 3.7MM **Privately Held**
WEB: www.septicsolutions.com
SIC: 5091 5039 3949 Exercise equipment; septic tanks; exercise equipment

(G-7879)
SRMD SOLUTIONS LLC
202 W Center St (62424-1012)
PHONE..................217 925-5773
Paul Romack, *CEO*
Brad Schumacher, *COO*
EMP: 7
SQ FT: 4,000
SALES (est): 367K **Privately Held**
WEB: www.srmdsolutions.com
SIC: 3559 7373 Electronic component making machinery; office computer automation systems integration

Divernon
Sangamon County

(G-7880)
LEONARD EMERSON
Also Called: Emerson Press
103 W Dodds St (62530-2301)
P.O. Box 437 (62530-0437)
PHONE..................217 628-3441
Leonard Emerson, *Owner*
EMP: 6
SQ FT: 3,000
SALES (est): 630.1K **Privately Held**
SIC: 2752 2791 2789 Commercial printing, offset; typesetting; bookbinding & related work

Dix
Jefferson County

(G-7881)
BOYD SAWMILL
Also Called: Garren Sawmill & Farm
19775 N Boyd Ln (62830-3406)
PHONE..................618 735-2056
Wendall Klockenga, *President*

EMP: 6 EST: 1956
SALES (est): 150K **Privately Held**
SIC: 0191 2421 2426 General farms, primarily crop; sawmills & planing mills, general; hardwood dimension & flooring mills

(G-7882)
ROYAL FIBERGLASS POOLS INC
Also Called: The Pool Center
312 Duncan Ln (62830-1467)
PHONE..................618 266-7089
EMP: 60
SQ FT: 5,000
SALES (est): 4.3MM **Privately Held**
SIC: 3949 1799 Mfg Sporting/Athletic Goods Trade Contractor

Dixmoor
Cook County

(G-7883)
CHICAGO MAGNESIUM
14050 Wood St (60426-1157)
PHONE..................708 926-9531
Deb Grasso, *President*
Robert Littlefield, *General Mgr*
EMP: 3
SALES (est): 229K **Privately Held**
SIC: 3356 Magnesium

(G-7884)
NATIONAL RAILWAY EQUIPMENT CO
Also Called: Alco Locomotive Company
14400 Robey Ave Ste 2 (60426-1042)
P.O. Box 2270, Harvey (60426-8270)
PHONE..................708 388-4781
Lenny Mysiewicz, *Superintendent*
Krishna Boggaram, *Engineer*
John Tooke, *Manager*
Kevin Russell, *Manager*
Pat Brown, *Director*
EMP: 60
SALES (corp-wide): 314MM **Privately Held**
WEB: www.nationalrailway.com
SIC: 3743 Railroad equipment
PA: National Railway Equipment Co.
1100 Shawnee St
Mount Vernon IL 62864
618 242-6590

(G-7885)
NATIONAL RAILWAY EQUIPMENT CO
Also Called: Nre
14400 Robey Ave Ste 2 (60426-1042)
PHONE..................708 388-6002
Robert Riley, *CFO*
Tammy Murphy, *Info Tech Mgr*
EMP: 30
SALES (corp-wide): 314MM **Privately Held**
SIC: 3743 Railroad equipment
PA: National Railway Equipment Co.
1100 Shawnee St
Mount Vernon IL 62864
618 242-6590

(G-7886)
ORIENT MACHINING & WELDING INC
14501 Wood St Ste A (60426-1617)
PHONE..................708 371-3500
Andrzej Plewa, *President*
Walter Koszarek, *Vice Pres*
EMP: 22
SQ FT: 100,000
SALES (est): 9.6MM **Privately Held**
SIC: 3599 3499 7692 Machine shop, jobbing & repair; welding tips, heat resistant: metal; welding repair

Dixon
Lee County

(G-7887)
AAA GALVANIZING - JOLIET INC
Also Called: AAA Galvanizing of Dixon
310 E Progress Dr (61021-9607)
PHONE..................815 284-5001
Mike Echebarria, *Senior VP*
Mike Echeabarria, *Branch Mgr*
EMP: 45
SALES (corp-wide): 1B **Publicly Held**
SIC: 3479 3441 Hot dip coating of metals or formed products; fabricated structural metal
HQ: Aaa Galvanizing - Joliet, Inc.
625 Mills Rd
Joliet IL 60433

(G-7888)
ALLIED-LOCKE INDUSTRIES INC
1020 Subic Rd (61021-8358)
PHONE..................800 435-7752
Joe Rock, *Sales Staff*
EMP: 50
SALES (corp-wide): 96.9MM **Privately Held**
SIC: 3568 Power transmission equipment
PA: Allied-Locke Industries, Incorporated
1088 Corregidor Rd
Dixon IL 61021
815 288-1471

(G-7889)
BELLINIS CUSTOM WELDING AND A
1577 Eldena Rd (61021-8329)
P.O. Box 953 (61021-0953)
PHONE..................815 284-4175
Leanne Bellini, *Owner*
Brian Bellini, *Co-Owner*
EMP: 5
SALES (est): 1MM **Privately Held**
SIC: 7692 Welding repair

(G-7890)
BONNELL INDUSTRIES INC
1385 Franklin Grove Rd (61021-9150)
PHONE..................815 284-3819
Joseph W Bonnell, *President*
Cindy Bonnell, *Corp Secy*
EMP: 87 EST: 1960
SQ FT: 37,000
SALES: 13MM **Privately Held**
SIC: 3531 5013 5012 Road construction & maintenance machinery; truck parts & accessories; truck bodies

(G-7891)
BORG WARNER AUTOMOTIVE - B
1350 Franklin Grove Rd (61021-9148)
PHONE..................248 754-9200
EMP: 22
SALES (est): 4.3MM **Privately Held**
SIC: 3714 Motor vehicle parts & accessories

(G-7892)
BORGWARNER INC
Also Called: Borg-Warner Emissions Systems
1350 Franklin Grove Rd (61021-9174)
PHONE..................815 288-1462
Ray Jones, *Materials Mgr*
Pat Lachat, *Safety Mgr*
Jennifer Adcock, *Purch Mgr*
Scott Hollywood, *Buyer*
Terry Winchell, *Buyer*
EMP: 250
SQ FT: 100,000
SALES (corp-wide): 10.1B **Publicly Held**
WEB: www.borgwarner.com
SIC: 3465 3592 3714 Automotive stampings; carburetors; fuel systems & parts, motor vehicle
PA: Borgwarner Inc.
3850 Hamlin Rd
Auburn Hills MI 48326
248 754-9200

GEOGRAPHIC SECTION
Dixon - Lee County (G-7918)

(G-7893)
CLARIOS
Also Called: Johnson Controls
629 N Galena Ave Ste 210 (61021-1664)
PHONE.....................................815 288-3859
William Perry, *Manager*
EMP: 200 **Privately Held**
WEB: www.johnsoncontrols.com
SIC: 2531 Seats, automobile
HQ: Johnson Controls, Inc.
5757 N Green Bay Ave
Milwaukee WI 53209
414 524-1200

(G-7894)
CROWN INDUSTRIAL
1020 Subic Rd (61021-8358)
PHONE.....................................607 745-8709
▲ **EMP:** 7 **EST:** 2010
SALES (est): 1.1MM **Privately Held**
WEB: www.crownindustrial.biz
SIC: 3462 Gear & chain forgings

(G-7895)
CUSTOM MACHINE INC
895 Shop Rd (61021-3281)
PHONE.....................................815 284-3820
Gary Haenitsch, *President*
William Haenitsch, *Vice Pres*
EMP: 8 **EST:** 1976
SQ FT: 8,500
SALES: 680K **Privately Held**
WEB: www.custommachinedixon.com
SIC: 3599 Machine shop, jobbing & repair

(G-7896)
DIXON DIRECT LLC (DH)
Also Called: Arcade Beauty
1226 W 7th St (61021-3412)
PHONE.....................................815 284-2211
Peter Lennox, *CEO*
EMP: 10
SALES (est): 3.7MM **Privately Held**
SIC: 2752 Commercial printing, offset

(G-7897)
DIXON TELEGRAPH
113 S Peoria Ave Ste 1 (61021-2905)
P.O. Box 498, Sterling (61081-0498)
PHONE.....................................815 284-2224
Ed Bushman, *General Mgr*
EMP: 3
SALES (est): 162.9K **Privately Held**
SIC: 2711 Newspapers, publishing & printing

(G-7898)
DONALDSON COMPANY INC
815 W Progress Dr (61021-9655)
PHONE.....................................815 288-3374
Brenda Walls, *Production*
Marc Tintori, *Engineer*
Jeff Carson, *Branch Mgr*
EMP: 50
SALES (corp-wide): 2.8B **Publicly Held**
SIC: 3564 3599 Purification & dust collection equipment; air intake filters, internal combustion engine, except auto
PA: Donaldson Company, Inc.
1400 W 94th St
Minneapolis MN 55431
952 887-3131

(G-7899)
FLEX-O-GLASS INC
1200 Warp Rd (61021-9166)
PHONE.....................................815 288-1424
Harold G Warp, *Branch Mgr*
EMP: 50
SALES (est): 7.4MM
SALES (corp-wide): 51.6MM **Privately Held**
SIC: 3081 3082 2821 2671 Plastic film & sheet; unsupported plastics profile shapes; plastics materials & resins; packaging paper & plastics film, coated & laminated
PA: Flex-O-Glass, Inc.
4647 W Augusta Blvd Ste 1
Chicago IL 60651
773 261-5200

(G-7900)
FRANKLIN MAINTENANCE
1597 Nachusa Rd (61021-8804)
PHONE.....................................815 284-6806
Larry Crawford, *Owner*
Maggie Crawford, *Co-Owner*
EMP: 3
SALES (est): 118.9K **Privately Held**
SIC: 7692 Cracked casting repair

(G-7901)
GRANITEWORKS
1220 S Galena Ave (61021-3844)
PHONE.....................................815 288-3350
Dan Johns, *Principal*
EMP: 2
SALES (est): 224.4K **Privately Held**
SIC: 2541 Counter & sink tops

(G-7902)
JOHN THOMAS INC
Also Called: John Thomas Company
1560 Lovett Dr (61021-9623)
PHONE.....................................815 288-2343
John Dvorak, *President*
Charlie Percival, *Research*
Kole Weaver, *CFO*
Blake Balzart, *Manager*
EMP: 30 **EST:** 1988
SQ FT: 18,000
SALES: 6.5MM **Privately Held**
WEB: www.jtitraffic.com
SIC: 5084 3669 7359 3499 Safety equipment; traffic signals, electric; work zone traffic equipment (flags, cones, barrels, etc.); automobile seat frames, metal; automotive parts, plastic

(G-7903)
KREIDER SERVICES INCORPORATED (PA)
Also Called: Hilltop Group Home
500 Anchor Rd (61021-8854)
P.O. Box 366 (61021-0366)
PHONE.....................................815 288-6691
Arlan L McClain, *CEO*
Tom Bowen, *Human Res Mgr*
Brian Gephart, *Program Mgr*
Annette Hatchett, *Manager*
Hilaree Lombardo, *Manager*
EMP: 70 **EST:** 1952
SQ FT: 60,000
SALES: 16.6MM **Privately Held**
SIC: 8331 8361 2875 4953 Sheltered workshop; residential care; fertilizers, mixing only; recycling, waste materials

(G-7904)
NEISEWANDER ENTERPRISES INC (PA)
Also Called: Raynor Garage Door
1101 E River Rd (61021-3252)
P.O. Box 448 (61021-0448)
PHONE.....................................815 288-1431
Ray H Neisewander III, *President*
EMP: 1000
SQ FT: 600,000
SALES (est): 311.8MM **Privately Held**
SIC: 3442 2431 3429 Garage doors, overhead: metal; garage doors, overhead: wood; manufactured hardware (general)

(G-7905)
OSMER WOODWORKING INC
406 E Bradshaw St (61021-1637)
PHONE.....................................815 973-5809
Adam Osmer, *President*
EMP: 2
SALES (est): 219.5K **Privately Held**
SIC: 2431 8711 1799 1521 Millwork; building construction consultant; home/office interiors finishing, furnishing & remodeling; kitchen & bathroom remodeling; single-family home remodeling, additions & repairs; general remodeling, single-family houses;

(G-7906)
PLEWS INC (PA)
Also Called: Plews & Edelmann
1550 Franklin Grove Rd (61021-9110)
PHONE.....................................815 288-3344
Brett Mueller, *President*
◆ **EMP:** 157
SQ FT: 350,000
SALES (est): 37.9MM **Privately Held**
SIC: 3714 3429 3492 Motor vehicle parts & accessories; manufactured hardware (general); fluid power valves & hose fittings

(G-7907)
QUALITY READY MIX CONCRETE CO
1569 Franklin Grove Rd (61021-9110)
P.O. Box 321 (61021-0321)
PHONE.....................................815 288-6416
Jason Dykema, *Manager*
EMP: 6
SALES (corp-wide): 3.7MM **Privately Held**
SIC: 3273 Ready-mixed concrete
PA: Quality Ready Mix Concrete Co.
14849 Lyndon Rd
Morrison IL 61270
815 772-7181

(G-7908)
RAYNOR MFG CO (HQ)
Also Called: Raynor Garage Doors
1101 E River Rd (61021-3277)
P.O. Box 448 (61021-0448)
PHONE.....................................815 288-1431
Ray N Heisewander III, *President*
Michael Setchell, *COO*
Joshua Brigl, *Buyer*
Warren Sherman, *Engineer*
Christopher Walter, *Regl Sales Mgr*
◆ **EMP:** 800
SQ FT: 900,000
SALES (est): 280.6MM
SALES (corp-wide): 311.8MM **Privately Held**
WEB: www.raynor.com
SIC: 3442 7011 3699 2431 Garage doors, overhead: metal; hotels; electrical equipment & supplies; millwork
PA: Neisewander Enterprises Inc.
1101 E River Rd
Dixon IL 61021
815 288-1431

(G-7909)
RAYOVAC CORP
200 E Corporate Dr (61021-9301)
PHONE.....................................815 285-6500
Donna Smith, *Exec VP*
EMP: 3
SALES (est): 353.7K **Privately Held**
SIC: 3691 Storage batteries

(G-7910)
RENNER QUARRIES LTD (PA)
1700 S Galena Ave Ste 116 (61021-9695)
PHONE.....................................815 288-6699
Robert Egert, *President*
Gary Egert, *Corp Secy*
Marty Egert, *Office Mgr*
EMP: 2
SQ FT: 500
SALES: 1MM **Privately Held**
SIC: 1422 Limestones, ground

(G-7911)
ROCK RIVER READY MIX INC (PA)
2320 S Galena Ave (61021-9608)
P.O. Box 384 (61021-0384)
PHONE.....................................815 288-2260
Adel A Mobarak, *President*
Mary Frances Mobarak, *Corp Secy*
George Mobarak, *Vice Pres*
Scott Mills, *Admin Sec*
EMP: 7
SQ FT: 800
SALES: 6.9MM **Privately Held**
WEB: www.rockriverreadymix.com
SIC: 1442 5032 Construction sand mining; gravel mining; concrete mixtures

(G-7912)
ROCK RIVER READY MIX INC
1905 Mound Hill Rd (61021-9735)
P.O. Box 384 (61021-0384)
PHONE.....................................815 625-1139
Donna Rodriguez, *Manager*
EMP: 9
SALES (corp-wide): 6.9MM **Privately Held**
SIC: 3273 Ready-mixed concrete
PA: Rock River Ready Mix, Inc.
2320 S Galena Ave
Dixon IL 61021
815 288-2260

(G-7913)
ROCK RIVER READY-MIX
2320 S Galena Ave (61021-9608)
P.O. Box 384 (61021-0384)
PHONE.....................................815 288-2269
Adel A Mobarak, *President*
Mary F Mobarak, *Corp Secy*
George Mobarak, *Vice Pres*
J Scott Mills, *Asst Sec*
EMP: 30 **EST:** 1948
SQ FT: 800
SALES (est): 2.2MM
SALES (corp-wide): 6.9MM **Privately Held**
SIC: 3273 5032 Ready-mixed concrete; gravel; sand, construction
PA: Rock River Ready Mix, Inc.
2320 S Galena Ave
Dixon IL 61021
815 288-2260

(G-7914)
SAUK VALLEY PRINTING
113 S Peoria Ave Ste 1 (61021-2905)
PHONE.....................................815 284-2222
Bob Clardie, *Owner*
EMP: 5
SALES (est): 213.2K **Privately Held**
SIC: 2711 Newspapers, publishing & printing

(G-7915)
SCHEFFLER CUSTOM WOODWORKING
Also Called: Freight House Kit & Bath Str
925 Depot Ave (61021-3548)
PHONE.....................................815 284-6564
Jerry Scheffler, *President*
Matthew J Scheffler, *Vice Pres*
EMP: 4
SALES (est): 548.3K **Privately Held**
SIC: 1521 5712 2431 Single-family housing construction; cabinet work, custom; millwork

(G-7916)
SCHRADER-BRIDGEPORT INTL INC
Also Called: Syracuse Guage
1550 Franklin Grove Rd (61021-9110)
PHONE.....................................815 288-3344
Kelly Mosher, *Principal*
EMP: 4
SALES (corp-wide): 3.5B **Privately Held**
WEB: www.schrader-bridgeport.com
SIC: 3491 3823 Industrial valves; industrial instrmnts msrmnt display/control process variable
HQ: Schrader-Bridgeport International Inc.
205 Frazier Rd
Altavista VA 24517
434 369-4741

(G-7917)
SEWER EQUIPMENT CO AMERICA
Also Called: Sewer Equipment of Canada
1590 Dutch Rd (61021-8624)
PHONE.....................................815 835-5566
Daniel J O'Brien, *President*
John Wichmann, *Exec VP*
Dave Loomis, *Vice Pres*
Joe Gennaro, *Prdtn Mgr*
Brenda Harris, *Purch Mgr*
EMP: 120 **EST:** 1974
SQ FT: 6,000
SALES (est): 39.9MM **Privately Held**
SIC: 3589 Sewer cleaning equipment, power

(G-7918)
SOUTHFIELD CORPORATION
Also Called: Dixon-Marquette Cement
1914 White Oak Ln (61021-9089)
P.O. Box 468 (61021-0468)
PHONE.....................................815 284-3357
Larry Setchell, *Opers-Prdtn-Mfg*
EMP: 150
SALES (corp-wide): 344.9MM **Privately Held**
SIC: 3273 3241 Ready-mixed concrete; cement, hydraulic

Dixon - Lee County (G-7919)

PA: Southfield Corporation
8995 W 95th St
Palos Hills IL 60465
708 344-1000

(G-7919)
SPECTRUM BRANDS INC
200 E Corporate Dr (61021-9301)
PHONE..................................815 285-6500
Steve Randorfer, *Branch Mgr*
EMP: 8
SALES (corp-wide): 3.8B **Publicly Held**
SIC: 3691 Alkaline cell storage batteries
HQ: Spectrum Brands, Inc.
3001 Deming Way
Middleton WI 53562
608 275-3340

(G-7920)
ST MARYS CEMENT INC (US)
1914 White Oak Ln (61021-9089)
P.O. Box 468 (61021-0468)
PHONE..................................313 842-4600
Mark Hill, *Opers Staff*
EMP: 50
SALES (corp-wide): 83.2MM **Privately Held**
SIC: 3241 Cement, hydraulic
PA: St. Marys Cement U.S. Llc
9333 Dearborn St
Detroit MI 48209
313 842-4600

(G-7921)
STERLING-ROCK FALLS READY MIX
1905 Mound Hill Rd (61021-9735)
P.O. Box 384 (61021-0384)
PHONE..................................815 288-3135
Adel Mobarak, *President*
Mary Francis Mobarak, *Corp Secy*
George Mobarak, *Vice Pres*
EMP: 12
SQ FT: 3,600
SALES: 1.2MM **Privately Held**
SIC: 3273 Ready-mixed concrete

(G-7922)
TIMBER INDUSTRIES LLC
900 Depot Ave (61021-3549)
PHONE..................................815 857-3674
Thomas May, *Principal*
EMP: 20
SALES (est): 1MM **Privately Held**
SIC: 3999 Manufacturing industries

(G-7923)
TLM ENTERPRISES INC
Also Called: Creative Printing
213 W 1st St (61021-3027)
PHONE..................................815 284-5040
Tracey L Montgomery, *President*
Toni L Montgomery, *Vice Pres*
EMP: 2
SQ FT: 2,000
SALES (est): 300.5K **Privately Held**
SIC: 2752 7699 2791 Commercial printing, offset; printing trades machinery & equipment repair; typesetting

(G-7924)
UPM RAFLATAC INC
101 E Corporate Dr (61021-9306)
PHONE..................................815 285-6100
Aaron Dewey, *Engineer*
April Kutz, *Engineer*
Barry King, *Sales Staff*
Jan-Erik Forsstrom, *Branch Mgr*
Annariikka Ostring, *Manager*
EMP: 118 **Privately Held**
SIC: 2672 3083 Coated & laminated paper; laminated plastics plate & sheet
HQ: Upm Raflatac, Inc.
400 Broadpointe Dr
Mills River NC 28759
828 651-4800

(G-7925)
UZHAVOOR FUELS INC
707 N Galena Ave (61021-1509)
PHONE..................................630 401-6173
Joy Ashish, *Principal*
EMP: 4
SALES (est): 215.3K **Privately Held**
SIC: 2869 Fuels

(G-7926)
WORLD GRANITE INC
1220 S Galena Ave (61021-3844)
PHONE..................................815 288-3350
Dan Johns, *President*
EMP: 2
SALES: 400K **Privately Held**
SIC: 3281 Cut stone & stone products

(G-7927)
ZIGLERS & MCH & METALWORKS LLC
629 Palmyra Rd (61021-9139)
PHONE..................................815 255-8200
John Zigler, *President*
Mike Skinner, *Engineer*
EMP: 14
SALES: 1.5MM **Privately Held**
SIC: 3599 Machine shop, jobbing & repair

Dolton
Cook County

(G-7928)
ABUNDANT LIVING CHRISTIAN CTR
14540 Lincoln Ave (60419-1810)
PHONE..................................708 896-6181
EMP: 8
SALES (est): 583K **Privately Held**
SIC: 2531 Mfg Public Building Furniture

(G-7929)
ARDAGH GLASS INC
13850 Cottage Grove Ave (60419-1052)
PHONE..................................708 849-4010
Vrian Houger, *Manager*
Jeremy Holiness, *Maintence Staff*
EMP: 100
SALES (corp-wide): 242.1K **Privately Held**
SIC: 3221 Glass containers
HQ: Ardagh Glass Inc.
10194 Crosspoint Blvd
Indianapolis IN 46256

(G-7930)
ASG-UNIAERO
13829 Park Ave (60419-1024)
PHONE..................................773 941-5053
Calvin Stinson, *Owner*
EMP: 6
SALES: 400K **Privately Held**
SIC: 3672 Printed circuit boards

(G-7931)
B A P ENTERPRISES INC
14235 Cottage Grove Ave (60419-1354)
P.O. Box 610 (60419-0610)
PHONE..................................708 849-0900
Bruce A Prokop, *President*
Debbie Prokop, *Corp Secy*
Louis A Prokop, *Vice Pres*
EMP: 4
SQ FT: 3,100
SALES (est): 1MM **Privately Held**
SIC: 1711 3599 Heating & air conditioning contractors; machine & other job shop work; machine shop, jobbing & repair

(G-7932)
BALL FOSTER GLASS CONTAINER
13850 Cottage Grove Ave (60419-1052)
PHONE..................................708 849-1500
EMP: 4 EST: 1980
SALES (est): 233.9K **Privately Held**
SIC: 3221 Mfg Glass Containers

(G-7933)
BELBOZ CORP
742 Evans Ct (60419-2115)
PHONE..................................708 856-6099
Kiana Belcher, *President*
EMP: 6
SQ FT: 200
SALES: 62K **Privately Held**
SIC: 6531 2759 Real estate managers; promotional printing

(G-7934)
CALUMET BRASS FOUNDRY INC
14610 Lakeside Ave (60419-2023)
P.O. Box 158 (60419-0158)
PHONE..................................708 849-3040
Catherine Dolan, *President*
Dawn Stromberg, *Sales Staff*
EMP: 12
SQ FT: 25,000
SALES (est): 1.3MM **Privately Held**
WEB: www.calbrass.com
SIC: 3366 Brass foundry

(G-7935)
CARAVAN INGREDIENTS INC
14622 Lakeside Ave (60419-2023)
PHONE..................................708 849-8590
Richard Hulfeld, *Manager*
EMP: 60
SQ FT: 40,000
SALES (corp-wide): 1B **Privately Held**
WEB: www.caravaningredients.com
SIC: 2099 2087 Food preparations; flavoring extracts & syrups
HQ: Caravan Ingredients Inc.
8250 Flint St
Lenexa KS 66214
913 890-5500

(G-7936)
HARRIS LUBRICANTS
14335 Dorchester Ave (60419-1328)
PHONE..................................708 849-1935
Carl Harris, *President*
EMP: 2
SQ FT: 6,000
SALES: 875K **Privately Held**
SIC: 2992 Oils & greases, blending & compounding

(G-7937)
HOLLAND MANUFACTURING CORP
13901 Indiana Ave (60419-1169)
P.O. Box 261, South Holland (60473-0261)
PHONE..................................708 849-1000
Kenneth Hoekstra, *President*
David Myroup, *Corp Secy*
John Nelson, *Vice Pres*
▲ EMP: 42
SQ FT: 60,000
SALES (est): 6.4MM **Privately Held**
WEB: www.refractoryshape.com
SIC: 3255 Clay refractories

(G-7938)
PDQ TOOL & STAMPING CO
14901 Greenwood Rd (60419-2238)
PHONE..................................708 841-3000
Thomas Miller, *President*
Joann Labarge, *Finance Mgr*
Jan Ehrlich, *Office Mgr*
Robert Smith, *Technician*
EMP: 30 EST: 1975
SQ FT: 23,000
SALES (est): 5MM **Privately Held**
WEB: www.pdqtoolandstamping.com
SIC: 3544 3469 Die sets for metal stamping (presses); metal stampings

(G-7939)
PROAM SPORTS PRODUCTS
435 Adams St (60419-1120)
PHONE..................................708 841-4200
Raymond McClinton Jr, *Principal*
EMP: 4
SALES (est): 217K **Privately Held**
SIC: 3949 Sporting & athletic goods

(G-7940)
T A U INC
Also Called: Die Cut Plates
14075 Lincoln Ave (60419-1021)
PHONE..................................708 841-5757
William Hinton, *President*
Curt Voss, *President*
Bill Hinton, *Vice Pres*
EMP: 3
SALES (est): 436.4K **Privately Held**
SIC: 3469 3354 Ornamental metal stampings; aluminum extruded products

(G-7941)
YUSRAA INC
14828 Cottage Grove Ave (60419-2108)
PHONE..................................312 608-1916
Tajmah Y Al-Faruqi, *Principal*
EMP: 2
SALES (est): 205K **Privately Held**
SIC: 3537 Trucks: freight, baggage, etc.: industrial, except mining

Dongola
Union County

(G-7942)
CHEERS FOOD FUEL
510 Ne Front St (62926-2349)
PHONE..................................618 827-4836
David Godfrey, *Manager*
EMP: 4
SALES (est): 203K **Privately Held**
WEB: www.acees.com
SIC: 2869 Fuels

Dorsey
Madison County

(G-7943)
AXON TELECOM LLC
Also Called: Csd
177 Snake Rd (62021-3007)
PHONE..................................618 278-4606
William Ludwig,
EMP: 1
SALES (est): 5MM **Privately Held**
SIC: 3661 Fiber optics communications equipment

(G-7944)
FARMERS MANUFACTURING COMPANY
5635 Loop Rd (62021-1111)
PHONE..................................618 377-6237
Wilfred F Aljets, *President*
Timothy A Thompson, *Admin Sec*
EMP: 2
SQ FT: 6,000
SALES (est): 203.7K **Privately Held**
WEB: www.cropresources.com
SIC: 2873 2879 Nitrogenous fertilizers; soil conditioners

(G-7945)
MCCANN CONCRETE PRODUCTS INC
8709 N State Route 159 (62021-1217)
PHONE..................................618 377-3888
Patrick McCann, *President*
Jack McCann, *Vice Pres*
Mark Melvin, *Vice Pres*
Chris McCann, *Sales Engr*
Debbie Christopher, *Sales Staff*
EMP: 20
SQ FT: 5,000
SALES (est): 4.3MM **Privately Held**
SIC: 3272 Concrete products, precast

Dow
Jersey County

(G-7946)
MORRIS PALLET SKIDS INC
15133 Newbern Rd (62022-3192)
PHONE..................................618 786-2241
John Abbott, *Exec Dir*
EMP: 4 EST: 2010
SALES (est): 459.7K **Privately Held**
SIC: 2448 Pallets, wood

(G-7947)
STINE WOODWORKING LLC
16376 Bartlett Rd (62022-3030)
PHONE..................................618 885-2229
David Stine, *Mng Member*
Stephanie Abbajay, *Manager*
EMP: 2
SALES: 250K **Privately Held**
SIC: 2431 Millwork

Downers Grove
Dupage County

(G-7948)
A LEN RADIATOR SHOPPE INC
Also Called: A Len Complete Auto Svc Ctr
333 Ogden Ave (60515-3142)
PHONE 630 852-5445
Leonard H Senicka, *President*
Cynthia Senicka, *Corp Secy*
EMP: 5
SQ FT: 10,000
SALES (est): 1MM **Privately Held**
SIC: 5531 5013 7539 7538 Automotive parts; automotive supplies & parts; radiator repair shop, automotive; general automotive repair shops; hose & tube fittings & assemblies, hydraulic/pneumatic

(G-7949)
ADVANCED OZONE TECH INC
Also Called: Cec, The Ozone Co
2743 Curtiss St (60515-4002)
PHONE 630 964-1300
Kathryn V Johnston, *President*
William R Johnston, *Vice Pres*
EMP: 10
SQ FT: 3,500
SALES (est): 1.8MM **Privately Held**
SIC: 3589 Water treatment equipment, industrial

(G-7950)
AMERICAN COMM & NETWORKS
Also Called: Acnc
2516 Wisconsin Ave (60515-4230)
PHONE 630 241-2800
Pao-Fan Liu, *Ch of Bd*
Paul Liu, *President*
▲ **EMP:** 40
SALES (est): 4.9MM **Privately Held**
SIC: 5045 3661 Computers, peripherals & software; telephones & telephone apparatus

(G-7951)
AMKUS INC
Also Called: Amkus Rescue Systems
2700 Wisconsin Ave (60515-4226)
P.O. Box 408, Bolingbrook (60440-1097)
PHONE 630 515-1800
Margaret Weigand, *President*
Judy Weigand, *Exec VP*
Rw Steingass, *Research*
Chuck Sheaffer, *Sales Mgr*
Alice Huball, *Sales Staff*
▲ **EMP:** 26 **EST:** 1973
SQ FT: 40,000
SALES (est): 5.5MM **Privately Held**
SIC: 3569 Firefighting apparatus

(G-7952)
APERGY ENERGY AUTOMATION LLC (HQ)
Also Called: Timberline Manufacturing
3005 Highland Pkwy (60515-5682)
PHONE 630 541-1540
Michael Martindale,
EMP: 32 **EST:** 2002
SQ FT: 11,000
SALES (est): 12MM
SALES (corp-wide): 1.1B **Publicly Held**
WEB: www.dovercorporation.com
SIC: 3561 3545 Pumps & pumping equipment; machine tool accessories
PA: Championx Corporation
   2445 Tech Frest Blvd Bldg
   The Woodlands TX 77381
   281 403-5772

(G-7953)
APOLLO AEROSOL INDUSTRIES LLC
2651 Warrenville Rd # 300 (60515-5544)
PHONE 770 433-0210
EMP: 3
SALES (est): 183K **Privately Held**
SIC: 3999 Manufacturing industries

(G-7954)
ARCHITECTURAL WDWKG DESIGN INC
4401 Roslyn Rd (60515)
PHONE 630 810-1604
David Pocci, *President*
EMP: 7
SALES (est): 953.9K **Privately Held**
SIC: 2431 Millwork

(G-7955)
ARROW GEAR COMPANY (PA)
2301 Curtiss St (60515-4036)
PHONE 630 969-7640
David Goodfellow, *CEO*
Brett Bodoh, *Mfg Spvr*
Peter Joerms, *Engineer*
Andrew Mazzarella, *CFO*
Sharon Buchanan, *Human Res Dir*
▲ **EMP:** 275 **EST:** 1947
SQ FT: 140,000
SALES (est): 69.3MM **Privately Held**
WEB: www.arrowgear.com
SIC: 3724 3566 3714 3568 Aircraft engines & engine parts; drives, high speed industrial, except hydrostatic; motor vehicle parts & accessories; power transmission equipment; iron & steel forgings; metal heat treating

(G-7956)
ARROW GEAR COMPANY
5240 Belmont Rd (60515-4340)
PHONE 630 969-7640
Joe Arzin, *President*
EMP: 25
SQ FT: 10,625
SALES (est): 1.1MM
SALES (corp-wide): 69.3MM **Privately Held**
WEB: www.arrowgear.com
SIC: 3599 Machine shop, jobbing & repair
PA: Arrow Gear Company
   2301 Curtiss St
   Downers Grove IL 60515
   630 969-7640

(G-7957)
BALES MOLD SERVICE INC
2824 Hitchcock Ave Ste A (60515-4030)
PHONE 630 852-4665
Stacey Bales, *President*
Genaro Garza, *QC Mgr*
Rich Wozniak, *Technical Mgr*
Jaime Santiago, *Engineer*
Matt Adams, *Sales Staff*
EMP: 40
SQ FT: 28,000
SALES (est): 6MM **Privately Held**
WEB: www.balesusa.com
SIC: 3471 7692 Polishing, metals or formed products; chromium plating of metals or formed products; electroplating of metals or formed products; welding repair

(G-7958)
BASELINE GRAPHICS INC
5424 Webster St (60515-4916)
PHONE 630 964-9566
Marry Joe Hobbs, *President*
Marijo Hobbs, *President*
EMP: 3
SQ FT: 10,000
SALES (est): 223.1K **Privately Held**
SIC: 2791 7336 Typesetting; graphic arts & related design

(G-7959)
BECTON DICKINSON AND COMPANY
Also Called: B D
1400 Opus Pl Ste 805 (60515-5754)
P.O. Box 5200, Rantoul (61866-5200)
PHONE 630 743-2006
Jim Meurer, *Manager*
EMP: 3
SALES (corp-wide): 17.2B **Publicly Held**
SIC: 3841 Diagnostic apparatus, medical
PA: Becton, Dickinson And Company
   1 Becton Dr
   Franklin Lakes NJ 07417
   201 847-6800

(G-7960)
BLUE DIAMOND ATHLETIC DISP INC
1933 Loomes Ave (60516-2432)
PHONE 847 414-9971
Nilmini Posmer, *President*
Kenneth Posmer, *Vice Pres*
EMP: 5
SALES: 54K **Privately Held**
SIC: 3993 Signs & advertising specialties

(G-7961)
C & C PRINTING CONTROLS INC
5015 Chase Ave (60515-4014)
PHONE 630 810-0484
Brian Chapas, *President*
EMP: 3
SQ FT: 2,400
SALES (est): 402.4K **Privately Held**
SIC: 3555 Printing trade parts & attachments; printing presses

(G-7962)
C AND C MACHINE TOOL SERVICE
5015 Chase Ave (60515-4014)
PHONE 630 810-0484
Kathleen Chapas, *President*
Richard Chapas, *Admin Sec*
EMP: 9
SQ FT: 5,400
SALES (est): 900K **Privately Held**
SIC: 7694 5084 Rebuilding motors, except automotive; printing trades machinery, equipment & supplies

(G-7963)
CAMPBELL CAMIE INC
2651 Warrenville Rd # 300 (60515-5772)
PHONE 314 968-3222
Vincent J Doder, *President*
Jim McLarty, *Vice Pres*
EMP: 21 **EST:** 1946
SQ FT: 18,000
SALES (est): 3MM
SALES (corp-wide): 283.8MM **Privately Held**
WEB: www.camie.com
SIC: 2819 2891 2992 2899 Industrial inorganic chemicals; adhesives; lubricating oils & greases; chemical preparations; industrial organic chemicals
HQ: Plaze, Inc.
   2651 Warrenville Rd # 300
   Downers Grove IL 60515
   630 628-4240

(G-7964)
CAMPBELL SOUP COMPANY
230 2nd St (60515-5282)
PHONE 630 241-6200
Chris Gardier, *Vice Pres*
EMP: 169
SALES (corp-wide): 8.1B **Publicly Held**
WEB: www.campbellsoupcompany.com
SIC: 5461 2038 2033 2052 Bakeries; frozen specialties; canned fruits & specialties; cookies & crackers; bread, cake & related products; potato chips & similar snacks
PA: Campbell Soup Company
   1 Campbell Pl
   Camden NJ 08103
   856 342-4800

(G-7965)
CANADA ORGANIZATION & DEV LLC (HQ)
3005 Highland Pkwy (60515-5682)
PHONE 630 743-2563
Robert A Livingston, *President*
EMP: 4 **EST:** 2002
SALES (est): 60.6MM
SALES (corp-wide): 7.1B **Publicly Held**
SIC: 3561 Pumps & pumping equipment
PA: Dover Corporation
   3005 Highland Pkwy # 200
   Downers Grove IL 60515
   630 541-1540

(G-7966)
CEMEC INC (PA)
1516 Centre Cir (60515-1019)
PHONE 630 495-9696
James C Klouda, *President*
Marilyn Klouda, *Corp Secy*
Rob Fredres, *Info Tech Dir*
EMP: 3
SQ FT: 3,500
SALES (est): 2.7MM **Privately Held**
SIC: 3677 8734 3621 Filtration devices, electronic; testing laboratories; motors & generators

(G-7967)
CHEMRING ENERGETIC DEVICES
2525 Curtiss St (60515-4060)
PHONE 310 784-2100
David K Shingledecker, *President*
Mike Cunningham, *Opers Staff*
Jan L Hauhe, *CFO*
Michael Walther, *Info Tech Mgr*
EMP: 130
SALES (est): 22.4MM
SALES (corp-wide): 414.1MM **Privately Held**
SIC: 3769 Guided missile & space vehicle parts & aux eqpt, rsch & dev
PA: Chemring Group Plc
   Roke Manor
   Romsey HANTS SO51
   179 483-3901

(G-7968)
CHEMRING ENERGETIC DEVICES INC
2525 Curtiss St (60515-4060)
PHONE 630 969-0620
William Currer, *President*
Michael Solch, *General Mgr*
Jonathan Bailey, *Vice Pres*
Robert Glembin, *Vice Pres*
Brian Lockhart, *Facilities Mgr*
EMP: 111
SQ FT: 55,000
SALES (est): 24.9MM
SALES (corp-wide): 414.1MM **Privately Held**
WEB: www.chemringenergeticdevices.com
SIC: 3812 3724 Missile guidance systems & equipment; aircraft engines & engine parts
PA: Chemring Group Plc
   Roke Manor
   Romsey HANTS SO51
   179 483-3901

(G-7969)
CHICAGO CRATE INC
440 Roe Ct (60516-3904)
PHONE 708 380-4716
Mark Harrington, *President*
EMP: 5
SALES (est): 471.5K **Privately Held**
SIC: 2449 Rectangular boxes & crates, wood

(G-7970)
CITGO PETROLEUM CORPORATION
1201 Ogden Ave (60515-2741)
PHONE 847 818-1800
Chuck Mavus, *Branch Mgr*
EMP: 5 **Privately Held**
SIC: 2911 Petroleum refining
HQ: Citgo Petroleum Corporation
   1293 Eldridge Pkwy
   Houston TX 77077
   832 486-4000

(G-7971)
CITRUS SYSTEMS
2001 Butterfield Rd # 600 (60515-1289)
PHONE 608 271-3000
Robert Voss, *Manager*
Janet Adamo, *Info Tech Mgr*
EMP: 3
SALES (est): 139.8K **Privately Held**
WEB: www.all-juice.com
SIC: 2037 Frozen fruits & vegetables

(G-7972)
CLAIRE-SPRAYWAY INC (DH)
Also Called: Claire Manufacturing
2651 Warrenville Rd # 300 (60515-5772)
PHONE 630 628-3000
Michael Rohl, *CEO*
Edward Byczynski, *President*

Downers Grove - Dupage County (G-7973)

Bob Potvin, *Vice Pres*
Olga Hernandez, *Sales Staff*
Deanna Mackiewicz, *Sales Staff*
▼ **EMP:** 50 **EST:** 1913
SQ FT: 100,000
SALES (est): 33.7MM
SALES (corp-wide): 283.8MM **Privately Held**
WEB: www.clairemfg.com
SIC: 2842 Cleaning or polishing preparations; deodorants, nonpersonal; disinfectants, household or industrial plant
HQ: Plaze, Inc.
2651 Warrenville Rd # 300
Downers Grove IL 60515
630 628-4240

(G-7973) CLAIRE-SPRAYWAY INC
2651 Warrenville Rd # 300 (60515-5772)
PHONE................................630 628-3000
Theresa Lavine, *Manager*
EMP: 80
SALES (corp-wide): 283.8MM **Privately Held**
SIC: 2813 2992 2899 2879 Aerosols; lubricating oils & greases; chemical preparations; agricultural chemicals; specialty cleaning, polishes & sanitation goods
HQ: Claire-Sprayway, Inc.
2651 Warrenville Rd # 300
Downers Grove IL 60515
630 628-3000

(G-7974) CLOUD 9 INFOSYSTEMS INC
1333 Butterfield Rd # 401 (60515-5609)
PHONE................................855 225-6839
Sonal C Malavia, *President*
Bert Parekh, *Vice Pres*
EMP: 112
SALES (est): 8MM **Privately Held**
WEB: www.cloud9infosystems.com
SIC: 7371 7372 7373 Computer software systems analysis & design, custom; computer software development & applications; business oriented computer software; computer integrated systems design; systems integration services

(G-7975) CLOVER US HOLDINGS LLC (HQ)
Also Called: Hearthside
3333 Finley Rd Ste 800 (60515-1298)
PHONE................................630 967-3600
Liam McClennon, *President*
Paul Kenny, *Treasurer*
Conor O'Leary, *Admin Sec*
▲ **EMP:** 72
SALES (est): 573.1MM **Privately Held**
SIC: 2043 Oatmeal: prepared as cereal breakfast food

(G-7976) COLLEGE BOUND ATHLETE LLC
2659 Wisconsin Ave (60515-4244)
PHONE................................708 259-7713
William Novak, *Mng Member*
Andrew Brauer, *Mng Member*
Matthew Buckley, *Mng Member*
Scott Lawler, *Mng Member*
EMP: 3
SALES (est): 127.1K **Privately Held**
SIC: 3949 Baseball equipment & supplies, general

(G-7977) COMPTIA LEARNING LLC
3500 Lacey Rd Ste 100 (60515-5439)
PHONE................................630 678-8490
EMP: 12
SQ FT: 35,000
SALES (est): 760K **Privately Held**
SIC: 7372 8611 Prepackaged Software Services Business Association

(G-7978) COMPUSYSTEMS INC (PA)
Also Called: C S I
2651 Warrenville Rd # 400 (60515-5544)
PHONE................................708 344-9070
Clark K Williams, *Ch of Bd*
Chris Williams, *President*
Pat Fallon, *President*
Kahle Williams, *COO*

Paul McCaffray, *Exec VP*
EMP: 103
SQ FT: 27,000
SALES (est): 55.4MM **Privately Held**
WEB: www.compusystems.com
SIC: 7372 Business oriented computer software

(G-7979) CONSCISYS CORP
1125 Mistwood Pl (60515-1205)
PHONE................................630 810-4444
Scott Carr, *President*
EMP: 25
SALES (est): 1.5MM **Privately Held**
SIC: 7372 Business oriented computer software

(G-7980) CONTEMPORARY CTRL SYSTEMS INC (PA)
2431 Curtiss St (60515-4006)
PHONE................................630 963-7070
George M Thomas, *President*
Judith L Thomas, *Admin Sec*
◆ **EMP:** 52 **EST:** 1975
SQ FT: 14,000
SALES (est): 12.6MM **Privately Held**
WEB: www.ccontrols.com
SIC: 3577 Computer peripheral equipment

(G-7981) COOPERS HAWK INTRMDATE HLDG LL (PA)
Also Called: Coopers Hawk Winery & Rest
3500 Lacey Rd Ste 1000 (60515-5441)
PHONE................................708 839-2920
Cara Mahler, *General Mgr*
Kat Szeszak, *General Mgr*
Walter Fisher, *Vice Pres*
Ben Hummer, *Vice Pres*
Jennifer Hammer, *Opers Staff*
EMP: 148
SALES (est): 246.9MM **Privately Held**
WEB: www.chwinery.com
SIC: 8741 2084 5182 5812 Restaurant management; wines; wine; eating places

(G-7982) D S PRECISION TOOL COMPANY
1420 Brook Dr (60515-1025)
PHONE................................630 627-0696
David Steininger II, *President*
Nancy Lott, *Admin Sec*
EMP: 5
SQ FT: 3,500
SALES (est): 500K **Privately Held**
SIC: 3544 Special dies & tools

(G-7983) DALLAS CORPORATION
4340 Cross St (60515-1715)
PHONE................................630 322-8000
Lance Haack, *President*
EMP: 18
SQ FT: 10,000
SALES (est): 3.5MM **Privately Held**
SIC: 5112 4225 2752 Manifold business forms; general warehousing; commercial printing, offset

(G-7984) DEAN B SCOTT
1319 Butterfield Rd # 524 (60515-5621)
P.O. Box 1509, Fort Myers FL (33902-1509)
PHONE................................630 960-4455
Dean B Scott, *Owner*
EMP: 3
SALES (est): 311.7K **Privately Held**
SIC: 3851 Eyes, glass & plastic

(G-7985) DEE ERECTORS INC
8314 Old Fence Ct (60517-4104)
PHONE................................630 327-1185
EMP: 2
SALES (est): 238.9K **Privately Held**
SIC: 3325 Steel Foundry

(G-7986) DFK AMERICA INC
2464 Wisconsin Ave (60515-4050)
PHONE................................630 324-6793
Dalibor Kanovsky, *President*

▲ **EMP:** 7
SALES (est): 1MM **Privately Held**
SIC: 3537 Cabs, for industrial trucks & tractors

(G-7987) DIAMOND WEB PRINTING LLC
2820 Hitchcock Ave (60515-4041)
PHONE................................630 663-0351
Gregg Herlin, *Principal*
Dawn Mellas, *Vice Pres*
Louis Sedivy, *CFO*
Charles J Gardella,
Mark Kramer,
EMP: 18
SQ FT: 26,000
SALES (est): 1.4MM **Privately Held**
SIC: 2752 2759 Commercial printing, offset; commercial printing

(G-7988) DICKE TOOL COMPANY (PA)
Also Called: Dicke Safety Products
1201 Warren Ave (60515-3548)
PHONE................................630 969-0050
Vera D Dicke, *President*
Lora Stesanski, *Traffic Mgr*
John Pasakarnis, *Engrg Dir*
Jim Kokenes, *Engineer*
Gina Horton, *Sales Staff*
▲ **EMP:** 60 **EST:** 1880
SQ FT: 25,000
SALES (est): 17.8MM **Privately Held**
WEB: www.dicketool.com
SIC: 3441 3993 Fabricated structural metal; signs & advertising specialties

(G-7989) DOVER CORPORATION (PA)
3005 Highland Pkwy # 200 (60515-5655)
PHONE................................630 541-1540
Michael F Johnston, *Ch of Bd*
Richard J Tobin, *President*
Erin Reiff, *Counsel*
James Moyle, *Exec VP*
Ivonne M Cabrera, *Senior VP*
◆ **EMP:** 150 **EST:** 1947
SALES: 7.1B **Publicly Held**
WEB: www.dovercorporation.com
SIC: 3585 3586 3533 3577 Refrigeration & heating equipment; refrigeration equipment, complete; measuring & dispensing pumps; oil & gas drilling rigs & equipment; computer peripheral equipment; bar code (magnetic ink) printers; semiconductors & related devices

(G-7990) DOVER CORPORATION
3005 Highland Pkwy # 200 (60515-5655)
PHONE................................212 922-1640
Bob Livingston, *General Mgr*
EMP: 5
SALES (corp-wide): 7.1B **Publicly Held**
WEB: www.dovercorporation.com
SIC: 3632 Household refrigerators & freezers
PA: Dover Corporation
3005 Highland Pkwy # 200
Downers Grove IL 60515
630 541-1540

(G-7991) DOVER EUROPE INC (HQ)
3005 Highland Pkwy # 200 (60515-5655)
PHONE................................630 541-1540
Robert A Livingston, *President*
John F Hartner, *President*
Jeffrey S Niew, *President*
William W Spurgeon, *President*
Michael Y Zhang, *President*
EMP: 5
SALES (est): 22.7MM
SALES (corp-wide): 7.1B **Publicly Held**
SIC: 3531 3542 3565 3534 Construction machinery; machine tools, metal forming type; packaging machinery; elevators & moving stairways
PA: Dover Corporation
3005 Highland Pkwy # 200
Downers Grove IL 60515
630 541-1540

(G-7992) DOVER PRTG IDENTIFICATION INC (HQ)
3005 Highland Pkwy # 200 (60515-5682)
PHONE................................630 541-1540
Lewis Burns, *CEO*
John F Hartner, *President*
◆ **EMP:** 90
SQ FT: 2,600
SALES (est): 1.8B
SALES (corp-wide): 7.1B **Publicly Held**
SIC: 3556 3565 3593 7699 Food products machinery; packaging machinery; fluid power cylinders, hydraulic or pneumatic; industrial equipment services
PA: Dover Corporation
3005 Highland Pkwy # 200
Downers Grove IL 60515
630 541-1540

(G-7993) DUPAGE PRODUCTS GROUP
2250 Curtiss St (60515-4054)
PHONE................................630 969-7200
Jerry Piper, *CEO*
EMP: 60
SALES (est): 4.6MM **Privately Held**
SIC: 3356 Nonferrous rolling & drawing

(G-7994) DURAVANT (PA)
3500 Lacey Rd Ste 290 (60515-5443)
PHONE................................630 635-3910
EMP: 9
SALES (est): 4.5MM **Privately Held**
SIC: 3565 3535 Mnaufacturing Packaging Machinery Conveyors/Equipment

(G-7995) DURAVANT LLC (HQ)
3500 Lacey Rd Ste 290 (60515-5443)
PHONE................................630 635-3910
Michael J Kachmer, *President*
Vivek Joshi, *Vice Pres*
Mike Labelle, *Vice Pres*
David Parker, *Vice Pres*
Eleni Yianas, *Vice Pres*
◆ **EMP:** 10
SALES (est): 206.4MM
SALES (corp-wide): 862.6MM **Privately Held**
SIC: 3559 3565 3535 Bag seaming & closing machines (sewing machinery); packaging machinery; belt conveyor systems, general industrial use
PA: Odyssey Capital Partners V, Llc
590 Madison Ave Fl 39
New York NY 10022
212 351-7900

(G-7996) EARTHGRAINS REFRIGERTD DOUGH P
Also Called: Refrigerated Dough Division
3250 Lacey Rd Ste 600 (60515-7918)
PHONE................................630 455-5200
Kevin Hunt, *CEO*
▼ **EMP:** 700 **EST:** 1957
SALES (est): 143.1MM
SALES (corp-wide): 4.2B **Publicly Held**
WEB: www.ralcorpartisanbreads.com
SIC: 2051 2053 2041 2035 Breads, rolls & buns; cakes, pies & pastries; frozen bakery products, except bread; doughs, frozen or refrigerated; dressings, salad: raw & cooked (except dry mixes); mayonnaise; frozen food & ice cream containers; food containers (liquid tight), including milk cartons
PA: Treehouse Foods, Inc.
2021 Spring Rd Ste 600
Oak Brook IL 60523
708 483-1300

(G-7997) ELGIN EQUIPMENT GROUP LLC (HQ)
2001 Bttrfield Rd Ste 1020 (60515)
PHONE................................630 434-7200
David Hall, *President*
Kerry Koch, *Vice Pres*
Karen Oshea, *Controller*
EMP: 7

▲ = Import ▼ = Export
◆ = Import/Export

GEOGRAPHIC SECTION
Downers Grove - Dupage County (G-8022)

SALES (est): 151.4MM
SALES (corp-wide): 1.7B **Privately Held**
SIC: 3532 Mining machinery
PA: Audax Group, L.P.
101 Huntington Ave # 2450
Boston MA 02199
617 859-1500

(G-7998)
ELGIN NATIONAL INDUSTRIES INC (PA)
2001 Bttrfeld Rd Ste 1020 (60515)
PHONE 630 434-7200
Fred C Schulte, *Ch of Bd*
David Hall, *President*
Charles D Hall, *President*
Marco Petracchini, *Sr Exec VP*
Lynn C Batory, *Vice Pres*
◆ EMP: 13
SQ FT: 6,470
SALES (est): 87.8MM **Privately Held**
WEB: www.clinchrivercorp.com
SIC: 3532 8711 Mining machinery; crushing, pulverizing & screening equipment; engineering services

(G-7999)
ELKAY MANUFACTURING COMPANY
1333 Butterfield Rd # 200 (60515-5613)
PHONE 800 223-5529
EMP: 3
SALES (corp-wide): 1B **Privately Held**
SIC: 3431 3585 3432 2434 Sinks: enameled iron, cast iron or pressed metal; coolers, milk & water: electric; faucets & spigots, metal & plastic; wood kitchen cabinets
PA: Elkay Manufacturing Company Inc
1333 Butterfield Rd # 200
Downers Grove IL 60515
630 574-8484

(G-8000)
EMMETTS TAVERN & BREWING CO
5200 Main St (60515-4688)
PHONE 630 434-8500
Kirsten Swanson, *Principal*
EMP: 5
SALES (corp-wide): 3.2MM **Privately Held**
WEB: www.emmettsbrewingco.com
SIC: 5812 2082 5182 Chicken restaurant; beer (alcoholic beverage); wine & distilled beverages
PA: Emmett's Tavern & Brewing Co.
128 W Main St
West Dundee IL 60118
847 428-4500

(G-8001)
FASTSIGNS LLC
408 75th St (60516-4454)
PHONE 630 541-8901
Janet Calahan, *Mng Member*
EMP: 5
SQ FT: 1,300
SALES: 300K **Privately Held**
SIC: 3993 Signs & advertising specialties

(G-8002)
FEMINA SPORT INC
5100 Walnut Ave (60515-4066)
PHONE 630 271-1876
Roberta Weimer, *President*
EMP: 6
SALES (est): 245K **Privately Held**
SIC: 2395 Embroidery products; except schiffli machine

(G-8003)
FIXTURE DISPLAYS
2333 Wisconsin Ave (60515-4022)
PHONE 630 296-4190
Gao Yang, *Principal*
▲ EMP: 2
SALES (est): 268.5K **Privately Held**
SIC: 3496 Miscellaneous fabricated wire products

(G-8004)
FLAVORCHEM CORPORATION (PA)
Also Called: Orchid Labs
1525 Brook Dr (60515-1024)
PHONE 630 932-8100
Jacqueline Sprovieri, *Corp Secy*
Ross Sprovieri, *Senior VP*
Phillip Sprovieri, *Vice Pres*
Drew Plunk, *Opers Dir*
Henry Van Denack, *Opers Mgr*
◆ EMP: 90
SQ FT: 70,000
SALES (est): 30.6MM **Privately Held**
SIC: 2087 Extracts, flavoring; syrups, flavoring (except drink)

(G-8005)
FOUNDATION LITHUANIAN MINOR
908 Rob Roy Pl (60516-3824)
PHONE 630 969-1316
Ramunas Buntinas, *Principal*
EMP: 5
SALES: 8.9K **Privately Held**
SIC: 2731 Book publishing

(G-8006)
FUSIBOND PIPING SYSTEMS INC
2615 Curtiss St (60515-4003)
PHONE 630 969-4488
Richard H Krause, *President*
Patricia Ann Krause, *Vice Pres*
Craig J Krause, *Treasurer*
Kyle Jo Manowsky, *Admin Sec*
Kyle Manowsky, *Admin Sec*
EMP: 18
SQ FT: 32,000
SALES (est): 3.6MM **Privately Held**
SIC: 3084 5084 Plastics pipe; industrial machinery & equipment

(G-8007)
GEOMENTUM INC (HQ)
Also Called: Geomentum Solutions
3025 Highland Pkwy # 700 (60515-5506)
P.O. Box 7063 (60515-7063)
PHONE 630 729-7500
Sean Finnegan, *CEO*
Larry Fuchs, *Vice Pres*
Robin Zeldin, *Vice Pres*
Adriana Bautista, *Auditor*
Tony Bombacino, *Chief Mktg Ofcr*
▲ EMP: 291
SQ FT: 73,500
SALES (est): 63.4MM
SALES (corp-wide): 10.2B **Publicly Held**
SIC: 2711 7311 Newspapers; advertising agencies
PA: The Interpublic Group Of Companies Inc
909 3rd Ave
New York NY 10022
212 704-1200

(G-8008)
GEOMENTUM INC
Magnet Media
3025 Highland Pkwy (60515-5506)
PHONE 630 729-7500
Randy Novak, *Branch Mgr*
EMP: 3
SALES (corp-wide): 10.2B **Publicly Held**
SIC: 2711 7311 Newspapers; advertising agencies
HQ: Geomentum Inc.
3025 Highland Pkwy # 700
Downers Grove IL 60515

(G-8009)
GH PRINTING CO INC
2820 Hitchcock Ave (60515-4041)
PHONE 630 663-0351
Gregg Herlin, *Principal*
EMP: 5
SALES (est): 489.4K
SALES (corp-wide): 4.5MM **Privately Held**
WEB: www.ghprinting.com
SIC: 2752 Commercial printing, offset
PA: Gh Printing Co., Inc.
5207 Walnut Ave
Downers Grove IL 60515
630 960-4115

(G-8010)
GH PRINTING CO INC (PA)
5207 Walnut Ave (60515-4025)
PHONE 630 960-4115
Gail Herlin, *President*
Gregg Herlin, *Vice Pres*
Todd Herlin, *Marketing Mgr*
EMP: 22
SQ FT: 12,500
SALES (est): 4.5MM **Privately Held**
SIC: 2752 7336 Commercial printing, offset; graphic arts & related design

(G-8011)
GIFT CHECK PROGRAM 2013 INC
Also Called: Holiday Gift Check Program
1400 Opus Pl Ste 810 (60515-5708)
PHONE 630 986-5081
Mary Avery, *Principal*
EMP: 4
SALES (est): 189.7K **Privately Held**
SIC: 2015 Turkey, processed

(G-8012)
GLANBIA PRFMCE NTRTN NA INC (DH)
Also Called: Optimum Nutrition
3500 Lacey Rd (60515-5422)
PHONE 630 236-0097
Thomas Tench, *CEO*
Paul Freeborn, *Counsel*
Patricia Kim, *Counsel*
Constancia Estrada, *Production*
Andrew Knox, *Production*
◆ EMP: 120
SQ FT: 140,000
SALES (est): 135.6MM **Privately Held**
SIC: 2833 5149 5122 Vitamins, natural or synthetic: bulk, uncompounded; health foods; vitamins & minerals

(G-8013)
GLOBAL GEAR & MACHINING LLC
2500 Curtiss St (60515-4058)
PHONE 630 969-9400
Harshad Gujarathi, *President*
Brad Rapciak, *Director*
▲ EMP: 127
SQ FT: 130,000
SALES: 31.1MM
SALES (corp-wide): 189.6MM **Privately Held**
SIC: 3599 Machine shop, jobbing & repair
PA: Ims Companies, Llc
1 Innovation Dr
Des Plaines IL 60016
847 391-8100

(G-8014)
GREEN BAY PACKAGING INC
Also Called: Chicago Sales & Dist Ctr
2200 Warrenville Rd (60515-1764)
PHONE 847 455-2553
Kevin Shields, *Manager*
EMP: 30
SALES (corp-wide): 1.3B **Privately Held**
WEB: www.gbpcoated.com
SIC: 2653 Boxes, corrugated: made from purchased materials
PA: Green Bay Packaging Inc.
1700 N Webster Ave
Green Bay WI 54302
920 433-5111

(G-8015)
GUE LIQUIDATION DELIVERY INC (DH)
3113 Woodcreek Dr (60515-5412)
PHONE 630 719-7800
Scott D Levin, *President*
Rhys J Hughes, *President*
Tom D Moeller, *Exec VP*
Dale Perrott, *Exec VP*
Steven Barnhart, *CFO*
▲ EMP: 1
SQ FT: 120,000
SALES (est): 326.7MM **Privately Held**
WEB: www.broadwayfloristny.com
SIC: 5193 7389 2771 Florists' supplies; florist telegraph service; greeting cards

(G-8016)
HARRIS BOOKBINDING LLC
5375 Walnut Ave (60515-4108)
PHONE 773 287-9414
Greg Goodman, *Mng Member*
EMP: 20
SALES (est): 2.1MM **Privately Held**
SIC: 2789 Binding only: books, pamphlets, magazines, etc.

(G-8017)
HARRY J TRAINOR
2113 Oxnard Dr (60516-2512)
PHONE 630 493-1163
Harry Trainor, *Principal*
EMP: 4
SALES (est): 386.9K **Privately Held**
SIC: 3823 Humidity instruments, industrial process type

(G-8018)
HAVI GLOBAL SOLUTIONS LLC (HQ)
3500 Lacey Rd Ste 600 (60515-5440)
PHONE 630 493-7400
Daniel Musachia, *President*
Joseph Herzer, *Analyst*
Kevin Rutkowski, *Analyst*
▲ EMP: 300
SALES (est): 203.2MM **Privately Held**
SIC: 7372 Business oriented computer software

(G-8019)
HEARTHSIDE FOOD SOLUTIONS LLC (PA)
3500 Lacey Rd Ste 300 (60515-8342)
PHONE 630 967-3600
Chuck Metzger, *CEO*
Richard Scalise, *Ch of Bd*
Bob Scalia, *Vice Pres*
Fred Jasse, *CFO*
Steve England, *VP Human Res*
▼ EMP: 50
SALES (est): 2.8B **Privately Held**
SIC: 2043 2038 Cereal breakfast foods; snacks, including onion rings, cheese sticks, etc.

(G-8020)
HEARTHSIDE USA LLC (DH)
Also Called: Clover Usa, Llc
3333 Finley Rd Ste 800 (60515-1298)
PHONE 978 716-2530
Anton Vincent, *President*
Liam McClennon, *CEO*
▲ EMP: 434
SALES (est): 183.8MM **Privately Held**
SIC: 2099 7389 Sandwiches, assembled & packaged: for wholesale market; salads, fresh or refrigerated; ready-to-eat meals, salads & sandwiches
HQ: Clover Us Holdings, Llc
3333 Finley Rd Ste 800
Downers Grove IL 60515
630 967-3600

(G-8021)
HEUFT USA INC
2820 Thatcher Rd (60515-4051)
PHONE 630 395-9521
Oscar Dominguez, *President*
Carl Bonnan, *General Mgr*
Daniel McKee, *Engineer*
Jeffrey Devoy, *Sales Staff*
Laura Quid, *Manager*
▲ EMP: 11
SQ FT: 7,500
SALES (est): 6.6MM
SALES (corp-wide): 113.6MM **Privately Held**
SIC: 5065 3699 Electronic parts & equipment; electrical equipment & supplies
HQ: Heuft Systemtechnik Gmbh
Am Wind 1
Burgbrohl 56659
263 656-0

(G-8022)
HILLSHIRE BRANDS COMPANY
Superior Coffee & Foods
3500 Lacey Rd (60515-5422)
PHONE 312 614-6000
Jeffrey Abbott, *Business Mgr*
Jimmy Yang, *Opers Dir*

Downers Grove - Dupage County (G-8023)

Jeff Kozak, *Branch Mgr*
Thomas Gates, *Manager*
Bob Johnson, *Info Tech Dir*
EMP: 30
SALES (corp-wide): 42.4B **Publicly Held**
SIC: 2013 2015 Sausages & other prepared meats; poultry slaughtering & processing
HQ: The Hillshire Brands Company
400 S Jefferson St Fl 1
Chicago IL 60607
312 614-6000

(G-8023)
HILLSHIRE BRANDS COMPANY
3131 Woodcreek Dr (60515-5400)
PHONE.................................630 991-5100
EMP: 11
SALES (corp-wide): 42.4B **Publicly Held**
SIC: 2013 Sausages & other prepared meats
HQ: The Hillshire Brands Company
400 S Jefferson St Fl 1
Chicago IL 60607
312 614-6000

(G-8024)
HIROSE ELECTRIC (USA) INC (HQ)
2300 Warrenville Rd # 150 (60515-1755)
PHONE.................................630 282-6700
Yasushi Nakamura, *President*
Rick Van Weezel, *VP Sales*
Akira Yoshida, *Administration*
EMP: 55
SQ FT: 40,000
SALES (est): 29.9MM **Privately Held**
WEB: www.hirose.com
SIC: 5065 3678 Electronic parts; electronic connectors

(G-8025)
HOLY COW SPORTS INCORPORATED
5004 Chase Ave (60515-4013)
PHONE.................................630 852-9001
Margaret Buhtanic, *President*
EMP: 10
SALES: 1.2MM **Privately Held**
SIC: 2261 Screen printing of cotton broadwoven fabrics

(G-8026)
IFASTGROUPE USA LLC
2626 Warrenville Rd # 400 (60515-1775)
PHONE.................................450 658-7148
E A Roskovensky, *Principal*
▲ **EMP:** 5
SALES (est): 455K **Privately Held**
SIC: 3315 Steel wire & related products

(G-8027)
IGD DISPLAY LLC
2804 Centre Cir (60515-1029)
PHONE.................................630 916-0700
Mark Kreymborg, *Executive*
Pamela J Hauser,
James L Hauser,
EMP: 18
SALES (est): 2.8MM **Privately Held**
WEB: www.igddisplay.com
SIC: 2542 2631 Office & store showcases & display fixtures; packaging board

(G-8028)
IMAGE PLUS INC
4248 Belle Aire Ln Ste 1 (60515-1914)
PHONE.................................630 852-4920
Ronald A Burzynski, *Manager*
EMP: 6
SALES (est): 855.2K **Privately Held**
SIC: 2262 5199 2759 2395 Screen printing: manmade fiber & silk broadwoven fabrics; advertising specialties; screen printing; embroidery products, except schiffli machine; automotive & apparel trimmings

(G-8029)
IMHEAR CORPORATION
2711 Curtiss St Ste B (60515-4002)
PHONE.................................630 395-9628
Kiki Liang, *CEO*
EMP: 6 **EST:** 2014
SQ FT: 1,500
SALES: 2.2MM **Privately Held**
WEB: www.imhearusa.com
SIC: 3842 Hearing aids

(G-8030)
IMS OLSON LLC
2500 Curtiss St (60515-4058)
PHONE.................................630 969-9400
Norman Sachs, *Mng Member*
EMP: 75
SALES (est): 5.6MM **Privately Held**
SIC: 3544 3469 Special dies & tools; metal stampings

(G-8031)
INDUSTRIAL KINETICS INC (PA)
2535 Curtiss St (60515-4059)
PHONE.................................630 655-0300
George Huber III, *President*
Dwight Pentzien, *Vice Pres*
Richard Robinson, *Project Mgr*
Rich Moldovan, *Mfg Mgr*
Jim Sevening, *Materials Mgr*
▼ **EMP:** 35
SQ FT: 90,000
SALES (est): 10.7MM **Privately Held**
WEB: www.iki.com
SIC: 3535 Unit handling conveying systems

(G-8032)
J J COLLINS SONS INC (PA)
Also Called: J. J. Collins Printers
2300 Warrenville Rd # 190 (60515-1702)
PHONE.................................630 960-2525
James F Collins Jr, *Ch of Bd*
Bob Collins, *Vice Pres*
Robert E Collins, *Vice Pres*
Robert Collins, *Vice Pres*
Kevin Rankin, *Vice Pres*
▲ **EMP:** 15
SQ FT: 5,000
SALES: 50MM **Privately Held**
WEB: www.jjcollins.com
SIC: 2752 Business forms, lithographed

(G-8033)
J WALLACE & ASSOCIATES INC
1409 Centre Cir (60515-1022)
PHONE.................................630 960-4221
John Wallace, *President*
Anna Marie Orseno, *Admin Asst*
Anna Orseno, *Assistant*
EMP: 2
SQ FT: 4,000
SALES (est): 1.2MM **Privately Held**
SIC: 7319 2653 Display advertising service; corrugated boxes, partitions, display items, sheets & pad

(G-8034)
JFB HART COATINGS INC (PA)
5337 Maplewood Pl (60515-4815)
PHONE.................................630 783-1917
James F Beedie, *President*
Timothy Kingsbury, *CFO*
EMP: 10
SALES (est): 2.4MM **Privately Held**
SIC: 2851 Paints & allied products

(G-8035)
JUSKIE PRINTING CORP
2820 Hitchcock Ave Ste E (60515-4062)
PHONE.................................630 663-8833
Mark Spash, *President*
EMP: 3
SQ FT: 2,500
SALES (est): 569.5K **Privately Held**
SIC: 2752 2789 Commercial printing, offset; bookbinding & related work

(G-8036)
K-G SPRAY-PAK INC
2651 Warrenville Rd # 300 (60515-5772)
PHONE.................................630 543-7600
Mike Magner, *Vice Pres*
EMP: 5
SALES (est): 198.5M **Privately Held**
SIC: 2813 Aerosols

(G-8037)
KA STEEL CHEMICALS INC
1001 31st St Ste 200 (60515-1364)
PHONE.................................630 257-3900
Brad Budner, *Opers Staff*
EMP: 42

SALES (corp-wide): 6.1B **Publicly Held**
SIC: 2812 Alkalies & chlorine
HQ: K.A. Steel Chemicals, Inc.
15185 Main St
Lemont IL 60439
630 257-3900

(G-8038)
KD-KIDZ DLIGHT INTERACTIVE LLC
1431 Opus Pl Ste 110 (60515-1164)
PHONE.................................630 724-0223
EMP: 8
SALES (est): 842.5K **Privately Held**
SIC: 3944 5092 5945 Games, toys & children's vehicles; toys & hobby goods & supplies; hobby, toy & game shops

(G-8039)
KENYERI CONSULTING LLC
Also Called: Kenyeri Engineering & Mfg
2300 Wscnsin Ave Ste 218 (60515)
PHONE.................................630 920-3497
Tracy Hauppa-Kenye, *CEO*
Tracy Kenyeri, *Project Mgr*
Ronald L Kenyeri,
EMP: 7 **EST:** 2002
SALES: 180K **Privately Held**
WEB: www.kenyeriengineering.com
SIC: 8711 3545 5084 3613 Consulting engineer; chucks: drill, lathe or magnetic (machine tool accessories); tool holders (chucks, turrets); control panels, electric

(G-8040)
KOI COMPUTERS INC
1341 Warren Ave Ste B (60515-3437)
PHONE.................................630 627-8811
Fanny Ho, *President*
Ayde Chavez, *Sales Staff*
EMP: 6
SQ FT: 3,500
SALES (est): 2.3MM **Privately Held**
SIC: 7373 3571 5045 5734 Computer integrated systems design; electronic computers; computers, peripherals & software; computer peripheral equipment

(G-8041)
KRICK ENTERPRISES INC
Also Called: Signs Now
1548 Ogden Ave (60515-2771)
PHONE.................................630 515-1085
Marlene Krick, *President*
James Krick, *Vice Pres*
EMP: 5
SQ FT: 1,800
SALES: 500K **Privately Held**
SIC: 3993 Signs & advertising specialties

(G-8042)
LAUNDRY SERVICES COMPANY
4805 Pershing Ave (60515-3346)
PHONE.................................630 327-9329
Karl Keefer, *President*
Kevin Mniszewski, *Technician*
EMP: 4
SALES (est): 554.8K **Privately Held**
SIC: 3452 Washers

(G-8043)
LED BUSINESS SOLUTIONS LLC
433 Maple Ave (60515-3806)
PHONE.................................844 464-5337
EMP: 10
SALES (est): 670K **Privately Held**
SIC: 3646 Mfg Commercial Lighting Fixtures

(G-8044)
LEXRAY LLC
3041 Woodcreek Dr Ste 200 (60515-5419)
PHONE.................................630 664-6740
Alex Bratton,
EMP: 10
SQ FT: 3,000
SALES (est): 1MM **Privately Held**
SIC: 7372 Application computer software

(G-8045)
LIXI INC
1438 Brook Dr (60515-1025)
PHONE.................................630 620-4646
Fax: 630 620-7776

EMP: 3 **EST:** 2008
SALES (est): 170K **Privately Held**
SIC: 3844 Mfg X-Ray Apparatus/Tubes

(G-8046)
LODAAT LLC
410 40th St (60515-2258)
PHONE.................................630 852-7544
Reggie Patel, *General Mgr*
EMP: 54
SALES (corp-wide): 50MM **Privately Held**
SIC: 2834 Pharmaceutical preparations
PA: Lodaat, Llc
1415 W 22nd St Ste Tower
Oak Brook IL 60523
630 248-2380

(G-8047)
LOFTHOUSE BAKERY PRODUCTS INC
3250 Lacey Rd Ste 600 (60515-7918)
PHONE.................................630 455-5229
EMP: 6
SALES (corp-wide): 4.2B **Privately Held**
SIC: 2052 Crackers, dry
HQ: Lofthouse Bakery Products, Inc.
215 N 700 W Ste A10
Ogden UT 84404

(G-8048)
LOVEJOY INC (HQ)
2655 Wisconsin Ave (60515-4299)
PHONE.................................630 852-0500
Mike Hennessey, *Ch of Bd*
Arif Syed, *Controller*
Jim Mueller, *Finance*
Judy Brannen, *Sales Staff*
Roger Bain, *Manager*
◆ **EMP:** 193
SQ FT: 75,000
SALES (est): 92.1MM
SALES (corp-wide): 3.7B **Publicly Held**
WEB: www.lovejoy-inc.com
SIC: 3568 Couplings, shaft: rigid, flexible, universal joint, etc.; pulleys, power transmission
PA: The Timken Company
4500 Mount Pleasant St Nw
North Canton OH 44720
234 262-3000

(G-8049)
MACHINE SOLUTION PROVIDERS INC
Also Called: MSP
2659 Wisconsin Ave (60515-4244)
PHONE.................................630 717-7040
William A Novak, *President*
Michael P O'Brien, *Vice Pres*
Mike O'Brien, *Vice Pres*
Jeremy Gierich, *Foreman/Supr*
Barry Tomsky, *Purch Mgr*
▲ **EMP:** 55
SQ FT: 45,000
SALES (est): 28.8MM **Privately Held**
SIC: 3531 Roofing equipment

(G-8050)
MANSCORE LLC
1239 Gilbert Ave (60515-4516)
PHONE.................................630 297-7502
James Stocki, *CEO*
EMP: 3
SALES (est): 150K **Privately Held**
SIC: 7372 Application computer software

(G-8051)
MAR COR PURIFICATION INC
Also Called: Marcor
2850 Hitchcock Ave (60515-4016)
PHONE.................................630 435-1017
Kevin Peers, *Manager*
Kevin Pierce, *Manager*
EMP: 8
SALES (corp-wide): 918.1MM **Publicly Held**
WEB: www.mcpur.com
SIC: 5999 2834 Water purification equipment; chlorination tablets & kits (water purification)
HQ: Mar Cor Purification, Inc.
4450 Township Line Rd
Skippack PA 19474
800 633-3080

GEOGRAPHIC SECTION — Downers Grove - Dupage County

(G-8052)
MARKETING CARD TECHNOLOGY LLC
1213 Butterfield Rd (60515-1032)
PHONE..................630 985-7900
Pushparaj Venkitsamy, *President*
SRI Lala, *Vice Pres*
EMP: 90
SQ FT: 181,985
SALES (est): 21.3MM **Privately Held**
SIC: 7331 2754 2396 Mailing service; cards, except greeting: gravure printing; printing & embossing on plastics fabric articles

(G-8053)
MAXIMUM PRTG & GRAPHICS INC
911 Burlington Ave (60515-4716)
PHONE..................630 737-0270
David Dipple, *President*
EMP: 10
SALES (est): 1.5MM **Privately Held**
SIC: 2752 Commercial printing, offset

(G-8054)
MICROGUIDE INC
1635 Plum Ct (60515-1325)
PHONE..................630 964-3335
Glenn Krol, *President*
EMP: 3 EST: 1981
SALES (est): 318.1K **Privately Held**
SIC: 3842 Surgical appliances & supplies

(G-8055)
MICROSOFT CORPORATION
3025 Highland Pkwy # 300 (60515-5533)
PHONE..................630 725-4000
Joey Avraham, *Accounts Exec*
Mike Graef, *Accounts Exec*
John Notta, *Accounts Exec*
Greg Tipsword, *Accounts Exec*
Branislav Filipovic, *Sales Staff*
EMP: 60
SALES (corp-wide): 125.8B **Publicly Held**
SIC: 7372 Application computer software
PA: Microsoft Corporation
1 Microsoft Way
Redmond WA 98052
425 882-8080

(G-8056)
MIDPOINT PACKAGING LLC
2512 Wisconsin Ave (60515-4230)
P.O. Box 947 (60515-0947)
PHONE..................630 613-9922
Cory Lee, *Mng Member*
Michael Flanagan,
EMP: 7
SALES: 2.5MM **Privately Held**
SIC: 3086 5199 Packaging & shipping materials, foamed plastic; packaging materials

(G-8057)
MIDWEST THEOLOGICAL FORUM INC
4340 Cross St 1 (60515-1715)
PHONE..................630 739-9750
James Socias, *Vice Pres*
EMP: 5
SQ FT: 15,000
SALES (est): 572.3K **Privately Held**
SIC: 2731 Books: publishing only

(G-8058)
MOLDTRONICS INC
703 Rogers St (60515-3735)
PHONE..................630 968-7000
Henry J Schmidt, *President*
Patrick Bishop, *QC Mgr*
Eileen Schmidt, *Admin Sec*
EMP: 43 EST: 1940
SQ FT: 23,000
SALES (est): 9.7MM **Privately Held**
WEB: www.moldtronics.com
SIC: 3089 3545 3442 Molding primary plastic; machine tool accessories; metal doors, sash & trim

(G-8059)
MOLEX LLC
Molex Fiber Optics
5224 Katrine Ave (60515-4070)
PHONE..................630 512-8787
Frederick A Krehbiel, *CEO*
EMP: 14
SALES (corp-wide): 48.9B **Privately Held**
SIC: 3678 3679 3643 3357 Electronic connectors; electronic switches; electronic circuits; connectors & terminals for electrical devices; communication wire; fiber optic cable (insulated)
HQ: Molex, Llc
2222 Wellington Ct
Lisle IL 60532
630 969-4550

(G-8060)
MOTEC INC
555 Rogers St Ste 5 (60515-3776)
PHONE..................630 241-9595
Joanne Cleaves, *President*
Thomas E Cleaves, *Vice Pres*
▲ EMP: 5
SALES (est): 759.2K **Privately Held**
SIC: 3679 3714 3613 Electronic switches; motor vehicle parts & accessories; switchgear & switchboard apparatus

(G-8061)
MOTOROLA SOLUTIONS INC
1411 Opus Pl Ste 350 (60515-5717)
PHONE..................630 353-8000
EMP: 5
SALES (corp-wide): 7.8B **Publicly Held**
SIC: 3663 Radio & TV communications equipment
PA: Motorola Solutions, Inc.
500 W Monroe St Ste 4400
Chicago IL 60661
847 576-5000

(G-8062)
MPS CHICAGO INC (DH)
Also Called: Fulfillment Center, The
1500 Centre Cir (60515-1019)
PHONE..................630 932-9000
George Bogdanovic, *President*
Donal Murray, *Production*
Ron Roginski, *VP Sales*
Randy Fox, *Chief Mktg Ofcr*
Andrea Plachy, *Marketing Mgr*
▲ EMP: 190 EST: 1962
SQ FT: 160,000
SALES (est): 36.4MM
SALES (corp-wide): 18.2B **Publicly Held**
WEB: www.multipkg.com
SIC: 2752 3499 Color lithography; novelties & giftware, including trophies

(G-8063)
NATIONAL SPORTING GOODS ASSN
Also Called: Nsga Retail Focus
3041 Woodcreek Dr Ste 210 (60515-5419)
PHONE..................847 296-6742
Matthew Carlson, *CEO*
Matt Carlson, *CEO*
Dan Wiersma, *CFO*
EMP: 18 EST: 1929
SQ FT: 9,697
SALES: 2MM **Privately Held**
WEB: www.nsga.org
SIC: 8611 2721 8742 Trade associations; magazines: publishing only, not printed on site; business consultant

(G-8064)
NEC DISPLAY SOLUTIONS AMER INC (DH)
3250 Lacey Rd Ste 500 (60515-8003)
PHONE..................630 467-3000
Todd Bouman, *President*
Paul Redding, *Business Mgr*
Jennifer Cheh, *Vice Pres*
Rich Ventura, *Vice Pres*
Kirt Yanke, *Vice Pres*
◆ EMP: 140
SQ FT: 45,000
SALES (est): 34MM **Privately Held**
SIC: 3575 Computer terminals, monitors & components

(G-8065)
NICKELS QUARTERS LLC
1651 Bolson Dr (60516-2637)
PHONE..................630 514-5779
John Nickels, *Principal*
EMP: 4
SALES (est): 369.2K **Privately Held**
SIC: 3356 Nickel

(G-8066)
NITE OWL PRINTS LLC
1323 Butterfield Rd # 102 (60515-5620)
PHONE..................630 541-6273
Sandip B Mehta, *Principal*
Sejal M Shah,
EMP: 2 EST: 2010
SALES (est): 369.5K **Privately Held**
SIC: 2752 Commercial printing, lithographic

(G-8067)
NUTHEME SIGN COMPANY
2659 Wisconsin Ave (60515-4244)
PHONE..................847 230-0067
Mary Ann Giovenco, *President*
Len Giovenco, *Principal*
James Borys, *VP Opers*
EMP: 6
SQ FT: 3,750
SALES: 150K **Privately Held**
WEB: www.nutheme.com
SIC: 3993 Signs, not made in custom sign painting shops

(G-8068)
OLIN CHLOR ALKALI PDTS VINYLS
1001 31st St (60515-1342)
PHONE..................844 238-3445
EMP: 4
SALES (est): 513.6K **Privately Held**
SIC: 2812 Alkalies & chlorine

(G-8069)
PAPERWORKS
904 62nd St (60516-1901)
PHONE..................630 969-3218
Ellen Arnold, *Owner*
EMP: 3
SALES (est): 150K **Privately Held**
SIC: 2741 Business service newsletters: publishing & printing

(G-8070)
PAUL D STARK & ASSOCIATES (PA)
Also Called: Stark Aire Fluid Bed Dryers
509 Blackburn Ct (60516-3919)
PHONE..................630 964-7111
Paul D Stark, *President*
Andy Stark, *Treasurer*
EMP: 12
SALES (est): 2.1MM **Privately Held**
SIC: 3567 3564 3443 Driers & redriers, industrial process; air purification equipment; cyclones, industrial: metal plate

(G-8071)
PENRAY COMPANIES INC (PA)
2651 Warrenville Rd # 300 (60515-5772)
PHONE..................800 323-6329
Rodney H McKenzie, *President*
Steve Abrams, *Vice Pres*
William Nonnamaker, *Vice Pres*
Dave Campbell, *Purchasing*
Shannon Flint, *Purchasing*
◆ EMP: 83 EST: 1916
SALES (est): 22.6MM **Privately Held**
WEB: www.penray.com
SIC: 2842 2851 2869 2899 Cleaning or polishing preparations; degreasing solvent; paints & allied products; undercoatings, paint; industrial organic chemicals; oil treating compounds

(G-8072)
PEPPERIDGE FARM INCORPORATED
230 2nd St (60515-5249)
PHONE..................630 241-6372
Paul Caton, *Branch Mgr*
Yvette Poole, *Manager*
Maria Bliznick, *Supervisor*
EMP: 3
SALES (corp-wide): 8.1B **Publicly Held**
WEB: www.pepperidgefarm.com
SIC: 5461 2052 2099 2053 Bakeries; cookies; bread crumbs, not made in bakeries; frozen bakery products, except bread
HQ: pepperidge Farm, Incorporated
595 Westport Ave
Norwalk CT 06851
203 846-7000

(G-8073)
PERKINELMER HLTH SCIENCES INC
Also Called: Perkinlmer Lf Anlytcal Scences
2200 Warrenville Rd (60515-1764)
PHONE..................630 969-6000
Kenneth H Clear, *Principal*
David Linster, *Principal*
Steve Schaich, *Branch Mgr*
EMP: 198
SALES (corp-wide): 2.8B **Publicly Held**
SIC: 3829 3824 3823 2819 Measuring & controlling devices; fluid meters & counting devices; industrial instrmnts msrmnt display/control process variable; industrial inorganic chemicals
HQ: Perkinelmer Health Sciences, Inc.
940 Winter St
Waltham MA 02451
781 663-6900

(G-8074)
PERRYCO INC (PA)
Also Called: Enterprise Printing
6920 Webster St (60516-3509)
PHONE..................303 652-8282
Wayne Perry, *President*
Lee Crispe, *CPA*
Donald A Perry, *CPA*
Dayna E Roane, *CPA*
Beverly Perry, *Admin Sec*
EMP: 24
SALES (est): 3MM **Privately Held**
SIC: 2711 Newspapers, publishing & printing

(G-8075)
PETRO PROP INC
7948 Highland Ave (60516-4328)
PHONE..................630 910-4738
EMP: 7
SALES (est): 550K **Privately Held**
SIC: 3366 Copper Foundry

(G-8076)
PLAZE INC (HQ)
Also Called: Plz Aerospience
2651 Warrenville Rd # 300 (60515-5772)
PHONE..................630 628-4240
John Ferring IV, *Ch of Bd*
Ben Lacroffe, *CFO*
Scott Bauer, *Manager*
Karina Rimas, *Manager*
Tracy Wadford, *Info Tech Mgr*
▲ EMP: 124 EST: 1940
SALES (est): 175.7MM
SALES (corp-wide): 283.8MM **Privately Held**
WEB: www.plaze.com
SIC: 5169 2819 Aerosols; charcoal (carbon), activated
PA: Plz Aeroscience Corporation
2651 Warrenville Rd # 300
Downers Grove IL 60515
630 628-3000

(G-8077)
PLUMROSE USA INC (DH)
1901 Butterfield Rd # 305 (60515-7912)
PHONE..................800 526-4909
Dave Schanzer, *CEO*
Mike Krieger, *Vice Pres*
Freddy Mortensen, *Vice Pres*
Marlon Bingham, *Traffic Mgr*
Craig Getty, *Production*
▲ EMP: 50
SALES (est): 380.5MM **Privately Held**
SIC: 2011 5147 2013 5149 Hams & picnics from meat slaughtered on site; bacon, slab & sliced from meat slaughtered on site; meats & meat products; sausages & other prepared meats; specialty food items

Downers Grove - Dupage County (G-8078)

HQ: Jbs Usa Food Company
1770 Promontory Cir
Greeley CO 80634
970 506-8000

(G-8078)
PLZ AEROSCIENCE CORPORATION (PA)
2651 Warrenville Rd # 300 (60515-5772)
PHONE..................................630 628-3000
Ed Byczynski, *President*
Ed Hribar, *Vice Pres*
Aaron Barringer, *Project Mgr*
Ben Lacrosse, *CFO*
Matt Keller, *Regl Sales Mgr*
EMP: 37
SQ FT: 250,000
SALES (est): 283.8MM **Privately Held**
WEB: www.plzaeroscience.com
SIC: 2813 Aerosols

(G-8079)
PORTOLA PACKAGING LLC
1140 31st St (60515-1212)
PHONE..................................630 515-8383
Anthony J Allot,
Joseph A Heaney,
Frank W III Hogan,
EMP: 24
SALES (est): 12.2MM **Publicly Held**
SIC: 3089 Closures, plastic
PA: Silgan Holdings Inc.
4 Landmark Sq Ste 400
Stamford CT 06901

(G-8080)
POWDERED METAL TECH LLC
Also Called: Love Joy Technology
2655 Wisconsin Ave (60515-4243)
PHONE..................................630 852-0500
Michael Hennessy, *Manager*
EMP: 3
SALES (est): 329.7K **Privately Held**
SIC: 3444 Sheet metalwork

(G-8081)
PRACTICE MANAGEMENT INFO CORP
2001 Butterfield Rd # 310 (60515-1050)
PHONE..................................800 633-7467
Meta Rias, *Branch Mgr*
EMP: 30
SALES (corp-wide): 4.3MM **Privately Held**
SIC: 2731 Book publishing
PA: Practice Management Information Corporation
4727 Wilshire Blvd # 302
Los Angeles CA 90010
323 954-0224

(G-8082)
PRECISION BRAND PRODUCTS INC
2250 Curtiss St (60515-4038)
PHONE..................................630 969-7200
Terry Piper, *President*
Larry Franczyk, *Vice Pres*
Raymond Luchetti, *Admin Sec*
◆ **EMP:** 44
SQ FT: 50,000
SALES (est): 9.7MM
SALES (corp-wide): 327.2B **Publicly Held**
SIC: 3499 3429 3545 Shims, metal; manufactured hardware (general); machine tool accessories; bits for use on lathes, planers, shapers, etc.; drills (machine tool accessories); gauges (machine tool accessories)
HQ: Precision Steel Warehouse, Incorporated
3500 Wolf Rd
Franklin Park IL 60131
800 323-0740

(G-8083)
PRECISION CIRCUITS INC
2538 Wisconsin Ave (60515-4230)
PHONE..................................630 515-9100
George Cepynsky, *President*
Tegan Hengle, *Executive Asst*
EMP: 19 **EST:** 2000
SQ FT: 3,400
SALES (est): 4.6MM **Privately Held**
WEB: www.precisioncircuitsinc.com
SIC: 3679 Electronic circuits

(G-8084)
PRECISION PRINTING INC
1422 Centre Cir (60515-1021)
PHONE..................................630 317-7004
Kevin Bauman, *President*
EMP: 3 **EST:** 2010
SALES (est): 11.7K **Privately Held**
SIC: 2752 Commercial printing, offset

(G-8085)
PRODUCT SERVICE CRAFT INC
5407 Walnut Ave (60515-4106)
PHONE..................................630 964-5160
Fax: 630 964-5161
EMP: 10
SQ FT: 15,000
SALES: 900K **Privately Held**
SIC: 3499 3613 3466 Mfg Misc Fabricated Metal Products Mfg Switchgear/Switchboards Mfg Crowns/Closures

(G-8086)
RAILDECKS INTERMODAL
1311 Palmer St (60516-2732)
PHONE..................................630 442-7676
EMP: 3 **EST:** 2012
SALES (est): 206.8K **Privately Held**
SIC: 2448 Cargo containers, wood & metal combination

(G-8087)
REXNORD INDUSTRIES LLC
2400 Curtiss St (60515-4037)
P.O. Box Caller # 1482 (60516)
PHONE..................................630 969-1770
Lee J Ruesch, *Branch Mgr*
EMP: 100
SQ FT: 500,000 **Publicly Held**
SIC: 3568 Power transmission equipment
HQ: Rexnord Industries, Llc
247 W Freshwater Way # 200
Milwaukee WI 53204
414 643-3000

(G-8088)
S G S INC
Also Called: Logic Printing
900 Ogden Ave Ste 190 (60515-2829)
PHONE..................................708 544-6061
Hema Gajiwala, *President*
EMP: 2 **EST:** 1984
SQ FT: 500
SALES: 200K **Privately Held**
SIC: 2752 7336 7334 Commercial printing, offset; commercial art & graphic design; photocopying & duplicating services

(G-8089)
SAP AMERICA INC
3010 Highland Pkwy # 900 (60515-5547)
PHONE..................................630 395-2700
Aaron Green, *Vice Pres*
Richard Palak, *Project Mgr*
Julie McElvogue, *Manager*
Gary Stoltz, *Manager*
Gregory Brown, *Director*
EMP: 22
SALES (corp-wide): 30.4B **Privately Held**
WEB: www.sap.com
SIC: 7372 Prepackaged software
HQ: Sap America, Inc.
3999 West Chester Pike
Newtown Square PA 19073
610 661-1000

(G-8090)
SAWIER
7517 Florence Ave (60516-4482)
PHONE..................................630 297-8588
Justin Sawier, *President*
EMP: 46
SALES: 13.9MM **Privately Held**
SIC: 5999 3524 Tents; lawn & garden equipment

(G-8091)
SCOT INC
2525 Curtiss St (60515-4039)
PHONE..................................630 969-0620
Jonathan Bailey, *Vice Pres*
Mark Fosdal, *Purchasing*
Eric Green, *Engineer*
Jacob Robbins, *Engineer*
Nancy Saurbaugh, *CFO*
EMP: 7 **EST:** 2014
SALES (est): 779K **Privately Held**
SIC: 3621 Motors, electric

(G-8092)
SERVICENOW INC
2001 Butterfield Rd # 240 (60515-1050)
PHONE..................................630 963-4608
Lisa Gantos, *Sales Staff*
EMP: 5 **Publicly Held**
SIC: 7372 Prepackaged software
PA: Servicenow, Inc.
2225 Lawson Ln
Santa Clara CA 95054

(G-8093)
SIEMENS INDUSTRY SOFTWARE INC
2001 Butterfield Rd # 630 (60515-1050)
PHONE..................................630 437-6700
Geoff Halliday, *Principal*
Andrea Molinari, *Sales Mgr*
Chris Becker, *Director*
EMP: 34
SALES (corp-wide): 96.9B **Privately Held**
SIC: 7372 Business oriented computer software
HQ: Siemens Industry Software Inc.
5800 Granite Pkwy Ste 600
Plano TX 75024
972 987-3000

(G-8094)
SIGN SHOP EXPRESS
1015 Maple Ave Ste 1 (60515-4978)
PHONE..................................630 964-3500
Ed Carroll, *Owner*
EMP: 2
SALES (est): 200.9K **Privately Held**
SIC: 3993 Signs, not made in custom sign painting shops

(G-8095)
SIGNATURE OF CHICAGO INC
8428 Brookridge Rd (60516-4823)
PHONE..................................630 271-1876
Roberta Weimer, *President*
EMP: 3
SALES: 250K **Privately Held**
SIC: 2395 Embroidery products, except schiffli machine

(G-8096)
SILGAN WHITE CAP AMERICAS LLC
Also Called: Silgan Plstic Clsure Solutions
1140 31st St (60515-1212)
PHONE..................................630 515-8383
Ray Torres, *President*
Christopher Roth, *CFO*
Jeff Emmerling, *Technical Staff*
EMP: 19
SALES (est): 2.5MM **Publicly Held**
SIC: 3411 3444 Food & beverage containers; metal housings, enclosures, casings & other containers
PA: Silgan Holdings Inc.
4 Landmark Sq Ste 400
Stamford CT 06901

(G-8097)
SNEAKY CLEAN LLC
5117 Main St Ste B (60515-4676)
PHONE..................................312 550-9654
Randy Haines, *Mng Member*
EMP: 4
SALES (est): 156.7K **Privately Held**
SIC: 2842 Sanitation preparations, disinfectants & deodorants

(G-8098)
SPANNAGEL TOOL & DIE
2732 Wisconsin Ave (60515-4226)
P.O. Box 22, Medinah (60157-0022)
PHONE..................................630 969-7575
Brian Spannagel, *President*
Margaret Spannagel, *Admin Sec*
EMP: 20 **EST:** 1920
SQ FT: 15,000
SALES (est): 1MM **Privately Held**
WEB: www.spannageltool.com
SIC: 3544 3469 Special dies & tools; metal stampings

(G-8099)
STANLEY BLACK & DECKER INC
2854 Hitchcock Ave (60515-4016)
PHONE..................................630 724-3632
James M Loree, *President*
EMP: 3
SALES (corp-wide): 14.4B **Publicly Held**
SIC: 3429 Builders' hardware
PA: Stanley Black & Decker, Inc.
1000 Stanley Dr
New Britain CT 06053
860 225-5111

(G-8100)
TEASE
4717 Seeley Ave (60515-3413)
PHONE..................................630 960-4950
Allan Harris, *Partner*
EMP: 4
SALES (est): 240K **Privately Held**
SIC: 2759 Screen printing

(G-8101)
TECHNICAL ORDNANCE INC
2525 Curtiss St (60515-4060)
PHONE..................................630 969-0620
Ebby Bryce, *Branch Mgr*
Gregg Eichwedel, *Manager*
EMP: 201
SALES (corp-wide): 42.5MM **Privately Held**
SIC: 2899 Pyrotechnic ammunition: flares, signals, rockets, etc.
PA: Technical Ordnance, Inc.
47600 180th St
Clear Lake SD 57226

(G-8102)
TREEHOUSE PRIVATE BRANDS INC
3250 Lacey Rd Ste 600 (60515-7918)
PHONE..................................630 455-5265
Mark Fleming, *Vice Pres*
Kelli Adams, *Sales Staff*
Charles G Huber, *Branch Mgr*
Bernie Hirsch, *Manager*
Salina Smith, *Manager*
EMP: 13
SALES (corp-wide): 4.2B **Publicly Held**
SIC: 2043 2052 2068 2035 Cereal breakfast foods; crackers, dry; cookies; nuts: dried, dehydrated, salted or roasted; dressings, salad: raw & cooked (except dry mixes); seasonings & sauces, except tomato & dry
HQ: Treehouse Private Brands, Inc.
2021 Spring Rd Ste 600
Oak Brook IL 60523

(G-8103)
UNIQUE ASSEMBLY & DECORATING
2550 Wisconsin Ave (60515-4242)
PHONE..................................630 241-4300
James Gerberich, *President*
George Brown, *Shareholder*
Lynn Gerberich, *Admin Sec*
▲ **EMP:** 40
SQ FT: 20,500
SALES: 3MM **Privately Held**
SIC: 3089 2759 2396 Coloring & finishing of plastic products; screen printing; fabric printing & stamping

(G-8104)
VERTEC BIOSOLVENTS INC
1441 Branding Ave Ste 100 (60515-5624)
PHONE..................................630 960-0600
Skip Laubach, *President*
Gerald Vasek, *Vice Pres*
EMP: 6 **EST:** 1997
SQ FT: 4,000
SALES (est): 2MM **Privately Held**
WEB: www.vertecbiosolvents.com
SIC: 2869 Industrial organic chemicals

(G-8105)
WALLACE/HASKIN CORP
900 Ogden Ave 181 (60515-2829)
PHONE..................................630 789-2882
Kenneth Eng, *President*
Ashley C Eng, *Chairman*
▲ **EMP:** 5 **EST:** 1896
SQ FT: 10,000

GEOGRAPHIC SECTION

Dundee - Kane County (G-8131)

SALES (est): 496.9K **Privately Held**
SIC: **3556** 3546 3646 5085 Grinders, commercial, food; fish & shellfish processing machinery; power-driven handtools; fluorescent lighting fixtures, commercial; industrial supplies; abrasives & adhesives; saw blades & handsaws; cutlery

(G-8106)
WALNECKS INC
Also Called: Walneck's Cycle Trader
7923 Janes Ave (60517-3800)
PHONE...............................630 985-2097
Buzz Walneck, *President*
EMP: 2 **EST:** 1981
SALES (est): 273.1K **Privately Held**
SIC: **2721** Magazines: publishing only, not printed on site

(G-8107)
WATERS WIRE EDM SERVICE
2719 Curtiss St (60515-4002)
PHONE...............................630 640-3534
Ron Vondrasek, *Owner*
EMP: 5
SQ FT: 35,000
SALES: 400K **Privately Held**
SIC: **3312** Tool & die steel

(G-8108)
WELKINS LLC
3000 Woodcreek Dr Ste 300 (60515-5408)
PHONE...............................877 319-3504
Bill Elkins, *Officer*
Christopher Blodgett,
EMP: 5
SALES (est): 455.1K **Privately Held**
SIC: **3949** 3841 3842 Sporting & athletic goods; surgical & medical instruments; surgical appliances & supplies

(G-8109)
WHITE GRAPHICS INC
1411 Centre Cir (60515-1022)
PHONE...............................630 791-0232
Richard T White Jr, *CEO*
Andrew White, *President*
Thomas White, *Vice Pres*
Joyce R White, *Admin Sec*
EMP: 10
SALES (est): 1.9MM **Privately Held**
WEB: www.whitegraphics.com
SIC: **2752** Commercial printing, offset

(G-8110)
WHITE GRAPHICS PRINTING SVCS
1411 Centre Cir (60515-1022)
PHONE...............................630 629-9300
Richard T White Jr, *President*
Dee Zaremba, *Plant Mgr*
Kate Arsenault, *Sales Staff*
Pamela Bukovsky, *Office Mgr*
Joyce White, *Admin Sec*
EMP: 5
SQ FT: 15,000
SALES (est): 720.1K **Privately Held**
WEB: www.whitegraphics.com
SIC: **2754** 2759 Commercial printing, gravure; commercial printing

(G-8111)
WINNER CUTTING & STAMPING CO
1245 Warren Ave (60515-3548)
PHONE...............................630 963-1800
John Berwanger, *President*
Robert A Simpson, *President*
Ernest Dix, *Vice Pres*
Kevin Phillips, *Vice Pres*
Thomas Slott, *Vice Pres*
EMP: 11
SQ FT: 10,000
SALES (est): 2.1MM **Privately Held**
SIC: **3053** Gaskets, all materials

Downs
Mclean County

(G-8112)
PRAIRIE WOODWORKS INC
311 S Lincoln St (61736-7567)
P.O. Box 21 (61736-0021)
PHONE...............................309 378-2418
Ronald Skidmore, *President*
Stephen Stenger, *Treasurer*
EMP: 7
SQ FT: 10,000
SALES: 350K **Privately Held**
SIC: **2511** 2434 2431 Wood household furniture; wood kitchen cabinets; millwork

(G-8113)
TRUELINE INC
7095 Shaffer Dr (61736-7547)
PHONE...............................309 378-2571
Kenneth Mysvka, *President*
EMP: 20
SALES (est): 2.3MM **Privately Held**
SIC: **3569** Assembly machines, non-metalworking

(G-8114)
UNITED OIL CO
405 S Seminary St (61736-7583)
P.O. Box 1263, Bloomington (61702-1263)
PHONE...............................309 378-3049
Bill Chaney, *Owner*
EMP: 5
SALES (est): 415.5K **Privately Held**
SIC: **1389** Oil field services

Du Quoin
Perry County

(G-8115)
AMERICAN FUR ENTERPRISES
413 S Greenwood Ave (62832-2564)
PHONE...............................618 542-2018
Tyrone Lindner, *Owner*
Tyrone Lindner, *Owner*
EMP: 3
SALES: 38K **Privately Held**
SIC: **3999** Furs, dressed: bleached, curried, scraped, tanned or dyed

(G-8116)
BURKE TOOL & MANUFACTURING INC
339 E Olive St (62832-2316)
PHONE...............................618 542-6441
John Burke, *President*
Jeannie Burke, *Vice Pres*
EMP: 8
SQ FT: 13,000
SALES (est): 1.1MM **Privately Held**
SIC: **3599** 7692 3625 Machine shop, jobbing & repair; welding repair; relays & industrial controls

(G-8117)
COCA-COLA REFRESHMENTS USA INC
Hwy 51 S (62832)
PHONE...............................618 542-2101
Jim Walter, *Branch Mgr*
EMP: 116
SALES (corp-wide): 37.2B **Publicly Held**
SIC: **2086** 2087 Bottled & canned soft drinks; soft drinks: packaged in cans, bottles, etc.; fruit drinks (less than 100% juice): packaged in cans, etc.; syrups, drink; concentrates, drink
HQ: Coca-Cola Refreshments Usa, Inc.
2500 Windy Ridge Pkwy Se
Atlanta GA 30339
770 989-3000

(G-8118)
DUQUOIN DENTAL ASSOCIATES
1266 S Washington St (62832-3853)
PHONE...............................618 542-8832
Isaac E Davison, *President*
EMP: 4
SALES (est): 383.5K **Privately Held**
SIC: **3843** Dental equipment & supplies

(G-8119)
E & R MEDIA LLC
Also Called: Wdqn Radio
104 E Main St (62832-1421)
P.O. Box 411 (62832-0411)
PHONE...............................618 790-9376
Jeff Egbert,
Jerry Reppert,
EMP: 12
SALES: 200K **Privately Held**
SIC: **2711** 4832 7371 Newspapers; radio broadcasting stations; computer software development & applications

(G-8120)
FIVE STAR INDUSTRIES INC (PA)
1308 Wells Street Rd (62832-4171)
P.O. Box 60 (62832-0060)
PHONE...............................618 542-4880
Byford Reidelberger, *President*
Helen Mayer, *Vice Pres*
Tom Emling, *Treasurer*
Susan Englehart, *Exec Dir*
Susan Engelhardt, *Exec Dir*
EMP: 70
SQ FT: 40,000
SALES: 3.4MM **Privately Held**
SIC: **2511** 8361 8331 Wood lawn & garden furniture; rehabilitation center, residential: health care incidental; sheltered workshop

(G-8121)
GE FAIRCHILD MINING EQUIPMENT
707 N Hickory St (62832-1238)
Rural Route 51 (62832)
PHONE...............................618 559-3216
Russell T Stokes, *Branch Mgr*
EMP: 78
SALES (corp-wide): 57.7MM **Privately Held**
SIC: **3532** 3535 Mining machinery; conveyors & conveying equipment
PA: Ge Fairchild Mining Equipment
200 Fairchild Ln
Glen Lyn VA 24093
540 921-8000

(G-8122)
GENERAL CABLE INDUSTRIES INC
Also Called: Du Quoin, IL Plant
1453 S Washington St (62832-3803)
PHONE...............................618 542-4761
Tony Cannizzaro, *Controller*
Tom Lang, *Controller*
Kathy Hanks, *Human Res Mgr*
Erik Perks, *Manager*
EMP: 200 **Privately Held**
WEB: www.generalcable.com
SIC: **3357** Building wire & cable, nonferrous
HQ: General Cable Industries, Inc.
4 Tesseneer Dr
Highland Heights KY 41076

(G-8123)
PERRY ADULT LIVING INC
1308 Wells Street Rd (62832-4171)
PHONE...............................618 542-5421
John Childs, *Manager*
EMP: 6
SALES (est): 327.1K **Privately Held**
SIC: **8322** 3949 Social services for the handicapped; baskets (creels), fish & bait

(G-8124)
ST NICHOLAS BREWING CO (PA)
12 S Oak St (62832-1515)
PHONE...............................618 790-9212
Theodore Wichmann, *President*
Gary Sullivan, *Partner*
Abby Ancell, *General Mgr*
Karen Hand, *Vice Pres*
Sarah Andrew, *Treasurer*
EMP: 5
SALES (est): 520.9K **Privately Held**
SIC: **2082** Beer (alcoholic beverage)

(G-8125)
TRI-J MACHINE WORKS
546 N Howard St (62832-1000)
PHONE...............................618 542-2663
David Haner, *Owner*
EMP: 2
SQ FT: 1,400
SALES (est): 216.6K **Privately Held**
SIC: **3599** Machine shop, jobbing & repair

Dundee
Kane County

(G-8126)
CJ DRILLING INC
19n041 Galligan Rd (60118-9536)
PHONE...............................847 669-8000
Tammie A Johnson, *President*
Dylan Welsh, *President*
Charlie Fitzpatrick, *Vice Pres*
Charlie Johnson, *Vice Pres*
Marty Mohr, *Safety Dir*
EMP: 100
SALES (est): 17.1MM **Privately Held**
SIC: **1629** 3441 4213 7389 Caisson drilling; fabricated structural metal; trucking, except local;

(G-8127)
ENERGY GROUP INC (PA)
14 N 679 Il Rt 25 Ste C (60118)
PHONE...............................847 836-2000
Lawrence R Buettner, *President*
Ronald Walblay, *Corp Secy*
EMP: 30
SQ FT: 3,500
SALES (est): 2.5MM **Privately Held**
SIC: **1382** Oil & gas exploration services

(G-8128)
MAYTEC INC
901 Wesemann Dr (60118-9407)
PHONE...............................847 429-0321
Harold Ley, *President*
Thomas Paskiewicz, *Manager*
Dieter Ley, *Admin Sec*
▲ **EMP:** 9
SALES (est): 2.1MM **Privately Held**
WEB: www.maytecinc.com
SIC: **3354** Aluminum extruded products

(G-8129)
MEASUREMENT DEVICES US LLC
1001 Wesemann Dr (60118-9409)
PHONE...............................281 646-0050
Stephen L Ball, *Mng Member*
Sandy Borthwick,
Mike Hutchison,
Wendy Peters,
EMP: 10
SALES (est): 1.2MM **Privately Held**
SIC: **3812** 5049 Navigational systems & instruments; surveyors' instruments

(G-8130)
NORTHERN ILLINOIS MOLD CORP
17n520 Adams Dr (60118-9526)
PHONE...............................847 669-2100
Bruce Niggemann, *President*
Bill Fox, *Buyer*
EMP: 15
SQ FT: 20,000
SALES (est): 2.2MM **Privately Held**
SIC: **3544** Forms (molds), for foundry & plastics working machinery

(G-8131)
RENISHAW INC (HQ)
1001 Wesemann Dr (60118-9409)
PHONE...............................847 286-9953
John Deer, *Ch of Bd*
Leo Somerville, *President*
Denis Zayia, *President*
Andy Huber, *Business Mgr*
David Bozich, *Vice Pres*
▲ **EMP:** 68
SQ FT: 50,000

SALES (est): 13.8MM
SALES (corp-wide): 726.9MM **Privately Held**
WEB: www.renishaw.com
SIC: **2759** 5084 Commercial printing; industrial machinery & equipment
PA: Renishaw P L C
New Mills
Wotton-Under-Edge GLOS
145 352-4524

Dunlap
Peoria County

(G-8132)
BAKER DRAPERY CORPORATION
Also Called: Snap-A-Pleat Drapery System
4211 W Simpson Dr (61525-9272)
PHONE.................................309 691-3295
Chad Baker Jr, *President*
EMP: 2
SQ FT: 16,000
SALES (est): 367.9K **Privately Held**
SIC: **5023** 3429 2591 2391 Draperies; manufactured hardware (general); drapery hardware & blinds & shades; curtains & draperies

(G-8133)
HIDDEN HOLLOW STABLES INC
9222 Brimfield Jubilee Rd (61525-9149)
PHONE.................................309 243-7979
Kathy Simpson, *President*
EMP: 4
SALES (est): 204.8K **Privately Held**
SIC: **7999** 5812 1711 3599 Riding stable; eating places; boiler & furnace contractors; machine shop, jobbing & repair

(G-8134)
ITC INC
11808 N Hickory Grove Rd (61525-9173)
PHONE.................................309 634-1825
Daniel Ferrari, *CEO*
Giacomo Baldini, *President*
EMP: 2
SALES (est): 256.1K **Privately Held**
SIC: **3599** Machine shop, jobbing & repair

Dupo
St. Clair County

(G-8135)
CUSTOM BLENDING & PCKAGING OF
108 Coulter Rd (62239)
PHONE.................................618 286-1140
Dale Horne, *Mng Member*
Judy Hamilton,
Seelman Craig A,
▲ EMP: 11
SALES (est): 2.9MM **Privately Held**
SIC: **2841** 2813 2843 Soap: granulated, liquid, cake, flaked or chip; aerosols; surface active agents

(G-8136)
EARTHWISE RECYCLED PALLET
336 Mcbride Ave (62239-1640)
P.O. Box 162 (62239-0162)
PHONE.................................618 286-6015
Daryll G Mallin, *Owner*
EMP: 3
SALES (est): 249.5K **Privately Held**
SIC: **2448** Pallets, wood

(G-8137)
FLOWERS FOODS INC
Also Called: Flowers Baking
731 Prairie Dupont Dr (62239-1819)
PHONE.................................618 286-3300
Michael Henricks, *Branch Mgr*
EMP: 14
SALES (corp-wide): 4.1B **Publicly Held**
WEB: www.flowersfoods.com
SIC: **2051** Bread, cake & related products
PA: Flowers Foods, Inc.
1919 Flowers Cir
Thomasville GA 31757
229 226-9110

(G-8138)
HUCKS FOOD FUEL
110 S Main St (62239-1348)
PHONE.................................618 286-5111
Amanda Feiser, *Principal*
EMP: 15
SALES (est): 1MM **Privately Held**
SIC: **2869** Fuels

(G-8139)
KUNA MEAT COMPANY INC
Also Called: Kuna Food Service
704 Kuna Industrial Ct (62239-1823)
PHONE.................................618 286-4000
Daniel F Bippen, *President*
Mike Wochner, *Business Mgr*
Larry Lammert, *Vice Pres*
Larry Rudolph, *Vice Pres*
Richard Garavaglia, *Warehouse Mgr*
▲ EMP: 105
SQ FT: 90,000
SALES (est): 36.1MM **Privately Held**
WEB: www.kunafoodservice.com
SIC: **2011** 5149 5169 5144 Meat packing plants; groceries & related products; specialty cleaning & sanitation preparations; sanitation preparations; poultry & poultry products; fresh fruits & vegetables; meats & meat products

(G-8140)
MILLER MANUFACTURING CO INC
Miller Group
1610 Design Way (62239-1826)
PHONE.................................636 343-5700
Randy Castle, *President*
EMP: 80
SQ FT: 100,000
SALES (corp-wide): 12.1MM **Privately Held**
SIC: **2541** Wood partitions & fixtures
PA: Miller Manufacturing Co Inc
3301 Castlewood Rd
Richmond VA 23234
804 232-4551

(G-8141)
MULTIPLEX DISPLAY FIXTURE CO
Also Called: Miller Group Multiplex Div
1610 Design Way (62239-1826)
PHONE.................................800 325-3350
Randy Castle, *President*
EMP: 50
SQ FT: 97,000
SALES (est): 9.9MM
SALES (corp-wide): 12.1MM **Privately Held**
WEB: www.multiplexdisplays.com
SIC: **2541** 2542 2434 Display fixtures, wood; partitions & fixtures, except wood; wood kitchen cabinets
PA: Miller Manufacturing Co Inc
3301 Castlewood Rd
Richmond VA 23234
804 232-4551

(G-8142)
PROGRESSIVE RECOVERY INC (PA)
700 Industrial Dr (62239-1827)
PHONE.................................618 286-5000
Daniel B Marks, *President*
Rich Meyer, *Opers Mgr*
Jim Welsch, *Purch Mgr*
Don Fluchel, *Engineer*
Justin Bowers, *Project Engr*
EMP: 60
SQ FT: 60,000
SALES (est): 18.9MM **Privately Held**
SIC: **3569** Liquid automation machinery & equipment

(G-8143)
R T P COMPANY
1610 Design Way Ste B (62239-1826)
PHONE.................................618 286-6100
Garry Johnson, *President*
EMP: 3
SALES (est): 158.4K **Privately Held**
SIC: **2821** Plastics materials & resins

(G-8144)
STELLAR BLENDING & PACKAGING
1556 Decoma Dr (62239-1824)
PHONE.................................314 520-7318
Daniel G Connelly,
Jerry Lewinski,
Jeffrey C Walker,
EMP: 19
SALES (est): 2.2MM **Privately Held**
SIC: **7389** 2842 Packaging & labeling services; cleaning or polishing preparations

(G-8145)
STERLING PHRM SVCS LLC (PA)
109 S 2nd St (62239-1351)
PHONE.................................618 286-6060
Robert G Flynn, *Mng Member*
Sarah Henry, *Director*
Robert T Flynn,
EMP: 7
SQ FT: 3,600
SALES: 4MM **Privately Held**
SIC: **2834** Pharmaceutical preparations

(G-8146)
STOLLE CASPER QUAR & CONTG CO
Also Called: Falling Springs Quarry
2901 Stolle Rd (62239-1635)
PHONE.................................618 337-5212
Sharon Dell, *Manager*
EMP: 25
SALES (corp-wide): 55.9MM **Privately Held**
SIC: **1422** 1411 Crushed & broken limestone; dimension stone
PA: Stolle, Casper Quarry & Contracting Co Inc
3003 Stolle Rd
Dupo IL
618 337-3343

(G-8147)
TRAUBE CANVAS PRODUCTS INC
1727 Bluffview Dr (62239-1488)
PHONE.................................618 281-0696
Todd Traube, *President*
Don Traube, *Vice Pres*
EMP: 12
SQ FT: 2,400
SALES (est): 1.2MM **Privately Held**
SIC: **2394** Awnings, fabric: made from purchased materials; tents: made from purchased materials

(G-8148)
UPCHURCH READY MIX CONCRETE
200 N 2nd St (62239-1231)
PHONE.................................618 286-4808
Jim Upchurch, *Executive*
EMP: 3
SALES (est): 189.5K **Privately Held**
SIC: **3273** Ready-mixed concrete

(G-8149)
VERTEX CHEMICAL CORPORATION
3101 Carondelet Ave (62239-1176)
P.O. Box 277 (62239-0277)
PHONE.................................618 286-5207
John Helebusch, *Manager*
EMP: 14
SALES (corp-wide): 540.2MM **Publicly Held**
SIC: **2819** Bleaching powder, lime bleaching compounds
HQ: Vertex Chemical Corporation
11685 Manchester Rd
Saint Louis MO 63131
314 471-0500

(G-8150)
WINNING STREAK INC
1580 Decoma Dr (62239-1824)
PHONE.................................618 277-8191
Chris Braun, *President*
EMP: 93
SQ FT: 10,000
SALES (est): 3.6MM **Privately Held**
SIC: **2759** 5941 2395 Screen printing; sporting goods & bicycle shops; embroidery & art needlework

Durand
Winnebago County

(G-8151)
FOLK RACE CARS
9027 Freeport Rd (61024-9721)
PHONE.................................815 629-2418
Ron Folk, *Owner*
EMP: 3
SQ FT: 2,700
SALES (est): 338.9K **Privately Held**
SIC: **3711** 5531 7692 3599 Chassis, motor vehicle; automotive accessories; welding repair; custom machinery; top & body repair & paint shops

(G-8152)
GLO HEAT TREAT SERVICES LLC
1207 Cameron Dr (61024-9004)
PHONE.................................815 601-5728
Burk Glogowski,
EMP: 3
SALES: 750K **Privately Held**
SIC: **3589** Service industry machinery

(G-8153)
KR MACHINE
15322 Eicks Rd (61024-9641)
PHONE.................................815 248-2250
Karen Judd, *President*
Laurence Judd Jr, *Vice Pres*
EMP: 5
SALES (est): 250K **Privately Held**
SIC: **3469** Machine parts, stamped or pressed metal

(G-8154)
MULVAIN WOODWORKS
14578 Center Rd (61024-9525)
PHONE.................................815 248-2305
Patricia Mulvain, *President*
EMP: 5
SALES (est): 618.1K **Privately Held**
SIC: **2421** 2431 Sawmills & planing mills, general; millwork

(G-8155)
ROCK VALLEY PUBLISHING LLC
1102 Ann St (61024)
PHONE.................................815 654-4854
EMP: 12
SALES (corp-wide): 5.2MM **Privately Held**
SIC: **2711** Newspapers: publishing only, not printed on site
PA: Rock Valley Publishing Llc
7124 Windsor Lake Pkwy # 4
Loves Park IL 61111
815 467-6397

Dwight
Livingston County

(G-8156)
NEW LENOX MACHINE CO INC
1200 E Mazon Ave Ste B (60420-8218)
P.O. Box 188 (60420-0188)
PHONE.................................815 584-4866
Alan G Seniw, *President*
Carol Seniw, *Corp Secy*
EMP: 10
SQ FT: 22,000
SALES: 1.2MM **Privately Held**
SIC: **3599** 8742 3542 Machine shop, jobbing & repair; maintenance management consultant; rebuilt machine tools, metal forming types

(G-8157)
PAPER
204 E Chippewa St (60420-1408)
P.O. Box 245 (60420-0245)
PHONE.................................815 584-1901
Mary Boma, *Owner*

EMP: 22 **EST:** 2000
SALES (est): 890.1K Privately Held
WEB: www.thepaper1901.com
SIC: 2711 Newspapers: publishing only, not printed on site

(G-8158)
R R DONNELLEY & SONS COMPANY
R R Donnelley
801 N Union St (60420-7032)
PHONE.................................815 584-2770
Denise Seeman, *Manager*
EMP: 900
SQ FT: 357,000
SALES (corp-wide): 6.2B Publicly Held
SIC: 2752 2789 2759 2732 Commercial printing, lithographic; bookbinding & related work; commercial printing; book printing; miscellaneous publishing
PA: R. R. Donnelley & Sons Company
  35 W Wacker Dr
  Chicago IL 60601
  312 326-8000

(G-8159)
RIBER CONSTRUCTION INC
405 S Old Route 66 (60420-1290)
PHONE.................................815 584-3337
Paul Riber, *President*
Patsy Riber, *Corp Secy*
Mark Riber, *Director*
EMP: 12
SQ FT: 2,400
SALES: 2.4MM Privately Held
SIC: 1622 3273 Bridge construction; ready-mixed concrete

Earlville
Lasalle County

(G-8160)
EARLVILLE COLD STOR LCKR LLC
101 N East St (60518-8094)
P.O. Box 51 (60518-0051)
PHONE.................................815 246-9469
Gene Coppes, *Owner*
Margie Coppes, *Co-Owner*
EMP: 5 **EST:** 1937
SQ FT: 1,000
SALES (est): 380.2K Privately Held
SIC: 2011 2013 Meat packing plants; sausages & other prepared meats

(G-8161)
FREEDOM SAUSAGE INC
4155 E 1650th Rd (60518-6192)
PHONE.................................815 792-8276
Mark Wiley, *President*
Jim Pfau, *Treasurer*
Dave Gast, *Admin Secy*
EMP: 10
SQ FT: 6,000
SALES (est): 797.8K Privately Held
SIC: 7299 2013 Butcher service, processing only; sausages & other prepared meats

East Alton
Madison County

(G-8162)
ACE PRINTING CO
615 E Airline Dr (62024-1913)
PHONE.................................618 259-2711
Donald J Mitchell, *Owner*
Carolyn Mitchell, *Owner*
Carolyn Mitchelle, *Co-Owner*
EMP: 3
SQ FT: 2,700
SALES: 145K Privately Held
SIC: 2759 Visiting cards (including business): printing

(G-8163)
BRYAN METALS LLC (DH)
305 Lewis And Clark Blvd (62024-1177)
PHONE.................................419 636-4571
Tony Norden, *Mng Member*

▲ **EMP:** 5 **EST:** 1955
SALES (est): 21.9MM
SALES (corp-wide): 4.8MM Privately Held
WEB: www.olinbrass.com
SIC: 3331 3351 Blocks, copper; copper & copper alloy sheet, strip, plate & products

(G-8164)
DUGAN TOOL AND DIE INC
1145 E Airline Dr (62024-2283)
PHONE.................................618 259-1351
Mark Willmore, *President*
EMP: 19
SQ FT: 25,000
SALES (est): 4.2MM Privately Held
SIC: 3599 Machine shop, jobbing & repair

(G-8165)
FLOWERS DISTRIBUTING INC
Also Called: 7 Up
4605 Hedge Rd (62024)
PHONE.................................618 255-1021
Harry Flowers Jr, *President*
EMP: 20
SQ FT: 5,000
SALES (est): 3.1MM Privately Held
SIC: 2086 Bottled & canned soft drinks

(G-8166)
GLOBAL BRASS AND COPPER INC (DH)
305 Lewis And Clark Blvd (62024-1177)
PHONE.................................502 873-3000
Michael Psaros, *Ch of Bd*
John Wasz, *President*
David Kern, *Human Res Dir*
David Hagenbrock, *VP Sales*
Scott B Hamilton, *Admin Sec*
EMP: 2
SALES (est): 653.5MM
SALES (corp-wide): 4.8MM Privately Held
SIC: 3351 3341 3469 1542 Brass rolling & drawing; copper smelting & refining (secondary); metal stampings; commercial & office building, new construction

(G-8167)
NEWSSOR MANUFACTURING INC
302 Dry St (62024-1010)
PHONE.................................618 259-1174
Wendell Ross, *President*
EMP: 9
SQ FT: 7,300
SALES (est): 1.1MM Privately Held
SIC: 3599 5084 Machine shop, jobbing & repair; industrial machinery & equipment

(G-8168)
OLIN CORPORATION
Also Called: Winchester Ammunition
600 Powder Mill Rd (62024-1273)
PHONE.................................618 258-2000
Matt Brueckner, *Plant Mgr*
Kim Flaugher, *Manager*
EMP: 150
SALES (corp-wide): 6.1B Publicly Held
SIC: 3484 Small arms
PA: Olin Corporation
  190 Carondelet Plz # 1530
  Saint Louis MO 63105
  314 480-1400

(G-8169)
OLIN ENGINEERED SYSTEMS INC
427 N Shamrock St (62024-1174)
PHONE.................................618 258-2874
EMP: 3
SALES (est): 198K
SALES (corp-wide): 6.2B Publicly Held
SIC: 3449 Mfg Misc Structural Metalwork
PA: Olin Corporation
  190 Carondelet Plz # 1530
  Saint Louis MO 63105
  314 480-1400

(G-8170)
RONALD S LEFORS BS CPO
214 W Saint Louis Ave (62024-1122)
PHONE.................................618 259-1969
EMP: 4
SQ FT: 3,500

SALES (est): 220K Privately Held
SIC: 3842 5999 Mfg Surgical Appliances/Supplies Ret Misc Merchandise

(G-8171)
STAAR BALES LESTARGE INC
Also Called: Neon Works of St Louis
450 W Saint Louis Ave (62024-1123)
PHONE.................................618 259-6366
Christopher Staar, *President*
Dave Kapper, *Principal*
EMP: 4
SQ FT: 3,200
SALES (est): 220K Privately Held
SIC: 3993 1799 5046 Neon signs; sign installation & maintenance; neon signs

East Carondelet
St. Clair County

(G-8172)
ERIC HARR
7508 Triple Lakes Rd (62240-1712)
PHONE.................................618 538-7889
Eric Harr, *Owner*
EMP: 30
SALES (est): 1.3MM Privately Held
SIC: 3442 Metal doors

(G-8173)
STERLING PHRM SVCS LLC
102 Coulter Rd (62240-1346)
PHONE.................................618 286-4116
Jaime Kennedy, *Branch Mgr*
EMP: 12 Privately Held
SIC: 2834 Pharmaceutical preparations
PA: Sterling Pharmaceutical Services, Llc
  109 S 2nd St
  Dupo IL 62239

East Dubuque
Jo Daviess County

(G-8174)
AGGREGATE MATERIALS COMPANY
18525 Us Highway 20 W (61025-8505)
PHONE.................................815 747-2430
Harvey Seiler, *Superintendent*
EMP: 7
SALES (corp-wide): 739.3K Privately Held
SIC: 1442 Construction sand & gravel
PA: Aggregate Materials Company Inc
  5 Jones St Ste 1
  Dubuque IA 52001
  563 583-6642

(G-8175)
AIR LIQUIDE AMERICA LP
Also Called: Air Liquide Industrial U S
16675 Us Highway 20 W # 1 (61025-8605)
PHONE.................................815 747-6803
Scott Flemming, *Manager*
EMP: 7
SALES (corp-wide): 129.8MM Privately Held
SIC: 2813 Industrial gases
HQ: Air Liquide America L.P.
  9811 Katy Fwy Ste 100
  Houston TX 77024
  713 624-8000

(G-8176)
EAST DBQUE NTRGN FRTLIZERS LLC
16675 Us Highway 20 W (61025-8605)
PHONE.................................815 747-3101
Mark A Pytosh, *President*
Bill White, *Exec VP*
John R Walter, *Senior VP*
Neal Barkley, *Vice Pres*
Benjamin Carryer, *Engineer*
▲ **EMP:** 145
SALES (est): 10MM Publicly Held
SIC: 2873 Ammonium nitrate, ammonium sulfate

HQ: Cvr Partners, Lp
  2277 Plaza Dr Ste 500
  Sugar Land TX 77479

(G-8177)
KATS MEOW
288 Sinsinawa Ave (61025-1221)
PHONE.................................815 747-2113
Kathy Runde, *Owner*
EMP: 4
SALES (est): 159.1K Privately Held
SIC: 2085 Cocktails, alcoholic

(G-8178)
LANGE SIGN GROUP
1780 Il Route 35 N (61025-9681)
PHONE.................................815 747-2448
Dan Lange, *Owner*
Daniel Lange, *Officer*
EMP: 5
SALES (est): 459.7K Privately Held
SIC: 3993 Electric signs

(G-8179)
RENTECH DEVELOPMENT CORP
16675 Us Highway 20 W (61025-8605)
P.O. Box 229 (61025-0229)
PHONE.................................815 747-3101
John Diesch, *Branch Mgr*
EMP: 115
SALES (corp-wide): 150.7MM Privately Held
SIC: 2873 Nitrogen solutions (fertilizer)
HQ: Rentech Development Corporation
  4949 S Syracuse St # 320
  Denver CO 80237

(G-8180)
RENTECH ENERGY MIDWEST CORP
16675 Us Highway 20 W Upper (61025-8605)
PHONE.................................815 747-3101
John Ambrose, *President*
EMP: 6
SALES (est): 108.9K Privately Held
SIC: 2873 Nitrogenous fertilizers

(G-8181)
S AND K PACKAGING INCORPORATED
120 N Frentress Lake Rd (61025-9529)
P.O. Box 1681, Dubuque IA (52004-1681)
PHONE.................................563 582-8895
Shawn Stackis, *President*
▲ **EMP:** 5 **EST:** 2005
SALES (est): 590K Privately Held
WEB: www.sandkpackaging.com
SIC: 5199 2621 Packaging materials; wrapping & packaging papers

(G-8182)
SCHMALZ PRECAST CONCRETE MFG
18363 Us Highway 20 W (61025-8514)
PHONE.................................815 747-3939
Michael Schmalz, *President*
Marlene Schmalz, *Vice Pres*
EMP: 7
SALES: 350K Privately Held
SIC: 3272 Burial vaults, concrete or precast terrazzo; septic tanks, concrete

(G-8183)
SMITHFIELD PACKAGED MEATS CORP
Also Called: Smithfield Food
18531 Us Highway 20 W (61025-8505)
PHONE.................................815 747-8809
Marlene Wand, *Branch Mgr*
EMP: 6 Privately Held
SIC: 2011 Meat packing plants
HQ: Smithfield Packaged Meats Corp.
  805 E Kemper Rd
  Cincinnati OH 45246
  513 782-3800

(G-8184)
SOCIALCLOAK INC
399 Sinsinawa Ave (61025-1222)
PHONE.................................650 549-4412
Heath Hutchinson, *CEO*
EMP: 5
SQ FT: 1,500

East Dubuque - Jo Daviess County (G-8185)

SALES (est): 170.5K **Privately Held**
SIC: 7372 Publishers' computer software

(G-8185)
TERRY TERRI MULGREW
521 Montgomery Ave (61025-1034)
PHONE...................................815 747-6248
Terry Mulgree, *Owner*
EMP: 4 **EST:** 2000
SALES (est): 356.4K **Privately Held**
SIC: 2951 Asphalt paving mixtures & blocks

East Dundee
Kane County

(G-8186)
A AND T CIGARETTES IMPORTS
105 Prairie Lake Rd (60118-9137)
PHONE...................................847 836-9134
Deepti Shah, *President*
◆ **EMP:** 3
SALES (est): 194.3K **Privately Held**
SIC: 3999 Cigarette & cigar products & accessories

(G-8187)
ALLIANCE CREATIVE GROUP INC (PA)
Also Called: St. Louis Packaging
160 Windsor Dr (60118-9169)
PHONE...................................847 885-1800
Steven M St Louis, *CEO*
Greg Kardasz, *Vice Pres*
Kevin Piemonte, *Vice Pres*
Travis Taplin, *Opers Staff*
Paul Sorkan, *Admin Sec*
EMP: 22
SQ FT: 13,000
SALES (est): 10MM **Publicly Held**
SIC: 5199 2752 8742 Packaging materials; commercial printing, lithographic; marketing consulting services

(G-8188)
BAVIUS TECHNOLOGIE INC
205 Prairie Lake Rd Ste B (60118-9112)
PHONE...................................847 844-3300
Andres Much, *President*
Sandra Ebel, *Admin Sec*
◆ **EMP:** 9
SALES (est): 1.7MM
SALES (corp-wide): 355.8K **Privately Held**
SIC: 3549 3541 Metalworking machinery; machine tools, metal cutting type
HQ: Bavius Technologie Gmbh
Eisenbahnstr. 17
Baienfurt 88255
751 507-90

(G-8189)
CARSON PRINTING INC
Also Called: Cpiprint
1110 Heinz Dr Ste C (60118-2451)
P.O. Box 1017, West Dundee (60118-7017)
PHONE...................................847 836-0900
Terrence P Carson, *President*
Joie Carson, *Admin Sec*
EMP: 2
SQ FT: 4,000
SALES (est): 200K **Privately Held**
SIC: 2752 2796 2791 2759 Lithographing on metal; commercial printing, offset; platemaking services; typesetting; commercial printing; die-cut paper & board

(G-8190)
CUTSHAW INSTLS INC
216 Dundee Ave (60118-1627)
PHONE...................................847 426-9208
Leo Cutshaw, *Principal*
EMP: 3 **EST:** 2007
SALES (est): 178.9K **Privately Held**
SIC: 3643 Lightning protection equipment

(G-8191)
DAVITZ MOLD CO INC
570 Rock Road Dr Ste D (60118-2448)
PHONE...................................847 426-4848
David Davitz, *President*
Marlis Davitz, *Vice Pres*
EMP: 6
SQ FT: 1,500
SALES: 900K **Privately Held**
SIC: 3544 Industrial molds; special dies & tools

(G-8192)
DPS DIGITAL PRINT SVC
555 Plate Dr Ste 4 (60118-2465)
PHONE...................................847 836-7734
David Cohn, *Owner*
EMP: 5
SALES (est): 483K **Privately Held**
SIC: 2752 Commercial printing, lithographic

(G-8193)
DTS AMERICA INC
Also Called: Mod Tech
427 E 4th St (60118-1308)
PHONE...................................847 783-0401
Terry Aschenbrenner, *President*
Bob Schmidt, *Engineer*
EMP: 4
SQ FT: 3,500
SALES (est): 865K **Privately Held**
SIC: 3569 5084 Liquid automation machinery & equipment; industrial machinery & equipment

(G-8194)
DUNDEE DESIGN LLC
570 Rock Road Dr Ste P (60118-2448)
PHONE...................................847 494-2360
Steve Swanson,
Linda Swanson,
EMP: 3
SQ FT: 2,750
SALES (est): 359.6K **Privately Held**
WEB: www.dundeedesign.com
SIC: 3822 Building services monitoring controls, automatic

(G-8195)
DUNDEE TRUCK & TRLR WORKS LLC
Also Called: Dundee Truck Repair & Wash
407 Christina Dr (60118-3541)
P.O. Box 328, Algonquin (60102-0328)
PHONE...................................224 484-8182
Tj Bhathal, *President*
MB Bhathal, *Opers Mgr*
EMP: 7 **EST:** 2016
SQ FT: 11,000
SALES (est): 511.3K **Privately Held**
SIC: 7538 7542 3715 General truck repair; truck wash; truck trailers

(G-8196)
FRIGEL NORTH AMERICA INC
150 Prairie Lake Rd Ste A (60118-9131)
PHONE...................................847 540-0160
Duccio Dorin, *CEO*
Matteo Gallerini, *President*
Jacek Branka, *General Mgr*
Randy Burgardt, *Opers Mgr*
Francesco Cipriani, *Controller*
▲ **EMP:** 25
SALES (est): 4.2MM **Privately Held**
SIC: 3585 5075 Heating equipment, complete; warm air heating & air conditioning

(G-8197)
GMC TECHNOLOGIES INC
215 Prairie Lake Rd Ste A (60118-9125)
PHONE...................................847 426-8618
Gabriela Alvarez, *President*
Maritza Jagusch, *Treasurer*
M Carolina Vargas, *Admin Sec*
EMP: 8
SALES (est): 300K **Privately Held**
SIC: 3549 Metalworking machinery

(G-8198)
GRADS INC
Also Called: Custom Flooring Insets
205 Prairie Lake Rd Ste C (60118-9112)
PHONE...................................847 426-3904
Alan Stensrud, *President*
Gordon Smith, *Principal*
Ron Diskin, *Vice Pres*
Sandy Stensrud, *Admin Sec*
EMP: 6 **EST:** 1946
SQ FT: 5,000
SALES (est): 393.7K **Privately Held**
WEB: www.customflooringinsets.com
SIC: 2426 1752 Flooring, hardwood; floor laying & floor work

(G-8199)
GREAT SPIRIT HARDWOODS LLC
7 Jackson St (60118-1318)
PHONE...................................224 801-1969
Don Gleichman Jr, *Manager*
Skip Gleichman, *Manager*
EMP: 9
SALES (est): 519.1K **Privately Held**
SIC: 5211 2511 Millwork & lumber; wood household furniture

(G-8200)
HUMIDITY 2 OPTIMIZATION LLC
Also Called: H2o
105 Prairie Lake Rd Ste D (60118-9133)
PHONE...................................847 991-7488
Jeff Bossong, *Mng Member*
Anthony Graffia,
Christopher Rosman,
EMP: 11
SALES (est): 1MM **Privately Held**
SIC: 3823 1731 Humidity instruments, industrial process type; electronic controls installation

(G-8201)
HYDROSIL INTERNATIONAL LTD
125 Prairie Lake Rd (60118-9126)
PHONE...................................847 741-1600
William Waldschmidt, *President*
▲ **EMP:** 8
SQ FT: 5,000
SALES (est): 1.6MM **Privately Held**
SIC: 3564 Air purification equipment

(G-8202)
INTELEX USA LLC
105 Prairie Lake Rd (60118-9137)
PHONE...................................844 927-6437
Anthony R Graffia, *Principal*
EMP: 3
SALES (est): 241.3K **Privately Held**
WEB: www.intelexusallc.com
SIC: 2259 Towels, knit

(G-8203)
J N MACHINERY CORP
1081 Rock Road Ln (60118-2444)
PHONE...................................224 699-9161
Daniel F Pierre III, *President*
▲ **EMP:** 5
SQ FT: 3,700
SALES (est): 986.6K **Privately Held**
SIC: 3567 Heating units & devices, industrial: electric

(G-8204)
LAKE COUNTY TECHNOLOGIES INC
120 Prairie Lake Rd Ste E (60118-9128)
PHONE...................................847 977-1330
Robert Weskamp, *President*
Maryl S Weskamp, *Admin Sec*
EMP: 15
SQ FT: 7,800
SALES (est): 1MM **Privately Held**
SIC: 3599 Amusement park equipment

(G-8205)
MAXI-VAC INC
120 Prairie Lake Rd Ste C (60118-9128)
P.O. Box 668, Dundee (60118-0668)
PHONE...................................630 620-6669
Jeff Lichthardt, *President*
EMP: 4
SALES (est): 252K **Privately Held**
SIC: 3699 Cleaning equipment, ultrasonic, except medical & dental

(G-8206)
NATIONAL TOOL & MFG CO
Also Called: Ntm
563 Rock Road Dr (60118-2446)
PHONE...................................847 806-9800
Jim Soderquist, *President*
Scott Farley, *Vice Pres*
Mitch Predki, *Vice Pres*
David Niedbalec, *Prdtn Mgr*
Mike Murtha, *Purch Mgr*
EMP: 100
SQ FT: 38,000
SALES (est): 21.3MM **Privately Held**
SIC: 3599 Ties, form: metal

(G-8207)
ORANGE CRUSH LLC
507 Rock Road Dr (60118-2446)
PHONE...................................847 428-6176
Phil Doherty, *Plant Supt*
Tim Daniell, *Branch Mgr*
EMP: 7
SALES (corp-wide): 104.2MM **Privately Held**
SIC: 2951 1795 Asphalt paving mixtures & blocks; concrete breaking for streets & highways
PA: Orange Crush, L.L.C.
321 Center St
Hillside IL 60162
708 544-9440

(G-8208)
PETER FOX
Also Called: Hqf Manufacturing
578 Rock Road Dr Ste 4 (60118-2450)
P.O. Box 6581, Aurora (60598-0581)
PHONE...................................847 428-2249
Peter Fox, *Owner*
EMP: 5
SQ FT: 6,500
SALES (est): 300K **Privately Held**
SIC: 3965 Fasteners, buttons, needles & pins

(G-8209)
REX RADIATOR AND WELDING CO
578 Rock Road Dr Ste 5 (60118-2450)
PHONE...................................847 428-1112
Joseph Garboyan, *Manager*
EMP: 5
SALES (est): 332K
SALES (corp-wide): 3.4MM **Privately Held**
SIC: 7692 7539 7538 Welding repair; radiator repair shop, automotive; general truck repair
PA: Rex Radiator And Welding Co Inc
1440 W 38th St
Chicago IL 60609
312 421-1531

(G-8210)
S4 INDUSTRIES INC
140 Prairie Lake Rd (60118-9134)
PHONE...................................224 699-9674
James Del RE, *President*
Michael P Howlett, *Admin Sec*
▲ **EMP:** 15
SQ FT: 21,000
SALES (est): 3MM **Privately Held**
SIC: 3089 Injection molding of plastics

(G-8211)
TELSER LIGHTING ASSOCIATES LLC
Also Called: Vertical Lighting Controls
558 Plate Dr Ste 1 (60118-2458)
PHONE...................................630 800-5312
Joshua Albrecht, *Mng Member*
Matt Reynolds, *Mng Member*
John Molak, *Manager*
EMP: 9
SALES: 1.5MM **Privately Held**
SIC: 3648 Lighting equipment

(G-8212)
TLK INDUSTRIES INC
130 Prairie Lake Rd Ste A (60118-9130)
PHONE...................................847 359-3200
Douglas Sarrazine Jr, *President*
Ron Schumacher, *Opers Mgr*
Beverly Sarrazine, *Admin Sec*
Kenneth Schumacher, *Administration*
EMP: 60 **EST:** 1971
SALES (est): 6.7MM **Privately Held**
SIC: 7389 3444 Design services; sheet metalwork

(G-8213)
TLK TOOL & STAMPING INC
130 Prairie Lake Rd Ste C (60118-9130)
P.O. Box 340, Carpentersville (60110-0340)
PHONE...................................224 293-6941

GEOGRAPHIC SECTION
East Moline - Rock Island County (G-8239)

Kevin Sarrazine, *President*
▲ **EMP:** 8
SALES (est): 1.1MM **Privately Held**
SIC: 3469 Metal stampings

(G-8214)
UPLAND CONCRETE
563 Commonwealth Dr # 1000
(60118-2443)
PHONE.................................224 699-9909
EMP: 6
SALES (est): 925K **Privately Held**
SIC: 5211 5032 3273 Cement; concrete & cinder building products; ready-mixed concrete

(G-8215)
XCO INTERNATIONAL INCORPORATED
1082 Rock Road Ln Ste A (60118-2481)
PHONE.................................847 428-2400
Deborah D Kious, *President*
Patrick D Ertel, *Admin Sec*
EMP: 10
SQ FT: 2,000
SALES (est): 985.5K **Privately Held**
SIC: 3823 Thermocouples, industrial process type

East Hazel Crest
Cook County

(G-8216)
ADVANCE IRON WORKS INC
1325 171st St (60429-1906)
P.O. Box 4169, Saint Charles (60174-9079)
PHONE.................................708 798-3540
Robert J Sutphen, *President*
Robert Sutphen, *Vice Pres*
EMP: 16
SQ FT: 10,000
SALES (est): 2.6MM **Privately Held**
SIC: 3441 1791 Fabricated structural metal; structural steel erection

(G-8217)
ALLOY SLING CHAINS INC (PA)
1406 175th St (60429-1820)
PHONE.................................708 647-4900
Duane Kaminski, *President*
Michelle Billows, *General Mgr*
Milton Kanellakes, *Purchasing*
Tony Fastuca, *VP Sales*
Larry Pommier, *Manager*
▲ **EMP:** 85
SQ FT: 40,000
SALES (est): 18.2MM **Privately Held**
WEB: www.ascindustries.com
SIC: 3496 Slings, lifting: made from purchased wire

(G-8218)
TOOL AUTOMATION ENTERPRISES
Also Called: T A E Signals Division
1516 175th St Ste A (60429-1892)
PHONE.................................708 799-6847
John Kut, *President*
Patrick Kut, *Vice Pres*
Bruce Moorhouse, *Vice Pres*
Patricia McCarthy, *Admin Sec*
EMP: 6 **EST:** 1961
SQ FT: 27,000
SALES (est): 490K **Privately Held**
SIC: 3669 3469 3647 Railroad signaling devices, electric; metal stampings; flasher lights, automotive

(G-8219)
WELDING SPECIALTIES
17300 Laflin Ave (60429-1844)
PHONE.................................708 798-5388
EMP: 4
SALES: 200K **Privately Held**
SIC: 7692 3444 Welding Repair Mfg Sheet Metalwork

East Lynn
Vermilion County

(G-8220)
GREENE WELDING & HARDWARE INC
Also Called: Galvanized Stairs
41774 N Main St (60932)
P.O. Box 191 (60932-0191)
PHONE.................................217 375-4244
Paul S Greene, *Ch of Bd*
Rex A Greene, *President*
Rhoda Greene, *Treasurer*
Sumer Horton, *Cust Mgr*
Mike Adams, *Sales Staff*
EMP: 25 **EST:** 1961
SQ FT: 45,000
SALES (est): 3.6MM **Privately Held**
WEB: www.greenebinstairs.com
SIC: 7699 1542 3446 5251 Farm machinery repair; farm building construction; stairs, staircases, stair treads: prefabricated metal; builders' hardware

East Moline
Rock Island County

(G-8221)
A1 SKILLED STAFFING
915 15th Ave (61244-2137)
P.O. Box 364 (61244-0364)
PHONE.................................309 281-1400
Shawn Garcia, *Owner*
EMP: 26
SALES (est): 3.7MM **Privately Held**
SIC: 3537 Lift trucks, industrial: fork, platform, straddle, etc.

(G-8222)
ATLAS ROOFING CORPORATION
Also Called: Atlas Energy Products
3110 Morton Dr (61244-1964)
PHONE.................................309 752-7121
Crystal Kitterman, *Accounts Mgr*
Jennifer Sansone, *Accounts Mgr*
Randell Shaffer, *Manager*
EMP: 21
SQ FT: 120,000 **Privately Held**
SIC: 3296 3086 2952 Fiberglass insulation; plastics foam products; asphalt felts & coatings
HQ: Atlas Roofing Corporation
    802 Highway 19 N Ste 190
    Meridian MS 39307
    601 484-8900

(G-8223)
BI STATE STEEL CO
503 7th St (61244-1459)
PHONE.................................309 755-0668
Paul Thomas, *President*
Dennis Ahrens, *Vice Pres*
EMP: 5
SQ FT: 12,000
SALES (est): 934.1K **Privately Held**
SIC: 3441 7692 Fabricated structural metal; welding repair

(G-8224)
CENTRO INC
1001 13th St (61244-1734)
PHONE.................................309 751-9700
Joyce Swanson, *President*
EMP: 8
SALES (corp-wide): 213.4MM **Privately Held**
SIC: 3089 Molding primary plastic
PA: Centro, Inc.
    1 Centro Way
    North Liberty IA 52317
    319 626-3200

(G-8225)
DERBYTECH INC
700 16th Ave (61244-2122)
P.O. Box 576 (61244-0576)
PHONE.................................309 755-2662
Alan Derbyshire, *President*
Mark Riedesel, *Software Dev*
EMP: 26
SALES (est): 4.3MM **Privately Held**
SIC: 3571 5045 5734 7378 Computers, digital, analog or hybrid; computers; computer & software stores; computer maintenance & repair

(G-8226)
FUN INDUSTRIES INC
627 15th Ave (61244-1323)
P.O. Box 458 (61244-0458)
PHONE.................................309 755-5021
Roy Johnston III, *President*
Brandi Gustafson, *Sales Associate*
Judy Bowser, *Manager*
EMP: 10
SQ FT: 17,000
SALES: 1MM **Privately Held**
SIC: 3999 Coin-operated amusement machines

(G-8227)
GLOBAL FIRE CONTROL INC
1033 7th St Ste 1 (61244-1461)
PHONE.................................309 755-6352
Jeffrey G Oppenheimer, *CEO*
EMP: 4
SALES: 1MM **Privately Held**
SIC: 3669 5063 Fire alarm apparatus, electric; fire alarm systems

(G-8228)
HC DUKE & SON LLC (DH)
Also Called: Electro Freeze
2116 8th Ave (61244-1800)
PHONE.................................309 755-4553
Dorothy Ball, *General Mgr*
Dick Bryant, *Purch Dir*
Gary Almblade, *Engineer*
James Hamann, *Engineer*
Jim Hamann, *Engineer*
◆ **EMP:** 111 **EST:** 1931
SQ FT: 110,000
SALES (est): 17.9MM
SALES (corp-wide): 2.6MM **Privately Held**
WEB: www.electrofreeze.com
SIC: 3556 Ice cream manufacturing machinery
HQ: Ali Group Srl
    Via Piero Gobetti 2/A
    Cernusco Sul Naviglio MI 20063
    029 219-9

(G-8229)
I-N-I MACHINING INC
17128 Route 2 & 92 (61244)
P.O. Box 101 (61244-0101)
PHONE.................................309 496-1002
Nikki Young, *President*
EMP: 6
SALES (est): 1.1MM **Privately Held**
WEB: www.inimachining.com
SIC: 3599 Machine shop, jobbing & repair

(G-8230)
JDIS DEALERS
1400 13th St (61244-1443)
PHONE.................................309 765-8000
EMP: 12
SALES (est): 2.5MM **Privately Held**
SIC: 3523 Farm machinery & equipment

(G-8231)
KVF-QUAD CORPORATION
808 13th St (61244-1628)
P.O. Box 795 (61244-0795)
PHONE.................................563 529-1916
Michael Crotty, *President*
Tim Cain, *General Mgr*
Eric Davis, *Opers Mgr*
Melody Watters, *Human Resources*
Jim Wells, *Sales Engr*
EMP: 45 **EST:** 1976
SQ FT: 60,000
SALES (est): 7MM **Privately Held**
WEB: www.kvfquad.com
SIC: 3479 Coating of metals & formed products

(G-8232)
LCV COMPANY
919 15th Ave (61244-2137)
PHONE.................................309 738-6452
Lambros C Mihalopoulos, *President*
EMP: 6

SALES (est): 64.7K **Privately Held**
WEB: www.lcvco.com
SIC: 2099 Food preparations

(G-8233)
MATERIAL CONTROL SYSTEMS INC (PA)
Also Called: Matcon
375 36th St (61244-9525)
P.O. Box 437, Port Byron (61275-0437)
PHONE.................................309 523-3774
Donn R Larson, *President*
Judy Scott, *CFO*
Brad Palmer, *Manager*
▲ **EMP:** 52
SALES (est): 28.7MM **Privately Held**
SIC: 5099 2542 Containers: glass, metal or plastic; racks, merchandise display or storage: except wood

(G-8234)
MCLAUGHLIN BODY CO
1400 5th St (61244)
PHONE.................................309 736-6105
T Beinke, *Branch Mgr*
EMP: 120
SALES (corp-wide): 13.8MM **Privately Held**
SIC: 3441 Fabricated structural metal
PA: Mclaughlin Body Co.
    2430 River Dr
    Moline IL 61265
    309 762-7755

(G-8235)
NIXALITE OF AMERICA INC
1025 16th Ave (61244-1424)
P.O. Box 727 (61244-0727)
PHONE.................................309 755-8771
Marie Gellerstedt, *Ch of Bd*
Cory A Gellerstedt, *President*
John Gellerstedt, *President*
Keith Gellerstedt, *Exec VP*
George Winthurst, *Engineer*
▲ **EMP:** 16 **EST:** 1950
SQ FT: 25,000
SALES (est): 3.6MM **Privately Held**
WEB: www.nixalite.com
SIC: 3496 Miscellaneous fabricated wire products

(G-8236)
POWER-SONIC CORPORATION
1300 19th St Ste 200 (61244-2338)
PHONE.................................309 752-7750
Roger Lyll, *Principal*
EMP: 6
SALES (corp-wide): 52.5MM **Privately Held**
SIC: 3442 Rolling doors for industrial buildings or warehouses, metal
PA: The Power-Sonic Corporation
    365 Cabela Dr Ste 300
    Reno NV 89523
    619 661-2020

(G-8237)
QC SERVICE ASSOCIATES INC
1300 90th St Ste 110 (61244)
P.O. Box 525 (61244-0525)
PHONE.................................309 755-6785
Carl McNair, *President*
EMP: 30
SALES (est): 2.1MM **Privately Held**
SIC: 3549 Assembly machines, including robotic

(G-8238)
QUAD CITY ENGINEERING COMPANY
3650 Morton Dr (61244-1918)
P.O. Box 377 (61244-0377)
PHONE.................................309 755-9762
Roger Dolleslager, *President*
Rodney Delp, *Manager*
EMP: 22 **EST:** 1944
SQ FT: 28,000
SALES (est): 3.4MM **Privately Held**
WEB: www.quadcityeng.com
SIC: 3544 Dies & die holders for metal cutting, forming, die casting; jigs & fixtures

(G-8239)
R K PRODUCTS INC
3802 Jean St (61244-9648)
PHONE.................................309 792-1927

East Moline - Rock Island County (G-8240)

Philip Kester, *President*
Marilyn Kaster, *Vice Pres*
EMP: 4
SALES (est): 300K **Privately Held**
SIC: 3523 Farm machinery & equipment

(G-8240)
SIGN TEAM INC
5417 180th St N (61244-9423)
PHONE 309 302-0017
Alison Rodriguez, *President*
EMP: 2
SALES (est): 222K **Privately Held**
SIC: 3993 Signs & advertising specialties

(G-8241)
SMALL NWSPPR GROUP SHRED SVCS (HQ)
Also Called: Moline Dispatch Pubg Co LLC
1033 7th St Ste 101 (61244-1462)
PHONE 309 764-4344
Len R Small,
Joseph Lacaeyse,
Jean Alice Small,
EMP: 2
SQ FT: 60,000
SALES (est): 66.9MM
SALES (corp-wide): 131.4MM **Privately Held**
WEB: www.qconline.com
SIC: 2711 2752 Newspapers, publishing & printing; commercial printing, lithographic
PA: Small Newspaper Group
8 Dearborn Sq
Kankakee IL 60901
815 937-3300

(G-8242)
SMALL NWSPPR GROUP SHRED SVCS
Also Called: Leader Newspaper
1033 7th St Ste 101 (61244-1462)
PHONE 309 757-8377
Len Small, *President*
EMP: 3
SALES (corp-wide): 131.4MM **Privately Held**
SIC: 2711 Newspapers, publishing & printing
HQ: Small Newspaper Group Shared Services, Llc
1033 7th St Ste 101
East Moline IL 61244
309 764-4344

(G-8243)
TIMBERLINE PALLET & SKID INC
2500 8th Ave (61244-1831)
P.O. Box 631 (61244-0631)
PHONE 309 752-1770
Joseph Tindall, *President*
Joseph R Tindall, *President*
Stephen Duff, *Admin Sec*
EMP: 13
SQ FT: 40,000
SALES: 1.7MM **Privately Held**
SIC: 2448 5031 Pallets, wood; skids, wood & wood with metal; lumber, plywood & millwork

(G-8244)
TOPPERT JETTING SERVICE INC (PA)
1350 10th St (61244-1446)
P.O. Box 838 (61244-0838)
PHONE 309 755-2240
Debra Toppert, *President*
Ali Toppert, *Vice Pres*
Larry Toppert, *Vice Pres*
EMP: 3
SQ FT: 150,000
SALES (est): 1.8MM **Privately Held**
SIC: 7699 7389 8999 3589 Sewer cleaning & rodding; sewer inspection service; earth science services; sewer cleaning equipment, power; excavating slush pits & cellars

(G-8245)
VALSPAR
3560 5th Ave (61244-9548)
PHONE 309 743-7133
EMP: 3

SALES (est): 340.2K **Privately Held**
SIC: 2851 Paints & allied products

(G-8246)
VAN PELT CORPORATION
Also Called: Service Steel Division
2930 Morton Dr (61244-1959)
PHONE 313 365-3600
Robert Schwarm, *Branch Mgr*
EMP: 22
SQ FT: 87,350
SALES (corp-wide): 31.4MM **Privately Held**
SIC: 5051 3441 3449 Structural shapes, iron or steel; fabricated structural metal; miscellaneous metalwork
PA: Van Pelt Corporation
36155 Mound Rd
Sterling Heights MI 48310
313 365-3600

(G-8247)
WALLACE ENTERPRISES INC
1812 21st Ave (61244-2350)
PHONE 309 496-1230
Kevin R Wallace, *President*
EMP: 4 EST: 2000
SALES (est): 439.8K **Privately Held**
WEB: www.wallace-enterprises.net
SIC: 3844 Radiographic X-ray apparatus & tubes

(G-8248)
YASH TECHNOLOGIES INC
Moline Semicon
841 42nd Ave (61244-4134)
PHONE 309 755-0433
Manoj Baheti, *Branch Mgr*
EMP: 40 **Privately Held**
SIC: 3674 Semiconductors & related devices
PA: Yash Technologies, Inc.
605 17th Ave
East Moline IL 61244

East Peoria
Peoria County

(G-8249)
CATERPILLAR INC
100 Tractor Dr (61630-1200)
PHONE 309 675-2545
James W Owens, *Principal*
Heather Pendleton, *Buyer*
Ryan Rumler, *Technical Mgr*
Shiva Kalidas, *Engineer*
Martin Rebec, *Engineer*
EMP: 90
SALES (corp-wide): 53.8B **Publicly Held**
WEB: www.caterpillar.com
SIC: 3531 Construction machinery
PA: Caterpillar Inc.
510 Lake Cook Rd Ste 100
Deerfield IL 60015
224 551-4000

East Peoria
Tazewell County

(G-8250)
AMERIGREEN PALLETS
280 Fondulac Dr (61611-2602)
PHONE 309 698-3463
EMP: 3 EST: 2009
SALES (est): 130K **Privately Held**
SIC: 2448 Mfg Wood Pallets/Skids

(G-8251)
ARMATURE MOTOR & PUMP COMPANY
3011 N Main St Ste B (61611-4979)
PHONE 309 829-3600
Craig Doerr, *President*
Richard Jackson, *Manager*
EMP: 2
SALES: 250K **Privately Held**
SIC: 7694 Electric motor repair

(G-8252)
BBQ SMOKEWAGON INC
245 Farmdale Rd (61611-3088)
PHONE 309 271-7002
Connie Marizetts, *President*
EMP: 8
SQ FT: 2,150
SALES (est): 419.6K **Privately Held**
SIC: 5812 3556 Restaurant, family: independent; barbecue restaurant; smokers, food processing equipment

(G-8253)
BESSLER WELDING INC
5313 N Main St (61611-1398)
PHONE 309 699-6224
Albert Durst, *President*
David Crumley, *Vice Pres*
EMP: 13
SQ FT: 2,500
SALES (est): 1MM **Privately Held**
SIC: 7692 Welding repair

(G-8254)
BOLEY TOOL & MACHINE WORKS INC
1044 Spring Bay Rd (61611-1395)
PHONE 309 694-2722
Warren M Boley, *President*
Dan Weston, *Plant Mgr*
Frank Boley, *Finance*
Leaann Liesse, *Human Res Mgr*
Steve Summa, *Sales Executive*
EMP: 125 **EST:** 1963
SQ FT: 99,000
SALES (est): 29.1MM **Privately Held**
WEB: www.boleytool.com
SIC: 3519 5013 3599 3569 Parts & accessories, internal combustion engines; automotive supplies & parts; machine shop, jobbing & repair; assembly machines, non-metalworking

(G-8255)
CATERPILLAR INC
2000 Carver Ln (61611)
PHONE 309 675-1000
Julie Jones, *Branch Mgr*
EMP: 355
SALES (corp-wide): 53.8B **Publicly Held**
WEB: www.caterpillar.com
SIC: 3531 Tractors, crawler
PA: Caterpillar Inc.
510 Lake Cook Rd Ste 100
Deerfield IL 60015
224 551-4000

(G-8256)
CATERPILLAR INC
600 W Washington St (61611-2054)
PHONE 309 675-1000
Fax: 309 633-8695
EMP: 355
SALES (corp-wide): 47B **Publicly Held**
SIC: 3531 Mfg Construction Machinery
PA: Caterpillar Inc.
100 Ne Adams St
Peoria IL 60015
309 675-1000

(G-8257)
CATERPILLAR INC
600 W Washington St (61611-2054)
PHONE 309 495-9216
Troy Sams, *Engineer*
Jyothi Parupalli, *Info Tech Mgr*
Paul Klaus, *Technology*
Brad Rozboril, *Technology*
Geoff Bucher, *Analyst*
EMP: 65
SALES (corp-wide): 53.8B **Publicly Held**
SIC: 3531 Construction machinery
PA: Caterpillar Inc.
510 Lake Cook Rd Ste 100
Deerfield IL 60015
224 551-4000

(G-8258)
CATERPILLAR INC
901 W Washington St (61611-2044)
PHONE 309 675-3183
EMP: 22
SALES (corp-wide): 53.8B **Publicly Held**
SIC: 3531 Construction machinery

PA: Caterpillar Inc.
510 Lake Cook Rd Ste 100
Deerfield IL 60015
224 551-4000

(G-8259)
CENTRAL MANUFACTURING COMPANY
4258 Springfield Rd (61611-9217)
P.O. Box 420, Groveland (61535-0420)
PHONE 309 387-6591
Michael D McLemore, *President*
EMP: 6
SALES (est): 1.6MM **Privately Held**
WEB: www.centralmhs.com
SIC: 3535 3443 Conveyors & conveying equipment; fabricated plate work (boiler shop)

(G-8260)
CHIPS ALEECES PITA
Also Called: Anthony's
308 Illini Dr (61611-1825)
PHONE 309 699-8859
Alice Anthony, *Owner*
EMP: 5
SQ FT: 1,500
SALES (est): 406.3K **Privately Held**
SIC: 2096 Potato chips & similar snacks

(G-8261)
CLARIOS
Also Called: Johnson Controls
3850 N Main St (61611-5512)
PHONE 309 427-2800
Claudius Anderson, *Branch Mgr*
EMP: 28 **Privately Held**
WEB: www.johnsoncontrols.com
SIC: 2531 5063 Seats, automobile; electrical supplies
HQ: Johnson Controls, Inc.
5757 N Green Bay Ave
Milwaukee WI 53209
414 524-1200

(G-8262)
COBALT CHAINS INC
200 Catherine St (61611-3128)
PHONE 309 698-9250
Cristopher Robinson, *President*
Mike Robinson, *General Mgr*
Terry Schaad, *Sales Mgr*
Priscilla Cooper, *Admin Sec*
▲ **EMP:** 10
SALES (est): 2.4MM **Privately Held**
SIC: 3568 Power transmission equipment

(G-8263)
COPE PLASTICS INC
630 High Point Ln (61611-9304)
PHONE 309 787-4465
Steve Riexinger, *Principal*
EMP: 6
SALES (corp-wide): 246.9MM **Privately Held**
WEB: www.copeplastics.com
SIC: 5162 2821 Plastics materials; plastics materials & resins
PA: Cope Plastics, Inc.
4441 Indl Dr
Alton IL 62002
618 466-0221

(G-8264)
CROWN TROPHY
235 E Washington St Ste C (61611-7004)
PHONE 309 699-1766
Shari Prather, *Owner*
EMP: 3
SALES (est): 130K **Privately Held**
SIC: 5999 3479 3993 Trophies & plaques; etching & engraving; signs & advertising specialties

(G-8265)
DAPPER DEFENSE LLC
232 Pershing Pl (61611-2761)
PHONE 309 922-9203
Ryan McDonald,
EMP: 4 EST: 2017
SALES (est): 289.5K **Privately Held**
SIC: 3812 Defense systems & equipment

GEOGRAPHIC SECTION

East Peoria - Tazewell County (G-8294)

(G-8266)
ENERCON ENGINEERING INC (PA)
201 Altorfer Ln (61611-2038)
PHONE..................800 218-8831
Lawrence Tangel, *CEO*
Edward J Tangel, *President*
Nicholas Keever, *Vice Pres*
Keith Lozeau, *Vice Pres*
Paul Madeley, *Vice Pres*
◆ **EMP:** 101
SQ FT: 160,000
SALES (est): 48.2MM **Privately Held**
SIC: 3613 3625 Control panels, electric; control equipment, electric

(G-8267)
ENERCON ENGINEERING INC
301 Altorfer Ln (61611-2039)
PHONE..................309 694-1418
Edward Tangel, *Branch Mgr*
EMP: 70
SALES (corp-wide): 48.2MM **Privately Held**
SIC: 3625 3613 Relays & industrial controls; switchgear & switchboard apparatus
PA: Enercon Engineering, Inc.
201 Altorfer Ln
East Peoria IL 61611
800 218-8831

(G-8268)
FOUR SEASONS GUTTER PROTE
1815 Meadow Ave (61611-3605)
PHONE..................309 694-4565
Jeff Harper, *Owner*
EMP: 4
SALES (est): 417.2K **Privately Held**
SIC: 1761 3089 Siding contractor; gutters (glass fiber reinforced), fiberglass or plastic

(G-8269)
GMH METAL FABRICATION INC
136 Fleur De Lis Dr (61611-2155)
PHONE..................309 253-6429
Terry Leong, *President*
Gary M Hagel, *Admin Sec*
EMP: 2
SALES (est): 221.3K **Privately Held**
SIC: 3449 Miscellaneous metalwork

(G-8270)
J H BENEDICT CO INC
3211 N Main St (61611-1790)
PHONE..................309 694-3111
Robert M Jones, *President*
Chad Miars, *COO*
David Gilbert, *Vice Pres*
Austin Jones, *Plant Mgr*
Ed Metts, *Purch Agent*
EMP: 53 **EST:** 1946
SQ FT: 26,500
SALES (est): 10.7MM **Privately Held**
WEB: www.jhbenedict.com
SIC: 3545 3544 Machine tool accessories; special dies & tools

(G-8271)
J&J READY MIX INC
100 Cass St (61611-2408)
PHONE..................309 676-0579
Dave Minor, *Principal*
EMP: 3
SALES (est): 203.8K **Privately Held**
SIC: 3273 Ready-mixed concrete

(G-8272)
JK WILLIAMS DISTILLING LLC (PA)
526 High Point Ln (61611-9327)
PHONE..................309 839-0591
Jonathan A Williams,
EMP: 5
SALES (est): 1.2MM **Privately Held**
WEB: www.jkwilliamsdistilling.com
SIC: 2085 Scotch whiskey; bourbon whiskey; rye whiskey

(G-8273)
JTEC INDUSTRIES INC
201 Carver Ln (61611-3016)
PHONE..................309 698-9301
Jonathan S Peterson, *President*

Joseph Knepp, *Admin Sec*
EMP: 50
SQ FT: 13,500
SALES (est): 15.8MM **Privately Held**
SIC: 3089 4213 Plastic containers, except foam; trailer or container on flat car (TOFC/COFC)

(G-8274)
KELLEY ORNAMENTAL IRON LLC (PA)
Also Called: Kelley Iron Works
4303 N Main St (61611-1455)
PHONE..................309 697-9870
Joel Hoerr, *Mng Member*
EMP: 25 **EST:** 1948
SALES (est): 3.2MM **Privately Held**
SIC: 3446 Ornamental metalwork

(G-8275)
KROGER CO
201 S Main St (61611-2458)
PHONE..................309 694-6298
April Smith, *Branch Mgr*
EMP: 130
SALES (corp-wide): 122.2B **Publicly Held**
SIC: 5411 5992 5912 2051 Supermarkets, chain; florists; drug stores & proprietary stores; bread, cake & related products
PA: The Kroger Co
1014 Vine St Ste 1000
Cincinnati OH 45202
513 762-4000

(G-8276)
LAHOOD CONSTRUCTION INC
3305 N Main St (61611-1566)
PHONE..................309 699-5080
Joe Lahood, *President*
EMP: 35 **EST:** 1991
SALES (est): 5.9MM **Privately Held**
WEB: www.lahoodconstruction.com
SIC: 3273 Ready-mixed concrete

(G-8277)
METROPOLITAN PRINTERS
109 E Washington St (61611-2566)
P.O. Box 2416 (61611-0416)
PHONE..................309 694-1114
Fax: 309 694-2871
EMP: 4
SQ FT: 1,500
SALES (est): 250K **Privately Held**
SIC: 2752 Lithographic Commercial Printing

(G-8278)
MEYER ENTERPRISES LLC (PA)
Also Called: ISI Building Products
401 Truck Haven Rd (61611-1356)
PHONE..................309 698-0062
Donald L Meyer,
Thomas Fahey,
Connie Klinkdradt,
James Klinkdradt,
Charles Meyer,
EMP: 3 **EST:** 1997
SQ FT: 40,000
SALES (est): 8MM **Privately Held**
SIC: 5033 2621 Insulation materials; insulation siding, paper

(G-8279)
NEO ORTHOTICS INC
100 Park Pl (61611-1493)
PHONE..................309 699-0354
Timothy W Potendyk, *President*
EMP: 2
SALES (est): 230K **Privately Held**
SIC: 3842 Orthopedic appliances

(G-8280)
OLYMPIA MANUFACTURING INC
101 Annie Ln (61611-9568)
PHONE..................309 387-2633
Richard Gedhardt, *President*
EMP: 8
SALES (est): 497.4K **Privately Held**
SIC: 3444 Sheet metalwork

(G-8281)
PAFCO TRUCK BODIES INC
1954 E Washington St (61611-2959)
PHONE..................309 699-4613

Max F Pfaffmann, *President*
Ida H Pfaffmann, *Corp Secy*
Robert W Pfaffmann, *Vice Pres*
EMP: 10
SQ FT: 12,000
SALES (est): 1.5MM **Privately Held**
WEB: www.e-pafco.com
SIC: 3713 Truck & bus bodies

(G-8282)
PARKER FABRICATION INC
3700 N Main St (61611-1447)
PHONE..................309 698-8080
Jim Zimmerman, *President*
EMP: 4
SALES (est): 260K **Privately Held**
WEB: www.parkerfabrication.com
SIC: 3498 Tube fabricating (contract bending & shaping)
PA: Parker Fabrication, Inc.
501 E Courtland St
Morton IL 61550

(G-8283)
PERDUE PAVEMENT SOLUTIONS INC
3202 E Washington St (61611-1955)
PHONE..................309 698-9440
Doug Perdue, *President*
Audra Perdue, *Vice Pres*
EMP: 10
SALES (est): 203.8K **Privately Held**
SIC: 2952 Sheathing, asphalt saturated

(G-8284)
PREMIER BEVERAGE SOLUTIONS LLC
805 Oakwood Rd (61611-1652)
PHONE..................309 369-7117
Pete Bennett, *Vice Pres*
EMP: 2
SALES (est): 200K **Privately Held**
SIC: 2037 Frozen fruits & vegetables

(G-8285)
QUICK PRINT SHOPPE
500 Fondulac Dr (61611-2161)
PHONE..................309 694-1204
David R Blair, *Owner*
EMP: 3 **EST:** 2001
SALES (est): 200K **Privately Held**
SIC: 2752 Commercial printing, offset

(G-8286)
RAYS MACHINE & MFG CO INC
419 Truck Haven Rd (61611-1356)
PHONE..................309 699-2121
Hylee Matthew Kemp, *President*
EMP: 10 **EST:** 1971
SALES: 3.8MM
SALES (corp-wide): 14.9MM **Privately Held**
SIC: 3599 Machine shop, jobbing & repair
PA: Kemp Manufacturing Company
4310 N Voss St
Peoria IL 61616
309 682-7292

(G-8287)
RJ DISTRIBUTING CO
410 High Point Ln (61611-9479)
PHONE..................309 685-2794
Robert A Jockisch, *President*
Gordon R Jockisch, *Vice Pres*
Brian Jockisch, *Manager*
▲ **EMP:** 35 **EST:** 1945
SQ FT: 20,000
SALES (est): 14.4MM **Privately Held**
WEB: www.mostrefreshingfriend.com
SIC: 5181 5182 2869 Beer & other fermented malt liquors; wine; alcohols, non-beverage

(G-8288)
ROANOKE CONCRETE PRODUCTS CO
1275 Spring Bay Rd (61611-9779)
PHONE..................309 698-7882
Gerald W Hodel Roanoke, *President*
EMP: 15
SALES (corp-wide): 9.7MM **Privately Held**
SIC: 3273 Ready-mixed concrete

PA: Roanoke Concrete Products Co.
1275 Springbay Rd E
Peoria IL 61611
309 698-7882

(G-8289)
SC2 INC
200 Carver Ln (61611-3029)
PHONE..................309 677-5980
Steve Baumann, *COO*
Lindsay Egel, *Opers Staff*
Randy Rarick, *Manager*
EMP: 2
SALES (est): 204.5K **Privately Held**
SIC: 3479 Metal coating & allied service

(G-8290)
SELNAR INC
Also Called: American Speedy Printing
240 Farmdale Rd (61611-3015)
PHONE..................309 699-3977
Keith Hopkins, *President*
Leslie A Hopkins, *Treasurer*
EMP: 3
SALES (est): 500.7K **Privately Held**
SIC: 5943 2752 Office forms & supplies; commercial printing, lithographic

(G-8291)
SOPHER DESIGN & MANUFACTURING
3312 Meadow Ave (61611-4639)
PHONE..................309 699-6419
Terry Sopher, *President*
Jennifer Stout, *Admin Sec*
EMP: 7
SQ FT: 4,500
SALES: 400K **Privately Held**
SIC: 3544 3523 3555 Special dies & tools; farm machinery & equipment; printing trades machinery

(G-8292)
TAG TOOL SERVICES INCORPORATED
Also Called: County Line Tool
3303 N Main St (61611-6009)
PHONE..................309 694-2400
Vonda Jones, *President*
Brock Jones, *Sales Engr*
Austin L Jones, *Admin Sec*
EMP: 23
SALES (est): 4MM **Privately Held**
SIC: 3545 Cutting tools for machine tools

(G-8293)
UNITED SEATING & MOBILITY LLC
125 Thunderbird Ln Ste 1 (61611-5536)
PHONE..................309 699-0509
Tamas Feitel, *CFO*
EMP: 4
SALES (corp-wide): 3.3B **Privately Held**
WEB: www.numotion.com
SIC: 3842 Wheelchairs
HQ: United Seating & Mobility Llc
975 Hornet Dr
Hazelwood MO 63042
800 500-9150

(G-8294)
VERSA PRESS INC
1465 Spring Bay Rd (61611-9788)
PHONE..................309 822-0260
Steven J Kennell, *President*
Kristine Losby, *Vice Pres*
Kelli Gatton, *Production*
Pam Larson, *Production*
Larry Miller, *Production*
EMP: 185
SQ FT: 145,000
SALES (est): 54.2MM **Privately Held**
WEB: www.versapress.com
SIC: 2752 Commercial printing, offset

East Saint Louis
St. Clair County

(G-8295)
ACCU-WRIGHT FIBERGLASS INC
2393 Carol St (62206-2722)
PHONE..................................618 337-3318
Steve Wright, *President*
EMP: 5
SALES (est): 512.7K **Privately Held**
SIC: **1799** 7699 2221 Fiberglass work; boat repair; fiberglass fabrics

(G-8296)
AFTON CHEMICAL CORPORATION
501 Monsanto Ave (62206-1138)
PHONE..................................618 583-1000
Christopher Conley, *Vice Pres*
Carolyn Garrett, *Plant Mgr*
Ken Shock, *Opers Mgr*
Greg Giedeman, *Safety Mgr*
Reggie Maclin, *Safety Mgr*
EMP: 292
SALES (corp-wide): 2.1B **Publicly Held**
SIC: **2869** 3566 2899 2841 Industrial organic chemicals; speed changers, drives & gears; chemical preparations; soap & other detergents
HQ: Afton Chemical Corporation
500 Spring St
Richmond VA 23219
804 788-5800

(G-8297)
ATLAS READY MIX INC
2901 Missouri Ave (62205-1122)
PHONE..................................618 271-0774
Greg Upchurch, *President*
EMP: 5
SALES (est): 213.5K **Privately Held**
SIC: **3273** Ready-mixed concrete

(G-8298)
AVTEC INC
6 Industrial Dr (62206-1023)
PHONE..................................618 337-7800
Bouchaib Ziadi, *President*
Chris Gresick, *VP Sales*
Susan Jumper, *Admin Asst*
EMP: 15
SQ FT: 4,000
SALES (est): 2.8MM **Privately Held**
SIC: **3646** Commercial indusl & institutional electric lighting fixtures

(G-8299)
BEELMAN READY-MIX INC (PA)
1 Racehorse Dr (62205-1001)
PHONE..................................618 646-5300
Frank Beelman III, *President*
Sam Beelman, *President*
Michele Haselhorst, *Mktg Dir*
EMP: 34
SALES (est): 14MM **Privately Held**
SIC: **3273** Ready-mixed concrete

(G-8300)
BLUE NILE TRUCKING LLC
404 N 27th St (62205-1708)
PHONE..................................618 215-1077
EMP: 3
SALES (est): 214.5K **Privately Held**
SIC: **3537** Mfg Industrial Trucks/Tractors

(G-8301)
CHEMTRADE CHEMICALS US LLC
2500 Kingshighway (62201-2446)
PHONE..................................618 274-4363
Don Brown, *Opers-Prdtn-Mfg*
Brian Wiese, *Director*
EMP: 25
SALES (corp-wide): 1.1B **Privately Held**
SIC: **2819** Aluminum sulfate
HQ: Chemtrade Chemicals Us Llc
90 E Halsey Rd
Parsippany NJ 07054

(G-8302)
CONCRETE SUPPLY LLC
Also Called: Concrete Supply of Illinois
1 Racehorse Dr (62205-1001)
PHONE..................................618 646-5300
Marianne Pelate, *Manager*
EMP: 1
SALES (est): 1,000K **Privately Held**
SIC: **3273** Ready-mixed concrete

(G-8303)
DELICIOUS TREATS LLC
1905 Marseilles Dr (62206-2605)
PHONE..................................618 410-6722
Janet Woolfolk,
EMP: 6
SALES (est): 75K **Privately Held**
SIC: **2024** Ice cream & frozen desserts

(G-8304)
DOUGHERTY E J OIL & STONE SUP
1501 Lincoln Ave (62204-1041)
PHONE..................................618 271-4414
E J Dougherty Jr, *President*
Deborah L Dougherty, *Admin Sec*
EMP: 7 EST: 1957
SQ FT: 5,000
SALES (est): 1.5MM **Privately Held**
SIC: **5172** 2951 Petroleum products; asphalt paving mixtures & blocks

(G-8305)
DOXA ENTERPRISES LLC
1798 Summit Ave (62205-2800)
PHONE..................................618 515-4470
Daneen Turner,
Chassidy Blackwell,
Barbara Taylor,
EMP: 3
SALES (est): 131.8K **Privately Held**
SIC: **8748** 2731 5961 7389 Business consulting; book publishing; women's apparel, mail order;

(G-8306)
EAST ST LOUIS TRML & STOR CO
1501 Lincoln Ave (62204-1041)
PHONE..................................618 271-2185
James A Dougherty, *President*
Edward J Dougherty Jr, *Vice Pres*
EMP: 25
SQ FT: 5,000
SALES (est): 2MM **Privately Held**
SIC: **4231** 1389 4226 Trucking terminal facilities; processing service, gas; petroleum & chemical bulk stations & terminals for hire

(G-8307)
ETHYL CORP
501 Monsanto Ave (62206-1138)
PHONE..................................618 583-1292
J Tiemann, *Human Res Mgr*
EMP: 3
SALES (est): 207.7K **Privately Held**
SIC: **2869** Industrial organic chemicals

(G-8308)
GASKET & SEAL FABRICATORS INC
1640 Sauget Indl Pkwy (62206-1449)
PHONE..................................314 241-3673
Gerald Johnson, *President*
Jason Tabares, *Sales Staff*
▲ EMP: 20
SQ FT: 40,000
SALES (est): 5MM **Privately Held**
SIC: **3053** Gaskets, all materials

(G-8309)
GATEWAY CRUSHING & SCREENING
3936 Mississippi Ave (62206-1060)
PHONE..................................618 337-1954
Johnny R Baur, *President*
EMP: 20
SALES (est): 1.7MM **Privately Held**
SIC: **1429** Igneous rock, crushed & broken-quarrying

(G-8310)
GATEWAY FABRICATORS INC
633 Collinsville Ave (62201-1309)
P.O. Box 2193 (62202-2193)
PHONE..................................618 271-5700
Kevin J Mocabee, *President*
EMP: 7
SQ FT: 18,000
SALES (est): 600K **Privately Held**
SIC: **3443** Fabricated plate work (boiler shop)

(G-8311)
ILLINI DIGITAL PRINTING CO
680 N 20th St (62205-1812)
PHONE..................................618 271-6622
John Eichelberger, *Principal*
EMP: 4
SALES (est): 379.8K **Privately Held**
SIC: **2752** Commercial printing, offset

(G-8312)
INDUSTRIAL GAS PRODUCTS INC
2350 Falling Springs Rd (62206-1102)
PHONE..................................618 337-1030
Robert Clarkson, *President*
Rick Clarkson, *Treasurer*
Rhonda Wheeler, *Bookkeeper*
EMP: 6
SQ FT: 6,500
SALES (est): 1.4MM **Privately Held**
SIC: **2813** Hydrogen

(G-8313)
LAUX GRAFIX INC
3709 Mississippi Ave (62206-1036)
PHONE..................................618 337-4558
Rich Laux, *Owner*
EMP: 4
SQ FT: 1,800
SALES (est): 275K **Privately Held**
SIC: **3993** 7389 Signs, not made in custom sign painting shops; printed circuitry graphic layout

(G-8314)
MEDICATE DME INC
1833 Kingshighway (62204-2135)
PHONE..................................618 874-3000
Michael Schaltenbrand, *President*
EMP: 12
SALES (est): 2.5MM **Privately Held**
SIC: **2813** 3841 Oxygen, compressed or liquefied; surgical & medical instruments

(G-8315)
MONITOR NEWSPAPER INC
Also Called: East St Louis Monitor Pubg Co
1501 State St (62205-2011)
P.O. Box 2137 (62202-2137)
PHONE..................................618 271-0468
Anne Jordan, *President*
Clyde Jordan Jr, *Principal*
Anthony Sanders, *Principal*
EMP: 6
SALES: 400K **Privately Held**
SIC: **2711** Newspapers: publishing only, not printed on site

(G-8316)
NATIONAL TOOL & MACHINE CO
1235 Piggott Ave (62201)
PHONE..................................618 271-6445
Fax: 618 874-3135
EMP: 10 EST: 1928
SQ FT: 6,500
SALES (est): 730K **Privately Held**
SIC: **3599** 7692 Mfg Industrial Machinery Welding Repair

(G-8317)
OLDCASTLE LAWN & GARDEN INC
Also Called: Oldcastle Lawn & Grdn Midwest
1130 Queeny Ave (62206-1150)
PHONE..................................618 274-1222
Tim Thomas, *Owner*
EMP: 22
SALES (corp-wide): 30.6B **Privately Held**
SIC: **3524** Lawn & garden equipment
HQ: Oldcastle Lawn & Garden, Inc.
400 Prmter Ctr Ter Ne Ste
Atlanta GA 30346

(G-8318)
PETER BUILT
2350 Sauget Indus Pkwy (62206-2937)
PHONE..................................618 337-4000
Claire Larson, *President*
EMP: 30
SALES (est): 5.1MM **Privately Held**
SIC: **3715** Trailer bodies

(G-8319)
REAGENT CHEMICAL & RES INC
1700 S 20th St (62207-1916)
PHONE..................................618 271-8140
Robert Merseman, *Branch Mgr*
EMP: 3
SALES (corp-wide): 517MM **Privately Held**
WEB: www.prosysfill.com
SIC: **2819** 3949 Sulfur, recovered or refined, incl. from sour natural gas; targets, archery & rifle shooting
PA: Reagent Chemical & Research, Inc.
115 Rte 202
Ringoes NJ 08551
908 284-2800

(G-8320)
RESCAR COMPANIES INC
501 Monsanto Ave (62206-1138)
PHONE..................................618 875-3234
Jeremy Speelman, *Manager*
EMP: 4
SALES (corp-wide): 24.3MM **Privately Held**
WEB: www.rescar.com
SIC: **3743** Railroad car rebuilding
PA: Rescar Companies, Inc.
1101 31st St Ste 250
Downers Grove IL 60515
630 963-1114

(G-8321)
SAFETY-KLEEN SYSTEMS INC
3000 Missouri Ave (62205-1125)
PHONE..................................618 875-8050
Steve Ogdenwald, *President*
EMP: 9
SALES (corp-wide): 3.4B **Publicly Held**
SIC: **2992** 4953 Re-refining lubricating oils & greases; refuse systems
HQ: Safety-Kleen Systems, Inc.
42 Longwater Dr
Richardson TX 02061
972 265-2000

(G-8322)
SOLVAY CHEMICALS INC
3500 Missouri Ave (62205-3104)
PHONE..................................618 274-0755
Milton Highhouse, *Branch Mgr*
Cindy Shirley, *Manager*
EMP: 41
SALES (corp-wide): 13.8MM **Privately Held**
WEB: www.solvay.us
SIC: **2819** 2869 2899 Fluorine, elemental; industrial organic chemicals; chemical preparations
HQ: Solvay Chemicals, Inc.
3737 Buffalo Speedway
Houston TX 77098
713 525-6800

(G-8323)
SOUTHERN COLOR COMPANY INC (DH)
Also Called: Southern Color N.A.
2051 Lynch Ave (62204-1717)
P.O. Box 1507, Cartersville GA (30120-1507)
PHONE..................................770 386-4766
Andy Ross, *CEO*
Bill Kagel, *Vice Pres*
◆ EMP: 8
SQ FT: 100,000
SALES (est): 2.2MM
SALES (corp-wide): 6.8B **Publicly Held**
SIC: **5198** 2865 2816 Colors & pigments; cyclic crudes & intermediates; inorganic pigments
HQ: Venator Americas Llc
10001 Woodloch Forest Dr
The Woodlands TX 77380
281 465-6700

GEOGRAPHIC SECTION

Edwardsville - Madison County (G-8347)

(G-8324)
ST LOUIS FLEXICORE INC
Also Called: Flexicore Slab
6351 Collinsville Rd (62201-2523)
PHONE..............................618 531-8691
Kim Moore, *President*
Marvin P Siegele, *President*
Denise Lyons, *Corp Secy*
Ken Moore, *Vice Pres*
EMP: 10 **EST:** 1956
SQ FT: 9,000
SALES (est): 2.5MM **Privately Held**
WEB: www.stlflexicore.com
SIC: 3272 2952 Floor slabs & tiles, precast concrete; roofing tile & slabs, concrete; asphalt felts & coatings

(G-8325)
STONETREE FABRICATION INC
9 Production Pkwy (62206-1081)
PHONE..............................618 332-1700
Thomas Smugala, *President*
EMP: 20
SALES: 2MM **Privately Held**
SIC: 2434 5712 Vanities, bathroom: wood; customized furniture & cabinets

(G-8326)
SWANSEA BUILDING PRODUCTS INC
494 N 33rd St (62205-1422)
PHONE..............................618 874-6282
Cletus Mueth, *President*
EMP: 18
SALES (est): 2.8MM **Privately Held**
SIC: 3271 Blocks, concrete or cinder: standard
PA: Building Products Corp.
950 Freeburg Ave
Belleville IL 62220
618 233-4427

(G-8327)
TOP METAL BUYERS INC (PA)
Also Called: Top Metal Recycling
808 Walnut Ave (62201-2940)
PHONE..............................314 421-2721
Norman Schultz, *President*
Brett Nickel, *Admin Sec*
EMP: 16
SQ FT: 60,000
SALES (est): 3.4MM **Privately Held**
WEB: www.topmetalbuyers.com
SIC: 5093 4953 3341 Junk & scrap; ferrous metal scrap & waste; refuse systems; secondary nonferrous metals

(G-8328)
UNIVERSAL AIR FILTER COMPANY (HQ)
1624 Sauget Indus Pkwy (62206-1451)
PHONE..............................618 271-7300
Todd C Deibel, *President*
Dan Krupp, *President*
Robert Haas, *Purch Mgr*
Jeffrey Bloese, *Engineer*
Jeff McDonnell, *Engineer*
EMP: 49
SQ FT: 45,000
SALES (est): 18MM
SALES (corp-wide): 50.9MM **Privately Held**
WEB: www.uaf.com
SIC: 3564 Filters, air: furnaces, air conditioning equipment, etc.
PA: Thompson Street Capital Manager Llc
7676 Forsyth Blvd
Saint Louis MO 63105
314 727-2112

(G-8329)
WASTEQUIP SAINT LOUIS
2701 Converse Ave (62207-1728)
PHONE..............................216 292-0625
Greg Podell, *President*
EMP: 28
SALES (est): 3.2MM **Privately Held**
SIC: 3537 Trucks, tractors, loaders, carriers & similar equipment

Easton
Mason County

(G-8330)
MAHANS FIBERGLASS
106 E Main St (62633-9324)
P.O. Box 112 (62633-0112)
PHONE..............................309 562-7349
Jim Mahan, *Owner*
EMP: 3
SALES (est): 212.9K **Privately Held**
SIC: 2221 Fiberglass fabrics

(G-8331)
ONKENS INCORPORATED
320 E Main St (62633-9325)
P.O. Box 72 (62633-0072)
PHONE..............................309 562-7477
James H Onken, *President*
Joseph D Onken, *Admin Sec*
▲ **EMP:** 15
SALES (est): 2.3MM **Privately Held**
SIC: 3441 Fabricated structural metal

Edelstein
Peoria County

(G-8332)
CUSTOM POWER PRODUCTS INC
Also Called: Cpp
19727 N State Route 40 (61526-9507)
P.O. Box 106 (61526-0106)
PHONE..............................309 249-2704
Lowell Langeland, *President*
EMP: 6
SQ FT: 25,000
SALES (est): 1.6MM **Privately Held**
SIC: 3613 Switchgear & switchgear accessories

(G-8333)
INTERNATIONAL SUPPLY CO
2717 N North St (61526-9530)
P.O. Box 17 (61526-0017)
PHONE..............................309 249-6211
E Lee Hofmann, *President*
Becky Hofmann, *Corp Secy*
Duane Dean, *Vice Pres*
EMP: 90
SQ FT: 100,000
SALES (est): 29.1MM
SALES (corp-wide): 150MM **Privately Held**
SIC: 3621 Control equipment for electric buses & locomotives
PA: Fibrebond Corporation
1300 Davenport Dr
Minden LA 71055
318 377-1030

Edgewood
Effingham County

(G-8334)
ARCHER-DANIELS-MIDLAND COMPANY
Also Called: ADM
406 Route 37 (62426-1116)
P.O. Box 248, Farina (62838-0248)
PHONE..............................618 238-4800
Darrell Schaal, *Manager*
EMP: 4
SALES (corp-wide): 64.6B **Publicly Held**
WEB: www.adm.com
SIC: 2041 Flour & other grain mill products
PA: Archer-Daniels-Midland Company
77 W Wacker Dr Ste 4600
Chicago IL 60601
312 634-8100

Edinburg
Christian County

(G-8335)
MIDWEST METER INC
200 E Franklin St (62531-9417)
P.O. Box 318 (62531-0318)
PHONE..............................217 623-4064
Donald L Luttrell, *President*
Steve Dauster, *Sales Mgr*
Paul Koepke, *Cust Mgr*
Nick Clark, *Sales Staff*
Dave Devaughn, *Sales Staff*
EMP: 20
SALES (est): 4.3MM **Privately Held**
SIC: 3824 Fluid meters & counting devices

Edwards
Peoria County

(G-8336)
AMERICAN BOTTLING COMPANY
7215 N Kckapoo Edwards Rd (61528-9705)
PHONE..............................309 693-2777
Paul Bersell, *Manager*
EMP: 40 **Publicly Held**
SIC: 2086 Soft drinks: packaged in cans, bottles, etc.
HQ: The American Bottling Company
5301 Legacy Dr
Plano TX 75024

(G-8337)
CATERPILLAR INC
5801 N Smith Rd (61528-9711)
PHONE..............................309 675-8327
Fred Dooley, *Manager*
Brent Allen, *Manager*
EMP: 13
SALES (corp-wide): 53.8B **Publicly Held**
SIC: 3531 Construction machinery
PA: Caterpillar Inc.
510 Lake Cook Rd Ste 100
Deerfield IL 60015
224 551-4000

(G-8338)
KICKAPOO CREEK WINERY
6605 N Smith Rd (61528-9631)
PHONE..............................309 495-9463
David Conner, *Owner*
Mary Conner, *Exec Dir*
EMP: 7
SALES (est): 768.4K **Privately Held**
WEB: www.kickapoocreekwinery.com
SIC: 2084 5921 5947 Wines; wine; gift shop

(G-8339)
MIDWEST PERMA-COLUMN INC
7407 N Kckapoo Edwards Rd (61528-9705)
PHONE..............................309 589-7949
Doug Streitmatter, *President*
Phil Ehnle, *Vice Pres*
David Ehnle, *Prdtn Mgr*
Ray Blunier, *Treasurer*
EMP: 4
SALES (est): 602K **Privately Held**
SIC: 3272 Concrete products, precast

(G-8340)
R/A HOERR INC
Also Called: Hoerr Racing Products
9804 W Primrose (61528-9306)
PHONE..............................309 691-8789
Irv Hoerr, *CEO*
Jason Mitchell, *President*
◆ **EMP:** 23
SQ FT: 10,000
SALES (est): 5.1MM **Privately Held**
SIC: 3711 7948 Motor vehicles & car bodies; race car owners

(G-8341)
WAYNE PRINTING COMPANY (PA)
7917 N Kckapoo Edwards Rd (61528-9579)
PHONE..............................309 691-2496
Kenneth E Hoerr, *President*
Scott M Hoerr, *Admin Sec*
EMP: 38 **EST:** 1990
SQ FT: 34,120
SALES (est): 8.9MM **Privately Held**
SIC: 2752 Commercial printing, offset

(G-8342)
WAYNE PRINTING COMPANY
Also Called: Wayne Wagoner Printing
7917 N Kckapoo Edwards Rd (61528-9579)
PHONE..............................309 691-2496
Eric Timm, *Branch Mgr*
EMP: 50
SALES (corp-wide): 8.9MM **Privately Held**
SIC: 2752 Commercial printing, offset
PA: Wayne Printing Company
7917 N Kckapoo Edwards Rd
Edwards IL 61528
309 691-2496

Edwardsville
Madison County

(G-8343)
510 HOLDINGS COMPANY LLC
Also Called: Minuteman Press
1019 Century Dr Ste 10 (62025-3772)
PHONE..............................618 659-8600
Jason R Hasquin,
Brooke M Hasquin,
EMP: 13
SALES (est): 1.8MM **Privately Held**
SIC: 2752 7389 Commercial printing, lithographic; document embossing

(G-8344)
A2 CREATIVE INC
1115 N 2nd St (62025-1069)
PHONE..............................855 344-5667
Andrew Mayhall, *President*
EMP: 3
SALES: 150K **Privately Held**
SIC: 2891 Adhesives, plastic

(G-8345)
ART HOUSE COFFEE LLC
Also Called: Goshen Coffee
206 E Linden St (62025-2044)
P.O. Box 652 (62025-0652)
PHONE..............................618 659-0571
Jay Beard,
EMP: 3 **EST:** 2012
SALES: 400K **Privately Held**
WEB: www.goshencoffee.com
SIC: 2095 Coffee roasting (except by wholesale grocers)

(G-8346)
B JS PRINTABLES
1501 Troy Rd B (62025-2534)
PHONE..............................618 656-8625
Brenda Schrage, *Owner*
EMP: 4
SALES: 160K **Privately Held**
SIC: 2396 5136 5611 5137 Screen printing on fabric articles; sportswear, men's & boys'; clothing, sportswear, men's & boys'; sportswear, women's & children's; women's sportswear; pleating & stitching

(G-8347)
B QUAD OIL INC
1405 Troy Rd Ste B (62025-2532)
P.O. Box 749 (62025-0749)
PHONE..............................618 656-4419
Bill Blythe, *President*
Robert Rohrkaste, *Corp Secy*
EMP: 3
SALES (est): 351.2K **Privately Held**
SIC: 1311 Crude petroleum production

Edwardsville - Madison County (G-8348)

(G-8348)
BC ENTERPRISES
99 Shore Dr Sw (62025-5338)
PHONE....................618 655-0784
Bret Seavers, *Partner*
Christopher McMiller, *Partner*
EMP: 2
SALES (est): 218.8K **Privately Held**
SIC: 3824 Water meters

(G-8349)
BEALL MANUFACTURING INC (PA)
Also Called: Supertuf
420 N Main St (62025-1618)
PHONE....................618 307-9589
Jim Speciale, *CEO*
Mark Speciale, *President*
Art Fultz, *Marketing Mgr*
Sally Speciale, *Admin Sec*
EMP: 50
SQ FT: 75,000
SALES (est): 15.6MM **Privately Held**
SIC: 3524 Lawn & garden equipment

(G-8350)
BEASTMAN TEA LLC
3815 Sequoia Dr (62025-7718)
PHONE....................636 362-4594
Brad Eastman, *Principal*
EMP: 3
SALES (est): 140.3K **Privately Held**
SIC: 2086 Bottled & canned soft drinks

(G-8351)
BUDGET PRINTING CENTER
3709 Edwardsville Rd # 1 (62025-7249)
PHONE....................618 655-1636
John Sharp, *President*
Jane Stahlhut, *Corp Secy*
EMP: 4
SALES (est): 150K **Privately Held**
SIC: 2752 2791 Commercial printing, offset; typesetting

(G-8352)
CITY OF EDWARDSVILLE
3735 Wanda Rd (62025-7401)
PHONE....................618 692-7053
Billy Sietz, *Branch Mgr*
EMP: 5 **Privately Held**
WEB: www.cityofedwardsville.com
SIC: 3589 Water treatment equipment, industrial
PA: City Of Edwardsville
    118 Hillsboro Ave
    Edwardsville IL 62025
    618 692-7500

(G-8353)
CSI CUTTING SPECIALIST INC
420 N Main St (62025-1618)
PHONE....................731 352-5351
Mark Speciale, *President*
EMP: 75
SALES (est): 8.2MM
SALES (corp-wide): 15.6MM **Privately Held**
SIC: 3469 Machine parts, stamped or pressed metal
PA: Beall Manufacturing, Inc.
    420 N Main St
    Edwardsville IL 62025
    618 307-9589

(G-8354)
CUSTOM FRAMEWORK INC
3865 Ridge View Rd (62025-7731)
PHONE....................618 401-8494
Clint Gipson, *President*
Jennie Gipson, *Vice Pres*
EMP: 7
SALES (est): 750K **Privately Held**
SIC: 2499 Picture frame molding, finished

(G-8355)
CUTTING SPECIALISTS INC
420 N Main St (62025-1618)
PHONE....................731 352-5351
Mark Speciale, *President*
Sally J Speciale, *Admin Sec*
EMP: 45
SALES (est): 9.3MM **Privately Held**
SIC: 3523 3524 Farm machinery & equipment; lawn & garden tractors & equipment

(G-8356)
DAVID YATES
Also Called: Yates Complete Concrete
6407 Sworm Ln (62025-4921)
PHONE....................618 656-7879
David Yates, *Owner*
EMP: 4
SALES (est): 165K **Privately Held**
SIC: 3273 Ready-mixed concrete

(G-8357)
DYNAMI SOLUTIONS LLC
2 Loggers Trl (62025-5743)
P.O. Box 976 (62025-0976)
PHONE....................618 363-2771
Kevin Ogle, *Mng Member*
J Scott Jagoe,
William R Jagoe IV,
EMP: 6
SALES (est): 383.5K **Privately Held**
SIC: 7372 Prepackaged software

(G-8358)
EAST SIDE JERSEY DAIRY INC
3744 Staunton Rd (62025-6936)
PHONE....................662 289-3344
EMP: 7
SALES (est): 592.9K
SALES (corp-wide): 1.7B **Privately Held**
SIC: 2026 Milk processing (pasteurizing, homogenizing, bottling)
HQ: East Side Jersey Dairy Inc
    1100 Broadway
    Carlinville IL 62626
    217 854-2547

(G-8359)
EBERHART SIGN & LIGHTING CO (PA)
104 1st Ave (62025-2574)
PHONE....................618 656-7256
Ronald P Eberhart, *President*
EMP: 8
SQ FT: 2,200
SALES (est): 1.1MM **Privately Held**
WEB: www.eberhartsigns.net
SIC: 3993 1731 Electric signs; electrical work

(G-8360)
EDWARDSVILLE MCH & WLDG CO INC
1509 Troy Rd (62025-2534)
PHONE....................618 656-5145
Richard L Hartnagel, *President*
George Hartnagel, *Vice Pres*
EMP: 4 EST: 1947
SQ FT: 6,500
SALES (est): 350K **Privately Held**
WEB: www.cityofedwardsvilleecondev.com
SIC: 3599 7692 Machine shop, jobbing & repair; welding repair

(G-8361)
EDWARDSVILLE PUBLISHING CO
Also Called: Edwardsville Intelligencer
116 N Main St (62025-1902)
P.O. Box 70 (62025-0070)
PHONE....................618 656-4700
Brittany Johnson, *Editor*
Bruce E Coury, *Vice Pres*
Denise Vonderhaar, *Controller*
Lacey Barnett, *Advt Staff*
Mary Cook, *Advt Staff*
EMP: 73
SALES (est): 5.3MM
SALES (corp-wide): 8.2B **Privately Held**
WEB: www.theintelligencer.com
SIC: 2711 2791 2752 Newspapers, publishing & printing; typesetting; commercial printing, lithographic
PA: The Hearst Corporation
    300 W 57th St Fl 42
    New York NY 10019
    212 649-2000

(G-8362)
FOSTER LEARNING LLC
900 Timberlake Dr (62025-4107)
PHONE....................618 656-6836
Ann Robertson, *Opers Staff*
Edwards Ackad, *Chief Engr*
Thomas Foster, *Treasurer*
EMP: 3
SALES (est): 90.6K **Privately Held**
SIC: 7372 Application computer software; educational computer software

(G-8363)
FRAMERY
216 E Park St (62025-1711)
PHONE....................618 656-5749
EMP: 3 EST: 1979
SALES (est): 160K **Privately Held**
SIC: 3499 Mfg Misc Fabricated Metal Products

(G-8364)
FUSION GATES LLC
2412 Little Round Top Dr (62025-3110)
PHONE....................618 650-9170
Shelly Wolfe, *Vice Pres*
Donna Potter, *Software Dev*
EMP: 2
SALES (est): 201.7K **Privately Held**
SIC: 3446 Fences, gates, posts & flagpoles

(G-8365)
HUBBELL POWER SYSTEMS INC
131 Enterprise Dr (62025-7436)
PHONE....................618 797-5000
EMP: 19
SALES (corp-wide): 4.5B **Publicly Held**
SIC: 3612 3679 3699 3691 Power transformers, electric; power supplies, all types: static; electrical equipment & supplies; nickel cadmium storage batteries
HQ: Hubbell Power Systems, Inc.
    200 Center Point Cir # 200
    Columbia SC 29210
    803 216-2600

(G-8366)
HUBBELL POWER SYSTEMS INC
Turner Electric
131 Enterprise Dr (62025-7436)
PHONE....................618 797-5000
EMP: 23
SALES (corp-wide): 3.3B **Publicly Held**
SIC: 3613 Mfg Switchgear/Switchboards
HQ: Hubbell Power Systems, Inc.
    200 Center Point Cir # 200
    Columbia SC 29210
    803 216-2600

(G-8367)
KSEM INC
6471 Miller Dr (62025-4927)
PHONE....................618 656-5388
Joan Ketcham, *President*
EMP: 3 EST: 1977
SQ FT: 4,800
SALES (est): 370.8K **Privately Held**
SIC: 3523 3993 7692 3441 Farm machinery & equipment; signs, not made in custom sign painting shops; welding repair; fabricated structural metal

(G-8368)
LIZOTTE SHEET METAL INC
632 W Schwarz St (62025-1564)
PHONE....................618 656-3066
Paul Lizotte, *President*
Aileen Lizotte, *Corp Secy*
EMP: 4
SQ FT: 3,000
SALES (est): 494.2K **Privately Held**
WEB: www.lizottesheetmetal.com
SIC: 1711 3446 3444 3443 Warm air heating & air conditioning contractor; ventilation & duct work contractor; architectural metalwork; sheet metalwork; fabricated plate work (boiler shop); fabricated structural metal

(G-8369)
MENASHA PACKAGING COMPANY LLC
21 W Gtwy Commerce Ctr Dr (62025-2814)
PHONE....................618 931-7805
Richard McFarland, *Branch Mgr*
EMP: 18
SALES (corp-wide): 2.2B **Privately Held**
SIC: 2653 Boxes, corrugated: made from purchased materials
HQ: Menasha Packaging Company, Llc
    1645 Bergstrom Rd
    Neenah WI 54956
    920 751-1000

(G-8370)
MENASHA PACKAGING COMPANY LLC
9 Gatway Cmmerce Ctr Dr E (62025-2810)
PHONE....................618 501-6040
EMP: 140
SALES (corp-wide): 2.2B **Privately Held**
SIC: 2653 Boxes, corrugated: made from purchased materials
HQ: Menasha Packaging Company, Llc
    1645 Bergstrom Rd
    Neenah WI 54956
    920 751-1000

(G-8371)
MIDWEST RAILCAR CORPORATION (HQ)
855 S Arbor Vitae (62025-3779)
PHONE....................618 692-5575
Rich Murphy, *President*
Corey Coil, *Vice Pres*
Richard M Folio, *CFO*
Michelle Nation, *Controller*
Matthew McFarlane, *Manager*
EMP: 21
SALES (est): 8.5MM **Privately Held**
SIC: 3743 Railroad equipment

(G-8372)
NIKKIN FLUX CORP
512 Phillipena St (62025-1007)
P.O. Box 402 (62025-0402)
PHONE....................618 656-2125
Steven Schoeffler, *President*
▲ EMP: 5
SALES (est): 792.5K **Privately Held**
SIC: 2819 Industrial inorganic chemicals

(G-8373)
OLIVE OILS & MORE LLC
1990 Troy Rd Ste A (62025-2596)
PHONE....................618 656-4645
Mary Burke, *Principal*
EMP: 3
SALES (est): 248.7K **Privately Held**
WEB: www.oliveoilsandmore.com
SIC: 2079 Olive oil

(G-8374)
RICHARDS BRICK COMPANY (PA)
234 Springer Ave (62025-1806)
PHONE....................618 656-0230
John R Motley, *President*
Mike Semanisin, *General Mgr*
James Richards, *Admin Sec*
Vickie Radcliffe, *Clerk*
EMP: 85 EST: 1890
SQ FT: 5,000
SALES (est): 31.8MM **Privately Held**
WEB: www.richardsbrick.com
SIC: 5032 3251 Brick, except refractory; brick clay: common face, glazed, vitrified or hollow

(G-8375)
SJD DIRECT MIDWEST LLC (PA)
Also Called: Rand Diversified Midwest
21 Gtewy Cmrc Ctr Dr W (62025-2814)
PHONE....................618 931-2151
Mike Waite, *President*
Vera McCarty, *Manager*
David Kauffman,
Stuart Sklovsky,
John P Wuensch,
▲ EMP: 6
SALES (est): 28.6MM **Privately Held**
SIC: 3565 Packing & wrapping machinery

GEOGRAPHIC SECTION

Effingham - Effingham County (G-8404)

(G-8376)
ST LOUIS SCRAP TRADING LLC
5 Sunset Hills Blvd N (62025-3732)
PHONE..................618 307-9002
Charles Fred Francis, *Mng Member*
EMP: 3
SALES (est): 302.7K **Privately Held**
SIC: 3312 8748 1795 Blast furnaces & steel mills; business consulting; wrecking & demolition work

(G-8377)
T J S EQUIPMENT INC
1514 Weber Dr (62025-4104)
PHONE..................618 656-8046
Terrence J Scheibal, *President*
EMP: 3
SALES (est): 410K **Privately Held**
SIC: 5046 3531 Commercial equipment; plows: construction, excavating & grading

(G-8378)
TINSLEY STEEL INC
2 Oasis Dr (62025-5939)
PHONE..................618 656-5231
Greg Tinsley, *President*
Cathy Tinsley, *Corp Secy*
EMP: 8
SQ FT: 12,000
SALES: 2MM **Privately Held**
SIC: 3316 3446 3444 3443 Bars, steel, cold finished, from purchased hot-rolled; architectural metalwork; sheet metalwork; fabricated plate work (boiler shop); fabricated structural metal; nonferrous rolling & drawing

(G-8379)
WESTROCK CONVERTING LLC
3101 Westway Dr (62025-7049)
PHONE..................618 709-5284
Megan Kearns, *Branch Mgr*
EMP: 31
SALES (corp-wide): 18.2B **Publicly Held**
SIC: 2653 Partitions, solid fiber: made from purchased materials; boxes, corrugated: made from purchased materials
HQ: Westrock Converting, Llc
1000 Abernathy Rd Ste 125
Atlanta GA 30328
770 448-2193

(G-8380)
WILSEYS HANDMADE SWEETS LLC
316 W Park St (62025-1942)
PHONE..................314 504-0851
Lindsey Wulfing, *Principal*
EMP: 6
SALES (est): 427.7K **Privately Held**
WEB: www.wilseyscakeballs.com
SIC: 2053 Cakes, bakery: frozen

Effingham
Effingham County

(G-8381)
4X4 HEADQUARTERS LLC
18086 N Highway 45 (62401-6957)
PHONE..................217 540-5337
James McHuge,
EMP: 6 **EST:** 2010
SALES (est): 702.9K **Privately Held**
WEB: www.4x4headquarters.net
SIC: 3711 Motor vehicles & car bodies

(G-8382)
AD WORKS INC
17866 N Us Highway 45 (62401-6708)
PHONE..................217 342-9688
David Campbell, *President*
EMP: 4
SQ FT: 4,000
SALES (est): 275K **Privately Held**
SIC: 2759 2752 Commercial printing; commercial printing, lithographic

(G-8383)
ADERMANNS WELDING & MCH & CO
1310 Pike Ave (62401-4270)
PHONE..................217 342-3234
Steve Bloemer, *President*
Kelly Lidy, *Corp Secy*
Paul Bloemer, *Vice Pres*
EMP: 5 **EST:** 1942
SALES (est): 330K **Privately Held**
SIC: 3599 7692 3441 Machine shop, jobbing & repair; automotive welding; fabricated structural metal

(G-8384)
AIR STAMPING INC
3 Legend Park (62401-9442)
P.O. Box 568 (62401-0568)
PHONE..................217 342-1283
Gene Williams, *President*
Larry Hines, *Vice Pres*
Ray Nuxoll, *Purchasing*
Kim Schmidt, *Executive*
▲ **EMP:** 12
SQ FT: 18,800
SALES (est): 3.3MM **Privately Held**
WEB: www.airstamping.com
SIC: 5072 3599 Screws; machine shop, jobbing & repair

(G-8385)
ARCHER-DANIELS-MIDLAND COMPANY
Also Called: ADM
1200 Mcgrath Ave (62401-4231)
P.O. Box 687 (62401-0687)
PHONE..................217 342-3986
Kyle Taylor, *Branch Mgr*
EMP: 44
SALES (corp-wide): 64.6B **Publicly Held**
SIC: 2048 Prepared feeds
PA: Archer-Daniels-Midland Company
77 W Wacker Dr Ste 4600
Chicago IL 60601
312 634-8100

(G-8386)
ATHLETIC IMAGE
510 W Jaycee Ave Ste 3 (62401-2967)
PHONE..................217 347-7377
Jim Smothers, *Owner*
EMP: 5
SALES (est): 180K **Privately Held**
SIC: 2759 Screen printing

(G-8387)
AXIOSONIC LLC
2600 S Raney St (62401-4219)
PHONE..................217 342-3412
Peter Bonutti, *CEO*
Justin Beyers, *Vice Pres*
EMP: 10
SQ FT: 5,000
SALES (est): 408.2K **Privately Held**
SIC: 3845 Ultrasonic medical equipment, except cleaning

(G-8388)
B & L MACHINE SALES INC
Also Called: B & L Machine & Design
1 Legend Park (62401-9442)
P.O. Box 743 (62401-0743)
PHONE..................217 342-3918
Larry Hines, *President*
Lara J Westjohn, *Admin Secy*
◆ **EMP:** 28
SQ FT: 50,000
SALES (est): 5.3MM **Privately Held**
SIC: 3599 Machine shop, jobbing & repair

(G-8389)
BIERMAN WELDING INC
1103 S Willow St (62401-4044)
P.O. Box 25 (62401-0025)
PHONE..................217 342-2050
James Bierman, *President*
Phillip Bierman, *Vice Pres*
Mark Bierman, *Treasurer*
Jerry Bierman, *Admin Sec*
EMP: 14
SQ FT: 4,000
SALES: 1.6MM **Privately Held**
WEB: www.biermanwelding.com
SIC: 7692 7539 Welding repair; trailer repair

(G-8390)
BUCKEYE PARTNERS LP
18264 N Highway 45 (62401-6958)
PHONE..................217 342-2336
Clark Smith, *Branch Mgr*
EMP: 5
SALES (corp-wide): 4.1B **Privately Held**
SIC: 1389 5085 Pipe testing, oil field service; pipeline wrappings, anti-corrosive
HQ: Buckeye Partners, L.P.
1 Greenway Plz Ste 600
Houston TX 77046
832 615-8600

(G-8391)
CNHI LLC
Also Called: Shelbyville Daily Union
201 N Banker St (62401-2304)
PHONE..................217 774-2161
Bob Dennis, *Manager*
EMP: 13 **Privately Held**
SIC: 2711 Commercial printing & newspaper publishing combined; newspapers, publishing & printing
HQ: Cnhi, Llc
445 Dexter Ave Ste 7000
Montgomery AL 36104

(G-8392)
CONTINENTAL MILLS INC
1200 Stevens Ave (62401-4264)
PHONE..................217 540-4000
Danielle Niebrugge, *Human Res Mgr*
EMP: 140
SALES (corp-wide): 223.6MM **Privately Held**
SIC: 2045 Flours & flour mixes, from purchased flour
PA: Continental Mills, Inc.
18100 Andover Park W
Tukwila WA 98188
206 816-7000

(G-8393)
CONTRACT TRANSPORTATION SYS CO
711 W Wabash Ave (62401-2605)
PHONE..................217 342-5757
Shawn Mohundro, *Manager*
EMP: 110
SALES (corp-wide): 17.9B **Publicly Held**
SIC: 2851 Paints & allied products
HQ: Contract Transportation System Co.
101 W Prospect Ave
Cleveland OH 44115
216 566-2000

(G-8394)
CONTRACTORS CONCRETE INC
Also Called: CCI Redi Mix
2604 N Haarmann St (62401-4272)
PHONE..................217 342-2299
Edward Grunloh, *President*
Gary Bartels, *President*
EMP: 50
SALES (est): 5.1MM **Privately Held**
SIC: 3273 5032 Ready-mixed concrete; concrete & cinder block

(G-8395)
DINGO INC
14480 N 1025th St (62401-6257)
PHONE..................217 868-5615
Kathy Witkowski, *President*
Kathleen A Witkowski, *President*
Gerald Crisman, *Admin Sec*
EMP: 4
SALES (est): 276.8K **Privately Held**
SIC: 2033 Barbecue sauce: packaged in cans, jars, etc.

(G-8396)
DUST LOGGING LLC
16666 E 2050th Ave (62401-6992)
PHONE..................217 844-2305
Ryan Dust, *Principal*
EMP: 3
SALES (est): 310.4K **Privately Held**
SIC: 2411 Logging camps & contractors

(G-8397)
EFFINGHAM MONUMENT CO INC
Rr 33 Box E (62401)
P.O. Box 899 (62401-0899)
PHONE..................217 857-6085
Bart Willenborg, *President*
Allen Koester, *Vice Pres*
EMP: 3
SQ FT: 2,400
SALES (est): 300K **Privately Held**
SIC: 5999 3281 Gravestones, finished; monuments, finished to custom order; cut stone & stone products

(G-8398)
EFFINGHAM SIGNS & GRAPHICS
1009 S Oak St (62401-1969)
PHONE..................217 347-8711
Alice Hahn, *Owner*
EMP: 7
SQ FT: 6,000
SALES (est): 700K **Privately Held**
SIC: 7389 3993 Lettering service; signs & advertising specialties

(G-8399)
EFFINGHAM TTPLIS NEWS RPORT IN
Also Called: E T News Report
1901 S 4th St (62401-4187)
PHONE..................217 342-5583
Stephen R Raymond, *President*
Steve Raymond, *Publisher*
Ruth A Raymond, *Admin Sec*
EMP: 4 **EST:** 2012
SALES (est): 76.2K **Privately Held**
SIC: 2711 Newspapers, publishing & printing

(G-8400)
FLOWERS FOODS INC
2305 Hoffman Dr (62401)
PHONE..................217 347-2308
EMP: 12
SALES (corp-wide): 4.1B **Publicly Held**
SIC: 2051 Bread, cake & related products
PA: Flowers Foods, Inc.
1919 Flowers Cir
Thomasville GA 31757
229 226-9110

(G-8401)
GOT 2B SCRAPPIN
1901 S 4th St Ste 11 (62401-4188)
PHONE..................217 347-3600
Bev Esgar, *Manager*
EMP: 3
SALES (est): 284.1K **Privately Held**
SIC: 2782 Scrapbooks

(G-8402)
HEARTLAND HARDWOODS INC
20871 N 1600th St (62401-7506)
P.O. Box 84 (62401-0084)
PHONE..................217 844-3312
Mark J Willenborg, *President*
Craig C Willenborg, *Vice Pres*
EMP: 20
SQ FT: 25,000
SALES (est): 2MM **Privately Held**
SIC: 2426 2431 2421 2411 Furniture stock & parts, hardwood; millwork; sawmills & planing mills, general; logging

(G-8403)
J M LUSTIG CUSTOM CABINETS CO
921 E Fayette Ave (62401-3657)
P.O. Box 26 (62401-0026)
PHONE..................217 342-6661
Isabel Lustig, *President*
EMP: 11 **EST:** 1925
SQ FT: 16,435
SALES (est): 1.2MM **Privately Held**
WEB: www.lustigcabinets.com
SIC: 2434 2511 2521 2421 Wood kitchen cabinets; wood household furniture; wood office furniture; sawmills & planing mills, general

(G-8404)
JBC HOLDING CO (PA)
3601 S Banker St (62401-2899)
P.O. Box 609 (62401-0609)
PHONE..................217 347-7701
Louis Kenter, *Chairman*
Tracy Worman, *COO*
Ted Gravenhorst Sr, *Director*
John Eisel, *Admin Sec*
◆ **EMP:** 4

Effingham - Effingham County (G-8405)

SALES (est): 63.2MM **Privately Held**
SIC: **2541** 2542 2511 2099 Wood partitions & fixtures; counters or counter display cases: except wood; wood household furniture; bread crumbs, not made in bakeries

(G-8405)
KINGERY PRINTING COMPANY (PA)
Also Called: M & D Printing Div
3012 S Banker St (62401-2900)
P.O. Box 727 (62401-0727)
PHONE..................217 347-5151
John Kingery, *Ch of Bd*
Michael C Kingery, *President*
Robert Broom, *Business Mgr*
Jeff Hoene, *Business Mgr*
John Wurtsbaugh, *COO*
EMP: 160
SQ FT: 100,000
SALES: 31MM **Privately Held**
WEB: www.kingeryprinting.com
SIC: **2752** Commercial printing, offset

(G-8406)
KUCHE FINE CABINETRY
814 E Fayette Ave (62401-3603)
PHONE..................217 342-2244
Amy Thoele, *President*
EMP: 4
SALES (est): 412.7K **Privately Held**
SIC: **2434** Wood kitchen cabinets

(G-8407)
LANGE ELECTRIC INC
912 E Fayette Ave (62401-3605)
PHONE..................217 347-7626
James H Lange, *President*
Linda Lange, *Corp Secy*
EMP: 3
SQ FT: 3,500
SALES (est): 350K **Privately Held**
SIC: **7694** 5063 Electric motor repair; motors, electric

(G-8408)
LUDWIG MEDICAL INC
1010 N Parkview St (62401-3152)
PHONE..................217 342-6570
Gerald E Ludwig, *President*
Diana Ludwig, *Corp Secy*
EMP: 3
SALES (est): 450.1K **Privately Held**
SIC: **3841** 3821 Surgical & medical instruments; laboratory apparatus & furniture

(G-8409)
MERZ AIR CONDITIONING AND HTG
509 S Willow St (62401-3756)
P.O. Box 1305 (62401-1305)
PHONE..................217 342-2323
Glen Freeman, *President*
EMP: 30
SALES: 5MM **Privately Held**
SIC: **1711** 3444 Warm air heating & air conditioning contractor; sheet metalwork

(G-8410)
METTES CABINET CORNER INC
3240 S Banker St (62401-2927)
P.O. Box 604 (62401-0604)
PHONE..................217 342-9552
John Mette, *President*
Janice Mette, *Treasurer*
Josh Robison, *IT/INT Sup*
EMP: 17
SQ FT: 13,000
SALES (est): 2.6MM **Privately Held**
SIC: **2434** Wood kitchen cabinets

(G-8411)
MIDTOWN FUELS
503 W Jefferson Ave (62401-2338)
P.O. Box 504 (62401-0504)
PHONE..................217 347-7191
Sandy Lewis, *Manager*
EMP: 3
SALES (est): 176.3K **Privately Held**
WEB: www.martinsiga.com
SIC: **2869** Fuels

(G-8412)
MIDWEST FINISHERS PWDRCTNG
10235 N 800th St (62401-6507)
PHONE..................217 536-9098
Richard Murphy, *Owner*
EMP: 3
SALES (est): 217.2K **Privately Held**
SIC: **3399** Powder, metal

(G-8413)
MORROW SHOE AND BOOT INC
320 W Jefferson Ave (62401-2352)
PHONE..................217 342-6833
William A Morrow, *President*
EMP: 1
SQ FT: 7,500
SALES: 348.2K **Privately Held**
SIC: **3069** 5661 Boot or shoe products, rubber; women's boots

(G-8414)
NEW YORK BLOWER COMPANY
Also Called: Mechanovent
1304 W Jaycee Ave (62401-4226)
PHONE..................217 347-3233
Greg Pelletier, *Manager*
EMP: 60
SALES (corp-wide): 117.7MM **Privately Held**
SIC: **3564** Ventilating fans: industrial or commercial
PA: The New York Blower Company
7660 S Quincy St
Willowbrook IL 60527
630 794-5700

(G-8415)
NEWSPAPER HOLDING INC
Also Called: Effingham Daily News
201 N Banker St (62401-2304)
P.O. Box 370 (62401-0370)
PHONE..................217 347-7151
Steve Raymond, *Principal*
EMP: 65 **Privately Held**
SIC: **2711** Newspapers, publishing & printing
HQ: Newspaper Holding, Inc.
425 Locust St
Johnstown PA 15901
814 532-5102

(G-8416)
NOVA SOLUTIONS INC (PA)
Also Called: Nova The Right Solution
421 Industrial Ave (62401-2835)
P.O. Box 725 (62401-0725)
PHONE..................217 342-7070
John Lechman, *President*
Suzanne Lechman, *Corp Secy*
Kelly McWhorter, *Mfg Staff*
Teresa Miller, *CFO*
Nicholas Lechman, *Manager*
◆ EMP: 30
SQ FT: 101,000
SALES (est): 4.5MM **Privately Held**
SIC: **2521** 5021 Wood office furniture; office furniture

(G-8417)
PATTON PRINTING AND GRAPHICS
902 W Wabash Ave B (62401-1908)
P.O. Box 683 (62401-0683)
PHONE..................217 347-0220
Dan Patton, *Owner*
Madonna Patton, *Co-Owner*
EMP: 8
SQ FT: 1,800
SALES (est): 500K **Privately Held**
SIC: **2752** 2791 2789 Commercial printing, offset; typesetting; bookbinding & related work

(G-8418)
PEERLESS AMERICA INCORPORATED
1201 W Wabash Ave (62401-1967)
PHONE..................217 342-0400
Mike Warkins, *President*
Roger Paulman, *President*
Frederick Paulman, *Chairman*
Scott Berty, *CFO*
Dave Murray, *Manager*
◆ EMP: 150 EST: 1912

SALES (est): 41.4MM **Privately Held**
WEB: www.peerlessofamerica.com
SIC: **3354** 3585 3498 3443 Coils, rod, extruded, aluminum; condensers, refrigeration; fabricated pipe & fittings; fabricated plate work (boiler shop)

(G-8419)
QG LLC
420 Industrial Ave (62401-2834)
PHONE..................217 347-7721
Brian Mulroney, *Branch Mgr*
EMP: 340
SALES (corp-wide): 3.9B **Publicly Held**
SIC: **2752** Color lithography
HQ: Qg, Llc
N61w23044 Harrys Way
Sussex WI 53089

(G-8420)
QG LLC
Also Called: Worldcolor Effingham
1200 W Niccum Ave (62401-4217)
PHONE..................217 347-7721
Dwaine Kinderkhecht, *Branch Mgr*
EMP: 60
SALES (corp-wide): 3.9B **Publicly Held**
SIC: **2754** 2759 Commercial printing, gravure; commercial printing
HQ: Qg, Llc
N61w23044 Harrys Way
Sussex WI 53089

(G-8421)
QUAD/GRAPHICS INC
420 Industrial Ave (62401-2834)
PHONE..................217 347-7721
Joel Quadracci, *Chairman*
Kenneth Erickson, *Engineer*
Kim McCain, *Human Resources*
Jeff Mayhaus, *Director*
EMP: 15
SALES (corp-wide): 3.9B **Publicly Held**
SIC: **2752** Commercial printing, offset
PA: Quad/Graphics Inc.
N61w23044 Harrys Way
Sussex WI 53089
414 566-6000

(G-8422)
R & G MACHINE SHOP INC
1303 Parker Ave (62401-4233)
PHONE..................217 342-6622
Mike Rieman, *President*
Curt Goeckner, *Admin Sec*
EMP: 10
SQ FT: 2,500
SALES: 1MM **Privately Held**
SIC: **3559** Semiconductor manufacturing machinery

(G-8423)
RUSTY & ANGELA BUZZARD
Also Called: Effingham Printing Company
801 N 3rd St 1 (62401-3137)
P.O. Box 71 (62401-0071)
PHONE..................217 342-9841
Rusty Buzzard, *Owner*
Angela Buzzard, *Co-Owner*
EMP: 3
SALES: 110K **Privately Held**
SIC: **2752** 2791 2789 2759 Commercial printing, offset; typesetting; bookbinding & related work; commercial printing

(G-8424)
SANTA CRUZ HOLDINGS LLC (PA)
1307 Kollmeyer Ln (62401-5234)
PHONE..................217 821-0304
John Dietzen,
EMP: 4
SALES (est): 164.2MM **Privately Held**
SIC: **2023** Dietary supplements, dairy & non-dairy based

(G-8425)
SC HOLDINGS LLC (HQ)
1307 Kollmeyer Ln (62401-5234)
PHONE..................217 821-0304
John Dietzen,
EMP: 497
SALES (est): 164.2MM **Privately Held**
SIC: **2834** Lozenges, pharmaceutical; antacids; tablets, pharmaceutical

PA: Santa Cruz Holdings, Llc
1307 Kollmeyer Ln
Effingham IL 62401
217 821-0304

(G-8426)
SPORTS DESIGNS & GRAPHICS
807 S Maple St (62401-2641)
PHONE..................217 342-2777
Robert Smothers, *President*
EMP: 25
SALES (est): 1.2MM **Privately Held**
SIC: **2759** Screen printing

(G-8427)
TUSCAN HILLS WINERY LLC
2200 Historic Hills Dr (62401-7009)
PHONE..................217 347-9463
Wanda L Pitcher, *Principal*
EMP: 3
SALES (est): 208.8K **Privately Held**
SIC: **2084** Wines

(G-8428)
VERSATECH LLC
1609 W Wernsing Ave Ste D (62401-4213)
PHONE..................217 342-3500
Kelly Fenton, *Project Mgr*
Curtis Garrard, *Project Mgr*
Paul Pugsley, *Purchasing*
Rodney Davidson, *Engineer*
Ryan Engel, *Engineer*
EMP: 130
SQ FT: 75,000
SALES (est): 27.9MM **Privately Held**
WEB: www.versatech1.com
SIC: **8711** 3542 Structural engineering; machine tools, metal forming type

(G-8429)
VOGEL MANUFACTURING CO INC
10862 N 1000th Rd (62401-6568)
PHONE..................217 536-6946
Charles Vogel, *President*
Virginia Vogel, *Corp Secy*
Kevin Vogel, *Vice Pres*
EMP: 3
SALES: 414K **Privately Held**
SIC: **3714** Motor vehicle engines & parts

(G-8430)
WAUPACA FOUNDRY INC
1500 Heartland Blvd (62401-4234)
PHONE..................217 347-0600
Bob Harter, *Plant Mgr*
Jordan Shields, *Purchasing*
Rob Pfeiffer, *Engineer*
J R Elder, *Manager*
Melvin Bates, *Supervisor*
EMP: 128 **Privately Held**
SIC: **3559** 3321 3465 Automotive related machinery; ductile iron castings; body parts, automobile: stamped metal
HQ: Waupaca Foundry, Inc.
1955 Brunner Dr
Waupaca WI 54981
715 258-6611

(G-8431)
WILLENBORG HARDWOOD INDS INC
15485 E 1900th Ave (62401-6972)
P.O. Box 632 (62401-0632)
PHONE..................217 844-2082
Dennis Willenborg, *CEO*
Russell Willenborg, *Vice Pres*
Kim Parker, *Treasurer*
EMP: 18 EST: 1960
SQ FT: 20,000
SALES (est): 2.8MM **Privately Held**
SIC: **2421** Sawmills & planing mills, general

(G-8432)
WORTMAN PRINTING COMPANY INC
1713 S Banker St (62401-2748)
P.O. Box 38 (62401-0038)
PHONE..................217 347-3775
Del Wortman, *President*
Diane Wortman, *Vice Pres*
James Wortman, *Vice Pres*
Lindsay Wagner, *Graphic Designe*
EMP: 8

El Paso
Woodford County

(G-8433)
AMERICAN BUILDINGS COMPANY
2101 E Main St (61738-1348)
P.O. Box 18 (61738-0018)
PHONE.................309 527-5420
Terry Kuper, *Branch Mgr*
EMP: 105
SQ FT: 133,000
SALES (corp-wide): 22.5B **Publicly Held**
SIC: 3448 Buildings, portable: prefabricated metal
HQ: American Buildings Company
1150 State Docks Rd
Eufaula AL 36027
334 687-2032

(G-8434)
CENTRAL HYDRAULICS INC
513 State Route 251 (61738-1791)
PHONE.................309 527-5238
Chris Porzelius, *President*
EMP: 3
SALES (est): 300K **Privately Held**
SIC: 3569 3714 3594 7699 Jacks, hydraulic; motor vehicle parts & accessories; fluid power pumps & motors; hydraulic equipment repair

(G-8435)
CUSTOM CRAFTED DOOR INC
2810 County Road 520 N (61738-1793)
PHONE.................309 527-5075
Jimmy D Young, *President*
Dennis Ortinac, *Vice Pres*
Bonnie Young, *Treasurer*
EMP: 15
SQ FT: 50,000
SALES (est): 2.1MM **Privately Held**
SIC: 2431 5211 Doors, wood; millwork & lumber

(G-8436)
E I DU PONT DE NEMOURS & CO
Also Called: Dupont
2830 Us Highway 24 (61738-1734)
PHONE.................309 527-5115
Kenneth Cook, *Manager*
EMP: 50
SALES (corp-wide): 21.5B **Publicly Held**
SIC: 2879 Fungicides, herbicides
HQ: E. I. Du Pont De Nemours And Company
974 Centre Rd Bldg 735
Wilmington DE 19805
302 485-3000

(G-8437)
EL PASO JOURNAL
51 W Front St (61738-1553)
PHONE.................309 527-8595
Kim Kearney, *President*
EMP: 3
SALES (est): 226.6K **Privately Held**
SIC: 2711 Newspapers, publishing & printing

(G-8438)
HILL REPORTER LLC
404 W 4th St (61738-1047)
PHONE.................309 532-4794
James Allen Kosur,
EMP: 3
SALES (est): 120K **Privately Held**
SIC: 2741

(G-8439)
INNOVATIVE INDUSTRIAL SVCS LLC
600 S Fayette St Ste 4 (61738-1478)
PHONE.................309 527-2035
Jack Widmer,
Mary Widmer,
EMP: 17
SQ FT: 7,000
SALES (est): 931.8K **Privately Held**
SIC: 2759 2791 2789 2752 Screen printing; typesetting; bookbinding & related work; commercial printing, lithographic

Elburn
Kane County

(G-8440)
A E FRASZ INC
1n545 Brundige Rd (60119-9412)
PHONE.................630 232-6223
Andrew E Frasz, *President*
Gail Frasz, *Admin Sec*
EMP: 12
SQ FT: 5,400
SALES (est): 2.2MM **Privately Held**
SIC: 1794 1442 Excavation work; gravel mining

(G-8441)
ACCURAIL INC
400 W Nebraska St (60119-8300)
P.O. Box 278 (60119-0278)
PHONE.................630 365-6400
Dennis Storzek, *President*
Robert B Walker Jr, *Vice Pres*
Robert Walker, *Vice Pres*
▲ EMP: 12
SQ FT: 5,000
SALES (est): 750K **Privately Held**
SIC: 3944 5092 Railroad models: toy & hobby; model kits

(G-8442)
ADVANCED MICRO LITES INC
205 Dempsey St Ste A (60119-7028)
PHONE.................630 365-5450
Shirley Jaeger, *President*
Dawn Kuefler, *Corp Secy*
Bob Jaeger, *Vice Pres*
▲ EMP: 6
SQ FT: 4,000
SALES: 2MM **Privately Held**
SIC: 3645 3641 5063 Residential lighting fixtures; electric lamps; light bulbs & related supplies

(G-8443)
AQUATROL INC
600 E North St (60119-9048)
P.O. Box 8012 (60119-8012)
PHONE.................630 365-2363
Bert Lowden, *President*
Eric Lambert, *Vice Pres*
Karl Witte, *Engineer*
Valerie Greisch,
▲ EMP: 14
SQ FT: 20,000
SALES (est): 3.6MM **Privately Held**
WEB: www.aquatrol.com
SIC: 3494 3491 Valves & pipe fittings; industrial valves

(G-8444)
ARCH CHEMICALS INC
Marine Bio Chemist
809 Hicks Dr Ste A (60119-9062)
PHONE.................630 365-1720
Doug Walls, *Opers Mgr*
John Cortell, *Manager*
EMP: 3
SALES (corp-wide): 5.5B **Privately Held**
SIC: 2899 Water treating compounds
HQ: Arch Chemicals, Inc.
1200 Bluegrass Lakes Pkwy
Alpharetta GA 30004
678 624-5800

(G-8445)
BARCAR MANUFACTURING INC
1 N 081 Thryselius Dr (60119)
P.O. Box 8042 (60119-8042)
PHONE.................630 365-5200
Dan Carson II, *President*
Dan D Carson Sr, *President*
Dan Carson Jr, *Corp Secy*
▲ EMP: 7 EST: 1979
SQ FT: 6,000
SALES: 1.3MM **Privately Held**
SIC: 3714 Automotive wiring harness sets

(G-8446)
BOGART INDUSTRIES LLC
315 E Reader St (60119-8936)
PHONE.................224 242-4578
Michael Henry Van Bogaert, *Principal*
EMP: 3
SALES (est): 102.2K **Privately Held**
SIC: 3999 Manufacturing industries

(G-8447)
BRIANNAS PANCAKE CAFE
151 Il Route 38 (60119-8879)
PHONE.................630 365-4770
Araceli Robelledo, *Owner*
EMP: 9
SALES (est): 652.5K **Privately Held**
SIC: 2099 5812 Pancake syrup, blended & mixed; coffee shop; family restaurants

(G-8448)
CROWN COATINGS COMPANY
215 W Nebraska St (60119-8309)
PHONE.................630 365-9925
Carolyn Popp, *President*
EMP: 12
SQ FT: 10,000
SALES (est): 250K **Privately Held**
SIC: 5033 2952 Roofing, asphalt & sheet metal; asphalt felts & coatings
PA: Drafting & Construction Services, Inc
55 Winthrop New Rd
Sugar Grove IL

(G-8449)
DRUMBEATERS OF AMERICA INC
215 W Nebraska St (60119-8309)
PHONE.................630 365-5527
Carolyn Popp, *President*
James Popp, *Vice Pres*
Mary Brown, *Executive*
▼ EMP: 16
SQ FT: 10,000
SALES (est): 5.4MM **Privately Held**
SIC: 3532 4953 Crushers, stationary; cleaning machinery, mineral; hazardous waste collection & disposal

(G-8450)
DU-CALL MILLER PLASTICS INC
704 E North St (60119-9049)
PHONE.................630 964-6020
William C Miller III, *President*
Linnea Miller, *Treasurer*
Harvey Hanig, *Manager*
EMP: 10
SQ FT: 15,730
SALES (est): 1.4MM **Privately Held**
WEB: www.du-call.com
SIC: 3089 3161 2441 Thermoformed finished plastic products; luggage; nailed wood boxes & shook

(G-8451)
ELBURN MARKET INC
Also Called: Ream's Meat Market
250 S Main St (60119-9426)
PHONE.................630 365-6461
Randall D Ream, *President*
Phyllis Ream, *Corp Secy*
Janelle Ream, *Vice Pres*
EMP: 25
SQ FT: 1,800
SALES (est): 2MM **Privately Held**
WEB: www.reamsmeatmarket.com
SIC: 5421 5411 2013 Meat markets, including freezer provisioners; fish markets; grocery stores; sausages from purchased meat

(G-8452)
ELBURN METAL STAMPING INC
44w210 Keslinger Rd (60119)
P.O. Box 947 (60119-0947)
PHONE.................630 365-2500
Steven P Porter, *President*
Lana Porter, *Treasurer*
Chad Porter, *Manager*
Rehanna Stout, *Supervisor*
▲ EMP: 30
SQ FT: 50,000
SALES (est): 4.5MM **Privately Held**
WEB: www.elburnstamping.com
SIC: 3599 3469 Custom machinery; stamping metal for the trade

(G-8453)
ELECTRIC CONDUIT CNSTR CO
816 Hicks Dr (60119-9060)
PHONE.................630 293-4474
EMP: 250
SALES (est): 57.7MM **Privately Held**
SIC: 1521 3644 1623 3272 Single-Family House Cnst Mfg Nonconductv Wire Dvc Water/Sewer/Utility Cnst Mfg Concrete Products

(G-8454)
ELECTRIC CONDUIT CONSTRUCTION
Also Called: Midwestern Contractors
601 E North St (60119-9048)
PHONE.................630 859-9310
Mark Schiavi, *Vice Pres*
EMP: 18 EST: 2008
SALES (est): 3.4MM **Privately Held**
WEB: www.midwesterncontractors.com
SIC: 3644 Electric conduits & fittings

(G-8455)
HARRY OTTO PRINTING COMPANY
Also Called: Exclusive Boarding
707 E North St Ste A (60119-9010)
PHONE.................630 365-6111
Thomas Otto, *President*
Cindy Otto, *Vice Pres*
EMP: 10 EST: 1954
SQ FT: 5,000
SALES (est): 1.3MM **Privately Held**
WEB: www.ottoprinting.com
SIC: 2759 2752 2789 2771 Letterpress printing; commercial printing, offset; edging books, cards or paper; greeting cards

(G-8456)
LABORATORY TECHNOLOGIES INC
4n645 Mohican Ln (60119-8841)
PHONE.................630 365-1000
Donald Oesterlin, *President*
EMP: 2 EST: 2015
SALES (est): 291K **Privately Held**
SIC: 3829 Nuclear instrument modules

(G-8457)
LAFARGE AGGREGATES ILL INC
1s194 Il Route 47 (60119-9678)
PHONE.................630 365-3600
EMP: 4
SALES (corp-wide): 4.5B **Privately Held**
SIC: 1411 1442 Limestone, dimension-quarrying; common sand mining; gravel mining
HQ: Lafarge Aggregates Illinois, Inc.
7n394 S Mclean Blvd
South Elgin IL 60177
847 742-6060

(G-8458)
LIGHTHOUSE MARKETING SERVICES
1484 Anderson Rd (60119-8407)
PHONE.................630 482-9900
Scott Salvati, *President*
Kim Salvati, *Vice Pres*
Kimberly Salvati, *Vice Pres*
EMP: 5 EST: 2000
SALES (est): 673.8K **Privately Held**
WEB: www.lighthousemktg.com
SIC: 2759 Commercial printing

(G-8459)
MANTICORE ARMS INC
747 Herra St Unit A (60119-8437)
PHONE.................630 715-0334
Sven G Jonsson, *President*
EMP: 8
SALES (est): 213.7K **Privately Held**
SIC: 3484 Guns (firearms) or gun parts, 30 mm. & below

(G-8460)
MEYER MATERIAL CO MERGER CORP
1s194 Il Route 47 (60119-9678)
PHONE.................847 824-4111
Dave Young, *Manager*
EMP: 50

Elburn - Kane County (G-8461)

SALES (corp-wide): 4.5B **Privately Held**
SIC: 3273 Ready-mixed concrete
HQ: Meyer Material Company Llc
580 S Wolf Rd
Des Plaines IL 60016
815 331-7200

(G-8461)
MITY INC (PA)
Also Called: Self-Cleaning Strainer Co
700 E North St Ste B (60119-7009)
P.O. Box 818 (60119-0818)
PHONE 630 365-5030
Melvin J Thryselius, *President*
Gerald Runge, *Vice Pres*
Jerry R Rundee, *Admin Sec*
EMP: 4
SQ FT: 600
SALES: 600K **Privately Held**
SIC: 3569 5084 3564 3494 Filters & strainers, pipeline; industrial machinery & equipment; blowers & fans; valves & pipe fittings; metal stampings

(G-8462)
MIWA LOCK CO
816 Hicks Dr (60119-9060)
PHONE 630 365-4261
EMP: 3
SALES (est): 161.4K **Privately Held**
SIC: 3429 Manufactured hardware (general)

(G-8463)
MONITOR TECHNOLOGIES LLC
44w320 Keslinger Rd (60119-9702)
PHONE 630 365-9403
Craig Arussell, *President*
Darrell Lundquist, *Mfg Mgr*
Stephen Odell, *Buyer*
Andy Bowman, *Engineer*
Jeff Cole, *Engineer*
▲ **EMP:** 40
SQ FT: 30,000
SALES (est): 13.9MM **Privately Held**
WEB: www.monitortech.com
SIC: 3823 Liquid level instruments, industrial process type; level & bulk measuring instruments, industrial process

(G-8464)
NEXPUMP INC
820 Stover Dr Unit B (60119-8424)
PHONE 630 365-4639
Daniel Gierke, *President*
Chris Gierke, *Vice Pres*
▲ **EMP:** 5
SALES (est): 975.5K **Privately Held**
SIC: 3561 Pumps, domestic: water or sump

(G-8465)
NOVALEX THERAPEUTICS INC
43w605 Willow Creek Dr (60119-9182)
PHONE 630 750-9334
Michael Johnson, *President*
Shahila Christie, *Principal*
Elizabeth Woods, *Vice Pres*
EMP: 4
SALES (est): 365.2K **Privately Held**
SIC: 2834 Druggists' preparations (pharmaceuticals)

(G-8466)
ODIN FABRICATION INC
Also Called: Odin Industries
740 Hicks Dr (60119-9059)
PHONE 630 365-2475
Matthew Tokarsky, *President*
EMP: 12
SALES (est): 476.5K **Privately Held**
SIC: 3444 Sheet metal specialties, not stamped

(G-8467)
ODIN INDUSTRIES INC
740 Hicks Dr (60119-9059)
PHONE 630 365-2475
David Anderson, *President*
Linda Anderson, *Corp Secy*
EMP: 15
SQ FT: 13,000
SALES (est): 2.6MM **Privately Held**
SIC: 3444 Sheet metal specialties, not stamped; forming machine work, sheet metal

(G-8468)
OPTIMAL CONSTRUCTION SVCS INC
843 Shepherd Ln (60119-7125)
P.O. Box 488 (60119-0488)
PHONE 630 365-5050
Jerald Meister, *President*
EMP: 1 EST: 2011
SALES: 380K **Privately Held**
WEB: www.optimal-construction.com
SIC: 3448 1761 Prefabricated metal buildings; roofing, siding & sheet metal work; gutter & downspout contractor; siding contractor

(G-8469)
PRECISION COMPUTER METHODS
801 Drover St (60119-8955)
PHONE 630 208-8000
Peter Hart Heinicke, *President*
Karen Heinicke, *Vice Pres*
EMP: 4
SQ FT: 750
SALES (est): 526.6K **Privately Held**
SIC: 7373 3577 5734 Computer systems analysis & design; data conversion equipment, media-to-media: computer; software, business & non-game

(G-8470)
PRO ACCESS SYSTEMS INC (PA)
116 Paul St (60119-7027)
PHONE 630 426-0022
Andrew M Faville, *CEO*
Leslie R Heerdt, *Ch of Bd*
Donald R Parrin, *President*
Michael Wroblewski, *General Mgr*
Ervin E Schlepp, *Exec VP*
▲ **EMP:** 10
SQ FT: 6,000
SALES (est): 3.3MM **Privately Held**
SIC: 3699 Door opening & closing devices, electrical

(G-8471)
R B EVANS CO
808 Hicks Dr (60119-9060)
PHONE 630 365-3554
Margaret Spelman, *President*
David G Evans, *Vice Pres*
Kenneth Evans, *Vice Pres*
Marsha Fazio, *Admin Sec*
EMP: 6
SQ FT: 10,000
SALES (est): 600K **Privately Held**
WEB: www.evanscustommachining.com
SIC: 3541 3451 Numerically controlled metal cutting machine tools; screw machine products

(G-8472)
RUNGE ENTERPRISES INC
1 N 020 Thryselius Dr (60119)
P.O. Box 157 (60119-0157)
PHONE 630 365-2000
Gerald Runge, *President*
Barbara Liljehorn, *Admin Sec*
EMP: 8
SQ FT: 20,000
SALES (est): 971.4K **Privately Held**
WEB: www.webs.com
SIC: 3599 3469 Machine shop, jobbing & repair; metal stampings

(G-8473)
SIMULATION TECHNOLOGY LLC
747 Herra St Unit B (60119-8437)
PHONE 630 365-3400
Leland George, *Mng Member*
EMP: 8
SALES (est): 970.4K **Privately Held**
WEB: www.simulationtechnologyllc.com
SIC: 3699 Automotive driving simulators (training aids), electronic

(G-8474)
TECH-WELD INC
801 E North St (60119-9084)
PHONE 630 365-3000
Gregory J Lesage, *President*
Linda Lesage, *Admin Sec*
EMP: 15

SQ FT: 10,000
SALES (est): 4.5MM **Privately Held**
SIC: 3443 3498 Tanks, standard or custom fabricated: metal plate; tube fabricating (contract bending & shaping)

(G-8475)
TERRAMAC LLC
724 Hicks Dr (60119-9059)
PHONE 630 365-4800
Lisa Crimaldi, *COO*
Jeff Goebel, *Parts Mgr*
Andrew Banas, *Regl Sales Mgr*
Jon Mix, *Regl Sales Mgr*
Matt Nelson, *Regl Sales Mgr*
EMP: 5
SQ FT: 10,000
SALES (est): 1.2MM **Privately Held**
WEB: www.terramac.com
SIC: 3531 Construction machinery

(G-8476)
THRYSELIUS MACHINING INC
44w480 Keslinger Rd (60119-9755)
P.O. Box 248 (60119-0248)
PHONE 630 365-9191
James Thryselius, *President*
Judy Thryselius, *Vice Pres*
EMP: 15
SQ FT: 21,000
SALES (est): 1.7MM **Privately Held**
SIC: 3599 Machine shop, jobbing & repair

(G-8477)
TIN MANS GARAGE INC
39w869 Midan Dr Unit B (60119-9472)
PHONE 630 262-0752
EMP: 4
SALES (est): 437.9K **Privately Held**
SIC: 3444 Sheet metalwork

(G-8478)
TURF INC
Also Called: Bulk-Strap
Os 951 953 Green Rd 951 Os (60119)
P.O. Box 262, Batavia (60510-0262)
PHONE 630 365-3903
Ralph Hernandez, *President*
Sunny Hernandez, *Owner*
EMP: 5
SQ FT: 6,000
SALES: 500K **Privately Held**
SIC: 2298 Cordage & twine

Eldorado
Saline County

(G-8479)
BECKS MEDICAL & INDUS GASES
1411 Locust St (62930-1629)
PHONE 618 273-9019
Carl V Kasiar, *President*
EMP: 15
SALES: 145K **Privately Held**
SIC: 3842 Prosthetic appliances

(G-8480)
CAP FACTORY
816 State St (62930-1220)
PHONE 618 273-9662
Susan Stevons, *Manager*
EMP: 15
SALES (est): 758.3K **Privately Held**
SIC: 2353 Hats, caps & millinery

(G-8481)
EXTREME WELDING & MACHINE SERV
1506 Us Highway 45 N (62930-3788)
PHONE 618 272-7237
Smith Thomason, *Principal*
EMP: 5
SALES (est): 430.5K **Privately Held**
SIC: 7692 Welding repair

(G-8482)
QUORUM LABS LLC
895 Grayson Rd (62930-3913)
P.O. Box 29 (62930-0029)
PHONE 618 525-5600
David Bartok,
EMP: 3 EST: 2015

SQ FT: 3,200
SALES (est): 160K **Privately Held**
SIC: 2836 Biological products, except diagnostic

(G-8483)
RDF INC
2909 Richardson St (62930-3559)
P.O. Box 1088, Mount Vernon (62864-0022)
PHONE 618 273-4141
Dale Kjensrud, *President*
Janet Melissen, *Admin Sec*
▲ **EMP:** 18
SQ FT: 16,000
SALES (est): 2.9MM **Privately Held**
SIC: 3069 4953 Reclaimed rubber (reworked by manufacturing processes); recycling, waste materials

(G-8484)
TOWNLEY ENGRG & MFG CO INC
607 Sutton Rd (62930)
P.O. Box 531 (62930-0531)
PHONE 618 273-8271
Virgil Sanders, *Manager*
Beth Bowers, *Admin Asst*
EMP: 15
SALES (corp-wide): 70.3MM **Privately Held**
SIC: 3561 3532 3356 Pump jacks & other pumping equipment; mining machinery; nonferrous rolling & drawing
PA: Townley Engineering And Manufacturing Company, Inc.
10551 Se 110th St Rd
Candler FL 32111
352 687-3001

(G-8485)
TRI-COUNTY CHEMICAL INC (PA)
2441 Public Rd (62930-1148)
PHONE 618 273-2071
H E Melton, *President*
EMP: 14 EST: 1956
SQ FT: 8,000
SALES (est): 10.9MM **Privately Held**
WEB: www.liquidnpk.com
SIC: 2873 Fertilizers: natural (organic), except compost

(G-8486)
WILDCAT HILLS
115 Grayson Ln (62930-3947)
PHONE 618 273-8600
EMP: 6 EST: 2010
SALES (est): 318.6K **Privately Held**
SIC: 1241 Coal mining services

Eldred
Greene County

(G-8487)
ASSOCIATED AGRI-BUSINESS INC (PA)
Also Called: Simfax Agri-Services
229 Elm St (62027-1002)
P.O. Box 82 (62027-0082)
PHONE 618 498-2977
G John Roundcount, *President*
Whitney McIver, *Admin Sec*
EMP: 1
SALES (est): 427.2K **Privately Held**
SIC: 6331 7372 Federal crop insurance corporation; prepackaged software

---
Elgin
Kane County

(G-8488)
2ND CINE INC
637 Frazier St Ste 2 (60123-2105)
PHONE 773 455-5808
Thomas S Ciciura, *Principal*
Rob Dolan, *Manager*
EMP: 3
SQ FT: 6,000

GEOGRAPHIC SECTION

Elgin - Kane County (G-8515)

SALES (est): 570.4K **Privately Held**
WEB: www.2ndcine.com
SIC: **7819** 5043 3861 Consultants, motion picture; equipment rental, motion picture; motion picture cameras, equipment & supplies; motion picture apparatus & equipment

(G-8489)
A J FUNK & CO
Also Called: Glass Cleaner
1471 Timber Dr (60123-1898)
PHONE.................................847 741-6760
Patrick Funk, *President*
Lou Carlotti, *Sales Dir*
Barbara Devfkf, *Admin Sec*
EMP: 1 **EST:** 1941
SQ FT: 24,000
SALES: 976.7K **Privately Held**
SIC: **2842** 5169 Window cleaning preparations; chemicals & allied products

(G-8490)
ABRASIVE TECHNOLOGY INC
1175 Bowes Rd (60123-5541)
PHONE.................................847 888-7100
Yefim Vernik, *Research*
Shahla Amiri, *Branch Mgr*
EMP: 50
SALES (corp-wide): 99.5MM **Privately Held**
SIC: **3291** Abrasive wheels & grindstones, not artificial
PA: Abrasive Technology, Inc.
 8400 Green Meadows Dr N
 Lewis Center OH 43035
 740 548-4100

(G-8491)
ACCU CAST 2 INC
412 N State St (60123-2877)
PHONE.................................423 622-4344
EMP: 5
SALES (est): 644.5K **Privately Held**
SIC: **3544** Special dies & tools

(G-8492)
ACME DESIGN INC
37 N Union St (60123-5334)
PHONE.................................847 841-7400
Clinton Borucki, *President*
EMP: 9
SALES (est): 914.2K **Privately Held**
SIC: **3999** Models, general, except toy

(G-8493)
ACOMTECH MOLD INC
39w433 Highland Ave Ste 1 (60124-4208)
P.O. Box 5153 (60121-5153)
PHONE.................................847 741-3537
Dave Malo, *President*
Judy Malo, *Vice Pres*
EMP: 9
SQ FT: 8,400
SALES (est): 1.4MM **Privately Held**
SIC: **2821** 3544 Molding compounds, plastics; special dies, tools, jigs & fixtures

(G-8494)
ACTION CABINET SALES INC
1150 Davis Rd Ste K (60123-1345)
PHONE.................................847 717-0011
Mary Weine, *President*
Edward J Weine, *President*
EMP: 7
SALES (est): 520K **Privately Held**
SIC: **2434** 1751 2541 Wood kitchen cabinets; cabinet building & installation; wood partitions & fixtures

(G-8495)
ADMO INC
2550 Decade Ct Ste A (60124-7861)
PHONE.................................847 741-5777
Matthew Krieps, *CEO*
Scott Hill, *Mfg Dir*
Vicki Wilder, *Purch Mgr*
Kurt Von Kampen, *QC Mgr*
Nicole Hurtado, *Accountant*
▲ **EMP:** 100
SQ FT: 40,000
SALES (est): 39.6MM **Privately Held**
SIC: **3089** 3544 Injection molding of plastics; industrial molds

(G-8496)
ADVANCE ENGINEERING CORP
Also Called: AEC
440 S Mclean Blvd (60123-7102)
PHONE.................................847 760-9421
Thomas Brown, *President*
Mike Legittino, *Vice Pres*
Brian Paszkiewicz, *Vice Pres*
John Roberts, *Purch Mgr*
Albert Claps, *QC Mgr*
◆ **EMP:** 40 **EST:** 1950
SQ FT: 75,000
SALES (est): 10.6MM **Privately Held**
WEB: www.advengcorp.net
SIC: **3824** Integrating & totalizing meters for gas & liquids

(G-8497)
ADVANCED REFR INSTLLATION TECH
1150 Davis Rd Ste G (60123-1345)
PHONE.................................847 741-3105
Gerald Galloway, *President*
EMP: 10 **EST:** 1995
SALES (est): 919.2K **Privately Held**
WEB: www.advancedrefractory.com
SIC: **3297** Nonclay refractories

(G-8498)
AEROMOTIVE SERVICES INC
345 Willard Ave (60120-6810)
PHONE.................................224 535-9220
Carl Dumele, *President*
Brian Rattanabapha, *Warehouse Mgr*
Rene Alaniz, *QC Mgr*
EMP: 10
SALES (est): 2MM **Privately Held**
SIC: **3694** Harness wiring sets, internal combustion engines

(G-8499)
AGNES & CHRIS GULIK
Also Called: Cds Engineering
408 W Amberside Dr (60124-7860)
PHONE.................................847 931-9641
Chris Gulik, *Principal*
EMP: 3
SALES (est): 427.4K **Privately Held**
SIC: **3613** Panel & distribution boards & other related apparatus

(G-8500)
AIR GAGE COMPANY
516 Slade Ave (60120-3028)
PHONE.................................847 695-0911
▲ **EMP:** 104
SQ FT: 60,000
SALES (est): 13.6MM **Privately Held**
SIC: **3545** 3823 3825 Gauges (machine tool accessories); industrial instrmnts msrmnt display/control process variable; instruments to measure electricity

(G-8501)
AKT CORPORATION
Also Called: Akt Corporation of Wisconsin
909 Grace St (60120-8419)
PHONE.................................414 475-5020
Tucker Schoenecker, *CEO*
Deborah Schoenecker, *President*
EMP: 2
SALES (est): 302.7K **Privately Held**
SIC: **3648** Reflectors for lighting equipment: metal

(G-8502)
ALLEGRA PRINT & IMAGING INC
Also Called: Alegra Printing
909 Davis Rd (60123-1311)
PHONE.................................847 697-1434
Robert S Hanson, *President*
Virginia Hanson, *Admin Sec*
EMP: 5
SQ FT: 5,500
SALES (est): 600K **Privately Held**
SIC: **2752** 2791 2789 2671 Commercial printing, offset; typesetting; bookbinding & related work; packaging paper & plastics film, coated & laminated; mailing service

(G-8503)
ALLIED ASPHALT PAVING CO INC (PA)
1100 Brandt Dr (60120)
PHONE.................................630 289-6080
Dan Plote, *President*
Raymond Plote, *Chairman*
Daniel R Plote, *Vice Pres*
EMP: 30 **EST:** 1949
SQ FT: 2,000
SALES (est): 6.4MM **Privately Held**
WEB: www.alliedapc.com
SIC: **1611** 2951 2952 Highway & street paving contractor; asphalt & asphaltic paving mixtures (not from refineries); asphalt felts & coatings

(G-8504)
ALPHA ASSEMBLY SOLUTIONS INC
2541 Technology Dr (60124-7845)
PHONE.................................847 426-4241
EMP: 109
SALES (corp-wide): 1.8B **Publicly Held**
SIC: **3356** Solder: wire, bar, acid core, & rosin core
HQ: Alpha Assembly Solutions Inc.
 300 Atrium Dr Fl 3
 Somerset NJ 08873
 908 791-3000

(G-8505)
ALPHABET SHOP INC
300 Elgin Ave (60120-8412)
PHONE.................................847 888-3150
Sheldon Bernstein, *President*
Paul Tylman, *Vice Pres*
Barbara Trager, *Treasurer*
Phil Genitoni, *Consultant*
Robert Smith, *Admin Sec*
EMP: 25 **EST:** 1963
SQ FT: 26,000
SALES (est): 4.1MM **Privately Held**
WEB: www.alphabetshop.com
SIC: **3993** 2759 Electric signs; displays & cutouts, window & lobby; letters for signs, metal; commercial printing

(G-8506)
AMERICAN COLLOID COMPANY
Metallurgical Alloy Division
3422 Cameron Dr (60124-8070)
PHONE.................................304 882-2123
EMP: 11
SALES (corp-wide): 1.7B **Publicly Held**
SIC: **1459** 2899 Clay/Related Mineral Mining Mfg Chemical Preparations
HQ: American Colloid Company
 2870 Forbs Ave
 Hoffman Estates IL 60192

(G-8507)
AMERICAN INDUSTRIAL DIRECT LLC (PA)
Also Called: Auto Body Tool Mart
2545 Millennium Dr (60124-7815)
PHONE.................................800 382-1200
Rosa Lazaro, *Sales Mgr*
Matthew Dorfman, *Mng Member*
Brian Henke,
◆ **EMP:** 31
SQ FT: 30,000
SALES: 16MM **Privately Held**
SIC: **5013** 5085 3559 Body repair or paint shop supplies, automotive; industrial supplies; frame straighteners, automobile (garage equipment)

(G-8508)
AMERICAN NTN BEARING MFG CORP (DH)
Also Called: Anbm
1525 Holmes Rd (60123-1205)
PHONE.................................847 741-4545
Andy Kitajima, *President*
Katsu Miyake, *President*
John Welch, *General Mgr*
Rick Hately, *Chief*
Bill Murray, *Foreman/Supr*
◆ **EMP:** 380 **EST:** 1971
SQ FT: 400,000
SALES (est): 83.1MM **Privately Held**
SIC: **3562** Ball bearings & parts; roller bearings & parts

(G-8509)
AMERICAN WILBERT VAULT CORP
954 Bluff City Blvd (60120-7594)
PHONE.................................847 741-3089
Marc Hejnosz, *Manager*
EMP: 3
SALES (est): 247.9K
SALES (corp-wide): 8.2MM **Privately Held**
SIC: **3272** Burial vaults, concrete or precast terrazzo
PA: American Wilbert Vault Corp
 4415 Harrison St Ste 246
 Hillside IL 60162
 708 366-3210

(G-8510)
AMTEC MOLDED PRODUCTS INC
1355 Holmes Rd Ste A (60123-1244)
PHONE.................................815 226-0187
Ganesh Subramanian, *President*
Jayakar Krishnamurphy, *Chairman*
Krushna C Pati, *Admin Sec*
EMP: 33 **EST:** 1998
SQ FT: 49,000
SALES (est): 4MM **Privately Held**
SIC: **3089** Molding primary plastic
HQ: Ucal Systems, Inc.
 1875 Holmes Rd
 Elgin IL 60123

(G-8511)
ANGSTEN GROUP INC
Also Called: Shopware
2175 Point Blvd Ste 100 (60123-9218)
PHONE.................................888 222-7126
John Young, *Sales Engr*
Jim Frick, *Sales Associate*
Ryan Mermall, *Director*
EMP: 8
SALES (est): 632.8K **Privately Held**
SIC: **7372** Prepackaged software

(G-8512)
AQUA COAT INC
1061 Davis Rd (60123-1313)
PHONE.................................815 209-0808
Sven Carstensen, *Principal*
EMP: 2
SALES (est): 202.8K **Privately Held**
WEB: www.aquacoat.com
SIC: **3479** Coating, rust preventive

(G-8513)
AQUA-TECH CO
1875 Big Timber Rd Ste C (60123-1150)
PHONE.................................847 383-7075
Mark Vera, *President*
Katherine Devine, *Admin Sec*
EMP: 9
SALES (est): 737.4K **Privately Held**
SIC: **2048** Fish food

(G-8514)
ARTHUR SCHUMAN INC
2589 Technology Dr (60124-7832)
PHONE.................................847 851-8500
Thomas Deangelo, *Branch Mgr*
EMP: 36
SALES (corp-wide): 181.1MM **Privately Held**
SIC: **2022** Cheese, natural & processed
PA: Arthur Schuman Inc.
 40 New Dutch Ln
 Fairfield NJ 07004
 973 227-0030

(G-8515)
ARTHUR SCHUMAN MIDWEST LLC
2589 Technology Dr (60124-7832)
PHONE.................................847 851-8500
Neil Schumann, *CEO*
Rich Phillips, *Exec VP*
Malin Benicek, *Vice Pres*
Mike Novacovici, *Purchasing*
Jim Gregori, *Regl Sales Mgr*
▲ **EMP:** 65
SALES (est): 26.9MM
SALES (corp-wide): 181.1MM **Privately Held**
SIC: **2022** Cheese, natural & processed

Elgin - Kane County (G-8516)

PA: Arthur Schuman Inc.
40 New Dutch Ln
Fairfield NJ 07004
973 227-0030

(G-8516)
ASSOCIATED PROFESSIONALS
665 Tollgate Rd Ste F (60123-9353)
PHONE..................847 931-0095
Fax: 847 931-0132
EMP: 3
SALES (est): 240K Privately Held
SIC: 3531 Mfg Construction Machinery

(G-8517)
ATLAS BOILER & WELDING COMPANY
424 N Grove Ave (60120-3612)
P.O. Box 202 (60121-0202)
PHONE..................815 963-3360
Justine Ackmann, *President*
EMP: 4
SQ FT: 4,800
SALES (est): 498.5K Privately Held
WEB: www.atlasboilerandwelding.com
SIC: 7699 7692 3443 Boiler repair shop; welding repair; fabricated plate work (boiler shop)

(G-8518)
AVERUS USA INC (PA)
2410 Vantage Dr (60124-7867)
PHONE..................800 913-7034
Daryl Mirza, *President*
John Collins, *Vice Pres*
Christie Kaye, *Admin Sec*
EMP: 85
SQ FT: 26,000
SALES (est): 56.2MM Privately Held
SIC: 3569 7349 Filters, general line: industrial; building component cleaning service

(G-8519)
B D C INC
1185 Jansen Farm Ct (60123-2595)
PHONE..................847 741-2233
Thom Carpenter, *President*
Carol Carpenter, *Corp Secy*
D Lee Carpenter, *Vice Pres*
Adriana Casarrubias, *Purch Dir*
◆ **EMP:** 30
SQ FT: 20,000
SALES (est): 5.5MM Privately Held
SIC: 3652 3679 Pre-recorded records & tapes; electronic circuits

(G-8520)
BELLEN CONTAINER CORPORATION
Also Called: Packaging By Design
1460 Bowes Rd (60123-5539)
P.O. Box 5125 (60121-5125)
PHONE..................847 741-5600
Joseph Graziano Sr, *President*
Charles J Graziano, *President*
Joseph Graziano Jr, *Vice Pres*
Kathleen Rutta, *Controller*
Michael Graziano, *Regl Sales Mgr*
EMP: 35
SQ FT: 34,970
SALES (est): 4.9MM Privately Held
SIC: 7389 2759 Laminating service; flexographic printing

(G-8521)
BFI WASTE SYSTEMS N AMER INC
Also Called: Site 933
1330 Gasket Dr (60120-7543)
PHONE..................847 429-7370
Kim Davis, *Principal*
EMP: 29
SALES (corp-wide): 10.3B Publicly Held
SIC: 4953 4212 3341 2611 Rubbish collection & disposal; local trucking, without storage; secondary nonferrous metals; pulp mills
HQ: Bfi Waste Systems Of North America, Inc.
2394 E Camelback Rd
Phoenix AZ 85016

(G-8522)
BOHLER
2505 Millennium Dr (60124-7815)
PHONE..................630 883-3000
EMP: 2
SALES (est): 290K Privately Held
SIC: 3449 Mfg Misc Structural Metalwork

(G-8523)
BOWL-TRONICS ENTERPRISES INC
1115 Sherwood Ave (60120-2444)
PHONE..................847 741-4500
Richard Mc Gehee, *President*
EMP: 8
SQ FT: 3,200
SALES (est): 764.8K Privately Held
SIC: 3949 7629 Bowling equipment & supplies; electronic equipment repair

(G-8524)
BRIGITFLEX INC
1725 Fleetwood Dr (60123-7130)
PHONE..................847 741-1452
Brigit Lawrence, *President*
EMP: 10
SQ FT: 15,000
SALES (est): 1.4MM Privately Held
SIC: 3672 Printed circuit boards

(G-8525)
BTR CONTROLS INC
1570 Todd Farm Dr (60123-1287)
PHONE..................847 608-9500
Ron Seyk, *President*
Rik Bruns, *CTO*
Alejandro Valdecasas, *Software Engr*
Mateusz Wielgos, *Software Engr*
Sandra Seyk, *Admin Sec*
EMP: 9
SQ FT: 15,000
SALES (est): 1.9MM Privately Held
SIC: 3625 Control equipment, electric; industrial controls: push button, selector switches, pilot

(G-8526)
BUCHER HYDRAULICS INC
2545 Northwest Pkwy (60124-7870)
PHONE..................847 429-0700
Dan Vaughan, *CEO*
Dan Leary, *Sales Staff*
Sylvia Veal, *Technology*
Vicky Schroeder, *Admin Sec*
EMP: 7
SALES (corp-wide): 3.1B Privately Held
SIC: 3594 Pumps, hydraulic power transfer
HQ: Bucher Hydraulics, Inc.
1363 Michigan St Ne
Grand Rapids MI 49503
616 458-1306

(G-8527)
C AND S CARPENTRY LLC
164 E Chicago St (60120-5518)
PHONE..................224 523-8064
Bryan Schmoldt, *Principal*
EMP: 4
SALES (est): 586.9K Privately Held
WEB: www.woodindustry.com
SIC: 2431 Millwork

(G-8528)
C&C SEALANTS
576 Covered Bridge Dr (60124-5613)
PHONE..................708 717-0686
Kevin Carey, *Principal*
EMP: 13
SALES (est): 950K Privately Held
SIC: 3011 Tires & inner tubes

(G-8529)
CAPSONIC AUTOMOTIVE INC
Also Called: Capsonic Group
495 Renner Dr (60123-6903)
PHONE..................847 888-7300
George Albrecht, *Branch Mgr*
EMP: 10 Privately Held
SIC: 3625 Motor controls & accessories; switches, electric power
PA: Capsonic Automotive, Inc.
460 2nd St
Elgin IL 60123

(G-8530)
CAPSONIC AUTOMOTIVE INC (PA)
460 2nd St (60123-7008)
PHONE..................847 888-7300
Gregory G Liautaud, *President*
Seth Gutkowski, *Vice Pres*
Raul Ramirez, *Controller*
Todd N Zangler, *Accounts Mgr*
Thomas J Gillespie, *Admin Sec*
▲ **EMP:** 10
SQ FT: 70,000
SALES (est): 111.7MM Privately Held
SIC: 3625 3679 3674 Motor controls & accessories; switches, electric power; harness assemblies for electronic use: wire or cable; radiation sensors

(G-8531)
CAPSONIC GROUP LLC (PA)
460 2nd St (60123-7008)
PHONE..................847 888-7264
Greg G Liautaud, *CEO*
George Albrecht, *Vice Pres*
Kotaro Furuichi, *Project Mgr*
Josue Mejia, *Purch Mgr*
Isidro Botello, *Engineer*
▲ **EMP:** 441
SQ FT: 72,000
SALES (est): 48.4MM Privately Held
WEB: www.capsonicgroup.com
SIC: 3089 Injection molded finished plastic products; injection molding of plastics

(G-8532)
CAR - MON PRODUCTS INC
1225 Davis Rd (60123-1365)
PHONE..................847 695-9000
Fred L Imming, *President*
Sandra K Imming, *Admin Sec*
EMP: 40
SQ FT: 46,000
SALES (est): 10MM Privately Held
WEB: www.car-mon.com
SIC: 3564 Exhaust fans: industrial or commercial; air cleaning systems; air purification equipment

(G-8533)
CARLSON STI INC
1875 Big Timber Rd Ste A (60123-1149)
PHONE..................630 232-2460
JC Carlson, *Principal*
EMP: 8 EST: 2009
SALES (est): 1MM Privately Held
WEB: www.carlson-tool.com
SIC: 3559 Bag seaming & closing machines (sewing machinery)

(G-8534)
CARLSON TOOL & MACHINE COMPANY
Also Called: Carlson STI
1875 Big Timber Rd Ste A (60123-1149)
PHONE..................630 232-2460
John M Carlson, *President*
John Wilson, *COO*
Sam Satish, *Vice Pres*
Mit Patel, *Opers Staff*
Jeff Bogda, *Engineer*
▲ **EMP:** 10
SQ FT: 45,000
SALES (est): 2MM Privately Held
WEB: www.carlson-tool.com
SIC: 3559 Broom making machinery

(G-8535)
CGK ENTERPRISES INC
Also Called: Tri-State Asphalt Emulsions
695 Church Rd (60123-9308)
PHONE..................847 888-1362
Todd Weist, *CEO*
Charles Kline, *President*
EMP: 4
SALES (est): 956.3K Privately Held
SIC: 2951 Asphalt & asphaltic paving mixtures (not from refineries)

(G-8536)
CHARTER PRECISION LLC
Also Called: Cmworks Acquisition LLC
1145 Jansen Farm Dr (60123-2596)
PHONE..................847 214-8400
John W Mellowes, *CEO*
EMP: 100

SALES (est): 7.3MM
SALES (corp-wide): 681.7MM Privately Held
SIC: 3451 Screw machine products
HQ: Charter Automotive Llc
7850 N 81st St
Milwaukee WI 53223
414 365-5000

(G-8537)
CHEMTECH PLASTICS INC
765 Church Rd (60123-9308)
PHONE..................630 503-6000
Ragnar Korthase, *CEO*
Derek N Popp, *President*
Jeff Nesslar, *Vice Pres*
Karyn Sandmann, *Purch Dir*
Katie Kovach, *Purch Agent*
▲ **EMP:** 100
SQ FT: 60,000
SALES (est): 32.5MM Privately Held
SIC: 3089 Injection molding of plastics

(G-8538)
CHICAGO DYE WORKS
18 N State St (60123-5484)
P.O. Box 703 (60121-0703)
PHONE..................847 931-7968
Tom Hodge, *Owner*
EMP: 6
SALES (est): 250K Privately Held
SIC: 2269 Linen fabrics: dyeing, finishing & printing

(G-8539)
CHURCH OF BRETHREN INC (PA)
Also Called: Denominational Headquarters
1451 Dundee Ave (60120-1694)
PHONE..................847 742-5100
Patrick C Starkey, *Ch of Bd*
Carl Fike, *Ch of Bd*
Roxane Hill, *Managing Dir*
Judy E Keyser, *CFO*
Leann Wine, *Treasurer*
EMP: 80
SQ FT: 70,000
SALES (est): 8.8MM Privately Held
SIC: 8661 2721 Brethren Church; magazines: publishing only, not printed on site

(G-8540)
CIRCUITRONICS
1300 Holmes Rd (60123-1202)
PHONE..................630 668-5407
Job Varghese, *Mng Member*
Manohar L Sharma, *President*
EMP: 40
SALES (est): 6.8MM Privately Held
SIC: 3672 Printed circuit boards

(G-8541)
CITY ORNAMENTAL IRON WORKS
Also Called: City Iron Works
1140 Morningside Dr (60123-1437)
PHONE..................847 888-8898
Tom Walton, *Owner*
EMP: 5
SQ FT: 3,000
SALES (est): 387.4K Privately Held
SIC: 3315 3446 Fence gates posts & fittings: steel; stairs, fire escapes, balconies, railings & ladders; railings, prefabricated metal

(G-8542)
CLARIDGE PRODUCTS
923 N State St (60123-2146)
PHONE..................847 991-8822
EMP: 2
SALES (est): 219.8K Privately Held
SIC: 2531 Public building & related furniture

(G-8543)
CLARIDGE PRODUCTS AND EQP INC
923 N State St (60123-2146)
PHONE..................847 991-8822
Mike Denker, *Division Mgr*
Mary Follensbee, *Office Mgr*
EMP: 6

GEOGRAPHIC SECTION

Elgin - Kane County (G-8568)

SALES (corp-wide): 109.3MM **Privately Held**
SIC: **2493** 2531 Reconstituted wood products; blackboards, wood
PA: Claridge Products And Equipment, Incorporated
601 Highway 62 65 S
Harrison AR 72601
870 743-2200

(G-8544)
COBRA METAL WORKS INC
1140 Jansen Farm Dr (60123-2550)
PHONE..................................847 214-8400
Anton Hirsch, *President*
Adrian Deleon, *Opers Staff*
Sullivan Matt, *Opers Staff*
Marcel Oros, *Engrg Dir*
Matt Sullivan, *Engineer*
▲ EMP: 180 EST: 1997
SALES (est): 76.7MM **Privately Held**
WEB: www.cobrametalworks.com
SIC: **3444** Sheet metalwork

(G-8545)
COLONY DISPLAY LLC (HQ)
2531 Tech Dr Ste 314 (60124)
PHONE..................................847 426-5300
Jerrold Zich, *President*
Scott Harrington, *Facilities Mgr*
Maira Cervantes, *Production*
Dave Rhodes, *Buyer*
Craig Lemon, *Project Engr*
◆ EMP: 25
SALES (est): 60.5MM **Privately Held**
SIC: **2542** 2541 Partitions & fixtures, except wood; wood partitions & fixtures
PA: Kinzie Capital Partners Llc
20 N Clark St Fl 36
Chicago IL 60602
312 809-2490

(G-8546)
COMPONENT PLASTICS INC
700 Tollgate Rd (60123-9338)
PHONE..................................847 695-9200
Joseph Valente, *President*
Justin Newlin, *Vice Pres*
Darrick Schlossmann, *Project Mgr*
Eric Ulbrich, *Project Mgr*
Kirit Shah, *QC Mgr*
▲ EMP: 100
SQ FT: 40,000
SALES (est): 23.3MM **Privately Held**
WEB: www.cpielgin.com
SIC: **3089** Injection molding of plastics

(G-8547)
COMPONENT SPECIALTY INC (HQ)
412 N State St (60123-2877)
PHONE..................................847 742-4400
Bruce J Carter, *President*
Andy Nuggehalli, *CFO*
Nand Kumar, *Executive*
▲ EMP: 18
SQ FT: 52,000
SALES (est): 7.9MM
SALES (corp-wide): 29.2MM **Privately Held**
SIC: **3599** Machine shop, jobbing & repair
PA: Uca Group, Inc
412 N State St
Elgin IL 60123
847 742-8870

(G-8548)
COMPUTERPROX
163 E Chicago St Fl 2 (60120-5523)
PHONE..................................847 516-8560
Greg Gliniecki, *CEO*
Mark Elliot, *Partner*
EMP: 10
SALES (est): 817.3K **Privately Held**
SIC: **3577** Computer peripheral equipment

(G-8549)
CONCRETE SPECIALTIES CO INC
1375 Gifford Rd (60120-7306)
PHONE..................................847 608-1200
Jim Nondorf, *President*
EMP: 40
SQ FT: 50,000

SALES (est): 2.8MM
SALES (corp-wide): 16.4MM **Privately Held**
SIC: **3272** Concrete products
PA: Concrete Specialties Co.
1375 Gifford Rd
Elgin IL 60120
847 608-1200

(G-8550)
CONCRETE SPECIALTIES CO (PA)
1375 Gifford Rd (60120-7306)
PHONE..................................847 608-1200
James Nondorf, *President*
▼ EMP: 44 EST: 1946
SALES (est): 16.4MM **Privately Held**
WEB: www.concretespecialtiescompany.com
SIC: **3272** Concrete products, precast

(G-8551)
CONDOR GRANITES INTL INC
1605 Dundee Ave Ste H (60120-1678)
PHONE..................................847 635-7214
Jayanti K Patel, *President*
Bharat K Thakkar, *Admin Sec*
▲ EMP: 3
SALES (est): 289.2K **Privately Held**
SIC: **3281** Granite, cut & shaped

(G-8552)
CONTINENTAL DATALABEL INC (PA)
1855 Fox Ln (60123-7815)
PHONE..................................847 742-1600
Timothy J Flynn, *CEO*
Michael P Nicholas, *President*
Meghan Flynn, *Vice Pres*
Brian Zimmerman, *Plant Mgr*
David Marino, *Facilities Mgr*
▲ EMP: 110
SQ FT: 120,000
SALES (est): 31.5MM **Privately Held**
WEB: www.datalabel.com
SIC: **2672** Tape, pressure sensitive: made from purchased materials

(G-8553)
CONTROL SYSTEM INNOVATORS INC
1760 Britannia Dr Ste 1 (60124-7814)
PHONE..................................847 741-0007
Darrell Whitmore, *President*
EMP: 9
SALES (est): 121.4K **Privately Held**
SIC: **3625** Relays & industrial controls

(G-8554)
CONTROLLINK INCORPORATED
1650 Cambridge Dr (60125-1143)
PHONE..................................847 622-1100
Gary Dembski, *President*
Boris Bednyak, *Corp Secy*
John Jackson, *Engineer*
EMP: 30
SQ FT: 20,000
SALES (est): 6.4MM **Privately Held**
SIC: **7373** 3625 Computer integrated systems design; relays & industrial controls

(G-8555)
CONTROLS GROUP USA INC
2521 Tech Dr Ste 203 (60124)
PHONE..................................847 551-5775
John Lamond, *General Mgr*
EMP: 5 EST: 2015
SQ FT: 4,000
SALES: 2MM
SALES (corp-wide): 177.9K **Privately Held**
SIC: **5013** 3829 Testing equipment, engine; testing equipment: abrasion, shearing strength, etc.
HQ: Controls Spa
Via Salvo D'acquisto 2/4
Liscate MI 20060
029 218-41

(G-8556)
COOK COMMUNICATIONS MINIS
Chariot Family Publishing
850 N Grove Ave (60120-2807)
PHONE..................................847 741-5168
David Orriss, *Manager*

EMP: 100
SALES (corp-wide): 13.1MM **Privately Held**
SIC: **2721** 2731 2754 Periodicals; book publishing; magazines: gravure printing, not published on site
PA: Cook Communications Ministries International, Inc.
4050 Lee Vance Vw
Colorado Springs CO 80918
719 536-0100

(G-8557)
COOK COMMUNICATIONS MINISTRIES
Also Called: Cook, David C
850 N Grove Ave (60120-2807)
PHONE..................................847 741-0800
Cris Doornbos, *CEO*
EMP: 150
SALES (corp-wide): 13.1MM **Privately Held**
SIC: **8661** 2721 2771 2731 Religious organizations; periodicals: publishing & printing; greeting cards; books: publishing & printing; book printing
PA: Cook Communications Ministries International, Inc.
4050 Lee Vance Vw
Colorado Springs CO 80918
719 536-0100

(G-8558)
CS LEGACY CORP
Also Called: Cap & Seal Co.
1591 Fleetwood Dr (60123-7126)
PHONE..................................847 741-3101
Thomas J Brown, *President*
EMP: 27 EST: 1957
SQ FT: 34,000
SALES (est): 3.5MM
SALES (corp-wide): 6.1MM **Privately Held**
WEB: www.capseal.com
SIC: **3469** Metal stampings
PA: Sealco Industries, Inc
1591 Fleetwood Dr
Elgin IL 60123
847 741-3101

(G-8559)
CUSTOM CABINET REFACERS INC
2482 Technology Dr (60124-7925)
PHONE..................................847 695-8800
David Solari, *President*
EMP: 9
SQ FT: 7,000
SALES (est): 850K **Privately Held**
SIC: **2434** Wood kitchen cabinets

(G-8560)
CUSTOM FABRICATIONS INC
1625 Weld Rd Ste B (60123-5800)
PHONE..................................847 531-5912
Scott McConaughay, *President*
EMP: 5
SALES (est): 836.6K **Privately Held**
SIC: **3444** Sheet metalwork

(G-8561)
CVP SYSTEMS LLC
1675 Todd Farm Dr (60123-1146)
PHONE..................................630 852-1190
Wesley Bork, *President*
Richard Kelly, *General Mgr*
Laurie Mykleby, *Vice Pres*
Pat Duranty, *Plant Mgr*
Patrick Duranty, *Opers Mgr*
◆ EMP: 52 EST: 1982
SALES (est): 14.3MM
SALES (corp-wide): 2.9B **Publicly Held**
SIC: **3556** 3565 3563 Food products machinery; packaging machinery; air & gas compressors
PA: The Middleby Corporation
1400 Toastmaster Dr
Elgin IL 60120
847 741-3300

(G-8562)
D & S COMMUNICATIONS INC (PA)
1355 N Mclean Blvd (60123-1245)
PHONE..................................847 628-4195

Jason Kaubasak, *President*
Guy Fortin, *Business Mgr*
Charls Grisham, *Engineer*
Adam Petrauskas, *Engineer*
Ivan Anastasov, *Senior Engr*
▲ EMP: 60
SQ FT: 54,000
SALES (est): 20.8MM **Privately Held**
SIC: **3661** 4812 4813 Telephone & telegraph apparatus; radio telephone communication; telephone communication, except radio

(G-8563)
DAVID H POOL
Also Called: Print Loop
1405 Timber Dr Ste B (60123-1809)
PHONE..................................847 695-5007
David H Pool, *Owner*
EMP: 4
SALES (est): 170K **Privately Held**
WEB: www.print-loop.com
SIC: **3552** 2262 8743 Silk screens for textile industry; screen printing: manmade fiber & silk broadwoven fabrics; promotion service

(G-8564)
DAXAM INC
1550 Executive Dr (60123-9311)
PHONE..................................847 214-1733
Janus Pukszta, *President*
Janus Drobek, *Vice Pres*
Andrew Schulingkamp, *Manager*
EMP: 19
SQ FT: 33,000
SALES: 2.2MM **Privately Held**
SIC: **7336** 7389 2752 Graphic arts & related design; design services; promotional printing, lithographic

(G-8565)
DENTSPLY SIRONA INC
Midwest Dental
385 Airport Rd Ste 104 (60123-9341)
PHONE..................................847 640-4800
Jami Stell, *Regional Mgr*
Gregory Sheehan, *Vice Pres*
Ken Keenan, *Controller*
Salvatore Disimone, *Financial Analy*
Dave Christian, *Regl Sales Mgr*
EMP: 175
SALES (corp-wide): 4B **Publicly Held**
SIC: **3843** Dental equipment & supplies
PA: Dentsply Sirona Inc.
13320 Bllntyne Crprtate P
Charlotte NC 28277
844 848-0137

(G-8566)
DIRECT PALLET INC
1144 Saint Charles St (60120-8443)
PHONE..................................847 697-1019
Tony Farainella, *President*
Anthony Farinella, *Vice Pres*
John Fabiano, *Opers Mgr*
EMP: 22
SALES (est): 3.8MM **Privately Held**
SIC: **2448** Pallets, wood

(G-8567)
DOCUMENT PUBLISHING GROUP
Also Called: Healthware Systems
2511 Tech Dr Ste 102 (60124)
PHONE..................................847 783-0670
Stephen Gruner, *President*
EMP: 24 EST: 1998
SQ FT: 7,100
SALES (est): 2MM **Privately Held**
SIC: **7371** 2759 Computer software development; laser printing

(G-8568)
DORMER PRAMET LLC
Also Called: Precision Dormer, LLC
2511 Tech Dr Ste 113 (60124)
PHONE..................................800 877-3745
Wendy Leon, *Superintendent*
Ryan Bysterbusch, *Engineer*
Jonas Roy, *Finance Mgr*
Bogdan Nica, *Sales Mgr*
Mark Damato, *Regl Sales Mgr*
◆ EMP: 217

Elgin - Kane County (G-8569) — GEOGRAPHIC SECTION

SALES (est): 41.3MM
SALES (corp-wide): 11.1B **Privately Held**
SIC: 3545 Drills (machine tool accessories); cutting tools for machine tools
HQ: Sandvik, Inc.
17-02 Nevins Rd
Fair Lawn NJ 07410
201 794-5000

(G-8569)
DOVEE MANUFACTURING INC
640 Church Rd (60123-9340)
PHONE..................847 437-8122
John Malina, *Principal*
Amy Malina, *Principal*
EMP: 15 **EST:** 1944
SQ FT: 10,000
SALES: 3.3MM **Privately Held**
WEB: www.dovee.com
SIC: 3544 3469 Special dies & tools; die sets for metal stamping (presses); metal stampings

(G-8570)
DSM DESOTECH INC (DH)
Also Called: DSM Functional Materials
1122 Saint Charles St (60120-8498)
PHONE..................847 697-0400
Steve Hartig, *President*
Les Nack, *Vice Pres*
Geri Gashkoff, *Admin Sec*
▲ **EMP:** 200
SQ FT: 80,000
SALES (est): 77MM
SALES (corp-wide): 10.6B **Privately Held**
SIC: 2821 2819 8731 2851 Plastics materials & resins; industrial inorganic chemicals; commercial physical research; paints & allied products

(G-8571)
DTV INNOVATIONS LLC (PA)
2402 Millennium Dr (60124-7827)
PHONE..................847 919-3550
Scott Lopresto, *Research*
Ray Bryant, *Engineer*
Benitius Handjojo,
EMP: 12
SQ FT: 7,000
SALES (est): 4MM **Privately Held**
SIC: 3663 Television broadcasting & communications equipment

(G-8572)
DYNACAST LLC
195 Corporate Dr (60123-9355)
PHONE..................847 608-2200
Frank Anaya, *Plant Mgr*
Larry Lawson, *Production*
Mark Nissen, *Project Engr*
Mike Poyner, *Branch Mgr*
Scott Witt, *Manager*
EMP: 105
SALES (corp-wide): 1.2B **Privately Held**
SIC: 3364 3369 3365 3363 Zinc & zinc-base alloy die-castings; nonferrous foundries; aluminum foundries; aluminum die-castings
HQ: Dynacast Us Holdings, Inc.
14045 Balntyn Corp Pl
Charlotte NC 28277
704 927-2790

(G-8573)
EDM SCORPIO INC
Also Called: Scorpio Elec Dschrge Machining
84 Joslyn Dr (60120-4578)
PHONE..................847 931-5164
James M Hickey, *President*
EMP: 7
SQ FT: 5,000
SALES (est): 210K **Privately Held**
SIC: 3599 Electrical discharge machining (EDM)

(G-8574)
ELGIN INDUSTRIES INC
Also Called: Elgin World Trade
1100 Jansen Farm Dr (60123-2555)
PHONE..................847 742-1720
Martin J Skok Jr, *Ch of Bd*
Chris Anderson, *Exec VP*
Tom Skok, *Exec VP*
Dan Gathman, *Vice Pres*
Cheryl Hogrewe, *Vice Pres*
▲ **EMP:** 250 **EST:** 1920
SQ FT: 150,000
SALES (est): 79.8MM **Privately Held**
WEB: www.elginind.com
SIC: 3714 5013 Motor vehicle engines & parts; motor vehicle supplies & new parts

(G-8575)
ELGIN INSTANT PRINT
293 S Aldine St (60123-7249)
PHONE..................847 931-9006
Bonnie Pacetti, *President*
Brian Pacetti, *President*
Kathy Brockner, *Vice Pres*
EMP: 5
SQ FT: 2,400
SALES: 350K **Privately Held**
SIC: 2752 7334 2791 2789 Commercial printing, offset; photocopying & duplicating services; typesetting; bookbinding & related work

(G-8576)
ELGIN MOLDED PLASTICS INC (PA)
Also Called: Empco-Lite Div
909 Grace St (60120-8419)
PHONE..................847 931-2455
Clarence Labar, *President*
Henry Lindner, *Vice Pres*
Jeff Wheeland, *Plant Mgr*
Betty Studt, *Human Res Mgr*
Raymond P Kriske, *Admin Sec*
▲ **EMP:** 100
SQ FT: 80,000
SALES (est): 35MM **Privately Held**
SIC: 3089 Injection molded finished plastic products; injection molding of plastics

(G-8577)
ELGIN SWEEPER COMPANY
1300 W Bartlett Rd (60120-7529)
PHONE..................847 741-5370
Robert Welding, *CEO*
Mark Weber, *President*
Gary Gembala, *General Mgr*
David Panizzi, *Business Mgr*
Julie Cook, *Vice Pres*
◆ **EMP:** 425 **EST:** 1903
SQ FT: 240,000
SALES (est): 132.8MM
SALES (corp-wide): 1.2B **Publicly Held**
WEB: www.elginsweeper.com
SIC: 3537 Industrial trucks & tractors
PA: Federal Signal Corporation
1415 W 22nd St Ste 1100
Oak Brook IL 60523
630 954-2000

(G-8578)
EMERSON ELECTRIC CO
1901 South St (60123-6939)
PHONE..................847 585-8300
Sharon Adams, *President*
EMP: 100
SQ FT: 25,000
SALES (corp-wide): 18.3B **Publicly Held**
WEB: www.emerson.com
SIC: 3823 Industrial instrmnts msrmnt display/control process variable
PA: Emerson Electric Co.
8000 West Florissant Ave
Saint Louis MO 63136
314 553-2000

(G-8579)
ENGINEERED COMPONENTS CO (PA)
1100 Davis Rd Ste A (60123-1316)
PHONE..................847 985-8000
Arne A Henriksen, *President*
Jeffrey Henriksen, *Vice Pres*
Jim Nicchia, *Sales Staff*
Diane E Coursey, *Admin Sec*
▲ **EMP:** 32
SALES: 20MM **Privately Held**
SIC: 3965 5085 Fasteners; fasteners, industrial: nuts, bolts, screws, etc.

(G-8580)
ENGINEERED PLASTIC SYSTEMS LLC
885 Church Rd (60123-9309)
PHONE..................800 480-2327
John Joyce,
Timothy Andrews,
David Cook,
◆ **EMP:** 16
SQ FT: 30,000
SALES (est): 4.7MM **Privately Held**
SIC: 3082 5211 Unsupported plastics profile shapes; lumber products

(G-8581)
ETON MACHINE CO LTD
1485 Davis Rd Ste B (60123-1351)
PHONE..................847 426-3380
Bob Adamek, *President*
Narandera Dhawan, *Vice Pres*
EMP: 10
SQ FT: 14,000
SALES: 1MM **Privately Held**
SIC: 3599 7692 Machine shop, jobbing & repair; welding repair

(G-8582)
EZ COMFORT HEATING & AC
1290 Evergreen Ln (60123-4101)
PHONE..................630 289-2020
Steven J Marks, *Principal*
EMP: 3
SALES (est): 250K **Privately Held**
SIC: 3585 Heating & air conditioning combination units

(G-8583)
FABRIC IMAGES INC
325 Corporate Dr (60123-9373)
PHONE..................847 488-9877
Marco Alvarez, *President*
Patrick W Hayes, *President*
Vince Graal, *Opers Mgr*
Dorrie Brunke, *Purch Mgr*
Mark Wisnevitz, *CFO*
▲ **EMP:** 80
SQ FT: 55,000
SALES (est): 14.5MM **Privately Held**
SIC: 2399 Banners, made from fabric

(G-8584)
FABRICATORS & MFRS ASSN INTL (PA)
Also Called: FMA
2135 Point Blvd (60123-7956)
PHONE..................815 399-8700
Gerald Shankel, *President*
EMP: 50 **EST:** 1970
SQ FT: 38,220
SALES: 14.3MM **Privately Held**
SIC: 8611 2721 Trade associations; trade journals: publishing only, not printed on site

(G-8585)
FINISH LINE USA INC
1750 Todd Farm Dr Ste A (60123-1137)
PHONE..................847 608-7800
Grace Vargas, *President*
William Diaz, *Co-Owner*
Patricio Izquierdo, *Co-Owner*
EMP: 15
SALES (est): 2.2MM **Privately Held**
SIC: 3399 Powder, metal

(G-8586)
FIRST AYD CORPORATION
1325 Gateway Dr (60124-7866)
PHONE..................847 622-0001
Thomas R Schreiner, *President*
James K Evans, *Admin Sec*
EMP: 7
SQ FT: 100,000
SALES (est): 29.6MM **Privately Held**
SIC: 2842 2841 Sanitation preparations; soap & other detergents

(G-8587)
FIRST PRIORITY INC (PA)
Also Called: Priority Care
1590 Todd Farm Dr (60123-1287)
PHONE..................847 531-1215
Lawrence F Schneider, *President*
Ray Letak, *Opers Staff*
Paul Gutierrez, *Production*
Keith Pinkonsly, *Purch Mgr*
Paul Madej, *Human Res Dir*
◆ **EMP:** 75
SQ FT: 99,000
SALES (est): 23.5MM **Privately Held**
SIC: 2834 5122 Veterinary pharmaceutical preparations; animal medicines

(G-8588)
FLENDER CORPORATION
1401 Madeline Ln (60124-7949)
PHONE..................847 931-1990
Robert Tepe, *CEO*
Anabel Martinez, *Production*
William Galdo, *CFO*
Kenneth Kelly, *Manager*
▲ **EMP:** 200
SALES (est): 93.5MM
SALES (corp-wide): 96.9B **Privately Held**
SIC: 3714 3494 5085 Gears, motor vehicle; couplings, except pressure & soil pipe; gears
HQ: Flender Gmbh
Alfred-Flender-Str. 77
Bocholt 46395
287 192-0

(G-8589)
FMA COMMUNICATONS INC
2135 Point Blvd (60123-7956)
PHONE..................815 227-8284
Ed Youdell, *President*
Mary Bohnsack, *Admin Sec*
EMP: 82
SQ FT: 15,000
SALES (est): 11.2MM
SALES (corp-wide): 14.3MM **Privately Held**
SIC: 2721 Trade journals: publishing only, not printed on site
PA: Fabricators & Manufacturers Association, International
2135 Point Blvd
Elgin IL 60123
815 399-8700

(G-8590)
FOUNTAIN PRODUCTS INC
2769 Cascade Falls Cir (60124-3116)
PHONE..................630 991-7237
Paul J Lamb Jr, *President*
Janette Lamb, *Treasurer*
EMP: 2 **EST:** 1930
SALES (est): 256.2K **Privately Held**
SIC: 3469 Kitchen fixtures & equipment, porcelain enameled

(G-8591)
GCB METAL BUILDING SYSTEMS LLC
800 Dundee Ave (60120-3068)
PHONE..................224 268-3792
EMP: 4
SALES (est): 334.8K **Privately Held**
SIC: 3444 Sheet metalwork

(G-8592)
GEKA MANUFACTURING CORPORATION
1690 Cambridge Dr (60123-1143)
PHONE..................224 238-5080
Brad Thompson, *President*
Franco Luca Waizendorf, *Admin Sec*
◆ **EMP:** 37
SALES (est): 11.4MM
SALES (corp-wide): 3.7B **Privately Held**
WEB: www.geka-world.com
SIC: 2844 Cosmetic preparations
HQ: Geka Gmbh
Waizendorf 3
Bechhofen 91572
982 287-01

(G-8593)
GERALI CUSTOM DESIGN INC
1482 Sheldon Dr (60120-8131)
PHONE..................847 760-0500
David Gerali, *President*
Ruth Gerali, *Corp Secy*
EMP: 65
SQ FT: 10,500
SALES (est): 10.1MM **Privately Held**
SIC: 2542 2541 1799 Counters or counter display cases: except wood; wood partitions & fixtures; counter top installation

(G-8594)
GIBSON BRANDS INC
Gibson Strings & Original Eqp
1150 Bowes Rd (60123-5537)
PHONE..................800 544-2766
Larry Hall, *Engineer*
Lee Farrell, *Enginr/R&D Mgr*

GEOGRAPHIC SECTION

Elgin - Kane County (G-8619)

David D Timmons, *Marketing Staff*
Kavin Van Pamel, *Branch Mgr*
EMP: 40
SALES (corp-wide): 479.1MM **Privately Held**
SIC: 3931 5736 Guitars & parts, electric & nonelectric; musical instrument stores
PA: Gibson Brands, Inc.
209 10th Ave S
Nashville TN 37203
615 871-4500

(G-8595)
GIVAUDAN FLAVORS CORPORATION
580 Tollgate Rd Ste A (60123-9320)
PHONE.................................847 608-6200
Dan McCafferty, *Manager*
Andrew Roush, *Director*
EMP: 133
SALES (corp-wide): 6.2B **Privately Held**
SIC: 2869 Flavors or flavoring materials, synthetic
HQ: Givaudan Flavors Corporation
1199 Edison Dr
Cincinnati OH 45216

(G-8596)
GIVAUDAN FRAGRANCES CORP
Givaudan-Quest International
580 Tollgate Rd Ste A (60123-9320)
PHONE.................................847 645-7000
Gilles Andrier, *President*
EMP: 5
SALES (corp-wide): 6.2B **Privately Held**
SIC: 2869 Industrial organic chemicals
HQ: Givaudan Fragrances Corporation
1199 Edison Dr Ste 1-2
Cincinnati OH 45216
973 448-6500

(G-8597)
GMT INC
180 S Melrose Ave (60123-6140)
PHONE.................................847 697-8161
Glenn Bolt, *President*
Jermiah Seah, *President*
Michelle Dubanowski, *Vice Pres*
Barbara Bolt, *Admin Sec*
Tammy Frusolone,
▲ **EMP:** 42
SQ FT: 30,000
SALES (est): 10.5MM **Privately Held**
SIC: 3089 Thermoformed finished plastic products; plastic processing

(G-8598)
GOOD LITE CO (PA)
1155 Jansen Farm Dr (60123-2596)
PHONE.................................847 841-1145
Robert Rodgers, *President*
Chris Greening, *General Mgr*
Ruth Keller, *Cust Mgr*
Tim Collins, *Marketing Staff*
▲ **EMP:** 6 **EST:** 1931
SQ FT: 10,000
SALES: 1MM **Privately Held**
WEB: www.good-lite.com
SIC: 5047 3841 Medical equipment & supplies; surgical & medical instruments

(G-8599)
GPI MIDWEST LLC (DH)
Also Called: Artistic Carton Company
1975 Big Timber Rd (60123-1139)
PHONE.................................847 741-0247
Michael P Doss, *CEO*
Jeff Zeedyk, *COO*
Dawn Tischauser, *Purch Agent*
Jeff Farnsworth, *Engineer*
Jerry Hartje, *Natl Sales Mgr*
EMP: 50 **EST:** 1935
SQ FT: 60,000
SALES (est): 67.6MM **Publicly Held**
WEB: www.artisticcarton.com
SIC: 2631 2675 2657 Folding boxboard; die-cut paper & board; folding paperboard boxes

(G-8600)
GRAZIANO TL INC (PA)
1450 Bowes Rd (60123-5539)
P.O. Box 5118 (60121-5118)
PHONE.................................847 741-1900
Terri Lynn Schuck, *President*
Mark E Graziano, *Corp Secy*

Charles J Graziano, *Vice Pres*
Joseph Graziano, *Purch Agent*
Greg Schroyer, *CFO*
▼ **EMP:** 35
SQ FT: 108,000
SALES (est): 11.7MM **Privately Held**
SIC: 2068 2064 2034 Salted & roasted nuts & seeds; candy & other confectionery products; dried & dehydrated fruits

(G-8601)
GREAT LAKES CLAY & SUPPLY INC
927 N State St (60123-2146)
P.O. Box 831, Park Ridge (60068-0831)
PHONE.................................224 535-8127
Timothy Pfiffner, *President*
Alado Marchetti, *Treasurer*
Stephanie Meyer, *Manager*
EMP: 5
SQ FT: 10,500
SALES: 1.4MM **Privately Held**
SIC: 5032 5719 3255 Ceramic wall & floor tile; pottery; clay refractories

(G-8602)
H H INTERANTIONAL INC
1010 Douglas Rd (60120-7507)
PHONE.................................847 697-7805
Hormoz Homozi, *President*
EMP: 3
SALES: 250K **Privately Held**
SIC: 3081 Unsupported plastics film & sheet

(G-8603)
HAIGHT COMPANY
Also Called: Haight, The
166 Symphony Way (60120-5589)
PHONE.................................224 407-0763
John Haight, *Principal*
Kari Goodmay, *Principal*
Doree Haight, *Principal*
EMP: 32
SALES (est): 7.8K **Privately Held**
SIC: 2499 Decorative wood & woodwork

(G-8604)
HANSEN PLASTICS CORP
2758 Alft Ln (60124-7899)
PHONE.................................847 741-4510
David Watermann, *CEO*
Roy D Lilly, *President*
Tim Bayer, *Vice Pres*
Taylor Reed, *Project Mgr*
Glenn Whitecotton, *Foreman/Supr*
▲ **EMP:** 65 **EST:** 1968
SQ FT: 60,000
SALES (est): 29.4MM **Privately Held**
SIC: 3089 Injection molding of plastics

(G-8605)
HANSEN PLASTICS CORP
1300 Abbott Dr (60123-1821)
PHONE.................................847 741-4510
EMP: 3
SALES (est): 170.2K **Privately Held**
SIC: 3089 Mfg Plastic Products

(G-8606)
HARDINGE GRINDING GROUP INC (DH)
Also Called: Usach Technologies, Inc.
1524 Davis Rd (60123-1359)
PHONE.................................847 888-0148
Giacomo Antonini, *President*
Richard L Simons, *President*
Edward J Gaio, *Admin Sec*
▲ **EMP:** 42
SQ FT: 34,000
SALES (est): 8.2MM
SALES (corp-wide): 317.9MM **Privately Held**
SIC: 3541 5084 7699 Grinding machines, metalworking; metalworking machinery; industrial machinery & equipment repair
HQ: Hardinge Inc.
1 Hardinge Dr
Elmira NY 14903
607 734-2281

(G-8607)
HARIG PRODUCTS INC
1875 Big Timber Rd (60123-1148)
PHONE.................................847 695-1000
EMP: 17

SQ FT: 40,000
SALES (est): 3.9MM **Privately Held**
SIC: 3531 Mfg Construction Machinery
PA: Tru Tech Systems, Inc.
24550 N River Rd
Mount Clemens MI 48043

(G-8608)
HARTING INC OF NORTH AMERICA
Also Called: Harting Elektronik
1375 Crispin Dr (60123)
PHONE.................................847 741-2700
Allan Dickson, *President*
Elizabeth McQuaid, *Regl Sales Mgr*
EMP: 25
SALES (corp-wide): 899.3MM **Privately Held**
SIC: 3678 Electronic connectors
HQ: Harting Inc. Of North America
1370 Bowes Rd
Elgin IL 60123
847 741-1500

(G-8609)
HARTING INC OF NORTH AMERICA (HQ)
1370 Bowes Rd (60123-5556)
PHONE.................................847 741-1500
Dietmar Harting, *Ch of Bd*
Edmund Garstkiewicz, *Business Mgr*
Jim Volkening, *Opers Staff*
Dan Galfi, *Engineer*
Jeff McGhee, *Asst Controller*
▲ **EMP:** 35
SQ FT: 50,000
SALES (est): 45.4MM
SALES (corp-wide): 899.3MM **Privately Held**
SIC: 5065 3678 Connectors, electronic; electronic connectors
PA: Harting Stiftung & Co. Kg
Marienwerder Str. 3
Espelkamp 32339
577 247-0

(G-8610)
HARTING MANUFACTURING INC
1370 Bowes Rd (60123-5538)
PHONE.................................847 741-1500
Philip Harting, *Ch of Bd*
Jose Vargas, *Facilities Mgr*
Michael Bushman, *Purch Mgr*
Richard Hansen, *Engineer*
Phill Shaw, *Engineer*
EMP: 8
SALES (est): 99K **Privately Held**
SIC: 3678 Electronic connectors

(G-8611)
HENDRICK MANUFACTURING
1320 Gateway Dr (60124-7825)
PHONE.................................847 608-2047
Sandy Winkelman, *Principal*
EMP: 2
SALES (est): 228.1K **Privately Held**
WEB: www.hendrickcorp.com
SIC: 3999 Manufacturing industries

(G-8612)
HENDRICK METAL PRODUCTS LLC
1320 Gateway Dr (60124-7825)
PHONE.................................847 742-7002
Mike Drake, *Principal*
Tracy Wickerheim, *Electrical Engi*
Rommel Malay, *Info Tech Mgr*
Darin Drake,
EMP: 55
SQ FT: 76,000
SALES (est): 12MM **Privately Held**
SIC: 3444 Sheet metalwork

(G-8613)
HENKEL US OPERATIONS CORP
1345 Gasket Dr (60120-7544)
PHONE.................................847 468-9200
Steve Roseti, *Sales/Mktg Mgr*
Brian Croissant, *Sales Staff*
Judy Zehr, *Sales Executive*
EMP: 100
SALES (corp-wide): 22.2B **Privately Held**
SIC: 2891 5169 Adhesives; chemicals & allied products

HQ: Henkel Us Operations Corporation
1 Henkel Way
Rocky Hill CT 06067
860 571-5100

(G-8614)
HERBS BAKERY INC
1020 Larkin Ave (60123-5240)
PHONE.................................847 741-0249
Lynn Schwartz, *President*
Wendy Wessel, *Vice Pres*
Erick Schwartz, *Admin Sec*
EMP: 19
SQ FT: 3,400
SALES (est): 822.7K **Privately Held**
WEB: www.herbsbakery.com
SIC: 5461 2051 Cakes; bread, cake & related products

(G-8615)
HEXAGON METROLOGY INC
755 Tollgate Rd (60123-9331)
PHONE.................................847 469-3344
William Fetter, *Branch Mgr*
EMP: 3
SALES (corp-wide): 4.3B **Privately Held**
SIC: 3823 Industrial instrmnts msrmnt display/control process variable
HQ: Hexagon Metrology, Inc.
250 Circuit Dr
North Kingstown RI 02852
401 886-2000

(G-8616)
HOWARD CUSTOM TRANSFERS INC
1925 Holmes Rd Ste 400 (60123-1204)
PHONE.................................847 695-8195
Jeff Howard, *President*
Quintin Howard, *Admin Sec*
EMP: 30
SALES (est): 4.7MM **Privately Held**
SIC: 2752 Transfers, decalcomania or dry; lithographed

(G-8617)
HUMBOLDT MFG CO (PA)
875 Tollgate Rd (60123-9351)
PHONE.................................708 456-6300
Dennis E Burgess, *President*
Joseph Bryk, *Corp Secy*
Joe Bryk, *CFO*
Grant Graff, *Sales Mgr*
Robin Bailey, *Mktg Dir*
◆ **EMP:** 38 **EST:** 1925
SQ FT: 45,000
SALES: 30MM **Privately Held**
WEB: www.humboldtmfg.com
SIC: 3829 3821 Surveying & drafting equipment; bunsen burners; laboratory equipment: fume hoods, distillation racks, etc.

(G-8618)
HYDROX CHEMICAL COMPANY INC
Also Called: Hydrox Laboratories
825 Tollgate Rd Ste B (60123-9326)
PHONE.................................847 468-9400
Kappana Ramanandan, *President*
John Polydoros, *COO*
Jack Conarchy, *Purchasing*
Brian Gaare, *CFO*
Cristina Carranza, *Human Res Mgr*
▲ **EMP:** 65 **EST:** 1913
SQ FT: 85,000
SALES (est): 38.8MM **Privately Held**
WEB: www.hydroxlabs.com
SIC: 2844 2819 2834 2869 Shampoos, rinses, conditioners; hair; peroxides, hydrogen peroxide; veterinary pharmaceutical preparations; industrial organic chemicals

(G-8619)
I W M CORPORATION
Also Called: Industrial Water Management
399 Hammond Ave (60120-8423)
PHONE.................................847 695-0700
Leonard Sneed, *President*
Larry McCarthy, *Engineer*
Brandon Palmer, *Office Mgr*
EMP: 9
SQ FT: 24,000

Elgin - Kane County (G-8620)

SALES (est): 1MM **Privately Held**
WEB: www.iwmcorporation.com
SIC: **8748** 5084 2899 Business consulting; industrial machinery & equipment; chemical preparations

(G-8620)
ILLINOIS TOOL WORKS INC
ITW Shakeproof Auto Div
1201 Saint Charles St (60120-8494)
PHONE..................................847 741-7900
Dave Hauner, *Branch Mgr*
EMP: 35
SALES (corp-wide): 14.1B **Publicly Held**
SIC: **3452** 3451 Bolts, nuts, rivets & washers; screw machine products
PA: Illinois Tool Works Inc.
   155 Harlem Ave
   Glenview IL 60025
   847 724-7500

(G-8621)
ILLINOIS TOOL WORKS INC
Also Called: ITW Paslode
2501 Galvin Dr (60124-8391)
PHONE..................................847 783-5500
EMP: 104
SALES (corp-wide): 14.1B **Publicly Held**
SIC: **3089** 3965 3499 2891 Injection molded finished plastic products; fasteners; strapping, metal; adhesives & sealants; refrigeration & heating equipment
PA: Illinois Tool Works Inc.
   155 Harlem Ave
   Glenview IL 60025
   847 724-7500

(G-8622)
IMAC ASSET SALES CORP
2521 Tech Dr Ste 212 (60124)
PHONE..................................847 741-4622
John Krezski, *President*
EMP: 5
SALES (est): 1MM **Privately Held**
SIC: **3861** Motion picture apparatus & equipment
PA: Triphase Automation, Inc.
   1251 E Wisconsin Ave
   Pewaukee WI 53072

(G-8623)
IN COLOR GRAPHICS COML PRTG
1855 Fox Ln (60123-7813)
PHONE..................................847 697-0003
Rich Philip, *Owner*
EMP: 10 EST: 1998
SALES (est): 981.6K **Privately Held**
SIC: **2759** 2752 Commercial printing; commercial printing, lithographic

(G-8624)
INCREDIBLE THREADS LLC
300 Moseley St (60123-7580)
PHONE..................................847 970-0183
Theresa Windisch,
John R Miers,
EMP: 4
SQ FT: 10,000
SALES (est): 1.5MM **Privately Held**
WEB: www.incrediblethreadsllc.com
SIC: **2395** Embroidery & art needlework

(G-8625)
INDUCTION INNOVATIONS INC
1175 Jansen Farm Ct (60123-2595)
PHONE..................................847 836-6933
Thomas M Gough, *President*
Steven Gough, *Vice Pres*
Dave Pacholok, *Vice Pres*
Johanna Smith, *Marketing Mgr*
▲ EMP: 5
SALES (est): 940.8K **Privately Held**
SIC: **3677** Inductors, electronic

(G-8626)
INLAND BROACHING AND TL CO LLC
1441 Timber Dr (60123-1827)
PHONE..................................847 233-0033
Amarnath Nuggehalli,
Nandkumar Nuggehalli,
Vijay Raichura,
EMP: 2

SALES (est): 240K **Privately Held**
SIC: **3541** Broaching machines

(G-8627)
INTECELLS INC
2541 Tech Dr Ste 407 (60124)
PHONE..................................586 612-9811
Xiaohong Gayden, *Principal*
EMP: 3
SALES (est): 33.8K **Privately Held**
SIC: **7389** 3552 ; textile machinery

(G-8628)
INTEGRITY TECHNOLOGIES LLC
Also Called: Integratech
1140 Peachtree Ln Unit B (60120-4803)
PHONE..................................850 240-6089
John Jinkins,
EMP: 3
SALES (est): 224.2K **Privately Held**
SIC: **3571** 5734 Electronic computers; modems, monitors, terminals & disk drives: computers

(G-8629)
INTELLISOURCE INC
2531 Tech Dr Ste 301 (60124)
PHONE..................................847 426-7400
Tamatha Kelleher, *President*
Cassandra Farrar, *Project Mgr*
Frank Rotundo, *Project Mgr*
Ron Weeks, *Sales Staff*
Cassandra Serrurier, *Manager*
EMP: 41 EST: 2004
SALES (est): 6.8MM **Privately Held**
WEB: www.intellisourcesolutions.com
SIC: **8742** 7819 3497 Marketing consulting services; visual effects production; developing & printing of commercial motion picture film; foil, laminated to paper or other materials

(G-8630)
J SCHNEERBERGER CORP
1160 Abbott Dr (60123-1817)
PHONE..................................847 888-3498
Jurg Schneerberger, *President*
Hans Peter Maurer, *Treasurer*
▲ EMP: 7
SALES (est): 1.9MM
SALES (corp-wide): 30.4MM **Privately Held**
SIC: **5084** 3541 Machine tools & metalworking machinery; grinding machines, metalworking
PA: J. Schneerberger Maschinen Ag
   Geissbergstrasse 2
   Roggwil BE 4914
   629 184-100

(G-8631)
JALOR COMPANY
545 Tollgate Rd Ste E (60123-9305)
PHONE..................................847 202-1172
John Goorsky, *Owner*
EMP: 3
SALES (est): 257.9K **Privately Held**
WEB: www.jalorcompany.com
SIC: **3441** Fabricated structural metal

(G-8632)
JOHN B SANFILIPPO & SON INC (PA)
1703 N Randall Rd (60123-7820)
PHONE..................................847 289-1800
Jeffrey T Sanfilippo, *Ch of Bd*
Jasper B Sanfilippo Jr, *President*
Michael J Valentine, *President*
Howard Brandeisky, *Senior VP*
Stephen C Chester, *Senior VP*
◆ EMP: 240
SQ FT: 400,000
SALES: 876.2MM **Publicly Held**
WEB: www.jbssinc.com
SIC: **2068** 2064 2099 2096 Nuts: dried, dehydrated, salted or roasted; candy & other confectionery products; peanut butter; dessert mixes & fillings; potato chips & similar snacks; chocolate & cocoa products

(G-8633)
JOHN B SANFILIPPO & SON INC
Fisher Division
2350 Fox Ln (60123)
PHONE..................................847 690-8432

Francisco Almazan, *Manager*
EMP: 150
SALES (corp-wide): 876.2MM **Publicly Held**
SIC: **2068** 2099 Nuts: dried, dehydrated, salted or roasted; food preparations
PA: John B. Sanfilippo & Son, Inc.
   1703 N Randall Rd
   Elgin IL 60123
   847 289-1800

(G-8634)
JOHN OMALLEY
Also Called: Ozark Industries
170 River Bluff Rd (60120-2109)
PHONE..................................847 924-8670
John Omalley, *Principal*
EMP: 2
SALES (est): 206.4K **Privately Held**
WEB: www.ozarkgroup.com
SIC: **3993** Signs & advertising specialties

(G-8635)
JR TECH INC
1600 Todd Farm Dr Ste A (60123-1141)
PHONE..................................847 214-8860
Dan Scully, *President*
Joseph Rick, *Vice Pres*
EMP: 8
SALES (est): 1.2MM **Privately Held**
WEB: www.jrtechinc.com
SIC: **3599** Machine shop, jobbing & repair

(G-8636)
KINNEY ELECTRICAL MFG CO
678 Buckeye St (60123-2827)
PHONE..................................847 742-9600
Lowell D Naber, *President*
Tim Shelton, *General Mgr*
Roger Shelton, *Purchasing*
Amber Williams, *Purchasing*
Richard Markovich, *Design Engr*
EMP: 80
SQ FT: 99,000
SALES (est): 38.1MM **Privately Held**
SIC: **3613** Panelboards & distribution boards, electric; switchboard apparatus, except instruments

(G-8637)
KNIGHT TOOL WORKS INC
1200 Abbott Dr Ste C (60123-1825)
PHONE..................................847 678-1237
Richard Peterson II, *President*
Elizabeth Peterson, *Corp Secy*
▲ EMP: 17 EST: 1964
SQ FT: 250,000
SALES (est): 1.4MM **Privately Held**
WEB: www.my-molding-website.com
SIC: **3544** Dies & die holders for metal cutting, forming, die casting

(G-8638)
KO-POLYMER INC
1380 Gateway Dr Ste 7 (60124-7891)
PHONE..................................847 742-7700
Natalia Kovari, *President*
Andrew Kovari, *Exec VP*
▲ EMP: 10
SQ FT: 20,000
SALES (est): 1.4MM **Privately Held**
SIC: **2821** Plastics materials & resins

(G-8639)
KREIS TOOL & MFG CO INC
1615 Cambridge Dr (60123-1144)
PHONE..................................847 289-3700
E Stephen Kreis, *President*
Valerie Kreis, *Corp Secy*
Siegfried Kreis, *Vice Pres*
Aldo Andrade, *Prdtn Mgr*
Pete Keller, *Prdtn Mgr*
EMP: 30
SQ FT: 35,000
SALES (est): 8.6MM **Privately Held**
SIC: **3544** 3599 Special dies & tools; machine shop, jobbing & repair

(G-8640)
LASER PRO
978 N Mclean Blvd (60123-2039)
PHONE..................................847 742-1055
William Grocke, *President*
William A Grocke, *Owner*
Shannon Pierce, *Sales Staff*
EMP: 5

SALES (est): 794.4K **Privately Held**
SIC: **3861** 5734 Toners, prepared photographic (not made in chemical plants); computer peripheral equipment

(G-8641)
LEHMAN FAST TECH
37w468 Elmer Ct (60124-4810)
P.O. Box 301, South Elgin (60177-0301)
PHONE..................................847 742-5202
James Lehman, *Owner*
EMP: 3
SQ FT: 300
SALES (est): 245.8K **Privately Held**
SIC: **3599** 3544 Machine shop, jobbing & repair; special dies, tools, jigs & fixtures

(G-8642)
LUBEQ CORPORATION
1380 Gateway Dr Ste 6 (60124-7891)
P.O. Box 6627 (60121-6627)
PHONE..................................847 931-1020
▲ EMP: 10
SQ FT: 17,500
SALES (est): 7.5MM **Privately Held**
SIC: **5172** 3561 Lubricating oils & greases; pumps & pumping equipment

(G-8643)
LYNK LABS INC
2511 Tech Dr Ste 108 (60124)
PHONE..................................847 783-0123
Mike Miskin, *President*
Bill Rodey, *Opers Mgr*
EMP: 6
SQ FT: 5,000
SALES (est): 4.5MM **Privately Held**
SIC: **3674** Light emitting diodes

(G-8644)
M2M ENTERPRISES LLC
361 N Alfred Ave (60123-3317)
PHONE..................................847 899-7565
Debra Sauder, *Mng Member*
EMP: 5
SALES (est): 451.2K **Privately Held**
SIC: **3842** Surgical appliances & supplies

(G-8645)
MACCARB INC
2430 Millennium Dr (60124-7827)
PHONE..................................877 427-2499
Adam McCarthy, *President*
David McCarthy, *Engineer*
EMP: 2
SQ FT: 1,500
SALES: 1MM **Privately Held**
SIC: **5169** 2813 3443 Industrial gases; carbon dioxide; cylinders, pressure: metal plate

(G-8646)
MACHINED CONCEPTS LLC
1760 Britannia Dr Ste 8 (60124-7814)
PHONE..................................847 708-4923
Albert Raczynski,
EMP: 3
SALES (est): 450.4K **Privately Held**
SIC: **3599** Machine shop, jobbing & repair

(G-8647)
MAKO NETWORKS SALES & MKTG INC
1355 N Mclean Blvd (60123-1239)
PHONE..................................847 752-5566
Jason Kubusak, *CEO*
Simon Gamble, *President*
Michael Bryniarski, *Vice Pres*
EMP: 100
SQ FT: 54,000
SALES: 15MM **Privately Held**
SIC: **7374** 5065 5999 3661 Computer processing services; telephone equipment; telephone & communication equipment; telephones & telephone apparatus

(G-8648)
MANGOLD NETWORKS
1068 Bayside Rd (60123-1535)
PHONE..................................224 402-0068
Joshua Mangold, *Principal*
EMP: 3
SALES (est): 147.5K **Privately Held**
SIC: **2011** Meat packing plants

Elgin - Kane County

(G-8649)
MARSHALL MIDDLEBY INC (HQ)
Also Called: Middleby Cooking Systems Group
1400 Toastmaster Dr (60120-9274)
PHONE..................847 741-3300
William F Whitman Jr, *Ch of Bd*
Selim A Bassoul, *President*
Todd Breiner, *Vice Pres*
Ray Hart, *Vice Pres*
David B Baker, *CFO*
◆ EMP: 200
SQ FT: 210,000
SALES (est): 972.6MM
SALES (corp-wide): 2.9B **Publicly Held**
SIC: **3556** 3585 3631 Ovens, bakery; mixers, feed, except agricultural; refrigeration equipment, complete; household cooking equipment
PA: The Middleby Corporation
1400 Toastmaster Dr
Elgin IL 60120
847 741-3300

(G-8650)
MASTER MACHINE GROUP INC
Also Called: Alpha Form Technologies
1515 Commerce Dr (60123-9304)
PHONE..................847 472-9940
M Glenn Burchett II, *President*
Amy Berchett, *Admin Sec*
EMP: 5
SALES (est): 713.3K **Privately Held**
SIC: **3541** Machine tools, metal cutting type

(G-8651)
MASTER MOLDED PRODUCTS LLC
1000 Davis Rd (60123-1314)
PHONE..................847 695-9700
Ken Slocum, *General Mgr*
Rachel Lewis, *Business Mgr*
Ken Mraz, *Vice Pres*
Bill Collins, *Vice Pres*
Jason Nelson, *Plant Mgr*
▲ EMP: 125 EST: 1945
SQ FT: 85,000
SALES (est): 39.7MM
SALES (corp-wide): 242.6MM **Privately Held**
WEB: www.mastermolded.com
SIC: **3089** Injection molding of plastics
PA: Qp Holdings, Llc
1000 Davis Rd
Elgin IL 60123
847 695-9700

(G-8652)
MATE TECHNOLOGIES INC
1695 Todd Farm Dr (60123-1146)
PHONE..................847 289-1010
Steven Matecki, *CEO*
Mark Matecki, *Principal*
Randy Matecki, *Vice Pres*
EMP: 10
SQ FT: 10,000
SALES (est): 1.1MM **Privately Held**
SIC: **5162** 3089 2851 Plastics products; injection molding of plastics; paints & allied products

(G-8653)
MAXI-VAC INC
1437 Holmes Rd (60123-1203)
P.O. Box 668, Dundee (60118-0668)
PHONE..................630 620-6669
Jeffrey Lichtardt, *President*
Janice Nolan, *Admin Sec*
EMP: 4
SQ FT: 4,000
SALES (est): 527.8K **Privately Held**
SIC: **3452** 5075 Washers, metal; air conditioning & ventilation equipment & supplies

(G-8654)
MB CORP & ASSOCIATES
Also Called: Mbc-Aerosol
445 Renner Dr (60120-6903)
P.O. Box 54, South Elgin (60177-0054)
PHONE..................847 214-8843
Jim McBride, *President*
Pete Burt, *Vice Pres*
EMP: 13
SQ FT: 14,000
SALES (est): 3.1MM **Privately Held**
WEB: www.mbc-aerosol.com
SIC: **3542** 3565 Crimping machinery, metal; bottling machinery: filling, capping, labeling; bag opening, filling & closing machines

(G-8655)
MEF CONSTRUCTION INC
707 Mariner Ct (60120-7606)
PHONE..................847 741-8601
Dianna Magana, *President*
EMP: 3 EST: 2014
SALES (est): 264.5K **Privately Held**
SIC: **1623** 1794 1799 3271 Water & sewer line construction; excavation & grading, building construction; athletic & recreation facilities construction; playground construction & equipment installation; blocks, concrete: landscape or retaining wall;

(G-8656)
META-MEG TOOL CORPORATION
1434 Davis Rd (60123-1322)
PHONE..................847 742-3600
Robert Schuld, *President*
Barbara Schuld, *Corp Secy*
EMP: 5 EST: 1975
SQ FT: 3,500
SALES (est): 500K **Privately Held**
SIC: **7699** 3544 Plastics products repair; special dies, tools, jigs & fixtures

(G-8657)
METAL FINISHING PROS CORP
41 N Union St (60123-5334)
PHONE..................630 883-8339
EMP: 4
SALES (est): 271.7K **Privately Held**
WEB: www.metal-pros.com
SIC: **3471** Electroplating of metals or formed products

(G-8658)
METAL IMAGES INC
325 Corporate Dr (60123-9373)
PHONE..................847 488-9877
Marco Alvarez, *President*
Patrick Hayes, *President*
EMP: 6
SALES (est): 530K **Privately Held**
SIC: **3471** Buffing for the trade

(G-8659)
MEYER METAL SYSTEMS INC
1111 Davis Rd (60123-1315)
PHONE..................847 468-0500
Craig Meyer, *President*
EMP: 12
SQ FT: 39,000
SALES (est): 2.5MM **Privately Held**
SIC: **3355** Aluminum rail & structural shapes

(G-8660)
MIDDLEBY CORPORATION (PA)
1400 Toastmaster Dr (60120-9274)
PHONE..................847 741-3300
Timothy J Fitzgerald, *CEO*
Adam McCollough, *General Mgr*
David Brewer, *COO*
Michael Potter, *Exec VP*
Meghan Daro, *Vice Pres*
EMP: 30
SQ FT: 207,000
SALES: 2.9B **Publicly Held**
SIC: **3589** 3556 Commercial cooking & foodwarming equipment; cooking equipment, commercial; food warming equipment, commercial; ovens, bakery

(G-8661)
MIDDLEBY CORPORATION
Also Called: Toastmaster
1400 Toastmaster Dr (60120-9274)
PHONE..................847 741-3300
EMP: 20
SALES (corp-wide): 2.9B **Publicly Held**
SIC: **3589** 3556 Cooking equipment, commercial; food warming equipment, commercial; ovens, bakery
PA: The Middleby Corporation
1400 Toastmaster Dr
Elgin IL 60120
847 741-3300

(G-8662)
MIDDLEBY PACKG SOLUTIONS LLC
Also Called: M-Tek
1675 Todd Farm Dr (60123-1146)
PHONE..................847 741-3500
EMP: 25
SALES (est): 1.2MM
SALES (corp-wide): 2.9B **Publicly Held**
SIC: **3565** Vacuum packaging machinery
PA: The Middleby Corporation
1400 Toastmaster Dr
Elgin IL 60120
847 741-3300

(G-8663)
MIDDLEBY WORLDWIDE INC (HQ)
1400 Toastmaster Dr (60120-9274)
PHONE..................847 741-3300
Tim Fitzgerald, *CFO*
Martin M Lindsay, *Treasurer*
◆ EMP: 7 EST: 1987
SALES (est): 1.2MM
SALES (corp-wide): 2.9B **Publicly Held**
SIC: **3556** Food products machinery
PA: The Middleby Corporation
1400 Toastmaster Dr
Elgin IL 60120
847 741-3300

(G-8664)
MORCOR INDUSTRIES INC
501 Davis Rd (60123-1303)
PHONE..................224 293-2000
Anthony Moran, *President*
Jane Moran, *Admin Sec*
▲ EMP: 4
SALES (est): 248.7K **Privately Held**
SIC: **2671** Plastic film, coated or laminated for packaging

(G-8665)
MOTOROLA SOLUTIONS INC
2520 Galvin Dr (60124-7928)
PHONE..................847 576-5000
Mark Seaborn, *Engineer*
Slaughter Josie, *Marketing Staff*
Mary Beth Northrup, *Branch Mgr*
Michael Fox, *Director*
Jerrold Lev, *Analyst*
EMP: 142
SALES (corp-wide): 7.8B **Publicly Held**
SIC: **3663** Radio & TV communications equipment
PA: Motorola Solutions, Inc.
500 W Monroe St Ste 4400
Chicago IL 60661
847 576-5000

(G-8666)
MPR PLASTICS INC
1551 Scottsdale Ct # 100 (60123-9336)
PHONE..................847 468-9950
Paul D Doran, *President*
Kashmir Singh, *Plant Mgr*
Adam Tyminski, *Engineer*
Kelly Feely, *Cust Mgr*
Don Wessendorf, *Manager*
▲ EMP: 30
SQ FT: 25,000
SALES (est): 7.3MM **Privately Held**
SIC: **3089** Injection molded finished plastic products; injection molding of plastics

(G-8667)
NEW VISION DISPLAY
25 S Grove Ave Ste 400 (60120-6400)
PHONE..................224 268-3345
EMP: 3 EST: 2016
SALES (est): 194.7K **Privately Held**
WEB: www.newvisiondisplay.com
SIC: **3674** Semiconductors & related devices

(G-8668)
NEWHAVEN DISPLAY INTL INC
2661 Galvin Ct (60124-8092)
PHONE..................847 844-8795
Gary Murrell, *President*
Laura Borek, *Purchasing*
Paul Bartek, *Engineer*
Curt Lagerstam, *Engineer*
Michael Lavine, *Engineer*
▲ EMP: 32
SALES (est): 6.4MM **Privately Held**
SIC: **3612** 3634 3651 3699 Transformers, except electric; electric housewares & fans; household audio & video equipment; electrical equipment & supplies

(G-8669)
NEWOVO PLASTICS LLC
345 Willard Ave (60120-6810)
PHONE..................224 535-8183
Carl Dumele, *CEO*
EMP: 6
SALES (est): 441.8K **Privately Held**
SIC: **3089** Injection molding of plastics

(G-8670)
NEXT GEN MANUFACTURING INC
1330 Crispin Dr Ste 205 (60123-5504)
PHONE..................847 289-8444
Carl Bonta, *President*
Kim Ponta, *Admin Sec*
EMP: 7 EST: 2012
SQ FT: 3,600
SALES (est): 560K **Privately Held**
WEB: www.nextgenmfginc.com
SIC: **2221** Textile warping, on a contract basis

(G-8671)
NEXUS OFFICE SYSTEMS INC
2250 Point Blvd Ste 125 (60123-7869)
PHONE..................847 836-1095
Fax: 847 836-1945
EMP: 12
SALES (corp-wide): 9.6MM **Privately Held**
SIC: **3861** Mfg Photographic Equipment/Supplies
PA: Nexus Office Systems, Inc.
898 Featherstone Rd
Rockford IL 61107
815 227-0170

(G-8672)
NGS PRINTING INC
1400 Crispin Dr (60123-5533)
PHONE..................847 741-4411
Gerhard Landrowski, *President*
Mark Landrowski, *COO*
Mike Jones, *Manager*
Dan Kramer, *Manager*
John Socha, *Executive*
▲ EMP: 45
SQ FT: 40,000
SALES (est): 8.6MM **Privately Held**
WEB: www.ngsprint.com
SIC: **2752** Commercial printing, lithographic

(G-8673)
NIDEC MOTOR CORPORATION
Also Called: Elgin Engineering Center
1901 South St (60123-6939)
PHONE..................847 585-8430
David Lass, *Engineer*
EMP: 415 **Privately Held**
SIC: **3621** Rotors, for motors
HQ: Nidec Motor Corporation
8050 West Florissant Ave
Saint Louis MO 63136

(G-8674)
NORTHGATE TECHNOLOGIES INC
1591 Scottsdale Ct (60123-9361)
PHONE..................847 608-8900
Robert Mantell, *President*
Barbara Meissner, *Production*
Brad Haber, *Engineer*
Daniel Washburn, *CFO*
Michael Fritz, *Controller*
EMP: 40
SQ FT: 19,000
SALES (est): 9.2MM
SALES (corp-wide): 5.6MM **Privately Held**
SIC: **3841** 5047 3845 Diagnostic apparatus, medical; medical equipment & supplies; electromedical equipment

Elgin - Kane County (G-8675) GEOGRAPHIC SECTION

PA: Trudell Medical Limited
725 Baransway Dr
London ON N5V 5
519 455-7060

(G-8675)
NUTRAID MANUFACTURING
420 Airport Rd (60123-9329)
PHONE..................847 214-4860
Rodelo Maglente, Vice Pres
James Rodriguez, Plant Mgr
EMP: 3
SALES (est): 205.5K Privately Held
SIC: 3999 Manufacturing industries

(G-8676)
ODORS AWAY LLC (PA)
368 Bluff City Blvd (60120-8398)
PHONE..................888 235-7559
Jericca Held, Mng Member
Jonathan Held,
EMP: 2
SALES (est): 354.6K Privately Held
SIC: 2842 Sanitation preparations

(G-8677)
OERLIKON BLZERS CATING USA INC
1181 Jansen Farm Ct (60123-2595)
PHONE..................847 695-5200
Sandy Gilton, Human Res Mgr
Thomas Schmalberger, Mktg Dir
Darin Swiger, Manager
EMP: 32
SALES (corp-wide): 2.6B Privately Held
SIC: 3479 Coating of metals & formed products
HQ: Oerlikon Balzers Coating Usa Inc.
1700 E Golf Rd Ste 200
Schaumburg IL 60173
847 619-5541

(G-8678)
OLYMPIC CONTROLS CORP
Also Called: Amperite Co.
1250 Crispin Dr (60123-5531)
PHONE..................847 742-3566
Matt Scandora, President
Albano Andreini, President
David Armon, Vice Pres
Donald Dumper, Vice Pres
John Scandora, Vice Pres
▲ EMP: 30
SQ FT: 18,000
SALES (est): 5.7MM Privately Held
WEB: www.occorp.com
SIC: 3677 3625 3714 Coil windings, electronic; relays & industrial controls; control equipment, electric; fuel pumps, motor vehicle

(G-8679)
OMNI CONTAINMENT SYSTEMS LLC
1501 Commerce Drive Elgin (60123)
P.O. Box 12, Algonquin (60102-0012)
PHONE..................847 468-1772
Brian Smith, COO
Gary Weldon, Opers Mgr
Scott Justis, Manager
Kevin Chwala,
Brian Chwala,
◆ EMP: 6
SQ FT: 4,000
SALES: 615K Privately Held
SIC: 3589 Commercial cooking & food-warming equipment

(G-8680)
ORR MARKETING CORP
Also Called: Great Holloween Stores
784 Scott Dr (60123-2640)
PHONE..................847 401-5171
Orrion Ferguson, President
EMP: 10
SALES: 400K Privately Held
SIC: 8742 2389 Marketing consulting services; costumes

(G-8681)
ORSTROM WOODWORKING LTD
1502 Sawgrass Ct (60123-6804)
PHONE..................847 697-1163
EMP: 3 EST: 1999
SALES (est): 170K Privately Held
SIC: 2431 Mfg Millwork

(G-8682)
OZINGA CONCRETE PRODUCTS INC
2521 Tech Dr Ste 212 (60124)
PHONE..................847 426-0920
Marty Ozinga, President
Dave Lapoint, Treasurer
EMP: 50
SQ FT: 4,000
SALES (est): 5.5MM Privately Held
SIC: 3272 Concrete products

(G-8683)
PADDOCK PUBLICATIONS INC
385 Airport Rd Ste A (60123-9341)
PHONE..................847 608-2700
EMP: 243
SALES (est): 4MM
SALES (corp-wide): 79.9MM Privately Held
SIC: 2711 Newspapers, publishing & printing
PA: Paddock Publications, Inc.
95 W Algonquin Rd Ste 300
Arlington Heights IL 60005
847 427-4300

(G-8684)
PALAPA COATINGS INC
325 Corporate Dr (60123-9373)
PHONE..................847 628-6360
Marco Alvarez, President
Kyle Hayes, Admin Sec
EMP: 5
SALES (est): 626.5K Privately Held
SIC: 3479 Coating of metals & formed products

(G-8685)
PARKER-HANNIFIN CORPORATION
Also Called: Engineered Polymer Systems Div
2565 Northwest Pkwy (60124-7870)
PHONE..................847 836-6859
Dale Burnett, Branch Mgr
EMP: 100
SALES (corp-wide): 14.3B Publicly Held
WEB: www.phtruck.com
SIC: 3087 Custom compound purchased resins
PA: Parker-Hannifin Corporation
6035 Parkland Blvd
Cleveland OH 44124
216 896-3000

(G-8686)
PATRICK MANUFACTURING INC
667 N State St (60123-2801)
PHONE..................847 697-5920
Susan Mc Grail, President
Jeanette Mc Grail, Corp Secy
Patricia Lane, Vice Pres
Jeanette Grail, Treasurer
Pattie Lane, VP Sales
EMP: 20
SQ FT: 45,000
SALES (est): 4.1MM Privately Held
SIC: 3495 Wire springs

(G-8687)
PLASMATREAT USA INC (PA)
Also Called: Plasma Technology Systems
2541 Tech Dr Ste 407 (60124)
PHONE..................847 783-0622
Andreas Stecher, President
Mercedes Escriva, Business Mgr
Nick Rollick, Vice Pres
Jeff Leighty, Sales Staff
John Clem, Manager
EMP: 19 EST: 2006
SALES: 3.5MM Privately Held
WEB: www.plasmatreat.com
SIC: 3694 Automotive electrical equipment

(G-8688)
PLASTIC TECHNOLOGIES INC
1200 Abbott Dr (60123-1825)
PHONE..................847 841-8610
Arthur P Schueler Jr, President
Gary Kinberg, Vice Pres
▲ EMP: 20
SQ FT: 13,600

SALES (est): 4MM Privately Held
SIC: 3648 3465 Reflectors for lighting equipment: metal; automotive stampings

(G-8689)
PLASTICS
39w446 Capulet Cir (60124-8110)
PHONE..................847 931-9391
Jennifer Schwab, Principal
EMP: 3
SALES (est): 207.6K Privately Held
SIC: 3089 Molding primary plastic

(G-8690)
PLASTIVAL INC
Also Called: Re-Source Building Products
1685 Holmes Rd (60123-5709)
PHONE..................847 931-4771
Guy David, President
Jim Quinn, Admin Sec
EMP: 500
SALES (est): 3.1MM Privately Held
SIC: 3089 Fences, gates & accessories: plastic
PA: Cyprium Investment Partners Llc
200 Public Sq Ste 2020
Cleveland OH 44114

(G-8691)
POLY COMPOUNDING LLC
1390 Gateway Dr Ste 6 (60124-7842)
PHONE..................847 488-0683
Steve Hagan, Engineer
Scott Crosby, Mng Member
John Wolfe,
▲ EMP: 9
SQ FT: 16,000
SALES (est): 1.1MM Privately Held
SIC: 2821 Plastics materials & resins

(G-8692)
POTHOLE PROS
3074 Chalkstone Ave (60124-8939)
PHONE..................847 815-5789
Andy Carter, Principal
EMP: 5 EST: 2010
SALES (est): 438.8K Privately Held
WEB: www.potholepros.com
SIC: 2951 Asphalt & asphaltic paving mixtures (not from refineries)

(G-8693)
PPG INDUSTRIES INC
Also Called: PPG 5534
266 Kimball St (60120-4202)
PHONE..................847 742-3340
Jeff Molicm, Branch Mgr
EMP: 24
SALES (corp-wide): 15.1B Publicly Held
SIC: 2851 Paints & allied products
PA: Ppg Industries, Inc.
1 Ppg Pl
Pittsburgh PA 15272
412 434-3131

(G-8694)
PRICE CIRCUITS LLC
1300 Holmes Rd (60123-1202)
PHONE..................847 742-4700
Wayne Price,
Sibi Varghese,
EMP: 40
SQ FT: 22,000
SALES (est): 7.9MM Privately Held
SIC: 3672 Printed circuit boards

(G-8695)
PRINCETON INDUSTRIAL PDTS INC
1485 Davis Rd Ste B (60123-1351)
PHONE..................847 839-8500
Elizabeth Lorance, CEO
Alec Schreiber, President
EMP: 10
SQ FT: 5,500
SALES (est): 1.8MM Privately Held
SIC: 3451 Screw machine products

(G-8696)
PRINTPACK INC
Flexible Packaging
1400 Abbott Dr (60123-1882)
PHONE..................847 888-7150
Jay Rotta, President
Deloach Jerry, Human Res Mgr
Donna McCoy, Human Resources

John Rosauer, Branch Mgr
Jeff Olson, Manager
EMP: 160
SALES (corp-wide): 1.3B Privately Held
WEB: www.printpack.com
SIC: 2673 3081 2671 Bags: plastic, laminated & coated; plastic film & sheet; packaging paper & plastics film, coated & laminated
HQ: Printpack, Inc.
2800 Overlook Pkwy Ne
Atlanta GA 30339
404 460-7000

(G-8697)
PROFILE FOOD INGREDIENTS LLC
1151 Timber Dr (60123-1861)
PHONE..................847 622-1700
Ted Benic, CEO
Eloy Diaz, Plant Mgr
▲ EMP: 46
SALES (est): 5.2MM
SALES (corp-wide): 5.5B Publicly Held
SIC: 2064 2051 2024 Candy & other confectionery products; bread, cake & related products; dairy based frozen desserts
HQ: Mantrose-Haeuser Co., Inc.
100 Nyala Farms Rd
Westport CT 06880

(G-8698)
PROFORMA-PPG INC
158 Dawson Dr (60120-6409)
PHONE..................847 429-9349
Katherine Labbe, President
EMP: 4
SALES (est): 360K Privately Held
SIC: 2754 Business form & card printing, gravure

(G-8699)
PROGRESSIVE PUBLICATIONS INC
Also Called: Coupon Magazine
85 Market St Ste 105 (60123-5083)
PHONE..................847 697-9181
David W Schmidt, President
Kimberly E Schmidt, Treasurer
EMP: 4
SQ FT: 800
SALES (est): 432.6K Privately Held
SIC: 2721 Magazines: publishing only, not printed on site

(G-8700)
PROQUIS INC
423 Walnut Ave (60123-7513)
PHONE..................847 278-3230
David Best, CEO
William P Best, President
Gil Hersh, Vice Pres
EMP: 11
SQ FT: 3,200
SALES: 1.8MM Privately Held
SIC: 7372 7371 7373 8243 Prepackaged software; computer software development & applications; systems software development services; software training, computer; general management consultant

(G-8701)
PROTON MULTIMEDIA INC
Also Called: Kult of Athena
1485 Davis Rd Ste A (60123-1351)
PHONE..................847 531-8664
Ryan Whittlinger, President
▲ EMP: 3
SQ FT: 23,000
SALES: 700K Privately Held
SIC: 3423 Hammers (hand tools)

(G-8702)
PROVEN PARTNERS GROUP LLC (HQ)
Also Called: PPG
1111 Bowes Rd (60123-5541)
PHONE..................847 488-1230
Dave Nelson, CEO
Ranjit Bahadur MBA, Agent
EMP: 88
SQ FT: 150,000

SALES (est): 62.7MM
SALES (corp-wide): 33.9MM **Privately Held**
SIC: 2099 Food preparations
PA: Tilia Holdings, Llc
  111 S Wacker Dr Ste 4960
  Chicago IL 60606
  312 535-0225

(G-8703)
PSIMET LLC (PA)
612 N Lyle Ave (60123-2608)
  PHONE.................................847 871-7005
Robert Curtis, *Principal*
EMP: 2
SALES (est): 236.2K **Privately Held**
WEB: www.psimet.com
SIC: 3999 Manufacturing industries

(G-8704)
PUSKAR PRECISION MACHINING CO
1610 Cambridge Dr (60123-1143)
  PHONE.................................847 888-2929
Asim Puskar, *President*
Fuad Puskar, *Vice Pres*
EMP: 15 EST: 1973
SQ FT: 24,000
SALES (est): 2.7MM **Privately Held**
SIC: 3599 Machine shop, jobbing & repair

(G-8705)
QP HOLDINGS LLC (PA)
1000 Davis Rd (60123-1314)
  PHONE.................................847 695-9700
Ron Embree, *CEO*
Morris Rowlett, *Ch of Bd*
Lisa Fiorenza, *CFO*
Maria Escamilla, *Manager*
EMP: 3 EST: 2014
SALES (est): 242.6MM **Privately Held**
SIC: 3089 Injection molded finished plastic products

(G-8706)
QUAD-ILLINOIS INC (PA)
Also Called: Shamrock Specialty Packaging
2760 Spectrum Dr (60124-7841)
  PHONE.................................847 836-1115
James M Owens, *President*
Michael Carroll, *Principal*
Gilbert Patton, *Principal*
Penny Seeds, *Principal*
Michael Sengstock, *Principal*
EMP: 15
SALES (est): 19.2MM **Privately Held**
SIC: 5113 3999 5084 4789 Shipping supplies; barber & beauty shop equipment; packaging machinery & equipment; cargo loading & unloading services

(G-8707)
QUALITY DIE CASTING CO
1760 Britannia Dr Ste 5 (60124-7814)
  PHONE.................................847 214-8840
Pamela Cavka, *Owner*
Mirsa Talic, *Vice Pres*
EMP: 14
SQ FT: 12,100
SALES (est): 2.4MM **Privately Held**
SIC: 3364 Zinc & zinc-base alloy die-castings

(G-8708)
QUALITY FASTENER PRODUCTS INC
1430 Davis Rd (60123-1322)
  PHONE.................................224 330-3162
EMP: 2 EST: 2011
SALES (est): 242.5K **Privately Held**
WEB: www.qualityfastenerproductsinc.com
SIC: 3559 Special industry machinery

(G-8709)
QUALITY TECHNOLOGY INTL INC
Also Called: Qti
1707 N Randall Rd Ste 300 (60123-9412)
  PHONE.................................847 649-9300
Dan Hammes, *President*
Steve Joloy, *CFO*
Kaz Nishida, *Admin Sec*
◆ EMP: 20
SQ FT: 4,000

SALES (est): 2.9MM **Privately Held**
SIC: 3999 Seeds, coated or treated, from purchased seeds
HQ: Itochu International Inc.
  1251 Ave Of The Amrcas 51
  New York NY 10020
  212 818-8000

(G-8710)
QUESTEK MANUFACTURING CORP
2570 Technology Dr (60124-7884)
  PHONE.................................847 428-0300
Dale R Krueger, *President*
▲ EMP: 70
SQ FT: 60,000
SALES (est): 12.8MM **Privately Held**
SIC: 3625 3644 Electric controls & control accessories, industrial; noncurrent-carrying wiring services

(G-8711)
R & S AUTOMOTIVE INC
88 Airport Rd (60123-9324)
  PHONE.................................847 622-8838
Huajun Xu, *President*
EMP: 3
SALES (est): 155.9K
SALES (corp-wide): 10.8MM **Privately Held**
SIC: 3711 Automobile bodies, passenger car, not including engine, etc.
HQ: Wanxiang America Corporation
  88 Airport Rd
  Elgin IL 60123

(G-8712)
R G SPRING COMPANY INC
2587 Millennium Dr Ste F (60124-5826)
  PHONE.................................847 695-2986
Elizabeth Hudec, *President*
Michael Hudec, *President*
Lacee Hudec, *Manager*
EMP: 4
SALES: 400K **Privately Held**
SIC: 3495 Wire springs

(G-8713)
R M TOOL & MANUFACTURING CO
368 Bluff City Blvd Ste 6 (60120-8398)
  PHONE.................................847 888-0433
Russell Mueller, *President*
Fred Mueller, *Corp Secy*
Paul Mueller, *Vice Pres*
EMP: 6
SQ FT: 3,600
SALES (est): 439.2K **Privately Held**
SIC: 3599 3312 3544 Machine shop, jobbing & repair; tool & die steel & alloys; special dies, tools, jigs & fixtures

(G-8714)
R R DONNELLEY & SONS COMPANY
Also Called: R R Donnelley
168 E Highland Ave Ste 2 (60120-5564)
  PHONE.................................847 622-1026
Tony Myrie, *Manager*
EMP: 45
SALES (corp-wide): 6.2B **Publicly Held**
SIC: 2754 2759 Commercial printing, gravure; commercial printing
PA: R. R. Donnelley & Sons Company
  35 W Wacker Dr
  Chicago IL 60601
  312 326-8000

(G-8715)
RAYS ELECTRICAL SERVICE LLC
37w904 Us Highway 20 (60124-8125)
  PHONE.................................847 214-2944
Lisa Sakolari, *Office Mgr*
Ray Sakolari,
EMP: 15
SALES (est): 1.8MM **Privately Held**
SIC: 1731 1381 7389 General electrical contractor; directional drilling oil & gas wells;

(G-8716)
REGAL STEEL ERECTORS LLC
850 Tollgate Rd (60123-9300)
  PHONE.................................847 888-3500

Michael Bates, *Mng Member*
Brian Bates,
EMP: 40
SALES (est): 7MM **Privately Held**
SIC: 1791 7692 Structural steel erection; welding repair

(G-8717)
REID COMMUNICATIONS INC
Also Called: Green Book Lenders Guide, The
450 Shepard Dr Ste 11 (60123-7033)
P.O. Box 5000 (60121-5000)
  PHONE.................................847 741-9700
David Sears, *President*
Paul Sears, *CFO*
EMP: 24
SALES (est): 3.2MM **Privately Held**
SIC: 2759 2741 Publication printing; miscellaneous publishing

(G-8718)
RELIANCE TOOL & MFG CO (PA)
Also Called: Rtm Trend
900 N State St Ste 101 (60123-2106)
  PHONE.................................847 695-1235
Paul Knowlton, *President*
EMP: 45 EST: 1947
SQ FT: 27,000
SALES (est): 24.1MM **Privately Held**
WEB: www.reliancetool.com
SIC: 3541 3469 Machine tools, metal cutting type; stamping metal for the trade

(G-8719)
RELYON METAL PRODUCTS CO
40w885 Chippewa Pass (60124-8290)
  PHONE.................................847 679-1510
Joseph Clouser, *President*
Laura Donaldson, *Vice Pres*
EMP: 5
SQ FT: 6,000
SALES (est): 544.5K **Privately Held**
SIC: 3469 3544 Stamping metal for the trade; special dies & tools

(G-8720)
RIEKE OFFICE INTERIORS INC
Also Called: R O I
2000 Fox Ln (60123-7814)
  PHONE.................................847 622-9711
Melissa Dotson, *President*
Carol Nelson, *Vice Pres*
Libby Rieke, *Vice Pres*
Margaret Whitted, *Controller*
Molly Stevenson, *Manager*
EMP: 78
SQ FT: 150,000
SALES (est): 24.1MM **Privately Held**
SIC: 2521 5932 Wood office furniture; office furniture, secondhand; store fixtures & equipment, secondhand

(G-8721)
RPS ENGINEERING INC
1300 Crispin Dr (60123-5532)
P.O. Box 5186 (60121-5186)
  PHONE.................................847 931-1950
Richard Stanis, *President*
Steven Kelly, *COO*
▲ EMP: 18
SQ FT: 40,000.
SALES (est): 6.4MM **Privately Held**
WEB: www.rpsengineering.com
SIC: 3444 3535 Siding, sheet metal; conveyors & conveying equipment

(G-8722)
S & S WELDING & FABRICATION
31w377 Spaulding Rd (60120-7577)
  PHONE.................................847 742-7344
Henry Eolz, *President*
EMP: 4
SQ FT: 12,000
SALES (est): 235K **Privately Held**
SIC: 7692 3441 3444 Welding repair; fabricated structural metal; sheet metalwork

(G-8723)
SAFE WATER TECHNOLOGIES INC
996 Bluff City Blvd (60120-7594)
  PHONE.................................847 888-6900
Brett Oleskow, *President*
▲ EMP: 8
SQ FT: 10,000

SALES (est): 1.6MM **Privately Held**
SIC: 3589 Water treatment equipment, industrial

(G-8724)
SCHWANOG LLC
1301 Bowes Rd Ste A (60123-5510)
  PHONE.................................847 289-1055
Clemens Guentert,
EMP: 11
SALES: 3MM **Privately Held**
SIC: 2819 Carbides

(G-8725)
SEALCO INDUSTRIES INC (PA)
Also Called: Cap & Seal Company
1591 Fleetwood Dr (60123-7126)
  PHONE.................................847 741-3101
Thomas J Brown, *President*
Gilbert Lee, *Controller*
▲ EMP: 27
SQ FT: 34,000
SALES (est): 6.1MM **Privately Held**
SIC: 3469 Stamping metal for the trade

(G-8726)
SEIGLES CABINET CENTER LLC (PA)
1331 Davis Rd (60123-1319)
  PHONE.................................224 535-7034
Mark S Seigle,
EMP: 4 EST: 2011
SALES (est): 644K **Privately Held**
SIC: 2434 Vanities, bathroom: wood

(G-8727)
SET SCREW & MFG CO
1210 Saint Charles St (60120-8445)
  PHONE.................................847 717-3700
James A Brown, *President*
Dale Engelking, *Vice Pres*
Kevin Brown, *Purch Mgr*
Kim Todd, *Sales Mgr*
Katie Kessell, *Sales Staff*
▲ EMP: 23
SQ FT: 25,000
SALES (est): 4.3MM **Privately Held**
WEB: www.setscrewmfg.com
SIC: 3452 5085 Bolts, nuts, rivets & washers; fasteners, industrial: nuts, bolts, screws, etc.

(G-8728)
SHARP DEFENSE LLC
Also Called: Sbg Illinois
226 Wing Park Blvd (60123-3341)
  PHONE.................................630 205-3502
Nichol Sharp,
EMP: 4 EST: 2018
SALES (est): 212.4K **Privately Held**
SIC: 3812 Defense systems & equipment

(G-8729)
SHAW INDUSTRIES
2410 Galvin Dr (60124-7883)
  PHONE.................................847 844-9190
EMP: 3
SALES (est): 189.3K **Privately Held**
SIC: 3999 Manufacturing industries

(G-8730)
SIGMATRON INTERNATIONAL INC
Also Called: Spitfire Controls
1901 South St (60123-6939)
  PHONE.................................847 586-5200
Robert Alvord, *Engineer*
Tom Musser, *Program Mgr*
Arif Mohammed, *Manager*
Lester Hensley, *Director*
EMP: 6 **Publicly Held**
SIC: 3672 3677 3679 3549 Printed circuit boards; electronic coils, transformers & other inductors; electronic circuits; assembly machines, including robotic; engine electrical test equipment
PA: Sigmatron International, Inc.
  2201 Landmeier Rd
  Elk Grove Village IL 60007

(G-8731)
SIGNS IN DUNDEE INC
Also Called: Signs By Tomorrow
1028 Dundee Ave (60120-2447)
  PHONE.................................847 742-9530

Elgin - Kane County (G-8732)

John Pendexter, *President*
EMP: 4
SALES (est): 270K **Privately Held**
SIC: 3993 2396 2752 2759 Signs & advertising specialties; fabric printing & stamping; poster & decal printing, lithographic; poster & decal printing & engraving

(G-8732)
SIKORA PRECISION INC
140 Will Scarlett Ln (60120-9524)
PHONE..................847 468-0900
Kurt Sikora, *President*
Margaret Sikora, *Admin Sec*
EMP: 4
SQ FT: 1,200
SALES (est): 175K **Privately Held**
SIC: 3089 3599 Injection molding of plastics; machine shop, jobbing & repair

(G-8733)
SIMPLOMATIC MANUFACTURING CO
1616 Berkley St Ste 100 (60123-7083)
PHONE..................773 342-7757
David Hahn, *President*
Joseph Margherone, *Engineer*
Valerie Crazybear, *Accountant*
Joanne Cipolla, *Shareholder*
Patricia Voller, *Admin Sec*
EMP: 30 **EST:** 1944
SQ FT: 25,000
SALES (est): 7MM **Privately Held**
WEB: www.simplomatic.com
SIC: 3469 3089 Metal stampings; plastic processing

(G-8734)
SKF USA INC
Also Called: SKF Arspace Sling Slutions Div
900 N State St (60123-2104)
PHONE..................847 742-0700
Jim Hasara, *District Mgr*
McCawley Brett, *Vice Pres*
Dianna Ortman, *Project Dir*
Kim Satterfield, *Project Dir*
Carl Kent, *Maint Spvr*
EMP: 88
SALES (corp-wide): 8.9B **Privately Held**
WEB: www.skfextranet.com
SIC: 3053 Gaskets, packing & sealing devices
HQ: Skf Usa Inc.
890 Forty Foot Rd
Lansdale PA 19446
267 436-6000

(G-8735)
SKF USA INC
Also Called: SKF Automotive Division
890 N State St Ste 200 (60123-2177)
PHONE..................847 742-0700
Jeff Guempel, *Regional Mgr*
Mike Macgrath, *Manager*
Bethany Jordan, *Manager*
EMP: 61
SALES (corp-wide): 8.9B **Privately Held**
SIC: 3562 3053 Ball & roller bearings; gaskets, packing & sealing devices
HQ: Skf Usa Inc.
890 Forty Foot Rd
Lansdale PA 19446
267 436-6000

(G-8736)
SKF USA INC
SKF Sealing Solutions Division
900 N State St (60123-2104)
PHONE..................847 742-0700
Christine J Kessler, *Manager*
Phil Balbi, *Director*
Trisha John,
John Rottjakob, *Representative*
EMP: 61
SALES (corp-wide): 8.9B **Privately Held**
SIC: 3053 3829 3714 3568 Gaskets & sealing devices; vibration meters, analyzers & calibrators; motor vehicle parts & accessories; power transmission equipment; ball bearings & parts
HQ: Skf Usa Inc.
890 Forty Foot Rd
Lansdale PA 19446
267 436-6000

(G-8737)
SKIMAN SALES INC
850 Villa St (60120-8073)
PHONE..................847 888-8200
Dee Pizer, *CEO*
EMP: 2
SALES (est): 750K **Privately Held**
SIC: 2451 Mobile homes, personal or private use

(G-8738)
SPINTEX INC
1439 Holmes Rd (60123-1203)
PHONE..................847 608-5411
Ken Katayama, *President*
Marie Katayama, *Corp Secy*
▲ **EMP:** 9
SQ FT: 23,000
SALES (est): 1.8MM **Privately Held**
SIC: 3089 Injection molding of plastics

(G-8739)
STARRO PRECISION PRODUCTS INC
1730 Todd Farm Dr (60123-1142)
PHONE..................847 741-9400
Bruce Stark Jr, *President*
EMP: 50
SQ FT: 37,000
SALES (est): 6.5MM **Privately Held**
WEB: www.hmmaskiner.com
SIC: 3599 Machine shop, jobbing & repair

(G-8740)
STELFAST INC
2780 Spectrum Dr (60124-7841)
PHONE..................847 783-0161
David Gawlik, *Branch Mgr*
EMP: 12
SALES (corp-wide): 158.7MM **Privately Held**
SIC: 3452 Bolts, nuts, rivets & washers
HQ: Stelfast Llc
22979 Stelfast Pkwy
Strongsville OH 44149
440 879-0077

(G-8741)
SULLIVAN TOOL AND REPAIR INC
370 Brook St Unit 3 (60120-4153)
PHONE..................224 856-5867
John P Sullivan, *President*
John Sullivan, *President*
EMP: 1 **EST:** 2009
SALES (est): 264.9K **Privately Held**
SIC: 3089 Injection molded finished plastic products

(G-8742)
SUNSTAR PHARMACEUTICAL INC
1300 Abbott Dr (60123-1821)
PHONE..................773 777-4000
Richard McMan, *Ch of Bd*
▲ **EMP:** 90
SALES (est): 12.4MM **Privately Held**
SIC: 2834 2844 7389 Tablets, pharmaceutical; vitamin preparations; toothpastes or powders, dentifrices; packaging & labeling services
HQ: Sunstar Americas, Inc.
301 E Central Rd
Schaumburg IL 60195
847 794-4157

(G-8743)
SUZLON WIND ENERGY CORPORATION
Suzlon Wind Trbine Trining Ctr
2583 Technology Dr (60124-7832)
PHONE..................773 328-5077
Charles Clayton, *President*
EMP: 9 **Privately Held**
WEB: www.suzlon.com
SIC: 3511 Turbines & turbine generator sets
HQ: Suzlon Wind Energy Corporation
8750 W Bryn Mawr Ave # 300
Chicago IL 60631
773 328-5077

(G-8744)
T C I VACUUM FORMING COMPANY
1620 Cambridge Dr (60123-1143)
PHONE..................847 622-9100
John Vinka, *President*
Maynard Ostrowski, *Vice Pres*
Bob Neuzil, *Plant Mgr*
Don Swiat, *Sales Mgr*
Joann Spellman, *Office Mgr*
EMP: 50 **EST:** 1989
SQ FT: 40,000
SALES (est): 6.7MM **Privately Held**
SIC: 3089 Molding primary plastic; plastic processing

(G-8745)
TAYKIT INC
Also Called: Creekside Printing
1175 Davis Rd (60123-1315)
PHONE..................847 888-1150
Steven Kittay, *President*
Don Anderson, *Accounts Exec*
Peggy Havery, *Manager*
EMP: 35
SQ FT: 22,000
SALES (est): 6MM **Privately Held**
SIC: 2752 Commercial printing, offset

(G-8746)
TECH GLOBAL INC
2759 Pinnacle Dr (60124-7943)
PHONE..................847 532-4882
James Rocheford, *President*
▲ **EMP:** 16
SQ FT: 11,000
SALES (est): 3.8MM **Privately Held**
SIC: 3577 Computer peripheral equipment

(G-8747)
TECH GLOBAL INC
2521 Tech Dr Ste 206 (60124)
PHONE..................224 623-2000
James Rocheford, *CEO*
EMP: 1
SALES: 1,000K **Privately Held**
SIC: 3571 Electronic computers

(G-8748)
TEK-CAST INC
195 Corporate Dr (60123-9355)
PHONE..................630 422-1458
John Cahill, *President*
Aiden Walsh, *President*
Simon Newman, *Principal*
Maureen Cahill, *Admin Sec*
▲ **EMP:** 60
SQ FT: 10,000
SALES (est): 9.8MM **Privately Held**
SIC: 3542 Machine tools, metal forming type

(G-8749)
TELEDYNE LECROY INC
Also Called: Quantum Data
2111 Big Timber Rd (60123-1123)
PHONE..................847 888-0450
Mark Stockfisch, *Vice Pres*
Sean Daugherty, *Engineer*
Jim Kimnetz, *CFO*
Jim Kimmetz, *Controller*
Neal Kendall, *Marketing Mgr*
EMP: 27
SALES (corp-wide): 3.1B **Publicly Held**
SIC: 3825 3829 3621 3577 Test equipment for electronic & electrical circuits; measuring & controlling devices; motors & generators; computer peripheral equipment; computer terminals
HQ: Teledyne Lecroy, Inc.
700 Chestnut Ridge Rd
Chestnut Ridge NY 10977
845 425-2000

(G-8750)
TEMP EXCEL PROPERTIES LLC
2520 Vantage Dr (60124-7881)
PHONE..................847 844-3845
Rick Powell, *Manager*
EMP: 5 **Privately Held**
SIC: 5075 3444 Warm air heating equipment & supplies; air conditioning & ventilation equipment & supplies; furnace casings, sheet metal
HQ: Temp Excel Properties, Llc
17725 Volbrecht Rd Ste 1
Lansing IL 60438

(G-8751)
TEMP-AIR INC
Temp Heat Division
39 W 107 Highland Ave (60123)
PHONE..................847 931-7700
Beth Shelby, *Manager*
EMP: 10
SQ FT: 12,000
SALES (corp-wide): 5.9B **Privately Held**
SIC: 3585 Refrigeration & heating equipment
HQ: Temp-Air, Inc.
3700 W Preserve Blvd
Burnsville MN 55337
800 836-7432

(G-8752)
TEMPERATURE EQUIPMENT CORP
Also Called: A Division of TEC
1313 Timber Dr (60123-1826)
PHONE..................847 429-0818
EMP: 8
SALES (corp-wide): 116.5MM **Privately Held**
SIC: 3822 Mfg Environmental Controls
HQ: Temperature Equipment Corporation
17725 Volbrecht Rd Ste 1
Lansing IL 60438
708 418-0900

(G-8753)
TENDER LOVING CARE INDS INC
Also Called: TLC Industries
1270 Abbott Dr (60123-1819)
PHONE..................847 891-0230
Edward Bender, *President*
Bob Goodman, *Vice Pres*
EMP: 70
SALES (est): 8.3MM **Privately Held**
SIC: 2511 2499 Juvenile furniture: wood; decorative wood & woodwork

(G-8754)
THOMAS RESEARCH PRODUCTS LLC
Also Called: Trp
1215 Bowes Rd Ste 1225 (60123-5542)
PHONE..................224 654-8626
Glenn Garbowicz, *CEO*
Warren Hecht, *President*
▲ **EMP:** 15
SQ FT: 4,000
SALES (est): 1.8MM
SALES (corp-wide): 4.5B **Publicly Held**
SIC: 3612 Power & distribution transformers
HQ: Varon Lighting Group, Llc
765 S Il Route 83
Elmhurst IL 60126
630 279-9800

(G-8755)
TLC DENTAL CARE LLC
Also Called: Stembox
344 Shadow Hill Dr (60124-3815)
PHONE..................425 442-9000
Dalvina Sharma, *CEO*
Ajay Sharma, *Principal*
EMP: 2 **EST:** 2017
SALES (est): 357.5K **Privately Held**
SIC: 5113 3612 2671 8021 Industrial & personal service paper; transformers, except electric; packaging paper & plastics film, coated & laminated; group & corporate practice dentists

(G-8756)
TOOLING SOLUTIONS INC
1515 Commerce Dr (60123-9304)
PHONE..................847 472-9940
Glenn Burchette, *President*
Amy Burchette, *Vice Pres*
EMP: 5
SQ FT: 3,000
SALES (est): 1.1MM **Privately Held**
SIC: 3541 Machine tools, metal cutting type

GEOGRAPHIC SECTION
Elgin - Kane County (G-8780)

(G-8757)
TRANSCONTINENTAL MULTIFILM INC (HQ)
Also Called: Multifoil Packaging
1040 N Mclean Blvd (60123-1709)
PHONE................................847 695-7600
Olle Mannertorp, *CEO*
Christopher Rogers, *President*
Dan Acevedo, *QC Mgr*
Dave Paetsch, *Plant Engr*
George Thibeault, *Sales Staff*
◆ **EMP:** 70
SQ FT: 82,200
SALES (est): 30MM
SALES (corp-wide): 2.2B **Privately Held**
WEB: www.multifilm.com
SIC: 3081 Packing materials, plastic sheet
PA: Transcontinental Inc
 1 Place Ville-Marie Bureau 3240
 Montreal QC H3B 0
 514 954-4000

(G-8758)
TRANSCONTINENTAL MULTIFILM INC
1700 Big Timber Rd (60123-1704)
PHONE................................847 695-7600
EMP: 3
SALES (corp-wide): 2.2B **Privately Held**
SIC: 3081 Unsupported plastics film & sheet
HQ: Transcontinental Multifilm Inc.
 1040 N Mclean Blvd
 Elgin IL 60123
 847 695-7600

(G-8759)
TRI-DIM FILTER CORPORATION
Also Called: I D T
999 Raymond St (60120-8364)
PHONE................................847 695-5822
Margaret Bingham, *Branch Mgr*
Tony Andolino, *Manager*
Bob Harken, *Manager*
EMP: 35
SALES (corp-wide): 4.5B **Privately Held**
SIC: 3569 3564 Filters, general line: industrial; blowers & fans
HQ: Tri-Dim Filter Corporation
 93 Industrial Dr
 Louisa VA 23093
 540 967-2600

(G-8760)
TRICOR SYSTEMS INC
1650 Todd Farm Dr (60123-1145)
PHONE................................847 742-5542
Tim Allen, *President*
Keith Jereb, *Vice Pres*
Tommy Erhardt, *Design Engr*
Tom Allen, *VP Mktg*
EMP: 45 **EST:** 1976
SQ FT: 24,000
SALES: 13.2MM **Privately Held**
SIC: 3829 3823 3699 8731 Measuring & controlling devices; industrial instrmnts msrmnt display/control process variable; electronic training devices; flight simulators (training aids), electronic; commercial research laboratory

(G-8761)
TRITECH INTERNATIONAL LLC
1710 Todd Farm Dr (60123-1142)
PHONE................................847 888-0333
Bernstein Yuki, *Admin Mgr*
Kazuyuki Toriyama,
▲ **EMP:** 8
SQ FT: 10,000
SALES (est): 1.5MM **Privately Held**
SIC: 3312 5084 Tool & die steel & alloys; tool & die makers' equipment

(G-8762)
TRIUMPH TRUSS & STEEL COMPANY
1250 Larkin Ave Ste 200 (60123-6078)
PHONE................................815 522-6000
David Watts, *Mng Member*
EMP: 10
SALES (corp-wide): 2.8MM **Privately Held**
SIC: 2439 Trusses, wooden roof

PA: Triumph Truss & Steel Company
 11804 S Il Route 47
 Huntley IL

(G-8763)
TUBE & PIPE ASSOCIATION INTL
Also Called: Fabricators and Mfrs Assn
2135 Point Blvd (60123-7956)
PHONE................................815 399-8700
Jerry Shankel, *President*
EMP: 75
SALES (est): 3.5MM **Privately Held**
SIC: 8611 2721 Trade associations; periodicals

(G-8764)
TYSON FRESH MEATS INC
2170 Point Blvd Ste 300 (60123-7875)
PHONE................................847 836-5550
Brad Bodine, *Manager*
EMP: 17
SALES (corp-wide): 42.4B **Publicly Held**
SIC: 2013 3111 4213 3556 Sausages & other prepared meats; prepared beef products from purchased beef; prepared pork products from purchased pork; ham, roasted; from purchased meat; leather tanning & finishing; trucking, except local; meat processing machinery; boxed beef from meat slaughtered on site
HQ: Tyson Fresh Meats, Inc.
 800 Stevens Port Dr
 Dakota Dunes SD 57049
 479 290-6397

(G-8765)
UCAL HOLDINGS INC (DH)
Also Called: Amtec Precision Products, Inc.
1875 Holmes Rd (60123-1298)
PHONE................................847 695-8030
Jay Krishnamurthy, *CEO*
Ganesh Subramanian, *President*
Krushna Pati, *Admin Sec*
▲ **EMP:** 62
SALES: 37MM **Privately Held**
SIC: 3714 3089 3469 Transmission housings or parts, motor vehicle; fuel systems & parts, motor vehicle; motor vehicle transmissions, drive assemblies & parts; injection molding of plastics; machine parts, stamped or pressed metal

(G-8766)
UCAL SYSTEMS INC
Also Called: Amtec Precision Products
1355 Holmes Rd (60123-1254)
PHONE................................847 695-8030
Church Russel, *CEO*
EMP: 100 **Privately Held**
SIC: 3451 Screw machine products
HQ: Ucal Systems, Inc.
 1875 Holmes Rd
 Elgin IL 60123

(G-8767)
UCAL SYSTEMS INC (DH)
Also Called: Amtec Precision Products
1875 Holmes Rd (60123-1298)
PHONE................................847 695-8030
Jaykar Krishnamurthy, *Ch of Bd*
Ganesh Subramanian, *President*
Kenneth Formanski, *Vice Pres*
Krushna C Pati, *Admin Sec*
▲ **EMP:** 126
SQ FT: 214,000
SALES (est): 33.4MM **Privately Held**
SIC: 3714 3089 3469 Transmission housings or parts, motor vehicle; fuel systems & parts, motor vehicle; motor vehicle transmissions, drive assemblies & parts; injection molding of plastics; machine parts, stamped or pressed metal

(G-8768)
ULTRA POLISHING
1320 Holmes Rd (60123-1202)
PHONE................................224 769-7140
EMP: 7 **EST:** 2018
SALES (est): 896K **Privately Held**
SIC: 3471 Plating of metals or formed products

(G-8769)
UNIVERSAL CHEM & COATINGS INC (PA)
Also Called: Unichem
1975 Fox Ln (60123-7839)
PHONE................................847 931-1700
Daniel Chin, *President*
Frederick V Chin, *Vice Pres*
Frederick Chin, *Vice Pres*
Elizabeth Lidster, *Marketing Mgr*
Andy Marck, *Manager*
▼ **EMP:** 25
SQ FT: 50,000
SALES (est): 9.7MM **Privately Held**
WEB: www.unicheminc.com
SIC: 2851 2891 Coating, air curing; adhesives & sealants

(G-8770)
UNIVERSAL-SPC INC
412 N State St (60123-2877)
PHONE................................847 742-4400
Nand Kumar, *President*
Bruce J Carter, *Vice Pres*
Amarnath Nuggehalli, *CFO*
EMP: 3
SALES (est): 380.7K
SALES (corp-wide): 29.2MM **Privately Held**
SIC: 3599 3471 Machine shop, jobbing & repair; plating & polishing
PA: Uca Group, Inc
 412 N State St
 Elgin IL 60123
 847 742-8870

(G-8771)
V AND F TRANSFORMER CORP (PA)
Also Called: V&F Transformer
2475 Millennium Dr (60124-7827)
PHONE................................630 497-8070
Dean Foderaro, *CEO*
Francis Foderaro, *President*
Leann Millar, *CFO*
▲ **EMP:** 85 **EST:** 1963
SALES (est): 20.7MM **Privately Held**
WEB: www.vf-transformer.com
SIC: 3612 3677 5063 Specialty transformers; electronic coils, transformers & other inductors; electrical apparatus & equipment

(G-8772)
VALUE ADDED SERVICES & TECH
Also Called: Vast
164 Division St Ste 315 (60120-5528)
PHONE................................847 888-8232
James Hanson, *President*
EMP: 5
SQ FT: 1,200
SALES (est): 544.5K **Privately Held**
WEB: www.vastproducts.net
SIC: 3625 Electric controls & control accessories, industrial

(G-8773)
VECCHIO MANUFACTURING OF ILL (PA)
Also Called: V M I
801d N State St Unit D (60123-2145)
PHONE................................847 742-8429
Sandra Vecchio, *President*
▲ **EMP:** 10
SQ FT: 21,000
SALES (est): 950K **Privately Held**
SIC: 3083 2493 3281 2531 Plastic finished products, laminated; bulletin boards, wood; blackboards, slate; public building & related furniture

(G-8774)
WALTER TOOL & MFG INC
1535 Commerce Dr (60123-9304)
PHONE................................847 697-7230
John Walter, *President*
Tony Walter, *Vice Pres*
EMP: 15
SQ FT: 15,000
SALES (est): 2.6MM **Privately Held**
SIC: 3541 3599 Numerically controlled metal cutting machine tools; machine shop, jobbing & repair

(G-8775)
WALTERS DISTRIBUTING COMPANY
1625 Dundee Ave Ste D (60120-1679)
PHONE................................847 468-0941
Neil J Fischer, *President*
Bruce L Fischer, *Vice Pres*
EMP: 7 **EST:** 1947
SQ FT: 5,500
SALES (est): 1MM **Privately Held**
SIC: 3714 Transmissions, motor vehicle

(G-8776)
WANXIANG USA HOLDINGS CORP (HQ)
88 Airport Rd Ste 100 (60123-9324)
PHONE................................847 622-8838
Weiding Lu, *CEO*
Gary Wetzel, *COO*
Pin Ni, *Vice Pres*
▲ **EMP:** 11
SQ FT: 1,000
SALES (est): 59.3MM
SALES (corp-wide): 10.8MM **Privately Held**
SIC: 3714 6211 Motor vehicle parts & accessories; investment firm, general brokerage
PA: Wanxiang Group Corporation
 Xiaoshan Economic And Technological Development Zone
 Hangzhou 31121
 571 828-3299

(G-8777)
WATER SERVICES COMPANY OF ILL
390 Sadler Ave (60120-8038)
PHONE................................847 697-6623
Michael J Pedone, *President*
Julie Termini, *Manager*
Margarette Pedone, *Admin Sec*
EMP: 8
SQ FT: 50,000
SALES (est): 1.2MM **Privately Held**
SIC: 3829 7699 Gauges, motor vehicle: oil pressure, water temperature; professional instrument repair services

(G-8778)
WEILER ENGINEERING INC
1395 Gateway Dr (60124-7866)
PHONE................................847 697-4900
Gerhard H Weiler, *President*
Carol Zolp, *President*
Arjun Ramrakhyani, *Vice Pres*
Scott Garrison, *Project Mgr*
Bill Lagro, *Maint Spvr*
▲ **EMP:** 100 **EST:** 1959
SQ FT: 120,000
SALES (est): 30.7MM **Privately Held**
WEB: www.weilerengineering.com
SIC: 3565 Packaging machinery

(G-8779)
WELCH BROS INC (PA)
1050 Saint Charles St (60120-8441)
P.O. Box 749 (60121-0749)
PHONE................................847 741-6134
David D Welch, *President*
Mark Welch, *Vice Pres*
Kevin Murphy, *Purchasing*
Denise Oltmann, *Human Res Mgr*
Kevin Johnson, *Mktg Dir*
▲ **EMP:** 118
SQ FT: 7,200
SALES (est): 20.1MM **Privately Held**
SIC: 3272 5211 Concrete products, pre-cast; septic tanks, concrete; manhole covers or frames, concrete; lumber & other building materials

(G-8780)
WELCH STEEL PRODUCTS INC
333 Hammond Ave (60120-8421)
P.O. Box 749 (60121-0749)
PHONE................................847 741-2623
David Welch, *President*
EMP: 12
SALES (est): 1.1MM **Privately Held**
SIC: 3462 Iron & steel forgings

Elgin - Kane County (G-8781)

(G-8781)
WENCO MANUFACTURING CO INC
11n261 Muirhead Rd (60124-8225)
PHONE....................630 377-7474
Bonnie Little, *President*
James Little, *Vice Pres*
EMP: 20
SALES (est): 2.3MM **Privately Held**
WEB: www.wencosimplex.com
SIC: 3452 3469 3545 3423 Bolts, metal; metal stampings; cutting tools for machine tools; hand & edge tools

(G-8782)
WILLIAMS HALTHCARE SYSTEMS LLC
158 N Edison Ave (60123-5215)
PHONE....................847 741-3650
Lisa Miller, *Buyer*
Vikki Broaddus, *Controller*
Thomas Kenny, *Info Tech Mgr*
Thomas J Kenny, *Administration*
▲ EMP: 60
SQ FT: 10,000
SALES (est): 8.8MM **Privately Held**
WEB: www.williamshealthcare.com
SIC: 3842 Surgical appliances & supplies

(G-8783)
WISDOM ADHESIVES LLC (HQ)
Also Called: H. E. Wisdom & Sons, Inc.
1575 Executive Dr (60123-9363)
PHONE....................847 841-7002
Ed Marzano, *President*
Tom Rolando, *COO*
Paul Preston, *Vice Pres*
Tereso Sanchez, *Vice Pres*
Andrea Steiger, *Vice Pres*
▲ EMP: 20
SQ FT: 12,000
SALES (est): 19.7MM
SALES (corp-wide): 2.9B **Publicly Held**
WEB: www.wisdomadhesives.com
SIC: 2295 2891 Resin or plastic coated fabrics; adhesives; glue
PA: H.B. Fuller Company
    1200 Willow Lake Blvd
    Saint Paul MN 55110
    651 236-5900

(G-8784)
WISDOM ADHESIVES LLC
1500 Scottsdale Ct (60123-9365)
PHONE....................847 841-7002
EMP: 6
SALES (corp-wide): 2.9B **Publicly Held**
SIC: 2891 Adhesives & sealants
HQ: Wisdom Adhesives, Llc
    1575 Executive Dr
    Elgin IL 60123
    847 841-7002

(G-8785)
WORLD RICHMAN MFG CORP
2505 Bath Rd (60124-7894)
PHONE....................847 468-8898
David D Huang, *President*
Colleen Hadson, *Accountant*
▲ EMP: 11
SQ FT: 40,000
SALES (est): 2.1MM **Privately Held**
SIC: 3172 Personal leather goods

Elizabeth
Jo Daviess County

(G-8786)
CIVIL CONSTRUCTORS INC
Also Called: Civil Constrs Inc Illinois
1307 W Longhollow Rd (61028-9487)
P.O. Box 750, Freeport (61032-0750)
PHONE....................815 858-2691
Dave Hermsen, *Manager*
EMP: 8
SALES (corp-wide): 163MM **Privately Held**
SIC: 1629 1422 Rock removal; crushed & broken limestone
HQ: Civil Constructors, Inc.
    2283 Us Highway 20 E
    Freeport IL 61032
    815 235-2200

(G-8787)
M & W FEED SERVICE
201 S Ash St (61028-9104)
P.O. Box 294 (61028-0294)
PHONE....................815 858-2412
Marvin J Wurster, *President*
Laurie Wuster, *Vice Pres*
EMP: 4
SQ FT: 3,600
SALES (est): 1.1MM **Privately Held**
SIC: 5191 2048 Feed; prepared feeds

(G-8788)
MD TECHNOLOGIES INC
6965 S Pleasant Hill Rd (61028-9315)
P.O. Box 60, Galena (61036-0060)
PHONE....................815 598-3143
Bill Merkle, *President*
Melissa Merkle, *Manager*
EMP: 10
SALES (est): 1.4MM **Privately Held**
SIC: 3841 Diagnostic apparatus, medical; ophthalmic instruments & apparatus

Elk Grove Village
Cook County

(G-8789)
24LAND EXPRESS INC
1460 Mark St (60007-6714)
PHONE....................630 766-2424
Kevin Cho, *President*
Paul Cho, *Principal*
◆ EMP: 4
SALES (est): 303.3K **Privately Held**
SIC: 2741 Miscellaneous publishing

(G-8790)
A & A MACHINE CO INC
1530 Jarvis Ave (60007-2459)
PHONE....................847 985-4619
Richard A Kehr, *President*
Daniel Kehr, *Vice Pres*
Eleanor Kehr, *Treasurer*
EMP: 2
SQ FT: 5,000
SALES (est): 207.3K **Privately Held**
SIC: 3599 Machine shop, jobbing & repair

(G-8791)
A J R INDUSTRIES INC
117 Gordon St (60007-1182)
PHONE....................847 439-0380
Alan Wojtowicz, *President*
Richard Simantz, *Vice Pres*
Gary Wojtowicz, *Vice Pres*
Pamela Simantz, *Treasurer*
Gregg Wojtowicz, *Sales Mgr*
EMP: 40 EST: 1965
SQ FT: 22,000
SALES: 12MM **Privately Held**
WEB: www.ajrindustries.com
SIC: 3728 Gears, aircraft power transmission

(G-8792)
A M P SOFTWARE INC
455 Vermont Dr (60007-2750)
PHONE....................630 240-5922
Adam M Pajerski, *Owner*
EMP: 1
SALES: 250K **Privately Held**
SIC: 7372 Prepackaged software

(G-8793)
ABBOTT LABORATORIES
Abbott Molecular
1800 Brummel Ave (60007-2121)
PHONE....................224 361-7129
EMP: 4
SALES (corp-wide): 31.9B **Publicly Held**
SIC: 2834 Pharmaceutical preparations
PA: Abbott Laboratories
    100 Abbott Park Rd
    Abbott Park IL 60064
    224 667-6100

(G-8794)
ABERDON ENTERPRISES
225 Bond St (60007-1220)
PHONE....................847 228-1300
Kim Komacki, *Principal*
EMP: 12

SALES (est): 1.6MM **Privately Held**
SIC: 3569 General industrial machinery

(G-8795)
ABILITY FASTENERS INC
685 Fargo Ave (60007-4742)
PHONE....................847 593-4230
John Larsen, *President*
Mary Ann Larsen, *Corp Secy*
▲ EMP: 10 EST: 1983
SQ FT: 11,000
SALES (est): 2.8MM **Privately Held**
SIC: 5072 3452 3451 Nuts (hardware); bolts; screws; rivets; bolts, nuts, rivets & washers; screw machine products

(G-8796)
ABILITY METAL COMPANY
1355 Greenleaf Ave (60007-5520)
PHONE....................847 437-7040
Tim Selleck, *President*
Steve Mucci, *President*
Ron Hansen, *COO*
Jim Kovacs, *QC Mgr*
Shannon Podgorski, *Engineer*
▲ EMP: 42
SQ FT: 40,000
SALES (est): 5.8MM **Privately Held**
WEB: www.abilitymetal.com
SIC: 3469 Stamping metal for the trade

(G-8797)
ABRAXIS BIOSCIENCE LLC
1300 Chase Ave (60007-4813)
PHONE....................310 437-7715
EMP: 4
SALES (corp-wide): 26.1B **Publicly Held**
WEB: www.abraxisbio.com
SIC: 2834 Pharmaceutical preparations
HQ: Abraxis Bioscience, Llc
    11755 Wilshire Blvd Fl 20
    Los Angeles CA 90025

(G-8798)
ACCELERATED ASSEMBLIES INC
725 Nicholas Blvd (60007-2508)
PHONE....................630 616-6680
Brian Steelglove, *President*
Michelle Hinca, *Shareholder*
EMP: 20
SQ FT: 13,500
SALES (est): 7.4MM **Privately Held**
WEB: www.acceleratedassemblies.com
SIC: 3679 3674 3571 3672 Electronic circuits; semiconductors & related devices; electronic computers; printed circuit boards

(G-8799)
ACCULIGHT LLC
2570 United Ln (60007-6819)
PHONE....................630 847-1000
Febin Mootheril, *President*
Jennifer Bonn, *Accounts Exec*
Joe Vallikalam, *Analyst*
EMP: 3
SALES (est): 230.4K **Privately Held**
SIC: 3641 5719 Tubes, electric light; lighting fixtures

(G-8800)
ACCURATE DIE CUTTING INC
120 Joey Dr (60007-1304)
PHONE....................847 437-7215
Laura Wolff, *President*
EMP: 4
SQ FT: 2,200
SALES (est): 515.9K **Privately Held**
WEB: www.accuratedie.com
SIC: 3544 Special dies & tools

(G-8801)
ACCUTRACE INC
2425 Touhy Ave (60007-5331)
PHONE....................847 290-9900
Ramzan Dhanji, *President*
EMP: 15
SALES (est): 990K **Privately Held**
SIC: 3672 Printed circuit boards

(G-8802)
ACE PRECISION TOOL & MFG CO
1612 Landmeier Rd (60007-2478)
PHONE....................847 690-0111
James A Glorioso Jr, *President*
EMP: 8
SALES (est): 1.2MM **Privately Held**
WEB: www.aceprecisiontool.com
SIC: 3599 Machine shop, jobbing & repair

(G-8803)
ACME FINISHING COMPANY LLC
1595 Oakton St (60007-2149)
PHONE....................847 640-7890
William Walters, *Principal*
Michal Kedryna, *Plant Mgr*
Andy Macari, *Plant Mgr*
Lisha Keener, *Controller*
Brian Liewergen, *Sales Staff*
EMP: 19
SALES (est): 1.2MM
SALES (corp-wide): 4.6MM **Privately Held**
SIC: 5199 3999 Packaging materials; atomizers, toiletry
PA: Acuity Capital Partners Llc
    180 N Stetson Ave
    Chicago IL
    312 268-5749

(G-8804)
ACME INDUSTRIES INC
1325 Pratt Blvd (60007-5710)
PHONE....................847 296-3346
Warren Young, *Ch of Bd*
Fred Young, *President*
Addison Mock, *Principal*
Gil Cates, *Vice Chairman*
Peter Brunk, *Vice Pres*
▲ EMP: 115 EST: 1948
SQ FT: 270,000
SALES (est): 41MM **Privately Held**
WEB: www.acmeind.com
SIC: 3599 Custom machinery; machine shop, jobbing & repair

(G-8805)
ACTEGA NORTH AMERICA INC
1550 Carmen Dr Bldg 7 (60007-6502)
PHONE....................847 690-9310
EMP: 5
SALES (corp-wide): 3.2B **Privately Held**
SIC: 2893 Printing ink
HQ: Actega North America, Inc.
    1450 Taylors Ln A
    Cinnaminson NJ 08077
    856 829-6300

(G-8806)
ACTIVE AUTOMATION INC
530 Bennett Rd (60007-1122)
PHONE....................847 427-8100
Sam V Marinkovich, *President*
Biba M Marinkovich, *Admin Sec*
EMP: 10
SQ FT: 11,000
SALES: 500K **Privately Held**
SIC: 3549 5084 7389 8742 Assembly machines, including robotic; industrial machinery & equipment; design, commercial & industrial; automation & robotics consultant

(G-8807)
ADEMCO INC
Also Called: ADI Global Distribution
509 Busse Rd (60007-2128)
PHONE....................847 472-2900
John Szeliga, *Sales Staff*
Juan Garcia, *Manager*
EMP: 45
SQ FT: 23,000
SALES (corp-wide): 4.9B **Publicly Held**
SIC: 5063 3669 3822 Electrical apparatus & equipment; emergency alarms; air conditioning & refrigeration controls
HQ: Ademco Inc.
    1985 Douglas Dr N
    Golden Valley MN 55422
    800 468-1502

GEOGRAPHIC SECTION
Elk Grove Village - Cook County (G-8834)

(G-8808)
ADK PRODUCTS INC
2821 Old Higgins Rd (60007-6416)
PHONE...................847 710-0021
EMP: 3
SALES: 100K **Privately Held**
SIC: 3499 Mfg Misc Fabricated Metal Products

(G-8809)
ADVANCED STEEL FABRICATION
181 Randall St (60007-1014)
PHONE...................847 956-6565
Alex Varga, *President*
EMP: 5
SQ FT: 5,000
SALES (est): 761.8K **Privately Held**
SIC: 3441 Fabricated structural metal

(G-8810)
ADVANCED VALVE TECH LLC (HQ)
Also Called: Valve Acquisition, LLC
800 Busse Rd (60007-2429)
PHONE...................847 364-3700
Frank Firsching, *CEO*
▲ **EMP:** 27
SQ FT: 25,000
SALES (est): 22.4MM **Privately Held**
SIC: 5074 3317 Pipes & fittings, plastic; steel pipe & tubes

(G-8811)
ADVANTAGE TOOL AND MOLD INC
1501 Kathleen Way (60007-3128)
PHONE...................847 301-9020
Bill Stack, *President*
EMP: 3
SQ FT: 3,600
SALES: 700K **Privately Held**
SIC: 3312 Forgings, iron & steel

(G-8812)
ADVERTISING PRODUCTS INC
Also Called: API
680 Fargo Ave (60007-4701)
PHONE...................847 758-0415
Glenn Rebechini, *CEO*
Doug McDonald, *Administration*
EMP: 3
SQ FT: 10,000
SALES (est): 324.2K **Privately Held**
SIC: 3993 Signs, not made in custom sign painting shops

(G-8813)
ALCONIX USA INC
25 Northwest Point Blvd # 800 (60007-1056)
PHONE...................847 717-7407
Kenji Ito, *President*
Frank W Jamieson, *Exec VP*
Yoshihiko Suzuki, *Treasurer*
Kazuo Nezaki, *Admin Sec*
▲ **EMP:** 7
SALES (est): 2.5MM **Privately Held**
SIC: 5051 3498 Copper sheets, plates, bars, rods, pipes, etc.; tube fabricating (contract bending & shaping)
PA: Alconix Corporation
2-11-1, Nagatacho
Chiyoda-Ku TKY 100-0

(G-8814)
ALL WEATHER PRODUCTS CO LLC
1500 Greenleaf Ave (60007-5525)
PHONE...................847 981-0386
John Blair, *Warehouse Mgr*
William S Rossi, *Mng Member*
Jessica Depaolis, *Administration*
Carla Hoag, *Administration*
Bill Rossi,
EMP: 13 **EST:** 1998
SQ FT: 30,000
SALES (est): 3.7MM **Privately Held**
WEB: www.awsubstrates.com
SIC: 2679 Paper products, converted; paperboard products, converted

(G-8815)
ALL-STATE INDUSTRIES INC
Also Called: Alert Manufacturing
2651 Carl Blvd (60007-6718)
PHONE...................847 350-0460
Greg Sage, *Branch Mgr*
EMP: 70
SALES (corp-wide): 78.8MM **Privately Held**
SIC: 5085 3061 3053 Hose, belting & packing; rubber goods, mechanical; mechanical rubber goods; gaskets, packing & sealing devices
PA: All-State Industries, Inc.
500 S 18th St
West Des Moines IA 50265
515 223-5843

(G-8816)
ALLSTAR FASTENERS INC
1550 Arthur Ave (60007-5733)
PHONE...................847 640-7827
Allan Vodicka, *CEO*
William Vodick, *President*
Bob Steinkellner, *Treasurer*
Bill Vodicka, *Sales Mgr*
Adam Anders, *Sales Staff*
▲ **EMP:** 50
SQ FT: 50,000
SALES (est): 10MM **Privately Held**
SIC: 3452 Bolts, nuts, rivets & washers

(G-8817)
ALPHA OMEGA PLASTICS COMPANY
1099 Touhy Ave (60007-4921)
PHONE...................847 956-8777
Lambros Kalamaris, *President*
Strat Kalamaris, *Vice Pres*
Lambros Brown, *Plant Mgr*
Maria Theodosis, *Treasurer*
Angeline Beladakis, *Admin Sec*
▼ **EMP:** 55 **EST:** 1975
SQ FT: 64,000
SALES (est): 11.5MM **Privately Held**
WEB: www.alphaomegaplastics.com
SIC: 3089 5162 Injection molding of plastics; plastics materials

(G-8818)
ALPHA OMEGA PROFILE EXTRUSION
1099 Touhy Ave (60007-4921)
PHONE...................847 956-8777
Angeline Beladakis, *CEO*
Lambros Kalamaris, *President*
Strat Kalamaris, *Vice Pres*
▼ **EMP:** 16
SALES (est): 1.6MM **Privately Held**
SIC: 3524 Edgers, lawn

(G-8819)
AMBER ENGINEERING AND MFG CO
2400 Brickvale Dr (60007-6809)
PHONE...................847 595-6966
Sigismund Paul, *President*
Bernard Paul, *Vice Pres*
EMP: 70 **EST:** 1960
SQ FT: 50,000
SALES (est): 11.5MM **Privately Held**
WEB: www.amberengineering.net
SIC: 8711 3549 3452 Designing: ship, boat, machine & product; assembly machines, including robotic; bolts, nuts, rivets & washers

(G-8820)
AMBRIT INC
Also Called: Taurus Engraving
1191 E Higgins Rd Ste 100 (60007-1563)
PHONE...................847 593-3301
B J Davis, *President*
Robin Dickerson, *Dean*
Robert Davis, *Vice Pres*
Elizabeth Gomez, *Treasurer*
Lisa Gehrke, *Advt Staff*
EMP: 3
SQ FT: 2,500
SALES (est): 264.5K **Privately Held**
SIC: 7629 5087 3965 2396 Business machine repair, electric; engraving equipment & supplies; fasteners, buttons, needles & pins; automotive & apparel trimmings; engraving service

(G-8821)
AMCRAFT MANUFACTURING INC
Also Called: Fabracraft Manufacturing
580 Lively Blvd (60007-2014)
PHONE...................847 439-4565
Mark Deutsch, *President*
James Rudins, *Manager*
▼ **EMP:** 14
SQ FT: 7,200
SALES (est): 2.8MM **Privately Held**
WEB: www.amcraftmanufacturing.com
SIC: 2393 Bags & containers, except sleeping bags: textile

(G-8822)
AMERICAN CIRCUIT SERVICES INC
80 Martin Ln (60007-1308)
PHONE...................847 895-0500
Nick Chaudhai, *President*
EMP: 6 **EST:** 2000
SQ FT: 2,500
SALES (est): 400K **Privately Held**
WEB: www.testpcb.net
SIC: 3672 Printed circuit boards

(G-8823)
AMERICAN DIGITAL CORPORATION
25 Northwest Point Blvd # 200 (60007-1056)
PHONE...................847 637-4300
Norbert Wojcik, *CEO*
Paul J Gute, *Senior VP*
Robert Panos, *Senior VP*
Michael Scoby, *Vice Pres*
David Shoffet, *Shareholder*
EMP: 38
SQ FT: 8,000
SALES (est): 17MM **Privately Held**
SIC: 3577 7373 Computer peripheral equipment; computer systems analysis & design

(G-8824)
AMERICAN MOLDING TECH INC
Also Called: A M T
2350 Lunt Ave (60007-5610)
PHONE...................847 437-6900
Dimitri Poulos, *President*
Steve Fernandez, *Production*
Tina Martinez, *Sales Staff*
EMP: 25
SALES (est): 5.6MM **Privately Held**
SIC: 3089 Injection molding of plastics

(G-8825)
AMERICAN TOOL DESIGN INC
680 Lunt Ave (60007-5015)
PHONE...................847 690-1010
Konrad Ostalowski, *President*
EMP: 6
SALES (est): 924.9K **Privately Held**
WEB: www.americantooldesign.com
SIC: 3599 Machine shop, jobbing & repair

(G-8826)
AMERICAN VULKO TREAD CORP
690 Chase Ave (60007-4802)
PHONE...................847 956-1300
Andrew C Bryniczka, *President*
Wayne Johnson, *Treasurer*
Carol Dalton, *Admin Sec*
▲ **EMP:** 12
SQ FT: 5,500
SALES (est): 2.4MM **Privately Held**
WEB: www.avt.us
SIC: 3714 Wheels, motor vehicle

(G-8827)
AMG INTERNATIONAL INC
Also Called: Freeman Products Worldwide
1480 E Devon Ave (60007-5801)
PHONE...................847 439-1001
Dave Shultz, *Manager*
EMP: 4 **Privately Held**
SIC: 3914 Trophies
PA: Amg International Inc
71 Walsh Dr Ste 101
Parsippany NJ 07054

(G-8828)
AMITRON INC
2001 Landmeier Rd (60007-2422)
PHONE...................847 290-9800
Bhagvan Patel, *President*
Milan Mortimer, *Corp Secy*
Nigel Warren, *Director*
▲ **EMP:** 137
SQ FT: 73,000
SALES (est): 29.3MM **Privately Held**
SIC: 3672 Circuit boards, television & radio printed

(G-8829)
AMPEL INCORPORATED (PA)
925 Estes Ave (60007-4905)
PHONE...................847 952-1900
Jay Gopani, *CEO*
Barry Weddington, *Manager*
EMP: 33
SQ FT: 34,000
SALES: 4MM **Privately Held**
SIC: 3672 Printed circuit boards

(G-8830)
ANAH MACHINE MFG CO
801 Pratt Blvd (60007-5116)
PHONE...................847 228-6450
Andrew Kolosa, *President*
EMP: 10
SQ FT: 17,500
SALES (est): 1MM **Privately Held**
WEB: www.anahmachine.com
SIC: 3599 Machine shop, jobbing & repair

(G-8831)
ANGLE METAL MANUFACTURING CO
Also Called: Angle Sheet Metal
1497 Tonne Rd (60007-5003)
PHONE...................847 437-8666
Jeff Nowak, *President*
Wayne Wittmeyer, *Vice Pres*
Brian Nowak, *Treasurer*
EMP: 4
SQ FT: 4,600
SALES (est): 575K **Privately Held**
SIC: 3444 Sheet metal specialties, not stamped

(G-8832)
ANGLE TOOL COMPANY
425 Crossen Ave (60007-2003)
PHONE...................847 593-7572
Fax: 847 593-7582
EMP: 5 **EST:** 1970
SQ FT: 8,000
SALES: 500K **Privately Held**
SIC: 3544 3469 Mfg Dies/Tools/Jigs/Fixtures Mfg Metal Stampings

(G-8833)
ANODIZING SPECIALISTS LTD
210 Crossen Ave (60007-1612)
PHONE...................847 437-9495
Mike Panoplos, *President*
EMP: 9 **EST:** 1981
SQ FT: 6,200
SALES (est): 146.4K **Privately Held**
SIC: 3471 Anodizing (plating) of metals or formed products; chromium plating of metals or formed products

(G-8834)
ANRITSU INFIVIS INC
Also Called: Anritsu Indus Slutions USA Inc
1001 Cambridge Dr (60007-2453)
PHONE...................847 419-9729
Eric Braner, *CEO*
Doug Dobben, *CFO*
Guy Wheeler, *Regl Sales Mgr*
Eva Bar, *Marketing Staff*
Carlos Freire, *Manager*
▲ **EMP:** 33
SQ FT: 20,000
SALES: 9.7MM **Privately Held**
SIC: 2834 Intravenous solutions
HQ: Anritsu Infivis Co., Ltd.
5-1-1, Onna
Atsugi KNG 243-0

Elk Grove Village - Cook County (G-8835)

(G-8835)
APHELION PRECISION TECH CORP
1800 Greenleaf Ave (60007-5502)
PHONE..............................847 215-7285
Jane Black, *President*
William Black, *Exec VP*
Michael Black, *Vice Pres*
Ruben Obregon, *Engineer*
Blake Taubman, *Engineer*
EMP: 45 **EST:** 1981
SQ FT: 25,000
SALES (est): 9.3MM **Privately Held**
WEB: www.aphelionptc.com
SIC: 3599 Machine shop, jobbing & repair

(G-8836)
AQUION PARTNERS LTD PARTNR
2080 Lunt Ave (60007-5606)
PHONE..............................847 437-9400
David Cole, *CEO*
Eddie Garmon, *Exec VP*
Patrick Steele, *Exec VP*
Diane Dzukola, *Purch Mgr*
Donald Miller, *VP Bus Dvlpt*
EMP: 5
SALES (est): 418.6K **Privately Held**
SIC: 2819 Industrial inorganic chemicals

(G-8837)
ARC-TRONICS INC
1150 Pagni Dr (60007-6686)
PHONE..............................847 437-0211
Conrad Goeringer, *CEO*
Michael Goeringer, *President*
Mark Goeringer, *Vice Pres*
Matthew Goeringer, *VP Mfg*
Steve Hrycko, *Mfg Staff*
▲ **EMP:** 210
SQ FT: 30,000
SALES (est): 66.2MM **Privately Held**
SIC: 3672 3824 3679 Printed circuit boards; mechanical & electromechanical counters & devices; electronic circuits; harness assemblies for electronic use: wire or cable

(G-8838)
ARMOR CONTRACT MFG INC
2301 Estes Ave (60007-5428)
PHONE..............................847 981-9800
David K Schmitt, *CEO*
EMP: 20
SALES (est): 874.8K
SALES (corp-wide): 60.8MM **Privately Held**
SIC: 3441 Fabricated structural metal
PA: Armor Consolidated, Inc.
4600 N Mson Montgomery Rd
Mason OH 45040
513 923-5260

(G-8839)
ARROW ROAD CONSTRUCTION CO (PA)
1445 Oakton St (60007-2023)
P.O. Box 334, Mount Prospect (60056-0334)
PHONE..............................847 437-0700
John F Healy, *President*
Eileen Healy, *Vice Pres*
Ann Neshek, *Vice Pres*
Anthony Somers, *Vice Pres*
Dan Jones, *Opers Mgr*
EMP: 125 **EST:** 1925
SALES (est): 42.7MM **Privately Held**
WEB: www.arrowroad.com
SIC: 1611 2951 Highway & street paving contractor; asphalt & asphaltic paving mixtures (not from refineries)

(G-8840)
ARTHUR/BUSSE PROPERTIES INC
2299 Busse Rd (60007-6012)
PHONE..............................847 289-1800
Jasper B Sanfilippo, *Principal*
EMP: 15
SALES (est): 1.8MM **Privately Held**
SIC: 2068 Salted & roasted nuts & seeds

(G-8841)
ASCENT MFG CO
123 Scott St (60007-1210)
PHONE..............................847 806-6600
George Daniel, *President*
Marie Daniel, *Corp Secy*
Andy Daniel, *Vice Pres*
Chet Daniel, *Vice Pres*
EMP: 20
SQ FT: 40,000
SALES (est): 4.8MM **Privately Held**
SIC: 3495 3496 7692 3469 Precision springs; miscellaneous fabricated wire products; welding repair; metal stampings; springs

(G-8842)
ASHLAND DOOR SOLUTIONS LLC
185 Martin Ln (60007-1309)
PHONE..............................773 348-5106
Anne Gruber,
EMP: 5
SALES (est): 183.1K **Privately Held**
SIC: 3429 7699 5251 1751 Manufactured hardware (general); repair services; hardware; carpentry work

(G-8843)
ASSA ABLOY ENTRANCE SYSTEMS US
Also Called: Besam Entrance Solutions
1630 Jarvis Ave (60007-2404)
PHONE..............................847 228-5600
Mike Sumrall, *Manager*
EMP: 10
SALES (corp-wide): 8.8B **Privately Held**
SIC: 3699 1796 3442 Door opening & closing devices, electrical; installing building equipment; metal doors
HQ: Assa Abloy Entrance Systems Us Inc.
1900 Airport Rd
Monroe NC 28110
704 290-5520

(G-8844)
ASTRO MACHINE CORPORATION
630 Lively Blvd (60007-2016)
PHONE..............................847 364-6363
George Selak, *President*
Martin Selak, *Chairman*
Martin M Selak, *Chairman*
Nancy Dedic, *Corp Secy*
Miryana Schubert, *Vice Pres*
◆ **EMP:** 42
SQ FT: 35,000
SALES (est): 12MM **Privately Held**
SIC: 3599 Machine shop, jobbing & repair; carnival machines & equipment, amusement park

(G-8845)
ATLAS COPCO COMPRESSORS LLC
2501 Landmeier Rd Ste 110 (60007-2622)
P.O. Box 91730, Chicago (60693-1730)
PHONE..............................847 640-6067
Bob Von Cloedt, *Manager*
EMP: 10
SALES (corp-wide): 10.5B **Privately Held**
SIC: 3563 Air & gas compressors
HQ: Atlas Copco Compressors Llc
300 Technology Center Way # 5
Rock Hill SC 29730
866 472-1015

(G-8846)
ATOMIC ENGINEERING CO
365 Kent Ave (60007-1901)
PHONE..............................847 228-1387
Jacqueline Redmond, *President*
EMP: 13 **EST:** 1952
SALES (est): 1.3MM **Privately Held**
WEB: www.atomiceng.com
SIC: 3599 3544 Machine shop, jobbing & repair; die sets for metal stamping (presses); jigs & fixtures

(G-8847)
ATOMIC INDUSTRIAL MACHINE INC
365 Kent Ave (60007-1901)
PHONE..............................847 228-1387
Rayna Gregurich, *President*
EMP: 10
SALES (est): 374.3K **Privately Held**
SIC: 3599 Machine shop, jobbing & repair

(G-8848)
AUTOMATIC PRODUCTION EQP INC
815 Touhy Ave (60007-4917)
PHONE..............................847 439-1448
Donald Schmucker, *President*
Helen Schmucker, *Treasurer*
EMP: 8 **EST:** 1974
SQ FT: 15,000
SALES (est): 2MM **Privately Held**
WEB: www.apeinc.com
SIC: 5084 3541 Machine tools & accessories; machine tools, metal cutting type

(G-8849)
AUTOMOTIVE ENGINE SPECIALTIES
173 Randall St (60007-1014)
PHONE..............................847 956-1244
Anthony Schroeder, *Owner*
EMP: 3
SQ FT: 3,700
SALES (est): 220K **Privately Held**
SIC: 3599 Machine shop, jobbing & repair

(G-8850)
AVANA ELECTRIC MOTORS INC
Also Called: Avana Electrotek
1445 Brummel Ave (60007-2110)
P.O. Box 644 (60009-0644)
PHONE..............................847 588-0400
Tom Hannay, *President*
Vivian Woodville, *Accounting Mgr*
Chuck Ramke, *Sales Associate*
Tom Ziemba, *Sales Associate*
Jim Holtzer, *Sales Executive*
EMP: 17 **EST:** 1943
SQ FT: 15,600
SALES (est): 7.5MM **Privately Held**
WEB: www.avanaelectrotek.com
SIC: 5063 7694 Motors, electric; motor controls, starters & relays: electric; generators; electric motor repair

(G-8851)
AWNINGS BY ZIP DEE INC
96 Crossen Ave (60007-1608)
PHONE..............................847 640-0460
James G Webb, *President*
Ron Mullins, *Plant Mgr*
Linda Johnson, *Cust Svc Dir*
▲ **EMP:** 26
SALES (est): 4.4MM **Privately Held**
SIC: 2394 Awnings, fabric: made from purchased materials

(G-8852)
AXIS MANUFACTURING INC
2436 Delta Ln (60007-6303)
PHONE..............................847 350-0200
Will Pavon, *President*
Alberto Del Gadillo, *Vice Pres*
Amparo Mendoza, *Treasurer*
Carmen Mendoza, *Admin Sec*
EMP: 14
SALES (est): 2.5MM **Privately Held**
WEB: www.axismfg.net
SIC: 3599 Custom machinery

(G-8853)
B & W MACHINE COMPANY INC
71 Gordon St (60007-1117)
PHONE..............................847 364-4500
P Bockstahler, *President*
Peter Bockstahler, *President*
Bernadette Bockstahler, *Admin Sec*
EMP: 5
SQ FT: 5,000
SALES (est): 300K **Privately Held**
WEB: www.bwmachinecoinc.com
SIC: 3599 7692 Machine shop, jobbing & repair; welding repair

(G-8854)
B S GRINDING INC
2535 United Ln (60007-6820)
PHONE..............................847 787-0770
Ted Boska, *President*
EMP: 5
SQ FT: 4,600
SALES (est): 479.1K **Privately Held**
SIC: 7389 3599 Grinding, precision: commercial or industrial; machine shop, jobbing & repair

(G-8855)
BAL-CRAFT SCREW MACHINE CO
985 Lively Blvd (60007-2206)
PHONE..............................847 398-7688
Marcus Bode, *President*
Eva Bode, *Admin Sec*
EMP: 3
SQ FT: 3,200
SALES (est): 250K **Privately Held**
SIC: 3451 Screw machine products

(G-8856)
BALANSTAR CORPORATION (PA)
Also Called: Balancing Services
170 Lively Blvd (60007-1621)
PHONE..............................773 261-5034
Erwin Schulz, *President*
Ivan Aguilar, *Manager*
EMP: 11
SQ FT: 25,000
SALES (est): 1.5MM **Privately Held**
SIC: 3545 Balancing machines (machine tool accessories)

(G-8857)
BALLY FOIL GRAPHICS INC
1701 Elmhurst Rd (60007-6407)
PHONE..............................847 427-1509
Allan L Bally, *President*
EMP: 4
SALES: 200K **Privately Held**
SIC: 2752 2791 2759 Commercial printing, offset; typesetting; commercial printing; publication printing

(G-8858)
BAYER CORPORATION
25 Northwest Point Blvd # 560 (60007-1069)
PHONE..............................847 725-6320
Sang Lyu, *Manager*
EMP: 3
SALES (corp-wide): 48.1B **Privately Held**
WEB: www.bayer.com
SIC: 2834 Pharmaceutical preparations
HQ: Bayer Corporation
100 Bayer Rd Bldg 14
Pittsburgh PA 15205
412 777-2000

(G-8859)
BEA ELECTRO SALES INC
Also Called: B E A Electro-Optics
1400 Howard St (60007-2221)
PHONE..............................847 238-1420
Ron Rutkowski, *President*
Joseph Sieracki, *Admin Sec*
EMP: 4 **EST:** 1999
SALES (est): 745K **Privately Held**
WEB: www.bea-eo.com
SIC: 5065 3821 Electronic parts; laser beam alignment devices

(G-8860)
BECKER SPECIALTY CORPORATION (DH)
2526 Delta Ln (60007-6305)
PHONE..............................847 766-3555
Jack McGrew, *Principal*
▲ **EMP:** 21
SALES (est): 34.2MM
SALES (corp-wide): 882MM **Privately Held**
SIC: 3677 Electronic coils, transformers & other inductors
HQ: Becker Industrial Coatings Holding Ab

Marsta 195 0
859 079-126

(G-8861)
BECKS LIGHT GAUGE ALUMINUM CO
1425 Tonne Rd (60007-5003)
PHONE..............................847 290-9990
Greg Beck, *President*
EMP: 10

GEOGRAPHIC SECTION
Elk Grove Village - Cook County (G-8890)

SALES (est): 3.7MM **Privately Held**
WEB: www.beckslight.net
SIC: 5051 3365 Miscellaneous nonferrous products; aluminum foundries

(G-8862)
BELL LITHO INC (PA)
Also Called: Glo Document Solutions
370 Crossen Ave (60007-2089)
PHONE..................................847 952-3300
Felix Ricci, *President*
Herman A Bellagamba, *Chairman*
Martin Bellagamba, *Vice Pres*
Nick Filip, *Opers Staff*
Laura Anderson, *Production*
▲ EMP: 82 EST: 1965
SQ FT: 30,000
SALES (est): 16.8MM **Privately Held**
WEB: www.bell-litho.com
SIC: 2752 2789 Commercial printing, offset; bookbinding & related work

(G-8863)
BELL LITHO INC
Also Called: Sun America
1820 Lunt Ave (60007-5602)
PHONE..................................847 290-9300
Gary Miller,
EMP: 6
SALES (corp-wide): 16.8MM **Privately Held**
PA: Bell Litho, Inc.
  370 Crossen Ave
  Elk Grove Village IL 60007
  847 952-3300

(G-8864)
BELMONT SAUSAGE COMPANY
2201 Estes Ave (60007-5426)
PHONE..................................847 357-1515
Walter Milica, *President*
Michael Mulica, *Project Mgr*
Elwira Blicharz, *QC Mgr*
Monika Chmiel, *Technology*
Jez Greg, *Maintence Staff*
▲ EMP: 25 EST: 1963
SALES (est): 5.9MM **Privately Held**
WEB: www.belmontsausage.com
SIC: 2013 2011 Sausages & other prepared meats; meat packing plants

(G-8865)
BEST METAL EXTRUSIONS INC
1900 E Devon Ave (60007-6022)
PHONE..................................847 981-0797
Terry Slade, *President*
EMP: 20
SQ FT: 7,000
SALES (est): 5MM **Privately Held**
WEB: www.bestmetalextrusion.com
SIC: 3544 Extrusion dies

(G-8866)
BEVWRAP LLC
420 Bonnie Ln (60007-1908)
PHONE..................................773 580-5434
Rafael Drozt, *Mng Member*
EMP: 3
SQ FT: 3,000
SALES (est): 200K **Privately Held**
SIC: 3565 Labeling machines, industrial

(G-8867)
BIOSYNERGY INC (PA)
1940 E Devon Ave (60007-6022)
PHONE..................................847 956-0471
Fred K Suzuki, *Ch of Bd*
Laurence Mead, *COO*
Mary K Friske, *Vice Pres*
Jennifer A Rieck, *Vice Pres*
Lauane C Addis, *Admin Sec*
EMP: 5
SQ FT: 10,400
SALES: 1.2MM **Privately Held**
SIC: 3829 3841 3822 3821 Thermometers & temperature sensors; temperature sensors, except industrial process & aircraft; surgical & medical instruments; auto controls regulating residntl & coml environmt & applncs; laboratory apparatus & furniture

(G-8868)
BLACK BOX CORPORATION
1850 Jarvis Ave (60007-2440)
PHONE..................................847 439-5000
Anita Fletcher, *Branch Mgr*
Jean Ryan, *Program Mgr*
EMP: 8 **Privately Held**
SIC: 3577 Computer peripheral equipment
HQ: Black Box Corporation
  1000 Park Dr
  Lawrence PA 15055
  724 746-5500

(G-8869)
BLOCKMASTER ELECTRONICS INC
1400 Howard St (60007-2221)
PHONE..................................847 956-1680
Joe Sieracki, *President*
▲ EMP: 8
SQ FT: 20,000
SALES (est): 640K **Privately Held**
SIC: 3679 Electronic circuits

(G-8870)
BROOKE GRAPHICS LLC
1331 Greenleaf Ave (60007-5520)
PHONE..................................847 593-1300
Kit Geary, *Production*
Thomas James B Bednarke,
Sheila L Bednarke,
EMP: 22
SQ FT: 35,000
SALES (est): 4.3MM **Privately Held**
SIC: 2759 Commercial printing

(G-8871)
BROWN PACKAGING LLC
Also Called: Brown Adhesives & Equipment
901 Cambridge Dr (60007-2434)
PHONE..................................224 415-3182
Todd Brown, *President*
EMP: 10
SALES: 5MM **Privately Held**
SIC: 2891 Adhesives & sealants

(G-8872)
BUCTHEL METAL FINISHING CORP
1945 Touhy Ave (60007-5315)
PHONE..................................847 427-8704
Abe Yousif, *President*
EMP: 12
SQ FT: 10,000
SALES (est): 1.6MM **Privately Held**
SIC: 3471 Buffing for the trade; polishing, metals or formed products; finishing, metals or formed products

(G-8873)
BUHRKE INDUSTRIES LLC
Also Called: IMS Buhrke-Olson
2771 Busse Rd (60007-6102)
PHONE..................................630 412-2028
EMP: 47
SALES (corp-wide): 189.6MM **Privately Held**
SIC: 3999 Barber & beauty shop equipment
HQ: Buhrke Industries, Llc
  511 W Algonquin Rd
  Arlington Heights IL 60005
  847 981-7550

(G-8874)
BURSTAN INC
2530 United Ln (60007-6819)
PHONE..................................847 787-0380
Santon Katka, *President*
EMP: 4 EST: 2011
SALES (est): 377.4K **Privately Held**
SIC: 2752 Commercial printing, lithographic

(G-8875)
BWAY CORPORATION
1350 Arthur Ave (60007-5707)
PHONE..................................847 956-0750
Samantha Desilva, *Warehouse Mgr*
Marcelo Osorio, *Manager*
EMP: 131
SALES (corp-wide): 1.2B **Privately Held**
SIC: 3089 3411 Plastic containers, except foam; tubs, plastic (containers); can lids & ends, metal
HQ: Bway Corporation
  375 Northridge Rd Ste 600
  Atlanta GA 30350

(G-8876)
C2 IMAGING LLC
Elk Grove Graphics
1200 Chase Ave (60007-4826)
PHONE..................................847 439-7834
Jim Stanley, *Vice Pres*
Cory Baldwin, *Production*
Ron Lindeen, *Accounts Exec*
Jose Avalos, *Manager*
EMP: 45
SALES (corp-wide): 108.4MM **Privately Held**
SIC: 2752 Commercial printing, lithographic
HQ: C2 Imaging, Llc
  201 Plaza Two
  Jersey City NJ 07311

(G-8877)
CABLE COMPANY (PA)
498 Bonnie Ln (60007-1908)
PHONE..................................847 437-5267
John S Lloyd, *President*
▲ EMP: 33
SQ FT: 12,000
SALES (est): 6.8MM **Privately Held**
SIC: 3663 5063 Television broadcasting & communications equipment; wire & cable

(G-8878)
CAMIS MOLD & TOOL CO
1350 Brummel Ave (60007-2109)
PHONE..................................847 593-6620
Theodore Camis, *President*
EMP: 3
SALES (est): 144.2K **Privately Held**
SIC: 3089 Injection molding of plastics

(G-8879)
CARR MACHINE & TOOL INC
1301 Jarvis Ave (60007-2387)
PHONE..................................847 593-8003
Richard Carr, *President*
James R Carr, *Vice Pres*
Serge Shelepov, *Mfg Mgr*
Linda Cobos, *Director*
Ryan Carr, *Technician*
EMP: 8
SQ FT: 7,500
SALES (est): 1.6MM **Privately Held**
SIC: 3599 Machine shop, jobbing & repair

(G-8880)
CATALINA COATING & PLAS INC
Also Called: Catalina Graphic Films
870 Greenleaf Ave (60007-5026)
PHONE..................................847 806-1340
EMP: 11
SALES (corp-wide): 22.7MM **Privately Held**
SIC: 3083 5162 3081 Mfg Laminated Plastic Plate/Sheet Whol Plastic Materials/Shapes Mfg Unsupported Plastic Film/Sheet
PA: Catalina Coating & Plastics, Inc.
  4855 W Harmon Ave Ste D
  Las Vegas NV 89103
  818 880-8060

(G-8881)
CATALOG DESIGNERS INC
106 Buckingham Ct (60007-3856)
PHONE..................................847 228-0025
Robert N Holzheimer, *CEO*
Kathleen Holzheimer, *Vice Pres*
EMP: 4
SALES (est): 444.3K **Privately Held**
SIC: 2741 7311 2759 Catalogs: publishing only, not printed on site; advertising agencies; commercial printing

(G-8882)
CATAPULT GLOBAL LLC
1000 Lee St (60007-1208)
PHONE..................................847 364-8149
Long S Shouchou,
Rocio Palma, *Executive Asst*
Frederick Kesselman,
▲ EMP: 10
SQ FT: 25,000
SALES (est): 1.9MM **Privately Held**
SIC: 3441 Fabricated structural metal

(G-8883)
CCC CHICAGO CABINET CENTER LLC
Also Called: CCC Cabinets
300 King St (60007-1115)
PHONE..................................855 508-5525
Bahri C Ozmen, *Principal*
EMP: 10
SALES (est): 814.6K **Privately Held**
WEB: www.ccccabinets.com
SIC: 2434 Wood kitchen cabinets

(G-8884)
CENTECH PLASTICS INC
Also Called: Cmt
855 Touhy Ave (60007-4917)
PHONE..................................847 364-4433
Mark Hendee, *CEO*
Gyongyi Varhegyi, *President*
Peter Varhegyi, *Vice Pres*
▲ EMP: 126
SQ FT: 31,500
SALES: 12MM **Privately Held**
SIC: 3089 Injection molding of plastics

(G-8885)
CENTRAL STATE FINDS
221 King St (60007-1112)
PHONE..................................630 359-4706
John Hornberger, *Owner*
Cody Nick, *Co-Owner*
EMP: 2
SALES (est): 351.1K **Privately Held**
SIC: 3993 Signs & advertising specialties

(G-8886)
CENTURY MOLD & TOOL CO
855 Touhy Ave (60007-4917)
PHONE..................................847 364-5858
Peter Varhegyi, *President*
Gyongyi Varhegyi, *Corp Secy*
EMP: 28
SQ FT: 12,500
SALES (est): 3.3MM **Privately Held**
SIC: 7389 3089 3544 Grinding, precision: commercial or industrial; injection molding of plastics; special dies, tools, jigs & fixtures

(G-8887)
CHALLENGE TOOL CO
60 Joey Dr (60007-1302)
PHONE..................................847 640-8085
Russell K Stoltz, *Owner*
EMP: 4
SQ FT: 6,000
SALES (est): 220K **Privately Held**
SIC: 3544 Industrial molds; dies, plastics forming; dies & die holders for metal cutting, forming, die casting

(G-8888)
CHAMBERS MARKETING OPTIONS
Also Called: Wedding Pages of Chicago, The
1008 Bonaventure Dr (60007-3277)
PHONE..................................847 584-2626
Joe Chambers, *President*
Suzan Chambers, *Admin Sec*
EMP: 6
SQ FT: 1,200
SALES (est): 580.4K **Privately Held**
SIC: 5621 7389 2721 Bridal shops; trade show arrangement; periodicals

(G-8889)
CHEM-PLATE INDUSTRIES INC (PA)
1800 Touhy Ave (60007-5314)
PHONE..................................847 640-1600
Martin Straus, *President*
Nevresa Mujcinovic, *Engineer*
Jose Pena, *Manager*
Aaron S Kolesar, *Technology*
Robert Miller, *Technology*
EMP: 80
SQ FT: 59,000
SALES (est): 56.1MM **Privately Held**
SIC: 3398 3471 Metal heat treating; plating & polishing

(G-8890)
CHERITH AGRO INC
921 Oakton St (60007-1905)
PHONE..................................847 258-3865

Elk Grove Village - Cook County (G-8891)

GEOGRAPHIC SECTION

Abraham Kim, *President*
EMP: 5
SQ FT: 6,000
SALES: 5MM **Privately Held**
SIC: 2075 Lecithin, soybean

(G-8891)
CHICAGO CIRCUITS CORPORATION
2685 United Ln (60007-6822)
PHONE 847 238-1623
Hari Kher, *President*
Mahendra Patel, *Exec VP*
Mike Patel, *Vice Pres*
Rakesh Patel, *Vice Pres*
EMP: 16
SQ FT: 15,000
SALES: 2.2MM **Privately Held**
SIC: 3672 5063 Printed circuit boards; circuit breakers

(G-8892)
CHICAGO PALLET SERVICE INC (HQ)
1875 Greenleaf Ave (60007-5501)
PHONE 847 439-8754
Leo Rodriguez, *President*
Araceli Rodriguez, *Vice Pres*
EMP: 32
SALES (est): 5.5MM **Privately Held**
SIC: 2448 Pallets, wood

(G-8893)
CHICAGO PALLET SERVICE II INC (PA)
1875 Greenleaf Ave (60007-5501)
PHONE 847 439-8330
Amparo Rodrigguez, *President*
EMP: 31
SALES (est): 10.5MM **Privately Held**
SIC: 2448 Pallets, wood

(G-8894)
CHICAGO PRESS CORPORATION
1880 Busse Rd (60007-5718)
PHONE 773 276-1500
Mitchell H Harrison, *President*
Rick Clement, *President*
Pat Mallo, *President*
Patrica Mallo, *President*
Paul Monsen, *COO*
EMP: 40 **EST:** 1927
SQ FT: 68,000
SALES (est): 8.5MM **Privately Held**
WEB: www.chicagopress.net
SIC: 2752 Commercial printing, offset

(G-8895)
CHICAGO VALVES & CONTROLS LLC
885 Cambridge Dr (60007-2436)
PHONE 312 637-3551
Alex Winkler, *President*
Carmel Winkler, *COO*
EMP: 5
SALES: 2MM **Privately Held**
SIC: 3491 Industrial valves

(G-8896)
CHICAGO WATERJET INC
42 Martin Ln (60007-1308)
PHONE 847 350-1898
Patrick Hill, *President*
EMP: 2 **EST:** 2000
SQ FT: 2,500
SALES (est): 356.9K **Privately Held**
WEB: www.chicagowaterjet.com
SIC: 3599 4941 Machine shop, jobbing & repair; water supply

(G-8897)
CHRISTOPHER R CLINE PRTG LTD
931 Oakton St (60007-1905)
PHONE 847 981-0500
Christopher R Cline, *President*
EMP: 12
SQ FT: 5,000
SALES (est): 1.1MM **Privately Held**
SIC: 2752 2791 2789 Commercial printing, offset; typesetting; bookbinding & related work

(G-8898)
CIM-TECH PLASTICS INC
2670 United Ln (60007-6821)
PHONE 847 350-0900
Charles Pertile, *President*
Anthony D'Angelo, *Admin Sec*
EMP: 16
SQ FT: 6,000
SALES (est): 2.8MM **Privately Held**
SIC: 3089 Injection molding of plastics

(G-8899)
CIRCUIT ENGINEERING LLC
1390 Lunt Ave (60007-5620)
PHONE 847 806-7777
Pradeep Jose, *Opers Mgr*
Dileep Thomas, *Opers Mgr*
Sue Pontanini, *VP Sales*
Tony Serpe, *VP Sales*
Dennis Dworzak, *Sales Mgr*
▲ **EMP:** 40 **EST:** 1999
SQ FT: 40,000
SALES (est): 7.7MM **Privately Held**
SIC: 3672 Printed circuit boards

(G-8900)
CMP ASSOCIATES INC
Also Called: Cmp Anodizing
1340 Howard St (60007-2214)
PHONE 847 956-1313
Werner Langenstrass, *President*
Jon Cordell, *QA Dir*
Leah Langenstrass, *Office Mgr*
Carol Langenstrass, *Admin Sec*
Lisa Nie,
EMP: 12 **EST:** 1994
SALES (est): 2.1MM **Privately Held**
WEB: www.cmpanodizing.com
SIC: 3471 Plating of metals or formed products

(G-8901)
COLORS FOR PLASTICS INC (PA)
2245 Pratt Blvd (60007-5916)
PHONE 847 437-0033
John Dalleska, *President*
Robert Dalleska, *President*
Matthew Halminiak, *Prdtn Mgr*
Deana Mirante, *Traffic Mgr*
Ashly Nummer, *Purch Agent*
EMP: 75
SQ FT: 45,000
SALES (est): 18.1MM **Privately Held**
SIC: 2816 2865 Inorganic pigments; cyclic crudes & intermediates

(G-8902)
COMET TOOL INC
880 Nicholas Blvd (60007-2511)
PHONE 847 956-0126
Constance Ray, *President*
Slawek Jodlowski, *Opers Mgr*
Kamil Swierzynski, *QC Mgr*
Andrea Moore, *Finance*
Connie Ray, *Office Mgr*
▲ **EMP:** 50 **EST:** 1968
SQ FT: 34,000
SALES (est): 1.7MM **Privately Held**
SIC: 3545 Precision tools, machinists'

(G-8903)
COMMERCIAL COPY PRINTING CTR
520 Bennett Rd (60007-1122)
PHONE 847 981-8590
EMP: 15 **EST:** 1979
SQ FT: 4,000
SALES: 1MM **Privately Held**
SIC: 2752 2796 2791 2789 Lithographic Coml Print Platemaking Services Typesetting Services Bookbinding/Related Work

(G-8904)
COMMERCIAL FINISHES CO LTD
540 Lively Blvd (60007-2014)
PHONE 847 981-9222
Sam Legittino, *President*
John Klodnicki, *Vice Pres*
Judith Legittino, *Admin Sec*
EMP: 23
SQ FT: 16,000
SALES (est): 1.2MM **Privately Held**
WEB: www.cfcpaint.com
SIC: 3479 Coating of metals & formed products

(G-8905)
COMMERCIAL MACHINE SERVICES
1099 Touhy Ave (60007-4921)
P.O. Box 835 (60009-0835)
PHONE 847 806-1901
Herbert R Gottelt, *President*
Robert Walser, *Vice Pres*
EMP: 10
SQ FT: 4,000
SALES (est): 1.4MM **Privately Held**
SIC: 7699 7692 3599 Industrial machinery & equipment repair; welding repair; machine shop, jobbing & repair

(G-8906)
COMMERCIAL STAINLESS SVCS INC
1201 Busse Rd (60007-4820)
PHONE 847 349-1560
Daniel Hansen, *President*
EMP: 19
SALES (est): 4.1MM **Privately Held**
WEB: www.commercialstainlessservices.com
SIC: 3312 Stainless steel

(G-8907)
CONCEPT INDUSTRIES INC
199 Gaylord St (60007-1106)
PHONE 847 258-3545
Robert Renner, *President*
Jack Krafcisin, *Admin Sec*
EMP: 4
SQ FT: 7,000
SALES (est): 895.7K **Privately Held**
SIC: 7692 Welding repair

(G-8908)
CONCORD PRINTING INC
1550 E Higgins Rd Ste 113 (60007-1627)
P.O. Box 118, Harvard (60033-0118)
PHONE 847 734-1616
Robert Ahern, *President*
Matt Witry, *Vice Pres*
EMP: 3
SQ FT: 750
SALES (est): 750K **Privately Held**
SIC: 2752 Commercial printing, offset

(G-8909)
CONSOLIDATED PRINTING CO INC
1715 Elmhurst Rd (60007-5924)
PHONE 773 631-2800
Marily K Jones, *President*
Marilyn K Jones, *President*
Kathy Anderson, *Vice Pres*
Shane Anderson, *CIO*
Kathlynn Anderson, *Admin Sec*
EMP: 11
SQ FT: 9,000
SALES (est): 2.4MM **Privately Held**
SIC: 2752 Commercial printing, offset

(G-8910)
CONTINENTAL BINDERY CORP
1250 Pratt Blvd (60007-5709)
PHONE 847 439-6811
Tim Hoffman, *President*
EMP: 100
SQ FT: 21,000
SALES (est): 11MM **Privately Held**
SIC: 2789 Binding only: books, pamphlets, magazines, etc.

(G-8911)
CONTOUR MACHINING INC
640 Fargo Ave (60007-4701)
PHONE 847 364-0111
Gertrude Schneider, *CEO*
Werner Schneider, *President*
EMP: 7
SQ FT: 5,000
SALES: 1MM **Privately Held**
WEB: www.contourmachining.net
SIC: 3599 Machine shop, jobbing & repair

(G-8912)
CONVERTING TECHNOLOGY INC
Also Called: CTI
1557 Carmen Dr (60007-6501)
PHONE 847 290-0590
John Norgard, *President*
Dave Bazdor, *Vice Pres*
Pat Callahan, *Technical Mgr*
William Crutchfield, *Treasurer*
Ken Paihr, *Manager*
▲ **EMP:** 57
SQ FT: 27,600
SALES (est): 10.9MM **Privately Held**
SIC: 3544 Dies, steel rule

(G-8913)
COOPER LIGHTING LLC
2550 United Ln (60007-6819)
PHONE 312 595-2770
Tony Tarello, *Branch Mgr*
EMP: 4
SALES (corp-wide): 7.2B **Privately Held**
SIC: 3645 Residential lighting fixtures
HQ: Cooper Lighting, Llc
1121 Highway 74 S
Peachtree City GA 30269
770 486-4800

(G-8914)
COOPER LIGHTING LLC
400 Busse Rd (60007-2195)
PHONE 847 956-8400
Dave Arnold, *Branch Mgr*
EMP: 100
SALES (corp-wide): 7.2B **Privately Held**
SIC: 3645 3646 Residential lighting fixtures; commercial indusl & institutional electric lighting fixtures
HQ: Cooper Lighting, Llc
1121 Highway 74 S
Peachtree City GA 30269
770 486-4800

(G-8915)
CORD SETS INC
1822 Elmhurst Rd (60007-5911)
PHONE 847 427-1185
EMP: 3
SALES (est): 153.1K **Privately Held**
SIC: 3678 Electronic connectors

(G-8916)
CORRO-SHIELD INTERNATIONAL INC
2575 United Ln (60007-6820)
PHONE 847 298-7770
M Grant Brown, *President*
Bret Sneider, *COO*
Bret Snider, *COO*
Hugh Mc Veigh, *Vice Pres*
Jesus Urbieta, *Plant Mgr*
EMP: 12
SQ FT: 11,000
SALES: 1.5MM **Privately Held**
SIC: 2821 Epoxy resins

(G-8917)
COZZINI LLC
2567 Greenleaf Ave (60007-5574)
PHONE 773 478-9700
Peter J Samson, *President*
EMP: 124
SALES (est): 24.1MM
SALES (corp-wide): 2.9B **Publicly Held**
SIC: 3556 Meat processing machinery
PA: The Middleby Corporation
1400 Toastmaster Dr
Elgin IL 60120
847 741-3300

(G-8918)
CRAFTSTECH INC
Also Called: Crafts Technology
91 Joey Dr (60007-1321)
PHONE 847 758-3100
Thomas Kuhl, *President*
David Le Maistre, *Vice Pres*
Susan Lustro, *Controller*
Joe Abbate, *Technical Staff*
Joseph Abbate, *Technical Staff*
EMP: 37 **EST:** 1996
SQ FT: 20,000

GEOGRAPHIC SECTION
Elk Grove Village - Cook County (G-8944)

SALES: 7.1MM **Privately Held**
WEB: www.craftstech.net
SIC: 3545 Cutting tools for machine tools

(G-8919)
CREATIVE LABEL INC (PA)
2450 Estes Ave (60007-5490)
PHONE.................847 956-6960
Jerry Koril, *CEO*
Gary Koril, *President*
Terri Koril, *Admin Sec*
EMP: 75
SQ FT: 50,000
SALES (est): 9.6MM **Privately Held**
WEB: www.labels-decals.com
SIC: 2796 2789 2675 Platemaking services; gold stamping on books; die-cut paper & board

(G-8920)
CREATIVE WERKS LLC (PA)
1460 Brummel Ave (60007-2111)
PHONE.................630 860-2222
Steve Schroeder, *CEO*
J Rgen Peters, *Principal*
Senada Dracic, *Buyer*
Brian Philipps, *Engineer*
Allison Socie, *Accountant*
▲ **EMP:** 45
SQ FT: 550,000
SALES (est): 54.6MM **Privately Held**
SIC: 3999 Novelties, bric-a-brac & hobby kits

(G-8921)
CRISTAUX INC
Also Called: Cristaux International
1343 Brummel Ave (60007-2108)
PHONE.................312 778-8800
Andre Janus, *President*
Robert Szafarowicz, *Vice Pres*
Renee Hickman, *Creative Dir*
▲ **EMP:** 2
SQ FT: 20,000
SALES (est): 303.4K **Privately Held**
WEB: www.cristaux.com
SIC: 3231 Products of purchased glass

(G-8922)
CROSS EXPRESS COMPANY
153 Crest Ave (60007-1731)
PHONE.................847 439-7457
Tihomir Mintchev, *President*
EMP: 2
SALES (est): 275.8K **Privately Held**
SIC: 2741 Miscellaneous publishing

(G-8923)
CSM TUBE USA INC
1599 Lunt Ave (60007-5628)
PHONE.................847 640-6447
Andrea Solimbergo, *CEO*
◆ **EMP:** 5
SQ FT: 35,000
SALES (est): 820.3K
SALES (corp-wide): 957.2K **Privately Held**
SIC: 3317 Steel pipe & tubes
PA: Csm Holding Spa
  Via Friuli 11
  San Vendemiano TV 31030

(G-8924)
CURATEK PHARMACEUTICALS LLC
1965 Pratt Blvd (60007-5905)
PHONE.................702 215-5700
Robert J Borgman, *President*
EMP: 3
SALES (corp-wide): 1MM **Privately Held**
SIC: 2834 Pharmaceutical preparations
PA: Curatek Pharmaceuticals, Llc
  8960 Spanish Ridge Ave
  Las Vegas NV 89148
  847 806-2930

(G-8925)
CURV GROUP LLC
Also Called: Key Smart
860 Bonnie Ln (60007-2223)
PHONE.................847 636-0101
Michael Tunney, *CEO*
Jason Grueter, *Sales Associate*
EMP: 33 **EST:** 2013

SALES (est): 4.8MM **Privately Held**
WEB: www.curvgroup.com
SIC: 3172 Key cases

(G-8926)
CUSTOM PLASTICS INC
Also Called: Custom Accents
1940 Lunt Ave (60007-5634)
PHONE.................847 439-6770
Peter Tisbo, *President*
William Morelock, *General Mgr*
Richard Kneisel, *Vice Pres*
David Phillips, *Vice Pres*
Trino Martinez, *Foreman/Supr*
▲ **EMP:** 220 **EST:** 1955
SQ FT: 150,000
SALES (est): 62.2MM **Privately Held**
WEB: www.customplasticsinc.com
SIC: 3089 Extruded finished plastic products; injection molded finished plastic products

(G-8927)
CUSTOM PLASTICS INC
1940 Lunt Ave (60007-5634)
PHONE.................847 439-6770
Peter Tisbo, *President*
EMP: 12
SALES (est): 1.6MM **Privately Held**
SIC: 3089 Injection molding of plastics; injection molded finished plastic products

(G-8928)
CUTTING EDGE MACHINING INC
105 Randall St Ste B (60007-1010)
PHONE.................847 427-1392
Steven Campos, *President*
Ron Gokan, *Vice Pres*
EMP: 4
SQ FT: 5,000
SALES (est): 549.8K **Privately Held**
WEB: www.cuttingedgemachininginc.com
SIC: 3599 Machine shop, jobbing & repair

(G-8929)
CWS CABINETS
225 Stanley St (60007-1558)
PHONE.................847 258-4468
EMP: 4
SALES (est): 352.7K **Privately Held**
SIC: 2434 Mfg Wood Kitchen Cabinets

(G-8930)
D & K CUSTOM MACHINE DESIGN
1795 Commerce Dr (60007-2119)
P.O. Box 1146 (60009-1146)
PHONE.................847 956-4757
Karl Singer, *President*
Christina Znorski, *Sls & Mktg Exec*
Yajaira Sanchez, *Human Resources*
Thomas Pidgeon, *VP Sales*
Sally Singer, *Admin Sec*
▲ **EMP:** 30
SQ FT: 50,000
SALES (est): 6.5MM
SALES (corp-wide): 35.7MM **Privately Held**
SIC: 3555 Printing trades machinery
PA: D & K Group, Inc.
  1795 Commerce Dr
  Elk Grove Village IL 60007
  847 956-0160

(G-8931)
D & K GROUP INC (PA)
1795 Commerce Dr (60007-2119)
P.O. Box 1146 (60009-1146)
PHONE.................847 956-0160
Karl Singer, *President*
Gerardo Silva, *Area Mgr*
James Broz, *COO*
Mary Nitscheider, *Vice Pres*
Tom Pidgeon, *Vice Pres*
◆ **EMP:** 40
SQ FT: 135,000
SALES (est): 35.7MM **Privately Held**
SIC: 2891 3555 Laminating compounds; printing trades machinery

(G-8932)
D & K INTERNATIONAL INC (HQ)
1795 Commerce Dr (60007-2119)
P.O. Box 1146 (60009-1146)
PHONE.................847 956-0160

James Broz, *CFO*
Sally Singer, *Admin Sec*
Tony Singer, *Admin Sec*
EMP: 51
SQ FT: 85,000
SALES (est): 22.4MM
SALES (corp-wide): 35.7MM **Privately Held**
SIC: 2891 Laminating compounds
PA: D & K Group, Inc.
  1795 Commerce Dr
  Elk Grove Village IL 60007
  847 956-0160

(G-8933)
D & K MACHINE AND TOOL INC
1080 Howard St (60007-2208)
PHONE.................847 439-8691
Artur Drewno, *President*
Oscar Romo, *Area Mgr*
Gloria Gallegos, *Sales Staff*
Gene Gajos, *Med Doctor*
Beth Strother, *Med Doctor*
EMP: 2 **EST:** 1997
SALES (est): 326K **Privately Held**
SIC: 3599 Machine shop, jobbing & repair

(G-8934)
D & S WIRE INC
2531 E Devon Ave (60007-6313)
PHONE.................847 766-5520
Perry Kospe, *President*
Joe Messina, *Prdtn Mgr*
Tom Alexander, *Treasurer*
Perry D Koste, *Treasurer*
Kristin Kospe, *Admin Sec*
EMP: 17 **EST:** 1963
SQ FT: 18,000
SALES (est): 4.1MM **Privately Held**
WEB: www.dswire.com
SIC: 3496 Miscellaneous fabricated wire products

(G-8935)
D/C EXPORT & DOMESTIC PKG INC (PA)
Also Called: D/C Group The
1300 E Devon Ave (60007-5831)
PHONE.................847 593-4200
Carol Cocciemiglio, *President*
Dominick Cocciemiglio Jr, *Corp Secy*
John Cocciemiglio, *Vice Pres*
Paul Michalak, *Vice Pres*
EMP: 34
SQ FT: 55,000
SALES (est): 12.5MM **Privately Held**
SIC: 4783 2449 2653 2441 Packing & crating; rectangular boxes & crates, wood; corrugated boxes, partitions, display items, sheets & pad; boxes, wood

(G-8936)
DAIRY DYNAMICS LLC
17820 Washington St (60007)
P.O. Box 283, Union (60180-0283)
PHONE.................847 758-7300
Herbert J Sewell,
EMP: 12
SALES (est): 3.4MM **Privately Held**
SIC: 2841 Soap & other detergents

(G-8937)
DAITO USA INC
1470 Elmhurst Rd (60007-6417)
PHONE.................847 437-6788
Shinichi Sugimoto, *President*
▲ **EMP:** 3
SALES (est): 1.1MM **Privately Held**
SIC: 5084 3541 Machine tools & accessories; drilling machine tools (metal cutting)
HQ: Daito Seiki Co., Ltd.
  2-26, Higashitsushimacho
  Amagasaki HYO 660-0

(G-8938)
DATASIS CORPORATION
1687 Elmhurst Rd (60007-6413)
PHONE.................847 427-0909
Joseph Hassen, *President*
David Bertz, *Exec VP*
Christina Hassen, *Marketing Mgr*
Robert Senne, *Executive*
EMP: 16
SQ FT: 12,000

SALES (est): 2.5MM **Privately Held**
SIC: 7373 3652 7377 Systems software development services; compact laser discs, prerecorded; computer hardware rental or leasing, except finance leasing; computer peripheral equipment rental & leasing

(G-8939)
DAYTON SUPERIOR CORPORATION (DH)
Also Called: Metal Acesories
2400 Arthur Ave (60007-6017)
PHONE.................847 391-4700
John Cicearelli, *President*
Jim Eenka, *Vice Pres*
Thomas Vintzel, *Vice Pres*
Catherine Gilbert, *Program Mgr*
Karen Barkan, *Manager*
◆ **EMP:** 300 **EST:** 1901
SQ FT: 25,000
SALES (est): 69.1MM
SALES (corp-wide): 50.9B **Publicly Held**
WEB: www.daytonsuperior.com
SIC: 3444 Concrete forms, sheet metal
HQ: Dayton Superior Corporation
  1125 Byers Rd
  Miamisburg OH 45342
  937 866-0711

(G-8940)
DEADLINE PRTG CLOR COPYING LLC
963 Kentucky Ln (60007-2935)
PHONE.................847 437-9000
George Samp, *Mng Member*
Alan Hugar,
EMP: 6
SALES: 1.2MM **Privately Held**
SIC: 2752 2789 Commercial printing, offset; bookbinding & related work

(G-8941)
DECO ADHESIVE PDTS 1985 LTD
Also Called: Deco Labels & Tags
500 Thorndale Ave Ste H (60007)
PHONE.................847 472-2100
Douglas B Ford, *President*
Kathy De Marco, *Opers Mgr*
EMP: 25
SALES (corp-wide): 10.5MM **Privately Held**
SIC: 2679 2675 2671 Tags & labels, paper; die-cut paper & board; packaging paper & plastics film, coated & laminated
PA: Deco Adhesive Products (1985) Limited
  28 Greensboro Dr
  Etobicoke ON M9W 1
  416 247-7878

(G-8942)
DELTA LABORATORIES INC
2690 Delta Ln (60007-6307)
PHONE.................630 351-1798
Dennis Fath, *President*
▲ **EMP:** 7 **EST:** 1999
SALES (est): 1.5MM **Privately Held**
SIC: 2844 Cosmetic preparations

(G-8943)
DELTA PRECISION CIRCUITS INC
1370 Lively Blvd (60007-4926)
PHONE.................847 758-8000
Mukesh Patel, *President*
Ashok Patel, *Vice Pres*
Adesh Patel, *Admin Sec*
▲ **EMP:** 33 **EST:** 1971
SQ FT: 35,000
SALES (est): 5.2MM **Privately Held**
WEB: www.deltapcb.com
SIC: 3672 Printed circuit boards

(G-8944)
DENOR GRAPHICS INC
665 Lunt Ave (60007-5014)
PHONE.................847 364-1130
Edward W De Luga, *President*
Arleen E De Luga, *Corp Secy*
EMP: 10
SQ FT: 8,000
SALES (est): 1.8MM **Privately Held**
SIC: 2752 2791 2789 Commercial printing, offset; typesetting; bookbinding & related work

Elk Grove Village - Cook County (G-8945)

(G-8945)
DESCO INC
Also Called: Desco Dryers
1240 Howard St (60007-2267)
PHONE..................847 439-2130
George J Gambini III, *President*
Lisa M Defily, *CFO*
EMP: 6 **EST:** 1971
SQ FT: 6,700
SALES: 730K **Privately Held**
SIC: 3559 Metal finishing equipment for plating, etc.

(G-8946)
DESIGN LOFT IMAGING INC
393 Bianco Dr (60007-4401)
PHONE..................847 439-2486
Jeffrey Hastings, *President*
Cindy Hastings, *Vice Pres*
EMP: 2
SALES: 200K **Privately Held**
SIC: 2395 Embroidery products, except schiffli machine

(G-8947)
DESIGNED EQP ACQUISITION CORP
1510 Lunt Ave (60007-5622)
PHONE..................847 647-5000
Jerrefry Hughart, *President*
Laura Petterson, *CFO*
EMP: 45 **EST:** 2007
SALES (est): 1.5MM **Privately Held**
SIC: 3446 5082 Scaffolds, mobile or stationary: metal; scaffolding

(G-8948)
DIAMOND SCREEN PROCESS INC
321 Bond St (60007-1222)
PHONE..................847 439-6200
Roddy Zukowski, *President*
Kate Nurkowski, *Marketing Staff*
EMP: 8
SQ FT: 10,000
SALES (est): 1MM **Privately Held**
WEB: www.diamondscreen.net
SIC: 2759 Screen printing

(G-8949)
DIE MOLD JIG GRINDING & MFG
1485 Landmeier Rd Ste M (60007-2464)
PHONE..................847 228-1444
EMP: 3 **EST:** 1982
SQ FT: 1,000
SALES (est): 250K **Privately Held**
SIC: 3544 Die & Mold Jig Grinding Service

(G-8950)
DIEMASTERS MANUFACTURING INC
2100 Touhy Ave (60007-5325)
PHONE..................847 640-9900
Virgil Dela, *President*
Charles Brewer, *Vice Pres*
Tom Haring, *Materials Dir*
Don A Morman, *Project Mgr*
Ben Perkins, *Materials Mgr*
▲ **EMP:** 125
SALES (est): 20.7MM **Privately Held**
WEB: www.thediemasters.com
SIC: 2396 3544 3469 3444 Fabric printing & stamping; special dies, tools, jigs & fixtures; metal stampings; sheet metalwork

(G-8951)
DIEMOLD SERVICE COMPANY
1591 Elmhurst Rd (60007-6414)
PHONE..................847 885-6007
Dave Bellperche, *CEO*
Bren Bellperche, *President*
Ian Hodgkinson, *Corp Secy*
▲ **EMP:** 16
SQ FT: 15,000
SALES (est): 1.6MM
SALES (corp-wide): 6MM **Privately Held**
SIC: 3544 Special dies, tools, jigs & fixtures
HQ: Diemould Service Company (Canada) Limited
1875 Blackacre Dr Rr 1
Oldcastle ON N0R 1
519 737-6743

(G-8952)
DLS CUSTOM EMBROIDERY INC
Also Called: DLS Printing & Promotions
1665 Tonne Rd (60007-5123)
PHONE..................847 593-5957
Edward K Schaefer, *President*
Melisa Hoberg, *Vice Pres*
EMP: 20
SQ FT: 5,000
SALES (est): 2.5MM **Privately Held**
SIC: 2211 Print cloths, cotton

(G-8953)
DOUMAK INC
2491 Estes Ave (60007-5422)
PHONE..................847 981-2180
Gary Conway, *VP Opers*
Adela Rada, *Human Res Mgr*
Tim Samson, *Branch Mgr*
EMP: 76
SALES (corp-wide): 72.2MM **Privately Held**
SIC: 2064 Marshmallows
PA: Doumak Inc.
1004 Fairway Dr
Bensenville IL 60106
800 323-0318

(G-8954)
DOW CHEMICAL COMPANY
2401 Pratt Blvd (60007-5920)
PHONE..................847 439-2240
David Sizka, *Branch Mgr*
EMP: 45
SALES (corp-wide): 42.9B **Publicly Held**
WEB: www.dow.com
SIC: 2819 2821 Industrial inorganic chemicals; plastics materials & resins
HQ: The Dow Chemical Company
2211 H H Dow Way
Midland MI 48642
989 636-1000

(G-8955)
DRESSER LLC
Becker Precision Equipment
1550 Greenleaf Ave (60007-5525)
PHONE..................847 437-5940
Narendra Desai, *General Mgr*
EMP: 55
SALES (corp-wide): 1.1B **Privately Held**
SIC: 3491 3625 3612 3593 Regulators (steam fittings); control equipment, electric; industrial controls: push button, selector switches, pilot; transformers, except electric; fluid power cylinders & actuators; valves & pipe fittings
PA: Dresser, Llc
4425 Westway Park Blvd
Houston TX 77041
262 549-2626

(G-8956)
DUO GRAPHICS
1612 Landmeier Rd Ste C (60007-2463)
PHONE..................847 228-7080
EMP: 4
SQ FT: 3,500
SALES: 170K **Privately Held**
SIC: 2759 2752 Letterpress

(G-8957)
DURABLE LONGLASTING
Also Called: Dlp Coating
2301 Eastern Ave (60007-6814)
PHONE..................847 350-0113
Richard Murphy, *President*
Jacqueline Murphy, *Treasurer*
EMP: 40
SQ FT: 20,000
SALES (est): 5.6MM **Privately Held**
SIC: 3479 Enameling, including porcelain, of metal products; japanning of metal

(G-8958)
DURABUILT DIE CORP
619 Woodview Ave (60007-4340)
PHONE..................847 437-2086
Dan Urbina, *President*
Raul Urbina, *Principal*
Evelyn Urbina, *Admin Sec*
EMP: 4
SQ FT: 2,460
SALES: 280K **Privately Held**
SIC: 3544 Dies, steel rule

(G-8959)
DURACREST FABRICS
2474 Delta Ln (60007-6303)
PHONE..................847 350-0030
Ralph Fortino, *President*
EMP: 5
SALES (est): 93.4K **Privately Held**
SIC: 5949 2399 Fabric stores piece goods; fabricated textile products

(G-8960)
DURATRACK INC
950 Morse Ave (60007-5108)
PHONE..................847 806-0202
Russell Scott, *President*
Jacek Janasek, *Plant Mgr*
Amidee Barnes, *Prdtn Mgr*
Amy Poulos, *Production*
Terrica Philpot, *Manager*
EMP: 25
SQ FT: 30,000
SALES (est): 1.7MM **Privately Held**
WEB: www.duratrack.com
SIC: 3444 Sheet metalwork

(G-8961)
DVA METAL FABRICATION INC
1427 Tonne Rd (60007-5003)
PHONE..................224 577-8217
Dimitar Atanassov, *Principal*
EMP: 4
SALES (est): 415.7K **Privately Held**
SIC: 3399 Powder, metal

(G-8962)
E B G B INC
Also Called: Chicago Sign Designs
220 Lively Blvd (60007-1623)
PHONE..................847 228-9333
Gary Becker, *President*
Eric Becker, *Vice Pres*
EMP: 2
SQ FT: 2,500
SALES (est): 283.9K **Privately Held**
SIC: 3993 Signs, not made in custom sign painting shops

(G-8963)
E C SCHULTZ & CO INC
333 Crossen Ave (60007-2050)
PHONE..................847 640-1190
Michael Pautz, *President*
James Pautz, *Vice Pres*
EMP: 16 **EST:** 1895
SQ FT: 8,000
SALES: 1.9MM **Privately Held**
WEB: www.ecschultz.com
SIC: 2796 3544 Engraving on copper, steel, wood or rubber: printing plates; special dies, tools, jigs & fixtures

(G-8964)
E J WELCH CO INC
2601 Lively Blvd (60007-6730)
PHONE..................847 238-0100
Mike Gee, *Manager*
EMP: 10
SALES (corp-wide): 348.7MM **Privately Held**
SIC: 3423 Hand & edge tools
HQ: E. J. Welch Co., Inc.
13735 Lakefront Dr
Earth City MO 63045
314 739-2273

(G-8965)
E-M METAL FABRICATOR
145 Joey Dr (60007-1303)
PHONE..................847 593-9970
Milton R Moscoso, *Principal*
Gladys Moscoso, *Sales Staff*
Elva Moscoso, *Post Master*
EMP: 3
SALES (est): 605.2K **Privately Held**
SIC: 3444 Metal housings, enclosures, casings & other containers

(G-8966)
E-Z ROTATIONAL MOLDER INC
1001 Nicholas Blvd Ste F (60007-2523)
PHONE..................847 806-1327
Edmund Zalewski, *President*
John Zalewski, *Vice Pres*
Theresa Zalewski, *Admin Sec*
EMP: 6
SQ FT: 5,000
SALES (est): 917.5K **Privately Held**
SIC: 3089 Injection molding of plastics

(G-8967)
ECOLAB INC
Rayburn Products
1060 Thorndale Ave (60007-6747)
PHONE..................847 350-2229
Michael Pena, *Branch Mgr*
EMP: 7
SALES (corp-wide): 14.9B **Publicly Held**
SIC: 2842 Specialty cleaning, polishes & sanitation goods
PA: Ecolab Inc.
1 Ecolab Pl
Saint Paul MN 55102
800 232-6522

(G-8968)
ECOLAB INC
Also Called: Johnson Contrls Authorized Dlr
1060 Thorndale Ave (60007-6747)
PHONE..................847 350-2229
Greg Powers, *Principal*
EMP: 35
SALES (corp-wide): 14.9B **Publicly Held**
SIC: 2842 5075 Specialty cleaning, polishes & sanitation goods; warm air heating & air conditioning
PA: Ecolab Inc.
1 Ecolab Pl
Saint Paul MN 55102
800 232-6522

(G-8969)
EDLONG CORPORATION (PA)
Also Called: Edlong Flavors
225 Scott St (60007-1212)
PHONE..................847 439-9230
Laurette Rondenet-Smith, *President*
Rick Schultz, *Vice Pres*
Bob Corbett, *Marketing Staff*
Ann Woolsoncroft, *Marketing Staff*
◆ **EMP:** 75
SQ FT: 120,000
SALES (est): 21.5MM **Privately Held**
WEB: www.edlong.com
SIC: 2087 Extracts, flavoring

(G-8970)
EJ PIEROGI
1700 Oakton St (60007-2103)
PHONE..................773 318-3383
Ewa Swagon, *Owner*
EMP: 10 **EST:** 2013
SALES (est): 808.3K **Privately Held**
WEB: www.polishfoodelkgrovevillage.com
SIC: 3321 Gray & ductile iron foundries

(G-8971)
ELECTRONIC INTERCONNECT CORP
2375 Estes Ave (60007-5428)
PHONE..................847 364-4848
Pratish Patel, *President*
Dr Bharad Barai, *Chairman*
Sunjay Shah, *Vice Pres*
EMP: 84
SQ FT: 25,000
SALES (est): 17.8MM **Privately Held**
SIC: 3672 Circuit boards, television & radio printed

(G-8972)
ELK GROVE CUSTOM SHEET METAL
106 N Lively Blvd (60007-1329)
PHONE..................847 352-2845
Thomas J Dahm, *President*
Kathleen Dahm, *Admin Sec*
EMP: 10
SQ FT: 3,500
SALES (est): 1.2MM **Privately Held**
SIC: 1796 1761 3444 1711 Pollution control equipment installation; sheet metalwork; sheet metalwork; heating & air conditioning contractors

(G-8973)
ELK GROVE SIGNS INC
Also Called: Signs Now
1670 Greenleaf Ave (60007-5527)
PHONE..................847 427-0005
Joe Danco, *President*
▲ **EMP:** 3
SQ FT: 1,350

GEOGRAPHIC SECTION
Elk Grove Village - Cook County (G-9002)

SALES (est): 403.6K **Privately Held**
SIC: 3993 Signs & advertising specialties

(G-8974)
ELLA ENGINEERING INCORPORATED
800 Morse Ave (60007-5106)
PHONE..............................847 354-4767
Randy Zitella, *President*
Charles Wulf, *Vice Pres*
EMP: 5 EST: 2014
SQ FT: 15,000
SALES (est): 736.4K **Privately Held**
SIC: 3451 Screw machine products

(G-8975)
EMCO GEARS INC (PA)
160 King St (60007-1111)
PHONE..............................847 220-4327
Richard R Wolfe Sr, *President*
Richard Wolfe, *COO*
Peter Koenen, *Chief Engr*
EMP: 30 EST: 1933
SQ FT: 20,000
SALES (est): 5.5MM **Privately Held**
WEB: www.emco-gears.com
SIC: 3462 Gear & chain forgings

(G-8976)
EMSUR USA LLC (HQ)
2800 Carl Blvd (60007-6721)
PHONE..............................847 367-8787
Cynthia Parcher, *CFO*
Ron Ramsey,
▲ EMP: 35
SALES (est): 6.5MM
SALES (corp-wide): 7.6MM **Privately Held**
SIC: 2759 Commercial printing
PA: Laninver Usa Inc
2800 Carl Bulevard
Elk Grove Village IL 60007
847 367-8787

(G-8977)
EN POINTE CABINETRY LLC (PA)
950 Thorndale Ave (60007-6759)
PHONE..............................847 787-0077
Jackey Lin,
Qiang Huang,
Jin Xiao Xin,
EMP: 9
SQ FT: 53,000
SALES: 1MM **Privately Held**
WEB: www.enpointecabinetry.com
SIC: 2434 Wood kitchen cabinets

(G-8978)
ENGELHARDT GEAR CO
2526 American Ln (60007-6265)
PHONE..............................847 766-7070
Armin Engelhardt, *President*
EMP: 20
SQ FT: 10,000
SALES (est): 4.4MM **Privately Held**
WEB: www.engelhardtgear.com
SIC: 3566 Gears, power transmission, except automotive

(G-8979)
EPCOR INDUSTRIAL INC
1325 Louis Ave (60007-2309)
PHONE..............................847 545-9212
Jolanta Lis, *CEO*
Jaroslaw Lis, *President*
EMP: 7
SQ FT: 5,000
SALES: 550K **Privately Held**
WEB: www.epcorind.com
SIC: 3542 Machine tools, metal forming type

(G-8980)
EPE INDUSTRIES USA INC
Also Called: Epe Industries USA Chicago
1109 Kirk St (60007-6738)
PHONE..............................800 315-0336
Jose Telles, *Branch Mgr*
EMP: 10 **Privately Held**
WEB: www.epeusa.com
SIC: 3086 Packaging & shipping materials, foamed plastic
HQ: Epe Industries Usa, Inc.
17835 Newhope St Ste G
Fountain Valley CA 92708

(G-8981)
ERA INDUSTRIES INC
1800 Greenleaf Ave (60007-5502)
PHONE..............................847 357-1320
Paul Podedworny, *President*
Gene Kline, *General Mgr*
Ziggy Skirucha, *Site Mgr*
Marcin Skirucha, *Opers Staff*
Clarke Cubbage, *Production*
▲ EMP: 130
SQ FT: 39,000
SALES (est): 41MM **Privately Held**
WEB: www.eraind.com
SIC: 3599 Machine shop, jobbing & repair

(G-8982)
ERELL MANUFACTURING COMPANY
2678 Coyle Ave (60007-6404)
PHONE..............................847 427-3000
Randy Silton, *President*
Dori Schnieder, *Vice Pres*
EMP: 5
SQ FT: 1,000
SALES (est): 1.4MM **Privately Held**
SIC: 3999 Advertising curtains

(G-8983)
ETLON ENTERPRISES
1441 Elmhurst Rd (60007-6400)
PHONE..............................847 258-5265
EMP: 2 EST: 2010
SALES (est): 207.3K **Privately Held**
SIC: 2759 Screen printing

(G-8984)
ETYMOTIC RESEARCH INC
61 Martin Ln (60007-1307)
PHONE..............................847 228-0006
Mark Piepenbrink, *CEO*
Mead C Killion PHD, *President*
Devan Dauber, *Engineer*
Canh Diep, *Engineer*
Dave Friesema, *Engineer*
EMP: 44
SQ FT: 25,000
SALES (est): 9.3MM **Privately Held**
SIC: 8732 3842 Research services, except laboratory; hearing aids

(G-8985)
EXCEL COLOR CORPORATION
220 Bond St (60007-1221)
PHONE..............................847 734-1270
William G Osborne, *President*
Bob Huegel, *Sales Staff*
Bill Osborne, *Manager*
EMP: 4
SQ FT: 16,000
SALES (est): 699.7K **Privately Held**
SIC: 2796 Color separations for printing

(G-8986)
EXCEL ELECTRO ASSEMBLY INC
1595 Brummel Ave (60007-2112)
PHONE..............................847 621-2500
Hiten Bhanderi, *President*
Rasik Bhanderi, *Vice Pres*
Trushar Patel, *Engrg Dir*
EMP: 12
SQ FT: 10,000
SALES: 1MM **Privately Held**
SIC: 3672 Printed circuit boards

(G-8987)
EXCEL PHOTONICS INC
1595 Brummel Ave (60007-2112)
PHONE..............................732 829-2667
EMP: 3
SALES (est): 167.1K **Privately Held**
SIC: 3661 Fiber optics communications equipment

(G-8988)
EXCELL ELECTRONICS CORPORATION
2425 American Ln (60007-6203)
PHONE..............................847 766-7455
Ushma Patel, *President*
Chandra Dave, *Vice Pres*
Sav Patel, *Vice Pres*
Harry Patel, *Treasurer*
Jon Vukovich, *Sales Mgr*
▲ EMP: 28
SQ FT: 20,000
SALES (est): 4.7MM **Privately Held**
SIC: 3672 Circuit boards, television & radio printed

(G-8989)
EXCLUSIVE STONE
1361 Jarvis Ave (60007-2303)
PHONE..............................847 593-6963
Jeff Mueller, *Principal*
EMP: 3 EST: 2007
SALES (est): 321.7K **Privately Held**
WEB: www.kitchencountertopschicago.com
SIC: 3469 5211 Kitchen fixtures & equipment, porcelain enameled; masonry materials & supplies

(G-8990)
EXECL MACHINE TECHNOLOGY
1625 Tonne Rd (60007-5123)
PHONE..............................847 439-8434
Casey Sokalski, *Owner*
EMP: 5
SQ FT: 3,000
SALES (est): 463.3K **Privately Held**
SIC: 3599 Machine shop, jobbing & repair

(G-8991)
EXECUTIVE PERFORMANCE FUEL LLC
1060 Talbots Ln (60007-7106)
PHONE..............................847 364-1933
Ann E Potts, *Principal*
EMP: 3 EST: 2010
SALES (est): 224K **Privately Held**
SIC: 2869 Fuels

(G-8992)
EXPRESS GRINDING INC
119 Joey Dr (60007-1303)
PHONE..............................847 434-5827
Bill Rosinski, *Principal*
EMP: 2
SALES (est): 346.4K **Privately Held**
SIC: 3599 Grinding castings for the trade; machine shop, jobbing & repair

(G-8993)
F P M LLC (PA)
Also Called: F P M Heat Treating
1501 Lively Blvd (60007-5029)
PHONE..............................847 228-2525
William Koziel, *President*
Steve Kinloch, *COO*
Jim Feltner, *Vice Pres*
Robert Ferry, *Vice Pres*
Mike Migala, *Plant Mgr*
EMP: 130
SQ FT: 88,000
SALES (est): 41.4MM **Privately Held**
SIC: 3398 Metal heat treating

(G-8994)
FABRICATED METALS CO
Also Called: Machined Products
2121 Landmeier Rd (60007-2506)
PHONE..............................847 718-1300
David Pingel, *CEO*
Sirinivas Ghejji, *President*
Mohammed Qureshi, *President*
Srinivas Ghejji, *Vice Pres*
▲ EMP: 108 EST: 1955
SQ FT: 98,500
SALES (est): 19.9MM **Privately Held**
SIC: 3714 Motor vehicle parts & accessories

(G-8995)
FANMAR INC
901 Greenleaf Ave (60007-5010)
PHONE..............................847 621-2010
Dill Grobes, *President*
John C Nalbach, *Corp Secy*
Juan Malave, *Opers Staff*
Sue Gutierrez, *Office Mgr*
Sonja O'Brien, *Manager*
EMP: 25 EST: 1965
SQ FT: 28,000
SALES (est): 6.1MM **Privately Held**
WEB: www.fanmar.com
SIC: 3599 3444 3645 3469 Machine shop, jobbing & repair; sheet metalwork; residential lighting fixtures; metal stampings; fabricated structural metal; office furniture, except wood

(G-8996)
FASPRO TECHNOLOGIES INC
165 King St (60007-1110)
PHONE..............................847 364-9999
EMP: 13
SALES (corp-wide): 30.7MM **Privately Held**
SIC: 3479 Etching, photochemical
PA: Faspro Technologies, Inc.
500 W Campus Dr
Arlington Heights IL 60004
847 392-9500

(G-8997)
FASTSIGNS
1701 Howard St Ste C (60007-2479)
PHONE..............................847 981-1965
Bob Rogers, *President*
Lorenia Martinez, *Sales Mgr*
Diane Prater, *Accounts Exec*
David Mattson, *Sales Staff*
Patrick Kimball, *Manager*
EMP: 3
SALES (est): 282.5K **Privately Held**
SIC: 3993 Signs & advertising specialties

(G-8998)
FISA NORTH AMERICA INC
260 Stanley St (60007-1557)
PHONE..............................847 593-2080
Phil Vaudeleau, *CEO*
Eduardo Cerrato, *Sales Engr*
▲ EMP: 5
SALES (est): 861.3K **Privately Held**
SIC: 3699 Cleaning equipment, ultrasonic, except medical & dental

(G-8999)
FL 1
Also Called: Chicago Offset
128 N Lively Blvd Fl 1 (60007-1330)
PHONE..............................847 956-9400
An Han Kim, *President*
EMP: 11
SQ FT: 8,400
SALES: 2.3MM **Privately Held**
SIC: 2752 Commercial printing, offset

(G-9000)
FLUID PUMP SERVICE INC
Also Called: Fluid Pump Systems
435 Bennett Rd (60007-1006)
PHONE..............................847 228-0750
Thomas Krzak, *President*
Laura Krzak, *Administration*
EMP: 7 EST: 1971
SQ FT: 10,000
SALES: 1.7MM **Privately Held**
SIC: 7699 5084 7694 Pumps & pumping equipment repair; pumps & pumping equipment; motor repair services

(G-9001)
FNA IP HOLDINGS INC
1825 Greenleaf Ave (60007-5501)
PHONE..............................847 348-1500
Gus Alexander, *President*
Daphne Alexander, *Corp Secy*
William Alexander, *Vice Pres*
EMP: 80
SALES (est): 13.1MM **Privately Held**
SIC: 3589 3563 3561 5722 High pressure cleaning equipment; vacuum (air extraction) systems, industrial; pumps & pumping equipment; electric household appliances, major; builders' hardware; cleaning equipment, high pressure, sand or steam

(G-9002)
FOODHANDLER INC (HQ)
2301 Lunt Ave (60007-5625)
PHONE..............................866 931-3613
Michael Mattos, *CEO*
Sherri Hager, *Vice Pres*
◆ EMP: 11
SQ FT: 30,000
SALES (est): 16.6MM
SALES (corp-wide): 12B **Privately Held**
SIC: 5162 2673 Plastics products; bags: plastic, laminated & coated
PA: Bunzl Public Limited Company
York House
London W1H 7
207 725-5000

Elk Grove Village - Cook County (G-9003)

(G-9003)
FOREST PACKAGING CORPORATION
1955 Estes Ave (60007-5415)
PHONE 847 981-7000
Gregory R Kula, *President*
EMP: 40 EST: 1965
SQ FT: 47,000
SALES (est): 16.2MM **Privately Held**
WEB: www.forestpkg.com
SIC: 2653 7336 Boxes, corrugated: made from purchased materials; package design

(G-9004)
FORMULA SYSTEMS NORTH AMERICA
2300 Eastern Ave (60007-6813)
PHONE 847 350-0655
John Curzon, *President*
Stephanie Cassidy, *Manager*
Cornelius Walls, *Director*
Graham Davies, *Admin Sec*
▲ EMP: 2
SALES (est): 360.4K **Privately Held**
SIC: 3534 Elevators & equipment

(G-9005)
FORTMAN & ASSOCIATES LTD
Also Called: Newmax
472 Potomac Ln (60007-2764)
PHONE 847 524-0741
Angelika K Fortman, *President*
Stephen A Fortman, *Admin Sec*
EMP: 10
SALES (est): 970K **Privately Held**
SIC: 7336 2752 Art design services; offset & photolithographic printing

(G-9006)
FOX MACHINE & TOOL INC
985 Lively Blvd (60007-2206)
PHONE 847 357-1845
Jozef Lisiecki, *President*
EMP: 9
SALES (est): 1MM **Privately Held**
SIC: 3599 3545 Custom machinery; machine tool accessories

(G-9007)
FUJI YUSOKI KOGYO CO LTD
Also Called: Fuji Robotics
1220 Landmeier Rd (60007-2410)
PHONE 425 522-0722
Haruo Fujishige, *President*
Chris Cleaver, *Principal*
▲ EMP: 3 EST: 2008
SALES (est): 448.2K **Privately Held**
WEB: www.fujirobotics.com
SIC: 3089 Pallets, plastic
PA: Fuji Yusoki Kogyo Co.,Ltd.
2327-1, Ichinoyokomichi, Higashitakatomari
San-Yoonoda YMG 756-0

(G-9008)
GAG INDUSTRIES INC
Also Called: Filter Services
1065 Chase Ave (60007-4827)
PHONE 847 616-8710
Gerald Gradek, *President*
Jeffrey Gradek, *President*
Brandon Ser Voss, *Manager*
EMP: 35
SQ FT: 40,000
SALES (est): 15.8MM **Privately Held**
SIC: 5085 7699 3564 Filters, industrial; filter cleaning; filters, air: furnaces, air conditioning equipment, etc.

(G-9009)
GAGE MANUFACTURING INC
820 Touhy Ave (60007-4918)
PHONE 847 228-7300
Jacqueline Gajewski, *President*
EMP: 15
SALES (est): 3MM **Privately Held**
WEB: www.gagemanufacturing.com
SIC: 3451 Screw machine products

(G-9010)
GAGE TOOL & MANUFACTURING INC
1025 Pauly Dr (60007-1314)
PHONE 847 640-1069
Paul Oroni, *President*
EMP: 2
SQ FT: 1,200
SALES (est): 356K **Privately Held**
SIC: 3544 Special dies & tools

(G-9011)
GALAXY PRECISION MFG INC
2636 United Ln (60007-6821)
PHONE 847 238-9066
Ellias Kademoglou, *President*
EMP: 15
SQ FT: 20,000
SALES (est): 2.8MM **Privately Held**
SIC: 3599 3544 Machine shop, jobbing & repair; special dies, tools, jigs & fixtures

(G-9012)
GENERAL PRECISION MFG LLC
2670 Greenleaf Ave (60007-5513)
PHONE 847 624-4969
Nancy Reuhi,
EMP: 10
SALES (est): 293.3K **Privately Held**
SIC: 3599 Machine shop, jobbing & repair

(G-9013)
GERARD PRINTING COMPANY
710 Bonnie Ln (60007-2201)
PHONE 847 437-6442
Bob Denbroeder, *President*
Robert Denbroeder, *President*
John Denbroeder, *Vice Pres*
Phil Desilva, *Opers Mgr*
Ja Denbroeder, *Bookkeeper*
EMP: 9
SQ FT: 4,200
SALES (est): 1.3MM **Privately Held**
WEB: www.gerardprinting.com
SIC: 2752 Commercial printing, offset

(G-9014)
GET A QUOTE FOR YOUR PCB
925 Estes Ave (60007-4905)
PHONE 847 952-1900
Jagdish Gopani, *Director*
EMP: 3
SALES (est): 190.3K **Privately Held**
SIC: 3672 Printed circuit boards

(G-9015)
GLOBAL ENDOSCOPY INC
878 Cass Ln (60007-3049)
PHONE 847 910-5836
Nick Mircea, *President*
Mary Ann Mircea, *Vice Pres*
EMP: 3
SQ FT: 2,500
SALES (est): 320K **Privately Held**
WEB: www.global-endo.com
SIC: 3841 Surgical & medical instruments

(G-9016)
GLOBAL TOOL & DIE INC
1355 Tonne Rd (60007-5002)
PHONE 847 956-1200
Frank Fudala, *President*
Genene Fudala, *Treasurer*
EMP: 5
SALES (est): 500K **Privately Held**
SIC: 3544 Special dies & tools

(G-9017)
GLOBAL WEB SYSTEMS INC
742 Cutter Ln (60007-6903)
PHONE 630 782-9690
C Doyle Sutherland, *President*
Daniel Kosrow, *Vice Pres*
◆ EMP: 15
SQ FT: 10,000
SALES (est): 2.8MM **Privately Held**
SIC: 3555 Printing trades machinery

(G-9018)
GLOBUS FOOD PRODUCTS LLC
Also Called: Mystic Pizza Food Company
2258 Landmeier Rd Ste A (60007-2637)
PHONE 847 378-8221
Patrick Pawlis, *President*
EMP: 3
SALES (est): 340.5K **Privately Held**
SIC: 2038 Frozen specialties

(G-9019)
GOLDMAX CARRIER INC
2625 Greenleaf Ave (60007-5512)
PHONE 773 366-1718
EMP: 4
SALES (est): 655.5K **Privately Held**
SIC: 3537 Trucks, tractors, loaders, carriers & similar equipment

(G-9020)
GRAND PRODUCTS INC (PA)
1718 Hampshire Dr (60007-2760)
PHONE 800 621-6101
David Marofske Jr, *President*
Nicholas Kallas, *President*
David Marofske Sr, *Chairman*
◆ EMP: 325
SQ FT: 92,608
SALES (est): 34.1MM **Privately Held**
SIC: 3999 3679 Coin-operated amusement machines; harness assemblies for electronic use: wire or cable

(G-9021)
GRAPHIC INNOVATORS INC
855 Morse Ave (60007-5105)
PHONE 847 718-1516
Michael J Kiley, *CEO*
Scott J Kiley, *President*
Stephan Carter, *COO*
Paul Minasian, *Vice Pres*
Tim Hanson, *Mfg Staff*
◆ EMP: 50
SQ FT: 91,000
SALES (est): 21.6MM **Privately Held**
SIC: 5084 3555 Printing trades machinery, equipment & supplies; printing presses

(G-9022)
GRECIAN DELIGHT FOODS INC (PA)
Also Called: Grecian Delight Foods, Inc Del
1201 Tonne Rd (60007-4925)
PHONE 847 364-1010
Peter Parthenis Jr, *President*
Joseph Palazzo, *Regional Mgr*
Michael Loukis, *Business Mgr*
Dale Ohman, *Business Mgr*
Anthony Taxakis, *Business Mgr*
◆ EMP: 180
SALES (est): 103.7MM **Privately Held**
SIC: 2051 2011 2099 2013 Bread, all types (white, wheat, rye, etc): fresh or frozen; lamb products from lamb slaughtered on site; food preparations; sausages & other prepared meats

(G-9023)
GREENLEE DIAMOND TOOL CO
2375 Touhy Ave (60007-5330)
PHONE 866 451-3316
Jim Long, *General Mgr*
Michael L Wilkie, *Principal*
Joe Sanders, *Engineer*
James Camp, *Natl Sales Mgr*
Jay Valley, *Manager*
EMP: 25
SALES (est): 4.7MM **Privately Held**
SIC: 3545 Machine tool accessories

(G-9024)
GREENRIDGE FARM INC
2355 Greenleaf Ave (60007-5508)
PHONE 847 434-1803
Michael Madej, *President*
Sebastian Madej, *Vice Pres*
▲ EMP: 26 EST: 2008
SALES (est): 5.5MM **Privately Held**
WEB: www.greenridgefarm.com
SIC: 2013 Boneless meat, from purchased meat

(G-9025)
H D A FANS INC
1455 Brummel Ave 300 (60007-2110)
PHONE 630 627-2087
Thomas Kubik, *President*
Martin Keller, *President*
Mike Murphy, *Vice Pres*
EMP: 6
SALES (est): 500K **Privately Held**
SIC: 3564 Aircurtains (blower)
PA: Mk Systems, Incorporated
1455 Brummel Ave
Elk Grove Village IL 60007

(G-9026)
H S I FIRE AND SAFETY GROUP (PA)
107 Garlisch Dr (60007-1322)
PHONE 847 427-8340
Tom Berricad, *President*
▲ EMP: 4
SQ FT: 10,000
SALES (est): 702.2K **Privately Held**
SIC: 3829 Fire detector systems, non-electric

(G-9027)
HANOVER DISPLAYS INC
1601 Tonne Rd (60007-5123)
PHONE 773 334-9934
Gavin Williams, *President*
Brent Anderson, *Opers Mgr*
Rian Phillips, *Sales Staff*
Thomas Thorelli, *Admin Sec*
▲ EMP: 15
SALES (est): 2.5MM **Privately Held**
SIC: 3993 Electric signs

(G-9028)
HASKRIS CO
100 Kelly St (60007-1012)
PHONE 847 956-6420
Daniel M Falotico, *President*
Ed Rowe, *Prdtn Mgr*
Paul Falotico, *Production*
Rob Baer, *Buyer*
Allen Dreyer, *Engineer*
EMP: 51 EST: 1944
SQ FT: 24,000
SALES (est): 14.4MM **Privately Held**
WEB: www.haskris.com
SIC: 3585 Coolers, milk & water: electric

(G-9029)
HAUSNER HARD - CHROME INC (PA)
670 Greenleaf Ave (60007-5084)
PHONE 847 439-6010
David J Hausner, *CEO*
Jeffrey Hausner, *President*
John David, *CFO*
Mike Gould, *Manager*
EMP: 47
SQ FT: 11,500
SALES: 15.5MM **Privately Held**
WEB: www.hausnerinc.com
SIC: 3471 Electroplating of metals or formed products

(G-9030)
HD TURBO LLC
352 Lively Blvd (60007-2010)
PHONE 847 636-7586
EMP: 2
SALES (est): 207.2K **Privately Held**
SIC: 3714 Motor vehicle parts & accessories

(G-9031)
HEADCO INDUSTRIES INC
Also Called: Bearing Headquarters Co
109 N Lively Blvd (60007-1324)
PHONE 847 640-6490
Jim Scardina, *Exec VP*
Mike Wheatley, *Sales Staff*
Carl Scolaro, *Marketing Staff*
Ron Brousseau, *Branch Mgr*
William Love, *Technical Staff*
EMP: 10
SALES (corp-wide): 162.5MM **Privately Held**
WEB: www.bearingheadquarters.com
SIC: 5085 5084 3599 Bearings; sprockets; hydraulic systems equipment & supplies; machine shop, jobbing & repair
PA: Headco Industries, Inc.
2601 Parkes Dr
Broadview IL 60155
708 681-4400

(G-9032)
HELITUNE INC
Also Called: Prosig
190 Gordon St (60007-1120)
PHONE 847 228-0985
Douglas Shoemaker, *Principal*
Peter Morrish, *Info Tech Mgr*
Andy Lobato, *Director*
EMP: 7

SALES (est): 500K
SALES (corp-wide): 12.3MM Privately
Held
SIC: 3728 Aircraft parts & equipment
PA: Condition Monitoring Group Limited
   Hatchmoor Industrial Estate
   Torrington EX38
   180 562-6697

(G-9033)
**HELM TOOL COMPANY
INCORPORATED**
1290 Brummel Ave (60007-2168)
PHONE..................................847 952-9528
Helmut Mueller, *President*
Ralf Mueller, *Vice Pres*
Manfred Heumann, *Plant Mgr*
Michael Smith, *Purchasing*
Piotr Niedoba, *Manager*
EMP: 20
SQ FT: 22,000
SALES (est): 3.3MM Privately Held
SIC: 3544 Special dies & tools

(G-9034)
HFO CHICAGO LLC
555 Busse Rd (60007-2116)
PHONE..................................847 258-2850
Chrissy Edelmann, *Parts Mgr*
Ryan Motto-Ross, *Sales Engr*
Kelly Potter, *Sales Engr*
Nick Schuchardt,
Przemyslaw Tomera, *Administration*
EMP: 17
SQ FT: 35,000
SALES (est): 3.6MM Privately Held
WEB: www.hfochicago.com
SIC: 3599 5084 Machine & other job shop
   work; industrial machinery & equipment
HQ: Midwest Manufacturing Resources,
   Inc.
   1993 Case Pkwy
   Twinsburg OH 44087
   330 405-4227

(G-9035)
HILLSHIRE BRANDS COMPANY
Superior Coffee & Foods
1325 Chase Ave (60007-4812)
PHONE..................................847 956-7575
Bob Budlow, *Branch Mgr*
EMP: 120
SALES (corp-wide): 42.4B Publicly Held
SIC: 2095 5149 Roasted coffee; groceries
   & related products
HQ: The Hillshire Brands Company
   400 S Jefferson St Fl 1
   Chicago IL 60607
   312 614-6000

(G-9036)
**HONTECH INTERNATIONAL
CORP**
1000 Lee St (60007-1208)
PHONE..................................847 364-9800
Chou Long Shou, *President*
Fred Kesselman, *Opers Mgr*
▲ EMP: 10
SQ FT: 25,000
SALES (est): 3.4MM Privately Held
WEB: www.hontechgroup.com
SIC: 3444 Sheet metalwork

(G-9037)
HST MATERIALS INC
1631 Brummel Ave (60007-2125)
PHONE..................................847 640-1803
Kathryn E Miller, *President*
EMP: 12
SALES (est): 2.2MM Privately Held
WEB: www.hstmaterials.com
SIC: 3069 Sponge rubber & sponge rubber
   products

(G-9038)
HUETONE IMPRINTS INC
90 N Lively Blvd (60007-1317)
PHONE..................................630 694-9610
Bimal Thakkar, *CEO*
EMP: 6
SQ FT: 6,500
SALES (est): 899.6K Privately Held
SIC: 2752 Commercial printing, lithographic

(G-9039)
**I TW DELTAR INSERT MOLDED
PDTS**
830 Lee St (60007-1205)
PHONE..................................847 593-8811
Robert L Hamilton Jr, *Principal*
EMP: 3
SALES (est): 237.7K Privately Held
SIC: 3089 Molding primary plastic

(G-9040)
ILLINOIS BOTTLE MFG CO
701 E Devon Ave (60007-6702)
PHONE..................................847 595-9000
Robert Klekauskas, *President*
John Homyak, *Superintendent*
Bruce Ronner, *VP Finance*
John Coursey, *VP Mktg*
Athina Gonzalez,
▲ EMP: 80
SQ FT: 225,000
SALES (est): 12.7MM Privately Held
WEB: www.illinoisbottle.com
SIC: 3089 3085 3999 Plastic containers,
   except foam; plastics bottles; atomizers,
   toiletry

(G-9041)
ILLINOIS TOOL WORKS INC
950 Pratt Blvd (60007-5119)
PHONE..................................630 787-3298
EMP: 91
SALES (corp-wide): 14.1B Publicly Held
SIC: 3089 Injection molded finished plastic
   products
PA: Illinois Tool Works Inc.
   155 Harlem Ave
   Glenview IL 60025
   847 724-7500

(G-9042)
ILLINOIS TOOL WORKS INC
Also Called: ITW Filtration
830 Lee St (60007-1205)
PHONE..................................847 593-8811
Chris Fredricks, *Manager*
EMP: 28
SALES (corp-wide): 14.1B Publicly Held
SIC: 2834 5122 Pharmaceutical preparations; drugs, proprietaries & sundries
PA: Illinois Tool Works Inc.
   155 Harlem Ave
   Glenview IL 60025
   847 724-7500

(G-9043)
ILLINOIS TOOL WORKS INC
Also Called: ITW Ramset Red Head
2471 Brickvale Dr (60007-6810)
PHONE..................................847 350-0193
EMP: 25
SALES (corp-wide): 14.3B Publicly Held
SIC: 2899 Chemical Blending
PA: Illinois Tool Works Inc.
   155 Harlem Ave
   Glenview IL 60025
   847 724-7500

(G-9044)
ILLINOIS TOOL WORKS INC
Also Called: ITW Shakeproof-Elk Grove
2700 York Rd (60007-6315)
PHONE..................................847 766-9000
Earl Dineen, *General Mgr*
EMP: 185
SALES (corp-wide): 14.1B Publicly Held
SIC: 3452 Bolts, nuts, rivets & washers
PA: Illinois Tool Works Inc.
   155 Harlem Ave
   Glenview IL 60025
   847 724-7500

(G-9045)
IMAGE CIRCUIT INC
925 Estes Ave (60007-4905)
PHONE..................................847 622-3300
Mohan Dungarani, *President*
EMP: 9
SALES: 850K Privately Held
SIC: 3672 Printed circuit boards

(G-9046)
**IMAGE SYSTEMS BUS
SLUTIONS LLC**
Also Called: Isbs
1776 Commerce Dr (60007-2120)
PHONE..................................847 378-8249
Donna Diekneit, *Sales Mgr*
Jenna Altobelli, *Accounts Exec*
Paul Pritchard, *Accounts Exec*
John Heggeland, *Sales Staff*
Robert Wichman, *Sales Staff*
EMP: 30
SQ FT: 50,000
SALES (est): 6.8MM Privately Held
SIC: 3299 Images, small: gypsum, clay or
   papier mache

(G-9047)
IMAGINEERING INC
2425 Touhy Ave (60007-5331)
PHONE..................................847 806-0003
Khurrum Dhanji, *CEO*
Parvin Dhanji, *President*
Sulaiman Roy, *COO*
Hasnain Patel, *Accounts Exec*
Zohra Tharani, *Accounts Exec*
EMP: 48
SQ FT: 38,000
SALES (est): 6.9MM Privately Held
SIC: 8711 3672 8731 Electrical or electronic engineering; printed circuit boards;
   circuit boards, television & radio printed;
   wiring boards; electronic research

(G-9048)
**IMPACT PRTRS &
LITHOGRAPHERS**
1370 E Higgins Rd (60007-1603)
PHONE..................................847 981-9676
Robert Serna, *President*
Vito Griseta, *Vice Pres*
EMP: 37
SQ FT: 20,000
SALES (est): 4.4MM Privately Held
WEB: www.impactprinters.com
SIC: 2752 Commercial printing, offset; lithographing on metal

(G-9049)
**INDIUM CORPORATION OF
AMERICA**
80 Scott St (60007-1228)
PHONE..................................847 439-9134
Matthew Norris, *Engineer*
Joann Warren, *Human Res Mgr*
Paul Gassensmith, *Manager*
EMP: 8
SALES (est): 201.6MM Privately
Held
SIC: 3356 Nonferrous rolling & drawing
PA: Indium Corporation Of America
   34 Robinson Rd
   Clinton NY 13323
   315 853-4900

(G-9050)
INDUSTRIAL MODERN PATTERN
970 Nicholas Blvd (60007-2513)
PHONE..................................847 296-4930
Jared Megleo, *President*
Brad Schneider, *Opers Mgr*
Natalia Guzman, *Sales Engr*
Jaimee Kinsman, *Office Mgr*
Megan Decker, *Admin Asst*
EMP: 9
SQ FT: 7,500
SALES: 1.1MM Privately Held
SIC: 3544 Forms (molds), for foundry &
   plastics working machinery

(G-9051)
INFINITYBOX LLC
1410 Brummel Ave (60007-2111)
PHONE..................................847 232-1991
Mike Weber, *Engineer*
Edwin Harris,
EMP: 4
SALES (est): 246.3K Privately Held
WEB: www.isispower.com
SIC: 3714 Automotive wiring harness sets

(G-9052)
INK SOLUTIONS LLC (PA)
800 Estes Ave (60007-4904)
PHONE..................................847 593-5200
Greg Bourucki, *Sales Associate*
John P Jilek Sr, *Mng Member*
Martin Morrissey, *Manager*
Alan Berna, *Technical Staff*
Carl Hirsch,
▲ EMP: 15
SQ FT: 19,700
SALES (est): 3.8MM Privately Held
SIC: 2893 Printing ink

(G-9053)
INK SYSTEMS INC
800 Estes Ave (60007-4904)
PHONE..................................847 427-2200
John Jilek, *President*
Dennis Pearson, *Exec VP*
EMP: 9
SALES (corp-wide): 59.7MM Privately
Held
SIC: 2893 Printing ink
PA: Ink Systems, Inc.
   2311 S Eastern Ave
   Commerce CA 90040
   323 720-4000

(G-9054)
INNOVO CORP
2385 United Ln (60007-6816)
PHONE..................................847 616-0063
Bob Kinsley, *President*
Jan Jakimiec, *Vice Pres*
Ron Bochat, *Engineer*
Jerry Kedzierski, *Design Engr*
Anna Turek, *Office Mgr*
EMP: 12
SQ FT: 10,000
SALES (est): 2.8MM Privately Held
SIC: 3552 Dyeing machinery, textile

(G-9055)
**INTEGRATED PACKG &
FASTENER**
1678 Carmen Dr (60007-6504)
PHONE..................................847 439-5730
Mark Ryan, *President*
Jill Rozehon, *Corp Secy*
Jill Louise, *Opers Mgr*
Jill Rozhon, *Sales Staff*
◆ EMP: 78
SALES (est): 11.4MM Privately Held
SIC: 3565 Packaging machinery

(G-9056)
INTERFLO INDUSTRIES INC
695 Lunt Ave (60007-5014)
PHONE..................................847 228-0606
Leonard Gluck, *President*
▼ EMP: 5
SQ FT: 3,000
SALES (est): 1MM Privately Held
SIC: 2842 2841 Industrial plant disinfectants or deodorants; soap & other detergents

(G-9057)
**INTERNATIONAL PAPER
COMPANY**
25 Northwest Point Blvd # 300
(60007-1033)
PHONE..................................847 228-7227
Tom Dupuis, *Manager*
Hal Turrentine, *Info Tech Mgr*
EMP: 139
SALES (corp-wide): 22.3B Publicly Held
SIC: 2621 Paper mills
PA: International Paper Company
   6400 Poplar Ave
   Memphis TN 38197
   901 419-9000

(G-9058)
**INTERNATIONAL PROC CO
AMER**
Also Called: Iosso Products
1485 Lively Blvd (60007-5094)
PHONE..................................847 437-8400
Richard C Iosso, *President*
Marianne Iosso, *Vice Pres*
Marianne Ortmann, *Vice Pres*
Grace Iosso, *Admin Sec*
Grace Nosko, *Admin Sec*
▲ EMP: 30
SQ FT: 26,000

Elk Grove Village - Cook County (G-9059)

SALES (est): 6.8MM **Privately Held**
WEB: www.iosso.com
SIC: 3398 3341 3471 Brazing (hardening) of metal; secondary nonferrous metals; plating & polishing

(G-9059)
INTRATEK INC
54 N Lively Blvd (60007-1317)
PHONE..........................847 640-0007
Ken Patel, *President*
Jignesh Patel, *Vice Pres*
EMP: 4
SQ FT: 4,000
SALES (est): 425.5K **Privately Held**
WEB: www.intratekpcb.com
SIC: 8711 3672 Professional engineer; printed circuit boards

(G-9060)
INX GROUP
651 Bonnie Ln (60007-1911)
PHONE..........................847 441-0600
Hiroshi Ota, *Principal*
EMP: 4
SALES (est): 400.9K **Privately Held**
SIC: 2893 Printing ink

(G-9061)
IRVING PRESS INC
2530 United Ln (60007-6180)
PHONE..........................847 595-6650
Gerald W Gaul, *President*
Kristen Wilding, *Controller*
EMP: 26
SQ FT: 20,000
SALES (est): 4.8MM **Privately Held**
WEB: www.irvingpress.com
SIC: 2752 Commercial printing, offset

(G-9062)
J & K CABINETRY INC
1655 Busse Rd (60007-5517)
PHONE..........................847 758-7808
Sal Abecasis, *President*
▲ EMP: 4
SALES (est): 446.9K **Privately Held**
WEB: www.jandkcabinetrychicago.com
SIC: 2434 Wood kitchen cabinets

(G-9063)
J D GRAPHIC CO INC
1101 Arthur Ave (60007-5289)
PHONE..........................847 364-4000
James De Blasio Jr, *President*
Nick Deblasio, *Opers Mgr*
Connie Santoro, *Opers Mgr*
John Schmidt, *Prdtn Mgr*
Crista Deblasio, *Admin Asst*
EMP: 40
SQ FT: 40,000
SALES (est): 8.6MM **Privately Held**
WEB: www.jdgraphic.com
SIC: 2752 2796 2789 Commercial printing, offset; platemaking services; bookbinding & related work

(G-9064)
J R FRIDRICH INC
1830 Lunt Ave (60007-5602)
P.O. Box 621, Wood Dale (60191-0621)
PHONE..........................847 439-1554
Fax: 847 439-3765
EMP: 14
SALES (est): 1.7MM **Privately Held**
SIC: 3993 Mfg Signs/Advertising Specialties

(G-9065)
JACKSON SPRING & MFG CO
299 Bond St (60007-1220)
PHONE..........................847 952-8850
Robert Kupczak, *President*
Robert Meyers, *General Mgr*
Robert Kunkle, *Vice Pres*
Jeff Kolozsy, *Plant Supt*
Al Matusiak, *Safety Mgr*
EMP: 58 EST: 1961
SQ FT: 55,000
SALES (est): 12.7MM **Privately Held**
WEB: www.jacksonspring.com
SIC: 3495 Mechanical springs, precision

(G-9066)
JDM ENGINES CHICAGO LLC
1583 Elmhurst Rd (60007-6414)
PHONE..........................214 235-5071
Habib Khairi, *Principal*
EMP: 3 EST: 2016
SALES (est): 218.2K **Privately Held**
SIC: 3519 Internal combustion engines

(G-9067)
JEROME REMIEN CORPORATION
409 Busse Rd (60007-2114)
P.O. Box 1067, Northbrook (60065-1067)
PHONE..........................847 806-0888
Jerome Remien, *President*
EMP: 11
SQ FT: 3,000
SALES (est): 500K **Privately Held**
SIC: 3499 3429 Locks, safe & vault: metal; manufactured hardware (general)

(G-9068)
JESCORP INC
1900 Pratt Blvd (60007-5906)
PHONE..........................847 378-1200
John E Sanfilippo, *President*
James J Sanfilippo, *Vice Pres*
EMP: 85
SQ FT: 60,000
SALES (est): 16.8MM
SALES (corp-wide): 5.3B **Publicly Held**
SIC: 3565 3699 Packing & wrapping machinery; electrical equipment & supplies
HQ: Grove Sonoco Elk Inc
1950 Pratt Blvd
Elk Grove Village IL 60007
847 439-8570

(G-9069)
JOHNSON & JOHNSON
1350 Estes Ave (60007-5404)
PHONE..........................847 640-5400
Fax: 847 640-4618
EMP: 3
SALES (corp-wide): 67.2B **Publicly Held**
SIC: 2676 Mfg Consumer Products
PA: Johnson & Johnson
1 Johnson And Johnson Plz
New Brunswick NJ 08933
732 524-0400

(G-9070)
JRD LABS LLC
2613 Greenleaf Ave (60007-5512)
PHONE..........................847 818-1076
Mark Weinberg, *President*
◆ EMP: 5
SQ FT: 1,000
SALES (est): 727.5K **Privately Held**
SIC: 3826 Analytical instruments

(G-9071)
JSC PRODUCTS INC
2270 Elmhurst Rd (60007-6309)
PHONE..........................847 290-9520
John M Carrol, *President*
EMP: 5
SALES (est): 809.1K **Privately Held**
WEB: www.jsc-products.com
SIC: 2631 Cardboard

(G-9072)
K & L LOOSELEAF PRODUCTS INC
425 Bonnie Ln (60007-1907)
PHONE..........................847 357-9733
Ken Fairbanks Jr, *President*
Jim Boeing, *Safety Mgr*
Cathy Elliott, *Accounts Exec*
Pat Monzel, *Accounts Exec*
EMP: 60
SQ FT: 16,000
SALES (est): 8.1MM **Privately Held**
SIC: 2782 5199 Looseleaf binders & devices; advertising specialties

(G-9073)
K V F COMPANY (PA)
950 Lively Blvd (60007-2254)
PHONE..........................847 437-5100
Luis A Luna, *President*
Larry Luna, *Vice Pres*
Madison Carrasco, *Director*
EMP: 48
SQ FT: 26,400
SALES (est): 5.9MM **Privately Held**
WEB: www.kvfcompany.com
SIC: 3471 3398 Finishing, metals or formed products; sand blasting of metal parts; metal heat treating

(G-9074)
K V F COMPANY
1325 Landmeier Rd (60007-2411)
PHONE..........................847 437-5019
Manuel Luna, *Manager*
EMP: 14
SALES (corp-wide): 5.9MM **Privately Held**
SIC: 3471 3398 Finishing, metals or formed products; sand blasting of metal parts; metal heat treating
PA: K V F Company
950 Lively Blvd
Elk Grove Village IL 60007
847 437-5100

(G-9075)
KAVALIERGLASS NORTH AMER INC
1301 Brummel Ave (60007-2108)
PHONE..........................847 364-7303
Greg Bittner, *President*
EMP: 10
SALES (est): 568.3K **Privately Held**
SIC: 3221 Glass containers

(G-9076)
KERRY INC
Also Called: Kerry Ingredients and Flavours
1301 Mark St (60007-6711)
PHONE..........................847 595-1003
EMP: 9 **Privately Held**
SIC: 2051 Bread, cake & related products
HQ: Kerry Inc.
3400 Millington Rd
Beloit WI 53511
608 363-1200

(G-9077)
KERRY INGREDIENTS & FLAVOURS
1301 Mark St (60007-6711)
PHONE..........................847 595-1003
Bill Day, *Principal*
EMP: 13
SALES (est): 2.3MM **Privately Held**
SIC: 2051 Bakery: wholesale or wholesale/retail combined

(G-9078)
KLEIN TOOLS INC
Also Called: Turn Key Forging
2300 E Devon Ave (60007-6120)
PHONE..........................847 228-6999
Ernest Pawelczyk, *Branch Mgr*
EMP: 78
SALES (corp-wide): 292.1MM **Privately Held**
SIC: 3423 3199 3469 2899 Hand & edge tools; belting for machinery: solid, twisted, flat, etc.: leather; safety belts, leather; metal stampings; chemical preparations; partitions & fixtures, except wood; fabric dress & work gloves
PA: Klein Tools, Inc.
450 Bond St
Lincolnshire IL 60069
847 821-5500

(G-9079)
KOPP WELDING INC
991 Oakton St (60007-1905)
PHONE..........................847 593-2070
Adam Kopp, *President*
Kathy Kopp, *Vice Pres*
EMP: 7
SALES (est): 1.4MM **Privately Held**
SIC: 7692 Welding repair

(G-9080)
KURZ TRANSFER PRODUCTS LP
220 Martin Ln (60007-1311)
PHONE..........................847 228-0001
Tony Flaim, *Branch Mgr*
EMP: 4
SALES (corp-wide): 967.3MM **Privately Held**
SIC: 4225 3497 General warehousing & storage; gold foil or leaf
HQ: Kurz Transfer Products, Lp
3200 Woodpark Blvd
Charlotte NC 28206
704 927-3700

(G-9081)
L & M TOOL & DIE CO INC
1570 Louis Ave (60007-2314)
PHONE..........................847 364-9760
Fax: 847 364-9771
EMP: 5 EST: 1979
SQ FT: 12,000
SALES: 1.3MM **Privately Held**
SIC: 3544 Mfg Tools & Dies

(G-9082)
LA-CO INDUSTRIES INC (PA)
Also Called: Markal Company
1201 Pratt Blvd (60007-5746)
PHONE..........................847 956-7600
Daniel Kleiman, *CEO*
George Bowman, *President*
Michael Goluszka, *Vice Pres*
Mark Thaxter, *Mfg Staff*
Margaret Gora, *Production*
◆ EMP: 143 EST: 1935
SQ FT: 80,000
SALES (est): 28.6MM **Privately Held**
WEB: www.markal.com
SIC: 2891 2899 Sealants; fluxes: brazing, soldering, galvanizing & welding

(G-9083)
LANDMEIER CORP
180 Martin Ln (60007-1310)
PHONE..........................847 709-2823
Rich Dominelli, *President*
EMP: 5 EST: 2009
SALES (est): 728.8K **Privately Held**
SIC: 3672 Printed circuit boards

(G-9084)
LANINVER USA INC (PA)
2800 Carl Bulevard (60007)
PHONE..........................847 367-8787
Clemente Gonzales, *President*
EMP: 6 EST: 2013
SALES (est): 7.6MM **Privately Held**
SIC: 2759 Commercial printing

(G-9085)
LARSEN ENVELOPE CO INC
165 Gaylord St (60007-1106)
PHONE..........................847 952-9020
Leonard R Larsen Jr, *President*
Helen Larsen, *Corp Secy*
Helen M Larsen, *Admin Sec*
EMP: 22
SQ FT: 7,500
SALES (est): 3.4MM **Privately Held**
SIC: 2759 Commercial printing

(G-9086)
LASER PLUS TECHNOLOGIES LLC
2450 American Ln (60007-6204)
PHONE..........................847 787-9017
Jason Schawrtz, *Mng Member*
EMP: 4
SQ FT: 10,000
SALES (est): 625.3K **Privately Held**
SIC: 7389 3441 Metal cutting services; fabricated structural metal

(G-9087)
LASER TECHNOLOGY GROUP INC
1029 Charlela Ln Apt 407 (60007-3225)
PHONE..........................847 524-4088
Don McNeil, *President*
EMP: 3
SALES: 200K **Privately Held**
SIC: 2893 Printing ink

(G-9088)
LAWRENCE FOODS INC
2200 Lunt Ave (60007-5685)
PHONE..........................847 437-2400
Lester Lawrence, *CEO*
Craig Barnhart, *Business Mgr*
Shawn Kincanon, *Maint Spvr*

GEOGRAPHIC SECTION

Elk Grove Village - Cook County (G-9115)

Marlene Perrucci, *Opers Staff*
Amanda Burgan, *Production*
▼ **EMP:** 250
SQ FT: 200,000
SALES (est): 107.3MM **Privately Held**
WEB: www.lawrencefoods.com
SIC: 2033 2099 Canned fruits & specialties; food preparations

(G-9089)
LC INDUSTRIES INC
Also Called: Lewis N Clark Travel ACC
2781 Katherine Way (60007-6746)
PHONE 312 455-0500
Michael Smerling, *President*
Rae L Smerling, *Admin Sec*
▲ **EMP:** 27
SQ FT: 30,000
SALES (est): 6MM **Privately Held**
SIC: 3161 Luggage

(G-9090)
LEGACY FOODS MFG LLC
498 Franklin Ln (60007-2702)
PHONE 224 639-5297
Phillip M Graff, *Mng Member*
EMP: 3
SALES (est): 242K **Privately Held**
WEB: www.legacyfoodsmanufacturing.com
SIC: 2099 Sauces: gravy, dressing & dip mixes

(G-9091)
LEGACY FOODS MFG LLC
1550 Greenleaf Ave (60007-5525)
PHONE 847 595-9106
Monica Reyes, *Purchasing*
Stephen Sallenback, *VP Sales*
Phillip Graff,
John Barajas,
Steve Sallenback,
EMP: 14
SALES (est): 3.9MM **Privately Held**
SIC: 2035 2033 Pickles, sauces & salad dressings; barbecue sauce: packaged in cans, jars, etc.

(G-9092)
LEGACY VULCAN LLC
Also Called: Elk Grove Recycle
1520 Midway Ct (60007-6605)
PHONE 847 437-4181
Dave Kwoznewski, *Principal*
EMP: 22 **Publicly Held**
WEB: www.vulcanmaterials.com
SIC: 3273 Ready-mixed concrete
HQ: Legacy Vulcan, Llc
1200 Urban Center Dr
Vestavia AL 35242
205 298-3000

(G-9093)
LENS LENTICLEAR LENTICULAR
Also Called: Jacobsen Lntclar Tl Cylnder En
2515 Pan Am Blvd (60007-6308)
P.O. Box 806 (60009-0806)
PHONE 630 467-0900
Gary A Jacobsen, *President*
EMP: 11
SQ FT: 6,500
SALES: 2MM **Privately Held**
SIC: 3089 3542 3827 3544 Engraving of plastic; extruding machines (machine tools), metal; lenses, optical: all types except ophthalmic; forms (molds), for foundry & plastics working machinery

(G-9094)
LIBERTY CHEMICAL CORP
1503 Carmen Dr (60007-6501)
PHONE 773 657-1282
EMP: 6
SALES (est): 902.4K **Privately Held**
SIC: 2822 Ethylene-propylene rubbers, EPDM polymers

(G-9095)
LIGHTOLIER GENLYTE INC
951 Busse Rd (60007-2400)
PHONE 847 364-8250
Gary Basista, *President*
EMP: 56
SALES (est): 3MM **Privately Held**
SIC: 3648 Lighting equipment

(G-9096)
LITTLE LADY FOODS INC (PA)
Also Called: Miracapo Pizza Company
2323 Pratt Blvd (60007-5918)
PHONE 847 806-1440
Rick Anderson, *CEO*
Dan Rich, *Vice Pres*
Steven Kunkle, *VP Opers*
Edward Mulloy, *Plant Mgr*
Brian Scardina, *Plant Mgr*
EMP: 230
SQ FT: 200,000
SALES (est): 102.5MM **Privately Held**
WEB: www.littleladyfoods.com
SIC: 2038 2099 Pizza, frozen; food preparations

(G-9097)
LLLB LLC
1200 Thorndale Ave (60007-6749)
PHONE 630 315-3300
Joe Kostelc, *CFO*
Patrick McCartin, *Sales Staff*
▲ **EMP:** 18
SQ FT: 70,000
SALES (est): 19.4MM **Privately Held**
SIC: 3645 3596 Residential lighting fixtures; bathroom scales

(G-9098)
LOYOLA PAPER COMPANY
951 Lunt Ave (60007-5091)
PHONE 847 956-7770
Joan Lavezzorio, *President*
Nicholas Lavezzorio, *President*
EMP: 40 **EST:** 1969
SQ FT: 75,000
SALES (est): 12.9MM **Privately Held**
SIC: 2679 7389 Paperboard products, converted; interior designer

(G-9099)
LT SECURITY INC
1459 Elmhurst Rd (60007-6400)
PHONE 630 348-8088
EMP: 27 **Privately Held**
SIC: 3699 5999 Security devices; alarm & safety equipment stores
PA: Lt Security, Inc.
18738 San Jose Ave
City Of Industry CA 91748

(G-9100)
M & J MANUFACTURING CO INC
1450 Jarvis Ave (60007-2380)
PHONE 847 364-6066
Joseph Soehn, *President*
Joe Soehn Jr, *Vice Pres*
Matt Soehn, *Vice Pres*
EMP: 10 **EST:** 1967
SQ FT: 8,000
SALES (est): 1MM **Privately Held**
SIC: 3599 7692 Machine shop, jobbing & repair; welding repair

(G-9101)
M & R PRECISION MACHINING INC
680 Lively Blvd (60007-2016)
PHONE 847 364-1050
Richard G Beunhauer, *Principal*
Richard Beinhauer, *Vice Pres*
Monica Richter, *QC Mgr*
Irma Beinhauer, *Treasurer*
▲ **EMP:** 30
SQ FT: 19,000
SALES (est): 6.7MM **Privately Held**
SIC: 3599 Machine shop, jobbing & repair

(G-9102)
M I E AMERICA INC
420 Bennett Rd (60007-1007)
PHONE 847 981-6100
Gunther Kuel, *President*
Norman Von Hollen, *Vice Pres*
▲ **EMP:** 11
SQ FT: 10,000
SALES (est): 2.3MM
SALES (corp-wide): 2.4MM **Privately Held**
SIC: 3829 Nuclear instrument modules
HQ: Mie Medical Imaging Electronics Gmbh
Hauptstr. 112
Seth 23845
419 499-770

(G-9103)
M S A PRINTING CO
850 Touhy Ave (60007-4918)
PHONE 847 593-5699
Ross Diederich, *President*
Peggy Diederich, *Admin Sec*
EMP: 3
SQ FT: 5,000
SALES (est): 270K **Privately Held**
SIC: 2759 2752 2796 2675 Letterpress printing; commercial printing, offset; platemaking services; die-cut paper & board

(G-9104)
MACHINE TOOL BEARING & ACC INC
590 Bonnie Ln (60007-1910)
PHONE 847 357-1793
Don Caruso Jr, *President*
EMP: 7 **EST:** 2000
SQ FT: 2,500
SALES (est): 1.1MM **Privately Held**
WEB: www.mtbainc.com
SIC: 3599 Machine shop, jobbing & repair

(G-9105)
MACHINED METALS MANUFACTURING
1450 Jarvis Ave (60007-2306)
PHONE 847 364-6116
Matthias Soehn, *President*
Joseph Soehn, *Admin Sec*
EMP: 30
SQ FT: 8,000
SALES (est): 1.6MM **Privately Held**
SIC: 3599 Machine shop, jobbing & repair

(G-9106)
MAGNETIC INSPECTION LAB INC
Also Called: M I L
1401 Greenleaf Ave (60007-5536)
PHONE 847 437-4488
Robert L Schiewe, *President*
Betty Viets, *Principal*
Mike Ulman, *COO*
Jay Gandhi, *Vice Pres*
Tim Schiewe, *Vice Pres*
EMP: 85
SQ FT: 35,000
SALES (est): 20MM **Privately Held**
SIC: 8734 7692 3471 2899 Metallurgical testing laboratory; welding repair; plating & polishing; chemical preparations

(G-9107)
MAIN STEEL POLISHING CO INC (PA)
Also Called: Main Steel - Corporate 6001
2200 Pratt Blvd (60007-5917)
PHONE 847 916-1220
Keith Medick, *CEO*
Michael Folley, *General Mgr*
Bob Haas, *General Mgr*
George Bogan, *Exec VP*
Mark McCool, *Vice Pres*
▲ **EMP:** 35 **EST:** 1980
SQ FT: 15,000
SALES (est): 26.3MM **Privately Held**
WEB: www.mainsteel.com
SIC: 3471 Finishing, metals or formed products; buffing for the trade

(G-9108)
MAJESTIC SPRING INC
Also Called: Coil It
1390 Jarvis Ave (60007-2304)
PHONE 847 593-8887
EMP: 10
SQ FT: 5,000
SALES (est): 875K **Privately Held**
SIC: 3495 Wire springs

(G-9109)
MAPES & SPROWL LLC
1100 E Devon Ave (60007-5225)
PHONE 847 364-0055
EMP: 6 **EST:** 2016
SALES (est): 387.5K
SALES (corp-wide): 386.2MM **Privately Held**
SIC: 3441 Fabricated structural metal
HQ: Mapes Holding Llc
1100 W Devon Ave
Elk Grove Village IL 60007
800 777-1025

(G-9110)
MAPES & SPROWL STEEL LLC
1100 E Devon Ave (60007-5274)
PHONE 800 777-1025
Paul D Douglass, *Principal*
Pete Recchia, *Sales Dir*
Coy Sitter, *Sales Staff*
Christopher Hutter,
EMP: 2
SALES (est): 983.4K
SALES (corp-wide): 386.2MM **Privately Held**
SIC: 3315 Steel wire & related products
HQ: Mapes Holding Llc
1100 W Devon Ave
Elk Grove Village IL 60007
800 777-1025

(G-9111)
MARATHON TECHNOLOGIES INC
Also Called: MTI
800 Nicholas Blvd (60007-2511)
P.O. Box 627 (60009-0627)
PHONE 847 378-8572
Jerry Kozlowski, *President*
EMP: 40
SQ FT: 15,000
SALES (est): 6.3MM **Privately Held**
SIC: 3599 Machine shop, jobbing & repair

(G-9112)
MATERIAL SCIENCES CORPORATION
2250 Pratt Blvd (60007-5917)
PHONE 847 439-2210
Bret Davis, *Engineer*
Daniel Fondriest, *Manager*
EMP: 25
SALES (corp-wide): 119.1MM **Privately Held**
SIC: 3479 Painting of metal products
PA: Material Sciences Corporation
6855 Commerce Blvd
Canton MI 48187
734 207-4444

(G-9113)
MATTHEW WARREN INC
Also Called: Rumco
989 Pauly Dr (60007-1312)
PHONE 847 364-5000
Dan Bishop, *Branch Mgr*
EMP: 20
SALES (corp-wide): 185.9MM **Privately Held**
SIC: 3452 Screws, metal
HQ: Matthew Warren, Inc.
9501 Tech Blvd Ste 401
Rosemont IL 60018
847 349-5760

(G-9114)
MEA INC
2600 American Ln (60007-6270)
PHONE 847 766-9040
Townes Comer, *President*
William T Comer, *Vice Pres*
Aaron Johnson, *Opers Staff*
Eileen Thonn, *Production*
Taras Dykun, *Engineer*
EMP: 23 **EST:** 1963
SQ FT: 13,000
SALES (est): 8.5MM **Privately Held**
WEB: www.meaincorporated.com
SIC: 3593 8711 3492 Fluid power actuators, hydraulic or pneumatic; mechanical engineering; electrohydraulic servo valves, metal

(G-9115)
MET PLASTICS
333 King St (60007-1114)
PHONE 847 228-5070
EMP: 5
SALES (est): 174.5K **Privately Held**
SIC: 3089 3544 Injection molding of plastics; special dies, tools, jigs & fixtures

Elk Grove Village - Cook County (G-9116)   GEOGRAPHIC SECTION

(G-9116)
MET2PLASTIC LLC
Also Called: Met Plastics
701 Lee St (60007-1121)
PHONE..................................847 228-5070
Michael Walter, *President*
Michael J Walter, *Vice Pres*
Michael P Walter, *Mng Member*
Arnaud Burckle, *Info Tech Dir*
EMP: 50
SQ FT: 30,000
SALES (est): 10.4MM
SALES (corp-wide): 866.4K **Privately Held**
SIC: 3089 Injection molding of plastics
HQ: Dedienne Multiplasturgy
Zac Des Champs Chouette 2
Saint-Aubin-Sur-Gaillon 27600
232 223-838

(G-9117)
METAL IMPACT LLC
1501 Oakton St (60007-2101)
PHONE..................................847 718-0192
Kevin Prunsky, *Ch of Bd*
Mike Schumi, *Prdtn Mgr*
Dong Yeom, *Engineer*
Dustin Lyons, *Project Engr*
Ryan Schumi, *Controller*
EMP: 100
SQ FT: 175,000
SALES (est): 28.5MM
SALES (corp-wide): 86.6MM **Privately Held**
SIC: 3354 Aluminum extruded products
PA: Thunderbird Llc
1501 Oakton St
Elk Grove Village IL 60007
847 718-9300

(G-9118)
METAL IMPACT SOUTH LLC
1501 Oakton St (60007-2101)
PHONE..................................847 718-9300
EMP: 12
SALES (corp-wide): 86.6MM **Privately Held**
SIC: 3354 Aluminum extruded products
HQ: Metal Impact South Llc
795 Sam T Barkley Dr
New Albany MS 38652
662 538-6500

(G-9119)
METAL RESOURCES INTL LLC
1965 Pratt Blvd (60007-5905)
PHONE..................................847 806-7200
Cyrus Tang, *President*
National Material,
▲ **EMP:** 14
SALES (est): 4.6MM **Privately Held**
SIC: 3325 Rolling mill rolls, cast steel

(G-9120)
METRIC MACHINE SHOP INC
101 Kelly St Ste D (60007-1029)
PHONE..................................847 439-9891
Edward Rybecki, *President*
EMP: 4
SALES (est): 350K **Privately Held**
SIC: 3599 Machine shop, jobbing & repair

(G-9121)
MGB ENGINEERING COMPANY (PA)
1099 Touhy Ave (60007-4921)
PHONE..................................847 956-7444
Michael Beladakis, *President*
Maria Theodosis, *Treasurer*
Angie Beladakis, *Admin Sec*
EMP: 22
SQ FT: 64,000
SALES (est): 7MM **Privately Held**
WEB: www.mgbengineering.com
SIC: 3559 Plastics working machinery; machine tools, metal forming type

(G-9122)
MICHAEL A GREENBERG MD LTD
Also Called: Illinois Dermatological Center
800 Biesterfield Rd # 3002 (60007-3364)
PHONE..................................847 364-4717
Michael Greenberg, *President*
Brooks Johnson, *Surgeon*
EMP: 10
SQ FT: 1,100
SALES (est): 1.4MM **Privately Held**
SIC: 8011 2731 Dermatologist; physicians' office, including specialists; book publishing

(G-9123)
MIDACO CORPORATION
2000 Touhy Ave (60007-5368)
PHONE..................................847 593-8420
Michael P Cayley, *President*
Malcolm Keith, *Vice Pres*
Mike Munao, *Vice Pres*
Paul Bottum, *Purchasing*
Eric Halvorsen, *Purchasing*
EMP: 40
SQ FT: 40,000
SALES (est): 9.5MM **Privately Held**
SIC: 3599 3537 Custom machinery; machine shop, jobbing & repair; pallets, metal

(G-9124)
MIDWAY GRINDING INC
1451 Lunt Ave (60007-5621)
PHONE..................................847 439-7424
Jerry Malachowski, *President*
Dorothy Malachowski, *Corp Secy*
EMP: 45 EST: 1978
SQ FT: 30,000
SALES (est): 8.2MM **Privately Held**
SIC: 3599 Machine shop, jobbing & repair; grinding castings for the trade

(G-9125)
MIDWAY MACHINE PRODUCTS & SVCS
2690 American Ln (60007-6208)
PHONE..................................847 860-8180
Juan D Guemez, *President*
EMP: 5
SALES (est): 630.2K **Privately Held**
SIC: 3451 Screw machine products

(G-9126)
MIDWEST ARCHITECTURAL MILLWORK
125 Joey Dr (60007-1303)
PHONE..................................847 621-2013
EMP: 2
SALES (est): 298.2K **Privately Held**
SIC: 2431 Millwork

(G-9127)
MISSION CONTROL SYSTEMS INC
700 Oakton St (60007-1903)
PHONE..................................847 956-7650
Scott Medford, *President*
Gary Chapman, *Principal*
Brad Kodl, *Principal*
EMP: 16
SQ FT: 10,300
SALES (est): 5MM **Privately Held**
SIC: 3625 Electric controls & control accessories, industrial

(G-9128)
MIYANO MACHINERY USA INC (DH)
2316 Touhy Ave (60007-5329)
PHONE..................................630 766-4141
Tsugio Sasaki, *President*
Sasaki Tsugio, *Treasurer*
Akihiko Menemura, *Admin Sec*
▲ **EMP:** 20
SQ FT: 182,450
SALES (est): 4.2MM **Privately Held**
SIC: 5084 3541 Metalworking machinery; numerically controlled metal cutting machine tools

(G-9129)
MK SYSTEMS INCORPORATED (PA)
1455 Brummel Ave (60007-2110)
PHONE..................................847 709-6180
Brien Buelow, *President*
Thomas Kubik, *Admin Sec*
EMP: 14
SALES (est): 3.1MM **Privately Held**
SIC: 3599 Machine & other job shop work

(G-9130)
MODERN AIDS INC
201 Bond St (60007-1220)
PHONE..................................847 437-8600
Douglas E Croft, *President*
Ron Andrews, *Natl Sales Mgr*
Douglas Croft, *Prgrmr*
Larry A Lewis, *Admin Sec*
EMP: 20
SQ FT: 11,000
SALES (est): 5.1MM **Privately Held**
SIC: 3842 Gauze, surgical

(G-9131)
MONOTYPE IMAGING INC
25 Northwest Point Blvd # 525 (60007-1056)
PHONE..................................847 631-1111
Steve Kuhlman, *General Mgr*
EMP: 15
SALES (corp-wide): 381.6MM **Privately Held**
SIC: 7372 Prepackaged software
HQ: Monotype Imaging Inc.
600 Unicorn Park Dr
Woburn MA 01801

(G-9132)
MOSS HOLDING COMPANY (HQ)
2600 Elmhurst Rd (60007-6312)
P.O. Box 36547 Treasury, Chicago (60694-0001)
PHONE..................................847 238-4200
Dan Patterson, *President*
Constance Brooks, *Manager*
▲ **EMP:** 160
SALES (est): 59.3MM **Privately Held**
SIC: 2399 2541 2211 Banners, pennants & flags; store & office display cases & fixtures; stretch fabrics, cotton

(G-9133)
MOSS INC (PA)
2600 Elmhurst Rd (60007-6312)
P.O. Box 248, Belfast ME (04915-0248)
PHONE..................................800 341-1557
Dan Patterson, *President*
Mark Ollinger, *CFO*
EMP: 9
SALES (est): 12.4MM **Privately Held**
SIC: 2759 Commercial printing

(G-9134)
MOTION ACCESS LLC
775 Nicholas Blvd (60007-2508)
PHONE..................................847 357-8832
Michael Valencia, *Marketing Staff*
Robert Oakley, *Mng Member*
▲ **EMP:** 30
SALES (est): 3.7MM **Privately Held**
SIC: 2431 Doors & door parts & trim, wood

(G-9135)
MOTOR OIL INC
2250 Arthur Ave (60007-6011)
PHONE..................................847 956-7550
Thomas G Sullivan, *President*
EMP: 10
SQ FT: 5,000
SALES (est): 1.1MM **Privately Held**
SIC: 2992 5172 Oils & greases, blending & compounding; lubricating oils & greases

(G-9136)
MR RAKESH AVICHAL
2649 Greenleaf Ave (60007-5512)
PHONE..................................224 735-0505
EMP: 3 EST: 2017
SALES (est): 188.5K **Privately Held**
SIC: 3672 Printed circuit boards

(G-9137)
MSC PRE FINISH METALS EGV INC (HQ)
2250 Pratt Blvd (60007-5917)
PHONE..................................847 439-2210
Gerald G Nadig, *Ch of Bd*
Douglas M Rose, *President*
Jim Augsburger, *Engineer*
James Waclawik Sr, *CFO*
EMP: 230
SQ FT: 233,000
SALES (est): 53MM
SALES (corp-wide): 119.1MM **Privately Held**
SIC: 3479 3471 3399 Coating of metals & formed products; electroplating of metals or formed products; laminating steel
PA: Material Sciences Corporation
6855 Commerce Blvd
Canton MI 48187
734 207-4444

(G-9138)
MTA USA CORP
501 Lively Blvd (60007-2013)
PHONE..................................847 847-5503
Antonio Falchetti, *President*
▲ **EMP:** 7
SQ FT: 7,000
SALES: 3MM
SALES (corp-wide): 195.3MM **Privately Held**
SIC: 3694 Engine electrical equipment
PA: Mta Spa
Viale Dell'industria 12
Codogno LO 26845
037 741-8493

(G-9139)
MUELLER MFG CORP (PA)
Also Called: Mueller Metal Products
300 Lively Blvd (60007-2010)
PHONE..................................847 640-1666
Anton Mueller, *President*
Anne Mueller, *Treasurer*
Ronald Mueller, *Admin Sec*
EMP: 30 EST: 1969
SQ FT: 90,000
SALES (est): 5.2MM **Privately Held**
SIC: 3469 5084 Stamping metal for the trade; industrial machinery & equipment

(G-9140)
MUELLER ORNAMENTAL IRON WORKS
655 Lively Blvd (60007-2015)
PHONE..................................847 758-9941
Robert C Mueller, *President*
Lyn Mueller, *Vice Pres*
Lynn Parquette, *Treasurer*
Marilyn Mueller, *Admin Sec*
EMP: 10 EST: 1933
SALES (est): 1.9MM **Privately Held**
WEB: www.ornamentaliron.net
SIC: 3446 Fences or posts, ornamental iron or steel; railings, prefabricated metal; gates, ornamental metal

(G-9141)
MWW FOOD PROCESSING USA LLC (HQ)
Also Called: Thurne USA
2567 Greenleaf Ave (60007-5511)
PHONE..................................773 478-9700
Pj Jongen, *President*
EMP: 6 EST: 2015
SALES (est): 826K
SALES (corp-wide): 2.9B **Publicly Held**
SIC: 3556 1796 Cutting, chopping, grinding, mixing & similar machinery; machinery installation
PA: The Middleby Corporation
1400 Toastmaster Dr
Elgin IL 60120
847 741-3300

(G-9142)
NACME STEEL PROCESSING LLC
1965 Pratt Blvd (60007-5905)
PHONE..................................847 806-7226
Grant Kottemeyer, *Principal*
EMP: 7
SALES (est): 510K **Privately Held**
SIC: 3312 Blast furnaces & steel mills

(G-9143)
NANTPHARMA LLC
1300 Chase Ave (60007-4813)
PHONE..................................847 243-1200
Kevin Forney, *Vice Pres*
Rachana Vyas, *Research*
Bob Pahl, *Director*
EMP: 154

GEOGRAPHIC SECTION — Elk Grove Village - Cook County (G-9169)

SALES (est): 8.7MM
SALES (corp-wide): 187.2MM **Publicly Held**
WEB: www.nantpharma.com
SIC: 2834 Adrenal pharmaceutical preparations
PA: Nantworks, Llc
  2040 E Mariposa Ave
  El Segundo CA 90245
  310 883-1300

(G-9144)
NATIONAL MATERIAL COMPANY LLC (HQ)
1965 Pratt Blvd (60007-5905)
PHONE.....................847 806-7200
Bruce Henderson, *Sales Staff*
Vytas P Ambutas,
Ray Cellucci, *Administration*
EMP: 50
SALES (est): 125.3MM
SALES (corp-wide): 824.7MM **Privately Held**
SIC: 3315 3341 3399 Wire, ferrous/iron; aluminum smelting & refining (secondary); aluminum atomized powder
PA: National Material L.P.
  1965 Pratt Blvd
  Elk Grove Village IL 60007
  847 806-7200

(G-9145)
NBS CORPORATION
1501 Tonne Rd (60007-5004)
PHONE.....................847 860-8856
Don Ou, *President*
EMP: 4
SALES (corp-wide): 7.3MM **Privately Held**
SIC: 3965 Fasteners
PA: Nbs Corporation
  3100 E Slauson Ave
  Vernon CA 90058
  323 923-1627

(G-9146)
NEW CHICAGO WHOLESALE BKY INC
Also Called: Chicago Gourmet Wholesale Bky
795 Touhy Ave (60007-4915)
PHONE.....................847 981-1600
Juliana Achimas, *President*
Marius Achimas, *Vice Pres*
EMP: 42
SQ FT: 20,000
SALES (est): 7.2MM **Privately Held**
SIC: 2051 Bagels, fresh or frozen; pastries, e.g. danish: except frozen; cakes, pies & pastries; croissants, except frozen

(G-9147)
NICHIDEN USA CORP
2228 Landmeier Rd (60007-2617)
PHONE.....................224 266-2928
EMP: 7
SALES (est): 1.2MM **Privately Held**
SIC: 3824 Mechanical & electromechanical counters & devices

(G-9148)
NIDEC MOTOR CORPORATION
Merkle-Korff Industries
25 Northwest Point Blvd # 900
(60007-1056)
PHONE.....................847 439-3760
Kevin Machalek, *Vice Pres*
Maria Sanchez, *Human Res Mgr*
EMP: 75 **Privately Held**
SIC: 3621 Motors, electric
HQ: Nidec Motor Corporation
  8050 West Florissant Ave
  Saint Louis MO 63136

(G-9149)
NISSEI AMERICA INC
721 Landmeier Rd (60007-4757)
PHONE.....................847 228-5000
Peter Pollack, *Manager*
EMP: 8 **Privately Held**
WEB: www.nisseiamerica.com
SIC: 5084 3089 Plastic products machinery; extruded finished plastic products
HQ: Nissei America, Inc.
  1480 N Hancock St
  Anaheim CA 92807
  714 693-3000

(G-9150)
NORDENT MANUFACTURING INC
610 Bonnie Ln (60007-2379)
PHONE.....................847 437-4780
Richard Martin, *President*
Peter Martin, *Principal*
Joe Martin, *Vice Pres*
Robert Tatum, *Vice Pres*
Thomas Stopka, *Prdtn Mgr*
EMP: 20 **EST:** 1969
SQ FT: 5,000
SALES: 5.5MM **Privately Held**
SIC: 3843 7699 3841 Dental equipment; dental instrument repair; surgical & medical instruments

(G-9151)
NORTH AMERICA PACKAGING CORP
2350 Lively Blvd (60007-6723)
PHONE.....................847 979-1625
Tamara Vasquez, *Branch Mgr*
EMP: 12
SALES (corp-wide): 1.2B **Privately Held**
WEB: www.bwaycorp.com
SIC: 3411 Metal cans
HQ: North America Packaging Corp
  1515 W 22nd St Ste 550
  Oak Brook IL 60523
  630 203-4100

(G-9152)
NORTH AMERICAN EN INC
776 Lunt Ave (60007-5025)
PHONE.....................847 952-3680
Louis Brosio, *CEO*
Michael Brosio, *President*
David Brosio, *Treasurer*
EMP: 17 **EST:** 1998
SQ FT: 5,000
SALES (est): 2.3MM **Privately Held**
WEB: www.northamericanen.com
SIC: 3471 Plating of metals or formed products

(G-9153)
NORTH SHORE CONSULTANTS INC
Also Called: En Es Cee Technology
613 Thorndale Ave (60007-4334)
PHONE.....................847 290-1599
Audrey Wojtecki, *President*
Dennis Wojtecki, *Treasurer*
EMP: 5
SALES (est): 460K **Privately Held**
SIC: 2891 8748 5169 Adhesives; business consulting; chemicals & allied products

(G-9154)
NORTHFIELD INDUSTRIES
160 N Lively Blvd (60007-1318)
PHONE.....................847 981-7530
EMP: 2
SALES (est): 208.2K **Privately Held**
SIC: 3999 Manufacturing industries

(G-9155)
NORTHWEST MOLD & MACHINE CORP
131 Martin Ln (60007-1309)
PHONE.....................847 690-1501
Stanouy Kaczor, *President*
EMP: 5
SQ FT: 2,000
SALES (est): 600K **Privately Held**
SIC: 3599 Machine shop, jobbing & repair

(G-9156)
NU-WAY ELECTRONICS INC
Also Called: Nuway Electronics
165 Martin Ln (60007-1309)
PHONE.....................847 437-7120
William N Aldeen, *President*
Alina Rymsza, *CFO*
EMP: 36
SQ FT: 15,000
SALES (est): 6.7MM **Privately Held**
SIC: 3679 5065 Harness assemblies for electronic use: wire or cable; electronic parts

(G-9157)
OAKLEY INDUSTRIAL MCHY INC
1601 Lunt Ave (60007-5616)
PHONE.....................847 966-0052
Andrea Solimbergo, *President*
Elisabetta Trolese, *Chairman*
Carl T Kamys, *COO*
Chris Gulik, *Chief Engr*
Mark Karr, *Sales Mgr*
▼ **EMP:** 25 **EST:** 2010
SALES: 4MM
SALES (corp-wide): 957.2K **Privately Held**
SIC: 3567 Heating units & devices, industrial: electric
PA: Csm Holding Spa
  Via Friuli 11
  San Vendemiano TV 31020

(G-9158)
OBERG MEDICAL PRODUCTS CO LLC
330 Crossen Ave (60007-2002)
PHONE.....................847 364-4750
Kurt Wendhack, *Manager*
EMP: 20
SALES (corp-wide): 217.4MM **Privately Held**
SIC: 3841 Surgical & medical instruments
HQ: Oberg Medical Products Company, Llc
  273 N Pike Rd
  Sarver PA 16055
  724 295-2121

(G-9159)
OCTAVIA TOOL & GAGE COMPANY
135 Kelly St (60007-1011)
PHONE.....................847 913-9233
Larry Rust, *President*
EMP: 4 **EST:** 1957
SQ FT: 1,500
SALES: 500K **Privately Held**
WEB: www.octaviatool.com
SIC: 3544 3469 Special dies & tools; metal stampings

(G-9160)
OHARE SPRING COMPANY INC
930 Lee St (60007-1207)
PHONE.....................847 298-1360
John Schneider, *President*
Jim Vyleta, *General Mgr*
Dan Shnieder, *Plant Mgr*
Kathy Schneider, *Treasurer*
Jeff Adams, *Manager*
EMP: 20 **EST:** 1964
SQ FT: 28,000
SALES (est): 3.9MM **Privately Held**
WEB: www.oharespring.com
SIC: 3495 3469 3496 Mechanical springs, precision; stamping metal for the trade; wire winding

(G-9161)
OLDCASTLE BUILDINGENVELOPE INC
2901 Lively Blvd (60007-6735)
PHONE.....................630 250-7270
Fred Stella, *Manager*
EMP: 20
SALES (corp-wide): 30.6B **Privately Held**
SIC: 3231 Tempered glass: made from purchased glass; insulating glass: made from purchased glass
HQ: Oldcastle Buildingenvelope, Inc.
  5005 Lyndon B Johnson Fwy # 1050
  Dallas TX 75244
  214 273-3400

(G-9162)
OMEGA MOULDING NORTH AMER INC
1420 Thorndale Ave (60007-6751)
PHONE.....................630 509-2397
Jose Avita, *Branch Mgr*
EMP: 4 **Privately Held**
SIC: 2431 Moldings, wood: unfinished & prefinished
PA: Omega Moulding North America, Inc.
  1 Sawgrass Dr
  Bellport NY 11713

(G-9163)
OMEGA ROYAL GRAPHICS INC
1621 Brummel Ave (60007-2125)
PHONE.....................847 952-8000
Kenneth Grimshaw, *President*
Kenneth David, *Vice Pres*
Ann Grimshaw, *Treasurer*
EMP: 10
SQ FT: 15,000
SALES: 1.3MM **Privately Held**
SIC: 2752 Commercial printing, offset

(G-9164)
ONLINE ELECTRONICS INC
Also Called: Overnite Protos
1261 Jarvis Ave (60007-2301)
PHONE.....................847 871-1700
Aziz Ajani, *CEO*
Dilkhush Bhayani, *President*
EMP: 35
SALES (est): 4.9MM **Privately Held**
SIC: 3672 8711 Circuit boards, television & radio printed; electrical or electronic engineering

(G-9165)
OPTIMAL AUTOMATICS CO
120 Stanley St (60007-1554)
PHONE.....................847 439-9110
John Georgis, *President*
▼ **EMP:** 7
SQ FT: 8,000
SALES (est): 1.2MM **Privately Held**
SIC: 3589 3556 Commercial cooking & foodwarming equipment; food products machinery

(G-9166)
P M S CONSOLIDATED
2400 E Devon Ave (60007-6034)
PHONE.....................847 364-0011
Kurt Walker, *Plant Mgr*
EMP: 4
SALES (est): 343.8K **Privately Held**
SIC: 2821 Plastics materials & resins

(G-9167)
P-AMERICAS LLC
Also Called: Pepsico
1500 Touhy Ave (60007-5308)
PHONE.....................847 437-1520
Mark Ladick, *General Mgr*
Dan Grdycowski, *Manager*
EMP: 95
SALES (corp-wide): 67.1B **Publicly Held**
SIC: 2086 Carbonated soft drinks, bottled & canned
HQ: P-Americas Llc
  1 Pepsi Way
  Somers NY 10589
  336 896-5740

(G-9168)
PACKAGING CORPORATION AMERICA
Also Called: Boise Paper
25 Northwest Point Blvd (60007-1056)
PHONE.....................224 404-6616
Suzi Palmer, *Analyst*
EMP: 6
SALES (corp-wide): 6.9B **Publicly Held**
WEB: www.boisepaper.com
SIC: 2621 Paper mills
PA: Packaging Corporation Of America
  1 N Field Ct
  Lake Forest IL 60045
  847 482-3000

(G-9169)
PARKER-HANNIFIN CORPORATION
Also Called: Mobile Systems
850 Arthur Ave (60007-5215)
PHONE.....................847 258-6200
Jason Coolick, *Engineer*
Robert Metsker, *Sales Staff*
Donald E Washkewicz, *Manager*
Anthony Wroblewski, *Manager*
Joan Hawthorne, *Administration*
EMP: 120
SALES (corp-wide): 14.3B **Publicly Held**
WEB: www.phtruck.com
SIC: 3594 Fluid power pumps & motors

(PA)=Parent Co (HQ)=Headquarters (DH)=Div Headquarters
✪ = New Business established in last 2 years

Elk Grove Village - Cook County (G-9170)

PA: Parker-Hannifin Corporation
6035 Parkland Blvd
Cleveland OH 44124
216 896-3000

(G-9170)
PAULSON PRESS INC
Also Called: Paulson's Litho
904 Cambridge Dr (60007-2435)
PHONE..................................847 290-0080
Ben Letto, *President*
Paul Letto, *Vice Pres*
Anthony Letto, *Treasurer*
Vince Letto, *Admin Sec*
EMP: 28
SQ FT: 20,000
SALES (est): 5.8MM **Privately Held**
WEB: www.paulsonpressinc
SIC: 2752 Commercial printing, offset; lithographing on metal

(G-9171)
PCB EXPRESS INC
600 E Higgins Rd Ste 2c (60007-1500)
PHONE..................................847 952-8896
Pragna Patel, *President*
Bobbie Goldberg, *Sales Executive*
EMP: 3
SALES: 1.5MM **Privately Held**
SIC: 3672 Printed circuit boards

(G-9172)
PERFECTION PLATING INC (PA)
775 Morse Ave (60007-5184)
PHONE..................................847 593-6506
Randy G Zitella, *President*
Chuck Wulf, *Vice Pres*
EMP: 54
SQ FT: 65,000
SALES (est): 14.3MM **Privately Held**
WEB: www.perfectionplate.com
SIC: 3471 Electroplating of metals or formed products

(G-9173)
PERFECTION PLATING INC
1521 Morse Ave (60007-5723)
PHONE..................................847 593-6506
EMP: 66
SALES (corp-wide): 14.3MM **Privately Held**
SIC: 3471 Electroplating of metals or formed products
PA: Perfection Plating Inc
775 Morse Ave
Elk Grove Village IL 60007
847 593-6506

(G-9174)
PERMATRON CORPORATION
2020 Touhy Ave (60007-5318)
PHONE..................................847 434-1421
Leslye Sandberg, *President*
Gayle Matthies, *President*
Matthew Jason, *Accounts Mgr*
Leslye Palmer, *Accounts Mgr*
Jim Moran, *Sales Staff*
▲ **EMP:** 20
SQ FT: 13,000
SALES (est): 4.5MM **Privately Held**
WEB: www.permatron.com
SIC: 1711 3564 Plumbing, heating, air-conditioning contractors; filters, air: furnaces, air conditioning equipment, etc.

(G-9175)
PETE FRCANO SONS CSTM HM BLDRS
1225 Howard St (60007-2219)
PHONE..................................847 258-4626
Pete Fricano, *President*
EMP: 11
SALES (est): 211.4K **Privately Held**
SIC: 1521 1542 2842 New construction, single-family houses; commercial & office buildings, renovation & repair; specialty cleaning preparations

(G-9176)
PETERSEN ALUMINUM CORPORATION (HQ)
Also Called: Pac-Clad Metal Roofing
1005 Tonne Rd (60007-4817)
PHONE..................................847 228-7150
Michael L Petersen, *President*
Greg Beane, *Regional Mgr*
Kevin Riordan, *Regional Mgr*
Mark Goyke, *Plant Mgr*
Joe Hertvik, *Project Mgr*
◆ **EMP:** 52
SQ FT: 80,000
SALES (est): 73.6MM
SALES (corp-wide): 4.8B **Publicly Held**
WEB: www.pac-clad.com
SIC: 3444 5033 Metal roofing & roof drainage equipment; roofing & siding materials
PA: Carlisle Companies Incorporated
16430 N Scottsdale Rd # 400
Scottsdale AZ 85254
480 781-5000

(G-9177)
PETERSEN FINISHING CORPORATION (PA)
1005 Tonne Rd (60007-4817)
PHONE..................................847 228-7150
John P Paleczny, *President*
Michael Petersen, *Vice Pres*
William Kurth, *Shareholder*
Ann Petersen, *Shareholder*
Kathryn Petersen, *Shareholder*
EMP: 3
SQ FT: 80,000
SALES (est): 1.1MM **Privately Held**
SIC: 3471 Anodizing (plating) of metals or formed products

(G-9178)
PHOENIX TOOL CORP
700 Lunt Ave (60007-5025)
PHONE..................................847 956-1886
Henry E Bauerle, *President*
Frieda Bauerle, *Admin Sec*
▲ **EMP:** 14 **EST:** 1972
SQ FT: 12,800
SALES (est): 2.4MM **Privately Held**
SIC: 3544 3599 Industrial molds; machine shop, jobbing & repair

(G-9179)
PILLARHOUSE USA INC
201 Lively Blvd (60007-1622)
PHONE..................................847 593-9080
Jonathan Wol, *President*
Adrian De'ath, *Vice Pres*
Jacqueline Wray, *Admin Sec*
EMP: 10
SQ FT: 15,000
SALES: 9MM **Privately Held**
SIC: 5084 7699 7694 Machine tools & metalworking machinery; industrial machinery & equipment repair; coil winding service

(G-9180)
PK CORPORATION
527 Newberry Dr (60007-2740)
PHONE..................................847 879-1070
Petre Kazakov, *President*
EMP: 7
SALES (est): 856.8K **Privately Held**
SIC: 3715 Truck trailers

(G-9181)
PMI CARTONING INC
Also Called: PMI Kyoto Packaging Systems
850 Pratt Blvd (60007-5117)
PHONE..................................847 437-1427
Branko Tisma, *President*
Branko Vukotic, *Managing Dir*
Lilly Tisma, *Vice Pres*
Zika Marjanovic, *Plant Engr Mgr*
Srdjan Marsenic, *Engineer*
EMP: 100
SQ FT: 110,000
SALES (est): 21.2MM **Privately Held**
SIC: 3565 Packaging machinery

(G-9182)
POLYFORM PRODUCTS COMPANY
1901 Estes Ave (60007-5415)
PHONE..................................847 427-0020
Denice Steinmann, *President*
Wayne Marsh, *Vice Pres*
Ray Simmons, *Vice Pres*
Colleen Holmquist, *Purchasing*
Joseph Croughan, *QC Mgr*
◆ **EMP:** 40
SQ FT: 58,000
SALES (est): 8.4MM **Privately Held**
WEB: www.sculpey.com
SIC: 3952 5945 3295 2821 Modeling clay; hobby, toy & game shops; minerals, ground or treated; plastics materials & resins

(G-9183)
POLYONE CORPORATION
2400 E Devon Ave (60007-6034)
PHONE..................................847 364-0011
Kurt Walker, *Branch Mgr*
Telesforo Castaneda, *Manager*
David Petrosius, *Technical Staff*
EMP: 89 **Publicly Held**
SIC: 2865 2851 2816 Dyes & pigments; paints & allied products; inorganic pigments
PA: Polyone Corporation
33587 Walker Rd
Avon Lake OH 44012

(G-9184)
POSSEHL CONNECTOR SVCS SC INC
1521 Morse Ave (60007-5781)
PHONE..................................803 366-8316
Al Davis, *Engineer*
Darrell Shaw, *Branch Mgr*
EMP: 40
SALES (corp-wide): 360.4K **Privately Held**
WEB: www.possehlconnector.com
SIC: 3643 3471 Electric connectors; plating & polishing
HQ: Possehl Connector Services S.C., Inc.
445 Bryant Blvd
Rock Hill SC 29732
803 366-8316

(G-9185)
POST PRESS PRODUCTION INC (PA)
Also Called: Pp3
2601 Lively Blvd (60007-6730)
PHONE..................................630 860-9833
Steven Olandese, *President*
John J Mascari, *Vice Pres*
Ajay Sharma, *Vice Pres*
EMP: 16
SQ FT: 68,000
SALES (est): 2.9MM **Privately Held**
SIC: 2782 Blankbooks & looseleaf binders

(G-9186)
POWELL TREE CARE INC
212 E Devon Ave (60007-4037)
P.O. Box 1514 (60009-1514)
PHONE..................................847 364-1181
David Powell, *President*
EMP: 4
SALES (est): 260K **Privately Held**
SIC: 0783 1629 2411 4959 Tree trimming services for public utility lines; removal services, bush & tree; land clearing contractor; wood chips, produced in the field; snowplowing; wood (fuel)

(G-9187)
POWER LUBE LLC
1461 Busse Rd (60007-5323)
PHONE..................................847 806-7022
Jeno Han, *Mng Member*
EMP: 5
SALES (est): 626.4K **Privately Held**
WEB: www.trucklubeandwash.com
SIC: 2911 Oils, lubricating

(G-9188)
PRE FNISH MTALS MRRISVILLE INC
2250 Pratt Blvd (60007-5917)
PHONE..................................847 439-2211
Gerald Nadig, *Ch of Bd*
Martin A Scott, *Sales Mgr*
▲ **EMP:** 75
SQ FT: 116,000
SALES (est): 7.8MM
SALES (corp-wide): 119.1MM **Privately Held**
SIC: 3479 3621 Painting, coating & hot dipping; coating of metals & formed products; coating of metals with plastic or resins; painting of metal products; motors & generators
HQ: Msc Pre Finish Metals (Egv) Inc.
2250 Pratt Blvd
Elk Grove Village IL 60007
847 439-2210

(G-9189)
PRECISION GRINDING INC
2375 American Ln (60007-6201)
PHONE..................................847 238-1000
Shamkant Shirsat, *President*
Walter Malek, *Vice Pres*
EMP: 8
SQ FT: 8,500
SALES: 850K **Privately Held**
SIC: 3599 Machine shop, jobbing & repair

(G-9190)
PRECISION INC
2210 Elmhurst Rd (60007-6309)
PHONE..................................847 593-2947
James De Roche, *President*
EMP: 3
SALES (est): 292.4K **Privately Held**
SIC: 3599 Machine shop, jobbing & repair

(G-9191)
PRECISION INK CORPORATION
151 Stanley St (60007-1555)
PHONE..................................847 952-1500
Rod Cartwright, *President*
Matt Cartwright, *Sales Staff*
Kyle Hermanny, *Sales Staff*
EMP: 10
SQ FT: 6,000
SALES (est): 2MM **Privately Held**
WEB: www.precisioninkcorp.com
SIC: 2893 Printing ink

(G-9192)
PRECISION PROCESS CORP
1401 Brummel Ave (60007-2110)
PHONE..................................847 640-9820
Vladimir A Moskin, *President*
Kris Parzatka, *Engineer*
Ellie Nikolaeva, *Executive Asst*
EMP: 26
SQ FT: 14,000
SALES (est): 5.2MM **Privately Held**
SIC: 3544 Special dies & tools

(G-9193)
PRECISION TOOL WELDING
991 Oakton St (60007-1905)
PHONE..................................630 285-9844
Gary Welther, *Owner*
EMP: 4
SALES (est): 444.6K **Privately Held**
SIC: 7692 Welding repair

(G-9194)
PREGEL AMERICA
915 Busse Rd (60007-2400)
PHONE..................................847 258-3725
EMP: 3 **EST:** 2017
SALES (est): 142.8K **Privately Held**
SIC: 2099 Food preparations

(G-9195)
PRESS AMERICA INC
661 Fargo Ave (60007-4742)
PHONE..................................847 228-0333
Martin D'Amico, *President*
Jeffrey Prenzno, *Manager*
Debra D'Amico, *Admin Sec*
▲ **EMP:** 30
SQ FT: 12,500
SALES (est): 5.6MM **Privately Held**
WEB: www.pressamerica.com
SIC: 2752 Commercial printing, offset

(G-9196)
PRIME BLEND LLC
1300 Pratt Blvd (60007-5711)
PHONE..................................866 217-3732
EMP: 14
SALES (corp-wide): 4.5MM **Privately Held**
SIC: 2891 Adhesives & sealants
PA: Prime Blend Llc
24 Louella Ct Ste 200
Wayne PA 19087
866 217-3732

Elk Grove Village - Cook County (G-9226)

(G-9197)
PRIMEDGE INC (PA)
1281 Arthur Ave (60007-5705)
PHONE.....................224 265-6600
Ivo Cozzini, *President*
Peter Samson, *Exec VP*
Marcelo Zocchi, *Exec VP*
Annette Tuzzolino, *Purch Mgr*
Kerry Struecker, *Design Engr*
◆ **EMP:** 160
SQ FT: 70,000
SALES (est): 45.1MM **Privately Held**
SIC: 3556 5072 Meat processing machinery; cutlery

(G-9198)
PRINTING WORKS INC
Also Called: Printing Works II, The
2485 E Devon Ave (60007-6212)
PHONE.....................847 860-1920
Paul Mulvey, *CEO*
EMP: 3
SALES (est): 115.1K **Privately Held**
SIC: 2752 Commercial printing, lithographic

(G-9199)
PROTEIN2O INC
815 Bonnie Ln (60007-2224)
PHONE.....................646 919-5320
Robert Kral, *CEO*
David Baum, *Founder*
Joey Suhey, *Founder*
Rob Kral, *Vice Pres*
EMP: 20
SQ FT: 18,000
SALES: 16MM **Privately Held**
SIC: 2086 Mineral water, carbonated: packaged in cans, bottles, etc.

(G-9200)
PROTEPO LTD (PA)
906 Mayfair Ct (60007-3478)
PHONE.....................847 466-1023
Lynette Sowler, *President*
Lynette Fowler, *President*
Vasilis Katsoulis, *CTO*
EMP: 5
SQ FT: 500
SALES: 1MM **Privately Held**
SIC: 7372 Prepackaged software

(G-9201)
PULSARLUBE USA INC
1480 Howard St (60007-2221)
PHONE.....................847 593-5300
Yun J Yang, *President*
Bill Zavala, *Vice Pres*
▲ **EMP:** 5
SALES (est): 400K **Privately Held**
SIC: 3569 Lubrication equipment, industrial

(G-9202)
PULVER INC
Also Called: Mailers Company
575 Bennett Rd (60007-1101)
PHONE.....................847 734-9000
Patrick Pulver, *President*
Nanci Thompson, *Vice Pres*
Ashley Clark, *Sales Staff*
Dawn Pulver, *Admin Sec*
EMP: 20
SQ FT: 50,000
SALES (est): 6.1MM **Privately Held**
SIC: 2631 Container, packaging & boxboard

(G-9203)
QCIRCUITS INC (PA)
2574 United Ln (60007-6819)
PHONE.....................847 797-6678
Jeffery Cosman, *President*
Ed Waytula, *Vice Pres*
▲ **EMP:** 65
SALES (est): 10.2MM **Privately Held**
WEB: www.qcircuits.com
SIC: 3677 3672 3679 Coil windings, electronic; printed circuit boards; electronic circuits

(G-9204)
QUALITY FINISHING SERVICE INC
1461 Mark St (60007-6716)
PHONE.....................847 616-0336
Jose Rincon, *President*
EMP: 1
SALES (est): 209.8K **Privately Held**
SIC: 2434 Wood kitchen cabinets

(G-9205)
QUALITY PAPER INC
1855 Greenleaf Ave (60007-5501)
PHONE.....................847 258-3999
EMP: 15 **EST:** 2012
SALES (est): 1.5MM **Privately Held**
SIC: 2679 Mfg Converted Paper Products

(G-9206)
QUANTUM STORAGE SYSTEMS
2600 United Ln (60007-6821)
PHONE.....................630 274-6610
Brett Conley, *President*
EMP: 2
SALES (est): 215.9K **Privately Held**
SIC: 2541 Shelving, office & store, wood

(G-9207)
QWIK-TIP INC
2415 E Higgins Rd (60007-2605)
PHONE.....................847 640-7387
Warren Osborn, *President*
EMP: 3
SALES (est): 284.5K **Privately Held**
SIC: 3714 Motor vehicle body components & frame

(G-9208)
R & G SPRING CO INC
1451 Landmeier Rd Ste L (60007-2462)
PHONE.....................847 228-5640
Roman Hudec, *Owner*
Elizabeth Hudec, *Vice Pres*
EMP: 4
SQ FT: 120,000
SALES: 280K **Privately Held**
SIC: 3493 3495 5085 Steel springs, except wire; wire springs; springs

(G-9209)
R B M TOOL INC
2545 American Ln (60007-6205)
P.O. Box 1467 (60009-1467)
PHONE.....................630 422-7065
Joseph Kowalczyk, *President*
Krystyna Kowalczyk, *Admin Sec*
EMP: 5
SQ FT: 12,500
SALES (est): 333.3K **Privately Held**
SIC: 3599 Machine shop, jobbing & repair

(G-9210)
R R DONNELLEY & SONS COMPANY
Also Called: Bruce Offset
1099 Greenleaf Ave (60007-5012)
PHONE.....................847 593-1200
Jeff Brusick, *Branch Mgr*
EMP: 56
SALES (corp-wide): 6.2B **Publicly Held**
WEB: www.rrdonnelley.com
SIC: 2761 5943 Computer forms, manifold or continuous; office forms & supplies
PA: R. R. Donnelley & Sons Company
35 W Wacker Dr
Chicago IL 60601
312 326-8000

(G-9211)
R R DONNELLEY & SONS COMPANY
Also Called: District 32820
2075 Busse Rd (60007-5738)
PHONE.....................847 956-4187
Jeff Berzek, *Manager*
EMP: 6
SALES (corp-wide): 6.2B **Publicly Held**
SIC: 2761 5943 Manifold business forms; office forms & supplies
PA: R. R. Donnelley & Sons Company
35 W Wacker Dr
Chicago IL 60601
312 326-8000

(G-9212)
RAINBOW COLORS INC
935 Lee St (60007-1206)
PHONE.....................847 640-7700
Pankaj Patel, *President*
Patrick McDonnell, *Sales Staff*
EMP: 12 **EST:** 2008
SALES (est): 2.2MM **Privately Held**
WEB: www.rainbowcolorsinc.com
SIC: 3083 Plastic finished products, laminated

(G-9213)
RANDALL PUBLICATIONS (PA)
1840 Jarvis Ave (60007-2440)
PHONE.....................847 437-6604
Michael Goldstein, *Editor*
Luann Harrold, *Accountant*
Dorothy Fiandaca, *Executive*
EMP: 15
SALES (est): 1.8MM **Privately Held**
SIC: 2721 Magazines: publishing only, not printed on site

(G-9214)
RANDALL PUBLISHING INC
Also Called: Gear Technology
1425 Lunt Ave (60007-5621)
P.O. Box 1426 (60009-1426)
PHONE.....................847 437-6604
Michael Goldstein, *President*
Richard Goldstein, *Vice Pres*
EMP: 12
SALES (est): 1.2MM **Privately Held**
SIC: 2721 5084 Magazines: publishing only, not printed on site; industrial machinery & equipment

(G-9215)
REBECHINI STUDIO INC
Also Called: 680 Design
680 Fargo Ave (60007-4701)
PHONE.....................847 437-9030
Glenn Rebechini, *Owner*
Vince Papp, *Foreman/Supr*
Tony Comerci, *Sales Associate*
EMP: 17
SQ FT: 20,000
SALES (est): 2.5MM **Privately Held**
SIC: 3479 3993 8999 Etching on metals; electric signs; letters for signs, metal; signs, not made in custom sign painting shops; sculptor's studio

(G-9216)
REDEEN ENGRAVING INC
670 Chase Ave (60007-4802)
PHONE.....................847 593-6500
Floyd Redeen, *President*
EMP: 8
SQ FT: 6,000
SALES (est): 741.9K **Privately Held**
SIC: 2759 3544 Embossing on paper; special dies, tools, jigs & fixtures

(G-9217)
REPRO-GRAPHICS INC
1900 Arthur Ave (60007-6005)
PHONE.....................847 439-1775
John Schiele, *President*
Steve Funk, *CFO*
Jim Bellavia, *Supervisor*
Andy Olcott, *Director*
EMP: 70
SQ FT: 50,000
SALES (est): 22.1MM **Privately Held**
WEB: www.schielegroup.com
SIC: 2752 Commercial printing, offset

(G-9218)
RJ STUCKEL CO INC
94 Garlisch Dr (60007-1316)
PHONE.....................800 789-7220
Robert W Stuckel, *President*
▲ **EMP:** 20 **EST:** 1952
SQ FT: 35,000
SALES (est): 4.1MM **Privately Held**
SIC: 3469 3544 Stamping metal for the trade; die sets for metal stamping (presses)

(G-9219)
RODE WELDING INC
1211 Louis Ave (60007-2307)
PHONE.....................847 439-0910
Ken Slattery, *Director*
EMP: 25
SALES: 2MM **Privately Held**
SIC: 3443 3449 Cylinders, pressure: metal plate; bars, concrete reinforcing: fabricated steel

(G-9220)
ROLLEX CORPORATION (PA)
800 Chase Ave (60007-4806)
PHONE.....................847 437-3000
Bruce Stevens, *Ch of Bd*
James L Brittingham, *President*
Edwin Figueroa, *Opers Mgr*
Mike Shield, *Mfg Staff*
John Foley, *CFO*
EMP: 125 **EST:** 1950
SQ FT: 120,000
SALES (est): 94.6MM **Privately Held**
WEB: www.rollex.com
SIC: 3444 Gutters, sheet metal; siding, sheet metal

(G-9221)
ROPAK CENTRAL INC
Also Called: Linpac Ropak Packaging Central
1350 Arthur Ave (60007-5741)
PHONE.....................847 956-0750
Kenneth Roessler, *President*
Ronald W Cameron, *Vice Pres*
Terry Drainer, *Plant Mgr*
Eria M Kalawski, *Admin Sec*
▲ **EMP:** 85 **EST:** 1979
SQ FT: 161,000
SALES: 18.6MM
SALES (corp-wide): 1.2B **Privately Held**
SIC: 3089 Blow molded finished plastic products; injection molded finished plastic products; plastic containers, except foam
HQ: Ropak Corporation
10540 Talbert Ave 200w
Fountain Valley CA 92708
714 845-2845

(G-9222)
ROYAL FOODS & FLAVORS INC
2456 American Ln (60007-6204)
PHONE.....................847 595-9166
Harish Gadhvi, *President*
Dan Bhagat, *Manager*
▲ **EMP:** 10
SQ FT: 10,000
SALES (est): 1.4MM **Privately Held**
SIC: 2099 2087 Seasonings: dry mixes; flavoring extracts & syrups

(G-9223)
RR DEFENSE SYSTEMS INC
341 Lively Blvd (60007-2009)
PHONE.....................773 529-6007
Merriellyn Kett, *CEO*
EMP: 17
SQ FT: 5,000
SALES (est): 143.1K **Privately Held**
SIC: 3482 3484 Small arms ammunition; small arms

(G-9224)
S AND S ASSOCIATES INC
Also Called: Trademark Products
1016 Bonaventure Dr (60007-3277)
PHONE.....................847 584-0033
Larry Scanlon, *President*
EMP: 6
SQ FT: 2,500
SALES (est): 551.2K **Privately Held**
SIC: 3993 3953 5999 Signs & advertising specialties; embossing seals & hand stamps; rubber stamps

(G-9225)
S B LIQUIDATING COMPANY
Also Called: Spiral Binding of Illinois
1100 Touhy Ave (60007-4924)
PHONE.....................847 758-9500
Bruce L Kappele, *President*
Robert Frankiewicz, *Corp Secy*
EMP: 65
SQ FT: 60,000
SALES (est): 4.5MM **Privately Held**
SIC: 2789 Bookbinding & related work

(G-9226)
S P INDUSTRIES INC
Also Called: Sp Industries
1455 Elmhurst Rd (60007-6400)
PHONE.....................847 228-2851
Brian Wright, *President*
EMP: 45
SALES (corp-wide): 1.5B **Privately Held**
SIC: 3231 Products of purchased glass

Elk Grove Village - Cook County (G-9227)

HQ: S P Industries, Inc.
935 Mearns Rd
Warminster PA 18974
215 672-7800

(G-9227)
S-P PRODUCTS INC
730 Pratt Blvd (60007-5115)
P.O. Box 128, Glenview (60025-0128)
PHONE.................................847 593-8595
Peter A Vrame, *President*
Suresh Patel, *VP Prdtn*
Marcos Garcia, *Sales Mgr*
EMP: 16
SQ FT: 15,000
SALES (est): 3.7MM **Privately Held**
SIC: 3646 3643 Commercial indusl & institutional electric lighting fixtures; current-carrying wiring devices

(G-9228)
SAMMY USA CORP
800 Arthur Ave (60007-5215)
PHONE.................................847 364-9787
Yoshiharu Suzuki, *President*
James Miskell, *Vice Pres*
EMP: 45
SQ FT: 70,000
SALES (est): 4.5MM **Privately Held**
SIC: 3695 Computer software tape & disks: blank, rigid & floppy
PA: Sammy Corp
4-1-1, Kandasurugadai
Chiyoda-Ku TKY 101-0

(G-9229)
SANFORD CHEMICAL CO INC
1945 Touhy Ave (60007-5369)
PHONE.................................847 437-3530
Sanford Arenberg, *President*
Sylve Schwartz, *Corp Secy*
Barbara Arenberg, *Vice Pres*
Andy Bielecki, *Project Mgr*
EMP: 10 EST: 1956
SALES (est): 1.5MM **Privately Held**
WEB: www.sanfordchemicalcompany.com
SIC: 2891 2841 2879 2843 Adhesives; detergents, synthetic organic or inorganic alkaline; fungicides, herbicides; leather finishing agents; chemical preparations; industrial inorganic chemicals

(G-9230)
SAVAGE BROS COMPANY
1825 Greenleaf Ave (60007-5501)
PHONE.................................847 981-3000
Robert Parmley, *President*
William Bauer, *Electrical Engi*
Javier Sanchez, *Sales Staff*
Barbara Susmel, *Sales Staff*
Jacques D Waele, *Sales Staff*
▼ EMP: 65 EST: 1855
SQ FT: 25,000
SALES: 10MM **Privately Held**
WEB: www.savagebros.com
SIC: 3556 Confectionery machinery; smokers, food processing equipment

(G-9231)
SAVE ON PRINTING INC
1451 Landmeier Rd (60007-2454)
PHONE.................................847 922-7855
Luis Trevino, *Owner*
EMP: 5
SALES: 250K **Privately Held**
SIC: 2752 Commercial printing, lithographic

(G-9232)
SAWS UNLIMITED INC
494 Bonnie Ln (60007-1908)
PHONE.................................847 640-7450
Horst Stange, *President*
EMP: 4
SQ FT: 5,000
SALES (est): 599.1K **Privately Held**
SIC: 3425 3546 Saw blades for hand or power saws; saws & sawing equipment

(G-9233)
SCHIELE GRAPHICS INC
Also Called: Schiele Group
1880 Busse Rd (60007-5718)
PHONE.................................847 434-5455
John Schiele, *President*
Frank Grana, *COO*
Ralph Dynek, *Vice Pres*
Willie Page, *Plant Mgr*
Brian Conlin, *Prdtn Mgr*
EMP: 60 EST: 1948
SQ FT: 40,000
SALES (est): 23.8MM **Privately Held**
WEB: www.schielegroup.com
SIC: 2752 2791 Commercial printing, offset; typesetting

(G-9234)
SCREEN MACHINE INCORPORATED
1025 Criss Cir (60007-1203)
PHONE.................................847 439-2233
Dave Rhyan, *President*
Norman Lysiak, *Vice Pres*
Alison Schaudenecker, *Manager*
EMP: 9
SQ FT: 4,000
SALES: 582.8K **Privately Held**
SIC: 2752 5137 5136 2396 Offset & photolithographic printing; sportswear, women's & children's; shirts, men's & boys'; automotive & apparel trimmings

(G-9235)
SELAH USA INC
1501 Jarvis Ave (60007-2401)
PHONE.................................847 758-0702
Jun Kim, *Owner*
▲ EMP: 6
SALES (est): 616.3K **Privately Held**
SIC: 2759 Screen printing

(G-9236)
SHARP METAL PRODUCTS
140 Joey Dr (60007-1304)
PHONE.................................847 439-5393
George W Prisching, *President*
Craig Prisching, *Vice Pres*
Cecilia A Prisching, *Admin Sec*
EMP: 8
SALES (est): 1.1MM **Privately Held**
WEB: www.sharpmetalproducts.com
SIC: 3469 Stamping metal for the trade

(G-9237)
SHOPPE DE LEE INC
2625 American Ln Ste A (60007-6214)
PHONE.................................847 350-0580
Thomas Lee, *President*
Dorothy Lee, *Corp Secy*
Gerald Lee, *Vice Pres*
EMP: 3 EST: 1972
SQ FT: 4,000
SALES: 200K **Privately Held**
WEB: www.shoppedelee.com
SIC: 2512 Upholstered household furniture

(G-9238)
SIGMATRON INTERNATIONAL INC (PA)
2201 Landmeier Rd (60007-2616)
PHONE.................................847 956-8000
Gary R Fairhead, *Ch of Bd*
Gregory A Fairhead, *Exec VP*
Daniel P Camp, *Vice Pres*
Hom-Ming Chang, *Vice Pres*
Tom Rovtar, *Vice Pres*
▲ EMP: 7
SQ FT: 124,300
SALES: 290.5MM **Publicly Held**
SIC: 3672 3677 3679 3549 Printed circuit boards; electronic coils, transformers & other inductors; electronic circuits; assembly machines, including robotic; engine electrical test equipment

(G-9239)
SIGN CENTRE
2422 Pan Am Blvd (60007-6210)
PHONE.................................847 595-7300
Guy Dismang, *Principal*
Robert Dismang, *Principal*
EMP: 8
SALES (est): 484.3K **Privately Held**
SIC: 5099 3993 2675 7389 Signs, except electric; signs & advertising specialties; letters for signs, metal; stencils & lettering materials: die-cut; sign painting & lettering shop; property operation, retail establishment
PA: Visual Commitments Ltd
5221 N Long Ave
Chicago IL

(G-9240)
SIGN PALACE INC
68 N Lively Blvd (60007-1317)
PHONE.................................847 228-7446
Joseph Holik, *President*
Ken Holik, *Prdtn Mgr*
Darlene Holik, *Admin Sec*
EMP: 6
SQ FT: 7,000
SALES (est): 865.5K **Privately Held**
SIC: 7389 3993 Sign painting & lettering shop; signs & advertising specialties

(G-9241)
SIGNATURE INNOVATIONS LLC
1171 Landmeier Rd (60007-2408)
P.O. Box 464, Wood Dale (60191-0464)
PHONE.................................847 758-9600
Thomas Koczur, *Mng Member*
▲ EMP: 5
SALES (est): 917K **Privately Held**
SIC: 5023 1752 2426 2511 Wood flooring; wood floor installation & refinishing; carvings, furniture: wood; flooring, hardwood; parquet flooring, hardwood; coffee tables: wood

(G-9242)
SIGNS NOW
1670 Greenleaf Ave (60007-5527)
PHONE.................................847 427-0005
Bonnie McCulla, *President*
James McCulla, *Vice Pres*
EMP: 4
SALES: 200K **Privately Held**
SIC: 3993 Signs & advertising specialties

(G-9243)
SKILD MANUFACTURING INC
160 Bond St Fl 1 (60007-1297)
PHONE.................................847 437-1717
Alison Graunke, *President*
Jim Graunke, *Vice Pres*
Wendy Maniscalco, *Vice Pres*
EMP: 24 EST: 1953
SQ FT: 20,000
SALES (est): 3.5MM **Privately Held**
WEB: www.skildmachining.com
SIC: 3599 Machine shop, jobbing & repair

(G-9244)
SMITH COOPER INTERNATIONAL INC
Also Called: SCI
2701 Busse Rd (60007-6102)
PHONE.................................847 595-7572
Chuck Neely, *Branch Mgr*
EMP: 80 **Privately Held**
SIC: 3494 Valves & pipe fittings
PA: Smith Cooper International, Inc.
2867 Vail Ave
Commerce CA 90040

(G-9245)
SOLAR SPRING COMPANY
Also Called: Solar Spring & Wire Forms
345 Criss Cir (60007-1224)
PHONE.................................847 437-7838
Oscar Diaz, *President*
Margarita Rodriguez, *Production*
Yarissa Diaz, *Supervisor*
▲ EMP: 103 EST: 1979
SQ FT: 80,000
SALES (est): 23.9MM **Privately Held**
WEB: www.solarspring.com
SIC: 3495 3496 Mechanical springs, precision; miscellaneous fabricated wire products

(G-9246)
SONIC MANUFACTURING CORP
Also Called: Sonic Tool Mfg
950 Lee St (60007-1207)
PHONE.................................847 228-0015
Frank Sommer, *President*
George Sommer, *President*
John Sommer, *Vice Pres*
Mark Sommer, *Vice Pres*
Irene Sommer, *Treasurer*
EMP: 15 EST: 1965
SQ FT: 18,000
SALES: 2.9MM **Privately Held**
WEB: www.sonicmfgcorp.com
SIC: 3599 Machine shop, jobbing & repair

(G-9247)
SONOSCAN INC
2149 Pratt Blvd (60007-5914)
PHONE.................................847 437-6400
John Ippen, *General Mgr*
Michael Durso, *Engineer*
Rebecca McCordic, *Engineer*
Timothy Polka, *Engineer*
Michael Weiler, *Engineer*
▼ EMP: 75 EST: 1973
SQ FT: 40,000
SALES: 2.2MM
SALES (corp-wide): 2.1B **Publicly Held**
SIC: 3829 8734 8731 Ultrasonic testing equipment; testing laboratories; commercial research laboratory
PA: Nordson Corporation
28601 Clemens Rd
Westlake OH 44145
440 892-1580

(G-9248)
SOURCE UNITED LLC
Also Called: C N Tool
825 Nicholas Blvd (60007-2510)
PHONE.................................847 956-1459
Kris Malorny,
Radosav Trninich,
EMP: 5
SQ FT: 1,300
SALES (est): 747.6K **Privately Held**
SIC: 3599 Machine shop, jobbing & repair

(G-9249)
SPF SUPPLIES INC
300 Scott St (60007-1215)
PHONE.................................847 454-9081
Richard Spiess, *President*
EMP: 4
SQ FT: 2,500
SALES: 200K **Privately Held**
SIC: 3559 Chemical machinery & equipment

(G-9250)
SPORT INCENTIVES INC
1050 Pauly Dr (60007-1315)
PHONE.................................847 427-8650
Susan Jesselson, *President*
Mark Jesselson, *Vice Pres*
EMP: 12
SQ FT: 10,000
SALES (est): 2.3MM **Privately Held**
SIC: 2599 Stools, factory

(G-9251)
SPX CORPORATION
Genfare, A Division of Spx.
800 Arthur Ave (60007-5215)
PHONE.................................847 593-8855
Kim Green, *Branch Mgr*
EMP: 108
SQ FT: 53,000
SALES (corp-wide): 1.5B **Publicly Held**
SIC: 3443 Cooling towers, metal plate
PA: Spx Corporation
13320a Balntyn Corp Pl
Charlotte NC 28277
980 474-3700

(G-9252)
STANDARD RUBBER PRODUCTS CO
Also Called: S R P
120 Seegers Ave (60007-1650)
P.O. Box 797 (60009-0797)
PHONE.................................847 593-5630
Larry Gualano, *President*
Rita Schmidt, *Corp Secy*
John Schmidt, *Vice Pres*
Al Golano, *VP Opers*
Terri Welch, *Buyer*
EMP: 48 EST: 1946
SQ FT: 14,500
SALES (est): 10.1MM **Privately Held**
WEB: www.srpco.com
SIC: 3069 3053 3087 3061 Sponge rubber & sponge rubber products; washers, rubber; gaskets, all materials; custom compound purchased resins; mechanical rubber goods; industrial organic chemicals; plastics materials & resins

GEOGRAPHIC SECTION

Elk Grove Village - Cook County (G-9282)

(G-9253)
STANGE INDUSTRIAL GROUP
494 Bonnie Ln (60007-1908)
PHONE..................847 640-8470
Horst Stange, *President*
Arif Jasarevic, *Sales Staff*
EMP: 8
SALES (est): 1.2MM Privately Held
SIC: 3546 Drill attachments, portable

(G-9254)
STAR CNC MACHINE TOOL CORP
375 Bennett Rd (60007-1004)
PHONE..................847 437-8300
Denu White, *Sales/Mktg Mgr*
EMP: 7 Privately Held
SIC: 3599 Machine shop, jobbing & repair
HQ: Star Cnc Machine Tool Corp.
 123 Powerhouse Rd
 Roslyn Heights NY 11577
 516 484-0500

(G-9255)
STAR DIE MOLDING INC
2741 Katherine Way (60007-6746)
PHONE..................847 766-7952
Johan Peterse, *President*
Betty Petersen, *President*
Tim Malak, *Controller*
Johan Petersen, *Admin Sec*
▲ EMP: 62 EST: 1957
SQ FT: 21,000
SALES (est): 21MM Privately Held
WEB: www.stardie.com
SIC: 3089 3544 Injection molding of plastics; industrial molds

(G-9256)
STARK TOOLS AND SUPPLY INC
1001 Fargo Ave Ste 105 (60007-4706)
P.O. Box 7454, Libertyville (60048-7454)
PHONE..................847 772-8974
Daniel Pahng, *President*
EMP: 5
SALES: 100K Privately Held
SIC: 3423 Hand & edge tools

(G-9257)
STYLENQUAZA LLC
750 Pratt Blvd (60007-5115)
PHONE..................847 981-0191
John Bozek, *Manager*
EMP: 5
SALES (corp-wide): 29.8MM Privately Held
SIC: 3281 Building stone products
HQ: Stylenquaza, Llc
 11620 Goodnight Ln # 100
 Dallas TX 75229

(G-9258)
SUNG JI USA INC
Also Called: Chicago Off Set
128 N Lively Blvd (60007-1330)
PHONE..................847 956-9400
Daniel Kim, *General Mgr*
EMP: 10
SALES (est): 1MM Privately Held
SIC: 2752 Commercial printing, offset

(G-9259)
SUNRISE DISTRIBUTORS INC
Also Called: Sunrise Foods
2411 United Ln (60007-6818)
PHONE..................630 400-8786
Yousuf Karim, *President*
Farhan Karim, *Vice Pres*
▲ EMP: 6
SQ FT: 28,000
SALES (est): 6MM Privately Held
SIC: 5149 3321 5499 2041 Rice, polished; cooking utensils, cast iron; spices & herbs; flour & other grain mill products

(G-9260)
SUNRISE ELECTRONICS INC
130 Martin Ln (60007-1310)
PHONE..................847 357-0500
Ashok Patel, *President*
Jigar Patel, *Vice Pres*
▲ EMP: 28 EST: 1997
SQ FT: 18,000
SALES (est): 4.4MM Privately Held
WEB: www.sunrisepcb.com
SIC: 3672 Printed circuit boards

(G-9261)
SUPREME TAMALE CO
1495 Brummel Ave (60007-2110)
PHONE..................773 622-3777
John Paklaian, *President*
EMP: 6
SQ FT: 6,250
SALES (est): 600K Privately Held
WEB: www.supremetamale.com
SIC: 2032 2038 Tamales: packaged in cans, jars, etc.; frozen specialties

(G-9262)
SYNERGY MECH SOLUTIONS INC
55 N Lively Blvd (60007-1323)
P.O. Box 1485 (60009-1485)
PHONE..................847 437-4500
Thomas R Sullivan, *President*
Alex Smoler, *Data Proc Staff*
EMP: 6
SQ FT: 2,000
SALES: 6MM Privately Held
SIC: 3585 Heating & air conditioning combination units

(G-9263)
SYSTEMS & ELECTRONICS INC
190 Gordon St (60007-1120)
PHONE..................847 228-0985
Andy Lobato, *President*
James Putman, *COO*
Doug Shoemaker, *Purch Mgr*
EMP: 20
SQ FT: 14,500
SALES (est): 2.6MM
SALES (corp-wide): 12.3MM Privately Held
SIC: 3728 8731 Aircraft parts & equipment; electronic research
PA: Condition Monitoring Group Limited
 Hatchmoor Industrial Estate
 Torrington EX38
 180 562-6697

(G-9264)
TAISEI LAMICK USA INC
1801 Howard St (60007-2484)
PHONE..................847 258-3283
Yoshinari Kimura, *President*
Noriko Cowen, *Manager*
▲ EMP: 10
SALES (est): 1.9MM Privately Held
WEB: www.taiseilamick.com
SIC: 3565 Packaging machinery

(G-9265)
TAPE CASE LTD
150 Gaylord St (60007-1107)
PHONE..................847 299-7880
Martin Lahart, *President*
Mary Grace Castillo, *Manager*
◆ EMP: 21 EST: 1972
SALES (est): 18.5MM Privately Held
SIC: 5085 2891 7389 Adhesives, tape & plasters; adhesives & sealants;

(G-9266)
TEAM IMPRESSIONS INC
Also Called: T E A M
360 Scott St (60007-1215)
PHONE..................847 357-9270
Ronald C Felici, *President*
EMP: 22
SQ FT: 12,000
SALES (est): 3.4MM Privately Held
SIC: 2759 Labels & seals: printing; flexographic printing

(G-9267)
TEAM PLAY INC
201 Crossen Ave (60007-1611)
PHONE..................847 952-7533
Frank Pellegrini, *President*
Ken Fedesna, *COO*
Ad Pellegrini, *Vice Pres*
Bobby Llereza, *Director*
▲ EMP: 15
SQ FT: 15,000
SALES (est): 4.2MM Privately Held
SIC: 3861 Printing equipment, photographic

(G-9268)
TECH STAR DESIGN AND MFG
116 N Lively Blvd (60007-1318)
PHONE..................847 290-8676
Frank Sedlasek, *President*
Lois Sedlasek, *Corp Secy*
EMP: 10
SALES (est): 1.1MM Privately Held
SIC: 3679 8731 Electronic circuits; electronic research

(G-9269)
TECHPRINT INC
2330 Eastern Ave (60007-6813)
PHONE..................847 616-0109
Michael Roth, *President*
Ronald Roth, *Vice Pres*
John Roth, *Engineer*
EMP: 17
SALES: 800K Privately Held
SIC: 2759 2752 2789 Commercial printing; commercial printing, lithographic; bookbinding & related work

(G-9270)
TEMPIL INC (HQ)
1201 Pratt Blvd (60007-5708)
PHONE..................908 757-8300
Daniel Kleiman, *CEO*
Roger Hornburger, *General Mgr*
◆ EMP: 20
SQ FT: 30,000
SALES (est): 1.7MM
SALES (corp-wide): 28.6MM Privately Held
SIC: 2869 Laboratory chemicals, organic
PA: La-Co Industries, Inc.
 1201 Pratt Blvd
 Elk Grove Village IL 60007
 847 956-7600

(G-9271)
THREE JS INDUSTRIES INC
701 Landmeier Rd (60007-4757)
PHONE..................847 640-6080
Joanne Marozza, *President*
Judy Garnmeister, *Vice Pres*
Jennifer Herz, *Vice Pres*
EMP: 19 EST: 1980
SQ FT: 15,000
SALES (est): 2.6MM Privately Held
SIC: 3471 Electroplating of metals or formed products

(G-9272)
THUNDERBIRD LLC (PA)
1501 Oakton St (60007-2101)
PHONE..................847 718-9300
Blake Prunsky, *Mng Member*
John Newell,
Kevin Prunsky,
EMP: 12
SALES (est): 86.6MM Privately Held
SIC: 3599 Machine shop, jobbing & repair

(G-9273)
TIGERFLEX CORPORATION
1551 Pratt Blvd (60007-5714)
PHONE..................847 439-1766
Hitoya Kodama, *President*
Fred Bobzien, *Admin Sec*
▲ EMP: 1120
SQ FT: 50,000
SALES (est): 164.1MM Privately Held
SIC: 3052 Plastic hose
PA: Tigers Polymer Corporation
 1-4-1, Higashimachi, Shinsenri
 Toyonaka OSK 560-0

(G-9274)
TIME EMBROIDERY
2201 Lively Blvd (60007-5209)
PHONE..................847 364-4371
Christina Clifton, *Principal*
EMP: 4
SALES (est): 424.3K Privately Held
SIC: 2395 Embroidery products, except schiffli machine

(G-9275)
TISHMA ENGINEERING LLC
850 Pratt Blvd (60007-5117)
PHONE..................847 755-1200
EMP: 4
SALES: 300K Privately Held
SIC: 3999 Mfg Misc Products

(G-9276)
TOPY AMERICA INC
1200 Mark St (60007-6708)
PHONE..................847 350-6399
EMP: 9 Privately Held
SIC: 3714 Wheels, motor vehicle
HQ: Topy America, Inc.
 980 Chenault Rd
 Frankfort KY 40601
 502 783-1250

(G-9277)
TOPY PRECISION MFG INC (DH)
1375 Lunt Ave (60007-5619)
PHONE..................847 228-5902
Koichi Kevin Maruyama, *President*
Toshi Oguchi, *President*
Hiromitsu Oshida, *Principal*
Nick Sasaki, *Vice Pres*
Mike Knowlton, *Plant Mgr*
▲ EMP: 51
SQ FT: 52,000
SALES (est): 21MM Privately Held
SIC: 3465 3399 Automotive stampings; metal fasteners

(G-9278)
TOTAL PLASTICS INC
505 Busse Rd (60007-2116)
PHONE..................847 593-5000
Jeff Zonsius, *General Mgr*
EMP: 10
SALES (corp-wide): 768.2MM Privately Held
SIC: 2821 5162 Plastics materials & resins; plastics materials & basic shapes
HQ: Total Plastics Resources Llc
 2810 N Burdick St Ste A
 Kalamazoo MI 49004
 269 344-0009

(G-9279)
TOTAL TOOLING TECHNOLOGY INC
1475 Elmhurst Rd (60007-6400)
PHONE..................847 437-5135
Paul Majerus, *President*
James Majerus, *Vice Pres*
EMP: 10
SQ FT: 5,000
SALES (est): 1.6MM Privately Held
SIC: 3541 7699 3553 3546 Machine tools, metal cutting type; industrial machinery & equipment repair; woodworking machinery; power-driven handtools

(G-9280)
TOWER METAL PRODUCTS LP (PA)
1965 Pratt Blvd (60007-5905)
PHONE..................847 806-7200
Audie Tang, *Partner*
Cyrus Tang,
EMP: 2
SQ FT: 100,000
SALES (est): 4.1MM Privately Held
SIC: 3341 Aluminum smelting & refining (secondary)

(G-9281)
TOYOTA TSUSHO AMERICA INC
25 Nw Point Boulev (60007)
PHONE..................847 439-8500
Glenn Gawlik, *Branch Mgr*
EMP: 56 Privately Held
SIC: 5153 5169 5031 5131 Grains; chemicals & allied products; lumber: rough, dressed & finished; plywood; textiles, woven; finishing plants, cotton
HQ: Toyota Tsusho America, Inc.
 805 3rd Ave Fl 17
 New York NY 10022
 212 355-3600

(G-9282)
TREND TECHNOLOGIES LLC
737 Fargo Ave (60007-4702)
PHONE..................847 640-2382
Ruben Barrios, *Mfg Staff*
Dan Precour, *Branch Mgr*
Carol Precour, *Manager*
Steve Merena, *IT/INT Sup*
EMP: 200 Privately Held
SIC: 3089 3544 Molding primary plastic; special dies, tools, jigs & fixtures

---

(PA)=Parent Co (HQ)=Headquarters (DH)=Div Headquarters
◯ = New Business established in last 2 years

Elk Grove Village - Cook County (G-9283)

HQ: Trend Technologies, Llc
4626 Eucalyptus Ave
Chino CA 91710
909 597-7861

(G-9283)
TRI GUARDS INC
80 N Lively Blvd (60007-1317)
PHONE...............................847 537-8444
George Triunfol, *President*
Anne Triunfol, *Vice Pres*
Mary Lou Hazell, *Accounting Mgr*
EMP: 15 **EST:** 1970
SQ FT: 10,000
SALES (est): 1.3MM **Privately Held**
SIC: 3089 Plastic hardware & building products

(G-9284)
TRI-FIN LLC
79 Bond St (60007-1216)
PHONE...............................630 467-0991
Russell Novak, *Principal*
Marvin Kagan, *Principal*
Fernando Sorto, *Sales Staff*
EMP: 25
SALES (est): 3.5MM **Privately Held**
SIC: 3471 Finishing, metals or formed products

(G-9285)
TRI-STAR ENGINEERING INC
2455 Pan Am Blvd (60007-6209)
PHONE...............................847 595-3377
Robert Lindstrom, *President*
Alan Wicker, *Treasurer*
Judy Lindstrom, *Admin Sec*
EMP: 33
SQ FT: 2,500
SALES (est): 5.2MM **Privately Held**
SIC: 3544 3545 Special dies & tools; machine tool accessories

(G-9286)
TRIMACO LLC
1215 Landmeier Rd (60007-2433)
P.O. Box 2300, Morrisville NC (27560)
PHONE...............................919 674-3476
Vito Ancona, *Manager*
EMP: 21
SALES (corp-wide): 115MM **Privately Held**
SIC: 2679 Paper products, converted
PA: Trimaco, Llc
2300 Gateway Centre Blvd # 300
Morrisville NC 27560
919 674-3460

(G-9287)
TRODAT USA INC
2630 Greenleaf Ave (60007-5513)
PHONE...............................847 806-1750
Mark Klage, *Regl Sales Mgr*
EMP: 20
SALES (corp-wide): 272.5MM **Privately Held**
SIC: 3953 Marking devices
HQ: Trodat Usa, Inc.
48 Heller Park Ln
Somerset NJ 08873

(G-9288)
TSD MANUFACTURING CO INC
825 Chase Ave (60007-4805)
PHONE...............................630 238-8750
Semyon Trakhtenburg, *President*
EMP: 12
SQ FT: 6,000
SALES (est): 1.6MM **Privately Held**
SIC: 3599 Custom machinery

(G-9289)
TWISTED TRACES INC
725 Nicholas Blvd (60007-2508)
PHONE...............................630 345-5400
Brian Steelglove, *President*
EMP: 4
SALES (est): 448.2K **Privately Held**
WEB: www.twistedtraces.com
SIC: 3672 Printed circuit boards

(G-9290)
ULRICH KAEPPLER
Also Called: Kaeppler Machining
1693 Elmhurst Rd (60007-6413)
PHONE...............................847 290-0220
Ulrich Kaeppler, *Owner*
▲ **EMP:** 7
SALES (est): 597.8K **Privately Held**
SIC: 3599 Machine shop, jobbing & repair

(G-9291)
ULTIMATE MILLWORK INC
350 Lively Blvd (60007-2010)
PHONE...............................773 343-3070
EMP: 3
SALES (est): 113.5K **Privately Held**
SIC: 2431 Millwork

(G-9292)
ULTRA SPECIALTIES INCORPORATED
Also Called: Zopel Engineering Co.
1360 Howard St (60007-2274)
PHONE...............................847 437-8110
Peter Zopel, *President*
Tony Phipps, *Opers-Prdtn-Mfg*
Ron Cary, *Marketing Staff*
EMP: 20
SQ FT: 7,500
SALES (est): 312.6K **Privately Held**
SIC: 3599 Machine shop, jobbing & repair

(G-9293)
ULTRA SPECIALTY HOLDINGS INC
1360 Howard St (60007-2214)
PHONE...............................847 437-8110
Hans Scheel, *President*
Thaddeus Haderspeck, *Vice Pres*
Victor Zarecky, *Treasurer*
EMP: 24 **EST:** 1964
SQ FT: 22,400
SALES (est): 4.6MM **Privately Held**
WEB: www.ultraspecialties.com
SIC: 3599 3544 Machine shop, jobbing & repair; special dies, tools, jigs & fixtures

(G-9294)
UNI-LABEL AND TAG CORPORATION
Also Called: Varimed Division
1121 Pagni Dr (60007-6602)
PHONE...............................847 956-8900
Donna J Zgonina, *CEO*
Frank Kmet, *Human Res Dir*
Diane Lewendowski, *Human Res Dir*
Dan Mallek, *Sales Staff*
Mike Laziewicz, *Sales Associate*
EMP: 35 **EST:** 1975
SQ FT: 20,000
SALES (est): 5.4MM **Privately Held**
SIC: 2759 2671 2241 Labels & seals: printing; packaging paper & plastics film, coated & laminated; narrow fabric mills

(G-9295)
UNITECH INDUSTRIES INC
1461 Elmhurst Rd (60007-6400)
PHONE...............................847 357-8800
Atamjit Singh, *President*
Holanda Singh, *Admin Sec*
EMP: 18
SQ FT: 7,000
SALES (est): 2.3MM **Privately Held**
SIC: 3471 Electroplating of metals or formed products

(G-9296)
UNITED CMRA BINOCULAR REPR LLC
2525 Busse Rd (60007-6118)
PHONE...............................630 595-2525
Steve Schuldt, *President*
Antoinette Sciacca, *Principal*
Renee Miastkowski, *Vice Pres*
Brad Purl, *Vice Pres*
Adam Reiter, *Vice Pres*
EMP: 20
SQ FT: 7,500
SALES (est): 4.2MM **Privately Held**
SIC: 7699 7819 3652 Photographic equipment repair; video tape or disk reproduction; pre-recorded records & tapes

(G-9297)
UNITED LETTER SERVICE INC
Also Called: United Graphics Mailing Group
898 Cambridge Dr (60007-2437)
PHONE...............................312 408-2404
Erin Grogan, *President*
John Hayner, *Corp Secy*
Scott Hayner, *Exec VP*
Bob Nickel, *Sales Staff*
EMP: 19
SQ FT: 52,000
SALES (est): 4.4MM **Privately Held**
WEB: www.unitedletter.com
SIC: 7331 2752 Mailing service; commercial printing, offset

(G-9298)
UNIVERSAL BROACHING INC
1203 Pagni Dr (60007-6604)
PHONE...............................847 228-1440
Frances Hehn, *President*
Frances A Hehn, *President*
Ronald Hehn, *President*
Ronald P Hehn Jr, *Vice Pres*
EMP: 12
SQ FT: 10,000
SALES: 1MM **Privately Held**
SIC: 3541 3545 7692 5085 Broaching machines; broaches (machine tool accessories); welding repair; industrial tools

(G-9299)
UNIVERSAL CHEM & COATINGS INC
1124 Elmhurst Rd (60007-2615)
PHONE...............................847 297-2001
Frederick Chun, *Vice Pres*
EMP: 25
SALES (corp-wide): 9.7MM **Privately Held**
SIC: 2819 2891 2851 Industrial inorganic chemicals; adhesives & sealants; paints & allied products
PA: Universal Chemicals And Coatings, Inc.
1975 Fox Ln
Elgin IL 60123
847 931-1700

(G-9300)
VALEE INC (PA)
Also Called: Insty-Prints
859 Oakton St (60007-1904)
PHONE...............................847 364-6464
Valerie Roesti, *President*
Lee Roesti, *Vice Pres*
EMP: 6
SQ FT: 6,000
SALES (est): 1.1MM **Privately Held**
SIC: 2752 7334 2791 2759 Commercial printing, offset; photocopying & duplicating services; typesetting; commercial printing

(G-9301)
VENTEC USA LLC
720 Lee St (60007-1116)
PHONE...............................847 621-2261
Jack Pattie, *Mng Member*
▲ **EMP:** 8
SALES: 8MM **Privately Held**
WEB: www.ventec-usa.com
SIC: 1021 Copper ore milling & preparation

(G-9302)
VERSON ENTERPRISES INC
870 Cambridge Dr (60007-2437)
PHONE...............................847 364-2600
James Glover, *President*
Roger Anderson, *Corp Secy*
EMP: 19
SQ FT: 5,000
SALES (est): 2.2MM **Privately Held**
SIC: 8734 3826 Calibration & certification; analytical instruments

(G-9303)
VERZENAY LLC
Also Called: Verzenay Patisserie
714 New Mexico Trl (60007-2821)
PHONE...............................817 875-0699
Arshiya Farheen, *Mng Member*
Aqeel Wahiduddin, *Mng Member*
EMP: 4
SALES: 220K **Privately Held**
WEB: www.verzenaypatisserie.com
SIC: 2051 5461 Cakes, pies & pastries; pastries

(G-9304)
VIDA CABINETS INC
225 Stanley St (60007-1558)
PHONE...............................847 258-4468
Andrzej Zorychta, *Principal*
EMP: 4 **EST:** 2015
SALES (est): 516.2K **Privately Held**
SIC: 2434 Wood kitchen cabinets

(G-9305)
VISION ASSESSMENT CORPORATION
2675 Coyle Ave (60007-6403)
PHONE...............................847 239-5889
Thomas J Judy, *CEO*
Ralph Craig, *President*
Jacqueline Judy, *VP Sales*
EMP: 4 **EST:** 2007
SALES (est): 500K **Privately Held**
WEB: www.visionassessment.com
SIC: 3851 Ophthalmic goods

(G-9306)
VOESTLPINE PRECISION STRIP LLC
901 Morse Ave (60007-5107)
PHONE...............................847 227-5272
Udeo Coehler, *Mng Member*
▲ **EMP:** 65
SALES (est): 19.1MM **Privately Held**
SIC: 3544 Special dies, tools, jigs & fixtures

(G-9307)
WEYERHAEUSER COMPANY
Also Called: Elk Grove Corrugated Plant
1800 Nicholas Blvd (60007-5903)
PHONE...............................847 439-1111
Paul Bosley, *Branch Mgr*
EMP: 147
SALES (corp-wide): 6.5B **Publicly Held**
WEB: www.weyerhaeuser.com
SIC: 2653 Corrugated boxes, partitions, display items, sheets & pad
PA: Weyerhaeuser Company
220 Occidental Ave S
Seattle WA 98104
206 539-3000

(G-9308)
WHITE RACKER CO INC
420 Lively Blvd (60007-2012)
PHONE...............................847 758-1640
Kenneth F Rogalski, *President*
▲ **EMP:** 5 **EST:** 1986
SALES (est): 713.2K **Privately Held**
WEB: www.whiteracker.com
SIC: 3599 3471 3432 Machine shop, jobbing & repair; plating & polishing; plumbing fixture fittings & trim

(G-9309)
WILCOR SOLID SURFACE INC
2371 United Ln (60007-6816)
PHONE...............................888 956-1001
John Bradford Reamer, *President*
EMP: 15
SQ FT: 5,000
SALES (est): 1MM **Privately Held**
WEB: www.wilcorusa.com
SIC: 1799 2541 2434 2821 Counter top installation; counters or counter display cases, wood; wood kitchen cabinets; plastics materials & resins

(G-9310)
WILLIE WASHER MFG CO
2101 Greenleaf Ave (60007-5507)
PHONE...............................847 956-1344
William Neumann, *President*
Bill Fortney, *COO*
Diane Newmann, *Treasurer*
Brad Mayer, *Manager*
David Barreca, *Info Tech Mgr*
EMP: 115 **EST:** 1973
SQ FT: 140,000
SALES (est): 23MM **Privately Held**
SIC: 3469 3452 Stamping metal for the trade; washers, metal

(G-9311)
WOODLOGIC CUSTOM MILLWORK INC
505 Bonnie Ln (60007-1909)
PHONE...............................847 640-4500
Richard Theis, *President*
EMP: 20
SALES (est): 3.4MM **Privately Held**
SIC: 2431 Millwork

GEOGRAPHIC SECTION

Elmhurst - Dupage County (G-9339)

(G-9312)
WOOGL CORPORATION
Also Called: Allegra Marketing Print & Mail
859 Oakton St (60007-1904)
PHONE..................................847 806-1160
Joseph W Smith, *President*
Christine Accardo, *General Mgr*
Tom Auge, *Marketing Staff*
Becky Crotty, *Receptionist*
EMP: 23
SQ FT: 7,000
SALES (est): 3.2MM **Privately Held**
SIC: 2752 2796 2791 2789 Commercial printing, offset; platemaking services; typesetting; bookbinding & related work

(G-9313)
WRIGHT TECHNOLOGIES INC
1380 Howard St (60007-2214)
PHONE..................................847 439-4150
Kazimierz Aleszczyk, *President*
EMP: 9
SQ FT: 8,400
SALES (est): 1MM **Privately Held**
SIC: 3599 Machine shop, jobbing & repair

(G-9314)
WUNDERLICH DIAMOND TOOL CORP
1330 Howard St (60007-2200)
PHONE..................................847 437-9904
Jakub Wunderlich, *President*
Mark Wunderlich, *Vice Pres*
EMP: 13
SQ FT: 10,000
SALES (est): 2.4MM **Privately Held**
SIC: 3545 Diamond cutting tools for turning, boring, burnishing, etc.

(G-9315)
Y 2 K ELECTRONICS INC
2574 United Ln (60007-6819)
PHONE..................................847 238-9024
Nalini J Patel, *President*
Sonia Patel, *Treasurer*
Suketu Patel, *Admin Sec*
▲ **EMP:** 15 **EST:** 2000
SQ FT: 15,000
SALES (est): 1.5MM **Privately Held**
WEB: www.y2kled.com
SIC: 3672 Printed circuit boards

(G-9316)
YE OLDE SIGN SHOPPE
68 N Lively Blvd (60007-1317)
PHONE..................................847 228-7446
Joe Hollick, *Owner*
EMP: 4
SALES (est): 134.8K **Privately Held**
SIC: 3993 Signs, not made in custom sign painting shops

(G-9317)
ZAPTEL CORPORATION
836 S Arlington Hts Rd (60007-3667)
PHONE..................................847 386-8050
Ron Reimann, *President*
▲ **EMP:** 8
SQ FT: 2,000
SALES (est): 692.9K **Privately Held**
SIC: 2741 7389 4813 ; advertising, promotional & trade show services; local & long distance telephone communications

Elkhart
Logan County

(G-9318)
ICG ILLINOIS
781 600th St (62634-6057)
PHONE..................................217 947-2332
EMP: 3
SALES (est): 240K **Privately Held**
SIC: 4731 1241 Freight Transportation Arrangement Coal Mining Services

Ellis Grove
Randolph County

(G-9319)
5H CONSULTING & DESIGN LLC
8211 Oakdale Rd (62241-1905)
PHONE..................................618 317-5822
David R Hamilton, *President*
EMP: 20
SALES (est): 673K **Privately Held**
SIC: 1711 7389 3312 Mechanical contractor; process piping contractor; design services; pipes, iron & steel

Ellisville
Fulton County

(G-9320)
B A PRECAST INC
29794 N County Highway 2 (61431-9444)
PHONE..................................309 645-0639
EMP: 3
SALES (est): 214.5K **Privately Held**
SIC: 3272 Concrete products, precast

Elmhurst
Dupage County

(G-9321)
A J MANUFACTURING CO INC
437 W Wrightwood Ave (60126-1011)
PHONE..................................630 832-2828
Joe Chrzanowski, *Branch Mgr*
Mike Nelli, *Manager*
EMP: 8 **Privately Held**
WEB: www.ajmanufacturing.com
SIC: 3545 Machine tool attachments & accessories
PA: A J Manufacturing Co., Inc.
449 W Wrightwood Ave
Elmhurst IL

(G-9322)
AIM INC
586 S Rex Blvd (60126-4259)
PHONE..................................630 941-0027
Bill Kawales, *Manager*
EMP: 2
SALES (est): 201.9K **Privately Held**
SIC: 3699 Electrical equipment & supplies

(G-9323)
ALBAX INC
521 W Wrightwood Ave (60126-1004)
PHONE..................................630 758-1072
William Picciotti, *President*
Marrey Picciotti, *Vice Pres*
EMP: 20
SQ FT: 5,000
SALES (est): 1.6MM **Privately Held**
SIC: 2394 5091 Canvas & related products; boat accessories & parts

(G-9324)
ALBERT F AMLING LLC (PA)
Also Called: Amling's Flowerland
331 N York St (60126-2371)
PHONE..................................630 333-1720
Carl R Hayes, *President*
Douglas Aniballi, *Vice Pres*
EMP: 176 **EST:** 1890
SALES (est): 27.7MM **Privately Held**
WEB: www.chicagoflowers.com
SIC: 5992 5261 7359 3999 Flowers, fresh; plants, potted; garden supplies & tools; fertilizer; nursery stock, seeds & bulbs; live plant rental; flowers, artificial & preserved; plants, artificial & preserved; landscape contractors

(G-9325)
ALPHA CIRCUIT CORPORATION
730 N Oaklawn Ave (60126-1406)
PHONE..................................630 617-5555
Bhagvan Vaghani, *President*
Ankit Dungrani, *Purchasing*
Natu Vaghani, *Engineer*
Nita Buccino, *CFO*
Nita Vaghani Buccino, *Controller*
◆ **EMP:** 45
SQ FT: 44,000
SALES (est): 5.5MM **Privately Held**
WEB: www.alphacircuit.com
SIC: 3672 Circuit boards, television & radio printed

(G-9326)
ASM SENSORS INC
650 W Grand Ave Ste 205 (60126-1025)
PHONE..................................630 832-3202
Ines Steinich, *Manager*
EMP: 10
SALES (est): 1.7MM **Privately Held**
SIC: 3829 Measuring & controlling devices

(G-9327)
AV STUMPFL USA CORP
Also Called: AV Franklin
960 N Industrial Dr Ste 3 (60126-1119)
PHONE..................................630 359-0999
Franklin Moore, *President*
Reinhold Stumpfl, *CFO*
Maria Zeiger, *Sales Staff*
Rudi Hradil, *Chief Mktg Ofcr*
Jane W Moore, *Admin Sec*
▲ **EMP:** 10
SQ FT: 5,000
SALES (est): 10MM **Privately Held**
SIC: 3861 Screens, projection

(G-9328)
BB SERVICES LLC
Also Called: UPS Store of Elmhurst, The
205 E Butterfield Rd (60126-5103)
PHONE..................................630 941-8122
Edward J Chrabaszcz,
EMP: 9
SQ FT: 2,000
SALES (est): 518.3K **Privately Held**
SIC: 4215 7334 2789 Courier services, except by air; photocopying & duplicating services; binding & repair of books, magazines & pamphlets

(G-9329)
BEGOUN INC
655 W Grand Ave Ste 200 (60126-1063)
PHONE..................................630 617-0200
Alan Bass, *President*
Martin Bekanon, *General Mgr*
EMP: 6
SQ FT: 4,000
SALES (est): 1.1MM **Privately Held**
SIC: 3451 Screw machine products

(G-9330)
BELDEN ENERGY SOLUTIONS INC
719 S Berkley Ave (60126-4203)
PHONE..................................800 235-3361
Jim Belden, *Managing Dir*
James Belden, *Principal*
EMP: 6
SALES (est): 467.1K **Privately Held**
SIC: 3643 3678 3363 Current-carrying wiring devices; electronic connectors; aluminum die-castings

(G-9331)
BEMA INC
744 N Oaklawn Ave (60126-1406)
PHONE..................................630 279-7800
Glen Galloway, *President*
Mike Jenkins, *Prdtn Mgr*
Leon Tasche, *Prdtn Mgr*
Eric Kainer, *QC Mgr*
Tom Matusik, *Chief Engr*
▲ **EMP:** 90
SQ FT: 37,500
SALES (est): 19.2MM
SALES (corp-wide): 7.9MM **Privately Held**
SIC: 2671 Packaging paper & plastics film, coated & laminated
PA: Galloway Consolidated Holdings, Inc.
744 N Oaklawn Ave
Elmhurst IL 60126
630 279-7800

(G-9332)
BEST IN PRINTING INC
114 N Walnut St (60126-2634)
PHONE..................................630 833-7366
John Nicoli, *Principal*
EMP: 2
SALES (est): 264K **Privately Held**
SIC: 2752 Commercial printing, offset

(G-9333)
BIG GAME SOFTWARE LLC
110 E Schiller St Ste 302 (60126-2823)
PHONE..................................630 592-8082
EMP: 10 **EST:** 2009
SALES (est): 836.3K **Privately Held**
SIC: 7372 Prepackaged Software Services

(G-9334)
BIRD-X INC
Also Called: Yates Motloid
845 N Larch Ave (60126-1114)
PHONE..................................312 226-2473
Dennis Tilles, *President*
Tia Bianchi, *Human Res Mgr*
Alison James, *Human Resources*
Dan Hall, *Accounts Mgr*
Tom Olmsted, *Accounts Mgr*
▲ **EMP:** 39 **EST:** 1964
SALES (est): 13.2MM **Privately Held**
WEB: www.bird-x.com
SIC: 5087 5075 5047 2899 Extermination & fumigation equipment & supplies; warm air heating equipment & supplies; dental laboratory equipment; chemical preparations

(G-9335)
BLAC INC
195 W Spangler Ave Ste A (60126-1505)
PHONE..................................630 279-6400
Phillip B Black, *President*
Lenz Counsil, *Vice Pres*
Robert Borck, *Purch Mgr*
Robert Siegerdt, *QC Mgr*
John N Dimaggio, *Sales Staff*
◆ **EMP:** 65
SQ FT: 22,000
SALES (est): 25.9MM **Privately Held**
SIC: 3593 Fluid power cylinders & actuators

(G-9336)
BLOWERS LLC
835 N Industrial Dr (60126-1107)
PHONE..................................708 594-1800
Sabit Inan, *CEO*
EMP: 23 **EST:** 1951
SQ FT: 30,000
SALES (est): 1MM **Privately Held**
WEB: www.blowersllc.com
SIC: 3564 Dust or fume collecting equipment, industrial

(G-9337)
BRITISH CONVERTING SOLUTIONS
650 W Grand Ave Ste 201 (60126-1025)
PHONE..................................630 219-1906
Kevin Boyer,
EMP: 3
SALES (est): 186.4K **Privately Held**
SIC: 3554 Box making machines, paper

(G-9338)
BST NORTH AMERICA INC (DH)
655 W Grand Ave Ste 220 (60126-1063)
PHONE..................................630 833-9900
Kristian Juenke, *President*
Christian Juenke, *Vice Pres*
John Thome, *Vice Pres*
Ryan Florek, *Engineer*
Robert Mackay, *Treasurer*
▼ **EMP:** 41
SQ FT: 27,000
SALES (est): 8.8MM
SALES (corp-wide): 144.1K **Privately Held**
SIC: 3555 Printing trades machinery
HQ: Bst Eltromat International Gmbh
Heidsieker Heide 53
Bielefeld 33739
520 699-90

(G-9339)
BULLSEYE IMPRINTING & EMB
846 N York St Ste C (60126-1239)
PHONE..................................630 834-8175
Angie Nelson, *President*
Nick Nelson, *Vice Pres*
EMP: 3 **EST:** 2000

Elmhurst - Dupage County (G-9340)

SALES: 300K *Privately Held*
SIC: 2395 Embroidery products, except schiffli machine

(G-9340)
C & C 1 LLC
159 S Kenmore Ave (60126-3517)
PHONE 630 903-6345
EMP: 3
SALES (est): 144.8K *Privately Held*
SIC: 3691 Storage batteries

(G-9341)
CARSON PROPERTIES INC (PA)
Also Called: Closet Works Division
953 N Larch Ave (60126-1128)
Michael D Carson, *CEO*
PHONE 630 832-3322
EMP: 47
SQ FT: 30,000
SALES (est): 7.6MM *Privately Held*
SIC: 2511 Wood household furniture

(G-9342)
CERTIFYNATION INC
650 W Grand Ave Ste 105 (60126-1024)
P.O. Box 390, Sussex WI (53089-0390)
PHONE 775 237-8439
Jerome L Miastkowski, *President*
EMP: 3
SALES (est): 338.5K *Privately Held*
SIC: 3728 Aircraft parts & equipment

(G-9343)
CHASE HOME FINANCE
Also Called: Chase Manhattan
163 N York St (60126-2814)
PHONE 630 617-4747
David Proudfoot, *Branch Mgr*
EMP: 9
SALES (corp-wide): 142.4B *Publicly Held*
SIC: 3578 6029 Automatic teller machines (ATM); commercial banks
HQ: Chase Home Finance Inc.
480 Washington Blvd Fl 12
Jersey City NJ 07310

(G-9344)
CHEMSTATION CHICAGO LLC
934 N Oaklawn Ave Ste 1 (60126-1032)
PHONE 630 279-2857
Andrew Lasker, *President*
EMP: 24 **EST:** 2014
SQ FT: 25,000
SALES: 7.5MM *Privately Held*
SIC: 2841 Soap & other detergents

(G-9345)
CHICAGO SWITCHBOARD CO INC
470 W Wrightwood Ave (60126-1016)
PHONE 630 833-2266
Richard Blomquist, *President*
Bill Eder, *Vice Pres*
William Blomquist, *Treasurer*
EMP: 34 **EST:** 1915
SQ FT: 20,000
SALES (est): 10.9MM *Privately Held*
WEB: www.chiswbd.com
SIC: 3644 3613 Noncurrent-carrying wiring services; switchboards & parts, power

(G-9346)
CHRISTOPHER GLASS & ALUMINUM
832 N Industrial Dr (60126-1132)
PHONE 312 256-8500
Abraham Asllani, *President*
Paul Rowan, *Exec VP*
John T Metz, *CFO*
EMP: 100
SQ FT: 50,000
SALES: 19.9MM *Privately Held*
SIC: 1793 3446 Glass & glazing work; architectural metalwork

(G-9347)
CLARIOS
Also Called: Johnson Controls
450 W Wrightwood Ave (60126-1016)
PHONE 630 279-0050
Sean Margiotta, *Branch Mgr*
EMP: 94 *Privately Held*

SALES: 3.5MM *Privately Held*
SIC: 2531 3714 Seats, automobile; motor vehicle body components & frame
HQ: Johnson Controls, Inc.
5757 N Green Bay Ave
Milwaukee WI 53209
414 524-1200

(G-9348)
CMP MILLWORK CO
601 S Il Route 83 Ste 100 (60126-4261)
PHONE 630 832-6462
Mark E Olson, *President*
EMP: 6
SALES (est): 579.3K *Privately Held*
SIC: 2521 5039 5031 2431 Cabinets, office: wood; doors, sliding; windows; millwork

(G-9349)
COLOR SMITHS INC
747 N Church Rd Ste E6 (60126-1440)
PHONE 708 562-0061
Calvin Hill, *President*
Lori Hill, *Vice Pres*
Jonas Benson, *Urology*
EMP: 20 **EST:** 1961
SQ FT: 11,000
SALES (est): 1.4MM *Privately Held*
SIC: 2796 3555 2791 Lithographic plates, positives or negatives; color separations for printing; printing plates; typesetting

(G-9350)
COMET DIE & ENGRAVING COMPANY
909 N Larch Ave (60126-1158)
PHONE 630 833-5600
Terence J Donlin Jr, *President*
Mary L Donlin, *Treasurer*
Ed Foreman, *Controller*
Tony Mariniello, *Sales Engr*
John Rosenberger, *Sales Engr*
▲ **EMP:** 65 **EST:** 1898
SQ FT: 35,000
SALES (est): 12.6MM *Privately Held*
WEB: www.cometdie.com
SIC: 3544 3479 Industrial molds; engraving jewelry silverware, or metal

(G-9351)
COMMON GOAL SYSTEMS INC
188 W Industrial Dr # 240 (60126-1610)
P.O. Box 392, Lake Forest (60045-0392)
PHONE 630 592-4200
Michael Xakellis, *President*
Joe Granda, *Vice Pres*
Pat Helmers, *Vice Pres*
Cindy Rose, *Accounts Mgr*
Marty Bennet, *Accounts Exec*
EMP: 25 **EST:** 2001
SQ FT: 3,500
SALES (est): 2.5MM *Privately Held*
WEB: www.common-goal.com
SIC: 7372 Prepackaged software

(G-9352)
COMPONENT PRODUCTS INC
764 N Oaklawn Ave (60126-1406)
PHONE 847 301-1000
Linda Guertler, *President*
James Guertler, *Principal*
Jim Kintz, *Sales Staff*
▲ **EMP:** 20
SQ FT: 12,000
SALES (est): 11.2MM *Privately Held*
SIC: 5085 3569 3599 Signmaker equipment & supplies; liquid automation machinery & equipment; machine shop, jobbing & repair

(G-9353)
CQ INDUSTRIES INC
Also Called: Crazy Quilt Patch Factory
477 W Fullerton Ave (60126-1404)
PHONE 630 530-0177
Paul Jemmi, *President*
EMP: 5
SALES (est): 370.7K *Privately Held*
SIC: 2395 Emblems, embroidered

(G-9354)
CRAFTWOOD INC
889 N Larch Ave Ste 100 (60126-1109)
PHONE 630 758-1740
Jakub J Razniak, *President*
EMP: 20

SALES (est): 3.5MM *Privately Held*
SIC: 1389 Construction, repair & dismantling services

(G-9355)
CROWN METAL MANUFACTURING CO
765 S Il Route 83 (60126-4228)
PHONE 630 279-9800
Steven Varon, *President*
Juan Lopez, *Opers Mgr*
Joseph Stipati, *Engineer*
Mary Ellen Bielawski, *Human Res Mgr*
Chris McDonald, *Sales Mgr*
◆ **EMP:** 125 **EST:** 1948
SQ FT: 140,000
SALES (est): 31.7MM *Privately Held*
WEB: www.crownmetal.com
SIC: 2542 Partitions & fixtures, except wood

(G-9356)
CRUISE BOILER AND REPR CO INC
Also Called: Delta Steel Boilers Div
824 N Addison Ave (60126-1218)
PHONE 630 279-7111
EMP: 12
SALES (est): 870K *Privately Held*
SIC: 7699 3433 Boiler Repair Service And Mfg Low Pressure Heating Boilers

(G-9357)
CUMMINS - ALLISON CORP
851 N Addison Ave (60126-1217)
PHONE 630 833-2285
Keith Garvey, *Manager*
EMP: 18
SALES (corp-wide): 3.2B *Publicly Held*
SIC: 3579 3519 Perforators (office machines); internal combustion engines
HQ: Cummins-Allison Corp.
852 Feehanville Dr
Mount Prospect IL 60056
800 786-5528

(G-9358)
EDM PRODUCTS LLC
484 W Wrightwood Ave (60126-1016)
PHONE 630 785-2554
Neal Otten, *Sales Staff*
Francisco Soto, *Mng Member*
EMP: 5
SALES (est): 524.8K *Privately Held*
WEB: www.hirschmannusa.com
SIC: 3544 Special dies, tools, jigs & fixtures

(G-9359)
EIS
752 N Larch Ave (60126-1522)
PHONE 630 530-7500
Jesse Quiles, *Principal*
EMP: 3
SALES (est): 122.7K *Privately Held*
SIC: 3677 Electronic coils, transformers & other inductors

(G-9360)
ELMHURST-CHICAGO STONE COMPANY (PA)
400 W 1st St (60126-2604)
P.O. Box 57 (60126-0057)
PHONE 630 832-4000
Charles Hammersmith Jr, *President*
Charles Hammersmith Sr, *Chairman*
Kenneth J Lahner, *Vice Pres*
Mark Kroeger, *Opers Staff*
Peter Stamatopoulos, *QC Mgr*
EMP: 30 **EST:** 1960
SQ FT: 21,000
SALES (est): 127.2MM *Privately Held*
WEB: www.ecstone.com
SIC: 1442 3273 3272 Gravel mining; ready-mixed concrete; pipe, concrete or lined with concrete

(G-9361)
ENGINEERING FINSHG SYSTEMS LLC (PA)
Also Called: Engineered Finishing Systems
202 E Bttrfield Rd Ste 20 (60126)
PHONE 815 893-6090
Kevin Coursin, *Mng Member*
Terrance Ray,

▲ **EMP:** 15
SQ FT: 4,900
SALES: 9MM *Privately Held*
SIC: 3559 8711 Paint making machinery; engineering services

(G-9362)
ENTROPY CAB SOLUTIONS INC USA
918 N Oaklawn Ave (60126-1015)
PHONE 630 834-3872
Henry Yeh, *President*
▲ **EMP:** 11
SQ FT: 5,000
SALES (est): 2.1MM *Privately Held*
SIC: 3469 Stamping metal for the trade
PA: Entropy Precision System Inc.
31f-12, 99, Xintai Wu Rd., Sec. 1,
Taipei City TAP 22161

(G-9363)
ETCH-TECH INC
494 W Wrightwood Ave (60126-1078)
PHONE 630 833-4234
Hans J Peskowits, *President*
Woodrow J Fisher, *Corp Secy*
Woodrow Fisher, *Treasurer*
EMP: 6
SQ FT: 3,300
SALES (est): 667.5K *Privately Held*
SIC: 3479 3544 Etching on metals; special dies, tools, jigs & fixtures

(G-9364)
EUROVIEW ENTERPRISES LLC
342 W Carol Ln (60126-1003)
PHONE 630 227-3300
Duman Adam, *Principal*
Arnie Harris, *Mng Member*
▲ **EMP:** 50
SALES (est): 15.4MM *Privately Held*
SIC: 5039 3211 1793 Glass construction materials; tempered glass; construction glass; glass & glazing work

(G-9365)
G&K-VIJUK INTERN CORP
715 N Church Rd (60126-1415)
PHONE 630 530-2203
Rick Jasnica, *Opers Staff*
Kevin Boivin, *Sales Mgr*
Timothy Ellis, *Manager*
Steve Kozak, *Manager*
Achim Rees, *Admin Sec*
EMP: 5
SALES (est): 264.3K
SALES (corp-wide): 53.1MM *Privately Held*
SIC: 3569 Robots, assembly line: industrial & commercial
PA: Guk-Falzmaschinen Griesser & Kunzmann Gmbh & Co. Kg
Bahnhofstr. 4
Wellendingen 78669
742 670-31

(G-9366)
GLASS AMERICA MIDWEST LLC (DH)
Also Called: Glass America Midwest Inc.
977 N Oaklawn Ave Ste 200 (60126-1028)
PHONE 877 743-7237
Michael G Barry, *CEO*
Bob Simpson, *Vice Pres*
Don Perillo, *Marketing Mgr*
Robbie Price, *Manager*
EMP: 6
SALES (est): 24.7MM
SALES (corp-wide): 1.7B *Privately Held*
SIC: 7536 3231 Automotive glass replacement shops; windshields, glass: made from purchased glass
HQ: Glass America Llc
977 N Oaklawn Ave Ste 200
Elmhurst IL 60126
877 220-1724

(G-9367)
GLIDEPATH POWER LLC
132 N York St Apt 3l (60126)
PHONE 312 375-6034
Dan Foley, *CEO*
Chris McKissack, *Vice Pres*
EMP: 4
SALES (est): 434.8K *Privately Held*
SIC: 3691 Storage batteries

GEOGRAPHIC SECTION

Elmhurst - Dupage County (G-9394)

(G-9368)
GLIDERA INC
188 W Industrial Dr # 240 (60126-1623)
PHONE..................................773 350-4000
David Ripley, *President*
Michael Xakellis, *Chief Engr*
EMP: 5
SALES (est): 335.2K **Privately Held**
SIC: 7372 Application computer software

(G-9369)
GREENLEAF FOODS SPC (HQ)
Also Called: Field Roast Grain Meat Co
180 E Park Ave Ste 300 (60126-3433)
PHONE..................................800 268-3708
Ken Komejan, *Vice Pres*
EMP: 25
SALES (est): 63.9MM
SALES (corp-wide): 2.9B **Privately Held**
SIC: 2013 Roast beef from purchased meat
PA: Maple Leaf Foods Inc
   6985 Financial Dr
   Mississauga ON L5N 0
   905 285-5000

(G-9370)
HEICO COMPANIES LLC
360 W Butterfield Rd (60126-5068)
PHONE..................................847 258-0300
Gregory Pace, *Branch Mgr*
EMP: 3 **Privately Held**
WEB: www.heicocompanies.com
SIC: 3625 Resistors & resistor units
PA: The Heico Companies L L C
   70 W Madison St Ste 5600
   Chicago IL 60602

(G-9371)
HENKELMAN INC
493 W Fullerton Ave (60126-1404)
PHONE..................................331 979-2013
Duncan Blowers, *President*
Meike Persons, *President*
David Mahan, *Sales Staff*
EMP: 7
SALES: 1.5MM **Privately Held**
SIC: 3565 Vacuum packaging machinery

(G-9372)
HILTI INC
135 W Diversey Ave (60126-1101)
PHONE..................................847 364-9818
Ron Beckstrom, *Branch Mgr*
EMP: 11
SALES (corp-wide): 242.1K **Privately Held**
SIC: 3545 3399 Tools & accessories for machine tools; drill bits, metalworking; drills (machine tool accessories); metal fasteners
HQ: Hilti, Inc.
   7250 Dallas Pkwy Ste 1000
   Plano TX 75024
   800 879-8000

(G-9373)
IDEK GRAPHICS LLC
926 S Prospect Ave (60126-5008)
PHONE..................................630 530-1232
Kristine Granstrom, *Mng Member*
EMP: 4
SQ FT: 2,400
SALES: 100K **Privately Held**
SIC: 3993 Signs & advertising specialties

(G-9374)
IGD GROUP LLC
140 E Saint Charles Rd (60126-3424)
PHONE..................................630 240-6736
Pamela Hauser,
EMP: 10
SALES (est): 311.4K **Privately Held**
SIC: 3999 Manufacturing industries

(G-9375)
ILLIANA FINANCIAL INC
833 N Church Rd (60126-1005)
P.O. Box 1127 (60126-8127)
PHONE..................................630 941-3838
Thomas Arnold, *President*
Robert A Osborn, *Vice Pres*
EMP: 19 **EST:** 1981
SQ FT: 14,000
SALES (est): 2MM **Privately Held**
WEB: www.illianafinancial.com
SIC: 2752 Commercial printing, offset

(G-9376)
ILLINOIS TOOL WORKS INC
Also Called: ITW Deltar Seat Component
935 N Oaklawn Ave (60126-1012)
PHONE..................................630 993-9990
EMP: 23
SALES (corp-wide): 14.1B **Publicly Held**
WEB: www.itw.com
SIC: 3714 Motor vehicle parts & accessories
PA: Illinois Tool Works Inc.
   155 Harlem Ave
   Glenview IL 60025
   847 724-7500

(G-9377)
ILLINOIS TOOL WORKS INC
Also Called: I T W Chronotherm
935 N Oaklawn Ave (60126-1012)
PHONE..................................630 993-9990
Michael Neenan, *Principal*
EMP: 66
SALES (corp-wide): 14.1B **Publicly Held**
SIC: 3714 Heaters, motor vehicle
PA: Illinois Tool Works Inc.
   155 Harlem Ave
   Glenview IL 60025
   847 724-7500

(G-9378)
INLAND MIDWEST CORPORATION (HQ)
Also Called: Medtorque
612 W Lamont Rd (60126-1022)
PHONE..................................773 775-2111
Steven Sundberg, *CEO*
Eric Parmacek, *Vice Pres*
Brian Bedford, *Engineer*
John Greb, *Engineer*
Michael Pekovitch, *Engineer*
EMP: 49 **EST:** 1959
SQ FT: 25,000
SALES (est): 9.3MM
SALES (corp-wide): 3.5MM **Privately Held**
WEB: www.inlandmidwest.com
SIC: 3841 Surgical & medical instruments
PA: Medtorque Holdings, L.P.
   1 Westminster Pl Ste 100
   Lake Forest IL 60045
   847 295-4410

(G-9379)
INNOVATIVE AV SYSTEMS INC
909 S Il Route 83 (60126-5922)
PHONE..................................312 265-6282
Jose Marquez Jr, *President*
Jaclyn Marquez, *Principal*
Paula Smith, *Director*
EMP: 5
SQ FT: 2,500
SALES (est): 510.7K **Privately Held**
SIC: 5999 5099 3663 8748 Audio-visual equipment & supplies; video & audio equipment; antennas, transmitting & communications; telecommunications consultant; teleconferencing services; radio, television & electronic stores

(G-9380)
IRECO LLC
577 W Lamont Rd (60126-1021)
PHONE..................................630 741-0155
Jace Frechette, *Sales Staff*
Robert Grandy,
Robert Holden,
EMP: 15
SALES (est): 3.4MM **Privately Held**
SIC: 3441 Railroad car racks, for transporting vehicles: steel

(G-9381)
IRISH DANCING MAGAZINE
110 E Schiller St Ste 206 (60126-2822)
PHONE..................................630 279-7521
Denise Keanegillette, *Manager*
EMP: 3
SALES (est): 228.5K **Privately Held**
SIC: 2721 Magazines: publishing only, not printed on site

(G-9382)
JINHAP US CORPORATION (HQ)
900 N Church Rd (60126-1014)
PHONE..................................630 833-2880
Lee Young-Sup, *CEO*
John Grimsby, *Mfg Staff*
EMP: 5
SALES (est): 43.1MM **Privately Held**
SIC: 3965 Fasteners, buttons, needles & pins

(G-9383)
JOHN SAKASH COMPANY INC (PA)
700 N Walnut St (60126-1517)
P.O. Box 210 (60126-0210)
PHONE..................................630 833-3940
John W Sakash, *President*
Paul Slavik, *Vice Pres*
Latoya Diangelo, *Purchasing*
Victor Vazquez, *Purchasing*
Greg Fortmann, *Sales Staff*
EMP: 50 **EST:** 1952
SQ FT: 60,000
SALES (est): 2.7MM **Privately Held**
WEB: www.johnsakash.com
SIC: 3496 Miscellaneous fabricated wire products

(G-9384)
K & S SERVICE & RENTAL CORP (PA)
Also Called: All Foam Industries
471 W Monroe St (60126-4755)
PHONE..................................630 279-4292
Robert W Kirchhoff, *President*
Carl Kirchhoff, *Vice Pres*
▲ **EMP:** 11 **EST:** 1965
SQ FT: 17,000
SALES (est): 1.5MM **Privately Held**
WEB: www.allfoamindustries.com
SIC: 3086 5074 Insulation or cushioning material, foamed plastic; heating equipment (hydronic)

(G-9385)
KEANE GILLETTE PUBLISHING LLC
110 E Schiller St Ste 206 (60126-2822)
PHONE..................................630 279-7521
Denise Gillette,
EMP: 3
SALES (est): 212.4K **Privately Held**
SIC: 2741 Miscellaneous publishing

(G-9386)
KEEBLER FOODS COMPANY (DH)
677 N Larch Ave (60126-1521)
PHONE..................................630 833-2900
Gloria A Cannon, *Principal*
James T Willard, *Vice Pres*
James Willard, *Vice Pres*
Mark Spliethoff, *VP Bus Dvlpt*
E Nichol McCully, *CFO*
EMP: 29
SALES (est): 79MM
SALES (corp-wide): 13.5B **Publicly Held**
SIC: 2052 Cookies

(G-9387)
KELLOGG COMPANY
Also Called: Kellogg's
545 W Lamont Rd (60126-1021)
PHONE..................................630 941-0300
Frank Costanza, *Opers Mgr*
Robin May, *Plant Engr Mgr*
Chelsey Merritt, *Marketing Staff*
Chirayu Patel, *Manager*
David Atkins, *Director*
EMP: 160
SALES (corp-wide): 13.5B **Publicly Held**
WEB: www.kelloggcompany.com
SIC: 2052 2051 Cookies; cones, ice cream; crackers, dry; pretzels; bread, cake & related products
PA: Kellogg Company
   1 Kellogg Sq
   Battle Creek MI 49017
   269 961-2000

(G-9388)
KIEFT BROS INC
837 S Riverside Dr (60126-4964)
PHONE..................................630 832-8090
Patrick Spriet, *President*
Larry W Kieft, *President*
George A Smith, *President*
Sue Owens, *Corp Secy*
EMP: 27 **EST:** 1948
SQ FT: 10,200
SALES (est): 8.1MM **Privately Held**
WEB: www.kieftbros.com
SIC: 3272 5032 3432 Septic tanks, concrete; manhole covers or frames, concrete; sewer pipe, clay; plumbing fixture fittings & trim

(G-9389)
KRUEGER AND COMPANY
Also Called: Krueger Steel & Wire
900 N Industrial Dr (60126-1181)
PHONE..................................630 833-5650
Phyllis K Gillespie, *President*
David Kissel, *QC Mgr*
Shauna Johnson, *Office Mgr*
Sole Ofrier, *Admin Sec*
▲ **EMP:** 35 **EST:** 1946
SQ FT: 55,000
SALES (est): 18.2MM **Privately Held**
WEB: www.kruegersteelandwire.com
SIC: 3315 3316 3479 3471 Wire, steel: insulated or armored; bars, steel, cold finished, from purchased hot-rolled; coating of metals & formed products; plating & polishing

(G-9390)
LABELQUEST INC
493 W Fullerton Ave (60126-1404)
P.O. Box 1107 (60126-8107)
PHONE..................................630 833-9400
Pat Vandenberg, *President*
Neil Vandenberg, *Vice Pres*
Steven Rubinow, *Officer*
EMP: 23
SQ FT: 2,000
SALES (est): 2MM **Privately Held**
SIC: 2741 Miscellaneous publishing

(G-9391)
LHS INC
188 W Industrial Dr # 26 (60126-1623)
PHONE..................................630 832-3875
Terry Healy, *Principal*
EMP: 3
SALES (est): 235.2K **Privately Held**
SIC: 3965 Fasteners

(G-9392)
LIGHTLIFE FOODS INC (HQ)
180 E Park Ave Ofc 1 (60126-3456)
PHONE..................................413 774-9000
Roy Lubetkin, *President*
Michael Morin, *CFO*
▲ **EMP:** 116
SQ FT: 5,000
SALES (est): 81.2MM
SALES (corp-wide): 2.9B **Privately Held**
SIC: 2099 2034 2032 Food preparations; dehydrated fruits, vegetables, soups; canned specialties
PA: Maple Leaf Foods Inc
   6985 Financial Dr
   Mississauga ON L5N 0
   905 285-5000

(G-9393)
LORETTE DIES INC
246 E 2nd St (60126-2940)
PHONE..................................630 279-9682
Timothy Lohan, *President*
Laurel Lohan, *Vice Pres*
EMP: 3 **EST:** 1945
SQ FT: 1,500
SALES (est): 250K **Privately Held**
SIC: 3423 3544 Rules or rulers, metal; special dies & tools

(G-9394)
LOUVERS INTERNATIONAL INC
851 N Church Ct (60126-1036)
PHONE..................................630 782-9977
Alfred Wall, *Ch of Bd*
Alfred J Wall, *Ch of Bd*
Carol Wall, *Admin Sec*
▲ **EMP:** 27
SQ FT: 32,000
SALES: 8.9MM **Privately Held**
SIC: 3646 Fluorescent lighting fixtures, commercial

Elmhurst - Dupage County (G-9395)

(G-9395)
LUMEN TECHNOLOGIES INC
423 N Emery Ln (60126-2201)
PHONE...............................708 363-7758
Joseph Domingo, *President*
EMP: 6
SALES: 500K **Privately Held**
SIC: 3999 Manufacturing industries

(G-9396)
M C F PRINTING COMPANY
118 S York St Ste 212 (60126-3449)
P.O. Box 1501 (60126-8501)
PHONE...............................630 279-0301
Hal Cahill, *President*
Valerie Cahill, *Admin Sec*
EMP: 3
SALES (est): 441.5K **Privately Held**
SIC: 5199 2752 Advertising specialties; commercial printing, lithographic

(G-9397)
MAFOMSIC INCORPORATED
756 N Industrial Dr (60126-1129)
PHONE...............................630 279-2005
Jerome Cismoski, *President*
▲ EMP: 14
SQ FT: 13,000
SALES (est): 3.5MM **Privately Held**
SIC: 2891 Adhesives

(G-9398)
MAHER PUBLICATIONS INC
Also Called: Music Inc. Magazine
102 N Haven Rd (60126-2970)
P.O. Box 906 (60126-0906)
PHONE...............................630 941-2030
Kevin Maher, *President*
Frank Alkyer, *Publisher*
Ed Enright, *Editor*
Evelyn Hawkins, *Bookkeeper*
Billy Heschl, *Sales Staff*
EMP: 16 EST: 1940
SALES (est): 2.2MM **Privately Held**
WEB: www.downbeat.com
SIC: 2721 Magazines: publishing only, not printed on site

(G-9399)
MATCON USA INC
832 N Industrial Dr (60126-1132)
PHONE...............................856 256-1330
▲ EMP: 13
SQ FT: 14,000
SALES (est): 5.1MM
SALES (corp-wide): 2B **Publicly Held**
SIC: 3536 Mfg Hoists/Cranes/Monorails
HQ: Matcon (R & D) Limited
Vale Park West
Evesham WORCS
160 865-1666

(G-9400)
MATERION BRUSH INC
606 W Lamont Rd (60126-1022)
PHONE...............................630 832-9650
Craig Kozlow, *Branch Mgr*
EMP: 15 **Publicly Held**
SIC: 3339 Primary nonferrous metals
HQ: Materion Brush Inc.
6070 Parkland Blvd Ste 1
Mayfield Heights OH 44124
216 486-4200

(G-9401)
MGSOLUTIONS INC
451 N York St (60126-2003)
PHONE...............................630 530-2005
Mike Grant, *Owner*
EMP: 3
SALES (est): 338K **Privately Held**
SIC: 2752 Commercial printing, lithographic

(G-9402)
MICRON FILTER CARTRIDGES CORP
Also Called: Micron Filter Cartridge Corp.
506 S Spring Rd Ste 3 (60126-3953)
PHONE...............................630 337-3877
Keith A Watts, *President*
Lisa A Watts, *Vice Pres*
▼ EMP: 4
SQ FT: 2,500
SALES: 150K **Privately Held**
SIC: 3569 5961 Filter elements, fluid, hydraulic line; general merchandise, mail order

(G-9403)
MONARCH TOOL & DIE CO
862 N Industrial Dr (60126-1121)
PHONE...............................630 530-8886
Stanley Kabat, *President*
Tim Rose, *Vice Pres*
Greg Rose, *Admin Sec*
EMP: 35
SQ FT: 20,000
SALES (est): 6.1MM **Privately Held**
SIC: 3544 Special dies & tools

(G-9404)
N & M TYPE & DESIGN
562 S Rex Blvd (60126-3739)
PHONE...............................630 834-3696
Nancy Moroney, *Partner*
Mark Moroney, *Partner*
EMP: 2
SALES (est): 200K **Privately Held**
SIC: 2791 Typesetting

(G-9405)
NORTH STAR LIGHTING LLC
835 N Industrial Dr (60126-1107)
PHONE...............................708 681-4330
Sabit Inan, *CEO*
Judy Smaczny, *Manager*
Judith Smatzny, *Admin Sec*
▲ EMP: 100
SQ FT: 50,000
SALES (est): 18.3MM **Privately Held**
SIC: 3646 Commercial indusl & institutional electric lighting fixtures

(G-9406)
NSA (CHI) LIQUIDATING CORP
Also Called: Milton Division
205 E Bttrfeld Rd Ste 238 (60126)
PHONE...............................708 728-2000
Christopher Picone, *CEO*
▲ EMP: 13
SQ FT: 200,000
SALES (est): 2.4MM **Privately Held**
SIC: 3728 Gears, aircraft power transmission; aircraft power transmission equipment

(G-9407)
OBERWEIS DAIRY INC
1018 S York St (60126-5122)
PHONE...............................630 782-0141
Cindy Dairy, *Branch Mgr*
EMP: 15
SALES (corp-wide): 249.7MM **Privately Held**
SIC: 2026 5963 5451 Milk processing (pasteurizing, homogenizing, bottling); milk delivery; milk; ice cream (packaged)
PA: Oberweis Dairy, Inc.
951 Ice Cream Dr
North Aurora IL 60542
630 801-6100

(G-9408)
PATIENTBOND LLC
126 N York St Ste 2 (60126-2888)
PHONE...............................312 445-8751
Anurag Juneja, *CEO*
Jonathan Phillips, *Ch of Bd*
Bill Paschen, *Vice Pres*
Mike Gianfrancesco, *Director*
EMP: 22
SALES (est): 604K **Privately Held**
SIC: 7372 Application computer software

(G-9409)
PATRIOT MATERIALS LLC
750 N Industrial Dr (60126-1129)
PHONE...............................630 501-0260
▲ EMP: 7
SALES (est): 804.2K **Privately Held**
SIC: 3672 Mfg Printed Circuit Boards

(G-9410)
PET CELEBRATIONS INC
269 N Highland Ave (60126-2554)
PHONE...............................630 832-6549
Robin Sparacino, *President*
Thomas Sparacino, *Vice Pres*
EMP: 6
SQ FT: 2,100
SALES (est): 586.4K **Privately Held**
SIC: 2047 Dog & cat food

(G-9411)
PRAIRIE DISPLAY CHICAGO INC
758 N Industrial Dr (60126-1129)
PHONE...............................630 834-8773
Steve Moskal, *President*
Steve Michals, *Corp Secy*
Marianne McGinn, *Marketing Staff*
EMP: 10
SALES (est): 1.5MM **Privately Held**
SIC: 5046 3993 Store fixtures & display equipment; signs & advertising specialties

(G-9412)
PRO-TECH METAL SPECIALTIES INC
233 W Diversey Ave (60126-1103)
PHONE...............................630 279-7094
Joseph R Tummillo, *President*
Jason S Sabala, *Purch Mgr*
Mark Tummillo, *Purchasing*
Bonnie Jones, *Manager*
EMP: 28
SQ FT: 30,000
SALES (est): 5.9MM **Privately Held**
SIC: 3544 3469 3444 3441 Special dies & tools; metal stampings; sheet metalwork; fabricated structural metal

(G-9413)
QUANTUM POLYMERS INC
100 S York St Ste 222 (60126-3440)
P.O. Box 754 (60126-0754)
PHONE...............................630 834-8427
Thomas M Hughes, *Principal*
EMP: 5
SALES (est): 2.8MM **Privately Held**
SIC: 2821 Plastics materials & resins

(G-9414)
RANDALL MANUFACTURING LLC
722 N Church Rd (60126-1402)
PHONE...............................630 782-0001
Debbie Decker, *Principal*
Charles Carey, *Vice Pres*
Artur Zemela, *Vice Pres*
Art Zemela, *Opers Mgr*
Michael Galati, *Sales Mgr*
◆ EMP: 60
SQ FT: 65,000
SALES (est): 19.2MM
SALES (corp-wide): 90.1MM **Privately Held**
SIC: 3714 Motor vehicle parts & accessories
PA: Safe Fleet Investments Llc
6800 E 163rd St
Belton MO 64012
844 258-8178

(G-9415)
RAYTHEON TECHNOLOGIES CORP
655 W Grand Ave Ste 320 (60126-1065)
PHONE...............................630 516-3460
Cliff Akey, *Branch Mgr*
Sean Murphy, *Manager*
Julie Glynn, *Director*
Hilary Kerkstra, *Technician*
EMP: 255
SALES (corp-wide): 77B **Publicly Held**
WEB: www.rtx.com
SIC: 3724 Aircraft engines & engine parts
PA: Raytheon Technologies Corporation
870 Winter St
Waltham MA 02451
781 522-3000

(G-9416)
READY INC
231 E Fremont Ave Apt 209 (60126-2469)
PHONE...............................630 501-1352
Nicole Trinidad, *Sales Mgr*
EMP: 10
SALES: 250K **Privately Held**
SIC: 2759 Letterpress & screen printing

(G-9417)
REHLING & ASSOCIATES INC
1010 S Swain Ave (60126-5004)
PHONE...............................630 941-3560
William Rehling, *President*
Jim Rehling, *Vice Pres*
EMP: 3 EST: 1995
SALES: 180K **Privately Held**
SIC: 3069 Fabricated rubber products

(G-9418)
RESIN8 INC
603 S Fairview Ave (60126-4204)
PHONE...............................773 551-3633
Roger Walsh, *President*
EMP: 3
SALES: 300K **Privately Held**
SIC: 2821 Epoxy resins

(G-9419)
ROHRER GRAPHIC ARTS INC
491 W Fullerton Ave (60126-1476)
PHONE...............................630 832-3434
Richard A Rohrer Jr, *President*
Ellen Rohrer, *Shareholder*
EMP: 12 EST: 1955
SQ FT: 4,000
SALES (est): 1.2MM **Privately Held**
WEB: www.rohrergraphicarts.com
SIC: 2731 2752 2796 2791 Pamphlets: publishing & printing; lithographing on metal; platemaking services; typesetting

(G-9420)
ROHRER LITHO INC
487 W Fullerton Ave (60126-1404)
PHONE...............................630 833-6610
Eric Rohrer, *President*
Pam Nazar, *Principal*
Cindy Rohrer, *Treasurer*
EMP: 4
SQ FT: 4,000
SALES (est): 567.9K **Privately Held**
SIC: 2752 2796 2791 2789 Commercial printing, offset; platemaking services; typesetting; bookbinding & related work

(G-9421)
SALMAN METAL
552 W Fay Ave (60126-2149)
PHONE...............................630 359-5110
Syed Iqbal, *Owner*
▼ EMP: 5
SALES (est): 474.2K **Privately Held**
SIC: 3398 Metal heat treating

(G-9422)
SANDBAGGER LLC
Also Called: Sb Acquisition
765 S State Route 83 (60126-4228)
PHONE...............................630 876-2400
Steven Varon, *CEO*
Timothy Vandergrift, *President*
▼ EMP: 70
SQ FT: 160,000
SALES (est): 2.6MM **Privately Held**
SIC: 3599 Custom machinery

(G-9423)
SANDBAGGER CORP
765 S Il Route 83 (60126-4228)
P.O. Box 5798, Villa Park (60181-5309)
PHONE...............................630 876-2400
Timothy J Vandergrift, *President*
Mindy Krissinger, *Sales Staff*
Paula Eaves, *Director*
EMP: 10
SQ FT: 2,300
SALES: 1MM **Privately Held**
SIC: 3599 Sand riddles (hand sifting or screening apparatus)

(G-9424)
SARATOGA SPECIALTIES CO INC
200 W Wrightwood Ave (60126-1113)
PHONE...............................630 833-3810
EMP: 3
SALES (est): 304.2K **Privately Held**
SIC: 2011 Meat packing plants

(G-9425)
SEMBLEX CORPORATION
370 W Carol Ln (60126-1003)
PHONE...............................630 833-2880
Jim Capasso, *Maint Mgr*
Gene Simpson, *Manager*
Noel Tabang, *Analyst*
EMP: 45 **Privately Held**
SIC: 3452 Screws, metal

GEOGRAPHIC SECTION

Elmwood Park - Cook County (G-9450)

HQ: Semblex Corporation
900 N Church Rd
Elmhurst IL 60126
630 833-2880

(G-9426)
SENTRY SEASONINGS INC
928 N Church Rd (60126-1014)
P.O. Box 1413, Park Ridge (60068-7413)
PHONE..................630 530-5370
Carla Staniec, *President*
Wayne Staniec, *General Mgr*
EMP: 20
SQ FT: 10,000
SALES (est): 4.2MM **Privately Held**
SIC: 2099 Spices, including grinding; seasonings & spices

(G-9427)
SHERWIN-WILLIAMS COMPANY
223 N York St (60126-2726)
PHONE..................630 834-1470
EMP: 3
SALES (corp-wide): 17.9B **Publicly Held**
SIC: 5198 2851 Paints, varnishes & supplies; wood fillers or sealers
PA: The Sherwin-Williams Company
101 W Prospect Ave # 1020
Cleveland OH 44115
216 566-2000

(G-9428)
SOUTH WATER SIGNS LLC
934 N Church Rd Ste B (60126-1048)
PHONE..................630 333-4900
Thomas R Merkel, *President*
Jim Hoss, *Vice Pres*
Lora Cecchini, *Production*
Tony Chiavola, *VP Bus Dvlpt*
Joanne Gonzalez, *Controller*
EMP: 36
SQ FT: 50,000
SALES: 20.5MM **Privately Held**
SIC: 3993 Signs, not made in custom sign painting shops

(G-9429)
STENOGRAPH LLC (DH)
596 W Lamont Rd (60126-1022)
PHONE..................630 532-5100
John Wenclawski, *President*
Robert J Panfil, *Vice Pres*
Jim Kuta, *Senior Mgr*
EMP: 100
SQ FT: 75,000
SALES (est): 27MM
SALES (corp-wide): 1.2B **Privately Held**
SIC: 7371 3669 3579 Computer software development; intercommunication systems, electric; shorthand machines
HQ: Pettibone L.L.C.
27501 Bella Vista Pkwy
Warrenville IL 60555
630 353-5000

(G-9430)
STENTECH INC
Also Called: Stentech-Chicago
853 N Industrial Dr (60126-1117)
PHONE..................630 833-4747
Raza Khan, *Branch Mgr*
EMP: 4
SALES (corp-wide): 11.2MM **Privately Held**
WEB: www.stentech.com
SIC: 3952 Pencils & pencil parts, artists'
HQ: Stentech, Inc.
22 Manchester Rd Unit 8b
Derry NH 03038
603 505-4470

(G-9431)
STEVENS GROUP LLC (PA)
Also Called: Business Graphics
188 W Indl Dr Ste 428 (60126)
PHONE..................331 209-2100
Noe Nunez, *Manager*
Jeff Schoner, *Executive*
Chris Gorski, *Administration*
EMP: 20
SALES (est): 2.5MM **Privately Held**
SIC: 2752 Commercial printing, offset

(G-9432)
SYNSEL ENERGY INC
445 W Fullerton Ave (60126-1404)
PHONE..................630 516-1284
Timothy Tawoda, *CEO*
Robert Brylski, *COO*
Michael Judd, *Chief Engr*
John Woodbury, *CFO*
EMP: 4
SQ FT: 1,500
SALES (est): 270.8K **Privately Held**
SIC: 2911 Diesel fuels

(G-9433)
TAYCORP INC
Also Called: Fay Electric Wire
752 N Larch Ave (60126-1522)
PHONE..................630 530-7500
Phillip D Gnolfo, *Manager*
EMP: 26
SALES (corp-wide): 10.6MM **Privately Held**
SIC: 3677 Electronic coils, transformers & other inductors
PA: Taycorp, Inc.
5700 W 120th St
Alsip IL 60803
708 629-0921

(G-9434)
TELE PRINT
494 E Atwood Ct (60126-4605)
PHONE..................630 941-7877
Frank Troila, *Partner*
Donald Troila, *Partner*
EMP: 5
SQ FT: 1,500
SALES: 400K **Privately Held**
SIC: 2752 Commercial printing, offset

(G-9435)
THATCHER OAKS INC
Also Called: Thatcher Retractbles
718 N Industrial Dr (60126-1526)
PHONE..................630 833-5700
James Patten, *President*
Bill Mola, *Opers Staff*
Kevin Eltoft, *Marketing Staff*
Alex Bechteler, *Manager*
Joanne Patten, *Manager*
EMP: 30
SALES (est): 4.1MM **Privately Held**
SIC: 2394 Canvas awnings & canopies

(G-9436)
TRANE TECHNOLOGIES COMPANY LLC
Also Called: Ingersoll-Rand
131 W Diversey Ave (60126-1101)
PHONE..................630 530-3800
Shaun Rigby, *Manager*
EMP: 50
SQ FT: 17,000 **Privately Held**
WEB: www.ingersollrand.com
SIC: 5085 5084 1081 Industrial supplies; processing & packaging equipment; metal mining services
HQ: Trane Technologies Company Llc
800 Beaty St
Davidson NC 28036
704 655-4000

(G-9437)
TREE TOWNS REPROGRAPHICS INC
Also Called: Tree Twns Imging Clor Graphics
1041 S Il Route 83 (60126-4973)
PHONE..................630 832-0209
Charles W Wingard Jr, *President*
Chris Szydlowski, *Accounts Mgr*
Bob Trimble, *Sales Staff*
Mark Wells, *Sales Staff*
Denise Wasielewski, *Office Mgr*
EMP: 16 **EST:** 1955
SQ FT: 2,400
SALES (est): 5.1MM **Privately Held**
WEB: www.treetowns.com
SIC: 7334 7384 2752 5999 Blueprinting service; photograph developing & retouching; commercial printing, offset; drafting equipment & supplies; artists' supplies & materials; bookbinding & related work; commercial printing

(G-9438)
TRI VANTAGE LLC
Also Called: Geo B Carpenter Co Division
957 N Oaklawn Ave (60126-1012)
PHONE..................630 530-5333
Keith Brauner, *Branch Mgr*
EMP: 18
SALES (corp-wide): 878.8MM **Privately Held**
SIC: 5085 2394 Cordage; canvas & related products
HQ: Trivantage, Llc
1831 N Park Ave
Burlington NC 27217
800 786-1876

(G-9439)
UICO LLC
650 W Grand Ave Ste 308 (60126-1026)
PHONE..................630 592-4400
Hiten Randhawa, *CEO*
Binay Bajaj, *Vice Pres*
Scott Hensley, *Vice Pres*
Jeff Kinnan, *Engineer*
Timothy Welch, *CFO*
▲ **EMP:** 50
SQ FT: 7,000
SALES (est): 11.4MM **Privately Held**
SIC: 3679 Electronic circuits

(G-9440)
VAL-MATIC VALVE AND MFG CORP (PA)
905 S Riverside Dr (60126-4900)
PHONE..................630 941-7600
John Ballun, *CEO*
Patricia Nuter, *Ch of Bd*
Rich Holroyd, *Materials Mgr*
James Svehla, *Production*
Bob Dela, *Purch Mgr*
◆ **EMP:** 115
SQ FT: 118,000
SALES (est): 28MM **Privately Held**
WEB: www.valmatic.com
SIC: 3491 Valves, automatic control; water works valves

(G-9441)
VIKING AWARDS INC
846 N York St Ste A (60126-1239)
PHONE..................630 833-1733
James Hamilton, *President*
EMP: 5
SQ FT: 4,300
SALES (est): 873.8K **Privately Held**
SIC: 5199 7336 3479 Advertising specialties; commercial art & graphic design; engraving jewelry silverware, or metal

(G-9442)
VITAL SIGNS USA
791 N Industrial Dr (60126-1107)
PHONE..................630 832-9600
Don Meyers, *President*
EMP: 5 **EST:** 1997
SALES (est): 591.6K **Privately Held**
WEB: www.vitalsignsusa.com
SIC: 3993 Signs & advertising specialties

(G-9443)
W R S INC
Also Called: Minuteman Press
675 W Saint Charles Rd (60126-3024)
PHONE..................630 279-0400
William R Sturm, *President*
EMP: 5
SQ FT: 6,000
SALES (est): 480K **Privately Held**
SIC: 2752 Commercial printing, lithographic

(G-9444)
WAGNER MIDWEST DIE SUPPLY INC
960 N Industrial Dr Ste 8 (60126-1119)
PHONE..................630 782-6230
Ellsworth D Knutson, *President*
Thomas Knutson, *Admin Sec*
▲ **EMP:** 6
SQ FT: 5,000
SALES: 609.4K
SALES (corp-wide): 8.2MM **Privately Held**
SIC: 3544 Special dies & tools

PA: Wagner Die Supply, Inc.
2041 Elm Ct
Ontario CA 91761
909 947-3044

(G-9445)
WESCO INTERNATIONAL INC
737 N Oaklawn Ave (60126-1405)
PHONE..................630 513-4864
EMP: 5
SALES (est): 939.5K **Privately Held**
SIC: 7361 5063 3699 Employment Agency Whol Electrical Equipment Mfg Electrical Equipment/Supplies

(G-9446)
WIRELESS CHAMBERLAIN PRODUCTS
845 N Larch Ave (60126-1114)
PHONE..................800 282-6225
Shary Nassimi, *President*
Isabel Soto, *Mfg Staff*
Scot Rutherford, *Finance*
Henri Bouyett, *Sales Staff*
Michael Sloncen, *Sales Staff*
▲ **EMP:** 22
SQ FT: 15,000
SALES (est): 1.4MM
SALES (corp-wide): 1.4B **Privately Held**
SIC: 3651 3663 3661 3669 Household audio & video equipment; television broadcasting & communications equipment; telephone & telegraph apparatus; emergency alarms
HQ: The Chamberlain Group Inc
300 Windsor Dr
Oak Brook IL 60523
630 279-3600

(G-9447)
WOODX LUMBER INC
471 W Wrightwood Ave (60126-1011)
PHONE..................331 979-2171
EMP: 4
SALES (est): 434.5K **Privately Held**
SIC: 5031 2426 Whol Lumber/Plywood/Millwork Hardwood Dimension/Floor Mill

Elmwood
Peoria County

(G-9448)
LAMPE PUBLICATIONS
401 W Main St (61529-9785)
P.O. Box 745 (61529-0745)
PHONE..................309 741-9790
Jeffrey D Lampe, *Owner*
EMP: 2 **EST:** 2010
SALES (est): 208.2K **Privately Held**
SIC: 2741 Miscellaneous publishing

(G-9449)
POWERS JOHN
Also Called: Elmwood Locker Service
214 S Magnolia St (61529-7902)
P.O. Box 603 (61529-0603)
PHONE..................309 742-8929
John Powers, *Owner*
EMP: 4 **EST:** 1957
SALES (est): 223.6K **Privately Held**
WEB: www.elmwoodil.com
SIC: 7299 2013 Butcher service, processing only; sausages & other prepared meats

Elmwood Park
Cook County

(G-9450)
D & R PRESS
7959 W Grand Ave (60707-1831)
PHONE..................708 452-0500
David Ransom Jr, *Owner*
Daryl Ransom, *Manager*
EMP: 8 **EST:** 1973
SQ FT: 8,000
SALES (est): 1.1MM **Privately Held**
SIC: 2759 2752 Letterpress printing; commercial printing, offset

Elmwood Park - Cook County (G-9451)

GEOGRAPHIC SECTION

(G-9451)
ELEGANT CONCEPTS LTD
7444 W Grand Ave (60707-1911)
PHONE..................708 456-9590
Joseph Faraone, *CEO*
EMP: 4
SALES: 1MM **Privately Held**
SIC: 2499 Bowls, wood

(G-9452)
FEDEX OFFICE & PRINT SVCS INC
1720 N Harlem Ave (60707-4304)
PHONE..................708 452-0149
EMP: 20
SALES (corp-wide): 69.6B **Publicly Held**
SIC: 7334 2791 2789 2759 Photocopying & duplicating services; typesetting; bookbinding & related work; commercial printing
HQ: Fedex Office And Print Services, Inc.
7900 Legacy Dr
Plano TX 75024
800 463-3339

(G-9453)
FOREMOST PLASTIC PDTS CO INC
Also Called: Foremost Plastics
7834 W Grand Ave (60707-1891)
PHONE..................708 452-5300
Kenneth Muszynski, *President*
Adrian Press, *QC Dir*
EMP: 44 **EST:** 1961
SQ FT: 37,500
SALES (est): 9.6MM **Privately Held**
WEB: www.foremostplastic.com
SIC: 3089 Injection molding of plastics

(G-9454)
ME AND GIA INC
7434 W North Ave (60707-4238)
PHONE..................708 583-1111
Angelo Lollino, *Principal*
EMP: 5
SALES (est): 389.9K **Privately Held**
SIC: 2024 Ice cream & frozen desserts

(G-9455)
MEDICAL LIABILITY MONITOR INC
7234 W North Ave Ste 101 (60707-4200)
P.O. Box 680, Oak Park (60303-0680)
PHONE..................312 944-7900
Barbara Dillard, *Principal*
James H Cunningham, *Principal*
Michael Matray, *Editor*
EMP: 4 **EST:** 1975
SALES (est): 258.7K **Privately Held**
WEB: www.medicalliabilitymonitor.com
SIC: 2721 Magazines: publishing only, not printed on site

(G-9456)
RECENDIZ WELDING INC
2626 N 77th Ct (60707-1801)
PHONE..................708 205-8759
EMP: 8
SALES (est): 88.7K **Privately Held**
SIC: 7692 Welding repair

(G-9457)
VAR GRAPHICS
1743 N 75th Ct (60707-4132)
PHONE..................708 456-2028
Orlando Vale, *President*
EMP: 5
SQ FT: 3,000
SALES (est): 500K **Privately Held**
SIC: 2759 Flexographic printing

Elsah
Jersey County

(G-9458)
JACOBS REPRODUCTION
25116 Beltrees Rd (62028-7031)
PHONE..................618 374-2198
Stewart J Becker, *Owner*
EMP: 3
SALES (est): 132K **Privately Held**
SIC: 2499 Decorative wood & woodwork

Elwin
Macon County

(G-9459)
ILLINOIS VALLEY PAVING CO INC
Rr 51 Box S (62532)
PHONE..................217 422-1010
Eric Roegge, *Vice Pres*
EMP: 37
SQ FT: 2,500
SALES (corp-wide): 9.1MM **Privately Held**
SIC: 2951 1611 Asphalt & asphaltic paving mixtures (not from refineries); highway & street construction
PA: Illinois Valley Paving Co Inc
Junction Rtes 100 & 106
Winchester IL 62694
217 742-3103

Elwood
Will County

(G-9460)
AUTOCUT MACHINE COMPANY INC
23702 S Vetter Rd (60421-9671)
PHONE..................815 436-1900
Daniel R Caskey, *President*
Rita Caskey, *Corp Secy*
Maude Caskey, *Vice Pres*
EMP: 7
SQ FT: 13,000
SALES (est): 827K **Privately Held**
SIC: 3599 3545 Machine shop, jobbing & repair; machine tool accessories

(G-9461)
BISSELL INC
20200 W Ira Morgan Rd (60421-6055)
PHONE..................815 423-1300
Brian Bissell, *Principal*
EMP: 5
SALES (corp-wide): 919.8MM **Privately Held**
WEB: www.bissell.com
SIC: 3589 Vacuum cleaners & sweepers, electric: industrial
HQ: Bissell Inc.
2345 Walker Ave Nw
Grand Rapids MI 49544
616 453-4451

(G-9462)
EXXONMOBIL PIPELINE COMPANY
Also Called: Joliet Refinery
Interstate 55 & Smth Brg (60421)
PHONE..................815 423-5571
Paullette Myers, *Branch Mgr*
EMP: 15
SALES (corp-wide): 264.9B **Publicly Held**
WEB: www.exxonmobilpipeline.com
SIC: 2911 Petroleum refining
HQ: Exxonmobil Pipeline Company
22777 Sprngwoods Vlg Pkwy
Spring TX 77389
713 656-3636

(G-9463)
GEORGIA-PACIFIC LLC
21837 W Mississippi Ave (60421-8004)
PHONE..................815 423-9990
EMP: 12
SALES (corp-wide): 48.9B **Privately Held**
WEB: www.gp.com
SIC: 2621 Paper mills
HQ: Georgia-Pacific Llc
133 Peachtree St Nw
Atlanta GA 30303
404 652-4000

(G-9464)
STEPAN COMPANY
Also Called: Millsdale Plant
22500 Stepan Rd (60421)
PHONE..................847 446-7500
Gary Traverso, *Plant Mgr*
Vince Schuller, *Production*
Jim Vescovi, *Production*
Tammy McCormick, *Purch Mgr*
Kathy Kohl, *Purch Agent*
EMP: 400
SALES (corp-wide): 1.8B **Publicly Held**
SIC: 2869 2865 2821 Industrial organic chemicals; cyclic crudes & intermediates; plastics materials & resins
PA: Stepan Company
22 W Frontage Rd
Northfield IL 60093
847 446-7500

(G-9465)
TRADEX INTERNATIONAL INC
21705 W Mississippi Ave (60421-8000)
P.O. Box 75746, Cleveland OH (44101-4202)
PHONE..................216 651-4788
Saji T Daniel, *President*
Philip Baseil, *COO*
Al Buccieri, *Exec VP*
◆ **EMP:** 65
SQ FT: 148,000
SALES (est): 23.2MM
SALES (corp-wide): 145.5B **Publicly Held**
SIC: 2822 3081 3999 3842 Butadiene-acrylonitrile, nitrile rubbers, NBR; vinyl film & sheet; hair nets; radiation shielding aprons, gloves, sheeting, etc.; gloves or mittens, plastic
PA: Cardinal Health, Inc.
7000 Cardinal Pl
Dublin OH 43017
614 757-5000

Emden
Logan County

(G-9466)
B B MILLING CO INC
Also Called: Bills Best Feeds
300 North St (62635-6427)
P.O. Box 289 (62635-0289)
PHONE..................217 376-3131
Lee E Komnick, *President*
Dorothy Komnick, *Corp Secy*
EMP: 3 **EST:** 1942
SQ FT: 2,400
SALES (est): 133.1K **Privately Held**
SIC: 5191 2048 Feed; seeds: field, garden & flower; prepared feeds

Energy
Williamson County

(G-9467)
CAVCO PRINTERS
Also Called: Cavco Printers Prtg & Copy Ctr
406 N Pershing St (62933-3620)
P.O. Box 340 (62933-0340)
PHONE..................618 988-8011
David J Normington, *Owner*
EMP: 6
SQ FT: 1,400
SALES (est): 465.8K **Privately Held**
SIC: 2752 2759 Commercial printing, offset; commercial printing

Enfield
White County

(G-9468)
BIG ALS MACHINES INC
204 Il Highway 14 (62835-2420)
P.O. Box 94 (62835-0094)
PHONE..................618 963-2619
Allan R Kemp, *President*
EMP: 7
SALES (est): 306K **Privately Held**
SIC: 3533 Oil field machinery & equipment

Eola
Dupage County

(G-9469)
ASBESTOS CONTROL & ENVMTL SVC
Also Called: Storage Dem Envmtl Consulting
31 W 780 Poss Rd (60519)
P.O. Box 511, Wheaton (60187-0511)
PHONE..................630 690-0189
Daniel Coyne, *President*
John Coyne, *Principal*
Todd Coyne, *Vice Pres*
EMP: 12
SQ FT: 9,000
SALES (est): 1MM **Privately Held**
SIC: 3292 3589 Insulation, molded asbestos; asbestos removal equipment

Equality
Gallatin County

(G-9470)
PEABODY ENERGY CORPORATION
420 Long Lane Rd (62934-2047)
PHONE..................314 342-3400
Max Haney, *Safety Mgr*
Wendy Raetz, *Analyst*
EMP: 4
SALES (corp-wide): 4.6B **Publicly Held**
SIC: 1221 Bituminous coal & lignite-surface mining
PA: Peabody Energy Corporation
701 Market St
Saint Louis MO 63101
314 342-3400

(G-9471)
PEABODY MIDWEST MINING LLC
Also Called: Wildcat Hlls Cottage Grove Pit
12250 Mclain Rd (62934-2310)
PHONE..................618 276-5006
EMP: 120
SALES (corp-wide): 5.6B **Publicly Held**
SIC: 1221 Bituminous Coal/Lignite Surface Mining
HQ: Peabody Midwest Mining, Llc
566 Dickeyville Rd
Lynnville IN 47619
812 434-8500

Erie
Whiteside County

(G-9472)
DEINES-NITZ SOLUTIONS LLC
721 Chase Rd (61250-9438)
PHONE..................309 658-9985
Greg J Deines, *President*
Mark S Nitz, *Vice Pres*
EMP: 45
SALES (est): 9.9MM **Privately Held**
SIC: 2621 Packaging paper; wrapping & packaging papers; specialty or chemically treated papers

(G-9473)
GOLD STAR FS INC
9087 Moline Rd (61250-9757)
PHONE..................309 659-2801
Jeff Wirth, *Manager*
EMP: 6
SALES (corp-wide): 224.2MM **Privately Held**
WEB: www.goldstarfs.com
SIC: 2873 Fertilizers: natural (organic), except compost
PA: Gold Star Fs, Inc.
13125 Il Hwy 81
Cambridge IL 61238
309 937-3369

▲ = Import ▼ = Export
◆ = Import/Export

(G-9474)
REVIEW
Also Called: Wns Publication
910 Albany St (61250-7766)
P.O. Box 357 (61250-0357)
PHONE..................309 659-2761
Tony Komlanc, *President*
EMP: 4
SALES (est): 178.3K **Privately Held**
SIC: 2711 Newspapers: publishing only, not printed on site

Esmond
Dekalb County

(G-9475)
BEE DESIGNS EMBROIDERY & SCREE
20733 E Welty Rd (60129-9365)
PHONE..................815 393-4593
Barbara Eychaner, *Owner*
EMP: 3
SALES (est): 229.1K **Privately Held**
SIC: 2395 2759 5941 Embroidery products, except schiffli machine; screen printing; sporting goods & bicycle shops

Essex
Kankakee County

(G-9476)
TATTY STICK LLC
Also Called: Axiomm
205 Highpoint Dr (60935-6160)
PHONE..................815 905-1023
Michelle Axium, *Mng Member*
EMP: 5
SALES (est): 304.3K **Privately Held**
SIC: 2911 Mineral oils, natural

Eureka
Woodford County

(G-9477)
C TRI CO
1035 W Center St (61530-9558)
PHONE..................309 467-4715
Richard D McCollum, *President*
Dan Hadfield, *General Mgr*
Ken Brown, *Prdtn Mgr*
Laurie Mounce, *Software Dev*
Ellen Krumholz, *Admin Sec*
EMP: 32
SQ FT: 21,000
SALES (est): 7.3MM **Privately Held**
SIC: 7373 3599 3544 Computer-aided design (CAD) systems service; machine shop, jobbing & repair; special dies, tools, jigs & fixtures

(G-9478)
COLUMBUS MCKINNON CORPORATION
Also Called: Washington Equipment Company
801 W Center St (61530-9501)
PHONE..................800 548-2930
Jeff Borders, *Branch Mgr*
EMP: 134
SALES (corp-wide): 809.1MM **Publicly Held**
WEB: www.cmworks.com
SIC: 3536 Hoists
PA: Columbus Mckinnon Corporation
205 Crosspoint Pkwy
Getzville NY 14068
716 689-5400

(G-9479)
CRANE EQUIPMENT & SERVICES INC (HQ)
Also Called: Ces Material Handling
801 W Center St (61530-9501)
PHONE..................309 467-6262
Susan Hayes, *General Mgr*
Sandy Jansen, *Technology*
Sherrie Buer, *Executive*
EMP: 30
SQ FT: 96,000
SALES: 13MM
SALES (corp-wide): 809.1MM **Publicly Held**
SIC: 5084 3536 Materials handling machinery; hoists, cranes & monorails
PA: Columbus Mckinnon Corporation
205 Crosspoint Pkwy
Getzville NY 14068
716 689-5400

(G-9480)
DIE DARRELL
106 W Burton Ave (61530-1302)
PHONE..................309 282-9112
E Dies, *Executive Asst*
EMP: 5 EST: 2007
SALES (est): 466.1K **Privately Held**
WEB: www.darrelldies.com
SIC: 3544 Special dies & tools

(G-9481)
DOMOR EQUIPMENT LLC
925 W Center St (61530-9505)
PHONE..................309 467-3483
Kevin Brickman, *Owner*
Ryan Deemer, *Opers Staff*
Molly Aiken, *Manager*
Lance Deemer, *Manager*
Vickey Brinkman,
EMP: 20
SALES (est): 4.6MM **Privately Held**
WEB: www.domorequipment.com
SIC: 3531 Construction machinery

(G-9482)
EUREKA LOCKER INC
110 4h Park Rd (61530-1706)
P.O. Box 194 (61530-0194)
PHONE..................309 467-2731
Scott Bittner, *Owner*
EMP: 10
SQ FT: 3,000
SALES (est): 402.6K **Privately Held**
SIC: 2011 4222 2013 Meat packing plants; storage, frozen or refrigerated goods; sausages & other prepared meats

(G-9483)
MCDOWELL INC
809 W Center St (61530-9501)
PHONE..................309 467-2335
William M Frederick, *President*
EMP: 6
SALES (est): 550K **Privately Held**
SIC: 3589 Sewage & water treatment equipment

(G-9484)
PAUL D BURTON
Also Called: Eureka Printing & Stationery
124 N Main St (61530-1157)
PHONE..................309 467-2613
Paul Burton, *Owner*
EMP: 3 EST: 1913
SQ FT: 2,000
SALES: 100K **Privately Held**
SIC: 2752 2759 Lithographing on metal; letterpress printing

Evanston
Cook County

(G-9485)
ABET TECHNOLOGIES LLC
9446 Hamlin Ave (60203-1304)
PHONE..................847 682-5541
Garry Woodward, *CEO*
EMP: 12
SALES (est): 714.9K **Privately Held**
SIC: 3827 Optical instruments & lenses

(G-9486)
ACCUITY INC (HQ)
1007 Church St Ste 600 (60201-5930)
PHONE..................847 676-9600
Hugh M Jones IV, *President*
Julie Goldweitz, *Senior VP*
Ken Thompson, *Senior VP*
Regina Brandys, *Manager*
Bryan Lubash, *Associate*
EMP: 294
SQ FT: 18,000
SALES (est): 42.6MM
SALES (corp-wide): 9.6B **Privately Held**
SIC: 7374 7372 Data processing service; application computer software
PA: Relx Plc
Grand Buildings
London WC2N
207 166-5500

(G-9487)
ACCUTONE HEARING AID INC
1580 Sherman Ave (60201-4465)
PHONE..................773 545-3279
Stege Kim, *Principal*
EMP: 3
SALES (est): 221.2K **Privately Held**
SIC: 3842 Hearing aids

(G-9488)
AGATE PUBLISHING INC
1328 Greenleaf St (60202-1153)
PHONE..................847 475-4457
Douglas Seibold, *President*
David Schlesinger, *Manager*
▲ EMP: 2
SALES (est): 298.5K **Privately Held**
SIC: 2731 Books: publishing only

(G-9489)
AGINITY INC
1007 Church St Ste 700 (60201-5915)
P.O. Box 8159 (60204-8159)
PHONE..................224 307-2656
Tzaras Christon, *CEO*
Geoff Trukenbrod, *CFO*
Stephen Zampino, *Sales Staff*
Daniel Kuhn, *CTO*
EMP: 78
SALES (est): 2.3MM **Privately Held**
SIC: 7372 Prepackaged software

(G-9490)
ALEXANDER TECHNIQUE
1830 Sherman Ave Ste 302 (60201-3772)
PHONE..................847 337-7926
John Henes, *Owner*
EMP: 3
SALES (est): 209.3K **Privately Held**
WEB: www.johnhenes.com
SIC: 3221 Medicine bottles, glass

(G-9491)
ALL FRESH FOOD PRODUCTS (PA)
2156 Green Bay Rd (60201-3046)
PHONE..................847 864-5030
Gulshan Wadhwa, *Owner*
Anil Wadhwa, *Vice Pres*
EMP: 1
SQ FT: 15,000
SALES (est): 21.8MM **Privately Held**
SIC: 2079 Edible fats & oils

(G-9492)
ALLFRESH FOOD PRODUCTS INC (HQ)
2156 Green Bay Rd (60201-3046)
PHONE..................847 869-3100
Gulshan Wadhwa, *President*
EMP: 19 EST: 1952
SQ FT: 15,000
SALES (est): 3MM
SALES (corp-wide): 21.8MM **Privately Held**
WEB: www.allfreshfoodproducts.com
SIC: 2079 Edible fats & oils
PA: All Fresh Food Products
2156 Green Bay Rd
Evanston IL 60201
847 864-5030

(G-9493)
AMERICAN BIOOPTICS LLC
1801 Maple Ave Ste 4316 (60201-3149)
PHONE..................847 467-0628
Erin Lavelle, *COO*
Andrew Cittadine,
▲ EMP: 5
SQ FT: 1,500
SALES (est): 380K **Privately Held**
SIC: 3841 Diagnostic apparatus, medical

(G-9494)
ANATOMICAL WORLDWIDE LLC
1630 Darrow Ave (60201-3418)
PHONE..................312 224-4772
Alicia Kull, *Finance*
Adam Cordell,
▲ EMP: 8
SQ FT: 30,000
SALES (est): 2.4MM **Privately Held**
SIC: 3842 5961 Models, anatomical; catalog & mail-order houses

(G-9495)
ARDAGH GLASS INC
1 Rotary Ctr (60201-4422)
PHONE..................847 869-7248
EMP: 4 **Privately Held**
SIC: 3221 Mfg Glass Containers
HQ: Ardagh Glass Inc.
10194 Crosspoint Blvd
Indianapolis IN 46256

(G-9496)
ASHLEY LAUREN
Also Called: Ashley Lauren Natural Products
636 Church St Ste 701 (60201-6031)
PHONE..................847 733-9470
Georgia Parker, *Owner*
EMP: 5
SALES (est): 437K **Privately Held**
SIC: 2841 Textile soap

(G-9497)
BAM OPERATING INC
2145 Pioneer Rd (60201-2564)
PHONE..................254 629-8561
Gerald W Bolfing, *Director*
EMP: 3
SALES (est): 122K **Privately Held**
SIC: 1311 Crude petroleum production

(G-9498)
BELGIAN CHOCOLATIER PIRON INC
509 Main St Fl A (60202-4539)
PHONE..................847 864-5504
Robert F Piron, *President*
Fred Piron, *Vice Pres*
Patricia Piron, *Retailers*
EMP: 3
SALES (est): 200K **Privately Held**
SIC: 5441 2064 2066 Candy; candy & other confectionery products; chocolate & cocoa products

(G-9499)
BERNARD FOOD INDUSTRIES INC (PA)
1125 Hartrey Ave (60202-1035)
P.O. Box 1497 (60204-1497)
PHONE..................847 869-5222
Steven F Bernard, *President*
Jules F Bernard, *President*
Lou Haan, *Manager*
Ron Lynn, *Vice Pres*
George Brodzki, *CFO*
EMP: 89
SQ FT: 42,000
SALES (est): 18MM **Privately Held**
WEB: www.bernardfoods.com
SIC: 2099 2034 Food preparations; dehydrated fruits, vegetables, soups

(G-9500)
BIOSPAWN LURE CO
9332 Hamlin Ave (60203-1302)
PHONE..................773 458-0752
EMP: 3 EST: 2015
SALES (est): 278.2K **Privately Held**
SIC: 3949 Lures, fishing: artificial

(G-9501)
BUILDERS READY-MIX CO
2525 Oakton St (60202-2759)
PHONE..................847 866-6300
Thomas Sobczak, *President*
Mark Ronan, *Vice Pres*
Maria Sobczak, *Treasurer*
Judy Ronan, *Admin Sec*
EMP: 25
SQ FT: 3,000
SALES (est): 5MM **Privately Held**
SIC: 3273 Ready-mixed concrete

Evanston - Cook County (G-9502) — GEOGRAPHIC SECTION

(G-9502)
CHARLES SHERIDAN AND SONS
2331 Church St (60201-3940)
PHONE.....................847 903-7209
Charles Sheridan, *Owner*
EMP: 5 **EST:** 2011
SALES: 100K **Privately Held**
SIC: 3442 1611 Window & door frames; general contractor, highway & street construction

(G-9503)
CHASE CORPORATION
Tapecoat Company
1527 Lyons St (60201-3551)
P.O. Box 631 (60204-9031)
PHONE.....................847 866-8500
Tamer Mindaye, *Engineer*
Dick Reeves, *Branch Mgr*
Juan Lopez, *Manager*
EMP: 50
SALES (corp-wide): 281.3MM **Publicly Held**
SIC: 2672 2891 2851 2241 Adhesive papers, labels or tapes: from purchased material; adhesives & sealants; paints & allied products; narrow fabric mills
PA: Chase Corporation
295 University Ave
Westwood MA 02090
781 332-0700

(G-9504)
CHICAGO TANK LINING SALES
3603 Hillside Rd (60201-4936)
PHONE.....................847 328-0500
Warren Brand, *President*
Kenneth Brand, *Vice Pres*
Sheila Brand, *Admin Sec*
EMP: 9 **EST:** 1959
SQ FT: 3,000
SALES: 1.1MM **Privately Held**
SIC: 7699 3479 3443 Tank repair & cleaning services; tank repair; painting, coating & hot dipping; liners/lining; liners, industrial: metal plate

(G-9505)
CHRISTIAN NATIONAL WOMANS (PA)
Also Called: SIGNAL PRESS DIVISION
1730 Chicago Ave Ste 4585 (60201-4502)
PHONE.....................847 864-1396
Sarah F Ward, *President*
EMP: 3 **EST:** 1874
SALES: 116.1K **Privately Held**
SIC: 8661 2731 Religious organizations; book publishing

(G-9506)
COMMON CULTURE BREWING CO
Also Called: Sketchbook Brewing Co.
821 Chicago Ave (60202-2307)
PHONE.....................847 584-2337
Cesar Marron, *President*
Shawn Decker, *Manager*
EMP: 10
SALES: 600K **Privately Held**
SIC: 2082 5813 Malt beverages; bars & lounges

(G-9507)
CRYSTAL L SMITH
636 Church St Ste 510 (60201-4581)
PHONE.....................773 817-2797
Crystal Smith, *Principal*
EMP: 3
SALES (est): 110.1K **Privately Held**
SIC: 2741 Miscellaneous publishing

(G-9508)
DEAN PRSTHTIC ORTHTIC SVCS LTD
Also Called: Dean P & O Services
2530 Crawford Ave Ste 218 (60201-4959)
PHONE.....................847 475-7080
Linda Dean, *Owner*
Linda Jernigan, *Owner*
EMP: 5
SQ FT: 1,500
SALES (est): 277.3K **Privately Held**
SIC: 8011 3842 Specialized medical practitioners, except internal; surgical appliances & supplies

(G-9509)
DEPTH ACTION MARKETING GROUP
2512 Lawndale Ave (60201-1158)
PHONE.....................847 475-7122
Walter Holdamf, *President*
Sylvia Holdamf, *Corp Secy*
EMP: 4
SALES: 500K **Privately Held**
SIC: 3299 Images, small: gypsum, clay or papier mache

(G-9510)
DFG MERCURY CORP
Also Called: Df Goldsmith
909 Pitner Ave (60202-1550)
PHONE.....................847 869-7800
Robert P Goldsmith, *President*
James Moran, *Vice Pres*
EMP: 5
SQ FT: 5,500
SALES (est): 860.2K
SALES (corp-wide): 4.2MM **Privately Held**
SIC: 2819 Mercury, redistilled
PA: D. F. Goldsmith Chemical & Metal Corporation
909 Pitner Ave
Evanston IL
847 869-7800

(G-9511)
DOUBLETAKE MARKETING INC
54 Williamsburg Rd (60203-1813)
PHONE.....................845 598-3175
EMP: 2
SALES (est): 217.1K **Privately Held**
SIC: 2752 Commercial printing, lithographic

(G-9512)
DYNAMIC COLORS INC
1019 Florence Ave (60202-1150)
PHONE.....................847 721-8834
Anthony Giangrossi, *President*
EMP: 4 **EST:** 2004
SALES (est): 33.3K **Privately Held**
WEB: www.dynamiccolorsinc.com
SIC: 2893 Printing ink

(G-9513)
ENHANCED PLASMONICS LLC
820 Davis St Ste 216 (60201-4445)
PHONE.....................904 238-9270
Nathan Greenelch,
Martin Blaber,
EMP: 4
SALES (est): 250K **Privately Held**
SIC: 3826 Infrared analytical instruments

(G-9514)
ERDCO ENGINEERING CORPORATION
721 Custer Ave (60202-2200)
P.O. Box 6318 (60204-6318)
PHONE.....................847 328-0550
Bruce Nesvig, *President*
Robert Jeske, *Admin Sec*
EMP: 50
SQ FT: 21,000
SALES: 9.4MM **Privately Held**
WEB: www.erdco.com
SIC: 3825 3824 3829 3823 Instruments to measure electricity; fluid meters & counting devices; measuring & controlling devices; flow instruments, industrial process type

(G-9515)
EVANSTON AWNING COMPANY
2801 Central St (60201-1200)
PHONE.....................847 864-4520
Ann Hunzinger, *President*
Edward P Hunzinger Jr, *President*
EMP: 9
SQ FT: 7,200
SALES: 1MM **Privately Held**
WEB: www.evanstonawnings.com
SIC: 2394 5999 Awnings, fabric: made from purchased materials; canvas products

(G-9516)
EVANSTON GRAPHIC IMAGING INC
Also Called: Allegra Print & Imaging
1255 Hartrey Ave (60202-1056)
PHONE.....................847 869-7446
Frank Muns, *President*
Kyle Kurz, *Vice Pres*
Charlene Oracion, *Marketing Staff*
Sharon Knipmeyer, *Department Mgr*
▲ **EMP:** 9 **EST:** 1962
SQ FT: 47,000
SALES (est): 1.7MM **Privately Held**
WEB: www.allegraevanston.com
SIC: 2752 3663 2759 Commercial printing, offset; digital encoders; letterpress printing

(G-9517)
EVANSTON WOMAN MAGAZINE
1881 Oak Ave Apt 513w (60201-7403)
PHONE.....................847 722-5654
EMP: 3
SALES (est): 122.5K **Privately Held**
SIC: 2721 Magazines: publishing only, not printed on site

(G-9518)
EVE J ALFILLE LTD
Also Called: Eve J Alfille Gallery & Studio
623 Grove St (60201-4403)
PHONE.....................847 869-7920
Eve J Alfille, *President*
Diane Alfille, *Vice Pres*
Matt Arden, *Vice Pres*
Cato Heinz, *Sales Mgr*
Maurice Alfille, *Admin Sec*
EMP: 20
SQ FT: 3,600
SALES: 2MM **Privately Held**
SIC: 5944 3911 Jewelry, precious stones & precious metals; jewel settings & mountings, precious metal

(G-9519)
FEDEX OFFICE & PRINT SVCS INC
2518 Green Bay Rd (60201-2231)
PHONE.....................847 475-8650
EMP: 15
SALES (corp-wide): 69.6B **Publicly Held**
WEB: www.fedex.com
SIC: 7334 2791 2789 Photocopying & duplicating services; typesetting; bookbinding & related work
HQ: Fedex Office And Print Services, Inc.
7900 Legacy Dr
Plano TX 75024
800 463-3339

(G-9520)
FILMFAX MAGAZINE INC
Also Called: Outre'
1320 Oakton St (60202-2719)
PHONE.....................847 866-7155
Michael Stein, *President*
EMP: 2
SALES (est): 229.6K **Privately Held**
SIC: 2721 5942 Magazines: publishing only, not printed on site; book stores

(G-9521)
FLOW VALVES INTERNATIONAL LLC
500 Davis St Ste 600 (60201-4622)
PHONE.....................847 866-1188
George Stevenson, *Mng Member*
Cliff Deremo, *Mng Member*
EMP: 2
SALES (est): 228.5K **Privately Held**
SIC: 3492 Fluid power valves & hose fittings

(G-9522)
FRANK S JOHNSON & COMPANY INC
Also Called: Franks Auto Insurance A Div BR
818 Lake St (60201-4317)
PHONE.....................847 492-1660
Frank S Johnson, *President*
Richard F Johnson, *Admin Sec*
EMP: 3
SALES: 1MM **Privately Held**
SIC: 2951 6411 Asphalt & asphaltic paving mixtures (not from refineries); insurance agents, brokers & service

(G-9523)
FRANKS MAINTENANCE & ENGRG
Also Called: Forking By Frank
945 Pitner Ave (60202-1550)
PHONE.....................847 475-1003
Mary Stankovich, *President*
Douglas Graham, *Admin Sec*
EMP: 6
SQ FT: 3,500
SALES: 400K **Privately Held**
WEB: www.forking-by-frank.com
SIC: 5013 3312 3751 Motorcycle parts; pipes, iron & steel; motorcycles, bicycles & parts

(G-9524)
GERMANN INSTRUMENTS INC
8845 Forestview Rd (60203-1924)
PHONE.....................847 329-9999
Claus Petersen, *President*
Mariana Lara, *Vice Pres*
Barry Petrigala, *Sales Staff*
EMP: 7
SALES (est): 1.2MM **Privately Held**
SIC: 3829 Surveying & drafting equipment

(G-9525)
GOOSE PRINTING CO
8833 Ewing Ave (60203-1904)
PHONE.....................847 673-1414
Stuart Garber, *Owner*
EMP: 3
SALES (est): 291.8K **Privately Held**
SIC: 2752 Commercial printing, lithographic

(G-9526)
GORDON BURKE JOHN PUBLISHER
1032 Cleveland St (60202-2113)
PHONE.....................847 866-8625
John Gordon Burke, *President*
EMP: 6
SALES (est): 420.6K **Privately Held**
WEB: www.jgburkepub.com
SIC: 2731 Textbooks: publishing only, not printed on site

(G-9527)
GREEN AROUND SILLS LLC
1233 Judson Ave (60202-1371)
PHONE.....................847 868-8957
Prost Ronald, *Principal*
EMP: 3
SALES (est): 131.3K **Privately Held**
SIC: 2731 Book publishing

(G-9528)
GTX SURGERY INC
848 Dodge Ave Unit 384 (60202-1506)
PHONE.....................847 920-8489
EMP: 3
SALES (est): 78.2K **Privately Held**
SIC: 7372 Prepackaged Software Services

(G-9529)
H & H PRINTING
1800 Dempster St (60202-1003)
PHONE.....................847 866-9520
William Holloway, *President*
EMP: 6 **EST:** 1970
SQ FT: 5,000
SALES (est): 528.4K **Privately Held**
WEB: www.hnhprinting.com
SIC: 2759 Screen printing

(G-9530)
HALPER PUBLISHING COMPANY
913 Forest Ave Apt 2s (60202-5408)
PHONE.....................847 542-9793
Rick Levine, *President*
EMP: 4 **EST:** 1930
SQ FT: 1,300
SALES (est): 363.9K **Privately Held**
WEB: www.kathyhalper.com
SIC: 2721 2741 Magazines: publishing only, not printed on site; directories: publishing only, not printed on site

▲ = Import ▼ = Export ◆ = Import/Export

GEOGRAPHIC SECTION
Evanston - Cook County (G-9560)

(G-9531)
HARDSCHELLREPORT
1246 Hinman Ave (60202-1313)
PHONE..................................773 972-2500
Timothy Schell, *Principal*
EMP: 3
SALES (est): 112K **Privately Held**
WEB: www.hardschellreport.com
SIC: 2711 Newspapers, publishing & printing

(G-9532)
HMH SPORTS LLC
2727 Eastwood Ave (60201-1519)
PHONE..................................773 330-3789
Lara Hamann, *Principal*
EMP: 3
SALES (est): 191.7K **Privately Held**
SIC: 2731 Book publishing

(G-9533)
HOUGHTON MIFFLIN HARCOURT CO
Also Called: Hmh
909 Davis St Ste 300 (60201-3645)
PHONE..................................800 225-5425
Ryan Hall, *Accounts Exec*
EMP: 4
SALES (corp-wide): 1.3B **Publicly Held**
SIC: 3999 2731 Education aids, devices & supplies; book publishing
PA: Houghton Mifflin Harcourt Company
125 High St Ste 900
Boston MA 02110
617 351-5000

(G-9534)
HOUGHTON MIFFLIN HARCOURT PUBG
909 Davis St Ste 300 (60201-3645)
PHONE..................................847 869-2300
Caroline Chen, *Manager*
EMP: 350
SALES (corp-wide): 1.3B **Publicly Held**
SIC: 2731 Books: publishing only
HQ: Houghton Mifflin Harcourt Publishing Company
125 High St Ste 900
Boston MA 02110
617 351-5000

(G-9535)
HOUGHTON MIFFLIN HARCOURT PUBG
McDougal Littell
909 Davis St Ste 300 (60201-3645)
PHONE..................................708 869-2300
Julie A Mc Gee, *President*
EMP: 300
SALES (corp-wide): 1.3B **Publicly Held**
SIC: 2731 Textbooks: publishing only, not printed on site
HQ: Houghton Mifflin Harcourt Publishing Company
125 High St Ste 900
Boston MA 02110
617 351-5000

(G-9536)
HOUSE OF ATLAS LLC
1578 Sherman Ave Fl 2 (60201-4484)
PHONE..................................847 491-1800
Matthew Berman,
Jason Moss,
EMP: 6
SALES (est): 632.7K **Privately Held**
SIC: 2591 Drapery hardware & blinds & shades

(G-9537)
INCLUSION SOLUTIONS LLC
2000 Greenleaf Ste 3 (60202-1083)
PHONE..................................847 869-2500
Lisa Henthorn, *Mktg Dir*
Patrick Hughes,
Dawn Betz, *Admin Asst*
Kathy Nickolaus, *Representative*
▲ EMP: 7
SALES (est): 990K **Privately Held**
SIC: 3663 Radio & TV communications equipment

(G-9538)
INDUSTRIAL OPPRTNITY PRTNERS L (PA)
Also Called: Iop
1603 Orrington Ave # 700 (60201-3841)
PHONE..................................847 556-3460
Kenneth Tallering,
Adam R Gottlieb,
Robert M Vedra,
EMP: 29
SALES (est): 142.1MM **Privately Held**
SIC: 3751 3714 Motorcycle accessories; manifolds, motor vehicle

(G-9539)
INNOVATIONS FOR LEARNING INC (PA)
Also Called: SOFTWARE FOR SUCCESS
518 Davis St (60201-4644)
PHONE..................................800 975-3452
Seth Weinburger, *President*
Brian Hides, *Info Tech Dir*
John Friedman, *Director*
▲ EMP: 5
SALES: 1.8MM **Privately Held**
SIC: 7372 Prepackaged software

(G-9540)
INNOVTIVE DESIGN GRAPHICS CORP
Also Called: Innovative Design & Graphics
1327 Greenleaf St 1 (60202-1152)
PHONE..................................847 475-7772
Tim Sonder, *President*
EMP: 4
SQ FT: 1,500
SALES (est): 656.6K **Privately Held**
SIC: 2791 7336 2752 Typesetting; graphic arts & related design; commercial printing, lithographic

(G-9541)
JAMES ROSENBAUM CO
425 Davis St Unit 903 (60201-4825)
PHONE..................................847 859-7660
James Rosenbaum, *Principal*
EMP: 3
SALES (est): 115.9K **Privately Held**
SIC: 2339 Women's & misses' outerwear

(G-9542)
JOHN HARDY CO
Also Called: Hardy Company, The
1728 Brummel St (60202-3738)
PHONE..................................847 864-8060
John Hardy, *President*
Charles R Goerth, *Admin Sec*
EMP: 5
SALES (est): 200K **Privately Held**
SIC: 3651 Audio electronic systems

(G-9543)
JUST YOUR TYPE INC
1800 Dempster St (60202-1003)
PHONE..................................847 864-8890
William Holloway, *President*
EMP: 5
SQ FT: 1,500
SALES (est): 372.9K **Privately Held**
SIC: 7336 2791 Graphic arts & related design; typesetting

(G-9544)
KNOCKOUT LLC EVANSTON
1029 Davis St (60201-3609)
PHONE..................................224 714-3007
EMP: 3
SALES (est): 105.9K **Privately Held**
SIC: 2711 Newspapers, publishing & printing

(G-9545)
L P M INC
Also Called: Minuteman Press
1553 Sherman Ave (60201-4421)
PHONE..................................847 866-9777
Lisa Pharris Moran, *President*
Peter Moran, *Vice Pres*
EMP: 6
SALES (est): 625.1K **Privately Held**
SIC: 2752 7334 7336 Commercial printing, lithographic; photocopying & duplicating services; commercial art & graphic design

(G-9546)
LAKELAND BOATING MAGAZINE
Also Called: O'Meara/Brown Publications
630 Davis St Ste 301 (60201-4480)
PHONE..................................312 276-0610
Walter B O'Meara, *President*
Linda Omeara, *Publisher*
Patti McCleery, *Sales Staff*
Kate Bush, *Director*
Christy Bauhs, *Art Dir*
EMP: 9
SALES (est): 953.4K **Privately Held**
SIC: 2721 Magazines: publishing only, not printed on site

(G-9547)
LOCHMAN REF SILK SCREEN CO
Also Called: R.E.F. Silk Screen Productions
2405 Oakton St (60202-2743)
PHONE..................................847 475-6266
Adeline Hatzel, *Ch of Bd*
Phillip J Koser, *President*
Richard Magis, *Exec VP*
Dan Koser, *Vice Pres*
Robert Fuchs, *Admin Sec*
EMP: 14 EST: 1934
SQ FT: 10,000
SALES (est): 900K **Privately Held**
WEB: www.phico-ref.com
SIC: 5085 3069 3861 2396 Seals, industrial; printers' rolls & blankets: rubber or rubberized fabric; photographic processing chemicals; automotive & apparel trimmings

(G-9548)
M WARD MANUFACTURING CO INC
2222 2230 Main St (60202)
PHONE..................................847 864-4786
Michael Ward Jr, *President*
EMP: 42 EST: 1943
SALES (est): 9.1MM **Privately Held**
WEB: www.wardmfgco.com
SIC: 3469 3544 Stamping metal for the trade; special dies, tools, jigs & fixtures

(G-9549)
MANUFACTURERS NEWS INC
Also Called: Mni
1633 Central St (60201-1569)
PHONE..................................847 864-7000
Thomas Dubin, *President*
Mitch Aronov, *Editor*
Howard S Dubin, *Chairman*
Geraldine Major, *Cust Mgr*
Bob Burke, *Accounts Exec*
EMP: 95 EST: 1912
SQ FT: 20,000
SALES (est): 13.3MM **Privately Held**
WEB: www.manufacturersnews.com
SIC: 7379 2741 Computer related consulting services; directories: publishing only, not printed on site

(G-9550)
METTLE SPORTS LLC
1555 Sherman Ave Ste 22 (60201-4421)
PHONE..................................312 757-6373
Niel Lavine, *CEO*
EMP: 4
SALES (est): 178.3K **Privately Held**
SIC: 3949 Team sports equipment

(G-9551)
MICHELE TERRELL
Also Called: Premiere Distribution
230 Dodge Ave Unit C (60202-3663)
PHONE..................................312 305-0876
Michele Terrell, *Owner*
EMP: 3
SALES (est): 175.8K **Privately Held**
SIC: 3677 3672 Coil windings, electronic; transformers power supply, electronic type; filtration devices, electronic; inductors, electronic; printed circuit boards

(G-9552)
MICROSOFT CORPORATION
1822 Ridge Ave Ste 210 (60201-5927)
PHONE..................................847 864-4777
David Ostrov, *Branch Mgr*
EMP: 35
SALES (corp-wide): 125.8B **Publicly Held**
SIC: 7372 Application computer software
PA: Microsoft Corporation
1 Microsoft Way
Redmond WA 98052
425 882-8080

(G-9553)
MINASIAN RUG CORPORATION
1244 Chicago Ave (60202-1338)
PHONE..................................847 864-1010
Armen Minasian, *President*
Minasian Carnig, *Advisor*
EMP: 3
SALES (est): 134.4K **Privately Held**
SIC: 2273 Carpets & rugs

(G-9554)
MINUTE MLCULAR DIAGNOSTICS INC
Hogan Blgcal Scnces Bldg (60208-0001)
PHONE..................................847 849-0263
David Kelso, *Mng Member*
EMP: 3 EST: 2017
SALES (est): 151.2K **Privately Held**
SIC: 3841 Surgical & medical instruments

(G-9555)
MONOGRAM OF EVANSTON INC
Also Called: Monogram Etched Crystal
727 Clinton Pl (60201-3093)
PHONE..................................847 864-8100
Philip C Holm, *President*
▲ EMP: 1 EST: 1936
SALES: 300K **Privately Held**
WEB: www.prismetchedawards.net
SIC: 3231 3479 Decorated glassware: chipped, engraved, etched, etc.; etching & engraving

(G-9556)
NANOCYTOMICS LLC
1801 Maple Ave Ste 19 (60201-3150)
PHONE..................................847 467-2868
Michael Verleye, *Engineer*
Vadim Backman,
EMP: 2
SALES (est): 230.4K **Privately Held**
SIC: 3845 Ultrasonic scanning devices, medical

(G-9557)
NAUREX INC
1801 Maple Ave Ste 70 (60201-5103)
PHONE..................................847 871-0377
Norbert G Riedel, *CEO*
Derek Small, *President*
Jam Leestma, *Chief Mktg Ofcr*
Mitchell Bloom, *Admin Sec*
EMP: 3
SQ FT: 1,000
SALES (est): 733.4K **Privately Held**
SIC: 8071 2834 Neurological laboratory; pharmaceutical preparations
PA: Allergan Limited
Clonshaugh Business And Technology Park
Dublin

(G-9558)
NEON DESIGN INC
519 Howard St (60202-4005)
PHONE..................................773 880-5020
Peter Schwaba, *President*
Joan Schwaba, *Admin Sec*
EMP: 3
SALES: 375K **Privately Held**
SIC: 5046 3993 Neon signs; signs & advertising specialties

(G-9559)
ODX MEDIA LLC
848 Dodge Ave (60202-1506)
PHONE..................................847 868-0548
Karla Figueroa,
EMP: 5
SALES (est): 240.9K **Privately Held**
SIC: 2741

(G-9560)
OFFICE EXPRESS INC
1555 Sherman Ave 129 (60201-4421)
PHONE..................................888 526-8438
Sarah Bruns, *President*
William Raspe, *President*

(PA)=Parent Co (HQ)=Headquarters (DH)=Div Headquarters
✪ = New Business established in last 2 years

2020 Harris Illinois Industrial Directory

Evanston - Cook County (G-9561)

EMP: 3
SQ FT: 3,000
SALES: 325K **Privately Held**
SIC: 2677 5112 Envelopes; envelopes

(G-9561)
OHMX CORPORATION
1801 Maple Ave Ste 18 (60201-3150)
PHONE..................847 491-8500
Charles Rowland, *CEO*
EMP: 12
SALES (est): 2.8MM **Privately Held**
SIC: 2835 In vitro & in vivo diagnostic substances

(G-9562)
OLD TOWN OIL EVANSTON
1924 Central St (60201-2228)
PHONE..................312 787-9595
John D Dine, *Principal*
EMP: 3 EST: 2011
SALES (est): 203.4K **Privately Held**
WEB: www.oldtownoil.com
SIC: 2079 Olive oil

(G-9563)
OPTICENT INC
600 Davis St Fl 3 (60201-4488)
PHONE..................410 829-7384
Kieren Patel, *CEO*
Roman Kuranov, *Engineer*
Cheng Sun, *CTO*
Hao Zhang, *CTO*
EMP: 5
SALES (est): 275.3K **Privately Held**
SIC: 3841 Ophthalmic instruments & apparatus

(G-9564)
OZINGA BROS INC
2525 Oakton St (60202-2759)
PHONE..................312 432-5700
Kevin Coburn, *Principal*
EMP: 61
SALES (corp-wide): 434.5MM **Privately Held**
SIC: 3273 Ready-mixed concrete
PA: Ozinga Bros., Inc.
  19001 Old Lagrange Rd # 30
  Mokena IL 60448
  708 326-4200

(G-9565)
PETERSON DERMOND DESIGN LLC
900 Grove St Ste 10 (60201-6523)
PHONE..................414 383-5029
Susan Peterson,
EMP: 3
SQ FT: 8,169
SALES (est): 287.1K **Privately Held**
SIC: 2392 Hassocks, textile: made from purchased materials

(G-9566)
PHALANX TRAINING INC
617 Grove St Ste A (60201-4478)
PHONE..................847 859-9156
Jordan Zoot, *CEO*
EMP: 3 EST: 2013
SALES (est): 207K **Privately Held**
SIC: 3484 Guns (firearms) or gun parts, 30 mm. & below

(G-9567)
PM WOODWIND REPAIR INC
822 Custer Ave (60202-2269)
PHONE..................847 869-7049
Paul Maslin, *President*
EMP: 8
SALES (est): 392K **Privately Held**
SIC: 7692 5099 Welding repair; musical instruments

(G-9568)
PNEU FAST COMPANY
Also Called: Pneu-Fast
2200 Greenleaf St (60202-1030)
PHONE..................847 866-8787
Edward Chester, *President*
Reno Joseph, *Vice Pres*
Kalin Richardson, *Opers Staff*
▲ EMP: 18
SQ FT: 40,000
SALES (est): 4.3MM **Privately Held**
WEB: www.pneufast.com
SIC: 3315 Nails, spikes, brads & similar items

(G-9569)
PRINT NINJA LLC
Also Called: Printninja
1603 Orrington Ave # 150 (60201-3841)
PHONE..................877 396-4652
Potterfield April, *Principal*
Jen Talvensaari, *Manager*
EMP: 7
SALES (est): 480.7K **Privately Held**
WEB: www.printninja.com
SIC: 2752 Commercial printing, offset

(G-9570)
PRINTED WORD INC
1807 Central St (60201-1509)
PHONE..................847 328-1511
Bernard Brady, *President*
EMP: 3 EST: 1983
SQ FT: 2,200
SALES (est): 230K **Privately Held**
SIC: 2752 7336 2791 2789 Lithographing on metal; commercial art & graphic design; typesetting; bookbinding & related work

(G-9571)
PRIVA MOBILITY INC
515 Sheridan Rd Apt 103 (60202-3109)
PHONE..................248 410-3702
Patrick Hunt, *President*
EMP: 3
SALES (est): 78.4K **Privately Held**
SIC: 4789 7372 Transportation services; application computer software

(G-9572)
PSYLOTECH INC
1616 Payne St (60201-3032)
PHONE..................847 328-7100
Alex Arzoumanidis, *President*
EMP: 9 EST: 2008
SQ FT: 2,000
SALES (est): 1.5MM **Privately Held**
WEB: www.psylotech.com
SIC: 3829 7371 Measuring & controlling devices; computer software development & applications

(G-9573)
S R BASTIEN CO
Also Called: Retailer Watch Newsletter
600 Davis St Rear (60201-4488)
P.O. Box 8196, Gurnee (60031-7011)
PHONE..................847 858-1175
EMP: 10
SQ FT: 6,000
SALES (est): 1.1MM **Privately Held**
SIC: 2731 7331 2721 Pamphlets: publishing only, not printed on site; direct mail advertising services; periodicals

(G-9574)
SEEK DESIGN
Also Called: Seek Sustainable Designs
1914 Darrow Ave (60201-3455)
PHONE..................312 804-6629
Renee Casagranda, *CEO*
EMP: 5
SALES: 620K **Privately Held**
SIC: 7389 1389 8742 5932 Interior design services; interior decorating; construction, repair & dismantling services; retail trade consultant; antiques

(G-9575)
SOCIUS INGREDIENTS LLC
1033 University Pl # 110 (60201-3196)
PHONE..................847 440-0156
Martin O'Donovan, *Mng Member*
▲ EMP: 13
SQ FT: 5,000
SALES (est): 3.8MM **Privately Held**
WEB: www.sociusingredients.com
SIC: 2026 Milk & cream, except fermented, cultured & flavored
PA: Lakeland Dairies Co-Operative Society Ltd
  Killeshandra
  Cavan

(G-9576)
SPIKED
1620 Fowler Ave (60201-3957)
PHONE..................469 235-8103
William Loden, *Principal*
EMP: 3
SALES (est): 148.8K **Privately Held**
SIC: 3411 Metal cans

(G-9577)
SRS GLOBAL RET SOLUTIONS LLC (PA)
Also Called: Only One Boutique
1001 Brown Ave (60202-1012)
PHONE..................773 888-3094
Shawna Spencer,
EMP: 1
SALES (est): 236.2K **Privately Held**
SIC: 3172 5137 5621 Personal leather goods; women's & children's clothing; women's clothing stores

(G-9578)
ST JOHNS UNITED CHURCH CHRIST
Also Called: St John S United Church of
1136 Wesley Ave (60202-1163)
PHONE..................847 491-6686
Charles Powell, *President*
Rev Todd Mushaney, *Pastor*
EMP: 3
SALES (est): 186.9K **Privately Held**
SIC: 2741 8661 Miscellaneous publishing; Church of Christ

(G-9579)
STUDENTS PUBLISHING COMPANY IN
Also Called: DAILY NORTHWESTERN NEWSPAPER
1999 Sheridan Rd (60201-2924)
PHONE..................847 491-7206
Charles Whitaker, *Chairman*
Mike Bass, *Manager*
Stacia G Campbell, *Manager*
Michael Kelley, *Technology*
EMP: 2
SQ FT: 1,200
SALES: 395K **Privately Held**
SIC: 2731 2711 Books: publishing only; newspapers: publishing only, not printed on site

(G-9580)
SURREY BOOKS INC
1501 Madison St (60202-2033)
PHONE..................847 475-4457
Susan Schwartz, *President*
EMP: 3
SQ FT: 1,000
SALES (est): 140K **Privately Held**
SIC: 2731 Books: publishing only

(G-9581)
SV FAMILY EVANSTON LLC
6 Martha Ln (60201-2121)
PHONE..................773 420-6767
Shannon Valko, *Principal*
EMP: 4 EST: 2017
SALES (est): 190.5K **Privately Held**
SIC: 2711 Newspapers, publishing & printing

(G-9582)
TAGS BAKERY INC
Also Called: Tag's Bakery & Pastry Shop
2010 Central St (60201-2218)
PHONE..................847 328-1200
Gregory Vetter, *President*
Donald J Vetter, *President*
Greg Vetter, *Vice Pres*
Gretchen Vetter, *Treasurer*
Jan Vetter, *Admin Sec*
EMP: 25
SQ FT: 2,500
SALES (est): 1.2MM **Privately Held**
WEB: www.evanstonbakery.com
SIC: 5461 2052 2051 Cakes; cookies & crackers; bread, cake & related products

(G-9583)
TEMPERANCE BEER COMPANY LLC
2000 Dempster St (60202-1072)
PHONE..................847 864-1000
Emily Kwasny, *Opers Staff*
Josh Dildert,
EMP: 8
SALES (est): 573.6K **Privately Held**
WEB: www.temperancebeer.com
SIC: 2041 Corn grits & flakes, for brewers' use

(G-9584)
THOMAS A DOAN
Also Called: Estima
2717 Harrison St (60201-1215)
PHONE..................847 864-8772
Thomas A Doan, *Owner*
EMP: 3
SALES (est): 362.6K **Privately Held**
SIC: 7372 7371 Business oriented computer software; custom computer programming services

(G-9585)
UBERLUBE INC
2611 Hartzell St (60201-1311)
PHONE..................847 372-3127
Jack A Magnusen, *President*
▲ EMP: 7 EST: 2011
SALES (est): 1.3MM **Privately Held**
WEB: www.uberlube.com
SIC: 2992 Lubricating oils & greases

(G-9586)
UBERLUBE INC
8833 Lincolnwood Dr (60203-1926)
PHONE..................847 644-4230
John Epler, *Principal*
EMP: 3
SALES (est): 259.5K **Privately Held**
SIC: 2869 Silicones

(G-9587)
WCTU PRESS (PA)
Also Called: Woman Christian Temperance Un
1730 Chicago Ave (60201-4502)
PHONE..................847 864-1396
Sarah F Ward, *President*
EMP: 9
SALES: 14.6K **Privately Held**
SIC: 2732 Pamphlets: printing only, not published on site

(G-9588)
WILLIAM HOLLOWAY LTD
Also Called: Sir Speedy
1800 Dempster St (60202-1003)
PHONE..................847 866-9520
William Holloway, *President*
EMP: 9
SQ FT: 2,400
SALES: 750K **Privately Held**
SIC: 2752 7334 2789 2759 Commercial printing, lithographic; photocopying & duplicating services; bookbinding & related work; commercial printing; coated & laminated paper

(G-9589)
WONDER KIDS INC
1719 Brummel St (60202-3737)
PHONE..................773 437-8025
Sarah White, *Principal*
EMP: 3
SALES (est): 185.1K **Privately Held**
WEB: www.wonderkidsinc.com
SIC: 3261 Bathroom accessories/fittings, vitreous china or earthenware

Evansville
Randolph County

(G-9590)
VOGES INC
Also Called: Ice Maid
502 Chestnut St (62242-1822)
PHONE..................618 233-2760
Kirk Howell, *Manager*
EMP: 13
SALES (corp-wide): 14.7MM **Privately Held**
SIC: 3469 5078 Metal stampings; ice making machines

GEOGRAPHIC SECTION

Fairfield - Wayne County (G-9618)

PA: Voges, Inc.
100 N 24th St
Belleville IL 62226
618 233-2760

(G-9591)
WOLTERS CUSTOM CABINETS LLC
8204 State Route 3 (62242-1020)
PHONE.....................618 282-3158
Glenn A Wolter, *Mng Member*
Glenn Wolter, *Mng Member*
EMP: 8 EST: 2001
SQ FT: 6,000
SALES: 1MM **Privately Held**
SIC: 2434 Wood kitchen cabinets

Evergreen Park
Cook County

(G-9592)
DELTA DESIGN INC
3140 W 92nd St (60805-1602)
PHONE.....................708 424-9400
Cynthia M Tallent, *President*
John H Gaden, *Vice Pres*
John Gaden, *Vice Pres*
▲ EMP: 12 EST: 1976
SQ FT: 4,000
SALES: 675K **Privately Held**
WEB: www.deltadesigncorp.com
SIC: 3599 5999 3679 Machine shop, jobbing & repair; electronic parts & equipment; harness assemblies for electronic use: wire or cable

(G-9593)
ECLIPSE AWNINGS INC
3609 W 95th St (60805-2119)
PHONE.....................708 636-3160
Rey Williams, *Manager*
EMP: 15
SALES (est): 790K **Privately Held**
SIC: 3444 2394 5999 Awnings & canopies; canvas awnings & canopies; awnings

(G-9594)
EVERGREEN MARATHON
2755 W 87th St (60805-1104)
PHONE.....................708 636-5700
EMP: 3
SALES (est): 153.3K **Privately Held**
SIC: 1389 Oil/Gas Field Services

(G-9595)
J GARVIN INDUSTRIES INC
Also Called: Chicago Cremation Supplies
3513 W 97th St (60805-3017)
PHONE.....................708 297-7400
Adrienne Garvin, *Manager*
EMP: 4
SALES (corp-wide): 989.8K **Privately Held**
SIC: 3995 Burial caskets
PA: J Garvin Industries Inc.
14750 S Campbell Ave
Posen IL 60469
708 297-7400

(G-9596)
KM CABINET SUPPLY
3841 W 95th St (60805-2020)
PHONE.....................312 927-8860
EMP: 2 EST: 2016
SALES (est): 210.4K **Privately Held**
WEB: www.mkcabinet.com
SIC: 2434 Wood kitchen cabinets

(G-9597)
MENARD INC
9100 S Western Ave (60805-2501)
PHONE.....................708 346-9144
Juan Horton, *President*
EMP: 68
SALES (corp-wide): 11.4B **Privately Held**
SIC: 2431 Millwork
PA: Menard, Inc.
5101 Menard Dr
Eau Claire WI 54703
715 876-5911

(G-9598)
ROBERT L MURPHY
9545 S Hamlin Ave (60805-2030)
PHONE.....................708 424-0277
Robert Murphy, *Principal*
EMP: 4
SALES (est): 378.9K **Privately Held**
SIC: 3565 Vacuum packaging machinery

(G-9599)
RYAN MEAT COMPANY
9620 S Millard Ave (60805-2909)
PHONE.....................773 783-3840
Corneilios Ryan, *President*
Gerald Ryan, *Corp Secy*
Jerry Crofton, *Vice Pres*
EMP: 7
SALES (est): 1.4MM **Privately Held**
WEB: www.ryansmeats.com
SIC: 5147 2013 2011 Meats, fresh; sausages & other prepared meats; meat packing plants

(G-9600)
SEASONAL MAGNETS
3133 W 102nd St (60805-3516)
PHONE.....................708 499-3235
EMP: 3
SALES (est): 195.4K **Privately Held**
SIC: 3674 Mfg Semiconductors/Related Devices

(G-9601)
TANGENT SCREEN PRINT INC
9041 S Albany Ave (60805-1331)
PHONE.....................773 342-1223
Donnell Hall, *President*
Robert Hamano, *Admin Sec*
Shirley Haythorn, *Administration*
EMP: 10
SQ FT: 12,000
SALES (est): 1.5MM **Privately Held**
SIC: 2752 Commercial printing, lithographic

Ewing
Franklin County

(G-9602)
K & K STORAGE BARNS LLC (PA)
Also Called: K & K Buildings
19867 Ketterman Ln (62836-1307)
PHONE.....................618 927-0533
Keith Ebersole, *Mng Member*
Gordon Ebersole,
EMP: 12
SQ FT: 9,600
SALES (est): 1MM **Privately Held**
SIC: 3448 Prefabricated metal buildings

Fairbury
Livingston County

(G-9603)
ARCHER-DANIELS-MIDLAND COMPANY
Also Called: ADM
Rr 24 Box E (61739)
P.O. Box 205 (61739-0205)
PHONE.....................815 692-2324
Chris Hamilton, *Branch Mgr*
EMP: 5
SALES (corp-wide): 64.6B **Publicly Held**
SIC: 2041 Flour & other grain mill products
PA: Archer-Daniels-Midland Company
77 W Wacker Dr Ste 4600
Chicago IL 60601
312 634-8100

(G-9604)
AVOCA RIDGE LTD
Also Called: Design and Woodworks
310 S 7th St Ste 2 (61739-1687)
PHONE.....................815 692-4772
James A Tipton, *Owner*
EMP: 2 EST: 1999
SALES (est): 250K **Privately Held**
WEB: www.avocaridge.com
SIC: 3429 Cabinet hardware

(G-9605)
DOUBLE M MACHINE INC
614 W Pine St (61739-1453)
PHONE.....................815 692-4676
Jim Meister, *President*
Martin Meister, *President*
EMP: 12
SQ FT: 5,600
SALES (est): 1.7MM **Privately Held**
SIC: 3544 Special dies & tools

(G-9606)
E-MOTION LLC
124 W Locust St (61739-1549)
PHONE.....................815 825-4411
John A Slagel,
EMP: 5 EST: 2006
SQ FT: 1,200
SALES (est): 900K **Privately Held**
SIC: 8711 3829 5084 Engineering services; gauges, motor vehicle: oil pressure, water temperature; controlling instruments & accessories

(G-9607)
FEHR CAB INTERIORS
10116 N 1900 East Rd (61739-9265)
PHONE.....................815 692-3355
Ron Fehr, *Owner*
Norma Fehrm, *Partner*
▲ EMP: 7
SQ FT: 8,100
SALES (est): 782.1K **Privately Held**
SIC: 7641 3523 Upholstery work; farm machinery & equipment

(G-9608)
HOFFMAN TOOL INC
1301 W Oak St (61739-1490)
PHONE.....................815 692-4643
Gerald Hoffman, *President*
EMP: 20
SQ FT: 32,000
SALES (est): 1.8MM **Privately Held**
SIC: 3544 Special dies & tools

(G-9609)
JENNER PRECISION INC
8735 N 2000 East Rd (61739-9101)
PHONE.....................815 692-6655
James L Fehr, *President*
Bryan Fehr, *General Mgr*
Clint B Hohenstein, *Admin Sec*
EMP: 10
SALES (est): 471.6K **Privately Held**
WEB: www.jennerprecision.com
SIC: 5999 3711 Farm equipment & supplies; truck & tractor truck assembly

(G-9610)
JOHN JODA POST 54
Also Called: Fairbury Fair Association
600 S 3rd St (61739-1586)
P.O. Box 74 (61739-0074)
PHONE.....................815 692-3222
Dennis Kaisner, *President*
EMP: 3
SALES (est): 1.2MM **Privately Held**
SIC: 8641 2499 Veterans' organization; bakers' equipment, wood

(G-9611)
L & W FUELS
5484 N 2100 East Rd (61739-9151)
PHONE.....................815 848-8360
James Waldbeser, *Owner*
EMP: 3
SALES (est): 215.8K **Privately Held**
SIC: 2869 Fuels

(G-9612)
PTC TUBULAR PRODUCTS LLC
Also Called: Fairbury Division
23041 E 800 North Rd (61739-8824)
PHONE.....................815 692-4900
Gabe Shafer, *Purchasing*
Daniel McMinn, *Branch Mgr*
Jill Davis, *Manager*
EMP: 112 **Privately Held**
SIC: 3312 3321 3317 3498 Tubes, steel & iron; gray & ductile iron foundries; steel pipe & tubes; tube fabricating (contract bending & shaping)
HQ: Ptc Tubular Products Llc
1480 Nw 11th St
Richmond IN 47374

(G-9613)
SLAGEL DRAPERY SERVICE
302 S 8th St (61739-1315)
PHONE.....................815 692-3834
Judy Slagel, *Owner*
EMP: 3
SALES (est): 246.6K **Privately Held**
SIC: 2391 2392 Draperies, plastic & textile: from purchased materials; household furnishings

(G-9614)
TECHNICAL METALS INC
Also Called: TMI
1301 W Oak St (61739-1490)
P.O. Box 140 (61739-0140)
PHONE.....................815 692-4643
Gerald Hoffman, *President*
Becky Hoffman, *Warehouse Mgr*
William Allonge, *Foreman/Supr*
Jennifer Bracken, *Purchasing*
Rosemary Hoffman, *Treasurer*
EMP: 100
SQ FT: 32,000
SALES (est): 25.5MM **Privately Held**
SIC: 3469 3599 Machine parts, stamped or pressed metal; stamping metal for the trade; machine shop, jobbing & repair

(G-9615)
U S CO-TRONICS CORP
403 E Locust St (61739-1652)
P.O. Box 168 (61739-0168)
PHONE.....................815 692-3204
Paul Bullard, *President*
Sharlene Bullard, *Admin Sec*
EMP: 40
SQ FT: 9,000
SALES (est): 6.2MM **Privately Held**
SIC: 3621 3677 3612 Coils, for electric motors or generators; electronic coils, transformers & other inductors; transformers, except electric

Fairfield
Wayne County

(G-9616)
ACE CUSTOM UPHOLSTERY & ROD SP
200 W Delaware St (62837-1712)
PHONE.....................618 842-2913
Amos Eckleberry, *Owner*
EMP: 3
SALES (est): 140K **Privately Held**
SIC: 3315 Steel wire & related products

(G-9617)
AIRTEX PRODUCTS LP (DH)
407 W Main St (62837-1622)
PHONE.....................618 842-2111
David Peace, *CEO*
Thomas Degnan, *Partner*
◆ EMP: 30
SALES (est): 69.4MM
SALES (corp-wide): 332.6MM **Privately Held**
SIC: 3714 Fuel pumps, motor vehicle
HQ: Trico Products Corporation
3255 W Hamlin Rd
Rochester Hills MI 48309
248 371-1700

(G-9618)
BALDWIN TECHNOLOGY COMPANY INC
Also Called: Baldwin Americas
600 Us Highway 45 Ste A (62837-2555)
PHONE.....................618 842-2664
Bruce Fetherling, *Vice Pres*
Greg McGrath, *Sales Staff*
Dennis McManus, *Sales Staff*
Frank Simonetti, *Manager*
Brett Reynolds, *Info Tech Mgr*
EMP: 110 **Privately Held**
SIC: 3555 3822 3625 Printing trades machinery; auto controls regulating residntl & coml environmt & applncs; relays & industrial controls
HQ: Baldwin Technology Company, Inc.
8040 Forsyth Blvd
Saint Louis MO 63105
314 726-2152

(PA)=Parent Co (HQ)=Headquarters (DH)=Div Headquarters
✪ = New Business established in last 2 years

Fairfield - Wayne County (G-9619)

(G-9619)
BASNETT INVESTMENTS
Also Called: Basnett, John
215 Se 3rd St Ste 208 (62837-2172)
PHONE..................................618 842-4040
John Basnett, *Partner*
Greg Basnett, *Partner*
EMP: 3
SQ FT: 600
SALES (est): 1.6MM **Privately Held**
SIC: 1311 Crude petroleum production

(G-9620)
BULLARDS BAKERY
906 E Main St (62837-2216)
PHONE..................................618 842-6666
Jennifer Collins, *Owner*
EMP: 3
SALES (est): 189.1K **Privately Held**
SIC: 2051 Bakery: wholesale or wholesale/retail combined

(G-9621)
CARDINAL CONSTRUCTION CO
705 S 1st St (62837-1804)
PHONE..................................618 842-5553
Melvin Clark, *President*
EMP: 4
SALES (est): 512.1K **Privately Held**
SIC: 3585 Room coolers, portable

(G-9622)
FAIRFIELD ACID AND FRAC CO
Hwy 15 W (62837)
PHONE..................................618 842-9186
Jerry Friend, *Partner*
Paul Friend, *Partner*
Gary Grove, *Partner*
EMP: 10
SQ FT: 7,000
SALES (est): 520K **Privately Held**
SIC: 1389 Acidizing wells; oil field services

(G-9623)
FAIRFIELD READY MIX INC
Also Called: Garman Trucking
County Rte 45 N (62837)
P.O. Box 5 (62837-0005)
PHONE..................................618 842-9462
Ed Musgrave, *President*
Robert Musgrave, *Corp Secy*
Robert P Musgrave, *Treasurer*
EMP: 5
SQ FT: 2,200
SALES (est): 569K **Privately Held**
SIC: 3273 Ready-mixed concrete

(G-9624)
FRIEND OIL CO
Enterprise Rd Rr 3 (62837)
P.O. Box 545 (62837-0545)
PHONE..................................618 842-9161
Jerry Friend, *Owner*
EMP: 5
SQ FT: 1,500
SALES (est): 376.8K **Privately Held**
SIC: 1311 Crude petroleum production

(G-9625)
GAIN WIRELINE SERVICES INC
306a Petroleum Blvd (62837)
PHONE..................................618 842-2914
Fax: 618 842-9131
EMP: 2
SQ FT: 3,200
SALES (est): 202.1K **Privately Held**
SIC: 1389 Oil Well Logging & Perforation

(G-9626)
GORDYS MACHINE AND TOOL INC
1101 Sw 3rd St (62837-1866)
P.O. Box 760 (62837-0760)
PHONE..................................618 842-9331
Gordon Toombs, *President*
Dianne Toombs, *Vice Pres*
EMP: 15
SALES (est): 2MM **Privately Held**
SIC: 3599 Machine shop, jobbing & repair

(G-9627)
JACK WALTERS & SONS CORP
Also Called: Walters Buildings
204 E Main St (62837-2002)
P.O. Box 455 (62837-0455)
PHONE..................................618 842-2642
Fred Gilbert, *Manager*
EMP: 20
SALES (corp-wide): 25.2MM **Privately Held**
SIC: 3448 Buildings, portable: prefabricated metal
PA: Jack Walters & Sons, Corp.
6600 Midland Ct
Allenton WI 53002
262 629-5521

(G-9628)
JHT ROBERTSON LUMBER INC
408 Airport Rd (62837-1377)
PHONE..................................618 842-2004
Harold Robertson, *President*
EMP: 9
SALES (est): 1MM **Privately Held**
SIC: 2421 Lumber: rough, sawed or planed

(G-9629)
JONES GARRISON SONS MCH WORKS
Hwy 15 W (62837)
P.O. Box 274 (62837-0274)
PHONE..................................618 847-2161
Carroll E Garrison, *President*
EMP: 3
SQ FT: 2,400
SALES: 250K **Privately Held**
SIC: 7699 5999 3599 7539 Engine repair & replacement, non-automotive; agricultural equipment repair services; industrial machinery & equipment repair; engine & motor equipment & supplies; machine shop, jobbing & repair; radiator repair shop, automotive

(G-9630)
LARRY MUSGRAVE LOGGING
414 Nw 6th St (62837-1510)
PHONE..................................618 842-6386
Larry Musgrave, *Owner*
EMP: 4
SALES (est): 291.9K **Privately Held**
SIC: 2421 2411 Sawmills & planing mills, general; logging

(G-9631)
LEGGS MANUFACTURING
900 W Delaware St (62837-1411)
PHONE..................................618 842-9847
David Legg, *Owner*
EMP: 7
SALES (est): 727.4K **Privately Held**
SIC: 3446 Architectural metalwork

(G-9632)
MID STATES SALVAGE
Also Called: Mid States Distributing
6 Petroleum Blvd (62837)
P.O. Box 111 (62837-0111)
PHONE..................................618 842-6741
Tom Taylor, *Owner*
EMP: 8
SQ FT: 1,000
SALES (est): 1MM **Privately Held**
SIC: 1382 Oil & gas exploration services

(G-9633)
MID-STATES SERVICES LLC
6 Petroleum Blvd (62837)
P.O. Box 111 (62837-0111)
PHONE..................................618 842-4726
Taylor Tommy J, *President*
EMP: 10
SALES (est): 348.4K **Privately Held**
SIC: 1389 Oil field services

(G-9634)
REEF DEVELOPMENT INC
Rr 3 (62837)
P.O. Box 666 (62837-0666)
PHONE..................................618 842-7711
Jerry E Friend, *President*
Kevin Scheuneman, *Corp Secy*
EMP: 12
SALES (est): 1MM **Privately Held**
SIC: 1381 Drilling oil & gas wells

(G-9635)
REPUBLIC OIL CO INC
1508 W Delaware St (62837-2333)
P.O. Box D (62837-0089)
PHONE..................................618 842-7591
Eldon Doty, *President*
EMP: 4
SQ FT: 1,000
SALES (est): 670.2K **Privately Held**
SIC: 1311 Crude petroleum production

(G-9636)
ROBINSON PRODUCTION INC
108 Ne 7th St (62837-2153)
P.O. Box 131 (62837-0131)
PHONE..................................618 842-6111
Ann B Robinson, *President*
EMP: 5
SALES (est): 2,000
SALES (est): 434.7K **Privately Held**
WEB: www.robinsonknife.com
SIC: 1311 Crude petroleum production

(G-9637)
STRATA EXPLORATION INC
201 Ne 7th St (62837-2154)
P.O. Box 401 (62837-0401)
PHONE..................................618 842-2610
John R Kinney, *President*
Sheila Kinney, *Treasurer*
EMP: 2 **EST:** 2001
SALES (est): 267.2K **Privately Held**
SIC: 1382 Geophysical exploration, oil & gas field

(G-9638)
VAUGHAN EQUIPMENT INC
1102 S 1st St (62837-1857)
PHONE..................................618 842-3500
Josh Vaughan, *President*
Carroll Howard, *Vice Pres*
Jansen Vaughan, *Admin Sec*
EMP: 3
SALES (est): 143.3K **Privately Held**
SIC: 3715 Truck trailers

(G-9639)
VAUGHN & SONS MACHINE SHOP
Hwy 45 (62837)
PHONE..................................618 842-9048
Robert T Vaughn, *Owner*
Rosina Vaughn, *Co-Owner*
EMP: 3
SALES: 250K **Privately Held**
SIC: 5082 7692 3541 Oil field equipment; welding repair; machine tools, metal cutting type

(G-9640)
WAYNE COUNTY PRESS INC
213 E Main St (62837-2028)
P.O. Box F (62837-0149)
PHONE..................................618 842-2662
C Preston Mathews, *President*
Thomas O Mathews Jr, *Vice Pres*
EMP: 31
SQ FT: 12,000
SALES (est): 2.4MM **Privately Held**
WEB: www.waycopress.com
SIC: 2711 Commercial printing & newspaper publishing combined; newspapers: publishing only, not printed on site

(G-9641)
WAYNE COUNTY WELL SURVEYS INC
2225 Industrial Dr (62837-2719)
P.O. Box 421 (62837-0421)
PHONE..................................618 842-9116
Danny Young, *President*
David J Watson, *Admin Sec*
EMP: 13
SALES: 1.2MM **Privately Held**
SIC: 1389 Oil field services

Fairmount
Vermilion County

(G-9642)
DECATUR AERATION AND TEMP
Also Called: Dat Metal Fabricating
101 N Main St (61841)
P.O. Box 1757, Decatur (62525-1757)
PHONE..................................217 733-2800
J Michael Strader, *President*
Brenda Strader, *Admin Sec*
EMP: 15
SQ FT: 6,000
SALES (est): 1.6MM **Privately Held**
SIC: 3823 Industrial instrmnts msrmnt display/control process variable

(G-9643)
FERBER GEORGE & SONS
Also Called: Fairmount Redi-Mix
102 S Pine St (61841-7030)
P.O. Box 200 (61841-0200)
PHONE..................................217 733-2184
Kurt Ferber, *Partner*
Mike Ferber, *General Mgr*
EMP: 7 **EST:** 1940
SQ FT: 2,880
SALES (est): 1MM **Privately Held**
WEB: www.fairmountredimix.com
SIC: 3273 3272 Ready-mixed concrete; concrete products

(G-9644)
P L R SALES INC
14187 N 850 E Rd (61841)
PHONE..................................217 733-2245
EMP: 3
SALES: 200K **Privately Held**
SIC: 3691 Mfg Storage Batteries

Fairview Heights
St. Clair County

(G-9645)
EAGLE PUBLICATIONS INC
Also Called: Hometown Phone Book
11 Executive Dr Ste 10 (62208-1357)
PHONE..................................618 345-5400
Martin L Norton, *President*
Tammy Norton, *Vice Pres*
EMP: 45
SQ FT: 65,775
SALES (est): 4.5MM **Privately Held**
SIC: 2711 2741 Newspapers: publishing only, not printed on site; miscellaneous publishing

(G-9646)
HEIL SOUND LTD
5800 N Illinois St (62208-3505)
PHONE..................................618 257-3000
Bob Heil, *CEO*
Sarah Heil, *President*
Greg Heil, *Technology*
▲ **EMP:** 11 **EST:** 1966
SALES (est): 2MM **Privately Held**
SIC: 3663 5731 1731 3651 Radio & TV communications equipment; radio, television & electronic stores; communications specialization; cable television installation; sound equipment specialization; household audio & video equipment; current-carrying wiring devices; nonferrous wiredrawing & insulating

(G-9647)
INK WELL
10603 Lincoln Trl (62208-1913)
PHONE..................................618 398-1427
Clark Medley, *Owner*
EMP: 4
SALES (est): 250K **Privately Held**
SIC: 2752 Commercial printing, lithographic

(G-9648)
SMART CONTROLS LLC
10000 Saint Clair Ave (62208-1726)
PHONE..................................618 394-0300
David Kniepkamp,
EMP: 5 **EST:** 2000

Flat Rock - Crawford County (G-9674)

SALES (est): 952.4K **Privately Held**
SIC: 3674 Integrated circuits, semiconductor networks, etc.

Farina
Fayette County

(G-9649)
ADVANCE MANUFACTURING
204 Through St (62838-3751)
PHONE..................................618 245-6515
Calvin Byers, *President*
EMP: 3 EST: 2008
SALES (est): 202.7K **Privately Held**
SIC: 3999 Manufacturing industries

(G-9650)
B&A LIVESTOCK FEED COMPANY LLC
201 E Jefferson Ave (62838-1334)
PHONE..................................618 245-6422
Brian Sigrist, *President*
EMP: 5
SALES (est): 244.9K **Privately Held**
SIC: 2048 Livestock feeds

(G-9651)
BLOMBERG BROS INC
Hwy 37 S (62838)
P.O. Box 99 (62838-0099)
PHONE..................................618 245-6321
Charles E Blomberg, *President*
Ed Blomberg, *Corp Secy*
Frank Blomberg, *Vice Pres*
EMP: 12 EST: 1948
SQ FT: 5,600
SALES: 900K **Privately Held**
SIC: 4212 3273 5191 Local trucking, without storage; ready-mixed concrete; limestone, agricultural

(G-9652)
FARINA NEWS
109 N Walnut St (62838-1326)
P.O. Box 245 (62838-0245)
PHONE..................................618 245-6216
Shirley Ann Quick, *Owner*
EMP: 3
SQ FT: 2,500
SALES (est): 80K **Privately Held**
SIC: 2711 Job printing & newspaper publishing combined

(G-9653)
QUALITY TARGETS
204 Through St (62838-3751)
PHONE..................................618 245-6515
EMP: 4
SALES (est): 258.1K **Privately Held**
SIC: 3949 Sporting & athletic goods

Farmer City
De Witt County

(G-9654)
BRANDT CONSOLIDATED INC
788 E 3070 North Rd (61842)
PHONE..................................217 626-1123
Steve Darrett, *Branch Mgr*
EMP: 7
SALES (corp-wide): 159MM **Privately Held**
SIC: 2875 5191 Fertilizers, mixing only; fertilizer & fertilizer materials
PA: Brandt Consolidated, Inc.
  2935 S Koke Mill Rd
  Springfield IL 62711
  217 547-5800

(G-9655)
MAXWELL COUNTERS INC
324 S Plum St (61842-1438)
P.O. Box 234 (61842-0234)
PHONE..................................309 928-2848
Kevin Maxwell, *President*
Morgan Brackenhoff, *Accounts Mgr*
Jonathan Phillips, *Sales Staff*
Janis Maxwell, *Admin Sec*
EMP: 30

SALES (est): 5MM **Privately Held**
SIC: 2541 2821 Counters or counter display cases, wood; plastics materials & resins

(G-9656)
NEW ALLIANCE PRODUCTION LLC
1701 N John St (61842-1076)
P.O. Box 79 (61842-0079)
PHONE..................................309 928-3123
Ronald White,
Thomas W Butler,
▼ EMP: 26
SALES (est): 2.7MM **Privately Held**
SIC: 2041 0723 0115 5191 Flour & other grain mill products; crop preparation services for market; corn; seeds & bulbs

(G-9657)
SALT CREEK ALPACAS INC
3605 N 3300 East Rd (61842-8304)
PHONE..................................309 530-7904
Dee Stielow, *Principal*
EMP: 3
SALES (est): 366.4K **Privately Held**
WEB: www.saltcreekalpacas.com
SIC: 2231 Alpacas, mohair: woven

(G-9658)
T&L INTERNATIONAL MFG/DIST INC
25833 Hillcrest Dr (61842-7804)
PHONE..................................309 830-7238
Thomas E Blalock, *President*
Leila Blalock, *Corp Secy*
Paris Blalock, *Vice Pres*
Nicole Vanderspool, *Vice Pres*
▲ EMP: 4
SQ FT: 18,000
SALES: 1MM **Privately Held**
SIC: 3679 Electronic loads & power supplies

Farmersville
Montgomery County

(G-9659)
CARTER PRINTING CO INC
607 Elevator St (62533-4414)
P.O. Box 289 (62533-0289)
PHONE..................................217 227-4464
Roy Carter Jr, *President*
Chris Holloway, *Sales Staff*
EMP: 8
SQ FT: 4,000
SALES (est): 1MM **Privately Held**
SIC: 2752 2759 2791 2789 Commercial printing, offset; letterpress printing; typesetting; bookbinding & related work

(G-9660)
TRANTER PHE INC
30241 W Frontage Rd (62533)
PHONE..................................217 227-3470
Donna Long, *Principal*
▲ EMP: 13
SALES (est): 2.2MM **Privately Held**
SIC: 3443 Fabricated plate work (boiler shop)

Farmington
Fulton County

(G-9661)
FARMINGTON LOCKER/ICE PLANT CO
101 W Fort St (61531-1117)
PHONE..................................309 245-4621
Michael Thurman, *Owner*
EMP: 4
SQ FT: 3,000
SALES: 300K **Privately Held**
SIC: 5421 0751 2013 2011 Meat markets, including freezer provisioners; slaughtering; custom livestock services; sausages & other prepared meats; meat packing plants

(G-9662)
FARMINGTON WILBERT VAULT CORP (PA)
Also Called: Farmington Crematory
22413 E State Route 116 (61531-9452)
P.O. Box 50 (61531-0050)
PHONE..................................309 245-2133
Louis D Hecox, *President*
Janet Hecox, *Treasurer*
Karen Hecox, *Admin Sec*
EMP: 10 EST: 1954
SQ FT: 7,000
SALES (est): 1.2MM **Privately Held**
WEB: www.farmingtonwilbertvault.com
SIC: 3272 Burial vaults, concrete or precast terrazzo; concrete products, precast; septic tanks, concrete

(G-9663)
PLATTS PRINTING COMPANY
25 E Fort St (61531-1216)
PHONE..................................309 228-1069
Travis Platt, *CEO*
EMP: 1
SALES (est): 203.2K **Privately Held**
SIC: 2752 2759 7336 7334 Commercial printing, offset; letterpress & screen printing; commercial art & graphic design; photocopying & duplicating services; signs & advertising specialties

(G-9664)
UTZ QUALITY FOODS LLC
Also Called: Kitchen Cooked
632 N Main St (61531-1076)
PHONE..................................309 245-2191
Michael W Rice, *President*
EMP: 85
SALES (corp-wide): 660.5MM **Privately Held**
SIC: 2096 Potato chips & other potato-based snacks
PA: Utz Quality Foods, Llc ,
  900 High St
  Hanover PA 17331
  800 367-7629

Fillmore
Montgomery County

(G-9665)
S&S RECOVERY
227 Baldknob Trl (62032-2029)
PHONE..................................217 538-2206
Steve Bell, *Owner*
EMP: 4 EST: 2008
SALES (est): 298.2K **Privately Held**
SIC: 3531 Automobile wrecker hoists

(G-9666)
UNIQUE NOVELTY & MANUFACTURING
Also Called: Unique Novelty Mfg & Sales
200 S Main St (62032-2348)
P.O. Box 98 (62032-0098)
PHONE..................................217 538-2014
Mary Jones, *President*
EMP: 3
SALES (est): 192.6K **Privately Held**
SIC: 7389 3942 Textile & apparel services; dolls & stuffed toys

Fisher
Champaign County

(G-9667)
PRAXSYM INC
120 S Third St (61843-4202)
PHONE..................................217 897-1744
David Heiser, *President*
Roger Heiser, *Admin Sec*
Walter Gordon,
EMP: 12
SQ FT: 4,500
SALES: 825.7K **Privately Held**
SIC: 3829 Measuring & controlling devices

(G-9668)
VESUVIUS U S A CORPORATION
Hwy 136 E (61843)
P.O. Box 639 (61843-0639)
PHONE..................................217 897-1145
Fax: 217 897-6532
EMP: 134
SALES (corp-wide): 2.3B **Privately Held**
SIC: 3297 Mfg Nonclay Refractories Mfg Valves/Pipe Fittings Mfg Industrial Valves Nonferrous Metal Foundry
HQ: Vesuvius U S A Corporation
  1404 Newton Dr
  Champaign IL 61822
  217 402-9204

Fithian
Vermilion County

(G-9669)
FORSYTH BROTHERS CONCRETE PDTS
104 E North Sherman St (61844-1000)
P.O. Box 65 (61844-0065)
PHONE..................................217 548-2770
Jeffrey Bell, *President*
EMP: 3
SALES (corp-wide): 941.2K **Privately Held**
WEB: www.forsyth-puttmann.com
SIC: 3272 Burial vaults, concrete or precast terrazzo; septic tanks, concrete
PA: Forsyth Brothers Concrete Products Inc
  4500 N Fruitridge Rd
  Terre Haute IN 47805
  812 466-4080

Flanagan
Livingston County

(G-9670)
HULSE EXCAVATING
20289 N 400 East Rd (61740-8968)
PHONE..................................815 796-4106
Marlan Hulse, *Owner*
EMP: 3
SALES (est): 200K **Privately Held**
SIC: 1794 3272 Excavation work; drain tile, concrete

Flat Rock
Crawford County

(G-9671)
DATAFORDUMMIES
32 N 1550th St (62427-2705)
PHONE..................................618 421-2323
EMP: 5 EST: 2010
SALES (est): 190K **Privately Held**
SIC: 7372 Prepackaged Software Services

(G-9672)
PEACEFUL VALLEY CABINETRY
2090 N 1000th St (62427-3231)
PHONE..................................618 584-3615
Joseph Beachy, *Owner*
EMP: 5
SALES (est): 422.5K **Privately Held**
WEB: www.trillian3.com
SIC: 2434 Wood kitchen cabinets

(G-9673)
RUSTIC WOODCRAFTS
10510 E 350th Ave (62427-2019)
PHONE..................................618 584-3912
David A Raber, *Owner*
EMP: 4
SALES: 360K **Privately Held**
SIC: 2519 Household furniture

(G-9674)
STAR ENERGY CORP INC
1675 N 1200 Rd (62427)
P.O. Box 584, Lawrenceville (62439-0584)
PHONE..................................618 584-3631
Frank Ruvolo, *President*
EMP: 3

Flat Rock - Crawford County (G-9675)

SALES (est): 267.4K **Privately Held**
SIC: **1311** Crude petroleum & natural gas

(G-9675)
SUGARCREEK WOODWORKING
1501 N 1300th St (62427-2623)
PHONE.................................618 584-3817
EMP: 4
SALES (est): 302.4K **Privately Held**
SIC: **2431** Millwork

Flora
Clay County

(G-9676)
BOOTH RESOURCES INC
Also Called: B R I Operations
7965 Old Highway 50 (62839-4106)
P.O. Box 720 (62839-0720)
PHONE.................................618 662-4955
Marcus P Booth, *President*
EMP: 9 EST: 1980
SQ FT: 4,000
SALES (est): 1.1MM **Privately Held**
SIC: **1311 1381** Crude petroleum production; directional drilling oil & gas wells

(G-9677)
CARGILL INCORPORATED
6 Industrial Park (62839-9700)
PHONE.................................618 662-8070
Jim Cartwright, *Manager*
EMP: 17
SALES (corp-wide): 113.4B **Privately Held**
SIC: **2048** Prepared feeds
PA: Cargill, Incorporated
  15407 Mcginty Rd W
  Wayzata MN 55391
  952 742-7575

(G-9678)
CLAY CNTY RHBILITATION CTR INC
Also Called: Clay County Industries
1 Commercial Dr (62839-9000)
PHONE.................................618 662-6607
Gary White, *Branch Mgr*
EMP: 10
SALES (est): 395.8K
SALES (corp-wide): 2.2MM **Privately Held**
WEB: www.claycountyhospital.org
SIC: **8331 3465** Vocational rehabilitation agency; automotive stampings
PA: Clay County Rehabilitation Center, Inc.
  1 Commercial Dr
  Flora IL 62839
  618 662-4916

(G-9679)
CRUSADE ENTERPRISES INC
Also Called: T Renee Productions
200 E North Ave (62839-2029)
PHONE.................................618 662-4461
Dolores Harris, *Partner*
Tammy R Pob, *Corp Secy*
EMP: 2 EST: 1961
SQ FT: 7,500
SALES (est): 238.9K **Privately Held**
SIC: **3652 8661** Pre-recorded records & tapes; religious organizations

(G-9680)
FLORA BOWL
927 W North Ave (62839-1221)
PHONE.................................618 662-4561
Steven Galloway, *President*
◆ EMP: 5 EST: 1975
SQ FT: 3,100
SALES (est): 130K **Privately Held**
SIC: **3949** Bowling alleys & accessories

(G-9681)
FLORA READY MIX INC
11170 Old Highway 50 (62839-3432)
PHONE.................................618 662-4818
Eddie Musgrave, *President*
William Kent Musgrave, *Vice Pres*
Robert P Musgrave, *Treasurer*
EMP: 7
SQ FT: 2,200
SALES: 1.2MM **Privately Held**
SIC: **3273** Ready-mixed concrete

(G-9682)
HELLA CORPORATE CENTER USA INC
Also Called: Hella Electronics
50 Industrial Park (62839-9700)
PHONE.................................734 414-0900
Bill Killeon, *Branch Mgr*
EMP: 350
SALES (corp-wide): 7.8B **Privately Held**
SIC: **3625 5013 5088** Relays & industrial controls; motor vehicle supplies & new parts; transportation equipment & supplies
HQ: Hella Corporate Center Usa, Inc.
  15951 Technology Dr
  Northville MI 48168
  586 232-4788

(G-9683)
HELLA CORPORATE CENTER USA INC
1101 Vincennes Ave (62839-3440)
P.O. Box 398 (62839-0398)
PHONE.................................618 662-4402
Bill Killion, *Plt & Fclts Mgr*
Jeff Kohn, *Engineer*
Eric Smith, *Engineer*
EMP: 350
SALES (corp-wide): 7.8B **Privately Held**
SIC: **3625** Relays & industrial controls
HQ: Hella Corporate Center Usa, Inc.
  15951 Technology Dr
  Northville MI 48168
  586 232-4788

(G-9684)
HELLA ELECTRONICS CORPORATION
1101 Vincennes Ave (62839-3440)
P.O. Box 398 (62839-0398)
PHONE.................................618 662-5186
Christine James, *Warehouse Mgr*
Anthony Browning, *Opers Staff*
Mike Saltsgaver, *Engineer*
Wade Williams, *Engineer*
Bill Killon, *Manager*
EMP: 540
SALES (corp-wide): 7.8B **Privately Held**
SIC: **3625** Relays & industrial controls
HQ: Hella Electronics Corporation
  15951 Technology Dr
  Northville MI 48168
  734 414-0900

(G-9685)
MEAGHER SIGN & GRAPHICS INC
225 Hagen Dr (62839-2338)
PHONE.................................618 662-7446
Lela Meagher, *President*
Norman Meagher, *Admin Sec*
EMP: 7
SALES (est): 925.1K **Privately Held**
WEB: www.meaghergraphics.com
SIC: **3993** Signs & advertising specialties

(G-9686)
NORTH AMERICAN LIGHTING INC
Also Called: N A L
20 Industrial Park (62839-9700)
PHONE.................................618 662-4483
Chad Lueking, *Plant Mgr*
Stan Stanford, *Opers Mgr*
Randy Flood, *Production*
Roger Eaton, *Purch Mgr*
Chris Barnfield, *Engineer*
EMP: 500 **Privately Held**
SIC: **3647** Automotive lighting fixtures
HQ: North American Lighting, Inc.
  2275 S Main St
  Paris IL 61944
  217 465-6600

(G-9687)
PACKAGING CORPORATION AMERICA
Also Called: PCA
32 Industrial Park (62839-9700)
PHONE.................................618 662-6700
Tom Krugsinger, *Branch Mgr*
Tom Krutsinger, *Director*
EMP: 7
SALES (corp-wide): 6.9B **Publicly Held**
SIC: **2653** Boxes, corrugated: made from purchased materials; boxes, solid fiber: made from purchased materials
PA: Packaging Corporation Of America
  1 N Field Ct
  Lake Forest IL 60045
  847 482-3000

(G-9688)
PICTURES & MORE
Also Called: Pictures & More/Shirt Tales
134 W North Ave (62839-1612)
PHONE.................................618 662-4572
Rick Slaughter, *Owner*
EMP: 3
SALES (est): 214.4K **Privately Held**
SIC: **7384 2395** Film developing & printing; embroidery products, except schiffli machine

(G-9689)
POSITIVE MAMA ENTERPRISES LLC
701 Martha Ln (62839-2422)
PHONE.................................618 508-1995
Janette R Krutsinger, *Principal*
EMP: 6 EST: 2016
SALES (est): 334.1K **Privately Held**
WEB: www.janettescustommeals.com
SIC: **2099** Food preparations

(G-9690)
QCIRCUITS INC
1 Industrial Park (62839-9700)
PHONE.................................618 662-8365
Eric Petty, *Manager*
EMP: 40
SALES (est): 4.8MM
SALES (corp-wide): 10.2MM **Privately Held**
WEB: www.qcircuits.com
SIC: **3677 3672 3621** Electronic coils, transformers & other inductors; printed circuit boards; motors & generators
PA: Qcircuits, Inc.
  2574 United Ln
  Elk Grove Village IL 60007
  847 797-6678

(G-9691)
SHERWIN-WILLIAMS COMPANY
14 Industrial Park (62839-9700)
PHONE.................................618 662-4415
Jim Taylor, *Manager*
Tim Stork, *Manager*
EMP: 126
SQ FT: 34,000
SALES (corp-wide): 17.9B **Publicly Held**
SIC: **5231 2851** Paint & painting supplies; paints & allied products
PA: The Sherwin-Williams Company
  101 W Prospect Ave # 1020
  Cleveland OH 44115
  216 566-2000

(G-9692)
SILGAN PLASTICS LLC
2 Industrial Park (62839-9700)
PHONE.................................618 662-4471
Brian Craig, *Branch Mgr*
Curt Ray, *Maintence Staff*
EMP: 85 **Publicly Held**
WEB: www.silganplastics.com
SIC: **3089 3085 2673** Molding primary plastic; plastics bottles; bags: plastic, laminated & coated
HQ: Silgan Plastics Llc
  14515 North Outer 40 Rd # 210
  Chesterfield MO 63017
  800 274-5426

(G-9693)
SMOCO INC
832 W North Ave Ste A1 (62839-1293)
P.O. Box 367 (62839-0367)
PHONE.................................618 662-6458
Milton Smith II, *President*
EMP: 2
SQ FT: 1,200
SALES: 200K **Privately Held**
SIC: **1311** Crude petroleum production

(G-9694)
SOUTHWIRE COMPANY LLC
Southwire Utility Products Div
Eash Rd (62839)
PHONE.................................618 662-8341
Howard Strauss, *Vice Pres*
Paul McCracken, *Engineer*
Kari Warren, *Manager*
EMP: 72
SALES (corp-wide): 2B **Privately Held**
WEB: www.southwire.com
SIC: **3315 3355** Cable, steel: insulated or armored; wire, aluminum: made in rolling mills
PA: Southwire Company, Llc
  1 Southwire Dr
  Carrollton GA 30119
  770 832-4242

(G-9695)
WARRIOR LOGGING & PERFORAGINE
174 Lincoln Rd (62839-3352)
P.O. Box 51 (62839-0051)
PHONE.................................618 662-7373
Russell E Waters, *Administration*
EMP: 6
SALES (est): 431.8K **Privately Held**
SIC: **2411** Logging camps & contractors

(G-9696)
WARRIOR WELL SERVICES INC
745 Cedardom Dr (62839)
P.O. Box 411 (62839-0411)
PHONE.................................618 662-7710
Brent Burgess, *President*
Tom Skinner, *Manager*
EMP: 9 EST: 1999
SQ FT: 1,000
SALES (est): 749.3K **Privately Held**
SIC: **2411** Logging

(G-9697)
WOODROW TODD
1502 N Olive Rd (62839-2347)
PHONE.................................618 838-9105
Todd Woodrow, *Principal*
EMP: 3 EST: 2010
SALES (est): 151.9K **Privately Held**
SIC: **1382** Oil & gas exploration services

Flossmoor
Cook County

(G-9698)
FLEETCHEM LLC (PA)
1222 Brassie Ave Ste 19 (60422-1623)
PHONE.................................708 957-5311
Thomas J Blakemore,
Kathy Blakemore,
EMP: 11
SALES (est): 1.6MM **Privately Held**
SIC: **2045** Blended flour: from purchased flour

(G-9699)
GREVAN ENTERPRISES INC
Also Called: Vcr Service Center
3007 Lawrence Cres (60422-2053)
PHONE.................................708 799-3422
John J Grevan, *President*
EMP: 9 EST: 1982
SALES (est): 568.8K **Privately Held**
SIC: **3999** Education aids, devices & supplies

(G-9700)
PIN HSIAO & ASSOCIATES LLC
Also Called: Zen Bakery, MA
1040 Sterling Ave (60422-1234)
PHONE.................................206 818-0155
Pin Hsiano,
EMP: 20 **Privately Held**
SIC: **2051** Bakery: wholesale or wholesale/retail combined
PA: Pin Hsiao & Associates L.L.C.
  5501 West Valley Hwy E A101
  Sumner WA 98390

GEOGRAPHIC SECTION

Forest Park - Cook County (G-9727)

(G-9701)
SNOW COMMAND INCORPORATED
1607 Tina Ln (60422-1952)
PHONE.....................708 991-7004
Nick Eeluca, *President*
EMP: 3
SALES (est): 261.8K **Privately Held**
SIC: 2851 Removers & cleaners

(G-9702)
SPRINGBOX INC
Also Called: Ink Solution
2842 Scott Cres (60422-1724)
PHONE.....................708 921-9944
Therone Watson, *President*
EMP: 3
SALES (est): 350.3K **Privately Held**
SIC: 2893 Printing ink

(G-9703)
STONE LIGHTING LLC
2630 Flossmoor Rd Ste 102 (60422-1560)
PHONE.....................312 240-0400
Adam Stone, *Vice Pres*
Susan Brazzale, *Accounting Mgr*
Jenn Kruse, *Cust Mgr*
Jenny Kruse, *Cust Mgr*
Ben Sanborn, *Business Anlyst*
EMP: 19 EST: 2010
SALES (est): 3.1MM **Privately Held**
WEB: www.stonelighting.net
SIC: 3645 5063 Boudoir lamps; chandeliers, residential; fluorescent lighting fixtures, residential; garden, patio, walkway & yard lighting fixtures: electric; light bulbs & related supplies; lighting fixtures, residential

(G-9704)
SWEET ANNIES BAKERY INC
19710 Governors Hwy Ste 6 (60422-2081)
PHONE.....................708 297-7066
Michele Williams, *President*
EMP: 10
SQ FT: 1,700
SALES (est): 771.5K **Privately Held**
SIC: 2051 Cakes, bakery: except frozen

Foosland
Champaign County

(G-9705)
HEDRICKS WELDING & FABRICATION
201 Main St (61845-9403)
P.O. Box 77 (61845-0077)
PHONE.....................217 846-3230
Greg H Hedrick, *President*
Amy Hedrick, *Manager*
EMP: 3
SQ FT: 5,200
SALES (est): 250K **Privately Held**
SIC: 7692 Welding repair

Ford Heights
Cook County

(G-9706)
FORD MOTOR COMPANY
1000 E Lincoln Hwy (60411-2997)
P.O. Box 6, Chicago Heights (60412-0020)
PHONE.....................708 757-5700
Lisa Recinella, *QC Mgr*
Claudio Battistini, *Engineer*
Brian Beard, *Engineer*
Shay Fox, *Engineer*
Randolph Griffin, *Branch Mgr*
EMP: 1920
SQ FT: 2,500,000
SALES (corp-wide): 155.9B **Publicly Held**
WEB: www.ford.com
SIC: 3465 3469 Automotive stampings; metal stampings
PA: Ford Motor Company
1 American Rd
Dearborn MI 48126
313 322-3000

Forest Park
Cook County

(G-9707)
ACCENTS BY FRED
7519 Madison St (60130-1407)
PHONE.....................708 366-9850
Frederick Bryant, *Owner*
EMP: 4
SALES (est): 349.5K **Privately Held**
SIC: 3911 Jewelry, precious metal

(G-9708)
BLUE MONKEY GRAPHICS INC
7540 Roosevelt Rd Ste 4 (60130-3054)
P.O. Box 56, Lyons (60534-0056)
PHONE.....................708 488-9501
EMP: 3
SALES (est): 253.1K **Privately Held**
SIC: 3953 Marking Devices, Nsk

(G-9709)
CHICAGO PRODUCERS INC
Also Called: Studio Out West
7507 Madison St Ste D4 (60130-3514)
PHONE.....................312 226-6900
William Vala, *President*
Jason Gill, *Vice Pres*
Bill Vala, *Creative Dir*
EMP: 13
SALES: 1MM **Privately Held**
SIC: 3652 2754 Pre-recorded records & tapes; visiting cards: gravure printing

(G-9710)
CLARK CASTER CO
Also Called: A & E Forge
7310 Roosevelt Rd (60130-2443)
P.O. Box 83, Cave In Rock (62919-0083)
PHONE.....................708 366-1913
James H Clark, *President*
Bernice Clark, *Admin Sec*
EMP: 5
SQ FT: 3,000
SALES (est): 853.1K **Privately Held**
WEB: www.clarkcaster.com
SIC: 5072 3537 Casters & glides; industrial trucks & tractors

(G-9711)
CLASSIC SCREEN PRINTING INC
1401 Circle Ave Ste 1n (60130-2649)
PHONE.....................708 771-9355
Robert Shaw, *President*
Laura Shaw, *Admin Sec*
EMP: 12
SQ FT: 5,400
SALES (est): 825K **Privately Held**
SIC: 2759 Screen printing

(G-9712)
DURACO SPECIALTY TAPES LLC (PA)
7400 Industrial Dr (60130-2536)
PHONE.....................866 800-0775
Joshua Adams, *Managing Dir*
Robert Wilcox, *Manager*
◆ EMP: 66 EST: 2018
SQ FT: 152,000
SALES (est): 20.5MM **Privately Held**
WEB: www.duracoinc.com
SIC: 3069 3086 Sponge rubber & sponge rubber products; plastics foam products

(G-9713)
ENERGY TEES
1401 Circle Ave Ste 1n (60130-2649)
PHONE.....................708 771-0000
Robert Shaw, *President*
Laura Shaw, *Vice Pres*
EMP: 6
SALES: 350K **Privately Held**
WEB: www.energytees.com
SIC: 2759 7389 Screen printing; embroidering of advertising on shirts, etc.

(G-9714)
FARMINGTON FOODS INC (PA)
7419 Franklin St (60130-1016)
PHONE.....................708 771-3600
Anthony Dijohn, *President*
Frank A Dijohn, *President*
Ray Reid, *Director*
Jack Vogt, *Director*
▼ EMP: 155 EST: 1972
SQ FT: 55,000
SALES (est): 96MM **Privately Held**
SIC: 2013 Prepared beef products from purchased beef; prepared pork products from purchased pork

(G-9715)
FERRARA CANDY COMPANY
Also Called: Ferrara Pan Candy Co
7301 Harrison St (60130-2083)
PHONE.....................630 366-0500
Natalie Hagstrom, *General Mgr*
Maurizio Ficarra, *CFO*
EMP: 272
SALES (corp-wide): 228MM **Privately Held**
SIC: 2064 Candy & other confectionery products
HQ: Ferrara Candy Company
404 W Harrison St 650s
Chicago IL 60607
708 366-0500

(G-9716)
FERRARA CANDY COMPANY
7525 Industrial Dr (60130-2515)
PHONE.....................708 488-1892
Sal Ferrara, *CEO*
EMP: 272
SALES (corp-wide): 228MM **Privately Held**
SIC: 2064 Chewing candy, not chewing gum
HQ: Ferrara Candy Company
404 W Harrison St 650s
Chicago IL 60607
708 366-0500

(G-9717)
FOREST PLATING CO
930 Des Plaines Ave (60130-2199)
PHONE.....................708 366-2071
Walter Mc Govern, *President*
William P Mc Govern, *President*
EMP: 6 EST: 1947
SQ FT: 4,800
SALES (est): 566.7K **Privately Held**
SIC: 3471 Plating of metals or formed products

(G-9718)
FOREST PRINTING CO
7214 Madison St Ste 1 (60130-3106)
P.O. Box 79 (60130-0079)
PHONE.....................708 366-5100
Randy Martini, *President*
Megan Bubenicek, *Technology*
EMP: 13
SQ FT: 3,000
SALES (est): 2.3MM **Privately Held**
SIC: 2752 Commercial printing, offset

(G-9719)
GC LASER SYSTEMS INC
900 Des Plaines Ave (60130-2104)
PHONE.....................844 532-1064
Magdalena Dajnowski, *CEO*
Bartosz Dajnowski, *President*
EMP: 4
SALES: 74.7K **Privately Held**
SIC: 7699 8999 7532 3471 Machinery cleaning; art restoration; antique & classic automobile restoration; cleaning, polishing & finishing; oil & gas field machinery rubber goods (mechanical)

(G-9720)
INDEPENDENT NETWORK TV LLC
1525 Circle Ave Ste 3 (60130-2647)
PHONE.....................312 953-8508
Rodger Jackson, *Mng Member*
EMP: 3
SALES (est): 71.1K **Privately Held**
SIC: 7372 Home entertainment computer software

(G-9721)
KAFKA MANUFACTURING CO
7600 Industrial Dr (60130-2518)
PHONE.....................708 771-0970
Jeffrey S Kafka, *President*
Karen Kafka, *Corp Secy*
EMP: 9
SQ FT: 21,000
SALES (est): 693K **Privately Held**
WEB: www.kafkamfg.com
SIC: 3534 Elevators & equipment

(G-9722)
NEW ARCHERY PRODUCTS LLC
Also Called: Quikfletch
7500 Industrial Dr (60130-2516)
P.O. Box 535189, Grand Prairie TX (75053-5189)
PHONE.....................708 488-2500
Mike Czemske, *Opers Mgr*
Greg Smith, *Site Mgr*
Chris Kozlik, *Design Engr*
Chris Hunter, *Regl Sales Mgr*
Robert Tatum, *Supervisor*
▲ EMP: 60 EST: 1975
SQ FT: 20,000
SALES: 7.2MM
SALES (corp-wide): 13.7MM **Privately Held**
SIC: 3949 Archery equipment, general; arrows, archery
PA: Brs Outdoor Sports Holdings Llc
126 E 56th St Fl 29
New York NY 10022
212 521-3700

(G-9723)
OFFICE FURNITURE PARTS LLC
7540 Roosevelt Rd (60130-3054)
PHONE.....................708 546-5841
EMP: 2
SALES (est): 209.4K **Privately Held**
SIC: 2521 Wood office furniture

(G-9724)
SIEVERT ELECTRIC SVC & SLS CO
1230 Hannah Ave (60130-2400)
PHONE.....................708 771-1600
Peter A Sievert, *President*
Scott Sievert, *Exec VP*
David Bishop, *Opers Mgr*
Calvin Kruder, *Foreman/Supr*
Jason Podolski, *Sales Staff*
EMP: 60
SQ FT: 20,000
SALES (est): 22.3MM **Privately Held**
SIC: 3536 1731 Hoists; cranes, industrial plant; general electrical contractor

(G-9725)
THULE INC
Also Called: Thule Chicago
7609 Industrial Dr (60130-2517)
PHONE.....................847 455-2420
Don Domanus, *Plant Mgr*
Ray Church, *Opers Staff*
Tom Howell, *Opers Staff*
Graham Jackson, *Manager*
Donald Domanus, *Director*
EMP: 120 **Privately Held**
WEB: www.thule.com
SIC: 3713 Truck & bus bodies
HQ: Thule, Inc.
42 Silvermine Rd
Seymour CT 06483

(G-9726)
TIFFANY STAINED GLASS LTD
428 Des Plaines Ave Ste 1 (60130-3195)
PHONE.....................312 642-0680
Robert Nugent,
EMP: 6 EST: 1975
SQ FT: 5,000
SALES (est): 597.9K **Privately Held**
SIC: 3231 7699 Stained glass: made from purchased glass; antique repair & restoration, except furniture, automobiles

(G-9727)
VM HOIST CRANE
1230 Hannah Ave (60130-2448)
PHONE.....................708 771-1600
Scott Sievert, *Manager*
EMP: 2
SALES (est): 311K **Privately Held**
SIC: 3536 Hoists, cranes & monorails

Forest Park - Cook County (G-9728)

(G-9728)
VOCO TOOL & MFG INC
1441 Circle Ave (60130-2697)
PHONE..................708 771-3800
Ralph Vogel, *President*
Bob Bennett, *Managing Prtnr*
Jim Bennett, *Managing Prtnr*
Mary Jane Bennett, *Vice Pres*
Nancy Vogel, *Treasurer*
EMP: 8
SQ FT: 15,000
SALES: 1MM **Privately Held**
WEB: www.vocotool.com
SIC: 3469 3544 Stamping metal for the trade; special dies, tools, jigs & fixtures

(G-9729)
WEST FUELS INC
7340 Harrison St (60130-2017)
PHONE..................708 488-8880
Deborah Stange, *President*
EMP: 3
SALES (est): 378.1K **Privately Held**
SIC: 2869 Fuels

Forest View
Cook County

(G-9730)
JDB MACHINING INC
4635 S Harlem Ave (60402-4252)
PHONE..................708 749-9596
William Dinon, *President*
Daniel Ziemkiewicz, *Treasurer*
▲ EMP: 5
SQ FT: 6,700
SALES (est): 596.8K **Privately Held**
SIC: 3599 Machine shop, jobbing & repair

(G-9731)
JDB MANUFACTURING COMPANY
4635 S Harlem Ave (60402-4252)
PHONE..................708 749-9596
William G Dinon, *President*
▲ EMP: 7
SQ FT: 15,000
SALES: 1.5MM **Privately Held**
SIC: 3599 Machine shop, jobbing & repair

Forrest
Livingston County

(G-9732)
CROSSROAD CRATING & PALLET
27700 E 700 North Rd (61741-9468)
P.O. Box 260 (61741-0260)
PHONE..................815 657-8409
Mark Haab, *President*
EMP: 9
SALES (est): 1.3MM **Privately Held**
SIC: 2448 Pallets, wood

(G-9733)
FORREST REDI-MIX INC
321 W Krack St (61741-9368)
P.O. Box 308 (61741-0308)
PHONE..................815 657-8241
Ron Steidinger, *President*
Scot Steidinger, *Vice Pres*
Pam Rieger, *CFO*
Pamela Rieger, *Admin Sec*
EMP: 6 EST: 1948
SQ FT: 800
SALES (est): 1.1MM **Privately Held**
WEB: www.rdemx.com
SIC: 3273 3272 Ready-mixed concrete; concrete products

(G-9734)
KNAPP INDUSTRIAL WOOD
820 N Center St (61741-9600)
P.O. Box 543 (61741-0543)
PHONE..................815 657-8854
Louie D Knapp, *Owner*
Ken Wooten, *General Mgr*
EMP: 12
SALES: 1.9MM **Privately Held**
SIC: 2426 Hardwood dimension & flooring mills

(G-9735)
SELIG S LLC
342 E Wabash Ave (61741-9500)
PHONE..................815 785-2100
Andrew Kauffman,
EMP: 3 EST: 2015
SALES (est): 142K **Privately Held**
SIC: 3089 Caps, plastic

(G-9736)
SELIG SEALING HOLDINGS INC (DH)
342 E Wabash Ave (61741-9500)
PHONE..................815 785-2100
Stephen Cassidy, *Principal*
Steve Brucker, *Vice Pres*
Jay Kelley, *Regl Sales Mgr*
Jay Kelly, *Regl Sales Mgr*
Bob Tobiason, *Sales Staff*
EMP: 12 EST: 2005
SALES (est): 32.9MM
SALES (corp-wide): 1.5B **Privately Held**
WEB: www.seligsealing.com
SIC: 3089 Caps, plastic
HQ: C C Industries, Inc.
 222 N La Salle St # 1000
 Chicago IL 60601
 312 855-4000

(G-9737)
SELIG SEALING PRODUCTS INC (DH)
342 E Wabash Ave (61741-9500)
PHONE..................815 785-2100
Steve Cassidy, *CEO*
Mark Bossong, *Exec VP*
Bill Radek, *Exec VP*
Steve Brucker, *Vice Pres*
Bob Woods, *Vice Pres*
▲ EMP: 2
SQ FT: 128,000
SALES (est): 32.9MM
SALES (corp-wide): 1.5B **Privately Held**
SIC: 2671 Paper coated or laminated for packaging
HQ: Selig Sealing Holdings, Inc.
 342 E Wabash Ave
 Forrest IL 61741
 815 785-2100

(G-9738)
SLAGEL MANUFACTURING INC
Also Called: Vulcan Equipment
2911 N 2700 East Rd (61741-9333)
PHONE..................815 688-3318
Mark Slagel, *President*
Donald Slagel, *Admin Sec*
▲ EMP: 40
SQ FT: 64,000
SALES (est): 5.6MM **Privately Held**
SIC: 3999 Novelties, bric-a-brac & hobby kits

Forreston
Ogle County

(G-9739)
DANLEE WOOD PRODUCTS INC
207 S Chestnut St (61030-8000)
P.O. Box 383 (61030-0383)
PHONE..................815 938-9016
Toll Free:.....................888 -
Daniel Reif, *President*
EMP: 2 EST: 1997
SQ FT: 3,200
SALES: 3MM **Privately Held**
WEB: www.danleewoodproducts.net
SIC: 2499 Laundry products, wood

(G-9740)
FORRESTON TOOL INC
400 E Avon St (61030-7712)
P.O. Box 119 (61030-0119)
PHONE..................815 938-3626
Paul W White, *President*
Danny Mc Kean, *Vice Pres*
EMP: 11
SQ FT: 4,560

SALES: 750K **Privately Held**
SIC: 3089 Injection molded finished plastic products

(G-9741)
MID-AMERICA PLASTIC COMPANY
500 E Avon St (61030-7713)
P.O. Box 667 (61030-0667)
PHONE..................815 938-3110
Patricia Erdmann, *CEO*
Eric Erdmann, *President*
EMP: 32 EST: 1968
SQ FT: 17,500
SALES (est): 5.5MM **Privately Held**
SIC: 3089 Injection molding of plastics

Fowler
Adams County

(G-9742)
B L I TOOL & DIE INC
1468 Highway 24 (62338-2309)
PHONE..................217 434-9106
David A Ley, *President*
EMP: 5
SALES (est): 360K **Privately Held**
SIC: 3544 Special dies & tools

Fox Lake
Lake County

(G-9743)
ABRASIVE RUBBER WHEEL CO
135 S Us Highway 12 (60020-1770)
PHONE..................847 587-0900
Evelynn Ortman, *President*
EMP: 10 EST: 1943
SQ FT: 5,000
SALES (est): 1.1MM **Privately Held**
SIC: 3291 Wheels, abrasive

(G-9744)
ALERT SCREW PRODUCTS CORP
100 Honing Rd (60020-1929)
PHONE..................847 587-1360
Joe Dvorak, *President*
EMP: 9
SALES (est): 1.4MM **Privately Held**
SIC: 3451 Screw machine products

(G-9745)
DEAN PRINTING SYSTEMS
166 Waltonian Ter (60020-1316)
PHONE..................847 526-9545
David Dean, *Owner*
EMP: 2
SALES (est): 227.1K **Privately Held**
SIC: 2752 Commercial printing, lithographic

(G-9746)
FABRY INC (PA)
8315 Evergreen Ct (60020-1048)
P.O. Box 601, Antioch (60002-0601)
PHONE..................847 395-1919
David J Fabry, *CEO*
David Gustav Fabry, *Vice Pres*
Patricia J Fabry, *Treasurer*
EMP: 9
SALES: 775K **Privately Held**
SIC: 7699 3931 Organ tuning & repair; organs, all types: pipe, reed, hand, electronic, etc.

(G-9747)
HAMSHER LAKESIDE FUNERALS
12 N Pistakee Lake Rd (60020-1208)
PHONE..................847 587-2100
EMP: 3 EST: 2015
SALES (est): 177.5K **Privately Held**
SIC: 2396 Veils & veiling: bridal, funeral, etc.

(G-9748)
MCINTYRE & ASSOCIATES
41 Nippersink Rd Apt 3 (60020-1468)
PHONE..................847 639-8050

Robert McIntyre, *Partner*
Robert Mc Intyre, *Partner*
Margo McIntyre, *Partner*
EMP: 3
SALES (est): 384K **Privately Held**
SIC: 2752 7311 Commercial printing, offset; advertising agencies

(G-9749)
NORTHERN ILLINOIS PALLET INC
1285 Wentworth Dr (60020-3417)
PHONE..................815 236-9242
Scott Ganan, *Principal*
EMP: 3
SALES (est): 199.6K **Privately Held**
SIC: 2448 Pallets, wood

(G-9750)
NOWUBA LLC - INVESTIO PRINT
Also Called: Minuteman Press
111 Nippersink Rd (60020-1328)
PHONE..................833 669-8221
Gregory Roby,
EMP: 5
SALES (est): 190.2K
SALES (corp-wide): 449K **Privately Held**
SIC: 2752 Commercial printing, lithographic
PA: Nowuba Llc
 111 Nippersink Rd
 Fox Lake IL 60020
 801 510-8086

(G-9751)
NOWUBA LLC (PA)
111 Nippersink Rd (60020-1328)
PHONE..................801 510-8086
Gregory Roby, *Mng Member*
Tyron Merrell,
Eric Williams,
EMP: 3
SALES (est): 449K **Privately Held**
SIC: 8748 2711 Business consulting; commercial printing & newspaper publishing combined

(G-9752)
POWERSOURCE GENERATOR RENTALS
119 Christopher Way (60020-1732)
P.O. Box 157 (60020-0157)
PHONE..................847 587-3991
Mark Anthony Rossi, *President*
EMP: 9
SALES: 2MM **Privately Held**
SIC: 3621 Motors & generators

(G-9753)
PRECISION CHROME INC
105 Precision Rd (60020-1999)
PHONE..................847 587-1515
Donald Hjortland, *President*
Cheryl Preece, *Admin Sec*
EMP: 25
SQ FT: 24,000
SALES (est): 2.8MM **Privately Held**
SIC: 3471 3541 3567 3398 Chromium plating of metals or formed products; grinding, polishing, buffing, lapping & honing machines; honing & lapping machines; induction heating equipment; metal heat treating

(G-9754)
SIGN APPEAL INC
20 E Grand Ave (60020-1217)
PHONE..................847 587-4300
Debra Busch, *Owner*
EMP: 6
SQ FT: 4,000
SALES (est): 440K **Privately Held**
SIC: 3993 Signs & advertising specialties

(G-9755)
SPRAYTECH LLC
89 S Us Highway 12 (60020-1750)
PHONE..................847 973-9432
Piotr T Gryz,
EMP: 6
SALES: 900K **Privately Held**
SIC: 3089 Automotive parts, plastic

Fox River Grove
Mchenry County

(G-9756)
A D SPECIALTY SEWING
410 Northwest Hwy (60021-1139)
PHONE..................................847 639-0390
Adele Migdal, *Owner*
EMP: 6
SQ FT: 6,000
SALES: 230K **Privately Held**
WEB: www.grovesofa.com
SIC: 2391 5714 5949 5999 Draperies, plastic & textile: from purchased materials; upholstery materials; fabric stores piece goods; foam & foam products; upholstery work; household furnishings

(G-9757)
ERGO-HELP INC
Also Called: Ergo-Help Pneumatics
728 Northwest Hwy # 152 (60021-1207)
PHONE..................................847 593-0722
Gene Vatel, *President*
EMP: 4
SALES (est): 1.8MM **Privately Held**
SIC: 3593 3423 5084 Fluid power cylinders & actuators; hand & edge tools; materials handling machinery

(G-9758)
FINISHERS EXCHANGE
744 Northwest Hwy (60021-1207)
P.O. Box 5 (60021-0005)
PHONE..................................847 462-0533
Nelson G Stevens, *Principal*
▲ **EMP:** 4
SALES (est): 288.7K **Privately Held**
WEB: www.finishersexchange.com
SIC: 3554 Paper industries machinery

(G-9759)
GROVE PLATING COMPANY INC
400 Algonquin Rd (60021-1498)
PHONE..................................847 639-7651
Richard Kostner, *President*
Bev Kostner, *Vice Pres*
Beverly Kostner, *Vice Pres*
Bob Mersch, *Plant Mgr*
Brian Feezel, *Manager*
EMP: 15
SQ FT: 16,000
SALES (est): 1.9MM **Privately Held**
WEB: www.groveplating.com
SIC: 3471 Plating of metals or formed products

(G-9760)
LEMAITRE VASCULAR INC
912 Northwest Hwy Ste 106 (60021-1925)
PHONE..................................847 462-2191
EMP: 16
SALES (corp-wide): 117.2MM **Publicly Held**
SIC: 8099 3842 Blood related health services; cosmetic restorations
PA: Lemaitre Vascular, Inc.
63 2nd Ave
Burlington MA 01803
781 221-2266

(G-9761)
SALES & MARKETING RESOURCES
Also Called: Sterling RE & Investments
21 Ashcroft Ct (60021-1864)
PHONE..................................847 910-9169
Rick Maningas, *Owner*
EMP: 4
SALES (est): 210K **Privately Held**
SIC: 7372 Prepackaged software

(G-9762)
SOFTTECH LLC
613 Barberry Trl (60021-1147)
PHONE..................................847 809-8591
Lokesh Gyanwali, *President*
EMP: 3
SALES (est): 81.3K **Privately Held**
SIC: 7372 Application computer software

Frankfort
Will County

(G-9763)
3D MANUFACTURING CORPORATION
9218 Corsair Rd Unit 5 (60423-2566)
PHONE..................................815 806-9200
Patrick Dalton, *President*
Michelle Dalton, *Admin Sec*
EMP: 8
SALES: 1MM **Privately Held**
SIC: 3599 Machine shop, jobbing & repair

(G-9764)
AKRYLIX INC (PA)
171 Ontario St (60423-1808)
PHONE..................................773 869-9005
Randy Janata, *President*
EMP: 12
SALES (est): 1.5MM **Privately Held**
SIC: 3089 2541 2821 Boxes, plastic; store & office display cases & fixtures; acrylic resins

(G-9765)
ALPS GROUP INC (PA)
Also Called: Alps Group, The
8779 W Laraway Rd (60423-9704)
PHONE..................................815 469-3800
EMP: 8
SALES (est): 825.8K **Privately Held**
WEB: www.thealpsgroup.com
SIC: 3421 Table & food cutlery, including butchers'

(G-9766)
AMERICAN PERFORATOR COMPANY
22803 S Mustang Rd Ste A (60423-2557)
PHONE..................................815 469-4300
Bryan Spencer, *President*
Carl V Spencer, *Corp Secy*
EMP: 2 **EST:** 1890
SQ FT: 5,000
SALES: 293.2K **Privately Held**
WEB: www.americanperforatorco.com
SIC: 3579 Perforators (office machines)

(G-9767)
ANDERSON COPPER & BRASS CO LLC (DH)
Also Called: Anderson Fittings
255 Industry Ave (60423-1640)
PHONE..................................708 535-9030
Douglas Marciniak, *President*
▲ **EMP:** 50 **EST:** 1986
SQ FT: 10,000
SALES (est): 11.6MM
SALES (corp-wide): 327.2B **Publicly Held**
SIC: 3432 Plumbing fixture fittings & trim
HQ: Marmon Holdings, Inc.
181 W Madison St Ste 2600
Chicago IL 60602
312 372-9500

(G-9768)
AREA MARKETING INC
Also Called: Family Time Magazine
10221 W Lincoln Hwy (60423-1279)
PHONE..................................815 806-8844
Caroline O'Connell, *President*
Mike O'Connell, *Vice Pres*
Roseanne Muzinic, *Sales Staff*
Carrie Nitsche, *Creative Dir*
EMP: 7
SALES (est): 824K **Privately Held**
SIC: 2721 7389 Magazines: publishing & printing; promoters of shows & exhibitions

(G-9769)
B CREATIVE SCREEN PRINT CO
8844 W Steger Rd (60423-8077)
PHONE..................................815 806-3037
Bob Stortako, *Owner*
Bob Storako, *Owner*
EMP: 4
SALES (est): 446.6K **Privately Held**
SIC: 2759 Screen printing

(G-9770)
BCR ELEVATORS INCORPORATED
20608 S Driftwood Dr (60423-8160)
PHONE..................................219 689-5951
Michael Berg, *Principal*
EMP: 12
SALES (est): 621.5K **Privately Held**
SIC: 3534 Elevators & moving stairways

(G-9771)
BIG GAME GUT GLOVE
19500 E Hillside Dr (60423-8825)
PHONE..................................847 544-8806
▲ **EMP:** 2
SALES (est): 207.5K **Privately Held**
WEB: www.unclefreddies.com
SIC: 3949 Sporting & athletic goods

(G-9772)
BIMBA MANUFACTURING COMPANY
9450 W Laraway Rd (60423-1902)
PHONE..................................708 534-8544
Dan Harris, *Marketing Staff*
EMP: 40
SQ FT: 45,000
SALES (corp-wide): 2.4B **Privately Held**
SIC: 3593 Fluid power cylinders, hydraulic or pneumatic
HQ: Bimba Manufacturing Company Inc
25150 S Governors Hwy
University Park IL 60484
708 534-8544

(G-9773)
BLACHFORD CORPORATION
401 Center Rd (60423-1630)
PHONE..................................815 464-2100
John L Blachford, *President*
Joe Borean, *Corp Secy*
Charles Moritz, *Vice Pres*
Larry Smith, *Manager*
◆ **EMP:** 25
SQ FT: 45,000
SALES (est): 5.8MM **Privately Held**
WEB: www.blachford.com
SIC: 2841 Soap & other detergents
PA: Blachford Enterprises, Inc.
1400 Nuclear Dr
West Chicago IL 60185

(G-9774)
BORG-WARNER AUTOMOTIVE INC
300 S Maple St (60423-1691)
PHONE..................................815 469-2721
James R Verrier, *CEO*
Alexis P Michas, *Chairman*
EMP: 5
SALES (est): 1.1MM **Privately Held**
SIC: 3714 Motor vehicle parts & accessories

(G-9775)
BORGWARNER INC
300 S Maple St (60423-1691)
PHONE..................................248 754-9200
Andy Mickus, *Plant Mgr*
David Podbielski, *Engineer*
Josh Lahrman, *Design Engr*
Lisa Beard, *Hum Res Coord*
Doug Czerwonka, *Human Resources*
EMP: 30
SALES (corp-wide): 10.1B **Publicly Held**
SIC: 3714 Motor vehicle parts & accessories
PA: Borgwarner Inc.
3850 Hamlin Rd
Auburn Hills MI 48326
248 754-9200

(G-9776)
BORGWARNER TRANSM SYSTEMS INC
300 S Maple St (60423-1691)
PHONE..................................815 469-2721
Bill Liacone, *Branch Mgr*
EMP: 450
SALES (corp-wide): 10.1B **Publicly Held**
SIC: 3714 Transmissions, motor vehicle
HQ: Borgwarner Transmission Systems Inc.
3800 Automation Ave # 500
Auburn Hills MI 48326
248 754-9200

(G-9777)
CARNEY FLOW TECHNICS LLC
181 Ontario St (60423-1646)
PHONE..................................815 277-2600
Patrick Carney, *Principal*
EMP: 6
SALES (est): 824.6K **Privately Held**
SIC: 3589 Water treatment equipment, industrial

(G-9778)
CARROLL DISTRG & CNSTR SUP INC
121 Industry Ave (60423-1639)
PHONE..................................815 464-0100
Theo Buys, *Manager*
EMP: 6
SALES (corp-wide): 128.2MM **Privately Held**
SIC: 3444 Concrete forms, sheet metal
PA: Carroll Distributing & Construction Supply, Inc.
207 W 2nd St Ste 3
Ottumwa IA 52501
641 683-1888

(G-9779)
CHEMICAL PUMP
23233 S Center Rd (60423-9793)
P.O. Box 1627 (60423-7627)
PHONE..................................815 464-1908
John Reynhout, *Owner*
EMP: 4 **EST:** 2007
SALES (est): 210K **Privately Held**
SIC: 3589 Water treatment equipment, industrial

(G-9780)
CLASSROOM TECHNOLOGIES LLC
9227 Gulfstream Rd (60423-2550)
P.O. Box 1506 (60423-7506)
PHONE..................................708 548-1642
Milos Klipic, *Principal*
EMP: 11 **EST:** 2013
SALES (est): 413.2K **Privately Held**
WEB: www.classroom-technologies.com
SIC: 7372 Educational computer software

(G-9781)
CROWN PREMIUMS INC (PA)
22774 Citation Rd Unit A (60423-2638)
PHONE..................................815 469-8789
Bill Maxwell, *President*
▲ **EMP:** 12
SALES (est): 1.5MM **Privately Held**
SIC: 3449 2821 3363 Miscellaneous metalwork; plastics materials & resins; aluminum die-castings

(G-9782)
DAS BROTHERS LLC
997 S Butternut Cir (60423-2102)
PHONE..................................925 980-6180
Das Suzanne, *Principal*
EMP: 4
SALES (est): 265.9K **Privately Held**
SIC: 3572 Computer storage devices

(G-9783)
DESIGN GRAPHICS INC
23007 Long Beach Dr (60423-8559)
P.O. Box 1120 (60423-7120)
PHONE..................................815 462-3323
Edward Gramza, *President*
Marlene Gramza, *Corp Secy*
Kathy Gramza, *Vice Pres*
EMP: 6
SALES (est): 538K **Privately Held**
SIC: 2752 2791 2789 2759 Commercial printing, offset; typesetting; bookbinding & related work; commercial printing

(G-9784)
DESIGN ON TIME
9645 Lincolnway Ln # 103 (60423-1869)
PHONE..................................815 464-5750
Vicky Elliott-Cullen, *Principal*
EMP: 4
SALES (est): 350.9K **Privately Held**
SIC: 2752 Commercial printing, offset

Frankfort - Will County (G-9785)

(G-9785)
DESK & DOOR NAMEPLATE COMPANY
9310 Gulfstream Rd (60423-2522)
PHONE.................815 806-8670
Jay Burrichter, *President*
Beverly Burrichter, *Corp Secy*
EMP: 10 **EST:** 1967
SQ FT: 8,600
SALES (est): 1.2MM **Privately Held**
WEB: www.deskndoorusa.com
SIC: 3993 3469 2396 Letters for signs, metal; metal stampings; automotive & apparel trimmings

(G-9786)
DJB CORPORATION
Also Called: Vees Collectibles
9527 Corsair Rd Ste 2w (60423-2531)
PHONE.................815 469-7533
Fax: 815 469-7590
EMP: 5
SALES (est): 502.4K **Privately Held**
SIC: 3542 Mfg Machine Tools-Forming

(G-9787)
DS SERVICES OF AMERICA INC
Also Called: Hinckley Springs
9409 Gulfstream Rd (60423-2518)
PHONE.................815 469-7100
Dale Sjoerdsma, *Site Mgr*
Amy Gerlech, *Branch Mgr*
EMP: 26
SALES (corp-wide): 2.3B **Publicly Held**
SIC: 5499 2086 Water: distilled mineral or spring; mineral water, carbonated: packaged in cans, bottles, etc.
HQ: Ds Services Of America, Inc.
2300 Windy Ridge Pkwy Se
Atlanta GA 30339
770 933-1400

(G-9788)
DUNHILL CORP
Also Called: Tuf-Guard
9218 Corsair Rd Unit 1 (60423-2566)
P.O. Box 581 (60423-0581)
PHONE.................815 806-8600
Gary Clarke, *Principal*
▲ **EMP:** 10
SALES (est): 1.8MM **Privately Held**
SIC: 2541 Store fixtures, wood

(G-9789)
DURA-CRAFTS CORP
9408 Gulfstream Rd (60423-2521)
PHONE.................815 464-3561
Timothy Digrazia, *President*
Tim Digrazia, *President*
EMP: 19
SQ FT: 30,000
SALES (est): 2.3MM **Privately Held**
SIC: 3999 3842 Pet supplies; surgical appliances & supplies; orthopedic appliances

(G-9790)
E-QUIP MANUFACTURING CO
230 Industry Ave (60423-1641)
PHONE.................815 464-0053
Millard Minyard, *President*
Ray Fantozzi, *Opers Mgr*
Dan Minyard, *Treasurer*
Margaret A Minyard, *Admin Sec*
▲ **EMP:** 40
SQ FT: 35,000
SALES (est): 10.1MM **Privately Held**
SIC: 3556 Meat processing machinery

(G-9791)
EAGLE BURIAL VAULT
9535 W Steger Rd (60423-7776)
PHONE.................815 722-8660
EMP: 6
SALES (est): 613.9K **Privately Held**
WEB: www.eagleburialvault.com
SIC: 3272 Burial vaults, concrete or precast terrazzo

(G-9792)
EXRESS MOTOR AND LIFT PARTS
1018 Lambrecht Dr (60423-1649)
PHONE.................630 327-2000
Ron Cogswell, *Owner*
EMP: 6
SALES (est): 405.4K **Privately Held**
SIC: 3714 Motor vehicle parts & accessories

(G-9793)
F VOGELMANN AND COMPANY
440 Center Rd (60423-1816)
P.O. Box 324 (60423-0324)
PHONE.................815 469-2285
Fred Vogelmann, *President*
Ilse Vogelmann, *Admin Sec*
EMP: 14
SQ FT: 20,000
SALES (est): 1.3MM **Privately Held**
WEB: www.fvogelmann.com
SIC: 1799 3441 7692 3444 Welding on site; fabricated structural metal; welding repair; sheet metalwork

(G-9794)
FKM USA LLC
21950 S La Grange Rd A (60423-9780)
PHONE.................815 469-2473
James S Rusczyk, *Mng Member*
Ulrich Freutenberg,
▲ **EMP:** 11 **EST:** 2000
SQ FT: 200,000
SALES (est): 2.8MM
SALES (corp-wide): 8.1MM **Privately Held**
WEB: www.fkmusa.com
SIC: 3547 Steel rolling machinery
PA: Fkm Walzentechnik Dr. Freudenberg Gmbh
Stempelstr. 2-4
Duisburg 47167
203 581-752

(G-9795)
FRA-MILCO CABINETS CO INC
386 Nevada A Ct (60423-1533)
EMP: 8 **EST:** 1953
SQ FT: 8,500
SALES (est): 650K **Privately Held**
SIC: 5712 2541 2434 Ret Furniture Mfg Wood Partitions/Fixtures Mfg Wood Kitchen Cabinets

(G-9796)
FRANKFORT MACHINE & TOOLS INC
285 Industry Ave (60423-1640)
PHONE.................815 469-9902
Angelo Rotondi, *President*
EMP: 6
SQ FT: 14,000
SALES (est): 1MM **Privately Held**
SIC: 3544 Special dies & tools

(G-9797)
GH CRANES CORPORATION
9134 Gulfstream Rd (60423-2582)
PHONE.................815 277-5328
Jose Antonio Guerra, *CEO*
John O' Toole, *Sales Mgr*
▲ **EMP:** 3
SQ FT: 7,200
SALES (est): 3.2MM **Privately Held**
SIC: 3536 Cranes, overhead traveling

(G-9798)
GULFSTREAM AEROSPACE CORP
9416 Gulfstream Rd Ste 1a (60423-2542)
PHONE.................815 469-1509
Stanley Cielec, *Branch Mgr*
Lee A Walker, *Executive*
EMP: 6
SALES (corp-wide): 39.3B **Publicly Held**
SIC: 3721 Aircraft
HQ: Gulfstream Aerospace Corporation
500 Gulfstream Rd
Savannah GA 31408

(G-9799)
H&H DIE MANUFACTURING INC
22772 Challenger Rd A (60423-2594)
PHONE.................708 479-6267
Andrew Mueller, *President*
Linda Mueller, *Corp Secy*
EMP: 9 **EST:** 1952
SQ FT: 11,000
SALES (est): 1.8MM **Privately Held**
WEB: www.hhdiemfg.com
SIC: 3544 3423 Special dies & tools; hand & edge tools

(G-9800)
HARBOR MANUFACTURING INC
458 Ohio Rd (60423-1158)
PHONE.................708 543-1740
John E Stratta, *President*
John G Stratta Sr, *Corp Secy*
EMP: 75
SQ FT: 85,000
SALES (est): 13.6MM **Privately Held**
WEB: www.harbormfg.com
SIC: 3599 7692 3544 Machine shop, jobbing & repair; welding repair; special dies, tools, jigs & fixtures

(G-9801)
HOLSOLUTIONS INC
21200 S La Grange Rd # 119 (60423-2003)
PHONE.................888 847-5467
Johnny Holliday, *President*
EMP: 3 **EST:** 2016
SALES (est): 85.7K **Privately Held**
SIC: 7374 7311 2741 5065 Computer graphics service; advertising agencies; miscellaneous publishing; tapes, audio & video recording

(G-9802)
HPP PRECISION MACHINE CO INC
22829 S Mustang Rd (60423-2561)
PHONE.................815 469-2608
Robert Harper, *President*
Lawrence Polselli, *President*
Lee Pickett, *Admin Sec*
EMP: 4
SQ FT: 5,600
SALES (est): 250K **Privately Held**
SIC: 3599 Machine shop, jobbing & repair

(G-9803)
ILLINOIS TOOL WORKS INC
Also Called: Norwood Marking Systems
250 Industry Ave (60423-1641)
PHONE.................708 720-0300
Larry Kulik, *Manager*
EMP: 15
SALES (corp-wide): 14.1B **Publicly Held**
WEB: www.itw.com
SIC: 3569 Filters
PA: Illinois Tool Works Inc.
155 Harlem Ave
Glenview IL 60025
847 724-7500

(G-9804)
ILLINOIS TOOL WORKS INC
Also Called: ITW Delpro
21601 S Harlem Ave (60423-6018)
PHONE.................708 720-0300
Chris Marnell, *Engineer*
Eric Parker, *Manager*
EMP: 100
SALES (corp-wide): 14.1B **Publicly Held**
WEB: www.itw.com
SIC: 3089 Injection molding of plastics
PA: Illinois Tool Works Inc.
155 Harlem Ave
Glenview IL 60025
847 724-7500

(G-9805)
ILLINOIS TOOL WORKS INC
ITW Deltar Fasteners
21555 S Harlem Ave (60423-6017)
PHONE.................708 720-2600
Karla Dearstyne, *Director*
EMP: 117
SALES (corp-wide): 14.1B **Publicly Held**
WEB: www.itw.com
SIC: 3089 Injection molded finished plastic products
PA: Illinois Tool Works Inc.
155 Harlem Ave
Glenview IL 60025
847 724-7500

(G-9806)
ILLINOIS TOOL WORKS INC
Also Called: ITW Deltar Ipac
21701 S Harlem Ave (60423-6020)
PHONE.................708 720-7070
EMP: 12
SALES (corp-wide): 14.3B **Publicly Held**
SIC: 5031 2499 Whol Lumber/Plywood/Millwork Mfg Wood Products
PA: Illinois Tool Works Inc.
155 Harlem Ave
Glenview IL 60025
847 724-7500

(G-9807)
ILLINOIS TOOL WORKS INC
Norwood Marking Systems
250 Industry Ave (60423-1641)
PHONE.................708 720-0300
Bhabin Vave, *Manager*
EMP: 36
SALES (corp-wide): 14.1B **Publicly Held**
SIC: 5045 3955 2789 3565 Computers; carbon paper & inked ribbons; bookbinding & related work; bag opening, filling & closing machines
PA: Illinois Tool Works Inc.
155 Harlem Ave
Glenview IL 60025
847 724-7500

(G-9808)
ILLINOIS TOOL WORKS INC
Also Called: Deltar Body Interior
21701 S Harlem Ave (60423-6020)
PHONE.................708 720-3541
Fax: 708 720-3961
EMP: 9
SALES (corp-wide): 14.3B **Publicly Held**
SIC: 3465 Mfg Automotive Stampings
PA: Illinois Tool Works Inc.
155 Harlem Ave
Glenview IL 60025
847 724-7500

(G-9809)
ITW MOTION
21601 S Harlem Ave (60423-6018)
PHONE.................708 720-0300
Adolph Galinski, *Principal*
Maeve Higham, *Sales Engr*
EMP: 20 **EST:** 2013
SALES (est): 3.8MM
SALES (corp-wide): 14.1B **Publicly Held**
SIC: 3822 Damper operators: pneumatic, thermostatic, electric
PA: Illinois Tool Works Inc.
155 Harlem Ave
Glenview IL 60025
847 724-7500

(G-9810)
JEWEL OSCO INC
Also Called: Jewel-Osco 3052
21164 N Lagrange Rd (60423-2010)
PHONE.................815 464-5352
George Rumbaugh, *Manager*
EMP: 125
SALES (corp-wide): 60.5B **Privately Held**
SIC: 5411 5421 2051 Supermarkets, chain; eating places; meat & fish markets; bread, cake & related products
HQ: Jewel Osco, Inc.
150 E Pierce Rd Ste 200
Itasca IL 60143
630 948-6000

(G-9811)
K&H FUEL
22193 Clove Dr (60423-7808)
PHONE.................815 405-4364
Keith Asare, *Principal*
EMP: 3
SALES (est): 193.9K **Privately Held**
SIC: 2869 Fuels

(G-9812)
KAVANAUGH ELECTRIC INC
9511 Corsair Rd Ste B (60423-2559)
PHONE.................708 503-1310
Alicia Kavanaugh, *President*
EMP: 5
SALES (est): 316.9K **Privately Held**
SIC: 3699 1731 Electrical equipment & supplies; electrical work

Frankfort - Will County (G-9843)

(G-9813)
KOSON TOOL INC
9235 Corsair Rd Ste B (60423-2578)
PHONE...............................815 277-2107
Andrew A Koson, *President*
Debra A Koson, *Admin Sec*
EMP: 4
SALES (est): 483.3K **Privately Held**
WEB: www.kosontool.com
SIC: 3544 5251 Special dies, tools, jigs & fixtures; hardware

(G-9814)
M H DETRICK COMPANY
7231 W Laraway Rd (60423-7767)
PHONE...............................708 479-5085
R J Pena, *President*
Eric Bloom, *Vice Pres*
K L Farrell, *Vice Pres*
Roger L Hosbein, *Vice Pres*
Jim Neely, *Vice Pres*
◆ EMP: 31 EST: 1914
SALES (est): 11.9MM **Privately Held**
WEB: www.mhdetrick.com
SIC: 3567 8711 3322 3321 Heating units & devices, industrial; electric; engineering services; malleable iron foundries; gray & ductile iron foundries; nonclay refractories; ceramic wall & floor tile

(G-9815)
MACE IRON WORKS INC (PA)
221 Industry Ave (60423-1687)
PHONE...............................708 479-2456
Casimer Macewicz Jr, *President*
John Schultz, *General Mgr*
Dennis Macewicz, *Vice Pres*
Casmier J Macewicz Sr, *Shareholder*
EMP: 25 EST: 1943
SQ FT: 20,000
SALES (est): 5.6MM **Privately Held**
WEB: www.maceiron.com
SIC: 3441 Fabricated structural metal

(G-9816)
MIDWEST CAGE COMPANY
9217 Gulfstream Rd # 101 (60423-2564)
PHONE...............................815 806-0005
Daniel Casey, *President*
Kathy Nicholson, *Vice Pres*
EMP: 9
SQ FT: 10,000
SALES (est): 1.8MM **Privately Held**
SIC: 3446 Gratings, tread: fabricated metal

(G-9817)
MINUTEMAN PRESS OF FRANKFORT
55 Bankview Dr (60423-1861)
PHONE...............................779 254-2912
John Regas, *Owner*
EMP: 4
SALES (est): 250K **Privately Held**
WEB: www.minutemanpress.com
SIC: 2752 Commercial printing, lithographic

(G-9818)
ORLAND PRECISION MACHINE LLC
9302 Gulfstream Rd Ste A (60423-2623)
PHONE...............................815 464-9210
Dave Sparks, *Prdtn Mgr*
Vicki Slusi, *Accounting Mgr*
Paul J Slusi,
EMP: 21
SALES (est): 3.7MM **Privately Held**
SIC: 3599 Machine shop, jobbing & repair

(G-9819)
PACTIV LLC
437 Center Rd (60423-1630)
P.O. Box 92590, Chicago (60675-2590)
PHONE...............................815 469-2112
Lee Dodd, *Technician*
EMP: 238 **Publicly Held**
SIC: 2673 3089 Food storage & trash bags (plastic); food storage & frozen food bags, plastic; food casings, plastic
HQ: Pactiv Llc
1900 W Field Ct
Lake Forest IL 60045
847 482-2000

(G-9820)
PAPER SPOT
11 S White St Ste 201 (60423-4011)
PHONE...............................815 464-8533
Maryann Wall, *Partner*
EMP: 2
SALES (est): 273.4K **Privately Held**
SIC: 2621 Stationery, envelope & tablet papers

(G-9821)
PARATECH INCORPORATED (PA)
Also Called: Femsa
1025 Lambrecht Dr (60423-1648)
P.O. Box 1000 (60423-7000)
PHONE...............................815 469-3911
Peter K Nielsen, *CEO*
Kenneth Nielsen, *President*
Chris Framsted, *Regional Mgr*
Ken Nielsen, *COO*
Doug Vernotzy, *Opers Mgr*
▲ EMP: 71 EST: 1963
SQ FT: 30,000
SALES (est): 26.3MM **Privately Held**
WEB: www.paratech-inc.com
SIC: 3569 Firefighting apparatus & related equipment

(G-9822)
PIP PRINTING INC
9218 Corsair Rd Unit 3 (60423-2566)
PHONE...............................815 464-0075
John Bitter, *President*
Dawn Bitter, *Vice Pres*
EMP: 2
SQ FT: 1,200
SALES (est): 300K **Privately Held**
SIC: 2752 7334 2791 2789 Commercial printing, offset; photocopying & duplicating services; typesetting; bookbinding & related work

(G-9823)
PRECISION CONVEYOR AND ERCT CO
9511 Corsair Rd Ste E (60423-2559)
PHONE...............................779 324-5269
Jeff Reis, *President*
Jeffrey Reis, *Vice Pres*
EMP: 10
SQ FT: 6,000
SALES (est): 1.5MM **Privately Held**
SIC: 3535 Conveyors & conveying equipment

(G-9824)
PRECISION TOOL
21200 S La Grange Rd (60423-2003)
PHONE...............................815 464-2428
William Pradelski, *Principal*
Ed Marshall, *Principal*
EMP: 10
SALES (est): 478K **Privately Held**
SIC: 3423 Hand & edge tools

(G-9825)
PREMIER PACKAGING CORP
9424 Gulfstream Rd (60423-2521)
PHONE...............................815 469-7951
Dick Ballot, *President*
Dan Brtis, *Vice Pres*
▲ EMP: 8 EST: 1995
SQ FT: 9,000
SALES (est): 1.4MM **Privately Held**
WEB: www.premierpkg.net
SIC: 3951 Markers, soft tip (felt, fabric, plastic, etc.)

(G-9826)
PRIME MARKET TARGETING INC
Also Called: Pmt
7777 W Lincoln Hwy Ste A (60423-9491)
PHONE...............................815 469-4555
Scott Duff, *President*
Daniel Hendrickson, *Vice Pres*
Michelle Duff, *Treasurer*
EMP: 35
SQ FT: 6,000
SALES (est): 8.4MM **Privately Held**
SIC: 7311 7336 2791 3993 Advertising consultant; graphic arts & related design; typesetting; signs & advertising specialties; platemaking services

(G-9827)
PRINCIPAL INSTRUMENTS INC
845 Basswood Ln (60423-1180)
PHONE...............................815 469-8159
Michael Rosandich, *President*
Christine Rosandich, *Vice Pres*
EMP: 4
SALES (est): 1MM **Privately Held**
SIC: 3823 Primary elements for process flow measurement

(G-9828)
PROFORMA
144 Hickory St (60423-1470)
P.O. Box 1392 (60423-7392)
PHONE...............................815 534-5461
Mark Adams, *Principal*
EMP: 4
SALES (est): 366.4K **Privately Held**
SIC: 2752 Commercial printing, offset

(G-9829)
QUANTUM TECHNICAL SERVICES INC
Also Called: Quantum Topping Systems
9524 Gulfstream Rd (60423-2520)
PHONE...............................815 464-1540
Mark Freudinger, *President*
David White, *Admin Sec*
EMP: 20
SALES (est): 6MM **Privately Held**
SIC: 3589 Commercial cooking & food-warming equipment

(G-9830)
QUINCEANERABOUTIQUECOM INC
7624 W Saint Francis Rd (60423-6931)
PHONE...............................779 324-5468
A J Solheim, *CEO*
Sylvia Solheim, *Admin Sec*
EMP: 2
SALES (est): 324.9K **Privately Held**
SIC: 3499 Novelties & giftware, including trophies

(G-9831)
RIECO-TITAN PRODUCTS INC
965 Lambrecht Dr (60423-1650)
PHONE...............................815 464-7400
Robert E Mc Carthy, *President*
Sharon McCarthy, *Info Tech Mgr*
Sharon M E Mc Carthy, *Admin Sec*
▲ EMP: 35
SQ FT: 31,000
SALES (est): 5MM **Privately Held**
SIC: 3423 3792 Jacks: lifting, screw or ratchet (hand tools); travel trailers & campers

(G-9832)
ROLL-KRAFT NORTHERN INC
9324 Gulfstream Rd Ste 1e (60423-2541)
PHONE...............................815 469-0205
EMP: 6
SALES (est): 410K **Privately Held**
SIC: 3599 Machine Shop

(G-9833)
ROYAL ADHESIVES & SEALANTS LLC
9411 Corsair Rd (60423-2513)
PHONE...............................815 464-5606
EMP: 3
SALES (est): 201.3K **Privately Held**
SIC: 2891 Adhesives & sealants

(G-9834)
ROYAL ADHESIVES AND SEALANTS
9001 W Fey Dr (60423-1959)
PHONE...............................815 464-3310
EMP: 3
SALES (est): 123.2K **Privately Held**
SIC: 2891 Sealants

(G-9835)
S&R PRECISION MACHINE LLC
9305 Corsair Rd Ste A (60423-2580)
PHONE...............................815 469-6544
Alan Redman,
Bogdan Struminski,
EMP: 10
SQ FT: 12,000
SALES (est): 880K **Privately Held**
SIC: 3599 3568 Machine shop, jobbing & repair; power transmission equipment

(G-9836)
SANDRA E GREENE
Also Called: Promotions Plus
228 N Locust St (60423-1263)
PHONE...............................815 469-0092
EMP: 4
SALES (est): 250K **Privately Held**
SIC: 3993 7336 Mfg Signs/Advertising Specialties Commercial Art/Graphic Design

(G-9837)
SCHWIDER SYSTEMS
7842 W Laurel Dr (60423-8359)
P.O. Box 18 (60423-0018)
PHONE...............................815 469-2834
Jacqueline Picha, *Owner*
EMP: 3
SALES (est): 231.5K **Privately Held**
SIC: 7373 7372 Computer integrated systems design; prepackaged software

(G-9838)
SHARN ENTERPRISES INC
540 Aberdeen Rd (60423-9712)
PHONE...............................815 464-9715
▲ EMP: 22
SQ FT: 26,000
SALES (est): 3.9MM **Privately Held**
SIC: 3993 Mfg Signs & Advertising Specialties

(G-9839)
SOLUBLEND TECHNOLOGIES LLC
11487 Amhearst Ct (60423-5123)
PHONE...............................815 534-5778
Richard Staack, *Mng Member*
EMP: 6 EST: 2011
SALES (est): 359K **Privately Held**
SIC: 2053 Frozen bakery products, except bread

(G-9840)
STURDI IRON INC
22405 S Center Rd (60423-1632)
PHONE...............................815 464-1173
Gregory A Szablewski, *President*
Wendi Szablewski, *Vice Pres*
EMP: 3 EST: 1997
SALES (est): 812.8K **Privately Held**
SIC: 3441 Fabricated structural metal

(G-9841)
SUPERIOR CABINET SUPPLY INC
19800 S Harlem Ave (60423-8861)
PHONE...............................815 464-2700
Frank Klauck, *President*
EMP: 3
SQ FT: 10,000
SALES (est): 600K **Privately Held**
SIC: 2434 Wood kitchen cabinets

(G-9842)
SUSTAINABLE INFRASTRUCTURES INC
20632 Abbey Dr (60423-3109)
PHONE...............................815 341-1447
Myron Brick, *President*
George Olsen, *Admin Sec*
EMP: 6
SALES: 150K **Privately Held**
SIC: 3699 Electrical equipment & supplies

(G-9843)
T R Z MOTORSPORTS INC
Also Called: Trz Race Cars
25045 S Center Rd (60423-8200)
PHONE...............................815 806-0838
Thomas R Zdancewicz, *Owner*
EMP: 3
SALES (est): 31.9K **Privately Held**
SIC: 3465 3711 Automotive stampings; automobile assembly, including specialty automobiles

Frankfort - Will County (G-9844)

(G-9844)
TARANDA SPECIALTIES INC
8746 W Manhattan Monee Rd
(60423-9799)
PHONE.....................815 469-3041
Richard M Taranda Jr, *President*
Richard M Taranda Sr Estate of, *President*
Irene Taranda, *Treasurer*
EMP: 6
SALES (est): 787.9K **Privately Held**
SIC: 3672 Printed circuit boards

(G-9845)
TRI-STATE CUT STONE CO
Also Called: Tri State Cut Stone & Brick Co
10333 Vans Dr (60423-8547)
P.O. Box 726 (60423-0726)
PHONE.....................815 469-7550
Gary Murino Jr, *President*
Carolyn Morris, *Manager*
EMP: 40 **EST:** 1963
SQ FT: 30,000
SALES (est): 5.9MM **Privately Held**
WEB: www.stone-brick.com
SIC: 3281 5032 1422 1411 Granite, cut & shaped; limestone, cut & shaped; flagstones; brick, stone & related material; masons' materials; crushed & broken limestone; dimension stone

(G-9846)
TRIO WIRE PRODUCTS INC
141 Ontario St (60423-1646)
PHONE.....................815 469-2148
Stephen Mikan, *CEO*
Adele Mikan, *Corp Secy*
John Mikan, *Shareholder*
EMP: 7
SQ FT: 5,600
SALES (est): 1.2MM **Privately Held**
SIC: 3496 3469 Miscellaneous fabricated wire products; metal stampings

(G-9847)
TSV ADHESIVE SYSTEMS INC
9411 Corsair Rd (60423-2513)
PHONE.....................815 464-5606
Edward Koziol, *President*
John Tatarinchik, *Sales Associate*
Gary Johnson, *Admin Sec*
◆ **EMP:** 50
SALES (est): 16MM
SALES (corp-wide): 2.9B **Publicly Held**
SIC: 2891 Adhesives
HQ: Royal Adhesives And Sealants Llc
   2001 W Washington St
   South Bend IN 46628
   574 246-5000

(G-9848)
U S INTERMODAL INC
20835 Abbey Woods Ct N # 201
(60423-3184)
PHONE.....................708 448-9862
Richard Lombardo, *President*
Matthew Lombardo, *General Mgr*
EMP: 20
SALES (est): 3.4MM **Privately Held**
WEB: www.usintermodalinc.com
SIC: 3715 Truck trailers

(G-9849)
VILUTIS AND CO INC
22535 S Center Rd (60423-1655)
P.O. Box 10 (60423-0010)
PHONE.....................815 469-2116
James M Vilutis, *President*
John Vilutis, *Treasurer*
▼ **EMP:** 31
SQ FT: 50,000
SALES (est): 10.1MM **Privately Held**
WEB: www.vilutisinc.com
SIC: 2673 3556 Plastic bags; made from purchased materials; food products machinery

(G-9850)
VINDEE INDUSTRIES INC
965 Lambrecht Dr (60423-1650)
PHONE.....................815 469-3300
Robert Mc Carthy, *President*
Sharon Mc Carthy, *Corp Secy*
Douglas Bakker, *Opers Mgr*
Gina Frighetto-Sakie,
▲ **EMP:** 30
SQ FT: 30,000
SALES (est): 5.4MM **Privately Held**
SIC: 3498 7692 3549 3993 Tube fabricating (contract bending & shaping); welding repair; metalworking machinery; signs & advertising specialties; stamping metal for the trade

(G-9851)
WARFIELD ELECTRIC COMPANY INC (PA)
175 Industry Ave (60423-1685)
PHONE.....................815 469-4094
Jerome H Warfield, *President*
Sandra K Warfield, *Vice Pres*
▲ **EMP:** 50 **EST:** 1974
SQ FT: 28,000
SALES: 6MM **Privately Held**
SIC: 7694 3621 Rewinding stators; rebuilding motors, except automotive; coil winding service; motors, electric

(G-9852)
WESTERN APPLIED ROBOTICS CORP
Also Called: Warcorp
22530 S.Center Rd (60423-1667)
P.O. Box 54, Manhattan (60442-0054)
PHONE.....................815 735-6476
Daniel Jeslis, *President*
David Jeslis, *Vice Pres*
EMP: 6 **EST:** 2010
SQ FT: 12,000
SALES: 2MM **Privately Held**
SIC: 3541 Machine tool replacement & repair parts, metal cutting types

(G-9853)
YOUR LOGO HERE
9525 W Laraway Rd (60423-1928)
PHONE.....................708 258-6666
David Polhill, *Owner*
EMP: 2
SALES (est): 230.5K **Privately Held**
SIC: 2759 Screen printing

Franklin
Morgan County

(G-9854)
COCAJO BLADES & LEATHER
481 Oxley Rd (62638-5031)
PHONE.....................217 370-6634
EMP: 3
SALES (est): 248.6K **Privately Held**
SIC: 3199 Leather goods

(G-9855)
FAITH PRINTING
Also Called: Its Easy With Jesus Printing
824 Bills Rd (62638-5144)
PHONE.....................217 675-2191
Lyle Janell, *Principal*
EMP: 6
SALES (est): 440K **Privately Held**
SIC: 2752 Commercial printing, offset

(G-9856)
MIDWEST LINEN RECOVERY LLC
115 Blaine St (62638-4947)
PHONE.....................217 675-2766
Bill Harris, *Mng Member*
Angie Harris,
EMP: 10
SQ FT: 2,500
SALES (est): 706.4K **Privately Held**
SIC: 2393 Bags & containers, except sleeping bags; textile

Franklin Park
Cook County

(G-9857)
A E MICEK ENGINEERING CORP
9239 Cherry Ave (60131-3009)
PHONE.....................847 455-8181
Ronald A Micek, *President*
Wayne J Micek, *Treasurer*
EMP: 26
SQ FT: 11,000
SALES (est): 4.2MM **Privately Held**
SIC: 3451 Screw machine products

(G-9858)
AARSTAR PRECISION GRINDING
9007 Exchange Ave (60131-2815)
PHONE.....................847 678-4880
Frank L Tarolla, *President*
EMP: 4 **EST:** 1965
SQ FT: 5,000
SALES (est): 596.1K **Privately Held**
SIC: 3599 Machine shop, jobbing & repair

(G-9859)
ABILITY CABINET CO INC
3503 Martens St (60131-2015)
PHONE.....................847 678-6678
Chuck Star, *Principal*
Teresa Vasquez, *Vice Pres*
Ron Cruise, *Treasurer*
EMP: 6 **EST:** 1953
SQ FT: 6,000
SALES (est): 850K **Privately Held**
WEB: www.abilitycabinet.com
SIC: 2541 2431 2434 Store fixtures, wood; cabinets, except refrigerated: show, display, etc.: wood; millwork; vanities, bathroom: wood

(G-9860)
ADVANCED CABINETS CORP
9200 Belmont Ave (60131-2808)
PHONE.....................847 928-0001
Mark Nyc, *President*
Monica Stanniz, *Vice Pres*
▲ **EMP:** 7
SALES (est): 840.5K **Privately Held**
SIC: 2434 Wood kitchen cabinets

(G-9861)
AERO APMC INC
Also Called: Aero Precision Machining
411 S County Line Rd (60131-1002)
PHONE.....................630 766-0910
Ark Maciaczek, *President*
Stanislaw Kapusciarz, *Vice Pres*
Lucjan Borowsky, *Treasurer*
Curtis Snyder, *Admin Sec*
EMP: 14
SQ FT: 5,000
SALES (est): 2.1MM **Privately Held**
SIC: 3599 Machine shop, jobbing & repair

(G-9862)
AJAX TOOL WORKS INC
Also Called: Ajax Tools
10801 Franklin Ave (60131-1407)
PHONE.....................847 455-5420
Robert J Benedict, *President*
Mike Malget, *VP Mfg*
Jim Szmanda, *Regl Sales Mgr*
Troy Lane, *Manager*
▲ **EMP:** 87
SQ FT: 120,000
SALES: 13MM **Privately Held**
WEB: www.ajaxtools.com
SIC: 3423 3546 3542 Hand & edge tools; power-driven handtools; mechanical (pneumatic or hydraulic) metal forming machines

(G-9863)
AJAX TOOL WORKS INC
10530 Anderson Pl (60131-2302)
PHONE.....................847 737-2600
EMP: 2
SALES (est): 224.5K **Privately Held**
SIC: 3599 Machine shop, jobbing & repair

(G-9864)
AL GELATO CHICAGO LLC
3220 Mannheim Rd (60131-1532)
PHONE.....................847 455-5355
Paula Dinardo,
EMP: 9
SALES (est): 2.2MM **Privately Held**
SIC: 5169 5451 5143 2024 Gelatin; ice cream (packaged); frozen dairy desserts; ice cream & frozen desserts; ice cream, packaged: molded, on sticks, etc.; dairy based frozen desserts

(G-9865)
ALL AMERICAN SPRING STAMPING
10220 Franklin Ave (60131-1528)
PHONE.....................847 928-9468
Mark Sobkowicz, *President*
Chris Sobkowicz, *Vice Pres*
Elizabeth Sobkowicz, *Admin Sec*
EMP: 8
SALES (est): 1.1MM **Privately Held**
SIC: 3495 3469 Wire springs; metal stampings

(G-9866)
AMERICAN METALCRAFT INC
3708 River Rd Ste 800 (60131-2158)
PHONE.....................800 333-9133
David Kahn, *President*
Susan Kahn, *Vice Pres*
Anthony Di Tusa, *QC Mgr*
Harvey D Kahn, *Treasurer*
Mark Humenansky, *Regl Sales Mgr*
◆ **EMP:** 100
SQ FT: 100,000
SALES (est): 19.8MM **Privately Held**
WEB: www.amnow.com
SIC: 2599 5087 Restaurant furniture, wood or metal; restaurant supplies

(G-9867)
AMERICAN PRECISION MACHINING
11135 Franklin Ave (60131-1411)
PHONE.....................847 455-1720
Naresh Patel, *President*
Ramesh Patel, *Vice Pres*
EMP: 10
SQ FT: 5,000
SALES (est): 265.7K **Privately Held**
SIC: 3599 Machine shop, jobbing & repair

(G-9868)
AMERICAN SCREW MACHINE CO
2833 N Comm St (60131)
PHONE.....................847 455-4308
Stephen Kocian, *Owner*
Sarah Alzamora, *Admin Sec*
Steve Williams,
EMP: 9 **EST:** 2006
SQ FT: 5,000
SALES: 800K
SALES (corp-wide): 12.5MM **Privately Held**
SIC: 3451 Screw machine products
PA: Komar Screw Corp.
   7790 N Merrimac Ave
   Niles IL 60714
   847 965-9090

(G-9869)
AMMENTORP TOOL COMPANY INC
9828 Franklin Ave (60131-1913)
PHONE.....................847 671-9290
Edward Ammentorp, *President*
Dale Ammentorp, *Vice Pres*
Wayne Ammentorp, *Vice Pres*
EMP: 5
SQ FT: 5,500
SALES: 200K **Privately Held**
SIC: 3545 3544 3469 Tools & accessories for machine tools; die sets for metal stamping (presses); metal stampings

(G-9870)
ANDSCOT CO INC
9117 Medill Ave (60131-3468)
PHONE.....................847 455-5800
Andrew Shaffer, *President*
J M Shaffer, *Treasurer*
EMP: 4
SQ FT: 4,000
SALES (est): 613K **Privately Held**
WEB: www.andscot.com
SIC: 3441 5051 Fabricated structural metal; metals service centers & offices

(G-9871)
APEX WIRE PRODUCTS COMPANY INC
9030 Gage Ave (60131-2102)
PHONE.....................847 671-1830
Richard Kosowski, *President*

GEOGRAPHIC SECTION

Franklin Park - Cook County (G-9897)

EMP: 15 **EST:** 1940
SQ FT: 24,000
SALES (est): 3.3MM **Privately Held**
WEB: www.apexwireproducts.com
SIC: 3496 3469 3315 2542 Woven wire products; metal stampings; steel wire & related products; partitions & fixtures, except wood

(G-9872)
ARCADIA PRESS INC
10915 Franklin Ave Ste L (60131-1431)
PHONE.................847 451-6390
Dan Rosen, *President*
EMP: 10 **EST:** 1937
SQ FT: 3,500
SALES (est): 1.3MM **Privately Held**
WEB: www.arcadiapress.net
SIC: 2754 2791 2759 2672 Labels: gravure printing; typesetting; commercial printing; coated & laminated paper; packaging paper & plastics film, coated & laminated

(G-9873)
ARCHER SCREW PRODUCTS INC (PA)
11341 Melrose Ave (60131-1322)
PHONE.................847 451-1150
Timothy Coffee, *President*
Kelly Metcalf, *Principal*
Jodie Coffee, *Admin Sec*
▲ **EMP:** 63
SQ FT: 49,000
SALES (est): 23.3MM **Privately Held**
SIC: 5072 3452 Screws; bolts, nuts, rivets & washers

(G-9874)
ART-CRAFT PRINTERS
9108 Belden Ave (60131-3506)
P.O. Box 3064, Melrose Park (60164-8064)
PHONE.................847 455-2201
Gary Nardiello, *Owner*
Jeanmarie Nardiello, *Bookkeeper*
EMP: 2
SALES (est): 300K **Privately Held**
SIC: 2752 2759 Commercial printing, offset; letterpress printing

(G-9875)
ASAP PALLETS INC (PA)
480 Podlin Dr (60131-1008)
PHONE.................630 350-7689
EMP: 14
SALES (est): 2.1MM **Privately Held**
WEB: www.asappalletsinc.com
SIC: 2448 Pallets, wood; pallets, wood & wood with metal

(G-9876)
ASSA ABLOY ACC DOOR CNTRLS GRO
Rixson
9100 Belmont Ave (60131-2806)
PHONE.................704 283-2101
Eric Tannhauser, *Manager*
EMP: 75
SQ FT: 100,000
SALES (corp-wide): 9.3B **Privately Held**
WEB: www.yalecommercial.com
SIC: 3699 7629 Door opening & closing devices, electrical; security control equipment & systems; electronic equipment repair
HQ: Assa Abloy Accessories And Door Controls Group, Inc.
1902 Airport Rd
Monroe NC 28110
704 283-2101

(G-9877)
ASSOCIATE GENERAL LABS INC
Also Called: Rowlar Tool & Die Div
9035 Exchange Ave (60131-2815)
PHONE.................847 678-2717
Arthur Schroeder III, *President*
Arthur Schroeder Jr, *General Mgr*
EMP: 5
SQ FT: 5,000
SALES (est): 250K **Privately Held**
SIC: 3548 8734 8731 3699 Welding & cutting apparatus & accessories; testing laboratories; commercial physical research; electrical equipment & supplies

(G-9878)
AST INDUSTRIES INC
Also Called: Anti-Seize Technology
2345 17th St (60131-3432)
PHONE.................847 455-2300
John H Heydt, *President*
Allen Majeski, *Vice Pres*
Katie Niesen, *Sales Mgr*
Harold Heydt, *Shareholder*
Thuy Heydt, *Shareholder*
▼ **EMP:** 12
SQ FT: 15,000
SALES (est): 3.8MM **Privately Held**
SIC: 2891 2869 Sealing compounds for pipe threads or joints; industrial organic chemicals

(G-9879)
AWNINGS OVER CHICAGOLAND INC
10204 Franklin Ave (60131-1528)
PHONE.................847 233-0310
James Girard, *President*
EMP: 5
SQ FT: 3,800
SALES (est): 596.6K **Privately Held**
SIC: 3444 Awnings & canopies

(G-9880)
B & M PLASTIC INC
3737 Acorn Ln (60131-1101)
PHONE.................847 258-4437
Miroslaw Grabowski, *Principal*
EMP: 11
SALES (est): 1.8MM **Privately Held**
SIC: 3089 Air mattresses, plastic

(G-9881)
B & R GRINDING CO
459 Podlin Dr (60131-1009)
PHONE.................630 595-7789
Richard Ruhl, *President*
Debbie Ruhl, *Admin Sec*
EMP: 4 **EST:** 1974
SQ FT: 3,500
SALES (est): 740.5K **Privately Held**
SIC: 3599 Grinding castings for the trade; machine shop, jobbing & repair

(G-9882)
B J PLASTIC MOLDING CO (PA)
435 S County Line Rd (60131-1092)
PHONE.................630 766-3200
Robert K Jacobsen Jr, *President*
Mary M Jacobsen, *Corp Secy*
Craig L Jacobson, *Vice Pres*
Craig Jacobsen, *Plant Mgr*
Bob Jacobsen, *Technology*
EMP: 38 **EST:** 1967
SQ FT: 35,000
SALES (est): 10.8MM **Privately Held**
WEB: www.bjplastic.com
SIC: 3089 Injection molded finished plastic products; bookbinding & related work

(G-9883)
BADGER AIR BRUSH CO
9128 Belmont Ave (60131-2895)
PHONE.................847 678-3104
Kenneth Schlotfeldt, *President*
Candy Carnes, *Treasurer*
▲ **EMP:** 90 **EST:** 1963
SQ FT: 26,000
SALES (est): 14.9MM **Privately Held**
WEB: www.badgerairbrush.com
SIC: 3952 Brushes, air, artists'; artists' materials, except pencils & leads

(G-9884)
BCE-USA LLC
3500 Martens St (60131-2016)
PHONE.................815 556-3007
Warren Bennie,
EMP: 3
SALES (est): 142.6K **Privately Held**
SIC: 3564 Blowers & fans

(G-9885)
BELMONT PLATING WORKS INC (PA)
9145 King St (60131-2109)
PHONE.................847 678-0200
Mark Toni, *President*
David Toni, *Vice Pres*
EMP: 120 **EST:** 1947
SQ FT: 35,000
SALES (est): 15.1MM **Privately Held**
WEB: www.belmontplatingworks.com
SIC: 3471 Plating of metals or formed products; polishing, metals or formed products

(G-9886)
BEST REP COMPANY CORPORATION
Also Called: Alca Industrial Instrs Svc
9224 Grand Ave Ste 2 (60131-3029)
PHONE.................847 451-6644
Larry Gulik, *President*
EMP: 2 **EST:** 1966
SQ FT: 1,500
SALES (est): 272.6K **Privately Held**
SIC: 3699 7699 Appliance cords for household electrical equipment; industrial machinery & equipment repair

(G-9887)
BINDER TOOL INC
9833 Franklin Ave (60131-1912)
PHONE.................847 678-4222
Hans Bittenbinder, *President*
Anna Bittenbinder, *Treasurer*
EMP: 7 **EST:** 1975
SQ FT: 6,000
SALES (est): 926.2K **Privately Held**
SIC: 3544 Special dies & tools

(G-9888)
BLG MCC ENTERPRISES INC
Also Called: Garvin Electrical Manufacturer
3700 Sandra St (60131-1114)
PHONE.................847 455-0188
Barton L Garvin, *President*
Craig Watson, *Controller*
Lisa Garvin, *Admin Sec*
◆ **EMP:** 30 **EST:** 1980
SQ FT: 65,000
SALES (corp-wide): 14MM **Privately Held**
WEB: www.garvinindustries.com
SIC: 3699 3645 3646 Electrical equipment & supplies; residential lighting fixtures; commercial indusl & institutional electric lighting fixtures
PA: Southwire Company, Llc
1 Southwire Dr
Carrollton GA 30119
770 832-4242

(G-9889)
BLOCKSMOY INC
10632 Grand Ave (60131-2211)
PHONE.................847 260-9070
Wolfgang Reichelt, *CEO*
Jorg Reichelt, *President*
Lars Ullenboom, *Treasurer*
EMP: 13
SALES (est): 239K **Privately Held**
SIC: 3677 Electronic coils, transformers & other inductors

(G-9890)
BLUEBERRY WOODWORKING INC
2824 Birch St (60131-3004)
PHONE.................773 230-7179
Krzysztof Jagoda, *Principal*
EMP: 2
SALES (est): 224.9K **Privately Held**
SIC: 2431 Millwork

(G-9891)
BONSAL AMERICAN INC
10352 Franklin Ave (60131-1530)
PHONE.................847 678-6220
Robert Main, *Principal*
EMP: 70
SALES (corp-wide): 30.6B **Privately Held**
SIC: 3272 2952 2951 2899 Dry mixture concrete; asphalt felts & coatings; asphalt paving mixtures & blocks; chemical preparations; cement, hydraulic
HQ: Bonsal American, Inc.
625 Griffith Rd Ste 100
Charlotte NC 28217
704 525-1621

(G-9892)
BRETFORD MANUFACTURING INC (PA)
11000 Seymour Ave (60131-1230)
P.O. Box 92170, Elk Grove Village (60009-2170)
PHONE.................847 678-2545
David C Petrick, *Ch of Bd*
Chris Petrick, *President*
Jerry Flynn, *Vice Pres*
David Raddatz, *Plant Mgr*
Daniel Berger, *Project Mgr*
◆ **EMP:** 300
SQ FT: 360,000
SALES (est): 79.8MM **Privately Held**
WEB: www.bretford.com
SIC: 2522 3861 2521 3651 Office furniture, except wood; photographic equipment & supplies; wood office furniture; household audio & video equipment

(G-9893)
BRISTAR
3541 Martens St Ste 304 (60131-2058)
PHONE.................847 678-5000
Paul G Keefe Sr, *Owner*
Betty Lou Keefe, *Partner*
EMP: 3 **EST:** 1996
SALES (est): 209.5K **Privately Held**
SIC: 3496 Miscellaneous fabricated wire products

(G-9894)
BRUNSWICK CORPORATION
Also Called: Life Fitness US
10600 Belmont Ave (60131-1548)
PHONE.................847 288-3300
Tri Tran, *Engineer*
Amy Lamontagne, *Regl Sales Mgr*
Todd Morris, *Sales Staff*
Chris Clewson, *Manager*
Leo Gershun, *Manager*
EMP: 394
SALES (corp-wide): 4.1B **Publicly Held**
SIC: 3949 Gymnasium equipment
PA: Brunswick Corporation
26125 N Riverwoods Blvd # 500
Mettawa IL 60045
847 735-4700

(G-9895)
C & F FORGE COMPANY (PA)
9100 Parklane Ave (60131-3054)
PHONE.................847 455-6609
Thomas Herbstritt Jr, *President*
John Gorski, *Manager*
EMP: 32 **EST:** 1938
SQ FT: 500
SALES (est): 6.6MM **Privately Held**
WEB: www.chicagohardware.com
SIC: 3312 3462 Forgings, iron & steel; iron & steel forgings

(G-9896)
C & J METAL PRODUCTS INC
11119 Franklin Ave (60131-1486)
PHONE.................847 455-0766
Henry Dolecki, *President*
James Dolecki, *Treasurer*
▲ **EMP:** 16
SQ FT: 10,000
SALES (est): 3.2MM **Privately Held**
SIC: 3469 3496 Stamping metal for the trade; miscellaneous fabricated wire products

(G-9897)
CALMA OPTIMA FOODS
10915 Franklin Ave Ste A (60131-1431)
PHONE.................847 962-8329
Paul Zielinski, *Principal*
Spiro Vlahopoulos, *Opers Mgr*
EMP: 6
SALES (est): 728.5K **Privately Held**
SIC: 2099 Sandwiches, assembled & packaged: for wholesale market

Franklin Park - Cook County (G-9898)

(G-9898)
CARLISLE CONSTRUCTION MTLS LLC
9201 Belmont Ave (60131-2842)
PHONE.....................847 671-2516
Vince Loiacono, *Manager*
EMP: 95
SALES (corp-wide): 4.8B **Publicly Held**
SIC: 3086 Insulation or cushioning material, foamed plastic
HQ: Carlisle Construction Materials, Llc
  1285 Ritner Hwy
  Carlisle PA 17013

(G-9899)
CASA NOSTRA BAKERY CO INC
3140 Mannheim Rd (60131-2375)
PHONE.....................847 455-5175
Mike Florio, *President*
Joe Catucci, *Treasurer*
EMP: 15
SQ FT: 10,000
SALES (est): 2.2MM **Privately Held**
SIC: 2051 2052 Bakery: wholesale or wholesale/retail combined; cookies & crackers

(G-9900)
CASTING IMPREGNATORS INC (PA)
11150 Addison Ave (60131-1404)
PHONE.....................847 455-1000
David Koehler, *President*
Sunisa Hukhan, *Prdtn Mgr*
EMP: 16 **EST:** 1950
SQ FT: 20,000
SALES (est): 1.5MM **Privately Held**
WEB: www.castingimpregnators.com
SIC: 3479 Coating of metals & formed products

(G-9901)
CB MACHINE & TOOL CORP
9321 Schiller Blvd (60131-2949)
PHONE.....................847 288-1807
Stanley Barnas, *President*
Ann Barnasv, *President*
EMP: 5
SQ FT: 3,000
SALES (est): 250K **Privately Held**
SIC: 3599 7692 7629 3544 Machine shop, jobbing & repair; welding repair; electrical repair shops; special dies, tools, jigs & fixtures; metal heat treating

(G-9902)
CENTERLESS GRINDING CO
2330 17th St Unit B (60131-3409)
PHONE.....................847 455-7660
Haribhai Patel, *President*
EMP: 18
SQ FT: 4,000
SALES (est): 1.9MM **Privately Held**
SIC: 3599 Machine shop, jobbing & repair

(G-9903)
CHARLES H LUCK ENVELOPE INC
10551 Anderson Pl (60131-2301)
PHONE.....................847 451-1500
Timothy Kennedy, *President*
Kevin Dean, *Vice Pres*
Denise Kennedy, *Admin Sec*
EMP: 15
SQ FT: 24,000
SALES (est): 4.5MM **Privately Held**
SIC: 2261 Finishing plants, cotton

(G-9904)
CHICAGO DIE CASTING MFG CO
9148 King St (60131-2188)
PHONE.....................847 671-5010
John C Brundige III, *President*
Marie Brundige, *Vice Pres*
EMP: 30 **EST:** 1919
SQ FT: 40,000
SALES (est): 7.5MM **Privately Held**
WEB: www.chicagodiecasting.com
SIC: 3568 3364 Pulleys, power transmission; zinc & zinc-base alloy die-castings

(G-9905)
CHICAGO HARDWARE AND FIX CO (PA)
9100 Parklane Ave (60131-3066)
PHONE.....................847 455-6609
Thomas A Herbstritt Jr, *President*
Brian Herbstritt, *General Mgr*
Gregg Carlevato, *Corp Secy*
Mitch Hull, *Prdtn Mgr*
Rory Glennon, *Foreman/Supr*
▲ **EMP:** 200 **EST:** 1914
SQ FT: 85,000
SALES (est): 37.5MM **Privately Held**
WEB: www.chicagohardware.com
SIC: 3429 3545 3496 3462 Manufactured hardware (general); machine tool accessories; miscellaneous fabricated wire products; iron & steel forgings; bolts, nuts, rivets & washers; copper rolling & drawing

(G-9906)
CHICAGOLAND METAL FABRICATORS
10355 Franklin Ave (60131-1542)
PHONE.....................847 260-5320
Robert Szczepanik, *President*
EMP: 5
SALES (est): 620K **Privately Held**
SIC: 1521 1542 3441 3444 Single-family housing construction; nonresidential construction; fabricated structural metal; sheet metalwork

(G-9907)
CHUCKING MACHINE PRODUCTS INC
3550 Birch St (60131-2099)
PHONE.....................847 678-1192
Tim Merrigan, *President*
Tom Wendel, *General Mgr*
Jerry R Iverson, *Corp Secy*
Kevin Sullivan, *Vice Pres*
Milton Ramos, *Maintenance Dir*
EMP: 74 **EST:** 1957
SALES (est): 16MM **Privately Held**
WEB: www.chucking.com
SIC: 3728 3714 3841 Aircraft parts & equipment; motor vehicle parts & accessories; surgical & medical instruments; ophthalmic instruments & apparatus

(G-9908)
CIRCLE CASTER ENGINEERING CO
10706 Grand Ave Ste 1 (60131-2215)
PHONE.....................847 455-2206
Michael Gianelli, *President*
Jeffrey Giannelli, *Admin Sec*
▲ **EMP:** 5 **EST:** 1991
SQ FT: 11,000
SALES (est): 1MM **Privately Held**
SIC: 3089 Tires, plastic

(G-9909)
CLAD-REX STEEL LLC
11500 King St (60131-1310)
PHONE.....................847 455-7373
Davies Peter G, *Mng Member*
Mark A Bounds,
Rick Luft,
Stuart Skinner,
EMP: 30
SQ FT: 60,000
SALES (est): 7.5MM **Privately Held**
SIC: 3479 Coating of metals & formed products

(G-9910)
CLEAR FOCUS IMAGING INC (PA)
9201 Belmont Ave Ste 100c (60131-2842)
PHONE.....................707 544-7990
Debbie Ross, *President*
Michael Wollberg, *Vice Pres*
Dustin Brown, *Plant Mgr*
James Keoborakot, *Prdtn Mgr*
Kristin Celeste, *Cust Mgr*
▲ **EMP:** 21
SQ FT: 22,000
SALES (est): 1.7MM **Privately Held**
SIC: 3081 Vinyl film & sheet

(G-9911)
CLEAR PACK COMPANY
Also Called: Division Sonoco Products Co
11610 Copenhagen Ct (60131-1302)
PHONE.....................847 957-6282
R Howard Coker, *President*
Ken Watkins, *Accounts Mgr*
Ritchie L Bond, *Admin Sec*
Linda Waszkiewicz, *Administration*
EMP: 130
SALES (est): 219.8K
SALES (corp-wide): 5.3B **Publicly Held**
WEB: www.sonoco.com
SIC: 3089 3081 Thermoformed finished plastic products; plastic film & sheet
PA: Sonoco Products Company
  1 N 2nd St
  Hartsville SC 29550
  843 383-7000

(G-9912)
COATINGS INTERNATIONAL INC
Also Called: Americoats
3429 Runge St (60131-1315)
PHONE.....................847 455-1400
Rajendra Patel, *President*
Anna Kita, *General Mgr*
Bharat Patel, *Exec VP*
Rafal Turek, *Research*
Luz Corral, *Sales Staff*
▲ **EMP:** 40 **EST:** 1998
SQ FT: 35,000
SALES (est): 19.8MM **Privately Held**
WEB: www.americoats.com
SIC: 2851 Paints & allied products

(G-9913)
CONSOLIDATED ELEC WIRE & CABLE
11044 King St (60131-1412)
PHONE.....................847 455-8830
Thomas A Mann, *CEO*
David J Duncan, *President*
◆ **EMP:** 60
SQ FT: 55,000
SALES (est): 14.1MM **Privately Held**
WEB: www.conwire.com
SIC: 3679 5065 Loads, electronic; harness assemblies for electronic use: wire or cable; electronic parts & equipment; coils, electronic; connectors, electronic

(G-9914)
CONTAINER SPECIALTIES INC
10800 Belmont Ave Ste 200 (60131-1562)
PHONE.....................708 615-1400
Ralph W Johnson, *President*
Priscilla Trippi, *Admin Sec*
EMP: 21
SALES (est): 5.4MM **Privately Held**
SIC: 3085 Plastics bottles

(G-9915)
CORPORATE BUSINESS CARD LTD
9611 Franklin Ave (60131-2703)
PHONE.....................847 455-5760
Patricia Letarte, *President*
Terrance H Zimmer, *Principal*
Marie Gallagher, *Technology*
EMP: 20
SQ FT: 5,300
SALES (est): 2.5MM **Privately Held**
SIC: 2752 2759 Business form & card printing, lithographic; commercial printing

(G-9916)
CORTINA COMPANIES INC
Also Called: Cortina Companies, The
10706 Grand Ave Ste 1 (60131-2215)
PHONE.....................847 455-2800
Jeffrey Giannelli, *President*
Micahel Giannelli, *Admin Sec*
EMP: 20
SALES (est): 3.4MM **Privately Held**
SIC: 3089 Injection molding of plastics

(G-9917)
CORTINA TOOL & MOLDING CO
Also Called: Cortina Safety Products
10706 Grand Ave Ste 1 (60131-2215)
PHONE.....................847 455-2800
Jeffrey M Giannelli, *President*
Michael Giannelli, *Principal*
Franca Giannelli, *Admin Sec*
▲ **EMP:** 200 **EST:** 1971
SQ FT: 125,000
SALES (est): 75.3MM **Privately Held**
SIC: 3089 Injection molding of plastics; blow molded finished plastic products

(G-9918)
COSMOS PLASTICS COMPANY
3630 Wolf Rd (60131-1426)
PHONE.....................847 451-1307
Deborah Park, *Merchandise Mgr*
▲ **EMP:** 41
SQ FT: 57,000
SALES (est): 4.8MM **Privately Held**
SIC: 3089 Injection molding of plastics

(G-9919)
CRM NORTH AMERICA LLC
2308 17th St (60131-3407)
PHONE.....................708 603-3475
EMP: 2
SALES (est): 242K **Privately Held**
SIC: 3556 Food products machinery

(G-9920)
CULINARY CO-PACK INC
9140 Belden Ave (60131-3506)
PHONE.....................847 451-1551
EMP: 6
SALES (est): 655.2K **Privately Held**
SIC: 2099 Mfg Food Preparations

(G-9921)
CULINARY CO-PACK INCORPORATED
2300 N 17th Ave (60131)
PHONE.....................847 451-1551
John J Capozzoli Sr, *President*
John J Capozzoli Jr, *Vice Pres*
Barbara Capozzoli, *Treasurer*
Stewart Riske, *Executive*
EMP: 25 **EST:** 1981
SALES (est): 4.5MM **Privately Held**
SIC: 2099 2087 Food preparations; syrups, drink

(G-9922)
CUSTOM DESIGNS BY GEORGIO
9955 Pacific Ave (60131-1920)
PHONE.....................847 233-0410
George Spyropoulos, *President*
EMP: 10
SALES (est): 400K **Privately Held**
SIC: 2511 Wood household furniture

(G-9923)
CUTTING EDGE INDUSTRIES INC
9015 Exchange Ave (60131-2815)
PHONE.....................847 678-1777
Richard Richter, *President*
Tom Javan, *Treasurer*
EMP: 7
SQ FT: 6,000
SALES: 1MM **Privately Held**
WEB: www.cuttingedgeind.com
SIC: 3544 3496 3542 Special dies & tools; miscellaneous fabricated wire products; die casting & extruding machines

(G-9924)
D & N DEBURRING CO INC
2919 Birch St (60131-3005)
PHONE.....................847 451-7702
Stephen Flemming, *President*
EMP: 9
SQ FT: 4,600
SALES (est): 860K **Privately Held**
SIC: 7699 3471 Industrial equipment services; plating & polishing

(G-9925)
D E SPECIALTY TOOL & MFG INC
9865 Franklin Ave (60131-1912)
PHONE.....................847 678-0004
Joseph Fuchs, *President*
Paul Fuchs, *Vice Pres*
Tony Fuchs, *Vice Pres*
▲ **EMP:** 20
SQ FT: 12,000
SALES: 1.2MM **Privately Held**
SIC: 3544 3599 Special dies & tools; machine & other job shop work

Franklin Park - Cook County

(G-9926)
DEALER TIRE LLC
3708 River Rd Ste 600 (60131-2158)
PHONE.................847 671-0683
EMP: 9
SALES (corp-wide): 143.7MM Privately Held
SIC: 3011 5014 Tires & inner tubes; tires & tubes
PA: Dealer Tire, Llc
7012 Euclid Ave
Cleveland OH 44103
216 432-0088

(G-9927)
DEAN DAIRY ICE CREAM LLC
3600 River Rd (60131-2152)
PHONE.................937 323-5777
Jennifer Monterroso, Credit Staff
Francis Acosta, Sales Staff
John Walker, Sales Staff
Steve Paasch, Branch Mgr
Gail Williams, Manager
EMP: 4
SALES (corp-wide): 15.8B Privately Held
SIC: 2026 Fluid milk
HQ: Dfa Dairy Brands Ice Cream, Llc
1405 N 98th St
Kansas City KS 66111
816 801-6455

(G-9928)
DEAN FOOD PRODUCTS COMPANY
Also Called: Mrs Weavers Salads
3600 River Rd (60131-2152)
PHONE.................847 678-1680
William D Fischer, President
Timothy J Bondy, Vice Pres
Mark Lehrer, Safety Mgr
Roger Westergren, Purch Agent
Dale I Hecox, Treasurer
EMP: 20
SQ FT: 2,500
SALES (est): 6.3MM Publicly Held
WEB: www.deanfoods.com
SIC: 2026 Fluid milk
HQ: Dean Holding Company
2711 N Haskell Ave # 340
Dallas TX 75204
214 303-3400

(G-9929)
DEL GREAT FRAME UP SYSTEMS INC (PA)
9335 Belmont Ave Ste 100 (60131-2802)
PHONE.................847 808-1955
David Klitzky, President
Marlowe Klitzky, Vice Pres
▲ EMP: 30
SQ FT: 50,000
SALES (est): 2.7MM Privately Held
SIC: 5999 7311 5023 3442 Art, picture frames & decorations; advertising agencies; home furnishings; metal doors, sash & trim; millwork

(G-9930)
DELTA CENTERLESS GRINDING INC
921820 W Chestnut Ave (60131)
PHONE.................847 288-0300
Nick Flores, President
EMP: 11
SALES (est): 1.4MM Privately Held
SIC: 3599 Machine shop, jobbing & repair

(G-9931)
DELUXE STITCHER COMPANY INC
Also Called: Deluxe Fixture
3747 Acorn Ln (60131-1101)
PHONE.................847 455-4400
Frank P Cangelosi, President
Robert Ventura, COO
Bill O'Leary, Plant Mgr
Mary Torres, Production
Rob Klemp, Engineer
◆ EMP: 60 EST: 1970
SQ FT: 19,000
SALES (est): 14.4MM Privately Held
WEB: www.deluxestitcher.com
SIC: 3579 3549 Binding machines, plastic & adhesive; metalworking machinery

(G-9932)
DEVON PRECISION MACHINE PDTS
10140 Pacific Ave (60131-1647)
PHONE.................847 233-9700
Steve Weingart, President
Jose Corona, Vice Pres
▲ EMP: 11 EST: 1958
SQ FT: 8,400
SALES (est): 1.8MM Privately Held
SIC: 3451 Screw machine products

(G-9933)
DUAL MFG CO INC
3522 Martens St (60131-2000)
PHONE.................773 267-4457
Mary E Newon, President
Bonnie Price, Corp Secy
Leonard J Newon Jr, Vice Pres
Eric Newon, Branch Mgr
EMP: 12 EST: 1942
SQ FT: 5,200
SALES (est): 2.4MM Privately Held
WEB: www.dualmfg.com
SIC: 3821 3829 Clinical laboratory instruments, except medical & dental; time interval measuring equipment, electric (lab type); balances, laboratory; measuring & controlling devices

(G-9934)
DURABLE ENGRAVERS INC
521 S County Line Rd (60131-1013)
PHONE.................630 766-6420
Theodore Maybach, President
Gary Berenger, Corp Secy
James L Maybach, Vice Pres
EMP: 21 EST: 1952
SQ FT: 10,000
SALES (est): 2.9MM Privately Held
WEB: www.durablemecco.com
SIC: 3479 Name plates: engraved, etched, etc.

(G-9935)
EAGLE FREIGHT INC
3710 River Rd Ste 200 (60131-2162)
PHONE.................708 202-0651
Lukasz Jedrejek, President
EMP: 1
SALES (est): 234.9K Privately Held
SIC: 3743 Freight cars & equipment

(G-9936)
ECLIPSE LIGHTING INC
3506 River Rd (60131-2151)
PHONE.................847 916-2623
Robert Fiermuga, President
EMP: 3 Privately Held
WEB: www.eclipselightinginc.com
SIC: 3648 Lighting equipment
PA: Eclipse Lighting, Inc.
9245 Ivanhoe St
Schiller Park IL 60176

(G-9937)
EDGARS CUSTOM CABINETS
3315 Dora St (60131-1815)
PHONE.................847 928-0922
Edgar Mallqui, Principal
EMP: 5
SALES (est): 737.6K Privately Held
SIC: 2434 Wood kitchen cabinets

(G-9938)
ELITE FIBER OPTICS LLC
10029 Pacific Ave (60131-1830)
PHONE.................630 225-9454
Shawn Burke, Managing Prtnr
Helliwell John A, Mng Member
EMP: 21 EST: 2014
SQ FT: 6,000
SALES (est): 432.7K Privately Held
WEB: www.elitefiberoptics.com
SIC: 3229 3661 Fiber optics strands; fiber optics communications equipment

(G-9939)
ERECT-O-VEYOR CORPORATION
421 S County Line Rd (60131-1002)
PHONE.................630 766-1200
John D Ulm, President
Julia Brunner, Admin Sec
EMP: 10
SQ FT: 11,000
SALES (est): 1.8MM Privately Held
WEB: www.erectoveyor.com
SIC: 3535 Belt conveyor systems, general industrial use

(G-9940)
EVERSHARP PEN COMPANY
9240 Belmont Ave Unit A (60131-2849)
PHONE.................847 366-5030
Bruce J Brizzolara, President
Paul A Smith, Vice Pres
Christine Mear, Admin Sec
▲ EMP: 28 EST: 1948
SQ FT: 50,000
SALES (est): 3.2MM Privately Held
SIC: 3951 Ball point pens & parts; cartridges, refill: ball point pens

(G-9941)
EX-CELL KAISER LLC
11240 Melrose Ave (60131-1332)
PHONE.................847 451-0451
Jeffrey Speizman, President
Mary Peterson, Warehouse Mgr
Kevin Gough, Engineer
Steve Kostal, Marketing Staff
Janet Kaiser, Mng Member
▲ EMP: 40
SQ FT: 70,000
SALES (est): 8.5MM Privately Held
SIC: 3441 Fabricated structural metal

(G-9942)
EXPRESS MACHINING & MOLDS
456 Dominic Ct (60131-1004)
PHONE.................630 350-8480
Steve Arnold, Owner
EMP: 2
SALES (est): 217.9K Privately Held
SIC: 3599 Machine shop, jobbing & repair

(G-9943)
FABTEC MANUFACTURING INC
9896 Franklin Ave (60131-1937)
PHONE.................847 671-4888
Frank Guerrero, President
EMP: 12
SQ FT: 16,500
SALES (est): 1.7MM Privately Held
SIC: 3599 Machine shop, jobbing & repair

(G-9944)
FLASH PRINTING INC
9224 Grand Ave Ste 1 (60131-3029)
PHONE.................847 288-9101
Mary Rix, President
Sean Rix, Vice Pres
EMP: 4
SQ FT: 1,600
SALES (est): 300K Privately Held
SIC: 2752 2791 2789 Commercial printing, offset; typesetting; bookbinding & related work

(G-9945)
FRANKLIN PARK BUILDING MTLS
9400 Chestnut Ave (60131-2911)
PHONE.................847 455-3985
James Kusta Jr, President
David Kusta, Vice Pres
Nancy Kusta, Admin Sec
EMP: 6 EST: 1952
SQ FT: 900
SALES (est): 1.2MM Privately Held
WEB: www.franklinparkbuildingmaterial.com
SIC: 5211 3273 Lumber & other building materials; ready-mixed concrete

(G-9946)
FURA INC
Also Called: Fura International
9224 Chestnut Ave (60131-3014)
PHONE.................847 451-0000
Peter Moraitis, Manager
▲ EMP: 4
SALES (est): 206.5K Privately Held
SIC: 3561 Pumps & pumping equipment

(G-9947)
G & M METAL FABRICATORS INC
9120 Gage Ave (60131-2191)
PHONE.................847 678-6501
Ralph C Disilvestro, Ch of Bd
Rafael Flores, Plant Mgr
Ken Cielocha, Marketing Staff
Anthony Disilvestro, Manager
EMP: 55 EST: 1950
SQ FT: 65,000
SALES (est): 15.5MM Privately Held
WEB: www.gmmetalfab.com
SIC: 3499 3469 Fire- or burglary-resistive products; stamping metal for the trade

(G-9948)
G & R STAINED GLASS
2919 Emerson St (60131-2616)
P.O. Box 219 (60131-0219)
PHONE.................847 455-7026
M R Gordon, Owner
Renata Thorn, Partner
EMP: 3
SALES (est): 95.4K Privately Held
SIC: 3231 Stained glass: made from purchased glass

(G-9949)
GAUNT INDUSTRIES INC
9828 Franklin Ave (60131-1913)
PHONE.................847 671-0776
Wayne Ammentorp, President
William E Gaunt, Owner
Dale Ammentorp, Vice Pres
EMP: 2 EST: 1948
SQ FT: 1,800
SALES (est): 300K Privately Held
WEB: www.gauntindustries.com
SIC: 3569 3423 Lubrication equipment, industrial; hand & edge tools

(G-9950)
GEMINI TOOL & MANUFACTURING
3541 Martens St (60131-2058)
PHONE.................847 678-5000
Paul G Keefe Jr, President
Betty Lou Keefe, Corp Secy
EMP: 17 EST: 1966
SQ FT: 13,000
SALES (est): 1.9MM Privately Held
WEB: www.geminitl.com
SIC: 3544 Dies & die holders for metal cutting, forming, die casting; jigs & fixtures

(G-9951)
GRAB BROTHERS IR WORKS CO CORP
2302 17th St (60131)
PHONE.................847 288-1055
Tadeusz Grab, President
Jozef Grab, Admin Sec
EMP: 10
SALES (est): 1.3MM Privately Held
SIC: 3312 Rods, iron & steel: made in steel mills

(G-9952)
GRANT PARK PACKING COMPANY INC
3434 Runge St (60131-1315)
PHONE.................312 421-4096
Joe Maffei, President
Vince Maffei, Vice Pres
Lucia Maffei, Admin Sec
EMP: 45
SQ FT: 17,500
SALES (est): 14.9MM Privately Held
SIC: 5147 2011 2015 5149 Meats, fresh; pork products from pork slaughtered on site; beef products from beef slaughtered on site; poultry slaughtering & processing; pizza supplies; restaurant supplies

(G-9953)
GRAPHIC PACKAGING CORPORATION
Also Called: Graph-Pak
11250 Addison Ave (60131-1199)
PHONE.................847 451-7400
John Hewitt, President
Steve Farley, Plant Mgr
Rick Daitchman, Accounts Exec

Franklin Park - Cook County (G-9954)

Jay Gonzalez, *Manager*
EMP: 120
SQ FT: 93,000
SALES (est): 39.1MM **Privately Held**
SIC: 2631 2752 Folding boxboard; commercial printing, offset

(G-9954)
GROVE PLASTIC INC
10352 Front Ave (60131-1540)
P.O. Box 163 (60131-0163)
PHONE 847 678-8244
Ernesto O'Rosco, *President*
Gerrik L Grove, *President*
Raul Orosco, *Vice Pres*
Jose Luis Orosco, *Treasurer*
EMP: 10 **EST:** 1965
SQ FT: 7,000
SALES (est): 1.1MM **Privately Held**
WEB: www.groveplastics.com
SIC: 3544 Jigs & fixtures; dies, plastics forming

(G-9955)
H & M THREAD ROLLING CO INC
9212 Grand Ave (60131-3002)
PHONE 847 451-1570
Hubert Monzel, *President*
EMP: 5
SQ FT: 6,500
SALES (est): 453.9K **Privately Held**
WEB: www.hmthread.com
SIC: 3599 3451 Machine shop, jobbing & repair; screw machine products

(G-9956)
HOME STYLE
11125 Franklin Ave (60131-1411)
PHONE 847 455-5000
Albert Cortez, *Manager*
EMP: 3 **EST:** 2001
SALES (est): 120K **Privately Held**
SIC: 2099 Dessert mixes & fillings

(G-9957)
HONEY FOODS INC
4028 Tugwell St (60131-1216)
PHONE 847 989-8186
Elizabeth Rosinski, *President*
EMP: 5
SALES (est): 2.2MM **Privately Held**
SIC: 5146 2011 Fish & seafoods; meat packing plants

(G-9958)
HUDSON TOOL & DIE CO
3845 Carnation St (60131-1201)
PHONE 847 678-8710
Linda Hellwig-Salerno, *President*
Peter A Salerno, *Vice Pres*
EMP: 18 **EST:** 1942
SQ FT: 45,000
SALES (est): 3.8MM **Privately Held**
SIC: 3469 3496 Stamping metal for the trade; miscellaneous fabricated wire products

(G-9959)
HUNTER-STEVENS COMPANY INC
4003 Fleetwood Dr (60131-1205)
PHONE 847 671-5014
John A Zizzo, *President*
EMP: 17
SQ FT: 4,400
SALES (est): 1.2MM **Privately Held**
SIC: 3429 3452 Metal fasteners; bolts, nuts, rivets & washers

(G-9960)
HUSAR ABATEMENT LTD
10215 Franklin Ave (60131-1527)
PHONE 847 349-9105
Janina Stogowska, *President*
EMP: 10
SQ FT: 1,937
SALES (est): 791K **Privately Held**
SIC: 1799 1446 Asbestos removal & encapsulation; molding sand mining

(G-9961)
ILLINOIS ELECTRO DEBURRING CO (PA)
2915 Birch St (60131-3005)
PHONE 847 678-5010
Ken Semerau, *President*
George Bull, *Treasurer*
EMP: 15 **EST:** 1963
SQ FT: 6,000
SALES (est): 1.9MM **Privately Held**
SIC: 3089 3471 3541 Injection molded finished plastic products; finishing, metals or formed products; machine tools, metal cutting type

(G-9962)
INDILAB INC
10367 Franklin Ave (60131-1542)
PHONE 847 928-1050
Robert Gavrick Jr, *President*
Catherine Gavrick, *COO*
Mark Espenscheid, *Vice Pres*
Robert Gavrick Sr, *Vice Pres*
Tom Griffin, *Vice Pres*
EMP: 20
SQ FT: 10,000
SALES (est): 5.3MM **Privately Held**
SIC: 5047 2911 8021 Medical equipment & supplies; non-aromatic chemical products; dental clinic

(G-9963)
INDUSTRIAL FINISHING INC
2337 17th St (60131-3432)
PHONE 847 451-4230
Stanley Styrczula, *President*
EMP: 10
SQ FT: 5,000
SALES: 900K **Privately Held**
SIC: 3479 Painting of metal products

(G-9964)
INDUSTRIAL GRAPHITE PRODUCTS
429 S County Line Rd (60131-1002)
P.O. Box 548, Bensenville (60106-0548)
PHONE 630 350-0155
Ronald Machaj, *President*
Frank Machaj, *General Mgr*
EMP: 4
SQ FT: 16,000
SALES (est): 648.8K **Privately Held**
SIC: 3599 Machine shop, jobbing & repair

(G-9965)
INTERNATIONAL PLATING SVC LLC (PA)
11142 Addison Ave (60131-1404)
P.O. Box 210310, Chula Vista CA (91921-0310)
PHONE 619 734-2335
Guillermo A Fernandez, *President*
Jeffrey Robert Adams, *
EMP: 16
SQ FT: 500
SALES (est): 10.6MM **Privately Held**
SIC: 3471 Plating of metals or formed products

(G-9966)
INTERPLEX DAYSTAR INC
11130 King St 1 (60131-1413)
PHONE 847 455-2424
Bob Hudson, *Principal*
Dan Larcher, *Engineer*
Alicia Perez, *Supervisor*
Jim Ciemny, *Admin Sec*
▼ **EMP:** 98
SQ FT: 55,000
SALES (est): 27.8MM **Privately Held**
SIC: 3469 3674 Stamping metal for the trade; semiconductors & related devices
HQ: Interplex Industries, Inc.
231 Ferris Ave
Rumford RI 02916
718 961-6212

(G-9967)
J & I SON TOOL COMPANY INC
Also Called: J&I Tool Company
9219 Parklane Ave (60131-2837)
PHONE 847 455-4200
John Wodzinski, *Partner*
Mike Myung, *Partner*
▲ **EMP:** 8
SQ FT: 8,000
SALES (est): 1.3MM **Privately Held**
WEB: www.janditool.com
SIC: 3599 7692 3444 Machine shop, jobbing & repair; welding repair; sheet metalwork

(G-9968)
J AND D INSTALLERS INC
9330 Franklin Ave (60131-2831)
PHONE 847 288-0783
Jeffrey Blazek, *
Dawn Blazek, *Admin Sec*
EMP: 6
SQ FT: 23,000
SALES: 800K **Privately Held**
SIC: 3449 Bars, concrete reinforcing: fabricated steel

(G-9969)
J S PALUCH CO INC (PA)
3708 River Rd Ste 400 (60131-2158)
P.O. Box 2703, Schiller Park (60176-0703)
PHONE 847 678-9300
William J Rafferty, *President*
Keith Kalemba, *Editor*
Ron Rendek, *Editor*
Anthony Brassil, *District Mgr*
Justin Willis, *District Mgr*
▼ **EMP:** 180 **EST:** 1913
SQ FT: 120,000
SALES (est): 87.6MM **Privately Held**
WEB: www.jspaluch.com
SIC: 2731 2721 7371 2741 Pamphlets: publishing & printing; periodicals; computer software development; miscellaneous publishing

(G-9970)
J S PRINTING INC
Also Called: Catholic Book Covers
9832 Franklin Ave (60131-1913)
PHONE 847 678-6300
John Sammarco, *CEO*
John H Sammarco, *CEO*
Paul J Sammarco, *President*
Phillip J Sammarco, *Vice Pres*
Mary Jane Sammarco, *Treasurer*
EMP: 6 **EST:** 1952
SQ FT: 5,000
SALES (est): 390K **Privately Held**
SIC: 2752 2759 Commercial printing, offset; letterpress printing

(G-9971)
JADAY INDUSTRIES
10002 Pacific Ave (60131-1831)
PHONE 847 928-1033
Jane Park, *President*
EMP: 10
SQ FT: 3,000
SALES (est): 1.3MM **Privately Held**
SIC: 3599 Machine shop, jobbing & repair

(G-9972)
JAMCO TOOL & CAMS INC
10151 Franklin Ave (60131-1889)
PHONE 847 678-0280
Michael Hohenzy, *President*
Joseph Hohenzy, *Vice Pres*
Arthur Hohenzy, *Treasurer*
EMP: 15
SQ FT: 3,500
SALES (est): 1.2MM **Privately Held**
SIC: 3544 3545 Special dies & tools; machine tool accessories

(G-9973)
JB MFG & SCREW MACHINE PR
9243 Parklane Ave (60131-2838)
PHONE 847 451-0892
Jarzi Rojincki, *Owner*
EMP: 3
SALES (est): 410.2K **Privately Held**
SIC: 3451 Screw machine products

(G-9974)
JBW MACHINING INC
2826 Birch St (60131-3004)
PHONE 847 451-0276
John Mroczek, *President*
Wesley Miszczyszyn, *Vice Pres*
Boleslaw Miszczyszyn, *Treasurer*
EMP: 25
SQ FT: 10,000
SALES (est): 1.5MM **Privately Held**
WEB: www.jbwmachining.com
SIC: 3599 3544 Custom machinery; industrial molds

(G-9975)
JOHNSON SIGN CO
Also Called: C Johnson Sign Co
9615 Waveland Ave (60131-1792)
PHONE 847 678-2092
John C Johnson, *Owner*
EMP: 8
SQ FT: 4,000
SALES (est): 1MM **Privately Held**
SIC: 7336 7389 3993 3264 Silk screen design; sign painting & lettering shop; signs & advertising specialties; porcelain electrical supplies

(G-9976)
KENSEN TOOL & DIE INC
9200 Parklane Ave (60131-2878)
PHONE 847 455-0150
Ronald F Kenyeri, *President*
EMP: 15
SQ FT: 10,000
SALES (est): 2.2MM **Privately Held**
SIC: 3544 3469 Special dies & tools; jigs & fixtures; jigs: inspection, gauging & checking; stamping metal for the trade

(G-9977)
KOCH POULTRY
2155 25th Ave (60131-3502)
PHONE 847 455-0902
Richard Barthel, *Manager*
▼ **EMP:** 4
SALES (est): 258.3K **Privately Held**
SIC: 2015 Poultry slaughtering & processing

(G-9978)
KOEHLER ENTERPRISES INC
Also Called: Raydyot US
2960 Hart Ct (60131-2214)
PHONE 847 451-4966
Peter Koehler, *President*
▲ **EMP:** 8
SQ FT: 27,000
SALES (est): 1.4MM **Privately Held**
SIC: 5013 3714 Motor vehicle supplies & new parts; motor vehicle parts & accessories

(G-9979)
KPS CAPITAL PARTNERS LP
Also Called: Life Fitness Mfg Fcilty
10601 Belmont Ave (60131-1545)
PHONE 847 288-3300
Joseph Pedone, *Branch Mgr*
EMP: 786
SALES (corp-wide): 2.4B **Privately Held**
SIC: 3949 Exercising cycles
PA: Kps Capital Partners, Lp
485 Lexington Ave Fl 31
New York NY 10017
212 338-5100

(G-9980)
LEGACY WOODWORK INC
9137 Cherry Ave (60131-3007)
PHONE 847 451-7602
EMP: 5
SQ FT: 8,000
SALES: 420K **Privately Held**
SIC: 2511 Mfg Wood Household Furniture

(G-9981)
LEOS GLUTEN FREE LLC
10130 Pacific Ave (60131-1624)
PHONE 847 233-9211
Leo Bucaro, *General Mgr*
Rose Ellen Bucaro, *Mng Member*
Anna Maria Bucaro, *
▲ **EMP:** 13
SQ FT: 5,200
SALES: 597.3K **Privately Held**
SIC: 2099 7389 Packaged combination products; pasta, rice & potato; packaging & labeling services

(G-9982)
LUMENITE CONTROL TECHNOLOGY
Also Called: Lumenite Electronic
2331 17th St (60131-3432)
PHONE 847 455-1450
Ronald V Calabrese, *President*
Ronald Calabrese, *Vice Pres*
Carol Calabrese, *Admin Sec*

GEOGRAPHIC SECTION

Franklin Park - Cook County (G-10011)

EMP: 15 EST: 1934
SQ FT: 6,500
SALES (est): 3.4MM Privately Held
WEB: www.lumenite.com
SIC: 3625 3873 3823 3613 Electric controls & control accessories, industrial; timing devices, electronic; watches, clocks, watchcases & parts; industrial instrmnts msrmnt display/control process variable; switchgear & switchboard apparatus

(G-9983)
MADE RITE BEDDING COMPANY
11221 Melrose Ave (60131-1331)
PHONE..............................847 349-5886
Perry Stricker, *President*
Corey Stricker, *Vice Pres*
EMP: 12 EST: 1946
SQ FT: 15,000
SALES (est): 2.4MM Privately Held
WEB: www.maderitebedding.com
SIC: 2515 Mattresses, innerspring or box spring; box springs, assembled

(G-9984)
MANDEL METALS INC (PA)
Also Called: US Standard Sign
11400 Addison Ave (60131-1124)
PHONE..............................847 455-6606
Richard Mandel, *CEO*
Mike Ward, *President*
Barbara Lindstrom, *Corp Secy*
Steve Fallon, *COO*
Roberto Jimenez, *QC Mgr*
◆ EMP: 102
SQ FT: 115,000
SALES (est): 56.1MM Privately Held
SIC: 5051 3353 Aluminum bars, rods, ingots, sheets, pipes, plates, etc.; aluminum sheet, plate & foil

(G-9985)
MATT PAK INC
2910 Commerce St (60131-2929)
PHONE..............................847 451-4018
Theodore S Kunach, *President*
Ted Kunach, *Technical Staff*
▲ EMP: 75
SALES (est): 17.5MM Privately Held
SIC: 2621 8711 Packaging paper; machine tool design

(G-9986)
MBS MANUFACTURING
1100 E Green St (60131-1005)
PHONE..............................630 227-0300
EMP: 2
SALES (est): 220.8K Privately Held
SIC: 3999 3544 Manufacturing industries; special dies, tools, jigs & fixtures

(G-9987)
MC LAMINATED CABINETS
3115 Dora St (60131-1811)
PHONE..............................773 301-0393
EMP: 3
SALES (est): 187.9K Privately Held
SIC: 2434 Wood kitchen cabinets

(G-9988)
MEADOR INDUSTRIES INC
10031 Franklin Ave (60131-1835)
PHONE..............................847 671-5042
Darla Meador, *President*
John Meador, *President*
Robert Meador, *Vice Pres*
Bob Meador, *Treasurer*
Darla Gryzwa, *Admin Sec*
EMP: 20 EST: 1964
SQ FT: 16,000
SALES (est): 3.6MM Privately Held
SIC: 3451 Screw machine products

(G-9989)
MEIER GRANITE COMPANY
9966 Pacific Ave (60131-1933)
PHONE..............................847 678-7300
Michael Kwiatkski, *President*
EMP: 6 EST: 1929
SQ FT: 2,500
SALES (est): 864.2K Privately Held
SIC: 5999 3281 3253 2541 Monuments & tombstones; cut stone & stone products; ceramic wall & floor tile; wood partitions & fixtures; wood household furniture

(G-9990)
MEJ 1933 INC (PA)
9233 King St (60131-2111)
PHONE..............................847 678-5151
Paul Just, *President*
Matthew E Just, *Treasurer*
Bruce Keclik, *Director*
Elizabeth Collins, *Admin Sec*
Gertrude Just, *Admin Sec*
▲ EMP: 140 EST: 1933
SQ FT: 175,000
SALES (est): 25MM Privately Held
WEB: www.justmfg.com
SIC: 3431 Sinks: enameled iron, cast iron or pressed metal; plumbing fixtures: enameled iron cast iron or pressed metal

(G-9991)
MELROSE MOLD & MACHINE CO INC
10085 Pacific Ave (60131-1830)
PHONE..............................847 233-9970
Mark Kawczynski, *President*
Chris Kawczynski, *Vice Pres*
EMP: 7 EST: 1960
SQ FT: 3,000
SALES (est): 1MM Privately Held
WEB: www.melrosemold.com
SIC: 3544 7692 Industrial molds; welding repair

(G-9992)
MERCURY EQP FABG & MACHINING
11415 Melrose Ave Bldg 1 (60131-1324)
PHONE..............................847 288-0079
Tom Orlani, *Manager*
EMP: 6 EST: 2009
SALES (est): 130K Privately Held
WEB: www.mercurymachiningandfabrication.com
SIC: 3599 Machine shop, jobbing & repair

(G-9993)
MERCURYS GREEN LLC
Also Called: Picture Frame Factory
9201 King St (60131-2111)
PHONE..............................708 865-9134
Jatin J Patel, *President*
Urmela Patel, *Admin Sec*
EMP: 40
SQ FT: 48,000
SALES (est): 18MM Privately Held
SIC: 5999 2499 7699 5023 Art, picture frames & decorations; picture frames, ready made; picture & mirror frames, wood; picture framing, custom; frames & framing, picture & mirror

(G-9994)
METAL BOX INTERNATIONAL LLC
11600 King St (60131-1311)
PHONE..............................847 455-8500
Bruce Saltzberg, *President*
Gary Green, *Safety Dir*
Karyn Saltzberg Liss, *Admin Sec*
▲ EMP: 200
SQ FT: 115,000
SALES (est): 31.1MM Privately Held
SIC: 2514 3993 3444 2542 Metal bookcases & stereo cabinets; signs & advertising specialties; sheet metalwork; partitions & fixtures, except wood; office furniture, except wood

(G-9995)
METAL CERAMICS INC
9306 Belmont Ave (60131-2810)
PHONE..............................847 678-2293
Fax: 847 678-2368
EMP: 2 EST: 2010
SALES (est): 200K Privately Held
SIC: 3568 Mfg Power Transmission Equipment

(G-9996)
MICHELE BAKING COMPANY
3140 Mannheim Rd (60131-2375)
PHONE..............................847 451-9481
Mark Torelli, *Principal*
Armando Mazzeo, *CFO*
EMP: 16
SALES (est): 2.3MM Privately Held
SIC: 2051 Bread, cake & related products

(G-9997)
MICRO LAPPING & GRINDING CO
2330 17th St Unit B (60131-3409)
PHONE..............................847 455-5446
Haribloi Patel, *President*
EMP: 25
SALES (est): 4.3MM Privately Held
SIC: 3541 3915 Lapping machines; grinding machines, metalworking; jewelers' materials & lapidary work

(G-9998)
MIDWEST BRASS FORGING CO
10015 Franklin Ave 21 (60131-1817)
PHONE..............................847 678-7023
John Chew, *President*
Barbara Chew, *Corp Secy*
Maria Constantino, *Asst Admin*
EMP: 20 EST: 1946
SQ FT: 15,000
SALES (est): 3.9MM Privately Held
WEB: www.midwestbrass.com
SIC: 3462 Iron & steel forgings

(G-9999)
MIDWEST FOODS MFG INC
11359 Franklin Ave (60131-1117)
PHONE..............................847 455-4636
Amrit Patel, *President*
Bianca Lebron, *Opers Staff*
▲ EMP: 32 EST: 2006
SALES (est): 7.6MM Privately Held
WEB: www.midwest-foods.com
SIC: 3999 Fruits, artificial & preserved

(G-10000)
MINT MASTERS INC
9136 Belden Ave (60131-3506)
PHONE..............................847 451-1133
Elke Timm, *President*
Kerstin Palumbo, *Vice Pres*
EMP: 20
SALES (est): 2.4MM Privately Held
SIC: 3999 3914 3911 3469 Badges, metal: policemen, firemen, etc.; trophies; medals, precious or semiprecious metal; metal stampings

(G-10001)
MIREK CABINETS
1086 Waveland Ave (60131)
PHONE..............................630 350-8336
Mirek Cientkiewicz, *Owner*
EMP: 2
SALES (est): 248.3K Privately Held
SIC: 2434 Wood kitchen cabinets

(G-10002)
MISSION PRESS INC
10265 Franklin Ave (60131-1541)
PHONE..............................312 455-9501
Michael Smith, *President*
John Machaj, *Production*
Sara Domdey, *Graphic Designe*
EMP: 5 EST: 1999
SQ FT: 4,000
SALES (est): 980.8K Privately Held
SIC: 2752 Commercial printing, offset

(G-10003)
MLA FRANKLIN PARK INC
2925 Lucy Ln (60131-2218)
PHONE..............................847 451-0279
Mike Kramer, *President*
Angel Llanes, *VP Sales*
EMP: 12
SQ FT: 13,000
SALES (est): 2.7MM Privately Held
SIC: 2851 Epoxy coatings; coating, air curing

(G-10004)
MRT SUREWAY INC (PA)
Also Called: Sureway Tool & Engineering Co
2959 Hart Ct (60131-2213)
PHONE..............................847 801-3010
M Richard Tetrault, *President*
Julian Burnley, *Vice Pres*
Nick Blumenthal, *Project Mgr*
Kyle Denhart, *Project Mgr*
Kevin Greco, *Project Mgr*
EMP: 95 EST: 1962
SQ FT: 82,000
SALES (est): 29.7MM Privately Held
WEB: www.surewaytool.com
SIC: 3444 Sheet metalwork

(G-10005)
NAMEPLATE ROBINSON & PRECISION
10129 Pacific Ave (60131-1623)
PHONE..............................847 678-2255
Lu Martin, *Principal*
EMP: 7
SALES (est): 347K Privately Held
SIC: 3479 3993 3953 3949 Name plates: engraved, etched, etc.; signs & advertising specialties; marking devices; sporting & athletic goods

(G-10006)
NATIONAL CONCRETE PIPE CO (PA)
11825 Franklin Ave (60131-1068)
PHONE..............................630 766-3600
John M Esposito, *President*
Jeff L Delia, *Admin Sec*
EMP: 35 EST: 1946
SQ FT: 38,000
SALES (est): 6.2MM Privately Held
WEB: www.nationalconcretepipe.com
SIC: 3272 4212 Sewer pipe, concrete; drain tile, concrete; pipe, concrete or lined with concrete; local trucking, without storage

(G-10007)
NELSEN STEEL AND WIRE LP
Also Called: Nelsen Steel Company
9400 Belmont Ave (60131-2800)
PHONE..............................847 671-9700
C Davis Nelsen II, *CEO*
William Geray, *President*
Bill Lundeberg, *Vice Pres*
John R Mc Vicker, *Vice Pres*
John R McVicker, *Vice Pres*
▲ EMP: 80 EST: 1939
SQ FT: 250,000
SALES (est): 52.1MM Privately Held
WEB: www.nelsensteel.com
SIC: 3312 Blast furnaces & steel mills

(G-10008)
NESTLE CHCLAT CNFCTONS A DIV N
3401 Mount Prospect Rd (60131-1304)
PHONE..............................847 957-7850
Michael Nelson, *Manager*
EMP: 3
SALES (est): 57.9K Privately Held
SIC: 2064 Candy & other confectionery products

(G-10009)
NESTLE USA INC
Also Called: Nestle Confections
3401 Mount Prospect Rd (60131-1304)
PHONE..............................847 957-7850
Michael Nelson, *Branch Mgr*
EMP: 70
SALES (corp-wide): 93.5B Privately Held
SIC: 2064 Candy & other confectionery products
HQ: Nestle Usa, Inc.
  1812 N Moore St Ste 118
  Rosslyn VA 22209
  440 264-7249

(G-10010)
NOVA-CHROME INC
3200 Wolf Rd (60131-1363)
PHONE..............................847 455-8200
Lynn Knoth, *President*
Melanie Coyne, *Manager*
▲ EMP: 11
SQ FT: 7,800
SALES (est): 1.9MM Privately Held
WEB: www.nova-chrome.com
SIC: 3471 Electroplating of metals or formed products

(G-10011)
OMNI PUMP REPAIRS INC
9224 Chestnut Ave (60131-3014)
PHONE..............................847 451-0000
Mary Moraitis, *President*
Dennis Moraitis, *Admin Sec*
Peter Moraitis, *Admin Sec*

Franklin Park - Cook County (G-10012)

▲ EMP: 12
SQ FT: 9,000
SALES (est): 2.3MM **Privately Held**
SIC: 7699 3561 Pumps & pumping equipment repair; industrial pumps & parts

(G-10012)
OPTICOTE INC
10455 Seymour Ave (60131-1234)
PHONE...............................847 678-8900
Bob Sypniewski, *President*
Don Ellefsen, *Vice Pres*
Elaine A Favaro, *Admin Sec*
◆ EMP: 27
SQ FT: 16,000
SALES (est): 5.3MM **Privately Held**
SIC: 2891 3851 Adhesives & sealants; lens coating, ophthalmic

(G-10013)
PARK ENGINEERING INC
9227 Parklane Ave (60131-2882)
PHONE...............................847 455-1424
Ed Swan, *President*
Mona Szwankowski, *Corp Secy*
Steve Patterson, *Vice Pres*
EMP: 20
SQ FT: 13,000
SALES (est): 1.5MM **Privately Held**
WEB: www.lappingcarriers.com
SIC: 3561 3542 3599 Pump jacks & other pumping equipment; die casting & extruding machines; custom machinery

(G-10014)
PARTEC INC
9301 Belmont Ave (60131-2809)
PHONE...............................847 678-9520
Brian Poklacki, *President*
Frank Rogers, *Vice Pres*
▲ EMP: 120
SQ FT: 70,000
SALES: 16.1MM **Privately Held**
SIC: 3581 3679 Automatic vending machines; harness assemblies for electronic use: wire or cable

(G-10015)
PATRICK INDUSTRIES INC
Also Called: Gravure Ink
1077 Sesame St (60131-1316)
PHONE...............................630 595-0595
Debbie Elderkin, *Plant Mgr*
Harold Gordon, *Supervisor*
EMP: 32
SALES (corp-wide): 2.3B **Publicly Held**
WEB: www.patrickind.com
SIC: 3275 Gypsum products
PA: Patrick Industries, Inc.
107 W Franklin St
Elkhart IN 46516
574 294-7511

(G-10016)
PHOENIX WELDING CO INC
9220 Parklane Ave (60131-2836)
PHONE...............................630 616-1700
Norman Gron, *President*
EMP: 15
SQ FT: 11,000
SALES (est): 2.1MM **Privately Held**
SIC: 7692 7699 3441 Welding repair; aircraft & heavy equipment repair services; construction equipment repair; fabricated structural metal

(G-10017)
PICTURE FRAME FULFILLMENT LLC
9201 King St (60131-2111)
PHONE...............................708 483-8537
Jay Patel,
Riten Patel,
EMP: 51
SALES (est): 5.4MM **Privately Held**
SIC: 5023 5719 2499 Frames & framing, picture & mirror; pictures, wall; pictures & mirrors; picture & mirror frames, wood

(G-10018)
PIONEER GRINDING & MFG CO
10011 Franklin Ave (60131-1817)
PHONE...............................847 678-6565
Charles Stephens, *Owner*
EMP: 3 EST: 1960

SALES: 300K **Privately Held**
SIC: 3599 Grinding castings for the trade

(G-10019)
PIONEER POWDER COATINGS LLC
9240 Belmont Ave Unit B (60131-2849)
PHONE...............................847 671-1100
John Bauchwitz, *Mng Member*
EMP: 20
SALES (est): 4.2MM **Privately Held**
WEB: www.pioneerpowder.com
SIC: 3479 Coating of metals & formed products

(G-10020)
PLATING INTERNATIONAL INC
11142 Addison Ave (60131-1404)
P.O. Box 81, Bensenville (60106-0081)
PHONE...............................847 451-2101
Matthew D Pankow, *President*
Kristian Villarreal, *Opers Mgr*
David Harris, *Engineer*
John Sullivan, *Engineer*
Hugh Day, *Sales Engr*
▲ EMP: 11 EST: 2007
SQ FT: 20,000
SALES (est): 9MM **Privately Held**
SIC: 2899 7699 3471 Plating compounds; industrial equipment services; gold plating

(G-10021)
POWER DISTRIBUTION EQP CO INC
3010 Willow St (60131-2835)
PHONE...............................847 455-2500
John Gandy, *President*
Steven Medinger, *Vice Pres*
Jenny Kaganovsky, *Sales Staff*
EMP: 25 EST: 1997
SQ FT: 10,000
SALES (est): 4.5MM **Privately Held**
WEB: www.powerdistribution.biz
SIC: 3613 5063 Switchboards & parts, power; panel & distribution boards & other related apparatus; switchboards

(G-10022)
PRAIRIE STATE GRAPHICS INC
11100 Addison Ave (60131-1404)
PHONE...............................847 801-3100
Richard A Heinzen, *President*
EMP: 75
SQ FT: 40,000
SALES (est): 19.3MM **Privately Held**
SIC: 2672 Gummed tape, cloth or paper base: from purchased materials

(G-10023)
PRAIRIE STATE IMPRESSIONS LLC
Also Called: P S G
11100 Addison Ave (60131-1404)
PHONE...............................847 801-3100
Richard Heinzen,
Graham Redding,
▲ EMP: 70
SALES (est): 19.3MM **Privately Held**
SIC: 2672 Adhesive backed films, foams & foils

(G-10024)
PRECISE FINISHING CO INC
2842 Birch St (60131-3004)
PHONE...............................847 451-2077
John R Rivera, *President*
Iris Rivera, *Vice Pres*
▲ EMP: 25
SQ FT: 11,000
SALES: 1MM **Privately Held**
WEB: www.precisefinishing.com
SIC: 3471 Electroplating of metals or formed products

(G-10025)
PRECISION PLASTIC BALL CO
Also Called: Robinson Name Plate
10129 Pacific Ave (60131-1623)
PHONE...............................847 678-2255
Lu Martin, *Vice Pres*
EMP: 4 EST: 1951
SQ FT: 7,000
SALES (est): 1.4MM **Privately Held**
SIC: 3562 Ball bearings & parts

(G-10026)
PRECISION STEEL WAREHOUSE INC (HQ)
3500 Wolf Rd (60131-1395)
PHONE...............................800 323-0740
Terry A Piper, *President*
Ron G Cornwell, *Vice Pres*
Raymond Luchetti, *Admin Sec*
▲ EMP: 104 EST: 1940
SQ FT: 140,000
SALES (est): 19.8MM
SALES (corp-wide): 327.2B **Publicly Held**
WEB: www.precisionsteel.com
SIC: 5051 3499 3451 3496 Steel; shims, metal; screw machine products; miscellaneous fabricated wire products
PA: Berkshire Hathaway Inc.
3555 Farnam St Ste 1140
Omaha NE 68131
402 346-1400

(G-10027)
PRODUCTION CHEMICAL CO INC
Also Called: Action Painting & Cleaning
9381 Schiller Blvd (60131-2949)
PHONE...............................847 455-8450
Daniel F Lane, *President*
Dan L Lane, *COO*
EMP: 25
SQ FT: 70,000
SALES (est): 2.7MM **Privately Held**
WEB: www.actionpaintingandcleaning.com
SIC: 3479 3471 Painting, coating & hot dipping; plating & polishing

(G-10028)
QC FINISHERS INC
10244 Franklin Ave (60131-1528)
PHONE...............................847 678-2660
John Zeinda, *President*
Paul Podedworney, *Corp Secy*
▲ EMP: 20
SQ FT: 25,000
SALES (est): 2.7MM **Privately Held**
SIC: 3479 7389 Painting of metal products; coating of metals & formed products; sign painting & lettering shop

(G-10029)
QUALITY CLEANING FLUIDS INC
9216 Grand Ave (60131-3002)
PHONE...............................847 451-1190
Vito Dellegrazie, *President*
Doris Dellegrazie, *Admin Sec*
EMP: 4
SQ FT: 3,000
SALES (est): 1MM **Privately Held**
SIC: 5169 3569 3564 Specialty cleaning & sanitation preparations; filters; blowers & fans

(G-10030)
QUALITY TOOL INC
9239 Parklane Ave (60131-2838)
PHONE...............................847 288-9330
RAO Kilani, *President*
▲ EMP: 1
SALES (est): 213.3K **Privately Held**
SIC: 3599 Machine shop, jobbing & repair

(G-10031)
RADIAD MANUFACTURING
3543 Martens St (60131-2058)
PHONE...............................847 678-5808
Paul G Keefe, *President*
EMP: 5
SQ FT: 13,000
SALES (est): 434.6K **Privately Held**
SIC: 3469 Stamping metal for the trade

(G-10032)
RAMAR INDUSTRIES INC
9211 Parklane Ave (60131-2837)
PHONE...............................847 451-0445
Mike Roberts, *President*
EMP: 4
SQ FT: 5,000
SALES (est): 999.3K **Privately Held**
SIC: 5162 2431 Plastics materials & basic shapes; millwork

(G-10033)
RCM INDUSTRIES INC (PA)
Also Called: Allied Die Casting Company III
3021 Cullerton St (60131-2204)
PHONE...............................847 455-1950
Robert C Marconi, *President*
Donald Kilburg, *Exec VP*
Scott Torphy, *VP Admin*
Jeff Good, *Vice Pres*
Cary Bautista, *Foreman/Supr*
▲ EMP: 250
SQ FT: 100,000
SALES (est): 162.8MM **Privately Held**
SIC: 3363 Aluminum die-castings

(G-10034)
RELIABLE METAL STAMPING CO INC
9244 Parklane Ave (60131-2836)
PHONE...............................773 625-1177
Clarence W Ruesch, *CEO*
Carl Ruesch, *President*
Karen Calkins, *Vice Pres*
EMP: 14 EST: 1945
SQ FT: 20,000
SALES (est): 4.4MM **Privately Held**
WEB: www.reliablemetalstamping.com
SIC: 3469 Stamping metal for the trade

(G-10035)
RELIANCE TOOL & MFG CO
Also Called: Mosedale Manufacturing
11333 W Melrose St (60131)
PHONE...............................847 455-4350
EMP: 6
SALES (est): 675.3K
SALES (corp-wide): 24.1MM **Privately Held**
SIC: 3541 Machine tools, metal cutting type
PA: Reliance Tool & Mfg. Co.
900 N State St Ste 101
Elgin IL 60123
847 695-1235

(G-10036)
RINGSPANN CORPORATION
10550 Anderson Pl (60131-2302)
PHONE...............................847 678-3581
Thomas L Werking, *CEO*
Jason Mears, *Regional Mgr*
Rich Collins, *Vice Pres*
Tom Maru, *Production*
George Straka, *Purchasing*
▲ EMP: 19
SQ FT: 3,000
SALES: 10MM
SALES (corp-wide): 78.8MM **Privately Held**
SIC: 3568 Clutches, except vehicular
PA: Ringspann Gmbh
Schaberweg 30-38
Bad Homburg 61348
617 227-50

(G-10037)
RJ CNC WORKS INC
10134 Pacific Ave (60131-1647)
PHONE...............................847 671-9120
Boguslaw Janczura, *Principal*
EMP: 7
SALES (est): 921K **Privately Held**
SIC: 3599 Machine shop, jobbing & repair

(G-10038)
RRP ENTERPRISES INC
9510 Fullerton Ave (60131-3340)
PHONE...............................847 455-5674
Richard Perales, *President*
Kurt Miller, *Purch Mgr*
Janet Flynn,
EMP: 2
SQ FT: 3,000
SALES (est): 576.6K **Privately Held**
SIC: 3561 Cylinders, pump

(G-10039)
S&L TOOL COMPANY INC
Also Called: Aero Tool & Stamping
2324 N 17th Ave (60131)
PHONE...............................847 455-5550
Patricia A Snook, *President*
EMP: 4 EST: 1964
SQ FT: 5,500

GEOGRAPHIC SECTION

Franklin Park - Cook County (G-10066)

SALES (est): 439.2K **Privately Held**
SIC: 3469 Machine parts, stamped or pressed metal

(G-10040)
SACCO-CAMEX INC
460 Dominic Ct (60131-1004)
PHONE 630 595-8090
Steve Sacco, *President*
EMP: 3 **EST:** 1971
SALES (est): 210K **Privately Held**
SIC: 3545 3541 Cams (machine tool accessories); machine tools, metal cutting type

(G-10041)
SAI ADVANCED PWR SOLUTIONS INC (PA)
Also Called: Switchboard Apparatus
11333 Addison Ave Apt 100 (60131-1103)
PHONE 708 450-0990
Bradley K Bell, *President*
Dale Hoppensteadt, *Chairman*
David Martin, *COO*
Kevin Hoppensteadt, *VP Mfg*
Jim Africh, *Engineer*
▲ **EMP:** 71
SALES (est): 15.7MM **Privately Held**
WEB: www.sai-aps.com
SIC: 3613 Switchboards & parts, power

(G-10042)
SANDEE MANUFACTURING CO (PA)
10520 Waveland Ave (60131-1288)
PHONE 847 671-1335
Michael Feeny, *President*
Nancy Adkins, *General Mgr*
James Kunkel, *Exec VP*
Erin McLeod, *Human Res Mgr*
Carmen Micklus, *Sales Staff*
EMP: 49
SQ FT: 35,000
SALES (est): 14.2MM **Privately Held**
WEB: www.sandeeplastics.com
SIC: 3089 3993 3082 3081 Extruded finished plastic products; signs & advertising specialties; unsupported plastics profile shapes; unsupported plastics film & sheet

(G-10043)
SARJ USA INC
Also Called: Picture Frame Factory
9201 King St (60131-2111)
PHONE 708 865-9134
Jatin Patel, *CEO*
Urmela Patel, *Admin Sec*
◆ **EMP:** 48
SQ FT: 48,600
SALES: 10.7MM **Privately Held**
SIC: 2499 3231 5023 5999 Picture & mirror frames, wood; framed mirrors; frames & framing, picture & mirror; art, picture frames & decorations; picture framing, custom

(G-10044)
SAS INDUSTRIAL MACHINERY INC
9212 Cherry Ave (60131-3010)
PHONE 847 455-5526
Stanley Niedbalec, *President*
EMP: 5
SQ FT: 14,500
SALES (est): 600K **Privately Held**
SIC: 3599 Machine shop, jobbing & repair

(G-10045)
SCOT FORGE COMPANY
9394 Belmont Ave (60131-2810)
PHONE 847 678-6000
Tony Hall, *Purchasing*
Mike Brock, *Engineer*
Steve Hughes, *Engineer*
Axel Stromberg, *Sales Engr*
Harry Clayton, *Manager*
EMP: 58
SALES (est): 9.2MM
SALES (corp-wide): 107MM **Privately Held**
SIC: 3462 3325 Iron & steel forgings; steel foundries

PA: Scot Forge Company
8001 Winn Rd
Spring Grove IL 60081
815 675-1000

(G-10046)
SEMLER INDUSTRIES INC
3800 Carnation St (60131-1202)
PHONE 847 671-5650
Loren H Semler, *Ch of Bd*
Loren W Semler, *President*
Joseph Palm, *General Mgr*
Katherine Felton, *Senior VP*
Joe Palm, *Vice Pres*
▲ **EMP:** 31 **EST:** 1905
SQ FT: 20,000
SALES (est): 19.1MM **Privately Held**
WEB: www.semlerindustries.com
SIC: 5084 3823 5085 Water pumps (industrial); meters, consumption registering; industrial instrmnts msrmnt display/control process variable; hose, belting & packing

(G-10047)
SKYLINE BEAUTY SUPPLY INC
Also Called: Nail Superstore
3804 Carnation St (60131-1202)
PHONE 773 275-6003
Kevin Bao Huynh, *President*
◆ **EMP:** 10
SQ FT: 20,000
SALES (est): 1.6MM **Privately Held**
SIC: 5087 2844 Beauty parlor equipment & supplies; cosmetic preparations

(G-10048)
SLOAN VALVE COMPANY (PA)
Also Called: Sloan Valve Co Fkp
10500 Seymour Ave (60131-1259)
PHONE 847 671-4300
Charles S Allen Jr, *President*
Grahm C Allen, *President*
James C Allen, *President*
James Cutler, *President*
Linda Higgins, *President*
◆ **EMP:** 100
SQ FT: 410,000
SALES (est): 199.1MM **Privately Held**
WEB: www.sloanvalve.com
SIC: 3432 3494 Plumbing fixture fittings & trim; valves & pipe fittings; pipe fittings

(G-10049)
SONOCO PRODUCTS COMPANY
Clear Pack Company
11608 Copenhagen Ct (60131-1348)
PHONE 847 957-6282
Fax: 847 957-1529
EMP: 130
SALES (corp-wide): 4.9B **Publicly Held**
SIC: 3089 3081 Plastics Products, Nec, Nsk
PA: Sonoco Products Company
1 N 2nd St
Hartsville SC 29550
843 383-7000

(G-10050)
SPECIALTY ENTERPRISES INC
1075 Waveland Ave (60131-1011)
PHONE 630 595-7808
John Finn III, *President*
Wayne Finn, *Vice Pres*
EMP: 9 **EST:** 1959
SQ FT: 8,000
SALES (est): 900K **Privately Held**
WEB: www.specialtyenterprise.com
SIC: 3541 3599 Machine tools, metal cutting type; machine shop, jobbing & repair

(G-10051)
SPOT WELDING PRODUCTS INC
406 Dominic Ct (60131-1004)
PHONE 630 238-0880
Arthur McCaskey, *President*
Ann Mc Caskey, *President*
Arthur Mc Caskey, *Principal*
Robert Donahue, *Vice Pres*
EMP: 10
SALES (est): 948.2K **Privately Held**
SIC: 5084 3548 3366 3331 Welding machinery & equipment; resistance welders, electric; copper foundries; primary copper

(G-10052)
STERIS CORPORATION
11457 Melrose Ave Ste B (60131-1303)
PHONE 847 455-2881
Harry Bala, *President*
EMP: 10 **EST:** 2001
SQ FT: 25,000
SALES (est): 1.6MM **Privately Held**
WEB: www.danaproducts.com
SIC: 3842 Surgical appliances & supplies

(G-10053)
STERLING EXTRACT COMPANY INC
10929 Franklin Ave Ste V (60131-1430)
PHONE 847 451-9728
Craig Wakefield, *President*
Marion Wakefield, *Corp Secy*
Deborah Pavone, *Mktg Dir*
EMP: 6 **EST:** 1949
SQ FT: 4,900
SALES (est): 1.5MM **Privately Held*
WEB: www.sterlingextractcompany.com
SIC: 2087 Extracts, flavoring; concentrates, flavoring (except drink)

(G-10054)
STUECKLEN MANUFACTURING CO
10022 Pacific Ave (60131-1837)
P.O. Box 190 (60131-0190)
PHONE 847 678-5130
Paul Davis, *President*
Alexandra Davis, *Vice Pres*
EMP: 7 **EST:** 1948
SQ FT: 14,500
SALES (est): 1MM **Privately Held**
WEB: www.stuecklenmfg.com
SIC: 3444 3469 Sheet metalwork; spinning metal for the trade

(G-10055)
SUBURBAN INDUSTRIES INC
1090 E Green St (60131-1015)
PHONE 630 766-3773
C Kenneth Pobloske Jr, *President*
EMP: 10 **EST:** 1946
SQ FT: 14,000
SALES (est): 1.8MM **Privately Held**
WEB: www.sub-ind.com
SIC: 3452 3356 Dowel pins, metal; nonferrous rolling & drawing

(G-10056)
SUBURBAN METALCRAFT INC
Also Called: Decor Rv Locks
9045 Exchange Ave (60131-2815)
PHONE 847 678-7550
Patricia Ragon, *President*
Richard Ragon, *Vice Pres*
EMP: 8 **EST:** 1946
SQ FT: 7,500
SALES (est): 1.4MM **Privately Held**
SIC: 3469 Stamping metal for the trade

(G-10057)
SUBURBAN WELDING & STEEL LLC
9820 Franklin Ave (60131-1913)
PHONE 847 678-1264
Karen Karner, *President*
Brian Kasmer,
EMP: 14 **EST:** 1951
SQ FT: 13,500
SALES (est): 1.3MM **Privately Held**
WEB: www.suburbanweldingandsteel.com
SIC: 3444 7692 Sheet metalwork; welding repair

(G-10058)
SURFACETEC CORP
471 Podlin Dr (60131-1007)
PHONE 630 521-0001
Luis Gonzales, *President*
Rey Garcia, *Superintendent*
Alberta Vasquez, *Principal*
Luis Gonzalez, *Opers Mgr*
EMP: 14 **EST:** 2013
SALES: 1.5MM **Privately Held**
SIC: 3544 Industrial molds

(G-10059)
TELEGARTNER INC
411 Dominic Ct (60131-1003)
PHONE 630 616-7600

Ralph Souders, *President*
Jeanette Reedy, *Treasurer*
Peter W Mitchell, *Admin Sec*
EMP: 22
SQ FT: 7,800
SALES: 4.2MM **Privately Held**
SIC: 3643 5063 Power line cable; electrical supplies

(G-10060)
TESLER COMPANY OF ILLINOIS INC
Also Called: Unique Checkout Systems
2312 17th St (60131-3407)
PHONE 773 522-4400
David C Maloy, *President*
Stanley Tesler, *Principal*
EMP: 2 **EST:** 1979
SALES (est): 1.4MM **Privately Held**
WEB: www.uniquecheckoutsystems.com
SIC: 3444 Sheet metalwork

(G-10061)
TITAN TOOL COMPANY INC
10001 Pacific Ave (60131-1830)
PHONE 847 671-0045
Jim Jaroch, *President*
Anne M Jaroch, *Corp Secy*
Peter Jaroch, *Vice Pres*
EMP: 5 **EST:** 1961
SQ FT: 4,000
SALES (est): 120K **Privately Held**
SIC: 3544 3549 Special dies & tools; industrial molds; metalworking machinery

(G-10062)
TITUS TOOL COMPANY INC
11056 Addison Ave (60131-1402)
PHONE 847 243-8801
▲ **EMP:** 4
SALES (est): 133.2K **Privately Held**
SIC: 3599 Industrial machinery

(G-10063)
TRANSCENDIA INC (PA)
9201 Belmont Ave Ste 100a (60131-2842)
PHONE 847 678-1800
John Bagnuo, *President*
Richard Locke, *President*
Nicole Shy, *Vice Pres*
Pam Piazza, *Opers Mgr*
Zac Kimball, *Materials Mgr*
◆ **EMP:** 125 **EST:** 1931
SQ FT: 147,000
SALES (est): 327.9MM **Privately Held**
WEB: www.transcendia.com
SIC: 3081 5162 Plastic film & sheet; plastics products

(G-10064)
TRANSCENDIA INC
Lamination/Id Securities Div
9201 Belmont Ave Ste 100a (60131-2842)
PHONE 847 678-1800
Dennis Kuta, *General Mgr*
EMP: 26
SALES (corp-wide): 327.9MM **Privately Held**
SIC: 3083 Plastic finished products, laminated
PA: Transcendia, Inc.
9201 Belmont Ave Ste 100a
Franklin Park IL 60131
847 678-1800

(G-10065)
TRAVEL CADDY INC
Also Called: Travelon
11333 Addison Ave Apt 200 (60131-1103)
PHONE 847 621-7000
Donald E Godshaw, *President*
Kathy Curtin, *Vice Pres*
Matthew Lyons, *CFO*
Doug Brunner, *Accounting Mgr*
Tanya Krivtsov, *Senior Mgr*
◆ **EMP:** 50 **EST:** 1978
SALES (est): 10.7MM **Privately Held**
SIC: 3161 3792 Traveling bags; travel trailers & campers

(G-10066)
TRIANGLE SCREEN PRINT INC
10353 Franklin Ave (60131-1529)
PHONE 847 678-9200
Dan Congine, *President*
EMP: 14

Franklin Park - Cook County (G-10067)

SALES (est): 985K **Privately Held**
SIC: 2759 2396 2395 Screen printing; automotive & apparel trimmings; pleating & stitching

(G-10067)
TRO MANUFACTURING COMPANY INC
2610 Edgington St (60131-3492)
P.O. Box 528 (60131-0528)
PHONE 847 455-3755
Scott Sanda, *President*
Brian Heatherington, *Plant Mgr*
Jeff Danhoff, *QC Mgr*
Kim Ogle, *QC Mgr*
Keith Cutts, *Sales Dir*
EMP: 48
SQ FT: 68,000
SALES (est): 20.9MM **Privately Held**
SIC: 3469 Stamping metal for the trade

(G-10068)
TUKAIZ LLC
2917 Latoria Ln (60131-2216)
PHONE 847 288-4804
Christopher Calabria, *Managing Prtnr*
EMP: 13
SALES (corp-wide): 37.5MM **Privately Held**
SIC: 2771 Greeting cards
PA: Tukaiz, Llc
2950 Hart Ct
Franklin Park IL 60131
847 455-1588

(G-10069)
UNITED ELECTRONICS CORP INC
3615 Wolf Rd (60131-1425)
PHONE 847 671-6034
Hemant Patel, *President*
Arvind Moradia, *Engineer*
Mangesh Patel, *Treasurer*
Joan Strauss, *Sales Staff*
▲ EMP: 70
SQ FT: 70,000
SALES: 7.5MM **Privately Held**
SIC: 3672 Circuit boards, television & radio printed

(G-10070)
US SMOKELESS TOB MFG CO LLC
11601 Copenhagen Ct (60131-1312)
PHONE 804 274-2000
Greg Ray, *VP Mfg*
EMP: 16
SALES (corp-wide): 25.1B **Publicly Held**
SIC: 2131 Smoking tobacco
HQ: U.S. Smokeless Tobacco Manufacturing Company Llc
800 Harrison St
Nashville TN 37203

(G-10071)
UST INC
11601 Copenhagen Ct (60131-1301)
PHONE 847 957-5104
EMP: 4 EST: 2015
SALES (est): 300.9K **Privately Held**
SIC: 2131 Mfg Chewing/Smoking Tobacco

(G-10072)
VALMONT COATINGS INC
10909 Franklin Ave (60131-1409)
PHONE 847 455-0884
Brent Toller, *General Mgr*
EMP: 4
SALES (est): 513.9K **Privately Held**
SIC: 3479 Coating of metals & formed products

(G-10073)
VALMONT INDUSTRIES INC
Also Called: Valmont Ctngs Empire Glvnizing
10909 Franklin Ave (60131-1409)
PHONE 773 625-0354
Gerald Hill, *Opers Mgr*
Carol Schlau, *Branch Mgr*
EMP: 75
SQ FT: 65,000
SALES (corp-wide): 2.7B **Publicly Held**
SIC: 3441 Fabricated structural metal

PA: Valmont Industries, Inc.
1 Valmont Plz Ste 500
Omaha NE 68154
402 963-1000

(G-10074)
VANART ENGINEERING COMPANY
3504 River Rd (60131-2193)
PHONE 847 678-6255
Jane Baptist, *CEO*
Daniel A Baptist, *President*
Don Noren, *Vice Pres*
EMP: 30 EST: 1949
SQ FT: 8,000
SALES (est): 5MM **Privately Held**
WEB: www.vanartengineering.com
SIC: 3469 3544 Stamping metal for the trade; special dies, tools, jigs & fixtures

(G-10075)
VAPOR POWER INTERNATIONAL LLC (PA)
551 S County Line Rd (60131-1013)
PHONE 630 694-5500
Jim Pawlak, *COO*
Rob Pawlak, *Opers Staff*
Marc Dupuis, *Sales Mgr*
Glenn Kuhlman, *Sales Staff*
Robert C Forslund,
▲ EMP: 75
SQ FT: 55,000
SALES (est): 7.4MM **Privately Held**
WEB: www.vaporpower.com
SIC: 3443 Fabricated plate work (boiler shop)

(G-10076)
VAREX IMAGING CORPORATION
Also Called: Claymount
3835 Carnation St (60131-1201)
PHONE 847 279-5121
Barry Smith, *Manager*
Thomas Wiak, *Manager*
EMP: 55
SQ FT: 61,200
SALES (corp-wide): 780.6MM **Publicly Held**
SIC: 3844 X-ray apparatus & tubes
PA: Varex Imaging Corporation
1678 S Pioneer Rd
Salt Lake City UT 84104
801 972-5000

(G-10077)
VENUS PROCESSING & STORAGE
2401 Rose St (60131-3322)
PHONE 847 455-0496
James Mayer, *President*
Shesfield Wolk, *Vice Pres*
EMP: 52
SALES (est): 5.3MM **Privately Held**
SIC: 4225 3444 3312 General warehousing & storage; sheet metalwork; blast furnaces & steel mills

(G-10078)
VICARI TOOL & PLASTICS INC
3350 Schierhorn Ct (60131-2125)
PHONE 847 671-9430
Lou Vicari, *President*
Mark Vicari, *Treasurer*
EMP: 4
SQ FT: 5,000
SALES (est): 380K **Privately Held**
SIC: 3599 Machine shop, jobbing & repair

(G-10079)
VISIMARK INC
Also Called: Durable Technologies
521 S County Line Rd (60131-1013)
PHONE 866 344-7721
Clem Malinowski, *General Mgr*
EMP: 17
SALES (corp-wide): 3.4MM **Privately Held**
SIC: 3542 Machine tools, metal forming type
PA: Visimark Inc
33 Arctic St Ste 2
Worcester MA 01604
866 344-7721

(G-10080)
VORTEQ COIL FINISHERS LLC
11440 W Addison St (60131)
PHONE 847 455-7200
Dave Kuiz, *Branch Mgr*
EMP: 50
SALES (corp-wide): 45.7MM **Privately Held**
SIC: 3444 Siding, sheet metal
PA: Vorteq Coil Finishers, Llc
930 Armour Rd
Oconomowoc WI 53066
262 567-1112

(G-10081)
W N G S INC
11415 Melrose Ave (60131-1324)
PHONE 847 451-1224
Anthony Grammatis, *Ch of Bd*
Daniel Grammatis, *President*
▼ EMP: 48
SQ FT: 25,000
SALES (est): 9.4MM **Privately Held**
SIC: 3531 5084 Cranes, locomotive; loaders, shovel: self-propelled; materials handling machinery

(G-10082)
WALTER H JELLY & CO INC
2822 Birch St (60131-3074)
PHONE 847 455-4235
Susan Jelly, *Principal*
▲ EMP: 4 EST: 2011
SALES (est): 341.5K **Privately Held**
SIC: 3466 Bottle caps & tops, stamped metal

(G-10083)
WARDZALA INDUSTRIES INC
9330 Grand Ave (60131-3411)
PHONE 847 288-9909
Walter Wardzala, *President*
EMP: 16
SQ FT: 40,000
SALES (est): 3.2MM **Privately Held**
SIC: 3542 7692 3544 3496 Machine tools, metal forming type; welding repair; special dies, tools, jigs & fixtures; miscellaneous fabricated wire products; metal stampings

(G-10084)
WESTERN LIGHTING INC
2349 17th St (60131-3432)
P.O. Box 178, Park Ridge (60068-0178)
PHONE 847 451-7200
Norma Heen, *President*
Victor Heen Sr, *Vice Pres*
Victor Heen Jr, *Vice Pres*
EMP: 15
SQ FT: 10,000
SALES (est): 600K **Privately Held**
WEB: www.westernlightinginc.com
SIC: 3993 3646 3648 3645 Electric signs; fluorescent lighting fixtures, commercial; lighting equipment; residential lighting fixtures

(G-10085)
WILCZAK INDUSTRIAL PARTS INC
9220 Chestnut Ave (60131-3014)
PHONE 847 260-5559
Eric Wilczak, *President*
Barbara Wilczak, *Admin Sec*
EMP: 7
SQ FT: 5,000
SALES (est): 816.2K **Privately Held**
SIC: 3599 Machine shop, jobbing & repair

(G-10086)
WILLERT COMPANY
1144 E Green St (60131-1005)
PHONE 630 860-1620
Edward John Butler Jr, *President*
EMP: 3 EST: 1933
SALES: 300K **Privately Held**
SIC: 2752 Lithographing on metal

(G-10087)
WORLD LIBRARY PUBLICATIONS
3708 River Rd Ste 400 (60131-2158)
PHONE 847 678-9300
William Rafferty, *President*

Israel Martinez, *Editor*
Christine Krzystofczyk, *Regional Mgr*
Mary Lou Rafferty, *Vice Pres*
Dan Schrader, *VP Opers*
EMP: 180
SQ FT: 10,000
SALES (est): 13.1MM **Privately Held**
SIC: 2741 Miscellaneous publishing

Freeburg
St. Clair County

(G-10088)
CUSTOM TOWELS INC
6410 Hilgard Memorial Dr (62243-2343)
PHONE 618 539-5005
Debbie Martin, *President*
Tom Martin, *Vice Pres*
EMP: 3
SALES: 1MM **Privately Held**
SIC: 2396 Screen printing on fabric articles

(G-10089)
FREEBURG PRINTING & PUBLISHING
820 S State St (62243-1548)
P.O. Box 98 (62243-0098)
PHONE 618 539-3320
Harold Carpenter, *President*
Harold C Carpenter, *Owner*
Thomas Carpenter, *Vice Pres*
Tom Carpenter, *Prdtn Mgr*
Hal Carpenter, *Graphic Designe*
EMP: 8
SQ FT: 2,500
SALES: 185K **Privately Held**
SIC: 2711 2759 Job printing & newspaper publishing combined; letterpress printing

(G-10090)
GENERAL MACHINE INC
6038 Schiermeier Rd (62243-2012)
PHONE 618 234-1919
Patti Kreher, *Corp Secy*
Joseph C Kreher Jr, *Officer*
EMP: 22 EST: 1980
SQ FT: 18,000
SALES (est): 3.5MM **Privately Held**
SIC: 3599 Machine shop, jobbing & repair

(G-10091)
LEE SAUZEK
316 Silverthorne Dr (62243-2680)
P.O. Box 36 (62243-0036)
PHONE 618 539-5815
Lee Sauzek, *CEO*
EMP: 4
SALES (est): 201.8K **Privately Held**
SIC: 3635 Household vacuum cleaners

(G-10092)
PROFESSIONAL METAL WORKS LLC
9 Industrial Dr (62243-3229)
PHONE 618 539-2214
Dennis J Kaiser, *Mng Member*
Rhonda Kaiser, *Mng Member*
Dennis Jkaiser,
EMP: 14
SQ FT: 15,000
SALES: 4MM **Privately Held**
SIC: 3441 7692 Fabricated structural metal; welding repair

(G-10093)
SENTINEL EMRGNCY SOLUTIONS LLC (PA)
502 S Richland St (62243-1533)
PHONE 618 539-3863
Chris Hurst, *Sales Mgr*
Ryan Steck, *Sales Staff*
Tamra Wiesemeyer, *Sales Staff*
Cynthia Hake, *Marketing Mgr*
Bill Franz, *Mng Member*
EMP: 22
SALES: 10MM **Privately Held**
WEB: www.sentineles.com
SIC: 3711 Fire department vehicles (motor vehicles), assembly of

GEOGRAPHIC SECTION

Freeport - Stephenson County (G-10121)

(G-10094)
SIEMENS MANUFACTURING CO INC (PA)
410 W Washington St (62243-1394)
P.O. Box 61 (62243-0061)
PHONE..................................618 539-3000
Joe Kaeser, *President*
John F Siemens III, *President*
Janet Siemens, *Vice Pres*
Kelli Lubenkov, *Opers Staff*
Jaime Quintero, *Opers Staff*
EMP: 200 **EST:** 1963
SQ FT: 50,000
SALES (est): 64.8MM **Privately Held**
WEB: www.siemensmfg.com
SIC: 3672 Printed circuit boards

(G-10095)
STANDARD LABORATORIES INC
Also Called: Standard Laboratory
8451 River King Dr (62243-2352)
PHONE..................................618 539-5836
Richard Wilburn, *Manager*
EMP: 28
SALES (corp-wide): 55.3MM **Privately Held**
SIC: 1221 8734 Bituminous coal & lignite-surface mining; testing laboratories
PA: Standard Laboratories, Inc.
147 11th Ave Ste 100
South Charleston WV 25303
304 744-6800

(G-10096)
STAR CUSHION PRODUCTS INC
5 Commerce Dr (62243-3228)
PHONE..................................618 539-7070
Janice Fraser, *President*
Sarah Pietroburgo, *Executive*
▲ **EMP:** 12
SQ FT: 6,700
SALES: 2.5MM **Privately Held**
SIC: 3841 3842 Surgical & medical instruments; ligatures, medical

Freeport
Stephenson County

(G-10097)
ADVANCE TECHNOLOGIES INC
430 Challenge St (61032-2540)
PHONE..................................815 297-1771
Steve Buss, *CEO*
Robert Horton, *Vice Pres*
EMP: 4
SALES: 500K **Privately Held**
SIC: 3663 Satellites, communications

(G-10098)
AIR PURE LLC
1103 Hillcrest Dr (61032-6623)
PHONE..................................815 275-8990
Eric Siegmeier, *Administration*
EMP: 3
SALES: 120K **Privately Held**
SIC: 1711 1389 Heating systems repair & maintenance; construction, repair & dismantling services

(G-10099)
ALTONA CO
Also Called: Mrs Mike's Potato Chips
70 E Monterey St (61032-3347)
PHONE..................................815 232-7819
Robert L Mordick, *President*
Mordick Robert, *IT/INT Sup*
EMP: 5 **EST:** 1931
SQ FT: 3,100
SALES (est): 266.2K **Privately Held**
SIC: 2096 5441 2099 Potato chips & similar snacks; confectionery produced for direct sale on the premises; food preparations

(G-10100)
ANCHOR-HARVEY COMPONENTS LLC
Also Called: Ah
600 W Lamm Rd (61032-9631)
PHONE..................................815 233-3833
Harold Brown Harvey, *President*
Tom Lefaivre, *President*
Kevin Kriebs, *CFO*
Kevin Tribley, *CFO*
Rick McLean, *Prgrmr*
EMP: 97 **EST:** 1923
SQ FT: 100,000
SALES (est): 37.1MM
SALES (corp-wide): 5MM **Privately Held**
SIC: 3462 Iron & steel forgings
PA: Boler Ventures Llc
500 Park Blvd Ste 1010
Itasca IL 60143
630 773-9111

(G-10101)
ANDERSEN MACHINE & WELDING INC
1441 W Demeter Dr (61032-6609)
PHONE..................................815 232-4664
Norma Andersen, *President*
EMP: 9
SQ FT: 6,000
SALES (est): 710K **Privately Held**
SIC: 3714 3441 7692 Motor vehicle engines & parts; fabricated structural metal; welding repair

(G-10102)
BEE LINE SERVICE INC
2291 Us Highway 20 E (61032-9643)
PHONE..................................815 233-1812
Michael Bauch, *President*
Phyllis Bauch, *Vice Pres*
EMP: 5 **EST:** 1946
SALES: 500K **Privately Held**
WEB: www.beelineservicefreeport.com
SIC: 3273 Ready-mixed concrete

(G-10103)
BLACKHAWK BIOFUELS LLC
210 W Spring St Ste 1 (61032-4346)
P.O. Box 888, Ames IA (50010-0888)
PHONE..................................217 431-6600
EMP: 30
SALES (est): 2.5MM
SALES (corp-wide): 1.2B **Publicly Held**
SIC: 2911 Petroleum Refiner
HQ: Reg Biofuels, Llc
416 S Bell Ave
Ames IA 50010
515 239-8000

(G-10104)
CONMAT INC (HQ)
2283 Us Highway 20 E (61032-9643)
PHONE..................................815 235-2200
Eric Helm, *President*
EMP: 35
SQ FT: 7,200
SALES (est): 6.5MM
SALES (corp-wide): 163MM **Privately Held**
WEB: www.helmgroup.com
SIC: 1422 4212 0711 1794 Crushed & broken limestone; dump truck haulage; lime spreading services; excavation work
PA: Helm Group Inc
2283 Business 20 E
Freeport IL 61032
815 235-2244

(G-10105)
DANFOSS POWER SOLUTIONS US CO
580 N Henderson Rd (61032-9017)
PHONE..................................815 233-4200
Bert Lohr, *Director*
EMP: 150
SALES (corp-wide): 250.7K **Privately Held**
SIC: 3594 3462 3714 Fluid power pumps & motors; pump, compressor & turbine forgings; motor vehicle parts & accessories
HQ: Danfoss Power Solutions (Us) Company
2800 E 13th St
Ames IA 50010
515 239-6000

(G-10106)
DOUGLAS GRAYBILL
Also Called: Deerland Dairy
3693 N Dakota Rd (61032-9178)
PHONE..................................815 218-1749
Douglas Graybill, *Owner*
EMP: 4
SALES (est): 127.7K **Privately Held**
SIC: 2026 Fermented & cultured milk products

(G-10107)
FAMOUS FOSSIL VINYARD & WINERY
395 W Cedarville Rd (61032-9156)
PHONE..................................815 563-4665
Pam Rosmann, *Executive*
EMP: 4
SALES (est): 419.3K **Privately Held**
WEB: www.famousfossilwinery.com
SIC: 2084 Wines

(G-10108)
FISCHER STONE & MATERIALS LLC
1567 N Heine Rd (61032-8402)
PHONE..................................815 233-3232
Wayne Fischer,
Joe Fischer,
Joseph Fischer,
EMP: 7
SALES (est): 1.1MM **Privately Held**
SIC: 3272 Cast stone, concrete

(G-10109)
FNH READY MIX INC
751 Il Route 26 N (61032-8302)
P.O. Box 747 (61032-0747)
PHONE..................................815 235-1400
Dean Briggs, *Principal*
EMP: 12
SALES (est): 2MM **Privately Held**
WEB: www.fnhreadymix.com
SIC: 3273 Ready-mixed concrete

(G-10110)
FORGE GROUP STAR LLC
Also Called: Star Freeport Company
1801 S Ihm Blvd (61032-9736)
PHONE..................................815 758-6400
Donald G Jones,
EMP: 50
SALES (est): 1.6MM **Privately Held**
SIC: 3499 Fabricated metal products

(G-10111)
FREEPORT PRESS INC
1031 W Empire St (61032-6267)
P.O. Box 916 (61032-0916)
PHONE..................................815 232-1181
Jack Barron, *President*
Debbie Barron, *Vice Pres*
EMP: 5
SQ FT: 8,000
SALES: 200K **Privately Held**
SIC: 2759 Commercial printing

(G-10112)
FURST-MCNESS COMPANY (PA)
120 E Clark St (61032-3300)
PHONE..................................800 435-5100
Matt Heinrich, *CEO*
Frank E Furst, *Ch of Bd*
Ray Goodwin, *General Mgr*
Webb Howerton, *Regional Mgr*
Kevin Gyland, *Exec VP*
◆ **EMP:** 52 **EST:** 1908
SQ FT: 165,000
SALES: 345.2MM **Privately Held**
WEB: www.mcness.com
SIC: 2048 5191 Feed premixes; feed

(G-10113)
GS CUSTOM WORKS INC
2110 Park Crest Dr (61032-3553)
PHONE..................................815 233-4724
Mark Spittler, *President*
EMP: 2
SALES (est): 200.2K **Privately Held**
WEB: www.gsextreme.com
SIC: 3714 3751 3465 Gas tanks, motor vehicle; motorcycle accessories; fenders, automobile: stamped or pressed metal

(G-10114)
HBP INC
Also Called: HB Plastics
107 N Henderson Rd (61032-3335)
P.O. Box 720 (61032-0720)
PHONE..................................815 235-3000
William R Bailey, *President*
Ted Neels, *General Mgr*
Lori Reed, *QC Mgr*
Melissa Curry, *Human Res Mgr*
James Hauck, *Manager*
▲ **EMP:** 100
SQ FT: 85,000
SALES (est): 21MM **Privately Held**
WEB: www.hbplasticsinc.net
SIC: 3089 Molding primary plastic; thermoformed finished plastic products

(G-10115)
HONEYWELL
315 E Stephenson St (61032-3340)
PHONE..................................815 235-5500
EMP: 26
SALES (est): 3.6MM **Privately Held**
SIC: 3724 Mfg Aircraft Engines/Parts

(G-10116)
HONEYWELL INTERNATIONAL INC
11 W Spring St (61032-4316)
P.O. Box 92173, Chicago (60675-2173)
PHONE..................................847 251-3510
EMP: 14
SALES (corp-wide): 36.7B **Publicly Held**
WEB: www.honeywell.com
SIC: 3724 Aircraft engines & engine parts
PA: Honeywell International Inc.
300 S Tryon St
Charlotte NC 28202
704 627-6200

(G-10117)
HONEYWELL INTERNATIONAL INC
670 N Greenfield Dr (61032-2915)
PHONE..................................815 266-3209
EMP: 98
SALES (corp-wide): 40.5B **Publicly Held**
SIC: 3724 Mfg Aircraft Engines/Parts
PA: Honeywell International Inc.
115 Tabor Rd
Morris Plains NJ 28202
973 455-2000

(G-10118)
HONEYWELL INTERNATIONAL INC
315 E Stephenson St (61032-3340)
P.O. Box 460, Mars Hill NC (28754-0460)
PHONE..................................815 235-5500
EMP: 65
SALES (corp-wide): 38.5B **Publicly Held**
SIC: 3613 Mfg Switchgear/Switchboards
PA: Honeywell International Inc.
115 Tabor Rd
Morris Plains NJ 28202
973 455-2000

(G-10119)
HOOKER CUSTOM HARNESS INC
Also Called: Hooker Harness
324 E Stephenson St (61032-3341)
PHONE..................................815 233-5478
Jack Hooker, *President*
Mike Showerman, *Vice Chairman*
Susanne Hooker, *Corp Secy*
Scott McPhillips, *Vice Pres*
EMP: 5
SQ FT: 3,500
SALES (est): 689.5K **Privately Held**
SIC: 2399 Seat belts, automobile & aircraft

(G-10120)
INKY PRINTERS (PA)
122 N Van Buren Ave (61032-4105)
PHONE..................................815 235-3700
James Dooley, *Owner*
EMP: 4
SQ FT: 6,000
SALES (est): 745K **Privately Held**
SIC: 2752 2791 7331 Commercial printing, offset; typesetting; mailing service

(G-10121)
IRWIN INDUSTRIAL TOOL COMPANY
29 E Stephenson St (61032-4235)
PHONE..................................815 235-4171
Jon D Chamberlain, *Principal*
EMP: 150

Freeport - Stephenson County (G-10122)

SALES (corp-wide): 14.4B **Publicly Held**
SIC: 3423 3545 3421 Screw drivers, pliers, chisels, etc. (hand tools); wrenches, hand tools; mechanics' hand tools; drill bits, metalworking; snips, tinners'
HQ: Irwin Industrial Tool Company
   8935 N Pointe Exec Pk Dr
   Huntersville NC 28078
   704 987-4555

(G-10122)
JOURNAL STANDARD
Also Called: Freeport Journal Standard
50 W Douglas St Ste 900 (61032-4141)
P.O. Box 330 (61032-0330)
PHONE.....................815 232-1171
Josh Crust, *Publisher*
The J Standard, *Manager*
EMP: 9
SALES (est): 732.8K
SALES (corp-wide): 509.8MM **Publicly Held**
SIC: 2711 Newspapers: publishing only, not printed on site; newspapers, publishing & printing
HQ: Lee Publications, Inc.
   4600 E 53rd St
   Davenport IA 52807
   563 383-2100

(G-10123)
K & S MANUFACTURING CO INC
24 S Hooker Ave (61032-5319)
P.O. Box 313 (61032-0313)
PHONE.....................815 232-7519
Leo Krueger, *President*
Jan Wagner, *Treasurer*
Richard Krueger, *Admin Sec*
EMP: 11
SQ FT: 4,500
SALES (est): 1.5MM **Privately Held**
SIC: 3089 Injection molding of plastics

(G-10124)
LEGGETT & PLATT INCORPORATED
Also Called: Leggett & Platt 0351
1555 Il Route 75 E Ste 2 (61032-8703)
PHONE.....................815 233-0022
EMP: 60
SALES (corp-wide): 3.7B **Publicly Held**
SIC: 2515 General Warehouse/Storage Mfg Mattresses/Bedsprings
PA: Leggett & Platt, Incorporated
   1 Leggett Rd
   Carthage MO 64836
   417 358-8131

(G-10125)
LEMANSKI HEATING & AC
1398 S Armstrong Ave (61032-2504)
PHONE.....................815 232-4519
James Lemanski, *President*
EMP: 7
SALES (est): 943.2K **Privately Held**
SIC: 1711 3444 Warm air heating & air conditioning contractor; sheet metalwork

(G-10126)
LEVELOR CORPORATION
29 E Stephenson St (61032-4235)
PHONE.....................815 233-8684
EMP: 6
SALES (est): 1.2MM **Privately Held**
SIC: 3365 Aluminum foundries

(G-10127)
MODERN PLATING CORPORATION
Also Called: Modern Pltg Coatings Finishes
701 S Hancock Ave (61032-5300)
P.O. Box 838 (61032-0838)
PHONE.....................815 235-1790
James R Stenberg, *President*
Lucille F Miller, *Chairman*
Colin McDonough, *CFO*
H Brian Christianson, *Sales Mgr*
Brandon Smith, *Maintence Staff*
▲ EMP: 100 EST: 1936
SQ FT: 100,000
SALES (est): 13.3MM **Privately Held**
WEB: www.modernplating.com
SIC: 3471 Electroplating of metals or formed products

(G-10128)
NEWELL BRANDS INC
29 E Stephenson St (61032-4235)
PHONE.....................815 266-0066
Mike Amrich, *Business Mgr*
Lisa Winger, *Counsel*
Marcos De Oliveira, *Vice Pres*
Scott Petersen, *Vice Pres*
Mike Serak, *Vice Pres*
EMP: 72
SALES (corp-wide): 9.7B **Publicly Held**
SIC: 3089 Plastic kitchenware, tableware & houseware
PA: Newell Brands Inc.
   6655 Pachtree Dunwoody Rd
   Atlanta GA 30328
   770 418-7000

(G-10129)
NEWELL OPERATING COMPANY (HQ)
29 E Stephenson St (61032-4235)
PHONE.....................815 235-4171
Mark D Ketchum, *President*
William A Burke III, *President*
Robert Thibault, *Business Mgr*
Dale L Matschullat, *Vice Pres*
Madeline Boyer, *Engineer*
◆ EMP: 250 EST: 1903
SQ FT: 41,900
SALES (est): 3.1B
SALES (corp-wide): 9.7B **Publicly Held**
WEB: www.newellco.com
SIC: 3365 3991 3089 2591 Cooking/kitchen utensils, cast aluminum; paint rollers; paint brushes; trays, plastic; shade, curtain & drapery hardware; shade pulls, window; window shade rollers & fittings; needles, hand or machine; hooks, crochet; bathroom scales
PA: Newell Brands Inc.
   6655 Pachtree Dunwoody Rd
   Atlanta GA 30328
   770 418-7000

(G-10130)
NOR SERVICE INC
215 S State Ave (61032-5150)
PHONE.....................815 232-8379
Steven Rouse, *President*
Sharon Rouse, *Corp Secy*
Barry O Rouse, *Vice Pres*
EMP: 24
SQ FT: 32,400
SALES (est): 801.1K **Privately Held**
SIC: 3599 3542 3547 Machine shop, jobbing & repair; rebuilt machine tools, metal forming types; sheet metalworking machines; rolling mill machinery

(G-10131)
NOVA WILDCAT AMEROCK LLC
Also Called: Piedmont Hardware Brands
1750 Lincoln Dr (61032-9712)
PHONE.....................815 266-6416
David Jacobs, *President*
EMP: 16
SALES (corp-wide): 139.1MM **Privately Held**
SIC: 3429 Cabinet hardware
HQ: Nova Wildcat Amerock, Llc
   10115 Kincey Ave Ste 210
   Huntersville NC 28078
   704 696-5110

(G-10132)
PERKINS CONSTRUCTION
4872 W Lily Creek Rd (61032-8877)
PHONE.....................815 233-9655
Pete Perkins, *Owner*
EMP: 2
SALES (est): 200K **Privately Held**
SIC: 1521 1799 2434 1751 Single-family home remodeling, additions & repairs; new construction, single-family houses; kitchen & bathroom remodeling; wood kitchen cabinets; carpentry work

(G-10133)
PRECISION DRIVE & CONTROL INC
1650 S Galena Ave (61032-2518)
PHONE.....................815 235-7595
Keith Jacobson, *Manager*
EMP: 9

SALES (corp-wide): 36.1MM **Privately Held**
SIC: 5063 7694 Electrical supplies; armature rewinding shops
PA: Precision Drive & Control, Inc.
   504 11th St
   Monroe WI 53566
   608 328-5600

(G-10134)
PROTO-CUTTER INC
101 S Liberty Ave Ste 1 (61032-5119)
PHONE.....................815 232-2300
Peter P Alber, *President*
Eshell Edler, *Purchasing*
Vince Alber, *Sales Engr*
▼ EMP: 18
SQ FT: 16,000
SALES (est): 2.2MM **Privately Held**
SIC: 3545 5084 Reamers, machine tool; industrial machinery & equipment

(G-10135)
R-SQUARED CONSTRUCTION INC
35 N Commercial Ave (61032-3308)
PHONE.....................815 232-7433
Harold Rood, *President*
Robert Rood, *Vice Pres*
Dan Baldauf, *Sales Staff*
EMP: 7
SQ FT: 12,000
SALES (est): 1.1MM **Privately Held**
SIC: 1521 2435 New construction, single-family houses; panels, hardwood plywood

(G-10136)
RE-MAID INCORPORATED
1440 Sylvan Ct (61032-6642)
PHONE.....................815 315-0500
Brian Potempa, *Mng Member*
EMP: 4
SALES (est): 230.2K **Privately Held**
SIC: 3991 Brooms & brushes

(G-10137)
RHINO PROS
4223 Autumn Ln (61032-8635)
PHONE.....................815 235-7767
EMP: 3
SALES (est): 203.3K **Privately Held**
SIC: 3465 Body parts, automobile: stamped metal

(G-10138)
ROGERS PRECISION MACHINING
5816 Us Highway 20 W (61032-8707)
PHONE.....................815 233-0065
Dorothy C Rogers, *President*
Larry Rogers, *Vice Pres*
Jim Rogers, *Prdtn Mgr*
▲ EMP: 10
SALES (est): 1.3MM **Privately Held**
SIC: 3599 3444 Machine shop, jobbing & repair; sheet metalwork

(G-10139)
S & J MACHINE INC
2171 E Yellow Creek Rd (61032-9696)
PHONE.....................815 297-1594
Troy Milks, *President*
Vicki Milks, *Treasurer*
EMP: 5
SQ FT: 1,600
SALES (est): 200K **Privately Held**
SIC: 3599 Machine shop, jobbing & repair

(G-10140)
SANDES QUYNETTA
752 W American St Apt 5 (61032-4974)
PHONE.....................815 275-4876
Quynnetta Sanders, *Owner*
EMP: 6
SALES (est): 240K **Privately Held**
SIC: 3679 7929 2732 5961 Recording heads, speech & musical equipment; popular music groups or artists; book music: printing & binding, not published on site; record &/or tape (music or video) club, mail order

(G-10141)
SEAGA MANUFACTURING INC (PA)
700 Seaga Dr (61032-9644)
PHONE.....................815 297-9500
Steven V Chesney, *President*
Travis King, *Warehouse Mgr*
Brandon Smith, *Purch Mgr*
Janelle Blomberg, *Controller*
Gary Partridge, *Sales Dir*
◆ EMP: 66
SQ FT: 104,000
SALES (est): 27.1MM **Privately Held**
SIC: 3581 Automatic vending machines

(G-10142)
SNAK-KING CORP
3133 Industrial Dr (61032-9690)
PHONE.....................815 232-6700
Jorge Nava, *Plant Mgr*
Larry King, *Manager*
Michael Gahm, *Technical Staff*
EMP: 140
SALES (corp-wide): 130.9MM **Privately Held**
SIC: 2096 2099 Corn chips & other corn-based snacks; food preparations
PA: Snak-King Corp.
   16150 Stephens St
   City Of Industry CA 91745
   626 336-7711

(G-10143)
SPG INTERNATIONAL LLC
1555 Il Route 75 E Ste 2 (61032-8703)
PHONE.....................815 233-0022
Steve Ellison, *Vice Pres*
EMP: 18 **Privately Held**
WEB: www.spgusa.com
SIC: 3441 Fabricated structural metal
PA: Spg International Llc
   3340 Peachtree Rd Ne # 1250
   Atlanta GA 30326

(G-10144)
STAR FORGE INC
Also Called: Star Manufacturing Company
1801 S Ihm Blvd (61032-9737)
PHONE.....................815 235-7750
C E Johnson, *CEO*
Clarence E Johnson Jr, *Ch of Bd*
John Lehnhard, *Vice Pres*
Dan F Johnson, *CFO*
Julie Folgate, *HR Admin*
▲ EMP: 75 EST: 1873
SQ FT: 110
SALES (est): 19MM **Privately Held**
SIC: 3523 3462 3444 Farm machinery & equipment; iron & steel forgings; sheet metalwork

(G-10145)
STAR FREEPORT COMPANY LLC
1801 S Ihm Blvd (61032-9736)
PHONE.....................815 758-6400
Donald G Jones, *President*
EMP: 50
SALES (est): 1.6MM **Privately Held**
SIC: 3499 3999 Fabricated metal products; manufacturing industries

(G-10146)
TITAN TYRE CORPORATION
3769 Us Highway 20 E (61032-9652)
PHONE.....................217 228-6011
Maurice Taylor, *President*
Julie Suttman, *Senior Buyer*
EMP: 3
SALES (est): 327.7K **Privately Held**
SIC: 3011 Tires & inner tubes

(G-10147)
TREBOR ENTERPRISES LTD
927 W Stephenson St (61032-4963)
P.O. Box 88 (61032-0088)
PHONE.....................815 235-1700
Robert J Drucker, *President*
EMP: 6 EST: 1959
SALES (est): 500K **Privately Held**
SIC: 3911 Rings, finger: precious metal

GEOGRAPHIC SECTION

Galena - Jo Daviess County (G-10172)

(G-10148)
ULTRASONIC POWER CORPORATION
239 E Stephenson St (61032-4213)
PHONE..................815 235-6020
Judith A Thompson, *President*
Robert F Schnoes, *Chairman*
Debora A Witcik, *Vice Pres*
Michael W Thompson, *Admin Sec*
Michael Thompson, *Admin Sec*
▼ **EMP:** 30
SQ FT: 10,000
SALES (est): 7.7MM **Privately Held**
SIC: 3443 3829 3621 Ultrasonic testing equipment; motors & generators

(G-10149)
VAN DIEST SUPPLY COMPANY
1771 Lincoln Dr (61032-9712)
P.O. Box 855 (61032-0855)
PHONE..................815 232-6053
Bill Edwardson, *Branch Mgr*
EMP: 5
SALES (corp-wide): 764.2MM **Privately Held**
SIC: 5191 2875 2879 Chemicals, agricultural; fertilizer & fertilizer materials; fertilizers, mixing only; agricultural chemicals
PA: Van Diest Supply Company
1434 220th St
Webster City IA 50595
515 832-2366

(G-10150)
WITTE KENDEL DIE & MOLD
Also Called: Kendel Witte Die & Mold
657 Youngs Ln (61032-6856)
PHONE..................815 233-9270
Kendel E Witte, *Owner*
Kendel Witte, *Owner*
EMP: 4
SALES: 160K **Privately Held**
SIC: 3544 Dies, plastics forming; forms (molds), for foundry & plastics working machinery

Fulton
Whiteside County

(G-10151)
FENIX MANUFACTURING LLC
2001 9th St (61252-1385)
PHONE..................815 208-0755
John Benson,
Randall Boonstra,
James Hegner,
EMP: 4
SQ FT: 10,000
SALES (est): 506.9K **Privately Held**
SIC: 3429 Manufactured hardware (general)

(G-10152)
FULTON CORPORATION (PA)
Also Called: Davies Mfg
303 8th Ave (61252-1636)
PHONE..................815 589-3211
Richard C Willoughby, *President*
Audrey Willoughby, *Admin Sec*
Mrs R J Willoughby, *Admin Sec*
EMP: 57 **EST:** 1894
SQ FT: 64,800
SALES (est): 11MM **Privately Held**
WEB: www.fultoncorp.com
SIC: 3469 3545 Boxes: tool, lunch, mail, etc.: stamped metal; machine tool accessories

(G-10153)
J & B WELDING LLC
11280 Elston Rd (61252-9620)
PHONE..................309 887-4151
J D Jackson, *President*
Carl Bier,
EMP: 11 **EST:** 1998
SALES (est): 1.1MM **Privately Held**
WEB: www.jandbwelldingllc.com
SIC: 7692 Welding repair

(G-10154)
JT CULLEN CO INC
901 31st Ave (61252-9609)
P.O. Box 311 (61252-0311)
PHONE..................815 589-2412
Eric N Johnson, *President*
Eric Johnson, *Exec VP*
Michl Peters, *Opers Mgr*
Janis Johnson, *Admin Sec*
EMP: 70 **EST:** 1900
SQ FT: 120,000
SALES (est): 26.4MM **Privately Held**
WEB: www.jtcullenco.com
SIC: 3443 5051 3444 Fabricated plate work (boiler shop); iron or steel flat products; sheet metalwork

(G-10155)
MB BOX INC
1201 4th St (61252-1719)
PHONE..................815 589-3043
Paul G Brown, *President*
David Martinez, *Vice Pres*
▲ **EMP:** 6 **EST:** 1997
SQ FT: 5,000
SALES (est): 450K **Privately Held**
WEB: www.mbboxcorp.com
SIC: 2657 Folding paperboard boxes

(G-10156)
QUALITY READY MIX CONCRETE CO
1415 14th Ave (61252-1185)
PHONE..................815 589-2013
Dave Poss, *Manager*
EMP: 4
SALES (corp-wide): 3.7MM **Privately Held**
SIC: 3273 Ready-mixed concrete
PA: Quality Ready Mix Concrete Co.
14849 Lyndon Rd
Morrison IL 61270
815 772-7181

(G-10157)
RIVERSIDE CUSTOM WOODWORKING
1225 22nd Ave (61252-2104)
PHONE..................815 589-3608
Mark Evers, *President*
EMP: 6
SALES (est): 550K **Privately Held**
SIC: 2434 2426 2431 2511 Wood kitchen cabinets; furniture stock & parts, hardwood; staircases & stairs, wood; wood household furniture

(G-10158)
TIMKEN DRIVES LLC (HQ)
901 19th Ave (61252-1366)
PHONE..................815 589-2211
James Lamb, *Principal*
Joseph Hesse, *Opers Mgr*
Jack Riewerts, *Opers Mgr*
Dita Wilcox, *Purch Agent*
Corey Langner, *Engineer*
◆ **EMP:** 97
SQ FT: 301,154
SALES (est): 72.3MM
SALES (corp-wide): 3.7B **Publicly Held**
WEB: www.drivesllc.com
SIC: 3462 5072 Chains, forged steel; chains
PA: The Timken Company
4500 Mount Pleasant St Nw
North Canton OH 44720
234 262-3000

(G-10159)
VISUAL MARKETING SOLUTIONS
Also Called: Visual Imaging
800 20th Ave (61252-1376)
PHONE..................815 589-3848
Michael J Ottens, *President*
Michael Ottens, *Corp Secy*
Eisenhauer John I, *Director*
Gary Holstein, *Shareholder*
EMP: 5
SQ FT: 5,000
SALES (est): 480K **Privately Held**
SIC: 3993 Signs & advertising specialties

Fults
Monroe County

(G-10160)
F S GATEWAY INC
Also Called: GATEWAY F. S. INC
3145 Maeystown Rd (62244-1733)
PHONE..................618 458-6588
Ronald Rodenberg, *Branch Mgr*
EMP: 5 **Privately Held**
WEB: www.home.gatewayfs.com
SIC: 5191 5153 2875 Fertilizer & fertilizer materials; grain elevators; fertilizers, mixing only
PA: Gateway Fs, Inc.
221 E Pine St
Red Bud IL 62278

Galatia
Saline County

(G-10161)
AMERICAN COAL COMPANY (DH)
9085 Highway 34 N (62935-2344)
PHONE..................618 268-6311
Robert E Murray, *CEO*
Amy Bailey, *Hum Res Coord*
James Mitchell, *Technology*
▲ **EMP:** 3
SALES (est): 427.2MM
SALES (corp-wide): 3.7B **Privately Held**
SIC: 1222 5052 Bituminous coal-underground mining; copper ore
HQ: Amcoal Holdings Inc
29525 Chagrin Blvd # 111
Cleveland OH 44122
216 464-4614

(G-10162)
APEX MFG & DESIGN INC
125 Highland Rd (62935-2634)
P.O. Box 191, Marion (62959-0191)
PHONE..................618 252-5529
Allan Brown, *Manager*
EMP: 5
SALES (corp-wide): 250K **Privately Held**
SIC: 3599 Machine shop, jobbing & repair
PA: Apex Manufacturing And Design, Inc.
1800 E Boyton St
Marion IL 62959
618 997-0512

Galena
Jo Daviess County

(G-10163)
A R B C INC
Also Called: Lindstrand Balloons USA
11440 Dandar St (61036-8102)
P.O. Box 6002 (61036-6002)
PHONE..................815 777-6006
Phil Thompson, *President*
EMP: 10
SALES: 1.5MM **Privately Held**
SIC: 3721 3069 Balloons, hot air (aircraft); balloons, advertising & toy: rubber

(G-10164)
BLAUM BROTHERS DISTILLING CO
9380 W Us Highway 20 (61036-9172)
PHONE..................815 777-1000
Matthew C Blaum, *Principal*
▲ **EMP:** 12
SALES (est): 1.4MM **Privately Held**
SIC: 2085 Distilled & blended liquors

(G-10165)
C & C EMBROIDERY INC
800 Spring St Ste 201 (61036-2003)
PHONE..................815 777-6167
Terry Carrol, *President*
Virginia Carroll, *Vice Pres*
EMP: 4
SALES (est): 258.4K **Privately Held**
SIC: 2395 Embroidery products, except schiffli machine

(G-10166)
CAMPECHE RESTAURANT INC
Also Called: Campeche Restaurant & Bar
230 N Commerce St (61036-2212)
PHONE..................815 776-9950
Alex Lopez, *President*
Isidra Lopez, *Admin Sec*
EMP: 7 **EST:** 2010
SALES (est): 639.7K **Privately Held**
WEB: www.campecheingalena.com
SIC: 2599 5812 Bar, restaurant & cafeteria furniture; eating places; Mexican restaurant

(G-10167)
CONMAT INC
1246 S River Rd (61036-9135)
PHONE..................815 238-3885
Jeff Bussan, *Principal*
EMP: 3
SALES (corp-wide): 163MM **Privately Held**
WEB: www.helmgroup.com
SIC: 1422 Crushed & broken limestone
HQ: Conmat, Inc.
2283 Us Highway 20 E
Freeport IL 61032
815 235-2200

(G-10168)
DUHACK LEHN & ASSOCIATES INC
1228 N Blackjack Rd (61036-9400)
P.O. Box 45 (61036-0045)
PHONE..................815 777-3460
Lehn Duhack, *President*
EMP: 2
SALES (est): 200K **Privately Held**
SIC: 1521 2431 General remodeling, single-family houses; millwork

(G-10169)
GALENA CELLARS WINERY (PA)
Also Called: Lawlor Family Winery
515 S Main St (61036-2352)
P.O. Box 207 (61036-0207)
PHONE..................815 777-3330
Christine Lawlor, *President*
Robert L Lawlor, *Corp Secy*
EMP: 39
SQ FT: 10,000
SALES (est): 5.1MM **Privately Held**
SIC: 2084 5813 5182 5947 Wines; wine bar; wine; gift shop; commercial & industrial building operation

(G-10170)
GALENA CELLARS WINERY
Also Called: Lawlor Family Winery
4746 N Ford Rd (61036)
PHONE..................815 777-3429
Christine Lawlor, *Branch Mgr*
EMP: 30
SALES (corp-wide): 5.1MM **Privately Held**
SIC: 2084 Wines
PA: Galena Cellars Winery
515 S Main St
Galena IL 61036
815 777-3330

(G-10171)
GALENAS KANDY KITCHEN
100 N Main St (61036-2222)
PHONE..................815 777-0241
George Paxton, *President*
EMP: 6 **EST:** 1974
SQ FT: 2,500
SALES (est): 609K **Privately Held**
SIC: 5441 2064 2066 Candy; candy & other confectionery products; chocolate & cocoa products

(G-10172)
GAZETTE (PA)
716 S Bench St (61036-2502)
P.O. Box 319 (61036-0319)
PHONE..................815 777-0105
Paul Newton, *President*
Sarah Newton, *Vice Pres*
Jay Dickerson, *Adv Mgr*
EMP: 20 **EST:** 1834

Galena - Jo Daviess County (G-10173)

SALES: 800K **Privately Held**
WEB: www.galenianonline.com
SIC: 2711 2721 Newspapers: publishing only, not printed on site; periodicals

(G-10173)
GREAT AMERICAN POPCORN COMPANY
110 S Main St (61036-2225)
PHONE...............815 777-4116
David A Lewis, *President*
Catherine Lewis, *Vice Pres*
EMP: 6
SALES (est): 670.8K **Privately Held**
SIC: 2096 2099 5441 Popcorn, already popped (except candy covered); popcorn, packaged: except already popped; popcorn, including caramel corn

(G-10174)
HONEYWELL INTERNATIONAL INC
11309 W Chetlain Ln (61036-9433)
PHONE...............815 777-2780
Russ Pilsner, *Manager*
EMP: 150
SALES (corp-wide): 36.7B **Publicly Held**
SIC: 3724 Aircraft engines & engine parts
PA: Honeywell International Inc.
   300 S Tryon St
   Charlotte NC 28202
   704 627-6200

(G-10175)
J P VINCENT & SONS INC
11340 W Us Highway 20 (61036-8210)
P.O. Box 326 (61036-0326)
PHONE...............815 777-2365
Steven F Vincent, *President*
Patti Vincent, *Corp Secy*
Stephanie Vincent, *Vice Pres*
Hans Weinert, *Manager*
EMP: 8 EST: 1884
SALES (est): 1.2MM **Privately Held**
WEB: www.jcwifi.com
SIC: 5999 3272 Monuments, finished to custom order; tombstones; burial vaults, concrete or precast terrazzo; septic tanks, concrete

(G-10176)
LEMFCO INC
100 S Comm St (61036)
P.O. Box 316 (61036-0316)
PHONE...............815 777-0242
John C Einsweiler, *President*
Dirk Einsweiler, *Treasurer*
EMP: 33 EST: 1912
SQ FT: 50,000
SALES (est): 7.1MM **Privately Held**
WEB: www.lemfco.com
SIC: 3321 3369 3714 Gray iron castings; nonferrous foundries; motor vehicle parts & accessories

(G-10177)
RJT WOOD SERVICES
1653 S Tippett Rd (61036-9359)
PHONE...............815 858-2081
Ron Tippett, *Principal*
EMP: 2
SALES (est): 242.5K **Privately Held**
SIC: 2421 Sawmills & planing mills, general

(G-10178)
SIGNCRAFT SCREENPRINT INC
100 A J Harle Dr (61036-9000)
PHONE...............815 777-3030
Sandra Redington, *President*
Ron Redington, *Vice Pres*
Ian Harris, *Treasurer*
Terry McGovern, *Office Mgr*
EMP: 120 EST: 1947
SQ FT: 50,000
SALES (est): 22.3MM **Privately Held**
WEB: www.signcraftinc.com
SIC: 3993 2399 2752 2672 Name plates: except engraved, etched, etc.: metal; signs, not made in custom sign painting shops; emblems, badges & insignia from purchased materials; commercial printing, lithographic; coated & laminated paper; automotive & apparel trimmings

(G-10179)
TECHNICAL SEALANTS INC
Also Called: T S I
11476 Technnical Dr (61036-8117)
P.O. Box 6565 (61036-6565)
PHONE...............815 777-9797
John Sedan, *President*
▲ EMP: 15
SALES (est): 1.9MM **Privately Held**
SIC: 2295 2241 Sealing or insulating tape for pipe: coated fiberglass; narrow fabric mills

(G-10180)
VINTAJ NATURAL BRASS CO
5140 W Us Highway 20 A (61036-9313)
PHONE...............815 776-9300
Doug Duplessis, *Manager*
EMP: 7
SALES (est): 999.5K **Privately Held**
SIC: 3911 Jewelry apparel

(G-10181)
WESTWICK FOUNDRY LTD
200 S Main St (61036-2227)
P.O. Box 315 (61036-0315)
PHONE...............815 777-0815
William P Friede, *President*
Mary L Friede, *Corp Secy*
EMP: 25
SQ FT: 90,000
SALES (est): 1.1MM **Privately Held**
SIC: 3321 Gray iron castings

(G-10182)
WOODED WONDERLAND
610 S Devils Ladder Rd (61036-9448)
PHONE...............815 777-1223
John Eisbach, *Owner*
EMP: 3 EST: 1977
SALES (est): 60K **Privately Held**
SIC: 2421 5211 5031 7033 Sawmills & planing mills, general; lumber & other building materials; lumber: rough, dressed & finished; campgrounds; hardwood dimension & flooring mills

(G-10183)
WORKSHOP (PA)
Also Called: Jo Davies County Transit
706 S West St (61036-2544)
P.O. Box 6087 (61036-6087)
PHONE...............815 777-2211
Mike Bieleinva, *Exec Dir*
Brian Spillane, *Director*
EMP: 31
SQ FT: 20,000
SALES: 2.5MM **Privately Held**
WEB: www.theworkshopgalena.org
SIC: 8331 5947 7211 7349 Sheltered workshop; gift shop; power laundries, family & commercial; janitorial service, contract basis; building cleaning service; lawn services; screen printing

Galesburg
Knox County

(G-10184)
ALUMINUM CASTINGS CORPORATION
340 S Kellogg St (61401-4918)
PHONE...............309 343-8910
Bart Markum, *President*
▲ EMP: 24
SQ FT: 27,000
SALES: 5.4MM
SALES (corp-wide): 36.1MM **Privately Held**
WEB: www.aluminumcastingscorp.com
SIC: 3363 Aluminum die-castings
PA: Alcast Company
   8821 N University St
   Peoria IL 61615
   309 691-5513

(G-10185)
BLACKBURN SAMPLING INC
77 S Henderson St (61401-4327)
PHONE...............309 342-8429
Bob Blackburn, *President*
Michelle Patterson, *Vice Pres*
EMP: 4

SQ FT: 1,900
SALES: 400K **Privately Held**
SIC: 3084 8748 Plastics pipe; environmental consultant

(G-10186)
BRADLEY SMOKER USA INC
644 Enterprise Ave (61401-5799)
PHONE...............309 343-1124
Wade Bradley, *President*
Robert Chandler, *Plant Mgr*
Bob Kufahl, *Sales Mgr*
Becky Good, *Manager*
EMP: 15
SALES (corp-wide): 318.4K **Privately Held**
WEB: www.bradleysmoker.com
SIC: 2861 Wood extract products
PA: Bradley Smoker Inc
   8380 River Rd
   Delta BC
   604 946-3848

(G-10187)
CANADIAN HARVEST LP
701 W 6th St (61401-5903)
PHONE...............309 343-7808
Elaine Thomas, *Branch Mgr*
EMP: 10
SALES (corp-wide): 355.8K **Privately Held**
SIC: 2099 Food preparations
HQ: Canadian Harvest Lp
   16369 Us Highway 131 S
   Schoolcraft MI 49087
   952 835-6429

(G-10188)
CARDINAL ENGINEERING INC
Also Called: Centroid and Cardinal Engrg
1640 N Kellogg St (61401-1845)
PHONE...............309 342-7474
R W Friestad, *President*
Hershel Statham, *Vice Pres*
Lynne E Friestad, *Admin Sec*
EMP: 7
SQ FT: 15,000
SALES (est): 900.5K **Privately Held**
SIC: 3469 3499 Metal stampings; novelties & giftware, including trophies

(G-10189)
CUSTOM FIBERGLASS OF ILLINOIS
875 Enterprise Ave (61401-9362)
PHONE...............309 344-7727
Jeannie Gumm, *President*
EMP: 2 EST: 1996
SALES (est): 224.8K **Privately Held**
SIC: 3732 Boats, fiberglass: building & repairing

(G-10190)
DENTAL ARTS LABORATORIES INC
1172 Monroe St Ste 5 (61401-2554)
P.O. Box 813 (61402-0813)
PHONE...............309 342-3117
Steve Baker, *Branch Mgr*
EMP: 7
SALES (corp-wide): 18.8MM **Privately Held**
SIC: 8072 3843 Crown & bridge production; dental equipment & supplies
PA: Dental Arts Laboratories, Inc.
   241 Ne Perry Ave
   Peoria IL 61603
   309 674-8191

(G-10191)
DUCKYS FORMAL WEAR INC
309 E Main St (61401-4812)
PHONE...............309 342-5914
Diane Peters, *Branch Mgr*
EMP: 4
SALES (corp-wide): 936.4K **Privately Held**
SIC: 7299 5611 5699 5621 Tuxedo rental; clothing accessories: men's & boys'; formal wear; bridal shops; invitation & stationery printing & engraving
PA: Ducky's Formal Wear, Inc
   1773 Copperfield Ln
   Crystal Lake IL

(G-10192)
GALESBURG MANUFACTURING CO (PA)
1835 Lacon Dr (61401-9017)
P.O. Box 710 (61402-0710)
PHONE...............309 342-3173
Steve Apsey, *President*
EMP: 38
SALES (est): 12.9MM **Privately Held**
SIC: 3589 Car washing machinery

(G-10193)
GALESBURG REGISTER-MAIL (DH)
Also Called: Weekly Extra
140 S Prairie St (61401-4636)
P.O. Box 310 (61402-0310)
PHONE...............309 343-7181
David Adam, *President*
Robyn Gautschy, *Editor*
Tom Martin, *Editor*
Mike Trueblood, *Editor*
Nancy Leonard, *Business Mgr*
EMP: 115 EST: 1898
SQ FT: 40,000
SALES (est): 8.7MM
SALES (corp-wide): 1.8B **Publicly Held**
WEB: www.galesburg.com
SIC: 2711 2752 Newspapers, publishing & printing; commercial printing, lithographic
HQ: Gatehouse Media, Llc
   175 Sullys Trl Fl 3
   Pittsford NY 14534
   585 598-0030

(G-10194)
GALESBURG SIGN & LIGHTING
1518 S Henderson St (61401-5708)
PHONE...............309 342-9798
Kenneth Pickrell, *President*
Carol Pickrell, *Vice Pres*
Jeffery Pickrell, *Treasurer*
Adam Pickrell, *Admin Sec*
EMP: 5
SQ FT: 7,524
SALES (est): 663.8K **Privately Held**
SIC: 3993 Electric signs; signs, not made in custom sign painting shops

(G-10195)
GATEHOUSE MEDIA - WSTN ILL DIV
140 S Prairie St (61401-4605)
PHONE...............309 299-6135
EMP: 4
SALES (est): 167.2K **Privately Held**
SIC: 2711 Newspapers, publishing & printing

(G-10196)
GATES CORPORATION
Also Called: Gates Rubber Co, The
630 Us Highway 150 E (61401-8311)
PHONE...............309 343-7171
Bob Atwood, *Manager*
EMP: 150
SALES (corp-wide): 3B **Publicly Held**
SIC: 3052 3714 Rubber hose; motor vehicle parts & accessories
HQ: The Gates Corporation
   1144 15th St Ste 1400
   Denver CO 80202
   303 744-1911

(G-10197)
GENERAL MILLS INC
1557 S Henderson St (61401-5707)
PHONE...............309 342-9165
Courtney Padgett, *Branch Mgr*
EMP: 50
SALES (corp-wide): 16.8B **Publicly Held**
SIC: 2041 Flour & other grain mill products
PA: General Mills, Inc.
   1 General Mills Blvd
   Minneapolis MN 55426
   763 764-7600

(G-10198)
GO VAN GOGHS TEE SHIRT
Also Called: T-Shirt Factory, The
237 E Tompkins St (61401-4710)
PHONE...............309 342-1112
Fakhry Azer, *Owner*
EMP: 4
SQ FT: 4,000

GEOGRAPHIC SECTION

Galesburg - Knox County

SALES (est): 311.4K **Privately Held**
SIC: **7336** 5136 5699 2396 Silk screen design; shirts, men's & boys'; uniforms, men's & boys'; shirts, custom made; uniforms; automotive & apparel trimmings

(G-10199) HARVEY BROS INC
2181 Grand Ave (61401-6484)
PHONE.....................309 342-3137
Gary Harvey, *President*
Paul Harvey, *Treasurer*
Dale Harvey, *Admin Sec*
EMP: 17
SQ FT: 14,400
SALES (est): 1.8MM **Privately Held**
SIC: **7694** 3694 3625 3621 Electric motor repair; engine electrical equipment; relays & industrial controls; motors & generators

(G-10200) HEAT AND CONTROL INC
Galesburg Division
1721 Us Highway 164 (61401)
PHONE.....................309 342-5518
Denise Leo, *Manager*
EMP: 65
SALES (corp-wide): 287.1MM **Privately Held**
SIC: **3556** Food products machinery
PA: Heat And Control, Inc.
  21121 Cabot Blvd
  Hayward CA 94545
  510 259-0500

(G-10201) ILPEA INDUSTRIES INC
611 S Linwood Rd (61401-9060)
P.O. Box 190 (61402-0190)
PHONE.....................309 343-3332
Tom Cagney, *Branch Mgr*
EMP: 72 **Privately Held**
SIC: **3089** 3053 Window frames & sash, plastic; gaskets, all materials
HQ: Ilpea Industries, Inc.
  745 S Gardner St
  Scottsburg IN 47170
  812 752-2526

(G-10202) J BRODIE MEAT PRODUCTS INC
Also Called: Brodie's
605 W 6th St (61401-5901)
PHONE.....................309 342-1500
Kay F Johnson, *President*
John Brodie, *Vice Pres*
Virgil Frye, *Vice Pres*
Bob Waight, *Vice Pres*
Roland D Johnson, *Treasurer*
EMP: 15
SQ FT: 16,000
SALES (est): 2.2MM **Privately Held**
SIC: **2013** 2011 Sausages & other prepared meats; pork products from pork slaughtered on site

(G-10203) JRS J RETTENMAIER AND SOH
701 W 6th St (61401-5903)
PHONE.....................309 343-7808
EMP: 6
SALES (est): 563.3K **Privately Held**
SIC: **2099** Food preparations

(G-10204) JUPITER MACHINE TOOL INC
1124 Enterprise Ave (61401-9800)
P.O. Box 1562 (61402-1562)
PHONE.....................309 297-1920
Ruth A Whitehead, *Principal*
EMP: 4 EST: 2017
SALES (est): 103.1K **Privately Held**
SIC: **3545** Machine tool accessories

(G-10205) KCCDD INC
Also Called: Phoenix Industries
1200 Monmouth Blvd (61401-5769)
PHONE.....................309 344-2030
Bob Paulsgrove, *Manager*
EMP: 60

SALES (corp-wide): 4.9MM **Privately Held**
SIC: **2448** 8331 2441 8322 Pallets, wood; sheltered workshop; work experience center; nailed wood boxes & shook; general counseling services; motor vehicle parts & accessories
PA: Kccdd, Inc.
  2015 Windish Dr
  Galesburg IL 61401
  309 344-2600

(G-10206) KOPPERS INDUSTRIES INC
Koppers RR & Utility Pdts Div
Rr 41 Box S (61402)
PHONE.....................309 343-5157
Ted Woerle, *Opers-Prdtn-Mfg*
James Evans, *Director*
EMP: 46 **Publicly Held**
SIC: **2491** 2421 Poles, posts & pilings: treated wood; railroad cross bridges & switch ties, treated wood; railroad crossties, treated wood; sawmills & planing mills, general
HQ: Koppers Industries Of Delaware Inc.
  436 7th Ave Ste 2026
  Pittsburgh PA 15219

(G-10207) LEE BROTHERS WELDING INC
575 Lincoln St (61401-4033)
PHONE.....................309 342-6017
Robert Brown, *President*
EMP: 3
SQ FT: 7,500
SALES (est): 304.4K **Privately Held**
SIC: **7692** Welding repair

(G-10208) MARNIC INC (PA)
Also Called: American Speedy Printing
439 N Henderson St (61401-3507)
PHONE.....................309 343-1418
Marvin Eberle, *President*
EMP: 4
SQ FT: 1,800
SALES (est): 368.7K **Privately Held**
SIC: **2752** Commercial printing, offset

(G-10209) MESIC VALE LLC
161 S Cherry St Ste 207 (61401-4519)
PHONE.....................309 335-8521
William Denton, *Mng Member*
EMP: 12
SALES (est): 446.8K **Privately Held**
SIC: **2421** Building & structural materials, wood

(G-10210) MIDSTATE MANUFACTURING COMPANY
Also Called: Steelweld Division
750 W 3rd St (61401-5829)
PHONE.....................309 342-9555
Curtis A Pitman, *President*
Russell Larson, *Vice Pres*
Ed Winter, *Engineer*
Karen Berrian, *Controller*
Cynthia Reynolds, *Controller*
EMP: 150 EST: 1979
SQ FT: 16,000
SALES (est): 32MM **Privately Held**
SIC: **3599** 5084 Machine shop, jobbing & repair; industrial machinery & equipment

(G-10211) MIDWEST HYDRA-LINE INC (HQ)
Also Called: Bemis Hydraulics
698 Us Highway 150 E (61401-8311)
P.O. Box 1265 (61402-1265)
PHONE.....................309 342-6171
Will Stewart, *President*
David Palmer, *Vice Pres*
David M Uhlmann, *Vice Pres*
EMP: 11
SQ FT: 6,000
SALES (corp-wide): 36.8MM **Privately Held**
SIC: **5085** 3443 Hose, belting & packing; tools; cylinders, pressure: metal plate

PA: Minnesota Flexible Corp.
  305 Bridgepoint Dr # 400
  South Saint Paul MN 55075
  651 645-7522

(G-10212) MONMOUTH READY MIX CORP
816 N Henderson St (61401-2518)
PHONE.....................309 734-3211
John Kovak, *President*
Bob Fulton, *Vice Pres*
EMP: 5
SALES (est): 592.6K
SALES (corp-wide): 117.9MM **Privately Held**
SIC: **3273** 3271 5211 Ready-mixed concrete; concrete block & brick; masonry materials & supplies
HQ: Gcc Liquidating Corp.
  816 N Henderson St
  Galesburg IL 61401

(G-10213) NATIONAL COATINGS INC (PA)
604 S Highway 150 E (61401-8311)
P.O. Box 1314 (61402-1314)
PHONE.....................309 342-4184
James W Hillhouse, *President*
▲ EMP: 45 EST: 1980
SQ FT: 35,000
SALES (est): 18MM **Privately Held**
WEB: www.natcoinc.com
SIC: **2851** Paints & paint additives

(G-10214) NIFFTY AG INC
427 Old Post Rd (61401-8875)
PHONE.....................309 343-7447
Steve Peterson, *Principal*
EMP: 4
SALES (est): 554.6K **Privately Held**
SIC: **3523** Farm machinery & equipment

(G-10215) PEGASUS MFG INC
1382 Enterprise Ave (61401-9380)
P.O. Box 1503 (61402-1503)
PHONE.....................309 342-9337
Ruth Whitehead, *President*
James Kinkade, *Director*
Lauretta Hayes, *Admin Sec*
EMP: 15 EST: 2013
SQ FT: 15,000
SALES (est): 2.1MM **Privately Held**
WEB: www.pegasusmfginc.com
SIC: **3999** Atomizers, toiletry

(G-10216) PROGRESS RAIL SERVICES CORP
618 Us Highway 150 E (61401-8311)
PHONE.....................309 343-6176
Billy Ainsworth, *Branch Mgr*
EMP: 10
SALES (corp-wide): 53.8B **Publicly Held**
SIC: **3743** Railroad equipment
HQ: Progress Rail Services Corporation
  1600 Progress Dr
  Albertville AL 35950
  256 505-6421

(G-10217) RBJ INC
Also Called: Robbins Pallets
796 S Pearl St (61401-6159)
PHONE.....................309 344-5066
Rich L Robbins, *President*
Jason Robbins, *Vice Pres*
EMP: 15
SALES (est): 3MM **Privately Held**
WEB: www.robbinspallets.net
SIC: **2448** Pallets, wood

(G-10218) RJ RACE CARS INC
300 N Linwood Rd (61401-3280)
PHONE.....................309 343-7575
Rick Jones, *President*
Bonnie Jones, *Treasurer*
Shaun Clark, *Sales Staff*
Josh Dixon, *Marketing Staff*
EMP: 11
SQ FT: 5,000

SALES (est): 2MM **Privately Held**
SIC: **3711** 3714 5531 Automobile assembly, including specialty automobiles; motor vehicle parts & accessories; speed shops, including race car supplies

(G-10219) ROYAL PUBLISHING INC
Also Called: Royal Publishing Co
311 E Main St Ste 220 (61401-4879)
PHONE.....................309 343-4007
John Nelson, *Branch Mgr*
Blanche Shoup, *Exec Dir*
EMP: 9
SALES (corp-wide): 7MM **Privately Held**
SIC: **2731** 7336 Pamphlets: publishing & printing; graphic arts & related design
PA: Royal Publishing, Inc.
  7620 N Harker Dr
  Peoria IL
  309 693-3171

(G-10220) SCHWARZ BROS MANUFACTURING CO
584 E Brooks St (61401-5075)
PHONE.....................309 342-5814
Steven Gray, *President*
C Gray, *Treasurer*
EMP: 6
SQ FT: 4,800
SALES (est): 858.2K **Privately Held**
SIC: **3544** Special dies & tools; jigs & fixtures

(G-10221) THE PARTS HOUSE
343 S Kellogg St (61401-4969)
PHONE.....................309 343-0146
Steven Fransene, *President*
Jason Fransene, *Vice Pres*
Teddi Shipp, *Treasurer*
EMP: 3
SQ FT: 23,000
SALES (est): 648K **Privately Held**
SIC: **3315** 3496 Steel wire & related products; miscellaneous fabricated wire products

(G-10222) WAYLAND READY MIX CONCRETE SVC
816 N Henderson St (61401-2518)
P.O. Box 207, Macomb (61455-0207)
PHONE.....................309 833-2064
Champ H Wayland, *President*
Pauline Wayland, *Treasurer*
Larry Wayland, *Admin Sec*
EMP: 13
SALES (est): 2MM **Privately Held**
WEB: www.ucm.biz
SIC: **3273** 1442 Ready-mixed concrete; construction sand & gravel

(G-10223) WEATHERFORD INTERNATIONAL LLC
961 Abingdon St (61401-5838)
PHONE.....................309 342-5154
EMP: 25 **Privately Held**
SIC: **3498** Fabricated pipe & fittings
HQ: Weatherford International, Llc
  2000 Saint James Pl
  Houston TX 77056
  713 693-4000

(G-10224) WESTROCK CP LLC
Also Called: Smurfit-Stone Container
775 S Linwood Rd (61401-9002)
P.O. Box 1268 (61402-1268)
PHONE.....................309 342-0121
Al Widman, *Manager*
EMP: 130
SALES (corp-wide): 18.2B **Publicly Held**
SIC: **2653** 2657 2631 5113 Boxes, corrugated: made from purchased materials; folding paperboard boxes; paperboard mills; corrugated & solid fiber boxes
HQ: Westrock Cp, Llc
  1000 Abernathy Rd Ste 125
  Atlanta GA 30328

(PA)=Parent Co (HQ)=Headquarters (DH)=Div Headquarters
✪ = New Business established in last 2 years

Galt
Whiteside County

(G-10225)
IFH GROUP INC
5505 Anne St (61037)
PHONE..............................815 380-2367
EMP: 6
SALES (corp-wide): 22.5MM **Privately Held**
SIC: 3594 3443 Fluid power pumps; fuel tanks (oil, gas, etc.): metal plate
PA: The Ifh Group Inc
3300 E Rock Falls Rd
Rock Falls IL 61071
800 435-7003

Galva
Henry County

(G-10226)
ALL-FEED PROC & PACKG INC
717 W Division St (61434-1636)
P.O. Box 71 (61434-0071)
PHONE..............................309 932-3119
Tim Shanahan, *Safety Dir*
Heather Anderson, *Branch Mgr*
EMP: 6
SALES (corp-wide): 2MM **Privately Held**
SIC: 2048 Canned pet food (except dog & cat)
PA: All-Feed Processing And Packaging, Inc.
210 S 1st St
Alpha IL 61413
309 629-0001

(G-10227)
BIG RIVER PRAIRIE GOLD LLC
1100 Se 2nd St (61434-8907)
PHONE..............................319 753-1100
Raymond E Defenbaugh,
Andy Brader,
Roger Hubele,
Floyd Schultz,
Eugene Youngquist,
EMP: 5
SALES: 29.2K **Privately Held**
SIC: 2869 Fuels

(G-10228)
BIG RIVER RESOURCES GALVA LLC
1100 Se 2nd St (61434-8907)
PHONE..............................309 932-2033
Ray Defenbaugh, *Mng Member*
Les Allen,
Andy Brader,
Gene Youngquist,
EMP: 238
SALES: 224.6MM **Privately Held**
SIC: 2869 Ethyl alcohol, ethanol
HQ: Big River Resources West Burlington, Llc
15210 103rd St
West Burlington IA 52655
319 753-1100

(G-10229)
BOB EVANS FARMS INC
1001 Sw 2nd St (61434-1605)
PHONE..............................309 932-2194
EMP: 62
SALES (corp-wide): 1.6B **Publicly Held**
SIC: 2013 Mfg Prepared Meats
PA: Bob Evans Farms, Inc.
8111 Smiths Mill Rd
New Albany OH 43054
614 491-2225

(G-10230)
DIXLINE CORPORATION (PA)
Also Called: Thomson Casual Furniture Co
136 Exchange St (61434-1710)
P.O. Box 166 (61434-0166)
PHONE..............................309 932-2011
David E Thomson, *President*
Martha Thomson, *Vice Pres*
Reid Varnold, *Maint Mgr*
Chris Kocan, *Controller*
Lindsay Goad, *Manager*
EMP: 15 EST: 1922
SQ FT: 2,000
SALES (est): 13.8MM **Privately Held**
WEB: www.dixline.com
SIC: 3469 3429 2514 3471 Metal stampings; casket hardware; lawn furniture: metal; finishing, metals or formed products; aluminum die-castings; miscellaneous metalwork

(G-10231)
DIXLINE CORPORATION
26 Sw 4th Ave (61434-1611)
P.O. Box 166 (61434-0166)
PHONE..............................309 932-2011
Willard Thomson, *President*
EMP: 80
SALES (corp-wide): 13.8MM **Privately Held**
SIC: 3429 3995 3471 3469 Casket hardware; burial caskets; plating & polishing; metal stampings; miscellaneous metalwork; aluminum die-castings
PA: Dixline Corporation
136 Exchange St
Galva IL 61434
309 932-2011

(G-10232)
GALVA IRON AND METAL CO INC
625 Se Industrial Ave (61434-8930)
P.O. Box 121 (61434-0121)
PHONE..............................309 932-3450
Jeff Schilling, *President*
EMP: 7
SQ FT: 5,000
SALES (est): 890.4K **Privately Held**
SIC: 5093 5051 5072 5531 Scrap & waste materials; steel; chains; automotive & home supply stores; secondary nonferrous metals

(G-10233)
J MAC METALS INC
330 Se Industrial Ave (61434-8921)
P.O. Box 277 (61434-0277)
PHONE..............................309 932-3001
Adam Baze, *President*
Gary Baze, *Vice Pres*
EMP: 2
SQ FT: 8,000
SALES (est): 729K **Privately Held**
WEB: www.jmacmetals.com
SIC: 3444 Metal roofing & roof drainage equipment

(G-10234)
JOHN H BEST & SONS INC
Also Called: Best Display Systems
1 Burlington Rd (61434-1481)
P.O. Box 293 (61434-0293)
PHONE..............................309 932-2124
Ronald A Pankau, *President*
Bob Hook, *CFO*
Teresa O Pankau, *Admin Sec*
EMP: 38 EST: 1892
SQ FT: 45,000
SALES (est): 7.3MM **Privately Held**
WEB: www.jhbest.com
SIC: 2542 3599 Racks, merchandise display or storage: except wood; machine shop, jobbing & repair

(G-10235)
LMT INC
1105 Se 2nd St (61434-8911)
PHONE..............................217 568-8265
Michael Fenneman, *President*
Natalie Pearson, *Admin Sec*
◆ EMP: 16
SQ FT: 33,000
SALES (est): 3.7MM **Privately Held**
SIC: 3523 3443 3531 3713 Farm machinery & equipment; fabricated plate work (boiler shop); construction machinery; truck & bus bodies

Garden Prairie
Boone County

(G-10236)
CCSI INTERNATIONAL INC
Also Called: Garden Prrie Pool Spa Enclsres
8642 Us Highway 20 (61038-9531)
PHONE..............................815 544-8385
Russell Caldwell, *Ch of Bd*
Heather Steines, *Exec VP*
Thomas Caldwell, *Vice Pres*
Cynthia Caldwell, *Treasurer*
Charles Caldwel, *Shareholder*
▲ EMP: 30 EST: 1964
SQ FT: 23,000
SALES (est): 4.2MM **Privately Held**
WEB: www.ccsiusa.com
SIC: 3949 1761 Water sports equipment; skylight installation

(G-10237)
MACHOLL METAL FABRICATION
6934 Garden Prairie Rd (61038-9702)
PHONE..............................815 597-1908
Jack Macholl, *Principal*
EMP: 2
SALES (est): 239.5K **Privately Held**
SIC: 3499 Fabricated metal products

Geneseo
Henry County

(G-10238)
ALL IN STITCHES
100 E Main St (61254-1566)
PHONE..............................309 944-4084
Jan Dahl, *Owner*
EMP: 8
SQ FT: 5,000
SALES (est): 746.6K **Privately Held**
SIC: 2395 5137 Embroidery & art needlework; embroidery products, except schiffli machine; women's & children's outerwear; women's & children's sportswear & swimsuits; women's & children's dresses, suits, skirts & blouses

(G-10239)
ALLQUIP CO INC
524 E Exchange St (61254-2108)
P.O. Box 347 (61254-0347)
PHONE..............................309 944-6153
Raymond Pribble, *President*
Lona Pribble, *Corp Secy*
EMP: 6
SQ FT: 11,000
SALES (est): 1MM **Privately Held**
WEB: www.allquipco.com
SIC: 5084 3325 3444 3443 Materials handling machinery; steel foundries; sheet metalwork; fabricated plate work (boiler shop); fabricated structural metal; manufactured hardware (general)

(G-10240)
BRIDGE CITY MECHANICAL INC
777 E Culver Ct (61254-1851)
P.O. Box 176 (61254-0176)
PHONE..............................309 944-4873
Martin Kauzlarich, *President*
Deborah Kauzlarich, *Treasurer*
EMP: 15 EST: 2001
SALES: 1.2MM **Privately Held**
SIC: 3441 Fabricated structural metal

(G-10241)
EDWARDS ACQUISITION CORP
Also Called: Edwards Readymix Co.
210 S Chicago St (61254-1456)
P.O. Box 49 (61254-0049)
PHONE..............................309 944-2117
Christopher A Rayburn, *CEO*
Wayne Lawson, *Vice Pres*
Kevin Venhuizen, *Controller*
Edwards Readymix, *Accountant*
Kathy Aden, *Administration*
EMP: 12 EST: 2005
SALES (est): 1.5MM **Privately Held**
SIC: 3273 5032 Ready-mixed concrete; concrete & cinder building products

(G-10242)
EMERSON AUTOMATION SOLUTIONS
121 W 1st St (61254-1341)
PHONE..............................309 946-5205
EMP: 3
SALES (corp-wide): 18.3B **Publicly Held**
SIC: 3491 Industrial valves
HQ: Emerson Automation Solutions Final Control Us Lp
10707 Clay Rd
Houston TX 77041

(G-10243)
GREAT REVIVALIST BREWING LLC
Also Called: Great Revivalist Brew Lab
1225 S Oakwood Ave (61254-1990)
PHONE..............................309 944-5466
Robert Richard Schwab,
EMP: 10
SALES (est): 319.8K **Privately Held**
SIC: 2082 Beer (alcoholic beverage)

(G-10244)
INNOVATIVE MACHINE INC
925 Dilenbeck Dr (61254-1650)
PHONE..............................309 945-9445
Kim M McCubbin, *President*
EMP: 7
SQ FT: 2,400
SALES (est): 1.2MM **Privately Held**
SIC: 3599 Machine shop, jobbing & repair

(G-10245)
LIBERTY GROUP PUBLISHING (PA)
Also Called: Geneseo Republic, The
108 W 1st St (61254-1342)
P.O. Box 209 (61254-0209)
PHONE..............................309 944-1779
Tim Evans, *Principal*
Cathy Terry, *Shareholder*
Karry Wheelhouse, *Admin Sec*
EMP: 15 EST: 1856
SALES (est): 1.6MM **Privately Held**
WEB: www.geneseorepublic.com
SIC: 2711 2741 Job printing & newspaper publishing combined; shopping news: publishing & printing

(G-10246)
M & B SUPPLY INC
208 W 1st St (61254-1344)
PHONE..............................309 944-3206
Scott Cocquit, *President*
William Heller, *Vice Pres*
EMP: 12
SQ FT: 5,600
SALES (est): 1.1MM **Privately Held**
SIC: 2721 8999 Statistical reports (periodicals): publishing only; technical manual preparation

(G-10247)
SIVCO WELDING COMPANY
624 E Prospect St (61254-1828)
PHONE..............................309 944-5171
Irvin Venter, *President*
Karen Venter, *Vice Pres*
EMP: 5
SQ FT: 10,000
SALES (est): 1MM **Privately Held**
SIC: 7692 3441 Welding repair; fabricated structural metal

(G-10248)
SPRINGFIELD INC
Also Called: Springfield Armory
420 W Main St (61254-1524)
PHONE..............................309 944-5631
Dennis Reese, *CEO*
Donna Rahn, *General Mgr*
Jared Eaton, *Project Mgr*
Mike Doy, *Facilities Mgr*
Keith Stage, *Warehouse Mgr*
▲ EMP: 220
SQ FT: 32,860
SALES (est): 69.1MM **Privately Held**
WEB: www.springfield-armory.com
SIC: 3484 Guns (firearms) or gun parts, 30 mm. & below

Geneva
Kane County

(G-10249)
AIR SOURCE CORP
825 W State St Ste 109 (60134-2099)
PHONE..................630 355-7655
Ila Shah, *President*
Govind Shah, *Admin Sec*
EMP: 4
SALES (est): 356.7K **Privately Held**
SIC: 3564 Blowers & fans

(G-10250)
ALL SIGNS & WONDERS CO
1020 W Fabyan Pkwy (60134-3104)
PHONE..................630 232-9019
Victor Covarrubias, *Owner*
EMP: 2
SALES (est): 810K **Privately Held**
SIC: 5099 3993 Signs, except electric; signs & advertising specialties

(G-10251)
ALLIED RIVET INC
1172 Commerce Dr (60134-2484)
PHONE..................630 208-0120
Steven O Hindi, *President*
Jacquelyn J Hindi, *Vice Pres*
EMP: 14
SQ FT: 17,500
SALES (est): 1.7MM **Privately Held**
SIC: 3452 Bolts, nuts, rivets & washers

(G-10252)
AMERICAN TRISTAR INC
2089 Pillsbury Dr (60134-3731)
PHONE..................630 262-5500
EMP: 3
SALES (corp-wide): 71.2B **Privately Held**
SIC: 2099 Mfg Food Preparations
HQ: American Tristar, Inc.
    525 Dunham Rd
    Saint Charles IL 60174
    920 872-2181

(G-10253)
ARGENTUM MEDICAL LLC
2571 Kaneville Ct (60134-2505)
PHONE..................888 551-0188
Raul Brizuela,
EMP: 20
SALES (est): 3.6MM **Privately Held**
SIC: 3842 3841 Surgical appliances & supplies; surgical & medical instruments

(G-10254)
BANNON ENTERPRISES INC
2627 Lorraine Cir (60134-4418)
PHONE..................847 529-9265
Gerald Bannon, *President*
Maureen Bannon, *Vice Pres*
EMP: 3
SALES (est): 100K **Privately Held**
SIC: 3089 Organizers for closets, drawers, etc.; plastic

(G-10255)
BLUE CHIP CONSTRUCTION INC
435 Stevens St (60134-1361)
PHONE..................630 208-5254
EMP: 11
SQ FT: 12,000
SALES (est): 1MM **Privately Held**
SIC: 2431 Architectural Woodwork

(G-10256)
BURGESS-NORTON MFG CO INC (HQ)
737 Peyton St (60134-2189)
PHONE..................630 232-4100
Brett E Vasseuer, *President*
Brian Dalisay, *Business Mgr*
M J Cook, *Vice Pres*
G M Randich, *Vice Pres*
Tom Schneider, *Vice Pres*
▲ **EMP:** 277
SALES (est): 155MM
SALES (corp-wide): 2.3B **Privately Held**
SIC: 3399 3592 3452 Powder, metal; pistons & piston rings; pins

PA: Amsted Industries Incorporated
    180 N Stetson Ave # 1800
    Chicago IL 60601
    312 645-1700

(G-10257)
BURGESS-NORTON MFG CO INC
500 Western Ave (60134-3083)
PHONE..................630 232-4100
Donni Hess, *Branch Mgr*
EMP: 25
SALES (corp-wide): 2.3B **Privately Held**
SIC: 3321 3363 3452 3463 Gray & ductile iron foundries; aluminum die-castings; bolts, nuts, rivets & washers; engine or turbine forgings, nonferrous
HQ: Burgess-Norton Mfg Co., Inc.
    737 Peyton St
    Geneva IL 60134

(G-10258)
C R KESNER COMPANY
1624 Kummer Ct (60134-2929)
PHONE..................630 232-8118
Rudy C Kesner, *President*
EMP: 7
SQ FT: 7,500
SALES (est): 2MM **Privately Held**
SIC: 5047 3842 Hospital equipment & supplies; surgical appliances & supplies

(G-10259)
CHRONICLE NEWSPAPERS INC
1000 Randall Rd (60134-2590)
PHONE..................630 845-5247
Lee Husfeldt, *Principal*
Kevin Elder, *Director*
EMP: 8
SALES (est): 413.6K **Privately Held**
SIC: 2711 Newspapers, publishing & printing

(G-10260)
CLARIOS LLC
Johnson Controls
300 S Glengarry Dr (60134-3803)
PHONE..................630 232-4270
Tom Kreider, *Manager*
EMP: 325
SALES (corp-wide): 50.9B **Publicly Held**
WEB: www.johnsoncontrols.com
SIC: 3691 5063 Storage batteries; storage batteries, industrial
HQ: Clarios, Llc
    5757 N Green Bay Ave
    Milwaukee WI 53209

(G-10261)
CLC LUBRICANTS COMPANY (PA)
0n902 Old Kirk Rd (60134)
P.O. Box 764 (60134-0764)
PHONE..................630 232-7900
Patrick T O'Brien, *President*
Michael O'Brien, *Purch Mgr*
Paul Blume, *CFO*
John Howard, *Sales Mgr*
Karen O'Brien, *Office Mgr*
EMP: 25
SQ FT: 27,000
SALES (est): 5.1MM **Privately Held**
SIC: 2992 2899 2842 Oils & greases, blending & compounding; cutting oils, blending; made from purchased materials; chemical preparations; specialty cleaning, polishes & sanitation goods

(G-10262)
COILFORM COMPANY (PA)
2571 Kaneville Ct (60134-2505)
PHONE..................630 232-8000
Richard M Mc Farlane, *President*
EMP: 45 **EST:** 1955
SQ FT: 25,000
SALES (est): 4.4MM **Privately Held**
WEB: www.coilform.com
SIC: 3677 3621 3083 Electronic coils, transformers & other inductors; motors & generators; laminated plastics plate & sheet

(G-10263)
CPR PRINTING INC (PA)
321 Stevens St Ste E (60134-1318)
PHONE..................630 377-8420

Pat Hofstetter, *President*
Mindy Hofstetter, *Vice Pres*
EMP: 15
SQ FT: 5,000
SALES (est): 600K **Privately Held**
SIC: 2752 2796 2791 2789 Commercial printing, offset; platemaking services; typesetting; bookbinding & related work

(G-10264)
CRIPPA USA LLC
65 N River Ln Ste 209 (60134-2268)
PHONE..................630 659-7720
Massimo Denipoti, *CEO*
EMP: 8
SALES (est): 128.3K
SALES (corp-wide): 296.8K **Privately Held**
SIC: 3545 Precision measuring tools
HQ: Crippa Spa
    Via Michelangelo Buonarroti 3
    Arosio CO 22060
    031 760-200

(G-10265)
DENTAL LABORATORY INC
Also Called: Merrimac Lab
37w391 Keslinger Rd (60134-3914)
PHONE..................630 262-3700
Paul I Ema, *President*
Connie Rempala, *Senior VP*
Andrea C Ema, *Admin Sec*
EMP: 39
SALES (est): 2.6MM **Privately Held**
SIC: 8072 5047 3843 Dental laboratories; dentists' professional supplies; dental equipment & supplies

(G-10266)
DERMATIQUE LASER & SKIN
407 S 3rd St Ste 240 (60134-2744)
PHONE..................630 262-2515
Gina Lesnik, *Owner*
EMP: 11
SALES (est): 1.3MM **Privately Held**
SIC: 3845 Laser systems & equipment, medical

(G-10267)
DYNAWAVE CORPORATION
1624 Kummer Ct (60134-2587)
PHONE..................630 232-4945
Rudy C Kesner, *President*
Keith Kesner, *Vice Pres*
EMP: 10
SQ FT: 7,500
SALES (est): 2MM **Privately Held**
SIC: 3674 Solid state electronic devices

(G-10268)
ELECTION WORKS
0s096 Catlin Sq (60134-4435)
PHONE..................630 232-4030
Sandra Hed, *President*
EMP: 5
SALES (est): 565.6K **Privately Held**
SIC: 3579 2541 5712 5087 Voting machines; cabinets, lockers & shelving; cabinet work, custom; voting machines

(G-10269)
FONA INTERNATIONAL INC (PA)
1900 Averill Rd (60134-1601)
PHONE..................630 578-8600
Joseph James Slawek, *CEO*
Luke Slawek, *COO*
Manon Daoust, *Exec VP*
Tj Widuch, *Exec VP*
Jim Ellis, *Vice Pres*
▲ **EMP:** 53
SQ FT: 82,000
SALES (est): 67.8MM **Privately Held**
SIC: 2087 Extracts, flavoring; syrups, flavoring (except drink)

(G-10270)
FONA UK LTD
1900 Averill Rd (60134-1601)
PHONE..................331 442-5779
Joseph Slawek, *CEO*
EMP: 200
SALES (corp-wide): 67.8MM **Privately Held**
SIC: 2087 Extracts, flavoring; syrups, flavoring (except drink)

HQ: Fona Uk Ltd
    4 Coleman Street
    London EC2R

(G-10271)
GENEVA CABINET GALLERY
321 Stevens St (60134-1311)
PHONE..................630 232-9500
Lynnea M Havlicek, *Principal*
Valerie Price, *Assistant*
EMP: 4
SALES (est): 369.4K **Privately Held**
SIC: 2434 Wood kitchen cabinets

(G-10272)
GENEVA RUNNING OUTFITTERS LLC
221 W State St (60134-2255)
PHONE..................331 248-0221
Elizabeth Ott, *Principal*
EMP: 6
SALES (est): 623.8K **Privately Held**
WEB: www.genevarunningoutfitters.com
SIC: 3949 Sporting & athletic goods

(G-10273)
GENEVA SIGN CORPORATION
Also Called: Signs Now
726 E State St (60134-2365)
PHONE..................630 262-1700
EMP: 4
SALES (est): 390.7K **Privately Held**
SIC: 3993 Signs And Advertising Specialties

(G-10274)
GINGER WINDMILL BREW LLC
2600 Keslinger Rd Ste 15 (60134-3908)
PHONE..................630 677-2850
Joanna Meliunas, *Mng Member*
Edward Meliunas,
EMP: 3
SQ FT: 3,400
SALES: 219K **Privately Held**
SIC: 2082 Beer (alcoholic beverage)

(G-10275)
HOUGHTON MIFFLIN HARCOURT
1900 S Batavia Ave (60134-3310)
PHONE..................928 467-9599
Gary Greenwood, *Principal*
◆ **EMP:** 21
SALES (est): 1.8MM **Privately Held**
WEB: www.hmhco.com
SIC: 2731 Book publishing

(G-10276)
HOUGHTON MIFFLIN HARCOURT CO
Also Called: Hmh
1900 S Batavia Ave (60134-3310)
PHONE..................303 504-9312
EMP: 3
SALES (corp-wide): 1.3B **Publicly Held**
SIC: 3999 2731 Education aids, devices & supplies; book publishing
PA: Houghton Mifflin Harcourt Company
    125 High St Ste 900
    Boston MA 02110
    617 351-5000

(G-10277)
HOUGHTON MIFFLIN HARCOURT PUBG
Holt McDougal
1900 S Batavia Ave (60134-3310)
PHONE..................630 208-5704
Jess Toland, *Vice Pres*
Annalisa Musacchio, *Accounts Exec*
Kayla Mycoff, *Accounts Exec*
Stephanie Cantu, *Sales Staff*
Kelly Friel, *Sales Staff*
EMP: 250
SALES (corp-wide): 1.3B **Publicly Held**
WEB: www.hmhco.com
SIC: 2731 Textbooks: publishing & printing
HQ: Houghton Mifflin Harcourt Publishing Company
    125 High St Ste 900
    Boston MA 02110
    617 351-5000

Geneva - Kane County (G-10278)

(G-10278)
INDUSTRIAL CONTROLS INC
512 Nelson Dr (60134-4695)
PHONE..................................630 752-8100
Ken Arnold, *President*
EMP: 4
SALES (est): 604.9K **Privately Held**
SIC: 8711 5063 3625 1622 Electrical or electronic engineering; electrical apparatus & equipment; motor control accessories, including overload relays; tunnel construction

(G-10279)
INDUSTRIAL HARD CHROME LTD
501 Fluid Power Dr (60134-1181)
PHONE..................................630 208-7000
C G Therkildsen, *President*
Rich Peterson, *COO*
Fred Parker, *VP Admin*
Dave Hahne, *Vice Pres*
Steve Schaus, *Vice Pres*
EMP: 120 **EST:** 1955
SQ FT: 84,000
SALES (est): 20.6MM **Privately Held**
WEB: www.industrialhardchrome.com
SIC: 3471 Electroplating of metals or formed products

(G-10280)
INDUSTRIAL STEEL CNSTR INC (PA)
413 Old Kirk Rd (60134)
PHONE..................................630 232-7473
Joseph R Hish, *President*
Michael Mariano, *Treasurer*
Dorothy Avigiano, *Admin Sec*
▲ **EMP:** 225
SALES (est): 55.1MM **Privately Held**
SIC: 3441 Fabricated structural metal for bridges

(G-10281)
INITIAL IMPRESSIONS INC
405 Stevens St (60134-1361)
PHONE..................................630 208-9399
Rick Carlson, *President*
Mary Carlson, *Vice Pres*
EMP: 5
SQ FT: 3,000
SALES: 400K **Privately Held**
SIC: 3552 Embroidery machines

(G-10282)
INNOVA PRINT FULFILLMENT INC
2000 S Batavia Ave # 310 (60134-3303)
PHONE..................................630 845-3215
Steve Kuhn, *President*
Bob Caser, *Sales Staff*
EMP: 6
SALES (est): 937.1K **Privately Held**
SIC: 2752 Commercial printing, offset

(G-10283)
INNOVATIVE MOLECULAR DIAGNOSTI
Also Called: Imds
1436 Fargo Blvd (60134-2979)
PHONE..................................630 845-8246
Vijai K Pasupuleti, *CEO*
EMP: 1
SALES: 260K **Privately Held**
SIC: 2835 5169 In vitro & in vivo diagnostic substances; industrial chemicals

(G-10284)
INTERNATIONAL CONVEYORS AMER
10 W State St Ste 108 (60134-4505)
PHONE..................................630 549-4007
EMP: 4
SALES (est): 302.1K **Privately Held**
SIC: 3535 Conveyors & conveying equipment

(G-10285)
INTERNTNAL INGREDIENT MALL LLC
Also Called: Fona International
1900 Averill Rd (60134-1601)
PHONE..................................630 462-1414
Bill Slawk, *CEO*
EMP: 3
SALES (est): 192.6K **Privately Held**
WEB: www.fona.com
SIC: 2087 Extracts, flavoring

(G-10286)
JAMES STREET DENTAL P C
22 James St Ste 3 (60134-4513)
PHONE..................................630 232-9535
Laurie Slavik, *Principal*
EMP: 8
SALES (est): 797.9K **Privately Held**
SIC: 3843 Enamels, dentists'

(G-10287)
JOHNSONS SCREEN PRINTING
419 Stevens St Ste C (60134-1392)
PHONE..................................630 262-8210
Tom Johnson, *Owner*
EMP: 4
SALES (est): 365.1K **Privately Held**
SIC: 2752 Commercial printing, lithographic

(G-10288)
LAKELAND PALLETS INC
2080 Gary Ln Ste 3 (60134-2582)
PHONE..................................616 949-9515
Bruce Kintop, *Sales Staff*
EMP: 3 **Privately Held**
SIC: 2448 Pallets, wood; pallets, wood & wood with metal
PA: Lakeland Pallets, Inc.
3801 Kraft Ave Se
Grand Rapids MI 49512

(G-10289)
LUCK E STRIKE CORPORATION
Also Called: Luck E Strike USA
2100 Enterprise Ave (60134-4101)
PHONE..................................630 313-2408
Jeffrey Lee, *President*
▲ **EMP:** 15
SQ FT: 30,000
SALES (est): 2.2MM **Privately Held**
SIC: 3949 Lures, fishing: artificial

(G-10290)
MINER ELASTOMER PRODUCTS CORP
1200 E State St (60134-2440)
P.O. Box 471 (60134-0471)
PHONE..................................630 232-3000
David W Withall, *Ch of Bd*
Richard J Beranek, *President*
Gary A Withall, *Exec VP*
Carrie Edwards, *Purchasing*
Josh Davis, *Engineer*
▲ **EMP:** 35
SQ FT: 22,000
SALES (est): 6.7MM
SALES (corp-wide): 128.9MM **Privately Held**
SIC: 2821 Elastomers, nonvulcanizable (plastics)
PA: Miner Enterprises Inc
1200 E State St
Geneva IL 60134
630 232-3000

(G-10291)
MURNANE SPECIALTIES INC
1507 Averill Rd (60134-1682)
PHONE..................................708 449-1200
Steve Adamson, *Manager*
EMP: 15
SALES (est): 3.3MM
SALES (corp-wide): 5.5MM **Privately Held**
SIC: 2653 Boxes, corrugated: made from purchased materials
PA: Murnane Specialties, Inc.
607 Northwest Ave
Northlake IL 60164
708 449-1200

(G-10292)
NATIONAL BINDING SUPS EQP INC
39w254 Sheldon Ct (60134-6043)
PHONE..................................630 801-7600
Ken Vedder, *President*
Maureen Vedder, *Vice Pres*
EMP: 6
SALES (est): 934.6K **Privately Held**
SIC: 2789 Binding & repair of books, magazines & pamphlets

(G-10293)
NEW YORK & COMPANY INC
Also Called: Lerner New York
410 Commons Dr (60134-2518)
PHONE..................................630 232-7693
Fax: 630 232-7693
EMP: 17
SALES (corp-wide): 929MM **Publicly Held**
SIC: 5621 2389 5137 Ret Women's Clothing Mfg Apparel/Accessories Whol Women's/Child's Clothing
PA: New York & Company, Inc.
330 W 34th St Fl 9
New York NY 10001
212 884-2000

(G-10294)
O BRIEN BILL
Also Called: K B Sales & Service
0n175 Alexander Dr (60134-6023)
PHONE..................................630 980-5571
Bill O'Brien, *Owner*
EMP: 3
SALES (est): 243.9K **Privately Held**
SIC: 5087 5051 3599 Cleaning & maintenance equipment & supplies; iron & steel (ferrous) products; machine shop, jobbing & repair

(G-10295)
OASIS INTERNATIONAL LIMITED
Also Called: Oak Foundation
1770 S Randall Rd Ste A (60134-4646)
PHONE..................................630 326-0045
Mathew Eliott, *President*
Edward Elliot, *Chairman*
EMP: 3
SQ FT: 400
SALES (est): 580.8K **Privately Held**
SIC: 2731 Books: publishing only

(G-10296)
OERLIKON BLZERS CATING USA INC
737 Peyton St (60134-2150)
PHONE..................................630 208-0958
EMP: 10
SALES (corp-wide): 2.6B **Privately Held**
SIC: 3479 Coating of metals & formed products
HQ: Oerlikon Balzers Coating Usa Inc.
1700 E Golf Rd Ste 200
Schaumburg IL 60173
847 619-5541

(G-10297)
OLIVE OIL STORE INC (PA)
Also Called: Olive Mill, The
315 James St (60134-2114)
PHONE..................................630 262-0210
Ed O Connell, *Principal*
EMP: 10
SALES (est): 921K **Privately Held**
SIC: 2079 Vegetable shortenings (except corn oil); olive oil

(G-10298)
OLON INDUSTRIES INC (US) (HQ)
Also Called: Olon Decoratives
411 Union St (60134-1367)
PHONE..................................630 232-4705
Don Hambly, *President*
John Kozuch, *Vice Pres*
Ernie Saberieno, *CFO*
Terry Elliott, *Manager*
Kayla Gengelbach, *Administration*
◆ **EMP:** 23
SQ FT: 40,000
SALES (est): 21.5MM
SALES (corp-wide): 38.4MM **Privately Held**
WEB: www.olonusa.com
SIC: 3083 Laminated plastic sheets
PA: Errion Group Inc
42 Armstrong Ave
Georgetown ON L7G 4
905 877-7300

(G-10299)
PHILLIP C COWEN
106 7th Pl (60134-2100)
PHONE..................................630 208-1848
Phillip Cowen, *Owner*
EMP: 40 **EST:** 1960
SALES (est): 2.6MM **Privately Held**
SIC: 3399 3316 Primary metal products; cold finishing of steel shapes

(G-10300)
PROVENA RANDALWOOD OPEN MRI
110 James St (60134-2242)
PHONE..................................630 587-9917
Derrick Oregon, *Principal*
EMP: 20
SALES (est): 1MM **Privately Held**
SIC: 3841 Diagnostic apparatus, medical

(G-10301)
R & R CREATIVE GRAPHICS INC
Also Called: Mid West Investors Solutions
111 N Northampton Dr (60134-1802)
PHONE..................................630 208-4724
Roger Brown, *President*
▲ **EMP:** 2
SALES (est): 1MM **Privately Held**
SIC: 5112 5199 7389 2752 Business forms; advertising specialties; packaging & labeling services; commercial printing, offset

(G-10302)
RICHARDSON RFPD INC (HQ)
1950 S Batavia Ave # 100 (60134-3332)
PHONE..................................630 262-6800
Rafael Salmi, *President*
Deann Carrington, *Sales Staff*
John Donarski, *Marketing Staff*
Rich Naslonski, *Director*
▲ **EMP:** 74
SALES (est): 3.4MM
SALES (corp-wide): 28.9B **Publicly Held**
SIC: 3825 Radio frequency measuring equipment
PA: Arrow Electronics, Inc.
9201 E Dry Creek Rd
Centennial CO 80112
303 824-4000

(G-10303)
RIVERBANK LABORATORIES INC
18 S 8th St (60134-2002)
P.O. Box 110 (60134-0110)
PHONE..................................630 232-2207
Robert Swanson, *President*
Jack Martin, *Vice Pres*
Mary Robinson, *Vice Pres*
EMP: 16 **EST:** 1904
SALES (est): 3MM **Privately Held**
WEB: www.riverbanklabs.com
SIC: 3841 Surgical & medical instruments

(G-10304)
ROQUETTE AMERICA INC
2211 Innovation Dr (60134-1602)
PHONE..................................630 232-2157
EMP: 17
SALES (est): 238.2K **Privately Held**
SIC: 2041 Mfg Flour/Grain Mill Prooducts

(G-10305)
SHADING SOLUTIONS GROUP INC
1770 S Randall Rd A172 (60134-4646)
PHONE..................................630 444-2102
Joseph F Diffendal, *President*
Jacqueline Diffendal, *Admin Sec*
EMP: 2
SALES: 200K **Privately Held**
WEB: www.shadingsolutionsgroup.net
SIC: 2394 8611 Shades, canvas: made from purchased materials; contractors' association

(G-10306)
SMITH & RICHARDSON MFG CO
727 May St (60134-1379)
P.O. Box 589 (60134-0589)
PHONE..................................630 232-2581
Phil Cowen, *CEO*
W Richard Hoster III, *President*
Richard Briggs, *Engineer*

GEOGRAPHIC SECTION

Matt Liebert, *Plant Engr*
Richard Brink, *Sales Associate*
▲ **EMP:** 38
SQ FT: 66,000
SALES (est): 8.8MM **Privately Held**
WEB: www.smithandrichardson.com
SIC: 3599 Machine shop, jobbing & repair

(G-10307)
STATE STREET JEWELERS INC
230 W State St (60134-2217)
PHONE.....................630 232-2085
Jeffrey Hampton, *President*
John Christensen, *Principal*
Louise Keen, *Principal*
Martha Sanchez, *Principal*
Judy Shipanik, *Principal*
EMP: 10
SQ FT: 2,100
SALES (est): 4MM **Privately Held**
WEB: www.statestreetjewelers.com
SIC: 5944 7631 3999 3231 Jewelry, precious stones & precious metals; watches; watch repair; jewelry repair services; stringing beads; ornamental glass: cut, engraved or otherwise decorated

(G-10308)
STEEL MANAGEMENT INC
716 Natwill Sq (60134-2073)
PHONE.....................630 397-5083
Robert Harrington, *President*
EMP: 1 **EST:** 1997
SALES (est): 237.6K **Privately Held**
SIC: 3441 Fabricated structural metal

(G-10309)
STRATHMORE COMPANY
2000 Gary Ln (60134-2515)
P.O. Box 87, Saint Charles (60174-0087)
PHONE.....................630 232-9677
Chang Park, *President*
Charles Bong, *CFO*
Charles B Ong, *Controller*
Jack Tinney, *Manager*
EMP: 47
SQ FT: 74,000
SALES (est): 9.2MM **Privately Held**
SIC: 2752 Commercial printing, offset

(G-10310)
TEAMDANCE ILLINOIS
215 Fulton St (60134-2747)
PHONE.....................815 463-9044
Ramona Kitching, *Principal*
EMP: 4
SALES (est): 85.2K **Privately Held**
SIC: 3221 Medicine bottles, glass

(G-10311)
THRYSELIUS STAMPING INC
28 S 8th St (60134-2002)
P.O. Box 443 (60134-0443)
PHONE.....................630 232-0795
Jason Thryselius, *President*
EMP: 4 **EST:** 1956
SQ FT: 8,500
SALES (est): 430K **Privately Held**
WEB: www.thryseliusstamping.com
SIC: 3469 Stamping metal for the trade

(G-10312)
TONJON COMPANY
1450 Meadows Rd (60134-3254)
PHONE.....................630 208-1173
Anthony Llewellyn, *Ch of Bd*
Allen Eberts, *President*
EMP: 11
SQ FT: 9,000
SALES (est): 1.7MM **Privately Held**
SIC: 3827 3231 3634 Mirrors, optical; products of purchased glass; hair dryers, electric

(G-10313)
TRI CITY SHEET METAL
701 May St (60134-1303)
P.O. Box 51 (60134-0051)
PHONE.....................630 232-4255
Ken Hiscox, *President*
Margie Hiscox, *Admin Sec*
EMP: 5 **EST:** 1954
SALES (est): 498.4K **Privately Held**
SIC: 1711 3444 Warm air heating & air conditioning contractor; sheet metalwork

(G-10314)
TWOINSPIREYOU LLC
39w890 Carney Ln (60134-4421)
PHONE.....................630 849-8214
Bice Tonya, *President*
EMP: 8
SALES (est): 750K **Privately Held**
SIC: 7389 5961 3999 ; ; wreaths, artificial

Genoa
Dekalb County

(G-10315)
BENZINGER PRINTING
673 Park Ave Ste 1 (60135-5408)
PHONE.....................815 784-6560
Tony Benzinger Sr, *Partner*
Patrick Crosby, *Partner*
David Miller, *Partner*
EMP: 4
SQ FT: 1,200
SALES (est): 468.6K **Privately Held**
SIC: 2759 7389 5999 2791 Screen printing; engraving service; rubber stamps; typesetting; bookbinding & related work; commercial printing, lithographic

(G-10316)
CUSTOM ALUMINUM PRODUCTS INC
312 Eureka St (60135-1012)
PHONE.....................847 717-5000
Tony Amendola, *Sales Staff*
Mark Thurlby, *Branch Mgr*
EMP: 100
SALES (est): 12.7MM
SALES (corp-wide): 80.9MM **Privately Held**
WEB: www.custom-aluminum.com
SIC: 3354 3442 Aluminum extruded products; metal doors, sash & trim; sash, door or window: metal
PA: Custom Aluminum Products, Inc.
  414 Division St
  South Elgin IL 60177
  847 717-5000

(G-10317)
FRANKLIN SCREW PRODUCTS INC
600 S Sycamore St Unit 1 (60135-1155)
PHONE.....................815 784-8500
Dave Rice, *President*
EMP: 3
SALES (est): 388.6K **Privately Held**
SIC: 3451 Screw machine products

(G-10318)
GREENLEE TEXTRON INC
Also Called: Genoa Manufacturing Center
702 W Main St (60135-1034)
PHONE.....................815 784-5127
David Johnson, *Branch Mgr*
EMP: 180
SALES (corp-wide): 18.3B **Publicly Held**
WEB: www.greenlee.textron.com
SIC: 3825 Battery testers, electrical
HQ: Greenlee Tools, Inc.
  4455 Boeing Dr
  Rockford IL 61109
  800 435-0786

(G-10319)
J6 POLYMERS LLC
601 Derby Line Rd (60135-8009)
P.O. Box 250 (60135-0250)
PHONE.....................815 517-1179
Sandra Wood, *Mng Member*
James Wood, *Administration*
EMP: 4
SQ FT: 36,625
SALES (est): 582.1K **Privately Held**
SIC: 2821 Plastics materials & resins

(G-10320)
NORDSON CORPORATION
416 Holly Ct (60135-1133)
PHONE.....................815 784-5025
Edward Campbell, *President*
EMP: 50
SALES (corp-wide): 2.1B **Publicly Held**
SIC: 3563 Air & gas compressors
PA: Nordson Corporation
  28601 Clemens Rd
  Westlake OH 44145
  440 892-1580

(G-10321)
POLAR TECH INDUSTRIES INC (PA)
415 E Railroad Ave (60135-1200)
PHONE.....................815 784-9000
Donald Santeler, *President*
Cindy Nunez, *Production*
Allen Cole, *Sales Staff*
Melissa Kriegl, *Representative*
EMP: 30
SQ FT: 405,000
SALES (est): 10.8MM **Privately Held**
SIC: 3089 3086 Plastic containers, except foam; packaging & shipping materials, foamed plastic

(G-10322)
PRAIRIE STATE WINERY (PA)
222 W Main St (60135-1146)
PHONE.....................815 784-4540
Richard Mamoser, *Owner*
Maria Mamoser, *Co-Owner*
EMP: 3 **EST:** 2002
SALES (est): 423.4K **Privately Held**
SIC: 2084 Wines

(G-10323)
R HANSEL & SON INC
221 N Sycamore St (60135-1071)
PHONE.....................815 784-5500
Don Hansel, *President*
Robert Hansel, *President*
EMP: 6
SQ FT: 7,500
SALES (est): 700K **Privately Held**
SIC: 3469 Machine parts, stamped or pressed metal

(G-10324)
SYCAMORE PRECISION
334 E 1st St Ste 1 (60135-1097)
PHONE.....................815 784-5151
Ernest Hirn, *President*
Karen Hirn, *Admin Sec*
▲ **EMP:** 85
SQ FT: 60,000
SALES (est): 20.9MM **Privately Held**
SIC: 3599 3491 3479 Machine shop, jobbing & repair; industrial valves; painting, coating & hot dipping

(G-10325)
SYCAMORE WELDING & FABG CO
675 Park Ave (60135-1100)
PHONE.....................815 784-2557
Richard J Freeman, *Owner*
EMP: 3
SQ FT: 3,150
SALES (est): 379.5K **Privately Held**
SIC: 3441 Fabricated structural metal

Georgetown
Vermilion County

(G-10326)
GEORGETOWN WASTE WATER
208 S Walnut St (61846-1956)
PHONE.....................217 662-2525
Ed Shirley, *Manager*
Dale Brooks, *Manager*
EMP: 3
SALES (est): 253.9K **Privately Held**
SIC: 3561 Pumps, domestic: water or sump

(G-10327)
GEORGETOWN WOOD AND PALLET CO
5781 State Route 1 (61846-6091)
P.O. Box 235 (61846-0235)
PHONE.....................217 662-2563
Gil A Winland, *President*
Eric K Winland, *Vice Pres*
Donald W Winland, *Admin Sec*
EMP: 21
SQ FT: 30,000
SALES (est): 3.7MM **Privately Held**
SIC: 2448 Pallets, wood

(G-10328)
HAMMER ENTERPRISES INC
5781 State Route 1 (61846-6091)
P.O. Box 235 (61846-0235)
PHONE.....................217 662-8225
Gil Alan Winland, *President*
EMP: 10
SQ FT: 300
SALES (est): 710K **Privately Held**
SIC: 2448 Wood pallets & skids

(G-10329)
NEWPORT PALLET
310 S Main St (61846-1825)
PHONE.....................217 662-6577
Adam Winland, *Principal*
EMP: 3
SALES (est): 150.2K **Privately Held**
SIC: 2448 Pallets, wood & wood with metal

Germantown
Clinton County

(G-10330)
KOHNENS CONCRETE PRODUCTS INC
503 Green St (62245-2719)
P.O. Box 276 (62245-0276)
PHONE.....................618 277-2120
Gregory Wilburn, *President*
Randy Gebke, *General Mgr*
Pat Kreke, *Plant Mgr*
Dan Kohnen, *Manager*
Kim Aubogat, *Officer*
EMP: 40
SQ FT: 10,000
SALES (est): 7MM **Privately Held**
WEB: www.kohnenconcrete.com
SIC: 3272 3443 1781 Septic tanks, concrete; tanks, concrete; pipe, concrete or lined with concrete; water tanks, metal plate; water well drilling

(G-10331)
LAKENBURGES MOTOR CO
806 Walnut St (62245-2737)
P.O. Box 248 (62245-0248)
PHONE.....................618 523-4231
Roger H Lakenburges, *Partner*
Florence M Lakenburges, *Partner*
EMP: 3 **EST:** 1900
SQ FT: 4,350
SALES (est): 200K **Privately Held**
SIC: 7538 5261 7699 5541 General automotive repair shops; lawnmowers & tractors; lawn mower repair shop; filling stations, gasoline; electric motor repair; automotive parts

(G-10332)
WHITE STAR SILO
8320 Wesclin Rd (62245-1614)
PHONE.....................618 523-4735
William Heimbecker, *President*
Marcy Heimbecker, *Corp Secy*
EMP: 7 **EST:** 1957
SALES (est): 785.6K **Privately Held**
SIC: 3272 3448 Silos, prefabricated concrete; prefabricated metal buildings

Germantown Hills
Woodford County

(G-10333)
ASKRIC LLC
406 Johnson Ct (61548-8796)
PHONE.....................309 360-3125
Michael McConnell,
EMP: 2
SALES: 250K **Privately Held**
SIC: 7372 Application computer software

(G-10334)
WHITE OAK TECHNOLOGY
524 Wedgewood Ter (61548-9062)
PHONE.....................309 228-4201
James W Sutton, *President*

Gibson City
Ford County

(G-10335)
BUNGE NORTH AMERICA FOUNDATION
Rts 9& 47 # 9 (60936)
P.O. Box 112 (60936-0112)
PHONE...................217 784-8261
Mick Sullivan, *Branch Mgr*
EMP: 150 **Privately Held**
WEB: www.bungenorthamerica.com
SIC: 2075 Soybean protein concentrates & isolates; soybean flour & grits; lecithin, soybean
HQ: Bunge North America Foundation
1391 Timberlk Mnr Pkwy # 31
Chesterfield MO 63017
314 872-3030

(G-10336)
DAVIS WELDING & MANFCTG INC
511 W 8th St (60936-1309)
P.O. Box 111 (60936-0111)
PHONE...................217 784-5480
Mike Davis, *President*
Thomas Davis, *Corp Secy*
EMP: 10 **EST:** 1945
SQ FT: 18,000
SALES (est): 1.7MM **Privately Held**
WEB: www.davisweldingmfg.com
SIC: 3561 3523 Cylinders, pump; barn cleaners; loaders, farm type: manure, general utility

(G-10337)
ENGRAVINGS PLUS
421 S Lott Blvd (60936-1675)
P.O. Box 463 (60936-0463)
PHONE...................217 784-8426
Edward Fuoss, *Owner*
Phyllis Fuoss, *Manager*
EMP: 3
SALES: 130K **Privately Held**
SIC: 7389 3993 Engraving service; signs & advertising specialties

(G-10338)
GDM SEEDS INC (PA)
454 E 300n Rd (60936-7127)
PHONE...................317 752-6783
Ignacio Bartolome, *President*
Bruce Bailey, *Vice Pres*
EMP: 12
SALES (est): 4.1MM **Privately Held**
SIC: 2879 Plant hormones

(G-10339)
HUSTEDT MANUFACTURING JEWELERS
113 N Sangamon Ave (60936-1342)
P.O. Box 124 (60936-0124)
PHONE...................217 784-8462
Kermit Larry Hustedt, *Owner*
Ursala Hustedt, *Manager*
EMP: 4
SALES (est): 207.8K **Privately Held**
SIC: 3911 7631 3961 Jewelry, precious metal; jewelry repair services; costume jewelry

(G-10340)
LOAD REDI INC
1124 S Sangamon Ave (60936-1762)
PHONE...................217 784-4200
Jerry Minion, *President*
EMP: 2
SQ FT: 8,000
SALES (est): 220K **Privately Held**
SIC: 7539 3715 Trailer repair; truck trailers

(G-10341)
ONE EARTH ENERGY LLC
202 Jordan Dr (60936-2203)
PHONE...................217 784-5321
Steven Kelly, *President*
Jack Murray, *President*

EMP: 2
SALES (est): 245.3K **Privately Held**
SIC: 3553 Saws, power: bench & table, except portable: woodworking

Scott Docherty, *Chairman*
Joseph Thompson, *Vice Pres*
Larry Brees, *CFO*
EMP: 48
SALES (est): 21.8MM
SALES (corp-wide): 418MM **Publicly Held**
SIC: 2869 Ethyl alcohol, ethanol
PA: Rex American Resources Corporation
7720 Paragon Rd
Dayton OH 45459
937 276-3931

(G-10342)
PRECISION PLASTIC PRODUCTS
111 E 8th St (60936-1454)
PHONE...................217 784-4920
William Tubbs, *Owner*
Sarah Tubbs, *Admin Sec*
EMP: 2
SALES (est): 1.2MM **Privately Held**
SIC: 3089 Injection molding of plastics

(G-10343)
RHINOAG INC
Also Called: M & W Gear Company
1020 S Sangamon Ave (60936-1700)
PHONE...................217 784-4261
Dan Samet, *Prdtn Mgr*
Roger Hackbarth, *Buyer*
Jerry Stanley, *Buyer*
Doug Parsons, *Technical Mgr*
Andy Rose, *Engineer*
EMP: 33
SALES (corp-wide): 1.1B **Publicly Held**
SIC: 3523 Farm machinery & equipment
HQ: Rhinoag, Inc.
1627 E Walnut St
Seguin TX 78155
800 882-5756

(G-10344)
SNC SOLUTIONS INC
496 N 600e Rd (60936-7218)
P.O. Box 305 (60936-0305)
PHONE...................217 784-5212
Mark Sizemore, *President*
Thomas Curtis, *COO*
Jordan Sizemore, *CFO*
EMP: 47
SALES (est): 5.6MM **Privately Held**
SIC: 3441 1731 1771 1794 Tower sections, radio & television transmission; general electrical contractor; concrete work; excavation work; communication line & transmission tower construction; transmitting tower (telecommunication) construction

(G-10345)
SOLAE
115 Jordan Dr (60936)
PHONE...................217 784-8261
Bill Miller, *Manager*
◆ **EMP:** 13
SALES (est): 1.9MM **Privately Held**
SIC: 2099 Food preparations

(G-10346)
SOLAE
509 W 1st St (60936-2201)
PHONE...................217 784-2085
Paul Hosack, *Plant Mgr*
EMP: 3 **EST:** 2013
SALES (est): 362.4K **Privately Held**
SIC: 2075 Soybean oil mills

(G-10347)
SOLAE LLC
Also Called: Dupont Nutrition & Health
124 S Rte 47 (60936-7125)
P.O. Box 112 (60936-0112)
PHONE...................217 784-8261
Bill Miller, *Manager*
Gary Hammond, *Executive*
EMP: 125
SALES (corp-wide): 21.5B **Publicly Held**
SIC: 2075 Soybean oil mills
HQ: Solae, Llc
4300 Duncan Ave
Saint Louis MO 63110
314 659-3000

Gifford
Champaign County

(G-10348)
SPREADER INC
2296 County Road 3000 N (61847-9725)
P.O. Box 189 (61847-0189)
PHONE...................217 568-7219
Armin Hesterberg, *President*
EMP: 7
SQ FT: 6,240
SALES (est): 1MM **Privately Held**
SIC: 3523 3531 3494 Spreaders, fertilizer; construction machinery; valves & pipe fittings

Gilberts
Kane County

(G-10349)
ACCURATE METAL FINISHING CO
359 Sola Dr (60136-9006)
PHONE...................847 428-7705
Arnel Arias, *President*
EMP: 8
SQ FT: 6,000
SALES (est): 908.6K **Privately Held**
SIC: 3471 Finishing, metals or formed products

(G-10350)
AMRON STAIR WORKS INC (PA)
152 Industrial Dr (60136-9752)
PHONE...................847 426-4800
Ron Thorson, *President*
Julie Anderson, *Executive*
EMP: 15
SQ FT: 20,000
SALES (est): 2MM **Privately Held**
SIC: 2431 3446 Staircases & stairs, wood; stair railings, wood; architectural metalwork

(G-10351)
BOALEECO INC
56 E End Dr (60136-9731)
PHONE...................847 428-3085
Marvin G Ness, *President*
EMP: 7
SALES (est): 364.2K **Privately Held**
SIC: 3699 3728 Electronic training devices; flight simulators (training aids), electronic; automotive driving simulators (training aids), electronic; aircraft training equipment; link trainers (aircraft training mechanisms)

(G-10352)
BW EXHIBITS
41 Prairie Pkwy (60136-4039)
PHONE...................847 697-9224
Bruce Barna, *Principal*
Mike Reese, *Admin Sec*
EMP: 4 **EST:** 2009
SALES (est): 501.6K **Privately Held**
SIC: 3553 Cabinet makers' machinery

(G-10353)
DONTECH INDUSTRIES INC
76 Center Dr (60136-9712)
PHONE...................847 428-8222
Don L Catton, *President*
Mark Mann, *Corp Secy*
Stephanie Richardson, *Vice Pres*
▲ **EMP:** 10
SQ FT: 13,500
SALES (est): 2.2MM **Privately Held**
WEB: www.dontechindustriesinc.com
SIC: 3556 3589 8711 1796 Food products machinery; sewage & water treatment equipment; designing: ship, boat, machine & product; machinery installation; electric lamps

(G-10354)
E-Z PRODUCTS INC
92 E End Dr (60136-9731)
PHONE...................847 551-9199
Geraldine Hall, *President*

William Hall, *Principal*
▲ **EMP:** 10
SQ FT: 10,000
SALES (est): 1.4MM **Privately Held**
SIC: 3081 2673 Unsupported plastics film & sheet; bags: plastic, laminated & coated

(G-10355)
GATOR PRODUCTS INC
Also Called: Microcut Engineering
80 Industrial Dr Unit 105 (60136-9103)
PHONE...................847 836-0581
Andrew Starrenburg, *President*
▲ **EMP:** 8
SQ FT: 4,000
SALES (est): 1.6MM **Privately Held**
SIC: 3546 3545 Power-driven handtools; machine tool accessories

(G-10356)
HARMONY METAL FABRICATION INC
148 Industrial Dr (60136-9752)
PHONE...................847 426-8900
Robert F Farnham, *President*
EMP: 25
SQ FT: 20,000
SALES: 5MM **Privately Held**
SIC: 3599 3441 Machine shop, jobbing & repair; fabricated structural metal

(G-10357)
HENDERSON PRODUCTS INC
Also Called: Henderson Truck Equipment
124 Industrial Dr (60136-9752)
PHONE...................847 836-4996
Scott Gilmore, *Principal*
EMP: 10 **Publicly Held**
WEB: www.henderson-mfg.com
SIC: 3531 Snow plow attachments
HQ: Henderson Products, Inc.
1085 S 3rd St
Manchester IA 52057
563 927-2828

(G-10358)
HUML INDUSTRIES INC
78 E End Dr (60136-9731)
P.O. Box 95 (60136-0095)
PHONE...................847 426-8061
Mollie Huml, *CEO*
Molly Huml, *President*
EMP: 7 **EST:** 1923
SQ FT: 5,000
SALES: 700K **Privately Held**
WEB: www.humlindustries.com
SIC: 3334 3541 Primary aluminum; cutoff machines (metalworking machinery)

(G-10359)
HYPERMAX ENGINEERING INC
255 Higgins Rd (60136-9795)
PHONE...................847 428-5655
Jerome A Lagod, *President*
Linda Lagod, *Vice Pres*
EMP: 17 **EST:** 1973
SQ FT: 12,000
SALES (est): 2.8MM **Privately Held**
WEB: www.gohypermax.com
SIC: 8711 5531 3523 Designing: ship, boat, machine & product; truck equipment & parts; farm machinery & equipment

(G-10360)
J D MACHINING
57 Center Dr Ste B (60136-9647)
PHONE...................847 428-8690
Jack Diehl, *Owner*
EMP: 5
SQ FT: 3,600
SALES (est): 464.5K **Privately Held**
SIC: 3599 Machine shop, jobbing & repair

(G-10361)
MIDWEST INTGRTED COMPANIES LLC
Also Called: Midwest Material Management
275 Sola Dr (60136-9003)
PHONE...................847 426-6354
Scott Villalobos, *Manager*
Steve Berglund,
Veronica Berglund,
Dana Stillson,
Debra Stillson,
EMP: 150
SQ FT: 100,000

GEOGRAPHIC SECTION

SALES (est): 30.4MM **Privately Held**
SIC: 2875 7699 2491 Compost; waste cleaning services; railroad cross-ties, treated wood

(G-10362)
MIDWEST TURNED PRODUCTS LLC
80 Prairie Pkwy (60136-4090)
PHONE..................847 551-4482
Mike Clark, *QC Mgr*
John Robert Lang,
EMP: 50
SALES (est): 3MM **Privately Held**
SIC: 3541 Drilling & boring machines

(G-10363)
N J TECH INC
160 Industrial Dr Ste 5 (60136-9100)
P.O. Box 103 (60136-0103)
PHONE..................847 428-1001
Phounsanath Nanthanong, *President*
Douglas Jacobs, *Vice Pres*
EMP: 5
SQ FT: 8,000
SALES (est): 715K **Privately Held**
SIC: 3599 Machine shop, jobbing & repair

(G-10364)
PAVER PROTECTOR INC
57 Railroad St 171 (60136-9670)
P.O. Box 171 (60136-0171)
PHONE..................630 488-0069
EMP: 2 EST: 2011
SALES (est): 243.3K **Privately Held**
WEB: www.paverprotector.com
SIC: 3531 Pavers

(G-10365)
PRAXAIR INC
330 Arrowhead Dr (60136-9602)
PHONE..................847 428-3405
EMP: 21
SALES (corp-wide): 10.5B **Publicly Held**
SIC: 2813 Mfg Industrial
PA: Praxair, Inc.
10 Riverview Dr
Danbury CT 06810
203 837-2000

(G-10366)
R & I ORNAMENTAL IRON INC
Also Called: M B E
96 Center Dr (60136-9712)
PHONE..................847 836-6934
Raul Valdez Sr, *President*
Rene Valdez, *Vice Pres*
Olga Valdez, *Admin Sec*
EMP: 26 EST: 1970
SQ FT: 14,000
SALES: 6MM **Privately Held**
SIC: 3446 1799 Architectural metalwork; ornamental metal work

(G-10367)
RON MEYER
Also Called: Meyer Signs & Graphics
341 Sola Dr (60136-9006)
PHONE..................847 844-9880
Ron Meyer, *Owner*
EMP: 2
SALES (est): 232K **Privately Held**
SIC: 7359 3993 Sign rental; signs & advertising specialties

(G-10368)
SAFETY SOCKET LLC
49 Prairie Pkwy (60136-4039)
PHONE..................224 484-6222
Jim Erbs, *President*
Steven Payne, *Vice Pres*
Jessica Dishman, *Purchasing*
Bob Lukowski, *Manager*
EMP: 43
SQ FT: 40,500
SALES: 4.3MM **Privately Held**
SIC: 3965 Fasteners

(G-10369)
SBS STEEL BELT SYSTEMS USA INC
59 Prairie Pkwy (60136-4039)
PHONE..................847 841-3300
Paolo Fasana, *President*
Teresa A Hill, *Admin Sec*
◆ EMP: 12
SALES (est): 5.2MM **Privately Held**
SIC: 3535 8711 3291 Conveyors & conveying equipment; engineering services; steel shot abrasive
HQ: Sbs Steel Belt Systems Srl
Via Mattei 3
Venegono Inferiore VA 21040
033 186-4841

(G-10370)
SCOTT INDUSTRIAL BLOWER CO
15 W End Dr (60136-9657)
P.O. Box 226 (60136-0226)
PHONE..................847 426-8800
Hermes Haralambous, *President*
Tom Sloan, *Vice Pres*
Marlene Haralambous, *Admin Sec*
EMP: 18 EST: 1968
SQ FT: 22,000
SALES (est): 3.2MM **Privately Held**
SIC: 3564 Blowers & fans; blowing fans; industrial or commercial

(G-10371)
SELEE CORPORATION
Selee Advanced Ceramics
24 W End Dr (60136-9657)
P.O. Box 365 (60136-0365)
PHONE..................847 428-4455
Robert Simpson, *Manager*
EMP: 40
SQ FT: 10,000
SALES (corp-wide): 186.3MM **Privately Held**
WEB: www.selee.com
SIC: 3251 Ceramic glazed brick, clay
HQ: Selee Corporation
700 Shepherd St
Hendersonville NC 28792
828 693-0256

(G-10372)
SRR MANUFACTURING SERVICES
205 Tyler Creek St (60136-9002)
PHONE..................847 404-3527
EMP: 3
SALES (est): 182.5K **Privately Held**
WEB: www.srrmfg.com
SIC: 3672 Printed circuit boards

(G-10373)
TII TECHNICAL EDUCATN SYSTEMS
56 E End Dr (60136-9731)
PHONE..................847 428-3085
Marvin Ness, *President*
EMP: 5
SQ FT: 6,000
SALES (est): 1.4MM **Privately Held**
SIC: 3999 3823 3699 Education aids, devices & supplies; industrial instrmnts msrmnt display/control process variable; electrical equipment & supplies

(G-10374)
VEGA MOLDED PRODUCTS INC
122 Industrial Dr (60136-9752)
P.O. Box 246 (60136-0246)
PHONE..................847 428-7761
Karl Weid, *President*
Doris Weid, *Vice Pres*
EMP: 7
SALES (est): 1MM **Privately Held**
SIC: 3089 3544 Injection molding of plastics; special dies, tools, jigs & fixtures

Gillespie
Macoupin County

(G-10375)
GILLESPIE CITY WATER
400 Pear St (62033-1137)
PHONE..................217 839-3279
Dan Fisher, *Mayor*
Don Shuey, *Manager*
EMP: 7
SALES (est): 637.3K **Privately Held**
SIC: 3589 Water treatment equipment, industrial

(G-10376)
PETE AJ CO
103 N Jersey St (62033-1403)
PHONE..................217 825-5822
Austin Peterson, *President*
EMP: 7 EST: 2014
SALES (est): 388.5K **Privately Held**
SIC: 2759 Commercial printing

Gilman
Iroquois County

(G-10377)
CLARK INDUSTRIAL PRPTS INC
104 E Butterfield Trl (60938)
P.O. Box 127 (60938-0127)
PHONE..................815 265-7210
Rick K Clark, *President*
Richard K Clark, *President*
Richard J Clark, *Admin Sec*
▲ EMP: 8
SQ FT: 30,000
SALES (est): 1.4MM **Privately Held**
SIC: 3743 Railroad equipment

(G-10378)
GILMAN STAR INC
203 N Central St 7 (60938-1218)
P.O. Box 7 (60938-0007)
PHONE..................815 265-7332
John Elliott, *President*
EMP: 4 EST: 1949
SQ FT: 3,000
SALES (est): 210K **Privately Held**
WEB: www.thegilmanstar.com
SIC: 2711 Newspapers: publishing only, not printed on site

(G-10379)
GREGORY MARTIN
Also Called: M & D Supplies
325 E Park Ct (60938-1621)
PHONE..................815 265-4527
Gregory Martin, *Owner*
EMP: 4 EST: 1994
SALES (est): 292.3K **Privately Held**
SIC: 3484 Rifles or rifle parts, 30 mm. & below

(G-10380)
INCOBRASA INDUSTRIES LTD
540 E Us Highway 24 (60938-6078)
P.O. Box 98 (60938-0098)
PHONE..................815 265-4803
R B Ribeiro D Pedro II, *President*
Sergio Baruffi, *Plant Mgr*
Jeff Seibert, *Senior Buyer*
Kerry Fogarty, *QC Mgr*
Rudimar Schaefer, *Engineer*
▲ EMP: 120
SALES (est): 37.1MM **Privately Held**
SIC: 2075 Soybean oil mills

Girard
Macoupin County

(G-10381)
FREEMAN UNITED COAL MINING CO
22393 Crown Two Mine Rd 2 Mine (62640)
P.O. Box 259, Farmersville (62533-0259)
PHONE..................217 627-2161
Don Dame, *General Mgr*
EMP: 250
SALES (corp-wide): 39.3B **Publicly Held**
SIC: 1241 Coal mining services
HQ: Freeman United Coal Mining Company
4440 Ash Grove Dr Ste A
Springfield IL 62711

(G-10382)
FUNERAL REGISTER BOOKS INC
499 Rachel Rd (62640-8652)
PHONE..................217 627-3235
Richard R Roberts, *President*
Robert Alan Mc Intire, *Treasurer*
EMP: 15
SQ FT: 10,000
SALES (est): 1.3MM **Privately Held**
SIC: 2782 Memorandum books, printed

(G-10383)
LANGHEIM READY MIX INC
110 E Jefferson St (62640-1106)
P.O. Box 297, Pawnee (62558-0297)
PHONE..................217 625-2351
Reese Langheim, *President*
EMP: 2
SALES (est): 246K **Privately Held**
SIC: 3273 1771 Ready-mixed concrete; concrete work

(G-10384)
R & R BINDERY SERVICE INC
499 Rachel Rd (62640-8652)
PHONE..................217 627-2143
Robert C Mullins, *President*
Robert A McIntire, *Corp Secy*
Richard Roberts, *Vice Pres*
EMP: 180
SQ FT: 72,000
SALES (est): 30MM **Privately Held**
SIC: 2789 Binding only: books, pamphlets, magazines, etc.

(G-10385)
ROBERT HARLAN ERNST
Also Called: Furniture Doctor, The
145 S 2nd St (62640-1608)
PHONE..................217 627-3401
Robert Harlan Ernst, *Owner*
Renae Ernst, *Co-Owner*
EMP: 9
SQ FT: 2,000
SALES (est): 695.4K **Privately Held**
SIC: 7641 2391 2211 2221 Reupholstery; furniture upholstery repair; furniture repair & maintenance; antique furniture repair & restoration; curtains & draperies; draperies & drapery fabrics, cotton; draperies & drapery fabrics, manmade fiber & silk; finish & trim carpentry; custom made furniture, except cabinets

(G-10386)
THERMAL CERAMICS INC
1st & Mound St (62640)
P.O. Box 138 (62640-0138)
PHONE..................217 627-2101
John Stang, *Branch Mgr*
EMP: 35
SALES (corp-wide): 1.3B **Privately Held**
WEB: www.dixieriverside.com
SIC: 3299 4225 3255 3229 Ceramic fiber; general warehousing; clay refractories; pressed & blown glass; flat glass
HQ: Thermal Ceramics Inc.
2102 Old Savannah Rd
Augusta GA 30906
706 796-4200

Glasford
Peoria County

(G-10387)
GAZETTE PRINTING CO
Also Called: Glasford Gazette
508 W Main St (61533-9793)
P.O. Box 260 (61533-0260)
PHONE..................309 389-2811
William Watkins, *Owner*
EMP: 3 EST: 1899
SALES (est): 255.6K **Privately Held**
WEB: www.glasfordil.com
SIC: 2711 2752 2791 Newspapers: publishing only, not printed on site; commercial printing, lithographic; typesetting

Glen Carbon
Madison County

(G-10388)
HOPCROFT ELECTRIC INC
606 Glen Crossing Rd (62034-4065)
PHONE..................618 288-7302
Lola Niebruegge, *President*
Paul E Niebruegge, *Treasurer*
EMP: 7 EST: 1932
SQ FT: 2,200

Glen Carbon - Madison County (G-10389)

SALES (est): 1MM **Privately Held**
SIC: 7694 5063 3699 3621 Electric motor repair; motors, electric; electrical equipment & supplies; motors & generators

(G-10389)
JOURNAL OF BANKING AND FIN
4 Oxford Ln (62034-1531)
PHONE.................................618 203-9074
EMP: 4
SALES (est): 209.2K **Privately Held**
SIC: 2711 Newspapers, publishing & printing

(G-10390)
MECHANICS PLANING MILL INC
Also Called: Mpm Industries
1 Cottonwood Indus Park (62034-2742)
PHONE.................................618 288-3000
Jeffrey W Hanselman, *President*
Randall Hettick, *Vice Pres*
Randy Hettick, *Vice Pres*
Jeff Hanselman, *Sales Executive*
Linda Hanselman, *Manager*
◆ EMP: 30
SQ FT: 42,000
SALES (est): 6.4MM **Privately Held**
WEB: www.mpm-industries.com
SIC: 2421 3442 5072 Flooring (dressed lumber); softwood; metal doors, sash & trim; hardware

(G-10391)
WOODEN NICKEL PUB AND GRILL
171 S Main St (62034-1416)
PHONE.................................618 288-2141
Kelly Fuesting, *Officer*
EMP: 5
SALES (est): 548.2K **Privately Held**
SIC: 3356 Nickel

Glen Ellyn
Dupage County

(G-10392)
A-RELIABLE PRINTING
604 Roosevelt Rd (60137-5737)
PHONE.................................630 790-2525
Sharon Meyer, *Owner*
Ken Meyer, *Principal*
EMP: 4 EST: 2007
SALES (est): 366.6K **Privately Held**
WEB: www.areliableprinting.com
SIC: 2752 Commercial printing, offset

(G-10393)
ACCUWARE INCORPORATED
799 Roosevelt Rd 3-218 (60137-5922)
PHONE.................................630 858-8409
Steve Morris, *President*
Carrie Morris, *Treasurer*
Bill Mercer, *Director*
EMP: 10
SQ FT: 1,300
SALES (est): 1.2MM **Privately Held**
SIC: 7372 Business oriented computer software

(G-10394)
ANAMET INC (PA)
799 Roosevelt Rd 4-313 (60137-5873)
PHONE.................................217 234-8844
Joseph Venzron, *CEO*
David Wright, *Treasurer*
William Cady, *Director*
John Thomas, *Director*
EMP: 2
SQ FT: 2,000
SALES (est): 72MM **Privately Held**
SIC: 3599 3644 3829 3441 Hose, flexible metallic; electric conduits & fittings; vibration meters, analyzers & calibrators; expansion joints (structural shapes), iron or steel

(G-10395)
ANDERSON HOUSE FOUNDATION
258 Harwarden St (60137-5305)
PHONE.................................630 461-7254
Yuri Mezenko, *Exec Dir*
EMP: 1
SALES: 500K **Privately Held**
SIC: 2721 Periodicals

(G-10396)
BANTIX TECHNOLOGIES LLC
490 Pennsylvania Ave (60137-4432)
P.O. Box 2968 (60138-2968)
PHONE.................................630 446-0886
Tony Andriacchi, *Vice Pres*
Nicholas J Howard, *Mng Member*
Terra C Howard,
EMP: 3
SALES: 1.5MM **Privately Held**
WEB: www.bantix.com
SIC: 5734 7379 7372 Computer software & accessories; computer related consulting services; prepackaged software

(G-10397)
BARCODESOURCE INC (PA)
Also Called: Barcodesupplies.com
435 Pennsylvania Ave # 147 (60137-4401)
PHONE.................................630 545-9590
Michael Galiga, *President*
EMP: 7 EST: 1998
SQ FT: 1,500
SALES (est): 1.2MM **Privately Held**
WEB: www.barcodesource.com
SIC: 7372 3578 3578 Prepackaged software; bar code (magnetic ink) printers; point-of-sale devices

(G-10398)
COLES CRAFT CORPORATION
868 Baker Ct (60137-6104)
PHONE.................................630 858-8171
Eric Coles, *President*
EMP: 4
SALES (est): 334.6K **Privately Held**
SIC: 3699 Appliance cords for household electrical equipment

(G-10399)
CT GROUP INC
408 Lawrence Ave (60137-4305)
PHONE.................................708 466-8277
Tim Bogosian, *President*
EMP: 2 EST: 2018
SALES: 400K **Privately Held**
SIC: 2298 Cable, fiber

(G-10400)
DIAMOND INDUSTRIAL SALES LTD
175 Cortland Ct (60137-6481)
PHONE.................................630 858-3687
Daniel Steinbach, *President*
EMP: 5
SALES (est): 414.1K **Privately Held**
SIC: 3599 5085 Amusement park equipment; diamonds, industrial: natural, crude

(G-10401)
DREISILKER ELECTRIC MOTORS INC (PA)
352 Roosevelt Rd (60137-5692)
PHONE.................................630 469-7510
Leo Dreisilker, *President*
Richard Proud, *COO*
Susan Muehlfelt, *Vice Pres*
Rich Sawisch, *Plant Mgr*
Larry Ninis, *Prdtn Mgr*
EMP: 120 EST: 1965
SQ FT: 72,800
SALES (est): 28.3MM **Privately Held**
WEB: www.dreisilker.com
SIC: 7694 5063 Electric motor repair; motor controls, starters & relays: electric

(G-10402)
DUPAGE CHROPRACTIC CENTRE LTD
45 S Park Blvd Ste 155 (60137-6298)
PHONE.................................630 858-9780
Sally A Pepping, *Principal*
EMP: 5
SALES (est): 435.9K **Privately Held**
SIC: 3845 Patient monitoring apparatus

(G-10403)
FORREST CONSULTING
479 N Main St Ste 220 (60137-5174)
PHONE.................................630 730-9619
Lee S Crumbaugh, *Owner*
Lee F Crumbaugh, *Owner*
EMP: 5
SQ FT: 900
SALES (est): 319.9K **Privately Held**
SIC: 8748 2711 8742 8743 Publishing consultant; newspapers; marketing consulting services; public relations services

(G-10404)
H2O POD INC
Also Called: Watermat Company
490 Pennsylvania Ave (60137-4432)
P.O. Box 882320, Steamboat Springs CO (80488-2320)
PHONE.................................630 240-1769
Jay Croockston, *Vice Pres*
Robert Pole, *Mng Member*
EMP: 5
SALES (est): 203.9K **Privately Held**
SIC: 3949 Water sports equipment

(G-10405)
ICON CO
1s640 Sunnybrook Rd (60137-6451)
PHONE.................................630 545-2345
Young Bahng, *Owner*
EMP: 7
SQ FT: 7,700
SALES (est): 458.1K **Privately Held**
SIC: 3535 Conveyors & conveying equipment

(G-10406)
ILLINOIS CONVEYOR SERVICE INC
21w161 Hill Ave (60137-4851)
PHONE.................................630 469-1300
Paul Nielsen, *President*
Edward Johnson, *Admin Sec*
EMP: 6
SALES (est): 1.1MM **Privately Held**
SIC: 3535 Conveyors & conveying equipment

(G-10407)
KOP INDUSTRIES CORPORATED INC
22w440 Armitage Ave (60137-2891)
PHONE.................................630 930-9516
Art Kopacek, *Vice Pres*
EMP: 5 EST: 2015
SALES: 1.5MM **Privately Held**
SIC: 3999 5199 Atomizers, toiletry; automobile fabrics

(G-10408)
LEDRETROFITTING INC
2n138 Bernice Ave (60137-3136)
PHONE.................................815 347-5047
EMP: 4
SALES: 100K **Privately Held**
SIC: 3999 Manufacturing Ofled Retrofits

(G-10409)
LEYDEN LAWN SPRINKLERS
23w274 North Ave (60137-3474)
PHONE.................................630 665-5520
Karen Lipscomb, *President*
EMP: 24
SALES (est): 2.6MM **Privately Held**
SIC: 3432 Lawn hose nozzles & sprinklers

(G-10410)
LOOP BELT INDUSTRIES INC
21w171 Hill Ave (60137-4851)
PHONE.................................630 469-1300
Kevin Blake, *President*
Tavia Oury, *Admin Sec*
EMP: 9
SALES (est): 844.7K **Privately Held**
SIC: 3535 Conveyors & conveying equipment

(G-10411)
MACHINE & DESIGN
767 Willis St (60137-4266)
PHONE.................................630 858-6416
William Hansen, *Partner*
EMP: 2
SALES (est): 238K **Privately Held**
WEB: www.customtripletrees.com
SIC: 3599 3281 Machine shop, jobbing & repair; cut stone & stone products

(G-10412)
MATTARUSKY INC
1n272 Pleasant Ave (60137-3751)
PHONE.................................630 469-4125
Ann M Litavsky, *President*
Matt Litavsky, *Vice Pres*
EMP: 2 EST: 1998
SALES: 2.4MM **Privately Held**
SIC: 5199 3229 Christmas novelties; Christmas tree ornaments, from glass produced on-site

(G-10413)
MIDWEST BIOFLUIDS INC
22w080 Glen Valley Dr (60137-6854)
PHONE.................................630 790-9708
Michael W Rooney, *President*
EMP: 6
SALES (est): 670K **Privately Held**
SIC: 2834 Pharmaceutical preparations

(G-10414)
NAMEONANYTHINGCOM LLC
23w328 Great Western Ave (60137-3632)
PHONE.................................630 545-2642
Seaborg Steve, *Principal*
EMP: 2 EST: 2015
SALES (est): 207.4K **Privately Held**
SIC: 2752 Commercial printing, lithographic

(G-10415)
OBERWEIS DAIRY INC
651 E Roosevelt St (60137)
PHONE.................................630 801-6100
Paul Davison, *Manager*
EMP: 25
SALES (corp-wide): 249.7MM **Privately Held**
SIC: 2026 5963 5451 Milk processing (pasteurizing, homogenizing, bottling); milk delivery; milk; ice cream (packaged)
PA: Oberweis Dairy, Inc.
  951 Ice Cream Dr
  North Aurora IL 60542
  630 801-6100

(G-10416)
OLIVE AND VINNIES
449 N Main St (60137-5123)
PHONE.................................630 534-6457
Gary Evanson, *Owner*
EMP: 3
SALES (est): 200K **Privately Held**
SIC: 2079 5149 Olive oil; specialty food items

(G-10417)
PARTNERS RESOURCE INC
831 Woodland Dr (60137-4246)
PHONE.................................630 620-9161
Gregory J Yangas, *President*
Richard J Yangas, *President*
Claudia Yangas, *Project Mgr*
Sabrena Ocasio, *Accounts Exec*
EMP: 3
SALES (est): 469K **Privately Held**
WEB: www.partnersresource.com
SIC: 2531 8742 Public building & related furniture; sales (including sales management) consultant

(G-10418)
PEANUT BUTTER PARTNERS LLC
564 Crescent Blvd (60137)
PHONE.................................847 489-5322
Lawrence Hanson, *Principal*
EMP: 3 EST: 2012
SALES (est): 364.9K **Privately Held**
SIC: 2099 Peanut butter

(G-10419)
SIGN IDENTITY INC
415 Taft Ave Ste 1b (60137-6214)
PHONE.................................630 942-1400
Tom Van Winkle, *President*
Steve Peterson, *Production*
EMP: 3
SQ FT: 2,200
SALES (est): 359K **Privately Held**
SIC: 3993 7389 Signs, not made in custom sign painting shops; laminating service

▲ = Import ▼=Export
◆ =Import/Export

GEOGRAPHIC SECTION

Glendale Heights - Dupage County (G-10447)

(G-10420)
STAR SLEIGH
716 Crescent Blvd (60137-4208)
PHONE.................................630 858-2576
Mike Wilson, *Owner*
EMP: 15
SALES (est): 1MM **Privately Held**
SIC: 3944 Child restraint seats, automotive

(G-10421)
TEKNO INDUSTRIES INC (PA)
1200 Roosevelt Rd Ste 200 (60137-7808)
PHONE.................................630 766-6960
Ernest C Karras, *President*
Joseph Vodraska, *Vice Pres*
John G Karones, *Admin Sec*
EMP: 16
SALES (est): 3.4MM **Privately Held**
SIC: 3661 Telephone & telegraph apparatus

(G-10422)
TOA RESOURCE
374 Sandhurst Cir Apt 3 (60137-6666)
PHONE.................................312 317-3957
Tom Adler, *Owner*
EMP: 4
SALES (est): 700K **Privately Held**
SIC: 2752 Commercial printing, offset

(G-10423)
VIBRA-TECH ENGINEERS INC
Also Called: Vibra Tech
777 Roosevelt Rd Ste 110 (60137-5911)
PHONE.................................630 858-0681
Dane Tittman, *Manager*
EMP: 5
SALES (corp-wide): 13.1MM **Privately Held**
SIC: 3829 8711 Measuring & controlling devices; professional engineer
PA: Vibra-Tech Engineers, Inc.
  109 E 1st St
  Hazleton PA 18201
  570 455-5861

(G-10424)
WARPHOLE LLC
364 Pnnsylvnia Ave Ste 20 (60137)
PHONE.................................866 471-6464
Arturo Angel, *President*
EMP: 6
SALES (est): 323.4K **Privately Held**
SIC: 3949 Sporting & athletic goods

Glenarm
Sangamon County

(G-10425)
GRECO GRAPHICS INC
22 Sugar Creek Ln (62536-6524)
PHONE.................................217 483-2877
David Greco, *President*
EMP: 5
SALES (est): 105.6K **Privately Held**
SIC: 7336 2284 2759 Commercial art & graphic design; embroidery thread; promotional printing

(G-10426)
LINCOLNLAND ARCHTCTRAL GRPHICS
Also Called: Lincolnland Graphics
12 Covered Bridge Acres (62536-6529)
PHONE.................................217 629-9009
Karen Moore, *President*
EMP: 3
SALES (est): 200K **Privately Held**
SIC: 3993 5999 Signs & advertising specialties; banners, flags, decals & posters

(G-10427)
RAYS COUNTERTOP SHOP INC
125 Robb St (62536)
P.O. Box 46 (62536-0046)
PHONE.................................217 483-2514
Raymond Drendel, *CEO*
EMP: 12
SQ FT: 15,000
SALES (est): 500K **Privately Held**
SIC: 3131 5211 2541 5023 Counters; counter tops; wood partitions & fixtures; kitchenware; kitchen & bathroom remodeling; cabinet & finish carpentry

Glencoe
Cook County

(G-10428)
ARBY GRAPHIC SERVICE INC
676 Willow Tree Ln (60022-1039)
PHONE.................................847 763-0900
Richard Baruch, *CEO*
EMP: 12 **EST:** 1956
SALES (est): 1.1MM **Privately Held**
SIC: 7389 2791 2752 Brokers' services; typesetting; commercial printing, lithographic

(G-10429)
ELLIOTT JSJ & ASSOCIATES INC
Also Called: Directions Magazine
194 Green Bay Rd (60022-2126)
PHONE.................................847 242-0412
Jane Elliott, *President*
Johnny Elliott, *Administration*
EMP: 6
SALES: 800K **Privately Held**
SIC: 2741

(G-10430)
INTERNATIONAL SILVER PLATING
Also Called: International Locksmith
364 Park Ave (60022-1553)
PHONE.................................847 835-0705
David Hartley, *President*
Joyce Hartley, *President*
EMP: 3
SALES (est): 235.1K **Privately Held**
WEB: www.isilverplating.com
SIC: 5932 3471 Art objects, antique; plating of metals or formed products

(G-10431)
INTERNTNAL ICE BGGING SYSTEMS
234 Dennis Ln (60022-1320)
PHONE.................................312 633-4000
David C Makowski, *Principal*
EMP: 6
SALES (est): 880.7K **Privately Held**
WEB: www.iibsllc.com
SIC: 5078 2097 Commercial refrigeration equipment; manufactured ice; ice cubes

(G-10432)
MI-TE FAST PRINTERS INC
Also Called: Mi-Te Printing & Graphics
311 Park Ave (60022-1525)
PHONE.................................312 236-3278
Susan Davis, *Manager*
EMP: 5 **Privately Held**
SIC: 2752 2759 Commercial printing, offset; commercial printing
PA: Mi-Te Fast Printers, Inc
  180 W Washington St Fl 2
  Chicago IL 60602

(G-10433)
PANACHE EDITIONS LTD
Also Called: Art of Running, The
234 Dennis Ln (60022-1320)
PHONE.................................847 921-8574
Donna Macleod, *Partner*
Andrew Macleod, *Partner*
EMP: 5
SALES (est): 390.4K **Privately Held**
SIC: 2741 7389 Posters: publishing only, not printed on site; interior designer

(G-10434)
WHITNEY FOODS INC
687 Country Ln (60022-2016)
PHONE.................................773 842-8511
Whitney Blake Fitzgerald, *President*
Brian Key, *Opers Dir*
Ed Princell, *Sales Staff*
EMP: 12
SALES (est): 2MM **Privately Held**
WEB: www.whitneyfoods.com
SIC: 2099 Food preparations

Glendale Heights
Dupage County

(G-10435)
A J R INTERNATIONAL INC (PA)
300 Regency Dr (60139-2283)
PHONE.........................800 232-3965
James Oesterreich, *President*
Mark Pustil, *Vice Pres*
Steve Wills, *Opers Mgr*
EMP: 58
SQ FT: 56,000
SALES: 21MM **Privately Held**
SIC: 7629 3629 7622 7699 Electrical repair shops; electronic generation equipment; radio & television repair; customizing services

(G-10436)
ATLAS DIE LLC
2000 Bloomingdale Rd # 235 (60139-2182)
PHONE.................................630 351-5140
Ed Singleton, *Branch Mgr*
EMP: 56
SALES (corp-wide): 82MM **Privately Held**
SIC: 3423 3544 Cutting dies, except metal cutting; industrial molds
HQ: Atlas Die, Llc
  2000 Middlebury St
  Elkhart IN 46516
  574 295-0050

(G-10437)
AVANTI ENGINEERING INC (PA)
200 W Lake Dr (60139-4825)
PHONE.................................630 260-1333
Rocco Bratta, *President*
Rita J Bratta, *Corp Secy*
Nick Bratta, *Vice Pres*
Don Maxwell, *QC Mgr*
EMP: 10
SQ FT: 55,000
SALES (est): 2.3MM **Privately Held**
SIC: 3451 Screw machine products

(G-10438)
BIMBO BAKERIES USA INC
1695 Glen Ellyn Rd (60139-2503)
PHONE.................................630 469-4579
Larry Bilello, *Branch Mgr*
EMP: 4 **Privately Held**
WEB: www.arnoldbread.com
SIC: 2051 Bread, cake & related products
HQ: Bimbo Bakeries Usa, Inc
  255 Business Center Dr # 200
  Horsham PA 19044
  215 347-5500

(G-10439)
BODYCOTE THERMAL PROC INC
194 Internationale Blvd (60139-2094)
PHONE.................................630 221-0385
Ian Nichols, *Branch Mgr*
EMP: 5
SALES (corp-wide): 929.6MM **Privately Held**
WEB: www.bodycote.com
SIC: 3398 Metal heat treating
HQ: Bodycote Thermal Processing, Inc.
  12750 Merit Dr Ste 1400
  Dallas TX 75251
  214 904-2420

(G-10440)
CAPITAL PTTERN MODEL WORKS INC
410 Windy Point Dr (60139-2177)
PHONE.................................630 469-8200
Douglas Steffey, *President*
Lynn Steffey, *Vice Pres*
EMP: 8 **EST:** 1990
SQ FT: 11,500
SALES: 2.3MM **Privately Held**
WEB: www.cpm-industries.com
SIC: 3999 3543 Models, general, except toy; industrial patterns

(G-10441)
CARD PRSNLZATION SOLUTIONS LLC
80 Internationale Blvd C (60139-2000)
PHONE.................................630 543-2630
Jim Cooney, *General Mgr*
Grace Garritano, *Manager*
Chris Fuchs, *Director*
EMP: 30
SALES (corp-wide): 25.8MM **Privately Held**
SIC: 2752 7331 2759 Commercial printing, lithographic; direct mail advertising services; commercial printing
PA: Card Personalization Solutions Co., Llc
  7520 Morris Ct Ste 100
  Allentown PA 18106
  610 231-1860

(G-10442)
CASTLE METAL PRODUCTS CORP
1947 Quincy Ct (60139-2045)
PHONE.................................847 806-4540
Gary M Castle, *President*
EMP: 5
SALES (est): 871.3K **Privately Held**
SIC: 3444 Roof deck, sheet metal

(G-10443)
CHOICE CABINET CHICAGO
2000 Bloomingdale Rd # 135 (60139-2100)
PHONE.................................630 599-1099
Barbara Regan, *Principal*
EMP: 6
SALES (est): 891.2K **Privately Held**
WEB: www.choicecabinetchicago.com
SIC: 2434 Wood kitchen cabinets

(G-10444)
COMMUNICATION TECHNOLOGIES INC
Also Called: Data Management Center
188 Internationale Blvd (60139-2094)
PHONE.................................630 384-0900
Dale Dembski, *President*
Don Havis, *President*
Sandeep Patel, *Prdtn Mgr*
Forest Mayberry, *Sales Staff*
EMP: 33
SQ FT: 20,000
SALES (est): 9MM **Privately Held**
SIC: 2752 7331 7389 Promotional printing, lithographic; direct mail advertising services; telemarketing services; subscription fulfillment services: magazine, newspaper, etc.

(G-10445)
CORNELIUS INC (DH)
101 Regency Dr (60139-2206)
PHONE.................................630 539-6850
Tim Hubbard, *CEO*
Alen Duncan, *President*
◆ **EMP:** 300 **EST:** 1935
SALES (est): 164MM
SALES (corp-wide): 327.2B **Publicly Held**
WEB: www.cornelius.com
SIC: 3585 3556 3586 Soda fountain & beverage dispensing equipment & parts; food products machinery; measuring & dispensing pumps

(G-10446)
CPM INDUSTRIES
410 Windy Point Dr (60139-2177)
PHONE.................................630 469-8200
Lance Steffey, *Vice Pres*
EMP: 2 **EST:** 2014
SALES (est): 200.2K **Privately Held**
SIC: 3999 Manufacturing industries

(G-10447)
DOUBLE IMAGE PRESS INC
151 N Brandon Dr (60139-2039)
PHONE.................................630 893-6777
Carole Anderson, *President*
EMP: 10
SALES (est): 613.6K **Privately Held**
SIC: 2752 Commercial printing, lithographic

Glendale Heights - Dupage County (G-10448)

(G-10448)
ELMED INCORPORATED
35 N Brandon Dr (60139-2024)
PHONE..................................224 353-6446
Werner Hausner, *President*
Hermine Hausner, *Shareholder*
Karl Hausner, *Shareholder*
EMP: 22
SQ FT: 25,000
SALES (est): 3.3MM **Privately Held**
WEB: www.elmed.com
SIC: 3842 3841 3827 3845 Surgical appliances & supplies; surgical & medical instruments; optical instruments & lenses; cardiographs

(G-10449)
ENDERS PROCESS EQUIPMENT CORP
Also Called: Enders Engineering
746 Armitage Ave (60139-3356)
P.O. Box 308, Glen Ellyn (60138-0308)
PHONE..................................630 469-3787
Joseph T Enders, *President*
EMP: 6
SQ FT: 250
SALES (est): 924.1K **Privately Held**
SIC: 5084 8711 3567 Pollution control equipment, air (environmental); pollution control equipment, water (environmental); consulting engineer; incinerators, metal: domestic or commercial

(G-10450)
FEDEX GROUND PACKAGE SYS INC
115 W Lake Dr Ste 100 (60139-4882)
PHONE..................................800 463-3339
EMP: 4
SALES (corp-wide): 69.6B **Publicly Held**
SIC: 2759 5099 7334 Commercial printing; signs, except electric; photocopying & duplicating services
HQ: Fedex Ground Package System, Inc.
1000 Fed Ex Dr
Coraopolis PA 15108
800 463-3339

(G-10451)
G T L TECHNOLOGIES INC
Also Called: G.T.L. International
413 2nd Pl Ste 100 (60139-3505)
P.O. Box 42, Glen Ellyn (60138-0042)
PHONE..................................630 469-9818
Brian Xue, *President*
WEI Song, *Admin Sec*
EMP: 4
SALES: 800K **Privately Held**
SIC: 3469 Machine parts, stamped or pressed metal

(G-10452)
GATEWAY SCREW & RIVET INC
301 High Grove Blvd (60139-2256)
PHONE..................................630 539-2232
Richard L Gunderson, *Owner*
Randall T Gunderson, *Admin Sec*
▲ **EMP:** 30 EST: 1954
SALES (est): 5.2MM **Privately Held**
WEB: www.gatewayscrew.com
SIC: 3452 5072 Screws, metal; screws

(G-10453)
GLENDALE WOODWORKING
641 E North Ave (60139-3561)
PHONE..................................630 545-1520
Ben Malekian, *Owner*
EMP: 4
SALES (est): 395.8K **Privately Held**
SIC: 2431 Millwork

(G-10454)
GLOBAL INDUSTRIES INC
1879 Internationale Blvd (60139-2097)
PHONE..................................630 681-2818
Derek Watson, *Warehouse Mgr*
Lynnette Poole, *Manager*
EMP: 11
SALES (corp-wide): 109.9MM **Privately Held**
SIC: 2521 Wood office furniture
PA: Global Industries, Inc.
17 W Stow Rd
Marlton NJ 08053
856 596-3390

(G-10455)
GODING ELECTRIC COMPANY
686 E Fullerton Ave (60139-2597)
PHONE..................................630 858-7700
James M Goding, *President*
David Goding, *Vice Pres*
John Goding, *Vice Pres*
Katherine Orourke, *Executive Asst*
Rosie Nelson, *Education*
EMP: 14
SQ FT: 13,000
SALES (est): 4.3MM **Privately Held**
WEB: www.goding.com
SIC: 7694 5999 5063 Electric motor repair; motors, electric; motors, electric; motor controls, starters & relays: electric

(G-10456)
HOERBIGER-ORIGA CORPORATION
100 W Lake Dr (60139-4818)
PHONE..................................800 283-1377
Joseph M Hughes, *President*
Joseph H Mihalko, *Corp Secy*
▲ **EMP:** 55 EST: 1978
SQ FT: 56,000
SALES (est): 8.5MM **Privately Held**
SIC: 3443 5084 Cylinders, pressure: metal plate; industrial machinery & equipment

(G-10457)
HUDAPACK MTAL TREATING ILL INC
550 Mitchell Rd (60139-2581)
PHONE..................................630 793-1916
Gary Huss, *President*
Earl Pack, *Vice Pres*
EMP: 40
SQ FT: 42,000
SALES (est): 9.5MM **Privately Held**
SIC: 3398 Metal heat treating

(G-10458)
HYDAC TECHNOLOGY CORP
Also Called: Hydraulic Division
445 Windy Point Dr (60139-2196)
PHONE..................................630 545-0800
Gordon Dow, *Engineer*
Andrew Krajnik, *Manager*
Paul Smith, *Manager*
EMP: 50
SALES (corp-wide): 224.4MM **Privately Held**
WEB: www.hydac-na.com
SIC: 3492 Hose & tube fittings & assemblies, hydraulic/pneumatic
HQ: Hydac Technology Corp.
2260 City Line Rd
Bethlehem PA 18017
610 266-0100

(G-10459)
I T W RAMSET
700 High Grove Blvd (60139-2277)
PHONE..................................630 825-7900
John Sulit, *Owner*
EMP: 2
SALES (est): 236.4K **Privately Held**
SIC: 3546 Power-driven handtools

(G-10460)
ILLINOIS TOOL WORKS INC
ITW Commercial Cnstr N Amer
700 High Grove Blvd (60139-2277)
PHONE..................................630 825-7900
Timm Fields, *General Mgr*
EMP: 40
SALES (corp-wide): 14.1B **Publicly Held**
WEB: www.itw.com
SIC: 3672 Printed circuit boards
PA: Illinois Tool Works Inc.
155 Harlem Ave
Glenview IL 60025
847 724-7500

(G-10461)
INDUSTRIAL PALLETS LLC
1462 Glen Ellyn Rd (60139-3304)
PHONE..................................708 351-8783
Anwar Cantarero,
EMP: 3
SALES (est): 298.5K **Privately Held**
SIC: 2448 Pallets, wood

(G-10462)
J N R CUSTO-MATIC SCREW INC
200 W Lake Dr (60139-4825)
PHONE..................................630 260-1333
Joseph J Bratta, *President*
Nicholas C Bratta, *Vice Pres*
Rocco J Bratta, *Vice Pres*
Briana Pape, *Asst Controller*
Rita J Bratta, *Admin Sec*
▲ **EMP:** 62
SQ FT: 55,000
SALES: 12.2MM **Privately Held**
SIC: 3451 Screw machine products

(G-10463)
JDS PRINTING INC
1709 President St (60139-2019)
PHONE..................................630 208-1195
Abdul Mandani, *President*
Mariam Mandani, *Director*
EMP: 4
SQ FT: 1,375
SALES (est): 100K **Privately Held**
SIC: 2752 2791 5943 Commercial printing, offset; typesetting; office forms & supplies

(G-10464)
KKSP PRECISION MACHINING LLC (PA)
1688 Glen Ellyn Rd (60139-2504)
PHONE..................................630 260-1735
Dave Dolan, *President*
Ken Duffy, *General Mgr*
Dave Beller, *Vice Pres*
Mark Murray, *Vice Pres*
Samual Forsyth, *Engineer*
▲ **EMP:** 100
SQ FT: 85,000
SALES (est): 41.9MM **Privately Held**
WEB: www.kksp.com
SIC: 3599 Machine shop, jobbing & repair

(G-10465)
KRONOS FOODS CORP (PA)
1 Kronos (60139-1965)
PHONE..................................224 353-5400
Howard C Eirinberg, *CEO*
Elena Gatti, *Vice Pres*
Barbara Mocherek, *Production*
Laura Wika, *Human Resources*
Katherine Kotowski, *Marketing Staff*
▼ **EMP:** 350
SQ FT: 210,000
SALES (est): 108MM **Privately Held**
SIC: 2013 Prepared beef products from purchased beef

(G-10466)
LECTRO STIK CORP
Also Called: Stikkiworks Co
1957 Quincy Ct (60139-2090)
PHONE..................................630 894-1355
Penny Press Crow, *President*
▲ **EMP:** 26
SQ FT: 25,000
SALES (est): 4.2MM **Privately Held**
WEB: www.stikkiworks.com
SIC: 3952 2891 Wax, artists'; adhesives & sealants

(G-10467)
LENZE AMERICAS
125 Wall St (60139-1956)
PHONE..................................224 653-8119
▲ **EMP:** 4 EST: 2011
SALES (est): 340.5K **Privately Held**
SIC: 3999 Manufacturing industries

(G-10468)
LIFT-ALL COMPANY INC
1620 Fullerton Ct Ste 400 (60139-2754)
PHONE..................................630 534-6860
Steve Pacilio, *Manager*
Don Hauswirth, *Executive*
EMP: 43 **Privately Held**
SIC: 3496 Miscellaneous fabricated wire products
HQ: Lift-All Company, Inc.
1909 Mcfarland Dr
Landisville PA 17538
717 898-6615

(G-10469)
LINDGREN FAMILY LLC
400 High Grove Blvd (60139-4019)
PHONE..................................630 307-7200
Wayne Martin, *Principal*
EMP: 2
SALES (est): 323K **Privately Held**
SIC: 3825 Instruments to measure electricity

(G-10470)
M-WAVE CONTROLS LLC (PA)
100 High Grove Blvd (60139-2276)
PHONE..................................630 562-5550
Turek Joseph, *Principal*
Robert Alanis, *Manager*
John Curcio, *Director*
EMP: 22 EST: 2014
SALES (est): 7.9MM **Privately Held**
WEB: www.mwav.com
SIC: 3672 Printed circuit boards

(G-10471)
M-WAVE INTERNATIONAL LLC
100 High Grove Blvd (60139-2276)
PHONE..................................630 562-5550
Joseph A Turek, *President*
Bob Duke, *Vice Pres*
Bill Joseph, *Vice Pres*
Robert Alanis, *Human Res Mgr*
Robert Duke,
▲ **EMP:** 24
SALES (est): 6.7MM **Privately Held**
SIC: 3672 Printed circuit boards

(G-10472)
MAKKAH PRINTING
1979 Bloomingdale Rd (60139-2171)
PHONE..................................630 980-2315
Mohammed Uzzaman, *Owner*
EMP: 5
SQ FT: 1,500
SALES (est): 458.4K **Privately Held**
WEB: www.makkahprinting.com
SIC: 2752 Commercial printing, offset

(G-10473)
MARSHALL MOLD INC
Also Called: Marshall Mold & Engineering
1934 Bentley Ct Ste A (60139-4200)
PHONE..................................630 582-1800
Dean Stout, *President*
Justin Stout, *Engineer*
EMP: 9 EST: 1987
SQ FT: 6,200
SALES: 1.3MM **Privately Held**
SIC: 3544 Industrial molds

(G-10474)
MEDEFIL INC (PA)
250 Windy Point Dr (60139-3805)
PHONE..................................630 682-4600
Pradeep Aggarwal, *President*
Sandeep Aggarwal, *Vice Pres*
Richard Rysavy, *QA Dir*
Riddhi Saiyad, *Research*
Randy Blackwell, *Sales Staff*
▲ **EMP:** 65
SALES (est): 15MM **Privately Held**
WEB: www.medefilinc.com
SIC: 2834 Pharmaceutical preparations

(G-10475)
MID-AMERICA TAPING REELING INC (PA)
Also Called: Mid-America Government Supply
121 Exchange Blvd (60139-2095)
PHONE..................................630 629-6646
Barbara Pauls, *President*
Sue Lauritzen, *Vice Pres*
Ed Walton, *Vice Pres*
Chris Pauls, *VP Sales*
Enrique Acquart, *Marketing Staff*
▲ **EMP:** 95
SQ FT: 18,800
SALES (est): 11.3MM **Privately Held**
SIC: 7694 Coil winding service; rewinding stators

(G-10476)
MOBILE AIR INC
380 Windy Point Dr (60139-2176)
PHONE..................................847 755-0586
Ryan Boyle, *Manager*
EMP: 12

Glendale Heights - Dupage County (G-10502)

SALES (est): 933.5K **Privately Held**
SIC: 7359 3479 Equipment rental & leasing; name plates: engraved, etched, etc.
PA: Mobile Air, Inc
 1821 Northwood Dr
 Troy MI 48084

(G-10477)
MORRELL INCORPORATED
340 Windy Point Dr (60139-2176)
PHONE.................................630 858-4600
Robert Halladay, *Sales Engr*
Mark Garrett, *Manager*
EMP: 10
SALES (corp-wide): 96.6MM **Privately Held**
WEB: www.morrellinc.com
SIC: 5084 5065 3621 3643 Hydraulic systems equipment & supplies; electronic parts; motors & generators; power line cable; metal finishing equipment for plating, etc.
PA: Morrell Incorporated
 3333 Bald Mountain Rd
 Auburn Hills MI 48326
 248 373-1600

(G-10478)
NESTLE PREPARED FOODS COMPANY
601 Wall St (60139-1906)
PHONE.................................630 671-3721
Scott Agan, *General Mgr*
EMP: 495
SALES (corp-wide): 93.5B **Privately Held**
WEB: www.nestle.com
SIC: 2038 Dinners, frozen & packaged
HQ: Nestle Prepared Foods Company
 30003 Bainbridge Rd
 Solon OH 44139
 440 248-3600

(G-10479)
NIDEC-SHIMPO AMERICA CORP
175 Wall St (60139-1956)
PHONE.................................630 924-7138
Jeff Williams, *President*
Masatoshi Onishi, *Vice Pres*
Kossi Aziaka, *Warehouse Mgr*
Dan Zupancic, *Opers Staff*
Tyler Miller, *Engineer*
▲ **EMP:** 48
SQ FT: 75,000
SALES (est): 31.3MM **Privately Held**
SIC: 5085 3566 5084 3825 Power transmission equipment & apparatus; speed changers, drives & gears; industrial machinery & equipment; instruments to measure electricity; ceramic construction materials, excluding refractory
HQ: Nidec-Shimpo Corporation
 1, Terada, Kotari
 Nagaokakyo KYO 617-0

(G-10480)
NORTHSTAR INDUSTRIES INC
Also Called: Northstar Metal Products
591 Mitchell Rd (60139-2582)
PHONE.................................630 446-7800
David Boggess, *CEO*
Linda C Boggess, *Ch of Bd*
Margarito Alvarez, *Opers Staff*
Jeff True, *Opers Staff*
Paul Caravello, *Production*
▲ **EMP:** 109 **EST:** 1994
SQ FT: 85,000
SALES (est): 25.4MM **Privately Held**
WEB: www.northstarmetal.com
SIC: 3444 Sheet metalwork

(G-10481)
OMNI VISION INC
2000 Bloomingdale Rd # 245 (60139-2198)
PHONE.................................630 893-1720
Thomas Fair, *President*
▲ **EMP:** 42
SQ FT: 15,000
SALES (est): 5.4MM **Privately Held**
SIC: 3663 3577 Television monitors; computer peripheral equipment

(G-10482)
OVAL FIRE PRODUCTS CORPORATION
Also Called: Oval Brand Fire Products
115 W Lake Dr Ste 300 (60139-4824)
PHONE.................................630 635-5000
Kevin Kozlowski, *President*
Travis Dukes, *Sales Mgr*
EMP: 8
SQ FT: 16,000
SALES (est): 197.1K **Privately Held**
SIC: 3999 5999 Fire extinguishers, portable; fire extinguishers; banners

(G-10483)
PELCO TOOL & MOLD INC
181 Exchange Blvd (60139-2095)
PHONE.................................630 871-1010
Richard Truhlar, *President*
Jim Griswold, *Business Mgr*
Roger Wittersheim, *Vice Pres*
Rick Hale, *Plant Mgr*
Joel Bianchi, *Project Mgr*
EMP: 30 **EST:** 1963
SQ FT: 16,000
SALES: 6.6MM **Privately Held**
WEB: www.pelcotoolinc.com
SIC: 3544 Special dies & tools

(G-10484)
PREFERRED PRESS INC
1934 Bentley Ct Ste D (60139-4200)
P.O. Box 773, Wayne (60184-0773)
PHONE.................................630 980-9799
Frank Fanella, *President*
Kenneth Bork, *Admin Sec*
EMP: 6
SQ FT: 3,200
SALES (est): 668.1K **Privately Held**
SIC: 2752 Commercial printing, offset

(G-10485)
PRINTING SYSTEM
1935 Brandon Ct Ste A (60139-2199)
P.O. Box 88296, Carol Stream (60188-0296)
PHONE.................................630 339-5900
Ruel Lacsam, *Principal*
EMP: 3
SALES (est): 160K **Privately Held**
SIC: 2759 Commercial printing

(G-10486)
R C COIL SPRING MFG CO INC
490 Mitchell Rd (60139-2580)
PHONE.................................630 790-3500
Paul Sawko, *President*
Chester Sawko, *Chairman*
Mitchell Sawko, *Exec VP*
Mark Sawko, *Vice Pres*
Gregory E Dembek, *Treasurer*
EMP: 40
SQ FT: 57,000
SALES: 4MM **Privately Held**
WEB: www.rccoilspring.com
SIC: 3495 3469 Wire springs; metal stampings

(G-10487)
RAIN CREEK BAKING CORP
1 Sexton Dr (60139-1965)
PHONE.................................559 347-9960
EMP: 4 **EST:** 2011
SALES (est): 231.5K **Privately Held**
SIC: 2051 Bread, cake & related products

(G-10488)
RIGHTWAY PRINTING INC
Also Called: Allegra Print & Imaging
460 Windy Point Dr (60139-2177)
PHONE.................................630 790-0444
Gary Blaski, *President*
Larry Naselli, *Sales Mgr*
Cynthia Blaski, *Admin Sec*
EMP: 12
SQ FT: 6,000
SALES (est): 1.7MM **Privately Held**
SIC: 2752 2791 2789 Commercial printing, offset; typesetting; bookbinding & related work

(G-10489)
ROBERT C WEISHEIT CO INC
999 Regency Dr (60139-2281)
PHONE.................................847 648-4991
Robert C Weisheit, *President*
Bill Brubaker, *Plant Supt*
Andy Weisheit, *Prdtn Mgr*
Bill Serritella, *Human Resources*
EMP: 50 **EST:** 1946
SQ FT: 47,000
SALES: 9MM **Privately Held**
WEB: www.weisheit.com
SIC: 3599 Machine shop, jobbing & repair

(G-10490)
SANDMANCOM INC
399 Wall St Ste B (60139-1987)
PHONE.................................630 980-7710
Charles Hall, *President*
Ronald Bailey, *Manager*
William Widmann, *Manager*
Andrew Tuszynski, *Admin Sec*
EMP: 7
SQ FT: 5,000
SALES (est): 460.6K **Privately Held**
SIC: 3661 Telephone station equipment & parts, wire

(G-10491)
SCHMIT LABORATORIES INC
500 Wall St (60139-1988)
PHONE.................................773 476-0072
Robert G Schmit, *President*
Cathy Barton, *Office Mgr*
EMP: 48
SQ FT: 100,000
SALES (est): 7.1MM **Privately Held**
SIC: 3999 7389 2844 Hair & hair-based products; packaging & labeling services; toilet preparations

(G-10492)
SCHUBERT ENVIRONMENTAL EQP INC
Also Called: Replace Air
2000 Bloomingdale Rd # 115 (60139-2181)
PHONE.................................630 307-9400
John Schubert, *President*
Tom Martus, *Vice Pres*
EMP: 12 **EST:** 1979
SQ FT: 12,000
SALES (est): 1.5MM **Privately Held**
SIC: 3444 3564 Sheet metalwork; air cleaning systems

(G-10493)
SCREWS INDUSTRIES INC
301 High Grove Blvd (60139-2256)
PHONE.................................630 539-9200
Dennis Fiedler, *President*
▲ **EMP:** 55
SQ FT: 75,000
SALES (est): 13.1MM **Privately Held**
SIC: 3452 3451 3316 Bolts, metal; nuts, metal; screws, metal; screw machine products; cold finishing of steel shapes

(G-10494)
SI ENTERPRISES INC
Also Called: American Fastening Systems
301 High Grove Blvd (60139-2256)
PHONE.................................630 539-9200
Dennis Fiedler, *President*
▲ **EMP:** 3
SALES (est): 172K **Privately Held**
SIC: 3452 Screws, metal

(G-10495)
SIGN
Also Called: Sign-A-Rama
399 Wall St Ste J (60139-1987)
PHONE.................................630 351-8400
Aaron Growski, *Owner*
EMP: 3
SALES (est): 427.5K **Privately Held**
SIC: 3993 Signs & advertising specialties

(G-10496)
SOUND ENHANCEMENT PRODUCTS INC
Also Called: S.E. P. I.
100 High Grove Blvd (60139-2276)
PHONE.................................847 639-4646
Randy Wright, *President*
Scott Flesher, *Vice Pres*
Ken Scott, *Vice Pres*
▲ **EMP:** 32
SQ FT: 38,000
SALES (est): 5.1MM **Privately Held**
SIC: 3651 Household audio equipment

(G-10497)
SPIROTHERM INC
25 N Brandon Dr (60139-2024)
PHONE.................................630 307-2662
Eric Roffelsen, *President*
Paul Middlebrook, *Regional Mgr*
Matt Pefley, *Regional Mgr*
Falke Bruinsma, *Exec VP*
John Coggins, *VP Sales*
▲ **EMP:** 9
SQ FT: 16,000
SALES: 4MM **Privately Held**
SIC: 3585 3433 Parts for heating, cooling & refrigeration equipment; heating equipment, except electric

(G-10498)
SPRAYING SYSTEMS CO (PA)
Also Called: Autojet Technologies
200 W North Ave (60139-3408)
PHONE.................................630 665-5000
James E Bramsen, *President*
Joe Ruelas, *President*
Mark Chanana, *Partner*
David Yates, *Area Mgr*
Dave Foley, *Vice Pres*
▲ **EMP:** 700 **EST:** 1935
SQ FT: 240,000
SALES (est): 320.3MM **Privately Held**
WEB: www.spray.com
SIC: 3499 Nozzles, spray: aerosol, paint or insecticide

(G-10499)
SPRAYING SYSTEMS MIDWEST INC
Also Called: Spraying Systems Co
N Ave And Schmale Rd (60139)
PHONE.................................630 665-5000
John A Shoemaker Jr, *President*
Dave Smith, *Vice Pres*
Don Fox, *VP Mfg*
Ronald Bonitatibus, *Sales Engr*
Brian Curtis, *Sales Engr*
◆ **EMP:** 8
SALES (est): 1.7MM
SALES (corp-wide): 320.3MM **Privately Held**
SIC: 3499 Nozzles, spray: aerosol, paint or insecticide
PA: Spraying Systems Co.
 200 W North Ave
 Glendale Heights IL 60139
 630 665-5000

(G-10500)
STERLING DIE INC
676 E Fullerton Ave (60139-2538)
PHONE.................................216 267-1300
EMP: 5
SALES (est): 270K **Privately Held**
SIC: 3544 Mfg Dies/Tools/Jigs/Fixtures

(G-10501)
STONE DESIGN INC
598 Mitchell Rd (60139-2581)
PHONE.................................630 790-5715
Jean Mitchell-Lockerbie, *Branch Mgr*
EMP: 16
SALES (est): 116.8K
SALES (corp-wide): 20.7MM **Privately Held**
SIC: 5032 3281 Marble building stone; cut stone & stone products
PA: Stone Design, Inc
 551 598 Mitchell Rd
 Glendale Heights IL 60139
 630 790-5715

(G-10502)
STONE DESIGN INC (PA)
551 598 Mitchell Rd (60139)
PHONE.................................630 790-5715
Jean Mitchell-Lockerbie, *President*
Steve Skroamovsky, *CFO*
Chris Sorrell, *Sales Staff*
Marilyn Lockerbie, *Shareholder*
Robert Lockerbie, *Admin Sec*
▲ **EMP:** 49
SQ FT: 19,500
SALES (est): 20.7MM **Privately Held**
SIC: 5032 3281 Marble building stone; cut stone & stone products

Glendale Heights - Dupage County (G-10503)

(G-10503)
STONE INSTALLATION & MAINT INC
598 Mitchell Rd (60139-2581)
PHONE.....................................630 545-2326
William Santello, *President*
EMP: 1
SALES (est): 233.1K **Privately Held**
SIC: 3272 Stone, cast concrete

(G-10504)
SUMITOMO MACHINERY CORP AMER
175 W Lake Dr (60139-4818)
PHONE.....................................630 752-0200
Steve Scott, *President*
Jeff Eggleston, *Regional Mgr*
Wade Walder, *Manager*
EMP: 25 **Privately Held**
SIC: 5063 3714 3625 3566 Power transmission equipment, electric; motor vehicle parts & accessories; relays & industrial controls; speed changers, drives & gears; iron & steel forgings
HQ: Sumitomo Machinery Corp Of America
4200 Holland Blvd
Chesapeake VA 23323
800 762-9256

(G-10505)
SUNBURST SPORTSWEAR INC (PA)
Also Called: Chicago T-Shirt Authority
95 N Brandon Dr (60139-2024)
PHONE.....................................630 717-8680
Jin-Yan Lin, *President*
John Smith, *Manager*
Judy Chun Chun Yeh Lin, *Admin Sec*
EMP: 11
SQ FT: 30,000
SALES (est): 2.6MM **Privately Held**
SIC: 7336 2759 Silk screen design; graphic arts & related design; screen printing

(G-10506)
SURGICAL INSTRUMENT SERVICE CO
Also Called: S I S
151 N Brandon Dr (60139-2039)
PHONE.....................................630 221-1988
Greg J Posdal, *CEO*
Keith Posdal, *Opers Staff*
Diane Posdal, *Treasurer*
Patricia Posdal, *Human Resources*
Bob Posdal, *Manager*
EMP: 19
SQ FT: 7,500
SALES (est): 3.5MM **Privately Held**
WEB: www.sis-usa.com
SIC: 3842 Surgical appliances & supplies

(G-10507)
SURYA ELECTRONICS INC
Also Called: Amtex
600 Windy Point Dr (60139-3802)
PHONE.....................................630 858-8000
Bharat R Patel, *President*
Bob Patel, *President*
Bill Jesse, *Opers Mgr*
William Jesse, *Senior Mgr*
▲ **EMP:** 120
SQ FT: 60,000
SALES (est): 28.8MM **Privately Held**
SIC: 3672 3823 Printed circuit boards; computer interface equipment for industrial process control

(G-10508)
SYR-TECH PERFORATING CO
325 Windy Point Dr (60139-3804)
PHONE.....................................630 942-7300
Gary T Heflen Sr, *President*
Annette Heflen, *Admin Sec*
EMP: 45
SQ FT: 40,000
SALES (est): 10.2MM **Privately Held**
SIC: 3469 Metal stampings

(G-10509)
SYSTEMSLOGIX LLC
140 W Lake Dr (60139-4818)
PHONE.....................................630 784-3113
Dennis Dicosola,
EMP: 3
SALES: 36K **Privately Held**
SIC: 7372 Business oriented computer software

(G-10510)
TARGET PLASTICS TECH CORP
400 Windy Point Dr (60139-2177)
PHONE.....................................630 545-1776
Ivan Racz, *President*
Richard Denning, *Vice Pres*
Chano Salgado, *Plant Mgr*
Tony Knatt, *Admin Sec*
EMP: 68
SQ FT: 15,000
SALES: 6MM **Privately Held**
SIC: 3089 Injection molding of plastics

(G-10511)
TIGER TOOL INC
Also Called: Tiger Tool Supply, Inc.
410 Windy Point Dr (60139-2177)
PHONE.....................................888 551-4490
Jason Steffey, *Principal*
EMP: 4
SALES (est): 445.5K **Privately Held**
SIC: 3541 Machine tools, metal cutting type

(G-10512)
TITAN METALS INC
180 W Lake Dr (60139-4818)
PHONE.....................................630 752-9700
Susan Kraus, *President*
Brad Nemec, *Treasurer*
EMP: 45
SQ FT: 37,500
SALES (est): 9MM **Privately Held**
SIC: 3444 Sheet metalwork

(G-10513)
UNITED STEEL PERFORATING/ARC
Also Called: Syr Tech Perforating
325 Windy Point Dr (60139-3804)
PHONE.....................................630 942-7300
Gary Heflen Sr, *President*
EMP: 40 **EST:** 1951
SQ FT: 40,000
SALES (est): 765.7K **Privately Held**
SIC: 3441 Fabricated structural metal

(G-10514)
VR PRINTING CO INC
1979 Bloomingdale Rd (60139-2171)
PHONE.....................................630 980-2315
Virgil Remot, *President*
EMP: 3
SQ FT: 700
SALES (est): 142.1K **Privately Held**
SIC: 2759 Commercial printing

(G-10515)
WEBSTER-HOFF CORPORATION
704 E Fullerton Ave (60139-2998)
PHONE.....................................630 858-8030
Jack T Webster, *Ch of Bd*
Bryan Webster, *President*
Tom Zwitter, *Vice Chairman*
Liaquat Babul, *Vice Pres*
Mike Winograd, *QC Dir*
▲ **EMP:** 52
SQ FT: 17,800
SALES: 8MM **Privately Held**
SIC: 3499 Friction material, made from powdered metal

(G-10516)
YORK CORRUGATED CONTAINER CORP
120 W Lake Dr (60139-4818)
PHONE.....................................630 260-2900
Arthur Bostelman Jr, *President*
William F Lewis, *Vice Pres*
Ken Neuffer, *Vice Pres*
EMP: 75 **EST:** 1962
SQ FT: 58,500
SALES (est): 20MM **Privately Held**
SIC: 2653 Boxes, corrugated: made from purchased materials

Glenview
Cook County

(G-10517)
ACRYLIC VENTURES INC
Also Called: Pease Plastics
1921 Pickwick Ln (60026-1308)
PHONE.....................................847 901-4440
Patrick Pease, *President*
Jeanne Pease, *Admin Sec*
EMP: 10
SALES: 2.2MM **Privately Held**
SIC: 3089 Plastic processing

(G-10518)
ADAMS APPLE DISTRIBUTING LP
2301 Ravine Way (60025-7627)
PHONE.....................................847 832-9900
Ellis Levin, *Partner*
Allan Kandelman, *Partner*
▲ **EMP:** 50
SALES (est): 6.5MM **Privately Held**
SIC: 3089 5199 Novelties, plastic; variety store merchandise

(G-10519)
ADDISON STEEL INC
1340 Bonnie Glen Ln (60025-3137)
PHONE.....................................847 998-9445
James Chapman, *President*
Carol Chapman, *Admin Sec*
EMP: 2
SQ FT: 1,500
SALES (est): 274.7K **Privately Held**
SIC: 3441 Fabricated structural metal

(G-10520)
ADVANCE TOOLS LLC (PA)
2456 Saranac Ln (60026-1061)
PHONE.....................................630 337-5904
Chiencheng Liu,
EMP: 2 **EST:** 2012
SALES (est): 879.3K **Privately Held**
SIC: 5137 5072 3651 2393 Handbags; hardware; loudspeakers, electrodynamic or magnetic; textile bags; duffle bags, canvas: made from purchased materials

(G-10521)
AMERICAN CLLEGE CHEST PHYSCANS (PA)
2595 Patriot Blvd (60026-8022)
PHONE.....................................224 521-9800
Robert A Musacchio, *CEO*
Stephen J Welch, *CEO*
Curt Sessler, *President*
Kate Henson, *Partner*
Carla Miller, *Editor*
EMP: 82
SQ FT: 48,500
SALES: 27.7MM **Privately Held**
SIC: 8621 2721 Medical field-related associations; periodicals

(G-10522)
AMERICAN GRAPHICS NETWORK INC
1625 Glenview Rd Unit 309 (60025-2973)
P.O. Box 869 (60025-0869)
PHONE.....................................847 729-7220
Wanda M Sclavenitis, *President*
Frank Sclavenitis, *Treasurer*
Kirk Guthrie, *Sales Staff*
EMP: 12
SQ FT: 4,200
SALES (est): 1.5MM **Privately Held**
SIC: 2759 2791 2761 2677 Screen printing; typesetting; manifold business forms; envelopes; packaging paper & plastics film, coated & laminated

(G-10523)
AMEROC EXPORT INC
Also Called: Ameroc Lubricants Export
4126 Miller Dr (60026-1026)
PHONE.....................................818 961-6169
EMP: 3 **EST:** 2010
SALES (est): 189.1K **Privately Held**
SIC: 3011 Industrial tires, pneumatic

(G-10524)
ANGEL EQUIPMENT LLC
1941 Johns Dr (60025-1615)
PHONE.....................................847 730-3938
Timothy Anderson, *Co-Owner*
EMP: 6
SALES (est): 229K **Privately Held**
SIC: 3556 Bakery machinery

(G-10525)
ANIXTER INC
2301 Patriot Blvd (60026-8020)
P.O. Box 609 (60025)
PHONE.....................................512 989-4254
EMP: 31
SALES (est): 11.6MM **Privately Held**
SIC: 3965 5251 Mfg Fasteners/Buttons/Pins Ret Hardware

(G-10526)
ANIXTER INC
2301 Patriot Blvd (60026-8020)
PHONE.....................................800 323-8167
EMP: 198
SALES (est): 104.2MM **Privately Held**
SIC: 3641 Mfg Electric Lamps

(G-10527)
APPLE RUSH COMPANY
4300 Dipaolo Ctr (60025)
PHONE.....................................847 730-5324
Robert J Corr, *Principal*
EMP: 4
SALES (est): 225.3K **Privately Held**
SIC: 2082 Malt beverages

(G-10528)
ASAHI KASEI BIOPROCESS INC
1855 Elmdale Ave (60026-1355)
PHONE.....................................847 834-0800
Osamu Matsuzaki, *President*
Nobuo Nakano, *Principal*
Tomoyuki Miyabayashi, *Vice Pres*
Christopher Nordhoff, *Vice Pres*
Kimo Sanderson, *Vice Pres*
EMP: 48
SQ FT: 24,000
SALES (est): 13.3MM **Privately Held**
SIC: 3559 5047 Pharmaceutical machinery; medical laboratory equipment
HQ: Asahi Kasei Medical Co., Ltd.
1-1-2, Yurakucho
Chiyoda-Ku TKY 100-0

(G-10529)
BELLA PHARMACEUTICALS INC
Also Called: 503b FDA Outsourcing Facility
4301 Regency Dr (60025-5209)
PHONE.....................................847 722-1692
Michael B Younan, *CEO*
EMP: 3 **EST:** 2016
SALES (est): 149.1K **Privately Held**
SIC: 2834 Pharmaceutical preparations

(G-10530)
BELTONE CORPORATION (DH)
2601 Patriot Blvd (60026-8023)
PHONE.....................................847 832-3300
Todd Murray, *President*
Dan Lanan, *Project Mgr*
Greg Kelley, *Site Mgr*
Paul Giampaolo, *Treasurer*
Ron Skubisz, *Marketing Staff*
EMP: 111
SALES (est): 62MM
SALES (corp-wide): 1.8B **Privately Held**
SIC: 3842 Hearing aids
HQ: Gn Hearing Care Corporation
8001 E Bloomington Fwy
Bloomington MN 55420
800 248-4327

(G-10531)
BERGMANN ORTHOTIC LABORATORY
1864 Johns Dr (60025-1657)
PHONE.....................................847 729-7923
David Bergmann, *Manager*
EMP: 3
SALES (est): 240.5K **Privately Held**
SIC: 3842 Orthopedic appliances

GEOGRAPHIC SECTION

Glenview - Cook County (G-10561)

(G-10532)
BOTTI STUDIO OF ARCHITECTURAL (PA)
1225 Harms Rd (60025-3253)
PHONE..................847 869-5933
Ettore C Botti, *CEO*
EMP: 40 **EST:** 1864
SALES (est): 7.8MM **Privately Held**
SIC: 3231 3446 3281 2431 Stained glass: made from purchased glass; architectural metalwork; marble, building: cut & shaped; ornamental woodwork: cornices, mantels, etc.; glass & glazing work; interior design services

(G-10533)
BOWS ARTS INC
1944 Lehigh Ave Ste C (60026-1661)
PHONE..................847 501-3161
Barbara McBride, *President*
Nilton Dasilva, *Treasurer*
Charles McBride, *Treasurer*
▲ **EMP:** 18
SALES (est): 750K **Privately Held**
SIC: 3069 7389 Rubber hair accessories;

(G-10534)
BRANMARK STRATEGY GROUP LLC
2013 Burr Oak Dr W (60025-1805)
PHONE..................847 849-9080
Richard Kerndt, *Managing Dir*
Sarah Kerndt, *Principal*
EMP: 3
SALES (est): 231.8K **Privately Held**
SIC: 3761 Guided missiles & space vehicles, research & development

(G-10535)
CHOCOLATE POTPOURRI LTD
Also Called: Chicago Toffee Co
3908 Kiess Dr (60026-1083)
PHONE..................847 729-8878
Richard Gordon, *President*
Marsha Gordon, *Vice Pres*
Robert Gordon, *Admin Sec*
EMP: 11
SQ FT: 7,800
SALES (est): 1.8MM **Privately Held**
SIC: 2066 2064 Chocolate; chocolate candy, except solid chocolate

(G-10536)
CHRISTIANICA CENTER
1807 Prairie St (60025-2921)
P.O. Box 685 (60025-0685)
PHONE..................847 657-3818
John P Gabriel, *Director*
▲ **EMP:** 4
SQ FT: 700
SALES (est): 78.3K **Privately Held**
SIC: 2731 Books: publishing only

(G-10537)
CIS SYSTEMS INC
Also Called: Ink2image
4338 Regency Dr (60025-5218)
P.O. Box 2431 (60025-6431)
PHONE..................847 827-0747
EMP: 5
SQ FT: 4,000
SALES (est): 900K **Privately Held**
SIC: 2851 5111 5085 2893 Mfg Paints/Allied Prdts Whol Print/Writing Paper Whol Industrial Supplies Mfg Printing Ink

(G-10538)
CORA LEE CANDIES INC
1844 Waukegan Rd (60025-2112)
PHONE..................847 724-2754
James Preibe, *President*
James A Priebe, *President*
EMP: 12
SQ FT: 2,600
SALES (est): 856.5K **Privately Held**
SIC: 5441 5145 2066 Candy; candy; chocolate & cocoa products

(G-10539)
CORPORATE PRINT SOURCE INC
1969 Johns Dr (60025-1615)
PHONE..................847 724-1150
James Martin, *President*
EMP: 2 **EST:** 2001

SQ FT: 500
SALES (est): 292.6K **Privately Held**
WEB: www.corprintsource.com
SIC: 2752 Commercial printing, lithographic

(G-10540)
CRYSTAL CAVE
1946 Lehigh Ave Ste E (60026-1662)
PHONE..................847 251-1160
Joseph Puehringer, *Owner*
Jenny Puehringer, *Vice Pres*
Bridgette Baggio, *Sales Associate*
EMP: 10
SQ FT: 3,400
SALES (est): 732K **Privately Held**
SIC: 3231 5719 Cut & engraved glassware: made from purchased glass; glassware

(G-10541)
DAILY MONEY MATTERS LLC
2200 Goldenrod Ln (60026-8008)
PHONE..................847 729-8393
Wendy Freimuth, *Principal*
EMP: 3 **EST:** 2010
SALES (est): 139.4K **Privately Held**
SIC: 2711 Newspapers, publishing & printing

(G-10542)
DANIELS JEWELRY & MFG CO
1436 Waukegan Rd (60025-2121)
PHONE..................847 998-5222
Albert Daniels, *President*
Esther Daniels, *Corp Secy*
EMP: 3
SQ FT: 1,200
SALES (est): 350K **Privately Held**
SIC: 5944 3961 Jewelry, precious stones & precious metals; costume jewelry

(G-10543)
DREAMWRKS GRPHIC CMMNCTONS LLC
2323 Ravine Way (60025-7627)
PHONE..................847 679-6710
John Perkins, *Exec VP*
Susan Blumer, *Vice Pres*
Caitlyn Isham, *Opers Dir*
Jason Elsner, *Project Mgr*
Rocky Sardo, *Project Mgr*
EMP: 55
SQ FT: 45,000
SALES (est): 17.3MM **Privately Held**
SIC: 2752 Commercial printing, offset

(G-10544)
EIESLAND BUILDERS INC
Also Called: Eiesland Woodwork
2041 Johns Dr (60025-1654)
PHONE..................847 998-1731
Arvid Eiesland, *President*
Lisa Eiesland, *Bookkeeper*
Cindy Beck, *Office Admin*
EMP: 20
SALES: 1.4MM **Privately Held**
SIC: 1751 2431 Cabinet & finish carpentry; millwork

(G-10545)
FEDEX OFFICE & PRINT SVCS INC
1623 Waukegan Rd (60025-2107)
PHONE..................847 729-3030
EMP: 28
SALES (corp-wide): 69.6B **Publicly Held**
SIC: 7334 2791 2789 Photocopying & duplicating services; typesetting; bookbinding & related work
HQ: Fedex Office And Print Services, Inc.
7900 Legacy Dr
Plano TX 75024
800 463-3339

(G-10546)
FITNESS WEAR INC
1940 Lehigh Ave Ste B (60026-1659)
PHONE..................847 486-1704
Carol Clanton, *Manager*
EMP: 3
SALES (corp-wide): 1.3MM **Privately Held**
SIC: 2396 2395 Screen printing on fabric articles; pleating & stitching

PA: Fitness Wear Inc
2714 Prairie Ave
Evanston IL 60201
847 486-1704

(G-10547)
GC CUSTOM WOODWORKING LLC
3418 Winchester Ln (60026-5753)
PHONE..................847 724-7292
Gregory J Caputo, *Principal*
EMP: 3 **EST:** 2016
SALES (est): 105.3K **Privately Held**
SIC: 2431 Millwork

(G-10548)
GCG CORP
Also Called: Stitchmine Custom Embroidery
4344 Regency Dr (60025-5218)
PHONE..................847 298-2285
Gary Glenn, *President*
Carolyn Glenn, *Vice Pres*
EMP: 2
SALES (est): 309.9K **Privately Held**
WEB: www.stitchmine.com
SIC: 5611 2396 Clothing accessories: men's & boys'; clothing, men's & boys': everyday, except suits & sportswear; clothing, sportswear, men's & boys'; cap fronts & visors; screen printing on fabric articles

(G-10549)
GEMWORLD INTERNATIONAL INC
2640 Patriot Blvd Ste 240 (60026-8075)
PHONE..................847 657-0555
Richard Drucker, *President*
Susan Drucker, *Treasurer*
EMP: 6
SALES (est): 838.8K **Privately Held**
SIC: 2721 Periodicals

(G-10550)
GLEN PRODUCTS
927 Harms Rd (60025-3246)
P.O. Box 956 (60025-0956)
PHONE..................847 998-1361
David Slaght, *Owner*
EMP: 1 **EST:** 1960
SALES: 250K **Privately Held**
SIC: 3545 Precision measuring tools

(G-10551)
GLENVIEW CUSTOM CABINETS INC
1921 Pickwick Ln (60026-1308)
PHONE..................847 345-5754
Wayne Belue, *President*
EMP: 9
SQ FT: 12,200
SALES (est): 988.9K **Privately Held**
SIC: 2599 5712 2541 2434 Cabinets, factory; cabinet work, custom; wood partitions & fixtures; wood kitchen cabinets

(G-10552)
GLENVIEW SYSTEMS INC
Also Called: Glenview Health Systems
3048 N Lake Ter (60025-1335)
PHONE..................847 724-2691
Michael Sciortino, *President*
▲ **EMP:** 10
SQ FT: 11,000
SALES (est): 1.8MM **Privately Held**
SIC: 3596 Scales & balances, except laboratory

(G-10553)
GREEK ART PRINTING & PUBG CO
Also Called: Chicago Menu Co
2921 Covert Rd (60025-4608)
PHONE..................847 724-8860
John A Damianos, *Owner*
EMP: 4 **EST:** 1914
SQ FT: 2,400
SALES: 900K **Privately Held**
SIC: 2759 2752 2732 2731 Letterpress printing; commercial printing, offset; book printing; book publishing

(G-10554)
GREEN ROOF SOLUTIONS INC
3126 W Lake Ave (60026-1207)
PHONE..................847 297-7936
Kate Horvath, *President*
Brian Barry, *Opers Mgr*
▼ **EMP:** 5
SALES (est): 947.5K **Privately Held**
SIC: 2952 Roof cement: asphalt, fibrous or plastic

(G-10555)
HAMMOND PRINTING
1622 Pickwick Ln (60026-1506)
PHONE..................847 724-1539
EMP: 5
SALES (est): 370K **Privately Held**
SIC: 2752 Commercial Printing

(G-10556)
HENES USA INC
125 Milwaukee Ave Ste 301 (60025)
PHONE..................312 448-6130
Kyung Kyun Min, *President*
Yung Hwa, *Vice Pres*
▲ **EMP:** 60
SQ FT: 833
SALES (est): 5.5MM **Privately Held**
SIC: 3944 Children's vehicles, except bicycles

(G-10557)
HERITAGE SHEET METAL INC
2049 Johns Dr (60025-1654)
PHONE..................847 724-8449
Michael A Witt, *President*
Richard H Witt III, *Admin Sec*
EMP: 2
SALES (est): 215.9K **Privately Held**
SIC: 3444 Sheet metalwork

(G-10558)
HUE CIRCLE INC
4259 Commercial Way (60025-3573)
PHONE..................224 567-8116
▲ **EMP:** 3 **EST:** 2009
SALES (est): 281K **Privately Held**
SIC: 5087 3999 Beauty salon & barber shop equipment & supplies; barber & beauty shop equipment

(G-10559)
ILLINOIS BONE & JOINT INST LLC
Also Called: Mri Department
2350 Ravine Way Ste 600 (60025-7657)
PHONE..................847 724-4470
Wayne M Goldstein,
EMP: 66 **Privately Held**
SIC: 3826 7374 Magnetic resonance imaging apparatus; optical scanning data service
PA: Illinois Bone And Joint Institute, Llc
900 Rand Rd Ste 300
Des Plaines IL 60016

(G-10560)
ILLINOIS TOOL WORKS INC (PA)
Also Called: ITW
155 Harlem Ave (60025-4075)
PHONE..................847 724-7500
E Scott Santi, *Ch of Bd*
Axel Beck, *Exec VP*
Kenneth Escoe, *Exec VP*
John R Hartnett, *Exec VP*
Steven L Martindale, *Exec VP*
EMP: 400 **EST:** 1912
SALES: 14.1B **Publicly Held**
WEB: www.itw.com
SIC: 3089 3965 3499 2891 Injection molded finished plastic products; closures, plastic; synthetic resin finished products; fasteners; strapping, metal; adhesives & sealants; refrigeration & heating equipment

(G-10561)
ILLINOIS TOOL WORKS INC
3640 W Lake Ave (60026-1215)
PHONE..................847 657-4639
Arthur Malin, *Manager*
EMP: 4
SALES (corp-wide): 14.1B **Publicly Held**
WEB: www.itw.com
SIC: 2621 Paper mills

(PA)=Parent Co (HQ)=Headquarters (DH)=Div Headquarters
✪ = New Business established in last 2 years

Glenview - Cook County (G-10562)

PA: Illinois Tool Works Inc.
155 Harlem Ave
Glenview IL 60025
847 724-7500

(G-10562)
ILLINOIS TOOL WORKS INC
Magnaflux
155 Harlem Ave (60025-4075)
PHONE 847 657-5300
Steve Groeninger, *General Mgr*
Bill Zumdome, *Plant Mgr*
Jyi-Jiin Luo, *Project Mgr*
Kristine Tobin, *Controller*
Greg Burdick, *Sales Staff*
EMP: 40
SALES (corp-wide): 14.1B **Publicly Held**
SIC: 3829 3825 Measuring & controlling devices; instruments to measure electricity
PA: Illinois Tool Works Inc.
155 Harlem Ave
Glenview IL 60025
847 724-7500

(G-10563)
ILLINOIS TOOL WORKS INC
Signode Packaging Systems
3650 W Lake Ave (60026-1215)
PHONE 847 724-6100
John Becker, *General Mgr*
Michael Loeschen, *Vice Pres*
Lary Ruud, *Engineer*
Alex Popovich, *Controller*
EMP: 300
SALES (corp-wide): 14.1B **Publicly Held**
SIC: 3089 Injection molded finished products; closures, plastic; synthetic resin finished products
PA: Illinois Tool Works Inc.
155 Harlem Ave
Glenview IL 60025
847 724-7500

(G-10564)
ILLINOIS TOOL WORKS INC
Also Called: Midwest Industrial Packaging
3700 W Lake Ave (60026-1217)
PHONE 563 422-5686
Larry Huinker, *Branch Mgr*
EMP: 23
SALES (corp-wide): 14.1B **Publicly Held**
SIC: 3423 Hand & edge tools
PA: Illinois Tool Works Inc.
155 Harlem Ave
Glenview IL 60025
847 724-7500

(G-10565)
ILLINOIS TOOL WORKS INC
3660 W Lake Ave (60026-1215)
PHONE 847 657-4022
EMP: 92
SALES (corp-wide): 14.1B **Publicly Held**
SIC: 3089 Injection molded finished products
PA: Illinois Tool Works Inc.
155 Harlem Ave
Glenview IL 60025
847 724-7500

(G-10566)
IMED GLENVIEW
1247 Milwaukee Ave # 100 (60025-2464)
PHONE 847 298-2200
Alexander Gorodetsky, *Principal*
EMP: 3 **EST:** 2007
SALES (est): 352.1K **Privately Held**
WEB: www.imedvein.com
SIC: 3826 Magnetic resonance imaging apparatus

(G-10567)
INK SPOT SILK SCREEN
84 Park Dr (60025-2721)
PHONE 847 724-6234
EMP: 2
SALES (est): 215.9K **Privately Held**
SIC: 2752 Commercial printing, offset

(G-10568)
INLITEN LLC
2350 Ravine Way Ste 300 (60025-7621)
PHONE 847 486-4200
Robert Braasch Jr, *Mng Member*
Michael Sugar, *Mng Member*
EMP: 18
SALES (est): 1.7MM **Privately Held**
SIC: 3648 Lighting equipment

(G-10569)
INSTITUTIONAL FOODS PACKING CO
Also Called: Leahy-Ifp Company
2350 Ravine Way Ste 200 (60025-7621)
PHONE 847 904-5250
Timothy Leahy, *CEO*
Michael Leahy, *President*
Greg Lojkutz, *President*
Margaret Leahy, *Corp Secy*
EMP: 40
SALES (est): 4.1MM
SALES (corp-wide): 68.6MM **Privately Held**
SIC: 2087 Fruit juices: concentrated for fountain use; powders, drink
PA: Wm. H Leahy Associates, Inc.
2350 Ravine Way Ste 200
Glenview IL 60025
847 904-5250

(G-10570)
INTER-MARKET INC
1946 Lehigh Ave Ste A (60026-1662)
PHONE 847 729-5330
Jerry O'Connor, *President*
EMP: 5
SQ FT: 2,100
SALES (est): 852.9K **Privately Held**
WEB: www.imlec.com
SIC: 5063 2542 Electrical apparatus & equipment; partitions & fixtures, except wood

(G-10571)
ITW BLDG COMPONENTS GROUP (PA)
Also Called: ITW Paslode
155 Harlem Ave (60025-4075)
PHONE 847 634-1900
David B Speer, *CEO*
Bill Krick, *Chief Engr*
Ron Findley, *Engineer*
Chris Huddleston, *Engineer*
Michael Fagan, *Marketing Staff*
▲ **EMP:** 8
SALES (est): 1.7MM **Privately Held**
SIC: 3999 3315 5072 Atomizers, toiletry; nails, spikes, brads & similar items; staples

(G-10572)
ITW COVID SECURITY GROUP INC (HQ)
155 Harlem Ave (60025-4075)
PHONE 847 724-7500
Kevin O'Leary, *President*
EMP: 19
SALES (est): 5.9MM
SALES (corp-wide): 14.1B **Publicly Held**
SIC: 3089 Injection molded finished products
PA: Illinois Tool Works Inc.
155 Harlem Ave
Glenview IL 60025
847 724-7500

(G-10573)
ITW DYNATEC
3600 W Lake Ave (60026-1215)
PHONE 847 657-4830
Scott Santi, *CEO*
EMP: 3
SALES (est): 167.7K
SALES (corp-wide): 14.1B **Publicly Held**
SIC: 2891 3465 Adhesives; body parts, automobile: stamped metal
PA: Illinois Tool Works Inc.
155 Harlem Ave
Glenview IL 60025
847 724-7500

(G-10574)
ITW GLOBAL INVESTMENTS LLC (HQ)
Also Called: ITW Global Investments Inc.
155 Harlem Ave (60025-4075)
PHONE 847 724-7500
Randall Scheuneman, *President*
Phillip J McGovern, *Vice Pres*
Joanna B Pasek, *Vice Pres*
David O Livingston, *Treasurer*
EMP: 1
SALES (est): 3.6MM
SALES (corp-wide): 14.1B **Publicly Held**
SIC: 3714 Motor vehicle parts & accessories
PA: Illinois Tool Works Inc.
155 Harlem Ave
Glenview IL 60025
847 724-7500

(G-10575)
ITW INTERNATIONAL HOLDINGS LLC (HQ)
Also Called: I T W Affrdbl Hsing Invstments
3600 W Lake Ave (60026-1215)
PHONE 847 724-7500
Harold Smith, *Ch of Bd*
David Livingston, *President*
David C Parry, *Principal*
E Scott Santi, *Principal*
Kelly Rezny, *Counsel*
EMP: 10
SALES (est): 17.5MM
SALES (corp-wide): 14.1B **Publicly Held**
WEB: www.itw.com
SIC: 3089 Injection molded finished plastic products; closures, plastic
PA: Illinois Tool Works Inc.
155 Harlem Ave
Glenview IL 60025
847 724-7500

(G-10576)
JOSEPHS PRINTING SERVICE
1739 Chestnut Ave Ste 107 (60025-1760)
PHONE 847 724-4429
M Terry Oswald, *President*
EMP: 5
SQ FT: 6,800
SALES (est): 479.4K **Privately Held**
SIC: 2752 7336 2791 Commercial printing, offset; graphic arts & related design; typesetting

(G-10577)
K & A PRECISION MACHINE INC
2500 Ravine Way (60025-7629)
PHONE 847 998-1933
Arie Zweig, *President*
Hava Frenkel, *Admin Sec*
EMP: 55
SQ FT: 17,000
SALES (est): 4.9MM **Privately Held**
SIC: 3599 Machine shop, jobbing & repair

(G-10578)
KOHLER CO
Also Called: Kohler K&B Store
1180 Milwaukee Ave (60025-2418)
PHONE 847 635-8071
Gar Trispell, *General Mgr*
EMP: 48
SALES (corp-wide): 8.3B **Privately Held**
SIC: 3431 7389 Plumbing fixtures: enameled iron cast iron or pressed metal; design services
PA: Kohler Co.
444 Highland Dr
Kohler WI 53044
920 457-4441

(G-10579)
KOREA TIMES
615 Milwaukee Ave Ste 12 (60025-3878)
PHONE 847 626-0388
Yung W Kim, *Owner*
Yong Tae Park, *Systems Staff*
▲ **EMP:** 66
SALES (est): 4MM **Privately Held**
SIC: 2721 2791 2759 2711 Periodicals; typesetting; commercial printing; newspapers

(G-10580)
KOREA TIMES CHICAGO INC
615 Milwaukee Ave Ste 12 (60025-3878)
PHONE 847 626-0388
John Lee, *President*
EMP: 33
SQ FT: 22,000
SALES (est): 1.7MM
SALES (corp-wide): 85.3MM **Privately Held**
SIC: 2711 Commercial printing & newspaper publishing combined

PA: The Korea Times Los Angeles Inc
3731 Wilshire Blvd
Los Angeles CA 90010
323 692-2000

(G-10581)
KRAFT HEINZ FOODS COMPANY
801 Waukegan Rd (60025-4391)
PHONE 847 646-3690
EMP: 210
SALES (corp-wide): 24.9B **Publicly Held**
SIC: 2033 Canned fruits & specialties
HQ: Kraft Heinz Foods Company
1 Ppg Pl Fl 34
Pittsburgh PA 15222
412 456-5700

(G-10582)
KRAFT HEINZ FOODS COMPANY
Also Called: Kraft Foods
801 Waukegan Rd (60025-4391)
PHONE 847 646-2000
Tricia Lee, *Engineer*
Jon Reeve, *Engineer*
Julio Quintana-Castil, *Senior Engr*
Adalgiza S Alai, *Manager*
EMP: 203
SALES (corp-wide): 24.9B **Publicly Held**
SIC: 2099 Food preparations
HQ: Kraft Heinz Foods Company
1 Ppg Pl Fl 34
Pittsburgh PA 15222
412 456-5700

(G-10583)
KRAM DIGITAL SOLUTIONS INC (PA)
1717 Chestnut Ave (60025-1720)
PHONE 312 222-0431
David Kohn, *President*
Bill Smith, *Production*
EMP: 4
SQ FT: 1,100
SALES (est): 366.6K **Privately Held**
SIC: 2752 7334 Commercial printing, offset; photocopying & duplicating services

(G-10584)
LCR HALLCREST LLC
1911 Pickwick Ln (60026-1308)
PHONE 847 998-8580
Paul Krueger, *Opers Mgr*
Marcy Gutan, *QC Dir*
Ray Losch, *Engineer*
Scott Szafraniec, *Natl Sales Mgr*
John Romano, *Sales Staff*
◆ **EMP:** 50
SQ FT: 25,000
SALES (est): 17.6MM **Privately Held**
SIC: 3829 Thermometers, liquid-in-glass & bimetal type

(G-10585)
LOTTUS INC
3216 Ronald Rd (60025-4563)
PHONE 847 691-9464
Artemio Marquez, *Manager*
EMP: 4
SALES (est): 366.1K **Privately Held**
SIC: 2448 Wood pallets & skids

(G-10586)
LYRE GLASS PRESS LLC
3616 Glenlake Dr (60026-1379)
PHONE 847 834-9643
Sharma Amita K, *Principal*
EMP: 4
SALES (est): 172.6K **Privately Held**
WEB: www.glasslyrepress.com
SIC: 2741 Miscellaneous publishing

(G-10587)
MARCH MANUFACTURING INC (PA)
Also Called: March Pumps
1819 Pickwick Ln (60026-1306)
PHONE 847 729-5300
Fredrick Zimmermann, *President*
Carl Zimmermann, *Vice Pres*
Hans Zimmermann, *Vice Pres*
Michelle Bellito, *Purch Mgr*
Susan Christian, *Purch Mgr*
▲ **EMP:** 56 **EST:** 1954
SQ FT: 120,000

GEOGRAPHIC SECTION
Glenview - Cook County (G-10617)

SALES (est): 13.7MM **Privately Held**
WEB: www.marchpump.com
SIC: **3561** 3586 Industrial pumps & parts; measuring & dispensing pumps

(G-10588)
MICROWARE INC
2418 Swainwood Dr (60025-2744)
PHONE.................847 943-9113
William Anderson, *President*
Barbara Anderson, *Corp Secy*
EMP: 2
SALES (est): 230K **Privately Held**
SIC: **3625** Control circuit relays, industrial

(G-10589)
MID AMERICA INTL INC
Also Called: Mid America Chemical
1245 Milwaukee Ave # 202 (60025-2400)
PHONE.................847 635-8303
John C MA, *President*
▲ EMP: 6
SALES (est): 841K **Privately Held**
SIC: **2899** Chemical supplies for foundries

(G-10590)
MONOGRAM CREATIVE GROUP INC
1723 Wildberry Dr Unit C (60025-1794)
PHONE.................312 802-1433
Pamela Vankirk-Schmidt, *President*
▲ EMP: 4
SALES (est): 697.3K **Privately Held**
SIC: **5046** 3069 Store fixtures & display equipment; flooring, rubber: tile or sheet

(G-10591)
MOSAIC LABEL & PRINT LLC (PA)
4346 Di Paolo Ctr (60025-5201)
PHONE.................847 904-1375
Steven Brownstone, *Mng Member*
EMP: 8 EST: 2015
SALES (est): 3.5MM **Privately Held**
SIC: **2759** Labels & seals: printing

(G-10592)
NAVMAN WIRELESS HOLDINGS LP
2701 Patriot Blvd Ste 200 (60026-8039)
PHONE.................866 527-9896
Tzau J Chung, *General Ptnr*
▲ EMP: 63
SALES (est): 82.1MM
SALES (corp-wide): 7.3B **Publicly Held**
SIC: **3812** Search & navigation equipment
PA: Fortive Corporation
  6920 Seaway Blvd
  Everett WA 98203
  425 446-5000

(G-10593)
NESTLE PIZZA COMPANY INC (DH)
Also Called: Kraft Pizza Company, Inc
1 Kraft Ct (60025)
PHONE.................847 646-2000
David S Johnson, *President*
Peter Boyle, *President*
Barbara M Ford, *President*
Tammy Wemple, *Business Mgr*
Gregory P Banks, *Vice Pres*
▼ EMP: 50 EST: 1962
SQ FT: 450,000
SALES (est): 313.1MM
SALES (corp-wide): 93.5B **Privately Held**
WEB: www.kraft.com
SIC: **2038** Pizza, frozen; snacks, including onion rings, cheese sticks, etc.
HQ: Nestle Usa, Inc.
  1812 N Moore St Ste 118
  Rosslyn VA 22209
  440 264-7249

(G-10594)
NEW CENTURY MFG
Also Called: NCM
1016 Pleasant Ln (60025-1936)
PHONE.................847 998-0960
Leland Miller, *President*
Cynthia Miller, *Vice Pres*
EMP: 2
SQ FT: 20,000
SALES (est): 255.8K **Privately Held**
SIC: **3822** Liquid level controls, residential or commercial heating

(G-10595)
OPTIMAS OE SOLUTIONS LLC (DH)
Also Called: Circle Bolt & Nut Company
2651 Compass Rd (60026-8004)
PHONE.................224 999-1000
Anesa Chaibi, *CEO*
Ian Clarke, *CEO*
Eric Baroyan, *President*
Matt Ackerman, *Principal*
Rebecca Goldman, *Principal*
▲ EMP: 5
SALES (est): 947.6MM
SALES (corp-wide): 961.1MM **Privately Held**
SIC: **3452** 5072 5063 Bolts, nuts, rivets & washers; hardware; wire & cable
HQ: Optimas Oe Solutions Holding, Llc
  2651 Compass Rd
  Glenview IL 60026
  224 999-1000

(G-10596)
ORION METALS CO
3318 Maple Leaf Dr (60026-1127)
PHONE.................847 412-9532
David Adams, *Principal*
EMP: 4 EST: 2009
SALES (est): 399.3K **Privately Held**
SIC: **3399** Primary metal products

(G-10597)
PALLET WRAPZ
2009 Johns Dr (60025-1616)
PHONE.................847 729-5850
EMP: 15
SALES (est): 2.4MM **Privately Held**
SIC: **2448** Mfg Wood Pallets/Skids

(G-10598)
PALLET WRAPZ INC
2009 Johns Dr (60025-1616)
PHONE.................847 729-5850
Mark Lato, *CEO*
Vivian Lato, *CFO*
EMP: 6
SALES (est): 80.1K **Privately Held**
SIC: **2448** Pallets, wood; pallets, wood & wood with metal

(G-10599)
PIONEER FORMS INC
4315 Regency Dr (60025-5219)
PHONE.................773 539-8587
Kwang Lim Rah, *President*
Yunhee Rah, *Vice Pres*
EMP: 5
SALES (est): 513K **Privately Held**
SIC: **2759** Business forms: printing

(G-10600)
PRACTECHAL MARKETING
1867 Waukegan Rd (60025-2158)
PHONE.................847 486-8600
April Perry, *Owner*
EMP: 3
SALES (est): 100K **Privately Held**
SIC: **3429** Locks or lock sets

(G-10601)
PRECISION CTNG TLS SVC MFG INC
3222 W Lake Ave (60026-1209)
PHONE.................847 901-6800
Krzysztof Rafalski, *President*
Chris Rafalski, *Principal*
EMP: 2
SALES (est): 214.2K **Privately Held**
SIC: **3541** Machine tools, metal cutting type

(G-10602)
PRECISION REPRODUCTIONS INC
4316 Regency Dr (60025-5200)
PHONE.................847 724-0182
Mike Miller, *President*
Sandy Miller, *Admin Sec*
EMP: 14
SQ FT: 5,000
SALES (est): 1.2MM **Privately Held**
SIC: **7374** 2752 7334 Service bureau, computer; commercial printing, lithographic; blueprinting service

(G-10603)
PRINTING SHOP
Also Called: PIP Printing
1220 Waukegan Rd (60025-3020)
PHONE.................847 998-6330
Alex Rozenblat, *Owner*
EMP: 3
SQ FT: 1,300
SALES (est): 330.8K **Privately Held**
SIC: **2752** 2789 Commercial printing, offset; binding only: books, pamphlets, magazines, etc.

(G-10604)
PYCAS DESIGN INNOVATIONS LLC
602 Hillside Rd (60025-3919)
PHONE.................847 656-5000
Biju Jacob, *CEO*
EMP: 42
SQ FT: 2,000
SALES (est): 950K **Privately Held**
SIC: **7371** 7379 7372 Custom computer programming services; computer software writing services; computer software development & applications; software programming applications; data processing consultant; application computer software

(G-10605)
QUALITY CUSTOM CLOSETS
4304 Di Paolo Ctr (60025-5201)
PHONE.................773 307-1105
EMP: 6 EST: 2012
SALES (est): 622.3K **Privately Held**
WEB: www.qcclosets.com
SIC: **3089** Organizers for closets, drawers, etc.: plastic

(G-10606)
QUIPP INC (PA)
3700 W Lake Ave (60026-1217)
PHONE.................305 623-8700
Cristina H Kepner, *Ch of Bd*
Michael S Kady, *President*
John Connors, *Vice Pres*
Angel Arrabal, *VP Sls/Mktg*
Eric Bello, *CFO*
▲ EMP: 12
SQ FT: 63,170
SALES (est): 8MM **Privately Held**
SIC: **3554** Paper industries machinery

(G-10607)
R A ZWEIG INC
2500 Ravine Way (60025-7629)
PHONE.................847 832-9001
Arie Zweig, *President*
Mike Gniot, *General Mgr*
Richard Schmidt, *Principal*
Michael Zebura, *Principal*
Inez Vega, *QC Mgr*
EMP: 110
SQ FT: 125,000
SALES (est): 22.8MM **Privately Held**
SIC: **3599** Machine shop, jobbing & repair

(G-10608)
RAINMAKER
1539 Palmgren Dr (60025-4341)
PHONE.................847 998-0838
R Shinkle, *Principal*
EMP: 2
SALES (est): 211.5K **Privately Held**
SIC: **3569** Sprinkler systems, fire: automatic

(G-10609)
REDDI-PAC INC (PA)
3700 W Lake Ave (60026-1217)
PHONE.................847 657-5222
Mike Loeschen, *Vice Pres*
Virgen M Dejesus,
EMP: 17
SQ FT: 10,000
SALES (est): 4.7MM **Privately Held**
SIC: **2652** Setup paperboard boxes

(G-10610)
REEDY INDUSTRIES INC (PA)
2440 Ravine Way Ste 200 (60025-7649)
PHONE.................847 729-9450
Bill Reedy, *CEO*
Jack Deichl, *President*
Amy Cunningham, *Principal*
Barbara Hall, *Business Mgr*
Coleen Reedy, *Corp Secy*
EMP: 15
SQ FT: 20,000
SALES: 1.6K **Privately Held**
WEB: www.northtownmechanical.com
SIC: **1711** 3585 5078 Warm air heating & air conditioning contractor; parts for heating, cooling & refrigerating equipment; commercial refrigeration equipment

(G-10611)
RELIABLE MAIL SERVICES INC
2733 Langley Cir (60026-7736)
PHONE.................847 677-6245
Mark Conton, *President*
EMP: 15
SALES (est): 2.8MM **Privately Held**
SIC: **7331** 2752 Mailing service; commercial printing, lithographic

(G-10612)
REPUBLIC GROUP INC (PA)
2301 Ravine Way (60025-7627)
PHONE.................800 288-8888
Donald R Levin, *CEO*
EMP: 9
SALES (est): 36.5MM **Privately Held**
SIC: **2131** Smoking tobacco

(G-10613)
ROCKYS BEVERAGES LLC
1813 Elmdale Ave (60026-1355)
PHONE.................312 561-3182
Peter Rocky Mosele,
EMP: 10
SALES (est): 1MM **Privately Held**
SIC: **2086** Carbonated soft drinks, bottled & canned

(G-10614)
ROGERS LOOSE LEAF CO
1013 Elmdale Rd (60025-2500)
PHONE.................312 226-1947
James Stuercke, *President*
EMP: 18
SALES (est): 2.2MM **Privately Held**
WEB: www.rogerslooseleaf.com
SIC: **2754** Music sheet: gravure printing, not published on site

(G-10615)
SHENGLONG INTL GROUP CORP
1939 Waukegan Rd Ste 205 (60025-1758)
PHONE.................312 388-2435
Chunxiang Zhang, *President*
Licai Yang, *Vice Pres*
Zhanhai Zhang, *Vice Pres*
◆ EMP: 7
SQ FT: 1,200
SALES (est): 520K **Privately Held**
SIC: **5047** 5021 3411 Hospital equipment & furniture; office & public building furniture; food & beverage containers

(G-10616)
SIGNODE
3700 W Lake Ave (60026-1278)
PHONE.................800 228-4744
EMP: 17
SALES (est): 3.7MM **Privately Held**
SIC: **3565** Packaging machinery

(G-10617)
SIGNODE INDUSTRIAL GROUP LLC
Also Called: Signode Packaging Systems
3624 W Lake Ave (60026-1215)
PHONE.................800 862-7997
Ramunas Venclovas, *General Mgr*
Ginger Huber, *Accountant*
Scott Thomas, *Sales Staff*
EMP: 38
SALES (corp-wide): 11.6B **Publicly Held**
WEB: www.signodegroup.com
SIC: **3565** Packaging machinery

Glenview - Cook County (G-10618)

HQ: Signode Industrial Group Llc
3650 W Lake Ave
Glenview IL 60026
847 724-7500

(G-10618)
SIGNODE INDUSTRIAL GROUP LLC (HQ)
Also Called: Insulated Transport Products
3650 W Lake Ave (60026-1215)
PHONE.................................847 724-7500
Mark Burgees, *CEO*
Ron Kropp, *CFO*
Jerry Horn, *Info Tech Mgr*
Judy Agee, *Assistant*
▲ **EMP:** 40 **EST:** 2013
SALES (est): 222.6MM
SALES (corp-wide): 11.6B **Publicly Held**
SIC: 2671 Resinous impregnated paper for packaging; thermoplastic coated paper for packaging
PA: Crown Holdings Inc.
770 Township Line Rd # 100
Yardley PA 19067
215 698-5100

(G-10619)
SIGNODE INDUSTRIAL GROUP LLC
Muller Lcs
3644 W Lake Ave (60026-1215)
PHONE.................................800 628-6787
Joe Albert, *General Mgr*
Tim Gardner, *Natl Sales Mgr*
Nicholas Antique, *Sales Staff*
Steve Shaffer, *Sales Staff*
Sheldon Orcutt, *Manager*
EMP: 45
SALES (corp-wide): 11.6B **Publicly Held**
SIC: 3565 3081 Packing & wrapping machinery; polyethylene film
HQ: Signode Industrial Group Llc
3650 W Lake Ave
Glenview IL 60026
847 724-7500

(G-10620)
SIGNODE INDUSTRIAL GROUP LLC
Also Called: Signode Consumable Plastics
3680 W Lake Ave (60026-1215)
PHONE.................................847 724-6100
John Becker, *Vice Pres*
EMP: 39
SALES (corp-wide): 11.6B **Publicly Held**
SIC: 2671 Thermoplastic coated paper for packaging
HQ: Signode Industrial Group Llc
3650 W Lake Ave
Glenview IL 60026
847 724-7500

(G-10621)
SIGNODE INTL HOLDINGS LLC (HQ)
3700 W Lake Ave (60026-1217)
PHONE.................................800 648-8864
EMP: 19
SALES (est): 46.8MM **Privately Held**
SIC: 5199 2671 Industrial Packaging

(G-10622)
SIRIUS PERFORMANCE COMPANY LLC
5 Glenview Rd (60025-3340)
PHONE.................................312 909-0775
Robert Holz, *Mng Member*
Allen Hoube, *Mng Member*
EMP: 6
SALES (est): 506.1K **Privately Held**
SIC: 2086 Bottled & canned soft drinks

(G-10623)
SOLOMON PLUMBING
3706 Winnetka Rd (60026-1354)
PHONE.................................847 498-6388
Solomon Altez, *Owner*
EMP: 2 **EST:** 1998
SALES (est): 243.6K **Privately Held**
WEB: www.solomonplumbing.com
SIC: 3494 Plumbing & heating valves

(G-10624)
STAGES CONSTRUCTION INC
4317 Regency Dr (60025-5219)
PHONE.................................773 619-2977
Nenus Oshana, *President*
Susan Pirsch, *Principal*
EMP: 4
SALES (est): 293.6K **Privately Held**
SIC: 1799 8711 8741 1389 Construction site cleanup; fence construction; building construction consultant; construction management; construction, repair & dismantling services

(G-10625)
STEEL TUBE INSTITUTE N AMER
2516 Waukegan Rd Ste 172 (60025-1774)
PHONE.................................847 461-1701
Joseph Anderson, *Exec Dir*
EMP: 6
SALES: 974.5K **Privately Held**
SIC: 3317 Conduit: welded, lock joint or heavy riveted

(G-10626)
STELLAR ORTHTICS PRSTHTICS LLC
2401 Ravine Way Ste 301 (60025-7645)
PHONE.................................847 410-2751
Sy Rosen, *Branch Mgr*
EMP: 10
SALES (est): 1.1MM
SALES (corp-wide): 174K **Privately Held**
SIC: 3842 Orthopedic appliances
PA: Stellar Orthotics & Prosthetics, Llc
3230 Executive Dr
Joliet IL 60431
815 207-4200

(G-10627)
SUBURBAN FABRICATORS INC
1119 Depot St (60025-2905)
PHONE.................................847 729-0866
Michael Nemmer, *President*
Tim Nemmer, *Corp Secy*
EMP: 3
SQ FT: 800
SALES (est): 432.7K **Privately Held**
WEB: www.suburbancountertops.com
SIC: 2541 Wood partitions & fixtures

(G-10628)
SUE PETERSON
Also Called: Sue P Knits
1100 Raleigh Rd (60025-3026)
PHONE.................................847 730-3035
Sue Paterson, *Owner*
Sue Peterson, *Owner*
EMP: 3
SALES (est): 190K **Privately Held**
SIC: 2253 Sweaters & sweater coats, knit

(G-10629)
SUMA AMERICA INC
2700 Patriot Blvd Ste 250 (60026-8021)
PHONE.................................847 427-7880
Suma Kpandhi, *Principal*
◆ **EMP:** 3
SALES (est): 341.8K **Privately Held**
SIC: 2911 Gases & liquefied petroleum gases

(G-10630)
TEITELBAUM BROTHERS INC
Also Called: Pixie Sparkle
1944 Lehigh Ave Ste D (60026-1661)
PHONE.................................847 729-3490
James R Lucas, *President*
Louisa A Lucas, *Corp Secy*
EMP: 2
SQ FT: 1,100
SALES (est): 242.2K **Privately Held**
SIC: 2842 Industrial plant disinfectants or deodorants

(G-10631)
TELETRAC NAVMAN US LTD (DH)
2700 Patriot Blvd Ste 200 (60026-8064)
PHONE.................................866 527-9896
Tj Chung, *President*
Mike Henn, *CFO*
▲ **EMP:** 22
SQ FT: 10,000
SALES (est): 5.9MM
SALES (corp-wide): 7.3B **Publicly Held**
SIC: 3812 Navigational systems & instruments
HQ: Vontier Corporation
5420 Wade Park Blvd # 206
Raleigh NC 27607
984 247-8308

(G-10632)
TIMEOUT DEVICES INC
2718 Covert Rd (60025-4605)
PHONE.................................847 729-6543
Jim Daniel, *President*
EMP: 10
SALES (est): 250K **Privately Held**
SIC: 3577 Computer peripheral equipment

(G-10633)
TOP TOBACCO LP (PA)
Also Called: Republic Tobacco
2301 Ravine Way (60025-7627)
PHONE.................................847 832-9700
Alan Kandelman, *CEO*
Donald R Levin, *President*
Seth Gold, *Exec VP*
Allan Kandelman, *CFO*
Jenny Kuffel, *Manager*
▲ **EMP:** 1
SQ FT: 150,000
SALES (est): 36.1MM **Privately Held**
SIC: 2131 Smoking tobacco

(G-10634)
TWO TRIBES LLC
3607 Lawson Rd (60026-1105)
P.O. Box 2367, Northbrook (60065-2367)
PHONE.................................847 272-7711
Diana Israel, *Mng Member*
EMP: 6
SALES (est): 500K **Privately Held**
SIC: 2022 Natural cheese

(G-10635)
UNITED STANDARD INDUSTRIES INC
2062 Lehigh Ave (60026-1619)
PHONE.................................847 724-0350
Sherwin E Feldstein, *President*
Susan Feldstein, *Admin Sec*
EMP: 63 **EST:** 1966
SQ FT: 37,500
SALES (est): 14.9MM **Privately Held**
WEB: www.unitedstandard.com
SIC: 3599 Machine shop, jobbing & repair

(G-10636)
UNITED STATES AUDIO CORP (PA)
Also Called: US Audio
411 Crabtree Ln (60025-5114)
PHONE.................................312 316-2929
John Kowalik, *President*
Frances Kowalik, *Admin Sec*
EMP: 12
SALES (est): 265K **Privately Held**
SIC: 3651 Household audio equipment

(G-10637)
WINDWARD BRANDS LLC
2550 Compass Rd Ste G (60026-1610)
PHONE.................................224 432-5704
Jerry Isaacson, *President*
EMP: 5
SALES (est): 153.8K **Privately Held**
SIC: 2099 Ready-to-eat meals, salads & sandwiches

(G-10638)
WINTEK ELECTRO-OPTICS CORP (HQ)
1132 Waukegan Rd Ste 101 (60025-3060)
PHONE.................................734 477-5480
Hyley Huang, *President*
▲ **EMP:** 13 **EST:** 2001
SALES (est): 1.8MM **Privately Held**
SIC: 3679 Liquid crystal displays (LCD)

Glenwood
Cook County

(G-10639)
CHEMIX CORP
330 W 194th St (60425-1502)
PHONE.................................708 754-2150
Arthur Danko, *President*
Andrienne Danko, *Admin Sec*
EMP: 15 **EST:** 1960
SQ FT: 3,000
SALES (est): 2.5MM **Privately Held**
SIC: 5169 3471 2992 2899 Chemicals & allied products; plating & polishing; lubricating oils & greases; chemical preparations; paints & allied products; specialty cleaning, polishes & sanitation goods

(G-10640)
E GEORGE SPECIAL SERVICES LLC
642 E 192nd St (60425-2002)
PHONE.................................773 934-7878
Erick George, *President*
EMP: 5
SALES (est): 239.7K **Privately Held**
SIC: 3822 Building services monitoring controls, automatic

(G-10641)
JAMES WALKER MFG CO
511 W 195th St (60425-1532)
P.O. Box 467 (60425-0467)
PHONE.................................708 754-4020
Peter Needham, *President*
Chris May, *General Mgr*
Steve Moss, *General Mgr*
Peter A Tompsett, *Principal*
Catherine Stalioraitis, *Controller*
▲ **EMP:** 43 **EST:** 1915
SQ FT: 30,000
SALES (est): 8.1MM
SALES (corp-wide): 256.5MM **Privately Held**
WEB: www.jameswalker.biz
SIC: 3053 3599 3492 3441 Oil seals, leather; oil seals, rubber; gaskets, all materials; bellows, industrial: metal; fluid power valves & hose fittings; fabricated structural metal; mechanical rubber goods
PA: James Walker Group Limited
Lion House
Woking GU22
148 374-6146

(G-10642)
LANDAUER INC (HQ)
2 Science Rd (60425-1586)
PHONE.................................708 755-7000
Mike Kaminski, *President*
Peter Cempellin, *President*
Raani Kissinger, *President*
Doug King, *Senior VP*
Douglas R Gipson, *Executive*
EMP: 134
SQ FT: 59,100
SALES: 149.2MM
SALES (corp-wide): 7.3B **Publicly Held**
SIC: 8734 5047 3829 Radiation laboratories; radiation dosimetry laboratory; instruments, surgical & medical; X-ray film & supplies; measuring & controlling devices
PA: Fortive Corporation
6920 Seaway Blvd
Everett WA 98203
425 446-5000

(G-10643)
MORRISON TIMING SCREW COMPANY
Also Called: Morrison Cont Hdlg Solutions
335 W 194th St (60425-1501)
PHONE.................................708 756-6660
Nick Wilson, *President*
Nancy Wilson, *Owner*
Lois Hayworth, *Vice Pres*
Chris Wilson, *Vice Pres*
Mike Norman, *Mfg Staff*
EMP: 75 **EST:** 1971
SQ FT: 30,000

SALES (est): 27.6MM **Privately Held**
SIC: 3535 Conveyors & conveying equipment

(G-10644)
NALCO WTR PRTRTMENT SLTONS LLC
320 W 194th St (60425-1502)
PHONE..............................708 754-2550
EMP: 4
SALES (corp-wide): 5.1B **Privately Held**
SIC: 5999 5074 5084 3443 Water purification equipment; water heaters & purification equipment; industrial machinery & equipment; fabricated plate work (boiler shop); plumbing, heating, air-conditioning contractors
HQ: Nalco Water Pretreatment Solutions, Llc
1601 W Diehl Rd
Naperville IL 60563
708 754-2550

(G-10645)
SWEET CREATION BY SHEILA
803 N Rainbow Dr (60425-1307)
PHONE..............................708 754-7938
Sheila Kimbrough, *Principal*
EMP: 3
SALES (est): 138.5K **Privately Held**
SIC: 2053 Cakes, bakery; frozen

Godfrey
Madison County

(G-10646)
AB MACHINE SHOP LLC
6344 Lake Dr (62035-2208)
PHONE..............................618 467-6474
Tim Kuebrich, *President*
EMP: 6
SQ FT: 7,000
SALES (est): 550K **Privately Held**
SIC: 3599 7539 Machine shop, jobbing & repair; electrical services

(G-10647)
ABBEY COPYING SUPPORT SVCS INC
3312 Godfrey Rd (62035-2558)
PHONE..............................618 466-3300
Sherie Schroeder, *President*
EMP: 3
SALES (est): 261K **Privately Held**
WEB: www.abbeyinc.com
SIC: 2759 Commercial printing

(G-10648)
ALFA-PET INC (PA)
7319 Ingham Ln (62035-2881)
PHONE..............................314 865-0400
Ben Schulein Jr, *Ch of Bd*
Marty Johnes, *President*
▲ EMP: 40
SALES (est): 7.3MM **Privately Held**
WEB: www.alfapetco.com
SIC: 2048 Livestock feeds

(G-10649)
ARROW SIGNS (PA)
4545 N Alby Rd (62035-1954)
PHONE..............................618 466-0818
Lance De Mond, *Principal*
EMP: 14 EST: 2013
SALES (est): 619.1K **Privately Held**
WEB: www.arrowsignsinc.com
SIC: 3993 Electric signs

(G-10650)
ARROW SIGNS
6203 Godfrey Rd (62035-2431)
PHONE..............................618 466-0818
Valerie Winchester, *Office Mgr*
Lance Demond, *Branch Mgr*
EMP: 9
SALES (est): 918.5K
SALES (corp-wide): 619.1K **Privately Held**
SIC: 3993 Signs & advertising specialties
PA: Arrow Signs
4545 N Alby Rd
Godfrey IL 62035
618 466-0818

(G-10651)
DAVID L KNOCHE
Also Called: Hgh Products
611 Armsway Blvd (62035-2734)
PHONE..............................618 466-7120
David L Knoche, *Owner*
EMP: 7
SQ FT: 2,400
SALES (est): 601.3K **Privately Held**
SIC: 3599 Custom machinery

(G-10652)
HAMILTON FBRCATION STL SUP INC
311 Tolle Ln (62035-2455)
PHONE..............................618 466-0012
John Hamilton, *President*
Mary Capps, *Accountant*
Jared Hamilton, *Admin Sec*
EMP: 8 EST: 2016
SALES: 1MM **Privately Held**
SIC: 3441 Fabricated structural metal

(G-10653)
IMC OUTDOOR LIVING
315 Tolle Ln (62035-2455)
PHONE..............................314 373-1171
EMP: 9
SALES (est): 1.7MM **Privately Held**
SIC: 2421 Outdoor wood structural products

(G-10654)
KEN ELLIOTT CO
3704 Riehl Ln (62035-1064)
PHONE..............................618 466-8200
Kent Elliot, *President*
Kent Elliott, *President*
Gary Elliott, *Vice Pres*
EMP: 3 EST: 1952
SQ FT: 20,000
SALES (est): 285.5K **Privately Held**
SIC: 3462 3593 Gears, forged steel; fluid power cylinders & actuators

(G-10655)
KIMMATERIALS INC
Also Called: Lohr Quarry
9434 Godfrey Rd (62035-3046)
PHONE..............................618 466-0352
Dave Bangert, *President*
EMP: 5 EST: 1939
SALES (est): 388K **Privately Held**
SIC: 1422 Crushed & broken limestone

(G-10656)
MAX FIRE TRAINING INC
Also Called: MAX FIRE BOX
901 Hampton Ct (62035-1800)
PHONE..............................618 210-2079
Shawn Bloemker, *President*
EMP: 13
SALES: 364K **Privately Held**
SIC: 3441 3429 9411 Building components, structural steel; nozzles, fire fighting;

(G-10657)
MIDLAND RAILWAY SUPPLY INC (PA)
1815 W Delmar Ave (62035-1352)
PHONE..............................618 467-6305
John Ferenbach, *President*
Eric Ferenbach, *Vice Pres*
Jason Ferenbach, *Info Tech Mgr*
EMP: 26 EST: 1946
SALES (est): 20MM **Privately Held**
WEB: www.midlandrailway.com
SIC: 5088 3743 Railroad equipment & supplies; railroad equipment

(G-10658)
NEW CENTURY PERFORMANCE INC
3704 Riehl Ln (62035-1064)
P.O. Box 727 (62035-0727)
PHONE..............................618 466-6383
Lowell Bodenbach, *General Mgr*
EMP: 4
SALES: 500K **Privately Held**
WEB: www.newcenturyperformance.com
SIC: 3334 Primary aluminum

(G-10659)
OLIVE OIL MARKET PLACE
1018 Richard Dr (62035-2574)
PHONE..............................618 304-3769
Safi Dani, *Branch Mgr*
EMP: 3
SALES (corp-wide): 18.2MM **Privately Held**
WEB: www.oliveoilmarketplace.com
SIC: 2079 Olive oil
PA: Olive Oil Marketplace Inc.
108 W 3rd St
Alton IL 62002
618 304-3769

(G-10660)
RINALLI BOAT CO INC
3406 W Delmar Ave (62035-1007)
PHONE..............................618 467-8850
Donald B Rhodes, *President*
EMP: 6
SALES: 250K **Privately Held**
SIC: 3732 7389 Boats, fiberglass: building & repairing;

(G-10661)
RIVIERA TAN SPA
Also Called: Riviera Tan Products
5114 Stiritz Ln (62035-1244)
PHONE..............................618 466-1012
Joyce Carroll, *President*
Harley Carroll, *Admin Sec*
EMP: 5
SALES (est): 265.2K **Privately Held**
SIC: 3999 5122 Barber & beauty shop equipment; toiletries

(G-10662)
ROTARY RAM INC
3704 Riehl Ln (62035-1064)
PHONE..............................618 466-2651
Kent Elliott, *President*
Gary Elliott, *Sales Executive*
EMP: 20 EST: 1951
SQ FT: 15,100
SALES (est): 5MM **Privately Held**
WEB: www.elliottgears.com
SIC: 3492 Control valves, fluid power: hydraulic & pneumatic

(G-10663)
SCHNUCK MARKETS INC
Also Called: Schnucks Pharmacy
2712 Godfrey Rd (62035-3311)
PHONE..............................618 466-0825
Phil Lunn, *Manager*
EMP: 200
SALES (corp-wide): 2.1B **Privately Held**
SIC: 5411 5812 5912 7841 Supermarkets, chain; eating places; drug stores & proprietary stores; video tape rental; florists; bread, cake & related products
PA: Schnuck Markets, Inc.
11420 Lackland Rd
Saint Louis MO 63146
314 994-9900

(G-10664)
TAW ENTERPRISES LLC
5100 Seminole Ct (62035-1543)
PHONE..............................618 466-0134
EMP: 4
SALES (est): 449.7K **Privately Held**
SIC: 3714 Mfg Motor Vehicle Parts/Accessories

Golconda
Pope County

(G-10665)
HOGG HOLLOW WINERY LLC
48 E Glendale Rd (62938-4018)
PHONE..............................618 695-9463
Steve Hogg, *Mng Member*
EMP: 4
SALES (est): 233.6K **Privately Held**
SIC: 2084 Wines

(G-10666)
LAFARGE NORTH AMERICA INC
501 Il Route 146 34 (62938-4439)
PHONE..............................773 372-1000
EMP: 29

SALES (corp-wide): 4.5B **Privately Held**
SIC: 3241 Cement, hydraulic
HQ: Lafarge North America Inc.
8700 W Bryn Mawr Ave
Chicago IL 60631
773 372-1000

(G-10667)
MARTIN MARIETTA MATERIALS INC
Also Called: Rosiclare Quarry
Missouri Portland Rd (62938)
PHONE..............................618 285-6267
Jimmy Mc Crary, *Branch Mgr*
EMP: 15 **Publicly Held**
SIC: 1423 Crushed & broken granite
PA: Martin Marietta Materials Inc
2710 Wycliff Rd
Raleigh NC 27607

(G-10668)
SOUTHERN ILL WINE TRAIL NFP
48 E Glendale Rd (62938-4018)
PHONE..............................618 695-9463
EMP: 4
SALES (est): 184K **Privately Held**
SIC: 2084 Winery Trail

(G-10669)
US DEPT AGRICULTURE FOREST SVC
345 Job Corps Rd (62938-4158)
PHONE..............................618 285-5211
EMP: 3 **Publicly Held**
SIC: 7692 Welding repair
HQ: Us Dept Of Agriculture Forest Service
201 14th St Sw
Washington DC 20024

Good Hope
Mcdonough County

(G-10670)
MIDWEST OIL LLC
135 S Chestnut St (61438-5028)
PHONE..............................309 456-3663
Jerry Lewis, *President*
Cindy Bricker, *Manager*
EMP: 4
SQ FT: 4,000
SALES: 4MM **Privately Held**
SIC: 1311 Crude petroleum & natural gas

Goodfield
Woodford County

(G-10671)
CNH AMERICA LLC
600 E Peoria St (61742-9705)
PHONE..............................309 965-2217
EMP: 13
SALES (est): 1.9MM **Privately Held**
SIC: 3523 Farm machinery & equipment

(G-10672)
CNH INDUSTRIAL AMERICA LLC
Also Called: Case/D M I
1498 Us Highway 150 (61742-7515)
P.O. Box 65 (61742-0065)
PHONE..............................309 965-2233
William Schmidgall, *Manager*
EMP: 20
SALES (corp-wide): 28B **Privately Held**
SIC: 3523 3599 3714 Farm machinery & equipment; machine shop, jobbing & repair; bumpers & bumperettes, motor vehicle
HQ: Cnh Industrial America Llc
700 State St
Racine WI 53404
262 636-6011

(G-10673)
CNH INDUSTRIAL AMERICA LLC
600 E Peoria St (61742-9705)
P.O. Box 65 (61742-0065)
PHONE..............................309 965-2217
Paul Rouse, *Manager*
EMP: 208

SALES (corp-wide): 28B **Privately Held**
SIC: 3523 Farm machinery & equipment
HQ: Cnh Industrial America Llc
  700 State St
  Racine WI 53404
  262 636-6011

(G-10674)
DR & DR PROPERTY LEASING LLC
Also Called: Goodfield Milling Co
211 N Eureka St (61742-9638)
PHONE.................309 965-3200
Dale Rhoades, *Mng Member*
Donna Dorsey,
Leo Dorsey,
Dorman Eureka,
EMP: 5
SALES (est): 470.8K **Privately Held**
SIC: 2047 2048 Dog & cat food; fish food

(G-10675)
DSI INC
401 State Route 117 (61742-7520)
PHONE.................309 965-5110
William Dietrich, *President*
EMP: 6
SALES (est): 794.7K **Privately Held**
SIC: 0115 0119 3523 Corn; bean (dry field & seed) farm; farm machinery & equipment

(G-10676)
PAUL WEVER CONSTRUCTION EQP CO
Also Called: P W C E
401 W Martin Dr (61742-7536)
P.O. Box 85 (61742-0085)
PHONE.................309 965-2005
Paul Wever, *President*
Karen Wever, *Admin Sec*
EMP: 10
SALES (est): 1.8MM **Privately Held**
SIC: 3531 3441 Construction machinery attachments; fabricated structural metal

(G-10677)
TCI COMPANIES INC
405 State Route 117 (61742-7520)
P.O. Box 290 (61742-0290)
PHONE.................309 965-2057
Mike Barth, *President*
Joe Barth, *Vice Pres*
EMP: 30
SQ FT: 10,000
SALES (est): 6MM **Privately Held**
SIC: 1711 1731 1781 1381 Irrigation sprinkler system installation; lighting contractor; water well drilling; geothermal drilling; service well drilling

(G-10678)
TYSON FRESH MEATS INC
Also Called: I B P
373 Hwy 117 N (61742)
P.O. Box 386 (61742-0386)
PHONE.................309 965-2565
Thad Heffren, *Manager*
EMP: 10
SALES (corp-wide): 42.4B **Publicly Held**
SIC: 2011 5154 Meat packing plants; livestock
HQ: Tyson Fresh Meats, Inc.
  800 Stevens Port Dr
  Dakota Dunes SD 57049
  479 290-6397

Goreville
Johnson County

(G-10679)
CHEERS FOOD AND FUEL 240
845 S Broadway (62939-2479)
PHONE.................618 995-9153
Lance Vickers, *Principal*
EMP: 5
SALES (est): 189.9K **Privately Held**
SIC: 2869 Fuels

(G-10680)
GOREVILLE AUTO PARTS & MCH SP
Also Called: NAPA Auto Parts
Rr 37 (62939)
P.O. Box 106 (62939-0106)
PHONE.................618 995-2375
Wendell Stokes, *Owner*
Scottsa Stokes, *Vice Pres*
EMP: 7
SALES (est): 460.4K **Privately Held**
SIC: 5531 3599 Automobile & truck equipment & parts; machine & other job shop work

(G-10681)
GOREVILLE CONCRETE INC
301 N Hubbard Ave (62939-2351)
P.O. Box 232 (62939-0232)
PHONE.................618 995-2670
Carl Henderson, *President*
Tammy Rowe, *Admin Sec*
EMP: 20 **EST:** 1945
SQ FT: 1,200
SALES (est): 2.3MM **Privately Held**
SIC: 3273 Ready-mixed concrete

Gorham
Jackson County

(G-10682)
JACKSON COUNTY SAND & GRAV CO
1 Sickler Rd (62940-2109)
P.O. Box 242, Chester (62233-0242)
PHONE.................618 763-4711
Spencer F Brown, *President*
Shelby Lawder, *Corp Secy*
Bruce Brown, *Vice Pres*
EMP: 3
SQ FT: 1,000
SALES (est): 245.1K **Privately Held**
SIC: 1442 5032 Construction sand mining; brick, stone & related material

Grafton
Jersey County

(G-10683)
AERIES RIVERVIEW WINERY INC
600 Timber Ridge Dr (62037-1157)
PHONE.................618 786-7477
Karla Machens, *President*
EMP: 3
SALES (est): 279.3K **Privately Held**
SIC: 2084 Wines

(G-10684)
GRAFTON WINERY INC
300 W Main St (62037-1124)
PHONE.................618 786-3001
Michael J Nikonovich, *President*
Dennis Bick, *Principal*
Lori A Nikonovich, *Admin Sec*
EMP: 13
SALES (est): 1.6MM **Privately Held**
WEB: www.thegraftonwinery.com
SIC: 2084 Wines

(G-10685)
KNOTTY BY NATURE
15 E Main St (62037-1119)
PHONE.................618 610-2481
Dan Bechtold, *Principal*
EMP: 4 **EST:** 2017
SALES (est): 320.6K **Privately Held**
SIC: 2431 Millwork

(G-10686)
LAWRENCE ALLEN
21031 State Highway 3 (62037-2440)
PHONE.................618 786-3794
Allen Lawrence, *Owner*
EMP: 3
SALES (est): 325.4K **Privately Held**
SIC: 3523 Driers (farm): grain, hay & seed

Grand Chain
Pulaski County

(G-10687)
LAFARGE NORTH AMERICA INC
2500 Portland Rd (62941-2306)
PHONE.................618 543-7541
Dale Smith, *Project Mgr*
Deborah McKinney, *Safety Mgr*
Joe Pennings, *Branch Mgr*
EMP: 150
SALES (corp-wide): 4.5B **Privately Held**
SIC: 3241 Cement, hydraulic
HQ: Lafarge North America Inc.
  8700 W Bryn Mawr Ave
  Chicago IL 60631
  773 372-1000

Grand Ridge
Lasalle County

(G-10688)
EPIC EYE
1869 E 19th Rd (61325-9765)
PHONE.................309 210-6212
Susan Rees, *Owner*
Sarah Christensen, *Officer*
EMP: 3 **EST:** 2011
SALES (est): 133.1K **Privately Held**
SIC: 7335 3651 Photographic studio, commercial; video camera-audio recorders, household use

Granite City
Madison County

(G-10689)
ACCURATE FABRICATORS INC
Also Called: G & M Steel Fabricating
1603 Cleveland Blvd (62040-4402)
PHONE.................618 451-1886
Craig Vance, *President*
Marc Plank, *Principal*
John Carlyle, *Vice Pres*
EMP: 7
SQ FT: 20,000
SALES (est): 1.4MM **Privately Held**
SIC: 3441 Fabricated structural metal

(G-10690)
AERO AVIATION COMPANY INC (PA)
3701 State Route 162 (62040-6628)
PHONE.................618 797-6630
John P Mc Namara, *President*
Catherine J McNamara, *Admin Sec*
EMP: 12
SQ FT: 12,000
SALES (est): 2.7MM **Privately Held**
SIC: 3728 Aircraft parts & equipment

(G-10691)
AIR PRODUCTS AND CHEMICALS INC
2200 Monroe St (62040-5426)
P.O. Box 695 (62040-0695)
PHONE.................618 452-5335
Kenneth Miller, *Branch Mgr*
EMP: 25
SALES (corp-wide): 8.9B **Publicly Held**
WEB: www.airproducts.com
SIC: 2813 Industrial gases
PA: Air Products And Chemicals, Inc.
  7201 Hamilton Blvd
  Allentown PA 18195
  610 481-4911

(G-10692)
AIR PRODUCTS AND CHEMICALS INC
35 N Gate Indus Dr (62040-6806)
PHONE.................618 451-0577
Tom Minor, *Branch Mgr*
EMP: 58
SALES (corp-wide): 8.9B **Publicly Held**
SIC: 2813 5169 Industrial gases; chemicals & allied products

PA: Air Products And Chemicals, Inc.
  7201 Hamilton Blvd
  Allentown PA 18195
  610 481-4911

(G-10693)
ALL PALLET SERVICE
1459 State St (62040-4433)
PHONE.................618 451-7545
Carrie Shrum, *Principal*
EMP: 9 **EST:** 2009
SALES (est): 1.4MM **Privately Held**
SIC: 2448 Pallets, wood

(G-10694)
AMERICAN COLLOID COMPANY
1601 Walnut St (62040-3117)
PHONE.................618 452-8143
Van Coates, *Opers-Prdtn-Mfg*
EMP: 23 **Publicly Held**
SIC: 1459 2899 Bentonite mining; chemical preparations
HQ: American Colloid Company
  2870 Forbs Ave
  Hoffman Estates IL 60192

(G-10695)
AMSTED RAIL COMPANY INC
1700 Walnut St (62040-3100)
PHONE.................618 452-2111
Donnie Chandler, *Branch Mgr*
EMP: 2000
SALES (corp-wide): 2.3B **Privately Held**
SIC: 3743 Railroad equipment
HQ: Amsted Rail Company, Inc.
  311 S Wacker Dr Ste 5300
  Chicago IL 60606

(G-10696)
AMSTED RAIL COMPANY INC
1078 19th St (62040)
PHONE.................618 225-6463
John Wories, *Branch Mgr*
EMP: 450
SALES (corp-wide): 2.3B **Privately Held**
SIC: 3743 Railroad equipment
HQ: Amsted Rail Company, Inc.
  311 S Wacker Dr Ste 5300
  Chicago IL 60606

(G-10697)
ARIZON STRCTURES WORLDWIDE LLC
1200 W 7th St (62040-1895)
PHONE.................618 451-7250
John A Brennan, *CFO*
EMP: 50
SALES (est): 6.6MM **Privately Held**
SIC: 3069 Air-supported rubber structures
PA: Arizon Companies, Inc.
  11880 Dorsett Rd
  Maryland Heights MO 63043

(G-10698)
ARNETTE PATTERN CO INC
Also Called: Midwest Machining & Fabg
3203 Missouri Ave (62040-6833)
PHONE.................618 451-7700
Gary Z Zimmer, *President*
Jon Hughey, *Engineer*
Mike Murphy, *Sales Engr*
Diane Zimmer, *Office Mgr*
Joe Stimac, *Manager*
EMP: 30
SQ FT: 30,000
SALES (est): 6.3MM **Privately Held**
WEB: www.arnettepattern.com
SIC: 3599 3543 3441 Machine shop, jobbing & repair; foundry patternmaking; fabricated structural metal

(G-10699)
BAILY INTERNATIONAL INC (PA)
2501 W 20th St (62040-3101)
PHONE.................618 451-8878
George Tsai, *President*
Max Tsai, *Vice Pres*
Sandy Tsai, *Vice Pres*
▲ **EMP:** 71
SQ FT: 45,000
SALES (est): 80.3MM **Privately Held**
SIC: 2052 Bakery products, dry

GEOGRAPHIC SECTION

Granite City - Madison County (G-10727)

(G-10700)
BOISE CASCADE COMPANY
1201 W 1st St Ste 310 (62040-1890)
PHONE 618 491-7030
Mark Corso, *Branch Mgr*
EMP: 25
SALES (corp-wide): 4.6B **Publicly Held**
SIC: 2421 Building & structural materials, wood
PA: Boise Cascade Company
 1111 W Jefferson St # 300
 Boise ID 83702
 208 384-6161

(G-10701)
CUSTOM FBRICATION COATINGS INC
1107 22nd St (62040-3306)
PHONE 618 452-9540
Terry Carron, *President*
Cathy Carron, *Principal*
EMP: 60
SQ FT: 130,000
SALES (est): 16.5MM **Privately Held**
SIC: 3441 Fabricated structural metal

(G-10702)
CUSTOM SYSTEMS INC
3660 State Route 111 (62040-6612)
P.O. Box 1738 (62040-1738)
PHONE 314 355-4575
Robert L Stanford, *President*
Carol Stanford, *Admin Sec*
EMP: 4
SALES (est): 2MM **Privately Held**
SIC: 3556 3564 Bakery machinery; dust or fume collecting equipment, industrial

(G-10703)
DICKEY SIGN CO
116 Springfield Dr (62040-2831)
PHONE 618 797-1262
Dale Dickey, *Owner*
EMP: 3
SALES: 300K **Privately Held**
SIC: 3993 Signs & advertising specialties

(G-10704)
EHRHARDT TOOL & MACHINE LLC
Also Called: Ehrhardt Engineered Solutions
25 Central Industrial Dr (62040-6802)
PHONE 314 436-6900
Ralph Phillips, *President*
Patrick Walsh, *Vice Pres*
Michael Walz, *Vice Pres*
Tom Werly, *CFO*
Rich Dauphin, *Manager*
▼ **EMP:** 150
SQ FT: 100,000
SALES (est): 4.5MM **Privately Held**
SIC: 7692 3544 8711 Brazing; die sets for metal stamping (presses); machine tool design

(G-10705)
EVOQUA WATER TECHNOLOGIES LLC
3202 W 20th St (62040-1820)
PHONE 618 451-1205
James Kopsic, *Manager*
EMP: 8
SALES (corp-wide): 1.4B **Publicly Held**
SIC: 3589 3569 Water treatment equipment, industrial; filters, general line: industrial
HQ: Evoqua Water Technologies Llc
 210 6th Ave Ste 3300
 Pittsburgh PA 15222
 724 772-0044

(G-10706)
FAIRFIELD PROCESSING CORP
1201 W 1st St (62040-1890)
PHONE 618 452-8404
EMP: 28
SALES (corp-wide): 45.4MM **Privately Held**
SIC: 2824 Mfg Organic Fiber-Noncellulosic
PA: Fairfield Processing Corp
 88 Rose Hill Ave
 Danbury CT 06810
 203 744-2090

(G-10707)
FULLER ASPHALT & LANDSCAPE
4353 Lake Dr (62040-3038)
PHONE 618 797-1169
Gary W Fuller, *President*
Paula Fuller, *Admin Sec*
EMP: 5
SALES (est): 389.5K **Privately Held**
SIC: 1771 0782 4212 2951 Driveway contractor; parking lot construction; landscape contractors; local trucking, without storage; asphalt paving mixtures & blocks

(G-10708)
G F PRINTING
2439 Hemlock Ave (62040-2902)
PHONE 618 797-0576
Laura Falter, *President*
Greg Falter, *Owner*
Glenn Falter, *Vice Pres*
EMP: 3
SQ FT: 4,400
SALES (est): 180K **Privately Held**
SIC: 2752 2791 2789 2759 Commercial printing, offset; typesetting; bookbinding & related work; commercial printing

(G-10709)
GATEWAY PACKAGING COMPANY LLC
20 Central Industrial Dr (62040-6801)
PHONE 618 451-0010
EMP: 8
SALES (corp-wide): 1.2B **Privately Held**
SIC: 2674 Shipping bags or sacks, including multiwall & heavy duty; paper bags: made from purchased materials
HQ: Gateway Packaging Company Llc
 605 Highway 76
 White House TN 37188

(G-10710)
GEBCO MACHINE INC
2900 Emzee Ave (62040-1999)
PHONE 618 452-6120
Gary Vogeller, *President*
George Vogeller, *President*
EMP: 12
SQ FT: 17,000
SALES (est): 1.6MM **Privately Held**
WEB: www.gebco1.com
SIC: 3599 Machine shop, jobbing & repair

(G-10711)
GRAIN DENSIFICATION INTL LLC
Also Called: Gdi
1350 4th St (62040-1888)
PHONE 618 823-5122
EMP: 3
SALES (est): 68.6K **Privately Held**
SIC: 2048 Livestock feeds

(G-10712)
H&S MACHINE & TOOLS INC
35 Central Industrial Dr (62040-6802)
PHONE 618 451-0164
Richard Hollshouser, *President*
EMP: 9
SALES (est): 843.2K **Privately Held**
SIC: 7539 3599 Machine shop, automotive; industrial machinery

(G-10713)
H2O SOLUTIONS LLC
40 Georgetown Dr (62040-3009)
PHONE 618 219-2905
Travis McGovern,
EMP: 3
SALES: 250K **Privately Held**
SIC: 3589 7389 Water purification equipment, household type;

(G-10714)
HEIDTMAN STEEL PRODUCTS INC
10 Northgate Indus Dr (62040-6842)
PHONE 618 451-0052
Tom Becherer, *Traffic Mgr*
Tim Berra, *Branch Mgr*
Dave Fedio, *Maintence Staff*
EMP: 100
SQ FT: 55,000

SALES (corp-wide): 256.5MM **Privately Held**
SIC: 3312 5051 3471 Blast furnaces & steel mills; metals service centers & offices; plating & polishing
HQ: Heidtman Steel Products, Inc.
 2401 Front St
 Toledo OH 43605
 419 691-4646

(G-10715)
HOLSHOUSER MACHINE & TOOL INC
35 Central Industrial Dr (62040-6802)
PHONE 618 451-0164
Richard J Holshouser, *President*
Diane Jacober, *Corp Secy*
EMP: 7 **EST:** 1966
SQ FT: 6,400
SALES (est): 450K **Privately Held**
SIC: 7692 3599 Welding repair; machine shop, jobbing & repair

(G-10716)
ICON MECH CNSTR & ENGRG LLC
1616 Cleveland Blvd (62040-4401)
PHONE 618 452-0035
Brandon Elzea, *Superintendent*
Tim Nehrt, *Sr Project Mgr*
Michael F Bieg,
Timothy Schaeffer,
EMP: 250
SQ FT: 22,500
SALES (est): 59MM **Privately Held**
SIC: 8711 3498 Engineering services; fabricated pipe & fittings

(G-10717)
ILLINOIS ELECTRIC WORKS INC
2161 Adams St (62040-3315)
PHONE 618 451-6900
Dale M Hamil, *President*
Ernie F Hodge, *Vice Pres*
Trent Hamil, *Treasurer*
Norman Harrison, *Supervisor*
Denise Isringhausen, *Data Admn*
▲ **EMP:** 50
SQ FT: 80,000
SALES (est): 12MM **Privately Held**
SIC: 7694 Electric motor repair

(G-10718)
KRAFT HEINZ FOODS COMPANY
Also Called: Kraft Foods
2901 Missouri Ave (62040-2032)
PHONE 618 451-4820
Dave Peterson, *Manager*
EMP: 324
SALES (corp-wide): 24.9B **Publicly Held**
SIC: 2099 Food preparations
HQ: Kraft Heinz Foods Company
 1 Ppg Pl Fl 34
 Pittsburgh PA 15222
 412 456-5700

(G-10719)
LAWRENCE BRAND SHOT
1200 16th St (62040-4444)
PHONE 618 798-6112
EMP: 3 **EST:** 2011
SALES (est): 209.3K **Privately Held**
SIC: 3356 Nonferrous rolling & drawing

(G-10720)
LOVES TRAVEL STOPS
1201 Denham Dr (62040-4714)
PHONE 618 931-1575
John Rosen, *Principal*
EMP: 22
SALES (corp-wide): 4.2B **Privately Held**
SIC: 2992 Lubricating oils
PA: Love's Travel Stops & Country Stores, Inc.
 10601 N Pennsylvania Ave
 Oklahoma City OK 73120
 405 302-6500

(G-10721)
MAYCO MANUFACTURING LLC
1200 16th St (62040-4444)
PHONE 618 451-4400
Bob Cook, *Manager*
EMP: 50

SALES (corp-wide): 6.2MM **Privately Held**
SIC: 3339 Primary nonferrous metals
HQ: Mayco Manufacturing, Llc
 18 W Oxmoor Rd
 Birmingham AL 35209
 205 942-4242

(G-10722)
MAYCO-GRANITE CITY INC
1200 16th St (62040-4444)
PHONE 618 451-4400
Michael Drury, *President*
Eric W Finlayson, *Corp Secy*
▲ **EMP:** 40 **EST:** 1979
SQ FT: 186,000
SALES (est): 8.8MM
SALES (corp-wide): 97.6MM **Privately Held**
WEB: www.maycoindustries.com
SIC: 3356 Lead & zinc
PA: Metalico, Inc.
 135 Dermody St
 Cranford NJ 07016
 908 497-9610

(G-10723)
MCS MIDWEST LLC
5506 Dial Dr (62040-7085)
PHONE 314 398-8107
EMP: 3
SALES (corp-wide): 4.3MM **Privately Held**
WEB: www.mcsmidwest.com
SIC: 3089 Garbage containers, plastic
PA: Mcs Midwest Llc
 3876 Hendrickson Rd
 Franklin OH 45005
 513 217-0805

(G-10724)
MIDWEST LIFTING PRODUCTS INC
1635 W 1st St Ste 312 (62040-1883)
PHONE 214 356-7102
Sheila Bean, *President*
Radiance Bean, *Vice Pres*
Gary Head, *Admin Sec*
EMP: 4
SALES (est): 181.9K **Privately Held**
SIC: 2499 Tackle blocks, wood

(G-10725)
MIDWEST METAL COATINGS LLC
9 Konzen Ct (62040-6855)
PHONE 618 451-2971
Jerry Luna, *Executive*
EMP: 40
SQ FT: 94,000
SALES (est): 7.3MM
SALES (corp-wide): 3.3B **Publicly Held**
SIC: 3479 Coating of metals & formed products
HQ: Precoat Metals Corp.
 1310 Papin St Ste 300
 Saint Louis MO 63103

(G-10726)
MIDWEST SUN-RAY LIGHTING & SIG
Also Called: Midwest Sun-Ray Ltg & Sign
4762 E Chain Of Rocks Rd (62040)
PHONE 618 656-2884
Fax: 618 656-3764
EMP: 15
SQ FT: 2,000
SALES (est): 2.2MM **Privately Held**
SIC: 1799 3993 3645 1731 Special Trade Contractor Mfg Signs/Ad Specialties Mfg Residentl Light Fixt Electrical Contractor

(G-10727)
MRC GLOBAL (US) INC
3672 State Route 111 (62040-6612)
P.O. Box 550 (62040-0550)
PHONE 314 231-3400
Rance Long, *Vice Pres*
EMP: 11 **Publicly Held**
WEB: www.mrcglobal.com
SIC: 1311 Crude petroleum & natural gas

HQ: Mrc Global (Us) Inc.
1301 Mckinney St Ste 2300
Houston TX 77010
877 294-7574

(G-10728)
NICHOLS NET & TWINE INC
2200 State Route 111 (62040-6581)
PHONE.................................618 797-0211
John J Rogenski, *President*
Patrick Dillon, *Vice Pres*
Charlene Rogenski, *Admin Sec*
EMP: 5 **EST:** 1959
SQ FT: 10,000
SALES (est): 440K **Privately Held**
SIC: 2298 3949 Fishing lines, nets, seines; made in cordage or twine mills; sporting & athletic goods

(G-10729)
OSSOLA INDUSTRIALS INC (PA)
400 A St Ste B (62040-1891)
PHONE.................................618 451-2621
Dan Ossola, *President*
Glenda Evan, *Manager*
▲ **EMP:** 11
SALES (est): 1.7MM **Privately Held**
SIC: 3297 Cement: high temperature, refractory (nonclay)

(G-10730)
PRAIRIE FARMS DAIRY INC
1800 Adams St (62040-3347)
PHONE.................................618 451-5600
Bob Kmetz, *General Mgr*
Jeff Lawler, *Marketing Mgr*
Dale Chapman, *Manager*
Paula Sutton, *Manager*
EMP: 9
SALES (corp-wide): 1.7B **Privately Held**
WEB: www.prairiefarmsdairy.com
SIC: 2026 Milk processing (pasteurizing, homogenizing, bottling)
PA: Prairie Farms Dairy, Inc.
3744 Staunton Rd
Edwardsville IL 62025
618 659-5700

(G-10731)
PRECOAT METALS CORP
25 Northgate Indus Dr (62040-6841)
PHONE.................................618 451-0909
Jeff Hoffmeister, *Plant Mgr*
Jerry Luna, *Plant Mgr*
Matt Murphy, *Plant Mgr*
Dennis Harper, *Manager*
Heath Daugherty, *Info Tech Dir*
EMP: 56
SALES (corp-wide): 3.3B **Publicly Held**
SIC: 3724 3479 Aircraft engines & engine parts; coating of metals & formed products
HQ: Precoat Metals Corp.
1310 Papin St Ste 300
Saint Louis MO 63103

(G-10732)
PREMIER CDL TRAINING SVCS LLC (PA)
5529 Dial Dr Ste 4 (62040-7092)
PHONE.................................618 797-1725
Ann Bauza,
EMP: 9
SALES (est): 1.3MM **Privately Held**
SIC: 3537 Industrial trucks & tractors

(G-10733)
PROAMPAC PG BORROWER LLC
20 Central Industrial Dr (62040-6801)
PHONE.................................618 451-0010
Greg Tucker, *CEO*
Tharrin Akers, *Manager*
EMP: 290
SALES (corp-wide): 444.2MM **Privately Held**
SIC: 2674 2679 Bags: uncoated paper & multiwall; labels, paper: made from purchased material
PA: Proampac Pg Borrower Llc
12025 Tricon Rd
Cincinnati OH 45246
513 671-1777

(G-10734)
PROGRESS RAIL SERVICES CORP
All Track Equipment
1900 Missouri Ave (62040-3218)
P.O. Box 1247 (62040-1247)
PHONE.................................618 451-0072
Joel Frank, *Manager*
EMP: 21
SALES (corp-wide): 53.8B **Publicly Held**
WEB: www.progressrail.com
SIC: 3743 Railroad equipment
HQ: Progress Rail Services Corporation
1600 Progress Dr
Albertville AL 35950
256 505-6421

(G-10735)
S & S PALLET CORP
1459 State St (62040-4433)
P.O. Box 1387 (62040-1387)
PHONE.................................618 219-3218
Donnye Shrum, *President*
Kim Shrum, *Admin Sec*
EMP: 38
SALES (est): 6.5MM **Privately Held**
SIC: 2448 Pallets, wood

(G-10736)
SHIRTS GALORE & MORE
4132 Pontoon Rd (62040-4344)
PHONE.................................618 797-9801
Laura Worthen, *Owner*
EMP: 2
SALES (est): 278.9K **Privately Held**
SIC: 2759 Screen printing

(G-10737)
SHUP TOOL & MACHINE CO
4158 State Route 162 (62040-6607)
PHONE.................................618 931-2596
Dennis Shup, *Owner*
EMP: 3 **EST:** 1974
SQ FT: 2,000
SALES (est): 113.3K **Privately Held**
SIC: 7692 3544 Welding repair; special dies & tools

(G-10738)
SHUTTERBOOTH SPECL EVNTS BY LA
10 Cobblestone Ct (62040-5183)
PHONE.................................618 973-1894
EMP: 3
SALES (est): 228.9K **Privately Held**
SIC: 3442 Shutters, door or window: metal

(G-10739)
STEIN INC
Also Called: Stein Still Mills
2201 Edwardsville Rd (62040-6311)
P.O. Box 1369 (62040-1369)
PHONE.................................618 452-0836
Alan Medford, *Branch Mgr*
EMP: 70
SALES (corp-wide): 83.5MM **Privately Held**
SIC: 3399 3312 5084 Iron ore recovery from open hearth slag; blast furnaces & steel mills; industrial machinery & equipment
PA: Stein, Inc.
1929 E Royalton Rd Ste C
Cleveland OH 44147
440 526-9301

(G-10740)
STRIPMASTERS ILLINOIS INC
1107 22nd St (62040-3306)
PHONE.................................618 452-1060
Terry Carron, *President*
Cathy Carron, *Admin Sec*
EMP: 6
SALES (est): 593.5K **Privately Held**
SIC: 1799 3479 Sandblasting of building exteriors; painting, coating & hot dipping

(G-10741)
SUPPLIED INDUS SOLUTIONS INC
550 Niedringhaus Ave (62040-1839)
PHONE.................................618 452-8151
Stephen Brock, *President*
Angela Brock, *Admin Sec*
EMP: 3

SQ FT: 2,500
SALES (est): 2.6MM **Privately Held**
SIC: 5085 1629 3498 Industrial supplies; waste water & sewage treatment plant construction; fabricated pipe & fittings

(G-10742)
TMS INTERNATIONAL LLC
22nd & Edwardsville Rd (62040)
P.O. Box 398 (62040-0398)
PHONE.................................618 451-7840
EMP: 55
SALES (corp-wide): 282.4MM **Privately Held**
SIC: 3295 Mfg Minerals-Ground/Treated
HQ: Tms International Group Llc
12 Monongahela Ave
Glassport PA 15203
412 678-6141

(G-10743)
TMS INTERNATIONAL LLC
2500 E 23rd St (62040-5635)
PHONE.................................618 451-9526
Kevin Rudman, *President*
EMP: 5 **Privately Held**
SIC: 3312 Blast furnaces & steel mills
HQ: Tms International, Llc
Southside Wrks Bldg 1 3f
Pittsburgh PA 15203
412 678-6141

(G-10744)
TOP BRASS INC
2700 Missouri Ave (62040-2029)
PHONE.................................719 539-7242
Dan Scharch, *President*
EMP: 4 **EST:** 2011
SALES (est): 358K **Privately Held**
WEB: www.topbrass-inc.com
SIC: 3559 5961 Ammunition & explosives, loading machinery; fitness & sporting goods, mail order

(G-10745)
TOP BRASS LLC
2700 Missouri Ave (62040-2029)
PHONE.................................800 836-4683
Dan Scharch, *President*
Kay Scharch, *Vice Pres*
EMP: 11
SQ FT: 14,000
SALES (est): 2.4MM **Privately Held**
SIC: 3559 5961 Ammunition & explosives, loading machinery; fitness & sporting goods, mail order

(G-10746)
TRI CITY CANVAS PRODUCTS INC (PA)
3240 W Chain Of Rocks Rd A (62040-7065)
PHONE.................................618 797-1662
Herman Schoeber, *Owner*
EMP: 18
SQ FT: 12,000
SALES (est): 8.8MM **Privately Held**
SIC: 5013 2394 Trailer parts & accessories; tarpaulins, fabric: made from purchased materials

(G-10747)
U S FILTER PRODUCTS
3202 W 20th St (62040-1820)
P.O. Box 98 (62040-0098)
PHONE.................................618 451-1205
Jim Kopsic, *Manager*
EMP: 2
SALES (est): 200K **Privately Held**
SIC: 3569 Filters

(G-10748)
UNITED STATES STEEL CORP
Also Called: Granite City Works
1951 State St (62040-4622)
PHONE.................................618 451-3456
Sharron Owen, *General Mgr*
Nichols Robert, *Safety Mgr*
Mark Frields, *Engineer*
Wayne Horrell, *Engineer*
Ryan Relleke, *Project Engr*
EMP: 100
SALES (corp-wide): 12.9B **Publicly Held**
SIC: 3312 Blast furnaces & steel mills

PA: United States Steel Corp
600 Grant St
Pittsburgh PA 15219
412 433-1121

(G-10749)
WALTERS METAL FABRICATION INC
3660 State Route 111 (62040-6612)
P.O. Box 1245 (62040-1245)
PHONE.................................618 931-5551
Laurence Dittmeier, *President*
Paul Benne, *CFO*
EMP: 100
SQ FT: 42,000
SALES (est): 39.2MM **Privately Held**
WEB: www.waltersmetalfab.com
SIC: 3441 8711 Fabricated structural metal; engineering services

Grant Park
Kankakee County

(G-10750)
PEORIA PACKING LTD
8372 N 12000e Rd (60940-5014)
P.O. Box 162 (60940-0162)
PHONE.................................815 465-9824
Eddie Lynch, *Branch Mgr*
EMP: 15
SALES (est): 1.4MM **Privately Held**
SIC: 2011 Meat packing plants
PA: Peoria Packing, Ltd.
1307 W Lake St
Chicago IL 60607

(G-10751)
REYNOLDS FOOD PACKAGING
304 Ne Main St (60940-6001)
P.O. Box 660 (60940-0660)
PHONE.................................815 465-2115
Peter Boevers, *Principal*
EMP: 11
SALES (est): 1.6MM **Privately Held**
SIC: 3353 Foil, aluminum

(G-10752)
ROYAL MACHINE WORKS INC
204 N Stanley St (60940-7269)
P.O. Box 507 (60940-0507)
PHONE.................................815 465-6879
Ricky Bird, *President*
Tammy Nies, *Corp Secy*
EMP: 2
SQ FT: 12,500
SALES (est): 200K **Privately Held**
SIC: 3599 Machine shop, jobbing & repair

(G-10753)
TOOL-MASTERS TOOL & STAMP INC
204 N Stanley St (60940-7269)
P.O. Box 507 (60940-0507)
PHONE.................................815 465-6830
Tammy Nief, *President*
Rick Bird, *Admin Sec*
EMP: 9
SQ FT: 12,523
SALES (est): 1.5MM **Privately Held**
SIC: 3599 Machine shop, jobbing & repair

Granville
Putnam County

(G-10754)
CONCRETE PRODUCTS
Also Called: Concrete Products Ziano
304 E Harper Ave (61326-9719)
P.O. Box 232 (61326-0232)
PHONE.................................815 339-6395
James Ziano, *Owner*
EMP: 4 **EST:** 1958
SQ FT: 3,200
SALES (est): 630K **Privately Held**
SIC: 3272 Concrete products, precast; septic tanks, concrete

GEOGRAPHIC SECTION

(G-10755)
J W OSSOLA COMPANY INC
Also Called: Granville Ready Mix
502 E Harper Ave (61326-9709)
P.O. Box 346 (61326-0346)
PHONE..................................815 339-6112
Robert Ossola, *President*
Douglas Ossola, *Vice Pres*
Jack Ossola, *Treasurer*
EMP: 6 EST: 1945
SQ FT: 4,000
SALES (est): 741.9K **Privately Held**
SIC: 1794 3273 Excavation work; ready-mixed concrete

(G-10756)
JW OSSOLA CO INC
Also Called: Granville Ready Mix
And Elm St Rr 71 (61326)
PHONE..................................815 339-6113
Robert Ossola, *President*
Douglas Ossola, *Vice Pres*
Jack Ossola, *Admin Sec*
EMP: 6
SALES: 6MM **Privately Held**
SIC: 3273 Ready-mixed concrete

(G-10757)
MENNIES MACHINE COMPANY
508 N Saint Paul St (61326-9653)
Rural Route 1 Box 131 (61326-9747)
PHONE..................................815 339-2227
Jennifer Smoode, *Treasurer*
Cheryl Mennie, *Branch Mgr*
EMP: 14
SALES (corp-wide): 74.2MM **Privately Held**
SIC: 3599 Machine shop, jobbing & repair
PA: Mennie's Machine Company
Mennie Dr Mark Rr 71
Mark IL 61340
815 339-2226

Grayslake
Lake County

(G-10758)
ABBVIE
480 S Us Highway 45 (60030-3910)
PHONE..................................847 548-1016
EMP: 5
SALES (est): 440.6K
SALES (corp-wide): 33.2B **Publicly Held**
SIC: 2834 Pharmaceutical preparations
PA: Abbvie Inc.
1 N Waukegan Rd
North Chicago IL 60064
847 932-7900

(G-10759)
ASAP SPECIALTIES INC DEL
888 E Belvidere Rd # 111 (60030-2568)
PHONE..................................847 223-7699
EMP: 6
SALES (est): 512.3K **Privately Held**
SIC: 5199 5065 5136 5137 Nondurable Goods, Nec, Nsk

(G-10760)
CANNY TOOL & MOLD CORPORATION
888 E Belvidere Rd # 207 (60030-2571)
PHONE..................................847 548-1573
Roland Schroeder, *President*
Gisela Schroeder, *Admin Sec*
▲ EMP: 5
SQ FT: 3,200
SALES: 600K **Privately Held**
WEB: www.cannyinc.com
SIC: 3544 Special dies & tools

(G-10761)
CAREY ELECTRIC CO INC
24809 W Chardon Rd (60030-9518)
PHONE..................................847 949-9294
Bill Fialkowski, *Manager*
EMP: 2
SALES (est): 257.5K **Privately Held**
SIC: 3699 1731 Electrical equipment & supplies; electrical work

(G-10762)
COLLEAGUES OF BEER INC
Also Called: Light The Lamp Brewery
520 Laurie Ct (60030-1572)
PHONE..................................847 727-3318
William Hermes, *CEO*
James Sheppard, *CFO*
Jeff Sheppard, *CFO*
Kurt Engdahl, *Sales Staff*
Donald Chatten, *Admin Sec*
EMP: 4
SQ FT: 2,300
SALES (est): 261.9K **Privately Held**
SIC: 2082 Ale (alcoholic beverage)

(G-10763)
COMPX SECURITY PRODUCTS INC
Also Called: Compx Timberline
715 Center St (60030-1651)
PHONE..................................847 234-1864
Scott C James, *President*
Gregg Walla, *Principal*
Andrew Louis, *Admin Sec*
▲ EMP: 85
SQ FT: 120,000
SALES (est): 11.7MM
SALES (corp-wide): 2.3B **Publicly Held**
SIC: 3429 5712 Furniture hardware; furniture stores
HQ: Compx International Inc.
5430 Lyndon B Johnson Fwy
Dallas TX 75240

(G-10764)
CREATIVE CLOTHING CREATED 4 U
488 Wood Duck Ct (60030-2794)
PHONE..................................847 543-0051
Joe Covelli, *President*
EMP: 6
SALES (est): 460K **Privately Held**
SIC: 2253 2396 2395 Warm weather knit outerwear, including beachwear; dresses & skirts; automotive & apparel trimmings; pleating & stitching

(G-10765)
DAESAM CORPORATION
888 E Belvidere Rd # 306 (60030-2568)
PHONE..................................917 653-2000
▲ EMP: 5 EST: 2010
SALES: 950K **Privately Held**
SIC: 3679 Mfg Electronic Components

(G-10766)
DANDELION DISTRIBUTORS INC
Also Called: Holly Press, The
888 E Belvidere Rd # 114 (60030-2568)
P.O. Box 234 (60030-0234)
PHONE..................................815 675-9800
David H Gerholdt, *President*
EMP: 3
SALES (est): 488.6K **Privately Held**
SIC: 2752 Commercial printing, offset

(G-10767)
DISTINCTIVE SIGNS& THE NEON EX
1868 E Belvidere Rd A (60030-2289)
PHONE..................................847 245-7159
Fax: 847 395-1582
EMP: 2
SALES: 300K **Privately Held**
SIC: 7389 3993 Business Services Mfg Signs/Advertising Specialties

(G-10768)
ENCAP TECHNOLOGIES INC
61 S Seymour Ave (60030-1541)
PHONE..................................847 202-3443
John Hanrahan, *Branch Mgr*
EMP: 157
SALES (corp-wide): 20MM **Privately Held**
WEB: www.encaptech.com
SIC: 3621 Motors & generators
PA: Encap Technologies, Inc.
707 S Vermont St
Palatine IL 60067
510 337-2700

(G-10769)
ENERGY-GLAZED SYSTEMS INC
350 Center St (60030-1624)
PHONE..................................847 223-4500
Wayman Tidwell, *President*
EMP: 8
SALES (est): 998.6K **Privately Held**
SIC: 3211 Window glass, clear & colored

(G-10770)
ENGINEERED MILLS INC
Also Called: EMI
888 E Belvidere Rd (60030-2568)
PHONE..................................847 548-0044
Dave Peterson, *President*
EMP: 5
SQ FT: 5,000
SALES (est): 805.7K **Privately Held**
WEB: www.emimills.com
SIC: 3541 Chemical milling machines

(G-10771)
EXCEL LTD INC
888 E Belvidere Rd # 105 (60030-2568)
PHONE..................................847 543-9138
James Bartus, *President*
Susan Eisert, *Vice Pres*
EMP: 6
SALES (est): 1.8MM **Privately Held**
SIC: 3613 Control panels, electric

(G-10772)
FABRICATORS UNLIMITED INC
55 S Barron Blvd (60030-7825)
PHONE..................................847 223-7986
Randall E Peters, *President*
EMP: 3
SQ FT: 8,200
SALES: 450K **Privately Held**
SIC: 3469 1799 3599 8731 Stamping metal for the trade; welding on site; machine shop, jobbing & repair; industrial laboratory, except testing

(G-10773)
FORT LOCK CORPORATION (DH)
Also Called: Compx Fort
715 Center St (60030-1651)
PHONE..................................708 456-1100
Jay A Fine, *President*
▲ EMP: 32 EST: 1954
SQ FT: 70,000
SALES (est): 12.6MM
SALES (corp-wide): 2.3B **Publicly Held**
WEB: www.compxelock.com
SIC: 3429 Locks or lock sets

(G-10774)
GFX INTERNATIONAL LLC (HQ)
333 Barron Blvd (60030-1638)
PHONE..................................847 543-7179
Charles Huttinger, *CEO*
Tim Nisbet, *President*
Mark Taylor, *COO*
Dan Hill, *Vice Pres*
Wade Adams, *Project Mgr*
EMP: 110
SQ FT: 88,000
SALES (est): 45.9MM
SALES (corp-wide): 391.8MM **Privately Held**
WEB: www.gfxi.com
SIC: 7336 2759 7335 7812 Graphic arts & related design; posters, including billboards: printing; commercial photography; commercials, television: tape or film
PA: The Imagine Group Llc
1000 Valley Park Dr
Shakopee MN 55379
952 903-4515

(G-10775)
GIFT OF GAMES LTD
Also Called: Gift of Games, The
82 Center St Unit W (60030-1595)
PHONE..................................847 370-1541
Tim Backstrom, *President*
EMP: 4
SQ FT: 1,800
SALES (est): 139.8K **Privately Held**
SIC: 3944 Board games, children's & adults'

(G-10776)
GLAZED STRUCTURES INC
350 Center St (60030-1624)
P.O. Box 243 (60030-0243)
PHONE..................................847 223-4560
Deann Twitchel, *President*
EMP: 15
SQ FT: 14,000
SALES (est): 1.4MM **Privately Held**
SIC: 3211 3444 3231 3083 Flat glass; sheet metalwork; products of purchased glass; laminated plastics plate & sheet

(G-10777)
GLUNZ FMLY WINERY CELLARS INC (PA)
Also Called: Glunz Cellars
888 E Belvidere Rd # 205 (60030-2571)
PHONE..................................847 548-9463
Helen T Glunz, *President*
EMP: 25
SQ FT: 3,873
SALES (est): 3.4MM **Privately Held**
SIC: 2084 2085 Wines; distilled & blended liquors

(G-10778)
GRAM COLOSSAL INC
888 E Belvidere Rd # 113 (60030-2570)
PHONE..................................847 223-5757
Marilyn Schleiden, *CEO*
Bruce Schleiden, *President*
EMP: 3
SALES (est): 290.4K **Privately Held**
SIC: 2771 Greeting cards

(G-10779)
GRAYSLAKE FEED SALES INC
81 E Belvidere Rd (60030-2438)
P.O. Box 327 (60030-0327)
PHONE..................................847 223-4855
Richard C De Meyer, *Manager*
EMP: 7
SALES (corp-wide): 6MM **Privately Held**
SIC: 3568 Power transmission equipment
PA: Grayslake Feed Sales, Inc.
21 N Seymour Ave
Grayslake IL
847 223-4855

(G-10780)
HARGER INC (PA)
Also Called: Harger Lightning & Grounding
301 Ziegler Dr (60030-1664)
PHONE..................................847 548-8700
Mark S Harger, *President*
Jeffrey A Harger, *Vice Pres*
Timothy R Harger, *Vice Pres*
Dave Dove, *Plant Mgr*
Spencer Heynis, *Mfg Mgr*
▲ EMP: 42
SQ FT: 50,000
SALES (est): 13.5MM **Privately Held**
WEB: www.harger.com
SIC: 3643 1799 5063 Lightning protection equipment; lightning conductor erection; power transmission equipment, electric

(G-10781)
HEISE INDUSTRIES INC
Also Called: Krug-Northwest Electric Motors
123 Hawley St (60030-1514)
PHONE..................................847 223-2410
Robert Heise, *President*
Andrew Heise, *Vice Pres*
EMP: 3 EST: 1971
SQ FT: 4,000
SALES (est): 450K **Privately Held**
SIC: 7694 5063 Electric motor repair; motors, electric

(G-10782)
ILLUMEN STUDIOS LLC
314 Lexington Ln (60030-3720)
P.O. Box 2074, Round Lake (60073-0623)
PHONE..................................847 440-2222
David Charney, *CEO*
EMP: 3
SALES: 350K **Privately Held**
SIC: 8742 7372 Training & development consultant; educational computer software

Grayslake - Lake County (G-10783)

(G-10783)
INTERNATIONAL MOLD & PROD LLC
Also Called: Imap
1397 Mayfair Ln (60030-3755)
PHONE.................................313 617-5251
Leonard Koren, *President*
EMP: 4
SALES (est): 357.5K **Privately Held**
SIC: 8711 3089 Engineering services; plastic containers, except foam; buckets, plastic; clothes hangers, plastic; injection molded finished plastic products

(G-10784)
IVES WAY PRODUCTS INC
683 Center St Ste E (60030-1686)
P.O. Box 70, Round Lake (60073-0070)
PHONE.................................847 223-1020
Glenn Ours, *President*
EMP: 2 EST: 1997
SALES (est): 209.1K **Privately Held**
SIC: 5084 3579 3556 Industrial machinery & equipment; office machines; food products machinery

(G-10785)
JAD GROUP INC
888 E Belvidere Rd # 213 (60030-2572)
PHONE.................................847 223-1804
Joseph Dibartolo, *CEO*
EMP: 2
SQ FT: 2,100
SALES (est): 417.5K **Privately Held**
SIC: 3674 Semiconductors & related devices

(G-10786)
KINESIS VACCINES LLC
1495 Colbee Benton Rd (60030-3527)
PHONE.................................847 543-7725
EMP: 3
SALES (est): 147.1K **Privately Held**
SIC: 2836 Vaccines

(G-10787)
LIQUA FIT INC (PA)
100 N Atkinson Rd Ste 102 (60030-7801)
PHONE.................................630 965-8067
EMP: 7
SQ FT: 1,400
SALES: 2.1MM **Privately Held**
SIC: 2023 Dietary Supplements

(G-10788)
LIVORSI MARINE INC
715 Center St (60030-1651)
PHONE.................................847 548-5900
Mike Livorsi, *President*
◆ EMP: 24
SQ FT: 120,000
SALES (est): 4.1MM
SALES (corp-wide): 2.3B **Publicly Held**
SIC: 3829 Measuring & controlling devices
HQ: Compx Security Products Inc.
26 Old Mill Rd
Greenville SC 29607
864 286-1122

(G-10789)
MODELS PLUS INC
888 E Belvidere Rd # 110 (60030-2569)
PHONE.................................847 231-4300
Mary Fogel, *President*
Jared Fogel, *Admin Sec*
EMP: 29 EST: 1995
SALES (est): 2.6MM **Privately Held**
WEB: www.modelsplusinc.com
SIC: 3999 Models, general, except toy

(G-10790)
MODERN MEDIA SERVICES
155 Wicks St Unit E (60030-2436)
PHONE.................................847 548-0408
Ralph Roland, *Owner*
EMP: 10
SALES (est): 935K **Privately Held**
SIC: 2752 Commercial printing, offset

(G-10791)
MOLD SEEKERS
319 Fairfax Ln (60030-3703)
PHONE.................................847 650-8025
Kevin Waldenstrom, *Principal*
EMP: 7
SALES (est): 697.9K **Privately Held**
SIC: 3442 Molding, trim & stripping

(G-10792)
MULTICOPY CORP
33207 N Cove Rd (60030-2106)
PHONE.................................847 446-7015
Mike Semmerling, *President*
Terry Jackson, *Admin Sec*
EMP: 9
SQ FT: 25,000
SALES (est): 1.4MM **Privately Held**
WEB: www.multicopy.us
SIC: 2752 2796 2791 2789 Commercial printing, offset; platemaking services; typesetting; bookbinding & related work

(G-10793)
NU GLO SIGN COMPANY
18880 W Gages Lake Rd (60030-1704)
PHONE.................................847 223-6160
John Samson, *Partner*
Bill Samson, *Partner*
Joan Samson, *Partner*
Tina Samson, *Partner*
EMP: 11
SQ FT: 4,500
SALES (est): 350K **Privately Held**
SIC: 3993 Neon signs

(G-10794)
NUTRITIONAL INSTITUTE LLC
75 Commerce Dr Unit 7010 (60030-7678)
P.O. Box 7010 (60030-7010)
PHONE.................................847 223-7676
Linda S Dowling,
EMP: 2
SALES (est): 396.3K **Privately Held**
SIC: 2833 Vitamins, natural or synthetic: bulk, uncompounded

(G-10795)
PAPER MOON RECYCLING INC
123 Bluff Ave (60030-2310)
PHONE.................................847 548-8875
Martin Christiansen, *Corp Secy*
Gerri Christiansen,
EMP: 2
SALES (est): 500K **Privately Held**
SIC: 2611 5947 Pulp mills, mechanical & recycling processing; party favors

(G-10796)
PRINT BUTLER INC
674 Indian Path Rd (60030-3517)
PHONE.................................312 296-2804
Keith Andersson, *President*
EMP: 10
SALES: 2MM **Privately Held**
SIC: 2752 Commercial printing, lithographic

(G-10797)
RETMAP INC
34435 N Bobolink Trl (60030-2883)
PHONE.................................312 224-8938
Tamas Ban, *President*
John R Hetling, *Vice Pres*
Safa Rahmani, *Vice Pres*
EMP: 3
SALES (est): 340.2K **Privately Held**
SIC: 3845 Electromedical equipment

(G-10798)
RJG ENTERPRISES LTD
888 E Belvidere Rd # 222 (60030-2568)
PHONE.................................847 752-2065
Rich Gapinski, *President*
▼ EMP: 6 EST: 1985
SQ FT: 5,000
SALES (est): 1.3MM **Privately Held**
SIC: 2631 5084 Packaging board; industrial machine parts

(G-10799)
SHEET METAL SUPPLY LTD
150 Pine St (60030-1436)
PHONE.................................847 478-8500
Harriet Sloma, *President*
Ben Kweton, *Vice Pres*
Phillip Kweton, *Vice Pres*
EMP: 7
SALES (est): 2.9MM **Privately Held**
SIC: 3444 3441 2952 Sheet metalwork; fabricated structural metal; asphalt felts & coatings

(G-10800)
SIGNARAMA
Also Called: Sign-A-Rama
888 E Belvidere Rd # 408 (60030-2577)
PHONE.................................847 543-4870
Mike Burcker, *President*
EMP: 4
SQ FT: 1,400
SALES (est): 473.1K **Privately Held**
SIC: 3993 Signs & advertising specialties

(G-10801)
SUREBONDER COM INC
23670 W Chardon Rd (60030-9588)
PHONE.................................847 270-0254
Michael Kamins, *President*
EMP: 3
SALES (est): 123.2K **Privately Held**
SIC: 2891 Adhesives

(G-10802)
TITANIUM INC
Also Called: Titanium Supply Co
888 E Belvidere Rd # 104 (60030-2568)
PHONE.................................847 691-5446
Mike Lombardo, *President*
EMP: 2
SQ FT: 1,700
SALES (est): 354.5K **Privately Held**
SIC: 7379 3567 ; heating units & devices, industrial: electric

(G-10803)
TVH PARTS CO
95 S Rte 83 (60030)
PHONE.................................847 223-1000
EMP: 22
SALES (corp-wide): 169.6MM **Privately Held**
SIC: 5084 5013 3469 3499 Lift trucks & parts; motor vehicle supplies & new parts; metal stampings; automobile seat frames, metal; electronic circuits; lift trucks, industrial: fork, platform, straddle, etc.
PA: Tvh Parts Co.
16355 S Lone Elm Rd
Olathe KS 66062
913 829-1000

(G-10804)
WHYTE GATE INCORPORATED
400 S Curran Rd Ste 1 (60030-9202)
PHONE.................................847 201-7000
John Manolas, *Co-Owner*
Elli Manolas, *Co-Owner*
Karen McKee, *Finance Mgr*
EMP: 10
SQ FT: 15,000
SALES (est): 1.5MM **Privately Held**
SIC: 3999 Pet supplies

(G-10805)
WINCADEMY INC
34331 N Stonebridge Ln (60030-2856)
PHONE.................................847 445-7886
Ryan Chiu, *Principal*
Jeffrey Fastow, *Principal*
Anthony Marquez, *Principal*
EMP: 3
SALES (est): 146.7K **Privately Held**
SIC: 7372 Educational computer software

(G-10806)
WINDSONG PRESS LTD
33403 N Greentree Rd (60030-1945)
PHONE.................................847 223-4586
Brian F Frederiksen, *President*
Arnold Jacobs, *Project Mgr*
EMP: 3
SALES: 15K **Privately Held**
SIC: 2731 7929 Books: publishing only; entertainers & entertainment groups

(G-10807)
XELLIA PHARACEUTICALS INC
34121 N Us Highway 45 # 207 (60030-1768)
PHONE.................................847 986-7980
Thomas Huske, *Business Mgr*
Anthony Eason, *Prdtn Mgr*
Jimmy Campbell, *Production*
Ken Ruggiero, *Manager*
Sarita Van Bruggen, *Manager*
EMP: 23 EST: 2016
SALES (est): 4.7MM **Privately Held**
SIC: 2834 Pharmaceutical preparations

Grayville
White County

(G-10808)
HARBISON-FISCHER INC
Also Called: Harbison Fischer Sales Co
1421 N Court St (62844-1813)
PHONE.................................618 375-3841
Wayne Middleton, *Manager*
EMP: 4
SALES (corp-wide): 1.1B **Publicly Held**
SIC: 3714 Oil pump, motor vehicle
HQ: Harbison-Fischer, Inc.
901 N Crowley Rd
Crowley TX 76036
817 297-2211

(G-10809)
HOOSIER STAMPING & MFG CORP
399 Industrial Park Dr (62844)
PHONE.................................812 426-2778
Christina Webb, *Principal*
EMP: 5
SALES (corp-wide): 15.5MM **Privately Held**
SIC: 3312 Wheels
PA: Hoosier Stamping & Mfg. Corp
1865 W Franklin St
Evansville IN 47712
812 426-2778

(G-10810)
HOOSIER STAMPING & MFG CORP
832 W Spring St (62844)
P.O. Box 191 (62844-0191)
PHONE.................................618 375-2057
Thomas Johnson, *Manager*
EMP: 30
SALES (corp-wide): 15.5MM **Privately Held**
SIC: 3469 3714 3494 Metal stampings; motor vehicle parts & accessories; valves & pipe fittings
PA: Hoosier Stamping & Mfg. Corp
1865 W Franklin St
Evansville IN 47712
812 426-2778

(G-10811)
KASHA INDUSTRIES INC
1 Plastic Ln (62844)
P.O. Box 160 (62844-0160)
PHONE.................................618 375-2511
E Edwin Kasha Jr, *President*
James L Kasha, *Admin Sec*
EMP: 30
SQ FT: 230,000
SALES (est): 5.7MM **Privately Held**
SIC: 2816 7389 Color pigments; grinding, precision: commercial or industrial

(G-10812)
KASHA INDUSTRIES INC
1 Plastics Ln (62844)
PHONE.................................618 375-2511
Edwin E Kasha Jr, *President*
James L Kasha, *Admin Sec*
EMP: 10
SALES (est): 1.2MM **Privately Held**
SIC: 2816 Color pigments

(G-10813)
MAP OIL CO INC
139 County Road 990 E (62844)
PHONE.................................618 375-7616
Mark Peach, *Owner*
EMP: 6
SALES (est): 845.8K **Privately Held**
SIC: 1382 Oil & gas exploration services

(G-10814)
S & R MEDIA LLC
Also Called: Navigator & Journal Register
113 N Middle St (62844-1408)
PHONE.................................618 375-7502
Patrick Seal,
Jerry Reppert,
EMP: 15

GEOGRAPHIC SECTION

Greenville - Bond County (G-10840)

SALES (est): 519.8K **Privately Held**
SIC: 2711 Newspapers, publishing & printing

(G-10815)
SIDS WELL SERVICE
1007 N Ct (62844)
P.O. Box 144 (62844-0144)
PHONE..................618 375-5411
Sid Gross, *Owner*
Sherry Gross, *Manager*
EMP: 4
SALES (est): 240K **Privately Held**
SIC: 1389 Servicing oil & gas wells

Green Valley
Tazewell County

(G-10816)
CENTRAL ILLINOIS HARDWOOD
15634 Toboggan Ave (61534-9047)
PHONE..................309 352-2363
David Nash, *Principal*
EMP: 3
SALES (est): 287.8K **Privately Held**
SIC: 2426 Hardwood dimension & flooring mills

(G-10817)
K D CUSTOM SAWING LOGGING
6570 Illinois Route 29 (61534-9058)
PHONE..................309 231-4805
Steven Nash, *Principal*
EMP: 3 EST: 2010
SALES (est): 233.3K **Privately Held**
SIC: 2411 Logging

Greenfield
Greene County

(G-10818)
SCHIRZ CONCRETE PRODUCTS INC
1251-1299 Prairie St (62044)
PHONE..................217 368-2153
Kathleen Schirz, *President*
Stephen Schirz, *Admin Sec*
EMP: 10
SALES (est): 1.5MM **Privately Held**
SIC: 3273 5032 Ready-mixed concrete; concrete & cinder building products

Greenup
Cumberland County

(G-10819)
DRUM MANUFACTURING
804 E York Rd (62428-3559)
PHONE..................217 923-5625
David Drum, *President*
EMP: 10
SALES (est): 1.3MM **Privately Held**
SIC: 2821 Polyvinyl chloride resins (PVC)

(G-10820)
EVAPCO INC
Also Called: Evapco Midwest
1723 E York Rd (62428-3573)
P.O. Box 247 (62428-0247)
PHONE..................217 923-3431
Walt Altman, *Branch Mgr*
Sam Vineyard, *Manager*
EMP: 115
SALES (corp-wide): 378.8MM **Privately Held**
SIC: 3585 3443 5078 Parts for heating, cooling & refrigerating equipment; fabricated plate work (boiler shop); commercial refrigeration equipment
PA: Evapco, Inc.
5151 Allendale Ln
Taneytown MD 21787
410 756-2600

(G-10821)
JALAA FIBERGLASS INC
1654 County Road 350n (62428-3408)
P.O. Box 379, Newton (62448-0379)
PHONE..................217 923-3433
John Antrim, *President*
Louanne Antrim, *Vice Pres*
EMP: 3
SALES (est): 270K **Privately Held**
SIC: 3089 3088 2221 Plastic & fiberglass tanks; plastics plumbing fixtures; fiberglass fabrics

(G-10822)
QUINN BROOM WORKS INC
1527 Il Route 121 (62428-3222)
P.O. Box 575 (62428-0575)
PHONE..................217 923-3181
Mark Quinn, *President*
Betty Quinn, *Vice Pres*
▲ EMP: 22 EST: 1925
SQ FT: 7,000
SALES (est): 2.1MM **Privately Held**
WEB: www.quinnbroomworks.com
SIC: 3991 Brooms

Greenview
Menard County

(G-10823)
J & J INC OF ILLINOIS
20224 Big Oak Ave (62642-9650)
PHONE..................217 306-0787
Jeff Johnston, *President*
Paul Jhonston, *Principal*
Ronda Johnston, *Admin Sec*
EMP: 12
SQ FT: 1,200
SALES: 1MM **Privately Held**
SIC: 1799 2591 Glass tinting, architectural or automotive; drapery hardware & blinds & shades; window shades

(G-10824)
ROBERT SWAAR
25903 Levee St (62642-9591)
PHONE..................217 968-2232
Robert Swaar, *CEO*
Sirah Jane, *President*
EMP: 2
SALES (est): 235K **Privately Held**
SIC: 3523 Driers (farm): grain, hay & seed

Greenville
Bond County

(G-10825)
3 POINT INK LLC
1550 E City Route 40 (62246-2578)
P.O. Box 519 (62246-0519)
PHONE..................618 664-1550
Sherry Schaefer,
EMP: 3
SALES (est): 412.6K **Privately Held**
WEB: www.3pointink.com
SIC: 2721 Magazines: publishing only, not printed on site

(G-10826)
BASS-MOLLETT PUBLISHERS INC
507 Monroe St (62246-2043)
P.O. Box 189 (62246-0189)
PHONE..................618 664-3141
John Flowers, *President*
Tad Flowers, *Vice Pres*
Duane Mollet, *Vice Pres*
Angie Helige, *Warehouse Mgr*
Linda Flowers, *Treasurer*
◆ EMP: 65 EST: 1951
SQ FT: 32,000
SALES: 16MM **Privately Held**
WEB: www.bass-mollett.com
SIC: 2741 2759 Miscellaneous publishing; announcements: engraved

(G-10827)
BOND & FAYETTE COUNTY SHOPPER
201 N 3rd St Ste Frnt (62246-1003)
P.O. Box 16 (62246-0016)
PHONE..................618 664-4566
Steve Holt, *Owner*
Janean Rehkemper, *Sales Staff*
Jill Tompkins, *Sales Staff*
EMP: 5
SALES (est): 305.8K **Privately Held**
WEB: www.bondfayetteshopper.com
SIC: 2711 Newspapers: publishing only, not printed on site

(G-10828)
BOND BROADCASTING INC
Also Called: Wgel Radio
309 W Main St (62246-1716)
P.O. Box 277 (62246-0277)
PHONE..................618 664-3300
EMP: 12
SALES (est): 587.3K **Privately Held**
SIC: 4832 2711 Radio broadcasting stations; newspapers

(G-10829)
CARLISLE SYN TEC INC
1825 E City Route 40 (62246-2403)
PHONE..................618 664-4540
Kathleen Sullivan, *Principal*
Rick Chase, *Purchasing*
Chris Ziemba, *Project Engr*
Danny Hinkle, *Admin Sec*
EMP: 15
SALES (est): 2.9MM **Privately Held**
SIC: 2952 Asphalt felts & coatings

(G-10830)
CENTRAL TOWNSHIP ROAD & BRIDGE
920 E Bowman Dr (62246-2583)
PHONE..................618 704-5517
EMP: 3
SALES (est): 310.7K **Privately Held**
SIC: 3531 Drags, road (construction & road maintenance equipment)

(G-10831)
COVIDIEN HOLDING INC
100 Louis Latzer Dr (62246-2154)
PHONE..................618 664-2111
Richard Meelia, *Principal*
EMP: 4 **Privately Held**
WEB: www.covidien.com
SIC: 3841 Surgical & medical instruments
HQ: Covidien Holding Inc.
710 Medtronic Pkwy
Minneapolis MN 55432

(G-10832)
DEMOULIN BROTHERS & COMPANY (PA)
1025 S 4th St (62246-2170)
PHONE..................618 664-2000
Donald R Adamski, *President*
Michael Coling, *CFO*
Diann King, *Cust Svc Dir*
Don Adamski, *Data Proc Staff*
Nancy Marsden, *Admin Sec*
▲ EMP: 200
SQ FT: 85,000
SALES: 16MM **Privately Held**
WEB: www.demoulin.com
SIC: 2389 2339 2337 2326 Band uniforms; women's & misses' outerwear; women's & misses' suits & coats; men's & boys' work clothing; men's & boys' suits & coats

(G-10833)
ENERTECH GLOBAL LLC
2506 S Elm St (62246-2626)
PHONE..................605 996-7180
Andy Ziehl, *Warehouse Mgr*
John Krauss, *Branch Mgr*
EMP: 45
SALES (corp-wide): 2.5B **Privately Held**
WEB: www.geocomfort.com
SIC: 3585 Parts for heating, cooling & refrigerating equipment
HQ: Enertech Global, Llc
5751 Airport Rd
Mitchell SD 57301

(G-10834)
FEDERAL PRISON INDUSTRIES
Also Called: Unicor
Us Rt 40 4th St (62246)
PHONE..................618 664-6361
John Grindstaff, *Superintendent*
EMP: 13 **Publicly Held**
SIC: 2299 9223 Textile mill waste & remnant processing; correctional institutions;
HQ: Federal Prison Industries, Inc
320 1st St Nw
Washington DC 20534

(G-10835)
GREENVILLE ADVOCATE INC
305 S 2nd St (62246-1726)
P.O. Box 9 (62246-0009)
PHONE..................618 664-3144
Jay Endress, *President*
Richard D Reeves, *Principal*
EMP: 8 EST: 1858
SQ FT: 5,000
SALES (est): 577.9K **Privately Held**
WEB: www.greenvilleadvocate.com
SIC: 2711 Newspapers: publishing only, not printed on site

(G-10836)
JKLEIN ENTERPRISES INC
Also Called: Jk Installs
505a W South Ave (62246-1620)
PHONE..................618 664-4554
Jason Klein, *President*
Stephen Klein, *Vice Pres*
Doneva Klein, *Admin Sec*
EMP: 6
SALES: 52K **Privately Held**
SIC: 3663 1623 5731 7622 Radio & TV communications equipment; underground utilities contractor; antennas, satellite dish; radio & television receiver installation; cable television installation; subscription television services

(G-10837)
MARCOOT JERSEY CREAMERY LLC
526 Dudleyville Rd (62246-3801)
PHONE..................618 664-1110
Amy Marcoot, *Mng Member*
Jeffrey Tottleben,
Audrea Wall,
Beth Marcoot Young,
EMP: 12
SQ FT: 3,200
SALES: 600K **Privately Held**
SIC: 2022 0241 Natural cheese; cheese spreads, dips, pastes & other cheese products; milk production

(G-10838)
MID-ILLINOIS CONCRETE INC
Also Called: Greenville Ready Mix
1311 S 4th St (62246-2191)
PHONE..................618 664-1340
Scott Sugg, *Manager*
EMP: 6
SALES (corp-wide): 17.2MM **Privately Held**
WEB: www.mid-illinoisconcrete.com
SIC: 3272 3273 Concrete products; ready-mixed concrete
PA: Mid-Illinois Concrete, Inc.
1805 S 4th St
Effingham IL
217 342-2498

(G-10839)
NACO PRINTING CO INC
202 S 2nd St (62246-1725)
PHONE..................618 664-0423
Larry Dieters, *President*
Tracy Jeffers, *Graphic Designe*
EMP: 6
SQ FT: 8,800
SALES (est): 1MM **Privately Held**
SIC: 2752 2796 Commercial printing, offset; platemaking services

(G-10840)
NEVCO SPORTS LLC (PA)
301 E Harris Ave (62246-2193)
PHONE..................618 664-0360
Michael Lane, *President*
James Johannpeter, *Plant Mgr*
Dan Phalen, *CFO*

Greenville - Bond County (G-10841) GEOGRAPHIC SECTION

Nicole McGrievy, *Controller*
Julie Kirbach, *Asst Controller*
◆ **EMP:** 92
SQ FT: 10,000
SALES (est): 26.2MM **Privately Held**
WEB: www.nevco.com
SIC: 3993 Scoreboards, electric

(G-10841)
PANTHER PRODUCTS
102 W Main St (62246-1735)
PHONE 618 664-1071
Pam Craig, *Owner*
EMP: 3 **EST:** 1997
SQ FT: 5,000
SALES (est): 300.2K **Privately Held**
SIC: 2759 Screen printing

(G-10842)
SPECGX LLC
100 Louis Latzer Dr (62246-2154)
PHONE 618 664-2111
Kevin Eversman, *Production*
Doug Lugge, *Manager*
EMP: 50 **Privately Held**
SIC: 2834 Pharmaceutical preparations
HQ: Specgx Llc
385 Marshall Ave
Webster Groves MO 63119
314 654-2000

Gridley
Mclean County

(G-10843)
DIVERSATECH METALFAB LLC
Also Called: Dtmf
108 S Center St (61744-4111)
PHONE 309 747-4159
Michael Surma, *President*
Jim Mattina, *Vice Pres*
Jose Estradera,
EMP: 30
SQ FT: 80,000
SALES (est): 10.4MM **Privately Held**
SIC: 3535 Conveyors & conveying equipment

(G-10844)
GRIDLEY MEAT PRODUCTS LLC
205 E 3rd St (61744-7715)
PHONE 309 747-2120
Syed Razavi, *Principal*
EMP: 5
SALES (est): 139.9K **Privately Held**
SIC: 2013 Sausages & other prepared meats

(G-10845)
GRIDLEY WELDING INC
Also Called: Gridley Welding Shop
116 E 3rd St (61744-7725)
P.O. Box 159 (61744-0159)
PHONE 309 747-2325
Charles Iverson, *President*
Laura Iverson, *Admin Sec*
EMP: 3 **EST:** 1959
SQ FT: 7,000
SALES (est): 368.3K **Privately Held**
WEB: www.villageofgridley.com
SIC: 7692 Welding repair

(G-10846)
OMNIMAX INTERNATIONAL INC
Fabral
17904 E 3100 North Rd (61744-7547)
PHONE 309 747-2937
Mitchell B Lewis, *CEO*
EMP: 35
SALES (corp-wide): 768.6MM **Privately Held**
WEB: www.omnimax.com
SIC: 3444 2952 Metal roofing & roof drainage equipment; asphalt felts & coatings
HQ: Omnimax International, Inc.
30 Technology Pkwy S # 400
Peachtree Corners GA 30092

(G-10847)
TRACOINSA USA
108 S Center St (61744-4111)
PHONE 309 287-7046
EMP: 8
SALES (est): 757.4K **Privately Held**
WEB: www.diversatech-metalfab.com
SIC: 3535 Conveyors & conveying equipment

(G-10848)
UNITED ANIMAL HEALTH INC
Also Called: Gridley Division
116 W 2nd St (61744-9783)
P.O. Box 340 (61744-0340)
PHONE 309 747-2196
Jim Weber, *Maint Spvr*
John Stella, *Manager*
EMP: 40
SALES (corp-wide): 135.8MM **Privately Held**
SIC: 2048 5191 Livestock feeds; animal feeds
PA: United Animal Health, Inc.
322 S Main St
Sheridan IN 46069
317 758-4495

Griggsville
Pike County

(G-10849)
HOFMEISTER WELDING INC
402 N Wall St (62340-1176)
P.O. Box 552 (62340-0552)
PHONE 217 407-4091
Mary Dee Wintjen, *President*
EMP: 5
SALES (est): 151.6K **Privately Held**
SIC: 7692 Welding repair

(G-10850)
NATURE HOUSE INC
30494 State Highway 107 (62340-2268)
P.O. Box 390 (62340-0390)
PHONE 217 833-2393
EMP: 100
SQ FT: 57,000
SALES (est): 6.6MM **Privately Held**
SIC: 3999 2731 2752 3444 Mfg Misc Products Book-Publishing/Printing Lithographic Coml Print Mfg Sheet Metalwork

(G-10851)
SPIRIT INDUSTRIES INC
39920 274th Ln (62340-2216)
PHONE 217 285-4500
Dan Mefford, *CEO*
Anita Mefford, *President*
EMP: 4 **EST:** 2007
SALES (est): 464.3K **Privately Held**
WEB: www.spiritlg.com
SIC: 3199 Equestrian related leather articles

Gurnee
Lake County

(G-10852)
ABBOTT LABORATORIES
1136 Laurel Ln (60031-5164)
PHONE 847 935-8130
Richard Zawadzki, *Branch Mgr*
EMP: 578
SALES (corp-wide): 31.9B **Publicly Held**
SIC: 2834 Medicines, capsuled or ampuled
PA: Abbott Laboratories
100 Abbott Park Rd
Abbott Park IL 60064
224 667-6100

(G-10853)
ABBOTT LABORATORIES
1175 Tri State Pkwy (60031-9141)
PHONE 847 855-9217
Jennifer Venable, *Branch Mgr*
EMP: 10
SALES (corp-wide): 31.9B **Publicly Held**
SIC: 2834 Pharmaceutical preparations
PA: Abbott Laboratories
100 Abbott Park Rd
Abbott Park IL 60064
224 667-6100

(G-10854)
AGROWTEK INC
173 Ambrogio Dr Ste A (60031-3324)
P.O. Box 1074, Waukegan (60079-1074)
PHONE 847 380-3009
Thomas James Theis, *President*
EMP: 3
SQ FT: 1,830
SALES (est): 116.9K **Privately Held**
WEB: www.agrowtek.com
SIC: 3699 Electrical equipment & supplies

(G-10855)
AID FOR WOMEN NORTHERN LK CNTY
4606 Old Grand Ave Apt 2 (60031-2607)
PHONE 847 249-2700
Carol Walsh, *Director*
EMP: 12
SALES (est): 78.2K **Privately Held**
SIC: 2835 Pregnancy test kits

(G-10856)
AKHAN SEMICONDUCTOR INC
940 Lakeside Dr (60031-2400)
PHONE 847 855-8400
Adam Khan, *CEO*
Carl Shurboff, *President*
Christopher Fox, *Principal*
Kristie King, *CFO*
Craig Shaffer, *Accountant*
EMP: 8 **EST:** 2012
SQ FT: 18,720
SALES (est): 1.4MM **Privately Held**
SIC: 3674 Wafers (semiconductor devices)

(G-10857)
AKORN INC
5605 Centerpoint Ct Ste B (60031-5278)
PHONE 847 625-1100
Raj Rai, *Branch Mgr*
EMP: 10
SALES (corp-wide): 682.4MM **Privately Held**
WEB: www.akorn.com
SIC: 2834 5047 Pharmaceutical preparations; surgical equipment & supplies
PA: Akorn, Inc.
1925 W Field Ct Ste 300
Lake Forest IL 60045
847 279-6100

(G-10858)
ALLERGAN INC
605 Tri State Pkwy (60031-5277)
PHONE 714 246-4500
EMP: 3 **Privately Held**
SIC: 2834 Drugs acting on the central nervous system & sense organs
HQ: Allergan, Inc.
5 Giralda Farms
Madison NJ 07940
862 261-7000

(G-10859)
AMERICAN INDUSTRIAL COMPANY
Also Called: Aic
1080 Tri State Pkwy (60031-5140)
PHONE 847 855-9200
David Dunn, *President*
Stacy Nellessen, *Corp Secy*
Dennis Dunn, *Purchasing*
Stacy Sutton, *Office Mgr*
Stacy N Nellessen, *Manager*
EMP: 19 **EST:** 1962
SQ FT: 25,000
SALES (est): 4.1MM **Privately Held**
SIC: 3469 Stamping metal for the trade

(G-10860)
AMERICAN ROTORS INC
3873 Clearview Ct (60031-1247)
PHONE 847 263-1300
Alan Stark, *President*
Glenn Stark, *General Mgr*
Charles Stark, *Chairman*
EMP: 20
SQ FT: 12,000
SALES (est): 1.2MM **Privately Held**
WEB: www.americanrotors.com
SIC: 3621 Rotors, for motors

(G-10861)
ARCHITECTURAL LIMESTONE INC
2180 Swanson Ct (60031-1276)
PHONE 847 623-0100
Mieczyslaw Mikrut, *President*
▲ **EMP:** 14
SQ FT: 9,000
SALES (est): 3.8MM **Privately Held**
SIC: 1411 Limestone & marble dimension stone; limestone, dimension-quarrying

(G-10862)
BASE-LINE II INC
2001 N Delany Rd (60031-1206)
PHONE 847 336-8403
Fax: 847 336-8624
EMP: 3
SALES (corp-wide): 3.4MM **Privately Held**
SIC: 3861 Manufacture Graphic Art
PA: Base-Line Ii, Inc.
30 Main St Ste 406
Danbury CT 06810
203 826-7031

(G-10863)
BURGESS & BURGESS INC
157 S Hunt Club Rd (60031-2555)
PHONE 847 855-1048
Joanna Burgess, *President*
Robert A Burgess, *Vice Pres*
EMP: 3
SQ FT: 1,200
SALES: 42MM **Privately Held**
SIC: 2098 Macaroni & spaghetti

(G-10864)
CLEVELAND FOLDER SERVICE
4330 Lee Ave (60031-2143)
PHONE 847 782-5850
Marie Lipo, *President*
EMP: 6
SALES (est): 943.1K **Privately Held**
SIC: 3555 Printing trades machinery

(G-10865)
CONTROL DESIGNS INC
4006 Grove Ave (60031-2119)
PHONE 847 672-9514
Robert J Ludwig, *President*
EMP: 6
SQ FT: 2,000
SALES: 350K **Privately Held**
SIC: 3625 Electric controls & control accessories, industrial

(G-10866)
CORRIGAN CORPORATION AMERICA
104 Ambrogio Dr (60031-3373)
PHONE 800 462-6478
J Michael Corrigan, *President*
Eric Ellingson, *COO*
Paul Jones, *Vice Pres*
Debbie Seger, *Purchasing*
Sarah Adams, *Sales Staff*
EMP: 18
SQ FT: 6,700
SALES (est): 3.6MM **Privately Held**
SIC: 3556 Food products machinery

(G-10867)
CR WELDING MET FABRICATION INC (PA)
4190 Grove Ave (60031-2133)
PHONE 224 789-7825
Chris Russell, *President*
EMP: 3 **EST:** 2015
SALES (est): 279.6K **Privately Held**
SIC: 7692 Welding repair

(G-10868)
DEWRICH INC
Also Called: Signs Now
1379 Saint Paul Ave (60031-2130)
PHONE 847 249-7445
Douglas Groat, *President*
Jule Groat, *Vice Pres*
Rene Gonzalez, *Human Res Mgr*
EMP: 5 **EST:** 1989
SALES (est): 300K **Privately Held*
WEB: www.signsnow.com
SIC: 3993 Signs & advertising specialties

GEOGRAPHIC SECTION

Gurnee - Lake County (G-10895)

(G-10869)
DOMINO AMJET INC
4321 Lee Ave (60031-2142)
PHONE.....................847 662-3148
Neils Kruse, *Manager*
EMP: 50
SQ FT: 6,000 **Privately Held**
SIC: 2899 3699 3577 2759 Ink or writing fluids; electrical equipment & supplies; computer peripheral equipment; commercial printing
HQ: Domino Amjet, Inc.
1290 Lakeside Dr
Gurnee IL 60031
847 244-2501

(G-10870)
DOMINO AMJET INC (DH)
1290 Lakeside Dr (60031-2499)
PHONE.....................847 244-2501
Michael J Brown, *President*
Rita Echevarria, *Opers Staff*
Julius Arceo, *Technical Mgr*
Kevin Oakes, *Sales Mgr*
Megan Metzger, *Sales Staff*
◆ **EMP:** 100
SQ FT: 72,000
SALES (est): 40.6MM **Privately Held**
SIC: 3555 2899 Printing trades machinery; ink or writing fluids
HQ: Domino Printing Sciences Public Limited Company
Domino House
Cambridge CAMBS CB23
195 478-2551

(G-10871)
DOMINO HOLDINGS INC (DH)
1290 Lakeside Dr (60031-2400)
PHONE.....................847 244-2501
Nigel Bond, *Ch of Bd*
EMP: 100
SQ FT: 87,000
SALES (est): 27MM **Privately Held**
SIC: 5084 2893 Printing trades machinery; equipment & supplies; printing ink
HQ: Domino Amjet, Inc.
1290 Lakeside Dr
Gurnee IL 60031
847 244-2501

(G-10872)
DOMINO LASERS INC
1290 Lakeside Dr (60031-2400)
PHONE.....................847 855-1364
Leroy Sutter Jr, *President*
Ignacio Lozano, *Corp Secy*
Paul P Lynch, *Vice Pres*
EMP: 42
SQ FT: 2,000
SALES (est): 5.2MM **Privately Held**
SIC: 3699 3845 3577 Laser systems & equipment; electromedical equipment; computer peripheral equipment
HQ: Domino Holdings, Inc.
1290 Lakeside Dr
Gurnee IL 60031

(G-10873)
DYNAPAR CORPORATION (HQ)
Also Called: Danaher Indus Sensors Contrls
1675 N Delany Rd (60031-1237)
PHONE.....................847 662-2666
Joseph Alexander, *President*
Prafulla Shahi, *Engineer*
Curtis Uhll, *Engineer*
Patrick Ronayne, *Controller*
Joy Lipscomb, *Sales Staff*
▲ **EMP:** 130 **EST:** 1952
SQ FT: 38,000
SALES (est): 240.6MM
SALES (corp-wide): 7.3B **Publicly Held**
SIC: 3824 Controls, revolution & timing instruments; electronic totalizing counters; mechanical counters
PA: Fortive Corporation
6920 Seaway Blvd
Everett WA 98203
425 446-5000

(G-10874)
EDMIK INC
Also Called: Edmik Plastics
3850 Grove Ave (60031-2127)
PHONE.....................847 263-0460
Haydee Knill, *President*
Donald E Knill, *Corp Secy*
EMP: 25 **EST:** 1952
SQ FT: 12,000
SALES: 4.8MM **Privately Held**
SIC: 3545 3443 5162 Machine tool attachments & accessories; gauges (machine tool accessories); fabricated plate work (boiler shop); plastics sheets & rods; plastics film

(G-10875)
EIRICH MACHINES INC
Also Called: American Process Systems Div
4033 Ryan Rd (60031-1255)
PHONE.....................847 336-2444
Ralf Rohmann Postfach, *Managing Dir*
Dino Chece, *Managing Dir*
Rich Zak, *Vice Pres*
Rob Marks, *Purch Mgr*
Raymond Sutter, *Buyer*
◆ **EMP:** 100
SQ FT: 55,000
SALES (est): 37.3MM **Privately Held**
WEB: www.eirichusa.com
SIC: 3556 3559 3535 3531 Food products machinery; cement making machinery; conveyors & conveying equipment; construction machinery; fabricated plate work (boiler shop)

(G-10876)
ELITE INDUSTRIES
5710 Des Plaines Ct (60031-3204)
PHONE.....................224 433-6988
Rick Alaimo, *Owner*
EMP: 2
SALES (est): 241.5K **Privately Held**
SIC: 3999 Manufacturing industries

(G-10877)
EXTREME FLIGHT SIMULATION
1350 Tri State Pkwy # 128 (60031-9135)
PHONE.....................224 656-5546
Melissa Zimmerman, *President*
EMP: 9
SALES (est): 448.6K **Privately Held**
SIC: 3699 Electrical equipment & supplies

(G-10878)
FLOLO CORPORATION
1401 N Delany Rd (60031-1233)
PHONE.....................847 249-0880
Larry Layne, *Sales/Mktg Mgr*
EMP: 5
SALES (est): 949.4K
SALES (corp-wide): 16.2MM **Privately Held**
SIC: 5063 7694 3625 3621 Motors, electric; armature rewinding shops; relays & industrial controls; motors & generators
PA: Flolo Corporation
1400 Harvester Rd
West Chicago IL 60185
630 595-1010

(G-10879)
FOURTH QUARTER HOLDINGS INC
Also Called: Image360 Gurnee
1379 Saint Paul Ave (60031-2130)
PHONE.....................847 249-7445
Denis Dubois, *President*
Debra Dubois, *Admin Sec*
EMP: 5
SQ FT: 3,000
SALES (est): 377.1K **Privately Held**
SIC: 3993 Signs & advertising specialties

(G-10880)
FSP LLC
Also Called: Federal Screw Products
245 Ambrogio Dr (60031-3374)
PHONE.....................773 992-2600
Rick Terry, *Vice Pres*
EMP: 6 **EST:** 2013
SALES (est): 34.5K **Privately Held**
WEB: www.federalscrewproducts.com
SIC: 3451 Screw machine products

(G-10881)
GALLAGHER CORPORATION
3908 Morrison Dr (60031-1241)
PHONE.....................847 249-3440
Mary Gallagher, *Ch of Bd*
Richard J Gallagher Jr, *President*
Sharon Krawiec, *Vice Pres*
Jim Yunker, *Manager*
Debbie Gallagher, *Administration*
EMP: 80 **EST:** 1964
SQ FT: 100,000
SALES: 14MM **Privately Held**
WEB: www.gallaghercorp.com
SIC: 2821 Plastics materials & resins

(G-10882)
GATE SYSTEMS CORPORATION
690 Chandler Rd Apt 401 (60031-3185)
PHONE.....................847 731-6700
John Hennessey, *President*
Sue Leverenz, *Admin Sec*
EMP: 5
SQ FT: 4,000
SALES (est): 673K **Privately Held**
SIC: 3699 Door opening & closing devices, electrical

(G-10883)
GRANDSTAND PUBLISHING LLC
Also Called: Baseball Digest
1800 Nations Dr Ste 117 (60031-9171)
PHONE.....................847 491-6440
Norman Jacobs, *Publisher*
EMP: 7
SQ FT: 1,200
SALES (est): 389.9K **Privately Held**
SIC: 2721 Magazines: publishing only, not printed on site

(G-10884)
GRIFFIN MACHINING INC
4170 Grove Ave (60031-2133)
PHONE.....................847 360-0098
Elvin Griffin, *President*
Rebecca Griffin, *Admin Sec*
EMP: 7
SALES (est): 665.5K **Privately Held**
SIC: 3599 Machine shop, jobbing & repair

(G-10885)
GROW MASTERS
4641 Old Grand Ave (60031-2623)
PHONE.....................224 399-9877
✪ **EMP:** 3 **EST:** 2010
SALES (est): 258.2K **Privately Held**
WEB: www.growmasters.com
SIC: 3645 Garden, patio, walkway & yard lighting fixtures: electric

(G-10886)
HANGER PROSTHETICS &
Also Called: Hanger Clinic
35 Tower Ct Ste C (60031-5712)
PHONE.....................847 623-6080
Sam Liang, *President*
Angelo Bernardi, *Manager*
EMP: 5
SALES (corp-wide): 1.1B **Publicly Held**
SIC: 5999 3842 Orthopedic & prosthesis applications; limbs, artificial
HQ: Hanger Prosthetics & Orthotics East, Inc.
33 North Ave Ste 101
Tallmadge OH 44278

(G-10887)
HOLMES ASSOCIATES INC
Also Called: Fastsigns
4949 Grand Ave Ste 2 (60031-1821)
PHONE.....................847 336-4515
Glenn Holmes, *President*
EMP: 3
SQ FT: 1,450
SALES (est): 451K **Privately Held**
SIC: 3993 Signs & advertising specialties

(G-10888)
JAMES W SMITH PRINTING COMPANY
1573 Saint Paul Ave (60031-2146)
PHONE.....................847 244-6486
James W Smith, *Ch of Bd*
Matthew J Smith, *President*
Brian Smith, *Vice Pres*
Lorne Zdenahlik, *Production*
David Smith, *Treasurer*
▲ **EMP:** 45 **EST:** 1973
SQ FT: 18,000
SALES (est): 10.9MM **Privately Held**
SIC: 2752 Commercial printing, offset

(G-10889)
JETPOWER LLC
880 Lakeside Dr Ste 3 (60031-4001)
PHONE.....................847 856-8359
Aaron Neff, *CEO*
Brian Tuman, *Vice Pres*
Michele Viani, *Vice Pres*
EMP: 16
SALES (est): 825.2K **Privately Held**
SIC: 3724 3728 Airfoils, aircraft engine; bodies, aircraft

(G-10890)
K AND A GRAPHICS INC
4090 Ryan Rd Ste A (60031-1201)
PHONE.....................847 244-2345
Kenneth Echtenacher, *President*
EMP: 3
SQ FT: 3,000
SALES (est): 393.5K **Privately Held**
SIC: 2759 3993 3953 2396 Screen printing; signs, not made in custom sign painting shops; marking devices; automotive & apparel trimmings

(G-10891)
K H M PLASTICS INC
Also Called: Khm
4090 Ryan Rd Ste B (60031-1201)
PHONE.....................847 249-4910
Dan Kloczkowski, *President*
Glenn Murphy, *Vice Pres*
EMP: 34
SQ FT: 50,000
SALES (est): 7.8MM **Privately Held**
WEB: www.khmplastics.com
SIC: 3089 Molding primary plastic; injection molding of plastics

(G-10892)
K M J ENTERPRISES INC
Also Called: Frontier Soups
2001 Swanson Ct (60031-1221)
PHONE.....................847 688-1200
Matt Anderson, *CEO*
Patricia Anderson, *President*
Jim Anderson, *Vice Pres*
Jon Anderson, *Vice Pres*
James D Anderson, *Treasurer*
EMP: 30
SQ FT: 25,000
SALES: 5.8MM **Privately Held**
SIC: 2099 Food preparations

(G-10893)
KALLE USA INC
5750 Centerpoint Ct Ste B (60031-5279)
PHONE.....................847 775-0781
John Lample, *CEO*
Joe Wallner, *Business Mgr*
Mike Nelson, *Vice Pres*
Jed Hwang, *Engineer*
Detlev Schauwecker, *CFO*
▲ **EMP:** 4
SALES (est): 1.8MM
SALES (corp-wide): 177.9K **Privately Held**
SIC: 3089 Plastic hardware & building products
HQ: Kalle Gmbh
Rheingaustr. 190-196
Wiesbaden 65203
611 962-07

(G-10894)
LAKESIDE PUBLISHING CO LLC
1800 Nations Dr Ste 117 (60031-9171)
PHONE.....................847 491-6440
Barry Jacobs, *Principal*
Dale Jacobs, *Prdtn Mgr*
EMP: 5
SALES (est): 548K **Privately Held**
SIC: 2721 Magazines: publishing only, not printed on site

(G-10895)
MASTER BUILDERS LLC
1810 Northwestern Ave (60031-1288)
PHONE.....................847 249-4080
Robert Bach, *Principal*
EMP: 6
SALES (corp-wide): 65.6B **Privately Held**
SIC: 2899 2851 Concrete curing & hardening compounds; epoxy coatings; vinyl coatings, strippable

Gurnee - Lake County (G-10896)

HQ: Master Builders, Llc
  23700 Chagrin Blvd
  Beachwood OH 44122
  216 831-5500

(G-10896)
METROPOLITAN GRAPHIC ARTS INC
Also Called: M G A
3818 Grandville Ave (60031-2332)
PHONE..........................847 566-9502
Joseph Szymanski, *President*
Brian Szymanski, *Vice Pres*
EMP: 45
SALES (est): 19.3MM Privately Held
SIC: 2752 7331 2791 Commercial printing, offset; mailing service; typesetting

(G-10897)
MGA INNOVATION INC
3818 Grandville Ave (60031-2332)
PHONE..........................847 672-9947
EMP: 2
SALES (est): 235.6K Privately Held
WEB: www.mgainnovation.com
SIC: 2752 Commercial printing, lithographic

(G-10898)
MIDWEST SIGNS & STRUCTURES INC (PA)
4215 Grove Ave (60031-2134)
PHONE..........................847 249-8398
Robert Stuckey, *President*
Diane Root, *Vice Pres*
EMP: 2
SQ FT: 450
SALES: 400K Privately Held
SIC: 3993 Signs & advertising specialties

(G-10899)
MINUS NINE TECHNOLOGIES
101 Ambrogio Dr (60031-3382)
PHONE..........................224 399-9393
EMP: 3 EST: 2016
SALES (est): 184.1K Privately Held
SIC: 2819 Industrial inorganic chemicals

(G-10900)
MINUTEMAN PRESS OF WAUKEGAN
3701 Grand Ave Ste A (60031-2966)
PHONE..........................847 244-6288
Karen Dzierzbicki, *President*
Martin Dzierzbicki, *Vice Pres*
EMP: 3
SQ FT: 1,100
SALES (est): 499.2K Privately Held
SIC: 2752 2791 Commercial printing, lithographic; typesetting

(G-10901)
MULTIMETAL PRODUCTS CORP
3965 Grove Ave (60031-2161)
PHONE..........................847 662-9110
Andrew Marsch, *President*
Scott Marsch, *Vice Pres*
Dominick Stevens, *Manager*
Katie Johnson, *Agent*
EMP: 28
SQ FT: 15,000
SALES (est): 6.4MM Privately Held
SIC: 3599 Machine shop, jobbing & repair

(G-10902)
NAGEL-CHASE INC
2377 N Delany Rd (60031-1212)
PHONE..........................847 336-4494
Rosemary Sullivan, *CEO*
Harold Sullivan III, *President*
Dewey Burke, *Opers Staff*
Jim Hollingshead, *Purch Agent*
Kathy Kuroski, *Controller*
EMP: 3
SQ FT: 131,000
SALES (est): 281.3K
SALES (corp-wide): 20.9MM Privately Held
SIC: 3568 3429 Power transmission equipment; chain, power transmission; pulleys, power transmission; pulleys metal

PA: Payson Casters, Inc.
  2323 N Delany Rd
  Gurnee IL 60031
  847 336-6200

(G-10903)
NOSCO INC
1400 Saint Paul Ave (60031-2129)
PHONE..........................847 336-4200
Jonathan Haapanen, *Branch Mgr*
EMP: 43
SALES (corp-wide): 314MM Privately Held
SIC: 7336 2752 Graphic arts & related design; commercial printing, lithographic
HQ: Nosco, Inc
  2199 N Delany Rd
  Gurnee IL 60031
  847 336-4200

(G-10904)
NOSCO INC (HQ)
2199 N Delany Rd (60031-1208)
PHONE..........................847 336-4200
Craig Curran, *President*
Darrin Schmidt, *President*
Greg Hamilton, *Corp Secy*
John McKeough, *Senior VP*
Mike Atwood, *Vice Pres*
▲ EMP: 333 EST: 1980
SALES (est): 146.7MM
SALES (corp-wide): 314MM Privately Held
WEB: www.nosco.com
SIC: 2752 2657 Commercial printing, lithographic; folding paperboard boxes
PA: Holden Industries, Inc.
  500 Lake Cook Rd Ste 400
  Deerfield IL 60015
  847 940-1500

(G-10905)
NYPROMOLD INC
955 Tri State Pkwy (60031-5113)
PHONE..........................847 855-2200
Gordon Lankton, *President*
Randy Greiner, *Plant Mgr*
Paul Diemer, *Controller*
Greg Johnson, *Manager*
Nicholas D Aznoian, *Admin Sec*
EMP: 125
SQ FT: 85,000
SALES: 41.2MM
SALES (corp-wide): 25.2B Publicly Held
SIC: 3089 Injection molding of plastics
HQ: Nypro Inc.
  101 Union St
  Clinton MA 01510
  978 365-8100

(G-10906)
ODRA INC
4310 Lee Ave (60031-2143)
PHONE..........................847 249-2910
Hamid Bastani, *President*
Max Bastini, *Shareholder*
EMP: 4
SQ FT: 6,000
SALES (est): 604.2K Privately Held
SIC: 3089 2671 Injection molded finished plastic products; packaging paper & plastics film, coated & laminated

(G-10907)
OHIO MEDICAL LLC (DH)
1111 Lakeside Dr (60031-2489)
PHONE..........................847 855-0500
Halden Zimmermann, *President*
Anthony Wieczorek, *President*
Louis Manetti, *COO*
Elizabeth Culotta, *Vice Pres*
John Giard, *Vice Pres*
◆ EMP: 100
SQ FT: 120,000
SALES (est): 3.9MM Privately Held
WEB: www.ohiomedical.com
SIC: 3841 3563 Surgical & medical instruments; suction therapy apparatus; air & gas compressors
HQ: Omc Investors, Llc
  1111 Lakeside Dr
  Gurnee IL 60031
  847 855-6220

(G-10908)
OMC INVESTORS LLC (HQ)
Also Called: Ohio Medical
1111 Lakeside Dr (60031-2489)
PHONE..........................847 855-6220
Halden Zimmerman, *President*
EMP: 8 EST: 2014
SQ FT: 82,000
SALES (est): 24.3MM Privately Held
SIC: 3841 6719 Surgical & medical instruments; investment holding companies, except banks

(G-10909)
ONLY CHILD BREWING COMPANY LLC
1350 Tri State Pkwy # 124 (60031-9135)
PHONE..........................847 877-9822
Benjamin Rossi, *Partner*
EMP: 3
SALES (est): 293.1K Privately Held
SIC: 2082 Beer (alcoholic beverage)

(G-10910)
PAYSON CASTERS INC
Rolla Way Conveyors
2335 N Delany Rd (60031-1212)
PHONE..........................847 336-5033
Harold Sullivan, *President*
Dan Sullivan, *Branch Mgr*
EMP: 120
SALES (corp-wide): 20.9MM Privately Held
SIC: 5084 3535 Conveyor systems; conveyors & conveying equipment
PA: Payson Casters, Inc.
  2323 N Delany Rd
  Gurnee IL 60031
  847 336-6200

(G-10911)
PERFECTION EQUIPMENT INC
4259 Lee Ave (60031-2175)
PHONE..........................847 244-7200
Kay Hahn, *Ch of Bd*
Sanford Hahn, *President*
EMP: 20
SQ FT: 15,200
SALES (est): 4.6MM Privately Held
WEB: www.perfectequip.com
SIC: 3585 Soda fountain & beverage dispensing equipment & parts

(G-10912)
PLASTIC SPECIALISTS AMERICA
4225 Tiger Lily Ln # 308 (60031-9639)
PHONE..........................847 406-7547
Mitch Rabushka, *Owner*
EMP: 4
SALES (est): 303.1K Privately Held
SIC: 3842 3021 Personal safety equipment; protective footwear, rubber or plastic

(G-10913)
PPG INDUSTRIES INC
Also Called: P P G Mazer Chemicals Group
3938 Porett Dr (60031-1244)
P.O. Box 72167, Chicago (60678-2167)
PHONE..........................847 244-3410
EMP: 6
SALES (corp-wide): 15.1B Publicly Held
SIC: 2851 Paints & allied products
PA: Ppg Industries, Inc.
  1 Ppg Pl
  Pittsburgh PA 15272
  412 434-3131

(G-10914)
PQ CORPORATION
1945 N Delany Rd (60031-1204)
PHONE..........................847 662-8566
Christine Salaiz, *Buyer*
Rob Pickens, *Engineer*
Robert Pickens, *Manager*
Ken Schulte, *Manager*
EMP: 13
SALES (corp-wide): 1.5B Publicly Held
SIC: 2819 Industrial inorganic chemicals
HQ: Pq Corporation
  300 Lindenwood Dr
  Malvern PA 19355
  610 651-4200

(G-10915)
PREMIERE DISTILLERY LLC
1503 Saint Paul Ave (60031-2146)
P.O. Box 232 (60031-0232)
PHONE..........................847 662-4444
Inna Feldman Gerber, *Mng Member*
▲ EMP: 8 EST: 2008
SQ FT: 4,000
SALES (est): 663K Privately Held
SIC: 2085 Distilled & blended liquors

(G-10916)
PROFORMA QUALITY BUSINESS SVCS
Also Called: Bonnie's Slick Printing
18582 W Judy Dr (60031-1323)
PHONE..........................847 356-1959
Bonnie Ross, *President*
EMP: 2 EST: 1993
SALES (est): 500K Privately Held
SIC: 2752 Promotional printing, lithographic

(G-10917)
PROSCO INC
3901 Grove Ave (60031-2118)
PHONE..........................847 336-1323
Stan Kubala, *President*
Jolanta Kubala, *Admin Sec*
▲ EMP: 8
SALES (est): 2.8MM Privately Held
SIC: 5084 3541 Industrial machinery & equipment; grinding machines, metalworking

(G-10918)
PROTOTECH INDUSTRIES INC
1479 Almaden Ln (60031-5625)
PHONE..........................847 223-9808
Edwin Paff, *President*
Mary Lou Paff, *Vice Pres*
EMP: 4
SALES: 160K Privately Held
SIC: 3949 Archery equipment, general

(G-10919)
PURO FUTBOL NEWSPAPER
4248 Lake Park Ave (60031-3035)
PHONE..........................847 858-7493
Alberto Teran, *Principal*
EMP: 5
SALES (est): 249.4K Privately Held
WEB: www.purofutbolonline.com
SIC: 2711 Newspapers

(G-10920)
QUALITEK MANUFACTURING INC
4240 Grove Ave (60031-2124)
PHONE..........................847 336-7570
Ken Tibor, *President*
Keith Tibor, *Vice Pres*
Paulette Tibor, *Admin Sec*
EMP: 20
SQ FT: 15,000
SALES (est): 4.5MM Privately Held
SIC: 3544 Special dies & tools

(G-10921)
QUALITY MOLDING PRODUCTS LLC
Also Called: Nothing
118 Nations Dr (60031)
PHONE..........................224 286-4555
James Thomas, *President*
EMP: 3
SALES (est): 150K Privately Held
SIC: 3299 1522 Moldings, architectural: plaster of paris; multi-family dwelling construction

(G-10922)
RADIUS MACHINE & TOOL INC
4290 Lee Ave (60031-2164)
PHONE..........................847 662-7690
Steve Fischer, *President*
Laura Fischer, *Vice Pres*
EMP: 10
SQ FT: 6,000
SALES (est): 920K Privately Held
SIC: 3599 3544 Machine shop, jobbing & repair; special dies & tools

GEOGRAPHIC SECTION

Hamel - Madison County (G-10949)

(G-10923)
REALWHEELS CORPORATION
3940 Tannahill Dr (60031-1223)
PHONE................847 662-7722
John Polka, *President*
Gregory Polka, *General Mgr*
Cheryl Polka, *Corp Secy*
Colleen Fredrick, *Accounts Mgr*
Colleen Collins, *Corp Comm Staff*
▲ EMP: 45
SQ FT: 20,000
SALES (est): 10.8MM **Privately Held**
WEB: www.realwheels.com
SIC: 3469 3714 3443 Metal stampings; motor vehicle parts & accessories; fabricated plate work (boiler shop)

(G-10924)
ROLL-A-WAY CONVEYORS INC
2335 N Delany Rd (60031-1212)
PHONE................847 336-5033
Dan Sullivan, *Manager*
EMP: 10
SALES (est): 750.6K **Privately Held**
SIC: 3535 7532 3999 Conveyors & conveying equipment; body shop, trucks; atomizers, toiletry

(G-10925)
SCARS PUBLICATIONS
829 Brian Ct (60031-3155)
PHONE................847 281-9070
Janet Kuypers, *Owner*
EMP: 3
SALES (est): 106.4K **Privately Held**
SIC: 2741 Miscellaneous publishing

(G-10926)
SEXTANT COMPANY
433 Inverness Dr (60031-5349)
PHONE................847 680-6550
Clark Neuhoff, *President*
EMP: 3
SALES (est): 103K **Privately Held**
WEB: www.sextant-us.com
SIC: 3812 Sextants

(G-10927)
SIGN GIRLS INC
Also Called: Sign-A-Rama
3608 Grand Ave Ste E (60031-3744)
PHONE................847 336-4002
Sharon Segovia, *Owner*
Robin Petit, *Co-Owner*
EMP: 2
SALES (est): 317.5K **Privately Held**
SIC: 3993 Signs & advertising specialties

(G-10928)
SMART SCAN MRI LLC
350 S Greenleaf St # 401 (60031-5709)
PHONE................847 623-4000
Jeffrey Rosengarten, *Mng Member*
Robert Breit,
Frank Kalmar,
Wendy Silcox,
EMP: 8
SALES (est): 1.1MM **Privately Held**
WEB: www.smartscanmri.com
SIC: 3845 8099 3826 Ultrasonic scanning devices, medical; medical services organization; magnetic resonance imaging apparatus

(G-10929)
SPEEDPRO IMAGING
Also Called: 2 Koi
1350 Tri State Pkwy (60031-9185)
PHONE................847 856-8220
Tom Kmieciak, *President*
Maureen Kmieciak, *Treasurer*
EMP: 4
SALES (est): 367.4K **Privately Held**
WEB: www.speedpro.com
SIC: 7336 2759 Graphic arts & related design; commercial printing

(G-10930)
STERIGENICS US LLC
1003 Lakeside Dr (60031-2489)
PHONE................847 855-0727
Pat Hope, *Branch Mgr*
Laura Hartman, *Manager*
Beatriz Guzman, *Administration*
Michael Wieczorek, *Technician*
EMP: 30

SALES (corp-wide): 823.5MM **Privately Held**
WEB: www.sterigenics.com
SIC: 7389 3821 Product sterilization service; sterilizers
HQ: Sterigenics U.S., Llc
    2015 Spring Rd Ste 650
    Oak Brook IL 60523
    630 928-1700

(G-10931)
STERLINE MANUFACTURING CORP
4000 Porett Dr Ste B (60031-1209)
PHONE................847 244-1234
Leslie Raffel, *President*
Michael Berger, *Vice Pres*
Anna Williams, *Admin Sec*
EMP: 25
SQ FT: 25,000
SALES (est): 1.7MM **Privately Held**
SIC: 3432 3261 Plumbers' brass goods: drain cocks, faucets, spigots, etc.; vitreous plumbing fixtures

(G-10932)
T & T MACHINE SHOP
4406 Lee Ave (60031-2150)
PHONE................847 244-2020
Tom Olsen, *Owner*
EMP: 3
SALES (est): 322.2K **Privately Held**
SIC: 3599 3714 Machine shop, jobbing & repair; motor vehicle parts & accessories

(G-10933)
TABLECRAFT PRODUCTS CO INC (PA)
801 Lakeside Dr (60031-2489)
PHONE................847 855-9000
Glen Davis, *President*
Pat Arber, *President*
John Temple, *General Mgr*
David Burnside, *Exec VP*
Omar Jimenez, *Vice Pres*
◆ EMP: 100
SQ FT: 100,000
SALES (est): 30.9MM **Privately Held**
WEB: www.tablecraft.com
SIC: 3639 Major kitchen appliances, except refrigerators & stoves

(G-10934)
TECH OASIS INTERNATIONAL INC
5652 Chapel Hl (60031-1079)
PHONE................847 302-1590
Arul Veeramani, *President*
EMP: 15
SALES: 550K **Privately Held**
SIC: 3674 Light emitting diodes

(G-10935)
TECHNICAL SALES MIDWEST INC
36149 N Edgewater Ct (60031-4510)
P.O. Box 7793 (60031-7004)
PHONE................847 855-2457
Lj Lewis, *President*
EMP: 1
SALES: 250K **Privately Held**
SIC: 3823 Industrial process measurement equipment

(G-10936)
TELEFLEX MEDICAL OEM LLC (HQ)
1425 Tr State Pkwy Ste 12 (60031)
PHONE................847 596-3100
Ed Boarini, *President*
Shandrea Hums, *Human Resources*
Mika Hulliberger, *Sales Mgr*
John Burns, *Manager*
EMP: 101 EST: 1995
SALES (est): 836.3K
SALES (corp-wide): 2.6B **Publicly Held**
SIC: 3841 Surgical & medical instruments
PA: Teleflex Incorporated
    550 E Swedesford Rd # 400
    Wayne PA 19087
    610 225-6800

(G-10937)
TR CHEM SOLUTIONS LLC
5250 Grand Ave Ste 14 (60031-1877)
PHONE................262 865-7228
EMP: 4
SALES (est): 361.8K **Privately Held**
SIC: 2819 Industrial inorganic chemicals

(G-10938)
TRICEL CORPORATION
2100 Swanson Ct (60031-1276)
PHONE................847 336-1321
Blaine Loudin, *CEO*
Stephen C Loudin, *President*
Sue Mesmer, *Cust Mgr*
Sally Loudin, *Shareholder*
▼ EMP: 16
SQ FT: 27,400
SALES (est): 3.9MM **Privately Held**
SIC: 2679 Honeycomb core & board: made from purchased material

(G-10939)
TRICO TECHNOLOGIES INC
209 Ambrogio Dr (60031-3374)
PHONE................847 662-9224
Philip E Cook, *President*
David B Cook, *Vice Pres*
Deborahh Cook, *Admin Sec*
EMP: 7
SQ FT: 15,000
SALES: 5MM **Privately Held**
SIC: 2819 Industrial inorganic chemicals

(G-10940)
TUXCO CORPORATION
4300 Grove Ave (60031-2155)
PHONE................847 244-2220
Oscar Blomgren Jr, *CEO*
Oscar Blomgren III, *President*
Terri Potesta, *Vice Pres*
Beryl Blomgren, *Treasurer*
◆ EMP: 10 EST: 1945
SQ FT: 9,000
SALES (est): 1.9MM **Privately Held**
WEB: www.tuxco.com
SIC: 3714 3594 3593 3423 Motor vehicle steering systems & parts; motor vehicle wheels & parts; fluid power pumps & motors; fluid power cylinders & actuators; hand & edge tools

(G-10941)
URBAN WOOD GOODS LTD
3815 Grandville Ave Ste C (60031-2310)
PHONE................248 310-7668
Jason True, *CEO*
Erin True, *President*
Melissa Whitebread, *Associate*
▼ EMP: 12
SALES (est): 1.3MM **Privately Held**
SIC: 2599 2511 Restaurant furniture, wood or metal; wood household furniture; console tables: wood; kitchen & dining room furniture; desks, household: wood

(G-10942)
VANTAGE SPECIALTIES INC
3938 Porett Dr (60031-1244)
PHONE................773 579-5842
Connie Hartnell, *Branch Mgr*
EMP: 11
SALES (corp-wide): 247.2MM **Privately Held**
SIC: 2843 Surface active agents
HQ: Vantage Specialties, Inc
    3938 Porett Dr
    Gurnee IL 60031
    773 376-9000

(G-10943)
VANTAGE SPECIALTIES INC (DH)
3938 Porett Dr (60031-1244)
PHONE................773 376-9000
Julien Steinberg, *CEO*
Don Ciancio, *Exec VP*
Chris Humberstone, *Exec VP*
Helen Scott, *CFO*
Christopher Furman, *Supervisor*
▲ EMP: 100
SQ FT: 1,000

SALES (est): 111.9MM
SALES (corp-wide): 247.2MM **Privately Held**
SIC: 4925 2869 Mixed natural & manufactured gas, distribution; fatty acid esters, aminos, etc.
HQ: Vantage Specialty Chemicals, Inc.
    4650 S Racine Ave
    Chicago IL 60609
    773 376-9000

(G-10944)
VERDASEE SOLUTIONS INC
17825 W Pond Ridge Cir (60031-1669)
PHONE................847 265-9441
EMP: 5 EST: 2001
SALES: 500K **Privately Held**
SIC: 3577 7371 Mfg Computer Peripheral Equipment Custom Computer Programing

(G-10945)
ZAPP TOOLING ALLOYS INC
1528 Saint Paul Ave (60031-2148)
PHONE................847 599-0351
Harry O'Brien, *General Mgr*
EMP: 4
SALES (corp-wide): 1.4MM **Privately Held**
SIC: 3317 Steel pipe & tubes
HQ: Zapp Tooling Alloys Inc.
    475 International Cir
    Summerville SC 29483

Hainesville
Lake County

(G-10946)
CLASSIC PRINTERY INC
Also Called: Classic Management
336 W Main St (60073-3644)
PHONE................847 546-6555
Mark Basel, *President*
Cynthia Kutz, *Vice Pres*
Laura L Polka, *Treasurer*
EMP: 5
SQ FT: 11,900
SALES (est): 577.5K **Privately Held**
SIC: 2752 Commercial printing, offset

(G-10947)
GROWER EQUIPMENT & SUPPLY CO
294 E Belvidere Rd (60030-1039)
PHONE................847 223-3100
Jerry De Bruyne, *President*
EMP: 13
SQ FT: 18,400
SALES: 2.8MM **Privately Held**
WEB: www.growerequipment.com
SIC: 7699 3524 5083 Agricultural equipment repair services; lawn & garden equipment; lawn & garden machinery & equipment

Hamburg
Calhoun County

(G-10948)
BETTY WATTERS
Also Called: Watters Fishmarket
Rr 1 Box 27 (62045)
P.O. Box 27 (62045-0027)
PHONE................618 232-1150
Betty Watters, *Owner*
EMP: 2
SALES (est): 247.7K **Privately Held**
SIC: 5146 2092 Fish, fresh; fresh or frozen packaged fish

Hamel
Madison County

(G-10949)
H & H SERVICES INC
391 N Old Us Route 66 (62046-1070)
P.O. Box 365 (62046-0365)
PHONE................618 633-2837
Kirby Harris, *President*

(PA)=Parent Co (HQ)=Headquarters (DH)=Div Headquarters
✪ = New Business established in last 2 years

Kathryn Harris, *Corp Secy*
EMP: 10
SALES (est): 1.1MM **Privately Held**
SIC: 1442 7692 Construction sand & gravel; welding repair

(G-10950)
HAMEL TIRE AND CONCRETE PDTS
Also Called: Hamel Tire Service
200 Hamel Ave (62046-1049)
P.O. Box 255 (62046-0255)
PHONE 618 633-2405
Howard Reising, *President*
Keith Behrhorst, *Vice Pres*
EMP: 3 **EST:** 1965
SQ FT: 4,800
SALES: 480K **Privately Held**
SIC: 5531 3272 5014 Automotive tires; concrete products; tires & tubes

Hamilton
Hancock County

(G-10951)
COOPER LAKE MILLWORKS INC
1202 N State Highway 96 (62341-3145)
PHONE 217 847-2681
Robin Carel, *President*
EMP: 4
SQ FT: 8,500
SALES: 500K **Privately Held**
SIC: 2431 2439 2541 2517 Millwork; timbers, structural: laminated lumber; wood partitions & fixtures; wood television & radio cabinets; wood kitchen cabinets; cabinet & finish carpentry

(G-10952)
CORES FOR YOU INC
160 Industrial Park (62341)
PHONE 217 847-3233
Robert Harmon, *President*
Josh Harmon, *Principal*
Tim Neumann, *Principal*
EMP: 28
SQ FT: 52,000
SALES: 2.4MM **Privately Held**
SIC: 3543 Foundry cores

(G-10953)
D E ASBURY INC (PA)
Also Called: Great River Printing
1479 Keokuk St (62341-1135)
PHONE 217 222-0617
Dan Asbury, *President*
EMP: 10
SQ FT: 8,000
SALES (est): 1.7MM **Privately Held**
SIC: 2752 2791 2789 Commercial printing, offset; typesetting; bookbinding & related work

(G-10954)
DADANT & SONS INC (PA)
Also Called: American Bee Journal, The
51 S 2nd St Ste 2 (62341-1397)
PHONE 217 847-3324
Tim C Dadant, *President*
Nicholas J Dadant, *Vice Pres*
Richard Reikowski, *Vice Pres*
Thomas G Ross, *Vice Pres*
Jordan Ruebush, *Foreman/Supr*
◆ **EMP:** 60 **EST:** 1863
SQ FT: 45,000
SALES (est): 27.4MM **Privately Held**
WEB: www.dadant.com
SIC: 3999 2721 Honeycomb foundations (beekeepers' supplies); candles; magazines: publishing, not printed on site

(G-10955)
GRAY QUARRIES INC
Also Called: Gary Quarries
750 E County Road 1220 (62341-3140)
P.O. Box 386 (62341-0386)
PHONE 217 847-2712
Robert Miller, *President*
EMP: 12 **EST:** 1952
SALES: 2MM **Privately Held**
SIC: 1422 Limestones, ground

(G-10956)
GREAT RIVER READY MIX INC
750 E County Road 1220 (62341-3140)
PHONE 217 847-3515
Trent Miller, *President*
Floyd Rahn, *General Mgr*
Ralph Froman, *Manager*
EMP: 10
SQ FT: 5,000
SALES (est): 201.3K **Privately Held**
SIC: 3273 Ready-mixed concrete

(G-10957)
H & M WOODWORKS
1610 N County Road 1200 (62341-3009)
PHONE 608 289-3141
D Laura Mosena, *Principal*
EMP: 2
SALES (est): 213.9K **Privately Held**
WEB: www.hmwoodworks.com
SIC: 2431 Millwork

(G-10958)
HAMILTON CONCRETE PRODUCTS CO
Also Called: Hamilton Construction Co
400 Windy Woods Dr (62341-3180)
PHONE 217 847-3118
Larry Schrader, *President*
EMP: 2
SQ FT: 5,000
SALES (est): 448.2K **Privately Held**
SIC: 5032 1771 1711 1794 Concrete & cinder building products; concrete work; plumbing contractors; excavation work; concrete products; concrete block & brick

(G-10959)
HANCOCK COUNTY SHOPPER
1830 Keokuk St (62341-1144)
PHONE 217 847-6628
EMP: 6
SALES (est): 281.1K **Privately Held**
SIC: 2711 2741 Newspapers-Publishing/Printing Misc Publishing

(G-10960)
PRECISION FOUNDRY TOOLING LTD
160 Hamilton Indus Park (62341-3169)
PHONE 217 847-3233
Robert Harmon, *President*
EMP: 11 **EST:** 1977
SQ FT: 5,400
SALES (est): 1MM **Privately Held**
SIC: 3543 Industrial patterns

(G-10961)
U S FREE PRESS LLC
950 E Us Highway 136 (62341-3159)
PHONE 319 524-3802
James M Helenthal,
EMP: 2
SALES (est): 211.4K **Privately Held**
SIC: 2741 Miscellaneous publishing

Hampshire
Kane County

(G-10962)
AUTOMATION SPECIALIST SVCS LLC
44w110 Us Highway 20 A (60140-6200)
PHONE 847 792-1692
Mark Pfeiffer,
EMP: 14 **EST:** 2014
SQ FT: 5,400
SALES (est): 3.7MM **Privately Held**
SIC: 3559 Automotive related machinery

(G-10963)
BANKMARK INC
46w299 Middleton Rd (60140-8536)
P.O. Box 365, Burlington (60109-0365)
PHONE 847 683-9834
Bob Gilman, *President*
EMP: 16
SALES (est): 2.9MM **Privately Held**
SIC: 3535 Pneumatic tube conveyor systems

(G-10964)
BESTAIR PRO
Also Called: Bestairpro
281 Keyes Ave (60140-9449)
PHONE 847 683-3400
Del Fields, *President*
Jim Fahey, *VP Sales*
▲ **EMP:** 3 **EST:** 1983
SALES (est): 270K **Privately Held**
WEB: www.bestairpro.com
SIC: 3634 Humidifiers, electric: household

(G-10965)
BLUE RIDGE FIBERBOARD
300 Industrial Dr (60140-7722)
PHONE 800 233-8721
James Pieczynski, *Administration*
EMP: 3
SALES (est): 151.9K **Privately Held**
WEB: www.blueridgefiberboard.com
SIC: 2493 Reconstituted wood products

(G-10966)
CENTER TOOL COMPANY
250 Industrial Dr (60140-7902)
PHONE 847 683-7559
Helmut Winter, *President*
Rose Marie Winter, *Corp Secy*
EMP: 4
SQ FT: 3,000
SALES (est): 510.4K **Privately Held**
SIC: 3544 3545 Special dies & tools; machine tool accessories

(G-10967)
COMBINED METALS CHICAGO LLC
Also Called: El Giloy Specialty Metals
1 Hauk Rd (60140-8239)
PHONE 847 683-0500
Jim Darrow, *Manager*
EMP: 11
SALES (corp-wide): 824.7MM **Privately Held**
WEB: www.combmet.com
SIC: 3315 3316 3547 Steel wire & related products; cold finishing of steel shapes; rolling mill machinery
HQ: Combined Metals Of Chicago Llc
2401 Grant Ave
Bellwood IL 60104
847 695-1900

(G-10968)
CROWN POLYMERS LLC
44w104 Us Highway 20 (60140-6200)
PHONE 847 683-0800
Floyd Dimmick, *Chairman*
EMP: 3 **EST:** 2017
SALES (est): 157K **Privately Held**
SIC: 2822 Synthetic rubber

(G-10969)
DREYMILLER & KRAY INC
140 S State St (60140-7000)
P.O. Box 238 (60140-0238)
PHONE 847 683-2271
Edward Reiser, *President*
EMP: 9
SQ FT: 1,200
SALES (est): 626.5K **Privately Held**
WEB: www.dreymillerandkray.com
SIC: 5421 5147 2013 Meat markets, including freezer provisioners; meats & meat products; sausages & other prepared meats

(G-10970)
ELECTRO-MAX INC
105 Rowell Rd Ste D (60140-9700)
PHONE 847 683-4100
Kevin R Grant, *President*
Jeremy Fawbush, *Manager*
EMP: 85 **EST:** 1997
SQ FT: 24,000
SALES: 22MM **Privately Held**
SIC: 3471 Finishing, metals or formed products

(G-10971)
ELGILOY SPECIALTY METALS
1 Hauk Rd (60140-8239)
PHONE 847 683-0500
Kristi Lewis, *Regl Sales Mgr*
Charlie Mills, *Sales Staff*

Jeremy Hein, *Supervisor*
John Blaszcyk, *Executive*
EMP: 5
SALES (est): 370.3K **Privately Held**
SIC: 3356 Nickel & nickel alloy pipe, plates, sheets, etc.

(G-10972)
FAIRBANKS WIRE CORPORATION
260 Industrial Dr Ste B (60140-7900)
PHONE 847 683-2600
Gunther Hank Holz, *President*
Barbara Holz, *Vice Pres*
Jeff Holz, *Sales Staff*
EMP: 5 **EST:** 1948
SQ FT: 18,000
SALES: 900K **Privately Held**
WEB: www.fairbankswire.com
SIC: 3315 5051 3351 Wire, steel: insulated or armored; metals service centers & offices; copper rolling & drawing

(G-10973)
HT LUMBER & CRATES INC
Also Called: Allenton Lumber Company
200 Industrial Dr Unit C (60140-7909)
PHONE 847 683-0200
Raymond J Horn III, *President*
Anthony Vecchiolla, *General Mgr*
EMP: 11
SALES (est): 1.3MM **Privately Held**
SIC: 2448 Pallets, wood

(G-10974)
HYTEL GROUP INC (PA)
290 Industrial Dr (60140-7907)
PHONE 847 683-9800
Scott Johansen, *CEO*
EMP: 40
SQ FT: 30,000
SALES (est): 5.6MM **Privately Held**
SIC: 3674 3672 Hybrid integrated circuits; printed circuit boards

(G-10975)
KLEHM FAMILY WINERY LLC
44w637 Il Route 72 (60140-8268)
PHONE 847 609-9997
Arnold Klehm,
EMP: 6
SALES (est): 390K **Privately Held**
SIC: 2084 Wines

(G-10976)
LEADING AMERICAS INC
130 Arrowhead Dr Unit 13 (60140-7653)
PHONE 815 568-2199
Tsukamoto Takahiro, *President*
Yutaka Amada, *Admin Sec*
EMP: 5
SALES (est): 143K **Privately Held**
SIC: 3569 Assembly machines, non-metal-working
PA: Leading Co.,Ltd.
1-42-14, Kameido
Koto-Ku TKY 136-0

(G-10977)
LED RITE LLC
120 Rowell Rd (60140-9713)
PHONE 847 683-8000
Yang Jean, *Principal*
Michael Yang, *Engineer*
EMP: 6
SALES (est): 603.7K **Privately Held**
SIC: 3674 Light emitting diodes

(G-10978)
MARCH INDUSTRIES INC
150 Arrowhead Dr (60140-7658)
PHONE 224 654-6500
Joseph Marchewka, *President*
Erik Bohrnell, *Sales Staff*
▼ **EMP:** 11
SQ FT: 15,000
SALES (est): 2.1MM **Privately Held**
SIC: 2273 5072 3069 5251 Mats & matting; hardware; mats or matting, rubber; hardware; industrial inorganic chemicals; industrial organic chemicals

(G-10979)
MINERALLAC COMPANY (PA)
100 Gast Rd (60140-7654)
PHONE 630 543-7080

James Hlavacek, *President*
Sonya Donald, *Executive*
Arthur J Ferguson, *Admin Sec*
▲ **EMP:** 50
SQ FT: 135,000
SALES (est): 12.9MM **Privately Held**
WEB: www.minerallac.com
SIC: 3496 3644 Staples, made from purchased wire; electric conduits & fittings

(G-10980)
MINUTEMAN INTERNATIONAL INC
14n845 Us Highway 20 (60140-8893)
PHONE...................................847 683-5210
John Cali, *Opers Staff*
Bob Jesse, *Branch Mgr*
EMP: 65
SALES (corp-wide): 360.4K **Privately Held**
SIC: 3589 Commercial cleaning equipment
HQ: Minuteman International, Inc.
14n845 Us Highway 20
Pingree Grove IL 60140
630 627-6900

(G-10981)
NUTRIAD INC
201 Flannigan Rd (60140-8245)
PHONE...................................847 214-4860
Keith Klanderman, *President*
◆ **EMP:** 20
SQ FT: 55,000
SALES (est): 5.2MM
SALES (corp-wide): 64.2B **Privately Held**
WEB: www.nutriad.com
SIC: 2048 Feed supplements
HQ: Bluestar Adisseo Nanjing Co., Ltd.
No.389, Changfenghe Road, Chemical Industry Park
Nanjing 21004
255 768-8189

(G-10982)
OZINGA CONCRETE PRODUCTS INC
401 Brier Hill Rd (60140-8103)
PHONE...................................708 479-9050
Ron Floit, *President*
EMP: 3
SALES (est): 227.4K **Privately Held**
SIC: 3273 Ready-mixed concrete

(G-10983)
PET-AG INC
Also Called: Pet AG
180 Ryan Dr (60140-1004)
PHONE...................................847 683-2288
Darlene A Frudakis, *President*
Lewis M Sutton, *Exec VP*
CPA D Rotolo, *Controller*
Emma Rodriguez, *Accountant*
William J Geary, *Admin Sec*
◆ **EMP:** 40
SALES (est): 11MM
SALES (corp-wide): 30.7MM **Privately Held**
SIC: 2048 2047 Feed supplements; dog food; cat food
PA: Pbi-Gordon Corporation
22701 W 68th Ter
Shawnee KS 66226
816 421-4070

(G-10984)
POLI-FILM AMERICA INC (DH)
1 Elgiloy Dr (60140-8238)
PHONE...................................847 453-8104
Dan Ulbert, *President*
Rich Rudecki, *Engrg Dir*
Tyson Meade, *Treasurer*
▲ **EMP:** 65
SQ FT: 84,000
SALES (est): 21.7MM
SALES (corp-wide): 177.9K **Privately Held**
SIC: 3081 Polyethylene film
HQ: Polifilm Gmbh
Waidmarkt 11a
Koln 50676
221 801-4460

(G-10985)
ROTEC INDUSTRIES INC (PA)
270 Industrial Dr (60140-7902)
PHONE...................................630 279-3300
Robert F Oury, *Ch of Bd*
Alan S Ledger, *President*
◆ **EMP:** 81
SQ FT: 50,000
SALES (est): 19.6MM **Privately Held**
WEB: www.rotec-usa.com
SIC: 3535 7353 Belt conveyor systems, general industrial use; heavy construction equipment rental

(G-10986)
RPS PRODUCTS INC (PA)
Also Called: Best Air
281 Keyes Ave (60140-9463)
PHONE...................................847 683-3400
Richard P Schuld, *CEO*
Daniel E Schuld, *President*
Tom Myers, *Exec VP*
Paul Schneider, *Engineer*
Patricia Panagakos, *Accounting Mgr*
▲ **EMP:** 25
SQ FT: 80,000
SALES (est): 8.2MM **Privately Held**
SIC: 3589 3089 7389 2899 Water filters & softeners, household type; plastic containers, except foam; packaging & labeling services; water treating compounds

(G-10987)
SECURITY METAL PRODUCTS CORP
1741 Kelley Ln (60140-5409)
PHONE...................................630 965-6355
Joan Aktabowski, *Branch Mgr*
EMP: 3
SALES (corp-wide): 9.3B **Privately Held**
WEB: www.secmet.com
SIC: 3442 Metal doors, sash & trim
HQ: Security Metal Products Corporation
5678 Concours
Ontario CA 91764
310 641-6690

(G-10988)
SMART INC
41w584 Us Highway 20 (60140-8865)
PHONE...................................847 464-4160
Danny Smart, *President*
James Christensen, *Vice Pres*
▲ **EMP:** 5 **EST:** 1978
SQ FT: 15,000
SALES (est): 1MM **Privately Held**
SIC: 3555 5084 7629 Bookbinding machinery; printing trades machinery, equipment & supplies; electrical repair shops

(G-10989)
VILLAGE HAMPSHIRE TRTMNT PLANT
350 Mill Ave (60140)
PHONE...................................847 683-2064
Jeffrey Magnussen, *President*
EMP: 3
SALES (est): 215.6K **Privately Held**
SIC: 3823 Water quality monitoring & control systems

(G-10990)
WESTERN SLATE COMPANY (PA)
Also Called: W S Hampshire
365 Keyes Ave (60140-9458)
PHONE...................................847 683-4400
Jeff Pope, *President*
Greg Waack, *General Mgr*
Dan Jankoski, *Controller*
EMP: 64 **EST:** 1986
SQ FT: 140,000
SALES (est): 15MM **Privately Held**
WEB: www.wshampshire.com
SIC: 3569 Assembly machines, non-metalworking

Hanna City
Peoria County

(G-10991)
CAPTAIN HOOK INC
5125 S Hnna Cy Glsford Rd (61536)
PHONE...................................309 565-7676
Di Wagehofp, *Principal*
EMP: 4

SALES (est): 352.9K **Privately Held**
SIC: 3443 Dumpsters, garbage

(G-10992)
ILLINOIS WELD & MACHINE INC
123 S 2nd St (61536-8034)
PHONE...................................309 565-0533
Irwin Julin, *Manager*
EMP: 10 **Privately Held**
SIC: 3312 Blast furnaces & steel mills
PA: Illinois Weld & Machine, Inc
101 S 2nd St
Hanna City IL 61536

(G-10993)
ILLINOIS WELD & MACHINE INC (PA)
101 S 2nd St (61536)
PHONE...................................309 565-0533
Irwin Julian, *President*
Everett Frazier, *Vice Pres*
EMP: 10
SQ FT: 1,680
SALES (est): 1.3MM **Privately Held**
SIC: 3599 Machine shop, jobbing & repair

(G-10994)
RAYMOND EARL FINE WOODWORKING
201 S Main St (61536)
PHONE...................................309 565-7661
Earl Raymond, *Owner*
EMP: 2
SQ FT: 2,000
SALES (est): 223.7K **Privately Held**
SIC: 1521 2434 General remodeling, single-family houses; wood kitchen cabinets

Hanover
Jo Daviess County

(G-10995)
BOURRETTE LOGGING
1012 Blackhawk B (61041)
P.O. Box 227 (61041-0227)
PHONE...................................815 591-3761
Thomas Bourrette, *Principal*
EMP: 3
SALES (est): 215.9K **Privately Held**
SIC: 2411 Logging camps & contractors

(G-10996)
K D WELDING INC
2 River Bend Dr (61041-9673)
PHONE...................................815 591-3545
Kevin C Loney, *President*
EMP: 9 **EST:** 1997
SALES (est): 1.1MM **Privately Held**
WEB: www.kdweldinginc.com
SIC: 7692 Welding repair

(G-10997)
ROBERTSHAW CONTROLS COMPANY
Also Called: Invensys Controls
107 N Washington St (61041-9620)
PHONE...................................815 591-2417
EMP: 24
SALES (corp-wide): 19.3B **Privately Held**
SIC: 3823 Mfg Process Control Instruments
HQ: Robertshaw Controls Company
1222 Hamilton Pkwy
Itasca IL 60143
956 554-4107

Hanover Park
Cook County

(G-10998)
AMPAC FLEXICON LLC
Ampac Flexibles
825 Turnberry Ct (60133-5477)
PHONE...................................630 439-3160
Timothy Piper, *QC Mgr*
Joseph Beuchanan, *Manager*
EMP: 24

SALES (corp-wide): 1.2B **Privately Held**
WEB: www.ampaconline.com
SIC: 2671 Plastic film, coated or laminated for packaging; paper coated or laminated for packaging
HQ: Ampac Flexicon, Llc
165 Chicago St
Cary IL 60013
847 639-3530

(G-10999)
AMPAC FLEXICON LLC
Also Called: Ampac Flexibles
825 Turnberry Ct (60133-5477)
PHONE...................................952 541-0730
EMP: 3
SALES (corp-wide): 1.3B **Privately Held**
SIC: 2671 Mfg Packaging Paper/Film
HQ: Ampac Flexicon, Llc
165 Chicago St
Cary IL 60013
847 639-3530

(G-11000)
B/E AEROSPACE INC
1220 Central Ave (60133-5420)
PHONE...................................561 791-5000
EMP: 143
SALES (corp-wide): 77B **Publicly Held**
SIC: 2531 Seats, aircraft
HQ: B/E Aerospace, Inc.
1400 Corporate Center Way
Wellington FL 33414
561 791-5000

(G-11001)
CAMCRAFT INC (PA)
1080 Muirfield Dr (60133-5474)
PHONE...................................630 582-6001
Michael Bertsche, *President*
Steve Olsen, *Exec VP*
Ray Ross, *Prdtn Mgr*
Luis Montes, *Maint Spvr*
Janusz Ksel, *Mfg Staff*
EMP: 148 **EST:** 1950
SQ FT: 83,000
SALES (est): 43.7MM **Privately Held**
WEB: www.camcraft.com
SIC: 3451 Screw machine products

(G-11002)
DULCE VIDA JUICE BAR LLC
2003 Irving Park Rd (60133-3164)
PHONE...................................224 236-5045
Gregorio Hernandez,
EMP: 3
SALES (est): 137.9K **Privately Held**
SIC: 2037 Fruit juices

(G-11003)
FISHER SCIENTIFIC COMPANY LLC
Also Called: Fisher Safety
4500 Turnberry Dr (60133-5491)
PHONE...................................412 490-8300
Panny Swoopes, *Branch Mgr*
EMP: 115
SALES (corp-wide): 25.5B **Publicly Held**
SIC: 3826 5049 5084 Analytical instruments; laboratory equipment, except medical or dental; safety equipment
HQ: Fisher Scientific Company Llc
300 Industry Dr
Pittsburgh PA 15275
724 517-1500

(G-11004)
FLODYNE INC
Also Called: Cma, Flodyne, Hydradyne
1000 Muirfield Dr (60133-5426)
PHONE...................................630 563-3600
Frank Machac, *President*
Mike Butler, *Engineer*
Greg Catalano, *Engineer*
Joe Gignac, *Engineer*
Mitchell Muffler, *Engineer*
EMP: 6
SALES (est): 4.8MM **Privately Held**
SIC: 5084 3824 Hydraulic systems equipment & supplies; crushing machinery & equipment; mechanical & electromechanical counters & devices

Hanover Park - Cook County (G-11005)

(G-11005)
FLOW CONTROL US HOLDING CORP
1040 Muirfield Dr (60133-5468)
PHONE.............................630 307-3000
Karl Stoltenberg, *Business Mgr*
Volker Haag, *Vice Pres*
Norma Maxstadt, *Senior Buyer*
Jim Scott, *Buyer*
Dennis Dunn, *Engineer*
EMP: 15
SALES (corp-wide): 18.3B **Publicly Held**
SIC: 3561 Pumps & pumping equipment
HQ: Flow Control Us Holding Corporation
5500 Wayzata Blvd Ste 800
Minneapolis MN 55416
763 545-1730

(G-11006)
FUJIFILM ELCTRNIC MTLS USA INC
Also Called: Fujifilm NDT Systems
850 Central Ave (60133-5422)
PHONE.............................312 924-5800
Louise Bauer, *Branch Mgr*
EMP: 3 **Privately Held**
SIC: 5043 3861 Photographic equipment & supplies; photographic equipment & supplies
HQ: Fujifilm Electronic Materials U.S.A., Inc.
80 Circuit Dr
North Kingstown RI 02852
401 522-9499

(G-11007)
INTEGRATED CIRCUITS RESEARCH
6600 Appletree St (60133-3902)
PHONE.............................630 830-9024
Mike Rebeschini, *President*
EMP: 2
SALES: 300K **Privately Held**
SIC: 3679 Electronic circuits

(G-11008)
KAPAK COMPANY LLC
825 Turnberry Ct (60133-5477)
PHONE.............................952 541-0730
EMP: 3 **EST:** 2015
SALES (est): 143.9K **Privately Held**
SIC: 2673 Bags: Plastic, Laminated, And Coated, Nsk

(G-11009)
MEDICAL SPECIALTIES DISTRS LLC
1549 Hunter Rd (60133-6772)
PHONE.............................630 307-6200
Steve Schaudenecker, *Branch Mgr*
EMP: 34
SALES (corp-wide): 231B **Publicly Held**
SIC: 3845 5047 Electromedical apparatus; electro-medical equipment
HQ: Medical Specialties Distributors, Llc
800 Technology Center Dr # 3
Stoughton MA 02072
781 344-6000

(G-11010)
NEFAB PACKAGING N CENTL LLC
1539 Hunter Rd (60133-6754)
PHONE.............................630 451-5314
Mike Pectorelli,
EMP: 172
SALES (est): 25MM
SALES (corp-wide): 496.7MM **Privately Held**
SIC: 2448 2449 2441 Pallets, wood; skids, wood & wood with metal; rectangular boxes & crates, wood; nailed wood boxes & shook
HQ: Nefab Packaging, Inc.
204 Airline Dr Ste 100
Coppell TX 75019
469 444-5264

(G-11011)
NYPRO INC
Also Called: Nypro Hanover Park
6325 Muirfield Dr (60133-5467)
PHONE.............................630 671-2000
Beata Pekalski, *Purchasing*
Matthew Goldenberg, *Project Engr*
Mark Gomulka, *Branch Mgr*
Jon Hursey, *Manager*
Ellen Klempier, *Administration*
EMP: 50
SALES (corp-wide): 25.2B **Publicly Held**
SIC: 3089 Injection molding of plastics
HQ: Nypro Inc.
101 Union St
Clinton MA 01510
978 365-8100

(G-11012)
PENTAIR FLTRTION SOLUTIONS LLC (DH)
Also Called: Everpure
1040 Muirfield Dr (60133-5468)
PHONE.............................630 307-3000
Randall J Hogan, *CEO*
Tim Reckinger, *Vice Pres*
Cynthia Martin, *Regl Sales Mgr*
Michael Madsen,
◆ **EMP:** 25 **EST:** 2007
SQ FT: 110,000
SALES (est): 48.5MM
SALES (corp-wide): 18.3B **Publicly Held**
WEB: www.pentair.com
SIC: 3589 Water purification equipment, household type; water treatment equipment, industrial
HQ: Flow Control Us Holding Corporation
5500 Wayzata Blvd Ste 800
Minneapolis MN 55416
763 545-1730

(G-11013)
SCHELLERER CORPORATION INC
Also Called: Er2 Image Group
4350 Chandler Dr (60133-6763)
PHONE.............................630 980-4567
Gary R Schellerer, *President*
Adam Wagner, *Production*
Carla Schellerer, *Treasurer*
Michele Pedre, *Accounts Exec*
Laura Petersen, *Accounts Exec*
EMP: 65
SALES (est): 8.8MM **Privately Held**
SIC: 3993 7532 7319 Signs & advertising specialties; truck painting & lettering; display advertising service

(G-11014)
STANDARD INDUS & AUTO EQP INC
6211 Church Rd (60133-4802)
PHONE.............................630 289-9500
John Woitel, *President*
John F Woitel, *President*
Larry Garcia, *Accounts Mgr*
Joe Pinkul, *Sales Staff*
Don Corty, *Manager*
EMP: 20 **EST:** 1927
SALES (est): 8.4MM **Privately Held**
WEB: www.standardus.com
SIC: 5013 2841 3569 7539 Automotive supplies & parts; soap & other detergents; lubrication equipment, industrial; automotive repair shops

(G-11015)
STANDARD LIFTS & EQUIPMENT INC
6211 Church Rd (60133-4802)
PHONE.............................414 444-1000
John Woitel, *President*
Frank Woitel, *Vice Pres*
▲ **EMP:** 4
SQ FT: 20,000
SALES (est): 461.6K **Privately Held**
SIC: 5531 3586 3563 Automotive parts; oil pumps, measuring or dispensing; air & gas compressors

Hardin
Calhoun County

(G-11016)
CALHOUN QUARRY INCORPORATED
Eldred Rd (62047)
PHONE.............................618 576-9223
Tony Sievers, *Branch Mgr*
EMP: 8
SALES (corp-wide): 1.2MM **Privately Held**
SIC: 1422 Limestones, ground
PA: Calhoun Quarry, Incorporated
25 Main St
Batchtown IL 62006
618 396-2229

(G-11017)
HARDIN READY MIX INC
19321 Illinois River Rd (62047-9745)
P.O. Box 329 (62047-0329)
PHONE.............................618 576-9313
Patricia Meseke, *President*
Richard Meseke, *Vice Pres*
EMP: 10
SQ FT: 10,140
SALES (est): 168K **Privately Held**
SIC: 3273 3272 Ready-mixed concrete; septic tanks, concrete

Harmon
Lee County

(G-11018)
J M FABRICATING INC
214 S 1st St (61042-9400)
PHONE.............................815 359-2024
Mike Dunn, *Principal*
EMP: 4
SALES (est): 397.2K **Privately Held**
SIC: 2295 Metallizing of fabrics

Harrisburg
Saline County

(G-11019)
A&W STONE MASONRY LLC
2005 Walnut Grove Rd (62946-4551)
PHONE.............................618 499-7239
Trent Wallace, *Manager*
EMP: 3
SALES (est): 91.3K **Privately Held**
SIC: 2024 Yogurt desserts, frozen

(G-11020)
BOB BARNETT REDI-MIX INC (PA)
Also Called: Barnett Bob Redi-Mix
285 Garden Heights Rd (62946-5200)
PHONE.............................618 252-3581
Sherry Denny, *President*
Jeff Denny, *Corp Secy*
Bret Denny, *Vice Pres*
EMP: 37 **EST:** 1960
SQ FT: 2,200
SALES (est): 4.8MM **Privately Held**
WEB: www.tisonandhall.com
SIC: 3273 4212 Ready-mixed concrete; local trucking, without storage

(G-11021)
CHERRY STREET PRINTING & AWARD
211 E Poplar St Ste 2 (62946-1544)
PHONE.............................618 252-6814
Paul Pyle, *Principal*
EMP: 2
SALES (est): 214.5K **Privately Held**
SIC: 2759 Commercial printing

(G-11022)
EDWARDS COUNTY CONCRETE LL
210 N Commercial St (62946-1331)
PHONE.............................618 445-2711
Scott Aud, *Principal*
EMP: 5
SALES (est): 472.7K **Privately Held**
SIC: 3273 Ready-mixed concrete

(G-11023)
FINITE RESOURCES LTD
520 S Mckinley St (62946-2217)
P.O. Box 536 (62946-0536)
PHONE.............................618 252-3733
Kevin Reimer, *Managing Prtnr*
EMP: 5
SALES (est): 495.8K **Privately Held**
SIC: 1389 Construction, repair & dismantling services

(G-11024)
GATEHOUSE MEDIA LLC
Also Called: Daily Register
35 S Vine St (62946-1725)
P.O. Box 248 (62946-0248)
PHONE.............................618 253-7146
George Wilson, *Manager*
EMP: 30
SALES (corp-wide): 1.8B **Publicly Held**
SIC: 2711 Newspapers, publishing & printing; newspapers: publishing only, not printed on site
HQ: Gatehouse Media, Llc
175 Sullys Trl Fl 3
Pittsford NY 14534
585 598-0030

(G-11025)
GRAF INK PRINTING INC
Also Called: Rocky's Advanced Printing
24 W Church St (62946-1602)
PHONE.............................618 273-4231
Christopher Beavers, *President*
EMP: 4
SQ FT: 1,080
SALES (est): 310K **Privately Held**
SIC: 2752 Commercial printing, offset

(G-11026)
MINERAL PRODUCTS INC
6 Atkins Dr (62946)
P.O. Box 445 (62946-0445)
PHONE.............................618 433-3150
Jerry Farmer, *President*
EMP: 4
SALES (est): 252.7K **Privately Held**
SIC: 3295 3531 3274 Minerals, ground or treated; barite, ground or otherwise treated; railway track equipment; building lime

(G-11027)
NATIONWIDE GLOVE CO INC (PA)
925 Bauman Ln (62946-3550)
P.O. Box K (62946-5010)
PHONE.............................618 252-7192
Nathan Applebaum, *President*
Samuel Appelbaum, *Vice Pres*
EMP: 70 **EST:** 1940
SQ FT: 24,000
SALES (est): 11.7MM **Privately Held**
WEB: www.alliedglove.com
SIC: 2381 3151 Gloves, work: woven or knit, made from purchased materials; gloves, leather: work

(G-11028)
REGISTER PUBLISHING CO
35 S Vine St (62946-1725)
P.O. Box 617, West Frankfort (62896-0617)
PHONE.............................618 253-7146
Ken Serota, *President*
George Q Wilson, *Publisher*
Kay Brandsasse, *Business Mgr*
EMP: 25 **EST:** 1908
SQ FT: 10,800
SALES (est): 1.5MM **Privately Held**
WEB: www.dailyregister.com
SIC: 2711 Newspapers, publishing & printing

(G-11029)
SOUTHERN TRUSS INC
5510 Highway 13 W (62946-4134)
P.O. Box 275 (62946-0275)
PHONE.............................618 252-8144
Dennis J Murphy, *President*
Charles A Murphy, *Vice Pres*
Joey Heflin, *Sales Staff*
Marilyn Stiles, *Executive Asst*
EMP: 50
SQ FT: 9,000
SALES (est): 7.6MM **Privately Held**
WEB: www.southerntrusscompany.com
SIC: 2439 Trusses, wooden roof; trusses, except roof: laminated lumber

GEOGRAPHIC SECTION

(G-11030)
TISON & HALL CONCRETE PRODUCTS
210 N Commercial St (62946-1397)
PHONE..................618 253-7808
Sherry Denny, *President*
Wayne Mears, *General Mgr*
Randy Gates, *Sheriff*
Brett Denny, *Vice Pres*
Jeff Denny, *Treasurer*
EMP: 17 **EST:** 1946
SQ FT: 8,000
SALES (est): 2.9MM
SALES (corp-wide): 4.8MM **Privately Held**
SIC: 3271 5211 Blocks, concrete or cinder: standard; brick
PA: Bob Barnett Redi-Mix Inc
285 Garden Heights Rd
Harrisburg IL 62946
618 252-3581

(G-11031)
WILSON KITCHENS INC
Also Called: Wki
1653 S Feazel St (62946-3536)
PHONE..................618 253-7449
Harold Wilson, *President*
Blake Wilson, *Executive*
EMP: 54
SQ FT: 26,000
SALES (est): 10MM **Privately Held**
SIC: 2541 2542 5211 Cabinets, except refrigerated: show, display, etc.: wood; cabinets: show, display or storage: except wood; cabinets, kitchen

Harristown
Macon County

(G-11032)
LEGACY VULCAN LLC
2855 Lincoln Pkwy (62537)
PHONE..................217 963-2196
Tom Heft, *Principal*
EMP: 7 **Publicly Held**
SIC: 1442 Construction sand & gravel
HQ: Legacy Vulcan, Llc
1200 Urban Center Dr
Vestavia AL 35242
205 298-3000

(G-11033)
STRAIGHTLINE AG INC
8990 W Us 36 (62537)
P.O. Box 44 (62537-0044)
PHONE..................217 963-1270
EMP: 4 **EST:** 2010
SALES (est): 317.8K **Privately Held**
SIC: 3523 Farm machinery & equipment

Hartford
Madison County

(G-11034)
DOOLING MACHINE PRODUCTS INC (PA)
107 N Delmar Ave (62048-1008)
P.O. Box 3487, Freeport TX (77542-1687)
PHONE..................618 254-0724
Joseph Dooling Jr, *President*
Joseph Dooling Sr, *Corp Secy*
Beverly Landolt, *Vice Pres*
EMP: 6
SALES (est): 1.7MM **Privately Held**
SIC: 3599 7692 3549 3544 Machine shop, jobbing & repair; welding repair; metalworking machinery; special dies, tools, jigs & fixtures

(G-11035)
MESSER LLC
1200 S Delmar Ave (62048-2502)
P.O. Box 37 (62048-0037)
PHONE..................618 251-5217
William Brown, *Branch Mgr*
Berin Wildt, *Manager*
EMP: 50
SALES (corp-wide): 1.1B **Privately Held**
SIC: 2813 Nitrogen

HQ: Messer Llc
200 Somerset Corp Blvd # 7000
Bridgewater NJ 08807
908 464-8100

(G-11036)
NATIONAL MAINT & REPR INC (HQ)
401 S Hawthorne St (62048-1052)
P.O. Box 38 (62048-0038)
PHONE..................618 254-7451
Bruce D McGinnis, *President*
Bill Jessie, *CFO*
▲ **EMP:** 250
SALES (est): 99.2MM **Privately Held**
SIC: 3731 7699 Shipbuilding & repairing; engine repair & replacement, non-automotive

(G-11037)
PREMCOR INCORPORATED
201 E Hawthorne St (62048-1126)
PHONE..................618 254-7301
Cliff Lowe, *Manager*
EMP: 3
SALES (est): 371.7K **Privately Held**
SIC: 2911 Petroleum refining

Harvard
Mchenry County

(G-11038)
A T PRODUCTS INC
1600 S Division St (60033-9043)
P.O. Box 625 (60033-0625)
PHONE..................815 943-3590
Mike Rose, *President*
EMP: 5
SQ FT: 4,000
SALES (est): 896.6K **Privately Held**
SIC: 3661 Telephones & telephone apparatus

(G-11039)
A-OK INC
Also Called: Harvard Building Products
711 W Brown St (60033-2344)
P.O. Box 358 (60033-0358)
PHONE..................815 943-7431
Orrin Kinney, *President*
Andy Cyrus, *Sales Staff*
EMP: 45
SQ FT: 30,000
SALES (est): 10.9MM **Privately Held**
SIC: 3442 5031 Window & door frames; doors & windows

(G-11040)
ACRO MAGNETICS INC
24005 Il Route 173 (60033-8610)
PHONE..................815 943-5018
Neil T Schultz, *President*
Neil C Schultz, *Vice Pres*
Cynthia Schultz, *Treasurer*
Marla Schultz, *Admin Sec*
EMP: 5
SQ FT: 6,000
SALES (est): 892.9K **Privately Held**
SIC: 3559 3695 3535 Separation equipment, magnetic; magnetic & optical recording media; conveyors & conveying equipment

(G-11041)
AERO INDUSTRIES INC
450 Commanche Cir (60033-3110)
PHONE..................800 747-3553
James L Clingingsmith, *President*
Gary Kinshofer, *Vice Pres*
Theresa Taylor, *Manager*
▲ **EMP:** 10
SQ FT: 22,500
SALES (est): 1.8MM **Privately Held**
WEB: www.aerographite.com
SIC: 3295 3624 Graphite, natural: ground, pulverized, refined or blended; carbon & graphite products

(G-11042)
ALTIUM PACKAGING
875 W Diggins St (60033-2370)
PHONE..................815 943-7828
Bill Weber, *Branch Mgr*

EMP: 120
SALES (corp-wide): 14.9B **Publicly Held**
WEB: www.cccllc.com
SIC: 3089 Plastic containers, except foam
HQ: Altium Packaging Llc
2500 Windy Ridge Pkwy Se # 1
Atlanta GA 30339
678 742-4600

(G-11043)
ALUM-I-TANK INC
201 Ratzlaff St (60033-2651)
PHONE..................800 652-6630
Kathleen Egre, *Office Mgr*
David Kirkpatrick, *Branch Mgr*
EMP: 10 **Privately Held**
SIC: 3443 Fuel tanks (oil, gas, etc.): metal plate
PA: Alum-I-Tank, Inc.
11317 N Us Highway 14
Harvard IL 60033

(G-11044)
ALUM-I-TANK INC (PA)
Also Called: Alumitank
11317 N Us Highway 14 (60033-9152)
PHONE..................815 943-6649
Terence Kirkpatrick, *President*
Robert Kirkpatrick, *Corp Secy*
Bob Kirkpatrick, *Treasurer*
EMP: 48
SALES (est): 11.6MM **Privately Held**
SIC: 3443 Fuel tanks (oil, gas, etc.): metal plate

(G-11045)
AMERICAN GRINDERS INC
3 Lincoln St Ste 3 # 3 (60033-3100)
PHONE..................815 943-4902
Ian McHattie, *Owner*
EMP: 3
SALES (est): 564.7K **Privately Held**
SIC: 2952 Coating compounds, tar

(G-11046)
AQUADINE INC (PA)
Also Called: Aquadine Nutritional System
495 Commanche Cir (60033-3110)
PHONE..................800 497-3463
Robert Weiss, *President*
Paul Butler, *CFO*
EMP: 5
SALES (est): 814.4K **Privately Held**
SIC: 3999 5961 Pet supplies; catalog & mail-order houses

(G-11047)
ATLAS MANUFACTURING LTD
1001 W Roosevelt St (60033-1660)
PHONE..................815 943-1400
Nick Leicht, *President*
EMP: 15 **EST:** 1977
SQ FT: 10,500
SALES (est): 2.1MM **Privately Held**
SIC: 3599 Machine shop, jobbing & repair

(G-11048)
BILL PETERSON
Also Called: Peterson Farms
25007 Flat Iron Rd (60033-8942)
PHONE..................815 378-8633
Bill Peterson, *Owner*
EMP: 1
SALES (est): 229.6K **Privately Held**
SIC: 3523 Driers (farm): grain, hay & seed

(G-11049)
CARTEL HOLDINGS INC (PA)
Also Called: Vincent Castillo
3 Lincoln St Ste 2a (60033-3100)
P.O. Box 151, Woodstock (60098-0151)
PHONE..................815 334-0250
Vincent Castillo, *President*
EMP: 4
SQ FT: 3,800
SALES (est): 556.9K **Privately Held**
SIC: 2911 2992 Fuel additives; brake fluid (hydraulic): made from purchased materials

(G-11050)
CINDYS POCKET KITCHEN
23802 Chemung St (60033-8915)
PHONE..................815 388-8385
Cynthia McGee, *President*
EMP: 3 **EST:** 2014

SALES (est): 110K **Privately Held**
SIC: 2099 5963 Food preparations; food service, mobile, except coffee-cart

(G-11051)
CUSTOM WINDOW ACCENTS
900 W Diggins St (60033-2378)
P.O. Box 66 (60033-0066)
PHONE..................815 943-7651
James Pagles, *President*
Karen Pack, *Admin Sec*
EMP: 19
SQ FT: 18,375
SALES (est): 900K **Privately Held**
SIC: 2591 2431 2511 2541 Window shades; ornamental woodwork: cornices, mantels, etc.; bed frames, except water bed frames: wood; headboards: wood; wood partitions & fixtures

(G-11052)
DEAN DAIRY FLUID LLC
6303 Maxon Rd (60033-8853)
PHONE..................815 943-7375
David Stis, *Vice Pres*
Paul Hill, *QA Dir*
Bill Hoyt, *Engineer*
Kevin Young, *Engineer*
Jody Vandebogert, *CPA*
EMP: 221
SALES (corp-wide): 15.8B **Privately Held**
WEB: www.deanfoods.com
SIC: 2026 Milk processing (pasteurizing, homogenizing, bottling)
HQ: Dfa Dairy Brands Fluid, Llc
1405 N 98th St
Kansas City KS 66111
816 801-6455

(G-11053)
DURR - ALL CORPORATION
1001 W Diggins St Ste 2 (60033-2387)
P.O. Box 2332, Crystal Lake (60039-2332)
PHONE..................815 943-1032
Eric Gusakow, *President*
EMP: 3
SALES (est): 389.3K **Privately Held**
SIC: 3599 3471 Machine shop, jobbing & repair; plating & polishing

(G-11054)
ERECT-A-TUBE INC
701 W Park St (60033-2600)
P.O. Box 100 (60033-0100)
PHONE..................815 943-4091
Susan M Wagner, *President*
Klaus H Herkert, *Vice Pres*
Randall M Kirk, *Vice Pres*
Edwin H Thurnau, *Vice Pres*
Wes Walker, *Engineer*
EMP: 45
SQ FT: 60,000
SALES (est): 11.7MM **Privately Held**
WEB: www.erect-a-tube.com
SIC: 3442 Hangar doors, metal

(G-11055)
FLOTEK INC
1000 Northfield Ave (60033-1668)
P.O. Box 609, Cary (60013-0609)
PHONE..................815 943-6816
Richard Ballot, *President*
Harry Joy, *Admin Sec*
EMP: 6
SALES (est): 1MM **Privately Held**
SIC: 3089 Injection molding of plastics

(G-11056)
HAWK MOLDING INC
435 Andrea Ct (60033-7806)
PHONE..................224 523-2888
Sean Wolfert, *Principal*
EMP: 3
SALES (est): 209.9K **Privately Held**
SIC: 3089 Molding primary plastic

(G-11057)
INDUSTRIAL GRAPHITE SALES LLC
450 Commanche Cir (60033-3110)
PHONE..................815 943-5502
Marilyn Skok,
EMP: 2
SALES (est): 363.8K **Privately Held**
SIC: 3624 Carbon & graphite products

Harvard - Mchenry County

(G-11058)
JONES PACKING CO
22701 Oak Grove Rd (60033-8205)
PHONE.................815 943-4488
Ray Jones, *Partner*
Robert Jones, *Partner*
Mary Ann Trebes, *Bookkeeper*
EMP: 8 **EST:** 1952
SQ FT: 8,000
SALES: 400K **Privately Held**
SIC: 2011 5421 5147 2013 Meat packing plants; meat markets, including freezer provisioners; meats, fresh; sausages & other prepared meats

(G-11059)
LOGAN ACTUATOR CO
550 Chippewa Rd (60033-2337)
PHONE.................815 943-9500
George Logan, *President*
Scott Logan, *Vice Pres*
Adeline Logan, *Admin Sec*
EMP: 6
SALES (est): 665.5K **Privately Held**
SIC: 3536 3532 3842 3728 Mine hoists; mining machinery; surgical appliances & supplies; aircraft parts & equipment; machine tool accessories

(G-11060)
MEYER MATERIAL CO MERGER CORP
20806 Mcguire Rd (60033-8353)
PHONE.................815 943-2605
EMP: 53
SALES (corp-wide): 26.4B **Privately Held**
SIC: 1422 3273 3272 Crushed/Broken Limestone Mfg Ready-Mixed Concrete Mfg Concrete Products
HQ: Meyer Material Co Merger Corp.
580 S Wolf Rd
Des Plaines IL 60016
815 331-7200

(G-11061)
NORTHWEST PRINTING INC
20 N Ayer St (60033-2861)
PHONE.................815 943-7977
Robert Schneider, *President*
Joy Schneider, *Corp Secy*
Jill Gaulkey, *Director*
Randy Schneider, *Director*
Rodger Schneider, *Director*
EMP: 5 **EST:** 1975
SQ FT: 4,000
SALES (est): 629.6K **Privately Held**
SIC: 2752 2791 2789 Commercial printing, offset; typesetting; bookbinding & related work

(G-11062)
PETDINE LLC
New 2 Dogs Way (60033)
PHONE.................815 770-0342
EMP: 3
SALES (corp-wide): 12MM **Privately Held**
SIC: 2048 Dry pet food (except dog & cat)
PA: Petdine Llc
4700 Innovation Dr Ste B3
Fort Collins CO 80525
800 497-3463

(G-11063)
PRACTICAL BAKER INC
600 Chippewa Rd (60033-2372)
PHONE.................815 943-6040
John Stricker, *President*
▲ **EMP:** 6
SQ FT: 15,000
SALES (est): 907.5K **Privately Held**
SIC: 3556 Bakery machinery

(G-11064)
PROALLIANCE CORP
300 W Front St Ste 203k (60033-2711)
P.O. Box 404 (60033-0404)
PHONE.................815 207-8556
Brian Kaunas, *President*
EMP: 6
SQ FT: 1,200
SALES: 2MM **Privately Held**
SIC: 3843 Dental equipment & supplies

(G-11065)
PROMMAR PLASTICS INC
1001 W Diggins St Ste 1 (60033-2387)
PHONE.................815 770-0555
EMP: 7
SQ FT: 4,000
SALES (est): 491.2K **Privately Held**
SIC: 3089 Injection molding of plastics

(G-11066)
ROYAL OAK FARM INC
15908 Hebron Rd (60033-9357)
PHONE.................815 648-4141
Peter Bianchini, *President*
Gloria B Bianchini, *Admin Sec*
EMP: 10
SQ FT: 12,000
SALES (est): 699.8K **Privately Held**
WEB: www.royaloakfarmorchard.com
SIC: 0175 5947 2051 5812 Apple orchard; gift shop; bread, cake & related products; eating places

(G-11067)
ST CHARLES SCREW PRODUCTS INC
404 E Park St (60033-2941)
PHONE.................815 943-8060
Joe Adams, *President*
Joseph Michaels Adams III, *Corp Secy*
S Yvonne Adams, *Vice Pres*
EMP: 4
SQ FT: 3,500
SALES (est): 170K **Privately Held**
SIC: 3599 3451 Machine shop, jobbing & repair; screw machine products

(G-11068)
STEEL SPAN INC
630 W Blackman St (60033-2331)
P.O. Box 368 (60033-0368)
PHONE.................815 943-9071
Orrin Kinney, *President*
EMP: 10
SALES (est): 1.6MM **Privately Held**
SIC: 3441 3448 3444 2452 Building components, structural steel; prefabricated metal buildings; sheet metalwork; prefabricated wood buildings

Harvey
Cook County

(G-11069)
ADVANAGE DIVERSIFIED PDTS INC
16615 Halsted St (60426-6112)
PHONE.................708 331-8390
Nathan T Edwards, *President*
Bowen Arnold, *Controller*
Moten Darvece, *Technology*
Diana M Byrd, *Admin Sec*
EMP: 15
SQ FT: 16,000
SALES: 1.6MM **Privately Held**
SIC: 2842 3589 Disinfectants, household or industrial plant; vacuum cleaners & sweepers, electric: industrial

(G-11070)
AFC CABLE SYSTEMS INC (DH)
Also Called: Communications Integrators
16100 Lathrop Ave (60426-6021)
P.O. Box 1675 (60426-7675)
PHONE.................508 998-1131
John P Williamson, *President*
Edward Arditte, *Vice Pres*
Carol Davidson, *Vice Pres*
James A Mallak, *Vice Pres*
Timothy Timmerman, *Vice Pres*
▲ **EMP:** 300 **EST:** 1993
SQ FT: 47,250
SALES (est): 437.5MM **Publicly Held**
WEB: www.afcweb.com
SIC: 3429 3444 3599 5085 Manufactured hardware (general); sheet metalwork; hose, flexible metallic; industrial supplies

(G-11071)
ALLIED TUBE & CONDUIT CORP (DH)
16100 Lathrop Ave (60426-6021)
P.O. Box Dept Ch 10415, Palatine (60055-0001)
PHONE.................708 339-1610
William Taylor, *President*
Jim Hays, *Vice Pres*
Ed Kurasz, *Vice Pres*
◆ **EMP:** 740
SQ FT: 500,000
SALES (est): 461.3MM **Publicly Held**
SIC: 3317 Welded pipe & tubes

(G-11072)
ALSIP MFG INC
16700 Carse Ave (60426-6169)
PHONE.................708 333-4446
Joseph Lewandowski, *President*
Mark Regan, *Vice Pres*
Tom Lewandowski, *Manager*
Judy Lewandowski, *Admin Sec*
EMP: 23 **EST:** 1970
SQ FT: 6,000
SALES (est): 3.9MM **Privately Held**
SIC: 3599 Machine shop, jobbing & repair

(G-11073)
AMERICAN KITCHEN DELIGHTS INC
15320 Cooper Ave (60426-2922)
PHONE.................708 210-3200
Shahnawaz Hasan, *President*
Nick Rossi, *Administration*
EMP: 100
SQ FT: 78,000
SALES (est): 18.1MM **Privately Held**
SIC: 2099 2051 1541 5149 Ready-to-eat meals, salads & sandwiches; bread, cake & related products; food products manufacturing or packing plant construction; specialty food items

(G-11074)
ATKORE INTERNATIONAL INC (DH)
16100 Lathrop Ave (60426-6021)
PHONE.................708 339-1610
John P Williamson, *President*
Mark Lamps, *President*
Bob Pereira, *President*
Fred Echeverri, *Business Mgr*
Courtney Young, *Counsel*
▲ **EMP:** 50
SALES (est): 1.1B **Publicly Held**
SIC: 3317 Steel pipe & tubes

(G-11075)
ATKORE INTERNATIONAL GROUP INC (PA)
16100 Lathrop Ave (60426-6021)
PHONE.................708 339-1610
Michael V Schroc, *Ch of Bd*
John P Williamson, *President*
William Waltz, *President*
Melissa Kidd, *Senior VP*
Kevin P Fitzpatrick, *Vice Pres*
EMP: 3000
SALES: 1.9B **Publicly Held**
SIC: 3441 1791 3446 3448 Fabricated structural metal; structural steel erection; architectural metalwork; prefabricated metal buildings; miscellaneous fabricated wire products

(G-11076)
ATKORE INTL HOLDINGS INC (HQ)
16100 Lathrop Ave (60426-6021)
PHONE.................708 225-2051
John Williamson, *CEO*
John P Williamson, *President*
Bob Pereira, *President*
Mike Schulte, *President*
William Waltz, *President*
EMP: 4
SALES (est): 1.4B **Publicly Held**
SIC: 6719 3441 1791 3446 Investment holding companies, except banks; fabricated structural metal; structural steel erection; architectural metalwork; prefabricated metal buildings; miscellaneous fabricated wire products

(G-11077)
ATKORE RMCP INC (HQ)
16100 Lathrop Ave (60426-6021)
PHONE.................708 339-1610
William Waltz, *President*
David Johnson, *Vice Pres*
Daniel Kelly, *Vice Pres*
Matthew Kline, *Vice Pres*
Angel Lowe, *Vice Pres*
EMP: 2
SALES (est): 2.4MM **Publicly Held**
SIC: 3084 Plastics pipe

(G-11078)
BELLA ARCHITECTURAL PRODUCTS
16910 Lathrop Ave (60426-6033)
PHONE.................708 339-4782
Mark Ingratta, *President*
Jason Rockhold, *Plant Mgr*
Joyce Bozzetti, *Production*
Kindy Bergman, *Sales Staff*
Ted Myers, *Products*
▲ **EMP:** 2
SALES (est): 430.8K **Privately Held**
SIC: 3429 Manufactured hardware (general)

(G-11079)
BLUE ISLAND NEWSPAPER PRTG INC
262 W 147th St (60426-1543)
PHONE.................708 333-1006
Gary Rice, *President*
Judy Rice, *Corp Secy*
EMP: 70
SQ FT: 25,000
SALES (est): 11.7MM **Privately Held**
SIC: 2752 Commercial printing, offset

(G-11080)
BREWER COMPANY
Also Called: Rae Supply
3852 W 159th Pl (60428-4411)
PHONE.................708 339-9000
Mike Doelly, *President*
EMP: 18
SALES (corp-wide): 50MM **Privately Held**
SIC: 2952 5211 2813 Coating compounds, tar; lumber & other building materials; industrial gases
PA: The Brewer Company
25 Whitney Dr Ste 104
Milford OH 45150
800 394-0017

(G-11081)
CROSBY GROUP LLC
16868 Lathrop Ave (60426-6031)
PHONE.................708 333-3005
John Gorski, *Manager*
EMP: 3
SALES (corp-wide): 307.9MM **Privately Held**
SIC: 3429 Manufactured hardware (general)
PA: The Crosby Group Llc
2801 Dawson Rd
Tulsa OK 74110
918 834-4611

(G-11082)
EAM PALLETS
15224 Dixie Hwy Ste A (60426-2932)
PHONE.................708 333-0596
Efrain Alba, *Owner*
EMP: 2
SALES (est): 253.5K **Privately Held**
SIC: 2448 Pallets, wood

(G-11083)
ENGILITY CORPORATION
16501 Kedzie Ave Ph Rm245 (60428-5556)
PHONE.................708 596-8245
Deanna Pammenel, *Manager*
EMP: 5
SALES (corp-wide): 6.3B **Publicly Held**
WEB: www.engilitycorp.com
SIC: 3812 Inertial guidance systems; navigational systems & instruments

GEOGRAPHIC SECTION

Harwood Heights - Cook County (G-11110)

HQ: Engility Corporation
35 New England Bus Ctr Dr
Andover MA 01810
703 633-8300

(G-11084)
FABCO ENTERPRISES INC
16812 Lathrop Ave (60426-6031)
PHONE..................................708 333-4644
Christian G Mercedes, *President*
Jeanne Erickson, *Admin Sec*
EMP: 6 **EST:** 1976
SQ FT: 9,000
SALES: 1MM **Privately Held**
WEB: www.fabco.com
SIC: 3449 7692 3441 Miscellaneous metalwork; welding repair; fabricated structural metal

(G-11085)
FOUR SEASON PALLETS INC
16140 Clinton St (60426-5909)
PHONE..................................708 940-5545
Yaneli Ceja, *Principal*
EMP: 4
SALES (est): 304.3K **Privately Held**
SIC: 2448 Pallets, wood

(G-11086)
FUCHS CORPORATION (HQ)
Also Called: Fuchs Lubricants Co
17050 Lathrop Ave (60426-6035)
PHONE..................................800 323-7755
Steven Puffpaff, *CEO*
Jonas Palm, *Managing Dir*
Ken Nakamura, *Business Mgr*
Jim Deodhar, *Vice Pres*
Pamela Watson, *Vice Pres*
◆ **EMP:** 2
SQ FT: 180,000
SALES (est): 113.5MM
SALES (corp-wide): 2.8B **Privately Held**
SIC: 2992 5172 2899 Lubricating oils & greases; lubricating oils & greases; metal treating compounds
PA: Fuchs Petrolub Se
Friesenheimer Str. 17
Mannheim 68169
621 380-20

(G-11087)
HARVEY CEMENT PRODUCTS INC
16030 Park Ave (60426-5069)
PHONE..................................708 333-1900
Philipe J Steck, *President*
Frank Steck Jr, *Corp Secy*
Craig Kick, *Sales Staff*
EMP: 12 **EST:** 1949
SQ FT: 22,000
SALES (est): 1.4MM **Privately Held**
WEB: www.harveycement.com
SIC: 3271 5032 Blocks, concrete or cinder: standard; brick, concrete; masons' materials

(G-11088)
HARVEY FUELS
2 E 159th St (60426-5004)
PHONE..................................708 339-0777
Joseph Abraham, *Principal*
EMP: 3
SALES (est): 295.9K **Privately Held**
SIC: 2869 Fuels

(G-11089)
HOGG WELDING INC
16201 Clinton St (60426-5910)
PHONE..................................708 339-0033
Benny Stauersboll, *President*
Carol Stauersboll, *Admin Sec*
EMP: 4 **EST:** 1950
SQ FT: 2,900
SALES (est): 571.5K **Privately Held**
SIC: 3842 7692 3444 Wheelchairs; welding repair; sheet metalwork

(G-11090)
IDEAS INC
16131 Clinton St (60426-5908)
PHONE..................................708 596-1055
Celine Bess, *Manager*
EMP: 8

SALES (est): 2MM
SALES (corp-wide): 2.4MM **Privately Held**
SIC: 2992 Lubricating oils & greases
PA: Ideas, Inc.
625 S Main St
Lombard IL 60148
630 620-2010

(G-11091)
LB METALS LLC
Also Called: Concord Steel
15700 Lathrop Ave (60426-5118)
PHONE..................................708 331-2600
Cindy Blau, *CEO*
EMP: 179
SQ FT: 450,000
SALES (est): 90.7MM **Privately Held**
SIC: 3547 Plate rolling mill machinery

(G-11092)
LB STEEL LLC
Also Called: Topeka Metal Specialties
15700 Lathrop Ave (60426-5118)
PHONE..................................708 331-2600
Pete Raketic, *Vice Pres*
Nick Stevens, *Mfg Dir*
Dave Abshire, *Opers Mgr*
Chris Persch, *Engineer*
Mike Kotch, *Accounts Exec*
▲ **EMP:** 350
SQ FT: 400,000
SALES (est): 3.5MM **Privately Held**
SIC: 3599 Machine shop, jobbing & repair

(G-11093)
MR T SHIRT AND DOLLAR PLUS
75 W 159th St (60426-4956)
PHONE..................................708 596-9150
Fred Abdel, *President*
EMP: 5
SALES: 770K **Privately Held**
SIC: 2253 T-shirts & tops, knit

(G-11094)
PROTECTIVE DOOR INDUSTRIES
15700 Lathrop Ave (60426-5118)
PHONE..................................773 375-0300
Pdi Lbsteel, *President*
EMP: 3
SALES (est): 139.2K **Privately Held**
SIC: 3442 Metal doors, sash & trim

(G-11095)
SKYLINE PROVISIONS INC
Also Called: Skyline Foods
374 E 167th St (60426-6102)
P.O. Box 1616 (60426-7616)
PHONE..................................708 331-1982
Steven Blumental, *President*
Gerry A Michalak, *Vice Pres*
Vanessa Morales, *Admin Sec*
EMP: 15
SQ FT: 22,500
SALES (est): 5.9MM **Privately Held**
SIC: 5147 2011 Meats, fresh; meat packing plants

(G-11096)
SOUTH SUBN LOGISTICS SUPS CORP
16610 Finch Ave (60426-6042)
PHONE..................................312 804-3401
Tanya Johnson, *President*
EMP: 3
SALES (est): 155.2K **Privately Held**
SIC: 3728 Aircraft parts & equipment

(G-11097)
SUMMIT LABORATORIES INC
17010 Halsted St (60426-6129)
PHONE..................................708 333-2995
Clyde Hammond Sr, *President*
Natalie Hutchinson, *Vice Pres*
Darryl Strait, *Controller*
EMP: 45
SQ FT: 152,000
SALES (est): 9.8MM **Privately Held**
SIC: 2844 Hair preparations, including shampoos; cosmetic preparations

(G-11098)
TRI-CITY GOLD EXCHANGE INC
470 E 147th St (60426-2461)
PHONE..................................708 331-5995
Aaron Lake, *President*
EMP: 10
SQ FT: 900
SALES (est): 787K **Privately Held**
SIC: 5944 3911 Jewelry, precious stones & precious metals; jewelry, precious metal

(G-11099)
UNISTRUT INTERNATIONAL CORP (DH)
16100 Lathrop Ave (60426-6021)
PHONE..................................800 882-5543
John P Williamson, *President*
Nelda J Connors, *Principal*
Karl J Schmidt, *Vice Pres*
James A Mallak, *Treasurer*
Eileen Tierney, *Admin Sec*
▲ **EMP:** 127
SALES (est): 159.2MM **Publicly Held**
SIC: 3441 1791 3446 3448 Fabricated structural metal; structural steel erection; partitions & supports/studs, including accoustical systems; trusses & framing: prefabricated metal; cable, uninsulated wire: made from purchased wire; manufactured hardware (general)

(G-11100)
VOSS ELECTRIC INC
15241 Commercial Ave (60426-2396)
PHONE..................................708 596-6000
Peter W Voss Jr, *President*
Dan Medrano, *Director*
EMP: 5 **EST:** 1974
SQ FT: 80,000
SALES (est): 286.2K **Privately Held**
SIC: 7694 3621 Electric motor repair; motors & generators

Harwood Heights
Cook County

(G-11101)
ADVANCED SPECIALTY LIGHTING
Also Called: Advanced Strobe Products
7227 W Wilson Ave (60706-4705)
PHONE..................................708 867-3140
Jarold Bijak, *President*
▲ **EMP:** 250
SALES (est): 24.6MM **Privately Held**
SIC: 3646 Commercial indusl & institutional electric lighting fixtures

(G-11102)
CJ ANDERSON & COMPANY
4751 N Olcott Ave (60706-4605)
PHONE..................................708 867-4002
Milton Sybert, *CEO*
Thomas Sybert, *President*
Joellen Toussaint, *Purch Mgr*
Janet Szczepanski, *Cust Mgr*
Kelsey Sybert, *Sales Staff*
EMP: 30 **EST:** 1910
SQ FT: 16,000
SALES (est): 2.9MM **Privately Held**
SIC: 3534 Elevators & equipment

(G-11103)
DABIR SURFACES INC (HQ)
7447 W Wilson Ave (60706-4548)
PHONE..................................708 867-6777
Dave Dzioba, *President*
Jerry Babich, *Regl Sales Mgr*
EMP: 15
SALES (est): 2.9MM
SALES (corp-wide): 1B **Publicly Held**
SIC: 3842 Surgical appliances & supplies
PA: Methode Electronics, Inc
8750 W Bryn Mawr Ave # 1000
Chicago IL 60631
708 867-6777

(G-11104)
FCL GRAPHICS INC
4600 N Olcott Ave (60706-4604)
PHONE..................................708 867-5500
Stephen Flood, *CEO*
Donna Caldarulo, *Vice Pres*

Michael McGuire, *CFO*
Keith Murphy, *Accounts Exec*
Jerry Sill, *Manager*
EMP: 150
SQ FT: 115,000
SALES (est): 39.6MM **Privately Held**
SIC: 2752 Commercial printing, offset

(G-11105)
FIRST AMERICAN RESTORATION INC
6935 W Gunnison St (60706-3966)
PHONE..................................800 209-3609
Oscar Bonilla, *President*
EMP: 18
SALES (est): 787.6K **Privately Held**
SIC: 8742 6411 1389 8741 Construction project management consultant; insurance claim processing, except medical; construction, repair & dismantling services; construction management

(G-11106)
NAVITOR INC
Cosco Industries
7220 W Wilson Ave (60706-4706)
PHONE..................................800 323-0253
Steve Silkaitis, *President*
Vinh Ta, *General Mgr*
Mehwish Mohammad, *Accountant*
Janna Flanders, *Natl Sales Mgr*
Keith Betti, *Regl Sales Mgr*
EMP: 500
SALES (corp-wide): 2.5B **Privately Held**
SIC: 3953 2396 3469 3089 Marking devices; screen printing on fabric articles; metal stampings; injection molding of plastics; advertising artwork; advertising novelties; labels (unprinted), gummed: made from purchased materials
HQ: Navitor, Inc.
1625 Roe Crest Dr
North Mankato MN 56003

(G-11107)
QCC LLC (PA)
7301 W Wilson Ave (60706-4707)
PHONE..................................708 867-5400
Jon Goreham, *CEO*
Tom Walendzewicz, *General Mgr*
Keith Lecompte, *COO*
Dominik Golec, *Mfg Staff*
Todor Dinev, *Engineer*
◆ **EMP:** 188 **EST:** 1951
SQ FT: 120,085
SALES (est): 45.5MM **Privately Held**
WEB: www.qccorp.com
SIC: 3053 3451 Gaskets & sealing devices; screw machine products

(G-11108)
QUALISEAL TECHNOLOGY LLC
7319 W Wilson Ave (60706-4707)
PHONE..................................708 887-6080
Wes Shull, *Vice Pres*
EMP: 37
SQ FT: 3,300
SALES (est): 2.1MM
SALES (corp-wide): 1.2B **Publicly Held**
SIC: 3728 Aircraft parts & equipment
PA: Enpro Industries, Inc.
5605 Carnegie Blvd # 500
Charlotte NC 28209
704 731-1500

(G-11109)
QUALITY CONTROL CORP
7315 W Wilson Ave (60706-4770)
PHONE..................................708 887-6239
John Cosentino, *Plant Mgr*
Julian Fernandez, *Engineer*
Richard Koskiewicz, *Engineer*
Syed Qasim, *Engineer*
Donald Bennett, *CFO*
EMP: 32 **EST:** 2017
SALES (est): 5.2MM **Privately Held**
SIC: 3451 Screw machine products

(G-11110)
STERLING PLATING INC
4629 N Ronald St (60706-4718)
PHONE..................................708 867-6587
Herbert Degrenier, *CEO*
Colette Sherwin, *President*
Marcia Jerzyk, *Admin Sec*
EMP: 20 **EST:** 1959

Harwood Heights - Cook County (G-11111)

SQ FT: 16,000
SALES (est): 2MM **Privately Held**
WEB: www.sterlingplating.com
SIC: 3471 Plating of metals or formed products

(G-11111)
TECHNETICS GROUP LLC
Also Called: Qualiseal Technology
7319 W Wilson Ave (60706-4707)
PHONE.................................708 887-6080
Jon Goreham, *Manager*
EMP: 7
SALES (corp-wide): 1.2B **Publicly Held**
SIC: 3053 3351 Gaskets & sealing devices; copper rolling & drawing
HQ: Technetics Group Llc
5605 Carnegie Blvd # 500
Charlotte NC 28209
704 731-1500

(G-11112)
WINZELER INC
Also Called: Winzeler Gear
7355 W Wilson Ave (60706-4785)
PHONE.................................708 867-7971
John Winzeler, *President*
Harry Soling, *Vice Pres*
Daniel Prysmiki, *Mfg Spvr*
Erich Fiedler, *Engineer*
Agnes Rendel, *Accountant*
▲ EMP: 33
SQ FT: 42,000
SALES: 15MM **Privately Held**
WEB: www.winzelergear.com
SIC: 3089 Molding primary plastic; injection molding of plastics

(G-11113)
X HALE
4811 N Olcott Ave # 504 (60706-3453)
PHONE.................................847 884-6250
Kiavash Sayar, *Principal*
EMP: 4
SALES (est): 220K **Privately Held**
WEB: www.x-halehookahlounge.com
SIC: 2599 Bar, restaurant & cafeteria furniture

Havana
Mason County

(G-11114)
HAVANAH FUEL
520 E Laurel Ave (62644-1525)
PHONE.................................309 543-2211
Brian Tracy, *Principal*
EMP: 3
SALES (est): 215.4K **Privately Held**
SIC: 2869 Fuels

(G-11115)
JAMES G CARTER
Also Called: Paddlewheel The
15907 Sr 97 (62644-6758)
PHONE.................................309 543-2634
James Carter, *Owner*
EMP: 3 EST: 1998
SALES: 200K **Privately Held**
SIC: 3949 Bowling alleys & accessories

(G-11116)
MARTIN PUBLISHING CO (PA)
Also Called: Mason County Democrat
217 W Market St (62644-1145)
P.O. Box 380 (62644-0380)
PHONE.................................309 543-2000
Robert Martin Jr, *President*
Wendy Martin, *Corp Secy*
EMP: 25 EST: 1849
SQ FT: 30,000
SALES (est): 2.5MM **Privately Held**
SIC: 2711 Newspapers: publishing only, not printed on site

(G-11117)
METAL CULVERTS INC
Also Called: Havana Metal Culverts Division
15732 Rte 97 S (62644)
P.O. Box 350 (62644-0350)
PHONE.................................309 543-2271
Paul Fliege, *Manager*
EMP: 20
SALES (corp-wide): 33.7MM **Privately Held**
SIC: 3444 Pipe, sheet metal
PA: Metal Culverts, Inc.
711 Heisinger Rd
Jefferson City MO 65109
573 636-7312

(G-11118)
MIDWEST FILLERS
16861 Ncr 1800 E (62644)
PHONE.................................309 567-2957
EMP: 4 EST: 2016
SALES (est): 322.5K **Privately Held**
SIC: 3565 Packaging machinery

(G-11119)
OTTER CREEK SAND & GRAVEL
4125 N Stoneyard Rd (62644-4512)
P.O. Box 281 (62644-0281)
PHONE.................................309 759-4293
David Clinard, *President*
EMP: 10
SALES (est): 591.6K **Privately Held**
SIC: 1442 Construction sand & gravel

(G-11120)
PROFILE SCREENS INCORPORATED
Also Called: PSI
901 S Water St (62644-1657)
P.O. Box 370, Maurice LA (70555-0370)
PHONE.................................309 543-2082
Jerry Messmer, *President*
EMP: 6
SQ FT: 12,000
SALES (est): 516K **Privately Held**
SIC: 3569 3532 Filters, general line: industrial; mining machinery

Hawthorn Woods
Lake County

(G-11121)
ALLPRINT INC
66 Tournament Dr S (60047-8114)
P.O. Box 208, Lake Zurich (60047-0208)
PHONE.................................847 726-0658
Paul Hutchings, *President*
Sue Hutchings, *Vice Pres*
EMP: 3
SALES (est): 423.4K **Privately Held**
SIC: 5111 2752 Printing paper; color lithography

(G-11122)
D G PRINTING INC
69 Falcon Dr (60047-7560)
PHONE.................................847 397-7779
Mark Gagliano, *President*
Anthony Gagliano, *Accounts Exec*
EMP: 20
SALES (est): 2.9MM **Privately Held**
WEB: www.dgprinting.com
SIC: 7331 2759 Mailing service; commercial printing

(G-11123)
FLORALSTAR ENTERPRISES
68 Tournament Dr N (60047-8401)
PHONE.................................847 726-0124
Debra Hillstrand, *Owner*
EMP: 3
SQ FT: 5,000
SALES: 340K **Privately Held**
SIC: 3999 Artificial flower arrangements; Christmas trees, artificial

(G-11124)
IT FOR WHATS INC
3 Cayuga Ct (60047-1903)
PHONE.................................847 949-6522
Keith Bishof, *Principal*
EMP: 2
SALES (est): 306.1K **Privately Held**
SIC: 3541 Brushing machines (metalworking machinery)

(G-11125)
NATIONAL AEROSPACE CORP
28 Sequoia Rd (60047-1902)
PHONE.................................847 566-5834
Eric Abbott, *Owner*
EMP: 3 EST: 2015
SALES (est): 159.3K **Privately Held**
SIC: 3812 Search & navigation equipment

(G-11126)
T9 GROUP LLC
25635 N Stoney Kirk Ct (60047-7539)
P.O. Box 777, Prospect Heights (60070-0777)
PHONE.................................847 912-8862
Steve Hadgisava,
EMP: 8
SALES: 1.2MM **Privately Held**
SIC: 2822 5169 7389 Synthetic rubber; chemicals & allied products;

(G-11127)
TAKEDA
8 Copperfield Dr (60047-7549)
PHONE.................................847 902-0659
Karla Mans Giroux, *Principal*
Julie Brisch, *Sales Staff*
George Foley, *Manager*
EMP: 3
SALES (est): 239.8K **Privately Held**
WEB: www.takeda.com
SIC: 2834 Pharmaceutical preparations

Hazel Crest
Cook County

(G-11128)
CREATIVE IMAGE INC
3615 Briar Ln (60429-2411)
PHONE.................................708 647-2860
Louis Taylor, *President*
Bessie Taylor, *Vice Pres*
EMP: 2
SALES: 200K **Privately Held**
SIC: 2791 Typesetting

(G-11129)
GREENFIELD PRODUCTS LLC (PA)
3111 167th St (60429-1025)
PHONE.................................708 596-5200
Jack Lanigan, *Mng Member*
EMP: 38
SALES (est): 29.3MM **Privately Held**
SIC: 3423 Jacks: lifting, screw or ratchet (hand tools)

(G-11130)
KEI KEIS KREATION KAFE
2801 Lexington Dr (60429-1746)
PHONE.................................708 982-6560
Lakeisha Brown, *Principal*
EMP: 10
SALES (est): 369.4K **Privately Held**
SIC: 3944 Craft & hobby kits & sets

(G-11131)
LANCO INTERNATIONAL INC (PA)
Also Called: Lantech Logistics
3111 167th St (60429-1025)
PHONE.................................708 596-5200
John J Lanigan Jr, *President*
C Rog, *General Mgr*
Mike T Lanigan, *Exec VP*
William P Lanigan, *Exec VP*
David Rademacher, *Vice Pres*
◆ EMP: 350
SQ FT: 200,000
SALES (est): 181.8MM **Privately Held**
WEB: www.thelancogroup.com
SIC: 3531 8711 5084 3536 Construction machinery; designing: ship, boat, machine & product; cranes, industrial; cranes, overhead traveling; heavy construction equipment rental; industrial trucks & tractors

(G-11132)
LANIGAN HOLDINGS LLC (PA)
3111 167th St (60429-1025)
PHONE.................................708 596-5200
John J Lanigan Sr, *Ch of Bd*
John J Lanigan Jr, *President*
Mike T Lanigan, *Exec VP*
William Lanigan, *Exec VP*
Stephen J Bayers, *CFO*
EMP: 14 EST: 2001
SALES (est): 29.4MM **Privately Held**
SIC: 5082 3531 7948 8743 General construction machinery & equipment; crane carriers; race track operation; promotion service

(G-11133)
MI-JACK PRODUCTS INC (HQ)
3111 167th St (60429-0975)
PHONE.................................708 596-5200
John J Lanigan Sr, *Ch of Bd*
Michael T Lanigan, *President*
Steven Bayers, *President*
William P Lanigan, *Exec VP*
Joe Belcastro, *Vice Pres*
◆ EMP: 277
SQ FT: 1,310
SALES (est): 161.9MM
SALES (corp-wide): 181.8MM **Privately Held**
SIC: 3531 8711 Construction machinery; designing: ship, boat, machine & product
PA: Lanco International Inc.
3111 167th St
Hazel Crest IL 60429
708 596-5200

(G-11134)
MI-JACK SYSTEMS & TECH LLC
3111 167th St (60429-1025)
PHONE.................................708 596-3780
Stephen J Bayers,
EMP: 14
SALES (est): 1.9MM **Privately Held**
SIC: 3699 Door opening & closing devices, electrical

(G-11135)
MJMC INC
3111 167th St (60429-1025)
PHONE.................................708 596-5200
John Boquist, *President*
Frank Calomino, *Exec VP*
Harvey E Schmidt, *Vice Pres*
Robert Rausch, *Credit Mgr*
Henry Gurion, *Admin Sec*
EMP: 43
SALES (est): 12.4MM **Privately Held**
SIC: 3531 Backhoes, tractors, cranes, plows & similar equipment

(G-11136)
Q SALES & LEASING LLC
16720 Mozart Ave Ste A (60429-1092)
PHONE.................................708 331-0094
Pete Mirabella, *Vice Pres*
John J Jr Lanigan, *Mng Member*
Michael Lanigan, *Mng Member*
Stephen J Bayers,
Daniel Lanigan,
◆ EMP: 13
SALES (est): 3.1MM **Privately Held**
SIC: 3497 Foil containers for bakery goods & frozen foods

(G-11137)
ROBBINS CONSTRUCTION SUP LLC
17043 Annetta Ave (60429-1231)
PHONE.................................708 574-5944
Marvin Wells,
EMP: 3
SALES (est): 182.7K **Privately Held**
SIC: 3531 Construction machinery

(G-11138)
TECHNICAL SERVICES INTL INC
3115 167th St (60429-1025)
PHONE.................................708 596-5200
Michael Lanigan Sr, *CEO*
EMP: 3
SALES (est): 138.9K
SALES (corp-wide): 181.8MM **Privately Held**
SIC: 3531 Construction machinery
HQ: Mi-Jack Products Inc.
3111 167th St
Hazel Crest IL 60429
708 596-5200

Hebron
Mchenry County

(G-11139)
BROTHERS DECORATING
10305 Vanderkarr Rd (60034-9527)
P.O. Box 396 (60034-0396)
PHONE...................................815 648-2214
EMP: 2
SALES (est): 204K **Privately Held**
SIC: 2621 1721 Paper Mill Painting/Paper Hanging Contractor

(G-11140)
CHAMPION FOODS LLC
Also Called: Champion Pizza
9910 Main St (60034-8903)
PHONE...................................815 648-2725
Daniel Fontana,
EMP: 9
SQ FT: 3,800
SALES (est): 890K **Privately Held**
SIC: 2038 Pizza, frozen

(G-11141)
COEUR INC
11411 Price Rd (60034-9664)
PHONE...................................815 648-1093
EMP: 14
SALES (corp-wide): 14.1B **Publicly Held**
SIC: 3841 Surgical & medical instruments
HQ: Coeur, Inc.
  100 Physicians Way # 200
  Lebanon TN 37090
  615 547-7923

(G-11142)
CULTIVATED ENERGY GROUP INC
10702 Seaman Rd (60034-9535)
PHONE...................................312 203-8833
Joseph E Shacter, *CEO*
EMP: 3
SALES (est): 103.9K **Privately Held**
SIC: 3999 Manufacturing industries

(G-11143)
FILTERTEK INC (HQ)
Also Called: ITW Flter Pdts Trnsm Fltration
11411 Price Rd (60034-8936)
PHONE...................................815 648-2410
David F Atkinson, *CEO*
Roland Martel, *President*
Burks Law, *President*
Esteban Sifuentes, *Project Engr*
Michael Leonard, *Design Engr*
◆ **EMP:** 290
SQ FT: 100,000
SALES (est): 122.5MM
SALES (corp-wide): 14.1B **Publicly Held**
SIC: 3089 3564 Injection molding of plastics; blowers & fans
PA: Illinois Tool Works Inc.
  155 Harlem Ave
  Glenview IL 60025
  847 724-7500

(G-11144)
KEYSTONE DISPLAY INC
11916 Maple Ave (60034-8869)
P.O. Box 427 (60034-0427)
PHONE...................................815 648-2456
James Peterson, *CEO*
John J Streit, *President*
EMP: 75 **EST:** 1948
SQ FT: 70,000
SALES (est): 14.5MM **Privately Held**
WEB: www.keystonedisplay.com
SIC: 2542 3993 Racks, merchandise display or storage: except wood; signs & advertising specialties

(G-11145)
LABEL GRAPHICS CO INC
12024 3rd Ave (60034-8923)
PHONE...................................815 648-2478
Emil Salmons, *Manager*
EMP: 10
SALES (corp-wide): 1.6MM **Privately Held**
WEB: www.labelgraphicscompany.com
SIC: 2672 2671 Labels (unprinted), gummed: made from purchased materials; packaging paper & plastics film, coated & laminated
PA: Label Graphics Co., Inc.
  1225 Carnegie St Ste 104b
  Rolling Meadows IL
  847 454-1005

(G-11146)
LAMINATED COMPONENTS INC
12204 Hansen Rd (60034-8889)
PHONE...................................815 648-4811
Mark Romme, *President*
Sandra Romme, *Corp Secy*
▲ **EMP:** 22
SQ FT: 35,000
SALES (est): 4.3MM **Privately Held**
SIC: 2541 Display fixtures, wood

(G-11147)
PERFECT SHUTTERS INC
12213 Il Route 173 (60034-9610)
PHONE...................................815 648-2401
Nikunj H Shah, *President*
EMP: 40 **EST:** 1976
SQ FT: 100,000
SALES (est): 8.9MM **Privately Held**
WEB: www.perfectshutters.com
SIC: 3089 Shutters, plastic

(G-11148)
POLYCAST
10103 Main St Ste B (60034-8950)
PHONE...................................815 648-4438
John Moffatt, *General Mgr*
Wayne Johnson, *Treasurer*
EMP: 10
SALES (est): 1.5MM **Privately Held**
SIC: 2821 Polyvinylidene chloride resins

(G-11149)
SHERWOOD TOOL INC
Also Called: M J Molding
12120 Il Route 173 (60034-9619)
PHONE...................................815 648-1463
William J Snyder, *President*
Bill Snyder, *President*
EMP: 12 **EST:** 1985
SALES (est): 1.5MM **Privately Held**
SIC: 3089 Molding primary plastic

(G-11150)
SIGNCRAFTERS ENTERPRISES INC
Also Called: Signs of The Times
10714 Il Route 47 (60034-9605)
P.O. Box 368 (60034-0368)
PHONE...................................815 648-4484
James Bryan, *President*
EMP: 2
SALES: 210K **Privately Held**
SIC: 3993 Signs, not made in custom sign painting shops

(G-11151)
TRISEAL CORPORATION
Also Called: Triseal Worldwide
11920 Price Rd (60034-8933)
PHONE...................................815 648-2473
Patricia H Wales, *President*
John L Porritt II, *CFO*
Patrick Leahy, *Officer*
▲ **EMP:** 35
SQ FT: 26,000
SALES (est): 6.4MM **Privately Held**
SIC: 3713 3053 Truck & bus bodies; oil seals, leather; oil seals, rubber

(G-11152)
TRUE LINE MOLD AND ENGRG CORP
12205 Hansen Rd (60034-8890)
PHONE...................................815 648-2739
Ray Adkins, *President*
Jason Adkins, *COO*
Curtis Larsen, *Vice Pres*
Amon Adkins, *Admin Sec*
EMP: 40 **EST:** 1965
SQ FT: 43,000
SALES: 2MM **Privately Held**
WEB: www.true-line.com
SIC: 3089 Injection molding of plastics

(G-11153)
VAUGHAN & BUSHNELL MFG CO (PA)
11414 Maple Ave (60034)
PHONE...................................815 648-2446
Charles S Vaughan, *President*
Howard Vaughan Jr, *Chairman*
Dan Caspall, *Vice Pres*
Ronald Miller, *Treasurer*
Daniel Herman, *Admin Sec*
▲ **EMP:** 12 **EST:** 1869
SQ FT: 36,000
SALES (est): 48.4MM **Privately Held**
WEB: www.vaughanmfg.com
SIC: 3423 2499 3524 Hammers (hand tools); axes & hatchets; handles, wood; lawn & garden equipment

(G-11154)
VILLAGE HEBRON WATER SEWAGE
12007 Prairie Ave (60034-8892)
P.O. Box 372 (60034-0372)
PHONE...................................815 648-2353
Tom Shrewsbury, *Director*
EMP: 1 **EST:** 2007
SALES (est): 215.8K **Privately Held**
WEB: www.villageofhebron.org
SIC: 3823 Water quality monitoring & control systems

Hecker
Monroe County

(G-11155)
HOTTENROTT COMPANY INC
Also Called: Basic Industries
351 S Main St (62248)
P.O. Box 127 (62248-0127)
PHONE...................................618 473-2531
Roger W Hottenrott, *President*
Catherine Hottenrott, *Corp Secy*
Richard Hottenrott, *Vice Pres*
EMP: 5
SQ FT: 6,336
SALES (est): 500K **Privately Held**
SIC: 3599 Machine shop, jobbing & repair

Hennepin
Putnam County

(G-11156)
ARCELORMITTAL HENNEPIN LLC (DH)
10726 Steel Dr (61327-9507)
PHONE...................................815 925-2311
Lakshmi Mittal, *President*
Kenneth Brown, *Chief*
Thomas Cayia, *Mfg Spvr*
Jeff Day, *Technician*
Joe Schweickert, *Technician*
EMP: 120
SALES (est): 436.7K **Privately Held**
SIC: 3316 Cold finishing of steel shapes
HQ: Arcelormittal Usa Llc
  1 S Dearborn St Ste 1800
  Chicago IL 60603
  312 346-0300

(G-11157)
D & D MANUFACTURING
6th St Rr 26 (61327)
P.O. Box 354 (61327-0354)
PHONE...................................815 339-9100
Robert Dockins, *Owner*
EMP: 3
SALES: 300K **Privately Held**
SIC: 3089 3443 Plastic processing; closures, plastic; fabricated plate work (boiler shop)

(G-11158)
MARQUIS ENERGY LLC
11953 Prairie Indus Pkwy (61327-5160)
PHONE...................................815 925-7300
D L Marquis, *CEO*
Perry Gruss, *Vice Pres*
Walter Horst, *Vice Pres*
Michael Larkin, *Vice Pres*
Jason W Marquis, *Vice Pres*
◆ **EMP:** 90
SALES (est): 33.3MM **Privately Held**
SIC: 2869 Ethylene

(G-11159)
MARQUIS MARINE INC
7548 W Power Plant Rd (61327)
P.O. Box 347 (61327-0347)
PHONE...................................815 925-9125
Darrell L Marquis, *President*
Thomas L Marquis, *Admin Sec*
EMP: 2
SALES (est): 253K **Privately Held**
SIC: 2869 Methyl alcohol, synthetic methanol

(G-11160)
WASHINGTON MILLS HENNEPIN INC
13230 Prairie Indl Pkwy (61327)
PHONE...................................815 925-7302
Armand Ladage, *VP Mfg*
Dave Piccinelli, *Plant Mgr*
Steven Kalman, *Purch Mgr*
Nancy E Gates, *Admin Sec*
◆ **EMP:** 60
SALES (est): 13.3MM **Privately Held**
WEB: www.washingtonmills.com
SIC: 3291 Abrasive products
PA: Washington Mills Group, Inc.
  20 N Main St
  North Grafton MA 01536

Henning
Vermilion County

(G-11161)
HENNING MACHINE & DIE WORKS
4 N Main St (61848-8034)
P.O. Box 128 (61848-0128)
PHONE...................................217 286-3393
Jenny Walters, *Owner*
EMP: 6
SQ FT: 8,000
SALES: 560K **Privately Held**
SIC: 3599 3544 Machine shop, jobbing & repair; special dies, tools, jigs & fixtures

Henry
Marshall County

(G-11162)
DERBYTEESCOM
622 Gateway Dr (61537-1002)
PHONE...................................309 264-1033
Mark Klein, *Principal*
EMP: 2
SALES (est): 293.8K **Privately Held**
WEB: www.derbytees.com
SIC: 2253 T-shirts & tops, knit

(G-11163)
ED HARTWIG TRUCKING & EXCVTG
Also Called: Hartwig Roll Off Containers
312 Jefferson St (61537-1322)
PHONE...................................309 364-3672
Edward Hartwig, *President*
Lori Hartwig, *Vice Pres*
EMP: 8
SALES (est): 1.1MM **Privately Held**
SIC: 1794 4213 1711 3599 Excavation work; trucking, except local; boiler & furnace contractors; machine shop, jobbing & repair; saws & sawing equipment

(G-11164)
EMERALD PERFORMANCE MTLS LLC
1550 County Road 1450 N (61537-9404)
PHONE...................................309 364-2311
Tom Newby, *Controller*
Candi Wagner, *Mng Member*
Traci Dunn, *Planning*
Sandy Daniels,
EMP: 38 **Privately Held**
SIC: 2821 Plastics materials & resins

Henry - Marshall County (G-11165)

PA: Emerald Performance Materials Llc
1499 Se Tech Center Pl # 3
Vancouver WA 98683

(G-11165)
EMERALD POLYMER ADDITIVES LLC
1550 County Road 1450 N (61537-9404)
PHONE 309 364-2311
Jeff Lee, *Manager*
Dave Hill, *Technical Staff*
EMP: 81 **Privately Held**
WEB: www.emeraldmaterials.com
SIC: 2899 Chemical preparations
HQ: Emerald Polymer Additives Llc
240 W Emerling Ave
Akron OH 44301

(G-11166)
HENRY NEWS REPUBLICAN
Also Called: Wenona Index
709 3rd St (61537-1446)
P.O. Box 190 (61537-0190)
PHONE 309 364-3250
Doug Ziegler, *President*
EMP: 8
SALES (est): 670.7K **Privately Held**
SIC: 2759 2711 Newspapers: printing; newspapers

(G-11167)
MEXICHEM SPECIALTY RESINS INC
1546 County Road 1450 N (61537-9404)
PHONE 309 364-2154
EMP: 16 **Privately Held**
SIC: 2822 Ethylene-propylene rubbers, EPDM polymers
HQ: Mexichem Specialty Resins Inc.
33653 Walker Rd
Avon Lake OH 44012
440 930-1435

(G-11168)
POLYONE CORPORATION
1546 County Road 1450 N (61537-9404)
PHONE 309 364-2154
Briana Collins, *Sales Staff*
Joel Lindahl, *Branch Mgr*
Brady O'Mary, *Senior Mgr*
EMP: 108 **Publicly Held**
SIC: 2821 Thermoplastic materials; polyvinyl chloride resins (PVC); vinyl resins
PA: Polyone Corporation
33587 Walker Rd
Avon Lake OH 44012

(G-11169)
UNITY ENVIROTECH ILLINOIS LLC
1557 County Road 1400 N (61537-9402)
P.O. Box 216 (61537-0216)
PHONE 309 364-2361
Jeff Ellison, *Project Mgr*
EMP: 26
SALES (est): 1MM **Privately Held**
SIC: 2873 Ammonia & ammonium salts

Herod
Pope County

(G-11170)
ILLINOIS FUEL COMPANY LLC
920 Gape Hollow Rd (62947)
P.O. Box 7 (62947-0007)
PHONE 618 275-4486
Kathy Smith,
EMP: 80
SALES (est): 2.4MM **Privately Held**
SIC: 1221 1222 Strip mining, bituminous; bituminous coal-underground mining

Herrin
Williamson County

(G-11171)
FRENCH STUDIO LTD
Also Called: Herrin News Litho
821 S Park Ave Stop 1 (62948-4174)
PHONE 618 942-5328
Louis A French, *President*
EMP: 5
SQ FT: 6,000
SALES: 150K **Privately Held**
WEB: www.frenchstudio.us
SIC: 7221 2752 2791 2789 Photographer, still or video; photolithographic printing; typesetting; bookbinding & related work

(G-11172)
HANGER PRSTHTICS ORTHTICS E IN
Also Called: Hanger Clinic
404 Rushing Dr (62948-3762)
PHONE 618 997-1451
Ivan Sabel, *President*
Sam Liang, *President*
EMP: 4
SALES (corp-wide): 1.1B **Publicly Held**
SIC: 3842 Surgical appliances & supplies
HQ: Hanger Prosthetics & Orthotics East, Inc.
33 North Ave Ste 101
Tallmadge OH 44278

(G-11173)
K R N MACHINE AND LASER CENTER
Also Called: K R N Machine & Laser Center
516 N Park Ave (62948-3113)
P.O. Box 2065 (62948-5265)
PHONE 618 942-6064
Ronald P Stewart, *CEO*
Ronald Stewart, *CEO*
Randy Stewart, *Principal*
Norma Jean Stewart, *Corp Secy*
EMP: 8
SQ FT: 16,000
SALES (est): 532.4K **Privately Held**
SIC: 3599 Machine shop, jobbing & repair

(G-11174)
LIQUITUBE INDUSTRIES LLC
721 E Herrin St (62948-3344)
P.O. Box 456 (62948-0456)
PHONE 618 985-4445
Mark Shasteen, *CEO*
Dennis Belanger, *Vice Pres*
EMP: 15
SALES (est): 149.1K **Privately Held**
SIC: 2891 Adhesives & sealants

(G-11175)
ODUM CONCRETE PRODUCTS INC
201 Rushing Dr (62948-3753)
PHONE 618 942-4572
Scott Aud, *Branch Mgr*
EMP: 6
SALES (corp-wide): 11.6MM **Privately Held**
WEB: www.odumcp.com
SIC: 3273 5211 Ready-mixed concrete; masonry materials & supplies
PA: Odum Concrete Products, Inc
1800 N Court St
Marion IL 62959
618 993-6211

(G-11176)
ORTHOTECH SPORTS - MED EQP INC (PA)
Also Called: Intek Strength
1211 Weaver Rd (62948-2621)
P.O. Box 430 (62948-0430)
PHONE 618 942-6611
Jim Vigiano, *President*
John Allsopp, *Sales Staff*
Randy Dawson, *Admin Sec*
▲ **EMP:** 15
SQ FT: 2,000
SALES: 6MM **Privately Held**
SIC: 5091 3949 Fitness equipment & supplies; dumbbells & other weightlifting equipment

(G-11177)
ROTH NEON SIGN COMPANY INC
Also Called: Roth Sign Company
1100 N 13th St (62948-2813)
P.O. Box 610 (62948-0610)
PHONE 618 942-6378
Daniel Roth, *President*
Joy Roth, *Corp Secy*
David Roth, *Vice Pres*
EMP: 9
SQ FT: 7,000
SALES (est): 1.8MM **Privately Held**
SIC: 5046 1799 3993 Signs, electrical; sign installation & maintenance; signs, not made in custom sign painting shops

(G-11178)
SAMUEL ROWELL
Also Called: Rowell Pure Water
2817 S Park Ave (62948-3700)
PHONE 618 942-6970
Samuel Rowell, *Owner*
EMP: 3
SALES (est): 245.9K **Privately Held**
SIC: 2899 5999 5963 Distilled water; water purification equipment; bottled water delivery

(G-11179)
SOLLAMI COMPANY
1200 Weaver Rd (62948-2626)
P.O. Box 627 (62948-0627)
PHONE 618 988-1521
Phillip A Sollami, *President*
Joanne Sollami, *Corp Secy*
Jim Sollami, *Vice Pres*
▲ **EMP:** 20
SQ FT: 50,000
SALES (est): 4.2MM **Privately Held**
SIC: 3599 3546 3545 3532 Machine shop, jobbing & repair; power-driven handtools; machine tool accessories; mining machinery

(G-11180)
SOUTHERN ILL WILBERT VLT CO
2221 N Park Ave (62948-3039)
PHONE 618 942-5845
Betty Humphrey, *President*
Dennis Sanders, *Vice Pres*
David Sanders, *Treasurer*
Pat King, *Admin Sec*
EMP: 17 **EST:** 1948
SALES (est): 1.8MM **Privately Held**
WEB: www.wilbertvaultco.com
SIC: 3272 5087 Burial vaults, concrete or precast terrazzo; concrete burial vaults & boxes

(G-11181)
SOUTHERN ILLINOIS VAULT CO INC
2221 N Park Ave (62948-3039)
PHONE 270 554-4436
Betty Humphrey, *President*
EMP: 5
SALES (est): 588.8K **Privately Held**
SIC: 3272 Burial vaults, concrete or precast terrazzo

(G-11182)
WICOFF INC
Also Called: Sterling Mattress Factory
3201 S Park Ave (62948-3711)
PHONE 618 988-8888
Michael Wicoff, *President*
EMP: 3
SQ FT: 10,000
SALES: 450K **Privately Held**
SIC: 5712 2515 5021 Mattresses; mattresses & foundations; mattresses

Herscher
Kankakee County

(G-11183)
F5D INC
70 Tobey Dr (60941-9407)
PHONE 815 953-9183
Jason A Haag, *President*
Rachel L Haag, *Admin Sec*
EMP: 2
SALES (est): 419.2K **Privately Held**
SIC: 2439 2821 3499 Structural wood members; plastics materials & resins; fabricated metal products

(G-11184)
L & N STRUCTURES INC (PA)
104 S Park Rd (60941-9584)
P.O. Box 588 (60941-0588)
PHONE 815 426-2164
Leonard Tobey, *President*
Norm Riordan, *Vice Pres*
EMP: 20
SQ FT: 9,600
SALES (est): 2.7MM **Privately Held**
SIC: 7353 3531 Heavy construction equipment rental; asphalt plant, including gravel-mix type

(G-11185)
NATURAL GAS PIPELINE AMER LLC
5611 S 12000w Rd (60941-6031)
P.O. Box 97 (60941-0097)
PHONE 815 426-2151
Joe Laughlin, *Manager*
EMP: 16 **Publicly Held**
SIC: 4922 1311 8741 Pipelines, natural gas; storage, natural gas; natural gas production; management services
HQ: Natural Gas Pipeline Company Of America Llc
1001 Louisiana St
Houston TX 77002
713 369-9000

(G-11186)
PILOT TOWNSHIP ROAD DISTRICT
300 E Kankakee Ave (60941-6153)
P.O. Box 394 (60941-0394)
PHONE 815 426-6221
Basil Kilbreth, *Vice Pres*
EMP: 6
SALES (est): 795.8K **Privately Held**
SIC: 3531 Road construction & maintenance machinery

(G-11187)
STREATOR ASPHALT INC (HQ)
104 S Park Rd (60941-9584)
P.O. Box 588 (60941-0588)
PHONE 815 426-2164
Norman C Riordan, *President*
Leonard J Tobey, *Admin Sec*
EMP: 3
SQ FT: 4,200
SALES (est): 2.7MM **Privately Held**
SIC: 3531 Asphalt plant, including gravel-mix type
PA: L & N Structures Inc
104 S Park Rd
Herscher IL 60941
815 426-2164

(G-11188)
T & E ENTERPRISES HERSCHER INC
Also Called: T & E Auto Haulers
80 Tobey Dr (60941-9472)
P.O. Box 237 (60941-0237)
PHONE 815 426-2761
Earl Datweiler, *President*
Todd Datweiler, *Treasurer*
EMP: 15 **EST:** 1980
SQ FT: 16,000
SALES (est): 3MM **Privately Held**
WEB: www.tande-racetrailers.com
SIC: 3799 3537 Automobile trailer chassis; industrial trucks & tractors

GEOGRAPHIC SECTION Highland - Madison County (G-11216)

Heyworth
Mclean County

(G-11189)
ASSEMBLE AND MAIL GROUP INC
508 S Buchanan St (61745-7689)
P.O. Box 235 (61745-0235)
PHONE 309 473-2006
Lisa Gambrel, *President*
Brian Smith, *Vice Pres*
EMP: 7
SQ FT: 20,000
SALES (est): 938.6K **Privately Held**
SIC: 7331 2678 2782 7389 Addressing service; mailing service; mailing list management; mailing list brokers; stationery products; blankbooks & looseleaf binders; cosmetic kits, assembling & packaging

(G-11190)
RANDOLPH AGRICULTURAL SERVICES
15125 E 625 North Rd (61745-7567)
PHONE 309 473-3256
Dee Hamilton, *President*
Richard Graves, *Treasurer*
Robert Anderson, *Director*
Virgil Harbaugh, *Director*
Ted Nixon, *Director*
EMP: 8
SQ FT: 1,500
SALES (est): 2.1MM **Privately Held**
SIC: 5191 2875 Fertilizer & fertilizer materials; chemicals, agricultural; fertilizers, mixing only

(G-11191)
TATE LYLE INGRDNTS AMRICAS LLC
Also Called: Tate and Lyle
702 S Vine St (61745-9179)
P.O. Box 200 (61745-0200)
PHONE 309 473-2721
Bruce Basterd, *Branch Mgr*
EMP: 5
SALES (corp-wide): 3.5B **Privately Held**
SIC: 2046 2869 2048 Wet corn milling; industrial organic chemicals; poultry feeds
HQ: Tate & Lyle Ingredients Americas Llc
2200 E Eldorado St
Decatur IL 62521
217 423-4411

(G-11192)
TOMAHAWK AG & INDUSTRIAL LLC
514 Prairie Meadows Dr (61745-9433)
PHONE 309 275-2874
Dawn F Hawkins,
EMP: 28
SALES (est): 6.5MM **Privately Held**
SIC: 3537 Industrial trucks & tractors

Hickory Hills
Cook County

(G-11193)
ADVANCED O&P SOLUTIONS
8647 W 95th St (60457-1730)
PHONE 708 878-2241
Michael Oros, *CEO*
John Angelico, *Ch of Bd*
Mike Angelico, *President*
Dan Hasso, *Principal*
David Rotter, *Principal*
EMP: 50
SALES (est): 8MM
SALES (corp-wide): 11.4MM **Privately Held**
SIC: 3842 Prosthetic appliances
PA: Scheck & Siress Prosthetics, Inc
1 S 376 Summit Ave Ct E
Oakbrook Terrace IL
708 383-2257

(G-11194)
CADORE-MILLER PRINTING INC
9901 S 78th Ave (60457-2334)
PHONE 708 430-7091
John Miller, *President*
Audrey Bednarz, *Vice Pres*
EMP: 10
SQ FT: 21,900
SALES (est): 1.6MM **Privately Held**
WEB: www.cadoremiller.com
SIC: 2752 2789 Commercial printing, offset; bookbinding & related work

(G-11195)
DOMINOS PASTRIES INC
Also Called: Domino's Pastry Shop
7731 W 98th St Ste E (60457-2371)
PHONE 773 889-3549
Vincent Claps, *President*
Vito Claps, *Vice Pres*
EMP: 8
SQ FT: 2,880
SALES (est): 832.5K **Privately Held**
SIC: 2051 Bakery: wholesale or wholesale/retail combined

(G-11196)
G & K BAKING LLC
Also Called: Buttercrumb Bakery
7731 W 98th St Ste E (60457-2371)
PHONE 708 741-7260
Kathleen Meyer, *Managing Prtnr*
Gina Errico, *Managing Prtnr*
EMP: 2 EST: 2015
SALES (est): 209K **Privately Held**
SIC: 2051 Bread, cake & related products

(G-11197)
HEAVENLY ENTERPRISES
8401 S 85th Ct (60457-1007)
P.O. Box 116, Flossmoor (60422-0116)
PHONE 773 783-2981
Marilyn Alexander, *Principal*
EMP: 2 EST: 2014
SALES (est): 205.4K **Privately Held**
SIC: 2752 Commercial printing, lithographic

(G-11198)
INFAMOUS INDUSTRIES INC
9253 S 89th Ct (60457-1626)
PHONE 708 789-2326
EMP: 3
SALES (est): 90.5K **Privately Held**
SIC: 3999 Mfg Misc Products

(G-11199)
KEVRON PRINTING & DESIGN INC
9831 S 78th Ave Ste F (60457-2370)
PHONE 708 229-7725
Kevin D Domenick, *President*
Ronald Longanecker, *Admin Sec*
EMP: 6
SQ FT: 2,400
SALES (est): 1.1MM **Privately Held**
WEB: www.kevronprint.com
SIC: 2759 7331 Screen printing; mailing service

(G-11200)
MINUTEMAN PRESS
8330 W 95th St Apt 1 (60457-3804)
PHONE 708 598-4915
Judy Riedel, *Owner*
EMP: 3
SALES (est): 270.6K **Privately Held**
SIC: 2752 Commercial printing, lithographic

(G-11201)
NIS EXPRESS INC (PA)
7667 W 95th St Ste 300 (60457-2284)
PHONE 708 880-4090
Nikola Martic, *Principal*
EMP: 1
SALES (est): 306.3K **Privately Held**
SIC: 3743 Train cars & equipment, freight or passenger

(G-11202)
REDHORSE PERFORMANCE INC
9911 S 78th Ave (60457-2334)
PHONE 708 430-1603
Allison Flamm, *Mktg Dir*
Brandi Baugh, *Manager*
Kelly Paroubek, *Admin Asst*
Kelly Marrotta, *Associate*
EMP: 8 EST: 2013
SALES (est): 899.3K **Privately Held**
WEB: www.redhorseperformance.com
SIC: 3714 Motor vehicle parts & accessories

(G-11203)
SMART CHOICE MOBILE INC (PA)
Also Called: T-Mobile
7667 W 95th St Ste 300 (60457-2284)
PHONE 708 581-4904
Bassel Joudeh, *President*
EMP: 15
SALES (est): 8.6MM **Privately Held**
SIC: 3661 Telephone sets, all types except cellular radio

Highland
Madison County

(G-11204)
AIRCRAFT PLYWOOD MFG INC
806 Cedar St (62249-1307)
P.O. Box 133 (62249-0133)
PHONE 618 654-6740
Jerome Hediger, *President*
▲ EMP: 3
SQ FT: 120
SALES (est): 200K **Privately Held**
SIC: 2435 Hardwood veneer & plywood

(G-11205)
BRECHTS DATABASE SOLUTIONS
1000 Broadway Ste 300 (62249-1966)
P.O. Box 305 (62249-0305)
PHONE 618 654-6960
August Brecht, *President*
Jeff Smith, *Regl Sales Mgr*
Chad Kruthoff, *Software Dev*
EMP: 5
SALES: 450K **Privately Held**
SIC: 7372 Prepackaged software

(G-11206)
BT STEELLE INVESTMENTS INC
Also Called: Aggressive Graphics
3649 George St (62249-2865)
PHONE 618 410-0534
Brian Steele, *Owner*
▼ EMP: 5 EST: 2007
SQ FT: 8,000
SALES (est): 461.3K **Privately Held**
SIC: 2759 7336 Commercial printing; graphic arts & related design

(G-11207)
CABINET GALLERY LLC
205 Madison St (62249-1318)
PHONE 618 882-4801
Paul Ray Capelle,
Marjorie Capelle,
EMP: 4
SALES (est): 473.5K **Privately Held**
SIC: 2521 Wood office filing cabinets & bookcases

(G-11208)
CCO HOLDINGS LLC
2762 Troxler Way (62249-1160)
PHONE 618 651-6486
EMP: 3
SALES (corp-wide): 45.7B **Publicly Held**
SIC: 5064 4841 3663 3651 Electrical appliances, television & radio; cable & other pay television services; radio & TV communications equipment; household audio & video equipment
HQ: Cco Holdings, Llc
400 Atlantic St
Stamford CT 06901
203 905-7801

(G-11209)
CHEVRON COMMERCIAL INC
3545 George St (62249-2845)
P.O. Box 99 (62249-0099)
PHONE 618 654-5555
Bill Cunagin, *President*
EMP: 1
SALES (est): 220K **Privately Held**
SIC: 3537 1796 Industrial trucks & tractors; installing building equipment

(G-11210)
COOPER B-LINE INC (DH)
Also Called: Eaton
509 W Monroe St (62249-1331)
PHONE 618 654-2184
Richard H Fearon, *President*
Joe Kline, *General Mgr*
Kevin C Kissling, *Principal*
Linda Iberg, *Senior Buyer*
Connie Winkeler, *Purchasing*
◆ EMP: 600 EST: 1971
SQ FT: 300,000
SALES (est): 362.8MM **Privately Held**
SIC: 3441 3443 3452 3444 Fabricated structural metal; cable trays, metal plate; bolts, nuts, rivets & washers; sheet metalwork; manufactured hardware (general); nonferrous rolling & drawing

(G-11211)
CREDIT & MANAGEMENT SYSTEMS
13648 Alpine Way (62249-5062)
PHONE 618 654-3500
John Sargent, *CEO*
EMP: 11
SALES (corp-wide): 1.8MM **Privately Held**
SIC: 7372 Business oriented computer software
PA: Credit & Management Systems Inc
4441 Sw Parkgate Blvd
Palm City FL 34990
847 735-9700

(G-11212)
D W MACHINE PRODUCTS INC
1111 6th St (62249-1408)
PHONE 618 654-2161
Donald E Weder, *President*
EMP: 6
SALES (est): 470K **Privately Held**
SIC: 3497 Metal foil & leaf

(G-11213)
DIGITAL ARTZ LLC
Also Called: Imageworks Creative Group
188 Woodcrest Dr (62249-1266)
PHONE 618 651-1500
Josiah Romoser, *Prdtn Mgr*
Aimee Aryal, *Office Mgr*
Chris Ebl,
Garrett Rquayate,
EMP: 6 EST: 1997
SALES (est): 605.3K **Privately Held**
WEB: www.digitalartz.us
SIC: 3993 Signs & advertising specialties

(G-11214)
DOW JONES & COMPANY INC
915 Hemlock St (62249-1329)
PHONE 618 651-2300
Chris Galassini, *Sales/Mktg Mgr*
Tim Goldsbury, *Manager*
EMP: 30
SALES (corp-wide): 10B **Publicly Held**
SIC: 2711 Newspapers, publishing & printing
HQ: Dow Jones & Company, Inc.
1211 Avenue Of The Americ
New York NY 10036
609 627-2999

(G-11215)
ELITE POWER BOATS INC
3645 George St (62249-2865)
PHONE 618 654-6292
Albert Meinen Jr, *President*
Cynthia Meinen, *Treasurer*
EMP: 3
SALES (est): 104K **Privately Held**
WEB: www.elitecomposites.net
SIC: 3732 Boats, fiberglass: building & repairing

(G-11216)
GRANT J GRAPPERHAUS
470 Pike Dr E (62249-1775)
PHONE 618 410-4428
Grant J Grapperhaus, *Principal*
EMP: 2 EST: 2009
SALES (est): 215.7K **Privately Held**
SIC: 3537 Forklift trucks

Highland - Madison County (G-11217)

(G-11217)
HIGHLAND JOURNAL PRINTING INC (PA)
1014 Laurel St (62249-1504)
P.O. Box 266 (62249-0266)
PHONE..................618 654-4131
Keith A Federer, *President*
Kerry Federer, *Vice Pres*
Pam Schmitt, *Treasurer*
EMP: 3
SQ FT: 2,300
SALES (est): 343.2K **Privately Held**
WEB: www.journalprinting.tripod.com
SIC: 2759 Letterpress printing; card printing & engraving, except greeting; business forms: printing; invitation & stationery printing & engraving

(G-11218)
HIGHLAND MCH & SCREW PDTS CO
700 5th St (62249-1213)
PHONE..................618 654-2103
Edwin M Frisse, *Ch of Bd*
William G Sullivan, *President*
Kevin Hemann, *Vice Pres*
Mike Herschbach, *Vice Pres*
Jennifer Crocker, *Engineer*
EMP: 90 **EST:** 1944
SQ FT: 140,000
SALES (est): 18.5MM **Privately Held**
WEB: www.highlandmachine.com
SIC: 3599 3451 3594 3444 Machine shop, jobbing & repair; screw machine products; fluid power pumps & motors; sheet metalwork

(G-11219)
HIGHLAND MFG & SLS CO (PA)
Also Called: Highland Supply
1111 6th St (62249-1408)
PHONE..................618 654-2161
Erwin H Weder, *Ch of Bd*
Donald E Weder, *President*
Bernard J Maliszewski, *Treasurer*
Wanda Weder, *Admin Sec*
▲ **EMP:** 60 **EST:** 1952
SQ FT: 15,000
SALES (est): 3.7MM **Privately Held**
SIC: 3081 Polyethylene film

(G-11220)
HIGHLAND NEWS LEADER
1 Woodcrest Prof Park (62249)
P.O. Box 427, Belleville (62222-0427)
PHONE..................618 654-2366
Jane Dotson, *Manager*
EMP: 5
SALES (est): 232.6K **Privately Held**
WEB: www.highlandillinois.com
SIC: 2711 Commercial printing & newspaper publishing combined; newspapers, publishing & printing

(G-11221)
HIGHLAND PRINTERS
1005 Broadway Ste A (62249-1965)
PHONE..................618 654-5880
Steve Mahlandt, *Owner*
Charlie Depew, *Manager*
EMP: 2
SQ FT: 4,500
SALES (est): 285K **Privately Held**
SIC: 2752 2791 2789 Commercial printing, offset; typesetting; bookbinding & related work

(G-11222)
HIGHLAND SOUTHERN WIRE INC (PA)
Also Called: Highland Supply
1111 6th St (62249-1408)
PHONE..................618 654-2161
Donald E Weder, *President*
Wanda M Weder, *Vice Pres*
EMP: 9
SQ FT: 75,000
SALES (est): 12.3MM **Privately Held**
SIC: 3312 3469 3496 Wire products, steel or iron; metal stampings; woven wire products

(G-11223)
HIGHLAND SPRING & SPECIALTY
150 Matter Dr (62249-1271)
PHONE..................618 654-3831
Michael Kilgore, *President*
Patricia Lohman, *Opers Mgr*
Eunice Hediger, *Exec Dir*
EMP: 10
SQ FT: 10,000
SALES (est): 1.2MM **Privately Held**
SIC: 3495 3493 Wire springs; steel springs, except wire

(G-11224)
HIGHLAND SUPPLY CORPORATION (PA)
1111 6th St (62249-1408)
PHONE..................618 654-2161
Donald Weder, *Ch of Bd*
Andrew Weder, *Vice Pres*
Erwin Weder, *Opers Mgr*
Brad Mann, *Purchasing*
Mike King, *Engineer*
◆ **EMP:** 325 **EST:** 1937
SALES (est): 53MM **Privately Held**
WEB: www.highlandsupply.com
SIC: 3497 2672 3081 2891 Metal foil & leaf; coated & laminated paper; unsupported plastics film & sheet; adhesives & sealants; bags: plastic, laminated & coated

(G-11225)
HIGHLAND WIRE INC (PA)
1111 6th St (62249-1408)
PHONE..................618 654-2161
Donald E Weder, *President*
EMP: 13
SQ FT: 15,000
SALES (est): 1.4MM **Privately Held**
SIC: 3315 Wire & fabricated wire products

(G-11226)
HOLT PUBLICATIONS INC
12047 Travis Ln (62249-3855)
PHONE..................618 654-6206
Stephen L Holt, *CEO*
Terri Holt, *President*
EMP: 6
SALES (est): 500K **Privately Held**
SIC: 2741 Miscellaneous publishing

(G-11227)
HOME & LEISURE LIFESTYLES LLC
907 Washington St (62249-1644)
P.O. Box 194 (62249-0194)
PHONE..................618 651-0358
Doug Holmstead, *Mng Member*
Tom Vice,
EMP: 3
SQ FT: 4,200
SALES (est): 366.6K
SALES (corp-wide): 21.5MM **Privately Held**
SIC: 3631 Barbecues, grills & braziers (outdoor cooking)
PA: Tangent Technologies Llc
1001 Sullivan Rd
Aurora IL 60506
630 264-1110

(G-11228)
JERRYS TACKLE AND GUNS
604 12th St (62249-1820)
PHONE..................618 654-3235
Mary Ann Simpson, *Owner*
EMP: 3
SQ FT: 2,280
SALES (est): 420K **Privately Held**
SIC: 5961 5941 3949 5091 Fishing, hunting & camping equipment & supplies: mail order; bait & tackle; hunting equipment; lures, fishing: artificial; fishing equipment & supplies

(G-11229)
JOINER SHEET METAL & ROOFG INC
205 Madison St (62249-1318)
PHONE..................618 664-9488
John Joiner, *Principal*
EMP: 8
SALES (est): 2.2MM **Privately Held**
SIC: 3444 1761 Sheet metalwork; roofing contractor

(G-11230)
KORTE MEAT PROCESSORS INC
Also Called: Korte Meat Processing
810 Deal St (62249-1313)
PHONE..................618 654-3813
David Korte, *President*
EMP: 9
SALES: 500K **Privately Held**
WEB: www.korte-meats.com
SIC: 5147 0751 5421 4222 Meats, fresh; slaughtering: custom livestock services; meat markets, including freezer provisioners; storage, frozen or refrigerated goods; sausages & other prepared meats; meat packing plants

(G-11231)
MCCLATCHY NEWSPAPERS INC
Also Called: Highlandnews Leader
1 Woodcrest Prof Park (62249)
PHONE..................618 654-2366
Jane Dotson, *Branch Mgr*
EMP: 95
SALES (corp-wide): 709.5MM **Publicly Held**
SIC: 2711 Newspapers, publishing & printing
HQ: Mcclatchy Newspapers, Inc.
2100 Q St
Sacramento CA 95816
916 321-1855

(G-11232)
MOTOR SPORT MARKETING GROUP
Also Called: McGinley Kawasaki
7 Shamrock Blvd (62249-1174)
P.O. Box 278 (62249-0278)
PHONE..................618 654-6750
Timothy McGinley, *President*
Tim McGinley, *Manager*
EMP: 20
SALES (est): 2.2MM **Privately Held**
SIC: 5511 3699 Automobiles, new & used; electrical equipment & supplies

(G-11233)
MOUNT VERNON MILLS
Also Called: Regal Linen
1001 Main St (62249-1685)
PHONE..................618 882-6300
Bill Josey, *President*
EMP: 3
SALES (est): 160.7K **Privately Held**
SIC: 2269 Embossing: linen broadwoven fabrics

(G-11234)
PATTY STYLE SHOP
Also Called: Patty's Style Shop
621 Broadway Apt 1 (62249-1855)
PHONE..................618 654-2015
Pat Frey, *Owner*
EMP: 4
SQ FT: 7,000
SALES (est): 95.8K **Privately Held**
SIC: 7231 6513 3648 Cosmetology & personal hygiene salons; apartment building operators; sun tanning equipment, incl. tanning beds

(G-11235)
PROINTEGRATION TECH LLC
13348 Koch Rd (62249-4548)
PHONE..................618 409-3233
Sheri L Eveland, *Principal*
James Eveland, *Co-Owner*
EMP: 1
SALES (est): 370K **Privately Held**
WEB: www.prointegrationtechnologiesllc.com
SIC: 3842 Personal safety equipment

(G-11236)
QUALITY FILTER SERVICES
14446 Baumann Rd (62249-5100)
PHONE..................618 654-3716
Anthony Tebbe, *Owner*
EMP: 3
SQ FT: 1,000
SALES (est): 600K **Privately Held**
SIC: 3585 5075 Refrigeration & heating equipment; warm air heating & air conditioning; air filters

(G-11237)
RED-E-MIX LLC
405 Main St (62249-1328)
PHONE..................618 654-2166
David Nepereny, *President*
Mark Goestenkors, *Vice Pres*
EMP: 82 **EST:** 2007
SALES (est): 12.5MM
SALES (corp-wide): 395.5MM **Privately Held**
SIC: 3273 Ready-mixed concrete
HQ: Midwest Material Industries Inc.
100 Brodhead Rd Ste 230
Bethlehem PA 18017
610 882-5000

(G-11238)
RED-E-MIX TRANSPORTATION LLC
405 Main St (62249-1328)
PHONE..................618 654-2166
David Nepereny, *President*
EMP: 25
SALES (est): 3MM
SALES (corp-wide): 395.5MM **Privately Held**
SIC: 3241 Portland cement
HQ: Midwest Material Industries Inc.
100 Brodhead Rd Ste 230
Bethlehem PA 18017
610 882-5000

(G-11239)
SCOPEDAWG OPTICS LLC
3115 Lake Ridge Dr (62249-4813)
PHONE..................618 401-3342
Joseph Lopinot, *Principal*
EMP: 3
SALES (est): 249.6K **Privately Held**
SIC: 3827 Optical instruments & lenses

(G-11240)
SOUTHERN STEEL AND WIRE INC (HQ)
1111 6th St (62249-1408)
PHONE..................618 654-2161
Don Weder, *President*
David Kendrick, *Vice Pres*
Joe Burris, *Treasurer*
▲ **EMP:** 5
SQ FT: 40,000
SALES (est): 12.3MM **Privately Held**
SIC: 3544 3312 3496 Wire drawing & straightening dies; wire products, steel or iron; woven wire products

(G-11241)
SOUTHWESTERN HEARING CENTERS
1328 Mercantile Dr (62249-1257)
PHONE..................618 651-4199
EMP: 8
SALES (est): 82.2K **Privately Held**
SIC: 8062 3841 General medical & surgical hospitals; surgical & medical instruments

(G-11242)
TRACK WORKS LLC
13790 Frey Acres Dr (62249-4877)
PHONE..................618 781-2375
Jason Wuebbels, *Managing Prtnr*
▲ **EMP:** 1 **EST:** 2008
SALES: 630K **Privately Held**
WEB: www.trackworks1.com
SIC: 3531 Construction machinery

(G-11243)
TRI FAMILY OIL CO (PA)
2103 Saint Michael Ct N (62249-2340)
P.O. Box 271 (62249-0271)
PHONE..................618 654-1137
Joseph A Fennell, *President*
Deb Fennell, *Vice Pres*
Jan White, *Admin Sec*
EMP: 2
SALES (est): 500.7K **Privately Held**
SIC: 1311 Crude petroleum production

GEOGRAPHIC SECTION

Highland Park - Lake County (G-11274)

(G-11244)
TROUW NUTRITION USA LLC
Trouw Nutrition Latam
115 Executive Dr (62249-1269)
PHONE..............................618 654-2070
EMP: 3 **Privately Held**
SIC: 2048 Prepared feeds
HQ: Trouw Nutrition Usa, Llc
115 Executive Dr
Highland IL 62249
618 654-2070

(G-11245)
TROUW NUTRITION USA LLC (DH)
115 Executive Dr (62249-1269)
P.O. Box 219 (62249-0219)
PHONE..............................618 654-2070
Andrew Hunt, *General Mgr*
Carlos Miranda, *Managing Dir*
Mariano Hernandez, *Principal*
Chuck Hayden, *Vice Pres*
Bradley Hovatter, *Vice Pres*
◆ **EMP:** 40 **EST:** 2001
SQ FT: 10,388
SALES (est): 82.6MM **Privately Held**
WEB: www.trouw-nutritionusa.com
SIC: 2048 Prepared feeds
HQ: Nutreco N.V.
Stationsstraat 77
Amersfoort
334 226-100

(G-11246)
TROUW NUTRITION USA LLC
1 Ultraway Dr (62249-1241)
PHONE..............................618 654-2070
Dan Rose, *Branch Mgr*
EMP: 20
SQ FT: 35,000 **Privately Held**
WEB: www.trouw-nutritionusa.com
SIC: 2048 Prepared feeds
HQ: Trouw Nutrition Usa, Llc
115 Executive Dr
Highland IL 62249
618 654-2070

(G-11247)
TROUW NUTRITION USA LLC
145 Matter Dr (62249-1354)
PHONE..............................618 654-2070
Dan Rose, *Principal*
Michael Pippin, *Production*
EMP: 20
SQ FT: 37,000 **Privately Held**
WEB: www.trouw-nutritionusa.com
SIC: 2048 Prepared feeds
HQ: Trouw Nutrition Usa, Llc
115 Executive Dr
Highland IL 62249
618 654-2070

(G-11248)
WESTROCK CP LLC
501 Zschokke St (62249-1460)
P.O. Box 190 (62249-0190)
PHONE..............................618 654-2141
Jerry McGraw, *Branch Mgr*
EMP: 120
SALES (corp-wide): 18.2B **Publicly Held**
WEB: www.westrock.com
SIC: 2653 Boxes, corrugated: made from purchased materials
HQ: Westrock Cp, Llc
1000 Abernathy Rd Ste 125
Atlanta GA 30328

(G-11249)
WICKS ORGAN COMPANY
Also Called: Wicks Pipe Organ Company
416 Pine St (62249-1243)
PHONE..............................618 654-2191
Barbara Wick, *Ch of Bd*
Mark H Wick, *President*
Cheryl Mueller, *Accountant*
▲ **EMP:** 29 **EST:** 1906
SQ FT: 140,000
SALES (est): 4.3MM **Privately Held**
WEB: www.wicksorgan.com
SIC: 3931 2511 Pipes, organ; wood household furniture

Highland Park
Lake County

(G-11250)
ABOUT FACE DESIGNS INC
1510 Old Deerfield Rd # 211 (60035-3070)
PHONE..............................847 914-9040
Robert J Ricciardi, *President*
▲ **EMP:** 5
SQ FT: 24,200
SALES (est): 788.2K **Privately Held**
SIC: 3499 Novelties & giftware, including trophies

(G-11251)
ACME AWNING CO
1500 Old Deerfield Rd # 21 (60035-3067)
P.O. Box 23, Winnetka (60093-0023)
PHONE..............................847 446-0153
Kristopher Arends, *President*
Alyce Arends, *Vice Pres*
EMP: 3 **EST:** 1935
SALES (est): 419.8K **Privately Held**
WEB: www.acmeawningonline.com
SIC: 5211 2394 Roofing material; canvas & related products

(G-11252)
ALTI LLC
826 Pleasant Ave (60035-4600)
PHONE..............................951 505-3148
James Hargrove, *CEO*
EMP: 6
SALES (est): 132.9K **Privately Held**
SIC: 3826 3823 Automatic chemical analyzers; absorption analyzers: infrared, X-ray, etc.: industrial

(G-11253)
AMER NITROGEN CO
184 Leonard Wood S # 107 (60035-5950)
PHONE..............................847 681-1068
James Horstman, *Principal*
EMP: 3
SALES (est): 184.7K **Privately Held**
SIC: 2813 Nitrogen

(G-11254)
BARCOR INC
1510 Old Deerfield Rd # 206 (60035-3071)
P.O. Box 517, Northbrook (60065-0517)
PHONE..............................847 831-2650
Judy Baria, *President*
Ed Baria, *Vice Pres*
EMP: 10
SALES (est): 1MM **Privately Held**
SIC: 3829 Measuring & controlling devices

(G-11255)
BKA INC
Also Called: Imaging Equipment Sales
1999 Castlewood Rd (60035-2907)
PHONE..............................847 831-3535
Barry Ades, *President*
EMP: 4
SALES (est): 230K **Privately Held**
SIC: 3861 Cameras & related equipment

(G-11256)
CAIBROS AMERICAS LLC
116 Deere Park Ct (60035-5309)
PHONE..............................312 593-3128
Doreen Tho, *Principal*
EMP: 3
SALES (est): 240K **Privately Held**
SIC: 2911 Fuel additives

(G-11257)
CAST GLASSWORKS
1975 Northland Ave (60035-2756)
PHONE..............................847 831-0222
EMP: 4 **EST:** 2015
SALES (est): 222.9K **Privately Held**
SIC: 3369 Nonferrous foundries

(G-11258)
CIRCLE STUDIO STAINED GLASS
946 Central Ave (60035-5624)
PHONE..............................847 432-7249
Joseph Badalpour, *President*
EMP: 4 **EST:** 1975
SALES (est): 300.8K **Privately Held**
SIC: 1793 3471 3231 Glass & glazing work; plating & polishing; products of purchased glass

(G-11259)
CLIQSTER LLC
212 Pine Point Dr (60035-5335)
PHONE..............................847 732-1457
Nicholas Wieczorek, *CEO*
EMP: 5
SALES (est): 256.6K **Privately Held**
SIC: 7372 Application computer software; business oriented computer software

(G-11260)
CREATIVE MACHINING TECH LLC
1949 Saint Johns Ave # 200 (60035-3105)
PHONE..............................309 755-7700
Jonathan Canel, *Managing Dir*
Scott Canel,
▲ **EMP:** 100
SQ FT: 115,000
SALES (est): 18.3MM **Privately Held**
SIC: 3599 Machine shop, jobbing & repair

(G-11261)
EISENDRATH INC
Also Called: Signs Now
716 Central Ave Apt B (60035-3294)
PHONE..............................847 432-3899
Sharon Eisendrath, *President*
Peter Eisendrath, *Vice Pres*
EMP: 6
SALES (est): 340K **Privately Held**
SIC: 3993 Signs & advertising specialties

(G-11262)
FASHION CRAFT CORPORATION
1421 Old Deerfield Rd (60035-3025)
PHONE..............................847 998-0092
Robert Blank, *President*
Stanley Kramer, *Vice Pres*
EMP: 20 **EST:** 1936
SQ FT: 4,500
SALES (est): 2.2MM **Privately Held**
SIC: 3911 Rings, finger: precious metal; earrings, precious metal; bracelets, precious metal; pins (jewelry), precious metal

(G-11263)
FORCERL
1350 Forest Ave (60035-3457)
PHONE..............................847 432-7588
Robert Pascal, *Principal*
EMP: 2
SALES (est): 220.1K **Privately Held**
WEB: www.forcerl.com
SIC: 2752 Commercial printing, lithographic

(G-11264)
G-FAST DISTRIBUTION INC
Also Called: Mrgfastman
1954 1st St 228 (60035-3104)
PHONE..............................847 926-0722
Steve Greenberg, *President*
EMP: 2
SQ FT: 1,000
SALES (est): 322.6K **Privately Held**
SIC: 3452 Bolts, nuts, rivets & washers

(G-11265)
GOOD IMPRESSIONS INC
3150 Skokie Valley Rd # 24 (60035-1079)
PHONE..............................847 831-4317
EMP: 6
SQ FT: 8,000
SALES (est): 623.2K **Privately Held**
SIC: 2759 2396 Commercial Printing Mfg Auto/Apparel Trimming

(G-11266)
GOURMET FROG PASTRY SHOP
316 Green Bay Rd (60035)
PHONE..............................847 433-7038
Terry Lese, *Owner*
EMP: 5
SALES (est): 292K **Privately Held**
SIC: 2051 Bread, cake & related products

(G-11267)
GREAT IDEAS INC
Also Called: Solution Comfortseat
1633 Ravine Ln (60035-3346)
PHONE..............................800 611-5515
Elliott Rubin, *CEO*
Marilee Rubin, *President*
EMP: 13 **EST:** 1971
SALES: 1.2MM **Privately Held**
SIC: 5199 5047 3842 Advertising specialties; technical aids for the handicapped; technical aids for the handicapped

(G-11268)
GULF COAST EXPLORATION INC
983 Harvard Ct (60035-2377)
PHONE..............................847 226-4654
Joseph L Fieger, *President*
EMP: 5
SALES (est): 366.9K **Privately Held**
SIC: 1311 Crude petroleum production

(G-11269)
GVW GROUP LLC (PA)
Also Called: Gvw Holdings
625 Roger Williams Ave (60035-4807)
PHONE..............................847 681-8417
Andrew Taitz, *Chairman*
James Maclaughlin, *CFO*
Sergiu Catirau, *Software Dev*
Jeffrey Leeb, *General Counsel*
Aaron Stenger, *Administration*
▲ **EMP:** 8 **EST:** 2005
SQ FT: 1,000
SALES (est): 165.2MM **Privately Held**
WEB: www.gvwgroup.com
SIC: 3713 Truck bodies (motor vehicles)

(G-11270)
HENRY-LEE & COMPANY LLC
909 Rollingwood Rd (60035-3957)
PHONE..............................312 242-2501
Becky Hinton, *General Mgr*
Sheldon Mann, *Chairman*
Robert Mann, *Mng Member*
▲ **EMP:** 10 **EST:** 1957
SALES (est): 2.5MM **Privately Held**
WEB: www.henryandbelle.com
SIC: 2221 Apparel & outerwear fabric, manmade fiber or silk

(G-11271)
I C INNOVATIONS INC
1101 Golf Ave (60035-3637)
P.O. Box 1263, Northbrook (60065-1263)
PHONE..............................847 279-7888
Donald Gaule, *President*
Ronald Yermack, *Vice Pres*
▲ **EMP:** 4
SQ FT: 2,500
SALES (est): 498.4K **Privately Held**
SIC: 3829 Thermometers & temperature sensors

(G-11272)
ILLUMINIGHT LIGHTING LLC
1954 1st St 394 (60035-3104)
PHONE..............................312 685-4448
Scott Parrish, *Principal*
EMP: 10
SALES (est): 761.6K **Privately Held**
WEB: www.illuminightlights.com
SIC: 3648 7389 Lighting equipment;

(G-11273)
IMAGES ALIVE LTD
875 Pleasant Ave (60035-4614)
PHONE..............................847 498-5550
Ellen Robinson, *President*
EMP: 6
SALES (est): 972.1K **Privately Held**
SIC: 3993 Signs & advertising specialties

(G-11274)
INVITATION CREATIONS INC
580 Roger Williams Ave # 24 (60035-4823)
PHONE..............................847 432-4441
Ellen Fiely, *President*
EMP: 2
SALES (est): 202.6K **Privately Held**
WEB: www.invitationcreations.net
SIC: 2759 Invitation & stationery printing & engraving

Highland Park - Lake County (G-11275) — GEOGRAPHIC SECTION

(G-11275)
J II INC
Also Called: Aqua Belle Manufacturing Co
1292 Old Skokie Rd (60035-3035)
P.O. Box 496 (60035-0496)
PHONE...................847 432-8979
Ben Israel, *President*
Dov Kahana, *Vice Pres*
EMP: 91
SQ FT: 15,000
SALES (est): 9.3MM **Privately Held**
SIC: 3589 Water filters & softeners, household type; water treatment equipment, industrial

(G-11276)
J K PRINTING & MAILING INC
2090 Green Bay Rd (60035-2482)
P.O. Box 1975 (60035-7975)
PHONE...................847 432-7717
Robert Stoeller, *President*
EMP: 4
SQ FT: 3,300
SALES: 500K **Privately Held**
SIC: 7331 2752 Addressing service; mailing service; commercial printing, offset

(G-11277)
KENS QUICK PRINT INC
1500 Old Deerfield Rd # 5 (60035-3067)
PHONE...................847 831-4410
Kenneth Erlander, *President*
EMP: 10
SQ FT: 2,400
SALES (est): 1.7MM **Privately Held**
SIC: 2752 2791 2789 2759 Commercial printing, offset; typesetting; bookbinding & related work; commercial printing

(G-11278)
KEWAUNEE SCIENTIFIC CORP
3150 Skokie Valley Rd # 8 (60035-1079)
P.O. Box 405, Evanston (60204-0405)
PHONE...................847 675-7744
EMP: 5
SALES (corp-wide): 158MM **Publicly Held**
SIC: 3821 2599 2541 2542 Mfg Scientific Laboratory & Technical Workstations & Equipment Shop & Vocational Equipment & Storage Cabinets
PA: Kewaunee Scientific Corporation
2700 W Front St
Statesville NC 28677
704 873-7202

(G-11279)
LAMICO DESIGNERS DEERFIELD INC
3300 Skokie Valley Rd (60035-1055)
PHONE...................847 465-8850
Ronald Zaar, *President*
Mary Zaar, *Vice Pres*
Mark Zaar, *Controller*
Eric Zaar, *Admin Sec*
EMP: 4
SQ FT: 1,700
SALES (est): 553.1K **Privately Held**
SIC: 2434 Wood kitchen cabinets

(G-11280)
LARRY & MYRA STONE
Also Called: H P Tops
667 Central Ave Ste 5 (60035-5620)
PHONE...................847 433-0540
Larry Stone, *Partner*
Myra Stone, *Partner*
▲ **EMP:** 4 EST: 1978
SQ FT: 400
SALES (est): 453K **Privately Held**
SIC: 2759 Screen printing

(G-11281)
LAUREL INDUSTRIES INC
Also Called: C R L
544 Michigan Ave (60035-1924)
PHONE...................847 432-8204
Carl R Lambrecht Jr, *President*
Catherine A Lambrecht, *Admin Sec*
EMP: 50 EST: 1978
SQ FT: 4,000
SALES (est): 7.4MM **Privately Held**
SIC: 3827 Optical instruments & apparatus

(G-11282)
LOVE ME TENDERS LLC
833 Laurel Ave Unit 202 (60035-5710)
PHONE...................773 502-8000
EMP: 3
SALES (est): 179.2K **Privately Held**
SIC: 2015 Chicken, processed: frozen

(G-11283)
MENONI & MOCOGNI INC
2160 Skokie Valley Rd (60035-1731)
P.O. Box 128 (60035-0128)
PHONE...................847 432-0850
Mike Miotti, *President*
Danny Loizzo, *Vice Pres*
Anthony A Loizzo, *Admin Sec*
EMP: 11 EST: 1947
SQ FT: 5,000
SALES (est): 2.6MM **Privately Held**
WEB: www.menoniandmocogni.com
SIC: 5211 3273 1442 Masonry materials & supplies; ready-mixed concrete; construction sand & gravel

(G-11284)
MIZRAHI GRILL
215 Skokie Valley Rd (60035-4405)
PHONE...................847 831-1400
Eliyahu Mizrahi, *Principal*
EMP: 11
SALES (est): 1.2MM **Privately Held**
WEB: www.mizrahigrill.com
SIC: 2599 Bar, restaurant & cafeteria furniture

(G-11285)
MOLDED DISPLAYS
739 Old Trail Rd (60035-1359)
PHONE...................773 892-4098
Henry Adderley, *President*
EMP: 3
SALES (est): 274.9K **Privately Held**
SIC: 3089 Molding primary plastic

(G-11286)
MORTON GROUP LTD
Also Called: Great Lakes Bag & Vinyl
1510 Old Deerfield Rd # 20 (60035-3068)
P.O. Box 1075 (60035-7075)
PHONE...................847 831-2766
Harrison Kranick, *President*
▲ **EMP:** 5
SQ FT: 5,000
SALES (est): 6MM **Privately Held**
SIC: 3081 5199 Vinyl film & sheet; packaging materials

(G-11287)
MUTUAL SVCS HIGHLAND PK INC
Also Called: Mutual Steel
2760 Skokie Valley Rd (60035-1043)
PHONE...................847 432-3815
Bruno Ori, *Branch Mgr*
EMP: 15
SALES (corp-wide): 12.7MM **Privately Held**
SIC: 5051 3441 Structural shapes, iron or steel; fabricated structural metal
PA: Mutual Services Of Highland Park, Inc.
1393 Half Day Rd
Highland Park IL 60035
847 432-0026

(G-11288)
NERD ISLAND STUDIOS LLC
1347 Ferndale Ave (60035-2809)
PHONE...................224 619-5361
Chris Bruce, *Principal*
Christopher Bruce, *Principal*
EMP: 4 EST: 2012
SALES (est): 173.3K **Privately Held**
SIC: 7372 Educational computer software; application computer software

(G-11289)
OIL AND GAS DISCOVERER LLC
1910 Browning Ct (60035-1657)
PHONE...................847 877-1257
James Combs, *Vice Pres*
Jeffery Drizin, *Mng Member*
EMP: 11 EST: 2014
SALES: 10MM **Privately Held**
SIC: 1382 Oil & gas exploration services

(G-11290)
OPPORTUNITY INC
1200 Old Skokie Rd (60035-3036)
P.O. Box 1349, Deerfield (60015-6005)
PHONE...................847 831-9400
Lawrence Rosser, *President*
EMP: 75
SQ FT: 150,000
SALES (est): 9.4MM **Privately Held**
SIC: 3842 Surgical appliances & supplies

(G-11291)
POLYDESIGNS LTD
731 Orleans Dr (60035-3915)
P.O. Box 522 (60035-0522)
PHONE...................847 433-9920
Ronald Morris, *Partner*
EMP: 2 EST: 1991
SALES (est): 212.3K **Privately Held**
SIC: 3089 Plastic processing

(G-11292)
PRINCETON CHEMICALS INC
988 Princeton Ave (60035-2380)
P.O. Box 428 (60035-0428)
PHONE...................847 975-6210
Richard Small, *President*
EMP: 1 EST: 2015
SQ FT: 300
SALES (est): 1.5MM **Privately Held**
SIC: 2844 Toilet preparations

(G-11293)
R P GROLLMAN CO INC
1811 Lawrence Ln (60035-4326)
P.O. Box 1080 (60035-7080)
PHONE...................847 607-0294
Ronald Grollman, *President*
EMP: 3
SALES (est): 283.2K **Privately Held**
SIC: 3565 Packaging machinery

(G-11294)
RIBBON PRINT COMPANY
Also Called: Ribbon Print USA
508 Central Ave Ste 208 (60035-3271)
PHONE...................847 421-8208
Sue C Monhait, *Principal*
▲ **EMP:** 2
SALES (est): 235.2K **Privately Held**
SIC: 2752 Commercial printing, offset

(G-11295)
ROSS DESIGNS LTD
210 Skokie Valley Rd # 5 (60035-4464)
PHONE...................847 831-7669
Mark Neumann, *President*
Abby Neumann, *Vice Pres*
EMP: 1
SALES (est): 250K **Privately Held**
SIC: 5944 3911 Jewelry, precious stones & precious metals; jewelry, precious metal

(G-11296)
SAFERSONIC US INC
2873 Arlington Ave # 110 (60035-1115)
PHONE...................847 274-1534
Leopold Lackner, *President*
David Seitelman, *Exec Dir*
▲ **EMP:** 2 EST: 2012
SALES: 500K **Privately Held**
SIC: 3069 Medical & laboratory rubber sundries & related products

(G-11297)
SENIOR CARE PHARMACY LLC
1630 Old Deerfield Rd # 202 (60035-3031)
PHONE...................847 579-0093
Mark Kass,
EMP: 5
SQ FT: 800
SALES: 100K **Privately Held**
SIC: 2834 Pharmaceutical preparations

(G-11298)
SMART CREATIONS INC
Also Called: Chelsea's Beads
1799 Saint Johns Ave (60035-3532)
PHONE...................847 433-3451
R Dubinsky, *President*
EMP: 8
SALES (est): 590.3K **Privately Held**
WEB: www.chelseabeads.com
SIC: 5945 3961 Arts & crafts supplies; costume jewelry

(G-11299)
SOFTLABZ CORPORATION (PA)
1180 Saint Johns Ave (60035-3423)
PHONE...................847 780-7076
Olexiy Miroshnichenko, *President*
Olena Miroshnichenko, *CFO*
EMP: 2
SQ FT: 400
SALES: 440K **Privately Held**
SIC: 7372 Prepackaged software

(G-11300)
STAR INDUSTRIES INC
Also Called: Star Industries Intl Div
2210 Skokie Valley Rd (60035-1733)
P.O. Box 178, La Grange (60525-0178)
PHONE...................708 240-4862
Robert E Morris, *President*
Jake Van Der Kooy Jr, *Vice Pres*
EMP: 20
SQ FT: 30,000
SALES (est): 2.5MM **Privately Held**
WEB: www.starhydrodyne.com
SIC: 3589 Floor washing & polishing machines, commercial

(G-11301)
SWITCHEE BANDZ USA LLC
Also Called: Switchee USA
804 Kimballwood Ln (60035-3624)
PHONE...................312 415-1100
Michael Spatz, *Principal*
Michael N Spatz, *Principal*
EMP: 5
SALES (est): 605.8K **Privately Held**
SIC: 3679 Electronic switches

(G-11302)
T2 SITE AMENITIES INCORPORATED
1805 Spruce St (60035-2150)
PHONE...................847 579-9003
Lori Tilkin, *President*
Stephen L Tilkin, *Vice Pres*
Gerri Madenberg, *Office Mgr*
▼ **EMP:** 5
SALES: 1.5MM **Privately Held**
WEB: www.t2-sa.com
SIC: 3089 2449 2531 5193 Garbage containers, plastic; flower pots, plastic; planters & window boxes, wood; benches for public buildings; planters & flower pots; office chairs, benches & stools, except wood; benches, office: except wood

(G-11303)
TEAM SIDER INC
Also Called: Greater Than
158 Hastings Ave (60035-5139)
PHONE...................847 767-0107
Jon Sider, *President*
Mark Sider, *Vice Pres*
EMP: 3
SALES (est): 450K **Privately Held**
WEB: www.drinkgt.com
SIC: 2086 7389 Mineral water, carbonated: packaged in cans, bottles, etc.;

(G-11304)
WAND ENTERPRISES INC (PA)
Also Called: Wand Tool Company
1029 Green Bay Rd (60035-4000)
PHONE...................847 433-0231
William N Anderson, *President*
Nancy Corbett, *Corp Secy*
Thomas Anderson, *Vice Pres*
EMP: 17
SQ FT: 14,000
SALES (est): 3.3MM **Privately Held**
SIC: 3544 3672 Special dies, tools, jigs & fixtures; printed circuit boards

(G-11305)
WAND TOOL ENTERPRISE
1029 Green Bay Rd (60035-4000)
PHONE...................847 433-0231
Todd Anderson, *President*
EMP: 3
SALES (est): 220K **Privately Held**
SIC: 3544 Special dies, tools, jigs & fixtures

Highwood
Lake County

(G-11306)
DORIS BRIDAL BOUTIQUE
448 Sheridan Rd Ste 1 (60040-1344)
PHONE..................847 433-2575
Doris Lindqvist, *Partner*
Annette Hebel, *Partner*
EMP: 6
SQ FT: 4,000
SALES (est): 876.6K **Privately Held**
SIC: 2335 5621 Bridal & formal gowns; bridal shops

(G-11307)
I KUSTOM CABINETS INC
220 Oakridge Ave (60040-1614)
PHONE..................773 343-6858
Paul Korzun, *President*
EMP: 2
SALES (est): 206.1K **Privately Held**
SIC: 2434 Wood kitchen cabinets

(G-11308)
LAX SHOP
108 Washington Ave (60040-1122)
PHONE..................847 945-8529
Justin Smith, *President*
Adam Stewart, *Executive*
EMP: 1
SALES (est): 203.1K **Privately Held**
WEB: www.thelaxshop.com
SIC: 3949 Lacrosse equipment & supplies, general

(G-11309)
MARIAS BAKERY INC
410 Sheridan Rd (60040-1343)
PHONE..................847 266-0811
Fillippa Pollari, *President*
EMP: 3
SALES (est): 78.6K **Privately Held**
SIC: 2051 Bakery: wholesale or wholesale/retail combined

Hillsboro
Montgomery County

(G-11310)
ELITE MONUMENT CO
Also Called: Hough General Homes
1119 School St (62049-1931)
PHONE..................217 532-6080
David Hough, *Partner*
Daniel Hough, *Partner*
Danny Hough, *Partner*
EMP: 3
SALES (est): 195.1K **Privately Held**
SIC: 3272 Monuments, concrete

(G-11311)
FRITO-LAY NORTH AMERICA INC
1400 E Tremont St (62049-1915)
PHONE..................217 532-5040
EMP: 160
SALES (corp-wide): 66.6B **Publicly Held**
SIC: 2096 Mfg Potato Chips/Snacks
HQ: Frito-Lay North America, Inc.
7701 Legacy Dr
Plano TX 75024

(G-11312)
FULLER BROTHERS READY MIX
935 Ash St (62049-1519)
PHONE..................217 532-2422
Lance Fuller, *President*
Harry Fuller, *Partner*
EMP: 6
SQ FT: 4,000
SALES (est): 1.2MM **Privately Held**
SIC: 3273 Ready-mixed concrete

(G-11313)
HAYES ABRASIVES INC
120 Smith Ln # 120 (62049)
P.O. Box 237 (62049-0237)
PHONE..................217 532-6850
David Hayes, *President*
EMP: 15
SQ FT: 9,000
SALES (est): 2.3MM **Privately Held**
SIC: 3291 5085 Wheels, abrasive; industrial wheels

(G-11314)
HILLERS SHEET METAL WORKS
150 N Oak St (62049-1107)
PHONE..................217 532-2595
H Dennis Hiller, *Owner*
EMP: 3
SQ FT: 1,500
SALES (est): 181.5K **Privately Held**
SIC: 1711 3599 Warm air heating & air conditioning contractor; machine shop, jobbing & repair

(G-11315)
HILLSBORO ENERGY LLC
925 S Main St Ste 2 (62049-1757)
P.O. Box 457 (62049-0457)
PHONE..................217 532-7310
Mike Beyer, *CEO*
John Mick, *CFO*
▲ **EMP:** 5
SALES (est): 534.2K
SALES (corp-wide): 841.5MM **Publicly Held**
SIC: 1221 Bituminous coal surface mining
HQ: Foresight Energy Llc
1 Metropolitan Sq
Saint Louis MO 63102
314 932-6160

(G-11316)
HILLSBORO JOURNAL INC
Also Called: Sorento News, Raymond News
431 S Main St (62049-1433)
P.O. Box 100 (62049-0100)
PHONE..................217 532-3933
Phillip C Galer, *President*
John Galler, *Vice Pres*
EMP: 40 **EST:** 1853
SQ FT: 4,000
SALES (est): 1.9MM **Privately Held**
WEB: www.thejournal-news.net
SIC: 2711 2759 2752 Newspapers: publishing only, not printed on site; commercial printing; commercial printing, lithographic

(G-11317)
JOURNAL NEWS
431 S Main St (62049-1433)
PHONE..................217 532-3933
Nancy Slepicka, *Principal*
EMP: 6 **EST:** 2010
SALES (est): 195.6K **Privately Held**
SIC: 2711 Commercial printing & newspaper publishing combined

(G-11318)
PARIS FROZEN FOODS INC
Also Called: Paris Frozen Foods Locker
305 Springfield Rd (62049-1150)
PHONE..................217 532-3822
Allen Hopper, *President*
Tom Compagni, *Vice Pres*
Pam Hopper, *Treasurer*
EMP: 5 **EST:** 1959
SQ FT: 4,800
SALES (est): 437.6K **Privately Held**
SIC: 2011 Meat packing plants

(G-11319)
PRO-BILT BUILDINGS LLC
9181 Illinois Route 127 (62049-4117)
P.O. Box 461 (62049-0461)
PHONE..................217 532-9331
Becky Lessman,
Barbara Bogel,
Richard Bogel,
Dean Lessman,
EMP: 14
SALES (est): 1.3MM **Privately Held**
WEB: www.buildingsbyprobilt.com
SIC: 3444 Metal roofing & roof drainage equipment

(G-11320)
SULLIVAN HOME HEALTH PRODUCTS
311 Berry St (62049-1201)
P.O. Box 9 (62049-0009)
PHONE..................217 532-6366
EMP: 3
SALES (corp-wide): 555.7K **Privately Held**
SIC: 5047 3845 Whol Medical/Hospital Equipment Mfg Electromedical Equipment
PA: Sullivan Home Health Products Inc
117 W Spruce St
Gillespie IL 62033
217 839-3228

Hillsdale
Rock Island County

(G-11321)
BOS MACHINE TOOL SERVICES INC
Also Called: Kemco Portable Machining
621 Main St (61257-9785)
P.O. Box 96 (61257-0096)
PHONE..................309 658-2223
Charles Bos, *President*
Diane Bos, *Vice Pres*
Tim Marsden, *Sales Mgr*
EMP: 14
SQ FT: 30,000
SALES (est): 1MM **Privately Held**
SIC: 3541 7699 Machine tools, metal cutting type; industrial machinery & equipment repair

(G-11322)
TYSON FOODS INC
28424 38th Ave N (61257-9656)
PHONE..................309 658-2291
Rose Thompson, *Purch Agent*
Allan Schuetze, *Branch Mgr*
Michael Hays, *Manager*
David Vanspeybroeck, *Technical Staff*
David Hayes, *Director*
EMP: 13
SALES (corp-wide): 42.4B **Publicly Held**
SIC: 2015 Poultry slaughtering & processing
PA: Tyson Foods, Inc.
2200 W Don Tyson Pkwy
Springdale AR 72762
479 290-4000

(G-11323)
TYSON FRESH MEATS INC
Also Called: Transcontinental Cold Storage
28424 38th Ave N (61257-9656)
PHONE..................309 658-3377
Steven Martet, *Branch Mgr*
EMP: 128
SALES (corp-wide): 42.4B **Publicly Held**
SIC: 2011 Meat packing plants
HQ: Tyson Fresh Meats, Inc.
800 Stevens Port Dr
Dakota Dunes SD 57049
479 290-6397

Hillside
Cook County

(G-11324)
ACE ANODIZING IMPREGNATING INC
4161 Butterfield Rd (60162-1185)
P.O. Box 639 (60162-0639)
PHONE..................708 547-6680
David B Vaughn, *President*
EMP: 60 **EST:** 1959
SQ FT: 36,000
SALES (est): 8MM **Privately Held**
WEB: www.acemetalfinishing.com
SIC: 3471 2295 Anodizing (plating) of metals or formed products; coated fabrics, not rubberized

(G-11325)
ACE COATING ENTERPRISES INC (PA)
4161 Butterfield Rd (60162-1118)
P.O. Box 639 (60162-0639)
PHONE..................708 547-6680
David Vaughn, *President*
Nancy Burdick Vaughn, *Vice Pres*
Raquel Wenzel, *Admin Sec*
EMP: 47
SQ FT: 18,000
SALES (est): 5.9MM **Privately Held**
SIC: 3599 Machine shop, jobbing & repair

(G-11326)
ALLIANCE DOOR AND HARDWARE LLC
225 Fencl Ln (60162-2001)
PHONE..................630 451-7070
Jimenez Arthur, *CEO*
EMP: 4 **EST:** 2013
SALES (est): 656.1K **Privately Held**
SIC: 5031 2431 3442 Doors; door frames, wood; window & door frames

(G-11327)
AMERICAN WILBERT VAULT CORP (PA)
4415 Harrison St Ste 246 (60162-1900)
P.O. Box 7245, Westchester (60154-7245)
PHONE..................708 366-3210
David Reichle, *President*
Eric Urbano, *CFO*
Camille Powell, *Admin Sec*
EMP: 49 **EST:** 1924
SQ FT: 1,500
SALES (est): 8.2MM **Privately Held**
SIC: 3272 Burial vaults, concrete or precast terrazzo

(G-11328)
AMERIGAS
4158 Division St (60162-1803)
PHONE..................708 544-1131
Barbara Trentadue, *Manager*
EMP: 54
SQ FT: 12,500
SALES (est): 16.3MM
SALES (corp-wide): 7.3B **Publicly Held**
WEB: www.amerigas.com
SIC: 5172 5984 5169 2813 Gases, liquefied petroleum (propane); liquefied petroleum gas dealers; chemicals & allied products; industrial gases
HQ: Amerigas Partners, L.P.
460 N Gulph Rd Ste 100
King Of Prussia PA 19406

(G-11329)
BELDEN TOOLS INC
Also Called: Belden Universal
4100 Madison St (60162-1768)
PHONE..................708 344-4600
Perry Sainati, *President*
◆ **EMP:** 30
SQ FT: 26,000
SALES (est): 6.3MM **Privately Held**
SIC: 3545 Machine tool attachments & accessories

(G-11330)
BIO SERVICES INC
4917 Butterfield Rd (60162-1413)
P.O. Box 6358, Villa Park (60181-5318)
PHONE..................630 808-2125
Shiji Chirayil, *President*
Luke Phiroeyil, *Office Mgr*
EMP: 4
SALES: 300K **Privately Held**
SIC: 3365 Hospital utensils, cast aluminum

(G-11331)
BISCO INTL INC
543 Granville Ave (60162-1754)
PHONE..................708 544-6308
Michael Rizzo, *President*
EMP: 8
SQ FT: 14,000
SALES (est): 1.7MM **Privately Held**
WEB: www.biscointernational.com
SIC: 3555 2672 5065 Printing plates; coated & laminated paper; electronic parts

(G-11332)
C2 PUBLISHING INC
Also Called: West Suburban Living Magazine
4415 Harrison St Ste 412 (60162-1921)
P.O. Box 111, Elmhurst (60126-0111)
PHONE..................630 834-4994
Chuck Cozette, *President*
Ken Cozette, *Vice Pres*
EMP: 10
SALES (est): 620K **Privately Held**
SIC: 2721 Magazines: publishing only, not printed on site

Hillside - Cook County (G-11333)

(G-11333)
CHEM RX - CHICAGO LLC
150 Fencl Ln (60162-2041)
PHONE...................708 449-7600
Paula Agoglia, *Exec VP*
Deborah Zucker, *Asst Mgr*
EMP: 3 **EST:** 2008
SALES (est): 190.1K **Privately Held**
SIC: 2834 Pharmaceutical preparations

(G-11334)
COMPRESSED AIR ADVISORS INC
2215 S Wolf Rd Ste 127 (60162-2212)
PHONE...................877 247-2381
Craig Parmele, *CEO*
Lindsay Parmele, *Admin Sec*
EMP: 3
SALES (est): 75K **Privately Held**
SIC: 5999 7699 3563 Air purification equipment; compressor repair; air & gas compressors including vacuum pumps

(G-11335)
DARWILL INC
11900 Roosevelt Rd (60162-2069)
PHONE...................708 449-7770
Janice Van Dyke, *CEO*
Brandon Van Dyke, *President*
Howard Van Dyke, *President*
Troy V Dyke, *Vice Pres*
Troy Van Dyke, *Vice Pres*
▲ **EMP:** 150 **EST:** 1951
SQ FT: 60,000
SALES: 165.3K **Privately Held**
WEB: www.darwill.com
SIC: 5963 8748 8742 2789 Direct sales, telemarketing; communications consulting; marketing consulting services; bookbinding & related work; commercial printing

(G-11336)
DYNAMIC MANUFACTURING INC (PA)
4201 Raymond Dr (60162-1705)
PHONE...................708 343-8753
Nancy Partipilo, *President*
John Paukovits, *General Mgr*
Gary R Noel, *Chairman*
Johnny Bellantuono, *Exec VP*
Tony Partipilo, *Exec VP*
▲ **EMP:** 70
SALES (est): 149.5MM
SALES (corp-wide): 164.4MM **Privately Held**
SIC: 3714 Transmissions, motor vehicle

(G-11337)
DYNAMIC MANUFACTURING INC
4300 Madison St (60162-1340)
PHONE...................708 547-7081
John Partipilo, *President*
Nick Dentamaro, *Plant Mgr*
Jesus Gonzalez, *Maintence Staff*
EMP: 100
SALES (corp-wide): 164.4MM **Privately Held**
SIC: 3714 7537 7539 Transmissions, motor vehicle; automotive transmission repair shops; torque converter repair, automotive
PA: Dynamic Manufacturing Inc
4201 Raymond Dr
Hillside IL 60162
708 343-8753

(G-11338)
DYNAMIC MANUFACTURING INC
Also Called: Plant 2
4211 Madison St (60162-1731)
PHONE...................708 547-9011
Tony Partipilo, *Exec VP*
Theresa Smolen, *Purch Mgr*
Lester Coimbra, *Engineer*
Dale Nickos, *Engineer*
Anthony Price, *Electrical Engi*
EMP: 300
SALES (corp-wide): 164.4MM **Privately Held**
SIC: 3714 Transmissions, motor vehicle
PA: Dynamic Manufacturing Inc
4201 Raymond Dr
Hillside IL 60162

(G-11339)
EASTLAND INDUSTRIES INC
4115 Washington Blvd (60162-1126)
PHONE...................708 547-6500
Marlene Teichart, *President*
Gary Jindra, *President*
Kathy Jindra, *Principal*
Justin Jindra, *Vice Pres*
Conor O'Brien, *Human Resources*
EMP: 16
SQ FT: 14,200
SALES (est): 4.2MM **Privately Held**
SIC: 7694 Electric motor repair

(G-11340)
GPE CONTROLS INC (HQ)
Also Called: Shand & Jurs
5911 Butterfield Rd (60162-1457)
PHONE...................708 236-6000
Louis Jannotta, *President*
James B Filip, *Controller*
Isaac Lim, *Sales Mgr*
Leo Gimeltarb, *Info Tech Mgr*
Jeff Clay, *Executive*
▼ **EMP:** 15
SALES (est): 11.9MM **Privately Held**
SIC: 3829 3491 3728 3625 Gauging instruments, thickness ultrasonic; industrial valves; aircraft parts & equipment; relays & industrial controls; fluid power cylinders & actuators; fabricated plate work (boiler shop)

(G-11341)
HERFF JONES LLC
Also Called: Replogle Globe Partners
125 Fencl Ln (60162-2040)
PHONE...................317 612-3705
Dave Reed, *Branch Mgr*
EMP: 180
SALES (corp-wide): 1.1B **Privately Held**
SIC: 2389 2384 3911 Academic vestments (caps & gowns); robes & dressing gowns; jewelry, precious metal
HQ: Herff Jones, Llc
4501 W 62nd St
Indianapolis IN 46268
800 419-5462

(G-11342)
HIGHLAND METAL INC
541 Hyde Park Ave (60162-1816)
PHONE...................708 544-6641
Kenneth Gerard Martin, *President*
David Miller, *Opers Staff*
EMP: 23
SQ FT: 20,000
SALES (est): 4.2MM **Privately Held**
WEB: www.highlandmetal.com
SIC: 3451 3599 Screw machine products; grinding castings for the trade

(G-11343)
K SYSTEMS CORPORATION
4931 Butterfield Rd (60162-1437)
PHONE...................708 449-0400
Kent Piche, *President*
EMP: 6
SQ FT: 3,000
SALES (est): 972.1K **Privately Held**
SIC: 3545 Gauges (machine tool accessories)

(G-11344)
L & J ENGINEERING INC (HQ)
Also Called: L & J Technologies
5911 Butterfield Rd (60162-1457)
PHONE...................708 236-6000
Louis J Jannotta, *President*
EMP: 40
SQ FT: 85,000
SALES (est): 11.3MM **Privately Held**
SIC: 3829 5084 Measuring & controlling devices; industrial machinery & equipment

(G-11345)
L & J HOLDING COMPANY LTD (PA)
Also Called: L & J Technologies
5911 Butterfield Rd (60162-1457)
PHONE...................708 236-6000
Louis Jannotta, *President*
David Wojcik, *Engineer*
Daniel Rankin, *Controller*
John Nagle, *Asst Controller*
Mike Pickett, *Accountant*
EMP: 100
SQ FT: 85,000
SALES (est): 26.4MM **Privately Held**
SIC: 3491 3829 Industrial valves; gauging instruments, thickness ultrasonic

(G-11346)
LENOVA INC (PA)
4580 Roosevelt Rd (60162-2053)
P.O. Box 4440, Lisle (60532-9440)
PHONE...................312 733-1098
Yu Guifang, *President*
▲ **EMP:** 5 **EST:** 2009
SALES (est): 1.4MM **Privately Held**
WEB: www.lenovasinks.com
SIC: 3431 Sinks: enameled iron, cast iron or pressed metal

(G-11347)
METRITRACK INC
4415 Harrison St Ste 243 (60162-1904)
P.O. Box 7115, Villa Park (60181-7115)
PHONE...................630 607-9311
Calin Caluser, *CEO*
Michael Cannizzaro,
Mario Donato,
EMP: 5
SQ FT: 1,750
SALES (est): 47K **Privately Held**
WEB: www.metritrack.com
SIC: 3845 Electromedical equipment

(G-11348)
MJT DESIGN AND PRTG ENTPS INC
Also Called: Suit Plus More
4219 Butterfield Rd 1a (60162-1171)
PHONE...................708 240-4323
Manasses Edwards, *President*
Takiyah Baines-Edwards, *Vice Pres*
Joyce Edwards, *Admin Sec*
EMP: 3 **EST:** 2012
SQ FT: 1,200
SALES (est): 193.7K **Privately Held**
SIC: 2759 5621 5632 5699 Advertising literature: printing; women's clothing stores; women's accessory & specialty stores; T-shirts, custom printed; personal shopping service

(G-11349)
MTH ENTERPRISES LLC
1 Mth Plz (60162-1436)
PHONE...................708 498-1100
Edwin Carey, *CFO*
Mike Swanberg,
EMP: 90
SALES (est): 14.6MM **Privately Held**
SIC: 3231 Products of purchased glass

(G-11350)
NFCA
4415 Harrison St Ste 540 (60162-1908)
PHONE...................708 236-3411
Nicholas Adams,
Shawn Hartt,
EMP: 1
SALES: 328.8K **Privately Held**
SIC: 2851 Paints & allied products

(G-11351)
ON TIME PRINTING AND FINISHING
4206 Warren Ave (60162-1727)
PHONE...................708 544-4500
Dave Clark, *President*
Chris Clark, *Admin Sec*
EMP: 5 **EST:** 1994
SQ FT: 5,200
SALES (est): 1MM **Privately Held**
WEB: www.ontimeprintinginc.com
SIC: 2752 2791 2789 Commercial printing, offset; typesetting; bookbinding & related work

(G-11352)
ORANGE CRUSH LLC (PA)
321 Center St (60162-1814)
PHONE...................708 544-9440
Sam Palumbo Jr, *CEO*
Chad Tira, *Superintendent*
Letta Hollingsworth, *Principal*
Don Deegan, *Vice Pres*
Linda Tiscareno, *Human Res Dir*
EMP: 200
SQ FT: 20,000
SALES (est): 104.2MM **Privately Held**
SIC: 2951 1795 Asphalt paving mixtures & blocks; concrete breaking for streets & highways

(G-11353)
POLY FILMS INC
4101 Washington Blvd (60162-1126)
PHONE...................708 547-7963
Randy Christie, *President*
Bob Christie, *Vice Pres*
Tom Christie, *Vice Pres*
William Christie, *Vice Pres*
EMP: 9
SQ FT: 19,000
SALES (est): 1.2MM **Privately Held**
SIC: 3081 Polyethylene film

(G-11354)
REPLOGLE GLOBES PARTNERS LLC
125 Fencl Ln (60162-2040)
PHONE...................708 593-3995
Edward Dieschbourg, *Principal*
EMP: 6
SALES (est): 94.8K **Privately Held**
WEB: www.replogleglobes.com
SIC: 3999 Globes, geographical

(G-11355)
RTS PACKAGING LLC
250 N Mannheim Rd (60162-1835)
PHONE...................708 338-2800
Ron Hartwig, *Branch Mgr*
EMP: 124
SQ FT: 30,000
SALES (corp-wide): 18.2B **Publicly Held**
SIC: 2679 2675 2631 Paper products, converted; die-cut paper & board; paperboard mills
HQ: Rts Packaging, Llc
504 Thrasher St
Norcross GA 30071
800 558-6984

(G-11356)
SHORELINE GLASS CO INC
Also Called: Midwest Glass Co
1 Mth Plz (60162-1436)
PHONE...................312 829-9500
Jerry M Schor, *President*
EMP: 50
SQ FT: 45,000
SALES (est): 3.6MM **Privately Held**
WEB: www.mthindustries.com
SIC: 1793 5039 5231 3442 Glass & glazing work; glass construction materials; glass; metal doors, sash & trim; products of purchased glass

Hinckley
Dekalb County

(G-11357)
CIRCLE SYSTEMS INC (PA)
479 W Lincoln Ave (60520-9209)
P.O. Box 1228 (60520-1228)
PHONE...................815 286-3271
R Marquiss Erlanson, *President*
Debra Shreve, *Vice Pres*
Harriet Cursio, *Treasurer*
R Steven Polachek, *Admin Sec*
EMP: 10
SQ FT: 20,000
SALES (est): 1.5MM **Privately Held**
WEB: www.circlesafe.com
SIC: 2819 2899 3829 Nonmetallic compounds; chemical preparations; measuring & controlling devices

(G-11358)
HINCKLEY CONCRETE PRODUCTS CO
540 W Lincoln Ave (60520-9205)
P.O. Box 1207 (60520-1207)
PHONE...................815 286-3235
Gerald C Nehring, *Owner*
EMP: 8 **EST:** 1946
SQ FT: 16,000

SALES (est): 996.4K **Privately Held**
WEB: www.hinckleyconcreteproductsil.com
SIC: 3272 Septic tanks, concrete; floor slabs & tiles, precast concrete

(G-11359)
STEP ONE STAIRWORKS INC
201 Somonauk Rd (60520-6254)
PHONE.................................815 286-7464
Gary Lambes Jr, *President*
Lisa Lambes, *CFO*
EMP: 12
SQ FT: 10,000
SALES: 2MM **Privately Held**
SIC: 2431 Staircases, stairs & railings

Hinsdale
Dupage County

(G-11360)
ACCURIDE CORPORATION
201 E Ogden Ave Ste 220 (60521-3661)
PHONE.................................630 568-3914
Dan McGivney, *Sales Staff*
EMP: 243
SALES (corp-wide): 685.5MM **Privately Held**
SIC: 3714 Wheels, motor vehicle
HQ: Accuride Corporation
7140 Office Cir
Evansville IN 47715
812 962-5000

(G-11361)
ARVAMONT
549 W 58th St (60521-5181)
PHONE.................................630 926-2468
Yannis Arvanitis, *Partner*
Newenka Dumont, *Partner*
Darcy Zoells, *Partner*
EMP: 3 EST: 2013
SALES (est): 187.6K **Privately Held**
SIC: 7372 2731 7389 Publishers' computer software; books: publishing only;

(G-11362)
ASHLEYS INC
Also Called: Ashley's Cutom Stationary
30 E 1st St (60521-4102)
PHONE.................................630 794-0804
Ashley Killpack, *President*
EMP: 5
SQ FT: 600
SALES: 500K **Privately Held**
SIC: 2621 5943 Stationery, envelope & tablet papers; stationery stores

(G-11363)
BEH IL CORP (PA)
15 Salt Creek Ln Ste 412 (60521-2965)
PHONE.................................630 616-1850
William Wilson, *President*
EMP: 3
SALES (est): 3.6MM **Privately Held**
SIC: 3312 Rods, iron & steel: made in steel mills

(G-11364)
BEH IL SUB LLC (HQ)
Also Called: Mri Steel
15 Salt Creek Ln Ste 412 (60521-2965)
PHONE.................................630 616-1850
William Wilson, *Mng Member*
Frank Eberwein,
Howard Pena,
EMP: 3
SALES (est): 716.8K **Privately Held**
SIC: 3448 Prefabricated metal buildings

(G-11365)
BELLA CASA
322 N Adams St (60521-3128)
PHONE.................................630 455-5900
Mary Cashman, *Owner*
EMP: 3
SALES (est): 270K **Privately Held**
SIC: 3999 5199 Fire extinguishers, portable; gifts & novelties

(G-11366)
BOSE CORPORATION
Also Called: Bose Showcase Store
65 Oakbrook Ctr (60523-1809)
PHONE.................................630 575-8044
Lee Phillips, *Branch Mgr*
EMP: 9
SALES (corp-wide): 2.1B **Privately Held**
SIC: 5731 3651 High fidelity stereo equipment; household audio equipment
PA: Bose Corporation
100 The Mountain Rd
Framingham MA 01701
508 879-7330

(G-11367)
BUYERSVINE INC
641 S Bodin St (60521-3916)
PHONE.................................630 235-6804
Louis Lamoureux, *President*
EMP: 1
SALES: 200K **Privately Held**
SIC: 7379 7372 7389 Computer related consulting services; application computer software;

(G-11368)
FINE GOLD MFG JEWELERS
777 N York Rd Ste 27 (60521-3562)
PHONE.................................630 323-9600
Jeff Rutt, *President*
Melissa Rutt, *Treasurer*
Julie Rutt, *Admin Sec*
EMP: 3
SALES (est): 600K **Privately Held**
SIC: 3911 7631 Jewel settings & mountings, precious metal; rings, finger: precious metal; necklaces, precious metal; watch, clock & jewelry repair

(G-11369)
LUXURIOUS LATHERS LTD
15 Spinning Wheel Rd (60521-2914)
PHONE.................................844 877-7627
EMP: 3
SQ FT: 1,900
SALES (est): 78K **Privately Held**
SIC: 5999 2844 Ret Misc Merchandise Mfg Toilet Preparations

(G-11370)
NEVERSTRIP LLC (PA)
111 S Hinsdale (60521)
PHONE.................................708 588-9707
David Beedie, *President*
David Klick, *Exec VP*
Robert Peterson, *Exec VP*
John Rothschild, *Exec VP*
EMP: 7
SQ FT: 30,000
SALES (est): 559K **Privately Held**
SIC: 2851 Epoxy coatings; polyurethane coatings; vinyl coatings, strippable

(G-11371)
NUCOR CORPORATION
201 E Ogden Ave Ste 216 (60521-3679)
PHONE.................................630 887-1400
Hank Krusec, *District Mgr*
Henry Krusec, *Manager*
EMP: 9
SALES (corp-wide): 22.5B **Publicly Held**
SIC: 3312 Blast furnaces & steel mills
PA: Nucor Corporation
1915 Rexford Rd Ste 400
Charlotte NC 28211
704 366-7000

(G-11372)
PETCO PETROLEUM CORPORATION (PA)
108 E Ogden Ave Ste 100 (60521-3874)
PHONE.................................630 654-1740
Jay D Bergman, *President*
Jay Harriman, *Admin Sec*
EMP: 7
SQ FT: 3,500
SALES (est): 82MM **Privately Held**
SIC: 1311 Crude petroleum production

(G-11373)
PICCOLINO INC
802 S Clay St (60521-4541)
PHONE.................................708 259-2072
Dana Fort, *President*

EMP: 3
SALES (est): 254.1K **Privately Held**
SIC: 2392 Pads & padding, table: except asbestos, felt or rattan

(G-11374)
PIONEER NEWSPAPERS INC
Also Called: Doings Newspaper
440 E Ogden Ave Ste 2 (60521-3691)
PHONE.................................630 887-0600
EMP: 40
SALES (corp-wide): 4.3MM **Privately Held**
SIC: 2711 Newspapers-Publishing/Printing
HQ: Pioneer Newspapers Inc.
350 N Orleans St Fl 10
Chicago IL 60654
847 486-0600

(G-11375)
PLAYGROUND POINTERS
109 S Quincy St (60521-3012)
PHONE.................................952 200-4168
Mistie Lucht, *Owner*
EMP: 4
SALES (est): 211.6K **Privately Held**
SIC: 7372 Application computer software

(G-11376)
S&J FOOD MANAGEMENT CORP
435 E 4th St (60521-4659)
PHONE.................................630 323-9296
John Scales, *Principal*
Mark Jennings, *CFO*
EMP: 4
SALES (est): 170K **Privately Held**
SIC: 2099 Food preparations

(G-11377)
SASS-N-CLASS INC
19 W 1st St Ste A (60521-4390)
PHONE.................................630 655-2420
Gretchen A Wasniewski, *President*
James T Wasniewski, *Admin Sec*
EMP: 5
SQ FT: 700
SALES (est): 532.3K **Privately Held**
WEB: www.sass-n-class.net
SIC: 2759 Invitations: printing; announcements: engraved

(G-11378)
SAVINO DISPLAYS INC
28 Bradford Ln (60523-2322)
PHONE.................................630 574-0777
Alfred Savino, *President*
EMP: 3 EST: 1946
SALES (est): 172.9K **Privately Held**
SIC: 3993 Signs, not made in custom sign painting shops

(G-11379)
SEVERSTAL US HOLDINGS II INC (HQ)
Also Called: Esmark
907 N Elm St Ste 100 (60521-3644)
PHONE.................................708 756-0400
James P Bouchard, *CEO*
Craig T Bouchard, *President*
Joel Mazur, *President*
David A Luptak, *Co-CEO*
Thomas A Modrowski, *Co-CEO*
◆ EMP: 34
SQ FT: 180,000
SALES (est): 200.7MM **Privately Held**
SIC: 3291 Abrasive metal & steel products

(G-11380)
STERLING BOOKS LIMITED
735 S Oak St (60521-4635)
PHONE.................................630 325-3853
Mary Sterling, *President*
David Sterling, *Vice Pres*
Thomas Sterling, *Vice Pres*
EMP: 3
SALES (est): 140K **Privately Held**
SIC: 2731 Book publishing

(G-11381)
TAG SALES CO INC
1000 Jorie Blvd Ste 26 (60523-3089)
PHONE.................................630 990-3434
Thomas E Rickleman, *President*
Tom Rickleman, *Vice Pres*
Patsy A Rickelman, *Treasurer*
Ken Clingen, *Admin Sec*

EMP: 4
SQ FT: 1,000
SALES (est): 503.3K **Privately Held**
SIC: 3545 Tools & accessories for machine tools; cutting tools for machine tools

(G-11382)
TRUDEAU APPROVED PRODUCTS INC
3 Grant Sq 332 (60521-3351)
PHONE.................................312 924-7230
Suneil Sant, *President*
EMP: 4
SALES (est): 363.9K **Privately Held**
SIC: 2834 Vitamin preparations

(G-11383)
XEROX CORPORATION
2301 W 22nd St Ste 300 (60523-1224)
PHONE.................................630 573-1000
Colleen Finlay, *Manager*
EMP: 35
SALES (corp-wide): 9B **Publicly Held**
SIC: 3861 3577 7629 7378 Photocopy machines; computer peripheral equipment; business machine repair, electric; computer maintenance & repair; office equipment
HQ: Xerox Corporation
201 Merritt 7
Norwalk CT 06851
800 835-6100

Hodgkins
Cook County

(G-11384)
ARRO CORPORATION
7250 Santa Fe Dr Ste 1 (60525-5075)
PHONE.................................708 352-8200
Patrick Gaughan, *Branch Mgr*
EMP: 117
SALES (corp-wide): 133.3MM **Privately Held**
SIC: 4225 2045 5141 General warehousing & storage; pancake mixes, prepared: from purchased flour; groceries, general line
PA: Arro Corporation
7440 Santa Fe Dr
Hodgkins IL 60525
708 352-8200

(G-11385)
ARRO CORPORATION
Also Called: Arro Liquid Division
7550 Santa Fe Dr (60525-5046)
PHONE.................................708 352-7412
Patrick Gaughan, *Branch Mgr*
EMP: 30
SALES (corp-wide): 133.3MM **Privately Held**
SIC: 2045 4225 5141 Pancake mixes, prepared: from purchased flour; general warehousing & storage; groceries, general line
PA: Arro Corporation
7440 Santa Fe Dr
Hodgkins IL 60525
708 352-8200

(G-11386)
CHICAGO CNC MACHINING CO
6880 River Rd Unit 2 (60525-3417)
PHONE.................................708 352-1255
Doug Miller, *President*
Paul Julius, *Vice Pres*
Ed Montalvo, *Admin Sec*
EMP: 5
SQ FT: 3,200
SALES: 500K **Privately Held**
SIC: 3599 Machine shop, jobbing & repair

(G-11387)
CUMMINS NPOWER LLC
Also Called: Cummins Diesel Sales
7145 Santa Fe Dr (60525-5181)
PHONE.................................708 579-9222
Michael Hoehn, *Branch Mgr*
EMP: 50
SALES (corp-wide): 23.7B **Publicly Held**
SIC: 5084 3519 Engines & parts, diesel; internal combustion engines

Hodgkins - Cook County (G-11388)

HQ: Cummins Npower Llc
1600 Buerkle Rd
White Bear Lake MN 55110
800 642-0085

(G-11388)
ETHOS SEAFOOD GROUP LLC
6800 Santa Fe Dr Ste L (60525-7645)
PHONE..................312 858-3474
EMP: 59
SALES (est): 68.6K
SALES (corp-wide): 238.6MM Privately Held
SIC: 2092 5146 Fresh or frozen packaged fish; fish & seafoods
PA: Santa Monica Seafood Company
18531 S Broadwick St
Rancho Dominguez CA 90220
310 886-7900

(G-11389)
GOSIA CARTAGE LTD
6400 River Rd (60525-4256)
PHONE..................312 613-8735
Margaret Malinin, President
EMP: 6
SALES (est): 667.7K Privately Held
SIC: 4212 3991 Moving services; street sweeping brooms, hand or machine

(G-11390)
JANIK CUSTOM MILLWORK INC
6017 Lenzi Ave Ste 1 (60525-4258)
PHONE..................708 482-4844
Stanley A Janik, President
Ed J Janik, Vice Pres
Pat Janik, Admin Sec
EMP: 5
SALES (est): 1.2MM Privately Held
SIC: 2431 2541 2434 Doors, wood; doors & door parts & trim, wood; windows & window parts & trim, wood; staircases, stairs & railings; wood partitions & fixtures; wood kitchen cabinets

(G-11391)
ODM TOOL & MFG CO INC
9550 Joliet Rd (60525-4148)
PHONE..................708 485-6130
Gary Kautz, Principal
Sandra Michaelsen, Corp Secy
Jay Michaelsen, Vice Pres
James Schwenn, Foreman/Supr
Chris Ericksen, Production
EMP: 75 EST: 1946
SQ FT: 153,000
SALES (est): 18.7MM Privately Held
WEB: www.odmtool.com
SIC: 3469 3544 Stamping metal for the trade; special dies, tools, jigs & fixtures

(G-11392)
OPW FUEL MGT SYSTEMS INC (DH)
6900 Santa Fe Dr (60525-7600)
PHONE..................708 352-9617
Steven Trabilsy, President
Scott Burkard, Treasurer
Teconish'e Hill, Supervisor
▲ EMP: 1
SQ FT: 55,000
SALES (est): 493.6K
SALES (corp-wide): 7.1B Publicly Held
SIC: 3824 Gasoline dispensing meters

(G-11393)
OPW FUELING COMPONENTS INC
Also Called: Opw Fueling Management Systems
6900 Santa Fe Dr (60525-7600)
PHONE..................708 485-4200
Elizabeth Ivancsits, Prdtn Mgr
EMP: 4
SALES (corp-wide): 7.1B Publicly Held
SIC: 2899 Fuel treating compounds
HQ: Opw Fueling Components Inc.
9393 Prnceton Glendale Rd
West Chester OH 45011

(G-11394)
RECONSERVE OF ILLINOIS INC
6160 River Rd (60525-4278)
PHONE..................708 354-4641
Meyer Luskin, CEO
Rida Hamed, Admin Sec
EMP: 23
SALES (est): 5.1MM
SALES (corp-wide): 203.7MM Privately Held
SIC: 2048 Prepared feeds
PA: Scope Industries
2811 Wilshire Blvd # 410
Santa Monica CA 90403
310 458-1574

(G-11395)
SCHULZE AND BURCH BISCUIT CO
9100 67th St (60525-7607)
PHONE..................708 354-7050
Fabian Guerra, Branch Mgr
EMP: 4
SALES (corp-wide): 111.6MM Privately Held
WEB: www.schulzeburch.com
SIC: 2051 Bread, cake & related products
PA: Schulze And Burch Biscuit Co.
1133 W 35th St
Chicago IL 60609
773 927-6622

(G-11396)
SEALED AIR CORPORATION
Packaging Products Div
7110 Santa Fe Dr (60525-5051)
PHONE..................708 352-8700
Maria Ortega, Purch Agent
Donna Bonder, Human Res Mgr
Lou Suffern, Sales Mgr
Rohn Shellenberger, Mktg Dir
Mike Hardy, Manager
EMP: 100
SALES (corp-wide): 4.7B Publicly Held
SIC: 3086 Packaging & shipping materials, foamed plastic
PA: Sealed Air Corporation
2415 Cascade Pointe Blvd
Charlotte NC 28208
980 221-3235

(G-11397)
SILBRICO CORPORATION
6300 River Rd (60525-5189)
PHONE..................708 354-3350
Steven B Garnett, President
Christopher Mendius, Vice Pres
Lawrence Mendius, Vice Pres
Mike Harland, Project Mgr
Frank Bunzell, Mfg Staff
◆ EMP: 89
SQ FT: 100,000
SALES (est): 24.6MM Privately Held
WEB: www.silbrico.com
SIC: 3296 Mineral wool

(G-11398)
TARA INTERNATIONAL LP
9100 67th St (60525-5183)
PHONE..................708 354-7050
Mark Meyer, General Mgr
Amy Jensen, Materials Mgr
David Hensler, Controller
Robert Karasek, Technical Staff
EMP: 100 EST: 1978
SQ FT: 110,000
SALES (est): 13.3MM Privately Held
SIC: 7389 2099 Packaging & labeling services; food preparations

(G-11399)
VEE PAK LLC (HQ)
Also Called: Voyant Beauty
6710 River Rd (60525-4310)
PHONE..................708 482-8881
Richard McEvoy, CEO
EMP: 100
SQ FT: 70,000
SALES: 250MM
SALES (corp-wide): 27.4MM Privately Held
SIC: 2844 4225 Cosmetic preparations; general warehousing
PA: Vpi Holding Company, Llc
676 N Michigan Ave
Chicago IL 60611
312 255-4800

(G-11400)
VOYANT BEAUTY LLC
6710 River Rd (60525-4310)
PHONE..................708 482-8881
Richard McEvoy, CEO
Bill Saracco, CFO
EMP: 6
SALES (est): 351.7K Privately Held
SIC: 2844 Toilet preparations

(G-11401)
WEI-CHUAN USA INC
6845 Santa Fe Dr (60525-7637)
PHONE..................708 352-8886
Eyao Sung, Manager
EMP: 13
SALES (corp-wide): 116.9MM Privately Held
WEB: www.weichuanusa.com
SIC: 5142 2038 Packaged frozen goods; dinners, frozen & packaged; ethnic foods, frozen
PA: Wei-Chuan U.S.A., Inc.
13031 Temple Ave
City Of Industry CA 91746
626 225-7168

Hoffman
Clinton County

(G-11402)
DON ANDERSON CO
101 S Hickory St (62250)
P.O. Box 227 (62250-0227)
PHONE..................618 495-2511
Donald L Anderson, President
Vicky Anderson, Corp Secy
Tom Anderson, Vice Pres
EMP: 5 EST: 1953
SQ FT: 2,000
SALES (est): 765.4K Privately Held
SIC: 1611 2952 2951 General contractor, highway & street construction; asphalt felts & coatings; asphalt paving mixtures & blocks

Hoffman Estates
Cook County

(G-11403)
AD IMAGES
1729 Pebble Beach Ct (60169-1159)
PHONE..................847 956-1887
Kenneth R Haycock, President
Donna Delinger, Admin Sec
EMP: 5
SALES: 300K Privately Held
SIC: 2759 7311 7389 Screen printing; advertising agencies; embroidering of advertising on shirts, etc.

(G-11404)
AMCOL HLTH BUTY SOLUTIONS INC (HQ)
2870 Forbs Ave (60192-3702)
PHONE..................847 851-1300
Gary Castagna, President
James W Ashley Jr, Admin Sec
◆ EMP: 15
SALES (est): 20.1MM Publicly Held
SIC: 2821 Polymethyl methacrylate resins (plexiglass)

(G-11405)
AMCOL INTERNATIONAL CORP (HQ)
2870 Forbs Ave (60192-3702)
PHONE..................847 851-1500
Ryan F McKendrick, President
Gary L Castagna, Senior VP
Jason St Onge, Research
Donald W Pearson, CFO
◆ EMP: 49 EST: 1959
SALES (est): 1.1B Publicly Held
WEB: www.amcol.com
SIC: 1459 5032 4213 4731 Bentonite mining; fuller's earth mining; clay construction materials, except refractory; trucking, except local; truck transportation brokers

(G-11406)
AMERICAN COLLOID COMPANY (DH)
Also Called: Amcol
2870 Forbs Ave (60192-3702)
P.O. Box 95411 (60195-0411)
PHONE..................847 851-1700
Gary Morrison, President
Jim Papp, Vice Pres
Jason St Onge, Research
Joel Penzick, Director
◆ EMP: 25
SQ FT: 7,300
SALES (est): 751.7MM Publicly Held
SIC: 1459 2899 Bentonite mining; chemical preparations
HQ: Amcol International Corp
2870 Forbs Ave
Hoffman Estates IL 60192
847 851-1500

(G-11407)
BEVERLY MATERIALS LLC
1100 Brandt Dr (60192-1676)
PHONE..................847 695-9300
David R Plote,
Daniel R Plote,
Raymond E Plote,
EMP: 3
SALES (est): 440.3K Privately Held
SIC: 1442 Construction sand & gravel

(G-11408)
BI SOFTWARE INC
808 Linden Cir (60169-3261)
PHONE..................224 622-4706
Dariusz Danielewski, President
EMP: 3
SALES: 500K Privately Held
WEB: www.bisoftware.com
SIC: 7372 Prepackaged software

(G-11409)
BIG KSER PRECISION TOOLING INC
2600 Huntington Blvd (60192-1574)
PHONE..................847 228-7660
Chris Kaiser, CEO
John Burley, Vice Pres
EMP: 33
SQ FT: 13,000
SALES (est): 7.7MM Privately Held
SIC: 3545 Cutting tools for machine tools
HQ: Big Daishowa K.K.
3-3-39, Nishiishikiricho
Higashi-Osaka OSK 579-8

(G-11410)
BYSTRONIC INC (DH)
2200 W Central Rd (60192)
PHONE..................847 214-0300
Robert St Aubin, President
Ulrich Troesch, Chairman
Peter Kyc, Vice Pres
Matthew Meade, Engineer
Christian Zuercher, Treasurer
◆ EMP: 110
SQ FT: 48,300
SALES (est): 39.3MM
SALES (corp-wide): 200.2MM Privately Held
SIC: 3559 3541 3699 Glass making machinery: blowing, molding, forming, etc.; machine tools, metal cutting type; laser welding, drilling & cutting equipment
HQ: Bystronic Maschinen Ag
Industriestrasse 5
BUtzberg BE 4922
629 587-777

(G-11411)
BYSTRONIC MFG AMERICAS LLC
2200 W Central Rd (60192)
PHONE..................847 214-0300
Robert St Aubin, President
EMP: 9
SALES (est): 116.6K
SALES (corp-wide): 200.2MM Privately Held
SIC: 3559 Glass making machinery: blowing, molding, forming, etc.

GEOGRAPHIC SECTION

Hoffman Estates - Cook County (G-11440)

HQ: Bystronic Inc.
2200 W Central Rd
Hoffman Estates IL 60192
847 214-0300

(G-11412)
CDK GLOBAL INC (PA)
1950 Hassell Rd (60169-6308)
PHONE.................847 397-1700
Brian Krzanich, *President*
Neil Packham, *President*
Leslie A Brun, *Principal*
Rajiv K Amar, *Exec VP*
Lee J Brunz, *Exec VP*
EMP: 700
SQ FT: 155,000
SALES: 1.9B **Publicly Held**
SIC: 7372 Business oriented computer software

(G-11413)
CHICAGO BOTTLING INDUSTRIES
2075 Stonington Ave (60169-2014)
PHONE.................847 885-8093
EMP: 4
SALES (est): 75.4K **Privately Held**
SIC: 2086 Bottled & canned soft drinks

(G-11414)
CLOVER TECHNOLOGIES GROUP LLC (DH)
Also Called: Ces
2700 W Higgins Rd Ste 100 (60169-2006)
PHONE.................866 734-6548
George Milton, *CEO*
Ron Skowronski, *COO*
Brent Sallee, *CFO*
Arnold Coku, *IT/INT Sup*
◆ **EMP:** 1200
SALES (est): 1.9B
SALES (corp-wide): 1.2B **Privately Held**
SIC: 3861 Printing equipment, photographic
HQ: 4l Technologies Inc.
122 W Madison St
Ottawa IL 61350
815 431-8100

(G-11415)
COLLOID ENVMTL TECH CO LLC (DH)
Also Called: Cetco
2870 Forbs Ave (60192-3702)
PHONE.................847 851-1500
Ryan F McKendrick, *President*
Meredith Koons, *Marketing Staff*
◆ **EMP:** 109
SQ FT: 72,000
SALES (est): 376MM **Publicly Held**
SIC: 3259 2899 Liner brick or plates for sewer/tank lining, vitrified clay; concrete curing & hardening compounds
HQ: Amcol International Corp
2870 Forbs Ave
Hoffman Estates IL 60192
847 851-1500

(G-11416)
CONVERGENT BILL ETE ORT T
2000 W Att Center Dr Rm 4 (60192-5005)
PHONE.................847 387-4059
EMP: 3
SALES (est): 210.4K **Privately Held**
SIC: 3674 Mfg Semiconductors/Related Devices

(G-11417)
DDN INDUSTRIES INC
2155 Stnngton Ave Ste 221 (60169)
PHONE.................847 885-8595
Dian Naugle, *President*
David Naugle, *Vice Pres*
EMP: 6
SQ FT: 1,350
SALES (est): 1.4MM **Privately Held**
SIC: 2653 Boxes, corrugated: made from purchased materials

(G-11418)
DMG CHARLOTTE LLC (DH)
2400 Huntington Blvd (60192-1564)
PHONE.................704 583-1193
▲ **EMP:** 14
SQ FT: 21,000
SALES (est): 3.6MM **Privately Held**
SIC: 3541 Machine tools, metal cutting type
HQ: Dmg America Inc.
2400 Huntington Blvd
Hoffman Estates IL 60192
630 227-3900

(G-11419)
DMG MORI USA INC (HQ)
Also Called: Dmg Mori Seiki U.S.a
2400 Huntington Blvd (60192-1564)
PHONE.................847 593-5400
Thorsten Schmidt, *President*
Mark H Mohr, *Principal*
JD Donald, *Area Mgr*
Randall S Harland, *Exec VP*
Marlow Knabach, *Exec VP*
▲ **EMP:** 100
SQ FT: 102,000
SALES (est): 332.1MM **Privately Held**
SIC: 3541 3545 Machine tools, metal cutting type; machine tool accessories

(G-11420)
ELITE RF LLC
2155 Stnngton Ave Ste 217 (60169)
PHONE.................847 592-6350
Timothy Avicola, *Principal*
▼ **EMP:** 20
SQ FT: 10,000
SALES: 5MM **Privately Held**
WEB: www.eliterfllc.com
SIC: 3663 Radio & TV communications equipment

(G-11421)
EXCLUSIVE PUBLICATIONS INC
3830 Bordeaux Dr (60192-1616)
PHONE.................847 963-0400
Christian M Jacobs, *Manager*
EMP: 3 **EST:** 2010
SALES (est): 145.5K **Privately Held**
SIC: 2741 Miscellaneous publishing

(G-11422)
FACT NA LLC
Also Called: Rototime
2125 Bonita Ln (60192-4629)
PHONE.................847 421-1125
Jacob Ninan, *Manager*
EMP: 7
SALES (est): 889.1K **Privately Held**
SIC: 3566 Gears, power transmission, except automotive

(G-11423)
FANUC AMERICA CORPORATION
1800 Lakewood Blvd (60192-5008)
PHONE.................847 898-5000
Joe Cvengros, *General Mgr*
Keith Gerhardt, *District Mgr*
Sean Murphy, *District Mgr*
Ryan Patterson, *District Mgr*
Kristine Belardinelli, *Project Mgr*
EMP: 34 **Privately Held**
SIC: 3559 3548 3569 Metal finishing equipment for plating, etc.; electric welding equipment; robots, assembly line: industrial & commercial
HQ: Fanuc America Corporation
3900 W Hamlin Rd
Rochester Hills MI 48309
248 377-7000

(G-11424)
FMS USA INC
2155 Stnngton Ave Ste 119 (60169)
PHONE.................847 519-4400
Joerg Inhelder, *President*
Steven Leibold, *Vice Pres*
EMP: 3
SQ FT: 1,500
SALES (est): 512.4K **Privately Held**
SIC: 3823 Flow instruments, industrial process type

(G-11425)
FORTUNE INTERNATIONAL TECH LLC
5883 Chatham Dr (60192-4637)
PHONE.................847 429-9791
Ronald Oberstar, *Mng Member*
Mary Beth Oberstar,
▲ **EMP:** 2

SALES (est): 332.1K **Privately Held**
SIC: 2816 5198 Inorganic pigments; colors & pigments

(G-11426)
FUTTERS NUT BUTTERS
2400 Hassell Rd Ste 300 (60169-2041)
P.O. Box 5677, Villa Park (60181-5307)
PHONE.................847 540-0565
Jody Futterman, *Principal*
EMP: 5
SALES (est): 515.7K **Privately Held**
SIC: 2099 Food preparations

(G-11427)
GANNETT STLLITE INFO NTWRK LLC
Also Called: Gannett Health Care Group
1721 Moon Lake Blvd # 540 (60169-1069)
PHONE.................847 839-1700
Eric Kalter, *CFO*
EMP: 70
SALES (corp-wide): 1.8B **Publicly Held**
SIC: 2711 Newspapers
HQ: Gannett Satellite Information Network, Llc
7950 Jones Branch Dr
Mc Lean VA 22102
703 854-6000

(G-11428)
GENERAL ELECTRIC COMPANY
2501 Barrington Rd (60192-2061)
PHONE.................847 304-7400
John Ruf, *Branch Mgr*
EMP: 400
SALES (corp-wide): 95.2B **Publicly Held**
SIC: 3845 Electromedical apparatus
PA: General Electric Company
5 Necco St
Boston MA 02210
617 443-3000

(G-11429)
INKJET INC
4225 Winston Dr (60192-1746)
PHONE.................800 280-3245
Pat Ventrello, *Manager*
EMP: 5
SALES (est): 676.5K **Privately Held**
SIC: 2844 Cosmetic preparations
PA: Inkjet, Inc.
11111 Inkjet Way
Willis TX 77378

(G-11430)
INNOLUX TECHNOLOGY USA INC (HQ)
2300 Barrington Rd # 400 (60169-2082)
PHONE.................847 490-5315
Jyh-Chau Wang, *President*
Brant White, *Vice Pres*
EMP: 1
SALES (est): 1.3MM **Privately Held**
SIC: 3679 Liquid crystal displays (LCD)

(G-11431)
INTEGRITY PRTG MCHY SVCS LLC
1650 Glen Lake Rd (60169-4025)
PHONE.................847 834-9484
Thomas Dieden, *Principal*
EMP: 3 **EST:** 2011
SALES (est): 352K **Privately Held**
SIC: 2752 Commercial printing, lithographic

(G-11432)
JEWEL OSCO INC
Also Called: Jewel - Osco 3316
1071 N Roselle Rd (60169-4929)
PHONE.................847 882-6477
Laura Simmons, *Sales Executive*
Charl Pecoraro, *Branch Mgr*
EMP: 149
SALES (corp-wide): 60.5B **Privately Held**
WEB: www.jewelosco.mywebgrocer.com
SIC: 5912 5122 2833 Drug stores; pharmaceuticals; medicinals & botanicals
HQ: Jewel Osco, Inc.
150 E Pierce Rd Ste 200
Itasca IL 60143
630 948-6000

(G-11433)
KEN YOUNG CONSTRUCTION CO
Also Called: K D R Productions
1185 Ash Rd (60169-4449)
PHONE.................847 358-3026
Ken Young, *Owner*
Ellen Chung, *Manager*
EMP: 2
SALES (est): 500K **Privately Held**
SIC: 1751 7389 3993 Carpentry work; recording studio, noncommercial records; advertising novelties

(G-11434)
METAMATION INC (PA)
1900 W Central Rd (60192-1900)
PHONE.................775 826-1717
Kartik Vaidyanathan, *President*
Anupam Chakraborty, *Vice Pres*
EMP: 10
SALES (est): 1.5MM **Privately Held**
SIC: 7372 Business oriented computer software

(G-11435)
MINERALS TECHNOLOGIES INC
2870 Forbs Ave (60192-3702)
PHONE.................847 851-1500
Jodi Lindsay, *General Mgr*
EMP: 12 **Publicly Held**
SIC: 3295 Minerals, ground or treated
PA: Minerals Technologies Inc.
622 3rd Ave Rm 3800
New York NY 10017

(G-11436)
MINUTE MAN PRESS
Also Called: Minuteman Press
1037 W Golf Rd (60169-1339)
PHONE.................847 839-9600
Steven Horton, *Principal*
EMP: 4
SALES (est): 260K **Privately Held**
WEB: www.he.minutemanpress.com
SIC: 2752 Commercial printing, lithographic

(G-11437)
MOISTURE DETECTION INC
2200 Stonington Ave (60169-2031)
PHONE.................847 426-0464
Richard Ward PHD, *President*
EMP: 6
SQ FT: 3,500
SALES: 300K **Privately Held**
SIC: 3826 Moisture analyzers

(G-11438)
NANOCOR LLC (DH)
2870 Forbs Ave (60192-3702)
PHONE.................847 851-1900
Gary Castagna, *CEO*
Peter Maul, *President*
Tie Lan, *Director*
James Ashley, *Admin Sec*
▼ **EMP:** 20
SQ FT: 72,000
SALES (est): 2.8MM **Publicly Held**
SIC: 2821 Plastics materials & resins
HQ: Amcol International Corp
2870 Forbs Ave
Hoffman Estates IL 60192
847 851-1500

(G-11439)
NILAN/PRIMARC TOOL & MOLD INC
Also Called: Nilan/Primarc Tool & Mold
2125 Stonington Ave (60169-2016)
PHONE.................847 885-2300
Wesley Pietrasik, *CEO*
Diane Pietrasik, *Business Mgr*
Gerald Calvacca, *Opers Staff*
EMP: 19
SALES (est): 1.2MM **Privately Held**
SIC: 3061 Mechanical rubber goods

(G-11440)
NSK-AMERICA CORPORATION
1800 Global Pkwy (60192-1578)
PHONE.................847 843-7664
Eiichi Nakanishi, *President*
Hirohiko Murasi, *Exec VP*
Mike Gabris, *Sales Mgr*

Hoffman Estates - Cook County (G-11441)

Diane Kulak, *Admin Mgr*
William Quirindongo, *Technical Staff*
▲ **EMP:** 15
SQ FT: 5,500
SALES (est): 4.2MM **Privately Held**
SIC: 3569 Filters

(G-11441)
NXP USA INC
2800 W Higgins Rd Ste 600 (60169-7247)
PHONE.................847 843-6824
Daniel Herdmann, *Manager*
EMP: 366
SALES (corp-wide): 8.8B **Privately Held**
SIC: 3674 Semiconductors & related devices
HQ: Nxp Usa, Inc.
6501 W William Cannon Dr
Austin TX 78735
512 933-8214

(G-11442)
OMRON ELECTRONICS LLC (HQ)
Also Called: O E I
2895 Grnspint Pkwy Ste 20 (60169)
PHONE.................847 843-7900
Nigel Blakeway, *CEO*
Michael Joy, *Regl Sales Mgr*
Adeel Baig, *Sales Engr*
Erica Martin, *Marketing Staff*
Michelle Bridges, *Supervisor*
EMP: 77
SQ FT: 53,000
SALES (est): 92MM **Privately Held**
SIC: 5065 3699 Electronic parts; electrical equipment & supplies

(G-11443)
PLATT G MOSTARDI
Also Called: Mostardi Platt
5595 Trillium Blvd (60192-3405)
PHONE.................630 993-2100
Robert Platt, *Owner*
EMP: 10
SALES (est): 895.9K **Privately Held**
SIC: 1389 Testing, measuring, surveying & analysis services

(G-11444)
PLOTE CONSTRUCTION INC
Also Called: Beverly Materials
1100 Brandt Dr (60192-1676)
PHONE.................847 695-0422
Daniel R Plote, *President*
EMP: 50
SALES (corp-wide): 19.9MM **Privately Held**
WEB: www.plote.com
SIC: 1442 1611 Gravel mining; highway & street paving contractor
PA: Plote Construction Inc.
1100 Brandt Dr
Hoffman Estates IL 60192
847 695-9300

(G-11445)
PLOTE CONSTRUCTION INC (PA)
Also Called: Allied Asphalt Paving Company
1100 Brandt Dr (60192-1676)
PHONE.................847 695-9300
Daniel R Plote, *President*
Karen Busch, *President*
John Lichty, *President*
Jake Nollin, *Superintendent*
Ty Ziller, *Superintendent*
EMP: 85
SALES (est): 19.9MM **Privately Held**
SIC: 2951 1531 1442 6552 Asphalt paving mixtures & blocks; speculative builder, single-family houses; speculative builder, multi-family dwellings; construction sand mining; gravel mining; subdividers & developers; highway & street paving contractor; excavation & grading, building construction

(G-11446)
PLOTE INC
1100 Brandt Dr (60192-1676)
PHONE.................847 695-9467
Raymond E Plote, *President*
Jay Kissack, *Superintendent*
Billy Wagner, *Superintendent*
Janice Plote, *Corp Secy*
Daniel R Plote, *Vice Pres*
EMP: 85 **EST:** 1957
SALES (est): 12.9MM **Privately Held**
WEB: www.plote.com
SIC: 1794 2952 2951 1442 Excavation & grading, building construction; asphalt felts & coatings; asphalt paving mixtures & blocks; construction sand & gravel

(G-11447)
PLUM GROVE PRINTERS INC
2160 Stonington Ave (60169-7204)
PHONE.................847 882-4020
Peter Lineal, *CEO*
Adam Haines, *Vice Pres*
Tracy Sadowski, *Manager*
EMP: 27 **EST:** 1980
SQ FT: 9,500
SALES (est): 6.8MM **Privately Held**
WEB: www.plumgroveinc.com
SIC: 2752 Commercial printing, offset

(G-11448)
PO FOOD SPECIALISTS LTD
1800 Huntington Blvd # 610 (60169-6743)
PHONE.................847 517-8315
EMP: 6
SALES (est): 290K **Privately Held**
SIC: 2099 Food Mfg/Product Development

(G-11449)
R & P FUELS
798 Barrington Rd (60169-1107)
PHONE.................630 855-2358
EMP: 3
SALES (est): 158K **Privately Held**
SIC: 2869 Fuels

(G-11450)
RESINS INC
2200 W Higgins Rd Ste 204 (60169-2400)
PHONE.................847 884-0025
Mark Cohen, *President*
EMP: 2
SALES (est): 378.1K **Privately Held**
SIC: 5162 3089 Resins; plastics resins; resins, synthetic; molding primary plastic

(G-11451)
ROYAL BEDDING COMPANY INC (PA)
Also Called: Serta Mattress Co
2600 Forbs Ave (60192-3723)
PHONE.................847 645-0200
Alva Moog Jr, *President*
EMP: 80
SQ FT: 75,000
SALES (est): 6.5MM **Privately Held**
SIC: 2515 Mattresses, innerspring or box spring; box springs, assembled

(G-11452)
S HIMMELSTEIN AND COMPANY
2490 Pembroke Ave (60169-2077)
P.O. Box 1134, Barrington (60011-1134)
PHONE.................847 843-3300
S Himmelstein, *President*
Geraldine Shamoon, *Purch Mgr*
Angela Woltman, *Accounting Mgr*
Steven Tveter, *Sales Mgr*
Allen Jacks, *Manager*
EMP: 48 **EST:** 1960
SQ FT: 40,000
SALES (est): 11.5MM **Privately Held**
WEB: www.himmelstein.com
SIC: 3825 Measuring instruments & meters, electric; test equipment for electronic & electrical circuits

(G-11453)
S VS INDUSTRIES INC
646 Wainsford Dr (60169-4544)
P.O. Box 681532, Schaumburg (60168-1532)
PHONE.................630 408-1083
Bob Vonschaumburg, *President*
Robert Vonschaumburg, *Principal*
Deborah Vonschaumburg, *Vice Pres*
EMP: 2
SALES: 1MM **Privately Held**
SIC: 3545 5199 7389 Machine tool attachments & accessories; packaging materials;

(G-11454)
SADELCO USA CORP
1120 Warwick Cir N (60169-2330)
PHONE.................847 781-8844
Piet Zandbergen, *President*
EMP: 2
SALES (est): 4.5MM **Privately Held**
SIC: 2843 Leather finishing agents

(G-11455)
SCV FLOORSMITH
720 Durham Ln (60169-4800)
PHONE.................661 476-5034
Nick Patel, *Owner*
EMP: 4
SALES (est): 150K **Privately Held**
WEB: www.santaclaritacaflooring.com
SIC: 2426 Hardwood dimension & flooring mills

(G-11456)
SENSIENT FLAVORS
5115 Sedge Blvd (60192-3708)
PHONE.................847 645-7002
Patrick Pingul, *Manager*
EMP: 140 **EST:** 2014
SALES (est): 26.9MM **Privately Held**
SIC: 2087 Flavoring extracts & syrups

(G-11457)
SENSIENT FLAVORS LLC (HQ)
2800 W Higgins Rd Ste 900 (60169-7288)
PHONE.................317 243-3521
Ralph Pickles, *President*
Amy M Agallar, *Vice Pres*
Steve Jacobs, *Production*
Richard Swetits, *Purchasing*
Michael Janik, *Accounts Mgr*
◆ **EMP:** 320
SQ FT: 200,000
SALES (est): 379.4MM
SALES (corp-wide): 1.3B **Publicly Held**
WEB: www.sensient.com
SIC: 2087 Extracts, flavoring
PA: Sensient Technologies Corporation
777 E Wisconsin Ave # 1100
Milwaukee WI 53202
414 271-6755

(G-11458)
SIEMENS MED SOLUTIONS USA INC
Also Called: Hoffman Nuclear Medicine Group
2501 Barrington Rd (60192-2061)
PHONE.................847 304-7700
Jodi Kaelin, *Partner*
Ron Brons, *Mfg Mgr*
Donald Bak, *Engineer*
Daniel Kizior, *Engineer*
Baul Kasulis, *Manager*
EMP: 60
SALES (corp-wide): 96.9B **Privately Held**
SIC: 3829 3845 Medical diagnostic systems, nuclear; electromedical equipment
HQ: Siemens Medical Solutions Usa, Inc.
40 Liberty Blvd
Malvern PA 19355
888 826-9702

(G-11459)
SILESIA FLAVORS INC
5250 Prairie Stone Pkwy (60192-3709)
PHONE.................847 645-0270
Fax: 847 645-0266
Clemons Hanke, *President*
Philip Roman, *Purchasing*
Casey Violand, *Accounts Mgr*
Frederic Schulders, *Sales Staff*
Margrit Zbrug, *Sales Staff*
▲ **EMP:** 25
SQ FT: 26,000
SALES (est): 6.3MM
SALES (corp-wide): 113.6MM **Privately Held**
WEB: www.silesiafl.com
SIC: 2087 Extracts, flavoring
PA: Silesia Gerhard Hanke Gmbh & Co. Kg
Am Alten Bach 20-24
Neuss 41470
213 778-40

(G-11460)
SOLIDYNE CORPORATION
2155 Stonington Ave # 105 (60169-2039)
PHONE.................847 394-3333
Baha Erturk, *CEO*
EMP: 4 **EST:** 1980
SALES (est): 343.4K **Privately Held**
SIC: 3822 Auto controls regulating residntl & coml environmt & applncs

(G-11461)
SOLUTIONS MANUFACTURING INC
2109 Stonington Ave (60169-2016)
PHONE.................847 310-4506
Michael Sosine, *President*
Tim Lucey, *Exec VP*
Jeff Lebelle, *Vice Pres*
Jeff Labelle, *VP Mfg*
EMP: 20
SQ FT: 5,000
SALES (est): 3.7MM **Privately Held**
WEB: www.solutionsmfg.net
SIC: 3599 Machine shop, jobbing & repair

(G-11462)
STAR SU FELLOWS CUTTER LLC
5200 Prairie Stone Pkwy (60192-3709)
PHONE.................847 649-1450
Jeffrey L Lawton,
David W Goodfellow,
EMP: 70
SALES (est): 186.6K
SALES (corp-wide): 224.7MM **Privately Held**
SIC: 3541 3545 3479 Drilling machine tools (metal cutting); cutting tools for machine tools; hobs; reamers, machine tool; drilling machine attachments & accessories; painting, coating & hot dipping
PA: Star Cutter Co.
23461 Industrial Park Dr
Farmington Hills MI 48335
248 474-8200

(G-11463)
STEVEN PLASTICS INC
2125 Stonington Ave (60169-2016)
PHONE.................847 885-2300
Wesley A Pietrasik, *President*
Diane Pietrasik, *Principal*
Donna Flemming, *Admin Sec*
EMP: 20 **EST:** 1976
SQ FT: 33,000
SALES (est): 2MM **Privately Held**
SIC: 3089 Injection molding of plastics

(G-11464)
STRICTLY STAINLESS INC
2108 Stonington Ave (60169-2017)
PHONE.................847 885-2890
Todd Hopp, *President*
EMP: 3
SALES (est): 600K **Privately Held**
SIC: 3312 7389 Stainless steel; artists' agents & brokers

(G-11465)
SUNGLASS OTFTTERS BY SNGLASS H
5225 Prairie Stone Pkwy (60192-3709)
PHONE.................847 645-0476
EMP: 3
SALES (est): 63.2K **Privately Held**
SIC: 5699 2389 Miscellaneous apparel & accessories; apparel & accessories

(G-11466)
TANGENT SYSTEMS INC
2155 Stnngton Ave Ste 107 (60169)
PHONE.................847 882-3833
Steve Mack, *President*
Joe Kabbes, *Prgrmr*
EMP: 16
SQ FT: 10,246
SALES (est): 1.7MM **Privately Held**
SIC: 7371 3577 Computer software development; magnetic ink & optical scanning devices; bar code (magnetic ink) printers; magnetic ink recognition devices; optical scanning devices

(G-11467)
TATE LYLE INGRDNTS AMRICAS LLC
5450 Prairie Stone Pkwy (60192-3403)
PHONE.................847 396-7500
John Schnake, *Branch Mgr*

EMP: 16
SALES (corp-wide): 3.5B **Privately Held**
WEB: www.tateandlyle.com
SIC: 2046 Corn & other vegetable starches
HQ: Tate & Lyle Ingredients Americas Llc
2200 E Eldorado St
Decatur IL 62521
217 423-4411

(G-11468)
TEGNA INC
Also Called: Oncourse Learning
1721 Moon Lake Blvd # 540 (60169-1069)
PHONE..........................847 490-6657
Cynthia Vlasich, *Branch Mgr*
EMP: 120
SALES (corp-wide): 2.3B **Publicly Held**
SIC: 2711 2721 Commercial printing & newspaper publishing combined; periodicals
PA: Tegna Inc.
8350 Broad St Ste 2000
Tysons VA 22102
703 873-6600

(G-11469)
THOMAS ENGINEERING INC (PA)
Also Called: Triangle Metals Div
575 W Central Rd (60192-1999)
PHONE..........................847 358-5800
Brian T Casey, *Ch of Bd*
Jean Y Lefloc'h, *Vice Pres*
Jennifer Sullivan, *Buyer*
Wes Mancoff, *Engineer*
Tim Rainer, *Engineer*
◆ **EMP:** 100 **EST:** 1959
SQ FT: 72,000
SALES: 17.2MM **Privately Held**
WEB: www.thomaseng.com
SIC: 3559 5084 Pharmaceutical machinery; industrial machinery & equipment

(G-11470)
UNIVERSAL HOLDINGS INC
2800 W Higgins Rd Ste 210 (60169-7284)
PHONE..........................224 353-6198
Dean Raschke, *President*
John Read, *Admin Sec*
EMP: 18
SALES (est): 3.9MM **Privately Held**
WEB: www.ucardsolutions.com
SIC: 5084 3845 5199 Plastic products machinery; electrocardiographs; cards, plastic: unprinted

(G-11471)
WELLNESS CENTER USA INC (PA)
2500 W Higgins Rd Ste 770 (60169-2047)
PHONE..........................847 925-1885
Andrew J Kandalepas, *Ch of Bd*
Ricky Howard, *President*
Paul D Jones, *President*
Jay Joshi, *Chief Mktg Ofcr*
Thomas E Scott, *Admin Sec*
EMP: 11
SALES: 33.3K **Publicly Held**
SIC: 8099 3829 2834 Nutrition services; medical services organization; measuring & controlling devices; pharmaceutical preparations

Hoffman Estates
Lake County

(G-11472)
CSI2D INC
4907 Turnberry Dr (60010-5678)
PHONE..........................312 282-7407
Steven Kroll, *CEO*
EMP: 4
SALES (est): 180K **Privately Held**
SIC: 3674 Semiconductors & related devices

(G-11473)
NORTHWEST MARBLE PRODUCTS INC
1229 Silver Pine Dr (60010-5877)
PHONE..........................630 860-2288
Keith Madelung, *President*
Maureen Madelung, *Corp Secy*

EMP: 30
SQ FT: 25,000
SALES (est): 2.1MM **Privately Held**
SIC: 3088 2541 2434 Bathroom fixtures, plastic; sinks, plastic; tubs (bath, shower & laundry), plastic; shower stalls, fiberglass & plastic; wood partitions & fixtures; wood kitchen cabinets

Homer
Champaign County

(G-11474)
ALLENS FARM QUALITY MEATS
Rr 49 (61849)
P.O. Box 24 (61849-0024)
PHONE..........................217 896-2532
Ronald D Allen, *President*
EMP: 5 **EST:** 1964
SQ FT: 11,700
SALES (est): 413.2K **Privately Held**
WEB: www.allensfarmqualitymeats.com
SIC: 5421 5147 2013 2011 Meat markets, including freezer provisioners; meats, fresh; sausages & other prepared meats; meat packing plants

(G-11475)
ALLERTON SUPPLY COMPANY
1050 N &Amp 2600 E (61849)
PHONE..........................217 896-2522
Fred Page, *Branch Mgr*
EMP: 12
SALES (corp-wide): 17.1MM **Privately Held**
SIC: 2875 5261 Fertilizers, mixing only; fertilizer
PA: Allerton Supply Company
309 E Yates
Allerton IL 61810
217 834-3301

(G-11476)
HOMER VINTAGE BAKERY
111 S Main St (61849-1232)
PHONE..........................217 896-2538
Crystal Allen, *Principal*
EMP: 5
SQ FT: 2,000
SALES (est): 139.9K **Privately Held**
SIC: 2051 5812 5499 Cakes, bakery: except frozen; pies, bakery: except frozen; fast-food restaurant, independent; soft drinks

Homer Glen
Will County

(G-11477)
ARTHUR R BAKER INC
13507 W Oakwood Ct (60491-8157)
PHONE..........................708 301-4828
Fax: 708 596-8230
EMP: 7
SQ FT: 3,600
SALES (est): 642.8K **Privately Held**
SIC: 5999 2752 Ret Misc Merchandise Lithographic Commercial Printing

(G-11478)
DRAPERY ROOM INC
15757 Annico Dr Ste 5 (60491-4738)
PHONE..........................708 301-3374
Lorraine Simard, *President*
EMP: 10 **EST:** 1979
SQ FT: 2,000
SALES (est): 800K **Privately Held**
SIC: 2211 2391 Draperies & drapery fabrics, cotton; curtains & draperies

(G-11479)
FLOORING WAREHOUSE DIRECT INC
14126 Camdan Rd (60491-8259)
PHONE..........................815 730-6767
EMP: 5 **EST:** 2010
SALES: 1.5MM **Privately Held**
SIC: 2426 Hardwood Dimension/Floor Mill

(G-11480)
FORKLIFT FIRM LLC
12139 White Pine Trl (60491-8350)
PHONE..........................708 770-7207
Joe Bippus, *Principal*
Kevin Overlin, *Mng Member*
Jameson Scheier, *Mng Member*
▼ **EMP:** 4
SALES (est): 176.5K **Privately Held**
SIC: 3537 Trucks, tractors, loaders, carriers & similar equipment

(G-11481)
FOURIER SYSTEMS INC
12610 W Hank Ct E (60491)
PHONE..........................708 478-5333
Tamar Antokol, *Principal*
EMP: 5 **EST:** 2011
SALES (est): 440.2K **Privately Held**
SIC: 5045 3571 Computers, peripherals & software; electronic computers

(G-11482)
GLITTER YOUR PALLET
14350 S Saddle Brook Ln (60491-8567)
PHONE..........................708 516-8494
Lisa Schultz, *Principal*
EMP: 3
SALES (est): 125.7K **Privately Held**
SIC: 2448 Pallets, wood & wood with metal

(G-11483)
LEAS BAKING COMPANY LLC
14660 Pebble Creek Ct (60491-9355)
PHONE..........................708 710-3404
Robert Trebe, *Principal*
EMP: 4
SALES (est): 208.2K **Privately Held**
WEB: www.leasbakingcompany.com
SIC: 2051 Bread, cake & related products

(G-11484)
NAMA GRAPHICS E LLC
15751 Annico Dr Ste 2 (60491-4739)
PHONE..........................262 966-3853
Rick Smith, *Principal*
John Griffin, *Principal*
EMP: 3
SALES (est): 276.3K **Privately Held**
SIC: 3555 Printing trades machinery

(G-11485)
OMNICARE GROUP INC
13557 Parkland Ct (60491-7577)
PHONE..........................708 949-8802
Abdullah H Darwish, *President*
EMP: 3
SQ FT: 1,800
SALES (est): 634.1K **Privately Held**
SIC: 3841 Surgical & medical instruments

(G-11486)
SIMPLY SALSA LLC (PA)
12630 W 159th St (60491-7855)
PHONE..........................815 514-3993
Deless Jennifer, *Mng Member*
EMP: 7 **EST:** 2015
SALES (est): 508.8K **Privately Held**
SIC: 2033 2035 Tomato sauce: packaged in cans, jars, etc.; seasonings, vegetable sauces (except tomato & dry)

Homewood
Cook County

(G-11487)
AB&D CUSTOM FURNITURE INC
Also Called: AB & D Custom Cabinets
17200 Palmer Blvd (60430-4601)
PHONE..........................708 922-9061
Randall Agate, *President*
Mike Koczor, *Mfg Staff*
Patrick Stone, *Treasurer*
Marie Agate, *Office Mgr*
EMP: 25
SQ FT: 40,000
SALES (est): 4.4MM **Privately Held**
SIC: 2541 2521 2511 Store & office display cases & fixtures; cabinets, lockers & shelving; wood office furniture; wood household furniture

(G-11488)
BOLZONI AURAMO INC (DH)
17635 Hoffman Way (60430-2186)
PHONE..........................708 957-8809
Roberto Scotti, *President*
Brian Cummings, *Buyer*
Dustin Decker, *Sales Staff*
Joost Fissette, *Sales Staff*
Michael Warner, *Manager*
▲ **EMP:** 48
SQ FT: 40,000
SALES (est): 25.3MM
SALES (corp-wide): 12.5MM **Privately Held**
SIC: 5084 3537 Lift trucks & parts; lift trucks, industrial: fork, platform, straddle, etc.
HQ: Bolzoni Spa
Via I Maggio 103
Podenzano PC 29027
052 355-5511

(G-11489)
CARL BUDDIG AND COMPANY (PA)
950 175th St (60430-2027)
PHONE..........................708 798-0900
Robert Budding, *President*
David Streeter, *General Mgr*
Thomas Buddig, *Co-CEO*
Mitch Aronson, *Regional Mgr*
Lynn Strauss, *Regional Mgr*
EMP: 50
SQ FT: 15,000
SALES (est): 195.4MM **Privately Held**
WEB: www.buddig.com
SIC: 2013 2022 Smoked meats from purchased meat; sausages from purchased meat; natural cheese

(G-11490)
CCL CONSTRUCTION INC (PA)
18161 Morris Ave Ste 204 (60430-2141)
PHONE..........................219 237-2911
Jolaine N Pellar, *President*
Joe Cotten, *Vice Pres*
Tom Hayes, *Associate*
▲ **EMP:** 4
SQ FT: 1,000
SALES (est): 708.8K **Privately Held**
WEB: www.cclconstruction.com
SIC: 3446 1761 Louvers, ventilating; roofing, siding & sheet metal work

(G-11491)
DUNIGAN CUSTOM WOODWORKING
1426 Ridge Rd (60430-1827)
PHONE..........................708 351-5213
Dustin Dunigan, *Principal*
EMP: 4
SALES (est): 387.8K **Privately Held**
WEB: www.dunigancustoms.com
SIC: 2431 Millwork

(G-11492)
DZRO-BANS INTERNATIONAL INC
3011 183rd St (60430-2804)
PHONE..........................779 324-2740
Emmanuel Bansa, *CEO*
Connie Bansa, *President*
Melishia Bansa, *Director*
EMP: 4
SQ FT: 800
SALES (est): 463.3K **Privately Held**
SIC: 5136 2844 5141 5137 Men's & boys' clothing; face creams or lotions; groceries, general line; women's & children's clothing; commercial art & graphic design

(G-11493)
ENTRIGUE DESIGNS
825 Maple Ave (60430-2031)
PHONE..........................708 647-6159
Carrol Jones, *Principal*
EMP: 3
SALES (est): 168.5K **Privately Held**
SIC: 3089 5932 Plastic hardware & building products; clothing & shoes, secondhand

Homewood - Cook County (G-11494) — GEOGRAPHIC SECTION

(G-11494)
FREE-FLOW PACKAGING INTL INC
Also Called: FP International
905 175th St Fl 3 (60430-2076)
PHONE..................................708 589-6500
Tom Anzur, *Plant Mgr*
Gabriel Macias, *Purchasing*
Scott Morrell, *Manager*
EMP: 75 **Privately Held**
SIC: 3086 Packaging & shipping materials, foamed plastic; insulation or cushioning material, foamed plastic
HQ: Free-Flow Packaging International, Inc.
1650 Lake Cook Rd Ste 400
Deerfield IL 60015
650 261-5300

(G-11495)
GILLONS INC
17341 Palmer Blvd (60430-4605)
PHONE..................................773 531-8900
Naveed Anwar, *President*
Haroon Sarwar, *President*
EMP: 21
SALES (est): 1.5MM **Privately Held**
SIC: 7389 3999 ; barber & beauty shop equipment

(G-11496)
HI TECH
1551 187th St (60430-3849)
PHONE..................................708 957-4210
EMP: 1 **EST:** 2009
SALES: 950K **Privately Held**
SIC: 3661 2517 Mfg Telephone/Telegraph Apparatus

(G-11497)
HOMEWOOD-FLOSSMOOR CHRONICLE
1361 Olive Rd (60430-2409)
PHONE..................................630 728-2661
Marilyn Thomas, *Principal*
Eric Crump, *Manager*
Michael Schlesinger,
EMP: 4 **EST:** 2015
SALES (est): 210.1K **Privately Held**
SIC: 2721 Magazines: publishing only, not printed on site

(G-11498)
INK SPOTS PRTG & MEIDA DESIGN
Also Called: Isp
1131 175th St Ste B (60430-4604)
PHONE..................................708 754-1300
William Tucker, *Owner*
EMP: 4
SQ FT: 1,600
SALES: 265K **Privately Held**
WEB: www.inkspotsonline.com
SIC: 2732 2759 2752 2721 Book printing; laser printing; commercial printing, lithographic; magazines: publishing & printing

(G-11499)
INX GROUP LTD
1000 Maple Rd (60430-2047)
PHONE..................................708 799-1993
James Kochanny, *Manager*
EMP: 8 **Privately Held**
WEB: www.inxinternational.com
SIC: 2893 Printing ink
HQ: The Inx Group Ltd
150 N Martingale Rd # 700
Schaumburg IL 60173
630 382-1800

(G-11500)
INX INTERNATIONAL INK CO
1000 Maple Rd (60430-2047)
PHONE..................................708 799-1993
Ed Hill, *Manager*
EMP: 16 **Privately Held**
WEB: www.inxinternational.com
SIC: 2893 Printing ink
HQ: Inx International Ink Co.
150 N Martingale Rd # 700
Schaumburg IL 60173
630 382-1800

(G-11501)
MITCHLLS CNDIES ICE CREAMS INC
18211 Dixie Hwy (60430-2205)
PHONE..................................708 799-3835
George E Mitchell, *President*
Mary Kay Mitchell, *Treasurer*
EMP: 14
SQ FT: 4,000
SALES (est): 640K **Privately Held**
SIC: 5441 5812 2024 5143 Candy; ice cream stands or dairy bars; ice cream & frozen desserts; ice cream & ices

(G-11502)
ROSS-GAGE INC
2346 Alexander Ter (60430-3102)
PHONE..................................708 347-3659
Thomas W Ross, *Branch Mgr*
EMP: 22
SALES (corp-wide): 12.6MM **Privately Held**
WEB: www.rossgage.com
SIC: 2675 Die-cut paper & board
PA: Ross-Gage Inc
4011 W 54th St
Indianapolis IN 46254
317 283-2323

(G-11503)
URPOINT LLC
1739 187th St (60430-3853)
PHONE..................................773 919-9002
Margaret Fitzpatrick, *Owner*
James McLaughlin, *Owner*
EMP: 4
SALES (est): 260.9K **Privately Held**
SIC: 3089 5092 7389 Holders: paper towel, grocery bag, etc.: plastic; toy novelties & amusements;

(G-11504)
WALTER LAGESTEE INC
Also Called: Walts Food Center
2345 183rd St Ste 2 (60430-3141)
PHONE..................................708 957-2974
Chuck Volanti, *General Mgr*
Jerry Scaffguard, *Manager*
EMP: 200
SQ FT: 4,800
SALES (est): 6.9MM
SALES (corp-wide): 71.8MM **Privately Held**
WEB: www.waltsfoods.com
SIC: 5411 5921 5992 5912 Grocery stores, independent; beer (packaged); florists; drug stores & proprietary stores; cookies & crackers; bread, cake & related products
PA: Walter Lagestee, Inc.
16145 State St
South Holland IL 60473
708 596-3166

Hoopeston
Vermilion County

(G-11505)
CLINE CONCRETE PRODUCTS
438 W Thompson Ave (60942-1067)
PHONE..................................217 283-5012
Gerald L Cline, *President*
Mae Dell Cline, *Vice Pres*
EMP: 10 **EST:** 1950
SQ FT: 10,000
SALES (est): 1.2MM **Privately Held**
SIC: 3272 3523 3281 Septic tanks, concrete; monuments, concrete; tile, precast terrazzo or concrete; farm machinery & equipment; cut stone & stone products

(G-11506)
CRAFTSMEN PRINTING
217 Bank St (60942-1510)
PHONE..................................217 283-9574
Daniel W De Neal, *Owner*
EMP: 3
SALES: 100K **Privately Held**
SIC: 2752 2791 2789 2759 Commercial printing, offset; typesetting; bookbinding & related work; commercial printing

(G-11507)
DAVES ELECTRONIC SERVICE
105 E Penn St (60942-1501)
PHONE..................................217 283-5010
David Coffman, *President*
EMP: 15
SALES (est): 870.2K **Privately Held**
SIC: 7699 3931 3672 Organ tuning & repair; organ parts & materials; printed circuit boards

(G-11508)
EZEE ROLL MANUFACTURING CO
20 N 3000 East Rd (60942-1473)
P.O. Box 47 (60942-0047)
PHONE..................................217 339-2279
Lucille Layden, *President*
Paul Layden, *Vice Pres*
Mark Layden, *Treasurer*
▲ **EMP:** 6
SQ FT: 700
SALES (est): 1.2MM **Privately Held**
SIC: 3537 3714 3548 3444 Trucks, tractors, loaders, carriers & similar equipment; motor vehicle parts & accessories; welding apparatus; sheet metalwork

(G-11509)
FELSTE CO INC
217 N 9th Ave (60942-1016)
PHONE..................................217 283-4884
Eugene Felstehausen, *President*
Kevin Moore, *President*
EMP: 5
SALES: 270K **Privately Held**
SIC: 3556 Food products machinery

(G-11510)
L S DIESEL REPAIR INC
220 N 10th Ave (60942-1024)
PHONE..................................217 283-5537
Layton Seggebruch, *President*
Kim Seggebruch, *Corp Secy*
EMP: 3
SALES (est): 410K **Privately Held**
SIC: 3519 Diesel engine rebuilding

(G-11511)
PERFORMANCE DIESEL SERVICE
7586 E 4200 North Rd (60942-6299)
PHONE..................................217 375-4429
Robert Marshall, *President*
EMP: 3
SALES (est): 463.2K **Privately Held**
SIC: 3519 Diesel, semi-diesel or duel-fuel engines, including marine

(G-11512)
SILGAN CONTAINERS MFG CORP
324 W Main St (60942-1130)
PHONE..................................217 283-5501
Colin Bertsch, *Branch Mgr*
EMP: 110 **Publicly Held**
WEB: www.silgancontainers.com
SIC: 3411 Can lids & ends, metal
HQ: Silgan Containers Manufacturing Corporation
21600 Oxnard St Ste 1600
Woodland Hills CA 91367

(G-11513)
SILVER BROS INC
105 E Washington St (60942-1698)
PHONE..................................217 283-7751
David Silver, *President*
Brian Silver, *Vice Pres*
Deanna Silver, *Admin Sec*
EMP: 6
SQ FT: 10,000
SALES (est): 1.1MM **Privately Held**
WEB: www.silverbrosinc.com
SIC: 1541 3273 Industrial buildings, new construction; warehouse construction; ready-mixed concrete

(G-11514)
TEASDALE FOODS INC
Also Called: Hoopeston Foods
215 W Washington St (60942-1145)
P.O. Box 405 (60942-0405)
PHONE..................................217 283-7771
Ted Goodner, *Branch Mgr*
EMP: 82
SALES (corp-wide): 285.9MM **Privately Held**
WEB: www.teasdalefoods.com
SIC: 2099 Food preparations
PA: Teasdale Foods, Inc.
901 Packers St
Atwater CA 95301
209 358-5616

(G-11515)
TIMES REPUBLIC
Also Called: The Chronicle
308 E Main St (60942-1505)
PHONE..................................217 283-5111
Kevin Armold, *Manager*
EMP: 4 **Privately Held**
SIC: 2711 Newspapers, publishing & printing
HQ: The Times Republic
1492 E Walnut St
Watseka IL 60970
815 432-5227

Hopedale
Tazewell County

(G-11516)
CARROLL DISTRG & CNSTR SUP INC
201 Ford Ave (61747-9492)
PHONE..................................309 449-6044
Dan Reed, *Branch Mgr*
EMP: 4
SALES (corp-wide): 128.2MM **Privately Held**
SIC: 5082 3444 Contractors' materials; concrete forms, sheet metal
PA: Carroll Distributing & Construction Supply, Inc.
207 W 2nd St Ste 3
Ottumwa IA 52501
641 683-1888

(G-11517)
J & J EQUIPMENT INC
260 4th Ave (61747)
P.O. Box 211 (61747-0211)
PHONE..................................309 449-5442
Joe Slager, *President*
Alice Slager, *Vice Pres*
EMP: 4
SQ FT: 4,000
SALES: 330K **Privately Held**
SIC: 3523 Farm machinery & equipment

Hudson
Mclean County

(G-11518)
HAMILTON MAURER INTL INC
Also Called: H M I
14431 E 2400 North Rd (61748-9307)
PHONE..................................713 468-6805
Rolf Maurer, *President*
EMP: 5
SALES: 500K **Privately Held**
SIC: 3829 Physical property testing equipment

(G-11519)
STARLIGHT SOFTWARE SYSTEM INC
25130 Arrowhead Ln (61748-7400)
P.O. Box 37, Normal (61761-0037)
PHONE..................................309 454-7349
Lee Green, *President*
EMP: 1
SALES: 500K **Privately Held**
SIC: 7372 Prepackaged software

(G-11520)
SUN AG INC
108 N Shiner St (61748-9393)
P.O. Box 195 (61748-0195)
PHONE..................................309 726-1331
Zach Bennis, *Facilities Mgr*
Eric Wahls, *Sales Staff*
John Layden, *Branch Mgr*
EMP: 5

GEOGRAPHIC SECTION

SQ FT: 1,200
SALES (corp-wide): 29.1MM Privately Held
SIC: 2873 2874 5261 Nitrogenous fertilizers; phosphatic fertilizers; fertilizer
PA: Sun Ag, Inc.
2702 County Road 800 N
El Paso IL 61738
309 527-6500

(G-11521)
WHITACRES COUNTRY OAKS SHOP
Also Called: Whitacres Handcrafted
704 S Broadway St (61748-9162)
PHONE..................309 726-1305
Rick Whitacre, Owner
Bob Brady, Co-Owner
Ed Brady, Co-Owner
William Brady, Co-Owner
Mike O'Grady, Co-Owner
EMP: 17
SQ FT: 40,000
SALES (est): 1MM Privately Held
SIC: 5712 2511 Furniture stores; desks, household: wood

Humboldt
Coles County

(G-11522)
BOBBIE HAYCRAFT
Also Called: Bidwells Candies
110 Homann Ct (61931-9735)
PHONE..................217 856-2194
Bobbie Haycraft, Owner
EMP: 3
SALES (est): 141.7K Privately Held
SIC: 2064 Candy & other confectionery products

(G-11523)
HEARTLAND NEWS
3240 E County Road 1550n (61931-8006)
PHONE..................217 856-2332
EMP: 3 EST: 2016
SALES (est): 69.2K Privately Held
SIC: 2711 Newspapers, publishing & printing

(G-11524)
NORTH OKAW WOODWORKING
2409 E County Road 1700n (61931-8009)
PHONE..................217 856-2178
Clarence Stutzman, Owner
EMP: 5
SALES (est): 245.6K Privately Held
SIC: 3931 Woodwind instruments & parts

(G-11525)
WILLIAMS WELDING SERVICE
14772 Cooks Mills Rd (61931-7972)
PHONE..................217 235-1758
Barry Williams, Owner
EMP: 5
SALES (est): 170K Privately Held
SIC: 7692 Welding repair

Hume
Edgar County

(G-11526)
ARCHER-DANIELS-MIDLAND COMPANY
Also Called: ADM
10 Center St (61932)
P.O. Box 135 (61932-0135)
PHONE..................217 887-2514
Mike Shultz, Manager
EMP: 3
SALES (corp-wide): 64.6B Publicly Held
SIC: 2041 5153 Flour & other grain mill products; grains
PA: Archer-Daniels-Midland Company
77 W Wacker Dr Ste 4600
Chicago IL 60601
312 634-8100

Huntley
Mchenry County

(G-11527)
ALUMAPRO INC
1 Union Special Plz (60142-7007)
PHONE..................224 569-3650
Ken Meyer, President
▲ EMP: 9
SALES (est): 1.2MM Privately Held
SIC: 3651 Speaker systems

(G-11528)
AQUARIUS METAL PRODUCTS INC (PA)
12795 Muir Dr (60142-7799)
PHONE..................847 659-9266
Allen J Treml, President
Judy Treml, Admin Sec
EMP: 13
SQ FT: 26,000
SALES (est): 1.8MM Privately Held
SIC: 3444 Sheet metalwork

(G-11529)
BG DIE MOLD INC
11520 Smith Dr (60142-9600)
PHONE..................847 961-5861
EMP: 7
SALES (est): 610K Privately Held
SIC: 3544 Mfg Special Dies/Tools/Jigs/Fixtures

(G-11530)
CELL PARTS MANUFACTURING CO
10675 Wolf Dr (60142-7032)
PHONE..................847 669-9690
Valerie Dorr, President
EMP: 5
SALES (est): 275.1K Privately Held
SIC: 3089 Injection molding of plastics

(G-11531)
CENTURY AUTOMATICS LLC
11962 Oak Creek Pkwy (60142-6728)
PHONE..................847 515-1188
EMP: 6
SALES (est): 879.5K Privately Held
SIC: 3451 Screw machine products

(G-11532)
CROWN POLYMERS CORPORATION
11111 Kiley Dr (60142-6940)
PHONE..................847 659-0300
Vinicio Tresin, President
EMP: 15
SALES (corp-wide): 25.4MM Privately Held
SIC: 2822 Ethylene-propylene rubbers, EPDM polymers
HQ: Crown Polymers Corporation
8550 W Desert Inn Rd # 1
Las Vegas NV 89117
847 659-0300

(G-11533)
DATA ACCESSORIES INC
40w735 Powers Rd (60142-8043)
PHONE..................847 669-3640
Bruce Rose, President
Bobbie Rose, Admin Sec
EMP: 4
SALES (est): 340K Privately Held
SIC: 1731 5063 3678 Computer installation; switches, except electronic; electronic connectors

(G-11534)
DEAN DAIRY FLUID LLC
11710 Mill St (60142-7356)
PHONE..................847 669-5508
EMP: 4
SALES (corp-wide): 15.8B Privately Held
SIC: 2026 Fluid milk
HQ: Dfa Dairy Brands Fluid, Llc
1405 N 98th St
Kansas City KS 66111
816 801-6455

(G-11535)
DOGA USA CORPORATION
12060 Raymond Ct (60142-8069)
P.O. Box 95 (60142-0095)
PHONE..................847 669-8529
Antonio Garcia, President
Manel Roure, Vice Pres
Marcel Molins, Admin Sec
◆ EMP: 15
SQ FT: 19,000
SALES (est): 9.2MM Privately Held
SIC: 3714 Motor vehicle parts & accessories

(G-11536)
EXTRUDE HONE LLC
Thermoburr Illinois
10663 Wolf Dr (60142-7032)
PHONE..................847 669-5355
Bryan Wallis, Principal
EMP: 25
SALES (corp-wide): 201.2MM Privately Held
SIC: 3541 Milling machines
HQ: Extrude Hone Llc
235 Industry Blvd
Irwin PA 15642
724 863-5900

(G-11537)
GLENRAVEN INC
40w260 Apache Ln (60142-8000)
PHONE..................847 515-1321
Alan Eant, CEO
John Von Wachenfeldt, Principal
EMP: 3
SALES (est): 154K Privately Held
SIC: 2299 Textile goods

(G-11538)
H S CROCKER COMPANY INC (PA)
12100 Smith Dr (60142-9618)
PHONE..................847 669-3600
Ronald J Giordano, President
John C Dai, Vice Pres
John Dai, Vice Pres
William Linehan, Vice Pres
John Narish, Prdtn Mgr
▲ EMP: 81 EST: 1856
SQ FT: 65,000
SALES (est): 21.2MM Privately Held
WEB: www.hscrocker.com
SIC: 2671 2672 Packaging paper & plastics film, coated & laminated; adhesive papers, labels or tapes: from purchased material

(G-11539)
HENDERSON PRODUCTS INC
11921 Smith Dr (60142-9604)
PHONE..................847 515-3482
EMP: 4 Publicly Held
SIC: 3537 Industrial trucks & tractors
HQ: Henderson Products, Inc.
1085 S 3rd St
Manchester IA 52057
563 927-2828

(G-11540)
HUNTING NETWORK LLC
Also Called: Bowhunting.com
11964 Oak Creek Pkwy (60142-6728)
PHONE..................847 659-8200
Todd Graf, President
EMP: 8
SQ FT: 5,600
SALES (est): 612.4K Privately Held
SIC: 2741

(G-11541)
IDEAL SUPPLY INC (PA)
11400 Kreutzer Rd (60142-8094)
P.O. Box 1102 (60142-1102)
PHONE..................847 961-5900
Elizabeth Oakes, President
Marc Lodi, General Mgr
Peggy McCune, Manager
▲ EMP: 8
SQ FT: 5,000
SALES (est): 1.5MM Privately Held
SIC: 3965 Fasteners

(G-11542)
IN-PLACE MACHINING CO INC
11414 Smith Dr Unit D (60142-9635)
PHONE..................847 669-3006
EMP: 8
SALES (corp-wide): 20.3MM Privately Held
SIC: 3599 Mfg Industrial Machinery
PA: In-Place Machining Co., Inc.
3811 N Holton St
Milwaukee WI 53212
414 562-2000

(G-11543)
INGLESE BOX CO LTD
13851 Prime Point Rd (60142-8015)
PHONE..................847 669-1700
Len Inglese, President
Calogero Inglese, Corp Secy
EMP: 28
SQ FT: 140,000
SALES (est): 6.6MM Privately Held
WEB: www.inglesebox.com
SIC: 2653 5113 Boxes, corrugated: made from purchased materials; corrugated & solid fiber boxes

(G-11544)
INTERNATIONAL WATER WERKS INC
11470 Kreutzer Rd (60142-8094)
PHONE..................847 669-1902
William Tobin, President
Nancy Tobin, Vice Pres
EMP: 6
SQ FT: 10,000
SALES (est): 1.6MM Privately Held
SIC: 5074 3589 Water purification equipment; water treatment equipment, industrial

(G-11545)
JGR COMMERCIAL SOLUTIONS INC
11414 Smith Dr Unit G (60142-9635)
PHONE..................847 669-7010
Ron Ludwig, President
Scott Dombrowski, Sales Staff
EMP: 7
SQ FT: 6,000
SALES (est): 1MM Privately Held
WEB: www.jgrinc.net
SIC: 3272 Door frames, concrete

(G-11546)
JIM JOLLY SALES INC
11225 Giordano Ct (60142-6805)
PHONE..................847 669-7570
James E Jolly, Owner
Celeste M Jolly, Admin Sec
EMP: 2
SALES (est): 639.2K Privately Held
SIC: 5074 3991 Plumbing fittings & supplies; brushes, except paint & varnish

(G-11547)
JOHNSON TOOL COMPANY
11528 Smith Dr 3 (60142-9600)
PHONE..................708 453-8600
Arvid I Johnson, President
James Carlson, Vice Pres
EMP: 4 EST: 1945
SQ FT: 10,000
SALES (est): 330K Privately Held
WEB: www.johnsontoolco.com
SIC: 3469 3496 3495 3493 Stamping metal for the trade; miscellaneous fabricated wire products; wire springs; steel springs, except wire

(G-11548)
KOHLER CO
11449 Morning Glory Ln (60142-7674)
PHONE..................847 734-1777
Reg G Garratt, Branch Mgr
Jim Meyer, Director
EMP: 90
SALES (corp-wide): 8.3B Privately Held
SIC: 3432 3431 3261 Plumbing fixture fittings & trim; metal sanitary ware; vitreous plumbing fixtures
PA: Kohler Co.
444 Highland Dr
Kohler WI 53044
920 457-4441

Huntley - Mchenry County (G-11549)

(G-11549)
KUNDE WOODWORK INC
11901 Smith Dr (60142)
PHONE..................847 669-2030
Tony Kunde, *President*
EMP: 4
SALES (est): 644.6K **Privately Held**
SIC: 2441 Cases, wood

(G-11550)
LDI INDUSTRIES INC
12901 Jim Dhamer Dr (60142-8053)
PHONE..................847 669-7510
Mark Lukas, *Branch Mgr*
Thomas Weatherhead, *Maintence Staff*
EMP: 70
SALES (corp-wide): 29.4MM **Privately Held**
SIC: 3569 Lubrication equipment, industrial
PA: Ldi Industries, Inc.
1864 Nagle Ave
Manitowoc WI 54220
920 682-6877

(G-11551)
LIFE SPINE INC
13951 Quality Dr (60142-8099)
PHONE..................847 884-6117
Michael S Butler, *CEO*
Jason Bazemore, *Vice Pres*
Keith Clements, *Vice Pres*
Jennifer Jesse, *Opers Staff*
Nicholas Tielke, *Purchasing*
EMP: 70
SALES (est): 16.3MM **Privately Held**
SIC: 3841 Medical instruments & equipment, blood & bone work

(G-11552)
LIONHEART CRITICAL POW
13151 Executive Ct (60142-8096)
PHONE..................847 291-1413
Ken Lenhart, *President*
Monty Hagberg, *Marketing Staff*
Donald Ritter, *Admin Sec*
EMP: 45
SQ FT: 9,500
SALES (est): 10.5MM **Privately Held**
SIC: 3621 5063 7629 Power generators; generators; generator repair

(G-11553)
MAASS - MIDWEST MFG INC (PA)
Also Called: Maass Midwest
11283 Dundee Rd (60142-9247)
P.O. Box 547 (60142-0547)
PHONE..................847 669-5135
John Surinak, *President*
Donna Surinak, *Treasurer*
▲ EMP: 49
SQ FT: 55,000
SALES (est): 17.2MM **Privately Held**
WEB: www.maassmidwest.com
SIC: 3533 Water well drilling equipment

(G-11554)
MALL GRAPHIC INC
Also Called: Mall Publishing
12693 Cold Springs Dr (60142-7427)
PHONE..................847 668-7600
Ernest Mall, *President*
EMP: 12
SQ FT: 9,000
SALES: 1.1MM **Privately Held**
SIC: 2752 2789 Commercial printing, offset; bookbinding & related work

(G-11555)
MC METALS & FABRICATING INC
10683 Wolf Dr (60142-7032)
PHONE..................847 961-5242
EMP: 4
SALES (est): 336.1K **Privately Held**
SIC: 3499 Mfg Misc Fabricated Metal Products

(G-11556)
NORTH AMERICAN PRESS INC
12203 Spring Creek Dr (60142-7727)
PHONE..................847 515-3882
Herman H Pump, *Principal*
EMP: 4
SALES (est): 271.9K **Privately Held**
SIC: 2741 Miscellaneous publishing

(G-11557)
PARADIGM COATINGS LLC
11259 Kiley Dr (60142-6940)
PHONE..................847 961-6466
Jim Riley,
EMP: 4
SALES (est): 275K **Privately Held**
SIC: 3479 3471 Coating of metals & formed products; sand blasting of metal parts

(G-11558)
PARTING LINE TOOL INC
11915 Smith Ct (60142-7300)
PHONE..................847 669-0331
Mike Hookom, *President*
EMP: 16
SQ FT: 6,400
SALES: 3MM **Privately Held**
SIC: 3089 3544 Injection molded finished plastic products; special dies, tools, jigs & fixtures

(G-11559)
PHOENIX UNLIMITED LTD
11514 Smith Dr Unit D (60142-9633)
P.O. Box 503 (60142-0503)
PHONE..................847 515-1263
Jonathan Treubig, *President*
Jill Holgerson, *Admin Sec*
EMP: 6
SQ FT: 5,500
SALES (est): 350K **Privately Held**
SIC: 3085 7389 Plastics bottles; packaging & labeling services

(G-11560)
PRELLA TECHNOLOGIES INC
11408 Kiley Dr (60142-6988)
PHONE..................630 400-0626
EMP: 4
SALES (est): 335.8K **Privately Held**
SIC: 3531 Construction machinery

(G-11561)
QUALITY CONVERTING INC
10611 Wolf Dr (60142-7032)
P.O. Box 99, Woodstock (60098-0099)
PHONE..................847 669-9094
Guy Spinelli, *Principal*
EMP: 5
SALES (est): 734.2K **Privately Held**
SIC: 3554 Paper industries machinery

(G-11562)
R M ARMSTRONG & SON INC
11006 Bakley St (60142-7125)
P.O. Box 56 (60142-0056)
PHONE..................847 669-3988
Leon E Tripp, *President*
EMP: 4 EST: 1941
SQ FT: 4,500
SALES (est): 500K **Privately Held**
SIC: 3599 Machine shop, jobbing & repair

(G-11563)
REVOLUTION BRANDS LLC
12327 Bartelt Ct (60142-6062)
PHONE..................847 902-3320
Ian Abbott,
Glenn Backus,
EMP: 3 EST: 2014
SALES: 400K **Privately Held**
SIC: 2099 7389 Food preparations;

(G-11564)
ROHRER CORPORATION
Also Called: Gateway Printing
13701 George Bush Ct (60142-0018)
P.O. Box 248 (60142-0248)
PHONE..................847 961-5920
Mark Skradski, *Superintendent*
Jennifer Graser, *Cust Mgr*
George Colletti, *Branch Mgr*
Dennis McCaffrey, *Info Tech Mgr*
Mark Daniels, *IT/INT Sup*
EMP: 80
SALES (corp-wide): 142.2MM **Privately Held**
SIC: 3089 2675 Blister or bubble formed packaging, plastic; die-cut paper & board
PA: Rohrer Corporation
717 Seville Rd
Wadsworth OH 44281
330 335-1541

(G-11565)
RONCIN CUSTOM DESIGN
11514 Smith Dr Unit B (60142-9633)
PHONE..................847 669-0260
Ronald Ludwig, *President*
Cynthia Ludwig, *Admin Sec*
EMP: 5
SQ FT: 4,500
SALES (est): 750K **Privately Held**
SIC: 2434 2511 2541 2517 Wood kitchen cabinets; wood household furniture; wood partitions & fixtures; wood television & radio cabinets

(G-11566)
SERVICE PRINTING CORPORATION
11960 Oak Creek Pkwy (60142-6728)
PHONE..................847 669-9620
Henry T Goers, *President*
Kevin Goers, *Vice Pres*
EMP: 7
SQ FT: 7,700
SALES (est): 1MM **Privately Held**
SIC: 2752 2789 Commercial printing, offset; bookbinding & related work

(G-11567)
TAMPOTECH DECORATING INC
10901 Union Special Plz (60142-7020)
PHONE..................847 515-2968
Karin Kleist, *President*
Egon Kleist, *Treasurer*
EMP: 8
SQ FT: 15,000
SALES (est): 3.1MM **Privately Held**
SIC: 5084 3569 Printing trades machinery, equipment & supplies; robots, assembly line; industrial & commercial

(G-11568)
THERMFORM ENGINEERED QULTY LLC (HQ)
Also Called: T E Q
11320 Main St (60142-7396)
P.O. Box 68 (60142-0068)
PHONE..................847 669-5291
Robert C Tiede, *President*
Delia Beltran, *Assistant*
▼ EMP: 65
SQ FT: 90,000
SALES: 16.6MM
SALES (corp-wide): 5.3B **Publicly Held**
SIC: 3089 Plastic kitchenware, tableware & houseware
PA: Sonoco Products Company
1 N 2nd St
Hartsville SC 29550
843 383-7000

(G-11569)
TRAXCO INC
11416 Kiley Dr (60142-7136)
PHONE..................847 669-1545
Rose Marie Traxler, *President*
Lisa Modich, *Admin Sec*
▲ EMP: 4
SQ FT: 6,000
SALES: 850K **Privately Held**
SIC: 3599 Machine & other job shop work

(G-11570)
TRI PAR DIE MOLD
12872 Bluebell Ave (60142-6368)
PHONE..................847 515-3801
EMP: 3
SALES (est): 183K **Privately Held**
SIC: 3089 Injection molding of plastics

(G-11571)
UNICHEM INTERNATIONAL INC
11530 Smith Dr (60142-9600)
PHONE..................630 302-1469
Khaleeq Ahmed, *President*
EMP: 22
SQ FT: 160,000
SALES: 3.7MM **Privately Held**
SIC: 2834 Vitamin, nutrient & hematinic preparations for human use

(G-11572)
UNION SPECIAL LLC
1 Union Special Plz (60142-7007)
PHONE..................847 669-5101
Dave Hampton, *Maint Spvr*
Ken Waser, *Mfg Staff*
Dave Wnek, *Engineer*
Scott Ziegler, *Engineer*
Margaret Travis, *Human Res Mgr*
▲ EMP: 110
SQ FT: 400,000
SALES (est): 24.9MM **Privately Held**
WEB: www.unionspecial.com
SIC: 3559 5084 5131 5063 Sewing machines & attachments, industrial; sewing machines, industrial; industrial machine parts; sewing accessories; motors, electric; sewing machine repair shop

(G-11573)
WEBER-STEPHEN PRODUCTS LLC
11811 Oak Creek Pkwy (60142-6704)
PHONE..................847 669-4900
Bill Geid, *General Mgr*
EMP: 19
SALES (corp-wide): 979.6MM **Privately Held**
SIC: 3631 Barbecues, grills & braziers (outdoor cooking)
PA: Weber-Stephen Products Llc
1415 S Roselle Rd
Palatine IL 60067
847 934-5700

Illiopolis
Sangamon County

(G-11574)
KINGFISHER CONTROLS LLC
Also Called: Kf Control
208 Prairie Run (62539-3795)
PHONE..................425 359-5601
Timothy Christensen, *Mng Member*
EMP: 1
SALES: 200K **Privately Held**
SIC: 8711 3822 Engineering services; thermostats & other environmental sensors

INA
Jefferson County

(G-11575)
CRAFT PALLET INC
1620 N Benton Ln (62846-2209)
PHONE..................618 437-5382
Bill Kniffen, *President*
Susan Kniffen, *Admin Sec*
EMP: 8 EST: 1992
SALES (est): 985.5K **Privately Held**
SIC: 2448 Pallets, wood

Indian Head Park
Cook County

(G-11576)
BEVEL GRANITE COMPANY INC
6544 Pontiac Dr (60525-4349)
PHONE..................708 371-4191
James Rogan, *President*
Thomas Rogan, *Vice Pres*
▲ EMP: 75 EST: 1927
SALES (est): 7.5MM **Privately Held**
WEB: www.heartstonememorials.com
SIC: 3281 5999 Monuments, cut stone (not finishing or lettering only); granite, cut & shaped; monuments, finished to custom order

(G-11577)
ROGAN GRANITINDUSTRIE INC
Also Called: Bevel Granite
6544 Pontiac Dr (60525-4349)
PHONE..................708 758-0050
James Rogan, *Manager*
EMP: 3 **Privately Held**
WEB: www.rogangranite.com

GEOGRAPHIC SECTION

Island Lake - Lake County (G-11606)

SIC: 3281 Monuments, cut stone (not finishing or lettering only); building stone products; furniture, cut stone
HQ: Rogan Granitindustrie Inc
21550 E Lincoln Hwy
Lynwood IL 60411
708 758-0050

Ingleside
Lake County

(G-11578)
AMERICAN TOTAL ENGINE CO
Also Called: Ateco Automotive
27804 W Concrete Dr Ste B (60041-9317)
PHONE..................847 623-2737
William Lawson, Owner
EMP: 5 EST: 1970
SQ FT: 4,000
SALES (est): 520.6K Privately Held
SIC: 3599 3621 3544 Machine shop, jobbing & repair; motors & generators; special dies, tools, jigs & fixtures

(G-11579)
BETTER GASKETS INC
Also Called: Better Gaskets Sealing Systems
26218 W Ingleside Ave (60041-9656)
PHONE..................847 276-7635
Sandy Gordon, President
Robert L Gordon, Admin Sec
EMP: 5
SQ FT: 5,000
SALES: 125K Privately Held
SIC: 3053 Gaskets, all materials

(G-11580)
CUSTOM CANVAS LLC
26463 W Grand Ave (60041-9785)
PHONE..................847 587-0225
Roy Gundelach,
Marie Gundelach,
EMP: 6 EST: 1974
SQ FT: 8,000
SALES (est): 365K Privately Held
SIC: 2394 5999 5065 7532 Convertible tops, canvas or boat: from purchased materials; awnings, fabric: made from purchased materials; telephone & communication equipment; telephone equipment; upholstery & trim shop, automotive

(G-11581)
FIBERTEX NONWOVENS LLC
27981 W Concrete Dr (60041-8835)
PHONE..................815 349-3200
Henrik Kjeldsen, Managing Dir
Nikolaj Klit, Business Mgr
Mark Schultz, Opers Mgr
Clayton Carter, CFO
Sandra Fernandes, Manager
◆ EMP: 1032
SQ FT: 100,000
SALES (est): 227.6MM
SALES (corp-wide): 3.1B Privately Held
SIC: 2297 Nonwoven fabrics
HQ: Fin North America Holding Inc.
27981 W Concrete Dr
Ingleside IL 60041
815 349-3219

(G-11582)
FIN NORTH AMERICA HOLDING INC (DH)
27981 W Concrete Dr (60041-8835)
PHONE..................815 349-3219
Darryl Fournier, President
Beth Wolfe, CFO
EMP: 96
SALES (est): 5.9MM
SALES (corp-wide): 3.1B Privately Held
SIC: 6719 2297 Public utility holding companies; nonwoven fabrics
HQ: Fibertex Nonwovens A/S
Svendborgvej 16a
Aalborg 9220
963 535-35

(G-11583)
GE GES INC
411 Garfield Rd (60041-9382)
PHONE..................815 307-0595

EMP: 3
SALES (est): 124.6K Privately Held
SIC: 3724 Aircraft engines & engine parts

(G-11584)
IDENTCO INTERNATIONAL CORP (PA)
28164 W Concrete Dr (60041-8836)
PHONE..................815 385-0011
Scott B Lucas, President
EMP: 85
SQ FT: 20,000
SALES (est): 31.4MM Privately Held
SIC: 2672 Coated & laminated paper

(G-11585)
IDENTCO WEST LLC
28164 W Concrete Dr (60041-8836)
PHONE..................815 385-0011
Scott Lucas, President
Brian Connolly, Vice Pres
EMP: 2 EST: 1999
SALES (est): 552.8K Privately Held
SIC: 2679 Converted paper products

(G-11586)
LAKE SHORE STAIR CO INC (PA)
28090 W Concrete Dr (60041-9329)
PHONE..................815 363-7777
Christopher M Jensen, President
Jaime Swensen, Sales Staff
Peter Jensen, Admin Sec
EMP: 50 EST: 1931
SQ FT: 5,200
SALES (est): 3.8MM Privately Held
WEB: www.lakeshorestair.com
SIC: 2431 Staircases & stairs, wood; stair railings, wood

(G-11587)
MAJESTY CASES INC
34550 N Wilson Rd (60041-9247)
PHONE..................847 546-2558
Adam Button, President
EMP: 20 EST: 1999
SALES (est): 2.4MM Privately Held
SIC: 3537 Containers (metal), air cargo

(G-11588)
NEOLIGHT LABS LLC
34768 N Elm St (60041-9103)
PHONE..................312 242-1773
Momir Milinovich, Principal
EMP: 3
SALES (est): 152.1K Privately Held
SIC: 3229 Fiber optics strands

(G-11589)
SHORELINE GRAPHICS INC
415 Washington St (60041-9291)
PHONE..................847 587-4804
Harold D Pfuehler, President
EMP: 4
SALES (est): 358.4K Privately Held
SIC: 7336 2791 2789 2752 Graphic arts & related design; typesetting; bookbinding & related work; commercial printing, lithographic

(G-11590)
SUPERIOR FELT & FILTRATION LLC
27709 W Concrete Dr (60041-9363)
PHONE..................815 331-6382
Frank Porto, Principal
EMP: 40
SALES (corp-wide): 25.8MM Privately Held
SIC: 2299 Batting, wadding, padding & fillings
PA: Superior Felt & Filtration Llc
1150 Ridgeview Dr
Mchenry IL 60050
800 255-3358

Ingraham
Clay County

(G-11591)
ARTHUR LEO KUHL
Also Called: Kuhl's Trailer Sales
1023 N 500th St (62434-2122)
PHONE..................618 752-5473

Phyllis Prosser, Owner
EMP: 4 EST: 1973
SQ FT: 1,400
SALES (est): 62.7K Privately Held
SIC: 3792 7033 0191 Camping trailers & chassis; campgrounds; general farms, primarily crop

Inverness
Cook County

(G-11592)
AERODINE MAGAZINE
1514 Banbury Rd (60067-4285)
P.O. Box 247, Palatine (60078-0247)
PHONE..................847 358-4355
Kenneth Keifer, President
EMP: 3
SALES (est): 167.9K Privately Held
SIC: 2741 Directories: publishing only, not printed on site

(G-11593)
ALMACEN INC
927 Kirkwood Dr (60067-4235)
PHONE..................847 934-7955
Lloyd Wolf, Principal
EMP: 4
SALES: 1,000K Privately Held
SIC: 2521 2522 Wood office furniture; office furniture, except wood

(G-11594)
ANTHOS AND CO LLC
2010 Dundee Rd (60067-1801)
PHONE..................773 744-6813
Tammy Stergio,
EMP: 7
SALES (est): 369.7K Privately Held
SIC: 3961 7389 5999 Rosaries & small religious articles, except precious metal; decoration service for special events; religious goods

(G-11595)
EXTENTEL WRLESS COMMUNICATIONS
90 Dirleton Ln (60067-4877)
PHONE..................847 809-3131
Michael Ghadaksaz, Principal
EMP: 4
SALES (est): 205.4K Privately Held
SIC: 3669 Communications equipment

(G-11596)
HAMILTON BEACH BRANDS INC
142 Crichton Ln (60067-8006)
PHONE..................847 252-7036
EMP: 38
SALES (corp-wide): 740.7MM Publicly Held
SIC: 3634 Mfg Elec Housewares/Fans
HQ: Hamilton Beach Brands, Inc.
4421 Waterfront Dr
Glen Allen VA 23060
804 273-9777

(G-11597)
MEI REALTY LTD
1601 W Colonial Pkwy (60067-4732)
PHONE..................847 358-5000
Paul W Ziegler, CEO
Irene Ziegler, Treasurer
Linda Schutz, Admin Sec
EMP: 5
SQ FT: 45,000
SALES (est): 804K Privately Held
SIC: 6512 3677 Commercial & industrial building operation; electronic transformers

(G-11598)
T L SWINT INDUSTRIES INC
2211 Banbury Rd (60067-4213)
P.O. Box 277, Palatine (60078-0277)
PHONE..................847 358-3834
Thomas L Swint, President
EMP: 3
SQ FT: 2,000
SALES (est): 405.6K Privately Held
SIC: 3089 Injection molding of plastics

Inverness
Lake County

(G-11599)
CARGO SUPPORT INDUSTRIES INC
242 Willow St (60010-5812)
PHONE..................847 744-0786
EMP: 3
SALES (est): 276K Privately Held
SIC: 3999 Manufacturing industries

(G-11600)
ENGELHARDT ENTERPRISES INC
710 Bradwell Rd (60010-5601)
PHONE..................847 277-7070
Dean Englehardt, President
EMP: 2
SALES (est): 283.5K Privately Held
SIC: 3599 Machine shop, jobbing & repair

(G-11601)
HEAT AND CONTROL INC
1027 Ridgeview Dr (60010-5339)
PHONE..................847 381-0290
EMP: 791
SALES (corp-wide): 287.1MM Privately Held
WEB: www.heatandcontrol.com
SIC: 3556 Food products machinery
PA: Heat And Control, Inc.
21121 Cabot Blvd
Hayward CA 94545
510 259-0500

(G-11602)
MASON ENGINEERING & DESIGNING
Also Called: Cloud 9 Division
505 W Lancaster Ct (60010-5664)
PHONE..................630 595-5000
Jon Spranger, President
EMP: 45 EST: 1971
SQ FT: 19,000
SALES (est): 6.3MM Privately Held
SIC: 3564 Air purification equipment

(G-11603)
PROMOTIONAL CO OF ILLINOIS
2222 Shetland Rd (60010-5412)
PHONE..................847 382-0239
Jay Morgan, Owner
EMP: 5 EST: 1990
SALES (est): 500K Privately Held
SIC: 3993 Advertising novelties

Island Lake
Lake County

(G-11604)
AJS PUBLICATIONS
229 Brier Ct (60042-9750)
PHONE..................847 526-5027
Alex J Schmidt, Owner
EMP: 3
SALES (est): 144.8K Privately Held
WEB: www.ajspublications.com
SIC: 2731 Books: publishing only

(G-11605)
COMPETITIVE EDGE OPPORTUNITIES
Also Called: High Performance Packaging
910 E Burnett Rd (60042-9167)
P.O. Box 817, Wauconda (60084-0817)
PHONE..................815 981-4060
Ron Crews, President
EMP: 5
SALES (est): 1.5MM Privately Held
SIC: 5521 7389 3565 Used car dealers; labeling bottles, cans, cartons, etc.; packaging machinery

(G-11606)
CONCENTRIC COMPONENTS INC
811 Longacre Ct (60042-9673)
PHONE..................224 422-0638

Island Lake - Lake County (G-11607)

EMP: 3
SALES (est): 210.3K **Privately Held**
SIC: 3599 Machine shop, jobbing & repair

(G-11607)
G & W TECHNICAL CORPORATION
578 E Burnett Rd (60042-9203)
PHONE 847 487-0990
Waclaw Wanduch, *President*
EMP: 2
SQ FT: 2,000
SALES (est): 561K **Privately Held**
WEB: www.gwtechnical.com
SIC: 3569 Assembly machines, non-metalworking

(G-11608)
G&R MACHINING INC
3205 Poplar Dr (60042-9484)
P.O. Box 585 (60042-0585)
PHONE 847 526-7364
George Rudolph, *Principal*
EMP: 2
SALES (est): 207.5K **Privately Held**
SIC: 3599 Machine shop, jobbing & repair

(G-11609)
KNIGHT PRTG & LITHO SVC LTD
Also Called: Knight Printing and Litho Svcs
706 E Burnett Rd (60042-9236)
PHONE 847 487-7700
John A Hansen, *President*
EMP: 8 **EST:** 1962
SQ FT: 13,000
SALES (est): 1.2MM **Privately Held**
WEB: www.oilstickersdirect.com
SIC: 2752 2759 2672 Commercial printing, offset; commercial printing; coated & laminated paper

(G-11610)
OLSEN WOODWORK CO (PA)
4709 Southhampton Dr (60042-8471)
PHONE 847 865-5054
Myles Olsen Jr, *Principal*
EMP: 3 **EST:** 2013
SALES: 2K **Privately Held**
SIC: 2541 Store fixtures, wood

(G-11611)
STANCY WOODWORKING CO INC
301 Fern Dr (60042-9456)
PHONE 847 526-0252
Teresa J Vazouez-Stancy, *President*
EMP: 10
SALES (est): 220K **Privately Held**
SIC: 2499 2511 2434 2431 Decorative wood & woodwork; wood household furniture; wood kitchen cabinets; millwork

(G-11612)
VANGUARD DEFENSE GROUP
3005 Max Ct (60042-9009)
PHONE 850 218-4323
Joseph Plazyk, *Principal*
EMP: 3
SALES (est): 201.3K **Privately Held**
SIC: 3812 Defense systems & equipment

(G-11613)
WAGNERS CUSTOM WOOD DESIGN
4035 Roberts Rd (60042-8505)
P.O. Box 283 (60042-0283)
PHONE 847 487-2788
William Wagner, *President*
Christopher Wagner, *Admin Sec*
EMP: 2
SQ FT: 1,600
SALES (est): 291.1K **Privately Held**
SIC: 5712 2431 1751 Cabinet work, custom; panel work, wood; cabinet & finish carpentry

Itasca
Dupage County

(G-11614)
ABBOTT LABEL INC
1414 Norwood Ave (60143-1129)
PHONE 630 773-3614
EMP: 36
SALES (corp-wide): 20.3MM **Privately Held**
WEB: www.abbottlabel.com
SIC: 2759 Labels & seals: printing
PA: Abbott Label, Inc.
11440 Hillguard Rd
Dallas TX 75243
866 228-0100

(G-11615)
ABS GRAPHICS INC (PA)
Also Called: ABS Equipment Division
900 N Rohlwing Rd (60143-1161)
PHONE 630 495-2400
Kenneth Vander Veen, *President*
Rick Brown, *President*
Steven Vanderveen, *Corp Secy*
Ed Anderson, *Vice Pres*
Tony Galatte, *Vice Pres*
▼ **EMP:** 120
SQ FT: 70,000
SALES (est): 47.1MM **Privately Held**
WEB: www.absgraphics.com
SIC: 2752 2759 2789 Commercial printing, offset; commercial printing; bookbinding & related work

(G-11616)
AGS PARTNERS LLC
905 W Irving Park Rd (60143-2023)
PHONE 630 446-7777
EMP: 53
SALES (corp-wide): 36.2MM **Privately Held**
SIC: 3944 Mfg Games/Toys
PA: Ags Partners, Llc
6680 Amelia Earhart Ct # 50
Las Vegas NV 89118
702 294-0440

(G-11617)
AJINOMOTO FOOD INGREDIENTS LLC
1300 N Arlington Hts Rd (60143-3108)
PHONE 773 714-1436
EMP: 8
SALES (est): 701.1K **Privately Held**
SIC: 2834 Pharmaceutical preparations

(G-11618)
ALICONA CORPORATION
150 E Pierce Rd Ste 130 (60143-1223)
PHONE 630 372-9900
Stefan Scherer, *President*
Mark Raleigh, *Vice Pres*
EMP: 3
SALES (est): 624K
SALES (corp-wide): 2B **Publicly Held**
WEB: www.alicona.com
SIC: 3827 Microscopes, except electron, proton & corneal
HQ: Alicona Imaging Gmbh
Dr.-Auner-StraBe 21a
Raaba 8074
316 403-0107

(G-11619)
ALLMETAL INC (PA)
1 Pierce Pl Ste 295w (60143-2695)
P.O. Box 850, Bensenville (60106-0850)
PHONE 630 250-8090
Philip Collin, *CEO*
Roland Cram, *President*
Bob Fulton, *General Mgr*
Rick Allen, *CFO*
Linda Edie, *Treasurer*
◆ **EMP:** 60
SQ FT: 8,300
SALES (est): 78.4MM **Privately Held**
WEB: www.allmetalinc.com
SIC: 3699 3089 Laser welding, drilling & cutting equipment; injection molding of plastics

(G-11620)
AMADA AMERICA INC
1091 W Hawthorn Dr (60143-2057)
PHONE 877 262-3287
Mike Zordan, *Branch Mgr*
EMP: 6 **Privately Held**
SIC: 7372 Prepackaged software
HQ: Amada America, Inc.
7025 Firestone Blvd
Buena Park CA 90621
714 739-2111

(G-11621)
AMCOR RIGID PACKAGING USA LLC
750 Expressway Dr (60143-1322)
PHONE 630 773-3235
Eric Ferguson, *Engineer*
Mark Salkensteen, *Branch Mgr*
Derek McKaig, *Maintence Staff*
Alex Scotidis, *Maintence Staff*
EMP: 100
SALES (corp-wide): 947.2K **Privately Held**
SIC: 3089 Plastic containers, except foam
HQ: Amcor Rigid Packaging Usa, Llc
40600 Ann Arbor Rd E # 201
Plymouth MI 48170

(G-11622)
AMERICAN SUPPLY ASSOCIATION (PA)
Also Called: Asa
1200 N Arlngton Hts 150 (60143-3178)
PHONE 630 467-0000
Don Maloney, *Ch of Bd*
John Hester, *President*
Inge Calderon, *General Mgr*
EMP: 14
SQ FT: 7,500
SALES (est): 2.5MM **Privately Held**
SIC: 8611 2731 Trade associations; book publishing

(G-11623)
AMERISUN INC
1131 W Bryn Mawr Ave (60143-1508)
PHONE 800 791-9458
Bill Godwin, *President*
Jim Weiskircher, *Admin Sec*
▲ **EMP:** 10
SALES (est): 5.2MM
SALES (corp-wide): 10.3MM **Privately Held**
SIC: 5083 3524 Mowers, power; snowblowers & throwers, residential
PA: Zhejiang Dobest Power Tools Co., Ltd.
No.9, Huacheng West Road,
Huachuan Industrial Zone
Yongkang 32139
579 892-8629

(G-11624)
BAMBERGER POLYMERS INC
1 Pierce Pl Ste 255c (60143-2613)
PHONE 630 773-8626
Michael Pignataro, *Manager*
EMP: 10 **Privately Held**
WEB: www.bambergerpolymers.com
SIC: 5162 2822 Plastics resins; synthetic rubber
HQ: Bamberger Polymers, Inc.
2 Jericho Plz Ste 109
Jericho NY 11753

(G-11625)
BANDO USA INC (HQ)
1149 W Bryn Mawr Ave (60143-1508)
PHONE 630 773-6600
Joseph Laudadio, *President*
Minoru Fukuda, *Chairman*
Elena Windsor, *Credit Mgr*
Ralph White, *Finance*
Stephanie Pennock, *Manager*
◆ **EMP:** 35
SALES (est): 42.1MM **Privately Held**
SIC: 3052 Rubber belting

(G-11626)
BARON MANUFACTURING CO LLC
730 Baker Dr (60143-1308)
PHONE 630 628-9110
Robert A McKinney Sr, *President*
Robert A Mc Kinney Jr, *VP Sales*
▲ **EMP:** 20 **EST:** 1964
SQ FT: 16,217
SALES (est): 4.4MM **Privately Held**
WEB: www.baronsnaps.com
SIC: 3429 Manufactured hardware (general)

(G-11627)
BDNA CORPORATION
300 Park Blvd Ste 500 (60143-2635)
PHONE 650 625-9530
Constantin Delivanis, *CEO*
Fred Hessabi, *CEO*
Ossama Hassanein, *Ch of Bd*
Walker White, *President*
James Shaak, *Vice Pres*
EMP: 75
SALES (est): 9.6MM **Privately Held**
SIC: 7372 Business oriented computer software

(G-11628)
BOLER COMPANY (PA)
500 Park Blvd Ste 1010 (60143-1285)
PHONE 630 773-9111
Matthew J Boler, *President*
Nancy B Coons, *Exec VP*
Michael J Boler, *Vice Pres*
Dennis Lubertozzi, *Asst Controller*
Jeffrey Gunnlaugson, *Manager*
◆ **EMP:** 15 **EST:** 1977
SQ FT: 7,000
SALES (est): 980.2MM **Privately Held**
SIC: 3493 3714 Leaf springs: automobile, locomotive, etc.; axles, motor vehicle

(G-11629)
BOLER VENTURES LLC (PA)
500 Park Blvd Ste 1010 (60143-2608)
PHONE 630 773-9111
Matthew Boler, *Partner*
James Boler, *Partner*
Michael Boler, *Partner*
EMP: 97
SQ FT: 6,000
SALES (est): 5MM **Privately Held**
SIC: 3714 Motor vehicle parts & accessories

(G-11630)
BUDAPEST TOOL
1300 Industrial Dr Ste A (60143-1876)
PHONE 630 250-0711
Karoly Nemeth, *Owner*
EMP: 2
SQ FT: 2,500
SALES (est): 450K **Privately Held**
SIC: 3599 Machine shop, jobbing & repair

(G-11631)
BUILDEX DIVISON OF ITW
1349 W Bryn Mawr Ave (60143-1313)
PHONE 630 595-3500
Timothy Gardner, *Principal*
▲ **EMP:** 6 **EST:** 2013
SALES (est): 783.6K **Privately Held**
SIC: 3965 Fasteners

(G-11632)
BULAW WELDING & ENGINEERING CO
Also Called: Aero Vac Brazing Heat Treating
750 N Rohlwing Rd (60143-1347)
PHONE 630 228-8300
Jay Bulaw, *President*
Michael Bulaw, *Vice Pres*
Teresa Archambault, *Manager*
Vaidas Jagelavicius, *Maintence Staff*
EMP: 70 **EST:** 1935
SQ FT: 37,500
SALES (est): 2.5MM **Privately Held**
WEB: www.bulawwelding.com
SIC: 1799 7692 3398 Welding on site; welding repair; metal heat treating

(G-11633)
CANON SOLUTIONS AMERICA INC
1800 Bruning Dr W (60143-1061)
PHONE 630 351-1227
Robert Bergin, *Accounts Exec*
Aggie Giovannini, *Accounts Exec*
Janet Piszyk, *Marketing Staff*
Jack Needham, *Manager*
David Balentine, *Manager*

GEOGRAPHIC SECTION

Itasca - Dupage County (G-11659)

EMP: 95 **Privately Held**
SIC: **3861** 7371 Photographic film, plate & paper holders; custom computer programming services
HQ: Canon Solutions America, Inc.
1 Canon Park
Melville NY 11747
631 330-5000

(G-11634)
CARDINAL COLORPRINT PRTG CORP
1270 Ardmore Ave (60143-1141)
PHONE.................................630 467-1000
Partick A Lebeau, *President*
Arthur Le Beau, *Vice Pres*
Theresa Zielinski, *Production*
Michael J Lebeau, *Treasurer*
Zack Hines, *Accounts Exec*
EMP: 46 EST: 1947
SQ FT: 50,000
SALES (est): 10.5MM **Privately Held**
WEB: www.cardinalcolorgroup.com
SIC: **2752** 2796 2791 2789 Commercial printing, offset; platemaking services; typesetting; bookbinding & related work

(G-11635)
CARL MANUFACTURING USA INC
100 E Pierce Rd Ste 100 # 100 (60143-2665)
PHONE.................................847 884-2842
Yuichi Mori, *Ch of Bd*
Alex Martinez, *President*
▲ EMP: 12
SQ FT: 6,000
SALES (est): 5MM **Privately Held**
SIC: **2678** Stationery products
HQ: Carl Manufacturing Co., Ltd.
3-7-9, Tateishi
Katsushika-Ku TKY 124-0

(G-11636)
CHURCH STREET BREWING CO LLC
1480 Industrial Dr Ste C (60143-1857)
PHONE.................................630 438-5725
Gregor Joseph H, *Business Mgr*
Lisa Gregor MD, *Mng Member*
Chet Brett, *Manager*
EMP: 14
SALES (est): 2MM **Privately Held**
SIC: **5181** 2082 Beer & ale; ale (alcoholic beverage)

(G-11637)
CIRCUIT WORLD INC
751 Hilltop Dr (60143-1325)
PHONE.................................630 250-1100
Vipan Patel, *President*
Vinod Patel Chicago, *Vice Pres*
Kanti Sanghani, *Vice Pres*
Jagdish Metha, *Treasurer*
▲ EMP: 42
SQ FT: 25,000
SALES (est): 7.8MM **Privately Held**
SIC: **3672** Circuit boards, television & radio printed

(G-11638)
CONCENTRIC ITASCA INC
800 Hollywood Ave (60143-1353)
PHONE.................................630 773-3355
David Woolley, *CEO*
Len Mason, *President*
Joe Garlick, *Vice Pres*
Stan Schultz, *Prdtn Mgr*
David Bessant, *CFO*
▲ EMP: 87
SQ FT: 50,000
SALES (est): 50.8MM
SALES (corp-wide): 267.6MM **Privately Held**
SIC: **5084** 3519 Engines & parts, diesel; governors, pump, for diesel engines
HQ: Concentric Birmingham Limited
40 Chapel Ash
Wolverhampton W MIDLANDS WV3 0
190 242-8008

(G-11639)
CONTINENTAL WEB PRESS INC (PA)
1430 Industrial Dr (60143-1858)
PHONE.................................630 773-1903
Diane K Field, *President*
Jerry Haywood, *COO*
Jim Arnold, *Exec VP*
Ed Zepernick, *Exec VP*
Robert Avers, *Vice Pres*
▲ EMP: 125
SQ FT: 230,000
SALES (est): 58.4MM **Privately Held**
SIC: **2752** Commercial printing, offset

(G-11640)
CONTINENTAL WEB PRESS KY INC (PA)
1430 Industrial Dr (60143-1858)
PHONE.................................630 773-1903
Diane K Field, *President*
Jim Arnold, *COO*
Ken Field Jr, *Vice Pres*
Kenneth W Field, *Vice Pres*
▲ EMP: 56
SQ FT: 225,000
SALES (est): 38.4MM **Privately Held**
SIC: **2752** Commercial printing, offset

(G-11641)
CREATIVE PANEL SYSTEMS INC
1401 Glenlake Ave (60143-1114)
PHONE.................................630 625-5002
Stephen P Borst, *Principal*
EMP: 3
SALES (est): 429.2K **Privately Held**
SIC: **3446** Architectural metalwork

(G-11642)
DICE MOLD & ENGINEERING INC
75 N Prospect Ave (60143-1867)
PHONE.................................630 773-3595
Raymond Dierking, *President*
Sergio Ciscolini, *Treasurer*
Ray Dierking, *Manager*
Kevin Dirking, *Technology*
EMP: 20
SQ FT: 8,000
SALES (est): 3.8MM **Privately Held**
SIC: **3089** 3544 Injection molding of plastics; special dies & tools

(G-11643)
DIVERSFIED LBLING SLUTIONS INC (HQ)
Also Called: D L S
1285 Hamilton Pkwy (60143-1150)
PHONE.................................630 625-1225
Jim Kersten, *CEO*
Bob Hakman, *President*
Charlie Zgrabik, *President*
Tommy Highton, *Prdtn Mgr*
Nora Chernak, *Safety Mgr*
EMP: 146
SQ FT: 140,000
SALES: 61MM **Privately Held**
SIC: **2679** 2754 Labels, paper: made from purchased material; commercial printing, gravure

(G-11644)
DPCAC LLC
Also Called: Dwyer Products & Services
1345 Norwood Ave (60143-1126)
PHONE.................................630 741-7900
Frank San Roman, *Mng Member*
EMP: 12
SALES (est): 940K **Privately Held**
SIC: **2434** 2514 3264 2541 Wood kitchen cabinets; kitchen cabinets: metal; porcelain electrical supplies; wood partitions & fixtures

(G-11645)
DU PONT DELAWARE INC
Also Called: Dupont
500 Park Blvd Ste 545 (60143-1267)
PHONE.................................630 285-2700
EMP: 7
SALES (corp-wide): 21.5B **Publicly Held**
SIC: **2879** Agricultural chemicals
HQ: Du Pont Delaware, Inc.
974 Centre Rd Chestnut
Wilmington DE 19805

(G-11646)
EBWAY INDUSTRIES INC
1201 Ardmore Ave (60143-1187)
PHONE.................................630 860-5959
Alan Jardis, *President*
EMP: 40
SQ FT: 22,750
SALES: 9.2MM **Privately Held**
WEB: www.jardis.com
SIC: **3555** Printing trades machinery
PA: Jardis Industries, Inc.
1201 Ardmore Ave
Itasca IL 60143
630 860-5959

(G-11647)
ELEMATEC USA CORPORATION
500 Park Blvd Ste 760 (60143-2623)
PHONE.................................858 527-1700
Kenichi Oshiva, *Branch Mgr*
EMP: 8 **Privately Held**
SIC: **3676** Electronic resistors
HQ: Elematec Usa Corporation
4909 Murphy Canyon Rd # 220
San Diego CA 92123

(G-11648)
ELLIS CORPORATION (PA)
1400 W Bryn Mawr Ave (60143-1384)
PHONE.................................630 250-9222
Robert H Fesmire, *President*
Tom Reese, *Materials Mgr*
Alan Burleson, *Engineer*
Robert Schmitz, *Engineer*
Dan Noltin, *Design Engr*
◆ EMP: 60 EST: 1931
SQ FT: 64,800
SALES (est): 13.1MM **Privately Held**
WEB: www.elliscorp.com
SIC: **3582** 3589 Commercial laundry equipment; water treatment equipment, industrial

(G-11649)
EMERSON INDUSTRIES LLC (PA)
680 Baker Dr (60143-1346)
PHONE.................................630 279-0920
Walter A Emerson, *Mng Member*
Judith Emerson,
EMP: 10 EST: 1969
SQ FT: 27,000
SALES (est): 1.7MM **Privately Held**
SIC: **3544** Industrial molds

(G-11650)
ENESCO LLC (PA)
225 Windsor Dr (60143-1225)
PHONE.................................630 875-5300
Todd Mavis, *CEO*
Bruce S Raiffe, *President*
Theodore Eischeid, *COO*
Anthony G Testolin, *CFO*
Kathi P Lentzsch, *Chief Mktg Ofcr*
◆ EMP: 400
SALES: 200MM **Privately Held**
SIC: **5947** 3942 3069 5945 Gift shop; souvenirs; dolls & stuffed toys; toys, rubber; toys & games; toys & hobby goods & supplies

(G-11651)
ENVIRONMENTAL SPECIALTIES INC
Also Called: E S I
1600 Glenlake Ave (60143-1005)
PHONE.................................630 860-7070
Michael T Miske, *President*
▲ EMP: 5
SQ FT: 24,000
SALES (est): 520K **Privately Held**
SIC: **3625** 3555 2899 2893 Industrial controls: push button, selector switches, pilot; printing trades machinery; chemical preparations; printing ink

(G-11652)
ERGO-TECH INCORPORATED
217 Catalpa Ave (60143-2027)
P.O. Box 8, Urbana (61803-0008)
PHONE.................................630 773-2222
Neal T Lilly, *President*
Matthew Leahy, *Vice Pres*
Brian P Lilly, *Admin Sec*
EMP: 3

SALES (est): 380K **Privately Held**
SIC: **3491** Water works valves

(G-11653)
EXCEL GROUP HOLDINGS INC (PA)
800 Baker Dr (60143-1310)
PHONE.................................630 773-1815
John R Iacono, *President*
Alec Kozuch, *Sales Staff*
Kendall Mancillas, *Sales Staff*
▲ EMP: 24
SALES (est): 4MM **Privately Held**
WEB: www.exceldowel.com
SIC: **2499** Dowels, wood

(G-11654)
FARM PLASTIC SUPPLY INC (PA)
1555 Industrial Dr (60143-1862)
PHONE.................................312 625-1024
Matthew Randazzo, *President*
EMP: 1
SALES (est): 298K **Privately Held**
SIC: **2671** Plastic film, coated or laminated for packaging

(G-11655)
FERRARA CANDY COMPANY
1445 Norwood Ave (60143-1128)
PHONE.................................800 323-1768
EMP: 4
SALES (est): 393.9K **Privately Held**
SIC: **2064** Candy & other confectionery products

(G-11656)
FILTER MONKEY LLC
424 S Lombard Rd (60143-2566)
PHONE.................................630 773-4402
Timothy D Krause,
EMP: 2
SALES (est): 203.7K **Privately Held**
SIC: **3569** Filters

(G-11657)
FINER LINE INC
Also Called: Finer Line Engraving
1701 Glenlake Ave (60143-1006)
PHONE.................................847 884-1611
Mark C Case, *President*
Ryan Wyzinski, *Prdtn Mgr*
Rick Loveisky, *Accounts Exec*
▲ EMP: 11
SQ FT: 7,800
SALES: 990K **Privately Held**
SIC: **7389** 5999 5199 3479 Engraving service; trophies & plaques; badges; engraving jewelry silverware, or metal; glassware, art or decorative; engraving equipment & supplies

(G-11658)
FITZ CHEM LLC (DH)
450 E Devon Ave Ste 300 (60143-1263)
PHONE.................................630 467-8383
Robert Becker, *CEO*
Donald Deihs, *President*
Edward Croco, *Exec VP*
Jan Barber, *Purch Agent*
Mary Milinko, *Technical Mgr*
▲ EMP: 39
SALES (est): 35MM **Privately Held**
WEB: www.fitzchem.com
SIC: **5169** 2821 2891 Chemicals, industrial & heavy; plastics materials & resins; adhesives & sealants
HQ: Nagase America Corporation
546 5th Ave Fl 19
New York NY 10036
212 703-1340

(G-11659)
FLEXERA HOLDINGS LP
300 Park Blvd Ste 500 (60143-2635)
PHONE.................................847 466-4000
EMP: 6
SALES (est): 212.7MM
SALES (corp-wide): 1.6MM **Privately Held**
SIC: **7371** 7372 Computer software development; prepackaged software
HQ: Flexera Software Llc
300 Park Blvd Ste 500
Itasca IL 60143

Itasca - Dupage County (G-11660)

(G-11660)
FLEXERA SOFTWARE LLC (DH)
300 Park Blvd Ste 500 (60143-2635)
PHONE.................847 466-4000
Jim Ryan, *President*
Elliott Robinson, *Counsel*
Dana Sacks, *Senior VP*
Toan Phamdang, *Engineer*
Joseph Freda, *CFO*
EMP: 527
SQ FT: 74,479
SALES (est): 284.3MM
SALES (corp-wide): 1.6MM **Privately Held**
SIC: 7371 7372 Computer software development; prepackaged software
HQ: Flexera Software Limited
14-18 Bell Street
Maidenhead BERKS SL6 1
370 871-1111

(G-11661)
GEORGE VAGGELATOS
Also Called: Apple Print
400 W Center St (60143-1710)
PHONE.................847 361-3880
George Vaggelatos, *Principal*
EMP: 2 **EST:** 2010
SALES (est): 203.2K **Privately Held**
SIC: 2752 Commercial printing, lithographic

(G-11662)
GRINDAL COMPANY
1551 Industrial Dr (60143-1861)
PHONE.................630 250-8950
Janice E Spooner, *President*
Wayne D Domke, *General Mgr*
Ed Jean, *Opers Staff*
Joyce Whipple, *Manager*
Herminio Llamas, *Technician*
▲ **EMP:** 20 **EST:** 1965
SQ FT: 20,000
SALES (est): 3.4MM **Privately Held**
WEB: www.grindal.com
SIC: 3599 Machine shop, jobbing & repair

(G-11663)
HELIX INTERNATIONAL INC (PA)
Also Called: Helix International Mch Div
900 Hollywood Ave (60143-1330)
PHONE.................847 709-0666
Jan Jorfald, *President*
Drew Naismith, *Vice Pres*
Aleksandr Antonyuk, *Sales Mgr*
◆ **EMP:** 2
SALES (est): 695.2K **Privately Held**
SIC: 3569 Filters

(G-11664)
HENDRICKSON HOLDINGS LLC
500 Park Blvd Ste 1010 (60143-2608)
PHONE.................630 910-2800
Brian Parisi, *Project Mgr*
Pat Duenas, *Maint Spvr*
Keith Pullen, *Senior Buyer*
Nikhil Bhasker, *Engineer*
Chris Cantagallo, *Engineer*
EMP: 4
SALES (est): 753.1K
SALES (corp-wide): 980.2MM **Privately Held**
SIC: 3714 Motor vehicle parts & accessories
PA: The Boler Company
500 Park Blvd Ste 1010
Itasca IL 60143
630 773-9111

(G-11665)
HENDRICKSON USA LLC (HQ)
500 Park Blvd Ste 450 (60143-3153)
PHONE.................630 874-9700
Gregory Gilbert, *Buyer*
Kelly Ragonese, *Controller*
Carey S Ellens, *Benefits Mgr*
Jeff Miller, *Manager*
Robert Perrin, *Manager*
◆ **EMP:** 50
SALES (est): 170.5MM
SALES (corp-wide): 980.2MM **Privately Held**
SIC: 3714 Motor vehicle parts & accessories

PA: The Boler Company
500 Park Blvd Ste 1010
Itasca IL 60143
630 773-9111

(G-11666)
HOUGHTON MIFFLIN HARCOURT CO
Also Called: Hmh
761 District Dr (60143-1319)
PHONE.................630 467-6049
EMP: 6
SALES (corp-wide): 1.3B **Publicly Held**
SIC: 3999 2731 Education aids, devices & supplies; book publishing
PA: Houghton Mifflin Harcourt Company
125 High St Ste 900
Boston MA 02110
617 351-5000

(G-11667)
HOUGHTON MIFFLIN HARCOURT PUBG
Also Called: Riverside Publishing
425 Spring Lake Dr (60143-2076)
PHONE.................630 467-6095
John Laramy, *President*
EMP: 300
SALES (corp-wide): 1.3B **Publicly Held**
SIC: 2731 Books: publishing only
HQ: Houghton Mifflin Harcourt Publishing Company
125 High St Ste 900
Boston MA 02110
617 351-5000

(G-11668)
ICP INDUSTRIAL INC (HQ)
Also Called: National Industrial Coatings
1600 Glenlake Ave (60143-1005)
P.O. Box 809137, Chicago (60680-9137)
PHONE.................630 227-1692
Paul Grzedielucha, *Division Pres*
Patrick Neurath, *CFO*
Karen Loring, *Human Resources*
Jorge Hasbun, *Regl Sales Mgr*
Mike Stevens, *Sales Staff*
◆ **EMP:** 35
SQ FT: 75,000
SALES (est): 11.8MM
SALES (corp-wide): 105.5MM **Privately Held**
SIC: 3479 2891 2869 Coating of metals & formed products; adhesives; silicones
PA: Innovative Chemical Products Group, Llc
150 Dascomb Rd
Andover MA 01810
978 623-9980

(G-11669)
ICP INDUSTRIES LLC
Also Called: Minusnine Technologies
1600 Glenlake Ave (60143-1005)
PHONE.................888 672-2123
EMP: 20
SALES (corp-wide): 105.5MM **Privately Held**
SIC: 3479 Coating of metals & formed products
HQ: Icp Industries Llc
100 Business Park Ave
San Antonio TX 78204

(G-11670)
IFS NORTH AMERICA INC (DH)
300 Park Blvd Ste 555 (60143-2635)
PHONE.................888 437-4968
Cindy Jaudon, *CEO*
Michael Gauna, *Business Mgr*
Katherine James, *Vice Pres*
Roy Almeida, *Engineer*
Michael Fleming, *Engineer*
EMP: 50
SQ FT: 15,888
SALES (est): 59.7MM **Privately Held**
SIC: 7372 7379 8243 Prepackaged software; data processing consultant; software training, computer
HQ: Industrial And Financial Systems, Ifs Ab
Tekniкringen 5
Linkoping 583 3
858 784-500

(G-11671)
ILLINOIS TOOL WORKS INC
HI Cone Div
1140 W Bryn Mawr Ave (60143-1509)
PHONE.................630 773-9300
Fax: 630 773-3015
EMP: 30
SALES (corp-wide): 14.3B **Publicly Held**
SIC: 3089 Mfg Multi Plastic Products
PA: Illinois Tool Works Inc.
155 Harlem Ave
Glenview IL 60025
847 724-7500

(G-11672)
ILLINOIS TOOL WORKS INC
ITW Commercial Cnstr N Amer
1349 W Bryn Mawr Ave (60143-1313)
PHONE.................630 595-3500
Timm Fields, *General Mgr*
EMP: 227
SALES (corp-wide): 14.1B **Publicly Held**
WEB: www.itw.com
SIC: 3452 3542 Bolts, nuts, rivets & washers; machine tools, metal forming type
PA: Illinois Tool Works Inc.
155 Harlem Ave
Glenview IL 60025
847 724-7500

(G-11673)
ILLINOIS TOOL WORKS INC
Also Called: Hi-Cone Div
1140 W Bryn Mawr Ave (60143-1509)
PHONE.................217 345-2166
Andrew Albin, *General Mgr*
Aneta Racheva, *Opers Mgr*
Andy Mazurek, *Controller*
Kelsey Vanagaitis, *Controller*
Ed Kaminski, *Cust Mgr*
EMP: 50
SALES (corp-wide): 14.1B **Publicly Held**
SIC: 3086 3565 5199 Packaging & shipping materials, foamed plastic; packaging machinery; packaging materials
PA: Illinois Tool Works Inc.
155 Harlem Ave
Glenview IL 60025
847 724-7500

(G-11674)
IMAGING SYSTEMS INC (PA)
Also Called: Integrated Document Tech
1009 W Hawthorn Dr (60143-2057)
PHONE.................630 875-1100
Paul E Szemplinski, *Ch of Bd*
Michael Nolfo, *President*
Jeff Krause, *Vice Pres*
Ed Berlin, *CFO*
James P Raboin, *CTO*
EMP: 14
SQ FT: 5,700
SALES (est): 3.6MM **Privately Held**
SIC: 7371 5045 7372 7374 Computer software writers, freelance; computer software; application computer software; business oriented computer software; data processing & preparation

(G-11675)
IMCP INC
900 N Arlington (60143)
P.O. Box 9 (60143-0009)
PHONE.................630 477-8600
Patrick Grant, *President*
Mark Ward, *CTO*
EMP: 3
SQ FT: 2,000
SALES (est): 486.2K **Privately Held**
SIC: 7379 7372 Computer related consulting services; prepackaged software

(G-11676)
INDUSTRIAL FINANCE SYSTEMS
300 Park Blvd (60143-2682)
PHONE.................847 592-0200
Bengt G Nilsson, *Principal*
Mark Hamilton, *IT/INT Sup*
EMP: 7
SALES (est): 634.5K **Privately Held**
SIC: 7372 Prepackaged software

(G-11677)
INTERNATIONAL PAPER COMPANY
1225 W Bryn Mawr Ave (60143-1311)
PHONE.................630 250-1300
Clare Anderson, *General Mgr*
EMP: 25
SALES (corp-wide): 22.3B **Publicly Held**
SIC: 2621 2611 Paper mills; pulp mills
PA: International Paper Company
6400 Poplar Ave
Memphis TN 38197
901 419-9000

(G-11678)
IRETIRED LLC
700 District Dr (60143-1320)
PHONE.................630 285-9500
Becky Rovik, *Production*
Eric Montanez, *Engineer*
Michael Larmon, *Mktg Dir*
Mary Eileen Levi, *Mng Member*
Michael A Levi, *Mng Member*
▲ **EMP:** 34
SQ FT: 49,000
SALES (est): 8.9MM **Privately Held**
SIC: 5046 2542 Display equipment, except refrigerated; partitions & fixtures, except wood

(G-11679)
J-TEC METAL PRODUCTS INC
1320 Ardmore Ave (60143-1105)
PHONE.................630 875-1300
Jesus Garza, *President*
Francisca Garza, *Admin Sec*
Jesse Garza Sr, *Products*
EMP: 18
SALES (est): 5.1MM **Privately Held**
SIC: 3353 3469 3444 Aluminum sheet & strip; metal stampings; sheet metalwork

(G-11680)
JARDIS INDUSTRIES INC (PA)
Also Called: Bachi Company Div
1201 Ardmore Ave (60143-1187)
PHONE.................630 860-5959
Alan W Jardis, *President*
Art Langosch, *Sales Mgr*
Adam Jardis, *Technician*
▲ **EMP:** 42
SQ FT: 32,500
SALES (est): 9.2MM **Privately Held**
SIC: 3555 5084 Printing trades machinery; industrial machinery & equipment

(G-11681)
JARDIS INDUSTRIES INC
Bachi Company
1201 Ardmore Ave (60143-1187)
PHONE.................630 773-5600
David Hansen, *Branch Mgr*
EMP: 10
SALES (corp-wide): 9.2MM **Privately Held**
SIC: 3549 5084 3699 3621 Coil winding machines for springs; printing trades machinery, equipment & supplies; electrical equipment & supplies; motors & generators
PA: Jardis Industries, Inc.
1201 Ardmore Ave
Itasca IL 60143
630 860-5959

(G-11682)
KEEPER CORP
1345 Industrial Dr (60143-1894)
PHONE.................630 773-9393
Edward Kryger, *President*
Ronald Kryger, *Vice Pres*
Tom Kryger, *Vice Pres*
EMP: 7
SQ FT: 10,500
SALES (est): 955.4K **Privately Held**
SIC: 3599 Machine shop, jobbing & repair

(G-11683)
KESTER LLC
940 W Thorndale Ave (60143-1339)
PHONE.................630 616-6882
EMP: 7 **Privately Held**
SIC: 3356 Solder: wire, bar, acid core, & rosin core

GEOGRAPHIC SECTION

Itasca - Dupage County (G-11707)

HQ: Kester Llc
800 W Thorndale Ave
Itasca IL 60143
630 616-4000

(G-11684)
KESTER LLC (DH)
800 W Thorndale Ave (60143-1341)
PHONE................630 616-4000
Steven L Martindale, *President*
Roger Savage, *President*
Larry Lane, *Purchasing*
Fabien Laillet, *QC Mgr*
Arturo Espejo, *Engineer*
◆ EMP: 65
SALES (est): 73.1MM **Privately Held**
SIC: 3356 Solder: wire, bar, acid core, & rosin core
HQ: Hgs Digital, Llc
651 W Washington Blvd # 303
Chicago IL 60661
312 755-1845

(G-11685)
KNOWLES CORPORATION (PA)
1151 Maplewood Dr (60143-2058)
PHONE................630 250-5100
Jeffrey S Niew, *President*
Thomas G Jackson, *Senior VP*
Ray Cabrera, *Vice Pres*
John Donovan, *Vice Pres*
Dan Harper, *Vice Pres*
EMP: 44
SALES: 854.8MM **Publicly Held**
SIC: 3651 3675 Household audio & video equipment; audio electronic systems; microphones; speaker systems; electronic capacitors

(G-11686)
KNOWLES CORPORATION
Knowles Capacitors
1151 Maplewood Dr (60143-2058)
PHONE................630 250-5100
EMP: 250
SALES (corp-wide): 854.8MM **Publicly Held**
SIC: 3675 Electronic capacitors
PA: Knowles Corporation
1151 Maplewood Dr
Itasca IL 60143
630 250-5100

(G-11687)
KNOWLES ELEC HOLDINGS INC
1151 Maplewood Dr (60143-2058)
PHONE................630 250-5100
Jean-Pierre M Ergas, *Ch of Bd*
Michael A Adell, *President*
Jeffrey S Niew, *President*
John J Zei, *Principal*
Raymond D Cabrera, *Senior VP*
EMP: 2420
SQ FT: 60,000
SALES (est): 205.9MM
SALES (corp-wide): 854.8MM **Publicly Held**
WEB: www.knowles.com
SIC: 3679 3625 3651 8731 Transducers, electrical; headphones, radio; solenoid switches (industrial controls); sound reproducing equipment; engineering laboratory, except testing; commercial research laboratory; loan institutions, general & industrial
PA: Knowles Corporation
1151 Maplewood Dr
Itasca IL 60143
630 250-5100

(G-11688)
KNOWLES ELECTRONICS LLC (HQ)
1151 Maplewood Dr (60143-2071)
PHONE................630 250-5100
Jeffrey Niew, *President*
Pete Loeppert, *President*
Charles King, *Vice Chairman*
Roland Bowler, *Counsel*
John Anderson, *Senior VP*
▲ EMP: 250
SQ FT: 60,000
SALES (est): 205.9MM
SALES (corp-wide): 854.8MM **Publicly Held**
WEB: www.knowles.com
SIC: 3679 3842 Transducers, electrical; hearing aids
PA: Knowles Corporation
1151 Maplewood Dr
Itasca IL 60143
630 250-5100

(G-11689)
KWIK PRINT INC
206 W Irving Park Rd (60143-2041)
PHONE................630 773-3225
Gary F Roback, *President*
Julie Roback, *Corp Secy*
EMP: 4
SALES (est): 606.9K **Privately Held**
SIC: 2752 2789 2759 Commercial printing, offset; bookbinding & related work; commercial printing

(G-11690)
L & W TOOL & SCREW MCH PDTS
1447 Ardmore Ave (60143-1142)
PHONE................847 238-1212
Walter Sowa, *President*
Joseph Sowa, *Admin Sec*
EMP: 25
SQ FT: 15,000
SALES (est): 4.1MM **Privately Held**
SIC: 3451 Screw machine products

(G-11691)
LIFELINE SCIENTIFIC INC (PA)
1 Pierce Pl Ste 475w (60143-2618)
PHONE................847 294-0300
David Kravitz, *President*
Dave Nelligan, *Info Tech Mgr*
EMP: 20
SALES (est): 3.4MM **Privately Held**
SIC: 3845 Electromedical equipment

(G-11692)
LIFT-ALL COMPANY INC
1414 Norwood Ave (60143-1129)
P.O. Box 496 (60143-0496)
PHONE................800 909-1964
Steve Pacilio, *Manager*
EMP: 28 **Privately Held**
SIC: 3496 2221 Slings, lifting: made from purchased wire; broadwoven fabric mills, manmade
HQ: Lift-All Company, Inc.
1909 Mcfarland Dr
Landisville PA 17538
717 898-6615

(G-11693)
LILLY AIR SYSTEMS CO INC
217 Catalpa Ave (60143-2027)
P.O. Box 173 (60143-0173)
PHONE................630 773-2225
Tim Lilly, *President*
John Lilly, *President*
EMP: 10 EST: 1976
SQ FT: 700
SALES (est): 1.6MM **Privately Held**
SIC: 3564 Filters, air: furnaces, air conditioning equipment, etc.

(G-11694)
LILLY INDUSTRIES INC
Also Called: Lilly Steam Trap
427 W Irving Park Rd (60143-2039)
P.O. Box 173 (60143-0173)
PHONE................630 773-2222
Timothy Lilly, *President*
John R Lilly, *Admin Sec*
▲ EMP: 10
SQ FT: 6,000
SALES (est): 1.1MM **Privately Held**
SIC: 3491 3494 Steam traps; valves & pipe fittings

(G-11695)
LITHO RESEARCH INCORPORATED
1600 Glenlake Ave (60143-1005)
PHONE................630 860-7070
Michael T Miske, *President*
Brian Miske, *General Mgr*
Stephen Kielblock, *Technical Staff*
EMP: 8
SALES (est): 205.9MM
SALES (corp-wide): 854.8MM **Publicly Held**
WEB: www.knowles.com
SIC: 3679 3842 Transducers, electrical; hearing aids
PA: Knowles Corporation
1151 Maplewood Dr
Itasca IL 60143
630 250-5100

(G-11696)
MAJOR DIE & ENGINEERING CO
1352 Industrial Dr (60143-1804)
PHONE................630 773-3444
James Fett Sr, *Owner*
James Fett Jr, *Vice Pres*
EMP: 11
SQ FT: 15,000
SALES (est): 2.4MM **Privately Held**
WEB: www.majordie.com
SIC: 3469 3544 Stamping metal for the trade; special dies, tools, jigs & fixtures

(G-11697)
MARTY LUNDEEN
311 Willow St (60143-1760)
PHONE................630 250-8917
Marty Lundeen, *Executive*
EMP: 3
SALES (est): 118.7K **Privately Held**
SIC: 3511 Turbines & turbine generator sets

(G-11698)
MASTER SPRING & WIRE FORM CO
1340 Ardmore Ave (60143-1105)
PHONE................708 453-2570
Jeff Burda, *President*
Steve Skolozynski, *Vice Pres*
Rick Moris, *Marketing Mgr*
Toni La Fonti, *Manager*
Sherry Anton, *Director*
EMP: 25 EST: 1945
SQ FT: 20,000
SALES (est): 4.5MM **Privately Held**
WEB: www.masterspring.com
SIC: 3496 3495 Miscellaneous fabricated wire products; wire springs

(G-11699)
MEI LLC
315 N Linden St (60143-1839)
PHONE................630 285-1505
Darin Edgecomb,
EMP: 1
SALES (est): 230.9K **Privately Held**
SIC: 2671 Thermoplastic coated paper for packaging

(G-11700)
METAL STRIP BUIDING PRODUCTS
1345 Norwood Ave (60143-1126)
PHONE................847 742-8500
Frank San Roman, *President*
Edward Swantek, *Corp Secy*
Gerald Pines, *Vice Pres*
EMP: 6 EST: 1946
SQ FT: 8,000
SALES (est): 868.8K
SALES (corp-wide): 78.6MM **Privately Held**
SIC: 3499 3449 3444 Novelties & specialties, metal; miscellaneous metalwork; sheet metalwork
PA: Millenia Products Group, Inc.
1345 Norwood Ave
Itasca IL 60143
630 458-0401

(G-11701)
MICROCHIP TECHNOLOGY INC
333 W Pierce Rd Ste 180 (60143-3120)
PHONE................630 285-0071
Shane Crandall, *Engineer*
Steve Rusnock, *Regl Sales Mgr*
Mike Milanas, *Manager*
EMP: 27
SALES (corp-wide): 5.2B **Publicly Held**
SIC: 3674 Integrated circuits, semiconductor networks, etc.
PA: Microchip Technology Inc
2355 W Chandler Blvd
Chandler AZ 85224
480 792-7200

(G-11702)
MICROS SYSTEMS INC
2 Pierce Pl Ste 1700 (60143-3124)
PHONE................443 285-6000
Stephen Vogel, *Sales Staff*
Jim Chapman, *Executive*
EMP: 17
SALES (corp-wide): 39.5B **Publicly Held**
SIC: 3578 5044 3577 Point-of-sale devices; cash registers; computer peripheral equipment
HQ: Micros Systems, Inc.
7031 Columbia Gateway Dr # 1
Columbia MD 21046
443 285-6000

(G-11703)
MILLENIA METALS LLC
Also Called: Ravinia Metals
1345 Norwood Ave (60143-1126)
PHONE................630 458-0401
James Carroll, *CFO*
Eva Andujar, *Human Res Mgr*
Frank San Roman, *Mng Member*
Kevin West, *Supervisor*
Gerald Pines,
EMP: 100
SALES (est): 5.8MM
SALES (corp-wide): 78.6MM **Privately Held**
SIC: 3469 5051 Metal stampings; iron & steel (ferrous) products
PA: Millenia Products Group, Inc.
1345 Norwood Ave
Itasca IL 60143
630 458-0401

(G-11704)
MILLENIA PRODUCTS GROUP INC (PA)
Also Called: Mill Tek Metals
1345 Norwood Ave (60143-1126)
PHONE................630 458-0401
Frank San Roman, *CEO*
Patrick Milet, *Vice Pres*
Cherise Jolly, *Purch Mgr*
Gerald Pines, *Treasurer*
Marlon Carney, *Controller*
▲ EMP: 130
SQ FT: 110,000
SALES (est): 78.6MM **Privately Held**
SIC: 3499 3469 Fire- or burglary-resistive products; machine bases, metal; metal stampings

(G-11705)
MOONS INDUSTRIES AMERICA INC
1113 N Prospect Ave (60143-1401)
PHONE................630 833-5940
James Chang, *President*
Robert Wester, *Opers Mgr*
Rob Cheatham, *Natl Sales Mgr*
Andy Sklierenko, *Sales Staff*
Dottie Griffin, *Supervisor*
▲ EMP: 520
SQ FT: 2,800
SALES (est): 71.3MM **Privately Held**
SIC: 3621 Motors, electric

(G-11706)
N HENRY & SON INC
900 N Rohlwing Rd (60143-1161)
PHONE................847 870-0797
Ben I Wolf, *President*
Alfred B Henry, *Chairman*
EMP: 85
SQ FT: 60,000
SALES (est): 9.4MM **Privately Held**
WEB: www.nhenryandson.com
SIC: 2399 Banners, pennants & flags

(G-11707)
NATIONAL SAFETY COUNCIL (PA)
Also Called: Nsc
1121 Spring Lake Dr (60143-3201)
PHONE................630 285-1121
Mark Vergnano, *Ch of Bd*
Lorraine M Martin, *President*

Itasca - Dupage County (G-11708)

Joseph Ucciferro, *President*
Paulette Moulos, *Exec VP*
Tom Bell, *Vice Pres*
EMP: 275
SQ FT: 90,200
SALES: 59.1MM **Privately Held**
WEB: www.nsc.org
SIC: 8399 2721 1731 5084 Health & welfare council; periodicals: publishing only; safety & security specialization; safety equipment

(G-11708)
NATIONAL TRACKWORK INC
1500 Industrial Dr (60143-1848)
PHONE.................................630 250-0600
Michelle Sargis, *President*
Melissa Sargis, *Admin Sec*
▲ EMP: 40
SALES (est): 5.4MM **Privately Held**
SIC: 3743 Railroad equipment

(G-11709)
NCAB GROUP USA INC
1300 Norwood Ave (60143-1127)
PHONE.................................630 562-5550
Berry Zielke, *Branch Mgr*
EMP: 14
SALES (corp-wide): 5.9MM **Privately Held**
SIC: 3672 Circuit boards, television & radio printed; wiring boards
PA: Ncab Group Usa, Inc.
   10 Starwood Dr
   Hampstead NH 03841
   603 329-4551

(G-11710)
NEOPOST R MEADOWS
1200 N Arlington Hts Rd (60143-1284)
PHONE.................................630 467-0604
Fax: 630 981-9117
EMP: 4 EST: 2006
SALES (est): 370K **Privately Held**
SIC: 3579 Mfg Office Machines

(G-11711)
NESTLE USA INC
Also Called: Willy Wonka Candy Factory
1445 Norwood Ave (60143-1128)
PHONE.................................630 773-2090
Louise Defalco, *Manager*
EMP: 139
SALES (corp-wide): 93.5B **Privately Held**
SIC: 2064 Candy & other confectionery products
HQ: Nestle Usa, Inc.
   1812 N Moore St Ste 118
   Rosslyn VA 22209
   440 264-7249

(G-11712)
NNT ENTERPRISES INCORPORATED
1320 Norwood Ave (60143-1127)
PHONE.................................630 875-9600
David Nyc, *President*
Michael Nyc, *Vice Pres*
▲ EMP: 32
SQ FT: 30,000
SALES (est): 3.8MM **Privately Held**
SIC: 3546 3545 3541 2819 Power-driven handtools; machine tool accessories; machine tools, metal cutting type; industrial inorganic chemicals; metalworking tools (such as drills, taps, dies, files)

(G-11713)
ORACLE CORPORATION
17th Fl 2 Pierce Pl Flr 17 (60143)
PHONE.................................630 931-6400
Steve Vogel, *Sales Dir*
Kathy Martin, *Branch Mgr*
Jeff Andersen, *Training Spec*
EMP: 302
SALES (corp-wide): 39.5B **Publicly Held**
SIC: 7372 Business oriented computer software
PA: Oracle Corporation
   500 Oracle Pkwy
   Redwood City CA 94065
   650 506-7000

(G-11714)
ORGAN RECOVERY SYSTEMS INC
1 Pierce Pl Ste 475w (60143-2618)
PHONE.................................847 824-2600
David Kravitz, *President*
Matthew Copithorne, *General Mgr*
Joseph Annicchiarico, *Managing Dir*
Kayla Andalina, *Engineer*
Chris Steinman, *Engineer*
▲ EMP: 10 EST: 1998
SQ FT: 3,000
SALES (est): 1.3MM **Privately Held**
SIC: 3841 Surgical & medical instruments
PA: Lifeline Scientific, Inc.
   1 Pierce Pl Ste 475w
   Itasca IL 60143

(G-11715)
OVERHEAD DOOR CORPORATION
Also Called: Genie Pro Sales Center
295 S Prospect Ave (60143-2337)
PHONE.................................630 775-9118
Glenn Kerley, *Branch Mgr*
EMP: 7 **Privately Held**
SIC: 3442 2431 Garage doors, overhead: metal; doors, wood
HQ: Overhead Door Corporation
   2501 S State Hwy 121 Ste
   Lewisville TX 75067
   469 549-7100

(G-11716)
PFIZER INC
1 Pierce Pl Ste 300e (60143-2617)
PHONE.................................630 634-3704
Philip H Rose, *Branch Mgr*
EMP: 121
SALES (corp-wide): 51.7B **Publicly Held**
SIC: 2834 Pharmaceutical preparations
PA: Pfizer Inc.
   235 E 42nd St Rm 107
   New York NY 10017
   212 733-2323

(G-11717)
PHOENIX BINDING CORP
Also Called: American Binding
690 Hilltop Dr (60143-1326)
PHONE.................................847 981-1111
Harry Isbell, *President*
EMP: 70
SQ FT: 35,000
SALES (est): 2.3MM **Privately Held**
SIC: 2789 Binding only: books, pamphlets, magazines, etc.

(G-11718)
PHOENIX CONVERTING INC
1251 Ardmore Ave (60143-1103)
PHONE.................................630 258-1500
Robin Bowen, *Controller*
Stanley S Budzinski,
Sheron Ortiz, *Assistant*
EMP: 60
SALES (est): 81.6K **Privately Held**
SIC: 2671 Packaging paper & plastics film, coated & laminated

(G-11719)
PITNEY BOWES INC
1025 Hilltop Dr (60143-1118)
PHONE.................................800 784-4224
EMP: 35
SALES (corp-wide): 3.5B **Publicly Held**
SIC: 3579 7359 3661 8744 Mfg Office Machines Equipment Rental/Leasing Mfg Telephone/Graph Eqip
PA: Pitney Bowes Inc.
   3001 Summer St Ste 3
   Stamford CT 06905
   203 356-5000

(G-11720)
PNA CONSTRUCTION TECH INC (PA)
Also Called: P.N.a Construction Tech
1349 W Bryn Mawr Ave (60143-1313)
PHONE.................................770 668-9500
Russ Boxall, *President*
Benjamin Nantasai, *Design Engr*
Missy Du Toit, *Human Res Dir*
▲ EMP: 12
SQ FT: 11,500

SALES (est): 9.9MM **Privately Held**
SIC: 3449 Miscellaneous metalwork

(G-11721)
POLYBILT BODY COMPANY LLC (PA)
325 Spring Lake Dr (60143-2072)
PHONE.................................708 345-8050
Timothy S Dean, *Mng Member*
Peter Darley, *Mng Member*
Daniel Owen, *Mng Member*
EMP: 3
SALES: 800K **Privately Held**
SIC: 2821 Plastics materials & resins

(G-11722)
PRECISION PRESS & LABEL INC
1285 Hamilton Pkwy (60143-1150)
P.O. Box 185524, Fort Worth TX (76181-0524)
PHONE.................................630 625-1225
Jim Kersten, *CEO*
Michael Richter, *CFO*
EMP: 2
SQ FT: 7,500
SALES (est): 1.8MM **Privately Held**
SIC: 2752 2679 Commercial printing, lithographic; labels, paper: made from purchased material
HQ: Diversified Labeling Solutions, Inc.
   1285 Hamilton Pkwy
   Itasca IL 60143
   630 625-1225

(G-11723)
QUALITAS MANUFACTURING INC (PA)
Also Called: Qmi Security Solutions
1661 Glenlake Ave (60143-1004)
PHONE.................................630 529-7111
James V Miller, *President*
Stephen Miller, *Vice Pres*
Larry Wedoff, *Vice Pres*
Guy Haukedahl, *Sales Staff*
Joanell M McKenna, *Admin Sec*
◆ EMP: 78
SQ FT: 20,000
SALES (est): 21MM **Privately Held**
SIC: 3442 3089 Shutters, door or window: metal; shutters, plastic

(G-11724)
RDI GROUP INC
Also Called: Chicago Slitter
1025 W Thorndale Ave (60143-1336)
PHONE.................................630 773-4900
Curtis Maas, *Ch of Bd*
Fred Kestler, *President*
Andy Walkowicz, *Plant Mgr*
Timothy Johnson, *Project Mgr*
Nolan Tubbs, *Engineer*
▲ EMP: 120 EST: 1902
SQ FT: 120,000
SALES (corp-wide): 63.7MM
SALES (est): 735K **Privately Held**
WEB: www.therdigroup.com
SIC: 3531 Roofing equipment
PA: Reichel & Drews Gmbh
   Am Weichselgarten 28
   Erlangen

(G-11725)
RIVERSIDE ASSESSMENTS LLC (PA)
1 Pierce Pl Ste 900w (60143-3103)
PHONE.................................800 767-8420
Rajib Roy, *President*
Graham Ballbach, *CFO*
EMP: 2
SALES (est): 575.3K **Privately Held**
SIC: 3999 2731 Education aids, devices & supplies; book publishing

(G-11726)
ROBERTS SWISS INC
1387 Ardmore Ave (60143-1104)
PHONE.................................630 467-9100
Robert C Armitage, *President*
Fernando Ortiz, *Vice Pres*
Lawrence Rutan, *Mfg Staff*
Patricia Morrison, *Accountant*
Patty Morrison, *Accountant*
EMP: 48
SQ FT: 12,200

SALES (est): 9.5MM **Privately Held**
WEB: www.rswiss.com
SIC: 3451 3562 3541 3452 Screw machine products; ball & roller bearings; machine tools, metal cutting type; bolts, nuts, rivets & washers

(G-11727)
ROBERTSHAW CONTROLS COMPANY (HQ)
1222 Hamilton Pkwy (60143-1160)
PHONE.................................630 260-3400
Mark Balcunas, *CEO*
Andy Culver, *Vice Pres*
Francisco Escobar, *Purch Mgr*
Oscar Zapata, *Purch Agent*
Brandon Flanigan, *Engineer*
◆ EMP: 150
SALES (est): 1B **Privately Held**
SIC: 3823 3822 3492 Industrial instrmnts msrmnt display/control process variable; auto controls regulating residntl & coml environmt & applncs; control valves, aircraft: hydraulic & pneumatic

(G-11728)
ROLL SOURCE PAPER
900 N Arlington Heights R (60143-2805)
PHONE.................................630 875-0308
Sue Kiewert, *Manager*
EMP: 9
SALES (est): 1.2MM **Privately Held**
SIC: 2621 5113 5111 Paper mills; paperboard & products; writing paper

(G-11729)
ROYALE INNOVATION GROUP LTD
794 Willow Ct (60143-2864)
P.O. Box 479 (60143-0479)
PHONE.................................312 339-1406
Lisa Liarakos, *President*
Nicholas Liarakos, *Vice Pres*
EMP: 2
SALES: 1MM **Privately Held**
SIC: 3432 8711 7389 Plumbing fixture fittings & trim; engineering services;

(G-11730)
RS OWENS DIV ST REGIS LLC
1612 Glenlake Ave (60143-1005)
PHONE.................................773 282-6000
Richard Sirkser, *President*
Mark Psaros, *Manager*
▲ EMP: 80 EST: 2012
SALES (est): 9.4MM **Privately Held**
SIC: 3914 Trophies, plated (all metals)

(G-11731)
SERENE ONE LLC
Also Called: Phoenix Converting
1251 Ardmore Ave (60143-1103)
PHONE.................................630 285-1500
Tim Burgess, *Plant Mgr*
Sarah Budzinski, *Cust Mgr*
Stanley Budzinski, *Mng Member*
Samantha A Budzinski,
▲ EMP: 15
SALES (est): 3.4MM **Privately Held**
SIC: 3825 Analog-digital converters, electronic instrumentation type

(G-11732)
SHIMA AMERICAN CORPORATION
Also Called: PERFORMANCE MATERIAL DIVISION
500 Park Blvd Ste 725 (60143-3146)
PHONE.................................630 760-4330
Shima Koshi, *Ch of Bd*
Shinichiro Taki, *President*
Motoyasu Momoki, *Vice Pres*
▲ EMP: 18 EST: 1963
SQ FT: 23,000
SALES: 56MM **Privately Held**
WEB: www.shimaamerican.com
SIC: 5013 2992 5085 Automotive supplies & parts; lubricating oils & greases; industrial supplies; bearings; industrial tools; industrial wheels
PA: Shima Trading Co., Ltd.
   2-12-14, Ginza
   Chuo-Ku TKY 104-0

GEOGRAPHIC SECTION

(G-11733)
SLEE CORPORATION
Also Called: Crystal Edge
1612 Glenlake Ave (60143-1005)
PHONE..................................773 777-2444
Barry Slee, *President*
Lesley Slee, *Vice Pres*
▲ EMP: 27
SQ FT: 42,000
SALES (est): 4.4MM Privately Held
SIC: 3231 Ornamental glass: cut, engraved or otherwise decorated; mirrored glass

(G-11734)
SMART SOLUTIONS INC
211 Catalpa Ave (60143-2027)
P.O. Box 568 (60143-0568)
PHONE..................................630 775-1517
Brian Lilly, *President*
EMP: 5
SALES (est): 447.1K Privately Held
SIC: 3061 Mechanical rubber goods

(G-11735)
SOLBERG INTERNATIONAL LTD (PA)
1151 Ardmore Ave (60143-1305)
PHONE..................................630 616-4400
Charles H Solberg, *President*
Joyce C Solberg, *Vice Pres*
Jason Cox, *Manager*
Art Garcia, *Manager*
▲ EMP: 5
SALES (est): 955.5K Privately Held
SIC: 3564 Filters, air: furnaces, air conditioning equipment, etc.

(G-11736)
SOLBERG MFG INC (PA)
1151 Ardmore Ave (60143-1387)
P.O. Box 5988, Carol Stream (60197-5988)
PHONE..................................630 616-4400
Charles H Solberg Jr, *CEO*
Arnold Tor Solberg, *President*
Raymond Kulpa, *General Mgr*
Marquerite B Solberg, *Corp Secy*
Clint Browning, *Vice Pres*
◆ EMP: 60 EST: 1968
SQ FT: 97,000
SALES (est): 19MM Privately Held
SIC: 3564 Filters, air: furnaces, air conditioning equipment, etc.

(G-11737)
SOLBERG MFG INC
680 Baker Dr (60143-1346)
PHONE..................................630 773-1363
Charles Solberg Jr, *President*
EMP: 40
SALES (corp-wide): 19MM Privately Held
SIC: 3564 Filters, air: furnaces, air conditioning equipment, etc.
PA: Solberg Mfg., Inc
   1151 Ardmore Ave
   Itasca IL 60143
   630 616-4400

(G-11738)
SPECTRAL DYNAMICS INC
Also Called: L.A.B. Equipment
1549 Ardmore Ave (60143-1108)
PHONE..................................630 595-4288
EMP: 24
SALES (corp-wide): 8.5MM Privately Held
SIC: 3559 3825 Rubber working machinery, including tires; lab standards, electric: resistance, inductance, capacitance
PA: Spectral Dynamics, Inc.
   2199 Zanker Rd
   San Jose CA 95131
   760 761-0440

(G-11739)
SPRING BROOK NATURE CENTER
Also Called: Village Itasca Nature Center
411 N Prospect Ave (60143-1605)
PHONE..................................630 773-5572
Fred Maier, *Director*
EMP: 6

SALES: 500K Privately Held
SIC: 3822 Auto controls regulating residntl & coml environmt & applncs

(G-11740)
STANDARD REGISTER INC
1 Pierce Pl Ste 270c (60143-2621)
PHONE..................................630 467-8300
EMP: 18
SALES (corp-wide): 3.8B Privately Held
SIC: 2754 Printing
HQ: Standard Register, Inc.
   600 Albany St
   Dayton OH
   937 221-1000

(G-11741)
SUBARU OF AMERICA INC
Also Called: Great Lakes Region
500 Park Blvd Ste 255c (60143-3126)
PHONE..................................630 250-4740
Linda Walter, *Administration*
EMP: 23 Privately Held
SIC: 5511 8741 3711 Automobiles, new & used; management services; motor vehicles & car bodies
HQ: Subaru Of America, Inc.
   1 Subaru Dr
   Camden NJ 08103
   856 488-8500

(G-11742)
SYSTEMATICS SCREEN PRINTING
1625 Norwood Ave (60143-1009)
PHONE..................................630 521-1123
Govind Sanghani, *President*
Nalini Sanghani, *Vice Pres*
Anand Sanghani, *Admin Sec*
EMP: 12
SQ FT: 15,000
SALES (est): 2.4MM Privately Held
SIC: 2759 Screen printing

(G-11743)
SYSTEMS UNLIMITED INC
1350 W Bryn Mawr Ave (60143-1314)
PHONE..................................630 285-0010
Russell S Omuro, *President*
▲ EMP: 140
SQ FT: 107,000
SALES (est): 14.3MM Privately Held
SIC: 1799 2521 Home/office interiors finishing, furnishing & remodeling; office furniture installation; desks, office: wood; chairs, office: padded, upholstered or plain: wood

(G-11744)
TECH-MAX MACHINE INC
1170 Ardmore Ave (60143-1306)
PHONE..................................630 875-0054
Richard Malek, *President*
Ted Morawa, *Exec VP*
Lukasz Borowiec, *Sales Staff*
EMP: 20
SQ FT: 40,000
SALES (est): 4.1MM Privately Held
SIC: 3599 Machine shop, jobbing & repair

(G-11745)
TELCOM INNOVATIONS GROUP LLC
125 N Prospect Ave (60143-1811)
PHONE..................................630 350-0700
Matt Schwartz, *Sales Mgr*
Cheri Beatty, *Accounts Exec*
Shannon Carroll, *Marketing Mgr*
Randall Borchardt, *Mng Member*
Bridget Baker,
EMP: 50
SQ FT: 25,000
SALES (est): 11.3MM Privately Held
SIC: 4813 3825 8999 7389 ; network analyzers; communication services; design services

(G-11746)
THE WEB CMMNICATIONS GROUP INC
Also Called: Animated Printing & Packaging
105 E Irving Park Rd (60143-2117)
PHONE..................................630 467-0900
Gary A Jacobsen, *President*
Mary J Jacobsen, *Vice Pres*

Darlene Jacobsen, *Treasurer*
James R Schirott, *Admin Sec*
▼ EMP: 4
SQ FT: 1,000
SALES (est): 410K Privately Held
SIC: 2752 8742 Promotional printing, lithographic; marketing consulting services

(G-11747)
TRADE LABEL & DECAL (PA)
1285 Hamilton Pkwy (60143-1150)
P.O. Box 821 (60143-0821)
PHONE..................................630 773-0447
Harry Blecker, *President*
Catherine Blecker, *Admin Sec*
EMP: 8
SQ FT: 1,000
SALES (est): 659.7K Privately Held
SIC: 2679 Labels, paper: made from purchased material

(G-11748)
TRIVIAL DEVELOPMENT CORP
1035 Hilltop Dr (60143-1118)
PHONE..................................630 860-2500
Lawrence J Balsamo, *President*
Charles Schmelzer, *Vice Pres*
▲ EMP: 25
SQ FT: 15,000
SALES (est): 6.7MM Privately Held
SIC: 5092 3944 Toys & games; board games, puzzles & models, except electronic

(G-11749)
TWO FOUR SEVEN METAL LASER
1428 Norwood Ave (60143-1129)
PHONE..................................847 250-5199
EMP: 3
SALES (est): 242.2K Privately Held
WEB: www.247metallaser.com
SIC: 3499 Welding tips, heat resistant: metal

(G-11750)
UNITED STEEL & FASTENERS INC
1500 Industrial Dr (60143-1800)
PHONE..................................630 250-0900
Isaac Sargis, *President*
Joseph Wieczorek, *General Mgr*
Bill Albert, *Traffic Mgr*
Angela Hedger, *Accounting Mgr*
Nick Blakemore, *Sales Mgr*
◆ EMP: 41 EST: 1975
SQ FT: 60,000
SALES (est): 10MM Privately Held
SIC: 3429 Metal fasteners

(G-11751)
VORNE INDUSTRIES INC
1445 Industrial Dr (60143-1849)
PHONE..................................630 875-3600
Ramon Vorne, *President*
Alfred Vorne, *Shareholder*
Norman Vorne, *Admin Sec*
EMP: 27
SQ FT: 12,000
SALES: 9MM Privately Held
WEB: www.vorne.com
SIC: 3823 Industrial process measurement equipment

(G-11752)
W S DARLEY & CO
Also Called: Odin Foam
325 Spring Lake Dr (60143-2072)
PHONE..................................630 735-3500
Jim Guse, *Manager*
EMP: 17
SALES (corp-wide): 200MM Privately Held
WEB: www.darley.com
SIC: 3561 Industrial pumps & parts
PA: W. S. Darley & Co.
   325 Spring Lake Dr
   Itasca IL 60143
   630 735-3500

(G-11753)
WEIDENMILLER CO
1464 Industrial Dr (60143-1848)
PHONE..................................630 250-2500
Kras Stephen, *Engineer*
Thomas E Weidenmiller, *Treasurer*

▲ EMP: 16 EST: 1903
SQ FT: 25,000
SALES (est): 3.7MM Privately Held
WEB: www.weidenmiller.com
SIC: 3556 Biscuit cutting dies

(G-11754)
WERNER CO
555 W Pierce Rd Ste 300 (60143-2649)
PHONE..................................847 455-8001
Craig Werner, *President*
EMP: 800 Privately Held
SIC: 3353 3446 3354 Aluminum sheet, plate & foil; architectural metalwork; aluminum extruded products
HQ: Werner Co.
   93 Werner Rd
   Greenville PA 16125

(G-11755)
XERTREX INTERNATIONAL INC (PA)
Also Called: Tabbies
1530 Glenlake Ave (60143-1171)
PHONE..................................630 773-4020
Dennis W Cunningham, *President*
Cheri Miroballi, *Corp Secy*
Christopher Cunningham, *Vice Pres*
Chris Cunningham, *CFO*
Michael Stanley, *Sales Staff*
▲ EMP: 40 EST: 1955
SQ FT: 42,000
SALES (est): 8.4MM Privately Held
WEB: www.tabbies.com
SIC: 2679 5943 Tags & labels, paper; office forms & supplies

Ivesdale
Champaign County

(G-11756)
DAVID MARTIN
Also Called: Martin Machine Co
504 E 4th St (61851)
P.O. Box 25 (61851-0025)
PHONE..................................217 564-2440
David Martin, *Owner*
Sue Martin, *Co-Owner*
EMP: 3
SALES (est): 180K Privately Held
SIC: 3821 Laboratory apparatus & furniture

Jacksonville
Morgan County

(G-11757)
BILL WEST ENTERPRISES INC
2170 Arcadia Rd (62650-6082)
PHONE..................................217 886-2591
William C West Sr, *President*
Kathy West, *Vice Pres*
EMP: 1
SQ FT: 5,500
SALES: 900K Privately Held
SIC: 7948 3694 3621 3444 Stock car racing; automotive electrical equipment; starting equipment, street cars; sheet metalwork; motor vehicles & car bodies

(G-11758)
BIRDCO FABRICATORS INC (PA)
500 Allen Ave (62650-1500)
PHONE..................................217 408-8744
Alexis Martin, *President*
EMP: 2
SALES (est): 236.2K Privately Held
SIC: 3441 Fabricated structural metal

(G-11759)
BIRDSELL MACHINE & ORNA INC
531 W Independence Ave (62650-1311)
P.O. Box 100 (62651-0100)
PHONE..................................217 243-5849
Kevin Birdsell, *President*
Doug Birdsell, *Corp Secy*
EMP: 5

Jacksonville - Morgan County (G-11760)

SALES (est): 484K **Privately Held**
SIC: 3441 3446 Fabricated structural metal; grillwork, ornamental metal

(G-11760)
BRANSTITER PRINTING CO
217 E Morgan St (62650-2508)
PHONE.................................217 245-6533
Glenn Kafer, *Owner*
Janet Kay Kafer, *Co-Owner*
EMP: 7
SQ FT: 1,800
SALES (est): 728.9K **Privately Held**
SIC: 2752 2791 2789 2759 Commercial printing, offset; typesetting; bookbinding & related work; commercial printing

(G-11761)
CCK AUTOMATIONS INC
500 Capitol Way (62650-1092)
PHONE.................................217 243-6040
J J Richardson, *President*
Mike Allan, *Opers Staff*
Sherri Richardson, *CFO*
Martin Copeland, *Associate*
▲ EMP: 49
SALES (est): 25.3MM **Privately Held**
SIC: 3672 Printed circuit boards

(G-11762)
COMMUNITY READYMIX INC
710 Brooklyn Ave (62650-3072)
PHONE.................................217 245-6668
Jay Beltman, *President*
EMP: 20 EST: 1994
SALES: 2.8MM **Privately Held**
SIC: 3273 Ready-mixed concrete

(G-11763)
CREATIVE IDEAS INC
Also Called: Theatre In The Park
4 Sunnydale Ave (62650-2656)
PHONE.................................217 245-1378
EMP: 4 EST: 1994
SALES (est): 170K **Privately Held**
SIC: 2741 Misc Publishing

(G-11764)
DAN MOY
806 Woodland Pl (62650-2745)
PHONE.................................217 243-2572
Dan Moy, *Principal*
EMP: 3
SALES (est): 172.5K **Privately Held**
SIC: 3482 Small arms ammunition

(G-11765)
GAITHER TOOL CO
2255 W Morton Ave (62650-2626)
PHONE.................................217 245-0545
Richard Brahler, *President*
Jeff Alexander, *Vice Pres*
▲ EMP: 6
SQ FT: 6,000
SALES: 1.7MM **Privately Held**
SIC: 3423 Hand & edge tools

(G-11766)
HEARST CORPORATION
Also Called: Journal-Courier
235 W State St (62650-2001)
PHONE.................................217 245-6121
Jeff Bergin, *Branch Mgr*
EMP: 3
SALES (corp-wide): 8.2B **Privately Held**
SIC: 2711 Newspapers, publishing & printing
PA: The Hearst Corporation
300 W 57th St Fl 42
New York NY 10019
212 649-2000

(G-11767)
HOLE IN THE WALL SCREEN ARTS
112 Park St (62650-2308)
PHONE.................................217 243-9100
James Jamison, *President*
Gary Goodwin, *Treasurer*
John Carpenter, *Admin Sec*
EMP: 3
SQ FT: 2,400
SALES: 120K **Privately Held**
SIC: 5699 2396 2759 T-shirts, custom printed; automotive & apparel trimmings; screen printing

(G-11768)
I T R INC
21 Harold Cox Dr (62650-6771)
PHONE.................................217 245-4478
Richard W Brahler III, *President*
▲ EMP: 30
SALES (est): 3.1MM **Privately Held**
SIC: 3559 Automotive related machinery

(G-11769)
ILLINOIS ROAD CONTRACTORS INC (PA)
520 N Webster Ave (62650-1115)
P.O. Box 1060 (62651-1060)
PHONE.................................217 245-6181
Devon Davidsmeyer, *CEO*
Jeffry Davidsmeyer, *President*
R Thomas Slayback, *Corp Secy*
Thomas L Atkins, *Exec VP*
Jay Hornbeek, *Vice Pres*
EMP: 40 EST: 1925
SQ FT: 2,500
SALES (est): 36MM **Privately Held**
WEB: www.ircgrp.com
SIC: 1611 2951 4213 Highway & street maintenance; asphalt & asphaltic paving mixtures (not from refineries); trucking, except local

(G-11770)
ILMO PRODUCTS COMPANY (PA)
7 Eastgate Dr (62650-6761)
P.O. Box 790 (62651-0790)
PHONE.................................217 245-2183
Linda Standley, *CEO*
Brad Floreth, *President*
Sunny Hart, *District Mgr*
Terry Jack, *Store Mgr*
Steve Ford, *Buyer*
◆ EMP: 45 EST: 1913
SQ FT: 40,000
SALES (est): 37.3MM **Privately Held**
WEB: www.ilmoproducts.com
SIC: 5084 2813 Welding machinery & equipment; industrial gases

(G-11771)
JACKSONVILLE MACHINE INC
2265 W Morton Ave (62650-2626)
PHONE.................................217 243-1119
Jeff Rodems, *President*
Robert Rodems, *Vice Pres*
Ryan Wood, *Opers Mgr*
Jamie Byus, *Purch Mgr*
Luke Cantrell, *QC Mgr*
EMP: 60 EST: 1919
SQ FT: 35,000
SALES: 6MM **Privately Held**
WEB: www.jmimachine.com
SIC: 3599 7692 Machine shop, jobbing & repair; machine & other job shop work; welding repair

(G-11772)
JACKSONVILLE MONUMENT CO
330 E State St (62650-2030)
PHONE.................................217 245-2514
Andy Burington, *Owner*
John Mahoney, *General Mgr*
EMP: 5
SQ FT: 3,000
SALES (est): 372.5K **Privately Held**
SIC: 5999 3281 Monuments, finished to custom order; cut stone & stone products

(G-11773)
LONELINO SIGN COMPANY INC
2122 E Morton Ave (62650-6431)
PHONE.................................217 243-2444
Thomas Lonelino, *President*
EMP: 3
SALES (est): 90K **Privately Held**
SIC: 3993 Signs & advertising specialties

(G-11774)
LYLE JAMES
880 S Main St (62650-3012)
PHONE.................................217 675-2191
James Lyle, *Principal*
EMP: 3 EST: 2017
SALES (est): 205.9K **Privately Held**
SIC: 2752 Commercial printing, lithographic

(G-11775)
MARK LAHEY
107 S Johnson St (62650-2542)
PHONE.................................217 243-4433
Mark Lahey, *Owner*
EMP: 3
SQ FT: 5,400
SALES: 500K **Privately Held**
SIC: 3599 7692 Machine shop, jobbing & repair; welding repair

(G-11776)
MOELLER READY MIX INC
300 Moeller Rd (62650)
P.O. Box 1086 (62651-1086)
PHONE.................................217 243-7471
Arminda Moeller, *President*
Cheryl Moeller, *Admin Sec*
EMP: 13
SALES (est): 1.8MM **Privately Held**
SIC: 3273 Ready-mixed concrete

(G-11777)
MONQUI SUDS LLC
907 W Morton Ave (62650-3145)
PHONE.................................217 479-0090
Ross Monk, *Mng Member*
EMP: 5
SALES: 240K **Privately Held**
SIC: 3633 Laundry dryers, household or coin-operated

(G-11778)
NESTLE USA INC
Also Called: Nestle Beverage Division
1111 Carnation Dr (62650-1144)
PHONE.................................217 243-9175
Ryan Johnston, *Branch Mgr*
EMP: 135
SALES (corp-wide): 93.5B **Privately Held**
WEB: www.nestleusa.com
SIC: 2023 Evaporated milk
HQ: Nestle Usa, Inc.
1812 N Moore St Ste 118
Rosslyn VA 22209
440 264-7249

(G-11779)
PACTIV LLC
2230 E Morton Ave (62650)
PHONE.................................217 479-1144
Jeff Phillips, *Manager*
EMP: 238 **Publicly Held**
SIC: 2673 3497 3089 2621 Food storage & trash bags (plastic); trash bags (plastic film); made from purchased materials; food storage & frozen food bags, plastic; metal foil & leaf; plastic containers, except foam; plastic kitchenware, tableware & houseware; pressed & molded pulp & fiber products; molded pulp products
HQ: Pactiv Llc
1900 W Field Ct
Lake Forest IL 60045
847 482-2000

(G-11780)
PALLET REPAIR SYSTEMS INC
Also Called: P R S
2 Eastgate Dr (62650-6268)
PHONE.................................217 291-0009
Carolyn Williams, *President*
Jeff Williams, *Vice Pres*
▲ EMP: 16
SQ FT: 25,000
SALES: 4.5MM **Privately Held**
SIC: 3441 Fabricated structural metal

(G-11781)
PRODUCTION PRESS INC (PA)
307 E Morgan St (62650-2546)
P.O. Box 940 (62651-0940)
PHONE.................................217 243-3353
Joseph Racey, *President*
Anthony Hall, *CFO*
Shelly Whewell, *Human Res Dir*
Bradney Racey, *Admin Sec*
EMP: 40 EST: 1998
SALES (est): 6.7MM **Privately Held**
WEB: www.productionpress.com
SIC: 2752 Commercial printing, offset

(G-11782)
REYNOLDS CONSUMER PRODUCTS LLC
500 E Superior Ave (62650-3355)
PHONE.................................217 479-1126
Stan Peter, *Buyer*
Steve Long, *Engineer*
Barry McCollom, *Engineer*
Stephen Holt, *Senior Engr*
Ron Robison, *Human Res Mgr*
EMP: 23 **Publicly Held**
SIC: 3353 Foil, aluminum
HQ: Reynolds Consumer Products Llc
1900 W Field Ct
Lake Forest IL 60045

(G-11783)
REYNOLDS CONSUMER PRODUCTS LLC
2226 E Morton Ave (62650-6204)
PHONE.................................217 479-1466
EMP: 9 **Publicly Held**
SIC: 3353 Foil, aluminum
HQ: Reynolds Consumer Products Llc
1900 W Field Ct
Lake Forest IL 60045

(G-11784)
UNITED GILSONITE LABS INC
550 Capitol Way (62650-1092)
P.O. Box 1182 (62651-1182)
PHONE.................................217 243-7878
George Crolly, *Branch Mgr*
EMP: 30
SQ FT: 34,000
SALES (corp-wide): 56.2MM **Privately Held**
SIC: 2851 2899 2891 2821 Varnishes; stains: varnish, oil or wax; chemical preparations; adhesives & sealants; plastics materials & resins; paints
PA: United Gilsonite Laboratories, Inc.
1396 Jefferson Ave
Dunmore PA 18509
570 344-1202

Jerseyville
Jersey County

(G-11785)
A STUCKI COMPANY
Also Called: American Inds A Div A Stucki
27128 Crystal Lake Rd (62052-7089)
PHONE.................................618 498-4442
Jeff Vodar, *Vice Pres*
EMP: 20
SALES (corp-wide): 48.5MM **Privately Held**
SIC: 3999 Barber & beauty shop equipment
PA: A. Stucki Company
360 Wright Brothers Dr
Coraopolis PA 15108
412 424-0560

(G-11786)
ASSOCIATED AGRI-BUSINESS INC
Also Called: Simfax Agri-Services
100 S State St (62052-1853)
PHONE.................................618 498-2977
Connie Blackorby, *Manager*
EMP: 3
SALES (corp-wide): 427.2K **Privately Held**
SIC: 6331 7372 Federal crop insurance corporation; prepackaged software
PA: Associated Agri-Business, Inc.
229 Elm St
Eldred IL 62027
618 498-2977

(G-11787)
ATLAS BUILDING COMPONENTS INC
Also Called: A B C Truss
5 Industrial Dr (62052-3612)
PHONE.................................618 639-0222
EMP: 20
SALES: 2MM **Privately Held**
SIC: 2439 Mfg Structural Wood Members

GEOGRAPHIC SECTION   **Joliet - Will County (G-11816)**

(G-11788)
CAMPBELL PUBLISHING CO INC
Also Called: Jersey County Journal
832 S State St (62052-2343)
P.O. Box 407 (62052-0407)
  PHONE..................................618 498-1234
  Bruce Campbell, *Branch Mgr*
  EMP: 10
  SALES (corp-wide): 2MM **Privately Held**
  SIC: 2711 Newspapers, publishing & printing
  PA: Campbell Publishing Co Inc
    310 S County Rd
    Hardin IL
    618 576-2345

(G-11789)
CUSTOM CHROME & POLISHING
18416 Stagecoach Rd (62052-6987)
  PHONE..................................618 885-9499
  Bill Sheck, *Manager*
  EMP: 5 **EST:** 2008
  SALES (est): 280K **Privately Held**
  SIC: 3471 Chromium plating of metals or formed products

(G-11790)
EXTREME FORCE VALVE INC
515 Mound St (62052-2843)
  PHONE..................................618 494-5795
  Mark Willmore, *President*
  Eric Linder, *Vice Pres*
  EMP: 4 **EST:** 2015
  SALES (est): 204.5K **Privately Held**
  SIC: 3592 7699 Valves; valve repair, industrial

(G-11791)
GORMAN BROTHERS READY MIX INC
Also Called: Gorman Ready Mix
721 S State St (62052-2357)
  PHONE..................................618 498-2173
  Jane Leonhardt, *President*
  Eric W Leonhardt, *Vice Pres*
  EMP: 18
  SQ FT: 100,000
  SALES: 2.3MM **Privately Held**
  WEB: www.gormanreadymix.com
  SIC: 3273 2951 1794 5211 Ready-mixed concrete; asphalt & asphaltic paving mixtures (not from refineries); excavation work; lumber & other building materials; local trucking, without storage

(G-11792)
HANSEN PACKING CO
807 State Highway 16 (62052-2813)
  PHONE..................................618 498-3714
  Dave Hansen, *President*
  David Hansen, *Vice Pres*
  Ryan Hansen, *Manager*
  EMP: 8
  SQ FT: 3,700
  SALES (est): 572K **Privately Held**
  WEB: www.hansenpackingmeats.com
  SIC: 2011 5147 2013 Meat packing plants; meats, fresh; sausages & other prepared meats

(G-11793)
HENDERSON WATER DISTRICT
1004 State Highway 16 (62052-2826)
  PHONE..................................618 498-6418
  Don Miller, *Owner*
  EMP: 2
  SALES: 551.6K **Privately Held**
  SIC: 2086 Pasteurized & mineral waters, bottled & canned

(G-11794)
MTS JERSEYVILLE INC
27065 Crystal Lake Rd (62052-7096)
  PHONE..................................618 639-2583
  Adam Heitzig, *Manager*
  EMP: 4 **EST:** 2014
  SALES (est): 417.3K **Privately Held**
  WEB: www.midwesttractorsales.com
  SIC: 3523 Farm machinery & equipment

(G-11795)
PHILLIP GRIGALANZ
Also Called: Grigalanz Software Enterprises
114 N Washington St (62052-1603)
  PHONE..................................219 628-6706
  Phillip Grigalanz, *Owner*
  EMP: 3
  SALES (est): 83.9K **Privately Held**
  SIC: 7371 7372 7373 Computer software systems analysis & design, custom; computer software development & applications; business oriented computer software; utility computer software; computer integrated systems design

(G-11796)
SMITH BROTHERS FABRICATING
Also Called: Smith Bros Engineering
406 Maple Ave (62052-2218)
  PHONE..................................618 498-5612
  John N Smith, *President*
  EMP: 3
  SQ FT: 2,000
  SALES (est): 230K **Privately Held**
  SIC: 3441 Fabricated structural metal

(G-11797)
UNIQUE CONCRETE CONCEPTS INC
Also Called: Ingram Vault Co
26860 State Highway 16 (62052-6555)
P.O. Box 188 (62052-0188)
  PHONE..................................618 466-0700
  Carol Spencer, *Owner*
  EMP: 10
  SQ FT: 6,000
  SALES: 1.5MM **Privately Held**
  SIC: 3272 7699 Manhole covers or frames, concrete; septic tanks, concrete; septic tank cleaning service

(G-11798)
W A RICE SEED COMPANY
1108 W Carpenter St (62052-1363)
  PHONE..................................618 498-5538
  William A Rice, *President*
  Pamela Rice Weber, *Admin Sec*
  ▲ **EMP:** 6 **EST:** 1898
  SQ FT: 9,000
  SALES (est): 1MM **Privately Held**
  WEB: www.wariceseed.com
  SIC: 5191 3523 Seeds: field, garden & flower; cleaning machines for fruits, grains & vegetables

(G-11799)
WEBE INK
103 Lincoln Ave (62052-1455)
  PHONE..................................618 498-7620
  Marty Baker, *Owner*
  EMP: 3
  SALES: 170K **Privately Held**
  SIC: 2759 Screen printing

Johnsburg
Mchenry County

(G-11800)
2BALD INC
3420 N Richmond Rd (60051-5446)
  PHONE..................................815 403-8870
  Tim Stewart, *Admin Sec*
  EMP: 3
  SALES: 50K **Privately Held**
  SIC: 2741

(G-11801)
ARBORTECH CORPORATION
3607 Chapel Hill Rd Ste M (60051-2515)
  PHONE..................................847 462-1111
  Raymond J Graffia, *President*
  Ray Graffia, *Vice Pres*
  EMP: 4
  SALES (est): 828.3K **Privately Held**
  SIC: 5074 3589 Water purification equipment; water treatment equipment, industrial

(G-11802)
CDC ENTERPRISES INC
1512 River Terrace Dr (60051-7568)
P.O. Box 202, Ringwood (60072-0202)
  PHONE..................................815 790-4205
  Paul Pieper, *President*
  EMP: 3
  SALES (est): 280K **Privately Held**
  SIC: 7371 7372 3822 Electrical equipment & supplies; systems integration services; incinerator control systems, residential & commercial type

(G-11803)
FOCUS MARKETING GROUP INC
3320 Rocky Beach Rd (60051-9669)
  PHONE..................................815 363-2525
  Mary Lou Hutchinson, *President*
  EMP: 3
  SQ FT: 900
  SALES (est): 300K **Privately Held**
  SIC: 3429 Furniture hardware

(G-11804)
GROVE INDUSTRIAL
3915 Spring Grove Rd (60051-5906)
  PHONE..................................815 385-4800
  Wendel Dschida, *Partner*
  Martin Dschida, *Partner*
  EMP: 5
  SQ FT: 3,000
  SALES (est): 80K **Privately Held**
  SIC: 3545 Boring machine attachments (machine tool accessories)

(G-11805)
ILLINOIS INSTRUMENTS INC
2401 Hiller Rdg Ste A (60051-7451)
P.O. Box 38, Fox Lake (60020-0038)
  PHONE..................................815 344-6212
  Bryan Cummings, *President*
  Richard Smith, *President*
  Michael Buckley, *Engineer*
  Hanna Wargo, *Sales Associate*
  Donna Palmer, *Office Mgr*
  EMP: 20
  SQ FT: 10,000
  SALES (est): 5.1MM **Privately Held**
  SIC: 3826 Analytical instruments

(G-11806)
JDI MOLD AND TOOL LLC
2510 Hiller Rdg (60051-7447)
  PHONE..................................815 759-5646
  Clinton Renji, *VP Opers*
  James T Jurinak,
  Richard D Minehart Jr,
  EMP: 15
  SQ FT: 16,000
  SALES (est): 2.8MM **Privately Held**
  SIC: 3089 Injection molding of plastics

(G-11807)
MIDWEST HOSE & FITTINGS INC
3218 N Richmond Rd Unit 5 (60051-5441)
  PHONE..................................815 578-9040
  Jon Walleck, *Branch Mgr*
  EMP: 4
  SALES (est): 274.2K **Privately Held**
  WEB: www.midhose.com
  SIC: 3492 Fluid power valves & hose fittings
  PA: Midwest Hose & Fittings, Inc
    1840 Industrial Dr # 300
    Libertyville IL 60048

(G-11808)
NANAS KITCHEN INC
1313 Old Bay Rd (60051-9652)
  PHONE..................................815 363-8500
  Sargon Boudakh, *President*
  EMP: 7
  SQ FT: 1,200
  SALES: 2MM **Privately Held**
  SIC: 2099 Seasonings & spices

(G-11809)
REMINGTON INDUSTRIES INC
3521 Chapel Hill Rd (60051-2504)
  PHONE..................................815 385-1987
  Tom Liston, *Owner*
  EMP: 15
  SQ FT: 1,500
  SALES (est): 1.7MM
  SALES (corp-wide): 3.5MM **Privately Held**
  SIC: 3549 Coiling machinery
  PA: Prem Magnetics, Inc.
    3521 Chapel Hill Rd
    Johnsburg IL 60051
    815 385-2700

(G-11810)
STICKER DUDE INC
3420 N Richmond Rd Unit A (60051-5446)
  PHONE..................................815 322-2480
  EMP: 5
  SALES (est): 423K **Privately Held**
  SIC: 3993 Signs & advertising specialties

Johnsonville
Wayne County

(G-11811)
BACK FORTY WD WORKS & NURS LLC
1431 County Road 740 E (62850-9047)
  PHONE..................................618 898-1241
  Rudy R Yoder,
  EMP: 4 **EST:** 2013
  SALES: 380K **Privately Held**
  SIC: 2431 Millwork

Johnston City
Williamson County

(G-11812)
SATELLINK INC
724 W 15th St (62951-2012)
  PHONE..................................618 983-5555
  Hugh Durham, *Owner*
  Kay Durham, *Co-Owner*
  EMP: 5
  SALES (est): 290K **Privately Held**
  SIC: 3679 Antennas, satellite: household use

(G-11813)
SOUTHERN MOLD FINISHING INC
500 Follis Ave (62951-1432)
P.O. Box 228 (62951-0228)
  PHONE..................................618 983-5049
  James Oxendine, *President*
  Sharon Beltz, *Corp Secy*
  Shannon Oxedine, *Vice Pres*
  EMP: 15 **EST:** 1979
  SQ FT: 8,000
  SALES: 1.4MM **Privately Held**
  SIC: 5031 3544 Molding, all materials; special dies, tools, jigs & fixtures

(G-11814)
SOUTHERN PLATING INC
500 Follis Ave (62951-1432)
  PHONE..................................618 983-6350
  Mark Willingham, *President*
  Ted Oxendine, *Principal*
  Angela McQuire, *Admin Asst*
  EMP: 3
  SALES (est): 213.2K **Privately Held**
  SIC: 3471 Plating of metals or formed products

(G-11815)
US FABG & MINE SVCS INC
11196 Illinois Steel Rd (62951-2614)
  PHONE..................................618 983-7850
  Kenneth Cobb, *President*
  Bill Cobb, *President*
  EMP: 4
  SQ FT: 1,000
  SALES: 200K **Privately Held**
  SIC: 3441 Fabricated structural metal

Joliet
Will County

(G-11816)
AAA GALVANIZING - JOLIET INC (HQ)
Also Called: A Z Z
625 Mills Rd (60433-2842)
  PHONE..................................815 723-5000
  David Dindus, *President*
  ▲ **EMP:** 60
  SQ FT: 100,000

Joliet - Will County (G-11817)

SALES (est): 23.5MM
SALES (corp-wide): 1B **Publicly Held**
SIC: 3479 Hot dip coating of metals or formed products; coating of metals & formed products
PA: Azz Inc.
3100 W 7th St Ste 500
Fort Worth TX 76107
817 810-0095

(G-11817)
ADVANTAGE COMPONENTS INC
2240 Oak Leaf St (60436-1868)
PHONE..................................815 725-8644
Kevin O'Sullivan, *President*
Tim Kucera, *Vice Pres*
Timothy Kucera, *Vice Pres*
Mike Burman, *Sales Staff*
▲ EMP: 50 EST: 1997
SQ FT: 14,000
SALES (est): 12.9MM **Privately Held**
WEB: www.aciwires.com
SIC: 3496 3678 Cable, uninsulated wire: made from purchased wire; electronic connectors

(G-11818)
AGRESEARCH INC
1 Genstar Ln (60435-2674)
PHONE..................................815 726-0410
Alissa Hawkins, *Research*
John Gribble, *Admin Sec*
▲ EMP: 15
SQ FT: 20,000
SALES (est): 2.8MM **Privately Held**
SIC: 2048 Prepared feeds

(G-11819)
AMERICAN CHUTE SYSTEMS INC
Also Called: Nicor Products
603 E Washington St (60433-1135)
PHONE..................................815 723-7632
Frank Stephens, *President*
Bonnie Reynolds, *Admin Sec*
EMP: 5
SALES (est): 844.7K **Privately Held**
SIC: 3444 3443 Sheet metalwork; chutes & troughs

(G-11820)
AMERICAN STEEL SERVICES INC
840 Brian Dr (60403-2482)
PHONE..................................815 774-0677
Jeff Hmura, *President*
Bob Forrester, *Admin Sec*
EMP: 10
SQ FT: 10,000
SALES (est): 2.1MM **Privately Held**
SIC: 3441 Fabricated structural metal

(G-11821)
AMERIPLATE INC
600 Joyce Rd (60436-1814)
P.O. Box 2129 (60434-2129)
PHONE..................................815 744-8585
Douglas I McCallister, *President*
Kathleen McCallister, *Vice Pres*
EMP: 20
SQ FT: 30,000
SALES (est): 2.8MM **Privately Held**
SIC: 3471 Electroplating of metals or formed products; electroplating & plating

(G-11822)
ANDREW CORPORATION
2700 Ellis Rd (60433-8459)
PHONE..................................779 435-6000
EMP: 24
SALES (est): 6.3MM **Publicly Held**
SIC: 3357 Nonferrous Wiredrawing/Insulating
HQ: Commscope Technologies Llc
4 Westbrook Corporate Ctr
Westchester IL 28602
708 236-6600

(G-11823)
ANDREW INTERNATIONAL SVCS CORP
2700 Ellis Rd (60433-8459)
PHONE..................................779 435-6000
Marvin S Edwards, *CEO*

Ralph Faison, *President*
EMP: 1400
SQ FT: 571,000
SALES (est): 68MM **Publicly Held**
SIC: 3663 Microwave communication equipment
HQ: Commscope Technologies Llc
1100 Commscope Pl Se
Hickory NC 28602
708 236-6600

(G-11824)
ANTIGUA CASA SHERRY-BRENER (PA)
2801 W Jefferson St Ofc C (60435-5352)
PHONE..................................773 737-1711
James Sherry, *Partner*
Thomas Boodel, *Partner*
Eve Warren, *Partner*
EMP: 2
SALES (est): 1MM **Privately Held**
SIC: 5099 2731 2721 Musical instruments; book music: publishing only, not printed on site; magazines: publishing only, not printed on site

(G-11825)
AVE INC
Also Called: Mr. Rooter Plumbing
126 S Des Plaines St (60436)
PHONE..................................815 727-0153
Adam Erickson, *CEO*
EMP: 3
SQ FT: 7,000
SALES (est): 2.5MM **Privately Held**
SIC: 7699 1711 1081 Sewer cleaning & rodding; plumbing contractors; heating & air conditioning contractors; draining or pumping of metal mines

(G-11826)
AZZ INCORPORATED
625 Mills Rd (60433-2842)
PHONE..................................815 723-5000
Laxman Alreja, *Branch Mgr*
EMP: 62
SALES (corp-wide): 1B **Publicly Held**
SIC: 3699 Electrical equipment & supplies
PA: Azz Inc.
3100 W 7th St Ste 500
Fort Worth TX 76107
817 810-0095

(G-11827)
BAR STOOL DEPOTCOM
Also Called: In Focus Restaurant & Bar Sup
816 Caton Ave (60435-5906)
P.O. Box 131 (60434-0131)
PHONE..................................815 727-7294
Ursala Martin, *President*
EMP: 6
SALES (est): 230K **Privately Held**
SIC: 2711 5021 2542 Newspapers, publishing & printing; bar furniture; partitions & fixtures, except wood

(G-11828)
BARNEYS ALUMINUM SPECIALTIES
340 Ruby St (60435-6272)
PHONE..................................815 723-5341
William Barney, *President*
EMP: 1
SQ FT: 1,000
SALES (est): 229.4K **Privately Held**
SIC: 5211 3442 Doors, storm: wood or metal; windows, storm: wood or metal; metal doors, sash & trim

(G-11829)
BEAVER CREEK ENTERPRISES INC (PA)
Also Called: Beaver Creek Golf Carts
801 Rowell Ave (60433-2524)
PHONE..................................815 723-9455
William Rulien, *President*
Warner Rulien, *Vice Pres*
Bonnie Rulien, *Treasurer*
EMP: 11
SQ FT: 8,500
SALES (est): 1.9MM **Privately Held**
SIC: 7692 3443 Welding repair; fabricated plate work (boiler shop)

(G-11830)
BERGERON GROUP INC
Also Called: Cedar Rustic Fence Co.
99 Republic Ave (60435-6513)
PHONE..................................815 741-1635
James Bergeron, *CEO*
Gregory Bergeron, *President*
Michael Olena, *Opers Staff*
Frank Juplo, *Technology*
EMP: 35
SQ FT: 86,000
SALES (est): 6.4MM **Privately Held**
WEB: www.cedarrustic.com
SIC: 2499 1799 1521 3496 Fencing, wood; fence construction; patio & deck construction & repair; miscellaneous fabricated wire products

(G-11831)
BERGSTROM INC
4060 Mound Rd (60436-8901)
PHONE..................................847 394-4013
Tod Baum, *Prdtn Mgr*
Peter Petroff, *Engineer*
Scott Cserep, *Design Engr*
Gus Anton, *Manager*
EMP: 100
SALES (corp-wide): 490MM **Privately Held**
SIC: 3714 3711 Heaters, motor vehicle; air conditioner parts, motor vehicle; motor vehicles & car bodies
PA: Bergstrom Inc.
2390 Blackhawk Rd
Rockford IL 61109
815 874-7821

(G-11832)
BIOBLEND LUBRICANTS INTL
2439 Reeves Rd (60436-9538)
PHONE..................................630 227-1800
Gary Dyal, *President*
David Gaulke, *VP Sales*
EMP: 7 EST: 2001
SQ FT: 3,000
SALES (est): 930K **Privately Held**
WEB: www.bioblend.com
SIC: 2992 Lubricating oils & greases

(G-11833)
BLUESTONE SPECIALTY CHEM LLC
10 Industry Ave (60435-2652)
PHONE..................................815 727-3010
Walter Vanloo, *Managing Dir*
Danile Holbert, *Plant Mgr*
Steven Oliver, *CFO*
EMP: 12
SALES: 3.3MM **Privately Held**
WEB: www.apexmattech.com
SIC: 3312 Chemicals & other products derived from coking

(G-11834)
BROCK INDUSTRIAL SERVICES LLC
United
2210 Oak Leaf St (60436-1894)
PHONE..................................815 730-3350
Mike Gantz, *Branch Mgr*
EMP: 30 **Privately Held**
SIC: 3599 Bellows, industrial: metal
HQ: Brock Industrial Services, Llc
2210 Oak Leaf St
Joliet IL 60436
815 730-3350

(G-11835)
BUZZI UNICEM USA INC
450 Railroad St (60436-2704)
PHONE..................................815 768-3660
Scott Richardson, *Manager*
EMP: 23
SALES (corp-wide): 395.5MM **Privately Held**
SIC: 3241 Portland cement
HQ: Buzzi Unicem Usa Inc.
100 Brodhead Rd Ste 230
Bethlehem PA 18017
610 882-5000

(G-11836)
C & C PUBLICATIONS
Also Called: Joliet Times Weekly
254 E Cass St (60432-2813)
P.O. Box 2277 (60434-2277)
PHONE..................................815 723-0325
Jayme Cain, *President*
EMP: 7
SALES (est): 477.3K **Privately Held**
SIC: 2711 Newspapers, publishing & printing

(G-11837)
C & S CHEMICALS INC
Also Called: C & R Industries
1306 Mckinley St (60436-2915)
P.O. Box 2877 (60434-2877)
PHONE..................................815 722-6671
EMP: 5
SALES (corp-wide): 7.6MM **Privately Held**
SIC: 2819 2836 3842 3841 Mfg Indstl Inorgan Chem Mfg Biological Products Mfg Surgical Appliances Mfg Surgical/Med Instr Mfg Ophthalmic Goods
PA: C & S Chemicals, Inc.
4180 Providence Rd # 310
Marietta GA 30062
770 977-2669

(G-11838)
CATERPILLAR INC
540 Joyce Rd (60436-1812)
P.O. Box 504 (60434-0504)
PHONE..................................815 729-5511
Robert Macier, *Vice Pres*
Stephen Berlien, *Engineer*
Mohamed Kerdjoudj, *Engineer*
Siddharth Nair, *Design Engr*
Mike McKanna, *MIS Mgr*
EMP: 355
SALES (corp-wide): 53.8B **Publicly Held**
WEB: www.caterpillar.com
SIC: 3531 3823 3822 3625 Construction machinery; industrial instrmnts msrmnt display/control process variable; auto controls regulating residntl & coml environmt & applncs; relays & industrial controls; fluid power pumps & motors; valves & pipe fittings
PA: Caterpillar Inc.
510 Lake Cook Rd Ste 100
Deerfield IL 60015
224 551-4000

(G-11839)
CHICAGO BLIND COMPANY
20607 Burl Ct (60433-9713)
PHONE..................................815 553-5525
Mark Sims, *President*
Allen Sims, *Admin Sec*
EMP: 3
SQ FT: 2,800
SALES (est): 511.9K **Privately Held**
SIC: 2591 Blinds vertical

(G-11840)
CHROME CRANKSHAFT COMPANY LLC
4166 Mound Rd (60436-9009)
PHONE..................................815 725-9030
William F Walen,
▲ EMP: 15
SQ FT: 22,500
SALES (est): 2.2MM **Privately Held**
SIC: 3599 Crankshafts & camshafts, machining

(G-11841)
CMA INC
929 Kelly Ave (60435-4648)
PHONE..................................847 848-0674
Robert Johnson, *Principal*
EMP: 45 **Privately Held**
SIC: 2499 Insulating material, cork
PA: Cma, Inc.
19 Stonehill Rd
Oswego IL 60543

(G-11842)
CMC AMERICA CORPORATION
Also Called: C M C
208 S Center St (60436-2202)
PHONE..................................815 726-4337
Edward Fay, *President*
Michael Baron, *Plant Mgr*

GEOGRAPHIC SECTION
Joliet - Will County (G-11869)

Joel Swidergal, *Project Engr*
Bryan Malmquist, *Design Engr*
Mary Moore, *Office Mgr*
▲ **EMP:** 15 **EST:** 1993
SQ FT: 40,000
SALES (est): 4.5MM **Privately Held**
WEB: www.cmc-america.com
SIC: 3556 Bakery machinery

(G-11843)
COMMSCOPE INC NORTH CAROLINA
2700 Ellis Rd (60433-8459)
PHONE.................................779 435-6000
Pete Dosen, *Vice Pres*
Gary Heitman, *Opers Mgr*
Stacey Boudouris, *Purch Mgr*
Pete Bisiules, *Engineer*
Robert Brickhouse, *Engineer*
EMP: 132
SQ FT: 690,000 **Publicly Held**
WEB: www.commscope.com
SIC: 3663 Radio & TV communications equipment
HQ: Commscope, Inc. Of North Carolina
1100 Commscope Pl Se
Hickory NC 28602
866 277-2410

(G-11844)
COMMSCOPE CONNECTIVITY LLC
2700 Ellis Rd (60433-8459)
PHONE.................................779 435-6000
EMP: 15 **Publicly Held**
SIC: 3663 Radio & TV communications equipment
HQ: Commscope Connectivity Llc
1100 Commscope Pl Se
Hickory NC 28602
828 324-2200

(G-11845)
COMMSCOPE TECHNOLOGIES LLC
Also Called: Andrew Solutions
2700 Ellis Rd (60433-8459)
PHONE.................................779 435-6000
Stan Catey, *Branch Mgr*
EMP: 260 **Publicly Held**
SIC: 3663 3357 3679 3577 Microwave communication equipment; coaxial cable, nonferrous; waveguides & fittings; computer peripheral equipment
HQ: Commscope Technologies Llc
1100 Commscope Pl Se
Hickory NC 28602
708 236-6600

(G-11846)
COMPLEX WOODWORK INC
601 N Chicago St (60432-1730)
PHONE.................................630 651-3637
Vasile Vrinceanu, *President*
EMP: 3 **EST:** 2007
SQ FT: 7,000
SALES: 200K **Privately Held**
SIC: 2434 Wood kitchen cabinets

(G-11847)
CONVEYOR SPECIALTIES INC
841 Brian Dr Ste A (60403-2360)
PHONE.................................815 727-7638
Christian Stevens, *President*
Jim Buckner, *Engineer*
Andrew Stevens, *Project Engr*
Diane Stevens, *Treasurer*
Jennifer Casey, *Bookkeeper*
EMP: 6
SQ FT: 3,000
SALES (est): 1.2MM **Privately Held**
SIC: 3535 Conveyors & conveying equipment

(G-11848)
CORSETTI STRUCTURAL STEEL INC
2515 New Lenox Rd (60433-9718)
PHONE.................................815 726-0186
Nino Corsetti, *President*
Anthony Corsetti, *Vice Pres*
Edward Corsetti, *Treasurer*
EMP: 20
SQ FT: 17,000
SALES: 11.7MM **Privately Held**
SIC: 1791 3441 Structural steel erection; fabricated structural metal

(G-11849)
CROWN EQUIPMENT CORPORATION
Also Called: Crown Lift Trucks
4100 Olympic Blvd (60431-7942)
PHONE.................................815 773-0022
Scott Furlow, *Principal*
EMP: 133
SQ FT: 5,000
SALES (corp-wide): 6.3B **Privately Held**
SIC: 3537 Lift trucks, industrial: fork, platform, straddle, etc.
PA: Crown Equipment Corporation
44 S Washington St
New Bremen OH 45869
419 629-2311

(G-11850)
CUSTOM WOOD & LAMINATE LTD
1102 Davison St (60433-8512)
PHONE.................................815 727-4168
EMP: 2 **EST:** 2001
SQ FT: 4,000
SALES (est): 200K **Privately Held**
SIC: 2599 Mfg Furniture/Fixtures

(G-11851)
DAILY KRATOM
4010 Brenton Dr (60431-9264)
PHONE.................................815 768-7104
Kevin Murdaugh, *Principal*
EMP: 3
SALES (est): 163.5K **Privately Held**
SIC: 2711 Newspapers, publishing & printing

(G-11852)
DAVID NELSON EXQUISITE JEWELRY
1312 W Jefferson St Ste 2 (60435-6888)
PHONE.................................815 741-4702
David Nelson, *President*
Ann Marie Nelson, *Vice Pres*
EMP: 6
SQ FT: 3,000
SALES (est): 870.8K **Privately Held**
SIC: 5944 3911 7631 Jewelry, precious stones & precious metals; rings, finger: precious metal; watch, clock & jewelry repair

(G-11853)
DAVID ROTTER PROSTHETICS LTD
121 Springfield Ave Ste 3 (60435-6561)
PHONE.................................815 255-3220
David Rotter, *Owner*
Nicole Wright, *Manager*
EMP: 3
SALES (est): 262.3K **Privately Held**
SIC: 3842 Prosthetic appliances

(G-11854)
DAVIS MACHINE COMPANY INC
312 Henderson Ave (60432-2537)
PHONE.................................815 723-9121
Richard L Davis, *President*
Dan M Davis, *Corp Secy*
EMP: 7
SQ FT: 4,000
SALES: 500K **Privately Held**
SIC: 3599 3544 Machine shop, jobbing & repair; special dies & tools

(G-11855)
DIETRICH INDUSTRIES INC
3901 Olympic Blvd (60431-7947)
PHONE.................................815 207-0110
Andy Rybowiak, *Branch Mgr*
EMP: 25
SALES (corp-wide): 3.7B **Publicly Held**
SIC: 3441 Building components, structural steel
HQ: Dietrich Industries, Inc.
200 W Old Wlson Bridge Rd
Worthington OH 43085
800 873-2604

(G-11856)
E & F TOOL COMPANY INC
213 Amendodge Dr (60404-9362)
PHONE.................................815 729-1305
Wilhelm Engelsbel, *CEO*
Margaret Engelsbel, *President*
▲ **EMP:** 12
SQ FT: 17,000
SALES: 1.1MM **Privately Held**
SIC: 3599 Machine shop, jobbing & repair

(G-11857)
ECOLAB INC
Also Called: Johnson Contrls Authorized Dlr
3001 Channahon Rd (60436-9581)
PHONE.................................815 729-7334
Paul Anderson, *Branch Mgr*
EMP: 38
SALES (corp-wide): 14.9B **Publicly Held**
SIC: 2842 5075 Specialty cleaning preparations; warm air heating & air conditioning
PA: Ecolab Inc.
1 Ecolab Pl
Saint Paul MN 55102
800 232-6522

(G-11858)
ECOSYSTEM PROTECTIVE COATINGS
1214 Colorado Ave (60435-3703)
PHONE.................................815 725-6343
John R Ditsch, *Principal*
EMP: 3 **EST:** 2010
SALES (est): 139.7K **Privately Held**
SIC: 3479 Metal coating & allied service

(G-11859)
ELLWOOD GROUP INC
4166 Mound Rd (60436-9009)
PHONE.................................815 725-9030
Brian Taylor, *President*
EMP: 17
SQ FT: 30,000
SALES (corp-wide): 736.4MM **Privately Held**
SIC: 3471 Chromium plating of metals or formed products
PA: Ellwood Group, Inc.
600 Commercial Ave
Ellwood City PA 16117
724 752-3680

(G-11860)
EMC INNOVATIONS INC
1252 Woodland Ct (60436-1926)
PHONE.................................815 741-2546
▲ **EMP:** 6
SALES (est): 571.9K **Privately Held**
SIC: 3089 Manufacture Cookie Cutters

(G-11861)
ENDURA PAINT CHICAGO
2239 Muriel Ct (60433-8437)
PHONE.................................815 630-5083
EMP: 3 **EST:** 2017
SALES (est): 177.9K **Privately Held**
SIC: 2851 Paints & allied products

(G-11862)
ENGINEERED PLUMBING SPC LLC
Also Called: Kamflex, LLC
2312 Oak Leaf St (60436-1065)
PHONE.................................630 682-1555
Michael Whiteside, *President*
Grant Branch, *General Mgr*
John Tomaka, *Vice Pres*
Chris Rampersaud, *Engineer*
EMP: 30
SQ FT: 60,000
SALES: 9.7MM **Privately Held**
SIC: 3535 Conveyors & conveying equipment
PA: Mifab, Inc.
1321 W 119th St
Chicago IL 60643

(G-11863)
EVERON POLYMERS LLC
420 Woodruff Rd (60432-1259)
PHONE.................................815 681-8800
Yee Chiu, *Mng Member*
EMP: 6
SALES (est): 758.8K **Privately Held**
SIC: 2822 Ethylene-propylene rubbers, EPDM polymers

(G-11864)
FAST PRINTING OF JOLIET INC
842 Plainfield Rd (60435-4686)
PHONE.................................815 723-0080
Jim Studer, *President*
Kenneth Studer Sr, *Vice Pres*
Kenneth Studer Jr, *Vice Pres*
Christopher M Studer, *Treasurer*
Denise Studer, *Treasurer*
EMP: 9
SALES (est): 1.2MM **Privately Held**
SIC: 7334 2752 2789 Photocopying & duplicating services; commercial printing, offset; bookbinding & related work

(G-11865)
FILTRATION GROUP LLC
912 E Washington St Ste 1 (60433-1286)
PHONE.................................815 726-4600
Lawrence Ost, *CEO*
EMP: 50
SALES (corp-wide): 320.9MM **Privately Held**
WEB: www.filtrationgroup.com
SIC: 3564 Blowers & fans
PA: Filtration Group Llc
912 E Washington St Ste 1
Joliet IL 60433
815 726-4600

(G-11866)
FORCE AMERICA INC
500 Brookforest Ave (60404-9706)
PHONE.................................815 730-3600
Michael Taylor, *Sales Staff*
Rich Wiklak, *Sales Staff*
Jack Donvanan, *Manager*
EMP: 10
SALES (corp-wide): 135.2MM **Privately Held**
WEB: www.forceamerica.com
SIC: 5084 3568 Hydraulic systems equipment & supplies; drives, chains & sprockets
PA: Force America Inc.
501 Cliff Rd E Ste 100
Burnsville MN 55337
952 707-1300

(G-11867)
GALLEON INDUSTRIES INC
Also Called: Galleon Printing Co
16714 Cherry Creek Ct (60433-8466)
PHONE.................................708 478-5444
Paul Turay, *President*
Craig Turay, *Vice Pres*
Jeff Turay, *Vice Pres*
Cindy Turay, *Sales Staff*
EMP: 5
SQ FT: 4,500
SALES (est): 836.2K **Privately Held**
SIC: 2759 7389 Screen printing; printing broker

(G-11868)
GAYTAN SIGNS & CO INC
317 Mcdonough St (60436-2235)
PHONE.................................815 726-2975
Pedro Garcia, *President*
Mayra Garcia, *Corp Secy*
EMP: 4 **EST:** 2001
SQ FT: 900
SALES (est): 300K **Privately Held**
SIC: 3993 Signs & advertising specialties

(G-11869)
GENERAL MACHINE AND TOOL INC
615 Mills Rd (60433-2842)
PHONE.................................815 727-5270
Matthew Gregurich, *Branch Mgr*
EMP: 6
SALES (est): 570.8K
SALES (corp-wide): 4MM **Privately Held**
WEB: www.generalmachine.net
SIC: 3599 Machine shop, jobbing & repair
PA: General Machine And Tool, Inc.
348 Caton Farm Rd
Lockport IL 60441
815 727-4342

Joliet - Will County (G-11870)

(G-11870)
GRATE SIGNS INC
4044 Mcdonough St (60431-8816)
P.O. Box 2714 (60434-2714)
PHONE.................................815 729-9700
Anton Grate, *President*
EMP: 25 **EST:** 1948
SQ FT: 50,000
SALES (est): 2.9MM **Privately Held**
WEB: www.gratesigns.com
SIC: 3993 7359 7389 Electric signs; equipment rental & leasing; sign painting & lettering shop

(G-11871)
GROOVY LOGISTICS INC
1120 Manhattan Rd (60433-8533)
PHONE.................................847 946-1491
Marta Gawel, *President*
Radoslaw Stoklosa, *Admin Sec*
EMP: 5
SQ FT: 1,100
SALES (est): 788.6K **Privately Held**
SIC: 3715 Truck trailers

(G-11872)
GUYS HI-DEF INC
1948 Essington Rd Ste C (60435-1615)
PHONE.................................708 261-7487
Bajram Memishofski, *President*
EMP: 4
SALES (est): 433.8K **Privately Held**
SIC: 3651 Speaker monitors

(G-11873)
HANGER PRSTHTICS ORTHOTICS INC
694 Essington Rd Unit B (60435-4904)
PHONE.................................815 744-9944
Karen Gamble, *Principal*
Lodi Gill, *Manager*
Robert Picken, *Manager*
EMP: 3
SALES (corp-wide): 1.1B **Publicly Held**
SIC: 3842 Orthopedic appliances
HQ: Hanger Prosthetics & Orthotics, Inc.
10910 Domain Dr Ste 300
Austin TX 78758
512 777-3800

(G-11874)
HARD RESET PRINTING INC
109 3rd Ave (60433-1828)
PHONE.................................773 850-9277
Anthony Williams, *President*
EMP: 5
SALES (est): 92.3K **Privately Held**
SIC: 2752 Commercial printing, lithographic

(G-11875)
HEADCO INDUSTRIES INC
Also Called: Bearing Headquarters Co
2104 Oak Leaf St Unit D (60436-1875)
PHONE.................................815 729-4016
Jennifer Thomas, *Manager*
EMP: 5
SALES (corp-wide): 162.5MM **Privately Held**
SIC: 5085 5084 3599 Bearings; sprockets; hydraulic systems equipment & supplies; machine shop, jobbing & repair
PA: Headco Industries, Inc.
2601 Parkes Dr
Broadview IL 60155
708 681-4400

(G-11876)
HENDRICKSON INTERNATIONAL CORP
Hendrickson Stamping Division
501 Caton Farm Rd (60434)
P.O. Box 458 (60434-0458)
PHONE.................................815 727-4031
Jeff Zawacki, *Opers Mgr*
Doug Stanford, *Branch Mgr*
Carlos Archila, *Manager*
EMP: 200
SQ FT: 100,000
SALES (corp-wide): 980.2MM **Privately Held**
SIC: 3714 3429 Bumpers & bumperettes, motor vehicle; manufactured hardware (general)
HQ: Hendrickson International Corporation
840 S Frontage Rd
Woodridge IL 60517

(G-11877)
HENDRICKSON USA LLC
Also Called: Hendrickson Bumper and Trim
501 Caton Farm Rd (60435)
PHONE.................................815 727-4031
Jeff Zawacki, *Manager*
EMP: 65
SALES (corp-wide): 980.2MM **Privately Held**
SIC: 3714 Motor vehicle parts & accessories
HQ: Hendrickson Usa, L.L.C.
800 S Frontage Rd
Woodridge IL 60517

(G-11878)
ILLCO INC
Also Called: Johnson Contrls Authorized Dlr
2106 Mcdonough St (60436-1840)
PHONE.................................815 725-9100
Mike Dauner, *Principal*
EMP: 4
SALES (corp-wide): 40MM **Privately Held**
SIC: 3498 5075 Pipe fittings, fabricated from purchased pipe; warm air heating & air conditioning
PA: Illco, Inc.
535 S River St
Aurora IL 60506
630 892-7904

(G-11879)
IMPRESS PRINTING & DESIGN INC
1325 W Jefferson St (60435-6862)
PHONE.................................815 730-9440
Ricardo Lozano, *President*
Richard Lozano, *President*
Katie Kosiek, *Graphic Designe*
EMP: 2
SALES (est): 221.6K **Privately Held**
WEB: www.myimpressprinting.com
SIC: 2752 Commercial printing, offset

(G-11880)
IN AAW HAIR EMPORIUM LLC
423 Buell Ave 1 (60435-7021)
PHONE.................................779 227-1450
EMP: 3
SALES (est): 97.8K **Privately Held**
SIC: 3999 Mfg Misc Products

(G-11881)
INCLINE CONSTRUCTION INC
Also Called: Incline Welding & Construction
131 Airport Dr Unit H (60431-4792)
P.O. Box 377, Plainfield (60544-0377)
PHONE.................................815 577-8881
Val Curlee, *President*
EMP: 1
SALES (est): 444K **Privately Held**
SIC: 7692 Automotive welding

(G-11882)
INTERACTIVE BLDG SOLUTIONS LLC
Also Called: Honeywell Authorized Dealer
1919 Cherry Hill Rd (60433-8440)
P.O. Box 186, New Lenox (60451-0186)
PHONE.................................815 724-0525
Todd Dunlap, *Engineer*
Frank Palazzolo, *Engineer*
London Duda, *Controller*
Kevin Gleeson, *Manager*
Eric Williams, *Manager*
EMP: 14
SALES: 950K **Privately Held**
WEB: www.ibs-chicago.com
SIC: 3822 Temperature controls, automatic

(G-11883)
J H BOTTS LLC
Also Called: J.H. Botts
253 Bruce St (60431-1281)
P.O. Box 128 (60434-0128)
PHONE.................................815 726-5885
Monica Hickey, *Vice Pres*
Dan Patel, *Sales Mgr*
Michael Friel, *Mng Member*
Dennis Davila, *Manager*
Patrick Sheffield, *Director*
EMP: 39
SQ FT: 51,000
SALES (est): 15.5MM **Privately Held**
SIC: 3441 3452 3446 3443 Fabricated structural metal; bolts, metal; architectural metalwork; fabricated plate work (boiler shop)

(G-11884)
J L M PLASTICS CORPORATION
1012 Collins St (60432-1215)
PHONE.................................815 722-0066
Frank C Mitchell, *President*
EMP: 16
SQ FT: 37,000
SALES (est): 3.9MM **Privately Held**
SIC: 2821 Plastics materials & resins

(G-11885)
JETIN SYSTEMS INC
800 Railroad St (60436-9524)
PHONE.................................815 726-4686
Stephen M Jacak, *President*
EMP: 12
SQ FT: 10,000
SALES (est): 1.9MM **Privately Held**
SIC: 3589 3582 High pressure cleaning equipment; commercial laundry equipment

(G-11886)
JOLIET HERALD NEWSPAPER
Also Called: Shaw Media
2175 Oneida St (60435-6560)
PHONE.................................815 280-4100
Bob Wall, *Administration*
EMP: 20 **EST:** 2013
SALES (est): 589.2K **Privately Held**
WEB: www.theherald-news.com
SIC: 2711 7379 Newspapers, publishing & printing; computer related services

(G-11887)
JSC FREIGHT SOLUTIONS LLC
1427 Regency Ridge Dr (60436-1385)
PHONE.................................708 731-0448
Juan Cook,
EMP: 1
SALES: 300K **Privately Held**
SIC: 3537 Trucks, tractors, loaders, carriers & similar equipment

(G-11888)
JSN PRINTING INC
Also Called: Minuteman Press
1400 Essington Rd (60435-2886)
PHONE.................................815 582-4014
Scott Nelson, *President*
EMP: 5
SALES (est): 548.6K **Privately Held**
SIC: 2752 Commercial printing, lithographic

(G-11889)
KAMFLEX CONVEYOR CORPORATION
2312 Oak Leaf St (60436-1065)
P.O. Box 913, Bolingbrook (60440-1083)
PHONE.................................630 682-1555
Roderick Barbee, *Principal*
EMP: 6 **EST:** 2016
SQ FT: 4,800
SALES (est): 357.5K **Privately Held**
SIC: 3535 Conveyors & conveying equipment

(G-11890)
KLEINHOFFER MANUFACTURING INC
1852 Terry Dr (60436-8541)
PHONE.................................815 725-3638
Dale Kleinhoffer, *President*
EMP: 4
SALES: 450K **Privately Held**
SIC: 3714 5531 Motor vehicle parts & accessories; truck equipment & parts

(G-11891)
KNAUER INDUSTRIES LTD
19505 Ne Frontage Rd (60404-3567)
PHONE.................................815 725-0246
Conrad Knauer Sr, *CEO*
Robert Knauer, *President*
Louis Knauer, *Treasurer*
EMP: 20
SQ FT: 7,500
SALES (est): 3.4MM **Privately Held**
SIC: 3281 Cut stone & stone products

(G-11892)
L SURGES CUSTOM WOODWORK
225 Maple St (60432-3040)
PHONE.................................815 774-9663
L Surges, *Owner*
EMP: 2
SALES (est): 369.4K **Privately Held**
WEB: www.lsurgeswoodwork.com
SIC: 2431 1751 Millwork; cabinet & finish carpentry

(G-11893)
L T P LLC
Also Called: Premier Laundry Technologies
490 Mills Rd (60433-2734)
PHONE.................................815 723-9400
Jerry E Lewin,
EMP: 120
SALES (est): 10.4MM **Privately Held**
SIC: 3582 8748 Commercial laundry equipment; business consulting

(G-11894)
LEGACY VULCAN LLC
Midwest Division
595 W Laraway Rd (60436-8560)
PHONE.................................815 726-6900
William Glusac, *Branch Mgr*
EMP: 15 **Publicly Held**
SIC: 3273 Ready-mixed concrete
HQ: Legacy Vulcan, Llc
1200 Urban Center Dr
Vestavia AL 35242
205 298-3000

(G-11895)
LUB-TEK PETROLEUM PRODUCTS (PA)
2439 Reeves Rd (60436-9538)
PHONE.................................815 741-0414
William Nehart, *President*
EMP: 8
SQ FT: 1,000
SALES (est): 9MM **Privately Held**
SIC: 2992 2911 Lubricating oils & greases; gases & liquefied petroleum gases

(G-11896)
MAHONEY ENVIRONMENTAL INC (PA)
712 Essington Rd (60435-4912)
PHONE.................................815 730-2087
John Mahoney, *President*
Rick Sabol, *President*
Dave Ciarlette, *Exec VP*
Robert Amicon, *Vice Pres*
Brian Conrad, *Vice Pres*
EMP: 30
SQ FT: 5,000
SALES (est): 62.3MM **Privately Held**
WEB: www.mahoneyenvironmental.com
SIC: 2079 Shortening & other solid edible fats

(G-11897)
MANCUSO CHEESE COMPANY
612 Mills Rd Ste 1 (60433-2897)
PHONE.................................815 722-2475
Michael Berta, *President*
Phillip Falbo, *Vice Pres*
EMP: 19 **EST:** 1917
SQ FT: 20,000
SALES (est): 3.5MM **Privately Held**
WEB: www.mancusocheese.com
SIC: 2022 5149 2033 Natural cheese; pizza supplies; canned fruits & specialties

(G-11898)
MASTERMOLDING INC
1715 Terry Dr (60436-8543)
PHONE.................................815 741-1230
Ray Steinhart, *President*
Kenneth R Steinhart, *Vice Pres*
▼**EMP:** 34
SQ FT: 13,000
SALES (est): 8.8MM **Privately Held**
SIC: 3089 Injection molding of plastics

GEOGRAPHIC SECTION

Joliet - Will County (G-11926)

(G-11899)
MATHESON TRI-GAS INC
200 Alessio Dr (60433-2975)
PHONE..................815 727-2202
Don Ramlow, *President*
G Cantrella, *Personnel*
W Kroll, *Marketing Staff*
C J Van, *Manager*
EMP: 26 **Privately Held**
SIC: 2813 5084 2911 Industrial gases; welding machinery & equipment; petroleum refining
HQ: Matheson Tri-Gas, Inc.
150 Allen Rd Ste 302
Basking Ridge NJ 07920
908 991-9200

(G-11900)
MEYER SYSTEMS
25035 W Black Rd (60404-8600)
PHONE..................815 436-7077
Bruce Meyer, *Owner*
EMP: 1
SQ FT: 2,000
SALES (est): 300K **Privately Held**
SIC: 8711 3625 Consulting engineer; control equipment, electric

(G-11901)
MI VAPE CO
1112 W Jefferson St (60435-6814)
PHONE..................815 582-3838
Javier Arroyo, *General Mgr*
Mario Jirjees, *Mng Member*
EMP: 12 **EST:** 2015
SALES (est): 114K **Privately Held**
WEB: www.mivapeco.com
SIC: 3999 Cigar & cigarette holders

(G-11902)
MID-AMERICAN ELEVATOR CO INC
Also Called: USA Hoist Company
1000 Sak Dr Unit A (60403-2562)
PHONE..................815 740-1204
Tom Haas, *Manager*
EMP: 35
SALES (corp-wide): 51MM **Privately Held**
SIC: 1796 7699 3823 3535 Elevator installation & conversion; elevators: inspection, service & repair; controllers for process variables, all types; conveyors & conveying equipment; elevators & moving stairways
PA: Mid-American Elevator Company, Inc.
820 N Wolcott Ave
Chicago IL 60622
773 486-6900

(G-11903)
MIDWEST INNOVATIVE PDTS LLC
Also Called: Twist and Seal
3225 Corporate Dr Unit C (60431-7961)
PHONE..................888 945-4545
Bryan Nooner, *President*
Jason Duzan,
EMP: 20 **EST:** 2012
SQ FT: 25,000
SALES (est): 2MM **Privately Held**
SIC: 2821 5162 Casein plastics; plastics products

(G-11904)
MIDWEST POWER EQUIPMENT
1933 Cherry Hill Rd (60433-8507)
PHONE..................815 669-6331
Sergio Padilla, *Owner*
EMP: 3 **EST:** 2008
SALES (est): 293K **Privately Held**
WEB: www.midwestpowerequipmentinc.com
SIC: 7538 3471 Truck engine repair, except industrial; electroplating & plating

(G-11905)
MILANO BAKERY INC
433 S Chicago St (60436-2268)
PHONE..................815 727-2253
Mario De Benedetti III, *President*
Darin De Benedetti, *Vice Pres*
Mario D Benedetti, *Shareholder*
Mario De Benedetti Sr, *Shareholder*
EMP: 50
SQ FT: 30,000
SALES (est): 15.1MM **Privately Held**
WEB: www.milanobaking.com
SIC: 5149 2051 5461 Bakery products; bread, cake & related products; bread

(G-11906)
MINING INTERNATIONAL LLC
1955 Patterson Rd (60436-9303)
PHONE..................815 722-0900
Alec Burnham, *Director*
EMP: 50
SALES (est): 1.6MM **Privately Held**
SIC: 1422 Agricultural limestone, ground

(G-11907)
NAVISTAR INC
2700 Haven Ave (60433-8469)
PHONE..................331 332-5000
Tom Barker, *Branch Mgr*
EMP: 140
SALES (corp-wide): 11.2B **Publicly Held**
SIC: 3711 Motor vehicles & car bodies
HQ: Navistar, Inc.
2701 Navistar Dr
Lisle IL 60532
331 332-5000

(G-11908)
NORTHERN ILLINOIS GAS COMPANY
Also Called: Nicor Gas
3000 E Cass St (60432-9713)
PHONE..................815 693-3907
Patricio Munoz, *Superintendent*
Richard Stutzman, *Branch Mgr*
EMP: 133
SALES (corp-wide): 21.4B **Publicly Held**
SIC: 4924 1382 4923 Natural gas distribution; oil & gas exploration services; gas transmission & distribution
HQ: Northern Illinois Gas Company
1844 W Ferry Rd
Naperville IL 60563
630 983-8676

(G-11909)
NT LIQUIDATING INC
Also Called: Norwalk Tank Co
2121 Maple Rd (60432-9642)
PHONE..................815 726-3351
Mark Minnick, *President*
Kevin Bethard, *Plant Supt*
EMP: 35 **EST:** 1967
SQ FT: 9,000
SALES (est): 6.7MM **Privately Held**
WEB: www.norwalktank.com
SIC: 3272 3084 Septic tanks, concrete; plastics pipe
PA: Minnick Services Corp.
222 N Thomas Rd
Fort Wayne IN 46808
260 432-5031

(G-11910)
NYCOR PRODUCTS INC
603 E Washington St (60433-1135)
PHONE..................815 727-9883
Lawrence Nyquist, *President*
EMP: 5
SALES (est): 230K **Privately Held**
SIC: 3993 2542 Signs & advertising specialties; racks, merchandise display or storage: except wood

(G-11911)
OMNI GEAR AND MACHINE CORP
90 Bissel St (60432-3052)
PHONE..................815 723-4327
John Hall, *President*
Valerie Franck, *Admin Sec*
Keith Mellen, *Admin Sec*
▲ **EMP:** 10
SQ FT: 11,000
SALES (est): 2MM **Privately Held**
SIC: 3566 5085 Gears, power transmission, except automotive; gears

(G-11912)
PAMPPERED PUPS
2011 Essington Rd (60435-1629)
PHONE..................815 782-8383
Rachell Tomswell, *Partner*
EMP: 3

SALES: 100K **Privately Held**
SIC: 0752 2047 Grooming services, pet & animal specialties; dog food

(G-11913)
PETER PERELLA & CO
600 N Scott St (60432-1758)
PHONE..................815 727-4526
Jack Perella, *President*
John M Perella, *Corp Secy*
Steve Bruno, *Project Mgr*
EMP: 10
SQ FT: 6,000
SALES (est): 3.6MM **Privately Held**
SIC: 3444 1711 Sheet metalwork; plumbing contractors; heating & air conditioning contractors

(G-11914)
PETRAK INDUSTRIES INCORPORATED
17250 New Lenox Rd Ste 3 (60433-9763)
PHONE..................815 483-2290
Thomas J Petrak, *President*
Janice Petrak, *Corp Secy*
Chris Petrak, *Vice Pres*
Christoher Petrak, *Vice Pres*
▲ **EMP:** 21
SQ FT: 12,000
SALES (est): 5.3MM **Privately Held**
SIC: 3542 Machine tools, metal forming type

(G-11915)
POWER HOUSE TOOL INC
626 Nicholson St (60435-6114)
PHONE..................815 727-6301
Laura Patterson, *CEO*
Michael W Kelly, *President*
▲ **EMP:** 25
SQ FT: 4,000
SALES (est): 4MM **Privately Held**
SIC: 3544 3829 3677 3612 Special dies, tools, jigs & fixtures; measuring & controlling devices; electronic coils, transformers & other inductors; transformers, except electric; hand & edge tools

(G-11916)
PRESENCE LEGACY ASSOCIATION
2000 Glenwood Ave Ste 102 (60435-5676)
PHONE..................815 741-7555
EMP: 10
SALES (corp-wide): 25.3B **Privately Held**
SIC: 8071 3826 Medical laboratories; magnetic resonance imaging apparatus
HQ: Presence Legacy Association
200 S Wacker Dr Fl 12
Chicago IL 60606
773 774-8000

(G-11917)
PRINTING CRAFTSMEN OF JOLIET
2101 New Port Dr (60431-0604)
PHONE..................815 254-3982
Reed Mott, *President*
EMP: 6
SQ FT: 35,500
SALES (est): 834.6K **Privately Held**
SIC: 2791 2789 2759 2752 Typesetting; bookbinding & related work; commercial printing; commercial printing, offset

(G-11918)
PRY-BAR COMPANY
18542 Nw Frontage Rd (60404-9654)
PHONE..................815 436-3383
Leonard F Baran, *President*
Scott Baran, *Vice Pres*
EMP: 16 **EST:** 1978
SQ FT: 14,000
SALES (est): 3.4MM **Privately Held**
SIC: 2653 5113 3993 2675 Boxes, corrugated: made from purchased materials; corrugated & solid fiber boxes; signs & advertising specialties; die-cut paper & board

(G-11919)
QUAD PLUS LLC (PA)
1921 Cherry Hill Rd (60403-8507)
PHONE..................815 740-0860
John Crosetto, *CEO*

Tom Engel, *President*
Steve Chasten, *Project Mgr*
Don Gilson, *Project Mgr*
Ilker Bizer, *Mfg Mgr*
EMP: 39
SQ FT: 10,000
SALES (est): 19.2MM **Privately Held**
SIC: 3566 Speed changers, drives & gears

(G-11920)
QUALITY QUICKPRINT INC
2405 Caton Farm Rd (60403-1302)
PHONE..................815 439-3430
EMP: 10
SALES (corp-wide): 1.3MM **Privately Held**
SIC: 2752 2791 2789 Lithographic Commercial Printing Typesetting Services Bookbinding/Related Work
PA: Quality Quickprint Inc
1258 Cronin Ct
Lemont IL 60439
815 723-0941

(G-11921)
R-SIGNS SERVICE AND DESIGN INC
720 Collins St Ste D (60432-1628)
PHONE..................815 722-0283
Ruben Franchini, *President*
Rosa M Esparza, *Admin Sec*
EMP: 5
SALES (est): 460K **Privately Held**
SIC: 3993 Signs & advertising specialties

(G-11922)
RAPID LINE INDUSTRIES INC
455 N Ottawa St Ste 1 (60432-1714)
PHONE..................815 727-4362
Thomas S Papesh, *President*
Rick Van Dis, *Senior VP*
EMP: 10
SQ FT: 12,000
SALES: 1MM **Privately Held**
SIC: 3559 Frame straighteners, automobile (garage equipment)

(G-11923)
RAVCO INCORPORATED
1313 Colorado Ave (60435-3704)
PHONE..................815 725-9095
Joseph Filisko, *President*
EMP: 2
SALES (est): 236.7K **Privately Held**
SIC: 3544 3423 Special dies & tools; hand & edge tools

(G-11924)
REMIN LABORATORIES INC
Also Called: Remin Kart A Bag
510 Manhattan Rd (60433-3099)
PHONE..................815 723-1940
Eugene A Kazmark Jr, *President*
Barbara Starner, *Vice Pres*
Mary Bruskotter, *Treasurer*
▲ **EMP:** 60 **EST:** 1967
SQ FT: 5,000
SALES (est): 10.4MM **Privately Held**
SIC: 3496 3429 3444 Miscellaneous fabricated wire products; luggage hardware; sheet metalwork

(G-11925)
RESIST-A-LINE INDUSTRIES INC
214 Elm St (60433-2432)
PHONE..................815 650-3177
Ron M Pinzker, *President*
Sandra M Pinkzer, *Admin Sec*
▲ **EMP:** 7
SALES: 600K **Privately Held**
SIC: 3443 Liners/lining

(G-11926)
RHO CHEMICAL COMPANY INC
30 Industry Ave (60435-2688)
P.O. Box 55 (60434-0055)
PHONE..................815 727-4791
Robert Rolih, *President*
Lorraine Rolih, *Corp Secy*
Mark Rolih, *Vice Pres*
▲ **EMP:** 13 **EST:** 1960
SQ FT: 100,000
SALES (est): 3.3MM **Privately Held**
WEB: www.rhochem.com
SIC: 2869 Industrial organic chemicals

Joliet - Will County (G-11927)

(G-11927)
ROBOTICS TECHNOLOGIES INC
20655 Burl Ct (60433-9713)
PHONE.................................815 722-7650
Allan Roberts, *President*
Tom Mavec, *CFO*
▲ EMP: 50
SQ FT: 16,600
SALES (est): 4MM **Privately Held**
SIC: 3861 3651 Cameras & related equipment; household audio & video equipment

(G-11928)
ROVANCO PIPING SYSTEMS INC
20535 Se Frontage Rd (60431-9357)
PHONE.................................815 741-6700
Larry Stonitsch, *President*
Richard Stonitsch, *Vice Pres*
Drew Kobus, *Engineer*
Kevin Wido, *Engineer*
Mary Lou Stonitsch, *Admin Sec*
▲ EMP: 88
SQ FT: 56,000
SALES (est): 18MM **Privately Held**
SIC: 3498 Piping systems for pulp paper & chemical industries

(G-11929)
RSVP TOOLING INC
227 Airport Dr (60431-7968)
PHONE.................................815 725-3310
Eric Palmer, *President*
EMP: 5
SALES (est): 589.7K **Privately Held**
SIC: 5251 3545 3542 3541 Tools; threading tools (machine tool accessories); chasers (machine tool accessories); machine tools, metal forming type; machine tools, metal cutting type; machine tools & accessories

(G-11930)
SIGN O RAMA
1107 Essington Rd (60435-2870)
PHONE.................................815 744-8702
Joren Apiquian, *President*
EMP: 3
SQ FT: 1,400
SALES (est): 304.2K **Privately Held**
SIC: 3993 Signs, not made in custom sign painting shops

(G-11931)
SMOLICH BROTHERS SAUSAGE INC
Also Called: Smolich Bros
760 Theodore St (60403-2380)
PHONE.................................815 727-2144
Joseph A Smolich, *President*
EMP: 2 EST: 1971
SQ FT: 1,500
SALES (est): 203K **Privately Held**
SIC: 2013 Sausages from purchased meat

(G-11932)
STANDARD TRUCK PARTS INC (PA)
566 N Chicago St (60432-1779)
PHONE.................................815 726-4486
John M Jones Jr, *President*
EMP: 3
SQ FT: 21,000
SALES (est): 1.7MM **Privately Held**
WEB: www.standardtruckparts.com
SIC: 5013 3492 3429 Truck parts & accessories; fluid power valves & hose fittings; manufactured hardware (general)

(G-11933)
STELLATO PRINTING INC
777 Joyce Rd (60436-1876)
PHONE.................................815 280-5664
Anthony Stellato, *Principal*
EMP: 12
SALES (est): 1.5MM
SALES (corp-wide): 452.9K **Privately Held**
SIC: 2759 Screen printing
PA: Stellato Printing Inc
1801 Jared Dr
Crest Hill IL 60403
815 280-5664

(G-11934)
SULZER PUMP SERVICES (US) INC
Also Called: Sulzer Midwest Service Center
2600 Citys Edge Dr (60436-4554)
PHONE.................................815 600-7355
Mike Ostrowski, *Principal*
EMP: 13
SQ FT: 750
SALES (corp-wide): 3.7B **Privately Held**
WEB: www.sulzer.com
SIC: 3561 Pumps & pumping equipment
HQ: Sulzer Pump Services (Us) Inc.
101 Old Underwood Rd G
La Porte TX 77571
281 417-7110

(G-11935)
SUPERIOR BAKING STONE INC
926 Plainfield Rd (60435-4473)
PHONE.................................815 726-4610
EMP: 4
SALES (est): 212.1K **Privately Held**
SIC: 2051 Mfg Bread/Related Products

(G-11936)
TIMBERLAND CUSTOM CAB & TOPS
1923 Cherry Hill Rd (60433-8507)
PHONE.................................815 722-0825
Richard Stull, *President*
EMP: 5
SQ FT: 5,000
SALES: 600K **Privately Held**
SIC: 2434 Wood kitchen cabinets

(G-11937)
UIC INC
16720 Cherry Creek Ct (60433-8466)
P.O. Box 3986 (60434-3986)
PHONE.................................815 744-4477
Jerold L Armstrong, *Ch of Bd*
Waver Armstrong, *President*
Helen Frazier, *Admin Sec*
EMP: 9 EST: 1971
SQ FT: 28,000
SALES: 1.2MM **Privately Held**
SIC: 5049 3567 3823 Scientific instruments; distillation ovens, charcoal & coke; coulometric analyzers, industrial process type

(G-11938)
UNITED GRANITE & MARBLE
321 Airport Dr (60431-4894)
PHONE.................................815 582-3345
Maria Ochoa, *Principal*
EMP: 3
SALES (est): 194.8K **Privately Held**
SIC: 3281 Granite, cut & shaped

(G-11939)
UNITED UNIVERSAL INDS INC
20620 Burl Ct Ste 1 (60433-9707)
PHONE.................................815 727-4445
Edward B Smith, *President*
Diana Smith, *Corp Secy*
EMP: 25
SQ FT: 10,000
SALES (est): 3.5MM **Privately Held**
WEB: www.uniteduniversal.com
SIC: 3643 3699 3678 3577 Current-carrying wiring devices; electrical equipment & supplies; electronic connectors; computer peripheral equipment; nonferrous wiredrawing & insulating

(G-11940)
VALLEY CONCRETE INC
19515 Ne Frontage Rd (60404-3567)
PHONE.................................815 725-2422
Tom Huiner, *President*
Bill Pommerening, *Vice Pres*
EMP: 60 EST: 1981
SALES (est): 910.5K **Privately Held**
SIC: 3273 Ready-mixed concrete

(G-11941)
VISION SIGNS INC
2104 Oak Leaf St Unit A (60436-1875)
PHONE.................................815 530-0870
Carlos Tinoco, *President*
Jason Stearman, *Vice Pres*
EMP: 4

SALES (est): 125.2K **Privately Held**
SIC: 3993 Signs & advertising specialties

(G-11942)
VISTA WOODWORKING
500 Joyce Rd Unit B (60436-1879)
PHONE.................................815 922-2297
Nancy Quattrochi, *President*
EMP: 5
SALES (est): 463K **Privately Held**
WEB: www.vistawoodworking.com
SIC: 2431 Millwork

(G-11943)
W E S INC
18530 Nw Frontage Rd (60404-9654)
PHONE.................................815 436-1732
Joel Niekamp, *President*
EMP: 10
SQ FT: 13,300
SALES: 2.5MM **Privately Held**
SIC: 3599 Machine shop, jobbing & repair

(G-11944)
WEIGH RIGHT AUTOMATIC SCALE CO
612a Mills Rd (60433)
PHONE.................................815 726-4626
Stephen N Almberg, *President*
John Greenan, *Design Engr*
Mike Phillips, *Marketing Staff*
EMP: 9 EST: 1932
SQ FT: 11,500
SALES (est): 2.1MM **Privately Held**
WEB: www.weighright.com
SIC: 3565 Packaging machinery

(G-11945)
WILTON BRANDS INC
Also Called: Wilton Industries
21350 Sw Frontage Rd (60404-4702)
PHONE.................................815 823-8547
◆ EMP: 10
SALES (est): 1.1MM **Privately Held**
SIC: 3999 Manufacturing industries

Jonesboro
Union County

(G-11946)
G & C ENTERPRISES INC
18837 County Line Rd (62952-5002)
PHONE.................................618 747-2272
Conrad Shepard, *President*
Glenda Shepard, *Corp Secy*
EMP: 4
SALES (est): 405.1K **Privately Held**
SIC: 2411 Logging

Joy
Mercer County

(G-11947)
ROBIN L BARNHOUSE
Also Called: G1 Industries Co
1106 120th Ave (61260-8558)
PHONE.................................309 737-5431
Robin L Barnhouse, *Owner*
Mike Barnhouse, *Principal*
EMP: 3
SALES: 50K **Privately Held**
SIC: 3499 Fabricated metal products

Junction
Gallatin County

(G-11948)
BARNETT REDI-MIX INC
11300 Highway 1 (62954-2103)
P.O. Box 207, Equality (62934-0207)
PHONE.................................618 276-4298
Shery Denny, *President*
Mike Bardos, *Manager*
EMP: 3
SALES (est): 182.9K **Privately Held**
SIC: 3273 Ready-mixed concrete

Justice
Cook County

(G-11949)
ABILITY PLASTICS INC
8721 Industrial Dr (60458-1765)
PHONE.................................708 458-4480
Michael L Nuzzo, *President*
EMP: 35 EST: 1973
SQ FT: 15,000
SALES (est): 11.7MM **Privately Held**
SIC: 5162 3993 Plastics products; signs, not made in custom sign painting shops

(G-11950)
CLASSIC ROADLINER CORPORATION
8027 Marion Dr Apt 1e (60458-1641)
PHONE.................................708 769-0666
Shadi Alnadi, *President*
EMP: 4
SALES (est): 330K **Privately Held**
SIC: 3715 Truck trailers

(G-11951)
CZARNIK MEMORIALS INC
7300 Archer Rd (60458-1141)
P.O. Box 333, Summit Argo (60501-0333)
PHONE.................................708 458-4443
Carrie Sewcyck, *President*
Irene Bucher, *Corp Secy*
EMP: 3 EST: 1920
SALES (est): 349.9K **Privately Held**
SIC: 5999 3281 Monuments, finished to custom order; tombstones; cut stone & stone products

(G-11952)
E C MACHINING INC
8267 S 86th Ct (60458-1767)
PHONE.................................708 496-0116
Edward A Czorniak, *President*
EMP: 27
SQ FT: 7,500
SALES (est): 4.5MM **Privately Held**
SIC: 3599 Machine shop, jobbing & repair

(G-11953)
PETER TROOST MONUMENT CO
7200 Archer Rd (60458-1140)
PHONE.................................773 585-0242
Frank Troost, *Manager*
EMP: 5
SALES (corp-wide): 14MM **Privately Held**
SIC: 3281 5999 Cut stone & stone products; monuments, finished to custom order
PA: Peter Troost Monument Co.
4300 Roosevelt Rd
Hillside IL
708 544-0916

Kaneville
Kane County

(G-11954)
ELMHURST-CHICAGO STONE COMPANY
45 W 371 Main (60144)
PHONE.................................630 557-2446
Glen Ulery, *Superintendent*
EMP: 15
SALES (corp-wide): 127.2MM **Privately Held**
SIC: 3272 1442 Concrete products; construction sand & gravel
PA: Elmhurst-Chicago Stone Company
400 W 1st St
Elmhurst IL 60126
630 832-4000

(G-11955)
NEEDHAM SHOP INC
46 W 840 Main (60144)
P.O. Box 144 (60144-0144)
PHONE.................................630 557-9019
Bart Needham, *President*
EMP: 7
SQ FT: 6,000

Kankakee
Kankakee County

(G-11956)
ADCRAFT PRINTERS INC
1355 W Jeffery St (60901-4626)
PHONE...............................815 932-6432
Dallas Wheeler, *President*
Erik Wheeler, *Corp Secy*
EMP: 17 EST: 1940
SQ FT: 8,500
SALES: 900K **Privately Held**
WEB: www.adcraftprinters.com
SIC: 2752 2791 2789 Commercial printing, offset; typesetting; bookbinding & related work

(G-11957)
ADVANCED LUBRICATION INC
(PA)
4517 E 2000n Rd (60901-7501)
PHONE...............................815 932-3288
David Ward, *President*
Mary Pawlak, *Manager*
EMP: 3 EST: 1993
SALES: 1.8MM **Privately Held**
WEB: www.advlubrication.com
SIC: 1389 Oil consultants

(G-11958)
ARMSTRONG FLOORING INC
Also Called: Armstrong USA
1401 N Hobbie Ave (60901-9311)
PHONE...............................815 939-2501
Paul Smith, *Plant Mgr*
EMP: 300
SALES (corp-wide): 626.3MM **Publicly Held**
WEB: www.armstrongflooring.com
SIC: 3996 Hard surface floor coverings
PA: Armstrong Flooring, Inc.
2500 Columbia Ave
Lancaster PA 17603
717 672-9611

(G-11959)
BASF CORPORATION
Kankakee Manufacturing Plant
2525 S Kensington Ave (60901-8243)
PHONE...............................815 932-6751
Denny Ohomansiek, *Manager*
Dan Hayes, *Manager*
John McGinnis, *Manager*
David Golz, *Technical Staff*
John C McGinnis, *MIS Staff*
EMP: 400
SALES (corp-wide): 65.6B **Privately Held**
WEB: www.basf.com
SIC: 2869 2899 2821 Industrial organic chemicals; chemical preparations; plastics materials & resins
HQ: Basf Corporation
100 Park Ave
Florham Park NJ 07932
973 245-6000

(G-11960)
BERENS INC
1650 E Sheridan St (60901-5662)
PHONE...............................815 932-0913
Mark Berens, *President*
Elvira Berens, *Corp Secy*
EMP: 6
SALES (est): 552.1K **Privately Held**
SIC: 3429 Clamps, metal

(G-11961)
COMMERCIAL METALS COMPANY
780 Eastgate Indus Pkwy (60901-2889)
PHONE...............................815 928-9600
EMP: 6
SALES (corp-wide): 5.8B **Publicly Held**
SIC: 3441 3312 5051 Fabricated structural metal; blast furnaces & steel mills; metals service centers & offices
PA: Commercial Metals Company
6565 N Macarthur Blvd # 800
Irving TX 75039
214 689-4300

(G-11962)
DAYTON SUPERIOR CORPORATION
2150b S Us Highway 45 52 (60901-7200)
PHONE...............................219 476-4106
EMP: 40
SALES (corp-wide): 2.8B **Privately Held**
SIC: 3315 3452 Mfg Steel Wire/Related Products Mfg Bolts/Screws/Rivets
PA: Dayton Superior Corporation
1125 Byers Rd
Miamisburg OH 45342
937 866-0711

(G-11963)
DAYTON SUPERIOR CORPORATION
2150b S Us Highway 45 52 (60901-7200)
PHONE...............................815 936-3300
Joe Bachta, *Controller*
Charley Read, *Branch Mgr*
EMP: 78
SALES (corp-wide): 50.9B **Publicly Held**
SIC: 3449 3441 Bars, concrete reinforcing: fabricated steel; fabricated structural metal
HQ: Dayton Superior Corporation
1125 Byers Rd
Miamisburg OH 45342
937 866-0711

(G-11964)
DAYTON SUPERIOR CORPORATION
American Highway Technology
2150 W Jeffery St (60901-8221)
PHONE...............................815 936-3300
Jesus Valdez, *Branch Mgr*
EMP: 150
SALES (corp-wide): 50.9B **Publicly Held**
SIC: 3315 3452 3462 3089 Steel wire & related products; dowel pins, metal; construction or mining equipment forgings, ferrous; plastic hardware & building products; chemical preparations; miscellaneous fabricated wire products
HQ: Dayton Superior Corporation
1125 Byers Rd
Miamisburg OH 45342
937 866-0711

(G-11965)
DICKS ASPHALT SERVICE
2695 E 3500s Rd (60901-7049)
PHONE...............................815 932-7157
Richard Panozzo, *Executive*
EMP: 3
SALES (est): 290K **Privately Held**
SIC: 2951 Asphalt paving mixtures & blocks

(G-11966)
DOW CHEMICAL COMPANY
1400 Harvard Dr (60901-9462)
PHONE...............................815 933-8900
Gary Mc Farland, *Branch Mgr*
EMP: 75
SALES (corp-wide): 42.9B **Publicly Held**
SIC: 2819 2821 Industrial inorganic chemicals; plastics materials & resins
HQ: The Dow Chemical Company
2211 H H Dow Way
Midland MI 48642
989 636-1000

(G-11967)
ELECTRON BEAM TECHNOLOGIES INC
1275 Harvard Dr (60901-9471)
PHONE...............................815 935-2211
Eric Franklin, *President*
Michael Murtha, *Vice Pres*
Craig Cahan, *Engineer*
Bob Tokoly, *CFO*
Robert Tokoly, *Admin Sec*
▲ **EMP:** 104 EST: 2005
SQ FT: 100,000
SALES (est): 24.9MM **Privately Held**
WEB: www.electronbeam.com
SIC: 3548 3541 7699 Welding wire, bare & coated; plasma process metal cutting machines; industrial equipment services

(G-11968)
EMD MILLIPORE CORPORATION
195 W Birch St (60901-2346)
PHONE...............................815 937-8270
Dave Leppert, *Manager*
EMP: 180
SALES (corp-wide): 17.8B **Privately Held**
SIC: 3826 Analytical instruments
HQ: Emd Millipore Corporation
400 Summit Dr
Burlington MA 01803
781 533-6000

(G-11969)
EMD MILLIPORE CORPORATION
2407 Eastgate Pkwy (60901)
PHONE...............................815 932-9017
EMP: 317
SALES (corp-wide): 16.4B **Privately Held**
SIC: 3826 Analytical Instruments, Nsk
HQ: Emd Millipore Corporation
400 Summit Dr
Burlington MA 01803
781 533-6000

(G-11970)
FAST SIGNS 590
Also Called: Fastsigns
601a N 5th Ave (60901-2344)
PHONE...............................815 937-1855
EMP: 5
SALES (est): 338K **Privately Held**
SIC: 3993 Signs & advertising specialties

(G-11971)
FIBRE DRUM COMPANY
1650 E Sheridan St (60901-5662)
P.O. Box 349 (60901-0349)
PHONE...............................815 933-3222
Mark Berens, *President*
William Cox, *Executive*
Arnold C Berens, *Admin Sec*
EMP: 28 EST: 1946
SQ FT: 45,000
SALES: 6MM **Privately Held**
WEB: www.fibredrumco.com
SIC: 2655 Drums, fiber: made from purchased material

(G-11972)
FOOD SERVICE
1501 E Maple St (60901-4371)
PHONE...............................815 933-0725
Cathy Breeck, *Exec Dir*
Beth Proctor, *Director*
EMP: 70
SALES (est): 3.9MM **Privately Held**
WEB: www.smsd.org
SIC: 2099 Food preparations

(G-11973)
FRIENDLY SIGNS INC
1281 N Schuyler Ave (60901-2108)
PHONE...............................815 933-7070
Dave Whitlow, *Partner*
Francis Gullquist, *Partner*
EMP: 4
SALES (est): 300K **Privately Held**
SIC: 1799 3993 Sign installation & maintenance; signs & advertising specialties

(G-11974)
GROFF TESTING CORPORATION
1410 Stanford Dr (60901-9474)
PHONE...............................815 939-1153
Ron Groff, *President*
EMP: 4
SQ FT: 4,800
SALES (est): 500K **Privately Held**
SIC: 3546 Drills & drilling tools

(G-11975)
HEARTLAND HARVEST INC
2401 Eastgate Indus Pkwy (60901-2856)
PHONE...............................815 932-2100
Warren Ouwenga, *President*
Dennis Bunck, *Vice Pres*
▲ **EMP:** 2
SALES (est): 635.3K **Privately Held**
SIC: 2038 Frozen specialties
HQ: Bunge North America, Inc.
1391 Tmberlake Manor Pkwy
Chesterfield MO 63017
314 292-2000

(G-11976)
HOSTMANN STEINBERG INC
(HQ)
2850 Festival Dr (60901-8937)
PHONE...............................502 968-5961
Winfred Gleue, *President*
Frank Shostack, *Admin Sec*
EMP: 18
SALES (est): 9.9MM
SALES (corp-wide): 1.3MM **Privately Held**
SIC: 2893 Printing ink
PA: Michael Huber Ohg
Bahnhofstr. 3
Bergen 83346
866 280-52

(G-11977)
INLAND PLASTICS INC
1310 E Birch St (60901-2621)
P.O. Box 803 (60901-0803)
PHONE...............................815 933-3500
John W Goudy, *President*
Lorna E Goudy, *Admin Sec*
▲ **EMP:** 6
SQ FT: 30,000
SALES (est): 495K **Privately Held**
SIC: 3089 Molding primary plastic

(G-11978)
INSYNC MANUFACTURING LLC
601a N 5th Ave (60901-2344)
PHONE...............................815 304-6300
▲ **EMP:** 10
SQ FT: 450,000
SALES (est): 2.4MM **Privately Held**
SIC: 3599 Mfg Industrial Machinery

(G-11979)
J R SHORT MILLING COMPANY
(PA)
1580 Grinnell Rd (60901-8246)
PHONE...............................800 544-8734
Craig R Petray, *President*
Jon E Luikar, *President*
Nick Ladin, *Vice Pres*
Scott Rennewanz, *Production*
Dennis Bryar, *Purch Mgr*
▲ **EMP:** 125 EST: 1910
SALES (est): 35.3MM **Privately Held**
WEB: www.shortmill.com
SIC: 2041 5149 Flour; corn grits & flakes, for brewers' use; hominy grits (except breakfast food); baking supplies

(G-11980)
J R SHORT MILLING COMPANY
Bunge Milling
1580 Grinnell Rd (60901-8246)
PHONE...............................815 937-2633
Dennis Bunck, *General Mgr*
EMP: 120
SALES (corp-wide): 35.3MM **Privately Held**
WEB: www.shortmill.com
SIC: 2041 Flour & other grain mill products
PA: J. R. Short Milling Company
1580 Grinnell Rd
Kankakee IL 60901
800 544-8734

(G-11981)
J&A MTCHELL STL FBRICATORS INC
2524 S 8000w Rd (60901-7932)
PHONE...............................815 939-2144
Adam J Mitchell, *President*
Jeremy Mitchell, *Vice Pres*
Jeremy M Mitchell, *Manager*
EMP: 8
SQ FT: 1,200
SALES (est): 500K **Privately Held**
SIC: 3441 Fabricated structural metal

(G-11982)
JOES AUTOMOTIVE INC
560 S Washington Ave (60901-3746)
PHONE...............................815 937-9281
Larry Nottke, *President*
Maurice Marcotte, *Vice Pres*
SALES: 400K **Privately Held**
SIC: 7692 7699 Welding repair; farm machinery repair

EMP: 9
SQ FT: 150
SALES (est): 1.2MM **Privately Held**
WEB: www.joesautomotivekankakee.com
SIC: **3694** 7694 5531 5013 Automotive electrical equipment; electric motor repair; automotive accessories; automotive supplies

(G-11983)
JOSEPH B PIGATO MD LTD
375 N Wall St Ste P630 (60901-3495)
PHONE...................................815 937-2122
Dr Joseph B Pigato, *Principal*
Joseph R Pigato, *Med Doctor*
EMP: 9
SALES (est): 884.8K **Privately Held**
SIC: **2834** Drugs acting on the gastrointestinal or genitourinary system

(G-11984)
JR EDWRDS BRSHES ROLLERS INC
1325 Harvard Dr (60901-9473)
PHONE...................................815 933-3742
James R Edwards, *Ch of Bd*
Gary G Kolbe, *President*
Gary Kolbe, *President*
Gaye Edwards, *Corp Secy*
▲ EMP: 20
SALES (est): 5.1MM **Privately Held**
SIC: **2851** Paints & allied products

(G-11985)
KANKAKEE DAILY JOURNAL CO LLC (HQ)
Also Called: Daily Journal, The
8 Dearborn Sq (60901-3945)
PHONE...................................815 937-3300
Len R Small,
Joseph Lacaeyse,
Thomas P Small,
EMP: 220
SQ FT: 15,000
SALES (est): 25MM
SALES (corp-wide): 131.4MM **Privately Held**
WEB: www.daily-journal.com
SIC: **2711** Commercial printing & newspaper publishing combined; newspapers, publishing & printing
PA: Small Newspaper Group
   8 Dearborn Sq
   Kankakee IL 60901
   815 937-3300

(G-11986)
KANKAKEE TENT & AWNING CO
679b W 2000s Rd (60901-7838)
PHONE...................................815 932-8000
Lee E Fredrickson, *Owner*
EMP: 4
SALES (est): 512.8K **Privately Held**
WEB: www.itsashadydeal.com
SIC: **7359** 2394 5999 Tent & tarpaulin rental; awnings, fabric: made from purchased materials; awnings

(G-11987)
KEY PRINTING
111 E Court St (60901-3823)
PHONE...................................815 933-1800
Norman Strasma, *Owner*
EMP: 5
SQ FT: 2,420
SALES (est): 442.1K **Privately Held**
SIC: **7334** 2789 2752 Photocopying & duplicating services; bookbinding & related work; commercial printing, lithographic

(G-11988)
KOERNER AVIATION INC
1520 S State Route 115 (60901-7792)
PHONE...................................815 932-4222
Roger Koerner Sr, *President*
EMP: 4
SALES: 100K **Privately Held**
WEB: www.koerneraviation.com
SIC: **3599** 8249 5088 7692 Machine shop, jobbing & repair; aviation school; aircraft equipment & supplies; welding repair

(G-11989)
LEGACY VULCAN LLC
Also Called: South Midwest Division
1277 S 7000w Rd (60901-7923)
PHONE...................................815 937-7928
Steve Novak, *Opers-Prdtn-Mfg*
EMP: 28 **Publicly Held**
SIC: **1442** Construction sand & gravel
HQ: Legacy Vulcan, Llc
   1200 Urban Center Dr
   Vestavia AL 35242
   205 298-3000

(G-11990)
M & C POWERSPORTS
1548 S 6th Ave (60901-4848)
PHONE...................................207 713-3128
Michael Bell, *Owner*
EMP: 3
SALES (est): 340.9K **Privately Held**
SIC: **3799** Recreational vehicles

(G-11991)
METZKA INC
Also Called: Woody's Ems
431 S Washington Ave (60901-3743)
PHONE...................................815 932-6363
Ronald Metzka, *President*
EMP: 3
SQ FT: 7,250
SALES (est): 450K **Privately Held**
SIC: **7694** 5063 Electric motor repair; motors, electric

(G-11992)
MURPHY USA INC
503 Riverstone Pkwy (60901-7227)
PHONE...................................815 936-6144
EMP: 16 **Publicly Held**
SIC: **5541** 1311 Filling stations, gasoline; crude petroleum & natural gas production
PA: Murphy Usa Inc.
   200 E Peach St
   El Dorado AR 71730

(G-11993)
NORTHERN ILLINOIS GAS COMPANY
Also Called: Nicor Gas
2704 Festival Dr (60901-8953)
PHONE...................................630 983-8676
Richard Stutzman, *Manager*
EMP: 48
SALES (corp-wide): 21.4B **Publicly Held**
SIC: **4924** 1382 4923 Natural gas distribution; oil & gas exploration services; gas transmission & distribution
HQ: Northern Illinois Gas Company
   1844 W Ferry Rd
   Naperville IL 60563
   630 983-8676

(G-11994)
OFFKO TOOL INC
1995 S Kensington Ave (60901-8244)
P.O. Box 1826 (60901-1826)
PHONE...................................815 933-9474
Wayne H Offerman, *President*
Charlotte Offerman, *Corp Secy*
Howard Offerman, *Manager*
EMP: 8 EST: 1968
SQ FT: 6,000
SALES (est): 774.4K **Privately Held**
SIC: **3312** 3469 Tool & die steel; metal stampings

(G-11995)
OPTECH ORTHO & PROSTH SVCS (PA)
119 E Court St Ste 100 (60901-3823)
PHONE...................................815 932-8564
Martin B McNab, *Principal*
EMP: 10
SALES (est): 1.6MM **Privately Held**
SIC: **3842** Orthopedic appliances; prosthetic appliances

(G-11996)
P-AMERICAS LLC
Also Called: Pepsico
1525 S Schuyler Ave (60901-8336)
PHONE...................................815 939-3123
Dave Zajc, *Principal*
Craig Foerg, *Site Mgr*
EMP: 60

SALES (corp-wide): 67.1B **Publicly Held**
SIC: **2086** 5149 Carbonated soft drinks, bottled & canned; groceries & related products
HQ: P-Americas Llc
   1 Pepsi Way
   Somers NY 10589
   336 896-5740

(G-11997)
PROVENA ENTERPRISES INC (HQ)
555 W Court St Ste 414 (60901-3675)
PHONE...................................708 478-3230
Ray Dewitte, *President*
EMP: 20
SALES (est): 97.7K
SALES (corp-wide): 311K **Privately Held**
SIC: **2752** Commercial printing, offset
PA: Provena Ventures, Inc
   200 E Court St Ste 200 # 200
   Kankakee IL
   815 933-4452

(G-11998)
RINGWOOD CONTAINERS LP
Also Called: Ring Can
1825 American Way (60901-9400)
PHONE...................................815 939-7270
Clarence Heber, *Plant Mgr*
Ronald Owen, *Branch Mgr*
Delores Hedge, *Exec Dir*
EMP: 23 **Privately Held**
SIC: **3085** Plastics bottles
PA: Ringwood Containers, L.P.
   1 Industrial Park
   Oakland TN 38060

(G-11999)
RIVERSIDE MEDI-CENTER INC
Also Called: Pharmacy Store
400 N Wall St Ste 1 (60901-2965)
PHONE...................................815 932-6632
Tom Marcotte, *Manager*
Amber Meltzer, *Nurse*
EMP: 4
SALES (corp-wide): 340.2MM **Privately Held**
SIC: **2834** Druggists' preparations (pharmaceuticals)
HQ: Riverside Medi-Center, Inc
   350 N Wall St
   Kankakee IL 60901
   815 933-1671

(G-12000)
RYAN METAL PRODUCTS INC
Also Called: Stor-Loc
880 N Washington Ave (60901-2004)
PHONE...................................815 936-0700
Michael J Ryan, *President*
Patrick Ryan, *Corp Secy*
EMP: 35
SQ FT: 12,200
SALES (est): 8MM **Privately Held**
SIC: **2542** Racks, merchandise display or storage: except wood; cabinets: show, display or storage: except wood

(G-12001)
SHOUP MANUFACTURING CO INC
3 Stuart Dr (60901-8947)
PHONE...................................815 933-4439
Raymond Lovell, *President*
Cheryl Baber, *Vice Pres*
Bruce Smith, *Admin Sec*
◆ EMP: 43
SALES (est): 19.1MM **Privately Held**
SIC: **3523** 5083 Farm machinery & equipment; farm equipment parts & supplies

(G-12002)
SIGNODE INDUSTRIAL GROUP LLC
Also Called: Plastic Packaging Systems
2150 S Us Highway 45 52 (60901-7200)
PHONE...................................815 939-6192
EMP: 39
SALES (corp-wide): 11.6B **Publicly Held**
SIC: **3565** Packaging machinery
HQ: Signode Industrial Group Llc
   3650 W Lake Ave
   Glenview IL 60026
   847 724-7500

(G-12003)
SIGNODE INDUSTRIAL GROUP LLC
Also Called: Angleboard
2150m S Us Highway 45 52 (60901-7200)
PHONE...................................815 939-0033
Lawrance Peck, *Manager*
EMP: 50
SALES (corp-wide): 11.6B **Publicly Held**
SIC: **2679** 2631 Paper products, converted; paperboard mills
HQ: Signode Industrial Group Llc
   3650 W Lake Ave
   Glenview IL 60026
   847 724-7500

(G-12004)
SMALL NEWSPAPER GROUP (PA)
Also Called: Journal
8 Dearborn Sq (60901-3909)
P.O. Box 632 (60901-0632)
PHONE...................................815 937-3300
Len R Small, *President*
Joseph Lacaeyse, *Treasurer*
Sally Hendron, *VP Finance*
Cindy Liptak, *Finance*
Thomas P Small, *Admin Sec*
EMP: 200
SQ FT: 15,000
SALES (est): 131.4MM **Privately Held**
SIC: **2711** 2791 2752 Newspapers, publishing & printing; typesetting; commercial printing, lithographic

(G-12005)
SPECCO INDUSTRIES INC
601 N 5th Ave (60901-2344)
PHONE...................................630 257-5060
Patrick Soler, *CEO*
Jeff C Bencsik, *President*
John W Bencsik, *Admin Sec*
▲ EMP: 10 EST: 1972
SQ FT: 10,000
SALES (est): 2.6MM **Privately Held**
WEB: www.specco.com
SIC: **2899** Chemical preparations

(G-12006)
SPRINKLES CONFETTI
46 Baker St (60901-8249)
PHONE...................................815 304-5974
EMP: 4
SALES (est): 197.5K **Privately Held**
SIC: **2051** Bread, cake & related products

(G-12007)
STARMONT MANUFACTURING CO
655 S Harrison Ave (60901-5107)
PHONE...................................815 939-1041
Arthur W Schumacher, *President*
Tamara K Diorio, *Corp Secy*
EMP: 7
SQ FT: 17,000
SALES (est): 415.7K **Privately Held**
SIC: **3444** 3599 3469 Concrete forms, sheet metal; machine shop, jobbing & repair; metal stampings

(G-12008)
STEELFAB INC
2045 S Kensington Ave (60901-7100)
PHONE...................................815 935-6540
Matt McLaren, *President*
Martha McLaren, *Vice Pres*
EMP: 20
SQ FT: 40,000
SALES (est): 5MM **Privately Held**
SIC: **3441** Building components, structural steel

(G-12009)
SUN CHEMICAL CORPORATION
3200 Festival Dr (60901-8945)
PHONE...................................815 939-0136
Charles Tapscott, *Mfg Spvr*
Jeff Gallis Torfer, *Manager*
Gordon Palmer, *Technician*
EMP: 52 **Privately Held**
SIC: **2893** Printing ink
HQ: Sun Chemical Corporation
   35 Waterview Blvd Ste 100
   Parsippany NJ 07054
   973 404-6000

GEOGRAPHIC SECTION

(G-12010)
TAIT MACHINE TOOL INC
417 S Schuyler Ave (60901-5131)
P.O. Box 134 (60901-0134)
PHONE..................................815 932-2011
Louis Schuh, *President*
Eric Thompson, *Vice Pres*
EMP: 6
SQ FT: 4,800
SALES (est): 550K **Privately Held**
SIC: 3599 7692 Machine shop, jobbing & repair; welding repair

(G-12011)
WEST LABORATORIES INC
1305 Harvard Dr (60901-9473)
PHONE..................................815 935-1630
Gary West, *President*
Scott West, *Vice Pres*
Jay West, *Treasurer*
Dana West, *Admin Sec*
▼ **EMP:** 22 **EST:** 1965
SQ FT: 20,000
SALES: 4.9MM **Privately Held**
SIC: 2836 Plasmas; serums

Keensburg
Wabash County

(G-12012)
ALPHA NATURAL RESOURCES INC
Also Called: Wabash Mines
1000 Beall Woods Dr (62852)
P.O. Box 144 (62852-0144)
PHONE..................................618 298-2394
William A Kelly, *Manager*
EMP: 205
SALES (corp-wide): 2.2B **Publicly Held**
SIC: 1221 1222 Bituminous coal & lignite-surface mining; bituminous coal-underground mining
HQ: Alpha Natural Resources, Inc.
636 Shelby St Ste 1c
Bristol TN 37620
423 574-5100

Kempton
Ford County

(G-12013)
ADVENTURES UNLIMITED (PA)
Also Called: World Explorer
303 Main St (60946-4115)
P.O. Box 74 (60946-0074)
PHONE..................................815 253-6390
David Childress, *Owner*
Jennifer Bolm, *Co-Owner*
EMP: 5
SALES (est): 450K **Privately Held**
SIC: 2731 5961 Books: publishing only; books, mail order (except book clubs)

Kenilworth
Cook County

(G-12014)
C2 WATER INC
732 Cummings Ave (60043-1013)
PHONE..................................312 550-1159
Kevin Buzard, *President*
EMP: 4
SALES: 822.2K **Privately Held**
SIC: 3589 Water treatment equipment, industrial

(G-12015)
SHERWIN-WILLIAMS COMPANY
614 Green Bay Rd (60043-1003)
PHONE..................................847 251-6115
EMP: 5
SALES (corp-wide): 17.9B **Publicly Held**
WEB: www.sherwin-williams.com
SIC: 5231 3991 Paint; push brooms
PA: The Sherwin-Williams Company
101 W Prospect Ave # 1020
Cleveland OH 44115
216 566-2000

Kenney
De Witt County

(G-12016)
SCHNEIDER PIPE ORGANS INC
104 S Johnston St (61749-9615)
P.O. Box 137 (61749-0137)
PHONE..................................217 871-4807
Richard M Schneider, *President*
Joan Schneider, *Admin Sec*
EMP: 6 **EST:** 1976
SQ FT: 20,000
SALES (est): 350K **Privately Held**
SIC: 3931 7699 Musical instruments, electric & electronic; organ tuning & repair

Kent
Stephenson County

(G-12017)
B T BROWN MANUFACTURING
14871 E Airport Rd (61044-9707)
PHONE..................................815 947-3633
Brian T Brown, *Owner*
EMP: 3
SALES (est): 200K **Privately Held**
SIC: 7692 3523 Welding repair; farm machinery & equipment

(G-12018)
NUESTRO QUESO LLC
752 N Kent Rd (61044-9636)
P.O. Box 101 (61044-0101)
PHONE..................................815 443-2100
Anthony Andrate, *Branch Mgr*
EMP: 135 **Privately Held**
WEB: www.hcmakers.com
SIC: 2022 Cheese, natural & processed
PA: Nuestro Queso, Llc
100 S Wacker Dr Ste 1950
Chicago IL 60606

Kewanee
Henry County

(G-12019)
ADVANCE METALWORKING COMPANY
Also Called: Lo Riser Trailers
3726 Us Highway 34 (61443-8315)
PHONE..................................309 853-3387
Leonard Kull, *Ch of Bd*
Richard D Kull, *President*
Annette K Kull, *Corp Secy*
Rich Rwitte, *Mfg Dir*
Denis Shenaut, *Purch Mgr*
▲ **EMP:** 20
SQ FT: 33,000
SALES (est): 4.2MM **Privately Held**
WEB: www.advancemetalworking.com
SIC: 3799 Trailers & trailer equipment

(G-12020)
AMERICAN STEEL CARPORTS INC
832 N East St (61443-1516)
PHONE..................................800 487-4010
Melton Castillo, *Manager*
EMP: 15
SALES (corp-wide): 22.7MM **Privately Held**
SIC: 3448 Carports: prefabricated metal
PA: American Steel Carports, Inc.
457 N Brwy St
Joshua TX 76058
866 471-8761

(G-12021)
BAILLEU & BAILLEU PRINTING INC
Also Called: B & B Printing
214 S Main St Ste A (61443-4006)
PHONE..................................309 852-2517
Robert Bailleu, *President*
Leann Bailleu, *Admin Sec*
EMP: 8
SQ FT: 10,000
SALES (est): 1.4MM **Privately Held**
SIC: 2752 2759 2791 2789 Commercial printing, offset; screen printing; typesetting; bookbinding & related work; automotive & apparel trimmings

(G-12022)
BOSS BALLOON COMPANY INC
1221 Page St (61443-3241)
PHONE..................................309 852-2131
Bruce Lancaster, *President*
Steve Pont, *Vice Pres*
EMP: 5
SQ FT: 15,700
SALES (est): 347.4K **Publicly Held**
SIC: 3069 Balloons, advertising & toy: rubber
HQ: Boss Manufacturing Company Inc
1221 Page St
Kewanee IL 61443
309 852-2131

(G-12023)
BOSS HOLDINGS INC (PA)
1221 Page St (61443-3241)
PHONE..................................309 852-2131
G Louis Graziadio III, *Ch of Bd*
Richard Bern, *COO*
Steven G Pont, *VP Finance*
Josh Miskinis, *Marketing Staff*
Donna Boardman, *Director*
▲ **EMP:** 70
SQ FT: 70,000
SALES (est): 99.1MM **Publicly Held**
SIC: 2381 3151 2385 3069 Gloves, work: woven or knit, made from purchased materials; gloves, leather: work; waterproof outerwear; balloons, advertising & toy: rubber

(G-12024)
BOSS MANUFACTURING COMPANY (DH)
1221 Page St (61443-3241)
PHONE..................................309 852-2131
G Louis Graziadio III, *President*
Steven Pont, *Vice Pres*
Steve Witte, *Controller*
Tabitha Ainley, *Sales Staff*
Robin Danielson, *Sales Staff*
◆ **EMP:** 40
SQ FT: 80,000
SALES (est): 23.6MM **Publicly Held**
WEB: www.bossgloves.com
SIC: 2381 3021 Fabric dress & work gloves; protective footwear, rubber or plastic
HQ: Boss Manufacturing Holdings Inc
1221 Page St
Kewanee IL 61443
309 852-2781

(G-12025)
BOSS MANUFACTURING HOLDINGS (HQ)
1221 Page St (61443-3241)
PHONE..................................309 852-2781
Bruce Lancaster, *CFO*
▲ **EMP:** 10
SALES (est): 26.2MM **Publicly Held**
SIC: 2381 3151 3842 3949 Fabric dress & work gloves; leather gloves & mittens; gloves, safety; gloves, sport & athletic: boxing, handball, etc.; waterproof outerwear; boot or shoe products, plastic

(G-12026)
BOSS MANUFACTURING HOLDINGS
Warren Pet Products
1221 Page St (61443-3241)
PHONE..................................309 852-2131
Bruce Lancaster, *President*
EMP: 4 **Publicly Held**
SIC: 3999 Pet supplies
HQ: Boss Manufacturing Holdings Inc
1221 Page St
Kewanee IL 61443
309 852-2781

(G-12027)
BOSS PET PRODUCTS INC
1501 Burlington Ave (61443-2553)
PHONE..................................216 332-0802
EMP: 3 **Publicly Held**
SIC: 3999 Pet supplies
HQ: Boss Pet Products, Inc.
7730 First Pl Ste E
Oakwood Village OH 44146
216 332-0832

(G-12028)
BREEDLOVE SPORTING GOODS INC (PA)
Also Called: Breedlove's
123 W 2nd St (61443-2259)
PHONE..................................309 852-2434
William Breedlove, *President*
Debbie Breedlove, *Corp Secy*
Daniel Breedlove, *Vice Pres*
Catherine E Breedlove, *Shareholder*
EMP: 10
SQ FT: 3,500
SALES (est): 3.3MM **Privately Held**
WEB: www.breedlovesports.com
SIC: 5941 2396 Sporting goods & bicycle shops; screen printing on fabric articles

(G-12029)
BREEDLOVE SPORTING GOODS INC
215 W 2nd St (61443-2149)
PHONE..................................309 852-2434
William Breedlove, *President*
EMP: 10
SALES (corp-wide): 3.3MM **Privately Held**
SIC: 5941 2396 Sporting goods & bicycle shops; screen printing on fabric articles
PA: Breedlove Sporting Goods, Inc.
123 W 2nd St
Kewanee IL 61443
309 852-2434

(G-12030)
DIERZEN-KEWANEE HEAVY INDS
101 Franklin St (61443-2608)
P.O. Box 524 (61443-0524)
PHONE..................................309 853-2316
Louie Dierzen, *Owner*
EMP: 80
SALES (est): 2MM **Privately Held**
SIC: 7532 3711 Truck painting & lettering; truck tractors for highway use, assembly of

(G-12031)
DOOLEY BROTHERS PLUMBING & HTG
306 N Tremont St (61443-2240)
P.O. Box 312 (61443-0312)
PHONE..................................309 852-2720
Patrick J Dooley, *President*
Dorothy Ann Dooley, *Vice Pres*
Irene Dooley, *Manager*
EMP: 8
SALES (est): 1.3MM **Privately Held**
SIC: 3494 7539 Plumbing & heating valves; electrical services

(G-12032)
ELM STREET INDUSTRIES INC
Also Called: R & T Enterprises
206 W 4th St (61443-2132)
PHONE..................................309 854-7000
Fred Butcher, *Manager*
EMP: 14
SALES (corp-wide): 2.9MM **Privately Held**
SIC: 2441 2449 5731 2653 Boxes, wood; food containers, wood: wirebound; sound equipment, automotive: corrugated & solid fiber boxes; wood television & radio cabinets
PA: Elm Street Industries, Inc.
1310 Elm Pl
Kelso WA
360 423-1840

(G-12033)
FLEX COURT INTERNATIONAL INC
Also Called: Flex Court Electronic
4328 Us Highway 34 (61443-8317)
P.O. Box 741 (61443-0741)
PHONE..................................309 852-0899
Mats Jonmarker, *President*
Teri Jonmarker, *Vice Pres*

Kewanee - Henry County (G-12034)

Christie Wilson, *Sales Staff*
▼ EMP: 12
SQ FT: 10,000
SALES (est): 1.2MM **Privately Held**
SIC: 3949 Sporting & athletic goods

(G-12034)
FRED STOLLENWERK
Also Called: Central Welding Shop
801 Elmwood Ave (61443-3039)
PHONE..................................309 852-3794
Fred Stollenwerk, *Owner*
EMP: 1
SALES: 360K **Privately Held**
SIC: 7692 Welding repair

(G-12035)
GATEHOUSE MEDIA LLC
Also Called: Kewanee Star Courier
105 E Central Blvd (61443-2245)
P.O. Box A (61443-0836)
PHONE..................................309 852-2181
Stu Griffith, *Principal*
EMP: 15
SALES (corp-wide): 1.8B **Publicly Held**
WEB: www.gatehousemedia.com
SIC: 2711 Newspapers, publishing & printing
HQ: Gatehouse Media, Llc
   175 Sullys Trl Fl 3
   Pittsford NY 14534
   585 598-0030

(G-12036)
GREAT DANE LLC
324 N Main St (61443-2226)
P.O. Box 364 (61443-0364)
PHONE..................................309 854-0407
Nick Johnson, *Manager*
EMP: 175
SALES (corp-wide): 1.5B **Privately Held**
SIC: 3715 Semitrailers for truck tractors
HQ: Great Dane Llc
   222 N Lasalle St Ste 920
   Chicago IL 60601

(G-12037)
GREAT DANE LLC
Also Called: Great Dane Trlrs-Kewanee Plant
2006 Kentville Rd (61443-1714)
PHONE..................................309 854-0407
Chris Stolfe, *Manager*
EMP: 309
SALES (corp-wide): 1.5B **Privately Held**
SIC: 3715 Demountable cargo containers
HQ: Great Dane Llc
   222 N Lasalle St Ste 920
   Chicago IL 60601

(G-12038)
GREAT DANE LLC
Also Called: Pines Trailer
2006 Kentville Rd (61443-1714)
PHONE..................................773 254-5533
Chris Stolfe, *Manager*
EMP: 81
SALES (corp-wide): 1.5B **Privately Held**
SIC: 3715 5511 Semitrailers for truck tractors; trucks, tractors & trailers: new & used
HQ: Great Dane Llc
   222 N Lasalle St Ste 920
   Chicago IL 60601

(G-12039)
HEARTFELT GIFTS INC
Also Called: Heartfelt Framing Gallery
224 N Main St (61443-2224)
PHONE..................................309 852-2296
Susan Sagmoen, *President*
EMP: 4
SQ FT: 4,500
SALES (est): 184K **Privately Held**
SIC: 5947 2253 5999 Gift shop; knit outerwear mills; picture frames, ready made

(G-12040)
RHINO TOOL COMPANY
Also Called: Ground Cover Marketing
1134 W South St (61443-8357)
P.O. Box 111 (61443-0111)
PHONE..................................309 853-5555
James Martin, *President*
Robert Conner, *Design Engr*
Steve Orrick, *Sales Mgr*
Ashley Haffner, *Marketing Mgr*

Julie Martin, *Admin Sec*
▲ EMP: 11 **EST:** 1975
SQ FT: 10,000
SALES (est): 3.5MM **Privately Held**
SIC: 3531 3594 3566 3546 Construction machinery; fluid power pumps & motors; speed changers, drives & gears; power-driven handtools; industrial valves; hand & edge tools

(G-12041)
SECURITY HOLDINGS LLC
212 E 1st St (61443-2302)
PHONE..................................309 856-6000
EMP: 4 **Privately Held**
SIC: 3442 Metal doors
PA: Security Holdings Llc
   111 Kero Rd
   Carlstadt NJ 07072

(G-12042)
TRIANGLE CONCRETE CO INC
Also Called: Kewanee Triangle Concrete
1201 New St (61443-1841)
P.O. Box 431 (61443-0431)
PHONE..................................309 853-4334
Thomas Ratliff, *President*
Tom Kazubowski, *Plant Mgr*
William Leaf, *Admin Sec*
EMP: 4 **EST:** 1961
SQ FT: 1,300
SALES (est): 200K **Privately Held**
SIC: 3273 Ready-mixed concrete

Keyesport
Clinton County

(G-12043)
KEYESPORT MANUFACTURING INC
1610 Mulberry St (62253-2140)
PHONE..................................618 749-5510
Charlie Kern, *President*
Glenda Kern, *Treasurer*
EMP: 5
SQ FT: 18,360
SALES (est): 639.6K **Privately Held**
SIC: 3993 Electric signs

Kilbourne
Mason County

(G-12044)
HARDWOOD LUMBER PRODUCTS CO
21046 E Cr 800n (62655-6547)
PHONE..................................309 538-4411
Gary Hodgson, *Partner*
Todd Hodgson, *Partner*
EMP: 5
SALES: 1MM **Privately Held**
SIC: 2448 2426 Pallets, wood; furniture dimension stock, hardwood

(G-12045)
SUNRISE AG SERVICE COMPANY
Rr 1 (62655)
PHONE..................................309 538-4287
Mike Willing, *Manager*
EMP: 7
SALES (corp-wide): 13.3MM **Privately Held**
SIC: 2873 Nitrogenous fertilizers
PA: Sunrise Ag Service Company
   104 S 1st St
   Easton IL 62633
   309 562-7296

Kildeer
Lake County

(G-12046)
DRYWEAR APPAREL LLC
21231 W Brandon Rd (60047-8619)
PHONE..................................847 687-8540
Peter Durment,

EMP: 6
SALES (est): 398K **Privately Held**
SIC: 2321 7389 Men's & boys' sports & polo shirts;

(G-12047)
ENSEMBLEIQ INC
20909 N Middleton Dr (60047-8698)
PHONE..................................847 438-7357
L Stagnito, *Branch Mgr*
EMP: 5
SALES (corp-wide): 28.6MM **Privately Held**
SIC: 2721 Magazines: publishing only, not printed on site
PA: Ensembleiq, Inc.
   8550 W Bryn Mawr Ave # 200
   Chicago IL 60631
   773 992-4450

(G-12048)
GROUND COVER INDUSTRIES INC (PA)
21333 N Middleton Dr (60047-8508)
P.O. Box 1201, Warrenville (60555-7201)
PHONE..................................800 550-4424
Steve Gambla, *President*
Jerry Campbell, *Vice Pres*
EMP: 1 **EST:** 1995
SQ FT: 26,000
SALES (est): 689.1K **Privately Held**
SIC: 3621 Rotary converters (electrical equipment)

(G-12049)
INTEREXPO LTD
Also Called: Mobileskin Imaging
22438 N Clayton Ct (60047-7947)
PHONE..................................847 489-7056
George Webb, *President*
EMP: 16 **EST:** 2007
SALES: 700K **Privately Held**
SIC: 3845 5047 5999 Electromedical equipment; electro-medical equipment; medical apparatus & supplies

(G-12050)
LBE LTD
21038 N Andover Rd (60047-8604)
P.O. Box 1852, Palatine (60078-1852)
PHONE..................................847 907-4959
Loyd Bostic, *President*
Steven Fisher, *Sales Staff*
Claudia Bostic, *Admin Sec*
EMP: 4
SQ FT: 1,000
SALES: 100K **Privately Held**
SIC: 7372 7389 Utility computer software; financial services

(G-12051)
PARKER SYSTEMS INC
20989 N Middleton Dr (60047-8698)
PHONE..................................847 726-8600
Clark Beverly, *President*
EMP: 5
SQ FT: 2,600
SALES (est): 144.2K **Privately Held**
SIC: 2759 Commercial printing; facsimile letters: printing

(G-12052)
SANCO INDUSTRIES INC
21800 N Andover Rd (60047-8523)
PHONE..................................847 243-8675
Edwin Sanchez, *President*
Edward Sanchez, *President*
EMP: 15
SQ FT: 14,000
SALES (est): 2.2MM **Privately Held**
SIC: 3965 3495 5072 3496 Fasteners; wire springs; bolts; nuts (hardware); rivets; miscellaneous fabricated wire products; bolts, nuts, rivets & washers

(G-12053)
SHOELACE INC
20505 N Rand Rd Ste 218 (60047-3004)
PHONE..................................847 854-2500
Robert J Guss, *President*
EMP: 6 **Privately Held**
SIC: 2241 Narrow fabric mills
PA: Shoelace, Inc.
   23 N Williams St
   Crystal Lake IL 60014

Kings
Ogle County

(G-12054)
SPRING SPECIALIST CORPORATION
14400 E Dutch Rd (61068-4535)
PHONE..................................815 562-7991
John Nichols, *President*
Wesley Nichols, *Vice Pres*
Nancy G Nichols, *Admin Sec*
EMP: 8
SQ FT: 5,000
SALES (est): 1.3MM **Privately Held**
SIC: 3495 3496 3493 Mechanical springs, precision; miscellaneous fabricated wire products; steel springs, except wire

Kingston
Dekalb County

(G-12055)
DECAL WORKS LLC
2021 Johnson Ct (60145-8345)
PHONE..................................815 784-4000
Ron Joynt, *President*
Margie Joynt, *Production*
Brandon Rehrig, *Graphic Designe*
▲ EMP: 25 **EST:** 1989
SQ FT: 12,000
SALES (est): 3.3MM **Privately Held**
WEB: www.decalmx.com
SIC: 2759 Screen printing

(G-12056)
NEWERA SOFTWARE INC
9505 Wolf Rd (60145-8169)
PHONE..................................815 784-3345
Glennon Bagsby, *President*
Mary King, *Office Mgr*
EMP: 9
SALES (est): 524.4K **Privately Held**
SIC: 7372 Business oriented computer software

(G-12057)
US CHROME CORP ILLINOIS
United States Chrome
305 Herbert Rd (60145-7008)
PHONE..................................815 544-3487
John Carpenter, *COO*
Carlos Adaes, *Opers Mgr*
John Leahy, *Manager*
EMP: 20
SALES (corp-wide): 30.5MM **Privately Held**
WEB: www.uschrome.com
SIC: 3471 Electroplating of metals or formed products; chromium plating of metals or formed products
HQ: U.S. Chrome Corporation Of Illinois
   175 Garfield Ave
   Stratford CT
   203 378-9622

Kinmundy
Marion County

(G-12058)
DEEP ROCK ENERGY CORPORATION
7601 Oleary Rd (62854-2621)
PHONE..................................618 548-2779
Benny D Webster, *President*
EMP: 20
SALES (est): 1.6MM **Privately Held**
SIC: 1389 Building oil & gas well foundations on site

Kirkland
Dekalb County

(G-12059)
DIVISION 5 METALS INC
2314 Old State Rd (60146-8724)
P.O. Box 52, Esmond (60129-0052)
PHONE..................815 901-5001
Timothy Gulotta, *President*
EMP: 8
SALES (est): 1.2MM **Privately Held**
SIC: 3531 Construction machinery

(G-12060)
EUCLID CHEMICAL COMPANY
Also Called: Epoxy Chemicals
3835 State Route 72 (60146-8635)
PHONE..................815 522-2308
Brad Nemunaitis, *Principal*
Ralph Gosorn, *Controller*
Stephen Scarpinato, *VP Mktg*
Doug Cole, *Info Tech Mgr*
EMP: 11
SALES (corp-wide): 5.5B **Publicly Held**
SIC: 2899 Concrete curing & hardening compounds
HQ: The Euclid Chemical Company
19218 Redwood Rd
Cleveland OH 44110
800 321-7628

(G-12061)
IL GREEN PASTURES FIBER CO-OP
28668 Bell Rd (60146-8736)
PHONE..................815 751-0887
Connie Gustafson, *Treasurer*
EMP: 3
SALES (est): 198.2K **Privately Held**
SIC: 3661 Fiber optics communications equipment

(G-12062)
KIRKLAND SAWMILL INC
606 W Main St (60146)
P.O. Box 245 (60146-0245)
PHONE..................815 522-6150
EMP: 3
SQ FT: 18,800
SALES (est): 274.8K **Privately Held**
SIC: 2421 Sawmill/Planing Mill

(G-12063)
LEE QUARRY INC
1473 Flora Church Rd (60146-8122)
PHONE..................815 547-7141
EMP: 5
SALES (est): 290.5K **Privately Held**
SIC: 1422 Limestones, ground

(G-12064)
NESTEROWICZ & ASSOCIATES INC
313 W Main St (60146-8438)
P.O. Box 50 (60146-0050)
PHONE..................815 522-4469
Phillip A Nesterowicz, *President*
Nancy S Nesterowicz, *Corp Secy*
EMP: 6
SQ FT: 8,000
SALES (est): 1.1MM **Privately Held**
SIC: 1761 3444 Architectural sheet metal work; sheet metalwork

(G-12065)
SHAPE-MASTER TOOL CO
801 W Main St (60146-8465)
P.O. Box 520 (60146-0520)
PHONE..................815 522-6186
Don Spolum Jr, *President*
Scott Chambers, *Purch Dir*
Brett Young, *Sales Mgr*
Dan Chambers, *Sales Staff*
▲ EMP: 30 EST: 1976
SALES (est): 5.1MM **Privately Held**
WEB: www.shapemastertool.com
SIC: 3545 Diamond cutting tools for turning, boring, burnishing, etc.

(G-12066)
TAMMS INDUSTRIES INC
3835 Il Route 72 (60146-8635)
PHONE..................815 522-3394
M Thomas McCall, *President*
EMP: 63
SQ FT: 80,000
SALES (est): 12.5MM **Privately Held**
SIC: 2851 2899 5211 Paints & allied products; waterproofing compounds; masonry materials & supplies

Kirkwood
Warren County

(G-12067)
KIRKWOOD CRATES LLC
335 W Depot St (61447)
P.O. Box 2 (61447-0002)
PHONE..................651 373-5945
Ryan Harley, *Mng Member*
Justin Allaman,
Josh Dean,
N Defenbaugh,
EMP: 5
SALES (est): 479.7K **Privately Held**
SIC: 2448 Pallets, wood

Knoxville
Knox County

(G-12068)
KASER POWER EQUIPMENT INC
480 Henderson Rd (61448-1066)
P.O. Box 216 (61448-0216)
PHONE..................309 289-2176
David Kaser, *President*
Carla Kaser, *Vice Pres*
EMP: 5
SQ FT: 1,680
SALES (est): 495K **Privately Held**
SIC: 5261 7699 5251 5084 Garden supplies & tools; general household repair services; door locks & lock sets; engines, gasoline; saws & sawing equipment

(G-12069)
RING SHEET METAL HEATING & AC
213 Grove St (61448-1227)
PHONE..................309 289-4213
Jon Nelson, *Owner*
EMP: 3
SALES (est): 242.6K **Privately Held**
SIC: 1711 3585 Warm air heating & air conditioning contractor; ventilation & duct work contractor; refrigeration & heating equipment

La Grange
Cook County

(G-12070)
AKEMA INC
637 S Waiola Ave (60525-2734)
PHONE..................708 482-3148
Gerald Rife III, *Principal*
EMP: 3
SALES (est): 158.9K **Privately Held**
SIC: 3732 Boat building & repairing

(G-12071)
ALPHADIGITAL INC
Also Called: AlphaGraphics
712 E Elm Ave (60525-6835)
PHONE..................708 482-4488
Albert Schnell, *President*
Janet Schnell, *Corp Secy*
Michael A Schnell, *Vice Pres*
EMP: 6
SQ FT: 3,800
SALES (est): 1.1MM **Privately Held**
SIC: 2752 7334 2791 2789 Commercial printing, lithographic; photocopying & duplicating services; typesetting; bookbinding & related work

(G-12072)
ANDREWS CONVERTING LLC
707 E 47th St (60525-3069)
PHONE..................708 352-2555
James Andrews, *President*
Scott Andrews, *Vice Pres*
EMP: 38
SQ FT: 33,000
SALES: 4.7MM **Privately Held**
SIC: 2675 Die-cut paper & board

(G-12073)
BLUE PEARL STONE TECH LLC
333 Washington Ave (60525-6831)
PHONE..................708 698-5700
Teresa Fister, *Mng Member*
Fister Teresa, *Manager*
EMP: 5
SALES (est): 471.7K **Privately Held**
SIC: 8731 1411 3272 Commercial physical research; granite dimension stone; art marble, concrete

(G-12074)
BOYER CORPORATION
9600 W Ogden Ave (60525)
P.O. Box 10 (60525-0010)
PHONE..................708 352-2553
Harold Hurwitz, *President*
EMP: 2
SQ FT: 5,000
SALES (est): 237.3K **Privately Held**
SIC: 2842 2992 2819 Specialty cleaning preparations; cleaning or polishing preparations; drain pipe solvents or cleaners; lubricating oils & greases; industrial inorganic chemicals

(G-12075)
CARVER PLASTIC PRODUCTS INC
512 W Burlington Ave # 208 (60525-2245)
PHONE..................708 588-0081
Nick Sotos, *President*
EMP: 4
SALES (est): 200K **Privately Held**
SIC: 2821 Plastics materials & resins

(G-12076)
CONSUMER VINEGAR AND SPICE
745 S Ashland Ave (60525-2816)
PHONE..................708 354-1144
Stan Zarnowiecki, *President*
EMP: 3
SALES (est): 224.7K **Privately Held**
SIC: 2099 Vinegar

(G-12077)
GRAYHILL INC (PA)
561 W Hillgrove Ave (60525-5997)
PHONE..................708 354-1040
Gene R Hill, *CEO*
Brian May, *President*
Lisa Audino, *Business Mgr*
Benjamin Bartz, *Business Mgr*
Sean Liu, *Business Mgr*
◆ EMP: 500 EST: 1976
SQ FT: 175,000
SALES (est): 155.3MM **Privately Held**
WEB: www.grayhill.com
SIC: 3613 3625 3679 3643 Switches, electric power except snap, push button, etc.; switches, electric power; switches, electronic applications; electronic switches; electric switches; keyboards, computer, office machine

(G-12078)
HOLTON FOOD PRODUCTS COMPANY
500 W Burlington Ave (60525-2227)
PHONE..................708 352-5599
Ross Holton, *President*
John E Holton, *Exec VP*
EMP: 12
SQ FT: 2,000
SALES (est): 2.5MM
SALES (corp-wide): 5.5B **Publicly Held**
SIC: 2099 Dessert mixes & fillings
HQ: Mantrose-Haeuser Co., Inc.
100 Nyala Farms Rd
Westport CT 06880

(G-12079)
ID ADDITIVES INC
512 W Burlington Ave # 208 (60525-2245)
PHONE..................708 588-0081
Nicholas Sotos, *President*
Ronald Bishop, *Technical Mgr*
EMP: 3
SALES (est): 599.7K **Privately Held**
SIC: 2821 Plastics materials & resins

(G-12080)
IMPACT SIGNS & GRAPHICS INC
Also Called: Impact Bronze Plaques
26 E Burlington Ave (60525-2430)
PHONE..................708 469-7178
Toll Free:..................866
Ammar Moosabhoy, *President*
Shabbir Moosabhoy, *Vice Pres*
EMP: 5 EST: 1999
SQ FT: 1,400
SALES (est): 861K **Privately Held**
SIC: 3993 Electric signs

(G-12081)
K & N LABORATORIES INC
633 S La Grange Rd (60525-6741)
P.O. Box 7226, Deerfield (60015-7226)
PHONE..................708 482-3240
June Sabin, *President*
EMP: 13
SALES (est): 1.8MM **Privately Held**
SIC: 2679 Converted paper products

(G-12082)
MAINTENANCE INC
Also Called: Infra Red Heating
11055 80th Pl (60525-5204)
PHONE..................708 598-1390
Michael Lindy, *President*
Nina Lindy, *Vice Pres*
Bryan Garney, *Manager*
EMP: 3
SQ FT: 1,170
SALES: 750K **Privately Held**
SIC: 3567 5084 3714 Infrared ovens, industrial; heat exchange equipment, industrial; processing & packaging equipment; exhaust systems & parts, motor vehicle

(G-12083)
NATURAL PACKAGING INC
550 Hillgrove Ave Ste 518 (60525)
PHONE..................708 246-3420
Jack B Rolff, *President*
EMP: 4 EST: 2005
SALES (est): 270K **Privately Held**
SIC: 2673 Bags: plastic, laminated & coated

(G-12084)
OLIVACETO
77 S La Grange Rd (60525-2469)
PHONE..................708 639-4408
Margarita Rubi Castro, *Principal*
EMP: 3
SALES (est): 193.1K **Privately Held**
SIC: 2079 Olive oil

(G-12085)
ONE WAY SAFETY LLC
418 Shawmut Ave Ste B (60526-2193)
PHONE..................708 579-0229
Meg Shanley,
EMP: 35
SALES: 7.9MM **Privately Held**
SIC: 3851 7389 3842 Goggles: sun, safety, industrial, underwater, etc.; safety inspection service; personal safety equipment

(G-12086)
PMB INDUSTRIES INC
8072 53rd St (60525)
PHONE..................708 442-4515
EMP: 8
SALES (est): 453K **Privately Held**
SIC: 7389 3599 Designs & Mfg Custom Machinery & Related Equipment

(G-12087)
PRO-QUIP INCORPORATED
418 Shawmut Ave Ste A (60526-2085)
PHONE..................708 352-5732
Robert S Lefley III, *CEO*

La Grange - Cook County (G-12088)

David Lefley, *President*
Robert S Lefley IV, *Vice Pres*
EMP: 10
SQ FT: 10,000
SALES (est): 2MM **Privately Held**
SIC: 3625 3494 5084 Relays & industrial controls; valves & pipe fittings; controlling instruments & accessories

(G-12088)
RLC INDUSTRIES INC
715 S 10th Ave (60525-3061)
PHONE.................................708 837-7300
Raymond J Strack Jr, *President*
EMP: 3 **EST:** 2010
SALES (est): 319.7K **Privately Held**
SIC: 3613 Control panels, electric

(G-12089)
SERGIO BARAJAS
Also Called: SBA
205 Washington Ave (60525-2569)
PHONE.................................708 238-7614
Sergio Barajas, *Owner*
EMP: 5
SALES (est): 175K **Privately Held**
SIC: 3432 Plastic plumbing fixture fittings, assembly

(G-12090)
UPS AUTHORIZED RETAILER
106 W Calendar Ave (60525-2325)
PHONE.................................708 354-8772
Jinit Patel, *President*
EMP: 5
SQ FT: 2,200
SALES (est): 426.2K **Privately Held**
SIC: 7389 2759 Mailbox rental & related service; commercial printing

La Grange Highlands
Cook County

(G-12091)
AMERICAN TIRE DISTRIBUTORS
9450 W Sergo Dr Ste A (60525-7123)
PHONE.................................708 680-5150
◆ **EMP:** 5
SALES (est): 289.9K **Privately Held**
SIC: 5531 5014 3011 Automotive tires; tires & tubes; tires & inner tubes

(G-12092)
D2 LIGHTING LLC
5718 Harvey Ave (60525-7008)
PHONE.................................708 243-9059
David E Doubek, *Principal*
Dave Doubek, *Info Tech Mgr*
EMP: 5 **EST:** 2008
SALES (est): 610.3K **Privately Held**
SIC: 3648 Lighting equipment

(G-12093)
QUALITY SLEEP SHOP INC (PA)
1519 W 55th St (60525-7014)
PHONE.................................708 246-2224
Timothy W Masters, *President*
◆ **EMP:** 6
SQ FT: 4,000
SALES (est): 514.2K **Privately Held**
SIC: 2515 Mattresses & foundations

La Grange Park
Cook County

(G-12094)
ABET INDUSTRIES CORPORATION
111 Kemman Ave (60526-6007)
PHONE.................................708 482-8282
Cindy V Mottl, *President*
Eileen Votava, *Treasurer*
Daniel J Mottl, *Admin Sec*
EMP: 5
SQ FT: 8,300
SALES (est): 780.1K **Privately Held**
SIC: 3599 Electrical discharge machining (EDM); machine shop, jobbing & repair

(G-12095)
DESLAURIERS INC (PA)
1245 Barnsdale Rd (60526-1276)
PHONE.................................708 544-4455
Gary Workman, *President*
Philip Cozza, *Vice Pres*
Lynn Stolpe, *Purch Mgr*
Paul Cozza, *CFO*
Conrad Graff, *Sales Staff*
▲ **EMP:** 50 **EST:** 1888
SQ FT: 120,000
SALES: 21MM **Privately Held**
SIC: 3089 5051 Plastic hardware & building products; forms, concrete construction (steel)

(G-12096)
DIE SPECIALTY CO
1510 Cleveland Ave (60526-1308)
PHONE.................................312 303-5738
Harold W Langeland, *President*
Glenn E Langeland, *Vice Pres*
EMP: 6 **EST:** 1946
SQ FT: 5,000
SALES (est): 529.1K **Privately Held**
SIC: 3544 3545 Special dies & tools; machine tool accessories

(G-12097)
INTERNATIONAL MOLDING MCH CO
1201 Barnsdale Rd Ste 1 (60526-1285)
P.O. Box 1366 (60526-9466)
PHONE.................................708 354-1380
Tyrrell B Eichler Jr, *President*
Robert Eichler, *Corp Secy*
EMP: 6 **EST:** 1891
SQ FT: 46,000
SALES: 1MM **Privately Held**
WEB: www.internationalmolding.com
SIC: 3559 Foundry machinery & equipment

(G-12098)
MARCY ENTERPRISES INC
Also Called: MEI
250 Kings Ct (60526-5307)
P.O. Box 1322 (60526-9422)
PHONE.................................708 352-7220
Marcy K Britigan, *President*
Stuart Goldsand, *Corp Secy*
EMP: 5
SQ FT: 3,000
SALES (est): 2MM **Privately Held**
SIC: 5078 2521 2541 Refrigeration equipment & supplies; wood office furniture; cabinets, except refrigerated: show, display, etc.: wood

La Place
Piatt County

(G-12099)
J & M CUSTOM CABINETS
202 W North 2nd St (61936-1030)
P.O. Box 17 (61936-0017)
PHONE.................................217 677-2229
Michael Jackson, *Owner*
EMP: 3
SQ FT: 2,000
SALES (est): 89.2K **Privately Held**
SIC: 2434 Wood kitchen cabinets

La Salle
Lasalle County

(G-12100)
AGRI-NEWS PUBLICATIONS INC (HQ)
Also Called: Www.agrinews-Pubs.com
426 2nd St (61301-2334)
PHONE.................................815 223-2558
Peter Miller, *President*
Tom Doran, *Editor*
Marguerite Allen, *Vice Pres*
EMP: 53
SALES (est): 16.3MM
SALES (corp-wide): 33.9MM **Privately Held**
SIC: 2711 Newspapers, publishing & printing
PA: Daily News Tribune, Inc
426 2nd St
La Salle IL 61301
815 223-2558

(G-12101)
AIR PRODUCTS AND CHEMICALS INC
318 Civic Rd (61301-9710)
P.O. Box 1249 (61301-3249)
PHONE.................................815 223-2924
John Hardy, *Plant Mgr*
Susan Mennie, *Office Mgr*
EMP: 50
SALES (corp-wide): 8.9B **Publicly Held**
WEB: www.airproducts.com
SIC: 2813 Industrial gases
PA: Air Products And Chemicals, Inc.
7201 Hamilton Blvd
Allentown PA 18195
610 481-4911

(G-12102)
AMERICAN BARE CONDUCTOR INC
2969 Chartres St (61301-1085)
PHONE.................................815 224-3422
Marcos C Ramalho, *President*
Jorge Kawamura, *Vice Pres*
George Scidmore, *Info Tech Mgr*
Ricardo Kawamura, *Shareholder*
EMP: 35
SQ FT: 80,000
SALES (est): 10.4MM **Privately Held**
SIC: 3351 3643 3366 Wire, copper & copper alloy; current-carrying wiring devices; copper foundries

(G-12103)
ANBEK INC
222 3rd St (61301-2336)
PHONE.................................815 672-6087
James C Olmsted, *Principal*
EMP: 8 **Privately Held**
SIC: 3993 Signs & advertising specialties
PA: Anbek, Inc
104 W Madison St
Ottawa IL 61350

(G-12104)
ANBEK INC
Also Called: Designs and Signs By Anderson
222 3rd St (61301-2336)
PHONE.................................815 223-0734
EMP: 12
SALES (corp-wide): 1.3MM **Privately Held**
SIC: 3993 Mfg Signs/Advertising Specialties
PA: Anbek, Inc
104 W Madison St
Ottawa IL 61350
815 434-7340

(G-12105)
CARUS CORPORATION
1500 8th St (61301-1978)
PHONE.................................815 223-1565
EMP: 94
SALES (corp-wide): 157.4MM **Privately Held**
SIC: 2819 Mfg Industrial Inorganic Chemicals
HQ: Carus Corporation
315 5th St
Peru IL 61354
815 223-1500

(G-12106)
CARUS LLC
Also Called: Carus Chemical Company
1500 8th St (61301-1978)
P.O. Box 1500 (61301-0150)
PHONE.................................815 223-1500
Sandi Grubich, *Branch Mgr*
EMP: 123
SALES (corp-wide): 60.6MM **Privately Held**
SIC: 2819 Industrial inorganic chemicals

HQ: Carus Llc
315 5th St
Peru IL 61354
815 223-1500

(G-12107)
CHRISTYS KITCHEN
2203 Aplington St (61301-1127)
PHONE.................................815 735-6791
Christopher Kuhn, *Principal*
EMP: 8
SALES (est): 586.8K **Privately Held**
SIC: 2051 Bakery: wholesale or wholesale/retail combined

(G-12108)
CIPP ROBOTICS LLC
320 Raccuglia Dr (61301-9723)
P.O. Box 1541 (61301-3541)
PHONE.................................815 202-6628
Jeremy Recklein, *President*
EMP: 3
SALES (est): 322.6K **Privately Held**
SIC: 3827 Optical instruments & lenses

(G-12109)
CYCLOPS WELDING CO
11 Joliet St (61301-2593)
PHONE.................................815 223-0685
Joseph R Piano, *President*
EMP: 7
SQ FT: 5,000
SALES (est): 1.2MM **Privately Held**
SIC: 3441 7692 3444 3443 Fabricated structural metal; welding repair; sheet metalwork; fabricated plate work (boiler shop)

(G-12110)
DAILY NEWS TRIBUNE INC (PA)
426 2nd St (61301-2334)
PHONE.................................815 223-2558
Joyce T McCullough, *President*
Lisa Entwistle, *Advt Staff*
Joe Zokal, *Manager*
Kathleen Cordeiro, *Director*
Jenn Mann, *Director*
EMP: 150
SQ FT: 11,700
SALES (est): 33.9MM **Privately Held**
WEB: www.newstrib.com
SIC: 2711 Newspapers, publishing & printing

(G-12111)
FAST PIPE LINING INC
320 Raccuglia Dr (61301-9723)
P.O. Box 1521 (61301-3521)
PHONE.................................815 712-8646
EMP: 5 **EST:** 2012
SALES (est): 586.2K **Privately Held**
WEB: www.fastpipelining.com
SIC: 3321 Sewer pipe, cast iron

(G-12112)
FORTE INCORPORATED
601 2nd St Ste 3 (61301-8850)
P.O. Box 10, Ladd (61329-0010)
PHONE.................................815 224-8300
Jim Love, *President*
Bernie Victor, *Vice Pres*
EMP: 7
SALES: 1.2MM **Privately Held**
SIC: 7372 Operating systems computer software

(G-12113)
ILLINOIS CEMENT COMPANY LLC (HQ)
1601 Rockwell Rd (61301-9600)
P.O. Box 442 (61301-0442)
PHONE.................................815 224-2112
Steven R Rowley, *President*
Wayne Emmer, *Mng Member*
Frank Koeppel,
▲ **EMP:** 149
SQ FT: 4,000
SALES (est): 33.5MM
SALES (corp-wide): 1.3B **Publicly Held**
SIC: 3241 5032 Masonry cement; cement
PA: Eagle Materials Inc.
5960 Berkshire Ln Ste 900
Dallas TX 75225
214 432-2000

GEOGRAPHIC SECTION

(G-12114)
INDIANA AGRI-NEWS INC
420 2nd St (61301-2334)
PHONE.................................317 726-5391
Peter Miller III, *Vice Pres*
Lynn Barker, *Director*
S C Miller, *Admin Sec*
EMP: 3
SQ FT: 1,600
SALES (est): 235.4K
SALES (corp-wide): 33.9MM **Privately Held**
SIC: 2711 Newspapers, publishing & printing
PA: Daily News Tribune, Inc
426 2nd St
La Salle IL 61301
815 223-2558

(G-12115)
INMAN ELECTRIC MOTORS INC
314 Civic Rd (61301-9710)
P.O. Box 1108 (61301-3108)
PHONE.................................815 223-2288
David Inman, *President*
Celeste Inman, *Corp Secy*
Pam Mignone, *Purch Dir*
EMP: 27 **EST:** 1967
SQ FT: 75,000
SALES (est): 7.6MM **Privately Held**
SIC: 7694 5063 3621 3613 Electric motor repair; rebuilding motors, except automotive; motors, electric; motors & generators; coils, for electric motors or generators; switchgear & switchboard apparatus; industrial pumps & parts

(G-12116)
JANE STODDEN BRIDALS LLC
955 Marquette St (61301-1869)
PHONE.................................815 223-2091
Jane Stodden, *Owner*
EMP: 3
SALES: 8K **Privately Held**
SIC: 2335 5621 5947 Wedding gowns & dresses; bridal shops; greeting cards

(G-12117)
LINK MEDIA FLORIDA LLC
2968 Saint Vincent Ave (61301-9707)
PHONE.................................815 224-4742
Ann Salz, *Sales/Mktg Mgr*
EMP: 4
SALES (corp-wide): 41.3MM **Publicly Held**
SIC: 7312 3993 Billboard advertising; signs & advertising specialties
HQ: Link Media Florida, Llc
200 Mansell Ct E
Roswell GA 30076
866 209-5617

(G-12118)
NEW CIE INC
Also Called: Special Products Division
85 Chartres St (61301-2313)
P.O. Box 529 (61301)
PHONE.................................815 224-1485
Donald Boken, *President*
Bob Baker, *Manager*
EMP: 12
SQ FT: 10,000
SALES (corp-wide): 15.9MM **Privately Held**
WEB: www.completeindustrial.com
SIC: 3613 3625 7694 5063 Switchgear & switchboard apparatus; relays & industrial controls; armature rewinding shops; electrical apparatus & equipment
PA: New Cie, Inc.
1220 Wenzel Rd
Peru IL 61354
815 224-1510

(G-12119)
ON SITE REPAIR SERVICES INC
340 Civic Rd (61301-9710)
P.O. Box 1486 (61301-3486)
PHONE.................................815 223-4058
Donald Kotecki, *President*
Kevin Kotecki, *Opers-Prdtn-Mfg*
Bernard Kleinman, *Admin Sec*
EMP: 19
SALES (est): 3MM **Privately Held**
SIC: 3541 Machine tool replacement & repair parts, metal cutting types

(G-12120)
QUALITY LIQUID FEEDS INC
75 Creve Coeur St (61301-2319)
PHONE.................................815 224-1553
Joe Saini, *Branch Mgr*
EMP: 10
SALES (corp-wide): 153.2MM **Privately Held**
WEB: www.qlf.com
SIC: 2048 Feed supplements
PA: Quality Liquid Feeds, Inc.
3586 State Road 23
Dodgeville WI 53533
608 935-2345

(G-12121)
REMURIATE LLC (PA)
Also Called: Remuriate Technologies
122 Marquette St (61301-2413)
PHONE.................................815 220-5050
Paul Carus, *CEO*
▲ **EMP:** 4 **EST:** 2013
SQ FT: 5,000
SALES: 3.2MM **Privately Held**
SIC: 2819 Hydrochloric acid

(G-12122)
RS DUCTLESS TECHNICAL SUPPORT
227 Bucklin St (61301-2343)
PHONE.................................815 223-7949
EMP: 7
SALES (est): 223.1K **Privately Held**
SIC: 2741 Misc Publishing

(G-12123)
VIAKABLE MANUFACTURING LLC
2969 Chartres St (61301-1085)
PHONE.................................815 615-8355
Marcela Renteria,
EMP: 3
SALES (est): 102.3K **Privately Held**
SIC: 3355 Aluminum wire & cable

(G-12124)
VOSS SANDWORKS WEST INC
418 N 35th Rd (61301-9644)
PHONE.................................815 474-4042
Joshua Voss, *Principal*
EMP: 3
SALES (est): 181.1K **Privately Held**
SIC: 1442 Construction sand & gravel

Lacon
Marshall County

(G-12125)
AS LAWN & LAND LLC
301 4th St (61540-1409)
P.O. Box 99 (61540-0099)
PHONE.................................309 246-5012
David Suffern, *Principal*
EMP: 3
SALES (est): 115.6K **Privately Held**
SIC: 3537 Industrial trucks & tractors

(G-12126)
DJH INDUSTRIES INC
400 N Commercial St (61540-1764)
PHONE.................................309 246-8456
Dale Hardin, *President*
Tim Fishel, *Train & Dev Mgr*
EMP: 37 **EST:** 1979
SQ FT: 50,000
SALES (est): 7.8MM **Privately Held**
WEB: www.hardin-inc.com
SIC: 3621 Electric motor & generator parts

(G-12127)
HARDIN INDUSTRIES LLC
400 N Commercial St (61540-1764)
PHONE.................................309 246-8456
Becki Salmon, *President*
Janet Hodge, *Director*
EMP: 38
SALES (est): 2.7MM **Privately Held**
SIC: 3621 Motors & generators

(G-12128)
LACON HOME JOURNAL
204 S Washington St (61540-1498)
PHONE.................................309 246-2865
William Sondag, *Principal*
EMP: 3
SALES (est): 76.2K **Privately Held**
WEB: www.laconhomejournal.com
SIC: 2711 Newspapers: publishing only, not printed on site

(G-12129)
MARSHALL COUNTY PUBLISHING CO
204 S Washington St (61540-1445)
PHONE.................................309 246-2865
William H Sondag, *President*
Esther Sondag, *Vice Pres*
EMP: 5
SQ FT: 3,870
SALES (est): 300K **Privately Held**
SIC: 2711 Newspapers, publishing & printing

(G-12130)
MCKEAN PALLET CO
1046 State Route 26 (61540-8906)
PHONE.................................309 246-7543
Frank McKean, *Owner*
EMP: 3
SALES (est): 395K **Privately Held**
SIC: 2448 Pallets, wood

(G-12131)
META TEC DEVELOPMENT INC (PA)
125 N Commercial St (61540-8820)
PHONE.................................309 246-2960
David Suffren, *President*
Becky Scott, *Purch Mgr*
Rita Ann Suffern, *Admin Sec*
▲ **EMP:** 3
SALES (est): 2.1MM **Privately Held**
SIC: 7699 3599 Industrial equipment services; machine shop, jobbing & repair

(G-12132)
META TEC OF ILLINOIS INC
125 N Commercial St (61540-8820)
PHONE.................................309 246-2960
David Suffren, *President*
Rita Ann Suffern, *Admin Sec*
EMP: 85
SQ FT: 17,200
SALES (est): 15.1MM **Privately Held**
SIC: 3321 3599 Gray iron castings; custom machinery

(G-12133)
POIGNANT LOGGING
857 State Route 26 (61540-8903)
PHONE.................................309 246-5647
Leroy Poignant, *Owner*
EMP: 4
SALES (est): 291.7K **Privately Held**
SIC: 2411 Logging camps & contractors

Ladd
Bureau County

(G-12134)
TEE GROUP FILMS INC
605 N Mn Ave (61329)
P.O. Box 425 (61329-0425)
PHONE.................................815 894-2331
Thomas H Malpass, *President*
Paula Fues, *Administration*
▲ **EMP:** 60
SQ FT: 60,000
SALES (est): 18.9MM **Privately Held**
SIC: 3081 Polyethylene film

Lafox
Kane County

(G-12135)
BI-TORQ VALVE AUTOMATION INC
1n046 Linlar Dr (60147)
P.O. Box 309 (60147-0309)
PHONE.................................630 208-9343
Chris Sharp, *Regional Mgr*
Dan Eckel, *CFO*
Rich Caudillo, *Sales Staff*
Amber Rohr, *Sales Staff*
Rebecca Carney, *Technical Staff*
EMP: 1 **EST:** 2015
SALES (est): 260K
SALES (corp-wide): 18.8MM **Privately Held**
SIC: 3494 Valves & pipe fittings
HQ: Strahman Holdings, Inc.
10201 N Illinois St # 200
Indianapolis IN 46290
317 818-5030

(G-12136)
LAFOX MANUFACTURING CORP
1 N 278 Lafox Rd (60147)
P.O. Box 399 (60147-0399)
PHONE.................................630 232-0266
Kurt Kranz, *President*
Mike Zoch, *Vice Pres*
EMP: 7
SALES: 1.3MM **Privately Held**
SIC: 3498 Pipe fittings, fabricated from purchased pipe

(G-12137)
RICHARDSON ELECTRONICS LTD
Canvys
40 W 267 Keslinger Rd (60147)
P.O. Box 393 (60147-0393)
PHONE.................................630 208-2278
Robert Ben, *Exec VP*
Pat Fitzgerald, *Exec VP*
Jens Ruppert, *Exec VP*
Brian Blanchette, *Vice Pres*
Kathleenm McNally, *Vice Pres*
EMP: 250
SALES (corp-wide): 166.6MM **Publicly Held**
WEB: www.rell.com
SIC: 5046 3679 3577 7371 Display equipment, except refrigerated; liquid crystal displays (LCD); data conversion equipment, media-to-media: computer; decoders, computer peripheral equipment; encoders, computer peripheral equipment; graphic displays, except graphic terminals; computer software systems analysis & design, custom; computer software development & applications
PA: Richardson Electronics, Ltd.
40w267 Keslinger Rd
Lafox IL 60147
630 208-2200

(G-12138)
RICHARDSON ELECTRONICS LTD (PA)
40w267 Keslinger Rd (60147)
P.O. Box 393 (60147-0393)
PHONE.................................630 208-2200
Edward J Richardson, *Ch of Bd*
Hector Munoz, *Managing Dir*
Mark Gorecki, *Superintendent*
Wendy S Diddell, *COO*
Kathleen Dvorak, *Exec VP*
◆ **EMP:** 191 **EST:** 1947
SQ FT: 242,000
SALES: 166.6MM **Publicly Held**
WEB: www.rell.com
SIC: 5065 7373 3671 3679 Electronic parts; semiconductor devices; closed-circuit television; computer integrated systems design; value-added resellers, computer systems; electronic tube parts, except glass blanks; electronic circuits

Lafox - Kane County (G-12139)

(G-12139)
STRAHMAN VALVES INC
Also Called: Bi-Torq Valve Automation
1n046 Linlar Dr (60147)
P.O. Box 309 (60147-0309)
PHONE..................................630 208-9343
EMP: 24
SALES (est): 4.6MM
SALES (corp-wide): 12MM **Privately Held**
SIC: 3491 3494 Automatic regulating & control valves; valves & pipe fittings
PA: Strahman Valves, Inc.
2801 Baglyos Cir
Bethlehem PA 18020
877 787-2462

Lake Barrington
Lake County

(G-12140)
AEROMAX INDUSTRIES INC
28 W079 Industrial Ave (60010)
PHONE..................................847 756-4085
Mark Levine, *President*
Sean Schipper, *COO*
Jim Gunderson, *VP Sales*
Jared Heidenreich, *Office Mgr*
▲ EMP: 6
SQ FT: 2,000
SALES: 3MM **Privately Held**
SIC: 3944 Games, toys & children's vehicles

(G-12141)
AMBER SOFT INC
28214 W Northwest Hwy (60010-2324)
PHONE..................................630 377-6945
H Wayne Roby, *President*
Doris Roby, *Corp Secy*
EMP: 12 EST: 1968
SQ FT: 3,000
SALES (est): 1.6MM **Privately Held**
WEB: www.ambersoftwater.com
SIC: 3589 5999 7359 Water filters & softeners, household type; water purification equipment, household type; water treatment equipment, industrial; water purification equipment; equipment rental & leasing

(G-12142)
BROADCOM CORPORATION
25949 Oak Hills Rd (60010-7023)
PHONE..................................773 965-1600
Michael Oberholtzer, *Manager*
EMP: 3
SALES (corp-wide): 22.6B **Publicly Held**
SIC: 3674 Semiconductors & related devices
HQ: Broadcom Corporation
1320 Ridder Park Dr
San Jose CA 95131

(G-12143)
C B FERRARI INCORPORATED
22179 N Pepper Rd (60010-2461)
PHONE..................................847 756-4100
Josef Blechner, *President*
▲ EMP: 2
SALES (est): 284.3K **Privately Held**
SIC: 3549 Wiredrawing & fabricating machinery & equipment, ex. die

(G-12144)
COLE-PARMER INSTRUMENT CO LLC
28092 W Commercial Ave (60010-2443)
PHONE..................................847 381-7050
Larry Jones, *Manager*
EMP: 140
SALES (corp-wide): 272.8MM **Privately Held**
SIC: 3821 Laboratory equipment: fume hoods, distillation racks, etc.
HQ: Cole-Parmer Instrument Company Llc
625 Bunker Ct
Vernon Hills IL 60061
847 549-7600

(G-12145)
CROWN GYM MATS INC
27929 W Industrial Ave (60010-2455)
PHONE..................................847 381-8282
Judy Eckert, *President*
Jon Eckert, *Treasurer*
Holly Chevopulos, *Sales Mgr*
EMP: 10 EST: 1945
SQ FT: 14,000
SALES (est): 1.6MM **Privately Held**
WEB: www.crowngymmats.com
SIC: 3949 7699 Gymnasium equipment; recreational sporting equipment repair services

(G-12146)
CTI INDUSTRIES CORPORATION (PA)
22160 N Pepper Rd (60010-2301)
PHONE..................................847 382-1000
Frank Cesario, *CEO*
John H Schwan, *Ch of Bd*
Jana Schwan, *Vice Pres*
Samuel Komar, *VP Sales*
Bill Halstead, *Manager*
▲ EMP: 129
SQ FT: 68,000
SALES: 40.5MM **Publicly Held**
WEB: www.ctiindustries.com
SIC: 3089 3069 Plastic containers, except foam; tubs, plastic (containers); plastic kitchenware, tableware & houseware; balloons, metal foil laminated with rubber; balloons, advertising & toy: rubber; balls, rubber

(G-12147)
D S ARMS INCORPORATED
Also Called: D S A
27996 W Industrial Ave # 1 (60010-2533)
PHONE..................................847 277-7258
Dave Selvaggio, *President*
Mark Horn, *Mfg Dir*
Dennis Selvaggio, *Sales Staff*
EMP: 30
SALES (est): 4.9MM **Privately Held**
SIC: 3484 5199 5099 5961 Guns (firearms) or gun parts, 30 mm. & below; general merchandise, non-durable; firearms & ammunition, except sporting; mail order house

(G-12148)
GUARDIAN ROLLFORM LLC
27951 W Industrial Ave (60010-2455)
PHONE..................................847 382-8074
Maurice Loeffel, *Manager*
EMP: 55
SALES (est): 4.8MM **Privately Held**
SIC: 3356 Nonferrous rolling & drawing

(G-12149)
H & K PRECISION MACHINING CO
7 Hillside Dr Ste B (60010-5992)
PHONE..................................847 382-0288
Mike Kowatsch, *President*
Richard Scully, *Vice Pres*
EMP: 2
SQ FT: 1,200
SALES (est): 339.3K **Privately Held**
SIC: 3599 Machine shop, jobbing & repair

(G-12150)
HOWW MANUFACTURING COMPANY INC
28020 W Commercial Ave (60010-2443)
P.O. Box 276, Barrington (60011-0276)
PHONE..................................847 382-4380
M P Kalamaras, *President*
Glenn Greenwood, *VP Sales*
Jim Kalamaras, *VP Sales*
Michelle Roth-Smoot, *Creative Dir*
James Kalamaras, *Admin Sec*
▲ EMP: 25
SALES (est): 3.8MM **Privately Held**
SIC: 3231 Novelties, glass: fruit, foliage, flowers, animals, etc.

(G-12151)
HUNZINGER WILLIAMS INC
27w982 Commercial Ave (60010)
PHONE..................................847 381-1878
Lee J Ford, *President*
William Hunzinger, *Vice Pres*
Debbie Hunzinger, *Treasurer*
EMP: 11
SALES (est): 1.1MM **Privately Held**
SIC: 2394 Awnings, fabric: made from purchased materials; canopies, fabric: made from purchased materials

(G-12152)
IPM PRECISION INC
22179 N Pepper Rd (60010-2461)
PHONE..................................847 304-7900
Joe Blechner, *President*
Oliver Blechner, *Vice Pres*
EMP: 6
SQ FT: 16,800
SALES (est): 1.1MM **Privately Held**
SIC: 3599 Machine shop, jobbing & repair

(G-12153)
JOHN C GRAFFT (PA)
Also Called: Foreclosure Report
28045 Roberts Rd (60010-1139)
PHONE..................................847 842-9200
John C Grafft, *Owner*
EMP: 12
SALES (est): 250K **Privately Held**
SIC: 2721 6531 2741 8748 Magazines: publishing only, not printed on site; real estate agents & managers; miscellaneous publishing; publishing consultant

(G-12154)
JOHN F MATE CO
27930 W Industrial Ave # 5 (60010-2531)
PHONE..................................847 381-8131
John C Mate, *Partner*
Russell Mate, *Partner*
EMP: 2
SQ FT: 2,400
SALES (est): 250K **Privately Held**
SIC: 3585 3446 2541 Cabinets, show & display, refrigerated; architectural metalwork; wood partitions & fixtures

(G-12155)
JONEM GRP INC DBA SIGN A RAMA
28039 W Coml Ave Ste 9 (60010)
PHONE..................................224 848-4620
Vernon Jones, *President*
EMP: 2 EST: 2011
SALES (est): 238.2K **Privately Held**
SIC: 3993 Signs & advertising specialties

(G-12156)
K C PRINTING SERVICES INC
22292 N Pepper Rd Ste A (60010-2544)
PHONE..................................847 382-8822
Phillip Claps, *President*
Paul Claps, *Vice Pres*
EMP: 10
SQ FT: 3,000
SALES (est): 2.5MM **Privately Held**
SIC: 2621 5111 7389 Printing paper; printing & writing paper; advertising, promotional & trade show services

(G-12157)
LAKE PROCESS SYSTEMS INC
27930 W Commercial Ave (60010-2442)
PHONE..................................847 381-7663
Paul Harris, *President*
Rebecca A Harris, *Treasurer*
EMP: 20
SQ FT: 11,100
SALES (est): 5MM **Privately Held**
SIC: 3443 1623 5085 8711 Tanks, standard or custom fabricated: metal plate; pipe laying construction; valves, pistons & fittings; designing: ship, boat, machine & product; mechanical contractor

(G-12158)
LOEFFEL STEEL PRODUCTS INC (PA)
27951 W Industrial Ave (60010-2455)
P.O. Box 2100, Barrington (60011-2100)
PHONE..................................847 382-6770
Maurice F Loeffel, *President*
Matthew Loeffel, *Vice Pres*
Timothy K Loeffel Sr, *Vice Pres*
Mary Jane Loeffel, *Admin Sec*
EMP: 40
SQ FT: 20,000
SALES (est): 17.2MM **Privately Held**
SIC: 3441 Fabricated structural metal

(G-12159)
MATTSN/WITT PRECISION PDTS INC
28005 W Industrial Ave (60010-2454)
PHONE..................................847 382-7810
Jeffrey Witt, *President*
Sharon Kohler, *Production*
James Meyer, *Engineer*
Ron Cope, *Supervisor*
Faith Witt, *Admin Sec*
▲ EMP: 20 EST: 1957
SQ FT: 28,000
SALES (est): 3.6MM **Privately Held**
WEB: www.mattsonwitt.com
SIC: 3599 Machine shop, jobbing & repair

(G-12160)
MCLEAN MANUFACTURING COMPANY
Also Called: McLean Machine Tools
28040 W Industrial Ave (60010-2454)
PHONE..................................847 277-9912
John Cherney, *President*
▲ EMP: 5 EST: 1945
SALES (est): 804K **Privately Held**
WEB: www.mcleanmfg.com
SIC: 3499 5084 Strapping, metal; metalworking machinery

(G-12161)
MK TEST SYSTEMS AMERICAS INC
22102 N Pepper Rd Ste 116 (60010-2548)
PHONE..................................773 569-3778
Joseph Kane, *Admin Sec*
EMP: 2
SALES (est): 2MM
SALES (corp-wide): 9.1MM **Privately Held**
SIC: 3679 Harness assemblies for electronic use: wire or cable
HQ: M.K. Test Systems Ltd.
Ate House Westpark
Wellington

(G-12162)
NORMAN P MOELLER
Also Called: Universal Instrument Company
372 Rolling Wood Ln Apt D (60010-1789)
P.O. Box 2776, Glenview (60025-6776)
PHONE..................................847 991-3933
Norman Moeller, *Owner*
EMP: 8 EST: 1936
SQ FT: 3,000
SALES (est): 1.1MM **Privately Held**
WEB: www.uicoglass.com
SIC: 3829 3821 3231 3229 Hydrometers, except industrial process type; thermometers, including digital: clinical; laboratory apparatus & furniture; products of purchased glass; pressed & blown glass

(G-12163)
PHOENIX TRADING CHICAGO INC
26809 W Lakeridge Dr (60010-1980)
PHONE..................................847 304-5181
EMP: 2
SALES: 4.3MM **Privately Held**
SIC: 3462 Scrap Iron And Steel Brokers

(G-12164)
POINTE INTERNATIONAL COMPANY
446 Valley View Rd (60010-7316)
PHONE..................................847 550-7001
Sheila Liao, *President*
▲ EMP: 16
SQ FT: 34,000
SALES (est): 3.4MM **Privately Held**
WEB: www.pointecompany.com
SIC: 2522 2531 Office furniture, except wood; school furniture

(G-12165)
SIGN CITY CORP
28144 W Industrial Ave # 104 (60010-2536)
PHONE..................................847 382-3838
Rob Prigge, *Principal*
EMP: 2 EST: 2009
SALES (est): 217.1K **Privately Held**
WEB: www.signcitycorp.com
SIC: 3993 Electric signs

(G-12166)
STRUT & SUPPLY INC
28005 W Commercial Ave (60010-2443)
PHONE.....................847 756-4337
Mike Dagostino, *President*
Greg Norton, *Manager*
▲ EMP: 2
SALES (est): 276.9K **Privately Held**
SIC: 3429 Clamps, metal

(G-12167)
U R ON IT
22172 N Hillview Dr (60010-2317)
PHONE.....................847 382-0182
Ralph Gualano, *Owner*
EMP: 3
SALES (est): 99.1K **Privately Held**
SIC: 5699 5231 2395 5999 Sports apparel; glass, leaded or stained; embroidery products, except schiffli machine; trophies & plaques

Lake Bluff
Lake County

(G-12168)
ADVANGENE CONSUMABLES INC
21 N Skokie Hwy Ste 104 (60044-1777)
PHONE.....................847 295-2539
Shau-Zou Lu, *President*
▲ EMP: 6
SALES: 150K **Privately Held**
SIC: 3089 Plastics products

(G-12169)
AMERICAN MEDICAL INDUSTRIES
Also Called: European American Industries
28915 N Herky Dr Ste 107 (60044-1466)
PHONE.....................847 918-9800
Jim Fiocchi, *Director*
EMP: 6 **Privately Held**
SIC: 3841 Veterinarians' instruments & apparatus
PA: American Medical Industries Inc
330 E 3rd St Ste 2
Dell Rapids SD 57022

(G-12170)
AMERICAN METAL FIBERS INC (PA)
Also Called: Amfi
13420 Rockland Rd (60044-1469)
PHONE.....................847 295-8166
Rose Marie Carlson, *President*
Robert Carlson, *Treasurer*
Arnold M Schili, *Admin Sec*
◆ EMP: 50
SQ FT: 57,000
SALES (est): 11.2MM **Privately Held**
WEB: www.amfi-usa.com
SIC: 3399 Metal powders, pastes & flakes

(G-12171)
APPAREL WORKS INTL LLC
51 Sherwood Ter Ste G (60044-2232)
PHONE.....................847 778-9559
Gregg Pavalon, *Managing Prtnr*
◆ EMP: 4
SALES: 3MM **Privately Held**
WEB: www.apparelworksllc.com
SIC: 2326 2331 Industrial garments, men's & boys'; women's & misses' blouses & shirts

(G-12172)
AUTOMATED SYSTEMS & CONTROL CO
11 N Skokie Hwy Ste 115 (60044-1776)
P.O. Box 7592, Algonquin (60102-7592)
PHONE.....................847 735-8310
William Schrieber, *President*
EMP: 3
SALES (est): 330K **Privately Held**
SIC: 3625 3577 8711 3613 Relays & industrial controls; computer peripheral equipment; engineering services; switchgear & switchboard apparatus

(G-12173)
BAKER MANUFACTURING LLC
1349 Rockland Rd (60044-1435)
PHONE.....................847 362-3663
Arthur M Baker II, *Principal*
▲ EMP: 2
SALES (est): 281.8K **Privately Held**
SIC: 3999 Manufacturing industries

(G-12174)
BRANDT ASSOC
1002 Muir Ave (60044-1538)
PHONE.....................847 362-0556
Dixon Brandt, *Partner*
Greg Jackson, *Sales Staff*
Brian Haschemeyer, *Manager*
EMP: 2 EST: 1990
SALES (est): 307K **Privately Held**
SIC: 3825 Network analyzers

(G-12175)
BRAVURA MOULDING COMPANY
28915 N Herky Dr Ste 103 (60044-1466)
PHONE.....................262 633-1882
Kent Parco, *President*
EMP: 5
SQ FT: 5,000
SALES (est): 1MM **Privately Held**
SIC: 2499 Picture frame molding, finished

(G-12176)
COMPX INTERNATIONAL INC
915 Sherwood Dr (60044-2203)
PHONE.....................847 234-1864
Gregg Walla, *Principal*
EMP: 3
SALES (corp-wide): 2.3B **Publicly Held**
SIC: 3429 Manufactured hardware (general)
HQ: Compx International Inc.
5430 Lyndon B Johnson Fwy
Dallas TX 75240

(G-12177)
CORKEN INC (HQ)
105 Albrecht Dr (60044-2252)
PHONE.....................405 946-5576
Art Laszio, *President*
◆ EMP: 70
SQ FT: 67,000
SALES: 40MM
SALES (corp-wide): 2.4B **Publicly Held**
SIC: 3563 3561 3491 Air & gas compressors; pumps & pumping equipment; gas valves & parts, industrial
PA: Idex Corporation
1925 W Field Ct Ste 200
Lake Forest IL 60045
847 498-7070

(G-12178)
DORMAKABA USA INC
924 Sherwood Dr (60044-2204)
PHONE.....................847 295-2700
Anthony Sullivan, *Branch Mgr*
Salwan Lazim, *Manager*
Pat Harris, *Consultant*
Bianca Van Niekerk, *Consultant*
EMP: 70
SALES (corp-wide): 2.7B **Privately Held**
SIC: 3442 Metal doors, sash & trim
HQ: Dormakaba Usa Inc.
100 Dorma Dr
Reamstown PA 17567
717 336-3881

(G-12179)
DUROWELD COMPANY INC
Also Called: Arctic Blast Co
1565 Rockland Rd (60044-1455)
PHONE.....................847 680-3064
Stephen R Austin, *President*
Richard Austin, *Vice Pres*
Claudia Austin, *Admin Sec*
EMP: 30 EST: 1968
SALES (est): 5.8MM **Privately Held**
SIC: 3449 3842 3648 3471 Bars, concrete reinforcing: fabricated steel; wheelchairs; lighting equipment; cleaning, polishing & finishing; welding repair; sheet metalwork

(G-12180)
E A M & J INC
Also Called: A&E Plastics
65 Waukegan Rd (60044-1665)
PHONE.....................847 622-9200
Maynard Ostrowski, *President*
John Vinka, *Admin Sec*
▲ EMP: 25 EST: 1982
SALES (est): 4.9MM **Privately Held**
SIC: 3089 Molding primary plastic; plastic processing

(G-12181)
FLUID MANUFACTURING SERVICES
105 Albrecht Dr (60044-2252)
PHONE.....................800 458-5262
Frederick Wacker, *Owner*
EMP: 2
SALES (est): 215.3K **Privately Held**
SIC: 3829 Measuring & controlling devices

(G-12182)
GENETICS DEVELOPMENT CORP
21 N Skokie Hwy Ste 104 (60044-1777)
PHONE.....................847 283-9780
K Y Chiu, *President*
EMP: 3
SALES: 10K **Privately Held**
SIC: 3999 Manufacturing industries

(G-12183)
GEORGE DROWNE CABINET SAND
517 Lincoln Ave (60044-2419)
PHONE.....................847 234-1487
George Drowne, *Principal*
EMP: 4
SALES (est): 481K **Privately Held**
SIC: 2431 Millwork

(G-12184)
GPI MANUFACTURING INC
Also Called: Gpi Prototype & Mfg Svcs
940 W North Shore Dr (60044-2202)
PHONE.....................847 615-8900
Scott Galloway, *CEO*
Adam Galloway, *President*
Terry Gladman, *Vice Pres*
Jonathan Green, *VP Mfg*
Michelle Mitchell, *Production*
▲ EMP: 35
SQ FT: 40,000
SALES (est): 9.6MM **Privately Held**
WEB: www.gpianatomicals.com
SIC: 3499 Friction material, made from powdered metal

(G-12185)
GPI PROTOTYPE & MFG SVCS LLC
940 N Shore Dr (60044-2202)
PHONE.....................847 615-8900
Scott Galloway, *Principal*
Adam Galloway, *Principal*
Nicole Benner, *Purchasing*
Doug Hardina, *Accounts Exec*
EMP: 23
SALES (est): 886K **Privately Held**
SIC: 3999 Manufacturing industries

(G-12186)
HELIO PRECISION PRODUCTS INC
Also Called: Hn Precision
601 N Skokie Hwy Ste A (60044-1500)
PHONE.....................585 697-5434
EMP: 22
SALES (corp-wide): 31.3MM **Privately Held**
SIC: 3592 Valves, engine
PA: Helio Precision Products, Inc
601 N Skokie Hwy Ste B
Lake Bluff IL 60044
847 473-1300

(G-12187)
HELIO PRECISION PRODUCTS INC (PA)
Also Called: Hn Precision
601 N Skokie Hwy Ste B (60044-1500)
PHONE.....................847 473-1300
Daniel Nash, *President*
Steve Moroney, *Vice Pres*
Leynard Dasalla, *Production*
Victor Kovach, *Engineer*
Carl Drake, *Project Engr*
▲ EMP: 112
SQ FT: 155,000
SALES (est): 31.3MM **Privately Held**
SIC: 3592 Valves, engine

(G-12188)
HOMEWERKS WORLDWIDE LLC
55 Albrecht Dr (60044-2226)
PHONE.....................224 543-1529
Peter Berkman, *President*
Jeff Pischke, *VP Sales*
Richard Wild, *General Counsel*
Sarah Chilton, *Admin Asst*
▲ EMP: 50
SQ FT: 190,000
SALES (est): 15.4MM **Privately Held**
SIC: 3491 3432 5021 Industrial valves; faucets & spigots, metal & plastic; household furniture

(G-12189)
ILLINOIS TOOL WORKS INC
Buehler
41 Waukegan Rd (60044-1691)
P.O. Box 1 (60044-0001)
PHONE.....................847 295-6500
Jill Dreschler, *Research*
Sandy Anderson, *Engineer*
Joe Butchart, *Engineer*
Stanislaw Cisowski, *Engineer*
Charles Ey, *Engineer*
EMP: 180
SALES (corp-wide): 14.1B **Publicly Held**
SIC: 5049 3821 3829 3827 Optical goods; sample preparation apparatus; measuring & controlling devices; optical instruments & lenses; analytical instruments; instruments to measure electricity
PA: Illinois Tool Works Inc.
155 Harlem Ave
Glenview IL 60025
847 724-7500

(G-12190)
JESSUP MANUFACTURING COMPANY
1701 Rockland Rd (60044-1450)
PHONE.....................847 362-0961
Richard T Merle, *Exec VP*
Richard Merle, *Exec VP*
Dan Moen, *Prdtn Mgr*
EMP: 35
SALES (corp-wide): 25.6MM **Privately Held**
WEB: www.jessupmfg.com
SIC: 3069 2295 Sponge rubber & sponge rubber products; coated fabrics, not rubberized
PA: Jessup Manufacturing Company Inc
2815 W Rte 120
Mchenry IL 60051
815 385-6650

(G-12191)
L R GREGORY AND SON INC
1233 Rockland Rd (60044-1433)
PHONE.....................847 247-0216
Jim Gregory, *President*
Gwen Gregory, *Admin Sec*
EMP: 20
SQ FT: 10,000
SALES (est): 2.2MM **Privately Held**
SIC: 1711 1761 3444 Warm air heating & air conditioning contractor; ventilation & duct work contractor; roofing contractor; sheet metalwork; sheet metalwork

(G-12192)
LEGACY VULCAN LLC
29821 N Skokie Hwy (60044-1117)
PHONE.....................847 578-9622
Mike McCollum, *Manager*
EMP: 6 **Publicly Held**
SIC: 1422 Crushed & broken limestone
HQ: Legacy Vulcan, Llc
1200 Urban Center Dr
Vestavia AL 35242
205 298-3000

Lake Bluff - Lake County (G-12193) — GEOGRAPHIC SECTION

(G-12193)
LINDEMANN CHIMNEY SERVICE INC (PA)
Also Called: Lindemann Chimney Co
86 Albrecht Dr (60044-2227)
PHONE...................847 918-7994
Robert Lindemann, *President*
Gary Lindeman, *Treasurer*
Michael Schaefer, *Manager*
Rob Fisher, *Products*
Brett Lasik, *Associate*
▲ EMP: 15
SALES (est): 866.5K **Privately Held**
SIC: 7349 3444 5087 Chimney cleaning; ducts, sheet metal; cleaning & maintenance equipment & supplies

(G-12194)
LIQUID CONTROLS LLC (HQ)
105 Albrecht Dr (60044-2252)
PHONE...................847 295-1050
Teri Gulke, *Project Engr*
Natalia Semrau, *Design Engr*
Charlotte Wilson, *Controller*
Giorgio Magni, *Director*
◆ EMP: 166 EST: 1954
SQ FT: 69,000
SALES (est): 33.9MM
SALES (corp-wide): 2.4B **Publicly Held**
WEB: www.lcmeter.com
SIC: 3823 Industrial instrmnts msrmnt display/control process variable
PA: Idex Corporation
  1925 W Field Ct Ste 200
  Lake Forest IL 60045
  847 498-7070

(G-12195)
MASTER CONTROL SYSTEMS INC (PA)
910 N Shore Dr (60044-2295)
P.O. Box 276 (60044-0276)
PHONE...................847 295-1010
Jon Beckstrand, *CEO*
William Stelter, *President*
Jeff Peck, *CFO*
Elizabeth Villa, *Sales Executive*
Brian Woerheide, *Admin Sec*
▼ EMP: 30 EST: 1965
SALES (est): 4.4MM **Privately Held**
WEB: www.mastercontrols.com
SIC: 3823 3629 3625 Industrial instrmnts msrmnt display/control process variable; battery chargers, rectifying or nonrotating; control circuit devices, magnet & solid state

(G-12196)
MEYER MATERIAL CO MERGER CORP
30288 N Skokie Hwy (60044)
PHONE...................847 689-9200
Steve Wernke, *General Mgr*
EMP: 40
SALES (corp-wide): 4.5B **Privately Held**
SIC: 3273 Ready-mixed concrete
HQ: Meyer Material Company Llc
  580 S Wolf Rd
  Des Plaines IL 60016
  815 331-7200

(G-12197)
NATIONWIDE PRECISION PDTS CORP
Also Called: Hn Precision-Ny
601 N Skokie Hwy Ste A (60044-1500)
PHONE...................585 272-7100
Dan Nash, *CEO*
Dan Brooks, *Vice Pres*
Rick Menaldino, *Vice Pres*
Sharon Pierce, *Vice Pres*
Paul Ainsworth, *CFO*
▲ EMP: 425 EST: 1999
SALES (est): 102.1MM **Privately Held**
WEB: www.hnprecision.com
SIC: 3599 Machine shop, jobbing & repair

(G-12198)
NATURAL STONE INC
611 Rockland Rd Ste 208 (60044-2000)
PHONE...................847 735-1129
Paul Piwowarczyk, *President*
Anna Piwowarczyk, *Admin Sec*
EMP: 7
SQ FT: 5,000
SALES (est): 727.1K **Privately Held**
SIC: 3281 Marble, building: cut & shaped; granite, cut & shaped

(G-12199)
NELSON - HARKINS INDS INC
411 E Scranton Ave (60044-2535)
PHONE...................773 478-6243
Thomas Harkins, *President*
Donald P Harkins Jr, *Vice Pres*
Randal P Harkins, *Treasurer*
EMP: 27
SALES (est): 3.5MM **Privately Held**
WEB: www.nelson-harkins.com
SIC: 3993 3953 3446 3365 Signs, not made in custom sign painting shops; letters for signs, metal; marking devices; architectural metalwork; aluminum foundries; wood partitions & fixtures

(G-12200)
NORTH SHORE STAIRS
100 N Skokie Hwy Ste D (60044-1790)
PHONE...................847 295-7906
Joan Boulet Lynch, *Principal*
EMP: 5
SALES (est): 602.6K **Privately Held**
WEB: www.northshorestairs.biz
SIC: 3534 Elevators & moving stairways

(G-12201)
NORTH SHORE TRUCK & EQUIPMENT
29800 N Skokie Hwy Ste B (60044-1101)
PHONE...................847 887-0200
Mike Bicanic, *President*
EMP: 12
SALES (est): 2MM **Privately Held**
SIC: 7538 7699 7692 5012 General truck repair; industrial equipment services; welding repair; automobiles & other motor vehicles; sheet metalwork

(G-12202)
NOURISHLIFE LLC
Also Called: Lifetrients
37 Sherwood Ter Ste 109 (60044-2200)
PHONE...................847 234-2334
Bill Froese, *General Mgr*
Betsy Moreno, *Office Mgr*
Joanna Szymoniak, *Manager*
EMP: 9
SALES (est): 1.3MM **Privately Held**
SIC: 2834 Vitamin, nutrient & hematinic preparations for human use

(G-12203)
OZINGA BROS INC
30285 N Skokie Hwy (60044-1120)
PHONE...................847 783-6500
EMP: 46
SALES (corp-wide): 434.5MM **Privately Held**
WEB: www.ozinga.com
SIC: 3273 Ready-mixed concrete
PA: Ozinga Bros., Inc.
  19001 Old Lagrange Rd # 30
  Mokena IL 60448
  708 326-4200

(G-12204)
PETER BAKER & SON CO (PA)
1349 Rockland Rd (60044-1498)
P.O. Box 187 (60044-0187)
PHONE...................847 362-3663
Arthura Baker II, *President*
Arthur M Baker II, *President*
John Crawford, *Superintendent*
Jeremy Huntington, *Superintendent*
John G Broecker, *Exec VP*
EMP: 100 EST: 1915
SQ FT: 6,000
SALES (est): 22.2MM **Privately Held**
WEB: www.peterbaker.com
SIC: 2951 3272 1611 Asphalt paving mixtures & blocks; paving materials, prefabricated concrete; highway & street paving contractor; resurfacing contractor

(G-12205)
PHARMANUTRIENTS INC
37 Sherwood Ter Ste 109 (60044-2200)
PHONE...................847 234-2334
Mark A Nottoli, *President*
EMP: 5
SALES (est): 784K **Privately Held**
SIC: 2834 Pharmaceutical preparations

(G-12206)
PLC CORP
220 Baker Rd (60044-1442)
P.O. Box 67 (60044-0067)
PHONE...................847 247-1900
Roger Risher, *President*
Dennis Moffatt, *Manager*
EMP: 6
SQ FT: 6,000
SALES (est): 1.3MM **Privately Held**
WEB: www.theplccorp.com
SIC: 2842 2841 Cleaning or polishing preparations; automobile polish; sanitation preparations, disinfectants & deodorants; soap & other detergents

(G-12207)
PROFILE PLASTICS INC (PA)
Also Called: Safety Security Products Co
65 Waukegan Rd (60044-1665)
PHONE...................847 604-5100
Stephen R Murrill, *President*
EMP: 80
SALES (est): 16.9MM **Privately Held**
WEB: www.vacform.com
SIC: 3089 Thermoformed finished plastic products; injection molding of plastics

(G-12208)
RONDOUT IRON & METAL CO INC
1501 Rockland Rd (60044-1446)
PHONE...................847 362-2750
Bob Miller, *President*
EMP: 7
SQ FT: 5,000
SALES (est): 830.4K **Privately Held**
WEB: www.simsmm.com
SIC: 5093 3341 Ferrous metal scrap & waste; secondary nonferrous metals

(G-12209)
SEXTON WIND POWER LLC
49 Sherwood Ter Ste A (60044-2231)
PHONE...................224 212-1250
Arthur Daniels, *Principal*
EMP: 3
SALES (est): 253K **Privately Held**
WEB: www.sextoncompanies.net
SIC: 3621 Windmills, electric generating

(G-12210)
TERLATO WINE GROUP LTD (PA)
Also Called: Local Wine Tours
900 Armour Dr (60044-1926)
PHONE...................847 604-8900
Anthony J Terlato, *Ch of Bd*
William A Terlato, *President*
John Terlato, *Vice Chairman*
Emily Meyer, *District Mgr*
John Bihun, *Vice Pres*
◆ EMP: 25
SQ FT: 26,000
SALES (est): 110.4MM **Privately Held**
SIC: 5182 2084 8743 Wine; wines; promotion service

(G-12211)
US FIREPLACE PRODUCTS INC
110 Albrecht Dr (60044-2247)
PHONE...................888 290-8181
Robert Lindemann, *President*
EMP: 5
SALES (est): 269.8K **Privately Held**
SIC: 3272 Fireplace & chimney material: concrete

(G-12212)
VILLAGE OPTICAL SHOP
237 Forest View Dr (60044-1303)
PHONE...................847 295-3290
George Wiegold, *Owner*
EMP: 2
SALES (est): 220.4K **Privately Held**
SIC: 3851 5995 Ophthalmic goods; opticians

(G-12213)
VRN WELDING & FABRICATION INC
102 Skokie Valley Rd (60044-1824)
PHONE...................847 735-7270
Vince Nannini, *President*
EMP: 3
SALES (est): 146.4K **Privately Held**
SIC: 7692 Welding repair

(G-12214)
WEC WELDING AND MACHINING LLC (DH)
Also Called: Westinghouse
1 Energy Dr (60044-1453)
PHONE...................847 680-8100
Jimmy Morgan, *President*
Lena Willman, *Vice Pres*
Yuemei Kyer, *Project Mgr*
Priscilla Guzman, *Production*
John Flahive, *Engineer*
EMP: 1
SALES (est): 59.6MM **Privately Held**
SIC: 3398 3541 1799 Metal heat treating; machine tools, metal cutting type; welding on site
HQ: Westinghouse Electric Company Llc
  1000 Wstnghuse Dr Ste 572
  Cranberry Township PA 16066
  412 374-2020

(G-12215)
WECO TRADING INC (PA)
21 N Skokie Hwy Ste 101 (60044-1777)
PHONE...................847 615-1020
Walter L Roth, *CEO*
W Theodore Roth, *President*
Robert F Roth, *Vice Pres*
EMP: 7
SQ FT: 1,000
SALES (est): 18.1MM **Privately Held**
SIC: 5093 3341 Ferrous metal scrap & waste; secondary nonferrous metals

(G-12216)
WESTERN RAILWAY DEVICES CORP
Also Called: Western Railway Equipment
28665 Braeloch Ct (60044-3004)
PHONE...................847 625-8500
Lockhart S Burnett, *President*
▲ EMP: 4
SALES: 23.6K **Privately Held**
SIC: 3743 5088 Railroad equipment; railroad equipment & supplies

(G-12217)
WOODLAND ENGINEERING COMPANY
122 Baker Rd (60044-1424)
P.O. Box 632, Libertyville (60048-0632)
PHONE...................847 362-0110
David Englund, *President*
Donald Englund, *Admin Sec*
EMP: 9 EST: 1960
SQ FT: 16,000
SALES: 810K **Privately Held**
WEB: www.woodlandengineering.com
SIC: 3089 3423 Injection molding of plastics; hand & edge tools

---

Lake Forest
Lake County

(G-12218)
ABBOTT LABORATORIES
Also Called: Abbott Nutrition
100 Saunders Rd (60045-2502)
PHONE...................800 551-5838
Aine Allen, *Mfg Staff*
EMP: 8
SALES (corp-wide): 31.9B **Publicly Held**
SIC: 2835 3841 3826 2834 In vitro & in vivo diagnostic substances; blood derivative diagnostic agents; hemotology diagnostic agents; microbiology & virology diagnostic products; diagnostic apparatus, medical; medical instruments & equipment, blood & bone work; IV transfusion apparatus; blood testing apparatus; druggists' preparations (pharmaceuticals)

▲ = Import ▼ = Export
◆ = Import/Export

GEOGRAPHIC SECTION

Lake Forest - Lake County (G-12245)

PA: Abbott Laboratories
100 Abbott Park Rd
Abbott Park IL 60064
224 667-6100

(G-12219)
ACQUIRED SALES CORP (PA)
31 N Suffolk Ln (60045-4908)
PHONE..............................847 915-2446
Gerard M Jacobs, *Ch of Bd*
William C Jacobs, *President*
Nicholas S Warrender, *COO*
EMP: 6
SALES (est): 1.2MM **Privately Held**
WEB: www.acquiredsalescorp.com
SIC: 3999

(G-12220)
ADAZON INC
1485 N Western Ave (60045-1218)
PHONE..............................847 235-2700
John Barth, *President*
Jill Barth, *CFO*
Rachel Snyder, *Accounts Mgr*
EMP: 4
SALES (est): 1.4MM **Privately Held**
SIC: 5131 3577 Piece goods & notions; computer peripheral equipment

(G-12221)
AIR-DRIVE INC
576 Stockbridge Ct (60045-2680)
PHONE..............................847 625-0226
James H Gilford, *President*
EMP: 30 **EST:** 1962
SALES (est): 6.8MM
SALES (corp-wide): 94.1MM **Privately Held**
WEB: www.air-drivel.mfgpages.com
SIC: 3564 Blowers & fans
PA: Revcor, Inc.
251 Edwards Ave
Carpentersville IL 60110
847 428-4411

(G-12222)
AKORN INC (PA)
Also Called: Akorn Pharmaceuticals
1925 W Field Ct Ste 300 (60045-4862)
PHONE..............................847 279-6100
Alan Weinstein, *Ch of Bd*
Douglas S Boothe, *President*
Melissa Miller, *Partner*
Michael Ioannou, *COO*
Bruce Kutinsky, *COO*
◆ **EMP:** 124
SQ FT: 70,000
SALES: 682.4MM **Privately Held**
SIC: 2834 5047 Pharmaceutical preparations; surgical equipment & supplies

(G-12223)
AKORN PHARMACEUTICALS ✪
1925 W Field Ct (60045-4862)
PHONE..............................800 932-5676
EMP: 4 **EST:** 2019
SALES (est): 320.4K **Privately Held**
SIC: 2834 Pharmaceutical preparations

(G-12224)
AMITY DIE AND STAMPING CO
Also Called: ADS
13870 W Polo Trail Dr (60045-5102)
PHONE..............................847 680-6600
Evelyn Westphal, *President*
Patrick Stevens, *President*
Brian Westphal, *Treasurer*
Glen R Westphal Jr, *Admin Sec*
EMP: 30
SQ FT: 30,000
SALES (est): 6.8MM **Privately Held**
WEB: www.amitydie.com
SIC: 3469 3544 Stamping metal for the trade; die sets for metal stamping (presses)

(G-12225)
ARCSEC DIGITAL LLC
717 Forest Ave Fl 2 (60045-1822)
PHONE..............................312 324-4794
EMP: 5
SALES (est): 143.5K **Privately Held**
WEB: www.arcsecdigital.com
SIC: 2741 8742 7336 ; marketing consulting services; graphic arts & related design

(G-12226)
ARNDT ENTERPRISE LTD
674 Timber Ln Ste 200 (60045-3118)
PHONE..............................847 234-5736
Raymond Puszczewicz, *President*
◆ **EMP:** 3
SALES (est): 100K **Privately Held**
WEB: www.ae-welding-industrial.com
SIC: 7699 7692 Picture framing, custom; welding repair

(G-12227)
ASSERTIO HOLDINGS INC (PA)
100 Saunders Rd Ste 300 (60045-2508)
PHONE..............................224 419-7106
Arthur J Higgins, *Ch of Bd*
Todd N Smith, *President*
Mark Strobeck, *COO*
Megan Timmins, *Senior VP*
Daniel A Peisert, *CFO*
EMP: 252
SALES (est): 8.9MM **Publicly Held**
SIC: 2834 Drugs acting on the central nervous system & sense organs

(G-12228)
ASSERTIO THERAPEUTICS INC (HQ)
100 Saunders Rd Ste 300 (60045-2508)
PHONE..............................224 419-7106
Todd N Smith, *President*
Daniel A Peisert, *CFO*
EMP: 55
SQ FT: 31,209
SALES: 229.5MM
SALES (corp-wide): 8.9MM **Publicly Held**
SIC: 2834 Drugs acting on the central nervous system & sense organs
PA: Assertio Holdings, Inc.
100 Saunders Rd Ste 300
Lake Forest IL 60045
224 419-7106

(G-12229)
ASSOCIATED RESEARCH INC
13860 W Laurel Dr (60045-4531)
PHONE..............................847 367-4077
Richard Inman, *Ch of Bd*
Michael Braverman, *President*
Joseph Guerriero, *Vice Pres*
Eric Snow, *Opers Mgr*
Suzanne Braverman, *Admin Sec*
▲ **EMP:** 35 **EST:** 1936
SALES (est): 10.2MM
SALES (corp-wide): 14.8MM **Privately Held**
WEB: www.arisafety.com
SIC: 3825 Test equipment for electronic & electric measurement
PA: Ikonix Group, Inc
28105 N Keith Dr
Lake Forest IL 60045
847 367-4671

(G-12230)
BARRIERSAFE SOLUTIONS INTL INC
Also Called: Bssi
150 N Field Dr Ste 210 (60045-4853)
PHONE..............................866 931-3613
Michael Mattos, *President*
EMP: 195
SALES (est): 689.8K **Privately Held**
SIC: 3069 Laboratory sundries: cases, covers, funnels, cups, etc.; medical sundries, rubber
HQ: Pacific Dunlop Holdings (Usa) Llc
200 Schulz Dr
Red Bank NJ 07701

(G-12231)
BLISSFUL BROWNIES INC
619 Highview Ter (60045-3226)
P.O. Box 949 (60045-0949)
PHONE..............................541 308-0226
Ambler Fitzsimons, *President*
EMP: 5
SQ FT: 2,500
SALES (est): 362.7K **Privately Held**
SIC: 5441 2052 5149 Candy; bakery products, dry; cookies

(G-12232)
BOISE WHITE PAPER LLC (HQ)
1 N Field Ct (60045-4810)
P.O. Box 990050, Boise ID (83799-0050)
PHONE..............................847 482-3000
W Thomas Stephens, *CEO*
Tom Carlisle, *CFO*
Wayne Rancourt, *Treasurer*
Rebecca Kaiser, *Supervisor*
Tom Tobin, *Information Mgr*
◆ **EMP:** 10
SALES (est): 391.7K
SALES (corp-wide): 6.9B **Publicly Held**
SIC: 2621 Paper mills
PA: Packaging Corporation Of America
1 N Field Ct
Lake Forest IL 60045
847 482-3000

(G-12233)
BOISE WHITE PAPER LLC
1955 W Field Ct (60045-4824)
PHONE..............................208 805-1424
Alexander Toeldte, *CEO*
EMP: 11
SALES (est): 1.9MM
SALES (corp-wide): 6.9B **Publicly Held**
SIC: 2621 Paper mills
PA: Packaging Corporation Of America
1 N Field Ct
Lake Forest IL 60045
847 482-3000

(G-12234)
BRUNSWICK FAMILY BOAT CO INC
1 N Field Ct (60045-4810)
PHONE..............................847 735-4700
Huw S Bower, *President*
EMP: 4
SALES (est): 110.8K
SALES (corp-wide): 4.1B **Publicly Held**
SIC: 3732 Boats, fiberglass: building & repairing
PA: Brunswick Corporation
26125 N Riverwoods Blvd # 500
Mettawa IL 60045
847 735-4700

(G-12235)
BURY INDUSTRIAL SERVICE LLC
222 E Wscnsin Ave Ste 206 (60045)
PHONE..............................847 235-2053
George Bury,
EMP: 1
SALES (est): 227.6K **Privately Held**
SIC: 3541 Machine tool replacement & repair parts, metal cutting types

(G-12236)
CARROLL INTERNATIONAL CORP
55 N Mayflower Rd (60045-2420)
PHONE..............................630 983-5979
Barry J Carroll, *President*
EMP: 209
SQ FT: 6,000
SALES (est): 19.6MM **Privately Held**
SIC: 3444 3532 Metal ventilating equipment; mineral beneficiation equipment

(G-12237)
CINDYS NAIL & HAIR CARE
Also Called: Bella Salon
950 N Western Ave Ste G (60045-1734)
PHONE..............................847 234-0780
Cindy Schultz, *Owner*
EMP: 3
SALES (est): 76.3K **Privately Held**
SIC: 7231 3999 Manicurist, pedicurist; hair curlers, designed for beauty parlors

(G-12238)
COLBERT PACKAGING CORPORATION (PA)
Also Called: C P
28355 N Bradley Rd (60045-1173)
PHONE..............................847 367-5990
James B Hamilton, *President*
John Lackner, *President*
Bradley Davis, *Vice Pres*
Nancy C Macdougall, *Vice Pres*
Bill Snyder, *VP Opers*
▲ **EMP:** 155

SQ FT: 95,000
SALES (est): 66.4MM **Privately Held**
WEB: www.colbertpkg.com
SIC: 2657 2652 Folding paperboard boxes; setup paperboard boxes

(G-12239)
COLBORNE ACQUISITION CO LLC
28495 N Ballard Dr (60045-4510)
PHONE..............................847 371-0101
Rick Hoskins, *Director*
EMP: 30 **EST:** 2009
SALES (est): 8.1MM **Privately Held**
WEB: www.colbornefoodbotics.com
SIC: 3556 Food products machinery

(G-12240)
CORETECHS CORP
245 Butler Dr (60045-3009)
PHONE..............................847 295-3720
Dr Nelson L Levy, *President*
Louisa Levy, *Admin Sec*
EMP: 17
SQ FT: 600
SALES (est): 1.4MM **Privately Held**
SIC: 2834 Pharmaceutical preparations

(G-12241)
CORRUGATED SOLUTIONS LLC
276 E Deerpath 421 (60045-1940)
PHONE..............................847 220-8348
Michael Prassel,
EMP: 3
SALES (est): 150K **Privately Held**
SIC: 2653 Corrugated & solid fiber boxes

(G-12242)
CRYSTAL RAIN DISTILLERY I
28468 N Ballard Dr (60045-4508)
PHONE..............................224 508-9361
EMP: 5
SALES (est): 427.4K **Privately Held**
SIC: 2085 Distilled & blended liquors

(G-12243)
DISTRIBUTION ENTERPRISES INC
Also Called: Graphic Marking Systems
28457 N Ballard Dr Ste A1 (60045-4545)
PHONE..............................847 582-9276
Marjorie Mc Cullough, *President*
Doug Goodloe, *Vice Pres*
Deborah Marett, *Art Dir*
EMP: 10
SQ FT: 18,000
SALES: 4MM **Privately Held**
WEB: www.shopgms.com
SIC: 3555 5084 Printing trades machinery; printing trades machinery, equipment & supplies

(G-12244)
DRIV AUTOMOTIVE INC
500 N Field Dr (60045-2595)
P.O. Box 40013, College Station TX (77842-4013)
PHONE..............................847 482-5000
Brian Kesseler, *CEO*
EMP: 4
SQ FT: 10,000
SALES (est): 299.4K
SALES (corp-wide): 17.4B **Publicly Held**
SIC: 3714 5013 Motor vehicle parts & accessories; automotive supplies & parts
HQ: Tenneco Automotive Operating Company, Inc.
500 N Field Dr
Lake Forest IL 60045
847 482-5000

(G-12245)
DRIV INCORPORATED
Also Called: Ride Performance
500 N Field Dr (60045-2595)
PHONE..............................857 842-5000
Brian Kesseler, *CEO*
EMP: 4
SQ FT: 10,000
SALES (est): 198K **Privately Held**
SIC: 3714 5013 Motor vehicle parts & accessories; automotive supplies & parts

---

(PA)=Parent Co (HQ)=Headquarters (DH)=Div Headquarters
✪ = New Business established in last 2 years

Lake Forest - Lake County (G-12246) — GEOGRAPHIC SECTION

(G-12246)
ENVISION INC
40 N Ahwahnee Rd (60045)
PHONE..................847 735-0789
Dan Schilling, *Partner*
Eric Arnson, *Principal*
EMP: 6
SALES (est): 485.6K **Privately Held**
SIC: 2673 Bags: plastic, laminated & coated

(G-12247)
ERIEM SURGICAL INC
28438 N Ballard Dr (60045-4548)
PHONE..................847 549-1410
Carol Teitz, *President*
EMP: 6
SALES: 1,000K **Privately Held**
SIC: 3841 Surgical & medical instruments

(G-12248)
EXCEL SPECIALTY CORP
Also Called: National Multi Products Co
28101 N Ballard Dr Ste A (60045-4544)
PHONE..................773 262-7575
Robert Kopf, *CEO*
Paul Kopf, *President*
Michelle Kopf, *Corp Secy*
▲ EMP: 25 EST: 1949
SQ FT: 20,000
SALES (est): 4MM **Privately Held**
WEB: www.excelspecialty.com
SIC: 3679 3694 3644 3643 Harness assemblies for electronic use: wire or cable; engine electrical equipment; noncurrent-carrying wiring services; current-carrying wiring devices; nonferrous wiredrawing & insulating; steel wire & related products

(G-12249)
FRAM GROUP HOLDINGS INC
1900 W Field Ct (60045-4828)
PHONE..................847 482-2045
Aimee Pittman, *Cust Svc Dir*
Gregory Allen Cole, *Mng Member*
Jessica Hyde, *Manager*
Mike Betz, *Director*
EMP: 2400
SALES (est): 89.8MM **Privately Held**
SIC: 3714 Motor vehicle parts & accessories

(G-12250)
GIVAUDAN FRAGRANCES CORP
1720 N Waukegan Rd (60045-1155)
PHONE..................847 735-0221
Christopher Johnson, *Vice Pres*
EMP: 5
SALES (corp-wide): 6.2B **Privately Held**
SIC: 5149 2844 Flavourings & fragrances; colognes
HQ: Givaudan Fragrances Corporation
1199 Edison Dr Ste 1-2
Cincinnati OH 45216
973 448-6500

(G-12251)
GLASER USA INC
14181 W Hawthorne Ave (60045-1086)
PHONE..................847 362-7878
Peter Glaser, *President*
Harry Haack, *Admin Sec*
Melanie Reinmuller, *Admin Sec*
EMP: 3 EST: 1999
SALES: 200K **Privately Held**
SIC: 3541 Buffing & polishing machines

(G-12252)
GOHEAR LLC
100 Saunders Rd (60045-2502)
PHONE..................847 574-7829
EMP: 3
SALES (est): 257.2K **Privately Held**
WEB: www.sonetik.us
SIC: 3842 5047 8099 Hearing aids; hearing aids; hearing testing service

(G-12253)
GREGOR JONSSON ASSOCIATES INC
13822 W Laurel Dr (60045-4529)
PHONE..................847 247-4200
Frank Heurich, *President*
Mike Dancy, *Vice Pres*
Scott Heurich, *Vice Pres*
Richard Heurich, *Admin Sec*
EMP: 25 EST: 1956
SQ FT: 13,600
SALES (est): 5.9MM **Privately Held**
WEB: www.jonsson.com
SIC: 3556 Fish & shellfish processing machinery

(G-12254)
HOOGWEGT US INC
100 Saunders Rd Ste 200 (60045-2502)
PHONE..................847 918-8787
Dalyn L Dye, *CEO*
Arthur A Rauch, *CFO*
Tiffany Kobeck, *Admin Asst*
◆ EMP: 62
SQ FT: 14,000
SALES (est): 30.3MM
SALES (corp-wide): 3.4B **Privately Held**
SIC: 2021 2022 2023 Creamery butter; cheese, natural & processed; powdered buttermilk; powdered cream; powdered milk; powdered skim milk
HQ: Hoogwegt Group B.V.
Groningensingel 1
Arnhem
263 884-802

(G-12255)
HORIZON MEDICINES LLC
150 Saunders Rd (60045-2509)
PHONE..................224 383-3110
James Gruber, *President*
EMP: 101
SALES (est): 3.1MM **Privately Held**
SIC: 2834 Pharmaceutical preparations
HQ: Horizon Therapeutics Usa, Inc.
150 Saunders Rd Ste 150 # 150
Lake Forest IL 60045

(G-12256)
HORIZON PHARMA INC (HQ)
150 Saunders Rd Ste 400 (60045-2523)
PHONE..................224 383-3000
Timothy P Walbert, *President*
Gary Geraghty, *District Mgr*
Lance Martin, *District Mgr*
Brian Pennington, *District Mgr*
Alex Yim, *District Mgr*
EMP: 106
SQ FT: 34,460
SALES: 296.9MM **Privately Held**
SIC: 2834 Pharmaceutical preparations

(G-12257)
HORIZON PHRMA RHEUMATOLOGY LLC
150 Saunders Rd Ste 150 # 150 (60045-2523)
PHONE..................224 383-3000
Lance Palo, *Opers Mgr*
Cheri Kieca, *Manager*
Jorge Areces, *Manager*
Graciela Gonzalez, *Executive Asst*
EMP: 12
SALES (corp-wide): 2MM **Privately Held**
SIC: 2834 Pharmaceutical preparations
PA: Horizon Pharma Rheumatology Llc
500 W Silver Spring Dr
Glendale WI

(G-12258)
HORIZON THERAPEUTICS USA INC (DH)
Also Called: Horizon Pharmaceuticals
150 Saunders Rd Ste 150 # 150 (60045-2523)
PHONE..................224 383-3000
Timothy P Walbert, *President*
Barry L Golombik, *Founder*
Michelle Kern, *Counsel*
Robert J De Vaere, *CFO*
Ed Cini, *Manager*
▲ EMP: 30
SALES (est): 18.5MM **Privately Held**
SIC: 2834 Pharmaceutical preparations

(G-12259)
HOSPIRA INC (HQ)
275 N Field Dr (60045-2510)
PHONE..................224 212-2000
F Michael Ball, *CEO*
Pamela Puryear, *Vice Pres*
Mary Thome-Shaw, *Plant Mgr*
Eric Johnson, *Warehouse Mgr*
Matthew Stober, *Opers Staff*
◆ EMP: 700
SALES: 3.2B
SALES (corp-wide): 51.7B **Publicly Held**
SIC: 3841 2834 Diagnostic apparatus, medical; medical instruments & equipment, blood & bone work; IV transfusion apparatus; proprietary drug products
PA: Pfizer Inc.
235 E 42nd St Rm 107
New York NY 10017
212 733-2323

(G-12260)
HOSPIRA INC
375 N Field Dr Bldg H3 (60045-2513)
PHONE..................224 212-6244
Jean Kirkeleit Davis, *Manager*
EMP: 154
SALES (corp-wide): 51.7B **Publicly Held**
SIC: 2834 3841 Druggists' preparations (pharmaceuticals); emulsions, pharmaceutical; proprietary drug products; tablets, pharmaceutical; diagnostic apparatus, medical; medical instruments & equipment, blood & bone work; IV transfusion apparatus
HQ: Hospira, Inc.
275 N Field Dr
Lake Forest IL 60045
224 212-2000

(G-12261)
HOSPIRA WORLDWIDE LLC (DH)
275 N Field Dr (60045-2510)
PHONE..................224 212-2000
F Michael Ball, *CEO*
Christopher Begley, *CEO*
John C Staley, *Ch of Bd*
Royce R Bedward, *Senior VP*
Richard Davies, *Senior VP*
◆ EMP: 2
SALES (est): 968.3K
SALES (corp-wide): 51.7B **Publicly Held**
SIC: 3841 Diagnostic apparatus, medical
HQ: Hospira, Inc.
275 N Field Dr
Lake Forest IL 60045
224 212-2000

(G-12262)
HUNTER MFG LLP
227 Northgate St Ste 3 (60045-1884)
PHONE..................859 254-7573
Mark Shepherd, *CEO*
Will Harward, *CFO*
▲ EMP: 95
SQ FT: 255,262
SALES (est): 15.8MM **Privately Held**
SIC: 3229 3949 3999 3942 Novelty glassware; sporting & athletic goods; pet supplies; stuffed toys, including animals

(G-12263)
HZNP USA INC
150 Saunders Rd Ste 200 (60045-2523)
PHONE..................224 383-3000
Tim Walbert, *CEO*
EMP: 18
SALES (est): 2.5MM **Privately Held**
SIC: 2834 Pharmaceutical preparations
PA: Vidara Therapeutics Holdings Llc
1000 Holcomb Woods Pkwy
Roswell GA 30076
678 205-5444

(G-12264)
IDENTIFICATION PRODUCTS MFG CO (PA)
13777 W Laurel Dr (60045-4530)
PHONE..................847 367-6452
Michael Klainos, *CEO*
Sandra Klainos, *Corp Secy*
Mark Klainos, *Vice Pres*
▲ EMP: 8 EST: 1974
SQ FT: 5,000
SALES (est): 1.7MM **Privately Held**
SIC: 3089 3579 Identification cards, plastic; laminating of plastic; binding machines, plastic & adhesive

(G-12265)
IDEX CORPORATION (PA)
1925 W Field Ct Ste 200 (60045-4862)
PHONE..................847 498-7070
Andrew K Silvernail, *Ch of Bd*
Sammy Pava, *Regional Mgr*
Denise R Cade, *Senior VP*
James Maclennan, *Senior VP*
Daniel J Salliotte, *Senior VP*
EMP: 163
SQ FT: 36,588
SALES: 2.4B **Publicly Held**
SIC: 3561 3563 3594 Industrial pumps & parts; air & gas compressors; fluid power pumps & motors

(G-12266)
IKONIX GROUP INC (PA)
Also Called: Electrical Safety Testing Eqp
28105 N Keith Dr (60045-4528)
PHONE..................847 367-4671
Michael R Braverman, *President*
Adam Mikos, *Sales Mgr*
Jim Kenesie, *Marketing Staff*
Nelson Toro, *Data Admn*
▲ EMP: 5
SQ FT: 12,000
SALES (est): 14.8MM **Privately Held**
SIC: 3679 Power supplies, all types: static

(G-12267)
INITIAL CHOICE
226 E Westminster (60045-1840)
PHONE..................847 234-5884
Margaret H Lambrecht, *Partner*
Sarah Lambrecht, *Partner*
EMP: 10 EST: 1981
SQ FT: 1,500
SALES (est): 754K **Privately Held**
SIC: 5947 5641 2395 Gift shop; children's wear; infants' wear; pleating & stitching

(G-12268)
KINGSPAN LIGHT & AIR LLC
28662 N Ballard Dr (60045-4500)
PHONE..................847 816-1060
EMP: 5
SALES (est): 91.6K **Privately Held**
SIC: 8399 3272 Community development groups; concrete stuctural support & building material
PA: Kingspan Group Public Limited Company
Kingspan Innovation Centre
Kingscourt A82 X

(G-12269)
KIRBY LESTER LLC (HQ)
13700 W Irma Lee Ct (60045-5123)
PHONE..................847 984-3377
Gary Zage, *President*
Karen Bergendorf, *COO*
Aleksandr Geltser, *Vice Pres*
Dave Johnson, *Vice Pres*
Christopher Thomsen, *Vice Pres*
▲ EMP: 70
SQ FT: 15,000
SALES (est): 15.6MM
SALES (corp-wide): 150MM **Privately Held**
SIC: 3559 Pharmaceutical machinery
PA: Capsa Solutions Llc
4253 Ne 189th Ave
Portland OR 97230
503 766-2324

(G-12270)
KLAI-CO IDNTIFICATION PDTS INC
13777 W Laurel Dr (60045-4530)
PHONE..................847 573-0375
Mark Klainos, *President*
◆ EMP: 23
SQ FT: 20,000
SALES (est): 5MM **Privately Held**
SIC: 3555 3579 5044 5112 Bookbinding machinery; binding machines, plastic & adhesive; office equipment; office supplies; business machines & equipment

(G-12271)
LAMINTING BNDING SOLUTIONS INC
27885 Irma Lee Cir (60045-5110)
PHONE..................847 573-0375
John Moorehouse, *President*
Amy Beth Moorehouse, *Vice Pres*
EMP: 9 EST: 2016
SQ FT: 6,000

▲ = Import ▼ = Export ◆ = Import/Export

GEOGRAPHIC SECTION

Lake Forest - Lake County (G-12296)

SALES: 7.5MM **Privately Held**
SIC: 3579 Binding machines, plastic & adhesive

(G-12272)
LANA UNLIMITED CO (PA)
Also Called: Lana Jewelry
736 N Western Ave Ste 308 (60045-1820)
PHONE..............................312 226-7050
Lana Fertelmeister, *President*
Naum Fertelmeister, *Vice Pres*
EMP: 8
SALES (est): 626.5K **Privately Held**
SIC: 3911 Jewelry, precious metal

(G-12273)
MIDWEST RESEARCH LABS LLC (PA)
476 Oakwood Ave (60045-1927)
PHONE..............................847 283-9176
James L Yeager, *Partner*
Nadir Buyuktimkim, *Partner*
Servet Buyuktimkim, *Partner*
Jean Yeager, *Partner*
EMP: 5
SQ FT: 1,000
SALES (est): 508.8K **Privately Held**
SIC: 2834 Pharmaceutical preparations

(G-12274)
MJM GRAPHICS
433 Greenwood Ave (60045-3917)
PHONE..............................847 234-1802
Michael J Mc Kiernan, *Owner*
Michael J McKiernan, *Owner*
EMP: 5 EST: 1979
SALES (est): 1MM **Privately Held**
SIC: 2752 2759 Commercial printing, offset; commercial printing

(G-12275)
NORTHWOODS WREATHS COMPANY
450 W Deerpath (60045-1618)
P.O. Box 682 (60045-0682)
PHONE..............................847 615-9491
Andy Barrie, *Owner*
EMP: 30
SALES (est): 1.8MM **Privately Held**
SIC: 3999 5961 Wreaths, artificial; catalog & mail-order houses

(G-12276)
OMRON HEALTHCARE INC (DH)
1925 W Field Ct (60045-4862)
PHONE..............................847 680-6200
Ranndy Kellogg, *CEO*
Karen Stenseth, *General Mgr*
Jill Person, *Manager*
◆ EMP: 80 EST: 1974
SQ FT: 145,000
SALES (est): 48MM **Privately Held**
SIC: 5047 3845 3841 3829 Hospital equipment & supplies; surgical equipment & supplies; electromedical equipment; surgical & medical instruments; measuring & controlling devices; industrial instrmnts msrmnt display/control process variable

(G-12277)
PACKAGING CORPORATION AMERICA (PA)
Also Called: PCA
1 N Field Ct (60045-4810)
PHONE..............................847 482-3000
Mark W Kowlzan, *Ch of Bd*
Pamela A Barnes, *Senior VP*
Charles J Carter, *Senior VP*
Kent A Pflederer, *Senior VP*
Bruce A Ridley, *Senior VP*
◆ EMP: 200
SALES: 6.9B **Publicly Held**
SIC: 2631 2653 Container board; container, packaging & boxboard; corrugated & solid fiber boxes

(G-12278)
PACTIV INTL HOLDINGS INC (DH)
1900 W Field Ct (60045-4828)
PHONE..............................847 482-2000
James D Morris, *President*
David P Brush, *Vice Pres*
James V Faulkner, *Vice Pres*
Kenneth C Hinnett, *Vice Pres*
Jan Reeves, *Vice Pres*
EMP: 9
SALES (est): 894.6K **Publicly Held**
WEB: www.pactiv.com
SIC: 2621 3089 2673 Paper mills; plastic processing; bags: plastic, laminated & coated
HQ: Pactiv Llc
   1900 W Field Ct
   Lake Forest IL 60045
   847 482-2000

(G-12279)
PACTIV LLC (DH)
Also Called: Earthchoice
1900 W Field Ct (60045-4828)
P.O. Box 5040 (60045-5040)
PHONE..............................847 482-2000
Richard L Wambold, *CEO*
Jacquelyne Huerta, *CEO*
Ron Osborn, *COO*
Peter J Lazaredes, *Exec VP*
John N Schwab, *Senior VP*
◆ EMP: 550 EST: 1965
SALES (est): 6.5B **Publicly Held**
WEB: www.pactiv.com
SIC: 5113 3089 2673 Containers, paper & disposable plastic; food casings, plastic; food storage & frozen food bags, plastic

(G-12280)
PACTIV LLC
Also Called: Pactiv Molded Products
1900 W Field Ct (60045-4828)
PHONE..............................219 924-4120
Ronald Bullock, *Branch Mgr*
EMP: 150 **Publicly Held**
WEB: www.pactiv.com
SIC: 2656 Sanitary food containers
HQ: Pactiv Llc
   1900 W Field Ct
   Lake Forest IL 60045
   847 482-2000

(G-12281)
PACTIV LLC
1900 W Field Ct (60045-4828)
P.O. Box 119, Wanatah IN (46390-0119)
PHONE..............................847 482-2000
Dana Nead, *President*
EMP: 50 **Publicly Held**
WEB: www.pactiv.com
SIC: 3353 3497 Foil, aluminum; metal foil & leaf
HQ: Pactiv Llc
   1900 W Field Ct
   Lake Forest IL 60045
   847 482-2000

(G-12282)
PATRICIA JENKINS
Also Called: Pmj Designs
40 Washington Cir (60045-2454)
PHONE..............................224 436-7547
Patricia Jenkins, *Owner*
Megan Vignocchi, *Administration*
EMP: 3 EST: 2018
SALES (est): 130.8K **Privately Held**
SIC: 3149 Ballet slippers

(G-12283)
PCA CENTRAL CAL CORRUGATED LLC (HQ)
1955 W Field Ct (60045-4824)
PHONE..............................847 482-3000
Mark Kowlza, *CEO*
EMP: 2
SALES (est): 11.8MM
SALES (corp-wide): 6.9B **Publicly Held**
SIC: 2631 2653 Paperboard mills; corrugated & solid fiber boxes
PA: Packaging Corporation Of America
   1 N Field Ct
   Lake Forest IL 60045
   847 482-3000

(G-12284)
PCA CORRUGATED AND DISPLAY LLC (HQ)
1955 W Field Ct (60045-4824)
PHONE..............................847 482-3000
Thomas A Hassfurther, *President*
Matthew J Heleva, *Vice Pres*
Steve McCurdy, *Controller*
Hillary Miller, *Human Resources*
Richard Segrave-Daly, *Sales Mgr*
◆ EMP: 850 EST: 1956
SQ FT: 14,000
SALES: 316MM
SALES (corp-wide): 6.9B **Publicly Held**
SIC: 2653 Boxes, corrugated: made from purchased materials
PA: Packaging Corporation Of America
   1 N Field Ct
   Lake Forest IL 60045
   847 482-3000

(G-12285)
PCA INTERNATIONAL INC (HQ)
1955 W Field Ct (60045-4824)
PHONE..............................847 482-3000
EMP: 8 EST: 2001
SALES (est): 476:8K
SALES (corp-wide): 6.9B **Publicly Held**
SIC: 2653 Boxes, corrugated: made from purchased materials
PA: Packaging Corporation Of America
   1 N Field Ct
   Lake Forest IL 60045
   847 482-3000

(G-12286)
PERFECT CIRCLE PROJECTILES LLC
Also Called: Ato Systems
28101 N Ballard Dr Ste C (60045-4544)
PHONE..............................847 367-8960
Gary Gibson, *Mng Member*
EMP: 15
SALES: 900K **Privately Held**
SIC: 3081 Tile, unsupported plastic

(G-12287)
PFIZER INC
275 N Field Dr (60045-2579)
PHONE..............................224 212-3129
Maureen Mullen, *Research*
Andrew Thiel, *Research*
Amy Stanford, *Engineer*
Carol Felsenthal, *Human Res Mgr*
Martha Pritcher, *Human Res Mgr*
EMP: 3
SALES (corp-wide): 51.7B **Publicly Held**
SIC: 2834 Pharmaceutical preparations
PA: Pfizer Inc.
   235 E 42nd St Rm 107
   New York NY 10017
   212 733-2323

(G-12288)
PHARMDIUM HLTHCARE HLDINGS INC (HQ)
2 Conway Prk 150 N (60045)
PHONE..............................800 523-7749
William R Spalding, *CEO*
Matthew D Anderson, *CFO*
Roger McVey, *Manager*
EMP: 8
SALES (est): 13.6MM
SALES (corp-wide): 179.5B **Publicly Held**
SIC: 2834 6719 Adrenal pharmaceutical preparations; personal holding companies, except banks
PA: Amerisourcebergen Corporation
   1300 Morris Dr Ste 100
   Chesterbrook PA 19087
   610 727-7000

(G-12289)
PHARMEDIUM HEALTHCARE CORP (DH)
150 N Field Dr Ste 350 (60045-2506)
PHONE..............................847 457-2300
David N Jonas, *CEO*
Richard Kruzynski, *President*
William R Spalding, *Exec VP*
Jennifer Adams, *Vice Pres*
Tom Cosentino, *Vice Pres*
EMP: 32
SALES (est): 15.1MM
SALES (corp-wide): 179.5B **Publicly Held**
SIC: 2834 Pharmaceutical preparations
HQ: Pharmedium Healthcare Holdings, Inc.
   2 Conway Prk 150 N
   Lake Forest IL 60045
   800 523-7749

(G-12290)
PHOSPHATE RESOURCE PTRS
100 Saunders Rd Ste 300 (60045-2508)
PHONE..............................847 739-1200
J Reid Porter, *CEO*
EMP: 2972
SALES (est): 30.1MM **Publicly Held**
SIC: 1311 1475 2819 1094 Crude petroleum production; phosphate rock; sulfuric acid, oleum; uranium ore mining; phosphoric acid
HQ: Mosaic Global Holdings Inc.
   3033 Campus Dr Ste E490
   Minneapolis MN 55441
   763 577-2700

(G-12291)
PLASTIC BINDING LAMINATING INC
27885 Irma Lee Cir # 105 (60045-5110)
PHONE..............................847 573-0375
Frederick Nief, *President*
▲ EMP: 9
SQ FT: 7,000
SALES (est): 7.5MM **Privately Held**
SIC: 3579 Binding machines, plastic & adhesive

(G-12292)
POLYURTHANE ENGRG TCHNQUES INC (PA)
Also Called: Petco
28041 N Bradley Rd (60045-1163)
PHONE..............................847 362-1820
Russell S Smith, *President*
Dale Smith, *Vice Pres*
Gregory Smith, *Vice Pres*
William F Smith III, *Vice Pres*
Alison Marella, *Human Res Mgr*
EMP: 47
SQ FT: 37,000
SALES (est): 13.4MM **Privately Held**
WEB: www.petcorolls.com
SIC: 3555 Printing trades machinery

(G-12293)
PULLMAN COMPANY (PA)
500 N Field Dr (60045-2595)
PHONE..............................847 482-5000
M J Rock, *Principal*
EMP: 4
SALES (est): 1.6MM **Privately Held**
SIC: 3823 Industrial process control instruments

(G-12294)
RECYCLED VINYLS LLC
825 S.Waukegan Rd Ste A8 (60045-2665)
PHONE..............................847 624-1880
Albert Cheris, *Mng Member*
EMP: 25
SALES (est): 1.1MM **Privately Held**
SIC: 2821 Plastics materials & resins

(G-12295)
RENAISSANCE SSP HOLDINGS INC (HQ)
272 E Deerpath Ste 350 (60045-5326)
PHONE..............................210 476-8194
Pierre Frechette, *President*
Glenn Kues, *Vice Pres*
Christine Woolgar, *Treasurer*
David Koo, *Asst Sec*
EMP: 4 EST: 2012
SQ FT: 5,000
SALES (est): 73.1MM
SALES (corp-wide): 248MM **Privately Held**
SIC: 2834 Pharmaceutical preparations
PA: Renaissance Acquisition Holdings, Llc
   272 E Deerpath Ste 206
   Lake Forest IL 60045
   847 283-7772

(G-12296)
REYNOLDS CONSUMER PRODUCTS INC (DH)
1900 W Field Ct (60045-4828)
PHONE..............................800 879-5067
Richard Noll, *Ch of Bd*
Lance Mitchell, *President*
Francis Arseneault, *President*
Rachel Bishop, *President*
Judith Buckner, *President*
EMP: 5100

Lake Forest - Lake County (G-12297)

SQ FT: 70,400
SALES: 3B **Publicly Held**
SIC: 2673 5162 5199 Bags: plastic, laminated & coated; plastics products; foil, aluminum: household

(G-12297)
REYNOLDS CONSUMER PRODUCTS LLC (DH)
Also Called: Reynolds Consumer Products Co
1900 W Field Ct (60045-4828)
P.O. Box 5040 (60045-5040)
PHONE..................847 482-3500
Lance Mitchell, *President*
Thomas J Degnan, *President*
Thomas Degnan, *President*
David Watson, *Principal*
Paul Thomas, *Senior VP*
▼ EMP: 277
SALES (est): 587MM **Publicly Held**
SIC: 3353 Foil, aluminum

(G-12298)
REYNOLDS FOOD PACKAGING LLC
1900 W Field Ct (60045-4828)
P.O. Box 1128, Grove City PA (16127-5128)
PHONE..................847 482-3500
James Herman, *Engineer*
James Gomoll, *Senior Engr*
Rick Holbrook, *Manager*
John Krempa, *Executive*
EMP: 232 **Publicly Held**
SIC: 3081 Unsupported plastics film & sheet
HQ: Reynolds Food Packaging Llc
   6601 W Broad St
   Richmond VA 23230

(G-12299)
ROUNDTBLE HLTHCARE PARTNERS LP (PA)
272 E Deerpath Ste 350 (60045-5326)
PHONE..................847 739-3200
Lester Knight, *Managing Prtnr*
Jawwad A Akhtar, *Partner*
Joseph Damico, *Partner*
Leonard G Kuhr, *Partner*
Jack McGinley, *Partner*
◆ EMP: 21
SALES (est): 240.9MM **Privately Held**
SIC: 6722 3699 2834 Management investment, open-end; electrical equipment & supplies; pills, pharmaceutical

(G-12300)
SALTER LABS (HQ)
272 E Deerpath Ste 302 (60045-1981)
PHONE..................847 739-3224
Greg Pritchard, *CEO*
Angela Perkins, *CFO*
Samantha Kinzie, *Sales Staff*
William Feather, *Admin Sec*
◆ EMP: 18 EST: 1975
SQ FT: 100,000
SALES (est): 47.2MM
SALES (corp-wide): 240.9MM **Privately Held**
SIC: 3841 Surgical & medical instruments
PA: Roundtable Healthcare Partners, Lp
   272 E Deerpath Ste 350
   Lake Forest IL 60045
   847 739-3200

(G-12301)
SALTER MEDICAL HOLDINGS CORP
Also Called: Salter Labs
272 E Deerpath Ste 302 (60045-1981)
PHONE..................800 421-0024
EMP: 31
SALES (est): 14.8MM **Privately Held**
WEB: www.salterlabs.com
SIC: 3841 Surgical & medical instruments

(G-12302)
SHERMAN MEDIA COMPANY INC
222 E Wisconsin Ave Ste 7 (60045-1701)
PHONE..................312 335-1962
Harry Sherman, *President*
Andrew Sherman, *Corp Secy*
Lison Sherman, *Vice Pres*
EMP: 3

SALES (est): 26.1K **Privately Held**
SIC: 2721 5192 Magazines: publishing only, not printed on site; magazines

(G-12303)
SLAUGHTER COMPANY INC
Also Called: Iconic USA
28105 N Keith Dr (60045-4528)
PHONE..................847 932-3662
Eve Gramer, *President*
▲ EMP: 35
SALES (est): 4.4MM
SALES (corp-wide): 14.8MM **Privately Held**
SIC: 3629 Electronic generation equipment
PA: Ikonix Group, Inc
   28105 N Keith Dr
   Lake Forest IL 60045
   847 367-4671

(G-12304)
SPHEROTECH INC
27845 Irma Lee Cir # 101 (60045-5100)
PHONE..................847 680-8922
Andrew Wang, *CEO*
Timothy Cattell, *Mfg Staff*
Henry Trausch, *Mfg Staff*
Angela Gloria, *QC Mgr*
Robert Wijas, *Manager*
EMP: 31
SQ FT: 15,000
SALES: 1.6MM **Privately Held**
SIC: 2821 Polystyrene resins

(G-12305)
SPIRIT FOODSERVICE INC
Also Called: Spirit Brands/ Zoo Piks
1900 W Field Ct (60045-4828)
PHONE..................214 634-1393
EMP: 125 **Privately Held**
SIC: 3089 Mfg Plastic Products
HQ: Spirit Foodservice, Llc
   200 Brickstone Sq Ste G05
   Andover MA 01810
   978 964-1551

(G-12306)
SRM INDUSTRIES INC (PA)
1009 S Green Bay Rd (60045-4041)
PHONE..................847 735-0077
Jay Jacobsen Jr, *Vice Pres*
EMP: 2
SALES (est): 327.8K **Privately Held**
SIC: 2221 Nylon broadwoven fabrics

(G-12307)
SUNSET FOOD MART INC
825 S Waukegan Rd Ste A8 (60045-2665)
PHONE..................847 234-0854
Steve Davis, *Manager*
EMP: 150
SALES (corp-wide): 171.6MM **Privately Held**
SIC: 5411 5992 5912 2051 Grocery stores, independent; florists; drug stores & proprietary stores; bread, cake & related products; bakeries
PA: Sunset Food Mart, Inc.
   777 Central Ave Ste 2
   Highland Park IL 60035
   847 234-8380

(G-12308)
TENNECO AUTOMOTIVE OPER CO INC (HQ)
500 N Field Dr (60045-2595)
PHONE..................847 482-5000
Brian Kesseler, *CEO*
Brandon Smith, *Vice Pres*
Jason Holler, *CFO*
Audrey Smith, *Controller*
Corina Smith, *Analyst*
◆ EMP: 150 EST: 1888
SQ FT: 90,000
SALES (est): 4.4B
SALES (corp-wide): 17.4B **Publicly Held**
SIC: 3714 3699 Motor vehicle parts & accessories; shock absorbers, motor vehicle; motor vehicle engines & parts; electrical equipment & supplies
PA: Tenneco Inc.
   500 N Field Dr
   Lake Forest IL 60045
   847 482-5000

(G-12309)
TENNECO AUTOMOTIVE RSA COMPANY
500 N Field Dr (60045-2595)
PHONE..................847 482-5000
EMP: 5
SALES (est): 373.6K
SALES (corp-wide): 17.4B **Publicly Held**
SIC: 3714 Motor vehicle parts & accessories
HQ: Tenneco Automotive Operating Company, Inc.
   500 N Field Dr
   Lake Forest IL 60045
   847 482-5000

(G-12310)
TENNECO EUROPE LIMITED
Also Called: Tenneco Automobile
500 N Field Dr (60045-2595)
PHONE..................847 482-5000
Gregg Sherrill, *President*
◆ EMP: 2
SALES (est): 1MM
SALES (corp-wide): 17.4B **Publicly Held**
SIC: 3714 Motor vehicle parts & accessories
PA: Tenneco Inc.
   500 N Field Dr
   Lake Forest IL 60045
   847 482-5000

(G-12311)
TENNECO GLOBAL HOLDINGS INC (DH)
500 N Field Dr (60045-2595)
PHONE..................847 482-5000
Gregg Sherrill, *Ch of Bd*
Hari N Nair, *COO*
Josep Fornos, *Exec VP*
Tim Jackson, *Exec VP*
Kenneth R Trammell, *CFO*
EMP: 8
SALES (est): 14.8MM
SALES (corp-wide): 17.4B **Publicly Held**
SIC: 3714 Motor vehicle engines & parts; shock absorbers, motor vehicle

(G-12312)
TENNECO INC (PA)
500 N Field Dr (60045-2595)
PHONE..................847 482-5000
Brian J Kesseler, *CEO*
Kaled Awada, *Senior VP*
Brandon B Smith, *Senior VP*
John S Patouhas, *Vice Pres*
◆ EMP: 80
SALES: 17.4B **Publicly Held**
SIC: 3714 Motor vehicle engines & parts

(G-12313)
TENNECO INTL HOLDG CORP (DH)
500 N Field Dr (60045-2595)
PHONE..................847 482-5000
Gregg Sherrill, *CEO*
Brian Kesseler, *COO*
Josep Fornos, *Exec VP*
Tim Jackson, *Exec VP*
Kenneth R Trammell, *CFO*
EMP: 10
SALES (est): 14.8MM
SALES (corp-wide): 17.4B **Publicly Held**
SIC: 3714 3743 3711 Shock absorbers, motor vehicle; locomotives & parts; automobile bodies, passenger car, not including engine, etc.
HQ: Tenneco Automotive Operating Company, Inc.
   500 N Field Dr
   Lake Forest IL 60045
   847 482-5000

(G-12314)
THE UNITED GROUP INC
Also Called: Ergonomic Office Chairs
13700 W Polo Trail Dr (60045-5101)
PHONE..................847 816-7100
Paul Monfardini, *President*
Fred Edmonds, *Corp Secy*
Donald Radtke, *Vice Pres*
◆ EMP: 32
SQ FT: 33,000
SALES (est): 6.6MM **Privately Held**
SIC: 2531 Seats, automobile

(G-12315)
TPF LIQUIDATION CO
28160 Keith Rd (60045)
PHONE..................847 362-0028
Cheryl Zatz, *Vice Pres*
EMP: 75 **Publicly Held**
SIC: 2096 2099 Popcorn, already popped (except candy covered); popcorn, packaged: except already popped
HQ: Tpf Acquisition Co.
   13970 W Laurel Dr
   Lake Forest IL 60045
   847 362-0028

(G-12316)
TRIUMPH PACKAGING GEORGIA LLC
736 N Western Ave Ste 352 (60045-1820)
PHONE..................312 251-9600
Connelly Roberts,
Michael Roberts,
EMP: 35
SALES: 950K **Privately Held**
SIC: 2671 Packaging paper & plastics film, coated & laminated

(G-12317)
TRIUMPH PACKAGING GROUP
736 N Western Ave Ste 352 (60045-1820)
PHONE..................312 251-9600
Connelly Roberts, *Principal*
EMP: 35
SALES: 950K **Privately Held**
SIC: 2671 Packaging paper & plastics film, coated & laminated

(G-12318)
TRIWATER HOLDINGS LLC
1915 Windridge Dr (60045-4613)
PHONE..................847 457-1812
EMP: 7 EST: 2015
SALES (est): 328.7K **Privately Held**
SIC: 3589 Water treatment equipment, industrial

(G-12319)
UNICORN DESIGNS
659 N Bank Ln (60045-1826)
PHONE..................847 295-5230
Lisa Bennett, *Owner*
EMP: 3
SALES (est): 180K **Privately Held**
SIC: 5944 7631 3911 Jewelry, precious stones & precious metals; jewelry repair services; jewelry, precious metal

(G-12320)
UNITED TACTICAL SYSTEMS LLC (PA)
Also Called: Pepperball Technologies
28101 N Ballard Dr Ste F (60045-4544)
PHONE..................260 478-2500
George Eurick, *CEO*
Cal Stuart, *CFO*
◆ EMP: 20
SALES (est): 21.6MM **Privately Held**
SIC: 3489 3441 Ordnance & accessories; fabricated structural metal

(G-12321)
VPI HOLDINGS CORP (HQ)
1925 W Field Ct Ste 300 (60045-4862)
PHONE..................770 499-8100
Kevin Connelly, *CEO*
EMP: 5
SALES (est): 689.6K
SALES (corp-wide): 682.4MM **Privately Held**
SIC: 2834 Pharmaceutical preparations
PA: Akorn, Inc.
   1925 W Field Ct Ste 300
   Lake Forest IL 60045
   847 279-6100

(G-12322)
WILMAR GROUP LLC
818 Larchmont Ln (60045-1647)
PHONE..................847 421-6595
Bruce Rylance,
EMP: 3
SALES: 200K **Privately Held**
SIC: 3674 Semiconductors & related devices

GEOGRAPHIC SECTION

(G-12323)
WISCONSIN WILDERNESS FOOD PDTS
918 Timber Ln (60045-3932)
PHONE..................847 735-8661
Margaret B Gunn, *President*
Robert Loveman, *Treasurer*
Neil Gunn, *Shareholder*
Reed Eberly, *Admin Sec*
Marsha Nusslock, *Asst Sec*
EMP: 5
SQ FT: 22,000
SALES (est): 490.5K **Privately Held**
SIC: 2035 2096 7389 2099 Pickles, sauces & salad dressings; potato chips & similar snacks; packaging & labeling services; food preparations; canned fruits & specialties

(G-12324)
YEAGER JL & ASSOCIATES INC
476 Oakwood Ave (60045-1927)
PHONE..................847 283-9162
EMP: 1
SALES: 400K **Privately Held**
SIC: 2834 7389 Mfg Pharmaceutical Preparations Business Services

(G-12325)
ZEDPHARMA
602 Academy Woods Dr (60045-5118)
PHONE..................847 295-1950
EMP: 3
SALES (est): 254.6K **Privately Held**
SIC: 2834 Pharmaceutical preparations

Lake In The Hills
Mchenry County

(G-12326)
ACCURATE SECURITY & LOCK CORP
5533 Danbury Cir (60156-6376)
PHONE..................815 455-0133
Bian D Nelson, *President*
EMP: 2
SALES (est): 331K **Privately Held**
SIC: 3699 1731 Security devices; fire detection & burglar alarm systems specialization

(G-12327)
ADVANCED FLXBLE COMPOSITES INC (PA)
Also Called: A F C
14 Walter Ct (60156-1586)
PHONE..................847 658-3938
W Christopher Lewis, *President*
▲ **EMP:** 90
SQ FT: 60,000
SALES: 20MM **Privately Held**
SIC: 2296 2295 Fabric for reinforcing industrial belting; coated fabrics, not rubberized

(G-12328)
AG MEDICAL SYSTEMS INC
Also Called: AMS
13 Prosper Ct Ste B (60156-9603)
PHONE..................847 458-3100
James M Conroy, *President*
EMP: 11
SALES (est): 2.4MM **Privately Held**
SIC: 3339 Primary nonferrous metals

(G-12329)
BARRINGTON AUTOMATION LTD
Also Called: Frame World
9116 Virginia Rd (60156-9600)
PHONE..................847 458-0900
Al Mueller, *President*
Michael Mueller, *Vice Pres*
Wanda Lashaure, *Purch Mgr*
Matt Mueller, *Engineer*
Gail Mueller, *Admin Sec*
EMP: 25
SQ FT: 23,000
SALES (est): 7.3MM **Privately Held**
WEB: www.barrington-atn.com
SIC: 3535 3469 3569 3494 Pneumatic tube conveyor systems; machine parts, stamped or pressed metal; assembly machines, non-metalworking; valves & pipe fittings

(G-12330)
BARRINGTON FINANCIAL SERVICES
3 Sunvalley Ct (60156-4473)
PHONE..................847 404-1767
Dennis Coll, *President*
EMP: 1
SALES: 1,000K **Privately Held**
SIC: 3715 Truck trailers

(G-12331)
CUCCHI-BLT AMERICA INC
1520 Industrial Dr Unit C (60156-1525)
PHONE..................224 829-1400
Edoardo Paolo Catteneo, *President*
EMP: 4
SALES (est): 88.5K
SALES (corp-wide): 1.3MM **Privately Held**
SIC: 2754 Magazines: gravure printing, not published on site
HQ: Cucchi Blt Srl
Via Monte Gran Sasso 15
Cinisello Balsamo MI 20092
029 524-311

(G-12332)
DOBRATZ SALES COMPANY INC
5945 Lucerne Ln (60156-6746)
PHONE..................224 569-3081
Walter G Dobratz, *President*
Nola K Dobratz, *Vice Pres*
EMP: 7
SALES (est): 1.2MM **Privately Held**
SIC: 5085 3423 Hose, belting & packing; tools; rubber goods, mechanical, hammers (hand tools)

(G-12333)
EMISSIONS SYSTEMS INCORPORATED
Also Called: E M S
480 Wright Dr (60156-6234)
P.O. Box 7086, Algonquin (60102-7086)
PHONE..................847 669-8044
Jon Palek, *President*
EMP: 3 **EST:** 1995
SALES (est): 493.1K **Privately Held**
WEB: www.emsgas.com
SIC: 3829 Aircraft & motor vehicle measurement equipment

(G-12334)
EMMEL INC
13 Baldwin Ct (60156-6718)
PHONE..................847 254-5178
Katherine Emmel, *Principal*
EMP: 3
SALES: 3MM **Privately Held**
SIC: 2013 Sausages & other prepared meats

(G-12335)
GENERAL PRODUCTS INTERNATIONAL
Also Called: G P I
9245 S Il Route 31 (60156-1670)
PHONE..................847 458-6357
Edward Mack, *President*
▲ **EMP:** 6
SALES (est): 8.1MM **Privately Held**
SIC: 3366 3312 3084 3674 Machinery castings: copper or copper-base alloy; forgings, iron & steel; plastics pipe; semiconductors & related devices

(G-12336)
GRAPHIC SOURCE GROUP INC
Also Called: American Apparels & Promotions
1119 W Algonquin Rd Ste B (60156-3560)
PHONE..................847 854-2670
Sharon Meyer, *President*
EMP: 4
SALES: 1MM **Privately Held**
SIC: 5112 2752 Office supplies; commercial printing, lithographic

(G-12337)
JODI MAURER
Also Called: Ebk Containers
5001 Princeton Ln (60156-6393)
PHONE..................847 961-5347
Jodi Mauer, *Owner*
EMP: 2
SALES (est): 206.6K **Privately Held**
SIC: 3089 3443 Plastic containers, except foam; industrial vessels, tanks & containers

(G-12338)
KOLD-BAN INTERNATIONAL LTD
8390 Pingree Rd (60156-9671)
PHONE..................847 658-8561
James W Burke, *President*
James O Burke, *Vice Pres*
Mike Guevara, *Plant Mgr*
Richard Burke, *Treasurer*
Rick Burke, *Controller*
▼ **EMP:** 21
SQ FT: 14,200
SALES (est): 5.4MM **Privately Held**
SIC: 3694 Engine electrical equipment

(G-12339)
LITH LIQURE
461 N Randall Rd (60156-6335)
PHONE..................847 458-5180
Sangeeta Patel, *Principal*
EMP: 4
SALES (est): 312.1K **Privately Held**
WEB: www.lith.org
SIC: 2752 Commercial printing, lithographic

(G-12340)
MASTERBOLT LLC
8015 Pyott Rd (60156)
PHONE..................847 834-5191
Richard W Del Olmo, *Mng Member*
EMP: 12
SALES (est): 329.6K **Privately Held**
SIC: 3999 Manufacturing industries

(G-12341)
MW HOPKINS & SONS INC
Also Called: Hopkins Grease Company
9150 Pyott Rd (60156-9765)
P.O. Box 7722 (60102-7722)
PHONE..................847 458-1010
Michael A Hopkins, *President*
Timothy Hopkins, *Vice Pres*
EMP: 3 **EST:** 1997
SALES (est): 344K **Privately Held**
WEB: www.hopkinsgrease.com
SIC: 2077 Rendering

(G-12342)
NORTH STAR STAMPING & TOOL INC
1264 Industrial Dr (60156-1500)
PHONE..................847 658-9400
Catherine O'Brien, *CEO*
EMP: 11
SQ FT: 15,000
SALES (est): 1.2MM **Privately Held**
SIC: 3469 Stamping metal for the trade

(G-12343)
SEAT TRANS INC
620 Joseph St (60156-5200)
PHONE..................224 522-1007
Petya I Marinova, *President*
EMP: 3
SALES (est): 220K **Privately Held**
SIC: 3715 7389 Truck trailers;

(G-12344)
TOUR INDUSTRIES INC
1188 Starwood Pass (60156-4892)
PHONE..................847 854-9400
Greg Squires, *President*
Donna Squires, *Admin Sec*
EMP: 36
SALES (est): 1.3MM **Privately Held**
SIC: 3452 Bolts, nuts, rivets & washers

Lake Villa
Lake County

(G-12345)
ALLAN BROOKS & ASSOCIATES INC
Also Called: Brooks Allan
95 W Grand Ave Ste 120 (60046-8609)
PHONE..................847 537-7500
Deborah L Dunne, *President*
Joseph Dunne, *CFO*
Stacy Riley, *Administration*
EMP: 13
SQ FT: 10,000
SALES (est): 2.9MM **Privately Held**
WEB: www.brooks-allan.com
SIC: 5112 2759 Business forms; commercial printing

(G-12346)
BRIAN K WATTLEWORTH
36345 N Yew Tree Dr (60046-7427)
PHONE..................847 356-2103
Brian K Wattleworth, *Principal*
EMP: 4
SALES (est): 290.7K **Privately Held**
SIC: 2834 Pharmaceutical preparations

(G-12347)
BUMPER SCUFFS
37254 N Piper Ln (60046-7363)
PHONE..................847 489-7926
Ryan Mendoza, *CEO*
EMP: 2
SALES (est): 214.6K **Privately Held**
SIC: 2842 Automobile polish

(G-12348)
C & F PACKING CO INC
Also Called: Arco Brand
515 Park Ave (60046-6512)
P.O. Box 209 (60046-0209)
PHONE..................847 245-2000
Joseph A Freda, *President*
Michael P Stock, *Vice Pres*
Michael Stock, *VP Opers*
Ned Fakhouri, *Plant Mgr*
Dariusz Szczepanek, *Parts Mgr*
EMP: 130 **EST:** 1945
SQ FT: 120,000
SALES (est): 33.2MM **Privately Held**
WEB: www.cfpacking.com
SIC: 2013 5147 Sausages from purchased meat; meats, fresh

(G-12349)
EMBROIDME
36595 N Yew Tree Dr (60046-7489)
PHONE..................847 301-1010
Kreg Swett, *Owner*
Carol Swett, *Co-Owner*
EMP: 4
SALES (est): 254.6K **Privately Held**
SIC: 2395 Embroidery & art needlework

(G-12350)
EMERGE TECHNOLOGY GROUP LLC
1600 N Milwaukee Ave # 708 (60046-8585)
P.O. Box 866, Antioch (60002-0866)
PHONE..................224 603-2161
Ramsey Matarieh,
▲ **EMP:** 7
SQ FT: 2,200
SALES (est): 786.3K **Privately Held**
SIC: 3672 3643 3357 3613 Printed circuit boards; electric switches; automotive wire & cable, except ignition sets: nonferrous; switches, electric power except snap, push button, etc.

(G-12351)
FORCE MANUFACTURING INC
266 Park Ave (60046-8915)
PHONE..................847 265-6500
Russell Valin, *President*
EMP: 7
SALES (est): 1.6MM **Privately Held**
SIC: 3469 7692 Machine parts, stamped or pressed metal; welding repair

Lake Villa - Lake County (G-12352)

(G-12352)
GALLIMORE INDUSTRIES INC
200 Park Ave Ste B (60046-8903)
P.O. Box 158 (60046-0158)
PHONE..............................847 356-3331
Claris C Gallimore, *President*
Kent Gallimore, *VP Engrg*
Dorothea J Gallimore, *Treasurer*
EMP: 15
SQ FT: 19,000
SALES (est): 2.4MM **Privately Held**
SIC: 2759 Coupons: printing

(G-12353)
HANSEN CUSTOM CABINET INC
23418 W Apollo Ct (60046-9699)
PHONE..............................847 356-1100
Keith Hansen, *President*
Fredrick Hansen, *Vice Pres*
Craig Regnier, *Production*
EMP: 5 EST: 1956
SQ FT: 4,000
SALES (est): 450K **Privately Held**
SIC: 5712 2541 2434 Cabinet work, custom; wood partitions & fixtures; wood kitchen cabinets

(G-12354)
HAVECO TOOL & MFG INC
1600 N Milwaukee Ave (60046-8585)
P.O. Box 159 (60046-0159)
PHONE..............................847 603-1893
Frank Ventrice Jr, *President*
Beverly Ventrice, *Corp Secy*
EMP: 9
SQ FT: 5,000
SALES (est): 900K **Privately Held**
SIC: 3599 Machine shop, jobbing & repair

(G-12355)
ID LABEL INC (PA)
425 Park Ave (60046-6540)
PHONE..............................847 265-1200
Neil P Johnston, *President*
John Regner, *Business Mgr*
Jeff Chandler, *COO*
Tom Morgan, *Vice Pres*
Kurt Wagner, *Engineer*
EMP: 35
SQ FT: 40,000
SALES (est): 11.3MM **Privately Held**
SIC: 2759 Commercial printing

(G-12356)
JACK & LIDIAS RESORT INC
3610 N Edgewood St (60046)
PHONE..............................847 356-1389
Jack Krupka, *President*
Lidia Oleksy, *Vice Pres*
EMP: 2
SALES (est): 207.5K **Privately Held**
SIC: 3949 7011 Fishing equipment; hotels & motels

(G-12357)
KEY RESOURCES INC
36467 S Nathan Hale Dr (60046-7767)
PHONE..............................800 574-1339
Cynthia Overby, *President*
Ray Overby, *President*
EMP: 7
SALES (est): 481.3K **Privately Held**
WEB: www.krisecurity.com
SIC: 7373 7379 7372 Systems software development services; computer related consulting services; operating systems computer software

(G-12358)
LTE-LITTLE TIMBER ENTERPRISES
1331 Carriage Ln (60046-7001)
PHONE..............................224 321-0361
Rocco Militelo II, *Principal*
EMP: 3
SALES (est): 252.5K **Privately Held**
SIC: 2411 Logging

(G-12359)
M & G SIMPLICITEES
39420 N Il Route 59 # 4 (60046-8141)
PHONE..............................224 372-7426
Gary Matthews, *Partner*
Marc Thompson, *Partner*
EMP: 3
SALES (est): 331.7K **Privately Held**
SIC: 2253 7389 T-shirts & tops, knit; design services

(G-12360)
MATRIX CIRCUITS LLC (PA)
37575 N Il Route 59 (60046-9148)
PHONE..............................319 367-5000
Paul Krumenacher,
Mike Forseen,
EMP: 4 EST: 2008
SQ FT: 6,000
SALES (est): 600K **Privately Held**
WEB: www.matrixcircuits.com
SIC: 3679 7373 Electronic circuits; computer integrated systems design

(G-12361)
NEW GEN AEROSPACE CORP
290 Park Ave (60046-8915)
PHONE..............................847 740-2216
Thomas R Klapperich, *CEO*
Chris Mahon, *Accounts Exec*
Dan Crespo, *Sales Staff*
Christy Henderson, *Sales Staff*
Blake Jones, *Marketing Staff*
EMP: 8
SQ FT: 17,000
SALES (est): 10MM **Privately Held**
SIC: 3728 Aircraft parts & equipment

(G-12362)
NEW VISION CSTM CABINETS MLLWK
23390 W Apollo Ct (60046-9638)
P.O. Box 168 (60046-0168)
PHONE..............................847 265-2723
Julie Fill, *President*
Matt Fill, *Vice Pres*
Hugh O'Connell, *Vice Pres*
Ann O'Connell, *Admin Sec*
EMP: 3
SQ FT: 3,000
SALES (est): 387K **Privately Held**
WEB: www.newviscab.com
SIC: 2434 Wood kitchen cabinets

(G-12363)
PRINT SOURCE FOR BUSINESS INC
38966 N Deep Lake Rd (60046-6705)
P.O. Box 368 (60046-0368)
PHONE..............................847 356-0190
George Richter, *President*
James Richter, *Corp Secy*
EMP: 6
SQ FT: 4,200
SALES (est): 662.8K **Privately Held**
SIC: 2752 Commercial printing, offset

(G-12364)
PRO PATCH SYSTEMS INC
25704 W Lehmann Blvd (60046-9717)
PHONE..............................847 356-8100
Dennis Hoffmann, *President*
Linda Hoffman, *Vice Pres*
EMP: 2
SALES (est): 1MM **Privately Held**
SIC: 5032 2672 Drywall materials; adhesive backed films, foams & foils

(G-12365)
R+D CUSTOM AUTOMATION INC
23411 W Wall St (60046-8140)
PHONE..............................847 395-3330
Loren Esch, *President*
James Marron, *Production*
Ken Monson, *Engineer*
Todd Newton, *Engineer*
Timothy Roshko, *Engineer*
▼ EMP: 42
SQ FT: 20,000
SALES (est): 9.8MM **Privately Held**
SIC: 3549 7373 8742 Assembly machines, including robotic; systems integration services; automation & robotics consultant

(G-12366)
RAPID MOTION CNC LLC
473 Park Ave Ste 100 (60046-6561)
PHONE..............................224 372-9000
Tines Joseph P, *Principal*
EMP: 3 EST: 2013

SALES (est): 407.8K **Privately Held**
WEB: www.rapidmotioncnc.com
SIC: 3599 Machine shop, jobbing & repair

(G-12367)
SHEAS IRON WORKS INC
735 N Milwaukee Ave A (60046-8567)
PHONE..............................847 356-2922
Judy Shea, *President*
Ryan Shea, *Corp Secy*
EMP: 30
SALES (est): 4.6MM **Privately Held**
SIC: 3441 7389 7692 3446 Building components, structural steel; crane & aerial lift service; welding repair; architectural metalwork; sheet metalwork

(G-12368)
STRATEGIC APPLICATIONS INC
Also Called: SAI
278 Park Ave (60046-8915)
PHONE..............................847 680-9385
Steven C Denault, *President*
Liane Pinkos, *Technical Staff*
EMP: 2 EST: 1996
SALES: 1.6MM **Privately Held**
WEB: www.sai-infusion.com
SIC: 2834 8748 Pharmaceutical preparations; business consulting

(G-12369)
TIERNEYS SIGNS INC
36701 N Il Route 83 Apt A (60046-5229)
PHONE..............................847 395-8224
John Tierney, *CEO*
EMP: 2
SALES (est): 211.7K **Privately Held**
SIC: 3993 Signs & advertising specialties

(G-12370)
TRI-TECH MOLDING
21547 W Morton Dr (60046-8246)
PHONE..............................847 263-7769
Keith Rosedall, *Co-Owner*
Jeff Jones, *Co-Owner*
Rob Regel, *Co-Owner*
EMP: 5
SALES (est): 266K **Privately Held**
SIC: 3089 Molding primary plastic

(G-12371)
WARMING SYSTEMS
7706 Industrial Dr Unit D (60046)
PHONE..............................800 663-7831
Mark Bowernan, *CEO*
EMP: 6
SALES (est): 388.6K **Privately Held**
SIC: 3625 Flow actuated electrical switches

(G-12372)
WORKS IN PROGRESS FOUNDATION
24978 W Lakeview Dr (60046-9618)
PHONE..............................847 997-8338
Daniela Gorsuch, *President*
Matthew Gorsuch, *Admin Sec*
EMP: 3 EST: 2015
SALES (est): 149.5K **Privately Held**
SIC: 3312 Primary finished or semifinished shapes

Lake Zurich
Lake County

(G-12373)
ACCO BRANDS INC
4 Corporate Dr (60047-8997)
PHONE..............................847 541-9500
Robert J Keller, *President*
Robert Alley, *General Mgr*
Neal V Fenwick, *Exec VP*
Jeffrey Turofsky, *Senior VP*
Steven Baker, *Vice Pres*
▲ EMP: 1484
SALES (est): 433.1MM
SALES (corp-wide): 1.9B **Publicly Held**
SIC: 2542 Fixtures: display, office or store; except wood
PA: Acco Brands Corporation
  4 Corporate Dr
  Lake Zurich IL 60047
  847 541-9500

(G-12374)
ACCO BRANDS CORPORATION (PA)
4 Corporate Dr (60047-8997)
PHONE..............................847 541-9500
Boris Elisman, *Ch of Bd*
Patrick H Buchenroth, *President*
Cezary L Monko, *President*
Thomas W Tedford, *President*
Thomas Tedford, *Exec VP*
EMP: 600 EST: 1970
SALES: 1.9B **Publicly Held**
WEB: www.accobrands.com
SIC: 2782 2083 2761 2672 Looseleaf binders & devices; paper ruling; laminated plastic sheets; computer forms, manifold or continuous; adhesive papers, labels or tapes: from purchased material

(G-12375)
ACCO BRANDS INTERNATIONAL INC
4 Corporate Dr (60047-8997)
PHONE..............................847 541-9500
Boris Elisman, *President*
EMP: 4
SALES (est): 1.1MM
SALES (corp-wide): 1.9B **Publicly Held**
SIC: 2782 3083 2761 2672 Looseleaf binders & devices; paper ruling; laminated plastic sheets; computer forms, manifold or continuous; adhesive papers, labels or tapes: from purchased material
PA: Acco Brands Corporation
  4 Corporate Dr
  Lake Zurich IL 60047
  847 541-9500

(G-12376)
ACCO BRANDS USA LLC (HQ)
4 Corporate Dr (60047-8997)
P.O. Box 1342, Brentwood NY (11717-0718)
PHONE..............................800 222-6462
Boris Elisman, *President*
Christopher Franey, *Vice Pres*
Jed Peters, *Vice Pres*
Thomas Tedford, *Vice Pres*
Laurie Keck, *Treasurer*
◆ EMP: 400 EST: 1970
SALES (est): 1.8B
SALES (corp-wide): 1.9B **Publicly Held**
WEB: www.accobrands.com
SIC: 3089 2761 3496 2675 Injection molding of plastics; manifold business forms; clips & fasteners, made from purchased wire; folders, filing, die-cut: made from purchased materials
PA: Acco Brands Corporation
  4 Corporate Dr
  Lake Zurich IL 60047
  847 541-9500

(G-12377)
ACCO EUROPE FIN HOLDINGS LLC
4 Corporate Dr (60047-8924)
PHONE..............................800 222-6462
EMP: 2
SALES (est): 583.7K
SALES (corp-wide): 1.9B **Publicly Held**
SIC: 2782 Blankbooks & looseleaf binders
PA: Acco Brands Corporation
  4 Corporate Dr
  Lake Zurich IL 60047
  847 541-9500

(G-12378)
ACCO INTL HOLDINGS INC
4 Corporate Dr (60047-8924)
PHONE..............................800 222-6462
EMP: 3
SALES (est): 875.6K
SALES (corp-wide): 1.9B **Publicly Held**
SIC: 2782 Looseleaf binders & devices
PA: Acco Brands Corporation
  4 Corporate Dr
  Lake Zurich IL 60047
  847 541-9500

(G-12379)
ACME AWNING CO INC
325 Pebblecreek Dr (60047-2755)
P.O. Box 23, Winnetka (60093-0023)
PHONE..............................847 446-0153

GEOGRAPHIC SECTION
Lake Zurich - Lake County (G-12407)

Kristopher Arands, *President*
EMP: 4
SALES: 125K **Privately Held**
SIC: 3089 5039 Awnings, fiberglass & plastic combination; awnings

(G-12380)
AFCO PRODUCTS INCORPORATED
1030 Commerce Dr (60047-1545)
PHONE 847 299-1055
Kenneth A Klancnik, *President*
Chris Klancnik, *Vice Pres*
Rob Klancnik, *Vice Pres*
Rob N Klancnik, *Vice Pres*
Rob Klancnik, *Vice Pres*
EMP: 35 **EST:** 1940
SQ FT: 40,000
SALES (est): 8.8MM **Privately Held**
WEB: www.afco-products.com
SIC: 3451 Screw machine products

(G-12381)
AFFIRMED LLC
280a N Rand Rd Ste A (60047-2282)
PHONE 847 550-0170
Terrence Canning, *Mng Member*
Nick Canning,
EMP: 7
SALES (est): 334.5K **Privately Held**
SIC: 2844 Manicure preparations

(G-12382)
ALL RITE INDUSTRIES INC
470 Oakwood Rd (60047-1515)
P.O. Box 189 (60047-0189)
PHONE 847 540-0300
Edward Bilik, *President*
Mary Bilik, *Corp Secy*
Kathy Muncer, *Vice Pres*
Joe Santori, *Engineer*
Kim Young, *Engineer*
EMP: 38
SQ FT: 40,000
SALES (est): 9.9MM **Privately Held**
SIC: 3089 Injection molding of plastics

(G-12383)
ALPHA BEDDING LLC
Also Called: Alpha Tekniko
1290 Ensell Rd (60047-1537)
PHONE 847 550-5110
Ted Lazakis, *CEO*
Felix Gutierrez, *Plant Mgr*
Lisa Ravnsbeck, *Manager*
Tia Lazakis,
EMP: 11
SQ FT: 10,000
SALES (est): 2.6MM **Privately Held**
SIC: 3634 2211 Bedcoverings, electric; bed sheeting, cotton

(G-12384)
ANDERSON MSNRY REFR SPCIALISTS
Also Called: Anderson Msnry Refr Spcialist I
25675 N Stoney Kirk Ct (60047-7539)
PHONE 847 540-8885
Cynthia L Anderson, *President*
Alan R Anderson, *Vice Pres*
EMP: 6
SQ FT: 500
SALES (est): 730K **Privately Held**
SIC: 4953 3567 5085 Incinerator operation; industrial furnaces & ovens; refractory material

(G-12385)
APEX DENTAL MATERIALS INC
330 Telser Rd (60047-6701)
PHONE 847 719-1133
Scott Lamerand, *Admin Sec*
EMP: 4
SALES (est): 493K **Privately Held**
WEB: www.apexdentalmaterials.com
SIC: 3843 Dental equipment & supplies

(G-12386)
ASTRON DENTAL CORPORATION
815 Oakwood Rd Ste G (60047-6704)
PHONE 847 726-8787
Robert E Muller Sr, *President*
Dr Robert E Muller Sr, *President*
Robert Muller, *Vice Pres*
Robert E Muller Jr, *Vice Pres*
Douglas Muller, *VP Opers*
▲ **EMP:** 15
SQ FT: 3,000
SALES (est): 2.3MM **Privately Held**
SIC: 3843 Denture materials

(G-12387)
BASEMENT FLOOD PROTECTOR INC
100 Oakwood Rd Ste F (60047-1524)
PHONE 847 438-6770
Hollie Sloss, *President*
Jeffery Sloss, *Owner*
John Sloss, *General Mgr*
▲ **EMP:** 10
SALES (est): 2.2MM **Privately Held**
SIC: 3561 7699 1799 Pumps, domestic: water or sump; industrial pumps & parts; pumps & pumping equipment repair; battery service & repair; waterproofing

(G-12388)
BISH CREATIVE DISPLAY INC
945 Telser Rd (60047-6752)
PHONE 847 438-1500
Jerrold E Fox, *President*
Eric Lawler, *Vice Pres*
Sharon Monahan, *Project Mgr*
Gini Fales, *Production*
Jerry Rauman, *CFO*
◆ **EMP:** 20
SALES (est): 22.7MM **Privately Held**
WEB: www.bishdisplay.com
SIC: 3993 Displays & cutouts, window & lobby

(G-12389)
BRIGHT LIGHT SIGN COMPANY INC
310 Telser Rd (60047-6701)
PHONE 847 550-8902
William Holley, *President*
EMP: 9
SALES (est): 1.2MM **Privately Held**
SIC: 3993 Electric signs

(G-12390)
CATALYTIC PRODUCTS INTL INC
980 Ensell Rd (60047-1557)
PHONE 847 438-0334
Julia Lincoln, *CEO*
Dennis W Lincoln, *President*
Mark A Betz, *Vice Pres*
Stephen Klostermeyer, *Vice Pres*
Chris Drake, *Project Mgr*
◆ **EMP:** 28
SQ FT: 10,000
SALES (est): 12.9MM **Privately Held**
SIC: 3822 3567 2819 3564 Auto controls regulating residntl & coml environmt & applncs; ; catalysts, chemical; blowers & fans

(G-12391)
CCTY USA BEARING CO
1111 Rose Rd (60047-1533)
PHONE 847 540-8196
Evan Poulakidas, *President*
David Olsen, *Admin Sec*
▲ **EMP:** 7
SALES (est): 2.1MM **Privately Held**
SIC: 5085 3562 Bearings; roller bearings & parts

(G-12392)
CHAMPION MEDICAL TECH INC
Also Called: Champion Healthcare Tech
765 Ela Rd Ste 200 (60047-6305)
PHONE 866 803-3720
Peter I Casady, *President*
Donna Smith, *Opers Staff*
Matt Clark, *Sales Staff*
Thomas E Casady, *CTO*
Amanda Butler, *Director*
EMP: 32
SALES: 5.4MM
SALES (corp-wide): 5.8MM **Privately Held**
SIC: 7372 Application computer software
PA: Hematerra Technologies, Llc
  135 2nd Ave N Ste 5
  Jacksonville FL 32250
  904 249-3700

(G-12393)
CHELSEA FRAMING PRODUCTS INC
333 Enterprise Pkwy (60047-6733)
PHONE 847 550-5556
Min Han, *Principal*
Min S Han, *Principal*
EMP: 4
SALES (est): 458.7K **Privately Held**
SIC: 3795 Tanks & tank components

(G-12394)
CLAY VOLLMAR PRODUCTS CO
124 N Buesching Rd (60047-1569)
PHONE 847 540-5850
Kurt Schulberg, *Manager*
EMP: 6
SALES (corp-wide): 2.9MM **Privately Held**
WEB: www.vollmarclayproducts.com
SIC: 5032 3272 7699 Brick, stone & related material; concrete products; septic tank cleaning service
PA: Clay Vollmar Products Co
  5835 W Touhy Ave
  Chicago IL 60646
  773 774-1234

(G-12395)
COBRACO MANUFACTURING INC (PA)
300 E Il Route 22 (60047-2572)
PHONE 847 726-5800
Sy Emalfarb, *CEO*
Brad Emalfarb, *President*
▲ **EMP:** 20
SQ FT: 106,000
SALES (est): 2.2MM **Privately Held**
SIC: 3999 5083 Coin-operated amusement machines; lawn & garden machinery & equipment

(G-12396)
COORDINATED KITCHEN DEV INC
Also Called: Ckd
1525 Coral Reef Way (60047-2921)
PHONE 847 847-7692
Martin J Aimone, *President*
EMP: 1 **EST:** 2011
SALES: 300K **Privately Held**
SIC: 2541 Cabinets, lockers & shelving

(G-12397)
COPPER FIDDLE DISTILERY
532 W Il Route 22 (60047-2545)
PHONE 847 847-7613
Jose Hernandez, *President*
EMP: 7
SALES (est): 684.3K **Privately Held**
WEB: www.copperfiddledistillery.com
SIC: 2085 Distilled & blended liquors

(G-12398)
CRD ENTERPRISES INC
549 Capital Dr (60047-6711)
PHONE 847 438-4299
Charles R Davidson, *President*
▼ **EMP:** 3
SQ FT: 3,000
SALES (est): 1.2MM **Privately Held**
SIC: 5084 3542 Metalworking machinery; die casting machines

(G-12399)
CREATIVE CONVENIENCES BY K&E
55 N Buesching Rd Apt 312 (60047-6110)
P.O. Box 759 (60047-0759)
PHONE 847 975-8526
Karen Rafalowitz, *President*
Ellen Jakubicek, *Vice Pres*
EMP: 4
SALES: 50K **Privately Held**
SIC: 3089 Automotive parts, plastic

(G-12400)
CTI INDUSTRIES CORPORATION
800 Church St (60047-1573)
PHONE 800 284-5605
Dorothy Gates, *CFO*
EMP: 75
SALES (corp-wide): 40.5MM **Publicly Held**
SIC: 3089 3069 Plastic containers, except foam; tubs, plastic (containers); plastic kitchenware, tableware & housewar; balloons, advertising & toy: rubber; balloons, metal foil laminated with rubber; balls, rubber
PA: Cti Industries Corporation
  22160 N Pepper Rd
  Lake Barrington IL 60010
  847 382-1000

(G-12401)
D&W FINE PACK LLC
800 Ela Rd (60047-2340)
PHONE 800 323-0422
EMP: 3
SALES (corp-wide): 614.5MM **Privately Held**
WEB: www.dwfinepack.com
SIC: 3089 Plastic kitchenware, tableware & houseware
HQ: D&W Fine Pack Llc
  777 Mark St
  Wood Dale IL 60191

(G-12402)
DEVIL DOG ARMS INC
650 Telser Rd (60047-1528)
PHONE 847 790-4004
Joseph J Lucania III, *President*
EMP: 2
SALES (est): 272.8K **Privately Held**
SIC: 3484 3489 5091 5941 Guns (firearms) or gun parts, 30 mm. & below; guns or gun parts, over 30 mm.; guns, howitzers, mortars & related equipment; firearms, sporting; firearms

(G-12403)
DMS INC
1120 Ensell Rd (60047-6718)
PHONE 847 726-2828
David Polkinghorn, *President*
Duane Polkinghorne, *Vice Pres*
EMP: 17
SQ FT: 12,000
SALES (est): 4.2MM **Privately Held**
SIC: 3555 3544 Printing trades machinery; die sets for metal stamping (presses)

(G-12404)
ECHO INCORPORATED (HQ)
400 Oakwood Rd (60047-1564)
PHONE 847 540-8400
Dan Obringer, *President*
Steve James, *Business Mgr*
Sophia Levy, *Project Mgr*
Andy Cheng, *Manager*
Marc Schuessler, *Manager*
◆ **EMP:** 830 **EST:** 1972
SQ FT: 400,000
SALES (est): 259.7MM **Privately Held**
SIC: 3524 Lawn & garden equipment

(G-12405)
ECHO INCORPORATED
1000 Rose Rd (60047)
PHONE 847 540-3500
Dan Obringer, *Branch Mgr*
EMP: 47 **Privately Held**
SIC: 3524 Lawn & garden equipment
HQ: Echo, Incorporated
  400 Oakwood Rd
  Lake Zurich IL 60047
  847 540-8400

(G-12406)
ELECTRONIC DESIGN & MFG INC
Also Called: E D M
1225 Flex Ct (60047-1578)
PHONE 847 550-1912
Anthony Trocano, *President*
Sandra Trocano, *Principal*
EMP: 100
SQ FT: 24,000
SALES (est): 12.9MM **Privately Held**
SIC: 3672 3679 Printed circuit boards; power supplies, all types: static

(G-12407)
ELEGANT EMBROIDERY INC
100 Oakwood Rd Ste C (60047-1524)
PHONE 847 540-8003

Lake Zurich - Lake County (G-12408)

Nancy Solomon, *President*
EMP: 6
SALES (est): 577.7K **Privately Held**
SIC: 2395 2759 Embroidery & art needlework; screen printing

(G-12408)
EOE INC
590 Telser Rd Ste A (60047-1584)
P.O. Box 909 (60047-0909)
PHONE 847 550-1665
Jim Hnilo, *President*
Alice Hnilo, *VP Finance*
▼ **EMP:** 10
SQ FT: 12,000
SALES (est): 1.8MM **Privately Held**
SIC: 3565 Packaging machinery

(G-12409)
FAIRCHILD INDUSTRIES INC
475 Capital Dr (60047-6732)
PHONE 847 550-9580
Robert W Schauer, *President*
Kathryn Schauer, *President*
Joel Schauer, *Admin Sec*
◆ **EMP:** 22
SQ FT: 20,000
SALES (est): 8.1MM
SALES (corp-wide): 4.6MM **Privately Held**
WEB: www.fairchildind.com
SIC: 5199 3061 Foams & rubber; mechanical rubber goods
PA: Mcclure Associates Inc
475 Capital Dr
Lake Zurich IL 60047
847 550-9570

(G-12410)
FALCON TECHNOLOGIES INC
1050 Ensell Rd (60047-6715)
PHONE 847 550-1866
Christopher Nowacki, *President*
Stanley Kielek, *Principal*
EMP: 7
SQ FT: 4,000
SALES (est): 800K **Privately Held**
SIC: 3549 8711 Metalworking machinery; industrial engineers

(G-12411)
FENWAL INC (DH)
3 Corporate Dr Ste 300 (60047-8930)
P.O. Box 816, Wauconda (60084-0816)
PHONE 800 333-6925
John Ducker, *CEO*
Dean A Gregory, *President*
Jannette Lugo, *Buyer*
Pattie Todd, *Research*
Colin Austin, *Engineer*
◆ **EMP:** 450
SQ FT: 25,000
SALES (est): 492.8MM
SALES (corp-wide): 39.1B **Privately Held**
SIC: 5047 3069 Medical equipment & supplies; medical & laboratory rubber sundries & related products
HQ: Fresenius Kabi Pharmaceuticals Holding, Llc
3 Corporate Dr
Lake Zurich IL 60047
847 550-2300

(G-12412)
FOOD EQUIPMENT TECHNOLOGIES CO
Also Called: Fetco
600 Rose Rd (60047-1560)
P.O. Box 429 (60047-0429)
PHONE 847 719-3000
Christopher Nowak, *President*
◆ **EMP:** 170
SQ FT: 160,000
SALES (est): 50.1MM **Privately Held**
SIC: 3556 Food products machinery; cream separators (food products machinery); butter making & butter working machinery

(G-12413)
FRESENIUS KABI LLC (DH)
3 Corporate Dr (60047-8930)
PHONE 847 550-2300
John Ducker, *CEO*
Marlon Vazquez, *Superintendent*
John Chuwang, *Regional Mgr*
Steven J Adams, *Exec VP*
Scott W Meacham, *Exec VP*
◆ **EMP:** 75
SALES (est): 18.6MM
SALES (corp-wide): 39.1B **Privately Held**
SIC: 2834 5122 Pharmaceutical preparations; drugs, proprietaries & sundries
HQ: Fresenius Kabi Pharmaceuticals Holding, Llc
3 Corporate Dr
Lake Zurich IL 60047
847 550-2300

(G-12414)
FRESENIUS KABI PHARM (DH)
3 Corporate Dr (60047-8930)
PHONE 847 550-2300
John Ducker, *CEO*
Manuel N Vicente, *Principal*
Steven J Adams, *Exec VP*
Jack C Silhavy, *Exec VP*
Wolfgang Salrein, *Vice Pres*
EMP: 5
SALES (est): 1.3B
SALES (corp-wide): 39.1B **Privately Held**
SIC: 2834 Pharmaceutical preparations
HQ: Fresenius Kabi Ag
Else-Kroner-Str. 1
Bad Homburg 61352
617 268-60

(G-12415)
FRESENIUS KABI USA LLC (DH)
3 Corporate Dr Fl 3 # 3 (60047-8930)
PHONE 847 550-2300
John Ducker, *President*
Steven J Adams, *Exec VP*
Jack Silhavy, *Exec VP*
Arthur Harms, *Project Mgr*
Pat Nassopoulos, *Project Mgr*
▲ **EMP:** 1500 **EST:** 2007
SALES (est): 826.3MM
SALES (corp-wide): 39.1B **Privately Held**
WEB: www.fresenius-kabi.us
SIC: 2834 Pharmaceutical preparations
HQ: Fresenius Kabi Pharmaceuticals Holding, Llc
3 Corporate Dr
Lake Zurich IL 60047
847 550-2300

(G-12416)
FRESENIUS KABI USA LLC
3 Corporate Dr Ste 300 (60047-8930)
PHONE 847 550-2300
Donald Kruto, *Treasurer*
Matt Martinez, *Marketing Staff*
Jennifer Bossany, *Manager*
Steve Lundell, *Senior Mgr*
Juan Ortega, *Supervisor*
EMP: 35
SALES (corp-wide): 39.1B **Privately Held**
SIC: 2834 Pharmaceutical preparations
HQ: Fresenius Kabi Usa, Llc
3 Corporate Dr Fl 3 # 3
Lake Zurich IL 60047
847 550-2300

(G-12417)
GLOBAL FASTENER ENGRG INC
505 Oakwood Rd Ste 200 (60047-1534)
PHONE 847 929-9563
Dasheng Jiang, *President*
EMP: 11 **EST:** 2013
SALES (est): 1.7MM
SALES (corp-wide): 17.9MM **Privately Held**
SIC: 3452 Bolts, nuts, rivets & washers
PA: Hubei Boshlong Technology Co., Ltd.
No.269, Chutian Avenue, Dongqiao Town
Zhongxiang 43190
724 439-5081

(G-12418)
GPM MFG INC
1199 Flex Ct (60047-1578)
PHONE 847 550-8200
Ted Godek, *President*
Steven Godek, *Opers Mgr*
Augustyna Godek, *Treasurer*
EMP: 15
SQ FT: 6,800
SALES (est): 2MM **Privately Held**
SIC: 3599 Machine shop, jobbing & repair

(G-12419)
HPL STAMPINGS INC (PA)
425 Enterprise Pkwy (60047-6710)
PHONE 847 540-1400
Roger E Hedberg Jr, *President*
Gene Jasionowski, *Plant Mgr*
Rich Suvak, *Sales Executive*
Thomas R Gdovin, *Admin Sec*
Rose Wojcicki,
EMP: 49
SQ FT: 79,000
SALES (est): 5.5MM **Privately Held**
WEB: www.hplstampings.com
SIC: 3444 3469 Sheet metal specialties, not stamped; stamping metal for the trade

(G-12420)
HUNTLEY & ASSOCIATES INC
47 Carolyn Ct (60047-1506)
PHONE 224 381-8500
Craig Herriges, *President*
EMP: 3
SALES (est): 293.8K **Privately Held**
SIC: 8742 3441 3442 Management consulting services; fabricated structural metal; molding, trim & stripping

(G-12421)
INDUSTRIAL WIRE & CABLE CORP
66 N Buesching Rd (60047-1514)
PHONE 847 726-8910
Carl Calabrese, *CEO*
Christine Graham, *Vice Pres*
Stephanie Hadzima, *Human Resources*
Tom Lacalamita, *Sales Mgr*
Deborah Creighton, *Sales Staff*
▲ **EMP:** 29
SQ FT: 110
SALES (est): 7.3MM **Privately Held**
SIC: 3357 3496 Nonferrous wiredrawing & insulating; cable, uninsulated wire: made from purchased wire

(G-12422)
INDUSTRIAL WIRE CABLE II CORP
66 N Buesching Rd (60047-1514)
PHONE 847 726-8910
Carl Calabrese, *President*
Christine A Graham, *Exec VP*
▲ **EMP:** 16
SQ FT: 10,000
SALES (est): 4.1MM **Privately Held**
SIC: 3357 3351 Coaxial cable, nonferrous; appliance fixture wire, nonferrous; wire, copper & copper alloy

(G-12423)
INSIDE BEVERAGES
635 Oakwood Rd (60047-1518)
PHONE 847 438-1338
Andy Burke, *President*
EMP: 110
SQ FT: 87,000
SALES (est): 14.8MM **Privately Held**
SIC: 2045 2087 2066 Cake mixes, prepared: from purchased flour; powders, drink; instant cocoa

(G-12424)
INSIGHT BEVERAGES INC
750 Oakwood Rd (60047-1519)
PHONE 847 438-1598
EMP: 3 **Privately Held**
SIC: 2087 Beverage bases
HQ: Insight Beverages, Inc.
635 Oakwood Rd
Lake Zurich IL 60047

(G-12425)
INSIGHT BEVERAGES INC (DH)
Also Called: Kerry Zurich
635 Oakwood Rd (60047-1518)
PHONE 847 438-1598
Andrew F Burke, *CEO*
Gerard A Behan, *President*
VI Cabel, *Accounting Mgr*
Lanny M Schimmel, *Admin Sec*
◆ **EMP:** 23
SQ FT: 196,000
SALES (est): 41.8MM **Privately Held**
SIC: 2087 2095 2099 5499 Beverage bases; coffee extracts; tea blending; beverage stores
HQ: Kerry Inc.
3400 Millington Rd
Beloit WI 53511
608 363-1200

(G-12426)
JAY ELKA
Also Called: Dunkin' Donuts
1180 Heather Dr (60047-6707)
PHONE 847 540-7776
Jay Patel, *President*
EMP: 15
SQ FT: 3,400
SALES (est): 780K **Privately Held**
SIC: 5461 2051 Doughnuts; doughnuts, except frozen

(G-12427)
JLJ CORP
Also Called: Georges Printwear
250 Telser Rd Ste D (60047-1543)
PHONE 847 726-9795
John George, *President*
EMP: 3
SALES: 250K **Privately Held**
SIC: 2759 Screen printing

(G-12428)
LEGEND PROMOTIONS
Also Called: Legend Creative Group
815 Oakwood Rd Ste B (60047-6704)
PHONE 847 438-3528
David Voitik, *President*
EMP: 6
SQ FT: 500
SALES (est): 629.9K **Privately Held**
SIC: 7336 2791 2759 2752 Graphic arts & related design; typesetting; commercial printing; commercial printing, lithographic; advertising consultant

(G-12429)
LOCH PRECISION TECHNOLOGIES
Also Called: L P T
1215 Berkley Rd (60047-1827)
PHONE 847 438-1400
Terry Loch, *Owner*
Kathleen A Loch, *Nurse*
EMP: 6
SALES (est): 420.3K **Privately Held**
SIC: 3462 Gear & chain forgings

(G-12430)
MARIE GERE CORPORATION
1275 Ensell Rd (60047-1532)
PHONE 847 540-1154
James G Schultz, *President*
David Ohman, *Maintenance Dir*
Paul Swanson, *Purchasing*
Jorge Amaya, *QC Mgr*
Sheri Principato, *CFO*
▲ **EMP:** 170 **EST:** 1997
SQ FT: 165,000
SALES (est): 56.8MM **Privately Held**
WEB: www.geremarie.com
SIC: 3479 7379 8711 Aluminum coating of metal products; computer related consulting services; consulting engineer

(G-12431)
MELON INK SCREEN PRINT
100 Oakwood Rd Ste B (60047-1524)
PHONE 847 726-0003
EMP: 1
SALES: 500K **Privately Held**
SIC: 2759 Commercial Printing

(G-12432)
METROM LLC (NOT LLC)
904 Donata Ct (60047-5025)
PHONE 847 847-7233
Tony Scala,
FL Griffin,
EMP: 4
SALES (est): 292.5K **Privately Held**
SIC: 3545 Scales, measuring (machinists' precision tools)

(G-12433)
MILLENNIUM MOLD & TOOL
1194 Heather Dr (60047-6707)
PHONE 847 438-5600
Irene Gorney, *Principal*
EMP: 5

GEOGRAPHIC SECTION
Lake Zurich - Lake County (G-12462)

SALES (est): 610.4K **Privately Held**
SIC: 3544 Industrial molds; special dies & tools

(G-12434)
MINDFUL MIX
15 Maple Ave (60047-2323)
PHONE.................847 284-4404
Claire Slattery, *President*
EMP: 7
SALES (est): 819.5K **Privately Held**
SIC: 3273 Ready-mixed concrete

(G-12435)
MORGAN BRONZE PRODUCTS INC
340 E Il Route 22 (60047-2572)
PHONE.................847 526-6000
Ron Rogers, *President*
Scott Doorn, *General Mgr*
Ben Chelini, *Vice Pres*
Fred Talbot, *Maint Spvr*
Angel Custodio, *Production*
▲ **EMP:** 85
SQ FT: 70,000
SALES: 23.3MM **Privately Held**
WEB: www.morganbronze.com
SIC: 3599 5051 Machine shop, jobbing & repair; metals service centers & offices

(G-12436)
MOTHERBOARD GIFTS & MORE LLC
Also Called: J&M Acrylics
75 Oakwood Rd (60047-1566)
PHONE.................847 550-2222
Jay Silver, *Mng Member*
EMP: 3
SALES (est): 385.2K **Privately Held**
SIC: 2796 5087 5947 Engraving platemaking services; engraving equipment & supplies; gift shop

(G-12437)
MTECH CNC MACHINING INC
925 Telser Rd (60047-6752)
PHONE.................224 848-0818
Witold Zbierowski, *President*
EMP: 9
SQ FT: 6,000
SALES: 1.4MM **Privately Held**
SIC: 3599 Machine shop, jobbing & repair

(G-12438)
NATIONAL BUSHING & MFG
505 Oakwood Rd Ste 240 (60047-1534)
PHONE.................847 847-1553
John Carr, *President*
Lesley Carr, *Admin Sec*
EMP: 4
SQ FT: 2,000
SALES (est): 219.6K **Privately Held**
SIC: 3545 Drill bushings (drilling jig)

(G-12439)
NORTH STAR PICKLE LLC
968 Donata Ct (60047-5025)
PHONE.................847 970-5555
Jeff Oziemkowski,
Mike Alexander,
Steve Spector,
EMP: 10 **EST:** 2008
SALES (est): 1.1MM **Privately Held**
WEB: www.northstarpickle.com
SIC: 2035 Pickles, vinegar

(G-12440)
NORTHSTAR GROUP INC
577 Capital Dr (60047-6711)
PHONE.................847 726-0880
Karl Heerdegen, *President*
Amy Flaherty, *Director*
EMP: 10
SALES (est): 2MM **Privately Held**
SIC: 5112 2752 Business forms; color lithography

(G-12441)
OLIVET WOODWORKING
316 Hickory Rd (60047-2142)
PHONE.................773 505-5225
EMP: 4 **EST:** 2013
SALES (est): 232.4K **Privately Held**
SIC: 2431 Millwork

(G-12442)
PERFECTION PROBES INC
24241 W Rose Ave (60047-9362)
PHONE.................847 726-8868
Paul Christensen, *President*
EMP: 4
SQ FT: 1,400
SALES (est): 260K **Privately Held**
SIC: 3829 Physical property testing equipment

(G-12443)
PERFORMANCE DESIGN INC
Also Called: Pdi
238 Telser Rd (60047-1525)
PHONE.................847 719-1535
John A Fioretto, *President*
Deborah Fioretto, *Admin Sec*
EMP: 5
SQ FT: 7,000
SALES: 108K **Privately Held**
SIC: 3549 8711 3544 Assembly machines, including robotic; designing: ship, boat, machine & product; special dies, tools, jigs & fixtures

(G-12444)
PIXEL PUSHERS INCORPORATED
1050 Ensell Rd Ste 108 (60047-6709)
P.O. Box 1067, Palatine (60078-1067)
PHONE.................847 550-6560
Ryan Burke, *President*
EMP: 6
SALES (est): 462K **Privately Held**
WEB: www.pixelpushersinc.com
SIC: 3545 Pushers

(G-12445)
POWERNAIL COMPANY
1300 Rose Rd (60047-1554)
PHONE.................800 323-1653
David A Anstett, *President*
Tom Anstett, *President*
Joe Allyn, *Vice Pres*
David Anstett, *Vice Pres*
Tim Willems, *Accounts Mgr*
▲ **EMP:** 50
SALES (est): 25.7MM **Privately Held**
WEB: www.powernail.com
SIC: 5084 3546 3315 Machine tools & metalworking machinery; power-driven handtools; steel wire & related products

(G-12446)
PROTIDE PHARMACEUTICALS INC
220 Telser Rd (60047-1525)
PHONE.................847 726-3100
Milo R Polovina, *Ch of Bd*
EMP: 3
SQ FT: 9,500
SALES (est): 452.4K **Privately Held**
SIC: 2834 Pharmaceutical preparations

(G-12447)
QUARTER MASTER INDUSTRIES INC
510 Telser Rd (60047-1500)
PHONE.................847 540-8999
Ron Weinberg, *President*
Mike Levin, *Plant Mgr*
Donna Brunell, *Office Mgr*
EMP: 24
SQ FT: 12,000
SALES (est): 5.5MM **Privately Held**
WEB: www.quartermasterusa.com
SIC: 3714 Drive shafts, motor vehicle
HQ: Competition Cams, Inc.
3406 Democrat Rd
Memphis TN 38118
901 795-2400

(G-12448)
R AND R BROKERAGE CO (PA)
Also Called: C M Products
800 Ela Rd (60047-2340)
PHONE.................847 438-4600
Dave Randall, *President*
Mark Faber, *President*
Richard D Barton, *Vice Pres*
Michael F Jenkins, *Vice Pres*
Joe Hartmann, *Plant Mgr*
◆ **EMP:** 140
SQ FT: 300,000

SALES (est): 35.5MM **Privately Held**
WEB: www.dwfinepack.com
SIC: 3497 3089 Foil containers for bakery goods & frozen foods; tubs, plastic (containers)

(G-12449)
RETURN ON INV SYSTEMS INC
Also Called: R. O. I. Systems
950 Ensell Rd (60047-1557)
PHONE.................847 726-0081
James M Lehtinen, *President*
Dorothea Lehtinen, *Corp Secy*
EMP: 6
SQ FT: 4,200
SALES (est): 1.3MM **Privately Held**
SIC: 3535 Pneumatic tube conveyor systems

(G-12450)
REYCO PRECISION WELDING INC (PA)
320 E Il Route 22 (60047-2572)
PHONE.................847 593-2947
Jose Reyes, *President*
Marciala Reyes, *Admin Sec*
EMP: 14
SQ FT: 15,000
SALES (est): 1.7MM **Privately Held**
SIC: 3599 1799 Machine shop, jobbing & repair; welding on site

(G-12451)
ROBBINS HDD LLC
1221 Flex Ct (60047-1578)
PHONE.................847 955-0050
Roman Petryshyn, *Prdtn Mgr*
Felix Voskoboynik, *Engineer*
Oleg Raskin, *Mng Member*
Michael Verbato, *Manager*
Alexander Murovanny,
EMP: 11
SALES (est): 3MM **Privately Held**
SIC: 3541 Drilling & boring machines

(G-12452)
ROMED INDUSTRIES CORPORATION
320 E Il Route 22 (60047-2572)
PHONE.................847 362-3900
Oliver Osterhues, *President*
Inam Khan, *CFO*
EMP: 7
SQ FT: 10,000
SALES (est): 1.7MM **Privately Held**
SIC: 3599 Custom machinery

(G-12453)
SCHAFF INTERNATIONAL LLC
Also Called: Schaff Piano Supply
451 Oakwood Rd (60047-1516)
PHONE.................847 438-4560
Mike Donovan, *Plant Mgr*
Kevin Dwyer, *Sales Executive*
Stephen L Johnson,
David S Johnson,
Herbert L Johnson,
▲ **EMP:** 40 **EST:** 1867
SQ FT: 80,000
SALES (est): 8.7MM **Privately Held**
WEB: www.schaffinternational.com
SIC: 3495 3931 3496 Wire springs; musical instruments; miscellaneous fabricated wire products

(G-12454)
SCHNEIDER GRAPHICS INC
885 Telser Rd (60047-1536)
PHONE.................847 550-4310
Gregory Schneider, *President*
Justin Hess, *Vice Pres*
EMP: 25
SQ FT: 35,000
SALES (est): 5.8MM **Privately Held**
WEB: www.schneider-graphics.com
SIC: 2752 Commercial printing, offset

(G-12455)
SCHWEITZER ENGRG LABS INC
Fault Indicator & Sensor Div
450 Enterprise Pkwy (60047-6722)
PHONE.................847 362-8304
EMP: 100
SALES (corp-wide): 823.7MM **Privately Held**
SIC: 3825 Indicating instruments, electric

PA: Schweitzer Engineering Laboratories Inc.
2350 Ne Hopkins Ct
Pullman WA 99163
509 332-1890

(G-12456)
SESHIN USA INC
Also Called: Hiwood USA
333 Enterprise Pkwy (60047-6733)
PHONE.................847 550-5556
Brian Moon, *President*
Max Hahn, *Vice Pres*
▲ **EMP:** 6
SALES (est): 1.1MM **Privately Held**
SIC: 5023 2671 Frames & framing, picture & mirror; packaging paper & plastics film, coated & laminated

(G-12457)
SIGNSCAPES INC
884 S Rand Rd Ste D (60047-3412)
PHONE.................847 719-2610
Richard Palmblad, *President*
Gloria Palmblad, *Admin Sec*
EMP: 3
SALES: 200K **Privately Held**
SIC: 3993 Signs, not made in custom sign painting shops

(G-12458)
SMALLEY STEEL RING CO (PA)
555 Oakwood Rd (60047-1558)
PHONE.................847 537-7600
Michael A Greenhill, *President*
Charles Greenhill, *President*
Balan Chidambaram, *Vice Pres*
Mark A Greenhill, *Vice Pres*
Michael Greenhill, *Vice Pres*
▲ **EMP:** 110 **EST:** 1918
SALES (est): 64.3MM **Privately Held**
WEB: www.smalley.com
SIC: 3493 3495 Steel springs, except wire; wire springs

(G-12459)
SPIROLOX INC
555 Oakwood Rd (60047-1558)
PHONE.................847 719-5900
Mark Reno, *President*
EMP: 450
SALES (est): 16K
SALES (corp-wide): 64.3MM **Privately Held**
SIC: 3493 3495 Steel springs, except wire; wire springs
PA: Smalley Steel Ring Co.
555 Oakwood Rd
Lake Zurich IL 60047
847 537-7600

(G-12460)
STANDARD CONTAINER CO OF EDGAR (PA)
Also Called: Badger Basket Co
717 N Old Rand Rd (60047-2209)
PHONE.................847 438-1510
Gary Rasmussen, *President*
Janet Rasmussen, *Vice Pres*
▲ **EMP:** 21
SQ FT: 1,000
SALES (est): 17.7MM **Privately Held**
SIC: 2519 3944 5719 Wicker furniture: padded or plain; doll carriages & carts; bedding (sheets, blankets, spreads & pillows); bath accessories

(G-12461)
STANICK TOOL MANUFACTURING CO
1190 Heather Dr (60047-6707)
PHONE.................847 726-7090
Stanley S Kosjer, *President*
Edie Kosjer, *Principal*
EMP: 3
SALES (est): 327.6K **Privately Held**
SIC: 3544 Special dies & tools

(G-12462)
SWB INC
529 Capital Dr (60047-6711)
PHONE.................847 438-1800
Scot Braunling, *President*
▲ **EMP:** 4
SALES: 3.2MM **Privately Held**
SIC: 3545 Machine tool accessories

Lake Zurich - Lake County (G-12463)

GEOGRAPHIC SECTION

(G-12463)
TERMAX LLC (DH)
200 Telser Rd (60047-1525)
PHONE..................847 519-1500
Wes Gardocki, *President*
Michael Smith, *Co-CEO*
William R Smith, *Co-CEO*
Ken Bird, *Opers Staff*
Kenneth Bird, *Opers Staff*
▲ **EMP:** 188
SQ FT: 120,000
SALES (est): 65.3MM
SALES (corp-wide): 177.9K **Privately Held**
SIC: 3429 Metal fasteners
HQ: Lisi Automotive
2 Rue Juvenal Viellard
Grandvillars 90600
384 586-300

(G-12464)
TERMAX LLC
1155 Rose Rd Ste A (60047-1547)
PHONE..................847 519-1500
Michael Smith, *Co-CEO*
EMP: 3
SALES (corp-wide): 177.9K **Privately Held**
SIC: 3429 Metal fasteners
HQ: Termax Llc
200 Telser Rd
Lake Zurich IL 60047
847 519-1500

(G-12465)
TREDEGAR FILM PRODUCTS CORP
351 Oakwood Rd (60047-1509)
PHONE..................847 438-2111
Tim Rogers, *Production*
Carol Gillespie, *Purch Mgr*
Becky Bailey, *Technical Staff*
EMP: 170
SALES (corp-wide): 1B **Publicly Held**
WEB: www.tredegar.com
SIC: 3081 3089 Polyethylene film; plastic processing
HQ: Tredegar Film Products Corporation
1100 Boulders Pkwy # 200
North Chesterfield VA 23225

(G-12466)
TRUE WOODS CABINETRY INC
1050 Ensell Rd Ste 100 (60047-6709)
PHONE..................847 550-1860
Brian Peterson, *President*
EMP: 3
SQ FT: 2,800
SALES (est): 378K **Privately Held**
SIC: 2434 Wood kitchen cabinets

(G-12467)
TUF-TITE INC
1200 Flex Ct (60047-1578)
PHONE..................847 550-1011
Theodore W Meyers, *President*
Don Kimble, *Manager*
Edward Sadogierski, *Manager*
◆ **EMP:** 12
SQ FT: 40,000
SALES (est): 5.1MM **Privately Held**
SIC: 3089 Plastic hardware & building products

(G-12468)
VRG CONTROLS LLC
1199 Flex Ct Ste B (60047-1578)
PHONE..................844 356-9874
James M Garvey, *Mng Member*
Vladimir Rimboym, *Mng Member*
EMP: 27
SALES: 11MM **Privately Held**
SIC: 3492 Control valves, fluid power: hydraulic & pneumatic

(G-12469)
W & W ASSOCIATES INC
704 Telser Rd (60047-1576)
PHONE..................847 719-1760
Walter Toben, *President*
Katherine Toben, *Corp Secy*
EMP: 8
SQ FT: 1,620
SALES (est): 2.4MM **Privately Held**
SIC: 5131 2241 Labels; labels, woven

(G-12470)
WESTHEIMER CORP
100 Oakwood Rd Ste B (60047-1524)
PHONE..................847 498-9850
EMP: 3
SALES (est): 228.1K **Privately Held**
SIC: 3931 Musical instruments

Lakemoor
Mchenry County

(G-12471)
DENDRO CO
481 Scotland Rd Unit 102 (60051-8754)
PHONE..................312 772-6836
Sergey Podrez, *CEO*
EMP: 1
SQ FT: 2,400
SALES (est): 202.3K **Privately Held**
SIC: 2511 2521 Dining room furniture: wood; kitchen & dining room furniture; wood office furniture

(G-12472)
ILLINOIS RACK ENTERPRISES INC
480 Scotland Rd Ste A (60051-3001)
PHONE..................815 385-5750
Brian Mooney, *President*
Jorge Martinez, *Vice Pres*
EMP: 20
SQ FT: 9,000
SALES: 1.4MM **Privately Held**
SIC: 2542 3443 Racks, merchandise display or storage: except wood; fabricated plate work (boiler shop)

(G-12473)
PETERSEN SAND & GRAVEL INC
914 Rand Rd Ste A (60051-8709)
PHONE..................815 344-1060
Raymond J Petersen, *President*
Dennis Petersen, *Vice Pres*
Mike Mooney, *CFO*
EMP: 13 **EST:** 1950
SQ FT: 20
SALES (est): 1.2MM **Privately Held**
SIC: 1442 5211 Gravel mining; lumber & other building materials

(G-12474)
PODREZ ENTERPRISE LLC
Also Called: JMS Manufacturing
481 Scotland Rd Unit 102 (60051-8754)
PHONE..................815 353-5893
Sergey Podrez, *Principal*
EMP: 3
SALES (est): 200.4K **Privately Held**
SIC: 3531 Construction machinery attachments

(G-12475)
PRECISION GROUND
548 Herbert Rd Ste 2 (60051-8829)
PHONE..................815 578-2613
Kurt Suda, *President*
Ken Royce, *Vice Pres*
EMP: 12
SALES (est): 1.7MM **Privately Held**
SIC: 3599 Grinding castings for the trade

(G-12476)
PRINTING IMPRESSION DIREC
31704 N Clearwater Dr (60051-2203)
PHONE..................815 385-6688
James Maczko, *Owner*
Regia Maczko, *Vice Pres*
EMP: 6
SALES (est): 460.8K **Privately Held**
SIC: 2752 Commercial printing, offset

(G-12477)
STONECRAFTERS INC
430 W Wegner Rd (60051-8653)
PHONE..................815 363-8730
David Hammerl, *President*
▲ **EMP:** 45
SQ FT: 15,000
SALES (est): 10.9MM **Privately Held**
SIC: 5031 5719 5999 3281 Kitchen cabinets; bath accessories; monuments & tombstones; marble, building: cut & shaped; granite, cut & shaped; marble installation, interior

Lanark
Carroll County

(G-12478)
CARROLL COUNTY LOCKER
122 E Carroll St (61046-1144)
PHONE..................815 493-2370
Nancy Byington, *Owner*
EMP: 6
SQ FT: 1,800
SALES (est): 613.6K **Privately Held**
SIC: 4222 2013 Warehousing, cold storage or refrigerated; sausages & other prepared meats

(G-12479)
EASTLAND FABRICATION LLC
14273 Il Route 73 (61046-8860)
PHONE..................815 493-8399
Roger Coultherd, *Mng Member*
Terry Blair,
EMP: 4
SQ FT: 6,800
SALES (est): 410K **Privately Held**
SIC: 3443 Tanks, standard or custom fabricated: metal plate

(G-12480)
ELKAY MANUFACTURING COMPANY
Water Cooler Division
105 N Rochester St (61046-1149)
PHONE..................815 493-8850
Ed Perz, *Opers-Prdtn-Mfg*
EMP: 250
SALES (corp-wide): 1B **Privately Held**
WEB: www.elkay.com
SIC: 3585 Coolers, milk & water: electric
PA: Elkay Manufacturing Company Inc
1333 Butterfield Rd # 200
Downers Grove IL 60515
630 574-8484

(G-12481)
FORSTER PRODUCTS INC
310 Se Lanark Ave (61046-9704)
PHONE..................815 493-6360
Rodney P Hartman, *President*
Robert R Ruch, *CFO*
Robert Ruch, *CFO*
EMP: 21
SQ FT: 22,000
SALES (est): 2.9MM **Privately Held**
SIC: 3544 3545 Special dies & tools; precision tools, machinists'

(G-12482)
HYGIENIC FABRICS & FILTERS INC (PA)
Also Called: Bandage, The Div
118 S Broad St (61046-1204)
P.O. Box 34 (61046-0034)
PHONE..................815 493-2502
John F Wilson Jr, *President*
Tom Laiken, *Vice Pres*
EMP: 9 **EST:** 1959
SQ FT: 3,000
SALES (est): 2MM **Privately Held**
WEB: www.hyfab.com
SIC: 2211 Filter cloth, cotton; bags & bagging, cotton

Lansing
Cook County

(G-12483)
3V PALLET
2205 Thornton Lansing Rd (60438-2114)
PHONE..................708 333-1113
EMP: 4
SALES (est): 366.9K **Privately Held**
SIC: 2448 Mfg Wood Pallets/Skids

(G-12484)
AMERICAN CAST PRODUCTS INC
Also Called: Beverly Fndry Prcsion McHining
17730 Chicago Ave Frnt (60438-1964)
PHONE..................708 895-5152
Gordon W Fortier, *President*
Paul Menzel, *VP Opers*
Valerica Patrascu, *Opers Mgr*
Peter Zych, *Engineer*
John Seaton, *Electrical Engi*
▲ **EMP:** 12
SALES (est): 1.6MM **Privately Held**
SIC: 3364 Nonferrous die-castings except aluminum

(G-12485)
BEDFORD RAKIM
Also Called: Passco Parts & Electronics
3022 Bernice Ave Apt 3s (60438-1396)
PHONE..................773 749-3086
EMP: 3
SALES (est): 102.7K **Privately Held**
SIC: 3599 Mfg Industrial Machinery

(G-12486)
BYTTOW ENTERPRISES INC
18683 Forest View Ln (60438-4512)
PHONE..................708 372-4450
Norman Byttow, *President*
Mark Byttow, *Treasurer*
EMP: 4
SQ FT: 8,000
SALES (est): 422.4K **Privately Held**
SIC: 2434 2431 Wood kitchen cabinets; millwork

(G-12487)
CALUMET MOTORSPORTS INC
3441 Washington St (60438-2317)
PHONE..................708 895-0398
Thomas Milton, *President*
EMP: 3
SALES (est): 289.1K **Privately Held**
SIC: 3721 Aircraft

(G-12488)
CHICAGOS FINEST IRONWORKS
17564 Chicago Ave (60438-1925)
PHONE..................708 895-4484
John Micun, *President*
Bryan Hardy, *Vice Pres*
EMP: 6
SALES (est): 898.1K **Privately Held**
SIC: 3446 3496 2514 2511 Ornamental metalwork; miscellaneous fabricated wire products; metal household furniture; wood household furniture

(G-12489)
CONSTRUCTION CONTG SVCS INC
Also Called: Ccsi
1965 Bernice Rd Ste 1nw (60438-6031)
PHONE..................219 779-0900
Calvin E Williams, *President*
Kyle Taylor, *Vice Pres*
EMP: 11
SALES (est): 105.9K **Privately Held**
SIC: 8741 1521 1389 1522 Construction management; single-family housing construction; construction, repair & dismantling services; hotel/motel & multi-family home construction; multi-family dwellings, new construction

(G-12490)
DELITEFUL TASTE FOODS INC
18241 West St Ste 205 (60438-3282)
PHONE..................708 251-5121
Darryl Brown, *President*
Michael Davis, *COO*
Robert Irvin, *Exec VP*
EMP: 3 **EST:** 2013
SALES (est): 204.7K **Privately Held**
WEB: www.tastydelite.com
SIC: 2099 Seasonings & spices

(G-12491)
DMS INDUSTRIES INC (PA)
Also Called: Deny Machine Shop
1925 177th St (60438-1566)
PHONE..................708 895-8000
Steve Cirjakovich, *President*
EMP: 15

GEOGRAPHIC SECTION

Lansing - Cook County (G-12518)

SQ FT: 3,500
SALES (est): 2.8MM **Privately Held**
SIC: 3599 Machine shop, jobbing & repair

(G-12492)
EENIGENBURG MFG INC
19530 Burnham Ave (60438)
P.O. Box 286 (60438-0286)
PHONE...................708 474-0850
Robert Eenigenburg, *President*
Drew Eenigenburg, *Engineer*
Randall Eenigenburg, *Treasurer*
EMP: 7 **EST:** 1947
SQ FT: 5,840
SALES (est): 1.3MM **Privately Held**
WEB: www.eburgmfg.com
SIC: 3599 7692 Machine shop, jobbing & repair; welding repair

(G-12493)
FORZA CUSTOMS
17809 Torrence Ave (60438-1835)
PHONE...................708 474-6625
Rick Torre, *Principal*
EMP: 2
SALES (est): 273K **Privately Held**
SIC: 3312 Wheels

(G-12494)
GAYETY CANDY CO INC (PA)
Also Called: Gayetys Chocolates & Ice Cream
3306 Ridge Rd (60438-3112)
PHONE...................708 418-0062
EMP: 20 **EST:** 1920
SALES: 1.5MM **Privately Held**
SIC: 5441 5812 2066 2024 Ret Candy/Confectionery Eating Place Mfg Chocolate/Cocoa Prdt Mfg Ice Cream/Desserts

(G-12495)
GOOSE ISLAND MFG & SUPPLY CORP
Also Called: National Excelsior Company
17725 Volbrecht Rd Ste 1 (60438-4543)
PHONE...................708 343-4225
John Brady, *President*
William Cotugno, *Corp Secy*
Tom Milostan, *Exec VP*
Mike Boris Jr, *Vice Pres*
Chuck Dolezal, *Vice Pres*
EMP: 1 **EST:** 1886
SQ FT: 120,000
SALES (est): 8.5MM **Privately Held**
WEB: www.excelsiorhvac.com
SIC: 3444 5075 3585 3564 Furnace casings, sheet metal; warm air heating equipment & supplies; air conditioning & ventilation equipment & supplies; refrigeration & heating equipment; blowers & fans; architectural metalwork; heating equipment, except electric
HQ: Temperature Equipment Corporation
17725 Volbrecht Rd Ste 1
Lansing IL 60438
708 418-0900

(G-12496)
HADADY MACHINING COMPANY INC (PA)
16730 Chicago Ave (60438-1113)
PHONE...................708 474-8620
Peter Lanman, *President*
EMP: 12 **EST:** 1947
SQ FT: 16,000
SALES (est): 5.4MM **Privately Held**
WEB: www.hadadyinc.com
SIC: 3599 3823 3593 Machine shop, jobbing & repair; industrial instrmnts msrmnt display/control process variable; fluid power cylinders & actuators

(G-12497)
HBM ELECTRO CHEMICAL COMPANY
2800 Bernice Rd Ste 18 (60438-1271)
PHONE...................708 895-7710
Olga Mandich, *President*
Nick Mandich, *Principal*
EMP: 4
SQ FT: 8,000
SALES (est): 250K **Privately Held**
SIC: 3471 7389 7699 Chromium plating of metals or formed products; grinding, precision: commercial or industrial; hydraulic equipment repair

(G-12498)
ILLINOIS EXPEDITED EXPRESS INC
18227 Olde Farm Rd (60438-2553)
PHONE...................217 926-2171
Scot Robnett, *CEO*
EMP: 20
SALES (est): 745.5K **Privately Held**
SIC: 3462 Construction or mining equipment forgings, ferrous

(G-12499)
INNOVATIVE AUTOMATION
3116 192nd St (60438-3724)
PHONE...................708 418-8720
Ronald Carine, *Owner*
Karen Carine, *Admin Sec*
EMP: 1
SALES (est): 310K **Privately Held**
SIC: 5084 3053 Robots, industrial; packing materials

(G-12500)
KAMSTRA DOOR SERVICE INC
2007 Thornton Lansing Rd (60438-2111)
PHONE...................708 895-9990
Bruce Kamstra, *President*
Linda Kamstra, *Admin Sec*
EMP: 2
SQ FT: 2,000
SALES (est): 250K **Privately Held**
SIC: 5211 3699 Garage doors, sale & installation; door opening & closing devices, electrical

(G-12501)
KINGERY STEEL FABRICATORS INC
16895 Chicago Ave (60438-1197)
PHONE...................708 474-6665
David R Ash Jr, *President*
Joanne Ash, *Admin Sec*
EMP: 36
SQ FT: 10,000
SALES (est): 15.3MM **Privately Held**
SIC: 3441 Fabricated structural metal

(G-12502)
LAND OFROST INC (PA)
16850 Chicago Ave (60438-1115)
PHONE...................708 474-7100
Donna Van Eekeren, *Ch of Bd*
David Van Eekeren, *President*
Cami Guba, *Business Mgr*
Peter Burke, *Vice Pres*
Dave Funk, *Vice Pres*
▲ **EMP:** 225
SQ FT: 100,000
SALES (est): 86.9MM **Privately Held**
WEB: www.landofrost.com
SIC: 2099 2013 Ready-to-eat meals, salads & sandwiches; smoked meats from purchased meat

(G-12503)
LANSING CUT STONE CO
3125 Glenwood Lansing Rd (60438)
P.O. Box 5178 (60438-5178)
PHONE...................708 474-7515
John Boersma, *President*
Darlene Boersma, *Admin Sec*
EMP: 10
SQ FT: 7,000
SALES (est): 1.4MM **Privately Held**
WEB: www.lansingcutstone.com
SIC: 5032 3281 Granite building stone; cut stone & stone products

(G-12504)
LANSING WINGS INC
3720 Ridge Rd (60438-3319)
PHONE...................708 895-3300
Alan D Krygier, *President*
EMP: 3
SALES (est): 141.9K **Privately Held**
SIC: 2087 Beverage bases

(G-12505)
LIFETIME CREATIONS
17838 Chappel Ave (60438-4523)
PHONE...................708 895-2770
Pat Jensen, *President*
Elizabeth Lopez, *Graphic Designe*
EMP: 4
SALES (est): 455.7K **Privately Held**
SIC: 3479 Etching on metals

(G-12506)
LITHO TYPE LLC
16710 Chicago Ave (60438-1118)
P.O. Box 332 (60438-0332)
PHONE...................708 895-3720
Victor Arana, *Supervisor*
Edward Dewitt, *Executive*
Edward De Witt,
Edward D Witt,
EMP: 50
SQ FT: 27,000
SALES (est): 6.5MM **Privately Held**
SIC: 2752 Commercial printing, offset

(G-12507)
MAGNUM INTERNATIONAL INC
1965 Bernice Rd Ste 2se (60438-6052)
P.O. Box 1727, Calumet City (60409-7727)
PHONE...................708 889-9999
David Creech, *President*
Thomas S Eisner, *Admin Sec*
◆ **EMP:** 6
SQ FT: 2,600
SALES (est): 1.7MM **Privately Held**
SIC: 2851 5162 5169 Coating, air curing; plastics materials; chemicals, industrial & heavy

(G-12508)
MEDICAL CMMNCTIONS SYSTEMS INC (PA)
17595 Paxton Ave (60438-1514)
PHONE...................708 895-4500
William P Wilson, *President*
Ray Christner, *Vice Pres*
EMP: 3 **EST:** 1973
SQ FT: 7,500
SALES: 2MM **Privately Held**
SIC: 1731 3661 Telephone & telephone equipment installation; telephone & telegraph apparatus

(G-12509)
MINUTEMAN PRESS OF LANSING
17930 Torrence Ave Ste A (60438-1987)
PHONE...................708 895-0505
Karen C Kleine, *Owner*
EMP: 6
SQ FT: 1,700
SALES (est): 595.1K **Privately Held**
SIC: 2752 Commercial printing, lithographic

(G-12510)
NB COATINGS INC (DH)
2701 E 170th St (60438-1107)
PHONE...................800 323-3224
Kristina Nelson, *CEO*
Richard Derrick, *Superintendent*
Mitsuo Yamada, *Chairman*
Alan Thomas, *Business Mgr*
Hidefumi Morita, *Corp Secy*
▲ **EMP:** 250 **EST:** 1945
SQ FT: 160,000
SALES (est): 119.8MM **Privately Held**
WEB: www.nbcoatings.com
SIC: 2851 2865 Plastics base paints & varnishes; coating, air curing; color pigments, organic

(G-12511)
PERKINS PENCIL CO
3059 192nd St (60438-3721)
P.O. Box 237 (60438-0237)
PHONE...................708 363-9249
Paul Reese, *Owner*
EMP: 4
SALES (est): 285.6K **Privately Held**
SIC: 5199 3952 3951 Advertising specialties; lead pencils & art goods; pens & mechanical pencils

(G-12512)
PRINTMEISTERS INC
3240 Ridge Rd (60438-3193)
PHONE...................708 474-8400
Christine Widstrand, *President*
EMP: 4
SQ FT: 1,250
SALES (est): 290K **Privately Held**
SIC: 2752 7334 2791 2789 Commercial printing, offset; photocopying & duplicating services; typesetting; bookbinding & related work; commercial printing

(G-12513)
QUICK QUALITY PRINTING INC
Also Called: Sign-A-Rama
17332 Torrence Ave (60438-1019)
PHONE...................708 895-5885
Virginia Jokubauskas, *President*
Peter Jokubauskas, *Vice Pres*
EMP: 3
SQ FT: 2,000
SALES (est): 300K **Privately Held**
SIC: 3993 Signs & advertising specialties

(G-12514)
SEALS & COMPONENTS INC
Also Called: Seal Jet Unlimited
17955 Chappel Ave (60438-4526)
PHONE...................708 895-5222
Barbara Baney, *President*
Michael Baney, *Treasurer*
Janice Clark, *Director*
John Clark, *Director*
EMP: 5
SQ FT: 2,000
SALES (est): 647.1K **Privately Held**
SIC: 3053 3089 3492 Gaskets, all materials; extruded finished plastic products; fluid power valves & hose fittings

(G-12515)
SECURECOM INC
3338 E 170th St (60438-1142)
P.O. Box 5302 (60438-5302)
PHONE...................219 314-4537
Michael Banach, *President*
EMP: 2
SALES (est): 200K **Privately Held**
SIC: 3669 Communications equipment

(G-12516)
SILVER LINE BUILDING PDTS LLC
Also Called: Silverline Windows
16801 Exchange Ave Ste 2 (60438-6040)
PHONE...................708 474-9100
Ken Silverman, *CEO*
Danny Hall, *Sales Staff*
EMP: 500
SALES (corp-wide): 4.8B **Publicly Held**
WEB: www.silverlinewindows.com
SIC: 3089 3442 Window screening, plastic; metal doors, sash & trim
HQ: Silver Line Building Products Llc
1 Silverline Dr
North Brunswick NJ 08902
732 435-1000

(G-12517)
STANDARD PRECISION GRINDING CO
2800 Bernice Rd Ste 1 (60438-1282)
PHONE...................708 474-1211
Cynthia Bauer, *President*
▲ **EMP:** 12 **EST:** 1947
SQ FT: 20,000
SALES (est): 1.9MM **Privately Held**
WEB: www.standardprecisiongrinding.com
SIC: 3599 Machine shop, jobbing & repair

(G-12518)
STATE LINE INTERNATIONAL INC
18107 Torrence Ave (60438-2157)
PHONE...................708 251-5772
Jamel Mitchell, *Vice Pres*
EMP: 6
SALES (est): 352.6K **Privately Held**
SIC: 3569 5331 Robots, assembly line: industrial & commercial; variety stores

Lansing - Cook County (G-12519)   **GEOGRAPHIC SECTION**

(G-12519)
STEEL SERVICES ENTERPRISES
17500 Paxton Ave (60438-1696)
PHONE.................................708 259-1181
Stephen H Leeson, *President*
Josh Leeson, *Vice Pres*
EMP: 30
SQ FT: 3,000
SALES: 18MM **Privately Held**
SIC: **1791** 7692 3444 Iron work, structural; storage tanks, metal: erection; welding repair; sheet metalwork

(G-12520)
SUPERIOR METALCRAFT INC
17655 Chappel Ave (60438-4544)
PHONE.................................708 418-8940
Joshua A Lesson, *President*
Charles Brent, *Vice Pres*
EMP: 14
SALES: 3.8MM **Privately Held**
SIC: **3441** Fabricated structural metal

(G-12521)
TARTE CUPCAKERY COMPANY
18509 School St Apt 1d (60438-2947)
P.O. Box 744 (60438-0744)
PHONE.................................312 898-2103
EMP: 5
SALES (est): 182.2K **Privately Held**
SIC: **2051** Bread, cake & related products

(G-12522)
TOTH AUTOMOTIVE
1621 Thornton Lansing Rd (60438-1595)
PHONE.................................708 474-5137
James Toth, *Owner*
EMP: 10
SQ FT: 7,200
SALES (est): 1.7MM **Privately Held**
SIC: **5013** 3599 Automotive supplies & parts; machine shop, jobbing & repair

(G-12523)
V & C CONVERTERS
3511 Illinois St (60438-3393)
PHONE.................................708 251-5635
EMP: 3
SALES (est): 236.3K **Privately Held**
SIC: **3535** Mfg Conveyors/Equipment

(G-12524)
VECTOR ENGINEERING & MFG CORP
17506 Chicago Ave (60438-1925)
PHONE.................................708 474-3900
Daryl P Sullivan, *President*
▲ EMP: 20
SQ FT: 21,600
SALES (est): 3.1MM **Privately Held**
SIC: **3599** 3536 Machine shop, jobbing & repair; hoists, cranes & monorails

(G-12525)
ZEGERS INC
16727 Chicago Ave (60438-1196)
PHONE.................................708 474-7700
William H Zegers, *President*
Nancy Z Mitros, *Vice Pres*
EMP: 15 EST: 1931
SQ FT: 65,000
SALES (est): 2.2MM **Privately Held**
WEB: www.zegers-inc.com
SIC: **3479** Coating of metals & formed products

Lawrenceville
Lawrence County

(G-12526)
AMBRAW ASPHALT MATERIALS INC
S 15th St (62439)
P.O. Box 551 (62439-0551)
PHONE.................................618 943-4716
Kenneth Kavanaugh, *President*
John B Kavanaugh, *Corp Secy*
Shirley K Kavanaugh, *Vice Pres*
Troy Zeigler, *Project Mgr*
EMP: 25 EST: 1954
SQ FT: 6,000
SALES (est): 4.2MM **Privately Held**
WEB: www.ambrawasphalt.com
SIC: **1611** 2951 General contractor, highway & street construction; asphalt paving mixtures & blocks

(G-12527)
ASPHALT PRODUCTS INC
Also Called: Amberaw Asphalt Materials
6574 Akin Rd (62439-4062)
P.O. Box 551 (62439-0551)
PHONE.................................618 943-4716
Kenneth Kavanaugh, *President*
John B Kavanough, *Corp Secy*
Shirley K Kavanaugh, *Vice Pres*
EMP: 25
SALES (est): 4.2MM **Privately Held**
SIC: **2951** Asphalt & asphaltic paving mixtures (not from refineries)

(G-12528)
CENTRAL INDUSTRIES OF INDIANA
13301 Tinker St (62439-4930)
PHONE.................................618 943-2311
Terry Silver, *President*
EMP: 3
SALES (est): 222.1K **Privately Held**
SIC: **3679** Harness assemblies for electronic use: wire or cable

(G-12529)
DAILY LAWRENCEVILLE RECORD
Also Called: The Daily Record
1209 State St (62439-2332)
P.O. Box 639, Robinson (62454-0639)
PHONE.................................618 943-2331
Mike Van Dorn, *Manager*
EMP: 12
SALES (corp-wide): 827.6K **Privately Held**
WEB: www.robdailynews.com
SIC: **2711** Newspapers: publishing only, not printed on site
PA: Daily Lawrenceville Record Inc
1209 State St
Lawrenceville IL 62439
618 544-2101

(G-12530)
DAILY LAWRENCEVILLE RECORD (PA)
Also Called: Daily News/Daily Record
1209 State St (62439-2332)
P.O. Box 639, Robinson (62454-0639)
PHONE.................................618 544-2101
Larry H Lewis, *President*
Kathy Lewis, *Admin Sec*
EMP: 2
SALES (est): 827.6K **Privately Held**
SIC: **2711** Newspapers: publishing only, not printed on site

(G-12531)
EMULSIONS INC
1105 Adams St (62439-2614)
P.O. Box 147 (62439-0147)
PHONE.................................618 943-2615
Earl Kavanaugh, *President*
Robert Kizer, *Admin Sec*
EMP: 7
SQ FT: 2,000
SALES (est): 1MM **Privately Held**
SIC: **2951** Asphalt & asphaltic paving mixtures (not from refineries)

(G-12532)
FRANKLIN WELL SERVICES INC
10483 May Chapel Rd (62439-4791)
P.O. Box 237, Vincennes IN (47591-0237)
PHONE.................................812 494-2800
Donald E Jones Jr, *President*
Brent Jones, *President*
Matt Donaldson, *Opers Mgr*
Mark A Jones, *Admin Sec*
EMP: 55
SALES (est): 5.4MM **Privately Held**
SIC: **1389** Oil field services

(G-12533)
GREGORY GRAVEL CO
Also Called: Gregory's Gravel Pit
11403 Club Kilroy Rd (62439-4308)
PHONE.................................618 943-2796
Hayward Gregory, *Owner*
EMP: 7
SALES (est): 144.1K **Privately Held**
SIC: **1442** Gravel mining; common sand mining

(G-12534)
HALTER MACHINE SHOP INC
9452 Peachtree Rd (62439-4812)
P.O. Box 867 (62439-0867)
PHONE.................................618 943-2224
Patrick Halter, *President*
Renee Halter, *Admin Sec*
EMP: 4 EST: 1975
SQ FT: 9,000
SALES: 500K **Privately Held**
SIC: **3599** 7692 Machine shop, jobbing & repair; welding repair

(G-12535)
HERMAN L LOEB LLC
Also Called: Loeb Oil
600 Country Club Rd (62439-3369)
P.O. Box 838 (62439-0838)
PHONE.................................618 943-2227
Janette Loeb, *Mng Member*
Dan McGrew, *Area Spvr*
Shane Pelton, *Area Spvr*
Diane Lebovitz,
Edward Loeb,
EMP: 50
SQ FT: 1,800
SALES (est): 45MM **Privately Held**
SIC: **1311** Crude petroleum production

(G-12536)
NU-LIFE INC OF ILLINOIS
Hwy 1 S (62439)
P.O. Box 450 (62439-0450)
PHONE.................................618 943-4500
Herman Brinkley, *President*
Frances Brinkley, *Admin Sec*
EMP: 7
SQ FT: 24,500
SALES (est): 750K **Privately Held**
SIC: **2389** Men's miscellaneous accessories

(G-12537)
TOYOTA BOSHOKU ILLINOIS LLC
Also Called: A T S
100 Trim Masters Dr (62439-9501)
PHONE.................................618 943-5300
Akira Furusawa, *CEO*
Shuhei Toyoda, *President*
Shigetoshi Miyoshi, *COO*
Mark Boren, *Mfg Dir*
▲ EMP: 470
SQ FT: 209,000
SALES (est): 126.4MM **Privately Held**
SIC: **3714** Motor vehicle parts & accessories
HQ: Toyota Boshoku America, Inc.
1360 Dolwick Dr Ste 125
Erlanger KY 41018
859 817-4000

(G-12538)
TRACY ELECTRIC INC
Also Called: T-P Electric & Manufacturing
1308 Jefferson St (62439-2418)
PHONE.................................618 943-6205
Robert W Tracy, *President*
Angie Sweeten, *Admin Sec*
EMP: 33
SQ FT: 12,200
SALES (est): 6.2MM **Privately Held**
SIC: **1731** 1711 7694 3621 General electrical contractor; refrigeration contractor; rewinding services; electric motor repair; phase or rotary converters (electrical equipment)

Le Roy
Mclean County

(G-12539)
DEN GRAPHIX INC
111 S Chestnut St (61752-1782)
PHONE.................................309 962-2000
Bill Frautchi, *President*
EMP: 15 EST: 1992
SALES (est): 1.3MM **Privately Held**
SIC: **2759** Screen printing

(G-12540)
OMNI-TECH SYSTEMS INC
Also Called: Permabilt of Illinois
7 Demma Dr (61752-9792)
PHONE.................................309 962-2281
Richard Janko, *President*
Dominic Pasquale, *Vice Pres*
Michael Janko, *Treasurer*
EMP: 20 EST: 1971
SQ FT: 12,000
SALES (est): 2.2MM **Privately Held**
SIC: **2452** Prefabricated buildings, wood

Leaf River
Ogle County

(G-12541)
ENGLE MANUFACTURING CO
214 Main St (61047-9797)
P.O. Box 220 (61047-0220)
PHONE.................................815 738-2282
Jeffery Engle, *Managing Prtnr*
Lester Engle, *Partner*
EMP: 10 EST: 1965
SQ FT: 16,000
SALES (est): 1.3MM **Privately Held**
SIC: **3599** Machine shop, jobbing & repair

(G-12542)
GLORIUS RENDITIONS
508 E Third St (61047-4500)
PHONE.................................815 315-0177
Patricia Marie Mitchell, *Partner*
Sharon Mitchell, *Partner*
EMP: 6
SALES (est): 241.8K **Privately Held**
SIC: **2741** Miscellaneous publishing

Lebanon
St. Clair County

(G-12543)
CHRIST BROS PRODUCTS LLC
820 S Fritz St (62254-1720)
P.O. Box 158 (62254-0158)
PHONE.................................618 537-6174
Mark Christ, *Mng Member*
EMP: 6
SALES (est): 770K **Privately Held**
SIC: **2951** Asphalt paving mixtures & blocks

(G-12544)
CUSTOM COATING INNOVATIONS INC
30 Commerce Dr (62254-2541)
PHONE.................................618 808-0500
Kyle McCarter, *President*
Sue Doncarlos, *Business Mgr*
Joe Behnken, *Vice Pres*
EMP: 15
SQ FT: 6,000
SALES (est): 2.1MM **Privately Held**
SIC: **3089** Injection molding of plastics

(G-12545)
CUSTOM PRODUCT INNOVATIONS
40 Commerce Dr (62254-2541)
PHONE.................................618 628-0111
Kyle Mc Carter, *President*
Victoria McCarter, *Vice Pres*
Carol Ashcraft, *Office Mgr*
▲ EMP: 7
SQ FT: 16,000
SALES (est): 1.7MM **Privately Held**
WEB: www.go2cpi.com
SIC: **3069** Rubber coated fabrics & clothing

(G-12546)
PRESCRIPTION PLUS LTD (PA)
Also Called: True Value
753 True Value Dr (62254-1593)
PHONE.................................618 537-6202
Louis Schlaefer, *President*
Jackie Schlaefer, *Admin Sec*

GEOGRAPHIC SECTION

Lemont - Cook County (G-12576)

EMP: 15 **EST:** 1979
SQ FT: 10,000
SALES (est): 2.2MM Privately Held
SIC: 5251 5912 2851 5021 Hardware; drug stores; paints & allied products; outdoor & lawn furniture; paint, glass & wallpaper

Leland
Lasalle County

(G-12547)
BILT-RITE METAL PRODUCTS INC
Also Called: Bilt-Rite Metal Products
100 E North St (60531-3138)
P.O. Box 97 (60531-0097)
PHONE.................................815 495-2211
EMP: 30 **EST:** 1950
SQ FT: 65,000
SALES (est): 2.5MM Privately Held
SIC: 3648 3469 2542 3444 Mfg Sheet Metalwork Mfg Lighting Equipment Mfg Metal Stampings

(G-12548)
CALCON MACHINE INC
210 E Lincoln Ave (60531-9748)
P.O. Box 9 (60531-0009)
PHONE.................................815 495-9227
Victor J Brown Jr, *President*
Phil Brown, *Vice Pres*
Thomas Brown, *Marketing Staff*
Irma Brown, *Admin Sec*
EMP: 8
SQ FT: 10,000
SALES (est): 500K Privately Held
SIC: 3451 Screw machine products

(G-12549)
PRODUCTION STAMPINGS INC
1864 N 4253rd Rd (60531-9772)
PHONE.................................815 495-2800
Michael E Mayton, *President*
EMP: 7
SQ FT: 6,500
SALES (est): 330K Privately Held
SIC: 3469 Stamping metal for the trade

Lemont
Cook County

(G-12550)
A BARR FTN BEVERAGE SLS & SVC
16300 103rd St (60439-9666)
PHONE.................................708 442-2000
Thomas Barc, *President*
EMP: 60
SALES (est): 5.6MM Privately Held
SIC: 2087 Syrups, drink

(G-12551)
A&B RELIABLE
190 Munster Rd (60439-4452)
PHONE.................................708 228-6148
Vilma Ratkeviciute, *Principal*
◆ **EMP:** 2 **EST:** 2008
SALES (est): 232.7K Privately Held
SIC: 3822 Water heater controls

(G-12552)
AMERICAN CAST STONE
14563 136th St (60439-7925)
PHONE.................................630 291-0250
Robert Blaho, *Principal*
EMP: 8
SALES (est): 811K Privately Held
SIC: 3272 Concrete products, precast

(G-12553)
AMFAB LLC
1385 101st St Ste A (60439-9631)
PHONE.................................630 783-2570
David A Oestermeyer,
▼ **EMP:** 8
SALES: 2.5MM Privately Held
SIC: 3743 Railroad locomotives & parts, electric or nonelectric

(G-12554)
ASHTON DIVERSIFIED ENTERPRISES
19w442 Deerpath Ln (60439-8898)
PHONE.................................630 739-0981
Lina J Schade, *President*
EMP: 6
SALES (est): 431.8K Privately Held
SIC: 2452 Farm & agricultural buildings, prefabricated wood

(G-12555)
B & B SPECIALTY COMPANY INC
139 Timberline Dr (60439-4425)
PHONE.................................708 652-9234
William Harrison, *President*
EMP: 4 **EST:** 1943
SQ FT: 6,250
SALES (est): 300K Privately Held
SIC: 3599 Machine shop, jobbing & repair

(G-12556)
BARTECH PRECISION MACHINING CO
16135 New Ave Ste 3 (60439-2648)
PHONE.................................630 243-9068
Abdul Labaran, *President*
Bart Hypta, *Vice Pres*
EMP: 15
SQ FT: 5,000
SALES (est): 2.2MM Privately Held
SIC: 3599 Machine shop, jobbing & repair

(G-12557)
BROMBEREKS FLAGSTONE CO INC (PA)
910 Singer Ave (60439-3929)
PHONE.................................630 257-0686
Ronald Bromberek, *President*
Larry Bromberek, *Vice Pres*
EMP: 9
SALES (est): 971.2K Privately Held
SIC: 3281 Stone, quarrying & processing of own stone products

(G-12558)
CARROLL DISTRG & CNSTR SUP INC
13087 Main St (60439-9373)
PHONE.................................630 243-0272
Mike Petkovich, *Branch Mgr*
EMP: 4
SALES (corp-wide): 128.2MM Privately Held
SIC: 5082 3444 Contractors' materials; concrete forms, sheet metal
PA: Carroll Distributing & Construction Supply, Inc.
207 W 2nd St Ste 3
Ottumwa IA 52501
641 683-1888

(G-12559)
CCI MANUFACTURING IL CORP
15550 Canal Bank Rd (60439-3885)
P.O. Box 339 (60439-0339)
PHONE.................................630 739-0606
Okabe Shuji, *CEO*
Tetsuya Okabe, *President*
◆ **EMP:** 38
SQ FT: 30,000
SALES (est): 16MM Privately Held
SIC: 2899 Chemical preparations
HQ: Cci Corporation
12, Shinhasama
Seki GIF 501-3

(G-12560)
CHALON WOOD PRODUCTS INC
12670 111th St (60439-9327)
PHONE.................................630 243-9793
EMP: 3 **EST:** 2003
SALES: 360K Privately Held
SIC: 2435 Mfg Hardwood Veneer/Plywood

(G-12561)
CHICAGO MATERIALS CORPORATION
13769 Main St (60439-9310)
PHONE.................................630 257-5600
EMP: 35
SALES (est): 6MM
SALES (corp-wide): 27.4MM Privately Held
SIC: 3531 Construction Machinery, Nsk
PA: K-Five Construction Corporation
999 Oakmont Plaza Dr # 200
Westmont IL 60559
630 257-5600

(G-12562)
D & B FABRICATORS & DISTRS
16w065 Jeans Rd Ste A (60439-8974)
PHONE.................................630 325-3811
John D Young Jr, *President*
EMP: 15
SALES (est): 2.5MM Privately Held
WEB: www.dbfabricators.com
SIC: 3411 3531 3523 3469 Metal cans; construction machinery; farm machinery & equipment; metal stampings; metal barrels, drums & pails

(G-12563)
DUNBAR SYSTEMS INC (PA)
1186 Walter St (60439-3993)
PHONE.................................630 257-2900
Michael Dunbar, *CEO*
Mark Dunbar, *President*
George Dunbar, *Chairman*
Charles Kazen, *Controller*
Kenneth Wisz, *Controller*
▲ **EMP:** 15
SQ FT: 6,000
SALES (est): 4.9MM Privately Held
SIC: 2051 2045 Bread, cake & related products; bread & bread type roll mixes: from purchased flour

(G-12564)
FULL CIRCLE SHIPYARD LLC
13108 Grant Rd (60439-7726)
PHONE.................................630 343-2264
EMP: 5 **EST:** 2008
SALES (est): 759.5K Privately Held
WEB: www.fullcircleterminal.com
SIC: 3731 Shipbuilding & repairing

(G-12565)
GREEN APU LLC
13067 Main St (60439-9373)
PHONE.................................310 736-2211
Arkadiusz Gruszka, *Principal*
EMP: 3
SALES (est): 417.5K Privately Held
WEB: www.greenapu.com
SIC: 3724 External power units, for hand inertia starters, aircraft

(G-12566)
IDI FABRICATION INC
1385 101st St (60439-9630)
PHONE.................................630 783-2246
Scott Doll, *Branch Mgr*
EMP: 10 Privately Held
WEB: www.idifabrication.com
SIC: 3567 Induction & dielectric heating equipment
PA: Idi Fabrication, Inc.
14444 Herriman Blvd
Noblesville IN 46060

(G-12567)
K TRANSCO INC
13207 W Hunt Master Ln (60439-8169)
PHONE.................................630 881-5411
Kristina Komijenko, *Principal*
EMP: 4
SALES (est): 403.1K Privately Held
SIC: 3535 Conveyors & conveying equipment

(G-12568)
KEY COLONY INC
Also Called: Red Parrot Juices
16300 103rd St (60439-9666)
PHONE.................................630 783-8572
James Behrens, *President*
Janice Baisden, *Admin Sec*
EMP: 6
SALES (est): 693.8K Privately Held
SIC: 2087 2086 2037 2033 Fruit juices: concentrated for fountain use; bottled & canned soft drinks; frozen fruits & vegetables; canned fruits & specialties

(G-12569)
LEMONT SCRAP PROCESSING
16229 New Ave (60439-3684)
PHONE.................................630 257-6532
Leslie A Dudek, *President*
Les Dudek, *Human Res Mgr*
EMP: 8
SALES (est): 2.1MM Privately Held
WEB: www.lemontscrap.com
SIC: 5093 3341 Ferrous metal scrap & waste; metal scrap & waste materials; secondary nonferrous metals

(G-12570)
MACHINING TECHNOLOGY INC
Also Called: Grem Machining Division
418 Keepataw Dr (60439-4341)
PHONE.................................815 469-0400
Tom Guimont, *President*
▼ **EMP:** 4
SQ FT: 4,500
SALES (est): 417.9K Privately Held
SIC: 3599 Machine shop, jobbing & repair

(G-12571)
MENO STONE CO INC
10800 Route 83 (60439-4700)
PHONE.................................630 257-9220
Michael Meno, *President*
Joseph Meno Jr, *Corp Secy*
Dan Wollenberg, *Sales Associate*
EMP: 35
SQ FT: 32,000
SALES (est): 6.6MM Privately Held
SIC: 3441 1741 3281 3271 Fabricated structural metal; stone masonry; cut stone & stone products; concrete block & brick

(G-12572)
MISSION SIGNS INC
1415 Chestnut Xing (60439-7488)
PHONE.................................630 243-6731
Fax: 708 226-8119
EMP: 2
SALES (est): 265.6K Privately Held
SIC: 3993 Mfg Signs/Advertising Specialties

(G-12573)
NORTHERN ILLINOIS REAL ESTATE
1244 State St Ste 351 (60439-4489)
PHONE.................................630 257-2480
Roger Krieg, *President*
Mary Ann Wilke, *Sales Mgr*
Maryann Krieg, *Sales Staff*
EMP: 7
SALES: 400K Privately Held
WEB: www.niremag.com
SIC: 2721 Magazines: publishing & printing

(G-12574)
OAKRIDGE CORPORATION
Also Called: Oakridge Hobbies
15800 New Ave (60439-3659)
P.O. Box 247 (60439-0247)
PHONE.................................630 435-5900
Terrance Robb, *President*
EMP: 4
SQ FT: 6,500
SALES (est): 574.7K Privately Held
SIC: 3944 5945 Trains & equipment, toy: electric & mechanical; hobby, toy & game shops

(G-12575)
OUTDOOR NOTEBOOK PUBLISHING
14805 131st St (60439-7444)
PHONE.................................630 257-6534
EMP: 10
SQ FT: 1,200
SALES (est): 600K Privately Held
SIC: 2721 Publishes Tabloid Magazine

(G-12576)
OXBOW CARBON LLC
Also Called: Oxbow Midwest
12308 New Ave (60439-3686)
PHONE.................................630 257-7751
Jessica Maldonado, *Marketing Mgr*
Brett Wiltshire, *Branch Mgr*
EMP: 22

Lemont - Cook County (G-12577) — GEOGRAPHIC SECTION

SALES (corp-wide): 446.2MM **Privately Held**
SIC: 2911 Coke, petroleum
HQ: Oxbow Carbon Llc
   1601 Forum Pl Ste 1400
   West Palm Beach FL 33401

(G-12577)
OXBOW MIDWEST CALCINING LLC
12308 New Ave (60439-3686)
PHONE..................630 257-7751
Steve Fried, *President*
Rich Callahan, *Vice Pres*
Tony Grimes, *Vice Pres*
Eric Johnson, *Vice Pres*
Zachery Shipley, *CFO*
EMP: 75
SALES (est): 11.1MM
SALES (corp-wide): 446.2MM **Privately Held**
SIC: 2911 Coke, petroleum
HQ: Oxbow Carbon Llc
   1601 Forum Pl Ste 1400
   West Palm Beach FL 33401

(G-12578)
PATRICK IMPRESSIONS LLC
Also Called: Rainbow Printing
16135 New Ave Ste 1a (60439-2605)
PHONE..................630 257-9336
Patrick O'Neil,
EMP: 3
SALES (est): 345.7K **Privately Held**
SIC: 2752 2791 2789 2759 Commercial printing, offset; typesetting; bookbinding & related work; commercial printing

(G-12579)
PATTI GROUP INCORPORATED (PA)
12301 New Ave Ste A (60439-3676)
PHONE..................630 243-6320
Dale Patti, *President*
Nick Patti, *Vice Pres*
▲ EMP: 10
SQ FT: 3,000
SALES (est): 2.5MM **Privately Held**
SIC: 2653 Solid fiber boxes, partitions, display items & sheets

(G-12580)
PAWZ & KLAWZ
12263 Walker Rd (60439-4558)
PHONE..................630 257-0245
Norb Siwek, *President*
EMP: 5
SALES (est): 406.4K **Privately Held**
SIC: 3999 Pet supplies

(G-12581)
PDV MIDWEST REFINING LLC
Also Called: Citgo Refinery
135th St New Ave (60439)
PHONE..................630 257-7761
Jenny Allums, *President*
Carlos Jorda,
Oswaldo Contreras Maza,
Andres Riera,
EMP: 540
SALES (est): 121.4MM **Privately Held**
SIC: 2992 2911 5171 4213 Lubricating oils & greases; petroleum refining; petroleum bulk stations & terminals; trucking, except local
HQ: Pdv America, Inc.
   1293 Eldridge Pkwy
   Houston TX 77077

(G-12582)
PHOENIX INKS AND COATINGS LLC
20w267 101st St (60439-9672)
PHONE..................630 972-2500
Sheryl A Desanto, *Principal*
EMP: 19
SALES (est): 4.3MM **Privately Held**
SIC: 2899 Ink or writing fluids

(G-12583)
PLASTIC FILM CORP AMERICA INC (PA)
Also Called: PFC
1011 State St Ste 140 (60439-4381)
PHONE..................630 887-0800
Joel Bittner, *President*
Janelle Bittner-Kittrid, *Vice Pres*
Felix Lanier, *Purchasing*
Jim Drake, *Manager*
Kim Lupescu, *Assistant*
◆ EMP: 15 EST: 1982
SALES (est): 5MM **Privately Held**
WEB: www.plasticfilmcorporation.com
SIC: 3089 5162 Plastic processing; plastics sheets & rods

(G-12584)
PODHALANSKA LLC
1304 Oakmont Dr Unit 10 (60439-6444)
PHONE..................630 247-9256
Rene T Skorusa,
EMP: 8
SALES (est): 562.6K **Privately Held**
SIC: 2085 Vodka (alcoholic beverage)

(G-12585)
PRESS DOUGH INC
22 Longwood Way (60439-4479)
PHONE..................630 243-6900
James Bartley, *Principal*
EMP: 4
SALES (est): 281K **Privately Held**
SIC: 2741 Miscellaneous publishing

(G-12586)
QUALITY QUICKPRINT INC (PA)
Also Called: Quick Print
1258 Cronin Ct (60439-8579)
PHONE..................815 723-0941
Janet Fisher, *President*
Jeffery Fisher, *Admin Sec*
EMP: 7
SALES (est): 1.1MM **Privately Held**
SIC: 2752 7334 Commercial printing, offset; photocopying & duplicating services

(G-12587)
QUANTUM MARKETING LLC
Also Called: Quantum Packaging
12305 New Ave Ste H (60439-2613)
PHONE..................630 257-7012
Joe Forst, *Accounts Exec*
Mike Gardner, *Sales Staff*
Patrick Gardner,
EMP: 1
SALES (est): 2.5MM **Privately Held**
SIC: 3572 Computer storage devices

(G-12588)
SALCO PRODUCTS INC (PA)
1385 101st St Ste A (60439-9631)
PHONE..................630 783-2570
David Oestermeyer, *President*
Edward Fox, *Engineer*
Susan Krohn, *Supervisor*
Chuck Simpson, *Director*
Thomas Turner, *Graphic Designe*
EMP: 60
SQ FT: 51,735
SALES (est): 49.3MM **Privately Held**
SIC: 5013 5088 3743 Truck parts & accessories; railroad equipment & supplies; railroad equipment

(G-12589)
SENECA PETROLEUM CO INC
12460 New Ave (60439-3669)
P.O. Box 219 (60439-0219)
PHONE..................630 257-2268
Bob Krissik, *Manager*
EMP: 50
SALES (corp-wide): 17.9MM **Privately Held**
SIC: 2951 Asphalt & asphaltic paving mixtures (not from refineries)
PA: Seneca Petroleum Co., Inc.
   13301 Cicero Ave
   Crestwood IL 60418
   708 396-1100

(G-12590)
SOLAR TRAFFIC SYSTEMS INC
16135 New Ave Ste 2 (60439-2605)
PHONE..................331 318-8500
Ray Gal, *Treasurer*
EMP: 4 EST: 2008
SQ FT: 3,100
SALES (est): 138.4K **Privately Held**
SIC: 3993 Electric signs

(G-12591)
SUPERIOR PRINT SERVICES INC
12305 New Ave Ste H (60439-2613)
PHONE..................630 257-7012
Patrick Gardner,
Suzanne Gardner, *Treasurer*
EMP: 8
SALES (est): 1.1MM **Privately Held**
SIC: 2752 Commercial printing, offset

(G-12592)
SWEET SPECIALTY SOLUTIONS LLC
1005 101st St Ste B (60439-9628)
PHONE..................630 739-9151
John B Yonover,
EMP: 40
SALES (est): 10.2MM **Privately Held**
SIC: 2063 Beet sugar

(G-12593)
TOMKO MACHINE WORKS INC
20w067 Pleasantdale Dr (60439-9618)
PHONE..................630 244-0902
John C Tomaskovic, *President*
Patricia J Tomaskovic, *Treasurer*
Judy Tomaskovic, *Admin Sec*
EMP: 9
SQ FT: 10,000
SALES (est): 876.9K **Privately Held**
SIC: 3599 7692 3462 3312 Machine shop, jobbing & repair; welding repair; iron & steel forgings; blast furnaces & steel mills

(G-12594)
WEST SIDE MACHINE INC
11201 S Boyer St (60439-8769)
P.O. Box 426 (60439-0426)
PHONE..................630 243-1069
Casey Sularski, *President*
Tim Sularski, *Asst Mgr*
Andy J Wilczek, *Admin Sec*
▲ EMP: 17
SQ FT: 20,000
SALES (est): 3.6MM **Privately Held**
SIC: 3599 Machine shop, jobbing & repair

(G-12595)
WILLOW FARM PRODUCTS INC
20w114 97th St (60439-9680)
PHONE..................630 430-7491
Sharon Polivka, *President*
EMP: 3
SALES (est): 292.8K **Privately Held**
SIC: 3545 3441 Machine tool accessories; fabricated structural metal

(G-12596)
XCELL INTERNATIONAL CORP
16400 103rd St (60439-9667)
P.O. Box 452, Westmont (60559-0452)
PHONE..................630 323-0107
Dean J Henning, *President*
Dean Henning, *Principal*
Brian Misevich, *Warehouse Mgr*
Howard Williams, *Purchasing*
Scott Henning, *Research*
▲ EMP: 100
SQ FT: 44,000
SALES (est): 21.1MM **Privately Held**
SIC: 3089 5023 Jars, plastic; kitchenware

Lena
Stephenson County

(G-12597)
ADKINS ENERGY LLC
4350 W Galena Rd (61048-8504)
P.O. Box 227 (61048-0227)
PHONE..................815 369-9173
Ray Baker, *General Mgr*
Jason Townsend, *Plant Mgr*
Nelson Krahmer, *Purchasing*
Joan Strong, *Controller*
Tina Bookman, *Accountant*
EMP: 35
SALES (est): 10.7MM **Privately Held**
SIC: 2869 Ethyl alcohol, ethanol

(G-12598)
BUSS BOYZ CUSTOMS INC
216 S Center St (61048-8708)
P.O. Box 750 (61048-0750)
PHONE..................815 369-2803
Ryan Buss, *President*
EMP: 2
SALES (est): 313.3K **Privately Held**
WEB: www.bussboyzcustoms.com
SIC: 3699 Automotive driving simulators (training aids), electronic

(G-12599)
CENTRAL RADIATOR CABINET CO (PA)
8857 N 5 Corners Rd (61048-9761)
PHONE..................773 539-1700
Jeffrey Bishop, *President*
EMP: 5 EST: 1932
SQ FT: 3,000
SALES: 1MM **Privately Held**
SIC: 3444 3469 2522 Radiator shields or enclosures, sheet metal; metal stampings; office furniture, except wood

(G-12600)
KOLB-LENA INC
Also Called: Kolb-Lena Bresse Bleu, Inc.
3990 N Sunnyside Rd (61048-9613)
PHONE..................815 369-4577
Jim Williams, *President*
Stephen Bouchayer, *Corp Secy*
▲ EMP: 65
SQ FT: 60,000
SALES (est): 11.7MM
SALES (corp-wide): 6.2B **Privately Held**
SIC: 2022 Natural cheese
HQ: Zausner Foods Corp.
   400 S Custer Ave
   New Holland PA 17557
   717 355-8505

(G-12601)
KRAFTY KABINETS
106 W Provost St (61048-9112)
PHONE..................815 369-5250
Chuck Kraft, *Principal*
EMP: 2
SALES (est): 230.1K **Privately Held**
SIC: 2434 Wood kitchen cabinets

(G-12602)
LENA AJS MAID MEATS
500 W Main St (61048-9726)
PHONE..................815 369-4522
Kevin Koning, *CEO*
Marcia Pax, *Owner*
EMP: 14 EST: 1952
SQ FT: 10,000
SALES (est): 820K **Privately Held**
SIC: 7299 2011 5147 5142 Butcher service, processing only; meat packing plants; meat & meat products; packaged frozen goods; sausages & other prepared meats

(G-12603)
LENA MERCANTILE
101 W Railroad St (61048-9038)
P.O. Box 188 (61048-0188)
PHONE..................815 369-9955
Larry Maedge, *Principal*
EMP: 15
SALES (est): 1.6MM **Privately Held**
SIC: 2599 Restaurant furniture, wood or metal

(G-12604)
LENA SIGN SHOP
109 W Railroad St (61048-9038)
P.O. Box 188 (61048-0188)
PHONE..................815 369-9090
Larry Maedge, *Owner*
EMP: 3
SALES (est): 236.1K **Privately Held**
SIC: 3993 Signs, not made in custom sign painting shops

(G-12605)
LINGLE DESIGN GROUP INC
158 W Main St (61048-9247)
PHONE..................815 369-9155
Carl Lingle, *President*
Lisa Donmeyer, *Division Mgr*
Tony Bolotnik, *Vice Pres*
Josh Cocagne, *Project Mgr*

GEOGRAPHIC SECTION

Ray Gable, *Project Mgr*
EMP: 20
SALES (est): 2.8MM **Privately Held**
WEB: www.lingledesign.com
SIC: 2211 8712 Crepes & other crinkled texture fabrics, cotton; architectural services

(G-12606)
MAHONEY PUBLISHING INC
707 Maple St (61048-9370)
P.O. Box 95 (61048-0095)
PHONE..............................815 369-5384
Mark Mahoney, *President*
EMP: 7
SALES (est): 198.8K **Privately Held**
SIC: 2711 Newspapers

(G-12607)
NORTHWESTERN ILLINOIS FARMER
119 W Railroad St (61048-9038)
P.O. Box 536 (61048-0536)
PHONE..............................815 369-2811
Norman Templin, *Owner*
Connie Kempel, *Manager*
EMP: 3
SALES (est): 109K **Privately Held**
SIC: 2711 2759 Newspapers, publishing & printing; commercial printing

(G-12608)
SAVENCIA CHEESE USA LLC
3990 N Sunnyside Rd (61048-9613)
PHONE..............................815 369-4577
Dino Constantine, *Technical Mgr*
Kay Larsen, *Branch Mgr*
Fred Demeter, *Manager*
EMP: 3
SALES (corp-wide): 6.2B **Privately Held**
SIC: 5143 2022 Cheese; cheese, natural & processed
HQ: Savencia Cheese Usa Llc
400 S Custer Ave
New Holland PA 17557

(G-12609)
SHOPPERS GUIDE
Also Called: Scope, The
213 S Center St (61048-8711)
PHONE..............................815 369-4112
David Bauer, *Editor*
Cyndi Jensen, *Controller*
Pete Kruger, *Mng Member*
EMP: 6
SALES (est): 276.3K **Privately Held**
SIC: 2711 Newspapers: publishing only, not printed on site

Lenzburg
St. Clair County

(G-12610)
DUMPSTER DAVE LLC
10121 Marissa Twp Line Rd (62255-1627)
PHONE..............................618 475-3835
David Julius, *Principal*
EMP: 2
SALES (est): 299.5K **Privately Held**
SIC: 3443 Dumpsters, garbage

Leonore
Lasalle County

(G-12611)
BRIAN BURCAR
Also Called: Double R Manufacturing Co
310 Walnut St (61332-1030)
P.O. Box 107 (61332-0107)
PHONE..............................815 856-2271
Brian Burcar, *Owner*
EMP: 4
SQ FT: 10,000
SALES (est): 412.2K **Privately Held**
WEB: www.double-rmfg.com
SIC: 3599 3596 3444 3423 Machine shop, jobbing & repair; scales & balances, except laboratory; sheet metalwork; hand & edge tools; planting machines, agricultural

(G-12612)
MARETA RAVIOLI INC
Also Called: Mareta Ravioli & Noodle
303 Gary St (61332-1011)
P.O. Box 163 (61332-0163)
PHONE..............................815 856-2621
Martha Mareta, *President*
Michael Villareal, *Vice Pres*
Esteban Villareal, *Admin Sec*
EMP: 10
SQ FT: 3,500
SALES: 300K **Privately Held**
SIC: 2099 Food preparations

Lerna
Coles County

(G-12613)
JAKES WORLD DESIGN
2736 N County Road 1100e (62440-2311)
PHONE..............................217 348-3043
EMP: 3
SALES (est): 352.6K **Privately Held**
SIC: 2821 Mfg Plastic Materials/Resins

(G-12614)
M J KULL LLC
1911 3rd St (62440-1100)
P.O. Box 1423, Mattoon (61938-1423)
PHONE..............................217 246-5952
Mark E Kull, *President*
EMP: 5
SALES (est): 362.3K **Privately Held**
SIC: 2611 Pulp manufactured from waste or recycled paper

Lewistown
Fulton County

(G-12615)
GOODMAN SAWMILL
114 N Broadway St (61542-1202)
PHONE..............................309 547-3597
David Goodman, *Owner*
EMP: 3
SALES (est): 100K **Privately Held**
SIC: 2421 Sawmills & planing mills, general

(G-12616)
INDEPENDENT SHOPPERS
Also Called: Havana Independent Shopper
154 W Washington Ave (61542-1421)
PHONE..............................309 647-5200
Jackie Caulkins, *President*
EMP: 4
SALES (est): 323.5K **Privately Held**
SIC: 2759 7313 Publication printing; newspaper advertising representative

Lexington
Mclean County

(G-12617)
ANVIL ACQUISITION CORP
500 S Spencer St (61753-1615)
PHONE..............................309 365-8270
Steven D Hoselton, *President*
EMP: 14
SALES (est): 553.7K **Privately Held**
SIC: 3462 Horseshoes

(G-12618)
BRANDT CONSOLIDATED INC
610 W Main St (61753-1226)
P.O. Box 107 (61753-0107)
PHONE..............................309 365-7201
Dennis Myer, *Manager*
EMP: 7
SALES (corp-wide): 159MM **Privately Held**
SIC: 2875 5191 Fertilizers, mixing only; farm supplies
PA: Brandt Consolidated, Inc.
2935 S Koke Mill Rd
Springfield IL 62711
217 547-5800

(G-12619)
H & H MACHINING
500 S Spencer St (61753-1615)
P.O. Box 116 (61753-0116)
PHONE..............................309 365-7010
Steve Hoselton, *President*
Stuart Hoselton, *Corp Secy*
EMP: 3
SQ FT: 7,000
SALES (est): 477.4K **Privately Held**
WEB: www.hnhmachining.com
SIC: 3599 Machine shop, jobbing & repair

(G-12620)
PIONEER PLASTICS INC
510 S Spencer St (61753-1615)
PHONE..............................309 365-2951
EMP: 122
SALES (corp-wide): 25MM **Privately Held**
SIC: 3083 Laminated plastics plate & sheet
PA: Pioneer Plastics Inc.
3660 Dodd Rd
Eagan MN 55123
651 209-6600

(G-12621)
SCHUMAKER PUBLICATIONS INC
Rr 2 Box 72a (61753)
PHONE..............................309 365-7105
Roland Schumaker, *Owner*
Sharla Ishmael, *Manager*
Ammie McGraw, *Director*
Amber Martin, *Creative Dir*
EMP: 3
SALES (est): 195.8K **Privately Held**
WEB: www.theshowcircuit.com
SIC: 2741 Miscellaneous publishing

Liberty
Adams County

(G-12622)
ELLIOTT PUBLISHING INC
Also Called: Liberty Bee
103 E Hannibal St (62347-1055)
PHONE..............................217 645-3033
James Elliott, *President*
EMP: 8
SQ FT: 1,200
SALES (est): 603.2K **Privately Held**
SIC: 2711 2789 2759 2752 Newspapers, publishing & printing; bookbinding & related work; commercial printing; commercial printing, lithographic

(G-12623)
LIBERTY FEED MILL
408 Liberty St (62347-1125)
PHONE..............................217 645-3441
Brad Kroencke, *President*
Cheryl Ann Kroencke, *Treasurer*
EMP: 12
SQ FT: 5,000
SALES (est): 2.3MM **Privately Held**
WEB: www.libertyfeedandbeanmeal.com
SIC: 5191 5153 2048 Feed; grains; prepared feeds

Libertyville
Lake County

(G-12624)
A-S MEDICATION SOLUTIONS LLC (PA)
2401 Commerce Dr (60048-4464)
PHONE..............................847 680-3515
Walter Hoff, *CEO*
Mark Chapman, *Warehouse Mgr*
Phil Mesi, *Purch Mgr*
Dawn Powless, *QC Mgr*
Brian Czochara, *VP Sales*
EMP: 75
SALES (est): 21.2MM **Privately Held**
SIC: 2834 Pharmaceutical preparations

(G-12625)
ABBOTT LABORATORIES
279 Adler Dr (60048-3922)
PHONE..............................224 330-0271
Kevin Dcluff, *Branch Mgr*
EMP: 752
SALES (corp-wide): 31.9B **Publicly Held**
WEB: www.abbott.com
SIC: 2834 Pharmaceutical preparations
PA: Abbott Laboratories
100 Abbott Park Rd
Abbott Park IL 60064
224 667-6100

(G-12626)
AIDAREX PHARMACEUTICALS LLC
2401 Commerce Dr (60048-4464)
PHONE..............................800 657-4724
Walter Hoff, *Mng Member*
Chris Martin,
EMP: 5
SQ FT: 10,000
SALES (est): 6.6MM **Privately Held**
SIC: 2834 Adrenal pharmaceutical preparations

(G-12627)
ALLFORM MANUFACTURING CO
342 4th St (60048-2312)
PHONE..............................847 680-0144
Deno Alexakos, *President*
EMP: 2
SALES (est): 500K **Privately Held**
SIC: 3315 3496 Steel wire & related products; miscellaneous fabricated wire products

(G-12628)
AMERICAN CUSTOM PUBLISHING
Also Called: Natl Senior Hlth & Fitnes Day
328 W Lincoln Ave (60048-2725)
PHONE..............................847 816-8660
Gary W Ford, *President*
Patricia Henze Ford, *Vice Pres*
Patricia Henze, *Exec Dir*
EMP: 9
SQ FT: 4,000
SALES (est): 997K **Privately Held**
SIC: 2721 2741 Magazines: publishing & printing; newsletter publishing

(G-12629)
APTARGROUP INC
901 Technology Way (60048-5348)
PHONE..............................847 816-9400
Tanner Faulkner, *Principal*
Jamie Samz, *Plant Mgr*
Cesar Alonso, *Opers Mgr*
Bob Edwards, *Manager*
Kevin Napieralski, *Manager*
EMP: 5 **Publicly Held**
WEB: www.aptar.com
SIC: 3089 3499 Closures, plastic; aerosol valves, metal
PA: Aptargroup, Inc.
265 Exchange Dr Ste 100
Crystal Lake IL 60014

(G-12630)
ARIA CORPORATION
29471 N Northwoods Dr (60048-1629)
PHONE..............................847 327-9000
EMP: 3
SQ FT: 1,500
SALES (est): 296.9K **Privately Held**
SIC: 8711 3679 Engineering Services

(G-12631)
ARMSTRONG WORLD INDUSTRIES INC
1821 Industrial Dr (60048-9727)
PHONE..............................847 362-8720
Michael Schaefer, *President*
EMP: 40
SALES (corp-wide): 1B **Publicly Held**
SIC: 3446 Partitions, ornamental metal
PA: Armstrong World Industries, Inc.
2500 Columbia Ave
Lancaster PA 17603
717 397-0611

Libertyville - Lake County (G-12632)

GEOGRAPHIC SECTION

(G-12632)
AUSTINS SALOON & EATERY
481 Peterson Rd (60048-1009)
PHONE..................847 549-1972
Mark Khayat, *Principal*
Gregg Kalble, *Opers Staff*
Krissie Ginas, *Executive*
EMP: 5
SALES (est): 344.7K **Privately Held**
WEB: www.austinsaloon.com
SIC: 2869 Fuels

(G-12633)
AVEXIS INC
1940 Usg Dr (60048-5346)
PHONE..................847 572-8280
Michael B Johannesen, *Senior VP*
Mary Glynn, *Executive Asst*
EMP: 150
SALES (corp-wide): 47.5B **Privately Held**
SIC: 2836 Biological products, except diagnostic
HQ: Avexis, Inc.
2275 Half Day Rd Ste 200
Bannockburn IL 60015
847 572-8280

(G-12634)
AVEXIS INC
600 N Us Highway 45 (60048-1286)
PHONE..................847 572-8280
Mary Glynn, *Executive Asst*
EMP: 50
SALES (corp-wide): 47.5B **Privately Held**
SIC: 2836 Biological products, except diagnostic
HQ: Avexis, Inc.
2275 Half Day Rd Ste 200
Bannockburn IL 60015
847 572-8280

(G-12635)
BACH PLASTIC WORKS INC
1711 Young Dr B (60048-3902)
PHONE..................847 680-4342
EMP: 4
SQ FT: 2,000
SALES: 42.3K **Privately Held**
SIC: 3087 5162 Custom Compounding-Purchased Resins Whol Plastic Materials/Shapes

(G-12636)
BCI ACRYLIC INC
Also Called: B C I
1800 Industrial Dr (60048-9439)
PHONE..................847 963-8827
Scott Rosenbach, *President*
Norm Murdock, *Vice Pres*
Rich Seneker, *Plant Mgr*
John Michnowski, *Purch Mgr*
Peggy Volker, *Cust Mgr*
EMP: 30
SQ FT: 50,000
SALES (est): 12.1MM **Privately Held**
SIC: 3088 Plastics plumbing fixtures

(G-12637)
BEACHWAVER CO
850 Technology Way (60048-5350)
PHONE..................201 751-5625
Erin Wall, *President*
Paula Rostkowski, *Cust Mgr*
Emma Dodd, *Admin Asst*
Anthony Lawless, *Admin Asst*
▲ **EMP:** 29
SALES (est): 2.4MM **Privately Held**
WEB: www.beachwaver.com
SIC: 3999 Hair & hair-based products

(G-12638)
BLUE SKY BIO LLC
800 Liberty Dr (60048-2345)
PHONE..................718 376-0422
Maureen Manley, *Vice Pres*
Michael Saltzman, *Manager*
Sheldon Lerner,
Dr Albert Zickmann,
EMP: 10
SALES (est): 237.9K **Privately Held**
SIC: 3842 5045 Implants, surgical; computer software

(G-12639)
BOX ENCLSRES ASSEMBLY SVCS INC
14092 W Lambs Ln (60048-9505)
PHONE..................847 932-4700
John Fiocchi, *President*
▲ **EMP:** 6
SQ FT: 5,500
SALES (est): 1.3MM **Privately Held**
SIC: 3089 Injection molding of plastics

(G-12640)
BRILLIANT COLOR CORP
14044 W Petronella Dr # 3 (60048-9656)
PHONE..................847 367-3300
James D Ozga, *President*
Joseph D Ozga, *Vice Pres*
EMP: 8
SQ FT: 5,000
SALES (est): 1MM **Privately Held**
SIC: 2752 2741 2796 Color lithography; miscellaneous publishing; platemaking services

(G-12641)
BURGESS MANUFACTURING INC
1911 Industrial Dr (60048-9731)
PHONE..................847 680-1724
Allen J Bassel Sr, *President*
Ann Bassel, *Corp Secy*
EMP: 15 **EST:** 1973
SQ FT: 15,000
SALES (est): 2.2MM **Privately Held**
SIC: 3599 7692 Machine shop, jobbing & repair; welding repair

(G-12642)
CECOMP ELECTRONICS INC
1220 American Way (60048-3936)
PHONE..................847 918-3510
Jan Ehrlich, *Admin Sec*
EMP: 32
SALES (est): 2.7MM **Privately Held**
SIC: 3699 Electrical equipment & supplies
PA: Absolute Process Instruments, Inc
1220 American Way
Libertyville IL 60048

(G-12643)
CLEAN CODERS LLC
1520 Artaius Pkwy # 7038 (60048-7900)
P.O. Box 7038 (60048-7038)
PHONE..................847 370-4098
Tadd Linderman, *CEO*
Micah Martin, *President*
EMP: 5
SALES (est): 324.4K **Privately Held**
SIC: 7372 Prepackaged software

(G-12644)
COLOR4
28100 N Ashley Cir Ste 10 (60048-9478)
PHONE..................847 996-6880
Steve Rokicki,
EMP: 10
SALES (est): 1.2MM **Privately Held**
SIC: 2759 Letterpress printing

(G-12645)
COMBINED TECHNOLOGIES INC (PA)
Also Called: CTI
732 Florsheim Dr Ste 14 (60048-3722)
PHONE..................847 968-4855
Jerry Thompson, *President*
Steve Giambi, *Project Mgr*
EMP: 9
SQ FT: 160,000
SALES: 4MM **Privately Held**
WEB: www.ctipack.com
SIC: 2631 2657 2653 3565 Container, packaging & boxboard; folding paperboard boxes; corrugated & solid fiber boxes; bottling machinery: filling, capping, labeling; bag opening, filling & closing machines; carton packing machines; sugar; confectionary

(G-12646)
CUSTOM COPPER HOODS INC
103 Harding Ave (60048-1762)
PHONE..................224 577-9000
EMP: 2

SALES (est): 240.9K **Privately Held**
SIC: 3444 Sheet metalwork

(G-12647)
DESSERTWERKS INC (PA)
1421 Allyson Ct (60048-1401)
PHONE..................847 487-8239
Raymond L King, *President*
EMP: 5
SALES (est): 951.1K **Privately Held**
SIC: 2051 5145 Cakes, pies & pastries; snack foods

(G-12648)
E-Z CUFF INC
1840 Industrial Dr # 260 (60048-9467)
PHONE..................847 549-1550
Lisa Kohn, *President*
EMP: 7
SALES (est): 694.1K **Privately Held**
SIC: 3842 Restraints, patient

(G-12649)
EWAB ENGINEERING INC
1971 Kelley Ct (60048-9639)
PHONE..................847 247-0015
Chris Bates, *Managing Dir*
Glyn Punter, *Managing Dir*
Ronald Gneiss, *Engineer*
Martin Lindeberg, *Project Engr*
Ulrich Probst, *Director*
▲ **EMP:** 25
SQ FT: 35,000
SALES (est): 9.1MM
SALES (corp-wide): 406.2K **Privately Held**
SIC: 3535 Unit handling conveying systems
HQ: Ewab Engineering Ab
Kungs Starbyvagen 8
Vadstena 592 9
143 750-00

(G-12650)
EYE SURGEONS OF LIBERTYVILLE
1880 W Winchester Rd # 105 (60048-5321)
PHONE..................847 362-3811
Sara Vegh, *President*
EMP: 8
SALES (est): 619.2K **Privately Held**
SIC: 3851 8042 Eyes, glass & plastic; offices & clinics of optometrists

(G-12651)
FASTSIGNS
1350 S Milwaukee Ave (60048-3795)
PHONE..................847 680-7446
Larry Kilpatrick, *President*
EMP: 5
SQ FT: 2,500
SALES (est): 706.4K **Privately Held**
SIC: 3993 Signs & advertising specialties

(G-12652)
FIRM OF JOHN DICKINSON
2000 Hollister Dr (60048-3746)
PHONE..................847 680-1000
V George Maliekel, *President*
Alan F Herbert, *Principal*
Sam Brilliant, *CFO*
Melissa G Brunette, *Admin Sec*
Jerome A Saxon, *Admin Sec*
◆ **EMP:** 53
SQ FT: 200,000
SALES (est): 8.4MM **Privately Held**
WEB: www.hilldickinson.com
SIC: 3842 Surgical appliances & supplies

(G-12653)
GENENTECH INC
329 Laurel Ave (60048-2129)
PHONE..................650 225-1045
EMP: 4
SALES (corp-wide): 64.2B **Privately Held**
WEB: www.gene.com
SIC: 2834 Pharmaceutical preparations
HQ: Genentech, Inc.
1 Dna Way
South San Francisco CA 94080
650 225-1000

(G-12654)
GENESIS MOLD CORP
854 Liberty Dr Ste C (60048-2330)
PHONE..................847 573-9431
Mike Robison, *President*
EMP: 4
SALES: 328.1K **Privately Held**
SIC: 3544 Special dies & tools

(G-12655)
GREAT IMPRESSIONS INC
19071 W Casey Rd (60048-1078)
PHONE..................847 367-6725
Fax: 847 816-0024
EMP: 4 **EST:** 1983
SQ FT: 2,500
SALES: 450K **Privately Held**
SIC: 2752 Offset Commercial Printer

(G-12656)
H AND D DISTRIBUTION INC
28045 N Ashley Cir Unit 1 (60048-9658)
PHONE..................847 247-2011
Christopher Hogstrom, *President*
John Daniels, *Vice Pres*
EMP: 3
SQ FT: 4,300
SALES (est): 199.7K **Privately Held**
SIC: 3999 Dock equipment & supplies, industrial

(G-12657)
HERITAGE PRESS INC
312 Peterson Rd (60048-1008)
PHONE..................847 362-9699
Connie Fiorelli, *President*
Paul Fiorelli, *Vice Pres*
Cathleen Frank, *Manager*
EMP: 5
SQ FT: 2,000
SALES (est): 700.2K **Privately Held**
SIC: 2752 2791 2789 Commercial printing, offset; typesetting; bookbinding & related work

(G-12658)
HERITAGE SIGNS LTD
1840 Industrial Dr # 240 (60048-9400)
PHONE..................847 549-1942
Cynthia Fitzpatrick, *Owner*
EMP: 4
SQ FT: 1,000
SALES (est): 300K **Privately Held**
SIC: 3993 Signs & advertising specialties

(G-12659)
HOLLAND SAFETY EQUIPMENT INC
726 Mckinley Ave (60048-2640)
PHONE..................847 680-9930
Gary Holland, *President*
Kathleen Holland, *Admin Sec*
▲ **EMP:** 4
SQ FT: 750
SALES: 1.7MM **Privately Held**
SIC: 3822 Air flow controllers, air conditioning & refrigeration

(G-12660)
HOLLISTER INCORPORATED (PA)
2000 Hollister Dr (60048-3781)
PHONE..................847 680-1000
George Maliekel, *President*
Stephan Bonnelycke, *Managing Dir*
John O'Malley, *Counsel*
Denis R Chevaleau, *Vice Pres*
Robert A Crowe, *Vice Pres*
◆ **EMP:** 350
SQ FT: 200,000
SALES (est): 796.2MM **Privately Held**
WEB: www.hollister.com
SIC: 3841 3842 Surgical & medical instruments; surgical appliances & supplies

(G-12661)
IGM SOLUTIONS INC
1900 Enterprise Ct (60048-9737)
PHONE..................847 918-1790
Paul Kelly, *President*
Tom Dahlen, *Vice Pres*
Edward J Kelly, *Admin Sec*
▲ **EMP:** 50
SQ FT: 55,000

▲ = Import ▼ = Export
◆ = Import/Export

SALES (est): 21.7MM **Privately Held**
SIC: **3441** Fabricated structural metal

(G-12662)
ILLINOIS TOOL WORKS INC
14050 W Lambs Ln Unit 1 (60048-9505)
PHONE.....................847 918-6473
Jeff Ford, *Branch Mgr*
EMP: 16
SALES (corp-wide): 14.1B **Publicly Held**
SIC: **3531** Roofing equipment
PA: Illinois Tool Works Inc.
  155 Harlem Ave
  Glenview IL 60025
  847 724-7500

(G-12663)
INTEGRA PRINT & DATA SERVICES
940 N Milwaukee Ave Ste C (60048-1971)
PHONE.....................708 337-6265
EMP: 2 EST: 2016
SALES (est): 243.8K **Privately Held**
SIC: **2752** Commercial printing, lithographic

(G-12664)
IRONWOOD INDUSTRIES INC
115 S Bradley Rd (60048-9509)
PHONE.....................847 362-8681
Robert Grala, *Principal*
Jason Grala, *Vice Pres*
Laurie Glauner, *Supervisor*
▲ EMP: 70
SQ FT: 51,000
SALES (est): 20.5MM **Privately Held**
SIC: **3089** Injection molded finished plastic products

(G-12665)
LAKE COUNTY GRADING CO LLC (PA)
32901 N Hwy 21 (60048)
P.O. Box L (60048-4912)
PHONE.....................847 362-2590
Tom Rosenquist, *President*
Richard Keller, *General Mgr*
Chris Brankey, *Superintendent*
Bob Keegan, *Superintendent*
Michael Wolff, *Vice Pres*
EMP: 100
SQ FT: 2,000
SALES (est): 20.6MM **Privately Held**
WEB: www.lcgc.com
SIC: **1794** 1442 1623 1795 Excavation work; gravel mining; water main construction; sewer line construction; wrecking & demolition work

(G-12666)
LAKE SHORE STAIR CO INC
615 E Park Ave (60048-2904)
PHONE.....................847 362-3262
Chris Jensen, *President*
Cassidy Douglas, *Purchasing*
EMP: 35
SALES (est): 2.8MM
SALES (corp-wide): 3.8MM **Privately Held**
SIC: **2431** Staircases, stairs & railings
PA: Lake Shore Stair Co Inc
  28090 W Concrete Dr
  Ingleside IL 60041
  815 363-7777

(G-12667)
LIBERTY CLASSICS INC
1860 W Winchester Rd # 103 (60048-5312)
PHONE.....................847 367-1288
▲ EMP: 5
SQ FT: 3,500
SALES (est): 1MM **Privately Held**
SIC: **3944** Games, Toys, Childrens Vehicles, Nec

(G-12668)
LIBERTYVILLE BREWING COMPANY
Also Called: Mickey Finns Brewery
345 N Milwaukee Ave (60048-2237)
PHONE.....................847 362-6688
Brian Grano, *President*
Bill Sugars, *President*
Kristen Christensen, *Relations*

EMP: 75
SQ FT: 12,000
SALES (est): 2.5MM **Privately Held**
SIC: **5812** 5813 2082 American restaurant; cocktail lounge; malt beverages

(G-12669)
LIBERTYVILLE MONUMENTS
120 W Park Ave (60048-2702)
P.O. Box 6434 (60048-6434)
PHONE.....................641 295-3506
Dustin Versteeg, *Owner*
EMP: 3
SALES (est): 209.7K **Privately Held**
SIC: **3272** Monuments & grave markers, except terrazo

(G-12670)
LIGHTSCAPE INC
342 4th St (60048-2312)
PHONE.....................847 247-8800
Steven Achtemeier, *President*
Alejandro Martinez, *Vice Pres*
Karen Achtemeier, *Admin Sec*
EMP: 20
SQ FT: 1,200
SALES (est): 3.6MM **Privately Held**
WEB: www.lsilighting.net
SIC: **3648** 1731 Outdoor lighting equipment; electrical work

(G-12671)
M & D INDUSTRIES INC
1821 Industrial Dr (60048-9727)
PHONE.....................847 362-8720
Michael Schaefer, *President*
Daniela Schaefer, *Vice Pres*
Eddie Garza, *Purchasing*
Rozycki Matthew, *Engineer*
▲ EMP: 40
SQ FT: 45,000
SALES (est): 7.1MM **Privately Held**
WEB: www.mrkindustries.com
SIC: **3446** Acoustical suspension systems, metal

(G-12672)
MARJO GRAPHICS INC
1510 Bull Creek Dr (60048-1028)
P.O. Box Q (60048-4917)
PHONE.....................847 367-1305
Adam Kimpler, *President*
Margaret Kimpler, *Vice Pres*
EMP: 2
SALES (est): 350K **Privately Held**
SIC: **2752** Commercial printing, lithographic

(G-12673)
MARYTOWN
Also Called: Knights of Immaculata
1600 W Park Ave (60048-2563)
PHONE.....................847 367-7800
Mrs Marcia O Connor, *Manager*
Stephen McKinley, *Director*
EMP: 21
SQ FT: 87,000
SALES (est): 1.8MM **Privately Held**
SIC: **8661** 2731 Monastery; shrines; books: publishing only; pamphlets: publishing only, not printed on site

(G-12674)
MATTHEWS-GERBAR LTD
Also Called: Mathews Fan Company
1881 Industrial Dr (60048-9783)
PHONE.....................847 680-9043
Charles Matthews, *Principal*
EMP: 7
SALES (corp-wide): 1.8MM **Privately Held**
WEB: www.matthewsfanco.com
SIC: **3634** Ceiling fans
PA: Matthews-Gerbar, Ltd
  1881 Industrial Dr
  Libertyville IL 60048
  847 680-9043

(G-12675)
MATTHEWS-GERBAR LTD (PA)
Also Called: Matthews Fan Company
1881 Industrial Dr (60048-9783)
PHONE.....................847 680-9043
Chuck Matthews, *President*
▲ EMP: 5
SQ FT: 10,000

SALES (est): 1.8MM **Privately Held**
SIC: **3634** Ceiling fans

(G-12676)
MAXXSONICS USA INC
Also Called: MB Quart Entertainment
851 E Park Ave (60048-2980)
PHONE.....................847 540-7700
Alden Stiefel, *President*
Brian Sherman, *Vice Pres*
◆ EMP: 25
SQ FT: 65,000
SALES (est): 6.4MM **Privately Held**
SIC: **3651** Audio electronic systems

(G-12677)
MEKTRONIX TECHNOLOGY INC
530 N Milwaukee Ave Ste B (60048-2008)
PHONE.....................847 680-3300
Gregory Mayworm, *President*
Suzanne Quinn, *Treasurer*
EMP: 5
SALES (est): 622.4K **Privately Held**
SIC: **3625** 3672 Controls for adjustable speed drives; printed circuit boards

(G-12678)
METALEX LLC
Also Called: Metalex Corporation
700 Liberty Dr (60048-2343)
PHONE.....................847 362-5400
Brian Kobylinski, *President*
Bob Birk, *Vice Pres*
Andy Glyman, *Plant Mgr*
Mathys Rick, *Opers Mgr*
Florin Boca, *Project Engr*
▲ EMP: 105
SALES (est): 34.8MM
SALES (corp-wide): 386.2MM **Privately Held**
SIC: **3469** 3449 Perforated metal, stamped; lath, expanded metal
PA: Upg Enterprises Llc
  1400 16th St Ste 250
  Oak Brook IL 60523
  630 822-7000

(G-12679)
MGS GROUP NORTH AMERICA INC
14050 W Lambs Ln Ste 4 (60048-9505)
PHONE.....................847 371-1158
Craig Hall, *CEO*
EMP: 100
SALES (corp-wide): 561.7MM **Privately Held**
SIC: **3089** Injection molding of plastics
HQ: Mgs Group North America, Inc.
  W190n11701 Moldmakers Way
  Germantown WI 53022
  262 250-2950

(G-12680)
MGS MFG GROUP INC
Also Called: Tecstar Mfg Company III Div
14050 Lands Ln Ste 2 (60048)
PHONE.....................847 968-4335
Chris Nevratil, *Manager*
EMP: 45
SALES (corp-wide): 561.7MM **Privately Held**
WEB: www.mgstech.com
SIC: **3089** Plastic kitchenware, tableware & houseware
PA: Mgs Mfg. Group, Inc.
  W188n11707 Maple Rd
  Germantown WI 53022
  262 255-5790

(G-12681)
MIMO DISPLAY LLC (PA)
Also Called: Mimo Monitors
14048 W Petronella Dr (60048-9699)
PHONE.....................855 937-6466
David Anderson, *CEO*
Michael Wells, *Manager*
Tyler Wells, *Manager*
EMP: 9
SQ FT: 3,000
SALES (est): 3.5MM **Privately Held**
SIC: **3575** Computer terminals, monitors & components

(G-12682)
MITSUBISHI CHEMICAL ADVNCD MTR
Also Called: Piper Plastics
1840 Enterprise Ct (60048-9725)
PHONE.....................847 367-0110
Dan Bay, *Branch Mgr*
EMP: 110 **Privately Held**
SIC: **3599** Machine shop, jobbing & repair
HQ: Mitsubishi Chemical Advanced Materials Inc.
  2120 Fairmont Ave
  Reading PA 19605
  610 320-6600

(G-12683)
MOTOROLA SOLUTIONS INC
1899 W Winchester Rd (60048-5367)
PHONE.....................847 523-5000
Michael McClaughry, *Manager*
EMP: 25
SALES (corp-wide): 7.8B **Publicly Held**
SIC: **3663** Radio & TV communications equipment
PA: Motorola Solutions, Inc.
  500 W Monroe St Ste 4400
  Chicago IL 60661
  847 576-5000

(G-12684)
MOTOROLA SOLUTIONS INC
622 N Us Highway 45 (60048-1286)
PHONE.....................847 523-5000
Fred Kuznik, *General Mgr*
Loraine Pelayo, *Engineer*
EMP: 6
SALES (corp-wide): 7.8B **Publicly Held**
SIC: **3663** Radio & TV communications equipment
PA: Motorola Solutions, Inc.
  500 W Monroe St Ste 4400
  Chicago IL 60661
  847 576-5000

(G-12685)
MOTOROLA SOLUTIONS INC
1200 Technology Way (60048-5369)
PHONE.....................847 523-5000
EMP: 8
SALES (corp-wide): 7.8B **Publicly Held**
SIC: **3663** Radio & TV communications equipment
PA: Motorola Solutions, Inc.
  500 W Monroe St Ste 4400
  Chicago IL 60661
  847 576-5000

(G-12686)
MPD INC
325 1st St (60048-2205)
PHONE.....................847 489-7705
Joe Hajnos, *President*
◆ EMP: 28
SQ FT: 6,500
SALES: 10.1MM **Privately Held**
SIC: **3089** Injection molding of plastics

(G-12687)
NAFM LLC
1580 S Milwaukee Ave # 505 (60048-3764)
PHONE.....................513 504-4333
EMP: 3
SALES (est): 189.8K **Privately Held**
SIC: **3565** Packaging machinery

(G-12688)
NOISE BARRIERS LLC
2001 Kelley Ct (60048-9610)
PHONE.....................847 843-0500
Mark Campbell, *President*
Michael Daut, *Engineer*
Mark Herdman, *Engineer*
James Thomas, *Engineer*
Dave Mitchell, *Finance*
EMP: 50
SALES (est): 17MM **Privately Held**
SIC: **3499** Fire- or burglary-resistive products; barricades, metal
HQ: Sound Seal Holdings, Inc.
  50 Hp Almgren Dr
  Agawam MA 01001
  413 789-1770

Libertyville - Lake County (G-12689)

(G-12689)
NORTH SHORE DISTILLERY LLC
13990 W Rockland Rd (60048-9724)
P.O. Box 279, Lake Bluff (60044-0279)
PHONE 847 574-2499
Sonja Kassebaum, *Mng Member*
Derek Kassebaum,
EMP: 9
SQ FT: 5,000
SALES (est): 560.8K **Privately Held**
SIC: 2085 Cocktails, alcoholic

(G-12690)
NORTH SHORE SIGN COMPANY
1925 Industrial Dr (60048-9731)
PHONE 847 816-7020
Duane Laska, *President*
Patrick Dooley, *Vice Pres*
Kevin Laska, *Vice Pres*
Skip Spanjer, *Sales Mgr*
Jeff Barmueller, *Sales Staff*
EMP: 35
SQ FT: 17,000
SALES: 2.2MM **Privately Held**
SIC: 3993 1799 Electric signs; sign installation & maintenance

(G-12691)
NORTH STAR STONE INC
1840 Industrial Dr # 180 (60048-9467)
PHONE 847 996-6850
Alan Andrews, *Principal*
EMP: 3
SALES (est): 365.3K **Privately Held**
SIC: 3272 1741 Siding, precast stone; stone masonry

(G-12692)
OLD SCHOOL TIMBER WORKS CO
15409 W Old School Rd (60048-9702)
PHONE 847 918-8626
Jeffrey Clark, *Principal*
EMP: 3
SALES (est): 230.4K **Privately Held**
SIC: 2421 Sawmills & planing mills, general

(G-12693)
PADDOCK PUBLICATIONS INC
Also Called: Daily Herald
1795 N Butterfield Rd # 100 (60048-1212)
PHONE 847 680-5800
Peter Nenni, *General Mgr*
EMP: 30
SALES (corp-wide): 79.9MM **Privately Held**
SIC: 2711 2741 Newspapers, publishing & printing; miscellaneous publishing
PA: Paddock Publications, Inc.
    95 W Algonquin Rd Ste 300
    Arlington Heights IL 60005
    847 427-4300

(G-12694)
PERFORMANCE MAILING & PRTG INC
777 N Milwaukee Ave (60048-1913)
PHONE 847 549-0500
Marianne Wilson, *Owner*
EMP: 3
SALES: 330K **Privately Held**
SIC: 2752 Commercial printing, offset

(G-12695)
PHARMASYN INC
1840 Industrial Dr # 140 (60048-9400)
PHONE 847 752-8405
John Pierpont III, *President*
Glenn Norley, *Exec VP*
EMP: 4
SQ FT: 5,000
SALES: 500K **Privately Held**
SIC: 2819 8731 Chemicals, high purity: refined from technical grade; commercial physical research

(G-12696)
PIERCE CRANDELL & CO INC
14047 W Petronella Dr # 103 (60048-9429)
PHONE 847 549-6015
Roy Crandall Sr, *Ch of Bd*
Roy L Crandall Jr, *President*
Roy L Crandall III, *Admin Sec*
EMP: 7
SALES (est): 711.1K **Privately Held**
SIC: 2721 2741 Statistical reports (periodicals): publishing only; miscellaneous publishing

(G-12697)
PLATIT INC
1840 Industrial Dr # 220 (60048-9412)
PHONE 847 680-5270
Bo Torp, *President*
Goran Bulaja, *General Mgr*
▲ **EMP:** 2
SALES (est): 470.1K **Privately Held**
SIC: 3554 Coating & finishing machinery, paper

(G-12698)
PRECISION METAL CRAFTERS INC
1840 Industrial Dr # 340 (60048-9466)
PHONE 847 816-3244
EMP: 14
SQ FT: 9,500
SALES (est): 1.1MM **Privately Held**
SIC: 3599 Precision Machine Shop

(G-12699)
PW MASONRY INC
1230 Hunters Ln (60048-3408)
PHONE 847 573-0510
Piotr Wyszkowski, *President*
EMP: 3
SALES (est): 346K **Privately Held**
WEB: www.pwmasonry.com
SIC: 2381 Fabric dress & work gloves

(G-12700)
R R DONNELLEY & SONS COMPANY
Moore Computer Supplies
850 Technology Way (60048-5350)
PHONE 847 393-3000
Hank Hamner, *Vice Pres*
EMP: 120
SQ FT: 28,000
SALES (corp-wide): 6.2B **Publicly Held**
SIC: 2741 Catalogs: publishing only, not printed on site
PA: R. R. Donnelley & Sons Company
    35 W Wacker Dr
    Chicago IL 60601
    312 326-8000

(G-12701)
RAILSHOP INC
902 Wexford Ct (60048-3059)
P.O. Box 7400 (60048-7400)
PHONE 847 816-0925
EMP: 4
SALES (est): 382K **Privately Held**
SIC: 3089 Mfg Plastic Products

(G-12702)
RHOPAC FABRICATED PRODUCTS LLC
1819 Industrial Dr (60048-9727)
P.O. Box 83008, Chicago (60691-3010)
PHONE 847 362-3300
Gregory Nemecek, *President*
Philip B Langlois, *Vice Pres*
Elen Maliuta, *Controller*
Susan Sponsler, *Admin Sec*
Kevin McCue, *Analyst*
EMP: 40 **EST:** 1932
SQ FT: 40,000
SALES (est): 10.7MM **Privately Held**
WEB: www.rhopac.com
SIC: 3053 2891 2821 2675 Gaskets, all materials; adhesives & sealants; plastics materials & resins; die-cut paper & board

(G-12703)
SAMSUNG SIGN CORP
1840 Industrial Dr # 230 (60048-9412)
PHONE 847 816-1374
Brandon Chin, *President*
EMP: 5
SALES: 200K **Privately Held**
SIC: 3993 Signs & advertising specialties

(G-12704)
SEC DESIGN TECHNOLOGIES INC
1800 Tempel Dr (60048-9443)
PHONE 847 680-0439
Rory Gahart, *President*
Kevin Johnson, *Manager*
Ellen Gahart, *Admin Sec*
EMP: 14
SQ FT: 6,000
SALES (est): 3.5MM **Privately Held**
SIC: 3599 Custom machinery

(G-12705)
SERRA LASER PRECISION LLC
2400 Commerce Dr (60048-4462)
PHONE 847 367-0282
Chris Krafft, *Plant Mgr*
Jason Ming, *Prdtn Mgr*
Jeff Adams, *Mng Member*
Jenny Torres, *Manager*
EMP: 75
SQ FT: 60,000
SALES (est): 26.3MM **Privately Held**
SIC: 3444 Sheet metalwork

(G-12706)
SHERWIN-WILLIAMS COMPANY
1618 S Milwaukee Ave (60048-3751)
PHONE 847 573-0240
EMP: 6
SALES (corp-wide): 17.9B **Publicly Held**
WEB: www.sherwin-williams.com
SIC: 5231 5198 2851 Paint; paints, varnishes & supplies; wood fillers or sealers
PA: The Sherwin-Williams Company
    101 W Prospect Ave # 1020
    Cleveland OH 44115
    216 566-2000

(G-12707)
SIGNS & WONDERS UNLIMITED LLC
28318 N Oak Ln (60048-9762)
P.O. Box 489 (60048-0489)
PHONE 847 816-9734
Nancy Powers,
EMP: 3
SALES (est): 166.2K **Privately Held**
SIC: 7372 Application computer software

(G-12708)
SMART SOLAR INC
Also Called: Smart Living Home & Garden
1203 Loyola Dr (60048-1290)
PHONE 813 343-5770
James Bologeorges, *President*
▲ **EMP:** 15
SALES (est): 2.2MM **Privately Held**
SIC: 5719 3799 5261 3645 Lamps & lamp shades; pushcarts; fountains, outdoor; garden, patio, walkway & yard lighting fixtures: electric; hammocks: metal or fabric & metal combination

(G-12709)
STAREX INC
1880 W Winchester Rd # 206 (60048-5336)
PHONE 847 918-5555
James Yan, *President*
▲ **EMP:** 6
SQ FT: 2,000
SALES: 10MM **Privately Held**
SIC: 3624 Electrodes, thermal & electrolytic uses: carbon, graphite

(G-12710)
STRUCTURAL DESIGN CORP
1133 Claridge Dr (60048-1240)
PHONE 847 816-3816
William Vanni, *President*
Deborah Vanni, *Admin Sec*
EMP: 6
SQ FT: 400
SALES (est): 581.3K **Privately Held**
SIC: 8711 3441 Structural engineering; consulting engineer; fabricated structural metal

(G-12711)
SURGICAL INNOVATION ASSOC INC
800 Liberty Dr (60048-2345)
PHONE 847 548-8499
Paul Serio, *Branch Mgr*
EMP: 5
SALES (corp-wide): 935.1K **Privately Held**
SIC: 3841 Surgical & medical instruments
PA: Surgical Innovation Associates, Inc.
    800 Liberty Dr
    Chicago IL 60601
    626 372-4884

(G-12712)
SWANSON WATER TREATMENT INC
509 E Park Ave Ste 101 (60048-2873)
P.O. Box 675, Mundelein (60060-0675)
PHONE 847 680-1113
Murner Swanson, *President*
EMP: 5
SQ FT: 1,500
SALES (est): 300K **Privately Held**
SIC: 2899 Water treating compounds

(G-12713)
T J BROOKS CO
804 E Park Ave Ste 104 (60048-2901)
PHONE 847 680-0350
EMP: 2 **EST:** 2009
SALES (est): 200K **Privately Held**
SIC: 3593 Mfg Fluid Power Cylinders

(G-12714)
TALOC USA INC
1915 Enterprise Ct (60048-9764)
PHONE 847 665-8222
Bryan Timmerman, *President*
EMP: 7 **EST:** 2013
SALES (est): 701K **Privately Held**
SIC: 3579 1761 8999 Canceling machinery, post office; architectural sheet metal work; actuarial consultant

(G-12715)
TAYLOR ENTERPRISES INC
5510 Fairmont Rd Ste A (60048-4806)
PHONE 847 367-1032
Dr Wayne A Taylor, *Chairman*
Dr Wayne Taylor, *Chairman*
Ann Taylor, *Treasurer*
EMP: 2
SALES: 800K **Privately Held**
SIC: 2731 Books: publishing only

(G-12716)
THERAPEUTIC ENVISIONS INC
Also Called: Braceunder
151 Blueberry Rd (60048-2161)
PHONE 720 323-7032
Charles Hodges, *Principal*
EMP: 5
SALES (est): 290.4K **Privately Held**
SIC: 3842 Braces, orthopedic

(G-12717)
TRI CABLE INC
Also Called: Tri Systmes
521 Sandy Ln (60048-3553)
PHONE 847 815-6082
Steven Vivacue, *President*
EMP: 3
SALES (est): 205.1K **Privately Held**
SIC: 3699 Security devices

(G-12718)
TRI R
1921 Industrial Dr (60048-9731)
PHONE 224 399-7786
Rory Hebel, *Principal*
EMP: 8
SALES (est): 1MM **Privately Held**
WEB: www.trirfabrication.com
SIC: 3842 Welders' hoods

(G-12719)
UNIQUE INDOOR COMFORT
624 2nd St (60048-2076)
PHONE 847 362-1910
Judy Henrich, *Owner*
Josh Henrich, *Opers Mgr*
Kelly Covert, *Sales Executive*
EMP: 15
SQ FT: 3,500

GEOGRAPHIC SECTION

Lincolnshire - Lake County (G-12741)

SALES (est): 1.5MM **Privately Held**
WEB: www.uniqueindoor.com
SIC: **1711** 5063 3639 3561 Warm air heating & air conditioning contractor; generators; hot water heaters, household; pumps, domestic: water or sump; geothermal drilling

(G-12720)
US ACRYLIC LLC
1320 Harris Rd (60048-2413)
PHONE.....................................847 837-4800
Anne O' Connel, *Controller*
Monique Hsu,
Tina Hsu,
Jerry Lee,
◆ EMP: 56
SQ FT: 85,000
SALES (est): 11.5MM **Privately Held**
SIC: **3089** Plastic kitchenware, tableware & houseware; novelties, plastic

(G-12721)
USG CORPORATION
Also Called: Research & Technology Center
700 N Us Highway 45 (60048-1268)
PHONE.....................................847 970-5200
Steve Campbell, *Opers Staff*
Michael Shake, *Research*
James Lehane, *Technical Staff*
EMP: 19
SALES (corp-wide): 8.2B **Privately Held**
WEB: www.usg.com
SIC: **3296** 3275 Mineral wool insulation products; acoustical board & tile, mineral wool; gypsum board
HQ: Usg Corporation
550 W Adams St
Chicago IL 60661
312 436-4000

(G-12722)
VALENT BIOSCIENCES LLC (DH)
Also Called: Valent USA
870 Technology Way # 100 (60048-5350)
PHONE.....................................800 323-9597
Michael D Donaldson, *President*
Peter Dechant, *Business Mgr*
Jim Petta, *Business Mgr*
Roger Storey, *Business Mgr*
Steve Wiest, *Business Mgr*
◆ EMP: 80
SQ FT: 20,000
SALES (est): 35.4MM **Privately Held**
SIC: **2879** Agricultural chemicals
HQ: Valent U.S.A. Llc
1600 Riviera Ave Ste 200
Walnut Creek CA 94596
925 256-2700

(G-12723)
VIDASYM INC
872 S Milwaukee Ave 213 (60048-3227)
PHONE.....................................847 549-3357
Kinfun Wong,
Allen Lau,
Jin Tian,
Jinshyun Wu-Wong,
EMP: 8
SALES (est): 845.4K **Privately Held**
SIC: **2833** Medicinals & botanicals

(G-12724)
VILLAGE PRESS INC
124 E Church St (60048-2218)
PHONE.....................................847 362-1856
Stuart Pyle, *President*
Elizabeth Pyle, *Corp Secy*
Howard Pyle, *Executive*
Elizabeth Goering, *Admin Sec*
EMP: 6
SQ FT: 1,200
SALES (est): 400K **Privately Held**
SIC: **2752** 3953 2759 2675 Commercial printing, offset; screens, textile printing; commercial printing; die-cut paper & board; printing broker; platemaking services

(G-12725)
WILLIAM FRICK & COMPANY (PA)
2600 Commerce Dr (60048-2494)
PHONE.....................................847 918-3700
William G Frick, *CEO*
Jeffrey H Brandt, *President*
Jonathon Petersen, *Business Mgr*
Kyle Wagner, *Business Mgr*
Evie Bennett, *Vice Pres*
◆ EMP: 34
SQ FT: 30,333
SALES (est): 5.3MM **Privately Held**
SIC: **3993** 7389 Signs, not made in custom sign painting shops; design, commercial & industrial

(G-12726)
WILLIAM W MEYER AND SONS (PA)
1700 Franklin Blvd (60048-4407)
PHONE.....................................847 918-0111
Gregory R Buric, *President*
Gayle Baird, *COO*
Mark Dunn, *Vice Pres*
John Thacker, *Opers Staff*
Ray Sarckees, *Purch Mgr*
▲ EMP: 90 EST: 1933
SQ FT: 60,000
SALES (est): 18.3MM **Privately Held**
WEB: www.wmwmeyer.com
SIC: **3535** 3589 3564 3537 Bulk handling conveyor systems; vacuum cleaners & sweepers, electric: industrial; blowers & fans; industrial trucks & tractors; air & gas compressors

(G-12727)
ZELLER PLASTIK USA INC (DH)
1515 Franklin Blvd (60048-4458)
PHONE.....................................847 247-7900
Christian Voegeli, *President*
Roger Sim, *Admin Sec*
◆ EMP: 95
SALES (est): 38.7MM
SALES (corp-wide): 177.9K **Privately Held**
SIC: **3089** Injection molding of plastics
HQ: Global Closure Systems Uk Limited
Sapphire House
Rushden NORTHANTS NN10
178 445-6400

Lincoln
Logan County

(G-12728)
CONTRACTORS READY-MIX INC (PA)
601 S Kickapoo St (62656-3007)
P.O. Box 56 (62656-0056)
PHONE.....................................217 735-2565
Dan Curry, *President*
Sue Curry, *Vice Pres*
Jessie Butler, *Treasurer*
EMP: 15
SALES (est): 3.1MM **Privately Held**
SIC: **3273** 3272 Ready-mixed concrete; concrete products

(G-12729)
EATON CORPORATION
Eaton Electrical
1725 1200th Ave (62656-5040)
PHONE.....................................217 732-3131
Vladimir Salazar, *Plant Mgr*
Mark Gunter, *Mfg Staff*
Ralph Dinges, *Engineer*
Robert Duvall, *Engineer*
Thomas Iseman, *Engineer*
EMP: 700 **Privately Held**
WEB: www.eatonelectrical.com
SIC: **3613** 3644 Switchgear & switchboard apparatus; noncurrent-carrying wiring services
HQ: Eaton Corporation
1000 Eaton Blvd
Cleveland OH 44122
440 523-5000

(G-12730)
HERITAGE PACKAGING LLC
2350 5th St (62656-9628)
PHONE.....................................217 735-4406
Gregory Basford, *General Mgr*
EMP: 29 EST: 1977
SQ FT: 39,000
SALES (est): 6MM
SALES (corp-wide): 353MM **Privately Held**
SIC: **2653** 5113 Boxes, corrugated: made from purchased materials; shipping supplies
PA: Welch Packaging Group, Inc.
1020 Herman St
Elkhart IN 46516
574 295-2460

(G-12731)
INTERNATIONAL PAPER COMPANY
1601 5th St (62656-9128)
PHONE.....................................217 735-1221
Debbie Conlin, *Branch Mgr*
Bradley Migneron, *Technical Staff*
EMP: 160
SALES (corp-wide): 22.3B **Publicly Held**
SIC: **2653** 2656 2631 2611 Boxes, corrugated: made from purchased materials; food containers (liquid tight), including milk cartons; cartons, milk: made from purchased material; container, packaging & boxboard; container board; packaging board; pulp mills; printing paper
PA: International Paper Company
6400 Poplar Ave
Memphis TN 38197
901 419-9000

(G-12732)
LAWRENCE SCREW PRODUCTS INC
437 8th St (62656-2561)
PHONE.....................................217 735-1230
John Mammen, *Warehouse Mgr*
Richard Schmidt, *Branch Mgr*
EMP: 6
SALES (corp-wide): 71.6MM **Privately Held**
SIC: **3451** Screw machine products
PA: Lawrence Screw Products, Inc.
7230 W Wilson Ave
Harwood Heights IL 60706
708 867-5150

(G-12733)
LINCOLN PRINTERS INC
711 Broadway St (62656-2837)
PHONE.....................................217 732-3121
Mike Dykman, *President*
Rachel Stroud, *Office Mgr*
Noah Atkinson, *Manager*
EMP: 3
SQ FT: 3,600
SALES (est): 557.8K **Privately Held**
SIC: **2752** Commercial printing, offset

(G-12734)
LINCOLNDAILYNEWSCOM
601 Keokuk St (62656-1730)
PHONE.....................................217 732-7443
Jim Youngquist, *Owner*
Roy Logan, *Advt Staff*
EMP: 6 EST: 2000
SALES (est): 169.9K **Privately Held**
WEB: www.lincolndailynews.com
SIC: **2711** Newspapers, publishing & printing

(G-12735)
MENTAL HEALTH CTRS CENTL ILL
Also Called: Logan Mason Rehabilitation
760 S Postville Dr (62656-2237)
PHONE.....................................217 735-1413
Gene Frioli, *Manager*
EMP: 100
SALES (corp-wide): 14.6MM **Privately Held**
WEB: www.mhcci.org
SIC: **8093** 8331 2448 8399 Mental health clinic, outpatient; job training & vocational rehabilitation services; wood pallets & skids; community development groups
PA: Mental Health Centers Of Central Illinois
710 N 8th St
Springfield IL 62702
217 525-4777

(G-12736)
NEALS TRAILER SALES
1670 1100th St (62656-5027)
PHONE.....................................217 792-5136
Donny Neal, *Owner*
EMP: 3
SALES (est): 244.1K **Privately Held**
SIC: **5013** 7692 Trailer parts & accessories; welding repair

(G-12737)
PRECISION PRODUCTS INC
316 Limit St (62656-2943)
PHONE.....................................217 735-1590
Mort Kay, *President*
Rick Clayton, *Prdtn Mgr*
Les Jannings, *QC Mgr*
Becky Juilfs, *Human Res Mgr*
◆ EMP: 200
SQ FT: 650,000
SALES (est): 48.3MM **Privately Held**
SIC: **3423** 3524 Hand & edge tools; lawn & garden equipment

(G-12738)
SHEWS CUSTOM WOODWORKING
1441 1200th St (62656-5049)
PHONE.....................................217 737-5543
Mark Shew, *Owner*
EMP: 3
SQ FT: 1,872
SALES (est): 125K **Privately Held**
SIC: **2434** 2511 Wood kitchen cabinets; wood household furniture

(G-12739)
VERNON MICHEAL
Also Called: Hardball Chemical Co
1100 Home Ave (62656-3056)
P.O. Box 306 (62656-0306)
PHONE.....................................217 735-4005
Michael Vernon, *Owner*
EMP: 7
SALES (est): 625.3K **Privately Held**
WEB: www.hardballchemical.net
SIC: **2819** Industrial inorganic chemicals

Lincolnshire
Lake County

(G-12740)
1883 PROPERTIES INC (HQ)
Also Called: E H Wachs Company
600 Knightsbridge Pkwy (60069-3617)
PHONE.....................................847 537-8800
Edward H Wachs, *Ch of Bd*
Ken Morency, *President*
Tim Sheehan, *Vice Pres*
Russell Hendrix, *Opers Staff*
Mike Lange, *Senior Buyer*
◆ EMP: 70
SQ FT: 80,000
SALES (est): 27.6MM
SALES (corp-wide): 14.1B **Publicly Held**
WEB: www.ehwachs.com
SIC: **1799** 3541 Welding on site; machine tools, metal cutting type; pipe cutting & threading machines
PA: Illinois Tool Works Inc.
155 Harlem Ave
Glenview IL 60025
847 724-7500

(G-12741)
ACCO BRANDS USA LLC
500 Bond St (60069-4207)
PHONE.....................................847 272-3700
Victor Finch, *Director*
EMP: 100
SALES (corp-wide): 1.9B **Publicly Held**
SIC: **3089** 2761 3496 2675 Injection molding of plastics; manifold business forms; clips & fasteners, made from purchased wire; letters, cardboard, die-cut: from purchased materials
HQ: Acco Brands Usa Llc
4 Corporate Dr
Lake Zurich IL 60047
800 222-6462

Lincolnshire - Lake County (G-12742)

(G-12742)
ADCO GLOBAL INC (DH)
100 Tri State Intl # 135 (60069-4425)
PHONE...................847 282-3485
John Knox, *Principal*
Michael Graf, *Vice Pres*
Peter Paulsen, *CFO*
Mike Graf, *Marketing Mgr*
◆ **EMP:** 3 **EST:** 1999
SALES (est): 246.3MM
SALES (corp-wide): 2.9B **Publicly Held**
SIC: 2891 Adhesives & sealants
HQ: Royal Adhesives And Sealants Llc
2001 W Washington St
South Bend IN 46628
574 246-5000

(G-12743)
AKSYS LTD
2 Marriott Dr (60069-3700)
PHONE...................847 229-2020
Howard J Lewin, *President*
Jerry D Fisher, *Senior VP*
Richard P Goldhaber, *Senior VP*
Lawrence A Rohrer, *Senior VP*
Karen Krumeich, *CFO*
EMP: 87
SQ FT: 41,500
SALES (est): 10.2MM **Privately Held**
SIC: 3841 Hemodialysis apparatus

(G-12744)
ALTAIR CORPORATION (HQ)
Also Called: Altair Corporation Del
350 Barclay Blvd (60069-3643)
PHONE...................847 634-9540
Garry Brainin, *CEO*
Kevin Shinn, *Vice Pres*
Philippe Wendling, *Vice Pres*
Thomas Morthorst, *CFO*
Amanda Bate, *Marketing Staff*
EMP: 35 **EST:** 1937
SQ FT: 17,000
SALES (est): 52.4MM **Privately Held**
WEB: www.altair.com
SIC: 3555 3564 2048 Printing trades machinery; air purification equipment; livestock feeds
PA: Chatham Corporation
350 Barclay Blvd
Lincolnshire IL 60069
847 634-5506

(G-12745)
AMPHENOL CORPORATION
Amphenol Mechconect
100 Tristate Intl (60069-4403)
PHONE...................847 478-5600
EMP: 5
SALES (corp-wide): 8.2B **Publicly Held**
SIC: 3678 Electronic connectors
PA: Amphenol Corporation
358 Hall Ave
Wallingford CT 06492
203 265-8900

(G-12746)
AMPHENOL T&M ANTENNAS INC (HQ)
100 Tri State Intl # 255 (60069-4405)
PHONE...................847 478-5600
Edward Jepson, *CFO*
▲ **EMP:** 10
SQ FT: 1,100
SALES (est): 1.3MM
SALES (corp-wide): 8.2B **Publicly Held**
SIC: 3663 Antennas, transmitting & communications
PA: Amphenol Corporation
358 Hall Ave
Wallingford CT 06492
203 265-8900

(G-12747)
BURGHOF ENGINEERING & MFG CO
16051 W Deerfield Pkwy # 1 (60069-9629)
PHONE...................847 634-0737
Kaspar Kammerer, *President*
EMP: 20
SQ FT: 10,000
SALES (est): 4.3MM **Privately Held**
SIC: 3565 Packaging machinery

(G-12748)
CEC INDUSTRIES LTD
599 Bond St (60069-4226)
PHONE...................847 821-1199
Warren Wen Lai, *President*
Wen Hsin Lai, *President*
Michael Kwan, *COO*
Pearl Lai, *Controller*
John Goetluck, *Natl Sales Mgr*
▲ **EMP:** 48
SALES (est): 10MM **Privately Held**
WEB: www.cecindustries.com
SIC: 3641 Electric lamps

(G-12749)
CHATHAM CORPORATION (PA)
350 Barclay Blvd (60069-3606)
PHONE...................847 634-5506
Garry Brainin, *President*
Thomas Morthorst, *Vice Pres*
EMP: 15
SALES (est): 52.4MM **Privately Held**
SIC: 3555 3559 3564 2048 Printing trades machinery; foundry machinery & equipment; air purification equipment; feeds, specialty: mice, guinea pig, etc.

(G-12750)
CHEMICAL PROCESSING & ACC
175 Old Hlf Day Rd 140-10 (60069-3087)
P.O. Box 6475, Libertyville (60048-6475)
PHONE...................847 793-2387
Rich Podolski, *Owner*
EMP: 7
SALES (est): 951.6K **Privately Held**
SIC: 2899 5084 Chemical preparations; metal refining machinery & equipment

(G-12751)
CO-RECT PRODUCTS INC (PA)
Also Called: Co-Rect Bar Products
300 Knightsbridge Pkwy # 400 (60069-3668)
PHONE...................763 542-9200
Michael B Pierce, *President*
Steve Ess, *Vice Pres*
Greg Loffler, *Vice Pres*
▲ **EMP:** 29
SQ FT: 45,000
SALES: 8MM **Privately Held**
WEB: www.co-rectproducts.com
SIC: 5046 2599 Restaurant equipment & supplies; bar, restaurant & cafeteria furniture

(G-12752)
COLEMAN CABLE LLC (HQ)
Also Called: Southwire
1 Overlook Pt Ste 265 (60069-4339)
PHONE...................847 672-2300
G Gary Yetman, *President*
Wes Coleman, *Principal*
Richard Carr, *Exec VP*
Michael A Frigo, *Exec VP*
Kathy Jo Van, *Exec VP*
◆ **EMP:** 66
SALES (est): 614.3MM
SALES (corp-wide): 2B **Privately Held**
WEB: www.colemancable.com
SIC: 3661 3357 3643 Telephone cords, jacks, adapters, etc.; nonferrous wire-drawing & insulating; power line cable
PA: Southwire Company, Llc
1 Southwire Dr
Carrollton GA 30119
770 832-4242

(G-12753)
COLEMAN CABLE LLC
1 Overlook Pt (60069-4331)
PHONE...................847 672-2300
Scott Callaghan, *Branch Mgr*
EMP: 75
SALES (corp-wide): 2B **Privately Held**
SIC: 3357 3661 3663 Communication wire; telephone & telegraph apparatus; radio & TV communications equipment
HQ: Coleman Cable, Llc
1 Overlook Pt Ste 265
Lincolnshire IL 60069
847 672-2300

(G-12754)
CONDOMINIUMS NORTHBROOK CORT 1
Also Called: Condominiums Northbrook Court
830 Audubon Way Apt 217 (60069-3846)
PHONE...................847 498-1640
David Levine, *President*
EMP: 5
SALES (est): 190K **Privately Held**
SIC: 8641 3273 Condominium association; ready-mixed concrete

(G-12755)
COUPLINGS COMPANY INC
570 Bond St (60069-4223)
PHONE...................847 634-8990
Lewis Kwate, *President*
Steven Kwate, *Vice Pres*
▲ **EMP:** 15
SQ FT: 40,000
SALES (est): 3.2MM **Privately Held**
WEB: www.brassfittings.com
SIC: 3494 3432 Valves & pipe fittings; plumbers' brass goods: drain cocks, faucets, spigots, etc.

(G-12756)
CREATIVE MERCHANDISING SYSTEMS
425 Village Grn Unit 307 (60069-3098)
PHONE...................847 955-9990
Norman E Topping, *Owner*
EMP: 7
SALES (est): 1.3MM **Privately Held**
SIC: 3578 5046 Point-of-sale devices; display equipment, except refrigerated; store fixtures

(G-12757)
CROWN BRANDS LLC (PA)
Also Called: Clp Foodservice
300 Knightsbridge Pkwy (60069-3625)
PHONE...................224 513-2917
Timothy Palmer, *Vice Pres*
Michelle Hayes, *Controller*
Gregg Lisatinski, *Sales Staff*
David Kreilein,
Chris Baron,
EMP: 32
SALES (est): 36.2MM **Privately Held**
SIC: 3469 2499 3914 Cooking ware, except porcelain enamelled; ladders & stepladders, wood; cutlery, stainless steel

(G-12758)
DART CONTAINER CORP ILLINOIS
300 Tri State Intl Ste 20 (60069-4413)
PHONE...................800 367-2877
Tunde Shoneye, *Business Anlyst*
Christina Hibner, *Data Admn*
EMP: 4
SALES (est): 351.4K **Privately Held**
SIC: 3086 Plastics foam products

(G-12759)
DIGI TRAX CORPORATION
650 Heathrow Dr (60069-4205)
PHONE...................847 613-2100
Richard Kriozere, *CEO*
Jeff Kriozere, *President*
EMP: 26
SQ FT: 15,000
SALES (est): 5MM **Privately Held**
SIC: 7371 7372 5734 Computer software systems analysis & design, custom; business oriented computer software; printers & plotters: computers

(G-12760)
DOUGHNUT BOY
Also Called: Little Miss Muffin
250 Parkway Dr Ste 270 (60069-4346)
PHONE...................773 463-6328
Fax: 773 463-7101
EMP: 40
SALES (est): 6.7MM **Privately Held**
SIC: 2051 Mfg Bread/Related Products

(G-12761)
E H WACHS
600 Knightsbridge Pkwy (60069-3617)
PHONE...................815 943-4785
EMP: 3 **EST:** 2017
SALES (est): 184.7K **Privately Held**
SIC: 3498 Mfg Fabricated Pipe/Fittings

(G-12762)
E H WACHS
Also Called: ITW
600 Knightsbridge Pkwy (60069-3617)
PHONE...................815 943-4785
David B Speer, *Principal*
Mark Wozniak, *Engineer*
EMP: 7
SALES: 1.2MM **Privately Held**
SIC: 3541 Saws & sawing machines

(G-12763)
FAXITRON X-RAY LLC
575 Bond St (60069-4226)
PHONE...................847 465-9729
Allan Little, *Mng Member*
Steve Sapot, *Regional*
EMP: 20
SQ FT: 10,000
SALES (est): 3.2MM **Privately Held**
SIC: 5047 3844 Hospital equipment & furniture; X-ray apparatus & tubes

(G-12764)
FLEXAN LLC (HQ)
Also Called: F M I
500 Bond St (60069-4207)
PHONE...................224 543-0003
Jim Fitzgerarld, *CEO*
Harold Sant, *Vice Pres*
Jonathan Wacks, *Vice Pres*
Connor Kelleher, *Engineer*
David Milner, *CFO*
▲ **EMP:** 128 **EST:** 1977
SQ FT: 65,000
SALES (est): 45.8MM
SALES (corp-wide): 208.3MM **Privately Held**
WEB: www.flexan.com
SIC: 3069 Molded rubber products
PA: Linden Capital Partners Ii Lp
150 N Riverside Plz # 5100
Chicago IL 60606
312 506-5600

(G-12765)
FMI LLC
500 Bond St (60069-4207)
PHONE...................847 350-1535
Jim Fitzgerald, *CEO*
Wesley Distad, *Engineer*
▲ **EMP:** 60
SALES (est): 22.9MM
SALES (corp-wide): 208.3MM **Privately Held**
SIC: 3061 Mechanical rubber goods
HQ: Flexan, Llc
500 Bond St
Lincolnshire IL 60069
224 543-0003

(G-12766)
GF MACHINING SOLUTIONS LLC (DH)
Also Called: Agie Charmilles
560 Bond St (60069-4207)
PHONE...................847 913-5300
Glynn Fletcher, *President*
Mark Sanhamel, *Business Mgr*
Darlene Regilio, *Human Res Dir*
Alain Dubois, *Manager*
Jody Cope,
◆ **EMP:** 100
SQ FT: 55,000
SALES (est): 45.1MM
SALES (corp-wide): 3.7B **Privately Held**
SIC: 3599 Machine shop, jobbing & repair
HQ: George Fischer, Inc.
3401 Aero Jet Ave
El Monte CA 91731
626 571-2770

(G-12767)
GOOD SAM ENTERPRISES LLC (DH)
Also Called: GSE
250 Parkway Dr Ste 270 (60069-4346)
PHONE...................847 229-6720
Stephen Adams, *Ch of Bd*
Marcus A Lemonis, *President*
Matthew Baden, *Exec VP*
Brent Moody, *Exec VP*
John A Sirpilla, *Exec VP*

EMP: 23
SALES: 481.4MM Privately Held
SIC: 5561 7997 2721 Recreational vehicle parts & accessories; membership sports & recreation clubs; magazines: publishing only, not printed on site
HQ: Affinity Group Holding, Llc
2750 Park View Ct Ste 240
Oxnard CA 93036
805 667-4100

(G-12768)
GREAT LAKES MECH SVCS INC
100 Tri State Intl (60069-4403)
PHONE.................708 672-5900
EMP: 12
SQ FT: 10,000
SALES (est): 1.3MM Privately Held
SIC: 7699 1796 7692 Repair Services Bldg Equip Installation Welding Repair

(G-12769)
HCS HAHN CALIBRATION SERVICE
20575 N William Ave (60069-9602)
PHONE.................847 567-2500
William Hahn, *President*
Laurie Hahn, *Vice Pres*
EMP: 1
SALES (est): 234.6K Privately Held
SIC: 3821 Laboratory apparatus & furniture

(G-12770)
HONEYWELL ANALYTICS INC (HQ)
405 Barclay Blvd (60069-3609)
PHONE.................847 955-8200
Carl Johnson, *President*
Paul H Brownstein, *Vice Pres*
John Hakanson, *Vice Pres*
John J Tus, *Treasurer*
David M Demeo, *Asst Treas*
▲ **EMP:** 175
SALES (est): 197.4MM
SALES (corp-wide): 36.7B Publicly Held
SIC: 3491 3829 Process control regulator valves; gas detectors
PA: Honeywell International Inc.
300 S Tryon St
Charlotte NC 28202
704 627-6200

(G-12771)
HONEYWELL INTERNATIONAL INC
405 Barclay Blvd (60069-3609)
PHONE.................847 634-2802
EMP: 9
SALES (corp-wide): 36.7B Publicly Held
SIC: 3724 Aircraft engines & engine parts
PA: Honeywell International Inc.
300 S Tryon St
Charlotte NC 28202
704 627-6200

(G-12772)
HYDRAFORCE INC (PA)
500 Barclay Blvd (60069-4314)
PHONE.................847 793-2300
James Brizzolara, *President*
Mike Schneider, *Production*
Debbie Nunn, *Purchasing*
Martin Birchon, *Engineer*
Alma Botello, *Engineer*
▲ **EMP:** 950
SQ FT: 130,000
SALES (est): 300.1MM Privately Held
SIC: 3492 Control valves, fluid power: hydraulic & pneumatic

(G-12773)
ICD PUBLICATIONS INC
Also Called: Home World Business
175 Old Hlf Day Rd # 240 (60069-3063)
PHONE.................847 913-8295
Allen Rolleri, *Advt Staff*
Cyndi Evans, *Manager*
EMP: 3 Privately Held
SIC: 8743 2721 Sales promotion; periodicals
PA: Icd Publications Inc
150 Motor Pkwy Ste 401
Hauppauge NY 11788

(G-12774)
ILLINOIS TOOL WORKS INC
Also Called: E H Wachs
600 Knightsbridge Pkwy (60069-3617)
PHONE.................815 943-4785
William Pence, *Senior Mgr*
Bill Pence, *Director*
EMP: 80
SALES (corp-wide): 14.1B Publicly Held
SIC: 3644 Insulators & insulation materials, electrical
PA: Illinois Tool Works Inc.
155 Harlem Ave
Glenview IL 60025
847 724-7500

(G-12775)
ION INC
14702 W Mayland Villa Rd (60069-2105)
PHONE.................224 875-1313
EMP: 2
SALES (est): 245.4K Privately Held
SIC: 1382 Oil & gas exploration services

(G-12776)
KIEFFER HOLDING CO (PA)
585 Bond St (60069-4226)
PHONE.................877 543-3337
Matthew Mele, *President*
Jeffrey Fuhrmann, *VP Mfg*
Mark Steffen, *Treasurer*
Larry Caracciolo, *VP Sales*
Stella Chaves, *Admin Sec*
EMP: 5 Privately Held
SIC: 3993 Electric signs; signs, not made in custom sign painting shops

(G-12777)
KLEIN PLASTICS COMPANY LLC
450 Bond St (60069-4225)
PHONE.................616 863-9900
Mathias Klein,
Ken Trupke,
EMP: 85 **EST:** 1967
SQ FT: 70,000
SALES (est): 10.7MM Privately Held
WEB: www.kleintools.com
SIC: 3089 Injection molded finished plastic products

(G-12778)
KLEIN TOOLS INC (PA)
450 Bond St (60069-4225)
P.O. Box 1418 (60069-1418)
PHONE.................847 821-5500
Mark Klein, *President*
Thomas R Klein, *Chairman*
Melody Smith, *Counsel*
Kerry Walsh, *Mfg Mgr*
David Stein, *Opers Staff*
◆ **EMP:** 380 **EST:** 1958
SQ FT: 210,000
SALES (est): 292.1MM Privately Held
WEB: www.kleintools.com
SIC: 3423 3199 Hand & edge tools; belting for machinery: solid, twisted, flat, etc.: leather; safety belts, leather

(G-12779)
KLEIN TOOLS INC
450 Bond St (60069-4225)
PHONE.................847 821-5500
EMP: 48
SALES (corp-wide): 346.8MM Privately Held
SIC: 3423 3199 3469 2899 Mfg Hand Edge Tools Leather Goods Metal Stampings And Chemical Preparation
PA: Klein Tools, Inc.
450 Bond St
Lincolnshire IL 60069
847 821-5500

(G-12780)
LG INNOTEK USA INC
2000 Millbrook Dr (60069-3630)
PHONE.................847 941-8713
EMP: 3 Privately Held
SIC: 3812 Defense systems & equipment
HQ: Lg Innotek Usa, Inc.
2540 N 1st St Ste 400
San Jose CA 95131
408 955-0364

(G-12781)
LIBERTY MACHINERY COMPANY
111 Schelter Rd (60069-3603)
PHONE.................847 276-2761
Peter Sonneborn, *President*
Jim Lucas, *Business Mgr*
▼ **EMP:** 10 **EST:** 1996
SQ FT: 23,000
SALES (est): 2MM Privately Held
SIC: 3441 5084 Fabricated structural metal; industrial machinery & equipment

(G-12782)
MCALLISTER EQUIPMENT CO
100 Tri State Intl # 215 (60069-4427)
PHONE.................217 789-0351
EMP: 28
SALES (corp-wide): 19.1MM Privately Held
SIC: 3053 Mfg Gaskets/Packing/Sealing Devices
PA: Mcallister Equipment Co.
12500 S Cicero Ave
Alsip IL 60069
708 389-7700

(G-12783)
MELINTA SUBSIDIARY CORP (HQ)
300 Tristate Intl Ste 272 (60069-4415)
PHONE.................203 624-5606
Jennifer Sanfilippo, *CEO*
Eugene Sun, *CEO*
Mary T Szela, *Ch of Bd*
John Temperato, *President*
Lyn Baranowski, *Senior VP*
EMP: 40
SQ FT: 27,000
SALES (est): 10.1MM
SALES (corp-wide): 96.4MM Privately Held
WEB: www.melinta.com
SIC: 2834 Pharmaceutical preparations
PA: Melinta Therapeutics, Inc.
44 Whippany Rd Ste 280
Morristown NJ 07960
908 617-1309

(G-12784)
MELINTA SUBSIDIARY CORP
300 Tristate Intl Ste 272 (60069-4415)
PHONE.................203 624-5606
EMP: 10
SALES (corp-wide): 96.4MM Privately Held
SIC: 2834 Pharmaceutical preparations
HQ: Melinta Subsidiary Corp.
300 Tristate Intl Ste 272
Lincolnshire IL 60069
203 624-5606

(G-12785)
MODERN SILICONE TECH INC (PA)
101 Schelter Rd Ste 102b (60069-3632)
PHONE.................727 507-9800
Rachel Grunfeld, *CEO*
Aron Grunfeld, *President*
Phillip Grunfeld, *Manager*
▲ **EMP:** 12
SALES (est): 16.3MM Privately Held
SIC: 3053 3061 2822 Gaskets, packing & sealing devices; mechanical rubber goods; synthetic rubber

(G-12786)
NEXUS PHARMACEUTICALS INC
400 Knightsbridge Pkwy (60069-3613)
PHONE.................847 996-3790
Mariam S Darsot, *President*
Aishe Ahmed, *Vice Pres*
Ayesha Ahmed, *Vice Pres*
Shahid Ahmed, *Vice Pres*
Usman Ahmed, *Vice Pres*
EMP: 57
SQ FT: 38,000
SALES: 79.6MM Privately Held
SIC: 2834 Pharmaceutical preparations

(G-12787)
NICHOLS ALUMINUM LLC
200 Schelter Rd (60069-3635)
P.O. Box 1401 (60069-1401)
PHONE.................847 634-3150
EMP: 106 Privately Held
SIC: 3354 3353 Shapes, extruded aluminum; aluminum sheet, plate & foil
HQ: Nichols Aluminum Llc
25825 Science Park Dr # 400
Beachwood OH 44122

(G-12788)
NILES AUTO PARTS
20734 N Elizabeth Ave (60069-9631)
PHONE.................847 215-2549
Paul Mitsui, *President*
Sheryl Mitsui, *Admin Sec*
EMP: 4 **EST:** 1968
SQ FT: 2,800
SALES (est): 550K Privately Held
SIC: 5531 5013 3694 3625 Automotive parts; automotive supplies & parts; engine electrical equipment; relays & industrial controls

(G-12789)
PANATECH COMPUTER MANAGEMENT
250 Parkway Dr Ste 150 (60069-4340)
PHONE.................847 678-8848
Henry G Fiorentini, *President*
EMP: 3
SALES (est): 486.2K Privately Held
WEB: www.panatechcomputer.com
SIC: 5045 7379 7372 Computers; computer related consulting services; business oriented computer software

(G-12790)
PAPER GRAPHICS INC
612 Heathrow Dr (60069-4205)
PHONE.................847 276-2727
Craig Funk, *President*
EMP: 3
SALES (est): 194.1K Privately Held
SIC: 2893 Printing ink

(G-12791)
PARALLELDIRECT LLC
Also Called: Magic Mist, The
103 Schelter Rd Ste 20 (60069-3657)
PHONE.................847 748-2025
Guru Charan,
Amit Aggarwal,
Sanjay Veerkar,
EMP: 7
SALES: 400.8K Privately Held
SIC: 2131 7389 Smoking tobacco;

(G-12792)
PARKER-HANNIFIN CORPORATION
Also Called: Hydralic Cartridge Systems Div
595 Schelter Rd Ste 100 (60069-4220)
PHONE.................847 955-5000
Antonio Morales, *Manager*
Allie Francisco, *Supervisor*
Matt Gillmore, *Technician*
EMP: 200
SALES (corp-wide): 14.3B Publicly Held
SIC: 3594 Fluid power pumps
PA: Parker-Hannifin Corporation
6035 Parkland Blvd
Cleveland OH 44124
216 896-3000

(G-12793)
PURAC AMERICA INC
111 Barclay Blvd (60069-3610)
PHONE.................847 634-6330
EMP: 3
SALES (est): 185.5K Privately Held
SIC: 2099 Food preparations

(G-12794)
SAPUTO CHEESE USA INC (DH)
1 Overlook Pt Ste 300 (60069-4327)
PHONE.................847 267-1100
Lino A Saputo Jr, *President*
Vincent Staiger, *Director*
Louis Philippe Carriere, *Admin Sec*
▲ **EMP:** 100
SALES (est): 5.8B
SALES (corp-wide): 3.7B Privately Held
SIC: 2022 Cheese spreads, dips, pastes & other cheese products
HQ: Saputo Inc
6869 Boul Metropolitain E
Saint-Leonard QC H1P 1
514 328-6662

Lincolnshire - Lake County (G-12795)

(G-12795)
SAPUTO INC
1 Overlook Pt Ste 300 (60069-4327)
PHONE..................715 755-3485
Mike Braut, *Branch Mgr*
Jennifer Zientek, *Manager*
EMP: 50
SALES (corp-wide): 3.7B **Privately Held**
SIC: 2022 Cheese, natural & processed
HQ: Saputo Inc
6869 Boul Metropolitain E
Saint-Leonard QC H1P 1
514 328-6662

(G-12796)
SWIRLCUP
255 Parkway Dr Ste B (60069-4311)
PHONE..................847 229-2200
EMP: 8
SALES (est): 250K **Privately Held**
SIC: 2051 Mfg Bread/Related Products

(G-12797)
SYSMEX AMERICA INC (HQ)
577 Aptakisic Rd (60069-4325)
PHONE..................847 996-4500
John Kershaw, *President*
Bill Troup, *District Mgr*
Maurice Parker, *COO*
Andre Ezers, *Exec VP*
David Arms, *Vice Pres*
◆ **EMP:** 125
SQ FT: 55,000
SALES (est): 359.5MM **Privately Held**
WEB: www.partecnorthamerica.com
SIC: 5047 3841 Instruments, surgical & medical; medical instruments & equipment, blood & bone work

(G-12798)
TENNECO AUTOMOTIVE OPER CO INC
605 Heathrow Dr (60069-4206)
PHONE..................847 821-0757
Dave Shanaberger, *Branch Mgr*
John Murray, *Technology*
EMP: 204
SALES (corp-wide): 17.4B **Publicly Held**
SIC: 3714 Motor vehicle parts & accessories
HQ: Tenneco Automotive Operating Company, Inc.
500 N Field Dr
Lake Forest IL 60045
847 482-5000

(G-12799)
UNITED PRESS INC
211 Northampton Ln (60069-2400)
PHONE..................847 482-0597
Robert Deer, *President*
EMP: 16
SALES: 1MM **Privately Held**
SIC: 2752 2771 2657 Commercial printing, offset; greeting cards; folding paperboard boxes

(G-12800)
VARIAN MEDICAL SYSTEMS INC
425 Barclay Blvd (60069-3609)
PHONE..................847 279-5100
David Nisius, *President*
James McNally, *Branch Mgr*
EMP: 15
SALES (corp-wide): 3.2B **Publicly Held**
WEB: www.varian.com
SIC: 3841 Surgical & medical instruments
PA: Varian Medical Systems, Inc.
3100 Hansen Way
Palo Alto CA 94304
650 493-4000

(G-12801)
VICTOR CONSULTING
42 Cumberland Dr 2a (60069-3109)
PHONE..................847 267-8012
Barry Tauber, *Principal*
Catherine Tauber, *Principal*
EMP: 9
SALES: 250K **Privately Held**
SIC: 7372 Educational computer software

(G-12802)
WOODHEAD INDUSTRIES LLC (DH)
333 Knightsbridge Pkwy # 200 (60069-3662)
PHONE..................847 353-2500
Philippe Lemaitre, *Ch of Bd*
Robert A Moulton, *Vice Pres*
Robert J Tortorello, *Vice Pres*
Robert H Fisher, *CFO*
Joseph P Nogal, *Treasurer*
▲ **EMP:** 500
SQ FT: 11,600
SALES (est): 122.7MM
SIC: 3678 3679 3643 3357 Electronic connectors; electronic switches; electronic circuits; connectors & terminals for electrical devices; communication wire; fiber optic cable (insulated)
HQ: Molex, Llc
2222 Wellington Ct
Lisle IL 60532
630 969-4550

(G-12803)
ZEBRA RETAIL SOLUTIONS LLC
3 Overlook Pt (60069-4302)
PHONE..................847 634-6700
EMP: 3
SALES (est): 125K
SALES (corp-wide): 4.4B **Publicly Held**
SIC: 3577 Computer peripheral equipment
PA: Zebra Technologies Corporation
3 Overlook Pt
Lincolnshire IL 60069
847 634-6700

(G-12804)
ZEBRA TECHNOLOGIES CORPORATION (PA)
3 Overlook Pt (60069-4302)
PHONE..................847 634-6700
Anders Gustafsson, *CEO*
Michael A Smith, *Ch of Bd*
Cristen Kogl, *Senior VP*
Olivier Leonetti, *CFO*
Michael H Terzich, *Officer*
▲ **EMP:** 265
SALES: 4.4B **Publicly Held**
WEB: www.zebra.com
SIC: 3577 2672 2679 5045 Bar code (magnetic ink) printers; adhesive papers, labels or tapes: from purchased material; labels (unprinted), gummed: made from purchased materials; tags, paper (unprinted): made from purchased paper; computers, peripherals & software

(G-12805)
ZEBRA TECHNOLOGIES INTL LLC (HQ)
3 Overlook Pt (60069-4302)
PHONE..................847 634-6700
Philip Gerskovich, *Principal*
Michael Smiley, *Mng Member*
David Crist,
Noel Elfant,
Kaput Jim,
◆ **EMP:** 6
SALES (est): 7.3MM
SALES (corp-wide): 4.4B **Publicly Held**
SIC: 3577 Bar code (magnetic ink) printers
PA: Zebra Technologies Corporation
3 Overlook Pt
Lincolnshire IL 60069
847 634-6700

(G-12806)
ZENITH ELECTRONICS CORPORATION (DH)
2000 Millbrook Dr (60069-3630)
PHONE..................847 941-8000
Tok Joo Lee, *Ch of Bd*
Glen Dickson, *Vice Pres*
Jason Fuchs, *Vice Pres*
Laura Meighan, *Vice Pres*
Beverley Wyckoff, *Vice Pres*
▲ **EMP:** 46 **EST:** 1918

SALES (est): 183.3MM **Privately Held**
WEB: www.zenith.com
SIC: 3651 3671 3663 3674 Audio electronic systems; television receiving sets; video cassette recorders/players & accessories; television tubes; television broadcasting & communications equipment; cable television equipment; microcircuits, integrated (semiconductor); television cabinets, wood; television cabinets, plastic
HQ: Lg Electronics U.S.A., Inc.
111 Sylvan Ave
Englewood Cliffs NJ 07632
201 816-2000

(G-12807)
ZIH CORP
3 Overlook Pt (60069-4302)
PHONE..................847 634-6700
Anders Gustafsson, *CEO*
Gerhard Cless, *Exec VP*
Michael C Smiley, *CFO*
▲ **EMP:** 8
SQ FT: 154,300
SALES (est): 1.5MM
SALES (corp-wide): 4.4B **Publicly Held**
SIC: 3577 2672 Bar code (magnetic ink) printers; adhesive papers, labels or tapes: from purchased material; labels (unprinted), gummed: made from purchased materials
PA: Zebra Technologies Corporation
3 Overlook Pt
Lincolnshire IL 60069
847 634-6700

(G-12808)
ZIH CORP
Also Called: Zebra
3 Overlook Pt (60069-4302)
PHONE..................847 634-6700
EMP: 26
SALES (est): 5.5MM
SALES (corp-wide): 3.6B **Publicly Held**
SIC: 3577 Mfg Computer Peripheral Equipment
PA: Zebra Technologies Corporation
3 Overlook Pt
Lincolnshire IL 60069
847 634-6700

Lincolnwood
Cook County

(G-12809)
6965 NORTH HAMLIN LLC
6965 N Hamlin Ave (60712-2549)
PHONE..................847 673-8900
Richard A Voss, *Principal*
EMP: 3
SALES (est): 164.5K **Privately Held**
WEB: www.vossbelting.com
SIC: 3052 Rubber & plastics hose & beltings

(G-12810)
ABCT CORPORATION
3924 W Devon Ave Ste 300 (60712-1040)
PHONE..................773 427-1010
EMP: 5 **Privately Held**
WEB: www.framefactory.com
SIC: 5999 3499 Art, picture frames & decorations; picture frames, metal
PA: Abct Corporation
1809 W Webster Ave
Chicago IL

(G-12811)
ADA METAL PRODUCTS INC
7120 N Capitol Dr (60712-2702)
PHONE..................847 673-1190
Peter Barkules, *President*
Byron Barkules, *Vice Pres*
Leo Shtern, *Chief Engr*
Rene Campos, *Engineer*
William Barkules, *Treasurer*
EMP: 38 **EST:** 1945
SQ FT: 63,000
SALES (est): 8.3MM **Privately Held**
WEB: www.adametal.com
SIC: 3469 Stamping metal for the trade

(G-12812)
ADVANCED PLASTIC CORP
3725 W Lunt Ave (60712-2615)
PHONE..................847 674-2070
Harold Koenig, *President*
Fred CAM-Koo, *Vice Pres*
Jim Stoesser, *Vice Pres*
Fermin Castro, *Plant Mgr*
Frederick Koo, *Plant Mgr*
▲ **EMP:** 80 **EST:** 1981
SQ FT: 80,000
SALES (est): 25.1MM **Privately Held**
SIC: 3082 Rods, unsupported plastic; tubes, unsupported plastic

(G-12813)
ALL CONTAINER INC
7060 N Lawndale Ave (60712-2610)
PHONE..................847 677-2100
Linda Worley, *Manager*
EMP: 8 **EST:** 1968
SALES (est): 796.4K **Privately Held**
SIC: 3411 Metal cans

(G-12814)
BROWN WOOD PRODUCTS COMPANY (PA)
Also Called: Gavel Company Div, The
7040 N Lawndale Ave (60712-2610)
P.O. Box 598052, Chicago (60659-8052)
PHONE..................847 673-4780
Terry D Gross, *President*
Kathryn Constantine, *Sales Staff*
Mark Grewe, *Sales Staff*
Linda Dodero, *Manager*
Terry Gross, *CIO*
▲ **EMP:** 14 **EST:** 1927
SQ FT: 18,000
SALES (est): 3.2MM **Privately Held**
WEB: www.brownwoodinc.com
SIC: 2499 2431 5199 Carved & turned wood; interior & ornamental woodwork & trim; advertising specialties

(G-12815)
CORPORATE TEXTILES INC
6529 N Lincoln Ave 5 (60712-3925)
PHONE..................847 433-4111
Arnold L Kapp, *President*
Rhonda Kapp, *CFO*
Theresa Srnick, *Marketing Staff*
▲ **EMP:** 2
SQ FT: 1,000
SALES (est): 218.1K **Privately Held**
SIC: 2323 Neckties, men's & boys': made from purchased materials

(G-12816)
DENTAL TECHNOLOGIES INC
6901 N Hamlin Ave (60712-2553)
PHONE..................847 677-5500
Stephen Erickson, *President*
Paula Erickson, *Admin Sec*
Kyle Kudelka, *Representative*
▲ **EMP:** 70
SQ FT: 40,000
SALES (est): 22.5MM **Privately Held**
SIC: 2834 3843 Pharmaceutical preparations; dental equipment & supplies

(G-12817)
DYNAMIC AUTOMATION INC
3445 W Arthur Ave (60712-3841)
PHONE..................312 782-8555
Shaun Nejati, *President*
EMP: 6
SALES (est): 420K **Privately Held**
SIC: 8711 3541 Mechanical engineering; screw machines, automatic; tapping machines

(G-12818)
FASTSIGNS
3450 W Devon Ave (60712-1304)
PHONE..................847 675-1600
Elizabeth Oconnor, *President*
EMP: 5
SQ FT: 1,800
SALES (est): 512.9K **Privately Held**
SIC: 3993 8712 Signs & advertising specialties; architectural services

GEOGRAPHIC SECTION

Lincolnwood - Cook County (G-12846)

(G-12819)
FEDEX OFFICE & PRINT SVCS INC
6829 N Lincoln Ave (60712-2623)
PHONE..................847 329-9464
EMP: 12
SALES (corp-wide): 69.6B Publicly Held
SIC: 7334 2791 2789 2672 Photocopying & duplicating services; typesetting; bookbinding & related work; coated & laminated paper
HQ: Fedex Office And Print Services, Inc.
7900 Legacy Dr
Plano TX 75024
800 463-3339

(G-12820)
GAGE ASSEMBLY CO
3771 W Morse Ave (60712-2684)
PHONE..................847 679-5180
Daniel Plodzeen, *President*
Brad Plodzeen, *COO*
Dawn Wittig, *Human Res Mgr*
EMP: 55 EST: 1953
SQ FT: 23,000
SALES (est): 9.6MM Privately Held
WEB: www.gageassembly.com
SIC: 3545 Gauges (machine tool accessories); threading tools (machine tool accessories)

(G-12821)
GENERAL CUTNG TL SVC & MFG INC
6440 N Ridgeway Ave (60712-4028)
PHONE..................847 677-8770
Les J Kasperek, *President*
Joseph Carone, *Vice Pres*
Robert Kasperek, *Mktg Dir*
Yolanda Kasperek, *Admin Sec*
EMP: 18 EST: 1978
SQ FT: 7,500
SALES (est): 5.7MM Privately Held
SIC: 5085 3545 Industrial tools; machine knives, metalworking; precision tools, machinists'; shaping tools (machine tool accessories)

(G-12822)
GERALD GRAFF
Also Called: Aaron Co
6818 N Kildare Ave (60712-4726)
PHONE..................312 343-2612
Gerald Graff, *Owner*
EMP: 20
SALES (est): 1.1MM Privately Held
SIC: 2451 Mobile homes

(G-12823)
GLENAIR INC
Also Called: Microway Systems Div Glenair
7000 N Lawndale Ave (60712-2610)
PHONE..................847 679-8833
Donald Carroll, *Branch Mgr*
EMP: 48
SALES (corp-wide): 382.9MM Privately Held
SIC: 3678 Electronic connectors
PA: Glenair, Inc.
1211 Air Way
Glendale CA 91201
818 247-6000

(G-12824)
JBSMWG CORP
7170 N Ridgeway Ave (60712-2622)
PHONE..................847 675-1865
Basil Jacobson, *President*
Frank Guihan, *Vice Pres*
Michael Shade, *Admin Sec*
▲ EMP: 10
SALES (est): 1.3MM Privately Held
SIC: 3675 Electronic capacitors

(G-12825)
JVI INC
7131 N Ridgeway Ave (60712-2621)
PHONE..................847 675-1560
James Voss, *President*
▼ EMP: 20
SQ FT: 12,000
SALES (est): 3.1MM Privately Held
WEB: www.jvi-inc.com
SIC: 3069 Molded rubber products

(G-12826)
K CHAE CORP
Also Called: Modern Card Co
3630 W Pratt Ave (60712-3724)
PHONE..................847 763-0077
EMP: 10
SALES (est): 1.1MM Privately Held
SIC: 2771 2752 Mfg Greeting Cards Lithographic Commercial Printing

(G-12827)
LAUREL METAL PRODUCTS INC
3500 W Touhy Ave (60712)
P.O. Box 14, Glenview (60025-0014)
PHONE..................847 674-0064
Patrick Kent, *President*
Chip Kent, *Vice Pres*
EMP: 20 EST: 1960
SQ FT: 17,500
SALES (est): 3.9MM Privately Held
WEB: www.laurelmetal.com
SIC: 3581 Mechanisms for coin-operated machines

(G-12828)
LOGAN SQUARE ALUMINUM SUP INC
Also Called: Studio 41
4767 N Touhy Ave (60712-1622)
PHONE..................847 676-4767
Evaristo Roman, *Branch Mgr*
EMP: 10
SALES (corp-wide): 113MM Privately Held
SIC: 3442 Window & door frames
PA: Logan Square Aluminum Supply, Inc.
2500 N Pulaski Rd
Chicago IL 60639
773 235-2500

(G-12829)
MARC BUSINESS FORMS INC
6416 N Ridgeway Ave (60712-4028)
PHONE..................847 568-9200
Barbara Faermark, *President*
Charlotte Marcuse, *Corp Secy*
EMP: 10
SQ FT: 2,400
SALES (est): 2MM Privately Held
WEB: www.marcprint.com
SIC: 5112 2761 2752 Business forms; manifold business forms; commercial printing, lithographic

(G-12830)
MICROWAY SYSTEMS INC
7000 N Lawndale Ave (60712-2610)
PHONE..................847 679-8833
Richard Zic, *President*
EMP: 44
SQ FT: 24,000
SALES (est): 6.6MM Privately Held
SIC: 3678 Electronic connectors

(G-12831)
MIDWEST TROPICAL ENTPS INC
3420 W Touhy Ave (60712)
PHONE..................847 679-6666
Ken Burnett, *President*
Mike Burnett, *Vice Pres*
Susan Burnett, *Vice Pres*
Michael Burnett, *Sales Staff*
Rose Lee, *Office Mgr*
EMP: 20 EST: 1976
SQ FT: 20,000
SALES (est): 3.5MM Privately Held
SIC: 3231 3089 Aquariums & reflectors, glass; aquarium accessories, plastic

(G-12832)
NEW METAL CRAFTS INC
6453 N Kilpatrick Ave (60712-3416)
PHONE..................312 787-6991
James R Neumann, *President*
Sol Biewiess, *Corp Secy*
▲ EMP: 50
SQ FT: 40,000
SALES (est): 6.3MM Privately Held
WEB: www.newmetalcrafts.com
SIC: 3646 3645 5063 7349 Ornamental lighting fixtures, commercial; residential lighting fixtures; lighting fixtures, commercial & industrial; lighting fixtures, residential; building maintenance services

(G-12833)
NIGHT VISION CORPORATION
4324 W Chase Ave (60712-1915)
PHONE..................847 677-7611
Danny Filipovich, *President*
Thomas J Karacic, *Vice Pres*
EMP: 5
SQ FT: 2,200
SALES (est): 820.2K Privately Held
SIC: 8732 3851 Commercial nonphysical research; ophthalmic goods

(G-12834)
NYLOK LLC
6465 W Proesel Ave (60712-3916)
PHONE..................847 674-9680
Pete Henley, *Vice Pres*
Vito Sperando, *Engineer*
EMP: 75
SALES (corp-wide): 18MM Privately Held
SIC: 3452 Screws, metal
PA: Nylok, Llc
15260 Hallmark Ct
Macomb MI 48042
586 786-0100

(G-12835)
OUTBOUND LIGHTING LLC
7080 N Mccormick Blvd (60712-2711)
PHONE..................314 330-0696
Matthew Conte,
Andrew Schechter,
EMP: 28
SALES (est): 2.2MM Privately Held
SIC: 3647 8711 5091 Bicycle lamps; engineering services; bicycle equipment & supplies

(G-12836)
QUAY CORPORATION INC (PA)
Also Called: Mgr Imports
7101 N Capitol Dr (60712-2701)
PHONE..................847 676-4233
Victor Cuellar, *Ch of Bd*
Margaret Cuellar, *Vice Pres*
Hector Cuellar, *Shareholder*
◆ EMP: 16
SQ FT: 20,000
SALES (est): 5.2MM Privately Held
SIC: 2032 5149 5147 Mexican foods: packaged in cans, jars, etc.; dairy products, dried or canned; meats & meat products

(G-12837)
RESEARCH TECHNOLOGY INTL CO (PA)
Also Called: R T I
4700 W Chase Ave (60712-1608)
P.O. Box 545, Arlington Heights (60006-0545)
PHONE..................847 677-3000
Ray L Short Jr, *President*
Tom Boyle, *Senior VP*
Bill Wolavka, *Vice Pres*
Matthew Malone, *CFO*
Cheryl Davis, *Administration*
EMP: 40
SQ FT: 54,000
SALES (est): 4.3MM Privately Held
SIC: 3861 Motion picture apparatus & equipment

(G-12838)
RF MAU CO
7140 N Lawndale Ave (60712-2612)
PHONE..................847 329-9731
Bruce Mau, *President*
Brian J Adams, *President*
Cliff Garcia, *Mfg Mgr*
Christian Arias, *Foreman/Supr*
Joe Latrofa, *QC Mgr*
EMP: 15
SQ FT: 10,000
SALES (est): 4.1MM Privately Held
WEB: www.rfmau.com
SIC: 3494 3451 3599 Couplings, except pressure & soil pipe; screw machine products; tubing, flexible metallic

(G-12839)
RIFAST SYSTEMS LLC (PA)
3600 W Pratt Ave (60712-3724)
PHONE..................847 933-8330
William Epple, *Opers Mgr*
Zach Mager, *Engineer*
Joseph Gobernatz, *Sales Dir*
Weiss Heiner, *Mng Member*
Mike McKinney, *Manager*
▲ EMP: 30
SALES (est): 4.8MM Privately Held
SIC: 3429 Metal fasteners

(G-12840)
ROLFS PATISSERIE INC
4343 W Touhy Ave (60712-1908)
PHONE..................847 675-6565
Lloyd Culbertson, *President*
Ford Culbertson, *Admin Sec*
EMP: 110
SQ FT: 20,000
SALES (est): 13.5MM Privately Held
SIC: 2051 Bakery: wholesale or wholesale/retail combined; pastries, e.g. danish: except frozen; cakes, bakery: except frozen; pies, bakery: except frozen

(G-12841)
RUTGERS ENTERPRISES INC (PA)
Also Called: MSI Southland
6511 W Proesel Ave (60712-3918)
PHONE..................847 674-7666
Rachel Grunfeld, *CEO*
Aaron Grunfeld, *President*
EMP: 5
SALES (est): 1.4MM Privately Held
SIC: 3053 3069 Gaskets & sealing devices; molded rubber products

(G-12842)
SAFE TRAFFIC SYSTEM INC
6600 N Lincoln Ave (60712-3620)
PHONE..................847 233-0365
Hyun Kim, *CEO*
Moon Kim, *Ch of Bd*
Hoon Y Kim, *President*
Paul Kim, *President*
▲ EMP: 5
SQ FT: 1,200
SALES (est): 450K Privately Held
SIC: 3944 Child restraint seats, automotive

(G-12843)
SHANIN COMPANY
6454 N Kimball Ave (60712-3814)
P.O. Box 577909, Chicago (60657-7341)
PHONE..................847 676-1200
Milton H Shanin, *President*
Raymond Shanin, *Vice Pres*
Greg Shanin, *Manager*
Jeffrey Shanin, *Admin Sec*
EMP: 60
SALES (est): 3.9MM Privately Held
SIC: 2752 2761 2759 Commercial printing, offset; business forms, lithographed; manifold business forms; commercial printing

(G-12844)
TENNECO INC
7001 N Central Park Ave (60712-2700)
PHONE..................847 774-1636
EMP: 3
SALES (corp-wide): 17.4B Publicly Held
SIC: 3714 Motor vehicle parts & accessories
PA: Tenneco Inc.
500 N Field Dr
Lake Forest IL 60045
847 482-5000

(G-12845)
TERRANEO MERCHANTS INC
6525 W Proesel Ave (60712-3918)
PHONE..................312 753-9134
Sasha Burekovic, *President*
EMP: 6
SQ FT: 2,000
SALES (est): 163.1K Privately Held
SIC: 2084 Wines

(G-12846)
TRIM-TEX INC (PA)
3700 W Pratt Ave (60712-2500)
PHONE..................847 679-3000
Karyn Newman, *CEO*
Joseph Koenig Jr, *President*
Mike Garcia, *Vice Pres*
Katie Koenig, *VP Opers*
Linda Khalil, *Prdtn Mgr*

Lincolnwood - Cook County (G-12847)

▲ **EMP:** 100
SQ FT: 218,000
SALES (est): 16.9MM **Privately Held**
SIC: 3089 Extruded finished plastic products

(G-12847)
UPMERCH LLC
6634 N Minnehaha Ave (60712-3024)
PHONE.............................847 674-8601
Alsterda Kevin, *Principal*
EMP: 2
SALES (est): 232.7K **Privately Held**
SIC: 2752 Commercial printing, lithographic

(G-12848)
VITAL TIMES
7301 N Lincoln Ave # 190 (60712-1709)
PHONE.............................847 675-2577
Ricky Schwartz, *Owner*
EMP: 3
SALES (est): 76.2K **Privately Held**
SIC: 2711 Newspapers: publishing only, not printed on site

(G-12849)
VOSS BELTING & SPECIALTY CO
6965 N Hamlin Ave Ste 1 (60712-2598)
PHONE.............................847 673-8900
Richard A Voss, *President*
EMP: 45 **EST:** 1934
SQ FT: 48,000
SALES (est): 9MM **Privately Held**
WEB: www.vossbelting.com
SIC: 3052 3069 2822 2821 Rubber belting; hard rubber products; silicone rubbers; polytetrafluoroethylene resins (teflon); coated & laminated paper; narrow fabric mills

(G-12850)
VOSS ENGINEERING INC
6965 N Hamlin Ave Ste 1 (60712-2549)
PHONE.............................847 673-8900
Richard A Voss, *President*
Brian Smith, *Treasurer*
EMP: 45 **EST:** 1956
SQ FT: 25,500
SALES (est): 6.9MM **Privately Held**
WEB: www.vossengineering.com
SIC: 3463 5085 Bearing & bearing race forgings, nonferrous; bearings; rubber goods, mechanical

(G-12851)
WHITE STOKES COMPANY INC
4433 W Touhy Ave Ste 207 (60712-1833)
P.O. Box 9623, Chicago (60609-0623)
PHONE.............................773 254-5000
Irene Tzakis, *President*
Marilyn Tzakis, *Controller*
Dino Collaros, *Manager*
Joanne Smith, *Director*
EMP: 40 **EST:** 1907
SQ FT: 80,000
SALES (est): 6MM **Privately Held**
SIC: 2064 2087 Cake ornaments, confectionery; syrups, flavoring (except drink)

(G-12852)
YAZDAN ESSIE
Also Called: Laminate Craft
3730 W Morse Ave (60712-2618)
PHONE.............................847 675-7916
Essie Yazdan, *Owner*
EMP: 2 **EST:** 1986
SALES (est): 467.5K **Privately Held**
WEB: www.laminatecraft.com
SIC: 3553 Cabinet makers' machinery

Lindenhurst
Lake County

(G-12853)
CROSSWIND PRINTING
588 Crosswind Ln (60046-6743)
PHONE.............................847 356-1009
Robert Clausing, *Owner*
EMP: 2 **EST:** 2001
SALES: 525K **Privately Held**
SIC: 2752 Commercial printing, offset

(G-12854)
SITEXPEDITE LLC
430 N Crooked Lake Ln (60046-6429)
PHONE.............................847 245-2185
Vinh Diep, *VP Opers*
John McDade,
EMP: 27
SQ FT: 5,000
SALES: 2.2MM **Privately Held**
WEB: www.sitexpedite.net
SIC: 7629 3449 Telecommunication equipment repair (except telephones); miscellaneous metalwork

(G-12855)
WATSON FOODS CO INC
1711 E Grand Ave (60046-7815)
PHONE.............................847 245-8404
EMP: 63
SALES (corp-wide): 60.5MM **Privately Held**
SIC: 2045 Mfg Prepared Flour Mixes
PA: Watson Foods Co., Inc.
301 Heffernan Dr
West Haven CT 06516
203 932-3000

Lisle
Dupage County

(G-12856)
AAIS SERVICES CORPORATION (PA)
701 Warrenville Rd # 100 (60532-1375)
PHONE.............................630 681-8347
Edmund Kelly, *CEO*
Joan Zerkovich, *COO*
Truman Esmond, *Vice Pres*
Robert Guevara, *Vice Pres*
John Kadous, *Vice Pres*
EMP: 50
SQ FT: 11,500
SALES: 18.1MM **Privately Held**
SIC: 6411 5112 2721 Professional standards services, insurance; business forms; trade journals: publishing only, not printed on site

(G-12857)
AAIS SERVICES CORPORATION
701 Wrrnvlle Rd Ste 100 (60532)
PHONE.............................630 457-3263
Edmund Kelly, *CEO*
Joan Zerkovich, *COO*
Michael Peters, *CFO*
EMP: 4
SQ FT: 11,000
SALES: 16.7K
SALES (corp-wide): 18.1MM **Privately Held**
SIC: 6411 5112 2721 Professional standards services, insurance; business forms; trade journals: publishing only, not printed on site
PA: Aais Services Corporation
701 Warrenville Rd # 100
Lisle IL 60532
630 681-8347

(G-12858)
ADVANTAGE PRESS INC
3033 Ogden Ave Ste 110 (60532-1976)
P.O. Box 3025 (60532-8025)
PHONE.............................630 960-5305
William Rowland, *President*
Rick Windsor, *Treasurer*
EMP: 8
SALES (est): 552.6K **Privately Held**
SIC: 2731 8748 Books: publishing & printing; business consulting

(G-12859)
AIR DUCT MANUFACTURING INC
4810 Venture St (60532-3500)
PHONE.............................630 620-9866
Amir Sharify, *President*
EMP: 8
SALES (est): 1MM **Privately Held**
SIC: 3585 1611 Parts for heating, cooling & refrigerating equipment; general contractor, highway & street construction

(G-12860)
ALLEGRA PRINT & IMAGING
2200 Ogden Ave Ste 500a (60532-1972)
PHONE.............................630 963-9100
Wayne Muhs, *Owner*
Tom Sherman, *Marketing Mgr*
EMP: 10
SALES (est): 1.2MM **Privately Held**
WEB: www.allegramarketingprint.com
SIC: 2752 Commercial printing, offset

(G-12861)
ALPHAGRAPHICS PRINTSHOPS
1997 Ohio St Ste B (60532-4131)
PHONE.............................630 964-9600
Lynn McKenzie, *President*
Susan McKenzie Vice President, *Admin Sec*
EMP: 4
SQ FT: 1,734
SALES (est): 546K **Privately Held**
SIC: 2752 7334 2791 2789 Commercial printing, lithographic; photocopying & duplicating services; typesetting; bookbinding & related work

(G-12862)
ALTMAN MANUFACTURING CO INC
1990 Ohio St (60532-2145)
PHONE.............................630 963-0031
Paul C Altman, *President*
Kathleen Altman, *Treasurer*
Paul Altman, *Persnl Dir*
Brian Altman, *VP Sales*
▲ **EMP:** 10 **EST:** 1942
SQ FT: 4,800
SALES (est): 979K **Privately Held**
SIC: 3544 3542 Special dies & tools; machine tools, metal forming type

(G-12863)
AMPHENOL CORPORATION
Amphenol Fiber Optic Products
2100 Western Ct Ste 300 (60532-1971)
PHONE.............................800 944-6446
Thomas J Ricko, *General Mgr*
EMP: 83
SALES (corp-wide): 8.2B **Publicly Held**
SIC: 3678 Electronic connectors
PA: Amphenol Corporation
358 Hall Ave
Wallingford CT 06492
203 265-8900

(G-12864)
AMPHENOL FIBER OPTIC PRODUCTS
2100 Western Ct Ste 300 (60532-1971)
PHONE.............................630 960-1010
Fax: 630 810-5600
▲ **EMP:** 25
SALES (est): 6.4MM
SALES (corp-wide): 5.5B **Publicly Held**
SIC: 3678 Mfg Electronic Connectors
PA: Amphenol Corporation
358 Hall Ave
Wallingford CT 06492
203 265-8900

(G-12865)
ANHEUSER-BUSCH LLC
1011 Warrenville Rd # 350 (60532-0934)
PHONE.............................630 512-9002
Kevin Feehan, *Vice Pres*
EMP: 162
SALES (corp-wide): 1.5B **Privately Held**
SIC: 2082 Beer (alcoholic beverage)
HQ: Anheuser-Busch, Llc
1 Busch Pl
Saint Louis MO 63118
800 342-5283

(G-12866)
ANJU SOFTWARE INC
Also Called: Online Business Applications
4343 Commerce Ct Ste 501 (60532-3672)
PHONE.............................630 243-9810
EMP: 46
SALES (corp-wide): 28.2MM **Privately Held**
SIC: 7372 Business oriented computer software

PA: Anju Software, Inc.
4500 S Lkshore Dr Ste 620
Tempe AZ 85282
630 246-2527

(G-12867)
ARBOR PRINTING & GRAPHICS INC
438 Angelo Ln (60532-3196)
PHONE.............................630 969-2277
Pam Shuta, *President*
Michael Shuta, *Vice Pres*
EMP: 6
SQ FT: 2,700
SALES: 700K **Privately Held**
SIC: 2752 Commercial printing, offset

(G-12868)
ARIBA INC
3333 Warrenville Rd # 130 (60532-1498)
PHONE.............................630 649-7600
Christine Morrissey, *Manager*
EMP: 5
SALES (corp-wide): 30.4B **Privately Held**
WEB: www.ariba.com
SIC: 7372 Business oriented computer software
HQ: Ariba, Inc.
3420 Hillview Ave Bldg 3
Palo Alto CA 94304

(G-12869)
ASTA SERVICE INC
5821 Iris Ln (60532-2731)
PHONE.............................630 271-0960
Curt Willeford, *President*
Susan Willeford, *Vice Pres*
EMP: 2
SALES (est): 647.1K **Privately Held**
SIC: 5051 3559 Foundry products; foundry machinery & equipment

(G-12870)
AUTOMATED LOGIC CORPORATION
Also Called: Automated Logic Chicago
2400 Ogden Ave Ste 100 (60532-3933)
PHONE.............................630 852-1700
Juan Loredo, *Engineer*
Chirag Parikh, *Engineer*
Michael Giblin, *Design Engr*
Mark Crow, *Accounts Exec*
Suzanne Fritz, *Marketing Staff*
EMP: 16
SALES (corp-wide): 11.2B **Publicly Held**
WEB: www.automatedlogic.com
SIC: 3823 Water quality monitoring & control systems
HQ: Automated Logic Corporation
1150 Roberts Blvd Nw
Kennesaw GA 30144
770 429-3000

(G-12871)
BIG JOES SEALCOATI
6563 Fernwood Dr (60532-3451)
PHONE.............................630 935-7032
Eric Rasmussen, *Principal*
EMP: 3
SALES (est): 262.7K **Privately Held**
SIC: 3679 Hermetic seals for electronic equipment

(G-12872)
BISHOP ENGINEERING COMPANY (PA)
6495 Bannister Ct (60532-3342)
PHONE.............................630 305-9538
Samuel Bishop, *President*
Jackie Bishop, *Admin Sec*
EMP: 12
SQ FT: 6,000
SALES (est): 1.2MM **Privately Held**
SIC: 8711 3672 2741 5734 Electrical or electronic engineering; printed circuit boards; technical manuals: publishing & printing; computer software & accessories

(G-12873)
BLUE LIGHT INC
1440 Maple Ave Ste 5b (60532-4136)
P.O. Box 1121, Westmont (60559-8321)
PHONE.............................630 400-4539
EMP: 20

GEOGRAPHIC SECTION

Lisle - Dupage County (G-12895)

SALES (est): 2MM **Privately Held**
SIC: 2842 Polishes And Sanitation Goods

(G-12874)
BOLINGBROOK COMMUNICATIONS INC
Also Called: CPI Satcom Division- Lisle
1938 University Ln Ste C (60532-2314)
PHONE....................................630 759-9500
Howard Hausman, *President*
Kim Craddock, *Vice Pres*
David Faverio, *CFO*
Hillar Kiiss, *Admin Sec*
▲ EMP: 510
SQ FT: 120,000
SALES (est): 68.1MM
SALES (corp-wide): 6.8B **Publicly Held**
SIC: 3825 3663 3812 3621 Instruments to measure electricity; satellites, communications; search & navigation equipment; motors & generators
HQ: L3 Technologies, Inc.
600 3rd Ave Fl 34
New York NY 10016
212 697-1111

(G-12875)
CANNON BALL MARKETING INC
Also Called: Press Express
701 59th St (60532-3116)
PHONE....................................630 971-2127
James Cannon, *President*
Stan Scazepink, *Manager*
Maureen Cannon, *Admin Sec*
EMP: 3 EST: 1977
SQ FT: 2,000
SALES: 450K **Privately Held**
SIC: 2752 2759 2789 Commercial printing, offset; commercial printing; bookbinding & related work

(G-12876)
CHAS LEVY CIRCULATING CO
815 Ogden Ave (60532-1337)
PHONE....................................630 353-2500
EMP: 4
SALES (corp-wide): 105.5MM **Privately Held**
SIC: 2721 Magazines: publishing only, not printed on site
PA: Chas. Levy Circulating Co.
1930 George St Ste 4
Melrose Park IL 60160
708 356-3600

(G-12877)
COGNIZANT TECH SOLUTIONS CORP
3333 Warrenville Rd # 350 (60532-1157)
PHONE....................................630 955-0617
Janine Martin, *Marketing Staff*
David Althoff, *Manager*
Monica Lummus, *Manager*
Carman Ruzicka, *Manager*
Roshan Sahu, *Technical Staff*
EMP: 23 **Publicly Held**
SIC: 7371 7372 Computer software development & applications; prepackaged software
PA: Cognizant Technology Solutions Corporation
500 Frank W Burr Blvd
Teaneck NJ 07666

(G-12878)
CONCORDE LABORATORIES INC
4504 Concorde Pl (60532-3707)
PHONE....................................630 717-5300
Bonnie Metallo, *President*
EMP: 9 EST: 1996
SALES (est): 1.1MM **Privately Held**
WEB: www.concordelabs.com
SIC: 3991 Brooms & brushes

(G-12879)
CTS ADVANCED MATERIALS LLC
4925 Indiana Ave (60532-1611)
PHONE....................................630 577-8800
Kieran O'Sullivan, *President*
Luis Francisco Machado, *Vice Pres*
Ashish Agrawal, *CFO*
▲ EMP: 33

SALES (est): 7MM
SALES (corp-wide): 469MM **Publicly Held**
SIC: 3531 3569 3541 3561 Construction machinery; assembly machines, non-metalworking; electrical discharge erosion machines; electron-discharge metal cutting machine tools; pumps & pumping equipment
HQ: Cts Electronic Components, Inc.
4925 Indiana Ave
Lisle IL 60532
630 577-8800

(G-12880)
CTS AUTOMOTIVE LLC (HQ)
4925 Indiana Ave (60532-1611)
PHONE....................................630 577-8800
Troy Herold, *Engineer*
Christina Shane,
David Hartley,
David B Purdie,
Anthony Urban,
◆ EMP: 146 EST: 1998
SQ FT: 50,000
SALES (est): 26.2MM
SALES (corp-wide): 469MM **Publicly Held**
WEB: www.ctscorp.com
SIC: 3625 3845 3714 3674 Switches, electronic applications; electromedical apparatus; motor vehicle parts & accessories; semiconductors & related devices; current-carrying wiring devices; blow molded finished plastic products
PA: Cts Corporation
4925 Indiana Ave
Lisle IL 60532
630 577-8800

(G-12881)
CTS CORPORATION (PA)
4925 Indiana Ave (60532-1611)
PHONE....................................630 577-8800
Kieran O'Sullivan, *Ch of Bd*
Mark Cassens, *General Mgr*
Luis Francisco Machado, *Vice Pres*
Luis Machado, *Vice Pres*
Angel Lopez, *Mfg Staff*
▲ EMP: 110 EST: 1896
SQ FT: 105,925
SALES: 469MM **Publicly Held**
WEB: www.ctscorp.com
SIC: 3678 3829 3676 3679 Electronic connectors; measuring & controlling devices; aircraft & motor vehicle measurement equipment; resistor networks; electronic switches; switches, stepping; semiconductors & related devices

(G-12882)
CTS ELECTRONIC COMPONENTS INC (HQ)
4925 Indiana Ave (60532-1611)
PHONE....................................630 577-8800
Vinod Khilnani, *CEO*
Kieran M O Sullivan, *President*
Leon Miernicki, *Design Engr Mgr*
Robert J Patton, *Admin Sec*
▲ EMP: 71
SALES (est): 188MM
SALES (corp-wide): 469MM **Publicly Held**
SIC: 3724 Research & development on aircraft engines & parts
PA: Cts Corporation
4925 Indiana Ave
Lisle IL 60532
630 577-8800

(G-12883)
DANA INCORPORATED
1945 Ohio St (60532-2169)
PHONE....................................630 271-0001
Charlie Olfig, *Vice Pres*
Mike Denio, *Mktg Dir*
Christina Edwards, *Analyst*
EMP: 23 **Publicly Held**
SIC: 3714 Motor vehicle parts & accessories
PA: Dana Incorporated
3939 Technology Dr
Maumee OH 43537

(G-12884)
DANA SEALING PRODUCTS LLC
1945 Ohio St (60532-2169)
PHONE....................................630 960-4200
Rich Kozerski, *Branch Mgr*
EMP: 100
SQ FT: 10,000 **Publicly Held**
SIC: 3714 Motor vehicle parts & accessories
HQ: Dana Sealing Products, Llc
3939 Technology Dr
Maumee OH 43537

(G-12885)
DEMATIC CORP
750 Warrenville Rd # 101 (60532-0901)
PHONE....................................630 852-9200
Prashant Ranade, *President*
Jeffrey R Heinze, *Admin Sec*
EMP: 13
SALES (est): 1.5MM
SALES (corp-wide): 9.7B **Privately Held**
SIC: 3535 Conveyors & conveying equipment
HQ: Dematic Corp.
3550 Lenox Rd Ne
Atlanta GA 30326

(G-12886)
E & J GALLO WINERY
4225 Naperville Rd # 330 (60532-3699)
PHONE....................................630 505-4000
Peter Makris, *Sales Dir*
Michael Brooks, *Sales Staff*
Jeremy Cutler, *Sales Staff*
Tom Gillespie, *Manager*
EMP: 25
SALES (corp-wide): 2.9B **Privately Held**
SIC: 5182 5149 2086 Wine; groceries & related products; bottled & canned soft drinks
PA: E. & J. Gallo Winery
600 Yosemite Blvd
Modesto CA 95354
209 341-3111

(G-12887)
EMC CORPORATION
4225 Naperville Rd # 500 (60532-3699)
PHONE....................................630 505-3273
Rick Hoffman, *Principal*
Gautam Bhatia, *Senior Engr*
Adam Maniak, *Technology*
EMP: 100 **Publicly Held**
WEB: www.emc.com
SIC: 7372 Business oriented computer software
HQ: Emc Corporation
176 South St
Hopkinton MA 01748
508 435-1000

(G-12888)
ENDOTRONIX INC (PA)
815 Ogden Ave (60532-1337)
PHONE....................................630 504-2861
Harry Rowland, *CEO*
Anthony Nunez, *President*
Jim Yearick, *Senior VP*
Michael Nagy, *Vice Pres*
Mike Dilworth, *VP Mfg*
EMP: 8
SALES (est): 2.1MM **Privately Held**
SIC: 3841 Blood pressure apparatus

(G-12889)
ENERSYS
801 Warrenville Rd # 250 (60532-1396)
PHONE....................................630 455-4872
John D Craig, *Ch of Bd*
Hal Smith, *Sales Engr*
Ed Kirk, *Representative*
EMP: 88
SALES (corp-wide): 3B **Publicly Held**
SIC: 3691 5063 Storage batteries; electrical apparatus & equipment
PA: Enersys
2366 Bernville Rd
Reading PA 19605
610 208-1991

(G-12890)
FCA US LLC
Also Called: Midwest Business Center
901 Warrenville Rd # 550 (60532-4301)
PHONE....................................630 724-2321
Phil Scroggin, *Branch Mgr*
EMP: 5
SALES (corp-wide): 126.4B **Privately Held**
SIC: 3714 3711 Motor vehicle parts & accessories; motor vehicle engines & parts; automobile assembly, including specialty automobiles
HQ: Fca Us Llc
1000 Chrysler Dr
Auburn Hills MI 48326

(G-12891)
FORMTEK INC (HQ)
711 Ogden Ave (60532-1845)
PHONE....................................630 285-1500
John E Reed, *Ch of Bd*
Bruce Dewey, *President*
Edward J Kay, *Vice Pres*
Richard Poots, *Cust Mgr*
Brian Kopack, *Manager*
▲ EMP: 15
SALES (est): 48.2MM
SALES (corp-wide): 629.1MM **Privately Held**
SIC: 3542 Machine tools, metal forming type
PA: Mestek, Inc.
260 N Elm St
Westfield MA 01085
470 898-4533

(G-12892)
FOX METER INC
5403 Patton Dr Ste 218 (60532-4625)
PHONE....................................630 968-3635
Lila Grant, *President*
John Grant, *Vice Pres*
EMP: 6
SQ FT: 4,800
SALES: 500K **Privately Held**
SIC: 3823 Industrial instrmnts msrmnt display/control process variable

(G-12893)
GATEWAY CABLE INC (PA)
1998 Ohio St Ste 100 (60532-2184)
PHONE....................................630 766-7969
Kenneth Flerlage, *President*
EMP: 11
SQ FT: 11,000
SALES (est): 1.9MM **Privately Held**
WEB: www.tgccompany.com
SIC: 3643 Current-carrying wiring devices

(G-12894)
GE INTELLIGENT PLATFORMS INC
Also Called: Smartsignal
901 Warrenville Rd # 300 (60532-4301)
PHONE....................................630 829-4000
EMP: 75
SALES (corp-wide): 122B **Publicly Held**
SIC: 7372 7373 Prepackaged Software Services Computer Systems Design
HQ: Ge Intelligent Platforms, Inc.
2500 Austin Dr
Charlottesville VA 22911

(G-12895)
GERB VIBRATION CONTROL SYSTEMS
1950 Ohio St (60532-2145)
PHONE....................................630 724-1660
Victor Salcedo, *President*
Dr Frank Barutzki, *Vice Pres*
Christoff Von Waldow, *Treasurer*
▲ EMP: 7
SQ FT: 6,000
SALES: 1.5MM
SALES (corp-wide): 114.2MM **Privately Held**
SIC: 3495 8711 Mechanical springs, precision; industrial engineers
HQ: Gerb Holding Gmbh
Roedernallee 174-176
Berlin
304 191-0

Lisle - Dupage County (G-12896)

(G-12896)
H2O FILTER INC
4407 Chelsea Ave (60532-1314)
PHONE..............................630 963-3303
EMP: 2
SALES (est): 242.4K **Privately Held**
SIC: 3569 Mfg General Industrial Machinery

(G-12897)
HERA CNSLTNG INTERNTNL OPRATN
4307 Westerhoff Dr (60532-4190)
PHONE..............................630 515-8819
EMP: 10
SALES: 300K **Privately Held**
SIC: 7372 Prepackaged Software Services

(G-12898)
HILSCHER NORTH AMERICA INC
2525 Cabot Dr Ste 200 (60532-3628)
PHONE..............................630 505-5301
Philip Marshall, *CEO*
Phil Marshall, *COO*
John Martin, *Sales Staff*
Craig Lentzkow, *Manager*
Uwe Zeier, *Manager*
EMP: 15
SQ FT: 1,500
SALES (est): 974.2K
SALES (corp-wide): 40MM **Privately Held**
SIC: 3549 Assembly machines, including robotic
PA: Hilscher Gesellschaft Fur Systemautomation Mit Beschrankter Haftung
Rheinstr. 15
Hattersheim Am Main 65795
619 099-070

(G-12899)
INDUSTRIES PUBLICATION INC
4412 Black Partridge Ln (60532-1035)
PHONE..............................630 357-5269
Leonard Butler, *President*
EMP: 38
SALES (est): 1.4MM **Privately Held**
SIC: 3433 Heating equipment, except electric

(G-12900)
INEOS AMERICAS LLC
Also Called: Ineos Technologies
3030 Warrenville Rd # 650 (60532-1000)
PHONE..............................630 857-7000
Martin Olavesen, *CFO*
Bob Sokol, *CFO*
Gregory Novak, *Manager*
Debbie Johnson, *Administration*
Jim Bergmann, *Maintence Staff*
EMP: 3
SALES (corp-wide): 1MM **Privately Held**
SIC: 2821 Plastics materials & resins
HQ: Ineos Americas Llc
2600 S Shore Blvd Ste 500
League City TX 77573
251 535-6600

(G-12901)
INFOSYS LIMITED
2300 Cabot Dr Ste 250 (60532-4619)
PHONE..............................630 482-5000
Steve Jeffries, *VP Human Res*
Paneesh Murthy, *Branch Mgr*
Mayank Ranjan, *Director*
Wendy Morris, *Admin Sec*
EMP: 50 **Privately Held**
SIC: 7371 7379 7372 Computer software development; computer related consulting services; prepackaged software
HQ: Infosys Limited
2400 N Glenville Dr # 150
Richardson TX 75082
214 306-2100

(G-12902)
ISOPRIME CORPORATION
505 Warrenville Rd # 104 (60532-1669)
P.O. Box 3751 (60532-8751)
PHONE..............................630 737-0963
Kenneth Modaff, *President*
Kenneth J Modaff, *Manager*
EMP: 7

SALES: 100K **Privately Held**
SIC: 7371 7372 Computer software development; prepackaged software

(G-12903)
JEWELL RESOURCES CORPORATION (HQ)
1011 Warrenville Rd # 600 (60532-0903)
PHONE..............................276 935-8810
Charles Ellis, *President*
Jack Allison, *Treasurer*
Kenneth Ritchie, *Admin Sec*
EMP: 3
SALES (est): 60.7MM **Publicly Held**
SIC: 1222 Bituminous coal-underground mining

(G-12904)
JORDAN SERVICES
2100 Scarlet Oak Ln (60532-2855)
PHONE..............................630 416-6701
Michael G Jordan, *Owner*
EMP: 5
SALES (est): 340K **Privately Held**
SIC: 3531 Asphalt plant, including gravel-mix type

(G-12905)
KANBO INTERNATIONAL (US) INC
650 Warrenville Rd # 100 (60532-4315)
PHONE..............................630 873-6320
Jianxin LI, *President*
James Hinkle, *Vice Pres*
Aling LI, *Administration*
EMP: 3 EST: 2017
SALES (est): 254.6K **Privately Held**
SIC: 2099 Food preparations

(G-12906)
KONE INC (HQ)
4225 Naperville Rd # 400 (60532-3699)
PHONE..............................630 577-1650
Larry Wash, *CEO*
Ali Shamsa, *Superintendent*
Dennis Gerard, *Senior VP*
David McFadden, *Senior VP*
Charles Moore, *Senior VP*
◆ EMP: 580 EST: 1956
SQ FT: 527,000
SALES (est): 448.3MM
SALES (corp-wide): 11B **Privately Held**
WEB: www.kone.us
SIC: 7699 3534 1796 Elevators: inspection, service & repair; escalators, passenger & freight; walkways, moving, dumbwaiters; elevator installation & conversion
PA: Kone Oyj
Keilasatama 3
Espoo 02150
204 751-

(G-12907)
KRAFT HEINZ FOODS COMPANY
3030 Warrenville Rd # 200 (60532-1000)
PHONE..............................630 505-0170
EMP: 25
SALES (corp-wide): 26.2B **Publicly Held**
SIC: 2033 Mfg Canned Fruits/Vegetables
HQ: Kraft Heinz Foods Company
1 Ppg Pl Ste 3200
Pittsburgh PA 15222
412 456-5700

(G-12908)
KWIKSET CORPORATION
4225 Naperville Rd # 340 (60532-3656)
PHONE..............................630 577-0500
EMP: 5
SALES (corp-wide): 5.9B **Publicly Held**
SIC: 3429 Mfg Hardware
HQ: Kwikset Corporation
19701 Da Vinci
Foothill Ranch CA 92610
949 672-4000

(G-12909)
LSSP CORPORATION
4300 Commerce Ct (60532-3709)
PHONE..............................630 428-0099
Patrick Caruso, *President*
EMP: 6
SALES (est): 991.1K **Privately Held**
SIC: 3695 Computer software tape & disks: blank, rigid & floppy

(G-12910)
MIDDLETOWN COKE COMPANY LLC
1011 Warrenville Rd # 600 (60532-0903)
PHONE..............................630 284-1755
Matt Schwarz, *Principal*
EMP: 1
SALES (est): 5.1MM **Publicly Held**
SIC: 3312 Blast furnaces & steel mills
PA: Suncoke Energy, Inc.
1011 Warrenville Rd # 600
Lisle IL 60532

(G-12911)
MOLEX LLC (HQ)
Also Called: Molex Connected Entp Solutions
2222 Wellington Ct (60532-1682)
PHONE..............................630 969-4550
Joe Nelligan, *CEO*
Scott Whicker, *President*
J Michael Nauman, *Division Pres*
Liam McCarthy, *COO*
Jeff Neiman, *COO*
◆ EMP: 1100
SALES (est): 15.1B
SALES (corp-wide): 48.9B **Privately Held**
WEB: www.molex.com
SIC: 3679 3643 3357 Antennas, receiving; electronic circuits; connectors & terminals for electrical devices; communication wire; fiber optic cable (insulated)
PA: Koch Industries, Inc.
4111 E 37th St N
Wichita KS 67220
316 828-5500

(G-12912)
MOLEX LLC
Also Called: Logistic Department
2200 Wellington Ct (60532-3831)
PHONE..............................630 527-4357
Jim Kicher, *Principal*
EMP: 3
SALES (corp-wide): 48.9B **Privately Held**
SIC: 3678 Electronic connectors
HQ: Molex, Llc
2222 Wellington Ct
Lisle IL 60532
630 969-4550

(G-12913)
MOLEX ELECTRONIC TECH LLC (DH)
2222 Wellington Ct (60532-1682)
PHONE..............................630 969-4550
Joe Nelligan, *CEO*
EMP: 1
SALES (est): 27.4MM
SALES (corp-wide): 48.9B **Privately Held**
SIC: 3678 Electronic connectors
HQ: Molex, Llc
2222 Wellington Ct
Lisle IL 60532
630 969-4550

(G-12914)
MOLEX INTERNATIONAL INC (DH)
2222 Wellington Ct (60532-1682)
PHONE..............................630 969-4550
Liam McCarthy, *Vice Pres*
David Johnson, *Treasurer*
Neil Lefort, *Admin Sec*
▲ EMP: 10
SQ FT: 20,000
SALES (est): 1.9MM
SALES (corp-wide): 48.9B **Privately Held**
SIC: 3678 3679 3643 3357 Electronic connectors; electronic switches; electronic circuits; connectors & terminals for electrical devices; communication wire; fiber optic cable (insulated)
HQ: Molex, Llc
2222 Wellington Ct
Lisle IL 60532
630 969-4550

(G-12915)
MOLEX PREMISE NETWORKS INC
2222 Wellington Ct (60532-1682)
PHONE..............................866 733-6659
Fax: 630 813-9770
▲ EMP: 10001

SALES (est): 126.8MM **Privately Held**
SIC: 3679 3643 3357 Mfg Elec Components Mfg Conductive Wire Dvcs Nonfrs Wiredrwng/Insltng

(G-12916)
MTS PUBLISHING CO
Also Called: Crosswords Club, The
5229 Cypress Ct (60532-2007)
PHONE..............................630 955-9750
EMP: 15
SQ FT: 3,500
SALES (est): 1.3MM **Privately Held**
SIC: 2721 Periodicals-Publishing/Printing

(G-12917)
NAVISTAR INC (HQ)
2701 Navistar Dr (60532-3637)
P.O. Box 1488, Warrenville (60555-7488)
PHONE..............................331 332-5000
Troy A Clarke, *CEO*
Persio V Lisboa, *President*
Persio Lisboa, *President*
Susan Welter, *General Mgr*
Pam Bacon, *Business Mgr*
◆ EMP: 200 EST: 1965
SALES: 919.5MM
SALES (corp-wide): 11.2B **Publicly Held**
WEB: www.internationaltrucks.com
SIC: 3711 3714 3519 6153 Motor vehicles & car bodies; chassis, motor vehicle; motor vehicle parts & accessories; engines, diesel & semi-diesel or dual-fuel; financing of dealers by motor vehicle manufacturers organ.; purchasers of accounts receivable & commercial paper; buying of installment notes; truck finance leasing; finance leasing, vehicles: except automobiles & trucks; property damage insurance; fire, marine & casualty insurance: stock
PA: Navistar International Corporation
2701 Navistar Dr
Lisle IL 60532
331 332-5000

(G-12918)
NAVISTAR INC
2701 Navistar Dr (60532-3637)
PHONE..............................331 332-5000
EMP: 64
SALES (corp-wide): 10.1B **Publicly Held**
SIC: 3711 Manufacturing Of Motor Vehicle Bodies
HQ: Navistar, Inc.
2701 Navistar Dr
Lisle IL 60532
331 332-5000

(G-12919)
NAVISTAR INC
2701 Navistar Dr (60532-3637)
PHONE..............................662 494-3421
Rick Robertson, *Branch Mgr*
EMP: 353
SALES (corp-wide): 11.2B **Publicly Held**
SIC: 3713 Truck & bus bodies
HQ: Navistar, Inc.
2701 Navistar Dr
Lisle IL 60532
331 332-5000

(G-12920)
NAVISTAR DEFENSE LLC
2701 Navistar Dr (60532-3637)
PHONE..............................662 494-3421
Vance Gardner, *Principal*
EMP: 4
SALES (corp-wide): 11.2B **Publicly Held**
SIC: 3711 Military motor vehicle assembly
HQ: Navistar Defense Llc
10400 W North Ave
Melrose Park IL 60160
708 617-4500

(G-12921)
NAVISTAR INTERNATIONAL CORP (PA)
2701 Navistar Dr (60532-3637)
PHONE..............................331 332-5000
Ted Wright, *CEO*
Troy A Clarke, *Ch of Bd*
William V McMenamin, *President*
Persio V Lisboa, *COO*
Jamila Covington, *Counsel*
◆ EMP: 1000

GEOGRAPHIC SECTION

Lisle - Dupage County (G-12947)

SALES: 11.2B **Publicly Held**
SIC: 3711 3714 3713 3519 Truck & tractor truck assembly; chassis, motor vehicle; motor homes, self-contained, assembly of; motor vehicle parts & accessories; truck & bus bodies; engines, diesel & semi-diesel or dual-fuel; automobile finance leasing

(G-12922)
NUCLEAR POWER OUTFITTERS LLC
1955 University Ln (60532-2161)
PHONE 630 963-0320
Michael Fern, *Mng Member*
EMP: 12
SALES (est): 1.8MM **Privately Held**
SIC: 3356 Lead & lead alloy bars, pipe, plates, shapes, etc.
HQ: Eichrom Technologies Llc
   1955 University Ln
   Lisle IL 60532

(G-12923)
OAG AVIATION WORLDWIDE LLC (PA)
801 Warrenville Rd # 555 (60532-1396)
PHONE 630 515-5300
Mike Benjamin, *COO*
Ben Hollins, *COO*
Mark Raggio, *Vice Pres*
Dave Hopkins, *Safety Mgr*
Ed Calahan, *Production*
▼ **EMP:** 2
SALES: 2.1MM **Privately Held**
WEB: www.oag.com
SIC: 2741 Guides: publishing & printing;

(G-12924)
OCCIDENTAL CHEMICAL CORP
3030 Warrenville Rd # 330 (60532-3647)
PHONE 630 505-3242
Hasham Mukadam, *Branch Mgr*
EMP: 4
SALES (corp-wide): 21.2B **Publicly Held**
SIC: 2819 Industrial inorganic chemicals
HQ: Occidental Chemical Corporation
   14555 Dallas Pkwy Ste 400
   Dallas TX 75254
   972 404-3800

(G-12925)
ONX USA LLC
1001 Warrenville Rd (60532-1391)
PHONE 630 343-8940
Rochelle Manns, *Accounts Exec*
Nicole Wayne, *Marketing Staff*
Mike Cox, *Branch Mgr*
EMP: 45
SALES (corp-wide): 1.5B **Publicly Held**
SIC: 7379 7372 Computer related consulting services; business oriented computer software
HQ: Onx Usa Llc
   5910 Landerbrook Dr # 250
   Cleveland OH 44124

(G-12926)
PHYSICIAN SOFTWARE SYSTEMS LLC
3333 Warrenville Rd # 200 (60532-1157)
PHONE 630 717-8192
Lewis Mitchell, *CEO*
Roelaf Boonstra, *Chief*
John Tolle, *Opers Mgr*
Roelof Boonstra, *CTO*
Matt Stiegert, *Software Engr*
EMP: 12
SQ FT: 1,500
SALES (est): 600K **Privately Held**
SIC: 7372 Application computer software

(G-12927)
PITNEY BOWES INC
750 Warrenville Rd # 300 (60532-0901)
PHONE 630 435-7500
Micheal Cooper, *Principal*
EMP: 100
SQ FT: 20,000
SALES (corp-wide): 3.2B **Publicly Held**
SIC: 3579 7359 Postage meters; business machine & electronic equipment rental services
PA: Pitney Bowes Inc.
   3001 Summer St Ste 3
   Stamford CT 06905
   203 356-5000

(G-12928)
PRECISION CONTROL SYSTEMS
1980 University Ln (60532-4015)
PHONE 630 521-0234
William B Gushurst, *President*
Michael Corcoran, *Engineer*
Andrew J Arnold, *Admin Sec*
EMP: 58
SQ FT: 8,000
SALES (est): 19.7MM **Privately Held**
SIC: 3822 Temperature controls, automatic

(G-12929)
PRIME INDUSTRIES INC
4611 Main St Ste A (60532-1260)
PHONE 630 725-9200
Robert Antonio, *President*
Karen M Antonio, *Corp Secy*
◆ **EMP:** 50
SALES (est): 7.9MM **Privately Held**
SIC: 3821 Laboratory furniture

(G-12930)
PYLON PLASTICS INC
2111 Ogden Ave (60532-1508)
P.O. Box 505 (60532-0505)
PHONE 630 968-6374
Debora Kolzow, *President*
Frank Charles Brand, *Vice Pres*
EMP: 6 EST: 1950
SQ FT: 16,700
SALES (est): 814.4K **Privately Held**
SIC: 3089 3953 Plastic containers, except foam; planters, plastic; marking devices

(G-12931)
R R DONNELLEY & SONS COMPANY
Also Called: R R Donnelley
750 Warrenville Rd (60532-0901)
PHONE 630 588-5000
Jim Graham, *Manager*
EMP: 468
SALES (corp-wide): 6.2B **Publicly Held**
SIC: 2732 2754 2759 Books: printing & binding; commercial printing, gravure; magazines: gravure printing, not published on site; catalogs: gravure printing, not published on site; directories: gravure printing, not published on site; letterpress printing
PA: R. R. Donnelley & Sons Company
   35 W Wacker Dr
   Chicago IL 60601
   312 326-8000

(G-12932)
R S BACON VENEER COMPANY (PA)
Also Called: Bvc Veneer
770 Front St (60532-2207)
PHONE 630 323-1414
James McCracken, *President*
George Wilhelm, *Shareholder*
Nancy McCracken, *Admin Sec*
◆ **EMP:** 117
SQ FT: 7,000
SALES (est): 11.1MM **Privately Held**
WEB: www.baconveneer.com
SIC: 2499 2435 5031 Decorative wood & woodwork; veneer stock, hardwood; veneer

(G-12933)
R S BACON VENEER COMPANY
770 Front St (60532-2207)
PHONE 331 777-4762
Dan Meyerson, *Sales/Mktg Mgr*
EMP: 3
SALES (corp-wide): 11.1MM **Privately Held**
SIC: 2435 Hardwood plywood, prefinished
PA: R. S. Bacon Veneer Company
   770 Front St
   Lisle IL 60532
   630 323-1414

(G-12934)
ROCKWELL AUTOMATION INC
4343 Commerce Ct Ste 200 (60532-3615)
PHONE 630 789-5900
Richard Kostrzewa, *Sales Engr*
Rick Johnston, *Branch Mgr*
David Kovac, *Program Mgr*
EMP: 75 **Publicly Held**
SIC: 3625 Relays & industrial controls
PA: Rockwell Automation, Inc.
   1201 S 2nd St
   Milwaukee WI 53204

(G-12935)
RUCKUS WIRELESS INC
2400 Ogden Ave Ste 180 (60532-3999)
PHONE 630 281-3000
Ken Russman, *Principal*
Jeff Howe, *Vice Pres*
Doug McBride, *Engineer*
Brian Barker, *Director*
EMP: 25 **Publicly Held**
SIC: 3661 3663 5063 3357 Modems; radio & TV communications equipment; lighting fixtures; fiber optic cable (insulated)
HQ: Ruckus Wireless, Inc.
   350 W Java Dr
   Sunnyvale CA 94089

(G-12936)
SARDEE INDUSTRIES INC (PA)
5100 Academy Dr Ste 400 (60532-4208)
PHONE 630 824-4200
Steven R Sarovich, *President*
Laura L Maran, *Admin Sec*
▲ **EMP:** 4
SQ FT: 4,500
SALES (est): 13.5MM **Privately Held**
SIC: 1796 3565 5084 3537 Machinery installation; packaging machinery; conveyor systems; industrial trucks & tractors; conveyors & conveying equipment

(G-12937)
SLEEPING BEAR INC
5401 Patton Dr Ste 115 (60532-4532)
PHONE 630 541-7220
Robert Kasinecz, *President*
Rebecca Wing, *Principal*
EMP: 8
SALES: 500K **Privately Held**
SIC: 1751 2434 Cabinet building & installation; wood kitchen cabinets

(G-12938)
SMITHFIELD PCKGED MATS SLS CORP
4225 Naperville Rd (60532-3656)
PHONE 757 365-3541
Jacqueline Shue, *Principal*
EMP: 18 EST: 2017
SALES (est): 8MM **Privately Held**
SIC: 2011 Meat packing plants

(G-12939)
SMITHFIELD PACKAGED MEATS CORP
John Morrell Food Group
4225 Naperville Rd # 600 (60532-3656)
PHONE 630 281-5224
Bruce Johnson, *Project Engr*
Keith Veale, *Branch Mgr*
Kelly Gillespie, *Director*
Todd Naab, *Director*
Dennis Page, *Director*
EMP: 33 **Privately Held**
SIC: 2011 Meat packing plants
HQ: Smithfield Packaged Meats Corp.
   805 E Kemper Rd
   Cincinnati OH 45246
   513 782-3800

(G-12940)
SPIRAX SARCO INC
1500 Eisenhower Ln # 600 (60532-2135)
PHONE 630 493-4525
Pierre Schmidt, *Branch Mgr*
EMP: 10
SALES (corp-wide): 1.4B **Privately Held**
SIC: 3491 3494 3561 Steam traps; pressure valves & regulators, industrial; line strainers, for use in piping systems; pumps & pumping equipment
HQ: Spirax Sarco, Inc.
   1150 Northpoint Blvd
   Blythewood SC 29016
   803 714-2000

(G-12941)
SSAB SALES INC
801 Warrenville Rd # 800 (60532-0912)
PHONE 630 810-4800
David Britten, *President*
Michele Klebuc-Simes, *Vice Pres*
Phillip Marusarz, *CFO*
Gregory Burnett, *Treasurer*
Jimmy Briseno, *Asst Sec*
▲ **EMP:** 15
SALES (est): 82.4K
SALES (corp-wide): 7.8B **Privately Held**
SIC: 3312 Pipes, iron & steel
HQ: Ssab Enterprises, Llc
   11 N Water St Ste 17000
   Mobile AL 36602

(G-12942)
SSAB TEXAS INC
801 Warrenville Rd # 800 (60532-1396)
PHONE 630 810-4800
EMP: 8 EST: 1998
SALES (est): 790K **Privately Held**
SIC: 3312 Blast furnaces & steel mills

(G-12943)
STONE CENTER INC
2127 Ogden Ave (60532-1508)
PHONE 630 971-2060
Charles Joseph Plasil, *President*
Arlene Plasil, *Admin Sec*
Becky Zar, *Administration*
EMP: 7 EST: 1967
SQ FT: 4,000
SALES (est): 458.2K **Privately Held**
WEB: www.stonecenterlisle.com
SIC: 0781 5032 3281 Landscape architects; brick, except refractory; stone, crushed or broken; cut stone & stone products

(G-12944)
SUN COKE INTERNATIONAL INC (HQ)
Also Called: Sun Coke Energy
1011 Warrenville Rd # 600 (60532-0904)
PHONE 630 824-1000
Michael J Thomson, *President*
Cleo Boyd, *Vice Pres*
Mark Maccormick, *Vice Pres*
▲ **EMP:** 79
SQ FT: 5,692
SALES (est): 56MM **Publicly Held**
WEB: www.suncoke.com
SIC: 1222 3312 1221 Bituminous coal-underground mining; blast furnaces & steel mills; bituminous coal & lignite-surface mining

(G-12945)
SUNCOKE ENERGY INC (PA)
1011 Warrenville Rd # 600 (60532-0903)
PHONE 630 824-1000
Michael G Rippey, *President*
Brian Bokovoy, *Safety Mgr*
Murphy Poche, *Terminal Mgr*
Nancy Tinsley, *Accountant*
Tonia Denney, *Manager*
EMP: 220
SALES: 1.6B **Publicly Held**
SIC: 3312 1241 Blast furnaces & steel mills; coal mining services

(G-12946)
SUNCOKE ENERGY PARTNERS LP (HQ)
1011 Warrenville Rd # 600 (60532-0903)
PHONE 630 824-1000
Michael G Rippey, *Ch of Bd*
Fay West, *CFO*
C Scott Hobbs, *Director*
Wayne Moore, *Director*
Nancy Snyder, *Director*
EMP: 8 EST: 2012
SALES: 892.1MM **Publicly Held**
SIC: 3312 Coke oven products (chemical recovery)

(G-12947)
SUNCOKE TECHNOLOGY AND DEV LLC
1011 Warrenville Rd Fl 6 (60532-0903)
PHONE 630 824-1000
Michael J Thomson,
Mark Newman,

Lisle - Dupage County (G-12948)

EMP: 2
SALES (est): 360.3K **Publicly Held**
SIC: 3312 Blast furnaces & steel mills
PA: Suncoke Energy, Inc.
1011 Warrenville Rd # 600
Lisle IL 60532

(G-12948)
TALARIS INC (DH)
3333 Warrenville Rd # 310 (60532-1157)
PHONE...................................630 577-1000
Joseph P Patten, *President*
Rebekah Pryor, *Human Res Mgr*
Joe Rossa, *Sales Staff*
Lisa Howard, *Manager*
Stephane Lafrance, *Consultant*
▲ EMP: 250
SALES (est): 226.7MM **Privately Held**
SIC: 3578 3499 Banking machines; safes & vaults, metal; safe deposit boxes or chests, metal

(G-12949)
TECHNICAL POWER SYSTEMS INC
4642 Western Ave (60532-1543)
P.O. Box 606 (60532-0606)
PHONE...................................630 719-1471
Joseph G Giovanatto, *President*
Kurt Padera, *Vice Pres*
Tony Giovanatto, *Engineer*
John R Brophy, *CFO*
Najib Habiby, *Sales Staff*
◆ EMP: 20
SQ FT: 8,000
SALES (est): 4.9MM **Privately Held**
SIC: 3691 3999 Batteries, rechargeable; barber & beauty shop equipment

(G-12950)
TERRACYCLE REGULATED WASTE LLC
2200 Ogden Ave Ste 100 (60532-1972)
PHONE...................................800 909-9709
Tom Szaky, *Mng Member*
EMP: 20
SQ FT: 10,000
SALES (est): 7MM **Privately Held**
SIC: 3599 Custom machinery

(G-12951)
THOMAS PROESTLER
5400 Patton Dr Ste 2c (60532-4003)
PHONE...................................630 971-0185
John Drousias, *Owner*
EMP: 3
SALES (est): 103.2K **Privately Held**
SIC: 2099 5141 Food preparations; groceries, general line

(G-12952)
TIANHE STEM CELL BIOTECHNOLGIE
6398 Holly Ct (60532-3312)
PHONE...................................630 723-1968
Yong Zhao, *President*
EMP: 17
SALES (est): 781.3K **Privately Held**
SIC: 3841 Medical instruments & equipment, blood & bone work

(G-12953)
TZEE INC
4343 Commerce Ct Ste 200 (60532-3615)
PHONE...................................630 857-3425
Venkata C Majeti, *President*
John Schwartz, *Director*
EMP: 3
SALES (est): 145.1K **Privately Held**
SIC: 7372 Prepackaged software

(G-12954)
VALID SECURE SOLUTIONS LLC
1011 Warrenville Rd # 450 (60532-0935)
PHONE...................................260 633-0728
Dean Warner, *President*
Ron Stott, *Vice Pres*
Bob Zick, *Vice Pres*
EMP: 19
SQ FT: 62,000
SALES (est): 304.3K **Privately Held**
SIC: 8999 2759 Communication services; commercial printing

(G-12955)
VALID USA INC (HQ)
1011 Warrenville Rd # 450 (60532-0935)
PHONE...................................630 852-8200
Carlos Alfonso Seigneur, *CEO*
Gary Hofeldt, *Vice Pres*
Joseph J Taylor, *Vice Pres*
Theresa Jensen, *Human Resources*
Lysa Romero, *Program Mgr*
EMP: 1
SQ FT: 106,000
SALES (est): 286.7MM **Privately Held**
SIC: 2752 Commercial printing, lithographic

(G-12956)
VERITAS STEEL LLC (PA)
2300 Cabot Dr Ste 425 (60532-4611)
PHONE...................................630 423-8708
Henrik Jensen, *Ch of Bd*
Tracy Glende, *President*
Rick Daniels, *President*
Lance Shaver, *General Mgr*
Richard Phillips, *Exec VP*
EMP: 216 EST: 2013
SALES (est): 86.4MM **Privately Held**
SIC: 3441 Fabricated structural metal for bridges

(G-12957)
WE DO TECH AMERICAS INC
3333 Warrenville Rd # 200 (60532-1157)
PHONE...................................630 217-8723
Maggie Georgieva, *Financial Analy*
Hulya Altinsoy, *Branch Mgr*
Pedro Duque, *Manager*
Luis Rebelo, *Director*
EMP: 12 **Privately Held**
SIC: 2741 Miscellaneous publishing
HQ: We Do Technologies Americas, Inc.
9711 Washingtonian Blvd
Gaithersburg MD 20878
240 223-8080

(G-12958)
ZEMAN MFG CO
1996 University Ln (60532-2152)
PHONE...................................630 960-2300
Robert Zeman, *President*
Chris Glowacki, *Sales Staff*
Matty Trujillo, *Sales Associate*
Christopher Glowacki, *Marketing Staff*
Shaun Murphy, *Maintence Staff*
◆ EMP: 25 EST: 1936
SQ FT: 15,000
SALES (est): 3.7MM **Privately Held**
WEB: www.zemanmfg.com
SIC: 3498 3567 Tube fabricating (contract bending & shaping); heating units & devices, industrial: electric

Litchfield
Montgomery County

(G-12959)
ALPLY INSULATED PANELS LLC
1401 Eilerman Ave (62056-3001)
PHONE...................................217 324-6700
EMP: 9 EST: 2012
SALES (est): 2.1MM **Privately Held**
SIC: 2452 Prefabricated buildings, wood

(G-12960)
AMERITEX INDUSTRIES INC
14 Litchfield Plz Ste 1a (62056-1095)
P.O. Box 430, Hillsboro (62049-0430)
PHONE...................................217 324-4044
Jerry L Ruckman, *President*
Aaron Ruckman, *Vice Pres*
Carrie Barnes, *Project Mgr*
EMP: 10
SQ FT: 10,000
SALES (est): 1.3MM **Privately Held**
SIC: 2392 Napkins, fabric & nonwoven: made from purchased materials; tablecloths: made from purchased materials; table mats, plastic & textile

(G-12961)
BRAKE PARTS INC LLC
725 Mckinley Ave (62056-2701)
P.O. Box 725 (62056-0725)
PHONE...................................217 324-2161
EMP: 6
SALES (corp-wide): 600MM **Privately Held**
SIC: 5013 3714 3593 Whol Auto Parts/Supplies Mfg Motor Vehicle Parts/Accessories Mfg Fluid Power Cylinders
HQ: Brake Parts Inc Llc
4400 Prime Pkwy
Mchenry IL 60050
815 363-9000

(G-12962)
COUNTY TOOL & DIE
1400 W Hudson Dr (62056-3016)
P.O. Box 186 (62056-0186)
PHONE...................................217 324-6527
Jim Garrett, *Owner*
EMP: 3
SALES (est): 260.4K **Privately Held**
SIC: 3544 7692 7389 3599 Special dies & tools; welding repair; personal service agents, brokers & bureaus; amusement park equipment

(G-12963)
GARTECH MANUFACTURING CO
1400 W Hudson Dr (62056-3016)
PHONE...................................217 324-6527
Janet Garrett, *President*
Jim Garrett, *Vice Pres*
Rhonda Braden, *Purch Mgr*
EMP: 30
SQ FT: 10,500
SALES (est): 4.5MM **Privately Held**
SIC: 3423 3599 3316 Knives, agricultural or industrial; machine shop, jobbing & repair; cold finishing of steel shapes

(G-12964)
GEORGE PRESS INC
905 N Old Route 66 (62056-1071)
PHONE...................................217 324-2242
Robert Corrado, *Owner*
EMP: 7
SQ FT: 9,000
SALES (est): 1MM **Privately Held**
SIC: 2759 3571 2752 Letterpress printing; invitation & stationery printing & engraving; computers, digital, analog or hybrid; commercial printing, lithographic; advertising posters, lithographed

(G-12965)
HOWMET AEROSPACE INC
108 Historic Old Rte 66 (62056)
PHONE...................................217 324-4469
EMP: 135
SALES (corp-wide): 14.1B **Publicly Held**
SIC: 3353 Aluminum sheet & strip
PA: Howmet Aerospace Inc.
201 Isabella St Ste 200
Pittsburgh PA 15212
412 553-1950

(G-12966)
INTERNATIONAL FILTER MFG CORP
Also Called: Ifm
713 W Columbian Blvd S (62056-3027)
P.O. Box 549 (62056-0099)
PHONE...................................217 324-2303
Cecilia Ewing, *President*
James R Hayes, *Vice Pres*
Cecilia Hayes, *Marketing Mgr*
EMP: 18
SQ FT: 20,000
SALES (est): 4.1MM **Privately Held**
SIC: 3564 Filters, air: furnaces, air conditioning equipment, etc.

(G-12967)
ITW BLDING CMPONENTS GROUP INC
ITW Alpine
7 Skyview Dr (62056-4654)
PHONE...................................217 324-0303
Ufgy Bratt, *Branch Mgr*
EMP: 40
SALES (corp-wide): 14.1B **Publicly Held**
SIC: 3443 3446 3441 Truss plates, metal; architectural metalwork; fabricated structural metal
HQ: Itw Building Components Group, Inc.
13389 Lakefront Dr
Earth City MO 63045
314 344-9121

(G-12968)
JOURNAL NEWS
510 N State St (62056-1568)
PHONE...................................217 324-6604
Nancy Slepicka, *Principal*
EMP: 4
SALES (est): 130.7K **Privately Held**
SIC: 2711 Commercial printing & newspaper publishing combined; newspapers, publishing & printing

(G-12969)
KRANOS CORPORATION (PA)
Also Called: Schutt Sports
710 Industrial Dr (62056-3030)
PHONE...................................217 324-3978
Robert Erb, *CEO*
Scott Gerdes, *Business Mgr*
Drew Harcharik, *Business Mgr*
Omare Lowe, *Business Mgr*
Brady Pisano, *Business Mgr*
▲ EMP: 118
SALES (est): 53MM **Privately Held**
SIC: 3949 Masks: hockey, baseball, football, etc.; baseball equipment & supplies, general; baseball, softball & cricket sports equipment; football equipment & supplies, general

(G-12970)
LAMBOO INC
311 W Edwards St (62056-1904)
P.O. Box 195 (62056-0195)
PHONE...................................866 966-2999
▲ EMP: 20
SALES (est): 3.9MM **Privately Held**
SIC: 2421 Sawmill/Planing Mill

(G-12971)
LAMBOO TECHNOLOGIES LLC
311 W Edwards St (62056-1904)
PHONE...................................866 966-2999
Gary Harvey, *CEO*
Luke D Schuette, *COO*
Jeran Hammann, *Exec VP*
EMP: 4
SQ FT: 17,000
SALES (est): 413.4K
SALES (corp-wide): 29.3MM **Privately Held**
SIC: 2439 Timbers, structural: laminated lumber
PA: Af Holding Co.
811 S Hamilton St
Sullivan IL 61951
217 728-8388

(G-12972)
LITCHFIELD NEWS HERALD INC
112 E Ryder St (62056-2031)
P.O. Box 160 (62056-0160)
PHONE...................................217 324-2121
John C Hanafin, *President*
Michelle Romanus, *Admin Sec*
EMP: 10 EST: 1856
SQ FT: 5,000
SALES (est): 792.4K **Privately Held**
WEB: www.litchfieldil.com
SIC: 2711 Newspapers: publishing only, not printed on site; job printing & newspaper publishing combined

(G-12973)
MARINE ACQUISITION CORP
Also Called: Seastar Solutions
1 Sierra Pl (62056-3029)
PHONE...................................217 324-9400
Yvan Cote, *President*
Greg House, *CFO*
Vincent Heidrich, *Manager*
Donald Sturgeon, *Manager*
▼ EMP: 1250
SQ FT: 170,000
SALES (est): 205.9MM
SALES (corp-wide): 2B **Privately Held**
SIC: 3531 Marine related equipment
HQ: Dometic Sweden Ab
Hemvarnsgatan 15
Solna

▲ = Import ▼ = Export
◆ = Import/Export

GEOGRAPHIC SECTION

Lockport - Will County (G-13004)

(G-12974)
QUALITY PLUS
Also Called: Supportstoreus
901 S Old Route 66 (62056-1879)
PHONE..................................618 779-4931
John D Shaw, *Owner*
EMP: 10
SALES (est): 50K **Privately Held**
SIC: 2499 Wood products

(G-12975)
RIVER BEND PRINTING
60 Flat School Ln (62056-4546)
PHONE..................................217 324-6056
Sam Weller, *Owner*
EMP: 4
SALES (est): 200K **Privately Held**
SIC: 2752 2791 2789 Commercial printing, offset; typesetting; bookbinding & related work

(G-12976)
ROLLER DERBY SKATE CORP (PA)
Also Called: Tour
311 W Edwards St (62056-1904)
P.O. Box 249 (62056-0249)
PHONE..................................217 324-3961
Edwin C Seltzer, *Ch of Bd*
Walter Frazier, *President*
John Chrisman, *Vice Pres*
David Kennedy, *Vice Pres*
David P Kennedy, *CFO*
◆ **EMP:** 45 **EST:** 1935
SQ FT: 7,000
SALES (est): 1MM **Privately Held**
WEB: www.rollerderby.com
SIC: 3949 Sporting & athletic goods

(G-12977)
SARCO HYDRAULICS INC (PA)
216 N Old Route 66 (62056-2626)
P.O. Box 248 (62056-0248)
PHONE..................................217 324-6577
Richard Sarver, *President*
Verla I Sarver, *Treasurer*
◆ **EMP:** 30 **EST:** 1975
SQ FT: 50,000
SALES (est): 3.1MM **Privately Held**
SIC: 7699 3593 Hydraulic equipment repair; fluid power cylinders & actuators

(G-12978)
W A M COMPUTERS INTERNATIONAL
211 N State St (62056-2036)
P.O. Box 261 (62056-0261)
PHONE..................................217 324-6926
William A Morgan Jr, *Owner*
Tyler Brandt, *Supervisor*
EMP: 5
SQ FT: 7,000
SALES (est): 346.9K **Privately Held**
SIC: 8611 7372 Business associations; prepackaged software

Lockport
Will County

(G-12979)
A & S STEEL SPECIALTIES INC
1001 Clinton St Ste A (60441-4838)
P.O. Box 97 (60441-0097)
PHONE..................................815 838-8188
EMP: 20 **EST:** 1964
SQ FT: 50,000
SALES (est): 208.2K **Privately Held**
SIC: 3449 3792 3743 3715 Mfg Misc Structural Mtl Mfg Trailers/Campers Mfg Railroad Equipment Mfg Truck Trailers Structural Metal Fabrctn

(G-12980)
AA RIGONI BROTHERS INC
112 Connor Ave (60441-4736)
PHONE..................................815 838-9770
Doug Rigoni, *President*
Mark Rigoni, *Admin Sec*
EMP: 8
SALES (est): 2.7MM **Privately Held**
WEB: www.aarigoni.com
SIC: 3281 Granite, cut & shaped; marble, building: cut & shaped

(G-12981)
AMERI ROLLS AND GUIDES
337 Clover Ridge Dr (60441-3299)
PHONE..................................815 588-0486
EMP: 1
SALES (est): 200K **Privately Held**
SIC: 3325 Steel Foundry

(G-12982)
AUTOMATED FORMS & GRAPHICS INC
200 W 11th St Ste 2sw (60441-2979)
PHONE..................................630 887-9811
Michael Field, *President*
Lauren Bubinas, *Principal*
Jan Lask, *Principal*
EMP: 6
SALES (est): 888.6K **Privately Held**
SIC: 2752 Commercial printing, lithographic

(G-12983)
BENDING SPECIALISTS LLC
Also Called: Wil Lan Company
3051 S State St (60441-5024)
PHONE..................................815 726-6281
Greg Radecki, *President*
Mark Sorby, *General Mgr*
EMP: 20
SQ FT: 12,000
SALES (est): 2.9MM **Privately Held**
SIC: 3441 Fabricated structural metal

(G-12984)
BINZEL INDUSTRIES LLC
3051 S State St (60441-5024)
PHONE..................................847 506-0003
Anthony Ditommaso,
Greg Radecki,
EMP: 2 **EST:** 2011
SALES (est): 280.5K **Privately Held**
WEB: www.binzelindustries.com
SIC: 3441 Fabricated structural metal

(G-12985)
BYRNE & SCHAEFER INC
1061 Caton Farm Rd (60441-6517)
P.O. Box 453, Lisle (60532-0453)
PHONE..................................815 727-5000
Timothy K Byrne, *President*
EMP: 4
SALES (est): 186.7K **Privately Held**
SIC: 3599 Air intake filters, internal combustion engine, except auto

(G-12986)
CHEMTECH SERVICES INC
20648 Gaskin Dr (60446-1910)
PHONE..................................815 838-4800
John Hart, *President*
EMP: 15
SQ FT: 15,000
SALES (est): 4.6MM **Privately Held**
SIC: 2819 3559 Chemicals, high purity: refined from technical grade; refinery, chemical processing & similar machinery

(G-12987)
DMK SPECIALTIES
17435 Tanglewood (60441-4664)
PHONE..................................815 919-7282
Dawn Gustafson, *Principal*
EMP: 4
SALES (est): 237.1K **Privately Held**
SIC: 3369 Nonferrous foundries

(G-12988)
DONALDSON & ASSOCIATES INC
12141 W 159th St Ste A (60491-7804)
PHONE..................................708 633-1090
Dave Donaldson, *President*
EMP: 9
SQ FT: 1,100
SALES (est): 1.2MM **Privately Held**
SIC: 5091 3949 Fishing equipment & supplies; hunting equipment & supplies; fishing equipment; hunting equipment

(G-12989)
DOVE PRODUCTS INC
3357 S State St (60441-5251)
P.O. Box 717 (60441-0717)
PHONE..................................815 727-4683
EMP: 25

SQ FT: 16,000
SALES (est): 240K **Privately Held**
SIC: 3089 Mfg Molded Plastic Parts

(G-12990)
DOVE STEEL INC
16035 W Red Cloud Dr (60441-4597)
PHONE..................................815 588-3772
Dan Blankenship, *President*
Beverly Blankenship, *Director*
EMP: 10
SALES (est): 1.2MM **Privately Held**
SIC: 3498 Tube fabricating (contract bending & shaping)

(G-12991)
DVORAKS CREATIONS INC
1521 Daviess Ave (60441-2890)
PHONE..................................815 838-2214
Gary Dvorak, *President*
EMP: 4
SQ FT: 6,300
SALES (est): 462.4K **Privately Held**
SIC: 2434 Wood kitchen cabinets

(G-12992)
DYNAMICSIGNALS LLC (PA)
900 N State St (60441-2230)
PHONE..................................815 838-0005
Andre Lareau, *President*
Andrew Dawson, *Vice Pres*
Wayne Coppe, *Purch Mgr*
Kevin Garrabrant, *Engineer*
Linda Murphy, *Engineer*
▼ **EMP:** 40 **EST:** 1970
SQ FT: 60,000
SALES (est): 18.6MM **Privately Held**
SIC: 3829 Measuring & controlling devices

(G-12993)
ENVIRONETICS INC
1201 Commerce St (60441-2879)
PHONE..................................815 838-8331
Raymond Winters, *Chairman*
Rosemary Winters, *Manager*
EMP: 10
SALES (est): 2.1MM **Privately Held**
SIC: 3081 2394 Unsupported plastics film & sheet; canvas & related products

(G-12994)
FUSION FABRICATION
627 E 10th St (60441-3617)
PHONE..................................815 214-9148
Steven Chlebicki, *Principal*
EMP: 8
SALES (est): 1.1MM **Privately Held**
WEB: www.fusionfabricationinc.com
SIC: 3441 Fabricated structural metal

(G-12995)
GAGE APPLIED TECHNOLOGIES LLC
900 N State St (60441-2230)
PHONE..................................815 838-0005
Ricky Goldstein, *Software Dev*
William A Boston,
Patrick A Cassady,
Eric Schroeder,
EMP: 40
SALES (est): 6.7MM
SALES (corp-wide): 18.6MM **Privately Held**
SIC: 3678 Electronic connectors
PA: Dynamicsignals Llc
900 N State St
Lockport IL 60441
815 838-0005

(G-12996)
GENERAL MACHINE AND TOOL INC (PA)
348 Caton Farm Rd (60441-9535)
PHONE..................................815 727-4342
Matt Gregurich, *President*
Jim Gregurich, *Engineer*
Toni Gregurich, *Office Mgr*
Kristina Smyk, *Admin Sec*
EMP: 2 **EST:** 1962
SQ FT: 1,200
SALES: 4MM **Privately Held**
WEB: www.generalmachine.net
SIC: 3599 Custom machinery; machine shop, jobbing & repair

(G-12997)
GOLF GAZETTE
428 S Washington St (60441-3037)
PHONE..................................815 838-0184
Joann North, *Principal*
EMP: 3
SALES (est): 115.9K **Privately Held**
WEB: www.gringogazette.com
SIC: 2711 Newspapers, publishing & printing

(G-12998)
GREIF INC
Industrial Container Division
1225 Daviess Ave (60441-2804)
PHONE..................................815 838-7210
Trevor Davies, *Plant Mgr*
Dean Babcock, *Manager*
Amadeo Lopez, *Manager*
Sergio Manzo, *Supervisor*
Jose Arreguin, *Maintence Staff*
EMP: 50
SALES (corp-wide): 4.6B **Publicly Held**
WEB: www.greif.com
SIC: 3089 Plastic containers, except foam
PA: Greif, Inc.
425 Winter Rd
Delaware OH 43015
740 549-6000

(G-12999)
GRIFFIN JOHN
15751 Annico Dr Ste 2 (60491-4739)
PHONE..................................708 301-2316
John Griffin, *Owner*
EMP: 3
SALES (est): 100.3K **Privately Held**
SIC: 2759 Commercial printing

(G-13000)
HOLLINGWORTH CANDIES INC
926 N State St (60441-2230)
PHONE..................................815 838-2275
Wendy Carver, *President*
Margaret Carlson, *Corp Secy*
EMP: 23
SALES (est): 2.3MM **Privately Held**
SIC: 2064 Candy & other confectionery products

(G-13001)
HUDSON BOILER & TANK COMPANY
3101 S State St (60441-5053)
PHONE..................................312 666-4780
Edward Hoveke, *President*
Brent Tillman, *Vice Pres*
Hank Klein, *Project Mgr*
Bob Taylor, *Project Mgr*
EMP: 15 **EST:** 1940
SQ FT: 20,000
SALES: 5MM **Privately Held**
SIC: 3443 1791 1711 Boiler & boiler shop work; structural steel erection; boiler maintenance contractor; boiler setting contractor

(G-13002)
INSTRUMENTS & TECHNOLOGY
700 N Glenmore St (60441-2780)
PHONE..................................815 838-5909
Jeffrey Moore, *Principal*
EMP: 3
SALES (est): 289.7K **Privately Held**
SIC: 3826 Analytical instruments

(G-13003)
JOLIET CABINET COMPANY INC
405 Caton Farm Rd (60441-6513)
PHONE..................................815 727-4096
Daryl Del Sasso, *President*
Rosemary P Del Sasso, *Corp Secy*
Robert Ostapkowicz, *Vice Pres*
Colleen Ford, *Administration*
EMP: 40
SQ FT: 33,000
SALES (est): 6.6MM **Privately Held**
WEB: www.arbormills.com
SIC: 2511 2434 Wood household furniture; vanities, bathroom: wood

(G-13004)
KURE STEEL INC
422 N State St (60441-2651)
PHONE..................................815 836-8027

Lockport - Will County (G-13005)

Elsie Kure, *President*
EMP: 6
SALES (est): 830.9K **Privately Held**
SIC: 3441 Fabricated structural metal

(G-13005)
LA DOLCE BELLA CUPCAKES
1228 Newbridge Ave (60441-2782)
PHONE.................................847 987-3738
Nicole Pacione, *Principal*
EMP: 4
SALES (est): 193.1K **Privately Held**
SIC: 2051 Bread, cake & related products

(G-13006)
LINDE GAS NORTH AMERICA LLC
810 E 135th St (60441-5804)
PHONE.................................630 257-3108
EMP: 11 **Privately Held**
SIC: 2813 Oxygen, compressed or liquefied
HQ: Linde Gas North America Llc
10 Riverview Dr
Danbury CT 06810

(G-13007)
LOCKPORT FISH PANTRY
604 E 9th St (60441-3604)
P.O. Box 42 (60441-0042)
PHONE.................................815 588-3543
Sylvia Wynveen, *Principal*
EMP: 2
SALES: 372.2K **Privately Held**
SIC: 2048 Fish food

(G-13008)
LOCKPORT STEEL FABRICATORS LLC
3051 S State St (60441-5024)
PHONE.................................815 726-6281
Greg Radecki, *President*
Dirk Pfeil, *Vice Pres*
Paul Bakun, *Opers Mgr*
Glenn Whittaker, *Mfg Staff*
Vincent Di Tommaso, *Supervisor*
EMP: 80
SQ FT: 75,000
SALES (est): 29.6MM **Privately Held**
SIC: 3441 Fabricated structural metal

(G-13009)
M R GLENN ELECTRIC INC
200 W 6th St (60441-2990)
PHONE.................................708 479-9200
Michael R Glenn, *President*
EMP: 30
SALES (est): 3.7MM **Privately Held**
SIC: 7694 5063 3621 Rebuilding motors, except automotive; motors, electric; motors & generators

(G-13010)
MAGENTA LLC (PA)
15160 New Ave (60441-2244)
PHONE.................................773 777-5050
Russell A Steele, *President*
Benauf Denise, *Principal*
David Schooley, *Principal*
Frank Ross, *Vice Pres*
Dave Ziegenhorn, *Engineer*
EMP: 92 **EST:** 2008
SQ FT: 120,000
SALES (est): 25.2MM **Privately Held**
WEB: www.magentallc.com
SIC: 3089 Injection molding of plastics

(G-13011)
MARTIN DENTAL LABORATORY INC
411 New Ave Unit 2 (60441-2213)
PHONE.................................708 597-8880
Martin Buchtenkirch Jr, *President*
EMP: 17
SQ FT: 5,200
SALES (est): 1.3MM **Privately Held**
SIC: 3843 8072 Teeth, artificial (not made in dental laboratories; dental laboratories

(G-13012)
MESSER NORTH AMERICA INC
810 E Romeo Rd (60441-5804)
P.O. Box 7068, Romeoville (60446-0968)
PHONE.................................630 257-3612
Jim Bates, *Branch Mgr*
EMP: 21
SALES (corp-wide): 1.1B **Privately Held**
SIC: 2813 8711 Industrial gases; engineering services
HQ: Messer North America, Inc.
200 Somerset Corporate Bl
Bridgewater NJ 08807
908 464-8100

(G-13013)
METAL PRODUCTS SALES CORP
15700 S Parker Rd (60491-5969)
PHONE.................................708 301-6844
William H Rehr, *President*
EMP: 6 **EST:** 1962
SQ FT: 6,264
SALES (est): 705.6K **Privately Held**
SIC: 5211 5039 5031 3442 Doors, storm: wood or metal; windows, storm: wood or metal; doors, wood or metal, except storm; doors, sliding; glass construction materials; windows; metal doors, sash & trim; products of purchased glass; millwork

(G-13014)
MONTY BURCENSKI
1213 S Lincoln St (60441-3655)
PHONE.................................815 838-0934
Monty Burcenski, *President*
EMP: 6
SALES (est): 365.7K **Privately Held**
SIC: 3999 Manufacturing industries

(G-13015)
MY BED INC
14040 S Shoshoni Dr (60491-8906)
PHONE.................................800 326-9233
EMP: 10
SQ FT: 68,000
SALES (est): 930K **Privately Held**
SIC: 2515 Mfg Mattresses/Bedsprings

(G-13016)
NETGAIN MOTORS INC
800 S State St Ste 4 (60441-3434)
PHONE.................................630 243-9100
George Hamstra, *President*
EMP: 7
SALES (est): 550K **Privately Held**
SIC: 3621 Motors & generators

(G-13017)
OMNI CRAFT INC
411 New Ave Unit 1 (60441-2213)
PHONE.................................815 838-1285
Preston Wakeland, *President*
EMP: 6 **EST:** 1973
SALES (est): 477.4K **Privately Held**
SIC: 2541 2791 Cabinets, except refrigerated: show, display, etc.: wood; typesetting

(G-13018)
PANDUIT CORP
16530 W 163rd St (60441-7607)
PHONE.................................815 836-1800
Jack Caveney, *President*
Michael Verbeek, *Engineer*
Thuc Vu, *Engineer*
EMP: 50
SALES (corp-wide): 1.4B **Privately Held**
SIC: 3644 3643 5063 3699 Electric conduits & fittings; connectors & terminals for electrical devices; electrical apparatus & equipment; electrical equipment & supplies
PA: Panduit Corp.
18900 Panduit Dr
Tinley Park IL 60487
708 532-1800

(G-13019)
PRINTING PLUS
Also Called: A Arbec Company
15751 Annico Dr Ste 5 (60491-4739)
PHONE.................................708 301-3900
Beth Mc Lane, *President*
EMP: 5
SQ FT: 4,000
SALES (est): 470K **Privately Held**
SIC: 2752 7331 2789 Commercial printing, offset; mailing service; bookbinding & related work

(G-13020)
QUALITY QUICKPRINT INC
909 E 9th St (60441-3216)
PHONE.................................815 838-1784
EMP: 10
SALES (corp-wide): 1.4MM **Privately Held**
SIC: 2752 7334 2791 2789 Lithographic Coml Print Photocopying Service Typesetting Services Bookbinding/Related Work
PA: Quality Quickprint Inc
1258 Cronin Ct
Lemont IL 60439
815 723-0941

(G-13021)
REGAL CONVERTING CO INC
14503 S Gougar Rd Unit 1 (60491-6402)
P.O. Box 723 (60441-0723)
PHONE.................................630 257-3581
George E Gross, *President*
Bob Schmidt, *Treasurer*
Gerry Surmitis, *Sales Staff*
▲ **EMP:** 15
SALES (est): 1.5MM **Privately Held**
SIC: 1011 Iron ores

(G-13022)
S & S MFG SOLUTIONS LLC
15509 Weber Rd # 3 (60446-3566)
PHONE.................................815 838-1960
EMP: 3
SALES (est): 200.8K **Privately Held**
SIC: 3999 Manufacturing industries

(G-13023)
SIMON BOX MFG CO
355 Caton Farm Rd (60441-6512)
PHONE.................................815 722-6661
Paul Hischier, *Vice Pres*
Jacqueline Edmonson, *Admin Sec*
EMP: 7 **EST:** 1931
SQ FT: 12,000
SALES (est): 1.2MM **Privately Held**
SIC: 2653 Boxes, corrugated: made from purchased materials

(G-13024)
SOURCE SOFTWARE INC (PA)
16525 W 159th St 200 (60441-7900)
PHONE.................................815 922-7717
Thomas Weinberger, *President*
Alex Kantas, *Principal*
Kevin Schmidt, *Vice Pres*
EMP: 3
SQ FT: 500
SALES (est): 216.3K **Privately Held**
SIC: 7299 3577 Personal document & information services; computer peripheral equipment

(G-13025)
TOYAL AMERICA INC (DH)
17401 Broadway St (60441-6508)
PHONE.................................630 505-2160
Bud Loprest, *President*
Stephen Fugulsang, *Vice Pres*
◆ **EMP:** 85
SQ FT: 3,000
SALES (est): 18.3MM **Privately Held**
SIC: 2816 3399 Inorganic pigments; powder, metal

(G-13026)
UNLIMITED GRAPHIX INC
Also Called: Ugx
1453 Caton Farm Rd (60441-3953)
PHONE.................................630 759-0007
Richard B Neubauer, *President*
Claudia Neubauer, *Admin Sec*
Martha McTherthon, *Administration*
EMP: 20
SALES (est): 2.7MM **Privately Held**
SIC: 2752 5199 5112 Commercial printing, lithographic; advertising specialties; office supplies

(G-13027)
WHEATON CABINETRY
17238 Weber Rd (60441-6525)
PHONE.................................815 729-1085
Ken Wheaton, *Owner*
EMP: 8
SALES (est): 1MM **Privately Held**
SIC: 2434 Wood kitchen cabinets

Loda
Iroquois County

(G-13028)
HYDRA FOLD AUGER INC
931 N 1600e Rd (60948-9428)
PHONE.................................217 379-2614
Wayne Niewold, *President*
Douglas Niewold, *Vice Pres*
Janet Niewold, *Treasurer*
Grace J Funk, *Manager*
Grace Funk, *Director*
EMP: 3
SQ FT: 1,000
SALES: 1MM **Privately Held**
SIC: 3532 3423 Auger mining equipment; hand & edge tools

(G-13029)
LODA ELECTRONICS CO
307 S Elm St (60948)
P.O. Box 207 (60948-0207)
PHONE.................................217 386-2554
Jack Sandford, *Partner*
Bruce Komadina, *Partner*
EMP: 4
SALES (est): 514.5K **Privately Held**
SIC: 3679 8711 3625 Electronic circuits; engineering services; relays & industrial controls

(G-13030)
MIDWEST POULTRY SERVICES LP
Also Called: Hi-Grade Egg Producers
Hwy 45 N Ste 2 (60948)
P.O. Box 69 (60948-0069)
PHONE.................................217 386-2313
David Garretls, *Manager*
EMP: 60
SQ FT: 40,000
SALES (corp-wide): 174.9MM **Privately Held**
SIC: 2015 Poultry slaughtering & processing
PA: Midwest Poultry Services, L.P.
800 Wabash Rd
North Manchester IN 46962
574 353-7651

(G-13031)
POWER PLANTER INC
931 N 1600e Rd (60948-9428)
PHONE.................................217 379-2614
Gregory Niewold, *President*
EMP: 1
SALES: 1.6MM **Privately Held**
SIC: 3423 Hand & edge tools

Logan
Franklin County

(G-13032)
T & T CARBIDE INC
17409 Lowry Ave (62856-2205)
P.O. Box 13 (62856-0013)
PHONE.................................618 439-7253
Rick Thomas, *President*
◆ **EMP:** 8
SQ FT: 8,500
SALES: 1.8MM **Privately Held**
SIC: 5084 3546 Drilling bits; oil refining machinery, equipment & supplies; power-driven handtools

Lombard
Dupage County

(G-13033)
A K TOOL & MANUFACTURING INC
260 Cortland Ave Ste 4 (60148-1223)
PHONE.................................630 889-9220
John Asan, *President*
Mike Kirch, *Vice Pres*
EMP: 4

GEOGRAPHIC SECTION
Lombard - Dupage County (G-13059)

SQ FT: 3,500
SALES (est): 567.8K **Privately Held**
SIC: 3599 3544 Machine shop, jobbing & repair; special dies, tools, jigs & fixtures

(G-13034)
ACE METAL REFINISHERS INC (PA)
978 N Dupage Ave (60148)
PHONE.................................630 778-9200
Gordon R Swanson, *President*
▲ EMP: 30 EST: 1950
SQ FT: 12,000
SALES (est): 3.8MM **Privately Held**
SIC: 3471 Finishing, metals or formed products; polishing, metals or formed products

(G-13035)
ADDITION TECHNOLOGY INC
820 Oak Creek Dr (60148-6405)
PHONE.................................847 297-8419
Pedro Salazar, *CEO*
Daniel Salazar, *General Mgr*
Mark Grzeskowiak, *Director*
EMP: 10
SQ FT: 2,500
SALES (est): 1.5MM **Privately Held**
SIC: 3841 0752 Diagnostic apparatus, medical; animal specialty services

(G-13036)
ADVANTAGE PRINTING INC
1920 S Highland Ave # 300 (60148-6149)
PHONE.................................630 627-7468
Shiv Mendiratta, *President*
EMP: 2
SQ FT: 20,000
SALES: 274K **Privately Held**
SIC: 2621 2752 2771 Business form paper; commercial printing, lithographic; greeting cards

(G-13037)
AESPHEPTICS MEDICAL LTD
Also Called: Skin and Laser Aesheptics
477 E Bttrfeld Rd Ste 408 (60148)
PHONE.................................630 416-1400
Selma Arain, *Principal*
EMP: 3
SALES (est): 260K **Privately Held**
SIC: 3845 Laser systems & equipment, medical

(G-13038)
AKZO NOBEL COATINGS INC
931 N Du Page Ave (60148-1214)
PHONE.................................630 792-1619
Rick Bulgrin, *Manager*
EMP: 20
SALES (corp-wide): 10.2B **Privately Held**
SIC: 2851 5198 2821 Paints: oil or alkyd vehicle or water thinned; lacquer: bases, dopes, thinner; varnishes; paints; plastics materials & resins
HQ: Akzo Nobel Coatings Inc.
8220 Mohawk Dr
Strongsville OH 44136
440 297-5100

(G-13039)
AMTEX CHEMICALS LLC
450 E 22nd St Ste 164 (60148-6175)
PHONE.................................630 268-0085
David Gazzera,
▲ EMP: 2
SALES (est): 240.3K **Privately Held**
SIC: 2869 5169 Industrial organic chemicals; industrial chemicals

(G-13040)
ART OF SHAVING - FL LLC
441 E Roosevelt Rd (60148-4629)
PHONE.................................630 495-7316
Jo Ann, *Principal*
EMP: 7
SALES (corp-wide): 67.6B **Publicly Held**
WEB: www.theartofshaving.com
SIC: 5999 2844 3421 5122 Hair care products; toilet preparations; razor blades & razors; razor blades
HQ: The Art Of Shaving - Fl Llc
6100 Blue Lagoon Dr # 150
Miami FL 33126

(G-13041)
AT&T CORP
851 Oak Creek Dr (60148-6426)
PHONE.................................630 693-5000
Dave Lobianco, *Branch Mgr*
EMP: 222
SALES (corp-wide): 181.1B **Publicly Held**
WEB: www.att.com
SIC: 2741 Telephone & other directory publishing
HQ: At&T Corp.
1 At&T Way
Bedminster NJ 07921
800 403-3302

(G-13042)
BIG LIFT LLC (PA)
Also Called: Big Joe Forklift
1060 N Garfield St (60148-1336)
PHONE.................................630 916-2600
Daniel Rosskamm, *President*
Chris Kuny, *Business Mgr*
Sang Tian, *Vice Pres*
Andrea Palombizio, *Opers Staff*
Jim Reeves, *Opers Staff*
▲ EMP: 25
SQ FT: 7,500
SALES: 50MM **Privately Held**
WEB: www.bigjoeforklifts.com
SIC: 3537 Industrial trucks & tractors

(G-13043)
BIGTIME FANTASY SPORTS INC
149 W Washington Blvd (60148-2544)
PHONE.................................630 605-7544
Joe Ream, *President*
EMP: 4
SALES (est): 375.2K **Privately Held**
WEB: www.btfsports.com
SIC: 3577 7371 Computer peripheral equipment; computer software development

(G-13044)
BILZ TOOL COMPANY
1140 N Main St (60148-1362)
PHONE.................................630 495-3996
Bill Sternberg, *Sales Engr*
Tim Drumheller, *Branch Mgr*
EMP: 16
SALES (corp-wide): 178.7MM **Privately Held**
SIC: 3541 Machine tools, metal cutting type
HQ: Bilz Tool Company
1351 Brummel Ave
Elk Grove Village IL 60007
847 734-9390

(G-13045)
BIOMERIEUX INC
1113 N Main St (60148-1360)
PHONE.................................630 600-5516
Douglas Maxwell, *Vice Pres*
EMP: 17
SALES (corp-wide): 7.5MM **Privately Held**
SIC: 2833 8734 Medicinals & botanicals; testing laboratories
HQ: Biomerieux, Inc.
100 Rodolphe St
Durham NC 27712
919 620-2000

(G-13046)
BIOMERIEUX INC
1105 N Main St (60148-1360)
PHONE.................................630 628-6055
Joy Dellaringa, *Business Mgr*
Douglas Maxwell, *Vice Pres*
Matthew Pinto, *Engineer*
Kelly Martin, *Technology*
Arvind Lakshman, *Director*
EMP: 30
SALES (corp-wide): 7.5MM **Privately Held**
SIC: 2833 8734 8071 3231 Medicinals & botanicals; testing laboratories; medical laboratories; products of purchased glass
HQ: Biomerieux, Inc.
100 Rodolphe St
Durham NC 27712
919 620-2000

(G-13047)
BLOOMING COLOR INC
230 Eisenhower Ln N (60148-5403)
PHONE.................................630 705-9200
John R Lehman, *President*
Ray Kinney, *Vice Pres*
Brian Scott, *Vice Pres*
Paul Yerges, *Branch Mgr*
Kevin P Brahler, *Admin Sec*
EMP: 60
SQ FT: 30,700
SALES (est): 4.1MM **Privately Held**
SIC: 2796 2752 2731 2759 Color separations for printing; business form & card printing, lithographic; pamphlets: publishing & printing; poster & decal printing & engraving

(G-13048)
BOWTIE INC
477 E Bttrfeld Rd Ste 200 (60148)
PHONE.................................630 515-9493
Tina Pelletier, *Manager*
EMP: 9
SALES (corp-wide): 56.1MM **Privately Held**
SIC: 2721 Periodicals
HQ: Bowtie, Inc.
500 N Brand Blvd Ste 600
Glendale CA 91203
213 385-2222

(G-13049)
BUSINESSMINE LLC
Also Called: Pledgemine
784 Oak Creek Dr (60148-6403)
PHONE.................................630 541-8480
Todd Moxley, *Managing Prtnr*
EMP: 7 EST: 2009
SALES (est): 233.5K **Privately Held**
WEB: www.pledgemine.com
SIC: 2741 4813 Business service newsletters: publishing & printing;

(G-13050)
CHEM-TAINER INDUSTRIES INC
2 N 225 Grace (60148)
PHONE.................................630 932-7778
George Karathanas, *Plant Mgr*
Rick Straub, *Branch Mgr*
EMP: 5
SQ FT: 10,000
SALES (corp-wide): 44.3MM **Privately Held**
SIC: 3089 Pallets, plastic; plastic containers, except foam
PA: Chem-Tainer Industries Inc.
361 Neptune Ave
West Babylon NY 11704
631 422-8300

(G-13051)
CHEMI-FLEX LLC
1040 N Ridge Ave (60148-1211)
PHONE.................................630 627-9650
Maryann Morrell, *Sales Staff*
Richard A Voss, *Mng Member*
James Borthwick,
EMP: 45
SQ FT: 40,000
SALES (est): 1.8MM **Privately Held**
SIC: 3052 Plastic belting

(G-13052)
CHICAGO ROLL CO INC
970 N Lombard Rd (60148-1231)
PHONE.................................630 627-8888
Chuck Gehrisch, *CEO*
San Gy Shing, *President*
Frank Deangelis, *Plant Supt*
EMP: 25
SQ FT: 48,000
SALES: 4.5MM
SALES (corp-wide): 19.4MM **Privately Held**
SIC: 3544 3547 Dies & die holders for metal cutting, forming, die casting; rolling mill machinery
PA: Rki, Inc.
8901 Tyler Blvd
Mentor OH 44060
888 953-9400

(G-13053)
CHROMETEC LLC
192 S Lombard Ave (60148-2750)
PHONE.................................630 792-8777
Brian Skerik, *Mng Member*
EMP: 3
SALES: 500K **Privately Held**
SIC: 2441 Packing cases, wood: nailed or lock corner

(G-13054)
CINCH CNNCTIVITY SOLUTIONS INC (HQ)
1700 S Finley Rd (60148-4884)
PHONE.................................630 705-6000
Pete Bittner, *President*
Scott Martin, *Finance*
Martin Charles, *Manager*
Matt Meares, *Director*
John G Shively, *Admin Sec*
▲ EMP: 174
SALES: 800MM
SALES (corp-wide): 492.4MM **Publicly Held**
SIC: 3678 3679 Electronic connectors; harness assemblies for electronic use: wire or cable
PA: Bel Fuse Inc.
206 Van Vorst St
Jersey City NJ 07302
201 432-0463

(G-13055)
CINCH CONNECTORS INC (HQ)
1700 S Finley Rd (60148-4890)
PHONE.................................630 705-6001
Michael Murray, *President*
Bob Cwynar, *Vice Pres*
Michael Stewart, *Buyer*
Mark Dvorak, *Engineer*
Hecham Elkhatib, *Engineer*
EMP: 100
SALES (est): 174.3MM
SALES (corp-wide): 492.4MM **Publicly Held**
WEB: www.cinch.com
SIC: 3643 3678 Connectors & terminals for electrical devices; electronic connectors
PA: Bel Fuse Inc.
206 Van Vorst St
Jersey City NJ 07302
201 432-0463

(G-13056)
COMET NEON
1120 N Ridge Ave (60148-1213)
PHONE.................................630 668-6366
Peter Wolak, *Owner*
EMP: 9
SALES: 1MM **Privately Held**
SIC: 3993 Electric signs

(G-13057)
COMPUTHINK INC
151 E 22nd St (60148-6226)
PHONE.................................630 705-9050
James Sivis, *President*
John Stelmach, *CFO*
EMP: 33
SALES (est): 4.7MM **Privately Held**
SIC: 7372 3089 Publishers' computer software; identification cards, plastic

(G-13058)
CONTRACTORS REGISTER INC
Also Called: Blue Book of Building & Cnstr
555 Waters Edge Ste 150 (60148-7046)
PHONE.................................630 519-3480
Todd Brown, *Manager*
EMP: 10
SALES (corp-wide): 73.4MM **Privately Held**
SIC: 2731 Book publishing
PA: Contractors Register, Inc.
800 E Main St
Jefferson Valley NY 10535
914 245-0200

(G-13059)
COUNTER CFT SVC SYSTEMS & PDTS
720 Concord Ln (60148-3719)
PHONE.................................630 629-7336
Phyllis C Whitlock, *President*

Lombard - Dupage County (G-13060)

Ed Kring, *Corp Secy*
EMP: 3
SALES (est): 125K **Privately Held**
SIC: 2782 Looseleaf binders & devices

(G-13060)
CUSTOM CALENDAR CORP
Also Called: Custom Calender
875 E 22nd St Apt 202 (60148-5025)
P.O. Box 912, Oak Park (60303-0912)
PHONE..................708 547-6191
Patrick Schumann, *President*
EMP: 3
SQ FT: 1,000
SALES (est): 1.5MM **Privately Held**
SIC: 2752 Calendars, lithographed

(G-13061)
CUSTOM CULINARY INC (DH)
2505 S Finley Rd Ste 100 (60148-4867)
PHONE..................630 928-4898
Dean L Griffith, *Ch of Bd*
T C Chatterjee, *President*
Herve De La Vauvre, *President*
Zaw Minn, *Superintendent*
Mark Mason, *Regional Mgr*
EMP: 80
SQ FT: 75,000
SALES (est): 17.5MM
SALES (corp-wide): 1B **Privately Held**
WEB: www.customculinary.com
SIC: 2034 2099 Soup mixes; gravy mixes, dry; seasonings: dry mixes
HQ: Griffith Foods Inc.
1 Griffith Ctr
Alsip IL 60803
708 371-0900

(G-13062)
CUTTING EDGE DOCUMENT DSTRCTN
10 E 22nd St (60148-4977)
PHONE..................630 620-0193
Larry Samples, *Principal*
EMP: 12
SALES (est): 1.7MM **Privately Held**
SIC: 3589 Shredders, industrial & commercial

(G-13063)
DE AMERTEK CORPORATION INC (PA)
2000 S Finley Rd (60148-4825)
PHONE..................630 572-0800
Jack C Chen, *CEO*
Jeremy Waldrop, *Engineer*
Laura Aiardo, *Agent*
Edward Ahr, *Director*
Theresa Chen, *Admin Sec*
◆ **EMP:** 60
SQ FT: 140,000
SALES (est): 30MM **Privately Held**
SIC: 3679 Electronic circuits; electronic crystals; oscillators

(G-13064)
DELTA STRUCTURES INC
18w675 18th St (60148-5076)
PHONE..................630 694-8700
Maria Chambers, *President*
Thomas Chambers, *Vice Pres*
▲ **EMP:** 19
SQ FT: 15,000
SALES (est): 3.3MM **Privately Held**
SIC: 3441 Fabricated structural metal

(G-13065)
DIE CUT GROUP INC
850 N Du Page Ave Ste 5 (60148-1250)
PHONE..................630 629-9211
Marvin A Cichlar, *President*
EMP: 10
SQ FT: 20,000
SALES: 2.5MM **Privately Held**
SIC: 3544 Dies, steel rule; special dies & tools

(G-13066)
DIGITAL IGNITE LLC (DH)
101 W 22nd St Ste 104 (60148-4997)
P.O. Box 9272 (60148-9272)
PHONE..................630 317-7904
Tamer Ali, *CEO*
John Sun, *CTO*
EMP: 10 **EST:** 2005
SQ FT: 10,000
SALES (est): 898.1K
SALES (corp-wide): 2.4B **Privately Held**
WEB: www.digitalignite.com
SIC: 7372 Educational computer software
HQ: Yourmembership.Com, Inc.
9620 Exec Ctr N 200
Saint Petersburg FL 33702
727 827-0046

(G-13067)
DIGITAL PRINTING & TOTAL GRAPH
70 Eisenhower Ln N (60148-5414)
PHONE..................630 627-7400
Andy Jaeckel, *President*
EMP: 4 **EST:** 2015
SALES (est): 452.7K **Privately Held**
SIC: 2752 Commercial printing, offset

(G-13068)
DIGITAL PRTG & TOTAL GRAPHICS
123 Eisenhower Ln N (60148)
PHONE..................630 627-7400
Gary Johnson, *President*
Andrew Jeakel, *Vice Pres*
EMP: 6
SQ FT: 3,000
SALES (est): 710K **Privately Held**
SIC: 2759 7336 Commercial printing; commercial art & graphic design

(G-13069)
DLUX BRAND LLC
1s072 Luther Ave (60148-4164)
PHONE..................630 215-5557
Jason Wencel, *Partner*
▲ **EMP:** 3
SALES (est): 152.6K **Privately Held**
WEB: www.dluxbrand.com
SIC: 2084 Wines, brandy & brandy spirits

(G-13070)
EA MACKAY ENTERPRISES INC
Also Called: Speak Out
104 N West Rd (60148-2120)
PHONE..................630 627-7010
Scott D Mackay, *President*
Bonnie Mackay, *Admin Sec*
EMP: 20
SQ FT: 2,500
SALES (est): 1.2MM **Privately Held**
SIC: 2711 2741 Newspapers: publishing only, not printed on site; miscellaneous publishing

(G-13071)
EASTGATE CLEANERS
837 Westmore-Myers Rd A10 (60148-3777)
PHONE..................630 627-9494
Yun D Shim, *Owner*
EMP: 3
SALES (est): 200K **Privately Held**
SIC: 3633 7216 Household laundry machines, including coin-operated; cleaning & dyeing, except rugs

(G-13072)
EDMPARTSCOM INC
958 N Du Page Ave (60148-1243)
PHONE..................630 427-1603
Iyad Aweidah, *President*
▲ **EMP:** 2
SALES (est): 450K **Privately Held**
SIC: 3541 Electrical discharge erosion machines

(G-13073)
EMPIRE BRONZE CORP
1130 N Ridge Ave (60148-1213)
PHONE..................630 916-9722
Luciano Mordini, *President*
Ed Bandola, *Vice Pres*
▲ **EMP:** 16 **EST:** 1958
SQ FT: 12,000
SALES (est): 2.7MM **Privately Held**
WEB: www.regalbronze.com
SIC: 3914 3446 3351 Ecclesiastical ware; architectural metalwork; copper rolling & drawing

(G-13074)
EXIDE TECHNOLOGIES
1051 N Main St Ste B (60148-1350)
PHONE..................630 862-2200
Waseem Humecki, *Engineer*
Charlie Bresnak, *Supervisor*
Mike Berger, *Exec Dir*
EMP: 2
SALES (est): 212.4K **Privately Held**
SIC: 5063 3691 Circuit breakers; storage batteries

(G-13075)
EXIDE TECHNOLOGIES LLC
Also Called: GNB Industrial Global Business
829 Parkview Blvd (60148-3230)
PHONE..................678 566-9000
John Bondy, *Branch Mgr*
EMP: 86
SALES (corp-wide): 3.1B **Privately Held**
SIC: 3691 3692 3629 Lead acid batteries (storage batteries); primary batteries, dry & wet; battery chargers, rectifying or non-rotating
PA: Exide Technologies, Llc
13000 Drfeld Pkwy Bldg 20
Milton GA 30004
678 566-9000

(G-13076)
FLOWSERVE CORPORATION
10 Eisenhower Ln N (60148-5414)
PHONE..................630 435-9596
Ed Hand, *Sales Mgr*
James Baker, *Manager*
EMP: 25
SALES (corp-wide): 3.9B **Publicly Held**
SIC: 3561 Pumps & pumping equipment
PA: Flowserve Corporation
5215 N Ocnnor Blvd Ste 23 Connor
Irving TX 75039
972 443-6500

(G-13077)
FLOYDWARE LLC
1020 Parkview Blvd (60148-3238)
PHONE..................630 469-1078
James Bower, *Manager*
EMP: 2
SALES (est): 292.4K **Privately Held**
SIC: 7372 Business oriented computer software

(G-13078)
FOOT LOCKER RETAIL INC
Also Called: Champs Sports
112 Yorktown Ctr (60148-5527)
PHONE..................630 678-0155
Bogdan Babek, *Branch Mgr*
EMP: 8 **Publicly Held**
SIC: 5661 2329 Footwear, athletic; athletic (warmup, sweat & jogging) suits: men's & boys'
HQ: Foot Locker Retail, Inc.
330 W 34th St
New York NY 10001
212 720-3700

(G-13079)
FRANK R WALKER COMPANY
Also Called: Callahan Industries
700 Springer Dr (60148-6411)
PHONE..................630 613-9312
Eugene Callahan, *President*
EMP: 6
SQ FT: 5,000
SALES (est): 559.7K **Privately Held**
SIC: 2741 2731 2761 2721 Miscellaneous publishing; books: publishing only; manifold business forms; periodicals

(G-13080)
FSI TECHNOLOGIES INC
Also Called: Fork Standards
668 E Western Ave (60148-2005)
PHONE..................630 932-9380
W Scott Tobey, *President*
Chuck Faivre, *President*
Paul Curatolo, *Treasurer*
Ferd Turek, *Officer*
Gloria Tobey, *Executive*
EMP: 20
SQ FT: 5,500
SALES (est): 3.5MM **Privately Held**
WEB: www.fsinet.com
SIC: 3825 3625 3823 3812 Oscillators, audio & radio frequency (instrument types); solenoid switches (industrial controls); industrial instrmnts msrmnt display/control process variable; search & navigation equipment; semiconductors & related devices; radio & TV communications equipment

(G-13081)
G & J HALL TOOLS INC
77 Eisenhower Ln S (60148-5409)
PHONE..................314 968-5040
Scott Jury, *Principal*
▲ **EMP:** 4 **EST:** 2010
SALES (est): 464.4K **Privately Held**
WEB: www.gjhalltools.com
SIC: 3544 Special dies & tools

(G-13082)
GCPRO LLC
Also Called: Gcpro Restoration
220 Eisenhower Ln N (60148-5403)
PHONE..................773 764-2776
Michael Smolyansky, *President*
Dmitry Ruderman, *President*
Michael Levberg, *Contractor*
EMP: 36
SALES (est): 2.1MM **Privately Held**
SIC: 1521 1389 6331 1541 General remodeling, single-family houses; repairing fire damage, single-family houses; construction, repair & dismantling services; property damage insurance; renovation, remodeling & repairs: industrial buildings; remodeling, multi-family dwellings

(G-13083)
GRIMM METAL FABRICATORS INC
1121 N Garfield St (60148-1336)
PHONE..................630 792-1710
Warren Buesching, *President*
Kathleen Buesching, *Vice Pres*
EMP: 21 **EST:** 1967
SQ FT: 20,000
SALES (est): 5.7MM **Privately Held**
SIC: 3441 7692 3444 Fabricated structural metal; welding repair; sheet metalwork

(G-13084)
HELANDER METAL SPINNING CO
931 N Ridge Ave (60148-1208)
P.O. Box 1824 (60148-8824)
PHONE..................630 268-9292
Samuel A Ibrahim, *President*
Dominic Fiorito, *Production*
Ken Tan, *Design Engr*
Bharti Patel, *Human Res Mgr*
▲ **EMP:** 48
SQ FT: 30,000
SALES: 8MM **Privately Held**
SIC: 3444 Sheet metalwork

(G-13085)
HOLLYWOOD TRADERS LLC
1154 E Addison Ave (60148-6504)
PHONE..................630 943-6461
Khan Shuaib H, *CEO*
EMP: 9 **EST:** 2014
SALES: 569.9K **Privately Held**
SIC: 5199 5122 3281 Nondurable goods; general merchandise, non-durable; vitamins & minerals; household articles, except furniture; cut stone

(G-13086)
HOUSE OF RATTAN INC (PA)
18w375 Roosevelt Rd (60148-4167)
P.O. Box 7125, Deerfield (60015-7125)
PHONE..................630 627-8160
Richard Sanders, *President*
Joann Sanders, *Treasurer*
Elizabeth Leonard, *Admin Sec*
▼ **EMP:** 28
SALES (est): 3.1MM **Privately Held**
SIC: 2519 5719 Rattan furniture: padded or plain; wicker, rattan or reed home furnishings

GEOGRAPHIC SECTION

Lombard - Dupage County (G-13115)

(G-13087)
IDEAS INC (PA)
625 S Main St (60148-3341)
PHONE.................................630 620-2010
Todd Ressa, *President*
Francis Ressa, *Corp Secy*
Carole M Ressa, *Vice Pres*
Tim Grant, *Sales Staff*
▲ **EMP:** 5 **EST:** 1974
SALES (est): 2.4MM **Privately Held**
SIC: 2992 Lubricating oils & greases

(G-13088)
J K CUSTOM COUNTERTOPS
820 N Ridge Ave Ste A (60148-1236)
PHONE.................................630 495-2324
Gary McKenna, *Owner*
EMP: 3 **EST:** 1974
SQ FT: 3,000
SALES (est): 173K **Privately Held**
SIC: 3231 2434 2431 2521 Furniture tops, glass: cut, beveled or polished; wood kitchen cabinets; doors & door parts & trim, wood; wood office furniture; wood partitions & fixtures

(G-13089)
JAMES J SANDOVAL
Also Called: JMS Auto Electric
333 N Grace St (60148-1817)
PHONE.................................734 717-7555
EMP: 4
SALES (est): 200K **Privately Held**
SIC: 5999 3699 Ret Misc Merchandise Mfg Electrical Equipment/Supplies

(G-13090)
JLS INDUSTRIES INC
1015 E Wilson Ave (60148-3765)
PHONE.................................630 261-9445
EMP: 1
SALES (est): 226.4K **Privately Held**
SIC: 3543 Industrial patterns

(G-13091)
JODAAT INC
Also Called: Signs Now
18w333 Roosevelt Rd Ste 1 (60148-4180)
PHONE.................................630 916-7776
Lori Pastuszak, *President*
EMP: 5
SQ FT: 2,200
SALES (est): 746.9K **Privately Held**
SIC: 3993 Signs & advertising specialties

(G-13092)
KLEAN-KO INC
952 N Du Page Ave (60148-1243)
PHONE.................................630 620-1860
Daniel E Marsh, *President*
Mary Lou Gregorio, *Vice Pres*
Vanda Marsh, *Shareholder*
Robert L Marsh, *Admin Sec*
EMP: 60
SQ FT: 5,000
SALES (est): 2MM **Privately Held**
WEB: www.kleankojanitorial.com
SIC: 7349 2819 Janitorial service, contract basis; industrial inorganic chemicals

(G-13093)
KORMEX METAL CRAFT INC
961 Dupage Ave (60148)
PHONE.................................630 953-8856
Chul Y Whang, *President*
Grace B Whang, *President*
Bok S Whang, *Vice Pres*
EMP: 30
SQ FT: 22,000
SALES (est): 6.4MM **Privately Held**
SIC: 3444 3599 3549 Sheet metal specialties, not stamped; machine shop, jobbing & repair; metalworking machinery

(G-13094)
LAUNCH PRESS
325 N Martha St (60148-2016)
PHONE.................................773 669-8372
Craig Hobson, *Principal*
EMP: 3 **EST:** 2015
SALES (est): 69.2K **Privately Held**
SIC: 2711 Newspapers

(G-13095)
LINE CRAFT INC
10 W North Ave (60148-1263)
PHONE.................................630 932-1182
John Lyons, *President*
David M Schmitt, *Admin Sec*
EMP: 18
SALES (est): 4.2MM **Privately Held**
SIC: 2672 Coated & laminated paper

(G-13096)
LINE CRAFT TOOL COMPANY INC
Also Called: Amstadt Industries
10 W North Ave (60148-1263)
PHONE.................................630 932-1182
Jakob Amstadt, *President*
Jack W Amstadt, *President*
Hildegard Amstadt, *Admin Sec*
EMP: 150 **EST:** 1976
SALES (est): 19MM
SALES (corp-wide): 0 **Privately Held**
WEB: www.linecraftinc.com
SIC: 3599 5251 5084 3714 Machine shop, jobbing & repair; tools; machine tools & accessories; motor vehicle parts & accessories
HQ: The Electric Materials Company
50 S Washington St
North East PA 16428
814 725-9621

(G-13097)
LIQUITECH INC
421 Eisenhower Ln S (60148-5706)
PHONE.................................630 693-0500
Steve Schira, *Chairman*
Tory Schira, *COO*
Michael Mashione, *Mfg Staff*
Charles Maw, *Sales Staff*
Mark Desanto, *Director*
▲ **EMP:** 40
SALES (est): 5.2MM **Privately Held**
SIC: 3589 3823 4971 5074 Water filters & softeners, household type; water treatment equipment, industrial; industrial instrmnts msrmnt display/control process variable; water distribution or supply systems for irrigation; plumbing & hydronic heating supplies

(G-13098)
LSA UNITED INC
1020 E Emerson Ave (60148-3142)
PHONE.................................773 476-7439
Richard W Gessner, *Ch of Bd*
Robert Brani, *Vice Pres*
Connie Rae Wimmermark, *Admin Sec*
▲ **EMP:** 140
SQ FT: 47,000
SALES (est): 15.7MM **Privately Held**
SIC: 3469 Stamping metal for the trade

(G-13099)
MEDTRONIC INC
1 E 22nd St Ste 407 (60148-6159)
PHONE.................................630 627-6677
EMP: 25 **Privately Held**
SIC: 3841 Surgical & medical instruments
HQ: Medtronic, Inc.
710 Medtronic Pkwy
Minneapolis MN 55432
763 514-4000

(G-13100)
METAL IMPROVEMENT COMPANY LLC
E/M Coatings Solutions
129 Eisenhower Ln S (60148-5408)
PHONE.................................630 620-6808
Kevin Kobus, *Manager*
EMP: 36
SALES (corp-wide): 2.4B **Publicly Held**
SIC: 3398 Shot peening (treating steel to reduce fatigue)
HQ: Metal Improvement Company, Llc
80 E Rte 4 Ste 310
Paramus NJ 07652
201 843-7800

(G-13101)
MIDWEST ENERGY MANAGEMENT INC
10 E 22nd St Ste 111 (60148-6107)
PHONE.................................630 759-6007
Lonnie Samples, *President*
Thomas Samples, *Vice Pres*
Mark Brown, *Manager*
EMP: 6
SQ FT: 1,500
SALES (est): 1.1MM **Privately Held**
SIC: 3823 Industrial process measurement equipment

(G-13102)
MK ENVIRONMENTAL INC (PA)
765 Springer Dr (60148-6412)
PHONE.................................630 848-0585
Edward Tung, *President*
EMP: 2
SALES (est): 626.9K **Privately Held**
SIC: 3826 Environmental testing equipment

(G-13103)
MONARCH MANUFACTURING
118 E Goebel Dr (60148-1736)
PHONE.................................630 519-4580
Dave Petrucci, *Owner*
EMP: 3 **EST:** 1958
SQ FT: 3,000
SALES (est): 300K **Privately Held**
SIC: 3544 Forms (molds), for foundry & plastics working machinery; industrial molds

(G-13104)
MORMOR INCORPORATED
Also Called: Ink Well
119 E Roosevelt Rd (60148-4506)
PHONE.................................630 268-0050
Carol Morgan, *President*
EMP: 1
SQ FT: 2,100
SALES (est): 200K **Privately Held**
SIC: 2791 2789 2752 Typesetting; bookbinding & related work; commercial printing, lithographic

(G-13105)
MUNTONS MALTED INGREDIENTS INC
2505 S Finley Rd Ste 130 (60148-4867)
PHONE.................................630 812-1600
Neil Pearmain, *President*
Terence McNeill, *Vice Pres*
Steve Szirmai, *CFO*
Andrew Blackmore, *Treasurer*
Jeff Loranger, *Sales Mgr*
◆ **EMP:** 5 **EST:** 2010
SALES (est): 452K
SALES (corp-wide): 135.7MM **Privately Held**
WEB: www.muntons-inc.com
SIC: 2083 Barley malt
HQ: Muntons Plc
Cedars Maltings
Stowmarket IP14
144 961-8300

(G-13106)
NANOLUBE INC
9 N Main St Ste 2 (60148-2351)
PHONE.................................630 706-1250
Christopher Arnold, *President*
Marijean Arnold, *Corp Secy*
Richard Nagel, *Vice Pres*
▼ **EMP:** 3
SALES (est): 243.8K **Privately Held**
SIC: 2992 Lubricating oils

(G-13107)
NATURE S AMERICAN CO
665 W North Ave Ste 105 (60148-1134)
PHONE.................................630 246-4776
Jason Samatas, *CEO*
Tyler Page, *General Mgr*
EMP: 2
SALES (est): 800K **Privately Held**
WEB: www.naturesamerican.com
SIC: 2064 Granola & muesli, bars & clusters

(G-13108)
NEXT GERNERATION
1052 N Du Page Ave (60148-1246)
PHONE.................................630 261-1477
Stuart Fishman, *Owner*
EMP: 10
SALES (est): 1.3MM **Privately Held**
SIC: 2759 Screen printing

(G-13109)
NORTHWEST SNOW TIMBER SVC LTD
Also Called: Northwest Snow and Timber Svc
1321 S School St (60148-4737)
P.O. Box 1296, Arlington Heights (60006-1296)
PHONE.................................847 778-4998
Kevin Lavin, *President*
EMP: 8
SALES (est): 115.3K **Privately Held**
SIC: 4959 2491 0781 Snowplowing; structural lumber & timber, treated wood; landscape services

(G-13110)
NOVAK BUSINESS FORMS INC
20 Eisenhower Ln N (60148-5414)
PHONE.................................630 932-9850
Mae Novak, *President*
Edward Novak, *Corp Secy*
EMP: 31
SQ FT: 10,000
SALES (est): 3.3MM **Privately Held**
SIC: 2752 2761 Business form & card printing, lithographic; manifold business forms

(G-13111)
OAK HILL BRANDS CORP
Also Called: Modularhose.com
1013 N Lombard Rd (60148-1238)
PHONE.................................630 922-5010
David Zebutis, *CEO*
EMP: 6
SALES (est): 315.4K **Privately Held**
SIC: 3085 Plastics bottles

(G-13112)
OLYMPIC SIGNS INC
1130 N Garfield St (60148-1336)
PHONE.................................630 424-6100
Rob Whitehead, *President*
Bill Pyter, *Vice Pres*
John Wozniak, *Commercial*
EMP: 48 **EST:** 1982
SQ FT: 35,000
SALES (est): 7.9MM **Privately Held**
WEB: www.olysigns.com
SIC: 3993 Electric signs

(G-13113)
OMIOTEK COIL SPRING CO (PA)
833 N Ridge Ave (60148-1286)
P.O. Box 986 (60148-0986)
PHONE.................................630 495-4056
Mike Omiotek, *President*
Diane Omiotek, *Vice Pres*
Edward Omiotek, *Vice Pres*
Victor Omiotek, *Vice Pres*
Margaret Omiotek, *Admin Sec*
▲ **EMP:** 80 **EST:** 1973
SQ FT: 32,000
SALES (est): 11.5MM **Privately Held**
SIC: 3493 3469 3549 Coiled flat springs; stamping metal for the trade; metalworking machinery

(G-13114)
ORORA NORTH AMERICA
Also Called: Landsberg Chicago
100 E Progress Rd (60148-1333)
PHONE.................................630 613-2600
Matt O-Brien, *Division Mgr*
David Niedelman, *Vice Pres*
David Forrest, *Opers Mgr*
Nancy Prather, *Opers Mgr*
Dan Thomas, *Opers Staff*
EMP: 80 **Privately Held**
SIC: 5113 2653 Paper & products, wrapping or coarse; boxes, corrugated: made from purchased materials
HQ: Orora Packaging Solutions
6600 Valley View St
Buena Park CA 90620
714 562-6000

(G-13115)
PACRIMSON FIRE RISK SVCS INC
920 N Ridge Ave Ste C2 (60148-1226)
PHONE.................................630 424-3400
Anna Grezenko, *Treasurer*
David Grezenko, *Technology*
EMP: 1

Lombard - Dupage County (G-13116)

SALES (est): 271.6K **Privately Held**
WEB: www.pacrimson.com
SIC: 3569 Firefighting apparatus & related equipment

(G-13116)
PANZER TOOL CORP
920 N Ridge Ave Ste A2 (60148-1226)
PHONE..................630 519-5214
Earl Proball, *President*
Charles Proball, *Vice Pres*
EMP: 4 **EST:** 1964
SQ FT: 9,000
SALES: 700K **Privately Held**
SIC: 3544 Special dies & tools; industrial molds

(G-13117)
PARTEX MARKING SYSTEMS INC
1155 N Main St (60148-1360)
PHONE..................630 516-0400
Lisa Pickett, *Bookkeeper*
Robert Roach, *Sales Mgr*
Craig Mitchell, *Sales Staff*
Heather Lindquist, *Marketing Staff*
Janet Torres, *Manager*
EMP: 4
SALES (est): 1.2MM
SALES (corp-wide): 31.6MM **Privately Held**
SIC: 5063 3496 Wire & cable; cable conduit; miscellaneous fabricated wire products
HQ: Partex Marking Systems Ab
  Tore Loofs Gata 2
  Gullspang 547 3
  551 280-00

(G-13118)
PATE COMPANY INC
245 Eisenhower Ln S (60148-5407)
PHONE..................630 705-1920
Micheal Pylypczak, *President*
John R Gritis, *Vice Pres*
Joseph Valente, *Treasurer*
Leon Richlak, *Natl Sales Mgr*
Craig Veselits, *Sales Engr*
EMP: 35 **EST:** 1963
SQ FT: 45,000
SALES (est): 8.2MM **Privately Held**
WEB: www.patecurbs.com
SIC: 3444 Roof deck, sheet metal

(G-13119)
PENTWATER FURNISHING INC
Also Called: Pentwater Cabinetry
920 N Lombard Rd (60148-1218)
PHONE..................630 984-4703
Jinehen Fan, *General Mgr*
▲ **EMP:** 19
SALES (est): 2.6MM **Privately Held**
SIC: 2434 Wood kitchen cabinets

(G-13120)
PINE ENVIRONMENTAL SVCS LLC
1153 N Main St (60148-1360)
PHONE..................847 718-1246
Brigitt Hinde, *Branch Mgr*
EMP: 4
SALES (corp-wide): 339.8MM **Privately Held**
SIC: 3826 Environmental testing equipment
HQ: Pine Environmental Services Llc
  92 N Main St Bldg 20
  Windsor NJ 08561

(G-13121)
PRECISION PRINTING INC
230 Eisenhower Ln N (60148-5403)
P.O. Box 427 (60148-0427)
PHONE..................630 737-0075
Kevin Bauman, *Principal*
EMP: 8 **EST:** 2010
SALES (est): 782.6K **Privately Held**
SIC: 2752 Commercial printing, lithographic

(G-13122)
PROCON PACIFIC LLC
436 Eisenhower Ln N (60148-5404)
PHONE..................630 575-0551
Steven Dry, *CEO*
Vanessa Rodriguez, *Manager*
Bob Heelan, *Executive*
▲ **EMP:** 11
SALES (est): 2.3MM **Privately Held**
SIC: 2673 Plastic & pliofilm bags

(G-13123)
PRS INC
434 S Ahrens Ave (60148-3006)
PHONE..................630 620-7259
Paul Sanko, *President*
EMP: 2 **EST:** 2000
SALES (est): 220.4K **Privately Held**
SIC: 3543 Foundry patternmaking

(G-13124)
QSRSOFT
1806 S Highland Ave (60148-4938)
PHONE..................630 995-9642
EMP: 7
SALES (est): 569.2K **Privately Held**
SIC: 3652 Pre-recorded records & tapes

(G-13125)
ROTO-DIE COMPANY INC
Also Called: Roto Die Company
1054 N Du Page Ave (60148-1246)
PHONE..................630 932-8605
EMP: 5
SALES (corp-wide): 190.8MM **Privately Held**
SIC: 3544 Special dies & tools
PA: Roto-Die Company, Inc.
  800 Howerton Ln
  Eureka MO 63025
  636 587-3600

(G-13126)
S A W CO
376 E Saint Charles Rd # 5 (60148-2376)
P.O. Box 233, Addison (60101-0233)
PHONE..................630 678-5400
Sylvester Wetle, *Owner*
EMP: 3
SALES (est): 170K **Privately Held**
SIC: 3641 Electric lamps & parts for generalized applications

(G-13127)
SAF-T-LOK INTERNATIONAL CORP
Also Called: Saf-T-Eze
300 Eisenhower Ln N (60148-5405)
PHONE..................630 495-2001
Helen C Sherry, *President*
Neal Sherry, *Purch Mgr*
Shaun Sherry, *Mktg Dir*
EMP: 20
SQ FT: 25,000
SALES (est): 4.6MM **Privately Held**
SIC: 2891 Adhesives & sealants

(G-13128)
SEAMLESS GUTTER CORP
Also Called: A Seamless Gutters
601 E Saint Charles Rd (60148-2099)
PHONE..................630 495-9800
Robert G Carter, *President*
Brian Carter, *Vice Pres*
Marlene Carter, *Admin Sec*
EMP: 50 **EST:** 1963
SALES (est): 5MM **Privately Held**
SIC: 1761 3444 3429 Siding contractor; gutter & downspout contractor; sheet metalwork; manufactured hardware (general)

(G-13129)
SHARPER IMAGE ENGRAVERS INC
261 Eisenhower Ln S (60148-5407)
PHONE..................630 403-1600
Kathryn S Behlburch, *President*
Kathryn S Behl-Burch, *President*
Tom Guilfoyle, *Corp Secy*
Tracy Bush, *Controller*
Tom Smith, *Manager*
EMP: 33
SQ FT: 10,162
SALES (est): 260.8K **Privately Held**
SIC: 2796 3555 Platemaking services; printing plates

(G-13130)
SINGLE PATH LLC
905 Parkview Blvd (60148-3267)
PHONE..................708 653-4100
Marybrigid Briggs, *Project Mgr*
Tracy Garcia, *Opers Staff*
Ken Garcia, *Sales Staff*
Marty Jensen, *Manager*
Jeff Gricus, *Technology*
EMP: 30
SQ FT: 8,000
SALES (est): 11.9MM
SALES (corp-wide): 35.3MM **Privately Held**
SIC: 7372 Prepackaged software
PA: Dyopath, Llc
  13430 Nw Fwy Ste 1000
  Houston TX 77040
  855 749-6758

(G-13131)
SPECIALIZED WOODWORK INC
Also Called: Plastic Art
74 Eisenhower Ln N (60148-5414)
PHONE..................630 627-0450
Fax: 630 627-0452
EMP: 3 **EST:** 1956
SQ FT: 2,500
SALES (est): 400K **Privately Held**
SIC: 3089 2541 2511 2434 Mfg Plastic Products Mfg Wood Partitions/Fixt Mfg Wood Household Furn Mfg Wood Kitchen Cabinet

(G-13132)
SPECIALTY FOODS GROUP LLC
Also Called: Scott Petersen & Company
477 E Bttrfeld Rd Ste 410 (60148)
PHONE..................630 599-5900
Jim Bolnius, *Manager*
EMP: 5 **Privately Held**
SIC: 2013 2011 Prepared beef products from purchased beef; meat packing plants
HQ: Specialty Foods Group, Llc
  6 Dublin Ln
  Owensboro KY 42301

(G-13133)
SPECTRACRAFTS LTD
Also Called: All Spun Metal Products
931 N Ridge Ave (60148-1208)
PHONE..................847 824-4117
Gianfranco Isaia, *President*
Maria Isaia, *Admin Sec*
EMP: 9
SQ FT: 10,000
SALES (est): 1MM **Privately Held**
SIC: 3469 3441 Spinning metal for the trade; fabricated structural metal

(G-13134)
SPEEDPRO OF DUPAGE
441 Eisenhower Ln S (60148-5706)
PHONE..................630 812-5080
Jim Delaney, *Owner*
EMP: 4 **EST:** 2010
SALES (est): 458.5K **Privately Held**
SIC: 3993 Signs & advertising specialties

(G-13135)
STURTEVANT INC
Also Called: Fcm Mills
959 N Garfield St (60148-1336)
PHONE..................630 613-8968
Tomas Johansson, *Branch Mgr*
EMP: 4
SALES (corp-wide): 8MM **Privately Held**
SIC: 3999 Custom pulverizing & grinding of plastic materials
PA: Sturtevant, Inc.
  348 Circuit St Ste 1
  Hanover MA 02339
  781 829-6501

(G-13136)
SUPERIOR BUMPERS INC
920 N Ridge Ave Ste C3 (60148-1226)
PHONE..................630 932-4910
John Lindquist, *President*
EMP: 5
SALES: 1MM **Privately Held**
SIC: 3069 Medical & laboratory rubber sundries & related products

(G-13137)
T G AUTOMOTIVE
901 N Ridge Ave Ste 1 (60148-1228)
P.O. Box 395 (60148-0395)
PHONE..................630 916-7818
EMP: 30
SQ FT: 1,600
SALES (est): 1MM **Privately Held**
SIC: 7536 5531 3714 Automotive glass replacement shops; automotive & home supply stores; motor vehicle wheels & parts

(G-13138)
TACTICAL LIGHTING SYSTEMS INC
1001 N Lombard Rd (60148-1254)
PHONE..................800 705-0518
James P McGee, *President*
Nicholas Dedio, *General Mgr*
Rick Mills, *Vice Pres*
John Polk, *CFO*
EMP: 17
SALES (est): 5MM **Privately Held**
SIC: 3648 Airport lighting fixtures: runway approach, taxi or ramp

(G-13139)
TASSOS METAL INC
950 N Lombard Rd (60148-1231)
PHONE..................630 953-1333
Tassos Dafnis, *President*
Kathryn Dafnis, *Admin Sec*
▲ **EMP:** 30
SQ FT: 30,000
SALES (est): 5.7MM **Privately Held**
SIC: 3444 Sheet metal specialties, not stamped

(G-13140)
TAURUS SAFETY PRODUCTS INC
39 S Glenview Ave (60148-2463)
P.O. Box 1002 (60148-8002)
PHONE..................630 620-7940
Joseph Wimberly, *President*
Deborah Wimberly, *Admin Sec*
EMP: 7
SALES (est): 712.6K **Privately Held**
SIC: 3272 3644 Chimney caps, concrete; noncurrent-carrying wiring services

(G-13141)
TEC REP CORPORATION
1919 S Highland Ave 330a (60148-4979)
PHONE..................630 627-9110
Ronald Kleinschmidt, *President*
Barb Simone, *Vice Pres*
Barbara Simone, *Vice Pres*
Nicholas Fallucca, *Project Mgr*
Mark Horner, *Sales Engr*
EMP: 11 **EST:** 1993
SALES (est): 57.9K **Privately Held**
WEB: www.tec-rep.com
SIC: 3825 Test equipment for electronic & electric measurement

(G-13142)
TELLA TOOL & MFG CO (PA)
Also Called: Tella Technology Div
1015 N Ridge Ave Ste 1 (60148-1258)
PHONE..................630 495-0545
Scott Prince, *President*
Robert Mikl, *Project Mgr*
Richard Wagy, *Opers Mgr*
Ed Hurtig, *Purch Mgr*
Joanne Anderson, *Purchasing*
EMP: 110
SQ FT: 65,000
SALES (est): 44.8MM **Privately Held**
SIC: 3544 3444 Special dies & tools; sheet metal specialties, not stamped

(G-13143)
THERAPEUTIC SKIN CARE
21w221 Hemstead Rd (60148-5148)
PHONE..................630 244-1833
Susie Fricano, *President*
EMP: 6
SALES: 266K **Privately Held**
SIC: 2834 Dermatologicals

(G-13144)
THOMAS GLENN HOLDINGS LLC
1000 N Main St (60148-1361)
PHONE..................630 916-8090
Joe Lane, *Vice Pres*
Micheal T Lane, *Mng Member*
Jeff Miller, *President*
EMP: 45

GEOGRAPHIC SECTION

SQ FT: 40,000
SALES (est): 7.3MM **Privately Held**
SIC: 2653 Boxes, corrugated; made from purchased materials

(G-13145)
TOWER PRINTING & DESIGN
2211 S Highland Ave 5a (60148-5333)
PHONE 630 495-1976
John Wimmer, *Owner*
EMP: 3
SQ FT: 2,000
SALES: 250K **Privately Held**
SIC: 2752 2791 2789 Commercial printing, lithographic; typesetting; bookbinding & related work

(G-13146)
TRIMARK SCREEN PRINTING INC
710 E Western Ave Ste C (60148-2164)
PHONE 630 629-2823
Debbie Martin, *President*
Keith Martin, *Vice Pres*
EMP: 5
SQ FT: 900
SALES: 200K **Privately Held**
SIC: 2759 2396 2395 Screen printing; automotive & apparel trimmings; pleating & stitching

(G-13147)
TRP ACQUISITION CORP (PA)
Also Called: Room Place, The
1000 N Rohlwing Rd Ste 46 (60148-1187)
PHONE 630 261-2380
Joe Connolly, *CEO*
Richard Cawley, *CFO*
▲ **EMP:** 8
SALES (est): 124.2MM **Privately Held**
SIC: 2512 Living room furniture; upholstered on wood frames

(G-13148)
TRUE LACROSSE LLC
131 Eisenhower Ln N (60148-5413)
PHONE 630 359-3857
Buetikofer Alex, *Managing Dir*
Ryan Covert, *Managing Dir*
Chris Koerner, *CFO*
Flannery Posner, *Marketing Staff*
Nathaniel Cain, *Director*
EMP: 4
SALES: 78.2K **Privately Held**
WEB: www.truelacrosse.com
SIC: 3949 Lacrosse equipment & supplies, general

(G-13149)
VELOCITY SOFTWARE LLC
1042 E Maple St (60148)
PHONE 800 351-6893
Brian Kramer, *Principal*
David D O'Sullivan, *Principal*
Colin Finn, *Executive*
EMP: 12
SALES: 1.3MM **Privately Held**
SIC: 7372 Business oriented computer software

(G-13150)
VERTIV GROUP CORPORATION
995 Oak Creek Dr (60148-6408)
PHONE 630 579-5000
Kevin Bailey, *Branch Mgr*
EMP: 33
SALES (corp-wide): 14.2MM **Publicly Held**
SIC: 3661 3644 Telephone & telegraph apparatus; noncurrent-carrying wiring services
HQ: Vertiv Group Corporation
1050 Dearborn Dr
Columbus OH 43085
614 888-0246

(G-13151)
VISKASE COMPANIES INC (HQ)
333 E Bttrfeld Rd Ste (60148)
PHONE 630 874-0700
Thomas D Davis, *Ch of Bd*
Henry Palacci, *COO*
John G Becker, *Vice Pres*
Maria Kozareva, *Vice Pres*
Christopher Meyers, *Vice Pres*
◆ **EMP:** 100 **EST:** 1970

SALES: 391.9MM
SALES (corp-wide): 8.9B **Publicly Held**
SIC: 3089 Celluloid products; cases, plastic; battery cases, plastic or plastic combination
PA: Icahn Enterprises L.P.
16690 Collins Ave
Sunny Isles Beach FL 33160
305 422-4000

(G-13152)
VISKASE CORPORATION (DH)
333 E Bttrfeld Rd Ste 400 (60148)
PHONE 630 874-0700
F Edward Gustafson, *Ch of Bd*
John F Weber, *President*
Gordon S Donovan, *Vice Pres*
Eugene I Davis, *Director*
Kimberly K Duttlinger, *Admin Sec*
▼ **EMP:** 80
SQ FT: 45,000
SALES (est): 190.3MM
SALES (corp-wide): 8.9B **Publicly Held**
SIC: 3089 Celluloid products
HQ: Viskase Companies, Inc.
333 E Bttrfeld Rd Ste
Lombard IL 60148
630 874-0700

(G-13153)
WATERCO OF CENTRAL STATES INC
Also Called: Culligan
1920 S Highland Ave # 113 (60148-4766)
PHONE 630 576-4782
Donald A Fuller, *President*
John Capone, *COO*
EMP: 181 **EST:** 2011
SALES (est): 9.7MM
SALES (corp-wide): 50.1MM **Privately Held**
SIC: 5999 5963 3589 5074 Water purification equipment; bottled water delivery; water treatment equipment, industrial; water purification equipment
HQ: Waterco Of The Midwest, Inc.
1920 S Highland Ave # 113
Lombard IL 60148
630 576-4782

(G-13154)
WESTMORE SUPPLY CO
250 Westmore Meyers Rd (60148-3088)
PHONE 630 627-0278
John A Bielenda, *President*
Mark Bielenda, *Vice Pres*
EMP: 10
SQ FT: 75,000
SALES: 1.6MM **Privately Held**
WEB: www.westmoresupply.net
SIC: 5983 3273 Fuel oil dealers; ready-mixed concrete

(G-13155)
WHALE MANUFACTURING INC
870 N Ridge Ave (60148-1215)
PHONE 847 357-9192
Ron Lepinski, *President*
EMP: 4
SQ FT: 2,000
SALES (est): 250K **Privately Held**
SIC: 3599 Custom machinery

(G-13156)
YORKE PRINTE SHOPPE INC
930 N Lombard Rd (60148-1231)
PHONE 630 627-4960
Bradley P Scull, *President*
Sharon L Scull, *Vice Pres*
Lindsey Meachum, *Production*
Philip E Scull, *Treasurer*
Michele Willis-Rosso, *Marketing Mgr*
EMP: 41
SQ FT: 20,500
SALES (est): 9.5MM **Privately Held**
SIC: 2752 Commercial printing, offset

Long Grove
Lake County

(G-13157)
BENTLEYS PET STUFF LLC
4196 Illinois Rte 83 (60047)
PHONE 847 793-0500
EMP: 5
SALES (corp-wide): 1.1MM **Privately Held**
SIC: 3999 Pet supplies
HQ: Bentley's Pet Stuff, Llc
4192 Ill Rte 83 Ste C
Long Grove IL 60047
224 567-4700

(G-13158)
BROKEN EARTH WINERY
219 Rbert Prker Coffin Rd (60047-9616)
PHONE 847 383-5052
Melissa Forsythe, *Principal*
EMP: 4
SALES (est): 305.1K **Privately Held**
WEB: www.brokenearthwinerylg.com
SIC: 2084 Wines

(G-13159)
CONTROL SYSTEMS INC
3603 Crestview Dr (60047-5231)
PHONE 847 438-6228
Gerhard Maier, *President*
Susanne Maier, *Corp Secy*
EMP: 7 **EST:** 2000
SALES (est): 1.4MM **Privately Held**
WEB: www.controlsystemsinc.us
SIC: 3625 Control equipment, electric

(G-13160)
INTERNATIONAL DRUG DEV CONS
Also Called: Iddc
1549 Rfd (60047-9532)
PHONE 847 634-9586
Esam Dajani, *President*
EMP: 1
SALES (est): 388K **Privately Held**
SIC: 2834 Druggists' preparations (pharmaceuticals)

(G-13161)
LORDAHL MANUFACTURING CO
Also Called: Lordahl Engineering
1571 Rfd (60047-9789)
PHONE 847 244-0448
Var Lordahl, *Owner*
Frank O'Sullivan, *Vice Pres*
Scott Koepsel, *Engrg Mgr*
EMP: 59
SALES (corp-wide): 7.6MM **Privately Held**
SIC: 4225 5074 3089 General warehousing; plumbing & hydronic heating supplies; molding primary plastic
PA: Lordahl Manufacturing Co.
1001 S Lewis Ave
Waukegan IL 60085
847 244-0448

(G-13162)
MANGEL AND CO
Also Called: Long Grove Apple Haus
230 Rbert Prker Coffin Rd (60047-9539)
PHONE 847 634-0730
John Blyth, *Manager*
EMP: 10
SALES (corp-wide): 4.6MM **Privately Held**
WEB: www.longrove.com
SIC: 5149 2099 2051 5499 Bakery products; food preparations; bread, cake & related products; juices, fruit or vegetable
PA: Mangel And Co.
333 Lexington Dr
Buffalo Grove IL 60089
847 459-3100

(G-13163)
MAT CAPITAL LLC (PA)
6700 Wildlife Way (60047)
PHONE 847 821-9630
Steve Wang,
EMP: 3

SALES (est): 548.1K **Privately Held**
SIC: 3089 3999 5141 6719 Plastic kitchenware, tableware & houseware; straw goods; food brokers; investment holding companies, except banks

(G-13164)
MAT ENGINE TECHNOLOGIES LLC (HQ)
6700 Wildlife Way (60047)
PHONE 847 821-9630
Steve Wang,
▲ **EMP:** 1
SALES: 23.2MM **Privately Held**
SIC: 3694 Engine electrical equipment

(G-13165)
MAT HOLDINGS INC (PA)
6700 Wildlife Way (60047)
PHONE 847 821-9630
Steve Wang, *CEO*
Christen Powers, *Vice Pres*
Steven Rovtar, *Vice Pres*
Kirk Hampton, *Opers Mgr*
Bob Trott, *Opers Mgr*
◆ **EMP:** 100
SQ FT: 54,000
SALES: 1.5B **Privately Held**
SIC: 3714 3563 3524 1796 Motor vehicle parts & accessories; air & gas compressors including vacuum pumps; lawn & garden mowers & accessories; power generating equipment installation; washing & polishing, automotive; nonferrous rolling & drawing

(G-13166)
MAT INDUSTRIES LLC (HQ)
6700 Wildlife Way (60047)
PHONE 847 821-9630
Steve Wang,
George Ruhl,
◆ **EMP:** 4
SALES: 112.3MM **Privately Held**
SIC: 3563 Air & gas compressors

(G-13167)
NATIONAL SCHOOL SERVICES INC
3254 Mayflower Ln (60047-5019)
PHONE 847 438-3859
Norman Olson, *President*
EMP: 30
SQ FT: 3,000
SALES (est): 1.9MM **Privately Held**
SIC: 7373 7313 2731 5999 Computer integrated systems design; radio, television, publisher representatives; textbooks; publishing only, not printed on site; education aids, devices & supplies

(G-13168)
OTHERNET INC
20535 Il 53 (60047)
PHONE 773 688-4320
Syed Karim, *CEO*
EMP: 4
SQ FT: 10,000
SALES: 116K **Privately Held**
SIC: 8748 3679 4841 3651 Telecommunications consultant; antennas, satellite; household use; direct broadcast satellite services (DBS); radio receiving sets; radio & TV communications equipment; radio broadcasting & communications equipment

(G-13169)
PATTERSON AVENUE TOOL COMPANY
6515 High Meadow Ct (60047-5109)
PHONE 847 949-8100
James M Clarke, *President*
Karen Ann Keane, *Corp Secy*
Margo M Clarke, *Vice Pres*
▲ **EMP:** 3
SALES: 120K **Privately Held**
SIC: 3423 Hand & edge tools

(G-13170)
SHERWIN-WILLIAMS COMPANY
4194 Il Route 83 (60047-9563)
PHONE 847 478-0677
Shawn Faulkner, *Site Mgr*
EMP: 6

Long Grove - Lake County (G-13171)

SALES (corp-wide): 17.9B **Publicly Held**
SIC: 5231 5198 2851 Paint; paints, varnishes & supplies; wood fillers or sealers
PA: The Sherwin-Williams Company
101 W Prospect Ave # 1020
Cleveland OH 44115
216 566-2000

(G-13171)
TIGER ACCESSORY GROUP LLC (HQ)
Also Called: Clean Rite Products
6700 Wildlife Way (60047)
PHONE..................847 821-9630
Terry Obrien, *CFO*
Steve Wang,
George Ruhl,
▲ **EMP:** 15
SQ FT: 2,500
SALES: 45.1MM **Privately Held**
SIC: 2842 2259 3647 Specialty cleaning preparations; towels, knit; motor vehicle lighting equipment

(G-13172)
TOM ZOSEL ASSOCIATES LTD
Also Called: Tza Consulting
3880 Salem Lake Dr Ste B (60047-5292)
PHONE..................847 540-6543
Evan Danner, *President*
Thomas W Zosel, *President*
Lisa Danner, *Vice Pres*
◆ **EMP:** 60
SQ FT: 10,000
SALES (est): 6.9MM **Privately Held**
SIC: 8742 7372 Business consultant; business oriented computer software

(G-13173)
VALENTINO VINEYARDS INC
Also Called: Valentino Vineyards & Winery
5175 Aptakisic Rd (60047-5186)
PHONE..................847 634-2831
Rudolph Valentino, *President*
EMP: 3
SALES (est): 173.5K **Privately Held**
SIC: 2084 Wines

(G-13174)
WEILAND FAST TRAC INC
3386 Rfd (60047-9724)
P.O. Box 1059, Lake Zurich (60047-1059)
PHONE..................847 438-7996
David Weiland, *President*
Terry Weiland, *Vice Pres*
Kathy Weiland, *Treasurer*
Norma Weiland, *Admin Sec*
EMP: 4
SALES (est): 420.3K **Privately Held**
SIC: 3069 5571 3061 Hard rubber & molded rubber products; motorcycle dealers; mechanical rubber goods

Longview
Champaign County

(G-13175)
RJD MACHINING LLC
244 County Road 1900 E (61852-9603)
PHONE..................217 684-5100
Dennis K McCormick,
EMP: 3
SALES: 191.4K **Privately Held**
SIC: 3599 Machine shop, jobbing & repair

Lostant
Lasalle County

(G-13176)
HART ELECTRIC LLC
102 S Main St (61334-9004)
P.O. Box 230 (61334-0230)
PHONE..................815 368-3341
Milton Hartenbower,
Catherine Hartenbower,
Milton Fred Hartenbower,
EMP: 45
SQ FT: 10,000
SALES (est): 10MM **Privately Held**
SIC: 3679 Harness assemblies for electronic use: wire or cable

(G-13177)
PORCH ELECTRIC LLC
205 N Main St (61334-9017)
P.O. Box 183 (61334-0183)
PHONE..................815 368-3230
Janet Porch,
Eric Porch,
EMP: 2
SALES: 500K **Privately Held**
SIC: 3643 Current-carrying wiring devices

Louisville
Clay County

(G-13178)
DANNY FENDER
Also Called: Clay County Republican
124 S Church St (62858-1226)
P.O. Box B (62858-0902)
PHONE..................618 665-3135
Danny Fender, *Owner*
EMP: 3 **EST:** 1800
SALES (est): 10.1K **Privately Held**
SIC: 2711 Newspapers

(G-13179)
KINCAID OIL PRODUCERS INC
6166 Bible Grove Ln (62858-2468)
PHONE..................618 686-3084
Aaron Kincaid, *President*
EMP: 3 **EST:** 1986
SALES (est): 105.1K **Privately Held**
WEB: www.kincaidoilproducers.com
SIC: 1389 1381 Oil field services; drilling oil & gas wells

(G-13180)
SIMS COMPANY INC
1431 Panther Creek Ln (62858-2573)
P.O. Box 129 (62858-0129)
PHONE..................618 665-3901
Scott Sims, *President*
Lori Sims, *Admin Sec*
EMP: 2
SQ FT: 5,500
SALES: 400K **Privately Held**
SIC: 1389 Chemically treating wells

Loves Park
Winnebago County

(G-13181)
A-L-L EQUIPMENT COMPANY
5619 Pike Rd (61111-4710)
P.O. Box 909, Moline (61266-0909)
PHONE..................815 877-7000
Erick Welser, *Manager*
EMP: 7
SALES (est): 556.7K
SALES (corp-wide): 6MM **Privately Held**
SIC: 5084 5075 3561 Pumps & pumping equipment; compressors, except air conditioning; compressors, air conditioning; pumps & pumping equipment
PA: A-L-L Equipment Company
204 38th St
Moline IL 61265
309 762-8096

(G-13182)
ADVANCED HEAT TREATING INC
980 Industrial Ct (61111-7512)
PHONE..................815 877-8593
Gloria Stuhr Pernacciaro, *CEO*
Chuck Pernacciaro, *President*
Jerry Otterson, *Plant Mgr*
Mary Pernacciaro, *Director*
Molly Nash, *Admin Asst*
EMP: 25
SALES (est): 5.6MM **Privately Held**
SIC: 3398 Metal heat treating

(G-13183)
AERO ALEHOUSE LLC
6164 E Riverside Blvd (61111-4468)
PHONE..................815 977-5602
Pendergrass Matthew,
EMP: 5
SALES (est): 223.3K **Privately Held**
WEB: www.aerolovespark.com
SIC: 2082 5812 Ale (alcoholic beverage); eating places

(G-13184)
AGI CORP
6075 Material Ave Ste 100 (61111-4242)
P.O. Box 2506 (61132-2506)
PHONE..................815 708-0502
Christopher C Weber, *President*
EMP: 10 **EST:** 2013
SALES (est): 926K **Privately Held**
WEB: www.agi-corporation.com
SIC: 2851 Polyurethane coatings

(G-13185)
AIRCRAFT GEAR CORPORATION (PA)
Also Called: Rockford Acromatic Products
611 Beacon St (61111-5902)
P.O. Box 2066 (61130-0066)
PHONE..................815 877-7473
Dean A Olson II, *Ch of Bd*
James N Olson, *President*
Rick G Grimes, *Vice Pres*
Lynn Stohlglen, *Vice Pres*
Kay Mullins, *Treasurer*
▲ **EMP:** 65 **EST:** 1965
SQ FT: 50,000
SALES (est): 32.8MM **Privately Held**
WEB: www.rockfordacromatic.com
SIC: 3714 3728 Universal joints, motor vehicle; gears, aircraft power transmission

(G-13186)
ALERT TUBING FABRICATORS INC
8019 Commercial Ave (61111-2702)
PHONE..................815 633-5065
Kevin Coffey, *President*
Amy Coffey, *Principal*
James Martin, *Vice Pres*
EMP: 8
SALES (est): 2.1MM **Privately Held**
SIC: 3498 Tube fabricating (contract bending & shaping)

(G-13187)
ALLIED SCORING TABLES INC
5417 Forest Hills Ct (61111-8318)
P.O. Box 833, Roscoe (61073-0833)
PHONE..................815 654-8807
John Rygh, *President*
Nancy Moate, *Marketing Staff*
EMP: 6
SQ FT: 4,800
SALES: 1MM **Privately Held**
SIC: 3949 Basketball equipment & supplies, general

(G-13188)
AMERICAN BOTTLING COMPANY
Also Called: 7-Up-The American Bottling Co
5300 Forest Hills Rd (61111-5210)
PHONE..................815 877-7777
Larry Heck, *Manager*
EMP: 50 **Publicly Held**
SIC: 2086 Soft drinks: packaged in cans, bottles, etc.
HQ: The American Bottling Company
5301 Legacy Dr
Plano TX 75024

(G-13189)
AMV INTERNATIONAL INC
7814 Forest Hills Rd (61111-3310)
PHONE..................815 282-9990
Jean-Thierry Catrice, *President*
▲ **EMP:** 11
SALES (est): 1.2MM **Privately Held**
SIC: 3425 Saw blades for hand or power saws

(G-13190)
ARACHNID 360 LLC (PA)
6212 Material Ave (61111-4244)
P.O. Box 2901 (61132-2901)
PHONE..................815 654-0212
Jeanne Penney, *Prdtn Mgr*
Matt Malmberg, *Design Engr*
Marcio Bonilla, *VP Sales*
Chad Zander, *Sales Staff*
Jina Tenney, *Adv Mgr*

◆ **EMP:** 50 **EST:** 1970
SQ FT: 35,000
SALES: 10MM **Privately Held**
SIC: 3949 Dartboards & accessories

(G-13191)
ARCHITECTURAL METALS LLC
6200 Forest Hills Rd (61111-4763)
PHONE..................815 654-2370
Michael Messinnk, *Mng Member*
David Wendler,
Jason Wendler,
EMP: 12
SALES (est): 1.5MM **Privately Held**
SIC: 3441 Fabricated structural metal

(G-13192)
ATOMETRIC INC
7320 Forest Hills Rd (61111-3984)
PHONE..................815 505-2582
Thomas N Lindem, *President*
EMP: 1
SALES (est): 213.9K **Privately Held**
SIC: 3541 Machine tools, metal cutting type

(G-13193)
AUDIO INSTALLERS INC
Also Called: A I Satellite Distributing
5061 Contractors Dr (61111-1907)
PHONE..................815 969-7500
Michael Roncke, *President*
Jeanette M Roncke, *Vice Pres*
▲ **EMP:** 10
SQ FT: 4,900
SALES (est): 1.5MM **Privately Held**
WEB: www.aisatellite.com
SIC: 5731 5064 5063 1731 Radios, two-way, citizens' band, weather, short-wave, etc.; high fidelity stereo equipment; antennas, satellite dish; radios, motor vehicle; high fidelity equipment; burglar alarm systems; antennas, receiving, satellite dishes; telephone & telephone equipment installation; electronic kits for home assembly: radio, TV, phonograph

(G-13194)
BEST PALLET COMPANY LLC
Also Called: Great Lakes Pallet Company
1110 Widsor Rd (61111)
PHONE..................815 637-1500
Mike Faas, *Manager*
EMP: 14
SALES (est): 1.3MM
SALES (corp-wide): 2.7MM **Privately Held**
WEB: www.greatlakespallet.com
SIC: 2448 Pallets, wood
PA: Best Pallet Company Llc
166 W Washington St # 300
Chicago IL 60602
312 242-4009

(G-13195)
CONVERGENCE FUEL SYSTEMS LLC
1 Woodward (61111-7700)
PHONE..................970 498-3430
EMP: 3 **EST:** 2015
SALES (est): 126.1K
SALES (corp-wide): 2.9B **Publicly Held**
SIC: 3829 Fuel densitometers, aircraft engine; fuel mixture indicators, aircraft engine; fuel system instruments, aircraft; fuel totalizers, aircraft engine
PA: Woodward, Inc.
1081 Woodward Way
Fort Collins CO 80524
970 482-5811

(G-13196)
CORPRO SCREEN TECH INC
5129 Forest Hills Ct (61111-8305)
PHONE..................815 633-1201
Jeffrey Foster, *President*
Scott Gesner, *Treasurer*
Mike White, *Admin Sec*
EMP: 8
SQ FT: 4,000
SALES (est): 1.2MM **Privately Held**
SIC: 3993 Advertising artwork

GEOGRAPHIC SECTION

Loves Park - Winnebago County (G-13226)

(G-13197)
COVACHEM LLC
6260 E Riverside Blvd (61111-4418)
PHONE..................815 714-8421
Tony Nooner, *Managing Dir*
Anthony Nooner,
EMP: 10 EST: 2012
SALES (est): 1.2MM **Privately Held**
SIC: 2869 High purity grade chemicals, organic; laboratory chemicals, organic

(G-13198)
CRAFT WORLD INC
Also Called: Alpine Imports
6836 Forest Hills Rd (61111-4367)
PHONE..................800 654-6114
Fax: 815 654-2746
EMP: 4 EST: 1974
SQ FT: 10,000
SALES (est): 399.9K **Privately Held**
SIC: 3944 Mfg Games/Toys

(G-13199)
CRYSTAL PRECISION DRILLING
5122 Torque Rd (61111-7165)
PHONE..................815 633-5460
Norman Fisher, *President*
EMP: 7
SALES (est): 1.9MM **Privately Held**
WEB: www.cpdinc.org
SIC: 1381 3469 Directional drilling oil & gas wells; machine parts, stamped or pressed metal

(G-13200)
CUSTOM CUTTING TOOLS INC
5405 Forest Hills Ct (61111-8318)
PHONE..................815 986-0320
William J Mc Kenzie, *President*
Prudence M Mc Kenzie, *Treasurer*
EMP: 4 EST: 1961
SQ FT: 6,000
SALES (est): 300K **Privately Held**
SIC: 3423 3546 3545 3541 Edge tools for woodworking: augers, bits, gimlets, etc.; power-driven handtools; machine tool accessories; machine tools, metal cutting type; cutlery

(G-13201)
CUSTOM FEEDER CO OF ROCKFORD
6207 Material Ave Ste 1 (61111-4284)
P.O. Box 2802 (61132-2802)
PHONE..................815 654-2444
James Stamm, *President*
Mike Stamm, *Vice Pres*
Sarah Johnson, *Opers Staff*
Michael J Stamm, *Treasurer*
Ryan Meseck, *Sales Mgr*
EMP: 20
SQ FT: 20,000
SALES (est): 3.5MM **Privately Held**
SIC: 3545 3441 Hopper feed devices; fabricated structural metal

(G-13202)
D & S MANUFACTURING INC
5604 Pike Rd (61111-4711)
PHONE..................815 637-8889
Eric Johnson, *President*
John Rodz, *Vice Pres*
EMP: 8
SQ FT: 5,000
SALES (est): 600K **Privately Held**
WEB: www.dandsmanufacturinginc.com
SIC: 3599 Machine shop, jobbing & repair

(G-13203)
D MACHINE INC
921 River Ln (61111-4712)
PHONE..................815 877-5991
Vern Meyer, *President*
Linda Meyer, *Admin Sec*
EMP: 5
SQ FT: 15,000
SALES (est): 834.5K **Privately Held**
WEB: www.dmachine-inc.com
SIC: 3599 Machine shop, jobbing & repair

(G-13204)
DANFOSS INC
7500 Beverage Blvd (61111-5601)
PHONE..................815 639-8600
Kim Fausing, *CEO*

▲ EMP: 4
SALES (est): 569.5K **Privately Held**
SIC: 3625 Motor controls & accessories

(G-13205)
DANFOSS LLC
4401 N Bell School Rd (61111-5600)
PHONE..................717 261-5000
EMP: 7
SALES (corp-wide): 250.7K **Privately Held**
SIC: 3585 3822 3625 Refrigeration & heating equipment; auto controls regulating residntl & coml environmt & applncs; relays & industrial controls
HQ: Danfoss, Llc
11655 Crossroads Cir
Baltimore MD 21220
410 931-8250

(G-13206)
DANFOSS LLC
Also Called: Danfoss Power Electronics
4401 N Bell School Rd (61111-5600)
PHONE..................888 326-3677
Arnaldo Ircca, *Branch Mgr*
EMP: 182
SALES (corp-wide): 250.7K **Privately Held**
SIC: 3625 3823 Motor controls & accessories; industrial instrmnts msrmnt display/control process variable
HQ: Danfoss, Llc
11655 Crossroads Cir
Baltimore MD 21220
410 931-8250

(G-13207)
DESIGNOVATIONS INC
8020 Commercial Ave (61111-2703)
P.O. Box 15914 (61132-5914)
PHONE..................815 645-8598
Janis E Anderson, *President*
EMP: 3
SQ FT: 5,000
SALES (est): 486.6K **Privately Held**
SIC: 3993 Signs & advertising specialties

(G-13208)
DURA FEED INC
7542 Forest Hills Rd (61111-3304)
PHONE..................815 395-1115
John Lapour, *President*
Henry Aniszewski, *General Mgr*
EMP: 2
SALES (est): 358.7K **Privately Held**
SIC: 3523 Farm machinery & equipment

(G-13209)
EKLUND METAL TREATING INC
721 Beacon St (61111-5993)
PHONE..................815 877-7436
Henry Adamski Sr, *President*
Todd Alton, *Vice Pres*
Cheryl Adamski, *Admin Sec*
EMP: 25
SQ FT: 26,500
SALES (est): 5.4MM **Privately Held**
SIC: 3398 Metal heat treating

(G-13210)
EQUUSTOCK LLC
Also Called: Guardian Horse Bedding
8179 Starwood Dr Ste 1 (61111-5718)
PHONE..................866 962-4686
Claire Brant, *Managing Prtnr*
Jim Peterson, *COO*
Jonathan Brant, *Mktg Dir*
▼ EMP: 10
SQ FT: 2,500
SALES (est): 3.1MM **Privately Held**
SIC: 2499 2448 Carved & turned wood; pallets, wood

(G-13211)
FORD TOOL & MACHINING INC (PA)
Also Called: Lathom Pin - Div
2205 Range Rd (61111-2724)
P.O. Box 2211 (61131-0211)
PHONE..................815 633-5727
Thomas Chustak, *President*
Robert Ford, *President*
David P Beto, *Chairman*
Ronald Roling, *CFO*
EMP: 75 EST: 1972

SQ FT: 39,000
SALES (est): 16.6MM **Privately Held**
SIC: 3544 Special dies & tools

(G-13212)
FOREST CITY COUNTER TOPS INC
6050 Broadcast Pkwy (61111-4486)
PHONE..................815 633-8602
Charles Markese, *President*
Joanne Markese, *Corp Secy*
Thomas Markese, *Vice Pres*
EMP: 11
SALES (est): 1.1MM **Privately Held**
SIC: 2541 2542 2434 Table or counter tops, plastic laminated; partitions & fixtures, except wood; wood kitchen cabinets

(G-13213)
FOREST CITY INDUSTRY INC
6100 Material Ave (61111-4242)
P.O. Box 2105 (61130-0105)
PHONE..................815 877-4084
Michael A Gaffney, *President*
EMP: 18
SQ FT: 30,000
SALES (est): 1.2MM **Privately Held**
SIC: 3452 Bolts, nuts, rivets & washers

(G-13214)
GE AVIATION SYSTEMS LLC
1354 Clifford Ave Ste 100 (61111-4733)
P.O. Box 2909 (61132-2909)
PHONE..................779 203-8100
Mitzi Streid, *Branch Mgr*
EMP: 168
SALES (corp-wide): 95.2B **Publicly Held**
SIC: 3728 Aircraft parts & equipment
HQ: Ge Aviation Systems Llc
1 Neumann Way
Cincinnati OH 45215
937 898-9600

(G-13215)
GRAFCOR PACKAGING INC
1030 River Ln (61111-4715)
PHONE..................815 639-2380
William E Hall, *Vice Pres*
EMP: 10
SALES (corp-wide): 5.9MM **Privately Held**
SIC: 2631 3412 2653 Paperboard mills; metal barrels, drums & pails; corrugated & solid fiber boxes
PA: Grafcor Packaging, Inc.
121 Loomis St
Rockford IL 61101
815 963-1300

(G-13216)
HI-TECH POLYMERS INC
7967 Crest Hills Dr (61111-8301)
PHONE..................815 282-2272
Larry Phippen, *President*
EMP: 14
SQ FT: 10,800
SALES (est): 2.5MM **Privately Held**
SIC: 3089 Injection molding of plastics

(G-13217)
IMA AUTOMATION USA INC
Also Called: Ima Automation North America
4608 Interstate Blvd (61111-5702)
PHONE..................815 885-8800
Andrew Bittman, *President*
Michael Bognar, *Controller*
John Williams, *Regl Sales Mgr*
EMP: 77
SQ FT: 55,861
SALES (est): 19.1MM **Privately Held**
SIC: 3569 Liquid automation machinery & equipment; robots, assembly line: industrial & commercial
HQ: I.M.A. Industria Macchine Automatiche Spa
Via Bruno Tosarelli 184
Castenaso BO 40055
051 651-4111

(G-13218)
IMAGE SIGNS INC
7323 N Alpine Rd (61111-3901)
PHONE..................815 282-4141
Bob Baker, *President*
Joann Baker, *Vice Pres*

EMP: 10
SQ FT: 5,000
SALES (est): 1.4MM **Privately Held**
SIC: 7532 5999 1799 3993 Truck painting & lettering; banners; sign installation & maintenance; electric signs

(G-13219)
INDEV GAUGING SYSTEMS INC
6830 Forest Hills Rd (61111-4367)
PHONE..................815 282-4463
Dan Hanrahan, *President*
Mark Woodworth, *Treasurer*
EMP: 5
SALES (est): 1.2MM **Privately Held**
SIC: 3823 Draft gauges, industrial process type

(G-13220)
J-INDUSTRIES INC
5129 Forest Hills Ct (61111-8305)
PHONE..................815 654-0055
Jeffrey L Foster, *President*
EMP: 10
SQ FT: 3,500
SALES: 1MM **Privately Held**
SIC: 2782 3161 3172 Library binders, looseleaf; briefcases; wallets

(G-13221)
JANSSEN MACHINE INC
Also Called: Janssen, Ron
985 Industrial Ct (61111-7512)
PHONE..................815 877-9901
Ron J Janssen, *President*
Jeff Reisetter, *Vice Pres*
EMP: 12
SALES: 907K **Privately Held**
WEB: www.janssenmachineinc.com
SIC: 3599 Machine shop, jobbing & repair

(G-13222)
JASCH NORTH AMERICA COMPANY
6830 Forest Hills Rd (61111-4367)
PHONE..................815 282-4463
EMP: 4
SALES (est): 192.7K **Privately Held**
SIC: 2821 Plastics materials & resins
PA: Jasch Industries Limited
43/5 Bahalgarh Road,
Sonepat HR 13102

(G-13223)
JAVAMANIA COFFEE ROASTERY INC
8179 Starwood Dr Ste 4 (61111-5718)
PHONE..................815 885-4661
Sandy Keller, *President*
William Keller, *Vice Pres*
EMP: 3
SALES (est): 266.1K **Privately Held**
SIC: 5812 2095 Coffee shop; roasted coffee

(G-13224)
JEFCO SCREW MACHINE PRODUCTS
6203 Material Ave (61111-4282)
P.O. Box 2625 (61132-2625)
PHONE..................815 282-2000
Bruce C Mayer, *President*
EMP: 16 EST: 1960
SQ FT: 9,000
SALES (est): 3.1MM **Privately Held**
WEB: www.jefco-inc.com
SIC: 3599 Machine shop, jobbing & repair

(G-13225)
JOHN & HELEN INC
988 Industrial Ct (61111-7512)
PHONE..................815 654-1070
John Czaczkowski, *President*
Helen Czaczkowski, *Vice Pres*
EMP: 16
SQ FT: 8,000
SALES (est): 2.4MM **Privately Held**
SIC: 3599 Machine shop, jobbing & repair

(G-13226)
JOHNSON & JOHNSON
5500 Forest Hills Rd (61111-5213)
PHONE..................815 282-5671
Patricia Murrin, *Principal*
EMP: 79

(PA)=Parent Co (HQ)=Headquarters (DH)=Div Headquarters
◌ = New Business established in last 2 years

Loves Park - Winnebago County (G-13227)

SALES (corp-wide): 82B **Publicly Held**
SIC: 2834 Pharmaceutical preparations
PA: Johnson & Johnson
1 Johnson And Johnson Plz
New Brunswick NJ 08933
732 524-0400

(G-13227)
JRM INTERNATIONAL INC
5701 Industrial Ave (61111-4706)
PHONE..............................815 282-9330
James R Mattox, *President*
Lisa Giedd, *Accountant*
▲ **EMP:** 9
SQ FT: 32,000
SALES (est): 3.6MM **Privately Held**
SIC: 5084 3545 Hydraulic systems equipment & supplies; vises, machine (machine tool accessories)

(G-13228)
KEURIG DR PEPPER INC
Also Called: Dr Pepper Snapple Group
5300 Forest Hills Rd (61111-5210)
PHONE..............................815 877-7777
Larry Heck, *Branch Mgr*
EMP: 4 **Publicly Held**
SIC: 2086 Soft drinks: packaged in cans, bottles, etc.
PA: Keurig Dr Pepper Inc.
53 South Ave
Burlington MA 01803

(G-13229)
KI MACHINE TOOLS & PRODUCTIONS
2107 Charmar Dr (61111-3975)
PHONE..............................815 484-9216
Som Inthabandith, *President*
Chansouk Inthabandith, *Vice Pres*
Cathie Imus-Mayer, *Office Mgr*
EMP: 7 EST: 2000
SQ FT: 4,000
SALES (est): 1MM **Privately Held**
WEB: www.kimachine.com
SIC: 3544 Special dies & tools

(G-13230)
L M SHEET METAL INC
6727 Elm Ave (61111-3817)
PHONE..............................815 654-1837
C Sue Middleton, *President*
Bruce Middleton, *Treasurer*
Susan Middleton, *Office Mgr*
Brad Holifield, *Manager*
Susan L Middleton, *Admin Sec*
EMP: 20
SQ FT: 19,500
SALES (est): 4.1MM **Privately Held**
SIC: 1711 3444 Warm air heating & air conditioning contractor; sheet metalwork

(G-13231)
LAH INC
Also Called: Luthers Form Grinding Company
6309 Material Ave Ste 2 (61111-4286)
PHONE..............................815 282-4939
Lewis A Hiilstad, *President*
Brandon Hillstad, *Manager*
EMP: 2
SQ FT: 1,600
SALES (est): 200K **Privately Held**
SIC: 3544 Special dies, tools, jigs & fixtures

(G-13232)
LASER ENERGY SYSTEMS
4924 Torque Rd (61111-7163)
PHONE..............................815 282-8200
Steve Schaede, *President*
EMP: 2 EST: 1998
SALES (est): 294.4K **Privately Held**
WEB: www.laserenergysystems.com
SIC: 3699 Laser systems & equipment

(G-13233)
LEGIBLE SIGNS GROUP CORP
2221 Nimtz Ave (61111-3928)
PHONE..............................815 654-0100
Dorthy Drummond, *President*
EMP: 15
SQ FT: 11,000
SALES (est): 1.7MM **Privately Held**
SIC: 3993 Signs, not made in custom sign painting shops; name plates: except engraved, etched, etc.: metal

(G-13234)
LSL PRECISION MACHINING INC
Also Called: Long Screw
2210 Nimtz Rd (61111-3929)
P.O. Box 2093 (61130-0093)
PHONE..............................815 633-4701
Brian Long, *President*
Bradley Long, *Vice Pres*
Norman J Long, *Treasurer*
Dwayne E Long, *Admin Sec*
EMP: 23
SQ FT: 30,000
SALES (est): 1.9MM **Privately Held**
SIC: 3492 3451 Fluid power valves & hose fittings; screw machine products

(G-13235)
MANNER PLATING INC
926 River Ln (61111-4795)
PHONE..............................815 877-7791
John Gruner, *President*
EMP: 5
SQ FT: 10,000
SALES (est): 400K **Privately Held**
SIC: 3471 Plating of metals or formed products; electroplating of metals or formed products

(G-13236)
METHOD MOLDS INC
5085 Contractors Dr (61111-1907)
PHONE..............................815 877-0191
M C Moore, *President*
Joanne L Moore, *Admin Sec*
EMP: 4
SQ FT: 7,000
SALES (est): 495K **Privately Held**
SIC: 3544 7692 3545 Forms (molds), for foundry & plastics working machinery; industrial molds; welding repair; machine tool accessories

(G-13237)
MINUTEMAN PRESS OF ROCKFORD
5128 N 2nd St (61111-5002)
PHONE..............................815 633-2992
Eugene D Syring, *President*
Patricia L Syring, *Admin Sec*
EMP: 8
SQ FT: 2,500
SALES (est): 1.4MM **Privately Held**
SIC: 2752 2791 2789 Commercial printing, lithographic; typesetting; bookbinding & related work

(G-13238)
MONDELEZ GLOBAL LLC
Also Called: Cadbury
5500 Forest Hills Rd (61111-5213)
PHONE..............................815 877-8081
EMP: 190 **Publicly Held**
WEB: www.mdlz.com
SIC: 2064 Candy & other confectionery products
HQ: Mondelez Global Llc
3 N Pkwy Ste 300
Deerfield IL 60015
847 943-4000

(G-13239)
NATIONAL METAL WORKS INC
Also Called: Honeywell Authorized Dealer
916 River Ln (61111-4713)
PHONE..............................815 282-5533
Mary Kisting, *President*
David Kisting, *Admin Sec*
EMP: 7
SQ FT: 6,600
SALES (est): 1.4MM **Privately Held**
WEB: www.hvacnational.com
SIC: 3444 1711 Sheet metalwork; heating & air conditioning contractors

(G-13240)
NATURAL CHOICE CORPORATION
4601 Interstate Blvd (61111-5702)
PHONE..............................815 874-4444
George Knoll, *President*
Gerta Knoll, *Admin Sec*
Teresa Rodriquez, *Admin Asst*
▲ **EMP:** 18
SALES (est): 4.6MM **Privately Held**
SIC: 3589 3585 5078 Water purification equipment, household type; soda fountain & beverage dispensing equipment & parts; drinking water coolers, mechanical

(G-13241)
OLE SALTYS OF ROCKFORD INC (PA)
1920 E Riverside Blvd (61111-4900)
P.O. Box 8433, Rockford (61126-8433)
PHONE..............................815 637-2447
Al Domico, *President*
EMP: 3
SQ FT: 2,000
SALES (est): 1MM **Privately Held**
WEB: www.olesaltys.com
SIC: 2096 Potato chips & other potato-based snacks

(G-13242)
ONSITE WOODWORK CORPORATION (PA)
4100 Rock Valley Pkwy (61111-4472)
PHONE..............................815 633-6400
Ralph E Peterson, *Chairman*
Joy Peterson, *Corp Secy*
Mark Peterson, *Exec VP*
Tim Fruin, *Vice Pres*
Richard Greene, *Vice Pres*
EMP: 115
SQ FT: 40,000
SALES (est): 24.1MM **Privately Held**
SIC: 2431 Woodwork, interior & ornamental

(G-13243)
PARK LICENSE SERVICE INC
6402 N 2nd St (61111-4110)
PHONE..............................815 633-5511
Hazel Lindblade, *President*
EMP: 6
SALES (est): 150K **Privately Held**
SIC: 3711 Cars, electric, assembly of

(G-13244)
PHILLIP RODGERS
Also Called: Precise Tool & Manufacturing
5366 Forest Hills Ct (61111-8319)
P.O. Box 16361 (61132-6361)
PHONE..............................815 877-5461
Phillip Rodgers, *Owner*
Debra Rodgers, *Co-Owner*
EMP: 2
SQ FT: 4,000
SALES (est): 300K **Privately Held**
SIC: 3599 Machine shop, jobbing & repair

(G-13245)
PIERCE PACKAGING CO (PA)
Also Called: Pierce Distribution Svcs Co
2028 E Riverside Blvd (61111-4804)
P.O. Box 15600 (61132-5600)
PHONE..............................815 636-6650
Kevin Hogan, *President*
Dino McNabb, *Vice Pres*
Kristi Taylor, *Vice Pres*
Tracey Strawn, *Purch Mgr*
Anthony Chiodini, *CFO*
EMP: 10
SQ FT: 3,500
SALES (est): 59.5MM **Privately Held**
WEB: www.piercedistribution.com
SIC: 4783 2441 Packing goods for shipping; crating goods for shipping; containerization of goods for shipping; boxes, wood

(G-13246)
PIERCE PACKAGING CO
1200 Windsor Rd (61111-4250)
PHONE..............................815 636-5656
Judy Spitson, *Branch Mgr*
EMP: 10
SALES (corp-wide): 59.5MM **Privately Held**
SIC: 4783 2441 Packing goods for shipping; crating goods for shipping; containerization of goods for shipping; boxes, wood
PA: Pierce Packaging Co.
2028 E Riverside Blvd
Loves Park IL 61111
815 636-5650

(G-13247)
PLANET EARTH ANTIFREEZE INC
6307 Material Ave (61111-4245)
PHONE..............................815 282-2463
Cynthia A Bloyer, *President*
Donald Bloyer, *Vice Pres*
EMP: 5
SQ FT: 4,500
SALES (est): 870.2K **Privately Held**
WEB: www.planetearthantifreeze.com
SIC: 2899 Antifreeze compounds

(G-13248)
POWERTRAIN ROCKFORD INC
1200 Windsor Rd Unit 1 (61111-4250)
PHONE..............................815 633-7460
Einar K Forsman, *President*
William Hefferman, *President*
Heidi M Garner, *COO*
Rhonda Brunette, *Vice Pres*
David Carter, *Vice Pres*
▲ **EMP:** 203
SQ FT: 621,000
SALES (est): 55.3MM
SALES (corp-wide): 242.1K **Privately Held**
SIC: 3714 Motor vehicle transmissions, drive assemblies & parts; clutches, motor vehicle; drive shafts, motor vehicle; universal joints, motor vehicle
HQ: Wpg Us Holdco Llc
330 N Wabash Ave Ste 3750
Chicago IL 60611
312 517-3750

(G-13249)
PRO ARC INC
7440 Forest Hills Rd (61111-3971)
P.O. Box 15007 (61132-5007)
PHONE..............................815 877-1804
Denny J Forni, *President*
Angela Forni, *Corp Secy*
Regina Snider, *VP Opers*
EMP: 32
SQ FT: 25,000
SALES (est): 4.9MM **Privately Held**
SIC: 7692 Welding repair

(G-13250)
PRO MACHINING INC
2131 Harlem Rd (61111-2751)
PHONE..............................815 633-4140
John McMullin, *President*
EMP: 13
SALES (est): 1.4MM **Privately Held**
SIC: 3469 1799 Machine parts, stamped or pressed metal; welding on site

(G-13251)
PROGRESSIVE STEEL TREATING INC
922 Lawn Dr (61111-5192)
PHONE..............................815 877-2571
James R Simonovich, *President*
Chris Durham, *Maint Spvr*
Bobby Leonard, *Manager*
Richard J Simonovich, *Manager*
Rick Freiman, *Administration*
EMP: 25 EST: 1956
SQ FT: 45,000
SALES (est): 7.1MM **Privately Held**
WEB: www.progressivesteeltreating.com
SIC: 3398 Annealing of metal

(G-13252)
RELIANCE TOOL INC
946 River Ln (61111-4713)
PHONE..............................815 636-2770
Larry Dilillo Esq, *Principal*
EMP: 5
SALES (est): 637K **Privately Held**
SIC: 3599 Machine shop, jobbing & repair

(G-13253)
RICHARD KING AND SONS
6735 Elm Ave (61111-3817)
PHONE..............................815 654-0226
Richard King, *President*
Wanetta King, *Corp Secy*
Dave King, *Vice Pres*
Tracy King, *Vice Pres*
EMP: 6
SQ FT: 6,500

GEOGRAPHIC SECTION

Loves Park - Winnebago County (G-13280)

SALES: 250K **Privately Held**
WEB: www.king-and-sons.com
SIC: 2434 2431 Wood kitchen cabinets; vanities, bathroom: wood; doors, wood

(G-13254)
ROCK VALLEY OIL & CHEMICAL CO (PA)
1911 Windsor Rd (61111-4253)
PHONE.................815 654-2400
Roger L Schramm, *President*
John Price, *Vice Pres*
Ron Stone, *Plant Mgr*
Rich Hinerichsen, *Maint Spvr*
Ron Starks, *Opers Staff*
EMP: 83 **EST:** 1970
SALES (est): 25.2MM **Privately Held**
SIC: 2992 5169 4953 Oils & greases, blending & compounding; cutting oils, blending: made from purchased materials; brake fluid (hydraulic): made from purchased materials; chemicals & allied products; chemical detoxification

(G-13255)
ROCK VALLEY PUBLISHING LLC (PA)
Also Called: Gazette Newspapers
7124 Windsor Lake Pkwy # 4 (61111-3802)
PHONE.................815 467-6397
Pete Cruger, *President*
Jack Crueger,
EMP: 20 **EST:** 1966
SALES (est): 5.2MM **Privately Held**
WEB: www.rvpnews.com
SIC: 2711 Newspapers: publishing only, not printed on site

(G-13256)
ROCKFORD METAL POLISHING CO
5700 Industrial Ave (61111-7503)
PHONE.................815 282-4448
Barbara Gagliano, *President*
Barbara A Gagliano, *Vice Pres*
EMP: 8
SQ FT: 5,000
SALES: 1MM **Privately Held**
SIC: 3471 Buffing for the trade; depolishing metal

(G-13257)
ROCKFORD MOLDED PRODUCTS INC
5600 Pike Rd (61111-4711)
PHONE.................815 637-0585
Wayne Rasner Jr, *CEO*
Gerald G Gustafson, *President*
Barbara Pearson, *QC Mgr*
Tom Thome, *Human Res Mgr*
EMP: 60 **EST:** 1943
SQ FT: 45,000
SALES (est): 13.3MM **Privately Held**
WEB: www.rockfordmolded.com
SIC: 3089 Injection molding of plastics; thermoformed finished plastic products

(G-13258)
ROCKFORD SAND & GRAVEL CO (HQ)
5290 Nimtz Rd (61111-3932)
P.O. Box 2071 (61130-0071)
PHONE.................815 654-4700
Myron Rafferty, *President*
Dan Fisher, *Vice Pres*
Neil Maloney, *Treasurer*
Charles Howard, *Director*
Wayne Schwalen, *Admin Sec*
EMP: 25
SALES (est): 3.6MM
SALES (corp-wide): 130.9MM **Privately Held**
SIC: 5211 1442 Sand & gravel; construction sand & gravel
PA: William Charles, Ltd.
    1401 N 2nd St
    Rockford IL 61107
    815 963-7400

(G-13259)
ROCKFORD SEWER CO INC
Also Called: Aqua Marine Pools
6204 Forest Hills Rd (61111-4763)
PHONE.................815 877-9060
Nicholas J Migliore, *President*

Audrey A Migliore, *Corp Secy*
EMP: 9 **EST:** 1962
SQ FT: 5,500
SALES (est): 1.1MM **Privately Held**
SIC: 3272 1711 7699 5999 Septic tanks, concrete; septic system construction; plumbing contractors; sewer cleaning & rodding; septic tank cleaning service; swimming pools, above ground; swimming pool chemicals, equipment & supplies; swimming pool construction

(G-13260)
ROTHENBERGER USA LLC
7130 Clinton Rd (61111-3872)
PHONE.................800 545-7698
Ed Certisimol, *CEO*
◆ **EMP:** 52
SALES (est): 6.8MM
SALES (corp-wide): 726.3K **Privately Held**
SIC: 5074 3423 Plumbing fittings & supplies; plumbers' hand tools
HQ: Dr. Helmut Rothenberger Holding Gmbh.
    GewerbeparkstraBe 9
    Anif 5081
    624 672-0912

(G-13261)
RRB FABRICATION INC
Also Called: Welding Fabrication
5430 Forest Hills Ct (61111-8317)
PHONE.................815 977-5603
Sharon Brunson, *President*
Robin Brunson, *President*
EMP: 12
SQ FT: 4,200
SALES: 250K **Privately Held**
WEB: www.rrbfab.com
SIC: 3441 Fabricated structural metal

(G-13262)
S & B JIG GRINDING INC
6820 Forest Hills Rd (61111-4367)
PHONE.................815 654-7907
Rick Spades, *President*
Carl Bradberry, *President*
Melba Bradberry, *Admin Sec*
EMP: 6 **EST:** 1981
SQ FT: 4,500
SALES (est): 806.1K **Privately Held**
SIC: 3599 Grinding castings for the trade

(G-13263)
SEROLA BIOMECHANICS INC
5406 Forest Hills Ct (61111-8317)
PHONE.................815 636-2780
Rick Serola, *President*
Lowell Gillia, *Principal*
Matt Johnson, *Vice Pres*
Melody Serola, *Vice Pres*
EMP: 10
SALES (est): 1.8MM **Privately Held**
SIC: 3842 5047 8041 Orthopedic appliances; orthopedic equipment & supplies; offices & clinics of chiropractors

(G-13264)
SERVICE MACHINE COMPANY INC
6205 Material Ave (61111-4243)
P.O. Box 2183 (61130-0183)
PHONE.................815 654-2310
Arthur L Kneller Jr, *President*
Frances Kneller, *Corp Secy*
EMP: 18
SQ FT: 18,500
SALES (est): 3.5MM **Privately Held**
SIC: 3599 Machine shop, jobbing & repair

(G-13265)
SOUTHERN IMPERIAL INC
7135 Clinton Rd (61111-3871)
PHONE.................815 877-7041
EMP: 7 **Privately Held**
WEB: www.southernimperial.com
SIC: 3452 Screw eyes & hooks
HQ: Southern Imperial, Inc.
    1400 Eddy Ave
    Rockford IL 61103
    815 877-7041

(G-13266)
STEINER IMPRESSIONS INC
5596 E Riverside Blvd # 2 (61111-4950)
P.O. Box 2430 (61132-0430)
PHONE.................815 633-4135
David Steiner, *President*
EMP: 5
SALES (est): 590.8K **Privately Held**
SIC: 2752 Commercial printing, offset

(G-13267)
STRYKER ENTERPRISES LLC
7307 Edward Dr (61111-3950)
PHONE.................815 975-5167
Elmazi James, *Principal*
EMP: 3
SALES (est): 221.1K **Privately Held**
SIC: 3841 Surgical & medical instruments

(G-13268)
SUPERIOR METAL FINISHING
Also Called: Northern Star Plating Division
962 Industrial Ct (61111-7512)
PHONE.................815 282-8888
Larry Walsh, *President*
EMP: 16
SALES (est): 1.2MM **Privately Held**
SIC: 3471 Plating of metals or formed products; sand blasting of metal parts; tumbling (cleaning & polishing) of machine parts

(G-13269)
TADS
10 E Riverside Blvd (61111-4500)
PHONE.................815 654-3500
Therese Dobson, *Owner*
Theresse Dobson, *Principal*
EMP: 4
SALES (est): 352.9K **Privately Held**
SIC: 2599 Bar, restaurant & cafeteria furniture

(G-13270)
TAPCO CUTTING TOOLS INC
5605 Pike Rd (61111-4710)
PHONE.................815 877-4039
Terry Brewster, *President*
EMP: 4
SALES (est): 444.1K **Privately Held**
SIC: 3545 Taps, machine tool

(G-13271)
TAPCO USA INC
5605 Pike Rd (61111-4710)
PHONE.................815 877-4039
Jackie Brewster, *Opers Mgr*
John A Cotton, *Manager*
EMP: 6 **EST:** 1969
SQ FT: 10,000
SALES (est): 750K **Privately Held**
SIC: 3545 5085 3546 3544 Taps, machine tool; industrial tools; power-driven handtools; special dies, tools, jigs & fixtures

(G-13272)
TEMCO GRINDING INC
1002 River Ln (61111-4715)
PHONE.................815 282-9405
Mike Mahoney, *President*
Dan Mahoney, *Vice Pres*
Jessica Dishman, *Manager*
EMP: 12
SQ FT: 25,000
SALES: 750K **Privately Held**
SIC: 3599 Machine shop, jobbing & repair

(G-13273)
TH FOODS INC
2154 Harlem Rd (61111-2752)
PHONE.................702 565-2816
Dennis Mower, *Branch Mgr*
EMP: 3 **Privately Held**
SIC: 2052 Crackers, dry
HQ: Th Foods, Inc.
    2134 Harlem Rd
    Loves Park IL 61111
    800 896-2396

(G-13274)
TH FOODS INC (DH)
2134 Harlem Rd (61111-2752)
PHONE.................800 896-2396
Terry Jessen, *President*
Jared Smith, *Business Mgr*

Nick Ramsey, *Safety Mgr*
Dennis Mower, *Warehouse Mgr*
Patrick Latino, *Mfg Spvr*
▲ **EMP:** 250
SQ FT: 200,000
SALES (est): 109.3MM **Privately Held**
SIC: 2099 Food preparations
HQ: Mitsubishi International Corporation
    655 3rd Ave Fl 5
    New York NY 10017
    212 605-2000

(G-13275)
TOOL FORM INC
2102 Margaret Dr (61111-3992)
P.O. Box 15831 (61132-5831)
PHONE.................815 654-0035
Richard Leach, *President*
Andre Kelly, *CFO*
EMP: 9
SQ FT: 8,400
SALES: 900K **Privately Held**
SIC: 3599 Machine shop, jobbing & repair

(G-13276)
TOP DOLLAR SLOTS
6590 N Alpine Rd (61111-4353)
PHONE.................779 210-4884
Frank Laudicina, *Owner*
EMP: 8
SALES (est): 120.1K **Privately Held**
SIC: 5812 3999 Italian restaurant; slot machines

(G-13277)
TRI STATE ALUMINUM PRODUCTS
Also Called: Tri-State Alum & Vinyl Pdts
6300 Forest Hills Rd (61111-4761)
P.O. Box 2614 (61132-2614)
PHONE.................815 877-6081
James Heidenreich, *President*
Norman Heidenreich, *Corp Secy*
Lawrence Heidenreich, *Vice Pres*
Michael Heidenreich, *Shareholder*
EMP: 10
SQ FT: 43,000
SALES (est): 2.1MM **Privately Held**
WEB: www.tsamcinnis.com
SIC: 5031 5039 3442 3444 Metal doors, sash & trim; windows; awnings; screen & storm doors & windows; awnings, sheet metal; roofing, siding & insulation; millwork

(G-13278)
TRIWIRE INC
Also Called: Ford-Tool
2201 Range Rd (61111)
P.O. Box 2211 (61131-0211)
PHONE.................815 633-7707
David P Beto, *CEO*
Ginger Elsasser, *General Mgr*
Brian Larson, *Plant Mgr*
Ronald Roling, *CFO*
Ron Rolling, *Controller*
EMP: 3
SQ FT: 5,000
SALES (est): 650K
SALES (corp-wide): 16.6MM **Privately Held**
SIC: 3599 Machine shop, jobbing & repair
PA: Ford Tool & Machining, Inc.
    2205 Range Rd
    Loves Park IL 61111
    815 633-5727

(G-13279)
UNITED TOOLERS OF ILLINOIS
7203 Clinton Rd (61111-3806)
PHONE.................779 423-0548
Daniel Baumann, *Principal*
Darrin Schmidt, *Prdtn Mgr*
EMP: 10
SALES (est): 1.4MM **Privately Held**
WEB: www.unitedtoolers.com
SIC: 3312 Stainless steel

(G-13280)
WARD CNC MACHINING
7480 Forest Hills Rd (61111-3971)
PHONE.................815 637-1490
Doug Sosnowskik, *Owner*
EMP: 6 **EST:** 2000
SQ FT: 3,600

Loves Park - Winnebago County (G-13281) — GEOGRAPHIC SECTION

SALES: 188K **Privately Held**
WEB: www.wardcncmachining.com
SIC: 3599 Machine shop, jobbing & repair

(G-13281)
WOODWARD INC
1 Woodward (61111-7700)
P.O. Box 7001, Rockford (61125-7001)
PHONE..................................815 877-7441
Sagar A Patel, *President*
Brian Barthel, *Opers Mgr*
Alicia Gronli, *Engineer*
Doug Smith, *Project Engr*
Terry Houghton, *Manager*
EMP: 468
SALES (corp-wide): 2.9B **Publicly Held**
SIC: 3728 Aircraft assemblies, subassemblies & parts
PA: Woodward, Inc.
1081 Woodward Way
Fort Collins CO 80524
970 482-5811

(G-13282)
WOODWARD INC
5001 N 2nd St (61111-5808)
P.O. Box 7001, Rockford (61125-7001)
PHONE..................................815 877-7441
Martin V Glass, *Vice Pres*
Mike Nevicosi, *Facilities Mgr*
Paul Blee, *Buyer*
Al Bollenbeck, *Engineer*
Jeanne Lasley, *Corp Comm Staff*
EMP: 1200
SALES (corp-wide): 2.9B **Publicly Held**
SIC: 3724 Aircraft engines & engine parts
PA: Woodward, Inc.
1081 Woodward Way
Fort Collins CO 80524
970 482-5811

(G-13283)
WOODWARD GOVERNOR HLTH SVCS TR
5001 N 2nd St (61111-5800)
PHONE..................................815 877-7441
Thomas A Gendron, *CEO*
EMP: 1
SALES: 1MM **Privately Held**
SIC: 3728 Aircraft parts & equipment

(G-13284)
ZNL CORPORATION
Also Called: Window Coverings
2120 Harlem Rd (61111-2752)
PHONE..................................815 654-0870
William Lapins, *Vice Pres*
EMP: 6 **Privately Held**
SIC: 2591 Blinds vertical
HQ: Znl Corporation
550 Quail Ridge Dr
Westmont IL 60559

Lovington
Moultrie County

(G-13285)
REEVES LURE CO
4165 Shaw Rd (61937-9777)
PHONE..................................217 864-3493
Pam Reeves, *Owner*
EMP: 8
SALES: 45K **Privately Held**
SIC: 3949 Lures, fishing: artificial

Lyndon
Whiteside County

(G-13286)
C & D MACHINING INC
207 E Commercial St (61261-7766)
P.O. Box 308 (61261-0308)
PHONE..................................815 778-4946
Keith Crady, *President*
Brian Dolieslager, *Vice Pres*
EMP: 10
SALES (est): 550K **Privately Held**
SIC: 3599 Machine shop, jobbing & repair

(G-13287)
PHILLIPS & JOHNSTON INC
Also Called: Rock River Fabrication
900 E Commercial St (61261-7767)
P.O. Box 338 (61261-0338)
PHONE..................................815 778-3355
Brandon Eads, *Office Mgr*
EMP: 11
SALES (corp-wide): 480.7MM **Privately Held**
SIC: 3312 Tubes, steel & iron
HQ: Phillips & Johnston, Inc.
21w179 Hill Ave
Glen Ellyn IL 60137
630 469-8150

Lynn Center
Henry County

(G-13288)
CALMER CORN HEADS INC
3056 N 700th Ave (61262-9581)
P.O. Box 9, Alpha (61413-0009)
PHONE..................................309 629-9000
Marion Calmer, *CEO*
Gregory Nimrick, *Admin Sec*
▲ EMP: 23
SALES (est): 5MM **Privately Held**
SIC: 3523 Farm machinery & equipment

(G-13289)
DARLING INGREDIENTS INC
202 Bengston St (61262-7703)
P.O. Box 40 (61262-0040)
PHONE..................................309 476-8111
Keith Fulton, *Manager*
EMP: 20
SALES (corp-wide): 3.3B **Publicly Held**
SIC: 2077 2048 Animal & marine fats & oils; prepared feeds
PA: Darling Ingredients Inc.
5601 N Macarthur Blvd
Irving TX 75038
972 717-0300

(G-13290)
EARNEST EARTH AGRICULTURE INC
4655 Il Hwy 81 (61262-9761)
PHONE..................................217 766-4401
Gabriel Price-Christenson, *President*
EMP: 2
SALES (est): 419.4K **Privately Held**
SIC: 5191 2875 Farm supplies; garden supplies; potting soil, mixed

Lynwood
Cook County

(G-13291)
AVAN PRECAST CONCRETE PDTS INC
3201 211th St (60411-8788)
PHONE..................................708 757-6200
Ann Vandergenugten, *CEO*
Roger Vandergenugten, *President*
Brian Vandergenugten, *Executive*
EMP: 15
SQ FT: 8,500
SALES (est): 1.5MM **Privately Held**
WEB: www.avanprecast.com
SIC: 3272 Concrete products, precast; steps, prefabricated concrete; slabs, crossing: concrete

(G-13292)
BEHR PROCESS CORPORATION
21399 Torrence Ave Ste 1 (60411-8709)
PHONE..................................708 753-1820
Andy Locke, *Sales Staff*
Jeffrey D Filley, *Branch Mgr*
Terry Berrier, *Director*
EMP: 62
SALES (corp-wide): 6.7B **Publicly Held**
SIC: 2851 Paints & paint additives
HQ: Behr Process Corporation
1801 E Saint Andrew Pl
Santa Ana CA 92705

(G-13293)
DDU MAGNETICS INC
20152 Cypress Ave (60411-6809)
PHONE..................................708 325-6587
Douglas Richard, *President*
Clara Richard, *Admin Sec*
EMP: 2
SALES (est): 248.8K **Privately Held**
SIC: 3621 8748 Motors, electric; testing services

(G-13294)
KOSWELL PATTERN WORKS INC
3149 Glenwood Dyer Rd H (60411-9747)
PHONE..................................708 757-5225
James Koselke, *President*
EMP: 4
SQ FT: 1,500
SALES (est): 494.2K **Privately Held**
SIC: 3543 Industrial patterns

(G-13295)
LANS PRINTING INC
2581 Glenwd Lansing Rd A (60411-1682)
PHONE..................................708 895-6226
Joe Jiampaulo, *President*
EMP: 3
SQ FT: 2,000
SALES (est): 393.6K **Privately Held**
SIC: 2752 2759 2791 2789 Commercial printing, offset; screen printing; typesetting; bookbinding & related work

(G-13296)
ON TARGET GRINDING AND MFG
2250 199th St Ste 3 (60411-9606)
PHONE..................................708 418-3905
Barry Bridgeford, *President*
Mal Dixon, *Vice Pres*
EMP: 2
SQ FT: 1,500
SALES (est): 304.9K **Privately Held**
WEB: www.on-target-mfg.com
SIC: 3599 Machine shop, jobbing & repair

(G-13297)
POUR IT AGAIN SAM INC
2200 198th Pl (60411-8501)
PHONE..................................708 474-1744
EMP: 3
SALES (est): 144.5K **Privately Held**
WEB: www.pouritagainsam.com
SIC: 2084 Wines

(G-13298)
ROGAN GRANITINDUSTRIE INC (HQ)
21550 E Lincoln Hwy (60411-8744)
PHONE..................................708 758-0050
Thomas R Rogan, *President*
Bernice Rogan, *Treasurer*
▲ EMP: 2
SALES (est): 663.8K **Privately Held**
SIC: 3281 2434 Monuments, cut stone (not finishing or lettering only); building stone products; furniture, cut stone; wood kitchen cabinets

(G-13299)
ROYAL CROWN TRESSES LLC
20325 Joy Ln (60411-1061)
PHONE..................................773 967-8409
Popoola Olashade, *Principal*
EMP: 4
SALES (est): 75.4K **Privately Held**
SIC: 2086 Soft drinks: packaged in cans, bottles, etc.

Lyons
Cook County

(G-13300)
ACCUSHIM INC (PA)
4601 Lawndale Ave (60534-1730)
P.O. Box 73 (60534-0073)
PHONE..................................708 442-6448
Daniel Mottl, *President*
George Hurtado, *General Mgr*
Gary Mottl, *Vice Pres*
Glen Mottl, *Vice Pres*
EMP: 5
SQ FT: 1,000
SALES: 1.2MM **Privately Held**
SIC: 3825 5084 Instruments to measure electricity; machine tools & metalworking machinery

(G-13301)
ART CRYSTAL II ENTERPRISES INC
7852 47th St (60534-1852)
PHONE..................................630 739-0222
Patrick Dorgan, *President*
Albert Dorgan, *Vice Pres*
▼ EMP: 17
SQ FT: 13,500
SALES: 1.9MM **Privately Held**
SIC: 3231 Cut & engraved glassware: made from purchased glass

(G-13302)
ATLAS TOOL & DIE WORKS INC
4633 Lawndale Ave (60534-1724)
P.O. Box 32 (60534-0032)
PHONE..................................708 442-1661
Daniel J Mottl, *President*
Zachary Mottl, *COO*
Gary R Mottl, *Vice Pres*
Curtis Snyder, *Vice Pres*
Zack Mottl, *Purch Mgr*
▲ EMP: 55 EST: 1918
SQ FT: 50,000
SALES (est): 13.5MM **Privately Held**
WEB: www.atlas-tool.com
SIC: 3469 3544 3443 Stamping metal for the trade; special dies, tools, jigs & fixtures; fabricated plate work (boiler shop)

(G-13303)
BOND BROTHERS & CO
7826 47th St (60534-1852)
PHONE..................................708 442-5510
Donald Jobb, *CEO*
Buddi Byinsky, *President*
Bruce Jobb, *Vice Pres*
Scott Jobb, *Vice Pres*
Anthony Bond, *Project Engr*
EMP: 12
SQ FT: 15,000
SALES (est): 1.9MM **Privately Held**
WEB: www.bondbrothers.net
SIC: 2759 2791 2752 Letterpress printing; typesetting; commercial printing, lithographic

(G-13304)
BUELL MANUFACTURING COMPANY
Also Called: Buell Airhorns
8125 47th St (60534-1835)
P.O. Box 303 (60534-0303)
PHONE..................................708 447-6320
Gary Buell, *President*
Rudy Andrew, *CFO*
EMP: 6 EST: 1912
SALES (est): 1.3MM **Privately Held**
WEB: www.buellairhorns.com
SIC: 3714 3669 3585 3563 Horns, motor vehicle; marine horns, electric; compressors for refrigeration & air conditioning equipment; air & gas compressors

(G-13305)
C E R MACHINING & TOOLING LTD
8214 47th St (60534-1715)
PHONE..................................708 442-9614
David Spencer Sr, *President*
EMP: 5
SQ FT: 4,000
SALES (est): 450K **Privately Held**
SIC: 3599 3825 3469 7692 Machine shop, jobbing & repair; instruments to measure electricity; metal stampings; welding repair; metalworking machinery

(G-13306)
CONTAINERS INC
4424 Prescott Ave (60534-1932)
PHONE..................................708 442-2000
Thomas Barc, *Branch Mgr*
EMP: 5

GEOGRAPHIC SECTION

Machesney Park - Winnebago County (G-13332)

SALES (corp-wide): 5.9MM **Privately Held**
WEB: www.abarrsales.com
SIC: 5149 2087 2086 Beverages, except coffee & tea; flavoring extracts & syrups; bottled & canned soft drinks
PA: Containers, Inc.
  16300 103rd St
  Lemont IL 60439
  708 447-7842

(G-13307)
DRIVE SHAFT UNLIMITED INC
4323 Joliet Rd (60534-1986)
PHONE 708 447-2211
Dan Swain, *President*
Karen Swain, *Vice Pres*
EMP: 4
SQ FT: 3,000
SALES (est): 550K **Privately Held**
SIC: 3714 Drive shafts, motor vehicle

(G-13308)
FILTER KLEEN INC
8432 44th Pl (60534-1744)
PHONE 708 447-4666
William Buckholtz, *President*
Natalie Buckholtz, *Corp Secy*
EMP: 8
SALES (est): 1MM **Privately Held**
SIC: 5085 2992 Filters, industrial; lubricating oils & greases

(G-13309)
FRASER MILLWORK INC
8109 Ogden Ave (60534-1125)
P.O. Box 95 (60534-0095)
PHONE 708 447-3262
Gale W Fraser, *President*
Marilyn Fraser, *Corp Secy*
EMP: 4
SALES (est): 364.3K **Privately Held**
SIC: 2434 2431 2421 Wood kitchen cabinets; millwork; sawmills & planing mills, general

(G-13310)
GROSSE&SONS HTG &SHEET MET INC
4236 Elm Ave (60534-1428)
PHONE 708 447-8397
Phillip Grosse, *President*
Gene Grosse, *Treasurer*
Arthur Grosse, *Shareholder*
EMP: 6
SQ FT: 1,200
SALES (est): 460K **Privately Held**
SIC: 1711 1761 3444 Warm air heating & air conditioning contractor; gutter & downspout contractor; sheet metalwork

(G-13311)
HOSPITAL HLTH CARE SYSTEMS INC (PA)
7830 47th St Ste 1 (60534-1870)
PHONE 708 863-3400
Albert J Paveza, *President*
Albertas Simokaitis, *Vice Pres*
Ron Banaszak, *Treasurer*
Hermann Reutter, *Admin Secy*
EMP: 20
SQ FT: 20,000
SALES: 3MM **Privately Held**
SIC: 2679 Labels, paper: made from purchased material

(G-13312)
PATT SUPPLY CORPORATION
8111 47th St (60534-1835)
PHONE 708 442-3901
Craig Behrendt, *Principal*
George Yurkovich, *Principal*
EMP: 11
SQ FT: 10,000
SALES (est): 1.7MM **Privately Held**
WEB: www.pattcorp.com
SIC: 5072 3993 7389 Security devices, locks; displays & cutouts, window & lobby; packaging & labeling services

(G-13313)
SPECIALTY TAPE & LABEL CO INC
7830 47th St (60534-1869)
PHONE 708 863-3800
Brian D Gale, *President*
EMP: 25
SQ FT: 7,500
SALES (est): 2.2MM **Privately Held**
WEB: www.specialtytapeandlabel.com
SIC: 2672 Tape, pressure sensitive: made from purchased materials; labels (unprinted), gummed: made from purchased materials
PA: I.D. Images Llc
  2991 Interstate Pkwy
  Brunswick OH 44212

(G-13314)
STAIRSLAND
8001 47th St Fl 4 (60534-1833)
PHONE 708 853-9593
Douglas Wojnicz, *Owner*
EMP: 8
SALES (est): 482.6K **Privately Held**
SIC: 2431 1751 Staircases & stairs, wood; cabinet & finish carpentry

(G-13315)
STEVE BORTMAN
Also Called: Minuteman Press
7937 Ogden Ave (60534-1337)
PHONE 708 442-1669
Steve Bortman, *Owner*
EMP: 5
SQ FT: 1,500
SALES (est): 524.2K **Privately Held**
SIC: 2752 2791 2789 Commercial printing, lithographic; typesetting; bookbinding & related work

(G-13316)
ZMF INC
Also Called: Zmf Headphones
8015 Salisbury Ave (60534-1114)
PHONE 603 667-1672
Zachary Mehrbach, *President*
EMP: 5
SALES (est): 314.2K **Privately Held**
SIC: 3651 Sound reproducing equipment

Macedonia
Hamilton County

(G-13317)
SENECA REBUILD LLC (DH)
11550 N Thompsonville Rd (62860-1175)
PHONE 618 435-9445
Dana Wilkerson,
EMP: 16
SALES (est): 1.3MM
SALES (corp-wide): 841.5MM **Publicly Held**
SIC: 1241 Anthracite mining services, contract basis
HQ: Foresight Energy Llc
  1 Metropolitan Sq
  Saint Louis MO 63102
  314 932-6160

(G-13318)
VIKING MINING LLC (HQ)
Mc1 Mine 11525 N Thmpsn St (62860)
PHONE 314 932-6140
Robert D Moore, *Mng Member*
EMP: 37 EST: 2012
SALES (est): 79.9K
SALES (corp-wide): 841.5MM **Publicly Held**
SIC: 3532 Mining machinery
PA: Foresight Energy Lp
  211 N Broadway Ste 2600
  Saint Louis MO 63102
  314 932-6160

Machesney Park
Boone County

(G-13319)
H M C PRODUCTS INC
7165 Greenlee Dr (61011-9613)
PHONE 815 885-1900
David R Kreissler, *President*
Chris Canfield, *Purch Dir*
Jeff Brown, *Engineer*
David Wise, *Design Engr*
Angela Dowson, *Office Mgr*
EMP: 50
SQ FT: 10,000
SALES (est): 13.4MM **Privately Held**
SIC: 3599 Machine shop, jobbing & repair

(G-13320)
KEENE TECHNOLOGY INC
7550 Quantum Ct (61011-7500)
PHONE 815 624-8989
Danny Pearse, *President*
Dave Culvey, *Vice Pres*
Terry Keene, *Treasurer*
Nicole Dhuse, *Regl Sales Mgr*
Kerri Wallace, *Admin Sec*
◆ **EMP:** 80
SALES (est): 14.2MM **Privately Held**
SIC: 3554 Paper industries machinery

(G-13321)
QUANTUM DESIGN INC (PA)
7550 Quantum Ct (61011-7500)
PHONE 815 885-1300
Danny S Pearse, *President*
David Culvey, *Exec VP*
Peter Geisser, *Vice Pres*
Vince Fernandez, *Purch Agent*
Nevagay Abel, *Engineer*
EMP: 63
SALES (est): 16.1MM **Privately Held**
SIC: 3613 Control panels, electric

Machesney Park
Winnebago County

(G-13322)
ABBACUS INJECTION MOLDING INC
1248 Shappert Dr (61115-1418)
PHONE 815 637-9222
Judith A Beall, *Principal*
Tony Beall, *Principal*
EMP: 33
SALES (est): 2.7MM **Privately Held**
SIC: 3089 Injection molding of plastics

(G-13323)
ACCURATE BUSINESS CONTROLS INC
7846 Burden Rd (61115-8201)
P.O. Box 2244, Loves Park (61131-0244)
PHONE 815 633-5500
Frank J Moran, *President*
Tim Moran, *Vice Pres*
Timothy B Moran, *Vice Pres*
EMP: 2 EST: 1969
SQ FT: 1,600
SALES: 850K **Privately Held**
SIC: 2752 5112 Commercial printing, offset; business forms

(G-13324)
AKD CONTROLS INC
10340 Product Dr (61115-1439)
PHONE 815 633-4586
Andy Ballinger, *President*
Kathleen Ballinger, *Corp Secy*
EMP: 7
SQ FT: 4,500
SALES: 800K **Privately Held**
SIC: 3613 Panelboards & distribution boards, electric

(G-13325)
ALCO MANUFACTURING CORP LLC
4950 Marlin Dr (61115-1410)
PHONE 815 708-5540
EMP: 10
SALES (corp-wide): 441.6MM **Privately Held**
WEB: www.alcomfgcorp.com
SIC: 3542 Machine tools, metal forming type
HQ: Alco Manufacturing Corporation Llc
  10584 Middle Ave
  Elyria OH 44035

(G-13326)
ALDI INC
1545 W Lane Rd (61115-1903)
PHONE 815 877-0861
EMP: 11 **Privately Held**
SIC: 2082 Mfg Malt Beverages
HQ: Aldi Inc.
  1200 N Kirk Rd
  Batavia IL 60510
  630 879-8100

(G-13327)
APPLIED PRODUCTS INC
12000 Product Dr (61115-1479)
P.O. Box 10229, Loves Park (61131-3129)
PHONE 815 633-3825
Steven R Nethery, *President*
Elizabeth A Nethery, *Corp Secy*
Jack Nethery, *Vice Pres*
Elizabeth Nethery, *CFO*
Horn Jackie VA, *Sales Staff*
EMP: 30 EST: 1967
SQ FT: 50,000
SALES (est): 10MM **Privately Held**
WEB: www.appliedproductsinc.com
SIC: 2671 Packaging paper & plastics film, coated & laminated

(G-13328)
ASTRO-PHYSICS INC
11250 Forest Hills Rd (61115-8238)
PHONE 815 282-1513
Roland Christen, *President*
Marjorie Christen, *Vice Pres*
Robert Watters, *Mfg Spvr*
Karen Christen, *Controller*
Christine Schmidt, *Office Mgr*
EMP: 18
SQ FT: 11,000
SALES (est): 4.3MM **Privately Held**
SIC: 3827 Telescopes: elbow, panoramic, sighting, fire control, etc.; lens mounts

(G-13329)
BIMBA MANUFACTURING COMPANY
Also Called: IMI Precision Engineering
10914 N 2nd St (61115-1400)
PHONE 815 654-7775
Curt Dahl, *Engineer*
Kerry Reinhardt, *Manager*
EMP: 3
SALES (corp-wide): 2.4B **Privately Held**
SIC: 3593 Fluid power cylinders & actuators
HQ: Bimba Manufacturing Company Inc
  25150 S Governors Hwy
  University Park IL 60484
  708 534-8544

(G-13330)
BOWL DOCTORS INC
7664 Hawks Rdg (61115-8269)
PHONE 815 282-6009
Jim Egert, *President*
Tanya Egert, *Vice Pres*
EMP: 7 EST: 1994
SQ FT: 6,000
SALES (est): 1.3MM **Privately Held**
SIC: 3569 Liquid automation machinery & equipment

(G-13331)
BUSINESS CARD SYSTEMS INC
Also Called: B C T
11025 Raleigh Ct (61115-1416)
P.O. Box 2002, Loves Park (61130-0002)
PHONE 815 877-0990
Thomas G Mc Neany, *President*
Jeri A Mc Neany, *Corp Secy*
EMP: 15
SQ FT: 4,000
SALES (est): 3.2MM **Privately Held**
SIC: 2752 Commercial printing, lithographic

(G-13332)
BUSINESS CARDS TOMORROW
Also Called: B C T
11025 Raleigh Ct (61115-1416)
PHONE 815 877-0990
Kenneth Johnson, *President*
Mary Johnson, *Vice Pres*
EMP: 14
SALES (est): 920K **Privately Held**
SIC: 2752 2759 Commercial printing, lithographic; thermography

Machesney Park - Winnebago County (G-13333)

(G-13333)
CHAMFERMATIC INC
7842 Burden Rd (61115-8201)
PHONE..................815 636-5082
Michael Magee, *President*
Dixie Magee, *Vice Pres*
EMP: 3
SALES (est): 327.6K **Privately Held**
SIC: 3599 Machine shop, jobbing & repair

(G-13334)
CLUTCH SYSTEMS INC
10901 N 2nd St (61115-1461)
P.O. Box 15130, Loves Park (61132-5130)
PHONE..................815 282-7960
Dan Lemmons, *President*
EMP: 3
SQ FT: 18,000
SALES (est): 387.2K **Privately Held**
SIC: 3714 7371 Clutches, motor vehicle; custom computer programming services

(G-13335)
COMPAK INC
Also Called: Action Packaging
539 Chicory St (61115-1526)
PHONE..................815 399-2699
Kyle Hultgren, *President*
Kathy Messink, *Treasurer*
Mary K Woollums, *Admin Sec*
EMP: 23
SALES (est): 5.6MM **Privately Held**
SIC: 2653 3599 5113 Boxes, corrugated: made from purchased materials; machine shop, jobbing & repair; shipping supplies

(G-13336)
CRANDALL STATS AND SENSORS INC
9918 N Alpine Rd (61115-8211)
P.O. Box 10189, Loves Park (61131-0189)
PHONE..................815 316-8600
Michael Crandall, *President*
Kathleen Crandall, *Human Res Mgr*
Sasha Lofquist, *Office Mgr*
EMP: 30
SQ FT: 22,000
SALES: 5MM **Privately Held**
SIC: 3822 Temperature sensors for motor windings; hydronic pressure or temperature controls; surface burner controls, temperature

(G-13337)
CURTIS METAL FINISHING COMPANY
Also Called: Curtis Thermal Processing
10911 N 2nd St (61115-1461)
PHONE..................815 282-1433
Matt Heystek, *Branch Mgr*
EMP: 13
SALES (corp-wide): 30MM **Privately Held**
WEB: www.curtismetal.com
SIC: 3398 Metal heat treating
HQ: Curtis Metal Finishing Company
   6645 Sims Dr
   Sterling Heights MI 48313
   586 939-2850

(G-13338)
CURTIS METAL FINISHING COMPANY
9917 N Alpine Rd (61115-8212)
PHONE..................815 633-6693
Steve Wasson, *President*
EMP: 70
SALES (corp-wide): 30MM **Privately Held**
SIC: 3479 3471 Coating of metals & formed products; plating & polishing
HQ: Curtis Metal Finishing Company
   6645 Sims Dr
   Sterling Heights MI 48313
   586 939-2850

(G-13339)
CUTN EDGE CSTM FABRICATION LLC
10469 Product Dr (61115-1444)
PHONE..................779 774-4991
Sterling Sally A, *Principal*
EMP: 3 **EST:** 2014
SALES (est): 150.8K **Privately Held**
SIC: 3089 Injection molded finished plastic products

(G-13340)
DIABLO FURNACES LLC
7723 Burden Rd (61115-8219)
PHONE..................815 636-7502
EMP: 12 **EST:** 2017
SALES: 1MM **Privately Held**
SIC: 3567 Industrial furnaces & ovens

(G-13341)
ELECTROFORM COMPANY
11070 Raleigh Ct (61115-1416)
PHONE..................815 633-1113
Wade Clark, *President*
▲ **EMP:** 27
SQ FT: 9,000
SALES (est): 4.5MM **Privately Held**
SIC: 3089 3599 Injection molding of plastics; electrical discharge machining (EDM)

(G-13342)
FERRELLGAS LP
10522 N 2nd St (61115-1405)
PHONE..................815 877-7333
Gregory West, *Branch Mgr*
EMP: 3 **Privately Held**
SIC: 5984 1321 Propane gas, bottled; natural gas liquids
HQ: Ferrellgas, L.P.
   7500 College Blvd # 1000
   Overland Park KS 66210

(G-13343)
FIRST HEADER DIE INC
1313 Anvil Rd (61115-1463)
PHONE..................815 282-5161
Mark Gritzmacher, *President*
Kathy Gritzmacher, *Vice Pres*
EMP: 21
SQ FT: 2,500
SALES (est): 3MM **Privately Held**
SIC: 3542 3544 Headers; special dies, tools, jigs & fixtures

(G-13344)
FORTE AUTOMATION SYSTEMS INC
8155 Burden Rd (61115-8208)
P.O. Box 10325, Loves Park (61131-0325)
PHONE..................815 316-6247
Toby Henderson, *President*
Jim Deemer, *Vice Pres*
Tami Henderson, *Vice Pres*
William Flower, *Engineer*
John Lindman, *Engineer*
◆ **EMP:** 50
SQ FT: 50,000
SALES (est): 18.3MM **Privately Held**
SIC: 3552 3535 Textile machinery; conveyors & conveying equipment

(G-13345)
G & E AUTOMATIC
10462 Product Dr Ste B (61115-1465)
PHONE..................815 654-7766
Kevin Merkle, *Owner*
EMP: 4
SALES (est): 579.8K **Privately Held**
SIC: 3451 Screw machine products

(G-13346)
H & M MACHINING INC
1209 Shappert Dr (61115-1417)
PHONE..................815 877-5623
Rodney Hendrix, *President*
Joseph R Muzzillo, *President*
Deborah R Muzzillo, *Vice Pres*
Joseph Muzzillo, *Vice Pres*
Sandy Ferguson, *Admin Sec*
EMP: 18
SQ FT: 15,000
SALES (est): 3.4MM **Privately Held**
SIC: 3599 Machine shop, jobbing & repair

(G-13347)
HENNIG INC (HQ)
9900 N Alpine Rd (61115-8211)
PHONE..................815 636-9900
Willy Goellner, *Ch of Bd*
Dietmar Goellner, *President*
Dietmer Goellner, *President*
Marika Mertz, *Corp Secy*
Greg Champion, *Vice Pres*
▲ **EMP:** 4
SQ FT: 73,000
SALES (est): 24.8MM **Privately Held**
SALES (corp-wide): 111.7MM **Privately Held**
SIC: 3444 Machine guards, sheet metal
PA: Goellner, Inc.
   2500 Latham St
   Rockford IL 61103
   815 962-6076

(G-13348)
ILLINOIS TOOL WORKS INC
Also Called: ITW Shakeproof Automotive
10818 N 2nd St (61115-1406)
PHONE..................815 654-1510
Keith Gasiorowski, *Plant Mgr*
EMP: 50
SQ FT: 24,000
SALES (corp-wide): 14.1B **Publicly Held**
SIC: 3451 Screw machine products
PA: Illinois Tool Works Inc.
   155 Harlem Ave
   Glenview IL 60025
   847 724-7500

(G-13349)
ILLINOIS TOOL WORKS INC
Also Called: ITW Shake Proof Auto Division
10818 N 2nd St (61115-1406)
PHONE..................815 654-1510
EMP: 12
SALES (corp-wide): 14.3B **Publicly Held**
SIC: 3452 Mfg Bolts/Screws/Rivets
PA: Illinois Tool Works Inc.
   155 Harlem Ave
   Glenview IL 60025
   847 724-7500

(G-13350)
INSTRUMENT SERVICES INC
4075 Steele Dr (61115-8358)
PHONE..................815 623-2993
Chuck Cruse, *President*
Lynn Nocifora, *Controller*
EMP: 8
SQ FT: 40,000
SALES (est): 930K **Privately Held**
SIC: 5013 3873 5944 Automotive supplies & parts; clocks, assembly of; clocks

(G-13351)
INTERSTATE GRAPHICS INC
7817 Burden Rd (61115-8241)
PHONE..................815 877-6777
John Norwood Jr, *President*
John V Norwood Sr, *President*
Jim Norwood, *Treasurer*
Philip Brockwell, *Art Dir*
Diane Ratcliff, *Admin Sec*
EMP: 21
SQ FT: 23,500
SALES (est): 3.6MM **Privately Held**
SIC: 3993 Signs & advertising specialties

(G-13352)
JC PRECISION MILLING LLC ⊙
1275 Turret Dr (61115-1451)
PHONE..................815 654-1070
Robert Crowell,
Dean Svarc,
Dominique Svarc,
EMP: 25 **EST:** 2020
SALES (est): 521.5K **Privately Held**
SIC: 3599 Machine shop, jobbing & repair

(G-13353)
KANNEBERG CUSTOM KITCHENS INC
1242 Shappert Dr (61115-1499)
PHONE..................815 654-1110
Roger E Kanneberg, *Owner*
EMP: 6
SQ FT: 4,000
SALES (est): 515.1K **Privately Held**
WEB: www.kannebergkitchens.com
SIC: 2434 Wood kitchen cabinets

(G-13354)
KERNEL KUTTER INC
10509 Tartan Ct (61115-1373)
PHONE..................815 877-1515
Patricia Caccia, *President*
Cathy Caccia, *President*
Dan Caccia, *Corp Secy*
EMP: 3
SQ FT: 5,000
SALES (est): 220K **Privately Held**
SIC: 3469 5812 3421 Utensils, household: metal, except cast; eating places; cutlery

(G-13355)
LAB TEN LLC
5029 Willow Creek Rd (61115-8218)
PHONE..................815 877-1410
Smith Clifford, *Mng Member*
Bye Patrick, *Mng Member*
Duane Wingate,
EMP: 40
SQ FT: 16,000
SALES (est): 5MM **Privately Held**
SIC: 3451 5084 Screw machine products; industrial machinery & equipment

(G-13356)
LAMINATED DESIGNS COUNTERTOPS
9731 N 2nd St (61115-1617)
PHONE..................815 877-7222
EMP: 5
SALES (est): 296.8K **Privately Held**
SIC: 2541 Wood partitions & fixtures

(G-13357)
LLOYD MIDWEST GRAPHICS
7103 N 2nd St (61115-3709)
PHONE..................815 282-8828
Deborah Swain, *President*
EMP: 5
SALES (est): 421.9K **Privately Held**
SIC: 2759 7336 2796 2791 Screen printing; graphic arts & related design; platemaking services; typesetting; commercial printing, lithographic; automotive & apparel trimmings

(G-13358)
MARK POWER INTERNATIONAL
7897 Burden Rd (61115-8220)
PHONE..................815 877-5984
Greg Powers, *Owner*
▲ **EMP:** 15
SALES (est): 1.2MM **Privately Held**
SIC: 3089 Injection molded finished plastic products

(G-13359)
MICRO MATIC USA INC
10726 N 2nd St (61115-1440)
PHONE..................815 968-7557
Kerri Hartje, *Sales Mgr*
Nikki Chilson, *Sales Staff*
Neio Kaclhill, *Manager*
EMP: 10
SALES (corp-wide): 260MM **Privately Held**
SIC: 3585 Refrigeration & heating equipment
HQ: Micro Matic Usa, Inc.
   2386 Simon Ct
   Brooksville FL 34604
   352 544-1081

(G-13360)
MIDWEST AERO SUPPORT INC
1303 Turret Dr (61115-1452)
PHONE..................815 398-9202
Brent R Johnson, *President*
Barbara Johnson, *Vice Pres*
Tari Flack, *Finance Mgr*
EMP: 29
SQ FT: 14,400
SALES (est): 5.2MM **Privately Held**
SIC: 7699 3812 3679 3694 Aircraft & heavy equipment repair services; aircraft control systems, electronic; electronic circuits; harness wiring sets, internal combustion engines

(G-13361)
MIDWEST PACKAGING & CONT INC
9718 Forest Hills Rd (61115-8214)
PHONE..................815 633-6800
Terry Young, *President*
Leslie Young, *Vice Pres*
Robert Young, *Vice Pres*
David Lay, *Manager*
James Waller, *Admin Sec*
EMP: 70
SQ FT: 92,500

SALES (est): 19MM Privately Held
SIC: 2653 7389 Boxes, corrugated: made from purchased materials; packaging & labeling services

(G-13362)
PARKER-HANNIFIN CORPORATION
Also Called: Hydraulic Accumulator
10711 N 2nd St (61115-1459)
PHONE 815 636-4100
Holly Brockway, *Purch Mgr*
Richard Delreal, *Engineer*
Rj Marotta, *Engineer*
Bob Rajabi, *Engineer*
Gary Falendysz, *Senior Engr*
EMP: 80
SQ FT: 20,000
SALES (corp-wide): 14.3B Publicly Held
SIC: 3594 Fluid power pumps & motors
PA: Parker-Hannifin Corporation
  6035 Parkland Blvd
  Cleveland OH 44124
  216 896-3000

(G-13363)
PDQ MACHINE INC
7909b Burden Rd Ste B (61115-8277)
PHONE 815 282-7575
Chris Eickstead, *General Mgr*
EMP: 8
SALES (est): 750K Privately Held
SIC: 3599 3545 Machine shop, jobbing & repair; machine tool accessories

(G-13364)
PLASTIC PARTS INTL INC
1248 Shappert Dr (61115-1418)
PHONE 815 637-9222
Anthony Beall, *President*
Chris Beall, *VP Sales*
Scott Danielson, *Media Spec*
Eric Danielson, *Relations*
▲ **EMP:** 24
SQ FT: 23,000
SALES (est): 7.2MM Privately Held
SIC: 3089 Injection molding of plastics

(G-13365)
POLY PLASTICS FILMS CORP
334 Northway Park Rd # 3 (61115-4040)
P.O. Box 427, Grand Island NY (14072-0427)
PHONE 815 636-0821
Merle Wilson, *President*
EMP: 7
SQ FT: 6,000
SALES (est): 773K Privately Held
SIC: 5113 2673 Bags, paper & disposable plastic; plastic & pliofilm bags

(G-13366)
PRECISION DYNAMICS INC
5029 Willow Creek Rd (61115-8218)
PHONE 815 877-1592
William Brook, *Vice Pres*
Robert Becker, *Vice Pres*
EMP: 12
SALES (est): 772K Privately Held
SIC: 3599 Crankshafts & camshafts, machining

(G-13367)
PREMIER PRINTING & PROMOTIONS
1338 Turret Dr Ste B (61115-3405)
P.O. Box 596, Roscoe (61073-0596)
PHONE 815 282-3890
Ron Einsel, *Owner*
EMP: 11
SALES (est): 1MM Privately Held
SIC: 2759 Commercial printing

(G-13368)
PRINTJET CORPORATION
7816 Burden Rd (61115-8201)
PHONE 815 877-7511
Pedro Sotelo, *President*
Jose Vega, *Engineer*
Michaela Villarreal, *Sales Staff*
Susan Sotelo, *Admin Sec*
◆ **EMP:** 15
SQ FT: 11,000
SALES (est): 4.6MM Privately Held
SIC: 3577 Bar code (magnetic ink) printers

(G-13369)
ROCK VALLEY PALLET COMPANY
3511 Mildred Ct (61115-3877)
PHONE 815 654-4850
EMP: 3
SALES (est): 131.9K Privately Held
SIC: 2448 Mfg Wood Pallets/Skids

(G-13370)
ROCKFORD AIR DEVICES INC
1201 Turret Dr (61115-1451)
P.O. Box 2497, Loves Park (61132-2497)
PHONE 815 654-3330
Scott Bosi, *President*
Scott J Bosi, *President*
EMP: 10
SQ FT: 20,000
SALES (est): 2.7MM Privately Held
SIC: 3443 Cylinders, pressure: metal plate

(G-13371)
ROCKFORD COMMERCIAL WHSE INC
Also Called: STC International
8105 Burden Rd (61115-8208)
P.O. Box 140, Roscoe (61073-0140)
PHONE 815 623-8400
Adam Clayton, *President*
▲ **EMP:** 7
SQ FT: 16,000
SALES (est): 2.6MM Privately Held
SIC: 5072 3546 Hand tools; miscellaneous fasteners; grinders, portable: electric or pneumatic

(G-13372)
RUSCO MANUFACTURING INC
1304 Anvil Rd (61115-1409)
PHONE 815 654-3930
Russell Winters Jr, *Owner*
Jason Winters, *Plant Mgr*
EMP: 14
SQ FT: 55,000
SALES (est): 3.3MM Privately Held
SIC: 3599 Machine shop, jobbing & repair

(G-13373)
SAWS INTERNATIONAL INC
Also Called: Amv International
4929 Marlin Dr (61115-1413)
PHONE 815 397-0985
Joop Dekinkelber, *Ch of Bd*
Michael Rans, *Vice Pres*
Jeff Glasgow, *Foreman/Supr*
Julie Reckinger, *Accountant*
Bill Thornton, *Sales Mgr*
EMP: 42 **EST:** 2003
SQ FT: 24,000
SALES (est): 5.2MM Privately Held
WEB: www.kinkelderusa.com
SIC: 3425 Saw blades & handsaws
HQ: Neill Tools Limited
  Atlas Way
  Sheffield S4 7Q
  114 281-4242

(G-13374)
SHAWCRAFT SIGN CO
7727 Burden Rd (61115-8219)
PHONE 815 282-4105
Jay A Schoepski, *President*
EMP: 4
SQ FT: 3,120
SALES (est): 467.1K Privately Held
SIC: 2499 3993 Signboards, wood; signs & advertising specialties

(G-13375)
SPARTACUS GROUP INC
Also Called: Spartaclean
925 Colonial Dr (61115-3801)
PHONE 815 637-1574
Clayton H Balmes, *Technology*
Clayton Balmes, *Director*
EMP: 10
SALES: 950K Privately Held
SIC: 2992 Lubricating oils & greases

(G-13376)
SUPERIOR JOINING TECH INC
Also Called: Sjti
1260 Turret Dr (61115-1442)
PHONE 815 282-7581
Teresa L Beach-Shelow, *President*

Thomas A Shelow, *Treasurer*
EMP: 26
SQ FT: 55,000
SALES (est): 2.5MM Privately Held
SIC: 7692 3444 3724 8734 Welding repair; culverts, flumes & pipes; aircraft engines & engine parts; product testing laboratories; fabricated structural metal; steel wool

(G-13377)
SWEBCO MFG INC
7909 Burden Rd (61115-8277)
PHONE 815 636-7160
Kirk Schwebke, *President*
Daniel Schwebke, *Vice Pres*
Patricia Schwebke, *Vice Pres*
Rick St Clair, *Opers Mgr*
Jodee Schober, *Sales Staff*
EMP: 50
SQ FT: 34,000
SALES (est): 7.2MM Privately Held
SIC: 3451 3599 Screw machine products; machine & other job shop work

(G-13378)
TOWER TOOL & ENGINEERING INC
11052 Raleigh Ct (61115-1416)
PHONE 815 654-1115
Daniel Noe, *President*
Gordon Akey, *Vice Pres*
EMP: 13
SQ FT: 10,000
SALES (est): 1.8MM Privately Held
SIC: 3544 3599 Special dies & tools; custom machinery

(G-13379)
TRD MANUFACTURING INC
10914 N 2nd St (61115-1400)
PHONE 815 654-7775
Jeffrey Brown, *President*
Mr Kerry Reinhardt, *General Mgr*
James S Meldeau, *Admin Sec*
EMP: 45
SQ FT: 75,000
SALES (est): 11.7MM
SALES (corp-wide): 2.4B Privately Held
SIC: 3561 Cylinders, pump
HQ: Bimba Manufacturing Company Inc
  25150 S Governors Hwy
  University Park IL 60484
  708 534-8544

(G-13380)
TRI-PART SCREW PRODUCTS INC
10739 N 2nd St (61115-1459)
PHONE 815 654-7311
Donald Schuur, *President*
Mark C Lender, *President*
Robert Flaningam, *Corp Secy*
EMP: 45
SQ FT: 16,600
SALES (est): 9MM Privately Held
WEB: www.tri-part.com
SIC: 3451 Screw machine products

(G-13381)
UNIVERSAL DIE CAST CORPORATION
11500 Summerwood Dr (61115-8338)
PHONE 815 633-1702
Harold Winebaugh, *President*
Edward Palsgrove, *Vice Pres*
EMP: 6
SQ FT: 10,000
SALES (est): 882.5K Privately Held
SIC: 3364 Zinc & zinc-base alloy die-castings

(G-13382)
UNIVERSAL FEEDER INC
5299 Irving Blvd (61115-8274)
PHONE 815 633-0752
Harold Winebaugh, *President*
Edward Polsgrove, *President*
EMP: 7
SALES (est): 580.5K Privately Held
SIC: 7389 3545 3537 Design, commercial & industrial; hopper feed devices; industrial trucks & tractors

(G-13383)
UNLIMITED SVCS WISCONSIN INC
Also Called: Kenwood Electrical Systems
10108 Forest Hills Rd (61115-8234)
P.O. Box 170, Oconto WI (54153-0170)
PHONE 815 399-0282
William Kessenich, *President*
EMP: 20
SALES (corp-wide): 99.5MM Privately Held
SIC: 3679 3643 Harness assemblies for electronic use: wire or cable; current-carrying wiring devices
PA: Unlimited Services Of Wisconsin, Inc.
  170 Evergreen Rd
  Oconto WI 54153
  920 834-4418

(G-13384)
YANKEE MOLD INC
1158 Power Rd (61115-1412)
PHONE 815 986-1776
Beth A Everitt, *President*
Patrick Everitt, *Admin Sec*
EMP: 4 **EST:** 1997
SQ FT: 4,500
SALES: 420K Privately Held
WEB: www.yankeemold.com
SIC: 1799 3089 2821 Coating of concrete structures with plastic; injection molding of plastics; molding compounds, plastics

Mackinaw
Tazewell County

(G-13385)
PLAYING WITH FUSION INC
31201 State Route 9 (61755-8758)
PHONE 309 258-7259
Justin Steinlage, *President*
EMP: 3
SALES (est): 243.7K Privately Held
SIC: 3599 Amusement park equipment

(G-13386)
US CONVEYOR TECH MFG INC
30000 State Route 9 (61755-9571)
PHONE 309 359-4088
Kent Graves, *President*
EMP: 34
SQ FT: 50,000
SALES (est): 8.6MM Privately Held
SIC: 3535 Conveyors & conveying equipment

(G-13387)
US CONVEYOR TECHNOLOGIES
30000 State Route 9 (61755-9571)
PHONE 309 359-4088
Kent Graves, *Principal*
◆ **EMP:** 18
SALES (est): 5.5MM Privately Held
SIC: 3535 Conveyors & conveying equipment

Macomb
Mcdonough County

(G-13388)
CHALLENGE PUBLICATIONS L T D
Also Called: Palaestra
1948 Riverview Dr (61455-1277)
P.O. Box 269, Bushnell (61422-0269)
PHONE 309 421-0392
Dr David Beaver, *President*
Joseph Huver, *Vice Pres*
EMP: 6
SALES: 25MM Privately Held
SIC: 2721 Magazines: publishing & printing

(G-13389)
CLUGSTON TIBBITTS FUNERAL HOME (PA)
Also Called: Clugston-Tibbots Monument Co
303 E Washington St (61455-2341)
PHONE 309 833-2188
Steve Tibbitts, *President*
EMP: 4 **EST:** 1926

Macomb - McDonough County (G-13390)

SALES: 500K **Privately Held**
WEB: www.clugston-tibbittsfh.com
SIC: **7261** 3281 Funeral home; funeral director; cut stone & stone products

(G-13390)
CROOKED CREEK OUTDOORS
1025 W Grant St (61455-2620)
PHONE..................................309 837-3000
EMP: 2
SALES (est): 213.8K **Privately Held**
WEB: www.crookedcreekoutdoor.com
SIC: **3949** Sporting & athletic goods

(G-13391)
DESIGNED FOR JUST FOR YOU
106 Pam Ln (61455-3304)
PHONE..................................309 221-2667
Gloria Castle, *Owner*
EMP: 3
SALES (est): 158K **Privately Held**
SIC: **3648** Lanterns: electric, gas, carbide, kerosene or gasoline

(G-13392)
HILLYER INC
Also Called: Hillyer's U-Store-It
1420 E Carroll St (61455-1819)
PHONE..................................309 837-6434
William H Hillyer Sr, *President*
David Hillyer, *Vice Pres*
William H Hillyer Jr, *Vice Pres*
Michael Hillyer, *Treasurer*
Elizabeth Hillyer, *Shareholder*
EMP: 85
SQ FT: 2,000
SALES (est): 7.5MM **Privately Held**
WEB: www.hillyersustoreit.com
SIC: **1611** 1622 1794 1623 Surfacing & paving; bridge construction; excavation & grading, building construction; water main construction; sewer line construction; asphalt paving mixtures & blocks

(G-13393)
MCDONOUGH COUNTY SHOPPER INC
Also Called: Liberty Publishing
26 W Side Sq (61455-2219)
PHONE..................................309 833-2114
Pam McDowell, *General Mgr*
Scott Holland, *Editor*
Michelle Ringenberger, *Adv Mgr*
Dusty Vaughn, *Manager*
EMP: 8
SQ FT: 1,500
SALES (est): 724.6K **Privately Held**
SIC: **2711** Newspapers, publishing & printing

(G-13394)
NORFORGE AND MACHINING INC
2007 S Madison St (61455-3340)
PHONE..................................309 772-3124
Patricia S Hayes, *President*
EMP: 70
SQ FT: 90,000
SALES (est): 18MM **Privately Held**
SIC: **3462** 3429 Iron & steel forgings; manufactured hardware (general)

(G-13395)
NTN BEARING CORPORATION
Also Called: NTN Warehouse
1805 E University Dr (61455-1842)
PHONE..................................847 298-7500
EMP: 7
SALES (est): 480.7K **Privately Held**
SIC: **3562** Roller bearings & parts

(G-13396)
NTN-BOWER CORPORATION
707 Bower Rd (61455-2511)
PHONE..................................309 833-4541
EMP: 3 **Privately Held**
SIC: **3562** Ball & roller bearings
HQ: Ntn-Bower Corporation
711 Bower Rd
Macomb IL 61455
309 837-0440

(G-13397)
NTN-BOWER CORPORATION (DH)
711 Bower Rd (61455-2511)
PHONE..................................309 837-0440
Kunio Kamo, *President*
Dean Curley, *Prdtn Mgr*
James Hare, *Engineer*
Mike Kelly, *Plant Engr*
Leonard Peddicord, *Accountant*
◆ EMP: 9
SQ FT: 20,000
SALES: 172MM **Privately Held**
SIC: **3562** Roller bearings & parts

(G-13398)
QUICKPRINTERS
Also Called: Signs Express
1120 E Jackson St (61455-2522)
PHONE..................................309 833-5250
Tammie Speer, *President*
Tim Speer, *Vice Pres*
EMP: 4
SQ FT: 2,000
SALES (est): 362K **Privately Held**
SIC: **2752** 2759 2791 2789 Commercial printing, offset; commercial printing; typesetting; bookbinding & related work

(G-13399)
QUINCY PEPSI-COLA BOTTLING CO
236 Collins St (61455)
P.O. Box 365 (61455-0365)
PHONE..................................309 833-4263
Greg John, *CFO*
EMP: 15
SALES (corp-wide): 7.2MM **Privately Held**
SIC: **2086** 5149 Carbonated soft drinks, bottled & canned; beverage concentrates
PA: Quincy Pepsi-Cola Bottling Co
1121 Locust St
Quincy IL 62301
217 223-8600

(G-13400)
ROYAL HAEGER LAMP CO
1300 W Piper St (61455-2741)
P.O. Box 503 (61455-0503)
PHONE..................................309 837-9966
Nicholas Estes, *President*
Nick Estes, *Manager*
David Estes, *Data Proc Mgr*
▼ EMP: 30
SQ FT: 130,000
SALES (est): 3.5MM **Privately Held**
SIC: **3645** 3641 Table lamps; electric lamps

(G-13401)
WESTERN ILINOIS OPTICAL INC
909 E Grant St (61455-3371)
PHONE..................................309 837-2000
Gary Distin, *President*
Dr David Anderson, *Vice Pres*
Dr Gary Crosby, *Treasurer*
Dr Dan Doyle, *Admin Sec*
EMP: 3
SQ FT: 2,000
SALES (est): 390.3K **Privately Held**
SIC: **3851** 5048 Frames & parts, eyeglass & spectacle; lenses, ophthalmic; ophthalmic goods

(G-13402)
WHALEN MANUFACTURING COMPANY
1270 E Murray St (61455-1800)
PHONE..................................309 836-1438
Bernard F Whalen, *President*
Patrick T Whalen, *Admin Sec*
▲ EMP: 1
SQ FT: 30,000
SALES (est): 293.6K
SALES (corp-wide): 28.2MM **Privately Held**
SIC: **3523** Farm machinery & equipment
PA: Yetter Manufacturing Company Inc
109 S Mcdonough St
Colchester IL 62326
309 776-3222

(G-13403)
YETTER MANUFACTURING COMPANY
1270 E Murray St (61455-1800)
P.O. Box 15, Colchester (62326-0015)
PHONE..................................309 833-1445
Brian Concannon, *Principal*
EMP: 32
SALES (corp-wide): 26.8MM **Privately Held**
WEB: www.yetterco.com
SIC: **3999** Atomizers, toiletry
PA: Yetter Manufacturing Company Inc
109 S Mcdonough St
Colchester IL 62326
309 776-3222

Macon
Macon County

(G-13404)
ARCHER-DANIELS-MIDLAND COMPANY
Also Called: ADM
200 Front St (62544)
P.O. Box 287 (62544-0287)
PHONE..................................217 764-3345
Mike Snyder, *Branch Mgr*
EMP: 5
SALES (corp-wide): 64.6B **Publicly Held**
WEB: www.adm.com
SIC: **2041** Flour & other grain mill products
PA: Archer-Daniels-Midland Company
77 W Wacker Dr Ste 4600
Chicago IL 60601
312 634-8100

Madison
Madison County

(G-13405)
BEELMAN SLAG SALES
2000 Edwardsville Rd (62060-1349)
PHONE..................................618 452-8120
Sam Beelman, *President*
EMP: 500
SALES (est): 20.2MM **Privately Held**
SIC: **3295** Slag, crushed or ground

(G-13406)
BLAST PRODUCTS INC
224 State St (62060-1114)
PHONE..................................618 452-4700
Kent Newell, *President*
Carol B Newell, *Vice Pres*
EMP: 4
SQ FT: 20,000
SALES: 600K **Privately Held**
SIC: **2841** Soap & other detergents

(G-13407)
DAMCO PRODUCTS INC
Also Called: Blast Products
224 State St (62060-1114)
PHONE..................................618 452-4700
Mark J Fleming, *President*
Dave Altman, *Admin Sec*
EMP: 4 EST: 2010
SALES (est): 545.7K **Privately Held**
SIC: **2841** 2842 Soap & other detergents; specialty cleaning, polishes & sanitation goods

(G-13408)
DIAMOND PLATING COMPANY INC
5 Caine Dr (62060-1574)
P.O. Box 129 (62060-0129)
PHONE..................................618 451-7740
Fax: 618 451-7756
EMP: 35
SQ FT: 20,000
SALES (est): 3.8MM **Privately Held**
SIC: **3471** Metal Plating

(G-13409)
DYNO MANUFACTURING INC
2 Fox Industrial Dr (62060-1155)
PHONE..................................618 451-6609
EMP: 4

SALES (est): 249.6K **Privately Held**
SIC: **3999** Mfg Misc Products

(G-13410)
ELEKTRON N MAGNESIUM AMER INC (DH)
Also Called: Luxfer Graphic Arts
1001 College St (62060-1084)
P.O. Box 258 (62060-0258)
PHONE..................................618 452-5190
Chris Barnes, *President*
Ken Clark, *Vice Pres*
Kim Banovz, *Admin Sec*
◆ EMP: 82
SQ FT: 538,900
SALES (est): 21.9MM
SALES (corp-wide): 487.9MM **Privately Held**
SIC: **3356** Magnesium; magnesium & magnesium alloy bars, sheets, shapes, etc.; magnesium & magnesium alloy: rolling, drawing or extruding

(G-13411)
FALL PROTECTION SYSTEMS INC (PA)
2901 Old Nickel Plate Rd (62060-1673)
P.O. Box 229 (62060-0229)
PHONE..................................618 452-7000
Thomas Morhaus, *President*
Ted Hart, *Purch Mgr*
EMP: 24
SQ FT: 5,000
SALES (est): 4.6MM **Privately Held**
SIC: **3842** Personal safety equipment

(G-13412)
GATEWAY RAIL SERVICES INC
1980 3rd St (62060-1556)
P.O. Box 9 (62060-0009)
PHONE..................................618 451-0100
Roger J Verbeeren Jr, *President*
Clyde Hetz, *President*
George Williams, *Admin Sec*
EMP: 15
SQ FT: 740,520
SALES: 1.4MM **Privately Held**
SIC: **3743** Railroad car rebuilding

(G-13413)
GREEN PLAINS PARTNERS LP
395 Bissell St (62060-1177)
PHONE..................................618 451-4420
EMP: 14
SALES (corp-wide): 50.9MM **Publicly Held**
SIC: **2869** Mfg Industrial Organic Chemicals
PA: Green Plains Partners Lp
450 Regency Pkwy Ste 400
Omaha NE 68106
402 884-8700

(G-13414)
HTS COATINGS LLC
932 Fairway Park Dr (62060-1900)
PHONE..................................618 215-8161
Jason Hunsaker, *President*
Ashley Hunsaker, *CFO*
EMP: 25 EST: 2015
SQ FT: 30,000
SALES (est): 459.2K **Privately Held**
SIC: **7699** 7692 Industrial machinery & equipment repair; aircraft & heavy equipment repair services; welding repair

(G-13415)
ILLINOIS TRANSIT ASSEMBLY CORP
1980 3rd St (62060-1556)
P.O. Box 9 (62060-0009)
PHONE..................................618 451-0100
Leslie Kasten, *President*
▲ EMP: 18
SQ FT: 7,000
SALES (est): 1.5MM **Privately Held**
SIC: **3743** Railroad car rebuilding

(G-13416)
KIENSTRA PIPE & PRECAST LLC
1072 Eagle Park Rd (62060-1666)
PHONE..................................618 482-3283
Chris Kienstra, *President*
Ron Voss, *General Mgr*

EMP: 26
SALES (est): 3MM **Privately Held**
SIC: 3272 Precast terrazo or concrete products

(G-13417)
SLSB LLC
Also Called: St Louis Screw & Bolt
2000 Access Rd (62060-1083)
P.O. Box 260 (62060-0260)
PHONE.................................618 219-4115
Jonathan Oster, *Regional Mgr*
Jeremy Elliott, *Sales Staff*
Michael Friel, *Mng Member*
Frank Supancic, *Supervisor*
◆ **EMP:** 52
SQ FT: 120,000
SALES (est): 13.8MM **Privately Held**
SIC: 3452 5072 Bolts, nuts, rivets & washers; bolts

(G-13418)
TRONOX INCORPORATED
2 Washington Ave (62060-1463)
P.O. Box 166 (62060-0166)
PHONE.................................203 705-3704
John Falcone, *Branch Mgr*
EMP: 30
SALES (corp-wide): 2.9MM **Privately Held**
WEB: www.tronox.com
SIC: 2491 2421 Wood products, creosoted; sawmills & planing mills, general
HQ: Tronox Incorporated
1 Stamford Plz
Stamford CT 06901
203 705-3800

(G-13419)
WESTWOOD LANDS INC
4 Caine Dr (62060-1574)
PHONE.................................618 877-4990
Peter O'Dovero, *President*
James O'Dovero, *Vice Pres*
Joe O'Dovero, *Vice Pres*
EMP: 4
SALES (est): 400K **Privately Held**
SIC: 3312 Blast furnaces & steel mills

Mahomet
Champaign County

(G-13420)
ALL PRO WELDING SERVICES INC
157 County Road 2300 N (61853-8902)
PHONE.................................217 586-5383
Pat Hayes, *President*
EMP: 2
SALES (est): 242.3K **Privately Held**
SIC: 7692 Welding repair

(G-13421)
AMERICAN DECK & SUNROOM C
2603 Appaloosa Ln (61853-9773)
PHONE.................................217 586-4840
Thomas Parker, *Manager*
EMP: 8
SALES (est): 812K **Privately Held**
SIC: 3448 Prefabricated metal buildings

(G-13422)
BORDERS METALS RECOVERY
1203 S Sunny Acres Rd (61853-3710)
PHONE.................................217 586-2501
James R Borders, *Principal*
EMP: 2
SALES (est): 205.9K **Privately Held**
SIC: 3341 Recovery & refining of nonferrous metals

(G-13423)
F & L ELECTRONICS LLC
103 N Prairieview Rd (61853-7031)
P.O. Box 19 (61853-0019)
PHONE.................................217 586-2132
Frank Luksander,
Louis Lucksander,
EMP: 10
SALES (est): 600K **Privately Held**
SIC: 3671 Electron tubes, transmitting

(G-13424)
ILLINOIS VALLEY PRESS EAST
Also Called: Muhammed Citizens
303 E Main St Ste D (61853-7448)
P.O. Box 919 (61853-0919)
PHONE.................................217 586-2512
Steve Hoffman, *General Mgr*
Berry Winterland, *Principal*
EMP: 5
SALES (est): 156.1K **Privately Held**
SIC: 2711 Newspapers, publishing & printing

(G-13425)
LL ELECTRONICS
103 S Prairieview Rd (61853)
PHONE.................................217 586-6477
Louis A Luksander, *Owner*
EMP: 6
SALES (est): 330K **Privately Held**
SIC: 3663 Transmitter-receivers, radio

(G-13426)
MID-AMERICA SAND & GRAVEL (PA)
Also Called: Mid America Recycling
250 County Rd 2050 N (61853)
P.O. Box 290 (61853-0290)
PHONE.................................217 586-4536
Hugh Gallivan, *President*
William Booker, *Vice Pres*
Karen O'Neil, *Vice Pres*
EMP: 7
SQ FT: 900
SALES (est): 2MM **Privately Held**
SIC: 1442 Sand mining; gravel mining

Makanda
Jackson County

(G-13427)
BLUE SKY VINEYARD
3150 S Rocky Comfort Rd (62958-4062)
PHONE.................................618 995-9463
Barrett Rochman, *Owner*
EMP: 7
SALES (est): 664.8K **Privately Held**
SIC: 2084 Wine cellars, bonded: engaged in blending wines; wines

(G-13428)
KINSER WOODWORKS
120 Old Lower Cobden Rd (62958)
PHONE.................................618 549-4540
Kyler Kinser, *Owner*
EMP: 3 **EST:** 1976
SALES (est): 122K **Privately Held**
SIC: 2511 Wood household furniture

(G-13429)
NIGHT VISION SPECIALISTS LLC
260 S Rocky Comfort Rd (62958-4056)
PHONE.................................618 614-8726
Fred J III Terbrak, *Principal*
EMP: 3
SALES (est): 197.9K **Privately Held**
SIC: 3827 Optical instruments & lenses

Malta
Dekalb County

(G-13430)
NEILAND CUSTOM PRODUCTS
400 Il Route 38 (60150-9590)
P.O. Box 96 (60150-0096)
PHONE.................................815 825-2233
Neil Anderson, *Owner*
EMP: 3
SALES (est): 40K **Privately Held**
SIC: 3479 3471 Painting, coating & hot dipping; coating of metals & formed products; finishing, metals or formed products

Manhattan
Will County

(G-13431)
BOLHUIS WOODWORKING CO
14250 W Joliet Rd (60442-8199)
P.O. Box 1109, South Holland (60473-7109)
PHONE.................................708 333-5100
Steve Couch, *Owner*
EMP: 9 **EST:** 1970
SQ FT: 4,000
SALES (est): 849.8K **Privately Held**
SIC: 5712 2541 2434 Cabinet work, custom; wood partitions & fixtures; wood kitchen cabinets

(G-13432)
ERBECK ONE CHEM & LAB SUP INC
16279 Celtic Cir (60442-6101)
PHONE.................................312 203-0078
Stephen Erbeck, *President*
Gregory Fuller, *Marketing Staff*
EMP: 2
SALES: 700K **Privately Held**
SIC: 5169 3677 Silicon lubricants; filtration devices, electronic

(G-13433)
LINCOLN GENERATING FCILTY LLC
27150 S Kankakee St (60442-9833)
PHONE.................................815 478-3799
Merle Churchill,
EMP: 9
SALES (est): 2.1MM
SALES (corp-wide): 8.4B **Privately Held**
SIC: 3089 Injection molding of plastics
PA: Tenaska, Inc.
14302 Fnb Pkwy
Omaha NE 68154
402 691-9500

(G-13434)
MANHATTAN MECHANICAL SVCS LLC
25630 S Gougar Rd 3 (60442-9502)
PHONE.................................815 478-9940
Tara Minard, *Business Anlyst*
Michael J Uremovich, *Manager*
Chris Hempen, *Manager*
Tim Buchanan, *Director*
EMP: 28 **EST:** 2010
SALES (est): 5.5MM **Privately Held**
SIC: 1711 3599 Mechanical contractor; hose, flexible metallic

(G-13435)
RESPECT INCORPORATED
15555 Tyndall Ct (60442-6227)
P.O. Box 160, Lemont (60439-0160)
PHONE.................................815 806-1907
Kent Mast, *President*
EMP: 5
SALES: 5K **Privately Held**
SIC: 2731 Textbooks: publishing only, not printed on site

(G-13436)
WINNING COLORS
345 Jan St Unit C (60442-9284)
PHONE.................................815 462-4810
Mark Cryer, *Owner*
EMP: 4
SALES (est): 384.1K **Privately Held**
SIC: 3399 7532 Metal powders, pastes & flakes; top & body repair & paint shops

Manito
Mason County

(G-13437)
DEL MONTE FOODS INC
812 S Adams St (61546-9397)
PHONE.................................309 968-7033
Gary Molid, *Manager*
EMP: 3 **Privately Held**
WEB: www.delmonte.com

SIC: 2033 Vegetables & vegetable products in cans, jars, etc.
HQ: Del Monte Foods, Inc.
205 N Wiget Ln
Walnut Creek CA 94598
925 949-2772

(G-13438)
DONS MEAT MARKET
203 W Market St (61546-9386)
PHONE.................................309 968-6026
Don Wilson, *Owner*
EMP: 4
SQ FT: 1,680
SALES (est): 262.4K **Privately Held**
SIC: 3556 2013 Meat, poultry & seafood processing machinery; sausages & other prepared meats

(G-13439)
SENECA FOODS CORPORATION
7757 Airport Rd (61546-8706)
PHONE.................................309 545-2233
Brent Akers, *Sales Staff*
Bob Held, *Manager*
EMP: 50
SALES (corp-wide): 1.2B **Publicly Held**
SIC: 2033 Canned fruits & specialties
PA: Seneca Foods Corporation
3736 S Main St
Marion NY 14505
315 926-8100

(G-13440)
TIM SNYDER
13520 Winfield Dr (61546-8010)
PHONE.................................309 657-4764
Tim Snyder, *Principal*
EMP: 3
SALES (est): 188.5K **Privately Held**
SIC: 3353 Aluminum sheet, plate & foil

(G-13441)
WILLETTS WINERY & CELLAR
105 E Market St (61546-9205)
PHONE.................................309 968-7070
Cris Willett, *Executive*
EMP: 4
SALES (est): 273.8K **Privately Held**
WEB: www.willettswine.com
SIC: 2084 Wines

Mansfield
Piatt County

(G-13442)
PIATT COUNTY SERVICE CO
1070 Old Us 150 (61854-6835)
PHONE.................................217 489-2411
Keith Niemeier, *Opers-Prdtn-Mfg*
EMP: 5
SALES (corp-wide): 4.2MM **Privately Held**
SIC: 5999 5261 2875 Insecticides; fertilizer; fertilizers, mixing only
PA: Piatt County Service Co (Inc)
427 W Marion St Ste 1
Monticello IL 61856
217 762-2133

Manteno
Kankakee County

(G-13443)
ABC COATING COMPANY ILL INC
1160 N Boudreau Rd (60950-3028)
PHONE.................................708 258-9633
Marcelo Acuna, *President*
EMP: 20
SALES (est): 549.2K **Privately Held**
SIC: 3479 Coating of metals with plastic or resins

(G-13444)
BIMBA MANUFACTURING COMPANY
500 S Spruce St (60950-9473)
PHONE.................................708 534-7997
Dave Rademacher, *Manager*

Manteno - Kankakee County (G-13445)

EMP: 50
SALES (corp-wide): 2.4B **Privately Held**
WEB: www.bimba.com
SIC: 3593 Fluid power cylinders & actuators
HQ: Bimba Manufacturing Company Inc
25150 S Governors Hwy
University Park IL 60484
708 534-8544

(G-13445)
CONQUEST SOUND INC
Also Called: Conquest Sound Company
209 Cypress Dr (60950-1074)
P.O. Box 268, Monee (60449-0268)
PHONE.....................................708 534-0309
Larry Spalla, *President*
Jeanna Jozaitis, *President*
Nick Kutzko, *Vice Pres*
Sue Woolum, *Sales Associate*
▲ **EMP:** 13
SALES (est): 215.3K **Privately Held**
SIC: 3663 Cable television equipment

(G-13446)
DAWN FOOD PRODUCTS INC
1340 W Sycamore Rd (60950-9364)
PHONE.....................................815 468-6286
Diana Suarez, *Sales Staff*
John Obrian, *Manager*
EMP: 36
SALES (corp-wide): 1.7B **Privately Held**
SIC: 2045 Prepared flour mixes & doughs
HQ: Dawn Food Products, Inc.
3333 Sargent Rd
Jackson MI 49201

(G-13447)
F WEBER PRINTING CO INC
450 N Locust St (60950-1225)
PHONE.....................................815 468-6152
Franklin Weber, *President*
Anna Weber, *Corp Secy*
EMP: 9
SQ FT: 5,000
SALES (est): 670K **Privately Held**
SIC: 2752 2759 7336 2791 Commercial printing, offset; letterpress printing; commercial art & graphic design; typesetting; bookbinding & related work

(G-13448)
FRITO-LAY NORTH AMERICA INC
450 N Grove St (60950)
PHONE.....................................815 468-3940
Don Middleton, *District Mgr*
EMP: 15
SALES (corp-wide): 67.1B **Publicly Held**
SIC: 2099 5145 Food preparations; potato chips
HQ: Frito-Lay North America, Inc.
7701 Legacy Dr
Plano TX 75024

(G-13449)
HIGH PERFORMANCE LUBR LLC
500 S Spruce St (60950-9473)
PHONE.....................................815 468-3535
David Stoiber, *Plant Mgr*
David Ward,
EMP: 11
SALES (est): 1.5MM **Privately Held**
WEB: www.hplubricants.com
SIC: 2992 Lubricating oils

(G-13450)
LEGACY VULCAN LLC
Also Called: Manteno Quarry
6141 N Rte 50 (60950-3491)
PHONE.....................................815 468-8141
Jerry Roth, *Manager*
EMP: 23 **Publicly Held**
WEB: www.vulcanmaterials.com
SIC: 1442 1422 Construction sand & gravel; crushed & broken limestone
HQ: Legacy Vulcan, Llc
1200 Urban Center Dr
Vestavia AL 35242
205 298-3000

(G-13451)
LLC URBAN FARMER
1551 N Boudreau Rd (60950-9386)
PHONE.....................................815 468-7200
David Foran, *General Mgr*
Ryan Sparrow, *Mng Member*
Warren Ouwenga,
▲ **EMP:** 53
SALES (est): 3.6MM **Privately Held**
SIC: 2041 Pizza dough, prepared

(G-13452)
MANTENO METAL WORKS
4192 E 7000n Rd (60950-3088)
PHONE.....................................815 468-6128
Michael Deruiter, *Principal*
EMP: 3
SALES (est): 321.4K **Privately Held**
SIC: 3599 Machine shop, jobbing & repair

(G-13453)
PERFORMANCE AUTO SALON INC
17 E Sixth St (60950-1210)
PHONE.....................................815 468-6882
Thomas Kopp, *President*
EMP: 20
SALES (est): 1.3MM **Privately Held**
SIC: 3471 Finishing, metals or formed products

(G-13454)
PLOCHMAN INC
1333 N Boudreau Rd (60950-9384)
PHONE.....................................815 468-3434
Carl Plochman III, *President*
David Nicholson, *President*
Markus Kahr, *Principal*
Carl M Plochman Jr, *Chairman*
Martin Faye, *Plant Mgr*
EMP: 50 **EST:** 1852
SQ FT: 106,000
SALES: 13MM
SALES (corp-wide): 455.1MM **Privately Held**
WEB: www.plochman.com
SIC: 2035 5812 Mustard, prepared (wet); eating places
PA: Haco Holding Ag
Worbstrasse 262
Muri Bei Bern BE 3074
319 501-111

(G-13455)
R S CRYO EQUIPMENT INC
629 N Grove St (60950-9345)
PHONE.....................................815 468-6115
Ronald L Stluka, *President*
Michele Stluka, *Treasurer*
▲ **EMP:** 8
SQ FT: 32,000
SALES (est): 2MM **Privately Held**
SIC: 3556 Smokers, food processing equipment

(G-13456)
SONO ITALIANO CORPORATION
Also Called: True Sun Dried Tomatoes
655 Mulberry St (60950-9219)
PHONE.....................................817 472-8903
EMP: 4
SALES (est): 300K **Privately Held**
SIC: 2034 2099 Mfg Dehydrated Fruits/Vegetables Mfg Food Preparations

(G-13457)
SOUTHFIELD CORPORATION
Also Called: Prairie North Central Mtls
8215c N Us Highway 45 52 (60950-3381)
PHONE.....................................815 468-8700
Jim Purdy, *Manager*
EMP: 15
SALES (corp-wide): 344.9MM **Privately Held**
SIC: 1422 Crushed & broken limestone
PA: Southfield Corporation
8995 W 95th St
Palos Hills IL 60465
708 344-1000

(G-13458)
STEVENSON FABRICATION SVCS INC
680 Mulberry St (60950-9218)
P.O. Box 713 (60950-0713)
PHONE.....................................815 468-7941
Mark Stevenson, *President*
Elizabeth Stevenson, *President*
EMP: 4
SQ FT: 6,000
SALES (est): 607.3K **Privately Held**
SIC: 3441 7692 3446 Fabricated structural metal; welding repair; architectural metalwork

Maple Park
Kane County

(G-13459)
ACQUAVIVA WINERY LLC
47 W 614 Rr 38 (60151)
PHONE.....................................630 365-0333
Vito Brandonisio, *Principal*
Joseph Brandonisio, *Vice Pres*
EMP: 7
SALES (est): 799.9K **Privately Held**
SIC: 2084 Wines

(G-13460)
BORK INDUSTRIES
44w508 Ic Trl (60151-8725)
PHONE.....................................630 365-5517
EMP: 4 **EST:** 2015
SALES (est): 424K **Privately Held**
SIC: 3999 Mfg Misc Products

(G-13461)
C A LARSON & SON INC
Also Called: Old World Millworks
5n200 Wooley Rd (60151-8303)
PHONE.....................................847 717-6010
Robert Larson, *President*
Claudia Larson, *Admin Sec*
EMP: 35 **EST:** 1985
SQ FT: 120,000
SALES (est): 6.5MM **Privately Held**
SIC: 2431 Newel posts, wood; stair railings, wood

(G-13462)
EMERGENCY MEDICAL INSTRUMENTS
Also Called: EMI
44 W 528 Rt 64 (60151)
PHONE.....................................630 365-2001
R Karl, *Owner*
▲ **EMP:** 2
SALES (est): 232.3K **Privately Held**
SIC: 3841 Surgical & medical instruments

(G-13463)
LINEAR KINETICS INC
48 W 989 Rr 64 (60151)
PHONE.....................................630 365-0075
EMP: 5
SQ FT: 7,500
SALES (est): 715.6K **Privately Held**
SIC: 3569 3441 Mfg General Industrial Machinery Structural Metal Fabrication

(G-13464)
LIVING LAMINATES INC
50w485 Il Route 64 (60151-9188)
PHONE.....................................847 741-2004
Joseph Medina, *Owner*
EMP: 4
SALES (est): 380.1K **Privately Held**
SIC: 2434 Wood kitchen cabinets

(G-13465)
MAPLE PARK TRUCKING INC
Also Called: Maple Park Landscape Supplies
50w 363 Isle Rr 64 St 50 (60151)
PHONE.....................................815 899-1958
Connie J Meyer, *President*
Alana Meyer, *Treasurer*
Jodi Meyer, *Bookkeeper*
Deborah Meyer, *Admin Sec*
EMP: 6
SQ FT: 2,500
SALES (est): 872.9K **Privately Held**
SIC: 3715 0782 Truck trailers; landscape contractors

(G-13466)
STOVERS FINE WOODWORKING INC
474 Harter Rd (60151)
PHONE.....................................630 557-0072
Mike Stover, *Principal*
EMP: 2
SALES (est): 210.3K **Privately Held**
SIC: 2431 Millwork

(G-13467)
TOWER WORKS INC
47w543 Perry Rd (60151-9797)
PHONE.....................................630 557-2221
Steven Svestha, *President*
Eddy Finley, *Vice Pres*
▼ **EMP:** 15
SALES (est): 3.2MM **Privately Held**
SIC: 3441 Fabricated structural metal

Mapleton
Peoria County

(G-13468)
CATERPILLAR INC
8826 W Us Highway 24 (61547-7503)
PHONE.....................................309 633-8788
S David Sanders, *Engineer*
Edward Grammy, *Manager*
Rich Frow, *Info Tech Mgr*
EMP: 650
SALES (corp-wide): 53.8B **Publicly Held**
SIC: 3531 Construction machinery
PA: Caterpillar Inc.
510 Lake Cook Rd Ste 100
Deerfield IL 60015
224 551-4000

(G-13469)
CHEMICAL SPECIALTIES MFG CORP
8316 W Route 24 (61547-7500)
PHONE.....................................309 697-5400
Jan Pribble, *Branch Mgr*
EMP: 3
SALES (corp-wide): 5.5B **Publicly Held**
SIC: 2842 Cleaning or polishing preparations
HQ: Chemical Specialties Manufacturing Corporation
901 N Newkirk St
Baltimore MD 21205
410 675-4800

(G-13470)
CHEMTURA CORPORATION
8220 W Us Highway 24 (61547-7509)
P.O. Box 10 (61547-0010)
PHONE.....................................309 633-9480
Don Stahlberg, *Manager*
EMP: 6
SALES (est): 564.3K **Privately Held**
SIC: 2869 Industrial organic chemicals

(G-13471)
COMMON SCENTS MOM
10812 W Timber Rd (61547-9478)
PHONE.....................................309 389-3216
EMP: 3
SALES (est): 187.8K **Privately Held**
SIC: 2844 Toilet preparations

(G-13472)
EVONIK CORPORATION
8300 W Route 24 (61547-7500)
P.O. Box 9 (61547-0009)
PHONE.....................................309 697-6220
Stacey Hall, *Human Res Mgr*
Carl Sima, *Branch Mgr*
Dale Myers, *Technology*
Jeffrey Ralph, *Executive*
EMP: 250
SALES (corp-wide): 2.6B **Privately Held**
SIC: 2869 Industrial organic chemicals
HQ: Evonik Corporation
299 Jefferson Rd
Parsippany NJ 07054
973 929-8000

(G-13473)
INGREDION INCORPORATED
8310 W Rte 24 (61547-7500)
PHONE.....................................309 550-9136
Bill Coyle, *Principal*
EMP: 100
SALES (corp-wide): 6.2B **Publicly Held**
WEB: www.ingredion.com
SIC: 2046 Corn starch
PA: Ingredion Incorporated
5 Westbrook Corporate Ctr # 500
Westchester IL 60154
708 551-2600

GEOGRAPHIC SECTION

(G-13474)
LANXESS SOLUTIONS US INC
8220 W Route 24 (61547-7509)
PHONE..................309 633-9480
Don Stahlberg, *Manager*
EMP: 19
SQ FT: 60,000
SALES (corp-wide): 7.5B **Privately Held**
SIC: 2821 Plastics materials & resins
HQ: Lanxess Solutions Us Inc.
2 Armstrong Rd Ste 101
Shelton CT 06484
203 573-2000

(G-13475)
LONZA LLC
8316 W Route 24 (61547-7500)
PHONE..................309 697-7200
Eric Daly, *Production*
Shujun Wang, *Research*
Robert Bourman, *Engineer*
Charlie Reagan, *Engineer*
Bruce Davey, *Manager*
EMP: 95
SALES (corp-wide): 5.5B **Privately Held**
WEB: www.lonza.com
SIC: 2833 2869 2819 Medicinals & botanicals; industrial organic chemicals; industrial inorganic chemicals
HQ: Lonza Llc
412 Mount Kemble Ave # 200
Morristown NJ 07960
201 316-9200

(G-13476)
MATHESON TRI-GAS INC
7700 W Wheeler Rd (61547-9302)
PHONE..................309 697-1933
Mike Boock, *Branch Mgr*
EMP: 15 **Privately Held**
SIC: 5084 2813 Welding machinery & equipment; safety equipment; nitrogen
HQ: Matheson Tri-Gas, Inc.
150 Allen Rd Ste 302
Basking Ridge NJ 07920
908 991-9200

Maquon
Knox County

(G-13477)
CHOPPER MM LLC
500 Knox Road 900 E (61458-9392)
PHONE..................309 875-3544
Andrea Scharfenberg, *Principal*
EMP: 3
SALES (est): 308.1K **Privately Held**
SIC: 3751 Motorcycles & related parts

Marengo
Mchenry County

(G-13478)
ALAN MANUFACTURING CORP
Also Called: Alan Stamping
5017 Ritz Rd (60152-9128)
PHONE..................815 568-6836
Lyle Elyea, *Owner*
EMP: 5
SQ FT: 4,000
SALES (est): 421.2K **Privately Held**
WEB: www.alanstamping.com
SIC: 3469 3643 3542 3452 Stamping metal for the trade; current-carrying wiring devices; machine tools, metal forming type; bolts, nuts, rivets & washers; manufactured hardware (general)

(G-13479)
ARNOLD ENGINEERING CO (DH)
300 N West St (60152-2103)
PHONE..................815 568-2000
Gordon McNeil, *Ch of Bd*
Tim Wilson, *President*
Rob Strahs, *Vice Pres*
Mike Stachura, *CFO*
David Goodwin, *Sales Staff*
▲ **EMP:** 100 **EST:** 1905
SQ FT: 90,000
SALES (est): 21.6MM **Publicly Held**
WEB: www.arnoldmagnetics.com
SIC: 3677 Electronic coils, transformers & other inductors
HQ: Arnold Magnetic Technologies Corporation
770 Linden Ave
Rochester NY 14625
585 385-9010

(G-13480)
ARNOLD MAGNETIC TECH CORP
300 N West St (60152-2103)
PHONE..................815 568-2000
Colleen Massheimer, *Opers Spvr*
Lois Haime, *Accountant*
Roy Hollon, *Branch Mgr*
Michael Motley, *Software Dev*
Tom Pace, *Master*
EMP: 27 **Publicly Held**
WEB: www.arnoldmagnetics.com
SIC: 3264 Magnets, permanent: ceramic or ferrite
HQ: Arnold Magnetic Technologies Corporation
770 Linden Ave
Rochester NY 14625
585 385-9010

(G-13481)
B & D MURRAY MANUFACTURING CO
3911 N Il Route 23 (60152-8629)
P.O. Box 102 (60152-0102)
PHONE..................815 568-6176
Bobby D Murray, *President*
David Murray, *Vice Pres*
Evelyn Murray, *Treasurer*
EMP: 3 **EST:** 1975
SQ FT: 5,000
SALES: 500K **Privately Held**
SIC: 3544 3469 Special dies & tools; metal stampings

(G-13482)
CONSOLIDATED MATERIALS INC (PA)
Also Called: Coral Lake
8920 S Rt 23 (60152)
PHONE..................815 568-1538
Thomas A Lee, *President*
Thomas Kelecius, *Admin Sec*
EMP: 7
SALES (est): 3.4MM **Privately Held**
SIC: 1442 Construction sand & gravel

(G-13483)
DANAHER CORPORATION
1300 N State St (60152-2204)
PHONE..................815 568-8001
Christopher McMahon, *Exec VP*
Terry Levin, *Vice Pres*
Ron Wendel, *Manager*
Chris Espinosa, *Network Tech*
EMP: 225
SALES (corp-wide): 17.9B **Publicly Held**
WEB: www.danaher.com
SIC: 3823 Liquid level instruments, industrial process type
PA: Danaher Corporation
2200 Penn Ave Nw Ste 800w
Washington DC 20037
202 828-0850

(G-13484)
EPSCCA
1400 N State St (60152-2206)
PHONE..................815 568-3020
Steve Lindberg, *CEO*
Kim Keefer, *Cust Mgr*
EMP: 50
SALES (est): 3.2MM **Privately Held**
SIC: 3479 Coating of metals with plastic or resins

(G-13485)
HYPERSTITCH
219 E Grant Hwy (60152-3339)
PHONE..................815 568-0590
Paticia Lawlor, *Officer*
EMP: 12
SALES (est): 720.7K **Privately Held**
SIC: 2395 Embroidery products, except schiffli machine; embroidery & art needlework

(G-13486)
J & M FAB METALS INC
6710 S Grant Hwy (60152-9441)
P.O. Box 427 (60152-0427)
PHONE..................815 758-0354
Keane Paradiso, *President*
EMP: 2
SQ FT: 5,000
SALES (est): 250K **Privately Held**
SIC: 7692 3444 Welding repair; sheet metalwork

(G-13487)
K TROX SALES INC
6807 Paulson Dr (60152-9361)
PHONE..................815 568-1521
Debra Troxell, *President*
Tom Troxell, *Admin Sec*
▲ **EMP:** 2
SALES: 1MM **Privately Held**
SIC: 3672 Printed circuit boards

(G-13488)
KOLLMORGEN CORP
1300 N State St (60152-2204)
PHONE..................815 568-8001
Vickie Stclair, *Buyer*
▲ **EMP:** 9 **EST:** 2009
SALES (est): 1.1MM **Privately Held**
SIC: 3827 Optical instruments & lenses

(G-13489)
MARENGO TOOL & DIE WORKS INC
201 E Railroad St (60152-3133)
P.O. Box 100 (60152-0100)
PHONE..................815 568-7411
Gilbert Tauck, *CEO*
Fred Struckmeier, *President*
Robert Rosulek, *Corp Secy*
EMP: 45
SQ FT: 70,000
SALES (est): 8.3MM **Privately Held**
WEB: www.marengotool.com
SIC: 3469 3452 3544 Stamping metal for the trade; bolts, nuts, rivets & washers; special dies, tools, jigs & fixtures

(G-13490)
MARENGO UNION TIMES
709 Lura Ln (60152-3382)
PHONE..................815 568-5400
Jennifer Blais, *Principal*
EMP: 3 **EST:** 2011
SALES (est): 157.5K **Privately Held**
WEB: www.marengo-uniontimes.com
SIC: 2711 Newspapers, publishing & printing

(G-13491)
OZINGA BROS INC
9204 S Il Route 23 (60152-8131)
PHONE..................815 568-2589
EMP: 46
SALES (corp-wide): 434.5MM **Privately Held**
WEB: www.ozinga.com
SIC: 3273 Ready-mixed concrete
PA: Ozinga Bros., Inc.
19001 Old Lagrange Rd # 30
Mokena IL 60448
708 326-4200

(G-13492)
PAVELOC INDUSTRIES INC
8302 S Il Route 23 (60152-9317)
PHONE..................815 568-4700
Mike Corteen, *President*
Bradley Le Gare, *Vice Pres*
EMP: 15
SALES (est): 2.1MM **Privately Held**
SIC: 3271 5032 Paving blocks, concrete; brick, stone & related material

(G-13493)
PRAIRIE PURE CHEESE
1405 N State St (60152-2215)
PHONE..................815 568-5000
Brian Gerloff, *Principal*
EMP: 5
SALES (est): 327.5K **Privately Held**
SIC: 2022 5143 Cheese, natural & processed; dairy products, except dried or canned

(G-13494)
SWIFT TECHNOLOGIES INC
8601 S Hill Rd (60152-8251)
PHONE..................815 568-8402
John Bussert, *President*
Patricia Bussert, *Vice Pres*
EMP: 9
SALES (est): 900K **Privately Held**
SIC: 7372 7373 5045 Prepackaged software; value-added resellers, computer systems; computers, peripherals & software

(G-13495)
THOMSON INDUSTRIES INC
1300 N State St (60152-2204)
PHONE..................815 568-4309
Scott Benigni, *President*
Robert C Magee, *Chairman*
David Hill, *Plant Mgr*
Kevin Hoem, *Buyer*
Norman Dickey, *Engineer*
▲ **EMP:** 2400
SQ FT: 175,000
SALES (est): 25K
SALES (corp-wide): 1.8B **Publicly Held**
WEB: www.thomsonlinear.com
SIC: 3562 Ball bearings & parts
PA: Altra Industrial Motion Corp.
300 Granite St Ste 201
Braintree MA 02184
781 917-0600

(G-13496)
UNICARRIERS AMERICAS CORP (DH)
Also Called: Nissan Forklift
240 N Prospect St (60152-3235)
PHONE..................800 871-5438
K Berry Mansfield, *President*
Dale Mark, *Vice Pres*
Rodney Jacobson, *Mfg Spvr*
Kurt Kruse, *Engineer*
Patrick Pugasa, *Engineer*
◆ **EMP:** 5 **EST:** 1966
SQ FT: 370,740
SALES (est): 172.5MM **Privately Held**
WEB: www.unicarriersamericas.com
SIC: 3519 5084 Gasoline engines; lift trucks & parts; engines, gasoline
HQ: Mitsubishi Logisnext Americas Inc.
2121 W Sam Houston Pkwy N
Houston TX 77043
713 365-1000

(G-13497)
YOUR SUPPLY DEPOT LIMITED
Also Called: Army Navy Supply Depot
207 E Grant Hwy (60152-3339)
PHONE..................815 568-4115
Robert Stewart, *President*
Thomas Stewart, *Vice Pres*
▲ **EMP:** 4
SQ FT: 1,200
SALES: 1MM **Privately Held**
SIC: 3579 5961 5087 Embossing machines for store & office use; catalog & mail-order houses; engraving equipment & supplies

Marine
Madison County

(G-13498)
HESS MACHINE INC
10724 Pocahontas Rd (62061-1232)
PHONE..................618 887-4444
Timothy Hess, *President*
Shelley Hess, *Admin Sec*
EMP: 7
SQ FT: 3,150
SALES (est): 1MM **Privately Held**
WEB: www.hessmachine.net
SIC: 3599 Custom machinery; machine shop, jobbing & repair

Marion
Williamson County

(G-13499)
AISIN ELECTRONICS ILLINOIS LLC (DH)
11000 Redco Dr (62959-5889)
PHONE..................618 997-9800
Yutaka Iguchi, *President*
◆ **EMP:** 118
SALES (est): 40.8MM **Privately Held**
SIC: 3714 Instrument board assemblies, motor vehicle
HQ: Aisin Holdings Of America, Inc.
1665 E 4th Street Rd
Seymour IN 47274
812 524-8144

(G-13500)
AISIN LIGHT METALS LLC
11000 Redco Dr (62959-5889)
PHONE..................618 997-9800
Fumihiko Sugiura, *President*
Ryouju Tsuji, *President*
EMP: 5
SALES (est): 2.1MM **Privately Held**
SIC: 3675 Electronic capacitors
HQ: Aisin Holdings Of America, Inc.
1665 E 4th Street Rd
Seymour IN 47274
812 524-8144

(G-13501)
AISIN MFG ILLINOIS LLC
1100 Glenn Clarida Dr (62959-5883)
PHONE..................618 998-8333
Patty Clark, *Branch Mgr*
EMP: 70 **Privately Held**
SIC: 3714 Motor vehicle parts & accessories
HQ: Aisin Mfg. Illinois, Llc
11000 Redco Dr
Marion IL 62959
618 998-8333

(G-13502)
AISIN MFG ILLINOIS LLC (DH)
11000 Redco Dr (62959-5889)
PHONE..................618 998-8333
Hiroyuki Kato, *President*
Glenn Edwards, *Exec VP*
Naoki Niimi, *Treasurer*
▲ **EMP:** 650
SQ FT: 160,000
SALES (est): 133.9MM **Privately Held**
SIC: 3714 Motor vehicle parts & accessories
HQ: Aisin U.S.A. Mfg., Inc.
1700 E 4th Street Rd
Seymour IN 47274
812 523-1969

(G-13503)
AMERICAN MONUMENT CO
306 S Court St (62959-2710)
PHONE..................618 993-8968
Edward Patterson, *President*
Tammy Patterson, *Vice Pres*
EMP: 8
SALES (est): 880.8K **Privately Held**
SIC: 3281 5999 Monuments, cut stone (not finishing or lettering only); monuments & tombstones

(G-13504)
APEX MFG & DESIGN INC (PA)
1800 E Boyton St (62959-4318)
P.O. Box 191 (62959-0191)
PHONE..................618 997-0512
Darrell Ross, *President*
Doug Ralph, *Vice Pres*
EMP: 2
SQ FT: 200
SALES: 250K **Privately Held**
SIC: 3599 Machine shop, jobbing & repair

(G-13505)
ASSOCIATE COMPUTER SYSTEMS
211 N Market St Ste A (62959-2427)
PHONE..................618 997-3653
Patrick L Devine, *Partner*
Doug Camden, *Partner*
Pat Devine, *Partner*
EMP: 4
SQ FT: 1,200
SALES (est): 700K **Privately Held**
SIC: 5734 7372 Computer & software stores; prepackaged software

(G-13506)
BUCKET MART INC
300 W Longstreet Rd (62959-5327)
P.O. Box 1240 (62959-7740)
PHONE..................813 390-8626
Jack Johnson, *President*
EMP: 2
SALES (est): 230K **Privately Held**
SIC: 3536 Hoists, cranes & monorails

(G-13507)
CAPE PROSTHETICS-ORTHOTICS INC
Also Called: Novacare Prosthetics Orthotics
118 Airway Dr (62959-5841)
PHONE..................618 457-4692
David S Chernow, *President*
Richard Thiele, *Branch Mgr*
EMP: 5 **Privately Held**
SIC: 5999 3842 Artificial limbs; orthopedic & prosthesis applications; surgical appliances & supplies
HQ: Cape Prosthetics-Orthotics, Inc.
44 Doctors Park
Cape Girardeau MO 63703
573 334-6401

(G-13508)
CRISP CONTAINER CORPORATION
Also Called: Pepsi Midamerica
700 Skyline Dr (62959-4871)
PHONE..................618 998-0400
Harry Crisp, *President*
EMP: 55
SQ FT: 100,000
SALES (est): 9.4MM **Privately Held**
SIC: 2086 Carbonated soft drinks, bottled & canned

(G-13509)
DANIEL & SONS MECH CONTRS INC
105 Hilltop Ln (62959-7027)
P.O. Box 126, Carterville (62918-0126)
PHONE..................618 997-2822
Daniel Sloam, *President*
EMP: 10
SALES (est): 1.2MM **Privately Held**
SIC: 3444 Ducts, sheet metal

(G-13510)
FAST PRINT SHOP
501 W Deyoung St Ste 7 (62959-1628)
PHONE..................618 997-1976
Lisa Mc Raven, *Partner*
Mitch McRaven, *Partner*
EMP: 4
SQ FT: 1,200
SALES (est): 514.1K **Privately Held**
SIC: 2752 5943 2761 2759 Commercial printing, offset; office forms & supplies; manifold business forms; commercial printing

(G-13511)
GENERAL DYNAMICS CORPORATION
6658 Route 148 (62959-6389)
PHONE..................618 993-9207
EMP: 50
SALES (est): 48.5K **Privately Held**
SIC: 3483 Ammunition, except for small arms

(G-13512)
GENERAL DYNAMICS ORDNANCE
6658 Route 148 (62959-6389)
P.O. Box 278 (62959-0278)
PHONE..................618 985-8211
Mark Doss, *Engineer*
Hank Gross, *Marketing Mgr*
Kym Hubert, *Manager*
Teresa Webb, *Technology*
EMP: 235
SALES (corp-wide): 39.3B **Publicly Held**
WEB: www.gd-ots.com
SIC: 2892 3489 3483 Explosives; ordnance & accessories; ammunition, except for small arms
HQ: General Dynamics Ordnance And Tactical Systems, Inc.
11399 16th Ct N Ste 200
Saint Petersburg FL 33716
727 578-8100

(G-13513)
GL DOWNS INC
1805 Wolff Dr (62959-1427)
P.O. Box 1164, Benton (62812-5164)
PHONE..................618 993-9777
Glen L Downs II, *President*
EMP: 1
SQ FT: 2,000
SALES (est): 213.6K **Privately Held**
SIC: 5169 5087 5099 3299 Chemicals & allied products; janitors' supplies; signs, except electric; mica products

(G-13514)
HAUHINCO LP
Also Called: Tiesenbach
810 Skyline Dr (62959-4874)
PHONE..................618 993-5399
Bennie Manion, *Exec VP*
EMP: 20
SALES (corp-wide): 22.7MM **Privately Held**
WEB: www.hauhinco.com
SIC: 4011 4899 3823 3643 Railroads, line-haul operating; communication signal enhancement network system; industrial instrmnts msrmnt display/control process variable; current-carrying wiring devices; electronic generation equipment; relays & industrial controls
HQ: Hauhinco, L.P.
1325 Evans City Rd
Evans City PA 16033
724 789-7050

(G-13515)
HORIZON PUBLICATIONS INC (PA)
1120 N Carbon St Ste 100 (62959-1055)
PHONE..................618 993-1711
David Radler, *President*
Roland McBride, *CFO*
Daren Youngblood, *Executive*
EMP: 194 **EST:** 1997
SALES (est): 71.5MM **Privately Held**
WEB: www.horizonpublicationsinc.com
SIC: 2711 Newspapers, publishing & printing

(G-13516)
HORIZON PUBLICATIONS (2003) (PA)
1120 N Carbon St Ste 100 (62959-1055)
PHONE..................618 993-1711
David Radler, *President*
Roland McBride, *Exec VP*
Mark Kipnis, *Vice Pres*
EMP: 3
SQ FT: 7,000
SALES (est): 29MM **Privately Held**
SIC: 2711 Newspapers

(G-13517)
HPC OF PENNSYLVANIA INC
1120 N Carbon St Ste 100 (62959-1055)
PHONE..................618 993-1711
David Radler, *President*
Roland McBride, *Exec VP*
EMP: 100
SQ FT: 7,000
SALES (est): 2.8MM
SALES (corp-wide): 29MM **Privately Held**
SIC: 2711 Newspapers
PA: Horizon Publications (2003) Inc
1120 N Carbon St Ste 100
Marion IL 62959
618 993-1711

(G-13518)
ILLINOIS TOOL WORKS INC
Also Called: Diagraph MSP & ITW Company
5307 Meadowland Pkwy (62959-5893)
PHONE..................618 997-1716
Robert Quarles, *Branch Mgr*
EMP: 65
SQ FT: 66,000
SALES (corp-wide): 14.1B **Publicly Held**
SIC: 3953 3577 3565 3549 Marking devices; computer peripheral equipment; packaging machinery; metalworking machinery
PA: Illinois Tool Works Inc.
155 Harlem Ave
Glenview IL 60025
847 724-7500

(G-13519)
LEE ENTERPRISES INCORPORATED
Also Called: Southern Illinoisan
3000 W Deyoung St Ste 336 (62959-4893)
PHONE..................618 998-8499
Tom Woolf, *Manager*
EMP: 4
SALES (corp-wide): 509.8MM **Publicly Held**
SIC: 2711 Commercial printing & newspaper publishing combined
PA: Lee Enterprises, Incorporated
4600 E 53rd St
Davenport IA 52807
563 383-2100

(G-13520)
MACH MINING LLC
16468 Liberty School Rd (62959-7537)
PHONE..................618 983-3020
David Jude,
Maxine Jude, *Admin Sec*
EMP: 9
SALES (est): 634.5K **Privately Held**
SIC: 1241 Coal mining services

(G-13521)
MARION STAR
1205 Tower Square Plz (62959-2634)
PHONE..................618 997-7827
EMP: 3
SALES (est): 158.3K **Privately Held**
SIC: 2711 Newspapers: publishing only, not printed on site

(G-13522)
MINOVA USA INC
809 Skyline Dr (62959-4875)
PHONE..................618 993-2611
William Resnik, *Branch Mgr*
EMP: 52 **Privately Held**
WEB: www.minovausa.com
SIC: 2821 Plastics materials & resins
HQ: Minova Usa Inc.
150 Summer Ct
Georgetown KY 40324
502 863-6800

(G-13523)
ODUM CONCRETE PRODUCTS INC (PA)
1800 N Court St (62959-5433)
P.O. Box 248 (62959-0248)
PHONE..................618 993-6211
Tim Odum, *President*
EMP: 25 **EST:** 1921
SQ FT: 4,500
SALES (est): 11.6MM **Privately Held**
WEB: www.odumcp.com
SIC: 3273 Ready-mixed concrete

(G-13524)
PARKS INDUSTRIES LLC
Also Called: Hp2000 Apu
15460 Crabtree School Rd (62959-6420)
PHONE..................618 997-9608
L Dianne Parks, *Mng Member*
Gary Parks,
EMP: 10
SQ FT: 18,000
SALES: 1.7MM **Privately Held**
SIC: 3585 Compressors for refrigeration & air conditioning equipment

(G-13525)
PEPSI MIDAMERICA CO (PA)
2605 W Main St (62959-4932)
P.O. Box 1070 (62959-7570)
PHONE..................618 997-1377
Harry L Crisp III, *President*
Harry L Crisp II, *Chairman*
Gale Beachum, *Vice Pres*
Larry Chambers, *Vice Pres*

Keith Dickens, *Vice Pres*
EMP: 695
SQ FT: 312,000
SALES (est): 264.2MM **Privately Held**
WEB: www.pepsimidamerica.com
SIC: 2086 Carbonated soft drinks, bottled & canned

(G-13526)
PIECES OF LEARNING INC
1112 N Carbon St Unit A (62959-1075)
PHONE 618 964-9426
Tyler Young, *President*
EMP: 4
SQ FT: 6,400
SALES (est): 731.6K **Privately Held**
SIC: 2731 8748 7812 Books: publishing only; educational consultant; video tape production

(G-13527)
PINTSCH TIEFENBACH US INC
810 Skyline Dr (62959-4874)
PHONE 618 993-8513
Bennie Manion, *President*
EMP: 5
SALES (est): 607.5K **Privately Held**
SIC: 3679 7371 3743 Static power supply converters for electronic applications; computer software development & applications; railroad equipment; railroad locomotives & parts, electric or nonelectric

(G-13528)
PORTERVILLE RECORDER INC
1120 N Carbon St Ste 100 (62959-1055)
PHONE 559 784-5000
Melanie Walsh, *CEO*
EMP: 4 **EST:** 2013
SALES (est): 174.3K **Privately Held**
WEB: www.recorderonline.com
SIC: 2711 Newspapers: publishing only, not printed on site

(G-13529)
POS PLUS LLC
Also Called: Pos Plus Solutions
606 N Van Buren St (62959-2342)
P.O. Box 1907 (62959-8107)
PHONE 618 993-7587
Bob Satterfield,
EMP: 15
SQ FT: 10,000
SALES (est): 2.6MM **Privately Held**
SIC: 3577 3578 Magnetic ink & optical scanning devices; point-of-sale devices

(G-13530)
PRECISION MACHINE AND
410 N Pentecost Dr (62959)
PHONE 618 997-8795
Tony Burdin, *President*
EMP: 14
SALES (est): 1.8MM **Privately Held**
SIC: 3599 Machine shop, jobbing & repair

(G-13531)
PRO CABINETS INC
11123 Skyline Dr (62959-8380)
PHONE 618 993-0008
Cody Stacey, *President*
EMP: 1
SALES (est): 297.3K **Privately Held**
SIC: 2434 Wood kitchen cabinets

(G-13532)
READY MIX SOLUTIONS LLC
1800 N Court St (62959-5433)
P.O. Box 9 (62959-0009)
PHONE 618 889-6188
Tim Odum, *Principal*
EMP: 4
SALES (est): 349.2K **Privately Held**
WEB: www.rdymixsolutions.com
SIC: 3273 Ready-mixed concrete

(G-13533)
REVIEW
Also Called: Horizon, The
1120 N Carbon St Ste 100 (62959-1055)
P.O. Box 111 (62959-0111)
PHONE 618 997-2222
EMP: 4
SALES (est): 216.1K **Privately Held**
SIC: 2711 Newspapers-Publishing/Printing

(G-13534)
SHEW BROTHERS INC
Also Called: Ron Shew Welding & Fabricating
812 W Longstreet Rd (62959-5421)
PHONE 618 997-4414
Ronald D Shew, *President*
EMP: 9
SALES (est): 800K **Privately Held**
SIC: 3441 5084 3498 3444 Fabricated structural metal; welding machinery & equipment; fabricated pipe & fittings; sheet metalwork; fabricated plate work (boiler shop)

(G-13535)
SIGLEY PRINTING & OFF SUP CO
Also Called: Hill Printing and Office Sup
110 N Print Ave (62959-2412)
PHONE 618 997-5304
Rita Sigley, *President*
Earl Sigley, *Vice Pres*
Tim Nation, *Accounting Dir*
EMP: 6 **EST:** 1998
SQ FT: 4,000
SALES (est): 787.2K **Privately Held**
SIC: 2752 5943 2791 2789 Commercial printing, offset; office forms & supplies; typesetting; bookbinding & related work; commercial printing

(G-13536)
SOUTHERN IL RACEWAY
11682 Macie Dr. (62959-1386)
PHONE 618 201-0500
EMP: 3 **EST:** 2014
SALES (est): 112.2K **Privately Held**
WEB: www.southernillinoisraceway.org
SIC: 3644 Raceways

(G-13537)
SOUTHERN ILL HELICOPTERS LLC
2405 Black Diamond Dr (62959-5279)
PHONE 618 997-0101
William Rodney Cabaness, *Principal*
EMP: 2 **EST:** 2012
SALES (est): 228.2K **Privately Held**
SIC: 3721 Airplanes, fixed or rotary wing

(G-13538)
SOUTHERN ILLINOIS MINERS
1000 Miners Dr (62959-5080)
PHONE 618 969-8506
Kyle Bass, *Principal*
Joe Klinger, *Opers Staff*
William Leitner, *Opers Staff*
Will Niermann, *Opers Staff*
Heath Hooker, *Production*
EMP: 14
SALES (est): 1.6MM **Privately Held**
WEB: www.southernillinoisminers.com
SIC: 3949 Bases, baseball

(G-13539)
SOUTHERN ILLINOIS REDIMIX INC (PA)
11039 Skyline Dr (62959-8371)
PHONE 618 993-3600
Sherri Denny, *President*
Bret Denny, *Vice Pres*
Jeff Denny, *Treasurer*
EMP: 10
SQ FT: 1,100
SALES (est): 950.8K **Privately Held**
SIC: 3273 5211 3272 Ready-mixed concrete; masonry materials & supplies; concrete products, precast

(G-13540)
TIME REC PUBG BBBY MRTIN PRDCT
2537 Wards Mill Rd (62959-8621)
PHONE 618 996-3803
Bobby Martin, *President*
Tabitha Martin, *Exec VP*
Marjalea Martin, *Vice Pres*
EMP: 3
SALES (est): 217.6K **Privately Held**
SIC: 7313 3089 7929 Radio, television, publisher representatives; cases, plastic; musical entertainers; gospel singers; popular music groups or artists

(G-13541)
TONDINIS WRECKER SERVICE
2200 S Court St (62959-3630)
PHONE 618 997-9884
Kevin Pondini, *Owner*
Kevin Tondini, *Owner*
EMP: 4
SALES (est): 400.5K **Privately Held**
WEB: www.tondinistowing.com
SIC: 7549 3713 Towing service, automotive; automobile wrecker truck bodies

(G-13542)
WARREN OIL MGT CO IL LLC
201 N 4th St (62959-4704)
PHONE 618 997-5951
▲ **EMP:** 3
SALES (est): 210K **Privately Held**
SIC: 1311 Crude Petroleum/Natural Gas Production

Marissa
St. Clair County

(G-13543)
MIDWEST METALS INC
1296 Green Diamond Rd (62257-2518)
PHONE 618 295-3444
Vicky L Neuwirth, *President*
EMP: 4
SQ FT: 8,400
SALES (est): 607K **Privately Held**
SIC: 3441 Fabricated structural metal

(G-13544)
QUAD-COUNTY READY MIX CORP
655 Wshngton Cnty Line Rd (62257)
PHONE 618 295-3000
Amy Birkalo, *Principal*
EMP: 6
SALES (corp-wide): 16.1MM **Privately Held**
SIC: 5211 3273 Sand & gravel; ready-mixed concrete
PA: Quad-County Ready Mix Corp.
300 W 12th St
Okawville IL 62271
618 243-6430

Mark
Putnam County

(G-13545)
MARK DEVELOPMENT CORPORATION
Mennie Dr Rr 71 (61340)
PHONE 815 339-2226
Hubert J Mennie, *President*
Cheryl Mennie, *Admin Sec*
EMP: 180
SQ FT: 200,000
SALES (est): 17.2MM **Privately Held**
SIC: 3469 Machine parts, stamped or pressed metal

(G-13546)
MENNIES MACHINE COMPANY (PA)
Also Called: MMC Armory
Mennie Dr Mark Rr 71 (61340)
P.O. Box 110 (61340-0110)
PHONE 815 339-2226
David Mennie, *Vice Pres*
Mark Stengel, *Vice Pres*
Joe Smoode, *Mfg Mgr*
Ron Lindner, *Materials Mgr*
Jacob Cimei, *Purch Mgr*
▲ **EMP:** 170
SALES (est): 74.2MM **Privately Held**
SIC: 3544 8742 Special dies, tools, jigs & fixtures; materials mgmt. (purchasing, handling, inventory) consultant

(G-13547)
TAYLOR MADE MACHINING INC
W Mark Indus Park Rr 71 (61340)
P.O. Box 177 (61340-0177)
PHONE 815 339-6267
Frank Niewinski, *President*

Julie Niewinski, *Admin Sec*
EMP: 5
SQ FT: 6,300
SALES (est): 676.7K **Privately Held**
SIC: 3599 Machine shop, jobbing & repair

Markham
Cook County

(G-13548)
EVANGERS DOG AND CAT FD CO INC
2210 W 162nd St (60428-5604)
PHONE 847 537-0102
Holly Sher, *President*
Joel Sher, *Vice Pres*
Cynthia Stoner, *Manager*
◆ **EMP:** 45 **EST:** 1935
SQ FT: 15,000
SALES (est): 14MM **Privately Held**
WEB: www.evangersdogfood.com
SIC: 2047 Dog & cat food

(G-13549)
NUTRIPACK LLC
2210 W 162nd St (60428-5604)
PHONE 847 537-0102
Andrew Wasmuth, *Principal*
EMP: 3
SALES (est): 206K **Privately Held**
SIC: 2047 Dog & cat food

(G-13550)
RACO STEEL COMPANY
2100 W 163rd Pl (60428-5649)
PHONE 708 339-2958
Denny Erickson, *President*
David B Daly, *President*
Dennis Erickson, *President*
Diane Rogers, *General Mgr*
Robert Bruce, *Vice Pres*
◆ **EMP:** 50 **EST:** 1953
SQ FT: 120,000
SALES (est): 14.3MM **Privately Held**
WEB: www.racosteel.com
SIC: 3312 5051 3544 Stainless steel; metals service centers & offices; special dies, tools, jigs & fixtures

(G-13551)
RR MULCH AND SOIL LLC
3900 W 167th St (60428-5307)
PHONE 708 596-7200
Christy Webber, *Mng Member*
EMP: 4
SALES (est): 942.4K **Privately Held**
SIC: 5039 2499 5191 5261 Soil erosion control fabrics; mulch, wood & bark; soil, potting & planting; top soil; blocks, concrete: landscape or retaining wall

Maroa
Macon County

(G-13552)
HARBACH GILLAN & NIXON INC
Also Called: Maroa AG
40 Ag Rd (61756)
P.O. Box 679 (61756-0679)
PHONE 217 794-5117
Tim Wolfe, *Manager*
EMP: 5
SALES (corp-wide): 13.7MM **Privately Held**
SIC: 5191 2873 Fertilizer & fertilizer materials; nitrogenous fertilizers
PA: Harbach, Gillan & Nixon, Inc.
618 W Van Buren St
Clinton IL 61727
217 935-8378

(G-13553)
MASHBURN WELL DRILLING
214 N Pine St (61756-9240)
P.O. Box 45 (61756-0045)
PHONE 217 794-3728
Robert Edwin Mashburn, *Owner*
EMP: 2

(G-13554)
PERFORMANCE WELDING LLC
10333 W Washington St Rd (61756-9116)
P.O. Box 388 (61756-0388)
PHONE....................................217 412-5722
Grey Hale Jr,
EMP: 2
SALES (est): 275.6K Privately Held
SIC: 7692 Welding repair

Marseilles
Lasalle County

(G-13555)
GLEN-GERY CORPORATION
1401 Broadway St (61341-2067)
P.O. Box 306 (61341-0306)
PHONE....................................815 795-6911
Eric Efchleman, CFO
EMP: 78 Privately Held
SIC: 3271 5211 Brick, concrete; brick
HQ: Glen-Gery Corporation
1166 Spring St
Reading PA 19610
610 374-4011

(G-13556)
ICON POWER ROLLER INC
2882 E 24th Rd (61341-9624)
P.O. Box 216 (61341-0216)
PHONE....................................630 545-2345
Eunice Kim, Principal
▲ EMP: 20
SALES (est): 1.5MM Privately Held
SIC: 3469 Machine parts, stamped or pressed metal

(G-13557)
ILLINI PRECAST
2649 E Us Highway 6 (61341-9401)
PHONE....................................815 795-6161
William Hubbard, Principal
EMP: 2
SALES (est): 276.1K Privately Held
WEB: www.illiniprecast.com
SIC: 3272 Concrete products, precast

(G-13558)
INVENERGY
2192 E 25th Rd (61341-9752)
PHONE....................................815 795-4964
Mark Geibel, Principal
EMP: 6
SALES (est): 917.8K Privately Held
SIC: 3511 Turbines & turbine generator sets

(G-13559)
JOINT FIELD SERVICES INC
1020 Broadway St (61341-2038)
PHONE....................................815 795-3714
George R Sandora, President
Tony Sandora, Vice Pres
EMP: 40
SQ FT: 35,000
SALES (est): 1.7MM
SALES (corp-wide): 6.6MM Privately Held
SIC: 7692 Welding repair
PA: Mti Power Services, Inc.
1020 Broadway St
Marseilles IL 61341
815 795-3714

(G-13560)
MACHINE TECHNOLOGY INC (PA)
Also Called: Machine Tech Services
1020 Broadway St (61341-2038)
PHONE....................................815 795-6818
George Sandorat, President
Tony Sandorat, Vice Pres
Joanna Button, QC Mgr
John Geis, VP Bus Dvlpt
J Cox, Assistant
EMP: 15

SALES (est): 2.4MM Privately Held
SIC: 3541 3599 5084 Machine tools, metal cutting type; machine shop, jobbing & repair; machine tools & accessories

(G-13561)
NUCOR TUBULAR PRODUCTS INC
1201 Broadway St (61341-2000)
PHONE....................................815 795-4400
John Koschwanez, Branch Mgr
EMP: 63
SALES (corp-wide): 22.5B Publicly Held
SIC: 3317 Steel pipe & tubes
HQ: Nucor Tubular Products, Inc.
6226 W 74th St
Chicago IL 60638
708 496-0380

(G-13562)
P & H PATTERN INC
225 Lincoln St (61341-1904)
PHONE....................................815 795-2449
Michael Garrison, President
Vicky Garrison, Vice Pres
EMP: 4 EST: 1962
SQ FT: 3,000
SALES (est): 300K Privately Held
SIC: 3543 Industrial patterns

(G-13563)
PCS PHOSPHATE COMPANY INC
2660 E Us Highway 6 (61341-9401)
P.O. Box 88 (61341-0088)
PHONE....................................815 795-5111
Robert Startzer, Manager
EMP: 38
SALES (corp-wide): 20B Privately Held
SIC: 2048 5191 Feed supplements; animal feeds
HQ: Pcs Phosphate Company, Inc.
1101 Skokie Blvd Ste 400
Northbrook IL 60062
847 849-4200

(G-13564)
RIVER REDI MIX INC
2195 E Bluff St (61341-9200)
PHONE....................................815 795-2025
Michael Dearth, President
Steven Dearth, Corp Secy
EMP: 7
SALES (est): 500K Privately Held
SIC: 3273 Ready-mixed concrete

Marshall
Clark County

(G-13565)
BIG CREEK FORESTRY & LOGGING L
75 Archer Ave (62441-1065)
PHONE....................................217 822-8282
Mark Strait, Principal
EMP: 3
SALES (est): 206.1K Privately Held
SIC: 2411 Logging camps & contractors

(G-13566)
CHARLES INDUSTRIES LLC
Also Called: Coil Sales and Manufacturing
16265 E National Rd (62441-4287)
P.O. Box 319 (62441-0319)
PHONE....................................217 826-2318
Debbie Johnson, Vice Pres
Trebbie Thome, Engineer
Tim Vencel, Engineer
Terry Gurley, Branch Mgr
EMP: 100
SQ FT: 44,000
SALES (corp-wide): 8.2B Publicly Held
SIC: 3661 8741 3677 3621 Telephones & telephone apparatus; administrative management; electronic coils, transformers & other inductors; motors & generators; nonferrous wiredrawing & insulating
HQ: Charles Industries, Llc
1450 American Ln Fl 20
Schaumburg IL 60173
847 806-6300

(G-13567)
CLASSIC METAL VAULTS
806 N 2nd St (62441-1087)
P.O. Box 10 (62441-0010)
PHONE....................................217 826-6302
EMP: 5
SALES (est): 388.9K Privately Held
SIC: 3272 Burial vaults, concrete or pre-cast terrazzo

(G-13568)
CONTRACTORS CONCRETE
Also Called: Contractor Concrete
16996 N Quality Lime Rd (62441-4443)
PHONE....................................217 826-2290
EMP: 4 Privately Held
WEB: www.cciredimix.com
SIC: 5211 3273 Cement; ready-mixed concrete
PA: Contractors Concrete
2604 Harmon Ave 4
Effingham IL

(G-13569)
CUSTOM FILMS INC
1400 Archer Ave (62441-4437)
PHONE....................................217 826-2326
EMP: 19
SQ FT: 10,000
SALES: 2MM Privately Held
SIC: 2821 3089 3083 3082 Mfg Plstc Material/Resin Mfg Plastic Products Mfg Lamnatd Plstc Plates Mfg Plstc Profile Shapes Mfg Unsupport Plstc Film

(G-13570)
DORIC PRODUCTS INC (PA)
201 W Us Highway 40 (62441)
P.O. Box 10 (62441-0010)
PHONE....................................217 826-6302
Steven F Vincent, President
Michael C Crummitt, Vice Pres
Kelly Grooms, Plant Mgr
James R Wiens, Treasurer
Denise Cox, Accountant
EMP: 71
SQ FT: 44,000
SALES (est): 12.6MM Privately Held
WEB: www.doric-vaults.com
SIC: 3272 Burial vaults, concrete or pre-cast terrazzo

(G-13571)
G & S ASPHALT INC
16870 N Quality Lime Rd (62441-4442)
PHONE....................................217 826-2421
Gary Peak, President
Nancy Peak, Admin Sec
EMP: 12
SALES: 1.2MM Privately Held
WEB: www.gandsasphaltinc.com
SIC: 1611 2951 Resurfacing contractor; asphalt paving mixtures & blocks

(G-13572)
HEARTLAND LABELS INC
17135 N Quality Lime Rd (62441-4460)
P.O. Box 299 (62441-0299)
PHONE....................................217 826-8324
James J Withrow, President
Janice Withrow, Treasurer
Daniel Burgess, Broker
Phil Freeman, Sales Staff
Nikki Fritchie, Manager
EMP: 20
SALES (est): 1MM Privately Held
SIC: 2759 Labels & seals: printing

(G-13573)
KEMPER INDUSTRIES
1017 Clarksville Rd (62441-3822)
P.O. Box 117 (62441-0117)
PHONE....................................217 826-5712
Lloyd Kemper, Owner
EMP: 6
SQ FT: 4,800
SALES (est): 636.2K Privately Held
SIC: 3599 3441 7692 3444 Machine shop, jobbing & repair; fabricated structural metal; welding repair; sheet metalwork; manufactured hardware (general); rubber & plastics hose & beltings

(G-13574)
KIMCO USA INC
Also Called: Kimco U S A
118 E Trefz Dr (62441-3974)
PHONE....................................800 788-1133
Max Coffey, President
Kimberly Coffey, Corp Secy
EMP: 12
SALES: 4MM Privately Held
SIC: 3535 Conveyors & conveying equipment

(G-13575)
MJ SNYDER IRONWORKS INC
15640 E National Rd (62441)
P.O. Box 357 (62441-0357)
PHONE....................................217 826-6440
Julie Snyder, President
Abigail Snyder, Vice Pres
Mark Snyder, Treasurer
EMP: 9
SALES (est): 484K Privately Held
SIC: 7699 3531 3446 3444 Industrial machinery & equipment repair; construction machinery; architectural metalwork; sheet metalwork; fabricated plate work (boiler shop); fabricated structural metal

(G-13576)
PEPSI MID AMERICA
202 Vine St (62441-1848)
PHONE....................................217 826-8118
Kenneth Cannady, Principal
EMP: 5
SALES (est): 270.8K Privately Held
SIC: 2086 Carbonated soft drinks, bottled & canned

(G-13577)
QUALITY LIME COMPANY
Also Called: Quality Line
14915 N Quality Lime Rd (62441)
P.O. Box 439 (62441-0439)
PHONE....................................217 826-2343
Jerald Tarble, President
John Tarble, Vice Pres
EMP: 15 EST: 1937
SQ FT: 1,000
SALES: 5.2MM Privately Held
WEB: www.qualitylimeco.com
SIC: 1422 Limestones, ground

(G-13578)
STROHM NEWSPAPERS INC
Also Called: Marshall Advocate
610 Archer Ave (62441-1268)
P.O. Box 433 (62441-0433)
PHONE....................................217 826-3600
Gary Strohm, President
Melody Strohm, Corp Secy
EMP: 2
SALES (est): 328K Privately Held
SIC: 2711 Newspapers, publishing & printing; newspapers: publishing only, not printed on site

(G-13579)
YARGUS MANUFACTURING INC
Also Called: Agi-Yargus
12285 E Main St (62441-4127)
P.O. Box 238 (62441-0238)
PHONE....................................217 826-6352
Larry D Yargus, President
Samuel Pendleton, Sales Staff
▼ EMP: 26
SQ FT: 80,000
SALES: 15MM
SALES (corp-wide): 747.8MM Privately Held
SIC: 3523 Fertilizing machinery, farm
PA: Ag Growth International Inc
198 Commerce Dr
Winnipeg MB R3P 0
204 489-1855

(G-13580)
ZF ACTIVE SAFETY & ELEC US LLC
Also Called: ZF TRW Active Pssive Sfety Tec
902 S 2nd St (62441-1854)
PHONE....................................217 826-3011
Ward Litchfield, Safety Mgr
Marilyn Trefz, Purch Agent
Chuck Barnhart, Engineer
Alexander Fraser Jr, Engineer
Jeffrey Hook, Engineer

GEOGRAPHIC SECTION

Mascoutah - St. Clair County (G-13606)

EMP: 500
SALES (corp-wide): 216.2K Privately Held
WEB: www.zf.com
SIC: 3469 3679 Metal stampings; electronic loads & power supplies
HQ: Zf Active Safety & Electronics Us Llc
12001 Tech Center Dr
Livonia MI 48150
734 855-2600

Martinsville
Clark County

(G-13581)
BEEMAN & SONS INC
5815 E Snake Trail Rd (62442-2635)
PHONE.....................217 232-4268
Larry L Beeman, *President*
EMP: 15
SALES (est): 1.8MM Privately Held
SIC: 2411 Logging

(G-13582)
COLORKRAFT ROLL PRODUCTS INC (PA)
1 Harry Glynn Dr (62442-2247)
P.O. Box N (62442-0169)
PHONE.....................217 382-4967
Scott Ware, *CEO*
Tom Hoffman, *President*
April Wade, *Manager*
▲ EMP: 20
SQ FT: 120,000
SALES (est): 3.3MM Privately Held
SIC: 2621 Paper mills

(G-13583)
E ROWE FOUNDRY & MACHINE CO
147 W Cumberland St (62442-1192)
P.O. Box 130 (62442-0130)
PHONE.....................217 382-4135
Ellen Norton, *President*
Larry Norton, *Vice Pres*
Kelly Norton, *Treasurer*
Tony Williams, *Admin Sec*
EMP: 87 EST: 1898
SQ FT: 107,000
SALES (est): 18.1MM Privately Held
WEB: www.rowefoundry.com
SIC: 3596 3321 Scales & balances, except laboratory; gray iron castings

(G-13584)
EVERGREEN MANUFACTURING INC
1 Harry Glynn Dr (62442-2247)
PHONE.....................217 382-5108
Scott Ware, *President*
Tom Hoffman, *Vice Pres*
EMP: 25 EST: 2008
SALES (est): 4.1MM Privately Held
WEB: www.napkinbands.com
SIC: 2676 Towels, napkins & tissue paper products

(G-13585)
HELENA AGRI-ENTERPRISES LLC
9666 E Angling Rd (62442-2837)
PHONE.....................217 382-4241
Michael Zachary, *Branch Mgr*
EMP: 15 Privately Held
SIC: 2819 Industrial inorganic chemicals
HQ: Helena Agri-Enterprises, Llc
255 Schilling Blvd # 300
Collierville TN 38017
901 761-0050

(G-13586)
MID-ILLINOIS CONCRETE INC
Also Called: Clark County Ready Mix
1001 N Ridgelawn Rd (62442-2548)
P.O. Box 386 (62442-0386)
PHONE.....................217 382-6650
Floyd Spraker, *Branch Mgr*
EMP: 4
SALES (corp-wide): 17.2MM Privately Held
WEB: www.mid-illinoisconcrete.com
SIC: 3272 3273 Concrete products, pre-cast; ready-mixed concrete
PA: Mid-Illinois Concrete, Inc.
1805 S 4th St
Effingham IL
217 342-2498

(G-13587)
PAP-R PRODUCTS COMPANY (PA)
Also Called: Counting House
1 Harry Glynn Dr (62442-2247)
PHONE.....................800 637-4937
K Scott Ware, *President*
Clayton Huckaba, *Engineer*
Jerome G Williams, *CFO*
Jerome Williams, *CFO*
Lori Turner, *Human Res Mgr*
▲ EMP: 100 EST: 1964
SALES (est): 32.9MM Privately Held
WEB: www.paprproducts.com
SIC: 2679 2752 Wrappers, paper (unprinted): made from purchased material; commercial printing, lithographic

(G-13588)
PAP-R-TAINER LLC
1 Harry Glynn Dr (62442-2247)
PHONE.....................217 382-4141
Dave Walters,
Scott Ware,
EMP: 2
SALES (est): 281.2K Privately Held
SIC: 2752 Commercial printing, lithographic

Martinton
Iroquois County

(G-13589)
ARCHER-DANIELS-MIDLAND COMPANY
Also Called: ADM
104 S 1st (60951)
P.O. Box 1470, Decatur (62525-1820)
PHONE.....................815 428-7513
Ike Lambert, *Branch Mgr*
EMP: 4
SQ FT: 1,000
SALES (corp-wide): 64.6B Publicly Held
WEB: www.adm.com
SIC: 2041 Flour & other grain mill products
PA: Archer-Daniels-Midland Company
77 W Wacker Dr Ste 4600
Chicago IL 60601
312 634-8100

Maryville
Madison County

(G-13590)
CFT PERFORMANCE INC
18 Schiber Ct (62062-5840)
PHONE.....................618 781-3981
Joshua Chapman, *Principal*
EMP: 5
SALES (est): 599.8K Privately Held
SIC: 3714 Motor vehicle parts & accessories

(G-13591)
KURTS CARSTAR COLLISION CTR
1 Mueller Dr (62062-6854)
PHONE.....................618 345-4519
Kurt Mueller, *Principal*
Kurt Nathan Mueller, *Principal*
EMP: 14
SALES (est): 1.1MM Privately Held
WEB: www.auto-body-maryville-il.com
SIC: 7532 3713 3711 Body shop, automotive; truck & bus bodies; automobile bodies, passenger car, not including engine, etc.

(G-13592)
NEW STEP ORTHOTIC LAB INC
Also Called: Allison's Comfort Shoes
14 Schiber Ct (62062-5625)
P.O. Box 669 (62062-0669)
PHONE.....................618 208-4444
Joshua Allison, *President*
EMP: 13
SQ FT: 4,752
SALES: 875.6K Privately Held
SIC: 5661 3842 Shoes, orthopedic; supports: abdominal, ankle, arch, kneecap, etc.

Mascoutah
St. Clair County

(G-13593)
BETTER NEWS PAPERS INC (PA)
Also Called: Mascoutah Herald
314 E Church St Ste 1 (62258-2100)
PHONE.....................618 566-8282
Cleon Birkemeyer, *Ch of Bd*
Greg Hoskins, *President*
EMP: 9
SQ FT: 4,500
SALES (est): 2.6MM Privately Held
SIC: 2711 7331 Newspapers, publishing & printing; mailing service

(G-13594)
BOBS TSHIRT STORE
419 Jackson St (62258-1043)
P.O. Box 63 (62258-0063)
PHONE.....................618 567-1730
Robert Schubert, *Owner*
EMP: 1
SQ FT: 2,000
SALES (est): 300K Privately Held
SIC: 2759 Screen printing

(G-13595)
CABLOFIL INC
Also Called: Cablofil/Legrand
8319 State Route 4 (62258-2824)
PHONE.....................618 566-3230
Timothy Place, *President*
Robert Julian, *Vice Pres*
Nicholas Hanna, *Mfg Spvr*
Joseph Healy, *Mfg Staff*
James Laperriere, *Treasurer*
▲ EMP: 500 EST: 1997
SQ FT: 80,000
SALES (est): 117.6MM
SALES (corp-wide): 27.3MM Privately Held
WEB: www.legrand.us
SIC: 3443 Cable trays, metal plate
HQ: Legrand Holding, Inc.
60 Woodlawn St
West Hartford CT 06110
860 233-6251

(G-13596)
CONTINENTAL TIRE AMERICAS LLC
10075 Progress Pkwy (62258-2825)
PHONE.....................618 246-2585
EMP: 5
SALES (corp-wide): 49.2B Privately Held
SIC: 3011 Tires & inner tubes
HQ: Continental Tire The Americas, Llc
1830 Macmillan Park Dr
Fort Mill SC 29707
800 847-3349

(G-13597)
GREY SHIRT GUYS LLC
419 Jackson St (62258-1043)
P.O. Box 63 (62258-0063)
PHONE.....................800 787-4478
Robert Schubert,
EMP: 1
SALES: 500K Privately Held
SIC: 2261 5699 Printing of cotton broadwoven fabrics; T-shirts, custom printed

(G-13598)
HASSEBROCK ASPHALT SEALING
111 W Poplar St (62258-1312)
PHONE.....................618 566-7214
EMP: 4 EST: 1998
SALES (est): 200K Privately Held
SIC: 2951 Mfg Asphalt Mixtures/Blocks

(G-13599)
HERALD PUBLICATIONS (PA)
Also Called: Fairview Heights Tribune
314 E Church St Ste 1 (62258-2100)
P.O. Box C (62258-0189)
PHONE.....................618 566-8282
Greg Hoskins, *President*
EMP: 14
SQ FT: 4,320
SALES (est): 310K Privately Held
SIC: 2711 7331 Newspapers, publishing & printing; mailing service

(G-13600)
JOSEPH B KRISHER
9950 Drum Hill Rd (62258-4532)
PHONE.....................618 677-2016
Joseph Krisher, *Principal*
EMP: 4
SALES (est): 307.2K Privately Held
SIC: 2448 Pallets, wood & wood with metal

(G-13601)
KASKASKIA MECHANICAL INSUL CO
6606 State Route 15 (62258-5128)
PHONE.....................618 768-4526
Jill Oeltjen, *President*
EMP: 6
SALES (est): 660K Privately Held
SIC: 2611 Mechanical pulp, including groundwood & thermomechanical

(G-13602)
MARTIN STEEL FABRICATION INC
508 S Railway St (62258-2334)
PHONE.....................618 410-7066
Martin M Athy, *President*
Tim Botkin, *Prdtn Mgr*
EMP: 8
SQ FT: 5,000
SALES (est): 1.6MM Privately Held
SIC: 3441 Fabricated structural metal

(G-13603)
MID-WEST MILLWORK WHOLESALE
9 W Green St (62258-2037)
PHONE.....................618 407-5940
Harry Horstman, *Owner*
EMP: 2
SALES (est): 417.9K Privately Held
SIC: 5031 3541 Millwork; milling machines

(G-13604)
MIDWEST RECUMBENT BICYCLES
Also Called: Mwrbents
109 W George St (62258-2310)
PHONE.....................618 343-1885
Carolee Wright, *Owner*
EMP: 3
SALES: 154K Privately Held
SIC: 3751 Motorcycles, bicycles & parts

(G-13605)
N W HORIZONTAL BORING
8100 Summerfield South Rd (62258-3010)
PHONE.....................618 566-9117
R Friederich, *CEO*
EMP: 4
SALES (est): 519.3K Privately Held
SIC: 3541 Drilling & boring machines

(G-13606)
PURCHASING SERVICES LTD INC
602 Industrial St (62258-1724)
PHONE.....................618 566-8100
Tracey Vernier, *President*
EMP: 25
SQ FT: 10,000
SALES: 900K Privately Held
SIC: 3565 Packaging machinery

Mascoutah - St. Clair County (G-13607)

(G-13607)
TRIPLE B MANUFACTURING CO INC
620 Industrial St (62258)
P.O. Box 139 (62258-0139)
PHONE..................618 566-2888
Steve Beimfohr, *President*
Janis Beimfohr, *Corp Secy*
Jeff Beimfour, *Corp Secy*
EMP: 3
SQ FT: 7,500
SALES (est): 300K **Privately Held**
WEB: www.triplebtrailers.com
SIC: **3799** 3537 Trailers & trailer equipment; industrial trucks & tractors

Mason
Effingham County

(G-13608)
MARVIN SUCKOW
5267 N 700th St (62443-2001)
PHONE..................618 483-5570
Marvin Suckow, *Owner*
EMP: 4 EST: 1927
SALES (est): 402.2K **Privately Held**
SIC: **0115** 0116 2421 Corn; soybeans; sawmills & planing mills, general

(G-13609)
RUNGE EQUIPMENT INC
2370 E 475th Ave (62443-2134)
PHONE..................618 322-5628
Jason Runge, *Owner*
EMP: 5 EST: 2013
SALES (est): 245.7K **Privately Held**
SIC: **3531** Forestry related equipment

Mason City
Mason County

(G-13610)
CONTRACTORS READY-MIX INC
Also Called: Curry Ready Mix of Mason City
210 E Elm St (62664-1435)
PHONE..................217 482-5530
Bob Harrison, *Manager*
EMP: 4 **Privately Held**
SIC: **3273** 3496 3281 3271 Ready-mixed concrete; miscellaneous fabricated wire products; cut stone & stone products; concrete block & brick; construction sand & gravel
PA: Contractor's Ready-Mix Inc
601 S Kickapoo St
Lincoln IL 62656

(G-13611)
DARLING INGREDIENTS INC
1000 S Main St (62664-1522)
P.O. Box 192 (62664-0192)
PHONE..................217 482-3261
Evan Weidhuner-Birch, *Buyer*
Robert L Griffin, *Branch Mgr*
EMP: 50
SALES (corp-wide): 3.3B **Publicly Held**
WEB: www.darlingii.com
SIC: **2077** 4953 2992 2079 Meat meal & tankage, except as animal feed; grease rendering, inedible; refuse systems; lubricating oils & greases; edible fats & oils
PA: Darling Ingredients Inc.
5601 N Macarthur Blvd
Irving TX 75038
972 717-0300

(G-13612)
MASON CITY BANNER TIMES
Also Called: W H A M
126 N Tonica St (62664-1115)
P.O. Box 71 (62664-0071)
PHONE..................217 482-3276
Lois Lee Rickard, *Owner*
EMP: 14 EST: 1920
SALES (est): 530.5K **Privately Held**
WEB: www.masoncityillinois.org
SIC: **2711** 2791 2789 2759 Job printing & newspaper publishing combined; typesetting; bookbinding & related work; commercial printing; commercial printing, lithographic

(G-13613)
RICKARD PUBLISHING
126 N Tonica St (62664-1115)
P.O. Box 71 (62664-0071)
PHONE..................217 482-3276
Lois Rickard, *Owner*
EMP: 15
SALES (est): 793.1K **Privately Held**
SIC: **2741** Miscellaneous publishing

Matherville
Mercer County

(G-13614)
BRANCHFIELD CASTING INC (PA)
2580 130th Ave (61263)
P.O. Box 116, Galva (61434-0116)
PHONE..................309 932-2278
Theodore B Hopping, *President*
D Mark Compton, *Corp Secy*
James B Hopping, *Vice Pres*
EMP: 6
SQ FT: 5,800
SALES (est): 663.8K **Privately Held**
WEB: www.branchfield.net
SIC: **3321** 3325 3341 Gray iron castings; alloy steel castings, except investment; secondary nonferrous metals

(G-13615)
SLAVISH INC
309 1st St (61263-9010)
P.O. Box 641 (61263-0641)
PHONE..................309 754-8233
Paul Slavish, *President*
Kristen Slavish, *Vice Pres*
EMP: 5 EST: 1940
SQ FT: 5,000
SALES (est): 899.4K **Privately Held**
SIC: **3272** Burial vaults, concrete or precast terrazzo; septic tanks, concrete

Matteson
Cook County

(G-13616)
AFFECTIONATELY YOURS ENT
609 Old Meadow Rd (60443-1335)
PHONE..................708 275-6333
Pamela P Mercer, *Owner*
EMP: 3
SALES (est): 201K **Privately Held**
WEB: www.affectionatelyyoursenterprises.com
SIC: **2741** Miscellaneous publishing

(G-13617)
AJS MINISTRY
632 Primrose Cir (60443-1720)
PHONE..................773 403-4166
EMP: 3
SALES (est): 98.7K **Privately Held**
WEB: www.ajsministry.com
SIC: **2741** Miscellaneous publishing

(G-13618)
ANDREA AND ME AND ME TOO
4206 Lindenwood Dr 1ne (60443-1686)
PHONE..................708 955-3850
Ann Finney, *Owner*
EMP: 5
SALES (est): 222.9K **Privately Held**
SIC: **2389** Apparel & accessories

(G-13619)
BATTERY SALES INC
5545 Miller Circle Dr (60443-1482)
PHONE..................708 489-6645
Thomas Hardiman, *President*
Kenneth Sova, *Admin Sec*
EMP: 2
SALES (est): 223.6K **Privately Held**
SIC: **3691** 5063 5531 Storage batteries; batteries; batteries, automotive & truck

(G-13620)
BRITE ONE INC
21649 Richmond Rd (60443-2615)
PHONE..................708 481-8005
Kevin Zara, *President*
EMP: 3
SALES (est): 175.8K **Privately Held**
SIC: **3471** Cleaning, polishing & finishing

(G-13621)
CREED GROUP LLC
66 Kenneth St (60443-3118)
PHONE..................708 261-8387
Gaila Charles,
EMP: 5
SALES (est): 250K **Privately Held**
SIC: **1389** Construction, repair & dismantling services

(G-13622)
CUSTOM GOLF BY TANIS
Also Called: Tanis Custom Golf
21750 Main St Unit 17 (60443-3717)
PHONE..................708 481-4433
Richard L Tanis, *President*
EMP: 3
SQ FT: 900
SALES (est): 291.5K **Privately Held**
SIC: **3949** 5941 7699 Golf equipment; golf goods & equipment; golf club & equipment repair

(G-13623)
E & H GRAPHIC SERVICE INC
21750 Main St Unit 21 (60443-3716)
PHONE..................708 748-5656
Errol Outarsingh, *President*
EMP: 2 EST: 1982
SALES (est): 250K **Privately Held**
SIC: **2759** 7699 2791 2789 Screen printing; industrial machinery & equipment repair; typesetting; bookbinding & related work; commercial printing, lithographic

(G-13624)
HANGER INC
Also Called: Hanger Clinic
4525 Lincoln Hwy (60443-2318)
PHONE..................708 679-1006
EMP: 16
SALES (corp-wide): 1.1B **Publicly Held**
SIC: **3842** Prosthetic appliances
PA: Hanger, Inc.
10910 Domain Dr Ste 300
Austin TX 78758
512 777-3800

(G-13625)
IMAGINE THAT CANDLE CO
4107 Applewood Ln (60443-1902)
PHONE..................708 481-6370
Joseph L Franklin, *Principal*
EMP: 3
SALES (est): 167K **Privately Held**
SIC: **3999** Candles

(G-13626)
KONZEN CHEMICALS INC
Also Called: Kci Chemical
4248 Oakwood Ln (60443-1923)
PHONE..................708 878-7636
Bernard Konzen, *President*
James Konzen, *Vice Pres*
Mark Konzen, *Vice Pres*
Mark R Konzen, *Vice Pres*
EMP: 18
SQ FT: 4,000
SALES (est): 3.5MM **Privately Held**
WEB: www.kcichemicals.com
SIC: **2992** 2819 Oils & greases, blending & compounding; industrial inorganic chemicals

(G-13627)
OAK TECHNICAL LLC (PA)
600 Holiday Plaza Dr # 130 (60443-2241)
PHONE..................931 455-7011
Nathan Buchanan, *President*
▲ EMP: 6
SALES (est): 3.4MM **Privately Held**
SIC: **3089** Gloves or mittens, plastic

(G-13628)
SENSIENT TECHNOLOGIES CORP
810 Carnation Ln (60443-1946)
PHONE..................708 481-0910
EMP: 37
SALES (corp-wide): 1.3B **Publicly Held**
SIC: **2087** 2099 Mfg Food Flavors & Colors Yeast Dehydrated Products And Vegetable Protein Extract
PA: Sensient Technologies Corporation
777 E Wisconsin Ave # 1100
Milwaukee WI 53202
414 271-6755

(G-13629)
SPIKE NANOTECH INC
1008 Donnington Dr (60443-2290)
PHONE..................847 504-6273
Patty Fu-Giles, *Principal*
Cary Giles, *Admin Sec*
EMP: 3
SALES (est): 174K **Privately Held**
SIC: **2844** Toilet preparations

Mattoon
Coles County

(G-13630)
ANAMET ELECTRICAL INC
1000 Broadway Ave E (61938-4677)
P.O. Box 39 (61938-0039)
PHONE..................217 234-8844
Kathy Syfert, *Treasurer*
Debbie McKay, *Cust Mgr*
▲ EMP: 120
SQ FT: 231,000
SALES (est): 33MM **Privately Held**
SIC: **3644** 3498 Electric conduits & fittings; fabricated pipe & fittings

(G-13631)
BIMBO BAKERIES USA INC
Lenders Bagels
3801 Dewitt Ave (61938-6616)
P.O. Box 687 (61938-0687)
PHONE..................217 235-3181
Alan Guyon, *Production*
Brad Sam, *Manager*
EMP: 350 **Privately Held**
SIC: **2051** 5461 Bagels, fresh or frozen; bagels
HQ: Bimbo Bakeries Usa, Inc
255 Business Center Dr # 200
Horsham PA 19044
215 347-5500

(G-13632)
BOCKS CATTLE-IDENTI CO INC
Also Called: Bock's Identi Co.
3101 Cedar Ave (61938-3612)
P.O. Box 614 (61938-0614)
PHONE..................217 234-6634
Craig Salak, *President*
▼ EMP: 7
SQ FT: 15,000
SALES (est): 751.5K **Privately Held**
WEB: www.bocksid.com
SIC: **3999** Identification tags, except paper

(G-13633)
BRIGHTON CABINETRY INC
2908 Lake Land Blvd (61938-9522)
PHONE..................217 235-1978
Heather Rauch, *Human Res Mgr*
EMP: 11
SALES (corp-wide): 5MM **Privately Held**
WEB: www.brightoncabinetry.com
SIC: **2434** Wood kitchen cabinets
PA: Brighton Cabinetry, Inc.
1095 Industrial Park Ave
Neoga IL 62447
217 895-3000

(G-13634)
COMMERCIAL RFRGN CENTL ILL INC
2020 Prairie Ave (61938-2836)
PHONE..................217 235-5016
Joe Gillette, *President*
Debbie Parkerson, *Admin Sec*
EMP: 23

SALES (est): 5.3MM **Privately Held**
SIC: 3585 Refrigeration & heating equipment

(G-13635)
HARRIS METALS & RECYCLING
1213 N 11th St (61938-3156)
PHONE..................217 235-1808
Toni Harris, *Owner*
EMP: 8
SQ FT: 12,000
SALES (est): 754.5K **Privately Held**
SIC: 3559 5051 Recycling machinery; nonferrous metal sheets, bars, rods, etc.

(G-13636)
HELENA AGRI-ENTERPRISES LLC
3559 E County Road 1000n (61938-6658)
PHONE..................217 234-2726
Randy Parman, *Branch Mgr*
EMP: 9 **Privately Held**
SIC: 5191 2819 Chemicals, agricultural; industrial inorganic chemicals
HQ: Helena Agri-Enterprises, Llc
255 Schilling Blvd # 300
Collierville TN 38017
901 761-0050

(G-13637)
HI-DEF COMMUNICATIONS
3116 Pine Ave (61938-3633)
PHONE..................217 258-6679
Toby Ferris, *Owner*
Sara Ferris, *Owner*
EMP: 5
SALES: 500K **Privately Held**
SIC: 3663 Satellites, communications

(G-13638)
J L LAWRENCE & CO
Also Called: Lawrence J L & Co Dental Labs
1921 Richmond Ave (61938-2843)
P.O. Box 728 (61938-0728)
PHONE..................217 235-3622
Jimmy R Lawrence, *Owner*
EMP: 4
SALES (est): 323.5K **Privately Held**
SIC: 8072 3843 Dental laboratories; dental equipment & supplies

(G-13639)
JELENIZ
1414 Broadway Ave (61938-4014)
PHONE..................217 235-6789
EMP: 2
SALES (est): 225.7K **Privately Held**
SIC: 2599 Mfg Furniture/Fixtures

(G-13640)
KELLOGG COMPANY
3801 Dewitt Ave (61938-6616)
PHONE..................217 258-3251
EMP: 10
SALES (corp-wide): 13.5B **Publicly Held**
SIC: 2043 Cereal breakfast foods
PA: Kellogg Company
1 Kellogg Sq
Battle Creek MI 49017
269 961-2000

(G-13641)
LSC COMMUNICATIONS INC
6821 E County Road 1100n (61938-3478)
PHONE..................217 258-2832
Chuck Fleischmann, *Branch Mgr*
EMP: 5
SALES (corp-wide): 3.3B **Publicly Held**
SIC: 2732 Book printing
PA: Lsc Communications, Inc.
191 N Wacker Dr Ste 1400
Chicago IL 60606
773 272-9200

(G-13642)
LSC COMMUNICATIONS US LLC
Also Called: Building Maintenance Dept
6821 1100n (61938)
PHONE..................217 235-0361
Glenn Baker, *Branch Mgr*
EMP: 109

SALES (corp-wide): 3.3B **Publicly Held**
SIC: 2759 2752 2732 7331 Letterpress printing; commercial printing, offset; books: printing & binding; direct mail advertising services; graphic arts & related design; catalogs: gravure printing, not published on site
HQ: Lsc Communications Us, Llc
191 N Wacker Dr Ste 1400
Chicago IL 60606
844 572-5720

(G-13643)
LUCO MOP COMPANY
Also Called: American Broom Company
1200 Moultrie Ave (61938-3123)
PHONE..................217 235-1992
Clarence Gillespie, *Manager*
EMP: 7
SALES (corp-wide): 5.6MM **Privately Held**
WEB: www.lucomop.com
SIC: 3991 5719 Brooms; brooms
PA: Luco Mop Company
3345 Morganford Rd
Saint Louis MO 63116
314 772-5656

(G-13644)
MASTERPIECE CABINETRY DESIGN
69 Kingswood (61938-9031)
PHONE..................217 258-6880
Dale Love, *Owner*
EMP: 2
SALES: 300K **Privately Held**
SIC: 2434 Wood kitchen cabinets

(G-13645)
MATTOON PRECISION MFG
2408 S 14th St (61938-5748)
PHONE..................217 235-6000
Robert Shamdin, *President*
Noriyoshi Nishida, *Chairman*
Takesi Nakani, *Corp Secy*
Rod Orr, *Prdtn Mgr*
Austin Nunamaker, *Engineer*
▲ **EMP:** 160
SQ FT: 134,000
SALES: 66.9MM **Privately Held**
SIC: 3714 3363 Axles, motor vehicle; motor vehicle brake systems & parts; aluminum die-castings
PA: Nukabe Corporation
2457-2, Kuraganomachi
Takasaki GNM 370-1

(G-13646)
MATTOON PRINTING CENTER
212 N 20th St (61938-2851)
P.O. Box 703 (61938-0703)
PHONE..................217 234-3100
Bruce Cavitt, *President*
Kathy Cavitt, *Admin Sec*
EMP: 4 **EST:** 1963
SQ FT: 3,700
SALES (est): 498.2K **Privately Held**
WEB: www.mattoonchamber.com
SIC: 2752 2791 2789 2759 Commercial printing, offset; typesetting; bookbinding & related work; commercial printing

(G-13647)
MATTSON LAMP PLANT
1501 S 19th St (61938-5956)
PHONE..................217 258-9390
▲ **EMP:** 2
SALES (est): 277.4K **Privately Held**
SIC: 3641 Electric lamps

(G-13648)
MERVIS INDUSTRIES INC
Also Called: General Steel & Materials
612 N Logan St (61938-3505)
P.O. Box 8 (61938-0008)
PHONE..................217 235-5575
Lou Mervis, *President*
Jennifer Kline, *CFO*
Paul Garrett, *Manager*
Carl Meece, *Manager*
EMP: 10
SQ FT: 3,000
SALES (corp-wide): 161.2MM **Privately Held**
SIC: 5093 3341 Ferrous metal scrap & waste; secondary nonferrous metals

PA: Mervis Industries, Inc.
3295 E Main St Ste C
Danville IL 61834
217 442-5300

(G-13649)
METZGER WELDING SERVICE
Also Called: Metzger Welding & Machine
2900 Marshall Ave (61938-4912)
PHONE..................217 234-2851
Fax: 217 234-2851
EMP: 4 **EST:** 1979
SQ FT: 7,900
SALES (est): 210K **Privately Held**
SIC: 7692 5521 Welding Shop And Ret Used Cars

(G-13650)
MID-ILLINOIS CONCRETE INC
Also Called: Mattoon-Charleston Ready Mix
1413 Dewitt Ave E (61938-3533)
PHONE..................217 235-5858
Bud Ervin, *Manager*
EMP: 20
SALES (corp-wide): 17.2MM **Privately Held**
WEB: www.mid-illinoisconcrete.com
SIC: 3273 3272 Ready-mixed concrete; concrete products
PA: Mid-Illinois Concrete, Inc.
1805 S 4th St
Effingham IL
217 342-2498

(G-13651)
MONITOR SIGN CO
316 N Division St (61938-4540)
P.O. Box 61 (61938-0061)
PHONE..................217 234-2412
David Cornell, *President*
Dennis Creasy, *Vice Pres*
Cindy Cornell, *Accounts Mgr*
Dave Cornell, *CIO*
EMP: 18
SQ FT: 12,000
SALES (est): 1.3MM **Privately Held**
SIC: 3993 1799 Electric signs; displays, paint process; sign installation & maintenance

(G-13652)
R R DONNELLEY & SONS COMPANY
Also Called: R R Donnelley
6821 E County Road 1100n (61938-3478)
PHONE..................217 258-2675
Isabell Day, *Manager*
EMP: 40
SALES (corp-wide): 6.2B **Publicly Held**
WEB: www.rrdonnelley.com
SIC: 2759 Commercial printing
PA: R. R. Donnelley & Sons Company
35 W Wacker Dr
Chicago IL 60601
312 326-8000

(G-13653)
RR DONNELLEY PRINTING CO LP
Manufacturing Division
6821 E County Road 1100n (61938-3478)
P.O. Box 1668 (61938-1668)
PHONE..................217 235-0561
Daon Knotts, *Branch Mgr*
EMP: 960
SALES (corp-wide): 548.5MM **Privately Held**
WEB: www.rrdonnelley.com
SIC: 2754 2752 Commercial printing, gravure; letters, circular or form: lithographed
PA: R.R. Donnelley Printing Company L.P.
35 W Wacker Dr Ste 3650
Chicago IL 60601
312 326-8000

(G-13654)
SPECTRUM MEDIA INC
921 S 19th St (61938-5218)
P.O. Box 611 (61938-0611)
PHONE..................217 234-2044
Kyle Jansen, *President*
EMP: 3
SQ FT: 4,200
SALES (est): 352.6K **Privately Held**
SIC: 2759 Commercial printing

(G-13655)
U S SOY LLC
Also Called: US Soy
2808 Thomason Dr (61938-9277)
PHONE..................217 235-1020
Jake Florey,
Larry Nichols,
▼ **EMP:** 16
SALES (est): 2.3MM **Privately Held**
SIC: 2041 Flour & other grain mill products

(G-13656)
UNITED GRAPHICS LLC
2916 Marshall Ave (61938-4912)
PHONE..................217 235-7161
Jeffery Scrimager, *Exec VP*
Kerry Considine, *Vice Pres*
Erica Stollard, *Treasurer*
▲ **EMP:** 130
SQ FT: 75,000
SALES (est): 32.7MM **Privately Held**
SIC: 2752 Commercial printing, offset

(G-13657)
WAVE GRAPHICS INC
320 N 2nd St (61938-4452)
PHONE..................217 234-8100
Dan Pulson, *Owner*
Tom Epperson, *Partner*
Danny Paulson, *Partner*
John Stanley, *Partner*
Aubrey Frank, *Sales Executive*
EMP: 3
SALES (est): 451.4K **Privately Held**
WEB: www.wave-graphics.com
SIC: 2759 Screen printing

Maywood
Cook County

(G-13658)
AETNA PLYWOOD INC (PA)
1401 Saint Charles Rd (60153-1208)
PHONE..................708 343-1515
Lawrence Rassin, *President*
Scott Halden, *Vice Pres*
Jon Minnaert, *Vice Pres*
Keith Weller, *Vice Pres*
John Chlebek, *Sales Mgr*
▲ **EMP:** 75 **EST:** 1947
SQ FT: 177,000
SALES (est): 57.6MM **Privately Held**
WEB: www.aetnaplywood.com
SIC: 5031 5211 2449 Lumber: rough, dressed & finished; building materials, exterior; building materials, interior; plywood; lumber & other building materials; wood containers

(G-13659)
ALECTO INDUSTRIES INC
148 S 8th Ave (60153-1330)
PHONE..................708 344-1488
Marta Szwaya, *President*
James E Szway, *Admin Sec*
EMP: 29
SALES: 6.7MM **Privately Held**
SIC: 3496 Miscellaneous fabricated wire products

(G-13660)
ALLIANCE TOOL & MANUFACTURING
91 Wilcox St (60153-2397)
PHONE..................708 345-5444
Carl Uzgiris, *President*
Ramesh Gandhi, *General Mgr*
EMP: 16 **EST:** 1945
SQ FT: 10,000
SALES: 2MM **Privately Held**
SIC: 3541 3545 Machine tools, metal cutting: exotic (explosive, etc.); machine tool accessories

(G-13661)
AVW EQUIPMENT COMPANY INC
105 S 9th Ave (60153-1340)
PHONE..................708 343-7738
Milovan Vidakovich, *President*
Dusan Ilic, *Engineer*
Mira Djordjevic, *Admin Sec*
▲ **EMP:** 25

Maywood - Cook County (G-13662)

SQ FT: 25,400
SALES (est): 7.6MM **Privately Held**
SIC: 3589 Car washing machinery

(G-13662)
BECKER BROTHERS GRAPHITE CORP
39 Legion St (60153-2321)
PHONE...................708 410-0700
Cheryl Ivanovich, *President*
EMP: 7
SALES: 325K **Privately Held**
SIC: 3624 Carbon specialties for electrical use

(G-13663)
BOST CORPORATION (PA)
601 Saint Charles Rd (60153-1315)
P.O. Box 698 (60153-0698)
PHONE...................708 344-7023
Bogdan Lodyga, *President*
Stefan Kaminski, *Vice Pres*
EMP: 20
SQ FT: 12,000
SALES (est): 5.1MM **Privately Held**
SIC: 3564 3535 Dust or fume collecting equipment, industrial; conveyors & conveying equipment

(G-13664)
BROWNS GLOBAL EXCHANGE
1928 S 21st Ave (60153-2916)
PHONE...................708 345-0955
Maurice Brown, *Owner*
EMP: 99
SALES: 500K **Privately Held**
SIC: 2389 Apparel & accessories

(G-13665)
CHEM-PLATE INDUSTRIES INC
30 N 8th Ave (60153-1319)
PHONE...................708 345-3588
Octavio Nava, *Branch Mgr*
EMP: 25
SALES (corp-wide): 56.1MM **Privately Held**
SIC: 3398 3471 Metal heat treating; plating of metals or formed products
PA: Chem-Plate Industries, Inc
    1800 Touhy Ave
    Elk Grove Village IL 60007
    847 640-1600

(G-13666)
CHICAGO PALLET SERVICE INC
1305 S 1st Ave (60153-2405)
PHONE...................847 439-8330
Araceli Rodriguez, *Vice Pres*
EMP: 28 **Privately Held**
SIC: 3537 Pallets, metal
HQ: Chicago Pallet Service, Inc.
    1875 Greenleaf Ave
    Elk Grove Village IL 60007

(G-13667)
CLIFFE PRINTING COMPANY
112 S 5th Ave (60153-1308)
PHONE...................708 345-1665
Larry Poyer, *President*
Lois Jacobson, *Vice Pres*
Carol Poyer, *Admin Sec*
EMP: 3
SQ FT: 2,500
SALES: 400K **Privately Held**
SIC: 2752 2759 Commercial printing, offset; commercial printing

(G-13668)
DELLEMAN ASSOCIATES & CORP
8 N 6th Ave (60153-1310)
PHONE...................708 345-9520
Dan Delleman, *Owner*
EMP: 3
SALES (est): 256.2K **Privately Held**
SIC: 2499 Decorative wood & woodwork

(G-13669)
HIGH RISE SPECIALTY PRODUCTS
912 N Maywood Dr (60153-1862)
PHONE...................708 343-9265
Foster Brown, *President*
EMP: 1

SALES: 880K **Privately Held**
SIC: 3634 Heaters, space electric

(G-13670)
JSN INC
Also Called: Wire Cloth Filter Mfg
611 Saint Charles Rd (60153-1315)
PHONE...................708 410-1800
Suryakant B Patel, *President*
Urvashi S Patel, *Admin Sec*
▲ EMP: 28
SQ FT: 17,000
SALES (est): 5.3MM **Privately Held**
SIC: 3496 3714 3728 3469 Wire cloth & woven wire products; filters: oil, fuel & air, motor vehicle; aircraft body & wing assemblies & parts; metal stampings: gaskets, packing & sealing devices

(G-13671)
KRAMER WINDOW CO
1219 Orchard Ave (60153-2330)
P.O. Box 576 (60153-0576)
PHONE...................708 343-4780
James Scolaro, *President*
Diane Scolaro, *Vice Pres*
EMP: 8 **EST:** 1955
SQ FT: 5,500
SALES (est): 850K **Privately Held**
WEB: www.kramerwindow.com
SIC: 3442 5031 Storm doors or windows, metal; metal doors; doors & windows

(G-13672)
MACKENZIE JOHNSON
Also Called: Sunshine Products
1826 S 10th Ave (60153-3102)
PHONE...................630 244-2367
Mackenzie Johnson, *Owner*
EMP: 2
SALES (est): 210K **Privately Held**
SIC: 2842 Specialty cleaning, polishes & sanitation goods

(G-13673)
MORRIS MEAT PACKING CO INC
1406 S 5th Ave (60153-2129)
PHONE...................708 865-8566
Frank Masellis, *Manager*
EMP: 6
SALES (corp-wide): 1.5MM **Privately Held**
SIC: 2011 2013 Meat packing plants; sausages & other prepared meats
PA: Morris Meat Packing Company, Inc.
    1611 N Division St
    Morris IL
    815 942-9284

(G-13674)
NATIONAL CYCLE INC
Also Called: Barry Electric Div
2200 S Maywood Dr (60153-1783)
P.O. Box 158 (60153-0158)
PHONE...................708 343-0400
Barry Willey, *President*
Gordon B Willey, *Vice Pres*
Gordon Willey, *Vice Pres*
Rudy Flores, *Production*
Karen Drennan, *CFO*
◆ EMP: 200 **EST:** 1937
SQ FT: 160,000
SALES (est): 31.4MM **Privately Held**
WEB: www.nationalcycle.com
SIC: 3714 3751 3451 3441 Motor vehicle parts & accessories; motorcycle accessories; screw machine products; fabricated structural metal

(G-13675)
NS PRECISION LATHE INC
519 Lake St (60153-1651)
PHONE...................708 867-5023
Nicolas Sacarelos, *President*
Alfredo Santos,
EMP: 7
SQ FT: 5,000
SALES (est): 600K **Privately Held**
SIC: 3599 Machine shop, jobbing & repair

(G-13676)
NU-PUTTIE CORPORATION
Also Called: Npc Sealants
1208 S 8th Ave (60153-1995)
P.O. Box 645 (60153-0645)
PHONE...................708 681-1040

Stephen F Stefely, *President*
Helen Walsh, *Vice Pres*
Helen A Stefely, *Admin Sec*
EMP: 35 **EST:** 1922
SQ FT: 20,000
SALES (est): 8.4MM **Privately Held**
SIC: 2851 2952 2891 Putty; asphalt felts & coatings; adhesives & sealants

(G-13677)
OJEDAS WELDING CO
312 S 3rd Ave (60153-1640)
PHONE...................708 595-3799
Cristino Ojeda, *Principal*
Jose Ojeda, *Mng Member*
EMP: 6
SALES: 209K **Privately Held**
WEB: www.ojedawelding.com
SIC: 3499 Ladder assemblies, combination workstand: metal

(G-13678)
TECH UPGRADERS
2007 S 9th Ave (60153-3232)
PHONE...................877 324-8940
Elijah Goodwin, *Principal*
EMP: 8 **EST:** 2010
SALES: 350K **Privately Held**
WEB: www.techupgraders.com
SIC: 7378 3651 Computer maintenance & repair; household audio & video equipment

(G-13679)
TRY OUR PALLETS INC
37 S 9th Ave (60153-1364)
P.O. Box 1571, Melrose Park (60161-1571)
PHONE...................708 343-0166
Jose Trujillo, *President*
Dawn Trujillo, *Vice Pres*
EMP: 9
SALES: 1.5MM **Privately Held**
SIC: 2448 4953 Pallets, wood; refuse systems

(G-13680)
WELDON CORPORATION
Also Called: Van Bergen & Greener
1818 Madison St (60153-1710)
PHONE...................708 343-4700
Paul J Weldon, *President*
EMP: 45 **EST:** 1919
SQ FT: 45,000
SALES (est): 9.2MM **Privately Held**
WEB: www.spraggusa.com
SIC: 3621 3679 3566 Frequency converters (electric generators); solenoids for electronic applications; speed changers, drives & gears

Mazon
Grundy County

(G-13681)
ILLINOIS TOOL WORKS INC
ITW Filtration Products Div
804 Commercial Dr (60444-6203)
PHONE...................815 448-7300
Fax: 815 448-2066
EMP: 125
SALES (corp-wide): 13.6B **Publicly Held**
SIC: 3089 3714 Mfg Plastic Products Mfg Motor Vehicle Parts/Accessories
PA: Illinois Tool Works Inc.
    155 Harlem Ave
    Glenview IL 60025
    847 724-7500

(G-13682)
LOCODOCS INC (PA)
1000 Front St (60444-3622)
P.O. Box 150, Morris (60450-0150)
PHONE...................815 448-2100
Robert Bekker, *President*
EMP: 7
SQ FT: 25,000
SALES: 1.5MM **Privately Held**
SIC: 3743 Locomotives & parts

(G-13683)
MUELLER CUSTOM CABINETRY INC
4730 S Old Mazon Rd (60444-6264)
P.O. Box 297 (60444-0297)
PHONE...................815 448-5448
Daniel Mueller, *Executive*
EMP: 4
SALES (est): 428.2K **Privately Held**
WEB: www.muellercustomcabinetry.com
SIC: 2434 Wood kitchen cabinets

(G-13684)
PERITUS PLASTICS LLC
804 Commercial Dr (60444-6203)
PHONE...................815 448-2005
Timothy Clasby, *President*
James Macier, *Vice Pres*
EMP: 20
SQ FT: 25,000
SALES (est): 811.7K **Privately Held**
SIC: 3089 Injection molding of plastics

(G-13685)
WILLOUGHBYS AUTO & MCH SP
615 East St (60444-6043)
P.O. Box 330 (60444-0330)
PHONE...................815 448-2281
Berton Willoughby, *Owner*
EMP: 5 **EST:** 2001
SALES (est): 474.5K **Privately Held**
SIC: 3599 Machine shop, jobbing & repair

Mc Clure
Alexander County

(G-13686)
CAHOKIA RICE
31778 Lynns Ln (62957-4018)
P.O. Box 275 (62957-0275)
PHONE...................618 661-1060
EMP: 3 **EST:** 2018
SALES (est): 152.6K **Privately Held**
WEB: www.cahokiarice.com
SIC: 2099 Food preparations

(G-13687)
MDT CUSTOMS LLC
34734 Grapevine Trl (62957-4145)
PHONE...................573 316-5995
Michael Taylor, *Manager*
EMP: 4
SALES (est): 360.4K **Privately Held**
SIC: 3441 Fabricated structural metal

Mc Connell
Stephenson County

(G-13688)
CONNELL MC MACHINE & WELDING
8934 N Korth Rd (61050-9705)
PHONE...................815 868-2275
Roger Klontz, *Owner*
EMP: 6 **EST:** 1974
SQ FT: 300
SALES (est): 146.4K **Privately Held**
SIC: 7692 3599 Welding repair; machine shop, jobbing & repair

Mc Cook
Cook County

(G-13689)
A&S MACHINING & WELDING INC
Also Called: Asmw
4828 S Lawndale Ave Ste 3 (60525-3106)
PHONE...................708 442-4544
Stanley Rafacz, *President*
Mary Rafacz, *Admin Sec*
EMP: 20
SQ FT: 23,000

SALES (est): 3.9MM **Privately Held**
SIC: 3599 1799 7692 3544 Machine shop, jobbing & repair; welding on site; welding repair; special dies, tools, jigs & fixtures; sheet metalwork

(G-13690)
CORR-PAK CORPORATION
8000 Joliet Rd Ste 100 (60525-3256)
PHONE.................................708 442-7806
Hal Taylor, *President*
Henry O Taylor, *President*
Dubak Jelena, *Purchasing*
Anne Taylor, *Shareholder*
EMP: 24 **EST:** 1965
SQ FT: 46,000
SALES (est): 5.9MM **Privately Held**
WEB: www.corr-pak.com
SIC: 2653 7336 7389 2448 Boxes, corrugated: made from purchased materials; display items, solid fiber: made from purchased materials; silk screen design; package design; packaging & labeling services; pallets, wood & wood with metal; freight transportation arrangement; general warehousing & storage

(G-13691)
GRAYHILL INC
4800 S Vernon Ave (60525-6004)
PHONE.................................708 482-1411
Gene R Hill, *CEO*
EMP: 3
SALES (est): 185.9K **Privately Held**
SIC: 3613 3625 3679 3643 Switchgear & switchboard apparatus; relays & industrial controls; electronic components; current-carrying wiring devices; computer terminals

(G-13692)
HANDLING SYSTEMS INTL INC
8000 Joliet Rd Bldg 1 (60525-3254)
P.O. Box 626, La Grange (60525-0626)
PHONE.................................708 352-1213
Mark Rehor, *President*
Jake Rehor, *Sales Mgr*
EMP: 20
SALES (est): 10.7MM **Privately Held**
WEB: www.handlingsystemsintl.com
SIC: 5084 3536 3537 Hoists; materials handling machinery; cranes, industrial plant; industrial trucks & tractors

(G-13693)
K & K IRON WORKS LLC (PA)
5100 S Lawndale Ave Ste 7 (60525-3311)
PHONE.................................708 924-0000
Jerry Kulhanek, *Mng Member*
Bob Sullivan,
EMP: 90
SQ FT: 35,000
SALES (est): 37MM **Privately Held**
SIC: 3441 3446 Fabricated structural metal; stairs, staircases, stair treads: prefabricated metal; railings, prefabricated metal

(G-13694)
KZ MANUFACTURING CO
8312 Joliet Rd Unit 6 (60525-3103)
PHONE.................................708 937-8097
Barbara Mulica, *President*
EMP: 4 **EST:** 2013
SALES (est): 204.5K **Privately Held**
SIC: 3365 3462 3469 3625 Machinery castings, aluminum; iron & steel forgings; machine parts, stamped or pressed metal; numerical controls

(G-13695)
LEGACY VULCAN LLC
Midwest Division
5500 Joliet Rd (60525-3113)
PHONE.................................708 485-6602
Jeff May, *Manager*
EMP: 75 **Publicly Held**
SIC: 3273 Ready-mixed concrete
HQ: Legacy Vulcan, Llc
   1200 Urban Center Dr
   Vestavia AL 35242
   205 298-3000

(G-13696)
MATERIAL SERVICE CORPORATION
9101 W 47th St (60525-3306)
PHONE.................................708 485-8211
James Goldberg, *Superintendent*
EMP: 60
SALES (corp-wide): 20.8B **Privately Held**
SIC: 1411 Limestone, dimension-quarrying
HQ: Material Service Corporation
   2235 Entp Dr Ste 3504
   Westchester IL 60154
   708 731-2600

(G-13697)
NORTH AMERICAN REFINING CO
7601 W 47th St (60525-3203)
PHONE.................................708 762-5117
Lowell D Aughenbaugh, *President*
EMP: 3
SALES (est): 365.3K **Privately Held**
SIC: 2911 Oils, partly refined: sold for re-running

(G-13698)
POWERSTOP
7950 Joliet Rd Ste 200 (60525-3206)
PHONE.................................708 442-6761
EMP: 3
SALES (est): 47.5K **Privately Held**
SIC: 7537 5013 3714 Automotive transmission repair shops; automotive brakes; motor vehicle brake systems & parts

(G-13699)
PROGRESS RAIL LOCOMOTIVE INC (DH)
Also Called: Electro Motive Diesel
9301 W 55th St (60525-3214)
P.O. Box 1037, Albertville AL (35950-0017)
PHONE.................................800 255-5355
William P Ainsworth, *CEO*
Craig McKeen, *General Mgr*
Tapas Chakravarty, *Opers Mgr*
Ryan Donnelly, *Facilities Mgr*
Tony Wings, *Production*
◆ **EMP:** 1850
SQ FT: 790,000
SALES (est): 660.7MM
SALES (corp-wide): 53.8B **Publicly Held**
SIC: 3621 3519 3647 Motors & generators; internal combustion engines; locomotive & railroad car lights
HQ: Progress Rail Services Corporation
   1600 Progress Dr
   Albertville AL 35950
   256 505-6421

(G-13700)
PROGRESS RAIL LOCOMOTIVE INC
Also Called: EMD
9301 W 55th St (60525-3214)
P.O. Box 2377, La Grange (60525-8477)
PHONE.................................708 387-5510
EMP: 13
SALES (corp-wide): 38.5B **Publicly Held**
SIC: 3621 3519 3647 Mfg Motors/Generators Mfg Internal Combustion Engines Mfg Vehicle Lighting Equipment
HQ: Progress Rail Locomotive Inc.
   9301 W 55th St
   Mc Cook IL 60525
   800 255-5355

(G-13701)
SIMU LTD (PA)
8900 W 50th St (60525-6005)
PHONE.................................708 688-2200
Craig Simon, *President*
◆ **EMP:** 11
SQ FT: 256,000
SALES (est): 446.9MM **Privately Held**
SIC: 5113 5141 5142 2782 Industrial & personal service paper; groceries, general line; packaged frozen goods; loose-leaf binders & devices; menus: printing; packaging paper

(G-13702)
SKYLINE
9200 W 55th St (60525-3654)
PHONE.................................312 300-4700
Mary Crowe, *Principal*

EMP: 2 **EST:** 2012
SALES (est): 237.8K **Privately Held**
WEB: www.skyline.com
SIC: 2759 Screen printing

(G-13703)
SUMMIT TANK & EQUIPMENT CO
7801 W 47th St (60525-3204)
P.O. Box 9, Summit Argo (60501-0009)
PHONE.................................708 594-3040
Al Majeres, *President*
Peter Majeres, *Vice Pres*
EMP: 15
SQ FT: 15,000
SALES (est): 1MM **Privately Held**
SIC: 7699 3715 3713 Tank repair; truck trailers; truck & bus bodies

(G-13704)
UOP LLC
Also Called: Mc Cook Manufacturing Plant
8400 Joliet Rd Ste 100 (60525-3310)
PHONE.................................708 442-7400
Fax: 708 442-8082
EMP: 75
SALES (corp-wide): 38.5B **Publicly Held**
SIC: 2833 2819 1311 Mfg Medicinal/Botanicals Mfg Indstl Inorgan Chem Petro/Natural Gas Prodn
HQ: Uop Llc
   25 E Algonquin Rd
   Des Plaines IL 60016
   847 391-2000

Mc Henry
Mchenry County

(G-13705)
PETER BAKER & SON CO
Also Called: Plant 6
914 W Illinois Rte 120 (60050)
PHONE.................................815 344-1640
Arthura Baker II, *Branch Mgr*
EMP: 10
SALES (corp-wide): 22.2MM **Privately Held**
SIC: 3531 1611 Asphalt plant, including gravel-mix type; highway & street construction
PA: Peter Baker & Son Co.
   1349 Rockland Rd
   Lake Bluff IL 60044
   847 362-3663

Mc Leansboro
Hamilton County

(G-13706)
HERITAGE STRUCTURES INC
6267 County Road 400 N (62859-1901)
PHONE.................................618 895-8028
Daniel Hostetler, *CEO*
EMP: 15
SALES (est): 538.2K **Privately Held**
SIC: 2449 Chicken coops (crates), wood: wirebound

(G-13707)
NEWSPAPER HOLDING INC
Also Called: Times-Leader
200 S Washinton St Ste 1 (62859)
PHONE.................................618 643-2387
EMP: 3
SQ FT: 8,000 **Privately Held**
SIC: 2711 Newspapers-Publishing/Printing
HQ: Newspaper Holding, Inc.
   425 Locust St
   Johnstown PA 15901
   814 532-5102

(G-13708)
STC INC
Also Called: Sun Transformer
1201 W Randolph St (62859-2028)
PHONE.................................618 643-2555
Brad Cross, *President*
Angie Calkins, *Vice Pres*
Lynn Vines, *Purchasing*
Kezya Newman, *Financial Exec*
Scott Kolts, *Corp Comm Staff*

▼ **EMP:** 30
SQ FT: 27,000
SALES: 5MM **Privately Held**
SIC: 3677 3663 Electronic coils, transformers & other inductors;

(G-13709)
TRADE INDUSTRIES
1020 E Randolph St (62859-2149)
P.O. Box 5 (62859-0005)
PHONE.................................618 643-4321
John Dean, *President*
EMP: 30 **EST:** 1967
SQ FT: 8,000
SALES: 1.6MM **Privately Held**
SIC: 8331 2448 2441 Vocational training agency; wood pallets & skids; nailed wood boxes & shook

(G-13710)
WUEBBELS REPAIR & SALES LLC
505 W Market St (62859-1069)
P.O. Box Rr3 184 (62859)
PHONE.................................618 648-2227
Shelly A Wuebbels, *Principal*
EMP: 7
SALES (est): 219.7K **Privately Held**
SIC: 3519 Parts & accessories, internal combustion engines

McCullom Lake
Mchenry County

(G-13711)
FILTER RENEW TECNOLOGIES
3205 Lakeside Ct (60050-1514)
PHONE.................................815 344-2200
John T Colomer, *Principal*
EMP: 2
SALES (est): 283.6K **Privately Held**
WEB: www.filterrenew.com
SIC: 3569 Filters

(G-13712)
SASSY PRIMITIVES LTD
3202 Lakeside Ct Unit 1 (60050-1512)
PHONE.................................815 385-9302
Wendy Patchett, *Principal*
Lisbeth Nielson, *Principal*
EMP: 2 **EST:** 1999
SALES (est): 231.3K **Privately Held**
WEB: www.sassyprimitives.com
SIC: 3999 Candles

McHenry
Mchenry County

(G-13713)
ACCURATE SPRING TECH INC
Also Called: Hill Design
5801 W Hill St (60050-7445)
PHONE.................................815 344-3333
EMP: 13
SALES (est): 920K **Privately Held**
SIC: 3542 Manufacturer Of Window Springs

(G-13714)
ACE ENGRAVING & SPECIALTIES CO
4204 Ponca St (60050-5340)
PHONE.................................815 759-2093
Brenda Singleton, *President*
Morris Singleton, *Vice Pres*
EMP: 3
SQ FT: 3,000
SALES (est): 400K **Privately Held**
SIC: 3479 Engraving jewelry silverware, or metal

(G-13715)
ADAMS STEEL SERVICE INC
2022 S Il Route 31 Ste A (60050-8211)
PHONE.................................815 385-9100
Mike Chambers, *President*
EMP: 22
SQ FT: 11,000

McHenry - Mchenry County (G-13716)

SALES (est): 6.1MM **Privately Held**
SIC: 3441 7692 3548 Fabricated structural metal; welding repair; welding apparatus

(G-13716)
AJI CUSTOM CABINETS
5720 Wilmot Rd (60051-8400)
PHONE................................847 312-7847
Jason Rodriguez, *President*
EMP: 4 EST: 2013
SALES (est): 227.4K **Privately Held**
SIC: 2434 Wood kitchen cabinets

(G-13717)
ALLIED DIE CASTING CORPORATION
3923 W West Ave (60050-4395)
PHONE................................815 385-9330
Michael J Albanese Jr, *President*
Adam Albanese, *Vice Pres*
Gayle Albanese, *Treasurer*
▲ EMP: 20 EST: 1966
SQ FT: 20,000
SALES (est): 3.9MM **Privately Held**
WEB: www.allieddiecasting.com
SIC: 3364 3993 Zinc & zinc-base alloy die-castings; signs & advertising specialties

(G-13718)
AMERICAN CONVENIENCE INC
Also Called: Riverside Chocolate Factory
2102 W Il Route 120 (60051-4759)
PHONE................................815 344-6040
Robert B Hunter, *President*
EMP: 12
SQ FT: 1,500
SALES (est): 1MM **Privately Held**
SIC: 5441 2064 2066 Candy; confectionery; candy & other confectionery products; fudge (candy); chocolate & cocoa products

(G-13719)
APTARGROUP INC
Aptar and Cary Illinois
4900 Prime Pkwy (60050-7019)
PHONE................................847 462-3900
Hank Pucci, *Engineer*
Marcia Thomas, *Human Res Dir*
Paula Brunner, *Cust Svc Dir*
Anne Stecker, *Business Anlyst*
Emily Leising, *Marketing Staff*
EMP: 50 **Publicly Held**
SIC: 3089 Injection molded finished plastic products
PA: Aptargroup, Inc.
265 Exchange Dr Ste 100
Crystal Lake IL 60014

(G-13720)
ARENA SPORTS USA INC
820 Black Partridge Rd (60051-9321)
PHONE................................847 809-7268
Mary Marshall, *President*
EMP: 11 EST: 2007
SALES (est): 1.3MM **Privately Held**
WEB: www.arenasportsusa.com
SIC: 2759 Screen printing

(G-13721)
ARTISTIC EMBROIDERY CREATIONS
5203 Home Ave (60050-3456)
PHONE................................815 385-8854
Linda Showens, *Owner*
Raleigh Showens, *Co-Owner*
EMP: 4
SALES: 125K **Privately Held**
SIC: 2395 7389 8743 Embroidery products, except schiffli machine; apparel designers, commercial; promotion service

(G-13722)
BPI HOLDINGS INTERNATIONAL INC (DH)
4400 Prime Pkwy (60050-7003)
PHONE................................815 363-9000
David Overbeeke, *President*
Phil Cutting, *CFO*
Stephanie Flatkin, *Admin Sec*
EMP: 200 EST: 2012
SQ FT: 100,000
SALES (est): 1.2B
SALES (corp-wide): 10.8MM **Privately Held**
SIC: 3714 Motor vehicle brake systems & parts

(G-13723)
BRAKE PARTS INC INDIA LLC (DH)
4400 Prime Pkwy (60050-7033)
PHONE................................815 363-9000
Terry R McCormack, *Mng Member*
◆ EMP: 9
SALES (est): 29.7MM
SALES (corp-wide): 10.8MM **Privately Held**
SIC: 5013 3714 Automotive supplies & parts; motor vehicle brake systems & parts
HQ: Bpi Holdings International, Inc.
4400 Prime Pkwy
Mchenry IL 60050
815 363-9000

(G-13724)
BRAKE PARTS INC LLC
1380 Corporate Dr (60050-7044)
PHONE................................815 363-8181
Gary Allen, *Branch Mgr*
Richard Johnson, *Supervisor*
EMP: 300
SALES (corp-wide): 10.8MM **Privately Held**
WEB: www.brakepartsinc.com
SIC: 3714 Motor vehicle parts & accessories
HQ: Brake Parts Inc Llc
4400 Prime Pkwy
Mchenry IL 60050

(G-13725)
BRAKE PARTS INC LLC (DH)
4400 Prime Pkwy (60050-7033)
PHONE................................815 363-9000
H David Overbeeke, *President*
Edward J West, *Vice Pres*
Jake Wegner, *VP Sales*
◆ EMP: 125
SQ FT: 40,000
SALES (est): 1.1B
SALES (corp-wide): 10.8MM **Privately Held**
SIC: 3714 Motor vehicle brake systems & parts; brake drums, motor vehicle
HQ: Bpi Holdings International, Inc.
4400 Prime Pkwy
Mchenry IL 60050
815 363-9000

(G-13726)
CHROMA COLOR CORPORATION (PA)
3900 W Dayton St (60050-8376)
P.O. Box 486, Salisbury NC (28145-0486)
PHONE................................877 385-8777
Thomas G Bolger, *CEO*
Jeff Smink, *President*
Matt Barr, *Vice Chairman*
Tom Jaeger, *Vice Pres*
Gerald Baillargeon, *CFO*
▲ EMP: 122 EST: 1967
SQ FT: 57,000
SALES (est): 53.3MM **Privately Held**
WEB: www.carolinacolor.com
SIC: 3089 2865 2816 Coloring & finishing of plastic products; cyclic crudes & intermediates; inorganic pigments

(G-13727)
CHROMOLD PLATING INC
1631 Oak Dr (60050-0305)
PHONE................................815 344-8644
Eric Coulter, *President*
EMP: 3
SALES (est): 273.4K **Privately Held**
WEB: www.chromold.net
SIC: 3471 Plating of metals or formed products; electroplating of metals or formed products

(G-13728)
CLASSIC PRODUCTS INC
Also Called: Mastercoil Spring
4010 W Albany St (60050-8301)
PHONE................................815 344-0051
Catherine Musielak Miller, *President*
Paul Wesinger, *Maint Spvr*
Cathy M Musielak, *Purch Mgr*
Paula Green, *QC Mgr*
Chris Murphy, *Engineer*
▲ EMP: 45
SQ FT: 45,000
SALES (est): 9.8MM **Privately Held**
WEB: www.mastercoil.com
SIC: 3495 Wire springs

(G-13729)
CONCORDE MFG & FABRICATION INC
1620 S Schroeder Ln (60050-8251)
PHONE................................815 344-3788
John West, *President*
John Silberbauer, *Vice Pres*
EMP: 19 EST: 1980
SQ FT: 12,000
SALES (est): 3.6MM **Privately Held**
SIC: 3599 Machine shop, jobbing & repair

(G-13730)
CORPORATE DISK COMPANY (PA)
Also Called: Disk.com
4610 Prime Pkwy (60050-7005)
PHONE................................800 634-3475
William Mahoney, *President*
Alan Gault, *President*
Joseph Foley, *Vice Pres*
David Gimbel, *Vice Pres*
Jason Hyde, *VP Mktg*
EMP: 90
SQ FT: 60,000
SALES (est): 17.5MM **Privately Held**
SIC: 3652 Compact laser discs, prerecorded

(G-13731)
CPM CO INC
1805 Dot St (60050-6586)
PHONE................................815 385-7700
Scott Smith, *CEO*
John Smith, *Owner*
Jim Szamlewski, *Vice Pres*
Janice Johnson, *Purchasing*
Thomas Uutala, *CFO*
▼ EMP: 29 EST: 1970
SQ FT: 54,900
SALES (est): 5.7MM **Privately Held**
WEB: www.millerformless.com
SIC: 3531 Construction machinery

(G-13732)
CREATIVE CURRICULA INC
1621 Park St (60050-4440)
PHONE................................815 363-9419
EMP: 7 EST: 1998
SALES: 250K **Privately Held**
SIC: 8299 2731 School/Educational Services Books-Publishing/Printing

(G-13733)
CRYSTAL NAILS MCHENRY
2030 N Richmond Rd (60051-5419)
PHONE................................815 363-5498
Giang Ta, *Owner*
EMP: 5
SALES (est): 304.4K **Privately Held**
SIC: 3999 Fingernails, artificial

(G-13734)
CTS AUTOMOTIVE LLC
Also Called: Fabrick Molded Plastic Div
5213 Prime Pkwy (60050-7034)
PHONE................................815 385-9480
Seth Wagner, *Branch Mgr*
EMP: 50
SALES (corp-wide): 469MM **Publicly Held**
SIC: 3625 3089 Switches, electronic applications; boxes, plastic
HQ: Cts Automotive, Llc
4925 Indiana Ave
Lisle IL 60532
630 577-8800

(G-13735)
DEATAK INC
Also Called: Frederick P Schall
4004 W Dayton St (60050-8376)
PHONE................................815 322-2013
Frederick P Schall, *President*
Michael Schall, *Vice Pres*
Carol Ann Schall, *Admin Sec*
▲ EMP: 10
SQ FT: 10,000
SALES (est): 2.2MM **Privately Held**
SIC: 3829 Measuring & controlling devices

(G-13736)
DIVERSIFIED FLEET MGT INC
776 Ridgeview Dr (60050-7054)
PHONE................................815 578-1051
Robert Ozimek, *President*
Dan Griggs, *Manager*
EMP: 28
SALES (est): 3.8MM **Privately Held**
SIC: 8741 3535 Business management; robotic conveyors

(G-13737)
DONS DRAPERY SERVICE
Also Called: Don's Custom Draperies
2210 Orchard Beach Rd (60050-2850)
PHONE................................815 385-4759
Donald Welch, *Owner*
EMP: 2 EST: 1974
SALES (est): 315K **Privately Held**
SIC: 5023 1799 2591 2391 Draperies; drapery track installation; drapery hardware & blinds & shades; curtains & draperies

(G-13738)
DREWRYS BREWING COMPANY
5402 Brittany Dr (60050-3354)
PHONE................................815 385-9115
Francis Manzo, *Principal*
EMP: 4
SALES (est): 263.4K **Privately Held**
SIC: 2082 Malt beverages

(G-13739)
DURA WAX COMPANY
4101 W Albany St (60050-4807)
PHONE................................815 385-5000
Brian Schwerman, *President*
Bryan Kennedy, *Mktg Dir*
Mark P Chianakas, *Admin Sec*
Cindy Schwerman, *Admin Sec*
▼ EMP: 12 EST: 1935
SQ FT: 16,000
SALES (est): 2.7MM **Privately Held**
WEB: www.durawax.com
SIC: 2842 5087 3291 Floor waxes; janitors' supplies; abrasive products

(G-13740)
E & J PRECISION MACHINING INC
4215 W Orleans St (60050-3999)
PHONE................................815 363-2522
Ed Przepalkowski, *President*
Joyce Przepalkowski, *Vice Pres*
EMP: 7
SQ FT: 12,500
SALES (est): 97.2K **Privately Held**
SIC: 3599 Machine shop, jobbing & repair

(G-13741)
ENGINRED MOLDING SOLUTIONS INC
4913 Prime Pkwy (60050-7016)
PHONE................................815 363-9600
Mike Jacobs, *President*
EMP: 26
SQ FT: 25,000
SALES (est): 5.3MM **Privately Held**
WEB: www.moldingsolutions.com
SIC: 3089 Injection molding of plastics

(G-13742)
EVSCO INC
2309 N Ringwood Rd Ste M (60050-1313)
PHONE................................847 362-7068
Michael Barrett, *President*
Ann Barrett, *Admin Sec*
EMP: 10
SALES (est): 1.2MM **Privately Held**
SIC: 3491 3494 Industrial valves; valves & pipe fittings

(G-13743)
FABRIK INDUSTRIES INC
Also Called: Fabrik Molded Plastics
5213 Prime Pkwy (60050-7038)
PHONE................................815 385-9480
Seth Wagner, *President*
Keith Wagner, *President*

Matthew Casper, *Engineer*
Jess Jones, *Engineer*
Dave Lamberti, *Engineer*
▲ **EMP:** 280
SQ FT: 120,000
SALES (est): 85.2MM **Privately Held**
SIC: 3089 3544 Injection molding of plastics; special dies & tools

(G-13744)
FIVE STAR PALLETS INC
3939 W Albany St (60050-8390)
PHONE.................................847 613-8488
EMP: 9
SALES (est): 896.1K **Privately Held**
SIC: 2421 Sawmills & planing mills, general

(G-13745)
FOLLETT SCHOOL SOLUTIONS INC
1340 Ridgeview Dr (60050-7047)
PHONE.................................815 759-1700
Tom Schenck, *President*
Timothy Henrichs, *Treasurer*
R Mark Sproat, *Admin Sec*
EMP: 200
SALES (est): 15.6MM
SALES (corp-wide): 4.7B **Privately Held**
SIC: 7371 7372 5999 5192 Computer software development & applications; educational computer software; educational aids & electronic training materials; books
HQ: Follett School Solutions, Inc.
1340 Ridgeview Dr
Mchenry IL 60050
708 884-5000

(G-13746)
GLASS HAUS
2412 S Justen Rd (60050-8180)
PHONE.................................815 459-5849
Leonard Wilson, *Owner*
Carolyn Wilson, *Owner*
EMP: 3
SALES: 150K **Privately Held**
SIC: 2653 3231 3221 Sheets, solid fiber: made from purchased materials; novelties, glass: fruit, foliage, flowers, animals, etc.; glass containers

(G-13747)
HANGER INC
649 Ridgeview Dr (60050-7012)
PHONE.................................847 695-6955
Tracey Moore, *Office Mgr*
EMP: 20
SALES (corp-wide): 1.1B **Publicly Held**
SIC: 3842 Prosthetic appliances; orthopedic appliances
PA: Hanger, Inc.
10910 Domain Dr Ste 300
Austin TX 78758
512 777-3800

(G-13748)
HILL DESIGN PRODUCTS INC
5801 W Hill St (60050-7445)
PHONE.................................815 344-3333
EMP: 15
SALES (est): 2.4MM **Privately Held**
SIC: 2431 Millwork, Nsk

(G-13749)
I P C AUTOMATION INC
4615 Prime Pkwy (60050-7001)
PHONE.................................815 759-3934
David F Geiser, *President*
Gerald Warnke, *COO*
Bill Soltmann, *Vice Pres*
▲ **EMP:** 6
SQ FT: 15,000
SALES (est): 1.4MM **Privately Held**
SIC: 3625 3825 Electric controls & control accessories, industrial; instruments to measure electricity
HQ: Bluffton Motor Works Llc
410 E Spring St
Bluffton IN 46714

(G-13750)
JARR PRINTING CO
5435 Bull Valley Rd # 300 (60050-7436)
PHONE.................................815 363-5435
Dennis C Jarr, *Owner*
EMP: 13 EST: 1976

SQ FT: 4,000
SALES (est): 1.4MM **Privately Held**
SIC: 2752 Commercial printing, offset

(G-13751)
JASCO TOOL & MANUFACTURING
6000 Tomlinson Dr (60050-1716)
PHONE.................................815 271-5158
John Snyders, *President*
Ross Ishima, *Exec VP*
EMP: 2 EST: 1980
SQ FT: 2,500
SALES (est): 261.4K **Privately Held**
SIC: 3544 Special dies & tools

(G-13752)
JEDI CORPORATION
4450 Bull Valley Rd Ste 2 (60050-7495)
P.O. Box 459 (60051-9007)
PHONE.................................815 344-5334
Robert Karolewski, *President*
Denise Karolewski, *Admin Sec*
EMP: 4
SALES (est): 500K **Privately Held**
SIC: 3451 Screw machine products

Mchenry
Mchenry County

(G-13753)
JESSUP MANUFACTURING COMPANY (PA)
2815 W Rte 120 (60051)
P.O. Box 366, McHenry (60051-0366)
PHONE.................................815 385-6650
Robert A Jessup, *President*
Michael Demartinis, *Business Mgr*
Jeff Harvey, *Business Mgr*
Michael Kilkenny, *Business Mgr*
Mike Richardson, *Business Mgr*
▲ **EMP:** 70 EST: 1956
SQ FT: 55,000
SALES (est): 25.6MM **Privately Held**
WEB: www.jessupmfg.com
SIC: 3089 Battery cases, plastic or plastic combination

McHenry
Mchenry County

(G-13754)
KREISCHER OPTICS LTD
1729 Oak Dr (60050-0306)
PHONE.................................815 344-4220
Cody Kreischer, *President*
Daniel Charland, *Sales Staff*
EMP: 18
SQ FT: 8,400
SALES: 3MM **Privately Held**
SIC: 3827 Optical elements & assemblies, except ophthalmic

(G-13755)
KWIK MARK INC
4071 W Albany St (60050-8390)
PHONE.................................815 363-8268
Emil Cindric, *President*
EMP: 6
SALES (est): 670K **Privately Held**
SIC: 3542 Marking machines

(G-13756)
LENCO ELECTRONICS INC
1330 S Belden St (60050-8381)
PHONE.................................815 344-2900
Lenard J Duncan, *President*
Bruce Thackwray, *Exec VP*
Brad Schwagerman, *Safety Mgr*
Lauretta Montgomery, *Purch Dir*
Scott Duncan, *Engineer*
▲ **EMP:** 40 EST: 1971
SQ FT: 22,000
SALES (est): 9.7MM **Privately Held**
SIC: 3612 3677 Transformers, except electric; electronic transformers

(G-13757)
LIBERTY LIMESTONE INC
430 W Wegner Rd (60051-8653)
PHONE.................................815 385-5011
Dave Hammerl, *President*
EMP: 7
SALES: 350K **Privately Held**
SIC: 3281 Limestone, cut & shaped

(G-13758)
LIMITLESS INNOVATIONS INC
4800 Metalmaster Dr (60050-7017)
PHONE.................................855 843-4828
Michael V Smeja, *Principal*
Daniel F Smeja, *Principal*
Rock M Smeja, *Principal*
Sabrina Bauer, *Accountant*
Lisa Robinson, *Manager*
▲ **EMP:** 20
SQ FT: 100,000
SALES (est): 2.2MM **Privately Held**
WEB: www.limitlessinnovations.com
SIC: 3679 5065 5023 3089 Electronic loads & power supplies; electronic parts & equipment; decorative home furnishings & supplies; kitchenware, plastic

(G-13759)
LINCOLNSHIRE PRINTING INC
4004 W Dayton St (60050-8376)
PHONE.................................815 578-0740
John Kunath, *President*
Bill Kunath, *Software Engr*
EMP: 9 EST: 1977
SALES (est): 1.2MM **Privately Held**
SIC: 2752 2759 Commercial printing, offset; commercial printing

(G-13760)
M S —ACTION MACHINING CORP
4061 W Dayton St (60050-8377)
PHONE.................................815 344-3770
Norman Stengel, *President*
Ralph Stengel, *Vice Pres*
Maureen Schmitt, *Office Mgr*
EMP: 35 EST: 1966
SQ FT: 12,000
SALES (est): 6.3MM **Privately Held**
WEB: www.ms-action.com
SIC: 3599 Machine shop, jobbing & repair

(G-13761)
M-1 TOOL WORKS INC
1419 S Belden St (60050-8399)
PHONE.................................815 344-1275
Martin Ryba, *President*
Karin Peter, *Treasurer*
Chuck Duhai, *Supervisor*
EMP: 40
SQ FT: 15,000
SALES (est): 8.6MM **Privately Held**
SIC: 3544 3625 Special dies & tools; control equipment, electric

(G-13762)
MANN+HUMMEL FILTRATION TECH
4500 Prime Pkwy (60050-2136)
PHONE.................................800 407-9263
EMP: 19
SALES (corp-wide): 3.4B **Privately Held**
SIC: 3714 5013 Mfg Vechicle Replacement Parts
HQ: Mann+Hummel Filtration Technology Group Inc.
1 Wix Way
Gastonia NC 28054
704 869-3300

(G-13763)
MANN+HUMMEL FILTRATION TECHNOL
1380 Corporate Dr (60050-7044)
PHONE.................................815 759-7744
Pat Keane, *Branch Mgr*
EMP: 7
SALES (corp-wide): 4.5B **Privately Held**
SIC: 3714 Motor vehicle brake systems & parts
HQ: Mann+Hummel Filtration Technology Group Inc.
1 Wix Way
Gastonia NC 28054
704 869-3300

(G-13764)
MASTER TECH TOOL INC
4539 Prime Pkwy (60050-7000)
PHONE.................................815 363-4001
Kathy Farwick, *Treasurer*
Glenn Farwick, *Treasurer*
EMP: 2
SQ FT: 2,500
SALES (est): 319.5K **Privately Held**
SIC: 3544 Special dies & tools

(G-13765)
MCHENRY PRINTING SERVICES
Also Called: Hanover Park Press
4901 Pyndale Dr (60050-5016)
PHONE.................................815 385-7600
Michael Lehman, *President*
Charles Lehman, *President*
EMP: 3
SQ FT: 3,200
SALES (est): 270K **Privately Held**
WEB: www.mchenryprinting.com
SIC: 2752 2791 2789 2759 Commercial printing, offset; typesetting; bookbinding & related work; commercial printing

(G-13766)
MCHENRY SCREW PRODUCTS INC
4515 Prime Pkwy (60050-7000)
PHONE.................................815 344-4638
Ronald Wenk, *President*
EMP: 3
SQ FT: 1,900
SALES (est): 199.6K **Privately Held**
SIC: 3451 Screw machine products

(G-13767)
MECC ALTE INC
1229 Adams Dr (60051-4562)
PHONE.................................815 344-0530
Pom Weber, *CEO*
Steve Sharpe, *Sales Dir*
Nikolay Bogdanov, *Sales Staff*
◆ **EMP:** 11 EST: 2008
SQ FT: 20,000
SALES (est): 2.2MM **Privately Held**
WEB: www.meccalte.com
SIC: 3621 Generating apparatus & parts, electrical; generators & sets, electric

(G-13768)
MEDELA LLC (DH)
1101 Corporate Dr (60050-7006)
P.O. Box 660 (60051-0660)
PHONE.................................800 435-8316
Melissa Gonzalez, *Exec VP*
Shari Heck, *Vice Pres*
Nancy Huff, *Prdtn Mgr*
David Johnson, *Opers Staff*
Crystal Kattner, *Production*
◆ **EMP:** 153
SQ FT: 135,000
SALES: 155.2MM
SALES (corp-wide): 355.8K **Privately Held**
SIC: 5047 3596 Medical equipment & supplies; scales & balances, except laboratory; baby products
HQ: Medela Ag
Lattichstrasse 4b
Baar ZG 6340
417 695-151

(G-13769)
MFS HOLDINGS LLC
Also Called: Miller Formers Co
1805 Dot St (60050-6586)
PHONE.................................815 385-7700
Scott Smith, *CEO*
EMP: 35 EST: 2015
SQ FT: 85,000
SALES (est): 6.4MM **Privately Held**
SIC: 3531 Drags, road (construction & road maintenance equipment)

(G-13770)
MIDWEST INNOVATIONS INC
4137 W Orleans St (60050-3973)
P.O. Box 221 (60051-9003)
PHONE.................................815 578-1401
Lindsay Trax, *President*
EMP: 2 EST: 2009
SALES: 1MM **Privately Held**
SIC: 3559 Plastics working machinery

McHenry - Mchenry County (G-13771)

(G-13771)
MITCHELL AIRCRAFT PRODUCTS
2309 N Ringwood Rd (60050-1313)
PHONE..................................815 331-8609
Bob Woasecki, *Principal*
EMP: 5 **EST:** 2013
SALES (est): 586K **Privately Held**
SIC: 3728 Aircraft parts & equipment

(G-13772)
OAKRIDGE PRODUCTS LLC
Also Called: Oak Ridge Molded Products
4612 Century Ct (60050-7018)
PHONE..................................815 363-4700
Conor O'Malley, *President*
Andrew Kovari, *Exec VP*
▲ **EMP:** 7
SQ FT: 17,000
SALES (est): 1.6MM **Privately Held**
SIC: 3841 Surgical & medical instruments
PA: Mr. Chips, Inc.
1380 Gateway Dr Ste 7
Elgin IL 60124
847 468-9000

(G-13773)
OMNI PRODUCTS INC (PA)
3911 W Dayton St (60050-8377)
PHONE..................................815 344-3100
William E Cook, *President*
John Hart, *Corp Secy*
Caleb Riechman, *Engineer*
James Clark, *CFO*
EMP: 40
SALES (est): 6.9MM **Privately Held**
SIC: 3069 Molded rubber products

(G-13774)
ONLINE INC
4071 W Albany St (60050-8390)
PHONE..................................815 363-8008
Emil Cindric, *President*
EMP: 12
SQ FT: 10,000
SALES (est): 3MM **Privately Held**
SIC: 3569 Liquid automation machinery & equipment

(G-13775)
PAN AMERICA ENVIRONMENTAL INC
2309 N Ringwood Rd Ste G (60050-1313)
PHONE..................................815 344-2960
Scott Spalding, *President*
▲ **EMP:** 4
SALES (est): 932.8K **Privately Held**
SIC: 3823 8748 Water quality monitoring & control systems; environmental consultant

(G-13776)
PAPYS FOODS INC
4131 W Albany St (60050-8390)
PHONE..................................815 385-3313
David L Gallimore, *Ch of Bd*
Matt Gallimore, *President*
John Becker, *QA Dir*
EMP: 25
SQ FT: 65,000
SALES (est): 3.9MM **Privately Held**
WEB: www.papys.com
SIC: 7389 2099 Packaging & labeling services; seasonings; dry mixes

(G-13777)
PAW OFFICE MACHINES INC
816 Madison Ave (60050-2414)
PHONE..................................815 363-9780
EMP: 2
SALES (est): 200K **Privately Held**
SIC: 3555 Mfg Printing Trades Machinery

(G-13778)
PINNACLE WOOD PRODUCTS INC
1703 S Schroeder Ln (60050-7028)
PHONE..................................815 385-0792
Wayne Lyons, *President*
Norman Evan, *Shareholder*
EMP: 7
SQ FT: 10,000
SALES (est): 700K **Privately Held**
SIC: 2431 Millwork

(G-13779)
PLASPROS INC (PA)
1143 Ridgeview Dr (60050-7013)
PHONE..................................815 430-2300
Norm Dusenberry, *President*
David Georgi, *President*
Debbie McQuaide, *Principal*
Phyllis Nelson, *COO*
Kate McHugh, *Vice Pres*
◆ **EMP:** 150
SQ FT: 76,500
SALES (est): 50.6MM **Privately Held**
WEB: www.plaspros.com
SIC: 3089 Injection molded finished plastic products; injection molding of plastics

(G-13780)
PLATINUM INC
Also Called: Fox Valley Tree Professionals
813 N Lillian St (60050-5323)
PHONE..................................815 385-0910
Nicole Lee, *Principal*
EMP: 5
SALES (est): 155K **Privately Held**
SIC: 1799 3537 Construction site cleanup; trucks: freight, baggage, etc.: industrial, except mining

(G-13781)
POINT READY MIX LLC (PA)
5435 Bull Valley Rd # 130 (60050-7434)
PHONE..................................815 578-9100
David Lapointe, *President*
EMP: 1
SALES (est): 7.1MM **Privately Held**
SIC: 3273 Ready-mixed concrete

(G-13782)
POLYONE CORPORATION
GLS Thrmplstic Elstmers N Amer
833 Ridgeview Dr (60050-7050)
PHONE..................................815 385-8500
James Albert, *Plant Mgr*
Bob Heffington, *Mfg Mgr*
Hochul Jung, *Research*
Andrew Orosz, *Engineer*
Osvaldo Hernandez, *Accounts Mgr*
EMP: 75 **Publicly Held**
SIC: 2821 3087 Thermoplastic materials; custom compound purchased resins
PA: Polyone Corporation
33587 Walker Rd
Avon Lake OH 44012

Mchenry
Mchenry County

(G-13783)
POLYONE CORPORATION
921 Ridgeview Dr (60050)
PHONE..................................815 385-8500
Walter Ripple, *Manager*
EMP: 10 **Publicly Held**
SIC: 2821 3087 Thermoplastic materials; custom compound purchased resins
PA: Polyone Corporation
33587 Walker Rd
Avon Lake OH 44012

McHenry
Mchenry County

(G-13784)
PROSTHETICS ORTHOTICS HAN
620 S Il Route 31 Ste 7 (60050-3134)
PHONE..................................847 695-6955
EMP: 3
SALES (est): 184.5K **Privately Held**
SIC: 3842 Mfg Surgical Appliances/Supplies

(G-13785)
RAM SYSTEMS & COMMUNICATION
6411 Round Up Rd (60050-6553)
PHONE..................................847 487-7575
Ronald Mitchell, *President*
Julie Mitchell, *Admin Sec*
EMP: 4 **EST:** 1983
SALES (est): 405K **Privately Held**
SIC: 3663 Radio & TV communications equipment

(G-13786)
REHOBOT INC
3980 W Albany St Ste 1 (60050-8397)
PHONE..................................815 385-7777
Kjell-Roger Holmstrom, *Ch of Bd*
Magnus Johnson, *Principal*
Trish Simpson, *Administration*
▲ **EMP:** 3
SQ FT: 1,200
SALES (est): 280.9K **Privately Held**
SALES (corp-wide): 10.6MM **Privately Held**
WEB: www.rehobot.us
SIC: 1799 3569 3593 3492 Hydraulic equipment, installation & service; jacks, hydraulic; fluid power actuators, hydraulic or pneumatic; fluid power valves & hose fittings; pumps, hydraulic power transfer
PA: Obadja Ab
Soderbyvagen 2
Arlandastad 195 6
708 400-800

(G-13787)
RELIABLE SAND AND GRAVEL CO
Also Called: Drr Construction
2121 S River Rd Ste B (60051-9228)
P.O. Box 707, Island Lake (60042-0707)
PHONE..................................815 385-5020
Donald R Roberts, *President*
EMP: 8
SQ FT: 600
SALES (est): 1.1MM **Privately Held**
WEB: www.docsriverroadstorage.com
SIC: 1442 Common sand mining; gravel mining

(G-13788)
RIVERSIDE BAKE SHOP
1309 N Riverside Dr (60050-4509)
PHONE..................................815 385-0044
Charles B Rice, *President*
Carol Rice, *Corp Secy*
EMP: 40 **EST:** 1973
SQ FT: 1,200
SALES (est): 1.6MM **Privately Held**
WEB: www.riversidebakeshop.com
SIC: 5461 5149 2051 Bread; bakery products; bread, cake & related products

(G-13789)
RUSH PRINTING ON OAK
1627 Oak Dr (60050-0305)
PHONE..................................815 344-8880
John De Fabio, *President*
EMP: 4
SALES (est): 357.5K **Privately Held**
SIC: 2752 Commercial printing, offset

(G-13790)
SALATAS SMOKED MEATS
1206 N Oakwood Dr (60050-4138)
PHONE..................................224 433-1205
Dariusz Salata, *Principal*
EMP: 3
SALES (est): 129.9K **Privately Held**
SIC: 2013 Smoked meats from purchased meat

(G-13791)
SCHOMMER INC
Also Called: Minuteman Press
3410 W Elm St (60050-4433)
PHONE..................................815 344-1404
Tom Schommer, *President*
EMP: 8
SQ FT: 2,500
SALES (est): 750K **Privately Held**
SIC: 2752 2791 2789 Commercial printing, lithographic; typesetting; bookbinding & related work

(G-13792)
SNO GEM INC
Also Called: Sno Gem Snow Guards
4800 Metalmaster Dr (60050-7017)
PHONE..................................888 766-4367
Michael V Smeja, *Principal*
Daniel F Smeja, *Principal*
James Carpenter, *Vice Pres*
David Kozial, *Controller*
Marisol Macias, *Accounts Exec*
EMP: 13
SQ FT: 100,000
SALES: 5MM **Privately Held**
SIC: 3354 3089 3446 Aluminum extruded products; plastic hardware & building products; architectural metalwork

(G-13793)
SPHERE LASER LLC (PA)
2020 Julia Way (60051-3778)
PHONE..................................317 752-1604
John Gonzales,
◆ **EMP:** 3
SQ FT: 5,000
SALES: 2MM **Privately Held**
SIC: 3699 Laser systems & equipment

Mchenry
Mchenry County

(G-13794)
SPLICE ENERGY SOLUTIONS LLC
2106 Stilling Ln (60050-8057)
PHONE..................................815 861-8402
Nolan Heatley,
EMP: 3
SALES (est): 125.5K **Privately Held**
SIC: 3714 Booster (jump-start) cables, automotive

McHenry
Mchenry County

(G-13795)
STANDARD SAFETY EQUIPMENT CO
1407 Ridgeview Dr (60050-7023)
P.O. Box 189 (60051-9003)
PHONE..................................815 363-8565
Scott R Olson, *President*
Steven A Medves, *Exec VP*
Cindy Burger, *Vice Pres*
Kim Jebens, *Mfg Staff*
Jim Krammen, *Engineer*
EMP: 32 **EST:** 1921
SQ FT: 35,000
SALES (est): 5.9MM **Privately Held**
WEB: www.standardsafety.com
SIC: 3842 3826 3021 2326 Personal safety equipment; welders' hoods; clothing, fire resistant & protective; environmental testing equipment; rubber & plastics footwear; men's & boys' work clothing

(G-13796)
SULLIVANS INC
5508 W Chasefield Cir (60050-5133)
PHONE..................................815 331-8347
EMP: 10
SALES (corp-wide): 12.2MM **Privately Held**
WEB: www.sullivansinc.com
SIC: 5131 3965 Notions; fasteners, buttons, needles & pins
PA: Sullivans, Inc.
121 Franklin St
Hanson MA
781 293-9430

(G-13797)
SUMMIT PLASTICS INC
1207 Adams Dr (60051-4562)
PHONE..................................815 578-8700
Michael Stekl, *President*
Michelle L Martin, *Vice Pres*
▲ **EMP:** 5
SQ FT: 4,500
SALES (est): 874.4K **Privately Held**
SIC: 3089 Injection molding of plastics

(G-13798)
SUMMIT TOOLING INC
1207 Adams Dr (60051-4562)
PHONE..................................815 385-7500
Dan Martin, *President*
Al Linden, *Foreman/Supr*
Michelle Martin, *CFO*

▲ = Import ▼ = Export
◆ = Import/Export

GEOGRAPHIC SECTION

Melrose Park - Cook County (G-13825)

EMP: 18
SQ FT: 3,000
SALES (est): 3.9MM **Privately Held**
SIC: 3544 Special dies & tools

(G-13799)
SUNNYWOOD INCORPORATED
2750 Barney Ct (60051-4565)
PHONE..............815 675-9777
William Woo, *President*
▲ EMP: 4
SALES (est): 972K **Privately Held**
SIC: 3944 2389 3961 Games, toys & children's vehicles; costumes; costume jewelry

(G-13800)
SUPER AGGREGATES INC (HQ)
Also Called: Super Mix
5435 Bull Valley Rd # 330 (60050-7434)
PHONE..............815 385-8000
Jack Pease, *President*
Andrea Jones, *Admin Sec*
EMP: 8
SALES (est): 2.4MM
SALES (corp-wide): 16.7MM **Privately Held**
SIC: 1442 Sand mining; gravel mining
PA: J. Pease Construction Co., Inc.
1001 Williams Rd
Genoa City WI 53128
815 790-1293

(G-13801)
SUPER MIX INC (PA)
Also Called: Negative
5435 Bull Valley Rd # 130 (60050-7433)
PHONE..............815 578-9100
Jack Pease, *President*
Thomas Ziemba, *General Mgr*
Tory Pease, *Principal*
Shelly Denkov, *Manager*
EMP: 57
SALES (est): 14.2MM **Privately Held**
SIC: 3273 Ready-mixed concrete

(G-13802)
SUPER MIX OF WISCONSIN INC
5435 Bull Valley Rd # 130 (60050-7433)
PHONE..............262 859-9000
Robert Epping, *President*
EMP: 3
SALES (est): 321.3K **Privately Held**
WEB: www.pointreadymix.com
SIC: 3273 Ready-mixed concrete

(G-13803)
SUPER MIX OF WISCONSIN INC
5435 Bull Valley Rd # 130 (60050-7433)
PHONE..............815 578-9100
EMP: 12
SALES (est): 1.8MM **Privately Held**
SIC: 3273 Mfg Ready-Mixed Concrete

(G-13804)
T AND T CABINET CO
5505 W Chasefield Cir (60050-5134)
PHONE..............815 245-6322
Mike Heinz, *Owner*
EMP: 2
SALES (est): 217.4K **Privately Held**
SIC: 2434 Wood kitchen cabinets

(G-13805)
T J VAN DER BOSCH & ASSOCIATES
430 W Wegner Rd (60051-8653)
P.O. Box 340, Wauconda (60084-0340)
PHONE..............815 344-3210
Thomas J Van Der Bosch, *President*
Cornelia M Van Der Bosch, *Treasurer*
EMP: 20
SQ FT: 15,000
SALES (est): 1.3MM **Privately Held**
SIC: 3711 3714 3088 2522 Automobile bodies, passenger car, not including engine, etc.; motor vehicle parts & accessories; plastics plumbing fixtures; office furniture, except wood

(G-13806)
VANDERBOSCH TJ & ASSOC INC
1614 S River Rd (60051-9251)
PHONE..............815 344-3210

Thomas Der Bosch, *President*
EMP: 3
SALES (est): 243.6K **Privately Held**
SIC: 3711 Automobile bodies, passenger car, not including engine, etc.

(G-13807)
VESTERGAARD COMPANY INC (PA)
1721 Oak Dr (60050-0306)
P.O. Box 280 (60051-9004)
PHONE..............815 759-9102
Godfrey Vestergaard, *President*
Brock Crocker, *Business Mgr*
Stefan Vestergaard, *Vice Pres*
Dave Madson, *Opers Staff*
Peter Haug, *Sales Mgr*
▲ EMP: 6
SQ FT: 10,000
SALES (est): 691K **Privately Held**
WEB: www.vestergaardcompany.com
SIC: 3728 Aircraft parts & equipment

(G-13808)
W M PLASTICS INC
Also Called: Novation Industries
5151 Bolger Ct (60050-7015)
PHONE..............815 578-8888
Chris Metz, *Ch of Bd*
Scott Baxter, *President*
David Butt, *President*
Russ Schweizer, *Vice Pres*
John Snyder, *Vice Pres*
▲ EMP: 87 EST: 1966
SQ FT: 105,000
SALES (est): 32.6MM **Privately Held**
WEB: www.wmplastics.com
SIC: 3089 Injection molding of plastics

(G-13809)
WIRFS INDUSTRIES INC
4021 Main St (60050-5244)
P.O. Box 2049 (60051-9034)
PHONE..............815 344-0635
Timothy Wirfs, *President*
EMP: 10
SQ FT: 6,500
SALES (est): 1.4MM **Privately Held**
SIC: 7538 7692 3444 General truck repair; welding repair; sheet metalwork

(G-13810)
WRIGHT TOOL & DIE INC
4829 Prime Pkwy (60050-7002)
PHONE..............815 669-2020
Dan Peterson, *President*
EMP: 12
SQ FT: 9,000
SALES (est): 1.2MM **Privately Held**
SIC: 3544 Forms (molds), for foundry & plastics working machinery; special dies & tools

Mechanicsburg
Sangamon County

(G-13811)
PRYCO INC (PA)
3rd And Garvey (62545)
P.O. Box 108 (62545-0108)
PHONE..............217 364-4467
Marjorie Bernhal, *President*
Bonnie Miller, *Partner*
Rolla Womack, *CIO*
Marjorie Bernahl, *MIS Dir*
▼ EMP: 30
SQ FT: 30,000
SALES (est): 3.8MM **Privately Held**
SIC: 3714 5661 3443 Fuel systems & parts, motor vehicle; men's boots; women's boots; fabricated plate work (boiler shop)

(G-13812)
QUANTUM HEALING
809 Timber Ridge Rd (62545-8101)
PHONE..............217 414-2412
EMP: 3
SALES (est): 171.9K **Privately Held**
SIC: 3572 Mfg Computer Storage Devices

Medinah
Dupage County

(G-13813)
GREAT GUY INC
Also Called: Ggi
22 W 220 Woodview Dr (60157)
P.O. Box 717, Itasca (60143-0717)
PHONE..............312 203-9872
Martin Gavac, *President*
Mike Messina, *Admin Sec*
EMP: 4
SQ FT: 140,000
SALES (est): 2.8MM **Privately Held**
SIC: 4225 7331 2759 General warehousing; mailing service; promotional printing

(G-13814)
INGENIOUS CONCEPTS INC
22w313 Temple Dr (60157-9707)
PHONE..............630 539-8059
Robert L Cucchi, *President*
Karen Cucchi, *Vice Pres*
EMP: 3
SQ FT: 500
SALES (est): 281.7K **Privately Held**
WEB: www.inconinc.com
SIC: 8711 3542 Machine tool design; machine tools, metal forming type

Medora
Jersey County

(G-13815)
PAULETTE COLSON
518 S Main St (62063-1012)
PHONE..............618 372-8888
Paulette M Colson, *Principal*
EMP: 13
SALES (est): 1.9MM **Privately Held**
WEB: www.colsontimber.com
SIC: 2421 Sawmills & planing mills, general

Melrose Park
Cook County

(G-13816)
A & L CONSTRUCTION INC
1951 Cornell Ave (60160)
PHONE..............708 343-1660
Angela Cook, *CEO*
Brice Schweitzer, *Real Est Agnt*
EMP: 30
SALES (est): 3.7MM **Privately Held**
SIC: 3273 Ready-mixed concrete

(G-13817)
A-1 TOOL CORPORATION
1425 Armitage Ave (60160-1424)
PHONE..............708 345-5000
Geoffrey Luther, *President*
Alfonso Arciniegas, *Vice Pres*
Monica Lucero, *Purch Agent*
Le Roy D Luther, *Treasurer*
Edward Schultz, *Sales Mgr*
▲ EMP: 80
SQ FT: 50,000
SALES (est): 12MM
SALES (corp-wide): 56.3MM **Privately Held**
SIC: 3544 Industrial molds
PA: Triangle Tool Corporation
8609 W Port Ave
Milwaukee WI 53224
414 357-7117

(G-13818)
ABOVE & BEYOND BLACK OXIDING
1029 N 27th Ave (60160-2940)
P.O. Box 1724 (60161-1724)
PHONE..............708 345-7100
Jack Cooper, *President*
EMP: 4
SALES (est): 516.9K **Privately Held**
SIC: 3541 Brushing machines (metalworking machinery)

(G-13819)
ABRAXIS BIOSCIENCE LLC
2020 N Ruby St (60160-1112)
PHONE..............310 883-1300
Barbara Relation, *Branch Mgr*
EMP: 5
SALES (corp-wide): 26.1B **Publicly Held**
SIC: 2834 Pharmaceutical preparations
HQ: Abraxis Bioscience, Llc
11755 Wilshire Blvd Fl 20
Los Angeles CA 90025

(G-13820)
ACCU-CHEM INDUSTRIES INC
1930 George St Ste 3 (60160-1501)
PHONE..............708 344-0900
Richard Ponx, *President*
EMP: 3
SQ FT: 12,000
SALES (est): 1.5MM **Privately Held**
SIC: 3555 Printing trades machinery

(G-13821)
ALIN MACHINING COMPANY INC (PA)
Also Called: Power Plant Services
3131 W Soffel Ave (60160-1718)
PHONE..............708 681-1043
Manish Gandhi, *CEO*
Sonia Gandhi, *Exec VP*
Don Haag, *Vice Pres*
Ray Bonilla, *Plant Supt*
Atiq Quadri, *Plant Mgr*
▲ EMP: 130
SQ FT: 100,000
SALES: 50MM **Privately Held**
SIC: 3621 5084 3511 3533 Electric motor & generator parts; power generators; electric motor & generator auxillary parts; industrial machinery & equipment; steam turbine generator set units, complete; gas field machinery & equipment; industrial machinery & equipment repair

(G-13822)
ALLOY WELDING CORP
2033 Janice Ave (60160-1076)
PHONE..............708 345-6756
John Troccoli, *President*
Mark Nausieda, *Design Engr*
Santo Urso, *Shareholder*
Elizabeth Schultz, *Admin Sec*
EMP: 30
SQ FT: 35,000
SALES (est): 5.8MM **Privately Held**
SIC: 3444 7692 Sheet metalwork; welding repair

(G-13823)
ALM DISTRIBUTORS LLC
Also Called: Racconto
2060 Janice Ave (60160-1011)
PHONE..............708 865-8000
Joe Mugnolo, *General Mgr*
Chris Hansen, *Vice Pres*
Andrea J Mugnolo, *Mng Member*
Steve Listecki,
Lee Mugnolo,
▲ EMP: 3
SALES (est): 606.3K **Privately Held**
SIC: 2032 Italian foods: packaged in cans, jars, etc.

(G-13824)
ALOIS BOX CO INC
2000 N Mannheim Rd (60160-1092)
PHONE..............708 681-4090
David G Jones, *President*
Bruna J Granato, *Vice Pres*
George Hurd, *Purch Mgr*
Robert Reid, *Controller*
Bruna Granato, *VP Sales*
EMP: 50
SQ FT: 55,000
SALES (est): 13.8MM **Privately Held**
WEB: www.aloisbox.com
SIC: 2653 Boxes, corrugated: made from purchased materials; display items, corrugated: made from purchased materials

(G-13825)
AMERICAN STEEL FABRICATORS INC
1985 Anson Dr (60160-1018)
PHONE..............847 807-4200

Melrose Park - Cook County (G-13826)

Mary Ann Parker, *President*
Terry Stoll, *Director*
EMP: 11 **EST:** 2005
SQ FT: 1,500
SALES: 4.7MM **Privately Held**
SIC: 5051 3449 Structural shapes, iron or steel; miscellaneous metalwork

(G-13826)
AP MACHINE INC
1975 N 17th Ave (60160-1348)
PHONE................................708 450-1010
Peter Konieczny, *CEO*
EMP: 19
SALES (est): 3MM **Privately Held**
SIC: 3599 Machine shop, jobbing & repair

(G-13827)
ATHENIAN FOODS CO
Also Called: Athenian Pastries & Food
1814 N 15th Ave (60160-2112)
PHONE................................708 343-6700
Kostas Thanopoulos, *President*
Polyxeni Thanopoulos, *Admin Sec*
EMP: 10
SALES (est): 3.8MM **Privately Held**
WEB: www.athenianfoods.com
SIC: 5149 5461 2099 2051 Bakery products; bakeries; food preparations; bread, cake & related products

(G-13828)
AUTOMATION SYSTEMS INC
2001 N 17th Ave (60160-1347)
PHONE................................847 671-9515
Carl Schanstra, *President*
EMP: 20 **EST:** 1960
SQ FT: 12,000
SALES (est): 3.2MM **Privately Held**
WEB: www.weassemble4u.com
SIC: 8711 3569 3451 3549 Designing: ship, boat, machine & product; assembly machines, non-metalworking; screw machine products; metalworking machinery

(G-13829)
AVLON INDUSTRIES INC
1999 N 15th Ave (60160-1402)
PHONE................................708 344-0709
Ali N Syed, *President*
Ned Washington, *Sales Dir*
Abbas Rizawi, *Director*
Dure S Syed, *Admin Sec*
◆ **EMP:** 90
SQ FT: 60,000
SALES (est): 56.6MM **Privately Held**
SIC: 5122 2844 5131 Cosmetics; hair preparations; toilet preparations; hair preparations, including shampoos; piece goods & notions

(G-13830)
BALEY ENTERPRISES INC
1206 N 31st Ave (60160-2969)
PHONE................................708 681-0900
James Baley, *President*
Jim Baley, *Owner*
Norma Baley, *Corp Secy*
EMP: 5
SQ FT: 6,000
SALES: 750K **Privately Held**
SIC: 3599 5084 7692 Machine shop, jobbing & repair; industrial machinery & equipment; welding repair

(G-13831)
BILLY CASH FOR GOLD INC
101 N 19th Ave (60160-3702)
PHONE................................773 905-2447
Aqel Harb, *Owner*
EMP: 3
SALES (est): 149.1K **Privately Held**
SIC: 1041 Gold ores

(G-13832)
BODYCOTE THERMAL PROC INC
1975 N Ruby St (60160-1109)
PHONE................................708 236-5360
Jill Long, *Vice Pres*
Gerald Ketchum, *Plant Supt*
Tim Veenbaas, *Branch Mgr*
William Iancau, *Director*
John Delong, *Maintence Staff*
EMP: 63
SQ FT: 150,000
SALES (corp-wide): 929.6MM **Privately Held**
WEB: www.bodycote.com
SIC: 3398 Metal heat treating
HQ: Bodycote Thermal Processing, Inc.
12750 Merit Dr Ste 1400
Dallas TX 75251
214 904-2420

(G-13833)
BORGWARNER INC
2437 W North Ave (60160-1120)
PHONE................................708 731-4540
Michelle Rosas, *Principal*
EMP: 18
SALES (corp-wide): 10.1B **Publicly Held**
SIC: 3559 Automotive maintenance equipment
PA: Borgwarner Inc.
3850 Hamlin Rd
Auburn Hills MI 48326
248 754-9200

(G-13834)
BORGWARNER TRANSM SYSTEMS INC
2437 W North Ave (60160-1120)
PHONE................................708 731-4540
Darlene Baldridge, *Branch Mgr*
EMP: 19
SALES (corp-wide): 10.1B **Publicly Held**
SIC: 3714 Motor vehicle parts & accessories
HQ: Borgwarner Transmission Systems Inc.
3800 Automation Ave # 500
Auburn Hills MI 48326
248 754-9200

(G-13835)
BOST CORPORATION
Also Called: Tax Collector
2780 Thomas St (60160-2900)
PHONE................................708 450-9234
Stefan Kiminski, *Manager*
EMP: 10
SALES (corp-wide): 5.1MM **Privately Held**
SIC: 3564 Blowers & fans
PA: Bost Corporation
601 Saint Charles Rd
Maywood IL 60153
708 344-7023

(G-13836)
BOYCE INDUSTRIES INC
4915 Division St (60160-2653)
PHONE................................708 345-0455
Robert L Boyce, *President*
EMP: 13
SQ FT: 10,000
SALES: 1.3MM **Privately Held**
WEB: www.boyceindustries.com
SIC: 3498 3714 Tube fabricating (contract bending & shaping); motor vehicle parts & accessories; frames, motor vehicle; exhaust systems & parts, motor vehicle

(G-13837)
BRISTOL HOSE & FITTING INC
Also Called: Hydraulic Hoses & Fittings
1950 N Mannheim Rd Ste 1 (60160-1038)
PHONE................................708 492-3456
Michael Tuminaro, *CEO*
Carol Tuminaro, *Vice Pres*
Peter Tuminaro, *Vice Pres*
Phillip Tuminaro, *Admin Sec*
EMP: 23
SALES: 6MM **Privately Held**
SIC: 5074 3492 3052 Plumbing fittings & supplies; fluid power valves & hose fittings; automobile hose, plastic

(G-13838)
BRISTOL TRANSPORT INC
Also Called: Bristol Towing & Transport
1950 N Mannheim Rd Ste 1 (60160-1038)
PHONE................................708 343-6411
Philip Tuminaro, *President*
Michael Tuminaro, *Vice Pres*
Peter Tuminaro, *Vice Pres*
Carol Tuminaro, *Admin Sec*
EMP: 26
SALES (est): 3.3MM **Privately Held**
SIC: 4212 3492 3052 Local trucking, without storage; fluid power valves & hose fittings; rubber & plastics hose & beltings

(G-13839)
CATCHING HYDRAULICS CO LTD
1733 N 25th Ave (60160-1823)
PHONE................................708 344-2334
Inderjit Sundal, *President*
Juanita B Sundal, *Corp Secy*
EMP: 20 **EST:** 1954
SQ FT: 1,000
SALES (est): 1MM **Privately Held**
WEB: www.catchingengineering.com
SIC: 3593 3494 3511 Fluid power cylinders, hydraulic or pneumatic; plumbing & heating valves; turbines & turbine generator sets

(G-13840)
CELGENE CORPORATION
2045 Cornell Ave (60160-1002)
PHONE................................908 673-9000
Sandre Knotts, *Mfg Staff*
Nathan Boersen, *Research*
Lalita Gardner, *Research*
Ho-Wah Hui, *Research*
Barbara Gluck, *Sales Staff*
EMP: 14
SALES (corp-wide): 26.1B **Publicly Held**
SIC: 2834 Pharmaceutical preparations
HQ: Celgene Corporation
86 Morris Ave
Summit NJ 07901
908 673-9000

(G-13841)
CHASE FASTENERS INC
1539 N 25th Ave (60160-1821)
PHONE................................708 345-0335
Kennith Chadwick, *CEO*
Kenneth Chadwick, *Finance*
Rios Pablo,
EMP: 40
SQ FT: 40,000
SALES (est): 9.1MM **Privately Held**
WEB: www.chasefasteners.com
SIC: 3316 3451 3452 5085 Cold finishing of steel shapes; screw machine products; screws, metal; industrial supplies

(G-13842)
CHICAGO ENCLOSURES
1975 N 17th Ave (60160-1348)
PHONE................................708 344-6600
Angela P Caulfield, *Principal*
Dan Waterloo, *Opers Staff*
EMP: 4
SALES (est): 604.6K **Privately Held**
WEB: www.chicagoenclosures.com
SIC: 3448 Screen enclosures

(G-13843)
CHICAGO GRINDING & MACHINE CO
1950 N 15th Ave (60160-1403)
PHONE................................708 343-4399
Leonard D Kreplin, *Principal*
Glen Micek, *Site Mgr*
Mike Kreplin, *CFO*
Len Kreplin, *Manager*
EMP: 47 **EST:** 1920
SQ FT: 22,000
SALES (est): 10.1MM **Privately Held**
WEB: www.chicagogrinding.com
SIC: 3599 3541 3441 3423 Machine shop, jobbing & repair; machine tools, metal cutting type; fabricated structural metal; hand & edge tools

(G-13844)
CONSUMERS PACKING CO INC
1301 Carson Dr (60160-2970)
PHONE................................708 344-0047
William Schutz, *President*
Mike McKee, *Plant Mgr*
John Schutz, *Maint Spvr*
EMP: 73 **EST:** 1953
SQ FT: 14,000
SALES (est): 40.6MM **Privately Held**
WEB: www.consumerspacking.com
SIC: 5147 5812 2013 2011 Meats, fresh; eating places; sausages & other prepared meats; meat packing plants

(G-13845)
CSL PLASMA INC
1977 N Mannheim Rd (60160-1012)
PHONE................................708 343-8845
Ingrid Cox, *Supervisor*
EMP: 44 **Privately Held**
SIC: 2836 Plasmas
HQ: Csl Plasma Inc.
900 Broken Sound Pkwy Nw # 400
Boca Raton FL 33487
561 981-3700

(G-13846)
CURTO-LIGONIER FOUNDRIES CO
1215 N 31st Ave (60160-2905)
PHONE................................708 345-2250
Mark Borneman, *President*
Darleen Helig, *Manager*
Robert Krencik, *Manager*
Holly N Borneman, *Admin Sec*
Stephen Payne, *Admin Sec*
EMP: 50 **EST:** 1946
SQ FT: 40,000
SALES (est): 6.5MM **Privately Held**
WEB: www.curto.com
SIC: 3364 3365 3363 3543 Magnesium & magnesium-base alloy die-castings; aluminum foundries; aluminum die-castings; industrial patterns; nonferrous foundries

(G-13847)
DELAIR PUBLISHING COMPANY INC
2085 Cornell Ave (60160-1002)
PHONE................................708 345-7000
Dan P Genovese, *President*
Ralph P Genovese, *President*
Nick Vergoth, *VP Sales*
Robert Flatow, *Admin Sec*
EMP: 250
SALES (est): 9.9MM **Privately Held**
SIC: 2741 Miscellaneous publishing

(G-13848)
DEMCO INC
2975 W Soffel Ave (60160-1714)
PHONE................................708 345-4822
Daniel Spata, *President*
Kara Destefano, *Manager*
EMP: 10
SQ FT: 4,500
SALES (est): 1.6MM **Privately Held**
SIC: 3444 Metal ventilating equipment

(G-13849)
DETREX CORPORATION
Solvents & Envmtl Svcs Div
2537 W Le Moyne St (60160-1830)
PHONE................................708 345-3806
David Cody, *Branch Mgr*
EMP: 5 **Privately Held**
SIC: 3589 2842 Commercial cleaning equipment; drain pipe solvents or cleaners
HQ: Detrex Corporation
1000 Belt Line Ave
Cleveland OH 44109
216 749-2605

(G-13850)
DIAMOND BLAST CORPORATION
1741 N 30th Ave (60160-1787)
PHONE................................708 681-2640
David Collignon, *President*
Bob Bulgarelli, *General Mgr*
EMP: 13 **EST:** 1958
SQ FT: 11,000
SALES (est): 1.8MM **Privately Held**
WEB: www.diamondblast.com
SIC: 3541 Machine tools, metal cutting type

(G-13851)
DIESEL RADIATOR CO (PA)
1990 Janice Ave (60160-1077)
PHONE................................800 345-9244
Brian P Cahill, *President*
Humberto Suarez, *Principal*
Lisa Burkhart, *Vice Pres*
Graciela Saldana, *Engineer*
Tibaire Suarez, *Engineer*
◆ **EMP:** 140

GEOGRAPHIC SECTION

Melrose Park - Cook County (G-13878)

SQ FT: 18,000
SALES (est): 40.3MM **Privately Held**
SIC: 3519 Radiators, stationary engine

(G-13852)
DIESEL RADIATOR CO
3030 W Hirsch St (60160-1739)
PHONE.................................708 865-7299
Wayne Gorham, *Manager*
EMP: 75
SALES (corp-wide): 40.3MM **Privately Held**
SIC: 3443 3519 Air coolers, metal plate; radiators, stationary engine
PA: Diesel Radiator Co.
 1990 Janice Ave
 Melrose Park IL 60160
 800 345-9244

(G-13853)
DOUBLE-DISC GRINDING CORP
2041 Janice Ave (60160-1010)
PHONE.................................708 410-1770
Mike Patel, *Principal*
EMP: 9
SQ FT: 17,000
SALES (est): 1.3MM **Privately Held**
WEB: www.preciselapping.com
SIC: 3599 Machine shop, jobbing & repair

(G-13854)
DUNE MANUFACTURING COMPANY
1800 N 15th Ave (60160-2112)
PHONE.................................708 681-2905
Denis Colht, *President*
EMP: 10 EST: 1980
SQ FT: 12,500
SALES (est): 1.7MM **Privately Held**
SIC: 3451 Screw machine products

(G-13855)
DYNAMIC MANUFACTURING INC
1800 N 30th Ave Ste 1 (60160-1702)
PHONE.................................708 681-0682
Mark Woday, *Branch Mgr*
EMP: 85
SALES (corp-wide): 164.4MM **Privately Held**
SIC: 3714 Transmissions, motor vehicle
PA: Dynamic Manufacturing Inc
 4201 Raymond Dr
 Hillside IL 60162
 708 343-8753

(G-13856)
DYNAMIC MANUFACTURING INC
Also Called: Dynamic Mfg Torque Converters
1930 N Mannheim Rd (60160-1013)
PHONE.................................708 343-8753
EMP: 36
SALES (corp-wide): 149.5MM **Privately Held**
SIC: 3714 Motor Vehicle Parts And Accessories
PA: Dynamic Manufacturing Inc
 4201 Raymond Dr
 Hillside IL 60162
 708 343-8753

(G-13857)
DYNAMIC MANUFACTURING INC
1801 N 32nd Ave (60160-1043)
PHONE.................................708 343-8753
Tony Falco, *Manager*
EMP: 29
SALES (corp-wide): 164.4MM **Privately Held**
SIC: 4225 3566 General warehousing & storage; speed changers, drives & gears
PA: Dynamic Manufacturing Inc
 4201 Raymond Dr
 Hillside IL 60162
 708 343-8753

(G-13858)
DYNAMIC POWERTRAIN REMAN LLC
3003 W Hirsch St (60160-1738)
PHONE.................................708 343-5444
EMP: 11
SALES (est): 1.9MM **Privately Held**
SIC: 3566 Torque converters, except automotive

(G-13859)
ECONOMY IRON INC
3132 N Hirsch St (60160-1741)
PHONE.................................708 343-1777
Donna Johnston, *President*
Dan Johnston, *Vice Pres*
EMP: 15
SQ FT: 6,000
SALES (est): 1MM **Privately Held**
SIC: 3312 3496 3446 Hot-rolled iron & steel products; miscellaneous fabricated wire products; architectural metalwork

(G-13860)
EDGEWATER PRODUCTS COMPANY INC
3315 W North Ave (60160-1016)
P.O. Box 8484 (60161-8484)
PHONE.................................708 345-9200
Edward D Rolf, *President*
Bill Rolf, *Vice Pres*
Eve Torre, *Manager*
Lois J Rolf, *Admin Sec*
▲ EMP: 18 EST: 1947
SQ FT: 14,000
SALES (est): 3.4MM **Privately Held**
WEB: www.edgewaterproducts.com
SIC: 3069 2499 Rubber hardware; washers, rubber; cork & cork products

(G-13861)
EDGEWELL PER CARE BRANDS LLC
5000 Proviso Dr (60163-1360)
PHONE.................................708 544-5550
Sue Eggersdorfer, *Manager*
EMP: 300
SALES (corp-wide): 2.1B **Publicly Held**
WEB: www.energizerholdings.com
SIC: 3421 Razor blades & razors
HQ: Edgewell Personal Care Brands, Llc
 6 Research Dr
 Shelton CT 06484
 203 944-5500

(G-13862)
EJ SOMERVILLE PLATING CO
Also Called: E J Somerville
1305 N 31st Ave (60160-2907)
PHONE.................................708 345-5100
Ralph Hauslein, *President*
Randy Hauslein, *Corp Secy*
Lori Cushion, *CFO*
EMP: 9 EST: 1955
SQ FT: 6,000
SALES (est): 800K **Privately Held**
SIC: 3471 Chromium plating of metals or formed products; plating of metals or formed products

(G-13863)
ELM TOOL AND MANUFACTURING CO
10257 Dickens Ave (60164-1912)
PHONE.................................847 455-6805
EMP: 3
SALES (est): 180K **Privately Held**
SIC: 3544 Mfg Dies/Tools/Jigs/Fixtures

(G-13864)
EN-CHRO PLATING INC
2755 W Lake St (60160-3041)
PHONE.................................708 450-1250
Milan Pecharich, *President*
▲ EMP: 50
SQ FT: 85,000
SALES (est): 6.5MM **Privately Held**
SIC: 3471 Electroplating of metals or formed products

(G-13865)
ENVIRO TECH INTERNATIONAL INC
1800 N 25th Ave (60160-1869)
PHONE.................................708 343-6641
Rich Morford, *CEO*
Salvatore Lamantia, *President*
▼ EMP: 9
SALES (est): 2.7MM **Privately Held**
SIC: 2899 Chemical preparations

(G-13866)
FASTRON CO
2040 Janice Ave (60160-1011)
PHONE.................................630 766-5000
Tracy Martin, *President*
▲ EMP: 25 EST: 1942
SQ FT: 40,000
SALES (est): 5.6MM **Privately Held**
WEB: www.fastron.com
SIC: 3452 Screws, metal; bolts, metal

(G-13867)
FIXTURE HARDWARE CO (PA)
Also Called: Product Emphasis
2800 W Lake St (60160-2933)
PHONE.................................773 777-6100
Roger Wolf, *President*
Todd Carmichael, *Vice Pres*
Robert Anderson, *Project Mgr*
Keith Billingsley, *Design Engr*
Anton Kurkalov, *Design Engr*
▲ EMP: 50 EST: 1920
SQ FT: 72,000
SALES (est): 7.6MM **Privately Held**
WEB: www.fhcmarketing.com
SIC: 2542 2591 Fixtures: display, office or store: except wood; showcases (not refrigerated): except wood; racks, merchandise display or storage: except wood; counters or counter display cases: except wood; shade, curtain & drapery hardware

(G-13868)
FOREST ELECTRIC COMPANY
Also Called: Felco
1301 Armitage Ave Ste B (60160-1423)
PHONE.................................708 681-0180
Charles C Meeks Jr, *President*
EER Loof, *Principal*
Jorge Alvarez, *Engineer*
▲ EMP: 22 EST: 1946
SQ FT: 25,000
SALES (est): 3.7MM **Privately Held**
WEB: www.forestelectric.com
SIC: 3677 3612 Electronic coils, transformers & other inductors; transformers, except electric
HQ: Kemet Electronics Corporation
 1 E Broward Blvd Ste 200
 Fort Lauderdale FL 33301
 864 963-6700

(G-13869)
FRESENIUS KABI USA INC
2020 N Ruby St (60160-1112)
PHONE.................................708 450-7500
Martha Urban, *QC Mgr*
Joel Stachura, *Engineer*
Zbigniew Goryl, *Project Engr*
John Goodfellow, *Marketing Mgr*
Steve Weltler, *Manager*
EMP: 400
SALES (corp-wide): 39.1B **Privately Held**
WEB: www.kabivenusa.com
SIC: 5122 2834 Pharmaceuticals; pharmaceutical preparations
HQ: Fresenius Kabi Usa, Inc.
 3 Corporate Dr
 Lake Zurich IL 60047

(G-13870)
FRESENIUS KABI USA INC
2020 N Ruby St (60160-1112)
PHONE.................................708 410-4761
Virgil Derencius, *Branch Mgr*
EMP: 166
SALES (corp-wide): 39.1B **Privately Held**
WEB: www.kabivenusa.com
SIC: 2834 Pharmaceutical preparations
HQ: Fresenius Kabi Usa, Inc.
 3 Corporate Dr
 Lake Zurich IL 60047

(G-13871)
FRESENIUS KABI USA INC
American Pharmaceutical
2020 N Ruby St (60160-1112)
PHONE.................................708 345-6170
Sam Trippie, *Principal*
EMP: 200
SALES (corp-wide): 39.1B **Privately Held**
SIC: 2834 Pharmaceutical preparations
HQ: Fresenius Kabi Usa, Inc.
 3 Corporate Dr
 Lake Zurich IL 60047

(G-13872)
FRIGID FLUID COMPANY
11631 W Grand Ave (60164-1302)
PHONE.................................708 836-1215
Robert Yeazel, *President*
John Yeazel, *Principal*
Marilyn Yeazel, *Chairman*
▲ EMP: 30 EST: 1892
SQ FT: 40,400
SALES: 4.1MM **Privately Held**
WEB: www.frigidfluid.com
SIC: 2869 5087 Embalming fluids; cemetery & funeral directors' equipment & supplies

(G-13873)
GENERAL MANUFACTURING LLC
1725 N 33rd Ave (60160-1707)
PHONE.................................708 345-8600
Shailja Gandhi, *CEO*
Earl Kaminski, *General Mgr*
Mike Netuik, *Principal*
Philip Sexauer, *Vice Pres*
Anthony McGee, *CFO*
▲ EMP: 70 EST: 2011
SALES (est): 16MM **Privately Held**
SIC: 3621 Motors & generators

(G-13874)
GLASS DIMENSIONS INC
Also Called: Extreme Glass
1942 N 15th Ave (60160-1403)
PHONE.................................708 410-2305
DOE Corsei, *President*
EMP: 15
SALES (est): 1.4MM **Privately Held**
SIC: 3231 Products of purchased glass

(G-13875)
GRAPHIC ARTS FINISHING COMPANY
Also Called: Gafco
1990 N Mannheim Rd (60160-1013)
PHONE.................................708 345-8484
William J Quinn, *President*
Mary Pat Quinn-Headley, *Corp Secy*
Robert D Quinn, *Vice Pres*
Bill Lodding, *Maint Spvr*
Emilio Flores, *Purchasing*
▲ EMP: 51 EST: 1945
SQ FT: 57,500
SALES (est): 12.4MM **Privately Held**
WEB: www.gafco.com
SIC: 2675 Paper die-cutting; paperboard die-cutting

(G-13876)
GRO-MAR INDUSTRIES INC
2725 Thomas St (60160-2934)
P.O. Box 1649 (60161-1649)
PHONE.................................708 343-5901
George E Molitor, *President*
EMP: 18
SQ FT: 20,000
SALES (est): 4.6MM **Privately Held**
SIC: 2679 Paper products, converted

(G-13877)
H J M P CORP (HQ)
Also Called: Home Juice Co of Memphis
1930 George St Ste 2 (60160-1501)
PHONE.................................708 345-5370
Stan Sheraton, *President*
Mike Hoeppel, *President*
Allen Domzalski, *Vice Pres*
EMP: 150
SQ FT: 65,000
SALES: 88MM
SALES (corp-wide): 1B **Publicly Held**
WEB: www.accuchemindustries.com
SIC: 2033 5149 0174 2037 Fruit juices: packaged in cans, jars, etc.; beverages, except coffee & tea; juices; orange grove; frozen fruits & vegetables
PA: National Beverage Corp.
 8100 Sw 10th St Ste 4000
 Plantation FL 33324
 954 581-0922

(G-13878)
HARRIS EQUIPMENT CORPORATION
2040 N Hawthorne Ave (60160-1106)
PHONE.................................708 343-0866
Gary Pollack, *President*
John Peterson, *COO*
Jeff Levin, *Vice Pres*
John Pearson, *Vice Pres*

Melrose Park - Cook County (G-13879)

Brenda Moelker, *Human Res Mgr*
◆ **EMP:** 42
SALES (est): 12.3MM **Privately Held**
SIC: 3563 Air & gas compressors

(G-13879)
HECKMANN BUILDING PRODUCTS INC
1501 N 31st Ave (60160-2911)
PHONE....................708 865-2403
Paul M Curtis, *CEO*
Paul G Curtis, *President*
▲ **EMP:** 20
SQ FT: 45,000
SALES (est): 3.8MM **Privately Held**
WEB: www.heckmannbuildingprods.com
SIC: 3429 5039 Builders' hardware; joists

(G-13880)
HOME JUICE CORP
1930 George St Ste 2 (60160-1501)
PHONE....................708 345-5370
EMP: 9
SALES (est): 121.5K
SALES (corp-wide): 1B **Publicly Held**
SIC: 2086 Iced tea & fruit drinks, bottled & canned
PA: National Beverage Corp.
  8100 Sw 10th St Ste 4000
  Plantation FL 33324
  954 581-0922

(G-13881)
IMPAC GROUP INC
1950 N Ruby St (60160-1110)
PHONE....................708 344-9100
Richard Block, *President*
EMP: 1526
SALES (est): 76MM
SALES (corp-wide): 18.2B **Publicly Held**
SIC: 2657 Folding paperboard boxes
HQ: Westrock Mwv, Llc
  501 S 5th St
  Richmond VA 23219
  804 444-1000

(G-13882)
INDUSTRIAL FIBERGLASS INC
Also Called: I F I
1100 Main St (60160-4130)
PHONE....................708 681-2707
Daryl Johnson, *President*
Dennis Johnson, *Admin Sec*
EMP: 10
SQ FT: 12,000
SALES: 1MM **Privately Held**
SIC: 3229 3564 3088 Glass fiber products; blowers & fans; plastics plumbing fixtures

(G-13883)
INTERLAKE MECALUX INC (DH)
1600 N 25th Ave (60160-1868)
PHONE....................708 344-9999
Angel De Arriba, *President*
Krzysztof Zygulski, *Purch Dir*
Jesus Casas, *Purchasing*
Ron Rhodes, *QC Dir*
Oleg Seroshtan, *Engineer*
◆ **EMP:** 289
SQ FT: 285,000
SALES (est): 294.1MM
SALES (corp-wide): 37.1MM **Privately Held**
SIC: 5084 2542 Materials handling machinery; partitions & fixtures, except wood
HQ: Mecalux, Sa
  Calle Silici, 1 -5
  Cornella De Llobregat 08940
  932 616-900

(G-13884)
INTERNATIONAL CUTTING DIE INC
2030 Janice Ave (60160-1027)
PHONE....................708 343-3333
Kevin McHenry, *President*
Timothy McEnery, *Admin Sec*
EMP: 30
SQ FT: 23,000
SALES (est): 6.2MM **Privately Held**
SIC: 3544 Special dies & tools

(G-13885)
J & S MACHINE WORKS INC
1733 N 25th Ave (60160-1823)
PHONE....................708 344-2101
Juanita B Sundal, *President*
EMP: 6
SALES (est): 605.8K **Privately Held**
SIC: 3599 Machine shop, jobbing & repair

(G-13886)
JKS VENTURES INC (PA)
2035 Indian Boundry Dr (60160-1136)
PHONE....................708 345-9344
Josephine Difronzo, *President*
EMP: 13
SALES (est): 1.1MM **Privately Held**
SIC: 1411 Limestone & marble dimension stone

(G-13887)
JOHN J MONACO PRODUCTS CO INC
3120 W Lake St (60160-2920)
P.O. Box 1816 (60161-1816)
PHONE....................708 344-3333
Louis Monaco, *President*
▼ **EMP:** 30 **EST:** 1959
SALES (est): 5.6MM **Privately Held**
WEB: www.monaco-packaging.com
SIC: 2653 Boxes, solid fiber: made from purchased materials; partitions, solid fiber: made from purchased materials

(G-13888)
KERRY INC
Also Called: Kerry Ingredients
3141 W North Ave (60160-1108)
PHONE....................708 450-3260
Jess Meyer, *Manager*
EMP: 100 **Privately Held**
SIC: 2045 2099 Bread & bread type roll mixes: from purchased flour; food preparations
HQ: Kerry Inc.
  3400 Millington Rd
  Beloit WI 53511
  608 363-1200

(G-13889)
KREG MEDICAL INC
1940 Janice Ave (60160-1009)
PHONE....................312 829-8904
Craig Poulos, *President*
Todd Poulos, *Vice Pres*
Alina Couret, *Sales Staff*
▲ **EMP:** 120
SQ FT: 5,000
SALES (est): 12.1MM **Privately Held**
SIC: 2599 Hospital beds

(G-13890)
LEWIS BROTHERS BAKERIES INC
Also Called: North Baking
1955 W North Ave (60160-1131)
PHONE....................708 531-6435
Doug Johnson, *Branch Mgr*
EMP: 40
SALES (corp-wide): 456.5MM **Privately Held**
WEB: www.lewisbakeries.net
SIC: 5411 5149 2051 Grocery stores; groceries & related products; bread, cake & related products
PA: Lewis Brothers Bakeries Inc
  500 N Fulton Ave
  Evansville IN 47710
  812 425-4642

(G-13891)
MECH-TRONICS CORPORATION (PA)
1635 N 25th Ave (60160-1860)
PHONE....................708 343-3333
Eugene R Demuro, *President*
Mike Janusz, *Purch Mgr*
Michael Miller, *Buyer*
Mike Miller, *Buyer*
Lorrie Wright, *QC Mgr*
▼ **EMP:** 98 **EST:** 1948
SQ FT: 50,000
SALES: 12.8MM **Privately Held**
SIC: 3444 3823 Sheet metalwork; industrial instrmnts msrmnt display/control process variable

(G-13892)
MECH-TRONICS CORPORATION
Also Called: Mech-Tronics Nucluear Div
1701 N 25th Ave (60160-1823)
PHONE....................708 344-0202
Vince Campobasso, *Manager*
EMP: 6
SALES (corp-wide): 12.8MM **Privately Held**
SIC: 4225 3829 General warehousing & storage; measuring & controlling devices
PA: Mech-Tronics Corporation
  1635 N 25th Ave
  Melrose Park IL 60160
  708 344-9823

(G-13893)
MILLWOOD INC
5000 Proviso Dr Ste 1 (60163-1360)
PHONE....................708 343-7341
Jayson Rhodes, *Branch Mgr*
EMP: 17 **Privately Held**
SIC: 2448 Pallets, wood
PA: Millwood, Inc.
  3708 International Blvd
  Vienna OH 44473

(G-13894)
NAVISTAR INC
10400 W North Ave (60160-1028)
PHONE....................317 352-4500
EMP: 290
SALES (corp-wide): 11.2B **Publicly Held**
SIC: 3519 Internal combustion engines
HQ: Navistar, Inc.
  2701 Navistar Dr
  Lisle IL 60532
  331 332-5000

(G-13895)
NAVISTAR INC
10400 W North Ave 3 (60160-1028)
PHONE....................708 865-3333
Bob Monroe, *Branch Mgr*
EMP: 66
SALES (corp-wide): 11.2B **Publicly Held**
SIC: 3711 3714 Truck & tractor truck assembly; motor vehicle parts & accessories
HQ: Navistar, Inc.
  2701 Navistar Dr
  Lisle IL 60532
  331 332-5000

(G-13896)
NAVISTAR DEFENSE LLC (HQ)
10400 W North Ave (60160-1028)
P.O. Box 1488, Warrenville (60555-7488)
PHONE....................708 617-4500
Ted Wright, *CEO*
Kevin Thomas, *President*
Mike Hawn, *Vice Pres*
Mark Stasell, *Vice Pres*
Jeffrey Byrdy, *Production*
◆ **EMP:** 50
SALES (est): 10.7MM
SALES (corp-wide): 11.2B **Publicly Held**
SIC: 3812 3795 Defense systems & equipment; tanks & tank components
PA: Navistar International Corporation
  2701 Navistar Dr
  Lisle IL 60532
  331 332-5000

(G-13897)
NB FINISHING INC
3131 W Soffel Ave (60160-1718)
PHONE....................847 364-7500
Bruce Nichols, *President*
EMP: 10
SQ FT: 6,000
SALES (est): 2MM **Privately Held**
SIC: 7389 3471 Grinding, precision: commercial or industrial; plating & polishing

(G-13898)
NEXUS INDUSTRIES CORP
520 Winston Dr (60160-2349)
PHONE....................708 673-9289
Ioan Romeo Molnar, *President*
EMP: 5
SALES (est): 380.1K **Privately Held**
WEB: www.nexusindustriescorp.com
SIC: 3365 Machinery castings, aluminum

(G-13899)
OMEGA MANUFACTURING LLC
1037 N 27th Ave (60160-2940)
PHONE....................708 345-8505
Jose Garcia, *CEO*
EMP: 3
SALES (est): 365.9K **Privately Held**
WEB: www.omegamanufacturingllc.com
SIC: 3599 Machine shop, jobbing & repair

(G-13900)
OTAK INTERNATIONAL INC
2080 N 16th Ave (60160)
PHONE....................630 373-9229
Taher Elashry, *President*
EMP: 3 **EST:** 2012
SQ FT: 46,000
SALES: 1.7MM **Privately Held**
WEB: www.otakhomeproducts.com
SIC: 3824 5082 Mechanical & electromechanical counters & devices; general construction machinery & equipment

(G-13901)
P & M ORNAMENTAL IR WORKS INC
1200 N 31st Ave (60160-2906)
PHONE....................708 267-2868
Michael Iovane, *President*
EMP: 15
SALES (est): 2.3MM **Privately Held**
SIC: 3446 Architectural metalwork

(G-13902)
PARAGON MANUFACTURING INC
2001 N 15th Ave (60160-1404)
PHONE....................708 345-1717
Peter J Wright, *President*
Sheila Wright, *Corp Secy*
EMP: 60 **EST:** 1953
SQ FT: 36,000
SALES (est): 21.3MM **Privately Held**
WEB: www.paragonmanufacturing.com
SIC: 3089 Plastic containers, except foam

(G-13903)
PARK MANUFACTURING CORP INC
Also Called: Park Industries
1819 N 30th Ave (60160-1701)
PHONE....................708 345-6090
Larry K Warren, *President*
Cynthia Bell, *Manager*
EMP: 12
SQ FT: 13,560
SALES (est): 2.4MM **Privately Held**
WEB: www.parkindustriesinc.com
SIC: 3493 3496 3469 Flat springs, sheet or strip stock; woven wire products; metal stampings

(G-13904)
PRECISE LAPPING GRINDING CORP
2041 Janice Ave (60160-1010)
PHONE....................708 615-0240
Balwant Patel, *President*
Mike Patel, *Vice Pres*
Upendra Patel, *Admin Sec*
▲ **EMP:** 16
SQ FT: 7,200
SALES (est): 2.9MM **Privately Held**
SIC: 3541 3915 Deburring machines; grinding machines, metalworking; lapping machines; diamond cutting & polishing

(G-13905)
PRIDE MACHINE & TOOL CO INC
1821 N 30th Ave (60160-1798)
PHONE....................708 343-7190
John Ilczyszyn, *President*
Paul Ciochon, *Vice Pres*
Wally Ciochon, *Manager*
EMP: 14
SQ FT: 16,500
SALES: 4.5MM **Privately Held**
WEB: www.pridemachinetool.com
SIC: 3599 Machine shop, jobbing & repair

GEOGRAPHIC SECTION

Mendota - Lasalle County (G-13933)

(G-13906)
RAPID COPY & DUPLICATING CO
1723 N 25th Ave (60160-1823)
PHONE.....................312 733-3353
Anthony Kara, *President*
Elissa Kara, *Corp Secy*
EMP: 4
SALES (est): 495.2K **Privately Held**
SIC: 2752 7334 Commercial printing, offset; photocopying & duplicating services

(G-13907)
RAPID ELECTROPLATING PROCESS
2901 W Soffel Ave (60160-1714)
PHONE.....................708 344-2504
Richard Rapids, *President*
Pauline Glinka, *Vice Pres*
Arlene Mickols, *Admin Sec*
EMP: 5 **EST:** 1938
SQ FT: 6,700
SALES: 600K **Privately Held**
WEB: www.rapidelectroplating-admin.com
SIC: 3559 Electroplating machinery & equipment

(G-13908)
REPUBLIC DRILL
2058 N 15th Ave (60160-1405)
P.O. Box 1606 (60161-1606)
PHONE.....................708 865-7666
Gary Poteshman, *Cust Mgr*
Luke Branchaw, *Sales Executive*
Donald Consitt, *Manager*
Nick Ayala, *Manager*
EMP: 2
SALES (est): 244.5K **Privately Held**
SIC: 3544 Jigs & fixtures

(G-13909)
ROMEL PRESS INC
1747 N 20th Ave (60160-1905)
PHONE.....................708 343-6090
Robert Zamboni, *President*
Laura Zamboni, *Treasurer*
EMP: 3
SQ FT: 1,600
SALES (est): 401.6K **Privately Held**
WEB: www.romelpressinc.com
SIC: 2752 2399 Commercial printing, offset; banners, pennants & flags

(G-13910)
ROMERO STEEL COMPANY INC
1300 Main St (60160-4020)
PHONE.....................708 216-0001
Jose G Romero, *President*
Jose Romero Jr, *Treasurer*
Jesse Jay Martinez, *Admin Sec*
▼ **EMP:** 30
SQ FT: 55,000
SALES (est): 8.7MM **Privately Held**
SIC: 3441 Building components, structural steel

(G-13911)
ROYAL MACHINING CORPORATION
1617 N 31st Ave (60160-1837)
PHONE.....................708 338-3387
Bob Branko, *President*
Branko Dragojlovich, *President*
Milka Dragojlovich, *Vice Pres*
Vladimir D Dragojlovich, *Plant Supt*
Vladimir Dragojlovich, *Manager*
EMP: 4
SQ FT: 10,000
SALES (est): 631.6K **Privately Held**
SIC: 3599 Machine shop, jobbing & repair

(G-13912)
SAND-RITE MANUFACTURING CO
3080 W Soffel Ave (60160-1717)
PHONE.....................312 997-2200
Meyer S Kaplan, *President*
Marcus Kaplan, *Vice Pres*
Sharon Barrera, *Admin Sec*
▲ **EMP:** 6
SQ FT: 5,000
SALES (est): 1MM **Privately Held**
SIC: 3553 3291 Sanding machines, except portable floor sanders: woodworking; abrasive products

(G-13913)
SCHILKE MUSIC PRODUCTS INC
4520 James Pl (60160-1007)
PHONE.....................708 343-8858
Andrew Naumann, *President*
Chris Jones, *Production*
Elizabeth Nowak, *Human Resources*
EMP: 31 **EST:** 1950
SQ FT: 12,000
SALES: 1MM **Privately Held**
WEB: www.schilkemusic.com
SIC: 3931 7699 Musical instruments; musical instrument repair services

(G-13914)
SCHRAM ENTERPRISES INC
5017 W Lake St (60160-2754)
PHONE.....................708 345-2252
Mark F Schram, *President*
Lorraine Schram, *Vice Pres*
EMP: 35 **EST:** 1954
SQ FT: 15,000
SALES (est): 7.1MM **Privately Held**
WEB: www.acegrinding.com
SIC: 3599 3541 3291 Machine shop, jobbing & repair; machine tools, metal cutting type; abrasive products

(G-13915)
SKEPTIC DISTILLERY CO
2525 W Le Moyne St (60160-1830)
PHONE.....................708 223-8286
Karl Loepke, *President*
EMP: 3
SALES: 300K **Privately Held**
SIC: 2085 Distilled & blended liquors

(G-13916)
STAIRS AND RAILS INC
1200 Main St Ste 2 (60160-4059)
PHONE.....................708 216-0078
Robert Srachta, *Principal*
EMP: 4
SALES (est): 456.1K **Privately Held**
SIC: 3441 Fabricated structural metal

(G-13917)
STRIKEFORCE BOWLING LLC
Also Called: Kr Strikeforce Bowling
2020 Indian Boundry Dr (60160-1132)
PHONE.....................800 297-8555
Brad Handelman, *Mng Member*
▲ **EMP:** 20
SQ FT: 80,000
SALES (est): 4.1MM **Privately Held**
SIC: 3949 Sporting & athletic goods

(G-13918)
SUBURBAN LAMINATING INC
908 W Lake St (60160-4145)
PHONE.....................708 389-6106
John Dixon, *President*
EMP: 9
SQ FT: 5,800
SALES (est): 940K **Privately Held**
SIC: 3083 2541 2511 Plastic finished products, laminated; wood partitions & fixtures; wood household furniture

(G-13919)
SUNSCAPE TIME INC
Also Called: Pets Stop
2001 Janice Ave (60160-1046)
P.O. Box 1975, Bolingbrook (60440-7711)
PHONE.....................708 345-8791
Hemant K Bhandari, *President*
Milan Bhandari, *Vice Pres*
▲ **EMP:** 7 **EST:** 2001
SALES (est): 592.1K **Privately Held**
SIC: 3999 0782 Pet supplies; lawn & garden services

(G-13920)
T & K PRECISION GRINDING
1301 Armitage Ave Ste C (60160-1423)
PHONE.....................708 450-0565
Chris Czapka, *Partner*
Ted Niepsuj, *Partner*
EMP: 2
SALES (est): 247.3K **Privately Held**
SIC: 3599 Grinding castings for the trade

(G-13921)
TAFCO CORPORATION
1953 N 17th Ave (60160-1348)
PHONE.....................847 678-8425
Frank J Tortorella Jr, *President*
Michael Keeley, *COO*
Wes Matheney, *Opers Staff*
▼ **EMP:** 25 **EST:** 1959
SQ FT: 23,000
SALES (est): 4.6MM **Privately Held**
WEB: www.tafco.com
SIC: 3442 5039 3231 Metal doors; storm doors or windows, metal; jalousies, metal; screens, window, metal; glass construction materials; products of purchased glass

(G-13922)
TARNOW LOGISTICS INC
1001 N 16th Ave (60160-3327)
PHONE.....................773 844-3203
Artur Tendera, *Owner*
EMP: 1 **EST:** 2015
SALES: 200K **Privately Held**
SIC: 3537 Trucks: freight, baggage, etc.: industrial, except mining

(G-13923)
TONE PRODUCTS INC
2129 N 15th Ave (60160-1406)
PHONE.....................708 681-3660
Tim Evon, *President*
Jerry Christopoulos, *Vice Pres*
Tom Evon, *Vice Pres*
Jason Larusso, *Opers Staff*
William H Hamen, *CFO*
▼ **EMP:** 45 **EST:** 1947
SQ FT: 72,000
SALES (est): 11MM **Privately Held**
WEB: www.toneproducts.com
SIC: 2087 Syrups, drink; fruit juices: concentrated for fountain use; extracts, flavoring

(G-13924)
VALLEY FASTENER GROUP LLC
Forgo Fastener Division
3302 Bloomingdale Ave (60160-1030)
P.O. Box 1521 (60161-1521)
PHONE.....................708 343-2496
Ed Belson, *Plant Mgr*
EMP: 10
SALES (corp-wide): 26.1MM **Privately Held**
SIC: 3452 Screws, metal; rivets, metal
PA: Valley Fastener Group, Llc
  1490 Mitchell Rd
  Aurora IL 60505
  630 299-8910

(G-13925)
VEECO MANUFACTURING INC
Also Called: Pet Groom Products Div
1930 George St Ste A (60160-1501)
PHONE.....................312 666-0900
Leonard S Cohen, *President*
Tanya Simenis, *General Mgr*
Laurie Cohen, *Vice Pres*
◆ **EMP:** 15 **EST:** 1944
SQ FT: 50,000
SALES (est): 1.5MM **Privately Held**
WEB: www.veecosalonfurniture.com
SIC: 3999 5021 Barber & beauty shop equipment; furniture

(G-13926)
WAGNER ZIP-CHANGE INC
3100 W Hirsch St (60160-1741)
PHONE.....................708 681-4100
Georgene A Bercier, *President*
Gary Delaquila, *Vice Pres*
Donald Kolkebeck, *Treasurer*
▲ **EMP:** 40 **EST:** 1930
SQ FT: 33,000
SALES (est): 12.9MM **Privately Held**
WEB: www.wagnerzip.com
SIC: 5099 3993 3953 3444 Signs, except electric; letters for signs, metal; marking devices; sheet metalwork; nonferrous rolling & drawing; automotive & apparel trimmings

(G-13927)
WALLYS PRECISION MACHINING
1025 N 27th Ave (60160-2940)
PHONE.....................708 205-2950
Wally Gorny, *President*
EMP: 5

SQ FT: 2,000
SALES: 500K **Privately Held**
SIC: 3599 Machine shop, jobbing & repair

(G-13928)
WESTROCK CNSMR PACKG GROUP LLC
1950 N Ruby St (60160-1110)
PHONE.....................804 444-1000
Rita Foley, *Mng Member*
Jacqueline M Barry,
John A Luke Jr,
Gretta Martinez,
Pat Schellinger,
◆ **EMP:** 799
SQ FT: 257,000
SALES (est): 1.4MM
SALES (corp-wide): 18.2B **Publicly Held**
SIC: 2671 Packaging paper & plastics film, coated & laminated
HQ: Westrock Mwv, Llc
  501 S 5th St
  Richmond VA 23219
  804 444-1000

(G-13929)
WISCON CORP (PA)
Also Called: Wisconsin Cheese
2050 N 15th Ave (60160-1405)
P.O. Box 5008 (60161-5008)
PHONE.....................708 450-0074
Pasquale Caputo, *CEO*
Natale Caputo, *President*
Brett Piccioni, *General Mgr*
Caterina Caputo, *Admin Sec*
◆ **EMP:** 30
SQ FT: 175,000
SALES (est): 91MM **Privately Held**
WEB: www.wisconcorp.com
SIC: 5143 2022 Cheese; cheese, natural & processed

(G-13930)
WISCON CORP
Also Called: Wisconsin Cheese
1931 N 15th Ave (60160-1402)
PHONE.....................708 450-0074
Natale Caputo, *President*
EMP: 39
SALES (corp-wide): 91MM **Privately Held**
SIC: 2022 5451 Cheese, natural & processed; dairy products stores
PA: Wiscon Corp.
  2050 N 15th Ave
  Melrose Park IL 60160
  708 450-0074

(G-13931)
YOUR CUSTOM CABINETRY CORP
1609 N 31st Ave (60160-1837)
PHONE.....................773 290-7247
Kacarzyna Pacholczyk, *President*
EMP: 2
SALES: 500K **Privately Held**
SIC: 2434 Wood kitchen cabinets

(G-13932)
ZAGONE STUDIOS LLC
Also Called: Be Something Studio
4533 W North Ave (60160-1022)
PHONE.....................773 509-0610
Phil Zagone, *President*
Margret Omano, *Vice Pres*
▲ **EMP:** 27 **EST:** 2005
SQ FT: 17,000
SALES (est): 901.8K **Privately Held**
SIC: 2389 Masquerade costumes

Mendota
Lasalle County

(G-13933)
ADVANCED DRAINAGE SYSTEMS INC
1600 Industrial Dr (61342-9409)
PHONE.....................815 539-2160
Joseph Chlapaty, *Manager*
EMP: 14
SALES (corp-wide): 1.6B **Publicly Held**
SIC: 3084 Plastics pipe

Mendota - Lasalle County (G-13934)

PA: Advanced Drainage Systems, Inc.
4640 Trueman Blvd
Hilliard OH 43026
614 658-0050

(G-13934)
AMERICAN MACHINE
215 E 12th St (61342-1878)
PHONE.................................815 539-6558
Michael Schuhler, *Owner*
EMP: 4
SQ FT: 4,000
SALES: 750K **Privately Held**
SIC: 3499 Welding tips, heat resistant: metal

(G-13935)
ANDOVER JUNCTION PUBLICATIONS
467 N 46th Rd (61342-9552)
P.O. Box 500 (61342-0500)
PHONE.................................815 538-3060
Stephen A Esposito, *Managing Prtnr*
Michael Schafer, *Partner*
EMP: 4
SQ FT: 2,000
SALES (est): 318.2K **Privately Held**
SIC: 2732 2721 7812 Book printing; magazines; publishing & printing; video tape production

(G-13936)
ARCHER-DANIELS-MIDLAND COMPANY
Also Called: ADM
3648 Meridian Rd (61342-9607)
P.O. Box 350 (61342-0350)
PHONE.................................815 538-3771
Tom Sondgeroth, *Branch Mgr*
EMP: 9
SALES (corp-wide): 64.6B **Publicly Held**
SIC: 2041 Flour & other grain mill products
PA: Archer-Daniels-Midland Company
77 W Wacker Dr Ste 4600
Chicago IL 60601
312 634-8100

(G-13937)
ARCHER-DANIELS-MIDLAND COMPANY
581 N 43rd Rd (61342)
P.O. Box 350 (61342-0350)
PHONE.................................815 539-6219
Matthew Moore, *Superintendent*
EMP: 7
SALES (corp-wide): 64.6B **Publicly Held**
SIC: 2041 2075 2074 5153 Wheat flour; soybean oil mills; cottonseed oil, cake or meal; grain elevators
PA: Archer-Daniels-Midland Company
77 W Wacker Dr Ste 4600
Chicago IL 60601
312 634-8100

(G-13938)
BLACK BROS CO (PA)
501 9th Ave (61342-1927)
P.O. Box 410 (61342-0410)
PHONE.................................815 539-7451
Matthew B Carroll, *President*
Brian Schultz, *Plant Mgr*
Pat Reeder, *Purchasing*
Dan Baxter, *Project Engr*
Jeff Simonton, *CFO*
◆ **EMP:** 63
SQ FT: 225,000
SALES: 16MM **Privately Held**
WEB: www.blackbros.com
SIC: 3553 3549 3554 3559 Woodworking machinery; metalworking machinery; paper industries machinery; plastics working machinery

(G-13939)
CLASSIC METAL COMPANY INC
115 16th St (61342-1315)
PHONE.................................815 252-0104
EMP: 3
SALES (est): 194K **Privately Held**
WEB: www.classicmetalcompany.com
SIC: 3471 Decorative plating & finishing of formed products

(G-13940)
E N P INC (PA)
Also Called: Smith Greenhouse & Supplies
603 14th St (61342-1219)
P.O. Box 618 (61342-0618)
PHONE.................................800 255-4906
Thomas J Smith, *President*
John Gruneisen, *Sales Staff*
EMP: 5
SQ FT: 6,400
SALES (est): 668.3K **Privately Held**
SIC: 2873 2879 2875 Nitrogenous fertilizers; agricultural chemicals; fertilizers, mixing only

(G-13941)
E N P INC
2001 E Main St (61342)
P.O. Box 618 (61342-0618)
PHONE.................................815 539-7471
Thomas Smith, *Branch Mgr*
EMP: 5
SALES (corp-wide): 668.3K **Privately Held**
SIC: 2873 2875 Nitrogenous fertilizers; fertilizers, mixing only
PA: E N P Inc
603 14th St
Mendota IL 61342
800 255-4906

(G-13942)
ENP INVESTMENTS LLC
Also Called: Foliar-Pak
2001 W Main St (61342-1099)
P.O. Box 618 (61342-0618)
PHONE.................................815 539-7471
EMP: 6
SALES (est): 298.2K **Privately Held**
WEB: www.enpturf.com
SIC: 6799 0782 2875 Investors; lawn & garden services; fertilizers, mixing only

(G-13943)
HCC INC
1501 1st Ave (61342-1385)
P.O. Box 952 (61342-0952)
PHONE.................................815 539-9371
Donald Bickel, *Ch of Bd*
Bryan Nelson, *President*
Jef Fields, *Opers Mgr*
Jim Legner, *Engineer*
Jason Schultz, *Engineer*
◆ **EMP:** 200
SQ FT: 150,000
SALES (est): 60.1MM **Privately Held**
SIC: 3523 Combines (harvester-threshers)

(G-13944)
KINDRED SPIRITS DISTILLERY
1701 Milwaukee Ave (61342-1383)
PHONE.................................815 910-7116
Kenneth Haun, *Principal*
EMP: 3 **EST:** 2014
SALES (est): 130.4K **Privately Held**
SIC: 2085 Distilled & blended liquors

(G-13945)
KUNZ ENGINEERING INC
2100 Welland Rd (61342-9139)
PHONE.................................815 539-6954
Gary L Kunz, *President*
Matthew A Kunz, *Vice Pres*
Wanda M Kunz, *Admin Sec*
▼ **EMP:** 3
SALES (est): 573.4K **Privately Held**
SIC: 3523 Farm machinery & equipment

(G-13946)
MENDOTA AGRI-PRODUCTS INC (PA)
448 N 3973rd Rd (61342-9305)
PHONE.................................815 539-5633
John T Mahoney, *President*
Scott Miller, *Corp Secy*
Denise Schmidt, *Human Res Mgr*
Brad Baird, *Director*
EMP: 33
SQ FT: 40,000
SALES (est): 4.7MM **Privately Held**
SIC: 2077 2048 Animal fats, oils & meals; prepared feeds

(G-13947)
MENDOTA MONUMENT CO
606 Main St (61342-1983)
P.O. Box 63 (61342-0063)
PHONE.................................815 539-7276
Eric Schmitt, *Partner*
Ronald Schmitt, *Partner*
Stephen Schmitt, *Partner*
EMP: 3 **EST:** 1913
SQ FT: 2,000
SALES (est): 254.6K **Privately Held**
WEB: www.mendotamonument.com
SIC: 5999 3281 Monuments, finished to custom order; cut stone & stone products

(G-13948)
MENDOTA REPORTER
Also Called: Reporter Money Saver
703 Illinois Ave (61342-1637)
P.O. Box 300 (61342-0300)
PHONE.................................815 539-9396
John Tompkins, *President*
Kip Cheek, *Publisher*
Mark Elston, *General Mgr*
Kip Sheek, *Principal*
Jennifer Sommer, *Editor*
EMP: 11
SALES (est): 986.6K **Privately Held**
SIC: 2711 2741 Commercial printing & newspaper publishing combined; miscellaneous publishing
HQ: Rochelle Newspapers, Inc.
211 E Illinois Rte 38
Rochelle IL 61068
815 562-4171

(G-13949)
MENDOTA WELDING & MFG
1605 One Half 13th Ave (61342)
PHONE.................................815 539-6944
Mark E Wujek, *Owner*
Debra Wujek, *Co-Owner*
EMP: 2
SQ FT: 4,000
SALES: 300K **Privately Held**
SIC: 7692 3714 3444 3443 Welding repair; bumpers & bumperettes, motor vehicle; sheet metalwork; fabricated plate work (boiler shop)

(G-13950)
MINNESOTA DIVERSIFIED PDTS INC
Also Called: Diversifoam Products
1101 Lori Ln (61342-9232)
P.O. Box 619 (61342-0619)
PHONE.................................815 539-3106
Jim Pestula, *Plant Mgr*
Jeanne Boardman, *Accountant*
Jim Postula, *Manager*
Mike Truebenbach, *Info Tech Mgr*
Paul Wolfgram, *Representative*
EMP: 30
SALES (est): 5.4MM
SALES (corp-wide): 19.6MM **Privately Held**
WEB: www.diversifoam.com
SIC: 3086 Insulation or cushioning material, foamed plastic
PA: Minnesota Diversified Products, Inc.
9091 County Road 50
Rockford MN 55373
763 477-5854

(G-13951)
NORTHERN ILLINOIS GAS COMPANY
Also Called: Nicor Gas
169 N 36th Rd (61342-9611)
PHONE.................................815 223-8097
Michael Fugate, *Regional Mgr*
Mike Fugate, *Branch Mgr*
EMP: 18
SALES (corp-wide): 21.4B **Publicly Held**
SIC: 4924 1382 Natural gas distribution; oil & gas exploration services
HQ: Northern Illinois Gas Company
1844 W Ferry Rd
Naperville IL 60563
630 983-8676

(G-13952)
PLANO MOLDING COMPANY LLC
1800 Hume Dr (61342-8906)
P.O. Box 440 (61342-0440)
PHONE.................................815 538-3111
Ron Jergenson, *Principal*
EMP: 170
SALES (corp-wide): 93.8MM **Privately Held**
SIC: 3089 3469 Molding primary plastic; metal stampings
HQ: Plano Molding Company, Llc
431 E South St
Plano IL 60545
630 552-3111

(G-13953)
PRAIRIE LAND MLLWRGHT SVCS INC
617 E Us Highway 34 (61342-9207)
PHONE.................................815 538-3085
Duane Chaon, *President*
Curt Chaon, *Treasurer*
EMP: 18 **EST:** 1997
SQ FT: 30,000
SALES (est): 4.4MM **Privately Held**
WEB: www.prairielandmillwright.com
SIC: 3523 Planting, haying, harvesting & processing machinery

(G-13954)
ROYAL SMOKE SHOP
1001 Main St (61342-1604)
PHONE.................................815 539-3499
Mike Ashour, *Owner*
EMP: 2
SALES (est): 212.9K **Privately Held**
SIC: 2111 Cigarettes

Meredosia
Morgan County

(G-13955)
ARCHER-DANIELS-MIDLAND COMPANY
Also Called: ADM
1673 Growmark Ln (62665-7207)
P.O. Box 560, Havana (62644-0560)
PHONE.................................217 754-3300
EMP: 8
SALES (corp-wide): 64.6B **Publicly Held**
SIC: 2041 Flour & other grain mill products
PA: Archer-Daniels-Midland Company
77 W Wacker Dr Ste 4600
Chicago IL 60601
312 634-8100

(G-13956)
PPG ARCHITECTURAL FINISHES INC
Also Called: Glidden Professional Paint Ctr
S Washington St (62665)
P.O. Box 500 (62665-0500)
PHONE.................................217 584-1323
Frank Mastria, *Dir Ops-Prd-Mfg*
Robbie N Sage, *Engineer*
Vithal Ayyagari, *Enginr/R&D Mgr*
EMP: 268
SALES (corp-wide): 15.1B **Publicly Held**
WEB: www.ppgpaints.com
SIC: 2821 2891 Plastics materials & resins; adhesives & sealants
HQ: Ppg Architectural Finishes, Inc.
1 Ppg Pl
Pittsburgh PA 15272
412 434-3131

(G-13957)
TARPS MANUFACTURING INC
1000 State Highway 104 (62665-7165)
P.O. Box 1060, Jacksonville (62651-1060)
PHONE.................................217 245-6181
Jeff Davidsmeyer, *President*
Tom Atkins, *Vice Pres*
Rich Ott, *Vice Pres*
R Thomas Slayback, *Treasurer*
Pdevon Davidsmeyer,
EMP: 10
SQ FT: 28,000

GEOGRAPHIC SECTION

Mettawa - Lake County (G-13982)

SALES: 661.9K
SALES (corp-wide): 36MM **Privately Held**
SIC: 2394 Tarpaulins, fabric: made from purchased materials
PA: Illinois Road Contractors, Inc.
520 N Webster Ave
Jacksonville IL 62650
217 245-6181

Metamora
Woodford County

(G-13958)
ARTS TAMALES
1453 Hickory Point Rd (61548-7803)
PHONE 309 367-2850
David Chinuge, *Owner*
EMP: 6
SQ FT: 4,200
SALES: 180K **Privately Held**
SIC: 2099 2035 2013 Food preparations; pickles, sauces & salad dressings; sausages & other prepared meats

(G-13959)
BENCHMARK ELECTRONICS INC
388 Riverview Blf (61548-9075)
PHONE 309 822-8587
Philip Bumbalough, *Principal*
EMP: 276
SALES (corp-wide): 2.2B **Publicly Held**
WEB: www.bench.com
SIC: 3672 Printed circuit boards
PA: Benchmark Electronics, Inc.
56 S Rockford Dr
Tempe AZ 85281
623 300-7000

(G-13960)
CENTRAL ILLINOIS GLASS &
506 W Mount Vernon St (61548-7074)
P.O. Box 80 (61548-0080)
PHONE 309 367-4242
Cristy Mooney, *Owner*
EMP: 8
SALES (est): 836.8K **Privately Held**
SIC: 3231 Products of purchased glass

(G-13961)
HONEYWELL INTERNATIONAL INC
539 Justa Rd (61548-7833)
PHONE 309 383-4045
EMP: 673
SALES (corp-wide): 40.5B **Publicly Held**
SIC: 3724 Mfg Aircraft Engines/Parts
PA: Honeywell International Inc.
115 Tabor Rd
Morris Plains NJ 28202
973 455-2000

(G-13962)
LOGO WEAR UNLIMITED INC
104 S Menard St (61548-7097)
P.O. Box 861 (61548-0861)
PHONE 309 367-2333
Andrew Martin, *CEO*
EMP: 2
SALES (est): 216.1K **Privately Held**
WEB: www.logowearunlimited.net
SIC: 2759 Screen printing

(G-13963)
MCBRIDE & SHOFF INC
723 N Wiedman St (61548-9614)
P.O. Box 650 (61548-0650)
PHONE 309 367-4193
Clifford D Shoff, *President*
Michael W Shoff, *Vice Pres*
Ryan Shoff, *Vice Pres*
Scott Shoff, *Vice Pres*
EMP: 50
SQ FT: 109,000
SALES (est): 8.4MM **Privately Held**
WEB: www.metamoraindustries.com
SIC: 3599 Machine shop, jobbing & repair

(G-13964)
METAMORA INDUSTRIES LLC
723 N Wiedman St (61548-9614)
P.O. Box 650 (61548-0650)
PHONE 309 367-2368
Michael Shoff, *COO*
Dale Ehringer, *Purchasing*
Cliff Shoff, *Mng Member*
Shoff Clifford D,
Mike Shoff,
▲ **EMP:** 40 **EST:** 1965
SQ FT: 50,000
SALES (est): 10.2MM **Privately Held**
WEB: www.metamoraindustries.com
SIC: 3441 3498 Fabricated structural metal; tube fabricating (contract bending & shaping)

(G-13965)
OLD MILL VINEYARD LLC
700 Coon Creek Rd (61548-7416)
PHONE 309 258-9954
Grohsmeyer Kurt, *Principal*
EMP: 4
SALES (est): 250K **Privately Held**
WEB: www.oldmillvineyard.com
SIC: 2084 Wines

(G-13966)
PEORIA WILBERT VAULT CO INC
510 Townhall Rd (61548-9405)
P.O. Box 27 (61548-0027)
PHONE 309 383-2882
William Buren, *President*
Bryant Defrance, *President*
EMP: 10
SALES (est): 1.5MM **Privately Held**
WEB: www.peoriawilbert.com
SIC: 3272 Burial vaults, concrete or precast terrazzo

(G-13967)
ROY WINNETT
303 W Pine St (61548-9687)
PHONE 309 367-4867
Roy Winnett, *Principal*
EMP: 3
SALES (est): 252.8K **Privately Held**
SIC: 2836 Toxins, viruses & similar substances, including venom

(G-13968)
SIMPLY SIGNS
1001 W Mount Vernon St D (61548-8411)
PHONE 309 849-9016
Nathan Connelly, *Principal*
EMP: 2 **EST:** 2011
SALES (est): 227.6K **Privately Held**
WEB: www.simplysignsandscreenprinting.com
SIC: 3993 Signs & advertising specialties

(G-13969)
SUPERIOR COATINGS ILLINOIS LLC
612 Outback Ln (61548-7704)
PHONE 309 367-9625
Craig Zimmerman, *Mng Member*
Keith Toone,
Chris Zimmerman,
EMP: 12
SALES (est): 1.7MM **Privately Held**
SIC: 3479 Coating, rust preventive

(G-13970)
WOODWRIGHTS SHOPPE INC
304 Townhall Rd (61548-9587)
PHONE 309 360-6603
Doug Rickard, *President*
EMP: 1
SALES: 250K **Privately Held**
SIC: 5712 2431 Customized furniture & cabinets; woodwork, interior & ornamental

Metropolis
Massac County

(G-13971)
GLOBAL MAINTENANCE LLC
5357 Industrial Park Dr (62960-4170)
PHONE 270 933-1281
James S Scourick, *Mng Member*
Steven Hibner,
EMP: 35
SALES (est): 3.9MM **Privately Held**
WEB: www.globalmaintenance1.com
SIC: 3498 7699 Fabricated pipe & fittings; industrial machinery & equipment repair

(G-13972)
HONEYWELL INTERNATIONAL INC
2768 N Us Hwy 45 N (62960)
P.O. Box 430 (62960-0430)
PHONE 618 524-2111
Mark J Byrne, *President*
EMP: 400
SALES (corp-wide): 36.7B **Publicly Held**
WEB: www.honeywell.com
SIC: 2819 2869 Industrial inorganic chemicals; industrial organic chemicals
PA: Honeywell International Inc.
300 S Tryon St
Charlotte NC 28202
704 627-6200

(G-13973)
METRO SERVICE CENTER
103 W 10th St Ste B (62960-1571)
P.O. Box 161 (62960-0161)
PHONE 618 524-8583
David Christian, *Owner*
EMP: 2
SALES (est): 234.2K **Privately Held**
SIC: 3663 Satellites, communications

(G-13974)
METROPOLIS READY MIX INC (PA)
Also Called: Kotter Ready Mix
1200 E 2nd St (62960-2289)
P.O. Box 107 (62960-0107)
PHONE 618 524-8221
Karl Kotter, *President*
Rick Kotter, *Admin Sec*
EMP: 25 **EST:** 1950
SQ FT: 1,800
SALES (est): 4.4MM **Privately Held**
SIC: 3273 4491 4222 4212 Ready-mixed concrete; loading vessels; unloading vessels; refrigerated warehousing & storage; local trucking, without storage

(G-13975)
MICHAELS EQUIPMENT CO
Also Called: Kubota Authorized Dealer
5481 Illinois 145 Rd (62960-3634)
PHONE 618 524-8560
Michael Reames, *Partner*
Rebecca Reames, *Partner*
EMP: 5
SQ FT: 3,600
SALES (est): 489K **Privately Held**
SIC: 5999 3546 5083 Farm equipment & supplies; saws & sawing equipment; farm & garden machinery

(G-13976)
R&R MEAT CO
5156 Old Marion Rd (62960-3527)
PHONE 270 898-6296
EMP: 5
SQ FT: 3,000
SALES (est): 600K **Privately Held**
SIC: 2013 Meat Processing

Mettawa
Lake County

(G-13977)
ABBOTT LABORATORIES
26525 N Riverwoods Blvd (60045-3440)
PHONE 847 735-0573
EMP: 817
SALES (corp-wide): 31.9B **Publicly Held**
SIC: 2834 Druggists' preparations (pharmaceuticals)
PA: Abbott Laboratories
100 Abbott Park Rd
Abbott Park IL 60064
224 667-6100

(G-13978)
BIRD PRODUCTS CORPORATION
26125 N Riverwoods Blvd (60045-3420)
PHONE 872 757-0114
Dave Mowry, *CEO*
EMP: 3
SALES (est): 99.3K
SALES (corp-wide): 353.3MM **Privately Held**
SIC: 3841 Surgical & medical instruments
HQ: Viasys Holdings Inc.
26125 N Riverwoods Blvd
Mettawa IL 60045

(G-13979)
BRUNSWICK CORPORATION (PA)
26125 N Riverwoods Blvd # 500 (60045-4811)
PHONE 847 735-4700
David M Foulkes, *CEO*
Manuel A Fernandez, *Ch of Bd*
Nancy Loube, *Assistant VP*
Michael Adams, *Vice Pres*
Randall S Altman, *Vice Pres*
◆ **EMP:** 329 **EST:** 1845
SALES: 4.1B **Publicly Held**
WEB: www.brunswick.com
SIC: 3519 3732 3949 7933 Outboard motors; marine engines; boats, fiberglass: building & repairing; motorboats, inboard or outboard: building & repairing; sporting & athletic goods; reels, fishing; rods & rod parts, fishing; bowling alleys & accessories; bowling centers; billiard equipment & supplies

(G-13980)
BRUNSWICK INTERNATIONAL LTD (HQ)
Also Called: B I L
26125 N Riverwoods Blvd # 500 (60045-4811)
PHONE 847 735-4700
Huw Bower, *President*
William Metzger, *Senior VP*
Judith Zelisko, *Vice Pres*
Randall Altman, *Vice Pres*
Fred Florjanick, *Vice Pres*
EMP: 23
SALES (est): 13.2MM
SALES (corp-wide): 4.1B **Publicly Held**
SIC: 3519 3732 3949 3728 Outboard motors; marine engines; boats, fiberglass: building & repairing; motorboats, inboard or outboard: building & repairing; reels, fishing; rods & rod parts, fishing; bowling alleys & accessories; aircraft body assemblies & parts; airframe assemblies, except for guided missiles; navigational systems & instruments
PA: Brunswick Corporation
26125 N Riverwoods Blvd # 500
Mettawa IL 60045
847 735-4700

(G-13981)
REVOLUTIONARY MEDICAL DVCS INC
Also Called: Superno2va
26125 N Riverwoods Blvd # 500 (60045-3422)
PHONE 520 464-4299
Dave Kane, *President*
Tom Reilly, *COO*
Kristine Kurilko, *Marketing Staff*
Michael Pedro MD, *Officer*
EMP: 10
SALES (est): 1.5MM
SALES (corp-wide): 353.3MM **Privately Held**
SIC: 3841 5047 Inhalators, surgical & medical; medical & hospital equipment
HQ: Vyaire Medical, Inc.
26125 N Riverwoods Blvd # 1
Mettawa IL 60045
833 327-3284

(G-13982)
SENSORMEDICS CORPORATION (DH)
26125 N Riverwoods Blvd (60045-3420)
PHONE 872 757-0114
Dave Mowry, *CEO*

Mettawa - Lake County (G-13983)

John De Santiago, *Technology*
EMP: 4
SALES (est): 777.9K
SALES (corp-wide): 353.3MM **Privately Held**
SIC: 3841 Diagnostic apparatus, medical

(G-13983)
VITAL SIGNS INC (DH)
26125 N Riverwoods Blvd (60045-3420)
PHONE..................872 757-0114
EMP: 3
SALES (est): 345.6K
SALES (corp-wide): 353.3MM **Privately Held**
SIC: 3841 Surgical & medical instruments
HQ: Vyaire Medical Llc
26125 N Riverwoods Blvd # 1
Mettawa IL 60045
833 327-3284

(G-13984)
VYAIRE COMPANY (HQ)
26125 N Riverwoods Blvd # 1 (60045-3422)
PHONE..................833 327-3284
Dave Mowry, *CEO*
EMP: 7
SALES (est): 800MM
SALES (corp-wide): 353.3MM **Privately Held**
SIC: 3841 Surgical & medical instruments
PA: Vyaire Holding Company
26125 N Riverwoods Blvd
Mettawa IL 60045
872 757-0114

(G-13985)
VYAIRE MEDICAL INC (DH)
26125 N Riverwoods Blvd # 1 (60045-3422)
PHONE..................833 327-3284
Gaurav Agarwal, *CEO*
Tommy Ung, *Engineer*
Randy Clare, *Sales Staff*
Obed Izquierdo, *Sales Staff*
Charity Schneider, *Sales Staff*
EMP: 200
SALES (est): 1.5B
SALES (corp-wide): 353.3MM **Privately Held**
SIC: 3841 Surgical & medical instruments
HQ: Vyaire Company
26125 N Riverwoods Blvd # 1
Mettawa IL 60045
833 327-3284

(G-13986)
VYAIRE MEDICAL LLC (DH)
26125 N Riverwoods Blvd # 1 (60045-3422)
PHONE..................833 327-3284
Dave Mowry, *CEO*
EMP: 7
SALES (est): 172.3MM
SALES (corp-wide): 353.3MM **Privately Held**
SIC: 3841 Surgical & medical instruments
HQ: Vyaire Medical, Inc.
26125 N Riverwoods Blvd # 1
Mettawa IL 60045
833 327-3284

(G-13987)
VYAIRE MEDICAL MX LLC (DH)
26125 N Riverwoods Blvd (60045-3420)
PHONE..................872 757-0114
EMP: 251
SALES (est): 5.5MM
SALES (corp-wide): 353.3MM **Privately Held**
SIC: 3841 Surgical & medical instruments
HQ: Vyaire Medical Llc
26125 N Riverwoods Blvd # 1
Mettawa IL 60045
833 327-3284

(G-13988)
VYAIRE MEDICAL PAYROLL LLC
26125 N Riverwoods Blvd # 1 (60045-3422)
PHONE..................224 544-5436
EMP: 39

SALES (est): 208.3K
SALES (corp-wide): 353.3MM **Privately Held**
SIC: 3841 Surgical & medical instruments
HQ: Vyaire Medical Llc
26125 N Riverwoods Blvd # 1
Mettawa IL 60045
833 327-3284

Midlothian
Cook County

(G-13989)
ACCURATE PRINTING INC
4749 W 136th St (60445)
PHONE..................708 824-0058
Thomas J Doyle, *President*
▲ **EMP:** 3 **EST:** 1996
SALES (est): 541.7K **Privately Held**
WEB: www.accurateprinting.net
SIC: 2752 Commercial printing, offset

(G-13990)
CHICAGO PREPRESS COLOR INC
14650 Kostner Ave (60445-2662)
PHONE..................708 385-3465
Larry Sargis, *President*
EMP: 3
SALES (est): 200K **Privately Held**
SIC: 2796 Color separations for printing

(G-13991)
FIX IT FAST LTD
14922 Lawndale Ave (60445-3533)
PHONE..................708 401-8320
Shawn Fuller, *President*
William Fuller, *Vice Pres*
EMP: 12 **EST:** 2012
SALES (est): 1.3MM **Privately Held**
SIC: 3442 1799 Fire doors, metal; dock equipment installation, industrial

(G-13992)
INSCERCO MFG INC
Also Called: Mailcrafters
4621 W 138th St (60445)
PHONE..................708 597-8777
Robert R Kruk, *President*
Anna M Kruk, *Corp Secy*
Robert R Kruk Jr, *Vice Pres*
Rusty Kruk, *Plant Mgr*
Herman Havinga, *Engineer*
EMP: 20 **EST:** 1968
SQ FT: 20,000
SALES (est): 4.8MM **Privately Held**
WEB: www.inscerco.com
SIC: 3579 Mailing, letter handling & addressing machines

(G-13993)
MARKHAM CABINET WORKS INC
4235 151st St (60445-3316)
PHONE..................708 687-3074
Gerhardt Reichel, *President*
Jack Reichel, *Vice Pres*
Alice Reichel, *Admin Sec*
EMP: 6 **EST:** 1946
SQ FT: 7,000
SALES (est): 300K **Privately Held**
SIC: 2434 2541 5211 Wood kitchen cabinets; table or counter tops, plastic laminated; cabinets, kitchen; counter tops

(G-13994)
METRO PAINT SUPPLIES
14032 Kostner Ave Unit G (60445)
PHONE..................708 385-7701
Melissa Rizzo, *Manager*
EMP: 3 **EST:** 2007
SALES (est): 281.9K **Privately Held**
SIC: 2851 5198 Paints & allied products; paints

(G-13995)
SECRETARY OF STATE ILLINOIS
14434 Pulaski Rd (60445-2895)
PHONE..................708 388-9199
EMP: 4 **Privately Held**
WEB: www.cyberdriveillinois.com

SIC: 3469 Automobile license tags, stamped metal
HQ: Secretary Of State, Illinois
213 State House
Springfield IL 62706
217 782-2201

(G-13996)
SOUTHWEST MESSENGER PRESS INC
Also Called: Alsip Express Newspaper
3840 147th St (60445-3452)
PHONE..................708 388-2425
Margaret D Lysen, *President*
Walter H Lysen, *President*
Margaret O Lysen, *Corp Secy*
Don Talac, *Vice Pres*
EMP: 46 **EST:** 1929
SQ FT: 3,750
SALES (est): 2.3MM **Privately Held**
WEB: www.southwestmessengerpress.com
SIC: 2711 Newspapers: publishing only, not printed on site

(G-13997)
TITANIUM INSULATION INC
14533 Turner Ave (60445-3029)
PHONE..................708 932-5927
Cesar Garcia, *President*
EMP: 1
SALES (est): 234.2K **Privately Held**
SIC: 3356 Titanium

(G-13998)
UNIVERSAL DIGITAL PRINTING
3314 147th St (60445-3612)
PHONE..................708 389-0133
EMP: 3
SALES (est): 259K **Privately Held**
SIC: 2759 Commercial printing

Milan
Rock Island County

(G-13999)
AGUSTA MILL WORKS
Also Called: Carver Custom Woodworks
117 17th St E (61264-2650)
PHONE..................309 787-4616
Ronald F Carver, *President*
Jan Carver, *President*
Rod Carver, *President*
EMP: 2 **EST:** 1946
SALES (est): 200K **Privately Held**
SIC: 2431 5211 5031 Moldings, wood: unfinished & prefinished; doors, wood; window frames, wood; lumber & other building materials; lumber, plywood & millwork

(G-14000)
BMS MANUFACTURING COMPANY INC
651 8th Ave W (61264-2332)
PHONE..................309 787-3158
Victoria J Bennett, *President*
Thomas Bennet, *Vice Pres*
Dan Bennett, *Vice Pres*
Daniel M Bennett, *Vice Pres*
Victoria Bennett, *Treasurer*
EMP: 25
SQ FT: 26,000
SALES (est): 9.5MM **Privately Held**
SIC: 3565 Packaging machinery

(G-14001)
BOHL MACHINE & TOOL COMPANY
4405 78th Ave (61264-3214)
PHONE..................309 799-5122
Carolyn Bohl, *President*
EMP: 1 **EST:** 1969
SALES (est): 4.7MM **Privately Held**
SIC: 3542 3544 Machine tools, metal forming type; special dies, tools, jigs & fixtures

(G-14002)
CHARNOR INC
1711 1st Ave E (61264-2610)
PHONE..................309 787-2427
Josh Hamilton, *Principal*
Anthony Stanley, *CFO*

Tony Stanley, *Controller*
Ray Inman, *Sales Mgr*
Brandee Viager, *Sales Mgr*
▲ **EMP:** 52
SALES: 6MM **Privately Held**
SIC: 3823 Industrial process control instruments

(G-14003)
CHICAGO TUBE AND IRON COMPANY
Also Called: Quad Cities Plant
1040 11th St W (61264-2243)
P.O. Box 1070 (61264-1070)
PHONE..................309 787-4947
Chris Prodoehl, *Vice Pres*
Randy Happ, *Purchasing*
Dan Deffenbaugh, *Marketing Staff*
EMP: 40
SQ FT: 30,000
SALES (corp-wide): 1.5B **Publicly Held**
SIC: 5051 4225 3498 Tubing, metal; pipe & tubing, steel; general warehousing; fabricated pipe & fittings
HQ: Chicago Tube and Iron Company
1 Chicago Tube Dr
Romeoville IL 60446
815 834-2500

(G-14004)
COLLINSON STONE CO (PA)
Also Called: Milan Stone Quarry
225 1st St E (61264-2509)
P.O. Box 290 (61264-0290)
PHONE..................309 787-7983
Kenneth Collinson, *President*
Robert Collinson, *Admin Sec*
EMP: 15
SQ FT: 1,500
SALES (est): 2MM **Privately Held**
SIC: 1422 Crushed & broken limestone

(G-14005)
COUNTRY STONE INC (PA)
6300 75th Ave Ste A (61264-3267)
P.O. Box 151 (61264-0151)
PHONE..................309 787-1744
Ronald D Bjustrom, *Owner*
EMP: 35
SQ FT: 1,000
SALES (est): 119.9MM **Privately Held**
SIC: 2499 2875 3273 3281 Mulch, wood & bark; potting soil, mixed; ready-mixed concrete; cut stone & stone products

(G-14006)
DELCO WEST LLC
7507 50th St (61264-3207)
PHONE..................309 799-7543
Zachary Honert, *Mng Member*
Zach Honert, *Manager*
EMP: 7
SQ FT: 10,000
SALES (est): 2MM **Privately Held**
WEB: www.delcowest.com
SIC: 3545 3541 Machine tool accessories; machine tools, metal cutting type

(G-14007)
EDWARDS CREATIVE SERVICES LLC
435 1st St E (61264-2740)
PHONE..................309 756-0199
Cathy Edwards,
Matt Nielsen, *Graphic Designe*
Steve Edwards,
EMP: 14
SQ FT: 14,000
SALES (est): 1.6MM **Privately Held**
SIC: 7336 7312 7319 7311 Graphic arts & related design; outdoor advertising services; transit advertising services; advertising agencies; commercial printing

(G-14008)
ELLIOTT AVIATION ARCFT SLS INC
6601 74th Ave (61264-3203)
P.O. Box 100, Moline (61266-0100)
PHONE..................309 799-3183
Wynn Elliott, *CEO*
Greg Sahr, *President*
Jeff Hyland, *CFO*
EMP: 1

SALES (est): 399.4K **Privately Held**
SIC: **8711** 7389 3553 Building construction consultant; interior design services; woodworking machinery
HQ: Elliott Aviation, Inc.
6601 74th Ave
Milan IL 61264
309 799-3183

(G-14009)
ETERNAL QUALITY GROUP
910 10th Ave W (61264-2233)
PHONE..................309 799-3800
Glenn Rohm, *President*
EMP: 4 EST: 2013
SALES (est): 371.2K **Privately Held**
WEB: www.qualitygroupprinting.com
SIC: **2759** Screen printing

(G-14010)
EXPORT PACKAGING CO INC (PA)
Also Called: Xpac
525 10th Ave E (61264-3117)
PHONE..................309 756-4288
Donald Ruggles, *CEO*
Gregory A Ruggies, *President*
John Beck, *Vice Pres*
Byron Fernald, *CFO*
Mike Groenenboom, *Admin Sec*
EMP: 800 EST: 1962
SQ FT: 1,500,000
SALES (est): 125.2MM **Privately Held**
WEB: www.xpac.com
SIC: **4783** 2448 2441 Packing goods for shipping; pallets, wood; shipping cases, wood: nailed or lock corner

(G-14011)
GAMETIME SNACKS LLC
2224 1st St W (61264-3343)
PHONE..................309 517-6342
Vince Grisha,
◆ EMP: 47
SALES: 7MM **Privately Held**
SIC: **2026** Milk, chocolate

(G-14012)
GETT INDUSTRIES LTD
Also Called: Machine Job Shop
7307 50th St (61264-3259)
PHONE..................309 799-5131
Patricia Edwards, *President*
Timothy Edwards, *President*
EMP: 55
SQ FT: 45,000
SALES (est): 12MM **Privately Held**
SIC: **3599** Machine shop, jobbing & repair

(G-14013)
GROUP O INC
Also Called: Group O Supply Chain Solution
7300 50th St (61264-3200)
P.O. Box 1220 (61264-1220)
PHONE..................309 736-8660
Ambrose Capell, *Branch Mgr*
Randal Goff, *Technical Staff*
EMP: 90 **Privately Held**
SIC: **3648** Decorative area lighting fixtures
PA: Group O, Inc.
4905 77th Ave E
Milan IL 61264

(G-14014)
GROUP O INC
Group O Supply Chain Solutions
120 4th Ave E (61264-2803)
PHONE..................309 736-8311
Robert Ontiveros, *Manager*
EMP: 280 **Privately Held**
SIC: **5013** 3479 5085 Automotive supplies; painting of metal products; bearings
PA: Group O, Inc.
4905 77th Ave E
Milan IL 61264

(G-14015)
GROUP O INC
Group O Direct Marketing Div
4905 77th Ave E (61264-3250)
PHONE..................309 736-8100
Gregg Ontiveros, *Branch Mgr*
EMP: 40 **Privately Held**

SIC: **7331** 7389 2789 8732 Direct mail advertising services; telephone answering service; binding only: books, pamphlets, magazines, etc.; commercial nonphysical research
PA: Group O, Inc.
4905 77th Ave E
Milan IL 61264

(G-14016)
HURST MANUFACTURING CO INC
823 9th St W (61264-2214)
P.O. Box 708 (61264-0708)
PHONE..................309 756-9960
Todd Hurst, *President*
William R Hurst, *President*
Patty Copeland, *Controller*
EMP: 18
SQ FT: 10,000
SALES: 1.5MM **Privately Held**
SIC: **3492** 3542 Hose & tube fittings & assemblies, hydraulic/pneumatic; bending machines

(G-14017)
MILL CREEK MINING INC
700 4th St W (61264-2725)
PHONE..................309 787-1414
Beau Brandt, *Exec VP*
EMP: 6 EST: 2015
SALES (est): 491.8K **Privately Held**
SIC: **1422** Dolomite, crushed & broken-quarrying

(G-14018)
MOLINE WELDING INC
3603 78th Ave (61264-3217)
PHONE..................309 756-0643
James Swinburn, *President*
Marilyn Swinburn, *President*
Kristofer Swinburn, *Vice Pres*
EMP: 17 EST: 1916
SQ FT: 36,000
SALES (est): 2.8MM **Privately Held**
WEB: www.molinewelding.com
SIC: **3469** 7692 3441 Metal stampings; welding repair; fabricated structural metal

(G-14019)
MORRISON WEIGHING SYSTEMS INC
7605 50th St (61264-3272)
P.O. Box 860 (61264-0860)
PHONE..................309 799-7311
Janice Morrison, *President*
Janice R Morrison, *Admin Sec*
EMP: 9
SQ FT: 8,500
SALES (est): 1.2MM **Privately Held**
SIC: **3596** Weighing machines & apparatus

(G-14020)
POOLS WELDING INC
816 10th Ave W (61264-2314)
PHONE..................309 787-2083
Doyle E Pool, *CFO*
EMP: 6 EST: 1973
SQ FT: 6,642
SALES (est): 804.2K **Privately Held**
SIC: **1799** 3441 3713 3537 Welding on site; fabricated structural metal; truck & bus bodies; industrial trucks & tractors; sheet metalwork; fabricated plate work (boiler shop)

(G-14021)
QUAD CITIES CONCRETE PDTS LLC
636 10th Ave W (61264-2309)
PHONE..................309 787-4919
Michael Banks,
Gregory Banks,
Jason Banks,
EMP: 9 EST: 2014
SQ FT: 24,172
SALES (est): 1.1MM **Privately Held**
SIC: **3272** Burial vaults, concrete or pre-cast terrazzo

(G-14022)
R & O SPECIALTIES INCORPORATED (HQ)
120 4th Ave E (61264-2803)
P.O. Box 1220 (61264-1220)
PHONE..................309 736-8660
Gregg Ontiveros, *CEO*
Robert Ontiveros, *President*
Kim Fox, *Vice Pres*
Alfred Ramirez, *Vice Pres*
Bob Marriott, *CFO*
▲ EMP: 55
SQ FT: 300,000
SALES (est): 174.7MM **Privately Held**
SIC: **5013** 3479 5085 Automotive supplies; painting of metal products; bearings

(G-14023)
R C INDUSTRIAL INC
Also Called: Rci
255 5th Ave W (61264-2709)
PHONE..................309 230-4631
Clayton H Weissenborn, *President*
Brenda Weisenborn, *Treasurer*
EMP: 7 EST: 2006
SQ FT: 5,280
SALES (est): 400K **Privately Held**
WEB: www.rcindustrialinc.com
SIC: **1796** 3441 Machinery installation; fabricated structural metal

(G-14024)
REFLEX FITNESS PRODUCTS INC
1130 15th Ave W (61264-2263)
PHONE..................309 756-1050
Mike Adolphson, *President*
Craig Askam, *Vice Pres*
EMP: 15
SALES: 1.5MM **Privately Held**
SIC: **3949** Exercise equipment; gymnasium equipment

(G-14025)
REYNOLDS MANUFACTURING COMPANY
630 4th St W (61264-2736)
PHONE..................309 787-8600
Larry Wilson, *General Mgr*
Larry E Wilson, *Mfg Staff*
EMP: 43
SALES (corp-wide): 11.6MM **Privately Held**
WEB: www.reynoldsmfg.com
SIC: **3544** 3599 3369 3366 Special dies & tools; machine shop, jobbing & repair; nonferrous foundries; copper foundries; aluminum foundries; gray & ductile iron foundries
PA: Reynolds Manufacturing
630 4th St W
Milan IL 61264
309 787-8600

(G-14026)
RIVERSTONE GROUP INC
Also Called: Allied Stone
601 Us Route 67 N (61264-2116)
PHONE..................309 787-3141
Jody Pace, *Finance Mgr*
Sean McKee, *IT/INT Sup*
EMP: 20
SALES (corp-wide): 2.5B **Privately Held**
WEB: www.riverstonegrp.com
SIC: **5032** 1422 Stone, crushed or broken; crushed & broken limestone
PA: Riverstone Group, Inc.
4640 E 56th St
Davenport IA 52807
309 757-8250

(G-14027)
ROTH PUMP COMPANY (HQ)
525 4th St W (61264-2722)
P.O. Box 4330, Rock Island (61204-4330)
PHONE..................309 787-1791
Peter Roth, *President*
Paul Roth, *Vice Pres*
Correen Montgomery, *Mfg Staff*
Dale Klapperich, *CFO*
Aaron Hoots, *Sales Engr*
EMP: 30
SQ FT: 98,700

SALES (est): 4.9MM
SALES (corp-wide): 10.2MM **Privately Held**
WEB: www.rothpump.com
SIC: **3561** Pumps & pumping equipment
PA: Roy E Roth Company Inc
6th Ave And 4th St
Milan IL 61264
309 787-1791

(G-14028)
ROY E ROTH COMPANY (PA)
Also Called: Roth's Pump Co.
6th Ave And 4th St (61264)
PHONE..................309 787-1791
Peter P Roth, *CEO*
Ed Mc Roberts, *Sales Mgr*
Dale Klapperich, *Admin Sec*
EMP: 3 EST: 1932
SQ FT: 98,700
SALES (est): 10.2MM **Privately Held**
WEB: www.rothpump.com
SIC: **3561** 5084 Pump jacks & other pumping equipment; pumps & pumping equipment

(G-14029)
TICKLE ASPHALT CO LTD
700 4th St W (61264-2725)
PHONE..................309 787-1308
Charles Brandt, *President*
Todd Brandt, *Treasurer*
Terrence Brandt, *Admin Sec*
EMP: 4
SALES (est): 580K
SALES (corp-wide): 10.3MM **Privately Held**
SIC: **3272** Paving materials, prefabricated concrete
PA: Brandt Construction Co.
700 4th St W
Milan IL 61264
309 787-4644

(G-14030)
WALMAN OPTICAL COMPANY
1280 11th St W (61264-2234)
PHONE..................309 787-0000
Shelly Watkins, *Cust Mgr*
Rhonda Whitcomb, *Branch Mgr*
EMP: 41
SALES (corp-wide): 446.8MM **Privately Held**
SIC: **3851** Ophthalmic goods
PA: The Walman Optical Company
801 12th Ave N Ste 1
Minneapolis MN 55411
612 520-6000

(G-14031)
WHIPPLES PRINTING PRESS INC
Also Called: Printing Press The
2410 119th Avenue Ct W (61264-4687)
PHONE..................309 787-3538
Christine D Whipple, *President*
EMP: 4
SALES (est): 344.8K **Privately Held**
SIC: **2752** Commercial printing, offset

(G-14032)
WILBERT VAULT COMPANY
Also Called: Milan, Wilbert Vault Co
636 10th Ave W (61264-2309)
PHONE..................309 787-5281
Michael Peterson, *President*
EMP: 10
SQ FT: 3,000
SALES (est): 1.2MM **Privately Held**
SIC: **3272** Burial vaults, concrete or precast terrazzo

Milford
Iroquois County

(G-14033)
CLOSET CONCEPT
1881 E 300 North Rd (60953-6323)
PHONE..................217 375-4214
Fax: 217 375-4214
EMP: 3
SALES (est): 208.6K **Privately Held**
SIC: **2673** Mfg Bags-Plastic/Coated Paper

(G-14034)
FIM ENGINEERING LLC
2199 E 1120 North Rd (60953-6106)
PHONE....................................773 880-8841
Marc Harris, *General Mgr*
EMP: 3
SALES (est): 157.4K **Privately Held**
SIC: 3484 Guns (firearms) or gun parts, 30 mm. & below

(G-14035)
ILLIANA REAL LOG HOMES INC
107 N Fritz Dr (60953-1017)
PHONE....................................815 471-4004
Steven W Cross, *Principal*
EMP: 5
SALES: 373.4K **Privately Held**
SIC: 2411 Logging

(G-14036)
ROBERT DAVIS & SON INC
Also Called: Davis Welding
832 N State Route 1 (60953-6347)
PHONE....................................815 889-4168
John Davis, *President*
Barbara Davis, *Manager*
EMP: 6 **EST:** 1928
SQ FT: 6,400
SALES (est): 620K **Privately Held**
WEB: www.fieldpup.com
SIC: 3715 7692 Truck trailers; automotive welding

(G-14037)
WAGNERS LLC
2812 E 1100 North Rd (60953-6053)
PHONE....................................815 889-4101
James Lundquist Jr, *Opers-Prdtn-Mfg*
EMP: 20
SALES (corp-wide): 50MM **Privately Held**
WEB: www.wagners.com
SIC: 2048 5199 Bird food, prepared; pet supplies
PA: Wagner's, Llc
366 N Broadway Ste 402
Jericho NY 11753
516 933-6580

Milledgeville
Carroll County

(G-14038)
CARROLL INDUSTRIAL MOLDS INC
202 N Washington St (61051-9274)
P.O. Box 429 (61051-0429)
PHONE....................................815 225-7250
Craig Dusing, *President*
Kaye A Dusing, *Corp Secy*
EMP: 19
SQ FT: 36,000
SALES (est): 3.1MM **Privately Held**
SIC: 3544 3543 Industrial molds; industrial patterns

(G-14039)
JSP MOLD LLC
404 E 4th St (61051-9104)
P.O. Box 669 (61051-0669)
PHONE....................................815 225-7110
Paul Sandefer, *General Mgr*
Susanne Ponto, *Human Res Mgr*
Pat Rich, *Sales Staff*
Tom Schweska, *Sales Staff*
Bob Frederick, *Info Tech Mgr*
EMP: 3 **EST:** 1977
SALES (est): 566.1K **Privately Held**
WEB: www.jspmold.com
SIC: 3544 3543 3365 Industrial molds; industrial patterns; aluminum foundries
HQ: Jsp International Llc
1285 Drummers Ln Ste 301
Wayne PA 19087

(G-14040)
SHANKS VETERINARY EQUIPMENT
505 E Old Mill St (61051-9264)
P.O. Box 397 (61051-0397)
PHONE....................................815 225-7700
Mark Dettman, *President*
Jennifer Dettman, *Corp Secy*
EMP: 8
SQ FT: 18,400
SALES: 857.3K **Privately Held**
SIC: 3841 7692 Veterinarians' instruments & apparatus; welding repair

Millstadt
St. Clair County

(G-14041)
ACE GREASE SERVICE INC (PA)
9035 State Route 163 (62260-3239)
PHONE....................................618 781-1207
Mike Costenak, *President*
Michael Kostelac III, *President*
Mike Kostelac, *President*
EMP: 3
SALES (est): 4.2MM **Privately Held**
SIC: 2077 Animal & marine fats & oils

(G-14042)
ACE GREASE SERVICE INC
9011 State Route 163 (62260)
PHONE....................................618 337-0974
Mike Kostelack, *Manager*
EMP: 6 **Privately Held**
SIC: 2077 Rendering
PA: Ace Grease Service, Inc.
9035 State Route 163
Millstadt IL 62260

(G-14043)
BASOR ELECTRIC INC (HQ)
604 S Mulberry St (62260-2088)
PHONE....................................618 476-6300
Tim Place, *President*
Jerry Nania, *VP Sales*
◆ **EMP:** 5 **EST:** 2012
SALES (est): 757.3K
SALES (corp-wide): 29.5MM **Privately Held**
SIC: 3317 Steel pipe & tubes
PA: Basor Electric Sa
Avenida Alcodar (Pg Ind Alcodar) 45
Gandia 46701
962 876-695

(G-14044)
BASOR ELECTRIC INC
900 W Adams St (62260)
PHONE....................................618 476-6300
Tim Place, *Branch Mgr*
EMP: 5
SALES (corp-wide): 29.5MM **Privately Held**
SIC: 3317 Steel pipe & tubes
HQ: Basor Electric, Inc.
604 S Mulberry St
Millstadt IL 62260
618 476-6300

(G-14045)
DOUBLE NICKEL LLC
Also Called: Detonics Defense Technologies
609 S Breese St Ste 101 (62260-2003)
PHONE....................................618 476-3200
Bruce Siddle, *Principal*
EMP: 3
SALES (est): 170K **Privately Held**
SIC: 7382 3484 Security systems services; machine guns & grenade launchers

(G-14046)
DOUBLE NICKEL HOLDINGS LLC
609 S Breese St Ste 101 (62260-2003)
PHONE....................................618 476-3200
Bruce Siddle, *Principal*
EMP: 3
SALES (est): 198.7K **Privately Held**
SIC: 3356 Nickel

(G-14047)
HUMAN FACTOR RES GROUP INC
609 Suth Brese St Ste 101 (62260)
PHONE....................................618 476-3200
Bruce K Siddle, *CEO*
EMP: 8
SALES (est): 634.5K **Privately Held**
SIC: 2731 Book publishing

(G-14048)
INLAND TECH HOLDINGS LLC
609 S Breese St (62260-2003)
PHONE....................................618 476-7678
Rick Jr Schmidt, *President*
EMP: 20 **EST:** 2015
SQ FT: 21,600
SALES (est): 1.9MM **Privately Held**
SIC: 3613 3674 Control panels, electric; modules, solid state

(G-14049)
LOGICON GROUP LLC
100 Traver Tine Cir (62260-2288)
PHONE....................................618 558-7757
Marc Whitney, *Mng Member*
EMP: 5
SQ FT: 3,000
SALES: 750K **Privately Held**
SIC: 8711 7373 3535 7389 Engineering services; computer integrated systems design; conveyors & conveying equipment;

(G-14050)
MAC CONSTRUCTION
10 Pine St (62260-2055)
PHONE....................................618 541-4092
Latoya McGruder, *Owner*
EMP: 30
SALES (est): 437.8K **Privately Held**
SIC: 1389 Construction, repair & dismantling services

(G-14051)
MAC MEDICAL INC
820 S Mulberry St (62260-2076)
PHONE....................................618 476-3550
Dennis W Cooper, *President*
Stacey A Cooper, *Vice Pres*
Joel Pottebaum, *Controller*
Kim Merchant, *Human Res Mgr*
◆ **EMP:** 130
SQ FT: 100,000
SALES (est): 20MM **Privately Held**
SIC: 3842 Surgical appliances & supplies

(G-14052)
METRO PRINTING & PUBG INC
Also Called: Record Printing & Publishing
109 W Washington St (62260-1155)
PHONE....................................618 476-9587
Paul Adrignola, *President*
EMP: 12
SQ FT: 11,500
SALES (est): 2.6MM **Privately Held**
SIC: 2752 2791 2789 2721 Commercial printing, offset; typesetting; bookbinding & related work; periodicals

(G-14053)
MILLSTADT TOWNSHIP
Also Called: Road District
18 E Harrison St (62260-2006)
P.O. Box 274 (62260-0274)
PHONE....................................618 476-3592
Stan Jarvis, *Commissioner*
EMP: 3 **Privately Held**
SIC: 3531 Road construction & maintenance machinery
PA: Millstadt Township
820 S Jefferson St
Millstadt IL 62260

Minier
Tazewell County

(G-14054)
LAUGHING DOG GRAPHICS
Also Called: Sudden Impact Sports
207 N Main Ave (61759-7524)
P.O. Box 889 (61759-0889)
PHONE....................................309 392-3330
Kenny Williams, *Owner*
EMP: 3
SQ FT: 3,500
SALES (est): 58.5K **Privately Held**
SIC: 2759 Screen printing

Minonk
Woodford County

(G-14055)
SMF INC (PA)
1550 N Industrial Park Rd (61760-9700)
PHONE....................................309 432-2586
Brian Brown, *CEO*
Ken Bauer, *COO*
Terence Manning, *Vice Pres*
Terry Manning, *Vice Pres*
Steven White, *Vice Pres*
EMP: 186
SQ FT: 160,000
SALES (est): 50.2MM **Privately Held**
SIC: 3441 Fabricated structural metal

(G-14056)
ZARC INTERNATIONAL INC
529 S Petri Dr (61760-7646)
P.O. Box 108 (61760-0108)
PHONE....................................309 807-2565
David T Froelich, *President*
EMP: 17
SQ FT: 15,000
SALES: 1.4MM **Privately Held**
SIC: 3949 Sporting & athletic goods

Minooka
Grundy County

(G-14057)
DOLLS LETTERING INC
110 Industrial Dr Unit A (60447-9130)
PHONE....................................815 467-8000
Jeffrey A Doll, *President*
EMP: 5
SALES (est): 300.3K **Privately Held**
SIC: 2759 Screen printing

(G-14058)
DYNE INC
7280 E Us Highway 6 (60447-9144)
P.O. Box 848 (60447-0848)
PHONE....................................815 521-1111
Roy Breaudoin, *President*
▲ **EMP:** 8
SQ FT: 100,000
SALES (est): 1MM **Privately Held**
SIC: 2221 Upholstery, tapestry & wall covering fabrics

(G-14059)
ELCON INC (PA)
600 Twin Rail Dr (60447-9465)
P.O. Box 910 (60447-0910)
PHONE....................................815 467-9500
Frank J Garrone Jr, *President*
Adam Wilhelmi, *Production*
Steven E Holic, *CFO*
Jose Santos, *Manager*
Lorraine Garrone, *Admin Sec*
EMP: 50 **EST:** 1988
SQ FT: 25,000
SALES (est): 9MM **Privately Held**
WEB: www.elconinc.net
SIC: 3625 7629 3829 3822 Control equipment, electric; electronic equipment repair; measuring & controlling devices; auto controls regulating residntl & coml environmt & applncs; printed circuit boards; switchgear & switchboard apparatus

(G-14060)
F C L KELLOGGS
6225 E Minooka Rd (60447-9339)
PHONE....................................815 467-8198
EMP: 5
SALES (est): 509.4K **Privately Held**
SIC: 2052 Cookies

(G-14061)
HALLMARK CABINET COMPANY
Also Called: Hallmark Surfaces
251 Switchgrass Dr (60447-8449)
PHONE....................................708 757-7807
Anthony S Pappas, *President*
Judith K Pappas, *Admin Sec*
EMP: 70 **EST:** 1980

GEOGRAPHIC SECTION

SALES (est): 8.5MM **Privately Held**
SIC: 2541 7389 Counters or counter display cases, wood;

(G-14062)
MENASHA PACKAGING COMPANY LLC
456 International Pkwy (60447-9414)
PHONE.................................630 391-1741
Vern Jackson, *Branch Mgr*
EMP: 450
SALES (corp-wide): 2.2B **Privately Held**
SIC: 2653 Sheets, corrugated: made from purchased materials
HQ: Menasha Packaging Company, Llc
   1645 Bergstrom Rd
   Neenah WI 54956
   920 751-1000

(G-14063)
METALSTAMP INC
6800 E Minooka Rd (60447-9445)
PHONE.................................815 467-7800
Leroy Hutchinson, *President*
John Talarico, *Purch Mgr*
Ben Hutchinson, *Engineer*
Jim Frieders, *Executive*
▲ EMP: 50
SQ FT: 12,000
SALES (est): 14.7MM **Privately Held**
SIC: 3469 Stamping metal for the trade

(G-14064)
NARVICK BROS LUMBER CO INC
Also Called: Narvick Bros Ready Mix
801 Rail Way Ct (60447-9242)
PHONE.................................815 521-1173
Tim Hardy, *Branch Mgr*
EMP: 20
SALES (est): 1.9MM
SALES (corp-wide): 18.3MM **Privately Held**
SIC: 3273 Ready-mixed concrete
PA: Narvick Bros. Lumber Co., Inc.
   1037 Armstrong St
   Morris IL 60450
   815 942-1173

(G-14065)
OAK COURT CREATIONS
202 Oak Ct (60447-9148)
P.O. Box 497 (60447-0497)
PHONE.................................815 467-7676
Beverly Sievers, *President*
EMP: 3
SALES (est): 364.3K **Privately Held**
SIC: 2844 Bath salts

(G-14066)
UPCYCLE PRODUCTS INC
400 E Wapella St (60447-9146)
P.O. Box 315, Channahon (60410-0315)
PHONE.................................815 383-6220
Richard Fielding, *President*
EMP: 2
SALES (est): 368.1K **Privately Held**
SIC: 2429 Barrels & barrel parts

Mode
Shelby County

(G-14067)
IOLA QUARRY INC
Also Called: Brush Creek Quarry
2671 County Hwy 6 (62444)
PHONE.................................217 682-3865
Bryan Hood, *President*
EMP: 10
SALES (corp-wide): 100MM **Privately Held**
SIC: 1422 Limestones, ground
HQ: Iola Quarry Inc
   202 W Main St Ste A
   Salem IL
   618 548-1585

Mokena
Will County

(G-14068)
ABOVE WAVES INC
11600 N Brightway Dr (60448-1412)
PHONE.................................708 341-9123
Ryan Hesslau, *President*
EMP: 4
SALES: 50K **Privately Held**
SIC: 8748 7372 7389 Communications consulting; educational computer software;

(G-14069)
ALINE INTERNATIONAL LLC
9100 W 191st St Ste 103 (60448-8773)
PHONE.................................708 478-2471
Liang Ruquan,
▲ EMP: 10
SALES (est): 1.3MM
SALES (corp-wide): 23.1MM **Privately Held**
SIC: 2599 Cabinets, factory
PA: Shouguang Sanyang Wood Industry Co., Ltd.
   The West Of Anqian Street, Beiluo Industrial Area
   Shouguang 26270
   536 559-8012

(G-14070)
ALPHA LASER OF CHICAGO
9632 194th Pl (60448-9344)
PHONE.................................708 478-0464
Jack McCallum, *Owner*
EMP: 2
SQ FT: 800
SALES (est): 250K **Privately Held**
SIC: 3861 Toners, prepared photographic (not made in chemical plants)

(G-14071)
AMERICAN MACHINE PDTS & SVCS
11863 W Josephine Dr (60448-8480)
PHONE.................................708 743-9088
Edward C Richerme, *President*
EMP: 3
SALES (est): 207.9K **Privately Held**
SIC: 3451 Screw machine products

(G-14072)
APPLIED ARTS & SCIENCES INC
Also Called: Hangerjack
21432 Prestancia Dr (60448-8404)
P.O. Box 3814, Winter Park FL (32790-3814)
PHONE.................................407 288-8228
Jack A Fugett, *President*
Dina Fugett, *Vice Pres*
Mark Fugett, *Vice Pres*
EMP: 4
SQ FT: 5,000
SALES (est): 304K **Privately Held**
SIC: 3089 Clothes hangers, plastic

(G-14073)
ASPEN CARPET DESIGNS
11335 Stratford Rd (60448-2007)
PHONE.................................815 483-8501
Gerald Krull, *Principal*
EMP: 3
SALES (est): 202.2K **Privately Held**
SIC: 2273 Carpets & rugs

(G-14074)
CALUMET SCREW MACHINE PRODUCTS
19600 97th Ave (60448-9388)
PHONE.................................708 479-1660
Louis J Bertoletti, *President*
Don Mertes, *Plant Mgr*
Deborah Bertoletti, *Human Res Mgr*
EMP: 70
SQ FT: 48,000
SALES (est): 15.7MM **Privately Held**
WEB: www.calscrew.com
SIC: 3451 Screw machine products

(G-14075)
CITIZENPRIME LLC
Also Called: Firepenny
8940 W 192nd St Ste I (60448-8137)
PHONE.................................708 995-1241
Brian Moke, *Mng Member*
EMP: 1
SQ FT: 1,600
SALES (est): 225K **Privately Held**
WEB: www.firepenny.com
SIC: 5023 3569 Fireplace equipment & accessories; firefighting apparatus & related equipment

(G-14076)
CONDATA GLOBAL INC (PA)
9830 W 190th St Ste M (60448-5603)
PHONE.................................708 390-2500
David Newberry, *President*
EMP: 50
SALES (est): 5.8MM **Privately Held**
SIC: 7372 Business oriented computer software

(G-14077)
CREAMERY INC
191000 Wolf Rd (60448)
PHONE.................................708 479-5706
Robyn Curbis, *Branch Mgr*
EMP: 3
SALES (est): 150.4K **Privately Held**
SIC: 2024 5143 Ice cream & frozen desserts; frozen dairy desserts
PA: The Creamery Inc
   459 W Nebraska St Ste 3
   Frankfort IL 60423

(G-14078)
DETAILS ETC
19256 85th Ct (60448-8854)
PHONE.................................708 932-5543
Phyllis Bauer, *President*
EMP: 16
SALES (est): 1.1MM **Privately Held**
SIC: 3272 Precast terrazo or concrete products

(G-14079)
EMBASSY SECURITY GROUP INC
9960 191st St Ste N (60448-8642)
PHONE.................................800 627-1325
Kenneth Boudreau, *CEO*
Mark Delia, *CEO*
EMP: 44 EST: 1995
SQ FT: 3,000
SALES: 170K **Privately Held**
WEB: www.embassysecurity.net
SIC: 7381 7372 Guard services; prepackaged software

(G-14080)
FAST SIGNS
Also Called: Fastsigns
19404 S La Grange Rd (60448-9316)
PHONE.................................815 730-7828
Bob Meyer, *Branch Mgr*
EMP: 3 **Privately Held**
SIC: 3993 Signs & advertising specialties
PA: Fast Signs
   8373 Southwest Fwy
   Houston TX 77074

(G-14081)
FIRE SYSTEMS HOLDINGS INC
Also Called: Automatic Fire Controls
8940 W 192nd St Ste M (60448-8137)
PHONE.................................708 333-4130
Charles S Cebula, *CEO*
Laura Johnson, *Technology*
EMP: 15
SALES (est): 2.6MM **Privately Held**
SIC: 3569 Sprinkler systems, fire: automatic

(G-14082)
FORMAX INC
9150 W 191st St (60448-1394)
P.O. Box 3 (60448-0003)
PHONE.................................708 479-3000
Mel Cohen, *President*
Cindy Bauer, *Export Mgr*
EMP: 36

SALES (est): 8.8MM
SALES (corp-wide): 1.5B **Privately Held**
WEB: www.formaxinc.com
SIC: 3556 Food products machinery
HQ: Provisur Technologies, Inc.
   9150 W 191st St
   Mokena IL 60448
   708 479-3500

(G-14083)
FRANK MILLER & SONS INC (PA)
Also Called: Fms of Wisconsin Div
10002 W 190th Pl (60448-8752)
P.O. Box 8215, South Bend IN (46660-8215)
PHONE.................................708 201-7200
Richard Miller, *President*
James A Miller Jr, *Vice Pres*
Johanna McInerney, *Admin Sec*
EMP: 30 EST: 1889
SQ FT: 87,000
SALES (est): 5MM **Privately Held**
WEB: www.icemelt.com
SIC: 2842 2899 2879 2819 Sweeping compounds, oil or water absorbent, clay or sawdust; cleaning or polishing preparations; chemical preparations; fungicides, herbicides; industrial inorganic chemicals

(G-14084)
FREEDOM DESIGN & DECALS INC
18811 90th Ave Ste G (60448-8030)
PHONE.................................815 806-8172
Julie Raduen, *Owner*
EMP: 3
SALES (est): 250.5K **Privately Held**
SIC: 3993 Signs & advertising specialties

(G-14085)
G H MEISER & CO
18770 88th Ave Unit B (60448-8777)
PHONE.................................708 388-7867
Brian Parduhn, *President*
Bruce Parduhn, *Vice Pres*
▲ EMP: 25 EST: 1906
SQ FT: 11,600
SALES (est): 4.2MM **Privately Held**
WEB: www.ghmeiser.com
SIC: 3824 3563 Gauges for computing pressure temperature corrections; tire inflators, hand or compressor operated

(G-14086)
GALLASI CUT STONE & MARBLE LLC
10001 191st St Ste (60448-8361)
PHONE.................................708 479-9494
Paul Gallasi,
EMP: 22
SQ FT: 13,000
SALES (est): 2.5MM **Privately Held**
WEB: www.gallasi.com
SIC: 5032 3281 Stone, crushed or broken; cut stone & stone products

(G-14087)
GEORGE PAGELS COMPANY
9910 W 190th Ave Ste H (60448-5607)
PHONE.................................708 478-7036
Richard Pagel, *CEO*
EMP: 3
SALES (est): 359.3K **Privately Held**
SIC: 2431 Millwork

(G-14088)
GFL ENVIRONMENTAL SVCS USA INC (HQ)
19701 97th Ave (60448-9391)
PHONE.................................866 579-6900
Patrick Dovigi, *President*
EMP: 48
SQ FT: 24,000
SALES: 6.3MM
SALES (corp-wide): 1.1B **Privately Held**
SIC: 2842 4953 Specialty cleaning preparations; recycling, waste materials
PA: Gfl Environmental Inc
   100 New Park Pl Suite 500
   Vaughan ON L4K 0
   905 326-0101

Mokena - Will County (G-14089)

(G-14089)
HUSKY INJECTION MOLDING
8845 W 192nd St Ste B (60448-8455)
PHONE..................708 479-9049
EMP: 17
SALES (est): 2.9MM Privately Held
SIC: 3089 Mfg Plastic Products

(G-14090)
ILLIANA MACHINE & MFG CORP
19700 97th Ave (60448-9396)
PHONE..................708 479-1333
Tito T Mattera, President
Anthony U Mattera, Corp Secy
George Born, VP Bus Dvlpt
▲ EMP: 60
SQ FT: 34,500
SALES (est): 7.9MM Privately Held
SIC: 3599 Machine shop, jobbing & repair

(G-14091)
ILLINOIS TOOL WORKS INC
ITW Deltar Fuel Systems Div
9629 197th St (60448-9351)
PHONE..................708 479-7200
EMP: 200
SQ FT: 50,000
SALES (corp-wide): 14.1B Publicly Held
SIC: 3089 3714 3544 Plastic hardware & building products; motor vehicle parts & accessories; special dies, tools, jigs & fixtures
PA: Illinois Tool Works Inc.
155 Harlem Ave
Glenview IL 60025
847 724-7500

(G-14092)
INTEGRITY SIGN COMPANY
18770 88th Ave Unit A (60448-8777)
PHONE..................708 532-5038
Ken Becvar, President
Keith Hlad, Vice Pres
EMP: 12
SALES (est): 1.3MM Privately Held
SIC: 3993 Electric signs

(G-14093)
LABEL DESIGN
19633 Snowmass Rd (60448-1654)
PHONE..................815 462-4949
John Sabados, President
EMP: 1
SALES: 1MM Privately Held
WEB: www.makelabel.com
SIC: 2759 Labels & seals: printing

(G-14094)
LANDQUIST & SON INC
Also Called: Magiglide
9850 W 190th St Ste L (60448-5606)
PHONE..................847 674-6600
Dennis Box, President
Tracy Koehler, Sales Staff
EMP: 20
SQ FT: 3,000
SALES (est): 3.2MM Privately Held
WEB: www.landquist.com
SIC: 2431 Doors, wood; interior & ornamental woodwork & trim

(G-14095)
LETTERMEN SIGNAGE INC
19912 Wolf Rd (60448-1318)
PHONE..................708 479-5161
Lawrence W Hansen, President
John Hansen, Vice Pres
EMP: 7 EST: 1973
SQ FT: 1,800
SALES (est): 800K Privately Held
WEB: www.lettermensign.com
SIC: 7389 3993 Sign painting & lettering shop; signs & advertising specialties

(G-14096)
LIGO PRODUCTS INC
9100 W 191st St Ste 101 (60448-8773)
PHONE..................708 478-1800
Ss Lee, President
Su-Tsen Lee, Admin Sec
▲ EMP: 34
SQ FT: 350,000
SALES (est): 4.1MM Privately Held
SIC: 2519 5021 Fiberglass furniture, household; padded or plain; household furniture

(G-14097)
MARLEY CANDLES
12525 187th St (60448-8278)
PHONE..................815 485-6604
Alice Fixari, Owner
EMP: 20
SQ FT: 4,784
SALES (est): 849.4K Privately Held
WEB: www.marleycandles.com
SIC: 5947 5999 3999 Gift shop; candle shops; candles

(G-14098)
MJ WORKS HOSE & FITTING LLC (PA)
11122 W 189th Pl Bldg C1 (60448-8963)
PHONE..................708 995-5723
Marty Martin, Mng Member
Lisa Martin,
EMP: 3
SQ FT: 1,500
SALES: 285K Privately Held
SIC: 5085 3492 Valves & fittings; fluid power valves & hose fittings

(G-14099)
NORTH AMERICAN SAFETY PDTS INC
8910 W 192nd St Ste C (60448-8111)
PHONE..................815 469-1144
Martin Mobeck, President
Cynthia Ruzon, Cust Mgr
John Dworak, Sales Staff
▲ EMP: 6
SQ FT: 12,000
SALES (est): 3MM Privately Held
SIC: 5084 5999 3499 Safety equipment; safety supplies & equipment; barricades, metal

(G-14100)
OZINGA BROS INC (PA)
19001 Old Lagrange Rd # 30 (60448-8012)
PHONE..................708 326-4200
Martin Ozinga III, Ch of Bd
James A Ozinga, Vice Pres
Richard Ozinga, Admin Sec
EMP: 20 EST: 1928
SALES (est): 434.5MM Privately Held
WEB: www.ozinga.com
SIC: 3273 Ready-mixed concrete

(G-14101)
OZINGA INDIANA RDYMX CON INC
19001 Old Lagrange Rd (60448-8012)
PHONE..................708 479-9050
EMP: 4
SALES (est): 414.3K Privately Held
SIC: 3273 Ready-mixed concrete

(G-14102)
OZINGA MATERIALS INC (HQ)
19001 Old Lagrange Rd (60448-8012)
PHONE..................309 364-3401
Martin Ozinga III, President
Barry N Voorn, Admin Sec
EMP: 205
SALES (est): 2.1MM
SALES (corp-wide): 434.5MM Privately Held
SIC: 3273 Ready-mixed concrete
PA: Ozinga Bros, Inc.
19001 Old Lagrange Rd # 30
Mokena IL 60448
708 326-4200

(G-14103)
OZINGA READY MIX CONCRETE INC (PA)
19001 Old Lagrange Rd # 300 (60448-8012)
PHONE..................708 326-4200
Justin Ozinga, President
Martin Ozinga, President
Barry N Voorn, Admin Sec
EMP: 46
SALES (est): 19.4MM Privately Held
SIC: 8711 3272 5999 3273 Building construction consultant; concrete products; concrete products, pre-cast; ready-mixed concrete

(G-14104)
OZINGA S SUBN RDYMX CON INC
18825 Old Lagrange Rd (60448-8350)
PHONE..................708 479-3080
Thomas Kerkstra, Branch Mgr
EMP: 10
SALES (corp-wide): 434.5MM Privately Held
SIC: 3273 Ready-mixed concrete
HQ: Ozinga South Suburban Ready Mix Concrete, Inc.
19001 Old Lagrange Rd # 300
Mokena IL 60448

(G-14105)
OZINGA S SUBN RDYMX CON INC (HQ)
Also Called: Ozinga South Suburban RMC
19001 Old Lagrange Rd # 300 (60448-8012)
PHONE..................708 326-4201
Justin Ozinga, President
EMP: 55
SALES (est): 31.2MM
SALES (corp-wide): 434.5MM Privately Held
SIC: 3273 Ready-mixed concrete
PA: Ozinga Bros., Inc.
19001 Old Lagrange Rd # 30
Mokena IL 60448
708 326-4200

(G-14106)
PEPPERIDGE FARM INCORPORATED
8910 W 192nd St (60448-8110)
PHONE..................708 478-7450
EMP: 3
SALES (corp-wide): 8.1B Publicly Held
WEB: www.pepperidgefarm.com
SIC: 5461 2052 2099 2053 Bakeries; cookies; bread crumbs, not made in bakeries; frozen bakery products, except bread
HQ: Pepperidge Farm, Incorporated
595 Westport Ave
Norwalk CT 06851
203 846-7000

(G-14107)
PHOENIX INDUSTRIES INC
10601 Saint John Dr (60448-1744)
PHONE..................708 478-5474
James Taylor-Gurley, Principal
▲ EMP: 3
SALES (est): 267.6K Privately Held
SIC: 3999 Manufacturing industries

(G-14108)
POLYENVIRO LABS INC
9960 191st St Ste K (60448-8642)
PHONE..................708 489-0195
Vishnu Gor, President
Kanak Gor, Treasurer
Allen Resnick, Admin Sec
EMP: 4
SQ FT: 11,000
SALES (est): 705K Privately Held
WEB: www.polyenviro.com
SIC: 2992 2869 3471 2899 Lubricating oils & greases; industrial organic chemicals; plating & polishing; chemical preparations

(G-14109)
PRINTING BY JOSEPH
19640 S La Grange Rd (60448-9321)
PHONE..................708 479-2669
Joseph Koszulinski, Owner
EMP: 3
SQ FT: 500
SALES (est): 343.6K Privately Held
SIC: 2752 2791 2789 Commercial printing, offset; typesetting; bookbinding & related work

(G-14110)
PRO-AM TEAM SPORTS LLC
8940 W 192nd St Ste J (60448-8137)
PHONE..................708 995-1511
Less Than, Principal
Joe Knudsen, Sales Staff
EMP: 15
SALES: 1MM Privately Held
SIC: 2329 3949 Men's & boys' sportswear & athletic clothing; men's & boys' athletic uniforms; team sports equipment

(G-14111)
PURIFIED LUBRICANTS INC
9629 194th St (60448-9301)
PHONE..................708 478-3500
Robert J Maloney, President
EMP: 21
SQ FT: 6,000
SALES (est): 2.1MM Privately Held
SIC: 1389 7353 Oil field services; oil equipment rental services

(G-14112)
REVERE METALS LLC
10014 W 190th Pl (60448-8752)
PHONE..................708 995-6131
Robert Lange, Mng Member
Rob Lange, Mng Member
EMP: 4
SQ FT: 5,000
SALES: 3MM Privately Held
SIC: 3312 Sheet or strip, steel, hot-rolled; sheet or strip, steel, cold-rolled: own hot-rolled

(G-14113)
ROTOSPRAY MFG INC
Also Called: Roto Spray Manufacturing
10315 Aileen Ave (60448-3331)
PHONE..................708 478-3307
Joseph R Kral, President
EMP: 4
SALES (est): 233.8K Privately Held
SIC: 7699 3569 Tool repair services; general industrial machinery

(G-14114)
RRR GRAPHICS & FILM CORP
Also Called: Triple R Graphics
19759 Westminster Dr (60448-2404)
PHONE..................708 478-4573
EMP: 8
SALES (est): 1MM Privately Held
SIC: 2752 2791 2789 Lithographic Commercial Printing Typesetting Services Bookbinding/Related Work

(G-14115)
SMS GROUP INC
Also Called: SMS Technical Services
19700 97th Ave (60448-9390)
PHONE..................708 479-1333
Tito T Mattera, Branch Mgr
Anthony Mattera, Admin Sec
EMP: 3
SALES (corp-wide): 144.1K Privately Held
SIC: 3559 Sewing machines & hat & zipper making machinery
HQ: Sms Group Inc.
100 Sandusky St
Pittsburgh PA 15212
412 231-1200

(G-14116)
SPECIFIC PRESS BRAKE DIES INC
9439 Enterprise Dr (60448-8319)
PHONE..................708 478-1776
Janett Pelech, President
Lynda Crites, Vice Pres
Bruno Pelech, Vice Pres
EMP: 11 EST: 1996
SQ FT: 3,200
SALES (est): 1.5MM Privately Held
WEB: www.specificbrakedies.com
SIC: 3544 Special dies & tools

(G-14117)
STORE 409 INC
Also Called: Image 360 - Mokena
9960 191st St Ste E (60448-8642)
PHONE..................708 478-5751
Fred Osborne, President
Jonathan Osborne, Vice Pres
Andy Kochel, Administration
Lynn Ingram, Representative
EMP: 10
SALES (est): 1.3MM Privately Held
SIC: 3993 Signs & advertising specialties

GEOGRAPHIC SECTION

Moline - Rock Island County (G-14146)

(G-14118)
SUBURBAN MACHINE & TOOL
8119 189th St (60448-8840)
PHONE.................815 469-2221
Alan Pokrzywa, *Owner*
EMP: 5 **EST:** 1977
SQ FT: 7,000
SALES (est): 487.9K **Privately Held**
SIC: 3599 Machine shop, jobbing & repair

(G-14119)
SURFACE SOLUTIONS ILLINOIS INC (PA)
9615 194th Pl (60448-9317)
PHONE.................708 571-3449
Mark Mercado, *President*
EMP: 8
SQ FT: 11,200
SALES (est): 2.9MM **Privately Held**
SIC: 1799 2541 1741 Counter top installation; counter & sink tops; masonry & other stonework

(G-14120)
SUSTAINABLE SOURCING LLC
19633 S La Grange Rd (60448-9360)
PHONE.................815 714-8055
John T Mahoney, *Mng Member*
EMP: 11
SALES (est): 1.8MM **Privately Held**
SIC: 2077 Animal & marine fats & oils

(G-14121)
TANYA SHIPLEY
Also Called: Decorators Vault
11344 Abbey Rd (60448-2437)
PHONE.................708 476-0433
Tanya Shipley, *Principal*
EMP: 3 **EST:** 2010
SALES (est): 167.9K **Privately Held**
SIC: 3272 Burial vaults, concrete or precast terrazzo

(G-14122)
TIMKEN GEARS & SERVICES INC
Also Called: Philadelphia Gear
8529 192nd St (60448-8874)
PHONE.................708 720-9400
Terry Dempsey, *Manager*
EMP: 10
SALES (corp-wide): 3.7B **Publicly Held**
SIC: 3462 Gear & chain forgings; gears, forged steel; anchors, forged
HQ: Timken Gears & Services Inc.
901 E 8th Ave Ste 100
King Of Prussia PA 19406

(G-14123)
TOMSONS PRODUCTS INC
Also Called: Tomson Railings
18800 Wolf Rd (60448-8933)
PHONE.................708 479-7030
Thomas Wisinski, *President*
EMP: 4
SALES (corp-wide): 500K **Privately Held**
SIC: 3599 Machine shop, jobbing & repair
PA: Tomson's Products Inc
13210 S 85th Ave
Orland Park IL 60462
708 479-7030

(G-14124)
TORRENCE MACHINE & TOOL CO
18830 82nd Ave (60448-9724)
PHONE.................815 469-1850
Scott Evans, *President*
▲ **EMP:** 9
SQ FT: 10,000
SALES (est): 451K **Privately Held**
SIC: 3599 7692 Machine shop, jobbing & repair; welding repair

(G-14125)
UNITED SYSTEMS INCORPORATED
9704 194th St (60448-9456)
P.O. Box 96 (60448-0096)
PHONE.................708 479-1450
Radovan Ilic, *President*
EMP: 16 **EST:** 1978
SQ FT: 20,000
SALES (est): 4.2MM **Privately Held**
SIC: 3535 Conveyors & conveying equipment

(G-14126)
VISUCOM
9910 W 190th St Ste C (60448-5607)
PHONE.................708 460-3001
Lisa Dedo, *Principal*
EMP: 3
SALES (est): 275.6K **Privately Held**
SIC: 3993 Signs & advertising specialties

(G-14127)
VOLFLEX INC
10920 Walnut Ln Ste 1 (60448-1615)
PHONE.................708 478-1117
Joseph A Bunch, *President*
Richard Bunch, *Co-Owner*
David Bunch, *Vice Pres*
Brian Meyer, *Production*
Tim Schoolman, *Sales Mgr*
▼ **EMP:** 31
SALES (est): 8.6MM **Privately Held**
WEB: www.volflex.com
SIC: 3086 Packaging & shipping materials, foamed plastic

(G-14128)
WOODSTREET CABINET
9951 W 190th St (60448-8332)
PHONE.................708 995-6077
EMP: 4
SALES (est): 128.1K **Privately Held**
SIC: 2434 Wood kitchen cabinets

(G-14129)
XYLEM WATER SOLUTIONS USA INC
9661 194th St (60448-9301)
PHONE.................856 467-3636
Christopher Tuinstra, *Sales Staff*
Michael Retter, *Branch Mgr*
Paul Weinert, *Technical Staff*
EMP: 11 **Publicly Held**
SIC: 7694 5531 Electric motor repair; automotive & home supply stores
HQ: Xylem Water Solutions U.S.A., Inc.
4828 Prkwy Plz Blvd 200
Charlotte NC 28217

Moline
Rock Island County

(G-14130)
A 1 MARKING PRODUCTS
Also Called: Des Moines Stamp Mfg Co
1801 5th Ave (61265-7902)
PHONE.................309 762-6096
Sheila Chess, *General Mgr*
Pam Talley, *Manager*
EMP: 4 **EST:** 1918
SALES (est): 329.8K **Privately Held**
SIC: 5943 3953 Stationery stores; marking devices

(G-14131)
AMERICAN SPEED ENTERPRISES
3006 Avenue Of The Cities (61265-4364)
PHONE.................309 764-3601
Gail Trent, *President*
EMP: 2 **EST:** 1973
SQ FT: 6,500
SALES: 350K **Privately Held**
SIC: 3714 5961 3519 Motor vehicle engines & parts; automotive supplies & equipment, mail order; internal combustion engines

(G-14132)
ANP INC
1515 5th Ave Ste 428 (61265-1367)
PHONE.................309 757-0372
Monte Bottens, *President*
Dawn Bull, *President*
EMP: 4
SQ FT: 900
SALES (est): 5.9MM **Privately Held**
SIC: 2875 Fertilizers, mixing only

(G-14133)
BENT RIVER BREWING CO (PA)
1413 5th Ave (61265-1335)
PHONE.................309 797-2722
Tom Merrill, *President*
EMP: 18
SQ FT: 4,200
SALES (est): 3.9MM **Privately Held**
SIC: 2082 5813 Malt beverages; bar (drinking places)

(G-14134)
BIMBO BAKERIES USA INC
5205 22nd Ave (61265-3626)
PHONE.................309 797-4968
Harrold Nelson, *Branch Mgr*
EMP: 24 **Privately Held**
SIC: 2051 Bakery: wholesale or wholesale/retail combined
HQ: Bimbo Bakeries Usa, Inc
255 Business Center Dr # 200
Horsham PA 19044
215 347-5500

(G-14135)
CAR SHOP INC
1214 17th Ave (61265-3925)
PHONE.................309 797-4188
Tim Ryherd, *Vice Pres*
EMP: 6
SALES (est): 794.3K **Privately Held**
SIC: 5531 3599 Speed shops, including race car supplies; automotive parts; automotive accessories; machine shop, jobbing & repair

(G-14136)
CLEAN ENERGY RENEWABLES LLC
4709 15th Street A (61265-7083)
PHONE.................309 797-4844
Bas Mattingly, *CEO*
Matthew Cumberworth Sr, *President*
EMP: 29
SQ FT: 7,500
SALES (est): 4MM **Privately Held**
SIC: 8748 8711 3829 3823 Energy conservation consultant; energy conservation engineering; wind direction indicators; industrial process measurement equipment

(G-14137)
DAVID HALL
1529 46th Ave (61265-7084)
PHONE.................309 797-9721
David Hall, *Owner*
EMP: 50
SALES (est): 1.5MM **Privately Held**
SIC: 3949 Swimming pools, except plastic

(G-14138)
DEERE & COMPANY (PA)
Also Called: John Deere
1 John Deere Pl (61265-8098)
PHONE.................309 765-8000
Samuel R Allen, *Ch of Bd*
James M Field, *President*
Rajesh Kalathur, *President*
John C May, *President*
Cory J Reed, *President*
EMP: 1400 **EST:** 1837
SALES: 39.2B **Publicly Held**
WEB: www.deere.com
SIC: 3531 3524 6159 3523 Construction machinery; tractors, crawler; dozers, tractor mounted: material moving; bulldozers (construction machinery); lawn & garden tractors & equipment; lawnmowers, residential: hand or power; rollers, lawn; agricultural credit institutions; tractors, farm

(G-14139)
DEERE & COMPANY
Also Called: John Deere Accounts Payble
John Deere (61266)
P.O. Box 8808 (61266-8808)
PHONE.................309 765-8275
Jan Lechner, *Accountant*
Tom Parker, *Marketing Staff*
Darrell Hess, *Manager*
Viacheslav Korsunov, *Manager*
Trudy Metcalfe, *Assistant*
EMP: 60
SALES (corp-wide): 39.2B **Publicly Held**
SIC: 3523 Farm machinery & equipment

PA: Deere & Company
1 John Deere Pl
Moline IL 61265
309 765-8000

(G-14140)
DEERE & COMPANY
1 John Deere Pl (61265-8098)
PHONE.................309 765-2960
EMP: 30
SALES (corp-wide): 36B **Publicly Held**
SIC: 3829 Mfg Measuring/Controlling Devices
PA: Deere & Company
1 John Deere Pl
Moline IL 61265
309 765-8000

(G-14141)
EAGLE PRINTING COMPANY
2957 12th Ave (61265-3302)
PHONE.................309 762-0771
Fax: 309 762-7705
EMP: 5
SQ FT: 2,300
SALES: 400K **Privately Held**
SIC: 5112 2752 Whol Business Forms & Offset Printing

(G-14142)
EAST MOLINE SHEET METAL CO
3001 48th Ave (61265-6326)
PHONE.................309 755-1422
Tod Luppen, *President*
Larry K Anderson, *Principal*
Carrel Sagon, *Admin Sec*
▲ **EMP:** 2
SALES (est): 500.6K **Privately Held**
SIC: 3441 Fabricated structural metal

(G-14143)
EVAC SYSTEMS FIRE & RESCUE
400 24th St (61265-1552)
P.O. Box 771 (61266-0771)
PHONE.................309 764-7812
Laurel McCune, *President*
Harold Defrieze, *Vice Pres*
Joan Mc Court, *Office Mgr*
Karen Defrieze, *Admin Sec*
EMP: 12
SQ FT: 3,000
SALES: 854.8K **Privately Held**
SIC: 3569 Firefighting apparatus & related equipment

(G-14144)
FARISS JOHN
Also Called: Fariss Step & Railing Co
3700 N Shore Dr (61265-6465)
PHONE.................815 433-3803
EMP: 3
SALES (est): 140K **Privately Held**
SIC: 3446 Mfg Architectural Metalwork

(G-14145)
FCA LLC (PA)
Also Called: FCA Packaging
7601 John Deere Pkwy (61265-8028)
P.O. Box 758 (61266-0758)
PHONE.................309 792-3444
David Wilsted, *President*
Jenny Dormire, *Vice Pres*
Glen Ringenberg, *Plant Supt*
Amber Bussert, *Purch Mgr*
Nathan Weeks, *Research*
EMP: 23
SQ FT: 3,000
SALES (est): 164.5MM **Privately Held**
SIC: 4783 5031 5085 2448 Packing goods for shipping; composite board products, woodboard; industrial supplies; pallets, wood

(G-14146)
FOSBINDER FABRICATION INC
130 35th St (61265-1742)
PHONE.................309 764-0913
Mike Fosbinder, *President*
▼ **EMP:** 23
SQ FT: 23,000
SALES (est): 4MM **Privately Held**
SIC: 3599 3544 Machine shop, jobbing & repair; special dies, tools, jigs & fixtures

Moline - Rock Island County (G-14147)

(G-14147)
GBA SYSTEMS INTEGRATORS LLC
1701 River Dr Ste 100 (61265-1384)
PHONE.................................913 492-0400
Michael L Smith, *CEO*
Shaun Kotwitz, *CFO*
EMP: 9
SALES: 1.6MM
SALES (corp-wide): 66.8MM **Privately Held**
WEB: www.gbateam.com
SIC: 3674 4899 Integrated circuits, semi-conductor networks, etc.; communication signal enhancement network system
PA: George Butler Associates, Inc.
9801 Renner Blvd Ste 300
Lenexa KS 66219
913 492-0400

(G-14148)
HARRINGTON SIGNAL INC
Also Called: Commercial Product Group
2519 4th Ave (61265-1527)
P.O. Box 590 (61266-0590)
PHONE.................................309 762-0731
Roy J Carver, *Ch of Bd*
Richard D Eisenlauer, *President*
Roy J Carver Jr, *Admin Sec*
▲ EMP: 50
SQ FT: 55,000
SALES: 12MM **Privately Held**
SIC: 3669 3625 Fire alarm apparatus, electric; electric controls & control accessories, industrial

(G-14149)
HONEYWELL INTERNATIONAL INC
2052 Ave (61265)
PHONE.................................401 573-6821
Harry Friedman, *Manager*
EMP: 673
SALES (corp-wide): 36.7B **Publicly Held**
SIC: 3724 3812 Aircraft engines & engine parts; aircraft control systems, electronic; cabin environment indicators; radar systems & equipment; aircraft flight instruments
PA: Honeywell International Inc.
300 S Tryon St
Charlotte NC 28202
704 627-6200

(G-14150)
INN INTL NEWSPAPER NETWORK
1521 47th Ave (61265-7022)
PHONE.................................309 764-5314
Marc Wilson, *CEO*
EMP: 3
SALES (est): 144.7K **Privately Held**
SIC: 2711 Newspapers, publishing & printing

(G-14151)
INVISIBLE FENCING OF QUAD CITY
5202 38th Ave Ste 2 (61265-6722)
PHONE.................................309 797-1688
Phil Vromen, *Owner*
EMP: 3
SALES (est): 228.3K **Privately Held**
SIC: 1799 3699 Fence construction; electric fence chargers

(G-14152)
JOHN DEERE AG HOLDINGS INC (HQ)
1 John Deere Pl (61265-8010)
PHONE.................................309 765-8000
Samuel R Allen, *CEO*
EMP: 5 EST: 1996
SALES (est): 5MM
SALES (corp-wide): 39.2B **Publicly Held**
SIC: 3531 3524 6159 3523 Construction machinery; tractors, crawler; dozers, tractor mounted: material moving; bulldozers (construction machinery); lawn & garden tractors & equipment; lawnmowers, residential: hand or power; rollers, lawn; agricultural credit institutions; tractors, farm
PA: Deere & Company
1 John Deere Pl
Moline IL 61265
309 765-8000

(G-14153)
JOSEPH TAYLOR INC
708 18th Avenue A (61265-3845)
PHONE.................................309 762-5323
Joseph Taylor, *Principal*
EMP: 2
SALES (est): 289.3K **Privately Held**
SIC: 3421 Table & food cutlery, including butchers'

(G-14154)
KONE ELEVATOR (DH)
1 Kone Ct (61265-1380)
PHONE.................................309 764-6771
▲ EMP: 200
SALES (est): 101.5MM
SALES (corp-wide): 11B **Privately Held**
SIC: 7699 3534 Elevators: inspection, service & repair; elevators & equipment
HQ: Kone Holland B.V.
Rijn 10
's-Gravenhage 2491
703 171-000

(G-14155)
L & W BEDDING INC
1211 16th Ave (61265-3035)
PHONE.................................309 762-6019
John A Wheatley, *President*
EMP: 3
SQ FT: 35,000
SALES: 393.7K **Privately Held**
SIC: 2392 5712 Mattress pads; mattresses; bedding & bedsprings

(G-14156)
L C INN PARTNERS (PA)
Also Called: Accudata
1510 47th Ave (61265-7021)
PHONE.................................309 743-0800
Spiro Dokolas, *Regional Mgr*
John Montgomery, *Regional Mgr*
Rick Rogers, *Vice Pres*
Patricia Bristol, *Opers Staff*
Laurie Verkruysse, *Sr Project Mgr*
EMP: 18
SALES: 3MM **Privately Held**
WEB: www.townnews365.com
SIC: 2741

(G-14157)
LAMCO SLINGS & RIGGING INC
4960 41st Street Ct (61265-7586)
PHONE.................................309 764-7400
Charles Lambrecht, *CEO*
Chuck Lambrecht, *Vice Pres*
EMP: 24
SALES (est): 12.4MM **Privately Held**
SIC: 5084 3496 3444 Materials handling machinery; hoists; slings, lifting: made from purchased wire; wire chain; sheet metalwork

(G-14158)
LEE ENTERPRISES INCORPORATED
1521 47th Ave (61265-7022)
PHONE.................................309 743-0800
Darcy Heist, *Manager*
EMP: 20
SALES (corp-wide): 509.8MM **Publicly Held**
WEB: www.lee.net
SIC: 2711 Newspapers, publishing & printing
PA: Lee Enterprises, Incorporated
4600 E 53rd St
Davenport IA 52807
563 383-2100

(G-14159)
MCLAUGHLIN BODY CO (PA)
2430 River Dr (61265-1500)
PHONE.................................309 762-7755
Raymond L Mc Laughlin, *Ch of Bd*
John Mann, *President*
Bob Anderson, *Vice Pres*
William Storm, *Vice Pres*
Michael Welch, *Opers Staff*
▲ EMP: 60 EST: 1902
SQ FT: 277,000
SALES (est): 13.8MM **Privately Held**
WEB: www.mclbody.com
SIC: 3713 3441 3559 3523 Truck & bus bodies; fabricated structural metal; frame straighteners, automobile (garage equipment); farm machinery & equipment

(G-14160)
MEGA EQUIPMENT INC
1834 46th St (61265-4527)
PHONE.................................309 764-5310
Thomas Pham, *President*
C Stanley Uskavitch, *Vice Pres*
EMP: 4
SQ FT: 1,225
SALES: 1MM **Privately Held**
SIC: 5083 5084 3523 2085 Farm & garden machinery; industrial machinery & equipment; turf equipment, commercial; distillers' dried grains & solubles & alcohol; winches

(G-14161)
MIDLAND DAVIS CORPORATION (PA)
3301 4th Ave (61265-1605)
PHONE.................................309 277-1617
Martin H Davis, *President*
Mitchell L Davis, *Vice Pres*
Eric Davis, *Admin Sec*
▼ EMP: 52 EST: 1892
SQ FT: 75,000
SALES: 35.7MM **Privately Held**
WEB: www.midland-davis.com
SIC: 5093 2679 3341 Metal scrap & waste materials; pressed & molded pulp products, purchased material; pressed fiber products from wood pulp: from purchased goods; secondary nonferrous metals

(G-14162)
MOLINE CONSUMERS CO
200 23rd Ave (61265-4616)
PHONE.................................309 757-8289
EMP: 13
SALES (est): 1.4MM **Privately Held**
SIC: 3273 Ready-mixed concrete

(G-14163)
MOLINE FORGE INC
4101 4th Ave (61265-1997)
PHONE.................................309 762-5506
Michael Schmooke, *CEO*
Michael H Schmooke, *Exec VP*
Keith Scrowther, *Opers Mgr*
Cory Calloway, *Manager*
Jeff Holtz, *Executive*
▲ EMP: 65 EST: 1915
SQ FT: 80,000
SALES (est): 11.6MM **Privately Held**
WEB: www.molineforge.com
SIC: 3462 Horseshoes

(G-14164)
OLFB CORPORATION
2128 5th Ave (61265-1411)
P.O. Box 6523, Rock Island (61204-6523)
PHONE.................................309 283-0825
Ray Williams, *President*
EMP: 3
SALES (est): 118.4K **Privately Held**
SIC: 3661 8331 Switching equipment, telephone; data sets, telephone or telegraph; job training & vocational rehabilitation services

(G-14165)
PARR INSTRUMENT COMPANY (PA)
211 53rd St (61265-1770)
PHONE.................................309 762-7716
James A Nelson, *President*
James Nelson, *COO*
Amie Cheline, *Accountant*
Joe Lambert, *Executive*
Carolina Saguilan, *Administration*
▼ EMP: 105 EST: 1899
SQ FT: 48,184
SALES: 30.7MM **Privately Held**
WEB: www.parrinst.com
SIC: 3821 3826 Calorimeters; laboratory measuring apparatus; analytical instruments

(G-14166)
PILOT CLUB OF MOLINE
3603 74th St (61265-8016)
P.O. Box 1171 (61266-1171)
PHONE.................................309 792-4102
Judy Blad, *President*
EMP: 10
SALES: 9.2K **Privately Held**
SIC: 2711 Newspapers, publishing & printing

(G-14167)
PLASTIC PRODUCTS COMPANY INC
4610 44th St (61265-7501)
PHONE.................................309 762-6532
Richard Klim, *Branch Mgr*
Heather Sanderson, *Manager*
Paul Tanghe, *Maintence Staff*
EMP: 125
SALES (corp-wide): 177.4MM **Privately Held**
SIC: 3089 3544 Injection molded finished plastic products; industrial molds
PA: Plastic Products Company, Inc.
13116 Lake Blvd
Lindstrom MN 55045
651 257-7879

(G-14168)
PURE ELEMENT
915 33rd Ave (61265-7117)
PHONE.................................309 269-7823
EMP: 3
SALES (est): 213.6K **Privately Held**
SIC: 2819 Mfg Industrial Inorganic Chemicals

(G-14169)
QCFEC LLC
4401 44th Ave (61265-6753)
PHONE.................................309 517-1158
Frank Miroballi, *Principal*
EMP: 4
SALES (est): 220K **Privately Held**
WEB: www.qcfec.com
SIC: 3949 Bowling alleys & accessories

(G-14170)
QUAD CITY PRESS
1325 15th St (61265-4059)
PHONE.................................309 764-8142
Daniel Brieser, *Owner*
EMP: 10
SQ FT: 3,000
SALES (est): 790K **Privately Held**
SIC: 2752 2791 2789 Commercial printing, offset; typesetting; bookbinding & related work

(G-14171)
QUAD CITY ULTRALIGHT AIRCRAFT
3810 34th St (61265-5300)
P.O. Box 370 (61266-0370)
PHONE.................................309 764-3515
Dave Goulet, *President*
William Ehlers, *Vice Pres*
Charles R Hamilton Sr, *Shareholder*
EMP: 12
SQ FT: 8,000
SALES (est): 1MM **Privately Held**
SIC: 3728 3721 Aircraft parts & equipment; aircraft

(G-14172)
REBELLION BREW HAUS
1525 3rd Avenue A (61265-1363)
PHONE.................................309 524-5219
EMP: 5
SALES (est): 269.6K **Privately Held**
SIC: 2082 Malt beverages

(G-14173)
RIVERSTONE GROUP INC
200 23rd Ave (61265-4616)
PHONE.................................309 757-8297
Chuck Ellis, *Branch Mgr*
EMP: 5
SALES (corp-wide): 2.5B **Privately Held**
SIC: 3273 Ready-mixed concrete
PA: Riverstone Group, Inc.
4640 E 56th St
Davenport IA 52807
309 757-8250

GEOGRAPHIC SECTION

(G-14174)
ROYAL PUBLISHING INC
1530 46th Ave (61265-7085)
PHONE.................309 797-6630
Duncan Royal, *Owner*
EMP: 10
SALES (corp-wide): 7MM **Privately Held**
SIC: 2741 Miscellaneous publishing
PA: Royal Publishing, Inc.
7620 N Harker Dr
Peoria IL
309 693-3171

(G-14175)
SALES MIDWEST PRTG & PACKG INC
426 37th St (61265-1629)
P.O. Box 653 (61266-0653)
PHONE.................309 764-5544
Jeffrey Wood, *President*
EMP: 4
SQ FT: 4,000
SALES: 77.7K **Privately Held**
SIC: 2752 3086 2675 Commercial printing, offset; packaging & shipping materials, foamed plastic; die-cut paper & board

(G-14176)
SEDONA INC (HQ)
Also Called: Sedona Group, The
612 Valley View Dr (61265-6100)
PHONE.................309 736-4104
Richard C John Jr, *President*
Don Schnauber, *Engineer*
Kayla Theofilis, *Accounts Mgr*
Carrie Duke, *Manager*
Mike Leinart, *Manager*
EMP: 120
SQ FT: 4,000
SALES: 20MM **Privately Held**
SIC: 7372 7379 Business oriented computer software; computer related consulting services

(G-14177)
SENTRY POOL & CHEMICAL SUPPLY
Also Called: Polar Paint Systems
1529 46th Ave Ste 1 (61265-7084)
PHONE.................309 797-9721
David E Hall, *President*
Sharon K Hall, *Corp Secy*
EMP: 37
SQ FT: 18,500
SALES (est): 8MM **Privately Held**
SIC: 5999 3949 5075 Swimming pool chemicals, equipment & supplies; air purification equipment; swimming pools, plastic; air filters

(G-14178)
SMITH FILTER CORPORATION
5000 41st Street Ct (61265-7583)
PHONE.................309 764-8324
Jana Lecander, *President*
Roger O Smith, *Principal*
Sharilyn Solis, *Corp Secy*
Jim Solis, *Vice Pres*
Nancy Gullette, *Purchasing*
▲ **EMP:** 44 **EST:** 1939
SQ FT: 72,000
SALES (est): 9.7MM **Privately Held**
WEB: www.smithfilter.com
SIC: 1711 3564 Plumbing, heating, air-conditioning contractors; filters, air: furnaces, air conditioning equipment, etc.

(G-14179)
STANDARD MACHINE & TOOL CORP
206 43rd St (61265-1930)
PHONE.................309 762-6431
Martin C Frederickson, *President*
Allen L Frederickson, *Vice Pres*
EMP: 18
SQ FT: 15,000
SALES: 1.2MM **Privately Held**
WEB: www.standardmachineandtool.com
SIC: 3599 3544 Machine shop, jobbing & repair; grinding castings for the trade; special dies & tools

(G-14180)
SUMMIT GRAPHICS INC
6810 34th Street Ct (61265-9756)
PHONE.................309 799-5100
David Deem, *President*
Deb Deem, *Vice Pres*
EMP: 10 **EST:** 1979
SQ FT: 7,000
SALES (est): 1.5MM **Privately Held**
SIC: 3552 5137 Silk screens for textile industry; women's & children's outerwear

(G-14181)
WILLIAMS WHITE & COMPANY
600 River Dr (61265-1178)
PHONE.................309 797-7650
Sunder Subbaroyan, *CEO*
David Takes, *President*
Robert Crane, *COO*
David Nesbitt, *Vice Pres*
Scott Law, *Project Mgr*
EMP: 130
SQ FT: 7,200
SALES (est): 37.6MM **Privately Held**
WEB: www.williamswhite.com
SIC: 3542 Mechanical (pneumatic or hydraulic) metal forming machines; presses: hydraulic & pneumatic, mechanical & manual; presses: forming, stamping, punching, sizing (machine tools); shearing machines, power

Momence
Kankakee County

(G-14182)
APPLIED MECHANICAL TECH LLC
135 Industrial Dr (60954-3903)
P.O. Box 530 (60954-0530)
PHONE.................815 472-2700
Carey Krefft, *President*
Chris Lynch, *Vice Pres*
Dave Criddle, *Engineer*
Sherrie Alexander, *Bookkeeper*
Linda Lynch, *Executive*
EMP: 7 **EST:** 1998
SQ FT: 8,450
SALES: 4.5MM **Privately Held**
WEB: www.appliedmechtech.com
SIC: 1629 3589 Waste water & sewage treatment plant construction; water treatment equipment, industrial
PA: Bulk Resources, Inc.
1507 S Alexander St # 102
Plant City FL 33563
813 764-8420

(G-14183)
BAKER & TAYLOR LLC
501 Gladiolus St (60954-1715)
PHONE.................815 802-2444
Gary Dayton, *Branch Mgr*
EMP: 500
SALES (corp-wide): 4.7B **Privately Held**
SIC: 5192 2732 Books; book printing
HQ: Baker & Taylor, Llc
2550 W Tyvola Rd Ste 300
Charlotte NC 28217

(G-14184)
D & J MACHINE SHOP INC
2120 N 11250e Rd (60954-3329)
PHONE.................815 472-6057
Donald Haut, *President*
Tim Haut, *Vice Pres*
EMP: 5
SQ FT: 10,000
SALES (est): 600K **Privately Held**
SIC: 3599 3544 3469 Machine shop, jobbing & repair; special dies, tools, jigs & fixtures; metal stampings

(G-14185)
GEMINI STEEL INC (PA)
1450 N 11250e Rd (60954-3326)
PHONE.................815 472-4762
INA Toma, *President*
Raymond J Toma, *Vice Pres*
EMP: 2 **EST:** 1981
SQ FT: 1,500
SALES (est): 725K **Privately Held**
SIC: 3446 3441 Fences or posts, ornamental iron or steel; fabricated structural metal

(G-14186)
LEE GILSTER-MARY CORPORATION
305 E Washington St (60954-1615)
PHONE.................815 472-6456
Gary Schultz, *Manager*
EMP: 84
SALES (corp-wide): 1B **Privately Held**
SIC: 2098 2047 2099 2045 Macaroni products (e.g. alphabets, rings & shells), dry; wet corn milling; popcorn, packaged: except already popped; blended flour: from purchased flour; plastic containers, except foam; bottled & canned soft drinks
HQ: Gilster-Mary Lee Corporation
1037 State St
Chester IL 62233
618 826-2361

(G-14187)
LN ENGINEERING LLC
125 Gladiolus St Ste A (60954-1781)
P.O. Box 401 (60954-0401)
PHONE.................815 472-2939
Charles Navarro, *President*
George Navarro, *Business Mgr*
Tammy Hellings,
▼ **EMP:** 10
SQ FT: 2,000
SALES (est): 2.7MM **Privately Held**
SIC: 5013 8711 7539 3599 Automotive supplies & parts; engineering services; mechanical engineering; machine shop, automotive; machine shop, jobbing & repair; automotive parts

(G-14188)
MOMENCE PACKING CO
334 W North St (60954-1157)
PHONE.................815 472-6485
Robert Salzwedel, *President*
EMP: 300 **EST:** 1982
SQ FT: 66,000
SALES (est): 39.7MM **Privately Held**
SIC: 2013 2011 Sausages from purchased meat; meat packing plants

(G-14189)
MOMENCE PALLET CORPORATION
11414 E State Route 114 (60954-3882)
P.O. Box 708 (60954-0708)
PHONE.................815 472-6451
Andrew Cryer, *President*
Patrick Cryer, *Vice Pres*
EMP: 40
SQ FT: 40,000
SALES (est): 6.7MM **Privately Held**
SIC: 2448 Pallets, wood

(G-14190)
PROGRESS REPORTER INC
Also Called: Progress Reporter Press
110 W River St (60954-1516)
PHONE.................815 472-2000
Anita Allison, *President*
Marilyn Lincoln, *Treasurer*
EMP: 5 **EST:** 1900
SQ FT: 3,000
SALES (est): 444.9K **Privately Held**
WEB: www.momenceprogressreporter.com
SIC: 2711 Commercial printing & newspaper publishing combined; job printing & newspaper publishing combined

(G-14191)
R J VAN DRUNEN & SONS INC (PA)
Also Called: Van Drunen Farms
300 W 6th St (60954-1136)
PHONE.................815 472-3100
Kevin Van Drunen, *President*
Andrew Wheeler, *Vice Pres*
Jeffrey Van Drunen, *Treasurer*
Debra Dobben, *Admin Sec*
Larry Wymore, *Technician*
◆ **EMP:** 52 **EST:** 1880
SQ FT: 30,000
SALES (est): 93.4MM **Privately Held**
WEB: www.vandrunenfarms.com
SIC: 2034 2037 0161 2099 Dried & dehydrated vegetables; frozen fruits & vegetables; rooted vegetable farms; seasonings & spices

(G-14192)
R J VAN DRUNEN & SONS INC
Also Called: Van Drunen Farms
214 Mechanic St (60954-1151)
PHONE.................830 422-2167
Kevin Van Drunen, *President*
EMP: 28
SALES (corp-wide): 93.4MM **Privately Held**
SIC: 2034 0161 0175 2099 Dried & dehydrated vegetables; rooted vegetable farms; deciduous tree fruits; seasonings & spices; frozen fruits & vegetables
PA: R. J. Van Drunen & Sons, Inc.
300 W 6th St
Momence IL 60954
815 472-3100

(G-14193)
R J VAN DRUNEN & SONS INC
3878 N Vincennes Trl (60954-3288)
PHONE.................815 472-3211
Jeff Van Drunen, *President*
EMP: 100
SALES (corp-wide): 93.4MM **Privately Held**
SIC: 2037 2099 0191 2034 Frozen fruits & vegetables; food preparations; general farms, primarily crop; dehydrated fruits, vegetables, soups
PA: R. J. Van Drunen & Sons, Inc.
300 W 6th St
Momence IL 60954
815 472-3100

Monee
Will County

(G-14194)
A PLUS SIGNS INC
25807 S Governors Hwy (60449-8650)
P.O. Box 508 (60449-0508)
PHONE.................708 534-2030
Joe Grasser, *Manager*
EMP: 3
SALES (est): 292.7K **Privately Held**
SIC: 3993 Signs & advertising specialties

(G-14195)
ADVANCED MOBILITY &
Also Called: Amst
6370 W Emerald Pkwy # 107 (60449-2405)
PHONE.................708 235-2800
Larry Sodomire, *CEO*
Robert Bachman, *President*
EMP: 30
SALES: 11.4MM
SALES (corp-wide): 9B **Publicly Held**
SIC: 3715 Truck trailers
HQ: R. C. Tway Company
7201 Logistics Dr
Louisville KY 40258
502 637-2551

(G-14196)
AQUAGREEN DISPOSITIONS LLC
25731 S Bristol Ln (60449-7207)
PHONE.................708 606-0211
Ryan Cattoni, *Principal*
EMP: 4
SALES (est): 500.8K **Privately Held**
WEB: www.aquagreendispositions.com
SIC: 3569 Cremating ovens

(G-14197)
ENTERPRISE PRODUCTS COMPANY
23313 S Ridgeland Ave (60449-9293)
PHONE.................708 534-6266
EMP: 4
SALES (est): 372.8K **Privately Held**
SIC: 1321 Natural gas liquids

Monee - Will County (G-14198)

(G-14198)
EVERGREEN TANK SOLUTIONS INC
25896 S Sunset Dr (60449-9394)
PHONE..................708 235-0487
Joe Fell, *Branch Mgr*
EMP: 3
SALES (corp-wide): 612.6MM **Publicly Held**
SIC: 3272 5084 Liquid catch basins, tanks & covers: concrete; tanks, storage
HQ: Evergreen Tank Solutions, Inc.
4646 E Van Buren St # 400
Phoenix AZ 85008
281 332-5170

(G-14199)
FAS-TRAK INDUSTRIES INC
4654 W Crocus Ave (60449-8771)
P.O. Box 757 (60449-0757)
PHONE..................708 570-0650
Mark Feldmeier, *President*
Mark Seldmeier, *President*
EMP: 8
SALES (est): 670K **Privately Held**
SIC: 2269 Finishing plants

(G-14200)
FUNK LINKO GROUP INC
26815 S Winfield Rd (60449-9229)
PHONE..................708 757-7421
Xochitl Valenvuela, *President*
William J Linko, *Admin Sec*
EMP: 2
SQ FT: 30,000
SALES (est): 755.8K **Privately Held**
SIC: 3441 Fabricated structural metal

(G-14201)
G K ENTERPRISES INC (PA)
26000 S Whiting Way Ste 2 (60449-8162)
PHONE..................708 587-2150
Kenneth Hoving, *President*
Jeffrey Kahn, *President*
Gene Kreider, *Principal*
Marilyn Platter, *Treasurer*
Greg Ciecierski, *VP Sales*
▲ **EMP:** 5
SQ FT: 200,000
SALES (est): 73.8MM **Privately Held**
SIC: 5812 3443 3559 3556 Ice cream stands or dairy bars; fabricated plate work (boiler shop); cupolas, metal plate; towers (bubble, cooling, fractionating, etc.): metal plate; ladles, metal plate; chemical machinery & equipment; food products machinery; hoists, cranes & monorails; cranes, overhead traveling; hoists

(G-14202)
HUGH COURTRIGHT & CO LTD
26749 S Governors Hwy (60449-9144)
PHONE..................708 534-8400
Patricia S Schoenbeck, *President*
Wayne Kozak, *Mktg Dir*
EMP: 10 **EST:** 1930
SQ FT: 6,000
SALES (est): 2.9MM **Privately Held**
WEB: www.right-tape.com
SIC: 5113 6794 5049 5084 Pressure sensitive tape; patent buying, licensing, leasing; laboratory equipment, except medical or dental; industrial machinery & equipment; coated & laminated paper

(G-14203)
K-MET INDUSTRIES INC
25911 S Ridgeland Ave (60449-9125)
PHONE..................708 534-3300
Carol Kranz, *President*
Steve Kranz, *Plant Mgr*
Sandra Putz, *Treasurer*
Gunther Kranz, *Admin Sec*
EMP: 18
SQ FT: 16,000
SALES (est): 8.3MM **Privately Held**
SIC: 5051 3441 Steel; fabricated structural metal

(G-14204)
R & C PATTERN WORKS INC
Also Called: R & C Castings
6370 W Emerald Pkwy # 111 (60449-2405)
PHONE..................708 331-1882
Shirl Paw, *President*
Kevin Paw, *Vice Pres*
EMP: 7 **EST:** 1968
SALES (est): 1.1MM **Privately Held**
WEB: www.rcpatterns.com
SIC: 3543 Industrial patterns

(G-14205)
R C CASTINGS INC
6370 W Emerald Pkwy # 111 (60449-2405)
PHONE..................708 331-1882
Shirl Paw, *President*
Kevin Paw, *Vice Pres*
EMP: 7
SALES (est): 1.5MM **Privately Held**
SIC: 5051 3543 Castings, rough: iron or steel; industrial patterns

(G-14206)
RAINBOW FARMS ENTERPRISES INC
25715 S Ridgeland Ave (60449-8963)
PHONE..................708 534-1070
Jacqueline Musch, *President*
EMP: 5
SALES (est): 500K **Privately Held**
SIC: 2499 Mulch, wood & bark

(G-14207)
REPLAY S DISC COOK-KANKAEE LLC
25526 S Devonshire Ln (60449-1606)
PHONE..................312 371-5018
Charles D Connolley,
EMP: 19
SALES (est): 950K **Privately Held**
SIC: 3652 Pre-recorded records & tapes

(G-14208)
SIGNALMASTERS INC
26120 S Governors Hwy (60449-8585)
PHONE..................708 534-3330
Ty Beoo, *President*
EMP: 12
SQ FT: 4,000
SALES (est): 1.2MM **Privately Held**
SIC: 3669 Railroad signaling devices, electric

(G-14209)
SOUTH HOLLAND MET FINSHG INC
26100 S Whiting Way (60449-8058)
PHONE..................708 235-0842
Robert J Meagher Sr, *President*
Deborah Jackson, *Vice Pres*
Debbie Jackson, *VP Opers*
James Meagher, *Prdtn Mgr*
Tom Langner, *Opers Staff*
EMP: 54
SQ FT: 90,000
SALES (est): 8.5MM **Privately Held**
WEB: www.shmf.com
SIC: 3471 Electroplating of metals or formed products

(G-14210)
TRITON MANUFACTURING CO INC (PA)
5700 W Triton Way (60449-8025)
PHONE..................708 587-4000
Michael Edwards Sr, *CEO*
Kyle Edwards, *President*
Colin Noone, *Opers Mgr*
Eunice Reed, *Buyer*
Tim Sheehy, *Research*
EMP: 144
SQ FT: 96,000
SALES (est): 33.2MM **Privately Held**
WEB: www.triton-mfg.com
SIC: 3643 3679 Bus bars (electrical conductors); harness assemblies for electronic use: wire or cable

(G-14211)
VINCOR LTD (PA)
5652 W Monee Manhattan Rd (60449-9611)
PHONE..................708 534-0008
Jeanne C Vinezeano, *CEO*
Anthony D Vinezeano, *President*
David E Basile, *Vice Pres*
Mark S Vinezeano, *Vice Pres*
Robert Vinezeano, *Vice Pres*
EMP: 17
SQ FT: 14,000
SALES (est): 3.4MM **Privately Held**
SIC: 3663 4812 1799 5065 Satellites, communications; radio telephone communication; antenna installation; electronic parts & equipment; video tape rental; radio, television & electronic stores

(G-14212)
WHITING CORPORATION (HQ)
26000 S Whiting Way Ste 1 (60449-8161)
PHONE..................800 861-5744
Toll Free:..................888 -
Jeff Kahn, *President*
Alan J Burke, *Vice Pres*
Ed Hain, *Project Mgr*
Robert O'Connor, *Opers Staff*
Donna Wess, *Production*
◆ **EMP:** 150 **EST:** 1983
SQ FT: 192,500
SALES (est): 56.3MM
SALES (corp-wide): 73.8MM **Privately Held**
WEB: www.whitingcorp.com
SIC: 3441 3743 3443 3536 Fabricated structural metal; railroad equipment; fabricated plate work (boiler shop); cupolas, metal plate: vessels, process or storage (from boiler shops): metal plate; ladles, metal plate; cranes, overhead traveling
PA: G. K. Enterprises, Inc.
26000 S Whiting Way Ste 2
Monee IL 60449
708 587-2150

(G-14213)
WILLE BROS CO (PA)
Also Called: Do It Best
11303 Manhattan Monee Rd (60449-9658)
PHONE..................708 535-4101
Curt Wille, *President*
Richard Shadle, *Vice Pres*
Rich Wille, *Vice Pres*
Richard E Wille, *Vice Pres*
Kris Ernest, *Human Res Dir*
EMP: 55
SQ FT: 35,000
SALES (est): 17.5MM **Privately Held**
WEB: www.willebrothers.com
SIC: 5251 3531 Hardware; bituminous, cement & concrete related products & equipment

Monmouth
Warren County

(G-14214)
BIG RVER RSRCES W BRLNGTON LLC
Also Called: Monmouth Grain & Dryer
903 S Sunny Ln (61462-2516)
PHONE..................309 734-8423
Raymond Defenbaugh, *Branch Mgr*
EMP: 8 **Privately Held**
SIC: 2869 Fuels
HQ: Big River Resources West Burlington, Llc
15210 103rd St
West Burlington IA 52655
319 753-1100

(G-14215)
CORNELIUS RENEW INC
1301 N Main St Ste 3 (61462-5223)
PHONE..................309 734-9505
Tim Hubbard, *President*
EMP: 12
SALES (est): 2.6MM **Privately Held**
SIC: 3556 Beverage machinery

(G-14216)
CUSTOM MILLERS SUPPLY INC
511 S 3rd St (61462-2235)
P.O. Box 617 (61462-0617)
PHONE..................309 734-6312
Howard White, *President*
Wanda White, *Treasurer*
EMP: 5
SQ FT: 6,000
SALES (est): 849.5K **Privately Held**
SIC: 3523 5063 3599 3799 Feed grinders, crushers & mixers; transformers & transmission equipment; machine shop, jobbing & repair; trailers & trailer equipment; automobile tires & tubes

(G-14217)
FORMAN CO INC
Also Called: Orion Enterprises
609 W Broadway (61462-1620)
P.O. Box 50 (61462-0050)
PHONE..................309 734-3413
Gary Judy, *President*
Robert Forman, *Chairman*
Marcia Judy, *Vice Pres*
EMP: 4 **EST:** 1856
SQ FT: 3,500
SALES (est): 110K **Privately Held**
SIC: 2789 7389 Binding only: books, pamphlets, magazines, etc.; microfilm recording & developing service

(G-14218)
IMI MCR INC
1301 N Main St Ste 3 (61462-5223)
PHONE..................309 734-6282
Tim Hubbard, *President*
▲ **EMP:** 26
SALES (est): 9.5MM
SALES (corp-wide): 2.4B **Privately Held**
SIC: 3556 Beverage machinery
PA: Imi Plc
4060 Lakeside
Birmingham W MIDLANDS B37 7
121 717-3700

(G-14219)
JIM COKEL WELDING
Also Called: Cokel Jim Prtble Wldg Sp Servi
204 E 6th Ave (61462-2612)
PHONE..................309 734-5063
James Cokel, *Owner*
EMP: 2
SQ FT: 3,000
SALES (est): 200K **Privately Held**
SIC: 7692 Welding repair

(G-14220)
KELLOGG PRINTING CO
95 Public Sq (61462-1772)
P.O. Box 437 (61462-0437)
PHONE..................309 734-8388
Buster L Kellogg Jr, *Owner*
EMP: 12 **EST:** 1924
SQ FT: 3,200
SALES (est): 1.5MM **Privately Held**
WEB: www.kelloggprinting.com
SIC: 2752 3953 2761 2759 Commercial printing, offset; marking devices; manifold business forms; commercial printing; book printing

(G-14221)
KIM GOUGH
Also Called: Metal Crafters
1201 N Main St Ste 2 (61462-5221)
PHONE..................309 734-3511
Kim Gough, *Owner*
EMP: 6
SALES (est): 386.5K **Privately Held**
SIC: 3441 7692 3444 Building components, structural steel; welding repair; sheet metalwork

(G-14222)
KIRKMAN COMPOSITES
1201 N Main St Ste 2 (61462-5221)
PHONE..................309 734-5606
Mark D Kirkman, *Owner*
EMP: 8
SALES (est): 748.3K **Privately Held**
SIC: 3624 Carbon & graphite products

(G-14223)
MIDWESTERN PET FOODS INC
Also Called: Wells Pet Stores
617 S D St (61462-2157)
P.O. Box 677 (61462-0677)
PHONE..................309 734-3121
Ed Cooper, *Branch Mgr*
EMP: 50
SALES (corp-wide): 24.1MM **Privately Held**
SIC: 2047 5199 Dog food; pet supplies

GEOGRAPHIC SECTION

Montgomery - Kendall County (G-14250)

PA: Midwestern Pet Foods Inc
9634 Hedden Rd
Evansville IN 47725
812 867-7466

(G-14224)
MONMOUTH STONE CO (PA)
1420 N Main St (61462-5224)
P.O. Box 733 (61462-0733)
PHONE 309 734-7951
Dan G Kistler, *President*
John Pratt, *Vice Pres*
James Howe, *Admin Sec*
EMP: 18 **EST:** 1935
SQ FT: 15,000
SALES (est): 1.2MM **Privately Held**
SIC: 1429 Igneous rock, crushed & broken-quarrying

(G-14225)
OLDCASTLE MATERIALS INC
Also Called: Sister Construction
2391 60th St (61462-9046)
PHONE 309 627-2111
Chad Ferguson, *Manager*
EMP: 12
SALES (corp-wide): 30.6B **Privately Held**
SIC: 3273 Ready-mixed concrete
HQ: Oldcastle Materials, Inc.
900 Ashwood Pkwy Ste 700
Atlanta GA 30338

(G-14226)
ROBBINS RESOURCE MGT INC
208 S Main St (61462-2160)
PHONE 309 734-8817
Jason Robbins, *CEO*
Teresa Armstrong, *Manager*
EMP: 43
SALES (est): 8.1MM **Privately Held**
SIC: 2448 Pallets, wood

(G-14227)
SMITHFIELD PACKAGED MEATS CORP
1220 N 6th St (61462-9674)
PHONE 309 734-5353
Dennis Simpson, *Purch Mgr*
Robin Scanlan, *Engineer*
Michelle Reyburn, *Human Res Dir*
Cliff Wiles, *Branch Mgr*
EMP: 600 **Privately Held**
SIC: 2011 5147 2013 Meat packing plants; meats & meat products; sausages & other prepared meats
HQ: Smithfield Packaged Meats Corp.
805 E Kemper Rd
Cincinnati OH 45246
513 782-3800

(G-14228)
WS INCORPORATED OF MANMOUTH (PA)
Also Called: Western Stoneware
220 W Franklin Ave (61462-1163)
P.O. Box 33 (61462-0033)
PHONE 309 734-2161
Dong SOO Chong, *President*
Dave Bates, *Vice Pres*
EMP: 15
SQ FT: 180,000
SALES (est): 1.2MM **Privately Held**
SIC: 3269 Stoneware pottery products

Montgomery
Kendall County

(G-14229)
A LAKIN & SONS INC (PA)
Also Called: Lakin General
2001 Greenfield Rd (60538-1183)
PHONE 773 871-6360
Ken Lakin, *President*
Lewis Lakin, *Chairman*
Rob Grammer, *Corp Secy*
Richard Gust, *Vice Pres*
Gib Younger, *Vice Pres*
▲ **EMP:** 30
SQ FT: 124,000
SALES (est): 34.4MM **Privately Held**
SIC: 5014 3069 5013 Tires, used; rubber automotive products; motor vehicle supplies & new parts

(G-14230)
AURORA BEARING COMPANY
901 Aucutt Rd (60538-1338)
PHONE 630 897-8941
Jesse F Maberry, *Ch of Bd*
David Richard, *President*
Harvey Sterkel, *Vice Pres*
John T Zinser, *Admin Sec*
◆ **EMP:** 252
SQ FT: 206,000
SALES (est): 95.9MM **Privately Held**
SIC: 3568 Power transmission equipment

(G-14231)
AURORA METALS DIVISION LLC
1995 Greenfield Rd (60538-1140)
PHONE 630 844-4900
Dave Bumbar, *Mfg Staff*
Alan Degarmo, *Engineer*
Jeff Mihalka, *Engineer*
Joyce Contos, *Sales Staff*
Brian Davis, *Manager*
◆ **EMP:** 120
SQ FT: 90,000
SALES (est): 32MM **Privately Held**
SIC: 3366 3599 Copper foundries; machine shop, jobbing & repair

(G-14232)
BENETECH INC
1851 Albright Rd (60538-1181)
PHONE 630 806-7888
EMP: 3
SALES (corp-wide): 70.3MM **Privately Held**
SIC: 3823 Combustion control instruments
HQ: Benetech, Inc.
2245 Sequoia Dr Ste 300
Aurora IL 60506
630 844-1300

(G-14233)
BINKS INDUSTRIES INC
1997a Aucutt Rd (60538-1135)
PHONE 630 801-1100
James D Calkins, *President*
Robert Wiersbe, *Purch Mgr*
◆ **EMP:** 4 **EST:** 1962
SQ FT: 5,000
SALES: 350K **Privately Held**
WEB: www.binksindustries.com
SIC: 3829 Measuring & controlling devices

(G-14234)
BIOLOGOS INC
2235 Cornell Ave (60538-3201)
PHONE 630 801-4740
Dennis Raine, *President*
EMP: 9
SQ FT: 15,000
SALES (est): 2MM **Privately Held**
SIC: 2836 Biological products, except diagnostic

(G-14235)
BOC GLOBAL HELIUM INC
1998 Albright Rd (60538-1158)
PHONE 630 897-1900
Mike Totteleer, *Principal*
EMP: 173
SALES (est): 10.3MM
SALES (corp-wide): 1.1B **Privately Held**
SIC: 2813 5169 Helium; industrial gases
HQ: Linde Gas Usa Llc
200 Somset Corp B 7000
Bridgewater NJ 08807
908 464-8100

(G-14236)
BUSATIS INC
1755 Aucutt Rd (60538-3025)
P.O. Box 1962, Arlington Heights (60006-1962)
PHONE 630 844-9803
Reinhard Jordan, *President*
Stephen Peck, *Admin Sec*
▲ **EMP:** 4
SALES (est): 310K **Privately Held**
SIC: 3444 8748 Sheet metalwork; agricultural consultant

(G-14237)
BUTTERBALL LLC
2125 Rochester Rd (60538-1066)
PHONE 800 575-3365
Ralph Caballero Sr, *President*
EMP: 375
SALES (corp-wide): 1.6B **Privately Held**
SIC: 2011 Meat packing plants
PA: Butterball, Llc
1 Butterball Ln
Garner NC 27529
919 255-7900

(G-14238)
CATERPILLAR INC
325 S Rte 31 (60538)
P.O. Box 348, Aurora (60507-0348)
PHONE 630 859-5000
Mark Mitchell, *Engineer*
Gerald Palmer, *Manager*
Diane Moncrief, *Comp Spec*
EMP: 3500
SALES (corp-wide): 53.8B **Publicly Held**
WEB: www.caterpillar.com
SIC: 3537 3531 Industrial trucks & tractors; excavators: cable, clamshell, crane, derrick; dragline, etc.
PA: Caterpillar Inc.
510 Lake Cook Rd Ste 100
Deerfield IL 60015
224 551-4000

(G-14239)
CERVANTES/SALGADO LLC
1001 Aucutt Rd Ste C (60538-1122)
PHONE 630 806-4864
Eduardo Salgado, *Principal*
EMP: 2 **EST:** 2016
SALES (est): 265.3K **Privately Held**
SIC: 2431 Millwork

(G-14240)
CHICAGO FLAMEPROOF WD SPC CORP (PA)
Also Called: Wisconsin Flameproof Shop
1200 S Lake St (60538-1400)
PHONE 630 859-0009
Vince Mancini, *President*
Maddy Rossobillo, *Vice Pres*
Melani Croft, *Administration*
EMP: 30
SQ FT: 80,000
SALES (est): 43.8MM **Privately Held**
SIC: 5031 2491 Building materials, exterior; building materials, interior; wood preserving

(G-14241)
COMERS WELDING SERVICE INC
1105 S Lake St (60538-1258)
P.O. Box 317 (60538-0317)
PHONE 630 892-0168
Gary Comer, *President*
Kay Comer, *Vice Pres*
Tom Comer, *Vice Pres*
William Comer, *Treasurer*
EMP: 8
SALES (est): 1MM **Privately Held**
WEB: www.comersweldingservice.com
SIC: 7692 Welding repair

(G-14242)
CTS OF ILLINOIS INC
Also Called: Cipher Tech Solutions
1556 Crescent Lake Dr (60538-1243)
PHONE 630 892-2355
Timothy Assell, *President*
Joe McElroy, *Opers Staff*
Eric Light, *Admin Sec*
EMP: 9 **EST:** 2010
SALES (est): 1.6MM **Privately Held**
SIC: 3699 7382 Security devices; security systems services

(G-14243)
DQM INC
Also Called: Sealtech
1551 Aucutt Rd (60538-1235)
PHONE 630 692-0633
Charles Herrera, *President*
Carla Herrera, *Vice Pres*
EMP: 11
SALES (est): 1.2MM **Privately Held**
SIC: 3643 Current-carrying wiring devices

(G-14244)
GENERAL MILLS INC
1370 Orchard Rd (60538-1065)
PHONE 630 844-1125
Mason Austin, *Branch Mgr*
EMP: 75
SALES (corp-wide): 16.8B **Publicly Held**
WEB: www.generalmills.com
SIC: 2043 Cereal breakfast foods
PA: General Mills, Inc.
1 General Mills Blvd
Minneapolis MN 55426
763 764-7600

(G-14245)
GENERAL MILLS OPERATIONS LLC
1370 Orchard Rd (60538-1065)
PHONE 630 844-1125
John R Church, *Mng Member*
EMP: 1
SALES (est): 204K **Privately Held**
SIC: 2043 Cereal breakfast foods

(G-14246)
HENKEL CONSUMER GOODS INC
2000 Aucutt Rd (60538-1133)
PHONE 630 892-4381
Dan Ahearn, *Purchasing*
Tom Hebert, *QC Dir*
Will Jensen, *Human Res Dir*
Byron Rimm, *Branch Mgr*
Linda Kavois, *Manager*
EMP: 200
SALES (corp-wide): 22.2B **Privately Held**
WEB: www.henkel-northamerica.com
SIC: 2844 2842 2032 5169 Toilet preparations; specialty cleaning, polishes & sanitation goods; canned specialties; detergents & soaps, except specialty cleaning; soap: granulated, liquid, cake, flaked or chip
HQ: Henkel Consumer Goods Inc.
200 Elm St
Stamford CT 06902

(G-14247)
HERTZ CORPORATION
1375 Bohr Ave (60538-1190)
PHONE 630 897-0956
EMP: 5
SALES (corp-wide): 9.7B **Publicly Held**
WEB: www.link.hertz.com
SIC: 7514 5012 3711 Rent-a-car service; automobiles & other motor vehicles; truck & tractor truck assembly
HQ: The Hertz Corporation
8501 Williams Rd
Estero FL 33928
239 301-7000

(G-14248)
HORMANN LLC (HQ)
5050 Baseline Rd (60538-1125)
PHONE 630 859-3000
Frank Weber, *President*
Camron Rudd, *Opers Staff*
Michael Adam, *Purchasing*
Steven Koehl, *Engineer*
Jeff Thomas, *Credit Mgr*
▲ **EMP:** 240
SQ FT: 181,000
SALES (est): 67.5MM
SALES (corp-wide): 81.1MM **Privately Held**
WEB: www.hormann.us
SIC: 3442 Garage doors, overhead: metal
PA: Hormann Kg Verkaufsgesellschaft
Upheider Weg 94-98
Steinhagen 33803
520 491-50

(G-14249)
ID SIGN AND LIGHTING INC
2287 Cornell Ave (60538-3201)
PHONE 630 844-3565
Ivica Stipetic, *President*
EMP: 2
SALES (est): 218.2K **Privately Held**
SIC: 3993 Signs & advertising specialties

(G-14250)
IDENTI-GRAPHICS INC
101 Knell St (60538-1248)
PHONE 630 801-4845
Terry Strong, *President*
Selena Semeraro, *Admin Sec*
EMP: 21

Montgomery - Kendall County (G-14251)

SALES (est): 988.9K **Privately Held**
SIC: **2759** 2679 Flexographic printing; labels, paper: made from purchased material

(G-14251)
INTERNATIONAL PAPER COMPANY
1001 Knell St (60538-1299)
PHONE.................................630 896-2061
Mary Proper, *Purchasing*
Jeff Novack, *Sales Staff*
Vito Goztziewicz, *Branch Mgr*
EMP: 125
SALES (corp-wide): 22.3B **Publicly Held**
WEB: www.internationalpaper.com
SIC: **2653** Boxes, corrugated: made from purchased materials
PA: International Paper Company
6400 Poplar Ave
Memphis TN 38197
901 419-9000

(G-14252)
L & D GROUP INC
Also Called: Lyon & Dittrich Holding Co
420 N Main St (60538-1367)
P.O. Box 671, Aurora (60507-0671)
PHONE.................................630 892-8941
R Peter Washington, *Ch of Bd*
Stephen Roberts, *District Mgr*
Douglas M Harrison, *COO*
Bob Miller, *Opers Staff*
Brice Hiner, *Sales Staff*
EMP: 500
SQ FT: 25,000
SALES (est): 62.4K **Privately Held**
SIC: **2542** 2522 2599 Shelving, office & store: except wood; lockers (not refrigerated): except wood; fixtures, office: except wood; desks, office: except wood; work benches, factory; stools, factory; cabinets, factory; tool stands, factory

(G-14253)
L & M SCREW MACHINE PRODUCTS
321 Webster St (60538-1252)
PHONE.................................630 801-0455
Louis Galarza, *President*
EMP: 10
SQ FT: 6,000
SALES (est): 350K **Privately Held**
SIC: **3965** 3714 3545 3452 Fasteners; motor vehicle parts & accessories; machine tool accessories; bolts, nuts, rivets & washers

(G-14254)
LABORATORY MEDIA CORPORATION
1731 Commerce Dr (60538-1232)
PHONE.................................630 897-8000
Daniel Micek, *President*
John Gawecki, *Vice Pres*
EMP: 11
SQ FT: 17,000
SALES: 3MM **Privately Held**
SIC: **2836** 5049 Culture media; bank equipment & supplies

(G-14255)
LAKIN GENERAL CORPORATION
2001 Greenfield Rd (60538-1183)
PHONE.................................773 871-6360
Lewis Lakin, *President*
Rob Grammer, *CFO*
EMP: 90
SALES: 20MM **Privately Held**
SIC: **5014** 5069 Tires, used; rubber automotive products
PA: A. Lakin & Sons, Inc.
2001 Greenfield Rd
Montgomery IL 60538

(G-14256)
LAKONE COMPANY
1003 Aucutt Rd (60538-1176)
PHONE.................................630 892-4251
Bruce Rhoades, *President*
▲ **EMP:** 100 **EST:** 1944
SQ FT: 51,000

SALES (est): 22.4MM **Privately Held**
WEB: www.lakoneco.com
SIC: **3089** 3083 Molding primary plastic; laminated plastics plate & sheet

(G-14257)
LION CONCRETE PRODUCTS INC
Also Called: Lion Ornamental Concrete Pdts
111 N Railroad St (60538-1214)
PHONE.................................630 892-7304
Scott E Neupert, *Owner*
Scott Neuprt, *Owner*
EMP: 3 **EST:** 2004
SALES (est): 333.7K **Privately Held**
WEB: www.lionconcrete.net
SIC: **5199** 3272 3271 5211 Statuary; concrete products; concrete block & brick; masonry materials & supplies

(G-14258)
LYON LLC (HQ)
420 N Main St (60538-1367)
P.O. Box 671, Aurora (60507-0671)
PHONE.................................630 892-8941
Louise E Berg, *CEO*
Maria Mojica, *General Mgr*
Bryan Lenz, *District Mgr*
William Guo, *Exec VP*
Matthew Zakaras, *Exec VP*
▲ **EMP:** 171 **EST:** 2013
SALES (est): 114.1MM **Privately Held**
SIC: **2542** Shelving, office & store: except wood
PA: Echelon Capital, Llc
121 W Wacker Dr
Chicago IL 60601
312 263-0263

(G-14259)
LYON WORKSPACE PRODUCTS INC
420 N Main St (60538-1367)
PHONE.................................630 892-8941
R Peter Washington, *President*
EMP: 5 **EST:** 2013
SALES (est): 633.3K **Privately Held**
SIC: **2542** Partitions & fixtures, except wood

(G-14260)
MAMATA ENTERPRISES INC (HQ)
2275 Cornell Ave (60538-3201)
PHONE.................................941 205-0227
Dharmisth Patel, *President*
Varun Patel, *Vice Pres*
Harshad Desai, *Admin Sec*
▲ **EMP:** 6
SQ FT: 5,000
SALES: 8MM **Privately Held**
SIC: **3559** 3565 Plastics working machinery; packaging machinery

(G-14261)
MARJAN INC
Also Called: Marjan Hot Tinning
1801 Albright Rd (60538-1194)
PHONE.................................630 906-0053
Bill Strobel, *Vice Pres*
EMP: 8
SALES (est): 966.1K **Privately Held**
SIC: **3471** Plating of metals or formed products

(G-14262)
MESSER NORTH AMERICA INC
1998 Albright Rd (60538-1158)
PHONE.................................630 897-1900
EMP: 9
SALES (corp-wide): 1.1B **Privately Held**
WEB: www.lindeus.com
SIC: **2813** Industrial gases
HQ: Messer North America, Inc.
200 Somerset Corporate Bl
Bridgewater NJ 08807
908 464-8100

(G-14263)
MULTIPLEX INDUSTRIES INC
1650 Se River Rd (60538-1500)
PHONE.................................630 906-9780
Ronald Potter, *President*
EMP: 2
SQ FT: 1,250

SALES (est): 619.7K **Privately Held**
SIC: **5051** 3316 3312 Steel; cold finishing of steel shapes; blast furnaces & steel mills

(G-14264)
MURPHY USA INC
1927 Us Route 30 (60538-7100)
PHONE.................................630 801-4950
Less Than, *Branch Mgr*
EMP: 4 **Publicly Held**
SIC: **1382** Oil & gas exploration services
PA: Murphy Usa Inc.
200 E Peach St
El Dorado AR 71730

(G-14265)
NORTHERN ILLINOIS LUMBER SPC
1200 S Lake St (60538-1400)
P.O. Box 318 (60538-0318)
PHONE.................................630 859-3226
EMP: 35
SQ FT: 75,000
SALES: 300K **Privately Held**
SIC: **2491** Wood Preserving, Nsk

(G-14266)
RAMPNOW LLC
2280 Cornell Ave (60538-3200)
PHONE.................................630 892-7267
John C S Sargent, *Mng Member*
Carlos Rogers-Lopez,
EMP: 8
SALES (est): 1.1MM **Privately Held**
SIC: **7699** 3448 7352 Medical equipment repair, non-electric; ramps: prefabricated metal; medical equipment rental

(G-14267)
ROCHESTER MIDLAND CORPORATION
2200 Rochester Rd (60538-1068)
PHONE.................................630 896-8543
John Schultz, *Principal*
Tim Bulthuis, *Regl Sales Mgr*
Jim Bruno, *Administration*
EMP: 40
SALES (corp-wide): 129.2MM **Privately Held**
WEB: www.rochestermidland.com
SIC: **2842** Specialty cleaning, polishes & sanitation goods
PA: Rochester Midland Corporation
155 Paragon Dr
Rochester NY 14624
585 336-2200

(G-14268)
SEALTEC
Also Called: Dqm
1551 Aucutt Rd (60538-1235)
PHONE.................................630 692-0633
Charles Herrera, *President*
Carla Herrera, *Vice Pres*
EMP: 13
SALES: 1MM **Privately Held**
SIC: **3053** Gaskets & sealing devices

(G-14269)
SHIRT OFF MY BACK CSTM TEES MO
26 Marnel Rd (60538-2015)
PHONE.................................331 999-2399
Jennifer Duque, *Principal*
EMP: 2
SALES (est): 203.2K **Privately Held**
WEB: www.shirtoffmybacktees.com
SIC: **2759** Screen printing

(G-14270)
SILENT W COMMUNICATIONS INC
Also Called: Keystroke Graphics
1651 Aucutt Rd (60538-1124)
PHONE.................................630 479-7950
Laura Wrasman, *President*
Mark Wrasman, *Vice Pres*
EMP: 8 **EST:** 1990
SALES (est): 1.6MM **Privately Held**
SIC: **2721** Magazines: publishing & printing

(G-14271)
TBC RETAIL GROUP INC
Also Called: Midas 8793
1971 Hill Ave (60538-7110)
PHONE.................................630 692-0232
Jay Moreno, *Branch Mgr*
EMP: 4 **Privately Held**
WEB: www.tirekingdom.com
SIC: **7533** 3714 3011 Muffler shop, sale or repair & installation; motor vehicle wheels & parts; tires & inner tubes
HQ: Tbc Retail Group, Inc.
4280 Prof Ctr Dr Ste 400
Palm Beach Gardens FL 33410
561 383-3000

(G-14272)
TRIO FOUNDRY INC (PA)
Also Called: Sandwich Casting & Machine Div
1985 Aucutt Rd (60538-1135)
PHONE.................................630 892-1676
Scott Rayfield, *President*
Ford Rayfield, *Vice Pres*
Austin Rayfield, *Officer*
Patricia Rayfield, *Admin Sec*
EMP: 38 **EST:** 1909
SQ FT: 70,000
SALES (est): 8.4MM **Privately Held**
WEB: www.triofoundry.com
SIC: **3366** 3365 3369 Brass foundry; bronze foundry; aluminum foundries; non-ferrous foundries

(G-14273)
VIKING METAL CABINET CO LLC
420 N Main St (60538-1367)
PHONE.................................800 776-7767
Bill Wilcoxson, *President*
Lisa Carpenter, *Director*
EMP: 90 **EST:** 2015
SALES (est): 3.4MM **Privately Held**
SIC: **3499** 3444 2522 2514 Fabricated metal products; sheet metalwork; office furniture, except wood; metal household furniture; wood kitchen cabinets

(G-14274)
VIKING METAL CABINET COMPANY
Also Called: A Divison of Da
420 N Main St (60538-1367)
PHONE.................................630 863-7234
Eugene Berg, *CEO*
Troy Berg, *President*
Jim Willis, *President*
Maureen Willis, *Admin Sec*
EMP: 100 **EST:** 2010
SQ FT: 70,000
SALES (est): 17.6MM **Privately Held**
WEB: www.vikingmetal.com
SIC: **3499** 3444 2522 2514 Fire- or burglary-resistive products; sheet metalwork; office furniture, except wood; metal household furniture; wood kitchen cabinets

(G-14275)
VVF ILLINOIS SERVICES LLC
2000 Aucutt Rd (60538-1133)
PHONE.................................630 892-4381
Rebecca Belmer, *Principal*
Jeanne Keach, *Executive*
▲ **EMP:** 450
SALES (est): 169.3MM **Privately Held**
WEB: www.vvfllc.com
SIC: **2841** Soap & other detergents
PA: V V F Limited
Plot No-109, Opp Sion Fort Garden,
Mumbai MH 40002

(G-14276)
WORKSPACE LYON PRODUCTS LLC
420 N Main St (60538-1367)
P.O. Box 671, Aurora (60507-0671)
PHONE.................................630 892-8941
Robert Brossell, *District Mgr*
Ray Fraser, *District Mgr*
Jeff Shuler, *District Mgr*
Mike Wilgus, *District Mgr*
Douglas M Harrison, *COO*
◆ **EMP:** 500 **EST:** 2015

Monticello
Piatt County

(G-14277)
B AND A SCREEN PRINTING
350 W Burnside Rd (61856-9574)
PHONE...................................217 762-2632
Alan Arney, *Owner*
EMP: 4
SQ FT: 10,000
SALES (est): 459.7K **Privately Held**
SIC: 2261 5137 5136 2396 Fire resistance finishing of cotton broadwoven fabrics; sportswear, women's & children's; sportswear, men's & boys'; automotive & apparel trimmings

(G-14278)
BIOANALYTICS INC
2067 Coyote Run Rd (61856-8059)
PHONE...................................217 649-6820
Lucas Smith, *CEO*
Michael Willard, *COO*
EMP: 5
SALES (est): 497.7K **Privately Held**
SIC: 2835 Enzyme & isoenzyme diagnostic agents

(G-14279)
BLUE RIDGE LAND AND CATTLE
1068 E 1765 North Rd (61856-8406)
P.O. Box 505 (61856-0505)
PHONE...................................217 762-9652
EMP: 5
SALES (est): 615.4K **Privately Held**
SIC: 3523 Mfg Farm Machinery/Equipment

(G-14280)
COUNTY OF PIATT
Also Called: Piatt County Clerk Recorder
101 W Washington St # 214 (61856-1672)
PHONE...................................217 762-7009
Pat Rhodes, *Principal*
Thomas Dobson, *Cnty Cmsnr*
EMP: 5 **Privately Held**
SIC: 3823 Panelboard indicators, recorders & controllers: receiver
PA: County Of Piatt
1020 N Market St
Monticello IL 61856
217 762-4002

(G-14281)
MCSHARES INC
Also Called: Viobin USA
226 W Livingston St (61856-1632)
PHONE...................................217 762-2561
Roger Mohr, *Branch Mgr*
EMP: 45
SALES (corp-wide): 24.7MM **Privately Held**
SIC: 2041 2819 2077 2032 Flour; peroxides, hydrogen peroxide; animal & marine fats & oils; canned specialties
PA: Mcshares, Inc.
1835 E North St
Salina KS 67401
785 825-2181

(G-14282)
NEWS-GAZETTE INC
Also Called: Piatt County Journal Repub
118 E Washington St (61856-1641)
P.O. Box 110 (61856-0110)
PHONE...................................217 762-2511
Ken Hartman, *Branch Mgr*
EMP: 4 **Privately Held**
SIC: 2711 Newspapers, publishing & printing
PA: The News-Gazette Inc
15 E Main St
Champaign IL 61820

SALES (est): 101MM **Privately Held**
WEB: www.lyonworkspace.com
SIC: 2542 Shelving, office & store: except wood; lockers (not refrigerated): except wood; cabinets: show, display or storage: except wood

(G-14283)
OBRIEN SCNTFIC GL BLOWING LLC
750 W Railroad St (61856-8180)
P.O. Box 495 (61856-0495)
PHONE...................................217 762-3636
Anne O'Brien-Murphy, *Mng Member*
EMP: 3
SALES: 150K **Privately Held**
SIC: 3229 3821 3231 Scientific glassware; laboratory apparatus & furniture; products of purchased glass

(G-14284)
PRAIRIE FIRE GLASS INC
217 W Washington St (61856-1683)
PHONE...................................217 762-3332
Jim Downey, *President*
EMP: 3
SALES (est): 296.8K **Privately Held**
SIC: 3229 Pressed & blown glass

(G-14285)
SCS ABSORBENT MFG INC
1086 S Market St (61856-1842)
PHONE...................................502 417-1365
David L Camfield, *Principal*
EMP: 2 **EST:** 2017
SALES (est): 211.2K **Privately Held**
SIC: 3999 Atomizers, toiletry

(G-14286)
SEBENS BACKHOE SERVICE INC
903 Madison St (61856-2239)
PHONE...................................217 762-7365
EMP: 2 **EST:** 2014
SALES (est): 266.3K **Privately Held**
SIC: 3531 Backhoes

(G-14287)
SOY CITY SOCK CO INC
1086 S Market St (61856-1842)
PHONE...................................217 762-2157
David Camfield, *President*
Rhonda Camfield, *Admin Sec*
EMP: 15
SALES (est): 1.8MM **Privately Held**
SIC: 2252 Socks

(G-14288)
TRACK MY FORECLOSURES LLC
Also Called: Bpo Assistant
107 N State St Ste 1 (61856)
PHONE...................................877 782-8187
Stacy Hall, *Principal*
EMP: 6
SALES (est): 177.1K **Privately Held**
SIC: 7372 Business oriented computer software

Montrose
Effingham County

(G-14289)
MEINHART GRAIN FARM INC
3546 E 1900th Ave (62445-2217)
PHONE...................................217 683-2692
Keith Meinhart, *President*
Denise Meinhart, *Admin Sec*
EMP: 2
SALES (est): 211.3K **Privately Held**
SIC: 3523 Driers (farm): grain, hay & seed

Morris
Grundy County

(G-14290)
ADVERT DISPLAY PRODUCTS INC
3727 N Division St (60450-9355)
PHONE...................................815 513-5432
Gary Chapman, *CEO*
EMP: 4

SALES: 362.5K **Privately Held**
SIC: 2542 5046 3089 Cabinets: show, display or storage: except wood; store fixtures & display equipment; molding primary plastic

(G-14291)
ATHLETIC OUTFITTERS INC
409 Liberty St (60450-2132)
PHONE...................................815 942-6696
Eric Gronski, *President*
Karen Gronski, *Admin Sec*
EMP: 5
SQ FT: 7,500
SALES (est): 773.9K **Privately Held**
SIC: 5661 2395 5999 5632 Footwear, athletic; embroidery & art needlework; trophies & plaques; apparel accessories

(G-14292)
AUX SABLE LIQUID PRODUCTS LP (PA)
6155 E Us Route 6 (60450-9020)
PHONE...................................815 941-5800
William McAdam, *Partner*
Dennis Kilhafner, *Foreman/Supr*
Duncan McGinnis, *Engineer*
Jody Henderson, *Accountant*
Larry Evans, *Manager*
▲ **EMP:** 30
SQ FT: 10,000
SALES (est): 96.7MM **Privately Held**
SIC: 1321 Natural gas liquids production

(G-14293)
AUX SABLE MIDSTREAM LLC
Also Called: Aux Sable Liquid Products
6155 E Us Route 6 (60450-9020)
PHONE...................................815 941-5800
Tim Stauft,
EMP: 50
SALES (est): 5.2MM
SALES (corp-wide): 3.7B **Privately Held**
SIC: 1321 Natural gas liquids production
PA: Enbridge Inc
425 1 St Sw Suite 200
Calgary AB T2P 3
403 231-3900

(G-14294)
BANNER EQUIPMENT CO
922 Armstrong St (60450-1921)
PHONE...................................815 941-9600
James K Groff, *President*
John E Kanaski, *Vice Pres*
Mike Tannhauser, *Vice Pres*
Carol Schull, *Purchasing*
Jordan Krugel, *CFO*
▲ **EMP:** 40 **EST:** 1937
SALES (est): 7.7MM **Privately Held**
WEB: www.bannerbeer.com
SIC: 3585 5078 Beer dispensing equipment; refrigerated beverage dispensers

(G-14295)
BLUE GEM COMPUTERS INC
822 East St (60450-2040)
PHONE...................................708 562-5524
David Latimer, *President*
Lori Latimer, *Vice Pres*
EMP: 2
SALES (est): 229.2K **Privately Held**
SIC: 3575 7378 Computer terminals, monitors & components; computer maintenance & repair

(G-14296)
CARGILL INCORPORATED
301 Griggs St (60450-2276)
PHONE...................................815 941-0932
Shane Cuddy, *Branch Mgr*
EMP: 6
SALES (corp-wide): 113.4B **Privately Held**
SIC: 5153 2075 Grains; soybean oil, cake or meal
PA: Cargill, Incorporated
15407 Mcginty Rd W
Wayzata MN 55391
952 742-7575

(G-14297)
CARROLL DISTRG & CNSTR SUP INC
460 Briscoe Dr (60450-6855)
PHONE...................................815 941-1548

Chuck Frazer, *Branch Mgr*
EMP: 3
SALES (corp-wide): 128.2MM **Privately Held**
SIC: 5082 3444 Contractors' materials; concrete forms, sheet metal
PA: Carroll Distributing & Construction Supply, Inc.
207 W 2nd St Ste 3
Ottumwa IA 52501
641 683-1888

(G-14298)
CENTRAL LIMESTONE COMPANY INC
16805 Quarry Rd (60450-9211)
PHONE...................................815 736-6341
John A Shaw, *President*
Kay M Shaw, *Corp Secy*
Jeff Shaw, *Opers Staff*
EMP: 13
SQ FT: 2,000
SALES (est): 1.5MM **Privately Held**
WEB: www.centrallimestone.com
SIC: 1422 Limestones, ground

(G-14299)
CROWN CONCEPTS CORPORATION
7080 Lisbon Rd (60450-8663)
PHONE...................................815 941-1081
James Sharwarko, *President*
Steven Sandstron, *Corp Secy*
Josh Kazmierczak, *Project Engr*
EMP: 21
SQ FT: 16,500
SALES: 3MM **Privately Held**
SIC: 3444 Sheet metalwork

(G-14300)
CROWN CUSTOM CABINETRY INC
1110 E Washington St (60450-2082)
PHONE...................................815 942-0432
Daniel Mueller, *President*
EMP: 4
SALES (est): 441.6K **Privately Held**
SIC: 2434 Wood kitchen cabinets

(G-14301)
D G BRANDT INC
Also Called: Brandt Printing
901 Liberty St (60450-1508)
PHONE...................................815 942-4064
Doug Brandt, *President*
EMP: 6
SQ FT: 4,000
SALES (est): 720.8K **Privately Held**
SIC: 2759 2789 2752 Letterpress printing; visiting cards (including business): printing; bookbinding & related work; commercial printing, lithographic

(G-14302)
DAZZLING DISPLAYS INC
3727 N Division St (60450-9355)
PHONE...................................708 262-6340
EMP: 10 **EST:** 2014
SQ FT: 1,500
SALES (est): 1.1MM **Privately Held**
SIC: 3993 Signs & advertising specialties

(G-14303)
EQUA STAR CHEMICAL CORP
8805 Tabler Rd (60450-9153)
PHONE...................................815 942-7011
Glenn Clarke, *President*
EMP: 3
SALES (est): 382.3K **Privately Held**
SIC: 2869 Industrial organic chemicals

(G-14304)
EVENSON EXPLOSIVES LLC
2019 Dunn Rd (60450-8335)
PHONE...................................815 942-5800
Ron Evenson,
EMP: 45 **EST:** 1996
SALES (est): 5.7MM **Privately Held**
SIC: 2892 Explosives

(G-14305)
FIRE & ICE IMPORTS LLC
1222 Andrea Ct (60450-2502)
PHONE...................................310 871-1695
Zachary Proctor, *President*

Morris - Grundy County (G-14306)

EMP: 5
SQ FT: 4,000
SALES (est): 142.1K **Privately Held**
SIC: 2085 Vodka (alcoholic beverage); scotch whiskey; rum (alcoholic beverage)

(G-14306)
FRESH LOOK & SONS
406 E Main St (60450-2231)
PHONE 815 325-9692
Larry Caroline, *Owner*
EMP: 3
SALES (est): 120K **Privately Held**
SIC: 3479 Painting, coating & hot dipping

(G-14307)
HB FULLER ADHESIVES LLC
7440 W Dupont Rd (60450-8375)
PHONE 815 357-6726
Brian Spetka, *Natl Sales Mgr*
John Raney II, *Branch Mgr*
EMP: 50
SALES (corp-wide): 2.9B **Publicly Held**
WEB: www.hbfuller.com
SIC: 2891 Adhesives
HQ: H.B. Fuller Adhesives, Llc
1200 Willow Lake Blvd
Saint Paul MN 55110
651 236-5823

(G-14308)
JC METALCRAFTERS INC
1360 East St (60450-1978)
PHONE 815 942-9891
Joseph Kapt, *President*
EMP: 3 **EST:** 2002
SALES (est): 200K **Privately Held**
SIC: 3449 Miscellaneous metalwork

(G-14309)
LAFARGE AUX SABLE LLC
Also Called: Aux Sable Sand & Gravel
4225 Dellos Rd (60450-9469)
P.O. Box 150 (60450-0150)
PHONE 815 941-1423
Nathan Creech,
EMP: 3
SALES (est): 397.1K
SALES (corp-wide): 2.8MM **Privately Held**
SIC: 1442 Construction sand & gravel
PA: Western Sand & Gravel Co. Llc
400 Old North Rd
Spring Valley IL
815 664-2341

(G-14310)
LOGO WORKS
824 Liberty St Ste A (60450-1965)
PHONE 815 942-4700
Dave Wiers, *Owner*
EMP: 7
SALES (est): 310K **Privately Held**
SIC: 2759 Screen printing

(G-14311)
LYONDELL CHEMICAL COMPANY
Also Called: Equistar
8805 Tabler Rd (60450-9153)
PHONE 815 942-7011
Emiliano Chavez, *Superintendent*
Josephine Hogue, *Safety Mgr*
Brian Angwin, *Site Mgr*
Robert Metroz, *Opers Staff*
Robert Osmond, *Opers Staff*
EMP: 312
SALES (corp-wide): 39.1B **Privately Held**
WEB: www.lyondellbasell.com
SIC: 2869 3087 2821 Industrial organic chemicals; custom compound purchased resins; plastics materials & resins
HQ: Lyondell Chemical Company
1221 Mckinney St Ste 300
Houston TX 77010
713 309-7200

(G-14312)
MICRO SURFACE CORPORATION
465 Briscoe Dr (60450-6802)
P.O. Box 788 (60450-0788)
PHONE 815 942-4221
Ed Fabiszak, *President*
▲ **EMP:** 17
SQ FT: 12,800
SALES (est): 2MM **Privately Held**
SIC: 3471 2899 2077 Plating & polishing; chemical preparations; animal & marine fats & oils

(G-14313)
MID RIVER MINERALS INC
4675 Weitz Rd (60450-8714)
PHONE 815 941-7524
Anthony Augius, *President*
Paul Augius, *Vice Pres*
▲ **EMP:** 9
SQ FT: 40,000
SALES (est): 1.6MM **Privately Held**
SIC: 3295 Minerals, ground or treated

(G-14314)
MIDWEST SIGNWORKS
307 Bedford Rd (60450-1339)
PHONE 815 942-3517
Rose Grossi, *Owner*
EMP: 4
SQ FT: 3,250
SALES (est): 200K **Privately Held**
SIC: 7389 3993 Sign painting & lettering shop; signs & advertising specialties

(G-14315)
MIKE MULCAHY MOTORSPORTS LLC
1801 Bruce St (60450-1118)
PHONE 630 567-0298
Michael Mulcahy, *President*
EMP: 3
SALES (est): 10MM **Privately Held**
SIC: 7532 7948 3714 Antique & classic automobile restoration; racing, including track operation; motor vehicle parts & accessories

(G-14316)
MONDELEZ INTERNATIONAL INC
100 Prologis Pkwy (60450-4501)
PHONE 815 710-2114
EMP: 5 **Publicly Held**
SIC: 2022 2013 2095 2043 Processed cheese; sausages & other prepared meats; coffee roasting (except by wholesale grocers); cereal breakfast foods
PA: Mondelez International, Inc.
905 W Fulton Market # 200
Chicago IL 60607

(G-14317)
MORRIS PUBLISHING COMPANY
Also Called: Morris Daily Herald Publisher
1802 N Div St Ste 314 (60450)
P.O. Box 749 (60450-0749)
PHONE 815 942-3221
Thomas D Shaw, *CEO*
Bob Wall, *General Mgr*
Robert Wall, *General Mgr*
Kim Warnell, *Assoc Editor*
Lisa Stroner, *Info Tech Dir*
EMP: 1870 **EST:** 1870
SQ FT: 13,000
SALES (est): 16.8MM
SALES (corp-wide): 73.4MM **Privately Held**
WEB: www.morrisherald-news.com
SIC: 2711 Newspapers, publishing & printing
PA: 'b. F. Shaw Printing Company, The'
3200 E Lincolnway
Sterling IL
815 284-4000

(G-14318)
NARVICK BROS LUMBER CO INC (PA)
Also Called: Narvick Bros Construction
1037 Armstrong St (60450-1922)
PHONE 815 942-1173
Arthur Narvick, *President*
Carla Ranz, *IT/INT Sup*
EMP: 50 **EST:** 1946
SQ FT: 55,000
SALES (est): 18.3MM **Privately Held**
WEB: www.narvickbrothers.com
SIC: 5211 3273 1542 7359 Lumber products; ready-mixed concrete; commercial & office building contractors; equipment rental & leasing

(G-14319)
NORTHFIELD BLOCK COMPANY
3400 Bungalow Rd (60450-8945)
PHONE 815 941-4100
Max Hunt, *Branch Mgr*
EMP: 35
SALES (corp-wide): 30.6B **Privately Held**
SIC: 3272 Concrete products
HQ: Northfield Block Company
1 Hunt Ct
Mundelein IL 60060
847 816-9000

(G-14320)
ORICA USA INC
Also Called: Orica Nitrogen
7700 W Dupont Rd (60450-8375)
PHONE 815 357-8711
Ben Vanveckhoves, *Principal*
EMP: 45 **Privately Held**
SIC: 5169 2892 2819 Explosives; explosives; industrial inorganic chemicals
HQ: Orica Usa Inc.
33101 E Quincy Ave
Watkins CO 80137

(G-14321)
POLYNT COMPOSITES USA INC
6350 E Collins Rd (60450-9735)
PHONE 815 942-4600
EMP: 3
SALES (est): 147.1K **Privately Held**
SIC: 2821 Plastics materials & resins

(G-14322)
PRINT SHOP OF MORRIS
1836 Unit B N Division St (60450)
PHONE 815 710-5030
EMP: 3
SQ FT: 1,500
SALES (est): 120K **Privately Held**
SIC: 2759 Commercial Printing

(G-14323)
PROFESSIONAL METERS INC
3605 N State Route 47 D (60450-8218)
P.O. Box 506 (60450-0506)
PHONE 815 942-7000
Robert T Dullard, *President*
Vickie Sajnaj, *General Mgr*
Joseph Zikan, *Opers Staff*
Dennis Brown, *Manager*
John R Cummings, *Admin Sec*
EMP: 130 **EST:** 1999
SQ FT: 15,000
SALES (est): 16.5MM **Privately Held**
WEB: www.prometers.com
SIC: 1799 3825 3824 Hydraulic equipment, installation & service; digital panel meters, electricity measuring; gasoline dispensing meters

(G-14324)
RBP SERVICES
1116 Liberty St Apt 6 (60450-1566)
PHONE 206 238-3526
EMP: 3
SALES (est): 191.8K **Privately Held**
WEB: www.rbpservices.com
SIC: 2721 Periodicals

(G-14325)
REICHHOLD INDUSTRIES INC
Reichhold Chemicals
6350 E Collins Rd (60450-9735)
PHONE 815 942-4600
David Earl, *Production*
Greg Liszka, *Engineer*
Tom Colwell, *Branch Mgr*
David Minkwitz, *Manager*
Todd Clark, *Planning*
EMP: 44 **Privately Held**
SIC: 2821 2851 Plastics materials & resins; paints & allied products
PA: Reichhold Industries, Inc.
100 E Cottage Ave
Carpentersville IL 60110

(G-14326)
SANDERS INC
2250 Wahoo Dr (60450-9424)
PHONE 815 634-4611
Scott Sanders, *President*
Deborah Sanders, *Admin Sec*
▲ **EMP:** 20
SALES (est): 2.2MM **Privately Held**
SIC: 3564 Air purification equipment

(G-14327)
SOUTH WEST OIL INC
7080 Highland Dr (60450-8649)
PHONE 815 416-0400
Gary Guster, *CEO*
EMP: 10
SALES (est): 988.3K **Privately Held**
WEB: www.swoinc.com
SIC: 2911 Petroleum refining

(G-14328)
SPONGE-CUSHION INC
Also Called: SCI
902 Armstrong St (60450-1921)
PHONE 815 942-2300
Scott S Douglas, *President*
Hugh McLaren, *General Mgr*
Gino Mancini, *Controller*
Marti Bafia, *Accountant*
John G Moore, *Admin Sec*
◆ **EMP:** 67 **EST:** 1961
SQ FT: 144,000
SALES (est): 12.9MM
SALES (corp-wide): 4.7B **Publicly Held**
WEB: www.commercial-carpetcushion.com
SIC: 3069 Sponge rubber & sponge rubber products
PA: Leggett & Platt, Incorporated
1 Leggett Rd
Carthage MO 64836
417 358-8131

(G-14329)
STOCKDALE BLOCK SYSTEMS LLC
4675 Weitz Rd (60450-8714)
PHONE 815 416-1030
Jon Marks, *Principal*
Paul Auguis, *Principal*
EMP: 2
SALES (est): 1MM **Privately Held**
SIC: 5032 5999 3272 Concrete building products; concrete products, pre-cast; concrete products

(G-14330)
SUBSTRATE TECHNOLOGY INC
1384 Bungalow Rd (60450-8847)
PHONE 815 941-4800
Lynn Jones, *President*
Julie Finger, *Opers Mgr*
Sally Turner, *Mktg Dir*
▲ **EMP:** 10
SALES (est): 1.6MM **Privately Held**
SIC: 1771 3559 Flooring contractor; concrete products machinery

(G-14331)
T H DAVIDSON & CO INC
Also Called: Welsch Ready Mix
1350 Bungalow Rd (60450-8929)
PHONE 815 941-0280
Michael J Dejong, *President*
Richard Chobar, *Admin Sec*
EMP: 5
SALES (est): 380.6K **Privately Held**
SIC: 3273 Ready-mixed concrete

(G-14332)
TECHNICAL PROPELLANTS INC
6440 E Collins Rd (60450-9735)
PHONE 815 942-2900
Paul G Kuehn, *President*
David Waterman, *Vice Pres*
Daphme Firestone, *CFO*
Kathy Mellendorf, *Admin Sec*
EMP: 16
SQ FT: 20,000
SALES (est): 3.3MM **Privately Held**
WEB: www.aeropres.com
SIC: 2813 Industrial gases

(G-14333)
TORBLO INC
Also Called: Quality Millwork and Trim
7075 Lisbon Rd (60450-7640)
PHONE 815 941-2684
Frank Olbrot, *President*
Brian Olbrot, *Admin Sec*
EMP: 4
SQ FT: 12,000

GEOGRAPHIC SECTION

Morton - Tazewell County (G-14360)

SALES (est): 620.8K **Privately Held**
SIC: 2431 Doors, wood; windows, wood; window frames, wood

(G-14334)
TUMINELLO ENTERPRIZES INC (PA)
Also Called: Quality Glass Block & Win Co
1347 East St (60450-1977)
PHONE..................................815 416-1007
Jennifer L Tuminello, *President*
Raymond Tuminello, *Admin Sec*
▲ EMP: 7
SQ FT: 3,000
SALES (est): 2.6MM **Privately Held**
WEB: www.qualitywindow.net
SIC: 5211 1793 3231 Windows, storm: wood or metal; glass & glazing work; products of purchased glass

(G-14335)
TUMINELLO ENTERPRIZES INC
Also Called: Quality Glass Block
1347 East St (60450-1977)
PHONE..................................815 416-1007
Chris Danek, *Branch Mgr*
Toni Hines, *Admin Asst*
EMP: 4
SALES (est): 416.5K
SALES (corp-wide): 2.6MM **Privately Held**
SIC: 5211 1793 3231 Windows, storm: wood or metal; glass & glazing work; products of purchased glass
PA: Tuminello Enterprizes Inc.
1347 East St
Morris IL 60450
815 416-1007

(G-14336)
UNION TANK CAR COMPANY
8805 Tabler Rd (60450-9153)
PHONE..................................815 942-7391
EMP: 3
SALES (corp-wide): 327.2B **Publicly Held**
WEB: www.utlx.com
SIC: 3743 Train cars & equipment, freight or passenger; railroad car rebuilding
HQ: Union Tank Car Company
175 W Jackson Blvd # 2100
Chicago IL 60604
312 431-3111

(G-14337)
US OIL MORRIS IL
105 E Main St (60450-2150)
PHONE..................................815 513-3496
EMP: 3
SALES (est): 118.5K **Privately Held**
SIC: 2711 Newspapers, publishing & printing

(G-14338)
UTILITY CONCRETE PRODUCTS LLC
Also Called: Ucp
2495 Bungalow Rd (60450-9038)
PHONE..................................815 416-1000
James Hawken, *Vice Pres*
Thomas Heraty, *Vice Pres*
Brian Dewalt, *Plant Mgr*
Pat Larson, *Project Mgr*
Nicky Johnson, *Safety Mgr*
EMP: 50
SQ FT: 30,000
SALES (est): 14MM **Privately Held**
SIC: 3272 Concrete products, precast

(G-14339)
VOSS SANDWORKS INC
3460 W Nettle Creek Dr (60450-8722)
P.O. Box 765 (60450-0765)
PHONE..................................815 795-9366
Joshua Voss, *President*
Kimberly Voss, *Corp Secy*
EMP: 2
SALES (est): 391.1K **Privately Held**
SIC: 1442 Construction sand & gravel

Morrison
Whiteside County

(G-14340)
AMERICAN PIPING GROUP INC
Also Called: Vegter Steel Fabrication
800 French Creek Rd (61270-9815)
PHONE..................................815 772-7470
Mike Vegter, *President*
EMP: 60
SQ FT: 30,000
SALES (est): 22.9MM **Privately Held**
SIC: 3498 3441 Piping systems for pulp paper & chemical industries; fabricated structural metal

(G-14341)
CANDLE-LICIOUS
634 E Lincolnway (61270-2964)
PHONE..................................847 488-9982
Sue Davey, *Principal*
EMP: 3
SALES (est): 222.7K **Privately Held**
SIC: 3999 Candles

(G-14342)
CLIMCO COILS COMPANY
701 Klimstra Ct (61270-3000)
PHONE..................................815 772-3717
Scott Salmon, *President*
Mills Chris, *Electrical Engi*
▲ EMP: 130
SALES (est): 44.2MM **Privately Held**
SIC: 3353 Coils, sheet aluminum

(G-14343)
HYPONEX CORPORATION
9349 Garden Plain Rd (61270-9631)
PHONE..................................815 772-2167
Steven Williams, *Opers-Prdtn-Mfg*
EMP: 25
SALES (corp-wide): 3.1B **Publicly Held**
SIC: 2873 3524 3423 2875 Plant foods, mixed; from plants making nitrog. fertilizers; lawn & garden equipment; hand & edge tools; fertilizers, mixing only
HQ: Hyponex Corporation
14111 Scottslawn Rd
Marysville OH 43040
937 644-0011

(G-14344)
KRUM KREATIONS
22585 Carroll Rd (61270-9407)
PHONE..................................815 772-8296
Mark Krum, *Owner*
EMP: 3 EST: 2008
SALES (est): 250K **Privately Held**
WEB: www.krumkreations.com
SIC: 3446 Brasswork, ornamental: structural

(G-14345)
MARKMAN PEAT CORP
13161 Fenton Rd (61270-9224)
PHONE..................................815 772-4014
Bobby Terry, *Manager*
Terry Kissner, *Manager*
EMP: 25
SALES (corp-wide): 55.2MM **Privately Held**
SIC: 1499 5261 Peat grinding; top soil
PA: Markman Peat Corp.
900 Eagle Ridge Rd
Le Claire IA 52753
563 289-3478

(G-14346)
OPEN HAND SELF DEFENSE
200 W North St (61270-2423)
PHONE..................................815 718-3994
Christopher Morris, *Principal*
EMP: 4 EST: 2017
SALES (est): 275.2K **Privately Held**
SIC: 3812 Defense systems & equipment

(G-14347)
QUALITY READY MIX CONCRETE CO (PA)
14849 Lyndon Rd (61270-9549)
PHONE..................................815 772-7181
Randy Holesinger, *President*
Dawn Bush, *Admin Sec*
EMP: 12
SQ FT: 8,000
SALES (est): 3.7MM **Privately Held**
SIC: 3273 Ready-mixed concrete

(G-14348)
SHAWVER PRESS INC (PA)
120 E Lincolnway (61270-2623)
P.O. Box 31 (61270-0031)
PHONE..................................815 772-4700
Ben Wolf, *President*
Darcy Houseman, *Vice Pres*
EMP: 6 EST: 1923
SQ FT: 5,520
SALES (est): 601.3K **Privately Held**
SIC: 2752 3953 2791 2789 Commercial printing, offset; marking devices; typesetting; bookbinding & related work; commercial printing

(G-14349)
WNS PUBLICATIONS INC
Also Called: Review, The
100 E Main St (61270-2638)
P.O. Box 31 (61270-0031)
PHONE..................................815 772-7244
Tony Komlanc, *President*
EMP: 21
SQ FT: 4,000
SALES (est): 950K **Privately Held**
SIC: 2711 Newspapers: publishing only, not printed on site

Morrisonville
Christian County

(G-14350)
BAIRD INC
577 Illinois Route 48 (62546-6371)
PHONE..................................217 526-3407
Jim Baird, *President*
EMP: 4
SALES (est): 337.5K **Privately Held**
SIC: 3531 Construction machinery attachments

(G-14351)
LOUIS MARSCH INC
601 Carlin St (62546-6457)
P.O. Box 42 (62546-0042)
PHONE..................................217 526-3723
Kirk Vocks, *President*
James Renner, *Vice Pres*
EMP: 20 EST: 1919
SQ FT: 2,400
SALES: 12MM **Privately Held**
SIC: 2951 1611 Asphalt & asphaltic paving mixtures (not from refineries); highway & street maintenance

Morton
Tazewell County

(G-14352)
360 YIELD CENTER LLC
Also Called: Yield360
180 Detroit Ave (61550-1532)
PHONE..................................309 263-4360
Tyler Wilson, *Prdtn Mgr*
Hass Jarrow, *Sales Staff*
Clinton Smith, *Manager*
Jeff Neihouser, *Exec Dir*
Tim Sauder,
EMP: 40
SQ FT: 6,000
SALES (est): 8.5MM **Privately Held**
SIC: 3523 Fertilizing, spraying, dusting & irrigation machinery; soil sampling machines

(G-14353)
AUTONOMOUS STUFF LLC (HQ)
Also Called: Autonomoustuff
306 Erie Ave (61550-9600)
PHONE..................................309 291-0966
Robert Hambrick, *CEO*
◆ EMP: 6

SALES (est): 1.6MM
SALES (corp-wide): 4.3B **Privately Held**
SIC: 3714 5063 5013 8711 Motor vehicle electrical equipment; signaling equipment, electrical; testing equipment, electrical: automotive; engineering services; prepackaged software
PA: Hexagon Ab
Lilla Bantorget 15
Stockholm 111 2
860 126-20

(G-14354)
BIG DOG TREESTAND INC
120 Detroit Pkwy (61550-1857)
P.O. Box 952 (61550-0952)
PHONE..................................309 263-6800
Douglas N Smith, *President*
◆ EMP: 7
SQ FT: 2,000
SALES (est): 865.6K **Privately Held**
SIC: 3949 Sporting & athletic goods

(G-14355)
CATERPILLAR INC
500 N Morton Ave (61550-1575)
PHONE..................................304 327-7793
EMP: 52
SALES (est): 22.6MM **Privately Held**
SIC: 3531 Construction machinery

(G-14356)
CENTRAL ILLINOIS TRUSS
919 Detroit Ct Ste 2 (61550-3701)
PHONE..................................309 266-8787
Mike Rassi, *Branch Mgr*
Michael J Rassi, *Branch Mgr*
EMP: 5 **Privately Held**
SIC: 2439 Trusses, wooden roof
PA: Central Illinois Truss
105 Prospect Dr
Deer Creek IL 61733

(G-14357)
D & D EMBROIDERY
140 S Main St (61550-2030)
PHONE..................................309 266-7092
Janna Grimm, *Owner*
EMP: 3
SALES (est): 215.1K **Privately Held**
SIC: 2395 Embroidery products, except schiffli machine; embroidery & art needlework

(G-14358)
DESIGN SYSTEMS INC
361 Erie Ave (61550-9607)
PHONE..................................309 263-7706
Anthony Dennis, *President*
Chad Seltvelt, *Vice Pres*
Philip L Graves, *Treasurer*
EMP: 35
SQ FT: 27,500
SALES (est): 5.1MM **Privately Held**
SIC: 8711 3545 3544 Machine tool design; machine tool accessories; special dies, tools, jigs & fixtures

(G-14359)
ENGINEERING DESIGN & DEV
1001 W Jefferson St (61550-1503)
PHONE..................................309 266-6298
Tad Wharram, *Vice Pres*
Linda Jenkins, *Vice Pres*
Jamey Bieneman, *Purchasing*
Janet Coots, *Treasurer*
Steve Huette, *Sales Staff*
EMP: 25 EST: 1977
SQ FT: 12,000
SALES (est): 4.6MM **Privately Held**
SIC: 3599 3544 Machine shop, jobbing & repair; special dies & tools

(G-14360)
FUGATE INC
Also Called: Fugate Instruments
1349 W Birchwood St (61550-9627)
PHONE..................................309 472-6830
Brett Fugate, *CEO*
EMP: 6
SALES (est): 204.7K **Privately Held**
SIC: 3931 5736 7699 Percussion instruments & parts; musical instrument stores; professional instrument repair services

Morton - Tazewell County (G-14361) — GEOGRAPHIC SECTION

(G-14361)
G&D INTEGRATED MFG LLC
50 Commerce Dr (61550-9196)
PHONE.................................309 284-6700
P Joseph O'Neill,
EMP: 50
SALES (est): 1.4MM Privately Held
SIC: 3599 Crankshafts & camshafts, machining

(G-14362)
G&D INTEGRATED SERVICES INC
50 Commerce Dr (61550-9196)
PHONE.................................309 284-6700
P Joseph O'Neill, President
Charles T Purcell, Vice Pres
Chris B Sanders, Treasurer
EMP: 46
SALES (est): 5MM Privately Held
SIC: 3532 Mining machinery

(G-14363)
IRON-A-WAY LLC
220 W Jackson St (61550-1588)
PHONE.................................309 266-7232
Reginald R Smidt,
Cignet LLC,
Lawrence Francetti,
William Lianos,
EMP: 30
SQ FT: 15,000
SALES (est): 5.6MM Privately Held
SIC: 3633 Household laundry equipment

(G-14364)
MARION TOOL & DIE INC
Also Called: Morton Machining
701 Flint Ave (61550-3603)
PHONE.................................309 266-6551
Tamara Marion, President
Jim Salyers, Engineer
EMP: 70 Privately Held
SIC: 3599 Machine shop, jobbing & repair
PA: Marion Tool & Die, Inc.
1126 W National Ave
West Terre Haute IN 47885

(G-14365)
MATCOR MTAL FBRICATION ILL INC (HQ)
Also Called: Matcor Metal Fabrication Group
1021 W Birchwood St (61550-9617)
PHONE.................................309 263-1707
Galliano Tiberin, President
Scott Tatlock, Plant Mgr
Todd Bennett, Materials Mgr
George Worel, Purchasing
Joseph Infusino, Controller
▲ EMP: 50
SALES (est): 17.7MM
SALES (corp-wide): 97.2MM Privately Held
SIC: 3441 Fabricated structural metal
PA: Matsu Manufacturing Inc
7657 Bramalea Rd
Brampton ON L6T 5
905 291-5000

(G-14366)
MIDWESTERN WOOD PRODUCTS CO
1500 W Jefferson St (61550-1321)
P.O. Box 434 (61550-0434)
PHONE.................................309 266-9771
Jerry Young, President
EMP: 6
SQ FT: 30,000
SALES (est): 808.9K Privately Held
SIC: 2431 Millwork

(G-14367)
MMC PRECISION HOLDINGS CORP
1021 W Birchwood St (61550-9617)
PHONE.................................309 266-7176
Frank C Lukacs, President
EMP: 1370
SQ FT: 284,000
SALES (est): 56.7MM Privately Held
SIC: 3449 Miscellaneous metalwork

(G-14368)
MODERN METHODS CREATIVE INC
408 N Nebraska Ave (61550-1740)
PHONE.................................309 263-4100
Dan Martin, President
EMP: 4
SALES (est): 525.7K Privately Held
SIC: 7319 5949 5199 2759 Advertising; sewing, needlework & piece goods; nondurable goods; commercial printing

(G-14369)
MORTON AUTOMATIC ELECTRIC CO
Also Called: General Methods Co
641 W David St (61550-1529)
PHONE.................................309 263-7577
Alan Rumbold, President
Alan J Rumbold, President
EMP: 9 EST: 1973
SQ FT: 5,544
SALES (est): 1.1MM Privately Held
SIC: 3613 3625 Control panels, electric; relays & industrial controls

(G-14370)
MORTON BUILDINGS INC
25 Erie Ct (61550-9702)
PHONE.................................309 263-3652
Chuck Love, Manager
EMP: 12
SALES (corp-wide): 462.5MM Privately Held
SIC: 3448 Prefabricated metal buildings
PA: Morton Buildings, Inc.
252 W Adams St
Morton IL 61550
800 447-7436

(G-14371)
MORTON INDUSTRIES LLC
70 Commerce Dr (61550-9198)
PHONE.................................309 263-2590
Russ Argadine, Vice Pres
Josh Bethel, Opers Staff
Jeremy Shaw, Buyer
Sam Wiegand, Engineer
Elaine Swigart, Human Res Mgr
▲ EMP: 750
SQ FT: 225,000
SALES (est): 60MM Privately Held
WEB: www.mortonind.com
SIC: 3441 Fabricated structural metal
PA: Nelson Global Products, Inc.
1560 Williams Dr
Stoughton WI 53589

(G-14372)
MULTAX CORPORATION
424 W Edgewood Ct (61550-2499)
P.O. Box 266 (61550-0266)
PHONE.................................309 266-9765
Don E Bigger, President
Doug Myers, Vice Pres
Mildred R Bigger, Admin Sec
▲ EMP: 63
SQ FT: 66,000
SALES (est): 11.1MM Privately Held
SIC: 3599 3728 Machine shop, jobbing & repair; aircraft parts & equipment

(G-14373)
NELSON GLOBAL PRODUCTS INC
231 Detroit Ave (61550-1533)
PHONE.................................309 263-8914
Steven Belser, President
EMP: 10 Privately Held
SIC: 3317 Steel pipe & tubes
PA: Nelson Global Products, Inc.
1560 Williams Dr
Stoughton WI 53589

(G-14374)
NESTLE USA INC
Nestle Confections Factory
216 N Morton Ave (61550-1830)
P.O. Box 198 (61550-0198)
PHONE.................................309 263-2651
Larry Popp, Branch Mgr
EMP: 200
SALES (corp-wide): 93.5B Privately Held
WEB: www.nestleusa.com
SIC: 2023 Evaporated milk
HQ: Nestle Usa, Inc.
1812 N Moore St Ste 118
Rosslyn VA 22209
440 264-7249

(G-14375)
P-AMERICAS LLC
Also Called: Pepsico
801 W Birchwood St (61550-9613)
PHONE.................................309 266-2400
Randy Ravens, Branch Mgr
EMP: 130
SALES (corp-wide): 67.1B Publicly Held
SIC: 2086 5149 Soft drinks: packaged in cans, bottles, etc.; carbonated beverages, nonalcoholic: bottled & canned; soft drinks
HQ: P-Americas Llc
1 Pepsi Way
Somers NY 10589
336 896-5740

(G-14376)
PARKER FABRICATION INC (PA)
501 E Courtland St (61550-9043)
PHONE.................................309 266-8413
Patrick A Parker, President
Matthew Parker, Vice Pres
Matt Lucas, Prdtn Mgr
Chuck Heerde, Purch Agent
Ben Binkele, Engineer
EMP: 35
SQ FT: 26,000
SALES (est): 5.4MM Privately Held
SIC: 3498 3714 7692 3444 Tube fabricating (contract bending & shaping); exhaust systems & parts, motor vehicle; welding repair; sheet metalwork

(G-14377)
PARKER-HANNIFIN CORPORATION
Also Called: Parker Hnnfin Elctrnic Contrls
1651 N Main St (61550-9058)
PHONE.................................309 266-2200
Pat Friend, Vice Pres
Tim Harris, Safety Mgr
Jim Lanigan, Manager
Chad Jewell, Technician
Mike Baker, Maintence Staff
EMP: 130
SALES (corp-wide): 14.3B Publicly Held
SIC: 3594 Fluid power pumps & motors
PA: Parker-Hannifin Corporation
6035 Parkland Blvd
Cleveland OH 44124
216 896-3000

(G-14378)
PIECE WORKS SPECIALISTS INC
300 W Adams St (61550-1988)
P.O. Box 5088 (61550-5088)
PHONE.................................309 266-7016
Charles Glover, President
EMP: 18
SQ FT: 6,000
SALES (est): 1.6MM Privately Held
SIC: 2448 Pallets, wood

(G-14379)
PRO-FAB INC
1050 W Jefferson St Ste A (61550-1585)
P.O. Box 449 (61550-0449)
PHONE.................................309 263-8454
Stephen R Kopetz, President
Jess Wallace, Vice Pres
Phil Young, Vice Pres
Matt Wiseman, Purch Mgr
Jess Wallis, VP Sales
EMP: 45
SQ FT: 30,000
SALES (est): 13.5MM Privately Held
SIC: 3441 Fabricated structural metal

(G-14380)
QUALITY TRAILER SALES INC
1701 N Main St (61550-9208)
PHONE.................................630 739-2495
Jeff Hendricks, Manager
EMP: 3
SALES (corp-wide): 30.2MM Privately Held
SIC: 3715 Semitrailers for truck tractors

PA: Quality Trailer Sales, Inc
1601 1st Ave E
Milan IL 61264
309 787-2179

(G-14381)
ROCKFORD RIGGING INC
1480 S Main St Ste A (61550-4513)
PHONE.................................309 263-0566
Brent Hart, Manager
EMP: 5
SALES (corp-wide): 9.9MM Privately Held
SIC: 3531 Construction machinery attachments
PA: Rockford Rigging, Inc.
5401 Mainsail Dr
Roscoe IL 61073
309 263-0566

(G-14382)
SOUTHFIELD CORPORATION
Also Called: Morton Ready Mix Concrete
775 W Birchwood St (61550-9605)
PHONE.................................309 676-6121
Dave Minor, Manager
EMP: 57
SALES (corp-wide): 344.9MM Privately Held
SIC: 3273 Ready-mixed concrete
PA: Southfield Corporation
8995 W 95th St
Palos Hills IL 60465
708 344-1000

(G-14383)
SPL SOFTWARE ALLIANCE LLC
Also Called: Caterpillar Authorized Dealer
500 N Morton Ave (61550-1527)
P.O. Box 474 (61550-0474)
PHONE.................................309 266-0304
EMP: 2
SALES (est): 760.5K
SALES (corp-wide): 45.4B Publicly Held
SIC: 7372 5082 Prepackaged Software Services Whol Construction/Mining Equipment
PA: Caterpillar Inc.
510 Lake Cook Rd Ste 100
Deerfield IL 60015
224 551-4000

(G-14384)
SUPER SUBLIMATION LLC
368 Erie Ave (61550-9600)
PHONE.................................309 256-0184
Robert W Super, Mng Member
EMP: 6
SALES: 450K Privately Held
SIC: 2396 Fabric printing & stamping

(G-14385)
SYNERGETIC INDUSTRIES
1060 W Jefferson St (61550-1504)
PHONE.................................309 321-8145
Jake Ludeman, Principal
EMP: 2
SALES (est): 250.4K Privately Held
SIC: 3999 Manufacturing industries

(G-14386)
TAZEWELL FLOOR COVERING INC
419 W Jefferson St (61550-1896)
PHONE.................................309 266-6371
Thomas Zimmerman, President
Steven Zimmerman, Vice Pres
EMP: 15
SQ FT: 11,000
SALES (est): 2.4MM Privately Held
WEB: www.tazewellfloors.com
SIC: 5713 5231 2391 Carpets; linoleum; floor tile; paint, glass & wallpaper; curtains & draperies

(G-14387)
YINLUN USA INC
77 Commerce Dr (61550-9197)
P.O. Box 5077 (61550-5077)
PHONE.................................309 291-0843
Xiaomin Xu, President
Marco Lambert, Vice Pres
Saul Torres, Manager
▲ EMP: 5

GEOGRAPHIC SECTION

Morton Grove - Cook County (G-14414)

SALES (est): 2.1MM
SALES (corp-wide): 723MM **Privately Held**
SIC: 3443 5075 Heat exchangers: coolers (after, inter), condensers, etc.; heat exchangers
PA: Zhejiang Yinlun Machinery Co., Ltd.
No.8, Shifeng East Rd., Fuxi Street,
Tiantai County
Taizhou 31720
576 839-3833

Morton Grove
Cook County

(G-14388)
ALFA MFG INDUSTRIES INC
Also Called: Alfa Tools
7845 Merrimac Ave (60053-2710)
PHONE..................847 470-9595
Diljit S Ahluwalia, *President*
Mohina A Sends, *Exec VP*
Shaan Ahluwalia, *Vice Pres*
EMP: 21
SQ FT: 12,000
SALES (est): 4.4MM **Privately Held**
SIC: 3545 5084 Cutting tools for machine tools; metalworking tools (such as drills, taps, dies, files)

(G-14389)
ALYCE DESIGNS INC (PA)
Also Called: Alyce Paris
7901 Caldwell Ave (60053-2701)
PHONE..................847 966-6933
Jean Paul Hamm, *President*
Claudine C Hamm, *Creative Dir*
▲ EMP: 30 EST: 1955
SQ FT: 97,000
SALES (est): 4.7MM **Privately Held**
WEB: www.alyceparis.com
SIC: 2335 Wedding gowns & dresses; gowns, formal; ensemble dresses: women's, misses' & juniors'; dresses, paper: cut & sewn

(G-14390)
AMERALLOY STEEL CORPORATION
7848 Merrimac Ave (60053-2737)
PHONE..................847 967-0600
Richard D Steele, *President*
Hannah Liberman, *Purchasing*
Joel Schmidt, *Engineer*
Dale C Altmin, *Admin Sec*
EMP: 50 EST: 1978
SQ FT: 22,600
SALES (est): 33.7MM **Privately Held**
SIC: 5051 3443 Steel; plate work for the metalworking trade

(G-14391)
BESTPYSANKY INC
6212 Madison Ct (60053-3218)
PHONE..................877 797-2659
Sergiy Lishchuk, *CEO*
▲ EMP: 9
SQ FT: 4,000
SALES: 869.3K **Privately Held**
WEB: www.bestpysanky.com
SIC: 5199 5947 3999 Gifts & novelties; gift shop; boutiquing: decorating gift items with sequins, fruit, etc.

(G-14392)
BUNZL RETAIL LLC
Also Called: Cdw Merchants
8338 Austin Ave (60053-3209)
PHONE..................847 733-1469
John Henry Flerx, *Manager*
EMP: 18
SALES (corp-wide): 12B **Privately Held**
SIC: 2542 Racks, merchandise display or storage: except wood
HQ: Bunzl Retail, L.L.C.
1 Cityplace Dr Ste 200
Saint Louis MO 63141
314 997-5959

(G-14393)
BUNZL RETAIL SERVICES LLC
Also Called: Schwarz
8338 Austin Ave (60053-3209)
PHONE..................847 966-2550
Judy Cooley, *Principal*
EMP: 30
SALES (corp-wide): 12B **Privately Held**
SIC: 5113 2759 Industrial & personal service paper; flexographic printing
HQ: Bunzl Retail Services, Llc
8338 Austin Ave
Morton Grove IL 60053
847 733-1469

(G-14394)
BUSINESS CARDS ETC
6437 Dempster St (60053-2604)
PHONE..................847 470-8848
Lawrence Strybel, *Owner*
EMP: 5
SQ FT: 2,000
SALES (est): 442.6K **Privately Held**
SIC: 2759 Commercial printing

(G-14395)
CHARGER WATER CONDITIONING INC (HQ)
8150 Lehigh Ave Ste A (60053-2600)
PHONE..................847 967-9558
Sig Feiger, *President*
Steve Feiger, *Vice Pres*
▲ EMP: 16
SQ FT: 3,500
SALES (est): 3.6MM
SALES (corp-wide): 113.4MM **Privately Held**
WEB: www.chargerwater.com
SIC: 3589 Water treatment equipment, industrial
PA: The Crawford Supply Group Inc
8150 Lehigh Ave Ste A
Morton Grove IL 60053
847 967-0550

(G-14396)
CLAESSENS KIDS INC
6350 Kirk St (60053-2705)
P.O. Box 7072, Evanston (60204-7072)
PHONE..................973 551-8528
Vincent Claessens, *Officer*
Monica Champignon, *Officer*
EMP: 3
SALES (est): 172.1K **Privately Held**
SIC: 3873 Watches, clocks, watchcases & parts

(G-14397)
CORNUCOPIA SUPPLY CORP
8305 Gross Point Rd (60053-3421)
PHONE..................847 532-9365
Saad Qureshi, *CEO*
EMP: 5
SALES (est): 328.5K **Privately Held**
SIC: 5999 3842 Medical apparatus & supplies; respiratory protection equipment, personal

(G-14398)
DAILY DOLLAR SAVINGS LLC
9448 Skokie Blvd (60053)
PHONE..................860 883-0351
Lababidi Michael, *Principal*
EMP: 5
SALES (est): 209.4K **Privately Held**
SIC: 2711 Newspapers, publishing & printing

(G-14399)
DEX BLUE CORP
6321 Dempster St 174 (60053-2848)
PHONE..................847 916-7744
Jerry Franco Piechowiak, *CEO*
EMP: 10
SALES: 500K **Privately Held**
SIC: 3612 Lighting transformers, fluorescent

(G-14400)
DINO DESIGN INCORPORATED
9023 Oriole Ave (60053-1855)
PHONE..................773 763-4223
Chris Kowalski, *President*
Christopher Kowarski, *Shareholder*
EMP: 4

SALES (est): 352.4K **Privately Held**
SIC: 2361 Girls' & children's dresses, blouses & shirts

(G-14401)
DOT SHARPER PRINTING INC
8120 River Dr Ste 1 (60053-2613)
PHONE..................847 581-9033
Steven R Clark, *President*
Jim Dravecky, *Admin Sec*
EMP: 6
SALES (est): 821.1K **Privately Held**
SIC: 2752 Commercial printing, offset

(G-14402)
E I DU PONT DE NEMOURS & CO
Also Called: Dupont
7828 Merrimac Ave (60053-2709)
PHONE..................847 965-6580
Renee Mignagaray, *Manager*
EMP: 20
SALES (corp-wide): 21.5B **Publicly Held**
SIC: 2819 Industrial inorganic chemicals
HQ: E. I. Du Pont De Nemours And Company
974 Centre Rd Bldg 735
Wilmington DE 19805
302 485-3000

(G-14403)
ECOLOCAP SOLUTIONS INC
6240 Oakton St (60053-2721)
PHONE..................312 585-6670
Jeung Kwak, *Ch of Bd*
James Kwak, *President*
Michel St-Pierre, *CFO*
Michael Siegel, *CTO*
EMP: 4 EST: 2004
SALES (est): 452.3K **Privately Held**
WEB: www.ecolocap.com
SIC: 2869 3691 Fuels; storage batteries

(G-14404)
ELAN FURS
Also Called: Barth Wind Elan Furs
3841 E 82nd St (60053)
PHONE..................317 255-6100
John Mitropoulos, *Owner*
Anna Miraupoulos, *Co-Owner*
EMP: 12
SALES (est): 423.5K **Privately Held**
SIC: 3999 5651 Furs; unisex clothing stores

(G-14405)
ENJOYLIFE INC
8244 Lehigh Ave (60053-2615)
P.O. Box 118, Lake Zurich (60047-0118)
PHONE..................847 966-3377
Marie-France Russell, *President*
Steven Russell, *Vice Pres*
▲ EMP: 8
SQ FT: 5,000
SALES: 1MM **Privately Held**
SIC: 3949 Sporting & athletic goods

(G-14406)
FAREVA MORTON GROVE INC
6901 Golf Rd (60053-1346)
PHONE..................847 966-0200
Jean-Paul David, *President*
EMP: 4
SALES (est): 301K
SALES (corp-wide): 299.6K **Privately Held**
SIC: 2844 Toilet preparations
PA: Fareva
Place De La Gare 28
Luxembourg
268 646-12

(G-14407)
FASTSIGNS INTERNATIONAL
7911 Golf Rd (60053-1040)
PHONE..................847 967-7222
Richard Goldberg, *President*
Janet Goldberg, *Admin Sec*
EMP: 7
SQ FT: 1,900
SALES (est): 1.5MM **Privately Held**
SIC: 3993 Signs & advertising specialties

(G-14408)
FLUID HANDLING LLC
Also Called: Bell & Gossett
8200 Austin Ave (60053-3205)
PHONE..................773 267-1600
Ken Napolitano, *President*
EMP: 500 **Publicly Held**
SIC: 3561 Pumps & pumping equipment
HQ: Fluid Handling, Llc
175 Standard Pkwy
Cheektowaga NY 14227
716 897-2800

(G-14409)
GAS DEPOT INC
8930 Waukegan Rd Ste 230 (60053-2132)
PHONE..................847 581-0303
George M Nediyakalayil, *President*
EMP: 3
SALES (est): 152.2K **Privately Held**
SIC: 1311 Natural gas production

(G-14410)
GRAPHIC PRESS INC
6511 Oakton St (60053-2728)
PHONE..................847 272-6000
Ronald Levine, *President*
Mark Swiatly, *Information Mgr*
Steve Colon, *Maintence Staff*
EMP: 8
SQ FT: 10,000
SALES (est): 585.6K **Privately Held**
SIC: 2759 Commercial printing

(G-14411)
HOWLAND TECHNOLOGY INC
Also Called: Evergreen Drive Systems
8129 Austin Ave (60053-3204)
PHONE..................847 965-9808
Thomas P Howland, *CEO*
Stephania Holland, *Vice Pres*
Britta Franck, *Marketing Staff*
Gaby Mancuso, *Marketing Staff*
◆ EMP: 10
SQ FT: 5,000
SALES (est): 10MM **Privately Held**
SIC: 3621 3799 Motors, electric; recreational vehicles

(G-14412)
ILLINI COOLANT MANAGEMENT CORP (PA)
8011 Parkside Ave (60053-3543)
PHONE..................847 966-1079
John Bailey, *President*
▲ EMP: 2
SALES (est): 2MM **Privately Held**
WEB: www.illinicoolant.com
SIC: 2992 Cutting oils, blending: made from purchased materials

(G-14413)
INTERNATIONAL SPRING COMPANY
Also Called: I S C O
7901 Nagle Ave (60053-2714)
PHONE..................847 470-8170
Joseph H Goldberg, *President*
Brett Goldberg, *General Mgr*
Brett Nudelman, *General Mgr*
Earl Peterson, *CFO*
Brett Nungleman, *Sales Mgr*
EMP: 100
SQ FT: 45,000
SALES (est): 15.5MM **Privately Held**
WEB: www.internationalspring.com
SIC: 3495 3469 Instrument springs, precision; stamping metal for the trade

(G-14414)
J & D INSTANT SIGNS
5614 Dempster St (60053-3108)
PHONE..................847 965-2800
John Swanson, *President*
EMP: 3
SQ FT: 2,500
SALES (est): 288.1K **Privately Held**
SIC: 7389 3993 2672 2396 Sign painting & lettering shop; signs & advertising specialties; coated & laminated paper; automotive & apparel trimmings

Morton Grove - Cook County (G-14415)

(G-14415)
JOHN CRANE INC
6400 Oakton St (60053-2725)
P.O. Box 91502, Chicago (60693-1502)
PHONE..................847 967-2400
Doug Harwick, *District Mgr*
Sam Rihani, *Business Mgr*
Marcio Costa, *Vice Pres*
Alistair Rogers, *Vice Pres*
Rick Albin, *Opers Mgr*
EMP: 9
SALES (corp-wide): 3.1B **Privately Held**
SIC: 3053 Gaskets & sealing devices; packing materials
HQ: John Crane Inc.
227 W Monroe St Ste 1800
Chicago IL 60606
312 605-7800

(G-14416)
K & B MACHINING
6206 Madison Ct (60053-3218)
PHONE..................847 663-9534
Robert J Zuttermeister Jr, *President*
Kurt Ericsson, *Vice Pres*
EMP: 6
SQ FT: 2,300
SALES (est): 300K **Privately Held**
SIC: 3599 3544 Machine shop, jobbing & repair; special dies, tools, jigs & fixtures

(G-14417)
KEENPAC LLC
8338 Austin Ave (60053-3209)
PHONE..................845 291-8680
Bruce Barton, *Branch Mgr*
EMP: 15
SALES (corp-wide): 12B **Privately Held**
SIC: 2673 Cellophane bags, unprinted: made from purchased materials
HQ: Keenpac, Llc
8338 Austin Ave
Morton Grove IL 60053

(G-14418)
KEENPAC LLC (DH)
Also Called: Bunzl
8338 Austin Ave (60053-3209)
PHONE..................845 291-8680
Bruce Barton, *General Mgr*
▲ **EMP:** 8
SALES (est): 2.1MM
SALES (corp-wide): 12B **Privately Held**
SIC: 2673 Cellophane bags, unprinted: made from purchased materials

(G-14419)
LICHTNWALD - JOHNSTON IR WORKS
Also Called: L J Iron Works
7840 Lehigh Ave (60053-2707)
P.O. Box 1328 (60053-7328)
PHONE..................847 966-1100
Ira Rosenberg, *President*
Patrick Cansler, *Vice Pres*
Paul Rosenberg, *Consultant*
EMP: 25
SQ FT: 120,000
SALES (est): 1.1MM **Privately Held**
WEB: www.lichtenwald-johnston.com
SIC: 3441 1791 Expansion joints (structural shapes), iron or steel; structural steel erection

(G-14420)
LIFEWAY FOODS INC (PA)
6431 Oakton St (60053-2727)
PHONE..................847 967-1010
Ludmila Smolyansky, *Ch of Bd*
Julie Smolyansky, *President*
Edward P Smolyansky, *COO*
Lana Mak, *Purch Mgr*
Eric Hanson, *CFO*
▲ **EMP:** 164
SALES: 93.6MM **Publicly Held**
SIC: 2023 2026 Dry, condensed, evaporated dairy products; fluid milk; kefir; yogurt; fermented & cultured milk products

(G-14421)
LIFEWAY KEFIR SHOP LLC
6431 Oakton St (60053-2727)
PHONE..................847 967-1010
Julie Smolyansky, *Manager*
Edward Smolyansky, *Manager*
EMP: 30

SALES (est): 1MM **Privately Held**
SIC: 2086 Iced tea & fruit drinks, bottled & canned

(G-14422)
LIGHTWORKS COMMUNCATION INC
Also Called: Monthly Aspectarian, The
5632 Carol Ave (60053-3101)
PHONE..................847 966-1110
Guy Spiro, *President*
EMP: 6
SALES (est): 335.1K **Privately Held**
SIC: 2721 Periodicals

(G-14423)
MAGRABAR LLC
6100 Madison Ct (60053-3216)
PHONE..................847 965-7550
Ravi Joshi, *President*
Colin J Hoather, *Vice Pres*
EMP: 16
SALES (est): 15MM
SALES (corp-wide): 328.7K **Privately Held**
SIC: 2819 Industrial inorganic chemicals
HQ: Munzing North America Lp
1455 Broad St Ste 3
Bloomfield NJ 07003

(G-14424)
MAIERS BAKERY
9328 Waukegan Rd (60053-1312)
PHONE..................847 967-8042
Gregg H Maier, *President*
John Koester, *Vice Pres*
EMP: 9
SQ FT: 1,800
SALES (est): 480K **Privately Held**
WEB: www.maiersbakery.com
SIC: 2051 2052 Bakery: wholesale or wholesale/retail combined; cookies & crackers

(G-14425)
MAIN STREET VISUALS INC
Also Called: Sign One
8340 Callie Ave Unit 110 (60053-3714)
PHONE..................847 869-7446
Henry Funkenbusch, *President*
Phyllis Funkenbusch, *Vice Pres*
EMP: 5
SALES (est): 589.2K **Privately Held**
SIC: 3993 Signs & advertising specialties

(G-14426)
MEDAOWVIEW VENTURES II INC (PA)
8350 Lehigh Ave (60053-2616)
PHONE..................847 965-1700
EMP: 30
SALES (est): 3.4MM **Privately Held**
SIC: 3911 Mfg Precious Metal Jewelry

(G-14427)
MEDIFIX INC
8727 Narragansett Ave (60053-2847)
PHONE..................847 965-1898
George Albulescu, *President*
EMP: 5
SALES (est): 850.1K **Privately Held**
SIC: 3841 5047 Surgical instruments & apparatus; hospital equipment & furniture

(G-14428)
MGP HOLDING CORP
6451 Main St (60053-2633)
PHONE..................847 967-5600
Frank Leo, *CEO*
Brian Tambi, *Ch of Bd*
William Goldberg, *President*
▲ **EMP:** 260
SALES (est): 35.6MM
SALES (corp-wide): 421.3MM **Privately Held**
SIC: 2834 Pharmaceutical preparations
PA: Gtcr Golder Rauner, L.L.C.
300 N La Salle Dr # 5600
Chicago IL 60654
312 329-0225

(G-14429)
MINUTEMAN PRESS MORTON GROVE
6038 Dempster St (60053-2942)
PHONE..................847 470-0212
Ken Lipski, *Owner*
Bea Lipski, *Co-Owner*
EMP: 4 **EST:** 1979
SALES (est): 140K **Privately Held**
SIC: 2752 2789 Commercial printing, lithographic; bookbinding & related work

(G-14430)
MORTON GROVE PHRMCEUTICALS INC
6451 Main St (60053-2633)
PHONE..................847 967-5600
Sunil Khera, *President*
Marc Mota, *Prdtn Mgr*
David Chovanec, *Manager*
Feroz Shaikh, *Asst Mgr*
Russell Budzicz, *Technology*
▲ **EMP:** 300
SQ FT: 125,000
SALES (est): 69.1MM **Privately Held**
SIC: 2834 Pharmaceutical preparations
HQ: Wockhardt Limited
Wockhardt Towers, Bandra Kurla Complex,
Mumbai MH 40005

(G-14431)
PDSS CONSTRUCTION
7516 Davis St (60053-1708)
PHONE..................847 980-6090
Sahir Isho, *Principal*
EMP: 10
SALES (est): 370K **Privately Held**
SIC: 1442 Construction sand & gravel

(G-14432)
PEARL PERFECT INC
8220 Austin Ave (60053-3207)
PHONE..................847 679-6251
Robert Gluck, *President*
Leah Gluck, *Admin Sec*
EMP: 26
SALES (est): 2MM **Privately Held**
SIC: 3961 5094 Costume jewelry, ex. precious metal & semiprecious stones; pearls

(G-14433)
PRINTING SOURCE INC
Also Called: ASAP Printing
8120 River Dr Ste 2 (60053-2613)
PHONE..................773 588-2930
David S Solomon, *President*
Priscilla Solomon, *Vice Pres*
EMP: 5 **EST:** 1972
SQ FT: 2,500
SALES (est): 640.9K **Privately Held**
SIC: 2752 2791 2789 Commercial printing, offset; typesetting; bookbinding & related work

(G-14434)
PUBLICATIONS INTERNATIONAL LTD (PA)
Also Called: Consumer Guide
8140 Lehigh Ave (60053-2627)
PHONE..................847 676-3470
Louis Weber, *President*
Su Bermingham, *President*
Ann Taylor, *President*
Barbara Rittenhouse, *Publisher*
John Biel, *Chief*
◆ **EMP:** 380
SQ FT: 125,000
SALES (est): 66.6MM **Privately Held**
WEB: www.pilbooks.com
SIC: 2731 2721 Books: publishing only; magazines: publishing only, not printed on site

(G-14435)
QUANTUM COLOR GRAPHICS LLC
6511 Oakton St (60053-2728)
PHONE..................847 967-3600
James Campise, *Exec VP*
Taylor Kobey, *Vice Pres*
Jay Garstecki, *VP Sls/Mktg*
Ray Barrett, *CFO*
Christine Vodnansky, *Human Res Mgr*

EMP: 155
SQ FT: 125,000
SALES (est): 63.1MM **Privately Held**
SIC: 2752 8741 7382 7389 Commercial printing, offset; management services; security systems services; finishing services

(G-14436)
R-B INDUSTRIES INC
6380 Oakton St (60053-2723)
PHONE..................847 647-4020
Ronald R Baade, *Ch of Bd*
Kris Baade, *Vice Pres*
Marsha K Baade, *Admin Sec*
◆ **EMP:** 25
SQ FT: 28,000
SALES (est): 5.1MM **Privately Held**
SIC: 5072 3965 Miscellaneous fasteners; fasteners, buttons, needles & pins

(G-14437)
RAO DESIGN INTERNATIONAL INC
Also Called: American Plastics Technoligies
9311 Osceola Ave (60053-1732)
PHONE..................847 671-6182
▲ **EMP:** 2
SQ FT: 62,000
SALES (est): 436.7K **Privately Held**
SIC: 3559 3544 Mfg Misc Industry Machinery Mfg Dies/Tools/Jigs/Fixtures

(G-14438)
RELIABLE APPLIANCE AND REF
7443 Emerson St (60053-1146)
PHONE..................847 581-9520
EMP: 2
SALES (est): 209.1K **Privately Held**
SIC: 3822 Appliance controls except air-conditioning & refrigeration

(G-14439)
SANDTECH INC
Also Called: Alfa Tools
7845 Merrimac Ave (60053-2710)
PHONE..................847 470-9595
Dilgit S Ahluwalia, *President*
Jocelyn Glynn, *Vice Pres*
Mohina Ahluwalia, *Treasurer*
▲ **EMP:** 13
SQ FT: 40,000
SALES (est): 48.7K **Privately Held**
SIC: 3545 3291 Cutting tools for machine tools; abrasive products

(G-14440)
SERVICE PACKAGING DESIGN INC
6238 Lincoln Ave (60053-2852)
PHONE..................847 966-6592
Norman Croft, *President*
Julie Okon, *Publisher*
EMP: 5
SQ FT: 2,500
SALES (est): 363.7K **Privately Held**
SIC: 2752 7389 2679 2672 Decals, lithographed; tag, ticket & schedule printing: lithographic; packaging & labeling services; tags & labels, paper; adhesive papers, labels or tapes: from purchased material

(G-14441)
STANDARD CONDENSER CORPORATION
5412 Keeney St (60053-3512)
PHONE..................847 965-2722
Bryan Mc Lean, *CEO*
Richard T Mc Lean, *President*
Marilynn Mc Lean, *Corp Secy*
Brian McLean, *Vice Pres*
EMP: 10
SQ FT: 10,000
SALES (est): 940K **Privately Held**
SIC: 3675 Electronic capacitors

(G-14442)
STEVEN BROWNSTEIN
Also Called: Background Investigator, The
5830 Lincoln Ave Unit A (60053-3304)
PHONE..................847 909-6677
Steven Brownstein, *Owner*
EMP: 3

GEOGRAPHIC SECTION

Mount Carmel - Wabash County (G-14465)

SALES (est): 105.5K Privately Held
SIC: 2711 Newspapers; publishing only, not printed on site

(G-14443)
STRANGE ENGINEERING INC
8300 Austin Ave (60053-3209)
PHONE.................................847 663-1701
Henry R Stange, *President*
Kevin Martinie, *Purch Mgr*
Richard Bickford, *Supervisor*
Jeffrey Stange, *Admin Sec*
Carol Fulara, *Clerk*
▲ EMP: 55
SQ FT: 50,000
SALES (est): 13.8MM Privately Held
WEB: www.strangeengineering.net
SIC: 3714 Axles, motor vehicle; motor vehicle brake systems & parts; steering mechanisms, motor vehicle; drive shafts, motor vehicle

(G-14444)
SUCCESS JOURNAL CORP
Also Called: Harmony House
7848 Foster St (60053-1034)
PHONE.................................847 583-9000
Chris Witting, *President*
EMP: 5
SALES (est): 294.3K Privately Held
SIC: 2711 Newspapers, publishing & printing

(G-14445)
TOP ACE INC
8440 Callie Ave Unit 612 (60053-5014)
PHONE.................................847 581-0550
▲ EMP: 3 EST: 2007
SALES (est): 160K Privately Held
SIC: 2254 Knit Underwear Mill

(G-14446)
VERLO MAT OF SKOKIE-EVANSTON
Also Called: Verlo Mattress Factory
7927 Golf Rd (60053-1040)
PHONE.................................847 966-9988
Fax: 847 966-4221
EMP: 7
SQ FT: 6,000
SALES (est): 994.4K Privately Held
SIC: 5712 2515 Mfg Mattresses And Ret Bedding And Accessories

(G-14447)
W R TYPESETTING CO
Also Called: W.R. Typesetting Co.
8120 River Dr Ste 2 (60053-2613)
PHONE.................................847 966-8327
Bob Rubino, *President*
Maureen Rubino, *Corp Secy*
EMP: 14
SQ FT: 2,900
SALES (est): 1.1MM Privately Held
SIC: 2791 7374 Typesetting; service bureau, computer

(G-14448)
WATTCORE INC
6208 Oakton St (60053-2721)
PHONE.................................571 482-6777
Chanty Khek, *President*
◆ EMP: 8
SQ FT: 3,000
SALES (est): 708.6K Privately Held
WEB: www.wattcore.com
SIC: 3677 Electronic coils, transformers & other inductors

(G-14449)
WOCKHARDT HOLDING CORP
6451 Main St (60053-2633)
PHONE.................................847 967-5600
Kurt Orlofski, *President*
Olivia Ho, *Associate*
EMP: 301
SALES (est): 36.6MM Privately Held
SIC: 2834 Pharmaceutical preparations
HQ: Wockhardt Limited
    Wockhardt Towers, Bandra Kurla Complex,
    Mumbai MH 40005

(G-14450)
XYLEM INC
Bell & Gossett
8200 Austin Ave (60053-3205)
PHONE.................................847 966-3700
Hanibal Acosta, *Production*
Andrew Cheng, *Plant Engr*
John Williamson, *Branch Mgr*
Glenn Huse, *Manager*
Bob Lutz, *Manager*
EMP: 58 Publicly Held
SIC: 3561 Pumps & pumping equipment
PA: Xylem Inc.
    1 International Dr
    Rye Brook NY 10573

(G-14451)
XYLEM LNC
8200 Austin Ave (60053-3205)
PHONE.................................847 966-3700
EMP: 6
SALES (corp-wide): 2.8B Publicly Held
WEB: www.wedeco.com
SIC: 3621 3613 3674 3511 Motors & generators; switchgear & switchboard apparatus; semiconductors & related devices; turbines & turbine generator sets
HQ: Xylem Lnc
    4828 Prkwy Plz Blvd 200
    Charlotte NC 28217
    704 409-9700

Mossville
Peoria County

(G-14452)
CATERPILLAR INC
48 Cranbarry (61552)
P.O. Box 116 (61552-0116)
PHONE.................................309 578-2185
Gary Leonard, *General Mgr*
Abron Staci, *Buyer*
Daniel Hodgen, *QC Mgr*
Ken Roat, *Engineer*
Tim Alcenius, *Technical Staff*
EMP: 9
SALES (corp-wide): 53.8B Publicly Held
WEB: www.caterpillar.com
SIC: 3531 3519 3511 6153 Construction machinery; engines, diesel & semi-diesel or dual-fuel; gas turbine generator set units, complete; mercantile financing; accident insurance carriers; fire, marine & casualty insurance: stock
PA: Caterpillar Inc.
    510 Lake Cook Rd Ste 100
    Deerfield IL 60015
    224 551-4000

(G-14453)
CATERPILLAR INC
14009 Old Galena Rd (61552-7547)
P.O. Box 1875 (61552-0875)
PHONE.................................309 578-6118
David Cooper, *Research*
Nick Arya, *Engineer*
Mark Hawkins, *Engineer*
Christopher Robbins, *Engineer*
John Endsley, *Manager*
EMP: 59
SALES (corp-wide): 53.8B Publicly Held
WEB: www.caterpillar.com
SIC: 3531 3519 3511 6531 Construction machinery; engines, diesel & semi-diesel or dual-fuel; gasoline engines; gas turbine generator set units, complete; hydraulic turbine generator set units, complete; fiduciary, real estate; accident insurance carriers; fire, marine & casualty insurance: stock
PA: Caterpillar Inc.
    510 Lake Cook Rd Ste 100
    Deerfield IL 60015
    224 551-4000

(G-14454)
CATERPILLAR INC
1900 E Old Galena Rd (61552)
PHONE.................................309 266-4294
Gifford Parsons, *Branch Mgr*
EMP: 355
SALES (corp-wide): 53.8B Publicly Held
SIC: 3531 Construction machinery

PA: Caterpillar Inc.
    510 Lake Cook Rd Ste 100
    Deerfield IL 60015
    224 551-4000

(G-14455)
CATERPILLAR INC
14009 Old Galena Rd (61552-7523)
PHONE.................................903 712-4505
EMP: 330
SALES (corp-wide): 53.8B Publicly Held
SIC: 3531 Construction machinery
PA: Caterpillar Inc.
    510 Lake Cook Rd Ste 100
    Deerfield IL 60015
    224 551-4000

(G-14456)
CATERPILLAR INC
Old Galena Rd Ste H (61552)
P.O. Box 4000 (61552-4000)
PHONE.................................309 578-2473
Mark Pflederer, *Principal*
EMP: 700
SALES (corp-wide): 53.8B Publicly Held
SIC: 3531 3429 3052 Construction machinery; manufactured hardware (general); rubber & plastics hose & beltings
PA: Caterpillar Inc.
    510 Lake Cook Rd Ste 100
    Deerfield IL 60015
    224 551-4000

(G-14457)
CATERPILLAR INC
14009 Old Galena Rd (61552-7547)
PHONE.................................309 675-1000
Dan Dunn, *Engineer*
Dan Henderson, *Engineer*
Paul Murphy, *Engineer*
Greg Stuckey, *Engineer*
Kenneth Rose, *Manager*
EMP: 437
SALES (corp-wide): 53.8B Publicly Held
SIC: 3531 Construction machinery
PA: Caterpillar Inc.
    510 Lake Cook Rd Ste 100
    Deerfield IL 60015
    224 551-4000

(G-14458)
CATERPILLAR INC
Illinois Rte 29 (61552)
P.O. Box 610 (61552-6100)
PHONE.................................309 675-6223
Mark Pflederer, *Branch Mgr*
EMP: 764
SALES (corp-wide): 53.8B Publicly Held
SIC: 1081 Metal mining services
PA: Caterpillar Inc.
    510 Lake Cook Rd Ste 100
    Deerfield IL 60015
    224 551-4000

(G-14459)
CATERPILLAR INC
Ac 6123 (61552)
P.O. Box 610 (61552-6100)
PHONE.................................309 578-1615
Dan Murphy, *Branch Mgr*
EMP: 1500
SALES (corp-wide): 53.8B Publicly Held
SIC: 3519 3511 3531 Engines, diesel & semi-diesel or dual-fuel; gasoline engines; gas turbine generator set units, complete; hydraulic turbine generator set units, complete; tractors, crawler
PA: Caterpillar Inc.
    510 Lake Cook Rd Ste 100
    Deerfield IL 60015
    224 551-4000

(G-14460)
KENNAMETAL INC
Olglena Rd (61552)
P.O. Box 610 (61552-6100)
PHONE.................................309 578-1888
Cat C Oltman, *Manager*
EMP: 14
SALES (corp-wide): 2.3B Publicly Held
WEB: www.kennametal.com
SIC: 3545 Cutting tools for machine tools
PA: Kennametal Inc.
    525 William Penn Pl # 3300
    Pittsburgh PA 15219
    412 248-8000

(G-14461)
PERKINS ENGINES INC (DH)
N4 Ac6160 # 6160 (61552)
P.O. Box 610 (61552-6100)
PHONE.................................309 578-7364
Frank Perkins, *Principal*
David Hollings, *Marketing Staff*
Laurie J Huxtable, *Admin Sec*
◆ EMP: 50 EST: 1932
SALES (est): 6MM
SALES (corp-wide): 751.7K Privately Held
SIC: 3519 Internal combustion engines
HQ: Perkins Engines Company Limited
    Frank Perkins Way
    Peterborough CAMBS PE1 5
    173 358-3000

(G-14462)
WHITE WHALE LLC
10639 State St (61552-7502)
P.O. Box 438 (61552-0438)
PHONE.................................309 303-0028
Dennis Owens, *Mng Member*
Frank Lovich,
EMP: 2
SALES: 700K Privately Held
SIC: 3949 Fishing equipment; hunting equipment

Mounds
Pulaski County

(G-14463)
OIL-DRI CORPORATION AMERICA
700 Industrial Park Rd (62964-2153)
P.O. Box 460 (62964-0460)
PHONE.................................618 745-6881
Wayne Gibson, *Manager*
James Warden, *Maintence Staff*
EMP: 88
SALES (corp-wide): 277MM Publicly Held
SIC: 1459 3295 2842 Clays, except kaolin & ball; minerals, ground or treated; specialty cleaning, polishes & sanitation goods
PA: Oil-Dri Corporation Of America
    410 N Michigan Ave # 400
    Chicago IL 60611
    312 321-1515

Mount Auburn
Christian County

(G-14464)
ARCHER-DANIELS-MIDLAND COMPANY
Also Called: ADM
503 S Auger St (62547)
P.O. Box 230 (62547-0230)
PHONE.................................217 676-3811
Jeff Gottman, *Manager*
EMP: 4
SALES (corp-wide): 64.6B Publicly Held
SIC: 2041 Flour & other grain mill products
PA: Archer-Daniels-Midland Company
    77 W Wacker Dr Ste 4600
    Chicago IL 60601
    312 634-8100

Mount Carmel
Wabash County

(G-14465)
B & D INDEPENDENCE INC
1024 Empire St (62863-5101)
PHONE.................................618 262-7117
John Evans, *President*
EMP: 20 EST: 1980
SQ FT: 20,000
SALES (est): 3.8MM Privately Held
SIC: 3842 3444 Wheelchairs; sheet metalwork

Mount Carmel - Wabash County (G-14466)

(G-14466)
B & G MACHINE INC
421 W 9th St (62863-1366)
PHONE..................618 262-2269
Greg Odom, *President*
Brady Cox, *Corp Secy*
EMP: 8
SQ FT: 4,800
SALES (est): 2.1MM **Privately Held**
SIC: 3599 Machine shop, jobbing & repair

(G-14467)
CEG SUBSIDIARY LLC (PA)
Also Called: Pacific Press Technologies
714 N Walnut St (62863-1466)
PHONE..................618 262-8666
Brian Evans, *Plant Mgr*
Clay Leek, *Production*
Chris Robinson, *Sales Mgr*
Andrea Nelson, *Mng Member*
Kay McCandless,
▲ EMP: 77
SQ FT: 150,000
SALES (est): 17MM **Privately Held**
SIC: 3542 Press brakes; presses: forming, stamping, punching, sizing (machine tools); shearing machines, power

(G-14468)
CEG SUBSIDIARY LLC
714 N Walnut St (62863-1466)
PHONE..................618 262-8666
Tim Johnson, *President*
David Strothers, *Principal*
EMP: 7
SALES (est): 793.6K **Privately Held**
SIC: 2741 Miscellaneous publishing

(G-14469)
CORWIN PRINTING
1004 Landes St (62863-1345)
PHONE..................618 263-3936
Kyle Day, *Owner*
Connie Day, *Owner*
EMP: 3
SQ FT: 2,450
SALES: 160K **Privately Held**
SIC: 2752 2791 2759 Commercial printing, offset; typesetting; commercial printing

(G-14470)
DEE DRILLING CO (PA)
431 N Market St (62863-1526)
P.O. Box 7 (62863-0007)
PHONE..................618 262-4136
J Roy Dee III, *President*
Jean Dee Fischer, *Treasurer*
EMP: 30 EST: 1949
SALES (est): 7.9MM **Privately Held**
WEB: www.wabashcountychamber.com
SIC: 1381 Drilling oil & gas wells

(G-14471)
HAGGARD WELL SERVICES INC
710 Poplar St (62863-1413)
P.O. Box 1056 (62863-1056)
PHONE..................618 262-5060
Barry Haggard, *President*
EMP: 6
SALES: 500K **Privately Held**
SIC: 1389 Haulage, oil field

(G-14472)
HOCKING OIL COMPANY INC
123 W 4th St Ste 103 (62863-1562)
P.O. Box 162 (62863-0162)
PHONE..................618 263-3258
Andy G Hocking, *President*
Patsy Hocking, *Vice Pres*
Andrea M Richardson, *Admin Sec*
EMP: 3
SQ FT: 3,000
SALES (est): 360K **Privately Held**
SIC: 1311 Crude petroleum production

(G-14473)
HOWARD ENERGY CORPORATION
519 W 3rd St (62863-1752)
P.O. Box 693 (62863-0693)
PHONE..................618 263-3000
Craig J Howard, *President*
Margaret Howard, *Admin Sec*
EMP: 3
SQ FT: 2,800
SALES: 300K **Privately Held**
SIC: 1382 1311 1389 Geological exploration, oil & gas field; crude petroleum production; oil consultants

(G-14474)
J & J QUALITY PALLETS INC
226 W 11th St (62863-1407)
PHONE..................618 262-6426
John Burton, *President*
EMP: 5
SALES (est): 236.7K **Privately Held**
SIC: 2448 Wood pallets & skids

(G-14475)
JACKSON OIL CORPORATION
809 W 9th St (62863-2414)
P.O. Box 95 (62863-0095)
PHONE..................618 263-6521
Fred Jackson, *President*
EMP: 3
SQ FT: 7,200
SALES: 200K **Privately Held**
SIC: 1381 5084 Directional drilling oil & gas wells; oil well machinery, equipment & supplies

(G-14476)
KEEPES FUNERAL HOME INC
1500 N Cherry St (62863-1879)
PHONE..................618 262-5200
Shaun Keepes, *President*
EMP: 10
SALES: 100K **Privately Held**
WEB: www.keepesfuneralhome.com
SIC: 7261 3281 Funeral home; monument or burial stone, cut & shaped

(G-14477)
LAWRENCE OIL COMPANY INC
801 W 9th St Rm 208 (62863-2446)
P.O. Box 251 (62863-0251)
PHONE..................618 262-4138
EMP: 5
SQ FT: 300
SALES (est): 540K **Privately Held**
SIC: 1311 Crude Oil Production

(G-14478)
M & S OIL WELL CEMENTING CO (PA)
Hwy 1 N (62863)
P.O. Box 344 (62863-0344)
PHONE..................618 262-7962
John D Morgan, *CEO*
Jeff Morgan, *President*
Teri Ewald, *Corp Secy*
Branda Morgan, *Corp Secy*
Patrick Morgan, *Vice Pres*
EMP: 3 EST: 1949
SQ FT: 5,000
SALES: 720K **Privately Held**
SIC: 1389 Oil field services

(G-14479)
MILLER TESTING SERVICE
1125 W 3rd St (62863)
P.O. Box 661 (62863-0661)
PHONE..................618 262-5911
Tim Schuler, *Owner*
EMP: 20
SQ FT: 4,000
SALES (est): 903.7K **Privately Held**
SIC: 1389 Testing, measuring, surveying & analysis services; oil field services

(G-14480)
MT CARMEL MACHINE SHOP INC
10011 N 1250th Blvd (62863)
P.O. Box 848 (62863-0848)
PHONE..................618 262-4591
David M Partee, *President*
Stephen F Partee, *Vice Pres*
David Partee, *Finance*
EMP: 14 EST: 1931
SQ FT: 6,000
SALES (est): 2.1MM **Privately Held**
WEB: www.bgmachine.net
SIC: 3599 3443 Machine shop, jobbing & repair; tanks, lined: metal plate

(G-14481)
MT CARMEL REGISTER CO INC
Also Called: Daily Republican Register
117 E 4th St (62863-2110)
P.O. Box 550 (62863-0550)
PHONE..................618 262-5144
Bill Brehm, *President*
Grant Essenmacher, *Editor*
A Philip Tofani, *Vice Pres*
EMP: 20
SQ FT: 10,000
SALES (est): 983.1K
SALES (corp-wide): 184MM **Privately Held**
WEB: www.mtcarmelregister.com
SIC: 2711 2752 Newspapers, publishing & printing; commercial printing, offset
PA: Brehm Communications, Inc.
16644 W Bernardo Dr # 300
San Diego CA 92127
858 451-6200

(G-14482)
MT CRMEL STBLZATION GROUP INC (PA)
1611 College Dr (62863-2614)
P.O. Box 458 (62863-0458)
PHONE..................618 262-5118
Mike McPherson, *President*
Greg Acree, *Superintendent*
Phil Hipsher, *Corp Secy*
Jack Fowler, *Counsel*
Doug McPherson, *Exec VP*
EMP: 30
SQ FT: 7,200
SALES: 106.7MM **Privately Held**
WEB: www.mtcsg.com
SIC: 1611 3273 General contractor, highway & street construction; ready-mixed concrete

(G-14483)
NEW TRIANGLE OIL COMPANY
Also Called: Southern Triangle Oil Co
600 Chestnut St (62863-1453)
P.O. Box 427 (62863-0427)
PHONE..................618 262-4131
Lester D Moore, *Partner*
EMP: 2 EST: 1955
SQ FT: 1,500
SALES (est): 3MM **Privately Held**
SIC: 1311 Crude petroleum production

(G-14484)
OMNI MATERIALS INC
1611 College Dr (62863-2614)
P.O. Box 458 (62863-0458)
PHONE..................618 262-5118
Michael McPherson, *President*
Phil Hipsher, *Corp Secy*
Doug McPherson, *Exec VP*
Neil Ryan, *Vice Pres*
EMP: 20 EST: 1999
SALES: 36.2MM **Privately Held**
SIC: 1422 Crushed & broken limestone

(G-14485)
PPT INDUSTRIAL MACHINES INC
Also Called: Pacific Press
714 N Walnut St (62863-1466)
PHONE..................800 851-3586
Richard Drexler, *CEO*
David A Somers, *President*
TAC D Kensler, *Admin Sec*
EMP: 50
SALES (est): 8.2MM
SALES (corp-wide): 24MM **Privately Held**
SIC: 3542 3541 Machine tools, metal forming type; machine tools, metal cutting type
PA: Quality Products, Inc.
1 Air Cargo Pkwy E
Swanton OH 43558
614 228-0185

(G-14486)
SOUTHERN TRIANGLE OIL COMPANY
600 Chestnut St (62863-1453)
P.O. Box 427 (62863-0427)
PHONE..................618 262-4131
Lester D Moore, *President*
Charley Campbell, *Treasurer*
Lynette Wiles, *Admin Sec*
EMP: 14 EST: 1957
SQ FT: 2,000
SALES: 1.7MM **Privately Held**
SIC: 1311 1381 Crude petroleum production; directional drilling oil & gas wells

(G-14487)
SPARTAN PETROLEUM COMPANY
328 N Market St (62863-1519)
P.O. Box 70 (62863-0070)
PHONE..................618 262-4197
James Capin, *President*
Carolyn Burwer, *Manager*
EMP: 2
SQ FT: 800
SALES (est): 235.9K **Privately Held**
SIC: 1381 1311 Drilling oil & gas wells; crude petroleum production

(G-14488)
TRANSCEDAR LIMITED
916 Empire St (62863-5102)
P.O. Box 667 (62863-0667)
PHONE..................618 262-4153
Mordi Fishman, *Principal*
Dan Young, *Vice Pres*
▲ EMP: 26
SALES (est): 4.1MM **Privately Held**
WEB: www.fishman-tt.com
SIC: 3599 3714 5531 Flexible metal hose, tubing & bellows; thermostats, motor vehicle; automotive parts

(G-14489)
TRI KOTE INC
1126 W 3rd St (62863)
P.O. Box 661 (62863-0661)
PHONE..................618 262-4156
Tim Schuler, *President*
EMP: 7 EST: 1965
SALES (est): 300K **Privately Held**
SIC: 1389 Oil field services

(G-14490)
VIGO COAL OPERATING CO INC
7790 Highway 15 (62863-4517)
PHONE..................618 262-7022
Ron Will, *Manager*
EMP: 5
SALES (est): 359.2K
SALES (corp-wide): 44.5MM **Privately Held**
SIC: 1481 6211 Nonmetallic mineral services; oil & gas lease brokers
PA: Vigo Coal Operating Co., Inc.
250 N Cross Pointe Blvd
Evansville IN 47715
812 759-8446

(G-14491)
WABASH CONTAINER CORPORATION
1015 W 9th St (62863-2437)
P.O. Box 127 (62863-0127)
PHONE..................618 263-3586
Steve Burton, *President*
Jack Fowler, *Admin Sec*
EMP: 30
SQ FT: 2,000
SALES (est): 8MM **Privately Held**
SIC: 2653 Boxes, corrugated: made from purchased materials

(G-14492)
WHITE LAND & MINERAL INC
526 N Market St (62863-1558)
P.O. Box 308 (62863-0308)
PHONE..................618 262-5102
Shad White, *President*
Clint White, *Corp Secy*
EMP: 6
SQ FT: 2,000
SALES (est): 1.5MM **Privately Held**
SIC: 1311 0191 Crude petroleum production; general farms, primarily crop

(G-14493)
ZANETIS OIL COMPANY
319 E 8th St (62863-2014)
P.O. Box 1026 (62863-1026)
PHONE..................618 262-4593
Chris Zanetis, *Manager*
EMP: 4

SALES (est): 362.9K **Privately Held**
SIC: 1311 Crude petroleum & natural gas

Mount Carroll
Carroll County

(G-14494)
CHARLES ELECTRONICS LLC
Also Called: Maco Antennas
302 S East St (61053-1448)
PHONE.................................815 244-7981
Thomas Charles, *Mng Member*
EMP: 6
SQ FT: 4,400
SALES (est): 483.1K **Privately Held**
SIC: 3663 Antennas, transmitting & communications

(G-14495)
METFORM LLC
Metform Machined Components
905 S Jackson St (61053-9764)
P.O. Box A, Savanna (61074-0501)
PHONE.................................815 273-2201
Robert Whitney, *Branch Mgr*
EMP: 20
SALES (corp-wide): 1.2B **Privately Held**
SIC: 3452 Bolts, metal
HQ: Metform, L.L.C.
    1000 Allanson Rd
    Mundelein IL 60060
    847 566-0010

(G-14496)
MIRROR-DEMOCRAT
Also Called: Savanna Times-Journal
308 N Main St (61053-1024)
P.O. Box 191 (61053-0191)
PHONE.................................815 244-2411
Robert Watson, *Owner*
Bob Watson, *Owner*
EMP: 8
SQ FT: 12,000
SALES (est): 412.4K **Privately Held**
SIC: 2711 Newspapers, publishing & printing

(G-14497)
TEAM PRODUCTS INC
636 S East St (61053-1459)
PHONE.................................815 244-6100
David R Johnston, *President*
Patti Shepard, *Office Mgr*
▲ EMP: 14
SALES (est): 2.1MM **Privately Held**
WEB: www.teamproductsinc.com
SIC: 3069 Bags, rubber or rubberized fabric

Mount Erie
Wayne County

(G-14498)
UNION DRAINAGE DISTRICT
Rr 1 (62446)
PHONE.................................618 445-2843
Robert Anniss, *Chairman*
EMP: 3
SALES: 72.1K **Privately Held**
SIC: 2843 Surface active agents

Mount Morris
Ogle County

(G-14499)
CUSTOM SEAL & RUBBER PRODUCTS
112 E Hitt St (61054-1220)
PHONE.................................888 356-2966
Brenda Getzendaner, *CEO*
Michael L Getzendaner, *President*
▼ EMP: 8
SQ FT: 8,500
SALES: 500K **Privately Held**
SIC: 3069 3061 2822 Molded rubber products; mechanical rubber goods; synthetic rubber

(G-14500)
QUAD/GRAPHICS INC
404 N Wesley Ave (61054-1199)
PHONE.................................815 734-4121
Jim Hayes, *Opers Mgr*
Troy Hendrickson, *Engineer*
Elena Palchikova, *Accounting Dir*
Lori Kaplan, *CPA*
Hall Bruce, *Accounts Mgr*
EMP: 509
SALES (corp-wide): 3.9B **Publicly Held**
WEB: www.qg.com
SIC: 2754 2752 2789 2759 Commercial printing, gravure; commercial printing, lithographic; bookbinding & related work; commercial printing; book printing
PA: Quad/Graphics Inc.
    N61w23044 Harrys Way
    Sussex WI 53089
    414 566-6000

(G-14501)
RESEARCH AND TESTING WORX INC
Also Called: Rat Worx
112 E Hitt St (61054-1220)
PHONE.................................815 734-7346
William H McKay III, *President*
EMP: 5
SALES (est): 660.9K **Privately Held**
WEB: www.ratworxusa.com
SIC: 7389 3592 3599 Inspection & testing services; valves; machine & other job shop work

(G-14502)
SPECTRUM PREFERRED MEATS INC
6194 W Pines Rd (61054-9755)
PHONE.................................815 946-3816
Kevin Rude, *President*
EMP: 60
SQ FT: 10,000
SALES (est): 10.9MM **Privately Held**
SIC: 2011 Meat packing plants

Mount Olive
Macoupin County

(G-14503)
GEORGIA-PACIFIC LLC
900 S Old Route 66 (62069-1559)
P.O. Box 100 (62069-0100)
PHONE.................................217 999-2511
Mike Augustine, *Branch Mgr*
EMP: 146
SALES (corp-wide): 48.9B **Privately Held**
SIC: 2653 5113 Boxes, corrugated: made from purchased materials; corrugated & solid fiber boxes
HQ: Georgia-Pacific Llc
    133 Peachtree St Nw
    Atlanta GA 30303
    404 652-4000

(G-14504)
HERALD MOUNT OLIVE
Also Called: Journal Fabrication
102 E Main St (62069-1702)
PHONE.................................217 999-3941
John Galer, *Owner*
EMP: 4
SALES (est): 176.8K **Privately Held**
SIC: 2711 Newspapers, publishing & printing

(G-14505)
IDEAL FABRICATORS INC
621 S Main St (62069-2712)
PHONE.................................217 999-7017
Mark Subick, *President*
Steve Subick, *Vice Pres*
EMP: 12 EST: 1965
SQ FT: 900
SALES (est): 1.8MM **Privately Held**
WEB: www.idealrolloffs.com
SIC: 3443 3441 3411 Trash racks, metal plate; fabricated structural metal; metal cans

(G-14506)
MENNEL MILLING CO
415 E Main St (62069-1709)
P.O. Box 255 (62069-0255)
PHONE.................................217 999-2161
Donald L Mennel, *President*
EMP: 12
SALES (est): 4MM
SALES (corp-wide): 158.7MM **Privately Held**
WEB: www.mennel.com
SIC: 2041 Wheat flour
PA: The Mennel Milling Company
    319 S Vine St
    Fostoria OH 44830
    419 435-8151

(G-14507)
NBS SYSTEMS INC (PA)
1000 S Old Route 66 (62069-1560)
PHONE.................................217 999-3472
Bill Gascon, *President*
Christy Bessemer, *Opers Mgr*
Gina Henrichs, *Accounts Mgr*
EMP: 35
SQ FT: 26,000
SALES (est): 6.8MM **Privately Held**
WEB: www.nbschecks.com
SIC: 2761 2759 Continuous forms, office & business; commercial printing

(G-14508)
RSB FUELS INC
701 W Main St (62069-1554)
PHONE.................................217 999-4409
Hardeep Bhalla, *Owner*
EMP: 5
SALES (est): 430.3K **Privately Held**
SIC: 2869 Fuels

Mount Prospect
Cook County

(G-14509)
ADVERTISING PREMIUMS INC
Also Called: Steakhouse Premium
800 W Central Rd Ste 162 (60056-6512)
PHONE.................................888 364-9710
Charles Feldman, *President*
Steven Goldstern, *Vice Pres*
EMP: 5
SQ FT: 2,500
SALES (est): 500K **Privately Held**
SIC: 5147 5961 3993 Meats & meat products; food, mail order; signs & advertising specialties

(G-14510)
ADVOCATE PRINT SHOP
799 Biermann Ct Ste 110 (60056-6059)
PHONE.................................847 390-3594
Jim Samp, *Superintendent*
EMP: 34 EST: 1975
SQ FT: 60,000
SALES (est): 12.4MM **Privately Held**
SIC: 2732 Book printing

(G-14511)
ALDEN & OTT PRINTING INKS CO
2050 S Carboy Rd (60056-5750)
PHONE.................................847 364-6817
Keith Elumann, *Branch Mgr*
EMP: 10
SALES (corp-wide): 355.8K **Privately Held**
SIC: 2893 Printing ink
HQ: Alden & Ott Printing Inks Co.
    616 E Brook Dr
    Arlington Heights IL 60005
    847 956-6830

(G-14512)
ATLAS MATERIAL TSTG TECH LLC (HQ)
Also Called: South Florida Test Service Div
1500 Bishop Ct (60056-6039)
PHONE.................................773 327-4520
Joergen Olsson, *President*
Scott Irvin, *Opers Staff*
Carter Greene, *Natl Sales Mgr*
Sarith Ven, *Director*
▲ EMP: 150 EST: 1917
SQ FT: 75,000
SALES: 123.4MM
SALES (corp-wide): 5.1B **Publicly Held**
WEB: www.atlas-mts.com
SIC: 3823 3569 3599 8734 Temperature measurement instruments, industrial; testing chambers for altitude, temperature, ordnance, power; machine shop, jobbing & repair; product testing laboratory, safety or performance; instruments to measure electricity; laboratory apparatus & furniture
PA: Ametek, Inc.
    1100 Cassatt Rd
    Berwyn PA 19312
    610 647-2121

(G-14513)
AVERY DENNISON CORPORATION
902 Feehanville Dr (60056-6003)
PHONE.................................847 824-7450
Carlos Hernandez, *Production*
Eric Shafer, *Branch Mgr*
Christina Finn, *Admin Sec*
EMP: 115
SALES (corp-wide): 7B **Publicly Held**
SIC: 2672 Coated paper, except photographic, carbon or abrasive
PA: Avery Dennison Corporation
    207 N Goode Ave
    Glendale CA 91203
    626 304-2000

(G-14514)
BRAUN MANUFACTURING CO INC
1350 Feehanville Dr (60056-6021)
PHONE.................................847 635-2050
Charles R Braun, *President*
Gloria Vasquez, *COO*
Michael J Braun, *Admin Sec*
Mike Braun, *Administration*
EMP: 30 EST: 1925
SQ FT: 62,000
SALES (est): 5.8MM **Privately Held**
WEB: www.hinge1.com
SIC: 3429 3469 Builders' hardware; stamping metal for the trade

(G-14515)
BREX-ARLINGTON INCORPORATED
800 W Central Rd Ste 101n (60056-2384)
PHONE.................................847 255-6284
Richard Brex, *President*
Tom Zolandek, *Vice Pres*
EMP: 15
SALES (est): 2.2MM **Privately Held**
SIC: 1711 3444 Warm air heating & air conditioning contractor; sheet metalwork

(G-14516)
C BECKY & COMPANY INC
Also Called: Crash Candles
708 S Na Wa Ta Ave (60056-3608)
PHONE.................................847 818-1021
Becky Corzilius, *President*
Robert Clauss, *Admin Sec*
EMP: 2
SQ FT: 1,300
SALES (est): 317.4K **Privately Held**
SIC: 5199 5112 3999 Gifts & novelties; greeting cards; candles

(G-14517)
C LINE PRODUCTS INC (PA)
1100 E Business Center Dr (60056-6053)
PHONE.................................847 827-6661
James E Krumwiede, *Ch of Bd*
Skip Robertson, *Exec VP*
Thomas E Robertson, *Exec VP*
Jennifer Krach, *Vice Pres*
Judi Krumwiede, *Vice Pres*
▲ EMP: 69
SQ FT: 108,000
SALES (est): 11.7MM **Privately Held**
WEB: www.c-lineproducts.com
SIC: 3089 3083 Holders: paper towel, grocery bag, etc.: plastic; laminated plastics plate & sheet

Mount Prospect - Cook County (G-14518)

(G-14518)
CABINETS CITY
1650 W Algonquin Rd (60056-5500)
PHONE..............847 440-3371
EMP: 2
SALES (est): 220.9K **Privately Held**
WEB: www.cabinetcity.com
SIC: 2434 Wood kitchen cabinets

(G-14519)
CONCEPT AND DESIGN SERVICES
807 S Golfview Pl (60056-4330)
PHONE..............847 259-1675
John S Glinka, *President*
EMP: 5
SALES (est): 698.8K **Privately Held**
SIC: 3569 8711 Assembly machines, non-metalworking; professional engineer; consulting engineer

(G-14520)
CONCEPTS MAGNET
515 S Edward St (60056-3909)
PHONE..............847 253-3351
EMP: 3 EST: 2012
SALES (est): 153K **Privately Held**
SIC: 7389 3993 Business Services Mfg Signs/Advertising Specialties

(G-14521)
CUMMINS - ALLISON CORP
891 Feehanville Dr (60056-6098)
PHONE..............847 299-9550
William J Jones, *Branch Mgr*
EMP: 64
SALES (corp-wide): 3.2B **Publicly Held**
SIC: 3579 3519 Perforators (office machines); paper cutters, trimmers & punches; check writing, endorsing or signing machines; internal combustion engines
HQ: Cummins-Allison Corp.
    852 Feehanville Dr
    Mount Prospect IL 60056
    800 786-5528

(G-14522)
CUMMINS - ALLISON CORP
851 Feehanville Dr (60056-6002)
PHONE..............847 299-9550
Douglas Mennie, *President*
EMP: 200
SALES (corp-wide): 3.2B **Publicly Held**
SIC: 3579 3519 Perforators (office machines); internal combustion engines
HQ: Cummins-Allison Corp.
    852 Feehanville Dr
    Mount Prospect IL 60056
    800 786-5528

(G-14523)
CUMMINS-ALLISON CORP (DH)
Also Called: Cummins Allison
852 Feehanville Dr (60056-6001)
P.O. Box 339 (60056-0339)
PHONE..............800 786-5528
Jan Hinrick Bauwe, *President*
John E Jones, *Chairman*
James Stearns, *Exec VP*
Tim Minor, *Senior VP*
Raymond Sherwood, *CFO*
◆ EMP: 350 EST: 1887
SQ FT: 110,000
SALES (est): 315.9MM
SALES (corp-wide): 3.2B **Publicly Held**
WEB: www.cumminsallison.com
SIC: 3578 3519 Automatic teller machines (ATM); internal combustion engines

(G-14524)
CUMMINS-AMERICAN CORP
852 Feehanville Dr (60056-6001)
PHONE..............847 299-9550
John E Jones, *CEO*
John Diedrich, *CFO*
EMP: 2 EST: 1957
SALES (est): 318.4K **Privately Held**
WEB: www.cumminsallison.com
SIC: 6163 3519 Mortgage brokers arranging for loans, using money of others; internal combustion engines

(G-14525)
CUSTOM MOLD SERVICES INC
1605 W Algonquin Rd (60056-5503)
PHONE..............847 364-6589
Ron Jackson, *President*
Janusz Majdzik, *Business Mgr*
EMP: 17
SALES (est): 3.2MM **Privately Held**
SIC: 3544 Special dies & tools

(G-14526)
ENGINEERED PLASTIC PDTS CORP
1848 S Elmhurst Rd (60056-5711)
PHONE..............847 952-8400
Alexander M Curtiss, *President*
Joe Pilolla, *Opers Mgr*
Pam Lechner, *Purch Agent*
Charles L Michod Jr, *Admin Sec*
EMP: 20 EST: 1976
SQ FT: 6,500
SALES (est): 4.6MM **Privately Held**
SIC: 3451 5162 3089 Screw machine products; plastics sheets & rods; plastic processing

(G-14527)
F & S ENGRAVING INC
1620 W Central Rd (60056-2269)
PHONE..............847 870-8400
James C Fromm, *President*
Clifford Fromm, *Chairman*
Scott Fromm, *Vice Pres*
Jerry Fontaine, *Engineer*
Dan Fromm, *Sales Staff*
EMP: 29 EST: 1922
SQ FT: 21,000
SALES (est): 5.6MM **Privately Held**
WEB: www.fandsengraving.com
SIC: 3544 2759 3556 Dies, steel rule; industrial molds; commercial printing; cracker making machines

(G-14528)
FEDEX OFFICE & PRINT SVCS INC
1 W Rand Rd Ste F (60056-1137)
PHONE..............847 670-7283
EMP: 4
SALES (corp-wide): 69.6B **Publicly Held**
SIC: 2759 7334 5099 Commercial printing; photocopying & duplicating services; signs, except electric
HQ: Fedex Office And Print Services, Inc.
    7900 Legacy Dr
    Plano TX 75024
    800 463-3339

(G-14529)
FIRST ELEMENT SOLUTIONS
505 S Henry St (60056-2426)
PHONE..............847 691-8381
Robert Sanger, *Principal*
EMP: 3 EST: 2018
SALES (est): 166.8K **Privately Held**
SIC: 2819 Elements

(G-14530)
GAM ENTERPRISES INC
901 E Business Center Dr (60056-2181)
PHONE..............847 649-2500
Gary A Michalek, *CEO*
Craig Van Den Avont, *President*
Rebecca K Michalek, *Admin Sec*
EMP: 20
SQ FT: 8,000
SALES (est): 5.3MM **Privately Held**
SIC: 3566 Reduction gears & gear units for turbines, except automotive

(G-14531)
GOOD EARTH LIGHTING INC
Also Called: Eco-Light
1400 E Business Center Dr # 108 (60056-6071)
PHONE..............847 808-1133
Marvin J Feig, *President*
Susan A Febles, *Principal*
Margaret M Hetzer, *Vice Pres*
Alexander Kowalenko, *Vice Pres*
Susan Gomez, *Supervisor*
▲ EMP: 23
SQ FT: 8,400
SALES (est): 9.3MM **Privately Held**
SIC: 5063 3648 Lighting fixtures; lighting equipment

(G-14532)
GROVAK INSTANT PRINTING CO
Also Called: Super Press Instant Prtg Co
701 S Meier Rd (60056-3546)
PHONE..............847 675-2414
Jeff Grovak, *Exec VP*
June Grovak, *Vice Pres*
EMP: 7 EST: 1971
SQ FT: 2,000
SALES: 1.1MM **Privately Held**
SIC: 2752 2789 Commercial printing, offset; bookbinding & related work

(G-14533)
HOBSOURCE
834 E Rand Rd Ste 2 (60056-2569)
PHONE..............847 229-9120
Andrea Mazur, *Manager*
Vladimir Polevoy, *Exec Dir*
EMP: 2
SALES (est): 243.6K **Privately Held**
SIC: 3541 Machine tools, metal cutting type

(G-14534)
INDIGO TIME
800 W Central Rd Ste 162 (60056-6512)
PHONE..............847 255-4818
Dean Resnekov, *Owner*
EMP: 6
SALES (est): 629.1K **Privately Held**
SIC: 3873 Watches, clocks, watchcases & parts

(G-14535)
INNOVATIVE HESS PRODUCTS LLC
Also Called: Milmour Products
1407 S Cypress Dr (60056-5005)
PHONE..............847 676-3260
Kevin Hess, *Mng Member*
▲ EMP: 406
SALES (est): 45.3MM **Privately Held**
SIC: 2821 Plastics materials & resins

(G-14536)
INTEL EAST
660 W Pickwick Ct Apt 1w (60056-5315)
PHONE..............312 725-2014
EMP: 3 EST: 2012
SALES (est): 185.3K **Privately Held**
SIC: 3674 Mfg Semiconductors/Related Devices

(G-14537)
INTER-CONTINENTAL TRDG USA INC
1601 W Algonquin Rd (60056-5503)
PHONE..............847 640-1777
Shrujal Patel, *President*
Rekha Shah, *Accountant*
◆ EMP: 80
SQ FT: 20,000
SALES (est): 6.4MM **Privately Held**
SIC: 2131 Chewing & smoking tobacco

(G-14538)
J & J INDUSTRIES INC
708 S Edgewood Ln (60056-3645)
PHONE..............630 595-8878
Jerry A Haug, *President*
Melanie Haug, *Admin Sec*
EMP: 8
SALES: 500K **Privately Held**
SIC: 3053 2891 3296 Gaskets, packing & sealing devices; adhesives & sealants; mineral wool

(G-14539)
JENCO METAL PRODUCTS INC
1690 W Imperial Ct (60056-5574)
PHONE..............847 956-0550
Gregory D Jensen, *President*
Mark D Jensen, *Corp Secy*
EMP: 12 EST: 1954
SQ FT: 16,000
SALES (est): 2.2MM **Privately Held**
WEB: www.jencomanufacturingsolutions.com
SIC: 3544 3469 3496 Die sets for metal stamping (presses); stamping metal for the trade; wire winding

(G-14540)
JINGDIAO NORTH AMERICA INC
Also Called: Beijing Jingdiao Group
1400 E Bus Ctr Dr Ste 103 (60056)
PHONE..............847 906-8888
EMP: 11
SALES (est): 1.3MM
SALES (corp-wide): 77.1MM **Privately Held**
SIC: 3599 7699 Air intake filters, internal combustion engine, except auto; industrial machinery & equipment repair
PA: Beijing Jingdiao Group Co., Ltd.
    No.10, Yong'an Rd., Shilong Industrial Zone, Mentougou District
    Beijing 10230
    106 080-1188

(G-14541)
KEANE INC
1697 W Imperial Ct (60056-5554)
PHONE..............847 952-9700
EMP: 12
SALES (est): 439.8K **Privately Held**
SIC: 2752 7389 Commercial printing, lithographic; courier or messenger service

(G-14542)
KEEBOMED INC
832 E Rand Rd Ste 22 (60056-2568)
PHONE..............630 888-2888
Stojan Bozinovski, *President*
Deborah Bozinovska, *Vice Pres*
EMP: 5
SALES (est): 355.7K **Privately Held**
WEB: www.keebomed.com
SIC: 3845 Ultrasonic medical equipment, except cleaning

(G-14543)
KOREA TRIBUNE INC
1699 Wall St Ste 200k (60056-5781)
PHONE..............847 956-9101
EMP: 3 EST: 2016
SALES (est): 92.2K **Privately Held**
SIC: 2711 Newspapers, publishing & printing

(G-14544)
LUTHERAN GENERAL PRINTING SVCS
799 Biermann Ct Ste 130 (60056-6059)
PHONE..............847 298-8040
James Skogsbergh, *Principal*
EMP: 4
SALES (est): 377K **Privately Held**
SIC: 2752 Commercial printing, lithographic

(G-14545)
MAILBOX PLUS
1516 N Elmhurst Rd (60056-1011)
PHONE..............847 577-1737
Donna Wolf, *Owner*
EMP: 3
SQ FT: 1,000
SALES (est): 224.4K **Privately Held**
SIC: 3086 Packaging & shipping materials, foamed plastic

(G-14546)
MARCRES MANUFACTURING INC
Also Called: Marcres Metal Works
600 W Carboy Rd (60056-5763)
PHONE..............847 439-1808
Marlene Palmer, *President*
EMP: 25
SQ FT: 22,500
SALES (est): 3MM **Privately Held**
SIC: 3444 Sheet metal specialties, not stamped

(G-14547)
MIZKAN AMERICA INC (DH)
Also Called: Nakano Foods
1661 Feehanville Dr # 200 (60056-6087)
PHONE..............847 590-0059

GEOGRAPHIC SECTION

Mount Prospect - Cook County (G-14572)

Koichi Yuki, *CEO*
Kevin Ponticelli, *President*
Craig Smith, *President*
Jack Kichura, *Business Mgr*
Mike Smith, *Exec VP*
◆ **EMP:** 50 **EST:** 1902
SQ FT: 13,000
SALES (est): 171MM **Privately Held**
SIC: 2099 2035 Vinegar; dressings, salad: raw & cooked (except dry mixes); mustard, prepared (wet)
HQ: Mizkan America Holdings, Inc
1661 Feehanville Dr # 300
Mount Prospect IL 60056
847 590-0059

(G-14548)
MIZKAN AMERICA HOLDINGS INC (HQ)
Also Called: Nakano Foods
1661 Feehanville Dr # 300 (60056-6087)
PHONE 847 590-0059
Hiroyasu Nakano, *President*
Kevin Ponticelli, *COO*
Michael Smith, *Exec VP*
Kenji Sano, *Vice Pres*
Ichiro Suzuki, *Vice Pres*
◆ **EMP:** 2
SALES (est): 715.1MM **Privately Held**
SIC: 2099 Vinegar

(G-14549)
MORTON SUGGESTION COMPANY LLC
800 W Central Rd Ste 101 (60056-2383)
P.O. Box 76 (60056-0076)
PHONE 847 255-4770
James Wade, *Sales Mgr*
Scott Kouri, *Sales Staff*
Marshall Smith,
Charles Marshall Smith,
Craig Smith,
▲ **EMP:** 8 **EST:** 1914
SQ FT: 35,000
SALES (est): 1.3MM **Privately Held**
SIC: 5199 2752 7336 Gifts & novelties; posters, lithographed; commercial art & illustration

(G-14550)
NELCO COIL SUPPLY COMPANY
1500 E Ironwood Dr (60056-1526)
PHONE 847 259-7517
Joanne Nelson Sime, *President*
EMP: 20
SQ FT: 14,000
SALES (est): 2MM **Privately Held**
SIC: 3677 3621 Coil windings, electronic; motors & generators

(G-14551)
NEW USN CHICAGO LLC (PA)
Also Called: Soluble Packaging Solutions
1804 W Central Rd (60056-2230)
PHONE 847 635-6772
Les Teague, *Partner*
Brian McInerney, *Partner*
Jeff Ostermeyer, *Vice Pres*
Samantha Bernardi, *Project Mgr*
Chris Benitez, *Maint Spvr*
EMP: 77 **EST:** 2010
SQ FT: 48,000
SALES (est): 58.6MM **Privately Held**
WEB: www.multipacksolutions.com
SIC: 7389 2844 Packaging & labeling services; towelettes, premoistened

(G-14552)
NOVA PRINTING AND LITHO CO
1621 E Dogwood Ln (60056-1519)
PHONE 773 486-8500
Jamie Thompson, *President*
Robert Ardisana, *Vice Pres*
EMP: 19
SQ FT: 13,000
SALES (est): 2.7MM **Privately Held**
SIC: 2752 Commercial printing, offset; lithographing on metal

(G-14553)
NOVOMATIC AMERICAS SALES LLC
1050 E Business Center Dr (60056-2180)
PHONE 224 802-2974
Rick Meitzler, *President*

Jakob Rothwangl, *CFO*
Paul Abbott, *Cust Mgr*
EMP: 10 **EST:** 2012
SALES (est): 681.6K
SALES (corp-wide): 2.9B **Privately Held**
SIC: 3944 Electronic game machines, except coin-operated
HQ: Novomatic Ag
Wiener StraBe 158
Gumpoldskirchen 2352
225 260-60

(G-14554)
NTN USA CORPORATION (HQ)
1600 Bishop Ct (60056-6055)
P.O. Box 7604 (60056-7604)
PHONE 847 298-4652
Masaaki Ayano, *President*
Makoto Kikukawa, *Admin Sec*
▼ **EMP:** 103
SQ FT: 88,000
SALES (est): 763.1MM **Privately Held**
SIC: 5085 3562 3568 Bearings; ball bearings & parts; roller bearings & parts; joints, swivel & universal, except aircraft & automotive

(G-14555)
OAKLAND INDUSTRIES LTD
Also Called: E-T-A Circuit Breakers
1551 Bishop Ct (60056-6039)
PHONE 847 827-7600
William Stewart, *President*
H Ellenberger, *Principal*
E Poensgen, *Principal*
William Sell, *Principal*
Mark Wise, *Engineer*
EMP: 46
SQ FT: 34,000
SALES (est): 16.2MM **Privately Held**
SIC: 5063 3823 3613 Circuit breakers; industrial instrmnts msrmnt display/control process variable; switchgear & switchboard apparatus

(G-14556)
ORCHARD PRODUCTS INC
500 W Huntington Cmns (60056-5277)
PHONE 847 818-6760
Betsy Ginocopolis, *Manager*
Sharon Geanakoplos, *Admin Sec*
EMP: 4
SALES (est): 240K **Privately Held**
SIC: 2833 Medicinals & botanicals

(G-14557)
P M ARMOR INC
237 E Prospect Ave (60056-3236)
PHONE 847 797-9940
Wilson Paul Mirza, *President*
Karl Sauer, *Corp Secy*
Joseph Mirza, *Vice Pres*
EMP: 32 **EST:** 1974
SQ FT: 6,000
SALES (est): 5.7MM **Privately Held**
SIC: 3599 Machine shop, jobbing & repair

(G-14558)
PARENTI & RAFFAELLI LTD
215 E Prospect Ave (60056-3236)
PHONE 847 253-5550
Robert Parenti, *President*
Don Parenti, *Vice Pres*
Robert G Parenti Jr, *Vice Pres*
Rob Naurath, *Project Mgr*
Louis Neri, *Project Mgr*
EMP: 170 **EST:** 1952
SQ FT: 45,000
SALES (est): 30.7MM **Privately Held**
WEB: www.parentiwoodwork.com
SIC: 2431 2434 Woodwork, interior & ornamental; wood kitchen cabinets

(G-14559)
PARENTI AND RAFFAELLI LTD
1401 Feehanville Dr (60056-6005)
PHONE 847 204-8116
EMP: 5
SALES (est): 476.2K **Privately Held**
SIC: 2431 Millwork

(G-14560)
PERFECTION SPRING STMPING CORP
1449 E Algonquin Rd (60056)
P.O. Box 275 (60056-0275)
PHONE 847 437-3900
David Kahn, *President*
Connie Nassif, *COO*
Joshua Kahn, *Exec VP*
Guido Heim, *Vice Pres*
Ken McLaren, *VP Opers*
▲ **EMP:** 100 **EST:** 1955
SQ FT: 70,000
SALES (est): 21.9MM **Privately Held**
WEB: www.pss-corp.com
SIC: 3465 3469 3495 3496 Automotive stampings; electronic enclosures, stamped or pressed metal; precision springs; miscellaneous fabricated wire products

(G-14561)
PHI GROUP INC
Also Called: Edoc Communications
555 E Business Center Dr (60056-2175)
PHONE 847 824-5610
Michael Frank, *President*
Micheal Frank, *President*
Brian Bending, *Vice Pres*
Glenn Grendzinski, *VP Opers*
Glenn Grendzinsi, *Opers Mgr*
EMP: 128
SQ FT: 35,000
SALES (est): 20MM **Privately Held**
SIC: 2759 Commercial printing

(G-14562)
PICTURE STONE INC
1431 W Greenbriar Dr (60056-3650)
PHONE 773 875-5021
Tomasz Parys, *Principal*
EMP: 3
SALES (est): 187.2K **Privately Held**
SIC: 1411 Granite dimension stone

(G-14563)
POLARIS GENOMICS CORPORATION
700 E Bus Ctr Dr 105 (60056)
PHONE 773 547-2350
Liang LI, *Principal*
EMP: 3
SALES (est): 123.2K **Privately Held**
SIC: 2835 Microbiology & virology diagnostic products

(G-14564)
R&B FOODS INC (DH)
1661 Feehanville Dr # 300 (60056-6087)
PHONE 847 590-0059
Ichizo Kobayashi, *President*
▼ **EMP:** 48
SALES (est): 28.5MM **Privately Held**
SIC: 2033 Spaghetti & other pasta sauce: packaged in cans, jars, etc.
HQ: Mizkan America, Inc.
1661 Feehanville Dr # 200
Mount Prospect IL 60056
847 590-0059

(G-14565)
R&R RESEARCH CO
300 N Prospect Manor Ave (60056-2334)
PHONE 847 345-5051
Randy R Hauslein, *Owner*
EMP: 8 **EST:** 1999
SALES (est): 509.9K **Privately Held**
SIC: 3471 Chromium plating of metals or formed products

(G-14566)
ROBERT BOSCH TOOL CORPORATION (DH)
Also Called: Garden Watering
1800 W Central Rd (60056-2230)
PHONE 224 232-2000
Heiko Fischer, *President*
Dan Hintze, *District Mgr*
Zoher Fatakdawala, *Business Mgr*
Pete Murphy, *Business Mgr*
Donna Wolf, *Opers Mgr*
◆ **EMP:** 600
SQ FT: 220,000

SALES (est): 1.2B
SALES (corp-wide): 294.8MM **Privately Held**
SIC: 3546 Cartridge-activated hand power tools
HQ: Scintilla Ag
Luterbachstrasse 10
Zuchwil SO 4528
326 863-111

(G-14567)
ROBERTS DRAPERIES CENTER INC
504 E Northwest Hwy (60056-3306)
PHONE 847 255-4040
Robert Lee Byers, *President*
Cheryl Lindholm, *Vice Pres*
EMP: 4 **EST:** 1950
SQ FT: 1,500
SALES (est): 370K **Privately Held**
WEB: www.robertsdraperycenter.com
SIC: 5714 5719 5231 2591 Draperies; window furnishings; wallpaper; drapery hardware & blinds & shades; curtains & draperies

(G-14568)
SAATI AMERICAS CORPORATION
Also Called: Saatiprint Div
901 E Business Center Dr (60056-2181)
PHONE 847 296-5090
EMP: 14
SALES (corp-wide): 16.4MM **Privately Held**
SIC: 2261 2262 3555 Cotton Finishing Plant Manmade Fiber & Silk Finishing Plant Mfg Printing Trades Machinery
PA: Saati Americas Corporation
201 Fairview Street Ext
Fountain Inn SC 29644
864 601-8300

(G-14569)
SCHUMACHER ELECTRIC CORP (PA)
801 E Business Center Dr (60056-2179)
PHONE 847 385-1600
Donald A Schumacher, *Ch of Bd*
John Waldron, *President*
Cory Watkins, *President*
Patrick Clarke, *Engineer*
Daniel Frano, *CFO*
◆ **EMP:** 80
SQ FT: 37,200
SALES (est): 34.2MM **Privately Held**
WEB: www.batterychargers.com
SIC: 3629 3677 Battery chargers, rectifying or nonrotating; transformers power supply, electronic type

(G-14570)
SILK ROAD LOGISTICS CO
2351 S Cannon Dr Apt G2 (60056-5973)
PHONE 773 432-5619
Zhakshylyk Tursunakunov, *Principal*
EMP: 2
SALES (est): 200K **Privately Held**
SIC: 2326 Medical & hospital uniforms, men's

(G-14571)
SIMPEX MEDICAL INC
401 E Prospect Ave (60056-3366)
PHONE 847 757-9928
Richard Gorski, *President*
EMP: 3
SALES (est): 286.6K **Privately Held**
SIC: 3841 5047 Surgical & medical instruments; medical equipment & supplies

(G-14572)
STERGO ROOFING
172 W Golf Rd Ste 299 (60056)
PHONE 312 640-9008
Steven Stergo, *President*
EMP: 36
SALES: 5MM **Privately Held**
WEB: www.chicagoindustrialroofing.com
SIC: 2621 Building & roofing paper, felts & insulation siding

Mount Prospect - Cook County (G-14573)

(G-14573)
SUN PROCESS CONVERTING INC
1660 W Kenneth Dr (60056-5515)
PHONE 847 593-0447
Michael J Moravectz, *President*
◆ EMP: 100
SQ FT: 138,000
SALES (est): 23.8MM **Privately Held**
WEB: www.sunprocess.com
SIC: 3081 3083 Vinyl film & sheet; laminated plastic sheets

(G-14574)
SURETINT TECHNOLOGIES LLC (PA)
411 E Bus Ctr Dr Ste 104 (60056)
PHONE 847 509-3625
Mitchell H Saranow,
Elizabeth Christie,
Vincent Davis,
Dina Elliot,
Patrick Parenty,
EMP: 7
SALES (est): 1.5MM **Privately Held**
SIC: 2844 Toilet preparations

(G-14575)
TECHNOTRANS AMERICA INC (HQ)
1441 E Business Center Dr (60056-2182)
PHONE 847 227-9200
Jeffrey Schneider, *President*
Tom Carbery, *Vice Pres*
Michael Reckamp, *Vice Pres*
Ralph Roling, *Vice Pres*
Bob Puleo, *Parts Mgr*
▲ EMP: 38
SQ FT: 35,000
SALES: 12MM
SALES (corp-wide): 230MM **Privately Held**
WEB: www.technotrans.com
SIC: 3555 Printing trades machinery
PA: Technotrans Se
Robert-Linnemann-Str. 17
Sassenberg 48336
258 330-1100

(G-14576)
TRI-TECH SLTONS CONSULTING INC
259 N Woodland Dr (60056-1936)
PHONE 847 941-0199
Dong Zhu, *President*
EMP: 3
SALES: 250K **Privately Held**
SIC: 7372 Prepackaged software

(G-14577)
TWO EAGLES DISTILLERY LLC
1852 S Elmhurst Rd (60056-5711)
PHONE 773 450-7575
Jesse Zien, *Mng Member*
EMP: 4
SALES (est): 289.5K **Privately Held**
SIC: 2085 Distilled & blended liquors

(G-14578)
U KEEP US IN STITCHES
1420 S Redwood Dr (60056-5018)
PHONE 847 427-8127
Cliff Higley, *Owner*
Diane Higley, *Co-Owner*
EMP: 4
SALES (est): 264.8K **Privately Held**
SIC: 2395 Embroidery products, except schiffli machine

(G-14579)
UNITEL TECHNOLOGIES INC
479 E Bus Ctr Dr Ste 105 (60056)
PHONE 847 297-2265
Serge Randhava, *CEO*
Ravi Randhava, *President*
Todd Harvey, *Vice Pres*
Richard KAO, *Vice Pres*
EMP: 15 EST: 1990
SQ FT: 3,500
SALES (est): 3.8MM **Privately Held**
WEB: www.uniteltech.com
SIC: 3559 8711 Petroleum refinery equipment; petroleum, mining & chemical engineers

(G-14580)
VANGUARD TOOL & ENGINEERING CO
555 W Carboy Rd (60056-5706)
PHONE 847 981-9595
Gary Donaldson, *President*
Kurt Donaldson, *Vice Pres*
Gertrude Slowik, *Office Mgr*
Richard Donaldson, *Director*
EMP: 20
SQ FT: 8,000
SALES (est): 3MM **Privately Held**
WEB: www.vanguard-tool.com
SIC: 3451 3545 Screw machine products; machine tool accessories

(G-14581)
VINS & VIGNOBLES LLC
40 E Northwest Hwy # 211 (60056-3214)
PHONE 312 375-7656
Taoufik Matty Iqbal,
EMP: 4
SALES (est): 91.3K **Privately Held**
SIC: 2084 5182 Wines; neutral spirits

(G-14582)
WIREFORMERS INC
500 W Carboy Rd (60056-5771)
PHONE 847 718-1920
Louis Lischko, *President*
Susan Kanellis, *Corp Secy*
Horst Lang, *Exec VP*
John Kanellis, *Vice Pres*
EMP: 20 EST: 1960
SQ FT: 15,000
SALES (est): 3.2MM **Privately Held**
WEB: www.wireformers.com
SIC: 3469 3544 3496 Stamping metal for the trade; die sets for metal stamping (presses); miscellaneous fabricated wire products

(G-14583)
WOOJIN PLAIMM INC
1693 W Imperial Ct (60056-5554)
PHONE 708 606-5536
Ick Whan Kim, *President*
EMP: 10
SQ FT: 10,000
SALES (est): 633.9K **Privately Held**
SIC: 3089 Injection molding of plastics

(G-14584)
XTTRIUM LABORATORIES INC (PA)
1200 E Business Center Dr (60056-6041)
PHONE 773 268-5800
Kevin S Creevy, *President*
Joan Bartosz, *Vice Pres*
Edilberto Gutierrez, *Prdtn Mgr*
Vijay Verma, *CFO*
Connie Nieves, *Office Mgr*
▲ EMP: 83 EST: 1939
SQ FT: 35,000
SALES: 50.5MM **Privately Held**
WEB: www.xttrium.com
SIC: 2834 Pharmaceutical preparations

(G-14585)
YS HEALTH CORPORATION
Also Called: Young Shin Honey Farm
411 Kingston Ct Ste A (60056-6022)
PHONE 847 391-9122
David Choi, *President*
Jae Heo, *Vice Pres*
Lilly Choi, *Manager*
Carol Lee, *Manager*
Ernie Lee, *Manager*
▲ EMP: 14
SQ FT: 9,000
SALES (est): 2.9MM **Privately Held**
SIC: 2099 2833 Honey, strained & bottled; vitamins, natural or synthetic: bulk, uncompounded

(G-14586)
ZZZSOCK LLC
501 N Pine St (60056-2056)
PHONE 224 330-7364
EMP: 3
SALES (est): 197.4K **Privately Held**
SIC: 2252 Socks

Mount Pulaski
Logan County

(G-14587)
GRO ALLIANCE LLC
247 1500th Ave (62548-6508)
PHONE 217 792-3355
Jason Thomas, *President*
EMP: 6
SALES (est): 479.3K **Privately Held**
WEB: www.groalliance.com
SIC: 2046 Corn milling by-products
PA: Gro Alliance Llc
613 N Randolph St
Cuba City WI 53807

(G-14588)
INLAND TOOL COMPANY
727 N Topper Dr (62548-6074)
P.O. Box 137 (62548-0137)
PHONE 217 792-3206
Kirk Evans, *President*
Susan Evans, *Admin Sec*
EMP: 50
SQ FT: 70,000
SALES (est): 18MM **Privately Held**
SIC: 3545 3469 3465 3544 Machine tool accessories; metal stampings; automotive stampings; special dies, tools, jigs & fixtures

---

Mount Sterling
Brown County

(G-14589)
BRUCE MCCULLOUGH
Also Called: Precision Oil Field Cnstr
1161 980n Ave (62353-4425)
PHONE 217 773-3130
Bruce McCullough, *Owner*
EMP: 2
SALES (est): 283.9K **Privately Held**
SIC: 1311 Crude petroleum production

(G-14590)
CLINARD READY MIX INC
Rr 24 Box West (62353)
P.O. Box 112 (62353-0112)
PHONE 217 773-3965
David Clinard, *President*
EMP: 40
SQ FT: 3,000
SALES (est): 4.4MM **Privately Held**
SIC: 3273 Ready-mixed concrete

(G-14591)
DEMOCRAT MESSAGE
Also Called: Colson Publications
123 W Main St (62353-1223)
P.O. Box 71 (62353-0071)
PHONE 217 773-3371
Warren Colson, *President*
EMP: 4
SALES (est): 172.2K **Privately Held**
SIC: 2711 Newspapers: publishing only, not printed on site

(G-14592)
R & D OIL PRODUCERS
709 N Capitol Ave (62353-1107)
PHONE 217 773-9299
Cloyd Drennan, *Principal*
EMP: 3
SALES (est): 196.4K **Privately Held**
SIC: 1311 Crude petroleum production

(G-14593)
SCHROCKS WOOD SHOP
356 650n Ave (62353-1718)
P.O. Box 4 (62353-0004)
PHONE 217 773-3842
Ray Schrock, *Owner*
EMP: 3
SALES (est): 210K **Privately Held**
SIC: 2452 Prefabricated wood buildings

(G-14594)
TWO RIVERS OIL & GAS CO INC
116 S Capitol Ave (62353-1502)
PHONE 217 773-3356
Edward B Tucker, *President*
Judith Tucker, *Treasurer*
EMP: 3
SQ FT: 1,000
SALES (est): 268.7K **Privately Held**
SIC: 1311 Crude petroleum production; natural gas production

Mount Vernon
Jefferson County

(G-14595)
ACCURATE AUTO MANUFACTURING CO
1804 S 8th St (62864-6108)
P.O. Box 847 (62864-0017)
PHONE 618 244-0727
Clarence Bonifacius, *Owner*
EMP: 5
SQ FT: 3,700
SALES (est): 240K **Privately Held**
SIC: 3714 7692 Cylinder heads, motor vehicle; motor vehicle engines & parts; welding repair

(G-14596)
AS FABRICATING INC
15518 N Il Highway 37 (62864-7856)
PHONE 618 242-7438
Addison Sharpe, *President*
Patricia Sharpe, *Corp Secy*
EMP: 5
SQ FT: 2,000
SALES (est): 220K **Privately Held**
SIC: 7692 3446 3444 3443 Welding repair; architectural metalwork; sheet metalwork; fabricated plate work (boiler shop); fabricated structural metal

(G-14597)
AZUSA INC
Also Called: Azusa Printing
15179 N Il Highway 37 (62864-7864)
PHONE 618 244-6591
Debi Trotter, *President*
EMP: 9
SALES (est): 968K **Privately Held**
WEB: www.azusaprinting.com
SIC: 2752 3993 2791 2761 Commercial printing, offset; signs & advertising specialties; typesetting; manifold business forms

(G-14598)
BEELMAN READY-MIX INC
13425 N Shiloh Dr (62864-7390)
PHONE 618 244-9600
Sam Beelman, *Owner*
EMP: 9 **Privately Held**
SIC: 3273 Ready-mixed concrete
PA: Beelman Ready-Mix, Inc.
1 Racehorse Dr
East Saint Louis IL 62205

(G-14599)
BENNETT METAL PRODUCTS INC
700 Rackaway St (62864)
P.O. Box 34 (62864-0001)
PHONE 618 244-1911
James C Bennett, *CEO*
Jim Stowers, *President*
Dale Winkeler, *Project Mgr*
Christina Cole, *Purch Agent*
Jeffrey Ceglinski, *Manager*
EMP: 58
SQ FT: 36,000
SALES: 6MM **Privately Held**
SIC: 3544 Special dies & tools

(G-14600)
BREHM OIL INC (PA)
Also Called: Beau-Brehm L Ranches
1915 Broadway St (62864-2980)
P.O. Box 648 (62864-0014)
PHONE 618 242-4620
Deborah Zielonki, *President*
Deborah Zielonkl, *President*
Micheal Alexander, *Vice Pres*
Carolyn Hayes, *Manager*
EMP: 12
SQ FT: 6,000

GEOGRAPHIC SECTION

Mount Vernon - Jefferson County (G-14629)

SALES (est): 2.5MM **Privately Held**
SIC: 1311 Crude petroleum production

(G-14601)
CENTRALIA PRESS LTD
Also Called: Mount Vernon Zone
1808 Broadway St (62864-2905)
PHONE..................618 246-2000
Tesa Culli, *Manager*
EMP: 10
SALES (corp-wide): 9.9MM **Privately Held**
SIC: 2711 Newspapers: publishing only, not printed on site
PA: Centralia Press, Ltd
232 E Broadway
Centralia IL 62801
618 532-5604

(G-14602)
COLLINS BROTHERS OIL CORP (PA)
Also Called: Collins Bros
218 N 9th St (62864-3937)
P.O. Box 689 (62864-0014)
PHONE..................618 244-1093
Michael O'Dea, *Manager*
EMP: 2
SQ FT: 5,000
SALES (est): 714.9K **Privately Held**
SIC: 1311 Crude petroleum production

(G-14603)
CONTINENTAL RESOURCES ILL INC (PA)
830 Il Highway 15 E (62864)
P.O. Box 749 (62864-0015)
PHONE..................618 242-1717
Richard Straeter, *President*
▲ EMP: 50 EST: 1962
SQ FT: 5,300
SALES (est): 5.4MM **Privately Held**
SIC: 1311 Crude petroleum production

(G-14604)
CONTINENTAL TIRE AMERICAS LLC
Also Called: Continental Tire Mt. Vernon
11525 N Il Highway 142 (62864-6600)
P.O. Box 1029 (62864-0022)
PHONE..................618 242-7100
Damon Haarmann, *Purch Mgr*
George Bradley, *Engineer*
Joshua Buhl, *Engineer*
Ivan Prada, *Engineer*
Tom Tompkins, *Engineer*
EMP: 100
SALES (corp-wide): 49.2B **Privately Held**
SIC: 3011 Tires & inner tubes
HQ: Continental Tire The Americas, Llc
1830 Macmillan Park Dr
Fort Mill SC 29707
800 847-3349

(G-14605)
DARRELL FICKAS
Also Called: Darrell Fickas Sawmill
16749 N Campground Ln (62864-8095)
PHONE..................618 599-3632
Darrell Sawmill, *Owner*
EMP: 9
SALES (est): 548.7K **Privately Held**
SIC: 2421 Sawmills & planing mills, general

(G-14606)
DECATUR CUSTOM TOOL INC
Also Called: Dct Mount Vernon
5101 Lake Ter Ne (62864-9666)
PHONE..................618 244-4078
Stacy Greenwalt, *Branch Mgr*
EMP: 5
SALES (corp-wide): 21.6MM **Privately Held**
SIC: 3546 Saws & sawing equipment
PA: Decatur Custom Tool, Llc
410 N Jasper St
Decatur IL 62521
217 423-3639

(G-14607)
DECATUR INDUSTRIAL ELC INC
Also Called: Mt Vernon Electric
1313 Harlan Rd (62864-6014)
P.O. Box 1548 (62864-0030)
PHONE..................618 244-1066
Mike Scott, *Branch Mgr*
Susan Bundy, *Director*
EMP: 35
SALES (corp-wide): 47.4MM **Privately Held**
WEB: www.decaturindustrial.com
SIC: 7694 5571 Motor repair services; motorcycle dealers
PA: Decatur Industrial Electric, Inc.
1650 E Garfield Ave
Decatur IL 62526
217 428-6621

(G-14608)
DENNIS CARNES
Also Called: Cartec
2118 Brownsville Rd (62864-6074)
PHONE..................618 244-1770
Dennis A Carnes, *Owner*
EMP: 3
SQ FT: 2,800
SALES (est): 314.2K **Privately Held**
SIC: 3069 Foam rubber

(G-14609)
DENTA TREET LLC
17707 E Angling Rd (62864-8027)
PHONE..................618 384-1028
Lee Willingham,
EMP: 4
SALES (est): 116.1K **Privately Held**
SIC: 2047 Dog & cat food

(G-14610)
EVERBRITE LLC
1 Neon Dr (62864-6723)
PHONE..................618 242-0645
David Meador, *Plant Mgr*
Joe Fryza, *Manager*
Betty Oliver, *MIS Mgr*
EMP: 3
SALES (est): 123.2K **Privately Held**
WEB: www.everbrite.com
SIC: 2813 Neon

(G-14611)
FRED PIGG DENTAL LAB
14544 N Wing Ln (62864-2048)
PHONE..................618 439-6829
Fred Pigg, *President*
EMP: 4
SALES (est): 328.2K **Privately Held**
SIC: 8072 3843 Denture production; dental equipment & supplies

(G-14612)
GUNNER ENERGY CORPORATION
Also Called: General Acrylics
1200 Hill St (62864-3270)
PHONE..................618 237-2829
Kenneth Roberts, *President*
EMP: 4
SALES (est): 250K **Privately Held**
SIC: 1389 1771 Oil field services; blacktop (asphalt) work

(G-14613)
HERMANN GENE SIGNS & SERVICE
12436 E Lakewood Dr (62864-1925)
PHONE..................618 244-3681
Gene Herrmann, *Owner*
EMP: 3
SALES (est): 151.4K **Privately Held**
SIC: 3993 Signs & advertising specialties

(G-14614)
HERRMANN SIGNS & SERVICE
12436 E Lakewood Dr (62864-1925)
PHONE..................618 246-6537
Gene Herrmann, *Owner*
EMP: 3
SALES (est): 261.9K **Privately Held**
SIC: 3993 Neon signs

(G-14615)
ILLINOI EYE SURGNS/QUANTM VISN
3000 Broadway St (62864-2340)
PHONE..................618 315-6560
EMP: 4 EST: 2014
SALES (est): 216K **Privately Held**
SIC: 3572 Computer storage devices

(G-14616)
INNOTECH MANUFACTURING LLC
915 S 13th St (62864-4818)
P.O. Box 963 (62864-0020)
PHONE..................618 244-6261
Joseph Collier, *Vice Pres*
Dan Black,
EMP: 24
SALES (est): 4.9MM **Privately Held**
WEB: www.innotechmfg.com
SIC: 3444 Sheet metalwork

(G-14617)
JACKSON MARKING PRODUCTS CO
9105 N Rainbow Ln (62864-6407)
PHONE..................618 242-7901
Coy Jackson, *President*
Sandra Jackson, *Treasurer*
Rhonda Poston, *Cust Mgr*
Gerald Mayo, *Manager*
Tom Jackson, *Admin Sec*
◆ EMP: 14
SQ FT: 6,400
SALES (est): 1.8MM **Privately Held**
SIC: 3953 2899 Embossing seals & hand stamps; chemical preparations

(G-14618)
JAX ASPHALT COMPANY INC
1800 Waterworks Rd (62864)
P.O. Box 1725 (62864-0034)
PHONE..................618 244-0500
Robert Metcalf, *President*
Sue Metcalf, *Treasurer*
EMP: 12
SQ FT: 1,500
SALES (est): 1.6MM **Privately Held**
WEB: www.jaxasphalt.net
SIC: 1731 4212 2952 2951 Communications specialization; fiber optic cable installation; sound equipment specialization; local trucking, without storage; asphalt felts & coatings; asphalt paving mixtures & blocks

(G-14619)
JOY GLOBAL UNDERGROUND MIN LLC
4111 N Water Tower Pl B (62864-6566)
PHONE..................618 242-3650
Don Biondi, *Manager*
EMP: 25
SQ FT: 100,000 **Privately Held**
SIC: 3535 Bucket type conveyor systems
HQ: Joy Global Underground Mining Llc
40 Pennwood Pl
Warrendale PA 15086
724 779-4500

(G-14620)
KM ENTERPRISES INC
Also Called: Entrac Systems
320 S 11th St Ste 2 (62864-4200)
PHONE..................618 204-0888
Rodney K Morgan, *President*
EMP: 11
SQ FT: 15,000
SALES (est): 7.5MM **Privately Held**
SIC: 3669 Pedestrian traffic control equipment

(G-14621)
LAYS MINING SERVICE INC
1121 S 10th St (62864-5401)
PHONE..................618 244-6570
James T Mellott, *President*
David G Mellott, *Admin Sec*
EMP: 35
SQ FT: 25,000
SALES (est): 6.2MM **Privately Held**
SIC: 3599 Machine shop, jobbing & repair

(G-14622)
MAGNUM STEEL WORKS INC
200 Shiloh Dr (62864-8347)
PHONE..................618 244-5190
Jim Czerwinski, *President*
Angela Czerwinski, *Corp Secy*
Josh Buchanan, *Purch Agent*
Johnny C Czerwinski, *Manager*
▲ EMP: 82
SALES: 9.5MM **Privately Held**
SIC: 3549 Metalworking machinery

(G-14623)
MAIN STREET RECORDS
313 S 10th St (62864-4235)
PHONE..................618 244-2737
John Ellis, *Owner*
EMP: 3
SQ FT: 288
SALES (est): 346.8K **Privately Held**
SIC: 2253 T-shirts & tops, knit

(G-14624)
MICHEL FERTILIZER & EQUIPMENT
1313 Shawnee St (62864-5457)
PHONE..................618 242-6000
Chris Michel, *Owner*
EMP: 6
SQ FT: 23,000
SALES (est): 1.3MM **Privately Held**
WEB: www.micheltanks.com
SIC: 5191 2873 Seeds & bulbs; chemicals, agricultural; fertilizer & fertilizer materials; nitrogenous fertilizers

(G-14625)
MIDWESTERN MCH HYDRAULICS INC
17265 N Timberline Ln (62864-8414)
P.O. Box 765 (62864-0015)
PHONE..................618 246-9440
Robin Stowers, *President*
James Stowers, *Corp Secy*
EMP: 11 EST: 1997
SQ FT: 30,000
SALES (est): 1.9MM **Privately Held**
SIC: 3599 7699 Machine shop, jobbing & repair; hydraulic equipment repair

(G-14626)
MOUNT VERNON NEON SIGN CO
1 Neon Dr (62864-6723)
PHONE..................618 242-0645
Bill Fritz, *President*
David Heger, *Treasurer*
Tom Donnelly, *Admin Sec*
EMP: 125 EST: 1933
SQ FT: 70,000
SALES: 13.7MM
SALES (corp-wide): 296.3MM **Privately Held**
SIC: 3993 Neon signs
PA: Everbrite, Llc
4949 S 110th St
Greenfield WI 53228
414 529-3500

(G-14627)
MOZ NUTRACEUTICALS LLC
14358 N Manhattan Ln (62864-9165)
PHONE..................314 315-2541
Filipe Muhale, *CEO*
EMP: 20
SALES (est): 1.8MM **Privately Held**
SIC: 2844 Lotions, shaving

(G-14628)
MT VERNON IRON WORKS LLC
Also Called: Mount Vernon Iron Works
10950 N Cactus Ln (62864-8260)
PHONE..................618 244-2313
Dave Black,
Kelsey Black, *Admin Sec*
David Black,
EMP: 6 EST: 2013
SALES (est): 968.2K **Privately Held**
SIC: 3399 Iron, powdered

(G-14629)
MT VERNON MOLD WORKS INC
15 Industrial Dr (62864)
P.O. Box 1761 (62864-0055)
PHONE..................618 242-6040

Mount Vernon - Jefferson County (G-14630)

Steve Zoumberakis, *President*
EMP: 21
SALES (est): 3.6MM
SALES (corp-wide): 72.9MM **Privately Held**
SIC: 3544 7692 Special dies & tools; welding repair
PA: Saehwa Imc Na, Inc.
2200 Massillon Rd
Akron OH 44312
330 645-6653

(G-14630)
NATIONAL RAILWAY EQUIPMENT CO
908 Shawnee St (62864-5451)
P.O. Box 1416 (62864-0029)
PHONE.................................. 618 241-9270
EMP: 3
SALES (corp-wide): 314MM **Privately Held**
SIC: 5088 3743 Railroad equipment & supplies; locomotives & parts
PA: National Railway Equipment Co.
1100 Shawnee St
Mount Vernon IL 62864
618 242-6590

(G-14631)
NUTHERM INTERNATIONAL INC
501 S 11th St (62864-4876)
PHONE.................................. 618 244-6000
Judy Hinson, *CEO*
Dave Massey, *President*
Wade Bowlin, *Principal*
Brittney Hefner, *Human Resources*
Eric Bussick, *Sales Engr*
▼ **EMP:** 33
SQ FT: 30,000
SALES (est): 10.6MM **Privately Held**
SIC: 3613 Time switches, electrical switchgear apparatus; control panels, electric; distribution boards, electric; metering panels, electric

(G-14632)
PARAGON OIL COMPANY INC
1726 Broadway St Ste B (62864-2930)
P.O. Box 885 (62864-0018)
PHONE.................................. 618 244-5541
Robert Herr, *President*
EMP: 2
SALES (est): 213.7K **Privately Held**
SIC: 1381 Drilling oil & gas wells

(G-14633)
PEACOCK PRINTING INC
1112 Jordan St (62864-3817)
PHONE.................................. 618 242-3157
Mark Smith, *President*
Carrie Smith, *Vice Pres*
EMP: 8 **EST:** 1946
SALES (est): 605K **Privately Held**
WEB: www.peacockprinting.com
SIC: 2752 2759 2262 5699 Commercial printing, offset; letterpress printing; screen printing: manmade fiber & silk broadwoven fabrics; T-shirts, custom printed; Army-Navy goods

(G-14634)
PEPSI MIDAMERICA CO
205 N Davidson St (62864-8338)
PHONE.................................. 618 242-6285
Randy Wright, *Manager*
Charles Jackson, *Analyst*
EMP: 417
SALES (corp-wide): 264.2MM **Privately Held**
SIC: 2086 Carbonated soft drinks, bottled & canned
PA: Pepsi Midamerica Co.
2605 W Main St
Marion IL 62959
618 997-1377

(G-14635)
QUAD-COUNTY READY MIX CORP
Also Called: Jefferson County Ready Mix
9240 Sahara Rd (62864-1924)
PHONE.................................. 618 244-6973
Herbert Hustedde, *Manager*
EMP: 20
SALES (corp-wide): 16.1MM **Privately Held**
WEB: www.qcrm4.com
SIC: 3273 Ready-mixed concrete
PA: Quad-County Ready Mix Corp.
300 W 12th St
Okawville IL 62271
618 243-6430

(G-14636)
SA NAT INDUSTRIAL CNSTR CO INC
103 E Perkins Ave (62864-5215)
P.O. Box 807 (62864-0017)
PHONE.................................. 618 246-9402
Mel Brookman, *President*
EMP: 28
SQ FT: 9,600
SALES (est): 6.3MM **Privately Held**
SIC: 3535 Conveyors & conveying equipment

(G-14637)
SCI BOX LLC
515 S 1st St (62864-5202)
PHONE.................................. 618 244-7244
Denise Wilson, *Mng Member*
EMP: 50
SQ FT: 100,000
SALES (est): 12.3MM **Privately Held**
SIC: 2653 Boxes, corrugated: made from purchased materials

(G-14638)
SHAPIRO BROS OF ILLINOIS INC
Also Called: Milano Metals & Recyling
510 S 6th St (62864-5300)
P.O. Box 1327 (62864-0027)
PHONE.................................. 618 244-3168
Gino Federici, *President*
Mike Federici, *General Mgr*
Mary Burgan, *Vice Pres*
Mia Barker, *Treasurer*
Debbie Storey, *Personnel*
EMP: 35 **EST:** 1955
SQ FT: 14,000
SALES: 8.6MM **Privately Held**
WEB: www.milanometals.com
SIC: 4225 3341 3312 General warehousing & storage; secondary nonferrous metals; blast furnaces & steel mills

(G-14639)
SHUTTERVIEW
9135 N Spring Garden Ln (62864-6624)
PHONE.................................. 618 244-0656
Tonya Lindsey, *President*
EMP: 3
SALES (est): 179.9K **Privately Held**
SIC: 3442 Shutters, door or window: metal

(G-14640)
STEWART PRODUCERS INC (PA)
Also Called: Stewart Well Service
301 N 27th St (62864-2943)
P.O. Box 546 (62864-0012)
PHONE.................................. 618 244-3754
Robert G Stewart, *President*
Mark Thompson, *Vice Pres*
April Johnson, *Admin Sec*
EMP: 5
SQ FT: 1,500
SALES (est): 1.6MM **Privately Held**
SIC: 1382 Oil & gas exploration services

(G-14641)
SUN CONTAINER INC
515 S 1st St (62864-5202)
PHONE.................................. 417 681-0503
Earl Bennett, *Owner*
EMP: 6
SALES (est): 990.2K **Privately Held**
SIC: 2653 Boxes, corrugated: made from purchased materials

(G-14642)
TONI FEDERICI
916 Main St (62864-4010)
PHONE.................................. 618 244-4842
Toni Federici, *Owner*
EMP: 15
SALES (est): 82K **Privately Held**
SIC: 2396 Veils & veiling: bridal, funeral, etc.

(G-14643)
VANEX INC
Also Called: Vanex Color
1700 Shawnee St (62864-5572)
P.O. Box 987 (62864-0020)
PHONE.................................. 618 244-1413
Jim W Montgomery, *President*
Kenneth Brandt, *Vice Pres*
Christina Campbell, *Vice Pres*
W Ray Grubb, *VP Mfg*
EMP: 25 **EST:** 1962
SQ FT: 40,000
SALES (est): 7.5MM
SALES (corp-wide): 15.1B **Publicly Held**
SIC: 2851 Paints: oil or alkyd vehicle or water thinned; enamels; epoxy coatings; undercoatings, paint
PA: Ppg Industries, Inc.
1 Ppg Pl
Pittsburgh PA 15272
412 434-3131

(G-14644)
WOOD ENERGY INC
3007 Broadway St (62864-2361)
P.O. Box 828 (62864-0017)
PHONE.................................. 618 244-1590
Charles P Wood, *President*
Velma R Wood, *Corp Secy*
J Nelson Wood, *Vice Pres*
EMP: 3
SQ FT: 2,000
SALES (est): 936.2K **Privately Held**
SIC: 1311 Crude petroleum production

Mount Zion
Macon County

(G-14645)
EDWARD HULL CABINET SHOP
1310 N State Route 121 (62549-1226)
PHONE.................................. 217 864-3011
Edward Hull, *Owner*
Franz Jones, *General Mgr*
EMP: 7
SALES (est): 1MM **Privately Held**
SIC: 5211 2434 Cabinets, kitchen; wood kitchen cabinets

(G-14646)
GIBSON INSURANCE INC
Also Called: Auto-Owners Insurance
300 N State Route 121 (62549-1513)
PHONE.................................. 217 864-4877
Jeffrey Gibson, *President*
Elaine Gibson, *Vice Pres*
EMP: 2
SALES (est): 264.9K **Privately Held**
SIC: 6411 6311 5261 3599 Insurance agents: life insurance; lawnmowers & tractors; machine shop, jobbing & repair; saws & sawing equipment

(G-14647)
GREEN VALLEY MFG ILL INC
100 Green Valley Dr (62549-1775)
PHONE.................................. 217 864-4125
Robert W Curry, *President*
Jonathan Simmons, *Admin Sec*
EMP: 33
SQ FT: 34,000
SALES (est): 2.5MM **Privately Held**
SIC: 3537 Industrial trucks & tractors

(G-14648)
JORDAN INDUSTRIAL CONTROLS INC
215 Casa Park Dr (62549-1289)
P.O. Box 108 (62549-0108)
PHONE.................................. 217 864-4444
Joseph Jordan, *President*
EMP: 22
SQ FT: 5,000
SALES (est): 5.7MM **Privately Held**
SIC: 3829 Measuring & controlling devices

(G-14649)
PRECISION TOOL & DIE COMPANY
445 W Main St (62549-1329)
P.O. Box 355 (62549-0355)
PHONE.................................. 217 864-3371
Bruce Harshman, *President*
John Harshman, *Treasurer*
Carrie Perry, *Admin Sec*
EMP: 14
SQ FT: 5,500
SALES (est): 2.5MM **Privately Held**
WEB: www.precisiontoolanddieinc.com
SIC: 3544 3549 3545 3541 Special dies & tools; jigs & fixtures; metalworking machinery; machine tool accessories; machine tools, metal cutting type

(G-14650)
VILLAGE OF MT ZION
Also Called: Atwoot Herald
433 N State Route 121 (62549-1514)
PHONE.................................. 217 864-4212
Don Robinson, *Branch Mgr*
EMP: 5
SALES (est): 218.3K **Privately Held**
SIC: 2711 Newspapers
PA: Village Of Mt Zion
1400 Mt Zion Pkwy
Mount Zion IL 62549
217 864-4012

Moweaqua
Christian County

(G-14651)
GRAIZED LLC
2912 N 645 East Rd (62550-8603)
PHONE.................................. 815 615-1012
Kolten Postin,
EMP: 3
SALES: 50K **Privately Held**
SIC: 2011 Beef products from beef slaughtered on site

(G-14652)
MOWEAQUA PACKING PLANT
601 N Main St (62550-3695)
PHONE.................................. 217 768-4714
Jerry Morehouse, *Owner*
Larry Baker, *Partner*
Jerry John Morehouse, *Principal*
EMP: 6 **EST:** 1964
SQ FT: 2,700
SALES (est): 320K **Privately Held**
WEB: www.mowpackingplant.com
SIC: 0751 5147 5421 2013 Slaughtering: custom livestock services; meats, fresh; meat markets, including freezer provisioners; sausages & other prepared meats; meat packing plants

Mulberry Grove
Bond County

(G-14653)
CREEKSIDE EXTERIOR SOLUTIONS
99 E 1300 Ave (62262-4010)
PHONE.................................. 618 326-7654
Steve Creek, *President*
EMP: 2 **EST:** 2016
SALES (est): 256K **Privately Held**
SIC: 2851 Removers & cleaners

(G-14654)
EAGLE PANEL SYSTEM INC
127 N Maple St (62262)
P.O. Box 247 (62262-0247)
PHONE.................................. 618 326-7132
Kenneth Disch, *President*
Vicki Disch, *Vice Pres*
EMP: 7
SQ FT: 60,000
SALES: 750K **Privately Held**
SIC: 3086 Prefabricated wood buildings

Mundelein
Lake County

(G-14655)
4 ELEMENTS COMPANY
520 Cardinal Pl (60060-2636)
PHONE..................773 236-2284
Charise Cowan-Leroy, *Principal*
Travis Leroy, *Co-Owner*
EMP: 2 **EST:** 2012
SALES (est): 246.5K **Privately Held**
SIC: 5122 2844 7389 Toilet soap; toilet preparations;

(G-14656)
9 DOTS SOLUTIONS LLC
Also Called: 9.solutions
112 Terrace Dr (60060-3826)
P.O. Box 157, Lake Bluff (60044-0157)
PHONE..................877 919-9349
Benjamin Shmitz, *Manager*
EMP: 5 **EST:** 2017
SALES (est): 242.5K
SALES (corp-wide): 656.2K **Privately Held**
SIC: 3861 Photographic equipment & supplies
PA: Koll Ltd.
 112 Terrace Dr
 Mundelein IL 60060
 224 544-5418

(G-14657)
A J KAY CO
304 Washington Blvd (60060-3106)
PHONE..................224 475-0370
Robert Schweda, *President*
Paul Kiscellus, *Corp Secy*
John Kiscellus, *Vice Pres*
EMP: 12
SQ FT: 4,500
SALES (est): 660K **Privately Held**
SIC: 3493 3496 3495 3452 Cold formed springs; coiled flat springs; miscellaneous fabricated wire products; wire springs; bolts, nuts, rivets & washers

(G-14658)
ABBVIE
1027 Aberdeen Ln (60060-1201)
PHONE..................847 946-8753
John Webb, *Principal*
EMP: 3
SALES (est): 179.6K **Privately Held**
SIC: 2834 Pharmaceutical preparations

(G-14659)
ACCESS ASSEMBLY LLC
1047 E High St (60060-3117)
PHONE..................847 894-1047
Jon Babii, *Mng Member*
▲ **EMP:** 5
SALES: 450K **Privately Held**
SIC: 3679 Electronic circuits

(G-14660)
AGRITECH WORLDWIDE INC (PA)
1011 Campus Dr (60060-3834)
PHONE..................847 549-6002
Edward Smith III, *President*
Edward B Smith III, *CEO*
Morris Garfinkle, *Ch of Bd*
Donald Wittmer, *CFO*
▲ **EMP:** 11
SQ FT: 44,000
SALES: 1.1MM **Publicly Held**
SIC: 2099 2041 Food preparations; flour & other grain mill products; corn flour

(G-14661)
ALL AMERICAN WASHER WERKS INC
912 E High St (60060-3120)
PHONE..................847 566-9091
Fred Nuemann, *President*
Michael Nuemann, *Vice Pres*
Mary Jane Neumann, *Admin Sec*
EMP: 24
SQ FT: 44,000
SALES (est): 5.7MM **Privately Held**
SIC: 3452 3469 3053 Bolts, metal; metal stampings; gaskets & sealing devices

(G-14662)
AMCOR FLEXIBLES LLC
Also Called: Amcor Flexibles Healthcare
1919 S Butterfield Rd (60060-9740)
PHONE..................847 362-9000
Ian Hayes, *Owner*
Siriporn Choosri, *Purchasing*
Marnie Hagan, *Engineer*
Bob Smith, *Engineer*
Sheila Stratton, *Manager*
EMP: 19
SALES (corp-wide): 947.2K **Privately Held**
SIC: 3845 Ultrasonic medical equipment, except cleaning
HQ: Amcor Flexibles Llc
 2150 E Lake Cook Rd
 Buffalo Grove IL 60089
 224 313-7000

(G-14663)
AMERI-TEX
1520 Mccormick Blvd (60060-4447)
PHONE..................847 247-0777
Larry Pasquesi, *President*
EMP: 9
SALES (est): 681.8K **Privately Held**
SIC: 7389 2395 Embroidering of advertising on shirts, etc.; emblems, embroidered

(G-14664)
ARJAY INSTANT PRINTING
26481 N Il Route 83 (60060-3488)
PHONE..................847 438-9059
Rick Fedor, *President*
Tim Carlson, *Vice Pres*
EMP: 3
SALES: 500K **Privately Held**
SIC: 2759 Commercial printing

(G-14665)
BARDS PRODUCTS INC (PA)
1427 Armour Blvd (60060-4403)
P.O. Box 852 (60060-0852)
PHONE..................800 323-5499
John Campbell, *President*
Heather Campbell, *Admin Sec*
▲ **EMP:** 23
SQ FT: 15,000
SALES (est): 2.8MM **Privately Held**
SIC: 3231 2541 3993 Novelties, glass: fruit, foliage, flowers, animals, etc.; ornamental glass: cut, engraved or otherwise decorated; wood partitions & fixtures; signs & advertising specialties

(G-14666)
BELLE-AIRE FRAGRANCES INC (PA)
Also Called: Belle Aire Creations
1600 Baskin Rd (60060-4602)
PHONE..................847 816-3500
Donald Conover, *CEO*
Jodi Vintartas, *COO*
Charles S David, *Vice Pres*
Richard David, *Vice Pres*
Gustavo Zepeda, *Export Mgr*
EMP: 50 **EST:** 1982
SQ FT: 22,000
SALES (est): 6.6MM **Privately Held**
WEB: www.belle-aire.com
SIC: 2869 2844 Perfume materials, synthetic; flavors or flavoring materials, synthetic; toilet preparations

(G-14667)
BODY WIPE CORPORATION
1027 E High St (60060-3117)
PHONE..................847 687-9321
Joel Saban, *Principal*
EMP: 2
SALES (est): 209.6K **Privately Held**
WEB: www.bodywipecompany.com
SIC: 2844 Towelettes, premoistened

(G-14668)
BOLCHAZY-CARDUCCI PUBLISHERS
1570 Baskin Rd (60060-4474)
PHONE..................847 526-4344
Marie J Bolchazy, *President*
Laurie Haight, *Editor*
Don Sprague, *Editor*
Donald Sprague, *Editor*
David Fiedelman, *Finance*
▲ **EMP:** 13 **EST:** 1979
SQ FT: 3,600
SALES (est): 1.9MM **Privately Held**
SIC: 2731 Books: publishing only; textbooks: publishing only, not printed on site

(G-14669)
BUTTERFIELD CLEANERS
1420 S Butterfield Rd (60060-9424)
PHONE..................847 816-7060
Yong Ho Lee, *Owner*
EMP: 2
SALES (est): 227.8K **Privately Held**
SIC: 3589 Servicing machines, except dry cleaning, laundry: coin-oper.

(G-14670)
CABINET CREATIONS PLUS
515 N Lake St (60060-1826)
PHONE..................847 245-3800
Christine Ciucci, *President*
EMP: 11
SQ FT: 6,000
SALES (est): 1.1MM **Privately Held**
WEB: www.cabinetcreationsplus.com
SIC: 2434 Wood kitchen cabinets

(G-14671)
CAMPANELLA CLG SOLUTIONS INC
Also Called: Aerus Electrolux
900 N Lake St Ste 100 (60060-1359)
PHONE..................847 949-4222
Thomas J Campanella, *President*
EMP: 6
SALES (est): 300.2K **Privately Held**
SIC: 3635 5722 Electric sweeper; vacuum cleaners

(G-14672)
CAMPBELL MANAGEMENT SERVICES
Also Called: Signs Now
25727 N Hillview Ct (60060-9437)
PHONE..................847 566-9020
Bruce J Campbell, *President*
EMP: 4
SQ FT: 2,500
SALES (est): 576.8K **Privately Held**
SIC: 3993 Signs & advertising specialties

(G-14673)
CARRERA STONE SYSTEMS OF CHICA
675 Tower Rd (60060-3819)
PHONE..................847 566-2277
Roberto Contreras, *President*
EMP: 50
SALES: 6MM
SALES (corp-wide): 4MM **Privately Held**
SIC: 3281 1799 Granite, cut & shaped; counter top installation
HQ: Stone Suppliers, Inc.
 13124 Trinity Dr
 Stafford TX

(G-14674)
CARTER HOFFMANN LLC
1551 Mccormick Blvd (60060-4491)
PHONE..................847 362-5500
Bob Fortmann, *President*
Mark Anderson, *Vice Pres*
David ABI, *Vice Pres*
Jeff Erber, *Vice Pres*
Jacqui Gustafson, *Vice Pres*
▲ **EMP:** 110
SQ FT: 80,000
SALES (est): 29.6MM
SALES (corp-wide): 2.9B **Publicly Held**
SIC: 3589 Food warming equipment, commercial
HQ: Marshall Middleby Inc
 1400 Toastmaster Dr
 Elgin IL 60120
 847 741-3300

(G-14675)
CHED MARKAY INC
1065 E High St (60060-3117)
PHONE..................847 566-3307
Garrett Holg, *President*
Lorraine M Holg, *Corp Secy*
Julie Holg, *Vice Pres*
EMP: 8
SQ FT: 2,260
SALES (est): 650K **Privately Held**
SIC: 3843 Dental equipment & supplies

(G-14676)
CHEROKEE PRINTING & SVCS INC
442 N Seymour Ave (60060-1835)
P.O. Box 722 (60060-0722)
PHONE..................847 566-6116
Patrick McGrath, *President*
Anita McGrath, *President*
EMP: 3 **EST:** 1977
SQ FT: 1,174
SALES (est): 433.2K **Privately Held**
SIC: 2752 Commercial printing, offset

(G-14677)
CIRCLE K INDUSTRIES INC
25563 N Gilmer Rd (60060-9410)
PHONE..................847 949-0363
Fax: 847 566-7309
EMP: 10
SQ FT: 14,000
SALES (est): 690K **Privately Held**
SIC: 3496 3523 2842 Mfg Misc Fabricated Wire Products Mfg Farm Machinery/Equipment Mfg Polish/Sanitation Goods

(G-14678)
CLARK WIRE & CABLE CO INC
408 Washington Blvd Ste A (60060-3102)
PHONE..................847 949-9944
Shane Collins, *President*
Patricia Collins, *Vice Pres*
Karen Tunison, *Purchasing*
Ken Bernd, *Natl Sales Mgr*
Dan Collins, *Sales Staff*
EMP: 22
SALES (est): 11.9MM **Privately Held**
SIC: 5063 2298 Electronic wire & cable; cable, fiber

(G-14679)
COMMERCIAL PLASTICS COMPANY (PA)
800 Allanson Rd (60060-3799)
Rural Route 72072, Chicago (60679)
PHONE..................847 566-1700
Matt O'Connor, *President*
Joseph Staniszewski, *Project Mgr*
Helmuth Fendel, *Prdtn Mgr*
Virgis Valeika, *Prdtn Mgr*
Michele Nielsen, *Purchasing*
▲ **EMP:** 105 **EST:** 1942
SQ FT: 100,000
SALES (est): 107.6MM **Privately Held**
WEB: www.ecommercialplastics.com
SIC: 3089 Injection molding of plastics; thermoformed finished plastic products

(G-14680)
CONNECTOR CONCEPTS INC
1530 Mccormick Blvd (60060-4447)
PHONE..................847 541-4020
EMP: 13
SQ FT: 8,500
SALES (est): 5.4MM **Privately Held**
SIC: 3643 Current-carrying wiring devices

(G-14681)
CRESTWOOD INDUSTRIES INC
1345 Wilhelm Rd (60060-4488)
PHONE..................847 680-9088
Paul Langer, *President*
Dale Langer, *Treasurer*
Marie Langer, *Admin Sec*
EMP: 16
SQ FT: 20,000
SALES (est): 3.4MM **Privately Held**
SIC: 3089 Injection molding of plastics

(G-14682)
DESIGN WOODWORKS
27266 N Owens Rd (60060-9512)
PHONE..................847 566-6603
Tim Mayer, *Owner*
EMP: 3
SALES (est): 176.6K **Privately Held**
SIC: 1751 2541 2434 Cabinet building & installation; wood partitions & fixtures; wood kitchen cabinets

Mundelein - Lake County (G-14683)

(G-14683)
DESIGNATION INC
1352 Armour Blvd Ste A (60060-4499)
PHONE..................847 367-9100
Margaret Hercek, *President*
Jerome Brunette, *Vice Pres*
Paul Brunette, *Vice Pres*
Vivian Brunette, *Vice Pres*
EMP: 11
SQ FT: 26,000
SALES (est): 2.7MM **Privately Held**
SIC: 5112 2752 Business forms; office supplies; commercial printing, lithographic; business forms, lithographed

(G-14684)
DVA METAL FABRICATION INC
1656 Brighton Dr (60060-4506)
PHONE..................224 577-8217
Dimitar Atanassov, *Principal*
EMP: 2
SALES (est): 202.4K **Privately Held**
SIC: 3499 Fabricated metal products

(G-14685)
ECOMED SOLUTIONS LLC
214 Terrace Dr (60060-3827)
PHONE..................866 817-7114
David Yurek, *CEO*
EMP: 20 **EST:** 2010
SQ FT: 3,400
SALES (est): 1.2MM **Privately Held**
SIC: 3842 Surgical appliances & supplies

(G-14686)
ENCOMPASS GROUP LLC
955 Campus Dr (60060-3830)
PHONE..................847 680-3388
Terry Voelker, *Mktg Dir*
Michael Green, *Branch Mgr*
EMP: 48
SALES (corp-wide): 159.7MM **Privately Held**
WEB: www.encompassgroup.net
SIC: 2392 Pillows, bed: made from purchased materials
HQ: Encompass Group, L.L.C.
615 Macon St
Mcdonough GA 30253
800 284-4540

(G-14687)
ENTREMATIC HPD NORTH AMER INC (HQ)
Also Called: Dynaco Door
935 Campus Dr (60060-3830)
PHONE..................847 562-4910
Bryan Gregory, *President*
Tim Arends, *General Mgr*
Dirk Wouters, *Admin Sec*
▲ **EMP:** 75
SQ FT: 20,000
SALES (est): 6.6MM
SALES (corp-wide): 9.3B **Privately Held**
SIC: 3442 Rolling doors for industrial buildings or warehouses, metal
PA: Assa Abloy Ab
Klarabergsviadukten 90
Stockholm 111 6
850 648-500

(G-14688)
FIBERGEL TECHNOLOGIES INC
1011 Campus Dr (60060-3834)
PHONE..................847 549-6002
Greg Halpern, *CEO*
Michael Theriult, *COO*
Dana Babney, *CFO*
EMP: 3
SQ FT: 22,000
SALES (est): 127.9K **Publicly Held**
SIC: 2099 Fat substitutes
PA: Agritech Worldwide, Inc.
1011 Campus Dr
Mundelein IL 60060

(G-14689)
FLATOUT GROUP LLC
Also Called: Flatout Gaskets
668 Tower Rd (60060-3820)
PHONE..................847 837-9200
Mark J Adelizzi, *President*
EMP: 3 **EST:** 2008
SQ FT: 10,000
SALES (est): 370K **Privately Held**
SIC: 3053 Gaskets, packing & sealing devices

(G-14690)
GO MANGO INTERACTIVE CORP
1664 Templeton Ct (60060-1479)
PHONE..................224 214-9528
Ajay Sharmam, *President*
EMP: 3
SALES (est): 71.1K **Privately Held**
WEB: www.gomango.io
SIC: 7372 Application computer software

(G-14691)
GRANTCO INC
102 Terrace Dr (60060-3826)
PHONE..................941 567-9259
Rachel Kachigian, *Owner*
EMP: 3 **EST:** 2018
SALES (est): 154.7K **Privately Held**
SIC: 2099 Food preparations

(G-14692)
GREGS FROZEN CUSTARD COMPANY
1490 S Lake St (60060-4260)
PHONE..................847 837-4175
George Orfanos, *President*
EMP: 8
SALES (est): 771K **Privately Held**
WEB: www.custardlist.com
SIC: 2024 Custard, frozen

(G-14693)
GURMAN FOOD CO
906 Tower Rd (60060-3812)
PHONE..................847 837-1100
Larisa Mikhailov, *President*
EMP: 13
SALES (est): 2.5MM **Privately Held**
SIC: 2011 Meat packing plants

(G-14694)
H&R BLOCK INC
Also Called: H & R Block
1527 S Lake St (60060-4210)
PHONE..................847 566-5557
Sue Elliot, *Branch Mgr*
EMP: 12
SALES (corp-wide): 3B **Publicly Held**
SIC: 7291 6794 7372 4822 Tax return preparation services; franchises, selling or licensing; application computer software; electronic mail
PA: H&R Block, Inc.
1 H&R Block Way
Kansas City MO 64105
816 854-3000

(G-14695)
HAMPSTER INDUSTRIES INC
Also Called: Big Time Bats
26400 N Pheasant Run (60060-9514)
PHONE..................866 280-2287
Margaret Obie, *CEO*
John Obie, *President*
EMP: 3
SALES (est): 1.8MM **Privately Held**
SIC: 3949 7389 Baseball, softball & cricket sports equipment;

(G-14696)
HENDRIX INDUSTRIAL GASTRUX INC
327 Rye Rd (60060-1143)
P.O. Box 638, Wauconda (60084-0638)
PHONE..................847 526-1700
Todd Hendrix, *President*
EMP: 6 **EST:** 1953
SQ FT: 7,000
SALES (est): 1.6MM **Privately Held**
WEB: www.propane-conversions.com
SIC: 5013 3714 Automotive engines & engine parts; exhaust systems (mufflers, tail pipes, etc.); exhaust systems & parts, motor vehicle

(G-14697)
HOLCOMB HOLLOW
580 Woodcrest Dr (60060-1525)
PHONE..................847 837-9123
Melissa Norton, *President*
EMP: 3
SALES (est): 200.3K **Privately Held**
SIC: 2099 Food preparations

(G-14698)
IFA INTERNATIONAL INC
Also Called: Alef Sausage & Deli
354356 Townline Rd (60060)
PHONE..................847 566-0008
Alex Mikhaylov, *President*
Lyubov Mikhaylov, *Vice Pres*
▲ **EMP:** 14 **EST:** 2000
SQ FT: 4,900
SALES (est): 1.9MM **Privately Held**
WEB: www.alefsausage.com
SIC: 2013 5812 Sausages & related products, from purchased meat; delicatessen (eating places)

(G-14699)
IN THE ATTIC INC
Also Called: Attic Gifts
1955 Buckingham Rd (60060-1461)
PHONE..................847 949-5077
Kimberly I Kelly, *President*
William P Kelly, *CFO*
EMP: 2
SQ FT: 500
SALES (est): 206.3K **Privately Held**
SIC: 7699 5947 5945 3269 Bicycle repair shop; gift shop; models, toy & hobby; art & ornamental ware, pottery; lawn ornaments

(G-14700)
INDUSTRIAL MOLDED PRODUCTS
800 Allanson Rd (60060-3711)
PHONE..................847 358-2160
Lee Benson, *Principal*
EMP: 2
SALES (est): 256K **Privately Held**
SIC: 3544 Industrial molds

(G-14701)
INNERWELD COVER CO
21227 W Coml Dr Ste E (60060)
PHONE..................847 497-3009
Tim Interrante, *President*
EMP: 10
SALES (est): 1.2MM **Privately Held**
SIC: 3533 3429 3499 Water well drilling equipment; fireplace equipment, hardware: andirons, grates, screens; metal ladders

(G-14702)
IVANHOE INDUSTRIES INC
3333 20th St (60060)
PHONE..................847 872-3311
Robert Wiese, *President*
Dawn Neilson, *Manager*
Daisy Gonzalez,
▲ **EMP:** 39 **EST:** 1979
SQ FT: 7,000
SALES (est): 11.8MM **Privately Held**
SIC: 2899 2843 Corrosion preventive lubricant; emulsifiers, except food & pharmaceutical

(G-14703)
JAY RS STEEL & WELDING INC
840 Tower Rd (60060-3810)
PHONE..................847 949-9353
Ronald R Nally, *President*
Randy Nally, *Corp Secy*
Roger Nally, *Vice Pres*
Ryan Nally, *Vice Pres*
EMP: 5
SQ FT: 6,300
SALES (est): 1.4MM **Privately Held**
SIC: 3441 3599 8734 Fabricated structural metal; machine shop, jobbing & repair; welded joint radiographing

(G-14704)
JMR PRECISION MACHINING INC
630 S Wheeling Rd (60060)
PHONE..................847 279-3982
Jose Marie Y Gonzales, *President*
Rowena Gonzales, *Admin Sec*
EMP: 2
SALES (est): 253.3K **Privately Held**
SIC: 3599 Machine shop, jobbing & repair

(G-14705)
JQL TECHNOLOGIES CORPORATION (PA)
1255 Armour Blvd (60060-4472)
PHONE..................800 236-9828
Jack Zhu, *President*
Christina Huan, *Vice Pres*
EMP: 10
SALES (est): 3.1MM **Privately Held**
SIC: 3674 3822 Optical isolators; hydronic circulator control, automatic

(G-14706)
JSTONE INC
Also Called: Endoplus
750 Tower Rd Spc A (60060-3813)
PHONE..................847 325-5660
Matthew Gudeman, *President*
John Schwab, *Admin Sec*
▲ **EMP:** 20
SQ FT: 10,000
SALES: 2MM **Privately Held**
SIC: 3841 Surgical & medical instruments

(G-14707)
KING MIDAS SEAFOOD ENTPS INC
309 N Lake St Ste 200 (60060-2253)
PHONE..................847 566-2192
Leon Trammell, *CEO*
Michael Meehan, *President*
EMP: 3
SQ FT: 800
SALES: 8MM **Privately Held**
SIC: 2092 Chowders, fish & seafood: frozen

(G-14708)
KOLL LTD (PA)
112 Terrace Dr (60060-3826)
P.O. Box 157, Lake Bluff (60044-0157)
PHONE..................224 544-5418
Christopher Harlocker, *President*
▲ **EMP:** 5
SALES (est): 656.2K **Privately Held**
WEB: www.koll-ltd.com
SIC: 3861 Photographic equipment & supplies

(G-14709)
LARSEN MANUFACTURING LLC (PA)
1201 Allanson Rd (60060-3807)
PHONE..................847 970-9600
Jim Lacroix, *General Mgr*
Jim Miles, *Sales Staff*
Dave Larsen,
Denis Larsen,
▲ **EMP:** 125
SQ FT: 65,000
SALES: 43MM **Privately Held**
SIC: 3469 Stamping metal for the trade

(G-14710)
MAC LEAN-FOGG COMPANY (PA)
Also Called: Maclean Fasteners
1000 Allanson Rd (60060-3804)
PHONE..................847 566-0010
Barry Maclean, *CEO*
Duncan A L Maclean, *President*
Margaret B Maclean, *Vice Pres*
Brad Southwood, *Vice Pres*
Rob Whitney, *Vice Pres*
◆ **EMP:** 92 **EST:** 1925
SQ FT: 3,500
SALES (est): 1.2B **Privately Held**
WEB: www.macleanfogg.com
SIC: 3678 3452 3089 3061 Electronic connectors; nuts, metal; bolts, metal; screws, metal; plastic processing; automotive rubber goods (mechanical); fluid power valves & hose fittings; screw machine products

(G-14711)
MACLEN-FOGG CMPNENT SLTONS LLC (HQ)
Also Called: Mvs Dynalink
1000 Allanson Rd (60060-3804)
PHONE..................248 853-2525
Duncan Maclean, *Vice Pres*
Tracey Herrington, *Vice Pres*
Kevin Lehmann, *Vice Pres*

GEOGRAPHIC SECTION

Mundelein - Lake County (G-14737)

Claudia Ortega, *Vice Pres*
George Pazdirek, *Vice Pres*
▲ **EMP:** 40
SQ FT: 28,000
SALES (est): 36.1MM
SALES (corp-wide): 1.2B **Privately Held**
SIC: 3452 Nuts, metal
PA: Mac Lean-Fogg Company
    1000 Allanson Rd
    Mundelein IL 60060
    847 566-0010

(G-14712)
MADDEN VENTURES INC
1045 Campus Dr Ste A (60060-3802)
PHONE.................................847 487-0644
Joseph Madden, *Principal*
Thomas Madden, *Principal*
EMP: 5
SQ FT: 28,000
SALES (est): 3MM **Privately Held**
SIC: 5084 3599 Machine tools & accessories; metalworking machinery; machine shop, jobbing & repair

(G-14713)
MARK TWAIN PRESS INC
3312 Sheridan Ln (60060-6029)
PHONE.................................847 255-2700
Linda Sloan, *President*
Jim Sloan, *Vice Pres*
EMP: 6
SQ FT: 4,800
SALES (est): 450K **Privately Held**
SIC: 2752 2791 2789 Commercial printing, offset; typesetting; bookbinding & related work

(G-14714)
MASTER MECHANIC MFG INC
970 Campus Dr (60060-3803)
PHONE.................................847 573-3812
Jerry Bost, *President*
EMP: 3
SALES (est): 216.9K **Privately Held**
SIC: 2621 5084 Catalog paper; hydraulic systems equipment & supplies

(G-14715)
MEDLINE INDUSTRIES INC
1200 Townline Rd (60060-4494)
PHONE.................................847 949-2056
Charles Mills, *President*
Angela Chaney, *Engineer*
Matthew Schlais, *Business Anlyst*
Jason Arnold, *Manager*
Viktoriya Gorlova, *Manager*
EMP: 500
SQ FT: 420,000
SALES (corp-wide): 7.4B **Privately Held**
SIC: 3841 Surgical & medical instruments
PA: Medline Industries, Inc.
    3 Lakes Dr
    Northfield IL 60093
    847 949-5500

(G-14716)
MERRY WALKER CORPORATION
21350 W Sylvan Dr S (60060-9442)
PHONE.................................847 837-9580
Mary M Harroun, *President*
EMP: 2
SQ FT: 5,000
SALES (est): 500K **Privately Held**
SIC: 3842 Surgical appliances & supplies

(G-14717)
METFORM LLC (HQ)
1000 Allanson Rd (60060-3804)
PHONE.................................847 566-0010
Dennis Keesey, *Vice Pres*
Gary Sullo, *Vice Pres*
Robert Whitney, *Vice Pres*
Thomas M Pruden, *Treasurer*
Daniel J Joyce,
▲ **EMP:** 5
SQ FT: 180,000
SALES (est): 81.2MM
SALES (corp-wide): 1.2B **Privately Held**
SIC: 3462 Iron & steel forgings
PA: Mac Lean-Fogg Company
    1000 Allanson Rd
    Mundelein IL 60060
    847 566-0010

(G-14718)
MUNTZ INDUSTRIES INC
Also Called: Afc Machining Division
710 Tower Rd (60060-3818)
PHONE.................................847 949-8280
David Muntz, *President*
Steve Muntz, *Vice Pres*
Steven Muntz, *Vice Pres*
Jean Ann Muntz, *Admin Sec*
◆ **EMP:** 50
SQ FT: 17,000
SALES (est): 36.5MM **Privately Held**
SIC: 5084 3677 Metalworking machinery; electronic coils, transformers & other inductors

(G-14719)
MURDOCK COMPANY INC
Also Called: Plasmag Pump Div
936 Turret Ct (60060-3821)
PHONE.................................847 566-0050
Frank J Olk, *President*
Betty R Olk, *Corp Secy*
John Olk, *Sales Mgr*
EMP: 6
SQ FT: 12,000
SALES (est): 1.1MM **Privately Held**
WEB: www.murdockcompany.com
SIC: 3564 3561 3443 5085 Filters, air: furnaces, air conditioning equipment, etc.; industrial pumps & parts; housings, pressure; filters, industrial; pumps & pumping equipment; industrial inorganic chemicals

(G-14720)
NETWORK PRINTING INC
109 Alexandra Ct (60060-2647)
PHONE.................................847 566-4146
Mike Murrow, *President*
EMP: 2
SALES (est): 237K **Privately Held**
SIC: 2752 Commercial printing, offset

(G-14721)
NORTHFIELD BLOCK COMPANY (DH)
1 Hunt Ct (60060-4487)
PHONE.................................847 816-9000
Craig M Belasco, *President*
◆ **EMP:** 200
SQ FT: 3,200
SALES (est): 90MM
SALES (corp-wide): 30.6B **Privately Held**
WEB: www.northfieldblock.com
SIC: 3272 Concrete products
HQ: Oldcastle Architectural, Inc.
    3 Glenlake Pkwy
    Atlanta GA 30328
    770 804-3363

(G-14722)
PACKAGING CORPORATION AMERICA
Also Called: PCA Tech Center
250 S Shaddle Ave (60060-3114)
PHONE.................................847 388-6000
Mike A Conley, *Plant Mgr*
Randy Cooley, *Prdtn Mgr*
Steve Huygens, *Engineer*
Desiree Booth, *Controller*
Fred Cordova, *Accounts Mgr*
EMP: 14
SALES (corp-wide): 6.9B **Publicly Held**
WEB: www.packagingcorp.com
SIC: 2653 Boxes, corrugated: made from purchased materials
PA: Packaging Corporation Of America
    1 N Field Ct
    Lake Forest IL 60045
    847 482-3000

(G-14723)
PARKER TOOL & DIE CO
20844 W Park Ave (60060-9109)
PHONE.................................847 566-2229
Tim Parker, *Owner*
EMP: 8
SQ FT: 4,500
SALES (est): 530K **Privately Held**
SIC: 3599 3544 Machine shop, jobbing & repair; special dies, tools, jigs & fixtures

(G-14724)
PET FACTORY INC
845 E High St (60060-3100)
PHONE.................................847 837-8900
Tom Miller, *President*
Doug Treeck, *Vice Pres*
Bhargavi Kanneganti, *QC Mgr*
Matt Bourseau, *Natl Sales Mgr*
Karla Arizmendi, *Sales Staff*
▲ **EMP:** 200
SQ FT: 117,000
SALES (est): 40.5MM **Privately Held**
SIC: 5149 3999 Pet foods; pet supplies

(G-14725)
PHARMA LOGISTICS
1050 E High St (60060-3118)
PHONE.................................847 388-3104
Michael Zaccaro, *Owner*
Ron Noel, *Accounts Exec*
Patricia Gaytan, *Associate*
▲ **EMP:** 61
SALES (est): 9.9MM **Privately Held**
SIC: 2834 Pharmaceutical preparations

(G-14726)
PHOENIX MARKETING SERVICES
104 Terrace Dr (60060-3826)
PHONE.................................630 616-8000
Lynn Gulbranson, *President*
Ann Sawicki, *Corp Secy*
EMP: 12
SALES (est): 1.7MM **Privately Held**
SIC: 7336 2759 Graphic arts & related design; screen printing

(G-14727)
PRECITEC CORPORATION
Also Called: Poly-Clip Systems
1000 Tower Rd (60060-3816)
PHONE.................................847 949-2800
Nicholas D Brasile, *President*
Gilbert Williams, *Principal*
Gil Williams, *Vice Pres*
Nicholas Brasile, *Finance*
Gregory Alex, *Regl Sales Mgr*
▲ **EMP:** 70
SQ FT: 35,000
SALES (est): 17.3MM
SALES (corp-wide): 156.5MM **Privately Held**
SIC: 3496 Clips & fasteners, made from purchased wire
PA: Poly-Clip System Gmbh & Co. Kg
    Niedeckerstr. 1
    Hattersheim Am Main 65795
    619 088-860

(G-14728)
PRINT TECH INC
Also Called: Printing Factory, The
407 Wshington Blvd Unit C (60060)
PHONE.................................847 949-5400
Brad Kington, *President*
John Petrovskis, *Corp Secy*
Fran Stephens, *Graphic Designe*
EMP: 12
SQ FT: 6,400
SALES (est): 2.1MM **Privately Held**
SIC: 2752 Commercial printing, offset

(G-14729)
PRINT-O-TAPE INC
755 Tower Rd (60060-3817)
P.O. Box 308, Libertyville, (60048-0308)
PHONE.................................847 362-1476
Carl Walliser, *President*
Jennifer Zemba, *General Mgr*
Jon Barrere, *Vice Pres*
Ron Cuba, *Vice Pres*
Bob Ryan, *Traffic Mgr*
EMP: 43 **EST:** 1947
SQ FT: 84,000
SALES (est): 22.3MM **Privately Held**
WEB: www.printotape.com
SIC: 2672 Tape, pressure sensitive: made from purchased materials; labels (unprinted), gummed: made from purchased materials

(G-14730)
R2C PERFORMANCE PRODUCTS LLC
605 Tower Rd (60060-3819)
PHONE.................................708 488-8211
Ryan Greenlees, *Opers Mgr*
Patrick Mooney, *Design Engr*
Ed Sroka, *Sales Executive*
Roy Greenlees, *Mng Member*
Pat Greenlees,
▲ **EMP:** 10
SALES (est): 1.7MM **Privately Held**
WEB: www.r2cperformance.com
SIC: 3714 Motor vehicle parts & accessories

(G-14731)
RAINBOW MANUFACTURING INC
Also Called: Rainbow Graphics, Inc.
933 Tower Rd (60060-3811)
PHONE.................................847 824-9600
Claude Koszuta, *CEO*
Jeff Koszuta, *President*
Scott Campbell, *Vice Pres*
Claude Koszuta Jr, *Vice Pres*
Len Karl, *Plant Mgr*
EMP: 44
SQ FT: 50,000
SALES (est): 15MM **Privately Held**
SIC: 2752 Commercial printing, offset

(G-14732)
ROSE CUSTOM CABINETS INC
Also Called: Rose Custom Builders
408 Washington Blvd Ste C (60060-3102)
PHONE.................................847 816-4800
Brian Rosenberg, *President*
EMP: 28
SQ FT: 26,000
SALES (est): 2.1MM **Privately Held**
SIC: 5712 2511 Cabinet work, custom; wood household furniture

(G-14733)
ROSES MOULDING BY DESIGN INC
408 Washington Blvd Ste C (60060-3102)
PHONE.................................847 549-9200
Tom Troush, *President*
Terry Allen, *Manager*
EMP: 30
SALES (est): 1MM **Privately Held**
SIC: 3999 Manufacturing industries

(G-14734)
SEAPORT DIGITAL LLC
112 Terrace Dr (60060-3826)
P.O. Box 157, Lake Bluff (60044-0157)
PHONE.................................847 235-2319
Benjamin Shmitz, *Manager*
EMP: 5
SALES (est): 203.2K
SALES (corp-wide): 656.2K **Privately Held**
SIC: 3861 Photographic equipment & supplies
PA: Koll Ltd.
    112 Terrace Dr
    Mundelein IL 60060
    224 544-5418

(G-14735)
SENJU COMTEK CORP
1322 Armour Blvd (60060-4402)
PHONE.................................847 549-5690
Ryoichi Suzuki, *Branch Mgr*
EMP: 6 **Privately Held**
SIC: 3399 Paste, metal
HQ: Senju Comtek Corp.
    2989 San Ysidro Way
    Santa Clara CA 95051

(G-14736)
SENSOR 21 INC
19541 W University Dr (60060-3485)
PHONE.................................847 561-6233
EMP: 5
SALES (est): 450K **Privately Held**
SIC: 3826 R&D Optical Sensor Systems

(G-14737)
SOMMERS FARE LLC
1301 Allanson Rd (60060-3835)
PHONE.................................877 377-9797

Mundelein - Lake County (G-14738)

Walter Sommers,
Lenny Lebovich,
EMP: 30
SALES (est): 3.8MM **Privately Held**
SIC: 2011 Canned meats (except baby food), meat slaughtered on site

(G-14738)
SPHERE INC
Also Called: Signal Graphics Printing
316 Washington Blvd (60060-3106)
PHONE................................847 566-4800
Diane C Donovan, *President*
Kevin M Donovan, *Vice Pres*
EMP: 3
SQ FT: 2,160
SALES (est): 490.2K **Privately Held**
WEB: www.signalgraphics.com
SIC: 2752 Commercial printing, offset

(G-14739)
STRAUSAK INC
1295 Armour Blvd (60060-4472)
PHONE................................847 281-8550
Joseph Kane, *President*
Joe Kane, *President*
▲ **EMP:** 4
SALES (est): 173.6K **Privately Held**
SIC: 3599 Machine shop, jobbing & repair

(G-14740)
STUART MOORE RACING LTD
Also Called: SMR Components
831 E Orchard St (60060-3019)
PHONE................................847 949-9100
Stuart Alan Moore, *President*
Stuart Moore, *Mktg Dir*
EMP: 8
SQ FT: 5,000
SALES (est): 1.1MM **Privately Held**
SIC: 3599 Machine shop, jobbing & repair

(G-14741)
SYSMEX REAGENTS AMERICA INC
2 Sysmex Way (60060-9528)
PHONE................................847 996-4500
▲ **EMP:** 30
SQ FT: 35,000
SALES (est): 608.1K
SALES (corp-wide): 2.1B **Privately Held**
SIC: 2835 Mfg Diagnostic Substances
HQ: Sysmex America, Inc.
577 Aptakisic Rd
Lincolnshire IL 60069
847 996-4500

(G-14742)
TE CONNECTIVITY CORPORATION
Also Called: Corcom
620 S Butterfield Rd (60060-9457)
PHONE................................847 680-7400
Michael P Raleigh, *President*
EMP: 85
SALES (corp-wide): 13.9B **Privately Held**
SIC: 3677 3678 Filtration devices, electronic; electronic connectors
HQ: Te Connectivity Corporation
1050 Westlakes Dr
Berwyn PA 19312
610 893-9800

(G-14743)
TEXMAC INC
224 Terrace Dr (60060-3827)
PHONE................................630 244-4702
Bill Mahon, *Manager*
EMP: 3 **Privately Held**
SIC: 3571 Electronic computers
HQ: Texmac Inc.
3001 Stafford Dr
Charlotte NC 28208
704 394-0314

(G-14744)
TICONA TECHNICAL POLYMERS
1301 Halifax Dr (60060-1045)
PHONE................................847 949-1444
Diane Blakey, *Principal*
EMP: 5
SALES (est): 365.2K **Privately Held**
SIC: 3087 3089 Custom compound purchased resins; plastics products

(G-14745)
ULTIMATE DISTRIBUTING INC
Also Called: Ultimate Screen Printing
436 Morris Ave (60060-1919)
PHONE................................847 566-2250
Don Hermestroff, *President*
Tracy Hermestroff, *Executive*
EMP: 6 **EST:** 1978
SALES (est): 845.7K **Privately Held**
SIC: 2262 2759 2396 2395 Screen printing: manmade fiber & silk broadwoven fabrics; screen printing; promotional printing; automotive & apparel trimmings; pleating & stitching

(G-14746)
WANDFLUH OF AMERICA INC
909 E High St (60060-3119)
PHONE................................847 566-5700
James R Brooks, *President*
Gary Getting, *Vice Pres*
Hansrudolph Wandfluh, *Vice Pres*
Shane Krupinski, *Opers Staff*
Dawn Wells, *Purch Agent*
▲ **EMP:** 15
SQ FT: 6,600
SALES (est): 2.8MM **Privately Held**
SIC: 3492 1799 Control valves, fluid power: hydraulic & pneumatic; hydraulic equipment, installation & service

(G-14747)
WW DISPLAYS INC
Also Called: Wood & Wire
401 Wshington Blvd Ste 10 (60060)
PHONE................................847 566-6979
William J Scarim, *President*
Jacqueline Scarim, *Corp Secy*
Robert Miller, *Vice Pres*
Sharon Plucinski, *Info Tech Mgr*
EMP: 16
SQ FT: 56,000
SALES (est): 3.1MM **Privately Held**
SIC: 2541 1751 2542 Display fixtures, wood; carpentry work; partitions & fixtures, except wood

(G-14748)
Z AUTOMATION COMPANY
163 N Archer Ave (60060-2301)
PHONE................................847 483-0120
Zoran Momich, *President*
Vesna Momich, *Vice Pres*
◆ **EMP:** 48
SQ FT: 56,000
SALES (est): 13.1MM **Privately Held**
SIC: 3565 Packaging machinery

Murphysboro
Jackson County

(G-14749)
ADVANCED CUSTOM SHAPES
550 N 19th St (62966-1704)
P.O. Box 384 (62966-0384)
PHONE................................618 684-2222
Fax: 618 684-2200
EMP: 18
SALES: 600K **Privately Held**
SIC: 2673 Mfg Bags-Plastic/Coated Paper

(G-14750)
ALSTAT WOOD PRODUCTS
456 Highway 4 (62966-4205)
PHONE................................618 684-5167
Dan Alstat, *Owner*
EMP: 10 **EST:** 1985
SALES (est): 1.5MM **Privately Held**
SIC: 2421 Sawmills & planing mills, general

(G-14751)
BLUFFS VINEYARD & WINERY L L C
1505 Business Highway 13 (62966-2972)
P.O. Box 236 (62966-0236)
PHONE................................618 763-4447
Steve Ellis, *Principal*
EMP: 4
SALES (est): 151.4K **Privately Held**
SIC: 2084 Wines

(G-14752)
BREES STUDIO INC
430 S 19th St (62966-2401)
P.O. Box 1120 (62966-1120)
PHONE................................618 687-3331
Gary Brees, *President*
Deborah Brees, *Executive*
EMP: 10
SQ FT: 18,000
SALES (est): 1.2MM **Privately Held**
SIC: 3999 Artificial trees & flowers

(G-14753)
BURKE WHISTLES INC
389 Wells St (62966-7023)
PHONE................................618 534-7953
Michael D Burke, *President*
Susan P Burke, *Admin Sec*
EMP: 2
SQ FT: 800
SALES: 240K **Privately Held**
SIC: 3999 Whistles

(G-14754)
CMT INTERNATIONAL INC
1400 N Wood Rd (62966-6290)
P.O. Box 3254, Carbondale (62902-3254)
PHONE................................618 549-1829
Ming-Tsang Chang, *President*
Monica Lien, *Corp Secy*
◆ **EMP:** 6
SQ FT: 1,300
SALES (est): 5.6MM **Privately Held**
SIC: 3089 Plastic processing

(G-14755)
HARTMANN
29 Steven Dr (62966-4236)
PHONE................................618 684-6814
EMP: 3
SALES (est): 250.1K **Privately Held**
SIC: 3161 Mfg Luggage

(G-14756)
PENN ALUMINUM INTL LLC (DH)
1117 N 2nd St (62966-3332)
PHONE................................618 684-2146
Bruce Hoffman, *Business Mgr*
Paul Crawford, *Safety Mgr*
James Martin,
EMP: 226
SQ FT: 200,000
SALES (est): 37.5MM
SALES (corp-wide): 327.2B **Publicly Held**
SIC: 3354 3334 3312 5051 Tube, extruded or drawn, aluminum; primary aluminum; blast furnaces & steel mills; aluminum bars, rods, ingots, sheets, pipes, plates, etc.
HQ: Marmon Group Llc
181 W Madison St Ste 2600
Chicago IL 60602
312 372-9500

(G-14757)
POPULAR RIDGE MACHINE MET CFT
134 S Jungle Rd (62966-6329)
PHONE................................618 687-1656
Michael Collins, *Principal*
EMP: 3 **EST:** 2007
SALES (est): 249.6K **Privately Held**
SIC: 3599 Machine shop, jobbing & repair

(G-14758)
SCHULZE & SCHULZE INC
3198 Town Creek Rd (62966-5375)
PHONE................................618 687-1106
David Schulze, *President*
EMP: 5
SALES (est): 594.1K **Privately Held**
SIC: 2951 1629 1611 Asphalt paving mixtures & blocks; tennis court construction; highway & street construction

(G-14759)
SCHWEBEL PRINTING
Also Called: Harold Printing & Graphics
1408 Walnut St (62966-2030)
PHONE................................618 684-3911
Cleon Birkemeyer, *President*
BJ Wyatt, *Corp Secy*
EMP: 2
SQ FT: 1,140
SALES (est): 237.2K **Privately Held**
WEB: www.schwebelprintingandgraphic.com
SIC: 2759 2752 2791 2789 Letterpress printing; commercial printing, offset; typesetting; bookbinding & related work

(G-14760)
SILKWORM INC
Also Called: Silkworm Screen Printing
102 S Sezmore Dr (62966-7046)
P.O. Box 340 (62966-0340)
PHONE................................618 687-4077
Robert Chambers, *President*
Cheryl Endres, *Vice Pres*
Racheal Hannel, *Accounts Mgr*
Elizabeth Hess, *Mktg Coord*
Shaad Schubert, *Director*
EMP: 56
SQ FT: 31,000
SALES (est): 7.7MM **Privately Held**
SIC: 2759 Screen printing

(G-14761)
THIRTEEN RF INC
Also Called: 13rf Rental & Fabrication
10 Alliance Ave (62966)
P.O. Box 1556 (62966-5056)
PHONE................................618 687-1313
Randall Fricke, *President*
Nancy Fricke, *President*
Renee Moniger, *Accountant*
EMP: 30
SALES (est): 2.3MM **Privately Held**
SIC: 3449 Bars, concrete reinforcing: fabricated steel

(G-14762)
WILDLIFE MATERIALS INC
1202 Walnut St (62966-2124)
PHONE................................618 687-3505
William Liao, *CEO*
Richard Blanchard, *President*
Lisa Filkins, *Production*
▲ **EMP:** 45
SQ FT: 15,000
SALES (est): 7.2MM **Privately Held**
SIC: 3699 Electrical equipment & supplies

Naperville
Dupage County

(G-14763)
ACCURATE REPRO INC
2368 Corporate Ln Ste 100 (60563-9631)
PHONE................................630 428-4433
Michael A Pavetto, *President*
Michael Merle, *General Mgr*
EMP: 14
SQ FT: 10,000
SALES (est): 2.4MM **Privately Held**
SIC: 3993 7334 Signs & advertising specialties; blueprinting service

(G-14764)
ACE GRAPHICS INC
2052 Corporate Ln (60563-9691)
PHONE................................630 357-2244
Rodney Kranz, *President*
Kaitlyn Battey, *Project Mgr*
Beth Kranz, *Treasurer*
Jessica Phelps, *Sr Project Mgr*
Sandy Boyles, *Admin Asst*
▲ **EMP:** 20
SQ FT: 22,000
SALES (est): 4.8MM **Privately Held**
SIC: 2752 Commercial printing, offset

(G-14765)
ADAMS MACHINE SHOP
1223 Arthur Rd (60540-6901)
PHONE................................630 851-6060
Casimir Adams, *Owner*
EMP: 4 **EST:** 1944
SQ FT: 5,000
SALES: 60K **Privately Held**
WEB: www.amspianotools.com
SIC: 3599 Machine shop, jobbing & repair

GEOGRAPHIC SECTION
Naperville - Dupage County (G-14792)

(G-14766)
ADVANCED ROBOTICS RESEARCH
791 Sigmund Rd (60563-1391)
PHONE..................630 544-0040
Bruce Taneja, *Principal*
Meena Taneja, *Principal*
EMP: 4
SALES (est): 180K **Privately Held**
SIC: 3549 8733 7389 Assembly machines, including robotic; scientific research agency;

(G-14767)
ADVANTAGE OPTICS INC
Also Called: Ao Corporate
1555 Bond St Ste 117 (60563-0100)
PHONE..................630 548-9870
Brian McConnell, *CEO*
Charles Parilla, *Sls & Mktg Exec*
EMP: 14
SALES (est): 3MM **Privately Held**
SIC: 3661 Fiber optics communications equipment

(G-14768)
AECHEM SCIENTIFIC CORPORATION (PA)
2055 University Dr (60565-2984)
PHONE..................630 364-5106
Jerry Wang, *Managing Prtnr*
Qiang MEI, *Principal*
EMP: 4
SALES (est): 518.4K **Privately Held**
WEB: www.aechemsc.com
SIC: 2834 Pharmaceutical preparations

(G-14769)
ALBRIGHT ENTERPRISES INC
Also Called: Signs Now
426 W 5th Ave (60563-2985)
PHONE..................630 357-2300
Stan Albright, *President*
Rachel Albright, *Admin Sec*
EMP: 8
SQ FT: 1,900
SALES (est): 1MM **Privately Held**
SIC: 3993 Signs & advertising specialties

(G-14770)
ALE USA INC
1960 Nperville Wheaton Rd (60563-1594)
PHONE..................630 713-5194
Priya Tamta, *Technology*
Manish Thakkar, *Technical Staff*
Ron Citta, *Maintence Staff*
EMP: 6
SALES (est): 392.5K **Privately Held**
WEB: www.alcatel-lucent.com
SIC: 3663 Radio & TV communications equipment

(G-14771)
ALL STAR CUSTOM AWARDS
1203 Hidden Spring Dr (60540-4113)
PHONE..................630 428-1515
Rick Belle, *Owner*
EMP: 1
SALES: 230K **Privately Held**
SIC: 3499 Novelties & giftware, including trophies

(G-14772)
ALL STAR PUBLISHING
1203 Hidden Spring Dr (60540-4113)
PHONE..................630 428-1515
Rick Belle, *Principal*
EMP: 3
SALES (est): 144.9K **Privately Held**
SIC: 2711 Newspapers: publishing only, not printed on site

(G-14773)
AMERICAN TECHNOLOGIES INC
1150 Shore Rd (60563-8759)
PHONE..................630 548-8150
John Lipke, *Opers Mgr*
Doug Fairless, *Manager*
Robert Sparks, *Executive*
EMP: 22 **Privately Held**
WEB: www.atirestoration.com
SIC: 2899 Water treating compounds
PA: American Technologies Inc.
3360 E La Palma Ave
Anaheim CA 92806

(G-14774)
ARCAM CAD TO METAL INC
55 Shuman Blvd Ste 850 (60563-7917)
PHONE..................630 357-5700
Glen Liddell, *Admin Sec*
▲ EMP: 3
SALES (est): 422.3K **Privately Held**
SIC: 3549 Metalworking machinery

(G-14775)
ASPEN PRINTING SERVICES LLC
405 S River Rd (60540-5036)
PHONE..................630 357-3203
Mark Botos, *Mng Member*
EMP: 5
SALES (est): 270.9K **Privately Held**
SIC: 2752 Commercial printing, offset

(G-14776)
BAKER LA RUSSO
Also Called: Baker's Custom Lettering
911 Joan Ct (60540-1931)
PHONE..................630 788-5108
La Russo Baker, *Owner*
EMP: 4
SALES (est): 170K **Privately Held**
SIC: 2759 Screen printing

(G-14777)
BATTERY SYSTEMS LLC
2135 City Gate Ln Ste 300 (60563-3066)
PHONE..................833 487-6937
Adam Smith,
Natalie Bertoglio,
EMP: 2
SALES (est): 318.7K **Privately Held**
SIC: 3629 Battery chargers, rectifying or nonrotating

(G-14778)
BELSON OUTDOORS LLC
627 Amersale Dr (60563-3602)
PHONE..................630 897-8489
Dennis Iverson, *Controller*
Brenda Wilmsen, *Cust Mgr*
Gavin McHugh, *Mng Member*
Xin Davies, *Director*
Geoffrey Munro, *Creative Dir*
◆ EMP: 32
SQ FT: 50,000
SALES (est): 7.5MM **Privately Held**
WEB: www.belson.com
SIC: 3631 2531 3639 Barbecues, grills & braziers (outdoor cooking); picnic tables or benches, park; trash compactors, household
HQ: Playcore Wisconsin, Inc.
544 Chestnut St
Chattanooga TN 37402
423 265-7529

(G-14779)
BERNARD CFFEY VTRANS FUNDATION
1634 Mulligan Dr (60563-1786)
PHONE..................630 687-0033
Bernard Coffey, *CEO*
EMP: 6
SALES (est): 434.7K **Privately Held**
SIC: 1521 3272 3585 7997 Single-family housing construction; housing components, prefabricated concrete; heating & air conditioning combination units; indoor/outdoor court clubs

(G-14780)
BLUCO CORPORATION
1510 Frontenac Rd (60563-1755)
PHONE..................630 637-1820
Robert W Ellig, *President*
John Born, *Opers Staff*
Ben Frola, *Mfg Staff*
Todd Bennett, *Engineer*
Kyle Lansford, *Engineer*
▲ EMP: 17
SALES (est): 3.8MM **Privately Held**
SIC: 3544 Special dies, tools, jigs & fixtures

(G-14781)
BLUE YONDER INC
280 Shuman Blvd Ste 105 (60563-8100)
PHONE..................630 701-1492
Seth Malley, *President*

Tim Karl, *Superintendent*
Bill Larson, *Superintendent*
Pat Vanhal, *Accounting Mgr*
Patricia Vanhal, *Manager*
EMP: 5
SALES (est): 890.3K **Privately Held**
SIC: 8741 1542 1541 1389 Management services; commercial & office building, new construction; school building construction; industrial buildings, new construction; construction, repair & dismantling services; highway & street construction

(G-14782)
BP AMOCO CHEMICAL COMPANY
150 W Warrenville Rd (60563-8473)
PHONE..................630 420-5111
N C Dunn, *President*
L M Sierra, *President*
Judy Ventura, *President*
Rebecca Raftery, *Counsel*
Rob Divalerio, *Vice Pres*
◆ EMP: 260 EST: 1945
SQ FT: 50,000
SALES (est): 8.6MM
SALES (corp-wide): 278.4B **Privately Held**
WEB: www.bp.com
SIC: 2221 2821 2869 2819 Broadwoven fabric mills, manmade; styrene resins; industrial organic chemicals; industrial inorganic chemicals; cyclic organic crudes
HQ: Bp Corporation North America Inc.
501 Westlake Park Blvd
Houston TX 77079
281 366-2000

(G-14783)
BP PRODUCTS NORTH AMERICA INC
Also Called: Amoco
150 W Warrenville Rd (60563-8473)
PHONE..................630 420-4300
Tom Bond, *Manager*
EMP: 5
SALES (corp-wide): 278.4B **Privately Held**
WEB: www.bp.com
SIC: 5541 5171 4612 4613 Filling stations, gasoline; petroleum bulk stations & terminals; crude petroleum pipelines; refined petroleum pipelines; crude petroleum & natural gas
HQ: Bp Products North America Inc.
501 Westlake Park Blvd
Houston TX 77079
281 366-2000

(G-14784)
BP SHIPPING
150 W Warrenville Rd (60563-8473)
PHONE..................630 393-1032
John Rigway, *President*
◆ EMP: 14
SALES (est): 1.7MM **Privately Held**
SIC: 2441 Shipping cases, wood: nailed or lock corner

(G-14785)
BP SOLAR INTERNATIONAL INC
150 W Warrenville Rd (60563-8473)
PHONE..................301 698-4200
Reyad Fezzani, *CEO*
Abhay Raichoora, *Vice Pres*
Ruben Mu Oz Aguilera, *Engineer*
R J Novaria, *Treasurer*
Lilly Baker, *Controller*
▲ EMP: 585
SQ FT: 100,000
SALES (est): 63.5MM
SALES (corp-wide): 278.4B **Privately Held**
SIC: 3674 3433 Solar cells; silicon wafers, chemically doped; heating equipment, except electric
HQ: Amoco Technology Company
200 E Randolph St # 3500
Chicago IL 60601
312 861-6000

(G-14786)
C H HANSON COMPANY (PA)
2000 N Aurora Rd (60563-8793)
PHONE..................630 848-2000

Craig F Hanson, *President*
Kimberly M Bork, *Corp Secy*
Gordon A Vogel, *VP Mfg*
Philip C Hanson, *Asst Treas*
Ernie Torkilsen, *VP Sales*
◆ EMP: 75
SALES (est): 63.2MM **Privately Held**
WEB: www.chhanson.com
SIC: 5085 5099 5112 5131 Adhesives, tape & plasters; signs, except electric; pens &/or pencils; piece goods & other fabrics; identification tags, except paper; stencils, painting & marking

(G-14787)
CALL POTENTIAL LLC
24047 W Lockport St (60540)
PHONE..................877 552-2557
Steve Kauffman, *Marketing Staff*
John Murphy, *Mng Member*
Michael Elberts, *Manager*
Wendy Pirkins, *Manager*
EMP: 13
SQ FT: 2,000
SALES (est): 382.3K **Privately Held**
SIC: 7372 Business oriented computer software

(G-14788)
CAPTIVATING SIGNS LLC (PA)
612 W 5th Ave Ste A (60563-4839)
PHONE..................630 470-6161
Atul Akhand,
EMP: 3
SALES (est): 474.6K **Privately Held**
WEB: www.captivatingsigns.com
SIC: 3993 Signs & advertising specialties

(G-14789)
CARLIN MFG A DIV GRS HOLDG LLC
131 W Jefferson Ave # 223 (60540-4682)
PHONE..................559 276-0123
Kari Franz, *Sales Staff*
Amy Lewis, *Marketing Staff*
Dave Damsen, *Senior Mgr*
Raul Reyes, *IT/INT Sup*
Ralph H Goldbeck,
EMP: 25
SALES: 3.5MM **Privately Held**
SIC: 2451 Mobile buildings: for commercial use

(G-14790)
CAROL ANDRZEJEWSKI
Also Called: Designer Blinds
2339 Kalamazoo Dr (60565-6361)
PHONE..................630 369-9711
Carol Andrzejewski, *Principal*
EMP: 4 EST: 2010
SALES (est): 361.8K **Privately Held**
SIC: 2591 Window blinds

(G-14791)
CARROLL DISTRG & CNSTR SUP INC
1700 Quincy Ave (60540-4176)
PHONE..................630 369-6520
Kurt Madsen, *Sales Staff*
Mike Kozacek, *Branch Mgr*
EMP: 18
SALES (corp-wide): 128.2MM **Privately Held**
SIC: 5082 3444 Contractors' materials; concrete forms, sheet metal
PA: Carroll Distributing & Construction Supply, Inc.
207 W 2nd St Ste 3
Ottumwa IA 52501
641 683-1888

(G-14792)
CASTROL INDUSTRIAL N AMER INC (DH)
150 W Warrenville Rd (60563-8473)
PHONE..................877 641-1600
Dave Feurst, *President*
Sanjay Srivastava, *Sales Mgr*
Bob Zoscsak, *Sales Staff*
Derek Ozbun, *Program Mgr*
Greg Hawes, *Manager*
◆ EMP: 225
SQ FT: 40,000

Naperville - Dupage County (G-14793)

SALES (est): 80.9MM
SALES (corp-wide): 278.4B **Privately Held**
SIC: 2992 2899 Lubricating oils & greases; corrosion preventive lubricant; rust resisting compounds
HQ: Bp America Inc
4101 Winfield Rd Ste 200
Warrenville IL 60555
630 420-5111

(G-14793)
CCS CONTRACTOR EQP & SUP INC (PA)
Also Called: Just Rite Rental
1567 Frontenac Rd (60563-1754)
PHONE..................630 393-9020
Ray Barthyolomae, *President*
Paul Koplin, *Opers Mgr*
Pete Colwell, *Purch Mgr*
Craig Helwig, *CFO*
Flamini Sr Jim, *Sales Staff*
▲ **EMP:** 33
SQ FT: 20,000
SALES (est): 23MM **Privately Held**
SIC: 5032 5082 7359 3444 Concrete building products; concrete processing equipment; equipment rental & leasing; concrete forms, sheet metal

(G-14794)
CDA INDUSTRIES INC
1228 Jane Ave (60540-5638)
PHONE..................630 357-7654
Mark Goralski, *Branch Mgr*
EMP: 3 **Privately Held**
SIC: 3496 Miscellaneous fabricated wire products
PA: Cda Industries Inc
1055 Squires Beach Rd
Pickering ON L1W 4
905 686-7000

(G-14795)
CENTRAL NEWSPAPER INCORPORATED
40 Shuman Blvd Ste 305 (60563-8656)
PHONE..................630 416-4191
Michael D Haddad, *Principal*
EMP: 3
SALES (est): 151.8K **Privately Held**
WEB: www.central-news.com
SIC: 2711 Newspapers, publishing & printing

(G-14796)
CHICAGO CHINESE TIMES
424 Fort Hill Dr Ste 100 (60540-3909)
PHONE..................630 717-4567
Danny Lee, *President*
Jwo Hwa Lee, *President*
Wea Lee, *Shareholder*
▲ **EMP:** 5
SALES (est): 390.2K **Privately Held**
SIC: 2711 Newspapers, publishing & printing

(G-14797)
CHICAGO CONTRACT BRIDGE ASSN (PA)
1624 Masters Ct (60563-1781)
P.O. Box 2858 (60567-2858)
PHONE..................630 355-5560
Jackie Addis, *President*
Sue Weinstein, *Admin Sec*
EMP: 5
SALES: 115.9K **Privately Held**
SIC: 2678 3944 Stationery: made from purchased materials; games, toys & children's vehicles

(G-14798)
CHICAGO RIVET & MACHINE CO (PA)
901 Frontenac Rd (60563-1744)
P.O. Box 3061 (60566-7061)
PHONE..................630 357-8500
Walter W Morrissey, *Ch of Bd*
Michael J Bourg, *President*
Diane Decker, *Purch Mgr*
Jeff Harrity, *Controller*
Jodi Bukovsky, *Sales Staff*
▼ **EMP:** 85
SALES: 32.8MM **Publicly Held**
WEB: www.chicagorivet.com
SIC: 3452 3542 7359 3451 Rivets, metal; riveting machines; equipment rental & leasing; screw machine products

(G-14799)
CHILD EVNGELISM FELLOWSHIP INC
365 Du Pahze St (60565-3052)
PHONE..................630 983-7708
Joshua Chang, *Branch Mgr*
EMP: 41
SALES (corp-wide): 24.4MM **Privately Held**
WEB: www.cefonline.com
SIC: 2752 Commercial printing, lithographic
PA: Child Evangelism Fellowship Incorporated
17482 Highway M
Warrenton MO 63383
636 456-4321

(G-14800)
CLEARSOUNDS COMMUNICATIONS INC (PA)
1743 Quincy Ave Ste 155 (60540-3995)
PHONE..................630 321-2300
Michele Ahlman, *President*
Mary Williams, *General Mgr*
Madelaine Uzuanis, *Vice Pres*
▲ **EMP:** 11
SQ FT: 5,000
SALES (est): 2.6MM **Privately Held**
SIC: 3651 Audio electronic systems

(G-14801)
COGNEX CORPORATION
800 E Diehl Rd Ste 125 (60563-7871)
PHONE..................630 505-9990
EMP: 3
SALES (corp-wide): 486.2MM **Publicly Held**
SIC: 3823 Mfg Process Control Instruments
PA: Cognex Corporation
1 Vision Dr
Natick MA 01760
508 650-3000

(G-14802)
COLBERT CUSTOM FRAMING INC
1283 S Naper Blvd (60540-8300)
PHONE..................630 717-1448
Kevin Colbert, *Owner*
EMP: 11
SQ FT: 2,000
SALES (est): 1MM **Privately Held**
SIC: 2499 5999 Picture & mirror frames, wood; picture frames, ready made

(G-14803)
CONAGRA BRANDS INC
Also Called: Hunt Foods Company
750 E Diehl Rd Ste 111 (60563-4804)
PHONE..................630 857-1000
EMP: 173
SALES (corp-wide): 9.5B **Publicly Held**
SIC: 2038 2013 2099 Frozen specialties; dinners, frozen & packaged; lunches, frozen & packaged; sausages & other prepared meats; dessert mixes & fillings
PA: Conagra Brands, Inc.
222 Mdse Mart Plz
Chicago IL 60654
312 549-5000

(G-14804)
CONCEPT ONE DESIGN INC
1034 Forest View Ct (60563-2248)
PHONE..................708 807-3111
Anna Virella-Kerwin, *President*
Joseph Kerwin, *Opers Staff*
EMP: 12
SALES (est): 380.6K **Privately Held**
SIC: 7221 7336 2759 Photographic studios, portrait; commercial art & graphic design; poster & decal printing & engraving

(G-14805)
CONCRETE 1 INC
Also Called: R & J Ready Mix
429 E 8th Ave (60563-3205)
PHONE..................630 357-1329
Richard Downs, *President*
Jakeda J Downs, *Admin Sec*
EMP: 7
SALES (est): 656.4K **Privately Held**
SIC: 3273 Ready-mixed concrete

(G-14806)
CORIANT NORTH AMERICA LLC
1415 W Diehl Rd (60563-2349)
PHONE..................630 798-8800
EMP: 2500
SALES (est): 900MM **Privately Held**
SIC: 3661 Telephone & telegraph apparatus
PA: Marlin Equity Partners, Llc
338 Pier Ave
Hermosa Beach CA 90254

(G-14807)
CORIANT OPERATIONS INC (PA)
1415 W Diehl Rd (60563-2349)
PHONE..................630 798-8800
Shaygan Kheradpir, *CEO*
Ken Craft, *Exec VP*
Uwe Fischer, *Exec VP*
Reza Ghaffari, *Exec VP*
Konrad Schtte, *Exec VP*
▲ **EMP:** 20
SQ FT: 850,000
SALES (est): 266MM **Privately Held**
SIC: 3661 Telephone & telegraph apparatus

(G-14808)
CORNERSTONE FDSRVICE GROUP INC (PA)
127 Ambassador Dr Ste 147 (60540-4079)
PHONE..................630 527-8600
EMP: 2
SALES (est): 13.7MM **Privately Held**
SIC: 3262 Dishes, commercial or household: vitreous china

(G-14809)
CORYDON CONVERTING COMPANY INC
1350 Shore Rd Ste 120 (60563-1099)
P.O. Box 1688, Aurora (60507-1688)
PHONE..................630 898-9896
William Dunbar, *Manager*
EMP: 12
SALES (corp-wide): 5.2MM **Privately Held**
SIC: 2679 Paper products, converted
PA: Corydon Converting Company, Inc.
932 E Benton St
Aurora IL 60505
630 983-1900

(G-14810)
COZENT LLC
2135 City Gate Ln Ste 300 (60563-3066)
PHONE..................630 781-2822
Al Kannan,
EMP: 9
SQ FT: 16,000
SALES (est): 1.4MM **Privately Held**
SIC: 7372 Application computer software

(G-14811)
CYMATICS INC
31w280 Diehl Rd Ste 104 (60563-1066)
P.O. Box 448 (60566-0448)
PHONE..................630 420-7117
Nancy Mikyska, *President*
Glenn E Mikyska, *President*
Lynn Mikyska, *Vice Pres*
EMP: 6
SQ FT: 5,000
SALES (est): 886.5K **Privately Held**
SIC: 3612 3613 3821 3825 Electronic meter transformers; control panels, electric; laboratory equipment: fume hoods, distillation racks, etc.; test equipment for electronic & electrical circuits

(G-14812)
DALEY AUTOMATION LLC (PA)
1111 S Washington St (60540-7953)
PHONE..................630 384-9900
Gregory T Mizen, *Principal*
Tom McKevitt, *Marketing Staff*
Gregory Mizen,
Kurt Richardson,
EMP: 5
SQ FT: 1,000
SALES (est): 512K **Privately Held**
SIC: 3599 3544 Custom machinery; special dies & tools

(G-14813)
DALY ENGINEERED FILTRATION INC
942 E Hillside Rd (60540-6809)
PHONE..................708 355-1550
William R Daly, *President*
EMP: 3
SALES (est): 367.1K **Privately Held**
SIC: 3677 Filtration devices, electronic

(G-14814)
DAMIEN CORPORATION
6s204 Cohasset Rd (60540-3535)
PHONE..................630 369-3549
Suzan N Anthaney, *President*
Rick Anthoney, *Sales Staff*
EMP: 5
SALES (est): 404.8K **Privately Held**
SIC: 2721 2741 2731 Periodicals: publishing only; miscellaneous publishing; book publishing

(G-14815)
DIAMOND READY MIX INC
27w742 North Ln (60540-6437)
PHONE..................630 355-5414
Robert Worley, *President*
EMP: 12
SALES (est): 1.5MM **Privately Held**
SIC: 3273 Ready-mixed concrete

(G-14816)
DIEHL METERING LLC
1813 N Mill St Ste C (60563-4872)
PHONE..................331 204-6540
Christof Bosbach, *President*
EMP: 3
SALES (est): 144.6K
SALES (corp-wide): 4.2B **Privately Held**
SIC: 3829 Measuring & controlling devices
PA: Diehl Stiftung & Co. Kg
Stephanstr. 49
Nurnberg 90478
911 947-0

(G-14817)
DIGITAL REALTY INC
303 N Mill St (60540-4051)
PHONE..................630 428-7979
Ken Carn, *President*
Scott Mills, *Vice Pres*
Cristen M Carn, *Admin Sec*
Elizabeth Leone, *Admin Asst*
EMP: 25
SALES (est): 2.2MM **Privately Held**
WEB: www.digitalrealty.net
SIC: 7372 6531 Prepackaged software; real estate agents & managers

(G-14818)
DU PAGE PRECISION PRODUCTS CO
433 Spring Ave (60540-4449)
PHONE..................630 849-2940
Dennis Flynn, *President*
EMP: 40
SALES (corp-wide): 16.8MM **Privately Held**
SIC: 3599 Machine shop, jobbing & repair
PA: Du Page Precision Products Co.
3695 Darlene Ct Ste 101
Aurora IL 60504
630 849-2940

(G-14819)
EAST PENN MANUFACTURING CO
1651 Frontenac Rd (60563-1756)
PHONE..................610 682-6361
Daniel Landon, *CEO*
EMP: 1600

GEOGRAPHIC SECTION

Naperville - Dupage County (G-14846)

SALES (est): 37MM **Privately Held**
SIC: 3691 Storage batteries

(G-14820)
ECODYNE WATER TREATMENT LLC
1270 Frontenac Rd (60563-1700)
P.O. Box 64420, Saint Paul MN (55164-0420)
PHONE................630 961-5043
Patrick Oneill,
◆ **EMP:** 20 **EST:** 1957
SQ FT: 40,000
SALES (est): 4.6MM
SALES (corp-wide): 327.2B **Publicly Held**
SIC: 3589 Water treatment equipment, industrial; sewage treatment equipment
HQ: Marmon Holdings, Inc.
181 W Madison St Ste 2600
Chicago IL 60602
312 372-9500

(G-14821)
EDGAR H FEY JEWELERS INC (PA)
Also Called: Fey & Company
833 N Washington St (60563-3168)
PHONE................708 352-4115
Thomas Fey, *President*
Edgar H Fey III, *Admin Sec*
EMP: 25 **EST:** 1945
SALES (est): 4.4MM **Privately Held**
SIC: 3911 5944 5094 Jewelry, precious metal; jewelry, precious stones & precious metals; jewelry & precious stones

(G-14822)
ELEMENT EVENTS LLC
123 Water St (60540-5450)
PHONE................630 717-2800
David Miller, *Managing Prtnr*
Cheryl Cady, *Sales Staff*
EMP: 4
SALES (est): 227.9K **Privately Held**
SIC: 2819 Elements

(G-14823)
ELITEGEN CORP
1112 Sheldon Ct (60540-1306)
PHONE................630 637-6917
Ken Chou, *President*
Minhui KAO, *Consultant*
EMP: 14
SALES (est): 1.3MM **Privately Held**
WEB: www.elitegen.com
SIC: 7372 Business oriented computer software

(G-14824)
EMINENT TECHNOLOGIES LLC
215 Shuman Blvd Ste 403 (60563-5100)
PHONE................630 416-2311
EMP: 3
SALES: 950K **Privately Held**
SIC: 3582 Mfg Commercial Laundry Equipment

(G-14825)
ENTRUST SERVICES LLC (PA)
608 S Washington St (60540-6663)
PHONE................630 699-9132
F Edward Gustafson, *President*
Steven Schuster, *Vice Pres*
J S Corcoran, *CFO*
EMP: 7
SQ FT: 4,000
SALES (est): 34.2MM **Privately Held**
SIC: 2051 2819 2869 Bread, cake & related products; industrial inorganic chemicals; industrial organic chemicals

(G-14826)
EXTREME TOOLS INC
740 Frontenac Rd (60563-1709)
PHONE................630 202-8324
Larry Grela, *President*
Larry Grela, *President*
▲ **EMP:** 7
SQ FT: 15,000
SALES (est): 1.5MM **Privately Held**
SIC: 2441 Boxes, wood

(G-14827)
FABRITEK LLC
Also Called: Fabri-Tek
216 Briarheath Ln (60565-2226)
PHONE................630 983-0211
Timothy Brown, *President*
Fred Bridge, *Vice Pres*
▲ **EMP:** 5
SQ FT: 2,000
SALES (est): 242.1K **Privately Held**
SIC: 2821 Plastics materials & resins; molding compounds, plastics

(G-14828)
FCA US LLC
1980 High Grove Ln (60540-3934)
PHONE................630 637-3000
EMP: 1126
SALES (corp-wide): 126.4B **Privately Held**
SIC: 3714 Motor vehicle parts & accessories
HQ: Fca Us Llc
1000 Chrysler Dr
Auburn Hills MI 48326

(G-14829)
FOOD PURVEYORS LOGISTICS
760 Inland Cir Apt 101 (60563-0213)
PHONE................630 229-6168
Andre Thomas, *Partner*
EMP: 15
SQ FT: 102,000
SALES (est): 1MM **Privately Held**
SIC: 2013 Smoked meats from purchased meat

(G-14830)
FORECAST 5 ANALYTICS INC (PA)
2135 City Gate Ln Ste 420 (60563-3062)
PHONE................630 955-7500
Vladimir Dragosavljevic, *President*
Jeff Carew, *Managing Dir*
Jason Rader, *Vice Pres*
Laura Griffith, *Opers Staff*
Drew Skarupa, *CFO*
EMP: 21
SALES (est): 7.9MM **Privately Held**
SIC: 7372 Business oriented computer software

(G-14831)
FRESH SOFTWARE SOLUTIONS LLC
1717 N Naper Blvd Ste 207 (60563-8808)
PHONE................630 995-4350
Steven Reilly, *Manager*
John Moore, *Prgrmr*
EMP: 6
SALES (est): 464.8K **Privately Held**
WEB: www.freshsoftwaresolutions.com
SIC: 7372 Prepackaged software

(G-14832)
G T C INDUSTRIES INC
609 Sara Ln (60565-1611)
P.O. Box 2493 (60567-2493)
PHONE................708 369-9815
Greg Weber, *President*
EMP: 4
SQ FT: 2,400
SALES (est): 200K **Privately Held**
SIC: 3679 8748 3651 3564 Electronic circuits; business consulting; household audio & video equipment; blowers & fans

(G-14833)
GEA FARM TECHNOLOGIES INC (HQ)
1880 Country Farm Dr (60563-1089)
PHONE................630 548-8200
Vern Foster, *President*
Matt Daley, *President*
Michael Fair, *Engineer*
Patrick Ferry, *CFO*
Claude Hoffman, *Accounts Mgr*
◆ **EMP:** 125 **EST:** 1906
SQ FT: 36,000
SALES (est): 214.5MM
SALES (corp-wide): 5.4B **Privately Held**
WEB: www.gea.com
SIC: 5083 3523 2841 2842 Dairy machinery & equipment; dairy equipment (farm); detergents, synthetic organic or inorganic alkaline; sanitation preparations
PA: Gea Group Ag
Peter-Muller-Str. 12
Dusseldorf 40468
211 913-60

(G-14834)
GEM MANUFACTURING CORPORATION
1922 Springside Dr (60565-2242)
PHONE................630 458-0014
Kirit Dave, *President*
EMP: 4
SALES (est): 492.8K **Privately Held**
SIC: 3714 Motor vehicle parts & accessories

(G-14835)
GEOCYN COMPANY INC
5s250 Frontenac Rd (60563-1711)
PHONE................331 213-2851
Bill Jesses, *President*
Ed Belson, *Plant Mgr*
Tim Bowers, *CFO*
Cynthia Bosco, *Treasurer*
Kristy Bosco-Sparacino, *VP Sales*
EMP: 50
SQ FT: 13,000
SALES (est): 13.8K
SALES (corp-wide): 26.1MM **Privately Held**
WEB: www.valleyfastener.com
SIC: 3452 3316 Screws, metal; rivets, metal; cold finishing of steel shapes
PA: Valley Fastener Group, Llc
1490 Mitchell Rd
Aurora IL 60505
630 299-8910

(G-14836)
GREIF INC
5s220 Frontenac Rd (60563-1711)
PHONE................630 753-1859
Harold Sechresst, *Manager*
EMP: 50
SALES (corp-wide): 4.6B **Publicly Held**
SIC: 2655 5085 Fiber cans, drums & similar products; commercial containers
PA: Greif, Inc.
425 Winter Rd
Delaware OH 43015
740 549-6000

(G-14837)
GREIF INC
5 S 220 Frontenace Rd (60540)
PHONE................630 961-1842
Harold Sechrest, *Manager*
EMP: 48
SALES (corp-wide): 4.6B **Publicly Held**
SIC: 2655 Drums, fiber: made from purchased material
PA: Greif, Inc.
425 Winter Rd
Delaware OH 43015
740 549-6000

(G-14838)
GRS HOLDING LLC (PA)
Also Called: Kitchens To Go Built By Carlin
131 W Jefferson Ave # 223 (60540-4682)
PHONE................630 355-1660
Stevin Rubin, *Partner*
Steven Rubin, *Principal*
Frederick Stowell,
EMP: 10
SALES (est): 4.5MM **Privately Held**
WEB: www.kitchenstogo.com
SIC: 3799 1541 2452 6512 Trailers & trailer equipment; industrial buildings, new construction; prefabricated buildings, wood; commercial & industrial building operation; truck rental & leasing, no drivers; equipment rental & leasing

(G-14839)
GULFSTREAM AEROSPACE CORP
472 Quail Dr (60565-4162)
PHONE................630 470-9146
Jim Guerin, *Branch Mgr*
EMP: 1173
SALES (corp-wide): 39.3B **Publicly Held**
WEB: www.gulfstream.com
SIC: 3721 Aircraft
HQ: Gulfstream Aerospace Corporation
500 Gulfstream Rd
Savannah GA 31408

(G-14840)
HEFFNER DESIGNS
2827 Aurora Ave (60540-0955)
PHONE................630 854-2852
EMP: 17
SALES (est): 1.9MM **Privately Held**
SIC: 3993 Signs & advertising specialties

(G-14841)
HEMMERLE JR IRVIN
Also Called: Caid Tronics
1526 Treeline Ct (60565-2013)
PHONE................630 334-4392
Mary Hemmerle, *President*
EMP: 2
SALES (est): 200K **Privately Held**
SIC: 3089 Identification cards, plastic

(G-14842)
I T C W INC
Also Called: Artganiks
584 Beaconsfield Ave (60565-4316)
PHONE................630 305-8849
Margaret Thomas, *President*
Dan Thomas, *Director*
EMP: 330
SALES (est): 17.1MM **Privately Held**
SIC: 8742 3999 Management consulting services; framed artwork

(G-14843)
I2C LLC
1708 Chepstow Ct (60540-0395)
PHONE................630 281-2330
Datta Ajjampur,
EMP: 5
SALES: 200K **Privately Held**
SIC: 7372 Prepackaged software

(G-14844)
IDEMIA AMERICA CORP
2764 Golfview Rd (60563-9156)
PHONE................630 551-0792
Ron Takacs, *General Mgr*
EMP: 100
SALES (corp-wide): 4.2B **Privately Held**
SIC: 3083 3089 Plastic finished products, laminated; identification cards, plastic
HQ: Idemia America Corp.
296 Concord Rd Ste 300
Billerica MA 01821
978 215-2400

(G-14845)
INEOS AMERICAS LLC
150 W Warrenville Rd (60563-8473)
PHONE................630 857-7463
Martin Olavesen, *CFO*
Steven Olson, *IT/INT Sup*
Carmella Marcello, *Admin Asst*
EMP: 3
SALES (corp-wide): 1MM **Privately Held**
WEB: www.ineos.com
SIC: 2821 Plastics materials & resins
HQ: Ineos Americas Llc
2600 S Shore Blvd Ste 500
League City TX 77573
251 535-6600

(G-14846)
INFOGIX INC (PA)
1240 E Diehl Rd Ste 400 (60563-4802)
PHONE................630 505-1800
Early Stephens, *President*
Angsuman Dutta, *Exec VP*
Paul Skordilis, *Exec VP*
John McDonell, *CFO*
Timothy Myszkowski, *Controller*
EMP: 155
SQ FT: 42,000
SALES: 64.6MM **Privately Held**
SIC: 7372 8742 Business oriented computer software; management consulting services

Naperville - Dupage County (G-14847)

(G-14847)
INFORMATICA LLC
2135 City Gate Ln Ste 340 (60563-3062)
PHONE..................360 393-7576
Juan Riojas, *Officer*
EMP: 4 **Privately Held**
SIC: 7372 Prepackaged software
PA: Informatica Llc
2100 Seaport Blvd
Redwood City CA 94063

(G-14848)
INNOVATIVE WERKS INC
800 W 5th Ave Ste 203c (60563-4923)
PHONE..................312 767-8618
Curtis P Porter, *President*
EMP: 3
SALES: 25K **Privately Held**
SIC: 8711 3823 1731 8748 Engineering services; computer interface equipment for industrial process control; computerized controls installation; systems engineering consultant, ex. computer or professional; custom computer programming services

(G-14849)
INPLEX CUSTOM EXTRUDERS LLC
1657 Frontenac Rd (60563-1756)
PHONE..................847 827-7046
Robert Anderson, *CEO*
Emily Wethy, *Plant Mgr*
Joe Tremback, *Controller*
Gene Panek, *Sales Staff*
Jessica Anderson, *Mktg Dir*
EMP: 58
SQ FT: 36,000
SALES: 12.5MM **Privately Held**
WEB: www.inplexllc.com
SIC: 3089 Injection molding of plastics; plastic processing

(G-14850)
IPC GROUP PURCHASING
1151 E Warrenville Rd M (60563-9340)
PHONE..................630 276-5485
Patrick Sonin, *Vice Pres*
EMP: 3
SALES (est): 183.4K **Privately Held**
WEB: www.ipcgrouppurchasing.com
SIC: 3799 Transportation equipment

(G-14851)
IRONSAFE LLC
1807 W Diehl Rd (60563-1890)
P.O. Box 241352, Apple Valley MN (55124-1352)
PHONE..................877 297-1833
Rick Ronchak, *CEO*
EMP: 4
SALES (est): 119K **Privately Held**
SIC: 7372 Prepackaged software

(G-14852)
J REAM MANUFACTURING
31w280 Diehl Rd Ste 101 (60563-9624)
PHONE..................630 983-6945
John R Fouser, *President*
EMP: 5
SQ FT: 5,000
SALES (est): 1MM **Privately Held**
SIC: 3624 5063 Brushes & brush stock contacts, electric; motors, electric

(G-14853)
JACKSON & PARTNERS LLC
1717 N Naper Blvd Ste 108 (60563-8837)
PHONE..................630 219-1598
Kristie Sams,
EMP: 7
SALES (est): 264K **Privately Held**
SIC: 5144 5146 2013 5142 Poultry & poultry products; fish & seafoods; sausages & other prepared meats; packaged frozen goods

(G-14854)
JEWEL OSCO INC
Also Called: Jewel-Osco 3059
1759 W Ogden Ave Ste A (60540-4205)
PHONE..................630 355-2172
Jim Davis, *Manager*
EMP: 152
SALES (corp-wide): 60.5B **Privately Held**
WEB: www.jewelosco.mywebgrocer.com
SIC: 5411 5912 2052 2051 Supermarkets, chain; drug stores & proprietary stores; cookies & crackers; bread, cake & related products
HQ: Jewel Osco, Inc.
150 E Pierce Rd Ste 200
Itasca IL 60143
630 948-6000

(G-14855)
JOHN CORNBLEET INC
Also Called: Fastsigns
931 E Ogden Ave Ste 127 (60563-4852)
PHONE..................630 357-3278
John Cornbleet, *President*
John Corbleet, *President*
EMP: 5
SQ FT: 1,500
SALES (est): 826K **Privately Held**
SIC: 3993 Signs & advertising specialties

(G-14856)
K & J PHILLIPS CORPORATION
Also Called: Sir Speedy
526 W 5th Ave (60563-2901)
PHONE..................630 355-0660
Kent Phillips, *President*
Julie Phillips, *Vice Pres*
EMP: 5
SQ FT: 3,500
SALES (est): 661.9K **Privately Held**
SIC: 2752 Commercial printing, lithographic

(G-14857)
K-C TOOL CO
552 S Washington St (60540-6658)
PHONE..................630 983-5960
George Stockin, *President*
EMP: 8
SALES (est): 590K **Privately Held**
SIC: 3546 3545 3423 Power-driven handtools; machine tool accessories; hand & edge tools

(G-14858)
KITCHENS TO GO LLC
131 W Jefferson Ave # 223 (60540-4683)
PHONE..................630 364-3083
Frederick C Stowell, *Partner*
Ralph H Goldbeck, *Partner*
Steven M Rubin, *Partner*
Susan Karoll, *Business Mgr*
Angel Lopez, *Project Mgr*
EMP: 20
SALES (est): 4.3MM **Privately Held**
WEB: www.kitchens-2-go.com
SIC: 6512 2452 Commercial & industrial building operation; prefabricated buildings, wood

(G-14859)
KOBAWALA POLY-PACK INC (PA)
Also Called: Fairdeal Jumbo Packaging USA
800 W 5th Ave Ste 212 (60563-4949)
PHONE..................312 664-3810
Ravindra Kobawala, *President*
James Oneill, *Vice Pres*
Ashwin Shah, *CTO*
Rupak Kobawala, *Director*
Nehao Shah, *Director*
▲ **EMP:** 4
SQ FT: 120,000
SALES (est): 2.6MM **Privately Held**
SIC: 2221 Polypropylene broadwoven fabrics

(G-14860)
LASER TECHNOLOGIES INC
1120 Frontenac Rd (60563-1749)
PHONE..................630 761-1200
Keri L Foster, *President*
Jeffrey Foster, *Vice Pres*
Michael Leali, *Controller*
Steve Cornelius, *Sales Staff*
Robert F Foster, *Admin Sec*
◆ **EMP:** 147
SQ FT: 160,000
SALES (est): 36.6MM **Privately Held**
SIC: 3541 3511 Machine tool replacement & repair parts, metal cutting types; numerically controlled metal cutting machine tools; turbines & turbine generator sets

(G-14861)
LE CHOCOLAT DU BOUCHARD LLC (PA)
Also Called: Le Chocolat Bky & Chocolates
127-129 S Washington St (60563)
PHONE..................630 355-5720
Cathy J Bouchard, *Mng Member*
David Hollingsworth, *Manager*
EMP: 3
SALES (est): 300.3K **Privately Held**
SIC: 5461 2053 Cakes; croissants, frozen

(G-14862)
LIAM BREX
222 S Main St (60540-5350)
PHONE..................630 848-0222
Liam Brex, *Principal*
EMP: 2
SALES (est): 249.8K **Privately Held**
WEB: www.liambrex.com
SIC: 2542 Cabinets: show, display or storage: except wood

(G-14863)
LIFETIME ROOFTILE COMPANY (PA)
Also Called: Lifetime Roof Tile
1805 High Grove Ln (60540-3931)
PHONE..................630 355-7922
Richard Wehrli, *President*
Robert L Hammerschmidt, *Admin Sec*
EMP: 3
SALES (est): 1.4MM **Privately Held**
SIC: 3272 2952 Roofing tile & slabs, concrete; asphalt felts & coatings

(G-14864)
LIGHTFOOT TECHNOLOGIES INC
Also Called: Bluesun Hitech
2135 City Gate Ln Ste 300 (60563-3066)
PHONE..................331 302-1297
Shankar Krishnamoorthy, *President*
EMP: 6
SQ FT: 1,200
SALES: 1.2MM **Privately Held**
SIC: 3575 7371 Computer terminals; software programming applications

(G-14865)
LOGICAL DESIGN SOLUTIONS INC
Also Called: Logicds
280 Shuman Blvd Ste 106 (60563-8100)
PHONE..................630 786-5999
Kyle Haroldsen, *CEO*
Tami Haroldsen, *Vice Pres*
EMP: 4
SALES (est): 54.5K **Privately Held**
SIC: 7371 8748 7372 7373 Computer software systems analysis & design, custom; systems engineering consultant, ex. computer or professional; business oriented computer software; operating systems computer software; office computer automation systems integration

(G-14866)
LUCREZIA LLC
Also Called: Lucrezia F. O'Brien
7 Baker Ln (60565-4313)
PHONE..................630 263-0088
Lucrezia F O'Brien, *Owner*
EMP: 3
SALES (est): 131.6K **Privately Held**
SIC: 2038 Frozen specialties

(G-14867)
MEDIA UNLIMITED INC
Also Called: Cygnet Midwest
1701 Quincy Ave Ste 25 (60540-6684)
PHONE..................630 527-0900
Laura Adamski, *President*
Colin Pritchard, *Art Dir*
John Adamski, *Real Est Agnt*
EMP: 8
SALES (est): 1.7MM **Privately Held**
SIC: 7311 7336 7334 5999 Advertising consultant; commercial art & graphic design; photocopying & duplicating services; banners, flags, decals & posters; poster & decal printing, lithographic

(G-14868)
MERIDIAN PARTS INC
445 Jackson Ave Ste 202 (60540-5258)
PHONE..................630 718-1995
Zhang Quan, *President*
Wang Yuhong, *Admin Sec*
▲ **EMP:** 3
SALES: 1.7MM **Privately Held**
WEB: www.meridianparts.com
SIC: 3469 Machine parts, stamped or pressed metal

(G-14869)
MESSER LLC
Boc Gases
1751 W Diehl Rd Ste 300 (60563-4800)
PHONE..................630 515-2576
Jay Slaughter, *Branch Mgr*
EMP: 25
SALES (corp-wide): 1.1B **Privately Held**
SIC: 2813 Nitrogen
HQ: Messer Llc
200 Somerset Corp Blvd # 7000
Bridgewater NJ 08807
908 464-8100

(G-14870)
MICRODYNAMICS CORPORATION (PA)
Also Called: Microdynamics Group
1400 Shore Rd (60563-8765)
PHONE..................630 276-0527
Thomas Harter Sr, *CEO*
Thomas Harter Jr, *Senior VP*
Chris Bartlett, *Vice Pres*
Tom Harter, *Vice Pres*
Rick Schaltegger, *Vice Pres*
▲ **EMP:** 146
SQ FT: 31,400
SALES (est): 45.5MM **Privately Held**
WEB: www.microdg.com
SIC: 7389 2759 2752 7374 Microfilm recording & developing service; laser printing; commercial printing, lithographic; data processing service

(G-14871)
MINELAB AMERICAS INC
123 Ambassador Dr Ste 123 # 123 (60540-3981)
PHONE..................630 401-8150
Peter Charlesworth, *President*
David Shields McGurk, *President*
Julieann Telford, *Corp Secy*
Maria Gabriela Olivarez, *Controller*
Linda Stvenson, *Finance*
▲ **EMP:** 17
SQ FT: 10,000
SALES (est): 4.1MM **Privately Held**
SIC: 3669 Metal detectors
HQ: Minelab Electronics Pty. Limited
Technology Park 2 Second Ave
Mawson Lakes SA 5095

(G-14872)
MINUTEMAN PRESS
1577 Nperville Wheaton Rd (60563-1556)
PHONE..................630 584-7383
Joe Tomsa, *President*
Jerry Prasse, *Vice Pres*
EMP: 8
SQ FT: 3,000
SALES (est): 1.4MM **Privately Held**
SIC: 2752 5112 2791 2759 Commercial printing, lithographic; business forms, lithographed; business forms; typesetting; commercial printing

(G-14873)
MOLEX LLC
Also Called: Molex Inc. Switch Division
1750 Country Farm Dr (60563-9175)
PHONE..................630 969-4550
Garry Thompson, *General Mgr*
EMP: 14
SALES (corp-wide): 48.9B **Privately Held**
SIC: 3678 Electronic connectors
HQ: Molex, Llc
2222 Wellington Ct
Lisle IL 60532
630 969-4550

GEOGRAPHIC SECTION

Naperville - Dupage County (G-14903)

(G-14874)
MONDELEZ GLOBAL LLC
Also Called: Kraft Foods
1555 W Ogden Ave (60540-3966)
PHONE.................................630 369-1909
Judy Czurylo, *Plant Mgr*
EMP: 300 **Publicly Held**
SIC: 2043 2052 Cereal breakfast foods; cookies & crackers
HQ: Mondelez Global Llc
   3 N Pkwy Ste 300
   Deerfield IL 60015
   847 943-4000

(G-14875)
MONONA HOLDINGS LLC (HQ)
1952 Mc Dowell Rd Ste 207 (60563-6506)
PHONE.................................630 946-0630
Roger Malatt,
Joseph Grote,
Stephen McConnell,
EMP: 9
SQ FT: 2,550
SALES (est): 201.1MM
SALES (corp-wide): 901.2MM **Publicly Held**
SIC: 3694 5063 Harness wiring sets, internal combustion engines; wire & cable
PA: Commercial Vehicle Group, Inc.
   7800 Walton Pkwy
   New Albany OH 43054
   614 289-5360

(G-14876)
MUDLARK PAPERS INC
1031 Shimer Ct (60565-3454)
PHONE.................................630 717-7616
Doug Hamilton, *President*
Kim Hamilton, *Treasurer*
▲ EMP: 20
SQ FT: 32,000
SALES (est): 3.3MM **Privately Held**
SIC: 2678 2679 Stationery products; gift wrap & novelties, paper

(G-14877)
NALCO HOLDING COMPANY (HQ)
1601 W Diehl Rd (60563-1198)
PHONE.................................630 305-1000
J Erik Fyrwald, *Ch of Bd*
Kristi Pegues, *Principal*
Lewis French, *District Mgr*
Brad Heath, *District Mgr*
Cyron Soyza, *District Mgr*
◆ EMP: 42
SALES (est): 2.7B
SALES (corp-wide): 14.9B **Publicly Held**
SIC: 2899 2992 Chemical preparations; corrosion preventive lubricant; water treating compounds; lubricating oils & greases
PA: Ecolab Inc.
   1 Ecolab Pl
   Saint Paul MN 55102
   800 232-6522

(G-14878)
NANOCHEM SOLUTIONS INC (PA)
1701 Quincy Ave Ste 10 (60540-6687)
PHONE.................................708 563-9200
Daniel O'Brien, *President*
▲ EMP: 15
SALES (est): 4MM **Privately Held**
SIC: 2819 Industrial inorganic chemicals

(G-14879)
NAPERSOFT INC
40 Shuman Blvd Ste 293 (60563-8670)
PHONE.................................630 420-1515
Bart Carlson, *President*
Edward Hebda, *Vice Pres*
Michael J D'Onofrio, *CFO*
Thomas F Grannan, *CTO*
EMP: 10
SQ FT: 9,500
SALES (est): 1.1MM **Privately Held**
SIC: 7372 Business oriented computer software

(G-14880)
NAPERVILLE HANNA ANDERSSON
140 W Jefferson Ave (60540-5007)
PHONE.................................331 250-7100
EMP: 3
SALES (est): 126.2K **Privately Held**
SIC: 2711 Newspapers

(G-14881)
NETGEAR INC
1000 E Warrenville Rd (60563-1867)
PHONE.................................630 955-0080
EMP: 4 **Publicly Held**
SIC: 3661 Mfg Networking Solution Products
PA: Netgear, Inc.
   350 E Plumeria Dr
   San Jose CA 95134

(G-14882)
NEW VISION PRINT & MARKETING
31w280 Diehl Rd Ste 104 (60563-1066)
P.O. Box 9487 (60567-0487)
PHONE.................................630 406-0509
Michael Frank, *Principal*
EMP: 8 EST: 2007
SALES (est): 895.3K **Privately Held**
WEB: www.newvisionprint.com
SIC: 2752 Commercial printing, offset

(G-14883)
NEWF LLC (PA)
Also Called: Delta Waseca
608 Driftwood Ct (60540-3200)
P.O. Box 4347 (60567-4347)
PHONE.................................630 330-5462
Dee Kapur, *President*
EMP: 4
SALES (est): 3.4MM **Privately Held**
SIC: 3713 Truck bodies & parts

(G-14884)
NHANCED SEMICONDUCTORS INC (PA)
1415 Bond St Ste 155 (60563-2769)
PHONE.................................408 759-4060
Robert Patti, *President*
EMP: 10 EST: 2016
SQ FT: 2,500
SALES: 2MM **Privately Held**
SIC: 3674 Semiconductor circuit networks

(G-14885)
NIVELCO USA LLC
1300 Iroquois Ave (60563-8553)
PHONE.................................630 848-2100
Peter Szollos, *President*
EMP: 4 EST: 2016
SALES (est): 377.1K **Privately Held**
SIC: 3714 Motor vehicle parts & accessories

(G-14886)
NORDIC A FILTRATION N AMER INC
507 Fairway Dr (60563-4051)
PHONE.................................331 457-5289
Andre Grundahl, *President*
Dean Riddle, *Admin Sec*
EMP: 2
SALES (est): 237.5K
SALES (corp-wide): 495MM **Privately Held**
SIC: 3564 Filters, air: furnaces, air conditioning equipment, air
HQ: Hengst Of North America, Inc.
   29 Hengst Blvd
   Camden SC 29020
   803 432-5992

(G-14887)
NORTH AMERICAN ENCLOSURES INC
1637 Windward Ct (60563-2365)
PHONE.................................630 290-7911
EMP: 2
SALES (est): 249.2K **Privately Held**
SIC: 3444 Sheet metalwork

(G-14888)
ODEN CORP
1119 Wickfield Ct (60563-3397)
PHONE.................................630 416-4543
Tom Sliwinski, *Principal*
EMP: 4
SALES (est): 475.6K **Privately Held**
SIC: 3565 Packaging machinery

(G-14889)
OROCHEM TECHNOLOGIES INC
340 Shuman Blvd (60563-1268)
PHONE.................................630 210-8300
Asha A Oroskar, *President*
Sangharsh Dongre, *Engineer*
Rahuljit Pal, *Engineer*
Dan Scanlan, *Engineer*
Anil Oroskar, *CFO*
▲ EMP: 37
SQ FT: 90,000
SALES (est): 9MM **Privately Held**
WEB: www.orochem.com
SIC: 3826 Analytical instruments

(G-14890)
OWP PHARMACEUTICALS INC
400 E Diehl Rd Ste 400 # 400 (60563-1388)
PHONE.................................331 871-7424
Scott Boyer, *President*
EMP: 16 EST: 2014
SQ FT: 1,000
SALES (est): 185.6K **Privately Held**
SIC: 2834 5122 Druggists' preparations (pharmaceuticals); pharmaceuticals

(G-14891)
P N K VENTURES INC
Also Called: Sign-A-Rama
1701 Quincy Ave Ste 24 (60540-6685)
PHONE.................................630 527-0500
Pat Sweeney, *President*
EMP: 4
SQ FT: 1,200
SALES: 500K **Privately Held**
SIC: 3993 7389 7336 Signs & advertising specialties; lettering & sign painting services; commercial art & graphic design

(G-14892)
PALM INTERNATIONAL INC (PA)
1159 Palmetto Ct Ste B (60540-6347)
P.O. Box 3923 (60567-3923)
PHONE.................................630 357-1437
Brian Palm, *President*
Donna Palm, *Principal*
EMP: 5
SALES (est): 237.1K **Privately Held**
SIC: 2741 7373 7379 8742 Miscellaneous publishing; computer integrated systems design; computer related maintenance services; ; marketing consulting services; market analysis, business & economic research

(G-14893)
PARATHON RECOVERY SERVICE LLC
1415 W Diehl Rd Ste 200n (60563-1102)
PHONE.................................630 689-0450
Krupa Martinez, *Principal*
Theresa Johnsen, *Vice Pres*
EMP: 6 EST: 2014
SALES (est): 487.3K **Privately Held**
SIC: 7372 Prepackaged software

(G-14894)
PAYLOCITY HOLDING CORPORATION
27w675 South Ln (60540-6413)
PHONE.................................331 701-7975
EMP: 244
SALES (corp-wide): 467.6MM **Publicly Held**
SIC: 7372 Prepackaged software
PA: Paylocity Holding Corporation
   1400 American Ln
   Schaumburg IL 60173
   847 463-3200

(G-14895)
PERKINELMER INC
1842 Centre Point Cir (60563-1445)
PHONE.................................331 229-3012
Richard Pelc, *Engineer*
EMP: 7
SALES (corp-wide): 2.8B **Publicly Held**
SIC: 3826 Analytical instruments
PA: Perkinelmer, Inc.
   940 Winter St
   Waltham MA 02451
   781 663-6900

(G-14896)
PERLE & SONS JEWELERS INC
8 W Jefferson Ave (60540-5309)
PHONE.................................630 357-3357
Janine Perle, *President*
Dean Perle, *Vice Pres*
EMP: 3 EST: 1971
SQ FT: 600
SALES (est): 800K **Privately Held**
SIC: 5944 3911 Jewelry, precious stones & precious metals; jewelry, precious metal

(G-14897)
PFEIFER INDUSTRIES LLC
2180 Corp Ln Unit 104 (60563)
PHONE.................................630 596-9000
James Danovan, *Mng Member*
Fredick Meyers,
Brian Nass,
▲ EMP: 1
SQ FT: 7,000
SALES (est): 1MM **Privately Held**
SIC: 3545 Precision tools, machinists'

(G-14898)
PHARMAZZ INC (PA)
608 Fawell Ct (60565-3569)
PHONE.................................630 780-6087
Anil Gulati, *Chairman*
EMP: 2
SALES (est): 229.9K **Privately Held**
SIC: 2834 Pharmaceutical preparations

(G-14899)
PHILIP REINISCH COMPANY
1555 Naperville Wheaton R (60563-8448)
PHONE.................................312 644-6776
Stanford J Reinisch, *President*
David Urbanick, *President*
Steve Reinisch, *Vice Pres*
▲ EMP: 11 EST: 1933
SQ FT: 5,000
SALES (est): 1.1MM **Privately Held**
SIC: 2511 Wood household furniture

(G-14900)
PNC FINANCIAL SVCS GROUP INC
1308 S Naper Blvd (60540-8362)
PHONE.................................630 420-8400
Sam Vardalos, *Branch Mgr*
Kelley Washington, *Manager*
EMP: 3
SALES (corp-wide): 21.6B **Publicly Held**
WEB: www.ryconinc.com
SIC: 3578 Automatic teller machines (ATM)
PA: The Pnc Financial Services Group Inc
   300 5th Ave
   Pittsburgh PA 15222
   888 762-2265

(G-14901)
POWER-IO INC
537 Braemar Ave (60563-1372)
PHONE.................................630 717-7335
Mary Ellen Cahill, *President*
EMP: 50
SALES: 2MM **Privately Held**
SIC: 3625 Relays & industrial controls

(G-14902)
PROCESS MECHANICAL INC
2208 Pontiac Cir (60565-3206)
PHONE.................................630 416-7021
John Pizzo, *President*
EMP: 1
SALES (est): 303.8K **Privately Held**
SIC: 5084 3823 Industrial machinery & equipment; industrial process measurement equipment

(G-14903)
PRP WINE INTERNATIONAL INC
Also Called: Golden Grape Estate
1323 Bond St Ste 179 (60563-2368)
PHONE.................................630 995-4500
Pad Bobbitt, *Branch Mgr*
EMP: 11

Naperville - Dupage County (G-14904)

SALES (corp-wide): 167.1K **Privately Held**
SIC: 2084 Wines
HQ: Prp Wine International, Inc.
1323 Bond St Ste 179
Naperville IL 60563

(G-14904)
R G H & ASSOCIATES INC
1783 S Washington St (60565-2462)
PHONE..................630 357-5915
Russ Haack, *President*
Cathy Sand, *Office Mgr*
EMP: 3 **Privately Held**
SIC: 3842 Personal safety equipment

(G-14905)
R R STREET & CO INC (PA)
Also Called: Street's
184 Shuman Blvd Ste 150 (60563-8428)
PHONE..................630 416-4244
L Ross Beard, *CEO*
J L Mayberry III, *Chairman*
Don Danner, *Vice Pres*
Dave Dawson, *Vice Pres*
EMP: 25 EST: 1876
SALES (est): 34MM **Privately Held**
WEB: www.4streets.com
SIC: 2842 Rug, upholstery, or dry cleaning detergents or spotters

(G-14906)
RADIO FREQUENCY SYSTEMS INC
2000 Nperville Wheaton Rd (60563-1443)
PHONE..................800 321-4700
Carrrie Lenkart, *Branch Mgr*
EMP: 25
SALES (corp-wide): 25.8B **Privately Held**
SIC: 3663 Radio & TV communications equipment
HQ: Radio Frequency Systems, Inc.
200 Pond View Dr
Meriden CT 06450
203 630-3311

(G-14907)
RAMONA SEDIVY
Also Called: Chickens & Things
1840 Auburn Ave (60565-6700)
PHONE..................630 983-1902
Ramona Sedivy, *Owner*
EMP: 3
SALES: 30K **Privately Held**
SIC: 3999 Novelties, bric-a-brac & hobby kits

(G-14908)
REILLY FOAM CORP
920 Frontenac Rd (60563-1745)
PHONE..................630 392-2680
Rob Quier, *Manager*
EMP: 42
SALES (corp-wide): 33MM **Privately Held**
WEB: www.reillyfoam.com
SIC: 3069 5199 Foam rubber; foam rubber
PA: Reilly Foam Corp.
751 5th Ave
King Of Prussia PA 19406
610 834-1900

(G-14909)
REX WORLDWIDE LTD
280 Shuman Blvd Ste 270 (60563-3187)
PHONE..................630 384-9361
EMP: 4
SALES (est): 336.8K **Privately Held**
SIC: 3441 Fabricated structural metal

(G-14910)
ROCK SOLID IMPORTS LLC
1004 Creekside Cir (60563-2420)
PHONE..................331 472-4522
Mark Warwick, *Mng Member*
▲ EMP: 1
SALES: 250K **Privately Held**
SIC: 3291 Stones, abrasive

(G-14911)
ROGER FRITZ & ASSOCIATES INC
1113 N Loomis St (60563-2745)
PHONE..................630 355-2614
Roger J Fritz, *President*
Kathryn Fritz, *Admin Sec*
EMP: 3
SQ FT: 1,000
SALES (est): 172.2K **Privately Held**
SIC: 2732 2741 8742 Book printing; miscellaneous publishing; corporation organizing

(G-14912)
SADANNAH GROUP LLC
Also Called: Signs Now Naperville
426 W 5th Ave (60563-2985)
PHONE..................630 357-2300
John Kelsheimer, *Owner*
David Groth, *Mng Member*
EMP: 2
SALES (est): 210.4K **Privately Held**
SIC: 3993 7336 7389 Signs & advertising specialties; graphic arts & related design; design services

(G-14913)
SHERMAN PLASTICS CORP (PA)
1650 Shore Rd (60563-8769)
PHONE..................630 369-6170
Lawrence Markin, *President*
Anthony Boose, *Vice Pres*
Cynthia Solovy, *Admin Sec*
▲ EMP: 27
SQ FT: 50,000
SALES (est): 29.1MM **Privately Held**
WEB: www.shermanplasticscorp.com
SIC: 5162 2821 Plastics materials; plastics materials & resins

(G-14914)
SHERTWINZ INC
1212 S Naper Blvd Ste 119 (60540-7349)
PHONE..................630 886-5681
EMP: 3
SALES (est): 169.3K **Privately Held**
SIC: 2323 Men's & boys' neckwear

(G-14915)
SMT LLC GROUP
Also Called: Smt Molding
2768 Golfview Rd (60563-9156)
PHONE..................630 961-3000
Monique Buchmann, *Controller*
Reinhard Buchmann,
EMP: 40
SQ FT: 15,000
SALES (est): 8.6MM **Privately Held**
SIC: 3089 Injection molding of plastics

(G-14916)
SOLAR TURBINES INCORPORATED
40 Shuman Blvd Ste 350 (60563-7973)
PHONE..................630 527-1700
Russle Bruno, *President*
EMP: 25
SALES (corp-wide): 53.8B **Publicly Held**
SIC: 3511 Gas turbine generator set units, complete
HQ: Solar Turbines Incorporated
2200 Pacific Hwy
San Diego CA 92101
619 544-5000

(G-14917)
SONNE INDUSTRIES LLC
5s528 Arlington Ave (60540-3819)
PHONE..................630 235-6734
William Dorn, *CEO*
EMP: 2
SALES (est): 238.6K **Privately Held**
SIC: 3822 Appliance controls except air-conditioning & refrigeration; energy cutoff controls, residential or commercial types

(G-14918)
SOURCEBOOKS LLC (PA)
1935 Brookdale Rd Ste 139 (60563-7994)
P.O. Box 4410 (60567-4410)
PHONE..................630 961-3900
Dominique Raccah, *President*
Mary Altman, *Editor*
Meg Gibbons, *Editor*
Brad Hentz, *Opers Mgr*
Rachel Gilmer, *Production*
◆ EMP: 70
SQ FT: 14,000
SALES (est): 57.6MM **Privately Held**
SIC: 2731 Books: publishing only

(G-14919)
SPELL IT WITH COLOR INC
Also Called: Allegra Mktg Print Mail
1644 Swallow St (60565-2332)
PHONE..................630 961-5617
Thomas Wilhelm, *President*
Daniel Spell, *Principal*
EMP: 3 EST: 2010
SALES (est): 315.7K **Privately Held**
SIC: 2752 Commercial printing, offset

(G-14920)
STREAMLINX LLC
387 Shuman Blvd Ste 205w (60563-8565)
PHONE..................630 864-3043
Jeff Seifert, *Mng Member*
Mike Seifert, *Mng Member*
EMP: 12
SALES: 2.8MM **Privately Held**
SIC: 7372 Business oriented computer software

(G-14921)
SUDPACK USA INC
937 N Washington St (60563-2762)
PHONE..................630 258-4015
EMP: 3
SALES (est): 137.4K **Privately Held**
SIC: 2092 Fresh or frozen packaged fish

(G-14922)
SUNCRAFT TECHNOLOGIES INC (PA)
1301 Frontenac Rd (60563-1710)
PHONE..................630 369-7900
Ronald F Desanto Sr, *President*
Eulalia Desanto, *Vice Pres*
Scott Hayes, *Vice Pres*
Lia Santo, *Vice Pres*
Ed Tinsley, *Vice Pres*
EMP: 110
SQ FT: 72,000
SALES (est): 27.5MM **Privately Held**
SIC: 2752 Commercial printing, offset

(G-14923)
SUNEMCO TECHNOLOGIES INC
500 Braemar Ave (60563-1369)
PHONE..................630 369-8947
Liang Hu, *President*
Hong Xue, *Treasurer*
Evelyn Lin, *Admin Sec*
EMP: 3
SALES (est): 317.6K **Privately Held**
SIC: 2821 7379 Plastics materials & resins;

(G-14924)
SUNNY DIRECT LLC (PA)
300 E 5th Ave Ste 465 (60563-3290)
PHONE..................630 795-0800
Steve Reinke, *Manager*
▲ EMP: 8
SALES (est): 2.3MM **Privately Held**
SIC: 2759 Commercial printing

(G-14925)
T C W F INC
Also Called: Minuteman Press
1577 Nperville Wheaton Rd (60563-1556)
PHONE..................630 369-1360
Kevin Brahler, *President*
Ray Kinney, *Vice Pres*
James Kelly, *Treasurer*
EMP: 28
SQ FT: 7,200
SALES (est): 5MM **Privately Held**
WEB: www.naperprinting.com
SIC: 2752 Commercial printing, lithographic

(G-14926)
T F N W INC
Also Called: Minuteman Press
1577 Nperville Wheaton Rd (60563-1556)
PHONE..................630 584-7383
Jerry Prasse, *President*
EMP: 4
SQ FT: 1,300
SALES (est): 364.1K **Privately Held**
SIC: 2752 2759 2791 2789 Commercial printing, lithographic; ready prints; typesetting; bookbinding & related work

(G-14927)
TBC CORPORATION
Also Called: Ntb
915 E Ogden Ave (60563-2836)
PHONE..................630 428-2233
Christopher Cruz, *Manager*
EMP: 3 **Privately Held**
SIC: 3011 Tires, cushion or solid rubber
HQ: Tbc Corporation
4300 Tbc Way
Palm Beach Gardens FL 33410
561 383-3000

(G-14928)
TELLABS MEXICO INC (DH)
1415 W Diehl Rd (60563-9950)
PHONE..................630 445-5333
Michael Birck, *President*
Brian Jackman, *Exec VP*
John Kohler, *Vice Pres*
Peter Guglielmi, *Treasurer*
EMP: 10
SALES (est): 3.5MM **Privately Held**
SIC: 3661 Telephones & telephone apparatus
HQ: Tellabs, Inc.
18583 Dallas Pkwy Ste 200
Dallas TX 75287
800 690-2324

(G-14929)
TELLABS TG INC
1415 W Diehl Rd (60563-9950)
PHONE..................630 798-8800
EMP: 3
SALES (est): 27.9K **Privately Held**
SIC: 3661 Telephone & telegraph apparatus
HQ: Tellabs, Inc.
18583 Dallas Pkwy Ste 200
Dallas TX 75287
800 690-2324

(G-14930)
TEXXON PLASTICS CORPORATION
424 Fort Hill Dr Ste 131 (60540-3913)
PHONE..................630 369-6850
Cheng Kaifu, *President*
▲ EMP: 3
SQ FT: 1,800
SALES: 5.7MM **Privately Held**
SIC: 2821 Plastics materials & resins

(G-14931)
TEZZARON SEMICONDUCTOR CORP
1415 Bond St Ste 111 (60563-2769)
PHONE..................630 505-0404
James Ayers, *CEO*
EMP: 110
SQ FT: 16,000 **Privately Held**
SIC: 3674 Integrated circuits, semiconductor networks, etc.
PA: Tezzaron Semiconductor Corporation
7600 Chevy Chase Dr
Austin TX 78752

(G-14932)
THE LIFEGUARD STORE INC
1212 S Naper Blvd Ste 109 (60540-8399)
PHONE..................630 548-5500
Art Eosseman, *Owner*
EMP: 7
SALES (corp-wide): 7.7MM **Privately Held**
WEB: www.thelifeguardstore.com
SIC: 2253 Bathing suits & swimwear, knit
PA: The Lifeguard Store Inc
903 Morrissey Dr Unit 2
Bloomington IL 61701
309 451-5858

(G-14933)
THRIFT MEDICAL PRODUCTS
1701 Quincy Ave (60540-3955)
PHONE..................630 857-3548
EMP: 3 EST: 2014
SALES (est): 218.3K **Privately Held**
SIC: 3841 Surgical & medical instruments

(G-14934)
TINY HUMAN FOOD INC
5s220 Beau Bien Blvd (60563-1633)
PHONE..................630 397-9936

Ashley Rossi, *CEO*
EMP: 1
SALES: 500K **Privately Held**
SIC: 3999 Manufacturing industries

(G-14935)
TOYAL AMERICA INC
1717 N Naper Blvd Ste 201 (60563-8838)
PHONE.................................630 505-2160
Bud Loprest, *Vice Pres*
Trish Wolf, *Director*
EMP: 6 **Privately Held**
WEB: www.toyala.com
SIC: 2816 3399 2819 Inorganic pigments; powder, metal; industrial inorganic chemicals
HQ: Toyal America, Inc.
   17401 Broadway St
   Lockport IL 60441
   630 505-2160

(G-14936)
TRACK GROUP INC (PA)
200 E 5th Ave Ste 100 (60563-3192)
PHONE.................................877 260-2010
Derek Cassell, *CEO*
Guy Dubois, *Ch of Bd*
Johan Elerud, *Vice Pres*
Aj Gigler, *Vice Pres*
Matt Swando, *Vice Pres*
▲ **EMP:** 37
SQ FT: 5,600
SALES: 34MM **Publicly Held**
SIC: 3669 7374 Visual communication systems; data processing & preparation

(G-14937)
TWOCANOES SOFTWARE INC
34 W Chicago Ave Ste A (60540-5397)
PHONE.................................630 305-9601
Timothy Perfitt, *President*
Tj Caracci, *Business Mgr*
Russell Scheil, *Manager*
Dave Lebbing, *Web Dvlpr*
EMP: 3
SQ FT: 1,200
SALES (est): 313.6K **Privately Held**
SIC: 7372 Application computer software

(G-14938)
UPM-KYMMENE INC (HQ)
Also Called: Upm North America
55 Shuman Blvd Ste 400 (60563-8248)
PHONE.................................630 922-2500
Angelo Lamantia, *General Mgr*
Terri Hable, *Business Mgr*
Bernd Eikens, *Exec VP*
ESA Retva, *Vice Pres*
Jussi Sarvikas, *Vice Pres*
▲ **EMP:** 90 **EST:** 1978
SALES (est): 56.8MM **Privately Held**
WEB: www.upm.com
SIC: 2621 5111 Paper mills; printing & writing paper

(G-14939)
VALLEY FASTENER GROUP LLC
Also Called: Valley Fasteners Group
5s250 Frontenac Rd (60563-1711)
PHONE.................................630 548-5679
EMP: 30
SALES (corp-wide): 26.1MM **Privately Held**
SIC: 3452 Bolts, nuts, rivets & washers
PA: Valley Fastener Group, Llc
   1490 Mitchell Rd
   Aurora IL 60505
   630 299-8910

(G-14940)
VEJ HOLDINGS LLC
1717 N Naper Blvd Ste 108 (60563-8837)
PHONE.................................630 219-1598
Vincent Jackson, *CEO*
EMP: 3
SALES (est): 745.2K **Privately Held**
SIC: 5142 5149 5147 2673 Frozen fish, meat & poultry; spices & seasonings; meats & meat products; food storage & frozen food bags, plastic; insurance agents, brokers & service

(G-14941)
VENTURE DESIGN INCORPORATED
2250 Allegany Dr (60565-3415)
PHONE.................................630 369-1148
EMP: 12
SQ FT: 5,280
SALES (est): 1.2MM **Privately Held**
SIC: 3613 8711 Mfg Electric And Pneumatic Control Panels & Designs Control Systems

(G-14942)
VORTEX MEDIA GROUP INC
1118 Knoll Dr (60565-2735)
PHONE.................................630 717-9541
James Vondruska, *President*
EMP: 6
SALES (est): 729K **Privately Held**
SIC: 2741

(G-14943)
VULCAN CONSTRUCTION MTLS LLC
1000 E Wrrnvlle Rd Ste 10 (60563)
PHONE.................................630 955-8500
Lenny Novak, *Manager*
EMP: 25 **Publicly Held**
WEB: www.vulcanmaterials.com
SIC: 1422 Crushed & broken limestone
HQ: Vulcan Construction Materials, Llc
   1200 Urban Center Dr
   Vestavia AL 35242
   205 298-3000

(G-14944)
WASHBURN GRAFICOLOR INC
1255 E Bailey Rd (60565-1646)
PHONE.................................630 596-0880
Gregory G Washburn, *President*
Sarah Washburn, *Admin Sec*
EMP: 5 **EST:** 1958
SQ FT: 1,350
SALES (est): 670.8K **Privately Held**
SIC: 2752 7336 2791 Commercial printing, offset; graphic arts & related design; typesetting

(G-14945)
WEBB-MASON INC
280 Shuman Blvd Ste 200 (60563-3187)
PHONE.................................630 428-5838
Dan Cahill, *Branch Mgr*
EMP: 10 **Privately Held**
WEB: www.webbmason.com
SIC: 2752 Commercial printing, lithographic
PA: Webb-Mason, Inc.
   10830 Gilroy Rd
   Hunt Valley MD 21031

(G-14946)
WEHRLI EQUIPMENT CO INC
1805 High Grove Ln # 117 (60540-3987)
PHONE.................................630 717-4150
Scott Wehrli, *President*
EMP: 10
SALES (est): 840.5K **Privately Held**
SIC: 3531 7699 5084 Bituminous, cement & concrete related products & equipment; industrial equipment services; industrial machinery & equipment

(G-14947)
WEYERHAEUSER COMPANY
Also Called: Weyerhauser
220 Brookshire Ct (60540-3911)
PHONE.................................630 778-7070
Fax: 630 778-7575
EMP: 60
SALES (corp-wide): 7B **Publicly Held**
SIC: 2611 Paper Mill
PA: Weyerhaeuser Company
   33663 Weyerhaeuser Way S
   Federal Way WA 98104
   253 924-2345

(G-14948)
WILTON BRANDS LLC (PA)
Also Called: K&Company
535 E Diehl Rd Ste 333 (60563-7723)
PHONE.................................630 963-7100
Sue Buchta, *CEO*
Anna Pulla, *Opers Mgr*
Roger Ruggeri, *Opers Staff*
Ida Rico, *Sales Staff*
Amily Tseng, *Sales Staff*
◆ **EMP:** 430
SQ FT: 38,000
SALES (est): 342.3MM **Privately Held**
SIC: 8299 5046 2051 5999 Cooking school; bakery equipment & supplies; cakes, pies & pastries; cake decorating supplies; cakes; baking supplies

(G-14949)
WILTON INDUSTRIES INC (HQ)
Also Called: Wilton Industries Co
535 E Diehl Rd Ste 333 (60563-7723)
PHONE.................................630 963-7100
Sue Buchta, *President*
Maya Bordeaux, *Vice Pres*
Marcos Cuzco, *Vice Pres*
Rich Ezra, *Vice Pres*
Richard Flores, *Vice Pres*
◆ **EMP:** 450
SQ FT: 38,000
SALES (est): 320.6MM **Privately Held**
SIC: 5023 2731 2721 7812 Kitchenware; kitchen tools & utensils; frames & framing, picture & mirror; books: publishing only; periodicals: publishing only; video tape production; candy making goods & supplies

(G-14950)
WILTON WW CO (PA)
Also Called: Simplicity Creative Group
535 E Diehl Rd Ste 300 (60563-2260)
PHONE.................................615 501-3000
Phil Handy, *CEO*
Jim Divizio, *CFO*
▲ **EMP:** 49
SQ FT: 34,000
SALES (est): 20.8MM **Privately Held**
SIC: 2395 5131 Pleating & stitching; sewing accessories

(G-14951)
XEROX CORPORATION
1435 Foxhill Rd (60563-2102)
PHONE.................................630 983-0172
Gary Zimmerman, *Project Mgr*
Chuck Sabino, *Manager*
Robert Bava, *Manager*
EMP: 74
SALES (corp-wide): 9B **Publicly Held**
WEB: www.xerox.com
SIC: 3861 Photographic equipment & supplies
HQ: Xerox Corporation
   201 Merritt 7
   Norwalk CT 06851
   800 835-6100

Naperville
Will County

(G-14952)
AGILE HEALTH TECHNOLOGIES INC
2728 Forgue Dr Ste 106 (60564-4192)
PHONE.................................331 457-5167
Sasikant Gandhamaneni, *President*
Dibyajyothi Mahanta, *Vice Pres*
Ravindran Nithyanandam, *Vice Pres*
EMP: 25
SALES: 3.5MM **Privately Held**
SIC: 7371 7372 7373 Computer software development; business oriented computer software; systems integration services

(G-14953)
AIKNOW INC
2243 Gloucester Ln (60564-8475)
PHONE.................................312 391-9452
Zuyi LI, *CEO*
Mengmeng Zhuang, *COO*
WEI Tian, *Vice Pres*
Zhen Bao, *Chief Engr*
EMP: 10
SALES (est): 549.9K **Privately Held**
SIC: 3825 Test equipment for electronic & electrical circuits

(G-14954)
AIM SCREEN PRINTING SUPPLY LLC
2731 Willow Ridge Dr (60564-8951)
P.O. Box 9645 (60567-0645)
PHONE.................................630 357-4293
Ben Goldstein, *Mng Member*
▲ **EMP:** 7
SQ FT: 3,000
SALES: 1.5MM **Privately Held**
SIC: 2759 Screen printing

(G-14955)
ALL LINE INC
31w310 91st St (60564-5615)
PHONE.................................630 820-1800
Alfonso Monraz, *Purch Mgr*
EMP: 5
SALES (corp-wide): 1.6MM **Privately Held**
SIC: 2298 3357 Cordage: abaca, sisal, henequen, hemp, jute or other fiber; aluminum wire & cable
PA: All Line Inc.
   16851 E Parkview Ave # 201
   Fountain Hills AZ 85268
   480 306-6001

(G-14956)
ALL STAR INJECTION MOLDERS INC
24w959 Ramm Dr Unit 5 (60564-3611)
PHONE.................................630 978-4046
Michael Tropinski, *President*
Marsha Tropinski, *Admin Sec*
EMP: 4
SALES (est): 487.2K **Privately Held**
SIC: 3089 Injection molding of plastics

(G-14957)
AMERICAN WATERSOURCE LLC
1228 Bards Ave (60564-3158)
P.O. Box 9548 (60567-0548)
PHONE.................................630 778-9900
Tom Sorensen, *Mng Member*
EMP: 50
SALES (est): 3MM **Privately Held**
SIC: 3589 7389 Water treatment equipment, industrial; water softener service

(G-14958)
AMERINET OF MICHIGAN INC
3909 White Eagle Dr W (60564-8283)
PHONE.................................708 466-0110
Mark Katsis, *Branch Mgr*
EMP: 4 **Privately Held**
SIC: 3825 8999 Network analyzers; technical manual preparation
PA: Amerinet Of Michigan, Inc.
   1241 S Maple Rd
   Ann Arbor MI 48103

(G-14959)
ANYTIME HEATING & AC
10s264 Schoger Dr Ste 2 (60564-8264)
PHONE.................................630 851-6696
Gary Murphy Sr, *President*
Michael Murphy, *Vice Pres*
Gary Murphy Jr, *Treasurer*
EMP: 10 **EST:** 1973
SQ FT: 3,000
SALES: 2.5MM **Privately Held**
SIC: 1711 5075 3444 Warm air heating & air conditioning contractor; air conditioning & ventilation equipment & supplies; sheet metalwork

(G-14960)
AVANTI MOTOR CARRIERS INC
4440 White Ash Ln (60564-1102)
PHONE.................................630 313-9160
EMP: 4
SALES (est): 370.7K **Privately Held**
SIC: 3531 Crane carriers

(G-14961)
BATTERY BUILDERS LLC
31w238 91st St (60564-5623)
PHONE.................................630 851-5800
Melissa Sachse, *CFO*
James Hanslik,
Mark Vesely,
EMP: 79
SQ FT: 54,517

Naperville - Will County (G-14962)

SALES (est): 2.5MM **Privately Held**
SIC: 3691 Lead acid batteries (storage batteries)

(G-14962)
CALX TRADING CORPORATION
1245 Amaranth Dr (60564-9336)
PHONE..................630 456-6721
Mohsen Abdelati, *CEO*
EMP: 25
SQ FT: 7,500
SALES: 1.2MM **Privately Held**
SIC: 3699 Security control equipment & systems

(G-14963)
CONTEMPRARY ENRGY SLUTIONS LLC
2951 Beth Ln (60564-4398)
PHONE..................630 768-3743
Antonio Vlastelica, *Mng Member*
EMP: 13 EST: 2011
SALES (est): 2.9MM **Privately Held**
WEB: www.ces-na.com
SIC: 3646 1731 Commercial indusl & institutional electric lighting fixtures; energy management controls

(G-14964)
CUTTING EDGE GRAPHICS LTD
Also Called: Signs and Designs
1329 Marengo Ct (60564-9505)
PHONE..................630 717-9233
Sherri Nagy, *President*
Jim Nagy, *Vice Pres*
EMP: 3
SALES (est): 299.5K **Privately Held**
WEB: www.cuttingedgegraphics.net
SIC: 3993 Signs & advertising specialties

(G-14965)
EDGO TECHNICAL SALES INC
9s131 Skylane Dr (60564-9450)
PHONE..................630 961-8398
Edwin A Goebel Jr, *President*
Ellen M Goebel, *Admin Sec*
EMP: 2
SALES (est): 265.3K **Privately Held**
SIC: 3672 Printed circuit boards

(G-14966)
FLURIDA GROUP INC
2439 Haider Ave (60564-5392)
PHONE..................310 513-0888
Jeff Ding, *President*
EMP: 5 **Privately Held**
WEB: www.fluridaappliances.com
SIC: 3632 Household refrigerators & freezers
PA: Flurida Group, Inc.
11220 Rojas Dr Ste C3
El Paso TX 79935

(G-14967)
GAME DAY INCENTIVES INC
1731 Princess Cir (60564-7130)
PHONE..................630 854-0581
Tracy Mazurek, *CEO*
Henry A Mazurek, *President*
Hank Mazurek, *President*
EMP: 2
SQ FT: 400
SALES (est): 208K **Privately Held**
SIC: 2759 Screen printing

(G-14968)
GARDNER DENVER NASH LLC
2808 Hillcrest Cir (60564-1134)
PHONE..................331 457-5377
Linda Scott, *Buyer*
Joseph Kowalski, *Engineer*
Robert Steeves, *Manager*
EMP: 11
SALES (corp-wide): 2.4B **Publicly Held**
WEB: www.gardnerdenver.com
SIC: 3563 Air & gas compressors
HQ: Gardner Denver Nash Llc
2 Trefoil Dr
Trumbull CT 06611
203 459-3923

(G-14969)
GLASSTEK INC
10s059 Schoger Dr Unit 40 (60564-3601)
PHONE..................630 978-9897
Torrence Caniglia, *President*

Robert Mortinsen, *Vice Pres*
EMP: 9 EST: 1992
SALES (est): 1.2MM **Privately Held**
SIC: 3089 Awnings, fiberglass & plastic combination

(G-14970)
GUARDIAN CONSTRUCTION PDTS INC
10s359 Normantown Rd (60564-5632)
PHONE..................630 820-8899
Gerald J Husarik, *President*
David Husarik, *Vice Pres*
Kathleen Husarik, *Treasurer*
Phillip Husarik, *Admin Sec*
▲ EMP: 28
SQ FT: 18,900
SALES (est): 4.7MM **Privately Held**
SIC: 1791 3312 Structural steel erection; structural & rail mill products

(G-14971)
HAKWOOD INC
2244 95th St Ste 200 (60564-8118)
PHONE..................630 219-3388
Cornelis Mannien, *President*
Francie Marchio, *Sales Staff*
Sandy Schroat, *Office Mgr*
Claire Hammock, *Manager*
Hans Alberts, *Director*
▲ EMP: 7 EST: 2012
SALES (est): 1.4MM
SALES (corp-wide): 183.7K **Privately Held**
SIC: 5023 2426 Floor coverings; flooring, hardwood
HQ: Hakwood B.V.
Leemansstraat 2
Werkendam 4251
183 504-266

(G-14972)
HIDALGO FINE CABINETRY
8952 Hanslik Ct Ste 22 (60564-5847)
PHONE..................630 753-9323
C Hidalgo, *Owner*
EMP: 3
SALES (est): 339.6K **Privately Held**
SIC: 2434 Wood kitchen cabinets

(G-14973)
HONEYWELL INTERNATIONAL INC
4412 Buttermilk Ct (60564-7107)
PHONE..................630 922-0138
EMP: 694
SALES (corp-wide): 40.5B **Publicly Held**
SIC: 3724 Mfg Aircraft Engines/Parts
PA: Honeywell International Inc.
115 Tabor Rd
Morris Plains NJ 28202
973 455-2000

(G-14974)
INLET & PIPE PROTECTION INC
24137 111th St Ste A (60564-8316)
PHONE..................630 355-3288
James Ringenbach, *President*
▲ EMP: 3
SALES (est): 863.6K
SALES (corp-wide): 1.6B **Publicly Held**
WEB: www.inletfilters.com
SIC: 5084 3589 3569 Industrial machinery & equipment; sewer cleaning equipment, power; filters
PA: Advanced Drainage Systems, Inc.
4640 Trueman Blvd
Hilliard OH 43026
614 658-0050

(G-14975)
IRONWOOD MANUFACTURING INC
Also Called: Hammer Source, The
2863 95th St Ste 14 (60564-9005)
PHONE..................630 969-1100
Jennifer Ayers, *CEO*
Andrew A Ayers, *President*
▼ EMP: 2
SQ FT: 500
SALES (est): 218.5K **Privately Held**
WEB: www.hammersource.com
SIC: 3423 3999 Hammers (hand tools); barber & beauty shop equipment

(G-14976)
KING S COURT EXTERIOR
2328 Skylane Dr (60564-8529)
PHONE..................630 904-4305
EMP: 3 EST: 2002
SALES (est): 180K **Privately Held**
SIC: 3671 Mfg Electron Tubes

(G-14977)
LESSY MESSY LLC
Also Called: Sourcing Solutions
3143 Aviara Ct (60564-4617)
PHONE..................708 790-7589
Shoaib S Khadri, *President*
Keith J Geitner,
EMP: 10
SALES (est): 6MM **Privately Held**
SIC: 2273 Mats & matting

(G-14978)
MACH MECHANICAL GROUP LLC
28w016 Country View Dr (60564-9643)
PHONE..................630 674-6224
Amy Reiser,
EMP: 1
SQ FT: 1,750
SALES (est): 250K **Privately Held**
SIC: 1711 3443 Heating & air conditioning contractors; ducting, metal plate

(G-14979)
MIDWEST STAIR PARTS
31w335 Schoger Dr (60564-5657)
PHONE..................630 723-3991
Mel Drendel, *President*
EMP: 3
SALES (est): 262.9K **Privately Held**
SIC: 3446 Stairs, staircases, stair treads: prefabricated metal

(G-14980)
NATIONAL DEF INTELLIGENCE INC
Also Called: Critical18
2863 95th St 143-380 (60564-9005)
PHONE..................312 233-2318
Daniel Sproul, *President*
Tom Leem, *Manager*
Andrea Sproul, *Administration*
EMP: 3
SALES (est): 657.5K **Privately Held**
SIC: 7373 1731 7381 7379 Local area network (LAN) systems integrator; voice, data & video wiring contractor; detective services; computer related consulting services; rockets, space & military, complete; personal investigation service

(G-14981)
NAVIPOINT GENOMICS LLC
2515 Dewes Ln (60564-8473)
PHONE..................630 464-8013
Utpal J Dave, *President*
EMP: 5 EST: 2016
SALES (est): 128.9K **Privately Held**
SIC: 7372 Business oriented computer software

(G-14982)
PANELSHOPNET INC
3460 Ohara Ter (60564-8167)
PHONE..................630 692-0214
Gregory Schoeck, *President*
EMP: 1
SALES (est): 244.6K **Privately Held**
WEB: www.panelshop.net
SIC: 3613 Control panels, electric

(G-14983)
PRESTIGE MOTOR WORKS INC
11258 S Route 59 Ste 1 (60564-8372)
PHONE..................630 780-6439
Alex Tovstanovsky, *Principal*
EMP: 5
SQ FT: 10,000
SALES (est): 1.2MM **Privately Held**
WEB: www.myprestigecar.com
SIC: 5599 3089 3069 3714 Automotive dealers; automotive parts, plastic; battery boxes, jars or parts, hard rubber; motor vehicle parts & accessories; motor vehicle engines & parts; high performance auto repair & service

(G-14984)
RADOVENT ILLINOIS LLC (PA)
10s187 Schoger Dr Ste 65 (60564-4679)
PHONE..................847 637-0297
Patrick Dwyer, *Regional Mgr*
Jay Cranney, *Sales Dir*
Travis Jewell, *Mng Member*
EMP: 8
SALES (est): 886.5K **Privately Held**
WEB: www.radovent.com
SIC: 3634 Air purifiers, portable

(G-14985)
SCREEN PRINT PLUS INC
8815 Ramm Dr Ste A (60564-9347)
P.O. Box 103, Eola (60519-0103)
PHONE..................630 236-0260
Robert Frances Jr, *President*
EMP: 2 EST: 1997
SQ FT: 3,600
SALES (est): 266.4K **Privately Held**
SIC: 2752 Commercial printing, lithographic

(G-14986)
SECOND CHANCE INC
Also Called: Craig Alan Salon
5320 Switch Grass Ln (60564-5369)
PHONE..................630 904-5955
EMP: 12
SALES (est): 730K **Privately Held**
SIC: 2395 Pleating/Stitching Services

(G-14987)
SHARPEDGE SOLUTIONS INC
2728 Forgue Dr Ste 106 (60564-4192)
PHONE..................630 792-9639
Bhaskara Katiki, *President*
Ramesh Addanki, *Director*
Sampath Murugan, *Associate*
EMP: 17
SALES (est): 1.8MM **Privately Held**
SIC: 7372 Prepackaged software

(G-14988)
SPRINTER COML PRINT LABEL CORP
Also Called: Proforma Coml Print Group
4820 Fesseneva Ln (60564-5769)
PHONE..................630 460-3492
Kevin J Springer, *President*
EMP: 6
SALES (est): 709.3K **Privately Held**
SIC: 2752 Commercial printing, lithographic

(G-14989)
SUGAR MONKEY CUPCAKES INC
2728 Wild Timothy Rd (60564-4357)
PHONE..................630 527-1869
Neda Darwish, *Owner*
EMP: 6 EST: 2008
SALES (est): 614.1K **Privately Held**
WEB: www.sugarmonkeycupcakes.com
SIC: 2051 Cakes, bakery: except frozen

(G-14990)
TIMKEN COMPANY
3155 Book Rd Ste 103 (60564-9546)
PHONE..................630 679-6756
Lawrence Warren, *Branch Mgr*
EMP: 163
SALES (corp-wide): 3.7B **Publicly Held**
SIC: 3562 Roller bearings & parts
PA: The Timken Company
4500 Mount Pleasant St Nw
North Canton OH 44720
234 262-3000

(G-14991)
VICTORIA AMPLIFIER COMPANY
1504 Newman Ct (60564-4132)
PHONE..................630 369-3527
Mark A Baier, *President*
Maureen Baier, *CFO*
EMP: 10
SALES: 1MM **Privately Held**
SIC: 3651 3699 Amplifiers: radio, public address or musical instrument; electric sound equipment

GEOGRAPHIC SECTION

(G-14992)
WILTEK INC
3819 Grassmere Rd (60564-8227)
P.O. Box 9330 (60567-0330)
PHONE..................................630 922-9200
Richard Wilinski, *President*
EMP: 3 **EST:** 1996
SALES (est): 280K **Privately Held**
SIC: 3444 Sheet metalwork

(G-14993)
ZEBRA TECHNOLOGIES CORPORATION
1116 Magenta Ct (60564-3115)
PHONE..................................630 548-1370
Bruce Winter, *Principal*
EMP: 3
SALES (corp-wide): 4.4B **Publicly Held**
SIC: 3577 Computer peripheral equipment
PA: Zebra Technologies Corporation
   3 Overlook Pt
   Lincolnshire IL 60069
   847 634-6700

Nashville
Washington County

(G-14994)
ANTOLIN INTERIORS USA INC
Also Called: Nashville Interior Systems Div
18355 Enterprise Ave (62263-1600)
PHONE..................................618 327-4416
Tim Staley, *Safety Mgr*
John Wall, *Engineer*
Mark Deterding, *Design Engr*
Wayne Broadwater, *Branch Mgr*
EMP: 291
SALES (corp-wide): 33.3MM **Privately Held**
SIC: 3714 Motor vehicle parts & accessories
HQ: Antolin Interiors Usa, Inc.
   1700 Atlantic Blvd
   Auburn Hills MI 48326
   248 373-1749

(G-14995)
BEELMAN READY-MIX INC
Also Called: Plant 06
17558 Mockingbird Rd (62263-3406)
PHONE..................................618 478-2044
Mike Hocking, *Manager*
EMP: 5 **Privately Held**
WEB: www.beelman.com
SIC: 5211 3273 Masonry materials & supplies; ready-mixed concrete
PA: Beelman Ready-Mix, Inc.
   1 Racehorse Dr
   East Saint Louis IL 62205

(G-14996)
EVANS TALAIHA
550 W Saint Louis St (62263-1110)
P.O. Box 287 (62263-0287)
PHONE..................................618 327-8200
Talaiha Evans, *Owner*
EMP: 3
SALES (est): 238K **Privately Held**
SIC: 1311 Crude petroleum production

(G-14997)
GATEWAY SEED COMPANY INC (PA)
5517 Van Buren Rd (62263-4812)
PHONE..................................618 327-8000
James Lutz, *President*
Dan Hish, *Vice Pres*
Matthew Heggemeir, *Admin Sec*
EMP: 4
SALES (est): 740.5K **Privately Held**
SIC: 3999 Seeds, coated or treated, from purchased seeds

(G-14998)
JC TOOLING COMPANY INC
560 National Mine Rd (62263-1677)
PHONE..................................618 327-9379
Jeffrey Cunningham, *CEO*
EMP: 10
SALES: 750K **Privately Held**
SIC: 3544 Special dies & tools

(G-14999)
MAGNA EXTERIORS AMERICA INC
18310 Enterprise Ave (62263-1619)
PHONE..................................618 327-4381
Art Stolle, *Purch Mgr*
Donnie Kroll, *Project Engr*
Gary Deering, *Administration*
EMP: 1000
SALES (corp-wide): 39.4B **Privately Held**
SIC: 3714 Bumpers & bumperettes, motor vehicle
HQ: Magna Exteriors Of America, Inc.
   750 Tower Dr
   Troy MI 48098
   248 631-1100

(G-15000)
MAGNA EXTERIORS AMERICA INC
Innertech - Nashville
18355 Enterprise Ave (62263-1600)
PHONE..................................618 327-2136
Renee Revermann, *Accountant*
Bob Shchwab, *Branch Mgr*
Janmarie Kent, *Exec Dir*
EMP: 350
SALES (corp-wide): 39.4B **Privately Held**
SIC: 3714 Motor vehicle parts & accessories
HQ: Magna Exteriors Of America, Inc.
   750 Tower Dr
   Troy MI 48098
   248 631-1100

(G-15001)
MARION OELZE (PA)
Also Called: Bits of Gold Jewelry
11872 County Highway 27 # 3 (62263-2606)
PHONE..................................618 327-9224
Marion Oelze, *Owner*
EMP: 8
SALES (est): 2.4MM **Privately Held**
SIC: 1381 5084 5944 5812 Drilling oil & gas wells; oil well machinery, equipment & supplies; jewelry stores; eating places

(G-15002)
NASCOTE INDUSTRIES INC (HQ)
18310 Enterprise Ave (62263-1619)
PHONE..................................618 327-4381
Andrew Barban, *President*
Jim Evilsizer, *Safety Mgr*
Neal Luehr, *Purchasing*
Mike Johannes, *Engineer*
Greg Kasban, *Engineer*
▲ **EMP:** 600
SALES (est): 258.4MM
SALES (corp-wide): 39.4B **Privately Held**
SIC: 3714 Bumpers & bumperettes, motor vehicle
PA: Magna International Inc
   337 Magna Dr
   Aurora ON L4G 7
   905 726-2462

(G-15003)
NASCOTE INDUSTRIES INC
17582 Mockingbird Rd (62263-3406)
PHONE..................................618 478-2092
Lee Suedmeyer, *Branch Mgr*
EMP: 200
SALES (corp-wide): 39.4B **Privately Held**
SIC: 3714 Bumpers & bumperettes, motor vehicle
HQ: Nascote Industries, Inc.
   18310 Enterprise Ave
   Nashville IL 62263
   618 327-4381

(G-15004)
NASHVILLE MEMORIAL CO
542 E Saint Louis St (62263-1706)
PHONE..................................618 327-8492
Jerome Lager, *President*
EMP: 3
SALES (est): 320K **Privately Held**
SIC: 3281 Monument or burial stone, cut & shaped

(G-15005)
NASHVILLE NEWS
Also Called: Nashville News, The
211 W Saint Louis St (62263-1161)
P.O. Box 47 (62263-0047)
PHONE..................................618 327-3411
Richard Tomaszewski, *President*
Constance Tomaszewski, *Treasurer*
EMP: 10
SALES (est): 704.4K **Privately Held**
WEB: www.nash-news.com
SIC: 2711 Commercial printing & newspaper publishing combined; newspapers, publishing & printing

(G-15006)
OELZE EQUIPMENT COMPANY LLC
11800 County Highway 27 (62263-2606)
P.O. Box 325 (62263-0325)
PHONE..................................618 327-9111
Kim Oelze,
Elmer Dean Oelze,
Jeffery E Oelze,
Wiliam A Oelze,
EMP: 25
SQ FT: 1,500
SALES (est): 2.2MM **Privately Held**
SIC: 1389 1311 Oil field services; crude petroleum & natural gas production

(G-15007)
PURINA ANIMAL NUTRITION LLC
17815 Mockingbird Rd (62263-3410)
PHONE..................................618 478-5555
Michael Brown, *Mfg Spvr*
EMP: 35
SALES (corp-wide): 6B **Privately Held**
SIC: 2048 Prepared feeds
HQ: Purina Animal Nutrition Llc
   100 Danforth Dr
   Gray Summit MO 63039

(G-15008)
QUAD-COUNTY READY MIX CORP
1050 N Washington St (62263-1000)
PHONE..................................618 327-3748
Herb Husteddi, *Manager*
EMP: 13
SALES (corp-wide): 16.1MM **Privately Held**
SIC: 3273 Ready-mixed concrete
PA: Quad-County Ready Mix Corp.
   300 W 12th St
   Okawville IL 62271
   618 243-6430

(G-15009)
REPUBLIC OF TEA INC
11051 N Mockingbird Rd A (62263-3436)
PHONE..................................618 478-5520
Dave Shrum, *Plant Mgr*
Barbara Graves, *Branch Mgr*
Debra Baldwin,
EMP: 6 **Privately Held**
SIC: 2099 Tea blending
PA: The Republic Of Tea Inc
   900 Larkspur Landing Cir # 275
   Larkspur CA 94939

(G-15010)
SISCO CORPORATION (PA)
Also Called: Southern Illinois State Cont
1520 S Mill St (62263-2077)
P.O. Box 51 (62263-0051)
PHONE..................................618 327-3066
Ronald D Whitener, *President*
Emanuel Whitener, *Corp Secy*
Joel Whitener, *Vice Pres*
Genie Ristick, *Treasurer*
EMP: 45
SQ FT: 80,000
SALES (est): 11.8MM **Privately Held**
SIC: 2653 3081 Boxes, corrugated: made from purchased materials; packing materials, plastic sheet

(G-15011)
STITCH TEC CO INC (PA)
887 N Washington St (62263-1050)
P.O. Box 253 (62263-0253)
PHONE..................................618 327-8054
H J Jones, *President*
Pat Jones, *Treasurer*
Tammy Jones, *Manager*
EMP: 6
SQ FT: 40,000
SALES (est): 1.6MM **Privately Held**
SIC: 2653 4225 Boxes, solid fiber: made from purchased materials; general warehousing & storage

National Stock Yards
St. Clair County

(G-15012)
DARLING INGREDIENTS INC
2 Exchange Ave (62071-1003)
P.O. Box 55 (62071-0055)
PHONE..................................618 271-8190
Garry Bryd, *Manager*
EMP: 42
SALES (corp-wide): 3.3B **Publicly Held**
WEB: www.darlingii.com
SIC: 2077 3111 Tallow rendering, inedible; leather tanning & finishing
PA: Darling Ingredients Inc.
   5601 N Macarthur Blvd
   Irving TX 75038
   972 717-0300

Nauvoo
Hancock County

(G-15013)
BAXTER VINEYARDS
2010 Parley St (62354-1355)
P.O. Box 342 (62354-0342)
PHONE..................................217 453-2528
Brenda Logan, *Owner*
Kelly Logan, *Owner*
EMP: 3 **EST:** 1857
SALES (est): 219.8K **Privately Held**
WEB: www.nauvoowinery.com
SIC: 2084 0172 0175 0111 Wines; grapes; apple orchard; pear orchard; wheat

(G-15014)
NAUVOO MILL & BAKERY
1530 Mulholland St (62354-1152)
PHONE..................................217 453-6734
Paul Brown, *Managing Prtnr*
Carol Brown, *Partner*
EMP: 7
SALES (est): 250K **Privately Held**
SIC: 0723 2051 2041 Flour milling custom services; bread, cake & related products; flour & other grain mill products

(G-15015)
NAUVOO PRODUCTS INC
1420 Mulholland St (62354-1006)
P.O. Box 176 (62354-0176)
PHONE..................................217 453-2817
Rose Poppe, *President*
Matthew Poppe, *Exec VP*
Jamie Poppe, *Director*
Sheila Poppe, *Director*
EMP: 11
SQ FT: 4,000
SALES: 1.3MM **Privately Held**
SIC: 2822 Synthetic rubber

Neoga
Cumberland County

(G-15016)
BRIGHTON CABINETRY INC (PA)
1095 Industrial Park Ave (62447-2421)
PHONE..................................217 895-3000
John Mikk, *President*
Tony Creek, *Vice Pres*
Dale Little, *Purch Agent*
Connie Easter, *Cust Mgr*
Erin Ledbetter, *Marketing Staff*
EMP: 35
SQ FT: 16,000
SALES (est): 5MM **Privately Held*
SIC: 2434 Wood kitchen cabinets

Neoga - Cumberland County (G-15017)

(G-15017)
GOLDA INC
Also Called: Leading Lady Company
100 Trowbridge Rd (62447-1120)
P.O. Box 850 (62447-0850)
PHONE.................................217 895-3602
Jerry Maddox, *Branch Mgr*
EMP: 108
SALES (est): 7.2MM
SALES (corp-wide): 20.4MM **Privately Held**
SIC: 2342 5621 2339 Maternity bras & corsets; maternity wear; maternity clothing
PA: Golda Inc.
24050 Commerce Park
Cleveland OH 44122
216 464-5490

Neponset
Bureau County

(G-15018)
MARTIN ENGINEERING COMPANY (PA)
Also Called: Martin Engineering USA
1 Martin Pl (61345-9766)
PHONE.................................309 852-2384
Robert J Nogaj, *President*
Edwin Peterson, *Chairman*
Dionisio Gomez, *Business Mgr*
Don Papini, *Business Mgr*
Clyde Smith, *Counsel*
◆ **EMP:** 235
SQ FT: 130,000
SALES (est): 183.7MM **Privately Held**
WEB: www.martin-eng.com
SIC: 3829 3532 Measuring & controlling devices; mining machinery; flotation machinery (mining machinery); cleaning machinery, mineral

New Athens
St. Clair County

(G-15019)
FORD MARBLE AND TILE INC
203 S Van Buren St (62264-1325)
PHONE.................................618 475-2987
Scott Ford, *President*
EMP: 18
SALES: 2.2MM **Privately Held**
WEB: www.fordmarble.com
SIC: 1743 3281 Tile installation, ceramic; granite, cut & shaped

(G-15020)
KASKASKIA TOOL AND MACHINE INC
107 S Benton St (62264-1311)
PHONE.................................618 475-3301
Roy Lee Albert, *President*
Brian Albert, *General Mgr*
Dave Albert, *General Mgr*
Dan Albert, *Vice Pres*
Terra Gabelman, *Personnel Assit*
EMP: 24 **EST:** 1971
SQ FT: 15,000
SALES (est): 2.5MM **Privately Held**
SIC: 3599 3544 3469 Machine shop, jobbing & repair; special dies, tools, jigs & fixtures; metal stampings

(G-15021)
SIEMENS MANUFACTURING CO INC
500 N Johnson St (62264-1157)
PHONE.................................618 475-3325
Dennis Allschied, *Manager*
Tim Smith, *Technician*
EMP: 198
SALES (corp-wide): 64.8MM **Privately Held**
SIC: 3672 Printed circuit boards
PA: Siemens Manufacturing Co. Inc.
410 W Washington St
Freeburg IL 62243
618 539-3000

New Baden
Clinton County

(G-15022)
QUAD-COUNTY READY MIX CORP
Also Called: Quad County Rdymx New Baden
7415 State Route 160 (62265-2713)
P.O. Box 18 (62265-0018)
PHONE.................................618 588-4656
Darrell Hewlett, *Branch Mgr*
EMP: 15
SALES (corp-wide): 16.1MM **Privately Held**
WEB: www.qcrm4.com
SIC: 3273 Ready-mixed concrete
PA: Quad-County Ready Mix Corp.
300 W 12th St
Okawville IL 62271
618 243-6430

(G-15023)
RELOAD SALES INC
Also Called: Roof Structures
418 Plum Ln (62265-1147)
PHONE.................................618 588-2866
Mike Rehkamper, *President*
Sandy Rehkamper, *Admin Sec*
EMP: 30
SALES (est): 3.7MM **Privately Held**
SIC: 3531 Roofing equipment

(G-15024)
SPAETH WELDING INC
321 W Missouri St (62265-1741)
PHONE.................................618 588-3596
Marvin J Spaeth, *President*
Darlene Spaeth, *Admin Sec*
EMP: 15 **EST:** 1974
SQ FT: 35,000
SALES (est): 2MM **Privately Held**
SIC: 7692 Welding repair

New Berlin
Sangamon County

(G-15025)
THOMAS TEES INC
210 S Oak St (62670-6468)
P.O. Box 47 (62670-0047)
PHONE.................................217 488-2288
Gregory A Thomas, *President*
Denise Thomas, *Corp Secy*
EMP: 6
SALES (est): 683K **Privately Held**
WEB: www.tpdink.com
SIC: 2752 Commercial printing, offset

New Boston
Mercer County

(G-15026)
CARGILL INCORPORATED
408 1st St (61272-5742)
PHONE.................................309 587-8111
Kim Bly, *General Mgr*
EMP: 6
SALES (corp-wide): 113.4B **Privately Held**
SIC: 2048 Prepared feeds
PA: Cargill, Incorporated
15407 Mcginty Rd W
Wayzata MN 55391
952 742-7575

New Lenox
Will County

(G-15027)
CHICAGO CABINET CO
22000 S Schoolhouse Rd (60451-3713)
PHONE.................................708 429-5100
Barb Schaaf, *Principal*
EMP: 2

SALES (est): 232.2K **Privately Held**
WEB: www.chicagocabinet.com
SIC: 2434 Wood kitchen cabinets

(G-15028)
CLASSICAL STATUARY & DECOR
21621 S Schoolhouse Rd (60451-3714)
PHONE.................................815 462-3408
Timothy Haggerty, *President*
Debra A Haggerty, *Vice Pres*
EMP: 8
SQ FT: 5,400
SALES (est): 1MM **Privately Held**
SIC: 3272 Concrete products

(G-15029)
COOLER CONCEPTS INC
21753 S Center Ave (60451-2803)
P.O. Box 1247, Frankfort (60423-7247)
PHONE.................................815 462-3866
William J Dunnett Jr, *President*
Diane Dunnett, *Vice Pres*
EMP: 6
SQ FT: 5,000
SALES: 1MM **Privately Held**
SIC: 3411 Metal cans

(G-15030)
DIRECT MAIL EQUIPMENT SERVICES
14460 W Edison Dr Ste D (60451-3776)
PHONE.................................815 485-7010
Gary Cullen, *Owner*
EMP: 2
SQ FT: 1,500
SALES (est): 250K **Privately Held**
SIC: 3579 Mailing machines

(G-15031)
DUNHAM DESIGNS INC
1043 Industry Rd (60451-2674)
PHONE.................................815 462-0100
George Carroll, *President*
EMP: 6
SQ FT: 6,000
SALES: 200K **Privately Held**
SIC: 3089 Thermoformed finished plastic products; plastic processing

(G-15032)
EJ USA INC
310 Garnet Dr (60451-3502)
PHONE.................................815 740-1640
Thomas Drown, *Manager*
EMP: 15 **Privately Held**
SIC: 3321 Manhole covers, metal
HQ: Ej Usa, Inc.
301 Spring St
East Jordan MI 49727
800 874-4100

(G-15033)
EMBROID ME
2399 E Joliet Hwy (60451-2578)
PHONE.................................815 485-4155
Bill Garrigan, *Owner*
EMP: 6
SALES (est): 628.2K **Privately Held**
SIC: 2759 5949 7319 7999 Screen printing; sewing & needlework; advertising; amusement & recreation

(G-15034)
EWW ENTERPRISE INC
1311 S Schoolhouse Rd # 2 (60451-3279)
PHONE.................................815 463-9607
Edward W Weiher, *President*
EMP: 5
SALES (est): 855.8K **Privately Held**
SIC: 3599 Machine shop, jobbing & repair

(G-15035)
GALMAR ENTERPRISES INC
Also Called: Humid-A-Mist
14408 W Edison Dr Ste F (60451-4501)
PHONE.................................815 463-9826
Gus Gallas, *President*
EMP: 3
SALES (est): 376.3K **Privately Held**
SIC: 3585 Humidifying equipment, except portable

(G-15036)
GRANITE MOUNTAIN INC
538 E Illinois Hwy Ste A (60451-2661)
PHONE.................................708 774-1442
Lisa Ritter, *President*
Mark Ritter, *General Mgr*
EMP: 5
SQ FT: 4,000
SALES (est): 249.4K **Privately Held**
SIC: 5211 3281 Counter tops; granite, cut & shaped

(G-15037)
INNOVATION SPECIALISTS INC
2328 E Lincoln Hwy # 356 (60451-9533)
PHONE.................................815 372-9001
Christopher Gambino, *President*
EMP: 5
SQ FT: 9,000
SALES (est): 758.5K **Privately Held**
SIC: 3496 3694 Miscellaneous fabricated wire products; engine electrical equipment

(G-15038)
KUCHAR PRODUCTS INC
12559 Old Plank Dr (60451-3274)
PHONE.................................815 405-3692
Erick Kuchar, *President*
EMP: 2
SALES (est): 200K **Privately Held**
SIC: 3599 Machine shop, jobbing & repair

(G-15039)
LIGHTHOUSE PRINTING INC
21754 S Center Ave (60451-2843)
P.O. Box 159 (60451-0159)
PHONE.................................708 479-7776
Mary J Rex, *President*
John D Rex, *Corp Secy*
EMP: 4
SQ FT: 100
SALES (est): 1.2MM **Privately Held**
SIC: 2759 7389 Screen printing; printing broker

(G-15040)
MAGNETIC OCCASIONS & MORE INC
21605 S Schoolhouse Rd (60451-3714)
PHONE.................................815 462-4141
Kevin Petrie, *President*
Cynthia Petrie, *Vice Pres*
EMP: 5
SQ FT: 1,200
SALES: 259K **Privately Held**
SIC: 2824 3695 Vinyl fibers; magnetic & optical recording media

(G-15041)
MERIT EMPLYMENT ASSSSMENT SVCS
Also Called: Tyler, Thomas A PHD
342 Alana Dr (60451-1784)
P.O. Box 193, Flossmoor (60422-0193)
PHONE.................................815 320-3680
Thomas A Tyler, *President*
Thomas A Tyler Jr, *Vice Pres*
Carol Tyler, *Admin Sec*
EMP: 3
SQ FT: 700
SALES (est): 310.8K **Privately Held**
WEB: www.measinc.us
SIC: 2741 8742 Miscellaneous publishing; human resource consulting services

(G-15042)
METRIE
2200 W Haven Ave (60451-2542)
PHONE.................................815 717-2660
Ted Eisses, *Principal*
Denise Tripamer, *Director*
Brian Czyl, *Representative*
▲ **EMP:** 26
SALES (est): 8.1MM **Privately Held**
SIC: 2431 Millwork

(G-15043)
MILLER PURCELL CO INC
244 W 3rd Ave (60451-1729)
P.O. Box 215 (60451-0215)
PHONE.................................815 485-2142
David Dyer, *President*
Donald Cordano, *Admin Sec*
EMP: 2 **EST:** 1922

SALES: 425K **Privately Held**
SIC: 2952 3297 2899 2891 Asphalt felts
& coatings; nonclay refractories; chemical
preparations; adhesives & sealants; cyclic
crudes & intermediates; paints & allied
products

(G-15044)
MURPHY USA INC
431 E Lincoln Hwy (60451-1973)
PHONE..................................815 463-9963
Robert Clyde, *CEO*
EMP: 9 **Publicly Held**
WEB: www.murphyusa.com
SIC: 5541 1311 Filling stations, gasoline;
crude petroleum & natural gas production
PA: Murphy Usa Inc.
200 E Peach St
El Dorado AR 71730

(G-15045)
OGORMAN SON CARPENTRY CONTRS
1930 Airway Ct (60451-2701)
PHONE..................................815 485-8997
Raymond O'Gorman, *President*
Patricia O'Gorman, *Vice Pres*
EMP: 22
SQ FT: 18,000
SALES (est): 2.2MM **Privately Held**
SIC: 1751 2541 2434 Cabinet building &
installation; wood partitions & fixtures;
wood kitchen cabinets

(G-15046)
ONOFFBLOCK INC
Also Called: Xenesis
2100 Cattleman Dr (60451-3131)
PHONE..................................312 899-6360
Mark Lapenna, *CEO*
EMP: 10
SALES (corp-wide): 1.6MM **Privately Held**
SIC: 7372 Prepackaged software
PA: Onoffblock, Inc.
2100 Cattleman Dr
New Lenox IL 60451
312 899-6360

(G-15047)
ONOFFBLOCK INC (PA)
Also Called: Xenesis
2100 Cattleman Dr (60451-3131)
PHONE..................................312 899-6360
Mark Lapenna, *CEO*
EMP: 10
SALES (est): 1.6MM **Privately Held**
SIC: 7372 Prepackaged software

(G-15048)
ORIN BRIANT INC
246 Stone Ct (60451-1598)
PHONE..................................779 206-2800
Ron Bordwine, *Principal*
EMP: 5 **EST:** 2018
SALES (est): 317K **Privately Held**
SIC: 2092 Fish sticks

(G-15049)
PEG N REDS
Also Called: Ramseys News Agency
212 S Main St (60451)
PHONE..................................618 586-2015
Rebecca Ramsey, *Owner*
EMP: 3
SQ FT: 1,600
SALES (est): 130K **Privately Held**
SIC: 2711 Newspapers

(G-15050)
PERMA GRAPHICS PRINTERS
216 N Marley Rd (60451-2096)
PHONE..................................815 485-6955
Gene Ludvik, *Owner*
EMP: 5
SALES (est): 750.4K **Privately Held**
SIC: 2752 2791 2789 Commercial printing, offset; typesetting; bookbinding & related work

(G-15051)
PREFERRED BUS PUBLICATIONS INC
1938 E Lincoln Hwy # 216 (60451-3835)
PHONE..................................815 717-6399
Joseph Farneti, *President*
EMP: 5
SALES (est): 427K **Privately Held**
SIC: 2741 Miscellaneous publishing

(G-15052)
QUEN-TEL COMMUNICATION SVC INC
2759 Meadow Path (60451-1808)
PHONE..................................815 463-1800
Thomas J Quenzel, *President*
EMP: 6
SALES (est): 550K **Privately Held**
SIC: 3661 Carrier equipment, telephone or telegraph

(G-15053)
R A E TOOL AND MANUFACTURING
1910 Clearing Ct Ste 2 (60451-3729)
PHONE..................................815 485-2506
Ron Abbott, *President*
Ed Dieringer, *Vice Pres*
EMP: 8 **EST:** 1996
SQ FT: 3,200
SALES (est): 1.4MM **Privately Held**
SIC: 3599 Machine shop, jobbing & repair

(G-15054)
R S CORCORAN CO
500 N Vine St (60451-2918)
PHONE..................................815 485-2156
William J Kramer, *President*
Gail K Swinson, *Treasurer*
Jerry Horvath, *Bookkeeper*
Joel Kramer, *Sales Associate*
Bill Kramer, *CTO*
EMP: 21 **EST:** 1945
SQ FT: 27,000
SALES (est): 4.5MM **Privately Held**
WEB: www.corcoranpumps.com
SIC: 3561 Industrial pumps & parts

(G-15055)
RISER MACHINE CORPORATION
1744 Ferro Dr (60451-3501)
PHONE..................................708 532-2313
Chris Lira, *President*
EMP: 12
SQ FT: 8,000
SALES (est): 1.1MM **Privately Held**
SIC: 3599 Crankshafts & camshafts, machining; electrical discharge machining (EDM)

(G-15056)
RIVERTON CABINET COMPANY
Also Called: Rivertoncabinets
22000 S Schoolhouse Rd (60451-3713)
PHONE..................................815 462-5300
Keith Hinshaw, *President*
Steve Hoerres, *Sales Staff*
▲ **EMP:** 31
SQ FT: 50,000
SALES (est): 3.7MM **Privately Held**
SIC: 1751 5712 2434 Cabinet building & installation; furniture stores; wood kitchen cabinets

(G-15057)
SAUDER INDUSTRIES LIMITED
Also Called: Moulding & Millwork Midwest
2200 W Haven Ave (60451-2542)
PHONE..................................815 717-2660
Ted Eisses, *Branch Mgr*
EMP: 25
SALES (corp-wide): 183.4MM **Privately Held**
SIC: 2431 Millwork
HQ: Metrie Canada Ltd
1055 Dunsmuir St Suite 3500
Vancouver BC V7X 1
604 691-9100

(G-15058)
SENDRA SERVICE CORP
309 Garnet Dr (60451-3503)
P.O. Box 957, Mokena (60448-0957)
PHONE..................................815 462-0061
Gary Sendra, *President*
Robert A Raycroft, *Admin Sec*
EMP: 1
SALES (est): 250.7K **Privately Held**
SIC: 3585 3443 Air conditioning equipment, complete; boilers: industrial, power, or marine

(G-15059)
STURDEE METAL PRODUCTS INC
1060 Grand Mesa Ave (60451-3133)
PHONE..................................773 523-3074
Howard Groves, *President*
Jeff Groves, *Vice Pres*
Thomas Kaliski, *Vice Pres*
Eileen Groves, *Admin Sec*
EMP: 7
SQ FT: 10,000
SALES (est): 1MM **Privately Held**
WEB: www.sturdeemetal.com
SIC: 3441 3444 Fabricated structural metal; sheet metalwork

(G-15060)
SUPERHEAT FGH SERVICES INC (PA)
313 Garnet Dr (60451-3503)
PHONE..................................708 478-0205
Norm Macarthur, *CEO*
Joe Borror, *Vice Pres*
Sundip Bajaj, *CFO*
EMP: 1
SQ FT: 10,000
SALES (est): 74.8MM **Privately Held**
SIC: 3398 Metal heat treating

(G-15061)
SUPERHEAT FGH SERVICES INC (PA)
313 Garnet Dr (60451-3503)
PHONE..................................708 478-0205
Norm Mac Arthur, *CEO*
Miles Brown, *President*
Ian Prudhoe, *Area Mgr*
Bob Dierkes, *Business Mgr*
Susan Murphy, *Business Mgr*
EMP: 2
SALES (est): 77.4MM **Privately Held**
SIC: 3398 Metal heat treating

(G-15062)
TEC SYSTEMS INC
Also Called: Nutec Manufacturing
908 Garnet Ct (60451-3569)
PHONE..................................815 722-2800
Zibe Gibson, *CEO*
Virginia Cagwin, *CFO*
EMP: 17
SALES (est): 3.8MM **Privately Held**
SIC: 3556 Meat processing machinery

(G-15063)
TEDDS CSTM INSTALLATIONS INC
Also Called: Tedds Custom Installations
21719 S Center Ave Ste A (60451-2818)
PHONE..................................815 485-6800
Tedd Vinciguerra, *CEO*
Heodore Vinciguerra, *President*
EMP: 3 **EST:** 2008
SALES (est): 270K **Privately Held**
WEB: www.teddscustom.com
SIC: 3679 Antennas, receiving

(G-15064)
TEES INK
1215 Revere Ct (60451-3172)
P.O. Box 694 (60451-0694)
PHONE..................................815 462-7300
Tim Opitz, *Principal*
EMP: 3
SALES (est): 221.3K **Privately Held**
WEB: www.teesink.net
SIC: 2759 Screen printing

(G-15065)
TRI STAR CABINET & TOP CO INC (PA)
1000 S Cedar Rd (60451-2646)
P.O. Box 338 (60451-0338)
PHONE..................................815 485-2564
Joseph E Wilda Jr, *President*
James H Thomas, *President*
Kathleen Lenci, *Vice Pres*
Becky Harvell, *Purchasing*
Cosmo Misischia, *Admin Sec*
EMP: 62 **EST:** 1966
SQ FT: 5,000
SALES (est): 9MM **Privately Held**
WEB: www.tristarcabinets.com
SIC: 2434 Wood kitchen cabinets

(G-15066)
TRINITY SERVICES INC
210 Haines Ave (60451-1604)
PHONE..................................815 485-5612
EMP: 3
SALES (est): 91.3K **Privately Held**
SIC: 2098 Macaroni & spaghetti

(G-15067)
V J MATTSON COMPANY
713 Jennifer Ct (60451-1300)
PHONE..................................708 479-1990
Thomas E Morack, *President*
Robert Morack, *Exec VP*
EMP: 100
SQ FT: 5,500
SALES (est): 15.1MM **Privately Held**
SIC: 3255 1741 Clay refractories; refractory or acid brick masonry

(G-15068)
WEST END TOOL & DIE INC
22020 Howell Dr (60451-3708)
PHONE..................................815 462-3040
Michael J Zambon, *President*
Robert W Lipka, *Admin Sec*
EMP: 3 **EST:** 1999
SALES (est): 643.8K **Privately Held**
SIC: 3544 7692 Special dies & tools; welding repair

(G-15069)
WILL COUNTY WELL & PUMP CO INC (PA)
1200 S Cedar Rd Ste 1a (60451-4400)
PHONE..................................815 485-2413
Jacqueline Rob, *President*
EMP: 9
SQ FT: 4,000
SALES (est): 1.3MM **Privately Held**
WEB: www.willcountywell.com
SIC: 3589 1781 Water treatment equipment, industrial; water well drilling

(G-15070)
WOODCRAFT ENTERPRISES INC
1928 Clearing Ct Ste A (60451-2979)
P.O. Box 26, Wilmington (60481-0026)
PHONE..................................815 485-2787
Dennis Jones, *President*
Thomas Avgeris, *Admin Sec*
EMP: 6
SQ FT: 8,000
SALES (est): 470K **Privately Held**
SIC: 2431 2511 2435 2434 Interior & ornamental woodwork & trim; wood household furniture; hardwood veneer & plywood; wood kitchen cabinets; hardwood dimension & flooring mills; sawmills & planing mills, general

New Windsor
Mercer County

(G-15071)
ANR PIPELINE COMPANY
296 N 600th Ave (61465-9433)
PHONE..................................309 667-2158
Tim Treece, *Manager*
EMP: 5
SALES (corp-wide): 9.9B **Privately Held**
SIC: 4922 1389 Pipelines, natural gas; gas compressing (natural gas) at the fields
HQ: Anr Pipeline Company
700 Louisiana St Ste 700 # 700
Houston TX 77002
832 320-2000

(G-15072)
DONALDSON COMPANY INC
3230 65th Ave (61465-9350)
PHONE..................................309 667-2885
EMP: 238
SALES (corp-wide): 2.8B **Publicly Held**
WEB: www.donaldson.com
SIC: 3599 Amusement park equipment
PA: Donaldson Company, Inc.
1400 W 94th St
Minneapolis MN 55431
952 887-3131

(G-15073)
ERICSON S LOG & LUMBER CO (PA)
11 State Highway 17 (61465-9452)
P.O. Box 37 (61465-0037)
PHONE 309 667-2147
Sam E Ericson, *Owner*
EMP: 8
SQ FT: 800
SALES (est): 989.9K **Privately Held**
SIC: 2421 5099 2426 2411 Sawmills & planing mills, general; logs, hewn ties, posts & poles; hardwood dimension & flooring mills; logging

Newark
Kendall County

(G-15074)
CA CUSTOM WOODWORKING
14690 County Line Rd (60541-9680)
PHONE 630 201-6154
Chris Ammenhauser, *Principal*
EMP: 3
SALES (est): 314.5K **Privately Held**
WEB: www.cacustomwoodworking.com
SIC: 2431 Millwork

(G-15075)
COMPLETE CONVEYING SVCS LLC
15583 State Route 71 (60541-8401)
P.O. Box 1051, Mokena (60448-2050)
PHONE 815 695-5176
John J Stocker,
EMP: 3
SALES (est): 582.6K **Privately Held**
SIC: 3535 Conveyors & conveying equipment

(G-15076)
DIERZEN TRAILER CO
101 N Fayette St (60541)
PHONE 815 695-5291
Louis Dierzen, *President*
Floyd Dierzen, *Vice Pres*
EMP: 60
SQ FT: 46,000
SALES (est): 9.9MM **Privately Held**
SIC: 3713 Truck bodies (motor vehicles)

(G-15077)
KEP WOODWORKING
12260 Lisbon Rd (60541-9488)
PHONE 847 480-9545
Kenneth E Papciak, *Owner*
EMP: 4
SALES (est): 536.5K **Privately Held**
SIC: 2431 1521 Millwork; single-family home remodeling, additions & repairs

(G-15078)
RYAN MANUFACTURING INC
11610 N La Salle Rd (60541-9626)
PHONE 815 695-5310
Gilbert Jacobs, *President*
Ryan Jacobs, *Manager*
EMP: 5
SQ FT: 12,000
SALES (est): 400K **Privately Held**
SIC: 3443 3563 3524 Weldments; air & gas compressors; lawn & garden equipment

Newton
Jasper County

(G-15079)
ADVANCED PLBG & PIPE FITTING
15498 N 1590th St (62448-3329)
PHONE 618 554-2677
Justin Griffith, *Principal*
EMP: 3
SALES (est): 232.3K **Privately Held**
SIC: 3494 Pipe fittings

(G-15080)
ARNDTS STORES INC (PA)
Also Called: Arndt's Hallmark Shop
106 W Washington St (62448-1256)
PHONE 618 783-2511
Tony B Arndt, *President*
William P Arndt, *Corp Secy*
Glenda Arndt, *Vice Pres*
Amber Shedelbower, *Marketing Mgr*
EMP: 6
SQ FT: 12,000
SALES (est): 1.1MM **Privately Held**
WEB: www.amish-buggy.com
SIC: 2064 Fudge (candy)

(G-15081)
BN NATIONAL TRAIL
8810 Commercial Ave (62448-4091)
PHONE 618 783-8709
EMP: 8
SALES (est): 540K **Privately Held**
SIC: 2836 Mfg Biological Products

(G-15082)
DON LEVENTHAL GROUP LLC
Also Called: Newton Broom & Brush Co
1508 W Jourdan St (62448-2006)
P.O. Box 358 (62448-0358)
PHONE 618 783-4424
Donald Leventhal, *Mng Member*
▲ **EMP:** 28 **EST:** 1954
SQ FT: 26,000
SALES: 2MM **Privately Held**
WEB: www.newtonbroom.com
SIC: 3991 2392 Brooms & brushes; mops, floor & dust

(G-15083)
GATEHOUSE MEDIA LLC
Also Called: Newton Press Mentor
700 W Washington St (62448-1129)
P.O. Box 151 (62448-0151)
PHONE 618 783-2324
Lynne Campbell, *President*
EMP: 3
SALES (corp-wide): 1.8B **Publicly Held**
WEB: www.gatehousemedia.com
SIC: 2711 Newspapers, publishing & printing
HQ: Gatehouse Media, Llc
    175 Sullys Trl Fl 3
    Pittsford NY 14534
    585 598-0030

(G-15084)
HEARTLAND CLASSICS INC
1705 W Jourdan St (62448-2022)
P.O. Box 227 (62448-0227)
PHONE 618 783-4444
Toll Free: .... 877 -
Anthony Griffith, *President*
EMP: 8
SALES (est): 1.1MM **Privately Held**
SIC: 3711 5521 5531 7532 Reconnaissance cars, assembly of; antique automobiles; automotive accessories; upholstery & trim shop, automotive

(G-15085)
JAYNE EXCAVATING & WELDING LLC
11477 E 1500th Ave (62448-3126)
PHONE 618 553-1149
Kelsey Jayne,
EMP: 6
SALES (est): 100.6K **Privately Held**
SIC: 7692 Welding repair

(G-15086)
JESSE B HOLT INC
Also Called: Holt Building
13 Hillcrest Dr (62448-1524)
P.O. Box 127 (62448-0127)
PHONE 618 783-3075
Ronald Lee Holt, *President*
EMP: 75 **EST:** 1948
SQ FT: 20,000
SALES (est): 6.5MM **Privately Held**
SIC: 2439 5211 Trusses, wooden roof; lumber & other building materials

(G-15087)
NEWTON IMPLEMENT PARTNERSHIP
9460 E State Highway 33 (62448-3916)
PHONE 618 783-8716
Jerry Newlin, *Partner*
Dennis Frichtl, *Partner*
EMP: 22
SALES (est): 12.6MM **Privately Held**
SIC: 3523 Farm machinery & equipment

(G-15088)
NEWTON READY MIX INC
Also Called: Ssi
8560 N State Highway 130 (62448-4067)
P.O. Box 40, Olney (62450-0040)
PHONE 618 783-8611
Terry Schrey, *President*
EMP: 10
SQ FT: 700
SALES (est): 1.3MM **Privately Held**
SIC: 3273 3281 1442 Ready-mixed concrete; cut stone & stone products; construction sand & gravel

(G-15089)
NOVANTA INC
106 Marshall Dr (62448-4093)
PHONE 781 266-5700
Anthony Lee, *Director*
EMP: 3 **Publicly Held**
SIC: 3699 Laser systems & equipment
PA: Novanta Inc.
    125 Middlesex Tpke
    Bedford MA 01730

(G-15090)
PETRON OIL PRODUCTION INC (PA)
405 E Jourdan St (62448-1517)
P.O. Box 232 (62448-0232)
PHONE 618 783-4486
John Kuebler, *President*
Ruth Parrish, *President*
Arlene Parrish Snyder, *Exec VP*
Carol Lyon, *Vice Pres*
Ilene Johnson, *Treasurer*
EMP: 18 **EST:** 1965
SQ FT: 3,500
SALES (est): 2.3MM **Privately Held**
SIC: 1311 Crude petroleum production

(G-15091)
RAYMOND D WRIGHT
35 Homestead Dr (62448-2004)
PHONE 618 783-2206
Raymond Wright, *Owner*
EMP: 1
SALES (est): 316K **Privately Held**
SIC: 2911 Petroleum refining

(G-15092)
REX VAULT CO
E Rte 33 (62448)
P.O. Box 323 (62448-0323)
PHONE 618 783-2416
Mark A Bolander, *President*
Keith Kocher, *Sales Mgr*
EMP: 17
SQ FT: 4,000
SALES (est): 2.6MM **Privately Held**
WEB: www.rexvault.com
SIC: 3272 6553 Burial vaults, concrete or precast terrazzo; septic tanks, concrete; cemetery subdividers & developers

(G-15093)
ST PIERRE OIL COMPANY INC
Also Called: Saint Pierre Oil
102 N Van Buren St (62448-1410)
P.O. Box 380 (62448-0380)
PHONE 618 783-4441
EMP: 5
SQ FT: 1,400
SALES (est): 451.5K **Privately Held**
SIC: 1311 Oil Production

(G-15094)
TPS ENTERPRISES INC
Also Called: Total Printing Systems
201 S Gregory Dr (62448-2111)
P.O. Box 375 (62448-0375)
PHONE 618 783-2978
Richard Lindemann II, *President*
Rick Wolfe, *Plant Mgr*
Jason Smith, *Traffic Mgr*
Michael Ammirata, *Sales Staff*
Dorette Ochs, *Manager*
▲ **EMP:** 44
SQ FT: 60,000
SALES: 5.5MM **Privately Held**
SIC: 2752 Commercial printing, offset

(G-15095)
TROJAN OIL INC
Also Called: Scott Oil
953 N 1300th St (62448-4939)
PHONE 618 754-3474
Larry L Scott, *Owner*
EMP: 3 **EST:** 1960
SALES (est): 268.8K **Privately Held**
SIC: 1311 Crude petroleum production

Niles
Cook County

(G-15096)
7 MILE SOLUTIONS INC
Also Called: Maxant Technologies
7540 N Caldwell Ave (60714-3808)
PHONE 847 588-2280
Robert Curran, *President*
Angela Witt, *Accountant*
▲ **EMP:** 31
SQ FT: 25,000
SALES (est): 7.4MM **Privately Held**
WEB: www.7milecompanies.com
SIC: 3829 3844 3625 Nuclear radiation & testing apparatus; X-ray apparatus & tubes; electric controls & control accessories, industrial

(G-15097)
9161 CORPORATION
Also Called: Vertical Blinds Factory
9161 N Milwaukee Ave (60714-1538)
PHONE 847 470-8828
Rosa Yaker, *President*
Barbara Finn, *Vice Pres*
EMP: 7
SQ FT: 2,500
SALES (est): 1.2MM **Privately Held**
SIC: 2591 5719 3429 Blinds vertical; window furnishings; venetian blinds; window shades; manufactured hardware (general)

(G-15098)
ABRASIC 90 INC
Also Called: Cgw Camel Grinding Wheels, USA
7525 N Oak Park Ave (60714-3819)
PHONE 847 647-5994
Joseph O'Mera, *President*
Ken Jelinek, *Opers Mgr*
Greg Geraci, *Purch Mgr*
Dan Kerrigan, *Purch Agent*
Rodney Finch, *Engineer*
▲ **EMP:** 44
SQ FT: 55,000
SALES (est): 7.5MM **Privately Held**
SIC: 3291 5085 Abrasive products; abrasives
HQ: Gamel Operated Grinding Sarid Ltd.
    Kibbutz
    Sarid 36589

(G-15099)
ACCURATE METAL COMPONENTS INC
Also Called: Columbia Tool & Gage Co.
7540 N Caldwell Ave (60714-3808)
PHONE 847 520-5900
Victor Herrera, *President*
Richard Tessitore, *Vice Pres*
Iris Tessitore, *Admin Sec*
EMP: 12
SQ FT: 14,000
SALES (est): 2.6MM **Privately Held**
SIC: 3599 Machine shop, jobbing & repair

(G-15100)
AFFY TAPPLE LLC
6300 W Gross Point Rd (60714-3916)
PHONE 773 338-1100
Stuart Sorkin, *CEO*
David Crosby, *President*
Mario Solano, *Safety Mgr*
John Kaney, *Opers Staff*

Eddie Delgado, *Production*
▲ **EMP:** 50 **EST:** 1948
SQ FT: 47,000
SALES (est): 18.6MM **Privately Held**
WEB: www.affytapple.com
SIC: 2064 Fruits: candied, crystallized, or glazed; fruit, chocolate covered (except dates)

(G-15101)
ALVA/MCO PHRMCAL COMPANIES INC
7711 N Merrimac Ave (60714-3423)
PHONE..................847 663-0700
Jeffery H Gerchenson, *President*
Emile H Gerchenson, *Chairman*
Terry Riddel, *Vice Pres*
EMP: 50 **EST:** 1940
SALES (est): 13.8MM **Privately Held**
WEB: www.alva-amco.com
SIC: 2834 Druggists' preparations (pharmaceuticals); diuretics; tranquilizers or mental drug preparations

(G-15102)
AMERICAN VACUUM COMPANY
Also Called: A R C O
6700 W Touhy Ave (60714-4518)
PHONE..................847 674-8383
Jack Person, *President*
Chad Johnson, *Area Mgr*
Person Tim, *Project Mgr*
▲ **EMP:** 5 **EST:** 1939
SALES (est): 3.5MM **Privately Held**
WEB: www.americanvacuum.com
SIC: 3589 3548 Vacuum cleaners & sweepers, electric; industrial; electric welding equipment

(G-15103)
AMT GROUP LLC
Also Called: Imbibe
7350 N Croname Rd (60714-3932)
PHONE..................847 324-4411
Sumner N Katz, *President*
Andrew Dratt,
Georgia S Katz,
Andrew J Rashkow,
EMP: 70
SQ FT: 5,000
SALES (est): 4.3MM **Privately Held**
SIC: 2087 Concentrates, drink

(G-15104)
AVERY DENNISON CORPORATION
7542 N Natchez Ave (60714-3804)
PHONE..................877 214-0909
Yasuhiro Masaka, *Manager*
EMP: 80
SALES (corp-wide): 7B **Publicly Held**
SIC: 3081 2672 Unsupported plastics film & sheet; coated & laminated paper
PA: Avery Dennison Corporation
207 N Goode Ave
Glendale CA 91203
626 304-2000

(G-15105)
BANKIER COMPANIES INC (PA)
6151 W Gross Point Rd (60714-3911)
PHONE..................847 647-6565
Jack D Bankier, *CEO*
James Schultz, *President*
Nina Mueller, *Vice Pres*
Alfonso Vazquez, *QC Mgr*
Lori Moros, *Human Res Dir*
▲ **EMP:** 35
SQ FT: 52,000
SALES: 12MM **Privately Held**
WEB: www.bankier.com
SIC: 3089 7389 Injection molding of plastics; packaging & labeling services

(G-15106)
BEE SALES COMPANY (PA)
Also Called: Riah Hair
6330 W Touhy Ave (60714-4624)
PHONE..................847 600-4400
Yong H Kim, *President*
Hae Kyung Kim, *Admin Sec*
Kathy Lee,
◆ **EMP:** 60
SQ FT: 70,000

SALES (est): 14MM **Privately Held**
SIC: 2353 5199 2252 5087 Baseball caps; general merchandise, non-durable; socks; beauty salon & barber shop equipment & supplies; girls' & children's outerwear; women's hosiery, except socks

(G-15107)
CANDY MANUFACTURING COMPANY
Also Called: Candy Controls
5633 W Howard St (60714-4011)
PHONE..................847 588-2639
Sarah Hendershot, *President*
Peter Murphy, *Mfg Staff*
Lisa Sacasa, *Manager*
▲ **EMP:** 10
SQ FT: 11,880
SALES (est): 1.8MM **Privately Held**
SIC: 3822 Auto controls regulating residntl & coml environmt & applncs

(G-15108)
CARNATION ENTERPRISES
8630 N National Ave (60714-2137)
PHONE..................847 804-5928
Simeon Khazin, *President*
Benjamin Glozman, *CFO*
▲ **EMP:** 5
SALES (est): 274K **Privately Held**
SIC: 5044 3694 Office equipment; automotive electrical equipment

(G-15109)
CHICAGO SPORTS MEDIA INC
Also Called: The Amateur Athlete Magazine
5940 W Touhy Ave Ste 230 (60714-4604)
PHONE..................847 676-1900
Elliot Wineberg, *Manager*
EMP: 6
SALES: 50K **Privately Held**
SIC: 2721 2741 Magazines: publishing only, not printed on site; miscellaneous publishing

(G-15110)
CISLAK MANUFACTURING INC
Also Called: Zoll-Dental
7450 N Natchez Ave (60714-3802)
PHONE..................847 647-1819
Karl Zoll, *President*
Ken Zoll, *Vice Pres*
Jeffrey Wornhoff, *VP Opers*
EMP: 24 **EST:** 1950
SQ FT: 3,800
SALES (est): 2.7MM **Privately Held*
WEB: www.zolldental.com
SIC: 2836 3843 Veterinary biological products; dental hand instruments

(G-15111)
COCA COLA FLEET SERVICE
Also Called: Coca-Cola
7500 N Oak Park Ave (60714-3820)
PHONE..................847 600-2279
EMP: 3
SALES (est): 134.7K **Privately Held**
SIC: 2086 Bottled & canned soft drinks

(G-15112)
COCA-COLA BTLG WISCONSIN DEL
7400 N Oak Park Ave (60714-3818)
PHONE..................847 647-0200
Marvin J Herb, *President*
Scott Briggs, *Vice Pres*
Evan Charles, *Finance Dir*
Susan Westling, *Finance Dir*
Shanti Brown, *Finance Mgr*
EMP: 400 **EST:** 2007
SALES (est): 51.7MM
SALES (corp-wide): 37.2B **Publicly Held**
WEB: www.coca-cola.com
SIC: 2086 Bottled & canned soft drinks
HQ: Coca-Cola Refreshments Usa, Inc.
2500 Windy Ridge Pkwy Se
Atlanta GA 30339
770 989-3000

(G-15113)
COCA-COLA COMPANY
7400 N Oak Park Ave (60714-3818)
PHONE..................847 647-0200
Roger Ruark, *Manager*
EMP: 70

SALES (corp-wide): 37.2B **Publicly Held**
SIC: 2086 Bottled & canned soft drinks
PA: The Coca-Cola Company
1 Coca Cola Plz Nw
Atlanta GA 30313
404 676-2121

(G-15114)
COCA-COLA REFRESHMENTS USA INC
7425 N Oak Park Ave (60714-3817)
PHONE..................847 647-0200
Jim Skarb, *Director*
EMP: 70
SALES (corp-wide): 37.2B **Publicly Held**
SIC: 2086 Bottled & canned soft drinks
HQ: Coca-Cola Refreshments Usa, Inc.
2500 Windy Ridge Pkwy Se
Atlanta GA 30339
770 989-3000

(G-15115)
D & J INTERNATIONAL INC
Also Called: Sharp Trading
7793 N Caldwell Ave (60714-3318)
PHONE..................847 966-9260
Jennifer Min, *President*
Don Min, *Vice Pres*
▲ **EMP:** 13 **EST:** 1996
SALES (est): 484K **Privately Held**
SIC: 2395 Embroidery & art needlework

(G-15116)
DOVE DENTAL STUDIO
6201 W Howard St Ste 202 (60714-3435)
PHONE..................847 679-2434
Michael Aiello, *Owner*
EMP: 3
SALES (est): 216.4K **Privately Held**
SIC: 8021 3843 Dental clinic; dental equipment & supplies

(G-15117)
ED GARVEY AND COMPANY (PA)
Also Called: Garvey Group, The
7400 N Lehigh Ave (60714-4024)
PHONE..................847 647-1900
Edward J Garvey Jr, *President*
Joe Kulis, *COO*
Brian Ritter, *Project Mgr*
Bob Garcia, *Prdtn Mgr*
Shaun Hill, *Production*
EMP: 52 **EST:** 1939
SQ FT: 100,000
SALES (est): 26.9MM **Privately Held**
WEB: www.thegarveygroup.com
SIC: 2752 Commercial printing, offset; promotional printing, lithographic

(G-15118)
EDWIN M KNOWLES CHINA COMPANY
9333 N Milwaukee Ave (60714-1303)
PHONE..................847 581-8354
Charles W Fennessy, *Vice Pres*
Charles W Femness, *Vice Pres*
Richard W Tinberg, *Treasurer*
Margaret G Ostoje, *Admin Sec*
▲ **EMP:** 18
SALES (est): 2.9MM **Privately Held**
SIC: 3262 Vitreous china table & kitchenware

(G-15119)
EINSTEIN CREST
9347 N Milwaukee Ave (60714-1303)
PHONE..................847 965-7791
Brian Borowski, *President*
Raymond Borowski, *Vice Pres*
EMP: 4
SQ FT: 2,500
SALES: 285K **Privately Held**
SIC: 2752 2791 2789 Photo-offset printing; typesetting; bookbinding & related work

(G-15120)
EMBROIDERY SERVICES INC
6287 W Howard St (60714-3403)
PHONE..................847 588-2660
John Reppert, *President*
Mark Reppert, *Vice Pres*
EMP: 4
SQ FT: 4,000
SALES: 350K **Privately Held**
SIC: 2395 Embroidery & art needlework

(G-15121)
FORT DEARBORN COMPANY
6035 W Gross Point Rd (60714-4045)
PHONE..................773 774-4321
Michael Anderson, *CEO*
EMP: 130
SALES (corp-wide): 4.2B **Privately Held**
SIC: 2759 Commercial printing
HQ: Fort Dearborn Company
1530 Morse Ave
Elk Grove Village IL 60007
847 357-9500

(G-15122)
FRANCIS SCREW PRODUCTS CO INC
7400 N Milwaukee Ave (60714-3708)
PHONE..................847 647-9462
John Francis, *President*
Charles Francis, *Corp Secy*
EMP: 1 **EST:** 1947
SQ FT: 3,000
SALES: 200K **Privately Held**
SIC: 3451 Screw machine products

(G-15123)
GARDNER DENVER INC
Welch-Ilmac
5621 W Howard St (60714-4011)
PHONE..................847 676-8800
Richard Fuksa, *Engineer*
Jim Barber, *Sales Staff*
Brad Barchus, *Sales Staff*
John Balamuta, *Branch Mgr*
EMP: 20
SALES (corp-wide): 2.4B **Publicly Held**
SIC: 3821 Vacuum pumps, laboratory
HQ: Gardner Denver, Inc.
222 E Erie St Ste 500
Milwaukee WI 53202

(G-15124)
GEO T SCHMIDT INC (PA)
Also Called: Schmidt Marking Systems
6151 W Howard St (60714-3401)
P.O. Box 480390 (60714-0390)
PHONE..................847 647-7117
Neal J O'Connor, *President*
Byrum Dickes, *Chairman*
Trevor Fawbush, *Vice Pres*
David Lacosse, *Plant Mgr*
Tucker Ashenfelter, *Engineer*
▲ **EMP:** 60
SQ FT: 45,000
SALES (est): 11.6MM **Privately Held**
SIC: 3544 3542 3599 Special dies & tools; marking machines; machine & other job shop work

(G-15125)
GHP GROUP INC (PA)
6440 W Howard St (60714-3302)
PHONE..................847 324-5900
Gus Haramaras, *President*
Steve Haramaras, *Business Mgr*
Michael Callen, *Vice Pres*
Dan Downing, *Vice Pres*
Ross Kutzler, *Purchasing*
▲ **EMP:** 41
SQ FT: 66,000
SALES (est): 7.7MM **Privately Held**
SIC: 3299 Tubing for electrical purposes, quartz

(G-15126)
GREAT LAKES GL & MIRROR CORP
6261 W Howard St (60714-3403)
PHONE..................847 647-1036
Robert Ginsburg, *President*
Marcy Nessenson, *Vice Pres*
EMP: 3
SQ FT: 2,500
SALES (est): 274.6K **Privately Held**
SIC: 3211 Flat glass

(G-15127)
GREENWOOD ASSOCIATES INC
6280 W Howard St (60714-3433)
PHONE..................847 579-5500
Ronald W Kaplan, *President*
Michael P Gard, *Admin Sec*
▲ **EMP:** 10
SQ FT: 2,000

Niles - Cook County (G-15128)

SALES (est): 1.7MM **Privately Held**
SIC: 2037 Fruit juice concentrates, frozen

(G-15128)
HALF PRICE BKS REC MGZINES INC
5605 W Touhy Ave (60714-4019)
PHONE...................................847 588-2286
Kathy Thomas, *Vice Pres*
Kent Hedtke, *Branch Mgr*
EMP: 26
SALES (corp-wide): 210.2MM **Privately Held**
WEB: www.halfpricebooks.com
SIC: 2721 5932 Magazines: publishing & printing; book stores, secondhand
PA: Half Price Books, Records, Magazines, Incorporated
5803 E Northwest Hwy
Dallas TX 75231
214 360-0833

(G-15129)
HORIZON METALS INC
5739 W Howard St (60714-4012)
PHONE...................................773 478-8888
Bruce Pinsof, *President*
Deborah Graff, *Office Admin*
Karen Pinsof, *Admin Sec*
EMP: 20
SALES (est): 3.8MM **Privately Held**
SIC: 3356 3339 Precious metals; primary nonferrous metals

(G-15130)
HOTVAPES LTD
7240 N Milwaukee Ave (60714)
PHONE...................................775 468-8273
Tim Roche, *President*
EMP: 15
SALES: 3MM **Privately Held**
WEB: www.hotvapes.com
SIC: 5993 3634 Cigarette store; cigarette lighters, electric

(G-15131)
IMAGININGS 3 INC
Also Called: Flix Candy
6401 W Gross Point Rd (60714-4507)
PHONE...................................847 647-1370
Sidney Diamond, *President*
Debbie Diamond, *Vice Pres*
Jeff Grossman, *Vice Pres*
Phyllis Diamond, *Admin Sec*
▲ EMP: 25
SQ FT: 55,000
SALES (est): 6MM **Privately Held**
SIC: 2064 Candy & other confectionery products

(G-15132)
IMBERT CONSTRUCTION INDS INC
7030 N Austin Ave (60714-4602)
PHONE...................................847 588-3170
John Grzeskowski, *President*
Lisa Acosta, *Controller*
Justin Burkhardt, *Director*
William S Toth, *Admin Sec*
EMP: 4
SQ FT: 4,800
SALES (est): 272.5K **Privately Held**
WEB: www.imbertconstruction.com
SIC: 1752 3443 Access flooring system installation; floating covers, metal plate

(G-15133)
INDUSTRIAL MARKET PLACE
Also Called: Imp
5940 W Touhy Ave Ste 230 (60714-4604)
PHONE...................................847 676-1900
Joel Wineberg, *President*
Harvey Wineberg, *Treasurer*
Dan Tepperman, *Sales Staff*
Ann Wineberg, *Admin Sec*
EMP: 25 EST: 1951
SALES (est): 2.2MM **Privately Held**
WEB: www.impmagazine.com
SIC: 2721 Trade journals: publishing only, not printed on site

(G-15134)
INVENTIVE DISPLAY GROUP LLC
Also Called: Inventex Medical
7415 N Melvina Ave (60714-3907)
PHONE...................................847 588-1100
Seth Bankir,
▲ EMP: 10
SALES (est): 1.3MM
SALES (corp-wide): 12MM **Privately Held**
SIC: 2542 Office & store showcases & display fixtures
PA: Bankier Companies, Inc.
6151 W Gross Point Rd
Niles IL 60714
847 647-6565

(G-15135)
JAHM INC
Also Called: Drawn Metal Products
6143 W Howard St (60714-3401)
PHONE...................................847 647-7650
Young Harris, *President*
Shawn Brady, *Vice Pres*
Diane Wall, *Sales Mgr*
EMP: 13
SQ FT: 35,000
SALES (est): 2MM **Privately Held**
SIC: 3465 3965 3469 Automotive stampings; fasteners, buttons, needles & pins; metal stampings

(G-15136)
JERON ELECTRONIC SYSTEMS INC
7501 N Natchez Ave (60714-3803)
PHONE...................................773 275-1900
Jerome J Chesnul, *President*
Ericka C Baran, *Vice Pres*
Joe Beckman, *Vice Pres*
Matthew Chesnul, *Vice Pres*
Tom Anderson, *Opers Mgr*
▲ EMP: 75 EST: 1964
SQ FT: 52,328
SALES (est): 15MM **Privately Held**
WEB: www.jeronnursecall.com
SIC: 3669 Emergency alarms

(G-15137)
JOHNS-BYRNE COMPANY (PA)
Also Called: Johnsbyrne
6701 W Oakton St (60714-3917)
PHONE...................................847 583-3100
Corey Gustafson, *President*
John Gustafson Jr, *COO*
James Pate Gustafson, *Exec VP*
Michael J Gustafson, *Exec VP*
Paul Morris, *Vice Pres*
EMP: 100
SQ FT: 40,000
SALES (est): 28.5MM **Privately Held**
WEB: www.johnsbyrne.com
SIC: 2752 2791 2789 Commercial printing, offset; typesetting; bookbinding & related work

(G-15138)
JOHNSBYRNE GRAPHIC TECH CORP
6701 W Oakton St (60714-3032)
PHONE...................................847 583-3100
Corey Gustafson, *President*
John B Gustason, *Admin Sec*
EMP: 1
SALES (est): 298.3K
SALES (corp-wide): 28.5MM **Privately Held**
SIC: 2752 Commercial printing, offset
PA: Johns-Byrne Company
6701 W Oakton St
Niles IL 60714
847 583-3100

(G-15139)
KOMAR SCREW CORP (PA)
7790 N Merrimac Ave (60714-3424)
PHONE...................................847 965-9090
Marvin Kocian, *President*
Steve Bagneschi, *QC Mgr*
Rose-Marie Beaster, *Sales Staff*
Brian Drwal, *Sales Staff*
Craig Wolfert, *Sales Staff*
▲ EMP: 50
SQ FT: 40,000
SALES: 12.5MM **Privately Held**
SIC: 5072 3452 Screws; nuts (hardware); bolts; screws, metal

(G-15140)
LEWIS SPRING AND MFG COMPANY (PA)
7500 N Natchez Ave (60714-3804)
PHONE...................................847 588-7030
James Robertson, *President*
Larry Gutowsky, *Vice Pres*
Jim Robertson, *Safety Mgr*
Luis Rodriguez, *Safety Mgr*
John Bold, *CFO*
EMP: 60
SQ FT: 60,000
SALES: 9MM **Privately Held**
SIC: 3495 3469 3496 3493 Instrument springs, precision; mechanical springs, precision; stamping metal for the trade; miscellaneous fabricated wire products; steel springs, except wire

(G-15141)
LSL INDUSTRIES INC
Also Called: Lsl Healthcare
6200 W Howard St (60714-3404)
P.O. Box 352, Northbrook (60065-0352)
PHONE...................................773 878-1100
Ashok Luthra, *President*
Michael Krysiak, *Vice Pres*
Ash Luthra, *Vice Pres*
Michael Jones, *Purchasing*
Michael Reeves, *Regl Sales Mgr*
◆ EMP: 84
SALES (est): 23.2MM **Privately Held**
WEB: www.lslhealthcare.com
SIC: 3841 3842 Surgical & medical instruments; surgical appliances & supplies

(G-15142)
M & S TECHNOLOGIES INC
5715 W Howard St (60714-4012)
PHONE...................................847 763-0500
Joseph Marino, *President*
▲ EMP: 14
SQ FT: 7,000
SALES (est): 2.4MM **Privately Held**
SIC: 3851 5045 Ophthalmic goods; computer peripheral equipment

(G-15143)
M R O SOLUTIONS LLC
5645 W Howard St (60714-4011)
PHONE...................................847 588-2480
James Gajewski,
Rob Burk,
Kevin Murphy,
Glen Stampnick,
◆ EMP: 20 EST: 1998
SALES (est): 3.9MM **Privately Held**
WEB: www.mrosolutions.com
SIC: 2899 Corrosion preventive lubricant

(G-15144)
MARIAS CHICKEN ATI ATIHAN
9054 W Golf Rd (60714-5805)
PHONE...................................847 699-3113
EMP: 3
SALES (est): 142.9K **Privately Held**
SIC: 3312 Stainless steel

(G-15145)
MICHELS FRAME SHOP
Also Called: Michel's Frame Shop & Gallery
7120 W Touhy Ave (60714-4526)
PHONE...................................847 647-7366
Margaret Michel, *Owner*
Maragaret Michel, *Principal*
Diane Hunn, *Manager*
EMP: 3 EST: 1965
SALES (est): 200K **Privately Held**
SIC: 2499 5999 5023 7389 Picture & mirror frames, wood; picture frames, ready made; frames & framing, picture & mirror; interior designer

(G-15146)
MICROLINK DEVICES INC
6457 W Howard St (60714-3301)
PHONE...................................847 588-3001
Dr Noren Pan, *CEO*
Glen Hillier, *Principal*
Dr Mark Osowski, *Vice Pres*
Andree Wibowo, *Production*
Todd Major, *Engineer*
EMP: 54
SQ FT: 30,000
SALES (est): 6.6MM **Privately Held**
SIC: 3674 Semiconductor circuit networks

(G-15147)
MILWAUKEE ELECTRIC TOOL CORP
6310 W Gross Point Rd (60714-3916)
PHONE...................................847 588-3356
Peter Weisell, *Branch Mgr*
EMP: 282 **Privately Held**
SIC: 3546 3425 Power-driven handtools; saw blades & handsaws
HQ: Milwaukee Electric Tool Corporation
13135 W Lisbon Rd
Brookfield WI 53005
800 729-3878

(G-15148)
MONETT METALS INC
Also Called: Horizon Metals
5739 W Howard St (60714-4012)
PHONE...................................773 478-8888
Steve Lamm, *Manager*
EMP: 5
SALES (corp-wide): 729.6MM **Privately Held**
SIC: 3325 Steel foundries
HQ: Monett Metals Inc.
101 Industrial Dr
Monett MO 65708
417 235-6053

(G-15149)
MPC PRODUCTS CORPORATION (HQ)
Also Called: Woodward Mpc, Inc.
6300 W Howard St (60714-3406)
PHONE...................................847 673-8300
Thomas Gendron, *CEO*
Martin Glass, *President*
Jeffrey Jarr, *Engineer*
Robert Webber Jr, *CFO*
Lilliana Gomez, *Business Anlyst*
◆ EMP: 512 EST: 1962
SQ FT: 100,000
SALES (est): 171MM
SALES (corp-wide): 2.9B **Publicly Held**
WEB: www.mpcproducts.com
SIC: 3728 3676 3621 3625 Aircraft body & wing assemblies & parts; aircraft assemblies, subassemblies & parts; electronic resistors; motors & generators; relays & industrial controls; aircraft/aerospace flight instruments & guidance systems
PA: Woodward, Inc.
1081 Woodward Way
Fort Collins CO 80524
970 482-5811

(G-15150)
MPC PRODUCTS CORPORATION
6300 W Howard St (60714-3406)
PHONE...................................847 673-8300
EMP: 3
SALES (corp-wide): 2.9B **Publicly Held**
SIC: 3625 3643 3613 Industrial electrical relays & switches; switches, electric power; switches, electronic applications; solenoid switches (industrial controls); current-carrying wiring devices; switchgear & switchboard apparatus
HQ: Mpc Products Corporation
6300 W Howard St
Niles IL 60714
847 673-8300

(G-15151)
NATURES SOURCES LLC
5665 W Howard St (60714-4011)
PHONE...................................847 663-9168
John Zapfel, *CEO*
Lee Frank, *Manager*
EMP: 5
SALES: 575.2K **Privately Held**
SIC: 5499 2869 5122 Vitamin food stores; enzymes; vitamins & minerals

(G-15152)
NEW PANEL BRICK COMPANY OF ILL
6959 N Milwaukee Ave (60714-4421)
PHONE...................................847 696-1686

GEOGRAPHIC SECTION

Niles - Cook County (G-15180)

Zeno Popa, *Principal*
EMP: 5 **EST:** 2016
SALES (est): 327.6K **Privately Held**
WEB: www.panelbrick.com
SIC: 3271 Brick, concrete

(G-15153)
OBERG MEDICAL PRODUCTS CO LLC
6150 W Mulford St (60714-3428)
PHONE.................................847 965-3030
David L Bonvenuto, *President*
EMP: 100
SALES (corp-wide): 217.4MM **Privately Held**
SIC: 3451 Screw machine products
HQ: Oberg Medical Products Company, Llc
273 N Pike Rd
Sarver PA 16055
724 295-2121

(G-15154)
ORORA VISUAL TX LLC
7400 N Lehigh Ave (60714-4024)
PHONE.................................414 423-2200
Roxann Black, *Manager*
EMP: 30 **Privately Held**
SIC: 2759 Screen printing
HQ: Orora Visual Tx Llc
3210 Innovative Way
Mesquite TX 75149
972 289-0705

(G-15155)
PEELMASTER PACKAGING CORP
Also Called: Peelmaster Medical Packaging
6153 W Mulford St (60714-3413)
PHONE.................................847 966-6161
William Sieck, *Principal*
Jim Bassing, *Sales Staff*
Elena Canizares, *Sales Staff*
EMP: 30
SQ FT: 16,700
SALES (est): 5.6MM **Privately Held**
SIC: 2673 Cellophane bags, unprinted: made from purchased materials

(G-15156)
PERFECTION CUSTOM CLOSETS & CO
7183 N Austin Ave (60714-4617)
PHONE.................................847 647-6461
Timothy Ohagan, *President*
EMP: 17
SALES (est): 3.5MM **Privately Held**
SIC: 2599 2541 Cabinets, factory; wood partitions & fixtures

(G-15157)
PERMA-PIPE INC (HQ)
Also Called: Permalert E S P
6410 W Howard St (60714-3302)
PHONE.................................847 966-1000
David Mansfield, *CEO*
◆ **EMP:** 40
SQ FT: 130,000
SALES (est): 75.5MM **Publicly Held**
SIC: 3498 Fabricated pipe & fittings

(G-15158)
PERMA-PIPE INTL HOLDINGS INC (PA)
6410 W Howard St (60714-3302)
PHONE.................................847 966-1000
David S Barrie, *Ch of Bd*
David J Mansfield, *President*
Bryan Norwood, *CFO*
D Bryan Norwood, *CFO*
Wayne Bosch, *Officer*
◆ **EMP:** 50
SQ FT: 31,650
SALES: 127.6MM **Publicly Held**
SIC: 3677 3564 3569 Filtration devices, electronic; blowers & fans; filters & strainers, pipeline

(G-15159)
PERMALERT ENVMTL SPCIALTY PDTS
6410 W Howard St (60714-3302)
PHONE.................................847 966-2190
EMP: 5 **EST:** 2016
SALES (est): 551.2K **Privately Held**
SIC: 3498 Fabricated pipe & fittings

(G-15160)
POLA COMPANY
8901 N Milwaukee Ave A (60714-1889)
PHONE.................................847 470-1182
EMP: 3
SALES (est): 215.5K **Privately Held**
SIC: 2339 Mfg Women's/Misses' Outerwear

(G-15161)
POLYSCIENCE INC
5709 W Howard St (60714-4012)
PHONE.................................847 647-0611
Phillip Preston, *CEO*
◆ **EMP:** 100
SALES (est): 12.4MM **Privately Held**
SIC: 3585 Refrigeration & heating equipment

(G-15162)
PRESTON INDUSTRIES INC
Also Called: Polyscience
6600 W Touhy Ave (60714-4516)
PHONE.................................847 647-0611
S Tinley Preston III, *President*
Philip K Preston, *President*
S Tinsley Preston, *Vice Pres*
Anabel Rojas, *Marketing Mgr*
Annabelle Rojas, *Marketing Mgr*
◆ **EMP:** 152
SQ FT: 60,000
SALES (est): 47.9MM **Privately Held**
SIC: 3821 2731 Laboratory apparatus & furniture; book publishing

(G-15163)
R & D ELECTRONICS INC
7948 W Oakton St (60714-2457)
PHONE.................................847 583-9080
Ernie Ruby, *President*
EMP: 2
SQ FT: 900
SALES (est): 200K **Privately Held**
SIC: 3625 3822 3433 Control equipment, electric; auto controls regulating residntl & coml environmt & applncs; heating equipment, except electric

(G-15164)
R Z TOOL INC
5691 W Howard St (60714-4011)
PHONE.................................847 647-2350
Samantha Jaber, *President*
Greg Sallecki, *Admin Sec*
EMP: 14
SQ FT: 6,500
SALES (est): 1.5MM **Privately Held**
SIC: 3469 Machine parts, stamped or pressed metal

(G-15165)
RICH PRODUCTS CORPORATION
6200 W Mulford St (60714-3430)
PHONE.................................847 581-1749
A Bogan, *Vice Pres*
Freddy Medina, *Production*
Will Flanagan, *Engineer*
Cristina Ng, *Engineer*
Mark Blaszkowski, *Controller*
EMP: 76
SALES (corp-wide): 5B **Privately Held**
SIC: 2092 2026 2023 Fresh or frozen packaged fish; shrimp, frozen: prepared; shellfish, frozen: prepared; fluid milk; whipped topping, dry mix
PA: Rich Products Corporation
1 Robert Rich Way
Buffalo NY 14213
716 878-8000

(G-15166)
RICO INDUSTRIES INC (PA)
Also Called: Rico Industries Tag Express
7000 N Austin Ave (60714-4602)
PHONE.................................312 427-0313
Cary S Schack, *President*
Jay Crawford, *COO*
Tom Schmit, *Vice Pres*
Todd Romano, *Production*
Bernard Schack, *Treasurer*
◆ **EMP:** 60
SQ FT: 55,000

SALES (est): 54MM **Privately Held**
WEB: www.ricoinc.com
SIC: 5199 3172 2396 3993 Leather goods, except footwear, gloves, luggage, belting; wallets; checkbook covers; key cases; automotive & apparel trimmings; signs & advertising specialties

(G-15167)
ROYAL KIT BTHROOM CABINETS INC (PA)
Also Called: Royal Kitchen & Bath Cabinets
7727 N Milwaukee Ave (60714-4733)
PHONE.................................847 588-0011
Agnieszka Hanusiak, *President*
EMP: 13
SALES (est): 2.4MM **Privately Held**
SIC: 3429 Cabinet hardware

(G-15168)
RV ENTERPRISES LTD
8926 N Greenwood Ave (60714-5163)
PHONE.................................847 509-8710
Linda L Vaccaro, *President*
EMP: 15
SALES (est): 1.5MM **Privately Held**
SIC: 2759 Promotional printing

(G-15169)
SERBIAN YELLOW PAGES INC
7400 N Waukegan Rd # 210 (60714-4353)
PHONE.................................847 588-0555
Goran Veselinovic, *President*
Dusan Delic, *Vice Pres*
EMP: 16
SALES (est): 978.7K **Privately Held**
SIC: 2741 Telephone & other directory publishing

(G-15170)
SHERWOOD INDUSTRIES INC
7800 N Merrimac Ave (60714-3426)
PHONE.................................847 626-0300
William Russin Sr, *Ch of Bd*
Robert Russin, *President*
Carole Studenroth, *Vice Pres*
Annette Ashbacher, *CFO*
Lorraine Russin Sr, *Shareholder*
▲ **EMP:** 10 **EST:** 1975
SQ FT: 33,000
SALES: 4MM **Privately Held**
SIC: 5085 3826 2512 Packing, industrial; analytical instruments; upholstered household furniture

(G-15171)
SHEVICK SALES CORP
Also Called: Sleep On Latex
5620 W Jarvis Ave (60714-4016)
PHONE.................................312 487-2865
Karl Shevick, *President*
▲ **EMP:** 2 **EST:** 2013
SALES (est): 402.6K **Privately Held**
WEB: www.sleeponlatex.com
SIC: 2515 Mattresses & bedsprings

(G-15172)
SMITHEREEN COMPANY
Also Called: Smithereen Pest Management
7400 N Melvina Ave (60714-3908)
PHONE.................................800 340-1888
Jack R Jennings, *President*
Leticia Fink, *Purch Mgr*
Scott Seifert, *Accounts Mgr*
Timothy Munyan, *Sales Staff*
John Anast, *Manager*
EMP: 60
SQ FT: 12,000
SALES: 8MM **Privately Held**
SIC: 7342 2879 Pest control in structures; agricultural chemicals

(G-15173)
SMITHEREEN COMPANY DEL (PA)
Also Called: Smithereen Exterminating Co
7400 N Melvina Ave (60714-3908)
PHONE.................................847 675-0010
Richard E Jennings, *President*
Chris Madsen, *Supervisor*
EMP: 60
SQ FT: 1,200
SALES (est): 7.8MM **Privately Held**
WEB: www.smithereen.com
SIC: 7342 2879 Exterminating & fumigating; agricultural chemicals

(G-15174)
SPECIALTY PROMOTIONS INC (PA)
Also Called: Specialty Printing Company
6019 W Howard St (60714-4801)
PHONE.................................847 588-2580
Paul B Lefebvre, *CEO*
Adam M Lefebvre, *President*
Rick Baruch, *Vice Pres*
Gil Bathgate, *Vice Pres*
Alex Crohn, *Vice Pres*
▲ **EMP:** 218
SQ FT: 103,000
SALES (est): 127MM **Privately Held**
SIC: 2752 Commercial printing, offset

(G-15175)
SRH HOLDINGS INC
6100 W Howard St (60714-3402)
PHONE.................................847 583-2295
Scott Harris, *President*
Cathy Spencer, *Admin Sec*
▲ **EMP:** 5
SQ FT: 2,000
SALES (est): 813.5K **Privately Held**
SIC: 2339 Mfg Women's/Misses' Outerwear

(G-15176)
SUMMIT INDUSTRIES LLC
7555 N Caldwell Ave (60714-3807)
PHONE.................................773 353-4000
Thomas Boon, *President*
Joe Flies, *President*
Don Matson, *Vice Pres*
Phuong Tran, *Electrical Engi*
Kurt Peterson, *CFO*
◆ **EMP:** 77
SQ FT: 25,000
SALES (est): 23.4MM **Privately Held**
SIC: 3841 Surgical & medical instruments

(G-15177)
SUPERIOR KNIFE INC
6235 W Howard St (60714-3403)
PHONE.................................847 982-2280
Claudio Cozzini, *President*
Marco Cozzini, *Vice Pres*
Silvano Cozzini, *Vice Pres*
Robert Cozzini, *Treasurer*
Ernie Christian, *Sales Staff*
▲ **EMP:** 40
SALES (est): 8.7MM **Privately Held**
WEB: www.superiorknife.com
SIC: 5023 3421 Kitchen tools & utensils; cutlery

(G-15178)
TALK-A-PHONE LLC
7530 N Natchez Ave (60714-3804)
PHONE.................................773 539-1100
Jim Hartney, *Opers Mgr*
Colleen Koroyanis, *Opers-Prdtn-Mfg*
Steve Liberman, *Chief Engr*
Jyoti Gianani, *Engineer*
Jyoti Mandalia, *Engineer*
EMP: 71 **EST:** 1927
SQ FT: 34,000
SALES (est): 13.5MM **Privately Held**
WEB: www.talkaphone.com
SIC: 3663 Radio & TV communications equipment

(G-15179)
TETRA MEDICAL SUPPLY CORP
6364 W Gross Point Rd (60714-3916)
PHONE.................................847 647-0590
Constance Shier, *President*
James A Shier Jr, *President*
Barb Hoffman, *Vice Pres*
Ollie Jackson, *Admin Sec*
▲ **EMP:** 12
SQ FT: 15,000
SALES (est): 1.4MM **Privately Held**
WEB: www.tetramed.com
SIC: 3842 5047 Surgical appliances & supplies; surgical equipment & supplies

(G-15180)
THERMAL CARE INC
5680 W Jarvis Ave (60714-3408)
PHONE.................................847 966-2260
Christopher S Keller, *Ch of Bd*
Lee Sobocinski, *President*
Drew Thomas, *Partner*
Steve Abbott, *General Mgr*

Niles - Cook County (G-15181)

Mike Duesenberg, *General Mgr*
◆ **EMP:** 120 **EST:** 1965
SQ FT: 135,227
SALES (est): 28MM
SALES (corp-wide): 229.1MM **Privately Held**
WEB: www.thermalcare.com
SIC: 3585 3555 Refrigeration & heating equipment; printing trades machinery
PA: Sewickley Capital Inc
  501 Silverside Rd Ste 67
  Wilmington DE 19809
  302 793-4964

(G-15181)
TMB PUBLISHING INC
Also Called: Plumbing Engineer Magazine
6201 W Howard St Ste 201 (60714-3435)
PHONE 847 564-1127
Tom M Brown Jr, *President*
Ruth Mitchell, *Editor*
Art Mazzone, *Sales Mgr*
Diane Spangler, *Sales Staff*
Ashlei Cooper, *Director*
EMP: 7
SALES (est): 862.6K **Privately Held**
SIC: 2721 Magazines: publishing only, not printed on site

(G-15182)
TRIDENT SOFTWARE CORP
1183 S Scoville Ave (60714)
PHONE 847 219-8777
Ramesh Vashi, *President*
EMP: 2
SALES: 204K **Privately Held**
SIC: 7372 Prepackaged software

(G-15183)
TRU LINE LITHOGRAPHING INC (HQ)
Also Called: Garvey Group, The
7400 N Lehigh Ave (60714-4024)
P.O. Box 565, Sturtevant WI (53177-0565)
PHONE 262 554-7300
Ed Garvey Jr, *President*
Donald R Ford, *Vice Pres*
Fran Angelini, *CFO*
EMP: 49
SQ FT: 41,400
SALES (est): 10.5MM
SALES (corp-wide): 26.9MM **Privately Held**
WEB: www.thegarveygroup.com
SIC: 2752 2796 2791 2789 Lithographing on metal; platemaking services; typesetting; bookbinding & related work; commercial printing
PA: Ed. Garvey And Company
  7400 N Lehigh Ave
  Niles IL 60714
  847 647-1900

(G-15184)
UMF CORPORATION
Also Called: Perfect Clean
5721 W Howard St (60714-4012)
PHONE 224 251-7822
Kim Roman, *Branch Mgr*
EMP: 3
SALES (corp-wide): 5MM **Privately Held**
SIC: 2842 3589 5087 Specialty cleaning, polishes & sanitation goods; commercial cleaning equipment; cleaning & maintenance equipment & supplies
PA: Umf Corporation
  4709 Golf Rd Ste 300a
  Skokie IL 60076
  847 920-0370

(G-15185)
UNITED GENERAL GRAPHICS LLC
7400 N Lehigh Ave (60714-4024)
PHONE 262 657-5054
Fax: 262 657-0325
EMP: 17
SQ FT: 29,000
SALES (est): 1.9MM
SALES (corp-wide): 29.9MM **Privately Held**
SIC: 2752 5112 Lithographic Commercial Printing Whol Stationery/Office Supplies Commercial Printing
PA: Ed. Garvey And Company
  7400 N Lehigh Ave
  Niles IL 60714
  847 647-1900

(G-15186)
WELD COTE METALS
7720 N Lehigh Ave (60714-3416)
PHONE 888 258-0121
Joe Onera, *CEO*
John Pandors, *CFO*
EMP: 3
SALES (est): 217.4K **Privately Held**
SIC: 3291 5085 Aluminum oxide (fused) abrasives; abrasives

(G-15187)
WHITNEY PRODUCTS INC
Also Called: Whitney Medical Solutions
5737 W Howard St (60714-4012)
PHONE 847 966-6161
Steven Whitney, *President*
Michael Whitney, *Assistant VP*
Lisa Gyori, *Vice Pres*
Sarah Whitney, *Admin Sec*
EMP: 18
SQ FT: 16,700
SALES (est): 3MM **Privately Held**
SIC: 3842 3841 3085 Surgical appliances & supplies; surgical & medical instruments; plastics bottles

Noble
Richland County

(G-15188)
BILL CHANDLER FARMS
5182 Bucktown Ln (62868-3013)
PHONE 618 752-7551
William R Chandler, *Owner*
EMP: 2
SALES: 900K **Privately Held**
SIC: 0212 0115 0116 0213 Beef cattle except feedlots; corn; soybeans; hogs; agricultural machinery & equipment; bird food, prepared

(G-15189)
CLARENCE HANCOCK SAWMILL INC
1191 E White Ln (62868-2709)
PHONE 618 854-2232
Dennis Hancock, *President*
EMP: 9
SALES (est): 530K **Privately Held**
SIC: 2421 Sawmills & planing mills, general

(G-15190)
MUHS FUNITURE MANUFACTURING
Also Called: Muhs Cabinet Creation
4808 N Passport Rd (62868-2101)
PHONE 618 723-2590
Von Muhs, *Owner*
Anjie Muhs, *Co-Owner*
EMP: 4
SALES (est): 210K **Privately Held**
SIC: 2511 Wood household furniture

(G-15191)
PATTERSON PRODUCTS
580 E Antioch Ln (62868-2221)
PHONE 618 723-2688
Gary Patterson, *Owner*
EMP: 7
SALES (est): 726.9K **Privately Held**
SIC: 3281 Table tops, marble

(G-15192)
SOUTHERN ILL SCALE & CNSTR INC
430 W South Ave (62868-1804)
PHONE 618 723-2303
Brad Fryburger, *President*
Susan Fryburger, *Vice Pres*
EMP: 5 **EST:** 1997
SQ FT: 1,340
SALES (est): 1.1MM **Privately Held**
WEB: www.southernilscale.com
SIC: 7699 3596 Scale repair service; truck (motor vehicle) scales

Nokomis
Montgomery County

(G-15193)
ALL PRECISION MFG LLC
Also Called: A P M
153 N 5th St (62075-1753)
P.O. Box 220 (62075-0220)
PHONE 217 563-7070
Jeffrey Howell,
Ralph Peifer,
EMP: 32
SQ FT: 20,000
SALES: 1.1MM **Privately Held**
SIC: 3599 Machine shop, jobbing & repair

(G-15194)
MATERIAL SERVICE CORPORATION
Also Called: Material Service Yard 12
22283 Taylorville Rd (62075-3812)
P.O. Box 6 (62075-0006)
PHONE 217 563-2531
Rich Ellis, *Manager*
EMP: 30
SALES (corp-wide): 20.8B **Privately Held**
SIC: 1422 Limestones, ground
HQ: Material Service Corporation
  2235 Entp Dr Ste 3504
  Westchester IL 60154
  708 731-2600

(G-15195)
NANO2 LLC
106 E State St (62075-1340)
P.O. Box 160 (62075-0160)
PHONE 217 563-2942
Kirk Brown, *Principal*
EMP: 2
SALES (est): 218.2K **Privately Held**
WEB: www.nano2.com
SIC: 3589 Water treatment equipment, industrial

(G-15196)
NOKOMIS QUARRY COMPANY
23311 Taylorville Rd (62075-3813)
P.O. Box 90 (62075-0090)
PHONE 217 563-2011
James A Dougherty, *President*
James H Prosser, *Corp Secy*
EMP: 15
SQ FT: 1,000
SALES (est): 2.1MM **Privately Held**
SIC: 1411 1422 Limestone, dimension-quarrying; crushed & broken limestone

(G-15197)
PROCESS SYSTEMS INC
316 E State St (62075-1324)
P.O. Box 188 (62075-0188)
PHONE 217 563-2872
Ralph Jones, *Manager*
EMP: 5 **Privately Held**
SIC: 3089 Injection molding of plastics
PA: Process Systems Inc.
  9160 Fishtrap Rd
  Crossroads TX 76227

(G-15198)
RONK ELECTRICAL INDUSTRIES INC
106 E State St (62075-1340)
P.O. Box 160 (62075-0160)
PHONE 217 563-8333
Daniel Dungan, *President*
Danny D Brady, *President*
Charlie O'Malley, *Controller*
Tom Giordano, *Marketing Mgr*
EMP: 40 **EST:** 1950
SQ FT: 8,400
SALES (est): 5.9MM
SALES (corp-wide): 256MM **Privately Held**
WEB: www.ronkelectrical.com
SIC: 3621 3613 Phase or rotary converters (electrical equipment); power switching equipment; panelboards & distribution boards, electric
PA: Springfield Electric Supply Company
  700 N 9th St
  Springfield IL 62702
  217 788-2100

Normal
Mclean County

(G-15199)
BLAC CULTIVATION LLC
1715 Rockingham Dr Apt B (61761-1052)
PHONE 309 532-6325
Bradley Brasher,
EMP: 9
SALES (est): 259.3K **Privately Held**
SIC: 3999

(G-15200)
BRIDGESTONE AMERICAS
1600 Fort Jesse Rd (61761-2200)
PHONE 309 452-4411
EMP: 21 **Privately Held**
SIC: 3011 5531 Tires & inner tubes; automotive tires
HQ: Bridgestone Americas Tire Operations, Llc
  200 4th Ave S Ste 100
  Nashville TN 37201
  615 937-1000

(G-15201)
CUMMINS CROSSPOINT LLC
450 W Northtown Rd (61761-4743)
PHONE 309 452-4454
Paul Krueger, *Sales Staff*
Deon Lindsay, *Branch Mgr*
EMP: 5
SALES (corp-wide): 23.5B **Publicly Held**
SIC: 3519 5084 Internal combustion engines; engines & parts, diesel
HQ: Cummins Crosspoint Llc
  2601 Fortune Cir E 300c
  Indianapolis IN 46241
  317 243-7979

(G-15202)
DOLL FURNITURE CO INC
400 N Beech St (61761-1815)
PHONE 309 452-2606
David Shutt, *President*
Nancy Shutt, *Vice Pres*
Jeff Shutt, *Treasurer*
James Shutt, *Admin Sec*
EMP: 3
SQ FT: 5,000
SALES (est): 276.1K **Privately Held**
WEB: www.dollfurniturecompany.com
SIC: 7641 5712 3553 7513 Furniture refinishing; furniture stores; woodworking machinery; truck rental & leasing, no drivers

(G-15203)
FRAME MART INC
Also Called: Wonderlin Galleries
1211 Silver Oak Cir (61761-9401)
PHONE 309 452-0658
Fax: 309 454-4406
EMP: 4
SALES (est): 294.6K **Privately Held**
SIC: 2499 5999 Mfg Wood Products Ret Misc Merchandise

(G-15204)
HANGER PRSTHETCS & ORTHO INC
211 Landmark Dr Ste A5 (61761-6165)
PHONE 309 585-2349
Shanie Scott, *Branch Mgr*
EMP: 4
SALES (corp-wide): 1.1B **Publicly Held**
SIC: 3842 Surgical appliances & supplies
HQ: Hanger Prosthetics & Orthotics, Inc.
  10910 Domain Dr Ste 300
  Austin TX 78758
  512 777-3800

(G-15205)
HARLAN VANCE COMPANY
1741 Hovey Ave (61761-4322)
PHONE 309 888-4804
Teresa J Vance, *President*
Drew S Vance, *Vice Pres*
Drew Vance, *Vice Pres*
Tom Hayslett, *Sales Staff*
Katie Vance, *Sales Staff*
EMP: 12

SQ FT: 11,000
SALES: 3.2MM **Privately Held**
WEB: www.harlanvance.com
SIC: 2395 2752 5112 Embroidery products, except schiffli machine; commercial printing, lithographic; looseleaf binders

(G-15206)
JLM WOODWORKING
500 Orlando Ave (61761-1233)
PHONE.................................309 275-8259
Joshua Moyer, *Principal*
EMP: 4 EST: 2010
SALES (est): 326.2K **Privately Held**
SIC: 2431 Millwork

(G-15207)
KONGSKILDE INDUSTRIES INC
1802 Industrial Park Dr A (61761-4363)
PHONE.................................309 452-3300
Catherine Lyssemko, *CFO*
◆ EMP: 16
SALES (est): 36.1MM
SALES (corp-wide): 1.9B **Privately Held**
SIC: 3535 3523 Pneumatic tube conveyor systems; farm machinery & equipment; fertilizing machinery, farm
HQ: Kk Denmark 2018 A/S
Skalskorvej 64
SorO
336 835-00

(G-15208)
LUTZ CORP
208 N Parkside Rd (61761-2346)
PHONE.................................800 203-7740
Lee Lutz, *President*
EMP: 3 EST: 2011
SALES (est): 316.5K **Privately Held**
WEB: www.lutzcorp.com
SIC: 3524 Lawn & garden equipment

(G-15209)
MEYER ELECTRONIC MFG SVCS INC
Also Called: Meyer E M S
440 Wylie Dr (61761-5405)
PHONE.................................309 808-4100
Gregory Meyer, *President*
Marsha Meyer, *Vice Pres*
EMP: 8
SQ FT: 1,000
SALES: 1MM **Privately Held**
SIC: 3672 Printed circuit boards

(G-15210)
MIRUS RESEARCH
618 E Lincoln St (61761-1889)
PHONE.................................309 828-3100
Matt Hughes, *Owner*
Don Spaulding, *Engineer*
EMP: 25
SALES (est): 2.3MM **Privately Held**
SIC: 7372 Prepackaged software

(G-15211)
MMMA
2601 W College Ave Ste A (61761-5920)
PHONE.................................309 888-8765
EMP: 17
SALES (est): 2.5MM **Privately Held**
SIC: 3465 Mfg Automotive Stampings

(G-15212)
NORMAL CORNBELTERS
1000 W Raab Rd (61761-9578)
PHONE.................................309 451-3432
Deana Roberts, *Business Mgr*
Ashlynne Solvie, *Manager*
EMP: 7
SALES (est): 616.9K **Privately Held**
SIC: 3949 Bases, baseball

(G-15213)
NORMALITE NEWSPAPER
1702 W College Ave Ste G (61761-2793)
P.O. Box 67 (61761-0067)
PHONE.................................309 454-5476
Ed Pyne, *Owner*
EMP: 10
SALES (est): 420.5K **Privately Held**
SIC: 2711 Newspapers: publishing only, not printed on site

(G-15214)
NUAIR FILTER COMPANY LLC
2219 W College Ave (61761-2375)
PHONE.................................309 888-4331
Kevin M McGinty, *President*
L Douglas Coartney, *Corp Secy*
EMP: 6
SQ FT: 105,000
SALES: 14MM
SALES (corp-wide): 183.7MM **Privately Held**
SIC: 5075 3443 Air filters; metal parts
PA: Superior Consolidated Industries, Inc.
801 Sw Jefferson Ave
Peoria IL 61605
309 677-5980

(G-15215)
OLDCASTLE INFRASTRUCTURE INC
1204 Aurora Way (61761-1260)
PHONE.................................309 661-4608
Matthew Buck, *Plant Mgr*
Brian Dill, *QC Mgr*
Dan Kozbiel, *Engineer*
Brent Anderson, *Treasurer*
Chris White, *Human Res Dir*
EMP: 15
SALES (corp-wide): 30.6B **Privately Held**
SIC: 3446 Open flooring & grating for construction
HQ: Oldcastle Infrastructure, Inc.
7000 Cntl Prkaway Ste 800
Atlanta GA 30328
470 602-2000

(G-15216)
PANTAGRAPH PUBLISHING CO
2551 W College Ave (61761-2597)
PHONE.................................309 451-0006
EMP: 5
SALES (corp-wide): 1MM **Privately Held**
SIC: 2711 Newspapers
PA: Pantagraph Publishing Co
301 W Washington St
Bloomington IL 61701
309 829-9000

(G-15217)
PEORIA MIDWEST EQUIPMENT INC
2150 W College Ave (61761-2372)
PHONE.................................309 454-6800
Steve Meyer, *Principal*
EMP: 6
SALES (corp-wide): 6.7MM **Privately Held**
SIC: 7699 5261 5063 3546 Lawn mower repair shop; lawnmowers & tractors; generators; saws & sawing equipment
PA: Peoria Midwest Equipment, Inc.
4826 W Farmington Rd
Peoria IL
309 676-5855

(G-15218)
PRAIRIE SIGNS INC
1215 Warriner St (61761-3334)
PHONE.................................309 452-0463
Andrew R Carby, *President*
Cassandra Mocilan, *President*
Diana Bubenik, *Treasurer*
Suzanne Anderson, *Admin Sec*
EMP: 13
SQ FT: 14,000
SALES: 1.9MM **Privately Held**
SIC: 3993 Electric signs

(G-15219)
PROSTHETIC ORTHOTIC SPECIALIST (PA)
303 Landmark Dr Ste 5a (61761-6164)
PHONE.................................309 454-8733
Kenneth W Ferencik, *President*
Rosemary D Ferencik, *Treasurer*
EMP: 12
SQ FT: 1,200
SALES (est): 45K **Privately Held**
SIC: 5999 3842 Orthopedic & prosthesis applications; orthopedic appliances

(G-15220)
R B WHITE INC
2011 Eagle Rd (61761-1001)
P.O. Box 538 (61761-0538)
PHONE.................................309 452-5816
Michael White, *President*
Robert White, *Chairman*
Stella White, *Vice Pres*
Dallas Wickenhauser, *Vice Pres*
John Bays, *CTO*
EMP: 40
SALES (est): 6.6MM **Privately Held**
SIC: 2542 3469 3444 Shelving, office & store: except wood; shelving angles or slotted bars: except wood; metal stampings; sheet metalwork

(G-15221)
R R DONNELLEY & SONS COMPANY
1821 Hovey Ave (61761-4315)
PHONE.................................309 808-3018
EMP: 3
SALES (corp-wide): 6.2B **Publicly Held**
WEB: www.rrdonnelley.com
SIC: 2754 Commercial printing, gravure
PA: R. R. Donnelley & Sons Company
35 W Wacker Dr
Chicago IL 60601
312 326-8000

(G-15222)
ROYAL PUBLISHING INC
1730 Bradford Ln Ste 185 (61761-5292)
PHONE.................................309 829-6191
Bryce Porter, *Branch Mgr*
EMP: 7
SALES (corp-wide): 7MM **Privately Held**
SIC: 2721 Magazines: publishing only, not printed on site
PA: Royal Publishing, Inc.
7620 N Harker Dr
Peoria IL
309 693-3171

(G-15223)
RUSSELL BRANDS LLC
2015 Eagle Rd (61761-1001)
P.O. Box 9 (61761-0009)
PHONE.................................309 454-6737
Dan Jurczak, *Branch Mgr*
EMP: 100
SALES (corp-wide): 327.2B **Publicly Held**
SIC: 2253 Jerseys, knit; jogging & warm-up suits, knit; T-shirts & tops, knit; pants, slacks or trousers, knit
HQ: Russell Brands, Llc
1 Fruit Of The Loom Dr
Bowling Green KY 42103
270 781-6400

(G-15224)
SCADAWARE INC
2023 Eagle Rd (61761-1001)
PHONE.................................309 665-0135
Richard J Caldwell, *President*
Tracy Morgan, *Project Mgr*
Scott Dappen, *Engineer*
Larry Miller, *Engineer*
Kurtis Liggett, *Project Engr*
EMP: 15 EST: 2000
SQ FT: 5,400
SALES (est): 4.2MM **Privately Held**
WEB: www.scadaware.com
SIC: 3577 7371 Input/output equipment, computer; computer software development & applications

(G-15225)
STAR TEST DYNAMOMETER INC
712 Thistlewood Cc Ct (61761-5301)
PHONE.................................309 452-0371
Michael E Barclay, *Principal*
EMP: 2
SALES (est): 233.4K **Privately Held**
SIC: 3829 Dynamometer instruments

(G-15226)
TWIN CITY AWARDS
1531 Fort Jesse Rd Ste 5b (61761-4742)
PHONE.................................309 452-9291
William M McGivern Jr, *Partner*
Carol McGivern, *Partner*
EMP: 2
SQ FT: 1,800
SALES (est): 200K **Privately Held**
SIC: 5999 5947 3993 Trophies & plaques; gift shop; signs & advertising specialties

(G-15227)
UNIQUE DESIGNS
408 Lumbertown Rd (61761-4744)
PHONE.................................309 454-1226
Mark Fagerland, *Owner*
EMP: 6
SQ FT: 12,000
SALES (est): 810K **Privately Held**
SIC: 3083 5712 1751 Plastic finished products, laminated; cabinet work, custom; custom made furniture, except cabinets; cabinet & finish carpentry

Norridge
Cook County

(G-15228)
ACCU-CUT DIAMOND TOOL COMPANY (PA)
423840 N Sayre Ave (60706)
P.O. Box 56186, Chicago (60656-0186)
PHONE.................................708 457-8800
Stan Domanski, *CEO*
Christine Domanski, *President*
Aneta Lysiak, *Purch Agent*
Carey Turner, *CFO*
Glenn Miller, *Director*
EMP: 19
SQ FT: 20,000
SALES (est): 10MM **Privately Held**
SIC: 3545 Diamond cutting tools for turning, boring, burnishing, etc.

(G-15229)
ACCU-CUT DMND BORE SZING SYSTE (HQ)
4238 N Sayre Ave (60706-7107)
PHONE.................................708 457-8800
Stanley Domanski, *CEO*
Christine Domanski, *President*
Andy Szremski, *Engineer*
John Wagner, *Engineer*
Cary Turner, *CFO*
EMP: 10
SQ FT: 20,000
SALES (est): 975K
SALES (corp-wide): 10MM **Privately Held**
SIC: 3541 Machine tools, metal cutting type
PA: Accu-Cut Diamond Tool Company, Inc
423840 N Sayre Ave
Norridge IL 60706
708 457-8800

(G-15230)
APPLIANCE REPAIR
4911 N Delphia Ave (60706-2808)
PHONE.................................708 456-1020
Jim Gagliano, *Owner*
EMP: 3
SALES (est): 268.1K **Privately Held**
SIC: 3639 5064 7629 Major kitchen appliances, except refrigerators & stoves; electrical appliances, major; electrical household appliance repair

(G-15231)
BUTERA FINER FOODS INC
Also Called: Butera Markets
4411 N Cumberland Ave (60706-4220)
PHONE.................................708 456-5939
Vito Trioa, *Manager*
EMP: 100
SALES (corp-wide): 77.6MM **Privately Held**
WEB: www.buteramarket.com
SIC: 5411 2051 Supermarkets, independent; bread, cake & related products
PA: Butera Finer Foods, Inc.
1 Clock Tower Plz Ste A
Elgin IL 60120
847 741-1010

(G-15232)
CAST PRODUCTS INC
Also Called: CPI
4200 N Nordica Ave (60706-1392)
PHONE.................................708 457-1500

Ron Paquet, *CEO*
Zoltan Salata, *President*
Dan Laurence, *Vice Pres*
Nicole Ferrero, *Opers Staff*
Jose Diaz, *Engineer*
▲ **EMP:** 115
SQ FT: 65,000
SALES (est): 34.1MM **Privately Held**
WEB: www.castproducts.com
SIC: 3363 Aluminum die-castings

(G-15233)
DISCO MACHINE & MFG INC
7327 W Agatite Ave (60706-4703)
PHONE.................................708 456-0835
Zbigniew Brzostowski, *President*
Monica Grzeda, *QC Mgr*
Helena Brzostowski, *Admin Sec*
EMP: 35
SQ FT: 13,500
SALES (est): 5.8MM **Privately Held**
SIC: 3599 Machine shop, jobbing & repair

(G-15234)
EXPRESS LLC
4122 N Harlem Ave (60706-1257)
PHONE.................................708 453-0566
EMP: 30 **Publicly Held**
SIC: 5621 2329 Womens Clothing Stores
HQ: Express, Llc
 1 Express Dr
 Columbus OH 43230
 800 474-7000

(G-15235)
GO TO STEEL INC (PA)
7625 W Norridge St (60706-3348)
PHONE.................................773 814-3017
Jerzy Krowiak, *President*
EMP: 3
SALES (est): 442.4K **Privately Held**
SIC: 3441 Fabricated structural metal

(G-15236)
HOT TOPIC INC
4104 N Harlem Ave Ste 132 (60706-1244)
PHONE.................................708 453-1216
EMP: 3 **Privately Held**
SIC: 2326 Men's & boys' work clothing
HQ: Hot Topic, Inc.
 18305 San Jose Ave
 City Of Industry CA 91748

(G-15237)
IGGYS AUTO PARTS
7230 W Montrose Ave (60706-1217)
PHONE.................................708 452-9790
Mike Ignoffo, *Owner*
EMP: 10
SALES (est): 822.3K **Privately Held**
SIC: 3714 5531 Motor vehicle parts & accessories; automobile & truck equipment & parts

(G-15238)
JOSEPH RINGELSTEIN
Also Called: Gamma Quality
4110 1/2 N Octavia Ave (60706-1208)
P.O. Box 56356, Chicago (60656-0356)
PHONE.................................708 955-7467
Joseph Ringelstein, *Owner*
EMP: 3
SALES (est): 162.9K **Privately Held**
SIC: 3829 Medical diagnostic systems, nuclear

(G-15239)
MAJOR WIRE INCORPORATED
7014 W Cullom Ave (60706-1397)
PHONE.................................708 457-0121
Kenneth G Michonski, *President*
Lynn Stepanovic, *Technology*
Donald Michonski, *Director*
Martin Michonski, *Director*
EMP: 10
SQ FT: 13,600
SALES (est): 1.7MM **Privately Held**
WEB: www.majorwire.com
SIC: 3357 3694 3315 Nonferrous wire-drawing & insulating; engine electrical equipment; wire & fabricated wire products

(G-15240)
MAKRAY MANUFACTURING COMPANY (PA)
4400 N Harlem Ave (60706-4774)
PHONE.................................708 456-7100
Paul Makray Jr, *President*
Patty Van Derpluym, *Persnl Mgr*
Christine Brownstein, *Admin Sec*
▲ **EMP:** 36
SQ FT: 100,000
SALES (est): 14.5MM **Privately Held**
WEB: www.makray.com
SIC: 3089 3544 Injection molded finished plastic products; special dies, tools, jigs & fixtures

(G-15241)
NATIONAL PUBLISHING COMPANY
Also Called: National Locksmith Magazine
7330 W Montrose Ave (60706-1158)
PHONE.................................630 837-2044
EMP: 10
SALES (est): 1.3MM **Privately Held**
SIC: 2721 Magazine Publisher

(G-15242)
OLTENIA INC
4905 N Opal Ave (60706-3219)
PHONE.................................773 987-2888
EMP: 3
SALES (est): 184.7K **Privately Held**
SIC: 2421 Flooring (dressed lumber), softwood

(G-15243)
SIGNA DEVELOPMENT GROUP INC (PA)
4641 N Oriole Ave (60706-4538)
PHONE.................................773 418-4506
John Signa, *President*
EMP: 2
SALES: 458.5K **Privately Held**
SIC: 3448 1541 1542 7389 Buildings, portable: prefabricated metal; prefabricated building erection, industrial; commercial & office buildings, renovation & repair;

(G-15244)
TESKO WELDING & MFG CO
Also Called: Tesko Enterprises
7350 W Montrose Ave (60706-1158)
PHONE.................................708 452-0045
Zbigniew Skoniecny, *President*
Theresa Borys, *Vice Pres*
Barbara Skoniecny, *Treasurer*
Maggie Adames, *Executive Asst*
Stella Skoniecny, *Admin Sec*
EMP: 70 **EST:** 1956
SQ FT: 53,000
SALES (est): 10.9MM **Privately Held**
WEB: www.teskoenterprises.com
SIC: 2542 2514 3498 Fixtures, store: except wood; showcases (not refrigerated) except wood; household furniture: upholstered on metal frames; fabricated pipe & fittings

(G-15245)
TRANSFORMER MANUFACTURERS INC
Also Called: TMI
7051 W Wilson Ave (60706-4784)
PHONE.................................708 457-1200
Alec K Gianaras Sr, *Ch of Bd*
Alexander Gianaras Jr, *President*
Alexander A Gianaras Jr, *President*
Viena P Gianaras, *Vice Pres*
Marin Marolli, *Chief Engr*
▲ **EMP:** 20
SQ FT: 25,000
SALES (est): 4.8MM **Privately Held**
WEB: www.tmitransformers.com
SIC: 3612 3825 3677 3621 Specialty transformers; instruments to measure electricity; electronic coils, transformers & other inductors; motors & generators

Norris City
White County

(G-15246)
B & B TANK TRUCK CONSTRUCTION (PA)
Also Called: Eastern Services
760 Us Highway 45 (62869-3001)
P.O. Box 276 (62869-0276)
PHONE.................................618 378-3337
William R Becker, *President*
William Becker, *President*
Phillys Becker, *Treasurer*
EMP: 10
SQ FT: 3,000
SALES (est): 2.1MM **Privately Held**
SIC: 1389 Acidizing wells; haulage, oil field; pumping of oil & gas wells; servicing oil & gas wells

(G-15247)
CATERPILLAR GLOBAL MINING LLC
635 Il Highway 1 (62869-3417)
PHONE.................................618 378-3441
Carrier Mills, *Manager*
EMP: 25
SALES (corp-wide): 53.8B **Publicly Held**
WEB: www.cat.com
SIC: 3531 Construction machinery
HQ: Caterpillar Global Mining Llc
 1118 Rawson Ave
 South Milwaukee WI 53172
 414 768-4000

(G-15248)
D R WALTERS
65 County Road 300 N (62869-3844)
PHONE.................................618 926-6337
D R Walters, *Principal*
EMP: 3
SALES (est): 305.7K **Privately Held**
SIC: 3131 Rands

(G-15249)
FABICK MINING LLC
635 Illinois Highway 1 (62869)
PHONE.................................618 982-9000
EMP: 12 **EST:** 2014
SALES (est): 1.4MM **Privately Held**
SIC: 1231 Anthracite Mining

(G-15250)
KINOCO INC
1000 County Road 300 E (62869-3163)
PHONE.................................618 378-3802
Richard Kingston, *President*
EMP: 5
SALES (est): 426.5K **Privately Held**
SIC: 1381 Drilling oil & gas wells

(G-15251)
VILLAGERS VOICE
103 E Main St (62869-1504)
PHONE.................................618 378-3094
Black Paul, *President*
EMP: 4 **EST:** 2014
SALES (est): 161.3K **Privately Held**
WEB: www.thevillagersvoice.com
SIC: 2711 Newspapers, publishing & printing

(G-15252)
WILLIAM R BECKER
Also Called: Brent Pumps Supply
760 Route 45 N (62869)
P.O. Box 276 (62869-0276)
PHONE.................................618 378-3337
William R Becker, *Owner*
Phyllis Becker, *Corp Secy*
EMP: 15
SQ FT: 3,000
SALES (est): 1MM **Privately Held**
SIC: 1311 5084 Crude petroleum production; oil well machinery, equipment & supplies

North Aurora
Kane County

(G-15253)
ABELEI INC
194 Alder Dr (60542-1485)
PHONE.................................630 859-1410
Karen R Criss, *President*
Marcia Criss, *Vice Pres*
EMP: 10
SQ FT: 12,000
SALES (est): 3.7MM **Privately Held**
SIC: 5149 2099 2087 Seasonings, sauces & extracts; food preparations; flavoring extracts & syrups

(G-15254)
ARCH PRINTING
710 Morton Ave (60542)
PHONE.................................630 896-6610
Tony Arch, *Owner*
Mary Arch, *Co-Owner*
EMP: 5 **EST:** 2013
SALES: 500K **Privately Held**
SIC: 2759 Screen printing

(G-15255)
AURORA PACKING COMPANY INC
125 S Grant St (60542-1603)
P.O. Box 209 (60542-0209)
PHONE.................................630 897-0551
Marvin Fagel, *Ch of Bd*
Mike Edmeier, *Manager*
Don Tanis, *Executive*
Michael Fagel, *Admin Sec*
EMP: 250 **EST:** 1939
SQ FT: 105,000
SALES (est): 40.8MM **Privately Held**
WEB: www.aurorapacking.com
SIC: 2011 Boxed beef from meat slaughtered on site

(G-15256)
CALO CORPORATION
Also Called: Recora Company
197 Alder Dr (60542-1471)
PHONE.................................630 879-2202
Balan Menon, *President*
Rob Falls, *Engineer*
Steve Hinterlong, *Engineer*
EMP: 25 **EST:** 1946
SQ FT: 55,000
SALES (est): 4.4MM **Privately Held**
WEB: www.recora-co.com
SIC: 3613 Switches, electric power except snap, push button, etc.

(G-15257)
CON-TEMP CABINETS INC
201 Poplar Pl (60542-1406)
PHONE.................................630 892-7300
Joe Marino, *President*
Brett Doranski, *Vice Pres*
Ann Hodyl, *Office Mgr*
EMP: 15
SQ FT: 12,500
SALES (est): 1.3MM **Privately Held**
WEB: www.con-tempcabinets.com
SIC: 2541 2434 Cabinets, except refrigerated: show, display, etc.: wood; wood kitchen cabinets

(G-15258)
DART CONTAINER CORP ILLINOIS
310 Evergreen Dr (60542-1702)
P.O. Box 500, Mason MI (48854-0500)
PHONE.................................630 896-4631
Robert C Dart, *CEO*
James D Lammers, *President*
Margo Burrage, *Corp Comm Staff*
Ron Haldeman, *Director*
EMP: 200 **EST:** 1966
SQ FT: 50,000
SALES (est): 35.3MM **Privately Held**
WEB: www.dart.biz
SIC: 3086 Cups & plates, foamed plastic

(G-15259)
EARTHGRAINS
321 Airport Rd (60542-1476)
PHONE.................................630 859-8782

GEOGRAPHIC SECTION

Richard Kline, *Executive*
EMP: 3
SALES (est): 221K **Privately Held**
SIC: 2032 Beans, baked without meat: packaged in cans, jars, etc.

(G-15260)
FAR WEST PRINT SOLUTIONS LLC
714 Fairfield Way (60542-8918)
PHONE...............................630 879-9500
Rebecca Dhuse, *Principal*
EMP: 6
SALES (est): 507.4K **Privately Held**
WEB: www.farwestprint.com
SIC: 2752 Commercial printing, offset

(G-15261)
GENEVA CONSTRUCTION COMPANY
216 Butterfield Rd (60542-1316)
PHONE...............................630 892-6536
Don Antich, *Branch Mgr*
EMP: 5
SALES (corp-wide): 4.2MM **Privately Held**
SIC: 1611 2951 Highway & street paving contractor; grading; asphalt paving mixtures & blocks
PA: Geneva Construction Company
1350 Aurora Ave
Aurora IL 60505
630 892-4357

(G-15262)
HARDSCAPE OUTPOST LLC
326 Butterfield Rd (60542-1318)
PHONE...............................630 551-6105
Mark R Schmitt, *Principal*
EMP: 3
SALES (est): 193.8K **Privately Held**
SIC: 2951 Asphalt paving mixtures & blocks

(G-15263)
HARNERS BAKERY RESTAURANT
10 W State St (60542-1620)
PHONE...............................630 892-5545
Darryl Harner, *President*
Sue Lavford, *General Mgr*
Karen Johnson, *Manager*
EMP: 90
SQ FT: 6,000
SALES (est): 2MM **Privately Held**
WEB: www.harnersbakery.com
SIC: 5812 5461 2051 Restaurant, family: independent; ice cream stands or dairy bars; bakeries; bread, cake & related products

(G-15264)
IYA FOODS LLC
Also Called: Naija Foods
348 Smoketree Bsn Dr (60542-1720)
PHONE...............................630 854-7107
Oluwatoyin Kolawole, *President*
EMP: 3
SALES (est): 178.8K **Privately Held**
SIC: 5149 2033 5141 Natural & organic foods; specialty food items; tomato products: packaged in cans, jars, etc.; groceries, general line

(G-15265)
JANSSEN AVENUE BOYS INC
Also Called: Fast Color
200 Alder Dr A (60542-1400)
PHONE...............................630 627-0202
Angela Muschong, *President*
Joe Muschong, *General Mgr*
Jeffrey Vitter, *Vice Pres*
EMP: 5
SQ FT: 3,700
SALES: 500K **Privately Held**
SIC: 2752 Commercial printing, offset

(G-15266)
LAFARGE NORTH AMERICA INC
105 Conco St (60542-1601)
PHONE...............................630 892-1616
Jason McNelis, *Plant Mgr*
EMP: 29
SALES (corp-wide): 4.5B **Privately Held**
SIC: 3241 Cement, hydraulic

HQ: Lafarge North America Inc.
8700 W Bryn Mawr Ave
Chicago IL 60631
773 372-1000

(G-15267)
LEGGETT & PLATT INCORPORATED
241 Airport Rd (60542-1816)
PHONE...............................630 801-0609
James Zaerr, *Branch Mgr*
EMP: 30
SQ FT: 106,000
SALES (corp-wide): 4.7B **Publicly Held**
WEB: www.leggett.com
SIC: 2515 2511 Bedsprings, assembled; wood household furniture
PA: Leggett & Platt, Incorporated
1 Leggett Rd
Carthage MO 64836
417 358-8131

(G-15268)
PENNASIS GROUP LLC
610 Oak Crest Dr (60542-9007)
PHONE...............................630 699-8390
H Hasana A Sisco, *Mng Member*
EMP: 6
SALES (est): 290.9K **Privately Held**
SIC: 1481 Nonmetallic minerals development & test boring

(G-15269)
PENTAIR FLOW TECHNOLOGIES LLC
Also Called: Aurora Pump
800 Airport Rd (60542-1403)
PHONE...............................630 859-7000
Jesus Cidello, *Branch Mgr*
EMP: 200 **Privately Held**
SIC: 3561 Pumps & pumping equipment
HQ: Pentair Flow Technologies, Llc
5500 Wayzata Blvd Ste 900
Minneapolis MN 55416
763 545-1730

(G-15270)
PERFTECH INC
251 Airport Rd (60542-1816)
PHONE...............................630 554-0010
Gerald Sullivan, *President*
Ken Gill, *Chief Mktg Ofcr*
Dave Pfeiffer, *Admin Sec*
▲ EMP: 31
SQ FT: 57,000
SALES (est): 4.8MM **Privately Held**
SIC: 2761 Manifold business forms

(G-15271)
PILLAR ENTERPRISES INC
121 S Lincolnway Ste 103 (60542-5117)
PHONE...............................630 966-2566
Raymond Pillar, *President*
EMP: 3
SALES (est): 260K **Privately Held**
SIC: 3299 Ceramic fiber

(G-15272)
PRECISE STAMPING INC
Also Called: Precise Lser Waterjet Stamping
202 Poplar Pl (60542-1407)
PHONE...............................630 897-6477
Christopher Goblet, *President*
Mary Brown, *Manager*
EMP: 28
SQ FT: 20,000
SALES: 3MM **Privately Held**
SIC: 3469 3312 Stamping metal for the trade; tool & die steel

(G-15273)
RECORA LLC
197 Alder Dr (60542-1471)
PHONE...............................630 879-2202
Rob Falls, *Engineer*
Steve Hinterlong, *Engineer*
Balan Menon, *Mng Member*
Sophia Meza, *Executive*
EMP: 2
SALES (est): 382.9K **Privately Held**
SIC: 3613 Switches, electric power except snap, push button, etc.

(G-15274)
SERVICE PALLET LLC
500 Overland Dr (60542-1839)
PHONE...............................708 458-9100
Frank Kratz, *Opers Mgr*
Dan Laughlin, *Sales Staff*
Jim Motsch, *Sales Staff*
Michael Soper, *Mng Member*
EMP: 7
SALES: 4.7MM **Privately Held**
SIC: 2448 Pallets, wood

(G-15275)
SOFRITO FOODS LLC
Also Called: Fillo's Frijoles
181 S Lincolnway (60542-1609)
P.O. Box 513, Geneva (60134-0513)
PHONE...............................224 535-9252
Daniel Caballero, *Mng Member*
EMP: 3
SQ FT: 100
SALES: 300K **Privately Held**
SIC: 2032 Canned specialties

(G-15276)
SOUND SEAL INC
IAC Acoustics
401 Airport Rd (60542-1818)
PHONE...............................630 844-1999
Mark Rubino, *General Mgr*
EMP: 31 **Privately Held**
SIC: 3625 Noise control equipment
HQ: Sound Seal, Inc.
50 Hp Almgren Dr
Agawam MA 01001
413 789-1770

(G-15277)
SPECIALTY BOX CORP
366 Smoketree Bsn Dr Pa (60542-1720)
PHONE...............................630 897-7278
Alan Vagoren, *President*
Bonnie L Zagoren, *Admin Sec*
EMP: 13
SALES (est): 1.4MM **Privately Held**
WEB: www.specialty-box.com
SIC: 2441 2657 2653 Boxes, wood; folding paperboard boxes; corrugated & solid fiber boxes

(G-15278)
STEPHENS PIPE & STEEL LLC
603 Oak Crest Dr (60542-9002)
PHONE...............................800 451-2612
EMP: 41 **Privately Held**
SIC: 5051 3315 3523 Pipe & tubing, steel; chain link fencing; cattle feeding, handling & watering equipment
HQ: Stephens Pipe & Steel, Llc
2224 E Highway 619
Russell Springs KY 42642
270 866-3331

(G-15279)
TELEHEALTH SENSORS LLC
197 Alder Dr (60542-1471)
PHONE...............................630 879-3101
Menon Balan, *President*
EMP: 25
SALES (est): 2.6MM **Privately Held**
WEB: www.telehealthsensors.com
SIC: 3674 Infrared sensors, solid state

(G-15280)
TUU DUC LE INC (PA)
Also Called: Aurora Orthopedic Laboratories
110 John St (60542-1632)
PHONE...............................630 897-6363
Tuu D Lee, *President*
EMP: 5
SQ FT: 2,400
SALES (est): 750K **Privately Held**
SIC: 3842 Limbs, artificial; braces, orthopedic

(G-15281)
VINYL LIFE NORTH
661 Dewig Ct (60542-9149)
PHONE...............................630 906-9686
Emil Kaderabek, *Owner*
EMP: 3
SALES (est): 211.9K **Privately Held**
SIC: 2599 2512 Bar, restaurant & cafeteria furniture; upholstered household furniture

North Barrington
Lake County

(G-15282)
COLUMBIAN HOME PRODUCTS LLC (PA)
Also Called: Snow River Products
404 N Rand Rd (60010-1496)
PHONE...............................847 307-8600
Brian Sinclair, *Plant Mgr*
Ray Akhavein, *Opers Staff*
Robert Prokuski, *CFO*
Dick Ryan, *Mng Member*
Rick Ryan, *Info Tech Dir*
◆ EMP: 120
SALES (est): 24.1MM **Privately Held**
WEB: www.columbianhp.com
SIC: 3469 Cooking ware, porcelain enameled

(G-15283)
DANIEL ZIMMER ASSOCIATES
77 Hillburn Ln (60010-6925)
PHONE...............................847 697-9393
Paul Daniel, *Owner*
EMP: 10
SALES (est): 1MM **Privately Held**
SIC: 3842 Orthopedic appliances

(G-15284)
HEALTHCARE LABELS INC
245 Honey Lake Ct (60010-6534)
PHONE...............................847 382-3993
Ronald F Gagnier, *President*
Constance Gagnier, *Corp Secy*
EMP: 19
SALES (est): 1.7MM **Privately Held**
SIC: 2759 Labels & seals: printing

(G-15285)
HOW TO BE GOOD FOR SANTA INC
261 Kimberly Rd (60010-2148)
PHONE...............................281 961-4002
Jordan Weiner, *Principal*
Lauren A Weiner, *Principal*
EMP: 5
SALES (est): 278.1K **Privately Held**
WEB: www.howtobegoodforsanta.com
SIC: 2731 2741 Book publishing; miscellaneous publishing

(G-15286)
HUFF & PUFF INDUSTRIES LTD
125 Arrowhead Ln (60010-6970)
PHONE...............................847 381-8255
Elaine Silets, *President*
EMP: 3
SALES (est): 336.9K **Privately Held**
SIC: 3944 Railroad models: toy & hobby

(G-15287)
MURRAY INC (PA)
Also Called: Medical Murray
400 N Rand Rd (60010-1496)
PHONE...............................847 620-7990
Phillip M Leopold, *President*
Samantha Brandel, *Opers Staff*
Andrew R Leopold, *Admin Sec*
EMP: 35
SQ FT: 10,000
SALES (est): 24MM **Privately Held**
SIC: 3841 8733 Medical instruments & equipment, blood & bone work; medical research

(G-15288)
MY KONJAC SPONGE INC
300 Lake View Pl (60010-1613)
PHONE...............................630 345-3653
Jimmy Setyo, *President*
Sandra Setyo, *Sales Mgr*
EMP: 10
SALES (est): 701.9K **Privately Held**
SIC: 2392 Washcloths & bath mitts: made from purchased materials

(G-15289)
TRADE-MARK COFFEE CORPORATION (PA)
8 Lakeside Ln (60010-6954)
PHONE...............................847 382-4200

North Chicago - Lake County (G-15290)

Fax: 847 382-4229
EMP: 12
SALES (est): 1.5MM Privately Held
SIC: 2095 Mfg Roasted Coffee

North Chicago
Lake County

(G-15290)
ABBOTT HEALTH PRODUCTS INC (HQ)
100 Abbott Park Rd (60064-3502)
PHONE.................847 937-6100
Miles D White, *CEO*
Thomas C Freyman, *CFO*
▲ EMP: 100 EST: 1970
SQ FT: 7,500
SALES (est): 46.3MM
SALES (corp-wide): 31.9B Publicly Held
SIC: 2834 Pharmaceutical preparations
PA: Abbott Laboratories
    100 Abbott Park Rd
    Abbott Park IL 60064
    224 667-6100

(G-15291)
ABBOTT LABORATORIES
Also Called: Receiving D84v K2 Complex
Mrtn Lthr Kng Dr Rr 41 (60064)
PHONE.................847 937-6100
EMP: 628
SALES (corp-wide): 31.9B Publicly Held
SIC: 2834 Pharmaceutical preparations
PA: Abbott Laboratories
    100 Abbott Park Rd
    Abbott Park IL 60064
    224 667-6100

(G-15292)
ABBOTT LABORATORIES
Bldg Ap 52 200 Ab Dept 36 (60064)
PHONE.................847 938-4196
Margaret Horner, *Engineer*
Glenn Roberts, *Manager*
Philip Geovanos, *Manager*
Charles Slattery, *Manager*
Peggy Rastovac, *Senior Mgr*
EMP: 60
SALES (corp-wide): 31.9B Publicly Held
SIC: 2834 Pharmaceutical preparations
PA: Abbott Laboratories
    100 Abbott Park Rd
    Abbott Park IL 60064
    224 667-6100

(G-15293)
ABBOTT LABORATORIES
1401 Sheridan Rd (60064-4000)
PHONE.................847 932-7900
John Langraf, *Branch Mgr*
EMP: 617
SALES (corp-wide): 31.9B Publicly Held
SIC: 2834 3844 2835 3841 Pharmaceutical preparations; X-ray apparatus & tubes; in vitro & in vivo diagnostic substances; surgical & medical instruments; analytical instruments; dry, condensed, evaporated dairy products
PA: Abbott Laboratories
    100 Abbott Park Rd
    Abbott Park IL 60064
    224 667-6100

(G-15294)
ABBOTT LABORATORIES
200 Abbott Park Rd (60064-3537)
PHONE.................847 937-6100
Cheryl Syslo, *Branch Mgr*
Jonathon Hamilton, *Director*
EMP: 5
SALES (corp-wide): 31.9B Publicly Held
SIC: 2834 3841 Pharmaceutical preparations; diagnostic apparatus, medical
PA: Abbott Laboratories
    100 Abbott Park Rd
    Abbott Park IL 60064
    224 667-6100

(G-15295)
ABBOTT LABORATORIES INTL CO (HQ)
100 Abbott Park Rd (60064-3500)
PHONE.................847 937-6100
Miles D White, *CEO*
EMP: 16
SALES (est): 14.2MM
SALES (corp-wide): 31.9B Publicly Held
SIC: 2834 Pharmaceutical preparations
PA: Abbott Laboratories
    100 Abbott Park Rd
    Abbott Park IL 60064
    224 667-6100

(G-15296)
ABBOTT LABORATORIES PCF LTD (HQ)
100 Abbott Park Rd (60064-3500)
P.O. Box 3020 (60064-9320)
PHONE.................847 937-6100
Miles D White, *CEO*
Robert Parkinson Jr, *President*
Frank Holas, *Principal*
Jason Staples, *Counsel*
Richard Ashley, *Exec VP*
◆ EMP: 15
SALES (est): 15.6MM
SALES (corp-wide): 31.9B Publicly Held
SIC: 2834 Pharmaceutical preparations
PA: Abbott Laboratories
    100 Abbott Park Rd
    Abbott Park IL 60064
    224 667-6100

(G-15297)
ABBOTT LABORATORIES SVCS CORP (HQ)
1 Abbott Park Rd (60064)
PHONE.................708 937-6100
Duane L Burnham, *Ch of Bd*
EMP: 4
SALES (est): 228.8K
SALES (corp-wide): 31.9B Publicly Held
SIC: 2834 Pharmaceutical preparations
PA: Abbott Laboratories
    100 Abbott Park Rd
    Abbott Park IL 60064
    224 667-6100

(G-15298)
ABBOTT-ABBVIE MULTIPLE EMPLOYE
100 Abbott Park Rd (60064-3502)
PHONE.................847 473-2053
EMP: 3
SALES (est): 154.9K Privately Held
SIC: 2834 Pharmaceutical preparations

(G-15299)
ABBVIE ENDOCRINOLOGY INC
Also Called: Pharmacy Solutions
1 N Waukegan Rd Apt 5ne (60064-1802)
PHONE.................888 857-0668
EMP: 19 EST: 2014
SALES (est): 2.3MM
SALES (corp-wide): 33.2B Publicly Held
SIC: 2834 Pharmaceutical preparations
PA: Abbvie Inc.
    1 N Waukegan Rd
    North Chicago IL 60064
    847 932-7900

(G-15300)
ABBVIE INC (PA)
1 N Waukegan Rd (60064-1802)
P.O. Box 210075, Dallas TX (75211-0075)
PHONE.................847 932-7900
Richard A Gonzalez, *Ch of Bd*
Michael E Severino, *President*
Azita Saleki-Gerhardt, *Exec VP*
Nicholas Donoghoe, *Senior VP*
Jeffrey R Stewart, *Senior VP*
◆ EMP: 230
SALES: 33.2B Publicly Held
SIC: 2834 2836 Druggists' preparations (pharmaceuticals); biological products, except diagnostic

(G-15301)
ABBVIE INC
1401 Sheridan Rd (60064-1803)
PHONE.................847 932-7900
Miles D White, *Ch of Bd*
James Foster, *Fire Chief*
John Glade, *Chief*
John Machak, *Opers Staff*
Jonathan Stikl, *Opers Staff*
EMP: 59
SALES (corp-wide): 33.2B Publicly Held
SIC: 2834 Druggists' preparations (pharmaceuticals)
PA: Abbott Laboratories
    100 Abbott Park Rd
    Abbott Park IL 60064
    224 667-6100

(G-15302)
ABBVIE INC
1675 Lakeside Ave J23 (60064)
PHONE.................847 938-2042
Georgina McLeod, *Principal*
James Erker, *Branch Mgr*
Arminda Montero, *Program Mgr*
Robert Hook, *Manager*
Gita Malladi, *Manager*
EMP: 7
SALES (corp-wide): 33.2B Publicly Held
SIC: 2834 Pharmaceutical preparations
PA: Abbvie Inc.
    1 N Waukegan Rd
    North Chicago IL 60064
    847 932-7900

(G-15303)
ABBVIE RESPIRATORY LLC
100 Abbott Park Rd (60064-3502)
PHONE.................847 937-6100
EMP: 3
SALES (est): 178.1K
SALES (corp-wide): 33.2B Publicly Held
SIC: 2834 Drugs acting on the respiratory system
PA: Abbvie Inc.
    1 N Waukegan Rd
    North Chicago IL 60064
    847 932-7900

(G-15304)
ABBVIE US LLC
1 N Waukegan Rd (60064-1802)
PHONE.................800 255-5162
Richard A Gonzalez, *CEO*
Michael Severino, *Vice Chairman*
Samantha Groeninger, *Counsel*
Laura J Schumacher, *Exec VP*
Laura Schumacher, *Exec VP*
▲ EMP: 6
SALES (est): 32MM
SALES (corp-wide): 33.2B Publicly Held
SIC: 2836 2834 Biological products, except diagnostic; pharmaceutical preparations
PA: Abbvie Inc.
    1 N Waukegan Rd
    North Chicago IL 60064
    847 932-7900

(G-15305)
ACM INC
2254 Commonwealth Ave (60064-3304)
PHONE.................847 473-1991
Art Zrimsek, *President*
Rita Zrimsek, *Corp Secy*
Martin Christoffel, *Vice Pres*
EMP: 9
SQ FT: 7,000
SALES (est): 732K Privately Held
SIC: 2851 Paints & allied products

(G-15306)
AEROPHARM TECHNOLOGY LLC
100 Abbott Park Rd (60064-3502)
PHONE.................847 937-6100
Chadwick Munz, *Principal*
EMP: 4 EST: 2010
SALES (est): 309K
SALES (corp-wide): 33.2B Publicly Held
SIC: 2834 Proprietary drug products
PA: Abbvie Inc.
    1 N Waukegan Rd
    North Chicago IL 60064
    847 932-7900

(G-15307)
BLACKJACK CUSTOMS
2920 Frontenac St (60064-3421)
PHONE.................847 361-5225
Quentin Jackson, *Owner*
EMP: 5
SALES (est): 321.5K Privately Held
SIC: 3711 Automobile assembly, including specialty automobiles

(G-15308)
C & M RECYCLING INC
1600 Morrow Ave (60064-3224)
PHONE.................847 578-1066
Michael Braus, *President*
Jennifer Turchany, *Human Res Dir*
Carole Braus, *Manager*
Carole A Braus, *Admin Sec*
EMP: 25
SALES (est): 9.2MM Privately Held
WEB: www.cmrecycle.com
SIC: 5093 4953 3341 2611 Waste paper; ferrous metal scrap & waste; refuse systems; secondary nonferrous metals; pulp mills

(G-15309)
CG NUTRITIONALS INC
100 Abbott Park Rd (60064-3502)
PHONE.................224 667-6100
EMP: 3
SALES (est): 166.5K
SALES (corp-wide): 31.9B Publicly Held
SIC: 2834 Pharmaceutical preparations
PA: Abbott Laboratories
    100 Abbott Park Rd
    Abbott Park IL 60064
    224 667-6100

(G-15310)
EMCO CHEMICAL DISTRIBUTORS INC
2100 Commonwealth Ave (60064-2725)
PHONE.................262 427-0400
Edward Polen, *President*
Rose Lipke, *Vice Pres*
Joe Lukanich, *Vice Pres*
Randy Schwab, *Vice Pres*
Dale Tebbe, *VP Opers*
EMP: 150
SALES (corp-wide): 473.8MM Privately Held
WEB: www.emcochem.com
SIC: 5169 7389 2819 Industrial chemicals; packaging & labeling services; industrial inorganic chemicals
PA: Emco Chemical Distributors, Inc.
    8601 95th St
    Pleasant Prairie WI 53158
    262 427-0400

(G-15311)
F K PATTERN & FOUNDRY COMPANY
1400 Morrow Ave (60064-3220)
PHONE.................847 578-5260
Frank Konigseder, *Principal*
EMP: 4 EST: 2008
SALES (est): 507.2K Privately Held
WEB: www.fkfoundries.com
SIC: 3354 Aluminum extruded products

(G-15312)
GILLETTE COMPANY
3500 16th St (60064-1599)
PHONE.................847 689-3111
Vernon Murdock, *Executive*
EMP: 65
SALES (corp-wide): 67.6B Publicly Held
WEB: www.gillette.com
SIC: 3421 2844 3951 2899 Razor blades & razors; toilet preparations; pens & mechanical pencils; correction fluid
HQ: The Gillette Company
    1 Gillette Park
    Boston MA 02127
    617 421-7000

(G-15313)
GOELITZ CONFECTIONERY COMPANY
1501 Morrow Ave (60064-3200)
PHONE.................847 689-2225
Herman G Rowland Sr, *Ch of Bd*
William H Kelley, *President*
EMP: 180 EST: 1898
SQ FT: 96,000
SALES (est): 26.2MM
SALES (corp-wide): 148.1MM Privately Held
SIC: 2064 Jellybeans
PA: Jelly Belly Candy Company
    1 Jelly Belly Ln
    Fairfield CA 94533
    707 428-2800

GEOGRAPHIC SECTION

(G-15314)
HMT MANUFACTURING INC
2323 Commonwealth Ave (60064-3390)
PHONE.....................847 473-2310
Burton Bucher, *President*
Ryan Bennet, *Division Mgr*
Glen J Bennett, *Plant Mgr*
Tim Bucher, *CFO*
Jessie Bennett, *Technology*
▲ **EMP:** 25
SQ FT: 30,500
SALES (est): 6MM **Privately Held**
SIC: 3559 3089 Plastics working machinery; laminating of plastic

(G-15315)
JELLY BELLY CANDY COMPANY
1501 Morrow Ave (60064-3221)
PHONE.....................847 689-2225
Mary Plebanek, *Manager*
Konstantin Kostadinov, *Technology*
EMP: 200
SALES (corp-wide): 148.1MM **Privately Held**
WEB: www.jellybelly.com
SIC: 5441 2064 Candy; candy & other confectionery products
PA: Jelly Belly Candy Company
1 Jelly Belly Ln
Fairfield CA 94533
707 428-2800

(G-15316)
LIBERTY COACH INC
1400 Morrow Ave (60064-3220)
PHONE.....................847 578-4600
Kurt Konigseder, *Corp Secy*
Frank Konigseder, *Vice Pres*
Thomas Hodgson, *Vice Pres*
Konigseder Frank, *Treasurer*
Carol Quinn, *Human Resources*
EMP: 68 **EST:** 1972
SQ FT: 12,000
SALES (est): 15.7MM **Privately Held**
SIC: 3711 3716 Motor buses, except trackless trollies, assembly of; motor homes

(G-15317)
NORTH CHICAGO IRON WORKS INC
1305 Morrow Ave (60064-3217)
P.O. Box 813 (60064-0813)
PHONE.....................847 689-2000
Mary Elaine Gallagher, *President*
John T Gallagher, *Vice Pres*
Mark Gallagher, *Vice Pres*
Jean Marie Humbrecht, *Vice Pres*
Mary Gallagher, *VP Purch*
EMP: 25
SQ FT: 12,000
SALES (est): 5.2MM **Privately Held**
WEB: www.nciron.com
SIC: 1791 3441 3446 Iron work, structural; fabricated structural metal; architectural metalwork

(G-15318)
NORTHSHORE GARDENS LTD
2925 22nd Pl (60064-2901)
PHONE.....................847 672-4391
Anastacio Montoya, *President*
Juan Montoya, *Vice Pres*
EMP: 5
SALES (est): 68.5K **Privately Held**
SIC: 0782 3251 Landscape contractors; paving brick, clay

(G-15319)
PROCTER & GAMBLE CO
3500 16th St (60064-1513)
PHONE.....................847 936-4621
Scott Mecher, *Plant Mgr*
EMP: 5
SALES (est): 690K **Privately Held**
SIC: 2676 Sanitary paper products

(G-15320)
R MADERITE INC
2306 Commonwealth Ave (60064-3306)
PHONE.....................847 785-0875
Rebecca Mellinger, *President*
EMP: 5
SQ FT: 12,000
SALES (est): 702K **Privately Held**
SIC: 2511 Wood household furniture

(G-15321)
STEVE O INC
Also Called: Steve Olson Printing & Design
1550 Green Bay Rd (60064-1522)
PHONE.....................847 473-4466
Steve Olson, *President*
Deborah Olson, *Corp Secy*
Darius Haring, *Graphic Designe*
EMP: 5 **EST:** 1941
SQ FT: 4,400
SALES (est): 902.3K **Privately Held**
WEB: www.steveoprinting.com
SIC: 2752 Commercial printing, offset

(G-15322)
TI INTERNATIONAL LTD
2260 Commonwealth Ave (60064-3304)
P.O. Box 670 (60064-0670)
PHONE.....................847 689-0233
Judith Krotz, *President*
EMP: 8 **EST:** 1914
SQ FT: 9,500
SALES (est): 950K **Privately Held**
SIC: 3728 Aircraft assemblies, subassemblies & parts

(G-15323)
WEAKLEY PRINTING & SIGN SHOP
1550 Green Bay Rd (60064-1522)
PHONE.....................847 473-4466
Michael Weakley, *President*
EMP: 5 **EST:** 1949
SQ FT: 5,400
SALES (est): 430K **Privately Held**
SIC: 2752 2759 3993 3953 Commercial printing, offset; letterpress printing; signs & advertising specialties; marking devices; typesetting; bookbinding & related work

(G-15324)
WESTROCK CP LLC
1900 Foss Park Ave (60064-2232)
PHONE.....................847 689-4200
Gordon Gerber, *Branch Mgr*
EMP: 230
SALES (corp-wide): 18.2B **Publicly Held**
WEB: www.westrock.com
SIC: 2653 3412 Boxes, corrugated: made from purchased materials; metal barrels, drums & pails
HQ: Westrock Cp, Llc
1000 Abernathy Rd Ste 125
Atlanta GA 30328

(G-15325)
WINNETKA SIGN CO INC
3338 Berwyn Ave Unit 93 (60064-3418)
PHONE.....................847 473-9378
Tom Gerhart, *President*
EMP: 4
SALES (est): 344.2K **Privately Held**
SIC: 5099 2759 Containers: glass, metal or plastic; decals: printing

North Pekin
Tazewell County

(G-15326)
AMEREX CORPORATION
Getz Manufacturing
540 S Main St (61554-1165)
P.O. Box 81, Trussville AL (35173-0081)
PHONE.....................309 382-4389
Kevin Rednour, *Branch Mgr*
EMP: 20
SALES (corp-wide): 1.2B **Privately Held**
SIC: 3999 3829 3714 3711 Fire extinguishers, portable; measuring & controlling devices; motor vehicle parts & accessories; motor vehicles & car bodies
HQ: Amerex Corporation
7595 Gadsden Hwy
Trussville AL 35173
205 655-3271

(G-15327)
PEKIN WELDORS INC
1525 Edgewater Dr (61554-7823)
P.O. Box 442, Pekin (61555-0442)
PHONE.....................309 382-3627
James T Carter, *CEO*
Carol J Carter, *President*
Gerald W Carter, *Vice Pres*
EMP: 14
SQ FT: 15,000
SALES (est): 1.1MM **Privately Held**
SIC: 7692 7699 Automotive welding; welding equipment repair

Northbrook
Cook County

(G-15328)
22ND CENTURY MEDIA
60 Revere Dr (60062-1563)
PHONE.....................847 272-4565
John Zeddies, *Sales Dir*
Orland P Adam, *Director*
Jeff Schouten, *Legal Staff*
EMP: 8 **Privately Held**
SIC: 2711 Newspapers: publishing only, not printed on site
PA: 22nd Century Media
11516 W 183rd St U Sw 3
Orland Park IL 60467

(G-15329)
A M LEE INC
Also Called: Charles Selon Associates
2778 Dundee Rd (60062-2609)
PHONE.....................847 291-1777
Albert Lee, *President*
Madiz Lee, *Corp Secy*
EMP: 3
SQ FT: 1,500
SALES (est): 315.9K **Privately Held**
WEB: www.amleejeweler.com
SIC: 3911 5944 Jewelry, precious metal; jewelry, precious stones & precious metals

(G-15330)
ACME ALLIANCE LLC (HQ)
Also Called: Acmealliance
3610 Commercial Ave (60062-1823)
PHONE.....................847 272-9520
Simon Ontiveros, *Engineer*
Rachel Sylverne, *Controller*
Daniel Twait, *Asst Controller*
Maria Chavez, *Human Resources*
Mary Lorenz, *Program Mgr*
▲ **EMP:** 36
SQ FT: 75,000
SALES (est): 15.4MM
SALES (corp-wide): 45MM **Privately Held**
WEB: www.acmealliance.com
SIC: 3363 Aluminum die-castings
PA: Lovejoy Industries, Inc.
3610 Commercial Ave
Northbrook IL 60062
859 873-6828

(G-15331)
ACME DIE CASTING LLC
Also Called: Acme Alliance
3610 Commercial Ave (60062-1823)
PHONE.....................847 272-9520
Chris Vazzana, *Vice Pres*
Roy Dusell, *Controller*
Denise Decman, *Manager*
Cari Hemmerling, *Manager*
Jesus Martinez, *Manager*
▲ **EMP:** 4
SALES (est): 789.2K
SALES (corp-wide): 45MM **Privately Held**
SIC: 3363 3364 3369 3365 Aluminum die-castings; zinc & zinc-base alloy die-castings; nonferrous foundries; aluminum foundries
PA: Lovejoy Industries, Inc.
3610 Commercial Ave
Northbrook IL 60062
859 873-6828

(G-15332)
ADVANCED DIAMOND TECH INC
2100 Sanders Rd Ste 170 (60062-6199)
PHONE.....................815 293-0900
John D Yerger III, *President*
EMP: 21
SALES (est): 6.4MM **Privately Held**
SIC: 2819 Industrial inorganic chemicals

(G-15333)
AERO METALS ALLIANCE INC (HQ)
555 Skokie Blvd Ste 555 # 555 (60062-2854)
PHONE.....................225 236-1441
Steven Altheide, *Vice Pres*
EMP: 15
SALES (est): 29.2MM
SALES (corp-wide): 55.6MM **Privately Held**
SIC: 3444 Sheet metal specialties, not stamped

(G-15334)
AGROCHEM INC
Also Called: Nature's Touch
3703 Pebble Beach Rd (60062-3111)
PHONE.....................847 564-1304
Donald Arenberg, *President*
Betty Beller, *Corp Secy*
Donna Arenberg, *Vice Pres*
EMP: 11
SQ FT: 10,000
SALES (est): 990K **Privately Held**
SIC: 2879 8734 Plant hormones; soil conditioners; testing laboratories

(G-15335)
ALL GEAR INC
3014 Commercial Ave (60062-1913)
PHONE.....................847 564-9016
Thomas Daly, *President*
EMP: 4
SALES (est): 552.6K **Privately Held**
SIC: 2298 Rope, except asbestos & wire

(G-15336)
AMPLIVOX SOUND SYSTEMS LLC (PA)
Also Called: Amplivox Prtable Sound Systems
650 Anthony Trl Ste D (60062-2512)
PHONE.....................800 267-5486
Don Roth, *President*
Jim Bungard, *Vice Pres*
Larry Stotts, *Mfg Staff*
Joe Yim, *Controller*
Tony Gatz, *Accounts Mgr*
◆ **EMP:** 23 **EST:** 1995
SQ FT: 18,000
SALES: 5.3MM **Privately Held**
WEB: www.ampli.com
SIC: 3663 5065 3651 Amplifiers, RF power & IF; sound equipment, electronic; household audio & video equipment

(G-15337)
ASTELLAS PHARMA GLOBAL DEV INC
1 Astellas Way (60062-6111)
PHONE.....................224 205-8800
Dr Steven Ryder, *President*
Robin J McGarry, *Vice Pres*
Steve Knowles, *Treasurer*
Linda Friedman, *Admin Sec*
EMP: 163
SALES (est): 44.9MM **Privately Held**
SIC: 2834 Pharmaceutical preparations
HQ: Astellas Us Holding, Inc.
1 Astellas Way
Northbrook IL 60062

(G-15338)
ASTELLAS PHARMA INC
1 Astellas Way (60062-6111)
PHONE.....................800 695-4321
Jane Dahlen, *Counsel*
Steve Knowles, *Vice Pres*
Kevin O'Toole, *Vice Pres*
Ramona Rorig, *Project Mgr*
Kate Marshall, *Research*
EMP: 34 **Privately Held**
WEB: www.astellas.com
SIC: 2834 Pharmaceutical preparations
PA: Astellas Pharma Inc.
2-5-1, Nihombashihoncho
Chuo-Ku TKY 103-0

(G-15339)
ASTELLAS PHARMA US INC (DH)
1 Astellas Way (60062-6111)
PHONE.....................800 888-7704
Masao Yoshida, *President*
Shontelle Dodson, *Senior VP*

Northbrook - Cook County (G-15340) GEOGRAPHIC SECTION

Joseph Fleishaker, *Senior VP*
Susanne Gronen, *Senior VP*
David Abbott, *Vice Pres*
▲ **EMP:** 271
SQ FT: 140,000
SALES (est): 651.4MM **Privately Held**
SIC: 2834 Pharmaceutical preparations

(G-15340)
ASTELLAS SCNTFIC MED AFFIRS IN
1 Astellas Way (60062-6111)
PHONE.................................224 205-5452
Masao Yoshida, *President*
Stanley Bukofzer, *Vice Pres*
EMP: 200
SALES (est): 10.5MM **Privately Held**
SIC: 2834 Pharmaceutical preparations

(G-15341)
ASTELLAS US HOLDING INC (HQ)
1 Astellas Way (60062-6111)
PHONE.................................224 205-8800
Yoshihiko Hatanaka, *CEO*
Geoff Towle, *Vice Pres*
Edward Gomez, *Director*
Jace Nielsen, *Associate Dir*
Bernhardt G Zeiher, *Officer*
EMP: 50
SALES (est): 810MM **Privately Held**
SIC: 2834 Pharmaceutical preparations

(G-15342)
ATLANTIC BEVERAGE COMPANY INC (PA)
1033 Skokie Blvd Ste 600 (60062-4101)
PHONE.................................847 412-6200
Merrick M Elfman, *Ch of Bd*
Thomas M Dalton, *President*
Steve Englander, *Exec VP*
Scott Brachmann, *Vice Pres*
EMP: 6
SALES (est): 84.7MM **Privately Held**
SIC: 5149 2013 5147 Beverages, except coffee & tea; juices; mineral or spring water bottling; soft drinks; sausages & other prepared meats; sausages & related products, from purchased meat; smoked meats from purchased meat; meats, cured or smoked

(G-15343)
ATLAS FIBRE COMPANY (PA)
3411 Woodhead Dr (60062-1812)
PHONE.................................847 674-1234
Richard Welch, *President*
Howard Natal, *Vice Pres*
Mark Russell, *Vice Pres*
Lori Lizak-Weiland, *Sales Engr*
Julie Marino, *Sales Staff*
▲ **EMP:** 53 **EST:** 1959
SQ FT: 42,000
SALES: 9MM **Privately Held**
SIC: 3083 5162 3082 2821 Thermoplastic laminates: rods, tubes, plates & sheet; plastics materials & basic shapes; unsupported plastics profile shapes; plastics materials & resins

(G-15344)
AUSTIN TOOL & DIE CO (PA)
3555 Woodhead Dr (60062-1814)
PHONE.................................847 509-5800
James R Archer, *President*
EMP: 55
SQ FT: 70,000
SALES: 9.2MM **Privately Held**
SIC: 3599 3469 3544 Machine shop, jobbing & repair; metal stampings; special dies & tools

(G-15345)
BARILLA AMERICA INC (DH)
885 Sunset Ridge Rd (60062-4006)
PHONE.................................515 956-4400
Jean Pierre Comte, *President*
Giannella Alvarez, *President*
Bill Nunn, *Vice Pres*
Sergio Periera, *Vice Pres*
Tom Dickerson, *Buyer*
◆ **EMP:** 75
SQ FT: 45,000
SALES (est): 90.1MM **Privately Held**
SIC: 2099 Food preparations

HQ: Barilla G. E. R. Fratelli Spa
Via Mantova 166
Parma PR 43122
052 126-21

(G-15346)
BELL FLAVORS & FRAGRANCES INC (PA)
Also Called: Bell Aromatics
500 Academy Dr (60062-2497)
PHONE.................................847 291-8300
James H Heinz, *President*
Ron Stark, *President*
Raymond J Heinz, *Exec VP*
Michael Heinz, *Vice Pres*
Noreen Lally, *Vice Pres*
◆ **EMP:** 130
SQ FT: 100,000
SALES (est): 64.2MM **Privately Held**
WEB: www.bellff.com
SIC: 2869 Perfumes, flavorings & food additives

(G-15347)
BELL FLAVORS & FRAGRANCES INC
501 Lindberg Ln (60062-2415)
PHONE.................................847 291-8300
EMP: 4
SALES (corp-wide): 64.2MM **Privately Held**
SIC: 2869 Perfumes, flavorings & food additives
PA: Bell Flavors And Fragrances, Inc.
500 Academy Dr
Northbrook IL 60062
847 291-8300

(G-15348)
BERNHARD WOODWORK LTD
3670 Woodhead Dr (60062-1817)
PHONE.................................847 291-1040
Herta Bernhard, *CEO*
Mark Bernhard, *President*
Brian Lowry, *Project Mgr*
Pete Schilling, *Project Mgr*
Les Westmoreland, *Project Mgr*
▼ **EMP:** 75
SQ FT: 100,000
SALES (est): 11.6MM **Privately Held**
WEB: www.bernhardwoodwork.com
SIC: 2541 2431 5712 Store fixtures, wood; woodwork, interior & ornamental; planing mill, millwork; customized furniture & cabinets

(G-15349)
BESLOW ASSOCIATES INC
633 Skokie Blvd Ste 200 (60062-2824)
PHONE.................................847 559-2703
John M Beslow, *President*
EMP: 2 **EST:** 1956
SQ FT: 1,500
SALES (est): 236.8K **Privately Held**
SIC: 2759 2791 2732 Publication printing; currency: engraved; typesetting; book printing

(G-15350)
BLACKFRIARS CORP (PA)
555 Skokie Blvd Ste 555 # 555 (60062-2854)
PHONE.................................818 597-3754
Keith W Colburn, *President*
David T Bradford, *Admin Sec*
EMP: 5
SALES (est): 225.4MM **Privately Held**
SIC: 3089 Windows, plastic

(G-15351)
CAMPUS CARDBOARD
600 Waukegan Rd (60062-1258)
PHONE.................................847 373-7673
Matthew Pope, *Principal*
EMP: 3
SALES (est): 253K **Privately Held**
SIC: 2631 Cardboard

(G-15352)
CARLEASE INC
1945 Techny Rd Ste 8 (60062-5306)
PHONE.................................847 714-1414
Andy O'Dower, *CEO*
Mike Mauceri, *Admin Sec*
EMP: 12

SALES (est): 154.5K **Privately Held**
SIC: 7515 7372 Passenger car leasing; application computer software

(G-15353)
CAROLS COOKIES INC
3184 Macarthur Blvd (60062-1904)
PHONE.................................847 831-4500
Carol Goldman, *President*
Jeff Goldman, *Vice Pres*
EMP: 5
SQ FT: 2,000
SALES (est): 732K **Privately Held**
SIC: 2052 5149 Cookies; cookies

(G-15354)
CASTINO & ASSOCIATES INC
Also Called: Fastsigns
3065 Dundee Rd (60062-2401)
PHONE.................................847 291-7446
Deborah Castino, *President*
Josh Sacchetti, *General Mgr*
Thomas Castino, *Vice Pres*
EMP: 9
SALES (est): 355.7K **Privately Held**
SIC: 3993 Signs & advertising specialties

(G-15355)
CHASE GROUP LLC
305 Era Dr (60062-1801)
PHONE.................................847 564-2000
Robert Chase Jr, *Mng Member*
▲ **EMP:** 14
SALES (est): 1.7MM **Privately Held**
SIC: 2741 5199 8999 Art copy: publishing & printing; art goods; artists & artists' studios

(G-15356)
CHESLEY LIMITED
3170 Macarthur Blvd (60062-1904)
PHONE.................................847 562-9292
Robert Chase, *Mng Member*
EMP: 8
SQ FT: 5,000
SALES (est): 700K **Privately Held**
SIC: 2741 Art copy: publishing only, not printed on site

(G-15357)
CHICAGO CUTTING DIE CO
3555 Woodhead Dr (60062-1814)
PHONE.................................847 509-5800
Newton L Archer Jr, *President*
Jim Archer, *Vice Pres*
Kyle Archer, *Vice Pres*
Ryan Archer, *Vice Pres*
James Stuper, *VP Mfg*
▲ **EMP:** 71
SQ FT: 60,000
SALES (est): 9.2MM **Privately Held*
WEB: www.chicagocuttingdie.com
SIC: 3544 3469 Dies & die holders for metal cutting, forming, die casting; stamping metal for the trade
PA: Austin Tool & Die Co
3555 Woodhead Dr
Northbrook IL 60062

(G-15358)
CHICAGO KNITTING MILLS
2424 Hampton Ln (60062-6942)
PHONE.................................773 463-1464
Robert Soll, *Owner*
EMP: 3
SQ FT: 3,800
SALES (est): 160K **Privately Held**
WEB: www.chicagoknitting.com
SIC: 2253 2395 5137 5136 Sweaters & sweater coats, knit; jackets, knit; emblems, embroidered; embroidery products, except schiffli machine; uniforms, women's & children's; uniforms, men's & boys'; women's & misses' outerwear; weft knit fabric mills

(G-15359)
CHRIS INDUSTRIES INC (PA)
2810 Old Willow Rd (60062-6809)
P.O. Box 8206, Northfield (60093-8206)
PHONE.................................847 729-9292
Creighton R Helms, *President*
Judy Muncer, *President*
Christy Helms, *Corp Secy*
▲ **EMP:** 20 **EST:** 1974
SQ FT: 38,000

SALES (est): 5.9MM **Privately Held**
SIC: 5051 3444 Copper products: sheets, metal; sheet metalwork

(G-15360)
CHRIS PLATING INC
2810 Old Willow Rd (60062-6809)
PHONE.................................847 729-9271
Christy Helms, *President*
EMP: 28
SALES (est): 3.1MM **Privately Held**
SIC: 3471 Electroplating of metals or formed products

(G-15361)
CLARUS THERAPEUTICS INC
555 Skokie Blvd Ste 340 (60062-2854)
PHONE.................................847 562-4300
Robert E Dudley, *President*
John P Gargiulo, *COO*
Wael A Salameh, *Vice Pres*
Patrick Shea, *Ch Credit Ofcr*
Theodore M Danoff, *Chief Mktg Ofcr*
EMP: 8
SALES (est): 986.6K **Privately Held**
SIC: 8733 2834 Medical research; pharmaceutical preparations

(G-15362)
CLOWN GLOBAL BRANDS LLC
3184 Doolittle Dr (60062-2409)
PHONE.................................847 564-5950
Mary Ellen Cahill, *CEO*
Martin Haver, *COO*
Cheryl Santucci, *Consultant*
Ni-Del Shubin, *Director*
EMP: 6
SQ FT: 2,000
SALES (est): 350K **Privately Held**
SIC: 2099 5411 3999 Food preparations; grocery stores; barber & beauty shop equipment

(G-15363)
COBIUS HALTHCARE SOLUTIONS LLC
853 Sanders Rd Ste 313 (60062-2901)
PHONE.................................847 656-8700
Doug Weinberg, *Mng Member*
EMP: 9
SALES (est): 996K **Privately Held**
WEB: www.cobius.com
SIC: 3577 Computer peripheral equipment

(G-15364)
CONCEP MACHINE CO INC
1800 Holste Rd (60062-7703)
PHONE.................................847 498-9740
Jefferey Fischer, *President*
Ronald Szostek, *Vice Pres*
Dave Schwind, *Project Mgr*
Steve French, *Electrical Engi*
Chris Lovendahl, *Sales Mgr*
EMP: 22
SQ FT: 13,000
SALES (est): 5.4MM **Privately Held**
WEB: www.concepmachine.com
SIC: 3569 Lubrication machinery, automatic

(G-15365)
CONSERVATION TECH ILL LLC
Also Called: Contech Lighting
725 Landwehr Rd (60062-2349)
PHONE.................................847 559-5500
John Ranshaw, *President*
Keyur Khambhati, *Supervisor*
EMP: 11
SALES (est): 208.4K
SALES (corp-wide): 1.3B **Privately Held**
SIC: 3646 Commercial indusl & institutional electric lighting fixtures
PA: Leviton Manufacturing Co., Inc.
201 N Service Rd
Melville NY 11747
631 812-6000

(G-15366)
CONSERVATION TECHNOLOGY LTD
Also Called: Con-Tech
725 Landwehr Rd (60062-2349)
PHONE.................................847 559-5500
John D Ranshaw, *President*
Glenn Konieczny, *Vice Pres*
Michael Lehman, *Vice Pres*

Mike Lehman, *Vice Pres*
Eva Ibrahim, *Purch Agent*
◆ **EMP:** 92
SALES (est): 30.2MM **Privately Held**
WEB: www.con-techlighting.com
SIC: 3646 3564 Commercial indusl & institutional electric lighting fixtures; ventilating fans: industrial or commercial

(G-15367)
COUR PHARMACEUTICALS DEV
2215 Sanders Rd Ste 428 (60062-6134)
PHONE.................................773 621-3241
John Tu, *President*
Samuel Magnuson, *Principal*
EMP: 4 **EST:** 2012
SALES (est): 388.1K **Privately Held**
SIC: 2834 Pharmaceutical preparations

(G-15368)
CREATIVE GRAPHIC ARTS INC
3690 Oak Ave (60062-4917)
PHONE.................................847 498-2678
Kathy Barnes, *President*
EMP: 4
SALES (est): 260K **Privately Held**
SIC: 2752 Commercial printing, offset

(G-15369)
CRYSTAL PRODUCTIONS CO
3701 Coml Ave Ste 10 (60062)
PHONE.................................847 657-8144
▲ **EMP:** 15
SALES (est): 1.8MM **Privately Held**
SIC: 2731 7812 Book Publishing & Video Production For Educational Institutions

(G-15370)
D D G INC (PA)
1955 Shermer Rd Ste 300 (60062-5363)
PHONE.................................847 412-0277
E A Goodman, *Ch of Bd*
Dd Goodman, *President*
▲ **EMP:** 4
SQ FT: 6,000
SALES (est): 193.8MM **Privately Held**
SIC: 3317 2511 6512 Steel pipe & tubes; wood bedroom furniture; nonresidential building operators

(G-15371)
D KERSEY CONSTRUCTION CO
4130 Timberlane Dr (60062-6123)
PHONE.................................847 919-4980
Doug Kersey, *President*
Virginia Ann Kersey, *Admin Sec*
EMP: 3
SALES (est): 344.3K **Privately Held**
SIC: 1389 1542 Construction, repair & dismantling services; nonresidential construction; institutional building construction

(G-15372)
DAITO PHARMACEUTICALS AMER INC
707 Skokie Blvd Ste 210 (60062-2837)
PHONE.................................847 205-0800
Kenji Fujita, *President*
Masamichi Oishi, *Admin Sec*
◆ **EMP:** 2
SQ FT: 1,500
SALES (est): 344.4K **Privately Held**
SIC: 5122 2834 2833 Pharmaceuticals; pharmaceutical preparations; medicinals & botanicals
PA: Daito Pharmaceutical Co.,Ltd.
   326, Yokamachi
   Toyama TYM 939-8

(G-15373)
DAMICO ASSOCIATES INC
Also Called: Fastsigns
3065 Dundee Rd (60062-2401)
PHONE.................................847 291-7446
Richard D'Amico, *President*
Saja D'Amico, *Vice Pres*
Josh Sacchetti, *Info Tech Mgr*
EMP: 8
SALES (est): 1MM **Privately Held**
SIC: 3993 2542 Signs & advertising specialties; partitions & fixtures, except wood

(G-15374)
DEC ART DESIGNS INC
2970 Maria Ave Ste 226 (60062-2024)
PHONE.................................312 329-0553
Gerald R Levy, *President*
Margaret Deshon, *Corp Secy*
Gloria Levy, *Vice Pres*
▲ **EMP:** 4
SQ FT: 2,000
SALES (est): 543K **Privately Held**
SIC: 2211 Bedspreads, cotton

(G-15375)
DIAMOND CELLOPHANE PDTS INC
Also Called: Diamond Bag & Print Co
2855 Shermer Rd (60062-7710)
PHONE.................................847 418-3000
Howard Diamond, *President*
Robin Diamond, *Principal*
Marion Diamond, *Admin Sec*
▲ **EMP:** 50
SQ FT: 85,000
SALES (est): 16.8MM **Privately Held**
WEB: www.diamondpack.com
SIC: 2673 3083 Plastic bags: made from purchased materials; laminated plastic sheets

(G-15376)
DIGITAL CHECK CORP (PA)
Also Called: Digital Check Technologies
630 Dundee Rd Ste 210 (60062-2792)
PHONE.................................847 446-2285
Thomas Anderson, *President*
Bruce Young, *Exec VP*
Fitz Anderson, *Vice Pres*
Jose Cardenas, *Vice Pres*
Rick Cusimano, *Vice Pres*
▲ **EMP:** 20
SQ FT: 6,000
SALES (est): 14.6MM **Privately Held**
SIC: 3577 Optical scanning devices

(G-15377)
DIVERSIFIED METAL PRODUCTS INC
Also Called: Dispense-Rite
2205 Carlson Dr (60062-6705)
PHONE.................................847 753-9595
Anton Gapp, *President*
Kevin Gapp, *Vice Pres*
Robert Gapp, *Vice Pres*
Paul Gapp, *CFO*
Mark Sutherland, *Manager*
▲ **EMP:** 25
SALES (est): 4.4MM **Privately Held**
WEB: www.dispense-rite.com
SIC: 2542 Cabinets: show, display or storage: except wood; office & store showcases & display fixtures

(G-15378)
EASYSHOW LLC
450 Skokie Blvd Ste 1200 (60062-7920)
PHONE.................................847 480-7177
Mike Gazdzik, *Info Tech Mgr*
Terese Penza,
EMP: 8 **EST:** 2008
SALES (est): 372.4K **Privately Held**
SIC: 2542 Mail racks & lock boxes, postal service: except wood

(G-15379)
ECF HOLDINGS LLC
Also Called: Encore Fastners
3550 Woodhead Dr (60062-1815)
PHONE.................................224 723-5524
Don Ayres, *Mng Member*
▲ **EMP:** 3 **EST:** 2006
SQ FT: 6,200
SALES (est): 635.5K **Privately Held**
WEB: www.encorefasteners.com
SIC: 3965 3399 Fasteners; metal fasteners

(G-15380)
ECO-TECH PLASTICS LLC
1519 Woodlark Dr (60062-4731)
PHONE.................................262 539-3811
Joseph Sadlier, *President*
Julie A Sadlier, *Admin Sec*
EMP: 40 **EST:** 1993
SALES (est): 7.9MM **Privately Held**
SIC: 3089 Injection molding of plastics

(G-15381)
EGG CREAM AMERICA INC (PA)
Also Called: Jeff's Soda
633 Skokie Blvd Ste 200 (60062-2824)
PHONE.................................847 559-2700
John Beslow, *CEO*
Adam Kurlander, *President*
EMP: 2
SQ FT: 1,200
SALES (est): 502.2K **Privately Held**
SIC: 2086 Soft drinks: packaged in cans, bottles, etc.

(G-15382)
ELONGATED PLASTICS INC
677 Alice Dr (60062-2517)
PHONE.................................224 456-0559
Kwang W Moon, *Principal*
▲ **EMP:** 4 **EST:** 2010
SALES (est): 531.3K **Privately Held**
SIC: 3086 Packaging & shipping materials, foamed plastic

(G-15383)
EMALEX BIOSCIENCES LLC (PA)
1033 Skokie Blvd (60062-4108)
PHONE.................................847 715-0577
Eric Messner, *CEO*
Atul Mahableshwarkar, *Senior VP*
EMP: 3
SALES (est): 339.2K **Privately Held**
SIC: 2834 Pharmaceutical preparations

(G-15384)
EMBROID ME
2845 Dundee Rd (60062-2501)
PHONE.................................847 272-9000
Greg Johnson, *Owner*
EMP: 3
SALES (est): 56.8K **Privately Held**
SIC: 2395 Embroidery & art needlework

(G-15385)
ER&R INC
Also Called: Equipment Rent and Royalty
800 Midway Rd Apt 2n (60062-3959)
PHONE.................................847 791-5671
Florence Berg, *President*
EMP: 6
SALES (est): 918.6K **Privately Held**
SIC: 3559 Recycling machinery

(G-15386)
EUROMARKET DESIGNS INC (DH)
Also Called: Cb2
1250 Techny Rd (60062-5419)
PHONE.................................847 272-2888
Steve Woodward, *President*
Ryan Turf, *Managing Dir*
John Olech, *Opers Mgr*
Jennifer Cutler, *Store Mgr*
Daniel Speller, *Purchasing*
◆ **EMP:** 600 **EST:** 1962
SQ FT: 190,000
SALES (est): 1.7B
SALES (corp-wide): 177.9K **Privately Held**
WEB: www.crateandbarrel.com
SIC: 5719 5947 5712 5961 Kitchenware; beddings & linens; gift shop; furniture stores; mail order house; boards: planning, display, notice
HQ: Otto (Gmbh & Co Kg)
   Werner-Otto-Str. 1-7
   Hamburg 22179
   406 461-0

(G-15387)
EYEWEARPLANET COM INC
3150 Commercial Ave (60062-1906)
PHONE.................................847 513-6203
EMP: 3 **EST:** 2010
SALES (est): 197.9K **Privately Held**
WEB: www.eyewearplanet.com
SIC: 3851 Eyes, glass & plastic

(G-15388)
FIELD HOLDINGS LLC (PA)
400 Skokie Blvd Ste 860 (60062-7936)
PHONE.................................847 509-2250
Lawrence I Field, *President*
EMP: 64
SQ FT: 5,000
SALES (est): 6.1MM **Privately Held**
SIC: 2754 Labels: gravure printing

(G-15389)
FIELD VENTURES LLC
400 Skokie Blvd Ste 860 (60062-7936)
PHONE.................................847 509-2250
Joseph Kaplin, *President*
EMP: 51
SALES (est): 3.5MM
SALES (corp-wide): 6.1MM **Privately Held**
SIC: 3083 Plastic finished products, laminated
PA: Field Holdings, Llc
   400 Skokie Blvd Ste 860
   Northbrook IL 60062
   847 509-2250

(G-15390)
FILE SYSTEM LABS LLC
3387 Commercial Ave (60062)
PHONE.................................617 431-4313
Robert Swartz,
Elan Pavlov,
EMP: 15
SALES (est): 1.2MM **Privately Held**
SIC: 3572 Computer storage devices

(G-15391)
FLINN & DREFFEIN ENGRG CO
4025 Michelline Ln (60062-2144)
PHONE.................................847 272-6374
J K Balaz, *President*
Rich Koomjian, *Vice Pres*
EMP: 30 **EST:** 1907
SQ FT: 30,000
SALES (est): 5.3MM **Privately Held**
WEB: www.flinndreffein.com
SIC: 3585 Heating equipment, complete

(G-15392)
GAIL MCGRATH & ASSOCIATES INC
Also Called: Chicago Wedding Resouce
3453 Commercial Ave (60062-1818)
PHONE.................................847 770-4620
Gail McGrath, *President*
Sheldon Levin, *Vice Pres*
Michelle Zebleckis, *Production*
Mike Hedge, *Marketing Mgr*
Lory Richards, *Graphic Designe*
EMP: 11
SALES (est): 2.4MM **Privately Held**
SIC: 2721 Magazines: publishing & printing

(G-15393)
GENNCO INTERNATIONAL INC
3162 Doriann Dr (60062-6910)
PHONE.................................847 541-3333
Kenneth Genender, *President*
Jerry Kushnir, *CFO*
▲ **EMP:** 15
SALES: 5.5MM **Privately Held**
SIC: 2339 2389 5094 Women's & misses' outerwear; men's miscellaneous accessories; watches & parts

(G-15394)
GLASS ARTISTRY
1908 Janke Dr (60062-6707)
P.O. Box 195, Deerfield (60015-0195)
PHONE.................................847 998-5800
Robert Helge, *Partner*
Ardith Harris, *Partner*
EMP: 4 **EST:** 2000
SALES (est): 399K **Privately Held**
SIC: 2519 5947 7231 Fiberglass furniture, household: padded or plain; gift, novelty & souvenir shop; beauty shops

(G-15395)
GLOBEPHARM INC
306 Basswood Dr (60062-1043)
PHONE.................................224 904-3352
Michael Anisfeld, *President*
Daryl Stone, *Vice Pres*
▼ **EMP:** 8
SALES (est): 500K **Privately Held**
SIC: 2834 8742 Pharmaceutical preparations; hospital & health services consultant

Northbrook - Cook County (G-15396)

(G-15396)
GRAPHTEK LLC (PA)
Also Called: Pennsylvania Carbon Products
600 Academy Dr Ste 100 (60062-2408)
PHONE 847 279-1925
Vladimir Novokhovsky,
Karina Novokhovsky,
▲ EMP: 12
SQ FT: 30,000
SALES (est): 2.2MM **Privately Held**
SIC: 3624 Carbon & graphite products

(G-15397)
HARRIS POTTERIES LP (PA)
Also Called: American Bakeware
707 Skokie Blvd Ste 220 (60062-2837)
PHONE 847 564-5544
Robert S Harris, *President*
▲ EMP: 3
SQ FT: 1,000
SALES (est): 19.3MM **Privately Held**
WEB: www.harrispotteries.com
SIC: 3229 Cooking utensils, glass or glass ceramic

(G-15398)
HAUSSERMANN USA LLC
425 Huehl Rd Bldg 10 (60062-2322)
PHONE 847 272-9850
Dale Haase,
EMP: 6
SALES (est): 768.5K **Privately Held**
SIC: 3559 Automotive related machinery

(G-15399)
HELLO DELICIOUS BRANDS LLC
707 Skokie Blvd Ste 580 (60062-2855)
PHONE 844 845-4544
EMP: 15
SALES (est): 4MM **Privately Held**
SIC: 2096 Potato chips & similar snacks

(G-15400)
HIGHLAND BAKING COMPANY INC
2301 Shermer Rd (60062-6721)
PHONE 847 677-2789
James Rosen, *President*
Andy Gorey, *Vice Pres*
Phillip Black, *IT/INT Sup*
EMP: 635
SQ FT: 38,000
SALES (est): 166.3MM **Privately Held**
SIC: 5149 2051 Bakery products; bread, cake & related products

(G-15401)
HPMILLWORK LLC
3007 Commercial Ave (60062-1912)
PHONE 630 220-4387
Stanley G Rousonelos, *Principal*
EMP: 4 EST: 2017
SALES (est): 350.7K **Privately Held**
SIC: 2431 Millwork

(G-15402)
ILLINOIS GLOVE COMPANY
650 Anthony Trl Ste A (60062-2512)
PHONE 847 291-1700
David Shmikler, *President*
Jonathan Shmikler, *Vice Pres*
▲ EMP: 9 EST: 1919
SQ FT: 4,200
SALES (est): 1.6MM **Privately Held**
WEB: www.illinoisglove.com
SIC: 2381 Fabric dress & work gloves

(G-15403)
IMADA INC
3100 Dundee Rd Ste 707 (60062-2442)
PHONE 847 562-0834
Akira Morita, *President*
EMP: 50
SQ FT: 5,000
SALES (est): 9.8MM **Privately Held**
WEB: www.imada.com
SIC: 3823 Industrial instrmnts msrmnt display/control process variable

(G-15404)
IMPOSSIBLE OBJECTS INC
3455 Commercial Ave (60062-1818)
PHONE 847 400-9582
Larry Kaplan, *CEO*
Robert Swartz, *CTO*
Liz Wolf, *Administration*
Darren Fill, *Technician*
EMP: 10
SALES (est): 1.7MM **Privately Held**
SIC: 2752 Offset & photolithographic printing

(G-15405)
INDUSTRIAL DIAMOND PRODUCTS
3045 Macarthur Blvd (60062-1901)
PHONE 847 272-7840
Vladimir Kompon, *President*
▲ EMP: 20
SALES (est): 1.4MM **Privately Held**
SIC: 3545 Dressers, abrasive wheel: diamond point or other

(G-15406)
INSTRUMENTALISTS INC
Also Called: Claviers Piano Explorer
1838 Techny Ct (60062-5474)
PHONE 847 446-5000
James T Rohner, *President*
EMP: 10
SALES (est): 1.2MM **Privately Held**
SIC: 2721 Magazines: publishing & printing

(G-15407)
INTERNTIONAL CMPT CONCEPTS INC
300 Wainwright Dr (60062-1911)
PHONE 847 808-7789
Raisa Stolyar, *President*
Yuriy Goncharov, *Warehouse Mgr*
Ian Stewart, *Accounts Exec*
Steven Osher, *Sales Staff*
Stefania Pascutti, *Sales Associate*
EMP: 30
SQ FT: 41,000
SALES: 30MM **Privately Held**
SIC: 3572 3571 Computer storage devices; computers, digital, analog or hybrid

(G-15408)
J H ROBISON & ASSOCIATES LTD (PA)
905 Voltz Rd (60062-4714)
PHONE 847 559-9662
EMP: 3
SQ FT: 1,300
SALES (est): 348.3K **Privately Held**
SIC: 1382 1381 Exploration Of Oil & Gas Fields & Drilling Of Oil & Gas Wells

(G-15409)
JADA SPECIALTIES INC
3834 Normandy Ln (60062-2120)
P.O. Box 753 (60065-0753)
PHONE 847 272-7799
David W Jacobson, *President*
EMP: 2
SALES (est): 259.9K **Privately Held**
SIC: 2869 Perfumes, flavorings & food additives; flavors or flavoring materials, synthetic

(G-15410)
JAMES INJECTION MOLDING CO
300 Pfingsten Rd (60062-2031)
PHONE 847 564-3820
Fax: 847 564-3965
EMP: 40
SQ FT: 23,400
SALES: 1.9MM **Privately Held**
SIC: 3089 3083 Mfg Plastic Products Mfg Laminated Plastic Plate/Sheet

(G-15411)
KAPSTONE KRAFT PAPER CORP (DH)
1101 Skokie Blvd Ste 300 (60062-4124)
PHONE 252 533-6000
Timothy Keneally, *President*
Michael Carter, *Business Mgr*
Randy Nebel, *Exec VP*
Mark Niehus, *Vice Pres*
Steven Tanzi, *Vice Pres*
▼ EMP: 10
SALES: 136MM
SALES (corp-wide): 18.2B **Publicly Held**
SIC: 2621 Packaging paper

(G-15412)
KINGPORT INDUSTRIES LLC
1912 Shermer Rd (60062-5320)
PHONE 847 480-5745
Claudia Chisholm, *Mng Member*
Anyuan Chang,
▲ EMP: 5
SALES (est): 856.6K **Privately Held**
SIC: 3161 Traveling bags; suitcases; cases, carrying

(G-15413)
KMP TOOL GRINDING INC
1808 Janke Dr Ste J (60062-6703)
PHONE 847 205-9640
Walt Mirco, *President*
Albert Koshaba, *Vice Pres*
EMP: 3
SQ FT: 2,400
SALES (est): 414K **Privately Held**
SIC: 3541 7699 3545 Grinding machines, metalworking; industrial tool grinding; machine tool accessories

(G-15414)
KOREAN MEDIA GROUP LLC
3520 Milwaukee Ave Fl 2 (60062-7130)
PHONE 847 391-4112
Ju Kyong,
▲ EMP: 12
SALES (est): 405.8K **Privately Held**
SIC: 2711 Newspapers, publishing & printing

(G-15415)
KRAFT HEINZ FOODS COMPANY
2301 Shermer Rd (60062-6721)
PHONE 847 291-3900
Steve Lagasse, *Principal*
EMP: 200
SALES (corp-wide): 24.9B **Publicly Held**
WEB: www.kraftfoodsgroup.com
SIC: 2033 2047 2091 2032 Canned fruits & specialties; dog & cat food; canned & cured fish & seafoods; canned specialties; frozen fruits & vegetables; frozen specialties
HQ: Kraft Heinz Foods Company
1 Ppg Pl Fl 34
Pittsburgh PA 15222
412 456-5700

(G-15416)
KULDISAK LLC
Also Called: Swag Golf
3342 Commercial Ave (60062-1909)
PHONE 847 772-7412
EMP: 6
SALES (est): 51.7K **Privately Held**
SIC: 3949 Golf equipment

(G-15417)
LANE INDUSTRIES INC (PA)
1200 Shermer Rd Ste 400 (60062-4561)
PHONE 847 498-6650
Forrest Schneider, *President*
William Keating, *Vice Pres*
EMP: 25
SQ FT: 12,000
SALES (est): 62.2MM **Privately Held**
SIC: 3579 3589 7011 1731 Binding machines, plastic & adhesive; shredders, industrial & commercial; hotels & motels; safety & security specialization

(G-15418)
LANMAR INC
3160 Doolittle Dr (60062-2409)
PHONE 800 233-5520
Martin Jacobs, *President*
EMP: 5
SQ FT: 1,800
SALES (est): 450K **Privately Held**
SIC: 2295 5085 3052 Tape, varnished: plastic & other coated (except magnetic); adhesives, tape & plasters; hose, belting & packing; rubber & plastics hose & beltings

(G-15419)
LINZ ELECTRIC INC
3005 Commercial Ave (60062-1912)
PHONE 847 595-1473
Sandro Alberghini, *President*
EMP: 10
SALES (est): 626.1K **Privately Held**
SIC: 3548 Arc welders, transformer-rectifier

(G-15420)
LJM EQUIPMENT CO
205 Huehl Rd (60062-1914)
PHONE 847 291-0162
Helen L Rivkin, *President*
EMP: 5
SQ FT: 81,000
SALES (est): 510K **Privately Held**
SIC: 3069 Rubber coated fabrics & clothing

(G-15421)
LOVEJOY INDUSTRIES INC (PA)
3610 Commercial Ave (60062-1823)
PHONE 859 873-6828
Walter R Lovejoy, *Ch of Bd*
Matthew Lovejoy, *President*
Mark Kepf, *CFO*
EMP: 4
SQ FT: 1,500
SALES (est): 45MM **Privately Held**
SIC: 3364 3363 3544 Zinc & zinc-base alloy die-castings; aluminum die-castings; special dies, tools, jigs & fixtures

(G-15422)
LUCKY GAMES INC
574 Alice Dr (60062-2516)
PHONE 773 549-9051
Heidi Sonen, *President*
David Sonen, *Corp Secy*
EMP: 17
SQ FT: 7,000
SALES (est): 2.6MM **Privately Held**
SIC: 2679 Pressed fiber & molded pulp products except food products

(G-15423)
LUMINEX CORPORATION
4088 Commercial Ave (60062-1829)
PHONE 847 400-9000
Michael McGarrity, *President*
Caleb White, *Sales Mgr*
James Chengary, *Manager*
Avery Vaughn, *Manager*
Brenda Higgins, *Software Engr*
EMP: 8 **Publicly Held**
SIC: 3841 Diagnostic apparatus, medical
PA: Luminex Corporation
12212 Technology Blvd
Austin TX 78727

(G-15424)
LUND INDUSTRIES INC
3175 Macarthur Blvd (60062-1903)
PHONE 847 459-1460
Paul A Lundberg, *President*
Mark J Lundberg, *Vice Pres*
Michael Malec, *Sales Staff*
Keith Mandic, *Sales Associate*
Mark Lundberg, *Manager*
▼ EMP: 30 EST: 1972
SQ FT: 16,000
SALES (est): 6.1MM **Privately Held**
SIC: 3669 Sirens, electric: vehicle, marine, industrial & air raid; signaling apparatus, electric

(G-15425)
M I T FINANCIAL GROUP INC
Also Called: General Lrng Communications
900 Skokie Blvd Ste 200 (60062-4031)
PHONE 847 205-3000
John E Cimba, *President*
Peggy Kane, *President*
David Husman, *Chairman*
Edward Conner, *Exec VP*
EMP: 45
SQ FT: 15,000
SALES (est): 6.6MM **Privately Held**
SIC: 2721 Magazines: publishing only, not printed on site

(G-15426)
MACLEE CHEMICAL COMPANY INC
1316 Edgewood Ln (60062-4716)
PHONE 847 480-0953
Joe Lee, *President*
▲ EMP: 3
SQ FT: 90,000

GEOGRAPHIC SECTION Northbrook - Cook County (G-15453)

SALES (est): 403.9K Privately Held
SIC: 2819 Industrial inorganic chemicals

(G-15427)
MARBLE EMPORIUM INC (PA)
2200 Carlson Dr (60062-6728)
PHONE..................................847 205-4000
Louiza Kourkouvis, President
Frank Gonzalez, Sales Staff
Loukas Pantelias, Manager
Tiffany Ponzo, Manager
Julie Keith, Director
▲ EMP: 20
SQ FT: 19,000
SALES (est): 4.3MM Privately Held
SIC: 5032 1743 3281 Marble building stone; granite building stone; marble installation, interior; marble, building: cut & shaped

(G-15428)
MAYLINE INVESTMENTS INC (PA)
555 Skokie Blvd (60062-2812)
PHONE..................................847 948-9340
Charles Barancik, Ch of Bd
Paul Simons, President
Chris Mc Namee, Exec VP
Eric Volcheff, Exec VP
Don Clements, Vice Pres
◆ EMP: 3
SQ FT: 2,200
SALES (est): 97MM Privately Held
WEB: www.mayline.com
SIC: 2521 2522 Wood office furniture; office cabinets & filing drawers: except wood

(G-15429)
MCKNIGHTS LONG TERM CARE NEWS
Also Called: McKnight's Assisted Living
900 Skokie Blvd Ste 114 (60062-4014)
PHONE..................................847 559-2884
William Pecover, CEO
Jim Berklan, Editor
Denise Devito, Manager
Diana Ernst, Director
Lois Bowers, Senior Editor
EMP: 7
SALES (est): 629.2K Privately Held
SIC: 2759 8051 Publication printing; skilled nursing care facilities

(G-15430)
MEDIARECALL HOLDINGS LLC
3363 Commercial Ave (60062-1908)
PHONE..................................847 513-6710
Scott Smith, Mng Member
Ryan E Kirch,
EMP: 5
SQ FT: 3,200
SALES: 500K Privately Held
SIC: 3577 Data conversion equipment, media-to-media: computer

(G-15431)
MEMORABLE INC
3336 Commercial Ave (60062-1909)
PHONE..................................847 272-8207
Eugene Gekhter, CEO
EMP: 6
SQ FT: 3,000
SALES: 30K Privately Held
SIC: 7371 7372 Computer software development & applications; application computer software

(G-15432)
MENASHA PACKAGING COMPANY LLC
1935 Techny Rd Ste 14 (60062-5305)
PHONE..................................773 489-8332
EMP: 5
SALES (corp-wide): 2.2B Privately Held
SIC: 2653 Boxes, corrugated: made from purchased materials
HQ: Menasha Packaging Company, Llc
   1645 Bergstrom Rd
   Neenah WI 54956
   920 751-1000

(G-15433)
MENGARELLI ENTERPRISES INC
2926 Macarthur Blvd (60062-2005)
PHONE..................................847 272-6980
Rocco Palmi, President
Craig Mengarelli, Vice Pres
Tim Booth, Chief Engr
Tim Happel, Design Engr
Jason Palmi, CFO
EMP: 62
SQ FT: 64,000
SALES: 29.1MM Privately Held
WEB: www.ramcel.com
SIC: 3469 Stamping metal for the trade

(G-15434)
MOBILE ENDOSCOPIX LLC
3330 Dundee Rd Ste C1 (60062-2328)
PHONE..................................847 380-8992
Roth Elizabeth C, Principal
EMP: 4
SALES (est): 207.6K Privately Held
SIC: 3845 Endoscopic equipment, electromedical

(G-15435)
MOOG INC
3650 Woodhead Dr (60062-1817)
PHONE..................................770 987-7550
EMP: 49
SALES (corp-wide): 2.7B Publicly Held
SIC: 7382 3699 Security Systems Services Mfg Electrical Equipment/Supplies
PA: Moog Inc.
   400 Jamison Rd
   Elma NY 14059
   716 652-2000

(G-15436)
MOOG INC
3650 Woodhead Dr (60062-1817)
PHONE..................................847 498-0704
Alfred Lazar, Controller
Pragnesh Patel, Software Engr
EMP: 102
SALES (corp-wide): 2.9B Publicly Held
SIC: 3861 Cameras & related equipment; tripods, camera & projector; cameras, still & motion picture (all types)
PA: Moog Inc.
   400 Jamison Rd
   Elma NY 14059
   716 805-2604

(G-15437)
MOSAIC CONSTRUCTION
Also Called: Charlie
425 Huehl Rd Bldg 15b (60062-2323)
PHONE..................................847 504-0177
Aaron Frazin, CEO
EMP: 6
SALES (est): 593.4K Privately Held
SIC: 7372 7389 Application computer software; business oriented computer software; interior designer

(G-15438)
NANOSPHERE LLC
4088 Commercial Ave (60062-1829)
PHONE..................................847 400-9000
Michael McGarrity, Chief Mktg Ofcr
Ryan Gould, Technical Staff
Ken Bahk, Security Dir
EMP: 148
SQ FT: 48,470
SALES (est): 28.8MM Publicly Held
SIC: 3841 Surgical & medical instruments
PA: Luminex Corporation
   12212 Technology Blvd
   Austin TX 78727

(G-15439)
NATURA PRODUCTS INC
3555 Woodhead Dr (60062-1814)
PHONE..................................847 509-5835
Newton L Archer Jr, President
James R Archer, Admin Sec
EMP: 15 EST: 1963
SQ FT: 10,000
SALES (est): 1.9MM Privately Held
WEB: www.naturaproducts.com
SIC: 3599 3544 3469 Machine shop, jobbing & repair; special dies & tools; metal stampings

PA: Austin Tool & Die Co
   3555 Woodhead Dr
   Northbrook IL 60062

(G-15440)
ND INDUSTRIES INC
N-D Industries Div
1840 Raymond Dr (60062-6779)
PHONE..................................847 498-3600
Sean Costin, COO
John Thramann, Engineer
Jane Castebens, Controller
Anthony Costa, Sales Staff
John J Thramann, Manager
EMP: 30
SALES (corp-wide): 80.5MM Privately Held
WEB: www.ndindustries.com
SIC: 3452 2891 Bolts, nuts, rivets & washers; adhesives & sealants
PA: Nd Industries, Inc.
   1000 N Crooks Rd
   Clawson MI 48017
   248 288-0000

(G-15441)
NEWMEDICAL TECHNOLOGY INC
310 Era Dr (60062-1834)
PHONE..................................847 412-1000
Amer Michael Hanna, Ch of Bd
Haitham Matloub, Vice Pres
Jeff Dziura, VP Sales
Nancy Buxbaum, Cust Mgr
Mark Chenoweth, Marketing Staff
▲ EMP: 24
SQ FT: 17,000
SALES (est): 442.8K Privately Held
SIC: 3842 3841 Bandages & dressings; tape, adhesive: medicated or non-medicated; surgical & medical instruments; operating tables

(G-15442)
O CHILLI FROZEN FOODS INC
1251 Shermer Rd (60062-4599)
PHONE..................................847 562-1991
Jeffrey L Rothschild, President
Odis Rothschild, Admin Sec
EMP: 27 EST: 1944
SQ FT: 50,000
SALES: 3MM Privately Held
SIC: 2038 2099 2013 Frozen specialties; food preparations; sausages & other prepared meats

(G-15443)
OCEANIC FOOD EXPRESS INC
1715 Longvalley Dr (60062-5117)
PHONE..................................847 480-7217
Yefim Mayzenberg, Principal
EMP: 3
SALES (est): 221.2K Privately Held
SIC: 2048 Fish food

(G-15444)
OFFICERS PRINTING INC
Also Called: Allegra Print & Imaging
710 Landwehr Rd Ste B (60062-2337)
PHONE..................................847 480-4663
Alan Wener, President
EMP: 4
SQ FT: 4,400
SALES (est): 368.5K Privately Held
SIC: 2752 Commercial printing, offset

(G-15445)
OLD WORLD GLOBAL LLC
4065 Commercial Ave (60062-1828)
PHONE..................................800 323-5440
Bryan Emrich, Vice Pres
▲ EMP: 4
SALES (est): 334.3K Privately Held
SIC: 3714 Motor vehicle parts & accessories

(G-15446)
OLD WORLD INDS HOLDINGS LLC
4065 Commercial Ave (60062-1828)
PHONE..................................800 323-5440
Sean Wheatley, Marketing Staff
Leonard Gazin,
EMP: 5 EST: 2012

SALES (est): 995.4K
SALES (corp-wide): 569.8MM Privately Held
SIC: 3714 Motor vehicle parts & accessories
PA: Old World Industries, Llc
   3100 Sanders Rd Fl 5
   Northbrook IL 60062
   847 559-2000

(G-15447)
ONEPLUS SYSTEMS INC
3182 Macarthur Blvd (60062-1904)
PHONE..................................847 498-0955
Jay Simon, President
Priya Emerson, Vice Pres
Morris Simon, Treasurer
Hazel Manks, Finance Mgr
Eoin Kettle, Marketing Staff
EMP: 20
SQ FT: 15,000
SALES (est): 5MM Privately Held
SIC: 3829 Measuring & controlling devices

(G-15448)
ORGANICS LLC
1935 Techny Rd Ste 14 (60062-5305)
PHONE..................................847 897-6000
Lawrence Hicks, Chairman
Elizabeth Hicks, Human Res Dir
EMP: 4
SALES (est): 271.9K Privately Held
SIC: 2834 Pharmaceutical preparations

(G-15449)
ORNAMENT SHOP CO INC
Also Called: Ornament Shop.com
2139 Claridge Ln (60062-8615)
PHONE..................................847 559-8844
Diane Weller, CEO
Russell Weller, Vice Pres
EMP: 75
SALES (est): 5.5MM Privately Held
SIC: 3231 Christmas tree ornaments: made from purchased glass

(G-15450)
OUTDOOR SOLUTIONS TEAM INC
1315 Southwind Dr (60062-4225)
PHONE..................................312 446-4220
John Reeves, President
Robert Neff, Admin Sec
EMP: 25
SQ FT: 13,000
SALES: 1.6MM Privately Held
SIC: 3993 Signs & advertising specialties

(G-15451)
PANEK PRECISION PRODUCTS CO
455 Academy Dr (60062-2416)
PHONE..................................847 291-9755
Gregg Panek, President
Josephine Panek, Corp Secy
Brian Panek, COO
Jesse Gomez, Warehouse Mgr
Andy Blach, Production
EMP: 178
SQ FT: 109,000
SALES (est): 58.7MM Privately Held
WEB: www.panekprecision.com
SIC: 3451 Screw machine products

(G-15452)
PCBL RETAIL HOLDINGS LLC
Also Called: Polaroid Store
5 Revere Dr Ste 206 (60062-1568)
PHONE..................................610 761-4838
Jeff Branman, Chairman
EMP: 2
SALES: 3MM Privately Held
SIC: 2759 Commercial printing

(G-15453)
PCS NITROGEN INC (DH)
1101 Skokie Blvd Ste 400 (60062-4123)
PHONE..................................847 849-4200
Tom Regan, President
Paul Dunbar, Engineer
Paula Gibson, Maintence Staff
◆ EMP: 90
SALES (est): 356.8MM
SALES (corp-wide): 20B Privately Held
SIC: 2874 2873 Phosphatic fertilizers; ammonia & ammonium salts

(PA)=Parent Co (HQ)=Headquarters (DH)=Div Headquarters
✪ = New Business established in last 2 years

Northbrook - Cook County (G-15454)

HQ: Potash Corporation Of Saskatchewan Inc
122 1st Ave S Suite 500
Saskatoon SK S7K 7
306 933-8500

(G-15454)
PCS NITROGEN FERTILIZER LP
1101 Skokie Blvd Ste 500 (60062-4126)
PHONE..................847 849-4200
Larry Obrien, *Partner*
Wayne R Brownley, *Partner*
G David Delaney, *Partner*
Rick Harnung, *Partner*
Brian E Johnson, *Partner*
EMP: 10
SALES (est): 1.8MM
SALES (corp-wide): 20B **Privately Held**
SIC: 2873 Nitrogenous fertilizers
HQ: Potash Corporation Of Saskatchewan Inc
122 1st Ave S Suite 500
Saskatoon SK S7K 7
306 933-8500

(G-15455)
PCS NITROGEN TRINIDAD CORP
1101 Skokie Blvd Ste 400 (60062-4123)
P.O. Box 3320 (60065-3320)
PHONE..................847 849-4200
Jim Dietz, *President*
EMP: 180 **EST:** 1993
SALES (est): 17.5MM
SALES (corp-wide): 20B **Privately Held**
WEB: www.potashcorp.com
SIC: 2873 Ammonia & ammonium salts; urea
HQ: Pcs Nitrogen, Inc.
1101 Skokie Blvd Ste 400
Northbrook IL 60062

(G-15456)
PCS NTRGEN FRTLZER OPRTONS INC (DH)
1101 Skokie Blvd Ste 400 (60062-4123)
PHONE..................847 849-4200
Brett Heimann, *President*
Bryan E Johnson, *Corp Secy*
David Delaney, *COO*
Fritz Bertz, *Vice Pres*
Wayne R Brownlee, *Treasurer*
▲ **EMP:** 100
SALES (est): 80.4MM
SALES (corp-wide): 20B **Privately Held**
SIC: 2873 Nitrogenous fertilizers
HQ: Potash Corporation Of Saskatchewan Inc
122 1st Ave S Suite 500
Saskatoon SK S7K 7
306 933-8500

(G-15457)
PCS PHOSPHATE COMPANY INC (DH)
Also Called: Pcs Sales
1101 Skokie Blvd Ste 400 (60062-4123)
PHONE..................847 849-4200
Brent Heimann, *President*
Thomas J Regan Jr, *President*
Doug Engel, *General Mgr*
Clint Roberts, *Technical Staff*
Joseph Podwika, *Admin Sec*
◆ **EMP:** 80 **EST:** 1981
SQ FT: 66,000
SALES (est): 16.6MM
SALES (corp-wide): 20B **Privately Held**
WEB: www.potashcorp.com
SIC: 1475 1474 2874 2819 Phosphate rock; potash mining; phosphatic fertilizers; phosphates, except fertilizers: defluorinated & ammoniated
HQ: Potash Corporation Of Saskatchewan Inc
122 1st Ave S Suite 500
Saskatoon SK S7K 7
306 933-8500

(G-15458)
PEN AT HAND
4120 Terri Lyn Ln (60062-4939)
PHONE..................847 498-9174
Ronnie Horrowitz, *Owner*
EMP: 5
SALES (est): 646.1K **Privately Held**
SIC: 2621 Writing paper

(G-15459)
PINGOTOPIA INC
Also Called: Pingoworld
3334 Commercial Ave (60062-1909)
PHONE..................847 503-9333
Alex Goldman, *COO*
Alexander Holden, *CFO*
EMP: 10
SQ FT: 5,000
SALES (est): 1MM **Privately Held**
SIC: 2754 5023 Post cards, picture: gravure printing; decorative home furnishings & supplies

(G-15460)
PLIBRICO COMPANY LLC (PA)
Also Called: Plibrico Refractory Cnstr
1935 Techny Rd Ste 16 (60062-5305)
PHONE..................312 337-9000
Fred Eck, *Ch of Bd*
Brad Taylor, *President*
Norm Phelps, *Vice Pres*
Dan Szynal, *Vice Pres*
Chris Smith, *Safety Mgr*
▼ **EMP:** 14
SQ FT: 11,460
SALES (est): 35MM **Privately Held**
SIC: 3297 Nonclay refractories

(G-15461)
POTASH CORP SSKTCHEWAN FLA INC (DH)
1101 Skokie Blvd Ste 400 (60062-4123)
PHONE..................847 849-4200
William Doyle, *CEO*
Stephen F Dowdle, *President*
Bart Hunt, *Regional Mgr*
Jessica Demonte, *Counsel*
Mark Etienne, *Vice Pres*
▼ **EMP:** 147
SALES (est): 80.4MM
SALES (corp-wide): 20B **Privately Held**
SIC: 2873 2874 2819 Nitrogenous fertilizers; phosphatic fertilizers; potash alum
HQ: Potash Corporation Of Saskatchewan Inc
122 1st Ave S Suite 500
Saskatoon SK S7K 7
306 933-8500

(G-15462)
POTASH HOLDING COMPANY INC
1101 Skokie Blvd Ste 400 (60062-4123)
PHONE..................847 849-4200
William J Bill Doyle, *President*
Wayne R Brownlee, *Vice Pres*
G David Delaney, *Vice Pres*
EMP: 3
SALES (est): 594.7K
SALES (corp-wide): 20B **Privately Held**
SIC: 5191 3999 Fertilizer & fertilizer materials; atomizers, toiletry
HQ: Potash Corporation Of Saskatchewan Inc
122 1st Ave S Suite 500
Saskatoon SK S7K 7
306 933-8500

(G-15463)
PRAIRIE STATE SCREW & BOLT CO
4219 Kayla Ln (60062-2167)
PHONE..................847 858-9551
Joseph Schyman, *President*
▲ **EMP:** 10
SALES (est): 129.2K **Privately Held**
SIC: 3452 Screws, metal

(G-15464)
PRESTIGE BRANDS INC
2100 Sanders Rd (60062-6139)
PHONE..................224 235-4049
EMP: 3
SALES (est): 188K **Privately Held**
SIC: 2834 Pharmaceutical preparations

(G-15465)
PRESTIGE DISTRIBUTION INC
720 Anthony Trl (60062-2542)
PHONE..................847 480-7667
David Waxman, *CEO*
Kevin Czerwiec, *Project Mgr*
Steve Dattilo, *Project Mgr*
Bryan Dolgin, *Project Mgr*
Bobby Robertson, *Project Mgr*
EMP: 8
SQ FT: 8,000
SALES (est): 1.6MM **Privately Held**
SIC: 2541 5039 Cabinets, lockers & shelving; lockers, construction

(G-15466)
PRIME PUBLISHING LLC
Also Called: llikecrochet.com
3400 Dundee Rd Ste 220 (60062-2338)
PHONE..................847 205-9375
Emily Artinian, *Editor*
Jenny Benoit, *Editor*
Jamie Garcia, *Editor*
Danielle Kamp, *Editor*
Tom Krawczyk, *Editor*
EMP: 45
SALES (est): 5.4MM **Privately Held**
SIC: 2741 Miscellaneous publishing

(G-15467)
PRISMATEC INC
1964 Raymond Dr (60062-6715)
PHONE..................847 562-9022
Erwin Gugolz, *President*
EMP: 4
SALES (est): 700K **Privately Held**
WEB: www.prismatecjet.com
SIC: 2759 Publication printing

(G-15468)
PRODUCTWORKS LLC
610 Academy Dr (60062-2421)
PHONE..................224 406-8810
Julie Jun, *Opers Mgr*
Mary Oconnor, *Accounting Mgr*
Marsailis Polk, *Accounts Mgr*
Sharon Roles, *Cust Mgr*
Sheri Schiff, *Sales Staff*
◆ **EMP:** 12
SALES (est): 1.3MM **Privately Held**
WEB: www.productworksllc.com
SIC: 3645 3646 3648 Residential lighting fixtures; commercial indusl & institutional electric lighting fixtures; lighting equipment

(G-15469)
PROTECT ASSOC
3215 Commercial Ave (60062-1920)
PHONE..................847 446-8664
Earl Bauer, *President*
EMP: 5 **EST:** 2013
SALES (est): 541.2K **Privately Held**
SIC: 2273 Floor coverings, textile fiber

(G-15470)
RAINBOW LIGHTING
3545 Commercial Ave (60062-1820)
PHONE..................847 480-1136
Mike Stern, *President*
Steve Kalish, *Vice Pres*
Keith Tucker, *Vice Pres*
Linda Stern, *Admin Sec*
◆ **EMP:** 20
SQ FT: 35,000
SALES (est): 5.3MM **Privately Held**
SIC: 5719 3646 Lamps & lamp shades; commercial indusl & institutional electric lighting fixtures

(G-15471)
REGIONAL EMERGENCY DISPATCH
Also Called: Red Center
1842 Shermer Rd (60062-5318)
PHONE..................847 498-5748
Jim Clausen, *Principal*
Chris Lienhardt, *Exec Dir*
EMP: 17
SALES (est): 1.7MM **Privately Held**
SIC: 3669 Emergency alarms

(G-15472)
RELIABLE GALVANIZING COMPANY
2541 Queens Way (60062-6542)
PHONE..................773 651-2500
Toll Free:..................888 -
Daniel D Sugarman, *Ch of Bd*
Michael Eisner, *President*
Dale Wolek, *Admin Sec*
EMP: 45

SALES (est): 5.5MM **Privately Held**
SIC: 3479 Galvanizing of iron, steel or end-formed products; hot dip coating of metals or formed products

(G-15473)
RICAR INDUSTRIES INC
2468 Greenview Rd (60062-7030)
PHONE..................847 914-9083
EMP: 3
SQ FT: 500
SALES: 1.5MM **Privately Held**
SIC: 3441 Structural Metal Fabrication

(G-15474)
ROBKO FLOCK COATING COMPANY
1935 Stanley St (60062-5324)
PHONE..................847 272-6202
Alison Kotlarz, *President*
Tracy Kotlarz, *Vice Pres*
Marcella Kotlarz, *Admin Sec*
EMP: 5
SQ FT: 7,000
SALES: 750K **Privately Held**
SIC: 3569 3564 Filters, general line: industrial; blowers & fans

(G-15475)
ROSENTHAL MANUFACTURING CO INC
Also Called: Smart-Slitters
1840 Janke Dr (60062-6704)
PHONE..................847 714-0404
Lorelei Rosenthal, *President*
David Rosenthal, *Exec VP*
Michael Rosenthal, *Exec VP*
Bosko Borjanovic, *Prdtn Mgr*
Sarah Passman, *Purchasing*
▲ **EMP:** 33 **EST:** 1926
SQ FT: 45,000
SALES (est): 9.6MM **Privately Held**
WEB: www.rosenthalmfg.com
SIC: 3554 3565 Cutting machines, paper; packaging machinery

(G-15476)
RUNWAY LIQUIDATION LLC
Also Called: Bcbg
400 Newport Center Dr (60062)
PHONE..................574 247-1500
EMP: 3
SALES (corp-wide): 559.4MM **Privately Held**
SIC: 2335 Women's, juniors' & misses' dresses
HQ: Runway Liquidation, Llc
2761 Fruitland Ave
Vernon CA 90058

(G-15477)
SCHOOL TOWN LLC
1340 Shermer Rd Ste 245 (60062-4598)
PHONE..................847 943-9115
Michael Kritzman,
EMP: 7
SALES: 600K **Privately Held**
SIC: 7372 Prepackaged software

(G-15478)
SEALMASTER INC
425 Huehl Rd Bldg 11b (60062-2340)
PHONE..................847 480-7325
Hannah Malin, *President*
EMP: 16
SQ FT: 2,300
SALES (est): 1.7MM **Privately Held**
SIC: 2951 5713 Asphalt paving mixtures & blocks; floor covering stores

(G-15479)
SELLERS COMMERCE LLC
633 Skokie Blvd Ste 490 (60062-2826)
PHONE..................858 345-1212
Ashook Reddy, *President*
Rick Levine, *Vice Pres*
David Sykes,
EMP: 12
SQ FT: 2,300
SALES: 2.5MM **Privately Held**
SIC: 7372 Application computer software

GEOGRAPHIC SECTION

(G-15480)
SERVICE ENVELOPE CORPORATION
1925 Holste Rd (60062-7704)
PHONE..................847 559-0004
Thomas Washburn, *President*
Marilyn Washburn, *Corp Secy*
Jim Washburn, *Vice Pres*
Carolina Aguilar, *Mfg Staff*
John Washburn, *Executive*
EMP: 25
SALES (est): 4.7MM Privately Held
SIC: 2759 Commercial printing

(G-15481)
SKYLINE PRINTING SALES
3004 Commercial Ave (60062-1913)
P.O. Box 4854, Buffalo Grove (60089-4854)
PHONE..................847 412-1931
Jeff Schultz, *Owner*
EMP: 4
SALES: 310K Privately Held
SIC: 2759 Commercial printing

(G-15482)
SOBOT TOOL & MANUFACTURING CO
3975 Commercial Ave (60062-1827)
PHONE..................847 480-0560
Steven Sobot, *President*
Mark Sobot, *Vice Pres*
Zofia Sobot, *Admin Sec*
EMP: 20
SQ FT: 48,000
SALES (est): 3.8MM Privately Held
WEB: www.sobottoolmfg.com
SIC: 3599 Machine shop, jobbing & repair

(G-15483)
SOCIAL QNECT LLC
666 Dundee Rd Ste 1904 (60062-2739)
PHONE..................847 997-0077
Gary Scheier,
EMP: 1 EST: 2012
SALES: 200K Privately Held
SIC: 7372 Application computer software

(G-15484)
SPENCER WELDING SERVICE INC
3215 Doolittle Dr (60062-2410)
PHONE..................847 272-0580
Steven C Spencer, *President*
EMP: 5
SQ FT: 3,000
SALES (est): 366.1K Privately Held
SIC: 7692 Welding repair

(G-15485)
SPORT ELECTRONICS INC
Also Called: Hass and Associates
1000 Skokie Blvd Unit 413 (60062)
PHONE..................847 564-5575
Debra M Hass, *President*
Joanne Meyerhoff, *Treasurer*
EMP: 4
SALES (est): 370.8K Privately Held
SIC: 3999 Stereographs, photographic

(G-15486)
SPURT INC
4033 Dana Ct (60062-3025)
PHONE..................847 571-6497
Mark Polin, *President*
EMP: 5
SALES: 900K Privately Held
SIC: 3699 3648 8711 Electrical equipment & supplies; lighting equipment; electrical or electronic engineering

(G-15487)
ST IMAGING INC
630 Dundee Rd Ste 210 (60062-2792)
PHONE..................847 501-3344
Tom Anderson, *President*
EMP: 13
SALES (est): 950K Privately Held
WEB: www.stimaging.com
SIC: 3826 Photomicrographic apparatus

(G-15488)
STRATEGIC MFG PARTNER LLC (PA)
Also Called: Jsa Tool & Engineering
3145 Elder Ct (60062-5831)
PHONE..................262 878-5213
Paul Yost, *Mng Member*
Joseph A Dipietro,
Jim Hendrickson,
EMP: 5
SQ FT: 10,000
SALES (est): 5.7MM Privately Held
SIC: 3599 Machine shop, jobbing & repair

(G-15489)
STRYTECH ADHESIVES
707 Skokie Blvd Ste 600 (60062-2841)
PHONE..................847 509-7566
Howard Neal, *Owner*
EMP: 3
SALES (est): 1.8MM Privately Held
SIC: 2891 Adhesives

(G-15490)
SUNSHINE METALS INC
555 Skokie Blvd Ste 555 # 555 (60062-2854)
PHONE..................304 422-0090
Sam Romeo, *President*
Brian Dees, *Vice Pres*
EMP: 8
SALES (est): 201.7K Privately Held
SIC: 3339 3341 Precious metals; recovery & refining of nonferrous metals

(G-15491)
TARGUN PLASTIC CO
899 Skokie Blvd Ste 334 (60062-4023)
PHONE..................847 509-9355
Jerome Targun, *Ch of Bd*
William Targun, *President*
Gloria Targun, *Admin Sec*
EMP: 5 EST: 1958
SQ FT: 1,200
SALES (est): 2.2MM Privately Held
WEB: www.targun.com
SIC: 2821 Plastics materials & resins

(G-15492)
TDY INDUSTRIES LLC
Also Called: ATI Wah Chang
700 Landwehr Rd (60062-2310)
PHONE..................847 564-0700
EMP: 100
SQ FT: 14,000 Publicly Held
SIC: 3312 Blast furnaces & steel mills
HQ: Tdy Industries, Llc
    1000 Six Ppg Pl
    Pittsburgh PA 15222
    412 394-2800

(G-15493)
TECHNY PLASTICS CORP
1919 Techny Rd (60062-5383)
PHONE..................847 498-2212
Roger D Mann, *President*
Tim Smith, *Plant Mgr*
Frederick Dibbern, *Engineer*
Robert W Jorgensen, *Treasurer*
Jill Brdecka, *Admin Sec*
EMP: 35
SQ FT: 10,000
SALES (est): 4.7MM Privately Held
SIC: 3089 Injection molding of plastics

(G-15494)
UK ABRASIVES INC
3045 Macarthur Blvd (60062-1901)
PHONE..................847 291-3566
Vladimir Kompan, *President*
Mark Gorelik, *CFO*
Vitaly Slobodsky, *Admin Sec*
▲ EMP: 21
SQ FT: 35,000
SALES (est): 3.7MM Privately Held
SIC: 3291 Abrasive products

(G-15495)
UNDERGROUND DEVICES INC
420 Academy Dr (60062-2417)
PHONE..................847 205-9000
Adrienne Greene, *President*
EMP: 17
SQ FT: 11,000
SALES (est): 5.3MM Privately Held
SIC: 2821 Molding compounds, plastics

(G-15496)
UNITROL ELECTRONICS INC
702 Landwehr Rd (60062-2310)
PHONE..................847 480-0115
Roger Hirsch, *President*
Carol Hirsch, *Exec VP*
Ronald Leibovitz, *Vice Pres*
Arman Leonar, *Research*
Grigory Ioffe, *Electrical Engi*
EMP: 20
SQ FT: 12,000
SALES (est): 2MM Privately Held
SIC: 3625 3822 Control equipment, electric; water heater controls

(G-15497)
USA INDUSTRIAL EXPORT CORP
Also Called: Industrialexport.net
707 Skokie Blvd Ste 600 (60062-2841)
PHONE..................312 391-5552
Charles Poremba, *CEO*
EMP: 2
SQ FT: 200,000
SALES (est): 207.9K Privately Held
SIC: 3599 Custom machinery

(G-15498)
WAGNER JOHN
Also Called: J F Wagner Printing Co
3004 Commercial Ave (60062-1913)
PHONE..................847 564-0017
John Wagner, *Owner*
John F Wagner, *Owner*
EMP: 5
SQ FT: 5,000
SALES: 1MM Privately Held
SIC: 2752 2759 2791 2789 Commercial printing, offset; commercial printing; typesetting; bookbinding & related work

(G-15499)
WALGREEN ASIA SERVICES SARL (HQ)
Also Called: Walgreen Intl Sarl - US BR
4010 Commercial Ave (60062-1829)
PHONE..................847 527-4341
Jack Mudde,
Gwenaelle Cousin,
Joseph H Greenberg,
EMP: 3 EST: 2014
SALES (est): 308.3K
SALES (corp-wide): 136.8B Publicly Held
SIC: 2844 Toilet preparations
PA: Walgreens Boots Alliance, Inc.
    108 Wilmot Rd
    Deerfield IL 60015
    847 315-2500

(G-15500)
WE INNOVEX INC
Also Called: Metal Works
3045 Macarthur Blvd (60062-1901)
PHONE..................847 291-3553
Vladimir Kompan, *President*
▲ EMP: 3
SQ FT: 22,000
SALES (est): 330K Privately Held
SIC: 3541 Machine tools, metal cutting type

(G-15501)
WESTROCK CONTAINER LLC (PA)
1101 Skokie Blvd Ste 300 (60062-4124)
PHONE..................847 239-8800
Roger W Stone, *CEO*
Theresa Lowry, *Vice Pres*
Brodie Jordan, *Sales Staff*
Robert Braeman, *Manager*
EMP: 84 EST: 2012
SALES (est): 31.5MM Privately Held
WEB: www.kapstonepaper.com
SIC: 2653 Boxes, corrugated: made from purchased materials

(G-15502)
WEXFORD HOME CORP
707 Skokie Blvd (60062-2857)
PHONE..................847 922-5738
John McGuire, *President*
▲ EMP: 4
SQ FT: 1,000
SALES: 500K Privately Held
SIC: 2679 Wallboard, decorated: made from purchased material

(G-15503)
XSHREDDERS INC (PA)
2855 Shermer Rd (60062-7710)
PHONE..................847 205-1875
David Klein, *President*
Howard Diamond, *Shareholder*
▲ EMP: 60
SQ FT: 84,000
SALES (est): 15.2MM Privately Held
SIC: 2671 Paper coated or laminated for packaging

Northfield
Cook County

(G-15504)
ALLIANCE TECHNOLOGY MGT CORP (PA)
790 W Frontage Rd Ste 716 (60093-1204)
PHONE..................847 574-9752
Vince Christy, *CEO*
Ryan Christy, *Vice Pres*
EMP: 5
SALES: 1MM Privately Held
SIC: 8741 7372 Management services; application computer software

(G-15505)
APAC UNLIMITED INC
790 W Frontage Rd Ste 214 (60093-1204)
PHONE..................847 441-4282
Saretta Joyner, *President*
EMP: 3
SALES (est): 256.6K Privately Held
SIC: 2653 Corrugated & solid fiber boxes

(G-15506)
APLICARE PRODUCTS LLC
3 Lakes Dr (60093-2753)
PHONE..................847 949-5500
Jay Tawil, *Vice Pres*
Johnny Hargrave, *Sales Staff*
John Henke, *Sales Staff*
Stacey Ledbetter, *Sales Staff*
Richard Epps, *Mktg Dir*
EMP: 4
SALES (corp-wide): 7.4B Privately Held
SIC: 3841 Surgical instruments & apparatus
HQ: Aplicare Products, Llc
    550 Research Pkwy
    Meriden CT 06450
    203 630-0500

(G-15507)
BEACON ANNUITY SOLUTIONS LLC
790 W Frontage Rd Ste 335 (60093-1204)
PHONE..................847 864-5447
Jeremy Alexander,
EMP: 1
SQ FT: 200
SALES: 700K Privately Held
SIC: 7372 Prepackaged software

(G-15508)
BERGMANN ORTHOTIC LAB INC
1730 Holder Ln (60093-3307)
PHONE..................847 446-3616
John N Bergmann, *President*
Susan C Simonetti, *Treasurer*
EMP: 3
SQ FT: 4,000
SALES (est): 1.2MM Privately Held
WEB: www.bergmannlab.com
SIC: 3842 Orthopedic appliances

(G-15509)
BODINE ELECTRIC COMPANY (PA)
201 Northfield Rd (60093-3311)
PHONE..................773 478-3515
Jeffrey P Bodine, *President*
Mike Gschwind, *Vice Pres*
Jim Johnson, *Vice Pres*

Northfield - Cook County (G-15510)

Dave Sima, *Safety Dir*
Robert Miller, *Project Mgr*
◆ **EMP:** 450 **EST:** 1905
SQ FT: 40,000
SALES (est): 170MM **Privately Held**
WEB: www.bodine-electric.com
SIC: 5063 3625 3621 Motors, electric; motor controls, electric; motors, electric

(G-15510)
CAP TODAY
325 Waukegan Rd (60093-2719)
PHONE...................847 832-7377
Robert McGonnagel, *Publisher*
Robert McGonnagle, *Publisher*
EMP: 12
SALES (est): 414.1K **Privately Held**
SIC: 2721 Magazines: publishing & printing

(G-15511)
CERTIFIED ASPHALT PAVING
540 W Frontage Rd # 3175 (60093-1281)
P.O. Box 8363 (60093-8363)
PHONE...................847 441-5000
Anthony G Harris, *President*
EMP: 7
SQ FT: 200
SALES (est): 2MM **Privately Held**
SIC: 2951 1794 1795 Asphalt & asphaltic paving mixtures (not from refineries); excavation work; demolition, buildings & other structures

(G-15512)
CHICAGO MLTLINGUA GRAPHICS INC (PA)
Also Called: Multi-Lngua Communications
550 W Frontage Rd # 2700 (60093-1202)
PHONE...................847 386-7187
Lizhe Sun, *President*
Yi Han, *Vice Pres*
Jane Zhang, *Manager*
EMP: 10
SQ FT: 8,000
SALES (est): 869.3K **Privately Held**
SIC: 7389 7336 2752 2791 Translation services; graphic arts & related design; commercial printing, lithographic; typesetting

(G-15513)
FINANCIAL PUBLISHING SVCS CO
Also Called: F P S
1883 Old Willow Rd (60093-2946)
PHONE...................847 501-4120
Ventsi Petrova, *President*
EMP: 11
SQ FT: 500
SALES: 500K **Privately Held**
SIC: 2741 2721 Business service newsletters: publishing & printing; periodicals: publishing only

(G-15514)
FRANK S BENDER INC
Also Called: Frank Bender Jewels
316 Happ Rd (60093-3419)
PHONE...................847 441-7370
Frank S Bender, *President*
Mona Bender, *Corp Secy*
Edward Rubin, *Vice Pres*
EMP: 5
SQ FT: 850
SALES (est): 450K **Privately Held**
SIC: 5944 3911 Jewelry, precious stones & precious metals; jewelry, precious metal

(G-15515)
GREENCYCLE OF INDIANA INC (HQ)
400 Central Ave Ste 115 (60093-3024)
PHONE...................847 441-6606
Caroline Repenning, *President*
David Wagner, *Corp Secy*
EMP: 3
SQ FT: 1,899
SALES (est): 2.6MM **Privately Held**
SIC: 4953 2499 Recycling, waste materials; mulch or sawdust products, wood; mulch, wood & bark

(G-15516)
H HAL KRAMER CO (PA)
1865 Old Willow Rd # 231 (60093-2954)
PHONE...................847 441-0213
Ilene Kramer, *President*
Peter Horwitz, *Vice Pres*
▲ **EMP:** 1 **EST:** 1962
SALES: 200K **Privately Held**
SIC: 3999 Plaques, picture, laminated

(G-15517)
IMPACT POLYMER LLC
790 W Frontage Rd (60093-1204)
PHONE...................847 441-2394
Adriano Pedrelli, *Manager*
John Espeland,
Wdig LLC,
Michael Olson,
EMP: 4 **EST:** 2016
SALES (est): 220K **Privately Held**
SIC: 3272 Concrete products, precast

(G-15518)
IONIT TECHNOLOGIES INC
2311 Dorina Dr (60093-2705)
PHONE...................847 205-9651
James Talbot, *CEO*
Tim Irwin, *President*
David Wedel, *Exec VP*
Brent Hamacheck, *CFO*
EMP: 30
SQ FT: 8,000
SALES (est): 5.2MM **Privately Held**
SIC: 3651 8711 5065 Video cassette recorders/players & accessories; engineering services; security control equipment & systems

(G-15519)
KARLIN FOODS CORP
1845 Oak St Ste 19 (60093-3022)
P.O. Box 8488 (60093-8488)
PHONE...................847 441-8330
Mitchell Karlin, *President*
Jacob Drew, *Opers Staff*
Jennifer Lemke, *QC Mgr*
Penny McNulty, *Research*
Ginny Palumbo, *Natl Sales Mgr*
◆ **EMP:** 17 **EST:** 1977
SQ FT: 9,000
SALES (est): 128.8MM **Privately Held**
SIC: 2034 Dehydrated fruits, vegetables, soups

(G-15520)
KELLER GROUP INC (PA)
1 Northfield Plz Ste 510 (60093-1216)
PHONE...................847 446-7550
John P Keller, *Ch of Bd*
David Spada, *Vice Pres*
EMP: 350
SQ FT: 2,700
SALES (est): 98.2MM **Privately Held**
SIC: 3462 1221 1222 Iron & steel forgings; bituminous coal & lignite-surface mining; bituminous coal-underground mining

(G-15521)
KRAFT HEINZ FOODS COMPANY
Also Called: Kraft Foods
3 Lakes Dr 2b (60093-2753)
PHONE...................847 646-2000
Georges El-Zoghbi, *Vice Chairman*
Wesley Cordner, *Business Mgr*
Mike Bokarae, *Vice Pres*
James M Klein, *Vice Pres*
Scott Frick, *Plant Mgr*
EMP: 225
SALES (corp-wide): 24.9B **Publicly Held**
SIC: 2022 Cheese, natural & processed
HQ: Kraft Heinz Foods Company
  1 Ppg Pl Fl 34
  Pittsburgh PA 15222
  412 456-5700

(G-15522)
MCILVAINE CO
191 Waukegan Rd Ste 208 (60093-2743)
PHONE...................847 784-0012
Robert Mc Ilvaine, *President*
E Lewis, *Manager*
Marilyn Mc Ilvaine, *Manager*
Robert McIlvaine, *CIO*
EMP: 40 **EST:** 1974
SQ FT: 6,000
SALES: 2MM **Privately Held**
WEB: www.mcilvainecompany.com
SIC: 2741 8748 8732 8742 Technical manuals: publishing only, not printed on site; catalogs: publishing only, not printed on site; newsletter publishing; guides: publishing only, not printed on site; business consulting; market analysis or research; management consulting services

(G-15523)
MEDLINE INDUSTRIES INC (PA)
3 Lakes Dr (60093-2753)
PHONE...................847 949-5500
Charles N Mills, *CEO*
Andrew Mills, *President*
Sarah Alasya, *Division Mgr*
John Raposo, *District Mgr*
Amin Setoodeh, *Senior VP*
◆ **EMP:** 1300 **EST:** 1910
SQ FT: 716,000
SALES (est): 7.4B **Privately Held**
WEB: www.medline.com
SIC: 3841 5047 5999 Surgical & medical instruments; instruments, surgical & medical; medical apparatus & supplies

(G-15524)
NORTHERN PALLET AND SUPPLY CO (PA)
464 Central Ave Ste 18 (60093-3030)
PHONE...................847 716-1400
Steven E Schultz, *President*
Craige Schultz, *Vice Pres*
EMP: 9 **EST:** 1954
SQ FT: 600
SALES (est): 6MM **Privately Held**
WEB: www.npallet.com
SIC: 5031 2448 Pallets, wood; pallets, wood

(G-15525)
OFFICENATION INC
Also Called: Pcnation
500 Central Ave (60093-3047)
PHONE...................847 504-3000
Medwin Dayan, *President*
EMP: 35
SQ FT: 30,000
SALES (est): 40.1MM **Privately Held**
SIC: 5044 5112 5571 7379 Office equipment; office supplies; electronic computers; computer related maintenance services

(G-15526)
ONE WAY SOLUTIONS LLC
400 Central Ave Ste 320 (60093-3024)
PHONE...................847 446-0872
Brian Pigott,
Lindsey Pigott,
▼ **EMP:** 3
SQ FT: 1,200
SALES: 646.2K **Privately Held**
SIC: 2448 Pallets, wood

(G-15527)
OZONOLOGY INC
790 W Frontage Rd Ste 522 (60093-1204)
PHONE...................847 998-8808
Allen Morr, *President*
EMP: 3
SQ FT: 5,600
SALES (est): 594K **Privately Held**
SIC: 3559 Ozone machines

(G-15528)
RAINBO SPORTS LLC
790 W Frontage Rd Ste 705 (60093-1204)
PHONE...................847 784-9857
Kevin Kasmar, *Branch Mgr*
EMP: 4
SALES (corp-wide): 1.5MM **Privately Held**
SIC: 3949 Ice skates, parts & accessories
PA: Rainbo Sports, Llc
  1440 Paddock Dr
  Northbrook IL

(G-15529)
SIGNA GROUP INC (PA)
540 W Frontage Rd # 2105 (60093-1250)
PHONE...................847 386-7639
Go Sugiura, *Ch of Bd*
William Henry, *CFO*
EMP: 2
SQ FT: 2,000
SALES (est): 25.7MM **Privately Held**
SIC: 3354 Aluminum extruded products

(G-15530)
SIMPLEMENT INC (PA)
1 Northfield Plz Ste 300 (60093-1214)
PHONE...................702 560-5332
Robert Maclain, *CEO*
Marjorie Zander, *President*
EMP: 3
SALES (est): 1.9MM **Privately Held**
SIC: 7372 8742 Business oriented computer software; business consultant

(G-15531)
STEPAN COMPANY (PA)
22 W Frontage Rd (60093-3470)
PHONE...................847 446-7500
F Quinn Stepan Jr, *Ch of Bd*
Scott R Behrens, *Vice Pres*
David G Kabbes, *Vice Pres*
Jason S Keiper, *Vice Pres*
Arthur W Mergner, *Vice Pres*
◆ **EMP:** 363 **EST:** 1932
SALES: 1.8B **Publicly Held**
WEB: www.stepan.com
SIC: 2821 2087 2865 2843 Polyurethane resins; phthalic anhydride resins; extracts, flavoring; cyclic organic intermediates; sulfonated oils, fats or greases

(G-15532)
STEPAN SPECIALTY PRODUCTS LLC
22 W Frontage Rd (60093-3407)
PHONE...................847 446-7500
EMP: 4
SALES (corp-wide): 1.8B **Publicly Held**
SIC: 2099 Food preparations
HQ: Stepan Specialty Products, Llc
  100 W Hunter Ave
  Maywood NJ 07607
  201 845-3030

(G-15533)
SURGICAL INSTRUMENT SVCS & SAV
3 Lakes Dr (60093-2753)
PHONE...................847 646-2000
EMP: 3
SALES (est): 124.2K **Privately Held**
SIC: 3841 Surgical & medical instruments

(G-15534)
TOWERS MEDIA HOLDINGS INC
Also Called: Towers Holdings
1 Northfield Plz Ste 300 (60093-1214)
PHONE...................312 993-1550
Jonathan Towers, *President*
▲ **EMP:** 78
SALES (est): 12.1MM **Privately Held**
SIC: 3652 7812 7819 Pre-recorded records & tapes; motion picture & video production; video tape or disk reproduction

(G-15535)
TRMG LLP
790 W Frontage Rd Ste 416 (60093-1204)
PHONE...................847 441-4122
Alisdair Martin, *Managing Prtnr*
Andy Odeh, *Executive*
Andrew Stevens, *Admin Sec*
Johnathon Fellows,
Amanda Stevens,
EMP: 10
SQ FT: 2,000
SALES: 1.2MM
SALES (corp-wide): 7.1MM **Privately Held**
SIC: 2721 Magazines: publishing only, not printed on site
PA: Trmg Limited
  Winchester Court
  Hatfield HERTS AL10
  170 727-3999

(G-15536)
TWR3 INC
400 Central Ave Ste 306 (60093-3025)
PHONE...................847 784-5251
EMP: 3
SALES (est): 157.9K **Privately Held**
SIC: 3663 Radio & TV communications equipment

GEOGRAPHIC SECTION

(G-15537)
VELOFLIP INC
540 W Frontage Rd # 2035 (60093-1250)
PHONE.....................847 757-4972
Jacob Weiskirch,
Thomas Torbik,
Dylan Weiskirch,
EMP: 3
SALES: 3K Privately Held
SIC: 7372 7371 Application computer software; computer software development & applications

Northlake
Cook County

(G-15538)
ABC BEVERAGE MFG INC
400 N Wolf Rd Ste A (60164-1659)
PHONE.....................708 449-2600
Roger Collins, Principal
EMP: 3
SALES (est): 355K Privately Held
SIC: 3999 Manufacturing industries

(G-15539)
ALL-BRITE ANODIZING CO INC (PA)
100 W Lake St (60164-2426)
PHONE.....................708 562-0502
Martin W Nieman, President
Bryan Bateman, Principal
EMP: 23
SQ FT: 7,500
SALES: 2.5MM Privately Held
SIC: 3471 Plating of metals or formed products

(G-15540)
AMERICAN BOTTLING COMPANY
400 N Wolf Rd Ste A (60164-1659)
PHONE.....................708 947-5000
Brad Troutman, Manager
EMP: 320 Publicly Held
SIC: 2086 5149 Soft drinks: packaged in cans, bottles, etc.; groceries & related products
HQ: The American Bottling Company
5301 Legacy Dr
Plano TX 75024

(G-15541)
AMERICAN CHEMICAL & EQP INC
128 W Lake St 130 (60164-2428)
P.O. Box 407, Ingleside (60041-0407)
PHONE.....................815 675-9199
Charles Connon, President
▲ EMP: 5
SQ FT: 31,000
SALES (est): 1.1MM Privately Held
SIC: 2899 5084 Chemical preparations; metal refining machinery & equipment

(G-15542)
AMERICAN METAL COIL WORKS INC
130 W Lake St (60164-2428)
P.O. Box 407, Ingleside (60041-0407)
PHONE.....................708 562-2645
EMP: 3
SALES (est): 310.1K Privately Held
SIC: 3559 Metal finishing equipment for plating, etc.

(G-15543)
BOX USA
401 Northwest Ave (60164-1698)
PHONE.....................708 562-6000
Jim McNeill, Principal
EMP: 4 EST: 2011
SALES (est): 616.3K Privately Held
SIC: 2653 Boxes, corrugated: made from purchased materials

(G-15544)
BWT LLC
Also Called: Bluewater Thermal Solutions
75 E Lake St (60164-2419)
PHONE.....................708 410-8000
Tyrone Pearson, General Mgr
Bob Bratsch, Business Mgr
Tom Tekiela, Plant Mgr
Jeff Hemmer, Opers Staff
Deborah Smith, Human Res Dir
EMP: 25 Privately Held
WEB: www.bluewaterthermal.com
SIC: 3398 Metal heat treating
HQ: Bwt Llc
201 Brookfield Pkwy
Greenville SC 29607

(G-15545)
DELTA-UNIBUS CORP
515 N Railroad Ave (60164-1652)
PHONE.....................708 409-1200
▲ EMP: 250
SALES (est): 60.8MM
SALES (corp-wide): 565.2MM Publicly Held
SIC: 3629 Mfg Electrical Industrial Apparatus
PA: Powell Industries, Inc.
8550 Mosley Rd
Houston TX 77075
713 944-6900

(G-15546)
DYNA-BURR CHICAGO INC
65 E Lake St (60164-2483)
PHONE.....................708 250-6744
Patrick McKenna, President
Robert Bea, Vice Pres
Warren H Dickinson, Shareholder
EMP: 15 EST: 1968
SQ FT: 15,000
SALES (est): 1.4MM Privately Held
SIC: 3471 Plating of metals or formed products; finishing, metals or formed products

(G-15547)
HOWARD PRESS PRINTING INC
303 E North Ave Lowr 100 (60164-2699)
P.O. Box 1186, Riverside (60546-0586)
PHONE.....................708 345-7437
Donald Baumruck, President
Shirley Phillips, Corp Secy
Howard Baumruck, Vice Pres
EMP: 5
SALES (est): 569.3K Privately Held
WEB: www.howardpressprinting.com
SIC: 2759 2752 Commercial printing; commercial printing, lithographic

(G-15548)
INTERNATIONAL PAPER COMPANY
401 Northwest Ave (60164-1605)
PHONE.....................708 562-6000
Jim McNeill, Principal
John Puglia, Site Mgr
Floyd Pierce, Info Tech Mgr
Miroslaw Kondracki, Maintence Staff
EMP: 100
SQ FT: 180,000
SALES (corp-wide): 22.3B Publicly Held
SIC: 2653 Boxes, corrugated: made from purchased materials
PA: International Paper Company
6400 Poplar Ave
Memphis TN 38197
901 419-9000

(G-15549)
KEURIG DR PEPPER INC
401 N Railroad Ave (60164-1666)
PHONE.....................708 947-5000
Dan Graham, Plant Mgr
David Vicik, Parts Mgr
John Luke, Manager
EMP: 100 Publicly Held
SIC: 2086 Soft drinks: packaged in cans, bottles, etc.
PA: Keurig Dr Pepper Inc.
53 South Ave
Burlington MA 01803

(G-15550)
KIMBERLY-CLARK CORPORATION
505 Northwest Ave Ste C (60164-1662)
PHONE.....................708 409-8500
John Musich, Manager
EMP: 30
SALES (corp-wide): 18.4B Publicly Held
SIC: 2621 2676 Sanitary tissue paper; infant & baby paper products
PA: Kimberly-Clark Corporation
351 Phelps Dr
Irving TX 75038
972 281-1200

(G-15551)
MICROSOFT CORPORATION
601 Northwest Ave (60164-1301)
PHONE.....................708 409-4759
EMP: 100
SALES (corp-wide): 125.8B Publicly Held
SIC: 7372 Application computer software
PA: Microsoft Corporation
1 Microsoft Way
Redmond WA 98052
425 882-8080

(G-15552)
MURNANE PACKAGING CORPORATION
Also Called: Murpack
607 Northwest Ave (60164-1301)
PHONE.....................708 449-1200
Frank J Murnane Sr, Ch of Bd
Frank J Murnane Jr, President
Patrick Murnane, Vice Pres
▼ EMP: 45 EST: 1919
SQ FT: 76,000
SALES (est): 11.7MM Privately Held
WEB: www.murnanecompanies.com
SIC: 2675 Cardboard cut-outs, panels & foundations: die-cut; food container products & parts, from die-cut paper

(G-15553)
MURNANE SPECIALTIES INC (PA)
607 Northwest Ave (60164-1301)
P.O. Box 631, Hinsdale (60522-0631)
PHONE.....................708 449-1200
Frank J Murnane Jr, President
Thomas Hanson, President
Patrick J Murnane, Exec VP
Frank J Murnane Sr, Treasurer
▲ EMP: 25
SQ FT: 76,000
SALES (est): 5.5MM Privately Held
SIC: 2653 Corrugated boxes, partitions, display items, sheets & pad

(G-15554)
OCTAPHARMA PLASMA INC
17 W North Ave (60164-2311)
PHONE.....................708 409-0900
EMP: 4
SALES (corp-wide): 2B Privately Held
WEB: www.octapharmaplasma.com
SIC: 2836 Plasmas
HQ: Octapharma Plasma, Inc.
10644 Westlake Dr
Charlotte NC 28273
704 654-4600

(G-15555)
POWELL ELECTRICAL SYSTEMS INC
Delta-Unibus Division
515 N Railroad Ave (60164-1652)
PHONE.....................708 409-1200
Blain Steh, Design Engr
Scott Scelfo, Train & Dev Mgr
Michael Bales, Manager
EMP: 200
SALES (corp-wide): 517.1MM Publicly Held
SIC: 3629 Electronic generation equipment
HQ: Powell Electrical Systems, Inc.
8550 Mosley Rd
Houston TX 77075
713 944-6900

(G-15556)
POWELL ELECTRICAL SYSTEMS INC
Delta-Unibus
515 N Railroad Ave (60164-1652)
PHONE.....................708 409-1200
EMP: 250
SALES (corp-wide): 517.1MM Publicly Held
SIC: 3629 Electronic generation equipment
HQ: Powell Electrical Systems, Inc.
8550 Mosley Rd
Houston TX 77075
713 944-6900

(G-15557)
POWELL INDUSTRIES INC
515 N Railroad Ave (60164-1652)
PHONE.....................708 409-1200
Art Zimecki, Materials Mgr
Shawn Eck, Mfg Spvr
Sharon Wendt, Production
Manda Nadkarni, Manager
Michael Dibeasi, Supervisor
EMP: 9
SALES (corp-wide): 517.1MM Publicly Held
WEB: www.powellind.com
SIC: 3612 Power & distribution transformers
PA: Powell Industries, Inc.
8550 Mosley Rd
Houston TX 77075
713 944-6900

(G-15558)
SCHOLLE IPN CORPORATION (PA)
Also Called: Scholle Packaging
200 W North Ave (60164-2402)
PHONE.....................708 562-7290
Thomas Bickford, CEO
Ross Bushnell, President
Peter Messacar, Business Mgr
Gracie Gamez, Adv Board Mem
Scott Cameron, Vice Pres
◆ EMP: 10
SQ FT: 3,000
SALES (est): 282.4MM Privately Held
WEB: www.scholle.com
SIC: 2819 3081 2821 3089 Industrial inorganic chemicals; packing materials, plastic sheet; cellulose derivative materials; plastic processing

(G-15559)
SCHOLLE PACKAGING INC
120 N Railroad Ave (60164-1607)
PHONE.....................708 273-3792
Leon Gianneschi, President
EMP: 4
SALES (est): 612.8K Privately Held
SIC: 3089 Plastic processing

(G-15560)
STEVENS SIGN CO INC
57 E Fullerton Ave (60164-1441)
PHONE.....................708 562-4888
Michael Stevens, President
▲ EMP: 2 EST: 1973
SQ FT: 3,000
SALES (est): 400K Privately Held
SIC: 7389 3993 2396 Sign painting & lettering shop; signs & advertising specialties; automotive & apparel trimmings

(G-15561)
SUN CHEMICAL CORPORATION
North American Inks
135 W Lake St Ste 2 (60164-2496)
PHONE.....................708 562-0550
Mike Murphy, Vice Pres
Tony Renzi, Vice Pres
Luigi Ribaudo, Purch Dir
Corey Soeldner, Purch Dir
A J Theros, Purchasing
EMP: 165
SQ FT: 160,000 Privately Held
SIC: 2893 Printing ink
HQ: Sun Chemical Corporation
35 Waterview Blvd Ste 100
Parsippany NJ 07054
973 404-6000

(G-15562)
TRI STATE RECYCLING SERVICE
301 W Lake St Frnt 1 (60164-2403)
PHONE.....................708 865-9939
Frank Ward, President
Gertrude Ward, Admin Sec
EMP: 25
SALES (est): 2.1MM Privately Held
SIC: 2611 Pulp manufactured from waste or recycled paper

Northlake - Cook County (G-15563)

(G-15563)
TRU-WAY INC
36 W Lake St (60164-2424)
P.O. Box 346127, Chicago (60634-6127)
PHONE.................................708 562-3690
EMP: 20
SQ FT: 10,000
SALES (est): 4.1MM **Privately Held**
SIC: 3469 3444 Mfg Metal Stampings Mfg Sheet Metalwork

(G-15564)
VACUMET CORP
200 W North Ave (60164-2402)
PHONE.................................708 562-7290
Wiiliam Scholle, *President*
Kent Kisselle, *Director*
Martin Bell, *Admin Sec*
EMP: 15
SALES (est): 2.6MM **Privately Held**
SIC: 3081 2819 2821 2295 Packing materials, plastic sheet; industrial inorganic chemicals; cellulose derivative materials; metallizing of fabrics

O Fallon
St. Clair County

(G-15565)
ANDRIAS FOOD GROUP INC (PA)
Also Called: Andria's Steak Sauce
6805 Old Collinsville Rd (62269-6916)
PHONE.................................618 632-4866
Larry Kenison, *President*
Sam Andria, *Vice Pres*
EMP: 40
SQ FT: 3,000
SALES (est): 1.7MM **Privately Held**
SIC: 5812 5813 2035 2033 Steak restaurant; drinking places; seasonings, meat sauces (except tomato & dry); barbecue sauce: packaged in cans, jars, etc.; spices & herbs; sauces

(G-15566)
ANDRIAS FOOD GROUP INC
Also Called: Andria's Steak Sauce
6813 Old Collinsville Rd (62269-6916)
PHONE.................................618 632-3118
Larry Kenison, *Owner*
EMP: 4
SALES (corp-wide): 1.7MM **Privately Held**
SIC: 2035 2033 Seasonings, meat sauces (except tomato & dry); barbecue sauce: packaged in cans, jars, etc.
PA: Andria's Food Group, Inc.
6805 Old Collinsville Rd
O Fallon IL 62269
618 632-4866

(G-15567)
ARINC INCORPORATED
8 Eagle Ctr Ste 4 (62269-1963)
PHONE.................................800 633-6882
Carol Laporte, *General Mgr*
EMP: 20
SALES (corp-wide): 77B **Publicly Held**
SIC: 8711 3812 Aviation &/or aeronautical engineering; search & navigation equipment
HQ: Arinc Incorporated
2551 Riva Rd
Annapolis MD 21401
410 266-4000

(G-15568)
ATK SERVICES INC
Also Called: Atk Home Services
1392 Frontage Rd Ste 9 (62269-2086)
PHONE.................................618 726-5114
Raymond Kelly, *President*
William Hassard, *Admin Sec*
EMP: 5
SQ FT: 5,500
SALES (est): 131.1K **Privately Held**
SIC: 1711 1389 Heating systems repair & maintenance; plumbing contractors; heating & air conditioning contractors; construction, repair & dismantling services

(G-15569)
C & C SPORT STOP
115 N Lincoln Ave (62269-1414)
PHONE.................................618 632-7812
Cathy Portell, *Owner*
Wayne Portell, *Co-Owner*
EMP: 3
SQ FT: 1,000
SALES (est): 202.8K **Privately Held**
SIC: 2396 5941 2395 7389 Screen printing on fabric articles; sporting goods & bicycle shops; pleating & stitching; embroidering of advertising on shirts, etc.

(G-15570)
CENTURY PRINTING
510 Pepperwood Ct (62269-3059)
PHONE.................................618 632-2486
Gary Weldbacher, *President*
EMP: 3
SQ FT: 4,000
SALES (est): 418.3K **Privately Held**
SIC: 2752 7334 2791 2789 Commercial printing, offset; photocopying & duplicating services; typesetting; bookbinding & related work; commercial printing

(G-15571)
DEMOND SIGNS INC
93 Betty Ln (62269-2234)
P.O. Box 414 (62269-0414)
PHONE.................................618 624-7260
Sue Demond, *President*
EMP: 10
SQ FT: 2,800
SALES (est): 1.4MM **Privately Held**
SIC: 3993 1799 Electric signs; sign installation & maintenance

(G-15572)
DKB PARTNERS INC
Also Called: AAA Tool and Machine
230 Obernuefemann Rd (62269-7105)
PHONE.................................618 632-6718
Brian Wort, *President*
EMP: 9 EST: 1969
SQ FT: 12,000
SALES (est): 1.4MM **Privately Held**
WEB: www.aaatoolandmachine.com
SIC: 3599 3544 3469 Machine shop, jobbing & repair; die sets for metal stamping (presses); metal stampings

(G-15573)
HIGHPOINT PUBLISHING INC
Also Called: High Pointe Publishing
305 Orange Jewel Ct (62269-6929)
PHONE.................................928 717-0100
Judy Dusman, *President*
Richard Dusman, *President*
Stan Miller, *Sales Staff*
Alex Popovics, *Sales Staff*
Inna Shames, *Marketing Staff*
EMP: 4
SALES (est): 281.4K **Privately Held**
WEB: www.homesandland.com
SIC: 2721 Magazines: publishing only, not printed on site

(G-15574)
ILER BRANDS INC
1350 Bossler Ln (62269-7128)
PHONE.................................314 799-3833
EMP: 4 EST: 2017
SALES (est): 346.8K **Privately Held**
SIC: 3949 Sporting & athletic goods

(G-15575)
JET PRECAST & REDIMIX INC
570 W 3rd St (62269-2091)
P.O. Box 8 (62269-0008)
PHONE.................................618 632-3594
John R Yoch, *President*
Michael Nuckolls, *Manager*
Sherry Yoch, *Admin Sec*
EMP: 7
SQ FT: 1,000
SALES (est): 1MM **Privately Held**
SIC: 3272 Concrete products

(G-15576)
K-PRO US LLC
475 Regency Park Ste 175 (62269-0119)
PHONE.................................872 529-5776
Erin Rockman, *Mng Member*
EMP: 3
SALES (est): 366.2K **Privately Held**
SIC: 8748 4731 2048 2077 Business consulting; freight transportation arrangement; bone meal, prepared as animal feed; feather meal, prepared as animal feed; fish meal, except as animal feed; animal feeds; commodity traders, contracts

(G-15577)
KVD ENTERPRISES LLC
Also Called: Kvd Sewer
1392 Frontage Rd Ste 10 (62269-2086)
PHONE.................................618 726-5114
Raymond Kelly,
EMP: 3 EST: 2008
SALES (est): 285K **Privately Held**
SIC: 1623 3531 1794 Water & sewer line construction; plows: construction, excavating & grading; excavation & grading, building construction

(G-15578)
LICKENBROCK & SONS INC
328 W State St (62269-1199)
PHONE.................................618 632-4977
Gary H Lickenbrock, *President*
Craig Lickenbrock, *Corp Secy*
EMP: 4 EST: 1946
SQ FT: 4,000
SALES (est): 100K **Privately Held**
WEB: www.lickenbrockandsonsinc.com
SIC: 5051 5084 3446 3441 Steel; welding machinery & equipment; architectural metalwork; fabricated structural metal

(G-15579)
LOCKHEED MARTIN CORPORATION
4 Eagle Ctr Ste 1 (62269-1800)
PHONE.................................618 628-0700
Greg Lovin, *Manager*
EMP: 3 **Publicly Held**
SIC: 3812 Search & navigation equipment
PA: Lockheed Martin Corporation
6801 Rockledge Dr
Bethesda MD 20817

(G-15580)
METROEAST MOTORSPORTS INC
1714 Frontage Rd (62269-1845)
PHONE.................................618 628-2466
Ladonna Boyd, *Co-Owner*
Bret Boyd, *Co-Owner*
EMP: 8
SQ FT: 5,000
SALES (est): 122.6K **Privately Held**
SIC: 7694 5561 5571 7699 Motor repair services; recreational vehicle dealers; motorcycle dealers; motorcycle repair service; engine repair & replacement, non-automotive

(G-15581)
OFALLON PRESSURE CAST CO
1418 Frontage Rd (62269-1807)
PHONE.................................618 632-8694
Raymond Leveling, *Owner*
Carolyn Leveling, *Treasurer*
Douglas Leveling, *Manager*
EMP: 5 EST: 1979
SQ FT: 2,920
SALES (est): 842.2K **Privately Held**
WEB: www.selfstorageofallon.com
SIC: 3363 Aluminum die-castings

(G-15582)
PPG INDUSTRIES INC
Also Called: PPG 4611
1333 Central Park Dr # 135 (62269-1775)
PHONE.................................618 206-2250
Hirchel Hill, *Branch Mgr*
EMP: 4
SALES (corp-wide): 15.1B **Publicly Held**
SIC: 2851 Paints & allied products
PA: Ppg Industries, Inc.
1 Ppg Pl
Pittsburgh PA 15272
412 434-3131

(G-15583)
SECURE DATA INC
640 Pierce Blvd Ste 200 (62269-2584)
PHONE.................................618 726-5225
Chris Nazetta, *President*
Aaron Broyles, *Vice Pres*
EMP: 13
SQ FT: 5,000
SALES (est): 1.9MM **Privately Held**
SIC: 7371 8741 7372 Computer software systems analysis & design, custom; business management; application computer software

(G-15584)
ST CLAIR TENNIS CLUB LLC
Also Called: Saint Clair Tennis Club
733 Hartman Ln (62269-1729)
P.O. Box 1034 (62269-8034)
PHONE.................................618 632-1400
David T Threlkeld,
Carolyn M Mc Laughlin,
William R Rusick,
EMP: 6 EST: 1969
SQ FT: 40,000
SALES (est): 227.8K **Privately Held**
WEB: www.stclairtennis.com
SIC: 7997 5941 7999 2951 Tennis club, membership; tennis goods & equipment; tennis courts, outdoor/indoor; non-membership; asphalt paving mixtures & blocks

(G-15585)
SUN INFRARED TECHNOLOGIES INC
808 Lakeshore Dr (62269-1215)
PHONE.................................618 632-3013
Chuck F Rolek, *President*
EMP: 5 EST: 2000
SQ FT: 1,200
SALES (est): 761.8K **Privately Held**
WEB: www.suninfrared.com
SIC: 3823 Industrial instrmnts msrmnt display/control process variable

(G-15586)
ZAPP NOODLE
1407 W Highway 50 Ste 106 (62269-1672)
PHONE.................................618 979-8863
EMP: 4 EST: 2010
SALES (est): 253K **Privately Held**
WEB: www.zappthai.com
SIC: 2098 Noodles (e.g. egg, plain & water), dry

Oak Brook
Dupage County

(G-15587)
2000PLUS GROUPS INC
2607 W 22nd St Ste 39 (60523-1231)
PHONE.................................630 528-3220
Ahmad A Adam, *President*
EMP: 5
SALES (est): 160.4K
SALES (corp-wide): 43.3MM **Privately Held**
SIC: 2015 Duck slaughtering & processing
PA: 2000plus Groups, Inc.
4343 W 44th Pl
Chicago IL 60632
800 939-6268

(G-15588)
ACE METAL REFINISHERS INC
2001 Spring Rd (60523-1812)
PHONE.................................800 323-7147
Gordon R Swanson, *Branch Mgr*
EMP: 3
SALES (est): 136.4K
SALES (corp-wide): 3.8MM **Privately Held**
WEB: www.ace-metal.com
SIC: 3471 Cleaning & descaling metal products
PA: Ace Metal Refinishers, Inc.
978 N Dupage Ave
Lombard IL 60148
630 778-9200

(G-15589)
AHEAD INC
1515 W 22nd St Ste 200 (60523-2012)
PHONE.................................312 753-7967
EMP: 2254
SALES (corp-wide): 6.1MM **Privately Held**
SIC: 7372 Prepackaged software

GEOGRAPHIC SECTION
Oak Brook - Dupage County (G-15616)

HQ: Ahead, Inc.
   401 N Michigan Ave # 3400
   Chicago IL 60611

(G-15590)
ALAN ROCCA LTD
Also Called: Alan Rocca Fine Jewelery
3824 York Rd Ste B (60523-2753)
PHONE..................630 323-5800
Alan Rocca, *President*
EMP: 20
SQ FT: 1,800
SALES: 3MM **Privately Held**
SIC: 3911 5944 Jewelry, precious metal; jewelry, precious stones & precious metals

(G-15591)
AMD INDUSTRIES INC (PA)
815 Saint Stephens Grn (60523-2567)
PHONE..................708 863-8900
David E Allen, *Chairman*
Lydia Allen, *Admin Sec*
Myrna Palmisano, *Admin Asst*
◆ **EMP:** 55
SALES (est): 9.9MM **Privately Held**
WEB: www.amdpop.com
SIC: 3993 Displays & cutouts, window & lobby

(G-15592)
AMERICAN ELECTRONIC PDTS INC
2001 Midwest Rd Ste 105 (60523-1377)
PHONE..................630 889-9977
▲ **EMP:** 10
SQ FT: 1,100
SALES (est): 1.1MM **Privately Held**
SIC: 3594 3621 3629 3321 Mfg Fluid Power Pump/Mtr Mfg Motors/Generators Mfg Elec Indstl Equip Gray/Ductile Iron Fndry Mfg Aluminum Die-Casting

(G-15593)
AMERICRAFT CARTON
2809 Butterfield Rd (60523-1151)
PHONE..................630 225-7311
EMP: 3
SALES (est): 177K **Privately Held**
SIC: 2657 Folding paperboard boxes

(G-15594)
ART OF SHAVING - FL LLC
100 Oakbrook Ctr (60523-1838)
PHONE..................630 684-0277
EMP: 5
SALES (corp-wide): 67.6B **Publicly Held**
SIC: 5999 2844 3421 5122 Hair care products; toilet preparations; razor blades & razors; razor blades
HQ: The Art Of Shaving - Fl Llc
   6100 Blue Lagoon Dr # 150
   Miami FL 33126

(G-15595)
AUDIO TECH BUS BK SUMMARIES
1314 Kensington Rd # 4953 (60523-2131)
PHONE..................630 734-0500
Fred Rogers, *President*
Eric Hambleton, *Regional Mgr*
Sue Carman, *Accountant*
Justin Spafford, *Mktg Dir*
Carlos Chacon, *Technology*
EMP: 5
SQ FT: 4,000
SALES: 750K **Privately Held**
SIC: 2731 Books: publishing only

(G-15596)
BENESSERE VINEYARD INC (PA)
2100 Clearwater Dr # 250 (60523-1927)
PHONE..................708 560-9840
John J Benish Jr, *CEO*
Marco Marino, *Vice Pres*
EMP: 1
SALES (est): 689.6K **Privately Held**
SIC: 2084 Wines

(G-15597)
BLISTEX GLOBAL INC
1800 Swift Dr (60523-1574)
PHONE..................630 571-2870
EMP: 3
SALES (est): 262.3K **Privately Held**
SIC: 2834 Pharmaceutical preparations

(G-15598)
BLISTEX INC (PA)
1800 Swift Dr (60523-1574)
PHONE..................630 571-2870
David C Arch, *Ch of Bd*
Michael J Donnantuono, *President*
Phillip J Hoolehan, *Vice Pres*
Michael A Wojcik, *Vice Pres*
Michael Sgarioto, *Technician*
◆ **EMP:** 175 **EST:** 1947
SQ FT: 87,500
SALES (est): 56.8MM **Privately Held**
WEB: www.blistex.com
SIC: 2834 Ointments; lip balms; antiseptics, medicinal

(G-15599)
BLISTEX INC
100 Windsor Dr (60523-1506)
PHONE..................630 571-2870
Jackie Elliott, *Manager*
EMP: 4
SALES (corp-wide): 56.8MM **Privately Held**
SIC: 2834 Ointments
PA: Blistex Inc.
   1800 Swift Dr
   Oak Brook IL 60523
   630 571-2870

(G-15600)
BMAC USA INC
1415 W 22nd St Towe Fl (60523-2074)
PHONE..................630 279-5500
Sen Yamanaka, *CEO*
EMP: 5 **EST:** 2012
SALES (est): 198.5K **Privately Held**
WEB: www.bmac.pro
SIC: 3421 Scissors, shears, clippers, snips & similar tools

(G-15601)
BUHLWORK DESIGN GUILD
320 Luthin Rd (60523-2791)
PHONE..................630 325-5340
Russell A Bulin, *President*
Russell Bulin, *President*
Ronald J Bulin, *Corp Secy*
Jeff Bulin, *Vice Pres*
EMP: 2
SQ FT: 7,600
SALES: 500K **Privately Held**
SIC: 2599 7389 Restaurant furniture, wood or metal; hotel furniture; bowling establishment furniture; interior design services

(G-15602)
BYELKAYCOM SALES INC
2222 Camden Ct (60523-4674)
PHONE..................630 574-8484
Timothy J Jahnke, *President*
EMP: 4
SALES (est): 52.8K
SALES (corp-wide): 1B **Privately Held**
SIC: 3431 Plumbing fixtures: enameled iron cast iron or pressed metal
PA: Elkay Manufacturing Company Inc
   1333 Butterfield Rd # 200
   Downers Grove IL 60515
   630 574-8484

(G-15603)
C B E INC
110 Oak Brook Rd (60523-2314)
PHONE..................630 571-2610
Clair Buffardi, *President*
Louis Buffardi,
EMP: 3
SALES (est): 493.3K **Privately Held**
SIC: 5199 2299 General merchandise, non-durable; gifts & novelties; fabrics: linen, jute, hemp, ramie

(G-15604)
CAINS FOODS INC (HQ)
2021 Spring Rd Ste 600 (60523-1860)
PHONE..................978 772-0300
Denis J Keaveny, *CEO*
EMP: 100
SALES (est): 29.1MM
SALES (corp-wide): 4.2B **Publicly Held**
SIC: 2035 Pickles, sauces & salad dressings
PA: Treehouse Foods, Inc.
   2021 Spring Rd Ste 600
   Oak Brook IL 60523
   708 483-1300

(G-15605)
CENTREX TECHNOLOGIES LLC
2021 Midwest Rd Ste 200 (60523-1370)
PHONE..................800 768-0700
Kevin George O'Hara, *Director*
Kathy Maniago, *Executive*
EMP: 8
SALES (est): 332.4K **Privately Held**
SIC: 7372 Business oriented computer software

(G-15606)
CHAMBERLAIN GROUP INC (DH)
Also Called: Liftmaster
300 Windsor Dr (60523-1510)
PHONE..................630 279-3600
Joanna Sohovich, *CEO*
Craig J Duchossois, *Ch of Bd*
Jeff Meredith, *President*
Robert I Baker, *President*
James J Roberts, *President*
◆ **EMP:** 340
SQ FT: 62,000
SALES (est): 1.5B
SALES (corp-wide): 1.4B **Privately Held**
SIC: 3699 Door opening & closing devices, electrical
HQ: Chamberlain Manufacturing Corporation
   300 Windsor Dr
   Oak Brook IL 60523
   630 279-3600

(G-15607)
CHAMBERLAIN GROUP INC
300 Windsor Dr (60523-1510)
PHONE..................630 279-3600
Larry Strait, *VP Engrg*
Andres Becerra, *Engineer*
Matthew Crane, *Engineer*
Claudia Bevilacqua, *Design Engr*
Souleymane Bah, *Electrical Engi*
EMP: 30
SALES (corp-wide): 1.4B **Privately Held**
SIC: 3699 Electrical equipment & supplies
HQ: The Chamberlain Group Inc
   300 Windsor Dr
   Oak Brook IL 60523
   630 279-3600

(G-15608)
CHAMBERLAIN MANUFACTURING CORP (HQ)
300 Windsor Dr (60523-1510)
PHONE..................630 279-3600
Merton L Townsend, *Principal*
Richard L Duchossois, *Chairman*
Craig J Duchossois, *Vice Pres*
Jeffrey Klein, *Vice Pres*
Kevin Anderson, *Manager*
◆ **EMP:** 865
SQ FT: 62,000
SALES (est): 1.5B
SALES (corp-wide): 1.4B **Privately Held**
WEB: www.chamberlaingroup.com
SIC: 3651 3625 3699 Household audio & video equipment; relays & industrial controls; door opening & closing devices, electrical
PA: The Duchossois Group Inc
   444 W Lake St Ste 2000
   Chicago IL 60606
   312 586-2110

(G-15609)
CHICOR INC
2021 Midwest Rd Ste 200 (60523-1370)
PHONE..................630 953-6154
Jeff Chimienti, *Principal*
EMP: 3 **EST:** 1999
SALES (est): 273.1K **Privately Held**
SIC: 2211 Apparel & outerwear fabrics, cotton

(G-15610)
CHINCHILLA SCIENTIFIC LLC
900 Jorie Blvd Ste 35 (60523-2268)
PHONE..................630 645-0600
Craig Chinchilla,
EMP: 4
SALES (est): 136.4K **Privately Held**
SIC: 3826 Analytical instruments

(G-15611)
CLARIOS
Also Called: Johnson Controls
78 Oakbrook Ctr (60523-1810)
PHONE..................630 573-0897
Dan Ellis, *Manager*
EMP: 91 **Privately Held**
WEB: www.johnsoncontrols.com
SIC: 2531 Seats, automobile
HQ: Johnson Controls, Inc.
   5757 N Green Bay Ave
   Milwaukee WI 53209
   414 524-1200

(G-15612)
CONFIGURE ONE INC (PA)
900 Jorie Blvd Ste 190 (60523-3853)
PHONE..................630 368-9950
Raymond J De Hont, *Ch of Bd*
Michael McDonnell, *President*
Dan Howe, *Vice Pres*
Aleks La Rosa, *Accounts Exec*
Eric Sandusky, *Technology*
EMP: 39
SQ FT: 2,700
SALES (est): 6.5MM **Privately Held**
SIC: 7372 Business oriented computer software

(G-15613)
CONTECH ENGNERED SOLUTIONS LLC
1200 Harger Rd Ste 707 (60523-1821)
PHONE..................630 573-1110
A J Margetis, *Sales/Mktg Mgr*
EMP: 6 **Privately Held**
WEB: www.conteches.com
SIC: 3443 Fabricated plate work (boiler shop)
HQ: Contech Engineered Solutions Llc
   9025 Centre Pointe Dr # 400
   West Chester OH 45069
   513 645-7000

(G-15614)
CSP INFORMATION GROUP INC
Also Called: CSP Magazine
1100 Jorie Blvd Ste 260 (60523-4431)
PHONE..................630 574-5075
Drayden McLane, *CEO*
Paul Reuder, *President*
EMP: 31
SQ FT: 3,200
SALES (est): 3.4MM **Privately Held**
SIC: 2721 Magazines: publishing only, not printed on site
PA: Ideal Media, Llc
   200 E Randolph St # 7000
   Chicago IL 60601

(G-15615)
CYBER TECH CORP
1301 W 22nd St Ste 308 (60523-2094)
PHONE..................630 472-3200
Edwin A Rodriguez, *President*
Pankaj Srivastava, *Senior VP*
Kiran Ramarao, *Manager*
EMP: 3
SALES (est): 126.1K **Privately Held**
SIC: 3825 Network analyzers

(G-15616)
ENERGY SERVICES GROUP LLC
700 Commerce Dr Ste 500 (60523-8736)
PHONE..................630 581-4840
Phil Galati, *CEO*
EMP: 3
SALES (corp-wide): 14.9MM **Privately Held**
SIC: 7372 Utility computer software
PA: Energy Services Group, Llc
   141 Longwater Dr Ste 113
   Norwell MA 02061
   781 347-9000

Oak Brook - Dupage County (G-15617)

(G-15617)
ENESPRO LLC
122 W 22nd St Ste 1 (60523-1562)
PHONE..................630 332-2801
Michael Enright, *Principal*
EMP: 8
SALES (est): 941.6K **Privately Held**
SIC: 3842 Gloves, safety

(G-15618)
FEDERAL SIGNAL CORPORATION (PA)
1415 W 22nd St Ste 1100 (60523-2004)
PHONE..................630 954-2000
Dennis J Martin, *Ch of Bd*
Jennifer L Sherman, *President*
Mark D Weber, *COO*
Daniel A Dupre, *Vice Pres*
Lauren B Elting, *Vice Pres*
◆ EMP: 54
SALES: 1.2B **Publicly Held**
WEB: www.federalsignal.com
SIC: 3647 3669 3559 3544 Motor vehicle lighting equipment; dome lights, automotive; flasher lights, automotive; sirens, electric: vehicle, marine, industrial & air raid; parking facility equipment & supplies; special dies & tools; die sets for metal stamping (presses); punches, forming & stamping; cutting tools for machine tools; fire department vehicles (motor vehicles), assembly of

(G-15619)
FILTRATION GROUP CORPORATION (PA)
600 W 22nd St Ste 300 (60523-1949)
PHONE..................512 593-7999
George Nolen, *President*
Bill Huber, *Senior VP*
John Lavorato, *Vice Pres*
Joseph Lynch, *Vice Pres*
Chris Koeppen, *VP Opers*
▲ EMP: 86 EST: 2010
SALES (est): 344.8MM **Privately Held**
SIC: 3564 Blowers & fans

(G-15620)
FIVECUBITS INC (HQ)
Also Called: Bmg Seltec
1315 W 22nd St Ste 300 (60523-2062)
PHONE..................630 749-4182
John Jazwiec, *President*
Alex Perstinski, *Software Engr*
Richard Haus, *Director*
Jordan Cox, *Executive*
John McDow, *Executive*
▲ EMP: 2
SQ FT: 3,800
SALES (est): 9.2MM
SALES (corp-wide): 87.3MM **Privately Held**
SIC: 7372 Business oriented computer software
PA: Command Alkon Incorporated
1800 Intl Pk Dr Ste 400
Birmingham AL 35243
205 879-3282

(G-15621)
FIVECUBITS INC
1315 W 22nd St Ste 300 (60523-2062)
PHONE..................925 273-1862
Bob Bratt, *Branch Mgr*
EMP: 12
SALES (corp-wide): 87.3MM **Privately Held**
SIC: 3625 Electric controls & control accessories, industrial
HQ: Fivecubits Inc.
1315 W 22nd St Ste 300
Oak Brook IL 60523

(G-15622)
FLYERINC CORPORATION
Also Called: Chicago Direct Mail
700 Commerce Dr Ste 500 (60523-8736)
PHONE..................630 655-3400
Scott Jonlich, *President*
Dan Jonlich, *Vice Pres*
EMP: 7
SQ FT: 1,200
SALES (est): 690.5K **Privately Held**
SIC: 2752 7331 8742 Promotional printing, lithographic; direct mail advertising services; marketing consulting services

(G-15623)
G & S PALLETS
66 Windsor Dr (60523-2365)
PHONE..................630 574-2741
John Salerno, *President*
EMP: 3 EST: 2011
SALES (est): 212.7K **Privately Held**
SIC: 2448 Pallets, wood & wood with metal

(G-15624)
GENERAL ELECTRIC COMPANY
2015 Spring Rd Ste 400 (60523-1865)
PHONE..................630 334-0054
David Chiesa, *Manager*
EMP: 50
SALES (corp-wide): 95.2B **Publicly Held**
SIC: 3613 Switches, electric power except snap, push button, etc.
PA: General Electric Company
5 Necco St
Boston MA 02210
617 443-3000

(G-15625)
GRAND SPECIALTIES CO
110 Oakbrook Ctr (60523-1808)
PHONE..................630 629-8000
Anthony M Sasgen Jr, *President*
George Sundheim, *Admin Sec*
EMP: 13 EST: 1920
SQ FT: 12,000
SALES (est): 920K **Privately Held**
SIC: 3537 3429 3594 Lift trucks, industrial: fork, platform, straddle, etc.; cranes, industrial truck; builders' hardware; fluid power pumps & motors

(G-15626)
IBS CONVERSIONS INC
2625 Bttrfield Rd Ste 114w (60523)
PHONE..................630 571-9100
Daniel Williams, *CEO*
EMP: 88
SALES (est): 6.6MM
SALES (corp-wide): 22MM **Privately Held**
SIC: 3577 7378 Data conversion equipment, media-to-media: computer; computer maintenance & repair
PA: Interactive Business Systems, Inc.
2625 Bttrfield Rd Ste 114w
Oak Brook IL 60523
630 571-9100

(G-15627)
JONES MEDICAL INSTRUMENT CO
200 Windsor Dr Ste A (60523-1597)
PHONE..................630 571-1980
Bill Jones, *President*
EMP: 20 EST: 1919
SQ FT: 20,000
SALES (est): 3.2MM **Privately Held**
WEB: www.jonesmedical.com
SIC: 3841 3845 3829 Surgical & medical instruments; electromedical equipment; measuring & controlling devices

(G-15628)
JRB ATTACHMENTS LLC
Also Called: Paladin
2211 York Rd Ste 320 (60523-4030)
PHONE..................319 378-3696
Dave Burdakin, *Manager*
EMP: 9
SALES (est): 2.2MM **Privately Held**
WEB: www.paladinattachments.com
SIC: 3531 Construction machinery

(G-15629)
KANAN FASHIONS INC (PA)
1010 Jorie Blvd Ste 324 (60523-2241)
PHONE..................630 240-1234
Mehul R Shah, *President*
Paresh R Joshi, *CFO*
▲ EMP: 24
SQ FT: 8,588
SALES (est): 2MM **Privately Held**
SIC: 2325 Men's & boys' trousers & slacks

(G-15630)
L & H COMPANY INC (PA)
Also Called: Meade Electric Co
1220 Kensington Rd 210 (60523-2113)
PHONE..................630 571-7200
John S Lizzadro, *President*
Alan L Shulman, *Admin Sec*
EMP: 10
SALES (est): 320.5MM **Privately Held**
WEB: www.lizzadrocre.com
SIC: 1611 1623 3621 1731 General contractor, highway & street construction; oil & gas pipeline construction; motors, electric; lighting contractor

(G-15631)
LAMINATION SPECIALTIES LLC (HQ)
1400 16th St (60523-1306)
PHONE..................312 243-2181
Lauane Addis,
EMP: 45
SALES (est): 8.9MM
SALES (corp-wide): 386.2MM **Privately Held**
SIC: 3531 3399 Ballast distributors; laminating steel
PA: Upg Enterprises Llc
1400 16th St Ste 250
Oak Brook IL 60523
630 822-7000

(G-15632)
LEARNING CURVE INTERNATIONAL (DH)
1111 W 22nd St Ste 320 (60523-1935)
PHONE..................630 573-7200
Richard E Rothcopf, *Ch of Bd*
Peter Henseler, *President*
Donald Toht, *Vice Pres*
Willie Wilkov, *Vice Pres*
Randy Peltier, *CIO*
◆ EMP: 50
SQ FT: 15,000
SALES (est): 27.2MM **Privately Held**
SIC: 5092 2389 Educational toys; costumes
HQ: Tomy International, Inc.
2021 9th St Se
Dyersville IA 52040
563 875-2000

(G-15633)
LEVOLOR INC
Also Called: Newell
2707 Butterfield Rd (60523-1278)
PHONE..................800 346-3278
EMP: 5 **Privately Held**
SIC: 2591 Window blinds
HQ: Levolor, Inc.
1 Blue Hill Plz
Pearl River NY 10965

(G-15634)
LEX HOLDING CO
1400 16th St Ste 250 (60523-8802)
PHONE..................708 594-9200
Robert S Douglass, *CEO*
Tim McFarland, *President*
Paul Douglass, *COO*
EMP: 6 EST: 2013
SALES (est): 550.5K **Privately Held**
SIC: 3317 Steel pipe & tubes

(G-15635)
LIBERTY SUBURBAN CHICAGO
709 Enterprise Dr (60523-8814)
PHONE..................630 368-1100
Gary Smith, *Administration*
EMP: 3
SALES (est): 121.3K **Privately Held**
SIC: 2711 Newspapers, publishing & printing

(G-15636)
LIFTSEAT CORPORATION
2001 Midwest Rd Ste 204 (60523-4308)
PHONE..................630 424-2840
Gregory C Kilgore, *Principal*
EMP: 20
SQ FT: 4,000
SALES (est): 3.2MM **Privately Held**
SIC: 2499 Seats, toilet

(G-15637)
LODAAT LLC (PA)
Also Called: Nutraceuticals and Pharma Tls
1415 W 22nd St Ste Tower (60523-2031)
PHONE..................630 248-2380
Yogeeta Khatau, *Opers Staff*
Ramila Khatau, *Mng Member*
EMP: 21 EST: 2007
SQ FT: 2,000
SALES: 50MM **Privately Held**
WEB: www.lodaat.com
SIC: 2834 Extracts of botanicals: powdered, pilular, solid or fluid

(G-15638)
LUTHERAN CHURCH-MISSOURI SYNOD
Also Called: Cais
1200 Jorie Blvd Ste 308 (60523-2254)
PHONE..................630 607-0300
Scott Hermanses, *Director*
EMP: 30
SALES (corp-wide): 145.2MM **Privately Held**
SIC: 7372 Educational computer software
PA: The Lutheran Church-Missouri Synod
1333 S Kirkwood Rd
Saint Louis MO 63122
314 965-9000

(G-15639)
MADE AS INTENDED INC
Also Called: MAI Apparel
3423 Spring Rd (60523-2739)
PHONE..................630 789-3494
Ray Sproug, *CEO*
EMP: 11
SALES (est): 1MM **Privately Held**
WEB: www.madeasintended.com
SIC: 3911 7389 Jewelry, precious metal;

(G-15640)
MAUSER PCKG SLTONS INTRMDATE I (PA)
1515 W 22nd St Ste 1100 (60523-2048)
PHONE..................770 645-4800
Kenneth M Roessler, *President*
Tarek Maguid, *COO*
Leslie L Bradshaw, *Exec VP*
Michael A Noel, *Exec VP*
EMP: 5
SALES (est): 544MM **Privately Held**
SIC: 3089 3411 Plastic containers, except foam; tubs, plastic (containers); can lids & ends, metal

(G-15641)
MC ADAMS MULTIGRAPHICS INC
900 Jorie Blvd Ste 26 (60523-3852)
PHONE..................630 990-1707
Dennis McAdams, *President*
Nancy M Adams, *Vice Pres*
Matt Plattenberger, *Sales Executive*
Meghan Plocinski, *Graphic Designe*
EMP: 5
SQ FT: 2,500
SALES: 520K **Privately Held**
WEB: www.mcadamsmultigraphics.com
SIC: 2752 2791 2759 7336 Commercial printing, offset; typesetting; promotional printing; commercial art & illustration

(G-15642)
MEDPLAST GROUP INC
1520 Kensington Rd # 313 (60523-2139)
PHONE..................630 706-5500
John Mitchell, *General Mgr*
EMP: 425
SALES (corp-wide): 456.1MM **Privately Held**
SIC: 3089 Injection molded finished plastic products
PA: Medplast Group, Inc.
7865 Northcourt Rd # 100
Houston TX 77040
480 553-6400

(G-15643)
METAL CENTER NEWS
1010 Jorie Blvd Ste 44 (60523-4451)
PHONE..................630 571-1067
Patrick Bernardo, *Publisher*
Nancy Hartley, *Principal*
Kerry Gottlieb, *Regl Sales Mgr*

GEOGRAPHIC SECTION

Oak Brook - Dupage County (G-15667)

Ed Sreniawski, *Accounts Exec*
Jonathan Samples, *Assoc Editor*
EMP: 12
SALES (est): 695K **Privately Held**
WEB: www.metalcenternews.com
SIC: 2721 Magazines: publishing & printing

(G-15644)
MICHAELS ROSS AND COLE INC (PA)
Also Called: M R C
2001 Midwest Rd Ste 310 (60523-1340)
PHONE..............................630 916-0662
Joseph Stangarone, *President*
Tyler Wassell, *Manager*
Rick Hurckes, *Director*
EMP: 13
SALES (est): 3.4MM **Privately Held**
SIC: 5045 7372 Computer software; prepackaged software

(G-15645)
MICRON INDUSTRIES CORPORATION (PA)
Also Called: Micron Power
1211 W 22nd St Ste 200 (60523-3226)
PHONE..............................630 516-1222
Donald R Clark, *President*
Dan Obrien, *Prdtn Mgr*
Mark Castonguay, *Opers Staff*
Dale Wagner, *QC Mgr*
Donna Griffin, *Human Res Dir*
▲ **EMP:** 105
SQ FT: 12,000
SALES (est): 41.9MM **Privately Held**
SIC: 3612 Control transformers; power transformers, electric; specialty transformers

(G-15646)
MINUTEMAN PRESS INTL INC
1301 W 22nd St Ste 709 (60523-2070)
PHONE..............................630 574-0090
Thomas E Davis, *Manager*
EMP: 3
SALES (corp-wide): 23.4MM **Privately Held**
SIC: 2752 Commercial printing, lithographic
PA: Minuteman Press International, Inc.
61 Executive Blvd
Farmingdale NY 11735
631 249-1370

(G-15647)
MOTOROLA SOLUTIONS INC
2301 W 22nd St Ste 102 (60523-1222)
PHONE..............................847 341-3485
Gary Birkland, *Branch Mgr*
EMP: 5
SALES (corp-wide): 7.8B **Publicly Held**
WEB: www.motorolasolutions.com
SIC: 3663 3674 3571 3812 Radio & TV communications equipment; semiconductors & related devices; electronic computers; search & navigation equipment
PA: Motorola Solutions, Inc.
500 W Monroe St Ste 4400
Chicago IL 60661
847 576-5000

(G-15648)
NORTH AMERICA PACKAGING CORP (DH)
Also Called: Nampac
1515 W 22nd St Ste 550 (60523-8742)
PHONE..............................630 203-4100
Tom Linton, *President*
Danny Byrne, *Vice Pres*
◆ **EMP:** 24
SQ FT: 8,100
SALES (est): 155.7MM
SALES (corp-wide): 1.2B **Privately Held**
SIC: 3089 Plastic containers, except foam

(G-15649)
NOVIPAX LLC (HQ)
2215 York Rd Ste 504 (60523-2379)
PHONE..............................630 686-2735
Ron Leach, *CEO*
Noel Leatherbury, *Vice Pres*
John Terrien, *Vice Pres*
Jeff Weingart, *VP Mfg*
Jeff Conrad, *Production*
EMP: 16 **EST:** 2015

SQ FT: 10,000
SALES (est): 186.7MM
SALES (corp-wide): 2.9B **Privately Held**
SIC: 2821 2299 Polystyrene resins; padding & wadding, textile
PA: Atlas Holdings, Llc
100 Northfield St
Greenwich CT 06830
203 622-9138

(G-15650)
NOVO SURGICAL INC
700 Comme Dr Ste 500 No 1 (60523)
PHONE..............................877 860-6686
Abed Moiduddin, *President*
EMP: 20
SQ FT: 7,500
SALES (est): 2.8MM **Privately Held**
WEB: www.novosurgical.com
SIC: 3841 Instruments, microsurgical: except electromedical

(G-15651)
NRR CORP
Also Called: Augustan
705 Deer Trail Ln (60523-2782)
PHONE..............................630 915-8388
N Athimoolan Naidu, *President*
Renu Naidu, *Vice Pres*
▲ **EMP:** 12 **EST:** 1990
SQ FT: 13,000
SALES (est): 1.9MM **Privately Held**
WEB: www.augustanusa.com
SIC: 5199 7213 2253 Bags, textile; apron supply; T-shirts & tops, knit

(G-15652)
OFFICE SNAX INC
125 Windsor Dr Ste 105 (60523-4075)
PHONE..............................630 789-1783
Todd Elmers, *CEO*
William Baker, *Exec VP*
Susan Burns, *Manager*
▲ **EMP:** 5 **EST:** 2001
SQ FT: 1,500
SALES (est): 438.8K **Privately Held**
SIC: 2064 Candy & other confectionery products

(G-15653)
ONETOUCHPOINT MTN STATES LLC
1200 Harger Rd Ste 419 (60523-1818)
PHONE..............................303 227-1400
Steve McConnell, *President*
Dan Rebro, *Opers Mgr*
James Greer, *Production*
Connie Hilburn, *Human Resources*
Manuel Saez, *VP Sales*
EMP: 3
SALES (corp-wide): 28.5MM **Privately Held**
WEB: www.1touchpoint.com
SIC: 2752 Commercial printing, lithographic
HQ: Onetouchpoint Mountain States, Llc
5280 Joliet St
Denver CO 80239
303 227-1400

(G-15654)
ORBIT ENTERPRISES INC
3525 S Cass Ct Unit T3n (60523-3727)
PHONE..............................630 469-3405
Joseph S Beda, *President*
EMP: 3
SQ FT: 1,300
SALES (est): 200K **Privately Held**
SIC: 7372 3993 Utility computer software; signs & advertising specialties

(G-15655)
PALADIN BRANDS INTERNATIONAL H
2211 York Rd Ste 320 (60523-4030)
PHONE..............................319 378-3696
Jeff Winters, *Principal*
▲ **EMP:** 6
SALES (est): 1.5MM **Privately Held**
SIC: 3531 Construction machinery

(G-15656)
POWBAB INC
1314 Kensington Rd # 3205 (60523-2131)
PHONE..............................630 481-6140
Tina Chan, *President*

EMP: 4 **EST:** 2012
SALES (est): 90K **Privately Held**
SIC: 2834 Pharmaceutical preparations

(G-15657)
PURECIRCLE USA INC
915 Harger Rd Ste 250 (60523-1492)
PHONE..............................866 960-8242
Magomet Malsagov, *CEO*
Jordi Ferre, *Vice Pres*
David Gallagher, *Vice Pres*
William Mitchell, *CFO*
Kamran Ghani, *Controller*
▲ **EMP:** 30
SQ FT: 7,000
SALES (est): 101MM **Privately Held**
SIC: 2869 Sweeteners, synthetic
HQ: Purecircle Sdn. Bhd.
Pt 23419 Lengkuk Technology Techpark
Seremban NSB

(G-15658)
RALSTON FOOD SALES INC
2021 Spring Rd Ste 600 (60523-1860)
PHONE..............................314 877-7000
Mark Oozzini, *Purch Agent*
Tim Snoke, *VP Finance*
Greg Dragan, *Sales Executive*
EMP: 4
SALES (est): 435.9K
SALES (corp-wide): 5.8B **Publicly Held**
SIC: 2043 Cereal breakfast foods
HQ: Treehouse Private Brands, Inc.
2021 Spring Rd Ste 600
Oak Brook IL 60523

(G-15659)
RANA MEAL SOLUTIONS LLC (HQ)
Also Called: Giovanni Rana
1400 16th St Ste 275 (60523-8801)
PHONE..............................630 581-4100
Angelo Iantosca, *President*
Barbara Cola, *Corp Secy*
▲ **EMP:** 277
SQ FT: 125,000
SALES: 300MM
SALES (corp-wide): 485.8MM **Privately Held**
SIC: 2033 Spaghetti & other pasta sauce: packaged in cans, jars, etc.
PA: Pastificio Rana Spa
Via Antonio Pacinotti 25
San Giovanni Lupatoto VR 37057
045 858-7311

(G-15660)
RICHARDSON & EDWARDS INC
303 Hambletonian Dr (60523-2619)
PHONE..............................630 543-1818
Edward Kolodziej, *President*
Michael Long, *Vice Pres*
Marie Long, *Admin Sec*
EMP: 38 **EST:** 1946
SQ FT: 48,000
SALES (est): 3.9MM
SALES (corp-wide): 142.2MM **Privately Held**
WEB: www.richanded.com
SIC: 2752 Commercial printing, offset
HQ: Transparent Container Co., Inc.
325 S Lombard Rd
Addison IL 60101
708 449-8520

(G-15661)
ROGER CANTU & ASSOCS
1100 Jorie Blvd Ste 215 (60523-3025)
PHONE..............................630 573-9215
Roger Cantu, *President*
John Miceli, *Vice Pres*
EMP: 5
SALES (est): 450K **Privately Held**
WEB: www.rcantu.com
SIC: 7372 Application computer software

(G-15662)
SCHREDER LIGHTING LLC
1415 W 22nd St Ste Tower (60523-2031)
PHONE..............................847 621-5130
Ricardo Lucchesi, *Manager*
John W Camp,
Keutgen Nicolas,
Gripp Wilson,
▲ **EMP:** 20

SQ FT: 7,600
SALES (est): 4.7MM
SALES (corp-wide): 177.9K **Privately Held**
SIC: 3648 Lighting equipment
HQ: Schreder
Rue De Lusambo 67
Bruxelles 1190
233 201-06

(G-15663)
TAYLOR COMMUNICATIONS INC
900 Jorie Blvd Ste 238 (60523-3838)
P.O. Box 238, Hinsdale (60522-0238)
PHONE..............................630 368-0336
David Cagatto, *Branch Mgr*
EMP: 9
SALES (corp-wide): 2.5B **Privately Held**
SIC: 2761 Manifold business forms
HQ: Taylor Communications, Inc.
1725 Roe Crest Dr
North Mankato MN 56003
866 541-0937

(G-15664)
TRADEBE ENVIRONMENTAL SVCS LLC
1301 W 22nd St (60523-2006)
PHONE..............................219 354-2452
Sheri Dewar, *Purchasing*
Robert Wilson, *Supervisor*
Christian Ebermayer, *Director*
EMP: 3 **EST:** 2011
SALES (est): 234.9K **Privately Held**
WEB: www.tradebeusa.com
SIC: 2611 Pulp mills, mechanical & recycling processing

(G-15665)
TREEHOUSE FOODS INC (PA)
2021 Spring Rd Ste 600 (60523-1860)
PHONE..............................708 483-1300
Gary D Smith, *Ch of Bd*
Steven Oakland, *President*
Kevin G Jackson, *President*
Maurice Alkemade, *Division Pres*
Mark A Fleming, *Division Pres*
◆ **EMP:** 173
SALES: 4.2B **Publicly Held**
SIC: 2035 2023 2032 2033 Pickles, sauces & salad dressings; cream substitutes; puddings, except meat: packaged in cans, jars, etc.; soups & broths: canned, jarred, etc.; jams, jellies & preserves: packaged in cans, jars, etc.; powders, drink

(G-15666)
TREEHOUSE PRIVATE BRANDS INC (HQ)
2021 Spring Rd Ste 600 (60523-1860)
PHONE..............................314 877-7300
Sean Connoly, *CEO*
Walt George, *President*
Ronald D Wilkinson, *President*
Gregory A Billhartz, *Vice Pres*
Scott Monette, *CFO*
◆ **EMP:** 250
SALES (est): 1.7B
SALES (corp-wide): 4.2B **Publicly Held**
SIC: 2043 2052 2068 2035 Cereal breakfast foods; crackers, dry; cookies; nuts: dried, dehydrated, salted or roasted; dressings, salad: raw & cooked (except dry mixes); seasonings & sauces, except tomato & dry
PA: Treehouse Foods, Inc.
2021 Spring Rd Ste 600
Oak Brook IL 60523
708 483-1300

(G-15667)
TWIN SUPPLIES LTD
1010 Jorie Blvd Ste 124 (60523-4447)
PHONE..............................630 590-5138
Chris Skokna, *President*
Nick Skokna, *Vice Pres*
Todd Soerens, *Opers Staff*
Karen Snow, *Accounts Exec*
EMP: 18 **EST:** 2009
SALES (est): 2.1MM **Privately Held**
SIC: 1731 3646 3648 General electrical contractor; commercial indusl & institutional electric lighting fixtures; lighting equipment

Oak Brook - Dupage County (G-15668)

(G-15668)
VECTOR USA INC (HQ)
Also Called: Vector Packaging
1900 Spring Rd Ste 450 (60523-1481)
PHONE..................................800 929-4516
Jaime Soroa, *CEO*
Cyndi Draski, *Opers Staff*
Liz Ventrella, *Controller*
Gabriel Pittelli, *Director*
◆ EMP: 15
SQ FT: 7,500
SALES (est): 12.3MM
SALES (corp-wide): 207.4MM **Privately Held**
SIC: 3089 Food casings, plastic
PA: Viscofan Sa
Calle Berroa (Tajonar), 15 - Piso 4
Aranguren 31192
948 198-444

(G-15669)
VERTEX INTERNATIONAL INC
2015 Spring Rd Ste 215 (60523-2073)
PHONE..................................312 242-1864
Ahmad Tayeh, *President*
EMP: 5
SQ FT: 1,008
SALES (est): 2.1MM **Privately Held**
SIC: 5136 5139 5087 2311 Uniforms; men's & boys'; footwear; firefighting equipment; military uniforms, men's & youths': purchased materials; field jackets, military

(G-15670)
WELLSKY CORPORATION
1900 Spring Rd Ste 450 (60523-1481)
PHONE..................................630 218-2700
EMP: 3
SALES (corp-wide): 115.1MM **Privately Held**
SIC: 7372 Prepackaged software
PA: Wellsky Corporation
11300 Switzer St
Overland Park KS 66210
913 307-1000

Oak Forest
Cook County

(G-15671)
AWI / TITANIUM
15146 Geoffrey Rd (60452-2022)
PHONE..................................708 263-9970
EMP: 3
SALES (est): 193.8K **Privately Held**
SIC: 3356 Titanium

(G-15672)
BABAK INC
Also Called: Ambassador Printing
15411 Cicero Ave (60452-2503)
PHONE..................................312 419-8686
Taha Hosseini Tabrizi, *President*
EMP: 2
SQ FT: 1,200
SALES (est): 210K **Privately Held**
SIC: 2752 2791 Commercial printing, offset; typesetting

(G-15673)
CITY SPORTS & STAGE DOOR DANCE
15801 Oak Park Ave (60452-1581)
PHONE..................................708 687-9950
Tom Starppeti, *Owner*
EMP: 20
SALES (est): 295.6K **Privately Held**
SIC: 7911 3949 Dance studios, schools & halls; sporting & athletic goods

(G-15674)
DANS PRINTING & OFF SUPS INC
Also Called: Daniels Printing & Office Sup
14800 Cicero Ave Ste 101 (60452-1458)
PHONE..................................708 687-3055
Pamela Vaclav, *President*
Daniel Vaclav Jr, *Admin Sec*
Pam Vaclav, *Administration*
EMP: 10
SQ FT: 8,800
SALES: 1.2MM **Privately Held**
WEB: www.danielspos.com
SIC: 5943 2752 2759 5999 Office forms & supplies; writing supplies; commercial printing, offset; letterpress printing; business machines & equipment

(G-15675)
E Z SIGN CO INC
15347 Cicero Ave Rear (60452-2555)
PHONE..................................815 469-4080
Madelon Meents, *President*
Frederick Meents, *Corp Secy*
EMP: 5
SQ FT: 3,200
SALES (est): 400K **Privately Held**
SIC: 3993 7389 Signs, not made in custom sign painting shops; sign painting & lettering shop; engraving service

(G-15676)
ELIA DAY SPA
5251 147th St Ste 3 (60452-1327)
PHONE..................................708 535-1450
Fax: 708 535-7611
EMP: 18
SALES (est): 800K **Privately Held**
SIC: 3999 5087 Mfg Misc Products Whol Service Establishment Equipment

(G-15677)
EMERSON PROCESS MANAGEMENT
4320 166th St (60452-4607)
PHONE..................................708 535-5120
Rich Perez, *Manager*
▲ EMP: 60
SALES (est): 5.6MM **Privately Held**
SIC: 3491 3494 Gas valves & parts, industrial; valves & pipe fittings

(G-15678)
FERNWOOD PRINTERS LTD
14955 Mission Ave (60452-1308)
PHONE..................................630 964-9449
Thomas Gregor, *President*
Marie Gregor, *Admin Sec*
EMP: 4
SQ FT: 1,500
SALES (est): 290K **Privately Held**
SIC: 2752 2789 Commercial printing, offset; bookbinding & related work

(G-15679)
FRITO-LAY NORTH AMERICA INC
4170 166th St (60452-4600)
PHONE..................................708 331-7200
Denise Starcovic, *Opers Mgr*
Taura Atkins, *Senior Buyer*
Lino Carrillo, *Sales Mgr*
EMP: 200
SALES (corp-wide): 67.1B **Publicly Held**
SIC: 5149 5145 2099 Pet foods; confectionery; food preparations
HQ: Frito-Lay North America, Inc.
7701 Legacy Dr
Plano TX 75024

(G-15680)
GRAFF-PINKERT & CO
4235 166th St (60452-4689)
PHONE..................................708 535-2200
Lloyd Graff, *President*
James Graff, *Corp Secy*
Rex Magagnotti, *Sales Mgr*
Noah Graff, *Sales Staff*
Kelly Born, *Office Mgr*
◆ EMP: 18 EST: 1941
SQ FT: 21,000
SALES (est): 3MM **Privately Held**
WEB: www.graffpinkert.com
SIC: 3541 Machine tools, metal cutting type

(G-15681)
HUNT ENTERPRISES INC
Also Called: Hunt Printing & Graphics
4201 166th St (60452-4608)
PHONE..................................708 354-8464
Doug May, *President*
EMP: 6
SQ FT: 2,000
SALES: 500K **Privately Held**
SIC: 2752 Commercial printing, offset

(G-15682)
IMPRESSION PRINTING
4901 Lorin Ln (60452-1445)
PHONE..................................708 614-8660
Katherine Drechsel, *Owner*
Kathryn Drechsel, *Owner*
Mary Kotnour, *Finance Mgr*
EMP: 10
SQ FT: 4,100
SALES (est): 1.2MM **Privately Held**
SIC: 2752 2759 2796 2789 Commercial printing, offset; letterpress printing; screen printing; platemaking services; bookbinding & related work; die-cut paper & board

(G-15683)
IN-PRINT GRAPHICS INC (PA)
Also Called: COPY WORKS
4201 166th St (60452-4608)
PHONE..................................708 396-1010
Joseph Racine Sr, *President*
John Vanderwey, *Principal*
Joseph Racine II, *Vice Pres*
John Rinozzi, *Vice Pres*
Mark Ruhnke, *Prdtn Mgr*
EMP: 30 EST: 1973
SQ FT: 20,000
SALES: 3.7MM **Privately Held**
SIC: 2752 7334 2789 2732 Commercial printing, offset; photocopying & duplicating services; bookbinding & related work; book printing

(G-15684)
INSTRUMENT & VALVE SERVICES CO
Also Called: Emerson
4320 166th St (60452-4607)
PHONE..................................708 535-5120
Reilly Patrick, *Director*
Jeff Acquaviva, *Director*
EMP: 54
SALES (corp-wide): 18.3B **Publicly Held**
SIC: 3823 Industrial instrmnts msrmnt display/control process variable
HQ: Instrument & Valve Services Company
205 S Center St
Marshalltown IA 50158

(G-15685)
KINGSBURY ENTERPRISES INC
15007 Moorings Ln (60452-6016)
PHONE..................................708 535-7590
Lynn Kingsbury, *President*
Thomas Kingsbury, *Vice Pres*
EMP: 2
SALES (est): 270K **Privately Held**
SIC: 2752 5199 Commercial printing, lithographic; advertising specialties

(G-15686)
MOLD SHIELDS INC
15309 Oak Rd (60452-1529)
PHONE..................................708 983-5931
Reginald Phillips, *President*
EMP: 4
SALES: 39K **Privately Held**
SIC: 3441 8299 Fabricated structural metal; educational services

(G-15687)
PREMIER LIGHTING AND SUP LLC
4161 166th St (60452-4614)
PHONE..................................708 612-9693
Bernard F McLaughlin, *President*
Michael Oremus, *Manager*
Denise Krivanec,
Kathy Winston,
EMP: 4
SALES (est): 191.5K **Privately Held**
SIC: 3646 Commercial indusl & institutional electric lighting fixtures

(G-15688)
SINGLETON PALLETS CO
15603 Waverly Ave (60452-3613)
P.O. Box 526 (60452-0526)
PHONE..................................708 687-7006
Joseph Singleton, *Principal*
EMP: 3 EST: 2011
SALES (est): 138.5K **Privately Held**
SIC: 2448 Pallets, wood

(G-15689)
SYSTEMS EQUIPMENT SERVICES
4314 166th St (60452-4607)
PHONE..................................708 535-1273
Robert Otterbacher, *President*
Susan Otterbacher, *Admin Sec*
EMP: 4
SQ FT: 26,000
SALES (est): 720.5K **Privately Held**
SIC: 3537 5084 Forklift trucks; lift trucks & parts

(G-15690)
T H DAVIDSON & CO INC (PA)
Also Called: Davidson Redi-Mix Concrete
4243 166th St (60452-4608)
PHONE..................................815 464-2000
Thomas W Davidson, *CEO*
Michael J Dejong, *President*
John Albinger, *President*
Richard Chobar, *Admin Sec*
James F Davidson, *Admin Sec*
EMP: 20
SQ FT: 3,000
SALES (est): 7.6MM **Privately Held**
WEB: www.welschreadymix.com
SIC: 3273 5032 Ready-mixed concrete; stone, crushed or broken; gravel; sand, construction

(G-15691)
TAYLOR COMMUNICATIONS INC
4849 167th St Ste 201 (60452-4551)
PHONE..................................708 560-7600
David Caquatto, *Branch Mgr*
EMP: 8
SALES (corp-wide): 2.5B **Privately Held**
SIC: 2761 Manifold business forms
HQ: Taylor Communications, Inc.
1725 Roe Crest Dr
North Mankato MN 56003
866 541-0937

(G-15692)
WE CLEAN
Also Called: Maria Salazar Rivas
5845 Victoria Dr (60452-2863)
PHONE..................................708 574-2551
Maria Salazar Rivas, *Owner*
EMP: 3
SALES: 40K **Privately Held**
SIC: 3589 Service industry machinery

Oak Lawn
Cook County

(G-15693)
ABSOLUTE WINDOWS INC
9630 S 76th Ave (60457-6625)
PHONE..................................708 599-9191
Ronald Baker, *President*
Larry Czachor, *Corp Secy*
Carl Maturo, *Vice Pres*
Gregory Seeber, *Shareholder*
EMP: 24
SQ FT: 15,000
SALES (est): 1.9MM **Privately Held**
SIC: 2431 5031 Windows & window parts & trim, wood; doors & windows

(G-15694)
ACCURATE CSTM SASH MLLWK CORP
5516 W 110th St Ste 1 (60453-4764)
PHONE..................................708 423-0423
Mark Sirvin, *President*
Patricia Sirvin, *Admin Sec*
EMP: 3 EST: 1981
SQ FT: 1,600
SALES (est): 360K **Privately Held**
WEB: www.accuratesash.com
SIC: 5211 2431 Doors, storm: wood or metal; windows, storm: wood or metal; millwork & lumber; sash, wood or metal; doors, wood; moldings, wood: unfinished & prefinished

(G-15695)
ACCURATE METALLIZING INC
5340 W 111th St Ste 2 (60453-5573)
PHONE..................................708 424-7747
Donald Vander Meulen, *President*

GEOGRAPHIC SECTION

Oak Lawn - Cook County (G-15726)

Shirley Vander Meulen, *Corp Secy*
EMP: 5
SQ FT: 9,000
SALES: 800K **Privately Held**
SIC: 3599 3479 Machine shop, jobbing & repair; painting, coating & hot dipping

(G-15696)
ACCUSOL INCORPORATED
9632 S Kildare Ave (60453-3225)
PHONE................................773 283-4686
David Anderson, *President*
EMP: 5
SALES (est): 424K **Privately Held**
SIC: 2899 Chemical preparations

(G-15697)
ACTIVE TOOL AND MACHINE INC
8445 Beloit Ave (60455-1717)
PHONE................................708 599-0022
Phillip D Nienhouse, *President*
Sherry A Nienhouse, *Corp Secy*
EMP: 12
SQ FT: 8,000
SALES (est): 2.3MM **Privately Held**
WEB: www.activetoolinc.com
SIC: 3621 3568 Armatures, industrial; power transmission equipment

(G-15698)
ALL-AMERICAN SIGN CO INC
5501 W 109th St Ste 1 (60453-2479)
PHONE................................708 422-2203
Richard P Santucci, *President*
Dave Monahan, *Vice Pres*
Gary Jerabek, *Marketing Staff*
Joseph Monahan, *Admin Sec*
▲ **EMP:** 20
SQ FT: 14,000
SALES (est): 2.8MM **Privately Held**
SIC: 3993 Electric signs

(G-15699)
ALPINE AMUSEMENT CO INC
8037 Neva Ave (60459-1616)
PHONE................................708 233-9131
Donald Massie III, *President*
Donald Massie Jr, *Treasurer*
EMP: 3
SALES (est): 310K **Privately Held**
SIC: 3599 7999 Carnival machines & equipment, amusement park; exhibition & carnival operation services

(G-15700)
AMBIENT LIGHTNING AND ELECTRIC
10033 Menard Ave (60453-3753)
PHONE................................708 529-3434
EMP: 4 **EST:** 2008
SALES (est): 515.8K **Privately Held**
SIC: 3699 Mfg Electrical Equipment/Supplies

(G-15701)
ARCO AUTOMOTIVE ELEC SVC CO
Also Called: Arco Automobile
10707 S Cicero Ave (60453-5401)
PHONE................................708 422-2976
Frank Malinowski Jr, *President*
Rich Malinowski, *Corp Secy*
EMP: 7 **EST:** 1958
SQ FT: 3,200
SALES: 500K **Privately Held**
SIC: 5013 7539 5531 3714 Automotive supplies & parts; automotive repair shops; automotive & home supply stores; motor vehicle parts & accessories

(G-15702)
BEFCO MANUFACTURING CO INC
Also Called: G N F
5555 W 109th St (60453-5001)
PHONE................................708 424-4170
Ron K Bais, *President*
EMP: 12 **EST:** 2000
SALES (est): 2.4MM **Privately Held**
SIC: 3443 Boiler shop products: boilers, smokestacks, steel tanks

(G-15703)
BIRON STUDIO GENERAL SVCS INC
Also Called: Seba Signs and Printing
6253 W 95th St Ste 1 (60453-2788)
PHONE................................708 229-2600
Wojciech Chramiec, *President*
EMP: 8
SALES: 600K **Privately Held**
SIC: 3993 Signs & advertising specialties

(G-15704)
C L VAULT & SAFE SRV
6754 W 89th Pl (60453-1028)
PHONE................................708 237-0039
Carlos Lopez, *Principal*
EMP: 4
SALES (est): 253.8K **Privately Held**
SIC: 3272 Burial vaults, concrete or pre-cast terrazzo

(G-15705)
C M J ASSOCIATES INC
10745 S Kolmar Ave (60453-5348)
P.O. Box 661 (60454-0661)
PHONE................................708 636-2995
James W Gilboy, *President*
Colleen Gilboy, *Corp Secy*
Michael Gilboy, *Vice Pres*
EMP: 1
SALES (est): 300K **Privately Held**
SIC: 5112 2752 Business forms; commercial printing, offset

(G-15706)
CABLE ELECTRIC COMPANY INC
7640 Archer Rd (60458-1144)
PHONE................................708 458-8900
David Goacher, *President*
Susan Goacher, *Admin Sec*
EMP: 6
SQ FT: 5,000
SALES: 1.2MM **Privately Held**
SIC: 1731 3613 General electrical contractor; control panels, electric

(G-15707)
CASTILLO LEATHER GOODS
9233 S 51st Ave (60453-1739)
PHONE................................773 491-0018
Gilbert Castillo, *Principal*
EMP: 4
SALES (est): 225.4K **Privately Held**
SIC: 3949 Sporting & athletic goods

(G-15708)
CHICAGO CARDINAL COMMUNICATION
Also Called: Video Surveillance
10232 S Kenton Ave # 204 (60453-4251)
PHONE................................708 424-1446
Kevin Bulger, *Owner*
EMP: 10
SQ FT: 1,500
SALES (est): 774K **Privately Held**
SIC: 4813 3679 4812 Telephone/video communications; hermetic seals for electronic equipment; paging services

(G-15709)
CINTAS CORPORATION NO 2
9525 S Cicero Ave (60453-3136)
PHONE................................708 424-4747
Nancy Armstrong, *Store Mgr*
EMP: 4
SALES (corp-wide): 6.8B **Publicly Held**
SIC: 2337 Uniforms, except athletic: women's, misses' & juniors'
HQ: Cintas Corporation No. 2
6800 Cintas Blvd
Mason OH 45040

(G-15710)
CUSTOM RAILZ & STAIRS INC
7808 La Crosse Ave (60459-1521)
PHONE................................773 592-7210
Andrei Pop, *Principal*
EMP: 3
SALES (est): 350.4K **Privately Held**
SIC: 3446 Stairs, staircases, stair treads: prefabricated metal

(G-15711)
CZARNIK PRECISION GRINDING MCH
5530 W 110th St Ste 8 (60453-2473)
PHONE................................708 229-9639
Wieslaw Czarnik, *CEO*
EMP: 2
SALES (est): 273.3K **Privately Held**
SIC: 3479 Coating of metals & formed products

(G-15712)
D & D PRINTING INC
9737 Southwest Hwy (60453-3614)
PHONE................................708 425-2080
Dan Perrino Jr, *President*
EMP: 2
SQ FT: 1,200
SALES (est): 366K **Privately Held**
SIC: 2752 Commercial printing, offset

(G-15713)
DEMCO PRODUCTS INC
4644 W 92nd St (60453-1802)
PHONE................................708 636-6240
Robert Dempster, *President*
Robert C Dempster, *Vice Pres*
Stephanie Dempster, *Treasurer*
William Dempster, *Admin Sec*
EMP: 12 **EST:** 1950
SQ FT: 15,300
SALES (est): 3MM **Privately Held**
WEB: www.demcoprod.com
SIC: 3451 3351 3321 Screw machine products; copper rolling & drawing; gray & ductile iron foundries

(G-15714)
EASTCO INC
5500 W 111th St (60453-5012)
PHONE................................708 499-1701
Earl A Silverman, *President*
George Pollack, *President*
▲ **EMP:** 4 **EST:** 1973
SQ FT: 28,000
SALES (est): 1.2MM **Privately Held**
SIC: 3678 3643 Electronic connectors; electric connectors

(G-15715)
F H LEINWEBER CO INC (PA)
9812 S Cicero Ave (60453-3104)
PHONE................................708 424-7000
Fred H Leinweber Sr, *President*
Fred H Leinweber, *Vice Pres*
Kip Nance, *Opers Staff*
Lillian Leinweber, *Treasurer*
Peggy Leinweber-Tallon, *Admin Sec*
EMP: 4
SQ FT: 1,000
SALES: 1.4MM **Privately Held**
WEB: www.leinwebercompany.com
SIC: 2891 1752 Sealants; floor laying & floor work

(G-15716)
G & F MANUFACTURING CO INC
Also Called: Befco Manufactoring Co.
5555 W 109th St (60453-5070)
PHONE................................708 424-4170
Ron Bias, *Principal*
Kiran Bais, *Family Practiti*
▼ **EMP:** 20
SQ FT: 14,000
SALES: 12MM **Privately Held**
WEB: www.gandf.com
SIC: 3613 3441 Panelboards & distribution boards, electric; fabricated structural metal

(G-15717)
G & M WOODWORKING INC
5656 W 88th Pl (60453-1215)
PHONE................................708 425-4013
Gene Marcinkowski, *Principal*
EMP: 3
SALES (est): 338K **Privately Held**
SIC: 2431 Millwork

(G-15718)
GENERAL MACHINING SERVICE INC
5521 W 110th St Ste 6 (60453-2604)
PHONE................................708 636-4848
Dennis Musial, *President*

Henry K Sziler, *Corp Secy*
Henry Sziler, *Vice Pres*
EMP: 6
SALES: 1.3MM **Privately Held**
WEB: www.generalmachiningservice.com
SIC: 3599 Machine shop, jobbing & repair

(G-15719)
HERFF JONES LLC
6305 W 95th St Ste 1w (60453-2780)
PHONE................................708 425-0130
Jim Cranley, *Manager*
EMP: 4
SALES (corp-wide): 1.1B **Privately Held**
SIC: 3911 Rings, finger: precious metal
HQ: Herff Jones, Llc
4501 W 62nd St
Indianapolis IN 46268
800 419-5462

(G-15720)
INTERSTATE BTRY SYS INTL INC
10336 S Cicero Ave (60453-4702)
PHONE................................708 424-2288
Ted Golebiowski, *Branch Mgr*
EMP: 8 **Privately Held**
WEB: www.interstatebatteries.com
SIC: 5531 5063 3691 Batteries, automotive & truck; batteries; storage batteries
PA: Interstate Battery System International, Inc.
12770 Merit Dr Ste 1400
Dallas TX 75251

(G-15721)
J AND K PRINTING
5629 W 84th Pl (60459-2629)
PHONE................................708 229-9558
Joseph Lorusso, *Owner*
EMP: 3
SALES: 85K **Privately Held**
SIC: 2752 6221 Commercial printing, offset; commodity contracts brokers, dealers

(G-15722)
JORDAN GOLD INC
Also Called: Ramallah Jewelry
8741 Ridgeland Ave (60453-1001)
PHONE................................708 430-7008
Elias Mseeh, *President*
Lina Mseeh, *Treasurer*
EMP: 3
SALES (est): 359.9K **Privately Held**
SIC: 5944 3961 Jewelry, precious stones & precious metals; costume jewelry

(G-15723)
KITCHY KOO GOURMET CO
7845 Lamon Ave (60459-1522)
PHONE................................708 499-5236
Sunai Limpanathon, *Principal*
EMP: 2
SALES (est): 248.2K **Privately Held**
SIC: 3556 Dehydrating equipment, food processing

(G-15724)
L A D SPECIALTIES
9010 Beloit Ave Ste F (60455-2611)
PHONE................................708 430-1588
Donald Grenier, *President*
EMP: 3
SALES (est): 417.2K **Privately Held**
SIC: 3053 Gaskets & sealing devices

(G-15725)
LMPL MANAGEMENT CORPORATION
Also Called: Southwest Denture Center
5757 W 95th St Ste 3 (60453-2385)
PHONE................................708 636-2443
Paul Lausch, *President*
EMP: 7
SALES (est): 476.2K **Privately Held**
SIC: 8021 8072 3843 Dental clinic; dental laboratories; dental equipment & supplies

(G-15726)
LO-KO PERFORMANCE COATINGS
5340 W 111th St Ste 1 (60453-5573)
PHONE................................708 424-7863
Donald Vander Meulen, *President*
EMP: 8

Oak Lawn - Cook County (G-15727)

SALES (est): 866.1K **Privately Held**
SIC: 3479 5571 Coating of metals & formed products; motorcycle dealers

(G-15727)
MEYER TOOL & MANUFACTURING INC
4601 Southwest Hwy (60453-1822)
PHONE..................708 425-9080
Eileen Cunningham, *President*
Kathryn M Meyer, *Chairman*
Edward Bonnema, *Vice Pres*
Julie Rios, *Administration*
EMP: 28 EST: 1969
SQ FT: 35,000
SALES (est): 8.2MM **Privately Held**
SIC: 3599 Machine shop, jobbing & repair

(G-15728)
MIDWEST IMPERIAL STEEL
5555 W 109th St (60453-5001)
PHONE..................815 469-1072
Ron Bais, *Mng Member*
EMP: 18
SALES (est): 4MM **Privately Held**
SIC: 3443 Fabricated plate work (boiler shop)

(G-15729)
N P D INC
Also Called: Printmart
4720 W 103rd St (60453-4706)
PHONE..................708 424-6788
Nick Hederman, *President*
Dawn Hederman, *Vice Pres*
EMP: 3 EST: 1978
SQ FT: 1,600
SALES (est): 547.6K **Privately Held**
SIC: 2752 2791 2789 Commercial printing, offset; typesetting; bookbinding & related work

(G-15730)
O & M ELECTRONIC INC
5451 W 110th St Ste 4 (60453-2389)
PHONE..................708 203-1947
Mohammad Salamah, *Principal*
EMP: 15 EST: 2014
SQ FT: 6,500
SALES (est): 1MM **Privately Held**
SIC: 4812 3661 Cellular telephone services; headsets, telephone

(G-15731)
PARK LAWN ASSOCIATION INC
5040 W 111th St (60453-5008)
PHONE..................708 425-7377
Frank Portada, *Manager*
EMP: 10 **Privately Held**
SIC: 7389 8331 3565 Packaging & labeling services; job training & vocational rehabilitation services; packaging machinery
PA: Park Lawn Association Inc
10833 Laporte Ave
Oak Lawn IL 60453

(G-15732)
PETERS MACHINE WORKS INC
8277 S 86th Ct (60458-1767)
PHONE..................708 496-3005
Delbert Peters, *President*
EMP: 10
SQ FT: 9,000
SALES (est): 384.1K **Privately Held**
SIC: 3599 Machine shop, jobbing & repair

(G-15733)
QUALITY MACHINE
5530 W 110th St Ste 8 (60453-2473)
PHONE..................708 499-0021
Chris Ren, *Owner*
EMP: 3
SALES (est): 326.8K **Privately Held**
SIC: 3599 Machine shop, jobbing & repair

(G-15734)
REEL MATE MFG CO
10113 Buell Ct (60453-3802)
P.O. Box 871 (60454-0871)
PHONE..................708 423-8005
Joseph Landgraf, *Partner*
Patricia A Landgraf, *Partner*
EMP: 4

SALES (est): 253.5K **Privately Held**
SIC: 2395 Embroidery products, except schiffli machine

(G-15735)
SOUTHFIELD CORPORATION
A 1 Express & Cartage Co Div
7601 W 79th St (60455-1115)
PHONE..................708 458-0400
John Zoback, *Manager*
EMP: 50
SALES (corp-wide): 344.9MM **Privately Held**
SIC: 5211 3273 5032 3271 Lumber & other building materials; ready-mixed concrete; stone, crushed or broken; concrete block & brick
PA: Southfield Corporation
8995 W 95th St
Palos Hills IL 60465
708 344-1000

(G-15736)
STRAIGHTLINE ERECTORS INC
7812 W 91st St (60457-2006)
PHONE..................708 430-5426
Don Engstrom, *President*
EMP: 3
SALES (est): 380K **Privately Held**
SIC: 3542 Sheet metalworking machines

(G-15737)
UGLY HOOKAH TOBACCO INC
5530 W 110th St Ste 10 (60453-2473)
PHONE..................708 724-9621
Jamal Ziadan, *President*
EMP: 5
SALES: 3MM **Privately Held**
SIC: 2131 5159 Smoking tobacco; tobacco distributors & products

(G-15738)
VAN CRAFT INDUSTRY OF DEL EDEL (DH)
8938 Ridgeland Ave (60453-1000)
PHONE..................708 430-6670
Norman Klein, *President*
Helene Jones, *Admin Sec*
EMP: 3
SQ FT: 100
SALES (est): 384.7K
SALES (corp-wide): 83.2MM **Privately Held**
SIC: 3429 Manufactured hardware (general)
HQ: Freight Consolidation Services Inc
8938 Ridgeland Ave # 200
Oak Lawn IL 60453
708 430-6670

(G-15739)
VAN NORMAN MOLDING COMPANY LLC
9615 S 76th Ave (60455-2373)
PHONE..................708 430-4343
Lynn Data, *Personnel*
Robert A Andre,
Richard L Andre,
EMP: 32
SQ FT: 30,000
SALES (est): 8.2MM **Privately Held**
WEB: www.vannormanmolding.com
SIC: 3089 Injection molded finished plastic products; molding primary plastic

Oak Park
Cook County

(G-15740)
ACTIVE SIMULATIONS INC
312 S Lombard Ave (60302-3524)
PHONE..................630 747-8393
Milos Zefran, *CEO*
Arnold Steinberg, *CFO*
EMP: 3
SALES (est): 69.8K **Privately Held**
SIC: 7371 7372 Computer software development & applications; educational computer software

(G-15741)
ADVANCE QUICK PRINT
900 Madison St (60302-4403)
PHONE..................708 848-2200
EMP: 3 EST: 1981
SALES: 100K **Privately Held**
SIC: 2752 Lithographic Commercial Printing

(G-15742)
ADVANCED RETINAL INSTITUTE INC
1123 N Oak Park Ave (60302-1222)
PHONE..................617 821-5597
Calvin A Grant, *President*
EMP: 4
SQ FT: 2,000
SALES: 600K **Privately Held**
SIC: 3841 Retinoscopes

(G-15743)
AIR CADDY
Also Called: Shipbikes.com
310 Lake St Ste 8 (60302-2641)
PHONE..................708 383-5541
Robert Lickton, *President*
Levana Lickton, *Treasurer*
EMP: 5
SALES (est): 548.1K **Privately Held**
SIC: 3444 Metal housings, enclosures, casings & other containers

(G-15744)
ALTAMIRA ART GLASS
202 And A Half S Mrion St (60302)
PHONE..................708 848-3799
Paul Damkoehler, *Owner*
EMP: 3
SQ FT: 1,000
SALES: 120K **Privately Held**
SIC: 5719 3229 Glassware; art, decorative & novelty glassware

(G-15745)
ARBETMAN & ASSOCIATES
635 S Humphrey Ave (60304-1714)
PHONE..................708 386-8586
Jay S Arbetman, *Owner*
EMP: 2
SALES: 250K **Privately Held**
SIC: 2396 Apparel findings & trimmings

(G-15746)
BAKER ELEMENTS INC
159 N Marion St (60301-1032)
PHONE..................630 660-8100
Paul Baker, *CEO*
EMP: 9
SALES (est): 1.1MM **Privately Held**
SIC: 2431 1751 2599 Millwork; cabinet building & installation; window & door installation & erection; bar, restaurant & cafeteria furniture; hotel furniture

(G-15747)
C E DIENBERG PRINTING COMPANY
114 Madison St Lowr 1 (60302-4252)
PHONE..................708 848-4406
EMP: 4
SQ FT: 3,000
SALES: 300K **Privately Held**
SIC: 2752 2759 Lithographic Commercial Printing Commercial Printing

(G-15748)
CAROLINE ROSE INC
741 Madison St (60302-4419)
PHONE..................708 386-1011
Rose Becker, *CEO*
Caroline Becker, *President*
EMP: 7
SQ FT: 12,000
SALES (est): 1.1MM **Privately Held**
SIC: 2339 2335 Sportswear, women's; women's, juniors' & misses' dresses

(G-15749)
CHARLES CHAUNCEY WELLS INC
Also Called: Wells Printing Co
735 N Grove Ave (60302-1551)
PHONE..................708 524-0695
Charles C Wells, *President*
Susan Austin Wells, *Admin Sec*

EMP: 2
SALES (est): 244.1K **Privately Held**
SIC: 2752 Commercial printing, offset

(G-15750)
DISTRICT 97
254 Pleasant St Apt 2 (60302-3365)
PHONE..................708 289-7064
EMP: 4
SALES (est): 195.2K **Privately Held**
WEB: www.op97.org
SIC: 2711 Newspapers, publishing & printing

(G-15751)
DOODY ENTERPRISES INC
1100 Lake St Ste LI25 (60301-1099)
PHONE..................312 239-6226
Dan Doody, *President*
Anne Hennessy, *Chief*
EMP: 4
SQ FT: 1,500
SALES: 500K **Privately Held**
SIC: 2741 Miscellaneous publishing

(G-15752)
EARTHCOMBER LLC
110 N Marion St (60301-1005)
PHONE..................708 366-1600
James Brady, *President*
Dana Sohr, *Vice Pres*
EMP: 10
SALES (est): 750K **Privately Held**
SIC: 2741 Miscellaneous publishing

(G-15753)
FRAME HOUSE INC
Also Called: Frame House Passport Photos
163 S Oak Park Ave (60302-2901)
PHONE..................708 383-1616
Fax: 708 383-4343
EMP: 9
SQ FT: 4,200
SALES (est): 620K **Privately Held**
SIC: 2499 5023 5999 Mfg Whol And Ret Picture Frames

(G-15754)
FREITAS P SABAH
Also Called: Lessabah Arts Center
6105 1/2 North Ave (60302-1124)
PHONE..................708 386-8934
Freitas P Sabah, *Owner*
EMP: 4
SALES (est): 197.3K **Privately Held**
SIC: 5092 3999 Arts & crafts equipment & supplies; manufacturing industries

(G-15755)
GENISYS DECISION CORPORATION
1150 S Taylor Ave Ste 200 (60304-2234)
P.O. Box 714 (60303-0714)
PHONE..................708 524-5100
David J Towne, *President*
Susan Towne, *Admin Sec*
EMP: 3
SALES (est): 500K **Privately Held**
SIC: 7372 Business oriented computer software

(G-15756)
H J MOHR & SONS COMPANY
915 S Maple Ave (60304-1893)
PHONE..................708 366-0338
Dolly Mohr, *President*
Steven E Mohr, *Vice Pres*
Karen Richards, *Vice Pres*
EMP: 15 EST: 1893
SQ FT: 33,000
SALES (est): 5.7MM **Privately Held**
SIC: 5031 5211 3273 Building materials, exterior; building materials, interior; lumber & other building materials; ready-mixed concrete

(G-15757)
HUMAGINARIUM LLC
325 S Grove Ave (60302-3501)
PHONE..................312 788-7719
Robert Becker, *CEO*
EMP: 5
SALES (est): 128.9K **Privately Held**
SIC: 7372 Educational computer software

(G-15758)
ITS A SIGN
6140 Roosevelt Rd (60304-2311)
PHONE..................................708 848-7446
Tim Rassmusin, *Managing Prtnr*
EMP: 4
SALES (est): 477.7K Privately Held
SIC: 3993 Signs & advertising specialties

(G-15759)
KAP HOLDINGS LLC (PA)
Also Called: Partscription
137 N Oak Park Ave # 214 (60301-1344)
PHONE..................................708 948-0226
Kevin Price, *Mng Member*
EMP: 10
SALES (est): 705.1K Privately Held
WEB: www.partscription.com
SIC: 3585 3564 3621 Refrigeration & heating equipment; blower filter units (furnaces, blowers); filters, air: furnaces, air conditioning equipment, etc.; electric motor & generator parts

(G-15760)
KATYS LLC (PA)
Also Called: Katy's Goodness
1040 S Maple Ave (60304-1805)
P.O. Box 6364, River Forest (60305-6364)
PHONE..................................708 522-9814
Kathleen Frantz, *Mng Member*
EMP: 2
SALES: 5MM Privately Held
SIC: 2052 5149 7389 Cookies & crackers; crackers, cookies & bakery products;

(G-15761)
KRUGER NORTH AMERICA INC
1010 Lake St Ste 106 (60301-1106)
PHONE..................................708 851-3670
Micheal De Vootd, *President*
Anton Straughun, *Vice Pres*
Judy Bradeen, *Accounting Mgr*
Jennifer Lieberman, *Manager*
▲ **EMP:** 10
SALES (est): 7.1MM
SALES (corp-wide): 1.7B Privately Held
SIC: 2087 2099 2066 Powders, drink; syrups, drink; food preparations; instant cocoa
PA: Kruger Gmbh & Co. Kg
Senefelderstr. 44
Bergisch Gladbach 51469
220 210-50

(G-15762)
LAURENCELESTE INC
230 Clinton Ave (60302-3114)
PHONE..................................708 383-3432
Lauren Murphy, *President*
Celeste Bayer, *Vice Pres*
EMP: 3
SALES (est): 210K Privately Held
SIC: 2369 Girls' & children's outerwear

(G-15763)
LITERACY RESOURCES LLC
Also Called: Heggerty Phonemic Awareness
711 South Blvd Ste 12 (60302-2926)
PHONE..................................708 366-5947
Andrew Follett, *Mng Member*
Jeremiah Kaye,
Marc Lonergan,
Alisa Vanhekken,
EMP: 7
SALES (est): 217K Privately Held
SIC: 2731 Book publishing

(G-15764)
MECK PRINT
830 S Kenilworth Ave (60304-1134)
PHONE..................................708 358-0600
Kristian Frumkin, *President*
EMP: 2 EST: 2007
SALES (est): 214K Privately Held
WEB: www.meckprint.com
SIC: 2752 Commercial printing, offset

(G-15765)
MINUTEMAN PRESS
6949 North Ave (60302-1046)
PHONE..................................708 524-4940
Laurie Freeman, *Owner*
EMP: 4 EST: 2009
SALES (est): 547.6K Privately Held
WEB: www.minutemanpress.com
SIC: 2752 Commercial printing, lithographic

(G-15766)
NORTHERN LIGHTING & POWER INC
1138 Woodbine Ave (60302-1212)
PHONE..................................708 383-9926
Fax: 847 671-9817
EMP: 3
SALES (est): 280K Privately Held
SIC: 3648 Mfg Lighting Equipment

(G-15767)
OBERWEIS DAIRY INC
124 N Oak Park Ave (60301-1304)
PHONE..................................708 660-1350
Patti Buchholv, *Branch Mgr*
EMP: 20
SALES (corp-wide): 249.7MM Privately Held
SIC: 2026 5963 5451 Milk processing (pasteurizing, homogenizing, bottling); milk delivery; milk; ice cream (packaged)
PA: Oberweis Dairy, Inc.
951 Ice Cream Dr
North Aurora IL 60542
630 801-6100

(G-15768)
PIONEER NEWSPAPERS INC
1010 Lake St Ste 104 (60301-1106)
PHONE..................................708 383-3200
Jennifer Clark, *Branch Mgr*
EMP: 20
SALES (corp-wide): 4.3MM Privately Held
SIC: 2711 Newspapers, publishing & printing
HQ: Pioneer Newspapers Inc.
350 N Orleans St Fl 10
Chicago IL 60654
847 486-0600

(G-15769)
POYNTING PRODUCTS INC
1011 Madison St (60302-4404)
P.O. Box 1564 (60304-0564)
PHONE..................................708 386-2139
Fax: 708 386-2517
EMP: 3
SQ FT: 3,000
SALES: 680.6K Privately Held
SIC: 7371 3577 Custom Computer Programing Mfg Computer Peripheral Equipment

(G-15770)
ROOKIE LLC
545 S Scolville Ave (60304)
PHONE..................................708 278-1628
Steven Gevinson,
EMP: 5
SALES (est): 612K Privately Held
SIC: 2721 2731 Magazines: publishing only, not printed on site; book clubs: publishing & printing

(G-15771)
SCHECK SIRESS PROSTHETICS INC
401 Harrison St (60304-1427)
PHONE..................................630 424-0392
James Kaiser, *CEO*
EMP: 120
SALES (corp-wide): 11.4MM Privately Held
SIC: 3842 Limbs, artificial
PA: Scheck & Siress Prosthetics, Inc
1 S 376 Summit Ave Ct E
Oakbrook Terrace IL
708 383-2257

(G-15772)
SHEDRAIN CORPORATION
715 Lake St Ste 269 (60301-1411)
PHONE..................................708 848-5212
Greg Liebreich, *Principal*
EMP: 9
SALES (corp-wide): 24.8MM Privately Held
SIC: 3999 5136 Umbrellas, canes & parts; umbrellas, men's & boys'
PA: Shedrain Corporation
8303 Ne Killingsworth St
Portland OR 97220
503 255-2200

(G-15773)
SIGN EXPRESS INC
900 S Oak Park Ave Ste 1 (60304-1936)
PHONE..................................708 524-8811
Bill David, *President*
EMP: 4
SQ FT: 850
SALES (est): 250K Privately Held
SIC: 3993 Signs & advertising specialties

(G-15774)
SPANNUTH BOILER CO
264 Madison St (60302-4112)
PHONE..................................708 386-1882
Keith Golz, *President*
Kirk Golz, *Vice Pres*
Scott Golz, *Admin Sec*
EMP: 7
SQ FT: 2,500
SALES (est): 730K Privately Held
WEB: www.spannuthboilers.com
SIC: 7699 7692 1542 Boiler repair shop; welding repair; nonresidential construction

(G-15775)
STITCHED CONVERSATION
404 N Marion St (60302-1856)
PHONE..................................312 966-1146
Angela Dear, *Principal*
EMP: 4
SALES (est): 50K Privately Held
SIC: 2395 Embroidery & art needlework

(G-15776)
SWEET THYME SOAPS
808 S Elmwood Ave (60304-1417)
PHONE..................................708 848-0234
Dianne Alexander, *Manager*
EMP: 3
SALES (est): 15K Privately Held
SIC: 2841 Soap & other detergents

(G-15777)
UNITEX INDUSTRIES INC (PA)
Also Called: Fashionaire
7001 North Ave Ste 2ne (60302-1040)
PHONE..................................708 524-0664
Robert C Sassetti, *President*
Bob Sassetti, *Vice Pres*
EMP: 5
SQ FT: 1,000
SALES (est): 2.2MM Privately Held
SIC: 2391 2392 2591 5023 Draperies, plastic & textile: from purchased materials; bedspreads & bed sets: made from purchased materials; drapery hardware & blinds & shades; vertical blinds

(G-15778)
VIGILANZ CORPORATION
137 N Oak Park Ave # 329 (60301-1375)
PHONE..................................708 383-3008
Craig Leischner, *Vice Pres*
Khilan Patel, *Project Mgr*
Randy Tofteland, *Director*
EMP: 23
SALES (corp-wide): 14MM Privately Held
WEB: www.vigilanzcorp.com
SIC: 7372 Prepackaged software
PA: Vigilanz Corporation
5775 Wayzata Blvd Ste 970
Minneapolis MN 55416
952 223-4010

Oakbrook Terrace
Dupage County

(G-15779)
AARDVARK PHARMA LLC
Also Called: Aardvark Pharmaceuticals
2 Mid America Plz Ste 800 (60181-4727)
PHONE..................................630 248-2380
Rajiv Khatau, *Mng Member*
◆ **EMP:** 32
SQ FT: 2,000
SALES (est): 1.5MM Privately Held
SIC: 2834 Druggists' preparations (pharmaceuticals)

(G-15780)
ACH FOOD COMPANIES INC
Also Called: Tones Brothers
1 Parkview Plz Ste 500 (60181-4495)
PHONE..................................866 386-8282
Jeff Atkins, *CFO*
EMP: 200
SALES (corp-wide): 20B Privately Held
SIC: 2079 Oil, hydrogenated: edible
HQ: Ach Food Companies, Inc.
1 Parkview Plz Ste 500
Oakbrook Terrace IL 60181

(G-15781)
ACH FOOD COMPANIES INC (HQ)
Also Called: A C H Retail Products
1 Parkview Plz Ste 500 (60181-4495)
PHONE..................................866 386-8282
Imad Bazzi, *CEO*
Stephen Zaruba, *CFO*
◆ **EMP:** 135
SALES (est): 533.6MM
SALES (corp-wide): 20B Privately Held
SIC: 2079 2099 Oil, hydrogenated: edible; spices, including grinding; dressings, salad: dry mixes
PA: Associated British Foods Plc
Fourth Floor
London W1K 4
207 399-6500

(G-15782)
AMANI FROYO LLC
2005 S Meyers Rd Apt 427 (60181-5269)
PHONE..................................941 744-1111
Malik Mustansir, *Principal*
EMP: 6
SALES (est): 453.2K Privately Held
SIC: 2024 Yogurt desserts, frozen

(G-15783)
AMEDICO LABORATORIES LLC
Also Called: Maylan Skincare
17w173 16th St (60181-4034)
PHONE..................................347 857-7546
Winnie Chan,
EMP: 4
SALES (est): 422.8K Privately Held
SIC: 2844 Cosmetic preparations

(G-15784)
AMIGO MOBILITY CENTER
Also Called: Mobility Center of Chicago
17w620 14th St Ste 101 (60181-3700)
PHONE..................................630 268-8670
EMP: 5
SALES (est): 33.3K Privately Held
SIC: 3845 Mfg Electromedical Equipment

(G-15785)
ANYLOGIC N AMER LTD LBLTY CO
1 Tower Ln Ste 2655 (60181-4666)
PHONE..................................312 635-3344
John Yedinak,
Timofey Popkov,
Andrei Vorshchez,
EMP: 12 EST: 2009
SQ FT: 3,300
SALES: 4.2MM Privately Held
WEB: www.anylogic.com
SIC: 7371 7372 Computer software development; prepackaged software

(G-15786)
APPRIZE PROMOTIONAL PDTS INC
18w100 22nd St Ste 125 (60181-4799)
PHONE..................................630 468-2043
Michelle James, *President*
Robin James, *Accounting Mgr*
EMP: 3
SALES (est): 195.4K Privately Held
SIC: 2752 Commercial printing, lithographic

Oakbrook Terrace - Dupage County (G-15787)

(G-15787)
BALDWIN RICHARDSON FOODS CO (PA)
1 Tower Ln Ste 2390 (60181-4693)
PHONE................815 464-9994
Eric Johnson, *President*
Pamela Johnson, *Vice Pres*
Jeff Phelan, *Sales Staff*
Anna Olsen, *Manager*
Erin Tolefree, *Admin Sec*
EMP: 7
SALES (est): 87.2MM **Privately Held**
SIC: 2024 Dairy based frozen desserts

(G-15788)
BIMEDA ANIMAL HEALTH INC
1 Tower Ln Ste 2250 (60181-4626)
PHONE................630 928-0361
Paul Brady, *Principal*
EMP: 3
SALES (est): 123.2K **Privately Held**
SIC: 2834 Pharmaceutical preparations

(G-15789)
BIO-BRIDGE SCIENCE INC
1801 S Meyers Rd Ste 220 (60181-5265)
P.O. Box 168081, Chicago (60616-8071)
PHONE................630 328-0213
Liang Qiao, *Ch of Bd*
EMP: 23
SQ FT: 2,203
SALES (est): 2.3MM **Privately Held**
SIC: 2834 Pharmaceutical preparations

(G-15790)
BMC SOFTWARE INC
18w140 Bttrfeld Rd Ste 10 (60181)
PHONE................331 777-8700
Al Arun, *Vice Pres*
Mark Graham, *Vice Pres*
Clement Chang, *Engineer*
Mike Merna, *Accounts Mgr*
Tom Lonergan, *Accounts Exec*
EMP: 40
SALES (corp-wide): 1.2B **Privately Held**
WEB: www.bmc.com
SIC: 7372 Utility computer software
HQ: Bmc Software, Inc.
 2103 Citywest Blvd # 2100
 Houston TX 77042
 713 918-8800

(G-15791)
CARDIAC IMAGING INC
2 Transam Plaza Dr # 420 (60181-4290)
PHONE................630 834-7100
Sam Kancherlapalli, *Director*
EMP: 18
SALES (est): 2.9MM **Privately Held**
WEB: www.mobilecardiacpet.com
SIC: 3845 Surgical support systems; heart-lung machine, exc. iron lung

(G-15792)
CHICAGO TECHNICAL SALES INC
17w755 Butterfield Rd (60181-4253)
PHONE................630 889-7121
James Moynihan, *President*
Thomas Bell, *Vice Pres*
Jim Moynihan, *Representative*
EMP: 2
SQ FT: 400
SALES: 3MM **Privately Held**
WEB: www.ctsalesinc.com
SIC: 3679 5063 Electronic switches; electrical apparatus & equipment

(G-15793)
CIMC LEASING USA INC
Also Called: Cimc Capital Inc.
2 Transam Plaza Dr # 320 (60181-4823)
PHONE................630 785-6875
Jeffrey Walker, *CEO*
Si Feng, *COO*
Mark Mason, *COO*
▲ **EMP:** 6
SALES (est): 882.1K **Privately Held**
SIC: 2448 Cargo containers, wood & metal combination
PA: China International Marine Containers (Group) Co., Ltd.
 8/F, Cimc R&D Center, No.2 Gangwan Avenue, Shekou Industrial Zon
 Shenzhen 51806

(G-15794)
COINSTAR PROCUREMENT LLC
1 Tower Ln Ste 900 (60181-4623)
PHONE................630 424-4788
Melanie Bonner, *Administration*
EMP: 5 **EST:** 2011
SALES (est): 309.6K **Privately Held**
SIC: 3674 3829 Modules, solid state; nuclear instrument modules

(G-15795)
COLSON GROUP HOLDINGS LLC (PA)
1815 S Meyers Rd Ste 750 (60181-5280)
PHONE................630 613-2941
Tom Blashill, *CEO*
Valerie Richardson, *Vice Pres*
Bruce Korp, *Director*
EMP: 42
SALES (est): 21MM **Privately Held**
WEB: www.colsongroup.com
SIC: 3325 Railroad car wheels, cast steel

(G-15796)
DOVER PMPS PRCESS SLTONS SGMEN (HQ)
Also Called: Dover Energy, Inc.
1815 S Meyers Rd (60181-5225)
PHONE................630 487-2240
John D Allen, *President*
Doug Cumpston, *Regional Mgr*
Jack Pitts, *Regional Mgr*
Jon Dora, *Business Mgr*
Rob Robbins, *Vice Pres*
EMP: 27
SALES (est): 72MM
SALES (corp-wide): 7.1B **Publicly Held**
WEB: www.psgdover.com
SIC: 3561 Pumps & pumping equipment
PA: Dover Corporation
 3005 Highland Pkwy # 200
 Downers Grove IL 60515
 630 541-1540

(G-15797)
ECOLOGIC LLC (PA)
18w140 Butterfield Rd # 1180 (60181-4845)
P.O. Box 477, Downers Grove (60515-0477)
PHONE................630 869-0495
EMP: 13
SALES (est): 1.3MM **Privately Held**
SIC: 2821 Mfg Plastic Materials/Resins

(G-15798)
FASTSIGNS
17w608 14th St (60181-3717)
PHONE................630 932-0001
Bob O'Hearn, *Owner*
EMP: 3 **EST:** 2015
SALES (est): 50.9K **Privately Held**
SIC: 3993 Signs & advertising specialties

(G-15799)
GATEHOUSE MEDIA LLC
Also Called: Metropolitan Newspapers, The
18w140 Butterfield Rd # 450 (60181-4843)
PHONE................585 598-0030
Alfredo Ricardo, *Auditor*
Toni Mann, *Manager*
Gilles Thierry, *Software Dev*
John Amspaugh, *Maintence Staff*
Steven Stout, *Maintence Staff*
EMP: 100
SALES (corp-wide): 1.8B **Publicly Held**
SIC: 2711 Commercial printing & newspaper publishing combined
HQ: Gatehouse Media, Llc
 175 Sullys Trl Fl 3
 Pittsford NY 14534
 585 598-0030

(G-15800)
GE ZENITH CONTROLS INC
18w140 Butterfield Rd # 350 (60181-4848)
PHONE................773 299-6600
Anne Brunsdale, *Human Res Mgr*
Robert Lamiot, *Manager*
Mark Serrano, *Manager*
Ray Prince, *Commercial*
EMP: 4

SALES (corp-wide): 95.2B **Publicly Held**
WEB: www.ge.com
SIC: 3613 Switchgear & switchboard apparatus
HQ: Ge Zenith Controls, Inc.
 601 Shiloh Rd
 Plano TX 75074
 800 637-1738

(G-15801)
HEAT TRANSFER LABORATORIES
2 Mid America Plz Ste 800 (60181-4727)
PHONE................708 715-4300
Bruce Green, *President*
EMP: 2
SALES (est): 205.3K **Privately Held**
SIC: 3589 Water treatment equipment, industrial

(G-15802)
HENG TUO USA INC (PA)
Also Called: Nci Technology
1 Transam Plaza Dr # 545 (60181-4822)
PHONE................630 317-7672
Weilong LI, *Principal*
James Xu, *Principal*
▲ **EMP:** 8
SQ FT: 4,800
SALES (est): 1.3MM **Privately Held**
SIC: 3823 3621 3596 Temperature measurement instruments, industrial; industrial process measurement equipment; storage battery chargers, motor & engine generator type; baby scales; industrial scales

(G-15803)
HIPSKIND TECH SLTONS GROUP INC
17w220 22nd St Ste 450 (60181-4471)
P.O. Box 840137, Hollywood FL (33084-2137)
PHONE................630 920-0960
Mark Amarant, *CEO*
Steven Roth, *President*
Brock Mowry, *CTO*
EMP: 55
SALES (est): 11.2MM
SALES (corp-wide): 16.2MM **Privately Held**
SIC: 7373 3825 7382 Value-added resellers, computer systems; network analyzers; security systems services
PA: Whoa Networks Inc
 7369 Sheridan St Ste 301
 Hollywood FL 33024
 954 449-4900

(G-15804)
JOHNSON MATTHEY INC
2 Transam Plaza Dr # 230 (60181-4296)
PHONE................630 268-6300
Karen Slehofer, *President*
Jamie Chisamore, *Sales Staff*
EMP: 20
SALES (corp-wide): 13.8B **Privately Held**
SIC: 2834 Pharmaceutical preparations
HQ: Johnson Matthey Inc.
 435 Devon Park Dr Ste 600
 Wayne PA 19087
 610 971-3000

(G-15805)
LEDCOR CONSTRUCTION INC
18w140 Bttrfeld Rd Ste 15 (60181)
PHONE................630 916-1200
John Helliwell, *Manager*
Steven Cullen, *Director*
Kristen Roberts, *Executive Asst*
EMP: 10
SALES (corp-wide): 39.8MM **Privately Held**
SIC: 3661 Fiber optics communications equipment
PA: Ledcor Construction, Inc.
 723 N Oaklawn Ave
 Elmhurst IL 60126
 312 971-9182

(G-15806)
MAC GRAPHICS GROUP INC
17w703 Butterfield Rd D (60181-4280)
P.O. Box 537, Elmhurst (60126-0537)
PHONE................630 620-7200
Robert J Cronin Jr, *President*

Robert Cronin Jr, *President*
EMP: 8
SQ FT: 2,500
SALES: 1MM **Privately Held**
SIC: 7331 2752 7336 2759 Direct mail advertising services; commercial printing, lithographic; commercial art & graphic design; publication printing

(G-15807)
MCCAIN FOODS USA INC (DH)
Also Called: McCain Foodservice
1 Tower Ln Fl 11 (60181-4671)
P.O. Box 2464, Carol Stream (60132-2464)
PHONE................630 955-0400
Frank Finn, *President*
Ian Mitchell, *Counsel*
Michael Campbell, *Vice Pres*
Mark Farrell, *Vice Pres*
Doug Fraser, *Vice Pres*
◆ **EMP:** 275 **EST:** 1952
SQ FT: 100,000
SALES (est): 1.1B
SALES (corp-wide): 19.5B **Privately Held**
WEB: www.mccainusa.com
SIC: 2037 Potato products, quick frozen & cold pack; vegetables, quick frozen & cold pack, excl. potato products

(G-15808)
MCCAIN FOODS USA INC
Also Called: Food Service Products Division
1 Tower Ln Ste Uppr (60181-4662)
PHONE................920 563-6625
Rick Pickruhn, *Manager*
EMP: 300
SQ FT: 38,000
SALES (corp-wide): 19.5B **Privately Held**
SIC: 2037 2038 Vegetables, quick frozen & cold pack, excl. potato products; frozen specialties
HQ: Mccain Foods Usa, Inc.
 1 Tower Ln Fl 11
 Oakbrook Terrace IL 60181
 630 955-0400

(G-15809)
MCCAIN USA INC (DH)
1 Tower Ln Ste Uppr (60181-4662)
PHONE................800 938-7799
Gilles Lessard, *President*
Rodney Norquay, *Plant Mgr*
Seth Williams, *Opers Mgr*
Grant Darric, *Production*
Parker Smith, *Engineer*
▼ **EMP:** 250
SQ FT: 50,000
SALES (est): 1.1B
SALES (corp-wide): 19.5B **Privately Held**
SIC: 2037 2038 5411 Potato products, quick frozen & cold pack; fruit juices; pizza, frozen; grocery stores
HQ: Mccain Foods Limited
 439 King St W Suite 500
 Toronto ON M5V 1
 416 955-1700

(G-15810)
ND FAIRMONT LLC (PA)
1901 S Meyers Rd Ste 600 (60181-5210)
PHONE................937 328-3870
Ken Liu, *CEO*
Simon Wang, *CFO*
Brian Burcham, *Controller*
EMP: 4
SALES (est): 19.3MM **Privately Held**
SIC: 2611 Pulp manufactured from waste or recycled paper

(G-15811)
ND PAPER INC (DH)
1901 S Meyers Rd Ste 600 (60181-5210)
PHONE................513 200-0908
Ken Liu, *CEO*
◆ **EMP:** 2
SQ FT: 18,015
SALES (est): 453.3MM **Privately Held**
SIC: 2621 Paper mills
HQ: Nd Paper Llc
 1901 S Meyers Rd Ste 600
 Oakbrook Terrace IL 60181
 937 528-3870

GEOGRAPHIC SECTION

Oglesby - Lasalle County (G-15840)

(G-15812)
ND PAPER LLC (HQ)
1901 S Meyers Rd Ste 600 (60181-5210)
PHONE..................937 528-3870
Ken Liu, *CEO*
Alexandra Foote, *Project Mgr*
EMP: 13
SQ FT: 18,015
SALES (est): 374.7MM **Privately Held**
SIC: 2621 Paper mills

(G-15813)
PRINTED IMPRESSIONS INC
Also Called: Commercial Prtg Graphics Arts
1640 S Ardmore Ave (60181-3742)
PHONE..................773 604-8585
Manish Patel, *President*
Anjana Patel, *Vice Pres*
EMP: 2
SQ FT: 6,500
SALES: 300K **Privately Held**
SIC: 2752 2791 Commercial printing, offset; typesetting

(G-15814)
RMKC INC
Also Called: Fastsigns
17w608 14th St (60181-3717)
PHONE..................630 932-0001
EMP: 3 **EST:** 2015
SALES (est): 215.7K **Privately Held**
SIC: 3993 Signs & advertising specialties

(G-15815)
S G C M CORP
Also Called: Spot Printing & Office Sups
1s171 Summit Ave (60181-3904)
PHONE..................630 953-2428
Sue Mehta, *President*
G C Mehta, *Vice Pres*
EMP: 4
SQ FT: 1,500
SALES (est): 583.7K **Privately Held**
SIC: 2752 5112 Commercial printing, offset; office supplies

(G-15816)
TENEXCO INC
17w715 Butterfield Rd C (60181-4203)
PHONE..................708 771-7870
Richard S Incandela, *President*
Richard Incandela II, *Vice Pres*
Sharon S Incandela, *Admin Sec*
EMP: 6
SQ FT: 1,700
SALES (est): 885.8K **Privately Held**
SIC: 1382 Oil & gas exploration services

(G-15817)
UNIVERSAL MFG CORPORATION
18 W 140 Butterfield Rd (60181)
PHONE..................630 613-7340
Arthur Mintz, *President*
Harvey Gossett, *Treasurer*
Harvey Grossett, *Manager*
Dale Odem, *Director*
Dale Frost, *Admin Sec*
◆ **EMP:** 175 **EST:** 1955
SQ FT: 195,000
SALES (est): 28MM **Privately Held**
WEB: www.universalmanufacturingcorp.com
SIC: 2384 Housecoats, except children's: from purchased materials

(G-15818)
VAUTO INC (DH)
1901 S Meyers Rd Ste 700 (60181-5211)
PHONE..................630 590-2000
Keith Jezek, *President*
Joshua Harrington, *General Mgr*
Jeff Stevenson, *Opers Staff*
Sharita Taylor, *Engineer*
Laurela Johnson, *Human Res Dir*
EMP: 30
SALES (est): 7.1MM
SALES (corp-wide): 31.8B **Privately Held**
SIC: 7372 Business oriented computer software
HQ: Autotrader.Com, Inc.
3003 Summit Blvd Fl 200
Brookhaven GA 30319
404 568-8000

Oakland
Coles County

(G-15819)
OAKLAND NOODLE COMPANY
10 W Main St (61943-7182)
P.O. Box 644 (61943-0644)
PHONE..................217 346-2322
Todd Ethington, *President*
EMP: 4
SALES (est): 399.8K **Privately Held**
SIC: 2099 8322 Noodles, fried (Chinese); geriatric social service

Oakwood
Vermilion County

(G-15820)
JAMESON STEEL FABRICATION INC
19965 Newtown Rd (61858-6272)
PHONE..................217 354-2205
Doug Cunningham, *President*
EMP: 8
SALES (est): 2.1MM **Privately Held**
SIC: 3441 Building components, structural steel

Oakwood Hills
Mchenry County

(G-15821)
NEIWEEM INDUSTRIES INC (PA)
21 Greenview Rd (60013-1061)
PHONE..................847 487-1239
Kurt Neiweem, *President*
EMP: 8
SQ FT: 4,000
SALES (est): 682K **Privately Held**
SIC: 3446 3441 1796 Fences or posts, ornamental iron or steel; fabricated structural metal; millwright

(G-15822)
SIMON ZELIKMAN
106 Meadow Ln (60013-1151)
PHONE..................847 338-8031
Simon Zelikman, *Owner*
EMP: 3 **EST:** 2011
SALES: 100K **Privately Held**
SIC: 3911 7631 Jewelry, precious metal; jewelry repair services

(G-15823)
UNCOMMON ELEMENTS LLC
22 Fawn Ridge Dr (60013-1069)
PHONE..................847 414-0708
Adela Crandell Durkee, *Principal*
EMP: 3
SALES (est): 212.2K **Privately Held**
SIC: 2819 Industrial inorganic chemicals

Oblong
Crawford County

(G-15824)
BULLETIN
103 W Main St Ste 4 (62449-1165)
P.O. Box 687, Olney (62450-0687)
PHONE..................618 553-9764
EMP: 4
SALES (est): 224.6K **Privately Held**
SIC: 2711 Newspapers, publishing & printing

(G-15825)
CROSS OIL & WELL SERVICE INC
104 E Missouri St (62449-1456)
PHONE..................618 592-4609
John O Cross, *President*
EMP: 11
SALES (est): 1MM **Privately Held**
SIC: 1389 Oil field services

(G-15826)
DEPENDABLE ELECTRIC
728 E State Hwy 33 (62449)
P.O. Box 202 (62449-0202)
PHONE..................618 592-3314
Phillip Rich, *Owner*
EMP: 2
SQ FT: 6,000
SALES (est): 200K **Privately Held**
SIC: 7694 5999 Electric motor repair; motors, electric

(G-15827)
ROBERT BOLDREY
8479 N 2250th St (62449-4113)
PHONE..................618 592-4892
Robert Boldrey, *Principal*
EMP: 3
SALES (est): 131.7K **Privately Held**
SIC: 2084 Wines

(G-15828)
ROSS OIL CO INC
11172 N 450th St (62449-2902)
PHONE..................618 592-3808
Curtis Ross, *President*
Sandra Ross, *Admin Sec*
EMP: 4 **EST:** 1970
SALES (est): 450K **Privately Held**
SIC: 1311 5172 Crude petroleum production; petroleum products

(G-15829)
SCHAEFFER ELECTRIC CO (PA)
400 S Taylor St (62449)
P.O. Box 52 (62449-0052)
PHONE..................618 592-3231
Gary Plumber, *Owner*
EMP: 3
SQ FT: 10,000
SALES (est): 1.7MM **Privately Held**
SIC: 7694 Electric motor repair

(G-15830)
T GRAPHICS
701 S Range St (62449-1606)
PHONE..................618 592-4145
Tony Madlem, *Owner*
EMP: 3
SQ FT: 5,000
SALES (est): 266.3K **Privately Held**
SIC: 2759 3993 2395 Screen printing; signs & advertising specialties; embroidery & art needlework

(G-15831)
THIRD DAY OIL & GAS LLC
210 S Range St (62449-1225)
P.O. Box 81, Casey (62420-0081)
PHONE..................618 553-5538
Danny Sheridan, *Mng Member*
David Sheridan,
EMP: 4
SALES (est): 183.3K **Privately Held**
SIC: 1382 7389 Oil & gas exploration services;

(G-15832)
WILLOWBROOK SAWMILL
1469 E 1600th Ave (62449-4704)
PHONE..................618 592-3806
EMP: 3
SALES (est): 196.4K **Privately Held**
SIC: 2421 Sawmills & planing mills, general

Odin
Marion County

(G-15833)
AAA TRASH
408 S Merritt St (62870-1190)
PHONE..................618 775-1365
V Stull, *Principal*
EMP: 5
SALES (est): 362.7K **Privately Held**
SIC: 3089 Garbage containers, plastic

(G-15834)
CITATION OIL & GAS CORP
2302 Hoots Chapel Rd (62870-2527)
PHONE..................618 548-2331
Michael Gorden, *Chief*
Steve Glassford, *Foreman/Supr*
EMP: 18
SALES (est): 948.6K **Privately Held**
SIC: 1382 Oil & gas exploration services

(G-15835)
ODIN FIRE PROTECTION DISTRICT
100 Perkins St (62870-1262)
P.O. Box 223 (62870-0223)
PHONE..................618 775-8292
Greg Miller, *Chief*
EMP: 25
SALES (est): 2.4MM **Privately Held**
SIC: 3711 Fire department vehicles (motor vehicles), assembly of

(G-15836)
WILSON & WILSON MONUMENT CO
406 W Poplar St (62870-1293)
P.O. Box 247 (62870-0247)
PHONE..................618 775-6488
Lindel Adams, *President*
EMP: 15 **EST:** 1946
SQ FT: 1,200
SALES (est): 1.1MM **Privately Held**
WEB: www.wilsonandwilsonmonuments.com
SIC: 3281 5999 Monuments, cut stone (not finishing or lettering only); gravestones, finished; monuments, finished to custom order

Ogden
Champaign County

(G-15837)
OGDEN METALWORKS INC
301 N Marilyn St (61859-5813)
P.O. Box 128 (61859-0128)
PHONE..................217 582-2552
Jeffrey L Mohr, *President*
▲ **EMP:** 15
SQ FT: 20,000
SALES (est): 3.6MM **Privately Held**
SIC: 3523 Farm machinery & equipment

(G-15838)
SHAPE MASTER INC
108 E Main St (61859-9527)
P.O. Box 372 (61859-0372)
PHONE..................217 582-2638
Kenneth Cooley, *CEO*
Pamela Cooley, *Corp Secy*
EMP: 8
SALES (est): 1.6MM **Privately Held**
SIC: 3089 Injection molding of plastics

Oglesby
Lasalle County

(G-15839)
BADGE-A-MINIT LTD (HQ)
345 N Lewis Ave (61348-1628)
PHONE..................815 883-8822
Malcolm Roebuck, *Ch of Bd*
Cindy Kurkowski, *President*
◆ **EMP:** 21
SQ FT: 85,000
SALES (est): 15MM
SALES (corp-wide): 21.4MM **Privately Held**
SIC: 5199 3999 Advertising specialties; badges, metal: policemen, firemen, etc.
PA: Malcolm Group, Inc
429 E North Water St
Chicago IL
815 883-8822

(G-15840)
COOKIE KINGDOM INC
1201 E Walnut St (61348-1344)
PHONE..................815 883-3331
Quentin G Pierce, *Ch of Bd*
Clifford A Sheppard, *President*
EMP: 100 **EST:** 1982
SQ FT: 38,000

Oglesby - Lasalle County (G-15841)

SALES (est): 21.1MM **Privately Held**
WEB: www.cookiekingdom.com
SIC: 2052 Cookies

(G-15841)
FIRST IMPRESSION
211 S Columbia Ave (61348-1415)
PHONE...................815 883-3357
Bill Quick, *Partner*
Robert Zetlis, *Partner*
EMP: 6
SALES (est): 100K **Privately Held**
SIC: 2395 2759 Embroidery & art needlework; commercial printing

(G-15842)
JASIEK MOTOR REBUILDING INC
451 E State Route 71 (61348-9720)
PHONE...................815 883-3678
Jeff Jasiek, *President*
Jerry Jasiek, *Corp Secy*
Bonnie Jasiek, *Vice Pres*
EMP: 4
SALES (est): 300K **Privately Held**
SIC: 7539 7694 7692 3714 Machine shop, automotive; armature rewinding shops; welding repair; motor vehicle parts & accessories; motors & generators; internal combustion engines

(G-15843)
LONE STAR INDUSTRIES INC
490 Portland Ave (61348-1334)
P.O. Box 130 (61348-0130)
PHONE...................815 883-3173
Richard Zimmell, *Manager*
EMP: 7
SALES (corp-wide): 395.5MM **Privately Held**
WEB: www.buzziunicemusa.com
SIC: 3241 Portland cement
HQ: Lone Star Industries Inc
   10401 N Meridian St # 120
   Indianapolis IN 46290
   317 706-3314

(G-15844)
WIRE MESH LLC
42 Marquette Ave (61348-1461)
PHONE...................815 579-8597
Romar De La Luz, *Manager*
Rafael Barrenechea,
Luis Barrenechea,
EMP: 7
SALES (est): 926.3K **Privately Held**
SIC: 3496 Miscellaneous fabricated wire products

Ohio
Bureau County

(G-15845)
SISLER DAIRY PRODUCTS COMPANY
Also Called: Sisler's Ice & Ice Cream Co
102 S Grove St (61349)
P.O. Box 128 (61349-0128)
PHONE...................815 376-2913
William M Sisler, *President*
Karen Anderson, *Corp Secy*
Brian Sisler, *Sales Staff*
Daniel G Thompson, *Shareholder*
Daniel Thompson, *Shareholder*
EMP: 5 EST: 1907
SQ FT: 10,500
SALES (est): 613.4K **Privately Held**
WEB: www.sislers.com
SIC: 2097 2024 Ice cubes; ice cream, packaged: molded, on sticks, etc.

Okawville
Washington County

(G-15846)
OKAWVILLE TIMES
Also Called: Putt and Times
109 E Walnut St (62271-1883)
P.O. Box 68 (62271-0068)
PHONE...................618 243-5563
Gary Stricker, *Owner*
EMP: 3 EST: 1893
SALES (est): 256.9K **Privately Held**
WEB: www.okawvilletimes.com
SIC: 2711 7999 2791 Commercial printing & newspaper publishing combined; miniature golf course operation; typesetting

(G-15847)
QUAD-COUNTY READY MIX CORP (PA)
300 W 12th St (62271-2137)
P.O. Box 158 (62271-0158)
PHONE...................618 243-6430
Herbert Hustedde, *President*
Carol Hustedde, *Vice Pres*
Barb Groennert, *Manager*
EMP: 17 EST: 1952
SQ FT: 1,500
SALES (est): 16.1MM **Privately Held**
WEB: www.qcrm4.com
SIC: 3273 Ready-mixed concrete

(G-15848)
US PALLETT SUPPLY INC (PA)
15340 Sawmill Rd (62271-1624)
PHONE...................618 243-6449
Leon Kuhl, *President*
Bill Gunderson, *Sales Staff*
EMP: 20
SQ FT: 1,800
SALES (est): 2.2MM **Privately Held**
SIC: 2448 Pallets, wood

Old Mill Creek
Lake County

(G-15849)
TEMPEL HOLDINGS INC
Also Called: Tempel Farms
17000 W Wadsworth Rd (60083-9761)
PHONE...................847 244-5330
Larry Leffingwell, *Manager*
EMP: 15
SQ FT: 1,500
SALES (corp-wide): 389MM **Privately Held**
SIC: 3313 Electrometallurgical products
PA: Tempel Holdings, Inc.
   5500 N Wolcott Ave
   Chicago IL 60640
   773 250-8000

Olmsted
Pulaski County

(G-15850)
AFCO INDUSTRIES INC
8161 State Highway 37 (62970-2240)
PHONE...................618 742-6469
EMP: 5
SALES (corp-wide): 76.4MM **Privately Held**
SIC: 3354 Aluminum extruded products
PA: Afco Industries, Inc.
   3400 Roy Ave
   Alexandria LA 71302
   318 448-1651

Olney
Richland County

(G-15851)
ALLANS WELDING & MACHINE INC
3815 E Illinois Hwy 250 (62450)
P.O. Box 343 (62450-0343)
PHONE...................618 392-3708
Allan May, *President*
Rhonda May, *Vice Pres*
EMP: 8
SQ FT: 200
SALES (est): 1.4MM **Privately Held**
SIC: 7692 3599 Welding repair; machine shop, jobbing & repair

(G-15852)
AMERICAN CIPS
4978 N Il 130 (62450-3740)
PHONE...................618 393-5641
Ron Bailey, *Principal*
EMP: 3
SALES (est): 140K **Privately Held**
SIC: 3612 Voltage regulators, transmission & distribution

(G-15853)
ANGEL ROSE ENERGY LLC
4368 N Holly Rd (62450-3318)
PHONE...................618 392-3700
EMP: 4 EST: 2007
SALES (est): 390K **Privately Held**
SIC: 1382 Oil/Gas Exploration Services

(G-15854)
BAKER HGHES OLFLD OPRTIONS LLC
Also Called: Baker Atlas
930 S West St (62450-1319)
PHONE...................618 393-2919
Donald Lapalne, *Manager*
EMP: 16 **Privately Held**
SIC: 1389 1381 1382 Oil field services; well logging; drilling oil & gas wells; seismograph surveys
PA: Baker Hughes Oilfield Operations Llc
   2001 Rankin Rd
   Houston TX 77073

(G-15855)
BENCHMARK PROPERTIES LTD
Also Called: Blumthal Gas Geologist
5076 N Il 130 (62450)
P.O. Box 419 (62450-0419)
PHONE...................618 395-7023
James Blumthal, *President*
EMP: 2
SQ FT: 2,400
SALES (est): 250K **Privately Held**
SIC: 1382 Oil & gas exploration services

(G-15856)
BILLS MACHINE & POWER TRANSM (PA)
Also Called: Bm Machine & Fabrication
4678 Weinmann Dr Ste B (62450-1845)
PHONE...................618 392-2500
James Harmon, *President*
Timothy Berry, *Vice Pres*
Sherry Inyart, *Treasurer*
William Barber, *Director*
Ron Urfer, *Admin Sec*
▲ EMP: 21
SQ FT: 12,000
SALES (est): 3.2MM **Privately Held**
SIC: 3599 Machine shop, jobbing & repair

(G-15857)
CONCORD OIL & GAS CORPORATION
1712 S Whittle Ave (62450-3426)
PHONE...................618 393-2124
Greg Gibson, *President*
EMP: 20
SALES (est): 1.1MM **Privately Held**
SIC: 1389 Oil field services; servicing oil & gas wells

(G-15858)
CONCORD WELL SERVICE INC
1102 N East St (62450-2489)
P.O. Box 448 (62450-0448)
PHONE...................618 395-4405
Peter Morse, *President*
EMP: 5
SALES (est): 500K **Privately Held**
SIC: 1311 Crude petroleum & natural gas

(G-15859)
EWELLIX USA LLC
3519 N Union Dr (62450-5141)
PHONE...................618 392-3647
Tammy Walten, *Branch Mgr*
EMP: 8 **Privately Held**
SIC: 3562 Ball & roller bearings
HQ: Ewellix Usa Llc
   3800 Sierra Cir 310
   Center Valley PA 18034
   267 436-6000

(G-15860)
FEHRENBACHER READY-MIX INC
1401 S Whittle Ave (62450-3444)
PHONE...................618 395-2306
Tom Fehrenbacher, *President*
Barbara Miller, *Manager*
EMP: 5
SALES (est): 470.8K **Privately Held**
SIC: 3273 Ready-mixed concrete

(G-15861)
FLOYDS WELDING SERVICE
3519 N Union Dr (62450-5141)
PHONE...................618 395-2414
Darrell Fehrenbacher, *Owner*
EMP: 4 EST: 1946
SQ FT: 3,200
SALES (est): 407.4K **Privately Held**
WEB: www.floydswelding.com
SIC: 7692 Automotive welding

(G-15862)
GATEHOUSE MEDIA LLC
Also Called: Olney Daily Reporter
206 S Whittle Ave (62450-2251)
P.O. Box 340 (62450-0340)
PHONE...................618 393-2931
Carol Garison, *General Mgr*
Cathy Slunaker, *Advt Staff*
EMP: 24
SALES (est): 1.8B **Publicly Held**
SIC: 2711 Newspapers: publishing only, not printed on site; newspapers, publishing & printing
HQ: Gatehouse Media, Llc
   175 Sullys Trl Fl 3
   Pittsford NY 14534
   585 598-0030

(G-15863)
GLOVER OIL FIELD SERVICE INC
4993 N Il 130 (62450-3741)
PHONE...................618 395-3624
Carmon L Glover Jr, *President*
Robert Swinson, *Manager*
EMP: 11 EST: 1960
SQ FT: 5,000
SALES: 500K **Privately Held**
SIC: 1381 1389 1311 Drilling oil & gas wells; cementing oil & gas well casings; crude petroleum & natural gas production

(G-15864)
HARRIS DRILLING FLUIDS INC
Also Called: 300 P S I
1015 S Whittle Ave (62450-3405)
P.O. Box 370 (62450-0370)
PHONE...................618 395-7395
Todd K Harris, *President*
Ken Harris, *President*
Lin Aguilar, *Admin Sec*
EMP: 7
SALES (est): 189.8K **Privately Held**
SIC: 1389 Oil field services

(G-15865)
HOUPT REVOLVING CUTTERS INC
516 W Butler St (62450-1407)
PHONE...................618 395-1913
Kenneth D Houpt, *President*
Katherine Houpt, *Treasurer*
Patricia Houpt, *Admin Sec*
EMP: 1
SQ FT: 3,200
SALES (est): 210.9K **Privately Held**
SIC: 3556 Cutting, chopping, grinding, mixing & similar machinery

(G-15866)
JOE HUNT
1911 E Main St (62450-3312)
PHONE...................618 392-2000
Joe Hunt, *Principal*
▲ EMP: 3
SALES (est): 334.8K **Privately Held**
SIC: 3751 5091 8748 Bicycles & related parts; bicycle equipment & supplies; business consulting

GEOGRAPHIC SECTION
Olney - Richland County (G-15895)

(G-15867)
KABINET KRAFT
536 E Cherry St (62450-2727)
PHONE 618 395-1047
EMP: 15
SALES (est): 1.8MM Privately Held
SIC: 5031 5211 2541 2434 Whol Lumber/Plywd/Millwk Ret Lumber/Building Mtrl Mfg Wood Partitions/Fixt Mfg Wood Kitchen Cabinet Mfg Millwork

(G-15868)
KAPP COMPANY LLC
3600 E White Ln (62450-5537)
PHONE 618 676-1000
Chesleigh Kapp,
EMP: 3
SALES (est): 310K Privately Held
SIC: 1381 Drilling oil & gas wells

(G-15869)
LIQUID RESIN INTERNATIONAL
4295 N Holly Rd (62450-4813)
P.O. Box 760 (62450-0760)
PHONE 618 392-3590
James Pottor, President
Thomas F Sloan, Vice Pres
Nathan Prevo, Sales Staff
EMP: 20
SQ FT: 7,800
SALES (est): 3.9MM Privately Held
SIC: 5169 2869 Chemicals & allied products; industrial organic chemicals

(G-15870)
M & L WELL SERVICE INC
3648 N Illinois 130 (62450)
P.O. Box 670 (62450-0670)
PHONE 618 393-7144
EMP: 20 EST: 1978
SALES (est): 930K Privately Held
SIC: 1389 Oil/Gas Field Services

(G-15871)
M & L WELL SERVICE INC
800 E Main St (62450-2620)
P.O. Box 670 (62450-0670)
PHONE 618 395-4538
Harold Murbarger, President
George Lambird, Treasurer
EMP: 9
SQ FT: 4,000
SALES: 600K Privately Held
SIC: 1389 1761 Servicing oil & gas wells; roofing, siding & sheet metal work

(G-15872)
MAC PLASTICS MANUFACTURING INC
715 N West St (62450-1033)
P.O. Box 38 (62450-0038)
PHONE 618 392-3010
Rod Michels, CEO
EMP: 37
SALES (est): 8.2MM Privately Held
SIC: 3089 Injection molding of plastics

(G-15873)
MASTER-HALCO INC
4633 E Radio Tower Ln (62450-4742)
PHONE 618 395-4365
Mike Uhl, Manager
EMP: 50 Privately Held
SIC: 3315 5031 3496 Chain link fencing; lumber, plywood & millwork; miscellaneous fabricated wire products
HQ: Master-Halco, Inc.
    3010 Lbj Fwy Ste 800
    Dallas TX 75234
    972 714-7300

(G-15874)
MOLDING SERVICES ILLINOIS INC
126 N West St (62450-1107)
PHONE 618 395-3888
Anthony King, CEO
Andy Scheutz, Vice Pres
▲ EMP: 28
SALES (est): 6MM Privately Held
SIC: 3089 Injection molding of plastics

(G-15875)
MOLDING SYSTEMS ENGRG CORP
126 N West St (62450-1107)
PHONE 618 395-3888
Anthony D King, President
EMP: 27
SQ FT: 12,000
SALES (est): 3.7MM Privately Held
SIC: 3089 Injection molding of plastics

(G-15876)
MURVIN & MEIR OIL CO
1102 N East St (62450-2489)
P.O. Box 396 (62450-0396)
PHONE 618 395-4405
Don Runyon, Corp Secy
Peter Morse, Exec VP
EMP: 7 EST: 1964
SALES (est): 946.7K Privately Held
SIC: 1382 Oil & gas exploration services

(G-15877)
MURVIN OIL COMPANY
1712 S Whittle Ave (62450-3426)
P.O. Box 297 (62450-0297)
PHONE 618 393-2124
Gregg C Gibson, President
Anthony C Gibson, Vice Pres
Lori Hundley, Office Mgr
Austin Bussard, Manager
Greg Gibson, Technology
EMP: 22
SALES (est): 4MM Privately Held
WEB: www.murvinoil.com
SIC: 1382 Oil & gas exploration services

(G-15878)
NATIONAL VINEGAR CO
203 W South Ave (62450-1776)
P.O. Box 495 (62450-0495)
PHONE 618 395-1011
Steve Wilson, Manager
EMP: 11
SALES (est): 319.7K Privately Held
SIC: 2099 Vinegar

(G-15879)
OLDE PRINT SHOPPE INC
Also Called: Print Shoppe Inc The Olde
1314 E Main St (62450-2630)
PHONE 618 395-3833
Max Balding, President
Velda Balding, Treasurer
Greg Balding, Manager
EMP: 8
SQ FT: 5,100
SALES (est): 1.1MM Privately Held
SIC: 2752 2759 2791 2789 Commercial printing, offset; letterpress printing; typesetting; bookbinding & related work

(G-15880)
OLNEY DAILY MAIL
206 S Whittle Ave (62450-2251)
PHONE 618 393-2931
Kerry Kocher, Owner
EMP: 50 EST: 2010
SALES (est): 1.5MM Privately Held
SIC: 2741 Miscellaneous publishing

(G-15881)
OLNEY MACHINE & DESIGN INC
4632 E Radio T (62450)
P.O. Box 66 (62450-0066)
PHONE 618 392-6634
Doug Walker, President
EMP: 10
SQ FT: 6,400
SALES (est): 2.3MM Privately Held
SIC: 3599 Machine shop, jobbing & repair

(G-15882)
PACIFIC CYCLE INC
4730 E Radio Tower Ln (62450-4743)
P.O. Box 344 (62450-0344)
PHONE 618 393-2508
Nicole Clodfelter, Financial Analy
Barbara Smith, Branch Mgr
James Holmes, Manager
Jessica Zwilling, Clerk
EMP: 200
SQ FT: 1,000,000
SALES (corp-wide): 2.6B Privately Held
SIC: 3751 3944 Bicycles & related parts; sleds, children's; wagons: coaster, express & play: children's
HQ: Pacific Cycle Inc.
    4902 Hammersley Rd
    Madison WI 53711
    608 268-2468

(G-15883)
PINNACLE EXPLORATION CORP
510 E Lafayette St (62450-2914)
P.O. Box 428 (62450-0428)
PHONE 618 395-8100
George Hagan, President
Jmaes Hagan, Vice Pres
Carletta Hagan, Admin Sec
EMP: 4
SQ FT: 5,000
SALES (est): 351.1K Privately Held
SIC: 1389 Oil field services

(G-15884)
PRECISION PLUGGING AND SLS INC
3978 N Elmdale Rd (62450-4746)
P.O. Box 22 (62450-0022)
PHONE 618 395-8510
John L Runyon, President
Jonathan Runyon, Vice Pres
EMP: 10
SALES (est): 1.6MM Privately Held
SIC: 1389 Oil field services

(G-15885)
PRINTFORCE INC
1409 E Main St (62450-3162)
PHONE 618 395-7746
Nancy McClenatham, President
Bob McClenatham, General Mgr
EMP: 4
SALES: 300K Privately Held
SIC: 2759 5099 2752 5999 Financial note & certificate printing & engraving; firearms & ammunition, except sporting; commercial printing, offset; alarm & safety equipment stores

(G-15886)
RICHLAND COUNTY MACHINE INC
302 N Walnut St (62450-2103)
P.O. Box 66 (62450-0066)
PHONE 618 392-2892
Douglas Walker, President
Timothy Fulk, Vice Pres
EMP: 5
SQ FT: 7,000
SALES: 400K Privately Held
SIC: 3599 Custom machinery

(G-15887)
RUNYON OIL PRODUCTION INC
208 Linn St (62450)
PHONE 618 395-8510
John Runyon, President
EMP: 4
SALES (est): 627.9K Privately Held
SIC: 1381 Drilling oil & gas wells

(G-15888)
RUNYON OIL TOOLS INC
331 Herman Dr (62450-4766)
PHONE 618 395-5045
Steven E Runyon, President
Mark Judge, Sales Staff
EMP: 8
SQ FT: 4,500
SALES (est): 720.2K Privately Held
SIC: 1389 7353 Grading oil & gas well foundations; oil field services; oil equipment rental services

(G-15889)
STEVEN A ZANETIS
1060 W Main St (62450-1100)
P.O. Box 99 (62450-0099)
PHONE 618 393-2176
Steven A Zanetis, Owner
EMP: 5
SALES (est): 249.3K Privately Held
SIC: 1311 Crude petroleum production

(G-15890)
TRI-STATE PRODUCING DEVELOPING
1060 W Main St (62450-1100)
P.O. Box 99 (62450-0099)
PHONE 618 393-2176
Steven A Zanetis, President
L Ronald Schwarzlose, Vice Pres
EMP: 5
SQ FT: 3,000
SALES (est): 707.9K Privately Held
SIC: 1311 Crude petroleum production

(G-15891)
U S WEIGHT INC
Also Called: Escalade Sports
4594 E Radio Tower Ln (62450-4748)
PHONE 618 392-0408
Robert E Griffin, President
▲ EMP: 35
SQ FT: 100,000
SALES: 9MM
SALES (corp-wide): 180.5MM Publicly Held
SIC: 3949 Dumbbells & other weightlifting equipment
HQ: Indian Industries Inc
    817 Maxwell Ave
    Evansville IN 47711
    812 467-1200

(G-15892)
VADA LLC
3723 N Van Rd (62450-4733)
P.O. Box 759 (62450-0759)
PHONE 407 572-4979
Sherry L Brookheart, Mng Member
Brian Brookheart, Mng Member
EMP: 12 EST: 2015
SALES (est): 925.8K Privately Held
SIC: 2952 Roofing materials

(G-15893)
WABASH VALLEY SERVICE CO
Also Called: Rich-Law
1201 S Whittle Ave (62450-3437)
P.O. Box 403 (62450-0403)
PHONE 618 393-2971
Ben Anderson, Manager
EMP: 10
SALES (corp-wide): 42.6MM Privately Held
WEB: www.wabashvalleyfs.com
SIC: 5171 5191 5199 5083 Petroleum bulk stations & terminals; feed; plant food; farm & garden machinery; fertilizers, mixing only
PA: Wabash Valley Service Co
    909 N Court St
    Grayville IL 62844
    888 869-8127

(G-15894)
XENIA MFG INC
1915 Miller Dr (62450-4744)
P.O. Box 237, Xenia (62899-0237)
PHONE 618 392-7212
Yancey Glassford, Manager
EMP: 40
SALES (est): 2.9MM
SALES (corp-wide): 22MM Privately Held
SIC: 3694 Harness wiring sets, internal combustion engines
PA: Xenia Mfg., Inc.
    1507 Church St
    Xenia IL 62899
    618 678-2218

(G-15895)
YOCKEY OIL INCORPORATED
1043 W Main St (62450-1156)
P.O. Box 70 (62450-0070)
PHONE 618 393-6236
Carolyn Ledtka-Crow, President
Donald Quillen, Vice Pres
Connie Shafer, Treasurer
EMP: 2 EST: 1968
SALES (est): 305.6K Privately Held
SIC: 1311 Crude petroleum production

Olympia Fields
Cook County

(G-15896)
NAS MEDIA GROUP INC (PA)
424 Brookwood Ter 2 (60461-1539)
PHONE..................................312 371-7499
Michael Gardner, *CEO*
Brandi McGhee, *CFO*
EMP: 6
SALES (est): 1.8MM **Privately Held**
SIC: 2741 8748 Business service newsletters: publishing & printing; business consulting

(G-15897)
OFGD INC
2401 Lincoln Hwy (60461-1901)
PHONE..................................708 283-7101
George Nediyakalayil, *President*
EMP: 2
SALES (est): 258.4K **Privately Held**
SIC: 1382 Oil & gas exploration services

(G-15898)
SHOPPERS PLANET
20915 Cambridge Ln (60461-1832)
PHONE..................................877 232-5435
Kacey Poe, *CEO*
EMP: 11
SALES (est): 399.9K **Privately Held**
SIC: 3955 Carbon paper for typewriters, sales books, etc.

(G-15899)
TIA TYNETTE DESIGNS INC
2600 Troy Cir (60461-1951)
PHONE..................................219 440-2859
Tia Rogers, *President*
EMP: 2 **EST:** 2008
SALES (est): 213.2K **Privately Held**
SIC: 3172 5094 Cases, jewelry; jewelry & precious stones

Omaha
Gallatin County

(G-15900)
HAYDEN MILLS INC
Also Called: Omaha Grain & Fertilizer
119 Washington Ave (62871-1147)
P.O. Box 98 (62871-0098)
PHONE..................................618 962-3136
David Sutton, *President*
Richard Sutton, *Vice Pres*
EMP: 33 **EST:** 1953
SQ FT: 3,000
SALES: 10MM **Privately Held**
SIC: 5191 2875 2041 Farm supplies; fertilizers, mixing only; flour & other grain mill products

Onarga
Iroquois County

(G-15901)
ANGEL WIND ENERGY INC
113 N Pine St (60955-1081)
PHONE..................................815 471-2020
Michael Harroun, *President*
Benjamin Harroun, *Vice Pres*
EMP: 3 **EST:** 2008
SALES (est): 293.6K **Privately Held**
SIC: 3511 Turbines & turbine generator sets

(G-15902)
PROCOMM INC HOOPESTON ILLINOIS
209 W Grant Ave (60955-1117)
P.O. Box 149 (60955-0149)
PHONE..................................815 268-4303
James M Bennett, *President*
Tondra Bennett, *Co-Owner*
▲ **EMP:** 34 **EST:** 1999
SQ FT: 25,000
SALES (est): 4.9MM **Privately Held**
WEB: www.procommproducts.com
SIC: 3669 5999 Intercommunication systems, electric; communication equipment

Oneida
Knox County

(G-15903)
KALB CORPORATION
110 W Depot St (61467)
P.O. Box 44 (61467-0044)
PHONE..................................309 483-3600
Mike Kalb, *CEO*
Rob Kalb, *Vice Pres*
Chad Walker, *VP Sales*
▼ **EMP:** 15
SQ FT: 1,000
SALES (est): 1.4MM **Privately Held**
SIC: 5033 3271 3634 Insulation, thermal; architectural concrete: block, split, fluted, screen, etc.; heating units, electric (radiant heat): baseboard or wall

Opdyke
Jefferson County

(G-15904)
CROOKED TRAILS SAWMILL
18058 E Il Highway 142 (62872-2405)
PHONE..................................618 244-1547
David Mast, *Owner*
EMP: 3 **EST:** 2008
SALES: 130K **Privately Held**
SIC: 2421 Sawmills & planing mills, general

(G-15905)
T HAM SIGN INC (PA)
7699 N Goshen Ln (62872-2707)
P.O. Box 155, Mount Vernon (62864-0004)
PHONE..................................618 242-2010
Todd Ham, *President*
Carmen Ham, *Vice Pres*
John Dungan, *Sales Staff*
Jason Suchomski, *Graphic Designe*
EMP: 31 **EST:** 1954
SQ FT: 3,800
SALES (est): 2.8MM **Privately Held**
WEB: www.thamsign.com
SIC: 1799 3993 Sign installation & maintenance; signs & advertising specialties

Oquawka
Henderson County

(G-15906)
OQUAWKA BOATS AND FABRICATIONS
1312 E State Highway 164 (61469-7017)
PHONE..................................309 867-2213
Carmen Thompson, *President*
EMP: 5
SQ FT: 9,000
SALES (est): 950.6K **Privately Held**
SIC: 3732 7699 Boats, fiberglass: building & repairing; boat repair

(G-15907)
PRO FUEL NINE INC
101 S 8th St (61469-9760)
PHONE..................................309 867-3375
Sean Chinna, *Principal*
EMP: 5 **EST:** 2011
SALES (est): 338.3K **Privately Held**
SIC: 2869 Fuels

Orangeville
Stephenson County

(G-15908)
COREFX INGREDIENTS LLC
12495 N Pleasant Hill Rd (61060-9758)
PHONE..................................773 271-2663
Michael Ernster, *Branch Mgr*
EMP: 15
SALES (corp-wide): 1.8B **Privately Held**
SIC: 2023 Dry, condensed, evaporated dairy products
HQ: Corefx Ingredients Llc
4725 W North Ave Ste 240
Chicago IL
773 271-2663

(G-15909)
HOGBACK HAVEN MAPLE FARM
Also Called: Hogback Hardwoods
13800 N Hogback Rd (61060-9794)
PHONE..................................815 291-9440
Scott E Elsasser, *Owner*
EMP: 9
SALES (est): 361.2K **Privately Held**
SIC: 2099 Sugar, industrial maple

Oreana
Macon County

(G-15910)
AKERS PACKAGING SOLUTIONS INC
Also Called: Akers Packg Solutions Decatur
7573 N State Route 48 (62554)
P.O. Box 248 (62554-0248)
PHONE..................................217 468-2396
David Econie, *General Mgr*
EMP: 28
SALES (corp-wide): 13.4MM **Privately Held**
SIC: 2653 Boxes, corrugated: made from purchased materials
PA: Akers Packaging Solutions, Inc.
2820 Lefferson Rd
Middletown OH 45044
513 422-6312

(G-15911)
GREIF INC
7573 N Rte 48 (62554)
P.O. Box 248 (62554-0248)
PHONE..................................217 468-2396
David Econie, *Manager*
EMP: 56
SALES (corp-wide): 4.6B **Publicly Held**
SIC: 2653 Boxes, corrugated: made from purchased materials; boxes, solid fiber: made from purchased materials
PA: Greif, Inc.
425 Winter Rd
Delaware OH 43015
740 549-6000

Oregon
Ogle County

(G-15912)
BEARMOON LLC
508 S 7th St (61061-1906)
PHONE..................................815 312-2327
Dean M Murray, *Principal*
EMP: 4 **EST:** 2017
SALES (est): 349.1K **Privately Held**
SIC: 2844 Toilet preparations

(G-15913)
BEESING WELDING & EQP REPR
2506 S Il Route 2 (61061-9504)
PHONE..................................815 732-7552
Dale Beesing, *Owner*
EMP: 4
SALES (est): 651K **Privately Held**
SIC: 7692 Welding repair

(G-15914)
BLOUNT INTERNATIONAL INC
2606 S Il Route 2 (61061-9685)
PHONE..................................800 319-6637
Sandra Stengel, *Branch Mgr*
EMP: 6
SALES (corp-wide): 1.4B **Privately Held**
SIC: 3531 Construction machinery
PA: Blount International, Inc.
4909 Se International Way
Portland OR 97222
503 653-8881

(G-15915)
COILCRAFT INCORPORATED
9 Clay St (61061-2030)
PHONE..................................815 288-7051
Scott Helfrich, *Branch Mgr*
EMP: 100
SALES (corp-wide): 844.1K **Privately Held**
SIC: 3677 Coil windings, electronic; electronic transformers; filtration devices, electronic
PA: Coilcraft, Incorporated
1102 Silver Lake Rd
Cary IL 60013
847 639-2361

(G-15916)
COVIA HOLDINGS CORPORATION
1446 N Devils Backbone Rd (61061-9583)
P.O. Box 156 (61061-0156)
PHONE..................................815 732-2121
Steve Bliton, *Plant Mgr*
EMP: 100
SALES (corp-wide): 125.5MM **Publicly Held**
SIC: 1446 Industrial sand
HQ: Covia Holdings Corporation
3 Summit Park Dr Ste 700
Independence OH 44131
440 214-3284

(G-15917)
ED ETNYRE & CO
Also Called: Oci Manufacturing Company
1333 S Daysville Rd (61061-9778)
PHONE..................................815 732-2116
Roger L Etnyre, *President*
Sharon Engel, *Vice Pres*
EMP: 375
SQ FT: 225,000
SALES (est): 56MM
SALES (corp-wide): 58.4MM **Privately Held**
SIC: 3531 3711 3537 Road construction & maintenance machinery; chip spreaders, self-propelled; motor vehicles & car bodies; industrial trucks & tractors
PA: Etnyre International, Ltd.
1333 S Daysville Rd
Oregon IL 61061
815 732-2116

(G-15918)
ETNYRE INTERNATIONAL LTD (PA)
1333 S Daysville Rd (61061-9783)
PHONE..................................815 732-2116
Roger L Etnyre, *Ch of Bd*
Thomas Brown, *President*
O'Brien Pat, *President*
Tim Krueger, *General Mgr*
Terry Stone, *General Mgr*
◆ **EMP:** 380
SQ FT: 250,000
SALES (est): 58.4MM **Privately Held**
WEB: www.etnyre.com
SIC: 3531 Road construction & maintenance machinery

(G-15919)
F N SMITH CORPORATION
1200 S 2nd St (61061-2330)
P.O. Box 179 (61061-0179)
PHONE..................................815 732-2171
Fred N Smith, *CEO*
Ed N Smith, *President*
Louise M Smith, *Corp Secy*
Gary Reding, *Plant Mgr*
Julie Kelly, *Purch Mgr*
EMP: 45 **EST:** 1972
SQ FT: 20,000
SALES (est): 10.5MM **Privately Held**
SIC: 3599 Custom machinery

(G-15920)
FAST TECHNOLOGIES CORP
4600 N River Rd (61061-9481)
PHONE..................................815 234-4744
Connie S Zimmerman, *President*
EMP: 1
SQ FT: 2,000

▲ = Import ▼ = Export
◆ = Import/Export

GEOGRAPHIC SECTION

Orland Park - Cook County (G-15946)

SALES: 350K **Privately Held**
SIC: **2033** Vegetables: packaged in cans, jars, etc.; fruit butters: packaged in cans, jars, etc.

(G-15921)
GENWOODS HOLDCO LLC
2606 S Illinois Rte 2 (61061)
P.O. Box 1000 (61061-1000)
PHONE..................................815 732-2141
Fred Korndorf,
Mark Miller,
EMP: 1250
SQ FT: 420,000
SALES (est): 56.2MM
SALES (corp-wide): 1.4B **Privately Held**
SIC: **3523** Farm machinery & equipment
PA: Blount International, Inc.
4909 Se International Way
Portland OR 97222
503 653-8881

(G-15922)
HA-INTERNATIONAL LLC
1449 W Devils Backbone Rd (61061-9583)
PHONE..................................815 732-3898
J Ebens, *Branch Mgr*
EMP: 30
SALES (corp-wide): 250.7K **Privately Held**
WEB: www.ha-international.com
SIC: **2869** Industrial organic chemicals
HQ: Ha-International, Llc
630 Oakmont Ln
Westmont IL 60559
630 575-5700

(G-15923)
LARRY PONTNACK
Also Called: Mo-Par City
6309 E Brick Rd (61061-9623)
PHONE..................................815 732-7751
Larry Pontnack, *Owner*
EMP: 3
SALES (est): 328.1K **Privately Held**
SIC: **7538 3714** General automotive repair shops; motor vehicle engines & parts

(G-15924)
MYERS CONCRETE & CONSTRUCTION
1100 Bennett Dr (61061-2140)
P.O. Box 96 (61061-0096)
PHONE..................................815 732-2591
Robert Diehl, *Owner*
EMP: 5 EST: 1936
SALES (est): 330K **Privately Held**
SIC: **3273 1771 4212 1794** Ready-mixed concrete; concrete work; dump truck haulage; excavation work; general warehousing

(G-15925)
OGLE COUNTY LIFE
311 W Washington St (61061-1621)
P.O. Box 378 (61061-0378)
PHONE..................................815 732-2156
Tina Ketter, *Principal*
Lesley Divers, *Advt Staff*
Lesley Sheffield, *Agent*
John Shank, *CTO*
EMP: 6
SALES (est): 203.7K **Privately Held**
SIC: **2711** Commercial printing & newspaper publishing combined

(G-15926)
ROGERS READY MIX & MTLS INC
Also Called: Byron Ready Mix
201 E Washington St (61061-9562)
P.O. Box 250, Byron (61010-0250)
PHONE..................................815 234-8044
Roger Corbitt, *Manager*
EMP: 4
SALES (corp-wide): 14.3MM **Privately Held**
SIC: **3273** Ready-mixed concrete
PA: Rogers Ready Mix & Materials, Inc.
8128 N Walnut St
Byron IL 61010
815 234-8212

(G-15927)
SPEECO INCORPORATED
Also Called: Special Products Company
2606 S Illinois Route 2 (61061)
PHONE..................................303 279-5544
Paul Valas, *President*
Ken Lehman, *CFO*
◆ EMP: 140
SQ FT: 120,000
SALES (est): 14.5MM
SALES (corp-wide): 1.4B **Privately Held**
WEB: www.speeco.com
SIC: **3523 3531** Farm machinery & equipment; log splitters
PA: Blount International, Inc.
4909 Se International Way
Portland OR 97222
503 653-8881

(G-15928)
THE B F SHAW PRINTING CO
Also Called: Ogle County Newspaper
121 S 4th St Ste A (61061-1628)
P.O. Box 8 (61061-0008)
PHONE..................................815 732-6166
Earleen Hinton, *Manager*
EMP: 8
SALES (corp-wide): 73.4MM **Privately Held**
SIC: **2711** Newspapers, publishing & printing
PA: 'b. F. Shaw Printing Company, The'
3200 E Lincolnway
Sterling IL
815 284-4000

(G-15929)
WOODS EQUIPMENT COMPANY
Gannon Manufacturing
2606 S Il Route 2 (61061-9685)
PHONE..................................815 732-2141
Tom Sieper, *Marketing Staff*
Eric Ritchie, *Manager*
Judy Navarrete, *Director*
EMP: 80
SQ FT: 80,883
SALES (corp-wide): 1.4B **Privately Held**
SIC: **3531 3412 5083** Construction machinery attachments; backhoe mounted, hydraulically powered attachments; buckets, excavating; clamshell, concrete, dragline, etc.; metal barrels, drums & pails; tractors, agricultural
HQ: Woods Equipment Company
2606 S Il Route 2
Oregon IL 61061

Orion
Henry County

(G-15930)
ORION TOOL DIE & MACHINE CO
1400 16th St (61273-7795)
P.O. Box 278 (61273-0278)
PHONE..................................309 526-3303
William Lange, *President*
Cory Lange, *General Mgr*
Sandra K Lange, *COO*
Kim Lange, *Office Mgr*
Megan Miles, *Admin Sec*
EMP: 23 EST: 1952
SQ FT: 14,000
SALES (est): 4.2MM **Privately Held**
WEB: www.oriontool.com
SIC: **3599** Machine shop, jobbing & repair

Orland Park
Cook County

(G-15931)
22ND CENTURY MEDIA (PA)
11516 W 183rd St U Sw 3 (60467)
PHONE..................................708 326-9170
Andrew Nicks, *Principal*
Nick Frazier, *Editor*
Michael Wojtychiw, *Editor*
Eric Degrechie, *Manager*
Katie Monahan, *Director*
EMP: 28
SALES (est): 4.8MM **Privately Held**
SIC: **2711** Newspapers: publishing only, not printed on site

(G-15932)
A AND P DIRECTIONAL DRLG LLC (PA)
10842 Eleanor Ln (60467-4592)
PHONE..................................708 715-1192
Larry Antone, *Principal*
EMP: 3
SALES (est): 912.6K **Privately Held**
SIC: **1381** Directional drilling oil & gas wells

(G-15933)
ACORN DIVERSIFIED INC
17809 New Jersey Ct # 14 (60467-9326)
PHONE..................................708 478-1051
EMP: 12
SALES (est): 1.2MM **Privately Held**
SIC: **2671** Mfg Release Liners And Films

(G-15934)
ADVANCE AWNAIR CORP
15418 S 70th Ct (60462-5133)
PHONE..................................708 422-2730
Joseph Jochheim, *President*
Billie Jochheim, *Vice Pres*
EMP: 10
SQ FT: 10,000
SALES (est): 1.2MM **Privately Held**
WEB: www.advancedawningsmfg.com
SIC: **3444** Awnings, sheet metal; canopies, sheet metal

(G-15935)
AEMM A ELECTRIC
8448 Camelia Ln (60462-4003)
PHONE..................................708 403-6700
Mark Czubiak, *Owner*
EMP: 2 EST: 2010
SALES (est): 228K **Privately Held**
SIC: **3699 1731** Electrical equipment & supplies; electrical work

(G-15936)
AIRBRAKE PRODUCTS INC
10334 Alveston St (60462-3072)
PHONE..................................708 594-1110
George Gajc, *President*
Richard J Murawski, *Corp Secy*
Peter Pasdach, *Vice Pres*
Rick Murawski, *Treasurer*
EMP: 15
SQ FT: 17,000
SALES: 1.5MM **Privately Held**
SIC: **3714** Air brakes, motor vehicle

(G-15937)
ALEX AND ANI LLC
544 Orland Square Dr E12 (60462-3217)
PHONE..................................708 403-4450
EMP: 3 **Privately Held**
SIC: **3915** Jewelers' materials & lapidary work
PA: Alex And Ani, Llc
2000 Chapel View Blvd # 360
Cranston RI 02920

(G-15938)
ALL-WAYS QUICK PRINT
14609 Birch St (60462-2619)
PHONE..................................708 403-8422
Bill Griffin, *President*
EMP: 1
SALES: 250K **Privately Held**
SIC: **2752 2791 2789** Commercial printing, offset; typesetting; bookbinding & related work

(G-15939)
AMERICAN ASP SURFC RECYCL INC
13301 Southwest Hwy Ste H (60462-1313)
PHONE..................................708 448-9540
Cheryl Jager, *President*
EMP: 13
SALES (est): 2.3MM **Privately Held**
SIC: **2952** Sheathing, asphalt saturated

(G-15940)
ANDREW NEW ZEALAND INC
10500 W 153rd St (60462-3071)
PHONE..................................708 873-3507
Jim Giacobazzi, *Vice Pres*
EMP: 40
SALES (est): 4.6MM **Publicly Held**
SIC: **3663 3357 3679 3812** Microwave communication equipment; antennas, transmitting & communications; television antennas (transmitting) & ground equipment; receiver-transmitter units (transceiver); coaxial cable, nonferrous; waveguides & fittings; search & navigation equipment; radar systems & equipment; computer peripheral equipment
HQ: Commscope Technologies Llc
1100 Commscope Pl Se
Hickory NC 28602
708 236-6600

(G-15941)
ANDREW SYSTEMS INC
10500 W 153rd St (60462-3071)
P.O. Box 962 (60462-0962)
PHONE..................................708 873-3855
Ralph Faifan, *President*
James Petelle, *Vice Pres*
Tom Gillett, *Engineer*
M Jeffery Gittleman, *Treasurer*
David Hagan, *Sales Staff*
▲ EMP: 50
SQ FT: 25,000
SALES (est): 6MM **Publicly Held**
SIC: **3663** Radio & TV communications equipment
HQ: Commscope Technologies Llc
1100 Commscope Pl Se
Hickory NC 28602
708 236-6600

(G-15942)
ARKADIAN GAMING LLC
11227 Distinctive Dr (60467-9458)
PHONE..................................708 377-5656
Nick Karounos,
Sam A Cappas,
EMP: 3 EST: 2010
SALES (est): 234.1K **Privately Held**
WEB: www.arkadiangaming.blogspot.com
SIC: **3944** Electronic game machines, except coin-operated

(G-15943)
CALDWELL LETTER SERVICE INC
10500 163rd Pl (60467-5444)
PHONE..................................773 847-0708
Patricia K Perry, *President*
Will J Perry, *Vice Pres*
Doug Ponsetti, *Sales Executive*
Patricia Perry, *Admin Sec*
▲ EMP: 25
SALES (est): 4.6MM **Privately Held**
WEB: www.cls4mail.com
SIC: **7331 2752** Mailing service; commercial printing, offset

(G-15944)
CALUTECH INC
Also Called: Old Chicago Coffee Co.
15646 S 70th Ct 1 (60462-5108)
PHONE..................................708 614-0228
Doug Freitag, *President*
EMP: 8
SQ FT: 5,000
SALES (est): 996K **Privately Held**
WEB: www.calutech.com
SIC: **5999 3564 7375** Air purification equipment; air purification equipment; online data base information retrieval

(G-15945)
CAM TEK LUBRICANTS INC
9540 W 144th Pl Ste 2a (60462-2554)
PHONE..................................708 477-3000
EMP: 4
SALES (est): 262.6K **Privately Held**
SIC: **2992** Lubricating oils

(G-15946)
CASWARD TOOL WORKS INC
8062 Pickens Dr (60462-1674)
PHONE..................................773 486-4900
Zdzislaw Szmajlo, *President*
Jessie Szamjlo, *Manager*
EMP: 6
SALES (est): 702.7K **Privately Held**
SIC: **3599 7692** Machine shop, jobbing & repair; welding repair

Orland Park - Cook County (G-15947)

(G-15947)
CGPROFESSIONAL SERVICES INC
10711 165th St Ste F (60467-8785)
PHONE 708 389-4110
Cheryl Gabriel, *President*
EMP: 6
SQ FT: 2,500
SALES: 950K **Privately Held**
SIC: 3621 Generators & sets, electric

(G-15948)
CONVEYORS PLUS INC
13301 Southwest Hwy Ste J (60462-1313)
P.O. Box 1038 (60462-8038)
PHONE 708 361-1512
Herbert Zimmermann, *President*
EMP: 5
SQ FT: 3,600
SALES (est): 944.3K **Privately Held**
SIC: 3535 3537 Conveyors & conveying equipment; industrial trucks & tractors

(G-15949)
COOPER OIL CO
9500 W 159th St (60467-5504)
PHONE 708 349-2893
Bill Cooper, *Principal*
EMP: 8
SALES (est): 927.2K **Privately Held**
SIC: 2869 Fuels

(G-15950)
DAX STEEL RULE DIES INC
13250 Jean Creek Dr (60462-1410)
PHONE 708 448-4436
Patricia Sczopanski, *President*
Leon Sczopanski, *Vice Pres*
EMP: 6 **EST:** 1970
SALES (est): 570K **Privately Held**
SIC: 3544 Dies, steel rule

(G-15951)
DIAGRIND INC
Also Called: T J Martin & Co Division
10491 164th Pl (60467-5438)
PHONE 708 460-4333
Donald Sommer, *President*
EMP: 13
SQ FT: 10,000
SALES (est): 2MM **Privately Held**
WEB: www.diagrind.com
SIC: 3291 5085 Wheels, abrasive; industrial wheels

(G-15952)
DONSON MACHINE
15440 S 70th Ct (60462-5133)
PHONE 708 468-8392
Nick Knowski, *Principal*
EMP: 2
SALES (est): 201.5K **Privately Held**
SIC: 3599 Machine shop, jobbing & repair

(G-15953)
DS PRODUCTION LLC
16101 108th Ave (60467-5337)
PHONE 708 873-3142
Derick Turl, *Director*
EMP: 6
SALES (est): 304K **Privately Held**
SIC: 2273 Carpets & rugs

(G-15954)
DUNKIN DONUTS
14461 S La Grange Rd (60462-2505)
PHONE 708 460-3088
John C Grivas, *President*
Roula Boorazanes, *Corp Secy*
Bill Boorazanes, *Vice Pres*
EMP: 22
SALES (est): 1MM **Privately Held**
SIC: 5461 2051 Doughnuts; doughnuts, except frozen

(G-15955)
GLOBAL GREEN PRODUCTS LLC (PA)
8617 Golfview Dr (60462-2852)
PHONE 708 341-3670
Larry P Koskan,
▲ **EMP:** 6 **EST:** 2004
SALES (est): 1.3MM **Privately Held**
WEB: www.globalgreenproducts.com
SIC: 3822 Auto controls regulating residntl & coml environmt & applncs

(G-15956)
GRAPHIC IMAGE CORPORATION
Also Called: G I C
10500 163rd Pl (60467-5444)
PHONE 312 829-7800
John Markasovic, *President*
Frank Markosovic, *Vice Pres*
Louise M Markasovic, *Admin Sec*
EMP: 12 **EST:** 1950
SALES (est): 2.3MM **Privately Held**
WEB: www.graphicimagecorp.com
SIC: 2752 2796 2791 Commercial printing, offset; platemaking services; typesetting

(G-15957)
GRAPHIC SCREEN PRINTING INC
15640 S 70th Ct (60462-5108)
PHONE 708 429-3330
Michael C Ahern, *President*
Mary Ahern, *Admin Sec*
EMP: 9
SQ FT: 2,000
SALES (est): 1.1MM **Privately Held**
SIC: 2759 2396 Screen printing; automotive & apparel trimmings

(G-15958)
HALANICK ENTERPRISES INC
Also Called: Eva's Bridal
14428 John Humphrey Dr (60462-2638)
PHONE 708 403-3334
Hala Samiri, *Principal*
Nick Ghusein, *Principal*
EMP: 20
SALES (est): 1.6MM **Privately Held**
SIC: 2335 2384 Wedding gowns & dresses; robes & dressing gowns

(G-15959)
HERRIS GROUP LLC
10410 163rd Pl (60467-5445)
PHONE 630 908-7393
Paul Michaels,
▲ **EMP:** 5
SALES (est): 258K **Privately Held**
WEB: www.herrisgroup.com
SIC: 2048 Feed premixes; feed supplements

(G-15960)
ICI FIBERITE
14342 Beacon Ave (60462-2422)
PHONE 708 403-3788
Susan Gonzalez, *Principal*
EMP: 3
SALES (est): 165.1K **Privately Held**
SIC: 3089 Injection molded finished plastic products

(G-15961)
IMPERIAL TECHNICAL SERVICES
14001 Thomas Dr (60462-2038)
PHONE 708 403-1564
EMP: 12
SQ FT: 1,400
SALES (est): 1.5MM **Privately Held**
SIC: 3695 Mfg Magnetic/Optical Recording Media

(G-15962)
JCW INVESTMENTS INC
Also Called: Tekky Toys
11415 183rd Pl Ste E (60467-5011)
PHONE 708 478-7323
James Wirt, *CEO*
Erika Demith, *Admin Sec*
◆ **EMP:** 5
SALES (est): 764.3K **Privately Held**
WEB: www.getcoolstuff.com
SIC: 3944 5092 Electronic toys; toy novelties & amusements

(G-15963)
K&G MENS COMPANY INC
Also Called: K & G Men's Superstore
180 Orland Park Pl (60462-3854)
PHONE 708 349-2579
Harvey Pearlstein, *Manager*
EMP: 7
SALES (corp-wide): 2.8B **Publicly Held**
SIC: 2389 Men's miscellaneous accessories
HQ: K&G Men's Company Inc.
6380 Rogerdale Rd
Houston TX 77072

(G-15964)
K-TRON INC
9704 Hummingbird Hill Dr (60467-5557)
PHONE 708 460-2128
Frank S Kasper, *President*
EMP: 3 **EST:** 1990
SALES (est): 250K **Privately Held**
SIC: 7372 Prepackaged software

(G-15965)
LIDS CORPORATION
416 Orland Square Dr (60462-3215)
PHONE 708 873-9606
Bob Fiore, *Manager*
EMP: 7 **Privately Held**
SIC: 2353 5661 Hats & caps; men's shoes
PA: Lids Corporation
7555 Woodland Dr
Indianapolis IN 46278

(G-15966)
LP SOFTWARE INC
15255 S 94th Ave Ste 500 (60462-3895)
PHONE 708 361-4310
Brian Eskra, *President*
Roy Haehnel, *Vice Pres*
EMP: 8
SALES (est): 1.2MM **Privately Held**
SIC: 7372 Prepackaged software
PA: Appriss Inc.
9901 Linn Station Rd # 500
Louisville KY 40223

(G-15967)
MC MECHANICAL CONTRACTORS INC
15774 S La Grange Rd # 245 (60462-4766)
PHONE 708 460-0075
Marcel Cairo Jr, *President*
Jamie B Penwitt, *Admin Sec*
EMP: 2 **EST:** 2010
SALES (est): 289K **Privately Held**
SIC: 2499 Cooling towers, wood or wood & sheet metal combination

(G-15968)
MIDWEST NAMEPLATE CORP
15127 S 73rd Ave Ste H (60462-3437)
PHONE 708 614-0606
Douglas Holgate, *President*
Susan Holgate, *Treasurer*
EMP: 5
SALES (est): 446.6K **Privately Held**
SIC: 3999 3993 3479 3469 Manufacturing industries; signs & advertising specialties; metal coating & allied service; metal stampings

(G-15969)
MOSTERT & FERGUSON SIGNS
Also Called: Artisan Signs
16249 107th Ave Ste 10 (60467-9027)
PHONE 815 485-1212
John F Mostert, *Owner*
EMP: 5
SQ FT: 10,000
SALES (est): 797.1K **Privately Held**
WEB: www.artisansignsandlighting.com
SIC: 3993 Neon signs

(G-15970)
MUHAMMAD SOTAVIA
9601 165th St (60467-5660)
PHONE 708 966-2262
Sotavia Muhammad, *Principal*
EMP: 3
SALES (est): 305.9K **Privately Held**
WEB: www.smuhammadlaw.com
SIC: 2835 Microbiology & virology diagnostic products

(G-15971)
NEXT DAY TONER SUPPLIES INC
Also Called: Next Day Plus
11411 183rd St Ste A (60467-9451)
PHONE 708 478-1000
Tom Kosloskus, *CEO*
Jeff Bollman, *President*
Beverly Bollman, *Vice Pres*
Jonathan Fiala, *Vice Pres*
Eric Zwartz, *Accounts Exec*
EMP: 30 **EST:** 1998
SALES (est): 8.5MM **Privately Held**
SIC: 5112 3955 5045 5044 Photocopying supplies; laserjet supplies; print cartridges for laser & other computer printers; printers, computer; office equipment

(G-15972)
OPTECH ORTHO & PROSTH SVCS
18016 Wolf Rd (60467-5407)
PHONE 708 364-9700
EMP: 9 **Privately Held**
SIC: 3842 Mfg Surgical Appliances/Supplies
PA: Optech Orthotics & Prosthetics Services, Ltd.
119 E Court St Ste 100
Kankakee IL 60901

(G-15973)
ORLAND PARK BAKERY LTD
14850 S La Grange Rd (60462-3229)
PHONE 708 349-8516
Thomas Major, *President*
Daniel Major, *General Mgr*
Kelly Sluis, *Sales Associate*
Tom Major, *Manager*
Kathleen Major, *Admin Sec*
EMP: 27
SQ FT: 2,000
SALES (est): 1.7MM **Privately Held**
WEB: www.orlandparkbakery.com
SIC: 5461 2051 Cakes; bread, cake & related products

(G-15974)
PELLEGRINI ENTERPRISES INC
Also Called: Artisan Signs & Lighting
16249 107th Ave Ste 10 (60467-9027)
PHONE 815 717-6408
Ruth Pelegrini, *President*
EMP: 4
SALES (est): 200K **Privately Held**
SIC: 3993 Electric signs

(G-15975)
PROTECTIVE COATINGS & WATERPRO
9320 136th St (60462-1344)
P.O. Box 127 (60462-0127)
PHONE 708 403-7650
Curtis Neeley, *Principal*
EMP: 2
SALES (est): 280.3K **Privately Held**
SIC: 1522 1799 3479 Residential construction; waterproofing; painting, coating & hot dipping

(G-15976)
ROSELAND II LLC
18410 115th Ave (60467-9488)
PHONE 708 479-5010
David M Lautenbach, *Principal*
EMP: 4 **EST:** 2010
SALES (est): 451.6K **Privately Held**
WEB: www.roselandstair.com
SIC: 2431 Staircases, stairs & railings

(G-15977)
RUTLEDGE PRINTING CO
11415 183rd Pl Ste C (60467-5011)
PHONE 708 479-8282
Richard W Marks, *President*
Linda Marks, *Corp Secy*
EMP: 12 **EST:** 1923
SQ FT: 2,800
SALES (est): 1.1MM **Privately Held**
WEB: www.rutledgeprinting.com
SIC: 2752 Commercial printing, offset

GEOGRAPHIC SECTION

Oswego - Kendall County (G-16007)

(G-15978)
SENSIBLE DESIGNS ONLINE INC
10556 Great Egret Dr (60467-8509)
PHONE 708 267-8924
Gintautas Burokas, *President*
▲ EMP: 8
SQ FT: 1,500
SALES (est): 749.4K **Privately Held**
SIC: 3634 Housewares, excluding cooking appliances & utensils

(G-15979)
SIR SPEEDY PRINTING CNTR 6129
9412 W 143rd St (60462-2031)
PHONE 708 349-7789
Gary Grohovena, *Owner*
EMP: 4
SQ FT: 1,500
SALES (est): 314.4K **Privately Held**
SIC: 2752 Commercial printing, lithographic

(G-15980)
SNOW CONTROL INC
7245 W 151st St (60462-2967)
PHONE 708 670-6269
EMP: 3
SALES (est): 230.1K **Privately Held**
WEB: www.snowcontrolinc.com
SIC: 2851 Removers & cleaners

(G-15981)
SOUTH SIDE BLER WLDG WORKS INC
Also Called: South Side Boiler & Wldg Work
10811 Minnesota Ct (60467-9341)
PHONE 708 478-1714
Edward Haavig, *President*
William Haavig, *Corp Secy*
EMP: 8
SALES: 750K **Privately Held**
SIC: 7699 7692 Boiler repair shop; welding repair

(G-15982)
SOUTHWEST TOOL & MACHINE
15600 116th Ct (60467-5884)
PHONE 708 349-4441
John Rekart, *Owner*
EMP: 4
SALES (est): 236K **Privately Held**
SIC: 3599 Machine shop, jobbing & repair

(G-15983)
SPIRIT WARRIOR INC
Also Called: New Life Screen Printing
15519 S 70th Ct (60462-5105)
P.O. Box 871 (60462-0871)
PHONE 708 614-0020
Richard Ryan, *President*
Nancy Jo Ryan, *Vice Pres*
EMP: 8
SQ FT: 2,700
SALES (est): 1MM **Privately Held**
SIC: 2759 5961 7389 Screen printing; mail order house; embroidering of advertising on shirts, etc.

(G-15984)
STAR OPHTHALMIC INSTRS INC
14038 Stonegate Ln (60467-7601)
PHONE 630 655-4500
Daniel R Reberski, *President*
Denise L Reberski, *Vice Pres*
EMP: 12
SQ FT: 3,500
SALES (est): 1.7MM
SALES (corp-wide): 10.3MM **Privately Held**
SIC: 3841 Surgical & medical instruments
PA: Eye Vision Technologies, Llc

    Saint Louis MO

(G-15985)
SWAROVSKI NORTH AMERICA LTD
288 Orland Square Dr (60462-3211)
PHONE 708 364-0090
EMP: 3
SALES (corp-wide): 4.7B **Privately Held**
WEB: www.swarovski.com
SIC: 3961 Costume jewelry

HQ: Swarovski North America Limited
    1 Kenney Dr
    Cranston RI 02920
    401 463-6400

(G-15986)
SWISSTRONICS CORP
16308 107th Ave Ste 8 (60467-4559)
PHONE 708 403-8877
EMP: 5 EST: 1966
SQ FT: 5,000
SALES (est): 450K **Privately Held**
SIC: 3451 3541 Mfg Screw Machine Products Mfg Machine Tools-Cutting

(G-15987)
TOMSONS PRODUCTS INC (PA)
13210 S 85th Ave (60462-1404)
PHONE 708 479-7030
Thomas J Wisinski, *President*
Mark A Wisinski, *Vice Pres*
EMP: 3
SQ FT: 7,500
SALES (est): 500K **Privately Held**
SIC: 3599 Machine shop, jobbing & repair

Osco
Henry County

(G-15988)
HELFTER ENTERPRISES INC
Also Called: Advanced Biological Concepts
301 Main St (61274-7001)
P.O. Box 27 (61274-0027)
PHONE 309 522-5505
Kendra Helfter, *President*
James Helfter, *Vice Pres*
EMP: 19
SQ FT: 135,000
SALES (est): 2.6MM **Privately Held**
SIC: 2048 Prepared feeds

Oswego
Kendall County

(G-15989)
ACQUAMED TECHNOLOGIES INC
195 Kendall Point Dr # 16 (60543-8518)
PHONE 630 728-4014
Hugh Palmer, *COO*
EMP: 8
SALES (est): 957K **Privately Held**
SIC: 3843 Dental equipment & supplies

(G-15990)
AERO-CABLES CORP
Also Called: S & M Products
114 Kirkland Cir Ste A (60543-8067)
PHONE 815 609-6600
Russell Coblentz, *President*
Susan Coblentz, *CFO*
▼ EMP: 4
SQ FT: 1,500
SALES (est): 370K **Privately Held**
SIC: 3724 Aircraft engines & engine parts

(G-15991)
AIR802 CORPORATION
1981d Wiesbrook Rd (60543-8311)
PHONE 630 966-2501
Lilian Bryant, *CEO*
Michael Bryant, *President*
▲ EMP: 5
SALES (est): 1.1MM **Privately Held**
SIC: 3679 Electronic circuits; attenuators; harness assemblies for electronic use: wire or cable

(G-15992)
ANFINSEN PLASTIC MOULDING INC
445b Treasure Dr Unit B (60543-7945)
PHONE 630 554-4100
Stephen R Laham, *President*
Kim Burks, *CFO*
▲ EMP: 25 EST: 1935
SQ FT: 40,000

SALES (est): 7.5MM **Privately Held**
WEB: www.anfinsen.com
SIC: 3089 3999 Molding primary plastic; barber & beauty shop equipment

(G-15993)
BLUE CHIP MFG LLC
37 Stonehill Rd (60543-9449)
PHONE 630 553-6321
Ronald K Gates,
Su Gates,
EMP: 3
SQ FT: 2,000
SALES (est): 296.4K **Privately Held**
SIC: 3469 Machine parts, stamped or pressed metal

(G-15994)
BONDFIRE LLC
133 Chapin Way (60543-4009)
PHONE 630 742-8022
Arthur Rucker, *Principal*
EMP: 3 EST: 2016
SALES (est): 182.8K **Privately Held**
SIC: 3571 Computers, digital, analog or hybrid

(G-15995)
CHRISTOPHER WAGNER
563 Cardinal Ave (60543-7741)
PHONE 630 205-9200
Christopher Wagner, *Principal*
EMP: 5
SALES (est): 746.5K **Privately Held**
SIC: 2752 Commercial printing, lithographic

(G-15996)
CMA INC (PA)
19 Stonehill Rd (60543-9449)
P.O. Box 9244, Naperville (60567-0244)
PHONE 630 551-3100
William Schultz, *CEO*
Bill Waterbury, *Opers Staff*
Marvin Peplo, *CFO*
EMP: 70
SALES (est): 10MM **Privately Held**
SIC: 2499 Insulating material, cork

(G-15997)
COMPU DOC INC
105 Theodore Dr Ste A (60543-6031)
PHONE 630 554-5800
James Mellema, *CEO*
Carol Mellema, *Admin Sec*
EMP: 5
SQ FT: 1,800
SALES (est): 669.3K **Privately Held**
SIC: 3679 Electronic components

(G-15998)
CONSOLIDATED DISPLAYS CO INC
1210 Us Highway 34 (60543-8939)
P.O. Box 4108, Naperville (60567-4108)
PHONE 630 851-8666
Sebastian Puccio, *President*
Anthony Puccio, *Vice Pres*
David L Miller, *CFO*
Rachael Puccio, *CFO*
EMP: 9
SQ FT: 13,000
SALES (est): 1MM **Privately Held**
SIC: 3993 3999 2542 Displays & cutouts, window & lobby; theatrical scenery; partitions & fixtures, except wood

(G-15999)
CULTURE MEDIA SUPPLIES INC
118 Kirkland Cir Ste D (60543-8069)
PHONE 630 499-5000
Irene Kenney, *President*
John Gura, *Executive*
EMP: 2
SALES (est): 257.7K **Privately Held**
SIC: 2836 5049 Culture media; laboratory equipment, except medical or dental

(G-16000)
CUSTOM CULINARY INC
Also Called: Custom Food Products
2100 Wiesbrook Rd (60543-8309)
PHONE 630 299-0500
Mike Fanselow, *Vice Pres*
George Levy, *Buyer*
Sargon Boudakh, *Branch Mgr*

Mike Rapaport, *Manager*
Paula Brown, *Director*
EMP: 70
SALES (corp-wide): 1B **Privately Held**
WEB: www.customculinary.com
SIC: 5141 2099 2087 Food brokers; food preparations; flavoring extracts & syrups
HQ: Custom Culinary, Inc.
    2505 S Finley Rd Ste 100
    Lombard IL 60148
    630 928-4898

(G-16001)
DEMONT GUITARS LLC (PA)
61a Stonehill Rd (60543-9449)
PHONE 347 433-6668
Nathaniel Demont, *Owner*
◆ EMP: 2
SALES (est): 470.4K **Privately Held**
SIC: 3931 5099 5736 Guitars & parts, electric & nonelectric; musical instruments; musical instruments parts & accessories; string instruments

(G-16002)
DISA HOLDING CORP (DH)
80 Kendall Point Dr (60543-8802)
PHONE 630 820-3000
Mike Lewis, *President*
Bob Grezlik, *Buyer*
Sandy Nelson, *Controller*
Robert Leffler, *Chief Mktg Ofcr*
Patrick Ganahl, *Department Mgr*
▲ EMP: 5
SALES (est): 30.5MM **Privately Held**
SIC: 3569 3559 5084 Blast cleaning equipment, dustless; foundry machinery & equipment; industrial machinery & equipment
HQ: Disa Holding Ag
    Kasernenstrasse 1
    BachenbUlach ZH 8184
    448 154-000

(G-16003)
EMPOWERED PRESS LLC
139 Pineridge Dr S (60543-7579)
PHONE 630 400-3127
Michael L Redd,
Kerri Redd,
EMP: 5
SALES: 75K **Privately Held**
SIC: 2731 Books: publishing only

(G-16004)
EUGENE EWBANK
Also Called: Flexo Prepress Solutions
118 Kirkland Cir Ste B (60543-8069)
PHONE 630 705-0400
Gene Ewbank, *Owner*
EMP: 4
SALES (est): 320K **Privately Held**
SIC: 2752 2796 2759 Commercial printing, lithographic; platemaking services; commercial printing

(G-16005)
FOX VALLEY WINERY INC
5600 Us Highway 34 (60543-9169)
PHONE 630 554-0404
Richard A Faltz, *President*
Tina Faltz, *Sales Staff*
Christine C Fatz, *Admin Sec*
EMP: 7
SALES (est): 724K **Privately Held**
SIC: 2084 Wines

(G-16006)
GUARDIAN PERSONAL DEFENSE TNG
403 Lennox Ct (60543-8353)
PHONE 630 272-9811
EMP: 3
SALES (est): 199.3K **Privately Held**
SIC: 3812 Defense systems & equipment

(G-16007)
HONEYWELL INTERNATIONAL INC
637 Salem Cir (60543-8667)
PHONE 630 554-5342
EMP: 4
SALES (corp-wide): 40.5B **Publicly Held**
SIC: 3724 Mfg Aircraft Engines/Parts

Oswego - Kendall County (G-16008)

(G-16008)
PA: Honeywell International Inc.
115 Tabor Rd
Morris Plains NJ 28202
973 455-2000

(G-16008)
INTEX SYSTEMS CORP
22 Crestview Dr (60543-9512)
PHONE..................................630 636-6594
Allen W Hametta, *Principal*
EMP: 3
SALES (est): 224.7K **Privately Held**
SIC: 3812 Detection apparatus: electronic/magnetic field, light/heat

(G-16009)
JAMES A FREUND LLC
Also Called: Fish Window Cleaning
26 Longford Ct (60543-8881)
PHONE..................................630 664-7692
James A Freund, *Mng Member*
EMP: 4
SALES: 100K **Privately Held**
WEB: www.fishwindowcleaning.com
SIC: 7349 3589 Window cleaning; high pressure cleaning equipment

(G-16010)
LARES TECHNOLOGIES LLC
748 Charismatic Dr (60543-7003)
PHONE..................................630 408-4368
Kevin L Hartman, *Manager*
Kevin Hartman,
EMP: 1
SALES: 600K **Privately Held**
SIC: 3669 Communications equipment

(G-16011)
LMD INDUSTRIES INC
316 Hemlock Ct (60543-3600)
PHONE..................................630 383-9546
EMP: 3
SALES (est): 155.9K **Privately Held**
SIC: 3999 Manufacturing industries

(G-16012)
MAB EQUIPMENT COMPANY
51 Stonehill Rd (60543-9449)
PHONE..................................630 551-4017
Mark Blanchflower, *President*
Dan Jaynes, *Sales Engr*
EMP: 4
SALES (est): 199.3K **Privately Held**
SIC: 1081 5084 Metal mining exploration & development services; industrial machinery & equipment

(G-16013)
MEDIGROUP INC
14a Stonehill Rd (60543-9400)
P.O. Box 950 (60543-0950)
PHONE..................................630 554-5533
Fax: 630 554-5535
EMP: 2
SALES (est): 262.4K **Privately Held**
SIC: 3841 Mfg Surgical/Medical Instruments

(G-16014)
MIDWEST PLASTICS SERVICES INC
6048 Dover Ct (60543-8560)
PHONE..................................630 551-4921
Steve Allread, *President*
EMP: 2 EST: 1985
SALES: 280K **Privately Held**
SIC: 1531 3089 Operative builders; injection molding of plastics

(G-16015)
MOLOR PRODUCTS COMPANY
73 Chippewa Dr (60543-8926)
P.O. Box 897 (60543-0897)
PHONE..................................630 375-5999
▲ EMP: 11
SQ FT: 50,000
SALES (est): 1.5MM **Privately Held**
SIC: 3999 3089 3714 Mfg Misc Products Mfg Plastic Products Mfg Motor Vehicle Parts

(G-16016)
NEWPORT MEDIA INC
Also Called: Hubba
439 Raintree Dr (60543-7931)
PHONE..................................630 551-1651
Frank Bernard, *President*
David Brandolino, *Admin Sec*
EMP: 3 EST: 2017
SALES (est): 71.1K
SALES (corp-wide): 125K **Privately Held**
SIC: 7372 Prepackaged software
PA: Newport International, Inc.
439 Raintree Dr
Oswego IL 60543
630 551-1651

(G-16017)
OBERWEIS DAIRY INC
2274 Us Highway 30 (60543-8972)
PHONE..................................630 906-6455
Darlene George, *Branch Mgr*
EMP: 21
SALES (corp-wide): 249.7MM **Privately Held**
WEB: www.oberweisdairy.com
SIC: 2026 5963 5451 Milk processing (pasteurizing, homogenizing, bottling); milk delivery; milk; ice cream (packaged)
PA: Oberweis Dairy, Inc.
951 Ice Cream Dr
North Aurora IL 60542
630 801-6100

(G-16018)
OSWEGO DIAMOND
3370 White Oak Dr (60543-7158)
PHONE..................................630 636-9617
EMP: 3
SALES (est): 135.3K **Privately Held**
SIC: 3291 Abrasive products

(G-16019)
OSWEGO VINYL
288 Devoe Dr (60543-4066)
PHONE..................................331 725-4801
Steven Weiss, *Principal*
EMP: 3 EST: 2016
SALES (est): 155.5K **Privately Held**
WEB: www.premiermailingink.com
SIC: 2752 Commercial printing, offset

(G-16020)
POWER PLANT REPAIR SVCS LLC
80 Kendall Point Dr (60543-8802)
PHONE..................................708 345-8600
Manny Gandhi, *CEO*
Shialja Gandhi, *President*
James Prete, *Project Engr*
EMP: 83
SALES (est): 9.3MM **Privately Held**
SIC: 3511 Gas turbines, mechanical drive; steam turbines

(G-16021)
PROFORMA AWARDS PRINT & PROMOT
403 Burr Oak Dr (60543-7503)
PHONE..................................630 897-9848
Gregory Siebert, *Principal*
EMP: 2
SALES (est): 372.9K **Privately Held**
SIC: 2752 Commercial printing, lithographic

(G-16022)
Q C H INCORPORATED
230 Kendall Point Dr (60543-8150)
PHONE..................................630 820-5550
Blair Pasternak, *President*
Nancy Wilson, *Purch Mgr*
Timothy Andrus, *Treasurer*
Mark Fueger, *Sales Mgr*
Trent Pankratz, *Manager*
EMP: 80
SQ FT: 53,000
SALES (est): 23.6MM **Privately Held**
WEB: www.hqcinc.com
SIC: 3089 Injection molding of plastics

(G-16023)
QUICK SIGNS INC
424 Treasure Dr (60543-7936)
PHONE..................................630 554-7370
Kevin Hanna, *President*
Michael Nielsen, *Vice Pres*
Mike Nielsen, *Opers Staff*
Deborah Hanna, *Shareholder*
EMP: 6
SQ FT: 5,000
SALES (est): 799.3K **Privately Held**
SIC: 3993 Signs, not made in custom sign painting shops

(G-16024)
RADIAC ABRASIVES INC
101 Kendall Point Dr (60543-8801)
PHONE..................................630 898-0315
Erin Wiencek, *Marketing Staff*
Jared Berkowitz, *Director*
EMP: 41
SALES (corp-wide): 797.8MM **Privately Held**
SIC: 3291 3541 Wheels, grinding: artificial; machine tools, metal cutting type
HQ: Radiac Abrasives, Inc.
1015 S College St
Salem IL 62881
618 548-4200

(G-16025)
SEGINUS INC
114 Kirkland Cir Ste B (60543-8067)
PHONE..................................630 800-2795
Erik Hatch, *President*
▼ EMP: 2
SQ FT: 3,500
SALES (est): 357.3K **Privately Held**
WEB: www.seginusinc.com
SIC: 3728 Aircraft parts & equipment

(G-16026)
TEMPLE DISPLAY LTD
114 Kirkland Cir Ste C (60543-8067)
P.O. Box 965 (60543-0965)
PHONE..................................630 851-3331
Tyler Temple, *President*
Maggie Washburn, *Sales Staff*
Dawn Franz, *Admin Asst*
▲ EMP: 9
SALES (est): 2.3MM **Privately Held**
SIC: 5199 3699 Christmas novelties; household electrical equipment

(G-16027)
TKS CONTROL SYSTEMS INC
88 Templeton Dr (60543-7000)
PHONE..................................630 554-3020
Timothy E Neal, *President*
Kimberly Neal, *Corp Secy*
EMP: 11
SQ FT: 12,000
SALES (est): 3.2MM **Privately Held**
SIC: 3567 Industrial furnaces & ovens

(G-16028)
TOOLS AVIATION LLC
Also Called: Personal Battery Caddy
101a Theodore Dr (60543-6031)
PHONE..................................630 377-7260
Shawnta Mateja,
Kathy Foreman,
Richard Foreman,
EMP: 3
SALES: 410K **Privately Held**
SIC: 3069 Battery boxes, jars or parts, hard rubber

(G-16029)
TYROLIT LIMITED
101 Kendall Point Dr (60543-8801)
PHONE..................................618 548-8314
EMP: 3 EST: 2015
SALES (est): 219.2K **Privately Held**
SIC: 3291 Abrasive products

(G-16030)
VEAL TECH INC
15 Stonehill Rd (60543-9449)
PHONE..................................630 554-0410
Richard Dennis, *President*
Connie Dennis, *Corp Secy*
Bernard Moe, *Vice Pres*
EMP: 7
SQ FT: 50,000
SALES (est): 807.2K **Privately Held**
SIC: 2048 Prepared feeds

(G-16031)
WALK 4 LIFE INC
1981c Wiesbrook Rd (60543-8311)
PHONE..................................815 439-2340
Ruthmarie Carver, *President*
Peggy Boris, *Finance Mgr*
Waldo Abreu, *Marketing Staff*
EMP: 19
SQ FT: 11,000
SALES: 3MM **Privately Held**
SIC: 3824 Pedometers

(G-16032)
WIN SOON CHICAGO INC
190 Kendall Point Dr (60543-8803)
PHONE..................................630 585-7090
Brian Ju, *General Mgr*
Young Kim, *CFO*
EMP: 193 EST: 2014
SALES (est): 62.6MM **Privately Held**
SIC: 2086 Carbonated beverages, nonalcoholic: bottled & canned

(G-16033)
WISDOM MEDICAL TECHNOLOGY LLC
19 Stonehill Rd (60543-9449)
P.O. Box 896 (60543-0896)
PHONE..................................630 803-6383
Jack Furcht, *Mng Member*
Anthony Jakubowski,
EMP: 7
SQ FT: 10,000
SALES: 1.8MM **Privately Held**
SIC: 3841 Surgical & medical instruments

(G-16034)
ZING ENTERPRISES LLC
83 Templeton Dr Ste G (60543-7026)
P.O. Box 789 (60543-0789)
PHONE..................................608 201-9490
Thomas R Prinzing,
EMP: 9
SALES: 1.7MM **Privately Held**
SIC: 3999 Identification plates

Ottawa
Lasalle County

(G-16035)
4L TECHNOLOGIES INC (HQ)
Also Called: Clover Global
122 W Madison St (61350-5006)
PHONE..................................815 431-8100
Dan Ruhl, *President*
James Cerkleski, *Admin Sec*
EMP: 1280
SALES (est): 1.6B
SALES (corp-wide): 1.2B **Privately Held**
SIC: 3555 Printing trades machinery

(G-16036)
A WILEY & ASSOCIATES
Also Called: Awa
707 E Dayton Rd (61350-9545)
P.O. Box 1040 (61350-6040)
PHONE..................................815 343-7401
Nicholas Crisler, *Owner*
EMP: 6
SALES: 950K **Privately Held**
SIC: 3999 Manufacturing industries

(G-16037)
AMERICAN FUEL ECONOMY INC
1772 N 2753rd Rd (61350-9701)
PHONE..................................815 433-3226
Diania K Heiss, *President*
EMP: 4 EST: 1975
SQ FT: 12,000
SALES (est): 489.2K **Privately Held**
SIC: 3585 3634 3444 3433 Heating equipment, complete; electric housewares & fans; sheet metalwork; heating equipment, except electric

(G-16038)
AMERICAN MACHINING INC
350 W Marquette St (61350-1916)
PHONE..................................815 498-1593
Rich Lindhout, *President*
Chris L Lindhout, *Manager*
EMP: 7

GEOGRAPHIC SECTION
Ottawa - Lasalle County (G-16064)

SALES (est): 1MM **Privately Held**
SIC: 3599 Machine shop, jobbing & repair

(G-16039)
ANBEK INC (PA)
Also Called: Designs & Signs By Anderson
104 W Madison St (61350-5006)
PHONE.............................815 434-7340
Toll Free:.........................888   -
Gene Anderson, *President*
Doug Beckman, *Vice Pres*
Sherlyn Beckman, *Treasurer*
Diane Anderson, *Admin Sec*
EMP: 12
SQ FT: 7,200
SALES (est): 2MM **Privately Held**
SIC: 3993 5199 Electric signs; advertising specialties

(G-16040)
B&BIMC LLC
707 E Dayton Rd (61350-9545)
P.O. Box 1040 (61350-6040)
PHONE..............................815 433-5100
Beth Nettles, *Controller*
EMP: 55 EST: 2012
SALES (est): 3.6MM **Privately Held**
SIC: 3629 Electronic generation equipment
HQ: B+B Smartworx Inc.
707 E Dayton Rd
Ottawa IL 61350
815 433-5100

(G-16041)
B+B SMARTWORX INC (HQ)
Also Called: Advantech Bb Smartworx
707 E Dayton Rd (61350-9545)
P.O. Box 1040 (61350-6040)
PHONE..............................815 433-5100
Jerry O'Gorman, *President*
Mike Fahrion, *Vice Pres*
Beth Nettles, *Controller*
Rich Czekanski, *Human Resources*
Gail Farlee, *VP Mktg*
▲ EMP: 99
SQ FT: 36,000
SALES (est): 47MM **Privately Held**
SIC: 3674 3825 Semiconductors & related devices; instruments to measure electricity

(G-16042)
BR MACHINE INC
3312 E 2153rd Rd (61350-9431)
P.O. Box 9, Wedron (60557-0009)
PHONE..............................815 434-0427
Bob Rogowski, *President*
Nancy Rogowski, *Vice Pres*
EMP: 10 EST: 1974
SQ FT: 10,000
SALES (est): 1.7MM **Privately Held**
SIC: 3599 3441 3631 3443 Machine shop, jobbing & repair; fabricated structural metal; household cooking equipment; fabricated plate work (boiler shop)

(G-16043)
BURMAC MANUFACTURING INC
4000 Burmac Rd (61350-9542)
P.O. Box 828 (61350-0828)
PHONE..............................815 434-1660
William E Burns Jr, *President*
John A Burns, *Treasurer*
Jan Cappellini, *Admin Sec*
EMP: 4
SQ FT: 28,000
SALES (est): 264.6K **Privately Held**
SIC: 3599 Machine shop, jobbing & repair
PA: Burns Machine Company
4000 Burmac Rd
Ottawa IL 61350

(G-16044)
BURNS MACHINE COMPANY
4000 Burmac Rd (61350-9542)
P.O. Box 828 (61350-0828)
PHONE..............................815 434-3131
William E Burns Jr, *President*
John A Burns, *Treasurer*
Jan Cappellini, *Admin Sec*
EMP: 30 EST: 1917
SQ FT: 33,000
SALES: 3MM **Privately Held**
WEB: www.burnsmachine.com
SIC: 3599 7692 3549 3544 Machine shop, jobbing & repair; welding repair; metalworking machinery; special dies, tools, jigs & fixtures
PA: Burns Machine Company
4000 Burmac Rd
Ottawa IL 61350

(G-16045)
BURNS MACHINE COMPANY (PA)
4000 Burmac Rd (61350-9542)
PHONE..............................815 434-1660
William E Burns Jr, *President*
Jerry Dauck, *Engineer*
Jan Cappellini, *Human Res Mgr*
John Burns, *Shareholder*
Jan Cappellina, *Admin Sec*
▲ EMP: 29
SQ FT: 33,000
SALES (est): 3.8MM **Privately Held**
SIC: 3599 3443 Machine shop, jobbing & repair; fabricated plate work (boiler shop)

(G-16046)
CLEAR PRINT INC
768 Adams St (61350-3806)
PHONE..............................815 795-6225
Jesse Fleming, *President*
EMP: 7 EST: 1996
SALES (est): 700K **Privately Held**
SIC: 2752 Commercial printing, lithographic

(G-16047)
CLIFFORD W ESTES CO INC
1289 W Marquette St (61350-1755)
PHONE..............................815 433-0944
Mick Lawsha, *Manager*
EMP: 16
SALES (corp-wide): 13.3MM **Privately Held**
SIC: 7389 1446 Personal service agents, brokers & bureaus; industrial sand
PA: Clifford W. Estes Co., Inc.
182 Fairfield Rd Ste 8
Fairfield NJ 07004
800 962-5128

(G-16048)
CLOVER IMAGING GROUP LLC
Also Called: Distribution Center
700 E Dayton Rd (61350-9062)
PHONE..............................815 431-8100
EMP: 433 **Privately Held**
SIC: 3861 Printing equipment, photographic

(G-16049)
COVIA HOLDINGS CORPORATION
776 Centennial Dr (61350-1002)
P.O. Box 9125 Dept 151, Stamford CT (06925)
PHONE..............................203 966-8880
Chad Storkel, *Maint Spvr*
Scott Schaffner, *Sr Project Mgr*
EMP: 32
SALES (corp-wide): 125.5MM **Publicly Held**
SIC: 1446 Industrial sand
HQ: Covia Holdings Corporation
3 Summit Park Dr Ste 700
Independence OH 44131
440 214-3284

(G-16050)
FAIRMONT CENTRAL LLC (PA)
776 Centennial Dr (61350-1002)
PHONE..............................815 433-2449
Michelle Pezanoski,
EMP: 31
SALES (est): 6.2MM **Privately Held**
SIC: 3295 Minerals, ground or treated

(G-16051)
FAIRMOUNT SANTROL INC
Also Called: Innovation Center
776 Centennial Dr (61350-1002)
PHONE..............................815 433-2449
Eric Peterson, *Project Mgr*
Kent Smith, *Project Mgr*
Janet Raber, *Branch Mgr*
EMP: 12
SALES (corp-wide): 125.5MM **Publicly Held**
WEB: www.fairmountsantrol.com
SIC: 1446 Industrial sand
HQ: Fairmount Santrol Inc.
3 Summit Park Dr Ste 700
Independence OH 44131
440 214-3200

(G-16052)
FAIRMOUNT SANTROL INC
776 Centennial Dr (61350-1002)
PHONE..............................815 587-4410
Daniel Gerber, *Exec VP*
Lynn Hiser, *Vice Pres*
Marco Payan, *Business Anlyst*
EMP: 18
SALES (corp-wide): 125.5MM **Publicly Held**
SIC: 1442 Construction sand & gravel
HQ: Fairmount Santrol Inc.
3 Summit Park Dr Ste 700
Independence OH 44131
440 214-3200

(G-16053)
FREQUENCY DEVICES INC
1784 Chessie Ln Unit 1 (61350-9626)
P.O. Box 218 (61350-0218)
PHONE..............................815 434-7800
William H Franklin III, *President*
Bill Franklin, *Vice Pres*
William Franklin Jr, *Vice Pres*
Dave Ross, *Purchasing*
Helena Ross, *Human Res Dir*
▼ EMP: 12 EST: 1968
SQ FT: 10,000
SALES (est): 2MM **Privately Held**
WEB: www.freqdev.com
SIC: 3825 3823 3564 Analog-digital converters, electronic instrumentation type; industrial instrmnts msrmnt display/control process variable; blowers & fans

(G-16054)
HEALTHY BODY LLC
2740 Columbus St Ste 300 (61350-3771)
P.O. Box 2093 (61350-6693)
PHONE..............................208 409-6602
Donald Wensek,
EMP: 3
SALES (est): 268.4K **Privately Held**
SIC: 2023 7389 Dietary supplements, dairy & non-dairy based; brokers, contract services

(G-16055)
HEISS WELDING INC
Also Called: HWI
260 W Marquette St (61350-1914)
PHONE..............................815 434-1838
Robert Heiss, *President*
EMP: 10 EST: 1980
SQ FT: 5,000
SALES (est): 1.7MM **Privately Held**
WEB: www.heisswelding.com
SIC: 7692 Welding repair

(G-16056)
ILLINOIS OFFICE SUP ELECT PRTG
1119 La Salle St (61350-2020)
P.O. Box 337 (61350-0337)
PHONE..............................815 434-0186
Robert J Keeney, *President*
Peggy Keeney, *Vice Pres*
EMP: 20
SALES (est): 3MM **Privately Held**
SIC: 2752 2791 2789 2759 Commercial printing, offset; typesetting; bookbinding & related work; commercial printing

(G-16057)
JOHNSON PATTERN & MCH WORKS
350 W Marquette St (61350-1916)
PHONE..............................815 433-2775
Esther Johnson, *President*
Stan Dale, *Treasurer*
Diane Dale, *Admin Sec*
EMP: 20
SQ FT: 32,000
SALES (est): 3.5MM **Privately Held**
WEB: www.johnsonmachine.com
SIC: 3599 3543 3545 Custom machinery; foundry cores; machine tool accessories

(G-16058)
LA SALLE CO ESDA
711 E Etna Rd (61350-1040)
PHONE..............................815 433-5622
EMP: 3
SALES (est): 208K **Privately Held**
WEB: www.lasallecounty.org
SIC: 3568 Joints & couplings

(G-16059)
LMK TECHNOLOGIES LLC
1779 Chessie Ln (61350-9687)
PHONE..............................815 433-1275
Michael J Reardon, *CEO*
Rick Gage, *Vice Pres*
James A Gordon, *Vice Pres*
Todd M Hamilton, *Vice Pres*
Cody Delmendo, *Corp Comm Staff*
EMP: 73
SQ FT: 20,000
SALES (est): 19.9MM **Privately Held**
SIC: 3552 Spindles, textile

(G-16060)
MARQUTTE STL SUP FBRCATION INC
800 W Marquette St (61350-1814)
PHONE..............................815 433-0178
James Sheridan Jr, *President*
William T Sheridan, *Vice Pres*
Charles Sheridan, *Admin Sec*
EMP: 12
SQ FT: 14,000
SALES (est): 2.6MM **Privately Held**
SIC: 3312 1791 3441 Structural shapes & pilings, steel; structural steel erection; fabricated structural metal

(G-16061)
MINIGRIP INC
Also Called: ITW Minigrip/Zip-Pak
1510 Warehouse Dr (61350-9003)
PHONE..............................845 680-2710
Jack Campbell, *President*
▲ EMP: 95 EST: 1951
SQ FT: 100,000
SALES (est): 14.1MM
SALES (corp-wide): 14.1B **Publicly Held**
WEB: www.zippak.com
SIC: 3081 3965 Unsupported plastics film & sheet; zipper
PA: Illinois Tool Works Inc.
155 Harlem Ave
Glenview IL 60025
847 724-7500

(G-16062)
MUCCI KIRKPATRICK SHEET METAL
1908 Ottawa Ave (61350-3443)
P.O. Box 2112 (61350-6712)
PHONE..............................815 433-3350
Debbie Mucci, *President*
Gary Kirkpatrick, *Vice Pres*
EMP: 9
SQ FT: 1,200
SALES (est): 644.2K **Privately Held**
SIC: 5075 7623 3444 Warm air heating & air conditioning; refrigeration service & repair; sheet metalwork

(G-16063)
MUFFYS INC
423 W Madison St (61350-2832)
PHONE..............................815 433-6839
Gerena Muffler, *Owner*
EMP: 4
SALES (est): 396.8K **Privately Held**
SIC: 2599 Bar, restaurant & cafeteria furniture

(G-16064)
NORTH RIDGE PROPERTIES LLC
Also Called: Frequency Devices
927 Fosse Rd (61350)
P.O. Box 218 (61350-0218)
PHONE..............................815 434-7800
William Franklin Jr,
EMP: 1
SQ FT: 800
SALES: 877K **Privately Held**
SIC: 3678 Electronic connectors

Ottawa - Lasalle County (G-16065)

(G-16065)
NORTHERN ILLINOIS GAS COMPANY
Also Called: Nicor Gas
1629 Champlain St (61350-1652)
PHONE..................................815 433-3850
Patricia McKibbon, *Branch Mgr*
EMP: 65
SALES (corp-wide): 21.4B **Publicly Held**
SIC: 4924 1382 4923 Natural gas distribution; oil & gas exploration services; gas transmission & distribution
HQ: Northern Illinois Gas Company
1844 W Ferry Rd
Naperville IL 60563
630 983-8676

(G-16066)
OAKWOOD MEMORIAL PARK INC
Also Called: Brooke Burial Vault Co
2405 Champlain St (61350-1260)
PHONE..................................815 433-0313
Richard Brooke, *President*
James Brooke, *Corp Secy*
EMP: 4 EST: 1938
SQ FT: 3,600
SALES (est): 289.4K **Privately Held**
WEB: www.oakwoodmemorialpark.net
SIC: 6553 3272 Cemeteries, real estate operation; burial vaults, concrete or precast terrazzo

(G-16067)
ODL INC (PA)
1304 Starfire Dr (61350-1624)
PHONE..................................815 434-0655
Luke Caruso III, *President*
Jim Caruso, *President*
Joanie Bretag, *Vice Pres*
John M Caruso, *Vice Pres*
Sandy Erwin, *Vice Pres*
▲ EMP: 60
SQ FT: 15,000
SALES (est): 8.5MM **Privately Held**
WEB: www.ottawadentallab.com
SIC: 8072 3843 Artificial teeth production; crown & bridge production; denture production; orthodontic appliance production; dental equipment & supplies

(G-16068)
OTTAWA PUBLISHING CO INC (HQ)
Also Called: Daily Times, The
110 W Jefferson St (61350-5018)
PHONE..................................815 433-2000
Len R Small, *President*
John A Newby, *Editor*
Joe La Caeyse, *Officer*
Betty Walsh, *Admin Sec*
EMP: 106 EST: 1844
SQ FT: 20,000
SALES (est): 7.9MM
SALES (corp-wide): 131.4MM **Privately Held**
WEB: www.mywebtimes.com
SIC: 2711 2752 Commercial printing & newspaper publishing combined; commercial printing, lithographic
PA: Small Newspaper Group
8 Dearborn Sq
Kankakee IL 60901
815 937-3300

(G-16069)
OTTAWA PUBLISHING CO INC
Also Called: Adventure Advertising
300 W Joliet St (61350-1925)
PHONE..................................815 434-3330
Harold Clemins, *Manager*
EMP: 13
SALES (corp-wide): 131.4MM **Privately Held**
SIC: 2711 2759 Commercial printing & newspaper publishing combined; commercial printing
HQ: Ottawa Publishing Co Inc
110 W Jefferson St
Ottawa IL 61350
815 433-2000

(G-16070)
PATIO PLUS
1624 W Main St (61350-2525)
PHONE..................................815 433-2399
Andy Ruger, *Owner*
EMP: 7
SQ FT: 11,000
SALES (est): 240K **Privately Held**
SIC: 2519 2531 2511 Fiberglass & plastic furniture; public building & related furniture; wood household furniture

(G-16071)
PERSONALIZED THREADS
2655 E 1559th Rd (61350-9290)
PHONE..................................815 431-1815
Peggy Enquist, *President*
EMP: 4
SALES (est): 188.9K **Privately Held**
SIC: 2395 Emblems, embroidered

(G-16072)
PILKINGTON NORTH AMERICA INC
300 Center 20th St (61350)
PHONE..................................815 433-0932
William Ebener, *Production*
Gave Perry, *Branch Mgr*
EMP: 238
SIC: 3211 3231 Flat glass; products of purchased glass
HQ: Pilkington North America, Inc.
811 Madison Ave Fl 3
Toledo OH 43604
419 247-3731

(G-16073)
POLANCICS MEATS & TENDERLOINS
412 W Norris Dr (61350-1435)
PHONE..................................815 433-0324
Jim Polancic, *President*
EMP: 7
SQ FT: 4,500
SALES (est): 806.6K **Privately Held**
WEB: www.polancicsmeats.com
SIC: 2013 5421 Prepared pork products from purchased pork; meat markets, including freezer provisioners

(G-16074)
R AND B DISTRIBUTORS INC
Also Called: Vitner Chips
1217 Saint Clair St (61350-2338)
PHONE..................................815 433-6843
Ronald E Chismarick, *President*
EMP: 2
SQ FT: 22,000
SALES: 475K **Privately Held**
SIC: 2096 Potato chips & similar snacks

(G-16075)
SABIC INNOVATIVE PLAS US LLC
2148 N 2753rd Rd (61350-9766)
P.O. Box 658 (61350-0658)
PHONE..................................815 434-7000
Russ Prechtl, *Safety Mgr*
Vern Lowry, *Engineer*
Brian Serby, *Human Resources*
Hugh Morton, *Branch Mgr*
Darren Mays, *Manager*
EMP: 450 **Privately Held**
SIC: 2821 Plastics materials & resins
HQ: Sabic Innovative Plastics Us Llc
2500 Citywest Blvd # 100
Houston TX 77042

(G-16076)
SIGAN AMERICA LLC
1111 W Mckinley Rd (61350-4732)
PHONE..................................815 431-9830
Selene Zimmer, *Maint Spvr*
Scott Wold, *Purchasing*
John Cinotto, *Controller*
Dean Gangbar, *Mng Member*
Greg Rubin,
▲ EMP: 62
SQ FT: 190,000
SALES (est): 10.5MM
SALES (corp-wide): 21.3MM **Privately Held**
SIC: 2844 Toilet preparations
HQ: Sigan America Holdings, Llc
1111 W Mckinley Rd
Ottawa IL 61350
815 431-9830

(G-16077)
SIGAN AMERICA HOLDINGS LLC (HQ)
1111 W Mckinley Rd (61350-4732)
PHONE..................................815 431-9830
Dean Gangbar, *Mng Member*
Greg Rubin,
Manjit Singh,
EMP: 2
SALES (est): 10.5MM
SALES (corp-wide): 21.3MM **Privately Held**
SIC: 2844 Toilet preparations
PA: Sigan Industries Inc
296 Orenda Rd
Brampton ON L6T 4
905 456-8888

(G-16078)
SIGMA GRAPHICS INC
4001 Baker Rd (61350-9536)
P.O. Box 260, Decatur (62525-0260)
PHONE..................................815 433-1000
Thomas W Kowa, *President*
Joe McCormick, *Mfg Staff*
EMP: 18
SQ FT: 24,000
SALES (est): 2.7MM **Privately Held**
SIC: 2752 Commercial printing, offset

(G-16079)
SIKA CORPORATION
1515 Titanium Dr (61350-8905)
PHONE..................................815 431-1080
Todd Stindler, *Branch Mgr*
EMP: 4
SALES (corp-wide): 8.1B **Privately Held**
SIC: 2891 2899 Epoxy adhesives; sealants; chemical preparations; concrete curing & hardening compounds
HQ: Sika Corporation
201 Polito Ave
Lyndhurst NJ 07071
201 933-8800

(G-16080)
TECHNISAND INC
776 Centennial Dr (61350-1002)
P.O. Box 736 (61350-0736)
PHONE..................................815 433-2449
Jenniffer Deckard, *President*
EMP: 4 EST: 2012
SALES (est): 1MM **Privately Held**
SIC: 2899 Chemical preparations

(G-16081)
THE TIMES
110 W Jefferson St (61350-5010)
PHONE..................................815 433-2000
Julie Barichello, *Editor*
Andy Tavegia, *Editor*
Charles Stanley, *Chief*
Anne Hinterlong, *Consultant*
Betty Walsh, *Admin Sec*
EMP: 9
SALES (est): 603.7K **Privately Held**
WEB: www.mywebtimes.com
SIC: 2711 Commercial printing & newspaper publishing combined

(G-16082)
U S SILICA COMPANY
701 Boyce Memorial Dr (61350-2561)
PHONE..................................800 635-7263
EMP: 8
SALES (corp-wide): 1.4B **Publicly Held**
SIC: 1446 Silica sand mining
HQ: U. S. Silica Company
24275 Katy Fwy Ste 100
Katy TX 77494
301 682-0600

(G-16083)
UNIMIN LIME CORPORATION (DH)
776 Centennial Dr (61350-1002)
PHONE..................................203 966-8880
Joseph Shapiro, *President*
EMP: 10
SALES (est): 13.8MM
SALES (corp-wide): 125.5MM **Publicly Held**
SIC: 1446 Industrial sand
HQ: Covia Holdings Corporation
3 Summit Park Dr Ste 700
Independence OH 44131
440 214-3284

(G-16084)
US SILICA HOLDINGS INC
Also Called: US Silica Co
701 Boyce Memorial Dr (61350-2561)
PHONE..................................815 667-7085
EMP: 16
SALES (corp-wide): 1.4B **Publicly Held**
SIC: 2819 Industrial inorganic chemicals
PA: U.S. Silica Holdings, Inc.
24275 Katy Fwy Ste 600
Katy TX 77494
281 258-2170

(G-16085)
WESTERN SAND & GRAVEL CO
4220 Mbl Dr (61350-9352)
PHONE..................................815 433-1600
Mike Sitterly, *Owner*
EMP: 10
SALES (est): 719.7K **Privately Held**
SIC: 5032 3999 Gravel; manufacturing industries

(G-16086)
WOODHILL CABINETRY DESIGN INC
3381 N State Route 23 (61350-9007)
PHONE..................................815 431-0545
Craig H Sweeney, *President*
Mary J Sweeney, *Admin Sec*
EMP: 7
SALES (est): 798.1K **Privately Held**
SIC: 2434 2541 2521 2517 Wood kitchen cabinets; wood partitions & fixtures; wood office furniture; wood television & radio cabinets

Ozark
Johnson County

(G-16087)
CORNERSTONE POLISHING COMPANY
85 Zach Ln (62972-1116)
PHONE..................................618 777-2754
Mark Kelton, *Owner*
EMP: 3
SALES (est): 178.2K **Privately Held**
SIC: 3471 Polishing, metals or formed products

Palatine
Cook County

(G-16088)
3 GOLDENSTAR INC
545 E Dundee Rd (60074-2815)
PHONE..................................847 963-0451
Abdul Zakir, *President*
EMP: 16
SALES: 687K **Privately Held**
SIC: 3999 Manufacturing industries

(G-16089)
ACURA PHARMACEUTICALS INC (PA)
616 N North Ct Ste 120 (60067-8121)
PHONE..................................847 705-7709
Robert B Jones, *President*
Albert W Brzeczko, *Vice Pres*
James F Emigh, *Vice Pres*
Peter A Clemens, *CFO*
Robert A Seiser, *Treasurer*
EMP: 14 EST: 1935
SQ FT: 1,600
SALES: 2.6MM **Publicly Held**
WEB: www.acurapharm.com
SIC: 2834 Tablets, pharmaceutical

GEOGRAPHIC SECTION

Palatine - Cook County (G-16118)

(G-16090)
ADVANCED PROTOTYPE MOLDING
263 N Woodwork Ln (60067-4930)
PHONE.................847 202-4200
Bruce Megleo, *President*
Mike Megleo, *Principal*
Laura Megleo, *Admin Sec*
▲ **EMP**: 6
SQ FT: 14,000
SALES: 600K **Privately Held**
SIC: 3542 3089 2821 2822 Machine tools, metal forming type; molding primary plastic; molding compounds, plastics; silicone rubbers

(G-16091)
AIMTRON CORPORATION (PA)
555 S Vermont St (60067-6947)
PHONE.................630 372-7500
Mukesh Vasani, *President*
Sameer Gokhale, *Materials Mgr*
Michael Patterson, *Engineer*
Bharat Sampat, *Controller*
Sejal Patel, *Finance*
▲ **EMP**: 85
SQ FT: 49,400
SALES (est): 46.5MM **Privately Held**
SIC: 3679 Electronic circuits

(G-16092)
AIMTRON SYSTEMS LLC
Also Called: Target
500 S Hicks Rd (60067-6943)
PHONE.................262 947-8400
Bhanu Vasani, *Mng Member*
Dhruti Vasani,
Mukesh Vasani,
EMP: 30 **EST**: 1964
SALES (est): 6.7MM **Privately Held**
WEB: www.targetcorporation.com
SIC: 3669 Intercommunication systems, electric

(G-16093)
AR CONCEPTS USA INC
520 N Hicks Rd Ste 120 (60067-3607)
PHONE.................847 392-4608
John Conti, *CEO*
EMP: 2 **EST**: 2000
SALES (est): 220K **Privately Held**
SIC: 3669 1629 Railroad signaling devices, electric; railroad & subway construction

(G-16094)
ARLINGTON PLATING COMPANY
600 S Vermont St (60067-6999)
P.O. Box 974 (60078-0974)
PHONE.................847 359-1490
Marvin E Gollob, *Ch of Bd*
Rich Macary, *President*
Lisa A Finke, *Admin Sec*
David Gollob, *Admin Sec*
▲ **EMP**: 180
SQ FT: 60,000
SALES (est): 24.8MM **Privately Held**
SIC: 3471 Electroplating of metals or formed products; polishing, metals or formed products; buffing for the trade

(G-16095)
AVASARALA INC
1 E Northwest Hwy Ste 214 (60067-1700)
PHONE.................847 969-0630
TT Mani, *President*
Narayana Raju Kothapalli, *Vice Pres*
EMP: 2
SQ FT: 500
SALES (est): 724.9K
SALES (corp-wide): 9.3MM **Privately Held**
SIC: 3535 5051 Conveyors & conveying equipment; rods, wire (not insulated)
PA: Avasarala Technologies Limited
No. 60, K Choodahalli Village, Somanahalli Gate,
Bengaluru KA 56000
802 668-3860

(G-16096)
B N BLANCE ENRGY SOLUTIONS LLC
2019 N Wainwright Ct (60074-1219)
PHONE.................847 287-7466
Brenda S Neumann,
EMP: 2
SALES (est): 241.4K **Privately Held**
SIC: 3511 Turbines & turbine generator sets

(G-16097)
CAB COMMUNICATIONS INC
Also Called: Recreation Management
50 N Brockway St Ste 4-11 (60067-5072)
PHONE.................847 963-8740
Chris Belbin, *President*
Sue Hetman, *Publisher*
Samantha Cronin, *Manager*
Robert Braschel, *Technology*
EMP: 5
SQ FT: 1,500
SALES (est): 594.1K **Privately Held**
SIC: 2741 Business service newsletters: publishing & printing

(G-16098)
CENTEC AUTOMATION INC
420 S Vermont St (60067-6946)
PHONE.................847 791-9430
Thomas Vrenios, *President*
EMP: 8
SQ FT: 3,000
SALES (est): 1.2MM **Privately Held**
SIC: 3569 5084 Assembly machines, non-metalworking; baling machines, for scrap metal, paper or similar material; conveyor systems

(G-16099)
CGR TECHNOLOGIES INC
350 W Colfax St (60067-2516)
PHONE.................847 934-7622
Gregory Muncer, *President*
Robert Muncer, *Admin Sec*
EMP: 20
SQ FT: 8,000
SALES (est): 4.4MM **Privately Held**
SIC: 3544 Die sets for metal stamping (presses)

(G-16100)
CLIFFORDS PUB INC
1503 N Rand Rd (60074-2931)
PHONE.................847 259-3000
Struckmon Carol, *Principal*
EMP: 5
SALES (est): 409.3K **Privately Held**
SIC: 2085 Cocktails, alcoholic

(G-16101)
COLFAX WELDING & FABRICATING
605 W Colfax St (60067-2374)
PHONE.................847 359-4433
Peter Altman, *President*
Lee Altman, *Corp Secy*
EMP: 4
SQ FT: 5,500
SALES (est): 588.9K **Privately Held**
SIC: 7692 3444 3443 Welding repair; sheet metalwork; fabricated plate work (boiler shop)

(G-16102)
COMPLETE LAWN AND SNOW SERVICE
Also Called: Class
544 W Colfax St Ste 5 (60067-2523)
P.O. Box 1442 (60078-1442)
PHONE.................847 776-7287
Paul Munagian, *President*
Brenda Munagian, *Vice Pres*
EMP: 14 **EST**: 1986
SALES (est): 860K **Privately Held**
WEB: www.classlandscaping.com
SIC: 0782 4959 0783 3251 Lawn care services; snowplowing; removal services, bush & tree; paving brick, clay

(G-16103)
CONNELLY & ASSOCIATES
892 E Glencoe St (60074-6435)
PHONE.................847 372-5001
Thomas Connelly, *Owner*
EMP: 25
SALES (est): 1.3MM **Privately Held**
SIC: 7372 Prepackaged software

(G-16104)
CONSOLIDATED MILL SUPPLY INC (PA)
Also Called: Vestis Group
1530 E Dundee Rd Ste 200 (60074-8318)
PHONE.................847 706-6715
Kenneth J Pies, *CEO*
Mark Kaplan, *President*
Andy Mass, *Vice Pres*
Michelle Mendenhall, *Vice Pres*
Adam Barshefski, *CFO*
◆ **EMP**: 5
SQ FT: 2,000
SALES (est): 2.9MM **Privately Held**
SIC: 3312 Blast furnaces & steel mills

(G-16105)
CONSTRUCTION BUS MEDIA LLC
579 N 1st Bank Dr Ste 220 (60067-8126)
PHONE.................847 359-6493
Tim Shea,
Gary Redmond,
EMP: 6
SALES (est): 1MM **Privately Held**
SIC: 2721 Magazines: publishing only, not printed on site

(G-16106)
CONTOUR TOOL WORKS INC
1712 N Lee Ct (60074-1117)
PHONE.................847 947-4700
Darrin Knuth, *President*
Wayne Knuth, *President*
EMP: 8
SQ FT: 5,500
SALES (est): 777.9K **Privately Held**
SIC: 7389 3312 Grinding, precision: commercial or industrial; tool & die steel

(G-16107)
DAILY FASTNER
1304 W Northwest Hwy (60067-1855)
PHONE.................847 907-9830
EMP: 3
SALES (est): 74.7K **Privately Held**
SIC: 2711 Newspapers, publishing & printing

(G-16108)
DANIEL BRUCE LLC
Also Called: Dibi Accessories
2365 N Irene Dr (60074-1036)
PHONE.................917 583-1538
Daniel Wimer,
▲ **EMP**: 10
SALES (est): 1.4MM **Privately Held**
SIC: 2339 2389 Women's & misses' accessories; men's miscellaneous accessories

(G-16109)
DARDA ENTERPRISES INC
Also Called: Midwest Foundry Products
301 N Dean Dr (60074-5541)
P.O. Box 91865, Elk Grove Village (60009-1865)
PHONE.................847 270-0410
Richard Darda, *President*
Robert L Carter, *Superintendent*
Roberta J Darda, *Vice Pres*
Linda Darda Smith, *Manager*
EMP: 15
SALES: 1MM **Privately Held**
SIC: 3369 3549 White metal castings (lead, tin, antimony), except die; metalworking machinery

(G-16110)
DELANEY SHEET METAL CO
Also Called: Delaney Sheetmetal
116 N Benton St (60067-5239)
PHONE.................847 991-9579
John P Delaney, *President*
Joan Delaney, *Vice Pres*
EMP: 4
SQ FT: 1,600
SALES (est): 450K **Privately Held**
SIC: 3444 Sheet metalwork

(G-16111)
DELTA PRESS INC
756 W Kimball Ave (60067-6776)
PHONE.................847 671-3200
Mark Masciola, *Ch of Bd*
Michael Naselli, *President*
John Masciola, *Vice Pres*
EMP: 27
SQ FT: 15,000
SALES (est): 3.1MM **Privately Held**
SIC: 7336 2796 2675 Commercial art & graphic design; platemaking services; die-cut paper & board

(G-16112)
DIX-MCGUIRE COMMODITIES - LLC
Also Called: Inc., Dix McGuire Intl
201 E Dundee Rd Ste 2 (60074-2806)
PHONE.................847 496-5320
Richard Feldman,
▼ **EMP**: 4
SALES (est): 374.5K **Privately Held**
SIC: 2041 Flour & other grain mill products

(G-16113)
DOLCHE TRUCKLOAD CORP
473 W Northwest Hwy 2e (60067-2452)
PHONE.................800 719-4921
Desi Evans, *President*
EMP: 4
SQ FT: 1,300
SALES (est): 2.5MM **Privately Held**
SIC: 3715 Truck trailers

(G-16114)
DROMONT CORPORATION
220 N Smith St Ste 414 (60067-2477)
PHONE.................404 615-2336
Mario Drocco, *Engineer*
Luca Drocco, *Finance*
Sandra Brangero, *Admin Sec*
EMP: 3 **EST**: 2017
SALES (est): 202.7K **Privately Held**
SIC: 3565 8731 3586 Packaging machinery; commercial physical research; measuring & dispensing pumps

(G-16115)
EMMETTS TAVERN & BREWING CO
Also Called: Emmett's Ale House
110 N Brockway St (60067-5063)
PHONE.................847 359-1533
EMP: 11
SALES (corp-wide): 3.2MM **Privately Held**
SIC: 5812 2082 5182 Chicken restaurant; beer (alcoholic beverage); wine & distilled beverages
PA: Emmett's Tavern & Brewing Co.
128 W Main St
West Dundee IL 60118
847 428-4500

(G-16116)
ENCAP TECHNOLOGIES INC (PA)
707 S Vermont St (60067-7138)
PHONE.................510 337-2700
Griffith Neal, *President*
John Hanrahan, *General Mgr*
EMP: 12
SQ FT: 70,000
SALES: 20MM **Privately Held**
SIC: 3621 Electric motor & generator parts

(G-16117)
ENCAP TECHNOLOGIES INC
640 S Vermont St (60067-6950)
PHONE.................510 337-2700
Griffith Neal, *President*
EMP: 314
SALES (corp-wide): 20MM **Privately Held**
SIC: 3621 Electric motor & generator parts
PA: Encap Technologies, Inc.
707 S Vermont St
Palatine IL 60067
510 337-2700

(G-16118)
EV INTERACTIVE LLC
675 N North Ct Ste 140 (60067-8130)
PHONE.................847 907-4689
EMP: 3 **EST**: 2018
SALES (est): 156.3K **Privately Held**
WEB: www.evinteractive.weebly.com
SIC: 3652 Pre-recorded records & tapes

Palatine - Cook County (G-16119)

(G-16119)
FJW OPTICAL SYSTEMS INC
322 N Woodwork Ln (60067-4933)
PHONE..................847 358-2500
Frank J Warzak, *President*
Barry F Warzak, *Vice Pres*
Georgy Das, *Engineer*
Mariann Kiraly, *Manager*
Gladys Everding, *Executive*
EMP: 10 **EST:** 1945
SQ FT: 8,000
SALES (est): 1.9MM **Privately Held**
WEB: www.findrscope.com
SIC: 3827 Optical instruments & lenses

(G-16120)
GREEN EARTH TECHNOLOGIES INC
617 S Middleton Ave (60067-6642)
PHONE..................847 991-0436
Mathew Zuckerman, *Ch of Bd*
Jeff Marshall, *President*
Lou Petrucci, *COO*
Greg D Adams, *CFO*
Jeffery Loch, *Chief Mktg Ofcr*
EMP: 4
SALES: 20MM **Privately Held**
SIC: 2875 Compost

(G-16121)
H-O-H WATER TECHNOLOGY INC (PA)
500 S Vermont St (60067-6948)
P.O. Box 487 (60078-0487)
PHONE..................847 358-7400
Thomas F Hutchison, *President*
Terry Brennan, *Division Mgr*
Paul Gleason, *Division Mgr*
Chris Lawson, *Division Mgr*
Nathan Rentschler, *Division Mgr*
EMP: 47
SQ FT: 39,300
SALES (est): 31.9MM **Privately Held**
WEB: www.hohwatertechnology.com
SIC: 3589 2899 Water treatment equipment, industrial; chemical preparations

(G-16122)
HARRIER INTERIOR PRODUCTS
319 W Colfax St (60067-2525)
PHONE..................847 934-1310
EMP: 2
SQ FT: 1,800
SALES (est): 210K **Privately Held**
SIC: 2531 Manufactures Library Shelving

(G-16123)
HAVOLINE XPRESS LUBE LLC
1402 N Rand Rd (60074-2923)
PHONE..................847 221-5724
EMP: 7
SALES (corp-wide): 9.1MM **Privately Held**
SIC: 2992 Mfg Lubricating Oils/Greases
PA: Havoline Xpress Lube Llc
  810 Sunset Dr
  Round Lake IL 60073
  224 757-5628

(G-16124)
HIGH-LIFE PRODUCTS INC
615 W Colfax St (60067-2340)
PHONE..................847 991-9449
EMP: 4 **EST:** 2010
SALES (est): 250K **Privately Held**
SIC: 3493 Mfg Steel Springs-Nonwire

(G-16125)
HONEYWELL INTERNATIONAL INC
407 N Quentin Rd (60067-4832)
PHONE..................847 701-3038
EMP: 699
SALES (corp-wide): 36.7B **Publicly Held**
SIC: 3724 Aircraft engines & engine parts
PA: Honeywell International Inc.
  300 S Tryon St
  Charlotte NC 28202
  704 627-6200

(G-16126)
IMACC LLC
500 W Wood St (60067-4929)
PHONE..................512 341-8189
William Walker, *President*
Troy Boley, *President*
Ralph Brewer, *Vice Pres*
EMP: 2
SALES (est): 1.1MM **Privately Held**
SIC: 3823 Industrial process measurement equipment

(G-16127)
IMPERIAL WOODWORKING COMPANY (PA)
310 N Woodwork Ln (60067-4933)
PHONE..................847 221-2107
Frank Huschitt Sr, *Ch of Bd*
Frank Huschitt III, *President*
Paul Garvin III, *Vice Pres*
Marion Huschitt, *Vice Pres*
Annette Purcell, *Vice Pres*
▲ **EMP:** 100
SQ FT: 65,000
SALES (est): 48.3MM **Privately Held**
WEB: www.imperialwoodworking.com
SIC: 2541 Store fixtures, wood; store fronts, prefabricated: wood

(G-16128)
IMPERIAL WOODWORKING ENTPS INC
310 N Woodwork Ln (60067-4933)
PHONE..................847 358-6920
Frank Huschitt Sr, *President*
Frank Huschitt III, *Exec VP*
Annette Huschitt, *Vice Pres*
EMP: 20
SALES (est): 215.6K **Privately Held**
SIC: 2431 Millwork

(G-16129)
INSTY PRINTS PALATINE INC
Also Called: Insty-Prints
453 S Vermont St Ste A (60067-6968)
PHONE..................847 963-0000
Lorraine Walsh, *President*
Brian Walsh, *Vice Pres*
Pat Walsh, *Vice Pres*
EMP: 10
SQ FT: 6,000
SALES (est): 51.4K **Privately Held**
SIC: 2752 2791 2789 Commercial printing, offset; typesetting; bookbinding & related work

(G-16130)
INTEC-MEXICO LLC
666 S Vermont St (60067-6950)
PHONE..................847 358-0088
Steven Perlman, *Mng Member*
Daryl Dishong, *Mng Member*
Michael Greeby, *Mng Member*
Scott Perlman, *Mng Member*
EMP: 360
SQ FT: 70,000
SALES (est): 68.7MM
SALES (corp-wide): 111.7MM **Privately Held**
SIC: 3089 Molding primary plastic
PA: The Intec Group Inc
  666 S Vermont St
  Palatine IL 60067
  847 358-0088

(G-16131)
INTERIOR FASHIONS CONTRACT
Also Called: Window Fashion Unlimited
120 S Northwest Hwy (60074-6233)
PHONE..................847 358-6050
Patricia McCormick, *President*
Randy McCormick, *Corp Secy*
Brian McCormick, *Vice Pres*
EMP: 3
SQ FT: 2,400
SALES: 500K **Privately Held**
WEB: www.windowfashionsultd.com
SIC: 2391 2392 Curtains & draperies; household furnishings

(G-16132)
J P GOLDENNE INCORPORATED
Also Called: Digital Homes Technologies
346 N Northwest Hwy (60067-5329)
PHONE..................847 776-5063
John P Goldenne, *President*
EMP: 10
SQ FT: 5,000
SALES (est): 1.7MM **Privately Held**
SIC: 3643 3651 Connectors & terminals for electrical devices; household audio & video equipment

(G-16133)
JAY PRINTING
553 N Hicks Rd (60067)
PHONE..................847 934-6103
EMP: 3 **EST:** 1994
SQ FT: 4,000
SALES: 250K **Privately Held**
SIC: 2752 2791 2789 Lithographic Commercial Printing Typesetting Services Bookbinding/Related Work

(G-16134)
K D IRON WORKS
542 W Colfax St Ste 5 (60067-2524)
PHONE..................847 991-3039
Karl Deutschmann, *President*
Michael Deutschmann, *Vice Pres*
EMP: 2
SQ FT: 1,400
SALES (est): 312.8K **Privately Held**
SIC: 3446 1799 Railings, bannisters, guards, etc.: made from metal pipe; ornamental metal work

(G-16135)
KSR SOFTWARE LLC
388 N Chalary Ct (60067-0920)
PHONE..................847 705-0100
EMP: 5
SALES (est): 390K **Privately Held**
SIC: 7372 Prepackaged Software Services

(G-16136)
LIGHT MATRIX INC
339 S Valor Ct (60074-6829)
PHONE..................847 590-0856
Xinliang Yang, *President*
▲ **EMP:** 2
SALES (est): 203.7K **Privately Held**
SIC: 3641 Electric lamps

(G-16137)
MAC STER INC
724 W Peregrine Dr (60067-7008)
PHONE..................847 359-3640
EMP: 2 **EST:** 2008
SALES (est): 269.3K **Privately Held**
SIC: 3444 Sheet metalwork

(G-16138)
MANUFASTENERS HOUSE IQ INC
427 S Middleton Ave (60067-5966)
PHONE..................847 705-6538
Tim Millar, *CEO*
▲ **EMP:** 3
SALES (est): 226.5K **Privately Held**
SIC: 3496 Clips & fasteners, made from purchased wire

(G-16139)
MAYFAIR METAL SPINNING CO INC
538 S Vermont St (60067-6948)
PHONE..................847 358-7450
John Janowski, *President*
Josephine Janowski, *Admin Sec*
EMP: 4 **EST:** 1955
SQ FT: 5,500
SALES (est): 500K **Privately Held**
WEB: www.mayfairmetalspinninginc.net
SIC: 3469 Spinning metal for the trade; stamping metal for the trade; machine parts, stamped or pressed metal

(G-16140)
MIDWEST FUEL INJCTION SVC CORP
543 S Vermont St Ste A (60067-6978)
PHONE..................847 991-7867
Dean Bismark, *Branch Mgr*
Paul Thons, *Manager*
Kevin Schmidt, *Manager*
EMP: 11
SALES (corp-wide): 6.6MM **Privately Held**
SIC: 5084 3724 3561 Engines & parts, diesel; aircraft engines & engine parts; pumps & pumping equipment
PA: Midwest Fuel Injection Service, Corp.
  1 Seidel Ct
  Bolingbrook IL
  708 532-1102

(G-16141)
MORKES INC
Also Called: Morkes Chocolates
1890 N Rand Rd (60074-1130)
PHONE..................847 359-3511
Rhonda Morkes, *President*
EMP: 15
SQ FT: 5,200
SALES (est): 3MM **Privately Held**
WEB: www.morkeschocolates.com
SIC: 2064 2066 5441 Chocolate candy, except solid chocolate; chocolate candy, solid; candy; confectionery

(G-16142)
NEWKO TOOL & ENGINEERING CO
Also Called: Newko Proto Type
720 S Vermont St (60067-7139)
PHONE..................847 359-1670
Scott Riddell, *President*
Gabriel Casanas, *Human Resources*
Barbara Newburg, *Admin Sec*
EMP: 25 **EST:** 1958
SQ FT: 1,400
SALES (est): 5MM **Privately Held**
WEB: www.newkogroup.com
SIC: 3544 3469 8711 3678 Special dies & tools; metal stampings; engineering services; electronic connectors

(G-16143)
NORTHLAKE INDUSTRIES
143 W Robertson St (60067-3525)
PHONE..................847 358-6875
EMP: 3
SALES (est): 175K **Privately Held**
SIC: 3999 Manufacturing industries

(G-16144)
NORTHWEST FRAME COMPANY INC
252 N Cady Dr (60074-5522)
PHONE..................847 359-0987
Steven M Chessin, *President*
Robert W Battaglia, *Admin Sec*
EMP: 4
SQ FT: 5,000
SALES (est): 249.6K **Privately Held**
SIC: 2499 Picture frame molding, finished

(G-16145)
NUEVOS SEMANA NEWSPAPER
1180 E Dundee Rd (60074-8305)
PHONE..................847 991-3939
Norma Vilcatoma, *President*
EMP: 4
SALES (est): 138.3K **Privately Held**
WEB: www.lanuevasemana.com
SIC: 2711 Newspapers

(G-16146)
OMNI-RINSE LLC
738 E Dundee Rd Ste 197 (60074-2858)
PHONE..................708 860-3250
Sonoda Naoki M, *Mng Member*
EMP: 3
SALES: 12K **Privately Held**
SIC: 3914 Stainless steel ware

(G-16147)
ORION STAR CORP
Also Called: Orion Offset
236 E Northwest Hwy Ste A (60067-8183)
PHONE..................847 776-2300
Joyce R Day, *President*
Kathleen Giardina, *Vice Pres*
Anita Zilis, *Consultant*
EMP: 10
SQ FT: 3,600
SALES (est): 1.1MM **Privately Held**
SIC: 2752 Commercial printing, offset

(G-16148)
PARALLEL MACHINE PRODUCTS INC
255 N Woodwork Ln (60067-4930)
PHONE..................847 359-1012
John Blyth, *President*
Donna Blyth, *Admin Sec*

EMP: 10
SQ FT: 4,800
SALES (est): 800K **Privately Held**
SIC: 3599 Machine shop, jobbing & repair

(G-16149)
PRESS BRAKE TOOL AND SUPPLY
850 N Virginia Lake Ct (60074-7249)
P.O. Box 217 (60078-0217)
PHONE 847 776-9201
Bob McOrmick, *President*
EMP: 3
SALES (est): 398.6K **Privately Held**
WEB: www.aaapressbrakedie.com
SIC: 3599 Machine shop, jobbing & repair

(G-16150)
PRIME VECTOR INTERNATIONAL LLC
349 S Circle Dr (60067-7705)
PHONE 847 348-1060
Tom Mazza, *Managing Prtnr*
Thomas A Mazza, *Principal*
▲ **EMP:** 3
SALES (est): 296.4K **Privately Held**
SIC: 3999 Manufacturing industries

(G-16151)
PROCAL INC
5721 Highland Dr (60067-2581)
PHONE 847 219-7257
Ashish Passi, *Principal*
EMP: 3
SALES (est): 75.7K **Privately Held**
SIC: 2048 Prepared feeds

(G-16152)
R & R CUSTOM CABINET MAKING
515 S Vermont St Ste B (60067-6919)
PHONE 847 358-6188
Phil Rybarczyk, *Mng Member*
Steve Rybarczyk, *Mng Member*
EMP: 4
SQ FT: 2,000
SALES (est): 405.8K **Privately Held**
SIC: 2434 2541 3083 1799 Wood kitchen cabinets; table or counter tops, plastic laminated; laminated plastics plate & sheet; counter top installation

(G-16153)
REMET CORPORATION
1540 E Dundee Rd Ste 170 (60074-8316)
PHONE 480 766-3464
John Paraszczak, *President*
▲ **EMP:** 20 **EST:** 1933
SQ FT: 95,000
SALES (est): 2.4MM
SALES (corp-wide): 61.8MM **Privately Held**
SIC: 2891 Sealing wax
PA: Remet Pic, Inc.
210 Commons Rd
Utica NY 13502
315 797-8700

(G-16154)
ROAD RUNNER SPORTS INC
20291 N Rand Rd Ste 105 (60074-2019)
PHONE 847 719-8941
EMP: 11
SALES (corp-wide): 82.1MM **Privately Held**
SIC: 5961 3949 5661 Mail order house; sporting & athletic goods; footwear, athletic
PA: Road Runner Sports, Inc.
5549 Copley Dr
San Diego CA 92111
858 974-4200

(G-16155)
ROSEWOOD SOFTWARE INC
1531 N Haven Dr (60074-2425)
PHONE 847 438-2185
Richard Lloyd, *President*
Laura Lloyd, *Admin Sec*
EMP: 8
SALES (est): 598.8K **Privately Held**
SIC: 7372 Application computer software

(G-16156)
S-P-D INCORPORATED
678 S Middleton Ave (60067-6678)
PHONE 847 882-9820
David M Whitfield, *President*
Nicholas Di Giovanni, *Vice Pres*
Betty Lauer, *Admin Sec*
EMP: 6
SQ FT: 3,000
SALES (est): 3MM **Privately Held**
SIC: 7629 3561 5084 Electrical repair shops; pumps, domestic: water or sump; instruments & control equipment; controlling instruments & accessories

(G-16157)
SHADY CREEK VINEYARD INC
1238 N Wellington Dr (60067-2455)
PHONE 847 275-7979
EMP: 3 **EST:** 2010
SALES (est): 125.2K **Privately Held**
SIC: 2037 Frozen fruits & vegetables

(G-16158)
SIGNS TODAY INC
342 W Colfax St (60067-2516)
PHONE 847 934-9777
John Theodore, *President*
EMP: 6
SQ FT: 2,700
SALES (est): 440K **Privately Held**
SIC: 7389 3993 2752 5999 Sign painting & lettering shop; signs & advertising specialties; commercial printing, lithographic; trophies & plaques

(G-16159)
SKYLINE INTERNATIONAL INC
4801 Emerson Ave Ste 202 (60067-0503)
PHONE 847 357-9077
Zain Subhani, *President*
Stacy L Shamberger, *Exec VP*
Shawn Gabbard, *Director*
▲ **EMP:** 18
SALES (est): 2.8MM **Privately Held**
WEB: www.skylineg.com
SIC: 3679 Electronic circuits

(G-16160)
SMARTBYTE SOLUTIONS INC
712 W Slippery Rock Dr (60067-2573)
PHONE 847 925-1870
Orlin Momchev, *President*
Tonya Momchev, *CFO*
EMP: 5
SALES: 250K **Privately Held**
WEB: www.smartbytesolutions.com
SIC: 7372 7373 Application computer software; systems software development services

(G-16161)
TANE CORPORATION
1122 W Partridge Dr (60067-7047)
PHONE 847 705-7125
Robert T Finegan, *President*
EMP: 5
SALES (est): 446.9K **Privately Held**
SIC: 3599 1711 Air intake filters, internal combustion engine, except auto; plumbing contractors

(G-16162)
THE INTEC GROUP INC (PA)
666 S Vermont St (60067-6950)
PHONE 847 358-0088
Steven M Perlman, *President*
Michael Gaines, *Vice Pres*
Tom Katchmar, *Opers Staff*
Rena Drewes, *QC Mgr*
Chad Archer, *CFO*
▲ **EMP:** 175
SQ FT: 60,000
SALES (est): 111.7MM **Privately Held**
WEB: www.intecgrp.com
SIC: 3089 Molding primary plastic; injection molding of plastics

(G-16163)
THREADS UP INC
461 N Jonathan Dr Apt 201 (60074-4190)
PHONE 630 595-2297
Art Barsella, *President*
EMP: 4
SALES (est): 535.4K **Privately Held**
SIC: 3599 Amusement park equipment

(G-16164)
THRIFT N SWIFT
309 Elmwood Ct (60067-7700)
PHONE 847 455-1350
William Denten, *President*
EMP: 7 **EST:** 1967
SQ FT: 2,500
SALES (est): 890.2K **Privately Held**
SIC: 2752 Commercial printing, offset

(G-16165)
TOWNE TOWING INC
400 S Vermont St (60067-6946)
PHONE 847 705-1710
John Heavey, *President*
Bruce Staley, *Vice Pres*
EMP: 3
SQ FT: 400
SALES (est): 569K **Privately Held**
SIC: 7549 3589 Towing service, automotive; asbestos removal equipment

(G-16166)
TRANSCENDA INC
Also Called: Brush Foil
923 W Sparrow Ct (60067-6602)
PHONE 847 705-6670
Andy Brewer, *President*
Fred Caruso, *Corp Secy*
Edward Koinskie, *Vice Pres*
Cynthia Simpler, *Vice Pres*
▲ **EMP:** 50
SQ FT: 89,000
SALES (est): 24.4MM
SALES (corp-wide): 327.9MM **Privately Held**
SIC: 3081 Plastic film & sheet
PA: Transcendia, Inc.
9201 Belmont Ave Ste 100a
Franklin Park IL 60131
847 678-1800

(G-16167)
TUFF SHED INC
1408 E Northwest Hwy (60074-7608)
PHONE 847 704-1147
EMP: 13
SALES (corp-wide): 292.4MM **Privately Held**
WEB: www.tuffshed.com
SIC: 2452 Prefabricated wood buildings
PA: Tuff Shed, Inc.
1777 S Harrison St # 600
Denver CO 80210
303 753-8833

(G-16168)
TURBO DRY LLC
873 N Martin Dr (60067-2025)
PHONE 847 702-4430
Cary Livingston, *Mng Member*
EMP: 2
SALES (est): 259.5K **Privately Held**
SIC: 3564 Blowers & fans

(G-16169)
UPHOLSTERED WALLS BY ANNE MARI
Also Called: Upholstred Walls By Anne Marie
419 S Rose St (60067-6855)
PHONE 847 202-0642
Anne Marie Scherlag, *President*
Bob Scherlag, *Admin Sec*
EMP: 7
SALES: 850K **Privately Held**
SIC: 2221 Upholstery, tapestry & wall covering fabrics

(G-16170)
VIDEO GAMING TECHNOLOGIES INC
963 N Carmel Dr (60074-3703)
PHONE 847 776-3516
Frank Fortunato, *Principal*
EMP: 3 **EST:** 2010
SALES (est): 174.2K **Privately Held**
SIC: 3944 7359 Electronic game machines, except coin-operated; video cassette recorder & accessory rental

(G-16171)
WAIST UP IMPRNTD SPRTSWEAR LLC
422 S Vermont St (60067-6946)
PHONE 847 963-1400
Don Banks,
Bill Banks,
EMP: 5
SALES: 300K **Privately Held**
WEB: www.waistup.com
SIC: 2395 2759 Embroidery products, except schiffli machine; screen printing

(G-16172)
WASOWSKI JACEK
Also Called: Midnight Marble
9a E Dundee Quarter Dr A (60074-1657)
PHONE 847 693-1878
Jacek Wasowski, *Owner*
EMP: 1
SALES (est): 800K **Privately Held**
SIC: 3281 Granite, cut & shaped

(G-16173)
WEBER-STEPHEN PRODUCTS LLC (PA)
Also Called: Weber Grills
1415 S Roselle Rd (60067-7337)
PHONE 847 934-5700
James C Stephen Sr, *President*
Michael J Kempster, *Exec VP*
Dale Wytiaz, *Exec VP*
Jim Forbes, *Vice Pres*
Brian Hendricks, *Vice Pres*
◆ **EMP:** 277 **EST:** 2010
SQ FT: 300,000
SALES (est): 979.6MM **Privately Held**
WEB: www.weber.com
SIC: 3631 Barbecues, grills & braziers (outdoor cooking)

(G-16174)
WEBER-STEPHEN PRODUCTS LLC
Also Called: Weber Grills
306 E Helen Rd (60067-6939)
PHONE 224 836-8536
EMP: 11
SALES (corp-wide): 979.6MM **Privately Held**
SIC: 3631 Barbecues, grills & braziers (outdoor cooking)
PA: Weber-Stephen Products Llc
1415 S Roselle Rd
Palatine IL 60067
847 934-5700

(G-16175)
WINDY CITY PUBLISHERS LLC
1051 S Hiddenbrook Trl (60067-9100)
PHONE 847 925-9434
Lise Marinelli, *President*
EMP: 3
SALES: 60K **Privately Held**
SIC: 2731 Book publishing

(G-16176)
WOLF CABINETRY & GANITE
1703 N Rand Rd (60074-2357)
PHONE 847 358-9922
Andy Huang, *Owner*
EMP: 4
SALES (est): 537.8K **Privately Held**
WEB: www.wolfcabinetsandgranites.com
SIC: 2434 Wood kitchen cabinets

(G-16177)
XLOGOTECH INC
1312 W Northwest Hwy (60067-1855)
PHONE 888 244-5152
Eugene Tensiper, *Principal*
Mark Furman, *Sales Staff*
EMP: 4
SALES (est): 1.1MM **Privately Held**
SIC: 5065 3572 Diskettes, computer; disk drives, computer

Palestine
Crawford County

(G-16178)
ILLIANA CORES INC
10156 N 1725th St (62451-2646)
P.O. Box 189 (62451-0189)
PHONE 618 586-9800
Randal L Burtch, *President*
Michael D Murray, *Vice Pres*
Michelle Hamilton,

EMP: 25
SQ FT: 28,000
SALES (est): 5.9MM **Privately Held**
SIC: 2655 Tubes, fiber or paper: made from purchased material

(G-16179)
S FLYING INC
Also Called: Flying S
17583 E 500th Ave (62451-2051)
PHONE..................618 586-9999
David Shaw, *Owner*
Peter Bowman, *Engineer*
Graham Parish, *Engineer*
Larry Zuber, *Engineer*
Barrett Robbins, *Supervisor*
EMP: 14
SQ FT: 16,000
SALES (est): 2.6MM **Privately Held**
SIC: 8711 3812 Engineering services; acceleration indicators & systems components, aerospace

Palmyra
Macoupin County

(G-16180)
PALMYRA MODESTO WATER COMM
9934 Water Plant Rd (62674-6324)
P.O. Box 104, Modesto (62667-0104)
PHONE..................217 436-2519
James Launer, *President*
Larry Garst, *Superintendent*
EMP: 5
SALES: 139K **Privately Held**
SIC: 3589 Water treatment equipment, industrial

Palos Heights
Cook County

(G-16181)
BLEW CHEMICAL COMPANY
12501 S Richard Ave (60463-1360)
P.O. Box 501 (60463-0501)
PHONE..................708 448-5780
Betsy Ochoa, *President*
Betsy Blew-Ochoa, *President*
William R Blew Jr, *Treasurer*
Besty Blew, *Admin Sec*
EMP: 5 EST: 1971
SALES: 1.2MM **Privately Held**
SIC: 2841 Soap: granulated, liquid, cake, flaked or chip; detergents, synthetic organic or inorganic alkaline

(G-16182)
CONTINENTAL SUPPLY CO
21 Carriage Trl (60463-1221)
PHONE..................708 448-2728
Joyce Moone, *President*
EMP: 3
SALES (est): 406K **Privately Held**
SIC: 2851 Lacquers, varnishes, enamels & other coatings

(G-16183)
ECOLAB INC
6236 W 124th Pl (60463-1864)
PHONE..................708 496-5378
EMP: 3
SALES (corp-wide): 14.9B **Publicly Held**
SIC: 2841 Soap & other detergents
PA: Ecolab Inc.
1 Ecolab Pl
Saint Paul MN 55102
800 232-6522

(G-16184)
GALVANIZE LABS INC
6728 W Highland Dr (60463-2219)
PHONE..................630 258-1476
Moria Hardek, *President*
Neal Hardek, *Chairman*
Matt Dyson, *COO*
EMP: 9
SALES: 800K **Privately Held**
SIC: 3999 Education aids, devices & supplies

(G-16185)
GOOD NEWS PRINTING
5535 W 131st St (60463)
P.O. Box 626 (60463-0626)
PHONE..................708 389-1127
Gerald Prosapio, *President*
EMP: 3
SALES (est): 299.9K **Privately Held**
SIC: 2752 Commercial printing, offset

(G-16186)
GRAPHIC COMMUNICATORS INC
Also Called: Family Record
12500 S Meade Ave (60463-1838)
PHONE..................708 385-7550
Edward Zapalik, *President*
EMP: 3
SALES (est): 200K **Privately Held**
SIC: 2741 Miscellaneous publishing

(G-16187)
GUERRERO INDUSTRIES LLC
12605 S Melvina Ave (60463-1800)
PHONE..................773 968-8648
Veronica Guerrero, *President*
EMP: 3 EST: 2016
SALES (est): 48K **Privately Held**
SIC: 3554 Paper industries machinery

(G-16188)
HICKMAN WILLIAMS & COMPANY
7800 W College Dr Ste 1e (60463-1007)
P.O. Box 5225, Oak Brook (60522-5225)
PHONE..................630 574-2150
Adrian Bethray, *General Mgr*
William Snyder, *Principal*
Robert Davis, *Sales Mgr*
Dave Barko, *Marketing Mgr*
James Ross, *Manager*
EMP: 12
SALES (corp-wide): 171.1MM **Privately Held**
WEB: www.hicwilco.com
SIC: 3313 5051 Alloys, additive, except copper: not made in blast furnaces; metals service centers & offices
PA: Hickman, Williams & Company
250 E 5th St Ste 300
Cincinnati OH 45202
513 621-1946

(G-16189)
HOPPER GRAPHICS INC
6106 W 127th St (60463-2370)
PHONE..................708 489-0459
John Stefanik, *President*
EMP: 6
SALES (est): 252.5K **Privately Held**
SIC: 7336 2732 2759 Graphic arts & related design; book printing; commercial printing

(G-16190)
MACHINE CONTROL SYSTEMS INC (PA)
12424 S Austin Ave (60463-1820)
PHONE..................708 389-2160
Bernard A Plummer, *President*
Margaret Plummer, *Admin Sec*
EMP: 2
SALES (est): 680.6K **Privately Held**
SIC: 3625 3613 Control equipment, electric; control panels, electric

(G-16191)
S I A INC (PA)
11743 Southwest Hwy (60463-1058)
PHONE..................708 361-3100
James M Regan, *President*
Joseph P Cairo, *Corp Secy*
Phillip G Regan, *Director*
Harry Clements, *Shareholder*
Thomas P Regan, *Shareholder*
EMP: 2
SQ FT: 2,000
SALES (est): 1.9MM **Privately Held**
SIC: 3728 Aircraft assemblies, subassemblies & parts

(G-16192)
SPACIL CONSTRUCTION CO
6018 W 123rd St (60463-1803)
PHONE..................708 448-3809
Frank Spacil, *President*
EMP: 5
SALES (est): 400K **Privately Held**
SIC: 3272 Building materials, except block or brick: concrete

(G-16193)
TERRAPIN XPRESS INC
7801 W 123rd Pl (60463-1217)
P.O. Box 366 (60463-0366)
PHONE..................866 823-7323
Priscilla Davis, *President*
EMP: 5
SALES (est): 301.8K **Privately Held**
SIC: 2679 5113 7389 Building, insulating & packaging paperboard; industrial & personal service paper; eating utensils, disposable plastic; bags, paper & disposable plastic; corrugated & solid fiber boxes;

(G-16194)
WALTER & KATHY ANCZEREWICZ (PA)
Also Called: Dunkin' Donuts
12807 S Harlem Ave (60463-2132)
PHONE..................708 448-3676
Walter Anczerewicz, *Partner*
Kathy Anczerewicz, *Partner*
EMP: 9
SALES (est): 1.5MM **Privately Held**
SIC: 5461 2051 5812 Doughnuts; doughnuts, except frozen; ice cream stands or dairy bars

Palos Hills
Cook County

(G-16195)
ASSOCIATED DESIGN INC
Also Called: Associated Design Service
11160 Southwest Hwy Ste B (60465-2473)
PHONE..................708 974-9100
Mary Noone, *President*
Mary C Kirby, *Corp Secy*
Thomas Noone, *Vice Pres*
EMP: 10 EST: 1947
SQ FT: 7,800
SALES (est): 904.7K **Privately Held**
WEB: www.associated-design.com
SIC: 8711 7389 8249 3999 Designing: ship, boat, machine & product; drafting service, except temporary help; vocational schools; models, general, except toy; commercial printing

(G-16196)
BELL CABINET & MILLWORK CO
10542 S Michael Dr (60465-1907)
PHONE..................708 425-1200
Joe Bellettiere, *President*
EMP: 6
SALES: 800K **Privately Held**
SIC: 2434 2511 Wood kitchen cabinets; wood household furniture

(G-16197)
CAROUSEL CHECKS INC
11152 Southwest Hwy Ste A (60465-2474)
PHONE..................708 613-2452
Andrew Crim, *President*
Jason Ward, *COO*
Heather Blackburn, *Vice Pres*
Dennis Crim, *Vice Pres*
Gail Martinez, *Opers Mgr*
▲ EMP: 10
SALES (est): 3.2MM **Privately Held**
SIC: 2782 Checkbooks

(G-16198)
COUNTER-INTELLIGENCE
8150 W 107th St (60465-1870)
PHONE..................708 974-3326
Mark Drong, *Principal*
EMP: 3
SALES (est): 228.6K **Privately Held**
SIC: 3131 Counters

(G-16199)
D L SHEET METAL
8717 W 98th Pl (60465-1137)
PHONE..................708 599-5538
Mary Barbour, *Owner*
EMP: 5
SALES (est): 549K **Privately Held**
SIC: 3444 Sheet metalwork

(G-16200)
DUO PLEX GLASS LTD (PA)
10655 S Michael Dr (60465-1908)
PHONE..................708 532-4422
Edward J Wytrwal, *President*
Cynthia M Wytrwal, *Corp Secy*
EMP: 3
SALES (est): 419.6K **Privately Held**
SIC: 3231 5231 3211 Insulating glass: made from purchased glass; glass; flat glass

(G-16201)
GAMMA PRODUCTS INC
7730 W 114th Pl Ste 1 (60465-2748)
P.O. Box 190, Palos Park (60464-0190)
PHONE..................708 974-4100
Nancy Meier, *CEO*
Walter Meier, *President*
Blake Meier, *Vice Pres*
EMP: 10 EST: 1965
SQ FT: 10,000
SALES (est): 1.7MM **Privately Held**
WEB: www.gammaproducts.com
SIC: 3829 Nuclear radiation & testing apparatus

(G-16202)
MIDWEST LASER INCORPORATED
10639 S 82nd Ct (60465-1848)
PHONE..................708 974-0084
Josie Tokarski, *President*
Mike Tokarski, *Vice Pres*
Michael Tokarski, *Treasurer*
EMP: 3
SQ FT: 1,500
SALES: 200K **Privately Held**
SIC: 3861 7378 Toners, prepared photographic (not made in chemical plants); computer peripheral equipment repair & maintenance

(G-16203)
PARK PRINTING INC (PA)
9903 S Roberts Rd (60465-1532)
PHONE..................708 430-4878
Carol Park, *President*
Tim Park, *Vice Pres*
▲ EMP: 5
SQ FT: 1,000
SALES (est): 542.3K **Privately Held**
SIC: 2752 2791 Commercial printing, offset; typesetting

(G-16204)
PEEPS INC
8945 W 103rd St (60465-1642)
PHONE..................708 935-4201
Rimvydas Tveras, *President*
EMP: 3
SALES (est): 181.5K **Privately Held**
SIC: 3089 Injection molded finished plastic products

(G-16205)
QUICK BUILDING SYSTEMS INC
9748 S Cambridge Ct (60465-1157)
PHONE..................708 598-6733
Joost Zerwijs, *President*
Anne Schipper, *Admin Sec*
EMP: 4
SALES: 265K **Privately Held**
SIC: 3272 Building materials, except block or brick: concrete

(G-16206)
R J S SILK SCREENING CO
Also Called: Rjs Silk Screening
10708 S Roberts Rd (60465-2314)
PHONE..................708 974-3009
Bob Stramaglia, *Owner*
EMP: 5
SQ FT: 1,500
SALES (est): 377.6K **Privately Held**
SIC: 7336 2396 Silk screen design; automotive & apparel trimmings

(G-16207)
SIGNS BY DESIGN
10330 S Harlem Ave (60465-2036)
PHONE..................708 599-9970
Mark King, *President*

GEOGRAPHIC SECTION

Paris - Edgar County (G-16235)

EMP: 7
SALES (est): 463.3K **Privately Held**
SIC: 3993 Signs, not made in custom sign painting shops

Palos Park
Cook County

(G-16208)
CARE EDUCATION GROUP INC
126 Commons Dr (60464-3106)
P.O. Box 180 (60464-0180)
PHONE.................................708 361-4110
Eric D Joseph, *President*
Nancy E Webster, *Vice Pres*
EMP: 3
SQ FT: 2,000
SALES: 750K **Privately Held**
SIC: 8299 8742 2721 Educational services; hospital & health services consultant; periodicals

(G-16209)
CONDOR LABELS INC
8506 W 119th Pl (60464-1228)
PHONE.................................708 429-0707
Robert Biel, *President*
EMP: 2
SALES (est): 275K **Privately Held**
SIC: 2759 2672 Flexographic printing; labels & seals: printing; coated & laminated paper

(G-16210)
EXTOL HYDRO TECHNOLOGIES INC
13020 Ridgewood Dr (60464-2513)
PHONE.................................708 717-4371
Ibrahim Taha, *Director*
EMP: 10
SALES: 500K **Privately Held**
SIC: 3589 Water treatment equipment, industrial

(G-16211)
H B PRODUCTS INCORPORATED
42 Parklane Dr (60464-2562)
PHONE.................................773 735-0936
James Hamann, *President*
George Hamann, *Treasurer*
EMP: 3 EST: 1978
SALES (est): 550K **Privately Held**
SIC: 3599 3544 Machine shop, jobbing & repair; special dies, tools, jigs & fixtures

(G-16212)
JOHN DAGYS MEDIA LLC
Also Called: Sportscar365
8011 W 125th St (60464-1924)
PHONE.................................708 373-0180
Jonathan Dagys, *President*
EMP: 4
SALES (est): 97.9K **Privately Held**
SIC: 2711 7389 Newspapers: publishing only, not printed on site;

(G-16213)
RESPIRONICS INC
12515 S 82nd Ave (60464-2011)
PHONE.................................708 923-6200
EMP: 164
SALES (corp-wide): 20.8B **Privately Held**
WEB: www.respironics.com
SIC: 3842 Surgical appliances & supplies
HQ: Respironics, Inc.
1001 Murry Ridge Ln
Murrysville PA 15668
724 387-5200

(G-16214)
SIMPLE CIRCUITS INC
12756 S 80th Ave (60464-2131)
P.O. Box 68 (60464-0068)
PHONE.................................708 671-9600
EMP: 5 EST: 2013
SALES (est): 608.4K **Privately Held**
SIC: 3679 Electronic circuits

(G-16215)
SPEC BUILT
11912 Southwest Hwy (60464-3101)
PHONE.................................312 623-5533
Michael J Guinta, *Principal*
EMP: 4
SALES (est): 434K **Privately Held**
WEB: www.specbuiltinc.com
SIC: 2431 Millwork

(G-16216)
VETERANS PRINT MANAGEMENT
35 Cherrywood Dr (60464-1576)
PHONE.................................630 816-0853
James Capuano, *Principal*
EMP: 3
SALES (est): 157.2K **Privately Held**
SIC: 2752 Commercial printing, offset

(G-16217)
WATER & GAS TECHNOLOGIES
Also Called: Wgt
8046 W 128th Pl (60464-2147)
PHONE.................................708 829-3254
Luis Simas, *Principal*
EMP: 4
SALES (est): 188.6K **Privately Held**
SIC: 1389 Impounding & storing salt water, oil & gas field

Pana
Christian County

(G-16218)
NEXUS CORPORATION
Also Called: National Greenhouse Company
6 Industrial Park Dr (62557-6814)
PHONE.................................217 303-5544
Arlen Helterbrand, *Manager*
EMP: 25
SALES (corp-wide): 1B **Publicly Held**
SIC: 3448 3231 Greenhouses: prefabricated metal; products of purchased glass
HQ: Nexus Corporation
10983 Leroy Dr
Northglenn CO 80233
303 457-9199

(G-16219)
PANA LIMESTONE COMPANY
325 N 1600 East Rd (62557-6843)
PHONE.................................217 562-4231
David Flatt, *President*
EMP: 3
SALES (est): 160K **Privately Held**
SIC: 1411 Limestone, dimension-quarrying

(G-16220)
PANA MONUMENT CO (PA)
Also Called: Adams & Masterson Memorials
2 N Poplar St (62557-1102)
PHONE.................................217 562-5121
Danny Adams, *Partner*
Richard Masterson, *Partner*
EMP: 4
SQ FT: 4,000
SALES (est): 499.1K **Privately Held**
SIC: 5999 3281 Monuments, finished to custom order; rock & stone specimens; monuments & tombstones; cut stone & stone products

(G-16221)
PANA NEWS INC (PA)
Also Called: Pana News Palladium
205 S Locust St (62557-1605)
P.O. Box 200 (62557-0200)
PHONE.................................217 562-2111
Thomas J Phillips, *President*
Beth Bennett, *Principal*
Cynthia Lotinis, *Principal*
Patricia Spracklen, *Principal*
Doris Phillips, *Vice Pres*
EMP: 15 EST: 1933
SQ FT: 14,000
SALES (est): 1.6MM **Privately Held**
SIC: 2752 2711 2759 Commercial printing, offset; newspapers, publishing & commercial printing

(G-16222)
PBI REDI MIX & TRUCKING
2 N Walnut St (62557-1186)
PHONE.................................217 562-3717
James Randolph, *President*
EMP: 25

SALES (est): 2.5MM **Privately Held**
SIC: 3273 Ready-mixed concrete

Paris
Edgar County

(G-16223)
ABITEC CORPORATION
1800 S Main St (61944-2945)
P.O. Box 878 (61944-0878)
PHONE.................................217 465-8577
Toby Wilson, *Opers Dir*
Robert Zulliger, *Opers Dir*
Mike Beesley, *QC Dir*
Peter Blagdon, *Manager*
Norma Pruiett, *Manager*
EMP: 21
SALES (corp-wide): 20.3B **Privately Held**
SIC: 5149 5141 2077 2076 Shortening, vegetable; groceries, general line; animal & marine fats & oils; vegetable oil mills
HQ: Abitec Corporation
501 W 1st Ave
Columbus OH 43215

(G-16224)
ALUMINITE OF PARIS
2009 S Main St (61944-2961)
PHONE.................................217 463-2233
▲ EMP: 4
SALES (est): 296.6K **Privately Held**
SIC: 3442 Screen & storm doors & windows

(G-16225)
CADILLAC PRODUCTS PACKAGING CO
Also Called: Cppc, Paris Plant
2005 S Main St (61944-2961)
PHONE.................................217 463-1444
Debra Osborn, *Manager*
EMP: 110 **Privately Held**
SIC: 3081 Polyethylene film
PA: Cadillac Products Packaging Company
5800 Crooks Rd
Troy MI 48098

(G-16226)
CARGILL DRY CORN INGRDENTS INC (HQ)
616 S Jefferson St (61944-2000)
PHONE.................................217 465-5331
Rex Winter, *President*
▼ EMP: 5 EST: 1934
SQ FT: 20,000
SALES (est): 16.4MM
SALES (corp-wide): 113.4B **Privately Held**
WEB: www.cargilldci.com
SIC: 2041 2048 5153 Corn meal; corn flour; corn grits & flakes, for brewers' use; grain mills (except rice); prepared feeds; grain elevators
PA: Cargill, Incorporated
15407 Mcginty Rd W
Wayzata MN 55391
952 742-7575

(G-16227)
CHRISMAN FUEL
102 Mcmillan St (61944-1302)
PHONE.................................217 463-3400
Randy Moore, *Manager*
EMP: 3
SALES (est): 137K **Privately Held**
SIC: 2869 Fuels

(G-16228)
CUSTOM TOOL INC
926 N Central Ave (61944-1172)
P.O. Box 817 (61944-0817)
PHONE.................................217 465-8538
Robert I Wilson, *President*
Carolyn Wilson, *Vice Pres*
EMP: 10 EST: 1974
SQ FT: 1,800
SALES (est): 1.6MM **Privately Held**
SIC: 3541 3699 3545 3544 Machine tools, metal cutting type; electrical equipment & supplies; machine tool accessories; special dies, tools, jigs & fixtures

(G-16229)
EDGAR COUNTY LOCKER SERVICE
116 E Steidl Rd (61944-5997)
PHONE.................................217 466-5000
Jim Dunn, *President*
Elizabeth Humphrey, *General Mgr*
Bill Moss, *Admin Sec*
EMP: 5 EST: 1944
SALES (est): 492.3K **Privately Held**
WEB: www.edgarcountylocker.com
SIC: 2011 4222 2013 Meat packing plants; storage, frozen or refrigerated goods; sausages & other prepared meats

(G-16230)
GSI GROUP LLC
Also Called: Grain Systems
13217 Illinois Hwy 133 W (61944)
PHONE.................................217 463-1612
Chuck Smith, *Branch Mgr*
Mary Denton, *Manager*
EMP: 200 **Publicly Held**
SIC: 5083 3535 3441 Livestock equipment; conveyors & conveying equipment; fabricated structural metal
HQ: The Gsi Group Llc
1004 E Illinois St
Assumption IL 62510
217 226-4421

(G-16231)
KEYS MANUFACTURING COMPANY INC
13338 N 1900th St (61944-8227)
PHONE.................................217 465-4001
Joseph Keys, *President*
Sheila Keys, *Admin Sec*
Sherrie Grimes, *Admin Asst*
▲ EMP: 20
SQ FT: 30,000
SALES: 7MM **Privately Held**
SIC: 3999 Pet supplies

(G-16232)
LYON LLC
13571 Il Highway 133 (61944-6953)
PHONE.................................217 465-6321
Roe Davidson, *President*
EMP: 3 EST: 2015
SALES (est): 519K **Privately Held**
SIC: 2542 Partitions & fixtures, except wood

(G-16233)
M & B SERVICES LTD INC
213 E Union St (61944-1810)
P.O. Box 1058 (61944-5058)
PHONE.................................217 463-2162
Michael J Bradley, *President*
EMP: 17
SALES (est): 1.5MM **Privately Held**
SIC: 3471 Electroplating of metals or formed products

(G-16234)
MECO COMPANY LLC
Also Called: Aerogen-Tek
2121 S Main St (61944-2965)
PHONE.................................217 465-5620
Alan Minnick, *Engineer*
Tim Hough,
EMP: 32
SALES (est): 35MM **Privately Held**
SIC: 3444 Sheet metalwork
PA: Cornerstone Capital
100 Wilshire Blvd # 1000
Santa Monica CA 90401
310 499-5670

(G-16235)
MORGAN ROBT INC
1914 S Central Ave (61944)
P.O. Box 877 (61944-0877)
PHONE.................................217 466-4777
Robert Morgan, *President*
Cathy Morgan, *Corp Secy*
▼ EMP: 40
SALES (est): 6.3MM **Privately Held**
SIC: 2048 Livestock feeds

Paris - Edgar County (G-16236)

(G-16236)
NORTH AMERICAN LIGHTING INC
2277 S Main St (61944-2963)
PHONE..................217 465-7800
Kem Cooley, *Manager*
EMP: 400 **Privately Held**
SIC: 3647 Automotive lighting fixtures
HQ: North American Lighting, Inc.
2275 S Main St
Paris IL 61944
217 465-6600

(G-16237)
NORTH AMERICAN LIGHTING INC (HQ)
2275 S Main St (61944-2963)
PHONE..................217 465-6600
Takashi Ohtake, *CEO*
Jun Toyota, *President*
Mike Harness, *General Mgr*
Randy Snyder, *General Mgr*
Ron Wheat, *General Mgr*
▲ **EMP:** 1000
SQ FT: 400,000
SALES (est): 1.4B **Privately Held**
SIC: 3647 Automotive lighting fixtures

(G-16238)
PARIS MACHINE & WELDING
13005 Illinois Hwy 133 (61944)
PHONE..................217 463-2894
Dale Martin, *Owner*
Russ Lawton, *General Mgr*
EMP: 4
SALES: 150K **Privately Held**
WEB: www.lawtons.com
SIC: 1799 3599 Welding on site; machine shop, jobbing & repair

(G-16239)
PARIS METAL PRODUCTS LLC
13571 Il Highway 133 (61944-6953)
PHONE..................217 465-6321
Corey Risden,
EMP: 76
SQ FT: 200,000
SALES (est): 12.5MM **Privately Held**
SIC: 3469 Boxes: tool, lunch, mail, etc.: stamped metal

(G-16240)
PRINTERS INK OF PARIS INC
Also Called: Printers The
124 W Court St (61944-1735)
PHONE..................217 463-2552
Carole Berl, *President*
EMP: 2
SALES (est): 225K **Privately Held**
SIC: 2752 5199 Commercial printing, offset; advertising specialties

(G-16241)
PVC CONTAINER CORPORATION
Also Called: Novapack
2015 S Main St (61944-2961)
PHONE..................217 463-6600
Dojai Hill, *Manager*
EMP: 150
SALES (corp-wide): 868.8MM **Privately Held**
SIC: 3085 Plastics bottles
HQ: Pvc Container Corporation
15450 South Outer 40 Rd # 12
Chesterfield MO 63017
732 542-0060

(G-16242)
QUANEX SCREENS LLC
13323 Illinois Hwy 133 (61944)
PHONE..................217 463-2233
Jeff Willaman, *Branch Mgr*
EMP: 8 **Publicly Held**
WEB: www.quanex.com
SIC: 3442 Screen doors, metal
HQ: Quanex Screens Llc
1800 West Loop S Ste 1500
Houston TX 77027
713 961-4600

(G-16243)
SECRETARY OF STATE ILLINOIS
714 Grandview St (61944-2039)
PHONE..................217 466-5220
EMP: 5 **Privately Held**
WEB: www.cyberdriveillinois.com
SIC: 3469 Automobile license tags, stamped metal
HQ: Secretary Of State, Illinois
213 State House
Springfield IL 62706
217 782-2201

(G-16244)
SIMONTON BUILDING PRODUCTS INC
Also Called: Simonton Windows
13263 Il Highway 133 (61944-6701)
PHONE..................217 466-2851
Fax: 217 465-2854
EMP: 350
SALES (corp-wide): 64.4MM **Privately Held**
SIC: 3089 Manufactures Window Products
HQ: Simonton Building Products, Inc.
5300 Briscoe Rd
Parkersburg WV 26105
304 659-2851

(G-16245)
TRIVAEO LLC
1 Regina Dr (61944-8502)
PHONE..................760 505-4751
Pat Graham, *President*
Mark Graham,
Connie Helton,
EMP: 3 **EST:** 2016
SALES (est): 104.1K **Privately Held**
SIC: 7371 7372 Computer software development & applications; business oriented computer software

(G-16246)
WHITE SHEET METAL
303 N Austin St (61944-1315)
PHONE..................217 465-3195
John White, *Owner*
Cheryl White, *Partner*
EMP: 3
SALES (est): 180.6K **Privately Held**
SIC: 1711 7623 3444 Boiler & furnace contractors; air conditioning repair; sheet metalwork

(G-16247)
YOTTA PET PRODUCTS INC
1977 S Central Ave (61944-2700)
P.O. Box 877 (61944-0877)
PHONE..................217 466-4777
Robert Morgan, *President*
EMP: 10
SALES (est): 646.8K **Privately Held**
SIC: 2047 Dog food

Park City
Lake County

(G-16248)
WILSON RAILING & METAL FABG CO
640 Wilson Ave (60085-5741)
PHONE..................847 662-1747
Steve Albert, *President*
Bruce Chevrette, *Sales Staff*
Gary Kratz, *Office Mgr*
EMP: 8
SQ FT: 3,200
SALES (est): 1.2MM **Privately Held**
SIC: 5999 3446 Alcoholic beverage making equipment & supplies; railings, bannisters, guards, etc.: made from metal pipe

Park Forest
Cook County

(G-16249)
ACS PARTS GROUP LLC
129 Hemlock St (60466-2117)
PHONE..................815 211-4707
EMP: 8
SALES (est): 299.2K **Privately Held**
SIC: 3728 Aircraft parts & equipment

(G-16250)
AGRATI INC (DH)
24000 S Western Ave (60466-3428)
PHONE..................704 747-1200
Phil Johnson, *President*
Mark Mariska, *Plant Mgr*
Chuck Beto, *CFO*
EMP: 1
SALES (est): 1.6MM **Privately Held**
SIC: 6719 3965 Investment holding companies, except banks; fasteners
HQ: A. Agrati Spa
Via Piave 28
Veduggio Con Colzano MB 20837
036 291-0863

(G-16251)
AGRATI - PARK FOREST LLC (DH)
Also Called: Continental/Midland, LLC
24000 S Western Ave (60466-3428)
PHONE..................708 228-5193
Philip Johnson, *CEO*
Fred Rake, *Vice Pres*
Anderson Gene, *Opers Mgr*
Ken Breiner, *Warehouse Mgr*
Tony Rivera, *Mfg Spvr*
EMP: 250
SALES (est): 280.5MM **Privately Held**
SIC: 3452 Screws, metal
HQ: Agrati, Inc.
24000 S Western Ave
Park Forest IL 60466
704 747-1200

(G-16252)
AGRATI USA CORP
24000 S Western Ave (60466-3428)
PHONE..................708 228-5193
Philip Johnson, *CEO*
Charles Beto, *CFO*
EMP: 500
SALES (est): 26.6MM **Privately Held**
SIC: 3452 Bolts, metal
HQ: A. Agrati Spa
Via Piave 28
Veduggio Con Colzano MB 20837
036 291-0863

(G-16253)
CONNIES HOME HEALTH CARE
453 Saugatuck St (60466-2208)
P.O. Box 164 (60466-0164)
PHONE..................708 790-4000
Linda Broadway, *Owner*
Ernest Broadway, *Co-Owner*
EMP: 5
SALES (est): 183.9K **Privately Held**
SIC: 8082 2759 3579 7374 Home health care services; business forms: printing; mailing, letter handling & addressing machines; data entry service; mailing service; business college or school

(G-16254)
CONTMID INC
24000 S Western Ave (60466-3428)
PHONE..................708 747-1200
Phil Johnson, *President*
Mike Delfin, *Vice Pres*
Fred Rake, *Vice Pres*
Doyle Tuttle, *QC Mgr*
Chuck Beto, *CFO*
EMP: 9
SALES (est): 329.8K **Privately Held**
SIC: 3452 Bolts, nuts, rivets & washers
HQ: Agrati, Inc.
24000 S Western Ave
Park Forest IL 60466
704 747-1200

(G-16255)
IMAGEWORKS MANUFACTURING INC
Also Called: Shipshapes Brands
49 South St (60466-1241)
PHONE..................708 503-1122
Thomas Becker, *President*
Tom Johnson, *Vice Pres*
Tiffany Narwick-Krivos, *Vice Pres*
Mark Zickert, *Vice Pres*
Tiffany Narwick, *VP Bus Dvlpt*
EMP: 45 **EST:** 1966
SQ FT: 35,000
SALES (est): 16MM **Privately Held**
WEB: www.imageworksmfg.com
SIC: 3577 3993 3442 3354 Computer peripheral equipment; signs & advertising specialties; name plates: except engraved, etched, etc.: metal; metal doors, sash & trim; aluminum extruded products

(G-16256)
JAI-S RECORD LABEL
22011 Central Park Ave (60466-1504)
PHONE..................708 351-4279
Jessica Hill, *Principal*
EMP: 4
SALES (est): 50K **Privately Held**
SIC: 3663 Studio equipment, radio & television broadcasting

(G-16257)
MARKHAM DIVISION 9 INC
2213 W Wolpers Rd (60466-3424)
PHONE..................708 503-0657
Tammie Cerf, *President*
Vern Paul, *Vice Pres*
Marc Cerf, *Admin Sec*
EMP: 25
SALES (est): 1.5MM **Privately Held**
SIC: 3589 Commercial cleaning equipment

(G-16258)
PURPLE ONYX LLC
420 N Orchard Dr (60466-1174)
PHONE..................708 756-1500
Kirby Ashley, *Manager*
EMP: 2 **EST:** 2001
SALES (est): 208.8K **Privately Held**
SIC: 3861 Motion picture film

(G-16259)
RONALD J NIXON
Also Called: Champion Silkscreen & EMB
56 South St (60466-1206)
PHONE..................708 748-8130
Sanford Nixon, *Manager*
EMP: 9
SALES (corp-wide): 867.2K **Privately Held**
SIC: 5136 2396 2395 Sportswear, men's & boys'; automotive & apparel trimmings; pleating & stitching
PA: Ronald J Nixon
2135 183rd St Ste 1
Homewood IL 60430
708 799-0240

(G-16260)
SOUTHLAND PAINTING
316 Forest Blvd (60466-2005)
PHONE..................833 724-6803
Tasha M Brown, *Principal*
Excell Brown Jr, *Principal*
EMP: 3
SALES (est): 113.9K **Privately Held**
SIC: 1742 1721 3253 1751 Plastering, drywall & insulation; painting & paper hanging; ceramic wall & floor tile; carpentry work

(G-16261)
WEI TO ASSOCIATES INC
224 Early St (60466-1216)
PHONE..................708 747-6660
Richard Daniel Smith, *President*
EMP: 6 **EST:** 1972
SQ FT: 3,600
SALES (est): 856.8K **Privately Held**
SIC: 3559 Chemical machinery & equipment

GEOGRAPHIC SECTION

Park Ridge
Cook County

(G-16262)
AANA PUBLISHING INC
222 S Prospect Ave (60068-4001)
PHONE..................847 692-7050
Christopher Betton, *President*
William Yeo, *Treasurer*
Luanne Irvin, *Officer*
EMP: 2
SALES (est): 900K
SALES (corp-wide): 23.8MM **Privately Held**
SIC: 2721 Trade journals: publishing only, not printed on site
PA: American Association Of Nurse Anesthetists
  222 S Prospect Ave
  Park Ridge IL 60068
  847 692-7050

(G-16263)
ADEL TOOL CO LLP
1516 Marguerite St (60068-1935)
PHONE..................708 867-8530
Casimir C Sobczak, *Partner*
Dorothy M Sobczak, *Partner*
EMP: 3 EST: 1954
SALES (est): 343.6K **Privately Held**
WEB: www.adelnibbler.com
SIC: 3423 Hand & edge tools

(G-16264)
ADVANCED TECHNOLOGIES INC
Also Called: Tekvend
310 Busse Hwy Ste 241 (60068-3251)
PHONE..................847 329-9875
Bob Mahoney, *President*
Vic Schlagman, *Vice Pres*
EMP: 5
SQ FT: 1,500
SALES: 610K **Privately Held**
SIC: 3679 3581 3823 3625 Harness assemblies for electronic use: wire or cable; mechanisms for coin-operated machines; industrial instrmnts msrmnt display/control process variable; relays & industrial controls

(G-16265)
AIRES PRESS INC
227 Murphy Lake Ln (60068-2832)
PHONE..................847 698-6813
William B Hameder, *President*
EMP: 5
SQ FT: 9,000
SALES (est): 410K **Privately Held**
SIC: 2752 Commercial printing, offset

(G-16266)
ALBERT WHITMAN & COMPANY
250 S Northwest Hwy # 320 (60068-4237)
PHONE..................847 232-2800
John Quattrocchi, *President*
Pat McPartland, *Vice Pres*
Patrick McPartland, *Vice Pres*
Sue Funari, *Supervisor*
Michelle Binks, *Administration*
▲ EMP: 23 EST: 1919
SQ FT: 20,000
SALES (est): 3.3MM **Privately Held**
WEB: www.albertwhitman.com
SIC: 2731 Books: publishing only

(G-16267)
ARBOR PRODUCTS
614 Wisner St (60068-3429)
PHONE..................847 653-6210
EMP: 4
SALES (est): 330.2K **Privately Held**
SIC: 2899 Mfg Chemical Preparations

(G-16268)
ASPEN FOODS INC
1300 Higgins Rd Ste 100 (60068-5766)
PHONE..................312 829-7282
Michael Fields, *President*
EMP: 150 EST: 1995
SQ FT: 45,000
SALES (est): 29.1MM
SALES (corp-wide): 2.2B **Privately Held**
SIC: 2015 Chicken, processed: fresh; chicken, processed: frozen; turkey, processed: fresh
HQ: Koch Meat Co., Inc.
  1300 Higgins Rd Ste 100
  Park Ridge IL 60068
  847 384-8018

(G-16269)
ATBC LLC
1580 N Northwest Hwy (60068-1444)
PHONE..................847 648-2822
Alex Mindich, *Principal*
EMP: 2
SALES (est): 214.1K **Privately Held**
SIC: 3535 Conveyors & conveying equipment

(G-16270)
BELLISARIO HOLDINGS LLC
117 Elmore St (60068-3519)
PHONE..................847 867-2960
Paul Bellisario,
Laura Bellisario,
EMP: 3
SALES: 300K **Privately Held**
SIC: 2099 Baking soda

(G-16271)
BOUND + D TERMINED INC
60 S Dee Rd Apt E (60068-3731)
PHONE..................847 696-1501
Janis M Boehm, *President*
▲ EMP: 3
SALES (est): 365.7K **Privately Held**
WEB: www.bound-determined.com
SIC: 2782 Scrapbooks, albums & diaries

(G-16272)
CASEY SPRING CO INC
1516 Marguerite St (60068-1935)
PHONE..................708 867-8949
Dorothy M Sobczak, *President*
Donna Barone, *Vice Pres*
EMP: 12 EST: 1957
SALES (est): 2.1MM **Privately Held**
WEB: www.caseyspring.com
SIC: 3493 3496 Coiled flat springs; miscellaneous fabricated wire products

(G-16273)
DIE CAST QUALITY SERVICES INC
438 S Dee Rd (60068-3738)
PHONE..................708 582-3584
Melany McCann, *CEO*
EMP: 5
SALES (est): 270.1K **Privately Held**
SIC: 3599 Machine shop, jobbing & repair

(G-16274)
FEDEX OFFICE & PRINT SVCS INC
678 N Northwest Hwy (60068-2540)
PHONE..................847 823-9360
EMP: 7
SALES (corp-wide): 69.6B **Publicly Held**
SIC: 7334 2791 2789 Photocopying & duplicating services; typesetting; bookbinding & related work
HQ: Fedex Office And Print Services, Inc.
  7900 Legacy Dr
  Plano TX 75024
  800 463-3339

(G-16275)
FEELSURE HEALTH CORPARATION
120 Columbia Ave (60068-4922)
PHONE..................847 823-0137
William Bartlett, *President*
Jim Habschmidt, *President*
EMP: 3
SALES (est): 176.4K **Privately Held**
SIC: 3841 Diagnostic apparatus, medical

(G-16276)
FOOD SERVICE PUBLISHING CO
1440 Renaissance Dr # 210 (60068-1356)
PHONE..................847 699-3300
Valerie Miller, *President*
EMP: 7
SALES (est): 159.2K **Privately Held**
SIC: 2741 Miscellaneous publishing

(G-16277)
FULLING MOTOR USA INC
1601 Park Ridge Pt (60068-1309)
P.O. Box 1101 (60068-7101)
PHONE..................847 894-6238
Brian Ranallo, *President*
Hanrong Zhang, *Treasurer*
Yufei Wang, *Admin Sec*
▲ EMP: 2
SQ FT: 1,000
SALES (est): 213.2K **Privately Held**
SIC: 3621 Collector rings, for electric motors or generators

(G-16278)
FUSION CHEMICAL CORPORATION
350 S Northwest Hwy # 300 (60068-4262)
PHONE..................847 656-5285
EMP: 3
SALES (est): 190.5K **Privately Held**
SIC: 2819 Industrial inorganic chemicals

(G-16279)
GAMMA ALPHA VISUAL COMMUNICATN
Also Called: AlphaGraphics
642 Busse Hwy (60068-2502)
PHONE..................847 956-0633
Gregory J Poulos, *Mng Member*
EMP: 7
SALES (est): 777.7K **Privately Held**
SIC: 2752 2791 2789 Commercial printing, lithographic; typesetting; bookbinding & related work

(G-16280)
GENERAL BANDAGES INC
717 N Washington Ave (60068-2716)
PHONE..................847 966-8383
John D Hinkamp, *President*
Philip Hinkamp, *Corp Secy*
Jim Hinkamp, *Vice Pres*
EMP: 19 EST: 1935
SQ FT: 20,000
SALES (est): 2.5MM **Privately Held**
WEB: www.generalbandages.com
SIC: 3842 5047 Adhesive tape & plasters, medicated or non-medicated; gauze, surgical; tape, adhesive: medicated or non-medicated; medical equipment & supplies

(G-16281)
GRAPHIC SCORE BOOK CO INC
306 Busse Hwy (60068-3251)
PHONE..................847 823-7382
William Smyrthe, *President*
EMP: 4
SALES (est): 210K **Privately Held**
SIC: 2731 5942 Books: publishing & printing; book stores

(G-16282)
GREAT LAKES LUMBER AND PALLET
2137 N Home Ave (60068-1021)
PHONE..................773 243-6839
EMP: 6 EST: 2015
SALES (est): 395.1K **Privately Held**
SIC: 2448 Pallets, wood & wood with metal

(G-16283)
HOMECONTROLPLUS INCORPORATED
1884 Fenton Ln (60068-1502)
PHONE..................847 823-8414
Jasna Ostojich, *President*
EMP: 2
SALES (est): 239.1K **Privately Held**
SIC: 3822 Auto controls regulating residntl & coml environmt & applncs

(G-16284)
HOORAY PUREE INC
310 Busse Hwy Ste 322 (60068-3251)
PHONE..................312 515-0266
Krista Ward, *CEO*
EMP: 5
SQ FT: 80,000
SALES (est): 430.4K **Privately Held**
SIC: 2033 Vegetable purees: packaged in cans, jars, etc.

(G-16285)
INTERRA GLOBAL CORPORATION
800 Busse Hwy Ste 101 (60068-2300)
P.O. Box 101 (60068-0101)
PHONE..................847 292-8600
William Wallace, *President*
Sara Curry, *Opers Staff*
Bill Wallace, *VP Sales*
Ron Naiser, *Business Dir*
Jason Skiersch, *Admin Sec*
◆ EMP: 11
SQ FT: 2,500
SALES (est): 9MM **Privately Held**
WEB: www.interraglobal.com
SIC: 5169 2899 2819 Industrial chemicals; chemical preparations; water treating compounds; aluminum compounds; silica gel

(G-16286)
JCG INDUSTRIES INC
Also Called: Aspen Foods
1300 Higgins Rd Ste 100 (60068-5766)
PHONE..................312 829-7282
Micheal Fields, *President*
EMP: 150
SALES (est): 12.2MM **Privately Held**
SIC: 2015 Chicken, processed: fresh; chicken, processed: frozen; turkey, processed: fresh
PA: Jcg Industries, Inc.
  4404 W Berteau Ave
  Chicago IL 60641

(G-16287)
LEGACY INTERNATIONAL ASSOC LLC
1420 Park Ridge Blvd (60068-5042)
PHONE..................847 823-1602
William Ristau, *President*
Pattie Risau, *Marketing Staff*
Mike Boychuck, *Manager*
Katie Ristau, *Analyst*
EMP: 6
SALES (est): 514.7K **Privately Held**
SIC: 3317 Steel pipe & tubes

(G-16288)
MORNINGFIELDS
800 Devon Ave Ste 7 (60068-4760)
PHONE..................847 309-8460
Marilyn Schuman, *Principal*
EMP: 9
SALES (est): 780.6K **Privately Held**
SIC: 2051 Cakes, bakery: except frozen

(G-16289)
NANTSOUND INC
Also Called: Sound World Solutions
960 N Northwest Hwy (60068-2358)
PHONE..................847 939-6101
Stavros P Basseas, *President*
Wayne Bayever, *Vice Pres*
Shawn Stahmer, *Vice Pres*
▲ EMP: 10
SALES (est): 1.8MM **Privately Held**
SIC: 3651 Amplifiers: radio, public address or musical instrument

(G-16290)
NICE CARD COMPANY
803 S Aldine Ave (60068-4416)
PHONE..................773 467-8450
Christopher Kean, *President*
EMP: 5
SQ FT: 2,000
SALES (est): 200K **Privately Held**
SIC: 2741 Miscellaneous publishing

(G-16291)
PALLETS PLUS INC
1000 Cedar St (60068-3203)
PHONE..................847 318-1853
Frank P Falzone, *Principal*
EMP: 4
SALES (est): 542K **Privately Held**
SIC: 2448 Pallets, wood

(G-16292)
PILOT CORPORATION OF AMERICA
1300 Higgins Rd Ste 214 (60068-5766)
PHONE..................773 792-1111
Jim Matese, *Vice Pres*

Park Ridge - Cook County (G-16293)

Mark Puppolo, *Sales Staff*
EMP: 3 **Privately Held**
SIC: 3951 Pens & mechanical pencils
HQ: Pilot Corporation Of America
3855 Regent Blvd
Jacksonville FL 32224
904 565-7600

(G-16293)
QUINN PRINT INC
508 Higgins Rd (60068-5732)
PHONE 847 823-9100
Eugene Walker, *President*
Mike Quinn, *Vice Pres*
EMP: 5
SQ FT: 1,600
SALES (est): 582.3K **Privately Held**
SIC: 2752 2791 2789 Commercial printing, offset; typesetting; bookbinding & related work

(G-16294)
ROYAL STAIRS CO
98 East Ave (60068-3504)
PHONE 847 685-9448
Krystyna Hryszko, *Principal*
EMP: 3
SALES (est): 247.7K **Privately Held**
SIC: 3446 Stairs, staircases, stair treads: prefabricated metal

(G-16295)
RUSSELL ENTERPRISES INC (PA)
865 Busse Hwy (60068-2359)
PHONE 847 692-6050
Richard Mathes, *President*
Don Popernik, *Corp Secy*
EMP: 500
SALES (est): 27.5MM **Privately Held**
SIC: 6141 8249 3743 3321 Personal finance licensed loan companies, small; trade school; freight cars & equipment; ductile iron castings; gray iron castings

(G-16296)
SOLARI R MFG JEWELERS
Also Called: Solari and Huntington
100 1/2 Main St (60068-4030)
PHONE 847 823-4354
Robert Solari, *Owner*
EMP: 6
SQ FT: 2,000
SALES (est): 616.6K **Privately Held**
SIC: 5944 3961 Jewelry, precious stones & precious metals; costume jewelry

(G-16297)
STRAUSS FACTER ASSOC INC
Also Called: 4 Seasons Sales and Marketing
1440 Renaissance Dr (60068-1356)
PHONE 847 759-1100
▲ **EMP:** 4 **EST:** 1975
SALES (est): 299.5K **Privately Held**
SIC: 3721 Mfg Aircraft

(G-16298)
SUBURBAN FIX & INSTALLATION
420 S Fairview Ave (60068-4753)
PHONE 847 823-4047
Robert Tamburrino, *President*
Martin K Sullivan, *Vice Pres*
Patricia G Tamburrino, *Vice Pres*
Marty Sullivan, *Manager*
EMP: 2
SALES (est): 1.5MM **Privately Held**
WEB: www.suburbanfixtures.com
SIC: 2541 1751 Store & office display cases & fixtures; store fixture installation

(G-16299)
TANCHER CORP
1493 Vernon Ave (60068-1593)
PHONE 847 668-8765
Mark Menarick, *CEO*
Joshua Barmey, *COO*
Anton Tyurin, *CFO*
Aleksey Voitovich, *Administration*
EMP: 15
SALES: 400K **Privately Held**
SIC: 3661 Telephones & telephone apparatus

(G-16300)
UNION STREET TIN CO
350 S Northwest Hwy (60068-4216)
PHONE 312 379-8200
John B Powers, *President*
▲ **EMP:** 8
SALES (est): 786K **Privately Held**
SIC: 3053 Packing, metallic

(G-16301)
UNITED RAWHIDE MFG CO
1315 Linden Ave (60068-5523)
PHONE 847 692-2791
Stefan F Palansky, *President*
Chester R Davis Jr, *Admin Sec*
EMP: 6 **EST:** 1950
SQ FT: 3,000
SALES (est): 510K **Privately Held**
SIC: 3111 Rawhide

Patoka
Marion County

(G-16302)
ARCHER-DANIELS-MIDLAND COMPANY
Also Called: ADM
408 S Railroad St (62875)
PHONE 618 432-7194
Scott Sporleder, *Branch Mgr*
EMP: 3
SALES (corp-wide): 64.6B **Publicly Held**
SIC: 2041 2048 Flour & other grain mill products; prepared feeds
PA: Archer-Daniels-Midland Company
77 W Wacker Dr Ste 4600
Chicago IL 60601
312 634-8100

(G-16303)
FOLTZ WELDING LTD
501 E Clinton Ave (62875-1153)
PHONE 618 432-7777
Jeff Foltz, *President*
EMP: 150
SQ FT: 1,800
SALES (est): 42.5MM **Privately Held**
SIC: 1389 1623 Pipe testing, oil field service; water, sewer & utility lines

Pawnee
Sangamon County

(G-16304)
HARSCO CORPORATION
226 E 1640 Rd (62558)
P.O. Box 652 (62558-0652)
PHONE 217 237-4335
Hary Marcorees, *Office Mgr*
EMP: 12
SALES (corp-wide): 1.5B **Publicly Held**
SIC: 3295 3291 2952 Minerals, ground or treated; abrasive products; asphalt felts & coatings
PA: Harsco Corporation
350 Poplar Church Rd
Camp Hill PA 17011
717 763-7064

(G-16305)
PINS & NEEDLES CONSINGMENT
7580 N Pawnee Rd (62558-4624)
PHONE 217 299-7365
Sally Neumann, *Partner*
EMP: 3
SALES (est): 213.3K **Privately Held**
SIC: 3452 Pins

(G-16306)
SLF MOTION LLC
1500 Horse Creek Trl (62558-4523)
PHONE 217 891-8384
Young Blake, *Principal*
EMP: 2 **EST:** 2016
SALES (est): 225.7K **Privately Held**
SIC: 3714 Motor vehicle parts & accessories

Paxton
Ford County

(G-16307)
BEE BOAT CO INC
209 E Green St (60957-1701)
P.O. Box 245 (60957-0245)
PHONE 217 379-2605
Philip Raymond Diskin, *President*
Dorcas Diskin, *Admin Sec*
EMP: 2
SQ FT: 30,000
SALES (est): 283K **Privately Held**
SIC: 3089 7699 Plastic boats & other marine equipment; boat repair

(G-16308)
HTS HANCOCK TRANSCRIPTIONS SVC (PA)
Also Called: Picket Fence Florist
136 S Market St (60957-1222)
PHONE 217 379-9241
Teri Hancock, *Owner*
EMP: 20
SALES (est): 1.5MM **Privately Held**
SIC: 2752 5992 Commercial printing, lithographic; florists

(G-16309)
NEXSTEP COMMERCIAL PDTS LLC
Also Called: Ncp Commercial
1450 W Ottawa Rd (60957-4205)
P.O. Box 71 (60957-0071)
PHONE 217 379-2377
Todd Leventhal,
Travis Deck, *Maintence Staff*
Stanley Koschnick,
◆ **EMP:** 8
SALES (est): 1.9MM **Privately Held**
SIC: 3991 Brooms & brushes

(G-16310)
NEXSTEP COMMERCIAL PRODUCTS
1450 W Ottawa Rd (60957-4205)
PHONE 217 379-2377
Todd Leventhal, *Principal*
Jeff Stewart, *Sales Staff*
EMP: 4
SALES (est): 230K **Privately Held**
SIC: 3423 Hand & edge tools

(G-16311)
O-CEDAR COMMERCIAL
131 N Railroad Ave (60957-1358)
P.O. Box 71 (60957-0071)
PHONE 217 379-2377
Frank Schossler, *Principal*
Bill Bouras, *Sales Staff*
EMP: 2 **EST:** 2011
SALES (est): 210K **Privately Held**
WEB: www.ocedarcommercial.com
SIC: 3532 Cleaning machinery, mineral

(G-16312)
PAXTON PACKING LLC
Also Called: Big Frontire
145 W State St (60957-1143)
PHONE 623 707-5604
Glen Kerby,
Tony Alford,
EMP: 11
SQ FT: 18,000
SALES (est): 1.1MM **Privately Held**
SIC: 2011 Meat packing plants

(G-16313)
PAXTON READY MIX INC
745 N Market St (60957-1023)
P.O. Box 177 (60957-0177)
PHONE 217 379-2303
Gregory Whitcomb, *President*
Carol Whitcomb, *Corp Secy*
Terry Whitcomb, *Vice Pres*
EMP: 8
SQ FT: 800
SALES (est): 1.3MM **Privately Held**
WEB: www.paxtonreadymix.com
SIC: 3273 Ready-mixed concrete

(G-16314)
PLASTIC DESIGNS INC
Also Called: AG Solutions
1330 S Vermillion St (60957-1700)
PHONE 217 379-9214
Steven G Glazik, *President*
Craig Coy, *Project Engr*
Bonnie Harrison, *Manager*
D Marcus Decker, *Admin Sec*
Gary B Glazik, *Admin Sec*
EMP: 35
SQ FT: 50,000
SALES: 5MM **Privately Held**
SIC: 3089 Molding primary plastic; injection molding of plastics

(G-16315)
PRO-TYPE PRINTING INC (PA)
130 N Market St (60957-1220)
PHONE 217 379-4715
Robin Niewold, *Principal*
EMP: 8
SALES (est): 725.1K **Privately Held**
SIC: 2752 2791 2789 Commercial printing, offset; typesetting; bookbinding & related work

(G-16316)
SOUTHFIELD CORPORATION
100 N 2280e Rd (60957-4186)
PHONE 217 379-3606
Eric Mills, *Manager*
EMP: 5
SALES (corp-wide): 344.9MM **Privately Held**
SIC: 1442 Common sand mining
PA: Southfield Corporation
8995 W 95th St
Palos Hills IL 60465
708 344-1000

Payson
Adams County

(G-16317)
PITTSFIELD MCH TL & WLDG CO
306 W State St (62360-1188)
PHONE 217 656-4000
Johnnie Leithoff, *President*
Darlene Leithoff, *Corp Secy*
EMP: 3 **EST:** 1964
SQ FT: 10,500
SALES (est): 344.7K **Privately Held**
SIC: 3599 3441 3444 Machine shop, jobbing & repair; fabricated structural metal; sheet metalwork

Pearl
Pike County

(G-16318)
MARTHA LACEY
Also Called: Lacey-Bauer
47424 212th Ave (62361-2016)
P.O. Box 53, Milton (62352-0053)
PHONE 217 723-4380
Martha Lacey, *Owner*
EMP: 3 **EST:** 1945
SQ FT: 600
SALES (est): 125K **Privately Held**
SIC: 1422 Crushed & broken limestone

Pearl City
Stephenson County

(G-16319)
EGGOLOGY INC
968 S Kent Rd (61062-9170)
PHONE 818 610-2222
Tony Gryack, *President*
Carl Orsorahage, *Vice Pres*
▲ **EMP:** 14
SQ FT: 4,500
SALES (est): 2.5MM **Privately Held**
SIC: 2015 2844 Egg substitutes made from eggs; toilet preparations

GEOGRAPHIC SECTION

Pecatonica
Winnebago County

(G-16320)
ANPEC INDUSTRIES INC
216 Main St (61063-9195)
P.O. Box 539 (61063-0539)
PHONE..................................815 239-2303
Douglas Allen, *President*
Brad Wagner, *Vice Pres*
EMP: 35 **EST:** 1968
SQ FT: 24,000
SALES (est): 6.9MM **Privately Held**
WEB: www.anpecindustries.com
SIC: 3599 Machine shop, jobbing & repair

(G-16321)
BAY VALLEY FOODS LLC
215 W 3rd St (61063-7001)
P.O. Box 359 (61063-0359)
PHONE..................................815 239-2631
Wade Deke, *Business Mgr*
Kristina Meneses, *Business Mgr*
William Vincent, *Business Mgr*
Brian Perry, *Vice Pres*
Craig Treankler, *Vice Pres*
EMP: 100
SALES (corp-wide): 4.2B **Publicly Held**
WEB: www.bayvalleyfoods.com
SIC: 2023 2026 Cream substitutes; fluid milk
HQ: Bay Valley Foods, Llc
3200 Riverside Dr Ste A
Green Bay WI 54301
800 558-4700

(G-16322)
IPSEN INC
Ipsen Ceramics Div
325 John St (61063-7735)
PHONE..................................815 239-2385
John Menne, *Principal*
Brenda Elliot, *Supervisor*
EMP: 20
SQ FT: 30,703
SALES (corp-wide): 240MM **Privately Held**
WEB: www.ipsenusa.com
SIC: 3269 3567 3297 3433 Laboratory & industrial pottery; industrial furnaces & ovens; nonclay refractories; heating equipment, except electric; nonferrous foundries
HQ: Ipsen, Inc.
984 Ipsen Rd
Cherry Valley IL 61016
815 332-4941

Pekin
Tazewell County

(G-16323)
AMERICAN MILLING COMPANY
1811 American St (61554-5419)
PHONE..................................309 347-6888
Stan Walshman, *Manager*
EMP: 12
SALES (corp-wide): 28.5MM **Privately Held**
SIC: 5191 2041 Feed; flour & other grain mill products
PA: The American Milling Company
3 Cargill Rd
Cahokia IL 62206
618 337-8877

(G-16324)
AVENTINE RNWBLE ENRGY HLDNGS L (HQ)
1300 S 2nd St (61554-5402)
PHONE..................................309 347-9200
Mark Beemer, *CEO*
Brian Steenhard, *CFO*
EMP: 32
SALES (est): 72.2MM
SALES (corp-wide): 1.4B **Publicly Held**
SIC: 2869 Ethyl alcohol, ethanol
PA: Pacific Ethanol, Inc.
400 Capitol Mall Ste 2060
Sacramento CA 95814
916 403-2123

(G-16325)
CITY OF PEKIN
Also Called: Street Dept
1208 Koch St (61554-5936)
PHONE..................................309 477-2325
John Abel, *Vice Chairman*
David Pagliaro, *Branch Mgr*
EMP: 16 **Privately Held**
SIC: 3648 9111 Street lighting fixtures; mayors' offices
PA: City Of Pekin
111 S Capitol St Ste 200
Pekin IL 61554
309 477-2300

(G-16326)
CONTINENTAL CARBONIC PDTS INC
140 Distillery Rd (61554-4075)
PHONE..................................309 346-7515
Tim Pleasant, *Branch Mgr*
EMP: 38 **Privately Held**
WEB: www.continentalcarbonic.com
SIC: 5169 2813 Dry ice; industrial gases
HQ: Continental Carbonic Products, Inc.
3985 E Harrison Ave
Decatur IL 62526
217 428-2068

(G-16327)
DCX-CHOL ENTERPRISES INC
Elecsys Division of Dcx-Chol
225 Enterprise Dr (61554-9311)
PHONE..................................309 353-4455
Mike Jamison, *General Mgr*
EMP: 50
SALES (corp-wide): 120.5MM **Privately Held**
WEB: www.dcxchol.com
SIC: 3671 3643 Electron tubes; current-carrying wiring devices
PA: Dcx-Chol Enterprises, Inc.
12831 S Figueroa St
Los Angeles CA 90061
310 516-1692

(G-16328)
DEUCE DEVELOPMENT CORP
100 Broadway St (61554-4014)
PHONE..................................309 353-6324
Tim Glass, *President*
EMP: 5
SALES (est): 802.2K **Privately Held**
SIC: 2434 Wood kitchen cabinets

(G-16329)
DISTILLERY WINE & ALLIED
300 Mclean St (61554-4414)
PHONE..................................309 347-1444
EMP: 6
SALES (est): 205.1K **Privately Held**
SIC: 2084 Mfg Wines/Brandy/Spirits

(G-16330)
DJ ILLINOIS RIVER VALLEY CALLS
7949 State Rte 78 (61554)
PHONE..................................309 348-2112
David Jackson, *CEO*
Randy Ruskey, *Administration*
EMP: 5
SALES (est): 320.4K **Privately Held**
SIC: 3949 Game calls

(G-16331)
ENVIRO-SAFE REFRIGERANTS INC
400 Hanna Dr (61554-8719)
PHONE..................................309 346-1110
Randy Price, *Vice Pres*
Melissa A King, *Admin Sec*
◆ **EMP:** 24
SQ FT: 10,000
SALES (est): 5MM **Privately Held**
WEB: www.es-refrigerants.com
SIC: 3221 Bottles for packing, bottling & canning: glass

(G-16332)
EXCEL FOUNDRY & MACHINE INC
1 Excel Way (61554-9313)
PHONE..................................309 347-6155
Doug Parsons, *President*
EMP: 1

SALES (est): 241.5K **Privately Held**
SIC: 3366 Copper foundries

(G-16333)
FEDERAL PRISON INDUSTRIES
Also Called: Unicor
2600 S 2nd St (61554-8297)
P.O. Box 7000 (61555-7000)
PHONE..................................309 346-8588
Peter Spartz, *Manager*
EMP: 175 **Publicly Held**
SIC: 2299 3621 3546 2353 Batting, wadding, padding & fillings; motors & generators; power-driven handtools; hats, caps & millinery; brooms & brushes; correctional institutions;
HQ: Federal Prison Industries, Inc
320 1st St Nw
Washington DC 20534

(G-16334)
FLSMIDTH INC
1 Excel Way (61554-9313)
PHONE..................................309 347-3031
Jim Ulrich, *Sales Mgr*
EMP: 3
SALES (corp-wide): 3B **Privately Held**
SIC: 5084 3564 Conveyor systems; air purification equipment
HQ: Flsmidth Inc.
16002 Winfield Rd
Fraziers Bottom WV 25082
610 264-6011

(G-16335)
FLSMIDTH PEKIN LLC (DH)
Also Called: FLS Pekin
14425 Wagonseller Rd (61554-8831)
P.O. Box 188 (61555-0188)
PHONE..................................309 347-3031
Fred Gross, *Mng Member*
◆ **EMP:** 59
SALES (est): 9MM
SALES (corp-wide): 3B **Privately Held**
SIC: 3531 Rock crushing machinery, portable
HQ: Flsmidth Inc.
16002 Winfield Rd
Fraziers Bottom WV 25082
610 264-6011

(G-16336)
HANNA STEEL CORPORATION
Also Called: Pekin Division
220 Hanna Dr (61554-8793)
PHONE..................................309 478-3800
Sergio Becerra, *General Mgr*
Michael Grube, *QC Mgr*
EMP: 110
SALES (corp-wide): 2MM **Privately Held**
WEB: www.hannasteel.com
SIC: 3317 Welded pipe & tubes
PA: Hanna Steel Corporation
4527 Southlake Pkwy
Hoover AL 35244
205 820-5200

(G-16337)
HARSCO CORPORATION
13090 E Manito Rd (61554)
PHONE..................................309 347-1962
Jonathan Watt, *Manager*
EMP: 9
SALES (corp-wide): 1.5B **Publicly Held**
WEB: www.harsco.com
SIC: 1481 Nonmetallic mineral services
PA: Harsco Corporation
350 Poplar Church Rd
Camp Hill PA 17011
717 763-7064

(G-16338)
HOME SCHOOL ENRICHMENT INC
124 Thrush Ave (61554-6462)
PHONE..................................309 347-1392
Frank Lewis, *CEO*
EMP: 3
SALES: 375K **Privately Held**
SIC: 2721 Magazines: publishing & printing

(G-16339)
ILLINOIS CORN PROCESSING LLC
1301 S Front St (61554-4065)
P.O. Box 10 (61555-0010)
PHONE..................................309 353-3990
Donald Oldham, *President*
Doug Leathers, *Mfg Staff*
Don Shippy, *Controller*
Jason King, *Director*
EMP: 75
SALES (est): 131.2MM
SALES (corp-wide): 1.4B **Publicly Held**
SIC: 2869 5169 Alcohols, industrial: denatured (non-beverage); alcohols
HQ: Pacific Ethanol Central, Llc
400 Capitol Mall Ste 2060
Sacramento CA 95814
916 403-2123

(G-16340)
ILLINOIS OIL MARKETING EQP INC (PA)
850 Brenkman Dr (61554-1523)
PHONE..................................309 347-1819
Kevin Lane, *President*
Mark McLaren, *Regional Mgr*
Joyce Hale, *Corp Secy*
Ron Jaegle, *Vice Pres*
Brad Rodgers, *Vice Pres*
EMP: 44 **EST:** 1954
SQ FT: 21,000
SALES: 22.5MM **Privately Held**
WEB: www.iome.com
SIC: 3443 Tanks, standard or custom fabricated: metal plate

(G-16341)
K D L MACHINING INC
1917 S 2nd St (61554-5413)
PHONE..................................309 477-3036
Deborah Lutz, *President*
EMP: 9
SQ FT: 14,000
SALES: 400K **Privately Held**
SIC: 3599 Machine shop, jobbing & repair

(G-16342)
KEGLEY MACHINE CO
615 Main St (61554-4305)
PHONE..................................309 346-8914
Chris Kegley, *Owner*
EMP: 2
SALES (est): 220K **Privately Held**
SIC: 3599 Machine shop, jobbing & repair

(G-16343)
MANUFCTRING MINT SOLUTIONS INC
14646 Watson Rd (61554-8849)
PHONE..................................309 263-6077
James Cochran, *President*
Wendell Good, *Treasurer*
EMP: 50
SQ FT: 30,000
SALES: 9.5MM **Privately Held**
SIC: 3599 Machine shop, jobbing & repair

(G-16344)
MESSER LLC
125 Distillery Rd (61554-4082)
PHONE..................................309 353-9717
Andy Harder, *Opers Staff*
Danny Osborn, *Branch Mgr*
EMP: 40
SALES (corp-wide): 1.1B **Privately Held**
WEB: www.lindeus.com
SIC: 2813 Carbon dioxide
HQ: Messer Llc
200 Somerset Corp Blvd # 7000
Bridgewater NJ 08807
908 464-8100

(G-16345)
MGP INGREDIENTS ILLINOIS INC
1301 S Front St (61554-4065)
P.O. Box 1069 (61555-1069)
PHONE..................................309 353-3990
Cloud L Cray, *Ch of Bd*
Ladd Seaberg, *President*
Dave Wilbur, *Vice Pres*
Brian Cahill, *Admin Sec*
EMP: 190

(PA)=Parent Co (HQ)=Headquarters (DH)=Div Headquarters
○ = New Business established in last 2 years

Pekin - Tazewell County (G-16346)

SALES: 385.2K
SALES (corp-wide): 362.7MM **Publicly Held**
SIC: 2046 2869 2085 2048 Gluten feed; alcohols, industrial: denatured (non-beverage); gin (alcoholic beverage); vodka (alcoholic beverage); prepared feeds
HQ: Mgpi Processing, Inc.
100 Commercial St
Atchison KS 66002
913 367-1480

(G-16346)
MGPI PROCESSING INC
Also Called: Midwest Grain Products
1301 S Front St (61554-4065)
PHONE..................................309 353-3990
Dave Wilbur, *General Mgr*
EMP: 150
SALES (corp-wide): 362.7MM **Publicly Held**
SIC: 2869 2085 2046 Ethyl alcohol, ethanol; ethyl alcohol for beverage purposes; gluten feed; gluten meal
HQ: Mgpi Processing, Inc.
100 Commercial St
Atchison KS 66002
913 367-1480

(G-16347)
NIKLI FUELS INC
801 S 2nd St (61554-4309)
PHONE..................................309 363-2425
EMP: 4
SALES (est): 295.9K **Privately Held**
SIC: 2869 Fuels

(G-16348)
OX PAPERBOARD LLC
Also Called: Pekin Mill
1525 S 2nd St (61554-5405)
PHONE..................................309 346-4118
Jeffrey Lyman, *VP Opers*
Joshua Woiwode, *Engineer*
Gary Pelech, *Plant Engr*
Katelyn Kegley, *Human Res Mgr*
Kevin J Hayward, *Branch Mgr*
EMP: 44 **Privately Held**
SIC: 2631 Container board
PA: Ox Paperboard, Llc
331 Maple Ave
Hanover PA 17331

(G-16349)
PACIFIC ETHANOL CANTON LLC
1300 S 2nd St (61554-5402)
P.O. Box 10 (61555-0010)
PHONE..................................309 347-9200
Neil Koehler, *President*
EMP: 4
SALES (est): 292.4K **Privately Held**
SIC: 2869 Ethyl alcohol, ethanol

(G-16350)
PACIFIC ETHANOL PEKIN LLC
Also Called: Aventine Rnwble Enrgy Holdings
1300 S 2nd St (61554-5402)
PHONE..................................309 347-9200
John Castle, *President*
Mark Beemer, *President*
Ronald H Miller, *President*
Daniel R Trunfio Jr, *COO*
Brian Steenhard, *Vice Pres*
EMP: 200
SALES (est): 58.7MM
SALES (corp-wide): 1.4B **Publicly Held**
SIC: 2869 Alcohols, industrial: denatured (non-beverage); ethyl alcohol, ethanol
PA: Pacific Ethanol, Inc.
400 Capitol Mall Ste 2060
Sacramento CA 95814
916 403-2123

(G-16351)
PAL HEALTH TECHNOLOGIES INC
Also Called: Podiatry Arts Lab
1805 Riverway Dr (61554-9309)
PHONE..................................309 347-8785
Jeff Schoenfeld, *Ch of Bd*
John Bouchey, *Purchasing*
Lori Cavitt, *Human Resources*
Brett Moore, *Consultant*
Kimberly Chaney, *Executive*
▲ EMP: 100
SQ FT: 40,000
SALES (est): 19MM **Privately Held**
WEB: www.palhealth.com
SIC: 3842 8011 Braces, orthopedic; offices & clinics of medical doctors

(G-16352)
PEKIN PAPERBOARD COMPANY LP
1525 S 2nd St (61554-5405)
P.O. Box 520 (61555-0520)
PHONE..................................309 346-4118
Larry Fields, *Partner*
Timothy Michaels, *VP Opers*
EMP: 50 EST: 1993
SALES (est): 10MM **Privately Held**
WEB: www.oxpaperboard.com
SIC: 2631 Paperboard mills

(G-16353)
PEKIN SAND AND GRAVEL LLC
13018 E Manito Rd (61554-8586)
PHONE..................................309 347-8917
Derrek Henry,
EMP: 7
SALES (est): 484.3K **Privately Held**
SIC: 1442 Construction sand & gravel

(G-16354)
PR MANUFACTURING ENTPS LLC
Also Called: Pal Health Technologies II
1805 Riverway Dr (61554-9309)
PHONE..................................309 347-8785
John Bouchey, *Purch Mgr*
David M Van Allen, *CFO*
Aaron Rossi, *Mng Member*
Sarah Linn, *Director*
Rod Dare,
EMP: 50
SALES (est): 164.1K **Privately Held**
SIC: 3842 Orthopedic appliances; foot appliances, orthopedic

(G-16355)
PRAIRE STATE FLOOR COVERING
333 South St (61554-5661)
PHONE..................................309 253-5982
Stephen L Collier, *Owner*
EMP: 3
SALES (est): 25.3K **Privately Held**
SIC: 3069 Rubber floor coverings, mats & wallcoverings

(G-16356)
PRAXAIR INC
1225 S Front St (61554-4063)
PHONE..................................309 347-5575
Jim Vierling, *Branch Mgr*
EMP: 10 **Privately Held**
SIC: 2813 Industrial gases
HQ: Praxair, Inc.
10 Riverview Dr
Danbury CT 06810
203 837-2000

(G-16357)
QUIKRETE COMPANIES LLC
Also Called: Quikrete of Peoria
11150 Garman Rd (61554-8181)
PHONE..................................309 346-1184
Dean M Cornick, *Manager*
EMP: 12 **Privately Held**
SIC: 3271 3272 2951 Concrete block & brick; concrete products; asphalt paving mixtures & blocks
HQ: The Quikrete Companies Llc
5 Concourse Pkwy Ste 1900
Atlanta GA 30328
404 634-9100

(G-16358)
R L LEWIS INDUSTRIES INC (PA)
14215 Towerline Rd (61554-8725)
PHONE..................................309 353-7670
Tracy Williams, *President*
Byron Young, *COO*
Shelly Nielsen, *Admin Sec*
EMP: 39
SQ FT: 22,000
SALES (est): 6.1MM **Privately Held**
SIC: 3599 Machine shop, jobbing & repair

(G-16359)
ROANOKE CONCRETE PRODUCTS CO
1675 S 2nd St (61554-5407)
PHONE..................................309 885-0250
EMP: 4
SALES (corp-wide): 9.7MM **Privately Held**
SIC: 3273 Ready-mixed concrete
PA: Roanoke Concrete Products Co.
1275 Springbay Rd E
Peoria IL 61611
309 698-7882

(G-16360)
SG SCREEN GRAPHICS INC
840 Kennedy Dr (61554-1534)
PHONE..................................309 699-8513
Jeff Ulrich, *President*
Daniel Jones, *President*
Patricia Jones, *Corp Secy*
Scott Ulrich, *Vice Pres*
EMP: 6
SQ FT: 3,660
SALES: 850K **Privately Held**
SIC: 2759 2752 2396 2395 Screen printing; commercial printing, lithographic; automotive & apparel trimmings; embroidery & art needlework

(G-16361)
SMB TOOLROOM INC
206 Derby St (61554-5504)
P.O. Box 326 (61555-0326)
PHONE..................................309 353-7396
William Baird, *CEO*
Sherry Baird, *Corp Secy*
EMP: 5
SALES: 150K **Privately Held**
SIC: 3569 Filters

(G-16362)
SUPERIOR INDUSTRIES INC
14425 Wagonseller Rd (61554-8831)
PHONE..................................309 346-1742
EMP: 10
SALES (corp-wide): 348.2MM **Privately Held**
SIC: 3535 Conveyors & conveying equipment
PA: Superior Industries, Inc.
315 State Highway 28
Morris MN 56267
320 589-2406

(G-16363)
SYNGENTA SEEDS LLC
18356 Rte 9 (61554)
PHONE..................................309 478-3686
Tyson Walters, *Branch Mgr*
EMP: 30
SALES (corp-wide): 64.2B **Privately Held**
SIC: 2075 Soybean protein concentrates & isolates
HQ: Syngenta Seeds, Llc
11055 Wayzata Blvd
Hopkins MN 55305
612 656-8600

(G-16364)
T & J ELECTRIC COMPANY INC
Also Called: Schwartz Electrical Co
2627 Allentown Rd (61554-8403)
PHONE..................................309 347-2196
Mike Taylor, *President*
Jayme Taylor, *Corp Secy*
EMP: 15
SQ FT: 5,000
SALES: 2MM **Privately Held**
SIC: 1731 3993 General electrical contractor; electric signs

(G-16365)
TAZEWELL MACHINE WORKS INC
2015 S 2nd St (61554-5465)
P.O. Box 895 (61555-0895)
PHONE..................................309 347-3181
Mack V Cakora, *President*
Alice F Cakora, *Corp Secy*
Daniel J Rose, *Vice Pres*
Mark Pankey, *Manager*
Timothy Snyder, *Info Tech Mgr*
EMP: 134
SQ FT: 104,000
SALES (est): 25.2MM **Privately Held**
WEB: www.tazewellmachine.com
SIC: 3365 3599 Aluminum & aluminum-based alloy castings; machine shop, jobbing & repair

(G-16366)
TROY MCDANIEL
Also Called: Guaranteed Ink
132 Court St (61554-3101)
P.O. Box 2222, East Peoria (61611-0222)
PHONE..................................309 369-6225
Troy McDaniel, *Owner*
EMP: 3
SQ FT: 1,200
SALES (est): 122.7K **Privately Held**
SIC: 3955 Print cartridges for laser & other computer printers

(G-16367)
VARSITY PUBLICATIONS INC
Also Called: Athletic Fundraising.com
309 Railroad Ave (61554-2732)
PHONE..................................309 353-4570
EMP: 4
SALES (est): 310K **Privately Held**
SIC: 2741 Misc Publishing

(G-16368)
WE-B-PRINT INC
Also Called: American Speedy Printing
1107 N 8th St (61554-2817)
PHONE..................................309 353-8801
Marvin Eberle, *President*
EMP: 9
SQ FT: 2,000
SALES (est): 1.4MM **Privately Held**
SIC: 2752 7334 2789 Commercial printing, offset; photocopying & duplicating services; bookbinding & related work

(G-16369)
WHEEL WORX NORTH LLC
200 Hanna Dr (61554-8793)
P.O. Box 641 (61555-0641)
PHONE..................................309 346-3535
Gary Schoenfeldt, *President*
Justin Schoefeldt, *Vice Pres*
Jerry Solt, *Vice Pres*
EMP: 2
SALES (est): 359.5K **Privately Held**
SIC: 3312 Wheels

(G-16370)
WINPAK HEAT SEAL CORP
1821 Riverway Dr (61554-9309)
PHONE..................................309 477-6600
Tanner Helm, *Sales Staff*
Bruce Hoerr, *Manager*
EMP: 55
SALES (corp-wide): 873.8MM **Privately Held**
SIC: 3497 Metal foil & leaf
HQ: Winpak Heat Seal Packaging Inc
21919 Ch Dumberry
Vaudreuil-Dorion QC J7V 8
450 424-0191

(G-16371)
WOODWORKERS SHOP INC (PA)
Also Called: Pekin Hardwood Lumber Co.
13587 E Manito Rd (61554-8593)
P.O. Box 277 (61555-0277)
PHONE..................................309 347-5111
Rick A Butler, *Principal*
Steve Barton, *Sales Staff*
Becky Griffin, *Sales Staff*
Jason Snyder, *Manager*
Guy Wickert, *Supervisor*
▲ EMP: 20 EST: 1935
SALES (est): 4.4MM **Privately Held**
WEB: www.woodworksshop.com
SIC: 2426 5031 5211 Lumber, hardwood dimension; lumber: rough, dressed & finished; lumber products

Peoria
Peoria County

(G-16372)
A LUCAS & SONS
1328 Sw Washington St (61602-1798)
PHONE................309 673-8547
Margaret A Hanley, *President*
John P Hanley, *President*
Terry Machetti, *Admin Sec*
EMP: 20
SALES (est): 5.8MM **Privately Held**
WEB: www.alucasandsons.com
SIC: 3441 Building components, structural steel

(G-16373)
AAA GALVANIZING - PEORIA INC
6718 W Plank Rd Ste 2 (61604-7218)
PHONE................309 697-4100
Sean Eogan, *President*
▲ **EMP:** 40
SALES (est): 3.5MM
SALES (corp-wide): 1B **Publicly Held**
SIC: 3479 Coating of metals & formed products
PA: Azz Inc.
3100 W 7th St Ste 500
Fort Worth TX 76107
817 810-0095

(G-16374)
ACADEMY SCREENPRINTING AWARDS
Also Called: Academy of Awards II
1316 E War Memorial Dr (61614-7725)
PHONE................309 686-0026
Dolores Hoop, *Owner*
EMP: 6
SQ FT: 7,000
SALES (est): 615.3K **Privately Held**
SIC: 5999 5699 5947 3993 Trophies & plaques; T-shirts, custom printed; gift shop; signs, not made in custom sign painting shops

(G-16375)
ADAMS OUTDOOR ADVG LTD PARTNR
Also Called: Adams Outdoor Advg Peoria
911 Sw Adams St (61602-1608)
PHONE................309 692-2482
Brad Creek, *Accounts Exec*
Brad Mitchell, *Manager*
Jim Youngman, *Manager*
EMP: 20
SALES (corp-wide): 47.1MM **Privately Held**
SIC: 7312 3993 Billboard advertising; signs & advertising specialties
PA: Adams Outdoor Advertising Limited Partnership
500 Colonial Center Pkwy # 1
Roswell GA 30076
770 333-0399

(G-16376)
AG-DEFENSE SYSTEMS INC
Also Called: ADS
801 W Main St Ste A118 (61606-1877)
PHONE................309 495-7258
Ken Owen, *CEO*
Beth S Turnbull-Dyer, *President*
Rex Dyer, *Principal*
EMP: 2
SALES (est): 284.7K **Privately Held**
SIC: 3826 Analytical instruments

(G-16377)
AGRISCIENCE INC
5115 N Martha St (61614-4946)
PHONE................212 365-4214
Robert Littmann, *Principal*
Kevin Riley, *Principal*
EMP: 3 **EST:** 2015
SALES (est): 202K **Privately Held**
SIC: 2879 4953 8711 Agricultural chemicals; recycling, waste materials; chemical engineering

(G-16378)
AIR VENT INC
7700 N Harker Dr Ste B (61615-5807)
PHONE................309 692-6969
Shelly Doubet, *Branch Mgr*
EMP: 8
SALES (corp-wide): 1B **Publicly Held**
SIC: 3444 Ventilators, sheet metal
HQ: Air Vent Inc.
4117 Pinnacle Point Dr # 400
Dallas TX 75211
800 247-8368

(G-16379)
AKR INDUSTRIES INC
9710 N Megan Ct (61615-7475)
PHONE................732 998-5662
Lakshman M Devarajan, *CEO*
EMP: 3
SALES (est): 116.1K **Privately Held**
SIC: 2211 Apparel & outerwear fabrics, cotton

(G-16380)
ALCAST COMPANY (PA)
8821 N University St (61615-1674)
PHONE................309 691-5513
Stephen Wessels, *President*
Brian A Holt, *Vice Pres*
Brian Holt, *Vice Pres*
Scott Kelsey, *Vice Pres*
Viston Batey, *Plant Mgr*
▲ **EMP:** 94
SQ FT: 42,688
SALES (est): 36.1MM **Privately Held**
SIC: 3365 Aluminum & aluminum-based alloy castings

(G-16381)
ALCAST COMPANY
8820 N Pioneer Rd (61615-1520)
PHONE................309 691-5513
Steve Wessels, *President*
EMP: 20
SALES (corp-wide): 36.1MM **Privately Held**
SIC: 3365 Aluminum & aluminum-based alloy castings
PA: Alcast Company
8821 N University St
Peoria IL 61615
309 691-5513

(G-16382)
ALCAST COMPANY
8600 N Industrial Rd (61615-1504)
PHONE................309 691-5513
EMP: 12
SALES (corp-wide): 36.1MM **Privately Held**
SIC: 3365 Aluminum & aluminum-based alloy castings
PA: Alcast Company
8821 N University St
Peoria IL 61615
309 691-5513

(G-16383)
ANNTAYLOR RETAIL INC
Also Called: Ann Taylor
5201 W War Memorial Dr # 54 (61615-9222)
PHONE................309 693-2762
Mary Beal, *Branch Mgr*
EMP: 4 **Publicly Held**
SIC: 5621 5137 2389 Women's specialty clothing stores; women's & children's outerwear; men's miscellaneous accessories
HQ: Anntaylor Retail, Inc.
933 Macarthur Blvd
Mahwah NJ 07430

(G-16384)
APANA INC
7201 N Drake Ct (61615-9291)
PHONE................309 303-4007
Diana Burritt, *Director*
EMP: 4
SALES (est): 204.9K **Privately Held**
SIC: 3845 Ultrasonic scanning devices, medical

(G-16385)
ARCHER-DANIELS-MIDLAND COMPANY
Also Called: ADM
1 Edmund St (61602-1775)
P.O. Box 99, Dunlap (61525-0099)
PHONE................309 673-7828
Corbin Adams, *Electrical Engi*
Jonovan Granger, *Electrical Engi*
Mark Resnik, *Manager*
Steve Ryan, *Manager*
EMP: 225
SALES (corp-wide): 64.6B **Publicly Held**
WEB: www.adm.com
SIC: 2041 Flour & other grain mill products.
PA: Archer-Daniels-Midland Company
77 W Wacker Dr Ste 4600
Chicago IL 60601
312 634-8100

(G-16386)
ARMITAGE MACHINE CO INC
6035 Washington St (61607-2501)
P.O. Box 1472 (61655-1472)
PHONE................309 697-9050
David A Armitage, *President*
Rich Terrian, *Manager*
EMP: 10 **EST:** 1969
SQ FT: 22,000
SALES (est): 1.5MM **Privately Held**
SIC: 3599 Machine shop, jobbing & repair

(G-16387)
ARVENS TECHNOLOGY INC
801 W Main St (61606-1877)
PHONE................650 776-5443
Sudhir Seth, *President*
EMP: 5
SALES (est): 202K **Privately Held**
SIC: 2869 Industrial organic chemicals

(G-16388)
ATS COMMUNICATIONS NETWRK CORP
1500 Ne Jefferson Ave (61603-3469)
PHONE................309 673-6733
EMP: 6
SALES (corp-wide): 608K **Privately Held**
SIC: 7372 Prepackaged Software Services
PA: Ats Communications Network Corporation
3102 N Gate Ave
Peoria IL
309 713-2094

(G-16389)
B & M AUTOMOTIVE
1811 S Oakwood Ave (61605-2649)
PHONE................309 637-4977
Marcia A Donahue, *Partner*
Bill Donahue, *Partner*
EMP: 3
SALES (est): 189K **Privately Held**
SIC: 3519 Marine engines

(G-16390)
BARNES & NOBLE COLLEGE
Also Called: Bradley University Bookstore
830 N Elmwood Ave (61606-1176)
PHONE................309 677-2320
Paul Kroenke, *Manager*
EMP: 20
SQ FT: 800
SALES (corp-wide): 2B **Publicly Held**
SIC: 5942 2395 College book stores; embroidery & art needlework
HQ: Barnes & Noble College Booksellers, Llc
120 Mountainview Blvd
Basking Ridge NJ 07920
908 991-2665

(G-16391)
BENCHMARK CABINETS & MLLWK INC
5913 W Plank Rd (61604-5226)
PHONE................309 697-5855
Joseph R Hart, *President*
Bryan Stoehr, *Opers Mgr*
Deanna McMurtry, *Office Mgr*
EMP: 20
SALES (est): 2.8MM **Privately Held**
SIC: 2434 2431 5712 Wood kitchen cabinets; brackets, wood; cabinet work, custom

(G-16392)
BETTER EARTH PREMIUM COMPOST
1400 S Cameron Ln (61607-9331)
PHONE................309 697-0963
Paul Rosebohm, *Owner*
Paul Rosenbohm, *Principal*
EMP: 6
SALES (est): 586.3K **Privately Held**
SIC: 2875 2611 Compost; pulp manufactured from waste or recycled paper

(G-16393)
BLACK BAND LLC
1000 Sw Adams St (61602-1611)
PHONE................309 208-0323
Christopher Ober, *CEO*
EMP: 3
SALES (est): 112.6K **Privately Held**
SIC: 2085 Distilled & blended liquors

(G-16394)
BOX MANUFACTURING INC
201 Spring St (61603-7002)
PHONE................309 637-6228
Fax: 309 637-1031
EMP: 5
SQ FT: 10,000
SALES (est): 200K **Privately Held**
SIC: 2653 Mfg Corrugated Boxes

(G-16395)
BUILDERS WAREHOUSE INC
2115 Sw Washington St (61602-1840)
PHONE................309 672-1760
Dan Holbrock, *President*
▲ **EMP:** 3
SALES (est): 533.8K **Privately Held**
WEB: www.builderswarehousepeoria.com
SIC: 2426 Hardwood dimension & flooring mills

(G-16396)
CALIHAN PORK PROCESSORS INC
1 South St (61602-1851)
P.O. Box 1155 (61653-1155)
PHONE................309 674-9175
Tom Landon, *CEO*
Louis M Landon, *President*
Al Schmid, *CFO*
Kathleen J Landon, *Treasurer*
EMP: 60
SQ FT: 26,000
SALES (est): 22.7MM **Privately Held**
SIC: 5147 2011 Meats & meat products; pork products from pork slaughtered on site

(G-16397)
CAPITOL IMPRESSIONS INC
1622 W Moss Ave (61606-1641)
PHONE................309 633-1400
Mark Matuszak, *President*
Morin Don, *Accountant*
Greenberg Michelle, *Manager*
Barbour Bernard, *Director*
Matt Daigle, *Admin Sec*
EMP: 23
SQ FT: 12,000
SALES (est): 2.7MM **Privately Held**
WEB: www.cimpress.com
SIC: 2752 2759 5943 2789 Commercial printing, offset; embossing on paper; office forms & supplies; bookbinding & related work

(G-16398)
CAST TECHNOLOGIES INC (PA)
1100 Sw Washington St (61602-1633)
P.O. Box 959 (61653-0959)
PHONE................309 676-1715
Mike McLaughlin, *President*
Clay D Canterbury, *President*
William J Carman, *CFO*
EMP: 141
SQ FT: 148,000
SALES (est): 34.9MM **Privately Held**
WEB: www.casttechnologies.net
SIC: 3365 3366 Aluminum & aluminum-based alloy castings; brass foundry

Peoria - Peoria County (G-16399)   GEOGRAPHIC SECTION

(G-16399)
CAST TECHNOLOGIES INC
2718 Sw Adams St (61602-1908)
PHONE.................................309 674-1402
EMP: 4
SALES (est): 177.3K **Privately Held**
WEB: www.casttechnologies.net
SIC: 3369 Nonferrous foundries

(G-16400)
CATERPILLAR BRAZIL LLC
100 Ne Adams St (61629-0002)
PHONE.................................309 675-1000
Luiz Carlos Calil, *Principal*
Douglas Vieira, *Buyer*
Charles Popp, *Consultant*
▼ EMP: 5701
SALES (est): 228.8MM
SALES (corp-wide): 53.8B **Publicly Held**
SIC: 3523 Farm machinery & equipment
PA: Caterpillar Inc.
  510 Lake Cook Rd Ste 100
  Deerfield IL 60015
  224 551-4000

(G-16401)
CATERPILLAR FOREST PDTS INC
330 Sw Adams St (61602-1527)
P.O. Box 999, Clayton NC (27528-0999)
PHONE.................................309 675-1000
John Carpenter, *CEO*
Diane Anderson, *Planning*
▲ EMP: 40
SALES (est): 12.8MM
SALES (corp-wide): 53.8B **Publicly Held**
SIC: 3531 Construction machinery
PA: Caterpillar Inc.
  510 Lake Cook Rd Ste 100
  Deerfield IL 60015
  224 551-4000

(G-16402)
CATERPILLAR FOUNDATION
100 Ne Adams St (61629-0002)
PHONE.................................309 675-4232
Caterpillar Foundation, *Principal*
EMP: 2
SALES: 43.6MM **Privately Held**
SIC: 3531 Construction machinery

(G-16403)
CATERPILLAR GB LLC
100 Ne Adams St (61629-0002)
PHONE.................................309 675-1000
David Thomas, *CEO*
EMP: 5
SALES (est): 386.8K
SALES (corp-wide): 53.8B **Publicly Held**
SIC: 3519 Internal combustion engines
PA: Caterpillar Inc.
  510 Lake Cook Rd Ste 100
  Deerfield IL 60015
  224 551-4000

(G-16404)
CATERPILLAR INC
100 Ne Adams St (61629-0002)
PHONE.................................309 675-1000
Mark Lang, *Accountant*
Minhua Zhao, *Accounts Mgr*
Tammy Romer, *Manager*
EMP: 277
SALES (corp-wide): 53.8B **Publicly Held**
WEB: www.caterpillar.com
SIC: 3531 Construction machinery
PA: Caterpillar Inc.
  510 Lake Cook Rd Ste 100
  Deerfield IL 60015
  224 551-4000

(G-16405)
CATERPILLAR INC
7022 W Middle Rd (61607-8446)
PHONE.................................309 675-5681
Mike Quimerson, *Manager*
EMP: 20
SALES (corp-wide): 53.8B **Publicly Held**
WEB: www.caterpillar.com
SIC: 3531 Construction machinery
PA: Caterpillar Inc.
  510 Lake Cook Rd Ste 100
  Deerfield IL 60015
  224 551-4000

(G-16406)
CATERPILLAR INC
8201 N University St # 2 (61615-1889)
PHONE.................................309 578-4643
EMP: 14
SALES (corp-wide): 53.8B **Publicly Held**
SIC: 3531 5082 Construction machinery; construction & mining machinery
PA: Caterpillar Inc.
  510 Lake Cook Rd Ste 100
  Deerfield IL 60015
  224 551-4000

(G-16407)
CATERPILLAR INC
501 Sw Jefferson Ave (61605-2500)
PHONE.................................888 614-4328
Brian Beggs, *COO*
Kevin Earle, *Counsel*
Kathleen Horchler, *Counsel*
Kelsey L Milman, *Counsel*
Andrew Triggs, *Counsel*
EMP: 360
SALES (corp-wide): 53.8B **Publicly Held**
SIC: 3531 3519 3511 6531 Construction machinery; engines, diesel & semi-diesel or dual-fuel; gasoline engines; gas turbine generator set units, complete; hydraulic turbine generator set units, complete; fiduciary, real estate; accident insurance carriers; fire, marine & casualty insurance: stock
PA: Caterpillar Inc.
  510 Lake Cook Rd Ste 100
  Deerfield IL 60015
  224 551-4000

(G-16408)
CATERPILLAR INC
100 Ne Adams St (61629-0002)
PHONE.................................309 675-1000
EMP: 3
SALES (corp-wide): 53.8B **Publicly Held**
SIC: 3531 Construction machinery
PA: Caterpillar Inc.
  510 Lake Cook Rd Ste 100
  Deerfield IL 60015
  224 551-4000

(G-16409)
CATERPILLAR INC
1335 Sw Washington St (61602-1705)
PHONE.................................309 675-1000
Bob Oliverius, *Manager*
EMP: 50
SALES (corp-wide): 53.8B **Publicly Held**
SIC: 3531 Construction machinery
PA: Caterpillar Inc.
  510 Lake Cook Rd Ste 100
  Deerfield IL 60015
  224 551-4000

(G-16410)
CATERPILLAR INC
100 Ne Adams St (61629-0002)
PHONE.................................309 675-1000
EMP: 355
SALES (corp-wide): 53.8B **Publicly Held**
SIC: 3531 Construction machinery
PA: Caterpillar Inc.
  510 Lake Cook Rd Ste 100
  Deerfield IL 60015
  224 551-4000

(G-16411)
CATERPILLAR INC
2400 Sw Washington St (61602-1846)
PHONE.................................309 675-6590
EMP: 355
SALES (corp-wide): 53.8B **Publicly Held**
SIC: 3519 3511 6153 6321 Engines, diesel & semi-diesel or dual-fuel; gasoline engines; gas turbine generator set units, complete; hydraulic turbine generator set units, complete; mercantile financing; accident insurance carriers; fire, marine & casualty insurance: stock; tractors, crawler
PA: Caterpillar Inc.
  510 Lake Cook Rd Ste 100
  Deerfield IL 60015
  224 551-4000

(G-16412)
CATERPILLAR INTL LSG LLC
100 Ne Adams St (61629-0002)
P.O. Box 6, Morton (61550-0006)
PHONE.................................309 675-1000
Glen Barton, *CEO*
David Bianchi, *Counsel*
Byron Buck II, *Counsel*
Shekar Palanivelu, *Vice Pres*
Martin Bina, *Opers Staff*
▲ EMP: 2
SALES (est): 583.6K
SALES (corp-wide): 53.8B **Publicly Held**
SIC: 3531 Construction machinery
PA: Caterpillar Inc.
  510 Lake Cook Rd Ste 100
  Deerfield IL 60015
  224 551-4000

(G-16413)
CATERPILLAR LUXEMBOURG LLC (HQ)
100 Ne Adams St (61629-0002)
PHONE.................................309 675-1000
▲ EMP: 4 EST: 2011
SALES (est): 2.7MM
SALES (corp-wide): 53.8B **Publicly Held**
SIC: 3531 Construction machinery
PA: Caterpillar Inc.
  510 Lake Cook Rd Ste 100
  Deerfield IL 60015
  224 551-4000

(G-16414)
CATERPILLAR POWER SYSTEMS INC
100 Ne Adams St (61629-0002)
PHONE.................................309 675-1000
Ringo Siu Keung Chow, *President*
Jerome Vannitamby, *Business Mgr*
Sean P Leuba, *Admin Sec*
EMP: 8
SALES (est): 1.5MM
SALES (corp-wide): 53.8B **Publicly Held**
SIC: 3531 Construction machinery
PA: Caterpillar Inc.
  510 Lake Cook Rd Ste 100
  Deerfield IL 60015
  224 551-4000

(G-16415)
CATERPILLAR WORLD TRADING CORP
100 Ne Adams St (61629-0002)
PHONE.................................309 675-1000
Charles Delph, *President*
EMP: 24
SALES (est): 9.9MM
SALES (corp-wide): 53.8B **Publicly Held**
SIC: 3531 Construction machinery
PA: Caterpillar Inc.
  510 Lake Cook Rd Ste 100
  Deerfield IL 60015
  224 551-4000

(G-16416)
CENTRAL ILLINOIS BUS PUBLS INC
5005 N Glen Park Place Rd (61614-4677)
PHONE.................................309 683-3060
Janet Wright, *CEO*
Michael Gudat, *VP Sales*
Jessica Moroz, *Manager*
Jan Benson Wright, *IT/INT Sup*
EMP: 5 EST: 1989
SQ FT: 2,000
SALES: 800K **Privately Held**
WEB: www.peoriamagazines.com
SIC: 2721 Magazines: publishing only, not printed on site

(G-16417)
CENTRAL ILLINOIS HOMES GUIDE
7307 N Willow Lake Ct (61614-8227)
PHONE.................................309 688-6419
Nancy Koch, *President*
▲ EMP: 7
SALES (est): 420K **Privately Held**
SIC: 2721 2741 Magazines: publishing only, not printed on site; miscellaneous publishing

(G-16418)
CENTRAL RC HOBBIES
Peoria Hts (61616)
PHONE.................................309 686-8004
Rick Jacobson, *Owner*
EMP: 8
SALES (est): 687K **Privately Held**
SIC: 3944 5092 5945 Board games, puzzles & models, except electronic; hobby supplies; hobbies; toys & games

(G-16419)
CERTIFIED HEAT TREATING CO
8917 N University St (61615-1637)
P.O. Box 5699 (61601-5699)
PHONE.................................309 693-7711
Joseph P O'Brien, *President*
Steven Matthew, *General Mgr*
Mary L Flanagan, *Corp Secy*
EMP: 18
SQ FT: 15,000
SALES (est): 3.2MM **Privately Held**
SIC: 3398 Metal heat treating

(G-16420)
CFS CRTIVE FBRCTION SLTONS LLC
5807 Washington St (61607-2043)
PHONE.................................309 264-3946
Lisa Eller, *Mng Member*
EMP: 3 EST: 2017
SALES (est): 270.1K **Privately Held**
SIC: 3441 Fabricated structural metal

(G-16421)
CHESTER WHITE SWINE RCORD ASSN
6320 N Sheridan Rd Ste A (61614-3053)
P.O. Box 9758 (61612-9758)
PHONE.................................309 691-0151
Jack Wall, *President*
EMP: 3 EST: 1894
SQ FT: 100
SALES: 282K **Privately Held**
WEB: www.cpsswine.com
SIC: 0751 2721 8611 Pedigree record services, livestock; magazines: publishing only, not printed on site; business associations

(G-16422)
CISCO HEATING & COOLING
3304 W Linda Ln (61605-2639)
PHONE.................................309 637-6809
Harry Cisco, *Owner*
Mary Cisco, *Co-Owner*
EMP: 4
SALES (est): 283.2K **Privately Held**
SIC: 3585 Refrigeration & heating equipment

(G-16423)
CITYBLUE TECHNOLOGIES LLC (PA)
404 Sw Adams St (61602-1520)
P.O. Box 1169 (61653-1169)
PHONE.................................309 550-5000
Nathan Peters, *Technology*
Michael McConnell,
EMP: 10
SQ FT: 13,000
SALES (est): 3.5MM **Privately Held**
SIC: 2759 5734 Commercial printing; printers & plotters: computers

(G-16424)
CJ SIGNS
4024 Sw Adams St (61605-3012)
PHONE.................................309 676-9999
Charles Johnson, *Principal*
EMP: 2
SALES (est): 300.7K **Privately Held**
WEB: www.cj-signs.com
SIC: 3993 Signs & advertising specialties

(G-16425)
COBATCO INC
1215 Ne Adams St (61603-4005)
PHONE.................................309 676-2663
Donald O Stephens, *President*
Amy Stephens, *Corp Secy*
Brian Fiddes, *Natl Sales Mgr*
◆ EMP: 19
SQ FT: 11,000

GEOGRAPHIC SECTION

Peoria - Peoria County (G-16454)

SALES (est): 4.7MM **Privately Held**
SIC: 3556 Food products machinery

(G-16426)
COMPONENTA USA LLC
8515 N University St (61615-1629)
PHONE 309 691-7000
Heikki Lehtonen, *Principal*
EMP: 6 **EST:** 2011
SALES (est): 791.2K **Privately Held**
SIC: 3325 Steel foundries

(G-16427)
CONSOLIDATED PAVING INC
6918 N Galena Rd (61614-3112)
PHONE 309 693-3505
EMP: 4
SALES: 750K **Privately Held**
SIC: 2951 Asphalt paving mixtures & blocks

(G-16428)
CUB FOODS INC
5001 N Big Hollow Rd (61615-3538)
PHONE 309 689-0140
Scott Presuhn, *Manager*
EMP: 160
SQ FT: 40,000 **Publicly Held**
SIC: 5411 5421 5921 5992 Supermarkets; meat markets, including freezer provisioners; liquor stores; florists; bread, cake & related products
HQ: Cub Foods, Inc
    421 3rd St S
    Stillwater MN 55082
    651 439-7200

(G-16429)
DENTAL SEALANTS & MORE
214 W Wolf Rd (61614-2156)
PHONE 309 692-6435
Clifford A Brown, *Principal*
EMP: 5
SALES (est): 489.6K **Privately Held**
SIC: 2891 Sealants

(G-16430)
DESIGN PLUS INDUSTRIES INC (PA)
6311 W Development Dr (61604-5283)
PHONE 309 697-9778
Michael Seibert, *President*
Laurie Dean, *Vice Pres*
▲ **EMP:** 15
SALES (est): 2MM **Privately Held**
SIC: 3999 1799 Coin-operated amusement machines; counter top installation

(G-16431)
DRUMHELLER BAG CORPORATION
1114 Sw Adams St (61602-1613)
PHONE 309 676-1006
David V Drumheller, *President*
Jackie Lampkin, *Treasurer*
EMP: 52
SQ FT: 4,500
SALES (est): 10.7MM **Privately Held**
SIC: 2673 Bags: plastic, laminated & coated

(G-16432)
DUST PATROL INC
Also Called: D.P. Filters
1620 W Chanute Rd Ste D (61615-1669)
PHONE 309 676-1161
Sean Donavan, *Opers Staff*
Jerry Swanson, *Branch Mgr*
EMP: 9
SALES (corp-wide): 3.8MM **Privately Held**
SIC: 5075 3564 Dust collecting equipment; blowers & fans
PA: Dust Patrol, Inc.
    1041 W Republic Dr
    Addison IL 60101
    630 543-5221

(G-16433)
EHS SOLUTIONS LLC (PA)
8800 N Allen Rd Ste 1 (61615-1595)
PHONE 309 282-9121
Benjamin Pfister, *Sales Engr*
Robert Herrmann, *Mng Member*
Ryan Hoerr,
Paul Sauder,
Nathan Steffen,
◆ **EMP:** 40
SALES: 5MM **Privately Held**
SIC: 8711 3535 Engineering services; unit handling conveying systems

(G-16434)
ELISE S ALLEN
Also Called: Traveler Printing
1600 Mrtn Lthr Kng Jr Dr (61605-1816)
PHONE 309 673-2613
Elise S Allen, *Owner*
EMP: 3
SALES (est): 188.3K **Privately Held**
SIC: 2752 2711 Commercial printing, lithographic; newspapers

(G-16435)
EM SMITH & CO
826 W Detweiller Dr (61615-2183)
PHONE 309 691-6812
Jack Cook, *President*
Dale Swearingen, *Exec VP*
Brian Davidson, *Treasurer*
EMP: 26
SQ FT: 40,000
SALES (est): 4.2MM **Privately Held**
SIC: 3599 Machine shop, jobbing & repair

(G-16436)
EVERYTHING XCLUSIVE
4010 N Brandywine Dr (61614-6866)
PHONE 309 370-7450
La'tisha Hughes, *Owner*
EMP: 3
SALES (est): 112K **Privately Held**
SIC: 2791 Typesetting

(G-16437)
FEDEX OFFICE & PRINT SVCS INC
3465 N University St (61604-1322)
PHONE 309 685-4093
Terri Ellenwood, *District Mgr*
William Jochum, *Accounts Exec*
Andrew Ferguson, *Manager*
Jeanne Steele, *Manager*
Barbara Veto, *Manager*
EMP: 24
SALES (corp-wide): 69.6B **Publicly Held**
SIC: 7334 3993 2789 2759 Photocopying & duplicating services; signs & advertising specialties; bookbinding & related work; commercial printing; coated & laminated paper; typesetting
HQ: Fedex Office And Print Services, Inc.
    7900 Legacy Dr
    Plano TX 75024
    800 463-3339

(G-16438)
FIREFLY INTERNATIONAL ENRGY CO (PA)
8306 N University St (61615-1626)
PHONE 309 402-0701
Mukesh Bhandari, *Ch of Bd*
Rajendra Patel, *COO*
Kurt Kelly, *CTO*
EMP: 1 **EST:** 2010
SQ FT: 54,000
SALES (est): 1.2MM **Privately Held**
SIC: 8731 3691 Energy research; storage batteries

(G-16439)
FORMS DESIGN PLUS COLEMAN PRTG
1105 E War Memorial Dr # 1 (61616-7772)
P.O. Box 9756 (61612-9756)
PHONE 309 685-6000
Lawrence J Dunn, *President*
Debra Dunn, *Corp Secy*
EMP: 4
SQ FT: 4,100
SALES: 980K **Privately Held**
SIC: 5112 2752 2789 Business forms; commercial printing, offset; bookbinding & related work

(G-16440)
FOUR-MOST INC (PA)
Also Called: Foremost Industrial Tech
6518 W Plank Rd (61604-5239)
PHONE 563 323-3233
Michael Moran, *President*
Brent Hubbard, *Manager*
Esther Tyler, *Executive*
EMP: 3
SALES (est): 959.6K **Privately Held**
WEB: www.foremost-fit.com
SIC: 5063 7694 Motors, electric; electric motor repair

(G-16441)
FREDMAN BROS FURNITURE CO INC
Also Called: Glideaway Bed Carriage Mf
908 Sw Washington St (61602-1629)
PHONE 309 674-2011
Carmi Fredman, *President*
EMP: 50
SALES (corp-wide): 99.9MM **Privately Held**
WEB: www.glideaway.com
SIC: 2515 2511 Sleep furniture; wood household furniture
PA: Fredman Bros. Furniture Company, Inc.
    8226 Lackland Rd
    Saint Louis MO 63114
    314 426-3999

(G-16442)
GATEHOUSE MEDIA ILL HOLDINGS
Also Called: Money Stretcher
1 News Plz (61643-0001)
P.O. Box 99, Galatia (62935-0099)
PHONE 585 598-0030
James Bond, *Principal*
Janette Bond, *Principal*
Garrett J Cummings,
EMP: 9
SALES: 1.2MM
SALES (corp-wide): 1.8B **Publicly Held**
SIC: 2711 2741 Newspapers: publishing only, not printed on site; miscellaneous publishing
PA: Gannett Co., Inc.
    7950 Jones Branch Dr
    Mc Lean VA 22102
    703 854-6000

(G-16443)
GEEBEES INC
Also Called: Fastsigns
3024 N University St (61604-2614)
PHONE 309 682-5300
Frank Smith, *President*
Scott Turk, *Executive*
EMP: 5
SQ FT: 2,500
SALES (est): 499.6K **Privately Held**
SIC: 3993 5999 Signs & advertising specialties; banners, flags, decals & posters

(G-16444)
GENACC LLC
60 State St Ste 101 (61602-5153)
PHONE 309 253-9034
James H Richmond, *Mng Member*
Eric Samuel Delgado,
Jill Rene Donahue,
Scott Thomas Gall,
Zachary Vernon Lloyd Holcomb,
EMP: 8
SALES (est): 1.1MM **Privately Held**
SIC: 3463 Engine or turbine forgings, non-ferrous

(G-16445)
GEO J ROTHAN CO
1200 W Johnson St (61605-2080)
PHONE 309 674-5189
George J Rothan Jr, *President*
Christopher H Rothan, *Admin Sec*
EMP: 20 **EST:** 1873
SQ FT: 4,000
SALES (est): 3.9MM **Privately Held**
WEB: www.rothanman.com
SIC: 2431 Doors, wood

(G-16446)
GORMAN & ASSOCIATES
7501 N University St # 122 (61614-1244)
PHONE 309 691-9087
Carol Gorman, *President*
EMP: 7
SQ FT: 2,000
SALES (est): 1MM **Privately Held**
SIC: 2791 2731 Typesetting; books: publishing & printing

(G-16447)
GUTTER MASTERS
2117 E Cornell St (61614-7921)
PHONE 309 686-1234
EMP: 4 **EST:** 2010
SALES (est): 455.9K **Privately Held**
WEB: www.peoriaguttermasters.com
SIC: 3569 Filters

(G-16448)
H & S MECHANICAL INC
5607 Washington St (61607-2075)
PHONE 309 696-7066
Tara Howard, *President*
Shaun P Howard, *President*
EMP: 65
SALES (est): 6.9MM **Privately Held**
WEB: www.hsmechanicalinc.com
SIC: 1711 3441 1791 1731 Mechanical contractor; building components, structural steel; structural steel erection; electrical work

(G-16449)
H FELDE TOOL & MACHINE CO
2324 W Altorfer Dr (61615-1810)
PHONE 309 692-5870
Heinrich Felde, *President*
EMP: 11
SQ FT: 6,250
SALES (est): 1.7MM **Privately Held**
SIC: 3599 Machine shop, jobbing & repair

(G-16450)
H3 GROUP LLC
900 Sw Adams St (61602-1609)
PHONE 309 222-6027
Lisa Kulavic,
Jay Kulavic,
Frank Mendoza,
EMP: 10
SQ FT: 18,000
SALES: 1.8MM **Privately Held**
SIC: 3441 Fabricated structural metal

(G-16451)
HANGER PRSTHTICS ORTHOTICS INC
311 W Romeo B Garrett Ave (61605-2504)
PHONE 309 637-6581
Jan Murzyn, *Manager*
EMP: 5
SALES (est): 1.1B **Publicly Held**
WEB: www.hanger.com
SIC: 3842 Surgical appliances & supplies
HQ: Hanger Prosthetics & Orthotics, Inc.
    10910 Domain Dr Ste 300
    Austin TX 78758
    512 777-3800

(G-16452)
HANLEY DESIGN INC
2519 N Rockwood Dr (61604-2215)
PHONE 309 682-9665
EMP: 9
SQ FT: 10,000
SALES: 275K **Privately Held**
SIC: 2541 5712 2531 2522 Mfg Wood Partitionsfixt Ret Furniture Mfg Public Building Furn Nonwood Office Furn & Wood Household Furn

(G-16453)
HOLLAND SPECIALTY CO
Also Called: Holland Laboratories
4611 W Middle Rd (61605-1055)
PHONE 309 697-9262
Stephen W Swanson, *President*
Eric Swanson, *Vice Pres*
EMP: 25
SQ FT: 2,688
SALES: 10MM **Privately Held**
SIC: 2844 3843 Denture cleaners; dental equipment & supplies

(G-16454)
HOWMET AEROSPACE INC
2616 Sw Jefferson Ave (61605-3542)
PHONE 309 674-0065
EMP: 135
SALES (corp-wide): 14.1B **Publicly Held**
SIC: 3353 Aluminum sheet & strip

Peoria - Peoria County (G-16455)

PA: Howmet Aerospace Inc.
201 Isabella St Ste 200
Pittsburgh PA 15212
412 553-1950

(G-16455)
IDEAL TURF INC
614 W Ravinwoods Rd (61615-1369)
PHONE.................................309 691-3362
Andy D Zeigler, *Principal*
Ronni Zeigler, *Marketing Mgr*
EMP: 2
SALES (est): 280.4K **Privately Held**
SIC: 3523 Turf equipment, commercial

(G-16456)
ILLINI FOUNDRY CO INC
6523 N Galena Rd (61614-3103)
PHONE.................................309 697-3142
William Bank, *President*
EMP: 5 **EST:** 1929
SQ FT: 10,000
SALES (est): 1MM **Privately Held**
WEB: www.illinifoundry.com
SIC: 3365 3366 3321 3369 Aluminum & aluminum-based alloy castings; brass foundry; gray iron castings; nonferrous foundries

(G-16457)
ILLINOIS VALLEY GLASS & MIRROR
3300 Ne Adams St Ste A (61603-2374)
PHONE.................................309 682-6603
Warren R Watkins, *President*
Mary A Watkins, *Vice Pres*
Regina Stanley, *Office Mgr*
EMP: 13
SQ FT: 20,000
SALES (est): 2.4MM **Privately Held**
WEB: www.illinoisvalleyglass.com
SIC: 1793 3231 7536 3444 Glass & glazing work; insulating glass: made from purchased glass; automotive glass replacement shops; sheet metalwork

(G-16458)
INDUSTRIAL TOOL AND REPAIR
218 S Starr Ln Ste A (61604-7204)
PHONE.................................309 633-0939
Ben Hamilton, *President*
EMP: 5
SQ FT: 7,000
SALES (est): 508K **Privately Held**
SIC: 3599 Machine shop, jobbing & repair

(G-16459)
INDUSTRIAL WASTE ELIMINATION
5115 N Martha St (61614-4946)
PHONE.................................312 498-0880
Robert Littmann, *CEO*
EMP: 10
SQ FT: 2,500
SALES (est): 450.4K **Privately Held**
SIC: 2899 Chemical preparations

(G-16460)
ISATES INC
Also Called: Signs Now
2251 W Altorfer Dr (61615-1807)
PHONE.................................309 691-8822
Irv Hodel, *President*
Sharon Hodel, *Corp Secy*
EMP: 6
SQ FT: 3,000
SALES: 600K **Privately Held**
SIC: 3993 Signs & advertising specialties

(G-16461)
IVEX SPECIALTY PAPER LLC
1 Sloan St (61603)
PHONE.................................309 686-3830
Thad R Edmonds, *CFO*
William Platt, *Mng Member*
EMP: 45
SALES (est): 2.5MM
SALES (corp-wide): 2.6MM **Privately Held**
SIC: 2621 Specialty papers
PA: Paper Investments, Llc
1 Sloan St
Peoria IL 61603
309 686-3830

(G-16462)
JIM MAUI INC
1 Aloha Ln (61615-1871)
PHONE.................................888 666-5905
Michael Dalton, *President*
Donna Ansell, *Opers Mgr*
Stacey Shoemaker, *Human Resources*
Anthony Manto, *Accounts Exec*
Beth Discepolo, *Sales Staff*
EMP: 7
SALES: 66.9K **Privately Held**
SIC: 5099 3851 Sunglasses; glasses, sun or glare

(G-16463)
JOANS TROPHY & PLAQUE CO
508 Ne Jefferson Ave (61603-3891)
P.O. Box 5939 (61601-5939)
PHONE.................................309 674-6500
Diana E Gustin, *CEO*
Donald R Gustin, *President*
Kim Baker, *Sales Associate*
▲ **EMP:** 21
SQ FT: 6,500
SALES (est): 3MM **Privately Held**
SIC: 5999 5094 3993 Trophies & plaques; trophies; signs & advertising specialties

(G-16464)
JOHNSON ROLAN CO INC
718 Sw Adams St (61602-1605)
PHONE.................................309 674-9671
Fred T Johnson, *President*
William Barr, *Vice Pres*
Pamela Barr, *Admin Sec*
EMP: 4
SQ FT: 4,800
SALES (est): 526K **Privately Held**
SIC: 7319 2396 Display advertising service; automotive & apparel trimmings

(G-16465)
KEMP MANUFACTURING COMPANY (PA)
4310 N Voss St (61616-6592)
PHONE.................................309 682-7292
Hylee F Kemp, *President*
Mary K Kemp, *Corp Secy*
Brian F Kemp, *Vice Pres*
Hylee M Kemp, *Vice Pres*
EMP: 40 **EST:** 1946
SALES (est): 14.9MM **Privately Held**
WEB: www.kempmfg.com
SIC: 3599 3999 Machine shop, jobbing & repair; custom pulverizing & grinding of plastic materials

(G-16466)
KEYSTONE CONSOLIDATED INDS INC
Keystone Energy
7000 S Adams St (61641-0002)
PHONE.................................309 697-7020
John Scheel, *Plant Mgr*
Jerry Rich, *Opers Mgr*
Kyle Ambroso, *Electrical Engi*
Chris Linnemeyer, *Sales Mgr*
Christopher Whitney, *Regl Sales Mgr*
EMP: 33
SALES (corp-wide): 633.2K **Privately Held**
SIC: 3312 3496 Billets, steel; miscellaneous fabricated wire products
HQ: Keystone Consolidated Industries, Inc.
5430 Lyndon B Johnson Fwy
Dallas TX 75240
800 441-0308

(G-16467)
KONICA MNLTA BUS SLTONS USA IN
401 Sw Water St (61602-1571)
PHONE.................................309 671-1360
Marty Schopp, *Branch Mgr*
EMP: 46 **Privately Held**
SIC: 7629 5045 5044 3571 Business machine repair, electric; computers, peripherals & software; copying equipment; electronic computers
HQ: Konica Minolta Business Solutions U.S.A., Inc.
11850 W Market Pl Ste P
Fulton MD 20759
201 825-4000

(G-16468)
LANGSTON BAG OF PEORIA LLC
1114 Sw Adams St (61602-1613)
PHONE.................................309 676-1006
Robert E Langston Jr, *CEO*
George T Parkey, *COO*
EMP: 63
SALES (est): 13.5MM
SALES (corp-wide): 69.6MM **Privately Held**
SIC: 2674 Shipping bags or sacks, including multiwall & heavy duty
PA: Langston Companies, Inc.
1760 S 3rd St
Memphis TN 38109
901 774-4440

(G-16469)
LEONARD A UNES PRINTING CO
619 Spring St (61603-4132)
P.O. Box 9573 (61612-9573)
PHONE.................................309 674-4942
Leonard A Unes II, *Owner*
Glenn Ogden, *Purch Dir*
Joann Ogden, *Treasurer*
Molly Ogden, *VP Sales*
EMP: 5
SQ FT: 12,500
SALES (est): 487.8K **Privately Held**
SIC: 2752 Commercial printing, offset

(G-16470)
LOUISVILLE LADDER INC
7921 N Hale Ave (61615-2047)
PHONE.................................309 692-1895
Lumis Craig, *Branch Mgr*
EMP: 8
SALES (corp-wide): 173.9MM **Privately Held**
SIC: 3499 Metal ladders
PA: Louisville Ladder Inc.
7765 National Tpke # 190
Louisville KY 40214
502 636-2811

(G-16471)
MACHINE MEDICS LLC
5726 W Plank Rd (61604-5223)
PHONE.................................309 633-5454
Eric Bruce,
Harry Murphy,
EMP: 3
SALES (est): 471.7K **Privately Held**
SIC: 3541 Machine tool replacement & repair parts, metal cutting types

(G-16472)
MICRO PRODUCTS COMPANY
Also Called: Summer Products
6523 N Galena Rd (61614-3103)
PHONE.................................630 406-9550
William W Banks, *CEO*
Bill Keiler, *Vice Pres*
▲ **EMP:** 50 **EST:** 1929
SQ FT: 5,000
SALES (est): 13MM **Privately Held**
WEB: www.micro-weld.com
SIC: 7692 Welding repair

(G-16473)
MICRO PRODUCTS COMPANY
6523 N Galena Rd (61614-3103)
PHONE.................................309 697-1216
William Banks, *President*
EMP: 3 **EST:** 2009
SALES (est): 535.2K **Privately Held**
WEB: www.micro-weld.com
SIC: 3548 5999 Electric welding equipment; welding supplies

(G-16474)
MID-CENTRAL BUSINESS FORMS
1413 W Sunnyview Dr (61614-4620)
PHONE.................................309 692-9090
Andy Matarelli, *President*
Rene Matarelli, *Admin Sec*
EMP: 2
SALES (est): 450K **Privately Held**
SIC: 5112 2752 5943 Business forms; commercial printing, lithographic; office forms & supplies

(G-16475)
MIDWEST HYDRA-LINE INC
Also Called: MFC
817 Ne Adams St (61603-3901)
PHONE.................................309 674-6570
Jason Drake, *Branch Mgr*
EMP: 5
SALES (corp-wide): 36.8MM **Privately Held**
WEB: www.mfchose.com
SIC: 5085 3443 Hose, belting & packing; cylinders, pressure; metal plate
HQ: Midwest Hydra-Line, Inc.
698 Us Highway 150 E
Galesburg IL 61401
309 342-6171

(G-16476)
MIDWEST MARKETING DISTRS INC (PA)
Also Called: Sun Gard Window Fashions
2000 E War Memorial Dr # 2 (61614-7918)
PHONE.................................309 688-8858
Jim House, *President*
Darla House, *Corp Secy*
▲ **EMP:** 19 **EST:** 1973
SQ FT: 18,000
SALES: 5MM **Privately Held**
SIC: 5719 3081 7549 Window shades; unsupported plastics film & sheet; automotive customizing services, non-factory basis

(G-16477)
MIDWESTERN FAMILY MAGAZINE LLC
3823 N Harmon Ave (61614-6630)
PHONE.................................309 303-7309
Ms Jennifer Rudd, *Principal*
EMP: 3
SALES (est): 153.7K **Privately Held**
SIC: 2721 Magazines: publishing & printing

(G-16478)
MODERN PATTERN WORKS INC
1100 Sw Washington St (61602-1633)
PHONE.................................309 676-2157
William B Mehlenbeck, *President*
James Collie, *Corp Secy*
Jack Harris, *Vice Pres*
Paul Markum, *Vice Pres*
EMP: 4
SQ FT: 80,000
SALES (est): 350.3K
SALES (corp-wide): 34.9MM **Privately Held**
SIC: 3543 Industrial patterns
PA: Cast Technologies, Inc.
1100 Sw Washington St
Peoria IL 61602
309 676-1715

(G-16479)
MONTEFUSCO HVAC INC
Also Called: Montefusco Heating Shtmtl Co
2200 W Altorfer Dr Ste D (61615-1874)
P.O. Box 9755 (61612-9755)
PHONE.................................309 691-7400
Eric Guenther, *President*
Lisa Rhoades, *Principal*
Dave Legrande, *Vice Pres*
EMP: 6 **EST:** 1940
SQ FT: 15,000
SALES (est): 1.2MM **Privately Held**
WEB: www.montefuscohvac.com
SIC: 1711 3446 3444 3443 Warm air heating & air conditioning contractor; ventilation & duct work contractor; architectural metalwork; sheet metalwork; fabricated plate work (boiler shop); fabricated structural metal

(G-16480)
MUIR OMNI GRAPHICS INC (PA)
908 W Main St (61606-1255)
PHONE.................................309 673-7034
Andrew S Muir, *President*
Rebecca Zentko, *Director*
Mary Sutton, *Admin Sec*
EMP: 46 **EST:** 1963
SQ FT: 30,000
SALES (est): 5.3MM **Privately Held**
WEB: www.muirgraphics.com
SIC: 2759 7389 Screen printing; lettering & sign painting services

GEOGRAPHIC SECTION

Peoria - Peoria County (G-16509)

(G-16481)
MURRAY CUSTOM CABINETRY
4310 N Sheridan Rd Ste A (61614-5937)
PHONE.....................309 966-0624
EMP: 2
SALES (est): 253.3K Privately Held
SIC: 2434 Wood kitchen cabinets

(G-16482)
NATURAL FIBER WELDING INC
801 W Main St Lab B206 (61606)
PHONE.....................309 685-3591
Luke Haverhals, *President*
Eric Pollitt, *Vice Pres*
EMP: 5
SALES (est): 228K Privately Held
SIC: 3552 Spinning machines, textile

(G-16483)
NATURAL FIBER WELDING INC
6533 N Galena Rd (61614-3120)
PHONE.....................309 339-7794
Luke Haverhals, *CEO*
EMP: 35
SALES (est): 27.6K Privately Held
SIC: 7692 Welding repair

(G-16484)
NEED TO KNOW INC
Also Called: Key Source
1723 W Detweiller Dr (61615-1611)
PHONE.....................309 691-3877
Jean Wyman, *President*
Rhonda Sherrod, *Med Doctor*
EMP: 5
SQ FT: 4,000
SALES (est): 612.3K Privately Held
SIC: 5961 2731 2752 2396 Catalog & mail-order houses; pamphlets: publishing only, not printed on site; commercial printing, lithographic; automotive & apparel trimmings; pleating & stitching

(G-16485)
NETWORK HARBOR INC
1230 N Candletree Dr D (61614-1574)
P.O. Box 4126 (61607-0126)
PHONE.....................309 633-9118
David Daxenbichler, *President*
Mike Daxenbichler, *Vice Pres*
Al Juraco, *Admin Sec*
EMP: 4
SALES (est): 736.3K Privately Held
SIC: 7372 Prepackaged software

(G-16486)
NICKELS ELECTRIC
1208 W Smith St (61605-2050)
PHONE.....................309 676-1350
Albert Nickels, *Principal*
EMP: 3
SALES (est): 164.8K Privately Held
SIC: 3356 Nickel

(G-16487)
ONEFIRE MEDIA GROUP INC
801 W Main St Peoria (61606)
PHONE.....................309 740-0345
Kristie Sparling, *CFO*
Lyndon Perry, *Ch Credit Ofcr*
Jason Parkinson, *Chief Mktg Ofcr*
Mark Hemmer, *Marketing Staff*
Chad Copeland, *Manager*
EMP: 24
SQ FT: 300
SALES (est): 599.9K Privately Held
SIC: 7372 Application computer software

(G-16488)
P & P PRESS INC
6513 N Galena Rd (61614-3119)
PHONE.....................309 691-8511
Arthur P Young, *President*
Linda Stewart, *Corp Secy*
Linda Stwesart, *Controller*
Josh Gullett, *Manager*
▼ EMP: 32
SQ FT: 30,000
SALES (est): 6.8MM Privately Held
SIC: 2752 Commercial printing, offset

(G-16489)
P & S COCHRAN PRINTERS INC (PA)
Also Called: PIP Printing
8325 N Allen Rd (61615-2076)
PHONE.....................309 691-6668
Paul L Cochran, *Ch of Bd*
Scott H Cochran, *President*
Chris Cochran, *Vice Pres*
Kris Davis, *Sales Staff*
Shamra Noy, *Admin Mgr*
EMP: 20 EST: 1978
SQ FT: 20,000
SALES: 2.5MM Privately Held
SIC: 2752 2791 2789 Commercial printing, offset; typesetting; bookbinding & related work

(G-16490)
PACE FOUNDATION
3528 W Chartwell Rd (61614-2326)
PHONE.....................309 691-3553
Sue Patterson, *President*
Becky Cassidy, *Vice Pres*
Susan Stockman, *Treasurer*
Jodi Garger, *Admin Sec*
EMP: 31
SALES: 21.3K Privately Held
SIC: 2515 Foundations & platforms

(G-16491)
PAPER INVESTMENTS LLC (PA)
Also Called: Paper Investments of Illinois
1 Sloan St (61603)
PHONE.....................309 686-3830
William Platt, *Mng Member*
EMP: 2
SALES (est): 2.6MM Privately Held
SIC: 2621 Paper mills

(G-16492)
PEORIA JOURNAL STAR CREDIT UN
1 News Plz (61643-0001)
PHONE.....................309 686-3191
Carol Ruben, *President*
EMP: 3
SQ FT: 200
SALES: 25.7K Privately Held
SIC: 2711 Newspapers, publishing & printing

(G-16493)
PEORIA JOURNAL STAR INC
1 News Plz (61643-0001)
PHONE.....................309 686-3000
Ken Mauser, *President*
Brenda Van Hoorn, *Human Res Mgr*
Donna Moore, *Advt Staff*
Tina Hartle, *Consultant*
Garrett J Cummings,
▲ EMP: 217
SQ FT: 129,000
SALES: 16.6MM
SALES (corp-wide): 1.8B Publicly Held
WEB: www.pjstar.com
SIC: 2711 Commercial printing & newspaper publishing combined; newspapers, publishing & printing
PA: Gannett Co., Inc.
7950 Jones Branch Dr
Mc Lean VA 22102
703 854-6000

(G-16494)
PEORIA OPEN M R I
6708 N Knoxville Ave # 2 (61614-2863)
PHONE.....................309 692-7674
Bob Gitomer, *President*
EMP: 4
SALES (est): 355.4K Privately Held
SIC: 3826 Magnetic resonance imaging apparatus

(G-16495)
PEORIA POST INC
Also Called: Tradin Post Newspaper
834 E Glen Ave (61616-5206)
P.O. Box 1547 (61655-1547)
PHONE.....................309 688-3628
Jack S Brisbin, *President*
Jack Brisbin, *Mktg Dir*
Patricia Brisbin, *Admin Sec*
EMP: 15
SQ FT: 800

SALES: 1.5MM Privately Held
SIC: 2711 Shopping news: publishing only, not printed on site; newspapers

(G-16496)
PERFORMANCE PATTERN & MCH INC
Also Called: Ppm
2421 Sw Adams St (61602-1852)
PHONE.....................309 676-0907
Tom Herman, *President*
Scott Herman, *Vice Pres*
EMP: 24
SQ FT: 25,000
SALES (est): 4.5MM Privately Held
SIC: 3599 8711 Machine shop, jobbing & repair; engineering services

(G-16497)
PIERCE PACKAGING CO
2130 W Townline Rd (61615-1547)
PHONE.....................815 636-5656
John McNabb, *Branch Mgr*
EMP: 5
SALES (corp-wide): 59.5MM Privately Held
SIC: 4783 2441 Packing goods for shipping; crating goods for shipping; containerization of goods for shipping; boxes, wood
PA: Pierce Packaging Co.
2028 E Riverside Blvd
Loves Park IL 61111
815 636-5650

(G-16498)
PIERSONS MATTRESS INC
Also Called: Piersons Mattress & Furn Co
1034 S Western Ave (61605-3353)
PHONE.....................309 637-8455
Conrad G Pierson, *President*
EMP: 4
SQ FT: 12,500
SALES: 250K Privately Held
WEB: www.piersonmattressinc.com
SIC: 2515 5712 Mattresses, innerspring or box spring; furniture stores

(G-16499)
PMP FERMENTATION PRODUCTS INC
900 Ne Adams St (61603-4200)
PHONE.....................309 637-0400
Yuzo Kono, *President*
Randy Niedermeier, *Corp Secy*
Dennis Huff, *Vice Pres*
◆ EMP: 50 EST: 1985
SQ FT: 15,000
SALES (est): 16.7MM Privately Held
SIC: 2869 5169 Industrial organic chemicals; food additives & preservatives
PA: Fuso Chemical Co., Ltd.
4-3-10, Koraibashi, Chuo-Ku
Osaka OSK 541-0

(G-16500)
PPG ARCHITECTURAL FINISHES INC
Also Called: Glidden Professional Paint Ctr
404 Sw Adams St (61602-1520)
PHONE.....................309 673-3761
Tim Klise, *Branch Mgr*
EMP: 4
SALES (corp-wide): 15.1B Publicly Held
SIC: 5231 5198 2851 Paint; paints, varnishes & supplies; paints & allied products
HQ: Ppg Architectural Finishes, Inc.
1 Ppg Pl
Pittsburgh PA 15272
412 434-3131

(G-16501)
PRAGER ASSOCIATES
4035 W Tangleoaks Ct (61615-8909)
PHONE.....................309 691-1565
Steve Prager, *Owner*
EMP: 4
SALES (est): 200K Privately Held
SIC: 3651 5064 Household video equipment; electrical entertainment equipment

(G-16502)
PREMIER SIGNS CREATIONS INC
710 Fayette St (61603-3612)
PHONE.....................309 637-6890
Adam Reiger, *Owner*
Adam Rieger, *Owner*
EMP: 4
SALES (est): 373K Privately Held
SIC: 3993 Signs & advertising specialties

(G-16503)
PROFORM
Also Called: Maco Business Forms
708 Fayette St (61603-3612)
PHONE.....................309 676-2535
Tom James, *Manager*
EMP: 5
SALES (corp-wide): 1MM Privately Held
SIC: 2752 2761 Fashion plates, lithographed; manifold business forms
PA: Proform
1315 E London Ave
Peoria IL 61603
309 685-5814

(G-16504)
PROFORMA BUSINESS BUILDERS
810 W Pioneer Pkwy (61615-2145)
PHONE.....................309 692-6390
Jeff Brooke, *President*
EMP: 4 EST: 1999
SQ FT: 1,700
SALES (est): 757.2K Privately Held
SIC: 2752 Commercial printing, offset

(G-16505)
QUALITY METAL PRODUCTS INC
7006 N Galena Rd (61614-2296)
PHONE.....................309 692-8014
Jo Ellen Dunbar, *President*
Tim Swise, *General Mgr*
Lori Gaskins, *Vice Pres*
Gina Begner, *Treasurer*
Mark Urban, *Manager*
EMP: 125
SQ FT: 62,000
SALES: 23MM Privately Held
SIC: 3599 Machine shop, jobbing & repair

(G-16506)
R LAMAR ACADEMY INC
1110 N Orange St (61606-1346)
PHONE.....................309 712-8100
Amanda Foster, *Vice Pres*
Elizabeth Foster, *Bd of Directors*
Stephen Foster, *Bd of Directors*
EMP: 3
SALES (est): 118.7K Privately Held
SIC: 3523 Incubators & brooders, farm

(G-16507)
RABER PACKING COMPANY
1320 N Wood Rd (61604-4790)
PHONE.....................309 673-0721
Henry Courdt, *President*
Carroll Wetteraur, *Admin Sec*
EMP: 22 EST: 1954
SALES (est): 1.6MM Privately Held
WEB: www.raberpacking.com
SIC: 5421 2011 Meat markets, including freezer provisioners; meat packing plants

(G-16508)
RAPID PRINT
934 N Bourland Ave (61606-1718)
PHONE.....................309 673-0826
Thomas Madigan, *Owner*
Cindy Madigan, *Co-Owner*
EMP: 3
SQ FT: 2,500
SALES: 200K Privately Held
SIC: 2752 7334 2789 Commercial printing, offset; photocopying & duplicating services; bookbinding & related work

(G-16509)
RELX INC
Lexisnexis
8512 N Allen Rd (61615-1527)
PHONE.....................309 689-1000
Chris Lemons, *Branch Mgr*
EMP: 49

Peoria - Peoria County (G-16510) GEOGRAPHIC SECTION

SALES (corp-wide): 9.6B **Privately Held**
SIC: 2721 Periodicals
HQ: Relx Inc.
230 Park Ave Ste 700
New York NY 10169
212 309-8100

(G-16510)
RIVER CITY OIL LLC
3310 W Chartwell Rd (61614-2322)
PHONE 309 693-2249
Chittaranjan Reddy, *Principal*
EMP: 3
SALES (est): 186K **Privately Held**
SIC: 1311 Crude petroleum & natural gas

(G-16511)
RIVERSIDE TOOL & DIE CO
1616 W Chanute Rd Ste A (61615-1670)
PHONE 309 689-0104
Jeff Davis, *President*
Hunt Taylor, *Vice Pres*
EMP: 14
SQ FT: 12,000
SALES (est): 2.3MM **Privately Held**
SIC: 3599 Machine shop, jobbing & repair

(G-16512)
RO-WEB INC
Also Called: Kwik Kopy Printing
4440 N Prospect Rd Ste C (61616-6580)
PHONE 309 688-2155
Roger G Weber, *President*
Beverly F Weber, *Admin Sec*
EMP: 4
SQ FT: 1,730
SALES (est): 460.5K **Privately Held**
SIC: 2752 7334 5943 2791 Commercial printing, offset; photocopying & duplicating services; office forms & supplies; typesetting; bookbinding & related work

(G-16513)
ROECKERS INC
6523 N Galena Rd (61614-3103)
PHONE 309 693-2929
Samuel R Parrott, *President*
Kim Lopatka, *Design Engr Mgr*
Stephanie Blair, *Design Engr*
Stephainy Blair, *Admin Sec*
EMP: 6
SALES (est): 662.7K **Privately Held**
SIC: 2434 Wood kitchen cabinets

(G-16514)
ROGER BURKE JEWELERS INC
Also Called: Burke, Roger G Jewelers
4700 N University St 6 (61614-5890)
PHONE 309 692-0210
Roger Burke, *President*
Kathy Burke, *Admin Sec*
EMP: 15
SQ FT: 1,800
SALES (est): 760K **Privately Held**
SIC: 5944 7631 3911 Jewelry, precious stones & precious metals; jewelry repair services; jewel settings & mountings, precious metal

(G-16515)
ROHN PRODUCTS LLC (PA)
1 Fairholm Ave (61603-2319)
P.O. Box 5999 (61601-5999)
PHONE 309 697-4400
Oskar Haschke, *Project Engr*
Dan Ludolph, *CFO*
Joseph P O'Brien, *Mng Member*
Michael J O'Brien,
▼ **EMP:** 80
SQ FT: 2,000
SALES: 30MM **Privately Held**
SIC: 3441 Tower sections, radio & television transmission

(G-16516)
ROHN PRODUCTS LLC
6718 W Plank Rd Ste 2 (61604-7218)
PHONE 309 566-3000
JD Long, *Project Mgr*
Joseph P O'Brien, *Branch Mgr*
EMP: 41 **Privately Held**
SIC: 3441 Tower sections, radio & television transmission
PA: Rohn Products, Llc
1 Fairholm Ave
Peoria IL 61603

(G-16517)
ROME INDUSTRIES INC (PA)
1703 W Detweiller Dr (61615-1688)
PHONE 309 691-7120
Rrichard O'Russa, *President*
John Orussa, *Opers Mgr*
Michael Orussa, *Marketing Staff*
Ted Stone, *Manager*
▲ **EMP:** 6
SQ FT: 12,000
SALES (est): 3MM **Privately Held**
WEB: www.romeindustries.com
SIC: 3999 3365 Lawn ornaments; cooking/kitchen utensils, cast aluminum

(G-16518)
RUYLE MECHANICAL SERVICES INC
201 Spring St Ste B (61603-7002)
PHONE 309 674-6644
Steven Foster, *President*
Chris Benson, *Treasurer*
EMP: 60
SQ FT: 10,000
SALES (est): 16.2MM **Privately Held**
SIC: 3444 Sheet metalwork

(G-16519)
SENN ENTERPRISES INC (PA)
Also Called: University Sport Shop
1309 W Main St (61606-1148)
PHONE 309 637-1147
Carol Senn, *President*
EMP: 10
SALES (est): 932.3K **Privately Held**
SIC: 5699 2395 Sports apparel; embroidery & art needlework

(G-16520)
SENN ENTERPRISES INC
Also Called: Embroidery House
1829 W Main St (61606-1071)
PHONE 309 673-4384
Carol Senn, *President*
EMP: 3
SALES (est): 196.7K **Privately Held**
SIC: 2395 Embroidery products, except schiffli machine
PA: Senn Enterprises, Inc
1309 W Main St
Peoria IL 61606

(G-16521)
SEW WRIGHT EMBROIDERY INC
Also Called: Embroid ME
7810 N University St (61614-1206)
PHONE 309 691-5780
Patricia R Wright, *President*
Kim Goodwin, *Treasurer*
Toni D Waldschmidt, *Admin Sec*
EMP: 4
SQ FT: 1,700
SALES (est): 310.4K **Privately Held**
SIC: 5949 2759 Sewing, needlework & piece goods; screen printing; promotional printing

(G-16522)
SHAMROCK PLASTICS INC
2615 Alta Ln (61615-9646)
P.O. Box 3530 (61612-3530)
PHONE 309 243-7723
Mary Cay Westphal, *President*
Michael Wilkinson, *General Mgr*
Dan Beaird, *Prdtn Mgr*
Rhonda Jones, *Sales Executive*
Catherine M Westphal PHD, *Admin Sec*
EMP: 30
SQ FT: 36,000
SALES (est): 4.8MM **Privately Held**
WEB: www.shamrockplastics.net
SIC: 3089 Injection molding of plastics; plastic processing

(G-16523)
SHERATON ROAD LUMBER
Also Called: Doubet Window & Door
6600 N Sheridan Rd (61614-2935)
PHONE 309 691-0858
Chuck Brown, *President*
Helen Unes, *President*
Robert Unes, *Corp Secy*
EMP: 15 **EST:** 1951
SALES (est): 1.8MM **Privately Held**
WEB: www.srlco.com
SIC: 5211 3442 Planing mill products & lumber; doors, storm: wood or metal; windows, storm: wood or metal; prefabricated buildings; metal doors, sash & trim

(G-16524)
SIMFORMOTION LLC (PA)
316 Sw Washington St # 300 (61602-1406)
PHONE 309 263-7595
Renee Gorrell, *CEO*
Lara Aaron, *Vice Pres*
Kim Dillard, *Accounts Mgr*
Kenneth Pflederer,
▼ **EMP:** 19
SALES (est): 3.3MM **Privately Held**
SIC: 3699 8331 Automotive driving simulators (training aids), electronic; job training & vocational rehabilitation services

(G-16525)
SOLAZYME
910 Ne Adams St (61603-3904)
PHONE 309 258-5695
EMP: 4 **EST:** 2011
SALES (est): 320K **Privately Held**
SIC: 2899 Mfg Chemical Preparations

(G-16526)
SOMMER PRODUCTS COMPANY INC
Also Called: Stryco Industries
6523 N Galena Rd (61614-3103)
PHONE 309 697-1216
William Banks, *President*
W E Stewart, *Admin Sec*
▲ **EMP:** 54 **EST:** 1937
SQ FT: 20,000
SALES (est): 11.7MM **Privately Held**
WEB: www.micro-weld.com
SIC: 3548 Electric welding equipment

(G-16527)
SOUTHFIELD CORPORATION
Also Called: Prairie Construction Material
100 W Cass St (61602-1724)
PHONE 309 676-0576
Dave Minor, *Manager*
EMP: 30
SALES (corp-wide): 344.9MM **Privately Held**
SIC: 3273 1442 Ready-mixed concrete; gravel mining
PA: Southfield Corporation
8995 W 95th St
Palos Hills IL 60465
708 344-1000

(G-16528)
STAFFCO INC
Also Called: River City Enterprises
3806 N Northwood Ave (61614-7342)
PHONE 309 688-3223
Stewart Boal Jr, *President*
S H Boal, *Vice Pres*
EMP: 4
SALES (est): 358K **Privately Held**
SIC: 2655 3443 3412 3411 Fiber cans, drums & containers; fabricated plate work (boiler shop); metal barrels, drums & pails; metal cans; plastics plumbing fixtures

(G-16529)
STAINED GLASS OF PEORIA
2215 W Arrowhead Ln (61604-2325)
PHONE 309 674-7929
EMP: 4 **EST:** 1976
SQ FT: 4,000
SALES (est): 401.4K **Privately Held**
SIC: 5231 5932 3231 Ret Paint/Glass/Wallpaper Ret Used Merchandise Mfg Products-Purchased Glass

(G-16530)
STANDARD SHEET METAL WORKS INC
220 N Commerce Pl (61604-5286)
PHONE 309 633-2300
Jay C Harms, *Ch of Bd*
Nancy Harms, *Vice Pres*
Thomas Subbert, *Purch Agent*
Tom Subbert, *Human Res Mgr*
Tom Hyde, *Sales Staff*
EMP: 50
SALES (est): 13.3MM **Privately Held**
WEB: www.standardsheet.com
SIC: 3441 Fabricated structural metal

(G-16531)
SUPERIOR WATER SERVICES INC
Also Called: Superior Water Systems
5831 N Knoxville Ave (61614-4332)
PHONE 309 691-9287
Steven Warfield, *President*
Elling Johnson, *Sales Staff*
EMP: 5
SALES (est): 700K **Privately Held**
SIC: 3589 5078 5074 7389 Water purification equipment, household type; drinking water coolers, mechanical; water softeners; water softener service

(G-16532)
SYNDIGO LLC
Also Called: Kwikee
1720 W Detweiller Dr (61615-1612)
PHONE 309 690-5231
Sarah Ohnemus, *Business Mgr*
Mary E Alig, *Plant Mgr*
James Howell, *Engineer*
Shari Kuepker, *Accountant*
Mike Irish, *Natl Sales Mgr*
EMP: 141
SALES (corp-wide): 1.3B **Privately Held**
SIC: 2741 7374 3993 Miscellaneous publishing; computer graphics service; signs & advertising specialties
HQ: Syndigo Llc
141 W Jackson Blvd # 122
Chicago IL 60604
312 766-4801

(G-16533)
SYNERGETIC HOLDINGS LLC
Also Called: Chip's Tool & Machine Works
3012 Sw Adams St (61602-1977)
PHONE 309 673-2437
Robert Reed,
Daniel Morgan,
EMP: 11
SALES (est): 2.4MM **Privately Held**
SIC: 3544 Special dies & tools

(G-16534)
T J P INVESTMENTS INC
Also Called: Kelch, Bob Floors
2522 W War Memorial Dr (61615-3506)
PHONE 309 673-8383
Ted Plotkin, *President*
EMP: 7
SALES (est): 1MM **Privately Held**
SIC: 2426 Flooring, hardwood

(G-16535)
TAYLOR COMMUNICATIONS INC
1100 W Glen Ave Ste 300 (61614-4823)
PHONE 309 693-3700
Brian Mahoney, *Sales/Mktg Mgr*
EMP: 8
SALES (corp-wide): 2.5B **Privately Held**
WEB: www.taylorcorp.com
SIC: 2761 Manifold business forms
HQ: Taylor Communications, Inc.
1725 Roe Crest Dr
North Mankato MN 56003
866 541-0937

(G-16536)
TECHGRAPHIC SOLUTIONS INC
Also Called: Stylus Mart
8824 N Industrial Rd (61615-1535)
PHONE 309 693-9400
Marc W Klass, *President*
Sheldon Katz, *Vice Pres*
▲ **EMP:** 10
SQ FT: 5,000
SALES (est): 1.9MM **Privately Held**
SIC: 5045 2721 Computer peripheral equipment; periodicals

(G-16537)
TECHNICRAFT SUPPLY CO (PA)
Also Called: Technicraft Display Graphics
419 Elm St (61605-3969)
PHONE 309 495-5245
Thomas J Whalen, *President*
Karen K Whalen, *Vice Pres*
EMP: 4 **EST:** 1969
SQ FT: 6,000

GEOGRAPHIC SECTION   Peru - Lasalle County (G-16566)

SALES (est): 861.3K **Privately Held**
SIC: 5999 2759 3993 Picture frames, ready made; commercial printing; signs & advertising specialties

(G-16538)
TRI COUNTY CONCRETE
2021 E Harvard Ave (61614-7925)
PHONE.................................309 222-4000
Dan Converse, *President*
EMP: 3
SALES (est): 163.1K **Privately Held**
SIC: 3273 Ready-mixed concrete

(G-16539)
TRUE ROYALTY SCENTS
2404 N Elmwood Ave (61604-3206)
PHONE.................................309 992-0688
EMP: 4
SALES (est): 332.4K **Privately Held**
SIC: 2844 Toilet preparations

(G-16540)
UNIQUEE TEES INC
1200 W Main St Ste 25 (61606-1218)
PHONE.................................309 839-0280
Shundra Parker, *Principal*
EMP: 4
SALES (est): 130.2K **Privately Held**
SIC: 2759 Commercial printing

(G-16541)
UNITED READY MIX INC (PA)
1 Leland St (61602-1818)
PHONE.................................309 676-3287
Jack Hoffman, *President*
Lowell Hoffman, *Vice Pres*
EMP: 25 EST: 1965
SQ FT: 15,000
SALES (est): 4.3MM **Privately Held**
SIC: 3273 Ready-mixed concrete

(G-16542)
US SHREDDER CASTINGS GROUP INC
4408 N Rockwood Dr (61615-3765)
PHONE.................................309 359-3151
William Tigner, *President*
Bill Tigner, *President*
▲ EMP: 2
SALES (est): 531.6K **Privately Held**
SIC: 3531 Construction machinery

(G-16543)
USA EMBROIDERY
1605 W Candletree Dr # 102 (61614-1658)
PHONE.................................309 692-1391
Bill White, *Owner*
EMP: 3
SALES (est): 100K **Privately Held**
SIC: 2395 Embroidery products, except schiffli machine

(G-16544)
VIRTUSENSE TECHNOLOGIES INC
801 W Main St Rm B216 (61606-1877)
PHONE.................................855 443-5744
Deepak K Gaddipati, *Principal*
David Park, *Principal*
Deepak Gaddipati, *CTO*
EMP: 50
SALES (est): 612.5K **Privately Held**
SIC: 3845 Electromedical equipment

(G-16545)
WALDOS SPORTS CORNER INC
Also Called: Sports Corner & Creations
1306 E Seiberling Ave (61616-6446)
PHONE.................................309 688-2425
Roger Waldo, *President*
Karen Waldo, *Admin Sec*
EMP: 3
SQ FT: 600
SALES (est): 295.8K **Privately Held**
SIC: 5699 5941 2396 2395 Uniforms; team sports equipment; automotive & apparel trimmings; pleating & stitching

(G-16546)
WCR INC
1610 W Altorfer Dr (61615-1923)
PHONE.................................309 697-0389
Melissa Carter, *Sales Associate*
Jeff Newman, *Branch Mgr*
EMP: 25
SALES (est): 4.5MM
SALES (corp-wide): 49.4MM **Privately Held**
SIC: 3443 Fabricated plate work (boiler shop)
PA: Wcr Incorporated
2377 Commerce Center Blvd B
Fairborn OH 45324
937 223-0703

(G-16547)
WIRELESS EXPRESS INC CENTRAL
4732 N University St (61614-5831)
PHONE.................................309 689-9933
Gary Anderson, *Principal*
EMP: 4
SALES (est): 210K **Privately Held**
SIC: 2741 Miscellaneous publishing

(G-16548)
ZANTECH INC
7501 N Harker Dr (61615-1848)
PHONE.................................309 692-8307
Marc Young, *CEO*
EMP: 4
SALES (est): 383.3K **Privately Held**
SIC: 3873 Watches, clocks, watchcases & parts

(G-16549)
ZENDAVOR SIGNS & GRAPHICS INC
2251 W Altorfer Dr (61615-1807)
PHONE.................................309 691-8822
Steve Hodel, *Principal*
EMP: 6
SALES (est): 984.8K **Privately Held**
WEB: www.zendavor.com
SIC: 3993 Signs & advertising specialties

Peotone
Will County

(G-16550)
BC WELDING INC
Also Called: Bc Welding Service and Repair
308 E Crawford St (60468-9274)
PHONE.................................708 258-0076
Robert Cragin, *President*
EMP: 2
SALES (est): 200K **Privately Held**
SIC: 7692 Welding repair

(G-16551)
CARLSON SCIENTIFIC INC
514 S Third St (60468-9208)
PHONE.................................708 258-6377
Jeffrey R Carlson, *President*
Dorothy Carlson, *Vice Pres*
EMP: 6
SQ FT: 8,000
SALES (est): 634.6K **Privately Held**
SIC: 3826 Analytical instruments

(G-16552)
CLEVELAND STEEL CONTAINER CORP
117 E Lincoln St (60468-8989)
PHONE.................................708 258-0700
Robert Harding, *Manager*
EMP: 50
SALES (corp-wide): 131.9MM **Privately Held**
SIC: 3412 Pails, shipping: metal
PA: Cleveland Steel Container Corporation
30310 Emerald Valley Pkwy # 400
Solon OH 44139
440 349-8000

(G-16553)
HAWKINS INC
32040 S Route 45 (60468-9731)
PHONE.................................708 258-3797
Mike Carroll, *Branch Mgr*
EMP: 4
SALES (corp-wide): 540.2MM **Publicly Held**
SIC: 2899 Chemical preparations
PA: Hawkins, Inc.
2381 Rosegate
Roseville MN 55113
612 331-6910

(G-16554)
KUSMIEREK INDUSTRIES INC
6434 W North Peotone Rd (60468-9390)
P.O. Box 415 (60468-0415)
PHONE.................................708 258-3100
James Kusmierek, *President*
EMP: 3
SALES (est): 400.7K **Privately Held**
SIC: 3312 Chemicals & other products derived from coking

(G-16555)
NORTH AMERICA PACKAGING CORP
Also Called: Bennett Industries
515 N First St (60468-8975)
P.O. Box 519 (60468-0519)
PHONE.................................630 845-8726
James Engebretson, *Branch Mgr*
EMP: 113
SALES (corp-wide): 1.2B **Privately Held**
WEB: www.bwaycorp.com
SIC: 3089 Pails, plastic
HQ: North America Packaging Corp
1515 W 22nd St Ste 550
Oak Brook IL 60523
630 203-4100

(G-16556)
PHOENIX FABRICATION & SUP INC
481 S Governors Hwy (60468-9116)
PHONE.................................708 754-5901
Steve Anderson, *CEO*
EMP: 8
SQ FT: 55,000
SALES (est): 1.6MM **Privately Held**
SIC: 3441 Fabricated structural metal

(G-16557)
RUSSELL PUBLICATIONS INC
Also Called: Peotone Vidette
120 W North St (60468-9226)
P.O. Box 429 (60468-0429)
PHONE.................................708 258-3473
Christopher L Russell, *President*
Gilbert L Russell Jr, *President*
Sharon Russell, *Corp Secy*
EMP: 20 EST: 1894
SQ FT: 1,500
SALES (est): 1.2MM **Privately Held**
WEB: www.russell-publications.com
SIC: 2711 Newspapers, publishing & printing

(G-16558)
TERESA FOODS INC
Also Called: Teresa Frozen Pizzas
116 Main St (60468-9265)
PHONE.................................708 258-6200
Robert T Nagel, *President*
Paul Nagel Jr, *Vice Pres*
EMP: 15
SQ FT: 8,000
SALES (est): 2.2MM **Privately Held**
SIC: 2038 2099 Pizza, frozen; food preparations

Percy
Randolph County

(G-16559)
KNIGHT HAWK COAL LLC (PA)
500 Cutler Trico Rd (62272-2716)
PHONE.................................618 426-3662
Keith Dailey, *General Mgr*
Dale Winter, *Plant Mgr*
Josh Carter, *Opers Staff*
Jim Smith, *CFO*
Josh Norton, *Accounting Mgr*
EMP: 7
SQ FT: 6,000
SALES (est): 544.3MM **Privately Held**
WEB: www.knighthawkcoal.com
SIC: 1241 1222 Coal mining services; bituminous coal-underground mining

(G-16560)
RUDY BRENNEMAN
Also Called: Brenneman Welding & Equipment
1117 Puxico Rd (62272-2609)
PHONE.................................618 317-2329
Rudy Brenneman, *Owner*
EMP: 3
SALES (est): 8K **Privately Held**
SIC: 3523 Balers, farm: hay, straw, cotton, etc.

(G-16561)
WILLIS PUBLISHING
Also Called: County Journal
1101 E Pine St (62272-1333)
P.O. Box 369 (62272-0369)
PHONE.................................618 497-8272
Gerald Willis, *President*
Larry R Willis, *Vice Pres*
EMP: 19
SQ FT: 7,000
SALES (est): 1.1MM **Privately Held**
SIC: 2711 2752 Newspapers: publishing only, not printed on site; commercial printing, offset

Perry
Pike County

(G-16562)
PIONEER EXPRESS
404 W Highway St (62362-1045)
P.O. Box 158 (62362-0158)
PHONE.................................217 236-3022
Cheryl White, *Principal*
EMP: 5
SALES (est): 404K **Privately Held**
SIC: 3567 Industrial furnaces & ovens

Peru
Lasalle County

(G-16563)
ACCUBOW LLC
350 5th St Ste 266 (61354-2813)
PHONE.................................815 250-0607
Matthew Pell, *CEO*
Cody Grandadam, *COO*
Robert Pell, *Vice Pres*
Tim Turczyn, *CFO*
EMP: 4 EST: 2016
SALES (est): 195.3K **Privately Held**
SIC: 3089 Injection molded finished plastic products

(G-16564)
ANDREW C ARNOLD
Also Called: Andys Pet Shop
2228 4th St (61354-3213)
PHONE.................................815 220-0282
Andrew C Arnold, *Owner*
EMP: 1 EST: 2010
SALES (est): 200K **Privately Held**
SIC: 3999 3949 Pet supplies; sporting & athletic goods

(G-16565)
APPLE PRESS INC
2428 4th St (61354-3112)
PHONE.................................815 224-1451
Greg Vaccaro, *Partner*
Chuck Allman, *Partner*
EMP: 4
SQ FT: 4,000
SALES (est): 210K **Privately Held**
SIC: 2759 2791 2789 2752 Commercial printing; typesetting; bookbinding & related work; commercial printing, lithographic

(G-16566)
ARCHER-DANIELS-MIDLAND COMPANY
Also Called: ADM
100 Foot Of Brunner St (61354)
P.O. Box 447, La Salle (61301-0447)
PHONE.................................815 223-7907
John Yucus, *Manager*
EMP: 15

Peru - Lasalle County (G-16567)

SALES (corp-wide): 64.6B **Publicly Held**
SIC: 2041 5191 Flour & other grain mill products; animal feeds
PA: Archer-Daniels-Midland Company
77 W Wacker Dr Ste 4600
Chicago IL 60601
312 634-8100

(G-16567)
AUGUST HILL WINERY
21 N 2551st Rd (61354-9411)
PHONE...............................815 224-8199
W August, *Principal*
▲ **EMP:** 7 **EST:** 2008
SALES (est): 688.8K **Privately Held**
SIC: 2084 Wines

(G-16568)
BAKERY MCHY & FABRICATION LLC
307 Bakery Ave (61354-3660)
PHONE...............................815 224-1306
Cloyd W Barnes,
EMP: 8
SQ FT: 175,000
SALES (est): 1.8MM **Privately Held**
SIC: 3556 Food products machinery

(G-16569)
CANAM STEEL CORPORATION
9 Unytite Dr (61354-9710)
PHONE...............................815 224-9588
Brad Wilke, *Traffic Mgr*
EMP: 3
SALES (corp-wide): 1B **Privately Held**
SIC: 3441 Building components, structural steel
HQ: Canam Steel Corporation
4010 Clay St
Point Of Rocks MD 21777
301 874-5141

(G-16570)
CARUS GROUP INC (PA)
315 5th St (61354-2859)
PHONE...............................815 223-1500
Inga Carus, *Principal*
Gregory G Thiess, *Vice Pres*
Judy Wierman, *Vice Pres*
M Blouke Carus, *Chm Emeritus*
Mary Stachowicz, *Asst Sec*
EMP: 57
SALES: 124.5MM **Privately Held**
SIC: 2819 Potassium compounds or salts, except hydroxide or carbonate

(G-16571)
CARUS LLC (HQ)
315 5th St (61354-2859)
P.O. Box 599 (61354-0599)
PHONE...............................815 223-1500
Inga Carus, *Ch of Bd*
David Kuzy, *President*
Susan Buchanan, *CFO*
Barbie Smith, *Sales Staff*
Brian Downing, *Manager*
◆ **EMP:** 56 **EST:** 1915
SQ FT: 56,000
SALES (est): 60.4MM
SALES (corp-wide): 60.6MM **Privately Held**
WEB: www.caruscorporation.com
SIC: 2819 Potassium compounds or salts, except hydroxide or carbonate
PA: Condy Holdings Llc
315 5th St
Peru IL 61354
815 223-1500

(G-16572)
CENTRAL STATE COCA-COLA PERU
3808 Progress Blvd (61354-1120)
PHONE...............................815 220-3100
EMP: 3 **EST:** 2017
SALES (est): 114.8K **Privately Held**
SIC: 2086 Bottled & canned soft drinks

(G-16573)
CONDY HOLDINGS LLC (PA)
315 5th St (61354-2859)
PHONE...............................815 223-1500
Inga Carus, *Ch of Bd*
EMP: 2

SALES (est): 60.6MM **Privately Held**
SIC: 2819 6719 Industrial inorganic chemicals; personal holding companies, except banks

(G-16574)
DRESBACH DISTRIBUTING CO
102 Pike St (61354-3477)
PHONE...............................815 223-0116
Robert Dresbach, *President*
EMP: 7
SQ FT: 18,000
SALES (est): 1.7MM **Privately Held**
WEB: www.dresbachdistributing.com
SIC: 5181 2671 Beer & other fermented malt liquors; packaging paper & plastics film, coated & laminated

(G-16575)
EAKAS CORPORATION
6251 State Route 251 (61354-9711)
PHONE...............................815 223-8811
Tomohisa Mori, *President*
Tony Mattiazza, *COO*
Cary Miller, *Plant Mgr*
Jeff Wagner, *Plant Mgr*
Susan Scheri, *Purch Agent*
▲ **EMP:** 275
SQ FT: 200,000
SALES (est): 79.4MM **Privately Held**
SIC: 3714 Motor vehicle parts & accessories
PA: Sakae Riken Kogyo Co., Ltd.
1-48, Nishibiwajimachomiyamae
Kiyosu AIC 452-0

(G-16576)
FLINT HILLS RESOURCES LP
501 Brunner St (61354-3638)
PHONE...............................815 224-5232
EMP: 3
SALES (corp-wide): 48.9B **Privately Held**
SIC: 2821 Polystyrene resins
HQ: Flint Hills Resources, Lp
4111 E 37th St N
Wichita KS 67220
800 292-3133

(G-16577)
HUNTSMAN EXPNDABLE POLYMERS LC
501 Brunner St (61354-3638)
PHONE...............................815 224-5463
Peter R Huntsman,
EMP: 111
SALES (est): 8MM
SALES (corp-wide): 6.8B **Publicly Held**
SIC: 3081 2821 Plastic film & sheet; plastics materials & resins; polyethylene resins; polypropylene resins; styrene resins
HQ: Huntsman-Cooper, L.L.C.
500 S Huntsman Way
Salt Lake City UT 84108
801 584-5700

(G-16578)
ILLINOIS VALLEY CONTAINER INC
2 Terminal Rd (61354-3700)
P.O. Box 49 (61354-0049)
PHONE...............................815 223-7200
Jay Alter, *President*
John Reinhardt, *Production*
Gary Wetsel, *Sales Staff*
EMP: 20
SQ FT: 40,000
SALES (est): 6MM **Privately Held**
WEB: www.ivcontainer.com
SIC: 2653 Boxes, corrugated: made from purchased materials

(G-16579)
KAWNEER COMPANY INC
2528 7th St (61354-2424)
PHONE...............................815 224-2708
EMP: 81
SALES (corp-wide): 23.9B **Publicly Held**
SIC: 3442 Mfg Metal Doors/Sash/Trim
HQ: Kawneer Company, Inc.
555 Guthridge Ct
Norcross GA 30092
770 449-5555

(G-16580)
LANGHAM ENGINEERING
1414 Shooting Park Rd (61354-1857)
PHONE...............................815 223-5250
J Michael Langham, *CEO*
Rob Pangicie, *Foreman/Supr*
EMP: 3
SQ FT: 4,000
SALES (est): 176.2K **Privately Held**
SIC: 8711 3825 3824 3663 Mechanical engineering; electrical or electronic engineering; instruments to measure electricity; fluid meters & counting devices; radio & TV communications equipment; switchgear & switchboard apparatus

(G-16581)
MERTEL GRAVEL COMPANY INC
2400 Water St (61354-3494)
PHONE...............................815 223-0468
Susan J Happ, *President*
Terry Mertel, *Vice Pres*
EMP: 10 **EST:** 1922
SQ FT: 800
SALES (est): 1.8MM **Privately Held**
WEB: www.mertelgravelreadymix.com
SIC: 3273 5032 1794 1442 Ready-mixed concrete; sand, construction; gravel; excavation work; construction sand & gravel

(G-16582)
METOKOTE CORPORATION
5750 State Route 251 (61354-9712)
PHONE...............................815 223-1190
James Kelly, *Manager*
EMP: 50
SALES (corp-wide): 15.1B **Publicly Held**
SIC: 3479 3471 Coating of metals & formed products; plating & polishing
HQ: Metokote Corporation
1340 Neubrecht Rd
Lima OH 45801
419 996-7800

(G-16583)
NANOCHEM SOLUTIONS INC
5350 Donlar Ave (61354-9622)
PHONE...............................815 224-8480
Don Anderson, *Manager*
EMP: 13
SALES (est): 2.6MM **Privately Held**
SIC: 2819 Industrial inorganic chemicals
PA: Nanochem Solutions Inc.
1701 Quincy Ave Ste 10
Naperville IL 60540

(G-16584)
NEW CIE INC
Motor Repair Division
3349 Becker Dr (61354-1161)
PHONE...............................815 224-1511
Harold Konieczki, *Manager*
EMP: 30
SALES (corp-wide): 15.9MM **Privately Held**
SIC: 3537 5063 7694 5999 Industrial trucks & tractors; electrical apparatus & equipment; armature rewinding shops; motors, electric; machine shop, jobbing & repair; machine moving & rigging
PA: New Cie, Inc.
1220 Wenzel Rd
Peru IL 61354
815 224-1510

(G-16585)
NICKS EMERGENCY LTG & MORE
3003 7th St (61354-2433)
PHONE...............................815 780-8327
Nicholas J Biagioni, *Owner*
EMP: 2
SALES (est): 293.3K **Privately Held**
SIC: 3648 Lighting equipment

(G-16586)
NOVA CHEMICALS INC
Also Called: Humpsman
501 Brunner St (61354-3638)
PHONE...............................815 224-1525
Brian Marcinkus, *Manager*
EMP: 53 **Privately Held**
SIC: 2821 Polystyrene resins

HQ: Nova Chemicals Inc.
1555 Coraopolis Hts Rd
Moon Township PA 15108
412 490-4000

(G-16587)
OZCUT INC
350 5th St Ste 266 (61354-2813)
PHONE...............................630 605-7398
Matthew Pell, *Principal*
EMP: 3
SALES (est): 83.9K **Privately Held**
SIC: 3999 Barber & beauty shop equipment

(G-16588)
P & D SIGN CO
1708 4th St (61354-3323)
PHONE...............................815 224-9220
Tim Iwanicki, *Branch Mgr*
EMP: 6
SALES (corp-wide): 1MM **Privately Held**
SIC: 3993 Signs & advertising specialties
PA: P & D Sign Co
411 S Main Ave
Ladd IL

(G-16589)
PGI MFG LLC
Also Called: Peru Plant
4747 Industrial Dr (61354-9329)
PHONE...............................815 224-7540
John Emmerling, *Branch Mgr*
EMP: 150
SALES (corp-wide): 39.1MM **Privately Held**
SIC: 3599 Machine shop, jobbing & repair
PA: Pgi Mfg., Llc
51565 Bittersweet Rd B
Granger IN 46530
574 968-3222

(G-16590)
PRETIUM PACKAGING LLC
4444 Hollerich Dr (61354-9334)
PHONE...............................815 224-2633
Robert Benton, *Plant Mgr*
Julie Perilla, *Marketing Staff*
John Kennedy, *Manager*
EMP: 80
SALES (corp-wide): 868.8MM **Privately Held**
SIC: 3089 3085 Molding primary plastic; plastics bottles
PA: Pretium Packaging, L.L.C.
15450 S Oter Frty Dr Ste
Chesterfield MO 63017
314 727-8200

(G-16591)
PROMIER PRODUCTS INC
350 5th St Ste 266 (61354-2813)
PHONE...............................815 223-3393
Cody Grandadam, *President*
Tim Turczyn, *CFO*
Prontip Larson, *Graphic Designe*
EMP: 10
SQ FT: 1,500
SALES: 8MM **Privately Held**
SIC: 3648 Flashlights

(G-16592)
ROYAL PUBLISHING INC
4375 Venture Dr (61354-1014)
PHONE...............................815 220-0400
John Shurtleff, *Branch Mgr*
EMP: 9
SALES (corp-wide): 7MM **Privately Held**
SIC: 2731 Pamphlets: publishing & printing
PA: Royal Publishing, Inc.
7620 N Harker Dr
Peoria IL
309 693-3171

(G-16593)
SALES STRETCHER ENTERPRISES
4920 E 103rd Rd (61354-9356)
P.O. Box 449 (61354-0049)
PHONE...............................815 223-9681
Rolif Loveland, *President*
▲ **EMP:** 18
SALES (est): 2.7MM **Privately Held**
SIC: 2952 5051 Coating compounds, tar; nails

GEOGRAPHIC SECTION

(G-16594)
T & T DISTRIBUTION INC
Also Called: T&T Hydraulics
304 5th St (61354-2813)
PHONE....................815 223-0715
Mike Turczyn, *President*
Tim Turczyn, *CFO*
Chester Turczyn, *Admin Sec*
EMP: 25
SQ FT: 18,000
SALES (est): 1.9MM **Privately Held**
SIC: 3492 5084 Hose & tube fittings & assemblies, hydraulic/pneumatic; drilling bits

(G-16595)
UNYTITE INC
1 Unytite Dr (61354-9710)
PHONE....................815 224-2221
Jun Hashimoto, *President*
Mike Hegland, *President*
Yuji Ozeki, *Vice Pres*
Andrew Liang, *Engineer*
Ron Pioli, *Engineer*
▲ **EMP:** 105
SQ FT: 125,000
SALES (est): 36MM **Privately Held**
SIC: 3452 Bolts, nuts, rivets & washers
PA: Unytite Corporation
  3-1-12, Takatsukadai, Nishi-Ku
  Kobe HYO 651-2

(G-16596)
W H MAZE COMPANY (PA)
Also Called: Maze Nails Div
1100 Water St (61354-3654)
P.O. Box 449 (61354-0449)
PHONE....................815 223-1742
Roelif Loveland, *President*
Pete Loveland, *General Mgr*
Roger Vaccaro, *Vice Pres*
Dave Munson, *Opers Mgr*
Chadd Kreofsky, *Engineer*
▲ **EMP:** 125
SQ FT: 15,700
SALES (est): 20.7MM **Privately Held**
WEB: www.mazenails.com
SIC: 3315 5211 Nails, steel: wire or cut; lumber & other building materials

(G-16597)
W H MAZE COMPANY
Maze Nails Division
100 Church St (61354-3498)
P.O. Box 449 (61354-0449)
PHONE....................815 223-8290
Len Kasperski, *Vice Pres*
Jamie Kreiser, *Vice Pres*
Jim Kaszynski, *Marketing Staff*
Roelif Loveland, *Manager*
Jim Loveland, *Manager*
EMP: 99
SALES (corp-wide): 20.7MM **Privately Held**
WEB: www.mazenails.com
SIC: 3315 Nails, steel: wire or cut
PA: W. H. Maze Company
  1100 Water St
  Peru IL 61354
  815 223-1742

(G-16598)
WILLIAM N PASULKA
Also Called: Home Water Products
15685 State Highway 71 (61354-5005)
PHONE....................815 339-6300
William Pasulka, *Owner*
Nick Pasulka, *Co-Owner*
EMP: 1 EST: 1977
SQ FT: 5,000
SALES: 5MM **Privately Held**
SIC: 3589 3651 Water purification equipment, household type; home entertainment equipment, electronic

Pesotum
Champaign County

(G-16599)
ROUTE 45 WAYSIDE
101 S Chestnut St (61863-9500)
PHONE....................217 867-2000
Christyn H Grassman, *Principal*
EMP: 4
SALES (est): 359.5K **Privately Held**
SIC: 2599 Bar, restaurant & cafeteria furniture

Petersburg
Menard County

(G-16600)
BACKYARD CREATIONS
14389 State Highway 97 (62675-6012)
PHONE....................217 836-5678
George Ford, *Owner*
EMP: 4
SALES: 350K **Privately Held**
SIC: 2421 4212 Building & structural materials, wood; moving services

(G-16601)
CURRY READY MIX OF PETERSBURG
1106 N 7th St (62675-1178)
PHONE....................217 632-2516
Dan Curry, *Owner*
EMP: 4
SALES (est): 349.1K **Privately Held**
SIC: 3273 Ready-mixed concrete

(G-16602)
INDESCO OVEN PRODUCTS INC
15935 Whisper Ln (62675-7200)
PHONE....................217 622-6345
Norman P Jones, *President*
EMP: 7
SALES (est): 750.6K **Privately Held**
SIC: 8742 3822 Automation & robotics consultant; gas burner, automatic controls

(G-16603)
PETERSBURG OBSERVER CO INC
235 E Sangamon Ave (62675-1245)
P.O. Box 350 (62675-0350)
PHONE....................217 632-2236
Harriett Shaw, *President*
Jane Cutright, *Corp Secy*
EMP: 7
SQ FT: 5,000
SALES (est): 350K **Privately Held**
WEB: www.petersburgil.com
SIC: 2711 2759 2752 Newspapers: publishing only, not printed on site; letterpress printing; commercial printing, lithographic

(G-16604)
SNAGAMON VALLEY LOG BUILDERS
21500 Old Farm Ave (62675-6072)
PHONE....................217 632-7609
Jeff Fore, *Owner*
EMP: 3
SALES (est): 222.2K **Privately Held**
SIC: 2452 Log cabins, prefabricated, wood

(G-16605)
WINERY WEST OF WISE
14096 State Highway 97 (62675-6017)
PHONE....................217 632-6003
Darrell Simmermaker, *Owner*
EMP: 3
SALES (est): 92.2K **Privately Held**
SIC: 2084 Wines

Philo
Champaign County

(G-16606)
JAMAICA PYROTECHNICS (PA)
Also Called: Jpi
212 Franks Dr (61864-9676)
PHONE....................217 649-2902
Todd Chew, *Partner*
EMP: 3
SALES (est): 329.5K **Privately Held**
SIC: 2899 Fireworks

(G-16607)
LOCKWOOD CUSTOM OPTICS INC
648 County Road 1700 E (61864-9724)
PHONE....................217 684-2170
Michael Lockwood, *Principal*
EMP: 3 EST: 2011
SALES (est): 204K **Privately Held**
SIC: 3827 Optical instruments & lenses

Phoenix
Cook County

(G-16608)
JOHN J RICKHOFF SHTMTL CO INC
320 E 152nd St (60426-2305)
PHONE....................708 331-2970
John E Rickhoff, *President*
Judy Rickhoff, *Principal*
Anthony Rickhoff, *Vice Pres*
Donna Rickhoff, *Admin Sec*
EMP: 10 EST: 1937
SQ FT: 12,000
SALES (est): 1.1MM **Privately Held**
SIC: 1761 3542 3444 Sheet metalwork; machine tools, metal forming type; sheet metalwork

(G-16609)
STERLING SITE ACCESS SOL (PA)
501 E 151st St (60426-2402)
PHONE....................708 388-2223
Carter Sterling, *CEO*
John Sterling, *CEO*
Michael O'Connell, *President*
Josh Warren, *Business Mgr*
John Capodice, *Exec VP*
◆ **EMP:** 250
SQ FT: 500,000
SALES (est): 138.6MM **Privately Held**
WEB: www.sterlingcranemats.com
SIC: 5031 7389 2448 Lumber: rough, dressed & finished; log & lumber broker; pallets, wood; skids, wood

Piasa
Macoupin County

(G-16610)
WAYMORE POWER CO INC
8334 Piasa Rd (62079-2024)
PHONE....................618 729-3876
Spencer Garrett, *President*
Julie Garrett, *Vice Pres*
EMP: 10
SALES (est): 1.1MM **Privately Held**
SIC: 7538 3519 Diesel engine repair: automotive; internal combustion engines

Pinckneyville
Perry County

(G-16611)
BEELMAN READY-MIX INC
5780 State Route 154 (62274-3420)
PHONE....................618 357-6120
Kiah McCance, *Manager*
EMP: 7 **Privately Held**
WEB: www.beelman.com
SIC: 3273 5211 Ready-mixed concrete; masonry materials & supplies
PA: Beelman Ready-Mix, Inc.
  1 Racehorse Dr
  East Saint Louis IL 62205

(G-16612)
COOPER B-LINE INC
Gs Metals
3764 Longspur Rd (62274-3103)
PHONE....................618 357-5353
Kenneth Alessi, *Branch Mgr*
EMP: 170 **Privately Held**
SIC: 3446 Gratings, tread: fabricated metal
HQ: Cooper B-Line, Inc.
  509 W Monroe St
  Highland IL 62249
  618 654-2184

(G-16613)
DESIGNS UNLIMITED
1242 S Main St (62274-3312)
PHONE....................618 357-6728
Steve R Tanner, *Owner*
EMP: 4
SALES (est): 296.9K **Privately Held**
SIC: 3993 Signs & advertising specialties

(G-16614)
FRESH FACS
612 County Rd (62274-1512)
PHONE....................618 357-9697
Ramona Hatch, *Owner*
EMP: 4
SALES (est): 297.4K **Privately Held**
WEB: www.freshfacs.com
SIC: 2741 Miscellaneous publishing

(G-16615)
FRIENDS PYRAMID STATE PARK INC
804 Belle Ave (62274-1506)
PHONE....................618 318-3992
Dr Charles Roe, *President*
Don Bigham, *Principal*
Josh Carter, *Principal*
Steve Carter, *Principal*
Peter Coppins, *Principal*
EMP: 19
SALES (est): 466.7K **Privately Held**
SIC: 2711 Newspapers

(G-16616)
GRAFFS TOOLING CENTER INC
801 S Main St (62274-1768)
PHONE....................618 357-5005
Marvin Graff, *President*
EMP: 6
SALES (est): 871.4K **Privately Held**
SIC: 3599 Machine shop, jobbing & repair

(G-16617)
GS METALS CORP
3764 Longspur Rd (62274-3103)
PHONE....................618 357-5353
Kenneth W Coco, *President*
Dennis J Gallitano, *Admin Sec*
▼ **EMP:** 170
SALES (est): 23.9MM **Privately Held**
SIC: 3446 Gratings, tread: fabricated metal

(G-16618)
PHOENIX GRAPHIX
4513 Swanwick Rice Rd (62274-2007)
PHONE....................618 531-3664
Christopher Wright, *Owner*
EMP: 4
SQ FT: 2,000
SALES: 250K **Privately Held**
SIC: 2241 5131 7336 Apparel webbing; trimmings, apparel; creative services to advertisers, except writers

(G-16619)
SIEMENS ENERGY INC
4646 White Walnut Rd (62274-2726)
PHONE....................618 357-6360
Tom Schrader, *Manager*
EMP: 209
SALES (corp-wide): 96.9B **Privately Held**
SIC: 3511 Turbines & turbine generator sets
HQ: Siemens Energy, Inc.
  444 Highway 49 S
  Richland MS 39218
  407 736-2000

(G-16620)
TREE-O LUMBER INC
5492 Woodhaven Rd (62274-2616)
P.O. Box 366 (62274-0366)
PHONE....................618 357-2576
Fred Kelly, *President*
Edreye Kelly, *Admin Sec*
EMP: 20
SALES (est): 2MM **Privately Held**
SIC: 2421 2431 2426 Sawmills & planing mills, general; millwork; hardwood dimension & flooring mills

Pingree Grove
Kane County

(G-16621)
ELGIN DIE MOLD CO
14n002 Prairie St (60140-6314)
PHONE...............................847 464-0140
John Sapiente, *President*
Rachael Heath, *General Mgr*
Bill Ruba, *Vice Pres*
Kent Wallace, *Production*
Jason Franklin, *Engineer*
EMP: 80 **EST:** 1967
SALES (est): 20MM **Privately Held**
WEB: www.elgindiemold.com
SIC: 3089 Molding primary plastic; injection molding of plastics

(G-16622)
MINUTEMAN INTERNATIONAL INC (DH)
14n845 Us Highway 20 (60140-8893)
PHONE...............................630 627-6900
Steve Liew, *CEO*
Mario Schreiber, *President*
John Troy, *Division Mgr*
Stephen Boebel, *Vice Pres*
Tim Vendegna, *Prdtn Mgr*
◆ **EMP:** 120 **EST:** 1951
SQ FT: 112,230
SALES (est): 36.5MM
SALES (corp-wide): 360.4K **Privately Held**
WEB: www.minutemanintl.com
SIC: 3589 2842 Commercial cleaning equipment; cleaning or polishing preparations
HQ: Hako Gmbh
Hamburger Str. 209-239
Bad Oldesloe 23843
453 180-60

(G-16623)
POWERBOSS INC
14n845 Us Highway 20 (60140-8893)
PHONE...............................630 627-6900
Steve Liew, *President*
Mario Schreiber, *Vice Pres*
▼ **EMP:** 125
SQ FT: 130,000
SALES (est): 16.9MM
SALES (corp-wide): 360.4K **Privately Held**
SIC: 3589 Vacuum cleaners & sweepers, electric: industrial
PA: Possehl-Stiftung
Beckergrube 38-52
Lubeck
451 148-200

(G-16624)
TRIDENT MANUFACTURING INC
14n2 Prairie St (60140)
PHONE...............................847 464-0140
John A Sapiente, *Chairman*
▲ **EMP:** 20 **Privately Held**
SIC: 3089 Injection molding of plastics

Piper City
Ford County

(G-16625)
ATS COMMERCIAL GROUP LLC
Also Called: Ats Acoustics
15 W Main St (60959-6031)
P.O. Box 260 (60959-0260)
PHONE...............................815 686-2705
Cynthia Starns, *Production*
Jordan Holliman, *Engineer*
Mark Aardsma,
▲ **EMP:** 11
SQ FT: 6,000
SALES: 1.3MM **Privately Held**
SIC: 7379 3695 Computer related consulting services; computer software tape & disks: blank, rigid & floppy

Pittsburg
Williamson County

(G-16626)
ANDERSON TRUSS COMPANY
12418 Poordo Rd (62974-1802)
PHONE...............................618 982-9228
Boyd Anderson, *President*
EMP: 4
SQ FT: 3,840
SALES (est): 420K **Privately Held**
SIC: 2439 Trusses, wooden roof

Pittsfield
Pike County

(G-16627)
AACTION PRINTING
652 Lowry St (62363-1768)
PHONE...............................951 788-5111
Judy Smith, *Owner*
EMP: 4
SALES (est): 293.8K **Privately Held**
SIC: 2759 Commercial printing

(G-16628)
B & B PRINTING COMPANY
115 E Washington St A (62363-1436)
PHONE...............................217 285-6072
Christopher Metcalf, *Owner*
EMP: 4 **EST:** 1967
SALES (est): 220K **Privately Held**
SIC: 2752 2791 2789 2761 Commercial printing, offset; typesetting; bookbinding & related work; manifold business forms; commercial printing; packaging paper & plastics film, coated & laminated

(G-16629)
BUCKLEY POWDER CO
1353 W Washington St (62363-9549)
PHONE...............................217 285-5531
EMP: 8
SALES (corp-wide): 49.5MM **Privately Held**
SIC: 2892 Explosives
PA: Buckley Powder Co.
42 Inverness Dr E Ste 200
Englewood CO 80112
303 790-7007

(G-16630)
CALLENDER CONSTRUCTION CO INC (PA)
928 W Washington St (62363-1356)
PHONE...............................217 285-2161
Bruce Callender, *President*
EMP: 10 **EST:** 1946
SQ FT: 5,000
SALES (est): 6.7MM **Privately Held**
SIC: 1422 4212 1794 Crushed & broken limestone; dump truck haulage; excavation & grading, building construction

(G-16631)
CAMPBELL PUBLISHING CO INC
Also Called: Pike Press
115 W Jefferson St (62363-1424)
P.O. Box 70 (62363-0070)
PHONE...............................217 285-2345
EMP: 6
SALES (corp-wide): 2MM **Privately Held**
SIC: 2711 Newspapers, publishing & printing
PA: Campbell Publishing Co Inc
310 S County Rd
Hardin IL
618 576-2345

(G-16632)
CENTRAL STONE COMPANY
26176 487th St (62363-2400)
PHONE...............................217 723-4410
Doug Brackett, *Manager*
EMP: 12
SALES (corp-wide): 2.5B **Privately Held**
SIC: 1422 Limestones, ground
HQ: Central Stone Company
4640 E 56th St
Davenport IA 52807
309 757-8250

(G-16633)
COMMUNITY RADY MIX OF PTTSFELD
Also Called: Community Ready Mix Pittsfield
1503 Kamar Dr (62363-2005)
PHONE...............................217 285-5548
Ray Curry, *President*
EMP: 5
SALES (est): 285.6K **Privately Held**
SIC: 3273 Ready-mixed concrete

(G-16634)
GOD FAMILY COUNTRY LLC
Also Called: Gfc
34273 210th Ave (62363-2716)
PHONE...............................217 285-6487
Owen Brown,
EMP: 13
SALES (est): 575K **Privately Held**
WEB: www.balebandit.com
SIC: 2011 Beef products from beef slaughtered on site

(G-16635)
KCI SATELLITE
101 N Industrial Park Dr (62363-2006)
PHONE...............................800 664-2602
Patrick Brian Shelton, *President*
EMP: 4
SALES (est): 519K **Privately Held**
SIC: 2599 Hospital beds

(G-16636)
OWEN WALKER
Also Called: Walker's Repair Shop
837 W Adams St (62363-1311)
PHONE...............................217 285-4012
Fax: 217 285-4456
EMP: 3
SQ FT: 1,000
SALES: 100K **Privately Held**
SIC: 7699 5251 5261 5084 Repair Services Ret Hardware Ret Nursery/Garden Supp Whol Industrial Equip

(G-16637)
PIKE COUNTY CONCRETE INC
1503 Kamar Dr (62363-2005)
PHONE...............................217 285-5548
Steve Dunham, *President*
Dwight Dunham, *Vice Pres*
Scott Dunham, *Treasurer*
EMP: 6
SALES (est): 644.2K **Privately Held**
SIC: 3273 Ready-mixed concrete

(G-16638)
PIKE COUNTY EXPRESS
Also Called: Coulson Publications
129 N Madison St (62363-1405)
P.O. Box 537 (62363-0537)
PHONE...............................217 285-5415
Robin Otiker, *Principal*
EMP: 16
SALES (est): 872.5K **Privately Held**
WEB: www.pikecountysd.org
SIC: 2711 Newspapers, publishing & printing

Plainfield
Will County

(G-16639)
A AND J DEVELOPMENT PLUS LLC
10101 S Mandel St Ste A (60585-6866)
PHONE...............................630 470-9539
Bill Shippy, *Owner*
EMP: 8 **EST:** 2010
SALES: 160K **Privately Held**
SIC: 2431 Millwork

(G-16640)
AK STEEL CORPORATION
24036 Nightingale Ct (60585-6170)
PHONE...............................815 267-3838
Mark Lambert, *Manager*
EMP: 298
SALES (corp-wide): 1.9B **Publicly Held**
SIC: 3312 Blast furnaces & steel mills
HQ: Ak Steel Corporation
9227 Centre Pointe Dr
West Chester OH 45069

(G-16641)
ALL TECH SYSTEMS & INSTALL
11952 S Spaulding Schl Dr (60585-9535)
PHONE...............................815 609-0685
Paul Allen, *President*
Karen Allen, *Vice Pres*
William Allen, *Admin Sec*
EMP: 4
SQ FT: 7,000
SALES (est): 540K **Privately Held**
SIC: 3669 Burglar alarm apparatus, electric

(G-16642)
AMS SEALS INC
12149 Rhea Dr (60585-9734)
PHONE...............................815 609-4977
Ernie Spiess, *President*
EMP: 7
SQ FT: 5,500
SALES (est): 2.2MM **Privately Held**
SIC: 5085 3624 Seals, industrial; carbon & graphite products

(G-16643)
AUTHORITY SCREENPRINT & EMB
10148 Clow Creek Rd Ste D (60585-6748)
PHONE...............................630 236-0289
Mandy Prendki, *President*
EMP: 2
SQ FT: 780
SALES (est): 251.1K **Privately Held**
WEB: www.authorityscreenprint.com
SIC: 2759 2396 Screen printing; automotive & apparel trimmings

(G-16644)
BEST TECHNOLOGY SYSTEMS INC
12024 S Aero Dr (60585-9702)
PHONE...............................815 254-9554
Gary Chinn, *President*
Barbra Crowder, *Admin Asst*
EMP: 22
SQ FT: 2,800
SALES (est): 1.9MM **Privately Held**
SIC: 7999 1799 3949 4959 Shooting range operation; decontamination services; sporting & athletic goods; shooting equipment & supplies, general; sanitary services

(G-16645)
BUILDINGPOINT MIDWEST LLC
12360 S Industrial Dr E # 1 (60585-8511)
PHONE...............................855 332-7527
Fisher Richard,
EMP: 2
SALES (est): 4.3MM **Privately Held**
SIC: 3429 Builders' hardware

(G-16646)
CALLIES CUTIES INC
24860 Madison St (60544-7444)
PHONE...............................815 566-6885
Laura Meehan, *President*
Thomas Meehan, *Admin Sec*
EMP: 4
SQ FT: 1,350
SALES (est): 280.1K **Privately Held**
SIC: 2051 5149 Cakes, bakery: except frozen; crackers, cookies & bakery products

(G-16647)
CAMBRIDGE SENSORS USA LLC
Also Called: Cambridge Sensor Limited
23866 W Industrial Dr N (60585-8567)
PHONE...............................877 374-4062
Scott Lefevre, *Vice Pres*
Engimann Frederick, *Mng Member*
EMP: 3
SALES (est): 769.5K **Privately Held**
SIC: 3826 8099 Blood testing apparatus; childbirth preparation clinic

GEOGRAPHIC SECTION
Plainfield - Will County (G-16679)

(G-16648)
CATHYS SWEET CREATIONS
519 W Lockport Rd (60544-1831)
PHONE.................................815 886-6769
Catherine M Deavila, *President*
Cathy Deavila, *Owner*
EMP: 4
SALES (est): 331.5K **Privately Held**
SIC: 2051 Bakery products, partially cooked (except frozen)

(G-16649)
CB&I TYLER LLC
14105 S Route 59 (60544-3890)
PHONE.................................281 774-2200
Gerald Glenn, *President*
Robert Wolfe, *Vice Pres*
Richard Goodrich, *CFO*
Richard A Byers, *Treasurer*
Scott Russell, *Admin Sec*
EMP: 3
SALES (est): 268.5K
SALES (corp-wide): 8.4B **Privately Held**
SIC: 3443 Industrial vessels, tanks & containers
HQ: Chicago Bridge & Iron Company
  757 N Eldridge Pkwy
  Houston TX 77079
  281 870-5000

(G-16650)
CHICAGO DSCOVERY SOLUTIONS LLC
23561 W Main St (60544-7601)
PHONE.................................815 609-2071
Anita Mehta, *General Mgr*
Arvind Mehta,
Mukund S Chorghade,
EMP: 4
SQ FT: 700
SALES (est): 412.8K **Privately Held**
SIC: 2834 8731 Pharmaceutical preparations; commercial physical research

(G-16651)
CITY UTILITY EQUIPMENT
22414 W 143rd St (60544-7622)
PHONE.................................815 254-6673
John Jacobs, *Principal*
EMP: 10
SALES (est): 1.1MM **Privately Held**
SIC: 3713 Utility truck bodies

(G-16652)
CLEAR VIEW INDUSTRIES INC
2429 Von Esch Rd Unit G (60586-9079)
PHONE.................................815 267-3593
EMP: 3
SALES (est): 350.4K **Privately Held**
SIC: 3231 Products Of Purchased Glass

(G-16653)
CNV ENTERPRISES INC
8282 Old Ridge Rd (60544-9140)
PHONE.................................815 405-6762
Vance Cryder, *President*
EMP: 3 EST: 2006
SALES (est): 262.2K **Privately Held**
SIC: 2411 Stumps, wood

(G-16654)
CUTTING EDGE GRAPHICS
10160 Clow Creek Rd (60585-6720)
PHONE.................................630 717-9333
EMP: 3
SALES (est): 282.5K **Privately Held**
WEB: www.cuttingedgegraphics.net
SIC: 3993 Signs & advertising specialties

(G-16655)
DIAGEO
24460 W 143rd St (60544-8704)
PHONE.................................815 267-4499
Socorro Cerero, *Principal*
EMP: 16
SALES (est): 2MM **Privately Held**
SIC: 2084 Wines, brandy & brandy spirits

(G-16656)
DIAGEO NORTH AMERICA INC
24440 W 143rd St (60544-8704)
PHONE.................................815 267-4400
Janelle Orozco, *Director*
EMP: 42

SALES (corp-wide): 16.3B **Privately Held**
SIC: 2085 2084 Gin (alcoholic beverage); vodka (alcoholic beverage); wines, brandy & brandy spirits
HQ: Diageo North America Inc.
  3 World Trade Ctr
  New York NY 10007
  212 202-1800

(G-16657)
DRP SOLUTIONS INC
24322 W 143rd St (60544-5533)
PHONE.................................815 782-2014
Daniel R Poston, *President*
EMP: 1
SALES (est): 205.5K **Privately Held**
SIC: 3089 Injection molding of plastics

(G-16658)
E&D PRINTING SERVICES INC
15857 Spanglers Farm Dr (60544-2160)
PHONE.................................815 609-8222
Evaristo Gallego, *President*
EMP: 3
SALES (est): 228.9K **Privately Held**
SIC: 2752 Commercial printing, offset

(G-16659)
ENGINEERING PRODUCTS COMPANY
Also Called: Epco
15125 S Meadow Ln (60544-1486)
PHONE.................................815 436-9055
Sharon Fazio-Mammosser, *President*
Robert R Herman, *VP Sales*
Lyle W Hughart, *Admin Sec*
EMP: 3
SQ FT: 1,000
SALES (est): 800K **Privately Held**
SIC: 5084 3545 3535 Conveyor systems; machine tool accessories; conveyors & conveying equipment

(G-16660)
ENTEC POLYMERS LLC
24210 W 143rd St (60544-8702)
PHONE.................................866 598-8941
Ronald Kohut, *Principal*
EMP: 8
SALES (corp-wide): 1.9MM **Privately Held**
SIC: 5162 1459 Plastics resins; plastic fire clay mining
HQ: Entec Polymers, Llc
  1900 Smmit Twr Blvd Ste 9
  Orlando FL 32810
  407 875-9595

(G-16661)
EURO-TECH CABINETRY RMDLG CORP
12515 Rhea Dr (60585-8507)
PHONE.................................815 254-3876
Kim Moriarty, *President*
EMP: 8
SALES (est): 659K **Privately Held**
WEB: www.etcrcorp.com
SIC: 2434 Wood kitchen cabinets

(G-16662)
F AND S ENTERPRISES PLAINFIELD
2035 Havenhill Dr (60586-6528)
P.O. Box 719 (60544-0719)
PHONE.................................815 439-9655
Feda Haleem, *CEO*
EMP: 2
SALES (est): 201.3K **Privately Held**
SIC: 3537 Forklift trucks

(G-16663)
F-C ENTERPRISES INC
12249 Rhea Dr Ste 3 (60585-8762)
PHONE.................................815 254-7295
Debra Fagel, *President*
EMP: 4 EST: 1979
SQ FT: 2,200
SALES: 213K **Privately Held**
SIC: 2759 Screen printing

(G-16664)
FAST FORWARD WELDING INC
23840 W Andrew Rd Ste 4 (60585-8769)
PHONE.................................815 254-1901
Aaron Stapleton, *Principal*

EMP: 2
SALES (est): 220.9K **Privately Held**
SIC: 7692 Welding repair

(G-16665)
FILL-WEIGH INC
Also Called: Liberty Systems
23900 W Industrial Dr S # 6 (60585-7296)
PHONE.................................815 254-4704
David Ierardi, *President*
EMP: 5
SQ FT: 2,000 **Privately Held**
SIC: 3569 5046 5084 Liquid automation machinery & equipment; scales, except laboratory; industrial machinery & equipment

(G-16666)
FLOLINE ARCHTCTRAL SYSTEMS LLC (PA)
16108 S Route 59 Ste 108 (60586-2932)
PHONE.................................630 922-0550
John Carron, *President*
Thomas Carron, *Principal*
EMP: 15
SALES (est): 3.9MM **Privately Held**
SIC: 3444 Sheet metalwork

(G-16667)
FRESH CONCEPT ENTERPRISES INC
12249 Rhea Dr (60585-9586)
PHONE.................................815 254-7295
Deborah Fagel, *President*
EMP: 3
SQ FT: 2,200
SALES: 300K **Privately Held**
SIC: 2396 2759 Printing & embossing on plastics fabric articles; engraving

(G-16668)
GLOBAL MEDICAL SERVICES LLC (PA)
12904 Rockfish Ln (60585-2544)
PHONE.................................847 460-8086
Kelvin Udogu,
Shunjonna Udeogu,
EMP: 4
SQ FT: 1,200
SALES (est): 511.3K **Privately Held**
SIC: 2834 Pharmaceutical preparations

(G-16669)
GRAPHIC PALLET & TRANSPORT
10225 Bode St (60585-6903)
PHONE.................................630 904-4951
Christy Furmaniak, *President*
John Krawisz, *Admin Sec*
▲ EMP: 20
SQ FT: 30,000
SALES: 23MM **Privately Held**
WEB: www.graphicpallet.com
SIC: 2448 5085 Pallets, wood; industrial supplies

(G-16670)
HEALTHDENTL LLC
10052 Bode St Ste E (60585-1973)
PHONE.................................800 845-5172
Steve Bevilacqua, *Mng Member*
Robert Bevilacqua,
EMP: 3
SQ FT: 1,996
SALES: 280.5K **Privately Held**
WEB: www.healthdentl.com
SIC: 3843 Dental equipment & supplies

(G-16671)
HEAVEN FRESH USA INC
10057 Bode St (60585-8701)
PHONE.................................800 642-0367
Taoufik Lahrache, *President*
Mohammad Kamal Anwar, *President*
Imran Bashir, *Vice Pres*
▲ EMP: 5
SALES (est): 617K **Privately Held**
SIC: 3634 3585 5722 Air purifiers, portable; humidifiers & dehumidifiers; electric household appliances, small

(G-16672)
HERITAGE MOULDING INC
10233 Clow Creek Rd (60585-7891)
PHONE.................................630 961-0001

Dominic J Imburgia, *President*
EMP: 2
SALES (est): 286.7K **Privately Held**
SIC: 2431 Millwork

(G-16673)
HPD LLC
Also Called: HPD Evporation Crystallization
23563 W Main St (60544-7660)
PHONE.................................815 609-2032
Jim Brown, *President*
Klaus Andersen, *COO*
Steven Kruger, *Vice Pres*
Mark Bavetz, *Research*
Andrew Kazana, *Engineer*
EMP: 165
SALES (est): 185MM
SALES (corp-wide): 559.3MM **Privately Held**
SIC: 3589 8711 Water treatment equipment, industrial; engineering services
HQ: Veolia Water Technologies, Inc.
  250 Airside Dr
  Moon Township PA 15108

(G-16674)
HUNTER-NUSPORT INC
24317 W 143rd St Ste 103 (60544-8715)
P.O. Box 321, Bloomingdale (60108-0321)
PHONE.................................815 254-7520
George Rogers, *General Mgr*
▲ EMP: 5
SALES (est): 368.1K **Privately Held**
SIC: 3949 2393 Bags, golf; duffle bags, canvas: made from purchased materials

(G-16675)
JEFFS SMALL ENGINE INC
12438 S Route 59 (60585-4607)
PHONE.................................630 904-6840
Jeff Witte, *CEO*
◆ EMP: 2
SQ FT: 2,000
SALES: 1.5MM **Privately Held**
SIC: 3524 Lawn & garden equipment

(G-16676)
JELINEK & SONS INC
25400 W Hafenrichter Rd (60585-9776)
PHONE.................................630 355-3474
Robert F Kovac Jr, *President*
Gloria M Kovac, *Admin Sec*
EMP: 6
SALES (est): 617.5K **Privately Held**
WEB: www.jelinekandsons.com
SIC: 1521 2431 2394 General remodeling, single-family houses; millwork; canvas & related products

(G-16677)
JEM SOLUTIONS INC
Also Called: Signs By Tomorrow
16200 S Lincoln Hwy # 100 (60586-5153)
PHONE.................................815 436-0880
Jodi Murray, *President*
Dawn Barber, *General Mgr*
Kelly Voss, *Business Mgr*
James Phinney, *COO*
EMP: 4
SALES (est): 179K **Privately Held**
WEB: www.signsbytomorrow.com
SIC: 3993 Signs & advertising specialties

(G-16678)
KARIMI SAIFUDDIN
Also Called: Karimi Enterprise
14017 S Lakeridge Dr (60544-6994)
PHONE.................................630 943-8808
Saifuddin Karimi, *Owner*
EMP: 1
SQ FT: 400
SALES: 1.1MM **Privately Held**
SIC: 2841 7373 Soap & other detergents; computer system selling services

(G-16679)
KASTELIC CANVAS INC
15940 S Lincoln Hwy (60586-5130)
PHONE.................................815 436-8160
Mark Muehlfelt, *President*
EMP: 2
SQ FT: 14,500

Plainfield - Will County (G-16680)

SALES (est): 265.6K **Privately Held**
SIC: 2394 Tents: made from purchased materials; tarpaulins, fabric: made from purchased materials; convertible tops, canvas or boat: from purchased materials

(G-16680)
KIT ARTISAN CAB REFINISHERS
10200 S Mandel St Ste D (60585-5372)
PHONE..................630 922-9714
EMP: 3 **EST:** 2010
SALES (est): 272.8K **Privately Held**
WEB: www.savewoodcabinets.com
SIC: 2434 Wood kitchen cabinets

(G-16681)
KUUSAKOSKI PHILADELPHIA LLC
13543 S Route 30 (60544-1100)
PHONE..................215 533-8323
Timo Kuusakoski, *Mng Member*
Harri Pulli,
▼ **EMP:** 77
SALES (est): 13.3MM **Privately Held**
SIC: 3559 Recycling machinery

(G-16682)
LEGACY VULCAN LLC
Midwest Division
Rr 126 (60544)
PHONE..................815 436-3535
Eric Steidl, *Manager*
EMP: 23 **Publicly Held**
SIC: 3273 Ready-mixed concrete
HQ: Legacy Vulcan, Llc
 1200 Urban Center Dr
 Vestavia AL 35242
 205 298-3000

(G-16683)
LEGACY VULCAN LLC
Also Called: Bolingbrook Quarry
22933 W Hassert Blvd (60585-9596)
PHONE..................630 904-1110
Phillip Hovis, *Manager*
EMP: 18 **Publicly Held**
SIC: 1422 Crushed & broken limestone
HQ: Legacy Vulcan, Llc
 1200 Urban Center Dr
 Vestavia AL 35242
 205 298-3000

(G-16684)
LOGOPLASTE CHICAGO LLC
14420 N Van Dyke Rd (60544-5867)
PHONE..................815 230-6961
Helder N Alves, *Project Mgr*
Katie Simms, *Controller*
Rui Abelho, *Manager*
EMP: 1
SALES (est): 5.3MM **Privately Held**
SIC: 3085 Plastics bottles
HQ: Logoplaste Usa, Inc.
 14420 N Van Dyke Rd
 Plainfield IL 60544
 815 230-6961

(G-16685)
LOGOPLASTE FORT WORTH LLC
14420 N Van Dyke Rd (60544-5867)
PHONE..................815 230-6961
Filipe De Botton, *CEO*
EMP: 1
SALES (est): 447K **Privately Held**
SIC: 3085 Plastics bottles
HQ: Logoplaste Usa, Inc.
 14420 N Van Dyke Rd
 Plainfield IL 60544
 815 230-6961

(G-16686)
LOGOPLASTE RACINE LLC
14420 N Van Dyke Rd (60544-5867)
PHONE..................815 230-6961
Filipe De Botton,
Renee Rogers, *Administration*
EMP: 1
SALES (est): 831.1K **Privately Held**
SIC: 3085 Plastics bottles
HQ: Logoplaste Usa, Inc.
 14420 N Van Dyke Rd
 Plainfield IL 60544
 815 230-6961

(G-16687)
LOGOPLASTE USA INC (DH)
14420 N Van Dyke Rd (60544-5867)
PHONE..................815 230-6961
Filipe De Botton, *CEO*
Rui Abelho, *Admin Sec*
▲ **EMP:** 95
SALES (est): 104.3MM **Privately Held**
SIC: 3085 Plastics bottles
HQ: Logoplaste Portugal, Lda
 Estrada Malveira Da Serra, 900
 Cascais 2750-
 214 858-500

(G-16688)
MIDWEST GROUND EFFECTS
1713 Fox Ridge Dr (60586-5831)
PHONE..................708 516-5874
EMP: 4 **EST:** 2011
SALES (est): 351.7K **Privately Held**
SIC: 2851 Removers & cleaners

(G-16689)
MIDWEST HOT RODS INC
23533 W Main St (60544-7660)
PHONE..................815 254-7637
Paul Quinn, *President*
Carol Thorne, *Corp Secy*
Dan Alrick, *Shareholder*
Randy Schwartz, *Shareholder*
EMP: 11
SALES (est): 1.8MM **Privately Held**
SIC: 3711 Automobile assembly, including specialty automobiles

(G-16690)
MIDWEST SPORT TURF SYSTEMS LLC
Also Called: Mwsts
10138 Bode St Ste E (60585-8779)
PHONE..................630 923-8342
Jeffrey Nelson, *Mng Member*
Jody Factor,
EMP: 12
SQ FT: 4,000
SALES (est): 506K **Privately Held**
SIC: 3523 Greens mowing equipment

(G-16691)
MIDWEST STONE SALES INC (PA)
11926 S Aero Dr (60585-9559)
PHONE..................815 254-6600
Christina Mercado, *President*
EMP: 11
SQ FT: 10,000
SALES (est): 1.6MM **Privately Held**
SIC: 3281 5032 Granite, cut & shaped; granite building stone

(G-16692)
MOTORSPORTS PUBLICATIONS HOUSE
24334 Blazing Star Ct (60585-5533)
PHONE..................630 699-7629
EMP: 3 **EST:** 2013
SALES (est): 45.4K **Privately Held**
SIC: 2741 Miscellaneous publishing

(G-16693)
NATURAL BEGINNINGS
15904 S Selfridge Cir (60586-7212)
PHONE..................773 457-0509
Phalice Benford, *Owner*
▲ **EMP:** 3
SQ FT: 2,500
SALES: 50K **Privately Held**
SIC: 2844 Hair preparations, including shampoos

(G-16694)
NEW WAVE LAX LLC
10204 Bode St Ste C (60585-9813)
PHONE..................630 219-3919
Anthony Amedei, *Principal*
Matt Benjamin, *Manager*
Kyle Sullivan, *Director*
Andy Thompson, *Director*
EMP: 3
SALES (est): 168.4K **Privately Held**
SIC: 3949 Sporting & athletic goods

(G-16695)
NEXT GENERATION INC
13304 Skyline Dr (60585-1467)
PHONE..................312 739-0520
Darrell Higueros, *President*
Heliza Higueros, *Admin Sec*
EMP: 4
SQ FT: 2,800
SALES: 1.2MM **Privately Held**
SIC: 7371 7372 Computer software development & applications; business oriented computer software

(G-16696)
NNM MANUFACTURING LLC
Also Called: Peterson Manufacturing Company
24133 W 143rd St (60544-8700)
PHONE..................815 436-9201
Maggie Urban, *Marketing Mgr*
Marija Goich,
EMP: 40
SALES (est): 7.6MM **Privately Held**
SIC: 3441 Fabricated structural metal

(G-16697)
OFF THE PRESS LLC
16041 S Lincoln Hwy # 103 (60586-5180)
PHONE..................815 436-9612
Paul Jackson,
Kimberly Jackson,
EMP: 6 **EST:** 1982
SQ FT: 4,500
SALES (est): 695.9K **Privately Held**
WEB: www.offthepressprinting.com
SIC: 2752 2791 2789 Commercial printing, offset; typesetting; bookbinding & related work

(G-16698)
OHRVALL MEDIA LLC
Also Called: Mbacase
13400 S Route 59 (60585-5826)
PHONE..................630 378-9738
David Ohrvall, *Mng Member*
Shiloah Ohrvall, *Mng Member*
EMP: 6
SALES (est): 36.8K **Privately Held**
SIC: 2731 8742 7389 Book publishing; training & development consultant;

(G-16699)
PANEL AUTHORITY INC
24121 W Theodore St Ste 1 (60586-7670)
PHONE..................815 838-0488
Preston Wakeland, *President*
Penelope Wendel, *President*
EMP: 12
SALES: 1.1MM **Privately Held**
SIC: 3613 Control panels, electric

(G-16700)
PERFORMANCE GEAR SYSTEMS INC
14309 S Route 59 (60544-3889)
PHONE..................630 739-6666
Patrick Odonnell, *President*
Tim Dorgan, *Purchasing*
Ed Jedlicka, *Manager*
EMP: 35 **EST:** 1997
SALES: 15MM **Privately Held**
WEB: www.performance-gear.com
SIC: 3714 Motor vehicle parts & accessories

(G-16701)
PERRYCO INC
Enterprise Newspaper
15507 S Route 59 (60544-2723)
P.O. Box 1613 (60544-3613)
PHONE..................815 436-2431
Wayne Perry, *Principal*
EMP: 16
SQ FT: 1,400
SALES (corp-wide): 3MM **Privately Held**
SIC: 2711 2752 2791 2789 Newspapers: publishing only, not printed on site; commercial printing, lithographic; typesetting; bookbinding & related work; commercial printing; packaging paper & plastics film, coated & laminated
PA: Perryco Inc
 6920 Webster St
 Downers Grove IL 60516
 303 652-8282

(G-16702)
PLAINFIELD SIGNS INC
219 W Main St (60544-1970)
PHONE..................815 439-1063
Thomas Bowen, *President*
EMP: 3
SQ FT: 3,000
SALES (est): 202.1K **Privately Held**
SIC: 3993 Signs, not made in custom sign painting shops

(G-16703)
POWERS SPORTS LLC
2425 Von Esch Rd Ste D (60586-2512)
PHONE..................815 436-6769
Tom Powers,
EMP: 2
SALES: 200K **Privately Held**
SIC: 3944 Electronic game machines, except coin-operated

(G-16704)
PRECISION ENGINE RBLDRS INC
Also Called: Per Race Engines
23807 W Andrew Rd Unit A (60585-4629)
PHONE..................815 254-2333
Thomas R Crowley, *President*
EMP: 3
SALES: 500K **Privately Held**
SIC: 3519 7538 7539 Gas engine rebuilding; engine rebuilding: automotive; machine shop, automotive

(G-16705)
PRECISION METAL CRAFTS INC
12201 Rhea Dr (60585-9713)
PHONE..................815 254-2306
Bozidar Skrlin, *President*
EMP: 2
SQ FT: 1,800
SALES (est): 391.6K **Privately Held**
SIC: 3471 Finishing, metals or formed products

(G-16706)
PREMIERE MOTORSPORTS LLC
16300 S Lincoln Hwy 1 (60586-5152)
PHONE..................708 634-0007
Czupta Christopher S, *Principal*
EMP: 2
SALES (est): 250.5K **Privately Held**
SIC: 3714 Motor vehicle engines & parts

(G-16707)
PRO BUILT TOOL & MOLD INC
23839 W Andrew Rd # 103 (60585-8764)
P.O. Box 829, Morris (60450-0829)
PHONE..................815 436-9088
Steve Bergmann, *President*
Robert Green, *Exec VP*
EMP: 5
SQ FT: 3,200
SALES (est): 537.9K **Privately Held**
SIC: 3544 Industrial molds

(G-16708)
PRO-BEAM USA INC
13900 S Van Dyke Rd # 106 (60544-5849)
PHONE..................630 327-6909
Rodwan Mourad, *President*
EMP: 5 **EST:** 2017
SALES (est): 123.8K **Privately Held**
SIC: 7699 3599 Repair services; industrial machinery

(G-16709)
RAVAGO AMERICAS LLC
24210 W 143rd St (60544-8702)
PHONE..................815 609-4800
Clarissa Vitacco, *Office Mgr*
EMP: 20
SALES (corp-wide): 1.9MM **Privately Held**
SIC: 2821 Plastics materials & resins
HQ: Ravago Americas Llc
 1900 Summit Tower Blvd
 Orlando FL 32810
 407 875-9595

GEOGRAPHIC SECTION

Plano - Kendall County (G-16737)

(G-16710)
RESPONSE GRAPHICS & EMB LLC
Also Called: Fireground Supply
23900 W Industrial Dr S # 4 (60585-7297)
PHONE.................................630 364-1471
Kevin L Yeazell, *Principal*
EMP: 7
SALES (est): 285.6K **Privately Held**
WEB: www.firegroundsupply.com
SIC: 2759 Screen printing

(G-16711)
ROCKDALE CONTROLS CO INC
2419 Von Esch Rd (60586-9079)
PHONE.................................815 436-6181
Peter G Gavankar, *President*
Shande Mohra Gavankar, *Corp Secy*
Mary Lee Horvath, *Accountant*
EMP: 10 EST: 1971
SQ FT: 8,000
SALES (est): 1.5MM **Privately Held**
SIC: 3625 Control equipment, electric

(G-16712)
ROW WINDOW COMPANY
13404 Wood Duck Dr (60585-7766)
PHONE.................................815 725-5491
Glen Brooks, *President*
William Gebhardt, *Vice Pres*
EMP: 1
SQ FT: 190,000
SALES (est): 210K **Privately Held**
SIC: 2431 Window frames, wood; window sashes, wood; doors & door parts & trim, wood

(G-16713)
SENNCO SOLUTIONS INC
14407 Coil Plus Dr # 101 (60544-7703)
PHONE.................................815 577-3400
Christopher Marszalek, *President*
Monika Marszalek, *Vice Pres*
Hannah Japp, *Buyer*
Andy Reynolds, *Engineer*
Jenn Byham, *Marketing Staff*
▲ EMP: 29 EST: 2000
SQ FT: 28,000
SALES (est): 7.5MM **Privately Held**
WEB: www.sennco.com
SIC: 3699 Security control equipment & systems

(G-16714)
SLICK SUGAR INC
Also Called: Slicksugar.com
24935 Heritage Oaks Dr (60585-5773)
PHONE.................................815 782-7101
Scott Mills, *President*
Jennifer Mills, *Vice Pres*
▼ EMP: 2
SALES (est): 224.1K **Privately Held**
SIC: 2369 5641 Girls' & children's outerwear; children's wear

(G-16715)
SOUND DESIGN INC
10104 S Mandel St Ste 1 (60585-8774)
PHONE.................................630 548-7000
Alfonso Marasco, *President*
Joseph Marasco, *Principal*
Jacqueline Mc Carthy, *Corp Secy*
Vince Marasco, *Vice Pres*
EMP: 5
SQ FT: 8,000
SALES (est): 1.2MM **Privately Held**
SIC: 3699 5999 5731 Electric sound equipment; alarm signal systems; high fidelity stereo equipment

(G-16716)
SPECIALTY PNTG SODA BLASTG INC
24031 W Winners Circle Ct (60585-6124)
PHONE.................................815 577-0006
Steven J Hackerson, *President*
EMP: 6
SALES (est): 690.1K **Privately Held**
SIC: 3479 3471 Painting of metal products; sand blasting of metal parts

(G-16717)
STOLP GORE COMPANY
10101 Bode St Ste A (60585-8731)
PHONE.................................630 904-5180
Robert Sepper, *President*
Mary C Sepper, *Admin Sec*
EMP: 3 EST: 1922
SQ FT: 6,000
SALES (est): 500K **Privately Held**
WEB: www.stolpgore.com
SIC: 3555 7699 Bookbinding machinery; industrial equipment services

(G-16718)
STRITZEL AWNNG SVC/AURRA TENT
Also Called: Aurora Tent & Awning Co
10206 Clow Creek Rd Ste A (60585-6891)
PHONE.................................630 420-2000
Norman Dial, *Partner*
Sande K Dial, *Partner*
EMP: 35 EST: 1952
SQ FT: 11,000
SALES (est): 3.4MM **Privately Held**
SIC: 2394 7359 Awnings, fabric: made from purchased materials; tent & tarpaulin rental

(G-16719)
STUHLMAN FAMILY LLC
Also Called: Stuhlman Engrg Manfacturin Co
12435 S Industrial Dr E (60585-8578)
P.O. Box 236 (60544-0236)
PHONE.................................815 436-2432
Tom Dravinski,
Pamela Dravinski,
EMP: 5
SQ FT: 8,000
SALES (est): 500K **Privately Held**
WEB: www.stuhlman.com
SIC: 3599 7692 Machine shop, jobbing & repair; welding repair

(G-16720)
SWEET SOLUTIONS LLC
25503 W Ruff St Unit A (60585-5487)
PHONE.................................630 364-2843
Brian Carben, *Opers Mgr*
Brian Bernard, *Mng Member*
▼ EMP: 9
SQ FT: 9,000
SALES (est): 1MM **Privately Held**
WEB: www.thesweetsolutions.com
SIC: 2099 Molasses, mixed or blended: from purchased ingredients

(G-16721)
TAILWINDS DISTILLERY
14912 S Eastern Ave (60544-3193)
PHONE.................................630 746-7526
EMP: 5
SALES (est): 394.1K **Privately Held**
SIC: 2085 Distilled & blended liquors

(G-16722)
TEESTYLER INC
4163 Oak Tree Ln (60586-4806)
PHONE.................................630 484-3104
EMP: 3 EST: 2016
SALES (est): 124K **Privately Held**
SIC: 2759 Screen printing

(G-16723)
THERMA-KLEEN INC
10212 S Mandel St Ste A (60585-5374)
P.O. Box 805, Au Gres MI (48703-0805)
PHONE.................................630 718-0212
Andrew Heller, *President*
Linda Heller, *Vice Pres*
▲ EMP: 7
SQ FT: 4,000
SALES (est): 1.3MM **Privately Held**
SIC: 3559 5084 1799 Degreasing machines, automotive & industrial; cleaning equipment, high pressure, sand or steam; steam cleaning of building exteriors

(G-16724)
ULTIMATE MACHINING & ENGRG INC
14015 S Van Dyke Rd (60544-3530)
PHONE.................................815 439-8361
John Kulczuga, *President*
Chris Borla, *Opers Mgr*
Rafal Nosek, *Production*
Caroline Kulczuga, *Business Dir*
Helga Lancaster, *Admin Asst*
EMP: 40
SQ FT: 30,000

(G-16725)
VEL-TYE LLC
23808 W Andrew Rd Ste 3 (60585-8767)
PHONE.................................757 518-5400
Steven Herring, *Principal*
EMP: 3
SALES (est): 191.3K **Privately Held**
SIC: 2399 Fabricated textile products

(G-16726)
VEOLIA WATER TECHNOLOGIES INC
Also Called: HPD Evporation Crystallization
23563 W Main St (60544-7660)
PHONE.................................815 609-2000
Robert Dawe, *Project Mgr*
Krauss Derek, *Project Mgr*
Mark Patterson, *Engineer*
Kelli Ehman, *Accountant*
Jim Brown, *Branch Mgr*
EMP: 23
SALES (corp-wide): 559.3MM **Privately Held**
SIC: 3589 Water treatment equipment, industrial
HQ: Veolia Water Technologies, Inc.
250 Airside Dr
Moon Township PA 15108

(G-16727)
VOYAGER ENTERPRISE INC
15507 S Route 59 (60544-2723)
PHONE.................................815 436-2431
Richard Masterson, *President*
EMP: 8
SALES (est): 1.1MM **Privately Held**
WEB: www.buglenewspapers.com
SIC: 2621 Lithograph paper

(G-16728)
WAVE PADS LLC
24121 W Theodore St 4-A (60586-8299)
PHONE.................................224 444-9283
Matthew Yassinger, *Owner*
◆ EMP: 2
SQ FT: 2,000
SALES (est): 550K **Privately Held**
SIC: 3086 3732 Plastics foam products; life rafts, noninflatable: rubber or plastic

---

Plainville
Adams County

(G-16729)
ED KABRICK BEEF INC
218 E Main St (62365-1016)
P.O. Box 158 (62365-0158)
PHONE.................................217 656-3263
Daren Rex Kabrick, *President*
Vicki Kabrick, *Vice Pres*
EMP: 6
SQ FT: 2,500
SALES (est): 630K **Privately Held**
SIC: 2011 5142 2013 Meat packing plants; packaged frozen goods; sausages & other prepared meats

---

Plano
Kendall County

(G-16730)
DLT ELECTRIC LLC
202 W Main St (60545-1433)
PHONE.................................630 552-4115
David L Tremain,
▲ EMP: 12
SQ FT: 5,000
SALES (est): 910K **Privately Held**
SIC: 3621 Motors, electric

(G-16731)
FOX VALLEY MOLDING INC (PA)
Also Called: F V M
113 S Center St (60545-1568)
PHONE.................................630 552-3176
Donald Haag, *CEO*
Lydia Flores, *Purch Mgr*
Beth Szabo, *Treasurer*
Lois K Haag, *Admin Sec*
▲ EMP: 150
SQ FT: 60,000
SALES (est): 31MM **Privately Held**
SIC: 3089 Injection molded finished plastic products; injection molding of plastics; molding primary plastic

(G-16732)
FRABILL INC
431 E South St (60545-1676)
PHONE.................................630 552-9426
Jeffery P Marble, *President*
Patricia Marble, *Vice Pres*
◆ EMP: 35
SALES (est): 3.8MM
SALES (corp-wide): 93.8MM **Privately Held**
SIC: 3949 Fishing equipment; fishing tackle, general; golf equipment; golf carts, hand
HQ: Plano Molding Company, Llc
431 E South St
Plano IL 60545
630 552-3111

(G-16733)
G FORCE LABELS & PRINTING INC
405 E South St (60545-1601)
PHONE.................................630 552-8911
Greg Gould, *President*
Norris H Gould, *Principal*
Michael Gould, *Vice Pres*
Todd Gould, *Vice Pres*
EMP: 11
SALES (est): 945.1K **Privately Held**
WEB: www.gforcelabels.net
SIC: 2759 Commercial printing

(G-16734)
MENARD INC
2611 Eldamain Rd (60545-9723)
PHONE.................................815 474-6767
Rene Hoffman, *Marketing Staff*
Kevin McCarty, *CIO*
EMP: 120
SALES (corp-wide): 11.4B **Privately Held**
WEB: www.menards.com
SIC: 2431 Millwork
PA: Menard, Inc.
5101 Menard Dr
Eau Claire WI 54703
715 876-5911

(G-16735)
MENARD INC
2619 Eldamain Rd Bldg 220 (60545-9706)
PHONE.................................715 876-5911
EMP: 68
SALES (corp-wide): 11.4B **Privately Held**
SIC: 2431 Millwork
PA: Menard, Inc.
5101 Menard Dr
Eau Claire WI 54703
715 876-5911

(G-16736)
NATIONAL TRACTOR PARTS INC
12127a Galena Rd (60545-9725)
P.O. Box 146 (60545-0146)
PHONE.................................630 552-4235
Christopher J Gunier, *President*
Charles Gunier Jr, *Principal*
Chuck Gunier, *Sales Staff*
Matt Gunier, *Manager*
Sue Norem, *Asst Office Mgr*
▲ EMP: 28
SQ FT: 28,000
SALES (est): 6.9MM **Privately Held**
SIC: 3531 7538 Backhoes, tractors, cranes, plows & similar equipment; general truck repair

(G-16737)
OT SYSTEMS LIMITED
18 W Main St (60545-1429)
PHONE.................................630 554-9178
Jeff Smith, *Technical Staff*
Joe Frank, *Director*
EMP: 1
SALES: 950K **Privately Held**
SIC: 3679 Electronic components

Plano - Kendall County (G-16738)

(G-16738)
PAGEPATH TECHNOLOGIES INC
13 E Main St (60545-1521)
PHONE 630 689-4111
Gregory Witek, *President*
Dakota Dunham, *Engineer*
Brandon Freeman, *Technical Staff*
EMP: 11
SQ FT: 1,800
SALES (est): 1.4MM **Privately Held**
SIC: 7372 7379 7371 Business oriented computer software; computer related consulting services; custom computer programming services

(G-16739)
PLANO HOLDING LLC (HQ)
431 E South St (60545-1676)
PHONE 630 552-3111
Thomas Hurt, *President*
EMP: 11
SALES (est): 53.1MM
SALES (corp-wide): 93.8MM **Privately Held**
SIC: 3089 Boxes, plastic
PA: Plano Synergy Holding Inc.
  602 Fountain Pkwy Ste C
  Grand Prairie TX 75050
  469 733-1868

(G-16740)
PLANO METAL SPECIALTIES INC
320 W State Rte 34 (60545)
P.O. Box 174 (60545-0174)
PHONE 630 552-8510
Ralph Whitecotton, *Ch of Bd*
Rick Whitecotton, *Vice Pres*
Audrey Whitecotton, *Treasurer*
EMP: 10 **EST:** 1981
SQ FT: 11,000
SALES (est): 800K **Privately Held**
SIC: 3471 3089 Plating of metals or formed products; polishing, metals or formed products; finishing, metals or formed products; plastic processing

(G-16741)
PLANO MOLDING COMPANY LLC (DH)
431 E South St (60545-1676)
PHONE 630 552-3111
Peter H Henning, *Ch of Bd*
Thomas Hurt, *President*
Christopher Leonard, *Vice Pres*
Robert Yarbrough, *Vice Pres*
Mike Edwards, *Project Mgr*
◆ **EMP:** 1 **EST:** 1932
SQ FT: 190,000
SALES (est): 58.4MM
SALES (corp-wide): 93.8MM **Privately Held**
WEB: www.planomolding.com
SIC: 3089 Boxes, plastic; molding primary plastic
HQ: Plano Holding Llc
  431 E South St
  Plano IL 60545
  630 552-3111

(G-16742)
PLANOS PAST INC
7050 Burroughs Ave (60545-7100)
P.O. Box 112 (60545-0112)
PHONE 630 552-9119
EMP: 3
SALES (est): 183K **Privately Held**
SIC: 3089 Plastic containers, except foam

(G-16743)
PRYDE GRAPHICS PLUS
306 Hubbard Cir (60545-1975)
PHONE 630 882-5103
Richard Pryde, *Principal*
David Homyak, *Vice Pres*
EMP: 2
SALES (est): 244.9K **Privately Held**
SIC: 2759 Commercial printing

(G-16744)
TALLWOOD
15751 Burr Oak Rd (60545-9811)
PHONE 815 786-8186
Ben T Stevenson, *Owner*
EMP: 4
SALES (est): 227.9K **Privately Held**
SIC: 2411 Timber, cut at logging camp

(G-16745)
TMF PLASTIC SOLUTIONS LLC
12127b Galena Rd (60545-9725)
PHONE 630 552-7575
Greg Kuppler, *President*
Dwight Priest, *Vice Pres*
Randy Johnson, *VP Opers*
Justin Guthrie, *Engineer*
Tim Raymond,
▲ **EMP:** 75
SQ FT: 14,000
SALES (est): 23.5MM **Privately Held**
SIC: 3089 Injection molding of plastics

(G-16746)
TMF POLYMER SOLUTIONS INC (PA)
12127b Galena Rd (60545-9725)
PHONE 630 552-7575
Greg Kuppler, *President*
Tim Raymond, *Exec VP*
Randy Johnson, *Vice Pres*
Corey Ryan, *QC Mgr*
Jackie Straub, *Accounting Mgr*
▲ **EMP:** 2
SQ FT: 14,000
SALES (est): 2.9MM **Privately Held**
SIC: 3089 Injection molding of plastics

(G-16747)
WGI INNOVATIONS LTD
431 E South St (60545-1676)
PHONE 800 847-8269
Gary F Wolz, *Principal*
EMP: 3
SALES (est): 193.9K **Privately Held**
SIC: 3625 Relays & industrial controls

Pleasant Hill
Pike County

(G-16748)
FRAME GAME
119 E Quincy St (62366-2415)
P.O. Box 454 (62366-0454)
PHONE 573 754-2385
Kevin Willis, *President*
EMP: 3
SALES (est): 261.7K **Privately Held**
SIC: 2499 Wood products

Pleasant Plains
Sangamon County

(G-16749)
ALPHA AG INC (PA)
8295 Bomke Rd (62677-3759)
PHONE 217 546-2724
Donald Trott, *President*
Robert Clark, *Manager*
Nanette Trott, *Manager*
◆ **EMP:** 3
SALES (est): 372.3K **Privately Held**
SIC: 5999 2879 Farm machinery; agricultural chemicals

Plymouth
Hancock County

(G-16750)
R L ONEAL & SONS INC
819 N County Road 3050 (62367-2220)
PHONE 309 458-3350
John C O'Neal, *President*
John C Jack O'Neal, *President*
Christen O'Neal, *Vice Pres*
EMP: 11
SQ FT: 800
SALES (est): 2MM **Privately Held**
SIC: 1422 Crushed & broken limestone

Pocahontas
Bond County

(G-16751)
COPPER DOCK
498 White Oak Ln (62275-3400)
PHONE 618 669-2675
Steven C Dugan, *Principal*
EMP: 5 **EST:** 2016
SALES (est): 27.7K **Privately Held**
WEB: www.copperdockwinery.com
SIC: 7299 5812 2084 Banquet hall facilities; eating places; brandy & brandy spirits

(G-16752)
JOSEPH C RAKERS
209 Pocahontas St (62275-1037)
P.O. Box 314 (62275-0314)
PHONE 618 670-6995
Joseph Rakers, *Owner*
EMP: 1
SALES (est): 300K **Privately Held**
SIC: 3679 Antennas, satellite: household use

(G-16753)
JWT FARMS INC
1072 Il Route 143 (62275-3811)
PHONE 618 664-3429
James W Tischhauser, *President*
Jeff Tischhauser, *Director*
EMP: 3
SALES (est): 50K **Privately Held**
SIC: 3523 Driers (farm): grain, hay & seed

(G-16754)
STAINLESS SPECIALTIES INC
329 Il Route 143 (62275-3649)
PHONE 618 654-7723
Victor Munie, *President*
Julius C Munie, *Vice Pres*
▲ **EMP:** 5
SQ FT: 7,200
SALES (est): 821.4K **Privately Held**
SIC: 1711 3444 Process piping contractor; restaurant sheet metalwork

Polo
Ogle County

(G-16755)
DESIGN ENHANCED MFG CO
9796 W Il Route 64 (61064-8982)
PHONE 815 946-3562
Roger Groves, *President*
EMP: 2
SALES (est): 229.3K **Privately Held**
SIC: 3599 Machine shop, jobbing & repair

(G-16756)
LEGACY PRINTS
607 S Division Ave (61064-1834)
PHONE 815 946-9112
Marty Cox, *Owner*
Peter Knipschield, *Production*
EMP: 9
SALES (est): 916.2K **Privately Held**
SIC: 2759 Screen printing

(G-16757)
NATIONAL BUS TRADER INC
Also Called: National Bus Trader Magazine
9698 W Judson Rd (61064-9015)
PHONE 815 946-2341
Larry J Plachno, *President*
Nancy Plachno, *Vice Pres*
EMP: 12
SQ FT: 2,500
SALES (est): 1.3MM **Privately Held**
SIC: 2721 2731 Magazines: publishing only, not printed on site; trade journals: publishing only, not printed on site; books: publishing only

(G-16758)
PNC INC (PA)
117 E Mason St (61064-1521)
PHONE 815 946-2328
C Keith Palmer, *President*
Keith Palmer, *Marketing Staff*
Daniel A Lawton, *Admin Sec*
Rich Lobdell, *Administration*
EMP: 51 **EST:** 1981
SQ FT: 22,000
SALES (est): 10.9MM **Privately Held**
SIC: 3677 3089 Coil windings, electronic; injection molding of plastics

(G-16759)
XENA INTERNATIONAL INC (PA)
910 S Division Ave (61064-1840)
PHONE 630 587-2734
Judith Sikorski, *CEO*
Richard Sikorski, *President*
Salvatore Ziccarelli, *Vice Pres*
▲ **EMP:** 70
SQ FT: 23,000
SALES (est): 10MM **Privately Held**
SIC: 2099 Food preparations

(G-16760)
XENA INTERNATIONAL INC
910 S Division Ave (61064-1840)
PHONE 815 946-2626
Timothy Wharton, *Branch Mgr*
EMP: 46
SALES (est): 5.7MM
SALES (corp-wide): 10MM **Privately Held**
SIC: 2819 5169 2869 Catalysts, chemical; chemicals & allied products; industrial organic chemicals
PA: Xena International, Inc.
  910 S Division Ave
  Polo IL 61064
  630 587-2734

(G-16761)
YORK INTERNATIONAL CORPORATION
3820 S Il Route 26 (61064-9006)
PHONE 815 946-2351
Mark Stencel, *Branch Mgr*
EMP: 94 **Privately Held**
WEB: www.shumakerwilliams.com
SIC: 3585 Compressors for refrigeration & air conditioning equipment
HQ: York International Corporation
  631 S Richland Ave
  York PA 17403
  717 771-7890

Pomona
Jackson County

(G-16762)
ABBEY RIDGE LLC
Also Called: Abbey Ridge Brewery & Tap Room
24 Brewster Vly (62975-0027)
P.O. Box 7, Alto Pass (62905-0007)
PHONE 618 713-2537
Terri Addison, *CEO*
Philip Royster, *President*
EMP: 6
SALES (est): 139K **Privately Held**
WEB: www.abbeyridgebrew.com
SIC: 5812 2082 Eating places; beer (alcoholic beverage)

(G-16763)
LONNIE HICKAM
2726 Sadler Rd (62975-2568)
PHONE 618 893-4223
Lonnie Hickam, *Executive*
EMP: 3
SALES (est): 240.7K **Privately Held**
SIC: 2411 Logging

(G-16764)
POMONA WINERY
2865 Hickory Ridge Rd (62975-2317)
PHONE 618 893-2623
Jayne Payne, *President*
George Majka, *Treasurer*
EMP: 7
SALES (est): 250K **Privately Held**
SIC: 2084 Wines

GEOGRAPHIC SECTION

Pontiac
Livingston County

(G-16765)
ANTHONY LIFTGATES INC
1037 W Howard St (61764-1666)
P.O. Box 615 (61764-0615)
PHONE..................815 842-3383
Thomas M Walker, *President*
Jeremy Walker, *Vice Pres*
Paul Walker, *Treasurer*
Dan Kusch, *Admin Sec*
◆ EMP: 200 EST: 1941
SQ FT: 100,000
SALES (est): 55.2MM
SALES (corp-wide): 83MM **Privately Held**
WEB: www.anthonyliftgates.com
SIC: **3537** 3714 Lift trucks, industrial: fork, platform, straddle, etc.; motor vehicle parts & accessories
HQ: Streator Industrial Handling, Inc.
1705 N Shabbona St
Streator IL 61364
815 672-0551

(G-16766)
AW DYNAMOMETER INC
1001 W North St (61764-1065)
PHONE..................815 844-6968
Delbert Robinson, *President*
Chris Robinson, *Vice Pres*
Trent Thedens, *Foreman/Supr*
Matt Robinson, *CFO*
Aaron Warsaw, *Data Proc Dir*
◆ EMP: 17 EST: 2008
SQ FT: 30,000
SALES (est): 3.8MM **Privately Held**
WEB: www.awdynamometer.com
SIC: **3829** Measuring & controlling devices

(G-16767)
CATERPILLAR INC
1300 4h Park Rd (61764-9254)
P.O. Box 740 (61764-0740)
PHONE..................815 842-6000
Scot Ward, *Engineer*
Tom Hazlett, *Manager*
Michael Duvall, *Supervisor*
Sridhar Krishnaswamy, *Supervisor*
EMP: 334
SALES (corp-wide): 53.8B **Publicly Held**
SIC: **3714** 5084 Radiators & radiator shells & cores, motor vehicle; fuel injection systems
PA: Caterpillar Inc.
510 Lake Cook Rd Ste 100
Deerfield IL 60015
224 551-4000

(G-16768)
DONNELLS PRINTING & OFF PDTS
708 W Howard St (61764-1602)
PHONE..................815 842-6541
Joseph Mehrkens, *President*
Peggy Mehrkens, *Treasurer*
Mark Mehrkens, *Graphic Designe*
EMP: 4
SQ FT: 4,000
SALES: 300K **Privately Held**
WEB: www.donnellsonline.com
SIC: **2754** 5943 2791 2789 Job printing, gravure; office forms & supplies; typesetting; bookbinding & related work; commercial printing; commercial printing, lithographic

(G-16769)
DOW AGROSCIENCES LLC
Also Called: Mycogen Seeds
18078 N 1500 East Rd (61764-2988)
PHONE..................815 844-3128
EMP: 9
SALES (corp-wide): 62.4B **Publicly Held**
SIC: **2879** 5191 0721 8731 Mfg Agricultural Chemcl Whol Farm Supplies Crops-Planting/Protect
HQ: Dow Agrosciences Llc
9330 Zionsville Rd
Indianapolis IN 46268
317 337-3000

(G-16770)
G P CONCRETE & IRON WORKS
1217 E Indiana Ave (61764-1205)
PHONE..................815 842-2270
Gary S Schulz, *Owner*
EMP: 3
SALES (est): 359.1K **Privately Held**
SIC: **3272** 3446 3442 Steps, prefabricated concrete; manhole covers or frames, concrete; septic tanks, concrete; railings, bannisters, guards, etc.: made from metal pipe; metal doors, sash & trim

(G-16771)
GATEHOUSE MEDIA LLC
Also Called: Daily Leader Newspaper
318 N Main St (61764-1930)
PHONE..................815 842-1153
Linda Stlye, *Manager*
EMP: 25
SALES (corp-wide): 1.8B **Publicly Held**
SIC: **2711** Newspapers, publishing & printing
HQ: Gatehouse Media, Llc
175 Sullys Trl Fl 3
Pittsford NY 14534
585 598-0030

(G-16772)
INTERLAKE MECALUX INC
701 N Interlake Dr (61764-9033)
PHONE..................815 844-7191
Ron Bakos, *Manager*
EMP: 246
SALES (corp-wide): 37.1MM **Privately Held**
SIC: **2542** Partitions & fixtures, except wood
HQ: Interlake Mecalux, Inc.
1600 N 25th Ave
Melrose Park IL 60160
708 344-9999

(G-16773)
JOHNSON PRESS AMERICA INC
800 N Court St (61764-1046)
P.O. Box 592 (61764-0592)
PHONE..................815 844-5161
Dale Flesburg, *President*
Ann Foley, *Human Res Dir*
Jill Rambo, *Sales Staff*
Tim Scarbrough, *Sales Staff*
Randy Schwartz, *Sales Staff*
EMP: 40 EST: 1945
SQ FT: 45,000
SALES (est): 7.7MM **Privately Held**
WEB: www.jpapontiac.com
SIC: **2721** 2791 2789 2752 Trade journals: publishing & printing; typesetting; bookbinding & related work; commercial printing, lithographic; book printing

(G-16774)
LSC COMMUNICATIONS US LLC
1600 N Main St (61764-1060)
PHONE..................815 844-5181
Bruce Mustard, *Manager*
EMP: 768
SALES (corp-wide): 3.3B **Publicly Held**
SIC: **2721** Magazines: publishing & printing
HQ: Lsc Communications Us, Llc
191 N Wacker Dr Ste 1400
Chicago IL 60606
844 572-5720

(G-16775)
MBI TOOLS LLC
Also Called: Mislich Bros
15116 E 2100 North Rd (61764-3261)
PHONE..................815 844-0937
Rja D-Orazio, *CEO*
Justin Wolfe, *President*
EMP: 5
SQ FT: 18,000
SALES: 750K **Privately Held**
WEB: www.mbitools.com
SIC: **3449** Miscellaneous metalwork

(G-16776)
PONTIAC GRANITE COMPANY INC
906 W North St (61764-1003)
P.O. Box 259 (61764-0259)
PHONE..................815 842-1384
Mark Ifft, *President*
EMP: 10

SQ FT: 2,400
SALES (est): 1MM **Privately Held**
WEB: www.pontiacgranite.com
SIC: **3281** 5999 Granite, cut & shaped; monuments & tombstones

(G-16777)
PONTIAC RECYCLERS INC
15355 E 1830 North Rd (61764-3634)
PHONE..................815 844-6419
Michael Crouch, *President*
Michael Freeman, *Corp Secy*
David Egley, *Vice Pres*
EMP: 8
SALES (est): 450.9K **Privately Held**
SIC: **3341** 3211 2621 4953 Aluminum smelting & refining (secondary); flat glass; paper mills; recycling, waste materials; metal scrap & waste materials

(G-16778)
PRINTING CRAFTSMEN OF PONTIAC
509 W Howard St (61764-1718)
P.O. Box 106 (61764-0106)
PHONE..................815 844-7118
Dean Hamilton, *President*
Mary Hamilton, *Admin Sec*
EMP: 3 EST: 1959
SQ FT: 2,800
SALES (est): 371.3K **Privately Held**
WEB: www.printsolutions4u.com
SIC: **2752** 2759 Commercial printing, offset; letterpress printing

(G-16779)
R R DONNELLEY & SONS COMPANY
Also Called: R R Donnelley
1600 N Main St (61764-1060)
PHONE..................815 844-5181
Joe Keenan, *Director*
EMP: 700
SQ FT: 9,000
SALES (corp-wide): 6.2B **Publicly Held**
SIC: **2752** 2789 2732 Commercial printing, lithographic; binding only: books, pamphlets, magazines, etc.; book printing
PA: R. R. Donnelley & Sons Company
35 W Wacker Dr
Chicago IL 60601
312 326-8000

(G-16780)
SOUTHFIELD CORPORATION
Also Called: Vcna Prairie
15887 E 1200 North Rd (61764-3652)
PHONE..................815 842-2333
Chris Bashan, *Manager*
EMP: 25
SALES (corp-wide): 344.9MM **Privately Held**
SIC: **1422** 5032 Crushed & broken limestone; stone, crushed or broken
PA: Southfield Corporation
8995 W 95th St
Palos Hills IL 60465
708 344-1000

Poplar Grove
Boone County

(G-16781)
JEWEL MACHINE INC
302 Kingsbury Dr Se (61065-8791)
PHONE..................815 765-3636
Jewel Kiefer, *Owner*
EMP: 2
SALES (est): 206.8K **Privately Held**
SIC: **3599** Machine shop, jobbing & repair

(G-16782)
MIDWEST PUB SAFETY OUTFITTERS
414 Redman Way Sw (61065-8964)
P.O. Box 391 (61065-0391)
PHONE..................866 985-0013
Tom Kronas, *President*
EMP: 10 EST: 2013

SALES (est): 897.5K **Privately Held**
WEB: www.mps-outfitters.com
SIC: **2389** 5941 5999 Uniforms & vestments; hunting equipment; safety supplies & equipment

(G-16783)
POLYONICS RUBBER CO
100 E Park St (61065-9789)
P.O. Box 100 (61065-0100)
PHONE..................815 765-2033
Bernard Hugus, *CEO*
Doug Stima, *President*
Christi Stima, *Vice Pres*
EMP: 6 EST: 1972
SQ FT: 10,000
SALES (est): 854.9K **Privately Held**
SIC: **3069** Molded rubber products

(G-16784)
STEVE FORREST
Also Called: Forrest Pallet Service
290 E Park St (61065-9798)
P.O. Box 363, Belvidere (61008-0363)
PHONE..................815 765-9040
EMP: 15
SQ FT: 4,000
SALES (est): 2.2MM **Privately Held**
SIC: **2448** Mfg Wood Pallets

Port Barrington
Lake County

(G-16785)
BROKEN OAR INC
614 Rawson Bridge Rd (60010-1011)
PHONE..................847 639-9468
Michael E Haber, *President*
Bonnie Miske, *General Mgr*
EMP: 3 EST: 1961
SQ FT: 3,000
SALES (est): 800K **Privately Held**
WEB: www.brokenoar.com
SIC: **5813** 2731 Tavern (drinking places); book publishing

Port Byron
Rock Island County

(G-16786)
CALVERT SYSTEMS
Also Called: Sound Master & Calvert Systems
21114 94th Ave N (61275-9623)
PHONE..................309 523-3262
Wade Calvert, *Owner*
EMP: 5
SALES (est): 307K **Privately Held**
SIC: **8711** 2298 Electrical or electronic engineering; designing: ship, boat, machine & product; cable, fiber

(G-16787)
SANDSTROM PRODUCTS COMPANY (PA)
224 S Main St (61275-9501)
P.O. Box 547 (61275-0547)
PHONE..................309 523-2121
Brian Suhl, *President*
Rick Hartsock, *President*
Nichole May, *General Mgr*
Scott Jacobs, *Safety Dir*
Sue Black, *Info Tech Mgr*
▲ EMP: 24
SQ FT: 50,000
SALES (est): 4.1MM **Privately Held**
WEB: www.sandstromproducts.com
SIC: **2851** 2842 2891 Paints & allied products; specialty cleaning, polishes & sanitation goods; adhesives

(G-16788)
SANDSTROM PRODUCTS COMPANY
218 S High St (61275-9531)
P.O. Box 547 (61275-0547)
PHONE..................309 523-2121
Rick Hartsock, *President*
EMP: 10

Posen - Cook County (G-16789)

SALES (est): 891K
SALES (corp-wide): 4.1MM **Privately Held**
SIC: 2851 2992 2891 2842 Paints & allied products; lubricating oils & greases; adhesives & sealants; specialty cleaning, polishes & sanitation goods
PA: Sandstrom Products Company
224 S Main St
Port Byron IL 61275
309 523-2121

Posen
Cook County

(G-16789)
A & A STEEL FABRICATING CO
14100 S Harrison Ave (60469-1047)
PHONE..............................708 389-4499
Sharon Poe, *President*
Wayne Mc Cartney, *Vice Pres*
Allen Poe, *Vice Pres*
Denise McCartney, *Info Tech Mgr*
EMP: 10 EST: 1961
SQ FT: 28,800
SALES (est): 2.3MM **Privately Held**
WEB: www.aasteelfab.com
SIC: 3312 3316 3444 3443 Blast furnaces & steel mills; bars, steel, cold finished, from purchased hot-rolled; sheet metalwork; fabricated plate work (boiler shop); fabricated structural metal

(G-16790)
ACCURATE GRINDING CO INC
14003 S Harrison Ave (60469-1022)
PHONE..............................708 371-1887
David M Niemeyer, *President*
Peter Niemeyer, *Vice Pres*
EMP: 8 EST: 1945
SQ FT: 3,500
SALES (est): 1.1MM **Privately Held**
SIC: 3544 Punches, forming & stamping; special dies & tools

(G-16791)
BIOCARE LABS INC
14800 S Mckinley Ave B (60469-1547)
PHONE..............................708 496-8657
Aisha R Chaudary, *President*
Sajjad Syed, *Applctn Conslt*
◆ EMP: 8
SALES (est): 1.7MM **Privately Held**
SIC: 2844 Hair preparations, including shampoos; cosmetic preparations

(G-16792)
CONFAB SYSTEMS INC
14831 S Mckinley Ave (60469-1524)
PHONE..............................708 388-4103
Daniel Rice, *President*
Michael Connor, *Admin Sec*
EMP: 10
SALES (est): 2MM **Privately Held**
SIC: 3535 Conveyors & conveying equipment

(G-16793)
DANDURAND CUSTOM WOODWORKING
2606 W Walter Zimny Dr (60469-1230)
PHONE..............................708 489-6440
Francis Dandurand, *Owner*
EMP: 2
SALES (est): 237.9K **Privately Held**
SIC: 2431 Millwork

(G-16794)
ENTECH FABRICATIONS INC
14002 S Harrison Ave (60469-1023)
P.O. Box 238 (60469-0238)
PHONE..............................708 597-5568
Harry W Workman, *President*
EMP: 5
SALES (est): 862.7K **Privately Held**
SIC: 3556 5084 Beverage machinery; conveyor systems

(G-16795)
GREMP STEEL CO
14100 S Western Ave Ste 2 (60469-1061)
PHONE..............................708 389-7393
Rod Samardzija, *President*
Bronny Samardzija, *Vice Pres*
Greg Koscielski, *Purch Mgr*
EMP: 25 EST: 1965
SQ FT: 55,000
SALES (est): 7.6MM **Privately Held**
WEB: www.grempsteel.com
SIC: 3441 Building components, structural steel

(G-16796)
J GARVIN INDUSTRIES INC (PA)
Also Called: Chicago Cremation Supplies
14750 S Campbell Ave (60469-1518)
PHONE..............................708 297-7400
John J Garvin, *President*
EMP: 5
SALES (est): 989.8K **Privately Held**
SIC: 3995 Burial caskets

(G-16797)
MID-OAK DISTILLERY INC
14800 S Mckinley Ave (60469-1547)
PHONE..............................708 926-9131
Matthew Altman, *President*
David Grotto, *Principal*
EMP: 15 EST: 2012
SALES (est): 988.4K **Privately Held**
WEB: www.cdvodka.com
SIC: 2085 Distillers' dried grains & solubles & alcohol

(G-16798)
MILK DESIGN COMPANY
14150 S Western Ave (60469-1030)
PHONE..............................312 563-6455
Joseph A Colosi, *President*
Jessica Houston, *CFO*
Jessica Colosi, *Admin Sec*
EMP: 5
SQ FT: 14,000
SALES (est): 1MM **Privately Held**
WEB: www.milkdesign.net
SIC: 3446 Stairs, staircases, stair treads: prefabricated metal

(G-16799)
NORTHSTAR CUSTOM CABINETRY
14825 S Mckinley Ave (60469-1524)
PHONE..............................708 597-2099
Edward J McGunn, *Manager*
EMP: 2
SALES (est): 328.1K **Privately Held**
SIC: 2434 Wood kitchen cabinets

(G-16800)
PARTS SPECIALISTS INC
Also Called: Lincoln Land Enterprises
14639 S Short St (60469-1327)
PHONE..............................708 371-2444
Glenn Duncan, *President*
Sharon Duncan, *Corp Secy*
◆ EMP: 7
SQ FT: 6,200
SALES (est): 1.1MM **Privately Held**
SIC: 5084 3661 Elevators; industrial machine parts; telephones & telephone apparatus

(G-16801)
SOUTH SUBN WLDG & FABG CO INC
14022 S Western Ave (60469-1029)
PHONE..............................708 385-7160
George Bender, *President*
EMP: 9 EST: 1946
SQ FT: 10,000
SALES (est): 1.4MM **Privately Held**
SIC: 3444 7692 3446 3443 Sheet metalwork; welding repair; architectural metalwork; fabricated plate work (boiler shop); fabricated structural metal

Potomac
Vermilion County

(G-16802)
ILLINI FS INC
Also Called: I F S
6637 E 3050 North Rd (61865-6506)
PHONE..............................217 442-4737
EMP: 4
SALES (corp-wide): 33MM **Privately Held**
SIC: 2869 5191 5169 Mfg Industrial Organic Chemicals Whol Farm Supplies Whol Chemicals/Products
PA: Illini Fs Inc
1509 E University Ave
Urbana IL 61802
217 384-8300

Princeton
Bureau County

(G-16803)
A & M PRODUCTS COMPANY
575 Elm Pl (61356-1458)
P.O. Box 266 (61356-0266)
PHONE..............................815 875-2667
Mark Austin, *President*
Jeanne Austin, *Corp Secy*
John Austin, *Vice Pres*
▲ EMP: 9
SQ FT: 4,750
SALES (est): 1.4MM **Privately Held**
WEB: www.aandmproducts.com
SIC: 2499 5947 Trophy bases, wood; gift, novelty & souvenir shop

(G-16804)
ADVANCED ASPHALT CO (PA)
308 W Railroad Ave (61356-1215)
P.O. Box 234 (61356-0234)
PHONE..............................815 872-9911
Steve Kelly, *COO*
Judith Nelson, *Vice Pres*
Skip Happ, *Project Mgr*
Todd Maynard, *Project Mgr*
Brad Bruins, *Executive*
EMP: 25 EST: 1961
SQ FT: 4,000
SALES (est): 8.5MM **Privately Held**
WEB: www.advasphalt.biz
SIC: 1611 2951 Surfacing & paving; asphalt paving mixtures & blocks

(G-16805)
ALLEGION S&S HOLDING CO INC
Also Called: Allegion Lcn & Falcon Closers
121 W Railroad Ave (61356-1201)
P.O. Box 100 (61356-0100)
PHONE..............................815 875-3311
Kristina Baldwin, *General Mgr*
Karen Suarez, *Buyer*
Christopher Smith, *Accounts Mgr*
Chris Karun, *Manager*
Barry Martell, *Manager*
EMP: 250
SQ FT: 200,000 **Privately Held**
WEB: www.allegion.com
SIC: 3561 3429 3546 3563 Pumps & pumping equipment; furniture builders' & other household hardware; keys, locks & related hardware; power-driven handtools; air & gas compressors including vacuum pumps; winches; roller bearings & parts
HQ: Allegion S&S Holding Company Inc.
11819 N Penn St
Carmel IN 46032
317 810-3700

(G-16806)
DENTAL CRAFTS LAB INC
211 S 5th St (61356-1817)
P.O. Box 389 (61356-0389)
PHONE..............................815 872-3221
Kenneth Nordstrom, *President*
Barry Nordstrom, *Vice Pres*
Nancy Nordstrom, *Bookkeeper*
EMP: 5 EST: 1945
SALES (est): 455.1K **Privately Held**
SIC: 8072 3843 Crown & bridge production; denture production; dental equipment & supplies

(G-16807)
EMPIRE ACOUSTICAL SYSTEMS INC
1111 Ace Rd (61356-9038)
PHONE..............................815 261-0072
Patrick McKeown, *President*
EMP: 20
SQ FT: 35,000
SALES (est): 113.4K **Privately Held**
SIC: 1442 Construction sand & gravel

(G-16808)
ENNIS INC
Also Called: GBS Document Solutions
200 W Railroad Ave (61356-1204)
PHONE..............................815 875-2000
David Crysler, *Branch Mgr*
EMP: 30
SALES (corp-wide): 438.4MM **Publicly Held**
SIC: 2752 2761 2671 Business forms, lithographed; manifold business forms; packaging paper & plastics film, coated & laminated
PA: Ennis, Inc.
2441 Presidential Pkwy
Midlothian TX 76065
972 775-9801

(G-16809)
FLIGHT MANUFACTURING CORP
2750 Tradition (61356-9402)
P.O. Box 502 (61356-0502)
PHONE..............................815 876-1616
Michael Hamilton, *President*
EMP: 6
SALES (est): 1.1MM **Privately Held**
SIC: 3999 Barber & beauty shop equipment

(G-16810)
GARDNER DENVER INC
Also Called: Champion A Gardner Denver Co
1301 N Euclid Ave (61356-9601)
PHONE..............................815 875-3321
Amber Dhesse, *Controller*
Mark Hoffman, *Branch Mgr*
Becky Butterfield, *Manager*
Dan Elias, *Info Tech Mgr*
EMP: 100
SALES (corp-wide): 2.4B **Publicly Held**
SIC: 3563 Air & gas compressors
HQ: Gardner Denver, Inc.
222 E Erie St Ste 500
Milwaukee WI 53202

(G-16811)
ITALVIBRAS USA INC
1940 Vans Way (61356-9037)
PHONE..............................815 872-1350
Paolo Silingardi, *President*
Mike Kargl, *General Mgr*
Carlo Silingardi, *Principal*
Rob Bradley, *Opers Staff*
Jeremy Skaggs, *Opers Staff*
▲ EMP: 6
SQ FT: 2,000
SALES (est): 1MM **Privately Held**
WEB: www.italvibrasusa.com
SIC: 3625 Industrial electrical relays & switches

(G-16812)
L W SCHNEIDER INC
1180 N 6th St (61356-9564)
PHONE..............................815 875-3835
Lloyd W Schneider, *CEO*
Beverly Schneider, *President*
Theresa Quezada, *COO*
Lisa Myers, *Vice Pres*
Bruce Stalter, *Vice Pres*
▲ EMP: 50 EST: 1971
SQ FT: 13,000
SALES (est): 11.5MM **Privately Held**
SIC: 3599 Machine shop, jobbing & repair

(G-16813)
MC HENRY MACHINE CO INC
1309 Il Highway 26 (61356-8341)
PHONE..............................815 875-1953
John Williams, *President*
EMP: 4
SQ FT: 2,652
SALES (est): 810K **Privately Held**
WEB: www.mchenrymachineco.com
SIC: 3599 Machine shop, jobbing & repair

(G-16814)
MISTIC METAL MOVER INC
1160 N 6th St (61356-9564)
PHONE..............................815 875-1371
Dwight K Thompson Jr, *President*

Hal Purky, *Vice Pres*
Brian Thompson, *Admin Sec*
Cynthia Thompson, *Admin Sec*
EMP: 4
SQ FT: 5,000
SALES (est): 591.8K **Privately Held**
SIC: 2992 Cutting oils, blending: made from purchased materials

(G-16815)
MONTEREY MUSHROOMS INC
27268 Us Highway 6 (61356-8959)
PHONE 815 875-4436
James Howard, *Branch Mgr*
Mike Abrahams, *Manager*
Sheryl Godina, *Telecomm Mgr*
EMP: 4
SALES (corp-wide): 777.4MM **Privately Held**
SIC: 0182 2099 Mushrooms grown under cover; food preparations
PA: Monterey Mushrooms, Inc.
260 Westgate Dr
Watsonville CA 95076
831 763-5300

(G-16816)
MTM JOSTENS INC
615 S 6th St (61356-1873)
PHONE 815 875-1111
Alm Dahms, *Principal*
EMP: 2
SALES (est): 282.7K **Privately Held**
SIC: 3911 Jewelry, precious metal

(G-16817)
MTM RECOGNITION CORPORATION
615 S 6th St (61356-1873)
PHONE 815 875-1111
Ashli Smith, *VP Admin*
Wes Temple, *Materials Mgr*
Tom Tester, *Enginr/R&D Mgr*
Chris Noll, *Controller*
Bob Conklin, *Accounts Mgr*
EMP: 250
SQ FT: 50,000
SALES (est): 36.7MM
SALES (corp-wide): 109MM **Privately Held**
WEB: www.mtmrecognition.com
SIC: 3911 3914 Jewelry, precious metal; trophies
PA: Mtm Recognition Corporation
3201 Se 29th St
Oklahoma City OK 73115
405 609-6900

(G-16818)
PRINCETON FAST STOP
720 N Main St (61356-1331)
PHONE 815 872-0706
Mark Orr, *President*
EMP: 14
SALES (est): 1.5MM **Privately Held**
SIC: 3589 Car washing machinery

(G-16819)
PRINCETON FLIGHTING CORP
Also Called: Express Flighting
145 W Progress Dr (61356-9723)
P.O. Box 599 (61356-0599)
PHONE 815 872-0945
Mike Hamilton, *President*
Darren Shaper, *Manager*
Lori Torri, *Manager*
EMP: 12
SALES: 3MM **Privately Held**
SIC: 3312 Hot-rolled iron & steel products

(G-16820)
PRINCETON READY-MIX INC
533 E Railroad Ave (61356-1392)
P.O. Box 9 (61356-0009)
PHONE 815 875-3359
Joan Perona, *President*
Gwen Walsh, *Admin Sec*
EMP: 16
SQ FT: 1,200
SALES (est): 450K **Privately Held**
SIC: 3273 Ready-mixed concrete

(G-16821)
PRINCETON SEALING WAX CO
106 W Long St (61356-1231)
PHONE 815 875-1943
Caroline Tompson, *Partner*
Carolyn A Lokay, *Partner*
EMP: 3 **EST:** 1907
SQ FT: 3,600
SALES (est): 434.7K **Privately Held**
WEB: www.princetonchamber-il.com
SIC: 2891 2842 Sealing wax; adhesives; specialty cleaning, polishes & sanitation goods

(G-16822)
QUALITY COATING CO
2955 N Main St (61356-9044)
PHONE 815 875-3228
Eldon Entwhistle, *President*
Marshann Entwhistle, *Vice Pres*
EMP: 18
SQ FT: 5,000
SALES (est): 2MM **Privately Held**
SIC: 3479 3229 2851 Coating of metals & formed products; pressed & blown glass; paints & allied products

(G-16823)
THE B F SHAW PRINTING CO
Also Called: Bureau County Republican
800 Ace Rd (61356-9201)
P.O. Box 340 (61356-0340)
PHONE 815 875-4461
Sam R Fisher, *Publisher*
Jim Dunn, *Editor*
Joanie Nichols, *Info Tech Dir*
EMP: 45
SQ FT: 11,250
SALES (corp-wide): 73.4MM **Privately Held**
SIC: 2711 2796 2791 2789 Commercial printing & newspaper publishing combined; platemaking services; typesetting; bookbinding & related work; commercial printing; commercial printing, lithographic
PA: 'b. F. Shaw Printing Company, The'
3200 E Lincolnway
Sterling IL
815 284-4000

(G-16824)
TRI-CON MATERIALS INC (PA)
308 W Railroad Ave (61356-1215)
P.O. Box 304 (61356-0304)
PHONE 815 872-3206
Richard L Nelson, *President*
Judith Nelson, *Vice Pres*
Steve Kelly, *Treasurer*
Steve Nelson, *Admin Sec*
EMP: 30
SQ FT: 4,000
SALES (est): 7.9MM **Privately Held**
WEB: www.triconmaterials.com
SIC: 1442 Construction sand & gravel

Princeville
Peoria County

(G-16825)
COKEL DJ WELDING BAY & MUFFLER
Also Called: Cokel D J Wldg Stl Fabricators
224 E Evans St (61559-7531)
PHONE 309 385-4567
Paul Cokel, *President*
EMP: 1
SQ FT: 4,500
SALES (est): 210.9K **Privately Held**
SIC: 3441 7692 Fabricated structural metal; welding repair

(G-16826)
EC HARMS MET FABRICATORS INC
1017 N Santa Fe Ave (61559-9279)
PHONE 309 385-2132
Dennis L Stoecker, *President*
EMP: 13
SQ FT: 25,000
SALES (est): 3.1MM **Privately Held**
SIC: 3441 Fabricated structural metal

(G-16827)
FCA LLC
610 S Walnut St (61559-9266)
PHONE 309 385-2588
Joe Cave, *Branch Mgr*
EMP: 46 **Privately Held**
WEB: www.fcapackaging.com
SIC: 5085 2448 2441 Industrial supplies; wood pallets & skids; nailed wood boxes & shook
PA: Fca, Llc
7601 John Deere Pkwy
Moline IL 61265

(G-16828)
GREENFIELD CONTRACTORS LLC
1012 N Santa Fe Ave Ste B (61559-9218)
PHONE 309 385-1859
Lucas D Young, *President*
EMP: 60
SALES (est): 1.1MM **Privately Held**
SIC: 2452 Farm & agricultural buildings, prefabricated wood

(G-16829)
SENECA FOODS CORPORATION
Also Called: Chiquita
606 S Tremont St (61559-9468)
PHONE 309 385-4301
Eric Martin, *Opers Mgr*
Wally Hochsprung, *Branch Mgr*
EMP: 36
SQ FT: 150,000
SALES (corp-wide): 1.2B **Publicly Held**
SIC: 2033 Vegetables: packaged in cans, jars, etc.
PA: Seneca Foods Corporation
3736 S Main St
Marion NY 14505
315 926-8100

Prophetstown
Whiteside County

(G-16830)
AMERICAN GEAR INC
910 Swanson Dr (61277-9524)
P.O. Box 156 (61277-0156)
PHONE 815 537-5111
Gregory W Scott, *President*
Pam Scott, *Treasurer*
Petrazio Heidi, *Manager*
EMP: 10
SALES: 1MM **Privately Held**
SIC: 3566 Gears, power transmission, except automotive

(G-16831)
GENESIS III INC
5575 Lyndon Rd (61277-9588)
P.O. Box 186 (61277-0186)
PHONE 815 537-7900
Roger Young, *Ch of Bd*
Jonathan Paul, *President*
EMP: 26
SQ FT: 18,000
SALES (est): 6.6MM **Privately Held**
WEB: www.g3hammers.com
SIC: 3531 Hammer mills (rock & ore crushing machines), portable

(G-16832)
HERITAGE PRINTING (PA)
219 Washington St (61277-1179)
P.O. Box 215 (61277-0215)
PHONE 815 537-2372
Randy Jacobs, *Partner*
Mark Jacobs, *Partner*
EMP: 4 **EST:** 1969
SQ FT: 1,800
SALES (est): 699.6K **Privately Held**
SIC: 2752 2791 Commercial printing, offset; typesetting

(G-16833)
IMH FABRICATION INC
Also Called: Sterling Multi-Products
326 W 5th St (61277-1006)
PHONE 815 537-2381
Eric Odmark, *President*
Earl Murphy, *Purch Mgr*
Michele Williams, *Manager*
EMP: 13
SALES (corp-wide): 11.6MM **Privately Held**
SIC: 3634 3599 3841 3531 Food mixers, electric: household; fryers, electric: household; machine shop, jobbing & repair; surgical & medical instruments; construction machinery; metal stampings; sheet metalwork
PA: Imh Fabrication Inc.
1929 Columbia Ave
Indianapolis IN 46202
317 508-7462

(G-16834)
PROPHET GEAR CO
46 Grove St (61277-9375)
P.O. Box 3 (61277-0003)
PHONE 815 537-2002
Kenneth Huizenga, *President*
Tom Green, *Sales Executive*
EMP: 25
SQ FT: 17,000
SALES (est): 4.7MM **Privately Held**
WEB: www.prophetgear.com
SIC: 3566 3568 Gears, power transmission, except automotive; pulleys, power transmission

Prospect Heights
Cook County

(G-16835)
ARCHITECTUAL WOODWORKING
305 Brian Ln (60070-1609)
PHONE 847 259-3331
Richard Kellerman, *Owner*
EMP: 2
SALES (est): 272.6K **Privately Held**
SIC: 2431 Millwork

(G-16836)
ARMSTRONG/ALAR INC
Also Called: Armstrong-Alar Chain
15 E Palatine Rd Ste 108 (60070-1871)
PHONE 847 808-8885
Allen Green, *President*
Larry Barabasz, *Vice Pres*
Candi Green, *Treasurer*
Davida Barabasz, *Admin Sec*
EMP: 6
SALES (est): 813.1K **Privately Held**
SIC: 3496 Miscellaneous fabricated wire products

(G-16837)
CREATIVE SCIENCE ACTIVITIES
Also Called: Esd
2 E Clarendon St (60070-1534)
PHONE 847 870-1746
Gerald T Anderson, *Owner*
EMP: 3
SALES: 300K **Privately Held**
SIC: 3825 Digital test equipment, electronic & electrical circuits

(G-16838)
DIRK VANDER NOOT
811 Andover Ct (60070-1169)
P.O. Box 438, Ingleside (60041-0438)
PHONE 224 558-1878
EMP: 3
SALES (est): 191K **Privately Held**
SIC: 3089 Mfg Plastic Products

(G-16839)
EARLY BIRD ADVERTISING INC
502 Grego Ct (60070-1634)
PHONE 847 253-1423
Wayne Vipond, *President*
Dorothy Vipond, *Treasurer*
Wayne Ter Haar, *Personnel Exec*
EMP: 3
SALES (est): 316.9K **Privately Held**
SIC: 7311 7335 2791 Advertising agencies; commercial photography; typesetting, computer controlled

(G-16840)
FIRE ORB LLC
300 Elm St (60070-1456)
PHONE 847 454-9198
Andrew Markow,

Prospect Heights - Cook County (G-16841)

EMP: 5 EST: 2011
SALES (est): 579.7K **Privately Held**
SIC: 3272 Fireplaces, concrete

(G-16841)
GEORGE WILSON
477 Greystone Ln (60070-2592)
PHONE....................847 342-1111
George Wilson Jr, *Partner*
EMP: 2
SALES: 400K **Privately Held**
SIC: 3861 Reproduction machines & equipment

(G-16842)
GERALD R PAGE CORPORATION (PA)
309 E Kenilworth Ave (60070-1316)
PHONE....................847 398-5575
Gerald R Page, *President*
Randy Randolph, *Principal*
Constance R Page, *Admin Sec*
EMP: 12
SQ FT: 10,000
SALES (est): 7.1MM **Privately Held**
SIC: 3312 1542 1541 8712 Structural shapes & pilings, steel; pipes & tubes; commercial & office building, new construction; industrial buildings, new construction; architectural services

(G-16843)
INSULATORS SUPPLY INC
741 Pinecrest Dr (60070-1807)
PHONE....................847 394-2836
William Melton, *President*
Ronald Lemmon, *Vice Pres*
EMP: 3
SQ FT: 6,000
SALES (est): 460K **Privately Held**
SIC: 5211 3442 5033 Insulation material, building; metal doors; insulation materials

(G-16844)
LEXPRESS INC
1176 Cove Dr (60070-1905)
PHONE....................773 517-7095
Eugeniu Dimbu, *Owner*
EMP: 5 EST: 2015
SALES (est): 233.7K **Privately Held**
SIC: 4212 3537 7389 Delivery service, vehicular; trucks: freight, baggage, etc.: industrial, except mining;

(G-16845)
PLATINUM TOOLING TECHNOLOGIES
16 Piper Ln Ste 129 (60070-1799)
PHONE....................847 749-0633
EMP: 3
SALES (est): 293.8K **Privately Held**
SIC: 3599 Machine shop, jobbing & repair

(G-16846)
STITCH BY STITCH INCORPORATED
Also Called: Stitch Plus
65 E Palatine Rd Ste 217 (60070-1845)
PHONE....................847 541-2543
Karen Locallo, *President*
Joanne Hansler, *Vice Pres*
EMP: 7
SALES (est): 653.2K **Privately Held**
SIC: 2395 Embroidery & art needlework

(G-16847)
SWISS E D M WIRECUT INC
743 Pinecrest Dr (60070-1807)
PHONE....................847 459-4310
John E Strahammer, *President*
Josef V Strahammer, *Admin Sec*
EMP: 10
SQ FT: 6,000
SALES (est): 1MM **Privately Held**
WEB: www.swissedm.com
SIC: 3599 Machine shop, jobbing & repair

(G-16848)
WOOLENWEAR CO
Also Called: Personalitee's
739 Pinecrest Dr (60070-1807)
PHONE....................847 520-9243
Jeffery Kroft, *President*
Gail Kroft, *Vice Pres*
EMP: 10

SQ FT: 6,000
SALES: 710K **Privately Held**
SIC: 2326 2339 2395 2759 Service apparel (baker, barber, lab, etc.), washable: men's; service apparel, washable: women's; embroidery products, except schiffli machine; screen printing

(G-16849)
XD INDUSTRIES INC
836 E Old Willow Rd (60070-2163)
PHONE....................847 293-0796
EMP: 2
SALES (est): 204.5K **Privately Held**
SIC: 3999 Manufacturing industries

Quincy
Adams County

(G-16850)
ADAMS TELEPHONE CO-OPERATIVE
Also Called: Adams Network
301 Oak St (62301-2516)
P.O. Box 247, Golden (62339-0247)
PHONE....................217 224-9566
Jim Broemmer, *Manager*
EMP: 30
SALES (corp-wide): 15.5MM **Privately Held**
SIC: 7372 Prepackaged software
PA: Adams Telephone Co-Operative
405 Emminga Rd
Golden IL 62339
217 696-4411

(G-16851)
AGCO RECYCLING LLC
4425 Gardner Expy (62305-7525)
PHONE....................217 224-9048
JD Albsmeyer, *Owner*
EMP: 17
SALES (est): 1.3MM **Privately Held**
SIC: 2448 5031 Pallets, wood; molding, all materials

(G-16852)
ALTER TRADING CORPORATION
Also Called: Alter Scrap
2834 Gardner Expy (62305-7529)
P.O. Box 766 (62306-0766)
PHONE....................217 223-0156
Ron Stephenson, *General Mgr*
EMP: 10
SALES (corp-wide): 740.9MM **Privately Held**
WEB: www.altertrading.com
SIC: 5093 5051 4953 3341 Ferrous metal scrap & waste; metals service centers & offices; refuse systems; secondary nonferrous metals
HQ: Alter Trading Corporation
700 Office Pkwy
Saint Louis MO 63141
314 872-2400

(G-16853)
ANIMAL CENTER INTERNATIONAL
4124 Kochs Ln (62305-7684)
PHONE....................217 214-0536
Flora Madey, *General Mgr*
▲ EMP: 8
SALES (est): 780.7K **Privately Held**
SIC: 2833 Animal based products

(G-16854)
ARCHER-DANIELS-MIDLAND COMPANY
ADM
1000 N 30th St (62301-3400)
PHONE....................217 222-7100
Dina Bell, *Superintendent*
Tim Schaal, *Vice Pres*
Erika Almeida, *Manager*
Shelly Bowman, *Manager*
Harold Bullard, *Manager*
EMP: 20
SALES (corp-wide): 64.6B **Publicly Held**
WEB: www.adm.com
SIC: 2048 Livestock feeds; feed supplements; mineral feed supplements

PA: Archer-Daniels-Midland Company
77 W Wacker Dr Ste 4600
Chicago IL 60601
312 634-8100

(G-16855)
ARCHER-DANIELS-MIDLAND COMPANY
ADM
436 S Front St (62305-3800)
P.O. Box 7001 (62305-7001)
PHONE....................217 228-0805
EMP: 7
SALES (corp-wide): 64.6B **Publicly Held**
SIC: 2041 Flour & other grain mill products
PA: Archer-Daniels-Midland Company
77 W Wacker Dr Ste 4600
Chicago IL 60601
312 634-8100

(G-16856)
ARCHER-DANIELS-MIDLAND COMPANY
Also Called: ADM
2100 Gardner Expy (62305-9376)
PHONE....................217 224-1800
EMP: 20
SALES (corp-wide): 64.6B **Publicly Held**
SIC: 2041 2079 2075 5153 Flour & other grain mill products; edible fats & oils; soybean oil mills; grain elevators
PA: Archer-Daniels-Midland Company
77 W Wacker Dr Ste 4600
Chicago IL 60601
312 634-8100

(G-16857)
ARCHER-DANIELS-MIDLAND COMPANY
Also Called: ADM
1900 Gardner Expy (62301)
PHONE....................217 224-1800
Todd Phillips, *Branch Mgr*
EMP: 58
SALES (corp-wide): 64.6B **Publicly Held**
SIC: 2041 Flour & other grain mill products
PA: Archer-Daniels-Midland Company
77 W Wacker Dr Ste 4600
Chicago IL 60601
312 634-8100

(G-16858)
ARCHER-DANIELS-MIDLAND COMPANY
Also Called: ADM
2701 Refinery Rd (62305-8700)
P.O. Box 1045 (62306-1045)
PHONE....................217 224-1875
Mike Pulliam, *Manager*
EMP: 80
SALES (corp-wide): 64.6B **Publicly Held**
SIC: 2041 5199 Flour & other grain mill products; oils, animal or vegetable
PA: Archer-Daniels-Midland Company
77 W Wacker Dr Ste 4600
Chicago IL 60601
312 634-8100

(G-16859)
AWERKAMP MACHINE CO (PA)
237 N 7th St (62301-3093)
PHONE....................217 222-3480
Toll Free:....................888 -
William J Awerkamp, *President*
Kevin Hukendick, *Office Mgr*
Donald T Awerkamp, *Admin Sec*
EMP: 49 EST: 1947
SQ FT: 45,000
SALES: 6MM **Privately Held**
WEB: www.awerkamp.com
SIC: 3599 7692 Machine shop, jobbing & repair; welding repair

(G-16860)
AWERKAMP MACHINE CO
Also Called: Awerkamp Steel
321 Broadway St (62301-2722)
PHONE....................217 222-3490
Toll Free:....................888 -
Mark Terwelp, *Manager*
Rod Snodgrass, *Systems Mgr*
EMP: 10
SALES (corp-wide): 6MM **Privately Held**
SIC: 3599 5051 Machine shop, jobbing & repair; steel

PA: Awerkamp Machine Co.
237 N 7th St
Quincy IL 62301
217 222-3480

(G-16861)
BEANS PRINTING INC
3710 Broadway St (62305-2822)
PHONE....................217 223-5555
Justin Hurayt, *President*
EMP: 4
SALES (est): 299.5K **Privately Held**
SIC: 2752 Commercial printing, lithographic

(G-16862)
BEAUTICONTROL
1702 Locust St (62301-1467)
PHONE....................217 223-0382
Kimberly Caster, *Principal*
EMP: 3
SALES (est): 202.3K **Privately Held**
SIC: 3562 Casters

(G-16863)
BEI ELECTRONICS LLC (HQ)
Also Called: Broadcast Electronics
4100 N 24th St (62305-7749)
PHONE....................217 224-9600
Elizabeth Keck,
EMP: 19
SALES (est): 22.1MM **Privately Held**
SIC: 3663 Transmitting apparatus, radio or television
PA: Broadcast Global Investment I, Inc.
4100 N 24th St
Quincy IL 62305
217 224-9600

(G-16864)
BEI HOLDING CORPORATION
Also Called: Broadcast Electronics
4100 N 24th St (62305-7749)
P.O. Box 3606 (62305-3606)
PHONE....................217 224-9600
John Tedlow, *President*
Ray Miklius, *Vice Pres*
Becky Keck, *CFO*
Elizabeth Keck, *CFO*
EMP: 2
SQ FT: 1,000
SALES (est): 254.1K **Privately Held**
SIC: 3663 Radio broadcasting & communications equipment

(G-16865)
BICK BROADCASTING INC
Also Called: Sign Pro
408 N 24th St (62301-3254)
PHONE....................217 223-9693
Tim Gottman, *Manager*
EMP: 4
SALES (est): 418.5K
SALES (corp-wide): 2.2MM **Privately Held**
SIC: 3993 Signs & advertising specialties
PA: Bick Broadcasting Inc
119 N 3rd St
Hannibal MO 63401
573 221-3450

(G-16866)
BLEIGH CONSTRUCTION COMPANY
Also Called: Quincy Ready Mix Co
3522 S 6th St (62305-7557)
PHONE....................217 222-5005
Mark E Tofall, *Branch Mgr*
EMP: 7
SQ FT: 1,000
SALES (corp-wide): 35.3MM **Privately Held**
WEB: www.bleigh.com
SIC: 3273 Ready-mixed concrete
PA: Bleigh Construction Company
9037 Highway 168
Palmyra MO 63461
573 221-2247

(G-16867)
BOWTREE INC
720 E Tolton Dr (62305-8379)
PHONE....................217 430-8884
Michael A Ray, *President*
Mike Ray, *Manager*
EMP: 3

GEOGRAPHIC SECTION
Quincy - Adams County (G-16892)

SALES (est): 70K **Privately Held**
SIC: 3949 Archery equipment, general

(G-16868)
BREWER UTILITY SYSTEMS INC
Also Called: Golfcar Utility Systems
1628 Madison St (62301-5558)
PHONE..........................217 224-5975
EMP: 5
SQ FT: 14,000
SALES (est): 520K **Privately Held**
SIC: 5941 3799 Mfg Transportation Equipment Ret Sporting Goods/Bicycles

(G-16869)
BROADCAST ELECTRONICS INC (HQ)
Also Called: B E
4100 N 24th St (62305-7749)
PHONE..........................217 224-9600
Tom Beck, *CEO*
Brian Lindemann, *President*
Chuck Edwards, *Materials Mgr*
Tim Whiston, *Safety Mgr*
Gene McAneny, *Engineer*
◆ EMP: 120 EST: 1959
SQ FT: 70,000
SALES (est): 17.7MM
SALES (corp-wide): 13.1MM **Privately Held**
WEB: www.bdcast.com
SIC: 3663 8742 Radio broadcasting & communications equipment; industry specialist consultants
PA: Elenos Srl
   Via Amendola 9
   Poggio Renatico FE 44028
   053 282-9965

(G-16870)
CENTRAL STONE COMPANY
Also Called: Crush Stone
8514 Rock Quarry Rd (62305-8025)
PHONE..........................217 224-7330
Ray Barry, *Superintendent*
EMP: 11
SALES (corp-wide): 2.5B **Privately Held**
SIC: 1422 Limestones, ground
HQ: Central Stone Company
   4640 E 56th St
   Davenport IA 52807
   309 757-8250

(G-16871)
CENTURY SIGNS INC
2704 N 30th St (62305-1231)
PHONE..........................217 224-7419
Stanley Helkey, *President*
EMP: 11
SQ FT: 14,000
SALES: 1MM **Privately Held**
SIC: 3993 7629 Neon signs; electrical repair shops

(G-16872)
CLASSIQUE SIGNS & ENGRV INC
1702 Harrison St (62301-6712)
PHONE..........................217 228-7446
Rodney Moore, *President*
Steven Moore, *Vice Pres*
EMP: 6
SQ FT: 4,000
SALES (est): 900K **Privately Held**
SIC: 5094 5199 2759 3993 Trophies; advertising specialties; commercial printing; signs & advertising specialties; trophies & plaques; coated & laminated paper

(G-16873)
CRAIG INDUSTRIES INC
Also Called: Enviro-Buildings
401 Delaware St (62301-4877)
PHONE..........................217 228-2421
Ellis Craig, *President*
Stephen Bowman, *COO*
Luke Craig, *COO*
Rachel Williams, *Counsel*
Allen Craig, *Vice Pres*
▼ EMP: 100
SQ FT: 40,000
SALES (est): 20.8MM **Privately Held**
SIC: 3448 3632 Prefabricated metal buildings; household refrigerators & freezers

(G-16874)
DAVID SCHUTTE
1226 N 14th St (62301-2037)
PHONE..........................217 223-5464
David Schutte, *President*
Mary Ruth Schutte, *Corp Secy*
EMP: 9
SALES (est): 389.7K **Privately Held**
SIC: 7699 7692 Industrial machinery & equipment repair; welding repair

(G-16875)
DAVID TAYLOR
Also Called: Selby Implement Company
2201 N 24th St (62301-1207)
PHONE..........................217 222-6480
David Taylor, *President*
EMP: 20
SALES (est): 1.3MM **Privately Held**
WEB: www.selbyimplement.com
SIC: 3523 3524 3751 Farm machinery & equipment; blowers & vacuums, lawn; gears, motorcycle & bicycle

(G-16876)
DE ASBURY INC
Also Called: Royal Printing Co
2615 Ellington Rd (62305-8830)
P.O. Box 3857 (62305-3857)
PHONE..........................217 222-0617
Dan E Asbury, *President*
Patrice Higgins, *General Mgr*
Andrew Asbury, *Vice Pres*
Eric Asbury, *VP Opers*
EMP: 30
SQ FT: 8,000
SALES (est): 5.3MM **Privately Held**
WEB: www.royal-printing.com
SIC: 2752 3993 2791 2789 Commercial printing, offset; signs & advertising specialties; typesetting; bookbinding & related work

(G-16877)
DYNEER CORPORATION
2701 Spruce St (62301-3473)
PHONE..........................217 228-6011
Maurice M Taylor Jr, *President*
EMP: 487
SQ FT: 1,000,000
SALES (est): 27.2MM
SALES (corp-wide): 1.4B **Publicly Held**
SIC: 3011 3069 3568 Tires, cushion or solid rubber; industrial tires, pneumatic; hard rubber & molded rubber products; hard rubber products; clutches, except vehicular
PA: Titan International, Inc.
   2701 Spruce St
   Quincy IL 62301
   217 228-6011

(G-16878)
E MC
906 Vermont St (62301-3050)
PHONE..........................217 228-1280
EMP: 3
SALES (est): 175.5K **Privately Held**
SIC: 3572 Computer storage devices

(G-16879)
EMCO WHEATON USA INC (DH)
1800 Gardner Expy (62305-9364)
PHONE..........................217 222-5400
Darren Sabino, *President*
Jerry Ludlum, *COO*
◆ EMP: 40
SALES (est): 9.1MM
SALES (corp-wide): 2.4B **Publicly Held**
SIC: 3561 1799 Pumps & pumping equipment; service station equipment installation & maintenance

(G-16880)
EMERALD CITY JEWELRY INC
Also Called: Emerald City Jewelers
3236 Broadway St (62301-3712)
PHONE..........................217 222-8896
Sheri Busse, *President*
Denise C Feldkamp, *Manager*
EMP: 6
SALES: 750K **Privately Held**
SIC: 3911 5944 7631 Jewelry, precious metal; jewelry stores; jewelry repair services

(G-16881)
EXPRESSIONS BY CHRISTINE INC
711 Maine St (62301-4012)
PHONE..........................217 223-2750
Christine Kaiser, *President*
EMP: 15
SQ FT: 3,000
SALES (est): 1MM **Privately Held**
SIC: 2395 Embroidery products, except schiffli machine; embroidery & art needlework

(G-16882)
FITZPATRICK BROS INC
309 Radio Rd (62305-7533)
PHONE..........................217 592-3500
Sandy Pontillo, *Branch Mgr*
EMP: 7
SALES (corp-wide): 23.3MM **Privately Held**
SIC: 3423 Plumbers' hand tools
HQ: Fitzpatrick Bros., Inc.
   10700 88th Ave
   Pleasant Prairie WI 53158
   262 947-3500

(G-16883)
GARDNER DENVER INC
Also Called: Hoffman Air & Filtration
1800 Gardner Expy (62305-9364)
PHONE..........................770 632-5000
Jason Brister, *Principal*
Gary Geiken, *Vice Pres*
Jim Perry, *Vice Pres*
Terry Hole, *Plant Mgr*
Trou Wiegand, *Plant Mgr*
EMP: 100
SALES (corp-wide): 2.4B **Publicly Held**
WEB: www.gardnerdenver.com
SIC: 3564 Blowers & fans
HQ: Gardner Denver, Inc.
   222 E Erie St Ste 500
   Milwaukee WI 53202

(G-16884)
GARDNER DENVER INC
1800 Gardner Expy (62305-9364)
P.O. Box 4024 (62305-4024)
PHONE..........................217 222-5400
Andrew Schiesl, *Vice Pres*
Addy Farou, *VP Mfg*
Marc Theune, *Plant Mgr*
Jeff Kon, *Project Mgr*
Nashu Barnard, *Production*
EMP: 52
SALES (corp-wide): 2.4B **Publicly Held**
SIC: 3563 Air & gas compressors
HQ: Gardner Denver, Inc.
   222 E Erie St Ste 500
   Milwaukee WI 53202

(G-16885)
GARDNER DENVER INC
1860 Gardner Expy (62305)
PHONE..........................800 231-3628
Elisha Samson, *Buyer*
EMP: 23
SALES (corp-wide): 2.4B **Publicly Held**
SIC: 3561 Pumps, domestic: water or sump
HQ: Gardner Denver, Inc.
   222 E Erie St Ste 500
   Milwaukee WI 53202

(G-16886)
GATESAIR INC
3200 Wisman Ln (62301-1252)
PHONE..........................800 622-0022
David Blickhan, *Engineer*
Jim Fenton, *Engineer*
Nick Smith, *Engineer*
Candice Kurk, *Accounting Mgr*
Jackie Drebes, *Credit Mgr*
EMP: 200
SALES (corp-wide): 3.8B **Privately Held**
SIC: 1731 3663 7371 Communications specialization; radio & TV communications equipment; computer software development & applications
HQ: Gatesair, Inc.
   5300 Kings Island Dr # 1
   Mason OH 45040
   513 459-3400

(G-16887)
GRIFFARD & ASSOCIATES LLC
Also Called: Rainmaker Brands
1022 Kochs Ln (62301-1336)
PHONE..........................217 316-1732
John Griffard, *Mng Member*
Gary Klingele
Tom Ries
▲ EMP: 3
SALES: 1MM **Privately Held**
SIC: 2421 7389 Outdoor wood structural products;

(G-16888)
H & B QUALITY TOOLING INC
2723 S Commercial Dr (62305-8807)
PHONE..........................217 223-2387
Roger Leenerts, *President*
Julie Leenerts, *Admin Sec*
EMP: 11
SQ FT: 14,000
SALES: 950K **Privately Held**
SIC: 3544 Dies & die holders for metal cutting, forming, die casting

(G-16889)
HARDY RADIATOR REPAIR
Also Called: Hardy's Auto Sales
1710 N 12th St (62301-1387)
PHONE..........................217 223-8320
Max Hardy, *Partner*
Rosemary Hardy, *Partner*
EMP: 11
SQ FT: 2,000
SALES (est): 650K **Privately Held**
SIC: 7539 3714 3433 Radiator repair shop, automotive; motor vehicle parts & accessories; heating equipment, except electric

(G-16890)
HEARTLAND COCA-COLA BTLG LLC
2620 Ellington Rd (62305-8829)
PHONE..........................217 223-3336
EMP: 3090
SALES (corp-wide): 23.9B **Privately Held**
SIC: 5149 2086 Beverages, except coffee & tea; carbonated beverages, nonalcoholic: bottled & canned
PA: Heartland Coca-Cola Bottling Company Llc
   9000 Marshall Dr
   Lenexa KS

(G-16891)
HERALD WHIG QUINCY
130 N 5th St (62301-2916)
P.O. Box 909 (62306-0909)
PHONE..........................217 222-7600
Tom Oakley, *CEO*
Whitney Allerheiligen, *Accounts Exec*
Shelly Bissell, *Advt Staff*
Jeannine Gilles, *Manager*
EMP: 2 EST: 2008
SALES (est): 207K **Privately Held**
WEB: www.whig.com
SIC: 5994 2711 Newsstand; newspapers, publishing & printing

(G-16892)
HOLLISTER-WHITNEY ELEV CO LLC
Also Called: Gsil Holding Corp
2603 N 24th St (62305-1215)
P.O. Box 4025 (62305-4025)
PHONE..........................217 222-0466
Brian Musholt, *President*
Herbert Glaser, *President*
Michael Graham, *Vice Pres*
Todd Leftwich, *President*
Donald Owens, *Engineer*
◆ EMP: 325 EST: 1959
SQ FT: 225,000
SALES (est): 126.7MM
SALES (corp-wide): 8.2B **Privately Held**
WEB: www.hollisterwhitney.com
SIC: 3534 Elevators & equipment
HQ: G.A.L. Manufacturing Company, Llc
   50 E 153rd St
   Bronx NY 10451
   718 292-9000

Quincy - Adams County (G-16893)

(G-16893)
HUBER CARBONATES LLC
3150 Gardner Expy (62305-9378)
PHONE.....................217 224-8737
Walter A Trott,
Douglas Grant,
David Riley,
EMP: 10
SALES (est): 723.3K
SALES (corp-wide): 860.2MM Privately Held
SIC: 1455 Kaolin mining
PA: J.M. Huber Corporation
499 Thornall St Ste 8
Edison NJ 08837
732 549-8600

(G-16894)
INTERSTATE ALL BATTERY CENTER
101 N 48th St (62305-0449)
PHONE.....................217 214-1069
Steve Leigh, President
EMP: 15 EST: 2011
SALES (est): 1.3MM Privately Held
SIC: 5531 5063 3691 Batteries, automotive & truck; batteries; storage batteries

(G-16895)
JM HUBER CORPORATION
Engineered Minerals Div
3150 Gardner Expy (62305-9378)
P.O. Box 4005 (62305-4005)
PHONE.....................217 224-1100
Michael Hughes, Purch Agent
Mike Morris, Branch Mgr
EMP: 32
SALES (corp-wide): 860.2MM Privately Held
SIC: 2819 2899 Industrial inorganic chemicals; chemical preparations
PA: J.M. Huber Corporation
499 Thornall St Ste 8
Edison NJ 08837
732 549-8600

(G-16896)
JM HUBER CORPORATION
1700 Turtle Lake Rd (62305-0730)
PHONE.....................217 224-1123
Kirk Bross, President
EMP: 87
SALES (corp-wide): 860.2MM Privately Held
SIC: 2819 Industrial inorganic chemicals
PA: J.M. Huber Corporation
499 Thornall St Ste 8
Edison NJ 08837
732 549-8600

(G-16897)
JOST & KIEFER PRINTING COMPANY
Also Called: J K Creative Printers
2029 Hllster Whitney Pkwy (62305-7601)
P.O. Box 2 (62306-0002)
PHONE.....................217 222-5145
Mike Nobis, President
Kevin Nobis, Vice Pres
Terri Brewer, Treasurer
Katherine Ridder, Admin Sec
Kathy Ridder, Admin Sec
EMP: 35
SQ FT: 35,000
SALES (est): 4.4MM Privately Held
SIC: 2752 Commercial printing, offset

(G-16898)
JP ORTHOTICS
9234 Broadway St (62305-8011)
PHONE.....................217 885-3047
Jonathan Horak, Principal
EMP: 3
SALES (est): 208.3K Privately Held
WEB: www.orthoticstoyou.com
SIC: 3842 Orthopedic appliances

(G-16899)
KEVIN KEWNEY
Also Called: Laser Images
410 S 10th St (62301-4152)
PHONE.....................217 228-7444
Kevin Kewney, Owner
EMP: 3
SALES (est): 190K Privately Held
SIC: 2759 2752 2791 2789 Commercial printing; commercial printing, lithographic; typesetting; bookbinding & related work

(G-16900)
KITCHEN & BATH GALLERY
615 Jersey St (62301-3905)
PHONE.....................217 214-0310
Kevin Bangert, Owner
EMP: 2
SQ FT: 2,000
SALES: 500K Privately Held
WEB: www.kitchenbathgallery.net
SIC: 5712 1711 3996 Cabinets, except custom made; kitchen; plumbing contractors; hard surface floor coverings

(G-16901)
KNAPHEIDE MANUFACTURING CO
436 S 6th St (62301-4118)
P.O. Box 7140 (62305-7140)
PHONE.....................217 222-7134
Jim Rubotton, Owner
Beth Katenin, Buyer
Adam Hendrian, Credit Staff
Teresa Fessler, Manager
Greg Schutte, Manager
EMP: 10
SALES (corp-wide): 71.9MM Privately Held
SIC: 3713 Truck & bus bodies
PA: The Knapheide Manufacturing Company
1848 Westphalia Strasse
Quincy IL 62305
217 222-7131

(G-16902)
KNAPHEIDE MANUFACTURING CO
1848 Westphalia Strasse (62305-7604)
P.O. Box 7140 (62305-7140)
PHONE.....................217 223-1848
Harold Knapheide, President
Carole Wiberg, Vice Pres
EMP: 50
SALES (corp-wide): 71.9MM Privately Held
SIC: 3469 5084 1799 Boxes: tool, lunch, mail, etc.: stamped metal; industrial machinery & equipment; swimming pool construction
PA: The Knapheide Manufacturing Company
1848 Westphalia Strasse
Quincy IL 62305
217 222-7131

(G-16903)
KNAPHEIDE MFG CO
3109 N 30th St (62305)
PHONE.....................217 223-1848
H Knapheide, Principal
Bill Quigley, Plant Mgr
Troy Hummel, Materials Mgr
Randy Stott, Production
Gary Wallace, Production
EMP: 25
SALES (est): 3.3MM Privately Held
SIC: 3999 Manufacturing industries

(G-16904)
KOENIG MACHINE & WELDING INC
2707 N 24th St (62305-1274)
PHONE.....................217 228-6538
Gary L Koening, President
EMP: 4 EST: 1998
SALES (est): 95.1K Privately Held
SIC: 3599 1799 Machine shop, jobbing & repair; welding on site

(G-16905)
KTM INDUSTRIES INC
2701 Weiss Ln (62305-1111)
PHONE.....................217 224-5861
Marian McKeon, President
Kathy Easterling, Vice Pres
EMP: 8
SQ FT: 22,000
SALES (est): 856.1K Privately Held
SIC: 2046 Starch

(G-16906)
LA QUINTA GAS PIPELINE COMPANY
1416 Donlee St (62305-1437)
PHONE.....................217 430-6781
Jerry McNay, President
Jeff Leenerts, Admin Sec
EMP: 2
SALES (est): 234.2K Privately Held
SIC: 1311 4924 Natural gas production; natural gas distribution

(G-16907)
LANDMARX SCREEN PRINTING
3902 Payson Rd (62305-6484)
PHONE.....................217 223-4601
Vincent Ed Moore, President
Jay Martin, Principal
EMP: 15
SQ FT: 8,000
SALES (est): 1.8MM Privately Held
SIC: 2759 Screen printing

(G-16908)
M J BURTON ENGRAVING CO
Also Called: Mj Burton Gifts & Engraving
824 Maine St (62304-4015)
PHONE.....................217 223-7273
Michael A Jenkins, Owner
EMP: 5
SALES (est): 423.3K Privately Held
SIC: 7389 5947 3479 Engraving service; gift shop; engraving jewelry silverware, or metal

(G-16909)
MANCHESTER TANK & EQUIPMENT CO
3400 Wisman Ln (62301-1256)
PHONE.....................217 224-7600
Mitch Dyel, Production
Mary Kendrick, Human Res Mgr
Connie Childs, Branch Mgr
John Washburn, Maintence Staff
EMP: 48
SALES (corp-wide): 1.2B Privately Held
SIC: 3443 Tanks, standard or custom fabricated: metal plate
HQ: Manchester Tank & Equipment Co Inc
1000 Corp Cntre Dr Ste 30
Franklin TN 37067
615 370-6104

(G-16910)
MARLBORO WIRE LTD
2403 N 24th St (62305-1211)
P.O. Box 5058 (62305-5058)
PHONE.....................217 224-7989
Don Brown, President
EMP: 30
SQ FT: 34,000
SALES (est): 5.6MM Privately Held
SIC: 3496 7692 3469 Miscellaneous fabricated wire products; welding repair; metal stampings

(G-16911)
MASTER FOUNDRY INC
4808 Ellington Rd (62305-8671)
PHONE.....................217 223-7396
Paul H Mast, President
Brian Guerin, Vice Pres
Joan Mast, Vice Pres
EMP: 15 EST: 1955
SALES (est): 790K Privately Held
WEB: www.mastercastfoundry.com
SIC: 3365 3543 3369 Aluminum & aluminum-based alloy castings; industrial patterns; nonferrous foundries

(G-16912)
MICHELMANN STEEL CNSTR CO
Also Called: Mid-States Door and Hardware
137 N 2nd St (62301-2999)
P.O. Box 609 (62306-0609)
PHONE.....................217 222-0555
Laura Gerdes Ehrhart, CEO
John Esselman, CFO
EMP: 41
SQ FT: 125,000
SALES (est): 26.7MM Privately Held
WEB: www.michelmann.us
SIC: 5051 3441 3442 Structural shapes, iron or steel; fabricated structural metal; metal doors, sash & trim

(G-16913)
MID-AMERICA CARBONATES LLC
520 N 30th St (62301-3618)
PHONE.....................217 222-3500
EMP: 7
SALES (est): 1.3MM
SALES (corp-wide): 1.8B Publicly Held
SIC: 1422 Crushed/Broken Limestone
HQ: White County Coal, Llc
1525 County Rd 1300 N
Carmi IL 62821
618 382-4651

(G-16914)
MIDWEST PATTERNS INC
4901 N 12th St (62305-8751)
PHONE.....................217 228-6900
Jeff Tushaus, President
Thomas Tushaus, President
Dennis Frericks, Vice Pres
Richard Tushaus, Vice Pres
EMP: 112 EST: 1956
SQ FT: 55,000
SALES (est): 20.9MM Privately Held
WEB: www.midwestpatterns.com
SIC: 3543 Industrial patterns

(G-16915)
MIDWEST TREASURE DETECTORS
2408 Cherry St Ste 1 (62305-3402)
PHONE.....................217 223-4769
Michael Zanger, President
EMP: 3 EST: 1975
SALES (est): 210K Privately Held
SIC: 3699 Security devices

(G-16916)
MIKE HOWERTON
1214 Huntleigh Rd (62305-6023)
PHONE.....................217 242-9676
Mike Howerton, Principal
EMP: 3
SALES (est): 204.5K Privately Held
SIC: 7372 Prepackaged software

(G-16917)
MODERN PRINTING OF QUINCY
2615 Ellington Rd (62305-8850)
PHONE.....................217 223-1063
Kevin Curran, Partner
David Rees, Partner
EMP: 10 EST: 1959
SQ FT: 8,000
SALES (est): 1.2MM Privately Held
SIC: 2752 2759 2789 Commercial printing, offset; letterpress printing; bookbinding & related work

(G-16918)
NIEMANN FOODS INC
Also Called: County Market
520 N 24th St (62301-3222)
PHONE.....................217 222-0190
Todd Musolino, Manager
EMP: 138
SALES (corp-wide): 79K Privately Held
SIC: 5411 5992 5812 2051 Grocery stores, chain; florists; eating places; bread, cake & related products
PA: Niemann Foods, Inc.
923 N 12th St
Quincy IL 62301
217 221-5600

(G-16919)
ORTMAN FLUID POWER INC
1400 N 30th St Ste 20 (62301-3476)
PHONE.....................217 277-0321
Francis K McGonigle, President
EMP: 25
SALES (est): 2.5MM
SALES (corp-wide): 12.8MM Privately Held
SIC: 3593 Fluid power cylinders, hydraulic or pneumatic
PA: Lehigh Fluid Power, Inc.
1413 Route 179
Lambertville NJ 08530
800 257-9515

GEOGRAPHIC SECTION

Quincy - Adams County (G-16947)

(G-16920)
OTR WHEEL ENGINEERING INC
4400 Kochs Ln (62305-7805)
P.O. Box 3743 (62305-3743)
PHONE..................217 223-7705
Fred Taylor, *President*
Mary Ann Ogle, *Purch Mgr*
Bob Owens, *CFO*
Chad Taylor, *Admin Sec*
▲ **EMP:** 28
SQ FT: 20,000
SALES (est): 2.5MM **Privately Held**
SIC: 3714 3011 5013 Wheels, motor vehicle; tires & inner tubes; wheels, motor vehicle
PA: Otr Wheel Engineering, Inc.
6 Riverside Indus Park Ne
Rome GA 30161

(G-16921)
OUTDOOR POWER INC
2703 Broadway St (62301-3638)
PHONE..................217 228-9890
Jeff W Waterman, *President*
Sandy Waterman, *Vice Pres*
Neil Howe, *Sales Mgr*
EMP: 11
SQ FT: 5,800
SALES (est): 1.1MM **Privately Held**
SIC: 5261 5251 5571 7699 Lawnmowers & tractors; chainsaws; all-terrain vehicles; lawn mower repair shop; knife, saw & tool sharpening & repair; recreational vehicle repair services; contractors' materials; saws & sawing equipment

(G-16922)
PAM PRINTERS AND PUBLS INC (PA)
Also Called: Sunday Missal Service
1012 Vermont St (62301-3052)
PHONE..................217 222-4030
Anaise Haubrich, *Ch of Bd*
Anthony Haubrich, *President*
Timothy Haubrich, *General Mgr*
Mike Haubrich, *Corp Secy*
EMP: 12
SQ FT: 27,000
SALES: 1.1MM **Privately Held**
WEB: www.sundaymissalservice.com
SIC: 2741 Miscellaneous publishing

(G-16923)
PRECISION PLATING OF QUINCY
2611 Locust St (62301-3329)
PHONE..................217 223-6590
William M Barnett, *President*
Eric Barnett, *Vice Pres*
Sandra Barnett, *Treasurer*
EMP: 8
SQ FT: 1,600
SALES (est): 430K **Privately Held**
SIC: 3471 Electroplating of metals or formed products

(G-16924)
PRINCE AGRI PRODUCTS INC
221 S Prince Agri Way St (62305-0004)
PHONE..................217 222-8854
Michael Escott, *Info Tech Mgr*
EMP: 4
SALES (corp-wide): 828MM **Publicly Held**
SIC: 2048 Feed supplements
HQ: Prince Agri Products, Inc.
300 Frank W Burr Blvd
Teaneck NJ 07666
201 329-7300

(G-16925)
PRINCE AGRI PRODUCTS INC
Also Called: Phibro Animal Health
229 Radio Rd (62305-7534)
PHONE..................217 222-8854
Clayton Lamkin, *Vice Pres*
David Kirk, *Technology*
Tim Costigan, *Director*
EMP: 50
SALES (corp-wide): 828MM **Publicly Held**
SIC: 2048 Feed supplements

HQ: Prince Agri Products, Inc.
300 Frank W Burr Blvd
Teaneck NJ 07666
201 329-7300

(G-16926)
PRINCE MINERALS LLC
223 Hampshire St (62301-2923)
P.O. Box 251 (62306-0251)
PHONE..................646 747-4222
Darryl Mayton, *General Mgr*
EMP: 3
SALES (corp-wide): 369K **Privately Held**
SIC: 2816 3313 Inorganic pigments; electrometallurgical products
HQ: Prince Minerals Llc
15311 Vantage Pkwy W
Houston TX 77032
646 747-4222

(G-16927)
PRINCE MINERALS LLC
401 N Prince Plz (62305-0084)
P.O. Box 251 (62306-0251)
PHONE..................646 747-4200
Marcus T Shumaker, *Manager*
EMP: 3
SALES (corp-wide): 369K **Privately Held**
SIC: 2816 3313 Inorganic pigments; electrometallurgical products
HQ: Prince Minerals Llc
15311 Vantage Pkwy W
Houston TX 77032
646 747-4222

(G-16928)
PRIORITY ONE PRINTING AND MAIL
Also Called: Priority One Prtg & Mailing
839 Jersey St (62301-4010)
PHONE..................217 224-8008
Tim Helgoth, *Owner*
EMP: 6 **EST:** 1976
SQ FT: 1,300
SALES (est): 1.1MM **Privately Held**
SIC: 7334 7331 2752 Photocopying & duplicating services; mailing service; commercial printing, lithographic; commercial printing, offset

(G-16929)
QUINCY BOW PRO
3110 Broadway St (62301-3710)
PHONE..................217 222-2222
Charles Whitcomb,
EMP: 5
SALES (est): 400K **Privately Held**
SIC: 3949 5941 Bows, archery; sporting goods & bicycle shops

(G-16930)
QUINCY ELECTRIC & SIGN COMPANY
1324 Spring Lake Cors (62305)
PHONE..................217 223-8404
James McEwen, *President*
EMP: 12
SALES (est): 1.8MM **Privately Held**
WEB: www.quincyelectricsign.com
SIC: 3993 Electric signs

(G-16931)
QUINCY FARM PRODUCTS LLC
3501 Wisman Ln (62301-1257)
PHONE..................217 214-1905
Jerrod Evans, *Mng Member*
Bryan Stokes, *Mng Member*
EMP: 16
SALES (est): 4MM **Privately Held**
SIC: 0191 2048 General farms, primarily crop; livestock feeds

(G-16932)
QUINCY FOUNDRY & PATTERN CO
435 S Front St (62301-3867)
PHONE..................217 222-0718
John W Juette, *President*
Sharon Juette, *Admin Sec*
EMP: 5 **EST:** 1945
SQ FT: 2,500
SALES (est): 370K **Privately Held**
SIC: 3543 3369 3365 Industrial patterns; nonferrous foundries; aluminum foundries

(G-16933)
QUINCY HERALD-WHIG LLC
130 S 5th St (62301-3916)
P.O. Box 909 (62306-0909)
PHONE..................217 223-5100
Deborah Husar, *Principal*
EMP: 17
SALES (est): 1.4MM **Privately Held**
SIC: 2711 Newspapers, publishing & printing

(G-16934)
QUINCY PEPSI-COLA BOTTLING CO (PA)
1121 Locust St (62301-1919)
P.O. Box 3035 (62305-3035)
PHONE..................217 223-8600
Mike Bartel, *President*
John Vecchie, *Principal*
Ronald Vecchie, *Vice Pres*
Shawn Vecchie, *Vice Pres*
EMP: 66
SQ FT: 100,000
SALES (est): 7.2MM **Privately Held**
SIC: 2086 Carbonated soft drinks, bottled & canned

(G-16935)
QUINCY SOCKS HOUSE
840 N 36th St (62301-4627)
PHONE..................217 506-6106
EMP: 3
SALES (est): 174.5K **Privately Held**
SIC: 2252 Socks

(G-16936)
R L HOENER CO
2923 Gardner Expy (62305-7528)
P.O. Box 1086 (62306-1086)
PHONE..................217 223-2190
Marty Jackson, *President*
Debbra Tritsch, *Vice Pres*
Kelly Jackson, *Shareholder*
EMP: 20
SQ FT: 26,000
SALES (est): 3.4MM **Privately Held**
SIC: 1799 5172 3443 5084 Service station equipment installation, maintenance & repair; service station supplies, petroleum; tanks, standard or custom fabricated: metal plate; petroleum industry machinery

(G-16937)
RACK BUILDERS INC (PA)
3809 Dye Rd (62305)
PHONE..................217 214-9482
Robert J Johannessen, *President*
EMP: 1
SALES (est): 511.7K **Privately Held**
SIC: 2542 Racks, merchandise display or storage: except wood

(G-16938)
RAH ENTERPRISES INC
2630 S Commercial Dr (62305-8317)
PHONE..................217 223-1970
Robert Huseman, *President*
Dorothy Huseman, *Admin Sec*
EMP: 8
SQ FT: 4,400
SALES (est): 800K **Privately Held**
SIC: 3599 Machine & other job shop work

(G-16939)
REFRESHMENT SERVICES INC (PA)
Also Called: Pepsico
1121 Locust St (62301-1919)
PHONE..................217 223-8600
Mike Bartel, *President*
Ronald J Vecchie, *Chairman*
Rodney Flowers, *Vice Pres*
Casey Hill, *Vice Pres*
Kyle Gossett, *Opers Mgr*
EMP: 16
SQ FT: 3,000
SALES (est): 88.8MM **Privately Held**
SIC: 2086 Carbonated soft drinks, bottled & canned

(G-16940)
RICHARDS ELECTRIC MOTOR CO (PA)
2028 Quintron Way (62305-1207)
PHONE..................217 222-7154
Bill Dietrich, *President*
Jim Keller, *Corp Secy*
EMP: 40 **EST:** 1954
SALES (est): 12.5MM **Privately Held**
WEB: www.richardselectricmotor.com
SIC: 5063 7699 7694 1731 Motors, electric; industrial equipment services; armature rewinding shops; electrical work

(G-16941)
RIETSCHLE INC
1800 Gardner Expy (62305-9364)
PHONE..................410 712-4100
Howard Barry, *Owner*
EMP: 3
SALES (est): 254.1K **Privately Held**
WEB: www.gardnerdenver.com
SIC: 3563 Air & gas compressors

(G-16942)
ROBUSCHI USA INC
1800 Gardner Expy (62305-9364)
PHONE..................704 424-1018
John Matela, *General Mgr*
▲ **EMP:** 4
SALES (est): 853.8K **Privately Held**
SIC: 3564 Purification & dust collection equipment

(G-16943)
ROSEWOOD CUSTOM FRAMING LLC
2114 S 40th St (62305-6025)
PHONE..................217 430-7669
Amber Bauer, *Principal*
EMP: 3
SALES (est): 208.9K **Privately Held**
SIC: 2499 Picture frame molding, finished

(G-16944)
SEM MINERALS LP (PA)
3806 Gardner Expy (62305-9343)
P.O. Box 1090, Bainbridge GA (39818-1090)
PHONE..................217 224-8766
Alec Poitevint, *President*
Terry Epley, *Controller*
▲ **EMP:** 55
SQ FT: 20,000
SALES (est): 16.8MM **Privately Held**
WEB: www.seminerals.com
SIC: 2048 3295 2879 Mineral feed supplements; minerals, ground or treated; trace elements (agricultural chemicals)

(G-16945)
SIGN PRO OF QUINCY INC
408 N 24th St (62301-3254)
PHONE..................217 223-9693
Evan Klauser, *Principal*
EMP: 1
SALES (est): 209K **Privately Held**
SIC: 3993 Signs & advertising specialties

(G-16946)
TEDS SHIRT SHACK INC
2811 Bluff Ridge Dr (62305-1391)
PHONE..................217 224-9705
Marty Tappe, *President*
Nicholas Tappe, *President*
Martin Tappe, *Owner*
Ted M Tappe, *Owner*
Steven Elmore, *Graphic Designe*
EMP: 7
SQ FT: 5,000
SALES: 750K **Privately Held**
SIC: 5651 2759 2396 3993 Family clothing stores; commercial printing; automotive & apparel trimmings; signs & advertising specialties; T-shirts, custom printed

(G-16947)
THOMAS GARDNER DENVER INC
1800 Gardner Expy (62305-9364)
PHONE..................217 222-5400
Michael McGrath, *President*
David J Antoniuk, *Admin Sec*
EMP: 26 **EST:** 1984

Quincy - Adams County (G-16948)   GEOGRAPHIC SECTION

SALES (est): 8.4MM **Privately Held**
SIC: 3563 Air & gas compressors including vacuum pumps; vacuum pumps, except laboratory

(G-16948)
TITAN INTERNATIONAL INC (PA)
2701 Spruce St (62301-3473)
PHONE.................................217 228-6011
Paul G Reitz, *President*
Shane Ort, *Area Mgr*
Bruce Walker, *Traffic Mgr*
David Kuhl, *VP Engrg*
Rich Sibbing, *Engineer*
EMP: 216
SQ FT: 1,205,000
SALES: 1.4B **Publicly Held**
SIC: 3312 3714 3011 Blast furnaces & steel mills; wheels, motor vehicle; wheel rims, motor vehicle; motor vehicle brake systems & parts; differentials & parts, motor vehicle; agricultural tires, pneumatic; pneumatic tires, all types

(G-16949)
TITAN TIRE CORPORATION
2701 Spruce St (62301-3473)
PHONE.................................217 228-6011
Jerry Holley, *Safety Mgr*
Justin Barnard, *Sales Staff*
Todd Shoot, *Branch Mgr*
Garry Hall, *Manager*
Alex Felde, *Technician*
EMP: 400
SALES (corp-wide): 1.4B **Publicly Held**
SIC: 3011 Tires & inner tubes
HQ: Titan Tire Corporation
    2345 E Market St
    Des Moines IA 50317

(G-16950)
TITAN WHEEL CORP ILLINOIS
2701 Spruce St (62301-3477)
PHONE.................................217 228-6023
P David Salen, *President*
Jim Walz, *QC Mgr*
Todd Fetter, *Engineer*
Rich Sibbing, *Engineer*
James Reed, *Electrical Engi*
◆ EMP: 900 EST: 1997
SALES: 158.4MM
SALES (corp-wide): 1.4B **Publicly Held**
SIC: 3714 Motor vehicle parts & accessories
PA: Titan International, Inc.
    2701 Spruce St
    Quincy IL 62301
    217 228-6011

(G-16951)
TRI-CITY SPORTS INC
4360 Broadway St (62305-9103)
PHONE.................................217 224-2489
Bruce Thomas, *President*
Kathy Thomas, *Corp Secy*
EMP: 5
SQ FT: 2,400
SALES (est): 390K **Privately Held**
SIC: 5941 5699 2759 Sporting goods & bicycle shops; sports apparel; screen printing

(G-16952)
TRI-STATE FOOD EQUIPMENT
1605 Chestnut St (62301-2115)
PHONE.................................217 228-1550
Kenny Miller, *Owner*
EMP: 1
SQ FT: 10,000
SALES (est): 225K **Privately Held**
SIC: 5719 5046 3632 3433 Kitchenware; commercial cooking & food service equipment; household refrigerators & freezers; heating equipment, except electric

(G-16953)
TWAIN MEDIA MARK PUBLISHING
617 Broadway St (62301-2706)
PHONE.................................217 223-7008
Harry Emrick, *President*
Sue Emrick, *Treasurer*
EMP: 7
SALES (est): 751.7K **Privately Held**
SIC: 2731 Books: publishing only

(G-16954)
WALTER LOUIS CHEM & ASSOC INC
Also Called: Walter Louis Fluid Tech
530 S 5th St (62301-4808)
PHONE.................................217 223-2017
Walter L Giesing, *President*
David Dreyer, *Regional Mgr*
Dianne Giesing, *Vice Pres*
Frank Murphy, *Opers Staff*
Roger Smith, *Engineer*
EMP: 10
SQ FT: 15,000
SALES (est): 2.2MM **Privately Held**
SIC: 3589 Water purification equipment, household type; water treatment equipment, industrial

(G-16955)
WEST ZWICK CORP
Also Called: Bauhaus Zwick Co
2132 Glenayre Way (62305-1258)
P.O. Box 527 (62306-0527)
PHONE.................................217 222-0228
James Vandiver, *President*
Ann Vandiver, *Corp Secy*
Joe Vandiver, *Foreman/Supr*
EMP: 4 EST: 1919
SQ FT: 11,000
SALES: 500K **Privately Held**
SIC: 3993 2431 2542 Signs, not made in custom sign painting shops; displays & cutouts, window & lobby; displays, paint process; millwork; partitions & fixtures, except wood

(G-16956)
WILBERT QUINCY VAULT CO
4128 Wisman Ln (62305-9554)
P.O. Box 3612 (62305-3612)
PHONE.................................217 224-8557
Steve Busch, *Owner*
EMP: 5
SALES (est): 428.8K **Privately Held**
SIC: 3272 5087 Burial vaults, concrete or precast terrazzo; concrete burial vaults & boxes

(G-16957)
WIRELESSUSA INC
Also Called: Wireless USA
2517 W Schneidman Dr E (62305-1237)
PHONE.................................217 222-4300
Toll Free:..............................866 -
George Brummell, *Branch Mgr*
EMP: 5
SALES (corp-wide): 26.7MM **Privately Held**
SIC: 3651 5065 FM & AM radio tuners; citizens band radios
PA: Wirelessusa, Inc.
    148 Weldon Pkwy
    Maryland Heights MO 63043
    888 615-3131

(G-16958)
WIS - PAK INC
Also Called: Wis-Pak of Quincy
2400 N 30th St (62301-1278)
PHONE.................................217 224-6800
Grant Gerth, *Warehouse Mgr*
Jim Schultz, *Maint Spvr*
Jeff Nickell, *QC Mgr*
Jeff Lamm, *Branch Mgr*
Bobbi Canavan, *Executive*
EMP: 91
SALES (corp-wide): 267.6MM **Privately Held**
SIC: 3221 2086 Bottles for packing, bottling & canning: glass; bottled & canned soft drinks
PA: Wis - Pak, Inc.
    860 West St
    Watertown WI 53094
    920 262-6300

Raleigh
Saline County

(G-16959)
CENTRIFUGAL SERVICES INC
Also Called: C S I
5595 Highway 34 N (62977-1430)
PHONE.................................618 268-4850
Dale R Martin, *President*
Fred C Schulte, *Vice Pres*
◆ EMP: 51
SQ FT: 16,166
SALES (est): 19.3MM
SALES (corp-wide): 1.7B **Privately Held**
SIC: 3532 Mineral beneficiation equipment
HQ: Elgin Equipment Group, Llc
    2001 Btterfield Rd Ste 1020
    Downers Grove IL 60515

(G-16960)
ELGIN NATIONAL INDUSTRIES INC
Also Called: Centrifugal & Mechanical Inds
5595 Highway 34 N (62977-1430)
PHONE.................................314 776-2848
Buddy Sebastino, *President*
EMP: 69
SALES (corp-wide): 87.8MM **Privately Held**
SIC: 3532 3567 Mineral beneficiation equipment; industrial furnaces & ovens
PA: Elgin National Industries, Inc.
    2001 Btterfield Rd Ste 1020
    Downers Grove IL 60515
    630 434-7200

(G-16961)
GARY & LARRY BROWN TRUCKING (PA)
Also Called: Raleigh Ready Mix
5525 Highway 34 N (62977-1430)
P.O. Box 218 (62977-0218)
PHONE.................................618 268-6377
Gary M Brown, *Partner*
Larry A Brown, *Partner*
EMP: 5
SQ FT: 7,200
SALES: 1.7MM **Privately Held**
SIC: 3273 5211 3272 1771 Ready-mixed concrete; masonry materials & supplies; concrete products, precast; concrete pumping; septic system construction

(G-16962)
PREVENTION HEALTH SCIENCES INC
5110 Highway 34 N (62977-1435)
P.O. Box 1916, Marion (62959-8124)
PHONE.................................618 252-6922
Dan Nicolosi, *President*
Wendy Sanders, *Vice Pres*
EMP: 3
SALES: 300.4K **Privately Held**
SIC: 2844 Mouthwashes

(G-16963)
SF CONTRACTING LLC
1030 Hamburg Rd (62977-1214)
PHONE.................................618 926-1477
Shannon D Burnett,
Charles E Slykhuis,
EMP: 45
SALES (est): 2.6MM **Privately Held**
SIC: 1081 1629 Metal mining services; land reclamation

Ramsey
Fayette County

(G-16964)
G L BEAUMONT LUMBER COMPANY (PA)
Also Called: Main Office
Rr 51 Box S (62080)
PHONE.................................618 423-2323
Dana Beaumont, *President*
Debbie Beaumont, *Corp Secy*
EMP: 17

SALES (est): 2.9MM **Privately Held**
SIC: 2421 2426 Sawmills & planing mills, general; hardwood dimension & flooring mills

Ransom
Lasalle County

(G-16965)
ILLINOIS VALLEY MACHINE SP INC
108 N Lincoln St (60470-8501)
P.O. Box 188 (60470-0188)
PHONE.................................815 586-4511
Mark Coonan, *President*
Leah Coonan, *Vice Pres*
EMP: 10 EST: 1972
SQ FT: 5,000
SALES (est): 1.8MM **Privately Held**
SIC: 3599 Machine shop, jobbing & repair

Rantoul
Champaign County

(G-16966)
ANALOG OUTFITTERS INC
701 Pacesetter Dr (61866-3659)
PHONE.................................217 202-6134
Ben B Juday, *President*
EMP: 6
SALES (est): 339.4K **Privately Held**
SIC: 3931 Musical instruments

(G-16967)
ARROW EDM INC
Also Called: Hansvedt
1120 Veterans Pkwy (61866-3449)
PHONE.................................217 893-4277
Chris Baskis, *President*
Kevin Vail, *Manager*
EMP: 10
SALES (corp-wide): 2MM **Privately Held**
SIC: 5063 3599 Electrical apparatus & equipment; flexible metal hose, tubing & bellows
PA: Arrow Edm, Inc.
    7512 Dr Phillips Blvd
    Orlando FL 32819
    217 893-4277

(G-16968)
BELL SPORTS INC
1001 Innovation Rd (61866-4200)
P.O. Box 6001 (61866-6001)
PHONE.................................217 893-9300
Bill Oldham, *Branch Mgr*
EMP: 82
SALES (corp-wide): 2B **Publicly Held**
SIC: 3949 Helmets, athletic
HQ: Bell Sports, Inc.
    5550 Scotts Valley Dr
    Scotts Valley CA 95066
    469 417-6600

(G-16969)
BRG SPORTS INC
Also Called: Easton Bell Sports
105 W Flessner Ave (61866-3600)
P.O. Box 6005 (61866-6005)
PHONE.................................217 892-4704
EMP: 14 **Privately Held**
SIC: 3949 Sporting & athletic goods
HQ: Brg Sports, Inc.
    1700 E Higgins Rd Ste 500
    Des Plaines IL 60018
    224 585-5200

(G-16970)
CHARLES INDUSTRIES LLC
201 Shellhouse Dr (61866-9711)
PHONE.................................217 893-8335
Joseph Charles, *President*
Bill Gray, *Manager*
EMP: 100
SALES (corp-wide): 8.2B **Publicly Held**
SIC: 3661 3444 Toll switching equipment, telephone; sheet metalwork
HQ: Charles Industries, Llc
    1450 American Ln Fl 20
    Schaumburg IL 60173
    847 806-6300

GEOGRAPHIC SECTION

(G-16971)
COMBE LABORATORIES INC
200 Shellhouse Dr (61866-9711)
PHONE..................217 893-4490
Keech Combe Shetty, *President*
Steve Thomas, *Plant Mgr*
Peggy Stanley, *Engineer*
James Keane, *VP Finance*
Sue Morelli, *Credit Staff*
◆ **EMP:** 110
SALES (est): 28.8MM
SALES (corp-wide): 174.7MM **Privately Held**
SIC: 2841 2844 Soap & other detergents; cosmetic preparations; toilet preparations
PA: Combe Incorporated
  1101 Westchester Ave
  White Plains NY 10604
  914 694-5454

(G-16972)
CONAIR CORPORATION
205 Shellhouse Dr (61866-9774)
PHONE..................203 351-9000
Ronald T Diamond, *President*
Jerry Perlmutter, *Regional Mgr*
Roberta Bacik, *Vice Pres*
Julie Granberg, *Nat'l Sales Mgr*
Angela Corrente, *Sales Staff*
◆ **EMP:** 3 **EST:** 1972
SALES (est): 10.4MM **Privately Held**
SIC: 3634 3999 Irons, electric: household; hair dryers, electric; curling irons, electric; hair curlers, electric; barber & beauty shop equipment

(G-16973)
CROWN PUBLICATIONS INC
Also Called: Kwik Kopy Printing
515 S Tanner St (61866-2923)
P.O. Box 1050 (61866-7050)
PHONE..................217 893-4856
Jack Briere, *President*
EMP: 2
SALES (est): 250K **Privately Held**
SIC: 2752 5199 3993 2759 Commercial printing, offset; advertising specialties; signs & advertising specialties; commercial printing

(G-16974)
EAGLE WINGS INDUSTRIES INC
Also Called: E W I
400 Shellhouse Dr (61866-9700)
PHONE..................217 892-4322
Tatsunori Shigeta, *President*
Hideki Hiraishi, *President*
Jim Schwartz, *Vice Pres*
Bob Ball, *Marketing Staff*
◆ **EMP:** 290
SQ FT: 314,200
SALES (est): 45MM **Privately Held**
SIC: 3714 Motor vehicle body components & frame
PA: Asteer Co.,Ltd.
  1597, Makabe
  Soja OKA 719-1

(G-16975)
EAST CENTRAL COMMUNICATIONS CO
Also Called: Target
1332 Harmon Dr (61866-3310)
P.O. Box 5110 (61866-5110)
PHONE..................217 892-9613
Dennis Kaster, *President*
EMP: 30 **EST:** 1880
SALES (est): 2.8MM **Privately Held**
WEB: www.rantoulpress.com
SIC: 2711 2752 Newspapers, publishing & printing; commercial printing, lithographic
PA: The News-Gazette Inc
  15 E Main St
  Champaign IL 61820

(G-16976)
G&G MACHINE SHOP INC
1580 E Grove Ave Ste 2 (61866-2777)
PHONE..................217 892-9696
Peter Good, *President*
Nicholas Jankowski, *Manager*
Kirk Gosser, *Admin Sec*
EMP: 3

SALES (est): 272.6K **Privately Held**
SIC: 7539 7538 3599 Machine shop, automotive; general automotive repair shops; machine shop, jobbing & repair

(G-16977)
JANCORP LLC (PA)
Also Called: Criss Cross Express Illinois
608 Kopman St (61866-3716)
P.O. Box 227, Norwalk WI (54648-0227)
PHONE..................217 892-4830
Frederick Stewart, *President*
EMP: 8
SALES (est): 1.1MM **Privately Held**
SIC: 2011 Meat packing plants

(G-16978)
JELD-WEN INC
Also Called: Jeld-Wen Windows
201 Evans Rd (61866-9778)
PHONE..................217 893-4444
Jody Wasser, *Vice Pres*
Julie Cribbett, *Sales Staff*
Linda Brandon, *Supervisor*
EMP: 64 **Publicly Held**
SIC: 2431 Doors, wood
HQ: Jeld-Wen, Inc.
  1162 Keystone Blvd
  Pottsville PA 17901
  800 535-3936

(G-16979)
JOHN PARKER ADVERTISING CO
520 E Grove Ave (61866-2429)
P.O. Box 918 (61866-0918)
PHONE..................217 892-4118
Carol A Parker, *Owner*
EMP: 3
SALES (est): 120K **Privately Held**
SIC: 5199 3993 Advertising specialties; signs & advertising specialties

(G-16980)
MIDWEST SILKSCREENING INC
104 N Century Blvd (61866-2305)
PHONE..................217 892-9596
Mark Seaman, *CEO*
EMP: 4
SALES (est): 325K **Privately Held**
SIC: 7336 2759 Silk screen design; screen printing

(G-16981)
RANTOUL FOODS LLC
205 Turner Dr (61866-9787)
PHONE..................217 892-4178
James Jendruczek, *President*
Alan Bressler, *Vice Pres*
David Bulgarelli, *Vice Pres*
Michael Lookingland, *Vice Pres*
David Piotrowski, *Vice Pres*
◆ **EMP:** 306
SQ FT: 300,000
SALES (est): 85.2MM **Privately Held**
WEB: www.rantoulfoods.com
SIC: 3556 0751 Meat processing machinery; slaughtering: custom livestock services

(G-16982)
RANTOUL YOUTH WRESTLING
920 Pinecrest Dr (61866-1126)
PHONE..................217 377-9523
EMP: 3
SALES (est): 101.2K **Privately Held**
SIC: 2711 Newspapers, publishing & printing

(G-16983)
SPORT REDI-MIX LLC
527 S Tanner St (61866-2923)
PHONE..................217 892-4222
Ken Demarse, *Manager*
EMP: 21
SALES (est): 1.2MM
SALES (corp-wide): 4.8MM **Privately Held**
WEB: www.sportredimix.com
SIC: 3273 Ready-mixed concrete
PA: Sport Redi-Mix, L.L.C.
  401 Wilbur Ave
  Champaign IL 61822
  217 355-4222

(G-16984)
TRANSOM SYMPHONY OPCO LLC
205 Shellhouse Dr (61866-9711)
PHONE..................203 951-1919
EMP: 178
SALES (corp-wide): 46.9MM **Privately Held**
SIC: 2844 Toilet preparations
PA: Transom Symphony Opco, Llc
  120 Long Ridge Rd
  Stamford CT 06902
  203 503-7938

(G-16985)
VISTA OUTDOOR INC
909 Pacesetter Dr (61866-3444)
PHONE..................309 693-2746
Tom Rettig, *Branch Mgr*
◆ **EMP:** 3
SALES (corp-wide): 2B **Publicly Held**
SIC: 2329 3949 Men's & boys' sportswear & athletic clothing; protective sporting equipment
PA: Vista Outdoor Inc.
  1 Vista Way
  Anoka MN 55303
  801 447-3000

(G-16986)
VISTA OUTDOOR INC
1001 Innovation Rd (61866-4200)
PHONE..................217 893-7254
Terri Braddock, *Branch Mgr*
EMP: 52
SALES (corp-wide): 2B **Publicly Held**
SIC: 3482 Small arms ammunition
PA: Vista Outdoor Inc.
  1 Vista Way
  Anoka MN 55303
  801 447-3000

(G-16987)
WARNER BROTHERS INC
1254 County Road 2700 N (61866-9725)
PHONE..................217 643-7950
Joseph Warner, *President*
Gene Warner, *Corp Secy*
Teresa S Schneider, *Manager*
EMP: 2
SALES (est): 632.3K **Privately Held**
SIC: 7692 Welding repair

Raymond
Montgomery County

(G-16988)
CREEKSTONE KETTLE WORKS LTD
509 S Obannon St (62560-5178)
P.O. Box 492 (62560-0492)
PHONE..................217 246-5355
Colleen Weir, *President*
EMP: 16
SALES (est): 502.6K **Privately Held**
SIC: 5145 2096 5441 Popcorn & supplies; popcorn, already popped (except candy covered); popcorn, including caramel corn

(G-16989)
ED WEITEKAMP INC
5046 N 23rd Ave (62560-5012)
PHONE..................217 229-4239
Greg Weitekamp, *President*
Kathy Johnson, *Admin Sec*
EMP: 3
SALES (est): 267.9K **Privately Held**
SIC: 3599 Machine shop, jobbing & repair

(G-16990)
POGGENPOHL LLC (PA)
Also Called: Poggenpohl Construction & Mtls
31 Sparks St (62560)
P.O. Box 581 (62560-0581)
PHONE..................217 229-3411
Russel Poggenpohl, *Mng Member*
Bruce Poggenpohl,
EMP: 6

SALES (est): 2.8MM **Privately Held**
SIC: 1521 1542 3273 Single-family housing construction; commercial & office building contractors; ready-mixed concrete

Red Bud
Randolph County

(G-16991)
COMWELL (PA)
Also Called: Human Service Center
10257 State Route 3 (62278-4418)
PHONE..................618 282-6233
Kimber Browne, *Finance*
Amy Bauer, *Manager*
Shea Haury, *Exec Dir*
Gary L Buatte, *Exec Dir*
Beth Nortin, *Executive*
EMP: 60
SQ FT: 7,200
SALES (est): 3.3MM **Privately Held**
SIC: 3471 2511 2448 8322 Plating & polishing; wood household furniture; wood pallets & skids; general counseling services; bakery products, dry

(G-16992)
DI STEFANI T SHIRT PRINTING
4716 Stefani Rd (62278-2756)
PHONE..................618 282-2380
Richard T Stefani, *Principal*
EMP: 2
SALES (est): 200.9K **Privately Held**
SIC: 2752 Commercial printing, lithographic

(G-16993)
EAGLE STONE AND BRICK INC
450 N Main St (62278-1023)
P.O. Box 103 (62278-0103)
PHONE..................618 282-6722
Glenn Gielow, *President*
EMP: 4
SALES (est): 1.3MM **Privately Held**
SIC: 5032 3272 Brick, stone & related material; stone, cast concrete

(G-16994)
FIRST STAGE FABRICATION INC
340 Kennedy Dr (62278-4218)
PHONE..................618 282-8320
Scott Dilley, *CEO*
EMP: 3
SALES: 1MM **Privately Held**
SIC: 3441 Fabricated structural metal

(G-16995)
G S FOUNDRY MFG
210 Kaskaskia Dr (62278-1386)
P.O. Box 771220, Saint Louis MO (63177-2220)
PHONE..................618 282-4114
Kate Wasem, *Vice Pres*
EMP: 4 **EST:** 2017
SALES (est): 109.9K **Privately Held**
SIC: 3325 Steel foundries

(G-16996)
INTEGRATED MFG TECH LLC
401 Randolph St (62278-1001)
PHONE..................618 282-8306
Rudi Roeslein, *President*
Joyce Fuhr, *Mng Member*
▲ **EMP:** 40
SALES (est): 6MM **Privately Held**
SIC: 3498 3999 3441 Coils, pipe: fabricated from purchased pipe; atomizers, toiletry; building components, structural steel

(G-16997)
LAU NAE WINERY INC
806 White Oak Dr (62278-2938)
PHONE..................618 282-9463
Matt Mollet, *President*
Brett Sintzel, *Vice Pres*
EMP: 4
SALES: 400K **Privately Held**
WEB: www.lau-naewinery.com
SIC: 2084 5812 Wines; eating places

Red Bud - Randolph County (G-16998)

(G-16998)
NORTH COUNTY NEWS INC
124 S Main St (62278-1103)
P.O. Box 68 (62278-0068)
PHONE 618 282-3803
Victor L Mohr, *President*
EMP: 6
SQ FT: 3,000
SALES: 400K **Privately Held**
WEB: www.northcountynews.org
SIC: 2711 2752 Newspapers: publishing only, not printed on site; commercial printing, lithographic

(G-16999)
R & D MACHINE LLC
126 Jackson St (62278-2104)
P.O. Box 182 (62278-0182)
PHONE 618 282-6262
Warren Snover,
EMP: 4
SQ FT: 4,500
SALES (est): 572.6K **Privately Held**
SIC: 3599 Machine shop, jobbing & repair

(G-17000)
RED BUD INDUSTRIES INC
Also Called: Red Bud Industries
200 B East Industrial Dr (62278)
PHONE 618 282-3801
Kalin Liefer, *President*
Dean Linders, *Vice Pres*
Jan Koudela, *Purch Dir*
Kathleen L Liefer, *Treasurer*
Kathy Liefer, *Treasurer*
▼ EMP: 172 EST: 1959
SALES (est): 35.4MM **Privately Held**
WEB: www.redbudindustries.com
SIC: 3549 5084 Metalworking machinery; industrial machinery & equipment

(G-17001)
SECON RUBBER AND PLASTICS INC (PA)
240 Kaskaskia Dr (62278-1386)
PHONE 618 282-2700
Doug Siebenberger, *President*
Rob Ewen, *Corp Secy*
Cherie Anderson, *Sales Staff*
EMP: 40 EST: 1997
SQ FT: 37,000
SALES (est): 9.4MM **Privately Held**
WEB: www.seconrubber.com
SIC: 3053 Gaskets, packing & sealing devices

(G-17002)
SOUTHERN IL CRANKSHAFT INC
225 Kaskaskia Dr (62278-1387)
PHONE 618 282-4100
Michael Schaefer, *President*
Jeannie Schaefer, *General Mgr*
Jeremy Schaefer, *Production*
EMP: 13
SQ FT: 30,000
SALES: 1MM **Privately Held**
SIC: 3599 Machine shop, jobbing & repair; crankshafts & camshafts, machining

(G-17003)
TOTAL TITANIUM INC
281 Kennedy Dr (62278-4217)
P.O. Box 10 (62278-0010)
PHONE 866 208-6446
Brian Casey, *President*
Ron D Casey, *Senior VP*
Ron Casey, *Vice Pres*
Patti Casey, *Manager*
EMP: 25
SQ FT: 14,000
SALES (est): 3.3MM **Privately Held**
SIC: 3841 3599 Surgical & medical instruments; machine & other job shop work

(G-17004)
ULTRA PLAY SYSTEMS INC (DH)
1675 Locust St (62278-1383)
PHONE 618 282-8200
Robert A Farnsworth, *President*
Douglas R Korn, *President*
Michael Moll, *Vice Pres*
▲ EMP: 50 EST: 1999
SQ FT: 12,500
SALES (est): 20.5MM **Privately Held**
WEB: www.ultraplay.com
SIC: 3949 Sporting & athletic goods; playground equipment; basketball equipment & supplies, general; soccer equipment & supplies
HQ: Playcore Wisconsin, Inc.
544 Chestnut St
Chattanooga TN 37402
423 265-7529

Reynolds
Rock Island County

(G-17005)
RURSCH SPECIALTIES INC
16420 132nd St W (61279-9760)
PHONE 309 795-1502
Darrin Rursch, *President*
EMP: 2
SALES (est): 258.6K **Privately Held**
SIC: 3469 5531 Machine parts, stamped or pressed metal; automobile & truck equipment & parts

Richmond
Mchenry County

(G-17006)
815 PALLETS INC
Also Called: Calco
11600 Sterling Pkwy (60071-7727)
P.O. Box 1922, Woodstock (60098-1922)
PHONE 815 678-0012
Matthew Calhoun, *President*
Greg Calhoun, *Opers Staff*
Jeff Elser, *Accounts Mgr*
EMP: 40
SALES (est): 9.6MM **Privately Held**
WEB: www.usacalco.com
SIC: 2448 Pallets, wood; pallets, wood & wood with metal

(G-17007)
ABLE AMERICAN PLASTICS INC
9703 Us Highway 12 Frnt Unit (60071-9204)
PHONE 815 678-4646
Tom Brown, *President*
Sheila Brown, *Vice Pres*
EMP: 10
SALES (est): 1.7MM **Privately Held**
SIC: 3089 Injection molding of plastics

(G-17008)
AMERICAN PALLET INDUSTRIES INC
9821 Route 12 (60071)
P.O. Box 550 (60071-0550)
PHONE 815 678-0680
Douglas Coley, *President*
EMP: 10
SALES (est): 464.4K **Privately Held**
SIC: 2448 Pallets, wood

(G-17009)
ANDERSONS CANDY SHOP INC (PA)
10301 N Main St (60071-7719)
P.O. Box 217 (60071-0217)
PHONE 815 678-6000
Lars Anderson, *President*
Leif Anderson, *Vice Pres*
Tracy Anderson, *Treasurer*
EMP: 15 EST: 1919
SQ FT: 2,000
SALES (est): 1.5MM **Privately Held**
WEB: www.andersonscandyshop.com
SIC: 2066 2064 Chocolate & cocoa products; candy & other confectionery products

(G-17010)
ATWOOD-HAMLIN MFG CO INC
5614 Kenosha St (60071-7708)
P.O. Box 578 (60071-0578)
PHONE 815 678-7291
Glen Hahnlein, *President*
EMP: 13
SQ FT: 12,000
SALES (est): 1.9MM **Privately Held**
SIC: 2531 Church furniture

(G-17011)
CHARLES ATWATER ASSOC INC
5705 George St (60071-9596)
P.O. Box 1188, Wheaton (60187-1188)
PHONE 815 678-4813
Carson Atwater, *President*
Clark Atwater, *Vice Pres*
EMP: 8
SALES (est): 565.7K **Privately Held**
SIC: 3444 Awnings, sheet metal

(G-17012)
EMS INDUSTRIAL AND SERVICE CO
10800 N Main St (60071-9654)
P.O. Box 548 (60071-0548)
PHONE 815 678-2700
Timothy Ellison, *President*
Judy Ellision, *Shareholder*
EMP: 20
SQ FT: 20,000
SALES (est): 5.5MM **Privately Held**
SIC: 3351 3469 Copper pipe; metal stampings

(G-17013)
EST LIGHTING INC
10305 Covell St (60071-9594)
PHONE 847 612-1705
Tim Tacheny, *Principal*
EMP: 2
SALES (est): 217.3K **Privately Held**
SIC: 3648 Lighting equipment

(G-17014)
HANSEL WALTER J & ASSOC INC (PA)
4311 Hill Rd (60071-9655)
PHONE 815 678-6065
Walter J Hansel, *President*
EMP: 1
SALES (est): 432.9K **Privately Held**
SIC: 3549 Metalworking machinery

(G-17015)
JAN-AIR INC
10815 Commercial St (60071-7703)
P.O. Box J (60071-0909)
PHONE 815 678-4516
Mark Sattersten, *President*
Steve Smith, *Mfg Mgr*
Kyle Pulvermacher, *Engineer*
Dave Nienhaus, *Prgrmr*
Jason Wootton, *Director*
EMP: 30 EST: 1949
SQ FT: 19,600
SALES (est): 3.8MM **Privately Held**
SIC: 3564 Blowers & fans

(G-17016)
KEYSTONE PRINTING & PUBLISHING
Also Called: Keystone Printing Service
5512 May Ave (60071-9541)
P.O. Box 467 (60071-0467)
PHONE 815 678-2591
William L Finney III, *Owner*
EMP: 3 EST: 1961
SQ FT: 2,000
SALES (est): 260.6K **Privately Held**
SIC: 2752 3993 2721 Commercial printing, offset; signs & advertising specialties; periodicals

(G-17017)
M & N DENTAL
9716 Ill Route 12 (60071)
PHONE 815 678-0036
David Domenella, *Owner*
EMP: 3
SALES (est): 176.9K **Privately Held**
WEB: www.domenelladentalcare.com
SIC: 3843 Dental hand instruments

(G-17018)
MAGNUM MACHINING LLC
11427 Coml Ave Unit 19 (60071)
PHONE 815 862-2040
Lynn A Pertler, *Mng Member*
EMP: 5
SALES: 700K **Privately Held**
SIC: 3599 Machine shop, jobbing & repair

(G-17019)
OLSUN ELECTRICS CORPORATION
10901 Commercial St (60071-9642)
P.O. Box 1 (60071-0001)
PHONE 815 678-2421
Cathleen Asta, *President*
Russell Schoenberger, *Production*
Tony Bruns, *Sales Engr*
Randy Rucker, *Admin Sec*
Georgia Fay-Radcliffe,
◆ EMP: 5
SQ FT: 100,000
SALES (est): 2.4MM **Privately Held**
WEB: www.olsun.com
SIC: 3612 Specialty transformers; saturable reactors

(G-17020)
R & S CUTTERHEAD MFG CO
11401 Commercial St Ste A (60071-9527)
P.O. Box 577 (60071-0577)
PHONE 815 678-2611
Christian W Fischer, *President*
Margot A Fischer, *Corp Secy*
Sylvia McClory, *Vice Pres*
Richard Fischer, *Manager*
EMP: 11
SQ FT: 16,000
SALES (est): 1.3MM **Privately Held**
SIC: 3425 3546 Saw blades & handsaws; power-driven handtools

(G-17021)
RODIFER ENTERPRISES INC
Also Called: R E I
5700 Walnut St (60071-9201)
PHONE 815 678-0100
EMP: 5
SALES (est): 450K **Privately Held**
SIC: 3541 Mfg Machine Tools-Cutting

(G-17022)
SCHULHOF COMPANY
5801 Ami Dr (60071-7704)
PHONE 773 348-1123
EMP: 11
SALES (est): 1.4MM
SALES (corp-wide): 19MM **Privately Held**
SIC: 3432 5074 Mfg Plumbing Fixture Fittings Whol Plumbing Equipment/Supplies
PA: Schulhof Company
4701 N Ravenwood
Manchester CT 60640
773 348-1123

(G-17023)
STEEL CONSTRUCTION SVCS INC
9618 Keystone Rd (60071-9322)
PHONE 815 678-7509
Alvin Ruck Jr, *President*
Melissa Ruck, *Admin Sec*
EMP: 5
SALES (est): 410K **Privately Held**
SIC: 3446 3441 Architectural metalwork; fabricated structural metal

(G-17024)
STITCHIN IMAGE
9203 Glacier Rdg (60071-9006)
PHONE 815 578-9890
Kathleen S Rechisky, *Partner*
Russ Hoppe, *Partner*
EMP: 5
SQ FT: 1,500
SALES (est): 403.7K **Privately Held**
SIC: 2395 Embroidery products, except schiffli machine

(G-17025)
WATLOW ELECTRIC MFG CO
5710 Kenosha St (60071-9411)
PHONE 314 878-4600
EMP: 3
SALES (corp-wide): 480.2MM **Privately Held**
SIC: 3829 Thermometers & temperature sensors
PA: Watlow Electric Manufacturing Company
12001 Lackland Rd
Saint Louis MO 63146
314 878-4600

▲ = Import ▼ = Export
◆ = Import/Export

GEOGRAPHIC SECTION

(G-17026)
WOODEN WORLD OF RICHMOND INC
7617 Il Route 31 (60071-9573)
P.O. Box 59 (60071-0059)
PHONE.................................815 405-4503
David C Dubs, *President*
EMP: 4
SQ FT: 6,000
SALES (est): 361.4K **Privately Held**
SIC: 2511 2431 Wood household furniture; millwork

Richton Park
Cook County

(G-17027)
AMELIO BROS MEATS
4322 Whitehall Ln (60471-1244)
PHONE.................................708 300-2920
Robert Ryan, *Manager*
EMP: 3
SALES (est): 231.3K **Privately Held**
SIC: 2011 Meat packing plants

(G-17028)
ILLINOIS TOOL WORKS INC
Also Called: ITW Deltar Bdy Intr Richton Pk
22501 Bohlmann Pkwy (60471-1200)
PHONE.................................708 720-7800
Doug Marciniak, *Manager*
EMP: 92
SQ FT: 62,000
SALES (corp-wide): 14.1B **Publicly Held**
SIC: 3089 Injection molding of plastics
PA: Illinois Tool Works Inc.
   155 Harlem Ave
   Glenview IL 60025
   847 724-7500

(G-17029)
JOE ANTHONY & ASSOCIATES
Also Called: Joe Chicken & Fish
5151 Sauk Trl (60471-1023)
PHONE.................................708 935-0804
Joe Webber, *Owner*
EMP: 5
SQ FT: 10,200
SALES: 100K **Privately Held**
SIC: 2599 5541 Bar, restaurant & cafeteria furniture; gasoline service stations

(G-17030)
KISHKNOWS INC
3831 Janis Dr (60471-2701)
PHONE.................................708 252-3648
Kisia Coleman, *President*
EMP: 3 **EST:** 2012
SALES (est): 172.7K **Privately Held**
SIC: 7379 8748 2731 Tape recertification service; business consulting; book publishing

(G-17031)
TOBY SMALL ENGINE REPAIR
22704 Millard Ave (60471-2529)
PHONE.................................708 699-6021
Lloyd Smith, *Owner*
EMP: 3
SALES (est): 178.9K **Privately Held**
SIC: 3423 Mechanics' hand tools

(G-17032)
UNIQUE PRODUCT PRODUCTIONS INC
22141 Woodbine Rd (60471-1162)
PHONE.................................708 259-1500
Eddie L Fisher, *President*
EMP: 5 **EST:** 2018
SALES: 80K **Privately Held**
SIC: 3699 7389 Security devices;

Richview
Washington County

(G-17033)
RAPCO LTD
Also Called: Rapco Building Pdts & Sup Co
405 E 1st South St (62877)
P.O. Box 94 (62877-0094)
PHONE.................................618 249-6614
Roger A Pierjok, *Owner*
EMP: 6
SQ FT: 2,500
SALES: 500K **Privately Held**
SIC: 3599 3273 7692 Machine shop, jobbing & repair; ready-mixed concrete; welding repair

(G-17034)
TA OIL FIELD SERVICE INC
27573 State Route 177 (62877-1015)
PHONE.................................618 249-9001
EMP: 5
SALES (est): 258.4K **Privately Held**
SIC: 1389 1381 Oil field services; drilling oil & gas wells

Ridgway
Gallatin County

(G-17035)
BOND BROTHERS HARDWOODS
412 W Main St (62979)
P.O. Box 208 (62979-0208)
PHONE.................................618 272-4811
Cleve Bond, *Partner*
Cletus Bond, *Partner*
EMP: 5
SQ FT: 30,000
SALES (est): 821.5K **Privately Held**
SIC: 5031 2431 2426 2421 Lumber, plywood & millwork; millwork; hardwood dimension & flooring mills; sawmills & planing mills, general

(G-17036)
DINGER BATS LLC
Also Called: Dinger Bat Company
109 S Kimbro St (62979-1135)
P.O. Box 71 (62979-0071)
PHONE.................................618 272-7250
Kyle Drone, *Mng Member*
Randy Drone,
EMP: 3
SALES (est): 254.4K **Privately Held**
SIC: 3949 Sporting & athletic goods

Ringwood
Mchenry County

(G-17037)
A&W TOOL INC
5309 Bus Pkwy Unit 101 (60072)
PHONE.................................815 653-1700
Gaylen Wester, *President*
EMP: 9
SQ FT: 5,000
SALES (est): 1.3MM **Privately Held**
SIC: 3541 3545 7699 Machine tools, metal cutting type; machine tool accessories; industrial tool grinding

(G-17038)
ADVANCED SEAL TECHNOLOGY INC
5306 Bus Pkwy Unit 107 (60072)
P.O. Box 1931, Evanston (60204-1931)
PHONE.................................815 861-4010
Steve Wieland, *President*
Thomas Doepker, *Manager*
EMP: 24
SALES (est): 2.6MM **Privately Held**
WEB: www.advancedsealtechus.com
SIC: 3561 Pumps & pumping equipment

(G-17039)
APEX MANUFACTURING INC
5409 Craftwell Dr Ste A (60072-9402)
PHONE.................................815 728-0108
David W Dowell, *President*
Kathy Dowell, *Admin Sec*
EMP: 4
SALES (est): 570.5K **Privately Held**
SIC: 3599 Machine shop, jobbing & repair

(G-17040)
BURNEX CORPORATION
5418 Business Pkwy (60072-9412)
PHONE.................................815 728-1317
Manfred Suhr, *CEO*
Scott Suhr, *President*
Matt Gilmore, *Regl Sales Mgr*
EMP: 30
SQ FT: 11,000
SALES (est): 6.5MM **Privately Held**
SIC: 3469 3493 3496 3545 Stamping metal for the trade; steel springs, except wire; woven wire products; tools & accessories for machine tools

(G-17041)
DENTAL CRAFT CORP
5414 Craftwell Dr (60072-9629)
P.O. Box 178 (60072-0178)
PHONE.................................815 385-7132
Jerome Wakitsch, *President*
Robert Wakitsch, *Vice Pres*
Mary Olson, *Treasurer*
EMP: 19
SQ FT: 3,200
SALES (est): 1MM **Privately Held**
SIC: 3842 8072 3843 Prosthetic appliances; denture production; dental equipment & supplies

(G-17042)
DOW CHEMICAL COMPANY
5005 Barnard Mill Rd (60072-9652)
P.O. Box 238 (60072-0238)
PHONE.................................815 653-2411
Sidney Martin, *Branch Mgr*
EMP: 210
SALES (corp-wide): 42.9B **Publicly Held**
SIC: 2819 2821 Industrial inorganic chemicals; plastics materials & resins
HQ: The Dow Chemical Company
   2211 H H Dow Way
   Midland MI 48642
   989 636-1000

(G-17043)
FOX VALLEY CHEMICAL COMPANY
5201 Mann Dr (60072-9664)
P.O. Box 129 (60072-0129)
PHONE.................................815 653-2660
Russell A Hopp, *President*
Matthew Hopp, *Vice Pres*
▲ **EMP:** 8 **EST:** 1979
SQ FT: 14,000
SALES (est): 1.2MM **Privately Held**
SIC: 2842 Wax removers; floor waxes

(G-17044)
HUNTSMAN INTERNATIONAL LLC
5015 Barnard Mill Rd (60072-9652)
P.O. Box 220 (60072-0220)
PHONE.................................815 653-1500
Peter Devries, *Principal*
Andrew Jaeger, *Executive*
Pat Holub, *Administration*
Haibo Zhao, *Administration*
David Cooper, *Maintence Staff*
EMP: 70
SALES (corp-wide): 6.8B **Publicly Held**
SIC: 2821 Polyurethane resins
HQ: Huntsman International Llc
   10003 Woodloch Forest Dr # 260
   The Woodlands TX 77380
   281 719-6000

(G-17045)
MORTON INTL INC ADHSVES SPCLTY
5005 Barnard Mill Rd (60072-9652)
PHONE.................................815 653-2042
Divyesh Patel, *Principal*
EMP: 3 **EST:** 2007
SALES (est): 223.4K **Privately Held**
SIC: 2891 Adhesives

(G-17046)
OBERRY ENTERPRISES INC (PA)
5306 Bsineil Pkwy Ste 110 (60072)
P.O. Box 130 (60072-0130)
PHONE.................................815 728-9480
Patrick O'Berry, *President*
Rita O'Berry, *Admin Sec*
▲ **EMP:** 3
SQ FT: 3,600
SALES: 1MM **Privately Held**
SIC: 3429 5072 Manufactured hardware (general); hardware

(G-17047)
ROHM AND HAAS COMPANY
5005 Barnard Mill Rd (60072-9652)
PHONE.................................815 728-4602
▲ **EMP:** 11
SALES (est): 3.4MM **Privately Held**
SIC: 2819 Industrial inorganic chemicals

(G-17048)
SURVYVN LTD
4613 Glacial Trl (60072-9503)
PHONE.................................847 977-8665
Gary Wiener, *President*
EMP: 2
SALES (est): 351K **Privately Held**
SIC: 3089 Injection molding of plastics

River Forest
Cook County

(G-17049)
ALLIED GEAR CO
1034 Keystone Ave (60305-1324)
PHONE.................................773 287-8742
Norman Teiber, *President*
Antoinette M Teiber, *Corp Secy*
EMP: 7 **EST:** 1946
SQ FT: 25,000
SALES (est): 1.3MM **Privately Held**
WEB: www.theallliedgearco.com
SIC: 3566 3568 3462 Gears, power transmission, except automotive; sprockets (power transmission equipment); iron & steel forgings

(G-17050)
BROKERASSIST LLC
31 Forest Ave (60305-2001)
PHONE.................................847 858-2357
Daniel Rm Beck, *Mng Member*
EMP: 2
SALES: 200K **Privately Held**
SIC: 6531 7372 7389 Real estate agents & managers; application computer software;

(G-17051)
DURABLE DESIGN PRODUCTS INC
1520 Franklin Ave (60305-1043)
PHONE.................................708 707-1147
Diane Herman, *President*
EMP: 1 **EST:** 2012
SALES: 1MM **Privately Held**
SIC: 2514 2522 2541 Beds, including folding & cabinet, household: metal; kitchen cabinets: metal; tables, household: metal; filing boxes, cabinets & cases: except wood; cabinets, lockers & shelving

(G-17052)
HALEYS CORKER INC
1323 Park Ave (60305-1020)
PHONE.................................708 228-1427
Jodie Tristano, *President*
Darren Tristano, *Vice Pres*
EMP: 3
SALES (est): 277.6K **Privately Held**
SIC: 2499 7389 Corks, bottle;

(G-17053)
LEOS DANCEWEAR INC
7601 North Ave (60305-1133)
PHONE.................................773 889-7700
Edward Harris, *Ch of Bd*
Glenn Baruck, *President*

River Forest - Cook County (G-17054)

▲ EMP: 75 EST: 1923
SQ FT: 45,000
SALES (est): 15.2MM **Privately Held**
WEB: www.leosdancewear.com
SIC: 5139 5137 3144 3143 Shoes; women's & children's clothing; women's footwear, except athletic; men's footwear, except athletic; rubber & plastics footwear

(G-17054)
PROTACTIC GOLF ENTERPRISES
504 River Oaks Dr (60305-1653)
PHONE..........................708 209-1120
Lee Paul Rosasco, *President*
▲ EMP: 15
SQ FT: 35,000
SALES (est): 810K **Privately Held**
SIC: 3949 Shafts, golf club

(G-17055)
SANTELLI CUSTOM CABINETRY
1531 Forest Ave Apt 3 (60305-1072)
PHONE..........................708 771-3884
Karen Diaferia Santelli, *Principal*
EMP: 4
SALES (est): 441.4K **Privately Held**
SIC: 2434 Wood kitchen cabinets

(G-17056)
SCIENTIFIC CMPT ASSOC CORP (PA)
Also Called: Sca
212 Lathrop Ave (60305-2121)
PHONE..........................708 771-4567
Chin Te Liu, *President*
Lon-Mu Liu, *Principal*
Mervin Muller, *Principal*
George C Tiao, *Principal*
William Lattyak, *Vice Pres*
EMP: 5
SQ FT: 2,200
SALES (est): 815.3K **Privately Held**
SIC: 7372 5734 Business oriented computer software; software, business & non-game

River Grove
Cook County

(G-17057)
BANNER MOULDED PRODUCTS
3050 River Rd (60171-1009)
PHONE..........................708 452-0033
Michael R Randazzo, *President*
Andy Randazzo, *Vice Pres*
Tony Randazzo, *Vice Pres*
Andrew Randazzo, *Admin Sec*
EMP: 35
SQ FT: 14,100
SALES (est): 5.3MM **Privately Held**
WEB: www.bannermp.com
SIC: 3555 3544 2796 Printing plates; special dies, tools, jigs & fixtures; platemaking services

(G-17058)
CHICAGO SALT COMPANY INC
2924 River Rd (60171-1327)
PHONE..........................708 906-4718
Leon Benish, *President*
Paul Benish, *General Mgr*
Denise Benish, *Treasurer*
EMP: 8 EST: 2014
SALES: 1.7MM **Privately Held**
WEB: www.bulksaltsaleschicago.com
SIC: 2819 1479 Sodium compounds or salts, inorg., ex. refined sod. chloride; rock salt mining

(G-17059)
EXPERT METAL FINISHING INC
2120 West St (60171-1904)
PHONE..........................708 583-2550
Gus Garza, *Manager*
EMP: 14
SALES (est): 1.8MM **Privately Held**
SIC: 3471 Finishing, metals or formed products

(G-17060)
G T EXPRESS LTD
2233 West St (60171-1817)
PHONE..........................708 338-0303
Tom Rzedzean, *President*
EMP: 8
SALES (est): 1.9MM **Privately Held**
SIC: 2655 Fiber shipping & mailing containers

(G-17061)
LIBORIO BAKING CO INC
8212 Grand Ave (60171-1518)
P.O. Box 328 (60171-0328)
PHONE..........................708 452-7222
Andrea Letizia, *President*
Rita Letizia, *Treasurer*
EMP: 6
SQ FT: 50,000
SALES (est): 825K **Privately Held**
SIC: 2051 2099 Bakery: wholesale or wholesale/retail combined; food preparations

(G-17062)
LUCMIA ENTERPRISES INC
8308 Fullerton Ave (60171-1747)
PHONE..........................800 785-3157
Timothy Caronti, *Principal*
EMP: 2
SALES (est): 245.6K **Privately Held**
SIC: 2752 Commercial printing, lithographic

(G-17063)
MATRIX MACHINE & TOOL MFG
8044 Grand Ave (60171-1597)
PHONE..........................708 452-8707
William Shekut, *President*
Roman Wojcik, *Vice Pres*
EMP: 5
SQ FT: 1,975
SALES (est): 596.5K **Privately Held**
WEB: www.matrixmachineandtool.com
SIC: 3599 7692 Machine shop, jobbing & repair; welding repair

(G-17064)
NOVA LINES INC
2314 River Rd Unit 1 (60171-1848)
PHONE..........................773 322-6262
EMP: 2 EST: 2018
SALES (est): 347.9K **Privately Held**
SIC: 3011 Truck or bus tires, pneumatic

(G-17065)
PALDO SIGN AND DISPLAY COMPANY
8110 Grand Ave (60171-1510)
PHONE..........................708 456-1711
Madeline Paldo, *President*
John Paldo, *Vice Pres*
Joseph Paldo, *Vice Pres*
EMP: 7
SQ FT: 5,000
SALES (est): 900K **Privately Held**
WEB: www.paldosigns.com
SIC: 3993 7532 Electric signs; neon signs; truck painting & lettering

(G-17066)
R N R PHOTOGRAPHERS INC
Also Called: R & R Lithography
8115 Grand Ave (60171-1509)
P.O. Box 32 (60171-0032)
PHONE..........................708 453-1868
Jan Ross, *President*
Jack Ross, *President*
Richard Ross, *Vice Pres*
Jaclynne Delarco, *Office Mgr*
Frank Noverini, *Admin Sec*
EMP: 7
SQ FT: 5,000
SALES (est): 1.2MM **Privately Held**
WEB: www.manorpressprinting.com
SIC: 2752 2759 2791 Commercial printing, offset; letterpress printing; typesetting

Riverdale
Cook County

(G-17067)
ARCELORMITTAL RIVERDALE LLC
13500 S Perry Ave (60827-1148)
PHONE..........................708 849-8803
Genuino M Christino, *Vice Pres*
Daniel Fairclough, *Vice Pres*
Ray Snyder, *Safety Mgr*
Michael Frankiewicz, *Engineer*
Rucker Odem, *Human Res Mgr*
▲ EMP: 320
SALES (est): 97.5MM **Privately Held**
SIC: 3316 Strip steel, flat bright, cold-rolled: purchased hot-rolled
HQ: Arcelormittal Usa Llc
  1 S Dearborn St Ste 1800
  Chicago IL 60603
  312 346-0300

(G-17068)
ATHERTON FOUNDRY PRODUCTS INC
13000 S Halsted St (60827-1119)
PHONE..........................708 849-4615
Owen Smith, *President*
Virginia Smith, *Corp Secy*
Larry Smith, *Vice Pres*
Mark Smith, *Vice Pres*
EMP: 9 EST: 1956
SQ FT: 10,000
SALES (est): 710K **Privately Held**
SIC: 3365 3366 Aluminum & aluminum-based alloy castings; castings (except die): brass; castings (except die): bronze

(G-17069)
BONELL MANUFACTURING COMPANY
13521 S Halsted St Fl 1 (60827-1190)
PHONE..........................708 849-1770
Thomas R Okleshen, *President*
Alex Okleshen, *Vice Pres*
Shannon Carroll, *Office Spvr*
Sheila Apel, *Admin Sec*
EMP: 40 EST: 1947
SQ FT: 64,500
SALES (est): 8.9MM **Privately Held**
WEB: www.bonellmfg.com
SIC: 3547 3398 3316 7699 Rolling mill machinery; metal heat treating; cold finishing of steel shapes; industrial machinery & equipment repair

(G-17070)
CALUMET ARMATURE AND ELC LLC
1050 W 134th St (60827-1097)
PHONE..........................708 841-6880
Hugh Scott, *President*
▲ EMP: 40
SQ FT: 33,000
SALES (est): 7.7MM **Publicly Held**
WEB: www.calumetarmature.com
SIC: 7694 3621 5063 Electric motor repair; rebuilding motors, except automotive; coils, for electric motors or generators; electrical apparatus & equipment
HQ: Ies Subsidiary Holdings, Inc
  5433 Westheimer Rd # 500
  Houston TX 77056
  713 860-1500

(G-17071)
E & E MACHINE & ENGINEERING CO
14016 S Indiana Ave (60827-2248)
PHONE..........................708 841-5208
Erwin Eiduk, *Owner*
EMP: 4
SQ FT: 12,000
SALES (est): 400K **Privately Held**
SIC: 3599 7692 Machine shop, jobbing & repair; welding repair

(G-17072)
JM INDUSTRIES LLC
Also Called: Standard Boiler Tank & Testing
1000 W 142nd St (60827-2343)
PHONE..........................708 849-4700
Nick Cimesa, *Chief Engr*
Mara Goich, *Mng Member*
Mary Beth Palka, *Manager*
Jenee Rinearson, *Info Tech Mgr*
EMP: 20
SQ FT: 26,000
SALES (est): 5.6MM **Privately Held**
WEB: www.standardboiler.com
SIC: 3443 7699 1791 Tanks, standard or custom fabricated: metal plate; vessels, process or storage (from boiler shops): metal plate; tanks, lined: metal plate; boiler repair shop; storage tanks, metal: erection

(G-17073)
MFI INDUSTRIES INC
14000 S Stewart Ave (60827-2163)
PHONE..........................708 841-0727
Christopher Matulajtys, *General Mgr*
EMP: 10
SALES (est): 1.6MM **Privately Held**
SIC: 3443 Fabricated plate work (boiler shop)

(G-17074)
PHOENIX SERVICES LLC
13500 S Perry Ave (60827-1148)
P.O. Box 277999 (60827-7999)
PHONE..........................708 849-3527
Jennifer Cunningham, *Office Mgr*
Vaughn Massey, *Branch Mgr*
EMP: 7 **Privately Held**
WEB: www.phxslag.com
SIC: 3295 Perlite, aggregate or expanded
HQ: Metal Services Llc
  148 W State St Ste 301
  Kennett Square PA 19348

(G-17075)
R & N MACHINE CO
14020 S Stewart Ave (60827-2163)
P.O. Box 563, South Holland (60473-0563)
PHONE..........................708 841-5555
Randy Zart, *President*
Carol Zart, *Treasurer*
EMP: 12
SQ FT: 7,000
SALES (est): 1.4MM **Privately Held**
SIC: 3599 3452 3451 Machine shop, jobbing & repair; bolts, nuts, rivets & washers; screw machine products

(G-17076)
RIVERDALE PLTG HEAT TRTING LLC
680 W 134th St (60827-1194)
PHONE..........................708 849-2050
James See, *President*
Rick Kaeding, *Plant Mgr*
Lisa McKinstry, *Treasurer*
Richard Kaeding,
Rico Mugnaini,
EMP: 50 EST: 1950
SQ FT: 125,000
SALES (est): 9MM **Privately Held**
WEB: www.riverdalepht.com
SIC: 3471 3398 Plating & polishing; annealing of metal

(G-17077)
TRI-STATE DISPOSAL INC
13903 S Ashland Ave (60827-3216)
PHONE..........................708 388-9910
Sheryl A Germany, *President*
Tommy Germany, *Vice Pres*
Jeff Germany, *Opers Mgr*
Katherine Bohse, *Librarian*
Jeffrey Germany, *Admin Sec*
EMP: 48
SQ FT: 2,800
SALES: 12.2MM **Privately Held**
WEB: www.tri-statedisposal.com
SIC: 4953 3443 Refuse collection & disposal services; dumpsters, garbage

GEOGRAPHIC SECTION

(G-17078)
WAGENATE ENTPS HOLDINGS LLC
14331 S Clark St (60827-2741)
PHONE...................773 503-1306
Nate Carson, *CEO*
Michael Striverson, *COO*
Sam McNabb, *Vice Pres*
Eddie Richards, *CFO*
EMP: 9
SALES (est): 352.6K **Privately Held**
SIC: 3621 8731 Power generators; energy research

(G-17079)
WALTER PAYTON POWER EQP LLC (HQ)
930 W 138th St (60827-1673)
PHONE...................708 656-7700
Pat Delis, *Sales Staff*
Dustin Louden, *Sales Staff*
Robert Johnson Sr, *Mng Member*
EMP: 30
SALES (est): 15.1MM
SALES (corp-wide): 29.4MM **Privately Held**
SIC: 3531 Crane carriers
PA: Lanigan Holdings Llc
   3111 167th St
   Hazel Crest IL 60429
   708 596-5200

Riverside
Cook County

(G-17080)
ANART INC
440 Repton Rd (60546-1622)
PHONE...................708 447-0225
Anna Maria Gallegos, *President*
EMP: 35
SALES (est): 1.6MM **Privately Held**
SIC: 2339 Women's & misses' outerwear

(G-17081)
ARCORP STRUCTURES LLC
7301 W 25th St Unit 199 (60546-1409)
PHONE...................773 791-1648
Daniel Zarco,
EMP: 22
SALES (est): 6.6MM **Privately Held**
WEB: www.arcorpgroup.com
SIC: 3441 Fabricated structural metal

(G-17082)
BIOCHEMICAL LAB
247 Addison Rd (60546-2003)
PHONE...................708 447-3923
Robert Novak, *Principal*
EMP: 3
SALES (est): 237.9K **Privately Held**
SIC: 3273 Ready-mixed concrete

(G-17083)
COLORSMITH STAINED GL STUDIO
8 E Quincy St (60546-2129)
PHONE...................708 447-8763
David Condon, *Owner*
Paul Damkoehler, *Partner*
EMP: 5
SQ FT: 1,000
SALES: 250K **Privately Held**
SIC: 3231 7699 Stained glass: made from purchased glass; china & glass repair

(G-17084)
HIGGINS GLASS STUDIO LLC
Also Called: Higgins Handcrafted Glass
33 E Quincy St Ste A (60546-2289)
PHONE...................708 447-2787
Louise Wimmer, *Owner*
Frances Higgins, *Owner*
EMP: 3
SQ FT: 3,125
SALES (est): 249.9K **Privately Held**
WEB: www.higginsglass.com
SIC: 5719 3211 Glassware; flat glass

(G-17085)
INK YOUR WEAR INC
3222 Harlem Ave (60546-1790)
PHONE...................708 329-4444
EMP: 2 EST: 2016
SALES (est): 220.4K **Privately Held**
WEB: www.inkyourwear.com
SIC: 2759 Screen printing

(G-17086)
KW FABRICATION INC
270 Maplewood Rd (60546-1846)
PHONE...................773 294-8584
Douglas Korslund, *President*
EMP: 7
SQ FT: 10,000
SALES: 1MM **Privately Held**
SIC: 3826 Analytical instruments

(G-17087)
OCULARIS PHARMA
2436 S 6th Ave (60546-1242)
PHONE...................708 712-6263
Alan R Meyer, *Principal*
EMP: 5
SALES (est): 467.8K **Privately Held**
WEB: www.ocularispharma.com
SIC: 2834 Druggists' preparations (pharmaceuticals)

(G-17088)
PELEGAN INC
277 Northwood Rd (60546-1882)
PHONE...................708 442-9797
Gayle J Egan, *President*
EMP: 3
SALES: 260K **Privately Held**
SIC: 2759 7336 Promotional printing; graphic arts & related design

Riverton
Sangamon County

(G-17089)
ROADSAFE TRAFFIC SYSTEMS INC
104 Douglas St (62561-6074)
PHONE...................217 629-7139
Richard Ricca, *Manager*
EMP: 4 **Privately Held**
SIC: 3531 Construction machinery
PA: Roadsafe Traffic Systems, Inc.
   3015 E Illini St
   Phoenix AZ 85040

Riverwoods
Lake County

(G-17090)
CCH INCORPORATED (DH)
2700 Lake Cook Rd (60015-3867)
PHONE...................847 267-7000
Jason Marx, *CEO*
Christopher F Kane, *President*
William Zale, *Principal*
Bruce C Lenz, *Corp Secy*
Teresa Mackintosh, *Exec VP*
▲ EMP: 600
SQ FT: 205,000
SALES (est): 845.1MM
SALES (corp-wide): 5.1B **Privately Held**
WEB: www.wolterskluwer.com
SIC: 2721 2731 7389 7338 Statistical reports (periodicals): publishing & printing; books: publishing & printing; pamphlets: publishing & printing; legal & tax services; secretarial & typing service; research services, except laboratory; computer software development
HQ: Wolters Kluwer United States Inc.
   2700 Lake Cook Rd
   Riverwoods IL 60015
   847 580-5000

(G-17091)
GUARDIAN ENERGY TECH INC
Also Called: Spray Foam Direct
2033 Milwaukee Ave # 136 (60015-3581)
PHONE...................800 516-0949
Janelle Munns, *President*
Mark Munns, *Principal*
EMP: 11
SALES (est): 2MM **Privately Held**
WEB: www.sprayfoamkit.com
SIC: 3644 5169 Insulators & insulation materials, electrical; polyurethane products

(G-17092)
INDORAMA VENTURES OXIDE & GLYL (DH)
2610 Lake Cook Rd Ste 133 (60015-5710)
PHONE...................800 365-0794
Satyanarayan Mohta, *President*
Tom Cholke, *Technical Mgr*
Conor Hegarty, *Sales Staff*
Frank Sullivan, *Sales Staff*
Craig Gullett, *Marketing Staff*
▼ EMP: 24
SALES (est): 17.2MM **Privately Held**
SIC: 2869 Industrial organic chemicals

(G-17093)
INDORAMA VNTRES USA HLDINGS LP (DH)
2610 Lake Cook Rd (60015-5711)
PHONE...................847 943-3100
Satyanarayan Mohta, *CEO*
EMP: 1
SALES (est): 101.9MM
SALES (corp-wide): 12.5MM **Privately Held**
SIC: 2899 5169 Oxidizers, inorganic; chemicals & allied products
HQ: Indorama Netherlands B.V.
   Markweg 201
   Europoort Rotterdam
   181 285-400

(G-17094)
JAM INTERNATIONAL CO LTD
Also Called: American Hao Feng Co
302 Saunders Rd Ste 200 (60015-3897)
PHONE...................847 827-6391
Ann Shen, *President*
Mary Bullock, *Vice Pres*
Jose Yu, *Director*
▲ EMP: 5
SQ FT: 1,800
SALES (est): 77.8K **Privately Held**
SIC: 2295 Metallizing of fabrics

(G-17095)
ROEVOLUTION 226 LLC (PA)
2610 Lake Cook Rd (60015-5711)
PHONE...................773 658-4022
Ramon Sandoval, *Manager*
Bernard Donaldson,
David Feder,
Mark Knepper,
Brian Lemay,
EMP: 0
SALES (est): 32.1MM **Privately Held**
SIC: 6719 5021 2521 Investment holding companies, except banks; office furniture; wood office furniture

(G-17096)
TORGO INC
2033 Milwaukee Ave # 352 (60015-3581)
PHONE...................800 360-5910
EMP: 4
SALES (est): 381.2K **Privately Held**
WEB: www.torgosoftware.com
SIC: 7372 Prepackaged software

(G-17097)
WOLTERS KLUWER US INC (DH)
2700 Lake Cook Rd (60015-3867)
PHONE...................847 580-5000
Richard Flynn, *CEO*
Deidra D Gold, *President*
Steven Hardy, *President*
Brian Kiernan, *President*
Nancy McKinstry, *President*
◆ EMP: 50
SALES (est): 2.8B
SALES (corp-wide): 5.1B **Privately Held**
SIC: 2731 2721 2741 2759 Books: publishing only; trade journals: publishing only, not printed on site; directories: publishing & printing; commercial printing
HQ: Wolters Kluwer International Holding B.V.
   Zuidpoolsingel 2
   Alphen Aan Den Rijn 2408
   172 641-400

Roanoke
Woodford County

(G-17098)
AMIGONI CONSTRUCTION
800 N State St (61561-7545)
P.O. Box 491 (61561-0491)
PHONE...................309 923-3701
Terry Monge, *Owner*
EMP: 3 EST: 1950
SALES (est): 214.4K **Privately Held**
WEB: www.roanokeil.org
SIC: 1794 1442 Excavation work; gravel mining

(G-17099)
B J FEHR MACHINE CO
209 N Main St (61561-7514)
P.O. Box 987 (61561-0987)
PHONE...................309 923-8691
Walter Fehr, *Owner*
EMP: 4
SQ FT: 8,160
SALES (est): 208.8K **Privately Held**
SIC: 7699 7692 7629 3523 Blacksmith shop; welding repair; electrical repair shops; farm machinery & equipment; welding on site

(G-17100)
GEM EQUIPMENT & MFG LLC
1503 W Front St (61561-7431)
PHONE...................309 923-7312
Andy Melton, *Principal*
EMP: 14
SALES (est): 609K **Privately Held**
SIC: 3523 Cabs, tractors & agricultural machinery

(G-17101)
GEM EQUIPMENT & MFG LLC
1503 W Front St (61561-7431)
PHONE...................309 923-7312
EMP: 37
SALES (est): 5.1MM **Privately Held**
SIC: 5531 5063 3469 Auto And Home Supply Stores, Nsk

(G-17102)
KEVS KANS INC
1501 W Front St (61561-7431)
PHONE...................309 303-3999
Kevin Wagner, *Principal*
EMP: 4
SALES (est): 405.3K **Privately Held**
SIC: 3089 Garbage containers, plastic

(G-17103)
LIFTS OF ILLINOIS INC
415 W Front St (61561-7817)
P.O. Box 289 (61561-0289)
PHONE...................309 923-7450
Jay Braker, *President*
EMP: 4
SALES (est): 630K **Privately Held**
SIC: 3534 5084 1796 Elevators & equipment; elevators; elevator installation & conversion

(G-17104)
PARSONS COMPANY INC
1386 State Route 117 (61561-7721)
PHONE...................309 467-9100
Robert Parsons, *President*
Kevin Trantina, *COO*
Patrick Weber, *CFO*
EMP: 270
SQ FT: 300,000
SALES (est): 53.2MM **Privately Held**
SIC: 3599 Custom machinery

Roberts
Ford County

(G-17105)
DCC PROPANE LLC (PA)
Also Called: Propane Central
204 N Highway 54 (60962-8094)
PHONE 217 395-2648
Evan Severson, *Principal*
Shawn Coady, *Principal*
EMP: 4
SALES (est): 24.2MM **Privately Held**
SIC: 1321 5172 5984 Propane (natural) production; gases, liquefied petroleum (propane); propane gas, bottled

Robinson
Crawford County

(G-17106)
BARRY CALLEBAUT USA LLC
1401 W Main St (62454-1263)
PHONE 312 496-7372
Lily Deforce, *Branch Mgr*
EMP: 7
SALES (corp-wide): 45.7MM **Privately Held**
SIC: 2066 Chocolate
HQ: Barry Callebaut U.S.A. Llc
600 W Chicago Ave Ste 860
Chicago IL 60654

(G-17107)
BELL BROTHERS
201 N Jefferson St (62454-2720)
PHONE 618 544-2157
Christopher B Pappageorge, *Owner*
EMP: 5
SQ FT: 3,000
SALES (est): 395.2K **Privately Held**
SIC: 1382 1311 Oil & gas exploration services; crude petroleum production

(G-17108)
BEST WAY CARPET & UPHL CLG
1401 N Johnson St (62454-1025)
PHONE 618 544-8585
Michael Dunlap, *Partner*
Sue Dunlap, *Partner*
EMP: 3
SALES: 65K **Privately Held**
SIC: 3589 7359 Carpet sweepers, except household electric vacuum sweepers; carpet & upholstery cleaning equipment rental

(G-17109)
CRAWFORD COUNTY OIL LLC
7005 E 1050th Ave (62454-4727)
P.O. Box 229 (62454-0229)
PHONE 618 544-3493
Larry Clark, *Mng Member*
EMP: 50
SALES (est): 9MM **Privately Held**
SIC: 1382 Oil & gas exploration services

(G-17110)
D & K TANKS
7875 N 600th St (62454-5115)
PHONE 618 553-3186
David L Goodwin, *Principal*
EMP: 3
SALES (est): 480.5K **Privately Held**
SIC: 3443 Fabricated plate work (boiler shop)

(G-17111)
DAILY ROBINSON NEWS INC
Also Called: Robinson Daily News
302 S Cross St (62454-2137)
P.O. Box 639 (62454-0639)
PHONE 618 544-2101
Larry H Lewis, *President*
Tom Osborne, *Editor*
Randy Harrison, *Systems Dir*
Kathy Lewis, *Admin Sec*
EMP: 30
SQ FT: 5,200
SALES (est): 1.7MM **Privately Held**
WEB: www.robdailynews.com
SIC: 2711 Commercial printing & newspaper publishing combined; newspapers: publishing only, not printed on site

(G-17112)
DANA SEALING MANUFACTURING LLC
Also Called: Victor Division Dana
1201 S Eaton St (62454-3607)
PHONE 618 544-8651
EMP: 4 **Publicly Held**
WEB: www.dana.com
SIC: 3714 Motor vehicle parts & accessories
HQ: Dana Sealing Manufacturing, Llc
3939 Technology Dr
Maumee OH 43537

(G-17113)
DANA SEALING MANUFACTURING LLC
Also Called: Dana Corp Power Tech Group
1201 E Victor Dana Rd (62454-5853)
P.O. Box 599 (62454-0599)
PHONE 618 544-8651
Doug Schultz, *Mfg Staff*
Martin Mockenhaupt, *Engineer*
Dave Kanofsky, *Senior Engr*
Steve Orey, *Branch Mgr*
EMP: 300 **Publicly Held**
WEB: www.dana.com
SIC: 3714 3053 Motor vehicle parts & accessories; gaskets, packing & sealing devices
HQ: Dana Sealing Manufacturing, Llc
3939 Technology Dr
Maumee OH 43537

(G-17114)
E H BAARE CORPORATION
500 S Heath Toffee Ave (62454-1699)
PHONE 618 546-1575
John Reynolds, *President*
Travis Crumrin, *Safety Mgr*
Cathy Bachelor, *Purch Agent*
Jerry Darnold, *Engineer*
Joel Owens, *Engineer*
EMP: 206
SALES (est): 46.8MM
SALES (corp-wide): 23.2MM **Privately Held**
SIC: 3315 3496 3469 3443 Wire & fabricated wire products; miscellaneous fabricated wire products; metal stampings; fabricated plate work (boiler shop); steel foundries; gray & ductile iron foundries
PA: E. H. Baare Corporation
3620 W 73rd St
Anderson IN 46011
765 778-7895

(G-17115)
GSG INDUSTRIES
1708 W Main St (62454-4845)
P.O. Box 429 (62454-0429)
PHONE 618 544-7976
Fax: 618 544-7976
EMP: 10
SALES (est): 550K **Privately Held**
SIC: 3677 3612 Mfg Electronic Coils/Transformers Mfg Transformers

(G-17116)
HERSHEY COMPANY
1401 W Main St (62454-1263)
P.O. Box 800 (62454-0800)
PHONE 618 544-3111
Bruce Frey, *Manager*
EMP: 750
SALES (corp-wide): 7.9B **Publicly Held**
SIC: 2064 2066 Candy & other confectionery products; chocolate & cocoa products
PA: Hershey Company
19 E Chocolate Ave
Hershey PA 17033
717 534-4200

(G-17117)
HONEYWELL INC
7656 E 700th Ave (62454-5124)
PHONE 618 546-1671
Giannantonio Ferrari, *President*
EMP: 11
SALES (est): 1.7MM
SALES (corp-wide): 36.7B **Publicly Held**
SIC: 3724 Aircraft engines & engine parts
PA: Honeywell International Inc.
300 S Tryon St
Charlotte NC 28202
704 627-6200

(G-17118)
L C NEELYDRILLING INC
702 N Jackson St (62454-3357)
PHONE 618 544-2726
Larry C Neely, *President*
Sue M Neely, *Treasurer*
EMP: 8
SQ FT: 2,500
SALES (est): 1.5MM **Privately Held**
SIC: 1382 Oil & gas exploration services

(G-17119)
MARATHON PETROLEUM COMPANY LP
400 S Marathon Ave (62454-3400)
P.O. Box 1200 (62454-1200)
PHONE 618 544-2121
Robbin List, *Project Mgr*
Mike Armbrester, *Manager*
William Potmesil, *Supervisor*
EMP: 600 **Publicly Held**
WEB: www.marathonpetroleum.com
SIC: 5172 2992 Petroleum products; re-refining lubricating oils & greases
HQ: Marathon Petroleum Company Lp
539 S Main St
Findlay OH 45840

(G-17120)
MORRIS CONSTRUCTION INC
Marathon Ave (62454)
P.O. Box 377 (62454-0377)
PHONE 618 544-8504
Kenneth Mattsey, *President*
EMP: 20
SALES (corp-wide): 13.7MM **Privately Held**
SIC: 1542 3498 3441 Commercial & office building, new construction; fabricated pipe & fittings; fabricated structural metal
PA: Morris Construction, Inc.
1406 S Eaton St
Robinson IL 62454
618 544-9215

(G-17121)
PIONEER LABELS INC
Also Called: Datamax Oneil Printer Supplies
7656 E 700th Ave (62454-5124)
PHONE 618 546-5418
Paul Sindoni, *President*
Christian Lefort, *President*
Carter Williams, *Admin Sec*
John Yuncza, *Admin Sec*
▼ **EMP:** 105
SQ FT: 65,000
SALES (est): 17.7MM
SALES (corp-wide): 36.7B **Publicly Held**
SIC: 2754 2672 2671 Labels: gravure printing; coated & laminated paper; packaging paper & plastics film, coated & laminated
HQ: Datamax-O'neil Corporation
4501 Pkwy Commerce Blvd
Orlando FL 32808

(G-17122)
POOL & POOL OIL PRODUCTIONS
1724 W Main St (62454-4845)
PHONE 618 544-7590
Stanley E Pool, *Owner*
EMP: 1 **EST:** 1982
SQ FT: 1,500
SALES (est): 450K **Privately Held**
SIC: 1311 Crude petroleum production

(G-17123)
R & L READY MIX INC
602 N Steel St (62454-3342)
PHONE 618 544-7514
Chadd Murray, *President*
EMP: 11 **EST:** 1953
SQ FT: 3,000
SALES: 350K **Privately Held**
WEB: www.rlreadymix.com
SIC: 3273 Ready-mixed concrete

(G-17124)
RAIN CII CARBON LLC
12187 E 950th Ave (62454-5844)
PHONE 618 544-2193
Trudy Ferguson, *President*
Steve Rowland, *Vice Pres*
Dan Fearday, *Plant Mgr*
Lonnie Samford, *CFO*
EMP: 26
SALES (est): 3.3MM **Privately Held**
SIC: 7389 3312 Petroleum refinery inspection service; blast furnaces & steel mills
HQ: Rain Cii Carbon Llc
2627 Chestnut Ridge Dr # 200
Kingwood TX 77339
281 318-2400

(G-17125)
S D CUSTOM MACHINING
9094 E 1050th Ave (62454-7400)
PHONE 618 544-7007
Glenn Wilson, *Owner*
EMP: 3
SQ FT: 3,800
SALES (est): 261.2K **Privately Held**
SIC: 3599 7692 3993 Machine shop, jobbing & repair; welding repair; signs & advertising specialties

(G-17126)
SUPERIOR WELDING INC
9172 E 1050th Ave (62454-4824)
PHONE 618 544-8822
Howard Bilyew, *President*
EMP: 12
SQ FT: 7,200
SALES (est): 1.4MM **Privately Held**
SIC: 7692 Welding repair

(G-17127)
TEMPCO PRODUCTS CO
301 E Tempco Ave (62454-2600)
P.O. Box 155 (62454-0155)
PHONE 618 544-3175
Steve Mc Gahey, *President*
Jerry Snider, *Admin Sec*
Kevin Letterle, *Representative*
EMP: 90 **EST:** 1952
SQ FT: 60,000
SALES (est): 15.6MM **Privately Held**
WEB: www.tempcoproducts.com
SIC: 3089 3442 Window frames & sash, plastic; storm doors or windows, metal

(G-17128)
WESTERN OIL & GAS DEV CO
9234 E 1050th Ave (62454-4825)
P.O. Box 165 (62454-0165)
PHONE 618 544-8646
Gregory Leavell, *President*
EMP: 14
SALES (est): 1.8MM **Privately Held**
SIC: 1311 Crude petroleum production

Rochelle
Ogle County

(G-17129)
A&G MANUFACTURING INC
Also Called: AG Manufacturing - Illinois
200 E Avenue G (61068-3502)
PHONE 815 562-2107
V C Edozien, *President*
Tonya Barton, *Info Tech Dir*
Chuck Hacker, *Maintence Staff*
▲ **EMP:** 13
SALES (est): 1.3MM **Privately Held**
SIC: 3714 Motor vehicle parts & accessories

(G-17130)
ALLOY ROD PRODUCTS INC
100 Quarry Rd (61068-3510)
PHONE 815 562-8200
Cristi A Hoffman, *President*
EMP: 12
SALES (est): 1.8MM **Privately Held**
SIC: 3356 Silver & silver alloy bars, rods, sheets, etc.

Rochelle - Ogle County (G-17157)

(G-17131)
ALM FINE CABINETRY INC
314 N 6th St (61068-1538)
PHONE..............................815 562-6667
Michael Arreguin, *President*
EMP: 4
SQ FT: 600
SALES (est): 502.3K **Privately Held**
SIC: 2434 Wood kitchen cabinets

(G-17132)
ARCHER-DANIELS-MIDLAND COMPANY
Rr 38 Box E (61068)
PHONE..............................815 384-4011
EMP: 3
SALES (corp-wide): 64.6B **Publicly Held**
SIC: 2041 Flour & other grain mill products
PA: Archer-Daniels-Midland Company
  77 W Wacker Dr Ste 4600
  Chicago IL 60601
  312 634-8100

(G-17133)
C U PLASTIC LLC
100 4th Ave (61068-1710)
PHONE..............................888 957-9993
Ll Rong Lin, *Mng Member*
Yu Tan Zheng,
▲ **EMP:** 6
SALES (est): 876.9K **Privately Held**
WEB: www.cuplastic.com
SIC: 2869 Ethylene

(G-17134)
CAIN MILLWORK INC
1 Cain Pkwy (61068-3501)
PHONE..............................815 561-9700
Daniel Levin, *CEO*
Don Lupa, *President*
Roger Cain, *Vice Pres*
Mike Leali, *Vice Pres*
Joe Sebek, *Vice Pres*
EMP: 67
SQ FT: 2,000
SALES (est): 15.2MM **Privately Held**
SIC: 2431 Millwork

(G-17135)
CLARKWESTERN DIETRICH BUILDING
501 S Steward Rd (61068-9304)
PHONE..............................815 561-2360
Mike Garrett, *Branch Mgr*
EMP: 23 **Privately Held**
SIC: 3441 Fabricated structural metal
HQ: Clarkwestern Dietrich Building Systems Llc
  9050 Cntre Pnte Dr Ste 40
  West Chester OH 45069

(G-17136)
CONTINUOUS CAST ALLOYS LLC
100 Quarry Rd (61068-3510)
PHONE..............................815 562-8200
Jason Fowler,
EMP: 15
SALES (est): 1.9MM **Privately Held**
SIC: 3356 Nickel

(G-17137)
E I DU PONT DE NEMOURS & CO
Also Called: Dupont
13239 E Il Route 38 (61068-9210)
P.O. Box 604 (61068-0604)
PHONE..............................815 562-7570
Larry Hageman, *Manager*
EMP: 8
SALES (corp-wide): 21.5B **Publicly Held**
SIC: 2819 Industrial inorganic chemicals
HQ: E. I. Du Pont De Nemours And Company
  974 Centre Rd Bldg 735
  Wilmington DE 19805
  302 485-3000

(G-17138)
EATON CORPORATION
Also Called: Eaton Cor Actuator & Sensor Di
200 E Avenue G (61068-3502)
PHONE..............................815 562-2107
Todd Brachta, *Branch Mgr*
EMP: 250 **Privately Held**
SIC: 3714 3625 5012 Motor vehicle parts & accessories; relays & industrial controls; automobiles
HQ: Eaton Corporation
  1000 Eaton Blvd
  Cleveland OH 44122
  440 523-5000

(G-17139)
ERIE GROUP INTERNATIONAL INC
1201 S Main St (61068-3515)
P.O. Box 30 (61068-0030)
PHONE..............................309 659-2233
James Jacoby, *Branch Mgr*
EMP: 60
SALES (corp-wide): 19.9MM **Privately Held**
WEB: www.eriefoods.com
SIC: 2023 2026 Dried milk preparations; fluid milk
PA: Erie Group International, Inc.
  401 7th Ave
  Erie IL 61250
  309 659-2233

(G-17140)
FBC INDUSTRIES INC
110 E Avenue H (61068-2193)
P.O. Box 173 (61068-0173)
PHONE..............................847 839-0880
Mike Pierce, *Manager*
EMP: 9
SALES (corp-wide): 5.2MM **Privately Held**
SIC: 2099 2087 2869 Emulsifiers, food; flavoring extracts & syrups; perfumes, flavorings & food additives
PA: F.B.C. Industries, Inc.
  1933 N Meacham Rd Ste 550
  Schaumburg IL 60173
  847 241-6143

(G-17141)
FIRE CHARIOT LLC
770 Wiscold Dr (61068-8502)
PHONE..............................815 561-3688
Jeffrey Brue, *Mng Member*
Allen Brue,
EMP: 2 **EST:** 2013
SALES (est): 237.1K **Privately Held**
SIC: 3714 Motor vehicle engines & parts

(G-17142)
GARDNER PRODUCTS INC
224 4th Ave (61068-1615)
PHONE..............................815 562-6011
Jack B Gardner, *President*
Sharon Gardner, *Corp Secy*
EMP: 12 **EST:** 1976
SQ FT: 15,000
SALES (est): 550K **Privately Held**
SIC: 3599 Machine shop, jobbing & repair

(G-17143)
GRAPHIC ARTS BINDERY LLC
1020 S Main St (61068-2174)
PHONE..............................708 416-4290
Christopher Love, *Mng Member*
EMP: 65
SALES (est): 858.7K **Privately Held**
SIC: 2789 Binding only: books, pamphlets, magazines, etc.

(G-17144)
HILLSHIRE BRANDS COMPANY
600 Wiscold Dr (61068-8519)
PHONE..............................800 727-2533
EMP: 255
SALES (corp-wide): 42.4B **Publicly Held**
SIC: 2013 Sausages & other prepared meats
HQ: The Hillshire Brands Company
  400 S Jefferson St Fl 1
  Chicago IL 60607
  312 614-6000

(G-17145)
HUB PRINTING COMPANY INC
Also Called: Hub Printing & Office Supplies
101 Maple Ave (61068-8927)
PHONE..............................815 562-7057
Chris Haas, *President*
Steve Haas, *President*
Catherine Haas, *Admin Sec*
EMP: 15
SALES (est): 3.1MM **Privately Held**
SIC: 2752 2791 2789 2672 Commercial printing, offset; office forms & supplies; typesetting; bookbinding & related work; commercial printing

(G-17146)
ILLINOIS RIVER ENERGY LLC
Also Called: CHS Rochelle
4000 N Division (61068)
PHONE..............................815 561-0650
Amir Saeed, *Mng Member*
Stanley R Blunier, *Mng Member*
Bradley A Riskedal, *Mng Member*
Richard Ruebe, *Mng Member*
Floyd A Schultz, *Mng Member*
▼ **EMP:** 60
SALES (est): 18.3MM
SALES (corp-wide): 31.9B **Publicly Held**
SIC: 2869 Ethyl alcohol, ethanol
PA: Chs Inc.
  5500 Cenex Dr
  Inver Grove Heights MN 55077
  651 355-6000

(G-17147)
MACKLIN INC (PA)
6089 Dement Rd (61068-8501)
PHONE..............................815 562-4803
Maryann Macklin, *President*
Keith Harvey, *Manager*
EMP: 11
SQ FT: 1,200
SALES (est): 1.7MM **Privately Held**
WEB: www.macklin-incorporated.hub.biz
SIC: 1422 Whiting mining, crushed & broken-quarrying

(G-17148)
MAPLEHURST FARMS INC (PA)
936 S Moore Rd (61068-9789)
PHONE..............................815 562-8723
Carol Hayenga, *CEO*
Lyn Carmichael, *President*
Barbara Koehnke, *CFO*
Jack Vandewoestyne, *Sales Staff*
Jerry Cowan, *Marketing Staff*
EMP: 10
SQ FT: 3,000
SALES (est): 129.9MM **Privately Held**
SIC: 5153 2879 4212 Grain elevators; agricultural chemicals; local trucking, without storage

(G-17149)
MASTER GRAPHICS LLC
1100 S Main St (61068-3509)
PHONE..............................815 562-5800
Christopher Barton Love,
Kenneth Barton Love,
EMP: 99
SQ FT: 225,000
SALES (est): 6MM **Privately Held**
SIC: 2752 Commercial printing, offset

(G-17150)
NEWS MEDIA CORPORATION (PA)
211 E Il Route 38 (61068-2303)
P.O. Box 46 (61068-0046)
PHONE..............................815 562-2061
John C Tompkins, *President*
Bonnie Morris, *Editor*
John Shank, *COO*
Mike Tompkins, *COO*
Bret Yager, *Vice Pres*
EMP: 30
SQ FT: 6,000
SALES (est): 91.3MM **Privately Held**
SIC: 2711 Newspapers, publishing & printing

(G-17151)
NIPPON SHARYO MFG LLC
1600 Ritchie Ct (61068-9306)
PHONE..............................815 562-8600
▲ **EMP:** 1 **EST:** 2010
SALES (est): 546.1K
SALES (corp-wide): 17.1B **Privately Held**
SIC: 3711 Mfg Motor Vehicle/Car Bodies
HQ: Nippon Sharyo U.S.A., Inc.
  2340 S Arlington Heights
  Arlington Heights IL 60005
  847 228-2700

(G-17152)
PRINTING ETC INC
1135 Lincoln Hwy (61068-1516)
PHONE..............................815 562-6151
Sherri Barber, *President*
Russ Barber, *Co-Owner*
EMP: 5
SQ FT: 2,000
SALES (est): 310K **Privately Held**
SIC: 2752 2791 2789 2672 Commercial printing, offset; typesetting; bookbinding & related work; coated & laminated paper

(G-17153)
QUICK START PDTS & SOLUTIONS
770 Wiscold Dr (61068-8502)
P.O. Box 665 (61068-0665)
PHONE..............................815 562-5414
Allen Brue, *President*
Jeff Brue, *Vice Pres*
EMP: 15
SQ FT: 15,000
SALES (est): 2.7MM **Privately Held**
SIC: 3694 Motors, starting: automotive & aircraft

(G-17154)
REGIONAL READY MIX LLC
15051 E Lind Rd (61068-9727)
PHONE..............................815 562-1901
Kevin Johnson, *Mng Member*
Brent Johnson,
Hugh McKiski,
Krista Watson,
EMP: 14
SALES (est): 2MM **Privately Held**
SIC: 3273 Ready-mixed concrete

(G-17155)
ROCHELLE FOODS LLC
1001 S Main St (61068-2190)
PHONE..............................815 562-4141
Paul Hardcastle, *Safety Mgr*
Mark Montieth, *Plant Engr*
Scott Morrison, *Human Res Dir*
Calvin Jacobs, *Mng Member*
EMP: 700
SALES (est): 90.9MM
SALES (corp-wide): 9.5B **Publicly Held**
SIC: 2013 2011 Sausages & other prepared meats; meat packing plants
PA: Hormel Foods Corporation
  1 Hormel Pl
  Austin MN 55912
  507 437-5611

(G-17156)
ROCHELLE NEWSPAPERS INC (HQ)
Also Called: Rochelle News Leader
211 E Illinois Rte 38 (61068)
P.O. Box 46 (61068-0046)
PHONE..............................815 562-4171
John C Tompkins, *President*
Michael Tompkins, *Vice Pres*
Nicole Cisneros, *Sales Staff*
Mike Feltes, *Sales Staff*
Janine Patterson, *Sales Staff*
EMP: 50 **EST:** 1933
SQ FT: 7,500
SALES (est): 37.7MM **Privately Held**
WEB: www.rochellenews-leader.com
SIC: 2711 2721 Newspapers: publishing only, not printed on site; periodicals: publishing only

(G-17157)
ROCHELLE NEWSPAPERS INC
Also Called: Rochelle News Leader
211 E State Route 38 (61068-1183)
PHONE..............................815 562-4171
John Thompkins, *CEO*
Janine Patterson, *Sales Staff*
Patrick Duffy, *Advt Staff*
EMP: 30 **Privately Held**
SIC: 2711 Newspapers, publishing & printing
HQ: Rochelle Newspapers, Inc.
  211 E Illinois Rte 38
  Rochelle IL 61068
  815 562-4171

Rochelle - Ogle County (G-17158)

(G-17158)
ROCHELLE VAULT CO
2119 S Il Route 251 (61068-9721)
P.O. Box 25 (61068-0025)
PHONE..................815 562-6484
David Williams, *President*
David Wiliiams, *President*
Margarite Allison, *Corp Secy*
Nancy Kranbuhl, *Admin Sec*
EMP: 5 **EST:** 1948
SQ FT: 5,000
SALES (est): 568.4K **Privately Held**
WEB: www.rochellevault.com
SIC: 1711 3272 Septic system construction; concrete products

(G-17159)
SILGAN CONTAINERS LLC
400 N 15th St (61068-1272)
PHONE..................815 562-1250
Terry Cooper, *Plant Mgr*
EMP: 80 **Publicly Held**
SIC: 3411 Metal cans
HQ: Silgan Containers Llc
    21600 Oxnard St Ste 1600
    Woodland Hills CA 91367
    818 710-3700

(G-17160)
SOUTHEAST WOOD TREATING INC
Also Called: Idaho Timber
300 E Avenue G (61068-3517)
PHONE..................815 562-5007
Belinda Seaton, *Manager*
EMP: 10
SALES (corp-wide): 127.5MM **Privately Held**
SIC: 2421 2491 5031 Lumber: rough, sawed or planed; structural lumber & timber, treated wood; lumber: rough, dressed & finished
PA: Southeast Wood Treating, Inc.
    3077 Carter Hill Rd
    Montgomery AL 36111
    321 631-1003

(G-17161)
T M T INDUSTRIES INC
770 Wiscold Dr (61068-8502)
PHONE..................815 562-0111
Thomas Takach, *President*
Marie Takach, *Corp Secy*
EMP: 30
SQ FT: 20,000
SALES: 1.4MM **Privately Held**
SIC: 3471 3544 Polishing, metals or formed products; chromium plating of metals or formed products; special dies, tools, jigs & fixtures

(G-17162)
TRANSWORLD PLASTIC FILMS INC
150 N 15th St (61068-1218)
PHONE..................815 561-7117
Ronald Mounts, *President*
Josephine Mounts, *President*
Beatrice Mounts, *Admin Sec*
▼ **EMP:** 10
SQ FT: 29,500
SALES (est): 2.8MM **Privately Held**
SIC: 3081 Plastic film & sheet

Rochester
Sangamon County

(G-17163)
APPLIANCE INFORMATION AND REPR
Also Called: A I R
10190 Buckhart Rd (62563)
P.O. Box 1150, Springfield (62705-1150)
PHONE..................217 698-8858
Michael Smith, *President*
EMP: 3
SALES: 72K **Privately Held**
SIC: 3694 Battery cable wiring sets for internal combustion engines

(G-17164)
COE EQUIPMENT INC
5953 Cherry St (62563-8078)
PHONE..................217 498-7200
Marty Coe, *President*
Debra Coe, *Corp Secy*
EMP: 4
SALES (est): 1.2MM **Privately Held**
SIC: 5084 7699 3589 Pumps & pumping equipment; sewer cleaning & rodding; sewer cleaning equipment, power

(G-17165)
EDWIN WALDMIRE & VIRGINIA
Also Called: Cardinal Hill Candles & Crafts
Hc 2 (62563)
PHONE..................217 498-9375
Arlene S Waldmire, *Partner*
Edwin S Waldmire, *Partner*
Virginia Waldmire, *Partner*
EMP: 4
SALES (est): 422.4K **Privately Held**
SIC: 3944 5999 Craft & hobby kits & sets; candle shops

(G-17166)
FEHRING ORNAMENTAL IRON WORKS
10685 E State Route 29 (62563-7977)
PHONE..................217 483-6727
Lewis Fehring, *President*
Jim Clanton, *Corp Secy*
William D Nickel, *Vice Pres*
EMP: 5
SQ FT: 30,000
SALES (est): 2.2MM **Privately Held**
WEB: www.fehringornamental.com
SIC: 3448 1799 7699 7692 Buildings, portable: prefabricated metal; ornamental metal work; blacksmith shop; welding repair; architectural metalwork; fabricated structural metal

(G-17167)
ILL DEPT NATURAL RESOURCES
Also Called: Sangchris Lake State Park
9898 Cascade Rd (62563-6048)
PHONE..................217 498-9208
Steven Kerry, *Manager*
EMP: 6 **Privately Held**
SIC: 2531 9512 Picnic tables or benches, park;
HQ: Illinois Department Of Natural Resources
    1 Natural Resources Way # 100
    Springfield IL 62702

(G-17168)
LEGACY VULCAN LLC
Also Called: Rochester Sand & Gravel
1200 Jostes Rd (62563-8421)
PHONE..................217 498-7263
Rob McMahan, *Principal*
Monica Colvin, *Clerk*
EMP: 22 **Publicly Held**
SIC: 1442 Construction sand & gravel
HQ: Legacy Vulcan, Llc
    1200 Urban Center Dr
    Vestavia AL 35242
    205 298-3000

(G-17169)
METRO CABINET REFINISHERS
7032 Ramblewood Dr (62563-9768)
PHONE..................217 498-7174
EMP: 3
SALES (est): 275K **Privately Held**
SIC: 2434 Wood kitchen cabinets

(G-17170)
NEW IMAGE DESIGNS
136 Roanoke Dr (62563-9236)
PHONE..................217 498-9830
Gary McBride, *Owner*
EMP: 3
SALES: 150K **Privately Held**
SIC: 2759 Screen printing

(G-17171)
SANGAMON VALLEY SAND & GRAVEL
102 Maple Ln (62563-9527)
PHONE..................217 498-7189
Dave Kilnard, *President*
EMP: 4 **EST:** 1973
SALES (est): 273.6K **Privately Held**
SIC: 1442 Construction sand & gravel

(G-17172)
TAILORED PRINTING INC
4855 Sage Rd (62563-9485)
PHONE..................217 498-1057
Kevin J Slot, *President*
Evelyn Slot, *CFO*
EMP: 4
SALES (est): 532.6K **Privately Held**
SIC: 2759 7389 Screen printing; brokers' services

(G-17173)
WALNUT ST WINERY PLUS SAUNAS
309 S Walnut St (62563-9703)
PHONE..................217 498-9800
Loren Shanle, *Owner*
EMP: 7
SALES (est): 542.5K **Privately Held**
WEB: www.walnutstreetwinery.com
SIC: 2084 Wines

Rock City
Stephenson County

(G-17174)
BERNER FOOD & BEVERAGE LLC
10010 N Rock City Rd (61070-9515)
PHONE..................815 865-5136
EMP: 50
SALES (corp-wide): 128.2MM **Privately Held**
SIC: 2022 2026 Cheese, natural & processed; fluid milk
PA: Berner Food & Beverage, Llc
    2034 E Factory Rd
    Dakota IL 61018
    815 563-4222

(G-17175)
DEVANSOY INC
10010 N Rock City Rd (61070-9515)
PHONE..................712 792-9665
Elmer Schettler, *President*
EMP: 5
SQ FT: 5,000
SALES (est): 586.6K **Privately Held**
SIC: 2075 Soybean powder

Rock Falls
Whiteside County

(G-17176)
BELT-WAY SCALES INC
1 Beltway Rd (61071-3169)
PHONE..................815 625-5573
Christopher McCoy, *President*
Colony Linville, *Opers Mgr*
Dockstader Doran, *Engineer*
Roy Meyer, *CFO*
EMP: 50
SQ FT: 16,000
SALES (est): 9.5MM **Privately Held**
SIC: 3596 Industrial scales

(G-17177)
BIMBO BAKERIES USA INC
1204 12th Ave (61071-2601)
PHONE..................815 626-6797
Groups Bcelery, *Principal*
EMP: 76 **Privately Held**
SIC: 2051 Bakery: wholesale or wholesale/retail combined
HQ: Bimbo Bakeries Usa, Inc
    255 Business Center Dr # 200
    Horsham PA 19044
    215 347-5500

(G-17178)
CHAMPION CHISEL WORKS INC (PA)
804 E 18th St (61071-2128)
PHONE..................815 535-0647
Bradley J Schreiner, *President*
Maggie Devries, *Purchasing*
Sheila Schreiner, *Sales Mgr*
Joey Cogdell, *Regl Sales Mgr*
Brandy Schuldt, *Manager*
◆ **EMP:** 11
SALES (est): 1.3MM **Privately Held**
SIC: 3545 3546 5072 Machine tool accessories; power-driven handtools; hardware

(G-17179)
CHAS O LARSON CO
Also Called: Larson Hardware Manufacturing
2602 E Rock Falls Rd (61071-3712)
PHONE..................815 625-0503
Richard Larson, *President*
John Larson, *Vice Pres*
EMP: 30
SQ FT: 69,000
SALES (est): 6MM **Privately Held**
WEB: www.larsonhardware.com
SIC: 3496 3452 3429 Miscellaneous fabricated wire products; bolts, nuts, rivets & washers; manufactured hardware (general)

(G-17180)
CUSTOM MONOGRAMMING
1204 Lincoln St (61071-1426)
PHONE..................815 625-9044
Barbara J Gillen, *Owner*
EMP: 3
SALES (est): 120K **Privately Held**
SIC: 2395 2396 Embroidery & art needlework; automotive & apparel trimmings

(G-17181)
FOLSOMS BAKERY INC
319 1st Ave (61071-1241)
PHONE..................815 622-7870
Gerald Folsom Jr, *President*
EMP: 13 **EST:** 2001
SALES (est): 1.5MM **Privately Held**
WEB: www.folsomsbakery.com
SIC: 2051 Bakery: wholesale or wholesale/retail combined

(G-17182)
HEAT SEAL TOOLING CORPORATION
300 Avenue A (61071-5111)
PHONE..................815 626-6009
Mike A Anderson, *President*
Karen L Anderson, *Admin Sec*
EMP: 3
SALES (est): 453K **Privately Held**
SIC: 3544 7389 Special dies, tools, jigs & fixtures; design services

(G-17183)
HILL HOLDINGS INC
Also Called: Tramec Hill Fastener
2700 E Hill Dr (61071-2000)
PHONE..................815 625-6600
Robert W Hill, *President*
Jerry Mammosser, *Purchasing*
Preston Boyd, *VP Sales*
Jerry L Anderson, *Admin Sec*
Nancy E Hill, *Admin Sec*
EMP: 40
SQ FT: 48,000
SALES: 13MM
SALES (corp-wide): 110MM **Privately Held**
WEB: www.hillfastener.com
SIC: 3452 Nuts, metal; bolts, metal
PA: Tramec, L.L.C.
    30 Davis St
    Iola KS 66749
    620 365-6977

(G-17184)
HILLS ELECTRIC MOTOR SERVICE
305 1st Ave (61071-1241)
P.O. Box 190 (61071-0190)
PHONE..................815 625-0305
Robert A Sandusky, *Owner*
EMP: 4
SQ FT: 5,000
SALES (est): 399K **Privately Held**
SIC: 7694 5063 5999 Electric motor repair; motors, electric; motors, electric

GEOGRAPHIC SECTION

Rock Island - Rock Island County (G-17212)

(G-17185)
HUEBER LLC
Also Called: United Animal Health
105 Dixon Ave (61071-1777)
PHONE..................815 625-4546
EMP: 8
SALES (corp-wide): 9.9MM **Privately Held**
SIC: 2048 Livestock feeds
PA: Hueber L.L.C.
110 S Main St
Creston IL 60113
815 393-4879

(G-17186)
I FORGE COMPANY LLC
Also Called: Illinois Forge Company
2900 E Rock Falls Rd (61071-3718)
PHONE..................815 535-0600
Jeffrey T Jones, *Mng Member*
EMP: 2
SALES (est): 344.6K **Privately Held**
SIC: 3462 Iron & steel forgings

(G-17187)
IFH GROUP INC (PA)
3300 E Rock Falls Rd (61071-3708)
P.O. Box 550 (61071-0550)
PHONE..................800 435-7003
Keith D Ellefsen, *President*
Brad Davis, *Vice Pres*
John Pope, *Vice Pres*
Tim Flessner, *Purchasing*
Sherri Hall, *Purchasing*
▼ EMP: 100
SQ FT: 106,000
SALES (est): 22.5MM **Privately Held**
WEB: www.ifhgroup.com
SIC: 3594 3443 Fluid power pumps; fuel tanks (oil, gas, etc.): metal plate

(G-17188)
INDUSTRIAL WELDING INC
805 Antec Rd (61071-2301)
P.O. Box 506 (61071-0506)
PHONE..................815 535-9300
Paul Heiss, *CEO*
Paul Prahl, *Corp Secy*
Mike Young, *COO*
EMP: 15
SQ FT: 16,000
SALES (est): 583.3K **Privately Held**
SIC: 7692 Welding repair

(G-17189)
METAL SPINNERS INC
Also Called: Rock Falls Div
802 E 11th St (61071-3157)
PHONE..................815 625-0390
James Baumgart, *Principal*
John Stephenson, *Technology*
EMP: 48
SALES (corp-wide): 44.2MM **Privately Held**
SIC: 3469 3444 Spinning metal for the trade; sheet metalwork
PA: Metal Spinners, Inc.
914 Wohlert St
Angola IN 46703
260 665-2158

(G-17190)
MIDWEST HARDFACING LLC
205 E 4th St (61071)
P.O. Box 506 (61071-0506)
PHONE..................815 622-9420
Mike Young, *President*
Arnie Nusbaum, *Vice Pres*
Kent Foster, *Materials Mgr*
EMP: 12
SALES (est): 2.1MM **Privately Held**
SIC: 3599 Machine shop, jobbing & repair

(G-17191)
PRODUCTS IN MOTION INC
804 Industrial Park Rd (61071-3157)
PHONE..................815 213-7251
Doug Krause, *President*
Jeff Frazer, *Principal*
EMP: 3
SALES (est): 331K **Privately Held**
SIC: 3462 Iron & steel forgings

(G-17192)
R&R RF INC
1104 E 17th St (61071-3156)
PHONE..................847 669-3720
Greg Ahsmann, *President*
EMP: 45 EST: 2008
SQ FT: 70,000
SALES (est): 7.6MM **Privately Held**
SIC: 3444 Sheet metalwork

(G-17193)
RIVERVIEW MFG HOUSE SA
901 Regan Rd (61071-2320)
PHONE..................815 625-1459
Frank De Haan, *Owner*
EMP: 3
SALES (est): 178K **Privately Held**
SIC: 3999 Manufacturing industries

(G-17194)
ROCK RIVER READY MIX INC
Also Called: Rock River Sand & Gravel
24261 Prophet Rd (61071)
P.O. Box 384, Dixon (61021-0384)
PHONE..................815 438-2510
Adel Moborak, *Branch Mgr*
EMP: 4
SALES (corp-wide): 6.9MM **Privately Held**
SIC: 1442 Gravel mining
PA: Rock River Ready Mix, Inc.
2320 S Galena Ave
Dixon IL 61021
815 288-2260

(G-17195)
SCUBA OPTICS INC
Also Called: Discount Eyewear
1405 8th Ave (61071-2814)
PHONE..................815 625-7272
Robert Klomann, *President*
▲ EMP: 7
SQ FT: 1,800
SALES (est): 914.7K **Privately Held**
SIC: 3851 Ophthalmic goods

(G-17196)
STERLING WIRE PRODUCTS INC
804 E 10th St (61071-1868)
P.O. Box 110 (61071-0110)
PHONE..................815 625-3015
Wayne A Moore, *President*
Hope Moore, *Corp Secy*
EMP: 8
SQ FT: 12,000
SALES (est): 1.4MM **Privately Held**
SIC: 3496 Miscellaneous fabricated wire products

(G-17197)
TOMPKINS ALUMINUM FOUNDRY INC
23876 Prophet Rd (61071-9635)
PHONE..................815 438-5578
David L Tompkins, *President*
Shirley Tompkins, *Treasurer*
Dale Tompkins, *Manager*
EMP: 3 EST: 1964
SQ FT: 8,800
SALES (est): 100K **Privately Held**
SIC: 3363 3369 3365 Aluminum die-castings; nonferrous foundries; aluminum foundries

(G-17198)
TURNROTH SIGN COMPANY INC
Also Called: Outdoor Advertising
1207 E Rock Falls Rd (61071-3115)
PHONE..................815 625-1155
Eric Turnroth, *President*
Richard Turnroth, *Vice Pres*
Barry Cox, *Sales Staff*
Kathy Wilhite, *Manager*
EMP: 10
SQ FT: 6,800
SALES (est): 1.2MM **Privately Held**
SIC: 3993 7312 Signs, not made in custom sign painting shops; outdoor advertising services

Rock Island
Rock Island County

(G-17199)
AD HUESING CORPORATION (PA)
Also Called: Pepsi Cola Btlg Co Rock Island
527 37th Ave (61201-5956)
P.O. Box 6880 (61204-6880)
PHONE..................309 788-5652
Esta Helpenstell, *President*
Jim Mills, *General Mgr*
Franz Helpenstell, *Chairman*
Jeff Tucker, *Business Mgr*
Corey Schultz, *Senior VP*
EMP: 42 EST: 1939
SQ FT: 25,000
SALES (est): 7.7MM **Privately Held**
WEB: www.huesing.com
SIC: 2086 Carbonated soft drinks, bottled & canned

(G-17200)
AFS CLASSICO LLC
Also Called: Mama Bosso Pizza
507 34th Ave (61201-5948)
PHONE..................309 786-8833
Scott Florence, *President*
Don Montgomery, *Production*
EMP: 50
SALES (est): 7MM **Privately Held**
SIC: 2038 Pizza, frozen

(G-17201)
ALM POSITIONERS INC
8080 Centennial Expy (61201-7316)
PHONE..................309 787-6200
Kevin Toft, *President*
Joshua Clare, *Principal*
Mark Ross, *Principal*
EMP: 7
SALES (est): 876K **Privately Held**
SIC: 3544 Welding positioners (jigs)

(G-17202)
B & B MACHINE INC
1221 2nd Ave (61201-8501)
PHONE..................309 786-3279
Chris Begyn, *President*
EMP: 8
SALES (est): 890K **Privately Held**
SIC: 3541 Home workshop machine tools, metalworking

(G-17203)
BEARDSLEY PRINTERY INC
1103 51st Ave (61201-6858)
PHONE..................309 788-4041
Charles D Van Blair, *President*
Loretta Van Blair, *Admin Sec*
EMP: 4 EST: 1967
SQ FT: 3,600
SALES (est): 555.7K **Privately Held**
SIC: 2752 Commercial printing, offset; letters, circular or form: lithographed

(G-17204)
BEDDING GROUP INC (PA)
Also Called: Bedding Group, The
2350 5th St (61201-4021)
PHONE..................309 788-0401
Jeffrey Sherman, *President*
Janice Reese, *Admin Sec*
▲ EMP: 89 EST: 1989
SQ FT: 80,000
SALES (est): 12.4MM **Privately Held**
WEB: www.thebeddinggroup.com
SIC: 2515 Mattresses, innerspring or box spring

(G-17205)
BELLOTA AGRSLTIONS TLS USA LLC
4415 85th Ave W (61201-7679)
PHONE..................309 787-2491
Patricio Echeverria,
◆ EMP: 26 EST: 2008
SALES (est): 6.4MM **Privately Held**
WEB: www.bellotaagrisolutions.com
SIC: 3469 3523 Metal stampings; planting, haying, harvesting & processing machinery

(G-17206)
BERGE PLATING WORKS INC (PA)
Also Called: Chrome Shop The
617 25th Ave (61201-5254)
PHONE..................309 788-2831
Douglas Matheson, *President*
Doug Mathason, *General Mgr*
Mike Penry, *Vice Pres*
Victor J Jackson, *Manager*
John P Matheson, *Shareholder*
EMP: 8
SQ FT: 10,600
SALES (est): 1.5MM **Privately Held**
SIC: 3471 Electroplating of metals or formed products

(G-17207)
BEUTEL CORPORATION (PA)
Also Called: Cambridge Monument Co
1800 11th St (61201-4310)
P.O. Box 4006 (61204-4006)
PHONE..................309 786-8134
Louis W Beutel, *President*
Mary Rita Beutel, *Vice Pres*
EMP: 5
SALES (est): 1MM **Privately Held**
SIC: 5999 3281 Monuments, finished to custom order; cut stone & stone products

(G-17208)
BOETJE FOODS INC
2736 12th St (61201-5330)
PHONE..................309 788-4352
Robert F Kropp, *President*
Dorothy Kropp, *Corp Secy*
Will Kropp, *Manager*
EMP: 5
SQ FT: 1,200
SALES (est): 286K **Privately Held**
SIC: 2035 Mustard, prepared (wet)

(G-17209)
BRIAN KINNEY
1529 28th St (61201-3724)
PHONE..................309 206-4219
Brian M Kinney, *Principal*
EMP: 3
SALES (est): 164.6K **Privately Held**
SIC: 2411 Logging

(G-17210)
BUZZI UNICEM USA INC
625 1st Ave (61201-8358)
PHONE..................610 882-5000
EMP: 3
SALES (corp-wide): 395.5MM **Privately Held**
SIC: 3241 Portland cement
HQ: Buzzi Unicem Usa Inc.
100 Brodhead Rd Ste 230
Bethlehem PA 18017
610 882-5000

(G-17211)
CRAWFORD HEATING & COOLING CO (PA)
Also Called: Crawford Company
1306 Mill St (61201-3266)
PHONE..................309 788-4573
Robert B Frink Jr, *President*
Ian A Frank, *Admin Mgr*
Michele Banaszek, *Admin Asst*
EMP: 75 EST: 1962
SALES (est): 58.5MM **Privately Held**
WEB: www.crawford-company.com
SIC: 6411 3444 1711 Insurance adjusters; ducts, sheet metal; heating & air conditioning contractors

(G-17212)
CRAWFORD HEATING & COOLING CO
Also Called: Division of Monoxivent
1306 Mill St (61201-3266)
PHONE..................309 794-1000
Ian Frink, *President*
Larry Anderson, *Controller*
Susan Reynolds, *Manager*
Jim Wischhusen, *Manager*
▲ EMP: 20
SQ FT: 21,000

Rock Island - Rock Island County (G-17213)

SALES (est): 1.8MM
SALES (corp-wide): 58.5MM **Privately Held**
SIC: 3714 5084 Mufflers (exhaust), motor vehicle; pollution control equipment, air (environmental)
PA: Crawford Heating & Cooling Co.
1306 Mill St
Rock Island IL 61201
309 788-4573

(G-17213)
CUMMINS DIST HOLDCO INC
Also Called: Cummins Great Plains Diesel
7820 42nd St W (61201-7319)
PHONE 309 787-4300
Dick Dearborn, *Manager*
EMP: 22
SALES (corp-wide): 23.5B **Publicly Held**
WEB: www.cummins.com
SIC: 5084 7538 3519 Engines & parts, air-cooled; truck engine repair, except industrial; internal combustion engines
HQ: Cummins Distribution Holdco Inc.
500 Jackson St
Columbus IN 47201
812 377-5000

(G-17214)
CUMMINS INC
7820 42nd St W (61201-7319)
PHONE 309 787-4300
Richard Dearborn, *Branch Mgr*
Rich Pasek, *Manager*
EMP: 20
SALES (corp-wide): 23.5B **Publicly Held**
SIC: 3519 Internal combustion engines
PA: Cummins Inc.
500 Jackson St
Columbus IN 47201
812 377-5000

(G-17215)
DEELONE DISTRIBUTING INC
1419 9th St (61201-3431)
PHONE 309 788-1444
Lc Dawson, *President*
EMP: 2
SALES: 405K **Privately Held**
SIC: 2299 Textile goods

(G-17216)
DELS METAL CO
1605 1st St (61201-3250)
P.O. Box 3586 (61204-3586)
PHONE 309 788-1993
Wanda Schumacher, *President*
Amadeo Diaz, *Vice Pres*
EMP: 16
SALES (est): 3.1MM **Privately Held**
SIC: 3341 5093 4953 Secondary nonferrous metals; metal scrap & waste materials; recycling, waste materials

(G-17217)
DEXTON ENTERPRISES
1324 2nd St (61201-3224)
PHONE 309 788-1881
Dave Thomas, *President*
EMP: 8
SQ FT: 168,000
SALES (est): 1.5MM **Privately Held**
SIC: 2448 2653 2441 Pallets, wood & metal combination; skids, wood & metal combination; corrugated & solid fiber boxes; nailed wood boxes & shook

(G-17218)
DIAMOND ICIC CORPORATION
916 21st St (61201-2765)
P.O. Box 4542 (61204-4542)
PHONE 309 269-8652
Angela Johnson, *President*
EMP: 50
SALES (est): 2.4MM **Privately Held**
SIC: 1499 7011 7389 5094 Gemstone & industrial diamond mining; casino hotel; apparel designers, commercial; jewelry & precious stones

(G-17219)
ESSILOR LABORATORIES AMER INC
Also Called: Customeyes
4470 48th Avenue Ct (61201-9213)
PHONE 309 787-2727
Robert Kane, *President*
EMP: 50
SALES (corp-wide): 1.7MM **Privately Held**
SIC: 3851 Eyeglasses, lenses & frames
HQ: Essilor Laboratories Of America, Inc.
13515 N Stemmons Fwy
Dallas TX 75234
972 241-4141

(G-17220)
GRAY MACHINE & WELDING INC
710 30th Ave (61201-5269)
PHONE 309 788-2501
Henry Gray, *President*
Lois Gray, *Corp Secy*
Martin Gray, *Vice Pres*
EMP: 10
SQ FT: 11,000
SALES (est): 1.9MM **Privately Held**
SIC: 3599 3714 Machine shop, jobbing & repair; motor vehicle transmissions, drive assemblies & parts

(G-17221)
HABEGGER CORPORATION
437 2nd St (61201-8211)
PHONE 309 793-7172
Brett Molfberry, *Branch Mgr*
EMP: 15
SALES (corp-wide): 78.3MM **Privately Held**
WEB: www.habeggercorp.com
SIC: 5075 3585 1711 Warm air heating equipment & supplies; heating equipment, complete; warm air heating & air conditioning contractor
PA: The Habegger Corporation
4995 Winton Rd
Cincinnati OH 45232
513 853-6644

(G-17222)
HERMANS INC
Also Called: Herman's World of Embroidery
2820 46th Ave (61201-6948)
PHONE 309 206-4892
Gary S Segal, *President*
Judith T Stroud, *Vice Pres*
Donn Stroud, *CFO*
▲ EMP: 24 EST: 1952
SQ FT: 43,000
SALES (est): 2.4MM **Privately Held**
WEB: www.hermansinc.com
SIC: 2395 5137 5136 Embroidery products, except schiffli machine; sportswear, women's & children's; underwear: women's, children's & infants'; hosiery: women's, children's & infants'; sportswear, men's & boys'; underwear, men's & boys'; hosiery, men's & boys'

(G-17223)
HONEYWELL SAFETY PDTS USA INC
101 13th Ave (61201-3207)
PHONE 309 786-7741
Tom Alger, *Manager*
EMP: 125
SALES (corp-wide): 36.7B **Publicly Held**
SIC: 3021 8748 Rubber & plastics footwear; business consulting
HQ: Honeywell Safety Products Usa, Inc.
300 S Tryon St Ste 500
Charlotte NC 28202
800 430-5490

(G-17224)
ILLINOIS OIL PRODUCTS INC
2715 36th St (61201-5642)
PHONE 309 788-1896
Robert Jackson, *President*
EMP: 16 EST: 1945
SQ FT: 165,000
SALES (est): 2.8MM **Privately Held**
SIC: 2992 2899 5084 Oils & greases, blending & compounding; antifreeze compounds; industrial machinery & equipment

(G-17225)
INPRO/SEAL LLC
4221 81st Ave W (61201-7336)
PHONE 309 787-8940
Peter T Francis, *President*
Mike Gunderson, *District Mgr*
Mike Becker, *Engineer*
Stephen Bouxsein, *Engineer*
Chandhini Gowthaman, *Engineer*
EMP: 135 EST: 1966
SALES (est): 55.4MM
SALES (corp-wide): 7.1B **Publicly Held**
WEB: www.inpro-seal.com
SIC: 5085 3053 Bearings; gaskets, packing & sealing devices
HQ: Waukesha Bearings Corporation
N17w24222 Rivrwood Dr
Waukesha WI 53188
262 506-3000

(G-17226)
JC AUTOMATION INC
Also Called: Hawk Technology
8072 Centennial Expy (61201-7316)
PHONE 309 270-7000
Joshua Clare, *President*
Robert Hurlburt, *Controller*
Liz Hartman, *Human Resources*
EMP: 25
SALES (est): 4.4MM **Privately Held**
SIC: 3544 Special dies, tools, jigs & fixtures

(G-17227)
LIBERTY DIVERSIFIED INTL INC
Also Called: Miller Container
3402 78th Ave W (61201-7331)
PHONE 309 787-6161
EMP: 250
SALES (corp-wide): 390.1MM **Privately Held**
SIC: 2653 Boxes, corrugated: made from purchased materials
PA: Liberty Diversified International, Inc.
5600 Highway 169 N
New Hope MN 55428
763 536-6600

(G-17228)
MANDUS GROUP LLC
2408 4th Ave (61201-9007)
PHONE 309 786-1507
Kevin M Jansen, *President*
Fred Jansen, *Principal*
Kyle Jensen, *Principal*
EMP: 15 EST: 1999
SQ FT: 2,500
SALES: 1.7MM **Privately Held**
SIC: 8742 3594 Foreign trade consultant; pumps, hydraulic power transfer

(G-17229)
MENASHA PACKAGING COMPANY LLC
7800 14th St W (61201-7402)
PHONE 309 787-1747
EMP: 300
SALES (corp-wide): 2.2B **Privately Held**
SIC: 2653 Boxes, corrugated: made from purchased materials
HQ: Menasha Packaging Company, Llc
1645 Bergstrom Rd
Neenah WI 54956
920 751-1000

(G-17230)
METAL SALES MANUFACTURING CORP
8111 29th St W (61201-7674)
PHONE 309 787-1200
Virgil Carol, *Manager*
EMP: 40
SALES (corp-wide): 390.6MM **Privately Held**
SIC: 3444 Siding, sheet metal
HQ: Metal Sales Manufacturing Corporation
545 S 3rd St Ste 200
Louisville KY 40202
502 855-4300

(G-17231)
PAK SOURCE INC
690 Mill St (61201-8200)
PHONE 309 786-7374
Brenda Gillman, *President*
Rob Gillman, *Vice Pres*
Jarrod Casteel, *Accounts Mgr*
Shannon Sellers, *Marketing Mgr*
Steve Pekios, *Representative*
▲ EMP: 20
SQ FT: 170,000
SALES (est): 8.1MM **Privately Held**
WEB: www.paksourceusa.com
SIC: 5199 2441 2448 2653 Packaging materials; nailed wood boxes & shook; wood pallets & skids; corrugated & solid fiber boxes; bags: plastic, laminated & coated

(G-17232)
PERFORMANCE FINISHES POWDER
1622 18th Ave Apt 23 (61201-4304)
PHONE 309 631-0664
EMP: 3
SALES (est): 206.3K **Privately Held**
SIC: 3471 Plating & polishing

(G-17233)
PREMIUM MANUFACTURING INC
Also Called: Evans Manufacturing
4608 78th Ave W (61201-7309)
P.O. Box 978, Milan (61264-0978)
PHONE 309 787-3882
Stephanie Acri, *President*
Mark Zude, *Safety Mgr*
Doug Gipe, *Purch Mgr*
Deb Ryckeghem, *Marketing Mgr*
Charles Pappas, *Prgrmr*
EMP: 40
SQ FT: 38,500
SALES (est): 5.6MM **Privately Held**
WEB: www.evanspremiumparts.com
SIC: 3599 Machine shop, jobbing & repair

(G-17234)
PRINTERS MARK
1512 4th Ave (61201-8614)
PHONE 309 732-1174
Gary Weinstein, *CEO*
EMP: 4
SALES (est): 352.4K **Privately Held**
SIC: 2752 Commercial printing, offset

(G-17235)
QUAD CITY CLOWN TROUPE INC
1601 25th St (61201-3716)
PHONE 309 788-1278
Sue Collins, *Principal*
EMP: 3
SALES (est): 122.7K **Privately Held**
WEB: www.qconline.com
SIC: 2711 Newspapers, publishing & printing

(G-17236)
QUAD CITY PROSTHETICS INC (PA)
Also Called: Quad Cy Prsthetic-Orthotic Lab
4730 44th St Ste 1 (61201-7152)
PHONE 309 676-2276
Amit Bhanti, *CEO*
Tara Ferencik, *President*
EMP: 10
SALES (est): 2.1MM **Privately Held**
SIC: 3842 Limbs, artificial; orthopedic appliances

(G-17237)
R & D CONCRETE PRODUCTS INC
8002 31st St W (61201-7408)
P.O. Box 1158, Milan (61264-1158)
PHONE 309 787-0264
Ronald D Bjustrom, *President*
Ron Bjustrom, *President*
Angela Bjustrom, *Admin Sec*
EMP: 40
SALES (est): 17.7MM **Privately Held**
SIC: 3271 Blocks, concrete: landscape or retaining wall

(G-17238)
RABBIT TOOL USA INC (PA)
105 9th St (61201-8353)
PHONE 309 793-4375
O J Birkestrand, *President*
EMP: 16
SQ FT: 13,000
SALES: 1MM **Privately Held**
SIC: 3541 Pipe cutting & threading machines

GEOGRAPHIC SECTION

(G-17239)
RCM SMITH INC
507 34th Ave (61201-5948)
PHONE.................................309 786-8833
Randy Smith, *President*
Chris Smith, *Vice Pres*
EMP: 10
SQ FT: 8,000
SALES: 690K **Privately Held**
SIC: 2038 Pizza, frozen

(G-17240)
RED HILL LAVA PRODUCTS INC (PA)
8002 31st St W (61201-7404)
P.O. Box 925, Milan (61264-0925)
PHONE.................................800 528-2765
Conner Bjustrom, *President*
EMP: 1
SALES (est): 276.4K **Privately Held**
SIC: 1411 Volcanic rock, dimension-quarrying

(G-17241)
REVIEW PRINTING CO INC
1326 40th St (61201-3116)
PHONE.................................309 788-7094
Michael Goodnight, *President*
EMP: 2 **EST:** 1955
SALES: 200K **Privately Held**
SIC: 2675 2752 2791 2789 Die-cut paper & board; commercial printing, lithographic; typesetting; bookbinding & related work; commercial printing

(G-17242)
RILCO FLUID CARE INC
1320 1st St (61201-3218)
PHONE.................................309 788-1854
Conrad Wagner, *President*
EMP: 50
SALES (est): 2.9MM **Privately Held**
SIC: 2992 Lubricating oils & greases

(G-17243)
RIVERSTONE GROUP INC
Also Called: General Sand & Gravel
Junction Of 280amp (61201)
PHONE.................................309 787-1415
Larry Stone, *Branch Mgr*
EMP: 6
SALES (corp-wide): 2.5B **Privately Held**
SIC: 1442 Sand mining
PA: Riverstone Group, Inc.
4640 E 56th St
Davenport IA 52807
309 757-8250

(G-17244)
RIVERSTONE GROUP INC
Also Called: Rock Island Ready Mixed
1603 Mill St (61201-3215)
PHONE.................................309 788-9543
Richard Cox, *Superintendent*
EMP: 10
SALES (corp-wide): 2.5B **Privately Held**
SIC: 3273 Ready-mixed concrete
PA: Riverstone Group, Inc.
4640 E 56th St
Davenport IA 52807
309 757-8250

(G-17245)
ROCK ISLAND CANNON COMPANY
2408 4th Ave (61201-9007)
PHONE.................................309 786-1507
Kevin Jansen, *President*
Keith Jansen, *Vice Pres*
Kris Jansen, *Vice Pres*
Sam Kupresin, *Vice Pres*
EMP: 4
SALES (est): 151.4K **Privately Held**
SIC: 3999 Models, except toy

(G-17246)
STECKER GRAPHICS INC
2215 4th Ave (61201-8903)
PHONE.................................309 786-4973
Robert G Stecker, *President*
EMP: 8 **EST:** 1977
SQ FT: 2,700
SALES (est): 1.4MM **Privately Held**
SIC: 2752 3993 Commercial printing, offset; signs & advertising specialties

(G-17247)
STEEL WHSE QUAD CITIES LLC
4305 81st Ave W (61201-7311)
PHONE.................................309 756-1089
David Lerman, *CEO*
Mike Lerman, *President*
Ron Wolfgang, *Human Res Dir*
Nancy Palmer, *Manager*
Melissa Daus, *Database Admin*
◆ **EMP:** 50
SQ FT: 84,000
SALES (est): 16.3MM **Privately Held**
WEB: www.steelwarehouse.com
SIC: 5051 3312 Steel; blast furnaces & steel mills
HQ: Steel Warehouse Company Llc
2722 Tucker Dr
South Bend IN 46619
574 236-5100

(G-17248)
TECHO-BLOC MIDWEST CORP
8111 31st St W (61201-7409)
PHONE.................................877 832-4625
EMP: 13
SALES (corp-wide): 27.3MM **Privately Held**
SIC: 3271 Concrete block & brick
HQ: Techo-Bloc Midwest Corp.
2397 County Road 27
Waterloo IN 46793
260 837-2597

(G-17249)
THER A PEDIC MIDWEST INC
2350 5th St (61201-4088)
PHONE.................................309 788-0401
Jeffrey Sherman, *Principal*
EMP: 3
SALES (est): 248.9K **Privately Held**
SIC: 2515 Mattresses & bedsprings

(G-17250)
TIBOR MACHINE PRODUCTS INC
2832 5th St Ste 2 (61201-4027)
PHONE.................................309 786-3052
Jeffery Mantyck, *Finance*
Dewey Behrle, *Manager*
EMP: 27
SALES (corp-wide): 24.9MM **Privately Held**
SIC: 3599 Machine shop, jobbing & repair
PA: Tibor Machine Products, Inc.
7400 W 100th Pl
Bridgeview IL 60455
708 499-0017

(G-17251)
TOFFEE TIME
2510 22 1/2 Ave (61201-4634)
PHONE.................................309 788-2466
Jody Schmitz, *Owner*
EMP: 3
SALES: 3K **Privately Held**
SIC: 2064 Candy & other confectionery products

(G-17252)
TRI-CITY HEAT TREAT CO INC
2020 5th St (61201-4090)
PHONE.................................309 786-2689
Ronald Damewood Jr, *President*
Gary I Damewood, *Vice Pres*
EMP: 56 **EST:** 1960
SQ FT: 52,000
SALES (est): 11.9MM **Privately Held**
WEB: www.tcht.com
SIC: 3398 Metal heat treating

(G-17253)
W W WILLIAMS COMPANY LLC
7800 14th St W (61201-7402)
PHONE.................................309 756-1068
Tammy Johnson, *Branch Mgr*
EMP: 10
SALES (corp-wide): 7.6B **Privately Held**
SIC: 3694 Engine electrical equipment
HQ: The W W Williams Company Llc
5025 Bradenton Ave # 130
Dublin OH 43017
614 228-5000

(G-17254)
WEAR-COTE INTERNATIONAL INC
101 10th St (61201-8445)
P.O. Box 4177 (61204-4177)
PHONE.................................309 793-1250
Jim Henry, *CEO*
Mark Henry, *COO*
EMP: 25 **EST:** 1946
SQ FT: 38,000
SALES (est): 1.1MM **Privately Held**
SIC: 3479 3471 Coating of metals & formed products; plating & polishing

---

Rockbridge
Greene County

(G-17255)
ROCKBRIDGE CASTING INC
25 State St (62081)
P.O. Box 266 (62081-0266)
PHONE.................................618 753-3188
Mark C Petersen, *President*
Kurt Petersen, *Vice Pres*
Linda V Kienstra, *Admin Sec*
EMP: 6
SQ FT: 20,000
SALES (est): 1.2MM **Privately Held**
WEB: www.rockbridgemfg.com
SIC: 3363 3364 3543 3369 Aluminum die-castings; nonferrous die-castings except aluminum; industrial patterns; nonferrous foundries

---

Rockdale
Will County

(G-17256)
ARCLINE FABRICATION LLC
12 Graham Dr Unit A (60436-2779)
PHONE.................................207 468-1997
Trevor Hein,
EMP: 2
SALES (est): 283K **Privately Held**
SIC: 3599 Machine shop, jobbing & repair

(G-17257)
COLUMBIA CHUTES LLC
610 Moen Ave (60436-2532)
PHONE.................................847 520-5989
Dombek John J III, *Mng Member*
EMP: 8
SALES (est): 1.3MM **Privately Held**
SIC: 3443 Chutes, metal plate

(G-17258)
CONTAINER SERVICE GROUP INC
2132 Gould Ct Unit A (60436-9545)
PHONE.................................815 744-8693
John Driscoll, *President*
Steven Sowski, *Vice Pres*
EMP: 15
SQ FT: 15,000
SALES (est): 3.3MM **Privately Held**
SIC: 3535 Conveyors & conveying equipment

(G-17259)
HOPE PALLET INC
936 Moen Ave Ste 16 (60436-2509)
PHONE.................................815 412-4606
EMP: 4
SALES (est): 339.9K **Privately Held**
SIC: 2448 Pallets, wood

(G-17260)
J & E SEATING LLC
Also Called: Mlp Seating
125 Connell Ave (60436-2466)
PHONE.................................847 956-1700
Ralph Samuel, *Mng Member*
EMP: 21
SQ FT: 32,000
SALES (est): 1.9MM **Privately Held**
SIC: 2522 Office chairs, benches & stools, except wood

(G-17261)
JOHNS MANVILLE CORPORATION
2151 Channahon Rd (60436-8559)
PHONE.................................815 744-1545
Joseph F Dionne Jr, *Principal*
Rashad Nuruddin, *Plant Engr*
EMP: 192
SALES (corp-wide): 327.2B **Publicly Held**
WEB: www.jm.com
SIC: 3296 Mineral wool
HQ: Johns Manville Corporation
717 17th St Ste 800
Denver CO 80202
303 978-2000

(G-17262)
JOLIET SAND AND GRAVEL COMPANY
2509 Mound Rd (60436-9028)
P.O. Box 254, Joliet (60434-0254)
PHONE.................................815 741-2090
George L Comerford, *President*
Glen A Weeks, *Vice Pres*
Mark Walsh, *Treasurer*
EMP: 70
SQ FT: 2,000
SALES (est): 5.5MM **Privately Held**
SIC: 1411 1442 Limestone, dimension-quarrying; construction sand & gravel

(G-17263)
KWM GUTTERMAN INC
795 S Larkin Ave (60426-2451)
PHONE.................................815 725-9205
Lois Minor, *President*
Keith Minor Jr, *COO*
Kenneth Minor Sr, *CFO*
Sara Dixon, *Director*
▼ **EMP:** 48 **EST:** 1961
SQ FT: 60,000
SALES (est): 10.8MM **Privately Held**
SIC: 1761 3542 Sheet metalwork; machine tools, metal forming type

(G-17264)
LAFARGE NORTH AMERICA INC
2509 Mound Rd (60436-9028)
PHONE.................................815 741-2090
EMP: 27
SALES (corp-wide): 4.5B **Privately Held**
SIC: 3241 Cement, hydraulic
HQ: Lafarge North America Inc.
8700 W Bryn Mawr Ave
Chicago IL 60631
773 372-1000

(G-17265)
LEONARDS UNIT STEP CO
1515 Channahon Rd (60436-9516)
PHONE.................................815 744-1263
George H Buck, *President*
Thomas W Buck, *Vice Pres*
Tim Buck, *Treasurer*
Joan Buck, *Admin Sec*
EMP: 5 **EST:** 1959
SQ FT: 11,000
SALES (est): 336.7K **Privately Held**
SIC: 3272 3446 Concrete products, precast; ornamental metalwork

(G-17266)
LESMARK TOOL COMPANY
1808 Moen Ave (60436)
PHONE.................................815 725-7430
Cheryl Merklein, *Owner*
EMP: 3
SALES (est): 203.1K **Privately Held**
SIC: 3599 Machine shop, jobbing & repair

(G-17267)
MC BRADY ENGINEERING INC
Also Called: Mc Brady Exports
1251 S Larkin Ave (60436-9326)
P.O. Box 2549, Joliet (60434-2549)
PHONE.................................815 744-8900
William Mc Brady, *President*
Patricia Mc Brady, *Treasurer*
Garrett W Mc Brady, *VP Sales*
◆ **EMP:** 18
SQ FT: 19,000
SALES (est): 3.9MM **Privately Held**
SIC: 3565 Packaging machinery

Rockdale - Will County (G-17268)

(G-17268)
MIDWEST RECYCLING CO
2324 Mound Rd (60436-9026)
PHONE..................................815 744-4922
David Kalumvy, *Vice Pres*
David Kaluznvy, *Vice Pres*
EMP: 40
SALES (est): 3.4MM Privately Held
SIC: 4953 2992 Recycling, waste materials; lubricating oils & greases

(G-17269)
MLP SEATING CORP
125 Connell Ave (60436-2466)
PHONE..................................847 956-1700
Ralph D Samuel, *President*
Laura Wdowiarz, *Sales Staff*
Michelle C Samuel, *Admin Sec*
▼ EMP: 25 EST: 1946
SQ FT: 43,000
SALES (est): 4.7MM Privately Held
WEB: www.mlpseating.com
SIC: 2522 2521 Chairs, office: padded or plain, except wood; stools, office: except wood; wood office furniture

(G-17270)
R & H PRODUCTS INC
800 Moen Ave Unit 7 (60436-2698)
P.O. Box 3787, Joliet (60434-3787)
PHONE..................................815 744-4110
Janice Rafac, *President*
John Hawkins, *Vice Pres*
Doug Shaughnessy, *Treasurer*
Robert Rambo, *Admin Sec*
EMP: 4
SALES (est): 483.9K Privately Held
SIC: 2449 2448 2441 Rectangular boxes & crates, wood; wood pallets & skids; nailed wood boxes & shook

(G-17271)
REX RADIATOR AND WELDING CO
14 Meadow Ave Unit 1 (60436-2694)
PHONE..................................815 725-6655
Jerry Baker, *Manager*
EMP: 5
SALES (est): 262.7K
SALES (corp-wide): 3.4MM Privately Held
SIC: 7539 7692 Radiator repair shop, automotive; welding repair
PA: Rex Radiator And Welding Co Inc
    1440 W 38th St
    Chicago IL 60609
    312 421-1531

(G-17272)
SANDENO INC
2115 Moen Ave (60436-9335)
PHONE..................................815 730-9415
Todd Sandeno, *President*
Tamara L Hansen, *Admin Sec*
EMP: 3
SALES (est): 270.1K Privately Held
SIC: 2951 Asphalt paving mixtures & blocks

(G-17273)
SCIENTIFIC COLORS INC (PA)
Also Called: Apollo Colors
1401 Mound Rd (60436-2859)
PHONE..................................815 741-1391
David Klebine, *President*
Richard P Milord, *Corp Secy*
Michele Brant, *COO*
Larry Bykerk, *Vice Pres*
Matt McClure, *Vice Pres*
▲ EMP: 170
SQ FT: 7,000
SALES (est): 55.9MM Privately Held
WEB: www.apollocolors.com
SIC: 2865 2816 Color pigments, organic; inorganic pigments

(G-17274)
SCIENTIFIC COLORS INC
Also Called: Apollo Colors Mfg Plant
1550 Mound Rd (60436-2800)
PHONE..................................815 744-5650
Bruce Wright, *Branch Mgr*
EMP: 170
SALES (corp-wide): 55.9MM Privately Held
WEB: www.apollocolors.com
SIC: 2893 2865 Lithographic ink; cyclic crudes & intermediates
PA: Scientific Colors, Inc.
    1401 Mound Rd
    Rockdale IL 60436
    815 741-1391

Rockford
Winnebago County

(G-17275)
11TH STREET EXPRESS PRTG INC
2135 11th St (61104-7214)
PHONE..................................815 968-0208
Gary Ehrhardt, *President*
EMP: 10 EST: 1972
SQ FT: 5,000
SALES: 1.4MM Privately Held
SIC: 2752 2791 7334 2789 Commercial printing, offset; hand composition typesetting; photocopying & duplicating services; bookbinding & related work; die-cut paper & board

(G-17276)
2ND AMENDMENT DEFENSE INC
4304 Maray Dr (61107-4966)
PHONE..................................815 218-2847
EMP: 3
SALES (est): 181.8K Privately Held
SIC: 3812 Defense systems & equipment

(G-17277)
425 MANUFACTURING
5004 27th Ave (61109-1711)
PHONE..................................815 873-7066
Mike Thomason, *Principal*
Felicia Dreher,
EMP: 7
SALES (est): 70.3K Privately Held
SIC: 3999 Manufacturing industries

(G-17278)
5 ALARM COIN LAUNDRY INC
3939 W Riverside Blvd E (61101-9507)
PHONE..................................815 298-0585
Matthew Felauer, *President*
EMP: 4
SALES: 100K Privately Held
SIC: 3633 Laundry dryers, household or coin-operated

(G-17279)
A & B MACHINE SHOP
1920 20th Ave (61104-7320)
PHONE..................................815 397-0495
Roy E Baumgardt, *Partner*
Timothy F Baumgardt, *Partner*
EMP: 5
SQ FT: 3,600
SALES (est): 549.1K Privately Held
WEB: www.abms1920.com
SIC: 3599 3544 Machine shop, jobbing & repair; special dies, tools, jigs & fixtures

(G-17280)
A E ISKRA INC
4814 American Rd (61109-2640)
PHONE..................................815 874-4022
Richard Schwartz, *President*
Ivan Lisjak, *Vice Pres*
Joyce Schwartz, *Admin Sec*
▲ EMP: 8
SQ FT: 600
SALES (est): 890.8K Privately Held
SIC: 3621 3694 Starters, for motors; alternators, automotive

(G-17281)
A&B APPAREL
1029 Broadway Frnt (61104-1433)
PHONE..................................815 962-5070
EMP: 3 EST: 2010
SALES (est): 231K Privately Held
SIC: 5621 5611 2844 2253 Ready-to-wear apparel, women's; men's & boys' clothing stores; perfumes & colognes; hats & headwear, knit; shoes

(G-17282)
A-1 LAPPING & MACHINE INC
539 Grable St (61109-2001)
PHONE..................................815 398-1465
Gordon A Greenberg, *President*
Bruce Greenberg, *Vice Pres*
Joanne Greenberg, *Treasurer*
EMP: 12
SQ FT: 10,000
SALES (est): 1.3MM Privately Held
SIC: 3599 Machine shop, jobbing & repair

(G-17283)
AARO ROLLER CORP
4338 11th St (61109-3028)
PHONE..................................815 398-7655
Ricky D Wilson, *President*
Jeffrey S Wilson, *Vice Pres*
Patricia Wilson, *Admin Sec*
EMP: 6
SQ FT: 10,000
SALES (est): 470K Privately Held
SIC: 3471 Plating of metals or formed products

(G-17284)
ABACUS MANUFACTURING GROUP INC
516 18th Ave (61104-5131)
PHONE..................................815 654-7050
Robert Voigtlander, *President*
Chantel Carlsson, *Office Mgr*
EMP: 4
SALES (est): 423.3K Privately Held
SIC: 3599 Machine shop, jobbing & repair

(G-17285)
ABBOTT PLASTICS & SUPPLY CO
3302 Lonergan Dr (61109-2670)
PHONE..................................815 874-8500
Robert C Nelson, *President*
Rodney Wright, *Purchasing*
Steve Forberg, *Sales Staff*
Cindy Wright, *Officer*
Jon Bengtson, *Administration*
EMP: 45
SQ FT: 25,000
SALES (est): 9.8MM Privately Held
WEB: www.abbottplastics.com
SIC: 3081 3082 3089 Unsupported plastics film & sheet; unsupported plastics profile shapes; vulcanized fiber plates, sheets, rods or tubes

(G-17286)
ABG BAG INC
Also Called: Alpha Bag Group
1925 Elmwood Rd (61103-1205)
PHONE..................................815 963-9525
William Bennett, *President*
Sandra Bennett, *Principal*
David Decastris, *Marketing Staff*
▲ EMP: 15
SQ FT: 20,000
SALES (est): 1.9MM Privately Held
SIC: 2393 2673 Bags & containers, except sleeping bags: textile; bags: plastic, laminated & coated

(G-17287)
ABLAZE WELDING & FABRICATING
2003 Kishwaukee St (61104-5123)
PHONE..................................815 965-0046
Charles Mc Clenthen, *President*
EMP: 7
SQ FT: 2,000
SALES (est): 303.5K Privately Held
SIC: 7692 3443 3444 3441 Welding repair; weldments; sheet metalwork; fabricated structural metal

(G-17288)
ABS TOOL & MACHINE INC
1202 20th Ave (61104-5355)
PHONE..................................815 968-4630
Robert Renwick, *President*
Jacqueline Renwick, *Treasurer*
EMP: 2
SQ FT: 2,500
SALES (est): 248.3K Privately Held
SIC: 3544 Special dies & tools

(G-17289)
ABSOLUTE GRINDING AND MFG
2400 11th St (61104-7218)
PHONE..................................815 964-1999
Gordon Rose, *President*
EMP: 18
SALES (est): 2.9MM Privately Held
SIC: 3599 Grinding castings for the trade; machine shop, jobbing & repair

(G-17290)
ACCELRTED MCH DESIGN ENGRG LLC
3044 Eastrock Ct (61109-1760)
PHONE..................................815 316-6381
Mike Longlois, *Engineer*
Michael Sullivan, *Director*
Mark C Tingley,
EMP: 24
SQ FT: 18,000
SALES (est): 2.3MM Privately Held
SIC: 8711 3569 3559 3541 Consulting engineer; robots, assembly line: industrial & commercial; pharmaceutical machinery; numerically controlled metal cutting machine tools; assembly machines, including robotic

(G-17291)
ACCU CUT INC
1617 Magnolia St (61104-5142)
PHONE..................................815 229-3525
Jason Bolen, *President*
EMP: 7
SALES (est): 1MM Privately Held
WEB: www.accucutproducts.com
SIC: 3599 Machine shop, jobbing & repair

(G-17292)
ACCUCAST INC
5113 27th Ave (61109-1712)
P.O. Box 5232 (61125-0232)
PHONE..................................815 394-1875
Judy Cottrell, *President*
EMP: 7
SQ FT: 6,000
SALES (est): 1.2MM Privately Held
SIC: 3364 Zinc & zinc-base alloy die-castings

(G-17293)
ACCURATE METALS ILLINOIS LLC
2524 11th St (61104-7220)
PHONE..................................815 966-6320
William Alverson, *President*
EMP: 18
SQ FT: 72,000
SALES (est): 3.2MM Privately Held
SIC: 7389 3312 Metal cutting services; structural shapes & pilings, steel

(G-17294)
ACTION TOOL & MFG INC
5573 Sandy Hollow Rd (61109-2793)
PHONE..................................815 874-5775
Troy Gay, *President*
Merle Keller, *Treasurer*
Eddy Kuball, *Sales Staff*
EMP: 20
SQ FT: 75,000
SALES (est): 5.2MM Privately Held
WEB: www.actiontool.com
SIC: 3469 3544 Stamping metal for the trade; special dies & tools

(G-17295)
ADEPT COALESCENCE LLC
3538 Golden Prairie Ave (61109-3842)
PHONE..................................440 503-1808
Maryam Palmer, *President*
Darryl Palmer, *Vice Pres*
EMP: 5
SALES (est): 269.7K Privately Held
SIC: 7371 7372 7373 7379 Custom computer programming services; prepackaged software; computer integrated systems design; computer related services

(G-17296)
ADVANCED MACHINE & ENGRG CO
2500 Latham St (61103-3972)
PHONE..................................815 962-6076

GEOGRAPHIC SECTION

Rockford - Winnebago County (G-17322)

Willy J Goellner, *Ch of Bd*
Dietmar Goellner, *President*
David Leezer, *CFO*
Marika Mertz, *Admin Sec*
▼ EMP: 110
SQ FT: 141,000
SALES (est): 16.7MM
SALES (corp-wide): 111.7MM **Privately Held**
SIC: 3599 3452 3429 3541 Machine shop, jobbing & repair; bolts, nuts, rivets & washers; manufactured hardware (general); drilling & boring machines
PA: Goellner, Inc.
2500 Latham St
Rockford IL 61103
815 962-6076

(G-17297)
AED ESSENTIALS (PA)
6775 Fincham Dr Ste 3 (61108-3018)
PHONE..................................815 977-5920
EMP: 8
SALES (est): 1.1MM **Privately Held**
SIC: 3845 Electromedical equipment

(G-17298)
AIM DISTRIBUTION INC
510 18th Ave (61104-5131)
PHONE..................................815 986-2770
Mark T Kofron, *President*
Gordy Hall, *Principal*
Wendy R Morris, *Admin Sec*
EMP: 10
SQ FT: 4,800
SALES (est): 2.4MM **Privately Held**
SIC: 2621 5162 Towels, tissues & napkins: paper & stock; plastics products

(G-17299)
ALPHAGAGE
5245 27th Ave (61109-1714)
PHONE..................................815 391-6400
EMP: 5
SQ FT: 12,000
SALES (est): 606.4K
SALES (corp-wide): 5.1MM **Privately Held**
SIC: 3829 Measuring And Controlling Devices, Nec
PA: Janco Industrial, Inc
5245 27th Ave
Rockford IL
815 399-0900

(G-17300)
AMBI-DESIGN INCORPORATED
4654 Crested Butte Trl (61114-7331)
PHONE..................................815 964-7568
Sivaraman S Sundaram, *President*
EMP: 4
SALES (est): 350K **Privately Held**
SIC: 3589 Water treatment equipment, industrial

(G-17301)
AMERICAN QUALITY MFG INC
3519 Kishwaukee St Ste 1 (61109-2000)
PHONE..................................815 226-9301
Mark Dzurisin, *President*
Mike Moncur, *Corp Secy*
Jason Barrett, *Vice Pres*
EMP: 34
SQ FT: 11,500
SALES (est): 5.5MM **Privately Held**
SIC: 3599 Machine shop, jobbing & repair

(G-17302)
AMJ INDUSTRIES INC
4000 Auburn St Unit 104 (61101-2473)
P.O. Box 246, Huntley (60142-0246)
PHONE..................................815 654-9000
▲ EMP: 12
SQ FT: 100,000
SALES (est): 1.6MM **Privately Held**
SIC: 7694 5084 Armature Rewinding Whol Industrial Equipment

(G-17303)
AMTECH INC
Also Called: American Header Tool Tech
1819 9th St (61104-5324)
PHONE..................................815 962-0500
Douglas Johnson, *President*
EMP: 12
SQ FT: 7,000

SALES: 1.2MM **Privately Held**
SIC: 3544 Special dies, tools, jigs & fixtures

(G-17304)
ANDERSON TAGE CO
2316 7th Ave (61104-3441)
PHONE..................................815 397-3040
Glen Ekberg, *President*
Jeff Lingel, *Manager*
EMP: 8 EST: 1949
SQ FT: 5,500
SALES (est): 600K **Privately Held**
SIC: 3599 Machine shop, jobbing & repair

(G-17305)
ANDROCK HARDWARE CORPORATION
711 19th St (61104-3434)
PHONE..................................815 229-1144
EMP: 19
SQ FT: 30,000
SALES (est): 3.2MM **Privately Held**
WEB: www.androckhardware.com
SIC: 3496 Miscellaneous fabricated wire products

(G-17306)
ARDEKIN PRECISION LLC
1300 Capital Dr (61109-3076)
PHONE..................................815 986-4359
Jeff Kaney, *CEO*
Ron Soave, *President*
Heather Spillare, *CFO*
Craig Legault,
Rick Ludwig,
EMP: 110 EST: 2008
SQ FT: 53,000
SALES (est): 2.7MM
SALES (corp-wide): 17.3MM **Privately Held**
WEB: www.ardekin.com
SIC: 3599 Machine shop, jobbing & repair
HQ: Kaney Aerospace, Inc.
1300 Capital Dr
Rockford IL 61109

(G-17307)
ARROW ENGINEERING INC
5191 27th Ave (61109-1770)
P.O. Box 5035 (61125-0035)
PHONE..................................815 397-0862
Timothy O Hawley, *President*
Nicholas J Hawley, *Vice Pres*
Steve Hagedorn, *Engineer*
EMP: 25
SQ FT: 8,000
SALES (est): 4.8MM **Privately Held**
WEB: www.arrow-eng.com
SIC: 3544 8711 3545 Special dies & tools; jigs & fixtures; designing: ship, boat, machine & product; machine tool accessories

(G-17308)
ARTLINE SCREEN PRINTING INC
1309 7th St (61104-4908)
PHONE..................................815 963-8125
Janet Hooker, *President*
Jason Smeltzer, *Vice Pres*
EMP: 3 EST: 1973
SQ FT: 2,400
SALES: 150K **Privately Held**
SIC: 2759 Screen printing

(G-17309)
AUXITROL SA
B V R Aero Precision
3358 N Publishers Dr (61109-6318)
PHONE..................................815 874-2471
Gary Frederick, *Manager*
EMP: 3
SALES (corp-wide): 5.2B **Publicly Held**
SIC: 3728 3812 Gears, aircraft power transmission; navigational systems & instruments
HQ: Auxitrol Sa
Zac De L Echangeur
Bourges 18000

(G-17310)
AZIMUTH CNC INC
4801 White Oak Ave (61114-6239)
PHONE..................................815 399-4433
James K Epperson, *President*

Larry Stapleton, *Vice Pres*
Jeanne Bergstrom, *Executive*
Andy Bergstrom, *Admin Sec*
EMP: 10
SALES (est): 1.8MM **Privately Held**
SIC: 3544 3599 3728 3769 Special dies & tools; machine shop, jobbing & repair; research & dev by manuf., aircraft parts & auxiliary equip; guided missile & space vehicle parts & aux eqpt, rsch & dev

(G-17311)
B & B TOOL CO
5005 27th Ave (61109-1710)
PHONE..................................815 229-5792
Kent L Akerman, *President*
Victoria J Akerman, *Corp Secy*
EMP: 20
SQ FT: 18,000
SALES (est): 3.3MM **Privately Held**
WEB: www.bbtoolcompany.com
SIC: 3599 3544 Machine shop, jobbing & repair; special dies, tools, jigs & fixtures

(G-17312)
BARNES INTERNATIONAL INC (PA)
814 Chestnut St (61102-2242)
P.O. Box 1203 (61105-1203)
PHONE..................................815 964-8661
David A Gollob, *Ch of Bd*
Marvin E Gollob, *Principal*
Bruce Larkin, *Vice Pres*
Jessica Allen, *Buyer*
Shaun Henry, *Engineer*
EMP: 122 EST: 1907
SQ FT: 70,000
SALES (est): 35MM **Privately Held**
WEB: www.barnesintl.com
SIC: 3677 5084 Filtration devices, electronic; metalworking machinery

(G-17313)
BARNSTORMER DISTILLERIES
Also Called: Grant View Distillery
6969 S Main St (61102-5109)
PHONE..................................314 397-1100
Timothy Ford, *Principal*
EMP: 3
SALES (est): 147.6K **Privately Held**
SIC: 2085 Distilled & blended liquors

(G-17314)
BARRON METAL FINISHING LLC
2219 Kishwaukee St (61104-7008)
PHONE..................................815 962-8053
Judy Barron,
Dennis Barron,
EMP: 12
SQ FT: 200
SALES: 700K **Privately Held**
WEB: www.barronfinishing.com
SIC: 3471 Polishing, metals or formed products; buffing for the trade

(G-17315)
BARUDAN AMERICA INC
6191 Abington Dr (61109-2701)
PHONE..................................815 227-1359
Ted Yamaue, *Branch Mgr*
EMP: 3 **Privately Held**
SIC: 3552 Embroidery machines
HQ: Barudan America, Inc.
30901 Carter St Frnt A
Solon OH 44139
440 248-8770

(G-17316)
BC MACHINE
1704 16th Ave (61104-5451)
PHONE..................................815 962-7884
William E Coon, *Owner*
EMP: 3
SALES (est): 248.4K **Privately Held**
SIC: 3599 Machine shop, jobbing & repair

(G-17317)
BEECHNER HEAT TREATING CO INC
905 Brooke Rd (61109-1165)
PHONE..................................815 397-4314
Gary Bagwell, *President*
Barbara Bagwell, *Vice Pres*
Brian Bagwell, *Admin Sec*
EMP: 5 EST: 1948
SQ FT: 11,250

SALES: 350K **Privately Held**
WEB: www.beechnerheat.com
SIC: 3398 Metal heat treating

(G-17318)
BERG INDUSTRIES INC
3455 S Mulford Rd (61109-2703)
PHONE..................................815 874-1588
Michael Stroud, *President*
EMP: 10 EST: 1920
SQ FT: 14,000
SALES (est): 1.2MM **Privately Held**
WEB: www.bergtents.com
SIC: 7359 2394 2391 Tent & tarpaulin rental; furniture rental; awnings, fabric: made from purchased materials; tarpaulins, fabric: made from purchased materials; convertible tops, canvas or boat: from purchased materials; curtains & draperies

(G-17319)
BERGSTROM CLIMATE SYSTEMS LLC (HQ)
2390 Blackhawk Rd (61109-3605)
P.O. Box 6007 (61125-1007)
PHONE..................................815 874-7821
Jack Shaffer, *President*
David Rydell, *Mng Member*
▲ EMP: 337
SQ FT: 250,000
SALES (est): 277MM
SALES (corp-wide): 490MM **Privately Held**
SIC: 3585 Air conditioning units, complete: domestic or industrial
PA: Bergstrom Inc.
2390 Blackhawk Rd
Rockford IL 61109
815 874-7821

(G-17320)
BERGSTROM ELCTRFIED SYSTEMS LL
2390 Blackhawk Rd (61109-3605)
PHONE..................................815 874-7821
EMP: 4 EST: 2015
SALES (est): 184.4K
SALES (corp-wide): 490MM **Privately Held**
SIC: 3531 Cabs, for construction machinery
PA: Bergstrom Inc.
2390 Blackhawk Rd
Rockford IL 61109
815 874-7821

(G-17321)
BERGSTROM INC (PA)
2390 Blackhawk Rd (61109-3605)
P.O. Box 6007 (61125-1007)
PHONE..................................815 874-7821
David Rydell, *Ch of Bd*
Dan Giovannetti, *President*
Sean Connell, *Managing Dir*
James Boone, *Business Mgr*
Steven L Boyle, *Vice Pres*
◆ EMP: 500 EST: 1949
SQ FT: 250,000
SALES (est): 490MM **Privately Held**
WEB: www.bergstrominc.com
SIC: 3531 Cabs, for construction machinery

(G-17322)
BERGSTROM INC
5910 Falcon Rd (61109-2916)
PHONE..................................815 874-7821
Jerry Rubitski, *Design Engr*
Steve Bennett, *Marketing Staff*
John Helms, *Branch Mgr*
Amanda Trier, *Program Mgr*
Joanne Gregg, *Director*
EMP: 100
SALES (corp-wide): 490MM **Privately Held**
WEB: www.bergstrominc.com
SIC: 3714 3585 Heaters, motor vehicle; air conditioning, motor vehicle
PA: Bergstrom Inc.
2390 Blackhawk Rd
Rockford IL 61109
815 874-7821

(PA)=Parent Co (HQ)=Headquarters (DH)=Div Headquarters
✪ = New Business established in last 2 years

Rockford - Winnebago County (G-17323)

(G-17323)
BERGSTROM PARTS LLC
5910 Falcon Rd (61109-2916)
PHONE.................................815 874-7821
▲ EMP: 7 EST: 1995
SALES (est): 203.4K
SALES (corp-wide): 490MM Privately Held
SIC: 3531 Cabs, for construction machinery
PA: Bergstrom Inc.
    2390 Blackhawk Rd
    Rockford IL 61109
    815 874-7821

(G-17324)
BIOAFFINITY INC
641 S Main St (61101-1410)
PHONE.................................815 988-5077
David Ayres, *President*
EMP: 1 EST: 2009
SQ FT: 20,000
SALES: 300K Privately Held
SIC: 2836 Biological products, except diagnostic

(G-17325)
BLAKE CO INC
Also Called: Blake Awning
1135 Charles St (61104-1220)
PHONE.................................815 962-3852
David Blake, *President*
EMP: 4
SQ FT: 10,000
SALES (est): 240K Privately Held
WEB: www.blakeawning.com
SIC: 2394 5999 Awnings, fabric: made from purchased materials; awnings

(G-17326)
BORING INDUSTRIES
2219 N Central Ave (61101-2347)
PHONE.................................815 986-1172
Leanne Alwood, *President*
EMP: 16
SALES (est): 1.3MM Privately Held
SIC: 3599 Machine shop, jobbing & repair

(G-17327)
BOURN & BOURN INC
2500 Kishwaukee St (61104-7010)
PHONE.................................815 965-4013
Tim Helle, *President*
EMP: 130
SQ FT: 130,000
SALES (est): 10MM Privately Held
SIC: 3542 3545 3541 Presses: forming, stamping, punching, sizing (machine tools); milling machine attachments (machine tool accessories); planers (metal cutting machine tools)

(G-17328)
BOURN & KOCH INC (PA)
2500 Kishwaukee St (61104-7010)
PHONE.................................815 965-4013
Terry Derrico, *President*
Loyd Koch, *General Mgr*
Lloyd L Koch, *Vice Pres*
Wayne Densmore, *Engineer*
Michael Malawski, *Engineer*
▲ EMP: 65
SQ FT: 130,000
SALES (est): 22.4MM Privately Held
WEB: www.bourn-koch.com
SIC: 7699 3541 Industrial machinery & equipment repair; gear cutting & finishing machines

(G-17329)
BRYNOLF MANUFACTURING INC
412 18th Ave (61104-5129)
PHONE.................................815 873-8878
Robert Brynolf, *CEO*
Daniel Brynolf, *President*
Ivan Ibarra, *Manager*
▲ EMP: 24
SQ FT: 38,000
SALES: 6MM Privately Held
SIC: 3452 Screws, metal

(G-17330)
BUWW COVERINGS INCORPORATED (PA)
4462 Boeing Dr (61109-2931)
PHONE.................................815 394-1985
Phil Zeilinger, *President*
EMP: 26
SQ FT: 30,000
SALES (est): 5.2MM Privately Held
SIC: 3444 Sheet metalwork

(G-17331)
BWT LLC
Also Called: Bluewater Thermal Solutions
5136 27th Ave (61109-1713)
PHONE.................................630 210-4577
Mike Lesiak, *Branch Mgr*
EMP: 25 Privately Held
SIC: 3398 Metal heat treating
HQ: Bwt Llc
    201 Brookfield Pkwy
    Greenville SC 29607

(G-17332)
C & E SPECIALTIES INC
2530 Laude Dr (61109-1446)
PHONE.................................815 229-9230
Chad C Endsley, *President*
EMP: 20
SQ FT: 18,000
SALES (est): 8.3MM Privately Held
SIC: 5199 2759 Advertising specialties; screen printing

(G-17333)
CAMPBELL SCIENCE CORP
641 S Main St (61101-1410)
PHONE.................................815 962-7415
Dave Ayres, *President*
Dave Ayers, *President*
EMP: 10
SALES (est): 1.9MM Privately Held
WEB: www.campbellscience.com
SIC: 2819 Chemicals, reagent grade: refined from technical grade

(G-17334)
CANDLE CREST LLC
604 N London Ave (61107-4433)
PHONE.................................815 704-3809
Judy Bieck, *Principal*
EMP: 3
SALES (est): 236.4K Privately Held
WEB: www.candlecrest.com
SIC: 3999 Candles

(G-17335)
CARLSON CAPITOL MFG CO
Also Called: Carlson Capitol Mfg Co
2319 23rd Ave (61104-7336)
P.O. Box 6165 (61125-1165)
PHONE.................................815 398-3110
Roger W Kjellstrom, *President*
EMP: 11 EST: 1945
SQ FT: 11,900
SALES (est): 2MM Privately Held
WEB: www.carlsoncapitol.com
SIC: 3469 Stamping metal for the trade

(G-17336)
CARLYLE BREWING CO
215 E State St (61104-1010)
PHONE.................................815 963-2739
Don Carlyle, *Owner*
EMP: 6
SALES (est): 407.4K Privately Held
SIC: 2082 Beer (alcoholic beverage)

(G-17337)
CARMONA GEAR CUTTING
1707 Magnolia St (61104-5144)
PHONE.................................815 963-8236
Frank A Carmona, *Owner*
EMP: 5
SQ FT: 2,000
SALES: 250K Privately Held
SIC: 3599 3462 Machine & other job shop work; iron & steel forgings

(G-17338)
CASA DI CASTRONOVO INC
Also Called: Castronovo's Bridal Shop
722 N Main St (61103-6904)
PHONE.................................815 962-4731
Frances Castronovo, *President*
Nino Castronovo, *Vice Pres*
EMP: 5
SQ FT: 2,500
SALES: 120K Privately Held
SIC: 5621 2335 Bridal shops; ready-to-wear apparel, women's; wedding gowns & dresses

(G-17339)
CDV CORP
Also Called: Precise Punch Products Co
5085 27th Ave (61109-1710)
P.O. Box 5085 (61125-0085)
PHONE.................................815 397-3903
Gary Kiely, *President*
EMP: 10
SQ FT: 12,800
SALES (est): 1.4MM Privately Held
SIC: 3544 3541 Special dies & tools; machine tools, metal cutting type

(G-17340)
CELINCO INC
Also Called: Ingram Gauge Co
2320 Kishwaukee St (61104-7006)
PHONE.................................815 964-2256
Ted Skrzypczak, *Sales Mgr*
EMP: 8
SALES (est): 958K
SALES (corp-wide): 300K Privately Held
SIC: 3545 Machine tool accessories
PA: Celinco, Inc
    2320 Kishwaukee St
    Rockford IL 61104
    815 964-2256

(G-17341)
CELINCO INC (PA)
Also Called: Ingram
2320 Kishwaukee St (61104-7006)
PHONE.................................815 964-2256
Celia Skrzypczak, *President*
Henry Skrzypczak, *Owner*
EMP: 8
SQ FT: 6,000
SALES (est): 300K Privately Held
SIC: 3821 3599 3829 3471 Laboratory apparatus, except heating & measuring; machine shop, jobbing & repair; measuring & controlling devices; plating & polishing

(G-17342)
CELLUSUEDE PRODUCTS INC
1515 Elmwood Rd (61103-1213)
PHONE.................................815 964-8619
Andrew Honkamp, *President*
Andy Honkamp, *Exec VP*
Diane Collins, *Production*
Steve Dorfman, *CFO*
Ruth Swain, *Admin Sec*
◆ EMP: 35 EST: 1938
SQ FT: 122,000
SALES (est): 7.3MM Privately Held
WEB: www.cellusuede.com
SIC: 2299 Flock (recovered textile fibers)

(G-17343)
CHAD MAZEIKA
Also Called: Rkfdcnc
3705 Burrmont Rd (61107-2167)
PHONE.................................815 298-8118
Chad Mazeika, *Owner*
EMP: 5
SALES (est): 302.2K Privately Held
SIC: 3541 8742 Machine tools, metal cutting type; management consulting services

(G-17344)
CHAMPION COMM SVCS INC
1090 Broadway (61104-1404)
P.O. Box 15398, Loves Park (61132-5398)
PHONE.................................815 654-8607
Ron Champion, *President*
Tammie Champion, *Admin Sec*
EMP: 3
SALES (est): 379.9K Privately Held
SIC: 3823 Combustion control instruments

(G-17345)
CHARLES R FRONTCZAK
Also Called: E M F Y & Associates
4816 Mohawk Rd (61107-2333)
PHONE.................................224 392-4151
Charles Frontczak, *Owner*
Charles Frontczak, *Owner*
EMP: 3
SALES: 248K Privately Held
SIC: 3621 Motors, electric

(G-17346)
CHEM PROCESSING INC (PA)
Also Called: CPI
3910 Linden Oaks Dr (61109-5552)
PHONE.................................815 874-8118
Curtis E Cedarleaf, *President*
Gardiner Rynne, *Business Mgr*
Matthew Smazik, *Opers Mgr*
Eleanor Denure, *Mfg Staff*
Rebecca Smith, *Purch Agent*
EMP: 65 EST: 1970
SQ FT: 45,600
SALES (est): 12.1MM Privately Held
SIC: 3471 3479 Electroplating of metals or formed products; coating of metals & formed products

(G-17347)
CHEM PROCESSING INC
715 N Madison St (61107-3933)
PHONE.................................815 965-1037
Linda Hunt, *Branch Mgr*
EMP: 10
SALES (est): 858.9K
SALES (corp-wide): 12.1MM Privately Held
SIC: 3479 3471 Coating of metals & formed products; electroplating of metals or formed products; anodizing (plating) of metals or formed products
PA: Chem Processing, Inc.
    3910 Linden Oaks Dr
    Rockford IL 61109
    815 874-8118

(G-17348)
CIRCLE BORING & MACHINE CO (PA)
3161 Forest View Rd (61109-1694)
PHONE.................................815 398-4150
Kurt Ekberg, *President*
Gary French, *Principal*
Ken Brown, *Purchasing*
John Ekberg, *Treasurer*
EMP: 1 EST: 1963
SQ FT: 24,000
SALES (est): 3.8MM Privately Held
WEB: www.circleboring.com
SIC: 3599 Machine shop, jobbing & repair

(G-17349)
CIRCLE BORING & MACHINE CO
2316 7th Ave (61104-3441)
PHONE.................................815 397-3040
Glen Ekberg, *Branch Mgr*
EMP: 7
SALES (corp-wide): 3.8MM Privately Held
SIC: 3599 Machine shop, jobbing & repair
PA: Circle Boring & Machine Co.
    3161 Forest View Rd
    Rockford IL 61109
    815 398-4150

(G-17350)
CIRCLE CUTTING TOOLS INC
3161 Forest View Rd (61109-1641)
PHONE.................................815 398-4153
Glen Ekberg, *President*
Rich Rugg, *President*
Kurt Ekberg, *Corp Secy*
EMP: 7
SQ FT: 3,600
SALES (est): 630K Privately Held
SIC: 3545 3541 Cutting tools for machine tools; machine tools, metal cutting type

(G-17351)
CLARIOS
Also Called: Johnson Controls
7316 Argus Dr 1 (61107-5864)
PHONE.................................815 397-5147
David Anderson, *Branch Mgr*
EMP: 30 Privately Held
SIC: 3822 Building services monitoring controls, automatic
HQ: Johnson Controls, Inc.
    5757 N Green Bay Ave
    Milwaukee WI 53209
    414 524-1200

GEOGRAPHIC SECTION

Rockford - Winnebago County (G-17380)

(G-17352)
CLASS A GRINDING
3704 Samuelson Rd (61109-3238)
PHONE 815 874-2118
Thomas Lawson, *Owner*
EMP: 4
SQ FT: 3,000
SALES (est): 200K **Privately Held**
SIC: 3599 Grinding castings for the trade

(G-17353)
CLEO COMMUNICATIONS INC (PA)
Also Called: Streem & Cleo Communications
4949 Harrison Ave Ste 200 (61108-7947)
P.O. Box 15835, Loves Park (61132-5835)
PHONE 815 654-8110
Mahesh Rajasekharan, *CEO*
Stuart Smith, *Vice Pres*
John Thielens, *Vice Pres*
Mike Dibaggio, *Engineer*
John Hardin, *Engineer*
EMP: 33
SQ FT: 11,870
SALES (est): 18.7MM **Privately Held**
SIC: 7373 7372 Systems software development services; prepackaged software

(G-17354)
COMET FABRICATING & WELDING CO
5620 Falcon Rd (61109-2985)
PHONE 815 229-0468
Anthony J Capricla Jr, *President*
Joseph A Capriola Jr, *President*
EMP: 50 **EST:** 1973
SQ FT: 68,000
SALES (est): 8.9MM **Privately Held**
SIC: 7692 3441 Welding repair; fabricated structural metal

(G-17355)
COMMERCIAL PRTG OF ROCKFORD
1120 2nd Ave (61104-2202)
PHONE 815 965-4759
Rebecca Hillburst, *President*
EMP: 5 **EST:** 1951
SQ FT: 1,600
SALES (est): 489.7K **Privately Held**
WEB: www.riverviewprinting.com
SIC: 2752 Commercial printing, offset

(G-17356)
COMPETITION ELECTRONICS INC
3469 Precision Dr (61109-2771)
PHONE 815 874-8001
James Bailey, *President*
Paula Bailey, *Vice Pres*
EMP: 6
SQ FT: 4,800
SALES (est): 1MM **Privately Held**
SIC: 3625 3823 Timing devices, electronic; industrial instrmnts msrmnt display/control process variable

(G-17357)
CONTROL PANELS INC
1350 Harder Ct (61103-1118)
PHONE 815 654-6000
Jeanette L Thompson, *President*
James P Nance, *Corp Secy*
David L Adkins, *Vice Pres*
EMP: 13
SQ FT: 19,000
SALES (est): 1.9MM **Privately Held**
SIC: 3613 1731 8711 Control panels, electric; general electrical contractor; consulting engineer

(G-17358)
CORRIGAN MANUFACTURING CO (PA)
1818 Christina St (61104-5139)
PHONE 815 399-9326
Douglas Corrigan, *Vice Pres*
Joseph Corrigan, *Vice Pres*
Roger Corrigan, *Treasurer*
EMP: 12 **EST:** 1927
SQ FT: 50,000
SALES (est): 1.6MM **Privately Held**
WEB: www.corriganmfg.com
SIC: 3599 Machine shop, jobbing & repair

(G-17359)
COVACHEM LLC
5055 28th Ave Ste 3 (61109-7511)
PHONE 779 500-0918
Anthony R Nooner, *Manager*
EMP: 3
SALES (est): 172.6K **Privately Held**
SIC: 2819 2833 Catalysts, chemical; chemicals, reagent grade: refined from technical grade; medicinal chemicals

(G-17360)
CREATIVE PIG MINDS DESIGNWEAR
105 Hall St (61107-4109)
PHONE 815 968-7447
Brian Endl, *Owner*
EMP: 3
SQ FT: 2,500
SALES (est): 316.1K **Privately Held**
SIC: 2759 Screen printing

(G-17361)
CROWN MACHINE INC
2707 N Main St (61103-3111)
PHONE 815 877-7700
Daniel J Glavin, *President*
John Peterson, *Vice Pres*
Patrick G Glavin, *Sales Mgr*
EMP: 30 **EST:** 1985
SQ FT: 27,000
SALES (est): 4.2MM **Privately Held**
SIC: 3599 Machine shop, jobbing & repair

(G-17362)
CUSTOM DESIGN SERVICES & ASSOC
220 E State St (61104-1035)
PHONE 815 226-9747
Frank Dajka, *President*
EMP: 15
SQ FT: 3,400
SALES (est): 1MM **Privately Held**
SIC: 2741 8999 Technical manuals: publishing only, not printed on site; technical manual preparation

(G-17363)
CYCLOPS INDUSTRIAL INC
126 Monroe St (61101-5027)
PHONE 815 962-1984
Matthew McGuire, *President*
Martha Kunz, *Treasurer*
Mysty Cowgill, *Admin Sec*
Matt McGuyre, *Admin Sec*
EMP: 9
SQ FT: 12,000
SALES (est): 800K **Privately Held**
SIC: 3648 Lighting equipment

(G-17364)
D & R AUTOCHUCK INC
5248 27th Ave (61109-1715)
PHONE 815 394-1744
Tod Kreissler, *President*
Jim Lewis, *Prdtn Mgr*
Tammy Ward, *Office Admin*
EMP: 25
SQ FT: 10,000
SALES (est): 1.1MM **Privately Held**
SIC: 3599 3444 3545 Machine shop, jobbing & repair; booths, spray: prefabricated sheet metal; cutting tools for machine tools

(G-17365)
D & R EKSTROM CARLSON CO
5248 27th Ave (61109-1715)
PHONE 815 394-1744
Todd Kreissler, *President*
Chris Waller, *QC Mgr*
EMP: 2 **EST:** 1997
SALES (est): 210K **Privately Held**
WEB: www.ekstromcarlson.com
SIC: 3545 Cutting tools for machine tools

(G-17366)
D AND S MOLDING & DCTG INC
2816 Kishwaukee St (61109-1019)
PHONE 815 399-2734
Melvin Wilton, *President*
EMP: 5
SQ FT: 7,000
SALES (est): 764.3K **Privately Held**
SIC: 3089 1711 Injection molded finished plastic products; injection molding of plastics; heating & air conditioning contractors

(G-17367)
DAR ENTERPRISES INC
Also Called: J & J Fish
217 7th St (61104-1208)
PHONE 815 961-8748
Darnel Watkins, *President*
EMP: 5
SALES (est): 333.8K **Privately Held**
SIC: 2092 Seafoods, fresh: prepared

(G-17368)
DASCO PRO INC
340 Blackhawk Park Ave (61104-5133)
PHONE 815 962-3727
Donald D Dray, *President*
Brad Groves, *General Mgr*
John R Bacher, *Vice Pres*
Rick Parker, *Vice Pres*
Karl Dundore, *Plant Mgr*
◆ **EMP:** 77
SQ FT: 220,000
SALES (est): 21.1MM
SALES (corp-wide): 48.4MM **Privately Held**
WEB: www.dascopro.com
SIC: 3423 Carpenters' hand tools, except saws: levels, chisels, etc.; mechanics' hand tools
PA: Vaughan & Bushnell Manufacturing Company
11414 Maple Ave
Hebron IL 60034
815 648-2446

(G-17369)
DATUM MACHINE WORKS INC
2219 N Central Ave (61101-2347)
PHONE 815 877-8502
Leon Wellwood, *President*
EMP: 12
SALES (est): 1.5MM **Privately Held**
SIC: 3599 Custom machinery

(G-17370)
DAVISON CO LTD
1812 Harlem Blvd (61103-6344)
PHONE 815 966-2905
James R Davison, *Owner*
▲ **EMP:** 3
SALES (est): 276.5K **Privately Held**
SIC: 3792 Travel trailers & campers

(G-17371)
DEAN DAIRY FLUID LLC
1126 Kilburn Ave (61101-5924)
PHONE 815 490-5578
Pamela Russell, *Dean*
Turner Adam, *Plant Mgr*
Paul Hooper, *Warehouse Mgr*
Steven Edwards, *Maint Spvr*
Christopher Lindsay, *Production*
EMP: 83
SALES (corp-wide): 15.8B **Privately Held**
WEB: www.deanfoods.com
SIC: 2026 Milk processing (pasteurizing, homogenizing, bottling)
HQ: Dfa Dairy Brands Fluid, Llc
1405 N 98th St
Kansas City KS 66111
816 801-6455

(G-17372)
DELTA POWER COMPANY (PA)
4484 Boeing Dr (61109-2998)
P.O. Box 5906 (61125-0906)
PHONE 815 397-6628
Joseph P Musial, *President*
Tobin Gimber, *Regional Mgr*
Brian Elmer, *COO*
Greg Brown, *Plant Mgr*
Joseph Musial, *Opers Mgr*
▲ **EMP:** 75 **EST:** 1966
SQ FT: 55,000
SALES (est): 17.2MM **Privately Held**
WEB: www.delta-power.com
SIC: 3492 Control valves, fluid power: hydraulic & pneumatic

(G-17373)
DEMUTH STEEL PRODUCTS INC
3939 S Central Ave (61102-4200)
PHONE 815 997-1116
Christopher De Muth, *Chairman*
EMP: 14
SALES (est): 2.6MM **Privately Held**
SIC: 3523 Farm machinery & equipment

(G-17374)
DG DIGITAL PRINTING
728 N Prospect St Ste 1 (61107-3155)
PHONE 815 961-0000
Don Giacone, *Principal*
EMP: 2 **EST:** 2009
SALES (est): 276.6K **Privately Held**
WEB: www.dgdplanroom.com
SIC: 2752 Commercial printing, lithographic

(G-17375)
DIAL INDUSTRIES INC
2902 Eastrock Dr (61109-1738)
P.O. Box 5246 (61125-0246)
PHONE 815 397-7994
Eric Anderberg, *President*
Jeffrey M Anderberg, *Corp Secy*
EMP: 15 **EST:** 1997
SQ FT: 45,000
SALES (est): 2.3MM **Privately Held**
SIC: 3599 Machine shop, jobbing & repair

(G-17376)
DIAL MACHINE INC
2902 Eastrock Dr (61109-1738)
P.O. Box 5246 (61125-0246)
PHONE 815 397-6660
Malcolm C Anderberg, *CEO*
Jeffrey M Anderberg, *President*
Leah Anderberg, *Corp Secy*
Steve Adam, *Controller*
Jeriene Gauthier, *Bookkeeper*
EMP: 50
SQ FT: 45,000
SALES (est): 9.6MM **Privately Held**
WEB: www.dialmachine.com
SIC: 3599 Machine shop, jobbing & repair

(G-17377)
DIAMOND HEAT TREAT INC
3691 Publishers Dr (61109-2773)
PHONE 815 873-1348
Carl D Neiber, *President*
Lewis Lance, *General Mgr*
Bill Akre, *Vice Pres*
Bill Denning, *Vice Pres*
William O Akre, *Admin Sec*
EMP: 35 **EST:** 1997
SQ FT: 25,000
SALES (est): 8.9MM **Privately Held**
WEB: www.diamondht.com
SIC: 3398 Metal heat treating

(G-17378)
DIE WORLD STEEL RULE DIES
2519 15th Ave (61108-5703)
PHONE 815 399-8675
Lindsey Earnest, *Owner*
EMP: 1
SALES (est): 270K **Privately Held**
SIC: 3544 Dies, steel rule

(G-17379)
DIP SEAL PLASTICS INC
2311 23rd Ave (61104-7392)
PHONE 815 398-3533
Jeffrey Holmgaard, *President*
Becky Ein, *Manager*
EMP: 5
SQ FT: 10,000
SALES (est): 2MM **Privately Held**
WEB: www.dipseal.com
SIC: 2821 3443 2891 2851 Plastics materials & resins; fabricated plate work (boiler shop); adhesives & sealants; paints & allied products

(G-17380)
DISPLAY LINK INC
311 S Main St (61101-1309)
PHONE 815 968-0778
Gary Severson, *CEO*
Fred H Ware, *Ch of Bd*
Jeffrey A Lindquist, *President*
EMP: 3 **EST:** 1949
SQ FT: 16,000

Rockford - Winnebago County (G-17381)

SALES: 221K **Privately Held**
SIC: **3993** 2759 Displays & cutouts, window & lobby; screen printing

(G-17381)
DIVERSIFIED MACHINING INC
6151 Montague Rd (61102-3724)
P.O. Box 250, Sun Prairie WI (53590-0250)
PHONE.....................815 316-8561
EMP: 2
SALES (est): 307.1K **Privately Held**
SIC: **3599** Machine shop, jobbing & repair

(G-17382)
DLM MANUFACTURING INC
919 Taylor St (61101-5859)
PHONE.....................815 964-3800
Duntai Mathews, *President*
EMP: 10
SALES (est): 1.5MM **Privately Held**
SIC: **2431** Millwork

(G-17383)
DMTG NORTH AMERICA LLC
1301 Eddy Ave (61103-3173)
PHONE.....................815 637-8500
Rich Ellison, *Principal*
Mike Throgmartin, *Opers Staff*
Dean Arnold, *Manager*
Jack Holthaus, *Manager*
▲ EMP: 4
SALES (est): 250K **Privately Held**
SIC: **3549** Metalworking machinery

(G-17384)
DOLLAR EXPRESS
4225 Charles St (61108-6230)
PHONE.....................815 399-9719
EMP: 3
SALES (est): 165K **Privately Held**
SIC: **3643** Mfg Conductive Wiring Devices

(G-17385)
DRAWING TECHNOLOGY INC
Also Called: Dti
1550 Elmwood Rd (61103-1217)
PHONE.....................815 877-5133
Charels Schooley, *President*
Mark Hawkinson, *Plant Mgr*
Lyle Strombeck, *Opers Mgr*
Jim Parus, *Purchasing*
Michael Yankaitis, *Admin Sec*
▲ EMP: 8 EST: 1999
SALES (est): 1.8MM **Privately Held**
WEB: www.drawingtechnology.com
SIC: **3549** Wiredrawing & fabricating machinery & equipment, ex. die

(G-17386)
DS SERVICES OF AMERICA INC
Also Called: Hinckley Spring
2425 Laude Dr (61109)
PHONE.....................800 322-6272
Mario Pseifer, *Branch Mgr*
EMP: 15
SALES (corp-wide): 2.3B **Publicly Held**
SIC: **2086** 5963 Mineral water, carbonated: packaged in cans, bottles, etc.; bottled water delivery
HQ: Ds Services Of America, Inc.
2300 Windy Ridge Pkwy Se
Atlanta GA 30339
770 933-1400

(G-17387)
DSPC COMPANY (PA)
3939 S Central Ave (61102-4200)
PHONE.....................815 997-1116
Christopher C De Muth, *Ch of Bd*
John Gazley, *President*
EMP: 20 EST: 1919
SQ FT: 33,000
SALES (est): 3.2MM **Privately Held**
SIC: **3523** 3448 3535 Silo fillers & unloaders; cattle feeding, handling & watering equipment; silos, metal; conveyors & conveying equipment

(G-17388)
ECLIPSE INC (HQ)
1665 Elmwood Rd (61103-1299)
PHONE.....................815 877-3031
David M Cote, *Ch of Bd*
Katherine L Adams, *Senior VP*
Thomas A Szlosek, *CFO*
◆ EMP: 64

SQ FT: 130,000
SALES: 125MM
SALES (corp-wide): 36.7B **Publicly Held**
WEB: www.eclipsenet.com
SIC: **3564** 3433 3822 3823 Blowing fans: industrial or commercial; gas-oil burners, combination; gas burners, industrial; gas burner, automatic controls; flame safety controls for furnaces & boilers; temperature instruments: industrial process type; heat exchangers, condensers & components; valves & pipe fittings
PA: Honeywell International Inc.
300 S Tryon St
Charlotte NC 28202
704 627-6200

(G-17389)
ECLIPSE COMBUSTION INC (DH)
1665 Elmwood Rd (61103-1299)
PHONE.....................815 877-3031
Douglas Perks, *CEO*
Lachlan L Perks, *President*
Chet Allen, *Vice Pres*
Greg Bubp, *Vice Pres*
▲ EMP: 220
SQ FT: 140,000
SALES (est): 93MM
SALES (corp-wide): 36.7B **Publicly Held**
SIC: **3433** Gas burners, industrial; gas-oil burners, combination; oil burners, domestic or industrial
HQ: Eclipse, Inc.
1665 Elmwood Rd
Rockford IL 61103
815 877-3031

(G-17390)
EDGEBROOK EYECARE
1603 N Alpine Rd Ste 121 (61107-1439)
PHONE.....................815 397-5959
David Nielsen, *Owner*
EMP: 10
SALES (est): 864.1K **Privately Held**
SIC: **5995** 3851 Eyeglasses, prescription; lens grinding, except prescription: ophthalmic

(G-17391)
EGD MANUFACTURING INC
2320 Kishwaukee St (61104-7006)
PHONE.....................815 964-2900
Henry Skrzypczak, *President*
Cecilia Skrzypczak, *Vice Pres*
EMP: 8
SQ FT: 2,200
SALES (est): 1.5MM **Privately Held**
WEB: www.egdmfg.com
SIC: **3569** Industrial shock absorbers

(G-17392)
EKSTROM CARLSON FABG CO INC
Also Called: Eccofab
1204 Milford Ave (61109-3692)
PHONE.....................815 226-1511
Gerald Bauer, *President*
▲ EMP: 5 EST: 1959
SQ FT: 10,000
SALES (est): 1.1MM **Privately Held**
WEB: www.eccofab.com
SIC: **7692** 3441 3444 3443 Welding repair; fabricated structural metal; sheet metalwork; fabricated plate work (boiler shop)

(G-17393)
ELAN EXPRESS INC
3815 N Mulford Rd Ste 4 (61114-5622)
PHONE.....................815 713-1190
Gregory Denning, *President*
EMP: 30 EST: 2011
SQ FT: 100
SALES (est): 2.2MM **Privately Held**
SIC: **3721** Aircraft

(G-17394)
ELECTION SYSTEMS & SFTWR LLC
Also Called: Election Services Division
929 S Alpine Rd Ste 301 (61108-3939)
PHONE.....................815 397-8144
Gary Webber, *Manager*
Eric Wall, *Director*

EMP: 16
SQ FT: 5,500
SALES (corp-wide): 115.5MM **Privately Held**
SIC: **3577** Computer peripheral equipment
PA: Election Systems & Software Llc
11208 John Galt Blvd
Omaha NE 68137
402 593-0101

(G-17395)
ELITE FASTENERS INC
2005 15th St (61104-5552)
PHONE.....................815 397-8848
John Lane, *President*
Mike Lane, *Vice Pres*
▲ EMP: 35
SQ FT: 20,000
SALES (est): 6.4MM **Privately Held**
SIC: **3452** Bolts, metal

(G-17396)
ENCHANTED SIGNS OF ROCKFORD
4626 Shropshire Dr (61109-3224)
PHONE.....................815 874-5100
Ragina Tomzak, *Owner*
Curtis Tomzak, *Co-Owner*
EMP: 4
SALES (est): 154K **Privately Held**
SIC: **3993** Signs & advertising specialties

(G-17397)
ENGINE SOLUTIONS INC
1928 12th St (61104-7308)
P.O. Box 1773, Belvidere (61008-1242)
PHONE.....................815 979-2312
Greg Tucker, *President*
▲ EMP: 1
SALES (est): 228.4K **Privately Held**
SIC: **3714** Motor vehicle engines & parts

(G-17398)
EQUILIBRIUM CONTACT CENTER INC
1410 Auburn St (61103-4679)
PHONE.....................888 708-1405
David Levi, *President*
EMP: 3
SQ FT: 1,500
SALES (est): 86K **Privately Held**
SIC: **7372** Business oriented computer software

(G-17399)
EQUITY CONCEPTS CO INC (PA)
5758 Elaine Dr (61108-3102)
PHONE.....................815 226-1300
EMP: 3
SQ FT: 1,550
SALES (est): 626.7K **Privately Held**
SIC: **6531** 6211 7372 7349 Real Estate Broker & Manager & Building Maintenance

(G-17400)
ERICKSON TOOL & MACHINE CO
1903 20th Ave (61104-7319)
PHONE.....................815 397-2653
Chris Erickson, *President*
EMP: 5 EST: 1953
SQ FT: 6,000
SALES (est): 788.4K **Privately Held**
WEB: www.ericksontool.com
SIC: **3599** 3544 3469 Machine shop, jobbing & repair; special dies, tools, jigs & fixtures; metal stampings

(G-17401)
ESSENTIAL LASER AND SKIN INST
534 Roxbury Rd (61107-5076)
PHONE.....................815 381-7005
Dr Lydia Savic, *Mng Member*
Stephanie Salcido, *Manager*
EMP: 2
SALES (est): 220.2K **Privately Held**
SIC: **2844** Cosmetic preparations

(G-17402)
ESTWING MANUFACTURING CO INC
2647 8th St (61109-1190)
PHONE.....................815 397-9521

Robert H Youngren, *President*
Steve Flosi, *Vice Pres*
John Ryan, *Vice Pres*
Mark Youngren, *Vice Pres*
Loyce Young, *Plant Supt*
◆ EMP: 500 EST: 1923
SQ FT: 110,200
SALES (est): 123.1MM **Privately Held**
WEB: www.estwing.com
SIC: **3423** 3546 3545 3429 Hammers (hand tools); axes & hatchets; garden & farm tools, including shovels; power-driven handtools; machine tool accessories; manufactured hardware (general); cutlery; saw blades & handsaws

(G-17403)
EVER READY PIN & MANUFACTURING
5560 International Dr (61109-2784)
PHONE.....................815 874-4949
Norma Whotton, *Corp Secy*
Steve Liphart, *Admin Sec*
EMP: 80
SQ FT: 40,000
SALES (est): 12.3MM **Privately Held**
WEB: www.everreadypin.com
SIC: **3544** 7389 Punches, forming & stamping; grinding, precision: commercial or industrial

(G-17404)
EVOQUA WATER TECHNOLOGIES LLC
4669 Shepherd Trl (61103-1294)
PHONE.....................815 921-8325
Gary Cappeline, *Principal*
Danny Mann, *Plant Mgr*
EMP: 24
SALES (corp-wide): 1.4B **Publicly Held**
SIC: **3589** Water treatment equipment, industrial
HQ: Evoqua Water Technologies Llc
210 6th Ave Ste 3300
Pittsburgh PA 15222
724 772-0044

(G-17405)
EWIKON MOLDING TECH INC
Also Called: Emt
5652 International Dr (61109-2778)
PHONE.....................815 874-7270
David Boxall, *President*
Catherine Boxall, *Admin Sec*
▲ EMP: 5
SALES (est): 1MM **Privately Held**
SIC: **3829** 3544 3559 Thermometers & temperature sensors; industrial molds; plastics working machinery

(G-17406)
EXACT MACHINE COMPANY INC
2502 Preston St (61102-1898)
PHONE.....................815 963-7905
Patricia Barnett, *President*
Michael Ferguson, *Vice Pres*
EMP: 4
SQ FT: 20,000
SALES: 1MM **Privately Held**
WEB: www.exactmachineco.com
SIC: **3599** Machine shop, jobbing & repair

(G-17407)
EXCELSIOR INC
4982 27th Ave (61109-1709)
PHONE.....................815 987-2900
Mike Abrahams, *President*
EMP: 25 EST: 1916
SALES (est): 4.2MM **Privately Held**
WEB: www.excelsiorinc.com
SIC: **3069** 3053 3086 3061 Washers, rubber; gaskets, all materials; packing, leather; packing, metallic; plastics foam products; mechanical rubber goods; synthetic rubber; plastics materials & resins

(G-17408)
EXCELSIOR INC
4982 27th Ave (61109-1709)
PHONE.....................815 987-2900
EMP: 3
SALES (est): 167.8K **Privately Held**
SIC: **3053** Mfg Gaskets/Packing/Sealing Devices

GEOGRAPHIC SECTION

Rockford - Winnebago County (G-17435)

(G-17409)
EXCLUSIVE PRO SPORTS LTD
5035 28th Ave (61109-1718)
PHONE.................. 815 877-8585
Terry D Taylor, *President*
Courtland Taylor, *Manager*
Lynette Taylor, *Executive*
EMP: 30
SQ FT: 5,200
SALES (est): 1.8MM **Privately Held**
SIC: 2339 2329 Uniforms, athletic: women's, misses' & juniors'; men's & boys' athletic uniforms

(G-17410)
EXPRESS CUTTING TOOLS INC
5026 27th Ave (61109-1711)
PHONE.................. 815 964-0410
Kate Buckner, *President*
Bruce Buckner, *Vice Pres*
▲ **EMP:** 6
SALES: 400K **Privately Held**
SIC: 3541 Machine tools, metal cutting type

(G-17411)
F AND F SCREW PRODUCTS
2136 12th St (61104-7365)
PHONE.................. 815 968-7330
Francisco Rosales, *Owner*
EMP: 3
SALES (est): 298K **Privately Held**
SIC: 3451 Screw machine products

(G-17412)
FEDEX OFFICE & PRINT SVCS INC
6234 Mulford Village Dr (61107-6615)
PHONE.................. 815 229-0033
EMP: 15
SALES (corp-wide): 69.6B **Publicly Held**
WEB: www.fedex.com
SIC: 7334 2791 2789 Photocopying & duplicating services; typesetting; bookbinding & related work
HQ: Fedex Office And Print Services, Inc.
   7900 Legacy Dr
   Plano TX 75024
   800 463-3339

(G-17413)
FIBERGLASS INNOVATIONS LLC
2219 Kishwaukee St (61104-7008)
PHONE.................. 815 962-9378
Al Smith, *Plant Mgr*
Donald D Dray,
Richard Provi,
Robert B Reitsch,
EMP: 10
SQ FT: 44,000
SALES (est): 4.3MM **Privately Held**
SIC: 3089 Plastic hardware & building products

(G-17414)
FIBERGLASS INNOVATIONS LLC
340 Blackhawk Park Ave (61104-5133)
PHONE.................. 815 962-3727
EMP: 3
SALES (est): 193.8K **Privately Held**
SIC: 3089 Plastics products

(G-17415)
FIBRO INC (DH)
Also Called: Fibromanta
139 Harrison Ave (61104-7044)
P.O. Box 5924 (61125-0924)
PHONE.................. 815 229-1300
Jurgen Gurt Postfach, *President*
H Schoenau, *President*
Wilfried Dehne, *Vice Pres*
Joe Ullrich, *Controller*
Mike Stewart, *Sales Staff*
▲ **EMP:** 12
SQ FT: 30,000
SALES: 12.4MM
SALES (corp-wide): 596.3MM **Privately Held**
SIC: 3532 5084 5013 Loading machines, underground; mobile; machine tools & accessories; materials handling machinery; tools & equipment, automotive
HQ: F I B R O GmbH
   Weidachstr. 41-43
   Weinsberg 74189
   713 473-0

(G-17416)
FLOW-EZE COMPANY
Also Called: McCarren Group, The
3209 Auburn St (61101-3399)
PHONE.................. 815 965-1062
Patrick D Mc Carren, *President*
Shaun Patrick Carren, *Admin Sec*
▲ **EMP:** 18 **EST:** 1947
SQ FT: 43,000
SALES (est): 2.9MM **Privately Held**
WEB: www.brewerybottles.com
SIC: 3993 5199 3089 5162 Advertising novelties; advertising specialties; plastic containers, except foam; closures, plastic; plastics products; commercial printing, offset; screen printing

(G-17417)
FOLKERTS MANUFACTURING INC
2229 23rd Ave (61104-7334)
PHONE.................. 815 968-7426
Ron Folkerts Jr, *President*
EMP: 7
SQ FT: 10,000
SALES (est): 1.1MM **Privately Held**
SIC: 3599 3452 3541 Machine shop, jobbing & repair; nuts, metal; screw & thread machines

(G-17418)
FOREST CITY AUTO ELECTRIC CO
Also Called: Western Motor Service Div
1255 23rd Ave (61104-7160)
PHONE.................. 815 963-4350
Richard Nicholls, *President*
Dave Venable, *Vice Pres*
▲ **EMP:** 14
SQ FT: 10,000
SALES: 2.4MM **Privately Held**
SIC: 3621 Motors, electric

(G-17419)
FOREST CITY GRINDING INC
Also Called: Nobleson and Associates
4844 Stenstrom Rd (61109-2628)
PHONE.................. 815 874-2424
Noble D Shepherd, *President*
David P Johnson, *Corp Secy*
EMP: 3
SQ FT: 9,000
SALES (est): 468K **Privately Held**
SIC: 3599 Machine shop, jobbing & repair

(G-17420)
FOREST CITY TECHNOLOGIES INC
892 Southrock Dr (61102-4298)
PHONE.................. 815 965-5880
John Cloud, *President*
EMP: 20
SALES (corp-wide): 291.7MM **Privately Held**
SIC: 3965 Fasteners
PA: Forest City Technologies, Inc.
   299 Clay St
   Wellington OH 44090
   440 647-2115

(G-17421)
FORGINGS & STAMPINGS INC (PA)
1025 23rd Ave (61104-7148)
PHONE.................. 815 962-5597
David Johnson, *President*
Pete Sireci, *Plant Mgr*
Daren Poppen, *Materials Mgr*
George Bohn, *Foreman/Supr*
Diann Johnson, *Treasurer*
EMP: 24
SQ FT: 7,620
SALES (est): 6.7MM **Privately Held**
WEB: www.forgingsandstampings.com
SIC: 3462 Iron & steel forgings

(G-17422)
FOUR-MOST INC
Also Called: Foremost Industrial Tech
1550 Elmwood Rd (61103-1217)
PHONE.................. 815 282-9788
Jeff Bonson, *Manager*
EMP: 7
SALES (corp-wide): 959.6K **Privately Held**
WEB: www.foremost-fit.com
SIC: 3625 Motor controls, electric
PA: Four-Most, Inc.
   6518 W Plank Rd
   Peoria IL 61604
   563 323-3233

(G-17423)
FRAZIER MANAGEMENT LLC
1635 New Milford Schl Rd (61109-4335)
PHONE.................. 815 484-8900
Tim Roberts, *Vice Pres*
Tris Evans, *Vice Pres*
Justin Schroeder, *Vice Pres*
EMP: 4 **Privately Held**
SIC: 2834 Pharmaceutical preparations
PA: Frazier Management, L.L.C.
   601 Union St Ste 3200
   Seattle WA 98101

(G-17424)
FRED KENNERLY
Also Called: Starline Communications
1619 Arden Ave (61107-2027)
PHONE.................. 815 398-6861
Fred Kennerly, *Owner*
EMP: 3
SALES (est): 241.5K **Privately Held**
SIC: 3663 4841 5999 Cable television equipment; cable television services; audio-visual equipment & supplies

(G-17425)
FREEWAY-ROCKFORD INC
4701 Boeing Dr (61109-2995)
PHONE.................. 815 397-6425
Raymond Scherler, *Ch of Bd*
Robb Scherler, *President*
Scott Sommers, *Vice Pres*
Michael Rosegger, *VP Finance*
EMP: 32
SQ FT: 23,000
SALES (est): 6.7MM
SALES (corp-wide): 50.9MM **Privately Held**
WEB: www.freewaycorp.com
SIC: 3452 Washers, metal
PA: Freeway Corporation
   9301 Allen Dr
   Cleveland OH 44125
   216 524-9700

(G-17426)
FUTURE TOOL INC
2029 23rd Ave (61104-7330)
PHONE.................. 815 395-0012
Michael R Bloom, *President*
Raymond Hodyniak Jr, *Vice Pres*
Judy Shervon, *Office Mgr*
EMP: 10
SQ FT: 8,000
SALES (est): 1.7MM **Privately Held**
SIC: 3599 3544 Machine shop, jobbing & repair; special dies, tools, jigs & fixtures

(G-17427)
GALACTIC TOOL CO
1402 18th Ave (61104-5437)
P.O. Box 3396 (61106-3396)
PHONE.................. 815 962-3420
Pat Healy, *Owner*
EMP: 6 **EST:** 1979
SQ FT: 12,000
SALES (est): 685.2K **Privately Held**
SIC: 3599 Machine shop, jobbing & repair

(G-17428)
GENERAL FORGING DIE CO INC
4635 Hydraulic Rd (61109-2615)
PHONE.................. 815 874-4224
Ralph A Morgan, *CEO*
EMP: 24 **EST:** 1966
SQ FT: 13,700
SALES (est): 4MM **Privately Held**
WEB: www.generalforgingdie.com
SIC: 3544 3462 Special dies & tools; iron & steel forgings

(G-17429)
GLOBAL DISPLAY SOLUTIONS INC
5217 28th Ave (61109-1722)
PHONE.................. 815 282-2328
Giovanni Cariolato, *President*
Thomas Lentz, *Chairman*
▲ **EMP:** 28
SALES: 26.3MM
SALES (corp-wide): 28.1K **Privately Held**
SIC: 3679 Liquid crystal displays (LCD)
HQ: Global Display Solutions Spa
   Via Tezze 20/A
   Cornedo Vicentino VI 36073

(G-17430)
GOELLNER INC (PA)
Also Called: Advanced Machine and Engrg
2500 Latham St (61103-3963)
PHONE.................. 815 962-6076
Willy Goellner, *CEO*
Dietmiar Goellner, *President*
David Leezer, *CFO*
Holly Hilby, *Manager*
Marika Mertz, *Admin Sec*
EMP: 224
SALES (est): 111.7MM **Privately Held**
SIC: 3599 Machine shop, jobbing & repair

(G-17431)
GOLFERS FAMILY CORPORATION
Also Called: Gfi Metal Treating
1531 Preston St (61102-2047)
PHONE.................. 815 968-0094
Richard G Francis, *President*
Denise J Francis, *Admin Sec*
EMP: 23
SALES (est): 5.5MM **Privately Held**
SIC: 3398 Metal heat treating

(G-17432)
GOODRICH CORPORATION
Also Called: UTC Aerospace Systems
4747 Harrison Ave (61108-7929)
PHONE.................. 815 226-6000
Juan D Celis, *Production*
Bruce Dunnett, *Sales Staff*
Ramses Jimenez, *Manager*
Alan R Smith, *Supervisor*
Susie Neal, *Director*
EMP: 63
SALES (corp-wide): 77B **Publicly Held**
SIC: 3823 Industrial instrmnts msrmnt display/control process variable
HQ: Goodrich Corporation
   2730 W Tyvola Rd
   Charlotte NC 28217
   704 423-7000

(G-17433)
GOODRICH CORPORATION
2421 11th St (61104-7217)
PHONE.................. 815 226-5915
Wayne Perrett, *Branch Mgr*
EMP: 11
SALES (corp-wide): 77B **Publicly Held**
SIC: 3728 Aircraft parts & equipment
HQ: Goodrich Corporation
   2730 W Tyvola Rd
   Charlotte NC 28217
   704 423-7000

(G-17434)
GRAFCOR PACKAGING INC (PA)
121 Loomis St (61101-1408)
PHONE.................. 815 963-1300
William E Hall, *President*
Thomas Wieland, *CFO*
Robert E Hall, *Shareholder*
EMP: 17
SQ FT: 60,000
SALES (est): 5.9MM **Privately Held**
SIC: 2631 3086 Container, packaging & boxboard; corrugating medium; folding boxboard; setup boxboard; packaging & shipping materials, foamed plastic

(G-17435)
GREENLEE TOOLS INC (HQ)
4455 Boeing Dr (61109-2932)
PHONE.................. 800 435-0786
Paul McAndrew, *Principal*
Mark Barmettler, *Vice Pres*

Rockford - Winnebago County (G-17436)

Joe Mallak, *Vice Pres*
Bill Shulha, *Vice Pres*
Alexandra Harris, *Production*
◆ **EMP:** 161
SQ FT: 60,000
SALES (est): 180.8MM
SALES (corp-wide): 18.3B **Publicly Held**
WEB: www.greenlee.textron.com
SIC: 3549 3541 3546 Metalworking machinery; machine tools, metal cutting type; power-driven handtools
PA: Emerson Electric Co.
 8000 West Florissant Ave
 Saint Louis MO 63136
 314 553-2000

(G-17436)
GUNITE CORPORATION (DH)
302 Peoples Ave (61104-7092)
PHONE 815 490-6260
James Cirar, *CEO*
Richard Dauch, *President*
Omar Fakhoury, *Vice Pres*
Jeff Elmer, *CFO*
Thomas Splinter, *VP Sales*
▲ **EMP:** 259
SQ FT: 619,113
SALES (est): 309.1MM
SALES (corp-wide): 685.5MM **Privately Held**
SIC: 3714 Motor vehicle brake systems & parts; brake drums, motor vehicle; wheels, motor vehicle
HQ: Truck Components, Inc.
 8819 N Brooks St
 Tampa FL 33604
 813 933-1166

(G-17437)
GUNITE CORPORATION
Also Called: Transportation Tech Industires
302 Peoples Ave (61104-7092)
PHONE 815 964-3301
James Cirar, *President*
EMP: 410
SALES (corp-wide): 685.5MM **Privately Held**
SIC: 3714 Motor vehicle parts & accessories
HQ: Gunite Corporation
 302 Peoples Ave
 Rockford IL 61104
 815 490-6260

(G-17438)
H&Z FUEL & FOOD INC
3420 E State St (61108-1808)
PHONE 815 399-9108
Aviz Choudry, *Regional Mgr*
EMP: 5 **EST:** 2007
SALES (est): 596.6K **Privately Held**
SIC: 2869 Fuels

(G-17439)
HAMILTON SNDSTRAND SPACE SYSTE (HQ)
4747 Harrison Ave (61108-7929)
PHONE 815 226-6000
EMP: 9
SALES (est): 573.4K
SALES (corp-wide): 77B **Publicly Held**
SIC: 3728 Aircraft parts & equipment
PA: Raytheon Technologies Corporation
 870 Winter St
 Waltham MA 02451
 781 522-3000

(G-17440)
HAMILTON SUNDSTRAND CORP
Also Called: United Tech Arospc Systems
2421 11th St (61104-7217)
P.O. Box 7002 (61125-7002)
PHONE 815 226-6000
Kaia Gottschalk, *Purchasing*
EMP: 16
SALES (corp-wide): 77B **Publicly Held**
WEB: www.utcaerospacesystems.com
SIC: 3625 3621 Actuators, industrial; frequency converters (electric generators)
HQ: Hamilton Sundstrand Corporation
 1 Hamilton Rd
 Windsor Locks CT 06096
 860 654-6000

(G-17441)
HAMILTON SUNDSTRAND CORP
Also Called: UTC Aerospace Systems
4747 Harrison Ave (61108-7900)
PHONE 815 226-6000
Charlie Antaya, *Facilities Mgr*
Alan Ackerman, *Engineer*
Christopher Batchelor, *Engineer*
Dave Frasure, *Engineer*
Michael Futrell, *Engineer*
EMP: 2300
SALES (corp-wide): 77B **Publicly Held**
SIC: 3728 7389 Aircraft assemblies, subassemblies & parts; telephone answering service
HQ: Hamilton Sundstrand Corporation
 1 Hamilton Rd
 Windsor Locks CT 06096
 860 654-6000

(G-17442)
HANSON AGGREGATES EAST LLC
5011 E State St (61108-2310)
PHONE 815 398-2300
Casey Singles, *Branch Mgr*
EMP: 30
SALES (corp-wide): 20.8B **Privately Held**
SIC: 3272 Concrete products
HQ: Hanson Aggregates East Llc
 3131 Rdu Center Dr
 Morrisville NC 27560
 919 380-2500

(G-17443)
HARDER SIGNS INC
4695 Stenstrom Rd (61109-2637)
PHONE 815 874-7777
John Harder, *President*
Donna D Harder, *Vice Pres*
EMP: 12 **EST:** 1900
SQ FT: 6,800
SALES (est): 1.3MM **Privately Held**
SIC: 3993 7389 2542 Neon signs; signs, not made in custom sign painting shops; displays & cutouts, window & lobby; sign painting & lettering shop; partitions & fixtures, except wood

(G-17444)
HD ELECTRIC COMPANY
4455 Boeing Dr (61109-2932)
PHONE 847 473-4980
◆ **EMP:** 29 **EST:** 1933
SALES (est): 6.5MM
SALES (corp-wide): 18.3B **Publicly Held**
WEB: www.hdelectriccompany.com
SIC: 3825 Meters: electric, pocket, portable, panelboard, etc.; test equipment for electronic & electrical circuits
HQ: Greenlee Tools, Inc.
 4455 Boeing Dr
 Rockford IL 61109
 800 435-0786

(G-17445)
HEADER DIE AND TOOL INC
3022 Eastrock Ct (61109-1760)
P.O. Box 5846 (61125-0846)
PHONE 815 397-0123
Lucas Derry, *President*
Richard Bried, *Vice Pres*
EMP: 60 **EST:** 1954
SQ FT: 23,650
SALES (est): 11.1MM **Privately Held**
WEB: www.header.com
SIC: 3544 Special dies & tools

(G-17446)
HEALING SCENTS
1986 Will James Rd (61109-4851)
PHONE 815 874-0924
Kathleen Hembree, *Principal*
EMP: 3
SALES (est): 264.5K **Privately Held**
SIC: 2844 Toilet preparations

(G-17447)
HEIMAN SIGN STUDIO
6909 Canter Ct (61108-4303)
PHONE 815 397-6909
Jon W Heiman, *Owner*
EMP: 3
SALES (est): 146.3K **Privately Held**
SIC: 3993 2399 Signs, not made in custom sign painting shops; fabricated textile products

(G-17448)
HERITAGE MOLD INCORPORATED
3170 Forest View Rd (61109-1642)
PHONE 815 397-1117
Bennett Franzen, *President*
Jaci Franzen, *Treasurer*
EMP: 15
SQ FT: 6,400
SALES (est): 3MM **Privately Held**
SIC: 3544 Industrial molds

(G-17449)
HG-FARLEY HOLDINGS LLC (PA)
6833 Stalter Dr (61108-2579)
PHONE 815 874-1400
John Johnson,
EMP: 10
SALES (est): 717.5K **Privately Held**
SIC: 3545 5082 Machine tool accessories; construction & mining machinery

(G-17450)
HG-FARLEY LASERLAB USA INC
4635 Colt Rd (61109-2609)
PHONE 815 874-1400
John Johnson, *President*
Jody Hickey, *Corp Secy*
▲ **EMP:** 9
SALES (est): 2.1MM **Privately Held**
SIC: 3545 5082 Machine tool accessories; construction & mining machinery
PA: Hg-Farley Holdings, L.L.C.
 6833 Stalter Dr
 Rockford IL 61108

(G-17451)
HOHLFLDER A H SHTMTL HTG COOLG
Also Called: AG Hohlfelder Sheet Metal
2911 Prairie Rd (61102-3960)
PHONE 815 965-9134
Theresa Hohlfelder, *President*
EMP: 4
SALES (est): 200K **Privately Held**
WEB: www.aghohlfelder.com
SIC: 1711 1761 3585 3444 Warm air heating & air conditioning contractor; ventilation & duct work contractor; sheet metalwork; refrigeration & heating equipment; sheet metalwork

(G-17452)
HOME FIRES INC
Also Called: Saffire Grill Co.
1102 10th St (61104-5007)
PHONE 815 967-4100
Stephen Benson, *President*
Jaron Benson, *Admin Sec*
◆ **EMP:** 3 **EST:** 2005
SALES (est): 2.1MM **Privately Held**
SIC: 3556 Smokers, food processing equipment

(G-17453)
HOT SHOTS NM LLC
Also Called: Pharmacy Services of Rockford
4330 Charles St (61108-6249)
PHONE 815 484-0500
Don Kapolnek, *Branch Mgr*
EMP: 8 **Privately Held**
SIC: 2834 Pharmaceutical preparations
PA: Hot Shots Nm, Llc
 2017 E Kimberly Rd
 Davenport IA 52807

(G-17454)
HURST CHEMICAL COMPANY
2020 Cunningham Rd (61102-2653)
PHONE 815 964-0451
Linda Rager, *Manager*
EMP: 4
SQ FT: 7,200
SALES (corp-wide): 4.1MM **Privately Held**
SIC: 2869 4226 5169 2893 Industrial organic chemicals; special warehousing & storage; chemicals & allied products; printing ink; specialty cleaning, polishes & sanitation goods; platemaking services
PA: Hurst Chemical Company
 167 Lambert St Ste 123
 Oxnard CA 93036
 800 723-2004

(G-17455)
IBANUM MANUFACTURING LLC
5963 Cambridge Chase (61107-2500)
PHONE 815 262-5373
Barlow Michael, *Mng Member*
Barlow Michael A, *Mng Member*
EMP: 1
SALES (est): 486K **Privately Held**
SIC: 3721 3541 3728 Aircraft; machine tools, metal cutting type; aircraft parts & equipment

(G-17456)
IDEAL ADVERTISING & PRINTING (PA)
Also Called: Vanco Printers Division
116 N Winnebago St (61101-1026)
PHONE 815 965-1713
John G Schmit, *Owner*
Charles Fricke, *Executive*
EMP: 10
SQ FT: 6,000
SALES (est): 7.8MM **Privately Held**
SIC: 2752 2759 7311 2791 Commercial printing, offset; letterpress printing; advertising agencies; typesetting; bookbinding & related work

(G-17457)
IMPERIAL PUNCH & MANUFACTURING
2016 23rd Ave (61104-7372)
PHONE 815 226-8200
Bruce A Keirn, *President*
Rosalynn M Keirn, *Vice Pres*
Rosalynn Keirn, *VP Finance*
EMP: 18
SQ FT: 9,000
SALES (est): 1.8MM **Privately Held**
SIC: 3544 3366 Special dies & tools; copper foundries

(G-17458)
INDUSTRIAL ELECTRONIC CONTRLS
Also Called: I E C
4689 Stenstrom Rd (61109-2637)
PHONE 815 873-1980
J Joseph Benjamin, *President*
EMP: 15
SQ FT: 6,000
SALES (est): 5.3MM **Privately Held**
SIC: 5065 3678 Electronic parts; electronic connectors

(G-17459)
INDUSTRIAL MOLDS INC (PA)
Also Called: True-Cut Wire EDM Div
5175 27th Ave (61109-1783)
PHONE 815 397-2971
Jack D Peterson, *President*
Eric Peterson, *Prdtn Mgr*
Andrew Peterson, *Production*
Randy Hanson, *Engineer*
Justin Carlson, *Design Engr*
▲ **EMP:** 60 **EST:** 1973
SQ FT: 44,000
SALES (est): 18.6MM **Privately Held**
WEB: www.industrialmolds.com
SIC: 3544 Forms (molds), for foundry & plastics working machinery

(G-17460)
INGENIUM AEROSPACE LLC
5389 International Dr (61109-2775)
PHONE 815 525-2000
Darrin Kopala,
Stephen Carter,
EMP: 22
SALES (est): 2.7MM **Privately Held**
SIC: 3728 Aircraft parts & equipment

GEOGRAPHIC SECTION

Rockford - Winnebago County (G-17485)

(G-17461)
INGERSOLL CUTTING TOOL COMPANY (HQ)
845 S Lyford Rd (61108-2749)
PHONE................815 387-6600
Charles Elder, *President*
Kevin Connelly, *Engineer*
James Deshazier, *Engineer*
James Plummer, *Engineer*
Kendall Smith, *Engineer*
▲ **EMP:** 320
SQ FT: 235,000
SALES (est): 74.4MM
SALES (corp-wide): 78.8MM **Privately Held**
SIC: 3545 Machine tool accessories
PA: Imc Group Usa Holdings Inc
 300 Westway Pl
 Arlington TX 76018
 817 258-3200

(G-17462)
INGERSOLL MACHINE TOOLS INC (DH)
707 Fulton Ave (61103-4069)
PHONE................815 987-6000
Tino Oldani, *President*
Paul Pipitone, *Purch Mgr*
Klaus Hoffmann, *Chief Engr*
John Dreher, *Engineer*
Nathan Haug, *Engineer*
◆ **EMP:** 220
SALES: 50.6MM
SALES (corp-wide): 177.9K **Privately Held**
SIC: 3541 3545 Machine tools, metal cutting type; machine tool accessories
HQ: Camozzi Automation Spa
 Via Eritrea 20/I
 Brescia BS 25126
 030 379-21

(G-17463)
INGERSOLL PROD SYSTEMS LLC (DH)
Also Called: I P S
1301 Eddy Ave (61103-3173)
PHONE................815 637-8500
Richard E Ellison,
Richard Ellison,
Chen Yong Long,
Jim Wang,
Chen Yonkai,
▲ **EMP:** 75
SQ FT: 100,000
SALES (est): 16.2MM
SALES (corp-wide): 66MM **Privately Held**
SIC: 3541 Machine tools, metal cutting type

(G-17464)
INNOVATECH IT SVC SOLUTIONS (PA)
730 N Church St Ste 201 (61103-6917)
PHONE................815 484-9940
EMP: 3 **EST:** 2018
SALES (est): 1MM **Privately Held**
WEB: www.innovatechweb.com
SIC: 3861 Photographic equipment & supplies

(G-17465)
INNOVATIVE FIX SOLUTIONS LLC
1122 Milford Ave (61109-3636)
PHONE................815 395-8500
EMP: 10 **EST:** 2014
SQ FT: 212,805
SALES (est): 590K **Privately Held**
SIC: 3496 Mfg Misc Fabricated Wire Products

(G-17466)
INNOVATIVE FIX SOLUTIONS LLC
1122 Milford Ave (61109-3636)
P.O. Box 1950, Catoosa OK (74015-1950)
PHONE................815 395-8500
Shaun Starbuck, *CEO*
Sherrie Bretl, *Controller*
EMP: 100
SALES (est): 26.4MM **Privately Held**
SIC: 2511 Magazine racks: wood

(G-17467)
INTEGRATED LABEL CORPORATION
3407 Pyramid Dr (61109-2737)
PHONE................815 874-2500
Marty Chowanski, *CEO*
Barret Ewing, *President*
Martin Chowanski, *Marketing Staff*
▲ **EMP:** 10
SQ FT: 10,000
SALES (est): 2.5MM **Privately Held**
SIC: 2679 Cardboard products, except diecut; labels, paper: made from purchased material

(G-17468)
INTER-STATE STUDIO & PUBG CO
3446 Colony Bay Dr (61109-2560)
PHONE................815 874-0342
Matt Waldschmidt, *Branch Mgr*
EMP: 39
SALES (corp-wide): 44.3MM **Privately Held**
SIC: 2741 Miscellaneous publishing
PA: Inter-State Studio & Publishing Co.
 3500 Snyder Ave
 Sedalia MO 65301
 660 826-1764

(G-17469)
INTERNATIONAL PAPER COMPANY
2100 23rd Ave (61104-7333)
P.O. Box 6227 (61125-1227)
PHONE................815 398-2100
Michelle Ponkratz, *Opers Mgr*
Michelle Ponkratz-Goncal, *Opers Staff*
John Liermann, *Manager*
Kevin Hainchek, *Manager*
Keith Palmer, *Manager*
EMP: 130
SQ FT: 125,000
SALES (corp-wide): 22.3B **Publicly Held**
WEB: www.internationalpaper.com
SIC: 2621 Paper mills
PA: International Paper Company
 6400 Poplar Ave
 Memphis TN 38197
 901 419-9000

(G-17470)
INTERSTATE POWER SYSTEMS INC
3736 11th St (61109-3019)
PHONE................952 854-2044
Gordon Galarneau, *Ch of Bd*
EMP: 99 **EST:** 2015
SQ FT: 50,000
SALES (est): 3.6MM **Privately Held**
SIC: 3714 5084 Motor vehicle parts & accessories; industrial machinery & equipment

(G-17471)
J & M PLATING INC
4500 Kishwaukee St (61109-2924)
PHONE................815 964-4975
Mark Morris, *President*
Rick Morris, *Vice Pres*
Jennifer Klemm, *Human Resources*
David Morris, *Admin Sec*
▲ **EMP:** 135
SQ FT: 185,000
SALES (est): 25.7MM **Privately Held**
SIC: 3471 Electroplating of metals or formed products; finishing, metals or formed products; polishing, metals or formed products

(G-17472)
JAEGER SAW AND CUTTER INC
Also Called: Jaeger Saw & Cutter Works
81005 5th Ave (61104)
PHONE................815 963-0313
Fax: 815 963-0313
EMP: 3
SQ FT: 1,500
SALES (est): 178.8K **Privately Held**
SIC: 7699 3425 Sharpens & Reconditions Saws & Metal Tools

(G-17473)
JERHEN INDUSTRIES INC
5196 27th Ave (61109-1713)
PHONE................815 397-0400
Roger Jerie, *President*
Tom Henderson, *Treasurer*
▲ **EMP:** 60
SALES (est): 10.2MM **Privately Held**
SIC: 3545 3549 Hopper feed devices; assembly machines, including robotic

(G-17474)
JIM STERNER MACHINES
Also Called: Sterner Screw Machine
2500 N Main St Ste 25 (61103-4078)
PHONE................815 962-8983
James Sterner, *Owner*
Laura Mason, *Co-Owner*
EMP: 5
SQ FT: 4,000
SALES (est): 466.4K **Privately Held**
SIC: 3599 3451 Machine shop, jobbing & repair; screw machine products

(G-17475)
JL CLARK LLC
2300 S 6th St (61104-7199)
PHONE................815 961-5677
Ray Rowland, *Chairman*
EMP: 6
SALES (corp-wide): 1.5B **Privately Held**
SIC: 3089 Plastic containers, except foam
HQ: J.L. Clark Llc
 923 23rd Ave
 Rockford IL 61104
 815 961-5609

(G-17476)
JL CLARK LLC (DH)
923 23rd Ave (61104-7173)
PHONE................815 961-5609
Phil Baerenwald, *President*
Philip Baerenwald, *Vice Pres*
Andrew Naclcovic, *Vice Pres*
Jim Fiddler, *Plant Mgr*
Bernie Houston, *Traffic Mgr*
▲ **EMP:** 219
SQ FT: 454,000
SALES (est): 88MM
SALES (corp-wide): 1.5B **Privately Held**
SIC: 3411 3499 2752 3089 Metal cans; magnetic shields, metal; lithographing on metal; plastic containers, except foam
HQ: C C Industries, Inc.
 222 N La Salle St # 1000
 Chicago IL 60601
 312 855-4000

(G-17477)
JOHNSON PUMPS AMERICA INC
5885 11th St (61109-3650)
PHONE................847 671-7867
Marc Michael, *President*
David Kowalski, *President*
Jerry Smeltser, *CFO*
▲ **EMP:** 44
SQ FT: 2,000
SALES (est): 9.9MM
SALES (corp-wide): 1.5B **Publicly Held**
SIC: 5084 3561 Pumps & pumping equipment; industrial pumps & parts; pumps, domestic: water or sump
PA: Spx Flow, Inc.
 13320 Balntyn Corp Pl
 Charlotte NC 28277
 704 752-4400

(G-17478)
K&J FINISHING INC
Also Called: Northern Illinois Metal Finshg
716 Cedar St (61102-2950)
PHONE................815 965-9655
Keith Beach, *President*
Pat Brunner, *Maintence Staff*
EMP: 16
SQ FT: 41,000
SALES (est): 3.2MM **Privately Held**
WEB: www.kjfinishing.com
SIC: 3471 Electroplating of metals or formed products

(G-17479)
KADON PRECISION MACHINING INC
5876 Sandy Hollow Rd (61109-2767)
PHONE................815 874-5850
Jeff Franklin, *President*
Cheryl L Spencer, *Corp Secy*
Cheryl Spencer, *COO*
EMP: 100
SQ FT: 19,000
SALES (est): 28.7MM **Privately Held**
SIC: 3599 Machine shop, jobbing & repair

(G-17480)
KANEY CAPITAL LLC
801 Airport Dr (61109-2945)
PHONE................815 986-4359
EMP: 3
SALES (est): 68.2K
SALES (corp-wide): 864.2K **Privately Held**
SIC: 3812 Mfg Search/Navigation Equipment
PA: Kaney Group, Llc
 1321 Capital Dr
 Rockford IL 61109
 815 986-4359

(G-17481)
KANEY GROUP LLC (PA)
1300 Capital Dr (61109-3076)
PHONE................815 986-4359
Jeffrey J Kaney Sr, *CEO*
Ronald J Soave, *President*
Dawn Johnson, *Human Res Dir*
EMP: 10 **EST:** 2009
SALES (est): 17.3MM **Privately Held**
SIC: 3812 Acceleration indicators & systems components, aerospace

(G-17482)
KENS STREET ROD REPAIR
5521 International Dr (61109-2783)
PHONE................815 874-1811
Ken Barnhart, *Owner*
EMP: 1
SALES: 375K **Privately Held**
SIC: 3711 Automobile assembly, including specialty automobiles

(G-17483)
KENT NUTRITION GROUP INC
1612 S Bend Rd (61109-4834)
PHONE................815 874-2411
Tom Smollen, *Branch Mgr*
EMP: 12
SALES (corp-wide): 459.4MM **Privately Held**
WEB: www.kentfeeds.com
SIC: 2048 Livestock feeds
HQ: Kent Nutrition Group, Inc.
 1600 Oregon St
 Muscatine IA 52761
 866 647-1212

(G-17484)
KLINCK INC
Also Called: Custom Metal Products
1827 Broadway (61104-5409)
PHONE................815 397-3306
Joseph P Klinck, *President*
Marilyn S Klinck, *Treasurer*
EMP: 30
SQ FT: 70,000
SALES (est): 4.8MM **Privately Held**
SIC: 3469 3452 Stamping metal for the trade; screws, metal

(G-17485)
KROGER CO
Also Called: Hilander 00805
2206 Barnes Blvd (61112-2000)
PHONE................815 332-7267
EMP: 116
SALES (corp-wide): 122.2B **Publicly Held**
WEB: www.thekrogerco.com
SIC: 5411 7384 5992 5912 Supermarkets, chain; photofinish laboratories; florists; drug stores & proprietary stores; cookies & crackers; bread, cake & related products
PA: The Kroger Co
 1014 Vine St Ste 1000
 Cincinnati OH 45202
 513 762-4000

Rockford - Winnebago County (G-17486) GEOGRAPHIC SECTION

(G-17486)
KRYDER WOOD PRODUCTS LLC
5150 8th St (61109-3662)
P.O. Box 7595 (61126-7595)
PHONE..................815 494-1208
Jonathan Kryder, *Mng Member*
EMP: 14
SALES (est): 2.3MM **Privately Held**
WEB: www.kryderwoodproducts.com
SIC: 2448 Pallets, wood

(G-17487)
L & T SERVICES INC
1004 Samuelson Rd (61109-3640)
PHONE..................815 397-6260
Toni R Seagren, *President*
EMP: 2
SALES (est): 400K **Privately Held**
SIC: 5013 5531 3647 Truck parts & accessories; automobile & truck equipment & parts; motor vehicle lighting equipment

(G-17488)
L T L CO
4801 American Rd (61109-2643)
PHONE..................815 874-0913
James Landquist, *President*
James F Landquist, *President*
Jeremy Landquist, *Vice Pres*
EMP: 13
SQ FT: 24,000
SALES: 1.5MM **Privately Held**
WEB: www.ltlmachining.com
SIC: 3544 Special dies & tools; jigs: inspection, gauging & checking

(G-17489)
L/J FABRICATORS INC
Also Called: Lj Fabricators
944 Research Pkwy (61109-2942)
PHONE..................815 397-9099
Gregory Johnson, *President*
Christopher Johnson, *Vice Pres*
Chuck Boan, *Prdtn Mgr*
Cesar Meza, *Engineer*
Kent Ogden, *VP Finance*
EMP: 35
SQ FT: 54,000
SALES (est): 10MM **Privately Held**
SIC: 3444 Sheet metal specialties, not stamped

(G-17490)
LAMSON OIL COMPANY (HQ)
2217 20th Ave (61104-7325)
P.O. Box 5303 (61125-0303)
PHONE..................815 226-8090
Raymond La Mantia, *President*
Greg La Mantia, *Vice Pres*
Bradley Lamantia, *Sales Mgr*
Angela Stahl, *Sales Staff*
Barbara La Mantia, *Admin Sec*
EMP: 2
SQ FT: 20,000
SALES: 2MM
SALES (corp-wide): 5.7MM **Privately Held**
SIC: 2911 Oils, lubricating
PA: Lsp Industries, Inc.
5060 27th Ave
Rockford IL 61109
815 226-8090

(G-17491)
LARRYS GARAGE & MACHINE SHOP
101 Vista Ter (61102-1775)
PHONE..................815 968-8416
Larry McCammond, *Partner*
Art McCammond, *Partner*
EMP: 3
SQ FT: 5,000
SALES: 35K **Privately Held**
SIC: 7538 7692 Engine rebuilding: automotive; automotive welding

(G-17492)
LEADING EDGE GROUP INC (PA)
Also Called: Leading Edge Hydraulics
1800 16th Ave (61104-5453)
PHONE..................815 316-3500
Russell Dennis, *CEO*
Russell Dennis Jr, *President*
John Dennis, *General Mgr*
Todd Dixon, *Sales Dir*
Hannah Kardell, *Sales Staff*
▲ EMP: 120 EST: 1966
SQ FT: 45,000
SALES (est): 27.2MM **Privately Held**
WEB: www.leadingedgegroupinc.com
SIC: 3599 3498 3594 3547 Machine shop, jobbing & repair; tube fabricating (contract bending & shaping); fluid power pumps & motors; rolling mill machinery; steel pipe & tubes

(G-17493)
LEGACY PLASTICS INC
5040 27th Ave (61109-1711)
PHONE..................815 226-3013
Bennett Franzen, *President*
Steve Dehart, *Mfg Mgr*
EMP: 9
SQ FT: 2,500
SALES (est): 1.4MM **Privately Held**
WEB: www.legacyplastics.net
SIC: 3089 Injection molding of plastics

(G-17494)
LEONARD ASSOCIATES INC
6733 Hedgewood Rd (61108-5633)
PHONE..................815 226-9609
Jayme J Leonard, *Branch Mgr*
EMP: 40
SALES (corp-wide): 11.2MM **Privately Held**
WEB: www.redleonard.com
SIC: 3559 Petroleum refinery equipment
PA: Rla, Inc.
1340 Kemper Meadow Dr
Cincinnati OH 45240
513 574-9500

(G-17495)
LESTER MANUFACTURING INC
2219 N Central Ave (61101-2347)
P.O. Box 1057 (61105-1057)
PHONE..................815 986-1172
Dai Bui, *President*
Sarah Eismueller, *Office Mgr*
EMP: 50
SALES (est): 5.7MM **Privately Held**
SIC: 3599 Machine shop, jobbing & repair

(G-17496)
LETRAW MANUFACTURING LLC
200 Quaker Rd Ste 2 (61104-7068)
PHONE..................815 987-9670
Ralph Wartell,
▲ EMP: 3
SQ FT: 4,000
SALES (est): 250K **Privately Held**
WEB: www.letraw.com
SIC: 3496 Miscellaneous fabricated wire products

(G-17497)
LSP INDUSTRIES INC (PA)
5060 27th Ave (61109-1711)
P.O. Box 5303 (61125-0303)
PHONE..................815 226-8090
Raymond La Mantia, *President*
Leroy Petersen, *Principal*
Brad La Mantia, *Vice Pres*
Greg La Mantia, *Vice Pres*
Mark Wessmann, *Purch Mgr*
EMP: 15
SQ FT: 12,000
SALES (est): 5.7MM **Privately Held**
WEB: www.lspind.com
SIC: 3569 2992 3423 Lubrication equipment, industrial; re-refining lubricating oils & greases; hammers (hand tools)

(G-17498)
LT CONSTRUCTION
1288 Anee Dr (61108-4364)
PHONE..................815 243-6807
Lorraine Weathers, *Owner*
EMP: 3
SALES: 180K **Privately Held**
SIC: 1442 Construction sand & gravel

(G-17499)
LUNQUIST MANUFACTURING CORP
5681 11th St (61109-3654)
PHONE..................815 874-2437
Johatan G Lunquist, *President*
Mark Dixon, *Vice Pres*
EMP: 28 EST: 1959
SQ FT: 20,000
SALES (est): 4.3MM **Privately Held**
WEB: www.lunquist.com
SIC: 3599 Machine shop, jobbing & repair

(G-17500)
M & W GRINDING OF ROCKFORD
4697 Hydraulic Rd (61109-2615)
PHONE..................815 874-9481
Scott R Monge, *President*
Maskey Heath, *Vice Pres*
EMP: 7
SQ FT: 4,800
SALES (est): 590K **Privately Held**
SIC: 3599 Machine shop, jobbing & repair; grinding castings for the trade

(G-17501)
M E F CORP
Also Called: Penguin Foods
1614 Christina St (61104-5137)
PHONE..................815 965-8604
Kathy Ciembronowicz, *President*
John Ciembronowicz, *Vice Pres*
EMP: 18
SQ FT: 4,615
SALES (est): 710K **Privately Held**
WEB: www.penguinfoods.net
SIC: 5812 5421 2013 Fast-food restaurant, chain; meat markets, including freezer provisioners; sausages & other prepared meats

(G-17502)
MACO-SYS LLC
3415 Precision Dr B (61109-2771)
PHONE..................779 888-3260
David Spahr, *Mng Member*
EMP: 14
SALES (est): 1.5MM **Privately Held**
SIC: 3699 Security control equipment & systems

(G-17503)
MAIN SOURCE MACHINING
2411 Latham St (61103-3953)
PHONE..................815 962-8770
Brian Heaslip, *President*
Polly Heaslip, *Vice Pres*
EMP: 4
SALES (est): 330K **Privately Held**
SIC: 3599 Machine shop, jobbing & repair

(G-17504)
MANUFACTURING TECH GROUP INC
3520 N Main St (61103-2116)
P.O. Box 93 (61105-0093)
PHONE..................815 966-2300
James Jackson, *President*
Daniel Rowe, *Engineer*
EMP: 3
SQ FT: 1,500
SALES (est): 240K **Privately Held**
SIC: 7372 7371 Prepackaged software; custom computer programming services

(G-17505)
MARTIN AUTOMATIC INC
1661 Northrock Ct (61103-1296)
PHONE..................815 654-4800
Roger Cederholm, *President*
John R Martin, *Chairman*
Bob Hoffman, *Regional Mgr*
Gavin Rittmeyer, *Regional Mgr*
Brian Sager, *Regional Mgr*
◆ EMP: 180
SQ FT: 165,000
SALES (est): 59.8MM **Privately Held**
SIC: 3565 3625 3823 3555 Packaging machinery; relays & industrial controls; industrial instrmnts msrmnt display/control process variable; presses, gravure

(G-17506)
MARTIN PRECISION INC
3230 Pyramid Dr (61109-2765)
PHONE..................815 873-1000
Jay M Lundberg, *President*
Karyn Lundberg, *Vice Pres*
EMP: 2
SALES (est): 459K **Privately Held**
SIC: 3599 Machine shop, jobbing & repair

(G-17507)
MASTER MACHINE CRAFT INC
6483 Falcon Rd (61109-4365)
PHONE..................815 874-3078
Randy Loomis, *CEO*
EMP: 4
SQ FT: 21,000
SALES (est): 591.6K **Privately Held**
SIC: 3549 Metalworking machinery

(G-17508)
MASTERS PLATING CO INC
2228 20th Ave (61104-7326)
PHONE..................815 226-8846
Larry R Farr, *President*
EMP: 5
SALES (est): 508K **Privately Held**
SIC: 3471 Plating of metals or formed products

(G-17509)
MASTERS YATES INC
Also Called: Masters & Yates Machine
1188 N Crest Dr (61107-6211)
PHONE..................815 227-9585
Dave J Masters, *President*
EMP: 3 EST: 1979
SALES (est): 750K **Privately Held**
SIC: 3451 Screw machine products

(G-17510)
MAXIMUM SEALANTS LLC
3086 Alliance Ave (61101-2302)
PHONE..................815 985-7183
Maximilian N Anderson, *Manager*
EMP: 3
SALES (est): 123.2K **Privately Held**
SIC: 2891 Sealants

(G-17511)
MC CHEMICAL COMPANY (PA)
Also Called: Lincoln State Steel Div
720 South St (61102-2126)
P.O. Box 1926 (61110-0426)
PHONE..................815 964-7687
Kathleen Hurka, *President*
Kathy Hurka, *COO*
Harry N Miller, *Opers Mgr*
Rebecca Dewane, *Finance*
Jim Krogh, *Info Tech Mgr*
EMP: 24 EST: 1969
SQ FT: 40,000
SALES (est): 4.9MM **Privately Held**
SIC: 2899 3312 Chemical preparations; blast furnaces & steel mills

(G-17512)
MDM CONSTRUCTION SUPPLY LLC
815 N Church St Ste 3 (61103-6983)
PHONE..................815 847-7340
Rosario Ocampo - Strategos,
EMP: 8
SALES (est): 719.5K **Privately Held**
SIC: 1389 Construction, repair & dismantling services

(G-17513)
MECHANICAL TOOL & ENGRG CO (PA)
Also Called: Mte Hydraulics
4701 Kishwaukee St (61109-2926)
P.O. Box 5906 (61125-0906)
PHONE..................815 397-4701
Richard D Nordlof, *President*
Gregory S Nordlof, *President*
John Fulton, *Principal*
Greg Nordlof, *Vice Pres*
Rich Thurman, *Vice Pres*
▲ EMP: 160 EST: 1946
SQ FT: 150,000
SALES (est): 69.1MM **Privately Held**
WEB: www.mtehydraulics.com
SIC: 3594 3542 Pumps, hydraulic power transfer; presses: forming, stamping, punching, sizing (machine tools)

(G-17514)
MECHANICAL TOOL & ENGRG CO
Also Called: M T E Hydraulics
4700 Boeing Dr (61109-2904)
P.O. Box 5906 (61125-0906)
PHONE..................815 397-4701
Randy Welch, *Superintendent*

GEOGRAPHIC SECTION

Rockford - Winnebago County (G-17541)

EMP: 200
SALES (corp-wide): 69.1MM **Privately Held**
WEB: www.mtehydraulics.com
SIC: 3594 3599 Pumps, hydraulic power transfer; machine shop, jobbing & repair
PA: Mechanical Tool & Engineering Co Inc
4701 Kishwaukee St
Rockford IL 61109
815 397-4701

(G-17515)
MEGA MANUFACTURING INC
Also Called: Piranha Fabrication
650 Race St (61101-1434)
PHONE.................................620 663-1127
Ronald Werth, *Branch Mgr*
EMP: 3
SALES (corp-wide): 18.4MM **Privately Held**
SIC: 3421 Cutlery
PA: Mega Manufacturing, Inc.
1 N Main St Ste 604
Hutchinson KS 67501
620 663-1127

(G-17516)
MENCARINI ENTERPRISES INC
Also Called: PIP Printing
4911 26th Ave (61109-1637)
P.O. Box 5403 (61125-0403)
PHONE.................................815 398-9565
Fax: 815 398-9568
EMP: 10
SQ FT: 4,000
SALES (est): 1.4MM **Privately Held**
SIC: 2752 2789 2791 Lithographic Commercial Printing Bookbinding/Related Work Typesetting Services

(G-17517)
MERIDIAN HEALTHCARE
1718 Northrock Ct (61103-1201)
PHONE.................................815 633-5326
Sherri Reicher, *Principal*
EMP: 3
SALES (est): 214.9K **Privately Held**
SIC: 2834 Pharmaceutical preparations

(G-17518)
MESSER MACHINE
2327 20th Ave (61104-7327)
PHONE.................................815 398-6248
David R Messer, *President*
EMP: 6
SQ FT: 3,500
SALES (est): 772K **Privately Held**
SIC: 3599 Machine shop, jobbing & repair

(G-17519)
METAL PREP SERVICES INC
5434 International Dr (61109-2776)
PHONE.................................815 874-7631
William R Wessel, *President*
EMP: 4
SQ FT: 5,000
SALES (est): 338.2K **Privately Held**
SIC: 1721 1799 3479 Industrial painting; sandblasting of building exteriors; painting, coating & hot dipping; coating of metals & formed products

(G-17520)
METROLOGY RESOURCE GROUP INC
316 Warren Ave (61107-4746)
P.O. Box 6436 (61125-1436)
PHONE.................................815 703-3141
Patrick Murphy, *President*
Wanda Alberts, *Executive Asst*
EMP: 3
SALES (est): 396.1K **Privately Held**
WEB: www.mrgprobing.com
SIC: 3823 Industrial process measurement equipment

(G-17521)
MICRO PUNCH & DIE CO
5536 International Dr (61109-2784)
P.O. Box 5252 (61125-0252)
PHONE.................................815 874-5544
Nordahl Kirking, *President*
Judith Kirking, *Corp Secy*
EMP: 15 **EST:** 1952
SQ FT: 8,000
SALES (est): 2.2MM **Privately Held**
WEB: www.micropunch.com
SIC: 3544 Dies & die holders for metal cutting, forming, die casting; punches, forming & stamping

(G-17522)
MICRO SCREW MACHINE CO INC
2115 15th St (61104-7310)
PHONE.................................815 397-2115
Ronald L Jacobson, *President*
Barbara L Jacobson, *Admin Sec*
EMP: 5
SQ FT: 3,000
SALES (est): 250K **Privately Held**
WEB: www.microscrewmachine.com
SIC: 3451 Screw machine products

(G-17523)
MICROGRAMS INC
Also Called: Micrograms Software
805 Hemlock Ln (61107-3551)
PHONE.................................815 877-4455
EMP: 5 **EST:** 1981
SALES (est): 356.7K **Privately Held**
SIC: 7372 7371 Prepackaged Software Services Custom Computer Programing

(G-17524)
MID-STATES FORGING DIE-TOOL
2844 Eastrock Dr (61109-1736)
P.O. Box 5025 (61125-0025)
PHONE.................................815 226-2313
Gregory P Heim, *President*
Richard Heim, *COO*
Joyce Young, *Office Mgr*
Virginia D Heim, *Admin Sec*
EMP: 6
SQ FT: 20,800
SALES (est): 87.1K
SALES (corp-wide): 8.8MM **Privately Held**
SIC: 3544 Special dies & tools
PA: Modern Drop Forge Company, Llc
8757 Colorado St
Merrillville IN 46410
708 489-4208

(G-17525)
MIDWEST CONVERTERS INC
5112 28th Ave (61109-1721)
PHONE.................................815 229-9808
Dennis G Sneath, *President*
Cathleen A Sneath, *Vice Pres*
EMP: 10
SQ FT: 20,000
SALES (est): 1.4MM **Privately Held**
SIC: 3714 3566 Motor vehicle transmissions, drive assemblies & parts; torque converters, except automotive

(G-17526)
MIDWEST DISPLAY & MFG INC
127 N Wyman St Apt 4 (61101-1114)
PHONE.................................815 962-2199
Kyle Bevers, *President*
EMP: 2
SQ FT: 2,400
SALES (est): 210K **Privately Held**
SIC: 2541 Cabinets, except refrigerated: show, display, etc.: wood; table or counter tops, plastic laminated; display fixtures, wood

(G-17527)
MIDWEST RAIL JUNCTION
1907 Cumberland St (61103-4763)
PHONE.................................815 963-0200
Scott Matejka, *Owner*
EMP: 2
SALES (est): 218K **Privately Held**
SIC: 3944 5092 5945 Board games, puzzles & models, except electronic; model kits; children's toys & games, except dolls

(G-17528)
MIDWEST STITCH
Also Called: D Castris
6767 Charles St (61108-6832)
PHONE.................................815 394-1516
Daniel De Castris, *Owner*
EMP: 7
SALES (est): 750K **Privately Held**
SIC: 2395 2396 Embroidery products, except schiffli machine; automotive & apparel trimmings

(G-17529)
MIDWEST WIRE WORKS LLC (PA)
4657 Stenstrom Rd (61109-2637)
PHONE.................................815 874-1701
Pete Dickerson, *Mng Member*
EMP: 10
SQ FT: 20,000
SALES (est): 1.3MM **Privately Held**
SIC: 3496 Miscellaneous fabricated wire products

(G-17530)
MNP PRECISION PARTS LLC (HQ)
1111 Samuelson Rd (61109-3620)
PHONE.................................815 391-5256
Loretta Dickey, *Human Res Dir*
Larry Berman, *President*
EMP: 189
SQ FT: 650,000
SALES: 25.2MM
SALES (corp-wide): 218.5MM **Privately Held**
SIC: 3452 3465 3469 Bolts, metal; automotive stampings; electronic enclosures, stamped or pressed metal
PA: Mnp Corporation
44225 Utica Rd
Utica MI 48317
586 254-1320

(G-17531)
MOBILITY CONNECTION INC
4100 E State St (61108-2008)
PHONE.................................815 965-8090
Roger Lichey, *President*
Becky Lichey, *Manager*
EMP: 5
SALES (est): 570.9K **Privately Held**
SIC: 3842 5047 Wheelchairs; medical equipment & supplies; therapy equipment

(G-17532)
MRS FISHERS INC
Also Called: Mrs. Fisher's Chips
1231 Fulton Ave (61103-4025)
PHONE.................................815 964-9114
Roma Hailman, *President*
Mark Hailman, *Corp Secy*
EMP: 11 **EST:** 1932
SQ FT: 10,000
SALES (est): 1.5MM **Privately Held**
WEB: www.mrsfisherschips.com
SIC: 2096 Potato chips & other potato-based snacks

(G-17533)
MULLER-PINEHURST DAIRY INC
Also Called: Prairie Farms Dairy
2110 Ogilby Rd (61102-3400)
P.O. Box 299 (61105-0299)
PHONE.................................815 968-0441
Neal L Rosinsky, *President*
EMP: 150
SALES (corp-wide): 20.1MM **Privately Held**
SIC: 2026 2024 2097 Milk processing (pasteurizing, homogenizing, bottling); ice cream & ice milk; manufactured ice
PA: Muller-Pinehurst Dairy, Inc.
1100 N Brdwy St
Carlinville IL 62626
217 854-2547

(G-17534)
MYLAN INSTITUTIONAL LLC
4901 Hiawatha Dr (61103-1287)
PHONE.................................724 514-1800
George Zorich, *Mng Member*
EMP: 26
SALES (est): 5.5MM
SALES (corp-wide): 204.1K **Privately Held**
SIC: 2834 Pharmaceutical preparations
HQ: Mylan Inc
1000 Mylan Blvd
Canonsburg PA 15317
724 514-1800

(G-17535)
N & S PATTERN CO
4911 Hydraulic Rd (61109-2620)
PHONE.................................815 874-6166
Lavern Neff, *President*
Blair Neff, *Treasurer*
EMP: 12
SQ FT: 9,000
SALES (est): 1.1MM **Privately Held**
SIC: 3543 Industrial patterns

(G-17536)
NATIONAL DETROIT INC
1590 Northrock Ct (61103-1234)
P.O. Box 2285, Loves Park (61131-0285)
PHONE.................................815 877-4041
Fax: 815 877-4050
EMP: 33 **EST:** 1939
SQ FT: 32,000
SALES (est): 6.1MM **Privately Held**
SIC: 3546 Mfg Power-Driven Handtools

(G-17537)
NELSON MANUFACTURING CO INC
2516 20th St (61104-7454)
PHONE.................................815 229-0161
Gordon S Nelson, *President*
Doris Nelson, *Corp Secy*
EMP: 15 **EST:** 1972
SQ FT: 10,000
SALES (est): 2.4MM **Privately Held**
SIC: 3469 3444 5093 Stamping metal for the trade; sheet metalwork; junk & scrap

(G-17538)
NORTHERN ILL BLOOD BNK INC (PA)
Also Called: ROCK RIVER VALLEY BLOOD CENTER
419 N 6th St (61107-4104)
P.O. Box 4305 (61110-0805)
PHONE.................................815 965-8751
Linda Garber, *CEO*
Heidi Ognibene, *General Mgr*
Thomas Mulcahy, *Facilities Mgr*
Lisa Entrikin, *Opers Staff*
Melissa Mason, *Credit Staff*
EMP: 14
SQ FT: 20,000
SALES: 9.2MM **Privately Held**
SIC: 2836 Blood derivatives; extracts; plasmas

(G-17539)
NORTHERN PROSTHETICS
2629 Charles St (61108-1608)
PHONE.................................815 226-0444
Erich Schulze, *President*
EMP: 8 **EST:** 1961
SQ FT: 5,738
SALES (est): 640K **Privately Held**
WEB: www.northernpo.com
SIC: 3842 Orthopedic appliances; limbs, artificial

(G-17540)
NYCLO SCREW MACHINE PDTS INC
3610 Mansfield St (61109-2007)
PHONE.................................815 229-7900
Timothy Clow, *President*
Peggy Clow, *Admin Sec*
EMP: 12
SQ FT: 14,000
SALES: 2MM **Privately Held**
WEB: www.nyclo.com
SIC: 3451 Screw machine products

(G-17541)
O & L MACHINE INC
1115 18th Ave (61104-5358)
PHONE.................................815 963-6600
Dan Olivotti, *President*
Nicholas Lamarca, *Admin Sec*
EMP: 8
SQ FT: 7,000
SALES: 610K **Privately Held**
SIC: 3599 Machine shop, jobbing & repair; machine & other job shop work

Rockford - Winnebago County (G-17542)

GEOGRAPHIC SECTION

(G-17542)
OBSIDIAN MFG INDS INC
5015 28th Ave (61109-1718)
P.O. Box 5045 (61125-0045)
PHONE 815 962-8700
David Nordman, *President*
▼ **EMP:** 11
SQ FT: 20,000
SALES (est): 2.1MM **Privately Held**
SIC: 3599 3545 Machine shop, jobbing & repair; rotary tables

(G-17543)
OLE SALTYS OF ROCKFORD INC
3131 Summerdale Ave (61101-3422)
PHONE 815 637-2447
Al Domico, *President*
EMP: 5
SALES (corp-wide): 1MM **Privately Held**
WEB: www.olesaltys.com
SIC: 2096 Potato chips & other potato-based snacks
PA: Ole Salty's Of Rockford, Inc.
1920 E Riverside Blvd
Loves Park IL 61111
815 637-2447

(G-17544)
OLSON ALUMINUM CASTINGS LTD
2135 15th St (61104-7310)
P.O. Box 6106 (61125-1106)
PHONE 815 229-3292
Tad L Olson, *President*
Laura Goodson, *Opers Staff*
Laura Myers, *Opers Staff*
Bill Cote, *QC Mgr*
Zac Utsinger, *Engineer*
EMP: 40
SQ FT: 39,000
SALES (est): 10.2MM **Privately Held**
WEB: www.olsonalum.com
SIC: 3365 3543 Aluminum & aluminum-based alloy castings; foundry patternmaking

(G-17545)
OWENS CORNING SALES LLC
2710 Laude Dr (61109-1448)
PHONE 815 226-4627
Joe Hanna, *Manager*
EMP: 81
SQ FT: 90,000 **Publicly Held**
WEB: www.owenscorning.com
SIC: 3275 3086 2821 Gypsum products; plastics foam products; plastics materials & resins
HQ: Owens Corning Sales, Llc
1 Owens Corning Pkwy
Toledo OH 43659
419 248-8000

(G-17546)
PAL MIDWEST LTD (PA)
1030 S Main St (61101-1418)
P.O. Box 624 (61105-0624)
PHONE 815 965-2981
Mary Lea Sagona Blum, *President*
David Blum, *Vice Pres*
EMP: 5
SQ FT: 20,000
SALES: 120K **Privately Held**
SIC: 2834 2844 Pharmaceutical preparations; toilet preparations

(G-17547)
PAMACHEYON PUBLISHING INC
305 Saint Louis Ave (61104-1522)
PHONE 815 395-0101
EMP: 5
SALES (est): 380K **Privately Held**
SIC: 2731 Books-Publishing/Printing

(G-17548)
PATKUS MACHINE CO
2607 Marshall St (61109-1334)
PHONE 815 398-7818
Terry Lynn Patkus, *President*
EMP: 6
SQ FT: 11,000
SALES (est): 1.1MM **Privately Held**
SIC: 5084 3599 7692 Tool & die makers' equipment; machine shop, jobbing & repair; welding repair

(G-17549)
PATRICK HOLDINGS INC (PA)
Also Called: Area Rigging & Millwright Svcs
5894 Sandy Hollow Rd (61109-2767)
PHONE 815 874-5300
James E Patrick, *President*
Linda Patrick, *Corp Secy*
EMP: 10
SQ FT: 18,000
SALES (est): 2.3MM **Privately Held**
SIC: 7699 3441 3446 7353 Industrial machinery & equipment repair; fabricated structural metal; railings, prefabricated metal; heavy construction equipment rental; installing building equipment

(G-17550)
PEARSON FASTENER CORPORATION
1400 Samuelson Rd (61109-3607)
PHONE 815 397-4460
Brad Pearson, *Chairman*
Lisbeth J Pearson, *Corp Secy*
David Pearson, *Vice Pres*
Paul Chandler, *Opers Staff*
Larry Fey, *Sales Staff*
EMP: 13
SQ FT: 56,000
SALES (est): 3.4MM **Privately Held**
SIC: 3452 Bolts, metal; rivets, metal; screws, metal

(G-17551)
PGI MFG LLC
Also Called: Deephole Drilling Service
614 Grable St (61109-2004)
PHONE 815 398-0313
John Razzano, *Mng Member*
Bill Wilfong, *Executive*
EMP: 6
SALES (corp-wide): 39.1MM **Privately Held**
SIC: 3546 Drills & drilling tools
PA: Pgi Mfg., Llc
51565 Bittersweet Rd B
Granger IN 46530
574 968-3222

(G-17552)
PGI MFG LLC
Also Called: La Salle Mfg & Mch Co
614 Grable St (61109-2004)
P.O. Box 625, Rochester IN (46975-0625)
PHONE 800 821-3475
Charles Chamberlain, *Engineer*
Tom Brown, *Manager*
EMP: 82
SALES (corp-wide): 39.1MM **Privately Held**
SIC: 3599 Custom machinery; machine shop, jobbing & repair
PA: Pgi Mfg., Llc
51565 Bittersweet Rd B
Granger IN 46530
574 968-3222

(G-17553)
PHELPS INDUSTRIES LLC
5213 26th Ave (61109-1707)
PHONE 815 397-0236
Douglas Nelson, *Manager*
Rich Bartuska, *Director*
EMP: 30
SQ FT: 20,000 **Privately Held**
WEB: www.phelpsindustries.com
SIC: 2047 Dog food
HQ: Phelps Industries Llc
599 North Ave Ste 9-4
Wakefield MA 01880

(G-17554)
PIETRO CARNAGHI USA INC
3445 Pyramid Dr (61109-2737)
PHONE 779 368-0564
Giuliano Radice, *Principal*
Larry Stegall, *Sales Staff*
EMP: 2
SALES (est): 334.1K **Privately Held**
WEB: www.pietrocarnaghi.com
SIC: 3541 3724 3511 Boring mills; aircraft engines & engine parts; gas turbine generator set units, complete; steam turbine generator set units, complete; turbines & turbine generator set units, complete

(G-17555)
PMI AEROSPACE INC
2801 Eastrock Dr (61109-7502)
PHONE 815 397-3894
EMP: 3
SALES (est): 195.4K **Privately Held**
WEB: www.pmiaerospace.com
SIC: 3599 Machine shop, jobbing & repair

(G-17556)
PRECISION GOVERNORS LLC
1715 Northrock Ct (61103-1201)
PHONE 815 229-5300
Ron Buck, *Vice Pres*
Chad Clendening, *Engineer*
Ryan Satterlee, *Engineer*
Smiljka Gavranovic, *Accounting Mgr*
Clif Jacobs, *VP Sales*
▲ **EMP:** 20 **EST:** 2001
SQ FT: 10,000
SALES (est): 4.5MM **Privately Held**
SIC: 3714 Governors, motor vehicle

(G-17557)
PRECISION HEADER TOOLING INC
3441 Precision Dr (61109-2771)
PHONE 815 874-9116
David Tollin, *President*
Dave Tollin, *President*
Charlotte Tollin, *Admin Sec*
EMP: 10
SQ FT: 9,000
SALES (est): 1.5MM **Privately Held**
SIC: 3545 3542 3544 Reamers, machine tool; headers; dies & die holders for metal cutting, forming, die casting

(G-17558)
PRECISION MASTERS INC
2801 Eastrock Dr (61109-7502)
PHONE 815 397-3894
James Baker, *President*
John W Kozyra, *Vice Pres*
Pat Cleeland, *Treasurer*
Pam Kozyra, *Admin Sec*
EMP: 32
SQ FT: 9,000
SALES (est): 6.6MM **Privately Held**
WEB: www.pmiaerospace.com
SIC: 3599 3545 Machine shop, jobbing & repair; precision measuring tools

(G-17559)
PREMIUM OIL COMPANY
923 Fairview Ct (61101-5952)
PHONE 815 963-3800
Richard A Fedeli, *President*
Kevin Fedeli, *Vice Pres*
Helen Fedeli, *Admin Sec*
EMP: 10
SQ FT: 14,000
SALES (est): 2.3MM **Privately Held**
SIC: 2992 5171 2842 Oils & greases, blending & compounding; petroleum bulk stations; specialty cleaning, polishes & sanitation goods

(G-17560)
PRINZINGS OF ROCKFORD
2046 Schell Dr (61109-4832)
PHONE 815 874-9654
Richard T Prinzing, *Owner*
EMP: 3
SALES: 1K **Privately Held**
SIC: 3589 Service industry machinery

(G-17561)
PROFESSIONAL GRAPHICS INC
Also Called: Prographics-Aka
4404 Boeing Dr (61109-2931)
PHONE 815 226-9422
Steven V Goley, *President*
Dave Goley, *Vice Pres*
▲ **EMP:** 45
SQ FT: 18,600
SALES (est): 7.3MM **Privately Held**
SIC: 2752 Commercial printing, offset

(G-17562)
PURE FLO BOTTLING INC
2430 N Main St (61103-4046)
PHONE 815 963-4797
Steve Souza, *President*
Carol Souza, *Vice Pres*
EMP: 3
SQ FT: 10,500
SALES: 250K **Privately Held**
SIC: 8748 2086 Business consulting; water, pasteurized: packaged in cans, bottles, etc.

(G-17563)
PWF
8123 Harrison Rd (61101-7309)
PHONE 815 967-0218
Michael Helwig, *Owner*
EMP: 2
SALES (est): 259.5K **Privately Held**
SIC: 3537 Forklift trucks

(G-17564)
R-TECH FEEDERS INC
5292 American Rd (61109-6311)
PHONE 815 874-2990
Jeffrey Richards, *President*
Tammy Richards, *Vice Pres*
Joshua Downs, *Sales Staff*
EMP: 22
SQ FT: 11,500
SALES (est): 4.7MM **Privately Held**
SIC: 3523 Feed grinders, crushers & mixers

(G-17565)
RAM PLASTIC CORP
1327 10th Ave (61104-5013)
PHONE 847 669-8003
Robert Anderson, *President*
EMP: 2 **EST:** 1971
SALES: 250K **Privately Held**
SIC: 3089 Injection molding of plastics

(G-17566)
RAYCAR GEAR & MACHINE COMPANY
6125 11th St (61109-4342)
PHONE 815 874-3948
Dan Schwartz, *President*
Don Abbott, *Prgrmr*
Joy Schwartz, *Executive*
EMP: 21 **EST:** 1964
SQ FT: 10,000
SALES: 3MM **Privately Held**
WEB: www.raycargear.com
SIC: 3566 3568 3543 3599 Speed changers, drives & gears; power transmission equipment; gears, forged steel; machine shop, jobbing & repair

(G-17567)
RAYTHEON TECHNOLOGIES CORP
4747 Harrison Ave (61108-7929)
PHONE 815 226-6000
Alan Nelson, *Principal*
Joseph Voss, *Engineer*
Liz Gullett, *Manager*
Lowell Meyer, *Sr Associate*
EMP: 268
SALES (corp-wide): 77B **Publicly Held**
SIC: 3585 3721 3534 3724 Refrigeration & heating equipment; helicopters; research & development on aircraft by the manufacturer; elevators & equipment; escalators, passenger & freight; aircraft engines & engine parts; research & development on aircraft engines & parts; high-energy particle physics equipment
PA: Raytheon Technologies Corporation
870 Winter St
Waltham MA 02451
781 522-3000

(G-17568)
RDH INC OF ROCKFORD
3445 Lonergan Dr (61109-2622)
PHONE 815 874-9421
Larry Bull, *President*
EMP: 18
SQ FT: 17,000
SALES (est): 3MM **Privately Held**
SIC: 3541 3594 3546 3545 Drilling & boring machines; tapping machines; fluid power pumps & motors; power-driven handtools; machine tool accessories

▲ = Import ▼ = Export
◆ = Import/Export

Rockford - Winnebago County (G-17596)

(G-17569)
REDIN PARTS INC
Also Called: Redin Production Machine
1922 7th St Ste 4d (61104-5391)
PHONE..................................815 398-1010
John Konopa, *President*
EMP: 5
SQ FT: 20,000
SALES (est): 889.9K **Privately Held**
SIC: 3541 Deburring machines

(G-17570)
RELIABLE MACHINE COMPANY
521 Schauer Ln (61107-2962)
PHONE..................................815 968-8803
Gloria Stuhr-Pernacciaro, *President*
David Weber, *Vice Pres*
EMP: 45 EST: 1921
SALES (est): 8.9MM **Privately Held**
WEB: www.reliablemachine.com
SIC: 3469 3429 Stamping metal for the trade; keys, locks & related hardware

(G-17571)
REMARK TECHNOLOGIES INC (PA)
10944 N State Route 2 (61102-9638)
PHONE..................................815 985-2972
Rod Kramer, *President*
Michael Jones, *Vice Pres*
EMP: 4
SQ FT: 4,000
SALES (est): 150K **Privately Held**
SIC: 5072 3423 Hand tools; hand & edge tools

(G-17572)
RING CONTAINER TECH LLC
Also Called: Ring Can of Illinois
4689 Assembly Dr (61109-3083)
PHONE..................................815 229-9110
Joe Ricks, *Prdtn Mgr*
Brian Best, *Sales Staff*
Steve Davis, *Manager*
Rob Romero, *Manager*
EMP: 30
SALES (corp-wide): 284.7MM **Privately Held**
SIC: 3085 Plastics bottles
PA: Ring Container Technologies, Llc.
1 Industrial Park
Oakland TN 38060
800 280-7464

(G-17573)
RIVER CITY MILLWORK INC
200 Quaker Rd Ste 3 (61104-7068)
PHONE..................................800 892-9297
William Sarbaugh, *President*
▲ EMP: 53
SQ FT: 95,000
SALES (est): 27.8MM **Privately Held**
SIC: 5031 3442 3231 2431 Millwork; building materials, exterior; building materials, interior; metal doors, sash & trim; products of purchased glass; millwork

(G-17574)
RIVERSIDE SPRING COMPANY
2136 12th St Ste 121 (61104-7374)
PHONE..................................815 963-3334
Charles A Davis Jr, *President*
Jerry Davis, *Vice Pres*
Charlotte Vincer, *Manager*
Charles A Davis Sr, *Admin Sec*
EMP: 6
SQ FT: 6,800
SALES (est): 700K **Privately Held**
SIC: 3495 3496 Wire springs; miscellaneous fabricated wire products

(G-17575)
RIVERVIEW PRINTING INC
99 E State St (61104-1009)
PHONE..................................815 987-1425
Steve Walker, *Manager*
EMP: 8
SALES: 400K **Privately Held**
SIC: 2752 Commercial printing, offset

(G-17576)
RJ LINK INTERNATIONAL INC
Also Called: Rj Link
3741 Publishers Dr (61109-6316)
PHONE..................................815 874-8110
Rodney J Link, *President*
Anne D Link, *Admin Sec*
▼ EMP: 16
SQ FT: 14,600
SALES (est): 3.2MM **Privately Held**
SIC: 3599 3566 3462 3321 Custom machinery; speed changers, drives & gears; iron & steel forgings; gray & ductile iron foundries

(G-17577)
RKFD LLC GRUA (PA)
500 18th Ave (61104-5131)
PHONE..................................815 414-2392
Peter Crane, *Mng Member*
EMP: 2
SALES (est): 1.1MM **Privately Held**
SIC: 3462 Iron & steel forgings

(G-17578)
RKFD LLC GRUA
2702 Preston St (61102)
PHONE..................................815 414-2392
Peter Crane, *Mng Member*
EMP: 3
SALES (corp-wide): 1.1MM **Privately Held**
SIC: 3462 Iron & steel forgings
PA: Rkfd Llc Grua
500 18th Ave
Rockford IL 61104
815 414-2392

(G-17579)
RMC IMAGING INC
780 Creek Bluff Ln (61114-6872)
PHONE..................................815 885-4521
Robert Czechowicz, *President*
EMP: 1
SALES: 300K **Privately Held**
SIC: 3571 Electronic computers

(G-17580)
RO PAL GRINDING INC
1916 20th Ave (61104-7320)
PHONE..................................815 964-5894
Ronald Nauschwander, *Vice Pres*
Ronald Neuschwander, *Vice Pres*
EMP: 10 EST: 1964
SQ FT: 5,200
SALES: 800K **Privately Held**
WEB: www.ropalgrind.com
SIC: 7389 3479 Grinding, precision, commercial or industrial; coating of metals & formed products

(G-17581)
ROCK RIVER BLENDING
1515 Cunningham St (61102-2601)
PHONE..................................815 968-7860
Daniel McLoraine, *Owner*
EMP: 6
SQ FT: 24,000
SALES (est): 702.9K **Privately Held**
SIC: 2841 Soap & other detergents

(G-17582)
ROCK RIVER TIMES
128 N Church St (61101-1002)
PHONE..................................815 964-9767
Frank Schier, *Information Mgr*
EMP: 13
SALES (est): 1MM **Privately Held**
SIC: 2711 Newspapers, publishing & printing

(G-17583)
ROCK ROAD COMPANIES INC
801 Beale Ct (61109-4308)
P.O. Box 1818, Janesville WI (53547-1818)
PHONE..................................815 874-2441
Mike Greenan, *Branch Mgr*
EMP: 10
SALES (corp-wide): 42.6MM **Privately Held**
SIC: 1611 2951 1771 Highway & street paving contractor; asphalt paving mixtures & blocks; concrete work
PA: Rock Road Companies, Inc.
301 W B R Townline Rd
Janesville WI 53545
608 752-8944

(G-17584)
ROCK VALLEY DIE SINKING INC
2457 Baxter Rd (61109-5079)
PHONE..................................815 874-8560
Timothy A Poshka, *President*
Patricia Vaughn, *Office Mgr*
EMP: 10 EST: 1975
SQ FT: 3,200
SALES (est): 1.6MM **Privately Held**
SIC: 3542 3544 Machine tools, metal forming type; special dies, tools, jigs & fixtures

(G-17585)
ROCKFORD BALL SCREW COMPANY
940 Southrock Dr (61102-4299)
PHONE..................................815 961-7700
Linda McGary, *President*
Linda Mc Gary, *President*
Randy Mc Bain, *Vice Pres*
Randy McBain, *Vice Pres*
Brian Allison, *Opers Staff*
EMP: 60
SQ FT: 56,000
SALES (est): 13.9MM **Privately Held**
SIC: 3452 Bolts, nuts, rivets & washers

(G-17586)
ROCKFORD BLACKTOP CNSTR CO
833 Featherstone Rd (61107-6301)
PHONE..................................815 654-4700
Ben Holmstrom, *President*
Wayne L Schwalen, *Treasurer*
EMP: 100 EST: 1892
SQ FT: 15,000
SALES (est): 39.1MM
SALES (corp-wide): 1.4B **Publicly Held**
WEB: www.williamcharlesconstruction.com
SIC: 1611 1623 1629 1794 Highway & street paving contractor; resurfacing contractor; highway & street maintenance; grading; sewer line construction; water main construction; drainage system construction; excavation & grading, building construction; asphalt paving mixtures & blocks; construction sand & gravel
HQ: Iea Energy Services Llc
8440 Woodfield Crossing B
Indianapolis IN 46240
800 688-3775

(G-17587)
ROCKFORD BOLT & STEEL CO
126 Mill St (61101-1491)
PHONE..................................815 968-0514
Michael G Rosman, *President*
John Moore, *Vice Pres*
Linda McComas, *Purch Mgr*
EMP: 48
SQ FT: 90,000
SALES (est): 12.2MM **Privately Held**
WEB: www.rockfordbolt.com
SIC: 3452 Bolts, metal; screws, metal

(G-17588)
ROCKFORD BROACH INC
4993 27th Ave (61109-1708)
PHONE..................................815 484-0409
Harold Hackworth, *President*
Janet Hackworth, *Vice Pres*
EMP: 12
SQ FT: 14,500
SALES (est): 990K **Privately Held**
SIC: 3541 Broaching machines

(G-17589)
ROCKFORD BURRALL MCH CO INC
4520 Shepherd Trl (61103-1238)
PHONE..................................815 877-7428
Raymond J Smith, *President*
Edmund P Freberg, *Vice Pres*
EMP: 28 EST: 1972
SQ FT: 12,000
SALES (est): 5.2MM **Privately Held**
SIC: 3599 Machine shop, jobbing & repair

(G-17590)
ROCKFORD CARBIDE DIE & TOOL
1920 20th Ave (61104-7320)
PHONE..................................815 394-0645
Tim Baumgardt, *Partner*
Roy Baumgardt, *Partner*
Doug Johnson, *Partner*
EMP: 5
SQ FT: 2,000
SALES (est): 586.1K **Privately Held**
SIC: 3544 Dies & die holders for metal cutting, forming, die casting

(G-17591)
ROCKFORD CEMENT PRODUCTS CO
315 Peoples Ave (61104-7034)
PHONE..................................815 965-0537
Robert C Beale, *President*
Rock Yachasz, *Corp Secy*
Jeremy Beale, *Vice Pres*
EMP: 14 EST: 1911
SQ FT: 10,000
SALES (est): 3MM **Privately Held**
WEB: www.rockfordcementproducts.com
SIC: 3272 3271 Covers, catch basin: concrete; manhole covers or frames, concrete; septic tanks, concrete; architectural concrete: block, split, fluted, screen, etc.; blocks, concrete or cinder: standard; brick, concrete; paving blocks, concrete

(G-17592)
ROCKFORD DROP FORGE COMPANY
2011 10th St (61104-5390)
P.O. Box 567, Dekalb (60115-0567)
PHONE..................................815 963-9611
Donald G Jones, *President*
Jeffrey T Jones, *Admin Sec*
EMP: 70 EST: 1903
SQ FT: 200,000
SALES (est): 11.2MM **Privately Held**
WEB: www.rockforddropforge.com
SIC: 3462 Iron & steel forgings

(G-17593)
ROCKFORD ELECTRIC EQUIPMENT CO
2010 Harrison Ave (61104-7343)
PHONE..................................815 398-4096
Bernard R Beishir, *President*
Stephan J Beishir, *Vice Pres*
EMP: 8
SQ FT: 10,000
SALES (est): 600K **Privately Held**
SIC: 7694 7629 5063 Electric motor repair; electronic equipment repair; electrical apparatus & equipment; motors, electric

(G-17594)
ROCKFORD FOUNDRIES INC
212 Mill St (61101-1490)
PHONE..................................815 965-7243
Peter Rundquist, *President*
John Rundquist, *Treasurer*
Linda Graham, *Office Mgr*
EMP: 12
SQ FT: 20,000
SALES (est): 1.8MM **Privately Held**
WEB: www.rockfordfoundries.com
SIC: 3365 3366 3369 Aluminum & aluminum-based alloy castings; castings (except die): brass; nonferrous foundries

(G-17595)
ROCKFORD HEAT TREATERS INC
4704 American Rd (61109-2629)
PHONE..................................815 874-0089
Bob Deutsch, *President*
Ted Deutsch, *Vice Pres*
Tom Deutsch, *Vice Pres*
Jim Buntjer, *Manager*
Don Shriver, *Admin Sec*
EMP: 24 EST: 1966
SQ FT: 36,600
SALES (est): 5.4MM **Privately Held**
WEB: www.rockfordheattreaters.com
SIC: 3398 Annealing of metal

(G-17596)
ROCKFORD JOBBING SERVICE INC
4955 28th Ave (61109-1716)
PHONE..................................815 398-8661
Brian D Hornbeck, *President*
EMP: 7 EST: 1964
SQ FT: 10,000

Rockford - Winnebago County (G-17597)   GEOGRAPHIC SECTION

SALES (est): 825K Privately Held
WEB: www.rockfordjobbing.com
SIC: 3599 3568 3566 3545 Machine shop, jobbing & repair; power transmission equipment; speed changers, drives & gears; machine tool accessories; iron & steel forgings

(G-17597)
ROCKFORD LINEAR ACTUATION
2111 23rd Ave (61104-7332)
PHONE..................................815 986-4400
Robert Trogan, *CEO*
EMP: 7
SALES (est): 1.1MM Privately Held
SIC: 3599 Custom machinery

(G-17598)
ROCKFORD LINEAR MOTION LLC
940 Southrock Dr (61102-4299)
PHONE..................................815 961-7900
Rick Sonneson, *Vice Pres*
Elaine Dyke, *Buyer*
Amy Hendrickson, *Accounting Mgr*
EMP: 4
SALES (est): 257.5K Privately Held
SIC: 3699 Linear accelerators

(G-17599)
ROCKFORD MAP PUBLISHERS INC
124 N Water St Ste 10 (61107-3970)
P.O. Box 6126 (61125-1126)
PHONE..................................815 708-6324
Suzanne Young, *President*
Charlie Lunn, *Vice Pres*
Donna Thompson, *Controller*
Bryan Marchione, *Sales Staff*
Brock Alekna, *Marketing Mgr*
EMP: 18 EST: 1944
SQ FT: 4,500
SALES (est): 1.7MM Privately Held
WEB: www.rockfordmap.com
SIC: 2741 Globe covers (maps): publishing only, not printed on site

(G-17600)
ROCKFORD NEWSPAPERS INC
Also Called: Rockford Register Star
99 E State St (61104-1009)
P.O. Box 439 (61105-0439)
PHONE..................................815 987-1200
Fredrick Jacobi, *President*
Shelby Gilliam, *Clerk*
EMP: 420
SQ FT: 10,000
SALES: 35.6MM
SALES (corp-wide): 1.8B Publicly Held
WEB: www.rrstar.com
SIC: 2711 2752 Newspapers, publishing & printing; commercial printing, lithographic
HQ: Gatehouse Media, Llc
   175 Sullys Trl Fl 3
   Pittsford NY 14534
   585 598-0030

(G-17601)
ROCKFORD PRECISION MACHINE
4729 Hydraulic Rd (61109-2617)
PHONE..................................815 873-1018
John D Casarotto Sr, *President*
John Casarotto Jr, *Vice Pres*
Theresa Casarotto, *Treasurer*
EMP: 10
SQ FT: 33,000
SALES (est): 1.6MM Privately Held
SIC: 3599 7692 Machine shop, jobbing & repair; welding repair

(G-17602)
ROCKFORD PROCESS CONTROL LLC
2020 7th St (61104-5353)
PHONE..................................815 966-2000
Gregory P Heim,
EMP: 125
SQ FT: 170,000
SALES (est): 4.5MM Privately Held
SIC: 3429 Door opening & closing devices, except electrical

(G-17603)
ROCKFORD QUALITY GRINDING INC
3160 Forest View Rd (61109-1642)
PHONE..................................815 227-9001
Todd Henning, *President*
Ann Henning, *Vice Pres*
EMP: 10
SALES (est): 500K Privately Held
SIC: 3599 Machine shop, jobbing & repair

(G-17604)
ROCKFORD RAMS PRODUCTS INC
2902 Eastrock Dr (61109-1738)
P.O. Box 5246 (61125-0246)
PHONE..................................815 226-0016
Malcolm Anderberg, *President*
Leah Anderberg, *Vice Pres*
Jeffrey Anderberg, *Admin Sec*
EMP: 6
SQ FT: 3,000
SALES (est): 200K Privately Held
SIC: 3829 Hardness testing equipment

(G-17605)
ROCKFORD SECONDARY CO
2424 Laude Dr (61109-1450)
PHONE..................................815 398-0401
Jimmie Clark, *Owner*
John Clark, *General Mgr*
EMP: 9
SQ FT: 20,000
SALES (est): 851.1K Privately Held
SIC: 3599 3316 Machine shop, jobbing & repair; cold finishing of steel shapes

(G-17606)
ROCKFORD SYSTEMS LLC
5795 Logistics Pkwy (61109-3608)
PHONE..................................815 874-7891
Brian Boes, *Opers Staff*
Melissa Trimble, *Sales Staff*
Jim Wilkinson, *Sales Staff*
Roger Harrison, *Training Dir*
Frederick Eck,
EMP: 52
SALES (est): 10.1MM
SALES (corp-wide): 10.6MM Privately Held
SIC: 3549 Wiredrawing & fabricating machinery & equipment, ex. die
PA: The Randolph Group Inc
   211 W Wacker Dr
   Chicago IL
   312 263-4900

(G-17607)
ROCKFORD TOOL AND MFG CO
3023 Eastrock Ct (61109-1761)
PHONE..................................815 398-5876
Gary McGregor, *President*
EMP: 10
SQ FT: 16,000
SALES (est): 1MM Privately Held
SIC: 3544 3599 Special dies & tools; machine shop, jobbing & repair

(G-17608)
ROCKFORD TOOLCRAFT INC (PA)
766 Research Pkwy 61109-2938)
PHONE..................................815 398-5507
Jerry Busse, *CEO*
Gerald A Busse, *President*
Thomas A Busse, *President*
Pete McKee, *Plant Mgr*
Tim Guentert, *Prdtn Mgr*
EMP: 175 EST: 1973
SQ FT: 200,000
SALES (est): 65.6MM Privately Held
SIC: 3469 3544 Stamping metal for the trade; special dies & tools; jigs & fixtures

(G-17609)
ROCKFORD TOOLCRAFT INC
5455 11th St (61109-3656)
PHONE..................................815 398-5507
John Fisher, *Manager*
EMP: 20
SALES (corp-wide): 65.6MM Privately Held
SIC: 3469 3544 Metal stampings; special dies & tools
PA: Rockford Toolcraft, Inc.
   766 Research Pkwy
   Rockford IL 61109
   815 398-5507

(G-17610)
ROCKFORM TOOLING & MACHINERY (PA)
2974 Eastrock Dr (61109-1738)
P.O. Box 4487, Canton GA (30114-0018)
PHONE..................................770 345-4624
Richard D Smith, *CEO*
James Erickson, *Vice Pres*
Sonia C Smith, *Treasurer*
▲ EMP: 30
SALES (est): 4MM Privately Held
WEB: www.rockform.com
SIC: 2819 Carbides

(G-17611)
ROCKFORM TOOLING & MACHINERY
Also Called: Gator Die Supplies
2974 Eastrock Dr (61109-1738)
P.O. Box 4487, Canton GA (30114-0018)
PHONE..................................815 398-7650
James Erickson, *Branch Mgr*
EMP: 4
SALES (corp-wide): 4MM Privately Held
SIC: 3545 5084 Cutting tools for machine tools; machine tools & accessories
PA: Rockform Tooling & Machinery, Inc
   2974 Eastrock Dr
   Rockford IL 61109
   770 345-4624

(G-17612)
ROCKWIND VENTURE PARTNERS LLC (PA)
8500 E State St (61108-2736)
PHONE..................................630 881-6664
Richard Johnson, *Mng Member*
Chet Kolodziej,
EMP: 2
SALES (est): 316.7K Privately Held
SIC: 3511 Turbines & turbine generator sets & parts

(G-17613)
ROGERS READY MIX & MTLS INC
5510 S Mulford Rd (61109-4156)
PHONE..................................815 874-6626
Toby Rogers, *Manager*
EMP: 25
SALES (corp-wide): 14.3MM Privately Held
SIC: 3273 Ready-mixed concrete
PA: Rogers Ready Mix & Materials, Inc.
   8128 N Walnut St
   Byron IL 61010
   815 234-8212

(G-17614)
ROMA BAKERIES INC
523 Marchesano Dr (61102-3518)
PHONE..................................815 964-6737
John Bowler, *President*
EMP: 14
SQ FT: 2,000
SALES: 1MM Privately Held
SIC: 5461 5149 2099 2051 Bread; bakery products; food preparations; bread, cake & related products; cookies & crackers

(G-17615)
RONDEX PRODUCTS INCORPORATED
324 N Gardiner Ave (61107-4337)
P.O. Box 1829 (61110-0329)
PHONE..................................815 226-0452
Gene Russell Baldwin, *President*
Marit Baldwin, *Admin Sec*
▲ EMP: 12
SALES (est): 1.5MM Privately Held
SIC: 3842 Respiratory protection equipment, personal

(G-17616)
RPC LEGACY INC (PA)
2020 7th St (61104-5353)
PHONE..................................815 966-2000
Patrick Derry, *President*
Shawn Curtis, *Vice Pres*

Dennis McInerney, *Vice Pres*
Dennis Swick, *Vice Pres*
Mark Priewe, *Purch Mgr*
▲ EMP: 75
SQ FT: 170,000
SALES (est): 16.1MM Privately Held
SIC: 3429 Manufactured hardware (general)

(G-17617)
RUST-OLEUM CORPORATION
615 Buckbee St (61104-4834)
PHONE..................................815 967-4258
Vonn Schopp, *Branch Mgr*
Kim Frazier, *Manager*
Megan Newton, *Manager*
Jim Weldon, *Manager*
Saul Echevarria, *Supervisor*
EMP: 60
SALES (corp-wide): 5.5B Publicly Held
SIC: 2851 2891 3089 3944 Enamels; lacquer: bases, dopes, thinner; adhesives; cement, except linoleum & tile; kits, plastic; games, toys & children's vehicles; brushes, air, artists'
HQ: Rust-Oleum Corporation
   11 E Hawthorn Pkwy
   Vernon Hills IL 60061
   847 367-7700

(G-17618)
S & J WOODPRODUCTS
5305 Forest Hills Rd (61114-5209)
PHONE..................................815 973-1970
Joyce Weiss, *Owner*
EMP: 3
SALES: 50K Privately Held
SIC: 2521 Wood office furniture

(G-17619)
S & K BORING INC
3360 Forest View Rd (61109-1645)
PHONE..................................815 227-4394
Mike Stupka, *President*
EMP: 2
SQ FT: 2,800
SALES (est): 307.7K Privately Held
SIC: 3599 Machine shop, jobbing & repair

(G-17620)
SAFEWAY PRODUCTS INC
1810 15th Ave (61104-5431)
PHONE..................................815 226-8322
Phil Fillweber, *President*
Renee Barker, *Manager*
EMP: 19 EST: 2000
SQ FT: 32,000
SALES (est): 1.8MM Privately Held
WEB: www.safewayproductsinc.com
SIC: 3089 Plastic containers, except foam

(G-17621)
SAFEWAY SERVICES ROCKFORD INC
1310 Samuelson Rd (61109-3646)
PHONE..................................815 986-1504
Thomas Lynde, *President*
Jamie Hanson, *Manager*
EMP: 22
SQ FT: 54,000
SALES: 950K Privately Held
SIC: 3479 Etching & engraving

(G-17622)
SCHNEIDER ELC BUILDINGS LLC (DH)
Also Called: Invensys Environmental Contrls
839 N Perryville Rd (61107-6202)
PHONE..................................815 381-5000
Jean-Pascal Tricoire, *CEO*
Barry Coflan, *Principal*
Aurelie Richard, *Principal*
Clemens Blum, *Exec VP*
Annette Clayton, *Exec VP*
▲ EMP: 500 EST: 1836
SQ FT: 500,000

SALES (est): 348.4MM
SALES (corp-wide): 177.9K **Privately Held**
WEB: www.schneider-electric.com
SIC: 3822 1711 3625 3823 Building services monitoring controls, automatic; mechanical contractor; relays & industrial controls; motor control accessories, including overload relays; motor controls, electric; actuators, industrial; industrial process control instruments; motors, electric

(G-17623)
SCHNEIDER ELC BUILDINGS LLC
Invensys Environmental Contrls
4104 Charles St (61108-6229)
PHONE.................................815 227-4000
L C Peterson, *Manager*
EMP: 50
SALES (corp-wide): 177.9K **Privately Held**
SIC: 3822 1711 Building services monitoring controls, automatic; mechanical contractor
HQ: Schneider Electric Buildings, Llc
839 N Perryville Rd
Rockford IL 61107
815 381-5000

(G-17624)
SENDELE WIRELESS SOLUTIONS
1475 Temple Cir (61108-4448)
PHONE.................................815 227-4212
Steve Sendele, *President*
EMP: 2
SALES (est): 1MM **Privately Held**
SIC: 3823 Computer interface equipment for industrial process control

(G-17625)
SEREEN LLC
Also Called: Sereen Boats
4543 Sable Ln (61109-4036)
PHONE.................................386 527-4876
Earl Eggert,
Logan Schnake,
EMP: 4
SALES (est): 262.4K **Privately Held**
SIC: 5551 3732 Outboard boats; outboard motors; motorboats, inboard or outboard: building & repairing

(G-17626)
SERVICE MACHINE JOBS
1308 Barnes St (61104-4721)
PHONE.................................815 986-3033
Bounnam Khempaseuth, *Owner*
EMP: 3
SQ FT: 4,000
SALES (est): 203.9K **Privately Held**
SIC: 3541 3544 3599 3542 Machine tools, metal cutting type; special dies, tools, jigs & fixtures; custom machinery; machine shop, jobbing & repair; die casting & extruding machines

(G-17627)
SHAARS INTERNATIONAL INC
129 Phelps Ave Ste 901a (61108-2484)
PHONE.................................815 315-0717
Shahid Naseer, *CEO*
EMP: 1
SALES (est): 317.3K **Privately Held**
SIC: 5099 5191 2834 8734 Firearms & ammunition, except sporting; animal feeds; veterinary pharmaceutical preparations; veterinary testing

(G-17628)
SHANER QUALITY MACHINING INC
4935 28th Ave (61109-1716)
PHONE.................................815 985-7209
Mike Shaner, *President*
Lori Conro, *Admin Sec*
EMP: 2
SALES (est): 219.1K **Privately Held**
SIC: 3599 Machine shop, jobbing & repair

(G-17629)
SHEET METAL CONNECTORS INC
5601 Sandy Hollow Rd (61109-2780)
PHONE.................................815 874-4600
Eric Lyzhoft, *CFO*
EMP: 17
SALES (est): 2.3MM
SALES (corp-wide): 25.5MM **Privately Held**
SIC: 3444 Ducts, sheet metal
PA: Sheet Metal Connectors, Inc.
5850 Main St Ne
Minneapolis MN 55432
763 572-0000

(G-17630)
SHERWIN-WILLIAMS COMPANY
1215 Nelson Blvd (61104-4773)
PHONE.................................815 987-3700
Rob Vanvleet, *Maint Spvr*
Chuck Matlock, *Branch Mgr*
EMP: 50
SALES (corp-wide): 17.9B **Publicly Held**
SIC: 2851 Paints & paint additives
PA: The Sherwin-Williams Company
101 W Prospect Ave # 1020
Cleveland OH 44115
216 566-2000

(G-17631)
SIGMA TOOL & MACHINING
2324 23rd Ave (61104-7337)
PHONE.................................815 874-0500
Jon Leid, *Principal*
EMP: 7
SALES (est): 1.3MM **Privately Held**
SIC: 3599 Machine shop, jobbing & repair

(G-17632)
SINGER EQUITIES INC
Also Called: Smith Industrial Rubber & Plas
5463 International Dr (61109-2777)
P.O. Box 5486 (61125-0486)
PHONE.................................815 874-5364
Robynn Scott, *Branch Mgr*
EMP: 12
SALES (corp-wide): 3.3B **Privately Held**
SIC: 3069 3999 Bags, rubber or rubberized fabric; atomizers, toiletry
HQ: Singer Equities, Inc.
125 Mccarty St
Houston TX 77029

(G-17633)
SKYWARD PROMOTIONS INC
1140 Charles St (61104-1219)
PHONE.................................815 969-0909
Timothy Dingus, *President*
EMP: 7
SQ FT: 6,600
SALES (est): 1.2MM **Privately Held**
SIC: 5199 3993 Advertising specialties; signs & advertising specialties

(G-17634)
SLIDEMATIC INDUSTRIES INC
1303 Samuelson Rd (61109-3645)
PHONE.................................815 986-0500
Randy Baker, *President*
Laura Duncan, *General Mgr*
Greg Jindrich, *QC Mgr*
Michael Kalajian, *Engineer*
Janet Kingsbury, *Human Res Mgr*
▲ EMP: 125 EST: 1983
SALES (est): 59.1MM **Privately Held**
WEB: www.slidematic.com
SIC: 3452 Nuts, metal

(G-17635)
SLIDEMTIC PRCSION CMPNENTS INC
1303 Samuelson Rd (61109-3645)
PHONE.................................815 986-0500
Randy Baker, *President*
Mark Woodbury, *Info Tech Mgr*
▲ EMP: 170
SALES (est): 232.5K **Privately Held**
SIC: 3452 Bolts, nuts, rivets & washers

(G-17636)
SMITH INDUSTRIAL RUBBER & PLAS
Also Called: Smith Industrial Rubber & Plas
5463 International Dr (61109-2777)
P.O. Box 5486 (61125-0486)
PHONE.................................815 874-5364
Sam Petillo, *President*
EMP: 14
SQ FT: 10,000
SALES (est): 1.6MM
SALES (corp-wide): 3.3B **Privately Held**
SIC: 3069 3999 Bags, rubber or rubberized fabric; atomizers, toiletry
HQ: Hampton Rubber Company
1669 W Pembroke Ave
Hampton VA 23661
757 722-9818

(G-17637)
SOUTHERN IMPERIAL INC (DH)
Also Called: Sunbelt Plastic Extrusions
1400 Eddy Ave (61103-3198)
PHONE.................................815 877-7041
Stanley Valiulis, *President*
Steven Vandemore, *President*
Gary Rothmeyer, *District Mgr*
Jeff Geron, *Business Mgr*
Brent Ewing, *Vice Pres*
▲ EMP: 250 EST: 1956
SQ FT: 320,000
SALES (est): 93.8MM **Privately Held**
WEB: www.southernimperial.com
SIC: 2542 5046 Fixtures: display, office or store: except wood; racks, merchandise display or storage: except wood; store fixtures & display equipment
HQ: Fasteners For Retail, Inc.
8181 Darrow Rd
Twinsburg OH 44087
330 998-7800

(G-17638)
SPECIALTY SCREW CORPORATION
2801 Huffman Blvd (61103-3997)
PHONE.................................815 969-4100
Russell Johansson, *President*
Bill Haas, *Engineer*
Kevin Van Briesen, *CFO*
Jim Gravunder, *Sales Staff*
Kayann Johansson, *Manager*
▲ EMP: 110
SQ FT: 100,000
SALES (est): 20.1MM **Privately Held**
SIC: 3451 Screw machine products

(G-17639)
SPENCER AND KRAHN MCH TL SLS (PA)
Also Called: S&K Machine
2621 Springdale Dr (61114-6451)
PHONE.................................815 282-3300
William Spencer, *President*
Ronald Krahn, *Corp Secy*
EMP: 5
SALES (est): 5MM **Privately Held**
SIC: 5084 3541 Machine tools & accessories; grinding machines, metalworking

(G-17640)
SPIDER COMPANY INC (PA)
Also Called: SCI
2340 11th Ave (61104-7246)
PHONE.................................815 961-8200
Thomas Diehl, *President*
Jack West, *Engineer*
Larry Cunningham, *Manager*
Jeff Johnson, *Manager*
Adam Wiemers, *IT/INT Sup*
EMP: 75
SQ FT: 72,000
SALES (est): 21.9MM **Privately Held**
SIC: 3441 Fabricated structural metal

(G-17641)
SPIDER COMPANY INC
2340 11th Ave (61104-7246)
PHONE.................................815 961-8200
Tim Troster, *Manager*
EMP: 100
SALES (corp-wide): 21.9MM **Privately Held**
SIC: 3471 Finishing, metals or formed products

PA: Spider Company, Inc.
2340 11th Ave
Rockford IL 61104
815 961-8200

(G-17642)
SPORTS RECREATION AND AP INC
623 E Jefferson St (61107-4025)
PHONE.................................815 962-7767
Mark Mannino, *Manager*
EMP: 3
SALES (est): 255.8K **Privately Held**
WEB: www.sportsrecreationandapparel.com
SIC: 2759 Screen printing

(G-17643)
SPX CORPORATION
5885 11th St (61109-3650)
PHONE.................................815 874-5556
Tom Farrell, *Principal*
EMP: 450
SALES (corp-wide): 1.5B **Publicly Held**
SIC: 3443 Cooling towers, metal plate
PA: Spx Corporation
13320a Balntyn Corp Pl
Charlotte NC 28277
980 474-3700

(G-17644)
SPX FLOW US LLC
5885 11th St (61109-3650)
PHONE.................................815 874-5556
Chris Kearney, *President*
Robert B Foreman, *Exec VP*
Jeremy Smeltzer, *CFO*
EMP: 8
SALES (est): 247.3K
SALES (corp-wide): 1.5B **Publicly Held**
SIC: 3494 Valves & pipe fittings
PA: Spx Flow, Inc.
13320 Balntyn Corp Pl
Charlotte NC 28277
704 752-4400

(G-17645)
STEEL FABRICATING INC
2806 22nd St (61109-1445)
P.O. Box 1057 (61105-1057)
PHONE.................................815 977-5355
Dai Bui, *President*
Jan Burgess, *General Mgr*
EMP: 12
SALES (est): 2.2MM **Privately Held**
SIC: 3449 Bars, concrete reinforcing: fabricated steel

(G-17646)
STEPHEN PAOLI MFG CORP
Also Called: Paoli, Stephen International
2531 11th St (61104-7219)
PHONE.................................815 965-0621
Louis Paoli, *President*
Shawn Lee, *General Mgr*
EMP: 10
SQ FT: 193,000
SALES (est): 1.5MM **Privately Held**
WEB: www.stephenpaoli.com
SIC: 3556 Meat processing machinery; poultry processing machinery

(G-17647)
STRICTLY DENTURES
3920 E State St Ste 2 (61108-2051)
PHONE.................................815 969-0531
Michael Peterson, *Owner*
Melissa Peterson, *Owner*
EMP: 5
SALES (est): 528.7K **Privately Held**
SIC: 3843 Dental laboratory equipment

(G-17648)
STUHR MANUFACTURING CO
Also Called: Cdv
5085 27th Ave (61109-1701)
P.O. Box 6246 (61125-1246)
PHONE.................................815 398-2460
Gary Kiely, *President*
EMP: 10 EST: 1964
SQ FT: 20,000
SALES (est): 1.3MM **Privately Held**
SIC: 3545 3541 3423 Balancing machines (machine tool accessories); centering machines; hand & edge tools

Rockford - Winnebago County (G-17649)

(G-17649)
SUB SOURCE INC
600 18th Ave (61104-5159)
PHONE..................815 968-7800
Kristen Reinhardt, *President*
Michael Reinhardt, *Admin Sec*
EMP: 40
SQ FT: 15,000
SALES (est): 5.2MM **Privately Held**
WEB: www.subsourceinc.com
SIC: 7389 3479 Inspection & testing services; coating of metals & formed products

(G-17650)
SUSTAINABLE INNOVATIONS INC
1491 S Bell School Rd (61108-1407)
PHONE..................815 713-1637
John Murray, *President*
Erik Carlson, *Corp Secy*
Joshua Gillan, *Manager*
EMP: 4
SALES (est): 147.6K **Privately Held**
SIC: 2299 2834 2051 2052 Textile goods; pharmaceutical preparations; bread, cake & related products; cookies & crackers

(G-17651)
T SHIRTZ ETC INC
1000 9th St Apt D (61104-4955)
PHONE..................815 962-5194
Laurie Lindell, *President*
EMP: 2
SALES (est): 253.5K **Privately Held**
SIC: 2759 Screen printing

(G-17652)
TARGET LASER & MACHINING INC
2433 Fremont St (61103-4071)
PHONE..................815 963-6706
Stephen B Reiter, *President*
Brent M Reiter, *Vice Pres*
EMP: 25
SQ FT: 50,000
SALES (est): 4.8MM **Privately Held**
SIC: 3599 Machine shop, jobbing & repair

(G-17653)
TAURUS 80 LLC
Also Called: Dynacast
5196 27th Ave (61109-1713)
P.O. Box 245, Stillman Valley (61084-0245)
PHONE..................704 927-2793
EMP: 4
SALES (est): 317.3K **Privately Held**
SIC: 3565 Packaging machinery

(G-17654)
TAURUS DIE CASTING LLC
5196 27th Ave (61109-1713)
P.O. Box 7391 (61126-7391)
PHONE..................815 316-6160
▲ EMP: 15 EST: 2015
SALES (est): 608.5K **Privately Held**
SIC: 3364 3465 Mfg Nonferrous Die-Castings Mfg Automotive Stampings

(G-17655)
TEMPERATURE EQUIPMENT CORP
1818 18th Ave (61104-7318)
PHONE..................815 229-2935
EMP: 4
SALES (corp-wide): 106.1MM **Privately Held**
SIC: 3585 Mfg Refrigeration/Heating Equipment
HQ: Temperature Equipment Corporation
17725 Volbrecht Rd Ste 1
Lansing IL 60438
708 418-0900

(G-17656)
TESTOR CORPORATION
615 Buckbee St (61104-4834)
PHONE..................815 962-6654
Charles Leichtweis, *President*
Jenny Brasfield, *Natl Sales Mgr*
Kathy Jolly, *Natl Sales Mgr*
Rick Hoffman, *Manager*
William Grocke, *Technician*
▲ EMP: 60 EST: 1983
SALES (est): 12.1MM
SALES (corp-wide): 5.5B **Publicly Held**
WEB: www.testors.com
SIC: 2851 2891 3089 3952 Enamels; lacquer: bases, dopes, thinner; adhesives; cement, except linoleum & tile; kits, plastic; brushes, air, artists'; games, toys & children's vehicles
HQ: Rpm Consumer Holding Company
2628 Pearl Rd
Medina OH 44256

(G-17657)
THERMO FISHER SCIENTIFIC INC
3747 N Meridian Rd (61101-9316)
PHONE..................815 968-7970
Dave Meadows, *Vice Pres*
Greg Kilmer, *Research*
David Piper, *Research*
Jeffery Wall, *Finance*
Karen Fait, *Human Resources*
EMP: 5
SALES (corp-wide): 25.5B **Publicly Held**
SIC: 3826 Analytical instruments
PA: Thermo Fisher Scientific Inc.
168 3rd Ave
Waltham MA 02451
781 622-1000

(G-17658)
THERMOPLASTEC INC
4755 Colt Rd (61109-2610)
PHONE..................815 873-9288
Shyam Singh, *President*
Sheela Singh, *Treasurer*
EMP: 10
SALES (est): 1.7MM **Privately Held**
SIC: 3545 Tools & accessories for machine tools

(G-17659)
THOMAS ENGINEERING INC
Also Called: Triangle Metals Division
2500 Harrison Ave (61108-7458)
PHONE..................815 398-0280
Michael Quiros, *Engineer*
Doug Kanne, *Branch Mgr*
Benjamin Barney, *Manager*
EMP: 20
SALES (corp-wide): 17.2MM **Privately Held**
SIC: 3444 3559 Sheet metal specialties, not stamped; pharmaceutical machinery
PA: Thomas Engineering Inc.
575 W Central Rd
Hoffman Estates IL 60192
847 358-5800

(G-17660)
THOMASON MACHINE WORKS INC (PA)
5459 11th St (61109-3656)
PHONE..................815 874-8217
James F Thomason, *President*
Rose Gypsy, *Accounting Mgr*
Shelly Triplett, *Sales Staff*
EMP: 12
SQ FT: 13,000
SALES (est): 2.3MM **Privately Held**
SIC: 3599 Machine shop, jobbing & repair

(G-17661)
THOROUGHBRED PLASTICS LLC
129 Phelps Ave Ste 838 (61108-2450)
PHONE..................815 985-5116
Tom Gustafson,
EMP: 5
SALES: 500K **Privately Held**
SIC: 3089 Injection molded finished plastic products

(G-17662)
THORWORKS INDUSTRIES INC
Also Called: Sealmaster
904 7th St (61104-4654)
PHONE..................815 969-0664
Kenneth Horton, *Branch Mgr*
EMP: 5 **Privately Held**
SIC: 2951 Asphalt paving mixtures & blocks
PA: Thorworks Industries, Inc.
2520 Campbell St
Sandusky OH 44870

(G-17663)
TIMOTHY ANDERSON CORPORATION
Also Called: Signs Now
700 20th St (61104-3505)
PHONE..................815 398-8371
Tim Anderson, *President*
Dave Pierson, *Graphic Designe*
EMP: 12
SQ FT: 17,000
SALES: 1.5MM **Privately Held**
SIC: 3993 Signs & advertising specialties

(G-17664)
TOLEDO SCREW MACHINE PRODUCTS
5257 Northrock Dr (61103-1235)
PHONE..................815 877-8213
William Bjork, *President*
Al Bjork, *General Mgr*
Alan Bjork, *Vice Pres*
Dorothy Bjork, *Admin Sec*
EMP: 9
SQ FT: 18,000
SALES (est): 1.8MM **Privately Held**
WEB: www.toledoscrew.com
SIC: 3451 Screw machine products

(G-17665)
TOMERMO INC
Also Called: Rockford Separators
5127 28th Ave (61109-1720)
PHONE..................815 229-5077
Merritt Mott, *President*
Jim Griffin, *VP Mfg*
Mike Timm, *Technical Staff*
▲ EMP: 35 EST: 1963
SQ FT: 35,000
SALES (est): 7.8MM **Privately Held**
WEB: www.rkfdseparators.com
SIC: 3569 Separators for steam, gas, vapor or air (machinery)

(G-17666)
TOOL ENGRG CONSULTING MFG LLC
2932 Eastrock Dr (61109-1738)
PHONE..................815 316-2304
Joel Zehrung, *Vice Pres*
Scott Cromwell, *Engineer*
EMP: 8 EST: 2006
SQ FT: 3,000
SALES: 700K **Privately Held**
WEB: www.tecmtools.com
SIC: 3545 Cutting tools for machine tools

(G-17667)
TOOLMASTERS LLC (PA)
1204 Milford Ave (61109-3638)
PHONE..................815 968-0961
EMP: 25 EST: 1996
SQ FT: 2,000
SALES (est): 2.7MM **Privately Held**
SIC: 3545 Mfg Machine Tool Accessories

(G-17668)
TRIDENT MACHINE CO
3491 N Meridian Rd (61101-9322)
PHONE..................815 968-1585
Lyle Sheley, *Partner*
Lylia Pierce, *Partner*
Mary Sheley, *Partner*
EMP: 8 EST: 1964
SQ FT: 5,000
SALES (est): 623.2K **Privately Held**
SIC: 3599 3812 3728 Machine shop, jobbing & repair; search & navigation equipment; aircraft parts & equipment

(G-17669)
TY PRECISION AUTOMATICS INC
2606 Falund St (61109-1042)
PHONE..................815 963-9668
John W Tallman, *President*
Todd T Tallman, *Vice Pres*
EMP: 16
SQ FT: 26,000
SALES: 150K **Privately Held**
SIC: 3451 Screw machine products

(G-17670)
ULTRA STAMPING & ASSEMBLY INC
4590 Hydraulic Rd (61109-2614)
PHONE..................815 874-9888
Charles Cushman, *President*
Tracy Cushman, *Vice Pres*
Paul Jones, *Safety Mgr*
Gordon Cushman, *Sales Executive*
Jon Legge, *Manager*
EMP: 21
SQ FT: 25,000
SALES (est): 5MM **Privately Held**
WEB: www.ultrastamping.com
SIC: 3441 3469 Fabricated structural metal; stamping metal for the trade

(G-17671)
UNITED SKILLED INC
3412 Precision Dr (61109-2770)
PHONE..................815 874-9696
Norman Tangerose, *President*
Jeremy Tangerose, *President*
EMP: 4 EST: 1973
SQ FT: 6,000
SALES (est): 241.5K **Privately Held**
SIC: 3544 Special dies & tools

(G-17672)
UNITED STATES FILTER/IWT
4669 Shepherd Trl (61103-1294)
PHONE..................815 877-3041
Marvin Deam, *Principal*
EMP: 7
SALES (est): 1MM **Privately Held**
SIC: 3569 Filters

(G-17673)
UNIVERSAL HOVERCRAFT AMER INC
1218 Buchanan St (61101-1404)
PHONE..................815 963-1200
William Zang, *President*
EMP: 12
SQ FT: 12,000
SALES (est): 1.1MM **Privately Held**
SIC: 3089 Kits, plastic

(G-17674)
UTC AEROSPACE SYSTEMS
4747 Harrison Ave (61108-7929)
PHONE..................877 808-7575
EMP: 3
SALES (est): 121.7K **Privately Held**
SIC: 3812 Mfg Search/Navigation Equipment

(G-17675)
VILLA FOODS LLC
8565 Jamesport Dr (61108-7032)
PHONE..................815 721-1136
Stephen Villacorta,
EMP: 3
SALES (est): 103.3K **Privately Held**
SIC: 2499 Food handling & processing products, wood

(G-17676)
WALERN FORM GRINDING INC
Also Called: Walern Form Grinding
4717 Colt Rd (61109-2610)
PHONE..................815 874-7000
Ernest Chisamore, *CEO*
James Chisamore, *President*
Hisako Chisamore, *Treasurer*
Carrie Harris, *Admin Sec*
EMP: 6 EST: 1970
SQ FT: 7,000
SALES: 600K **Privately Held**
SIC: 3599 3544 Grinding castings for the trade; special dies, tools, jigs & fixtures

(G-17677)
WARTHOG INC
2615 Yonge St (61101-4265)
PHONE..................815 540-7197
Michael Clayton, *President*
EMP: 4
SALES (est): 307.5K **Privately Held**
SIC: 3949 Sporting & athletic goods

(G-17678)
WATT PUBLISHING CO (PA)
Also Called: Watt Global Media
401 E State St Fl 3 (61104-1027)
PHONE.................................815 966-5400
James W Watt, *Ch of Bd*
Gregory A Watt, *President*
Roy Leidahl, *Vice Pres*
Bruce Plantz, *Vice Pres*
Steve Slakis, *Vice Pres*
EMP: 50 **EST:** 1917
SQ FT: 32,000
SALES (est): 9.3MM **Privately Held**
WEB: www.wattagnet.com
SIC: 2721 Magazines: publishing only, not printed on site

(G-17679)
WELLIVER & SONS INC
1540 New Milford Schl Rd (61109-4399)
PHONE.................................815 874-2400
Barry Welliver, *President*
EMP: 25 **EST:** 1945
SQ FT: 18,000
SALES (est): 2.8MM **Privately Held**
SIC: 3546 Power-driven handtools

(G-17680)
WEST SIDE TRACTOR SALES CO
Also Called: John Deere Authorized Dealer
3110 Prairie Rd (61102-3948)
PHONE.................................815 961-3160
Roger Svartoien, *Manager*
EMP: 20
SALES (corp-wide): 201.5MM **Privately Held**
SIC: 3531 5261 5082 Construction machinery; lawnmowers & tractors; construction & mining machinery
PA: West Side Tractor Sales Co.
1400 W Ogden Ave
Naperville IL 60563
630 355-7150

(G-17681)
WESTERN MOTOR MFG CO
1211 23rd Ave (61104-7160)
PHONE.................................815 986-2214
Marianne Anderson, *President*
Janet Champlin, *Regional Mgr*
Greg Sundeen, *Vice Pres*
Marty Anderson, *Manager*
▲ **EMP:** 3
SQ FT: 30,000
SALES (est): 405.1K **Privately Held**
SIC: 3621 Motors & generators

(G-17682)
WEYERHAEUSER COMPANY
1753 23rd Ave (61104-7356)
PHONE.................................815 987-0395
Robert Schultz, *Branch Mgr*
EMP: 6
SALES (corp-wide): 6.5B **Publicly Held**
WEB: www.weyerhaeuser.com
SIC: 4783 2621 Containerization of goods for shipping; paper mills
PA: Weyerhaeuser Company
220 Occidental Ave S
Seattle WA 98104
206 539-3000

(G-17683)
WHITNEY ROPER LLC
Also Called: Roper Whitney
2833 Huffman Blvd (61103-3906)
PHONE.................................815 962-3011
Mark Smith, *President*
Brad Smith, *Vice Pres*
Mike Smith, *Vice Pres*
◆ **EMP:** 56
SQ FT: 125,000
SALES: 15.8MM **Privately Held**
SIC: 3542 3546 3544 3423 Metal deposit forming machines; power-driven handtools; special dies, tools, jigs & fixtures; hand & edge tools; cutlery

(G-17684)
WHITNEY ROPER ROCKFORD INC
Also Called: Rw Acquisition
2833 Huffman Blvd (61103-3906)
PHONE.................................815 962-3011
Mark Smith, *President*
Brad Smith, *Vice Pres*
Mike Smith, *Vice Pres*
Jason Smoak, *Vice Pres*
Rick Keister, *Buyer*
▲ **EMP:** 56
SQ FT: 125,000
SALES (est): 69.8K **Privately Held**
SIC: 3542 3546 3544 3423 Sheet metalworking machines; power-driven handtools; special dies, tools, jigs & fixtures; hand & edge tools; cutlery

(G-17685)
WILLIAM DACH
Also Called: Dach Fence Co
4901 W State St (61102-1242)
PHONE.................................815 962-3455
William Dach, *Owner*
EMP: 10
SALES (est): 925K **Privately Held**
SIC: 1799 5211 3496 3354 Fence construction; fencing; miscellaneous fabricated wire products; aluminum extruded products; steel wire & related products

(G-17686)
WILSON MFG SCREW MCH PDTS
4004 Auburn St (61101-2505)
PHONE.................................815 964-8724
Michael Wilson Sr, *President*
Sharon Wilson, *Corp Secy*
EMP: 10
SALES (est): 825K **Privately Held**
WEB: www.wilson-mfg.com
SIC: 3451 Screw machine products

(G-17687)
WILSON TOOL CORPORATION
2401 20th St (61104-7451)
PHONE.................................815 226-0147
Virginia A Wilson, *President*
Kimberly Bradford, *General Mgr*
Frank Lasala, *Vice Pres*
Brad Wilson, *Purchasing*
David W Wilson, *Admin Sec*
EMP: 25
SQ FT: 25,000
SALES (est): 4.8MM **Privately Held**
SIC: 3599 3769 Machine shop, jobbing & repair; guided missile & space vehicle parts & aux eqpt, rsch & dev

(G-17688)
WIRETECH INC
521 18th Ave (61104-5130)
PHONE.................................815 986-9614
Gary Goodson, *Exec VP*
Mark Nelson, *Branch Mgr*
EMP: 3
SALES (corp-wide): 33.3MM **Privately Held**
SIC: 3315 Steel wire & related products
PA: Wiretech, Inc.
6440 Canning St
Commerce CA 90040
323 722-4933

(G-17689)
WNTA STUDIO LINE
830 Sandy Hollow Rd (61109-2027)
PHONE.................................815 874-7861
EMP: 3
SALES (est): 157.5K **Privately Held**
SIC: 2711 4832 Newspapers-Publishing/Printing Radio Broadcast Station

(G-17690)
WOODS EQUIPMENT COMPANY
Also Called: Tisco Parts
1818 Elmwood Rd Ste 2 (61103-1210)
PHONE.................................815 732-2141
Robert Mudloff, *Manager*
EMP: 56
SALES (corp-wide): 1.4B **Privately Held**
SIC: 3523 Turf & grounds equipment
HQ: Woods Equipment Company
2606 S Il Route 2
Oregon IL 61061

(G-17691)
X-TECH INNOVATIONS INC
424 18th Ave (61104-5129)
PHONE.................................815 962-4127
Jordan Kingsbury, *President*
EMP: 5
SALES (est): 783.9K **Privately Held**
SIC: 3599 7389 Custom machinery; industrial & commercial equipment inspection service

Rockton
Winnebago County

(G-17692)
BALSLEY PRINTING INC (PA)
Also Called: Balsley Fast Printing
119 E Main St (61072-2519)
PHONE.................................815 624-7515
James E Balsley, *President*
Tim Deberry, *Prdtn Mgr*
Denise Balsley, *Treasurer*
Billie Balsley, *Manager*
Judy Balsley, *Director*
EMP: 13 **EST:** 1979
SQ FT: 8,500
SALES (est): 1.9MM **Privately Held**
SIC: 2752 Commercial printing, offset

(G-17693)
BALSLEY PRINTING INC
119 E Main St (61072-2519)
PHONE.................................815 624-7515
Sam Balsley, *Branch Mgr*
EMP: 15
SQ FT: 1,500
SALES (est): 1.9MM **Privately Held**
SIC: 7334 2752 Photocopying & duplicating services; commercial printing, offset
PA: Balsley Printing, Inc.
119 E Main St
Rockton IL 61072
815 624-7515

(G-17694)
CHEMTOOL INCORPORATED (DH)
801 W Rockton Rd (61072-1647)
PHONE.................................815 957-4140
Charles Robinson, *President*
◆ **EMP:** 125 **EST:** 1963
SQ FT: 100,000
SALES: 126.8MM
SALES (corp-wide): 327.2B **Publicly Held**
WEB: www.chemtool.com
SIC: 2899 2842 2841 2992 Rust resisting compounds; water treating compounds; specialty cleaning, polishes & sanitation goods; soap & other detergents; cutting oils, blending: made from purchased materials
HQ: The Lubrizol Corporation
29400 Lakeland Blvd
Wickliffe OH 44092
440 943-4200

(G-17695)
CHEMTOOL INCORPORATED
1165 Prairie Hill Rd (61072-1545)
PHONE.................................815 389-0250
Sean Staedler, *Plant Mgr*
EMP: 3
SALES (corp-wide): 327.2B **Publicly Held**
SIC: 2992 Lubricating oils & greases
HQ: Chemtool Incorporated
801 W Rockton Rd
Rockton IL 61072
815 957-4140

(G-17696)
CREATIVE CONTROLS SYSTEMS INC
15929 Hauley Rd (61072-9769)
PHONE.................................815 629-2358
Allen R Holecek, *President*
Doris Holecek, *Corp Secy*
Dan Ebneter, *Vice Pres*
EMP: 6 **EST:** 1972
SQ FT: 3,100
SALES: 500K **Privately Held**
SIC: 3823 7371 3822 3625 Computer interface equipment for industrial process control; custom computer programming services; auto controls regulating residntl & coml environmt & applncs; relays & industrial controls

(G-17697)
EXPANDABLE HABITATS
11022 N Main St (61072-9458)
PHONE.................................815 624-6784
Tricia David, *Owner*
Gregory David, *Co-Owner*
EMP: 5
SQ FT: 3,600
SALES (est): 330K **Privately Held**
SIC: 3496 3316 Miscellaneous fabricated wire products; cold finishing of steel shapes

(G-17698)
GREEN TECHNOLOGIES INC
112 Hawick St (61072-2415)
P.O. Box 328 (61072-0328)
PHONE.................................815 624-8011
Barbara Green, *Principal*
EMP: 3
SALES (est): 279.3K **Privately Held**
WEB: www.greentechnologies.biz
SIC: 3599 Machine shop, jobbing & repair

(G-17699)
KENENT SCREW MACHINE PRODUCTS
4843 Yale Bridge Rd (61072-9503)
PHONE.................................815 624-7216
Mary Linda Kennedy, *Owner*
Tony Kennedy, *Co-Owner*
EMP: 10
SQ FT: 5,000
SALES: 500K **Privately Held**
SIC: 3451 Screw machine products

(G-17700)
NOVEL PRODUCTS INC
3266 Yale Bridge Rd (61072-9635)
P.O. Box 408 (61072-0408)
PHONE.................................815 624-4888
EMP: 3 **EST:** 1975
SALES: 600K **Privately Held**
SIC: 3821 Mfg Laboratory Apparatus & Furniture

(G-17701)
SENTRO PRINTING EQUIP N MOVERS
332 Harwich Pl (61072-2989)
PHONE.................................779 423-0255
Keith Sessler, *Principal*
EMP: 3
SALES (est): 217.8K **Privately Held**
SIC: 2759 Commercial printing

(G-17702)
TAYLOR CO ASUESS TAYLOR
750 N Blackhawk Blvd (61072-2104)
PHONE.................................815 624-8333
Clark Wangaard, *Principal*
Denise Baum, *Site Mgr*
Dean Bladom, *Purchasing*
Ken Moshier, *Engineer*
Michael Thompson, *Senior Engr*
▲ **EMP:** 2
SALES (est): 240K **Privately Held**
SIC: 3556 Food products machinery

(G-17703)
TAYLOR COML FOODSERVICE INC (DH)
Also Called: Beverage-Air, A Div of
750 N Blackhawk Blvd (61072-2104)
P.O. Box 410 (61072-0410)
PHONE.................................815 624-8333
◆ **EMP:** 15

Rockton - Winnebago County (G-17704)

SALES (est): 849.9MM
SALES (corp-wide): 2.9B **Publicly Held**
SIC: 3556 3631 3585 3589 Ice cream manufacturing machinery; dairy & milk machinery; household cooking equipment; refrigeration equipment, complete; beer dispensing equipment; food warming equipment, commercial; cooking equipment, commercial; coffee brewing equipment; dryers, electric: hand & face; hair dryers, electric
HQ: Marshall Middleby Inc
1400 Toastmaster Dr
Elgin IL 60120
847 741-3300

(G-17704)
TAYLOR COML FOODSERVICE INC
98 Autumnwood Dr (61072-3227)
PHONE.....................815 624-8333
EMP: 627
SALES (corp-wide): 2.9B **Publicly Held**
SIC: 3556 Ice cream manufacturing machinery
HQ: Taylor Commercial Foodservice Inc.
750 N Blackhawk Blvd
Rockton IL 61072
815 624-8333

(G-17705)
TWO CARDS INNOVATION LLC
1294 Dixie Trl (61072-9453)
PHONE.....................815 793-2517
Scott Danielson,
EMP: 4
SALES (est): 125.1K **Privately Held**
SIC: 3999 Manufacturing industries

Rockwood
Randolph County

(G-17706)
JONES WOOD PRODUCTS
11801 Ebenezer Rd (62280)
PHONE.....................618 826-2682
Harry M Jones, Owner
EMP: 4
SALES (est): 209.4K **Privately Held**
SIC: 2499 Wood products

Rolling Meadows
Cook County

(G-17707)
4200 KIRCHOFF CORP
Also Called: Marathon Gas
4200 Kirchoff Rd (60008-2006)
PHONE.....................773 551-1541
Jose Mathew, President
EMP: 5
SALES (est): 242.3K **Privately Held**
SIC: 2911 Petroleum refining

(G-17708)
A M TOOL & DIE
1000 Carnegie St (60008-1007)
PHONE.....................847 398-7530
Alan Mortenson, Owner
▲ EMP: 30 EST: 1972
SQ FT: 6,000
SALES (est): 5MM **Privately Held**
SIC: 3544 Special dies & tools

(G-17709)
ADESSO SOLUTIONS LLC
3701 Algonquin Rd Ste 270 (60008-3188)
PHONE.....................847 342-1095
Ron Reed, CEO
Fred Schroeder, President
Tom Utgard, Principal
Rich Jones, Exec VP
Jim Charles, Vice Pres
EMP: 13
SALES (est): 2.2MM **Privately Held**
SIC: 7372 Business oriented computer software

(G-17710)
AMERICAN ASSN NUROSURGEONS INC (PA)
Also Called: A A N S
5550 Meadowbrook Dr (60008)
PHONE.....................847 378-0500
Christopher I Shaffrey, President
Robert Heary, Vice Pres
Jon N Mau, Marketing Mgr
Adrienne Mortimer, Senior Mgr
Kathleen Craig, Exec Dir
▲ EMP: 40 EST: 1931
SQ FT: 33,000
SALES (est): 21.1MM **Privately Held**
SIC: 8621 2721 Medical field-related associations; periodicals

(G-17711)
ANGLE PRESS INC
3701 Algonquin Rd Ste 340 (60008-3189)
PHONE.....................847 439-6388
Fujio Nakagawa, President
EMP: 9
SALES (est): 680K **Privately Held**
SIC: 2741 Miscellaneous publishing

(G-17712)
APEX TOOL WORKS INC
Also Called: Wangren Machine
3200 Tollview Dr (60008-3706)
PHONE.....................847 394-5810
Michael C Collins, President
William Collins, Vice Pres
Phillip Whittenhall, Vice Pres
Rob Runyard, Foreman/Supr
Inge Ohnona, Purchasing
▲ EMP: 46 EST: 1919
SQ FT: 48,364
SALES (est): 9.6MM **Privately Held**
WEB: www.apextool.com
SIC: 3544 Special dies & tools

(G-17713)
ATS SORTIMAT USA LLC
Also Called: Sortimat Techonology
5655 Meadowbrook Indus Ct (60008-3833)
PHONE.....................847 925-1234
Hans Dieter Baumtrog, CEO
Brian Garside, Manager
◆ EMP: 60
SQ FT: 35,000
SALES (est): 22.6MM **Privately Held**
SIC: 3569 3549 3599 7692 Assembly machines, non-metalworking; assembly machines, including robotic; custom machinery; welding repair; packaging machinery

(G-17714)
AUTOMATIC BUILDING CONTRLS LLC (PA)
3315 Algonquin Rd Ste 550 (60008-3240)
PHONE.....................847 296-4000
Mark Bevill, CEO
Grant Bevill, President
Patrick McKinney, Engineer
▲ EMP: 75 EST: 1988
SQ FT: 8,000
SALES (est): 13MM **Privately Held**
SIC: 3822 Temperature controls, automatic

(G-17715)
AUTOTYPE AMERICAS INCORPORATED
1675 Winnetka Cir (60008-1372)
PHONE.....................847 818-8262
Frank Monteiro, Principal
EMP: 3
SALES (est): 240K **Privately Held**
SIC: 2796 5084 Lithographic plates, positives or negatives; printing trades machinery, equipment & supplies

(G-17716)
BANDJWET ENTERPRISES INC
Also Called: B.E.S.t
3603 Edison Pl (60008-1012)
PHONE.....................847 797-9250
Robert Wetterman, President
James Barnhart, Principal
EMP: 1
SALES (est): 226.8K **Privately Held**
SIC: 3672 Printed circuit boards

(G-17717)
BANDJWET ENTERPRISES INC
Also Called: B & J Wet Enterprises
3603 Edison Pl (60008-1012)
PHONE.....................847 797-9250
Robert Wettermann, President
Christine Kraner, CFO
Alexander Conley, Corp Comm Staff
EMP: 30
SQ FT: 24,000
SALES (est): 4.4MM **Privately Held**
SIC: 8249 3672 Vocational apprentice training; circuit boards, television & radio printed

(G-17718)
BAPS INVESTORS GROUP LLC
Also Called: Midwest Insert Composite Mold
3940 Industrial Ave (60008-1024)
PHONE.....................847 818-8444
Ripan Sheth, President
Kanti Patel,
▲ EMP: 25
SQ FT: 35,000
SALES (est): 5.1MM **Privately Held**
SIC: 3089 Injection molding of plastics

(G-17719)
BINGAMN-PRCSION MTAL SPNNING C
Also Called: Bingaman Metal Spinning
1000 Carnegie St (60008-1007)
PHONE.....................847 392-5620
Dorothy L Doumakes, President
EMP: 40
SQ FT: 35,000
SALES (est): 4.7MM **Privately Held**
SIC: 3469 Stamping metal for the trade

(G-17720)
CARMEN MATTHEW LLC
Also Called: Norlux
2100 Golf Rd Ste 460 (60008-4704)
PHONE.....................630 784-7500
Brad Lipinski, Purch Mgr
Greg Bobeczko, Engineer
Mahesh Patel, Engineer
John Dinardi,
Doug Hamilton,
▲ EMP: 56
SALES (est): 13.5MM **Privately Held**
SIC: 3648 Lighting equipment

(G-17721)
CIC NORTH AMERICA INC
5410 Newport Dr Ste 40 (60008-3722)
PHONE.....................847 873-0860
Jason Lim, Vice Pres
▲ EMP: 10
SALES (est): 593.2K **Privately Held**
SIC: 3559 Electronic component making machinery

(G-17722)
CLEAN AND SCIENCE USA CO LTD
2775 Algonquin Rd Ste 110 (60008-3899)
PHONE.....................847 461-9292
Jaewon Choi, President
▲ EMP: 4
SALES (est): 1MM **Privately Held**
WEB: www.cleanandscience.com
SIC: 5075 3564 3599 Air filters; blower filter units (furnace blowers); air intake filters, internal combustion engine, except auto

(G-17723)
CLICK-BLOCK CORPORATION
Also Called: Click Block
1100 Hicks Rd (60008-1016)
PHONE.....................847 749-1651
Byung Whang, President
Sungwhan Kim, Principal
▲ EMP: 36
SALES: 500K **Privately Held**
SIC: 3944 Blocks, toy

(G-17724)
COTTAGE DOOR PRESS LLC
5005 Newport Dr Ste 300 (60008-3839)
PHONE.....................224 228-6000
Jared Svoboda, Mfg Staff
Nadine Mims, Sales Dir
Eric Peterson, Sales Dir
Megan Reilly, Sales Staff
Maddrell Richard, Mng Member
EMP: 10
SALES (est): 1.7MM **Privately Held**
SIC: 2741 Miscellaneous publishing

(G-17725)
CRYSTAL DIE AND MOLD INC
5521 Meadowbrook Indus Ct (60008-3818)
PHONE.....................847 658-6535
Mike Biangardi, President
Maria Sanmiguel, Controller
Nancy Krahn, Director
▲ EMP: 50 EST: 1966
SQ FT: 24,000
SALES (est): 7.8MM **Privately Held**
WEB: www.cdmsolutions.com
SIC: 3089 3544 Injection molding of plastics; industrial molds

(G-17726)
DESIGNERS POINT INC
2150 Plum Grove Rd (60008-1932)
PHONE.....................224 578-7043
Dick Minar, President
Karen Schone, Partner
EMP: 7
SQ FT: 2,300
SALES (est): 847K **Privately Held**
WEB: www.designers-point.com
SIC: 2434 Vanities, bathroom: wood

(G-17727)
DIGITAL OPTICS TECH INC
1645 Hicks Rd Ste H (60008-1222)
PHONE.....................847 358-2592
Selim Shahriar, President
Nicholas Condon, Vice Pres
EMP: 4
SALES (est): 400K **Privately Held**
SIC: 3674 8731 Microprocessors; computer (hardware) development

(G-17728)
DYTEC MIDWEST INC (PA)
1855 Rohlwing Rd Ste C (60008-1474)
PHONE.....................847 255-3200
James D Okon, President
Armando Prado, Sales Engr
EMP: 6
SQ FT: 3,000
SALES (est): 1.2MM **Privately Held**
SIC: 5065 5045 3825 Electronic parts; computers, peripherals & software; test equipment for electronic & electric measurement

(G-17729)
ELIM PDTRIC PHRMACEUTICALS INC (PA)
Corp Ctr 1600 (60008)
PHONE.....................412 266-5968
Moji Adeyeye, CEO
EMP: 7
SALES (est): 4.3MM **Privately Held**
WEB: www.elimpedpharma.com
SIC: 2834 Pharmaceutical preparations

(G-17730)
ELIM PDTRIC PHRMACEUTICALS INC
Eppi and Consulting
Corp Ctr 1600 Glf Rd 12 (60008)
PHONE.....................412 266-5968
Dr Moji Adeyeye, Branch Mgr
EMP: 3
SALES (corp-wide): 4.3MM **Privately Held**
SIC: 2834 Pharmaceutical preparations
PA: Elim Pediatric Pharmaceuticals Inc.
Corp Ctr 1600
Rolling Meadows IL 60008
412 266-5968

(G-17731)
EMBEDUR SYSTEMS INC
3601 Algonquin Rd Ste 608 (60008-3110)
PHONE.....................847 749-3665
EMP: 3
SALES (est): 121.7K **Privately Held**
WEB: www.embedur.com
SIC: 7372 Prepackaged software
PA: Embedur Systems, Inc.
42808 Christy St Ste 102
Fremont CA

GEOGRAPHIC SECTION

Rolling Meadows - Cook County (G-17758)

(G-17732)
FELIX PARTNERS LLC
1845 Hicks Rd Ste C (60008-1269)
PHONE.................847 648-8449
Michael Lichter,
Felicia Shelfo,
EMP: 2 EST: 2007
SALES (est): 229.4K Privately Held
SIC: 3559 Electronic component making machinery

(G-17733)
FOUR STAR TOOL INC
5521 Meadowbrook Ct (60008)
PHONE.................224 735-2419
Helmut Hoppe, CEO
Mike Biangardi, President
Matthias Biangardi, CFO
▲ EMP: 100 EST: 1966
SQ FT: 36,000
SALES (est): 12.7MM Privately Held
WEB: www.injectit.com
SIC: 3679 3469 3089 Electronic circuits; metal stampings; injection molded finished plastic products

(G-17734)
GLOBAL TECH & RESOURCES INC
Also Called: Db Professionals
3601 Algonquin Rd Ste 650 (60008-3184)
PHONE.................630 364-4260
EMP: 2
SALES (est): 1.2MM Privately Held
SIC: 7372 8748 Prepackaged Software

(G-17735)
HUAWEI TECHNOLOGIES USA INC
3601 Algonquin Rd (60008-3126)
PHONE.................425 463-8275
EMP: 3
SALES (corp-wide): 103.8B Privately Held
WEB: www.huawei.com
SIC: 3663 Radio & TV communications equipment
HQ: Huawei Technologies Usa Inc.
5700 Tennyson Pkwy # 500
Plano TX 75024
214 545-3700

(G-17736)
HUBBELL LIGHTING INC
Also Called: Hubbell Lighting Components
2100 Golf Rd Ste 460 (60008-4704)
PHONE.................847 515-3057
EMP: 3
SALES (corp-wide): 4.5B Publicly Held
SIC: 3648 Outdoor lighting equipment
HQ: Hubbell Lighting, Inc.
701 Millennium Blvd
Greenville SC 29607

(G-17737)
HUBERGROUP USA INC (DH)
Also Called: Hubergroup North America
1701 Golf Rd Ste 3-201 (60008-4260)
PHONE.................815 929-9293
Martin Weber, CEO
Mark Wilson, COO
Reginal Smith, Vice Pres
Angela Hunt, Production
Venkat Subrahmanian, Finance Dir
◆ EMP: 90
SALES (est): 64.5MM
SALES (corp-wide): 355.8K Privately Held
SIC: 2893 Printing ink

(G-17738)
ICON IDENTITY SOLUTIONS INC (HQ)
1701 Golf Rd Ste 1-900 (60008-4246)
PHONE.................847 364-2250
Tim Eippert, CEO
Kurt Ripkey, President
Dave Walters, President
Kevin Hughes, Exec VP
Tom Hunt, Exec VP
EMP: 197 EST: 1925
SQ FT: 100,000
SALES: 168.7MM Privately Held
WEB: www.iconid.com
SIC: 3993 Neon signs

PA: Mc Sign Llc
8959 Tyler Blvd Unit 1
Mentor OH 44060
440 209-6200

(G-17739)
IMAGECARE MAINTENANCE SVCS LLC
1701 Golf Rd Ste 1-900 (60008-4246)
PHONE.................847 631-3306
Kurt W Ripkey, President
EMP: 17
SALES (est): 2MM
SALES (corp-wide): 168.7MM Privately Held
SIC: 3993 Signs & advertising specialties
HQ: Icon Identity Solutions, Inc.
1701 Golf Rd Ste 1-900
Rolling Meadows IL 60008
847 364-2250

(G-17740)
INDUSTRIAL THERMO PRODUCTS
1051 Rohlwing Rd Ste C (60008-1051)
PHONE.................847 398-8600
Francis E Worland, President
EMP: 8
SALES (est): 3MM Privately Held
SIC: 3585 3823 3822 3829 Heating equipment, complete; temperature instruments: industrial process type; temperature controls, automatic; thermometers & temperature sensors

(G-17741)
INSIGNIA DESIGN LTD
2118 Plum Grove Rd 191 (60008-1932)
PHONE.................301 254-9221
Pamela Roark, President
James M Roark, Principal
EMP: 2
SALES: 250K Privately Held
SIC: 3993 2262 Signs & advertising specialties; printing: manmade fiber & silk broadwoven fabrics

(G-17742)
JAMES COLEMAN COMPANY
1500 Hicks Rd (60008-1200)
PHONE.................847 963-8100
Chris Wade, President
Matthew Wade, Vice Pres
◆ EMP: 14 EST: 1972
SQ FT: 5,000
SALES (est): 2MM Privately Held
WEB: www.jimcolemanstore.com
SIC: 3999 Advertising display products

(G-17743)
JOONG-ANG DAILY NEWS
Also Called: The Korea Centl Daily Chicago
3501 Algonquin Rd Ste 250 (60008-3147)
PHONE.................847 228-7200
Gwang Jang, President
Daniel Um, Vice Pres
▲ EMP: 35 EST: 1975
SALES (est): 2.1MM Privately Held
SIC: 2711 2741 Commercial printing & newspaper publishing combined; miscellaneous publishing

(G-17744)
KOMATSU FORKLIFT USA LLC (HQ)
Also Called: Kfi
1701 Golf Rd Ste 1 (60008-4234)
PHONE.................847 437-5800
Patrick King, Finance Mgr
Scott Greene, Senior Mgr
Luke Waitkus, Director
Akira Yamakawa,
▲ EMP: 30
SALES (est): 24.4MM Privately Held
SIC: 3537 5084 Forklift trucks; lift trucks & parts

(G-17745)
KOMORI AMERICA CORPORATION (HQ)
5520 Meadowbrook Indus Ct (60008-3898)
PHONE.................847 806-9000
Kazuyoshi Miyao, President
Hiro Hoshino, Exec VP
Robert J Rath, Exec VP

Jacki Hudmon, Senior VP
Jerrold E Fink, Admin Sec
▲ EMP: 65
SQ FT: 48,000
SALES (est): 42.2MM Privately Held
WEB: www.komori-america.us
SIC: 5044 3542 3555 Office equipment; machine tools, metal forming type; printing trades machinery

(G-17746)
L C MOLD INC
3640 Edison Pl (60008-1013)
PHONE.................847 593-5004
Leonid Danushevsky, President
Margaret Danushevsky, Admin Sec
EMP: 36
SQ FT: 15,000
SALES (est): 5.4MM Privately Held
SIC: 3089 3544 8742 Injection molding of plastics; special dies, tools, jigs & fixtures; training & development consultant

(G-17747)
L3 TECHNOLOGIES INC
1200 Hicks Rd (60008-1017)
PHONE.................212 697-1111
Kai Liu, Electrical Engi
EMP: 14
SALES (corp-wide): 6.8B Publicly Held
SIC: 3663 Radio & TV communications equipment
HQ: L3 Technologies, Inc.
600 3rd Ave Fl 34
New York NY 10016
212 697-1111

(G-17748)
LION TRANS GROUP INC
5300 Carriageway Dr (60008-3990)
PHONE.................970 402-8073
Adrian Staver, President
EMP: 5
SALES: 400K Privately Held
SIC: 3537 Trucks: freight, baggage, etc.: industrial, except mining

(G-17749)
M & R PRINTING INC
Also Called: Allegra Print & Imaging
5100 Newport Dr Ste 4 (60008-3825)
PHONE.................847 398-2500
Michael E Tarpinian, President
EMP: 6
SQ FT: 2,800
SALES (est): 894.6K Privately Held
SIC: 2752 7389 2791 Commercial printing, offset; design, commercial & industrial; typesetting

(G-17750)
METHODE ELECTRONICS INC
Power Solutions Group
1700 Hicks Rd (60008-1229)
PHONE.................847 577-9545
Andrew Urda, General Mgr
EMP: 158
SQ FT: 1,145
SALES (corp-wide): 1B Publicly Held
WEB: www.methode.com
SIC: 3678 3643 Electronic connectors; current-carrying wiring devices
PA: Methode Electronics, Inc
8750 W Bryn Mawr Ave # 1000
Chicago IL 60631
708 867-6777

(G-17751)
MITSUTOYO-KIKO USA INC
1600 Golf Rd Ste 1200 (60008-4229)
PHONE.................847 981-5200
Tamotsu Ozaki, President
EMP: 4
SALES: 600K Privately Held
SIC: 3462 Machinery forgings, ferrous
PA: Mitsutoyo-Kiko Co.,Ltd.
1-4-12, Higashinoshinmachi
Kasugai AIC 486-0

(G-17752)
NATIONAL TECHNOLOGY INC
1101 Carnegie St (60008-1008)
PHONE.................847 506-1300
Roger Patel, CEO
Robert Keisler, President
Sudhir Pandya, Engineer

Vijay Patel, Treasurer
Jeff Phillips, Controller
◆ EMP: 40
SQ FT: 55,000
SALES (est): 8.7MM Privately Held
SIC: 3672 Printed circuit boards

(G-17753)
NITEK INTERNATIONAL LLC
5410 Newport Dr Ste 24 (60008-3722)
PHONE.................847 259-8900
Ed Planek,
▲ EMP: 4
SALES (est): 740.9K Privately Held
SIC: 3699 Security control equipment & systems

(G-17754)
NORTHERN INFORMATION TECH
Also Called: I Tech
5410 Newport Dr Ste 24 (60008-3722)
PHONE.................800 528-4343
Edward Polanek, President
EMP: 16 EST: 1984
SQ FT: 6,400
SALES (est): 1.7MM Privately Held
WEB: www.nitek.net
SIC: 3663 Television closed circuit equipment

(G-17755)
NORTHROP GRUMMAN SYSTEMS CORP
600 Hicks Rd (60008-1015)
PHONE.................847 259-9600
Jennifer Perkins, Vice Pres
James Drwal, Mfg Mgr
David Fulton, Opers Staff
James Sukowicz, Opers Staff
Tom Hopkins, Purchasing
EMP: 637
SQ FT: 400,000 Publicly Held
WEB: www.northropgrumman.com
SIC: 3663 3679 3671 3651 Radio broadcasting & communications equipment; electronic circuits; electron tubes; household audio & video equipment; motors & generators; electronic computers
HQ: Northrop Grumman Systems Corporation
2980 Fairview Park Dr
Falls Church VA 22042
703 280-2900

(G-17756)
NORTHROP GRUMMAN SYSTEMS CORP
1605 Rohlwing Rd (60008-1337)
PHONE.................847 259-9600
Roland Marquis, Branch Mgr
Kimberly Michalsen, Program Mgr
EMP: 65 Publicly Held
SIC: 3812 Search & navigation equipment
HQ: Northrop Grumman Systems Corporation
2980 Fairview Park Dr
Falls Church VA 22042
703 280-2900

(G-17757)
OBERWEIS DAIRY INC
1735 Algonquin Rd (60008-4112)
PHONE.................847 290-9222
Jen Shabec, Manager
EMP: 10
SALES (corp-wide): 249.7MM Privately Held
SIC: 2026 5963 5451 Milk processing (pasteurizing, homogenizing, bottling); milk delivery; milk; ice cream (packaged)
PA: Oberweis Dairy, Inc.
951 Ice Cream Dr
North Aurora IL 60542
630 801-6100

(G-17758)
P K NEUSES INCORPORATED
Also Called: Neuses Tools
1401 Rohlwing Rd (60008-1398)
P.O. Box 100, Arlington Heights (60006-0100)
PHONE.................847 253-6555
Gary B Neuses, President
Guy Neuses, Vice Pres

Rolling Meadows - Cook County (G-17759)

Kathy Neuses, *Admin Sec*
EMP: 6 **EST:** 1944
SQ FT: 8,000
SALES (est): 1.2MM **Privately Held**
WEB: www.pkneuses.com
SIC: 3825 3678 3545 3423 Measuring instruments & meters, electric; electronic connectors; machine tool accessories; hand & edge tools

(G-17759)
PALATINE WELDING COMPANY
3848 Berdnick St (60008-1003)
PHONE.................................847 358-1075
Dana Piacenza, *President*
Don Ellis, *Sales Staff*
Garrett Braun, *Manager*
Robin Piacenza, *Manager*
Carl S Piacenza, *Admin Sec*
EMP: 26 **EST:** 1973
SQ FT: 40,000
SALES (est): 4.4MM **Privately Held**
SIC: 7692 Welding repair

(G-17760)
PEPSI COLA GEN BTTLERS OF LIMA (DH)
Also Called: Pepsico
3501 Algonquin Rd Ste 700 (60008-3133)
PHONE.................................847 253-1000
EMP: 6
SQ FT: 55,000
SALES (est): 49.5MM
SALES (corp-wide): 63B **Publicly Held**
SIC: 2086 5149 Mfg Bottled/Canned Soft Drinks Whol Groceries
HQ: Pepsi-Cola General Bottlers, Inc.
1475 E Wdfeld Rd Ste 1300
Schaumburg IL 60173
847 598-3000

(G-17761)
PLIANT LLC
Also Called: Roll-O-Sheets
1701 Golf Rd Ste 2-900 (60008-4255)
PHONE.................................812 424-2904
Harold Davis, *President*
Len Azzaro, *President*
R David Corey, *COO*
Greg E Gard, *Senior VP*
Joseph J Kwederis, *Senior VP*
◆ **EMP:** 2800
SALES (est): 205MM **Publicly Held**
SIC: 3081 2673 3089 Plastic film & sheet; bags: plastic, laminated & coated; food storage & frozen food bags, plastic; air mattresses, plastic
HQ: Berry Global, Inc.
101 Oakley St
Evansville IN 47710

(G-17762)
PLIANT CORP INTERNATIONAL
1701 Golf Rd Ste 2-900 (60008-4255)
PHONE.................................847 969-3300
Harold C Bevis, *President*
Michelle Wilson, *President*
Stephen T Auburn, *Vice Pres*
R David Corey, *Vice Pres*
EMP: 3
SALES (est): 340K **Privately Held**
SIC: 3081 Plastic film & sheet

(G-17763)
POSITIVE PACKAGING INC
Also Called: Positive Packaging & Graphics
1100 Hicks Rd (60008-1016)
PHONE.................................708 560-3028
Todd Beidler, *President*
▲ **EMP:** 3
SALES (est): 567.5K **Privately Held**
SIC: 3086 Packaging & shipping materials, foamed plastic

(G-17764)
PRECISION METAL SPINNING CORP
Also Called: A M Tool
1000 Carnegie St (60008-1007)
PHONE.................................847 392-5672
Dorothy L Doumakes, *President*
Al Doumakes, *Vice Pres*
EMP: 38 **EST:** 1974
SALES (est): 4.1MM **Privately Held**
SIC: 3469 Spinning metal for the trade

(G-17765)
PRECISION METAL TECHNOLOGIES
2255 Lois Dr Ste 2 (60008-4100)
PHONE.................................847 228-6630
Timothy Perry, *President*
Donna Palmer, *Admin Sec*
EMP: 10
SQ FT: 5,000
SALES: 1MM **Privately Held**
SIC: 3469 8711 3398 Metal stampings; engineering services; metal heat treating

(G-17766)
PREMIER PRINTING AND PACKG INC
1881 Hicks Rd Ste B (60008-1214)
PHONE.................................847 970-9434
P Nuzzo, *Vice Pres*
EMP: 2
SALES (est): 275.5K **Privately Held**
SIC: 2752 Commercial printing, offset

(G-17767)
PROBLEND-EUROGERM LLC
1801 Hicks Rd Ste H (60008-1226)
PHONE.................................847 221-5004
Sebastien Jollet, *CEO*
Rick Gizzi, *Business Mgr*
EMP: 8
SALES (est): 269.2K **Privately Held**
SIC: 2041 Flour & other grain mill products

(G-17768)
PROOFING TECHNOLOGIES LTD
5400 Newport Dr Ste 14 (60008-3721)
PHONE.................................847 222-7100
Ronald D Edhlund, *President*
Troy Edhlund, *Vice Pres*
EMP: 7
SQ FT: 5,000
SALES: 1.5MM **Privately Held**
SIC: 2621 3861 5162 5111 Printing paper; photographic film, plate & paper holders; plastics film; printing paper

(G-17769)
RATIONAL COOKING SYSTEMS INC
1701 Golf Rd Ste C-LI (60008-4236)
PHONE.................................224 366-3500
Gunter Blaschke, *CEO*
Chris Koehler, *President*
Bjoern Rowland, *President*
John Ulrich, *Vice Pres*
Justin X Hoehn, *Regl Sales Mgr*
▲ **EMP:** 73
SQ FT: 2,000
SALES (est): 19MM
SALES (corp-wide): 933.3MM **Privately Held**
SIC: 3556 Ovens, bakery
PA: Rational Ag
Siegfried-Meister-Str. 1
Landsberg Am Lech 86899
819 132-70

(G-17770)
RAYTHEON COMPANY
4110 Winnetka Ave (60008-1375)
PHONE.................................630 295-6394
EMP: 450
SALES (corp-wide): 77B **Publicly Held**
WEB: www.rtx.com
SIC: 3812 Defense systems & equipment
HQ: Raytheon Company
870 Winter St
Waltham MA 02451
781 522-3000

(G-17771)
RF IDEAS INC (HQ)
4020 Winnetka Ave (60008-1374)
PHONE.................................847 870-1723
David Cottingham, *President*
Harvey Kuehn, *Controller*
Tim Collins, *CTO*
Gregory J Gliniecki, *Admin Sec*
▲ **EMP:** 61
SQ FT: 8,000
SALES (est): 15MM
SALES (corp-wide): 5.3B **Publicly Held**
SIC: 3699 5734 Security devices; personal computers

PA: Roper Technologies, Inc.
6901 Prof Pkwy E Ste 200
Sarasota FL 34240
941 556-2601

(G-17772)
SAFEMOBILE INC
3601 Algonquin Rd Ste 320 (60008-3107)
PHONE.................................847 818-1649
Dorel Nasui, *CEO*
Shayna Thompson, *Vice Pres*
Leslie Wick, *Opers Staff*
Christopher Enea, *Software Engr*
EMP: 12
SALES (est): 5MM **Privately Held**
SIC: 3679 3663 Electronic circuits;

(G-17773)
SAM ELECTRONICS WORLDWIDE INC
Also Called: Worldwide Voltage
3410 Newport Dr Unit 34 (60008)
PHONE.................................847 290-1720
Arvind Pandey, *CEO*
Santosh Pandey, *President*
EMP: 11
SQ FT: 3,500
SALES: 30K **Privately Held**
SIC: 5731 3677 Radio, television & electronic stores; electronic coils, transformers & other inductors

(G-17774)
SCREEN NORTH AMER HOLDINGS INC (HQ)
5110 Tollview Dr (60008-3715)
PHONE.................................847 870-7400
Hiroshi Hara, *President*
EMP: 12 **EST:** 1996
SALES (est): 89.4MM **Privately Held**
WEB: www.screenamericas.com
SIC: 7371 3861 7699 8742 Computer software development; graphic arts plates, sensitized; photographic & optical goods equipment repair services; management consulting services; survey service: marketing, location, etc.

(G-17775)
SOLIDYNE CORPORATION
4731 Woodland Ct (60008-2243)
PHONE.................................847 394-3333
Baha Erturk, *CEO*
Joann Golbeck, *Opers Mgr*
Adem Erturk, *Technical Mgr*
Jo Ann Konnen, *Controller*
▲ **EMP:** 15 **EST:** 1969
SQ FT: 6,000
SALES (est): 1.5MM **Privately Held**
SIC: 3822 Auto controls regulating residntl & coml environmt & applncs

(G-17776)
SORTIMAT TECHNOLOGY LP
5655 Meadowbrook Indus Ct (60008-3833)
PHONE.................................847 925-1234
Eric Pasman, *President*
Tom Kramer, *Partner*
Hans-Dieter Baumtrog, *Partner*
Ulrich Kloepfer, *Partner*
David Kruse, *Facilities Mgr*
◆ **EMP:** 61
SALES (est): 9.5MM **Privately Held**
SIC: 3549 Assembly machines, including robotic

(G-17777)
SPARTANICS LTD
3605 Edison Pl (60008-1077)
PHONE.................................847 394-5700
Thomas Kleeman, *CEO*
Thomas O'Hara, *President*
David Birch, *Business Mgr*
William Gillen, *COO*
Nazir Syed, *QC Mgr*
▲ **EMP:** 38
SQ FT: 25,000
SALES (est): 10.6MM **Privately Held**
WEB: www.spartanics.com
SIC: 3577 3824 3699 Optical scanning devices; mechanical & electromechanical counters & devices; teaching machines & aids, electronic

(G-17778)
SUBURBAN ACCENTS INC
3701 Berdnick St Ste A (60008-1043)
PHONE.................................847 776-7474
Raymond Sisi Jr, *President*
Donna Sisi, *Corp Secy*
EMP: 6
SALES: 675K **Privately Held**
SIC: 3993 Signs & advertising specialties

(G-17779)
THOMAS PACKAGING LLC
Also Called: Service Industries, LLC
3885 Industrial Ave (60008-1038)
PHONE.................................847 392-1652
Wesley Mancoff, *President*
▲ **EMP:** 13
SALES: 2.8MM
SALES (corp-wide): 17.2MM **Privately Held**
SIC: 3545 Machine tool accessories
PA: Thomas Engineering Inc.
575 W Central Rd
Hoffman Estates IL 60192
847 358-5800

(G-17780)
TKK USA INC (DH)
2550 Golf Rd Ste 800 (60008-4026)
PHONE.................................847 439-7821
Brad Niwa, *Corp Secy*
◆ **EMP:** 200
SQ FT: 15,000
SALES (est): 949.1K **Privately Held**
SIC: 3429 3086 Vacuum bottles or jugs; ice chests or coolers (portable), foamed plastic

(G-17781)
TRANSLOGIC CORPORATION
Also Called: Swisslog Consulting
1951 Rohlwing Rd Ste C (60008-1300)
PHONE.................................847 392-3700
Fax: 847 392-3738
EMP: 15
SALES (corp-wide): 2.6B **Privately Held**
SIC: 3535 Mfg Conveyors/Equipment
HQ: Translogic Corporation
10825 E 47th Ave
Denver CO 80020
303 371-7770

(G-17782)
TRI-TOWER PRINTING INC
Also Called: Printing/Typesetting
1701 Golf Rd Ste L01 (60008-4233)
PHONE.................................847 640-6633
Joseph Mulae, *President*
EMP: 4 **EST:** 1947
SQ FT: 2,500
SALES (est): 600K **Privately Held**
SIC: 2752 2791 7334 2791 2789 Commercial printing, offset; multilithing; mimeographing; typesetting, computer controlled; bookbinding & related work; commercial printing

(G-17783)
UNITED CHEMI-CON INC (HQ)
Also Called: 847 696-9278
1701 Golf Rd Ste 1-1200 (60008-4245)
PHONE.................................847 696-2000
Masatoshi Boi, *President*
Tsuneo Ohta, *President*
Steve Watlock, *General Mgr*
Jim Chavez, *Warehouse Mgr*
Sue Wagner, *Opers Staff*
▲ **EMP:** 40 **EST:** 1970
SQ FT: 10,692
SALES (est): 59MM **Privately Held**
SIC: 3675 Electronic capacitors

(G-17784)
VALUE ENGINEERED PRODUCTS
Also Called: Vep
1700 Hicks Rd (60008-1229)
PHONE.................................708 867-6777
Ed Luzader, *President*
Ms Tracy Shemwell, *Opers Mgr*
EMP: 30
SQ FT: 30,000
SALES (est): 3.4MM **Privately Held**
SIC: 3429 3674 Clamps, metal; semiconductors & related devices

▲ = Import ▼ = Export
◆ = Import/Export

GEOGRAPHIC SECTION

Romeoville - Will County (G-17811)

(G-17785)
VONBERG VALVE INC
3800 Industrial Ave (60008-1085)
PHONE..................847 259-3800
Joseph M Levon, *CEO*
Michael D Levon, *President*
Randall Hess, *Plant Mgr*
Randy Hess, *Plant Mgr*
James Carucio, *Chief Engr*
EMP: 30 **EST:** 1971
SQ FT: 20,000
SALES (est): 6.9MM **Privately Held**
SIC: 3492 3728 3494 3491 Control valves, aircraft: hydraulic & pneumatic; aircraft parts & equipment; valves & pipe fittings; industrial valves

(G-17786)
ZIV USA INC
5410 Newport Dr Ste 38 (60008-3722)
PHONE..................224 735-3961
Norberto Santiago, *President*
Oscar Bolado, *Manager*
Covadonga Coca, *Admin Sec*
▲ **EMP:** 5
SQ FT: 2,000
SALES (est): 1.6MM **Privately Held**
SIC: 3829 Measuring & controlling devices
HQ: Ziv Aplicaciones Y Tecnologia Sociedad Limitada
Poligono Teknologi Elkartegia, Ed 210
Zamudio 48170

Romeoville
Will County

(G-17787)
ADEL WOODWORKS (PA)
15523 Weber Rd Ste 104 (60446-3502)
PHONE..................815 886-9006
Gerimangas Saputis, *President*
EMP: 2
SALES (est): 292.5K **Privately Held**
SIC: 2431 Millwork

(G-17788)
ADVANCED GRAPHICS TECH INC
Also Called: Rotadyne-Decorative Tech GP
1101 Windham Pkwy (60446-1790)
PHONE..................817 481-8561
Thomas Gilson, *CEO*
EMP: 200
SQ FT: 30,000
SALES (est): 13.8MM
SALES (corp-wide): 145.7MM **Privately Held**
SIC: 3471 3479 Plating of metals or formed products; coating of metals & formed products
PA: Rotation Dynamics Corporation
1101 Windham Pkwy
Romeoville IL 60446
630 769-9255

(G-17789)
ALL PRODUCTS GASKET
618 Anderson Dr Ste B (60446-1293)
PHONE..................877 255-8700
EMP: 5
SALES (est): 373.3K **Privately Held**
WEB: www.apgasket.com
SIC: 3053 Gaskets, all materials

(G-17790)
ALL STONE INC
1525 Azalea Cir (60446-4987)
PHONE..................815 529-1754
Gerald Jagodzinski, *Principal*
EMP: 2
SALES (est): 257.5K **Privately Held**
SIC: 2541 Counter & sink tops

(G-17791)
ALLEGRA NETWORK LLC (PA)
Also Called: Allegra Marketing Print Mail
1340 Enterprise Dr (60446-1016)
PHONE..................331 253-2775
Thomas J Wilhelm, *President*
Linda Wilhelm, *Vice Pres*
Jessica Eng, *Marketing Staff*
Andrea Stapleton, *Marketing Staff*
Laura Pierce-Marutz, *Administration*
EMP: 6
SALES (est): 826.5K **Privately Held**
SIC: 2752 Commercial printing, offset

(G-17792)
ALWAYS THERE EXPRESS CORP
29 Forestwood Ct Ste 6 (60446-1477)
PHONE..................773 931-3744
Tadas Jurgaitis, *President*
EMP: 39
SALES (est): 4.2MM **Privately Held**
SIC: 3537 Trucks: freight, baggage, etc.: industrial, except mining

(G-17793)
AMERICAN INKS AND COATINGS CO
1225 Lakeside Dr 1 (60446-3971)
PHONE..................630 226-0994
Jerry Mosley, *President*
Robert Raeke, *Admin Sec*
EMP: 6 **EST:** 2012
SALES (est): 833.9K **Privately Held**
SIC: 2752 Lithographing on metal

(G-17794)
AMSYSCO INC
1200 Windham Pkwy (60446-1673)
PHONE..................630 296-8383
Rattan L Khosa, *President*
Neel Khosa, *Treasurer*
EMP: 23
SQ FT: 55,000
SALES (est): 7.2MM **Privately Held**
WEB: www.amsyscoinc.com
SIC: 3496 Cable, uninsulated wire: made from purchased wire

(G-17795)
APEX INDUSTRIAL AUTOMATION LLC (PA)
Also Called: Peoria Bearing
737 Oakridge Dr (60446-1371)
PHONE..................866 924-2808
Ryan J Watts,
Jennifer A Watts,
EMP: 7
SALES (est): 2MM **Privately Held**
SIC: 7694 Electric motor repair

(G-17796)
ARYZTA LLC
Also Called: Aryzta Great Kitchens
300 Innovation Dr (60446-4612)
PHONE..................815 306-7171
David Alcott, *President*
Ruth Meyer-Hawkins, *Superintendent*
Nancy Kirksey, *Vice Pres*
Anthony Corica, *Project Mgr*
Joseph Oceguera, *Maint Spvr*
EMP: 130
SALES (corp-wide): 3.4B **Privately Held**
SIC: 2038 Frozen specialties
HQ: Aryzta Llc
6080 Center Dr Ste 900
Los Angeles CA 90045
310 417-4700

(G-17797)
AUTOMATED DESIGN CORP
Also Called: ADC 360
1404 N Joliet Rd Ste D (60446-4410)
PHONE..................630 783-1150
Thomas C Bitsky, *President*
Joseph Bitsky, *Vice Pres*
Lisa Bitsky, *Vice Pres*
EMP: 9
SQ FT: 12,000
SALES: 1.5MM **Privately Held**
SIC: 7699 5063 3599 Recreational sporting equipment repair services; electrical apparatus & equipment; custom machinery

(G-17798)
BARRY-WHMLLER CONT SYSTEMS INC (DH)
Also Called: Bw Integrated Systems
1305 Lakeview Dr (60446-3900)
PHONE..................630 759-6800
Phillip G Ostapowicz, *President*
Robert H Chapman, *Chairman*
Pete Carlson, *Vice Pres*
Richard Cranston, *Vice Pres*
David M Gianini, *Vice Pres*
◆ **EMP:** 165
SQ FT: 121,000
SALES (est): 146.6MM **Privately Held**
SIC: 3535 Conveyors & conveying equipment
HQ: Barry-Wehmiller Companies, Inc.
8020 Forsyth Blvd
Saint Louis MO 63105
314 862-8000

(G-17799)
BOSCH AUTO SVC SOLUTIONS INC
1385 N Weber Rd (60446-4307)
PHONE..................815 407-3900
Mike Tuttle, *Manager*
EMP: 16
SALES (corp-wide): 294.8MM **Privately Held**
SIC: 3465 Body parts, automobile: stamped metal
HQ: Bosch Automotive Service Solutions Inc.
28635 Mound Rd
Warren MI 48092
586 574-2332

(G-17800)
C K NORTH AMERICA INC
1243 Naperville Dr (60446-1041)
PHONE..................815 524-4246
EMP: 10
SALES (est): 740K **Privately Held**
SIC: 3423 Mfg Hand/Edge Tools

(G-17801)
C P ENVIRONMENTAL INC
Also Called: Micronics Engineered Filtrtion
1336 Enterprise Dr Ste 2 (60446-2018)
PHONE..................630 759-8866
Thomas J Carr, *President*
Mike Schmidt, *Vice Pres*
Terri Schackle, *Manager*
Melissa Buehler, *Admin Sec*
EMP: 10
SALES (est): 3.9MM **Privately Held**
WEB: www.cp-environmental.com
SIC: 7699 5084 8711 3564 Industrial equipment services; pollution control equipment, air (environmental); pollution control engineering; blowers & fans
HQ: Micronics Filtration, Llc
300 Constitution Ave # 201
Portsmouth NH 03801
603 433-1299

(G-17802)
C4 PETROLUM TRANSPORT INC
1624 Arborwood Cir (60446-5103)
PHONE..................815 690-0356
Nathaniel Cooper, *President*
Jacquelyn Lee, *Admin Sec*
EMP: 5
SALES (est): 161.4K **Privately Held**
SIC: 1321 Liquefied petroleum gases (natural) production

(G-17803)
CARD DYNAMIX LLC
1120 Windham Pkwy (60446-1692)
PHONE..................630 685-4060
Connie Sanfilippo, *CEO*
Ray Brian, *Controller*
Cyze James, *Mng Member*
Doherty Thomas B, *Mng Member*
Duncan Joe, *Mng Member*
▲ **EMP:** 105
SALES (est): 15.6MM **Privately Held**
SIC: 3083 8999 Laminated plastics plate & sheet; greeting card painting by hand
PA: Psa Equity, Llc
485 E Half Day Rd Ste 500
Buffalo Grove IL 60089

(G-17804)
CENTRAL GRAPHICS CORP
1302 Enterprise Dr (60446-1016)
PHONE..................630 759-1696
James Crivellone, *President*
▲ **EMP:** 12
SQ FT: 10,000
SALES (est): 2.6MM **Privately Held**
SIC: 3555 Printing trades machinery

(G-17805)
CGI AUTOMATED MFG INC
275 Innovation Dr (60446-4613)
PHONE..................815 221-5300
Janice M Nieman, *President*
Gary Gurzynski, *Admin Sec*
EMP: 45
SQ FT: 62,500
SALES: 8MM **Privately Held**
SIC: 3444 Sheet metalwork

(G-17806)
CHECKPOINT SYSTEMS INC
1140 Windham Pkwy (60446-1692)
PHONE..................630 771-4240
Cliff Denzy, *Manager*
EMP: 80
SALES (corp-wide): 4B **Privately Held**
SIC: 3699 3812 3663 Security control equipment & systems; detection apparatus: electronic/magnetic field, light/heat; television closed circuit equipment
HQ: Checkpoint Systems, Inc.
101 Wolf Dr
West Deptford NJ 08086
800 257-5540

(G-17807)
CHICAGO TUBE AND IRON COMPANY
Also Called: Boiler Tube & Fabrication Div
1 Chicago Tube Dr (60446-2402)
PHONE..................815 834-2500
Bruce Butterfield, *General Mgr*
EMP: 25
SALES (corp-wide): 1.5B **Publicly Held**
SIC: 3498 7692 5051 3317 Tube fabricating (contract bending & shaping); welding repair; metals service centers & offices; steel pipe & tubes
HQ: Chicago Tube And Iron Company
1 Chicago Tube Dr
Romeoville IL 60446
815 834-2500

(G-17808)
CICERO PLASTIC PRODUCTS INC
121 Anton Dr (60446-4074)
PHONE..................815 886-9522
George Driggers, *President*
Dave Driggers, *Vice Pres*
Linda Driggers, *Treasurer*
EMP: 21 **EST:** 1943
SQ FT: 12,000
SALES: 2.5MM **Privately Held**
WEB: www.ciceroplastics.com
SIC: 3469 3089 Machine parts, stamped or pressed metal; plastic processing

(G-17809)
CIRCUITRON INC
Also Called: Progressive Model Design
211 Rocbaar Dr (60446-1163)
PHONE..................815 886-9010
Steve Worack, *President*
Katherine Yendrek, *Admin Sec*
EMP: 9
SQ FT: 11,000
SALES (est): 500K **Privately Held**
SIC: 3944 Electronic toys

(G-17810)
CMG PRECISION MACHINING CO INC
1342 Enterprise Dr (60446-1016)
PHONE..................630 759-8080
Craig Grinolds, *President*
Valarie Grinolds, *Vice Pres*
EMP: 9
SQ FT: 8,000
SALES (est): 1.4MM **Privately Held**
SIC: 3599 Machine shop, jobbing & repair

(G-17811)
CORPLEX USA LLC
Also Called: Ds Smith
208 Suth Pnnacle Dr Ste D (60446)
PHONE..................630 755-3132
Jeff Murray, *Mng Member*
John McCurdy, *Mng Member*
EMP: 25
SALES (est): 107.6K **Privately Held**
SIC: 3089 Extruded finished plastic products; automotive parts, plastic

Romeoville - Will County (G-17812)

(G-17812)
DATA CABLE TECHNOLOGIES INC
1306 Enterprise Dr Ste E (60446-4408)
PHONE.................................630 226-5600
Lionel Hawkins, *President*
Joe Mika, *Treasurer*
EMP: 18 EST: 1996
SQ FT: 4,000
SALES: 2MM Privately Held
WEB: www.datacabletech.com
SIC: 3357 Nonferrous wiredrawing & insulating

(G-17813)
DAVID S SMITH HLDINGS AMER INC (PA)
1201 Windham Pkwy (60446-1698)
PHONE.................................630 296-2000
David Smith, *Principal*
Jonathan Edmunds, *Business Mgr*
Marynic Foster, *Vice Pres*
Kristin Reim, *Marketing Staff*
Danelle Litchert, *Administration*
EMP: 11
SALES (est): 3.6MM Privately Held
WEB: www.dssmith.com
SIC: 3565 Packaging machinery

(G-17814)
DSS RAPAK INC
1201 Windham Pkwy Ste D (60446-1699)
PHONE.................................630 296-2000
EMP: 8
SALES: 650.9K Privately Held
SIC: 3089 Plastic processing

(G-17815)
ECO-PUR SOLUTIONS LLC
1245 Naperville Dr (60446-1041)
PHONE.................................630 226-2300
David Frank, *Mng Member*
EMP: 9 EST: 2012
SALES (est): 1.7MM Privately Held
SIC: 8748 2891 Business consulting; adhesives & sealants

(G-17816)
EMECOLE INC
50 Montrose (60446-1475)
P.O. Box 7486 (60446-0486)
PHONE.................................815 372-2493
Louis F Cole, *President*
Timothy Merkel, *Business Mgr*
Ryan Earley, *Technical Staff*
Maureen Cole, *Admin Sec*
▼ EMP: 12
SQ FT: 10,000
SALES (est): 3.7MM Privately Held
SIC: 2891 Adhesives & sealants

(G-17817)
ESSEN NUTRITION CORPORATION
1414 Sherman Rd (60446-4046)
PHONE.................................630 739-6700
Madhavan Aniruhan, *President*
Arun Aniruhan, *Vice Pres*
Tom Grandys, *Vice Pres*
Mike Holland, *Vice Pres*
Mina Siva, *Site Mgr*
▲ EMP: 22
SQ FT: 38,000
SALES: 6.4MM Privately Held
SIC: 2099 2032 2035 2086 Desserts, ready-to-mix; soups & broths: canned, jarred, etc.; pickles, sauces & salad dressings; bottled & canned soft drinks; food additives & preservatives

(G-17818)
EXCLUSIVELY EXPO (PA)
1225 Naperville Dr (60446-1041)
PHONE.................................630 378-4600
James F Buehner, *President*
Mike Florczak, *Technology*
Gerald L Czaban,
Kim E Stevenson,
◆ EMP: 65
SQ FT: 34,900
SALES (est): 19MM Privately Held
WEB: www.exclusivelyexpo.com
SIC: 5046 3081 5131 Display equipment, except refrigerated; unsupported plastics film & sheet; drapery material, woven

(G-17819)
EXCLUSIVELY EXPO
Bone Safety Signs
1201 Naperville Dr (60446-1041)
PHONE.................................630 378-4600
Herman Brown, *Division Mgr*
EMP: 15
SALES (corp-wide): 19MM Privately Held
SIC: 3993 Signs & advertising specialties
PA: Exclusively Expo
    1225 Naperville Dr
    Romeoville IL 60446
    630 378-4600

(G-17820)
EXEX HOLDING CORPORATION
Also Called: Online Eei
1201 Naperville Dr (60446-1041)
PHONE.................................815 703-7295
James F Buehner, *President*
Kevin Kriebs, *CFO*
EMP: 2
SALES (est): 260.9K Privately Held
SIC: 3993 Signs & advertising specialties

(G-17821)
FABRICATED METAL SYSTEMS INC
646 Forestwood Dr Ste C (60446-1379)
PHONE.................................815 886-6200
Brian Filipiak, *President*
EMP: 6
SALES: 1MM Privately Held
SIC: 3441 Fabricated structural metal

(G-17822)
FGWA
1305 Lakeview Dr (60446-3900)
PHONE.................................630 759-6800
Rich Hoinacki, *Engineer*
Brian Patrick, *Engineer*
Ross McKenzie, *Sales Staff*
Daniel Black, *Executive*
EMP: 4 EST: 2010
SALES (est): 468.3K Privately Held
WEB: www.bwcontainersystems.com
SIC: 3565 Packaging machinery

(G-17823)
FLINT GROUP US LLC
Also Called: Flint Ink North America Div
1225 Lakeside Dr 1 (60446-3971)
PHONE.................................920 725-0101
Brad Baerwald, *Plant Mgr*
Dave Schwatrz, *Manager*
EMP: 15
SALES (corp-wide): 53.9B Publicly Held
SIC: 2893 2899 Printing ink; ink or writing fluids
HQ: Flint Group Us Llc
    17177 N Laurel Park Dr # 300
    Livonia MI 48152
    734 781-4600

(G-17824)
FLOOR-CHEM INC
1313 Enterprise Dr Ste D (60446-1183)
PHONE.................................630 789-2152
Ike Basir, *President*
EMP: 3
SQ FT: 3,000
SALES: 250K Privately Held
WEB: www.floor-chem.com
SIC: 3471 2841 2842 Cleaning, polishing & finishing; soap & other detergents; cleaning or polishing preparations

(G-17825)
FLOW PRO PRODUCTS INC
618 Anderson Dr Ste A (60446-1293)
PHONE.................................815 836-1900
John Ruesch, *President*
Turhan Tiley, *Admin Sec*
▲ EMP: 13
SQ FT: 9,000
SALES (est): 3.9MM Privately Held
SIC: 3569 Filters

(G-17826)
G K L CORPORATION
Also Called: National Bathing Products
5 Greenwood Ave (60446-1340)
PHONE.................................815 886-5900
Kenneth J Salach, *President*
Diane Salach, *Treasurer*
EMP: 80
SQ FT: 30,000
SALES (est): 15.3MM Privately Held
SIC: 3088 Tubs (bath, shower & laundry), plastic; shower stalls, fiberglass & plastic

(G-17827)
GARY GALASSI AND SONS INC
Also Called: Gary Galassi Stone & Steel
44 Devonwood Ave (60446-1349)
PHONE.................................815 886-3906
Gary Galassi, *President*
Dave Downey, *Vice Pres*
Adam Pleszka, *Safety Mgr*
EMP: 32
SALES (est): 6.3MM Privately Held
SIC: 1411 Dimension stone

(G-17828)
GEA FARM TECHNOLOGIES INC
Chemical Division
1354 Enterprise Dr (60446-1069)
PHONE.................................630 369-8100
Carl Hoffman, *Opers-Prdtn-Mfg*
EMP: 50
SALES (corp-wide): 5.4B Privately Held
WEB: www.gea.com
SIC: 2841 2842 Soap & other detergents; specialty cleaning, polishes & sanitation goods
HQ: Gea Farm Technologies, Inc.
    1880 Country Farm Dr
    Naperville IL 60563
    630 548-8200

(G-17829)
GREEN PRODUCTS LLC
221 Rocbaar Dr (60446-1163)
PHONE.................................815 407-0900
Jim Hoselton,
James D Hoselton,
EMP: 15
SALES: 1,000K Privately Held
SIC: 2891 Adhesives & sealants

(G-17830)
HARRIS BMO BANK NATIONAL ASSN
630 N Independence Blvd (60446-1374)
PHONE.................................815 886-1900
Albert D Ottavio, *CEO*
David Glasscock, *Administration*
EMP: 50
SALES (corp-wide): 19.2B Privately Held
SIC: 6022 2782 State trust companies accepting deposits, commercial; passbooks: bank, etc.
HQ: Harris Bmo Bank National Association
    111 W Monroe St Ste 1200
    Chicago IL 60603
    312 461-2323

(G-17831)
IESCO INC
737 Oakridge Dr (60446-1371)
PHONE.................................708 594-1250
John M Doody, *President*
Barbara Doody, *Admin Sec*
EMP: 20
SALES (est): 5MM Privately Held
WEB: www.iescoelec.com
SIC: 7694 Electric motor repair

(G-17832)
INTEGRITY MANUFACTURING INC
1351 Enterprise Dr (60446-1015)
PHONE.................................815 514-8230
Cheryl Wellman, *CEO*
EMP: 3
SALES (est): 1.1MM Privately Held
SIC: 3469 Metal stampings

(G-17833)
INTEGRITY METALS LLC
1351 Enterprise Dr (60446-1015)
PHONE.................................630 963-4126
Cheryl Wellman, *President*
Holly Barajas, *Vice Pres*
Sean Stack, *Plant Mgr*
▼ EMP: 22
SQ FT: 34,500
SALES: 3MM Privately Held
SIC: 3469 Metal stampings

(G-17834)
ISOVAC PRODUCTS LLC
1306 Enterprise Dr Ste A (60446-4408)
P.O. Box 400, Hinsdale (60522-0400)
PHONE.................................630 679-1740
James Gauger, *Vice Pres*
Chris Schultz, *Vice Pres*
Peter Jenkner, *Sales Mgr*
Pete Jenkner, *Mng Member*
Joseph Petrovic,
EMP: 6
SALES: 10K Privately Held
SIC: 3089 3085 8731 3845 Plastic containers, except foam; plastics bottles; biological research; electromedical apparatus

(G-17835)
JIGSAW SOLUTIONS INC
1296 Lakeview Dr (60446-3901)
PHONE.................................630 926-1948
▲ EMP: 6
SALES (est): 751.6K Privately Held
SIC: 3089 Bottle caps, molded plastic

(G-17836)
JOHN HARLAND COMPANY
1003 Birch Ln (60446-3949)
PHONE.................................815 293-4350
John Harland, *Principal*
EMP: 3
SALES (est): 233.3K Privately Held
SIC: 3577 Printers & plotters

(G-17837)
KENEAL INDUSTRIES INC
Also Called: Keneal Graphic Solutions
679 Parkwood Ave (60446-1348)
PHONE.................................815 886-1300
Wayne R Cassells, *President*
Kent Cassells, *Vice Pres*
Claudia Cassells, *Admin Sec*
EMP: 12
SQ FT: 15,000
SALES (est): 1.8MM Privately Held
WEB: www.keneal.com
SIC: 2759 2752 3953 2761 Letterpress printing; flexographic printing; lithographing on metal; marking devices; manifold business forms; coated & laminated paper; pleating & stitching

(G-17838)
KIMBERLY-CLARK CORPORATION
740 Pro Logis Pkwy (60446-4502)
PHONE.................................815 886-7872
EMP: 213
SALES (corp-wide): 18.4B Publicly Held
SIC: 2621 2676 Sanitary tissue paper; infant & baby paper products
PA: Kimberly-Clark Corporation
    351 Phelps Dr
    Irving TX 75038
    972 281-1200

(G-17839)
LASER PRODUCTS INDUSTRIES INC
1344 Enterprise Dr (60446-1016)
PHONE.................................877 679-1300
Daniel Louis, *President*
Erik Louis, *Vice Pres*
Jim Hoffman, *Regl Sales Mgr*
Jeff Larson, *Regl Sales Mgr*
Matt Thomson, *Regl Sales Mgr*
EMP: 8
SQ FT: 3,000
SALES (est): 3MM Privately Held
SIC: 3826 Laser scientific & engineering instruments

(G-17840)
LASERSKETCH LTD
1319 Enterprise Dr (60446-1050)
PHONE.................................630 243-6360
Judy Mc Creary, *Owner*
◆ EMP: 15
SALES (est): 2.1MM Privately Held
SIC: 2759 5999 Embossing on paper; miscellaneous retail stores

GEOGRAPHIC SECTION

Romeoville - Will County (G-17865)

(G-17841)
LEGACY VULCAN LLC
Midwest Division
1361 N Joliet Rd (60446-4053)
PHONE..................................630 739-0182
Corey Fries, *Director*
EMP: 17 Publicly Held
SIC: 3273 Ready-mixed concrete
HQ: Legacy Vulcan, Llc
1200 Urban Center Dr
Vestavia AL 35242
205 298-3000

(G-17842)
LENNOX INDUSTRIES INC
187 S South Creek Pkwy (60446-4608)
PHONE..................................630 378-7054
Nate Slynn, *Branch Mgr*
EMP: 68
SALES (corp-wide): 3.8B Publicly Held
SIC: 5075 3585 Warm air heating & air conditioning; air conditioning units, complete: domestic or industrial; furnaces, warm air: electric
HQ: Lennox Industries Inc.
2100 Lake Park Blvd
Richardson TX 75080
972 497-5000

(G-17843)
LI GEAR INC
1292 Lakeview Dr (60446-3901)
PHONE..................................630 226-1688
Yumin Li, *President*
▲ **EMP: 2**
SALES (est): 393.3K Privately Held
SIC: 3566 Gears, power transmission, except automotive

(G-17844)
MAGID GLOVE SAFETY MFG CO LLC (PA)
1300 Naperville Dr (60446-1043)
PHONE..................................773 384-2070
Carol Anthony, *District Mgr*
Brenda Campbell, *District Mgr*
Pam Danner, *District Mgr*
Jobeth Ethington, *District Mgr*
Patricia Hester, *District Mgr*
◆ **EMP: 377 EST: 1946**
SQ FT: 500,000
SALES (est): 96.7MM Privately Held
WEB: www.magidgloveretail.com
SIC: 3151 2381 5699 3842 Gloves, leather: work; gloves, work: woven or knit, made from purchased materials; work clothing; surgical appliances & supplies; men's & boys' work clothing

(G-17845)
MASTER FOG LLC
148 S Pinnacle Dr (60446-4614)
PHONE..................................773 918-9080
Vincent Camerano, *Mng Member*
EMP: 3
SALES (est): 439.3K Privately Held
SIC: 3647 Fog lights

(G-17846)
MATERIAL SERVICE CORPORATION
Also Called: Hanson Material Service
681 S Material Rd (60446-2203)
P.O. Box 188, Lockport (60441-0188)
PHONE..................................815 838-2400
Jim Vallera, *Principal*
EMP: 20
SALES (corp-wide): 20.8B Privately Held
SIC: 3272 3273 5032 1442 Concrete products; ready-mixed concrete; concrete mixtures; construction sand & gravel
HQ: Material Service Corporation
2235 Entp Dr Ste 3504
Westchester IL 60154
708 731-2600

(G-17847)
MATERIAL SERVICE CORPORATION
125 N Independence Blvd (60446-1834)
PHONE..................................815 942-1830
EMP: 20
SALES (corp-wide): 20.3B Privately Held
SIC: 1442 Construction Sand/Gravel

HQ: Material Service Corporation
2235 Entp Dr Ste 3504
Westchester IL 60154
708 731-2600

(G-17848)
MATERIAL SERVICE CORPORATION
Also Called: Material Svc Yard 67
125 N Independence Blvd (60446-1834)
P.O. Box 158, Lockport (60441-0158)
PHONE..................................815 838-3420
Ed Senn, *Manager*
EMP: 50
SALES (corp-wide): 20.8B Privately Held
SIC: 1442 Construction sand & gravel
HQ: Material Service Corporation
2235 Entp Dr Ste 3504
Westchester IL 60154
708 731-2600

(G-17849)
MEGA POLYMERS INC
1343 Enterprise Dr (60446-1015)
P.O. Box 1205, New Lenox (60451-6205)
PHONE..................................815 230-0092
Bret Garrison, *President*
Shawn Mock, *Vice Pres*
Christine Zarbock, *Opers Mgr*
Luis Castellanos, *Sales Staff*
Bart Heath, *Sales Staff*
EMP: 14
SQ FT: 30,000
SALES (est): 4.4MM Privately Held
WEB: www.megapolymers.com
SIC: 2821 Plastics materials & resins

(G-17850)
METAL EDGE INC
624 Anderson Dr Ste A (60446-1372)
PHONE..................................708 756-4696
Thomas Brueck, *President*
EMP: 17
SALES (est): 4.7MM Privately Held
SIC: 3446 Architectural metalwork

(G-17851)
METROPOLITAN INDUSTRIES INC
Also Called: Metropolitan Pump Company
37 Forestwood Dr (60446-1343)
PHONE..................................815 886-9200
John R Kochan Jr, *President*
Mike Hancock, *Plant Mgr*
Brian Drafke, *Sales Dir*
Carla Harris, *Sales Staff*
Phil Luhn, *Manager*
▲ **EMP: 130**
SQ FT: 100,000
SALES (est): 59.9MM Privately Held
SIC: 3561 5064 7699 Pump jacks & other pumping equipment; water heaters, electric; pumps & pumping equipment repair

(G-17852)
MICROPRINT INC
1294 Lakeview Dr (60446-3901)
PHONE..................................630 969-1710
Arvin Bhargava, *President*
Neelam Bhargava, *Director*
EMP: 4
SQ FT: 5,000
SALES (est): 625.1K Privately Held
SIC: 2752 Commercial printing, offset

(G-17853)
MID-WEST SPRING & STAMPING INC (HQ)
1404 N Joliet Rd Ste C (60446-4407)
PHONE..................................630 739-3800
Jeffrey Ellison, *President*
Michael Curran, *CFO*
EMP: 5 EST: 1928
SQ FT: 3,000
SALES (est): 12.2MM
SALES (corp-wide): 17.6MM Privately Held
WEB: www.mwspring.com
SIC: 3495 3493 3469 Wire springs; torsion bar springs; automobile springs; coiled flat springs; metal stampings

PA: Spring Mid-West Manufacturing Company
1404 N Joliet Rd Ste C
Romeoville IL 60446
630 739-3800

(G-17854)
MID-WEST SPRING & STAMPING INC
Also Called: Mid-West Spring Mfg Co
1404 Joliet Rd Ste C (60446-4407)
PHONE..................................630 739-3800
Henry Orlawski, *Branch Mgr*
EMP: 8
SALES (corp-wide): 17.6MM Privately Held
WEB: www.mwspring.com
SIC: 3493 3495 5085 Steel springs, except wire; wire springs; springs
HQ: Spring Mid-West And Stamping Inc
1404 N Joliet Rd Ste C
Romeoville IL 60446
630 739-3800

(G-17855)
MID-WEST SPRING MFG CO (PA)
Also Called: Mid-West Spring and Stamping
1404 N Joliet Rd Ste C (60446-4407)
PHONE..................................630 739-3800
Jeffery Ellison, *President*
CJ Overmyer, *VP Mfg*
Michael Curran, *CFO*
Cathie Lukens, *Accounts Exec*
EMP: 130
SQ FT: 2,000
SALES (est): 17.6MM Privately Held
SIC: 3493 3495 Torsion bar springs; automobile springs; coiled flat springs; wire springs

(G-17856)
MONDI BAGS USA LLC
Also Called: Altivity Packaging
1198 Arbor Dr (60446-1176)
P.O. Box 37020, Louisville KY (40233)
PHONE..................................502 361-1371
Tim Wilhoit, *Branch Mgr*
Jason McCarty, *Manager*
EMP: 200 Privately Held
SIC: 2393 Textile bags
HQ: Mondi Bags Usa, Llc
1200 Abernathy Rd Ste 450
Atlanta GA 30328
770 243-5410

(G-17857)
MONDI ROMEOVILLE INC
1140 Arbor Dr (60446-1188)
PHONE..................................630 378-9886
Peter Windeit, *Managing Dir*
Carol Hunt, *Vice Pres*
Holly Martin, *Vice Pres*
Nathan Shepard, *Buyer*
Franco Messer, *Engineer*
◆ **EMP: 67 EST: 2003**
SQ FT: 125,000
SALES (est): 29.9MM Privately Held
WEB: www.mondigroup.com
SIC: 2674 Bags: uncoated paper & multi-wall
PA: Mondi Plc
1st Floor
Addlestone KT15

(G-17858)
NAFISCO INC
Also Called: Flexible Safety Zoning Co
808 Forestwood Dr (60446-1165)
PHONE..................................815 372-3300
John G Knox Sr, *President*
EMP: 10 EST: 1954
SQ FT: 2,400
SALES (est): 1.4MM Privately Held
WEB: www.nafiscoinc.com
SIC: 5063 3669 3499 3993 Signaling equipment, electrical; signaling apparatus, electric; barricades, metal; signs & advertising specialties

(G-17859)
NANOPHASE TECHNOLOGIES CORP (PA)
1319 Marquette Dr (60446-4011)
PHONE..................................630 771-6700
Jess A Jankowski, *President*
Nancy Baldwin, *VP Human Res*

Luis Lemus, *Manager*
Cristian Avalos, *Technician*
EMP: 54
SQ FT: 36,000
SALES: 12.5MM Publicly Held
SIC: 3399 3299 Powder, metal; ceramic fiber

(G-17860)
NATL KTCHN AND BATH CABINETRY
1811 W Normantown Rd (60446-4329)
PHONE..................................815 733-8888
EMP: 2
SALES (est): 201.3K Privately Held
SIC: 2434 Wood kitchen cabinets

(G-17861)
NEW AGE SURFACES LLC
1237 Naperville Dr (60446-1041)
PHONE..................................630 226-0011
Matt Domanico, *Mng Member*
Joanne Domanico,
▲ **EMP: 5**
SALES: 700K Privately Held
SIC: 2541 Counter & sink tops

(G-17862)
ORANGE CRUSH LLC
1001 N Independence Blvd (60446-4054)
PHONE..................................630 739-5560
Ed Lebau, *Branch Mgr*
EMP: 3
SALES (corp-wide): 104.2MM Privately Held
SIC: 2951 1795 Asphalt paving mixtures & blocks; concrete breaking for streets & highways
PA: Orange Crush, L.L.C.
321 Center St
Hillside IL 60162
708 544-9440

(G-17863)
PLUG POWER INC CTC
1160 Naperville Dr (60446-1375)
PHONE..................................518 782-7700
EMP: 3
SALES (est): 233.8K Privately Held
SIC: 3674 Semiconductors & related devices

(G-17864)
POLLMANN NORTH AMERICA INC
950 Chicago Tube Dr (60446-2202)
PHONE..................................815 834-1122
Marcos Cielak, *CEO*
Sintia Martinez, *Buyer*
David Auer, *Engineer*
Matt Macaluso, *Engineer*
Christian Bentz, *Design Engr*
▲ **EMP: 41**
SQ FT: 34,000
SALES (est): 13.9MM
SALES (corp-wide): 196.4MM Privately Held
WEB: www.pollmann-na.com
SIC: 3559 Automotive related machinery
PA: Pollmann International Gmbh
Raabser StraBe 1
Karlstein An Der Thaya 3822
284 422-30

(G-17865)
POLYONE CORPORATION
Polyone Distribution Company
1252 Windham Pkwy (60446-1673)
PHONE..................................630 972-0505
John Rubinic, *Branch Mgr*
Laura Mulcahy, *Manager*
Maryann Russell, *Administration*
EMP: 75 Publicly Held
SIC: 3087 5162 2865 2851 Custom compound purchased resins; plastics resins; cyclic crudes & intermediates; paints & allied products; plastics materials & resins
PA: Polyone Corporation
33587 Walker Rd
Avon Lake OH 44012

Romeoville - Will County (G-17866)

(G-17866)
PRECISION MCHNED CMPONENTS INC
Also Called: P M C
1348 Enterprise Dr (60446-1016)
PHONE.................................630 759-5555
Steven Wunar, *President*
Robert Wunar, *President*
▲ **EMP:** 25 **EST:** 1945
SQ FT: 15,500
SALES (est): 4.9MM **Privately Held**
WEB: www.precisionmachinedcomponents.com
SIC: 3451 3541 Screw machine products; machine tools, metal cutting type

(G-17867)
PRINT & MAILING SOLUTIONS LLC (PA)
1053 N Schmidt Rd (60446-1181)
PHONE.................................708 544-9400
James Hezinger,
Patrick Delmonico III,
EMP: 4 **EST:** 2006
SALES (est): 518.4K **Privately Held**
WEB: www.printmailingsolutions.com
SIC: 2752 Commercial printing, lithographic

(G-17868)
RAPAK LLC (HQ)
Also Called: Packaging Systems
1201 Windham Pkwy Ste D (60446-1699)
PHONE.................................630 296-2000
David Smith, *Principal*
Paul Georgelos, *Vice Pres*
Mike Sloan, *Plant Mgr*
Jose Pena, *Foreman/Supr*
Phil Furmanski, *Engineer*
▲ **EMP:** 140
SQ FT: 121,000
SALES (est): 56.1MM
SALES (corp-wide): 8.1B **Privately Held**
WEB: www.rapak.com
SIC: 2671 Plastic film, coated or laminated for packaging
PA: Ds Smith Plc
    350 Euston Road
    London NW1 3
    207 756-1800

(G-17869)
REYNOLDS HOLDINGS INC
Also Called: Signarama Bolingbrook
684 S Phillips Unit 2 (60446)
PHONE.................................630 739-0110
John Reynolds, *CEO*
EMP: 2
SALES: 300K **Privately Held**
WEB: www.signaramabb.com
SIC: 2499 Signboards, wood

(G-17870)
ROLL MCHNING TECH SLUTIONS INC
Also Called: Rmts
641 Forestwood Dr (60446-1392)
PHONE.................................815 372-9100
Joseph Olson, *CEO*
Rick Olson, *President*
Bekki Pickering, *Controller*
▲ **EMP:** 30
SQ FT: 20,000
SALES (est): 7.5MM **Privately Held**
WEB: www.rollsolutions.com
SIC: 3317 3545 Steel pipe & tubes; machine tool accessories

(G-17871)
ROTATION DYNAMICS CORPORATION
Also Called: Rotadyne-Roll Group
1101 Windham Pkwy (60446-1790)
PHONE.................................630 679-7053
Kirby Savage, *Branch Mgr*
EMP: 36
SALES (corp-wide): 145.7MM **Privately Held**
SIC: 3069 Printers' rolls & blankets: rubber or rubberized fabric
PA: Rotation Dynamics Corporation
    1101 Windham Pkwy
    Romeoville IL 60446
    630 769-9255

(G-17872)
RX VIALS USA
1296 Lakeview Dr (60446-3901)
PHONE.................................630 378-4417
Harrick Bhatia, *President*
EMP: 3
SALES (est): 238.8K **Privately Held**
SIC: 3089 Plastics products

(G-17873)
SATO LBLING SOLUTIONS AMER INC
Also Called: Sato America
1140 Windham Pkwy (60446-1692)
PHONE.................................630 771-4200
Joseph Podsedly, *President*
Dan Blackwelder, *Purch Mgr*
▲ **EMP:** 15 **EST:** 2015
SALES (est): 2MM **Privately Held**
SIC: 2759 Labels & seals: printing

(G-17874)
SATO LBLING SOLUTIONS AMER INC (PA)
1140 Windham Pkwy (60446-1692)
PHONE.................................630 771-4200
Joseph Podsedly, *President*
Eric Preisler, *Production*
Barbara Calabrese, *Accounting Mgr*
▲ **EMP:** 76
SQ FT: 200,000
SALES (est): 20.3MM **Privately Held**
SIC: 2759 2269 Labels & seals: printing; labels, cotton: printed

(G-17875)
SCHWAB PAPER PRODUCTS COMPANY
636 Schwab Cir (60446-1144)
PHONE.................................815 372-2233
Katherine S Obrien, *President*
Michael Schwab, *Owner*
Tom Schwab, *CFO*
Mary Rebellato, *Treasurer*
EMP: 32 **EST:** 1969
SQ FT: 55,000
SALES (est): 9.3MM **Privately Held**
WEB: www.schwabpaper.com
SIC: 2679 Paperboard products, converted

(G-17876)
SHERWIN-WILLIAMS COMPANY
664 S Weber Rd (60446-4999)
PHONE.................................815 254-3559
EMP: 6
SALES (corp-wide): 17.9B **Publicly Held**
SIC: 5231 5198 2851 Paint; paints, varnishes & supplies; wood fillers or sealers
PA: The Sherwin-Williams Company
    101 W Prospect Ave # 1020
    Cleveland OH 44115
    216 566-2000

(G-17877)
STEPAC USA CORPORATION (HQ)
1201 Windham Pkwy (60446-1698)
PHONE.................................630 296-2000
Don Stidham, *President*
Karen De Leon, *Controller*
◆ **EMP:** 4
SQ FT: 121,000
SALES (est): 821.5K
SALES (corp-wide): 8.1B **Privately Held**
SIC: 0723 2671 Fruit (fresh) packing services; vegetable packing services; packaging paper & plastics film, coated & laminated
PA: Ds Smith Plc
    350 Euston Road
    London NW1 3
    207 756-1800

(G-17878)
STUCCHI USA INC
1105 Windham Pkwy (60446-1790)
PHONE.................................847 956-9720
Scott Rolston, *President*
Lucas Stucchi, *Vice Pres*
Denzil Dsouza, *CFO*
Lorenzo Zaffaroni, *Admin Sec*
▲ **EMP:** 19
SQ FT: 15,000
SALES (est): 4.4MM **Privately Held**
SIC: 3429 Clamps, couplings, nozzles & other metal hose fittings

(G-17879)
SUPREME SCREW INC
Also Called: S S I
1224 N Independence Blvd (60446-1057)
PHONE.................................630 226-9000
Debbie Wood, *President*
Tommy Wood, *Sales Mgr*
▲ **EMP:** 8
SALES (est): 1.3MM **Privately Held**
SIC: 5943 3965 5072 Office forms & supplies; fasteners; bolts, nuts & screws; washers (hardware)

(G-17880)
TDW SERVICES INC
Also Called: Great Lakes Service Center
565 Anderson Dr Ste A (60446-1762)
PHONE.................................815 407-0675
Gary Buckles, *Branch Mgr*
EMP: 12
SALES (corp-wide): 306.7MM **Privately Held**
SIC: 1389 Oil field services
HQ: Tdw Services, Inc.
    6801 S 65th West Ave
    Tulsa OK 74131
    918 447-5000

(G-17881)
TRAMCO PUMP CO
1428 Sherman Rd (60446-4046)
PHONE.................................312 243-5800
John P Obermaier, *President*
Tayat Rashid, *Purch Mgr*
Marko Petrovich, *Sales Mgr*
Gloria Marrero, *Representative*
EMP: 26 **EST:** 1924
SQ FT: 20,000
SALES (est): 11.8MM **Privately Held**
WEB: www.tramcopump.com
SIC: 3561 5084 3594 Industrial pumps & parts; processing & packaging equipment; fluid power pumps & motors

(G-17882)
UNITED FLEXIBLE INC (PA)
815 Forestwood Dr (60446-1167)
PHONE.................................815 886-1140
EMP: 19
SALES (est): 40.2MM **Privately Held**
SIC: 3317 Seamless pipes & tubes

(G-17883)
US HOSE CORP (HQ)
815 Forestwood Dr (60446-1167)
PHONE.................................815 886-1140
John Devine, *President*
Duane McPeak, *Manager*
Tom Long, *Info Tech Mgr*
Nancy Hamilton,
◆ **EMP:** 79
SQ FT: 75,000
SALES (est): 23.5MM
SALES (corp-wide): 40.2MM **Privately Held**
SIC: 3599 Flexible metal hose, tubing & bellows; hose, flexible metallic
PA: United Flexible, Inc.
    815 Forestwood Dr
    Romeoville IL 60446
    815 886-1140

(G-17884)
V & N CONCRETE PRODUCTS INC
35 Forestwood Dr (60446-1343)
PHONE.................................815 293-0315
Charles Voss, *President*
EMP: 12 **EST:** 1977
SQ FT: 38,000
SALES (est): 1.8MM **Privately Held**
SIC: 3272 Covers, catch basin: concrete

(G-17885)
VLASICI HARDWOOD FLOORS CO
1959 Somerset Dr (60446-3987)
PHONE.................................815 505-4308
Svetlana Vlasici, *Owner*
EMP: 5
SALES (est): 349.6K **Privately Held**
SIC: 2426 Flooring, hardwood

(G-17886)
WALCO TOOL & ENGINEERING CORP
18954 W Airport Rd (60446-3531)
PHONE.................................815 834-0225
Dave Walsh, *CEO*
Bill Bucciarelli, *President*
Dawn Washburn, *CFO*
Dennis Rothermel, *Controller*
Brandi Campbell, *Human Res Mgr*
▲ **EMP:** 100
SQ FT: 65,000
SALES (est): 22MM **Privately Held**
WEB: www.walcotool.com
SIC: 3599 7692 Machine shop, jobbing & repair; welding repair

(G-17887)
WESTFALIA-SURGE INC
1354 Enterprise Dr (60446-1069)
PHONE.................................630 759-7346
Bob Lewis, *President*
EMP: 2
SALES (est): 218.8K **Privately Held**
SIC: 2841 Soap & other detergents

(G-17888)
WILTON INDUSTRIES INC
1125 Taylor Rd (60446-4215)
PHONE.................................815 834-9390
Seteria Bain, *Manager*
Karen Belgrad, *Director*
EMP: 10 **Privately Held**
SIC: 5023 2731 2721 7812 Kitchenware; kitchen tools & utensils; frames & framing, picture & mirror; books: publishing only; periodicals: publishing only; video tape production; water purification equipment; candy making goods & supplies
HQ: Wilton Industries, Inc.
    535 E Diehl Rd Ste 333
    Naperville IL 60563
    630 963-7100

(G-17889)
WM WRIGLEY JR COMPANY
Also Called: Wrigley Midwest
825 W Bluff Rd (60446-4007)
PHONE.................................312 644-2121
EMP: 214
SALES (corp-wide): 38.5B **Privately Held**
SIC: 2067 Chewing gum base
HQ: Wm. Wrigley Jr. Company
    930 W Evergreen Ave
    Chicago IL 60642
    312 280-4710

(G-17890)
WOOD GRAPHICS INC
Also Called: United Engraving
1101 Windham Pkwy (60446-1790)
PHONE.................................704 872-5798
John Pragar, *Manager*
EMP: 10
SALES (corp-wide): 145.7MM **Privately Held**
SIC: 3471 Chromium plating of metals or formed products
HQ: Wood Graphics, Inc.
    8075 Reading Rd Ste 301
    Cincinnati OH 45237
    513 771-6300

(G-17891)
ZAINAB ENTERPRISES INC
Also Called: Sign-A-Rama
684 Phelps Ave (60446-1533)
PHONE.................................630 739-0110
Qusai Tyebjee, *President*
EMP: 3
SALES: 300K **Privately Held**
SIC: 3993 Signs & advertising specialties

Roodhouse
Greene County

(G-17892)
CLOVERLEAF FEED CO INC
Rr 267 Box S (62082)
PHONE.................................217 589-5010
Martin Rhodes, *Partner*
Nancy Rhodes, *Partner*
Tony Rhodes, *Partner*

GEOGRAPHIC SECTION
Roscoe - Winnebago County (G-17921)

EMP: 4
SALES (est): 391K Privately Held
WEB: www.cloverleaffeed.com
SIC: 2048 5191 Prepared feeds; farm supplies

(G-17893)
MILLER PALLET
162 E Patterson Rd (62082-4418)
PHONE.............................217 589-4411
Norman Miller, *Owner*
EMP: 10
SALES (est): 868.5K Privately Held
SIC: 3952 Pallettes, artists'

(G-17894)
ROODHOUSE ENVELOPE CO
Also Called: Reco
414 S State St (62082-1544)
PHONE.............................217 589-4321
Gary Randall, *President*
Charles Strain, *Vice Pres*
John Strain, *Vice Pres*
Thomas A Martin, *Treasurer*
EMP: 70 EST: 1911
SQ FT: 26,200
SALES (est): 9.7MM Privately Held
SIC: 2677 Envelopes

(G-17895)
ROODHOUSE FIRE PROTECTION DST
1140 S State St (62082-1669)
P.O. Box 112 (62082-0112)
PHONE.............................217 589-5134
Bob Hart, *Principal*
Terry Hawkins, *Chief*
Thomas Meehan, *Corp Secy*
EMP: 25
SQ FT: 2,000
SALES (est): 2.8MM Privately Held
SIC: 3569 Firefighting apparatus & related equipment

Roscoe
Winnebago County

(G-17896)
3DP UNLIMITED LLC
Also Called: 3d Platform
6402 E Rockton Rd (61073-8812)
PHONE.............................815 389-5667
Kecheng Lu, *Principal*
EMP: 3
SALES (est): 261K Privately Held
SIC: 5045 7389 3999 Printers, computer; printers' services: folding, collating; atomizers, toiletry

(G-17897)
ACCURATE CNC MACHINING INC
Also Called: Accurate Cnc Machine
5365 Edith Ln (61073-9573)
PHONE.............................815 623-6516
Richard Fluegel, *President*
Daniel Fluegel, *Shareholder*
Phillip Fluegel, *Shareholder*
EMP: 9 EST: 1993
SQ FT: 12,000
SALES (est): 1.1MM Privately Held
SIC: 3599 Machine shop, jobbing & repair

(G-17898)
AMERICAN ALUM EXTRUSION CO LLC
5253 Mccurry Rd (61073-9552)
PHONE.............................815 525-3100
Vance Arnold, *Manager*
Tim Rood, *Manager*
Samuel Popa,
Diane M Henricks,
Lou Leggero,
EMP: 200
SQ FT: 90,000
SALES (est): 26.3MM Privately Held
SIC: 3354 Aluminum extruded products

(G-17899)
AMERICAN BELL SCREEN PRTG CO
11447 2nd St Ste 1 (61073-9522)
PHONE.............................815 623-5522
Vanessa Knipp, *President*
Tamara Shoevlin, *Corp Secy*
EMP: 4
SQ FT: 4,000
SALES (est): 527.2K Privately Held
SIC: 2759 Screen printing

(G-17900)
CABINETS BY CUSTOM CRAFT INC
5261 Swanson Rd (61073-9457)
PHONE.............................815 637-4001
Steve Levins, *President*
Glenn Hammock, *Vice Pres*
Merle Hammock, *Admin Sec*
EMP: 4
SQ FT: 3,600
SALES (est): 445.7K Privately Held
SIC: 2541 2517 2434 Cabinets, lockers & shelving; wood television & radio cabinets; wood kitchen cabinets

(G-17901)
CRAZY LLAMA BREWING CO LLC
5312 Williams Dr (61073-7320)
PHONE.............................779 200-1878
Alexander Mitkusevitch,
EMP: 3
SALES (est): 91.3K Privately Held
SIC: 2082 Beer (alcoholic beverage)

(G-17902)
DECISION SYSTEMS COMPANY
8937 Sheringham Dr (61073-8040)
P.O. Box 636 (61073-0636)
PHONE.............................815 885-3000
Laverne Ohlwine, *Owner*
EMP: 3
SALES (est): 208.3K Privately Held
SIC: 7372 5045 Operating systems computer software; computers

(G-17903)
DELLS RACEWAY PARK INC
13750 Metric Rd (61073-7638)
PHONE.............................815 494-0074
Matt Panure, *Principal*
EMP: 4 EST: 2012
SALES (est): 321.3K Privately Held
SIC: 3644 Raceways

(G-17904)
DGM ELECTRONICS INC
13654 Metric Rd (61073-7636)
PHONE.............................815 389-2040
Dennis Makovec, *President*
Connie Makovec, *Corp Secy*
EMP: 6
SQ FT: 3,000
SALES (est): 850.1K Privately Held
SIC: 3825 3625 Time code generators; relays & industrial controls

(G-17905)
ECOLAB INC
5151 E Rockton Rd (61073-7649)
PHONE.............................815 389-3441
Michael Buchko, *Project Mgr*
Michele Dawson, *Purchasing*
Robert Zoeller, *Branch Mgr*
Jared Kehl, *Manager*
Mark Reagan, *Manager*
EMP: 38
SALES (corp-wide): 14.9B Publicly Held
WEB: www.ecolab.com
SIC: 2842 Sanitation preparations, disinfectants & deodorants
PA: Ecolab Inc.
   1 Ecolab Pl
   Saint Paul MN 55102
   800 232-6522

(G-17906)
EXCEL GEAR INC
11865 Main St (61073-8276)
PHONE.............................815 623-3414
N K Chinnusamy, *President*
Ingrid West, *Production*
Willy Goellner, *Admin Sec*
▲ EMP: 25
SQ FT: 35,000
SALES (est): 4.6MM Privately Held
SIC: 3462 Gears, forged steel

(G-17907)
G & M FABRICATING INC
9014 Swanson Dr (61073-9415)
P.O. Box 399 (61073-0399)
PHONE.............................815 282-1744
George Owen, *President*
EMP: 5
SQ FT: 13,000
SALES (est): 800K Privately Held
SIC: 3499 3567 3446 3444 Machine bases, metal; industrial furnaces & ovens; architectural metalwork; sheet metalwork; fabricated plate work (boiler shop); fabricated structural metal

(G-17908)
GT FLOW TECHNOLOGY INC
5364 Mainsail Dr (61073-7212)
PHONE.............................815 636-9982
Thomas Rogers, *President*
EMP: 4
SQ FT: 4,000
SALES (est): 1.4MM Privately Held
SIC: 3554 Pulp mill machinery

(G-17909)
HANDCRAFTED BY JACKIE TURBOT
671 Purple Sage Dr (61073-6378)
PHONE.............................815 708-7200
Jackie Turbot, *Principal*
EMP: 4
SALES (est): 281.2K Privately Held
WEB: www.jackiesoap.com
SIC: 2844 Toilet preparations

(G-17910)
ILLINOIS PNEUMATIC INC
9325 Starboard Dr Ste B (61073-6908)
PHONE.............................815 654-9301
Kurt Eversole, *President*
Sheila Eversole, *Corp Secy*
Steve Pissow, *Manager*
EMP: 6
SQ FT: 5,400
SALES (est): 1MM Privately Held
SIC: 3593 Fluid power cylinders, hydraulic or pneumatic

(G-17911)
ILLINOIS WATER TECH INC
5443 Swanson Ct (61073-7174)
P.O. Box 19 (61073-0019)
PHONE.............................815 636-8884
Bill Helman, *Principal*
Scott J Lipke, *CFO*
◆ EMP: 22
SQ FT: 21,000
SALES (est): 7.1MM Privately Held
SIC: 3589 Water treatment equipment, industrial

(G-17912)
LIBCO INDUSTRIES INC
Also Called: Liberty Engineering Company
10567 Main St (61073-8830)
P.O. Box 470 (61073-0470)
PHONE.............................815 623-7677
Brian Belardi, *Vice Pres*
David Belardi, *Vice Pres*
John Akelaitis, *Plant Mgr*
EMP: 12 EST: 1942
SQ FT: 23,000
SALES (est): 2.9MM Privately Held
WEB: www.libertyengineering.com
SIC: 3829 3544 3565 3369 Testing equipment: abrasion, shearing strength, etc.; industrial molds; packaging machinery; nonferrous foundries

(G-17913)
LIGHTNING GRAPHIC
10444 Rock Ln (61073-9422)
PHONE.............................815 623-1937
Jeff Boelkes, *Owner*
EMP: 2 EST: 1990
SALES (est): 210K Privately Held
SIC: 3993 Signs & advertising specialties

(G-17914)
MAGNA-FLUX INTERNATIONAL
11898 Burnside Ln (61073-8632)
PHONE.............................815 623-7634
Bruce Handy, *Owner*
EMP: 2
SALES (est): 200K Privately Held
SIC: 3695 Magnetic disks & drums

(G-17915)
MAIN STREET MARKET ROSCOE INC
Also Called: Main Street Meat Co
9515 N 2nd St (61073-7205)
PHONE.............................815 623-6328
James A King, *President*
Amy J King, *Admin Sec*
EMP: 2
SALES (est): 246.6K Privately Held
SIC: 2011 2084 Beef products from beef slaughtered on site; bacon, slab & sliced from meat slaughtered on site; wines

(G-17916)
MAKERITE MFG CO INC
13571 Metric Rd (61073-9712)
P.O. Box 700 (61073-0700)
PHONE.............................815 389-3902
Paul Burke Sr, *President*
Paul Burke Jr, *Vice Pres*
Paul M Burke Jr, *Vice Pres*
Beverly Burke, *Treasurer*
EMP: 31
SQ FT: 14,000
SALES (est): 6.5MM Privately Held
SIC: 3451 3714 3728 Screw machine products; motor vehicle parts & accessories; aircraft parts & equipment

(G-17917)
MEISTER INDUSTRIES INC
6608 Saladino Dr (61073-9258)
P.O. Box 535 (61073-0535)
PHONE.............................815 623-8919
William Dickson, *President*
EMP: 3
SALES (est): 289.4K Privately Held
SIC: 3625 Electric controls & control accessories, industrial

(G-17918)
MOLDWORKS INC
11052 Jasmine Dr (61073-9414)
P.O. Box 802 (61073-0802)
PHONE.............................815 520-8819
EMP: 3 EST: 2015
SALES (est): 202.1K Privately Held
SIC: 3952 Lead pencils & art goods

(G-17919)
MZM MANUFACTURING INC
5409 Swanson Ct (61073-7174)
PHONE.............................815 624-8666
Jeffrey Marotta, *President*
EMP: 7 EST: 1997
SQ FT: 6,500
SALES: 1.5MM Privately Held
WEB: www.mzmmfg.com
SIC: 3542 Machine tools, metal forming type

(G-17920)
NELSON ENTERPRISES INC
5447 Mainsail Dr (61073-9460)
PHONE.............................815 633-1100
Allen Nelson, *President*
EMP: 5
SALES (est): 574.8K Privately Held
SIC: 5531 3519 2395 Speed shops, including race car supplies; parts & accessories, internal combustion engines; embroidery & art needlework

(G-17921)
PACIFIC BEARING CORP (PA)
Also Called: Pbc Linear
6402 E Rockton Rd (61073-8812)
P.O. Box 6980, Rockford (61125-1980)
PHONE.............................815 389-5600
Robert Schroeder, *President*
Tom Schroeder, *Vice Pres*
Ann Schroeder, *Officer*
▲ EMP: 130
SQ FT: 100,000

Roscoe - Winnebago County (G-17922)

SALES (est): 27.8MM **Privately Held**
SIC: 3562 3599 Ball bearings & parts; custom machinery

(G-17922)
PROFESSIONAL RR SOLUTIONS LLC
6678 Saladino Dr (61073-9258)
PHONE..................815 209-7473
Chad Smith,
EMP: 1
SALES: 1.2MM **Privately Held**
SIC: 3743 7371 Railroad locomotives & parts, electric or nonelectric; computer software development & applications

(G-17923)
REGAL BELOIT CORPORATION
Also Called: Regal Cutting Tools
5330 E Rockton Rd (61073-7652)
P.O. Box 38, South Beloit (61080-0038)
PHONE..................844 527-8392
Bobbi Tadder, *Regional Mgr*
J B Conway, *Vice Pres*
S Schneier, *Vice Pres*
Steven Smith, *Vice Pres*
Jim L Dhom, *VP Mfg*
EMP: 160
SALES (corp-wide): 3.2B **Publicly Held**
SIC: 5085 3545 3541 5063 Industrial tools; machine tool accessories; machine tools, metal cutting type; power transmission equipment, electric
PA: Regal Beloit Corporation
200 State St
Beloit WI 53511
608 364-8800

(G-17924)
REGAL CUTTING TOOLS INC
5330 E Rockton Rd (61073-7652)
PHONE..................815 389-3461
Ho K Song, *President*
Richard Hartnett, *General Mgr*
Dick Hartnett, *Vice Pres*
Todd Moran, *Engineer*
▲ EMP: 200
SALES (est): 33MM **Privately Held**
SIC: 3545 Cutting tools for machine tools
PA: Yg-1 Co., Ltd.
211 Sewolcheon-Ro, Bupyeong-Gu
Incheon 21300

(G-17925)
REVIEW GRAPHICS INC (PA)
10760 Main St (61073-8337)
P.O. Box 116 (61073-0116)
PHONE..................815 623-2570
Bill Johnson, *CEO*
EMP: 3
SQ FT: 2,400
SALES (est): 280.3K **Privately Held**
SIC: 2752 2791 Commercial printing, offset; typesetting

(G-17926)
ROCKFORD RIGGING INC (PA)
5401 Mainsail Dr (61073-8669)
PHONE..................309 263-0566
John Malcotte, *President*
Phil Herra, *Vice Pres*
James Alexander, *Admin Sec*
▲ EMP: 15
SQ FT: 35,000
SALES (est): 9.9MM **Privately Held**
SIC: 3643 3496 3339 3315 Current-carrying wiring devices; miscellaneous fabricated wire products; primary nonferrous metals; steel wire & related products

(G-17927)
ROGERS READY MIX & MTLS INC
14615 N 2nd St (61073)
P.O. Box 703 (61073-0703)
PHONE..................815 389-2223
Gary Bronkema, *Manager*
EMP: 16
SALES (corp-wide): 14.3MM **Privately Held**
SIC: 3273 1442 5032 Ready-mixed concrete; construction sand & gravel; stone, crushed or broken
PA: Rogers Ready Mix & Materials, Inc.
8128 N Walnut St
Byron IL 61010
815 234-8212

(G-17928)
ROSCOE GLASS CO
11212 Main St (61073-8854)
PHONE..................815 623-6268
Michael Flowers, *President*
Duane Flowers, *Vice Pres*
EMP: 3
SQ FT: 3,600
SALES (est): 100K **Privately Held**
SIC: 3231 7536 Products of purchased glass; automotive glass replacement shops

(G-17929)
ROSCOE TOOL & MANUFACTURING
5339 Stern Dr (61073-8341)
PHONE..................815 633-8808
EMP: 20
SQ FT: 6,000
SALES (est): 1.9MM **Privately Held**
SIC: 3544 3545 3599 Mfg Jigs Fixtures Gauges & Machine Parts

(G-17930)
RWS DESIGN AND CONTROLS INC
13979 Willowbrook Rd (61073-9700)
PHONE..................815 654-6000
Edison S Wirth Jr, *President*
Scott Lindvall, *Opers Mgr*
Richard Fox, *Engineer*
Jim Kipfer, *Engineer*
Greg Lynn, *Engineer*
EMP: 40
SQ FT: 6,000
SALES: 16MM **Privately Held**
SIC: 8711 3613 Electrical or electronic engineering; control panels, electric

(G-17931)
SCHAFER GEAR WORKS ROSCOE LLC
5466 E Rockton Rd (61073-7606)
PHONE..................815 874-4327
Stanley Blenke, *Mng Member*
Stan Blenke,
Bepin Doshi,
▲ EMP: 110
SQ FT: 42,000
SALES (est): 24.7MM
SALES (corp-wide): 38MM **Privately Held**
SIC: 3462 Iron & steel forgings
PA: Schafer Industries, Inc.
4701 Nimtz Pkwy
South Bend IN 46628
574 234-4116

(G-17932)
SCOTT SAWVEL
Also Called: Sweet As Sin
6112 Schaumburg Ln (61073-9900)
PHONE..................815 543-4136
Scott Sawvel, *Owner*
EMP: 3
SALES (est): 123.2K **Privately Held**
SIC: 2841 Soap & other detergents

(G-17933)
SHADE AIRE COMPANY
Also Called: Shade Aire Decorating
7511 Grace Dr (61073-8163)
PHONE..................815 623-7597
Roger H Stoeckel, *Partner*
Gail Stoeckel, *Partner*
Roger Stoeckel, *Partner*
EMP: 2
SALES: 300K **Privately Held**
SIC: 7389 2591 2391 Interior designer; drapery hardware & blinds & shades; curtains & draperies

(G-17934)
STATE LINE FOUNDRIES INC
13227 N 2nd St (61073-7729)
P.O. Box 530 (61073-0530)
PHONE..................815 389-3921
Steve Holdeman, *President*
Jesse Milks, *General Mgr*
Aaron Nevalainen, *Maint Spvr*
Dave Murphy, *Sales Mgr*
David Murphy, *Sales Mgr*
EMP: 54
SQ FT: 67,000
SALES (est): 11.3MM **Privately Held**
WEB: www.slfcastings.com
SIC: 3321 Gray iron castings; ductile iron castings

(G-17935)
STATELINE SWISS MFG LLC
5326 Stern Dr Ste C (61073-8363)
PHONE..................815 282-5181
EMP: 10
SALES (est): 507.8K **Privately Held**
SIC: 3599 Machine shop, jobbing & repair

(G-17936)
TAYLOR DESIGN INC
5375 E Rockton Rd (61073-7651)
PHONE..................815 389-3991
John G Taylor, *President*
EMP: 7 EST: 1959
SQ FT: 10,000
SALES (est): 1.1MM **Privately Held**
SIC: 3544 3599 8711 7692 Special dies & tools; custom machinery; designing: ship, boat, machine & product; welding repair

(G-17937)
UWD INC
9135 N 2nd St Ste 100 (61073-8517)
PHONE..................815 316-3080
EMP: 10
SALES (est): 1.5MM **Privately Held**
SIC: 3089 Mfg Plastic Products

Roselle
Dupage County

(G-17938)
AQUION INC (DH)
101 S Gary Ave Unit A (60172-1672)
PHONE..................847 725-3000
Karl R Frykman, *President*
▼ EMP: 103
SQ FT: 160,000
SALES (est): 56MM **Privately Held**
SIC: 3589 Water filters & softeners, household type; water purification equipment, household type; water treatment equipment, industrial
HQ: Water Ingenuity Holdings Corp.
5500 Wayzata Blvd Ste 900
Golden Valley MN 55416
763 545-1730

(G-17939)
BATHWRAPS
Also Called: Liners Direct
401 S Gary Ave Unit A (60172-1655)
PHONE..................630 227-1737
Jeffrey B Conner, *President*
EMP: 40
SQ FT: 56,000
SALES (est): 14.7MM **Privately Held**
SIC: 3088 Tubs (bath, shower & laundry), plastic; bathroom fixtures, plastic
HQ: Jacuzzi Brands Llc
13925 City Center Dr # 200
Chino Hills CA 91709
909 606-1416

(G-17940)
BELLA SIGN CO
9 Presidential Dr (60172-3914)
PHONE..................630 539-0343
Lou Porcaro, *Owner*
EMP: 3
SALES (est): 290.5K **Privately Held**
SIC: 3993 1799 Signs & advertising specialties; sign installation & maintenance

(G-17941)
BRIDGE PRINTING & PROMOTIONAL (PA)
52 Congress Cir W (60172-3911)
PHONE..................847 776-0200
Richard Stienstra, *President*
Richard Stienstra III, *Vice Pres*
Derek Stienstra, *Director*
Linda Stienstra, *Admin Sec*
EMP: 14
SALES (est): 1.5MM **Privately Held**
WEB: www.bridgeprinting.com
SIC: 2752 Commercial printing, lithographic

(G-17942)
BRISCOE SIGNS LLC
119 N Bokelman St (60172-1543)
PHONE..................630 529-1616
Tim Briscoe,
EMP: 3
SQ FT: 1,600
SALES (est): 231.8K **Privately Held**
SIC: 3993 Signs, not made in custom sign painting shops

(G-17943)
CATER CHEMICAL CO
30 Monaco Dr (60172-1955)
PHONE..................630 980-2300
Vinod M Patel, *President*
Jack Patel, *Treasurer*
Abhi Patel, *Sales Associate*
▲ EMP: 6
SQ FT: 5,000
SALES (est): 1.2MM **Privately Held**
SIC: 2841 5169 2899 2842 Soap & other detergents; chemicals & allied products; chemical preparations; specialty cleaning, polishes & sanitation goods; industrial inorganic chemicals

(G-17944)
CD MAGIC INC
116 S Prospect St (60172-2049)
P.O. Box 126, Bloomingdale (60108-0126)
PHONE..................708 582-3496
Tom Price, *President*
Edward V Edens, *Shareholder*
Lawrence M Taggart, *Shareholder*
EMP: 5
SQ FT: 1,500
SALES (est): 200K **Privately Held**
SIC: 2899 Chemical preparations

(G-17945)
CIGTECHS (PA)
173 W Irving Park Rd (60172-1119)
PHONE..................630 855-6513
Chris Ray, *Owner*
EMP: 10
SALES (est): 1.2MM **Privately Held**
SIC: 2111 Cigarettes

(G-17946)
COMPOSITION ONE INC
Also Called: Document Centre
400 Lake St Ste 110b (60172-3571)
PHONE..................630 588-1900
David R Rohe, *President*
Robin A Rohe, *Admin Sec*
EMP: 20
SALES (est): 2.4MM **Privately Held**
SIC: 2791 Photocomposition, for the printing trade

(G-17947)
COORDINATE MACHINE COMPANY
59 Congress Cir W (60172-3912)
PHONE..................630 894-9880
Shirley Luschen, *President*
Michael Gaffney, *QC Mgr*
Scott Luschen, *Admin Sec*
EMP: 25
SALES (est): 4.6MM **Privately Held**
SIC: 3545 Tools & accessories for machine tools

(G-17948)
CORPORATE SIGN SYSTEMS INC
900 Central Ave (60172-1742)
PHONE..................847 882-6100
Erik Olsen, *President*
EMP: 10
SQ FT: 5,000
SALES: 10MM **Privately Held**
SIC: 3993 Signs, not made in custom sign painting shops

Roselle - Dupage County

(G-17949)
CROWN COVERINGS INC
814 Central Ave (60172-1849)
PHONE..................630 546-2959
Rocco Molfese, *President*
Cheryl Molfese, *Admin Sec*
EMP: 20
SALES (est): 3.4MM Privately Held
WEB: www.crowncoverings.com
SIC: 2434 2541 Vanities, bathroom: wood; counter & sink tops

(G-17950)
CUSTOM DIRECT INC
715 E Irving Park Rd (60172-4332)
PHONE..................630 529-1936
John Georgas, *President*
Jeff Maniglia, *Creative Dir*
Timothy Williams, *Analyst*
EMP: 11
SQ FT: 6,000
SALES (est): 1.5MM Privately Held
SIC: 8742 7336 7335 2791 Marketing consulting services; commercial art & graphic design; commercial photography; typesetting

(G-17951)
D & J PLASTICS INC
1775 Illinois St (60172-4104)
PHONE..................847 534-0601
Dianne Wiseman, *President*
▲ EMP: 8 EST: 1999
SALES (est): 968.4K Privately Held
WEB: www.dandjplastics.com
SIC: 3089 Thermoformed finished plastic products

(G-17952)
ELECTRI-FLEX COMPANY
222 Central Ave (60172-1902)
P.O. Box 72260 (60172-0260)
PHONE..................630 529-2920
Jason Kinander, *CEO*
Edward Marinelli, *President*
Jan Jesernik Ruthe, *COO*
Alexandria Kinander Kelly, *Vice Pres*
Donna Brandonisio, *Buyer*
◆ EMP: 95
SQ FT: 115,000
SALES (est): 31.1MM Privately Held
WEB: www.electriflex.com
SIC: 3644 3599 3699 Electric conduits & fittings; hose, flexible metallic; electrical equipment & supplies

(G-17953)
EQUIPSOLUTIONS LLC (PA)
Also Called: Chemical Mgmt Systems
31 Presidential Dr (60172-3914)
PHONE..................630 351-9070
Mike Radel, *President*
EMP: 44
SALES (est): 18.7MM Privately Held
SIC: 5046 3589 Commercial equipment; water treatment equipment, industrial

(G-17954)
GEMINI DIGITAL INC
860 Lake St Ste 606 (60172-2891)
PHONE..................630 894-9430
Edward Baran, *President*
Cynthia Baran, *Corp Secy*
EMP: 3
SQ FT: 1,500
SALES (est): 349.4K Privately Held
SIC: 2752 Commercial printing, offset

(G-17955)
GENESIS INC (PA)
980 Central Ave (60172-1742)
PHONE..................630 351-4400
Tom Stringfellow, *General Mgr*
Thomas M Stringfellow, *Principal*
Scott Stringfellow, *Vice Pres*
▲ EMP: 90 EST: 1977
SQ FT: 60,000
SALES (est): 25.7MM Privately Held
SIC: 3444 Sheet metal specialties, not stamped

(G-17956)
GZ SIGN DESIGNS INC
912 Central Ave (60172-1742)
PHONE..................630 307-7446
Iolanda D Molnar, *President*
EMP: 2
SQ FT: 1,926
SALES (est): 208.4K Privately Held
WEB: www.gzsigndesigns.com
SIC: 7549 3993 Automotive maintenance services; signs & advertising specialties

(G-17957)
I C T W INK (PA)
968 Lake St Ste A (60172-3305)
PHONE..................630 893-4658
Dee Leonard, *COO*
Timothy McCants, *Marketing Staff*
▲ EMP: 3
SALES (est): 650.7K Privately Held
SIC: 2893 Printing ink

(G-17958)
ILLINOIS TOOL WORKS INC
Also Called: ITW Buildex
86 Chancellor Dr (60172-3903)
PHONE..................630 595-3500
Mark Fontana, *Manager*
EMP: 275
SALES (corp-wide): 14.1B Publicly Held
WEB: www.itw.com
SIC: 5072 3089 Screws; injection molded finished plastic products
PA: Illinois Tool Works Inc.
  155 Harlem Ave
  Glenview IL 60025
  847 724-7500

(G-17959)
INSTRMNTATION CTRL SYSTEMS INC
Also Called: I C S
360 Heritage Dr (60172-2978)
PHONE..................630 543-6200
Marion L Servos, *President*
Julie McDearman, *Engineer*
Alan Servos, *Treasurer*
MEI Wang, *Finance Mgr*
Susan Servos, *Admin Sec*
EMP: 10 EST: 1964
SQ FT: 20,000
SALES: 1MM Privately Held
WEB: www.ics-timers.com
SIC: 3625 Electric controls & control accessories, industrial

(G-17960)
IPS & LUGGAGE CO INC
685 Washington Ct (60172-5034)
PHONE..................630 894-2414
Paul Park, *President*
EMP: 2
SALES (est): 260K Privately Held
WEB: www.ipsluggage.com
SIC: 3161 Luggage

(G-17961)
KELLSTROM COML AROSPC INC (DH)
Also Called: Kellstrom Aerospace
450 Medinah Rd (60172-2329)
PHONE..................847 233-5800
Jeffrey Lund, *CEO*
Oscar Torres, *CFO*
EMP: 35
SQ FT: 162,000
SALES (est): 21.5MM
SALES (corp-wide): 1B Privately Held
SIC: 3728 Aircraft parts & equipment
HQ: Kellstrom Aerospace Group, Inc.
  2500 N Military Trl
  Boca Raton FL 33431
  954 538-2482

(G-17962)
KONICA MINOLTA
1000 Stevenson Ct Ste 109 (60172-4314)
PHONE..................630 893-8238
Eva Branch, *Owner*
EMP: 5
SALES (est): 428.5K Privately Held
WEB: www.kmbs.konicaminolta.us
SIC: 7629 5045 5044 3571 Business machine repair, electric; computers, peripherals & software; copying equipment; electronic computers

(G-17963)
LARSON-JUHL US LLC
550 Congress Cir N (60172-3905)
PHONE..................630 307-9700
Sheldon Schur, *General Mgr*
EMP: 25
SALES (corp-wide): 327.2B Publicly Held
SIC: 2499 5023 Picture frame molding, finished; home furnishings
HQ: Larson-Juhl Us Llc
  3900 Steve Reynolds Blvd
  Norcross GA 30093
  770 279-5200

(G-17964)
LEGNA IRON WORKS INC
80 Central Ave (60172-1904)
PHONE..................630 894-8056
Mike Gonzalez, *President*
Dawn Sanchez, *Manager*
Leticia Gonzalez, *Admin Sec*
EMP: 25
SQ FT: 11,000
SALES (est): 5.4MM Privately Held
SIC: 3446 1521 7692 1799 Architectural metalwork; general remodeling, single-family houses; welding repair; ornamental metal work

(G-17965)
LYNFRED WINERY INC (PA)
15 S Roselle Rd (60172-2043)
PHONE..................630 529-9463
Fred E Koehler, *President*
Diane Schramer, *Corp Secy*
Matt Phillips, *Store Mgr*
Gregory Hayes, *Sales Staff*
Lisa Klus, *Director*
▲ EMP: 45
SQ FT: 28,800
SALES (est): 5.4MM Privately Held
SIC: 2084 5812 2033 2032 Wines; eating places; canned fruits & specialties; canned specialties

(G-17966)
M & R PRINTING EQUIPMENT INC (HQ)
Also Called: M & R Sales and Service
440 Medinah Rd (60172-2329)
PHONE..................630 858-6101
Danny Sweem, *CEO*
Ronnie Riggs, *President*
John Carroll, *Regional Mgr*
Elizabeth Hoffman, *Exec VP*
Richard Nesladek, *Vice Pres*
▲ EMP: 375
SALES (est): 166.1MM Privately Held
SIC: 3555 3552 5084 Printing trades machinery; printing machinery, textile; printing trades machinery, equipment & supplies

(G-17967)
M&R HOLDINGS INC (PA)
Also Called: M&R Printing
440 Medinah Rd (60172-2329)
PHONE..................630 858-6101
Richard Hoffman, *President*
Howard Bloom, *Vice Pres*
Richard Nesladek, *Vice Pres*
Darek Sadowski, *Engineer*
Simi Deneufbourg, *Admin Sec*
▲ EMP: 200
SQ FT: 120,000
SALES (est): 166.1MM Privately Held
SIC: 3552 Printing machinery, textile

(G-17968)
MARKS CUSTOM SEATING
Also Called: MCS Booths
816 Central Ave (60172-1849)
PHONE..................630 980-8270
Mark Ehlers, *Owner*
EMP: 5
SALES (est): 376K Privately Held
SIC: 7641 2599 Furniture upholstery repair; bar, restaurant & cafeteria furniture

(G-17969)
METAL TECH INC
80 Monaco Dr (60172-1955)
P.O. Box 72907 (60172-0907)
PHONE..................630 529-7400
Lohtar Schick, *President*
Tony Castrovillari, *Vice Pres*
Carlene Schick, *Admin Sec*
EMP: 22
SQ FT: 15,000
SALES (est): 5.2MM Privately Held
SIC: 3441 Fabricated structural metal

(G-17970)
MIDLAND PLASTICS INC
295 W Walnut St (60172-3801)
PHONE..................262 938-7000
Joseph B Tremback, *President*
Joseph S Tremback, *Vice Pres*
EMP: 32 EST: 1962
SQ FT: 24,000
SALES (est): 5.5MM Privately Held
WEB: www.midlandplastics.com
SIC: 3089 Injection molding of plastics

(G-17971)
MORRIS MIDWEST LLC
68 Congress Cir W (60172-3911)
PHONE..................630 351-1901
Dean Brazgel, *Engineer*
Brian Bylls, *Engineer*
Mitch Fontana, *Sales Engr*
Scott Gilbert, *Sales Engr*
Al Gow, *Sales Engr*
EMP: 2
SALES (est): 239.4K Privately Held
WEB: www.morrismidwest.com
SIC: 3599 Machine shop, jobbing & repair
PA: Morris Midwest Llc
  2323 Corporate Dr
  Waukesha WI 53189

(G-17972)
NOW HEALTH GROUP INC
Also Called: Now Foods
1620 Central Ave (60172-1602)
PHONE..................888 669-3663
Elwood Richard, *Ch of Bd*
Matt Hancher, *Info Tech Dir*
EMP: 5
SALES (corp-wide): 454.3MM Privately Held
WEB: www.nowfoods.com
SIC: 2834 Vitamin, nutrient & hematinic preparations for human use
PA: Now Health Group, Inc.
  244 Knollwood Dr Ste 300
  Bloomingdale IL 60108
  888 669-3663

(G-17973)
NYPRO HANOVER PARK
401 S Gary Ave (60172-1654)
PHONE..................630 868-3517
EMP: 3 EST: 2011
SALES (est): 176.8K Privately Held
SIC: 3083 Plastic finished products, laminated

(G-17974)
PRINTING PLUS OF ROSELLE INC
205 E Irving Park Rd (60172-2057)
PHONE..................630 893-0410
Mark Borough, *President*
EMP: 9
SQ FT: 3,000
SALES (est): 1.4MM Privately Held
SIC: 5199 7334 2752 3993 Advertising specialties; photocopying & duplicating services; commercial printing, offset; signs & advertising specialties; typesetting; bookbinding & related work

(G-17975)
PRO-MOLD INCORPORATED
Also Called: Pro Mold & Die
55 Chancellor Dr (60172-3900)
PHONE..................630 893-3594
Walter Schaub, *President*
David Long, *CFO*
Michael Hurt, *Department Mgr*
Mike Duda, *Supervisor*
Edward Wiemer, *Programmer Anys*
EMP: 56
SQ FT: 35,000
SALES (est): 10.9MM Privately Held
SIC: 3544 Industrial molds; dies, plastics forming

(G-17976)
QUALITY SEALANTS INC
7n131 Willow St (60172-2183)
P.O. Box 72306 (60172-0306)
PHONE..................815 342-0409
EMP: 3 EST: 2014

Roselle - Dupage County (G-17977)

SALES (est): 135.6K **Privately Held**
SIC: 2891 Sealants

(G-17977)
RASOI RESTURAUNT
15 Clair Ct (60172-4517)
PHONE.................................847 455-8888
Sam Lakhia, *Owner*
EMP: 4
SALES (est): 293.4K **Privately Held**
SIC: 3949 Indian clubs

(G-17978)
REDI-STRIP COMPANY INC
100 Central Ave (60172-1950)
P.O. Box 72199 (60172-0199)
PHONE.................................630 529-2442
John Carlisle, *President*
Robert Kernan, *Vice Pres*
Barbara A Carlisle, *Admin Sec*
EMP: 9 EST: 1995
SQ FT: 44,000
SALES: 1.2MM **Privately Held**
WEB: www.redistripco.com
SIC: 3471 Plating & polishing

(G-17979)
ROMUS INCORPORATED
932 Central Ave (60172-1742)
PHONE.................................414 350-6233
Jay Schabelski, *President*
Kathleen Schabelski, *Treasurer*
EMP: 2 EST: 2000
SALES (est): 330K **Privately Held**
SIC: 3829 Hardness testing equipment

(G-17980)
ROSELLE CUSTOM WOODWORK LLC
57 N Garden Ave (60172-1733)
PHONE.................................630 980-5655
Steve Wright,
John Valentine,
EMP: 3
SQ FT: 4,500
SALES (est): 310K **Privately Held**
SIC: 2499 Decorative wood & woodwork

(G-17981)
RR DONNELLEY LOGISTICS SE
Also Called: D L S
200 N Gary Ave (60172-1681)
PHONE.................................630 672-2500
EMP: 18
SALES (corp-wide): 6.2B **Publicly Held**
WEB: www.dls-ww.com
SIC: 2759 2741 Commercial printing; miscellaneous publishing
HQ: Rr Donnelley Logistics Services Worldwide, Inc.
1000 Windham Pkwy
Bolingbrook IL 60490

(G-17982)
SAACHI INC
Also Called: Www.vltg-Cnvrtr-Transformer-com
364 Jennifer Ln (60172-4927)
PHONE.................................630 775-1700
Khushjiwan Kaur, *CEO*
▲ EMP: 7
SQ FT: 8,000
SALES: 4MM **Privately Held**
SIC: 3612 7389 Transformers, except electric;

(G-17983)
SATURN ELECTRICAL SERVICES INC
380 Monaco Dr (60172-1954)
PHONE.................................630 980-0300
George Schembari, *President*
EMP: 5
SALES (est): 638.3K **Privately Held**
SIC: 1731 3612 General electrical contractor; generator voltage regulators

(G-17984)
SCHOLASTIC INC
301 S Gary Ave Unit A (60172-1659)
PHONE.................................630 671-0601
Christy Lavine, *Sales Staff*
Greg Carter, *Branch Mgr*
EMP: 28

SALES (corp-wide): 1.6B **Publicly Held**
SIC: 2731 Textbooks: publishing only, not printed on site
HQ: Scholastic Inc.
557 Broadway Lbby 1
New York NY 10012
212 343-6100

(G-17985)
SCIENTIFIC METAL TREATING CO
106 Chancellor Dr (60172-3903)
PHONE.................................630 582-0071
Wayne Harelson, *CEO*
Kevin Harelson, *President*
Andy Evans, *Sales Mgr*
EMP: 28
SALES (est): 6.5MM **Privately Held**
SIC: 3398 Metal heat treating

(G-17986)
SELECT TOOL & DIE INC
324 Pinecroft Dr (60172-2469)
PHONE.................................630 980-8458
Robert Siemers, *President*
EMP: 3
SALES: 550K **Privately Held**
SIC: 3544 Special dies & tools

(G-17987)
SERVICE STAMPINGS OF IL INC
251 Central Ave (60172-1901)
P.O. Box 72157 (60172-0157)
PHONE.................................630 894-7880
Michael Grant, *President*
Timothy Grant, *Vice Pres*
Jim Zay, *Treasurer*
James Christensen, *Admin Sec*
EMP: 20 EST: 1963
SQ FT: 30,000
SALES (est): 3.8MM **Privately Held**
WEB: www.servicestampingsil.com
SIC: 3469 Stamping metal for the trade

(G-17988)
SHEPARD MEDICAL PRODUCTS INC
675 E Irving Park Rd # 201 (60172-2349)
PHONE.................................630 539-7790
Chris Wright, *President*
▲ EMP: 4
SQ FT: 1,000
SALES (est): 871.1K **Privately Held**
SIC: 3069 Medical & laboratory rubber sundries & related products

(G-17989)
SIGNIFY NORTH AMERICA CORP
Also Called: Philips Lighting
440 Medinah Rd (60172-2329)
PHONE.................................708 307-3000
Ed Shamsabad, *Principal*
EMP: 32
SALES (corp-wide): 7.2B **Privately Held**
WEB: www.colorkinetics.com
SIC: 3651 5063 Household audio & video equipment; transformers, electric
HQ: Signify North America Corporation
200 Franklin Square Dr # 4
Somerset NJ 08873
732 563-3000

(G-17990)
SPORT CONNECTION
741 E Nerge Rd (60172-1061)
PHONE.................................630 980-1787
Sharon M Mattioda, *President*
Barbara Butt, *Vice Pres*
EMP: 4 EST: 1978
SQ FT: 2,000
SALES (est): 217.8K **Privately Held**
SIC: 5699 2396 Sports apparel; uniforms; T-shirts, custom printed; automotive & apparel trimmings

(G-17991)
STERNBERG LANTERNS INC (DH)
Also Called: Sternberg Lighting
555 Lawrence Ave (60172-1568)
PHONE.................................847 588-3400
Joseph Waldau, *President*
Mark Dean, *Vice Pres*
Michael Manicone, *Vice Pres*
Dan Radochonski, *Vice Pres*

Tim Scharnagle, *Vice Pres*
▲ EMP: 106 EST: 1923
SQ FT: 130,000
SALES: 33.4MM
SALES (corp-wide): 36.6B **Privately Held**
WEB: www.sternberglighting.com
SIC: 3646 3648 3645 3354 Ornamental lighting fixtures, commercial; lighting equipment; residential lighting fixtures; aluminum extruded products
HQ: Groupe Lumenpulse Inc
1220 Boul Marie-Victorin
Longueuil QC J4G 2
514 937-3003

(G-17992)
TECH-TOOL ENTERPRISE
100 Monaco Dr (60172-1955)
PHONE.................................630 639-9425
EMP: 2
SALES (est): 313K **Privately Held**
SIC: 3599 Machine shop, jobbing & repair

(G-17993)
THRICE PUBLISHING NFP
734 Berwick Pl (60172-2734)
P.O. Box 725114 (60172-5114)
PHONE.................................630 776-0478
Robert Spryszak, *President*
EMP: 3
SALES (est): 107.9K **Privately Held**
SIC: 2741 Miscellaneous publishing

(G-17994)
TRIM SUITS BY SHOW-OFF INC
Also Called: Show Off
48 Congress Cir W (60172-3911)
PHONE.................................630 894-0100
Ena Fenn, *President*
EMP: 9
SALES (est): 1.2MM **Privately Held**
SIC: 2339 2369 5961 Athletic clothing: women's, misses' & juniors'; warm-up, jogging & sweat suits: girls' & children's; women's apparel, mail order; clothing, mail order (except women's)

(G-17995)
WINGS OF ROSELLE LLC
840 Lake St Ste 414 (60172-2894)
PHONE.................................630 529-5700
Denise Romano, *Principal*
EMP: 7
SALES (est): 758.5K **Privately Held**
SIC: 3421 Table & food cutlery, including butchers'

(G-17996)
WRITTEN WORD INC
986 Lake St Ste 108 (60172-3390)
PHONE.................................630 671-9803
Albert Chin-A-Young, *Owner*
EMP: 2
SQ FT: 700
SALES (est): 214.7K **Privately Held**
WEB: www.thewrittenword.com
SIC: 7372 Prepackaged software

(G-17997)
XPRESS PRINTING & COPYING CO
147 W Irving Park Rd (60172-1119)
PHONE.................................630 980-9600
Byron Myrhe, *President*
EMP: 3 EST: 1999
SQ FT: 2,400
SALES (est): 500K **Privately Held**
SIC: 2754 Commercial printing, gravure

(G-17998)
YKK AP AMERICA INC
1000 Stevenson Ct Ste 101 (60172-4314)
PHONE.................................630 582-9602
Max Mazoto, *Branch Mgr*
EMP: 15 **Privately Held**
SIC: 3442 Sash, door or window: metal
HQ: Ykk Ap America Inc.
270 Riverside Pkwy Sw # 100
Austell GA 30168

Rosemont
Cook County

(G-17999)
APPLETON GRP LLC (DH)
Also Called: Appleton Group
9377 W Higgins Rd (60018-4973)
PHONE.................................847 268-6000
Scott Anderson, *President*
Jerry Mc Quade, *Vice Pres*
Andy Schwegel, *Vice Pres*
Harley M Smith, *Vice Pres*
Michael Bryant, *CFO*
◆ EMP: 120 EST: 1997
SQ FT: 750,000
SALES (est): 694.6MM
SALES (corp-wide): 18.3B **Publicly Held**
WEB: www.emersonindustrial.com
SIC: 3644 3643 3613 3646 Junction boxes, electric; electric conduits & fittings; plugs, electric; electric switches; starting switches, fluorescent; switchgear & switchgear accessories; power circuit breakers; panelboards & distribution boards, electric; commercial indusl & institutional electric lighting fixtures; extension cords
HQ: Apple Jv Holding Corp.
8000 West Florissant Ave
Saint Louis MO 63136
314 553-2000

(G-18000)
BARBER STEEL FOUNDRY CORP
6400 Shafer Ct Ste 450 (60018-4948)
PHONE.................................231 894-1830
EMP: 17
SALES (est): 4.5MM **Publicly Held**
WEB: www.wabtec.com
SIC: 3324 Steel investment foundries
HQ: Wabtec Corporation
30 Isabella St
Pittsburgh PA 15212

(G-18001)
BUILDERS CHICAGO CORPORATION
9820 W Foster Ave (60018-5306)
PHONE.................................224 654-2122
Richard C Crandall Jr, *President*
Michael Kerley, *General Mgr*
Alex Humann, *Opers Mgr*
Mike Kilbridge, *Controller*
Christine Wachna, *Executive Asst*
EMP: 60 EST: 1927
SQ FT: 15,000
SALES (est): 8MM **Privately Held**
WEB: www.builderschicago.com
SIC: 7699 1791 3442 1751 Garage door repair; structural steel erection; garage doors, overhead: metal; garage door, installation or erection; window & door (prefabricated) installation; barricades, metal; dock equipment installation, industrial

(G-18002)
CAPSTONE DEV SVCS CO LLC
9450 Bryn Mawr Ave # 200 (60018-5271)
PHONE.................................847 999-0131
Dan Robins, *President*
EMP: 4 EST: 2015
SALES (est): 81.8K **Privately Held**
SIC: 2834 Pharmaceutical preparations

(G-18003)
CELERITY PHARMACEUTICALS LLC
9450 Bryn Mawr Ave # 200 (60018-5271)
PHONE.................................847 999-0131
Dan Robins, *Mng Member*
Alan Heller,
Peter Strothman,
EMP: 9 EST: 2013
SQ FT: 3,000
SALES (est): 1.7MM **Privately Held**
SIC: 2834 Pharmaceutical preparations

(G-18004)
CHEMALLOY COMPANY LLC
Also Called: Metal Briquetters
9550 W Higgins Rd Ste 380 (60018-4906)
PHONE.................................847 696-2400

▲ = Import ▼ = Export
◆ = Import/Export

Rosemont - Cook County (G-18030)

Jim Davis, *Manager*
EMP: 25
SALES (corp-wide): 177.9K **Privately Held**
SIC: 2999 Fuel briquettes or boulets: made with petroleum binder
HQ: Chemalloy Company Llc
1301 Conshohocken Rd
Conshohocken PA 19428
610 527-3700

(G-18005)
CJT AUTOMOTIVE INC
10275 W Higgins Rd # 470 (60018-5625)
PHONE 847 671-0800
Raymond Chan, *President*
EMP: 4
SALES (est): 161.4K **Privately Held**
SIC: 3089 Automotive parts, plastic

(G-18006)
COCA COLA BOTTLING COMPAN
9700 W Higgins Rd (60018-4796)
PHONE 847 227-6766
EMP: 3
SALES (est): 140K **Privately Held**
SIC: 2086 Bottled & canned soft drinks

(G-18007)
COCA-COLA REFRESHMENTS USA INC
6250 N River Rd Ste 9000 (60018-4241)
PHONE 813 298-1000
EMP: 116
SALES (corp-wide): 37.2B **Publicly Held**
SIC: 2086 Bottled & canned soft drinks
HQ: Coca-Cola Refreshments Usa, Inc.
2500 Windy Ridge Pkwy Se
Atlanta GA 30339
770 989-3000

(G-18008)
COPYCO PRINTING INC
9500 Bryn Mawr Ave # 130 (60018-5219)
PHONE 847 824-4400
Leonard F Thomas, *CEO*
Andrew Thomas, *President*
Alan Czarnik, *Exec VP*
David Piper, *Vice Pres*
David C Piper, *Vice Pres*
▲ **EMP:** 48 **EST:** 1968
SQ FT: 18,000
SALES (est): 7.7MM **Privately Held**
WEB: www.shift365.com
SIC: 2752 Commercial printing, offset

(G-18009)
CORELLE BRANDS HOLDINGS INC (PA)
9525 Bryn Mawr Ave Ste 30 (60018-5249)
PHONE 847 233-8600
Kenneth G Wilkes, *President*
Jon Freeman, *Vice Pres*
Kaveh Shamloo, *Vice Pres*
Michael Shafer, *Maint Spvr*
Craig Beams, *Engineer*
◆ **EMP:** 65
SQ FT: 60,000
SALES (est): 851.8MM **Privately Held**
SIC: 3229 3469 Pressed & blown glass; household cooking & kitchen utensils, metal

(G-18010)
CORELLE BRANDS LLC (HQ)
Also Called: Pyrex
9525 Bryn Mawr Ave (60018-5249)
PHONE 847 233-8600
Kenneth Wilkes, *President*
David Reeve, *Regional Mgr*
Preston Resue, *Maint Spvr*
Leo Spada, *Maint Spvr*
Linda Tchoryk, *Opers Staff*
◆ **EMP:** 175
SALES (est): 937MM **Privately Held**
SIC: 3229 5961 Tableware, glass or glass ceramic;

(G-18011)
CSITEQ LLC (PA)
Also Called: Csiteq Group
5600 N River Rd (60018-6705)
PHONE 312 265-1509
Olatunde Omosebi,
▼ **EMP:** 11
SALES (est): 10MM **Privately Held**
SIC: 4899 8742 7373 1623 Communication signal enhancement network system; management consulting services; local area network (LAN) systems integrator; oil & gas pipeline construction; filters & strainers, pipeline; aircraft/aerospace flight instruments & guidance systems

(G-18012)
CSITEQ STUDIO LLC
5600 N River Rd (60018-6705)
PHONE 312 265-1509
Donald Omosebi, *Officer*
Olatunde Omosebi,
EMP: 15
SALES (est): 161.8K **Privately Held**
SIC: 7819 7829 3652 7922 Services allied to motion pictures; motion picture distribution services; pre-recorded records & tapes; agent or manager for entertainers; artists' agents & brokers; motion picture & video production
PA: Csiteq, Llc
5600 N River Rd
Rosemont IL 60018

(G-18013)
CULLIGAN INTERNATIONAL COMPANY (PA)
9399 W Higgins Rd # 1100 (60018-4940)
PHONE 847 430-2800
Scott G Clawson, *CEO*
David Rich, *President*
Paula Jastper, *Business Mgr*
Ramona Cibas, *Vice Pres*
John Griffith, *Vice Pres*
◆ **EMP:** 150 **EST:** 1986
SALES (est): 797.6MM **Privately Held**
WEB: www.culligan.com
SIC: 3589 Sewage & water treatment equipment; water treatment equipment, industrial; water filters & softeners, household type

(G-18014)
CURLEE MFG
9377 W Higgins Rd (60018-4973)
PHONE 847 268-6517
EMP: 8 **EST:** 2009
SALES (est): 540K **Privately Held**
SIC: 3999 Mfg Misc Products

(G-18015)
CUSTOM HARD CHROME SERVICE CO
7083 Barry St (60018-3401)
P.O. Box 1234, Oak Park (60304-0234)
PHONE 847 759-1420
Philip Bolas, *President*
Craig Bolas, *Vice Pres*
EMP: 5
SQ FT: 11,500
SALES (est): 598.5K **Privately Held**
SIC: 3471 Electroplating of metals or formed products; chromium plating of metals or formed products; finishing, metals or formed products

(G-18016)
CUSTOM SUPERFINISHING GRINDING
Also Called: Horizon Sperfinishing Grinding
7083 Barry St (60018-3401)
PHONE 847 699-9710
Fax: 847 699-9326
EMP: 4
SQ FT: 5,000
SALES (est): 260K **Privately Held**
SIC: 3599 Grinding And Superfinishing Job Shop

(G-18017)
DIGITAL MINDS INC
Also Called: Touch Quest
9501 W Devon Ave Ste 603 (60018-4818)
PHONE 847 430-3390
Joseph P Fiduccia, *President*
EMP: 4
SQ FT: 1,700
SALES (est): 1MM **Privately Held**
SIC: 3993 7372 Signs & advertising specialties; prepackaged software

(G-18018)
DIRECT SELLING STRATEGIES
5600 N River Rd Ste 800 (60018-5166)
PHONE 847 993-3188
EMP: 3 **EST:** 2010
SALES (est): 150K **Privately Held**
SIC: 3399 Mfg Primary Metal Products

(G-18019)
DOMETIC CORPORATION
Also Called: Dometic Group
5600 N River Rd Ste 250 (60018-5118)
PHONE 847 447-7190
Roger Johannson, *CEO*
Frank Marciano, *President*
Steve McElwain, *Treasurer*
Jeff Johns, *Sales Staff*
Daniel Fuller, *Admin Sec*
◆ **EMP:** 1050 **EST:** 2005
SQ FT: 13,000
SALES (est): 413.1MM
SALES (corp-wide): 2B **Privately Held**
WEB: www.dometic.com
SIC: 3089 3443 3444 3822 Plastic boats & other marine equipment; heat exchangers, condensers & components; sheet metalwork; auto controls regulating residntl & coml environmt & applncs; industrial instrmnts msrmnt display/control process variable; combs, except hard rubber
PA: Dometic Group Ab (Publ)
Hemvarnsgatan 15
Solna 171 5
850 102-500

(G-18020)
DRIG CORPORATION
5600 N River Rd (60018-6705)
PHONE 312 265-1509
Olatunde Omosebi, *Principal*
EMP: 75 **EST:** 2012
SALES (est): 1MM **Privately Held**
SIC: 2911 5171 5172 1311 Diesel fuels; jet fuels; oils, fuel; petroleum bulk stations & terminals; petroleum terminals; gases, liquefied petroleum (propane); aircraft fueling services; crude petroleum & natural gas; drilling oil & gas wells; oil & gas exploration services

(G-18021)
DUBOIS CHEMICALS INC
5600 N River Rd Ste 800 (60018-5166)
PHONE 847 457-1813
EMP: 99 **Privately Held**
SIC: 3589 Water treatment equipment, industrial
PA: Dubois Chemicals, Inc.
3630 E Kemper Rd
Sharonville OH 45241

(G-18022)
EASY HEAT INC
9377 W Higgins Rd (60018-4973)
PHONE 847 268-6000
Michael O'Toole, *President*
▲ **EMP:** 40
SALES (est): 4.7MM
SALES (corp-wide): 18.3B **Publicly Held**
SIC: 3433 Heating equipment, except electric
HQ: Appleton Grp Llc
9377 W Higgins Rd
Rosemont IL 60018
847 268-6000

(G-18023)
EMERSON ELECTRIC CO
9377 W Higgins Rd (60018-4973)
PHONE 847 268-6000
Gary Karnes, *Principal*
Mark Dziedzic, *Marketing Staff*
Maya Jordan, *Marketing Staff*
Anna Maria Caponigri, *Manager*
Anthony Di Domenico, *Senior Mgr*
EMP: 23
SALES (corp-wide): 18.3B **Publicly Held**
SIC: 3823 Industrial instrmnts msrmnt display/control process variable
PA: Emerson Electric Co.
8000 West Florissant Ave
Saint Louis MO 63136
314 553-2000

(G-18024)
FRIEDMAN CORPORATION (HQ)
Also Called: Fog Software Group
10275 W Higgins Rd Ste 250 (60018-5625)
PHONE 847 948-7180
Mark Thompson, *President*
Cliff Caines, *Opers Staff*
Florence Debello, *Research*
Bridget Moran, *Research*
Eric Herrmann, *CFO*
EMP: 46
SALES (est): 13.8MM
SALES (corp-wide): 928K **Privately Held**
WEB: www.friedmancorp.com
SIC: 7372 Prepackaged software
PA: Vela Software International Inc
26 Soho St Suite 400
Toronto ON M5T 1
416 861-2279

(G-18025)
GREAT LAKES COCA-COLA DIST LLC (HQ)
6250 N River Rd Ste 9000 (60018-4241)
PHONE 847 227-6500
David Reyes, *Mng Member*
EMP: 53
SALES (est): 130MM **Privately Held**
SIC: 2086 5142 5149 Bottled & canned soft drinks; packaged frozen goods; soft drinks

(G-18026)
HW HOLDCO LLC
Also Called: Aberdeen Group
5600 N River Rd Ste 250 (60018-5118)
PHONE 773 824-2400
Mary Skelnik, *Manager*
EMP: 100
SALES (corp-wide): 166.8MM **Privately Held**
SIC: 2721 Trade journals: publishing only, not printed on site
PA: Hw Holdco, Llc
1 Thomas Cir Nw Ste 600
Washington DC 20005
202 452-0800

(G-18027)
HYDRO EXTRUSION USA LLC (DH)
6250 N River Rd Ste 5000 (60018-4214)
PHONE 877 710-7272
Charlie Straface, *President*
Eigil Madsen, *Vice Pres*
Joe Nickles, *Purch Mgr*
Amanda Potts, *Purchasing*
Chris Walters, *QC Mgr*
▲ **EMP:** 154
SALES (est): 1.1B
SALES (corp-wide): 16.5B **Privately Held**
SIC: 3354 Aluminum extruded products
HQ: Hydro Extrusion Sweden Ab
Metallvagen 10
Vetlanda 574 3
383 941-00

(G-18028)
JING MEI INDUSTRIAL USA INC (PA)
10275 W Higgins Rd # 470 (60018-3886)
PHONE 847 671-0800
Raymond C Wai, *President*
▲ **EMP:** 22
SQ FT: 50,000
SALES (est): 3.5MM **Privately Held**
SIC: 3999 Coins & tokens, non-currency

(G-18029)
KAAS INDUSTRIES INC
7035 Barry St (60018-3401)
PHONE 847 298-9106
Jakub Koeller-Kmicikiewicz, *President*
Jan Malarz, *Vice Pres*
▲ **EMP:** 7
SQ FT: 7,000
SALES (est): 1MM **Privately Held**
SIC: 3599 Machine shop, jobbing & repair

(G-18030)
LEXMARK INTERNATIONAL INC
9700 W Higgins Rd Ste 930 (60018-4713)
PHONE 847 318-5700
Dennis Valadez, *Manager*
EMP: 40

Rosemont - Cook County (G-18031)

SALES (corp-wide): 441.3K **Privately Held**
SIC: 3577 Printers, computer
HQ: Lexmark International Inc.
740 W New Circle Rd
Lexington KY 40511

(G-18031)
LIFEWATCH CORP (HQ)
10255 W Higgins Rd # 100 (60018-5608)
PHONE..................847 720-2100
Brent Cohen, *President*
Chris Kurtenbach, *Senior VP*
Chris Calhoun, *Vice Pres*
Paul Hanneman, *Vice Pres*
Erik Leverenz, *Vice Pres*
EMP: 4
SQ FT: 32,000
SALES (est): 147.3MM
SALES (corp-wide): 439.1MM **Publicly Held**
SIC: 8099 5047 3845 Physical examination & testing services; patient monitoring equipment; electro-medical equipment; electrocardiographs
PA: Biotelemetry, Inc.
1000 Cedar Hollow Rd # 10
Malvern PA 19355
610 729-7000

(G-18032)
LIFEWATCH SERVICES INC (HQ)
10255 W Higgins Rd # 100 (60018-5608)
PHONE..................847 720-2100
Stephan Rietiker, *CEO*
Roger K Richardson, *President*
Yacov Geva, *Principal*
George Michelson, *Vice Pres*
Kobi Ben Efraim, *CFO*
EMP: 370
SQ FT: 56,000
SALES (est): 147.1MM
SALES (corp-wide): 439.1MM **Publicly Held**
SIC: 5047 8099 3845 8071 Patient monitoring equipment; electro-medical equipment; physical examination service, insurance; health screening service; physical examination & testing services; electrocardiographs; testing laboratories
PA: Biotelemetry, Inc.
1000 Cedar Hollow Rd # 10
Malvern PA 19355
610 729-7000

(G-18033)
LIFEWATCH TECHNOLOGIES INC
Also Called: Instrumentics
10255 W Higgins Rd # 100 (60018-5606)
PHONE..................847 720-2100
Frederick Mindermann, *President*
Roger K Richardson, *COO*
Meg McGilley, *Vice Pres*
Francis Leonard, *CFO*
John M Tumblin, *Officer*
▲ EMP: 95 EST: 2000
SALES (est): 9.2MM
SALES (corp-wide): 439.1MM **Publicly Held**
WEB: www.lifewatch.com
SIC: 3845 5047 Electromedical equipment; electro-medical equipment
HQ: Lifewatch Corp
10255 W Higgins Rd # 100
Rosemont IL 60018

(G-18034)
LUMOS HOLDINGS US ACQUISITION (DH)
9525 Bryn Mawr Ave (60018-5249)
PHONE..................847 288-3300
Chris Clawson, *CEO*
Steve Klyn, *CFO*
EMP: 5
SALES (est): 45.4MM
SALES (corp-wide): 355.8K **Privately Held**
SIC: 6719 3949 Investment holding companies, except banks; exercise equipment
HQ: Lumos International Holdings B.V.
Keizersgracht 555
Amsterdam
202 050-142

(G-18035)
MATTHEW WARREN INC (DH)
Also Called: Mw Industries
9501 Tech Blvd Ste 401 (60018)
PHONE..................847 349-5760
William Marcum, *CEO*
Ken Garbellini, *Purch Mgr*
Chester Kwasniak, *CFO*
EMP: 30
SALES (est): 384.8MM
SALES (corp-wide): 185.9MM **Privately Held**
SIC: 3493 Coiled flat springs; cold formed springs; helical springs, hot wound; railroad equipment etc.; hot wound springs, except wire
HQ: Mw Industries, Inc.
9501 Tech Blvd Ste 401
Rosemont IL 60018
847 349-5760

(G-18036)
MILK PRODUCTS HOLDINGS N AMER
9525 Bryn Mawr Ave (60018-5249)
PHONE..................847 928-1600
Martin Bates, *President*
Teresa Smart, *Administration*
◆ EMP: 150
SQ FT: 30,000
SALES (est): 20.7MM **Privately Held**
SIC: 5143 2023 Dairy products, except dried or canned; dry, condensed, evaporated dairy products
PA: Fonterra Co-Operative Group Limited
109 Fanshawe St
Auckland 1010

(G-18037)
MILLER AND COMPANY LLC (DH)
9550 W Higgins Rd Ste 380 (60018-4906)
PHONE..................847 696-2400
John A Adcock, *President*
Mark Bielick, *Opers Staff*
Dimitra Kotsinonos, *CFO*
Colen Hansen, *Credit Mgr*
Fred Fudge, *Sales Staff*
◆ EMP: 35 EST: 1919
SQ FT: 10,500
SALES (est): 39.7MM
SALES (corp-wide): 177.9K **Privately Held**
WEB: www.millerandco.com
SIC: 5051 3313 Pig iron; ferroalloys; alloys, additive, except copper: not made in blast furnaces
HQ: Nizi International
Parc D'activites Capellen 89e

442 221-1

(G-18038)
NICHOLAS MACHINE & TOOL INC
7027 Barry St (60018-3401)
PHONE..................847 298-2035
Eugene Bereza, *President*
Josephine Bereza, *Vice Pres*
Diane Bereza, *Admin Sec*
▲ EMP: 6
SALES (est): 887.3K **Privately Held**
SIC: 3599 3544 3541 Machine shop, jobbing & repair; special dies, tools, jigs & fixtures; machine tools, metal cutting type

(G-18039)
PERQ/HCI LLC (DH)
Also Called: Srds
5600 N River Rd Ste 900 (60018-5167)
PHONE..................847 268-1600
Dave Emery, *CEO*
Benito Sumang, *Production*
Chandra Menconi, *Finance*
Tara Clifford, *Advt Staff*
Debbie Dunkleberger, *Director*
EMP: 100 EST: 1919
SALES: 40MM
SALES (corp-wide): 20B **Privately Held**
WEB: www.srds.com
SIC: 2741 Directories: publishing only, not printed on site

HQ: Young & Rubicam Llc
3 Columbus Cir
New York NY 10019
212 210-3000

(G-18040)
PERRY ELLIS INTERNATIONAL INC
5220 Fashion Outlets Way # 2265 (60018-5327)
PHONE..................847 678-7108
EMP: 3
SALES (corp-wide): 874.8MM **Privately Held**
SIC: 2321 Men's & boys' furnishings
HQ: Perry Ellis International Inc
3000 Nw 107th Ave
Doral FL 33172
305 592-2830

(G-18041)
PERRY JOHNSON INC
Also Called: Perry Johnson Consulting
10255 W Higgins Rd # 140 (60018-5606)
PHONE..................847 635-0010
Jeff Goldsher, *Manager*
EMP: 13
SALES (corp-wide): 27.3MM **Privately Held**
SIC: 7389 2731 8748 7812 Speakers' bureau; inspection & testing services; textbooks: publishing & printing; books: publishing & printing; business consulting; video tape production; business oriented computer software
PA: Perry Johnson, Inc
755 W Big Beaver Rd # 1300
Troy MI 48084
248 356-4410

(G-18042)
PICIS CLINICAL SOLUTIONS INC
9500 W Higgins Rd # 1100 (60018-4963)
PHONE..................847 993-2200
EMP: 10
SALES (corp-wide): 60.1MM **Privately Held**
SIC: 7372 7371 Prepackaged Software Services Custom Computer Programing
PA: Picis Clinical Solutions, Inc.
100 Quannapowitt Pkwy # 405
Wakefield MA 01880
336 397-5336

(G-18043)
PRESTONE PRODUCTS CORPORATION (DH)
6250 N River Rd Ste 6000 (60018-4217)
PHONE..................888 282-8960
Steven Clancy, *President*
David Lundstedt, *COO*
Leonard A Dececchis, *Exec VP*
Ricardo F Alvergue, *CFO*
Joe Doyle, *Admin Sec*
▼ EMP: 157
SQ FT: 25,000
SALES (est): 111.9MM
SALES (corp-wide): 3.2MM **Privately Held**
SIC: 2899 Antifreeze compounds

(G-18044)
PROSPAN MANUFACTURING
10013 Norwood St (60018-4326)
P.O. Box 899, Huntley (60142-0899)
PHONE..................847 815-0191
Jim Sullivan, *President*
EMP: 5
SALES (est): 339.5K **Privately Held**
SIC: 3999 Manufacturing industries

(G-18045)
PROTEINTECH GROUP INC
5400 Pearl St Ste 300 (60018-5305)
PHONE..................312 455-8498
Jianxun LI, *CEO*
Jeff Lee, *COO*
William Olds, *Officer*
Jeff Papp, *Executive*
EMP: 35

GEOGRAPHIC SECTION

SALES: 4.2MM **Privately Held**
WEB: www.ptglab.com
SIC: 2836 8733 Biological products, except diagnostic; biotechnical research, noncommercial

(G-18046)
RANDA ACCESSORIES LEA GDS LLC (PA)
5600 N River Rd Ste 500 (60018-5188)
PHONE..................847 292-8300
Patrick Moore, *Vice Pres*
Jerry Wu, *Vice Pres*
Marsha Labranche, *Opers Staff*
Wissam Hafidh, *Senior Engr*
Stephanie Xu, *Accountant*
◆ EMP: 90
SQ FT: 26,000
SALES (est): 147.8MM **Privately Held**
WEB: www.randa.net
SIC: 5136 5948 3172 Apparel belts, men's & boys'; luggage & leather goods stores; personal leather goods

(G-18047)
RELIEFBAND TECHNOLOGIES LLC
5600 N River Rd Ste 800 (60018-5166)
PHONE..................877 735-2263
Melanie Brothers, *General Mgr*
EMP: 3
SALES (est): 452.3K **Privately Held**
SIC: 3829 Measuring & controlling devices

(G-18048)
REYES HOLDINGS LLC (PA)
6250 N River Rd Ste 9000 (60018-4241)
PHONE..................847 227-6500
David Reyes, *Owner*
Kathleen Byrne, *Counsel*
Paola Alvarez, *Vice Pres*
Abzu Ceisel Caroline, *Vice Pres*
Jessica Muskey, *Vice Pres*
◆ EMP: 50
SQ FT: 100,000
SALES (est): 5.3B **Privately Held**
SIC: 2086 5142 Bottled & canned soft drinks; packaged frozen goods

(G-18049)
SAPA EXTRUSIONS NORTH AMER LLC
6250 N River Rd Ste 5000 (60018-4214)
PHONE..................877 922-7272
Andrea Bauer-Kuczma, *Principal*
EMP: 8
SALES (est): 650.2K **Privately Held**
SIC: 3354 Aluminum extruded products

(G-18050)
SOUTHERN GRAPHIC SYSTEMS LLC
5500 Pearl St Ste 100 (60018-5303)
PHONE..................847 695-9515
Pat Ryan, *General Mgr*
Mark Von, *Vice Pres*
Ken Wasserman, *Vice Pres*
Jeff Aker, *Accounts Mgr*
Bruce Gilbank, *Regl Sales Mgr*
EMP: 50
SALES (corp-wide): 272.7MM **Privately Held**
SIC: 2796 Platemaking services
HQ: Southern Graphic Systems, Llc
626 W Main St Ste 500
Louisville KY 40202
502 637-5443

(G-18051)
STANDARD CAR TRUCK COMPANY (DH)
6400 Shafer Ct Ste 450 (60018-4948)
PHONE..................847 692-6050
Richard A Mathes, *President*
Donald Popernik, *Corp Secy*
Daniel Schroeder, *Vice Pres*
Ron Golembiewski, *Engineer*
Don Popernik, *Treasurer*
◆ EMP: 40 EST: 1970
SQ FT: 12,000
SALES (est): 94.3MM **Publicly Held**
SIC: 3743 3321 Freight cars & equipment; ductile iron castings; gray iron castings

GEOGRAPHIC SECTION

Round Lake - Lake County (G-18077)

(G-18052)
SUN STEEL TRADING LLC (PA)
10275 W Higgins Rd # 410 (60018-5625)
PHONE...................614 439-3390
Matthew Clark, *Mng Member*
Sean Hecker, *Exec Dir*
EMP: 2
SALES (est): 534.3K **Privately Held**
SIC: 3312 Tinplate

(G-18053)
TERRELL MATERIALS CORPORATION
10600 W Higgins Rd # 300 (60018-3706)
PHONE...................847 635-8530
Patrick C Terrell, *President*
Tiffany Jones, *Accounts Mgr*
EMP: 20
SALES (est): 6MM **Privately Held**
SIC: 3271 3272 Blocks, concrete or cinder: standard; precast terrazo or concrete products

(G-18054)
TRAFALGAR COMPANY LLC
Also Called: Randa Accessories
5600 N River Rd Ste 500 (60018-5188)
PHONE...................847 292-8300
EMP: 3
SALES (corp-wide): 147.8MM **Privately Held**
SIC: 2323 Men's & boys' scarves
HQ: Trafalgar, The Company Llc
417 5th Ave Fl 11
New York NY 10016
212 768-8800

(G-18055)
TRANSPORTATION EQP ADVISORS
6250 N River Rd Ste 5000 (60018-4214)
PHONE...................847 318-7575
Jack Thomas, *President*
EMP: 80
SALES (est): 4MM
SALES (corp-wide): 103.9B **Publicly Held**
SIC: 2721 Trade journals: publishing only, not printed on site
HQ: Wells Fargo Rail Corporation
9377 W Higgins Rd Fl 6
Rosemont IL 60018

(G-18056)
ULTIMATE SOFTWARE GROUP INC
9450 Bryn Mawr Ave # 650 (60018-5268)
PHONE...................847 273-1701
George Poulos, *Sales Mgr*
Scott Goodell, *Business Anlyst*
Richard Torrance, *Manager*
Marla Craven, *Manager*
Cathy Law, *Manager*
EMP: 20
SALES (corp-wide): 1.1B **Privately Held**
SIC: 7372 Prepackaged software
HQ: The Ultimate Software Group Inc
2000 Ultimate Way
Weston FL 33326

(G-18057)
US FOODS CULINARY EQP SUPS LLC (HQ)
9399 W Higgins Rd # 100 (60018-6900)
PHONE...................847 720-8000
James Pyle, *Principal*
EMP: 1 **EST:** 2009
SALES (est): 1.4MM **Publicly Held**
SIC: 5719 2514 Kitchenware; metal kitchen & dining room furniture

(G-18058)
USP HOLDINGS INC
6250 N Rver Rd Ste 10100 (60018)
PHONE...................847 604-6100
John A Hatherly, *Managing Prtnr*
Meri Adler, *Partner*
Frank G Hayes, *Partner*
Terry M Theodore, *Partner*
Stephanie Schaeffer, *Executive Asst*
EMP: 1101
SALES (est): 60.8MM **Privately Held**
SIC: 3321 3491 Cast iron pipe & fittings; industrial valves

(G-18059)
VARSITY LOGISTICS INC
10275 W Higgins Rd # 250 (60018-5625)
PHONE...................650 392-7979
Madeline Bottari, *President*
Stephanie Roundtree, *Programmer Anys*
Laura Heindel, *Prgrmr*
Roberto Ansaloni, *Director*
EMP: 30
SALES (est): 3.2MM **Privately Held**
SIC: 7372 Business oriented computer software; application computer software

(G-18060)
VELSICOL CHEMICAL LLC (HQ)
10400 W Higgins Rd # 303 (60018-3705)
PHONE...................847 813-7888
Dennis Leu,
◆ **EMP:** 1
SALES (est): 14.1MM
SALES (corp-wide): 318.8MM **Privately Held**
WEB: www.velsicol.com
SIC: 2819 Industrial inorganic chemicals

(G-18061)
ZOTOS INTERNATIONAL INC
10600 W Higgins Rd # 415 (60018-3706)
PHONE...................847 390-0984
Bruce Selan, *Branch Mgr*
Lisa Huber, *Surgery Dir*
EMP: 107
SALES (corp-wide): 22.2B **Privately Held**
SIC: 2844 Hair preparations, including shampoos
HQ: Zotos International, Inc.
100 Tokeneke Rd
Darien CT 06820
203 655-8911

Roseville
Warren County

(G-18062)
FUSION TECH INTEGRATED INC (PA)
218 20th Ave (61473-9144)
PHONE...................309 774-4275
Kathryn Bentz, *President*
Bryan Ahee, *Vice Pres*
Brandon Bentz, *Vice Pres*
Dan Bentz, *Vice Pres*
Greg Decker, *Electrical Engi*
EMP: 53
SQ FT: 25,000
SALES (est): 12.9MM **Privately Held**
SIC: 3914 Plated ware (all metals)

Rosiclare
Hardin County

(G-18063)
HASTIE MINING & TRUCKING
68 Bohn St (62982)
PHONE...................618 285-3600
Donnie Oxford, *Branch Mgr*
EMP: 9
SALES (est): 19.2MM **Privately Held**
SIC: 1481 Nonmetallic mineral services
PA: Hastie Mining & Trucking, Limited Partnership
Hwy 146
Cave In Rock IL 62919
618 289-4536

(G-18064)
IMERYS REFRACTORY MNRL USA INC
Ferrell Rd (62982)
PHONE...................618 285-6558
Fred Bressel, *Opers-Prdtn-Mfg*
EMP: 25
SALES (corp-wide): 3MM **Privately Held**
SIC: 3295 Minerals, ground or treated
HQ: Imerys Refractory Minerals Usa, Inc.
100 Mansell Ct E Ste 615
Roswell GA 30076

(G-18065)
PRINCE MINERALS INC
Ferrell St (62982)
PHONE...................618 285-6558
J Willson Ropp, *President*
Charles Belt, *Principal*
▼ **EMP:** 17
SALES (est): 2MM **Privately Held**
SIC: 3295 Minerals, ground or otherwise treated

Rossville
Vermilion County

(G-18066)
NORTON MACHINE CO
711 S Chicago St (60963-9704)
P.O. Box 204 (60963-0204)
PHONE...................217 748-6115
Mark Norton, *Owner*
▲ **EMP:** 4
SQ FT: 1,500
SALES (est): 160K **Privately Held**
SIC: 3599 7692 Machine shop, jobbing & repair; welding repair

Round Lake
Lake County

(G-18067)
AIR MITE DEVICES INC
Also Called: Airmite Devices Inc Cylndrs
606 Long Lake Dr (60073-2812)
PHONE...................224 338-0071
Bert Stryker, *President*
Rose Wrobel, *Admin Sec*
EMP: 25 **EST:** 1945
SQ FT: 15,000
SALES (est): 4.4MM **Privately Held**
WEB: www.airmite.com
SIC: 3541 5084 Home workshop machine tools, metalworking; industrial machinery & equipment

(G-18068)
BAXALTA US INC
25212 W Il Route 120 (60073-9610)
PHONE...................847 948-2000
Sue Scott, *President*
Jeff Reading, *Opers Staff*
Benjamin Montano, *Engrg Dir*
Robin Reynolds, *Research*
John Hembree, *Engineer*
EMP: 92
SALES (corp-wide): 15.1B **Privately Held**
SIC: 2834 Pharmaceutical preparations
HQ: Baxalta Us Inc.
1200 Lakeside Dr
Bannockburn IL 60015
224 948-2000

(G-18069)
BAXTER HEALTHCARE CORPORATION
Also Called: Baxter Gene Therapy Unit
Wilson Rd Rr 120 (60073)
PHONE...................847 270-5720
Dori Egan, *Purchasing*
Joel Ruggaber, *Research*
Christina Szabo, *Research*
Benjamin Safron, *Engineer*
Jenny Thompson, *Supervisor*
EMP: 62
SALES (corp-wide): 11.3B **Publicly Held**
WEB: www.baxter.com
SIC: 3841 Surgical & medical instruments
HQ: Baxter Healthcare Corporation
1 Baxter Pkwy
Deerfield IL 60015
224 948-2000

(G-18070)
BAXTER HEALTHCARE CORPORATION
Baxter Biopharma Solutions
25212 W Il Route 120 (60073-9799)
PHONE...................847 948-4770
Robert Felicelli, *General Mgr*
Scott Hogan, *Engineer*
Tania Marvaki, *Manager*
Pulin Parikh, *Manager*
Colleen Wibbe, *Info Tech Mgr*
EMP: 19
SALES (corp-wide): 11.3B **Publicly Held**
SIC: 3841 Surgical & medical instruments
HQ: Baxter Healthcare Corporation
1 Baxter Pkwy
Deerfield IL 60015
224 948-2000

(G-18071)
BAXTER HEALTHCARE CORPORATION
32360 N Wilson Rd (60073-9401)
PHONE...................224 270-6300
Henk Bolm, *Research*
Karen Adams, *Human Res Dir*
Gary Hnline, *Branch Mgr*
Greg Hartke, *Manager*
Eddie Vasquez, *Info Tech Dir*
EMP: 900
SALES (corp-wide): 11.3B **Publicly Held**
SIC: 2834 Pharmaceutical preparations
HQ: Baxter Healthcare Corporation
1 Baxter Pkwy
Deerfield IL 60015
224 948-2000

(G-18072)
BAXTER HEALTHCARE CORPORATION
25212 W Illinois Rte 120 (60073)
PHONE...................847 940-6599
David Drohan, *President*
Robert Garber, *Research*
Jean Guyader, *Auditor*
Karen Ebdon, *Business Anlyst*
Colleen Wibbe, *Info Tech Mgr*
EMP: 300
SALES (corp-wide): 11.3B **Publicly Held**
SIC: 3841 Surgical & medical instruments
HQ: Baxter Healthcare Corporation
1 Baxter Pkwy
Deerfield IL 60015
224 948-2000

(G-18073)
CHRONX GLOBAL INDUSTRIES LTD
1787 S Hamlin Ln (60073-4286)
PHONE...................773 770-5753
Bob Gabrovski, *CEO*
EMP: 3
SALES (est): 95K **Privately Held**
SIC: 3999 Manufacturing industries

(G-18074)
EXTREME WOODWORKING INC
24650 W Luther Ave Apt B (60073-1409)
PHONE...................224 338-8179
Mike Spychal, *President*
EMP: 3
SQ FT: 2,000
SALES (est): 250K **Privately Held**
SIC: 2431 Woodwork, interior & ornamental

(G-18075)
G M SIGN INC
704 Sunset Dr (60073-2826)
PHONE...................847 546-0424
George Matiasek Jr, *President*
Beverly Kelly, *Corp Secy*
EMP: 51
SQ FT: 30,000
SALES (est): 5.6MM **Privately Held**
SIC: 3993 Electric signs; neon signs

(G-18076)
GENERAL MOTOR SIGN
704 Sunset Dr (60073-2826)
PHONE...................847 546-0424
George Matiasek Jr, *Owner*
EMP: 3
SALES (est): 336.9K **Privately Held**
SIC: 3993 Signs & advertising specialties

(G-18077)
GOODRICH SENSOR SYSTEMS
34232 N Bluestem Rd (60073-5245)
PHONE...................847 546-5749
Tyler Reid, *Principal*
EMP: 2

SALES (est): 226.9K **Privately Held**
SIC: 3822 Built-in thermostats, filled system & bimetal types

(G-18078)
GRIEVE CORPORATION
500 Hart Rd (60073-2898)
PHONE..................................847 546-8225
D V Grieve, *CEO*
Pat J Calabrese, *President*
Frank Calabrese, *Vice Pres*
Andy Luther, *Engineer*
Gayle Teltz, *Manager*
▼ EMP: 90
SQ FT: 110,000
SALES (est): 27.4MM **Privately Held**
WEB: www.grievecorp.com
SIC: 3567 3821 3433 Industrial furnaces & ovens; ovens, laboratory; furnaces, laboratory; heating equipment, except electric

(G-18079)
LA LUC BAKERY INC
246 N Cedar Lake Rd Frnt (60073-3284)
PHONE..................................847 740-0303
Montes Veoca, *President*
EMP: 6
SALES (est): 644.4K **Privately Held**
SIC: 2051 Bakery: wholesale or wholesale/retail combined

(G-18080)
MVS MOLDING INC
701 Long Lake Dr (60073-2813)
PHONE..................................847 740-7700
Miroslav Smid, *President*
Marie Smid, *Corp Secy*
EMP: 9
SQ FT: 14,200
SALES (est): 980K **Privately Held**
SIC: 3089 Injection molding of plastics

(G-18081)
ROUND LAKE PALLETS INC
740 Sunset Dr (60073-2826)
PHONE..................................847 637-6162
Juvenal Garcia, *President*
EMP: 3
SALES (est): 169.9K **Privately Held**
SIC: 2448 7699 Pallets, wood; pallet repair

(G-18082)
SAE CUSTOMS INC
27764 Volo Village Rd F (60073-9680)
PHONE..................................855 723-2878
Eric Schildkraut, *President*
EMP: 6 EST: 2009
SALES (est): 904.5K **Privately Held**
WEB: www.saecustoms.com
SIC: 3711 Motor vehicles & car bodies

(G-18083)
SIGN CENTRAL
34039 N Hainesville Rd (60073-9711)
PHONE..................................847 543-7600
Rita Buttacavola, *Owner*
EMP: 4
SQ FT: 1,012
SALES (est): 473.5K **Privately Held**
WEB: www.signcentral.com
SIC: 3993 7532 Electric signs; truck painting & lettering

(G-18084)
THREE R PLASTICS INC
310 W Nippersink Rd (60073-3553)
PHONE..................................847 740-2845
Michael Gore, *Principal*
EMP: 4 EST: 2010
SALES (est): 371.6K **Privately Held**
SIC: 3089 Injection molding of plastics

(G-18085)
TRI-COUNTY TRUCK TOPS INC
1218 W Rollins Rd (60073-1073)
PHONE..................................847 740-4004
Bill Silva, *Owner*
EMP: 8
SALES (corp-wide): 3.3MM **Privately Held**
SIC: 3713 Truck tops

PA: Tri-County Truck Tops, Inc.
    2240 E Algonquin Rd
    Algonquin IL
    847 658-5648

(G-18086)
WEST MACHINE PRODUCTS INC
606 Long Lake Dr (60073-2812)
PHONE..................................847 740-2404
Robert Szwaya, *President*
Amy Szwaya, *Vice Pres*
EMP: 20
SQ FT: 2,300
SALES (est): 2.9MM **Privately Held**
SIC: 3599 Machine shop, jobbing & repair

Round Lake Beach
Lake County

(G-18087)
BLUE BROTHERS COATINGS
2415 N Quaker Hollow Ln (60073-4854)
PHONE..................................847 265-5400
John Blue, *Owner*
EMP: 4
SALES (est): 296.9K **Privately Held**
SIC: 3479 Painting, coating & hot dipping

(G-18088)
DRG MOLDING & PAD PRINTING INC
1631 Wood St (60073-2250)
PHONE..................................847 223-3398
Dave Geborek, *President*
EMP: 10
SQ FT: 10,000
SALES (est): 628.7K **Privately Held**
SIC: 3089 Injection molding of plastics

(G-18089)
HOWARD SCHWARTZ
Also Called: Controlweigh
2189 N Rte 83 Ste 335 (60073)
PHONE..................................847 540-8260
Howard Schwartz, *Owner*
EMP: 5
SALES (est): 354.3K **Privately Held**
SIC: 3596 5084 Industrial scales; industrial machinery & equipment

(G-18090)
IVES-WAY PRODUCTS INC
2030 N Nicole Ln (60073-2288)
P.O. Box 70, Round Lake (60073-0070)
PHONE..................................847 740-0658
Glenn R Ours, *President*
Laura Ours, *Vice Pres*
EMP: 2
SQ FT: 2,000
SALES (est): 210K **Privately Held**
SIC: 3542 Metal container making machines: cans, etc.

(G-18091)
MURPHY USA INC
2676 N Il Route 83 (60073-4983)
PHONE..................................847 245-3283
EMP: 9 **Publicly Held**
WEB: www.murphyusa.com
SIC: 5541 2911 Filling stations, gasoline; petroleum refining
PA: Murphy Usa Inc.
    200 E Peach St
    El Dorado AR 71730

(G-18092)
RADIO CONTROLLED MODELS INC
Also Called: Ram R-C Models
229 E Rollins Rd (60073-1329)
PHONE..................................847 740-8726
Ralph P Warner, *President*
Elizabeth Warner, *Treasurer*
EMP: 8
SQ FT: 5,000
SALES (est): 1MM **Privately Held**
SIC: 3825 Oscillators, audio & radio frequency (instrument types); radio frequency measuring equipment

(G-18093)
VELASQUEZ & SONS MUFFLER SHOP
507 W Rollins Rd (60073-1220)
PHONE..................................847 740-6990
Juan Velasquez, *Principal*
EMP: 2
SALES (est): 238.2K **Privately Held**
SIC: 7533 3714 5015 Muffler shop, sale or repair & installation; mufflers (exhaust), motor vehicle; automotive parts & supplies, used

Round Lake Heights
Lake County

(G-18094)
M MARTINEZ INC
828 Warrior St (60073-1145)
PHONE..................................847 740-6364
Munuel Martinez, *President*
EMP: 2
SALES (est): 208.7K **Privately Held**
SIC: 3524 Grass catchers, lawn mower

Round Lake Park
Lake County

(G-18095)
B RADTKE AND SONS INC
101 W Main St Ste 2 (60073-3510)
PHONE..................................847 546-3999
John A Radtke, *President*
EMP: 6 EST: 1938
SQ FT: 7,500
SALES (est): 826.6K **Privately Held**
SIC: 3544 3469 3451 3599 Special dies & tools; metal stampings; screw machine products; machine shop, jobbing & repair

(G-18096)
DORIS COMPANY
30 Porter Dr (60073-3601)
PHONE..................................224 302-5605
Mike Sawant, *Admin Sec*
EMP: 5 EST: 2016
SALES (est): 278K **Privately Held**
SIC: 2842 Specialty cleaning preparations

(G-18097)
MARKET READY INC
30 Porter Dr (60073-3601)
PHONE..................................847 689-1000
Michael Sawant, *President*
Clayton Bolke, *Treasurer*
EMP: 4
SALES (est): 1.2MM **Privately Held**
SIC: 2844 Hair preparations, including shampoos

(G-18098)
SMALL DIFFERENT BETTER INC
Also Called: Sdb Products
30 Porter Dr (60073-3601)
PHONE..................................224 302-5163
Jason Dhaliwal, *President*
EMP: 4
SALES (est): 241.4K **Privately Held**
SIC: 3565 Packaging machinery

(G-18099)
TRUMANS BRANDS LLC
30 Porter Dr (60073-3601)
PHONE..................................224 302-5605
Michael Sawant,
John Esposito,
EMP: 10 EST: 2016
SALES (est): 450.4K **Privately Held**
SIC: 2844 Toilet preparations

Roxana
Madison County

(G-18100)
GEMINI INDUSTRIES INC
1 Gemini Industrial Dr (62084-2747)
PHONE..................................618 251-3352
Christopher Schaeffer, *Admin Sec*
▲ EMP: 75
SQ FT: 150,000
SALES (est): 10.1MM **Privately Held**
SIC: 3993 Advertising novelties

(G-18101)
RS USED OIL SERVICES INC
4559 Wagon Wheel Rd (62084-2715)
PHONE..................................618 781-1717
EMP: 4
SALES (corp-wide): 3.4B **Publicly Held**
SIC: 2992 Lubricating oils & greases
HQ: Rs Used Oil Services, Inc.
    2932 N Ohio St
    Wichita KS 67219

(G-18102)
SPECIALTY PRINTING MIDWEST
1 Gemini Industrial Dr (62084-2747)
PHONE..................................618 799-8472
EMP: 2
SALES (est): 229.4K **Privately Held**
SIC: 2752 Commercial Printing, Lithographic

(G-18103)
SUPERHEAT FGH SERVICES INC
4767 Signature Industrial (62084)
PHONE..................................618 251-9450
Jamie Cox, *Opers Mgr*
EMP: 11
SALES (corp-wide): 74.8MM **Privately Held**
WEB: www.superheatfgh.com
SIC: 3569 Heaters, swimming pool: electric
PA: Superheat Fgh Services, Inc.
    313 Garnet Dr
    New Lenox IL 60451
    708 478-0205

(G-18104)
W R B REFINERY LLC
900 S Central Ave (62084-1337)
PHONE..................................618 255-2345
Jerry Knoyle, *Plant Mgr*
▲ EMP: 31
SALES (est): 13.6MM
SALES (corp-wide): 109.5B **Publicly Held**
SIC: 2911 Petroleum refining
PA: Phillips 66
    2331 Citywest Blvd
    Houston TX 77042
    281 293-6600

Ruma
Randolph County

(G-18105)
RED BUD WINERY INC
214 Main St (62278-2606)
PHONE..................................618 282-9463
EMP: 4
SALES (est): 283.1K **Privately Held**
SIC: 2084 Wines, brandy & brandy spirits

(G-18106)
ROGERS REDI-MIX INC (PA)
55 E Mill St (62278-2715)
PHONE..................................618 282-3844
Roger Koester, *President*
Barbara A Koester, *Corp Secy*
EMP: 18 EST: 1965
SALES (est): 2.5MM **Privately Held**
SIC: 3273 1442 Ready-mixed concrete; construction sand & gravel

GEOGRAPHIC SECTION

(G-18107)
SOUTHERN ILLINOIS CRANKSHAFTS
225 Kaskaskia St (62278)
PHONE..................618 282-4100
Michael Schaefer, *President*
Lisa Koester, *Purch Mgr*
Sarah Schaefer, *Accounting Mgr*
EMP: 10 **EST:** 2009
SALES (est): 1.1MM **Privately Held**
WEB: www.sicrankshaft.com
SIC: 3599 Crankshafts & camshafts, machining

Rushville
Schuyler County

(G-18108)
B T TECHNOLOGY INC
Also Called: BT Tech
320 N Railroad Rd (62681-1284)
P.O. Box 49 (62681-0049)
PHONE..................217 322-3768
Brian D Tomlinson, *President*
Mackenzie E Malcomson, *Vice Pres*
Michael Tomlinson, *Opers Mgr*
EMP: 7
SQ FT: 500
SALES (est): 553K **Privately Held**
SIC: 3825 3821 Test equipment for electronic & electric measurement; laboratory apparatus & furniture

(G-18109)
HALL FABRICATION INC
121 N Liberty St (62681-1416)
PHONE..................217 322-2212
Jamie Lane, *Manager*
EMP: 3
SALES (est): 247.5K **Privately Held**
SIC: 3399 Primary metal products

(G-18110)
HOUSER MEATS
180 Rr 2 (62681)
PHONE..................217 322-4994
Doug Houser, *Partner*
Terri Houser, *General Ptnr*
EMP: 7
SQ FT: 1,000
SALES: 350K **Privately Held**
SIC: 0751 2013 Slaughtering: custom livestock services; sausages & other prepared meats

(G-18111)
INNOVATIVE DESIGN AND RES INC
Also Called: Idrc
338 W Lafayette St (62681-1324)
PHONE..................217 322-3907
Daniel J Meyer, *President*
EMP: 3
SALES: 100K **Privately Held**
SIC: 3724 Research & development on aircraft engines & parts

(G-18112)
PERRYCO INC
Also Called: Rushville Times
110 E Lafayette St (62681-1412)
P.O. Box 226 (62681-0226)
PHONE..................217 322-3321
Alan Icenogle, *General Mgr*
Teresa Haines, *Adv Mgr*
EMP: 9
SALES (est): 339.8K
SALES (corp-wide): 3MM **Privately Held**
SIC: 2711 Job printing & newspaper publishing combined
PA: Perryco Inc
6920 Webster St
Downers Grove IL 60516
303 652-8282

(G-18113)
STITCHABLES EMBROIDERY
Also Called: J Gayleen Hammond
416 Silverleaf St (62681-1231)
P.O. Box 406 (62681-0406)
PHONE..................217 322-3000
Janet Gayleen Hammond, *Partner*
Janet Gayleenhammond, *Partner*
Julie Zorn, *Partner*
EMP: 3
SALES: 81K **Privately Held**
SIC: 2395 Emblems, embroidered

Russell
Lake County

(G-18114)
I94 RV LLC
16125 Russel Rd (60075)
P.O. Box 332 (60075-0332)
PHONE..................847 395-9500
Ed Collier, *Principal*
Greg Stadlin, *Sales Mgr*
EMP: 17 **EST:** 2016
SALES (est): 126K **Privately Held**
SIC: 3792 7032 Travel trailers & campers; recreational camps

S Chicago Hts
Cook County

(G-18115)
ACME AUTO ELECTRIC CO
2626 Chicago Rd (60411-4760)
PHONE..................708 754-5420
Kenneth Eatinger, *President*
Garrett Eatinger, *Plant Mgr*
EMP: 9
SQ FT: 3,600
SALES (est): 500K **Privately Held**
SIC: 3714 7539 Motor vehicle engines & parts; automotive repair shops

(G-18116)
ALLOYS TECH INC
3305 Butler St (60411-5506)
PHONE..................708 248-5041
Surendra Daga, *Principal*
EMP: 5
SALES (est): 241.9K **Privately Held**
SIC: 3325 Alloy steel castings, except investment

(G-18117)
ARROW PIN AND PRODUCTS INC
51 E 34th St (60411-5501)
PHONE..................708 755-7575
Charles R Prucha Jr, *President*
Laura J Prucha, *Treasurer*
EMP: 11
SQ FT: 10,000
SALES (est): 2MM **Privately Held**
SIC: 3452 Pins

(G-18118)
COATING SPECIALTY INC
3311 Holeman Ave Ste 7 (60411-5559)
PHONE..................708 754-3311
Robert Buckley, *President*
EMP: 9
SQ FT: 5,500
SALES (est): 600K **Privately Held**
SIC: 3471 5531 Cleaning, polishing & finishing; automotive & home supply stores

(G-18119)
COSMOS MANUFACTURING INC
111 E 34th St (60411-5502)
PHONE..................708 756-1400
John Michelon, *President*
Gabriella Michelon, *Corp Secy*
Mike Jemilo, *Plant Mgr*
Walter Casey, *CFO*
Colleen Lusk, *Manager*
◆ **EMP:** 135
SQ FT: 60,000
SALES (est): 37.3MM **Privately Held**
SIC: 3469 Stamping metal for the trade

(G-18120)
DO-RITE DIE & ENGINEERING CO
3344 Butler St (60411-5507)
PHONE..................708 754-4355
Alan R Szymanski, *President*
Edward B Szymanski, *Vice Pres*
Cynthia S Szymanski, *Admin Sec*
EMP: 12 **EST:** 1953
SQ FT: 10,000
SALES: 2.8MM **Privately Held**
WEB: www.do-ritedie.com
SIC: 3544 Special dies & tools; dies & die holders for metal cutting, forming, die casting

(G-18121)
HENNESSY SHEET METAL
3256 Butler St (60411-5505)
PHONE..................708 754-6342
Pat Hennessey, *President*
EMP: 7
SQ FT: 6,000
SALES (est): 986.7K **Privately Held**
SIC: 3444 Sheet metal specialties, not stamped

(G-18122)
INDUSTRIAL PARK MACHINE & TOOL
3326 Butler St (60411-5507)
PHONE..................708 754-7080
Sergio Zorzi, *President*
Todd Schutte, *Vice Pres*
EMP: 10
SQ FT: 12,000
SALES (est): 500K **Privately Held**
SIC: 3544 3469 Special dies & tools; stamping metal for the trade

(G-18123)
MASON WELDING INC
3321 Holeman Ave (60411-5517)
PHONE..................708 755-0621
Bret Mason, *President*
Kathy Mason, *Admin Sec*
EMP: 3
SALES (est): 394K **Privately Held**
SIC: 7692 Welding repair

(G-18124)
MAX MILLER
Also Called: Miller's Ready Mix
3000 State St (60411-4844)
PHONE..................708 758-7760
Max Miller, *Owner*
EMP: 12 **EST:** 1974
SQ FT: 3,500
SALES: 2MM **Privately Held**
SIC: 3273 Ready-mixed concrete

(G-18125)
MID STATES CORPORATION
3245 Holeman Ave (60411-5599)
PHONE..................708 754-1760
Donald Bartolini, *President*
Robert Bartolini, *Vice Pres*
Thomas Bartolini, *Sales Staff*
Peter Bartolini, *Admin Sec*
EMP: 30 **EST:** 1978
SQ FT: 18,000
SALES (est): 7.6MM **Privately Held**
SIC: 3535 Conveyors & conveying equipment

(G-18126)
PRODUCTION FABG & STAMPING INC
3311 Butler St (60411-5588)
PHONE..................708 755-5468
Paul Gilliam, *President*
EMP: 15 **EST:** 1971
SQ FT: 26,000
SALES (est): 3.6MM **Privately Held**
SIC: 3469 3444 3544 7692 Stamping metal for the trade; sheet metalwork; special dies & tools; welding repair; metal cutting services

(G-18127)
R W G MANUFACTURING INC
3309 Holeman Ave Ste 7 (60411-5558)
PHONE..................708 755-8035
Ron Giannantonia, *President*
EMP: 7
SQ FT: 5,000
SALES (est): 250K **Privately Held**
SIC: 3842 2431 Technical aids for the handicapped; millwork

(G-18128)
UNIVERSIAL CAT LLC
111 E 34th St (60411-5502)
PHONE..................708 753-8070
John Michelon, *President*
John M Michelon, *Manager*
◆ **EMP:** 49
SALES (est): 3.9MM **Privately Held**
SIC: 2819 Catalysts, chemical

(G-18129)
WAXSTAR INC
3224 Butler St (60411-5505)
PHONE..................708 755-3530
Lawrence J Czaszwicz Jr, *President*
Noreen Czaszwicz, *Admin Sec*
EMP: 1 **EST:** 1970
SQ FT: 49,000
SALES (est): 270.6K **Privately Held**
SIC: 2673 2671 2674 Bags: plastic, laminated & coated; waxed paper: made from purchased material; bags: uncoated paper & multiwall

(G-18130)
WOODMAC INDUSTRIES INC
3233 Holeman Ave (60411-5515)
PHONE..................708 755-3545
James T McLaughlin, *President*
EMP: 16
SQ FT: 26,000
SALES (est): 1.8MM **Privately Held**
WEB: www.woodmacind.com
SIC: 2499 2426 Picture frame molding, finished; stepladders, wood; hardwood dimension & flooring mills

Sadorus
Champaign County

(G-18131)
DEEDRICK MACHINE INC
105 E Market St (61872-7505)
P.O. Box 50 (61872-0050)
PHONE..................217 598-2366
Donald Deedrick, *President*
John Deedrick, *Vice Pres*
Robin Fonner, *Marketing Staff*
EMP: 20
SQ FT: 20,000
SALES (est): 3.5MM **Privately Held**
SIC: 3599 Machine shop, jobbing & repair

Saint Anne
Kankakee County

(G-18132)
BERENS INC
1269 E 5000s Rd (60964-4231)
PHONE..................815 935-3237
Mark A Berens, *President*
EMP: 7 **EST:** 1988
SALES (est): 600K **Privately Held**
SIC: 3315 Steel wire & related products

(G-18133)
EASTERN ILLINOIS CLAY COMPANY (PA)
Also Called: Dom Plastic Div
460 S Elm Ave (60964-7245)
P.O. Box 657 (60964-0657)
PHONE..................815 427-8144
Ronald Meier, *President*
Dennis Meier, *Corp Secy*
Duane Meier, *Vice Pres*
EMP: 10
SQ FT: 19,500
SALES: 3.6MM **Privately Held**
SIC: 3084 Plastics pipe

(G-18134)
F & L DRAPERY INC
6279 Warren St (60964-5306)
PHONE..................815 932-8997
Lynn Wagner, *President*
EMP: 3
SALES (est): 213K **Privately Held**
SIC: 2211 5714 Draperies & drapery fabrics, cotton; drapery & upholstery stores

Saint Anne - Kankakee County (G-18135)

(G-18135)
JDL GRAPHICS
4489a S 4500e Rd (60964-4072)
PHONE.................................815 401-1120
EMP: 3
SALES (est): 194.8K Privately Held
WEB: www.jdlgraphics.com
SIC: 2759 Screen printing

(G-18136)
MIDWEST MACHINE TOOL INC
485 S Oak St (60964-7292)
P.O. Box 457 (60964-0457)
PHONE.................................815 427-8665
Myron D Wendt, President
Alyssa Wendt, Corp Secy
EMP: 5
SALES (est): 631.8K Privately Held
SIC: 3544 3545 3532 3599 Special dies & tools; vises, machine (machine tool accessories); drills & drilling equipment, mining (except oil & gas); machine shop, jobbing & repair; farm machinery repair; industrial machinery & equipment repair; drill presses

(G-18137)
RDA INC
400 N 3rd Ave (60964-7326)
P.O. Box 229 (60964-0229)
PHONE.................................815 427-8444
Raymond Hubert, President
Regina Hubert, Admin Sec
EMP: 18
SALES (est): 2.8MM Privately Held
SIC: 2899 Patching plaster, household

(G-18138)
TRU-CUT MACHINE INCORPORATED
480 S Oak St (60964-5357)
P.O. Box 497 (60964-0497)
PHONE.................................815 422-5047
Jim Butler, President
EMP: 5
SQ FT: 9,500
SALES (est): 400K Privately Held
SIC: 3599 Machine shop, jobbing & repair

Saint Augustine
Knox County

(G-18139)
RIVERSTONE GROUP INC
772 175th St (61474-9744)
PHONE.................................309 462-3003
Harry Flessner, Branch Mgr
EMP: 7
SALES (corp-wide): 2.5B Privately Held
SIC: 1422 Cement rock, crushed & broken-quarrying
PA: Riverstone Group, Inc.
4640 E 56th St
Davenport IA 52807
309 757-8250

Saint Charles
Kane County

(G-18140)
8 ELECTRONIC CIGARETTE INC
Also Called: 8 Electronic Cigarettes
1830 Wallace Ave Ste 201 (60174-3417)
PHONE.................................630 708-6803
Michael Goduco, CEO
EMP: 4
SALES (est): 359.3K Privately Held
SIC: 2111 7389 5194 Cigarettes; ; tobacco & tobacco products

(G-18141)
A & C MOLD COMPANY INC
Also Called: AC Mold
3870 Swenson Ave (60174-3438)
PHONE.................................630 587-0177
Andrew Mendala, President
Christine Mendala, Admin Sec
▲ EMP: 45
SQ FT: 20,000
SALES (est): 9.1MM Privately Held
SIC: 3544 Industrial molds

(G-18142)
ADVANCED COOLER INC
515 Illinois St (60174-2751)
PHONE.................................630 443-8933
Anthony Kotsy, President
EMP: 2
SALES (est): 645K Privately Held
WEB: www.advancedcooler.com
SIC: 7623 1711 3585 5078 Refrigeration repair service; refrigeration contractor; refrigeration equipment, complete; commercial refrigeration equipment

(G-18143)
AJR ENTERPRISES INC
1200 Rukel Way (60174-3427)
PHONE.................................630 377-8886
Jacob Rukel, CEO
Angelo Rukel, President
John Rukel, COO
Jason Dworak, Opers Mgr
Mike Doyle, Sales Staff
EMP: 250 EST: 1997
SQ FT: 450,000
SALES (est): 35.5MM Privately Held
WEB: www.ajrfiltration.com
SIC: 2393 5085 Textile bags; industrial supplies

(G-18144)
ALWAYS FAITFHUL DOG TRANING
73 Highgate Crse (60174-1422)
P.O. Box 771 (60174-0771)
PHONE.................................630 696-2572
EMP: 3
SALES (est): 137.6K Privately Held
WEB: www.kcchronicle.com
SIC: 2711 Newspapers

(G-18145)
AMERICAN CHURCH SUPPLY
Also Called: C Rockelmann Co
41w699 Foxtail Cir (60175-8466)
PHONE.................................847 464-4140
Steve Zanis, Owner
Beth Zanis, Co-Owner
Deth Zanis, Co-Owner
▲ EMP: 3
SALES: 200K Privately Held
SIC: 2389 5049 Clergymen's vestments; religious supplies

(G-18146)
AMERICAN POWDER COATINGS INC
420 38th Ave (60174-5426)
PHONE.................................630 762-0100
Brett Suvagia, President
Dave Suvagia, Vice Pres
Joe Alisia, Manager
▲ EMP: 50
SQ FT: 40,000
SALES (est): 14.2MM Privately Held
SIC: 2851 Enamels

(G-18147)
ARCTURUS PERFORMANCE PDTS LLC
3955 Commerce Dr (60174-5321)
P.O. Box 268 (60174-0268)
PHONE.................................630 204-0211
John R Palmer, Principal
Hugh V Palmer, Mng Member
EMP: 4
SALES (est): 263.1K Privately Held
SIC: 2819 Catalysts, chemical

(G-18148)
ARK DE MEXICO LLC (PA)
Also Called: ADM
902 S Randall Rd (60174-1781)
PHONE.................................630 240-9483
Anthony Urban, President
Tony Urban, President
EMP: 390
SALES: 6MM Privately Held
SIC: 3714 3694 Automotive wiring harness sets; automotive electrical equipment

(G-18149)
ARK TECHNOLOGIES INC (PA)
Also Called: A R K
3655 Ohio Ave (60174-5445)
PHONE.................................630 377-8855
Alfonso Cepeda, Plant Mgr
Natalie Ciska, Purchasing
Paul Daniels, Engineer
Lorin Holzbauer, Engineer
Mary Periman, Engineer
◆ EMP: 55
SALES (est): 7.7MM Privately Held
WEB: www.arktechno.com
SIC: 3495 3694 3469 Instrument springs, precision; engine electrical equipment; metal stampings

(G-18150)
ARTISAN MILLWORK LLC
902 S Randall Rd Ste C335 (60174-1781)
PHONE.................................847 417-5236
Daniel Glod, Mng Member
EMP: 7
SALES (est): 200.3K Privately Held
WEB: www.artisan-millwork.com
SIC: 2431 Millwork

(G-18151)
ASSURANCE CLG RESTORATION LLC
3740 Stern Ave (60174-5404)
PHONE.................................630 444-3600
Thomas Kollar, Mng Member
Lee Godinez,
EMP: 18
SQ FT: 24,000
SALES (est): 1.5MM Privately Held
SIC: 3544 Industrial molds

(G-18152)
AVID OF ILLINOIS INC
Also Called: AlphaGraphics
2740 E Main St (60174-2445)
PHONE.................................847 698-2775
Mari Connelly, President
EMP: 10
SQ FT: 4,300
SALES: 1.5MM Privately Held
SIC: 2752 2791 2789 Commercial printing, lithographic; typesetting; bookbinding & related work

(G-18153)
AWARD CONCEPTS INC
Also Called: Award Concepts Mfg Co
110 S 11th Ave (60174-2226)
P.O. Box 4305 (60174-9075)
PHONE.................................630 513-7801
Gordon L Campbell, President
Donald H Martens, Vice Pres
Julie Kettelkamp, Design Engr
Darren Jaenis, Manager
Craig Bonifas, Director
▲ EMP: 50
SQ FT: 20,000
SALES (est): 9.3MM Privately Held
SIC: 3911 5199 Jewelry, precious metal; gifts & novelties

(G-18154)
BENDPLEX COMPAND
36w610 Marguerite St A (60174-1135)
PHONE.................................630 797-5808
EMP: 2 EST: 2016
SALES (est): 229.4K Privately Held
SIC: 3599 Machine shop, jobbing & repair

(G-18155)
BESTAR TECHNOLOGIES INC
761 N 17th St Ste 4 (60174-1664)
PHONE.................................847 261-2850
Paul Gillespie, President
▲ EMP: 7
SQ FT: 4,800
SALES: 3MM Privately Held
SIC: 3679 Electronic circuits

(G-18156)
BISON GEAR & ENGINEERING CORP (PA)
3850 Ohio Ave (60174-5462)
PHONE.................................630 377-4327
Martin Swarbrick, President
George E Thomas, Exec VP
Andrew Burnette, Vice Pres
Ted Lat, Engineer
Robert Lewton, Design Engr
◆ EMP: 175
SQ FT: 114,200
SALES (est): 35.5MM Privately Held
SIC: 3621 3714 4789 Motors & generators; air conditioner parts, motor vehicle; cargo loading & unloading services

(G-18157)
BLACK START LABS INC
1500 Foundry St Ste 8 (60174-1555)
P.O. Box 1308 (60174-7308)
PHONE.................................630 444-1800
EMP: 3
SALES (est): 185.3K Privately Held
SIC: 2834 Pills, pharmaceutical

(G-18158)
BLUEGRASS ENTERPRISES LLC
1501 Indiana Ave (60174-3124)
PHONE.................................630 544-3781
Daniel T Flanagan, Principal
EMP: 2
SALES (est): 243.4K Privately Held
SIC: 2752 Commercial printing, lithographic

(G-18159)
BRADLEY ADHSIVE APPLCTIONS INC (PA)
Also Called: Bradley Group, The
3635 Swenson Ave (60174-3441)
PHONE.................................630 443-8424
Bradley Stefan, President
Bruce Stefan, Treasurer
Mark Sweeney, Executive
EMP: 124 EST: 1983
SQ FT: 65,000
SALES (est): 32.1MM Privately Held
SIC: 2891 Adhesives

(G-18160)
BUTTON MAN PRINTING INC
7 E Main St (60174-1925)
PHONE.................................630 549-0438
Jacob Martens, President
Mark Burger, Admin Sec
EMP: 8 EST: 2013
SALES (est): 148.6K Privately Held
SIC: 2752 Commercial printing, offset

(G-18161)
C M C INDUSTRIES INC
Also Called: Cutco Abrasive Co
2525 Production Dr (60174-3349)
PHONE.................................630 377-0530
William C Mc Cormick, President
Suzanne Mc Cormick, Admin Sec
EMP: 12
SQ FT: 10,000
SALES (est): 935.6K Privately Held
SIC: 3291 Grindstones, artificial

(G-18162)
CAIN TUBULAR PRODUCTS INC
310 Kirk Rd (60174-3430)
PHONE.................................630 584-5330
John Cain, President
Michael Cain, Treasurer
Robert Cain, Admin Sec
EMP: 9 EST: 1966
SQ FT: 16,000
SALES (est): 2MM Privately Held
WEB: www.caintubular.com
SIC: 3498 Tube fabricating (contract bending & shaping)

(G-18163)
CARA ANAM ENTERPRISES INC
Also Called: Embroidme-Fox River Valley
216 Kirk Rd (60174-2429)
PHONE.................................630 587-8700
Terence Aaron, President
Candice Aaron, Vice Pres
EMP: 3
SALES (est): 289.6K Privately Held
SIC: 2759 Screen printing

(G-18164)
CARBCO MANUFACTURING INC
2525 Production Dr (60174-3349)
P.O. Box 135, Geneva (60134-0135)
PHONE.................................630 377-1410
William C Mc Cormick, President
EMP: 19

GEOGRAPHIC SECTION

Saint Charles - Kane County (G-18192)

SALES (est): 2.9MM **Privately Held**
SIC: 3291 3545 Tungsten carbide abrasive; machine tool accessories

(G-18165)
CHICAGO MOLD ENGRG CO INC
615 Stetson Ave (60174-3458)
PHONE..................630 584-1311
Ralph Oswald, *CEO*
Richard Laverty, *President*
Jeffrey Oswald, *President*
Thomas E Heindl, *Corp Secy*
Jeff Oswald, *Vice Pres*
EMP: 58
SQ FT: 39,000
SALES (est): 14MM **Privately Held**
WEB: www.chicagomold.com
SIC: 3544 7699 Forms (molds), for foundry & plastics working machinery; plastics products repair

(G-18166)
CINO INCORPORATED
3n264 Loretta Dr (60175-7608)
PHONE..................630 377-7242
Thomas A Sparacino, *President*
Jodi Sparacino, *Vice Pres*
EMP: 2
SQ FT: 400
SALES (est): 502.7K **Privately Held**
SIC: 5047 3944 Medical equipment & supplies; games, toys & children's vehicles

(G-18167)
CLARKE AQUATIC SERVICES INC
675 Sidwell Ct (60174-3492)
PHONE..................630 894-2000
J Lyell Clarke III, *CEO*
Kevin Magro, *Exec VP*
Joel Fruendt, *Vice Pres*
Terry Phillips, *Vice Pres*
Julie Reiter, *Vice Pres*
EMP: 99
SALES (est): 12.1MM **Privately Held**
SIC: 2879 Agricultural chemicals

(G-18168)
CLARKE GROUP INC
675 Sidwell Ct (60174-3492)
PHONE..................630 894-2000
J Lyell Clarke III, *President*
Sue Stout, *Manager*
EMP: 160
SALES (est): 15.5MM **Privately Held**
SIC: 2879 Insecticides & pesticides

(G-18169)
CLARKE MOSQUITO CTRL PDTS INC (PA)
675 Sidwell Ct (60174-3492)
P.O. Box 72197, Roselle (60172-0197)
PHONE..................630 894-2000
J Lyell Clarke III, *President*
Kevin Magro, *Exec VP*
Joel Fruendt, *Vice Pres*
Karen Larson, *Vice Pres*
Terry Phillips, *Vice Pres*
◆ EMP: 102
SQ FT: 27,000
SALES (est): 44.8MM **Privately Held**
SIC: 2879 Insecticides & pesticides

(G-18170)
CLASSIC FASTENERS LLC
3540 Stern Ave (60174-5409)
PHONE..................630 605-0195
Bennett Jordan, *President*
Cheryl Jordan,
▲ EMP: 9
SQ FT: 2,000
SALES (est): 1.1MM **Privately Held**
SIC: 3965 3089 3569 5085 Fasteners, buttons, needles & pins; billfold inserts, plastic; sifting & screening machines; fasteners, industrial: nuts, bolts, screws, etc.; bolts, nuts, rivets & washers; washers; bolts, nuts & screws

(G-18171)
COCA-COLA REFRESHMENTS USA INC
105 Industrial Dr (60174-2428)
PHONE..................630 513-5247
Jeff Scarb, *Manager*
EMP: 250
SALES (corp-wide): 37.2B **Publicly Held**
WEB: www.cokecce.com
SIC: 2086 5149 Bottled & canned soft drinks; groceries & related products
HQ: Coca-Cola Refreshments Usa, Inc.
2500 Windy Ridge Pkwy Se
Atlanta GA 30339
770 989-3000

(G-18172)
COMET ROLL & MACHINE COMPANY
405 Stone Dr (60174-3301)
PHONE..................630 268-1407
Pasek Gregory, *President*
Juan Rios, *Vice Pres*
Greg Pasek, *Controller*
Kolleen Monahan, *Manager*
Dan Mennecke, *Executive*
EMP: 20
SQ FT: 32,000
SALES (est): 4.2MM **Privately Held**
SIC: 3444 3599 3353 Forming machine work, sheet metal; machine shop, jobbing & repair; aluminum sheet, plate & foil

(G-18173)
COMPACT INDUSTRIES INC
3945 Ohio Ave (60174-5467)
PHONE..................630 513-9600
Dale Brown, *CEO*
Mike Brown, *President*
Daniel Lamphier, *Opers Mgr*
Alfredo Guerrero, *Production*
Kevin Macarthur, *Production*
◆ EMP: 110
SQ FT: 150,000
SALES (est): 17.6MM **Privately Held**
SIC: 7389 2066 2087 2095 Packaging & labeling services; powdered cocoa; powders, drink; instant coffee

(G-18174)
CONTROL WORKS INC
2701 Dukane Dr Ste B (60174-3343)
PHONE..................630 444-1942
David Cossey, *President*
David Locke, *Vice Pres*
EMP: 6
SQ FT: 2,000
SALES (est): 1MM **Privately Held**
SIC: 3613 8711 7699 Control panels, electric; electrical or electronic engineering; industrial machinery & equipment repair

(G-18175)
COOPERS HAWK WINERY
3710 E M St (60174)
PHONE..................630 940-1000
EMP: 13
SALES (est): 321.1K **Privately Held**
SIC: 2084 Wines

(G-18176)
CORPORATE GRAPHICS INC
3710 Illinois Ave (60174-2421)
PHONE..................630 762-9000
EMP: 4
SQ FT: 10,000
SALES (est): 320K **Privately Held**
SIC: 3577 7336 Mfg Computer Peripheral Equipment Commercial Art/Graphic Design

(G-18177)
CREATIVE CONCEPTS FABRICATION
3725 Stern Ave (60174-5403)
PHONE..................630 940-0500
Brian Koestner, *President*
EMP: 10
SALES (est): 2.2MM **Privately Held**
SIC: 3089 Injection molding of plastics; plastic processing

(G-18178)
CREATIVE MILLWORK LLC
3700 Illinois Ave (60174-2421)
PHONE..................630 762-0002
Jim Behles, *Sales Staff*
Michael Behles, *Sales Staff*
Rich Behles, *Mng Member*
Cindy Filip,
EMP: 27
SQ FT: 10,000
SALES (est): 3.9MM **Privately Held**
WEB: www.creativemillworkllc.com
SIC: 2431 Millwork

(G-18179)
DASHER DEPENDABLE REINDEER LLC
3010 Royal Queens Ct (60174-8713)
PHONE..................630 513-7737
Alan Jania, *Mng Member*
Patrcik Henning, *Mng Member*
Carmelita Linden, *Mng Member*
EMP: 3
SQ FT: 180
SALES (est): 109.5K **Privately Held**
SIC: 2731 Books: publishing & printing

(G-18180)
DAVID JESKEY
Also Called: Rj45s.com
1523 Banbury Ave (60174-4453)
PHONE..................630 659-6337
David Jeskey, *Owner*
Lynn Jeskey, *Admin Sec*
EMP: 6
SALES (est): 6MM **Privately Held**
SIC: 5065 3613 3643 3678 Communication equipment; connectors, electronic; power connectors, electric; connectors & terminals for electrical devices; solderless connectors (electric wiring devices); electronic connectors; electrical services

(G-18181)
DEC TOOL CORP
2651 Dukane Dr (60174-3341)
PHONE..................630 513-9883
Jeff Decore, *President*
Jeffery A Decore, *Principal*
Robert Decore, *Vice Pres*
EMP: 25
SQ FT: 3,000
SALES (est): 5.3MM **Privately Held**
SIC: 3544 Special dies & tools

(G-18182)
DIAGER USA INC
1820 Wallace Ave Ste 122 (60174-3413)
PHONE..................630 762-8443
Francois Defougeres, *CEO*
Patti Lemke, *Treasurer*
Mark Lemke, *Director*
◆ EMP: 6
SQ FT: 3,500
SALES (est): 585.1K **Privately Held**
SIC: 3532 Drills, bits & similar equipment

(G-18183)
DIAMOND SPRAY PAINTING INC
1840 Production Dr (60174-2473)
P.O. Box 3130 (60174-9097)
PHONE..................630 513-5600
Stephanie Schmidt, *President*
Ted Schnidt, *President*
▲ EMP: 8
SQ FT: 21,000
SALES (est): 750K **Privately Held**
SIC: 3479 3471 Coating of metals & formed products; plating & polishing

(G-18184)
DIAMONDAIRE CORP
117 W Main St Ste 110 (60174-1860)
PHONE..................630 355-7464
Lauren Stallings, *President*
William Metzger, *Buyer*
▲ EMP: 6 EST: 2011
SALES (est): 527.8K **Privately Held**
SIC: 5094 7631 3961 Jewelry; jewelry repair services; costume jewelry

(G-18185)
DOMINICKS FINER FOODS INC
2063 Lincoln Hwy (60174-1580)
PHONE..................630 584-1750
EMP: 70
SALES (corp-wide): 44.2B **Publicly Held**
SIC: 5411 5912 2051 Ret Groceries Ret Drugs/Sundries Mfg Bread/Related Prdts
HQ: Dominick's Finer Foods Inc
711 Jorie Blvd Ste 1
Oak Brook IL 60523
630 891-5000

(G-18186)
DORAN SCALES INC
883 Enterprise Ct (60174-3445)
PHONE..................630 879-1200
Mark Podl, *CEO*
Shani Podl, *Vice Pres*
Peter Siegrist, *Vice Pres*
Jerry Thielman, *QC Mgr*
◆ EMP: 23
SQ FT: 20,000
SALES (est): 8.6MM **Privately Held**
WEB: www.doranscales.com
SIC: 5046 3596 Scales, except laboratory; industrial scales

(G-18187)
DSS INC
Also Called: Dss Competition Engines
3550 Stern Ave (60174-5408)
PHONE..................630 587-1169
Ronald Raffanti, *President*
Thomas Naegele, *Treasurer*
Tom Naegele, *VP Sales*
EMP: 8
SQ FT: 20,000
SALES (est): 1.8MM **Privately Held**
SIC: 5531 7538 3462 Automotive accessories; automotive parts; engine rebuilding: automotive; automotive & internal combustion engine forgings

(G-18188)
DTC PRODUCTS INC
2651 Dukane Dr (60174-3341)
PHONE..................630 513-3323
Jeffrey Decore, *President*
EMP: 3
SALES (est): 60K **Privately Held**
SIC: 3569 General industrial machinery

(G-18189)
DUKANE CORPORATION (PA)
2900 Dukane Dr (60174-3395)
PHONE..................630 797-4900
Michael W Ritschdorff, *CEO*
Mark Iannantuoni, *Regional Mgr*
Aaron O'Toole, *Regional Mgr*
Terry Goldman, *Vice Pres*
Jane Glyzewski, *Opers Mgr*
▲ EMP: 215 EST: 1922
SQ FT: 298,000
SALES (est): 46.8MM **Privately Held**
WEB: www.dukane.com
SIC: 3861 3699 Projectors, still or motion picture, silent or sound; welding machines & equipment, ultrasonic

(G-18190)
DUKANE CORPORATION
Dukane Intelligent Assembly
2900 Dukane Dr (60174-3395)
PHONE..................630 797-4900
Michael Ritschdorff, *President*
EMP: 4
SALES (corp-wide): 46.8MM **Privately Held**
SIC: 3612 Feeder voltage boosters (electric transformers)
PA: Dukane Corporation
2900 Dukane Dr
Saint Charles IL 60174
630 797-4900

(G-18191)
DUKANE IAS LLC (PA)
2900 Dukane Dr (60174-3348)
PHONE..................630 797-4900
Michael Johnston,
Andrew W Byrd,
Kenneth W Weaver,
EMP: 28
SALES: 10.2MM **Privately Held**
SIC: 3089 Plastic hardware & building products

(G-18192)
EAGLESTONE INC
3705 Swenson Ave (60174-3439)
PHONE..................630 587-1115
Carmen Sammauro, *President*
Richard Payne, *Engineer*
Gerry Ness, *Supervisor*
David Summers, *Admin Sec*
EMP: 15
SQ FT: 20,000

Saint Charles - Kane County (G-18193)   GEOGRAPHIC SECTION

SALES (est): 6MM **Privately Held**
SIC: 3535 3599 Conveyors & conveying equipment; machine shop, jobbing & repair

(G-18193)
EFFICIENT ENERGY LIGHTING INC
35w912 Rock Glen Rd (60175-6379)
PHONE..................................630 272-9388
EMP: 2
SALES (est): 201.8K **Privately Held**
SIC: 3648 Lighting equipment

(G-18194)
EIFELER COATINGS TECH INC
Also Called: Voestlpine High Prfmce Mtls Co
3800 Commerce Dr (60174-5323)
PHONE..................................630 587-1220
Hanz Eifeler, *CEO*
Luigi Parenti, *President*
Wibke Eifeler, *Vice Pres*
Wiebke Yovanovic, *VP Finance*
Niel Hillstrom, *Manager*
▲ EMP: 25 EST: 2001
SALES (est): 4MM
SALES (corp-wide): 15.3B **Privately Held**
WEB: www.eifeler.us
SIC: 3471 Finishing, metals or formed products
HQ: Voestalpine High Performance Metals Corporation
2505 Millennium Dr
Elgin IL 60124
877 992-8764

(G-18195)
ELITE EXTRUSION TECHNOLOGY INC
3620 Ohio Ave (60174-5446)
PHONE..................................630 485-2020
Glen Galloway, *President*
Fred Gross, *General Mgr*
EMP: 1
SALES (est): 1.4MM
SALES (corp-wide): 7.9MM **Privately Held**
SIC: 7819 2671 Film processing, editing & titling: motion picture; plastic film, coated or laminated for packaging
PA: Galloway Consolidated Holdings, Inc.
744 N Oaklawn Ave
Elmhurst IL 60126
630 279-7800

(G-18196)
ELKAY MANUFACTURING COMPANY
Aquaflow Div
2530 Production Dr (60174-3350)
PHONE..................................630 377-0150
Thomas E Hudock, *Enginr/R&D Mgr*
Sherry Chism, *Director*
EMP: 45
SALES (corp-wide): 1B **Privately Held**
WEB: www.elkay.com
SIC: 3432 Faucets & spigots, metal & plastic
PA: Elkay Manufacturing Company Inc
1333 Butterfield Rd # 200
Downers Grove IL 60515
630 574-8484

(G-18197)
ENDEAVOR TECHNOLOGIES INC
417 Stone Dr (60174-3301)
PHONE..................................630 562-0300
Charles Nichols, *President*
Scott Applehoff, *Vice Pres*
Jeffrey Mackey, *Production*
Thomas Mayer, *Admin Sec*
Rome Nichols, *Assistant*
EMP: 25
SQ FT: 15,685
SALES: 5MM **Privately Held**
SIC: 7694 Rebuilding motors, except automotive

(G-18198)
ENGINUITY COMMUNICATIONS CORP
3545 Stern Ave (60174-5407)
PHONE..................................630 444-0778
Sean Iwasaki, *President*
Stephen Todd, *General Mgr*
EMP: 40
SQ FT: 25,000
SALES (est): 8.4MM **Privately Held**
SIC: 3699 Electrical equipment & supplies

(G-18199)
FIRST & MAIN INC
2400 E Main St Ste 103-35 (60174-2436)
PHONE..................................630 587-1000
Brad Holes, *President*
Nancy Buckles, *Vice Pres*
◆ EMP: 25
SQ FT: 60,000
SALES (est): 7.5MM **Privately Held**
SIC: 5092 3942 Toys; stuffed toys, including animals

(G-18200)
FONA INTERNATIONAL INC
Also Called: Fona Distribution Center
3940 Swenson Ave (60174-3446)
PHONE..................................630 578-8600
Stephanie Paredes, *Branch Mgr*
EMP: 3
SALES (corp-wide): 67.8MM **Privately Held**
SIC: 2087 Extracts, flavoring; syrups, flavoring (except drink)
PA: Fona International Inc.
1900 Averill Rd
Geneva IL 60134
630 578-8600

(G-18201)
FOREMAN TOOL & MOLD CORP
Also Called: Plastic Injection Molding
3850 Swenson Ave (60174-3438)
PHONE..................................630 377-6389
Richard W Foreman, *President*
Kathleen C Foreman, *Corp Secy*
Piotr Kedzierski, *Vice Pres*
Rich Jarosinski, *QC Dir*
Frank Kowalski, *QC Mgr*
EMP: 50
SQ FT: 33,000
SALES (est): 1.2MM **Privately Held**
SIC: 3089 Injection molding of plastics

(G-18202)
FOREMAN TOOL AND MOLD
3627 Stern Ave (60174-5405)
PHONE..................................630 377-6389
EMP: 3
SALES (est): 257.9K **Privately Held**
SIC: 3089 Injection molding of plastics

(G-18203)
FORM PLASTICS COMPANY
Also Called: Pappas & Pappas Enterprises
3825 Stern Ave (60174-5457)
PHONE..................................630 443-1400
James D Pappas, *Principal*
James Pappas, *Principal*
John Gross, *Engineer*
Dawn Vitale, *Accountant*
Nancy Clausen, *Human Res Mgr*
▲ EMP: 100
SQ FT: 120,000
SALES (est): 22MM **Privately Held**
WEB: www.formplastics.com
SIC: 3089 Injection molding of plastics

(G-18204)
GIG KARASEK LLC
3955 Commerce Dr (60174-5321)
P.O. Box 268 (60174-0268)
PHONE..................................630 549-0394
Hugh Palmer,
Andreas Karasek,
John Palmer,
EMP: 10 EST: 2013
SALES (est): 1.7MM **Privately Held**
WEB: www.gigkarasekusa.com
SIC: 8711 1629 2824 Chemical engineering; waste water & sewage treatment plant construction; organic fibers, noncellulosic

(G-18205)
HAIRY ANT INC
601 Sidwell Ct Ste F (60174-3415)
PHONE..................................630 338-7194
EMP: 2 EST: 2016
SALES (est): 206.2K **Privately Held**
WEB: www.thehairyant.com
SIC: 2759 Screen printing

(G-18206)
HI TECH COLORANTS
5n634 Lostview Ln (60175-8218)
PHONE..................................630 762-0368
George Scarpelli, *Owner*
EMP: 2 EST: 1989
SALES (est): 300K **Privately Held**
SIC: 2865 Color pigments, organic

(G-18207)
HONEYWELL INTERNATIONAL INC
3825 Ohio Ave (60174-5467)
PHONE..................................630 377-6580
Ed Kurtz, *Engineer*
Cindy Edwards, *Controller*
EMP: 500
SALES (corp-wide): 36.7B **Publicly Held**
SIC: 3724 Aircraft engines & engine parts
PA: Honeywell International Inc.
300 S Tryon St
Charlotte NC 28202
704 627-6200

(G-18208)
HRB AMERICA CORPORATION
3485 Swenson Ave (60174-3449)
PHONE..................................630 513-1800
Xiangyang LI, *President*
Clayton Chang, *Vice Pres*
▲ EMP: 4
SQ FT: 10,000
SALES (est): 440K **Privately Held**
SIC: 3562 Ball & roller bearings

(G-18209)
ICT POWER USA INC
3960 Commerce Dr (60174-5319)
PHONE..................................630 313-4941
Afshin Montazeri, *President*
Dan Keen, *Principal*
EMP: 10
SALES (est): 1.3MM **Privately Held**
SIC: 3625 Switches, electric power

(G-18210)
ILLINOIS TICKET DEFENSE FIRM
39w745 Goldenrod Dr (60175-7959)
PHONE..................................954 467-1965
Michael Salazar, *Principal*
EMP: 3
SALES (est): 162.3K **Privately Held**
SIC: 3812 Defense systems & equipment

(G-18211)
INCON INDUSTRIES INC
3955 Commerce Dr (60174-5321)
P.O. Box 268 (60174-0268)
PHONE..................................630 728-4014
Hugh Palmer, *President*
Hugh Palmesr, *President*
John Palmer III, *Vice Pres*
EMP: 5
SQ FT: 6,000
SALES (est): 1MM **Privately Held**
SIC: 2819 Chemicals, high purity: refined from technical grade

(G-18212)
INNOVATE TECHNOLOGIES INC
761 N 17th St (60174-1664)
PHONE..................................630 587-4220
Joseph Talarczyk, *President*
Sean Altergott, *Engineer*
EMP: 4 EST: 1998
SQ FT: 3,000
SALES (est): 1.1MM **Privately Held**
WEB: www.innovatetec.com
SIC: 3542 High energy rate metal forming machines

(G-18213)
INNOVATION PLUS POWER SYSTEMS
3960 Commerce Dr (60174-5319)
PHONE..................................630 457-1105
Afshin Montazeri, *President*
EMP: 12
SALES (est): 2.2MM
SALES (corp-wide): 1.9MM **Privately Held**
WEB: www.innovationplususa.com
SIC: 3629 Capacitors, a.c., for motors or fluorescent lamp ballasts; capacitors, fixed or variable
PA: Innovation Plus Power Systems Inc
1220 Corporate Dr
Burlington ON L7L 5
905 331-1839

(G-18214)
INTELLIGENT FLRG SYSTEMS LLC
3830 Commerce Dr (60174-5323)
PHONE..................................630 587-1800
Thomas J Lutz, *President*
EMP: 8
SALES (est): 164.8K **Privately Held**
SIC: 1752 2421 Floor laying & floor work; flooring (dressed lumber), softwood

(G-18215)
INTERNATIONAL GRAPHICS & ASSOC
38w598 Clubhouse Dr (60175-6179)
PHONE..................................630 584-2248
EMP: 12
SQ FT: 5,000
SALES: 1.5MM **Privately Held**
SIC: 2754 2791 2789 2752 Commercial Printing, Gravure, Nsk

(G-18216)
ITASCA PLASTICS INC
3750 Ohio Ave (60174-5438)
PHONE..................................630 443-4446
Eric Fields, *President*
Eric Field, *President*
Duncan Mathieson, *Vice Pres*
Fred Morris, *Vice Pres*
Susan Field, *Admin Sec*
▲ EMP: 29
SQ FT: 81,000
SALES (est): 9.5MM **Privately Held**
SIC: 3089 Injection molding of plastics

(G-18217)
J STILLING ENTERPRISES INC
Also Called: Rice Chem
330 S 2nd St Ste A (60174-2868)
P.O. Box 310 (60174-0310)
PHONE..................................630 584-5050
Jim Stilling, *President*
Barbara Stilling, *Treasurer*
EMP: 3
SQ FT: 2,600
SALES (est): 376.3K **Privately Held**
SIC: 2819 Industrial inorganic chemicals

(G-18218)
JEWEL OSCO INC
Also Called: Jewel-Osco 3331
2073 Prairie St (60174-3594)
PHONE..................................630 584-4594
Jim Mc Kay, *General Mgr*
EMP: 175
SALES (corp-wide): 60.5B **Privately Held**
SIC: 5411 5149 2051 Supermarkets, chain; groceries & related products; bread, cake & related products
HQ: Jewel Osco, Inc.
150 E Pierce Rd Ste 200
Itasca IL 60143
630 948-6000

(G-18219)
KABAT AMERICAN INC
410 38th Ave (60174-5426)
PHONE..................................870 739-1430
Chaohui Xu, *President*
▲ EMP: 8
SALES (est): 1.5MM **Privately Held**
WEB: www.kabat-machinery.com
SIC: 3365 4731 Machinery castings, aluminum; brokers, shipping

(G-18220)
KANELAND PUBLICATIONS INC
Also Called: Elburn Herald
333 N Randall Rd Ste 111 (60174-1500)
PHONE..................................630 365-6446
Stephen Cooper, *President*
Richard Cooper, *Vice Pres*
EMP: 10 EST: 1908

GEOGRAPHIC SECTION

Saint Charles - Kane County (G-18247)

SALES (est): 853.2K **Privately Held**
WEB: www.elburnherald.com
SIC: 2711 Job printing & newspaper publishing combined

(G-18221)
KOHLERT MANUFACTURING CORP
2851 Dukane Dr (60174-3345)
PHONE 630 584-0013
John Kohlert, *President*
EMP: 4
SQ FT: 3,000
SALES (est): 661.9K **Privately Held**
SIC: 3599 Machine shop, jobbing & repair

(G-18222)
KRISTEL LIMITED PARTNERSHIP
Also Called: Kristel Displays
555 Kirk Rd Unit C (60174-3406)
PHONE 630 443-1290
Chris Petri, *Partner*
George Kinney, *Partner*
Keith Petri, *Partner*
▲ **EMP:** 100
SQ FT: 100,000
SALES (est): 32.9MM **Privately Held**
SIC: 3575 Cathode ray tube (CRT), computer terminal

(G-18223)
LABELS & SPECIALTY PDTS LLC
Also Called: Packaging Printing Specialists
3915 Stern Ave (60174-5441)
PHONE 630 513-8060
Thomas Tyndall, *President*
Alyssa Azzarelli, *Mktg Dir*
▲ **EMP:** 20
SQ FT: 24,000
SALES: 10MM **Privately Held**
WEB: www.ppsofil.com
SIC: 2759 2671 Flexographic printing; packaging paper & plastics film, coated & laminated

(G-18224)
LAMP CO OF AMERICA INC
214 S 13th Ave (60174-3119)
PHONE 630 584-4001
Lawrence Denna, *President*
EMP: 3
SALES (est): 386.7K **Privately Held**
SIC: 3646 3645 Commercial indusl & institutional electric lighting fixtures; residential lighting fixtures

(G-18225)
LECHLER INC
445 Kautz Rd (60174-5301)
PHONE 630 377-6611
Adolf Pfeiffer, *President*
Allen Harmon, *Division Mgr*
Dinesh Patel, *Vice Pres*
Andrew Mills, *Production*
Gil Ramirez, *Purch Mgr*
▲ **EMP:** 69 **EST:** 1912
SQ FT: 45,000
SALES: 18MM
SALES (corp-wide): 257.2K **Privately Held**
WEB: www.lechlerusa.com
SIC: 3499 Nozzles, spray: aerosol, paint or insecticide
HQ: Lechler International Gesellschaft Mit Beschrankter Haftung
   Ulmer Str. 128
   Metzingen 72555
   712 396-20

(G-18226)
LEVITON MANUFACTURING CO INC
3837 E Main St Ste 331 (60174-2424)
PHONE 630 443-0500
EMP: 150
SALES (corp-wide): 1.3B **Privately Held**
SIC: 3643 Current-carrying wiring devices
PA: Leviton Manufacturing Co., Inc.
   201 N Service Rd
   Melville NY 11747
   631 812-6000

(G-18227)
LFA INDUSTRIES INC
1820 Wallace Ave Ste 122 (60174-3413)
PHONE 630 762-7391
Mark Lemke, *President*
Patti Jo Lemke, *Vice Pres*
Carol Lemke, *Treasurer*
Patty Lemke, *Director*
▲ **EMP:** 6
SQ FT: 3,500
SALES (est): 805.4K **Privately Held**
SIC: 3545 Chucks: drill, lathe or magnetic (machine tool accessories)

(G-18228)
LIGHTING INNOVATIONS INC
Also Called: Fc Lighting
3609 Swenson Ave (60174-3441)
PHONE 630 889-8100
Bruce Bukas, *President*
Ryan Peterson, *Engineer*
Mark Macauley, *Controller*
Scott Bukas, *Sales Mgr*
Joe Freehill, *Marketing Mgr*
▲ **EMP:** 30
SQ FT: 58,000
SALES: 6.3MM **Privately Held**
SIC: 3648 Lighting equipment

(G-18229)
MAKO MOLD CORPORATION
3820 Ohio Ave Ste 7 (60174-5461)
PHONE 630 377-9010
Philip Denemark, *President*
EMP: 4
SQ FT: 3,000
SALES: 600K **Privately Held**
WEB: www.makomold.com
SIC: 3089 Injection molded finished plastic products

(G-18230)
MANUFACTURED SPECIALTIES INC
Also Called: MSI
3575 Stern Ave (60174-5412)
PHONE 630 444-1992
Cynthia J Jagmin, *CEO*
Michael A Jagmin, *President*
Cindy Jagmin, *Finance*
Mike Mallak, *Manager*
Donald Palomaki, *Admin Sec*
▲ **EMP:** 14
SQ FT: 25,000
SALES (est): 3.7MM **Privately Held**
WEB: www.msi-products.com
SIC: 3498 Fabricated pipe & fittings

(G-18231)
MCC TECHNOLOGY INC
2422 W Main St Unit 4d (60175-1010)
PHONE 630 377-7200
James J Kunzer, *President*
John Kunzer, *Vice Pres*
Mark Wildasin, *Engineer*
EMP: 10 **EST:** 1979
SQ FT: 4,000
SALES: 1.4MM **Privately Held**
SIC: 5045 5063 3669 Computers, peripherals & software; transformers & transmission equipment; intercommunication systems, electric

(G-18232)
MELT DESIGN INC
3803 Illinois Ave (60174-2422)
PHONE 630 443-4000
Panos Trakas, *President*
Joanna Accetta, *Director*
Emmy Trakas, *Admin Sec*
EMP: 11
SQ FT: 12,100
SALES (est): 1.1MM **Privately Held**
SIC: 3829 Thermometers & temperature sensors

(G-18233)
MSYSTEMS GROUP LLC
38w426 Mallard Lake Rd (60175-5445)
PHONE 630 567-3930
Calvin Moy, *Owner*
EMP: 3 **EST:** 2015
SALES (est): 107.9K **Privately Held**
SIC: 3355 Aluminum rolling & drawing

(G-18234)
NIDEC MOBILITY AMERICA CORP (HQ)
Also Called: Omron Global
3709 Ohio Ave (60174-5437)
PHONE 630 443-6800
Katsuhiro Wada, *Ch of Bd*
Randy Wara, *President*
Jim Eberhart, *Vice Pres*
Michael Rose, *Purchasing*
Seiichiro Osaki, *Treasurer*
▲ **EMP:** 565
SQ FT: 100,000
SALES (est): 377.5MM **Privately Held**
SIC: 5065 3625 3714 8742 Electronic parts; relays & industrial controls; motor vehicle parts & accessories; real estate consultant

(G-18235)
O-LIMINATOR LLC (PA)
902 S Randall Rd Ste C240 (60174-1781)
PHONE 630 400-0373
Peter A Bogle,
Margaret S Bogle,
William Y Bogle,
EMP: 3
SQ FT: 3,000
SALES (est): 330K **Privately Held**
SIC: 2074 Cottonseed oil, deodorized

(G-18236)
ODORITE INTERNATIONAL INC
Also Called: Fragrance Master
320 37th Ave (60174-5414)
PHONE 816 920-5000
Dan Bunch, *Ch of Bd*
▲ **EMP:** 16 **EST:** 1934
SQ FT: 45,000
SALES (est): 2.1MM **Privately Held**
SIC: 2842 Deodorants, nonpersonal

(G-18237)
OLCOTT PLASTICS INC
95 N 17th St (60174-1636)
PHONE 630 584-0555
Joseph Mark Brodner, *President*
Andre Greene, *Opers Mgr*
Ken Johnston, *Prdtn Mgr*
Hector Hernandez, *Maint Spvr*
Sarah Lindo, *Sales Staff*
EMP: 95
SQ FT: 60,000
SALES (est): 27.4MM
SALES (corp-wide): 868.8MM **Privately Held**
SIC: 3089 Plastic containers, except foam
PA: Pretium Packaging, L.L.C.
   15450 S Oter Frty Dr Ste
   Chesterfield MO 63017
   314 727-8200

(G-18238)
ORAT INC
761 N 17th St Ste 4 (60174-1664)
P.O. Box 417 (60174-0417)
PHONE 630 567-6728
Doug Turner, *President*
EMP: 4
SALES (est): 413.9K **Privately Held**
SIC: 3599 Custom machinery

(G-18239)
OSG USA INC
620 Stetson Ave (60174-3457)
P.O. Box A 3938, Chicago (60690)
PHONE 800 837-2223
Mike Grzybowski, *Regional Mgr*
Tom Patterson, *Regional Mgr*
Mark Coryea, *District Mgr*
Matt Dahlberg, *District Mgr*
Chris Dravis, *District Mgr*
EMP: 40 **Privately Held**
SIC: 3545 Machine tool accessories
HQ: Osg Usa, Inc.
   1945 W Walnut Hill Ln
   Irving TX 75038
   800 837-2223

(G-18240)
OUTBACK USA INC
5n825 Prairie Springs Dr (60175-6944)
PHONE 863 699-2220
Kay Johnston, *President*
Darrel Johnston, *Vice Pres*
EMP: 7

SQ FT: 1,800
SALES: 1.2MM **Privately Held**
SIC: 3732 4499 5199 5091 Pontoons, except aircraft & inflatable; motorboats, inboard or outboard: building & repairing; boat & ship rental & leasing, except pleasure; bait, fishing; fishing tackle; propane gas, bottled

(G-18241)
PACTIV LLC
315 Kirk Rd (60174-3429)
PHONE 630 262-6335
Bob Reschke, *Branch Mgr*
EMP: 200 **Publicly Held**
SIC: 2657 2656 Food containers, folding: made from purchased material; sanitary food containers
HQ: Pactiv Llc
   1900 W Field Ct
   Lake Forest IL 60045
   847 482-2000

(G-18242)
PERFECT PLASTIC PRINTING CORP (PA)
311 Kautz Rd Ste 1 (60174-5304)
PHONE 630 584-1600
Chris Smoczynski, *President*
Margaret White, *President*
Bob Stram, *Exec VP*
David Maresca, *Vice Pres*
Dave Moser, *Vice Pres*
▲ **EMP:** 143
SQ FT: 47,000
SALES (est): 34MM **Privately Held**
WEB: www.perfectplastic.com
SIC: 2752 3089 Commercial printing, offset; identification cards, plastic

(G-18243)
PERFECT PLASTIC PRINTING CORP
345 Kautz Rd (60174-5326)
PHONE 630 584-1600
Chris Smoczynski, *President*
EMP: 67
SALES (corp-wide): 34MM **Privately Held**
SIC: 2752 Commercial printing, lithographic
PA: Perfect Plastic Printing Corp.
   311 Kautz Rd Ste 1
   Saint Charles IL 60174
   630 584-1600

(G-18244)
PETAIRAPY LLC
3820 Ohio Ave Ste 9 (60174-5461)
PHONE 630 377-0348
Annette Uda,
Mamoru Uda,
EMP: 2
SALES (est): 410K **Privately Held**
SIC: 3564 Air purification equipment

(G-18245)
PETROCHEM INC
333 N Randall Rd Ste 25 (60174-1500)
PHONE 630 513-6350
Carole J Sluski, *President*
Jill E Dohner, *Vice Pres*
EMP: 5
SALES (est): 2.8MM **Privately Held**
SIC: 5172 2851 Lubricating oils & greases; removers & cleaners

(G-18246)
POLYTEC PLASTICS INC
3730 Stern Ave (60174-5404)
PHONE 630 584-8282
Karl R Blum, *President*
Paul Medrano, *Vice Pres*
EMP: 40
SQ FT: 16,000
SALES (est): 6MM **Privately Held**
SIC: 3089 Injection molding of plastics

(G-18247)
POLYTECH INDUSTRIES INC
1755 Wallace Ave (60174-3402)
P.O. Box 551, Geneva (60134-0551)
PHONE 630 443-6030
Richard J Walls, *President*
Timothy S Walls, *Vice Pres*
Carmon Taylor, *Design Engr*

Saint Charles - Kane County (G-18248)

GEOGRAPHIC SECTION

Wilma Walls, *Treasurer*
EMP: 25
SQ FT: 20,000
SALES (est): 3.8MM **Privately Held**
SIC: 3089 Injection molding of plastics

(G-18248)
POWERONE CORP
Also Called: Powerone Environmental
2325 Dean St Ste 200 (60175-4810)
PHONE..........................630 443-6500
James Chaggaris, *President*
EMP: 3
SALES (est): 353.6K **Privately Held**
SIC: 3629 5199 3443 Electrical industrial apparatus; ice, manufactured or natural; reactor containment vessels, metal plate

(G-18249)
PRECISION COMPONENTS INC
1020 Cedar Ave Ste 215 (60174-2279)
P.O. Box 323, Sycamore (60178-0323)
PHONE..........................630 462-9110
William J Gray Jr, *President*
Lou Battistoni, *Exec VP*
EMP: 90
SQ FT: 900
SALES (est): 4.5MM **Privately Held**
WEB: www.pcitransformers.com
SIC: 3661 3612 Telephones & telephone apparatus; transformers, except electric

(G-18250)
PRECISION SCREEN SPECIALTIES
3905 Commerce Dr (60174-5321)
PHONE..........................630 220-1361
Garry R Duber, *President*
Terry C Duber, *Vice Pres*
EMP: 8 **EST:** 1957
SQ FT: 8,000
SALES (est): 850K **Privately Held**
WEB: www.precisionscreenspecialties.com
SIC: 2759 3555 3231 2396 Screen printing; printing trades machinery; products of purchased glass; automotive & apparel trimmings

(G-18251)
PROELL INC
2751 Dukane Dr (60174-3343)
PHONE..........................630 587-2300
Werner Port, *President*
Reinhard Port, *Exec VP*
Edwin Brooks, *Asst Treas*
Karl Aschacher, *Sales Mgr*
Diane Moylan, *Sales Mgr*
EMP: 8
SQ FT: 13,500
SALES (est): 1MM **Privately Held**
WEB: www.proell.us
SIC: 2759 2261 Screen printing; screen printing of cotton broadwoven fabrics

(G-18252)
PROTEK INC
Also Called: Pro-Tek
209 S 3rd St (60174-2839)
PHONE..........................888 536-5466
Pamela Hendricks, *President*
EMP: 4
SQ FT: 10,500
SALES (est): 220K **Privately Held**
SIC: 2782 Looseleaf binders & devices

(G-18253)
PS3 TOOL MOLD & ASSEMBLY LLC
Also Called: Foreman Tool and Mold
3850 Swenson Ave (60174-3438)
PHONE..........................630 802-9462
Ripan Sheth,
EMP: 52
SALES (est): 10MM **Privately Held**
SIC: 3544 Industrial molds

(G-18254)
PYRAMID MANUFACTURING CORP
3815 Illinois Ave (60174-2422)
PHONE..........................630 443-0141
Paul Hernandez, *President*
John Hernandez, *Vice Pres*
▲ **EMP:** 100 **EST:** 1972
SQ FT: 50,000
SALES (est): 19.3MM **Privately Held**
SIC: 3444 Sheet metal specialties, not stamped

(G-18255)
QUALITY BAKERIES LLC
Also Called: Burry Foodservice
1750 E Main St Ste 280 (60174-4729)
PHONE..........................630 553-7377
Gary Gittleson, *Partner*
Patrick Shay, *Partner*
Brad Guimont, *Vice Pres*
EMP: 10
SALES: 65MM **Privately Held**
SIC: 2053 Frozen bakery products, except bread

(G-18256)
QUALITY SPRAYING SCREEN PRTG
3815 Illinois Ave (60174-2422)
PHONE..........................630 584-8324
Paul Hernandez, *Partner*
John Hernandez, *Partner*
EMP: 40
SQ FT: 50,000
SALES (est): 1.2MM **Privately Held**
WEB: www.qualityspraying.com
SIC: 7532 2396 Lettering & painting services; automotive & apparel trimmings

(G-18257)
R R DONNELLEY & SONS COMPANY
Also Called: W C S
1750 Wallace Ave (60174-3401)
PHONE..........................630 377-2586
Keith Gonnerman, *VP Mfg*
Philip Bykowski, *Network Enginr*
EMP: 175
SALES (corp-wide): 6.2B **Publicly Held**
SIC: 2752 Commercial printing, lithographic
PA: R. R. Donnelley & Sons Company
35 W Wacker Dr
Chicago IL 60601
312 326-8000

(G-18258)
R R DONNELLEY & SONS COMPANY
Also Called: RR Donnelley
3626 Stern Ave (60174-5406)
PHONE..........................630 762-7600
Troy Lancor, *Plant Mgr*
EMP: 60
SALES (corp-wide): 6.2B **Publicly Held**
SIC: 2752 2671 2396 Commercial printing, lithographic; packaging paper & plastics film, coated & laminated; automotive & apparel trimmings
PA: R. R. Donnelley & Sons Company
35 W Wacker Dr
Chicago IL 60601
312 326-8000

(G-18259)
RAVENSCROFT INC
473 Dunham Rd Ste 209 (60174-1427)
PHONE..........................630 513-9911
Peter Biagioni, *President*
Lisa Miller, *Human Res Dir*
Greg Warren, *Director*
Jennifer Baccus, *Asst Director*
Chuck Vitello, *Asst Director*
▲ **EMP:** 5
SALES (est): 530.8K **Privately Held**
SIC: 3089 Extruded finished plastic products

(G-18260)
RAY TOOL & ENGINEERING INC
Also Called: Rte
2440 Production Dr (60174-2455)
PHONE..........................630 587-0000
Michael Almgren, *President*
Mike Selmer, *Vice Pres*
Fred Martin, *Admin Sec*
EMP: 24
SQ FT: 10,000
SALES (est): 3.7MM **Privately Held**
WEB: www.rtestcharles.com
SIC: 3544 Special dies & tools

(G-18261)
REICHEL HARDWARE COMPANY INC
1820 Wallace Ave Ste 122 (60174-3413)
PHONE..........................630 762-7394
Patti Jo Lemke, *President*
▲ **EMP:** 4
SALES (est): 469.6K **Privately Held**
SIC: 3429 3545 Manufactured hardware (general); chucks: drill, lathe or magnetic (machine tool accessories)

(G-18262)
RUKEL MANAGEMENT LLC
1200 Rukel Way (60174-3427)
PHONE..........................630 377-8886
Jakob Rukel, *Principal*
EMP: 516
SALES (est): 32.4MM **Privately Held**
SIC: 3585 Refrigeration & heating equipment

(G-18263)
SAASOOM LLC
7n063 Plymouth Ct (60175-5801)
PHONE..........................630 561-7300
Maung Aung Khin, *Principal*
Maung Khin,
EMP: 3
SALES (est): 121.6K **Privately Held**
SIC: 2023 Dietary supplements, dairy & non-dairy based

(G-18264)
SC AVIATION INC
1433 Lancaster Ave (60174-3321)
PHONE..........................800 416-4176
John Bullock, *Manager*
EMP: 3
SALES (est): 220K **Privately Held**
SIC: 3721 Aircraft

(G-18265)
SCANLAB AMERICA INC
100 Illinois St Ste 200 (60174-1867)
PHONE..........................630 797-2044
Georg Hofner, *CEO*
Christian Huttenloher, *Vice Pres*
Dale Sabo, *Vice Pres*
Dirk Thomas, *Admin Sec*
EMP: 4
SQ FT: 1,200
SALES: 10MM
SALES (corp-wide): 168MM **Privately Held**
SIC: 3821 Laser beam alignment devices
HQ: Scanlab Gmbh
Siemensstr. 2a
Puchheim 82178
898 007-460

(G-18266)
SCHAFFER TOOL & DESIGN INC
3555 Stern Ave (60174-5407)
PHONE..........................630 876-3800
Steven Schaffer, *President*
Michael Schaffer, *Mfg Dir*
EMP: 7
SQ FT: 12,000
SALES: 1.6MM **Privately Held**
SIC: 3599 Machine shop, jobbing & repair

(G-18267)
SCHOLASTIC INC
2315 Dean St Ste 600 (60175-4823)
PHONE..........................630 443-8197
Carol Chanter, *Vice Pres*
Deborah Kurosz, *Project Mgr*
Gaye Masanjak, *Manager*
Melissa Coppert, *Supervisor*
Lynne Karppi, *Director*
EMP: 28
SALES (corp-wide): 1.6B **Publicly Held**
SIC: 2731 8742 Books: publishing only; sales (including sales management) consultant
HQ: Scholastic Inc.
557 Broadway Lbby 1
New York NY 10012
212 343-6100

(G-18268)
SEK CORPORATION (PA)
Also Called: Snap Edge
3925 Stern Ave (60174-5441)
PHONE..........................630 762-0606
Fred Strobl, *President*
Brad Le Gare, *Vice Pres*
Dave McCullough, *Vice Pres*
Lonny Shook, *Sales Staff*
▲ **EMP:** 37
SQ FT: 1,500
SALES (est): 7.5MM **Privately Held**
SIC: 3089 Flat panels, plastic

(G-18269)
SIEMENS INDUSTRY INC
580 Slawin Ct (60174)
PHONE..........................630 444-4316
Steve Clark, *Branch Mgr*
EMP: 87
SALES (corp-wide): 96.9B **Privately Held**
SIC: 3822 3669 Temperature controls, automatic; fire alarm apparatus, electric
HQ: Siemens Industry, Inc.
1000 Deerfield Pkwy
Buffalo Grove IL 60089
847 215-1000

(G-18270)
SKYJACK EQUIPMENT INC (HQ)
3451 Swenson Ave (60174-3449)
PHONE..........................630 797-3299
Linda Hasenfratz, *President*
Blake Sutter, *Research*
Vito Anello, *Engineer*
Bill Eisenhofer, *Engineer*
Omar Naeem, *Engineer*
▼ **EMP:** 38
SQ FT: 25,000
SALES: 26.6MM
SALES (corp-wide): 5.5B **Privately Held**
SIC: 3531 3441 Aerial work platforms: hydraulic/elec. truck/carrier mounted; fabricated structural metal
PA: Linamar Corporation
287 Speedvale Ave W
Guelph ON N1H 1
519 836-7550

(G-18271)
SKYJACK INC
Also Called: Skyjack Parts & Svc Skyjack
3451 Swenson Ave (60174-3449)
PHONE..........................630 262-0005
Chuck Burls, *General Mgr*
Linda Moritz, *Accountant*
Todd Hawkins, *Cust Mgr*
Courtney Piekarz, *Sales Staff*
EMP: 9
SALES (corp-wide): 5.5B **Privately Held**
WEB: www.skyjack.com
SIC: 3531 Aerial work platforms: hydraulic/elec. truck/carrier mounted
HQ: Skyjack Inc
55 Campbell Rd Suite 1
Guelph ON N1H 1
519 837-0888

(G-18272)
SOLID STATE LUMINAIRES LLC
3609 Swenson Ave (60174-3441)
PHONE..........................877 775-4733
Bruce J Bukas, *Mng Member*
▲ **EMP:** 5
SALES (est): 648.5K **Privately Held**
SIC: 3674 Light emitting diodes

(G-18273)
SPECIALTY GRAPHICS SUPPLY INC
3875 Commerce Dr (60174-5325)
PHONE..........................630 584-8202
David Lawrence, *President*
EMP: 5
SALES (est): 320K **Privately Held**
SIC: 3993 Signs & advertising specialties

(G-18274)
SPHERE LASER LLC
392 38th Ave (60174-5458)
PHONE..........................317 752-1604
John Gonzales, *Branch Mgr*
EMP: 14
SQ FT: 40,000
SALES (corp-wide): 2MM **Privately Held**
SIC: 3699 Laser systems & equipment

GEOGRAPHIC SECTION
Saint Charles - Kane County (G-18302)

PA: Sphere Laser Llc
2020 Julia Way
Mchenry IL 60051
317 752-1604

(G-18275)
ST CHARLES MEMORIAL WORKS INC (PA)
Also Called: Elgin Granite Works
1640 W Main St (60174-1630)
PHONE..................630 584-0183
Terry Carlson, *President*
Susan Carlson, *Corp Secy*
Christian Carlson, *Vice Pres*
EMP: 4 **EST:** 1955
SQ FT: 3,000
SALES (est): 822.1K **Privately Held**
WEB: www.stcharlesmemorialworks.com
SIC: 5999 7261 1542 3281 Monuments, finished to custom order; funeral service & crematories; mausoleum construction; cut stone & stone products

(G-18276)
ST CHARLES STAMPING INC
318 N 4th St (60174-1824)
P.O. Box 1029 (60174-7029)
PHONE..................630 584-2029
Bernie W Klein, *President*
Dave Blankenship, *President*
Gunter L Steves, *Corp Secy*
Sharon Russell, *Vice Pres*
EMP: 19 **EST:** 1958
SQ FT: 25,000
SALES (est): 3.9MM **Privately Held**
WEB: www.scstamping.com
SIC: 3469 Stamping metal for the trade

(G-18277)
STELLAR PLASTICS CORPORATION
3627 Stern Ave (60174-5405)
PHONE..................630 443-1200
Greg Freimuth, *President*
EMP: 70
SQ FT: 30,000
SALES: 6MM **Privately Held**
SIC: 3089 Injection molding of plastics

(G-18278)
STERLING SYSTEMS SALES CORP
3745 Stern Ave (60174-5403)
PHONE..................630 584-3580
Jerome D Schultz, *President*
Ruth Schultz, *Admin Sec*
▲ **EMP:** 6
SQ FT: 20,000
SALES: 1.4MM **Privately Held**
SIC: 3559 Electroplating machinery & equipment

(G-18279)
STRATA-TAC INC
3980 Swenson Ave (60174-3446)
PHONE..................630 879-9388
Charles L Casagrande, *President*
Andrew Schwarzbauer, *Vice Pres*
Thomas Yeager, *Vice Pres*
Tom Yeager, *VP Sls/Mktg*
Kari Necas, *Accountant*
▲ **EMP:** 17
SQ FT: 12,750
SALES (est): 6.1MM **Privately Held**
WEB: www.stratatac.com
SIC: 2672 5085 5113 5131 Labels (unprinted), gummed: made from purchased materials; tape, pressure sensitive: made from purchased materials; adhesives, tape & plasters; pressure sensitive tape; synthetic fabrics

(G-18280)
STRATHMORE PRESS
Also Called: C N F
2400 E Main St (60174-2436)
PHONE..................513 483-3600
EMP: 29
SQ FT: 25,000
SALES: 4.8MM
SALES (corp-wide): 8.7MM **Privately Held**
SIC: 2759 Commercial Printing

PA: Cns Inc
3716 Montgomery Rd
Cincinnati OH 45207
513 631-7073

(G-18281)
SUN CHEMICAL CORPORATION
Also Called: Coates Screen
2445 Production Dr (60174-2454)
PHONE..................630 513-5348
Dennis Haiman, *Opers Mgr*
Carmen Saracco, *Accounts Exec*
Brian Breidigan, *Branch Mgr*
Pete Bosque, *Manager*
Jon Conboy, *Manager*
EMP: 160 **Privately Held**
SIC: 2899 5085 Ink or writing fluids; ink, printers'
HQ: Sun Chemical Corporation
35 Waterview Blvd Ste 100
Parsippany NJ 07054
973 404-6000

(G-18282)
SUREBOND INC
3925 Stern Ave (60174-5441)
PHONE..................630 762-0606
Todd Asmuth, *President*
EMP: 26
SQ FT: 2,000
SALES (est): 5.2MM **Privately Held**
WEB: www.sek.us.com
SIC: 2891 Adhesives; glue; caulking compounds; sealing compounds, synthetic rubber or plastic
PA: Sek Corporation
3925 Stern Ave
Saint Charles IL 60174

(G-18283)
SWIFTY PRINT
210 W Main St (60174-1812)
P.O. Box 281 (60174-0281)
PHONE..................630 584-9063
Gordon Brown, *President*
Anne C Brown, *Admin Sec*
EMP: 5
SQ FT: 1,200
SALES (est): 649.2K **Privately Held**
WEB: www.swiftyprintinc.com
SIC: 2752 2791 2789 2759 Commercial printing, offset; typesetting; bookbinding & related work; commercial printing

(G-18284)
T P R RESOURCES INC
3604 Greenwood Ln (60175-5638)
PHONE..................630 443-9060
EMP: 4 **EST:** 1996
SALES (est): 230K **Privately Held**
SIC: 3999 Mfg Misc Products

(G-18285)
TANDEM INDUSTRIES INC
3820 Ohio Ave Ste 16 (60174-5463)
PHONE..................630 761-6615
James Burian, *President*
Lois Burian, *Officer*
EMP: 6
SQ FT: 4,250
SALES: 600K **Privately Held**
SIC: 3448 3444 Ramps: prefabricated metal; sheet metalwork

(G-18286)
TEAM CNC INC
761 N 17th St Ste 22 (60174-1667)
PHONE..................630 377-2723
Gary Carpenter, *President*
EMP: 5
SALES (est): 645K **Privately Held**
SIC: 3545 Precision tools, machinists'

(G-18287)
TEK PAK INC
707 Kautz Rd (60174-5302)
PHONE..................331 901-5570
EMP: 3
SALES (est): 206.1K **Privately Held**
SIC: 3089 Injection molding of plastics

(G-18288)
THUROW TOOL WORKS INC
41 W 523 Rte 64 (60175)
PHONE..................630 377-6403
Mark Thurow, *President*

EMP: 3 **EST:** 1989
SQ FT: 1,500
SALES (est): 370K **Privately Held**
SIC: 3089 Injection molding of plastics

(G-18289)
TIGER DRYLAC USA INC (DH)
3945 Swenson Ave (60174-3446)
PHONE..................630 587-2918
Larry McNeely, *President*
Karl Rijkse, *Vice Pres*
Dan Simovic, *Vice Pres*
Mark Grewe, *Maint Spvr*
Eric Staine, *Production*
◆ **EMP:** 18
SALES (est): 17.4MM
SALES (corp-wide): 242.1K **Privately Held**
SIC: 3479 Coating of metals & formed products
HQ: Tiger Coatings Gmbh & Co.Kg
NegrellistraBe 36
Wels 4600
724 240-00

(G-18290)
TOMS SIGNS
Also Called: Acclaim Sign Company
6n592 Il Route 25 (60174-5630)
PHONE..................630 377-8525
Tom Deppe, *Owner*
EMP: 2
SALES (est): 311.4K **Privately Held**
SIC: 3993 2759 Signs, not made in custom sign painting shops; screen printing

(G-18291)
TRIAD CONTROLS INC (PA)
3715 Swenson Ave (60174-3439)
PHONE..................630 443-9320
Kenneth L Barron Jr, *President*
F Gary Kovac, *Vice Pres*
EMP: 60
SALES (est): 6MM **Privately Held**
SIC: 3842 Personal safety equipment

(G-18292)
TRYAD SPECIALTIES INC (PA)
2015 Dean St Ste 6 (60174-1577)
PHONE..................630 549-0079
Randy Norris, *President*
Jody Harness, *Vice Pres*
EMP: 11
SQ FT: 2,250
SALES (est): 5.5MM **Privately Held**
SIC: 5199 2395 7371 Advertising specialties; emblems, embroidered; embroidery products, except schiffli machine; computer software systems analysis & design, custom

(G-18293)
TWO WILD SEEDS BAKING COMPANY
320 W Main St (60174-1814)
PHONE..................630 797-5350
EMP: 4
SALES (est): 267.3K **Privately Held**
SIC: 2051 Bread, cake & related products

(G-18294)
UNIPHASE INC
425 38th Ave (60174-5425)
PHONE..................630 584-4747
William Morici, *President*
EMP: 50
SQ FT: 35,000
SALES: 9MM **Privately Held**
SIC: 3089 Injection molding of plastics

(G-18295)
UNITED LABORATORIES INC (PA)
320 37th Ave (60174-5464)
P.O. Box 410 (60174-0410)
PHONE..................630 377-0900
Daniel Young, *Ch of Bd*
Eric Frazier, *President*
Julie Benson, *Vice Pres*
Michael Cusumano, *Vice Pres*
Dana Killmer, *Vice Pres*
◆ **EMP:** 65 **EST:** 1964
SQ FT: 80,000

SALES (est): 44.5MM **Privately Held**
WEB: www.unitedlabsinc.com
SIC: 2842 5169 Specialty cleaning preparations; specialty cleaning & sanitation preparations

(G-18296)
WARWICK PUBLISHING COMPANY
2601 E Main St (60174-4289)
PHONE..................630 584-3871
Robert H Paschal, *CEO*
James P Paschal, *Principal*
Don F Paschal, *Principal*
Jim Paschal, *Vice Pres*
Sandy Peterman, *Purch Mgr*
▲ **EMP:** 100 **EST:** 1881
SQ FT: 115,000
SALES (est): 19MM **Privately Held**
WEB: www.warwickpublishing.com
SIC: 2752 2675 Calendars, lithographed; folders, filing, die-cut: made from purchased materials

(G-18297)
WATER DYNAMICS INC (PA)
Also Called: Leasing Dynamics
1553 Allen Ln (60174-2319)
PHONE..................630 584-8475
William E Bergmann Jr, *President*
Mary E Collins, *Vice Pres*
James L Collins, *Treasurer*
Mary M Bergmann, *Admin Sec*
EMP: 6
SQ FT: 3,500
SALES: 920K **Privately Held**
SIC: 3589 7389 Water treatment equipment, industrial; water softener service

(G-18298)
WEST VLY GRAPHICS & PRINT INC
Also Called: Kwik Kopy Printing
201 S 3rd St (60174-2839)
PHONE..................630 377-7575
William R Ledvora, *President*
Margaret M Ledvora, *Admin Sec*
EMP: 9
SQ FT: 2,500
SALES (est): 1.7MM **Privately Held**
SIC: 2752 2796 2789 Commercial printing, offset; platemaking services; bookbinding & related work

(G-18299)
WESTROCK CP LLC
415 37th Ave (60174-5415)
PHONE..................630 443-3538
Robert Curran, *Branch Mgr*
EMP: 60
SALES (corp-wide): 18.2B **Publicly Held**
WEB: www.westrock.com
SIC: 2631 Paperboard mills
HQ: Westrock Cp, Llc
1000 Abernathy Rd Ste 125
Atlanta GA 30328

(G-18300)
WINDY POLYMERS INC
3701 Illinois Ave (60174-2420)
PHONE..................630 272-7453
EMP: 6
SALES (est): 991.8K **Privately Held**
SIC: 2673 Plastic & pliofilm bags

(G-18301)
WINFIELD TECHNOLOGY INC
53 Stirrup Cup Ct (60174-1432)
PHONE..................630 584-0475
James E Spitzer, *President*
Roberta L Spitzer, *Corp Secy*
EMP: 13
SQ FT: 11,000
SALES (est): 893.5K **Privately Held**
SIC: 3069 Tape, pressure sensitive: rubber

(G-18302)
WISE PLASTICS TECHNOLOGIES INC (PA)
Also Called: Wise Hamlin Plastics
3810 Stern Ave (60174-5402)
PHONE..................847 697-2840
Fred W Wise, *President*
Dave Laboda, *Vice Pres*
Lenore J Tocki, *Vice Pres*

Saint Charles - Kane County (G-18303)

John Mora, *Engineer*
Meghan Timke, *Engineer*
▲ **EMP:** 125
SQ FT: 100,000
SALES (est): 36.8MM **Privately Held**
SIC: 3089 Injection molding of plastics

(G-18303)
WRITE STUFF
5n465 Hazelwood Ct (60175-8168)
PHONE 630 365-4425
EMP: 4
SALES (est): 80.4K **Privately Held**
SIC: 5943 5112 3999 Office forms & supplies; stationery & office supplies; manufacturing industries

(G-18304)
ZELLER + GMELIN CORPORATION
3820 Ohio Ave Ste 1 (60174-5461)
PHONE 630 443-8800
Katrina Herrera, *Branch Mgr*
EMP: 5
SALES (corp-wide): 270.7MM **Privately Held**
SIC: 5085 2899 Ink, printers'; ink or writing fluids
HQ: Zeller + Gmelin Corporation
4801 Audubon Dr
Richmond VA 23231
800 848-8465

Saint Elmo
Fayette County

(G-18305)
BASIN TRANSPORTS
112 E 4th St (62458-1609)
PHONE 618 829-3323
EMP: 4
SQ FT: 1,000
SALES (est): 347.7K **Privately Held**
SIC: 1311 Crude Oil Producer

(G-18306)
BELDEN ENTERPRISES LP
801 N Elm St (62458-1362)
P.O. Box 159 (62458-0159)
PHONE 618 829-3274
David Belden, *Partner*
Susan Belden, *Partner*
EMP: 10
SQ FT: 1,800
SALES (est): 1.1MM **Privately Held**
SIC: 1311 Crude petroleum production

(G-18307)
D & Z EXPLORATION INC
901 N Elm St (62458-1361)
P.O. Box 159 (62458-0159)
PHONE 618 829-3274
Zane Belden, *Treasurer*
EMP: 3
SALES: 950K **Privately Held**
SIC: 1311 Crude petroleum production

(G-18308)
FELLER OILFIELD SERVICE INC
Hwy 40 W (62458)
P.O. Box 67 (62458-0067)
PHONE 618 267-5650
Kirk V Feller, *President*
EMP: 10
SQ FT: 7,200
SALES (est): 3.4MM **Privately Held**
SIC: 1389 Oil field services

(G-18309)
MARATHON PETROLEUM COMPANY LP
200 E 4th St (62458-1611)
P.O. Box 35 (62458-0035)
PHONE 618 829-3288
Jeremy Dilley, *Branch Mgr*
EMP: 6 **Publicly Held**
SIC: 5172 5032 2951 Petroleum products; asphalt mixture; asphalt paving mixtures & blocks
HQ: Marathon Petroleum Company Lp
539 S Main St
Findlay OH 45840

(G-18310)
NATURAL GAS PIPELINE AMER LLC
6 Miles N On Elm St (62458)
PHONE 618 829-3224
Gary Buchler, *Principal*
EMP: 23 **Publicly Held**
SIC: 4922 1311 Natural gas transmission; crude petroleum & natural gas
HQ: Natural Gas Pipeline Company Of America Llc
1001 Louisiana St
Houston TX 77002
713 369-9000

(G-18311)
PINNACLE FOODS GROUP LLC
1000 Brewbaker Dr (62458-1234)
PHONE 618 829-3275
Thomas Perkins, *Plant Mgr*
Laura Wharton, *Branch Mgr*
Brenda Welling, *Manager*
EMP: 300
SALES (corp-wide): 9.5B **Publicly Held**
WEB: www.pinnaclefoods.com
SIC: 4225 2038 General warehousing & storage; breakfasts, frozen & packaged
HQ: Pinnacle Foods Group Llc
399 Jefferson Rd
Parsippany NJ 07054

(G-18312)
SMITH WELDING LLC
2238 N 2225 St (62458-4054)
P.O. Box 2 (62458-0002)
PHONE 618 829-5414
Terry Smith, *Principal*
EMP: 3 **EST:** 1976
SQ FT: 4,400
SALES (est): 309.9K **Privately Held**
SIC: 7692 Welding repair

Saint Francisville
Lawrence County

(G-18313)
D LITTLE DRILLING
4734 Country Club Rd (62460-3042)
PHONE 618 943-3721
David Hulfachor, *Owner*
Denise Hulfachor, *Co-Owner*
EMP: 3
SALES (est): 278.7K **Privately Held**
SIC: 1311 Crude petroleum production

(G-18314)
GRAYS CABINET CO
Rr 1 (62460-9801)
P.O. Box 310 (62460-0310)
PHONE 618 948-2211
Shane Gray, *President*
Helen Gray, *Admin Sec*
EMP: 1 **EST:** 1945
SQ FT: 1,200
SALES (est): 202.9K **Privately Held**
SIC: 2521 2431 2517 2434 Cabinets, office: wood; millwork; wood television & radio cabinets; wood kitchen cabinets

(G-18315)
TUSSEY G K OIL EXPLRTN & PRDC
4th & Main St (62460)
P.O. Box 69 (62460-0069)
PHONE 618 948-2871
Gary K Tussey, *Owner*
Cindy Hasler, *Manager*
EMP: 3
SALES (est): 258.3K **Privately Held**
SIC: 1311 1381 Crude petroleum production; drilling oil & gas wells

Saint Jacob
Madison County

(G-18316)
FIFTH QUARTER
1770 Triad Rd (62281-1108)
PHONE 618 346-6659
EMP: 3

SALES (est): 339.9K **Privately Held**
SIC: 3131 Mfg Footwear Cut Stock

Saint Joseph
Champaign County

(G-18317)
HONEYWELL INTERNATIONAL INC
3737 Red Arrow Hwy (61873)
PHONE 269 428-6305
Dave Aschliman, *Branch Mgr*
EMP: 300
SALES (corp-wide): 36.7B **Publicly Held**
SIC: 3714 Motor vehicle brake systems & parts
PA: Honeywell International Inc.
300 S Tryon St
Charlotte NC 28202
704 627-6200

(G-18318)
PIONEER HI-BRED INTL INC
2112 County Road 1600 N (61873-9614)
PHONE 309 962-2931
Van Luck, *Vice Pres*
Joseph C Bandy, *Branch Mgr*
Mark Mead, *Info Tech Mgr*
EMP: 17
SALES (corp-wide): 21.5B **Publicly Held**
SIC: 8734 2075 5191 Seed testing laboratory; soybean oil mills; seeds & bulbs
HQ: Pioneer Hi-Bred International, Inc.
7100 Nw 62nd Ave
Johnston IA 50131
515 535-3200

(G-18319)
RIVER BEND WILD GAME & SAUSAGE
1161 County Road 2400 E (61873-9726)
PHONE 217 688-3337
Mary Ellen Stites, *Owner*
EMP: 4
SALES (est): 340.4K **Privately Held**
SIC: 3421 Table & food cutlery, including butchers'

(G-18320)
SHAPE MASTER INC
704 E Lincoln St (61873-9028)
PHONE 217 469-7027
Kenneth Cooley Jr, *Principal*
EMP: 4
SALES (est): 247.7K **Privately Held**
SIC: 3082 Unsupported plastics profile shapes

(G-18321)
WYLDEWOOD CELLARS 2 LLC
218 E Lincoln St (61873)
PHONE 217 469-9463
Tracie Trotter,
EMP: 3 **EST:** 2010
SALES (est): 262.4K **Privately Held**
WEB: www.wyldewoodillinois.com
SIC: 2084 Wines

Saint Peter
Fayette County

(G-18322)
AUTHENTIC STREET SIGNS INC
183 Main St (62880)
P.O. Box 183 (62880-0183)
PHONE 618 349-8878
Mark Wollin, *CEO*
◆ **EMP:** 4
SQ FT: 35,000
SALES (est): 470.2K **Privately Held**
SIC: 3993 Signs & advertising specialties

(G-18323)
COURSONS CORING & DRILLING
Nr Hwy 185 (62880)
PHONE 618 349-8765
Richard Courson, *President*
Doris Courson, *Admin Sec*
EMP: 3

SALES (est): 286K **Privately Held**
SIC: 1381 1781 Directional drilling oil & gas wells; water well drilling

(G-18324)
FLINT GROUP US LLC
619 N 2200 St (62880-0222)
PHONE 618 349-8384
David Frescon, *Principal*
EMP: 19
SALES (corp-wide): 53.9B **Publicly Held**
SIC: 2893 Printing ink
HQ: Flint Group Us Llc
17177 N Laurel Park Dr # 300
Livonia MI 48152
734 781-4600

Sainte Marie
Jasper County

(G-18325)
D M MANUFACTURING 2 INC
490 S Main St (62459)
P.O. Box 8 (62459-0008)
PHONE 618 455-3550
Don E Geltz, *President*
Barbara Geltz, *Admin Sec*
EMP: 8
SQ FT: 18,000
SALES (est): 1.7MM **Privately Held**
SIC: 3523 7692 Hog feeding, handling & watering equipment; welding repair

(G-18326)
HARTRICH MEATS INC
326 W Embarras St (62459-1003)
P.O. Box 27 (62459-0027)
PHONE 618 455-3172
Mark Hartrich, *President*
Lucy Hartrich, *Treasurer*
Tony Hartrich, *Admin Sec*
EMP: 9 **EST:** 1952
SQ FT: 6,000
SALES: 500K **Privately Held**
WEB: www.hartrichmeats.com
SIC: 2011 5421 5411 2013 Meat packing plants; meat & fish markets; grocery stores; sausages & other prepared meats

(G-18327)
MONT EAGLE PRODUCTS INC (PA)
219 S Main St (62459-1011)
P.O. Box 176 (62459-0176)
PHONE 618 455-3344
Rick Seamon, *President*
Kent Deisher, *Admin Sec*
EMP: 6
SQ FT: 7,200
SALES (est): 839.4K **Privately Held**
SIC: 2048 5191 Feed premixes; farm supplies

Salem
Marion County

(G-18328)
AMERICANA BUILDING PDTS INC (PA)
2 Industrial Dr (62881-5865)
P.O. Box 1290 (62881-6290)
PHONE 618 548-2800
Gerald G Purcell, *President*
David Allen, *Vice Pres*
Mark Peradotti, *Engineer*
Melanie Johnson, *Treasurer*
Melissa Ortiz, *Credit Mgr*
◆ **EMP:** 75 **EST:** 1949
SQ FT: 117,000
SALES (est): 2.9MM **Privately Held**
WEB: www.americana.com
SIC: 2394 3444 3448 Awnings, fabric: made from purchased materials; awnings, sheet metal; carports: prefabricated metal

GEOGRAPHIC SECTION

Salem - Marion County (G-18355)

(G-18329)
AMERICANA POWDER FINISHING LLC
Also Called: Americana Building Products
2 Industrial Dr (62881-5865)
P.O. Box 1290 (62881-6290)
PHONE 618 548-2800
Melissa Ortiz, *Credit Mgr*
Gerald Purcell,
EMP: 60
SALES (est): 5.4MM **Privately Held**
SIC: 3479 Painting, coating & hot dipping

(G-18330)
BAILEY BUSINESS GROUP
3089 State Route 37 (62881-3667)
PHONE 618 548-3566
Keith Bailey, *Owner*
Rachel Bailey, *Co-Owner*
EMP: 2
SALES (est): 203K **Privately Held**
WEB: www.baileybusinessgroup.com
SIC: 8741 2421 7389 3559 Business management; sawmills & planing mills, general; music recording producer; kilns

(G-18331)
BETTENDORF STANFORD INC
1370 W Main St (62881-3802)
P.O. Box 790 (62881-0790)
PHONE 618 548-3555
John Stanford, *President*
Mike Bays, *Engineer*
Matt Bledsoe, *Engineer*
Shannon McDanald, *Accountant*
Linny Bookhout, *Sales Staff*
▲ **EMP:** 52
SQ FT: 15,000
SALES (est): 15.3MM **Privately Held**
WEB: www.bettendorfstanford.com
SIC: 3556 3535 Food products machinery; conveyors & conveying equipment

(G-18332)
BOATMAN SIGNS
1700 E Main St (62881-3535)
PHONE 618 548-6567
Dale Boatman, *Owner*
EMP: 3 **EST:** 2010
SALES (est): 251.6K **Privately Held**
SIC: 3993 Signs, not made in custom sign painting shops

(G-18333)
CAMPBELL SOUP COMPANY
1824 W Main St (62881-5838)
PHONE 618 548-3001
Jerry Bateman, *Branch Mgr*
EMP: 5
SALES (corp-wide): 8.1B **Publicly Held**
WEB: www.campbellsoupcompany.com
SIC: 5461 2038 2033 2052 Bakeries; frozen specialties; canned fruits & specialties; cookies & crackers; bread, cake & related products; potato chips & similar snacks
PA: Campbell Soup Company
1 Campbell Pl
Camden NJ 08103
856 342-4800

(G-18334)
CHAMPIONX LLC
Also Called: Nalco Champion
3340 Selmaville Rd (62881-6606)
PHONE 618 740-1279
Lance Date, *Branch Mgr*
EMP: 3
SALES (corp-wide): 5.1B **Privately Held**
WEB: www.nalco.com
SIC: 2899 Chemical preparations
PA: Championx Llc
11177 S Stadium Dr
Sugar Land TX 77478
630 305-1000

(G-18335)
DEEP ROCK ENERGY CORPORATION
631 S Broadway Ave (62881-2210)
P.O. Box 160, Kinmundy (62854-0160)
PHONE 618 548-2779
Ben Webster, *President*
EMP: 15
SQ FT: 1,500
SALES (est): 1.8MM **Privately Held**
SIC: 1311 Crude petroleum production

(G-18336)
DUNCAN OIL COMPANY INC
Also Called: Precision Pump & Valve Service
300 S Washington St (62881-3027)
P.O. Box 218 (62881-0218)
PHONE 618 548-2923
Gene L Duncan, *President*
Mary Duncan, *Vice Pres*
EMP: 8 **EST:** 1957
SQ FT: 1,800
SALES (est): 800K **Privately Held**
SIC: 1311 1389 Crude petroleum production; oil field services

(G-18337)
ENTRANS INTERNATIONAL LLC
Also Called: Jarco
1414 S Broadway Ave (62881-2437)
P.O. Box 56 (62881-0056)
PHONE 618 548-3660
William Soulon, *Manager*
Don Haiker, *Director*
EMP: 25 **Privately Held**
SIC: 3715 7538 5531 5084 Truck trailers; general automotive repair shops; automotive & home supply stores; industrial machinery & equipment; truck & bus bodies
HQ: Entrans International, Llc
1145 Congress Pkwy N
Athens TN 37303
404 845-0083

(G-18338)
ESI STEEL & FABRICATION
Also Called: E S I Steel Fabrication
1645 N Broadway Ave (62881-4234)
PHONE 618 548-3017
Marshall C Smith, *President*
Kerry Smith, *Vice Pres*
Stephanie Conner, *Plant Mgr*
Billie Smith, *Admin Sec*
EMP: 12 **EST:** 1977
SQ FT: 37,000
SALES (est): 2.1MM **Privately Held**
SIC: 3441 3448 3444 Building components, structural steel; prefabricated metal buildings; sheet metalwork

(G-18339)
FINKS OIL CO INC
519 W Boone St (62881-1222)
PHONE 618 548-5757
EMP: 3 **EST:** 1974
SQ FT: 2,000
SALES (est): 270K **Privately Held**
SIC: 1311 Crude Oil Producer

(G-18340)
GEMTAR INC
138 Woodland Dr (62881-2635)
PHONE 618 548-1353
Jim Rainwater, *President*
Betty Rainwater, *Admin Sec*
EMP: 4
SALES (est): 565.3K **Privately Held**
SIC: 3533 3536 3531 Oil field machinery & equipment; drilling tools for gas, oil or water wells; hoists, cranes & monorails; construction machinery

(G-18341)
GOSSETT PRINTING INC
2100 Old Texas Ln (62881-5835)
P.O. Box 631 (62881-0631)
PHONE 618 548-2583
Jayson Gossett, *President*
EMP: 3
SQ FT: 2,400
SALES (est): 333K **Privately Held**
SIC: 2752 2791 2789 Commercial printing, offset; typesetting; bookbinding & related work

(G-18342)
HAROLD PREFINISHED WOOD INC
5318 State Route 37 (62881-4754)
PHONE 618 548-1414
Harold Smith, *Owner*
Kay Smith, *Corp Secy*
Tony Boyles, *Vice Pres*
EMP: 15
SQ FT: 30,000
SALES (est): 880K **Privately Held**
SIC: 2431 Doors, wood

(G-18343)
JARCO INC
8 Carpenter Dr (62881-3898)
PHONE 888 681-3660
Edward Peters Jarvis, *President*
Helen E Jarvis, *Corp Secy*
EMP: 25
SALES (est): 1MM **Privately Held**
SIC: 3713 Truck bodies (motor vehicles)

(G-18344)
JERRY D GRAHAM OIL
Also Called: Indian Point Oil & Gas
1213 S Broadway Ave (62881-2406)
P.O. Box 1118 (62881-6118)
PHONE 618 548-5540
Jerry Graham, *Owner*
EMP: 3
SALES (est): 168K **Privately Held**
SIC: 1381 Drilling oil & gas wells

(G-18345)
MERZ VAULT COMPANY INC
2918 State Route 37 (62881-3664)
P.O. Box 382 (62881-0382)
PHONE 618 548-2859
William Randy Vogt, *President*
Jan Vogt, *Admin Sec*
EMP: 23 **EST:** 1947
SQ FT: 28,000
SALES (est): 3.3MM **Privately Held**
SIC: 3272 7261 Burial vaults, concrete or precast terrazzo; funeral service & crematories

(G-18346)
MIDWEST INNOVATIVE TECH INC
400 S Broadway Ave (62881-2205)
PHONE 618 740-0074
Kim Cantrell, *President*
EMP: 4
SALES (est): 219.3K **Privately Held**
WEB: www.mitimfg.com
SIC: 3491 Fire hydrant valves

(G-18347)
MINOR LEAGUE INC
905 E Main St (62881-2940)
PHONE 618 548-8040
Jeff Morgan, *President*
Michael Bolton, *Corp Secy*
EMP: 3
SQ FT: 3,400
SALES (est): 410K **Privately Held**
SIC: 5941 2395 5999 Team sports equipment; embroidery & art needlework; trophies & plaques

(G-18348)
NORTH AMERICAN LIGHTING INC
Also Called: Signal Lighting Operations
1875 W Main St (62881-5839)
PHONE 618 548-6249
Eric Huddlestun, *Business Mgr*
Mike Blackburn, *Engineer*
Gordon Hansen, *Engineer*
Wayne Howard, *Engineer*
Shannon Iffert, *Engineer*
EMP: 900 **Privately Held**
SIC: 3647 3641 Automotive lighting fixtures; electric lamps
HQ: North American Lighting, Inc.
2275 S Main St
Paris IL 61944
217 465-6600

(G-18349)
P J REPAIR SERVICE INC
108 S Missouri St (62881-2008)
P.O. Box 426 (62881-0426)
PHONE 618 548-5690
Phill Dial, *President*
Kim Dial, *Vice Pres*
EMP: 13
SQ FT: 8,885
SALES: 1MM **Privately Held**
SIC: 7699 1389 Aircraft & heavy equipment repair services; oil field services

(G-18350)
PARK VIEW MANUFACTURING CORP
2510 S Broadway Ave (62881-3650)
PHONE 618 548-9054
Juliette I Nimmons, *Ch of Bd*
John Mansfield, *President*
James Walker, *Vice Pres*
Barb Crispens, *Controller*
Ron Scharf, *Admin Sec*
▲ **EMP:** 100
SQ FT: 106,000
SALES (est): 5.8MM **Privately Held**
SIC: 3949 8732 Helmets, athletic; pads: football, basketball, soccer, lacrosse, etc.; research services, except laboratory

(G-18351)
PRECISION CONTAINER INC
1370 W Main St (62881-3802)
PHONE 618 548-2830
Daniel Ackman, *President*
Ryan Thomas, *Marketing Staff*
EMP: 9
SALES (est): 770K **Privately Held**
SIC: 3089 Plastic containers, except foam

(G-18352)
PRECISION TRUCK PRODUCTS INC
2625 S Broadway Ave (62881-3601)
P.O. Box 1224 (62881-6224)
PHONE 618 548-9011
Dave Burdin, *CEO*
David McIntosh, *VP Sales*
Adam Ansberry, *Sales Staff*
Taylor Burdin, *Agent*
EMP: 40
SALES: 5.6MM **Privately Held**
SIC: 3714 Trailer hitches, motor vehicle

(G-18353)
QUAD-COUNTY READY MIX CORP
3782 Hotze Rd (62881-2443)
PHONE 618 548-2477
Jan Hubbell, *Manager*
EMP: 7
SALES (corp-wide): 16.1MM **Privately Held**
SIC: 3273 Ready-mixed concrete
PA: Quad-County Ready Mix Corp.
300 W 12th St
Okawville IL 62271
618 243-6430

(G-18354)
RADIAC ABRASIVES INC (HQ)
Also Called: National Grinding Wheel
1015 S College St (62881-2499)
P.O. Box 1410 (62881-7410)
PHONE 618 548-4200
Chris Dashiell, *Plant Mgr*
Todd Clark, *Maint Spvr*
Jason Wozniak, *Production*
Kristi Lobek, *Buyer*
Tim Bathon, *Engineer*
◆ **EMP:** 196
SQ FT: 150,000
SALES (est): 143.9MM
SALES (corp-wide): 797.8MM **Privately Held**
SIC: 3291 Grindstones, artificial; wheels, abrasive
PA: Tyrolit - Schleifmittelwerke Swarovski K.G.
SwarovskistraBe 33
Schwaz 6130
524 260-60

(G-18355)
RONNIE JOE GRAHAM
Also Called: R J Graham Oil Company
420 W Schwartz St (62881-1552)
P.O. Box 474 (62881-0474)
PHONE 618 548-5544
Fax: 618 548-3736
EMP: 2
SQ FT: 1,800
SALES (est): 288.7K **Privately Held**
SIC: 1311 Crude Oil Production

Salem - Marion County (G-18356)

(G-18356)
S CARPENTER LOGGING
3555 Country Ln (62881-6625)
PHONE..................618 548-6187
Glenn Carpenter, *Partner*
Mike Carpenter, *Partner*
EMP: 2
SALES (est): 203.1K **Privately Held**
SIC: 2411 Logging camps & contractors

(G-18357)
SALEM BUILDING MATERIALS INC
1217 S Broadway Ave (62881-2406)
PHONE..................618 548-3221
Nancy Broom, *President*
Gerald Broom, *President*
Kathy Rose, *Vice Pres*
EMP: 9 **EST:** 1953
SQ FT: 2,500
SALES: 1.6MM **Privately Held**
WEB: www.salembuilding.net
SIC: 5211 5031 3442 Door & window products; millwork & lumber; doors & windows; window & door frames

(G-18358)
SALEM TIMES-COMMONER INC (HQ)
Also Called: Tc Printers
120 S Broadway Ave (62881-1610)
P.O. Box 548 (62881-0548)
PHONE..................618 548-3330
John Perrine, *President*
William Perrine, *Admin Sec*
EMP: 25 **EST:** 1946
SQ FT: 70,000
SALES (est): 6.2MM
SALES (corp-wide): 9.9MM **Privately Held**
WEB: www.salemil.us
SIC: 2711 2791 2789 2752 Newspapers, publishing & printing; typesetting; bookbinding & related work; commercial printing, lithographic
PA: Centralia Press, Ltd
232 E Broadway
Centralia IL 62801
618 532-5604

(G-18359)
SHAWNEE STONE LLC (PA)
202 W Main St (62881-1519)
PHONE..................618 548-1585
Steve Stein, *Sales Mgr*
Bryan Temple Hood,
Doug Alberson,
Rebecca S Weber,
EMP: 15
SQ FT: 15,600
SALES: 2MM **Privately Held**
WEB: www.shakespeare-oil.com
SIC: 1422 Crushed & broken limestone

(G-18360)
SQUIBB TANK COMPANY
1001 S Broadway Ave (62881-2402)
P.O. Box 40 (62881-0040)
PHONE..................618 548-0141
Stephen M Squibb, *President*
Wayne T Puricelli, *Vice Pres*
EMP: 10 **EST:** 1961
SQ FT: 19,000
SALES (est): 1.4MM **Privately Held**
WEB: www.squibbtank.com
SIC: 3533 3443 Oil field machinery & equipment; fabricated plate work (boiler shop)

(G-18361)
STANFORD PRODUCTS LLC (HQ)
1139 S Broadway Ave (62881-2404)
P.O. Box 578 (62881-0578)
PHONE..................618 548-2600
Chris Dekalb, *Purch Mgr*
Maurens Gomes, *Engineer*
Tim Andrews, *Accounts Exec*
Shamus Lafferty,
◆ **EMP:** 33
SQ FT: 12,000
SALES (est): 4.4MM **Privately Held**
SIC: 2679 Paperboard products, converted

Sandoval
Marion County

(G-18362)
BEELMAN READY-MIX INC
100 Cemetery Rd (62882-1429)
PHONE..................618 247-3866
Kirk Becker, *Manager*
EMP: 8 **Privately Held**
SIC: 3273 3271 Ready-mixed concrete; concrete block & brick
PA: Beelman Ready-Mix, Inc.
1 Racehorse Dr
East Saint Louis IL 62205

(G-18363)
EVERGREEN POOL & SPA LLC
Also Called: Evergreen Pool & Spa Center
Us Hwys 50 & 51 (62882)
P.O. Box 70 (62882-0070)
PHONE..................618 247-3555
Michael Stock, *Owner*
Geralyn Dock, *COO*
EMP: 4
SQ FT: 15,000
SALES (est): 250K **Privately Held**
SIC: 3949 5999 5091 Swimming pools, except plastic; swimming pools, above ground; sauna equipment & supplies; swimming pools, equipment & supplies; spa equipment & supplies

(G-18364)
GENERAL CONTRACTOR INC
190 Industrial Park Dr (62882)
PHONE..................618 533-5213
Darryl Souger, *Manager*
EMP: 5
SALES (corp-wide): 1.5MM **Privately Held**
SIC: 2951 Asphalt paving mixtures & blocks
PA: General Contractor Inc
1 Industrial Dr
Salem IL

(G-18365)
SYNERGY POWER GROUP LLC
Also Called: Team Fenex
610 E Illinois Ave (62882-1430)
PHONE..................618 247-3200
Michelle Warner, *Purch Mgr*
Dave Smith, *Engineer*
Luciano Rapa, *Sales Staff*
James M Cleary,
Lori Peters,
EMP: 35
SALES: 13MM **Privately Held**
SIC: 3537 3621 3799 Industrial trucks & tractors; motors & generators; trailers & trailer equipment

Sandwich
Dekalb County

(G-18366)
BLACK MAGIC CUSTOMS INC
4686 E 29th Rd (60548-9104)
PHONE..................815 786-1977
Phil Hoffman, *President*
Tom Wade, *Vice Pres*
EMP: 4
SALES: 125K **Privately Held**
SIC: 3751 Motorcycles & related parts

(G-18367)
DESIGNED STAIRS INC (PA)
Also Called: Heartland Bench and Pew
1480 E 6th St (60548-7021)
PHONE..................815 786-2021
Robert S Ducharme, *Ch of Bd*
Michelle Ducharme, *President*
Kim Jansen, *Technology*
John Ressler, *Admin Sec*
EMP: 30
SQ FT: 50,000
SALES (est): 5.1MM **Privately Held**
SIC: 2431 Staircases & stairs, wood

(G-18368)
ELGINEX CORPORATION
1002 E 3rd St (60548-1873)
PHONE..................815 786-8406
Randy Holver, *Manager*
EMP: 8
SALES (corp-wide): 1.4MM **Privately Held**
SIC: 3842 Surgical appliances & supplies
PA: Elginex Corporation
200 S Frontage Rd Ste 101
Burr Ridge IL 60527
800 279-5955

(G-18369)
FABTEK AERO LTD
775 Duvick Ave (60548-7098)
PHONE..................630 552-3622
Michael A Chesnutt, *President*
Dave Tremain, *President*
Scott Chesnutt, *Principal*
Timothy Tremain, *Vice Pres*
Justin Dotson, *Engineer*
▲ **EMP:** 13
SQ FT: 10,000
SALES: 2.5MM **Privately Held**
SIC: 3443 Fabricated plate work (boiler shop)

(G-18370)
FORTUNE METAL MIDWEST LLC
1212 E 6th St (60548-1864)
PHONE..................630 778-7776
Victor Ng, *Mng Member*
Mark Matza,
John Ng,
EMP: 50
SQ FT: 53,000
SALES (est): 7.5MM **Privately Held**
SIC: 3559 Recycling machinery

(G-18371)
GAVIN WOODWORKING INC
Also Called: Gavin Machine & Manufacturing
16119 Chicago Rd (60548-4017)
P.O. Box 46 (60548-0046)
PHONE..................815 786-2242
Elizabeth Gavin, *President*
Gregory Gavin, *Vice Pres*
EMP: 4
SALES: 638.1K **Privately Held**
SIC: 7641 3599 2499 2511 Office furniture repair & maintenance; reupholstery; machine shop, jobbing & repair; spools, wood; wood household furniture; millwork

(G-18372)
GORD INDUSTRIAL PLASTICS INC
1310 E 6th St (60548-7018)
PHONE..................815 786-9494
James Gord, *President*
James F Gord, *President*
Wendy S Gord, *Corp Secy*
▲ **EMP:** 10
SQ FT: 31,000
SALES (est): 5MM **Privately Held**
WEB: www.gordplastics.com
SIC: 3089 Injection molding of plastics

(G-18373)
HADDOCK TOOL & MANUFACTURING
917 E Railroad St (60548-1823)
P.O. Box 67 (60548-0067)
PHONE..................815 786-2739
John Haddock, *President*
EMP: 3
SQ FT: 6,640
SALES (est): 200K **Privately Held**
SIC: 3429 3469 3452 Furniture hardware; metal stampings; bolts, nuts, rivets & washers

(G-18374)
HENDERSON ENGINEERING CO INC (PA)
Also Called: Sahara Air Dryers
95 N Main St (60548-1597)
PHONE..................815 786-9471
Terry D Henderson, *President*
Kevin Stern, *Vice Pres*
Rob Saitta, *Foreman/Supr*
Shawna Wheeler, *Purch Agent*
Heather Carr, *Project Engr*

EMP: 1 **EST:** 1956
SQ FT: 157,000
SALES (est): 16.3MM **Privately Held**
WEB: www.saharahenderson.com
SIC: 3564 3567 3845 Filters, air: furnaces, air conditioning equipment, etc.; driers & redriers, industrial process; electromedical equipment

(G-18375)
JK AUDIO INC
Also Called: Telecom Audio
1311 E 6th St (60548-7022)
PHONE..................815 786-2929
Joseph Klinger, *President*
Wayne Reed, *Technical Staff*
Linda M Klinger, *Admin Sec*
Linda Klinger, *Admin Sec*
EMP: 17
SQ FT: 12,500
SALES (est): 3.6MM **Privately Held**
SIC: 3699 Sound signaling devices, electrical

(G-18376)
KING & SONS MONUMENTS
131 E Center St Ste 1 (60548-1689)
PHONE..................815 786-6321
William R King, *Owner*
Linda King, *Co-Owner*
EMP: 4
SQ FT: 6,500
SALES (est): 280K **Privately Held**
SIC: 3281 Monuments, cut stone (not finishing or lettering only)

(G-18377)
MEADOWVALE INC
1305 E 6th St (60548-1868)
PHONE..................630 553-0202
Steve Steinwart, *President*
Jason Leslie, *Vice Pres*
Marl Kloster, *Plant Mgr*
Eddie Cajina, *Purch Agent*
Heather Foss, *Purch Agent*
EMP: 35 **EST:** 1967
SALES (est): 6MM **Privately Held**
WEB: www.meadowvale-inc.com
SIC: 2023 Ice cream mix, unfrozen: liquid or dry; milkshake mix

(G-18378)
OFFWORLD DESIGNS
624 W Center St (60548-1429)
PHONE..................815 786-7080
Barbara Van Tilburg, *President*
Raymond Van Tilburg, *Vice Pres*
Raymond Vantilburg, *Art Dir*
EMP: 6
SALES: 600K **Privately Held**
SIC: 2759 2396 Screen printing; automotive & apparel trimmings

(G-18379)
PLANO MOLDING COMPANY LLC
510 Duvick Ave (60548-7032)
PHONE..................630 552-9557
Dean Boatman, *Manager*
EMP: 124
SALES (corp-wide): 93.8MM **Privately Held**
SIC: 3089 Plastic containers, except foam
HQ: Plano Molding Company, Llc
431 E South St
Plano IL 60545
630 552-3111

(G-18380)
PLANO MOLDING COMPANY LLC
500 Duvick Ave (60548-7032)
PHONE..................815 786-3331
Dean Boatman, *Manager*
Mike Franklin, *Maintence Staff*
EMP: 200
SALES (corp-wide): 93.8MM **Privately Held**
SIC: 3089 3161 Plastic containers, except foam; luggage
HQ: Plano Molding Company, Llc
431 E South St
Plano IL 60545
630 552-3111

GEOGRAPHIC SECTION

Savanna - Carroll County (G-18405)

(G-18381)
PRINT SHOP
17 E Center St (60548-1562)
PHONE...............................815 786-8278
Maury Killui, *Owner*
EMP: 3
SALES (est): 236.6K **Privately Held**
SIC: 2752 Commercial printing, offset

(G-18382)
Q PRODUCTS
814 Lake Holiday Dr (60548-9314)
P.O. Box 87 (60548-0087)
PHONE...............................815 498-6356
Michael D Toner, *Principal*
EMP: 4
SALES (est): 363.1K **Privately Held**
SIC: 3565 Packaging machinery

(G-18383)
QUICK NIC JUICE LLC
122 Indian Springs Dr # 5 (60548-1987)
PHONE...............................815 315-8523
Richard M Schure,
Adele Schure,
EMP: 11 **EST:** 2013
SQ FT: 6,000
SALES (est): 1.1MM **Privately Held**
SIC: 3634 Vaporizers, electric: household

(G-18384)
SANDWICH MILLWORKS INC
700 W Center St (60548-1442)
PHONE...............................815 786-2700
John G Knur, *President*
Thomas Freiders, *Shareholder*
EMP: 6
SQ FT: 7,500
SALES: 360K **Privately Held**
WEB: www.sandwichmillworks.com
SIC: 2431 Moldings, wood: unfinished & prefinished

(G-18385)
TRI-COUNTY CONCRETE INC
331 W Church St (60548-2007)
P.O. Box 26 (60548-0026)
PHONE...............................815 786-2179
Michael Zerby, *President*
Craig Chapman, *Vice Pres*
EMP: 8 **EST:** 1973
SQ FT: 2,400
SALES (est): 1MM **Privately Held**
SIC: 3273 Ready-mixed concrete

(G-18386)
TRIO FOUNDRY INC
Also Called: Sandwich Casting & Machine
924 W Church St (60548-2058)
PHONE...............................815 786-6616
EMP: 24
SALES (est): 3.8MM
SALES (corp-wide): 6.9MM **Privately Held**
SIC: 3365 3369 Aluminum Foundry Nonferrous Metal Foundry
PA: Trio Foundry, Inc.
1985 Aucutt Rd
Montgomery IL 60538
630 892-1676

Sauget
St. Clair County

(G-18387)
AEROSPACE METALS LLC
2401 Mississippi Ave (62201-1078)
P.O. Box 460122, Saint Louis MO (63146-7122)
PHONE...............................888 600-7811
Paul J Fredericks,
Paul Fredericks, *Administration*
EMP: 3 **EST:** 2015
SQ FT: 30,000
SALES (est): 168.6K **Privately Held**
SIC: 3471 Anodizing (plating) of metals or formed products

(G-18388)
AFFTON FABG & WLDG CO INC
1635 Sauget Business Blvd (62206-1455)
PHONE...............................314 781-4100
Matt Tucker, *President*
Larry Henson, *Principal*
Ronald Pfeil, *Principal*
Matthew Tucker, *Principal*
Tom Henson, *Vice Pres*
EMP: 26 **EST:** 1956
SQ FT: 46,500
SALES (est): 24MM **Privately Held**
WEB: www.afwc.com
SIC: 3441 3449 3446 Building components, structural steel; miscellaneous metalwork; architectural metalwork

(G-18389)
BIG RIVER ZINC CORPORATION
2401 Mississippi Ave (62201-1078)
PHONE...............................618 274-5000
George M Obeldobel, *President*
John Likarish, *Vice Pres*
Dale Lattina, *Engineer*
Lawrence S Thaier, *CFO*
◆ **EMP:** 7
SQ FT: 200,000
SALES (est): 1.6MM **Privately Held**
SIC: 3356 3369 3341 3339 Lead & zinc; lead, zinc & white metal; secondary nonferrous metals; primary nonferrous metals; industrial inorganic chemicals; lead & zinc ores
PA: Zincox Resources Limited
Crown House, High Street
Hook HANTS
127 645-0100

(G-18390)
BRANDING IRON HOLDINGS INC (PA)
1682 Sauget Business Blvd (62206-1454)
PHONE...............................618 337-8400
R Scott Hudspeth, *CEO*
Michael H Holten, *President*
Andy Touchette, *Senior VP*
Mari Bertelsman, *Purchasing*
Ric Smith, *VP Sales*
EMP: 3
SALES (est): 59.5MM **Privately Held**
SIC: 2013 5147 Sausages & other prepared meats; meats & meat products

(G-18391)
CENTER ETHANOL COMPANY LLC
231 Monsanto Ave (62201-1010)
PHONE...............................618 875-3008
Barry W Frazier, *President*
Sandi Hill, *Controller*
Gary Barker, *Mng Member*
Keith Zarczynski, *Manager*
EMP: 47
SQ FT: 25,000
SALES (est): 13MM **Privately Held**
WEB: www.centerethanol.com
SIC: 2869 Ethyl alcohol, ethanol

(G-18392)
CERRO FLOW PRODUCTS LLC (DH)
3000 Mississippi Ave (62206-1057)
P.O. Box 66800, Saint Louis MO (63166-6800)
PHONE...............................618 337-6000
Gary Ewing, *President*
Michael Duggan, *President*
Robert C Gluth, *Treasurer*
Eric Pilas,
◆ **EMP:** 200 **EST:** 1908
SALES (est): 212.1MM
SALES (corp-wide): 327.2B **Publicly Held**
SIC: 3351 3331 3498 3585 Tubing, copper & copper alloy; primary copper; fabricated pipe & fittings; refrigeration & heating equipment; metals service centers & offices; copper sheets, plates, bars, rods, pipes, etc.; tubing, metal
HQ: Marmon Holdings, Inc.
181 W Madison St Ste 2600
Chicago IL 60602
312 372-9500

(G-18393)
EASTMAN CHEMICAL COMPANY
500 Monsanto Ave (62206-1137)
PHONE...............................618 482-6409
Evan Shippee, *Analyst*
EMP: 12 **Publicly Held**
WEB: www.eastman.com
SIC: 2821 Plastics materials & resins
PA: Eastman Chemical Company
200 S Wilcox Dr
Kingsport TN 37660

(G-18394)
HOLTEN MEAT INC
1682 Sauget Business Blvd (62206-1454)
PHONE...............................618 337-8400
Michael Holten, *President*
Craig Allen, *CFO*
EMP: 90
SQ FT: 82,000
SALES (est): 24.2MM **Privately Held**
WEB: www.holtenmeat.com
SIC: 2013 Frozen meats from purchased meat
PA: Branding Iron Holdings, Inc.
1682 Sauget Business Blvd
Sauget IL 62206

(G-18395)
MIDWEST NONWOVENS LLC
1642 Sauget Business Blvd (62206-1454)
PHONE...............................618 337-9662
Bryan Speight,
Christopher Look,
▲ **EMP:** 25
SQ FT: 80,000
SALES (est): 6.5MM **Privately Held**
SIC: 2297 Nonwoven fabrics

(G-18396)
NGL CRUDE LOGISTICS LLC
Also Called: Peavey
6 Pitzman Ave (62201-1066)
PHONE...............................618 274-4306
Ray Keating, *Branch Mgr*
EMP: 15 **Publicly Held**
SIC: 2037 Vegetables, quick frozen & cold pack, excl. potato products
HQ: Ngl Crude Logistics, Llc
6120 S Yale Ave Ste 805
Tulsa OK 74136

(G-18397)
OCCIDENTAL CHEMICAL CORP
Also Called: OXY Chem
520 Monsanto Ave (62206)
PHONE...............................618 482-6346
Rick Rauler, *Manager*
EMP: 12
SALES (corp-wide): 21.2B **Publicly Held**
SIC: 2812 Alkalies & chlorine
HQ: Occidental Chemical Corporation
14555 Dallas Pkwy Ste 400
Dallas TX 75254
972 404-3800

(G-18398)
SCF SERVICES LLC
8 Pitzman Ave (62201-1066)
PHONE...............................314 436-7559
Tim Power,
Kenneth Gillum,
Myron McDonough,
EMP: 30 **EST:** 2010
SALES (est): 4.1MM **Privately Held**
SIC: 3732 Boat building & repairing

(G-18399)
SOLUTIA INC
500 Monsanto Ave (62206-1137)
PHONE...............................618 482-6536
Bill Lashley, *Branch Mgr*
EMP: 560 **Publicly Held**
SIC: 2869 Industrial organic chemicals
HQ: Solutia Inc.
575 Maryville Centre Dr
Saint Louis MO 63141
423 229-2000

Sauk Village
Cook County

(G-18400)
HERR DISPLAY VANS INC
22401 Joshua Dr (60411-5667)
PHONE...............................708 755-7926
Timothy Herr, *President*
James Herr, *Vice Pres*
Carol Herr, *Treasurer*
Steve Herr, *Admin Sec*
EMP: 6
SQ FT: 6,000
SALES (est): 1.1MM **Privately Held**
SIC: 3713 Truck bodies & parts

(G-18401)
WINPAK PORTION PACKAGING INC (HQ)
1111 Winpak Way (60411-6111)
PHONE...............................708 753-5700
David Lacey, *President*
Glenn Van Derwende, *Engineer*
Mark Smith, *Controller*
Sam Perry, *Credit Staff*
Bill Romig, *Sales Dir*
◆ **EMP:** 55
SALES (est): 73.2MM
SALES (corp-wide): 873.8MM **Privately Held**
SIC: 3565 2671 Packaging machinery; plastic film, coated or laminated for packaging
PA: Winpak Ltd
100 Saulteaux Cres
Winnipeg MB R3J 3
204 889-1015

Saunemin
Livingston County

(G-18402)
QUAD COUNTY FIRE EQUIPMENT
37 Main St (61769-6110)
P.O. Box 155 (61769-0155)
PHONE...............................815 832-4475
Denist Moore, *President*
EMP: 5 **EST:** 1993
SALES (est): 723.8K **Privately Held**
SIC: 3713 Specialty motor vehicle bodies

Savanna
Carroll County

(G-18403)
BISON AEROSPACE AND DEF LLC
3297 Crim Dr (61074-8675)
PHONE...............................618 795-2678
Daniel Holcomb,
▲ **EMP:** 5
SALES (est): 258.4K **Privately Held**
SIC: 3482 3484 4522 8744 Small arms ammunition; small arms; air cargo carriers, nonscheduled; facilities support services; military aircraft equipment & armament

(G-18404)
ELKAY MANUFACTURING COMPANY
6400 Penn Ave (61074-2923)
PHONE...............................815 273-7001
Corly Tempright
Ed Perz, *Opers-Prdtn-Mfg*
Angela Determan, *Purch Mgr*
Mary Pasekel, *Analyst*
EMP: 300
SALES (corp-wide): 1B **Privately Held**
SIC: 3443 3431 3585 Air coolers, metal plate; drinking fountains, metal; refrigeration & heating equipment
PA: Elkay Manufacturing Company Inc
1333 Butterfield Rd # 200
Downers Grove IL 60515
630 574-8484

(G-18405)
FACEMAKERS INC (PA)
140 N 5th St (61074-1902)
PHONE...............................815 273-3944
Alan St George, *President*
Adrianne St George, *Vice Pres*
EMP: 12
SQ FT: 9,000
SALES (est): 3.4MM **Privately Held**
SIC: 2389 Theatrical costumes

Savanna - Carroll County (G-18406)

(G-18406)
FACEMAKERS INC
800 Chicago Ave (61074-2208)
PHONE...............................815 273-3944
Nancy Willis, Manager
EMP: 42
SALES (corp-wide): 3.4MM Privately Held
SIC: 2389 Theatrical costumes
PA: Facemakers, Inc
140 N 5th St
Savanna IL 61074
815 273-3944

(G-18407)
METFORM LLC
Also Called: Extrusion Science
2551 Wacker Rd (61074-2898)
PHONE...............................815 273-2201
Dennis Keesey, Vice Pres
Steven Dykstra, Maint Spvr
Danielle Lippens, Engineer
Aaron Mix, Project Engr
Phil Schaver, Project Engr
EMP: 190
SALES (corp-wide): 1.2B Privately Held
SIC: 3462 3452 Iron & steel forgings; bolts, nuts, rivets & washers
HQ: Metform, L.L.C.
1000 Allanson Rd
Mundelein IL 60060
847 566-0010

(G-18408)
METFORM LLC
7034 Rte 84 S (61074)
PHONE...............................815 273-0230
Matthias Praus, Vice Pres
Steve Whiting, Plant Mgr
EMP: 32
SALES (corp-wide): 1.2B Privately Held
SIC: 3398 3462 3452 Metal heat treating; iron & steel forgings; bolts, nuts, rivets & washers
HQ: Metform, L.L.C.
1000 Allanson Rd
Mundelein IL 60060
847 566-0010

(G-18409)
MILLS MACHINE INC
Also Called: Savanna Gas and Welding Sups
2416 Jackson St (61074-2836)
PHONE...............................815 273-4707
Phillip Mills, President
EMP: 8
SQ FT: 13,500
SALES: 1.1MM Privately Held
SIC: 3599 5984 Machine shop, jobbing & repair; liquefied petroleum gas dealers

(G-18410)
POWERLAB INC
9741 Powerlab Rd (61074)
P.O. Box 308 (61074-0308)
PHONE...............................815 273-7718
Don Rabon, Engineer
Robert Themas, Manager
EMP: 14
SALES (corp-wide): 13.1MM Privately Held
SIC: 2819 3339 Lead compounds or salts, inorganic, not used in pigments; primary nonferrous metals
PA: Powerlab, Inc.
1145 Highway 34 S
Terrell TX 75160
972 563-1477

(G-18411)
SAVANNA QUARRY INC
9859 Scenic Bluff Rd (61074-8416)
PHONE...............................815 273-4208
Charles Brandt, President
Kelly Bisby, CFO
Terence Brandt, Admin Sec
EMP: 3
SQ FT: 2,800
SALES (est): 338.5K Privately Held
WEB: www.savannaquarry.com
SIC: 1422 2951 Limestones, ground; asphalt & asphaltic paving mixtures (not from refineries)

(G-18412)
SAVANNA TIMES JOURNAL
121 Main St (61074-1931)
P.O. Box 218 (61074-0218)
PHONE...............................815 273-2277
Bob Watson, Owner
EMP: 6
SALES (est): 237.9K Privately Held
SIC: 2711 Newspapers, publishing & printing

(G-18413)
WILKOS INDUSTRIES
3199 School Dr (61074-8671)
PHONE...............................563 249-6691
Quinn Wilkin, Vice Pres
EMP: 3
SALES (est): 200K Privately Held
SIC: 3443 Fabricated plate work (boiler shop)

Savoy
Champaign County

(G-18414)
INNOVATIVE SEC SYSTEMS INC
Also Called: Argus Systems Group
1809 Woodfield Dr (61874-3915)
P.O. Box 187, Effingham (62401-0187)
PHONE...............................217 355-6308
Andrew Jones, President
N E Macgregor, Vice Pres
Dennis Beard, Director
Mike Beck, Director
Robert Kyle, Director
EMP: 16
SALES (est): 1.5MM Privately Held
SIC: 7372 Prepackaged software

(G-18415)
LUON ENERGY LLC
605 Buttercup Dr (61874-9465)
PHONE...............................217 419-2678
Nie Luo,
Lizhang Yang,
◆ EMP: 4
SALES (est): 247.5K Privately Held
SIC: 3621 7389 Storage battery chargers, motor & engine generator type;

(G-18416)
SHERWIN-WILLIAMS COMPANY
109 E Curtis Rd (61874)
PHONE...............................217 359-4934
EMP: 3
SALES (corp-wide): 17.9B Publicly Held
SIC: 5198 2851 Paints, varnishes & supplies; wood fillers or sealers
PA: The Sherwin-Williams Company
101 W Prospect Ave # 1020
Cleveland OH 44115
216 566-2000

(G-18417)
THERMAL SOLUTIONS INC
1706 Lyndhurst Dr (61874-9522)
PHONE...............................217 352-7019
EMP: 2 EST: 2001
SALES (est): 210K Privately Held
SIC: 3567 Mfg Industrial Furnaces/Ovens

Saybrook
Mclean County

(G-18418)
AGRO-CHEM INC
Also Called: Agro Chem West
127 S Center St (61770-9664)
P.O. Box 289 (61770-0289)
PHONE...............................309 475-8311
Jim Dunham, Manager
EMP: 10
SALES (corp-wide): 19.2MM Privately Held
SIC: 0782 3563 Fertilizing services, lawn; air & gas compressors
PA: Agro-Chem, Inc
2045 S Wabash St
Wabash IN 46992
800 686-5680

(G-18419)
PRO TECH ENGINEERING
129 W Lincoln St (61770-7558)
P.O. Box 50 (61770-0050)
PHONE...............................309 475-2502
Jim Gravitt, President
EMP: 2
SALES (est): 260.6K Privately Held
SIC: 3484 Machine guns or machine gun parts, 30 mm. & below

Scales Mound
Jo Daviess County

(G-18420)
GUIDE LINE INDUSTRIES INC
1453 W Schapville Rd (61075-9551)
PHONE...............................815 777-3722
Dave Pingel, President
Hans A Pingel, Principal
Hella Pingel, Admin Sec
EMP: 18
SQ FT: 4,000
SALES (est): 2.7MM Privately Held
SIC: 3496 3545 Miscellaneous fabricated wire products; machine tool accessories

(G-18421)
MILLER MACHINE
299 W Stagecoach Trl (61075-9562)
PHONE...............................815 845-2508
Herb Miller, Owner
EMP: 2
SALES (est): 204.7K Privately Held
WEB: www.millermachining.com
SIC: 3599 Machine shop, jobbing & repair

(G-18422)
WEEKLY VISITOR
101 E Burrall Ave (61075-9567)
PHONE...............................815 845-2328
EMP: 3
SALES (est): 149.2K Privately Held
SIC: 2711 Newspapers

Schaumburg
Cook County

(G-18423)
A & J FINISHERS
623 Lunt Ave (60193-4410)
PHONE...............................847 352-5408
Charlie Kalaria, Owner
EMP: 7
SQ FT: 8,200
SALES (est): 695.7K Privately Held
SIC: 3471 Finishing, metals or formed products

(G-18424)
A A SWIFT PRINT INC
30 Standish Ln (60193-1263)
PHONE...............................847 301-1122
Fax: 847 301-1093
EMP: 5
SALES: 240K Privately Held
SIC: 2752 7334 2789 Lithographic Commercial Printing Photocopying Services Bookbinding/Related Work

(G-18425)
ACCESS MEDICAL SUPPLY INC
658 Albion Ave (60193-4519)
PHONE...............................847 891-6210
John Hamparian, President
Ben Hamparian, Sales Staff
EMP: 3
SALES (est): 418.6K Privately Held
SIC: 2834 3841 Medicines, capsuled or ampuled; surgical & medical instruments

(G-18426)
ACRESSO SOFTWARE INC
1000 E Wdfield Rd Ste 400 (60173)
PHONE...............................408 642-3865
Sridevi Ravuri, Principal
Mike Snyders, Senior Mgr
EMP: 3
SALES (est): 121K Privately Held
WEB: www.flexerasoftware.com
SIC: 7372 Prepackaged software

(G-18427)
ACTION CARBIDE GRINDING CO
Also Called: Action Prcsion Crbide Grinding
1118 Lunt Ave Ste B (60193-4441)
PHONE...............................847 891-9026
Louis Pacini, President
Jean Pacini, Corp Secy
Terry Pacini, Vice Pres
EMP: 3 EST: 1978
SQ FT: 1,200
SALES: 130K Privately Held
SIC: 3599 Grinding castings for the trade

(G-18428)
ADVANCED MICRODERM INC
904 S Roselle Rd 302 (60193-3963)
PHONE...............................630 980-3300
Andrew Goodwin, Exec VP
EMP: 21
SALES (est): 3MM Privately Held
SIC: 3841 Surgical instruments & apparatus

(G-18429)
AERO PRODUCTS HOLDINGS INC
Also Called: Aero Products International
1834 Walden Office Sq # 300 (60173-4292)
P.O. Box 2931, Wichita KS (67201-2931)
PHONE...............................847 485-3200
▲ EMP: 45
SALES (est): 4.1MM Privately Held
SIC: 2599 5712 Mfg Furniture/Fixtures Ret Furniture

(G-18430)
AERO-TECH LIGHT BULB CO (PA)
534 Pratt Ave N (60193-4555)
PHONE...............................847 352-4900
Raymond M Schlosser, President
Kathy M Schlosser, Vice Pres
▲ EMP: 58
SQ FT: 15,000
SALES (est): 8.3MM Privately Held
SIC: 3641 5063 Lamps, incandescent filament, electric; light bulbs & related supplies

(G-18431)
ALLEGRA MARKETING PRINT MAIL
1945 Wright Blvd (60193-4567)
PHONE...............................630 790-0444
Gary Blaski, Owner
Cindy Blaski, Owner
EMP: 8
SALES (est): 74.3K Privately Held
SIC: 8742 2759 Marketing consulting services; commercial printing

(G-18432)
ALLFAVOR TECHNOLOGIES INC
905 Albion Ave (60193-4550)
PHONE...............................630 913-4263
EMP: 5
SALES (est): 542.8K Privately Held
SIC: 3672 Printed circuit boards

(G-18433)
ALLPRINT GRAPHICS INC
Also Called: Class Printing
1034 National Pkwy (60173-4519)
PHONE...............................847 519-9898
Walter Nagel Jr, President
Gary Parker, President
Walter Nagle Sr, Vice Pres
Carl Nagle, Admin Sec
EMP: 3
SQ FT: 2,500
SALES (est): 550K Privately Held
SIC: 2759 2752 Commercial printing; commercial printing, lithographic

(G-18434)
ALLTECH PLASTICS INC
821 Thornton Ct Apt 2b (60193-4854)
PHONE...............................847 352-2309
Ingemar Alexander, President
EMP: 4

▲ = Import ▼ = Export
◆ = Import/Export

SALES (est): 285.8K **Privately Held**
SIC: **3089** Plastics products

(G-18435)
ALTERA CORPORATION
425 N Martingale Rd # 1320 (60173-2297)
PHONE..............................847 240-0313
EMP: 4
SALES (corp-wide): 70.8B **Publicly Held**
SIC: **3674** Mfg Semiconductors/Related Devices
HQ: Altera Corporation
   101 Innovation Dr
   San Jose CA 95134
   408 544-7000

(G-18436)
AM PRECISION MACHINE INC
Also Called: Millusions
1310 Lorraine Pl (60173-6561)
PHONE..............................847 439-9955
Margaret Kozlowski, *CEO*
Stanley Kozlowski, *President*
Andy G Kozlowski, *Senior VP*
Krystina Kozlowski, *Vice Pres*
▲ EMP: 25 EST: 1983
SQ FT: 33,500
SALES: 4MM **Privately Held**
SIC: **3599** Machine shop, jobbing & repair

(G-18437)
AMERICAN LABEL COMPANY
1678 Wright Blvd Ste D (60193-4512)
PHONE..............................630 830-4444
Mohammed Saleem, *Vice Pres*
EMP: 3
SALES (est): 108K **Privately Held**
SIC: **2759** Labels & seals: printing

(G-18438)
AMERICAN PHRM PARTNERS INC
1501 E Woodfield Rd (60173-6052)
PHONE..............................847 969-2700
EMP: 19
SALES (est): 3.8MM **Privately Held**
SIC: **2834** Mfg Pharmaceutical Preparations

(G-18439)
ANALOG DEVICES INC
1901 N Roselle Rd Ste 100 (60195-3178)
PHONE..............................847 519-3669
Greg Wolf, *Engineer*
Bill Wison, *Branch Mgr*
EMP: 8
SALES (corp-wide): 5.9B **Publicly Held**
WEB: www.analog.com
SIC: **3674** Integrated circuits, semiconductor networks, etc.
PA: Analog Devices, Inc.
   1 Technology Way
   Norwood MA 02062
   781 329-4700

(G-18440)
ANSELMO DIE AND INDEX CO INC
Also Called: Anselmo Index
2235 Hammond Dr Ste F (60173-3848)
PHONE..............................847 397-1200
John Anselmo, *President*
EMP: 12
SQ FT: 10,000
SALES (est): 2.4MM **Privately Held**
SIC: **2675** Index cards, die-cut: made from purchased materials

(G-18441)
ANTENEX INC
1751 Wilkening Ct (60173-5310)
PHONE..............................847 839-6910
Don Cislo, *President*
Andrea Casebeer, *Admin Sec*
▲ EMP: 85
SQ FT: 25,000
SALES (est): 9.2MM
SALES (corp-wide): 177.9K **Privately Held**
SIC: **3663** Antennas, transmitting & communications
HQ: Laird Technologies, Inc.
   16401 Swingley Ridge Rd # 700
   Chesterfield MO 63017
   636 898-6000

(G-18442)
APP PHARMACEUTICALS INC
1501 E Woodfield Rd 300e (60173-6029)
PHONE..............................847 969-2700
EMP: 4 EST: 2015
SALES (est): 90K **Privately Held**
SIC: **2834** Pharmaceutical Preparations

(G-18443)
APPLIED POLYMER SYSTEM INC
507 Estes Ave (60193-4428)
PHONE..............................847 301-1712
Kevin Murray, *President*
EMP: 3
SALES (est): 362.5K **Privately Held**
SIC: **3089** Injection molded finished plastic products

(G-18444)
ARC INDUSTRIES INC
2020 Hammond Dr (60173-3810)
PHONE..............................847 303-5005
Dennis A Sjodin, *President*
Carolyn Sjodin, *Admin Sec*
EMP: 35
SQ FT: 58,000
SALES (est): 4.9MM **Privately Held**
WEB: www.arcmold.com
SIC: **3544** Industrial molds; dies & die holders for metal cutting, forming, die casting

(G-18445)
ASCENT INNOVATIONS LLC
475 N Martingale Rd # 820 (60173-2435)
PHONE..............................847 572-8000
Sohena Hafizy, *President*
Robert Sterling, *Manager*
EMP: 38 EST: 2009
SQ FT: 2,148
SALES (est): 6.3MM **Privately Held**
WEB: www.ascent365.com
SIC: **8748** 7373 7371 7379 Business consulting; computer integrated systems design; computer software systems analysis & design, custom; computer software development & applications; computer related consulting services; application computer software; business oriented computer software

(G-18446)
ASPEN SHUTTERS INC
2235 Hammond Dr Ste F (60173-3848)
PHONE..............................847 979-0166
Douglas Plager, *President*
EMP: 5 EST: 2008
SQ FT: 3,500
SALES (est): 482K **Privately Held**
SIC: **2431** Blinds (shutters), wood

(G-18447)
ASSOCIATED EQUIPMENT DISTRS (PA)
Also Called: NON-FOR PROFIT NATIONAL TRADE
650 E Algonquin Rd # 305 (60173-3853)
PHONE..............................630 574-0650
Jonathan Mack, *President*
EMP: 23 EST: 1919
SQ FT: 12,000
SALES: 5.1MM **Privately Held**
WEB: www.aednet.org
SIC: **8611** 2721 7389 8621 Trade associations; trade journals: publishing only, not printed on site; trade show arrangement; professional membership organizations

(G-18448)
ATHENEX PHARMACEUTICAL DIV LLC
10 N Martingale Rd # 230 (60173-2099)
PHONE..............................847 922-8041
John Romano, *Director*
Jon Turnquest, *Director*
Jeff Wojtynek, *Director*
EMP: 16
SALES (corp-wide): 2.9MM **Privately Held**
SIC: **2834** Powders, pharmaceutical; solutions, pharmaceutical
PA: Athenex Pharmaceutical Division, Llc
   1001 Main St Ste 600
   Buffalo NY 14203
   877 463-7823

(G-18449)
AUTOMATIC FEEDER COMPANY INC
921 Albion Ave (60193-4550)
PHONE..............................847 534-2300
Jack Verhasselt, *CEO*
Ken Eversole, *President*
Kirk Verhasselt, *Vice Pres*
EMP: 15 EST: 1954
SQ FT: 24,000
SALES: 4.9MM **Privately Held**
SIC: **3569** 3535 Assembly machines, non-metalworking; conveyors & conveying equipment

(G-18450)
AUTROL CORPORATION OF AMERICA
Also Called: Autrol America
10 N Martingale Rd # 470 (60173-2099)
PHONE..............................847 779-5000
Hermant Narayan, *President*
Unni Ken, *Principal*
▲ EMP: 10
SALES (est): 1.3MM **Privately Held**
SIC: **3823** Transmitters of process variables, stand. signal conversion

(G-18451)
AVALIGN GRMAN SPECIALTY INSTRS
626 Cooper Ct (60173-4537)
PHONE..............................847 908-0292
Rick Gutierrez, *President*
EMP: 27
SALES (est): 3MM **Privately Held**
SIC: **3841** Medical instruments & equipment, blood & bone work

(G-18452)
AVAYA INC
2500 W Higgins Rd (60195)
PHONE..............................847 885-3598
Becky Runes, *Branch Mgr*
EMP: 11 **Publicly Held**
SIC: **7372** Prepackaged software
HQ: Avaya Inc.
   4655 Great America Pkwy
   Santa Clara CA 95054
   908 953-6000

(G-18453)
AVI-SPL EMPLOYEE
2266 Palmer Dr (60173-3822)
PHONE..............................847 437-7712
EMP: 350
SALES (corp-wide): 596.9MM **Privately Held**
SIC: **3669** 3861 3663 3651 Mfg Communications Equip Mfg Photo Equip/Supplies Mfg Radio/Tv Comm Equip Mfg Home Audio/Video Eqp Whol Photo Equip/Supply
HQ: Avi-Spl Employee Emergency Relief Fund, Inc.
   6301 Benjamin Rd Ste 101
   Tampa FL 33634
   813 884-7168

(G-18454)
AXON CABLE INC (HQ)
1316 N Plum Grove Rd (60173-4546)
PHONE..............................847 230-7813
Joseph P Puzo, *President*
Gaetano Battaglia, *Manager*
Dominic Morrone, *Director*
▲ EMP: 16
SQ FT: 5,000
SALES: 3.7MM
SALES (corp-wide): 111.8MM **Privately Held**
SIC: **3357** Nonferrous wiredrawing & insulating
PA: Axon Cable
   2 Route De Chalons
   Montmirail 51210
   977 484-514

(G-18455)
AZILSA INC
1425 W Schaumburg Rd (60194-4051)
PHONE..............................312 919-1741
Pierre Schimper, *President*
EMP: 23

SALES (est): 1.7MM **Privately Held**
SIC: **3699** Security control equipment & systems

(G-18456)
BARRON 2M INC
1031 S Braintree Dr (60193-3646)
PHONE..............................847 219-3650
Stanislava N Dimitrova, *President*
Petko Dimitrov, *Vice Pres*
EMP: 3
SALES: 550K **Privately Held**
SIC: **3715** Truck trailers

(G-18457)
BEE CLEAN SPECIALTIES LLC
550 Albion Ave Ste 50 (60193-4547)
PHONE..............................847 451-0844
Phil Diener, *Marketing Staff*
Craig D McAbery,
Scott McAbery,
EMP: 14
SALES (est): 1.4MM **Privately Held**
SIC: **5075** 3564 Air pollution control equipment & supplies; air filters; air purification equipment; air cleaning systems

(G-18458)
BELMONTE PRINTING CO
525 W Wise Rd Ste D (60193-3882)
PHONE..............................847 352-8841
Anthony J Belmonte, *Partner*
Linda Belmonte, *Partner*
EMP: 5
SQ FT: 1,800
SALES (est): 668.5K **Privately Held**
SIC: **2759** 2791 2752 Commercial printing; typesetting; commercial printing, lithographic

(G-18459)
BEM MOLD INC
Also Called: Bem Cnc
410 Remington Rd (60173-4540)
PHONE..............................847 805-9750
Eugene Bozek, *President*
Mark Bozek, *Vice Pres*
Bogdan Falat, *Vice Pres*
EMP: 45
SQ FT: 20,000
SALES (est): 11.5MM **Privately Held**
SIC: **3599** Machine shop, jobbing & repair

(G-18460)
BEM WIRELESS LLC
1325 Remington Rd Ste H (60173-4815)
PHONE..............................815 337-0541
Michael Nakamura, *Mng Member*
Sheng-Huei Jou,
▲ EMP: 10
SALES: 15MM **Privately Held**
SIC: **3651** 3679 Speaker systems; headphones, radio

(G-18461)
BERRY GLOBAL INC
1228 Tower Rd (60173-4308)
PHONE..............................847 884-1200
Andy Poole, *Plant Mgr*
Bruce Garwood, *Purch Mgr*
Gary McDaniel, *Branch Mgr*
EMP: 125 **Publicly Held**
SIC: **3089** 3081 Bottle caps, molded plastic; unsupported plastics film & sheet
HQ: Berry Global, Inc.
   101 Oakley St
   Evansville IN 47710

(G-18462)
BIRCHER AMERICA INC
870 Pratt Ave N (60193-4561)
PHONE..............................847 952-3730
Barac Bieri, *President*
Roland Shibli, *President*
▲ EMP: 6
SQ FT: 5,000
SALES (est): 2MM
SALES (corp-wide): 213.5MM **Privately Held**
SIC: **5063** 3679 Safety switches; switches, stepping
HQ: Bbc Bircher Ag
   Wiesengasse 20
   Beringen SH 8222
   526 871-111

Schaumburg - Cook County (G-18463)

(G-18463)
BISCO ENTERPRISE INC
550 Albion Ave Ste 40 (60193-4547)
PHONE..................................630 628-1831
Martin Diener, *President*
John Diener, *Opers Mgr*
Hannah Diener, *Executive Asst*
Gregory Diener, *Admin Sec*
EMP: 10
SQ FT: 10,000
SALES (est): 3.7MM **Privately Held**
SIC: 5085 5075 5039 3564 Filters, industrial; air filters; air ducts, sheet metal; purification & dust collection equipment

(G-18464)
BISCO INC
1100 W Irving Park Rd (60193-3569)
PHONE..................................847 534-6000
Byoung I Suh, *President*
Julie Suh, *Vice Pres*
Larry Cohen, *Purch Agent*
Rich Nagel, *Engineer*
Byoung Suh, *Human Res Dir*
▲ **EMP:** 100 **EST:** 1981
SQ FT: 90,000
SALES (est): 18.2MM **Privately Held**
SIC: 3843 8021 Dental materials; cement, dental; compounds, dental; offices & clinics of dentists

(G-18465)
BROCADE CMMNCTIONS SYSTEMS LLC
20 N Martingale Rd # 290 (60173-2412)
PHONE..................................630 273-5530
Armando Pena, *Manager*
Vidya Renganarayanan, *Manager*
Kristine Wedum, *Manager*
EMP: 15
SALES (corp-wide): 22.6B **Publicly Held**
WEB: www.brocade.com
SIC: 3674 Semiconductors & related devices
HQ: Brocade Communications Systems Llc
130 Holger Way
San Jose CA 95134

(G-18466)
CACINI INC
Also Called: Sign-A-Rama
711 E Golf Rd (60173-4511)
PHONE..................................847 884-1162
Kim Brancamp, *President*
Vern Brancamp, *Vice Pres*
EMP: 8
SQ FT: 2,000
SALES (est): 788.3K **Privately Held**
SIC: 3993 5199 Signs & advertising specialties; advertising specialties

(G-18467)
CAPITOL COIL INC
821 Albion Ave Ste B (60193-4522)
PHONE..................................847 891-1390
David Jablonski, *President*
Edwin Jablonski, *President*
Michael Jablonski, *Treasurer*
▲ **EMP:** 15 **EST:** 1932
SQ FT: 6,500
SALES: 1.3MM **Privately Held**
WEB: www.capitolcoil.com
SIC: 3495 3496 3493 Mechanical springs, precision; miscellaneous fabricated wire products; steel springs, except wire

(G-18468)
CATAPULT COMMUNICATIONS CORP
1821 Walden Office Sq # 120 (60173-4295)
PHONE..................................847 884-0048
Toni Biesterfeld, *Manager*
EMP: 7
SALES (corp-wide): 4.3B **Publicly Held**
SIC: 7372 7371 Prepackaged software; computer software development
HQ: Catapult Communications Corporation
26601 Agoura Rd
Calabasas CA 91302
818 871-1800

(G-18469)
CERATIZIT CHICAGO HOLDING INC (DH)
Also Called: Komet of America Holding, Inc.
2050 Mitchell Blvd (60193-4544)
PHONE..................................847 923-8400
Dietmar Bolkhart, *President*
F Hans Grandin, *Principal*
Dan Corrigan, *Engineer*
Tim Lewerenz, *Engineer*
John Catanzaro, *Design Engr*
EMP: 13
SQ FT: 67,000
SALES (est): 25.1MM
SALES (corp-wide): 5.2MM **Privately Held**
SIC: 3541 3365 Machine tools, metal cutting type; aerospace castings, aluminum
HQ: Komet Deutschland Gmbh
Zeppelinstr. 3
Besigheim 74354
714 337-30

(G-18470)
CERATIZIT CHICAGO INC
Also Called: Komet of America, Inc.
2050 Mitchell Blvd (60193-4544)
PHONE..................................847 923-8400
Jan Pflugfelder, *President*
Dietmar Bolkhart, *Vice Pres*
Thomas Brand, *Vice Pres*
Peter Hoeger, *CFO*
Bob Karl, *Technology*
▲ **EMP:** 180 **EST:** 1982
SQ FT: 90,000
SALES (est): 22.4MM
SALES (corp-wide): 5.2MM **Privately Held**
SIC: 3541 Machine tools, metal cutting type
HQ: Ceratizit Chicago Holding Inc.
2050 Mitchell Blvd
Schaumburg IL 60193
847 923-8400

(G-18471)
CERVONES WELDING SERVICE INC
1104 Lunt Ave (60193-4421)
PHONE..................................847 985-6865
Michael Cervone, *President*
EMP: 5
SQ FT: 3,500
SALES (est): 466.6K **Privately Held**
SIC: 7692 3441 Welding repair; fabricated structural metal

(G-18472)
CF SOLUTIONS CO
725 E Weathersfield Way (60193-4311)
PHONE..................................630 413-9058
Fidanka Timova, *Principal*
EMP: 2
SALES (est): 204.1K **Privately Held**
SIC: 3537 Cranes, industrial truck

(G-18473)
CH GROUP HOLDINGS INC
Also Called: Procura, LLC
900 National Pkwy Ste 100 (60173-5146)
PHONE..................................888 428-6614
Christopher Junker, *CEO*
Kathy Pruitt, *Vice Pres*
John Walles, *CFO*
Chris Azar, *CIO*
EMP: 9
SALES (est): 582.5K
SALES (corp-wide): 12.9MM **Privately Held**
SIC: 7372 Prepackaged software
PA: Develus Systems Inc
1112 Fort St Suite 600
Victoria BC
250 388-0880

(G-18474)
CHARLES INDUSTRIES LLC (HQ)
1450 American Ln Fl 20 (60173-6090)
PHONE..................................847 806-6300
Richard Adam Norwitt, *CEO*
Dennis Bednar, *Vice Pres*
Minesh Patel, *Vice Pres*
Jason Vincent, *Foreman/Supr*
Jim Kasman, *Purch Mgr*
◆ **EMP:** 60
SQ FT: 30,000
SALES (est): 114.4MM
SALES (corp-wide): 8.2B **Publicly Held**
WEB: www.charlesindustries.com
SIC: 3661 3629 3677 Telephones & telephone apparatus; electronic generation equipment; electronic transformers
PA: Amphenol Corporation
358 Hall Ave
Wallingford CT 06492
203 265-8900

(G-18475)
CHICAGO FREIGHT CAR LEASING CO (HQ)
Also Called: Cfcl
425 N Martingale Rd Fl 6 (60173-2301)
P.O. Box 75129, Chicago (60675-5129)
PHONE..................................847 318-8000
Fred Sasser, *CEO*
Paul Deasy, *President*
Shad Peterson, *COO*
Josh Chesser, *Vice Pres*
John Cooney, *Vice Pres*
EMP: 59 **EST:** 1947
SQ FT: 9,500
SALES (est): 70.7MM
SALES (corp-wide): 105.2MM **Privately Held**
WEB: www.crdx.com
SIC: 4741 3643 Rental of railroad cars; electric switches
PA: Sasser Family Holdings, Inc.
425 N Martingale Rd Fl 8
Schaumburg IL 60173
800 517-0455

(G-18476)
CHILL PASSION (PA)
760 N Brookdale Dr (60194-4521)
PHONE..................................847 778-6121
▲ **EMP:** 3
SALES (est): 319.9K **Privately Held**
WEB: www.chillpassion.com
SIC: 3585 Refrigeration & heating equipment

(G-18477)
CIFUENTES LUIS & NICOLE INC
Also Called: AlphaGraphics
636 Remington Rd Ste D (60173-5612)
PHONE..................................847 490-3660
Luis Cifuentes, *President*
Catherine Cifuntes, *General Mgr*
Nicole Cifuentes, *Admin Sec*
EMP: 9
SALES (est): 1.5MM **Privately Held**
SIC: 2752 2791 2789 2759 Commercial printing, lithographic; typesetting; bookbinding & related work; commercial printing

(G-18478)
CKD USA CORPORATION (HQ)
1605 N Penny Ln (60173-4555)
PHONE..................................847 368-0539
Atsumi Nonoda, *President*
Tim Cochrane, *Corp Secy*
Scott Abbamonte, *Regl Sales Mgr*
Mick Ishimaru, *Sales Staff*
Jay Majima, *Sales Staff*
▲ **EMP:** 28
SQ FT: 13,000
SALES (est): 5MM **Privately Held**
WEB: www.ckdusa.com
SIC: 3492 3572 Control valves, aircraft: hydraulic & pneumatic; control valves, fluid power: hydraulic & pneumatic; disk drives, computer

(G-18479)
CLOOS ROBOTIC WELDING INC (DH)
Also Called: Cloos Robotics De Mexico
911 Albion Ave (60193-4550)
PHONE..................................847 923-9988
Hartmut Boegel, *President*
Manuel Petry, *Project Engr*
▲ **EMP:** 16
SQ FT: 14,000
SALES: 12MM
SALES (corp-wide): 355.8K **Privately Held**
SIC: 3542 7699 Robots for metal forming: pressing, extruding, etc.; industrial machinery & equipment repair
HQ: Carl Cloos SchweiBtechnik Gesellschaft Mit Beschrankter Haftung
Carl-Cloos-Str. 1
Haiger 35708
277 385-0

(G-18480)
CNE INC
Also Called: Sign Max
1018 Lunt Ave (60193-4419)
PHONE..................................847 534-7135
Gokan Oner, *President*
EMP: 4
SQ FT: 5,000
SALES (est): 498.7K **Privately Held**
SIC: 3993 Electric signs; neon signs

(G-18481)
COMMSCOPE TECHNOLOGIES LLC
1821 Walden Office Sq # 400 (60173-4295)
PHONE..................................847 397-6307
Ken Czosnowski, *Branch Mgr*
EMP: 4 **Publicly Held**
SIC: 3663 Radio & TV communications equipment
HQ: Commscope Technologies Llc
1100 Commscope Pl Se
Hickory NC 28602
708 236-6600

(G-18482)
COMMUNICATIONS RESOURCE INC
Also Called: Microlink Graphics
1175 Tower Rd (60173-4305)
PHONE..................................630 860-1661
Jim Noon, *President*
Michael Keyes, *Vice Pres*
EMP: 6
SQ FT: 5,600
SALES (est): 720K **Privately Held**
SIC: 7336 2741 2791 7311 Graphic arts & related design; miscellaneous publishing; typesetting; advertising agencies; outdoor advertising services; poster advertising service, except outdoor

(G-18483)
CON FORM INDUSTRY INC
561 Estes Ave (60193-4428)
PHONE..................................847 278-1143
Martin Walker, *President*
EMP: 10
SALES (est): 597.4K **Privately Held**
SIC: 3545 Precision tools, machinists'

(G-18484)
CONFORM INDUSTRIES INC
561 Estes Ave (60193-4428)
PHONE..................................630 285-0272
Marty Walker, *President*
David Selenis, *Opers Mgr*
EMP: 10
SQ FT: 7,500
SALES: 2MM **Privately Held**
SIC: 3599 3544 Grinding castings for the trade; special dies, tools, jigs & fixtures

(G-18485)
CONNOR ELECTRIC SERVICES INC
Also Called: Connor Voice and Data Tech
649 Estes Ave (60193-4402)
PHONE..................................630 823-8230
Lisa Szlenk, *President*
John Szlenk Jr, *Principal*
Frank Zator, *Vice Pres*
Paul Pratscher, *Technician*
EMP: 24
SALES (est): 6.7MM **Privately Held**
SIC: 3699 1731 Electrical equipment & supplies; electrical work

(G-18486)
CONTAINER GRAPHICS CORP
492 Lunt Ave (60193-4408)
PHONE..................................847 584-0299

GEOGRAPHIC SECTION

Schaumburg - Cook County (G-18514)

Wayne Wisinski, *Branch Mgr*
EMP: 25
SALES (corp-wide): 3MM **Privately Held**
WEB: www.containergraphics.com
SIC: 3555 Printing trades machinery
PA: Container Graphics Corp.
114 Ednbrgh S Dr Ste 104
Cary NC 27511
919 481-4200

(G-18487)
CONTROL EQUIPMENT COMPANY INC
1115 Morse Ave (60193-4505)
PHONE.................847 891-7500
James M Pish, *President*
Jerry J Pish, *Admin Sec*
EMP: 10
SQ FT: 19,000
SALES (est): 1.3MM **Privately Held**
SIC: 3822 3494 3444 Damper operators; pneumatic, thermostatic, electric; valves & pipe fittings; sheet metalwork

(G-18488)
CONTROL RESEARCH INC
908 Albion Ave (60193-4551)
P.O. Box 4103, Redondo Beach CA (90277-1745)
PHONE.................847 352-4920
Lars Malmborg, *President*
EMP: 4
SQ FT: 6,000
SALES (est): 380K **Privately Held**
SIC: 3625 Electric controls & control accessories, industrial

(G-18489)
CONVERTING SYSTEMS INC
1045 Remington Rd (60173-4517)
PHONE.................847 519-0232
William Englehardt, *President*
Bonnie Engelhardt, *Director*
Marty Nixon, *Admin Sec*
EMP: 4
SALES (est): 897.4K **Privately Held**
SIC: 7373 3829 Systems engineering, computer related; measuring & controlling devices

(G-18490)
CONVR ENTERPRISES INC
425 N Martingale Rd # 700 (60173-2406)
PHONE.................888 507-9793
Bruce Simpson, *President*
Phil Alampi, *Vice Pres*
Ramesh Natarajan, *Engineer*
Rikin Mehta, *Manager*
Graham Gudmestad, *Director*
EMP: 30 **EST:** 2015
SALES (est): 133.3K **Privately Held**
SIC: 7372 Prepackaged software

(G-18491)
CORUS AMERICA INC
475 N Martingale Rd # 400 (60173-2257)
PHONE.................847 585-2599
Dean Blakeney, *General Mgr*
EMP: 24
SQ FT: 800
SALES (est): 1.6MM **Privately Held**
SIC: 3355 Aluminum rolling & drawing

(G-18492)
CREATIVE HI-TECH LTD
710 Cooper Ct (60173-4537)
PHONE.................224 653-4000
Popatlal Radadia, *President*
Mukesh Vasani, *Vice Pres*
Gopal Radadia, *Opers Mgr*
Mitali Shah, *Project Engr*
EMP: 50
SQ FT: 30,000
SALES (est): 7.8MM **Privately Held**
WEB: www.creativehitech.com
SIC: 3672 Printed circuit boards

(G-18493)
CREATIVE LITHOCRAFT INC (PA)
1730 Wright Blvd (60193-4514)
PHONE.................847 352-7002
Charles Horist, *President*
Carol Horist, *Treasurer*
EMP: 14 **EST:** 1981
SALES (est): 1.1MM **Privately Held**
WEB: www.creativelithocraft.com
SIC: 2759 2752 Embossing on paper; commercial printing, offset

(G-18494)
CRESCEND TECHNOLOGIES LLC (PA)
140 E State Pkwy (60173-5335)
PHONE.................847 908-5400
Jim Hougo, *President*
Lawrence Fitzgerald, *Vice Pres*
Grace Lopez, *Purch Mgr*
Duda Markovic, *Purch Mgr*
Arkady Kostukovsky, *Engineer*
▲ **EMP:** 21
SQ FT: 15,000
SALES (est): 7.8MM **Privately Held**
WEB: www.crescendtech.com
SIC: 3663 Amplifiers, RF power & IF

(G-18495)
CRESTWOOD ASSOCIATES LLC
1501 E Wdfeld Rd Ste 113e (60173)
PHONE.................847 394-8820
Brian J McGuckin,
Diane Grayson, *Sr Consultant*
EMP: 16
SALES (est): 2.5MM **Privately Held**
SIC: 7372 Business oriented computer software

(G-18496)
CRONUS TECHNOLOGIES INC
424 E State Pkwy (60173-6405)
PHONE.................847 839-0088
EMP: 93 **EST:** 1994
SALES (est): 9.8MM **Privately Held**
SIC: 7373 3661 Computer Systems Design Mfg Telephone/Telegraph Apparatus

(G-18497)
CROWN EQUIPMENT CORPORATION
Also Called: Crown Lift Trucks
2055 Hammond Dr (60173-3809)
PHONE.................847 397-1900
Pat Cvengros, *Sales Staff*
Kevin Miller, *Manager*
EMP: 110
SALES (corp-wide): 6.3B **Privately Held**
SIC: 3537 Lift trucks, industrial: fork, platform, straddle, etc.
PA: Crown Equipment Corporation
44 S Washington St
New Bremen OH 45869
419 629-2311

(G-18498)
CRYSTAL PARTNERS INC
838 Prince Charles Ct (60195-2933)
PHONE.................847 882-0467
William Russell, *President*
EMP: 1
SQ FT: 2,400
SALES (est): 240.2K **Privately Held**
SIC: 3651 Household audio equipment

(G-18499)
CUBE TOMATO INC
636 Remington Rd Ste B (60173-5612)
PHONE.................224 653-2655
EMP: 3
SALES (est): 240K **Privately Held**
SIC: 2721 Periodicals-Publishing/Printing

(G-18500)
CUMBERLAND ENGRG ENTPS INC
1100 E Wdfield Rd Ste 550 (60173)
PHONE.................314 727-5550
Sam Fox, *CEO*
Tom Breslin, *President*
EMP: 300
SALES (est): 1.9MM
SALES (corp-wide): 1.5B **Privately Held**
SIC: 3559 Plastics working machinery
PA: Harbour Group Ltd.
7733 Forsyth Blvd Fl 23
Saint Louis MO 63105
314 727-5550

(G-18501)
CUSTOM ASSEMBLY SOLUTIONS INC
Also Called: Nortech, Inc.
101 E State Pkwy (60173-5336)
PHONE.................847 224-5800
Bojan Jovanovic, *President*
Sarah Taylor, *Vice Pres*
Joanne Schulman, *Office Mgr*
Petar Premovic, *Maintence Staff*
▲ **EMP:** 12
SQ FT: 2,500
SALES (est): 3MM
SALES (corp-wide): 1.1B **Privately Held**
SIC: 3549 Assembly machines, including robotic
HQ: Intertape Polymer Woven Usa Inc.
100 Paramount Dr Ste 300
Sarasota FL 34232
800 474-8273

(G-18502)
CUSTOM PRECISION INC
555 Estes Ave (60193-4428)
PHONE.................847 278-7877
Andreas Joerg, *President*
EMP: 3 **EST:** 2016
SALES (est): 355.8K **Privately Held**
SIC: 3599 Machine shop, jobbing & repair

(G-18503)
D AND R TECH
1118 Lunt Ave Ste F (60193-4441)
PHONE.................224 353-6693
John Traple, *Principal*
EMP: 3
SALES (est): 269.4K **Privately Held**
SIC: 2851 Paints & allied products

(G-18504)
DANA PLASTIC CONTAINER CORP
200 W Central Rd (60195-1909)
P.O. Box 545, Arlington Heights (60006-0545)
PHONE.................630 529-7878
Daniel Hiddings, *Manager*
EMP: 21
SALES (corp-wide): 15.6MM **Privately Held**
SIC: 3085 3083 Plastics bottles; laminated plastics plate & sheet
HQ: Dana Plastic Container Corp
6 N Hickory Ave
Arlington Heights IL 60004

(G-18505)
DEPT 28 INC
1169 Tower Rd (60173-4305)
P.O. Box 3722, Barrington (60011-3722)
PHONE.................847 285-1343
Andrzej Ciesielski, *Principal*
▲ **EMP:** 4
SALES (est): 213.7K **Privately Held**
WEB: www.dep28.com
SIC: 2082 Malt liquors

(G-18506)
DIEBOLD NIXDORF INCORPORATED
900 National Pkwy Ste 420 (60173-5168)
PHONE.................847 598-3300
Brad Browder, *General Mgr*
John Lodolce, *Manager*
EMP: 60
SALES (corp-wide): 4.4B **Publicly Held**
WEB: www.dieboldnixdorf.com
SIC: 3578 5044 Automatic teller machines (ATM); vaults & safes
PA: Diebold Nixdorf, Incorporated
5995 Mayfair Rd
North Canton OH 44720
330 490-4000

(G-18507)
DIVINE SIGNS INC
Also Called: Divine Signs & Graphics
601 Estes Ave (60193-4402)
PHONE.................847 534-9220
Jeffrey W Miller, *CEO*
Michele M Miller, *Admin Sec*
EMP: 6
SALES (est): 966.4K **Privately Held**
SIC: 3993 Signs & advertising specialties

(G-18508)
DK PRECISION INC
614 Lunt Ave (60193-4411)
PHONE.................847 985-8008
Donald F Knapp Sr, *President*
Donald E Knapp Jr, *Vice Pres*
EMP: 6
SQ FT: 4,400
SALES (est): 892.4K **Privately Held**
SIC: 3599 Machine shop, jobbing & repair

(G-18509)
DML DISTRIBUTION INC
Also Called: D M L
1814 W Weathersfield Way (60193-2338)
PHONE.................630 839-9041
Dan Long, *President*
▲ **EMP:** 16 **EST:** 2007
SALES (est): 1.4MM **Privately Held**
SIC: 3452 Screws, metal

(G-18510)
DYSON INC
1025 E Golf Rd (60173-4505)
PHONE.................847 995-8010
Georgina Jackson, *Advt Staff*
Richard Pityinski, *Manager*
EMP: 4 **Privately Held**
WEB: www.dyson.com
SIC: 3635 Household vacuum cleaners
HQ: Dyson, Inc.
1330 W Fulton St Fl 5
Chicago IL 60607
312 469-5950

(G-18511)
E+E ELEKTRONIK CORPORATION
333 E State Pkwy (60173-5337)
PHONE.................847 490-0520
Rick Korte, *President*
Martin Bussert, *CFO*
Veenstra Dan, *Sales Staff*
EMP: 7
SALES (est): 630.1K
SALES (corp-wide): 72K **Privately Held**
SIC: 3823 Industrial instrmnts msrmnt display/control process variable
PA: Dr. Johannes Heidenhain-Stiftung Gmbh
Dr.-Johannes-Heidenhain-Str. 5
Traunreut
866 931-0

(G-18512)
EAGLE CAPITAL GROUP INC
Also Called: Eagle Electronics
1735 Mitchell Blvd (60193-4528)
PHONE.................847 891-5800
Mike Kalaria, *President*
Madhukar S Kalaria, *Principal*
Brett McCoy, *Vice Pres*
Mavjibhai Lakhani, *Shareholder*
Ghanshyam Patel, *Shareholder*
EMP: 90
SQ FT: 45,000
SALES (est): 14.6MM **Privately Held**
SIC: 3672 Circuit boards, television & radio printed

(G-18513)
EBOOKS2GO
1111 N Plaza Dr Ste 652 (60173-4951)
PHONE.................847 598-1145
Ramana Abbaraju, *Principal*
John Bean, *Mktg Coord*
Leslie Chirchirillo, *Manager*
Suresh Sermugasamy, *Technical Staff*
EMP: 5 **EST:** 2011
SALES (est): 177.4K **Privately Held**
WEB: www.ebooks2go.net
SIC: 2731 Book publishing

(G-18514)
ECMC INC
1517 Wright Blvd (60193-4509)
PHONE.................847 352-5015
Daniel T Olson, *President*
G J Gordy Kissner, *General Mgr*
Arvind Patel, *President*
Jitu Shah, *Finance Mgr*
Warren Barnes, *Technical Staff*
EMP: 28
SALES (est): 3.1MM **Privately Held**
SIC: 3672 Printed circuit boards

Schaumburg - Cook County (G-18515)

(G-18515)
EFFICI INC
939 N Plum Grove Rd (60173-5183)
PHONE.....................401 584-2266
Michael Stolarz, *CEO*
EMP: 6 EST: 2017
SALES (est): 135.3K **Privately Held**
SIC: 7372 Application computer software

(G-18516)
ELECTRO-CIRCUITS INC
1651 Mitchell Blvd (60193-4526)
PHONE.....................630 339-3389
Dal Vaghasiya, *President*
EMP: 35 EST: 1981
SQ FT: 50,000
SALES (est): 4.9MM **Privately Held**
SIC: 3672 Printed circuit boards

(G-18517)
ELIM PDTRIC PHRMACEUTICALS INC
1141 Tower Rd (60173-4305)
PHONE.....................412 266-5968
EMP: 50
SALES (corp-wide): 4.3MM **Privately Held**
SIC: 2834 Pharmaceutical preparations
PA: Elim Pediatric Pharmaceuticals Inc.
   Corp Ctr 1600
   Rolling Meadows IL 60008
   412 266-5968

(G-18518)
ENERGY PARTS SOLUTIONS INC
820 Estes Ave (60193-4407)
PHONE.....................224 653-9412
Marek Przepiorka, *President*
Dan McCarthy, *Admin Sec*
EMP: 12 EST: 2005
SQ FT: 18,500
SALES (est): 3.4MM **Privately Held**
WEB: www.energypartssolutions.com
SIC: 3511 Steam turbines

(G-18519)
EQUUS POWER I LP (PA)
1900 E Golf Rd Ste 1030 (60173-5076)
PHONE.....................847 908-2878
Tk Komiyama, *Principal*
Equus GP Holdco LLC, *General Ptnr*
EMP: 3
SALES (est): 733K **Privately Held**
WEB: www.jpowerusa.com
SIC: 3612 Transformers, except electric

(G-18520)
ESPEE BIOPHARMA & FINECHEM LLC
1701 E Wdfield Rd Ste 636 (60173)
PHONE.....................224 355-5950
Dru West, *Principal*
David Everett, *Principal*
EMP: 4
SALES (est): 314.1K **Privately Held**
SIC: 2834 Druggists' preparations (pharmaceuticals)

(G-18521)
ESPEE BIOPHARMA & FINECHEM LLC
1701 E Woodfield Rd # 636 (60173-5905)
PHONE.....................888 851-6667
Ravi Patel,
Alka Shah,
▲ EMP: 4
SALES (est): 2.5MM **Privately Held**
SIC: 5122 2834 Pharmaceuticals; pharmaceutical preparations

(G-18522)
ESSEX ELECTRO ENGINEERS INC
2015 Mitchell Blvd (60193-4563)
PHONE.....................847 891-4444
Frank Pawlowski, *CEO*
Glenn F Pawlowski, *President*
Mark Pichla, *Purch Mgr*
John Loo, *Electrical Engi*
Mary Lou Pawlowski, *Admin Sec*
▲ EMP: 30 EST: 1964
SQ FT: 50,000
SALES (est): 14MM **Privately Held**
WEB: www.essexelectro.com
SIC: 3679 3724 3625 7389 Power supplies, all types: static; nonelectric starters, aircraft; control circuit relays, industrial; control equipment, electric; interior designer

(G-18523)
ESTES LASER & MFG INC
930 Lunt Ave (60193-4417)
PHONE.....................847 301-8231
Peter Tararo, *President*
EMP: 13
SQ FT: 7,500
SALES (est): 2.5MM **Privately Held**
SIC: 3444 Sheet metalwork

(G-18524)
ETEL INC
333 E State Pkwy (60173-5337)
PHONE.....................847 519-3380
Rick Korte, *President*
Arthur Holvknecht, *Vice Pres*
▲ EMP: 6 EST: 1999
SQ FT: 1,000
SALES: 3MM
SALES (corp-wide): 72K **Privately Held**
SIC: 3559 Electronic component making machinery
HQ: Heidenhain Corporation
   333 E State Pkwy
   Schaumburg IL 60173
   847 490-1191

(G-18525)
FASTWAY PRINTING INC
Also Called: Fastway Printing Service
14 E Schaumburg Rd Ste 3 (60194-3555)
PHONE.....................847 882-0950
Chirag N Patel, *President*
Shilpa C Patel, *Admin Sec*
EMP: 3
SALES (est): 134.9K **Privately Held**
SIC: 2752 2789 Commercial printing, offset; bookbinding & related work

(G-18526)
FBC INDUSTRIES INC (PA)
1933 N Meacham Rd Ste 550 (60173-4342)
PHONE.....................847 241-6143
Robert W Bloom, *President*
Felicia S Bloom, *Corp Secy*
▲ EMP: 6
SQ FT: 3,500
SALES (est): 5.2MM **Privately Held**
SIC: 2099 Emulsifiers, food

(G-18527)
FETZER SURGICAL LLC
1019 W Wise Rd Ste 201 (60193-3754)
PHONE.....................630 635-2520
Chad Fetzer,
Max Fetzer,
EMP: 5
SALES (est): 218.2M **Privately Held**
SIC: 3841 Surgical & medical instruments

(G-18528)
FINISHING GROUP
1300 Basswood Rd Ste 200r (60173-4522)
PHONE.....................847 884-4890
Terry Reed, *Owner*
EMP: 7 EST: 2011
SALES (est): 360K **Privately Held**
WEB: www.thefinishinggroup.com
SIC: 2732 Books: printing & binding

(G-18529)
FIREFLY MOBILE INC
1325 Remington Rd Ste H (60173-4815)
PHONE.....................305 538-2777
Patrick Marry, *President*
Don Deubler, *Vice Pres*
Donald Deubler Jr, *Vice Pres*
James Heagney, *CFO*
▲ EMP: 25
SQ FT: 3,000
SALES (est): 1.9MM **Privately Held**
SIC: 5999 3661 Mobile telephones & equipment; telephone sets, all types except cellular radio

(G-18530)
FLUID-AIRE DYNAMICS INC
Also Called: Pneutech Products
530 Albion Ave (60193-4594)
PHONE.....................847 678-8388
Garth Taylor, *President*
Kevin Taylor, *General Mgr*
Derrick Taylor, *Vice Pres*
Terry Pomer, *Accounts Exec*
Matthew Barnas, *Sales Engr*
▲ EMP: 28
SQ FT: 15,000
SALES (est): 8.9MM **Privately Held**
SIC: 3563 7699 3053 Air & gas compressors; compressor repair; packing: steam engines, pipe joints, air compressors, etc.

(G-18531)
FUJI OOZX AMERICA INC
1051 Perimeter Dr # 1175 (60173-5075)
PHONE.....................281 888-2247
AP Jyunko, *President*
EMP: 3
SALES (est): 170K **Privately Held**
SIC: 3711 Automobile assembly, including specialty automobiles

(G-18532)
FUTABA CORPORATION OF AMERICA (HQ)
711 E State Pkwy (60173-4530)
PHONE.....................847 884-1444
Takahiro Kuroda, *President*
Drew Haight, *Engineer*
Craig Henry, *CFO*
Akihiro Kishima, *Sales Staff*
Irma Boada, *Manager*
▲ EMP: 15
SQ FT: 27,000
SALES (est): 28.4MM **Privately Held**
SIC: 3671 Vacuum tubes

(G-18533)
GANNON GRAPHICS
1025 Morse Ave (60193-4503)
PHONE.....................847 895-1043
Gannon Marty, *Principal*
Martin Gannon, *Principal*
Joanie Gannon, *Office Mgr*
Carol Hulsey, *Supervisor*
EMP: 2 EST: 2012
SALES (est): 270.1K **Privately Held**
SIC: 2752 Commercial printing, offset

(G-18534)
GANTEC PUBG SOLUTIONS LLC
1827 Walden Office Sq # 260 (60173-4294)
PHONE.....................847 598-1144
Ramana Abbaraju, *CEO*
Lakshmi Abbaraju,
Krishna Mannuru,
EMP: 17
SQ FT: 3,000
SALES: 2MM **Privately Held**
SIC: 2741 Technical manual & paper publishing

(G-18535)
GLOBAL BRASS COP HOLDINGS INC (DH)
475 N Martingale Rd # 1050 (60173-2256)
PHONE.....................847 240-4700
John H Walker, *Ch of Bd*
John J Wasz, *President*
Kevin W Bense, *President*
Devin K Denner, *President*
William G Toler, *President*
EMP: 25
SALES: 1.7B
SALES (corp-wide): 4.8MM **Privately Held**
SIC: 3341 3469 3351 Copper smelting & refining (secondary); metal stampings; brass rolling & drawing
HQ: Wieland Holdings, Inc.
   567 Northgate Pkwy
   Wheeling IL 60090
   847 537-3990

(G-18536)
GM PARTNERS
219 Lundy Ln (60193-1709)
PHONE.....................847 895-7627
Steve Gorfsmin, *Partner*
Steve Grossman, *Partner*
Jeff Kuhn, *Partner*
EMP: 3
SALES: 150K **Privately Held**
WEB: www.gmpartners.com
SIC: 4226 3999 Household goods, warehousing; pet supplies

(G-18537)
GOLF TEE PRINTERS INC
550 Pratt Ave N (60193-4555)
PHONE.....................973 328-4008
Tony Rossi, *President*
Stacey Riley,
EMP: 6
SALES (est): 390.3K **Privately Held**
SIC: 2759 Screen printing

(G-18538)
GONNELLA BAKING CO (PA)
1117 Wiley Rd (60173-4337)
PHONE.....................312 733-2020
Nick Marcucci, *President*
Steve Hanrahan, *General Mgr*
Larry Klasen, *District Mgr*
Dave Gonnella, *Vice Pres*
Robert Gonnella Jr, *Vice Pres*
▲ EMP: 60 EST: 1886
SQ FT: 35,000
SALES (est): 113.6MM **Privately Held**
WEB: www.gonnella.com
SIC: 2051 5812 2099 2038 Bread, all types (white, wheat, rye, etc): fresh or frozen; eating places; food preparations; frozen specialties

(G-18539)
GONNELLA BAKING CO
Gonnella Frozen Products Div
1117 Wiley Rd (60173-4337)
PHONE.....................312 733-2020
Kenneth Gonnella, *Manager*
EMP: 90
SALES (corp-wide): 113.6MM **Privately Held**
WEB: www.gonnella.com
SIC: 2051 Bread, all types (white, wheat, rye, etc): fresh or frozen; pastries, e.g. danish: except frozen
PA: Gonnella Baking Co.
   1117 Wiley Rd
   Schaumburg IL 60173
   312 733-2020

(G-18540)
GONNELLA FROZEN PRODUCTS LLC (HQ)
1117 Wiley Rd (60173-4337)
PHONE.....................847 884-8829
Nicholas Marcucci, *President*
Kent Beernink, *Plant Mgr*
Anthony Mazukelli, *Sales Mgr*
Meg Donnell, *Sales Staff*
Gina Christophe, *Manager*
EMP: 154 EST: 1886
SALES (est): 79.5MM
SALES (corp-wide): 113.6MM **Privately Held**
WEB: www.gonnella.com
SIC: 2051 Bread, all types (white, wheat, rye, etc): fresh or frozen; rolls, bread type: fresh or frozen
PA: Gonnella Baking Co.
   1117 Wiley Rd
   Schaumburg IL 60173
   312 733-2020

(G-18541)
GREEN BOX AMERICA INC
1900 E Golf Rd Ste 950 (60173-5034)
PHONE.....................630 616-5400
Sasha Logan, *President*
Michael Teysar, *Sales Staff*
Michael Peyser, *Director*
▲ EMP: 3 EST: 2009
SALES: 1MM **Privately Held**
WEB: www.greenboxamerica.com
SIC: 3585 Parts for heating, cooling & refrigerating equipment

(G-18542)
HAMALOT INC (PA)
Also Called: Electrowire
933 Remington Rd (60173-4515)
PHONE.....................847 944-1500
Mickey M Hamano, *President*

GEOGRAPHIC SECTION

Schaumburg - Cook County (G-18569)

Kevin Mc Namara, *Vice Pres*
Jen Gilbert, *Purch Mgr*
Thomas Fair, *Engrg Mgr*
Patrick McNamara, *Sales Staff*
▲ **EMP:** 25
SQ FT: 116,000
SALES (est): 71MM **Privately Held**
SIC: 5063 3496 3315 Wire & cable; electronic wire & cable; miscellaneous fabricated wire products; steel wire & related products

(G-18543)
HAVING A GOOD TIME
1710 E Woodfield Rd (60173-5153)
PHONE...................................847 330-8460
EMP: 3
SALES (est): 294.7K **Privately Held**
SIC: 2131 Smoking tobacco

(G-18544)
HEALTHLIGHT LLC
920 E State Pkwy Unit B (60173-4527)
PHONE...................................224 231-0342
Warren Graber, *President*
Donald Baldwin, *CFO*
EMP: 11
SALES (est): 2MM **Privately Held**
SIC: 3845 Electromedical apparatus

(G-18545)
HEIDENHAIN CORPORATION (DH)
333 E State Pkwy (60173-5337)
PHONE...................................847 490-1191
Ludwig Wagatha, *Ch of Bd*
Rick J Korte, *President*
David Doyle, *Vice Pres*
Kathleen Stoneski, *Pub Rel Mgr*
David Armstrong, *CFO*
▲ **EMP:** 68
SQ FT: 110,000
SALES (est): 25.7MM
SALES (corp-wide): 72K **Privately Held**
WEB: www.heidenhain.com
SIC: 5084 3825 Measuring & testing equipment, electrical; instruments to measure electricity

(G-18546)
HEIDENHAIN HOLDING INC (DH)
333 E State Pkwy (60173-5337)
PHONE...................................716 661-1700
Rainer Burkhard, *Ch of Bd*
Dr Thomas Sesselmann, *Systems Staff*
Sally Overend, *Admin Sec*
▲ **EMP:** 2
SQ FT: 118,000
SALES (est): 49.6MM
SALES (corp-wide): 72K **Privately Held**
SIC: 3545 5084 Machine tool accessories; measuring & testing equipment, electrical
HQ: Dr. Johannes Heidenhain Gesellschaft Mit Beschrankter Haftung
Dr.-Johannes-Heidenhain-Str. 5
Traunreut 83301
866 931-0

(G-18547)
HELP/SYSTEMS LLC
1920 Thoreau Dr N Ste 165 (60173-4151)
PHONE...................................847 605-1311
EMP: 4
SALES (corp-wide): 79.8MM **Privately Held**
SIC: 7372 Prepackaged Software Services
PA: Help/Systems, Llc
6455 City West Pkwy
Eden Prairie MN 55344
952 933-0209

(G-18548)
HI-GRADE WELDING AND MFG LLC
Also Called: Hi-Grade Welding & Mfg
140 Commerce Dr (60173-5328)
PHONE...................................847 640-8172
Jon Frejd, *Vice Pres*
Broun Stephen, *Mng Member*
Krafcisin John, *Mng Member*
▼ **EMP:** 44
SQ FT: 48,000
SALES (est): 10.6MM
SALES (corp-wide): 1.4B **Publicly Held**
SIC: 3599 Machine shop, jobbing & repair

HQ: Capital For Business, Inc.
11 S Meramec Ave Ste 1330
Saint Louis MO 63105
314 746-7427

(G-18549)
HILLSHIRE BRANDS COMPANY
Bil Mar Foods
1355 Remington Rd Ste U (60173-4818)
PHONE...................................847 310-9400
Denis Raptata, *Branch Mgr*
EMP: 8
SALES (corp-wide): 42.4B **Publicly Held**
SIC: 2013 Sausages from purchased meat
HQ: The Hillshire Brands Company
400 S Jefferson St Fl 1
Chicago IL 60607
312 614-6000

(G-18550)
HK PAPER (USA) INC (PA)
943 N Plum Grove Rd Ste A (60173-4779)
PHONE...................................847 969-9600
Youshinori Kawaashima, *President*
Mike Ozawa, *Vice Pres*
EMP: 5
SALES (est): 850.5K **Privately Held**
SIC: 3089 Vulcanized fiber plates, sheets, rods or tubes

(G-18551)
HP INC
1124 Tower Rd (60173-4306)
PHONE...................................650 857-1501
Denitra Morris, *Branch Mgr*
EMP: 135
SALES (corp-wide): 58.7B **Publicly Held**
SIC: 3571 Personal computers (microcomputers)
PA: Hp, Inc.
1501 Page Mill Rd
Palo Alto CA 94304
650 857-1501

(G-18552)
HUGO BOSS USA INC
5 Woodfield Mall (60173-5012)
PHONE...................................847 517-1461
EMP: 19
SALES (corp-wide): 3.1B **Privately Held**
SIC: 5611 2299 Clothing accessories: men's & boys'; broadwoven fabrics: linen, jute, hemp & ramie
HQ: Hugo Boss Usa, Inc.
55 Water St Fl 48
New York NY 10041
212 940-0600

(G-18553)
HUNTER FOUNDRY MACHINERY CORP
2222 Hammond Dr (60196-3814)
PHONE...................................847 397-5110
William G Hunter, *President*
Jim Fitzgerald, *Vice Pres*
Linda Jones, *Vice Pres*
Kevin Purdy, *Vice Pres*
Amy Heinzl, *Senior Buyer*
◆ **EMP:** 53 **EST:** 1964
SQ FT: 120,000
SALES (est): 15.2MM **Privately Held**
WEB: www.hunterfoundry.com
SIC: 3559 Foundry machinery & equipment

(G-18554)
IDENTITI RESOURCES LTD
425 N Martingale Rd # 1800 (60173-2216)
PHONE...................................866 477-4467
Zack Sicher, *President*
Jessica Mudra, *Manager*
Susanna Donovan,
EMP: 42
SALES (est): 3.7MM **Privately Held**
SIC: 3993 8742 Signs & advertising specialties; management consulting services

(G-18555)
IDOT NORTH SIDE SIGN SHOP
201 Center Ct (60196-1096)
PHONE...................................847 705-4033
EMP: 5
SALES (est): 353.1K **Privately Held**
SIC: 3993 Signs & advertising specialties

(G-18556)
ILLINOIS PULLEY & GEAR INC
611 Lunt Ave Ste C (60193-4437)
PHONE...................................847 407-9595
Richard Wolter, *President*
Jose Flores, *Vice Pres*
Raul Flores Jr, *Treasurer*
Raul Flores, *Admin Sec*
▼ **EMP:** 6
SQ FT: 500
SALES (est): 1.9MM **Privately Held**
WEB: www.ipgbiz.com
SIC: 5085 5088 3568 Gears; pulleys; pulleys, power transmission

(G-18557)
INC MIDWEST DIE MOLD
624 Lunt Ave (60193-4411)
PHONE...................................224 353-6417
Gary Little, *Principal*
EMP: 5
SALES (est): 454.7K **Privately Held**
SIC: 3544 Industrial molds

(G-18558)
INFORMATION BUILDERS INC
20 N Martingale Rd # 430 (60173-2438)
PHONE...................................630 971-6700
Sandy Dwyer, *Accounts Exec*
Tom McKenzie, *Manager*
EMP: 40
SQ FT: 1,600
SALES (corp-wide): 217.9MM **Privately Held**
WEB: www.informationbuilders.com
SIC: 7377 5734 7372 7371 Computer rental & leasing; computer software & accessories; prepackaged software; custom computer programming services
PA: Information Builders, Inc.
2 Penn Plz Fl 28
New York NY 10121
212 736-4433

(G-18559)
INK WELL PRINTING & DESIGN LTD
604 Albion Ave (60193-4519)
PHONE...................................847 923-8060
Pete Costanza, *President*
Laurine Johnson, *Corp Secy*
EMP: 5
SQ FT: 10,000
SALES (est): 682.6K **Privately Held**
SIC: 2752 2789 Commercial printing, offset; bookbinding & related work

(G-18560)
INNOVATIVE COMPONENTS INC
1050 National Pkwy (60173-4519)
PHONE...................................847 885-9050
Mike Connor, *President*
Allison Morse, *Cust Mgr*
▲ **EMP:** 50
SQ FT: 30,326
SALES (est): 10.8MM
SALES (corp-wide): 1.2B **Privately Held**
SIC: 3089 3429 5072 Injection molding of plastics; furniture hardware; furniture hardware
PA: Essentra Plc
Avebury House
Milton Keynes BUCKS
190 835-9100

(G-18561)
INNOVATIVE MKTG SOLUTIONS INC
1320 N Plum Grove Rd (60173-4546)
PHONE...................................630 227-4300
Benjamin E Van Amerongen, *President*
John Sotos, *Admin Sec*
EMP: 12
SQ FT: 13,000
SALES (est): 3.1MM **Privately Held**
SIC: 2542 2511 Office & store showcases & display fixtures; wood household furniture

(G-18562)
INNOVATIVE PROJECTS LAB INC
150 N Martingale Rd # 838 (60173-2408)
PHONE...................................847 605-2125
Christopher Galassi, *President*

Hugh M Martin, *Director*
EMP: 2
SALES (est): 225.6K **Privately Held**
SIC: 3821 Laboratory apparatus, except heating & measuring

(G-18563)
INTERMET METALS SERVICES INC
1375 E Wdfield Rd Ste 520 (60173)
PHONE...................................847 605-1300
Timothy R Jaster, *President*
▲ **EMP:** 20
SALES (est): 5.8MM **Privately Held**
SIC: 5051 3366 Steel; bronze foundry

(G-18564)
INTERMOLDING TECHNOLOGY LLC
1420 Wright Blvd (60193-4508)
PHONE...................................847 376-8517
Helmut Mueller, *President*
EMP: 15
SALES (est): 2.1MM **Privately Held**
WEB: www.intermolding.com
SIC: 3089 Injection molding of plastics

(G-18565)
INTERNATIONAL TECHNOLOGIES INC
627 Estes Ave (60193-4402)
PHONE...................................847 301-9005
Al Gildemeister, *President*
▲ **EMP:** 2
SALES (est): 380.1K **Privately Held**
SIC: 3549 Wiredrawing & fabricating machinery & equipment, ex. die

(G-18566)
INTEX LIGHTING LLC
1300 E Wdfield Rd Ste 400 (60173)
PHONE...................................847 380-2027
Charles Gavzer, *Principal*
EMP: 4
SALES (est): 295.6K **Privately Held**
SIC: 3648 Lighting equipment

(G-18567)
INX DIGITAL INTERNATIONAL CO
150 N Martingale Rd # 700 (60173-2009)
PHONE...................................630 382-1800
◆ **EMP:** 14 **Privately Held**
SIC: 2893 Printing ink
HQ: The Inx Group Ltd
150 N Martingale Rd # 700
Schaumburg IL 60173
630 382-1800

(G-18568)
INX GROUP LTD (HQ)
150 N Martingale Rd # 700 (60173-2408)
PHONE...................................630 382-1800
Hiroshi Ota, *Ch of Bd*
Kotaro Morita, *President*
Richard Clendenning, *President*
Greg Polasik, *COO*
Akio Miyata, *Treasurer*
◆ **EMP:** 3
SQ FT: 21,000
SALES (est): 425.6MM **Privately Held**
SIC: 2893 Printing ink

(G-18569)
INX INTERNATIONAL INK CO (DH)
150 N Martingale Rd # 700 (60173-2009)
PHONE...................................630 382-1800
John Hrdlick, *CEO*
Kotaro Morita, *Ch of Bd*
Shane Bertsch, *Vice Pres*
Matthew Mason, *Vice Pres*
Ste'phan Nolla, *Production*
◆ **EMP:** 100
SQ FT: 21,000
SALES (est): 434.1MM **Privately Held**
WEB: www.inxinternational.com
SIC: 2893 Printing ink
HQ: The Inx Group Ltd
150 N Martingale Rd # 700
Schaumburg IL 60173
630 382-1800

Schaumburg - Cook County (G-18570)

(G-18570)
INX INTERNATIONAL INK CO
150 N Martingale Rd # 700 (60173-2009)
PHONE 800 233-4657
Rick Clendenning, *President*
EMP: 21 **Privately Held**
SIC: 2893 Printing ink
HQ: Inx International Ink Co.
150 N Martingale Rd # 700
Schaumburg IL 60173
630 382-1800

(G-18571)
INX INTERNATIONAL INK CO
150 N Martingale Rd # 700 (60173-2009)
PHONE 630 382-1800
Greg Hazen, *Manager*
EMP: 18 **Privately Held**
SIC: 2893 2899 Printing ink; ink or writing fluids
HQ: Inx International Ink Co.
150 N Martingale Rd # 700
Schaumburg IL 60173
630 382-1800

(G-18572)
ISCO INTERNATIONAL INC (PA)
444 E State Pkwy Ste A (60173-6424)
PHONE 630 283-3100
Gordon Reichard Jr, *CEO*
Ralph Pini, *Ch of Bd*
George Calhoun, *Principal*
Torbjorn Folkebrant, *Principal*
Stephen McCarthy, *Principal*
EMP: 4
SQ FT: 15,000
SALES (est): 12.1MM **Privately Held**
SIC: 3663 Radio receiver networks

(G-18573)
ITALIA FOODS INC
2127 Hammond Dr (60173-3811)
PHONE 847 397-4479
Arsenio Carabetta, *Ch of Bd*
Filippo Carabetta, *President*
Micolina Carabetta, *Corp Secy*
Maria Carabetta, *Exec VP*
Maria Arjmand, *Vice Pres*
▲ **EMP:** 26
SQ FT: 6,000
SALES (est): 6MM **Privately Held**
SIC: 2038 5812 2099 Ethnic foods, frozen; eating places; food preparations

(G-18574)
J R FINISHERS INC
616 Albion Ave (60193-4519)
PHONE 847 301-2556
Joe Rocco, *President*
Len Isbella, *Vice Pres*
Joe Rocco, *CFO*
EMP: 75
SQ FT: 23,000
SALES: 2MM **Privately Held**
SIC: 2789 Binding only: books, pamphlets, magazines, etc.

(G-18575)
JARVIS CORP
Also Called: Jarvis Lighting
1078 National Pkwy (60173)
PHONE 800 363-1075
Kirby Corkill, *CEO*
Sawyer Hopps, *Librarian*
▲ **EMP:** 27
SALES: 7.2MM **Privately Held**
WEB: www.jarvislights.com
SIC: 3646 Commercial indusl & institutional electric lighting fixtures

(G-18576)
JEWERLY AND BEYOND
608 Newbury Ln B (60173-4746)
PHONE 312 833-6785
Marlo Gardner, *Owner*
EMP: 4 **EST:** 2013
SALES (est): 91K **Privately Held**
SIC: 3961 7389 Costume jewelry;

(G-18577)
JJS TECHNICAL SERVICES
1900 E Golf Rd Ste 950 (60173-5034)
PHONE 847 999-4313
Joe Spratley, *Principal*
Greg Christopher, *Engineer*
EMP: 4 **EST:** 2000
SALES (est): 792.4K **Privately Held**
WEB: www.jjstech.com
SIC: 3823 Industrial instrmnts msrmnt display/control process variable

(G-18578)
JOSHI BROTHERS INC
Also Called: Country Donut
1218 S Roselle Rd (60193-4633)
PHONE 847 895-0200
Indrani Joshi, *President*
Manan Joshi, *Admin Sec*
▲ **EMP:** 23
SQ FT: 2,600
SALES: 1MM **Privately Held**
WEB: www.countydonuts.com
SIC: 2045 5812 Doughnut mixes, prepared: from purchased flour; coffee shop

(G-18579)
JOURNEY CIRCUITS INC
830 E Higgins Rd Ste 111h (60173-4792)
PHONE 630 283-0604
Sarah Fatima, *President*
Farhana Sofia, *Principal*
EMP: 3
SALES (est): 367.7K **Privately Held**
WEB: www.pcbjc.com
SIC: 3679 3672 Electronic circuits; printed circuit boards

(G-18580)
JUPITER INDUSTRIES INC (PA)
1821 Walden Office Sq # 400 (60173-4295)
PHONE 847 925-5120
George E Murphy, *President*
EMP: 1
SALES (est): 1.9MM **Privately Held**
SIC: 1711 3452 Plumbing contractors; fire sprinkler system installation; mechanical contractor; warm air heating & air conditioning contractor; bolts, nuts, rivets & washers

(G-18581)
JVC ADVANCED MEDIA USA INC
10 N Martingale Rd # 575 (60173-2298)
PHONE 630 237-2439
◆ **EMP:** 3
SALES (est): 196.5K
SALES (corp-wide): 1.9B **Privately Held**
SIC: 3695 Mfg Magnetic/Optical Recording Media
HQ: Victor Advanced Media Co.,Ltd.
2-26-5, Nihombashiningyocho
Chuo-Ku TKY
368 927-879

(G-18582)
JX NIPPON OIL & ENERGY LUBRICA
20 N Martingale Rd # 300 (60173-2412)
PHONE 847 413-2188
Sunami Motoshi, *President*
Takahashi Tomohiro, *Treasurer*
Yamaguchi Kenji, *Admin Sec*
▲ **EMP:** 16
SALES (est): 3.3MM **Privately Held**
SIC: 2992 Lubricating oils & greases
PA: Jx Group Kenko Hoken Kumiai
2-6-3, Otemachi
Chiyoda-Ku TKY 100-0

(G-18583)
JX NIPPON OIL & ENERGY USA INC (DH)
Also Called: Eneos
20 N Martingale Rd # 325 (60173-2412)
PHONE 847 413-2188
Motoshi Sunami, *President*
Hiroyuki Ishikawa, *Corp Secy*
Tomohiro Takahashi, *Vice Pres*
Thomas Hunt, *Sales Mgr*
Hiromi Takahashi, *Sales Staff*
◆ **EMP:** 20
SQ FT: 3,178
SALES (est): 65.6MM **Privately Held**
WEB: www.eneos.us
SIC: 2992 5172 Lubricating oils; lubricating oils & greases

(G-18584)
K & M PRINTING COMPANY INC
Also Called: Spotlight Graphics
1410 N Meacham Rd Frnt (60173-4845)
PHONE 847 884-1100
Ken J Stobart, *President*
Michael Stobart, *Vice Pres*
Chris Kelly, *Prdtn Mgr*
Gary Kinsman, *Prdtn Mgr*
Bonnie Weiss, *Human Res Mgr*
EMP: 95
SQ FT: 36,000
SALES (est): 25.9MM **Privately Held**
SIC: 2752 2791 2789 Commercial printing, offset; typesetting; bookbinding & related work

(G-18585)
KATO USA INC
100 Remington Rd (60173-3705)
PHONE 847 781-9500
Hiroshi Kato, *CEO*
Yuji Kato, *President*
Michael Conway, *Marketing Staff*
Nancy Sasamoto, *Admin Sec*
▲ **EMP:** 6
SALES (est): 1MM **Privately Held**
SIC: 3944 Games, toys & children's vehicles
HQ: Sekisui Kinzoku Co., Ltd.
1-24-10, Nishiochiai
Shinjuku-Ku TKY 161-0

(G-18586)
KING CIRCUIT
1651 Mitchell Blvd (60193-4526)
PHONE 630 629-7300
EMP: 35
SQ FT: 10,500
SALES (est): 2.1MM **Privately Held**
SIC: 3672 Mfg Printed Circuit Boards

(G-18587)
KITAGAWA USA INC
301 Commerce Dr (60173-5305)
PHONE 847 310-8198
Kazuya Kitagawa, *President*
Frank Fujikawa, *Vice Pres*
▲ **EMP:** 21
SQ FT: 30,000
SALES (est): 2.8MM **Privately Held**
SIC: 3545 3593 Chucks: drill, lathe or magnetic (machine tool accessories); fluid power cylinders & actuators
PA: Kitagawa Corporation
77-1, Motomachi
Fuchu HIR 726-0

(G-18588)
KITAGAWA-NORTHTECH INC
Also Called: Northtech Work Holding
301 Commerce Dr (60173-5305)
PHONE 847 310-8787
Mike Mizumoto, *President*
Yocharu Shimizu, *President*
Tim Winard, *COO*
Kenichiro Shichi, *Treasurer*
Eisuke Kondo, *Admin Sec*
▲ **EMP:** 30
SQ FT: 30,000
SALES (est): 5.2MM **Privately Held**
SIC: 3545 Chucks: drill, lathe or magnetic (machine tool accessories)
HQ: Nippon Steel Trading Americas, Inc.
200 N Martingale Rd # 801
Schaumburg IL 60173
847 882-6700

(G-18589)
KOKOKU RUBBER INC (HQ)
1375 E Wdfield Rd Ste 560 (60173)
PHONE 847 517-6770
Shinichiro Eno, *CEO*
Tomoki Eno, *President*
Toba Takashi, *Treasurer*
Charlie Hobbs, *Sales Mgr*
Yasuo Hashimoto, *Admin Sec*
▲ **EMP:** 7
SQ FT: 1,500
SALES (est): 16.6MM **Privately Held**
SIC: 3061 Automotive rubber goods (mechanical)

(G-18590)
KORHUMEL INC
Also Called: Kory Farm Equipment Division
230 Parktrail Ct (60173-2150)
PHONE 847 330-0335
Irene Korhumel, *President*
Charlotte Whetstone, *Vice Pres*
EMP: 2
SQ FT: 6,200
SALES (est): 365.5K **Privately Held**
SIC: 3523 3312 Farm machinery & equipment; tubes, steel & iron

(G-18591)
KORNICK ENTERPRISES LLC
711 E Golf Rd (60173-4511)
PHONE 847 884-1162
Philip Kornick,
Helen Kornick,
EMP: 5
SALES (est): 379.4K **Privately Held**
SIC: 3993 Signs & advertising specialties

(G-18592)
KRONOS INCORPORATED
475 N Martingale Rd # 900 (60173-2227)
PHONE 847 969-6501
Marcy Downer, *Partner*
Susan Cyr, *Vice Pres*
Carrie Norden, *Vice Pres*
Nick Ordon, *Vice Pres*
Martha Strittmater, *Vice Pres*
EMP: 15
SALES (corp-wide): 749.2MM **Privately Held**
WEB: www.kronos.com
SIC: 7372 Business oriented computer software
HQ: Kronos Incorporated
900 Chelmsford St # 312
Lowell MA 01851
978 250-9800

(G-18593)
KTM LAB SERVICE CO INC
716 Morse Ave (60193-4534)
P.O. Box 68219 (60168-0219)
PHONE 708 351-6780
Scott Kegarise, *President*
Art Mann, *Vice Pres*
Tom Turner, *Vice Pres*
EMP: 2
SQ FT: 1,000
SALES: 325K **Privately Held**
SIC: 1389 Testing, measuring, surveying & analysis services

(G-18594)
KURIYAMA OF AMERICA INC (HQ)
360 E State Pkwy (60173-5335)
PHONE 847 755-0360
Brian Dutton, *President*
Jay Henthorn, *Plant Mgr*
Tony Persico, *Opers Mgr*
Chantell Van Leer, *Opers Mgr*
Bobbi Gross, *Purchasing*
◆ **EMP:** 80 **EST:** 1968
SQ FT: 170,000
SALES (est): 89.9MM **Privately Held**
SIC: 5085 3052 Hose, belting & packing; rubber & plastics hose & beltings

(G-18595)
L K BEUTEL MACHINING CO INC
536 Morse Ave (60193-4530)
PHONE 847 895-5310
Ludwig K Beutel, *President*
EMP: 3
SQ FT: 2,500
SALES (est): 426.3K **Privately Held**
SIC: 3599 Machine shop, jobbing & repair

(G-18596)
LAIRD CONNECTIVITY INC
1751 Wilkening Ct (60173-5310)
PHONE 847 839-6000
Scott Lordo, *CEO*
Alexis Reggie, *Finance Mgr*
EMP: 3
SALES (corp-wide): 177.9K **Privately Held**
SIC: 3674 Computer logic modules

GEOGRAPHIC SECTION

Schaumburg - Cook County (G-18624)

HQ: Laird Connectivity, Inc.
50 S Main St Ste 1100
Akron OH 44308
330 434-7929

(G-18597)
LAIRD TECHNOLOGIES INC
1751 Wilkening Ct (60173-5310)
PHONE.................847 839-6000
John Sturm, *General Mgr*
EMP: 140
SALES (corp-wide): 177.9K **Privately Held**
SIC: 3499 Magnetic shields, metal
HQ: Laird Technologies, Inc.
16401 Swingley Ridge Rd # 700
Chesterfield MO 63017
636 898-6000

(G-18598)
LAMIN-ART LLC
1670 Basswood Rd (60173-5307)
PHONE.................800 323-7624
Kevin Geijer, *Site Mgr*
James Sorensen, *Opers Staff*
Paul S Micek, *Controller*
Lisa Curatti, *Finance*
Bill Newburn, *Supervisor*
◆ **EMP:** 15
SQ FT: 30,000
SALES: 14MM
SALES (corp-wide): 14.1B **Publicly Held**
WEB: www.laminart.com
SIC: 5085 5162 3083 Industrial supplies; plastics materials & basic shapes; thermoplastic laminates: rods, tubes, plates & sheet; thermosetting laminates: rods, tubes, plates & sheet
HQ: Wilsonart Llc
2501 Wilsonart Dr
Temple TX 76504
254 207-7000

(G-18599)
LAMINARP
1670 Basswood Rd (60173-5307)
PHONE.................847 884-9298
Donald Krog, *Owner*
EMP: 48 **EST:** 1982
SALES (est): 2.8MM **Privately Held**
SIC: 3089 Plastics products

(G-18600)
LARSEN & TOUBRO INFOTECH LTD
1821 Walden Office Sq # 400 (60173-4273)
PHONE.................847 303-3900
A M Nik, *CEO*
EMP: 5
SALES (est): 516.3K **Privately Held**
SIC: 7372 Prepackaged software

(G-18601)
LASER CENTER CORPORATION
1001 Morse Ave (60193-4503)
PHONE.................630 523-1600
Yun Chon Kwak, *President*
Chris Park, *General Mgr*
John Morse, *Sales Mgr*
EMP: 37
SALES (est): 8.3MM **Privately Held**
WEB: www.lasercentercorp.com
SIC: 3444 Sheet metalwork

(G-18602)
LEGEND RACING ENTERPRISES INC
Also Called: Lre
616 Morse Ave (60193-4532)
PHONE.................847 923-8979
Doug Roden, *President*
EMP: 3
SQ FT: 5,000
SALES (est): 422K **Privately Held**
SIC: 7538 7549 3711 Engine repair; high performance auto repair & service; automobile assembly, including specialty automobiles

(G-18603)
LEMKO CORPORATION
846 E Algonquin Rd # 101 (60173-3854)
PHONE.................630 948-3025
Nicholas Labun, *Ch of Bd*
Robert Condon, *President*

Bohdan Pyskir, *President*
David Dombrowski, *Vice Pres*
Joseph Barr, *CFO*
◆ **EMP:** 35
SQ FT: 22,000
SALES (est): 5.7MM **Privately Held**
SIC: 7371 3663 Computer software development; cellular radio telephone

(G-18604)
LETTERS UNLIMITED INC
1010 Morse Ave Ste E (60193-4584)
PHONE.................847 891-7811
Steve Koestler, *Principal*
EMP: 4
SALES (est): 452.4K **Privately Held**
SIC: 3081 3953 3993 Vinyl film & sheet; marking devices; signs & advertising specialties

(G-18605)
LEVI STRAUSS & CO
5 Woodfeld Shopg Ctr 11 # 114 (60173)
PHONE.................847 619-0655
EMP: 94
SALES (corp-wide): 5.7B **Publicly Held**
SIC: 2325 Jeans: men's, youths' & boys'
PA: Levi Strauss & Co.
1155 Battery St
San Francisco CA 94111
415 501-6000

(G-18606)
LIBERTY SPCLITY STELS AMER INC
20 N Martingale Rd # 200 (60173-2412)
PHONE.................847 521-6464
Rebecca C Ceto, *Principal*
EMP: 3
SALES (est): 184.2K **Privately Held**
SIC: 3462 Iron & steel forgings

(G-18607)
LINEAR TECHNOLOGY LLC
2040 E Algonquin Rd (60173-4187)
PHONE.................847 925-0860
Tom Buffo, *Manager*
EMP: 7
SALES (corp-wide): 5.9B **Publicly Held**
SIC: 3674 Semiconductors & related devices
HQ: Linear Technology Llc
1630 Mccarthy Blvd
Milpitas CA 95035
408 432-1900

(G-18608)
LINTEC OF AMERICA INC
935 National Pkwy # 93553 (60173-5334)
PHONE.................847 229-0547
Chooka Kaoru, *President*
Kazuyshio Node, *President*
▲ **EMP:** 7
SALES (est): 1.3MM **Privately Held**
SIC: 2891 Adhesives

(G-18609)
LITTELL LLC
1211 Tower Rd (60193-4307)
PHONE.................630 916-6662
Kevin Roberts,
▲ **EMP:** 40
SQ FT: 37,000
SALES (est): 8.9MM **Privately Held**
SIC: 3547 3549 3599 3537 Rolling mill machinery; metalworking machinery; machine & other job shop work; industrial trucks & tractors

(G-18610)
LITTELL INTERNATIONAL INC
1211 Tower Rd (60193-4307)
PHONE.................630 622-4950
Sterling Stevenson, *President*
Paul Raimondi, *Vice Pres*
Don Noesen, *Mfg Staff*
Cindy Lwin, *Purchasing*
Michael O'Day, *VP Engrg*
▲ **EMP:** 45 **EST:** 1918
SALES (est): 7.5MM **Privately Held**
SIC: 3542 3441 3549 3548 Machine tools, metal forming type; fabricated structural metal; metalworking machinery; welding apparatus

(G-18611)
LOGAN SQUARE ALUMINUM SUP INC
Also Called: Studio 41
1450 Mitchell Blvd (60193-4542)
PHONE.................847 985-1700
Bill Schmitt, *Branch Mgr*
EMP: 67
SALES (corp-wide): 113MM **Privately Held**
SIC: 3442 3444 5031 Window & door frames; awnings, sheet metal; building materials, exterior
PA: Logan Square Aluminum Supply, Inc.
2500 N Pulaski Rd
Chicago IL 60639
773 235-2500

(G-18612)
LORBERN MFG INC
708 Morse Ave (60193-4534)
PHONE.................847 301-8600
Bernard Treffy, *President*
Lorraine Treffy, *Corp Secy*
Laura Treffy, *Vice Pres*
Robert Treffy, *Vice Pres*
EMP: 21
SQ FT: 10,000
SALES (est): 3.8MM **Privately Held**
SIC: 3469 3599 Machine parts, stamped or pressed metal; machine shop, jobbing & repair

(G-18613)
LUVO USA LLC (PA)
2095 Hammond Dr (60173-3809)
PHONE.................847 485-8595
David Negus, *President*
EMP: 49
SALES (est): 10.6MM **Privately Held**
SIC: 2038 Lunches, frozen & packaged

(G-18614)
LUVO USA LLC
2095 Hammond Dr (60173-3809)
PHONE.................847 485-8595
EMP: 21
SALES (corp-wide): 10.6MM **Privately Held**
SIC: 2038 Mfg Frozen Specialties
PA: Luvo Usa, Llc
2095 Hammond Dr
Schaumburg IL 60173
847 485-8595

(G-18615)
LYNDA HERVAS
Also Called: Tri Star Manufacturing
800 Morse Ave (60193-4583)
PHONE.................847 985-1690
Lynda Hervas, *Owner*
EMP: 4
SQ FT: 3,000
SALES (est): 183.5K **Privately Held**
SIC: 3499 Novelties & specialties, metal

(G-18616)
M & R MEDIA INC
Also Called: Fastsigns
1084 National Pkwy (60193-4519)
PHONE.................847 884-6300
Merle Silverstein, *President*
EMP: 5
SALES (est): 340K **Privately Held**
SIC: 3993 Signs & advertising specialties

(G-18617)
M13 INC
Also Called: M13 Graphics
1300 Basswood Rd Ste 100 (60173-4522)
PHONE.................847 310-1913
Daniel Banakis, *President*
Rene Sanchez, *Cust Mgr*
Dominique Hadley, *Sales Staff*
EMP: 43
SQ FT: 50,000
SALES (est): 11MM **Privately Held**
SIC: 7373 2752 Computer integrated systems design; commercial printing, lithographic

(G-18618)
MANU INDUSTRIES INC
977 Lunt Ave (60193-4416)
PHONE.................847 891-6412

Manu Jayswal, *President*
Shawn Quillen, *Sales Staff*
EMP: 10
SQ FT: 8,000
SALES (est): 1.2MM **Privately Held**
SIC: 3672 5063 Printed circuit boards; wire & cable

(G-18619)
MARTIN TOOL WORKS INC
Also Called: Komet
2050 Mitchell Blvd (60193-4544)
PHONE.................847 923-8400
F Hans Grandin, *President*
Kevin McCoy, *Vice Pres*
Kaustav Roy, *Design Engr*
Jargen Juffa, *VP Finance*
Al Jenzeh, *Cust Mgr*
EMP: 14 **EST:** 1956
SQ FT: 67,000
SALES (est): 1.3MM
SALES (corp-wide): 5.2MM **Privately Held**
WEB: www.komet.com
SIC: 3365 Aerospace castings, aluminum
HQ: Ceratizit Chicago Holding Inc.
2050 Mitchell Blvd
Schaumburg IL 60193
847 923-8400

(G-18620)
MARTY GANNON
Also Called: Gannon Graphics
1025 Morse Ave (60193-4503)
PHONE.................847 895-1059
Marty Gannon, *CEO*
Galen Beck, *Production*
Carol Hulsey, *Cust Mgr*
Brian Huey, *Sales Staff*
Joanie Gannon, *Office Mgr*
EMP: 25 **EST:** 2001
SALES (est): 3MM **Privately Held**
SIC: 2732 2752 Book printing; commercial printing, lithographic

(G-18621)
MASCO CORPORATION
1821 Walden Office Sq # 400 (60173-4273)
PHONE.................847 303-3088
Jimmy Hsu, *Branch Mgr*
EMP: 94
SALES (corp-wide): 6.7B **Publicly Held**
SIC: 2434 Wood kitchen cabinets
PA: Masco Corporation
17450 College Pkwy
Livonia MI 48152
313 274-7400

(G-18622)
MASTER CUT E D M INC
1025 Lunt Ave Ste C (60193-4472)
PHONE.................847 534-0343
Scott Phillips, *President*
Harold Bartman, *Vice Pres*
EMP: 5
SQ FT: 2,500
SALES (est): 672.2K **Privately Held**
WEB: www.mastercutedm.com
SIC: 3599 Electrical discharge machining (EDM); machine shop, jobbing & repair

(G-18623)
MASTER HYDRAULICS & MACHINING
540 Morse Ave (60193-4530)
PHONE.................847 895-5578
Harold J Schafer, *President*
Diana Schafer, *Vice Pres*
EMP: 11
SQ FT: 5,000
SALES (est): 1MM **Privately Held**
SIC: 7699 3599 3593 Hydraulic equipment repair; machine shop, jobbing & repair; fluid power cylinders & actuators

(G-18624)
MCGILL MACHINE WORKS INC
638 Lunt Ave (60193-4411)
PHONE.................847 301-8000
Doug McGill, *President*
EMP: 3
SALES (est): 511.3K **Privately Held**
WEB: www.mmw-inc.com
SIC: 3599 Machine shop, jobbing & repair

Schaumburg - Cook County (G-18625)

(G-18625)
MEADOWORKS LLC
935 National Pkwy # 93510
PHONE 847 640-8580
Brian Walsh,
EMP: 15 **EST:** 2008
SALES (est): 2MM **Privately Held**
SIC: 3086 Plastics foam products

(G-18626)
MEGA CORPORATION
516 Morse Ave (60193-4530)
P.O. Box 3036, Barrington (60011-3036)
PHONE 847 985-1900
A William Van Meter, *President*
Patti A Rein, *Director*
Beth Fleury Van Meter, *Admin Sec*
▲ **EMP:** 20 **EST:** 1980
SQ FT: 5,000
SALES (est): 3.6MM **Privately Held**
SIC: 3089 Injection molding of plastics

(G-18627)
MERCURY PRODUCTS CORP (PA)
1201 Mercury Dr (60193-3513)
PHONE 847 524-4400
Bruce C Hael, *President*
Jack Ehlinger, *Managing Dir*
Bob Koltvedt, *Vice Pres*
Maria Jimenez, *Purch Mgr*
Luis Mellado, *QC Mgr*
▲ **EMP:** 200
SQ FT: 93,280
SALES (est): 87.1MM **Privately Held**
WEB: www.mercprod.com
SIC: 3465 3469 3714 Automotive stampings; machine parts, stamped or pressed metal; motor vehicle engines & parts; exhaust systems & parts, motor vehicle

(G-18628)
MERICHEM CHEM RFINERY SVCS LLC
Also Called: Merichem Catalyst & Tech Sls
650 E Algonquin Rd (60173-3846)
PHONE 847 285-3850
Kenneth F Currie, *CEO*
Laura Lampe, *Administration*
EMP: 150
SALES (est): 460.3K
SALES (corp-wide): 88.3MM **Privately Held**
SIC: 2819 Catalysts, chemical
PA: Merichem Company
5455 Old Spanish Trl
Houston TX 77023
713 428-5000

(G-18629)
MIDDLETONS MOULDINGS INC
1325 Remington Rd Ste H (60173-4815)
PHONE 517 278-6610
Jim Brock, *President*
▲ **EMP:** 53
SQ FT: 19,800
SALES (est): 10.2MM **Privately Held**
SIC: 2431 3442 2542 2434 Stair railings, wood; moldings & baseboards, ornamental & trim; metal doors, sash & trim; partitions & fixtures, except wood; wood kitchen cabinets

(G-18630)
MIDWEST SKYLITE SERVICE INC
907 Lunt Ave (60193-4416)
PHONE 847 214-9505
John Harris, *President*
EMP: 4
SQ FT: 11,000
SALES (est): 346.8K **Privately Held**
SIC: 3444 Sheet metalwork

(G-18631)
MIN SHENG TECHNOLOGY INC
461 Kerri Ct (60173-6592)
PHONE 815 569-4496
Shui Feng LI, *Director*
◆ **EMP:** 9
SALES: 100K **Privately Held**
SIC: 5211 3699 5063 Electrical construction materials; electrical welding equipment; electrical apparatus & equipment

(G-18632)
MITSUBISHI MATERIALS USA CORP
1314 N Plum Grove Rd (60173-4546)
PHONE 847 519-1601
Y Murakami, *Manager*
EMP: 10 **Privately Held**
SIC: 5511 3545 Automobiles, new & used; cutting tools for machine tools
HQ: Mitsubishi Materials Usa Corp
3535 Hyland Ave Ste 200
Costa Mesa CA 92626
714 352-6100

(G-18633)
MOSSAN INC
28 Ashburn Ct Unit Z1 (60193-5757)
PHONE 857 247-4122
Gustavo Frederico Mosquero, *CEO*
Gustavo Jesuf Mosquero, *CFO*
Gustavo Armando Mosquero, *Marketing Staff*
EMP: 3
SALES: 90K **Privately Held**
SIC: 2821 Molding compounds, plastics

(G-18634)
MOTOROLA INTERNATIONAL CAPITAL
1303 E Algonquin Rd (60196-1079)
PHONE 847 576-5000
EMP: 1
SALES (est): 340.2K
SALES (corp-wide): 6.3B **Publicly Held**
SIC: 3674 Mfg Semiconductors
PA: Motorola Solutions, Inc.
500 W Monroe St Ste 4400
Chicago IL 60661
847 576-5000

(G-18635)
MOTOROLA INTL DEV CORP (HQ)
2000 Progress Pkwy (60196-1079)
PHONE 847 576-5000
Kevin Sweet, *Opers Mgr*
Ken Russman, *Facilities Mgr*
Hai Nguyen, *Purchasing*
Rich Chomko, *Engineer*
Steve Gump, *Engineer*
EMP: 50
SQ FT: 2,000
SALES (est): 7.3MM
SALES (corp-wide): 7.8B **Publicly Held**
SIC: 3663 Radio & TV communications equipment
PA: Motorola Solutions, Inc.
500 W Monroe St Ste 4400
Chicago IL 60661
847 576-5000

(G-18636)
MOTOROLA SOLUTIONS INC
2100 Progress Pkwy (60196-1077)
PHONE 630 308-9394
Rick Osterloh, *Branch Mgr*
EMP: 139
SALES (corp-wide): 7.8B **Publicly Held**
SIC: 3663 Radio & TV communications equipment
PA: Motorola Solutions, Inc.
500 W Monroe St Ste 4400
Chicago IL 60661
847 576-5000

(G-18637)
MOTOROLA SOLUTIONS INC
1295 E Algonquin Rd (60196-1097)
PHONE 847 576-8600
Tom Guthrie, *Vice Pres*
Chris Ouimet, *Vice Pres*
Janet Robinson, *Vice Pres*
Sanjay Dhar, *Engineer*
James Jenkins, *Engineer*
EMP: 142

SALES (corp-wide): 7.8B **Publicly Held**
SIC: 3674 3571 3812 3661 Semiconductors & related devices; metal oxide silicon (MOS) devices; random access memory (RAM); microprocessors; personal computers (microcomputers); radar systems & equipment; position indicators for aircraft equipment; navigational systems & instruments; warfare counter-measure equipment; modems; multiplex equipment, telephone & telegraph; ignition apparatus, internal combustion engines; mobile communication equipment
PA: Motorola Solutions, Inc.
500 W Monroe St Ste 4400
Chicago IL 60661
847 576-5000

(G-18638)
MOTOROLA SOLUTIONS INC
1100 E Woodfield Rd # 535 (60173-5116)
PHONE 708 476-8226
Kirk Guy, *Principal*
Gerry Mita, *Branch Mgr*
EMP: 142
SALES (corp-wide): 7.8B **Publicly Held**
SIC: 3663 Radio & TV communications equipment
PA: Motorola Solutions, Inc.
500 W Monroe St Ste 4400
Chicago IL 60661
847 576-5000

(G-18639)
MOTOROLA SOLUTIONS INC
2000 Progress Pkwy (60196-1079)
P.O. Box 804358, Chicago (60680-4105)
PHONE 800 331-6456
EMP: 142
SALES (corp-wide): 7.3B **Publicly Held**
SIC: 3663 Radio And Tv Communications Equipment, Nsk
PA: Motorola Solutions, Inc.
500 W Monroe St Ste 4400
Chicago IL 60661
847 576-5000

(G-18640)
MT TOOL AND MANUFACTURING INC
1118 Lunt Ave Ste E (60193-4441)
PHONE 847 985-6211
Thomas J Lechner, *President*
Margaret H Lechner, *Admin Sec*
EMP: 2
SQ FT: 1,000
SALES (est): 307K **Privately Held**
SIC: 3312 Tool & die steel

(G-18641)
MURATA ELECTRONICS N AMER INC
425 N Martingale Rd # 1540 (60173-2213)
PHONE 847 330-9200
Anthony Swartz, *Engineer*
Chris Borawski, *Sales Staff*
Randall Michaels, *Marketing Staff*
Chris Borwski, *Manager*
Greg Taylor, *Manager*
EMP: 8 **Privately Held**
WEB: www.murataamericas.com
SIC: 3675 3679 7629 Electronic capacitors; electronic circuits; electronic equipment repair
HQ: Murata Electronics North America, Inc.
2200 Lake Park Dr Se
Smyrna GA 30080
770 436-1300

(G-18642)
MURRAY PRINTING SERVICE INC
635 Remington Rd Ste F (60173-4578)
PHONE 847 310-8959
David Koltonuk, *President*
EMP: 5 **EST:** 1963
SALES: 750K **Privately Held**
SIC: 2752 Commercial printing, offset

(G-18643)
N BUJARSKI INC
Also Called: Quiet Graphics
725 E Golf Rd (60173-4511)
PHONE 847 884-1600
Norvell Bujarski, *President*

EMP: 6
SQ FT: 2,100
SALES (est): 786K **Privately Held**
SIC: 2752 3993 2796 2791 Commercial printing, offset; signs & advertising specialties; platemaking services; typesetting; bookbinding & related work; manifold business forms

(G-18644)
NATION PIZZA PRODUCTS LP
Also Called: Nation Pizza and Foods
601 E Algonquin Rd (60173-3803)
PHONE 847 397-3320
Marshall Bauer, *Co-CEO*
Jay Bauer, *Co-CEO*
Joseph Giglio, *Exec VP*
Jack Campolo, *Vice Pres*
Teresa Martinez, *Vice Pres*
EMP: 700
SQ FT: 200,000
SALES (est): 179.6MM **Privately Held**
SIC: 2038 2045 2033 Pizza, frozen; pizza doughs, prepared: from purchased flour; pizza sauce: packaged in cans, jars, etc.

(G-18645)
NAVATEK RESOURCES INC
1505 Wright Blvd (60193-4509)
PHONE 847 301-0174
Giuseppe Paelmo, *President*
Gary Paelmo, *Admin Sec*
EMP: 3
SALES (est): 1MM **Privately Held**
SIC: 3679 Electronic circuits

(G-18646)
NE DESKTOP SOFTWARE INC
Also Called: Trugrid.com
1100 E Wdfield Rd Ste 100a (60173)
PHONE 800 211-8332
Peter Aydun, *CEO*
EMP: 15
SALES (est): 305.2K **Privately Held**
SIC: 7372 Prepackaged software

(G-18647)
NEPTUNE USA INC
983 W Wise Rd Ste 101 (60193-3883)
PHONE 847 987-3804
Jay Shah, *President*
▲ **EMP:** 1
SALES (est): 6.3MM **Privately Held**
SIC: 2221 3081 Polypropylene broadwoven fabrics; polypropylene film & sheet

(G-18648)
NEWPORT PRINTING SERVICES INC
1250 Remington Rd (60173-4812)
PHONE 847 632-1000
Michael Parla, *CEO*
EMP: 2
SALES: 500K **Privately Held**
SIC: 2759 3993 Screen printing; signs & advertising specialties

(G-18649)
NIPPON ELECTRIC GLASS AMER INC (HQ)
Also Called: Nega
1515 E Wdfield Rd Ste 720 (60173)
PHONE 630 285-8500
Tsuyoshi, *President*
Hidenari Tsuzuki, *Controller*
Makoto Nishimura, *Admin Sec*
▲ **EMP:** 8
SQ FT: 3,000
SALES (est): 350MM **Privately Held**
SIC: 3229 Glassware, industrial

(G-18650)
NISSHA USA INC (HQ)
1051 Perimeter Dr Ste 600 (60173-5853)
PHONE 847 413-2665
Junya Suzuki, *President*
Rocky Tsuruta, *CFO*
Ayumu Takashiba, *Admin Sec*
Sumiko Malek, *Administration*
◆ **EMP:** 20
SQ FT: 3,000
SALES: 30MM **Privately Held**
SIC: 2759 2752 Commercial printing; commercial printing, lithographic

GEOGRAPHIC SECTION

Schaumburg - Cook County (G-18677)

(G-18651)
NORTECH PACKAGING LLC
Also Called: Tishma Technologies
101 E State Pkwy (60173-5336)
PHONE..............................847 884-1805
David Showman, *Mng Member*
EMP: 60
SALES (est): 1.1MM **Privately Held**
SIC: 3565 Packaging machinery

(G-18652)
NORTHFIELD HOLDINGS LLC
700 Wiley Farm Ct (60173-5342)
PHONE..............................847 755-0700
Charles J Vogle,
▲ **EMP:** 26
SQ FT: 30,000
SALES (est): 6.5MM **Privately Held**
SIC: 3469 Machine parts, stamped or pressed metal

(G-18653)
NOVASPECT INC (PA)
1124 Tower Rd (60173-4306)
PHONE..............................847 956-8020
Terry Voigt, *President*
Timothy Holcer, *President*
Dave Fossier, *General Mgr*
Angela Musial, *General Mgr*
Keith Bentley, *Business Mgr*
EMP: 140
SQ FT: 19,000
SALES (est): 80.9MM **Privately Held**
SIC: 7372 5084 Prepackaged software; controlling instruments & accessories

(G-18654)
NTT AMERICA SOLUTIONS INC
1700 E Golf Rd Ste 1100 (60173-5864)
PHONE..............................847 278-6413
John Freres, *Branch Mgr*
EMP: 10 **Privately Held**
SIC: 7372 7373 Application computer software; systems integration services
HQ: Ntt America Solutions, Inc.
1 Penn Plz Fl 18
New York NY 10119
704 969-2784

(G-18655)
O E M MARKETING INC (PA)
1015 Lunt Ave (60193-4418)
P.O. Box 8444, Bartlett (60103-8444)
PHONE..............................847 985-9490
Scott Sutter, *President*
Claudia Sutter, *Treasurer*
▲ **EMP:** 10
SQ FT: 10,000
SALES (est): 1.5MM **Privately Held**
SIC: 3824 5084 Odometers; measuring & testing equipment, electrical

(G-18656)
OERLIKON BLZERS CATING USA INC (DH)
1700 E Golf Rd Ste 200 (60173-5801)
PHONE..............................847 619-5541
Natahan Olds, *CEO*
Tom Vaeth, *Plant Mgr*
Paul Faiken, *Opers Mgr*
Paul Olore, *Opers Staff*
Dan Johns, *Research*
▲ **EMP:** 12
SALES (est): 104.8MM
SALES (corp-wide): 2.6B **Privately Held**
SIC: 3479 3471 Coating of metals & formed products; finishing, metals or formed products
HQ: Oerlikon Balzers Coating Ag
Iramali 18
Balzers
423 388-5701

(G-18657)
OLYMPIC PETROLEUM CORPORATION
1171 Tower Rd (60173-4305)
PHONE..............................847 995-0996
Wendy Pierson, *Manager*
EMP: 5
SALES (corp-wide): 4.6B **Publicly Held**
SIC: 2992 Lubricating oils & greases

HQ: Olympic Petroleum Corporation
5000 W 41st St
Cicero IL 60804
708 876-7900

(G-18658)
OLYMPIC STEEL INC
1901 Mitchell Blvd (60193-4538)
PHONE..............................847 584-4000
Brad Clifford, *General Mgr*
Charles Latour, *Opers Mgr*
Amber Schnecke, *Sales Staff*
EMP: 20
SALES (corp-wide): 1.5B **Publicly Held**
SIC: 5051 3441 3312 Steel; fabricated structural metal; blast furnaces & steel mills
PA: Olympic Steel, Inc.
22901 Millcreek Blvd # 650
Cleveland OH 44122
216 292-3800

(G-18659)
OREILLY AUTOMOTIVE STORES INC
38 E Golf Rd Ste C (60173-3708)
PHONE..............................847 882-4384
Ed Pavon, *Branch Mgr*
EMP: 3 **Publicly Held**
SIC: 7699 7694 7538 5531 Engine repair & replacement, non-automotive; rebuilding motors, except automotive; engine repair; automotive parts
HQ: O'reilly Automotive Stores, Inc.
233 S Patterson Ave
Springfield MO 65802
417 862-2674

(G-18660)
ORTHO ARCH COMPANY INC
1107 Tower Rd (60173-4305)
PHONE..............................847 885-7805
Lindsay Brehm, *CEO*
Michael Zerafa, *President*
Robert Dunlap, *Vice Pres*
EMP: 22
SQ FT: 2,200
SALES (est): 674.4K **Privately Held**
WEB: www.orthoarch.com
SIC: 5999 3843 Medical apparatus & supplies; dental equipment & supplies

(G-18661)
P & J TECHNOLOGIES
1356 Saint Claire Pl (60173-6186)
PHONE..............................847 995-1108
David Ballotto, *Owner*
EMP: 4
SALES: 200K **Privately Held**
SIC: 3699 Security control equipment & systems

(G-18662)
PADDOCK PUBLICATIONS INC
Also Called: Daily Herald
1000 Albion Ave (60193-4549)
P.O. Box 280, Arlington Heights (60006-0280)
PHONE..............................847 427-5545
Don Stamper, *Opers Staff*
Jerry Schur, *Manager*
EMP: 250
SALES (corp-wide): 79.9MM **Privately Held**
SIC: 2711 Commercial printing & newspaper publishing combined
PA: Paddock Publications, Inc.
95 W Algonquin Rd Ste 300
Arlington Heights IL 60005
847 427-4300

(G-18663)
PAR GOLF SUPPLY INC
550 Pratt Ave N (60193-4555)
PHONE..............................847 891-1222
Mike Gallichio, *President*
Vicki Hartigan, *Manager*
▼ **EMP:** 28
SQ FT: 8,000
SALES (est): 6.5MM **Privately Held**
SIC: 5091 3949 Golf equipment; golf equipment

(G-18664)
PARAGON INTERNATIONAL INC
Also Called: Paragon Valuation Group
1901 N Roselle Rd Ste 711 (60195-5711)
PHONE..............................847 240-2981
Richard R Swarts, *President*
Scott R Swarts, *Vice Pres*
Shelle Danek, *Admin Sec*
EMP: 16
SQ FT: 3,600
SALES (est): 2.2MM **Privately Held**
SIC: 7372 7373 8721 8748 Business oriented computer software; value-added resellers, computer systems; accounting services, except auditing; business consulting; inventory computing service

(G-18665)
PARALLEL SOLUTIONS LLC
1251 N Plum Grove Rd # 160 (60173-5603)
PHONE..............................847 708-9227
Vince Panico, *Principal*
Brian Faster, *Sales Staff*
Rick Kleba, *Sales Staff*
Cammy Mann, *Sales Staff*
EMP: 2
SALES (est): 327K **Privately Held**
SIC: 7372 Prepackaged software

(G-18666)
PARKING SYSTEMS INC
911 Estes Ct (60193-4427)
P.O. Box 72031, Roselle (60172-0031)
PHONE..............................847 891-3819
Larry A Landis, *President*
Faye Landis, *Vice Pres*
Gary Montelione, *Mktg Dir*
EMP: 3 **EST:** 1974
SQ FT: 5,000
SALES (est): 300K **Privately Held**
SIC: 3625 3559 3829 Control equipment, electric; parking facility equipment & supplies; measuring & controlling devices

(G-18667)
PARTH CONSULTANTS INC
Also Called: Brijen Electronics
2385 Hammond Dr Ste 9 (60173-3844)
P.O. Box 331, Mount Prospect (60056-0331)
PHONE..............................847 758-1400
Maya Patel, *President*
Sam Patel, *Vice Pres*
EMP: 21
SQ FT: 5,000
SALES (est): 1.6MM **Privately Held**
SIC: 8742 3672 Management consulting services; circuit boards, television & radio printed

(G-18668)
PARTNERS MANUFACTURING INC
625 Lunt Ave (60193-4410)
PHONE..............................847 352-1080
Michael Lagioia, *President*
EMP: 25
SALES (est): 2MM **Privately Held**
SIC: 3544 Special dies & tools

(G-18669)
PATEL DISHABEN
Also Called: Valaji Pharma Chem
57 Bright Ridge Dr (60194-3681)
PHONE..............................312 880-8746
Dishaben Patel, *Owner*
EMP: 3
SALES (est): 158.6K **Privately Held**
SIC: 2834 Pharmaceutical preparations

(G-18670)
PAYLOCITY HOLDING CORPORATION (PA)
1400 American Ln (60173-5452)
PHONE..............................847 463-3200
Steven R Beauchamp, *CEO*
Steven I Sarowitz, *Ch of Bd*
Michael R Haske, *President*
Matt Fleming, *Partner*
John Mason-Smith, *District Mgr*
EMP: 134
SQ FT: 200,000

SALES: 467.6MM **Publicly Held**
SIC: 7372 Prepackaged software; business oriented computer software

(G-18671)
PECORA TOOL & DIE CO INC
520 Morse Ave (60193-4530)
PHONE..............................847 524-1275
Mario Pecora, *President*
Mary Pecora, *Admin Sec*
EMP: 4
SQ FT: 5,000
SALES (est): 583.9K **Privately Held**
SIC: 3544 Die sets for metal stamping (presses); jigs & fixtures

(G-18672)
PECORA TOOL SERVICE INC
520 Morse Ave (60193-4530)
PHONE..............................847 524-1275
Mario Pecora, *President*
EMP: 4
SALES (est): 414.9K **Privately Held**
SIC: 3469 Metal stampings

(G-18673)
PHILIP MORRIS USA INC
300 N Martingale Rd # 700 (60173-2407)
PHONE..............................847 605-9595
Andy Macray, *Vice Pres*
EMP: 100
SALES (corp-wide): 25.1B **Publicly Held**
SIC: 2111 Cigarettes
HQ: Philip Morris Usa Inc.
6601 W Brd St
Richmond VA 23230
804 274-2000

(G-18674)
PITNEY BOWES INC
2330 Hammond Dr Ste G (60173-3869)
PHONE..............................312 209-2216
Steve Pace, *Manager*
EMP: 20
SALES (corp-wide): 3.2B **Publicly Held**
WEB: www.pitneybowes.com
SIC: 3579 7359 Postage meters; business machine & electronic equipment rental services
PA: Pitney Bowes Inc.
3001 Summer St Ste 3
Stamford CT 06905
203 356-5000

(G-18675)
PLASTIC SPECIALTIES & TECH INC
Also Called: American Gasket & Rubber
119 Commerce Dr (60173-5311)
PHONE..............................847 781-2414
James Carosella, *General Mgr*
Angela Nava, *Opers Staff*
EMP: 3
SQ FT: 60,000
SALES (corp-wide): 1.3B **Privately Held**
SIC: 3053 5085 3242 Gaskets, packing & sealing devices; gaskets; synthetic rubber
HQ: Plastic Specialties And Technologies Inc.
101 Railroad Ave
Ridgefield NJ 07657
201 941-2900

(G-18676)
PLATE AND PRE-PRESS MANAGEMENT
431 Westover Ln (60193-2428)
PHONE..............................847 352-0462
Joe Babich, *President*
Barbara Babich, *Admin Sec*
EMP: 5
SQ FT: 2,300
SALES (est): 214.3K **Privately Held**
SIC: 3861 3555 Photographic film, plate & paper holders; printing plates

(G-18677)
PLIANT INVESTMENT INC
1475 E Wdfield Rd Ste 600 (60173)
PHONE..............................847 969-3300
EMP: 3
SALES (est): 194.5K **Privately Held**
SIC: 3081 Plastic film & sheet

(PA)=Parent Co (HQ)=Headquarters (DH)=Div Headquarters
✪ = New Business established in last 2 years

Schaumburg - Cook County (G-18678)

(G-18678)
PLIANT SOLUTIONS CORPORATION
1475 E Wdfield Rd Ste 600 (60173)
PHONE.....................847 969-3300
Craig Miller, *President*
Michelle Wilson, *President*
Gary Penna, *Owner*
EMP: 33
SALES (est): 6.6MM **Privately Held**
SIC: 3081 Plastic film & sheet

(G-18679)
PLUSTECH INC
735 Remington Rd (60173-4552)
PHONE.....................847 490-8130
Koji Yamauchi, *President*
Kohei Shinohara, *General Mgr*
Len Hampton, *Regl Sales Mgr*
R Scott Fernandez, *Admin Sec*
▲ EMP: 7
SQ FT: 3,500
SALES: 10MM **Privately Held**
SIC: 3089 Injection molding of plastics
PA: Yamazen Corporation
2-3-16, Itachibori, Nishi-Ku
Osaka OSK 550-0

(G-18680)
PM MOLD COMPANY
800 Estes Ave (60193-4407)
PHONE.....................847 923-5400
Lawrence Hauck, *President*
Larry Hauck, *General Mgr*
Melissa Tripoli, *QC Mgr*
David Bradley, *Treasurer*
Carlos Islas, *Finance*
▲ EMP: 45 EST: 1963
SQ FT: 45,000
SALES (est): 17.1MM **Privately Held**
WEB: www.pmmold.com
SIC: 3544 Forms (molds), for foundry & plastics working machinery; industrial molds

(G-18681)
PRACTICAL COMMUNICATIONS INC
Also Called: Outside Plant Magazine
1900 E Golf Rd Ste 950 (60173-5034)
PHONE.....................773 754-3250
Sharon Vollman, *President*
Janice Oliva, *Senior VP*
Carrie Naber, *Vice Pres*
Diane Roberts, *Sales & Mktg St*
Tina Senatra-Anderson, *Manager*
EMP: 29
SALES (est): 3.5MM **Privately Held**
SIC: 2721 7331 Trade journals: publishing only, not printed on site; mailing service

(G-18682)
PRECISEPOWER LLC
140 E State Pkwy (60173-5335)
PHONE.....................847 908-5400
James Hougo,
EMP: 48
SALES (est): 1.7MM **Privately Held**
SIC: 3559 Semiconductor manufacturing machinery

(G-18683)
PRIME WOOD CRAFT INC (HQ)
Also Called: P W C
1450 American Ln Ste 700 (60173-6016)
PHONE.....................216 738-2222
Ansir Junaid, *President*
Ijaz SA, *President*
Robert Campbell, *Vice Pres*
Ej Hughes, *Natl Sales Mgr*
Samantha Sheperd, *Office Mgr*
▲ EMP: 48
SALES (est): 14.4MM **Privately Held**
WEB: www.primewoodcraft.com
SIC: 2448 Pallets, wood

(G-18684)
PRIME WOOD CRAFT INC
1450 American Ln Ste 700 (60173-6016)
PHONE.....................716 803-3425
EMP: 3 **Privately Held**
SIC: 2448 Wood pallets & skids

HQ: Prime Wood Craft, Inc.
1450 American Ln Ste 700
Schaumburg IL 60173
216 738-2222

(G-18685)
PROMOFRAMES LLC
1113 Tower Rd (60173-4305)
PHONE.....................866 566-7224
Steve Lim,
▼ EMP: 5
SQ FT: 5,100
SALES: 500K **Privately Held**
SIC: 5043 7389 3953 2752 Cameras & photographic equipment; advertising, promotional & trade show services; stationery embossers, personal; offset & photolithographic printing

(G-18686)
PROTEC EQUIPMENT RESOURCES INC
1501 Wright Blvd (60193-4509)
PHONE.....................847 434-5808
Dan Allison, *Branch Mgr*
EMP: 3
SALES (corp-wide): 6MM **Privately Held**
SIC: 3825 Engine electrical test equipment
PA: Protec Equipment Resources, Inc.
1517 W North Carrier 11
Grand Prairie TX 75050
972 352-5550

(G-18687)
PRU DENT MFG INC
1929 Wright Blvd (60193-4567)
PHONE.....................847 301-1170
Tim Prusaitis, *President*
EMP: 8
SALES (est): 948.5K **Privately Held**
SIC: 3999 Barber & beauty shop equipment

(G-18688)
PULLR HOLDING COMPANY LLC
Also Called: Maasdam Pow'r-Pull
415 E State Pkwy (60173-4539)
PHONE.....................224 366-2500
Mark Lin, *General Mgr*
Jason Liu, *CFO*
Tyra Ciesielczyk, *Accounting Mgr*
Agnes Kieda, *Accounting Mgr*
Sharon Lin, *Accounting Mgr*
▲ EMP: 35
SALES (est): 7.1MM **Privately Held**
WEB: www.pullr.com
SIC: 3423 Hand & edge tools

(G-18689)
PUTMAN MEDIA INC (PA)
Also Called: Food Processing Magazine
1501 E Wdfeld Rd Ste 400n (60173)
PHONE.....................630 467-1301
John Cappelletti, *CEO*
Jim Maddox, *Publisher*
Brian Marz, *Publisher*
Traci Purdum, *Editor*
Mark Rosenzweig, *Editor*
▼ EMP: 51 EST: 1938
SQ FT: 16,000
SALES: 13MM **Privately Held**
WEB: www.putmanmedia.com
SIC: 2721 2731 Trade journals: publishing only, not printed on site; book publishing

(G-18690)
QT SIGN INC
1391 Wright Blvd (60193-4425)
PHONE.....................847 524-7950
William Chase Jr, *President*
EMP: 8
SALES (est): 1.2MM **Privately Held**
SIC: 3993 Signs & advertising specialties

(G-18691)
QUADRANT TOOL AND MFG CO
1720 W Irving Park Rd (60193-5477)
PHONE.....................847 352-6977
Kenneth G Kraemer, *President*
Lillian Kraemer, *Vice Pres*
Mike Fregeau, *Engineer*
Helayne Przeslicke, *Treasurer*
Kathryn Good, *Admin Sec*
EMP: 25
SQ FT: 18,500

SALES: 5.7MM **Privately Held**
WEB: www.quadranttool.com
SIC: 3599 Machine shop, jobbing & repair

(G-18692)
QUALITY MACHINE TOOL SERVICES
2385 Hammond Dr Ste 12 (60173-3844)
PHONE.....................847 776-0073
Dave Polido, *Owner*
EMP: 2 EST: 2011
SALES (est): 214.6K **Privately Held**
SIC: 7699 3599 Industrial machinery & equipment repair; machine shop, jobbing & repair

(G-18693)
QUALITY SERVICE & INSTALLATION
923 Sharon Ln (60193-1348)
PHONE.....................847 352-4000
Jeff Ficarrotta, *President*
EMP: 3
SALES: 100K **Privately Held**
SIC: 3669 Communications equipment

(G-18694)
QUINTUM TECHNOLOGIES INC
1821 Walden Office Sq # 200 (60173-4271)
PHONE.....................847 348-7730
Melissa Rohring, *Manager*
EMP: 15
SALES (corp-wide): 563.1MM **Publicly Held**
SIC: 3661 Telephone & telegraph apparatus
HQ: Quintum Technologies, Inc.
71 James Way
Eatontown NJ 07724
732 460-9000

(G-18695)
RAAJRTNA STINLESS WIRE USA INC
1015 W Wise Rd Ste 201 (60193-3777)
PHONE.....................823 923-8000
Samrat Brahmbhatt, *Business Mgr*
Baiju Sumathy, *Manager*
▲ EMP: 15 EST: 2007
SALES (est): 2.4MM **Privately Held**
SIC: 3315 Steel wire & related products
PA: Raajratan Metal Industries
Mittal Court, No 126, Nariman Point
Mumbai MH 40002

(G-18696)
REVLON INC
1900 E Golf Rd Ste 900 (60173-5093)
PHONE.....................847 240-1558
EMP: 4 **Publicly Held**
SIC: 2844 Cosmetic preparations
HQ: Revlon, Inc.
1 New York Plz Fl 49
New York NY 10004

(G-18697)
RITTAL NORTH AMERICA LLC (HQ)
425 N Martingale Rd # 1540 (60173-2213)
PHONE.....................847 240-4600
Michael Freund, *Managing Dir*
Brian Brink, *Vice Pres*
Vilmos Polgar, *Vice Pres*
Sandy Weber, *Buyer*
Nathan Xavier, *Technical Mgr*
◆ EMP: 635
SQ FT: 25,000
SALES (est): 194.6MM
SALES (corp-wide): 1.4B **Privately Held**
WEB: www.rittal.com
SIC: 3469 5065 Electronic enclosures, stamped or pressed metal; electronic parts & equipment
PA: Rittal Gmbh & Co. Kg
Auf Dem Stutzelberg
Herborn 35745
277 250-50

(G-18698)
ROBERT MCCORMICK TRIBUNE LBRRY
1400 N Roosevelt Blvd (60173-4377)
PHONE.....................847 619-7980
Yvette Garcia, *Manager*

Francie Bauer, *Director*
Lauren Chill, *Executive*
Nancy Michaels, *Executive*
Lee Earle, *Assoc Prof*
EMP: 3
SALES (est): 109.7K **Privately Held**
WEB: www.roosevelt.edu
SIC: 2711 Newspapers, publishing & printing

(G-18699)
RUBY AUTOMATION LLC
1261 Wiley Rd Ste A (60173-4353)
PHONE.....................847 273-9050
Den Lucas, *Branch Mgr*
EMP: 11
SALES (corp-wide): 735.6MM **Privately Held**
SIC: 5063 3621 Motors, electric; electric motor & generator auxillary parts
HQ: Ruby Automation, Llc
1 Vision Way
Bloomfield CT 06002
860 687-5000

(G-18700)
SAGENT LOGISTICS LP
1901 N Roselle Rd Ste 450 (60195-3181)
PHONE.....................847 908-1600
Peter Kaemmerer, *CEO*
Sean Brynjelsen, *Exec VP*
Donald Bullock, *Exec VP*
Frank Harmon, *Exec VP*
Jonathon Singer, *CFO*
EMP: 10
SALES (est): 409.5K **Privately Held**
SIC: 2834 Pharmaceutical preparations

(G-18701)
SAGENT PHARMACEUTICALS INC
1901 N Roselle Rd Ste 400 (60195-3167)
PHONE.....................847 908-1600
Jeff Grevee, *Branch Mgr*
EMP: 250 **Privately Held**
SIC: 2834 5122 Druggists' preparations (pharmaceuticals); pharmaceuticals
HQ: Sagent Pharmaceuticals, Inc.
1901 N Roselle Rd Ste 450
Schaumburg IL 60195

(G-18702)
SAGENT PHARMACEUTICALS INC (HQ)
1901 N Roselle Rd Ste 450 (60195-3181)
PHONE.....................847 908-1600
Peter Kaemmerer, *CEO*
Eileen Epstein, *Business Mgr*
Chad Fox, *Business Mgr*
Gina Iuni, *Business Mgr*
Bryn Jackson, *Business Mgr*
▲ EMP: 100
SQ FT: 23,500
SALES: 325.4MM **Privately Held**
SIC: 2834 5122 Druggists' preparations (pharmaceuticals); pharmaceuticals

(G-18703)
SANDVIK INC
Also Called: Sandvik Crmant Prductivity Ctr
1665 N Penny Ln (60173-4593)
PHONE.....................847 519-1737
Jim Gondeck, *President*
EMP: 100
SALES (corp-wide): 11.1B **Privately Held**
WEB: www.sandvik.com
SIC: 3316 Strip steel, cold-rolled: from purchased hot-rolled; wire, flat, cold-rolled strip: not made in hot-rolled mills
HQ: Sandvik, Inc.
17-02 Nevins Rd
Fair Lawn NJ 07410
201 794-5000

(G-18704)
SBIC AMERICA INC
205 Travis Ct Apt 304 (60195-5116)
PHONE.....................847 303-5430
Samuel Kim, *Principal*
EMP: 5 EST: 2007
SALES (est): 490K **Privately Held**
SIC: 3462 Iron & steel forgings

GEOGRAPHIC SECTION
Schaumburg - Cook County (G-18730)

(G-18705)
SC LIGHTING
607 W Wise Rd (60193-3865)
PHONE 630 849-3384
EMP: 4
SALES (est): 383.1K *Privately Held*
SIC: 3648 Lighting equipment

(G-18706)
SCHAUMBURG SPECIALTIES CO
550 Albion Ave Ste 30 (60193-4547)
PHONE 847 451-0070
Charles Schaumburg, *President*
Joel Bidmead, *Vice Pres*
Eric Schaumburg, *Vice Pres*
Jeff Schaumburg, *Sales Staff*
▼ EMP: 7
SQ FT: 5,000
SALES (est): 1.2MM *Privately Held*
WEB: www.shopcraftracks.com
SIC: 5084 2542 Materials handling machinery; office & store showcases & display fixtures

(G-18707)
SCHNEIDER ELC HOLDINGS INC (HQ)
200 N Martingale Rd # 100 (60173-2033)
PHONE 717 944-5460
Jean-Pascal Tricoire, *CEO*
Pat Cowart, *Regional Mgr*
Stephen Brown, *Exec VP*
Richard Korthaur, *Exec VP*
Scott Fleck, *Vice Pres*
▲ EMP: 4619
SALES (est): 7B
SALES (corp-wide): 177.9K *Privately Held*
SIC: 3822 1711 3625 3823 Building services monitoring controls, automatic; mechanical contractor; relays & industrial controls; motor control accessories, including overload relays; motor controls, electric; industrial process control instruments; motors, electric
PA: Schneider Electric Se
35 Rue Joseph Monier
Rueil Malmaison
146 046-982

(G-18708)
SCHNEIDER ELECTRIC USA INC
200 N Martingale Rd # 1000 (60173-2035)
PHONE 847 441-2526
Shelley Franzak, *Opers Staff*
Maichou Yang, *Buyer*
Piyush Shah, *Research*
David Daines, *Engineer*
Erik Davis, *Engineer*
EMP: 25
SALES (corp-wide): 177.9K *Privately Held*
SIC: 3643 3613 Bus bars (electrical conductors); switchgear & switchboard apparatus
HQ: Schneider Electric Usa, Inc.
201 Wshington St Ste 2700
Boston MA 02108
978 975-9600

(G-18709)
SCIENTIFIC INSTRUMENTS INC
622 Lunt Ave (60193-4411)
PHONE 847 679-1242
Jean Falk, *President*
Greg Falk, *Engineer*
EMP: 7 EST: 1962
SALES (est): 605K *Privately Held*
WEB: www.scientificinstrumentsinc.com
SIC: 7389 3826 3829 3822 Design, commercial & industrial; analytical instruments; measuring & controlling devices; auto controls regulating residntl & coml environmt & applncs; laboratory apparatus & furniture; relays & industrial controls

(G-18710)
SE RELAYS LLC (DH)
Also Called: Schneider Electric Relays
200 N Martingale Rd # 100 (60173-2033)
PHONE 847 441-2540
James Steinback, *Mng Member*
▲ EMP: 9
SQ FT: 4,200
SALES: 15MM
SALES (corp-wide): 177.9K *Privately Held*
SIC: 3625 Relays & industrial controls
HQ: Schneider Electric Usa, Inc.
201 Wshington St Ste 2700
Boston MA 02108
978 975-9600

(G-18711)
SENARIO LLC
1325 Remington Rd Ste H (60173-4815)
PHONE 847 882-0677
Mike Nakamura,
▲ EMP: 18
SQ FT: 17,600
SALES (est): 14.1MM *Privately Held*
SIC: 3651 5942 Home entertainment equipment, electronic; children's books

(G-18712)
SIEMENS MED SOLUTIONS USA INC
Also Called: Dosimetry Medicine Group
2501 N Barrington Rd (60195)
PHONE 847 304-7700
Steve Wille, *Manager*
EMP: 70
SALES (corp-wide): 96.9B *Privately Held*
SIC: 3841 Diagnostic apparatus, medical
HQ: Siemens Medical Solutions Usa, Inc.
40 Liberty Blvd
Malvern PA 19355
888 826-9702

(G-18713)
SK HYNIX AMERICA INC
Also Called: Hsa Chicago Office
1920 Thoreau Dr N (60173-4176)
PHONE 847 925-0196
EMP: 4 *Privately Held*
SIC: 3825 Mfg Electrical Measuring Instruments
HQ: Sk Hynix America Inc.
3101 N 1st St
San Jose CA 95134
408 232-8000

(G-18714)
SOFT O SOFT INC
1701 E Wdfield Rd Ste 215 (60173)
PHONE 630 741-4414
Syam C Thotakura, *President*
EMP: 20
SALES (est): 1.6MM *Privately Held*
WEB: www.softosoft.com
SIC: 7372 Prepackaged software

(G-18715)
SOOSAN USA INC
1261 Wiley Rd Ste B (60173-4353)
PHONE 224 653-8916
Suk Hyun Chung, *Principal*
Sung Jong Kee, *Admin Sec*
▲ EMP: 6 EST: 2015
SALES (est): 1MM *Privately Held*
SIC: 3531 Construction machinery

(G-18716)
SPARTON AYDIN LLC
Also Called: Aydin Displays
425 N Martingale Rd (60173-2406)
PHONE 800 772-7866
Cary B Wood, *CEO*
EMP: 3
SALES (est): 278.2K
SALES (corp-wide): 374.9MM *Privately Held*
SIC: 3577 3625 Computer peripheral equipment; control equipment, electric
HQ: Sparton Corporation
425 N Martingale Rd # 100
Schaumburg IL 60173
847 762-5800

(G-18717)
SPARTON CORPORATION (HQ)
425 N Martingale Rd # 100 (60173-2406)
PHONE 847 762-5800
Joseph G McCormack, *CEO*
Steven M Korwin, *Senior VP*
Gordon B Madlock, *Senior VP*
Michael A Gaul, *Vice Pres*
James M Lackemacher, *Vice Pres*
▲ EMP: 272 EST: 1900
SQ FT: 22,000
SALES (est): 412.4MM
SALES (corp-wide): 374.9MM *Privately Held*
WEB: www.sparton.com
SIC: 3672 Printed circuit boards
PA: Sparton Parent, Inc.
425 N Martingale Rd
Schaumburg IL 60173
847 762-5800

(G-18718)
SPARTON DESIGN SERVICES LLC (DH)
425 N Martingale Rd # 2050 (60173-2406)
PHONE 847 762-5800
EMP: 4 EST: 2015
SALES (est): 2.7MM
SALES (corp-wide): 374.9MM *Privately Held*
SIC: 3674 3672 Microprocessors; printed circuit boards
HQ: Sparton Corporation
425 N Martingale Rd # 100
Schaumburg IL 60173
847 762-5800

(G-18719)
SPARTON EMT LLC (DH)
425 N Martingale Rd Ste 2 (60173-2406)
PHONE 800 772-7866
EMP: 7
SALES (est): 297.1MM
SALES (corp-wide): 374.9MM *Privately Held*
SIC: 3674 Microprocessors
HQ: Sparton Corporation
425 N Martingale Rd # 100
Schaumburg IL 60173
847 762-5800

(G-18720)
SPARTON ONYX HOLDINGS LLC (DH)
425 N Martingale Rd (60173-2406)
PHONE 847 762-5800
David Molfenter, *Opers Staff*
James Fast, *Director*
Joseph Hartnett, *Director*
Charles Kummeth, *Director*
EMP: 6
SALES (est): 46.4MM
SALES (corp-wide): 374.9MM *Privately Held*
WEB: www.sparton.com
SIC: 3841 3699 3625 Surgical & medical instruments; electrical equipment & supplies; relays & industrial controls
HQ: Sparton Corporation
425 N Martingale Rd # 100
Schaumburg IL 60173
847 762-5800

(G-18721)
SPARTON PARENT INC (PA)
425 N Martingale Rd (60173-2406)
PHONE 847 762-5800
Joseph G McCormack, *CEO*
EMP: 4
SALES (est): 374.9MM *Privately Held*
SIC: 3674 3672 Microprocessors; printed circuit boards

(G-18722)
SPECTRUM METALS INC
890 E Higgins Rd Ste 150d (60173-4749)
PHONE 847 969-0887
Brian Zimmer, *Branch Mgr*
EMP: 11
SALES (corp-wide): 5MM *Privately Held*
WEB: www.spectrummetalsinc.com
SIC: 3541 Planers (metal cutting machine tools)
PA: Spectrum Metals, Inc.
39200 S Groesbeck Hwy
Clinton Township MI 48036
586 783-7840

(G-18723)
SPG USA INC
1726 Wright Blvd (60193-4514)
PHONE 847 439-4949
Daniel Kim, *CEO*
Chang Ho Kim, *President*
▲ EMP: 5
SQ FT: 9,000
SALES (est): 12.9MM *Privately Held*
SIC: 3821 5063 Motors, electric; motors, electric

(G-18724)
SPIE TOOL CO
1350 Wright Blvd (60193-4456)
PHONE 847 891-6556
Mabel Khoshaba, *President*
David Khoshaba, *Vice Pres*
Dorothy Loughlin, *Vice Pres*
Amy Khoshoba, *Cust Mgr*
Mabel Shannon, *Info Tech Mgr*
▲ EMP: 45 EST: 1976
SQ FT: 10,000
SALES (est): 7MM *Privately Held*
SIC: 3545 Cutting tools for machine tools

(G-18725)
SPOTLIGHT GRAPHIC SOLUTIONS
1400 Wilkening Rd (60173-5341)
PHONE 847 944-9600
Chris Kelly, *Principal*
EMP: 2
SALES (est): 203.5K *Privately Held*
SIC: 2759 Commercial printing

(G-18726)
SRJ INC (PA)
2242 Palmer Dr (60173-3822)
P.O. Box 59098 (60159-0098)
PHONE 630 351-0639
Woo Young Jee, *President*
Dennis Jee, *Vice Pres*
Sung R Jee, *Treasurer*
Anne Marie Derosa, *Human Resources*
▲ EMP: 18
SALES: 16MM *Privately Held*
SIC: 5083 2951 3052 Farm & garden machinery; asphalt paving mixtures & blocks; rubber & plastics hose & beltings

(G-18727)
SRV PROFESSIONAL PUBLICATIONS
235 Monson Ct (60173-2113)
PHONE 847 330-1260
S RAO Vallabhaneni, *President*
EMP: 2
SALES: 500K *Privately Held*
SIC: 7372 8742 Publishers' computer software; marketing consulting services

(G-18728)
STREAMWOOD PLASTICS LTD
979 Lunt Ave (60193-4416)
P.O. Box 427, Streamwood (60107-0427)
PHONE 847 895-9190
Richard L Monson, *President*
Robert Monson, *Corp Secy*
Larry Maty, *Vice Pres*
EMP: 5 EST: 1976
SALES (est): 1.1MM *Privately Held*
SIC: 5162 3082 Plastics materials; unsupported plastics profile shapes

(G-18729)
SUMIDA AMERICA INC
1251 N Plum Grove Rd # 150 (60173-5603)
PHONE 847 545-6700
Dan Chiu, *President*
Franz Friedl, *Vice Pres*
Douglas Malcolm, *Vice Pres*
Peter Rutkowski, *Engineer*
William Ng, *Treasurer*
EMP: 25
SQ FT: 4,000
SALES (est): 30K *Privately Held*
SIC: 3679 5065 Electronic loads & power supplies; electronic parts & equipment
PA: Sumida Corporation
1-8-10, Harumi
Chuo-Ku TKY 104-0

(G-18730)
SUNSTAR AMERICAS INC (HQ)
301 E Central Rd (60195-1901)
PHONE 847 794-4157
Daniel Descary, *President*
Yoshihiro Kaneda, *Vice Pres*
David Barcus, *VP Opers*
Greg Williams, *Mfg Mgr*
Carmen Keady, *Buyer*
◆ EMP: 460 EST: 1923

Schaumburg - Cook County (G-18731)

SALES (est): 125.1MM **Privately Held**
WEB: www.gumbrand.com
SIC: 2844 3843 Toilet preparations; dental equipment & supplies

(G-18731)
SUPERIOR BIOLOGICS IL INC
2050 E Algonquin Rd # 606 (60173-4161)
PHONE.................................847 469-2400
Kamyar Ghazvini, *President*
Kam Ghazvini, *Vice Pres*
Sheila Sheppard, *Vice Pres*
EMP: 8
SALES (est): 1.2MM **Privately Held**
SIC: 2834 Pharmaceutical preparations

(G-18732)
SURUGA USA CORP
1717 N Penny Ln Ste 200 (60173-5627)
PHONE.................................630 628-0989
▲ EMP: 35
SQ FT: 10,200
SALES: 3.1MM
SALES (corp-wide): 2.2B **Privately Held**
SIC: 3544 Mfg Dies/Tools/Jigs/Fixtures
HQ: Suruga Production Platform Co.,Ltd.
505, Nanatsushin-Ya, Shimizu-Ku
Shizuoka SZO 424-0
543 440-311

(G-18733)
SWAROVSKI NORTH AMERICA LTD
D344 Woodfield Mall (60173-5010)
PHONE.................................847 413-9960
John Tollins, *Branch Mgr*
EMP: 4
SALES (corp-wide): 4.7B **Privately Held**
SIC: 3961 Costume jewelry
HQ: Swarovski North America Limited
1 Kenney Dr
Cranston RI 02920
401 463-6400

(G-18734)
SYNOPSYS INC
10 N Martingale Rd # 400 (60173-2411)
PHONE.................................847 706-2000
John Kapinos, *Branch Mgr*
Raj Joshi, *Manager*
Vinay Vishwanatha, *Manager*
EMP: 12
SALES (corp-wide): 3.3B **Publicly Held**
SIC: 7372 Application computer software
PA: Synopsys, Inc.
690 E Middlefield Rd
Mountain View CA 94043
650 584-5000

(G-18735)
T H K HOLDINGS OF AMERICA LLC (HQ)
200 Commerce Dr (60173-5340)
PHONE.................................847 310-1111
Mikio Matsui, *President*
Corey Lamb, *General Mgr*
Chris Wilson, *Manager*
Takeki Shirai, *Director*
Toshihiro Teramachi, *Director*
EMP: 6
SALES (est): 48.6MM **Privately Held**
WEB: www.thk.com
SIC: 6712 3469 Bank holding companies; metal stampings

(G-18736)
TACMINA USA CORPORATION
105 W Central Rd (60195-1945)
PHONE.................................312 810-8128
Joseph S Parisi, *Principal*
EMP: 5
SALES (est): 394.1K **Privately Held**
SIC: 3561 Pumps, domestic: water or sump
PA: Tacmina Korea Co., Ltd.
Rm 616, 617 6/F Graduate School Of Dankook Univ.
Yongin-Gun 16890

(G-18737)
TANAKA KIKINZOKU INTL AMER INC
475 N Martingale Rd # 150 (60173-2405)
PHONE.................................224 653-8309
Atfushi Nozawa, *Director*
EMP: 4
SALES (est): 581.1K **Privately Held**
SIC: 3339 Precious metals

(G-18738)
TANAKA KKNZOKU INTRNATIONAL KK
Also Called: Tanaka Kikinzoku International
425 N Martingale Rd # 1550 (60173-2406)
PHONE.................................224 653-8309
Andrew Farry, *Branch Mgr*
EMP: 3 **Privately Held**
SIC: 3339 Precious metals
PA: Tanaka Holdings Co., Ltd.
2-7-3, Marunouchi
Chiyoda-Ku TKY 100-0

(G-18739)
TANDEM USA LLC
518 Lunt Ave (60193-4408)
PHONE.................................224 653-8840
Pentchev Kalin Tiholov, *Principal*
EMP: 3
SALES (est): 195.7K **Privately Held**
SIC: 2013 Sausages & other prepared meats

(G-18740)
TBW MACHINING INC
1030 Morse Ave (60193-4504)
PHONE.................................847 524-1501
Bernard Panski, *Owner*
EMP: 10
SALES (est): 1.3MM **Privately Held**
SIC: 3599 Machine shop, jobbing & repair

(G-18741)
TC ELECTRIC CONTROLS LLC (PA)
1320 Tower Rd (60173-4309)
PHONE.................................815 213-7680
Amer M Jaber,
EMP: 1
SQ FT: 144
SALES (est): 642.2K **Privately Held**
SIC: 3625 Relays & industrial controls

(G-18742)
TDM SYSTEMS INC
1901 N Roselle Rd Ste 800 (60195-3186)
PHONE.................................847 605-1269
Harald Kaiser, *Vice Pres*
Eric Graber, *Engineer*
Dan Speidel, *Sales Staff*
Patrick Bliki, *Manager*
Henry Miller, *Manager*
EMP: 4
SALES: 500K
SALES (corp-wide): 10.5B **Privately Held**
SIC: 3695 Computer software tape & disks: blank, rigid & floppy
PA: Sandvik Ab
Hogbovagen 45
Sandviken 811 3
262 600-00

(G-18743)
TEGRATECS DEVELOPMENT CORP
1320 Tower Rd (60173-4309)
PHONE.................................847 397-0088
F Rexford Smith II, *President*
Paul Wampach, *Vice Pres*
EMP: 8
SALES (est): 1MM **Privately Held**
SIC: 5734 7372 7379 Computer software & accessories; prepackaged software; computer related consulting services

(G-18744)
TELEMEDICINE SOLUTIONS LLC
Also Called: Wound Rounds
425 N Martingale Rd # 1250 (60173-2406)
PHONE.................................847 519-3500
John Croghan MD, *Chairman*
Rhett Gustafson, *Exec VP*
Mike Diamond, *Mng Member*
Betty Czowiecki, *Director*
Philip Sheridan Jr, *Director*
EMP: 16
SQ FT: 4,592
SALES (est): 1.1MM **Privately Held**
SIC: 7372 Prepackaged software

(G-18745)
THERMOS LLC (DH)
475 N Martingale Rd # 1100 (60173-2051)
PHONE.................................847 439-7821
Alex Huang, *CEO*
Rick Dias, *President*
Tom Lewis, *Vice Pres*
Mike Yeager, *Plant Mgr*
John Golden, *Prdtn Mgr*
◆ EMP: 55
SALES (est): 30.6MM **Privately Held**
SIC: 3429 3086 Manufactured hardware (general); plastics foam products

(G-18746)
THIESSEN COMMUNICATIONS INC
Also Called: T C
1300 Basswood Rd (60173-4522)
PHONE.................................847 884-0980
Allen Steinberg, *President*
EMP: 29 EST: 2008
SALES (est): 5.6MM **Privately Held**
WEB: www.thiessencommunications.com
SIC: 2752 Commercial printing, offset

(G-18747)
THK AMERICA INC (DH)
200 Commerce Dr (60173-5340)
PHONE.................................847 310-1111
Masaki Sugita, *President*
Ed Johnson, *General Mgr*
Casey Montena, *District Mgr*
Joe Timpone, *District Mgr*
Yoshitaka Kinoshita, *Engineer*
▲ EMP: 125
SQ FT: 105,000
SALES (est): 60.8MM **Privately Held**
SIC: 3568 Bearings, bushings & blocks; joints & couplings
HQ: T H K Holdings Of America Llc
200 Commerce Dr
Schaumburg IL 60173
847 310-1111

(G-18748)
TI SQUARED TECHNOLOGIES INC
1019 W Wise Rd Ste 101 (60193-3754)
PHONE.................................541 367-2929
Ronald E Shadle, *President*
EMP: 11
SALES (est): 1.6MM **Privately Held**
SIC: 3364 Titanium die-castings

(G-18749)
TISHMA TECHNOLOGY LLC
101 E State Pkwy (60173-5336)
PHONE.................................847 884-1805
David Showman,
EMP: 10
SALES (est): 1.8MM **Privately Held**
SIC: 3565 Packaging machinery

(G-18750)
TOWERLEAF LLC
1680 Wright Blvd (60193-4512)
PHONE.................................847 985-1937
Christine Thornblad, *Mng Member*
▲ EMP: 9
SALES (est): 1.3MM **Privately Held**
SIC: 2421 Sawmills & planing mills, general

(G-18751)
TPR AMERICA INC
10 N Martingale Rd # 145 (60173-2291)
PHONE.................................847 446-5336
Kazuhiro Haneishi, *President*
Shinichiro Kondo, *Vice Pres*
Toru Takahashi, *Vice Pres*
▲ EMP: 9
SQ FT: 3,500
SALES: 70MM **Privately Held**
SIC: 3519 5013 Parts & accessories, internal combustion engines; automotive engines & engine parts
PA: Tpr Co., Ltd.
1-6-2, Marunouchi
Chiyoda-Ku TKY 100-0

(G-18752)
TRANSPAC USA INC
1515 E Wdfield Rd Ste 340 (60173)
PHONE.................................847 605-1616
Karim Klat, *President*
Gregory Handrahan, *Vice Pres*
▲ EMP: 8
SALES (est): 1.6MM
SALES (corp-wide): 3.4MM **Privately Held**
SIC: 2621 Book paper
PA: Codefine International Sa
Avenue Du Leman 21
Lausanne VD 1005
213 458-211

(G-18753)
TRELLBORG SLING SLTIONS US INC
Also Called: Lutz Sales Company
20 N Martingale Rd # 210 (60173-2412)
PHONE.................................630 539-5500
Richard Banks, *Principal*
Mike Aronson, *Purch Mgr*
EMP: 14
SALES (corp-wide): 3.7B **Privately Held**
SIC: 3089 Plastic processing; bearings, plastic
HQ: Trelleborg Sealing Solutions Us, Inc.
2531 Bremer Rd
Fort Wayne IN 46803
260 749-9631

(G-18754)
TRI SECT CORPORATION
717 Morse Ave (60193-4533)
PHONE.................................847 524-1119
Joseph Barna, *President*
Jim Tobin, *Vice Pres*
EMP: 10
SQ FT: 13,000
SALES (est): 2.1MM **Privately Held**
SIC: 2841 2842 Soap & other detergents; cleaning or polishing preparations

(G-18755)
TRI STAR PLOWING
876 Asbury Ln (60193-4101)
PHONE.................................847 584-5070
Linda Johnson, *Principal*
EMP: 5 EST: 2001
SALES (est): 259.5K **Privately Held**
WEB: www.tristarsnow.com
SIC: 4959 2759 Snowplowing; screen printing

(G-18756)
TRIAD CUTTING TOOLS SVC & MFG
1025 Lunt Ave Ste E (60193-4472)
PHONE.................................847 352-0459
Mark Morris, *President*
Visilis Papateodoru, *Vice Pres*
EMP: 8
SQ FT: 2,000
SALES (est): 1MM **Privately Held**
SIC: 3545 Cutting tools for machine tools

(G-18757)
TRIDENT INDUSTRIES
1900 E Golf Rd (60173-5834)
PHONE.................................847 285-1316
EMP: 10
SALES (est): 2.2MM **Privately Held**
SIC: 3999 Barber & beauty shop equipment

(G-18758)
TRUFAB GROUP USA LLC (PA)
550 Albion Ave Ste 90 (60193-4547)
PHONE.................................630 994-3286
Gareth Trewarn, *Vice Pres*
Stuart Trewarn, *Mng Member*
Charles Schaumburg,
In Trewarn,
Maville Trewarn,
▲ EMP: 20
SQ FT: 30,000
SALES: 8MM **Privately Held**
SIC: 3599 Machine & other job shop work

(G-18759)
TRUSTAR HOLDINGS LLC
1515 E Wdfield Rd Ste 740 (60173)
PHONE.................................847 598-8800
James Sanfilippo,
EMP: 4
SALES: 350K **Privately Held**
SIC: 3999 Manufacturing industries

GEOGRAPHIC SECTION

Schiller Park - Cook County (G-18789)

(G-18760)
TSM NORTH AMERICA INC
Also Called: L-R Systems
1320 Tower Rd (60173-4309)
  PHONE...................815 372-1600
  EMP: 7
  SALES (est): 336.3K **Privately Held**
  SIC: 3531 Construction machinery

(G-18761)
TWR SERVICE CORPORATION
940 Lunt Ave (60193-4417)
  PHONE...................847 923-0692
  Daniel Moore, *President*
  Scott Hiestand, *Treasurer*
  EMP: 14
  SQ FT: 10,000
  SALES (est): 2.1MM **Privately Held**
  SIC: 3471 Electroplating of metals or formed products

(G-18762)
ULTRA POLISHING INC
640 Pratt Ave N (60193-4557)
  PHONE...................630 635-2926
  Casey Gwozdz, *President*
  Lester Doniec, *Treasurer*
  Sheri Richards, *Manager*
  EMP: 40
  SQ FT: 9,000
  SALES (est): 7.7MM **Privately Held**
  SIC: 3544 3471 Special dies & tools; plating & polishing

(G-18763)
UMW INC
601 Lunt Ave (60193-4410)
  PHONE...................847 352-5252
  Arina Muradyan, *CEO*
  Boris Muradyan, *President*
  EMP: 15
  SQ FT: 20,000
  SALES (est): 4.6MM **Privately Held**
  SIC: 3599 Machine shop, jobbing & repair

(G-18764)
UNIFLEX OF AMERICA LLC
1088 National Pkwy (60173-4519)
  PHONE...................847 519-1100
  Casey Carter, *Technical Mgr*
  Dr Friedrich Von Waitz, *Mng Member*
  ▲ **EMP:** 7 EST: 1999
  SQ FT: 8,000
  SALES (est): 1.1MM
  SALES (corp-wide): 355.8K **Privately Held**
  WEB: www.uniflexusa.com
  SIC: 3542 Crimping machinery, metal
  HQ: Uniflex-Hydraulik Gmbh
    Robert-Bosch-Str. 50-52
    Karben 61184
    603 991-710

(G-18765)
UNITED ENGRAVERS INC
618 Pratt Ave N (60193-4557)
  PHONE...................847 301-3740
  Peter P Cappas, *President*
  Peter Cappas, *President*
  EMP: 50
  SALES (est): 8.5MM **Privately Held**
  SIC: 2759 Commercial printing

(G-18766)
UNITED MACHINE WORKS INC
601 Lunt Ave (60193-4410)
  PHONE...................847 352-5252
  Boris Muradyan, *President*
  EMP: 3
  SQ FT: 6,000
  SALES (est): 540K **Privately Held**
  SIC: 3599 7692 Machine shop, jobbing & repair; welding repair

(G-18767)
UNITED WOODWORKING INC
729 Lunt Ave (60193-4412)
  PHONE...................847 352-3066
  Stanley Chraca, *President*
  Angie Chraca, *Vice Pres*
  EMP: 30
  SQ FT: 16,000
  SALES (est): 4.1MM **Privately Held**
  SIC: 2511 Wood household furniture

(G-18768)
URBAN SERVICES OF AMERICA (PA)
1901 N Roselle Rd Ste 740 (60195-3194)
  PHONE...................847 278-3210
  Douglas Ritter, *President*
  Gordon Mc Tavish, *Treasurer*
  EMP: 8
  SALES (est): 4.1MM **Privately Held**
  SIC: 3089 Toilets, portable chemical: plastic

(G-18769)
V2 SOLUTIONS INC
636 Remington Rd Ste B (60173-5612)
  PHONE...................312 528-9050
  Andre Van Vuren, *CEO*
  EMP: 6
  SALES (est): 750K **Privately Held**
  SIC: 8711 7372 Engineering services; application computer software

(G-18770)
VENUS PRINTING INC
549 Morse Ave (60193-4529)
  PHONE...................847 985-7510
  Phillip Touzios, *President*
  Pat Touzios, *Principal*
  EMP: 3
  SQ FT: 3,000
  SALES (est): 350K **Privately Held**
  SIC: 2752 Commercial printing, offset

(G-18771)
VERTEX CONSULTING SERVICES INC
935 N Plum Grove Rd Ste D (60173-4770)
  PHONE...................313 492-5154
  Abdul Mohammad, *President*
  Abdul Mannan Khan, *Vice Pres*
  Eloise Robinson, *Manager*
  EMP: 10 EST: 2011
  SALES (est): 310.5K **Privately Held**
  SIC: 7372 7373 7374 7371 Prepackaged software; computer integrated systems design; data processing & preparation; computer software development

(G-18772)
VLC SOLUTIONS LLC
718 Killarney Ct Apt 2b (60193-3252)
  PHONE...................630 447-9852
  Lanka Reddy, *Manager*
  Chandana Veerareddy,
  EMP: 90
  SQ FT: 12,000
  SALES: 7MM **Privately Held**
  SIC: 7372 Prepackaged software

(G-18773)
WIDE IMAGE INCORPORATED
Also Called: Chicago Printing Center
1187 Tower Rd (60173-4305)
  PHONE...................773 279-9183
  Tudor Fartaes, *President*
  EMP: 3
  SALES (est): 220.1K **Privately Held**
  WEB: www.chicagoprintingcenter.com
  SIC: 2759 Commercial printing

(G-18774)
WISE EQUIPMENT & RENTALS INC
1475 Rodenburg Rd (60193-3532)
  PHONE...................847 895-5555
  Edward J Zawilla, *President*
  ◆ **EMP:** 11
  SALES (est): 3.3MM **Privately Held**
  SIC: 5261 7699 7359 5999 Lawn & garden equipment; lawn mower repair shop; party supplies rental services; tents; trailers & trailer equipment

(G-18775)
WJ DIE MOLD INC
Also Called: Unique Plastics
915 Estes Ct (60193-4427)
  PHONE...................847 895-6561
  Wayne Johnson, *President*
  James Goddyn, *Vice Pres*
  EMP: 10
  SQ FT: 6,000
  SALES (est): 1.2MM **Privately Held**
  SIC: 3544 Special dies & tools

(G-18776)
WOZNIAK INDUSTRIES INC (PA)
Also Called: Gmp Metal Products
1901 N Roselle Rd Ste 750 (60195-3175)
  PHONE...................630 954-3400
  Sandra Wozniak, *Ch of Bd*
  Michael Wozniak, *President*
  Michael Powers, *CFO*
  Robert Gamboa, *Manager*
  Timothy Smith, *Manager*
  ◆ **EMP:** 9
  SQ FT: 3,000
  SALES (est): 81.3MM **Privately Held**
  SIC: 3469 3444 3462 Metal stampings; sheet metalwork; iron & steel forgings

(G-18777)
XINGFA USA CORPORATION
20 N Martingale Rd # 140 (60173-2423)
  PHONE...................630 305-9097
  Yong Zhao, *President*
  ▲ **EMP:** 11 EST: 2011
  SALES: 50MM
  SALES (corp-wide): 2.5B **Privately Held**
  SIC: 2819 Hydrochloric acid; sodium & potassium compounds, exc. bleaches, alkalies, alum.
  PA: Hubei Xingfa Chemicals Group Co., Ltd.
    Room-2110, Yuehe Building, No.62, Fazhan Avenue
    Yichang 44300
    717 676-0850

(G-18778)
XTREMEDATA INC
999 N Plaza Dr Ste 570 (60173-5407)
  PHONE...................847 871-0379
  Ravi Chandran, *President*
  Jay Desai, *Vice Pres*
  Geno Valente, *Safety Mgr*
  Radoslaw Garbacz, *Software Dev*
  Oleg Ostrozhansky, *Software Dev*
  EMP: 20
  SQ FT: 6,062
  SALES (est): 3.5MM **Privately Held**
  SIC: 3674 Integrated circuits, semiconductor networks, etc.

(G-18779)
YOUNG SHIN USA LIMITED
1320 Tower Rd Ste 111 (60173-4309)
  PHONE...................847 598-3611
  Richard Lee, *President*
  Phillip Mack, *Admin Sec*
  ▲ **EMP:** 3
  SALES (est): 390.7K **Privately Held**
  SIC: 2675 Die-cut paper & board

(G-18780)
YOUR IMAGES GROUP INC
1300 Basswood Rd Ste 200 (60173-4522)
  PHONE...................847 437-6688
  Bryan Tillmanns, *President*
  EMP: 4
  SALES: 900K **Privately Held**
  SIC: 2759 7331 Commercial printing; mailing service

Schiller Park
Cook County

(G-18781)
ABLE DIE CASTING CORPORATION
3907 Wesley Ter (60176-2131)
  PHONE...................847 678-1991
  Nestor Hernandez, *President*
  Robert Stout, *Vice Pres*
  Fredy Aguilar, *Prdtn Mgr*
  Scott Richter, *Purch Mgr*
  Nes Hernandez, *VP Mktg*
  EMP: 54 EST: 1920
  SQ FT: 14,000
  SALES (est): 12.7MM **Privately Held**
  WEB: www.ablediecasting.com
  SIC: 3369 3363 3365 Zinc & zinc-base alloy castings, except die-castings; aluminum die-castings; aluminum foundries

(G-18782)
ACCENT METAL FINISHING INC
9331 Byron St (60176-2303)
  PHONE...................847 678-7420
  Douglas Mangino, *President*
  EMP: 10
  SQ FT: 9,500
  SALES (est): 1MM **Privately Held**
  SIC: 3479 3471 Coating of metals & formed products; anodizing (plating) of metals or formed products

(G-18783)
AJ AUTO
4918 River Rd (60176-1120)
  PHONE...................847 678-8200
  John Jacnick, *Owner*
  John Janick, *Owner*
  EMP: 4
  SALES (est): 337.8K **Privately Held**
  SIC: 2741 Miscellaneous publishing

(G-18784)
ALLOY CHROME INC
9328 Bernice Ave (60176-2302)
  PHONE...................847 678-2880
  Richard Feign, *President*
  EMP: 9
  SQ FT: 5,000
  SALES (est): 1.2MM **Privately Held**
  SIC: 3471 2899 Chromium plating of metals or formed products; chemical preparations

(G-18785)
AMERICAN NTN BEARING MFG CORP
9515 Winona Ave (60176-1083)
  PHONE...................847 671-5450
  Elizabeth E Rotenberry, *HR Admin*
  Jen Dorbich, *Administration*
  EMP: 40 **Privately Held**
  SIC: 3562 Ball bearings & parts
  HQ: American Ntn Bearing Manufacturing Corporation
    1525 Holmes Rd
    Elgin IL 60123
    847 741-4545

(G-18786)
AMERLINE ENTERPRISES CO INC
9509 Winona Ave (60176-1024)
  PHONE...................847 671-6554
  Thomas A Krepelka, *President*
  Carmen Rompala, *Buyer*
  Patricia Krepelka, *Admin Sec*
  ▲ **EMP:** 42
  SQ FT: 30,000
  SALES (est): 7.9MM **Privately Held**
  WEB: www.amerline.com
  SIC: 3643 3694 3357 Connectors & terminals for electrical devices; engine electrical equipment; nonferrous wiredrawing & insulating

(G-18787)
ARPAC LLC (PA)
9555 Irving Park Rd (60176-1960)
  PHONE...................847 678-9034
  Richard Allegretti, *President*
  Gary Ehmka, *Vice Pres*
  John Wolf, *Vice Pres*
  Paul Szalek, *Mfg Staff*
  Armando Aguirre, *Purch Agent*
  ◆ **EMP:** 240
  SQ FT: 250,000
  SALES (est): 59.4MM **Privately Held**
  SIC: 3565 Wrapping machines

(G-18788)
AVERS MACHINE & MFG INC
3999 25th Ave (60176-2175)
  PHONE...................847 447-3430
  Chris Wellman, *President*
  EMP: 22
  SQ FT: 12,000
  SALES (est): 1.8MM **Privately Held**
  SIC: 3599 Machine shop, jobbing & repair

(G-18789)
BRANER USA INC (PA)
9301 W Bernice St (60176)
  PHONE...................847 671-6210
  Charles Damore, *President*

Schiller Park - Cook County (G-18790)

Douglas Matsunaga, *President*
Rosemarie Gervais, *Exec VP*
Mike De Young, *Engineer*
Craig Muehlfelder, *Director*
◆ **EMP:** 50
SQ FT: 60,000
SALES (est): 13.6MM **Privately Held**
SIC: 3549 Rotary slitters (metalworking machines)

(G-18790)
BURDZY TOOL & DIE CO
9355 Byron St (60176-2303)
PHONE..................847 671-6666
Boytek Burdzy, *President*
EMP: 12
SALES (est): 1.2MM **Privately Held**
SIC: 3544 Special dies & tools

(G-18791)
CASTLE METAL FINISHING CORP
4631 25th Ave (60176-1302)
P.O. Box 2221 (60176-0221)
PHONE..................847 678-6041
Phillip Meier, *President*
Dale Weter, *Vice Pres*
Betty Meier, *Admin Sec*
EMP: 17 **EST:** 1960
SQ FT: 22,000
SALES (est): 1.4MM **Privately Held**
WEB: www.castlemetalfinishing.com
SIC: 3471 Electroplating of metals or formed products

(G-18792)
CELCO TOOL & ENGINEERING INC
9300 Bernice Ave (60176-2302)
PHONE..................847 671-2520
John Cielak, *President*
Stanley Cielak, *Corp Secy*
Adam Cielak, *Vice Pres*
EMP: 19 **EST:** 1965
SQ FT: 10,000
SALES (est): 2.3MM **Privately Held**
WEB: www.mjcelco.com
SIC: 3469 Stamping metal for the trade

(G-18793)
CHICAGO POWDERED METAL PDTS CO
Also Called: Camet
9700 Waveland Ave (60131-1773)
P.O. Box 2128 (60176-0128)
PHONE..................847 678-2836
Thomas J Miller, *President*
Tom Miller, *VP Mfg*
Martin Hower, *Engineer*
Richard Wendel, *Engineer*
Michael F Miller, *Treasurer*
▼ **EMP:** 89 **EST:** 1948
SQ FT: 200,000
SALES (est): 21.1MM **Privately Held**
WEB: www.chipm.com
SIC: 3599 Machine shop, jobbing & repair

(G-18794)
CLASSIC MOLDING CO INC
3800 Wesley Ter (60176-2130)
PHONE..................847 671-7888
Thomas G Gebhardt, *President*
William P Koehn, *Admin Sec*
EMP: 80
SQ FT: 35,000
SALES (est): 28.6MM **Privately Held**
SIC: 3089 Injection molding of plastics
PA: Corporate Group, Inc.
7123 W Calumet Rd
Milwaukee WI 53223

(G-18795)
COMMUNICATION COIL INC
9601 Soreng Ave (60176-2104)
P.O. Box 111, Gowanda NY (14070-0111)
PHONE..................847 671-1333
Elliot Goldman, *President*
EMP: 65
SQ FT: 20,000
SALES (est): 7.6MM **Privately Held**
SIC: 5065 3621 3612 3564 Electronic parts & equipment; motors & generators; transformers, except electric; blowers & fans; inductors, electronic

(G-18796)
COOLEY WIRE PRODUCTS MFG CO
5025 River Rd (60176-1016)
PHONE..................847 678-8585
Duane Halleck, *President*
Harold Young, *Vice Pres*
Debbie Bergman, *Office Mgr*
▲ **EMP:** 25 **EST:** 1893
SQ FT: 21,000
SALES (est): 5.3MM **Privately Held**
WEB: www.cooleywire.com
SIC: 3496 3471 3398 Woven wire products; plating & polishing; metal heat treating

(G-18797)
CRAFTSMAN CUSTOM METALS LLC
3838 River Rd (60176-2307)
PHONE..................847 655-0040
Julio Gesklin, *President*
Eric Siegal, *Vice Pres*
Ren E Adam, *Purch Mgr*
Renee Adam, *Purch Mgr*
Roman Kramarz, *Engineer*
▼ **EMP:** 56
SQ FT: 65,000
SALES (est): 10.5MM
SALES (corp-wide): 178.1MM **Privately Held**
SIC: 3444 3469 3312 Sheet metalwork; metal stampings; tool & die steel
PA: Speyside Equity Fund I Lp
430 E 86th St
New York NY 10028
212 994-0308

(G-18798)
DAMY CORP
Also Called: Atlas Screen Supply Co.
9353 Seymour Ave (60176-2206)
PHONE..................847 233-0515
David Gayton, *President*
Kayla Gayton, *Marketing Staff*
EMP: 11
SQ FT: 11,000
SALES (est): 1.7MM **Privately Held**
SIC: 2752 Commercial printing, lithographic

(G-18799)
DAVID V MICHALS
9505 Winona Ave (60176-1024)
PHONE..................847 671-6767
David V Michals, *President*
Carl Smigiel, *General Mgr*
Kathy Michals, *Vice Pres*
EMP: 80 **EST:** 2001
SALES (est): 4.9MM **Privately Held**
SIC: 3495 Wire springs

(G-18800)
E J BASLER CO
9511 Ainslie St (60176-1115)
P.O. Box 87618, Chicago (60680-0618)
PHONE..................847 678-8880
Ed Basler, *CEO*
Edwin J Basler, *CEO*
Dennis E Basler, *President*
Brian Basler, *Vice Pres*
Gary Kautz, *Purch Mgr*
▲ **EMP:** 100 **EST:** 1940
SQ FT: 55,000
SALES (est): 39.9MM **Privately Held**
WEB: www.ejbasler.com
SIC: 3451 Screw machine products

(G-18801)
EARTH STONE PRODUCTS ILL INC
4535 25th Ave (60176-1455)
PHONE..................847 671-3000
Dorota Rajch, *President*
EMP: 3
SQ FT: 1,000
SALES (est): 450K **Privately Held**
SIC: 3281 Granite, cut & shaped

(G-18802)
ECLIPSE LIGHTING INC (PA)
9245 Ivanhoe St (60176-2305)
P.O. Box 2351 (60176-0351)
PHONE..................847 260-0333
Robert Fiermuga, *President*
▲ **EMP:** 34
SQ FT: 20,000
SALES (est): 4.8MM **Privately Held**
SIC: 3646 3645 Commercial indusl & institutional electric lighting fixtures; residential lighting fixtures

(G-18803)
ENCLOSURES INC (HQ)
9200 Ivanhoe St (60176-2306)
PHONE..................847 678-2020
Lee Simeone, *CEO*
Thomas J Simeone, *President*
Kenneth M Galeno, *Vice Pres*
Linda Galeno, *Director*
Milton Ross, *Director*
EMP: 2
SQ FT: 32,050
SALES (est): 4.5MM
SALES (corp-wide): 10MM **Privately Held**
SIC: 2542 Telephone booths: except wood
PA: Manor Tool And Manufacturing Co. Inc
9200 Ivanhoe St
Schiller Park IL 60176
847 678-2020

(G-18804)
ENROLLMENT RX LLC
9511 River St Ste 100 (60176-1019)
PHONE..................847 233-0088
Tim Bailey, *Sales Dir*
Karmel Kifarkis, *Accounts Mgr*
Jon Hazelgren, *Sales Staff*
Jon Hazelgren, *Sales Staff*
Xian Zhang, *Sales Staff*
EMP: 18
SALES (est): 2.5MM **Privately Held**
WEB: www.enrollmentrx.com
SIC: 7372 Application computer software

(G-18805)
ESPE MANUFACTURING CO
9220 Ivanhoe St (60176-2474)
PHONE..................847 678-8950
Robert Pethes Jr, *President*
Pat Pethes, *Vice Pres*
EMP: 12 **EST:** 1948
SQ FT: 30,000
SALES (est): 2.3MM **Privately Held**
WEB: www.espemfg.com
SIC: 3299 Non-metallic mineral statuary & other decorative products

(G-18806)
EURO MARBLE SUPPLY LTD
4552 Ruby St (60176-1443)
PHONE..................847 233-0700
Wojciech Rajch, *President*
Kostas Forligas, *Vice Pres*
Alexander Wolak, *Maintence Staff*
EMP: 10
SALES (est): 178K **Privately Held**
SIC: 3272 Floor slabs & tiles, precast concrete

(G-18807)
EXCEL GLASS INC
10507 Delta Pkwy (60176-1721)
PHONE..................847 801-5200
Enrique Badani, *CEO*
Leon Johnson, *CEO*
George Cutro, *Accountant*
EMP: 1
SQ FT: 12,200
SALES (est): 1.6MM **Privately Held**
SIC: 2759 Imprinting

(G-18808)
EXCEL SCREEN PRTG & EMB INC
10507 Delta Pkwy (60176-1721)
PHONE..................847 801-5200
Leon Johnson, *President*
Enrique Badani, *Admin Sec*
▲ **EMP:** 88
SQ FT: 49,150
SALES (est): 10MM **Privately Held**
SIC: 2396 Screen printing on fabric articles

(G-18809)
GAYTON GROUP INC
Also Called: Ameribest Fasteners
9353 Seymour Ave (60176-2206)
PHONE..................847 233-0509
Dan Gayton, *President*
Melanie Gayton, *Vice Pres*
EMP: 5
SALES (est): 729.9K **Privately Held**
SIC: 3089 Injection molding of plastics

(G-18810)
GGC CORP
4300 United Pkwy (60176-1712)
PHONE..................847 671-6500
Warren Hanssen, *Ch of Bd*
Catherine Moritz, *President*
Dan Caithamer, *CFO*
Craig Hanssen, *Admin Sec*
▲ **EMP:** 100 **EST:** 1967
SQ FT: 125,000
SALES (est): 11.2MM **Privately Held**
SIC: 2771 Greeting cards

(G-18811)
GLO-MOLD INC
3800 Wesley Ter (60176-2130)
PHONE..................847 671-1762
Larry Caldrone, *President*
Gloria Caldrone, *Vice Pres*
EMP: 14
SQ FT: 35,500
SALES (est): 2MM **Privately Held**
SIC: 3089 Injection molding of plastics
PA: Corporate Group, Inc.
7123 W Calumet Rd
Milwaukee WI 53223

(G-18812)
HI-TECH MANUFACTURING LLC
Also Called: Gcm Chicago
9815 Leland Ave (60176-1328)
PHONE..................847 678-1616
Darrell Schuyler, *General Mgr*
Todd Arcari, *Sales Staff*
Barton Vanberburg, *Mng Member*
Neoma Arcari, *Executive Asst*
Ford Bartholow,
EMP: 130
SQ FT: 47,000
SALES (est): 31.1MM **Privately Held**
SIC: 3599 Machine shop, jobbing & repair

(G-18813)
HOFFMAN J&M FARM HOLDINGS INC
3999 25th Ave (60176-2175)
PHONE..................847 671-6280
Francine F Hoffman, *President*
Maida E Hoffman, *Corp Secy*
Alan Blitstein, *Vice Pres*
▲ **EMP:** 85
SQ FT: 60,000
SALES (est): 15.9MM **Privately Held**
WEB: www.hpcworld.com
SIC: 3541 3577 5087 Keysetting machines; computer peripheral equipment; locksmith equipment & supplies

(G-18814)
HOUSE GRANITE & MARBLE CORP
5136 Pearl St (60176-1051)
PHONE..................847 928-1111
Henryk Zajkowski, *President*
Piotr Topolewicz, *Admin Sec*
▲ **EMP:** 3
SALES (est): 260K **Privately Held**
SIC: 3281 5032 Granite, cut & shaped; marble building stone

(G-18815)
ILLINOIS BROACHING COMPANY (PA)
4200 Grace St (60176-1981)
PHONE..................847 678-3080
Jonathan Crabtree, *President*
Jack Crabtree, *Vice Pres*
Patrick Kelly, *Treasurer*
Gregory Crabtree, *Admin Sec*
EMP: 24 **EST:** 1945
SQ FT: 16,600
SALES (est): 2.1MM **Privately Held**
WEB: www.ilbroach.com
SIC: 3541 3545 Broaching machines; machine tool accessories

Schiller Park - Cook County (G-18845)

(G-18816)
JOSEPH WOODWORKING CORPORATION
4226 Grace St (60176-1912)
PHONE..................847 233-9766
James P Helm, *President*
Terry N Lee, *Vice Pres*
EMP: 18
SQ FT: 11,000
SALES (est): 1.8MM **Privately Held**
SIC: 2499 Decorative wood & woodwork

(G-18817)
KAYLEN INDUSTRIES INC (PA)
9505 Winona Ave (60176-1024)
PHONE..................847 671-6767
David V Michals, *President*
James Strok, *Vice Pres*
Kathleen Michals, *Admin Sec*
EMP: 55 **EST:** 1960
SQ FT: 40,000
SALES (est): 12.4MM **Privately Held**
WEB: www.mw-ind.com
SIC: 3495 Mechanical springs, precision

(G-18818)
M J CELCO INC (PA)
3900 Wesley Ter (60176-2132)
PHONE..................847 671-1900
Michael Cielak, *President*
Steve Mikalakis, *General Mgr*
Don Mayo, *Mfg Dir*
Gregory Cholewinski, *Prdtn Mgr*
Annette Zabel, *Purch Agent*
▲ **EMP:** 80
SQ FT: 100,000
SALES (est): 50MM **Privately Held**
SIC: 3469 Stamping metal for the trade

(G-18819)
MAKRAY MANUFACTURING COMPANY
9515 Seymour Ave (60176-2125)
PHONE..................847 260-5408
EMP: 64
SALES (corp-wide): 14.5MM **Privately Held**
SIC: 3089 Injection molding of plastics
PA: Makray Manufacturing Company Inc
4400 N Harlem Ave
Norridge IL 60706
708 456-7100

(G-18820)
MANOR TOOL AND MFG CO (PA)
9200 Ivanhoe St (60176-2306)
PHONE..................847 678-2020
Thomas Simeone, *President*
Tom Simeone, *President*
Kenneth Galeno, *Vice Pres*
Steve Schneider, *Purchasing*
EMP: 78
SQ FT: 47,000
SALES (est): 10MM **Privately Held**
WEB: www.manortool.com
SIC: 3469 3544 Stamping metal for the trade; special dies & tools

(G-18821)
MATTHEW WARREN INC
Also Called: Mohawk Spring
9505 Winona Ave (60176-1024)
PHONE..................847 671-6767
EMP: 5
SALES (corp-wide): 185.9MM **Privately Held**
SIC: 3495 Mechanical springs, precision
HQ: Matthew Warren, Inc.
9501 Tech Blvd Ste 401
Rosemont IL 60018
847 349-5760

(G-18822)
MBR TOOL INC
5118 Pearl St (60176-1051)
PHONE..................847 671-4491
Raymond Stanis, *President*
EMP: 6
SQ FT: 4,000
SALES (est): 708.3K **Privately Held**
SIC: 3599 Machine shop, jobbing & repair

(G-18823)
MENNON RBR & SAFETY PDTS INC
4932 River Rd (60176-1120)
PHONE..................847 678-8250
Mary A Cibulka, *President*
James F Cibulka, *Vice Pres*
EMP: 5
SQ FT: 3,000
SALES (est): 2MM **Privately Held**
WEB: www.mennonsafety.com
SIC: 5139 5136 5661 5699 Shoes; men's & boys' clothing; men's shoes; work clothing; men's & boys' work clothing

(G-18824)
MIDAMERICAN PRTG SYSTEMS INC
3838 River Rd (60176-2307)
PHONE..................312 663-4720
Jerry Freund, *President*
Joel Amettis, *Vice Pres*
Art Chiappetta, *Vice Pres*
Leo Douglas, *Vice Pres*
Bruce Miller, *Vice Pres*
EMP: 50
SQ FT: 27,000
SALES (est): 11.6MM **Privately Held**
SIC: 2752 2759 Commercial printing, offset; business forms; printing; envelopes: printing

(G-18825)
MIDLAND STAMPING AND FABG CORP (PA)
9521 Ainslie St (60176-1115)
PHONE..................847 678-7573
Alan Blankshain, *President*
John Ehlers, *Opers Staff*
EMP: 56
SALES (est): 34.8MM **Privately Held**
SIC: 3469 3499 Stamping metal for the trade; novelties & specialties, metal

(G-18826)
MIDWEST OIL CO INC
9739 Irving Park Rd (60176-1938)
PHONE..................847 928-9999
Irfan Bhagat, *President*
Mohammed Ahmed, *Admin Sec*
EMP: 7
SQ FT: 2,000
SALES (est): 698.3K **Privately Held**
SIC: 1382 Oil & gas exploration services

(G-18827)
MJ CELCO INTERNATIONAL LLC
3900 Wesley Ter (60176-2132)
PHONE..................847 671-1900
Michael Cielak,
Patrick Cielak,
▲ **EMP:** 25
SALES (est): 2.3MM **Privately Held**
SIC: 3444 3469 Sheet metalwork; ornamental metal stampings

(G-18828)
MOFFITT CO
9347 Seymour Ave (60176-2206)
PHONE..................847 678-5450
Fax: 847 678-5463
EMP: 4
SALES (est): 397K **Privately Held**
SIC: 3567 Mfg Industrial Furnaces/Ovens

(G-18829)
OHARE SHELL PARTNERS INC
4111 Mannheim Rd (60176-1840)
PHONE..................847 678-1900
Ashanti Tippins, *Principal*
EMP: 5
SALES (est): 950.8K **Privately Held**
SIC: 3578 Automatic teller machines (ATM)

(G-18830)
ORBIT MACHINING COMPANY
9440 Ainslie St (60176-1140)
PHONE..................847 678-1050
George Zarytsky, *President*
Brian Kowal, *Plant Mgr*
Susan Marino, *Comp Spec*
EMP: 20 **EST:** 1967
SALES (est): 4.5MM **Privately Held**
WEB: www.orbitmachining.com
SIC: 3599 Machine shop, jobbing & repair

(G-18831)
PEOPLE & PLACES NEWSPAPER
4303 Atlantic Ave (60176-1950)
PHONE..................847 804-6985
Barbara Piltaver, *Publisher*
EMP: 5 **EST:** 2014
SALES (est): 167.6K **Privately Held**
SIC: 2711 Newspapers, publishing & printing

(G-18832)
PLASTIC POWER EXTRUSIONS CORP
3860 River Rd (60176-2307)
PHONE..................847 233-9901
Peter Cackowski, *President*
EMP: 20
SQ FT: 42,000
SALES (est): 5MM **Privately Held**
SIC: 3355 Extrusion ingot, aluminum: made in rolling mills

(G-18833)
POINT FIVE PACKAGING LLC
9435 River St (60176-1017)
PHONE..................847 531-4787
Bogdan Kumala, *Engineer*
Paul Kincaid, *Sales Mgr*
Bruce Devilling, *Sales Staff*
Greg Levy, *Mng Member*
◆ **EMP:** 6 **EST:** 2010
SQ FT: 10,000
SALES (est): 2.3MM **Privately Held**
SIC: 3565 Packing & wrapping machinery

(G-18834)
PRECISE ROTARY DIE INC
9250 Ivanhoe St (60176-2306)
PHONE..................847 678-0001
Ray Barak, *President*
EMP: 40
SQ FT: 19,024
SALES (est): 6.9MM **Privately Held**
SIC: 3544 Dies, steel rule

(G-18835)
PRECISION STAMPING PDTS INC
4848 River Rd (60176-1119)
PHONE..................847 678-0800
John J Sharkey, *President*
Dennis Sharkey, *VP Opers*
Jake Demars, *Sales Staff*
▲ **EMP:** 30 **EST:** 1919
SQ FT: 75,000
SALES (est): 10.2MM **Privately Held**
WEB: www.precisionstamp.com
SIC: 3469 Stamping metal for the trade

(G-18836)
PRIME STAINLESS PRODUCTS LLC
4848 River Rd (60176-1119)
PHONE..................847 678-0800
Dean Sharkey,
Michael Sharkey,
◆ **EMP:** 2
SALES (est): 812K **Privately Held**
SIC: 5051 3462 Steel; armor plate, forged iron or steel

(G-18837)
PRINT MANAGEMENT GROUP INC
1253 Pagni Dr (60176)
PHONE..................847 671-0900
Steven Mazza, *President*
Maria Mazza, *Vice Pres*
EMP: 3
SQ FT: 2,000
SALES (est): 530.2K **Privately Held**
SIC: 2752 Commercial printing, offset

(G-18838)
R B HAYWARD COMPANY
9556 River St (60176-1020)
PHONE..................847 671-0400
Robert Kuechenberg, *CEO*
Donald R Malzahn, *President*
Jeff Laskey, *Vice Pres*
Randal Novak, *Vice Pres*
Thomas Salomoun, *Sr Project Mgr*
EMP: 50 **EST:** 1915
SQ FT: 35,000
SALES (est): 9.4MM **Privately Held**
WEB: www.haywardhvac.com
SIC: 1711 3444 Mechanical contractor; metal ventilating equipment; ducts, sheet metal

(G-18839)
REX MORIOKA
Also Called: Railroad Electronics
4257 Wesley Ter (60176-1925)
PHONE..................847 651-9400
Rex Morioka, *Owner*
EMP: 1
SALES (est): 500K **Privately Held**
SIC: 3559 Electronic component making machinery

(G-18840)
ROENTGEN USA LLC
3725 25th Ave (60176-2147)
PHONE..................847 787-0135
Ken Forest, *Regl Sales Mgr*
Egon Arntz,
▲ **EMP:** 5
SQ FT: 5,200
SALES (est): 1.8MM
SALES (corp-wide): 54.3MM **Privately Held**
SIC: 3425 Saw blades for hand or power saws
PA: Robert Rontgen Gmbh & Co. Kg.
Auf Dem Knapp 44
Remscheid 42855
219 137-301

(G-18841)
RT WHOLESALE (PA)
Also Called: Food Evolution
4242 Old River Rd Ste 1a (60176-1659)
PHONE..................847 678-3663
Bret Schultz, *Mng Member*
Jeronimo Maldonado, *Mng Member*
Judd Rosenberg, *Mng Member*
EMP: 100
SALES (est): 12.6MM **Privately Held**
SIC: 5812 2099 Caterers; food preparations

(G-18842)
RUSH IMPRESSIONS INC
3941 25th Ave (60176-2117)
PHONE..................847 671-0622
Russell Dolhun, *President*
EMP: 4
SALES (est): 378.3K **Privately Held**
SIC: 2752 Commercial printing, offset

(G-18843)
SCIS AIR SECURITY CORPORATION
4321 United Pkwy (60176-1711)
PHONE..................847 671-9502
Steve Skogland, *President*
EMP: 4
SALES (corp-wide): 40.3B **Privately Held**
SIC: 3699 Electrical equipment & supplies
HQ: Scis Air Security Corporation
1521 N Cooper St Ste 300
Arlington TX 76011
817 792-4500

(G-18844)
SOLDY MANUFACTURING INC
Also Called: Aluminum and Zinc Die
9370 Byron St (60176-2304)
PHONE..................847 671-3396
Alex Gemignani, *President*
Alexander Gemignani, *President*
Sandra Steiner, *Admin Sec*
EMP: 80 **EST:** 1982
SQ FT: 22,000
SALES (est): 13.2MM **Privately Held**
WEB: www.soldy.com
SIC: 3544 3364 3363 Industrial molds; zinc & zinc-base alloy die-castings; aluminum die-castings

(G-18845)
SPECO INC
3946 Willow St (60176-2311)
PHONE..................847 678-4240
Craig W Hess, *President*

Schiller Park - Cook County (G-18846)
GEOGRAPHIC SECTION

Ron Schulmeister, *Vice Pres*
Jaclyn M Hess, *Purch Agent*
Dan Morgan, *Engineer*
Nadine Britton, *Treasurer*
▲ **EMP:** 49 **EST:** 1924
SQ FT: 25,000
SALES (est): 10.3MM **Privately Held**
WEB: www.speco.com
SIC: 3421 3544 3556 Knives: butchers', hunting, pocket, etc.; special dies, tools, jigs & fixtures; food products machinery

(G-18846)
SUNRISE PRINTING INC
9701 Cary Ave (60176-2436)
PHONE.................847 928-1800
Michael Martin, *President*
Anna Martin, *Treasurer*
EMP: 16
SQ FT: 8,000
SALES (est): 3MM **Privately Held**
SIC: 2752 Commercial printing, offset

(G-18847)
TDS INC
Also Called: Anscor
9225 Ivanhoe St (60176-2305)
PHONE.................847 678-2084
Ted R Campbell, *President*
Donald W Ruback Jr, *Vice Pres*
Ildefonso Solis, *Admin Sec*
EMP: 20 **EST:** 1958
SQ FT: 36,000
SALES: 1.7MM **Privately Held**
WEB: www.andersonsnowcoils.com
SIC: 3585 Parts for heating, cooling & refrigerating equipment

(G-18848)
UNIFIED TOOL DIE & MFG CO INC
9331 Seymour Ave (60176-2292)
PHONE.................847 678-3773
Steve Sciurba, *President*
Steven Sciurba, *Vice Pres*
EMP: 15
SQ FT: 8,700
SALES (est): 3MM **Privately Held**
WEB: www.unifiedtool.com
SIC: 3544 3469 3699 Special dies & tools; stamping metal for the trade; electrical equipment & supplies

(G-18849)
UNITED CARBURETOR INC (PA)
Also Called: United Carburator
9550 Soreng Ave (60176-2128)
PHONE.................773 777-1223
Robert Portman, *CEO*
Alan Portman, *Vice Pres*
David Portman, *Vice Pres*
EMP: 40
SQ FT: 20,000
SALES (est): 7.1MM **Privately Held**
SIC: 3592 3714 Carburetors; motor vehicle steering systems & parts; fuel systems & parts, motor vehicle

(G-18850)
UNITED REMANUFACTURING CO INC (HQ)
Also Called: UNITED CARBURATOR
9550 Soreng Ave (60176-2128)
PHONE.................773 777-1223
David Portman, *Vice Pres*
Alan Portman, *Vice Pres*
Scott Portman, *VP Sales*
▲ **EMP:** 32
SQ FT: 20,000
SALES: 3.2MM **Privately Held**
SIC: 3592 3714 5085 5013 Carburetors; motor vehicle steering systems & parts; fuel systems & parts, motor vehicle; industrial supplies; automotive supplies & parts

(G-18851)
UNITED REMANUFACTURING CO INC
Also Called: United Carborator
9550 Soreng Ave (60176-2128)
PHONE.................847 678-2233
Jerry Portman, *President*
Alan Portman, *General Mgr*
EMP: 30

SQ FT: 20,000 **Privately Held**
SIC: 3592 3714 Carburetors; steering mechanisms, motor vehicle
HQ: United Remanufacturing Co Inc
9550 Soreng Ave
Schiller Park IL 60176
773 777-1223

(G-18852)
VYSE GELATIN LLC
5010 Rose St (60176-1023)
PHONE.................847 678-4780
Rich Rossini, *Mng Member*
EMP: 20 **EST:** 2016
SALES (est): 13.5MM **Privately Held**
SIC: 2899 Gelatin
HQ: Nitta Gelatin Na, Inc.
598 Airport Blvd Ste 900
Morrisville NC 27560
919 238-3300

(G-18853)
W D MOLD FINISHING INC
3923 Wesley Ter (60176-2131)
PHONE.................847 678-8449
Thomas Dinkel, *President*
Walter J Dinkel, *Consultant*
Agnes Dinkel, *Admin Sec*
EMP: 3 **EST:** 1972
SQ FT: 7,200
SALES (est): 358.7K **Privately Held**
SIC: 3471 Polishing, metals or formed products

(G-18854)
WESTERN PRINTING MACHINERY CO (PA)
Also Called: Wpm
9229 Ivanhoe St (60176-2305)
PHONE.................847 678-1740
Paul G Kapolnek, *CEO*
Paul Kaponek, *CEO*
Roman Guzek, *Engineer*
Elmer Piper, *Engineer*
Chin Chung, *Electrical Engi*
▲ **EMP:** 30 **EST:** 1933
SALES (est): 11.1MM **Privately Held**
WEB: www.wpm.com
SIC: 3555 7371 Printing trades machinery; computer software writing services

(G-18855)
WESTERN PRINTING MACHINERY CO
9228 Ivanhoe St (60176-2306)
PHONE.................847 678-1740
Michael K Musgrave, *President*
EMP: 25
SALES (corp-wide): 11.1MM **Privately Held**
SIC: 3555 7371 Printing trades machinery; computer software writing services
PA: Western Printing Machinery Company
9229 Ivanhoe St
Schiller Park IL 60176
847 678-1740

Scott Afb
St. Clair County

(G-18856)
BOEING COMPANY
205 Hangar Rd Bldg 470 (62225)
PHONE.................618 746-4062
Bavan Holloway, *Vice Pres*
Michael Manning, *Manager*
EMP: 3
SALES (corp-wide): 76.5B **Publicly Held**
SIC: 3721 Airplanes, fixed or rotary wing
PA: The Boeing Company
100 N Riverside Plz
Chicago IL 60606
312 544-2000

Scott Air Force Base
St. Clair County

(G-18857)
DLA DOCUMENT SERVICES
901 South Dr Bldg 700e (62225-5103)
PHONE.................618 256-4686
Lenny Exavier, *Director*
EMP: 10 **Publicly Held**
SIC: 2752 9711 Commercial printing, lithographic; national security;
HQ: Dla Document Services
5450 Carlisle Pike Bldg 9
Mechanicsburg PA 17050
717 605-2362

Seneca
Lasalle County

(G-18858)
GRIFFIN INDUSTRIES LLC
Also Called: Bakery Feeds
410 Shipyard Rd (61360-9305)
PHONE.................815 357-8200
David Grassl, *Branch Mgr*
EMP: 5
SALES (corp-wide): 3.3B **Publicly Held**
SIC: 2843 2053 2052 Oils & greases; frozen bakery products, except bread; bakery products, dry
HQ: Griffin Industries Llc
4221 Alexandria Pike
Cold Spring KY 41076
859 781-2010

(G-18859)
JOHN A BIEWER LUMBER COMPANY
Also Called: Biewer John A Co of Seneca
524 E Union St (61360-9493)
PHONE.................815 357-6792
Richard Hales, *Manager*
EMP: 15
SALES (corp-wide): 53.8MM **Privately Held**
SIC: 2491 Structural lumber & timber, treated wood
PA: John A. Biewer Lumber Company
812 S Riverside Ave
Saint Clair MI 48079
810 329-4789

(G-18860)
REG SENECA LLC
614 Shipyard Rd (61360-9469)
P.O. Box 888, Ames IA (50010-0888)
PHONE.................888 734-8686
Natalie Lischer, *Corp Secy*
Brad Albin, *Vice Pres*
EMP: 35
SALES (est): 8.7MM
SALES (corp-wide): 2.6B **Publicly Held**
SIC: 2869 Industrial organic chemicals
PA: Renewable Energy Group, Inc.
416 S Bell Ave
Ames IA 50010
515 239-8000

(G-18861)
SENECA CUSTOM CABINETRY
2957 Us Highway 6 (61360-9520)
PHONE.................815 357-1322
Ken Bertrand, *Owner*
EMP: 7
SALES: 300K **Privately Held**
SIC: 2434 Wood kitchen cabinets

(G-18862)
SENECA SAND & GRAVEL LLC
2962 N 2553rd Rd (61360)
PHONE.................630 746-9183
Brandon S Boughton, *Partner*
EMP: 4 **EST:** 2009
SALES (est): 592.6K **Privately Held**
SIC: 1442 Construction sand & gravel

Serena
Lasalle County

(G-18863)
BLACK LAB LLC
3624 E 2351st Rd (60549-9730)
PHONE.................440 285-3189
Daryl Deckard, *Mng Member*
EMP: 5
SALES (est): 602.3K
SALES (corp-wide): 125.5MM **Publicly Held**
SIC: 3531 Concrete grouting equipment
HQ: Covia Holdings Corporation
3 Summit Park Dr Ste 700
Independence OH 44131
440 214-3284

(G-18864)
MIDAMERICAN TECHNOLOGY INC
3708 E 25th Rd (60549-9734)
PHONE.................815 496-2400
Kevin E Bailey, *President*
John Rauch, *Opers Mgr*
EMP: 4
SQ FT: 4,200
SALES: 700K **Privately Held**
SIC: 3812 Search & detection systems & instruments

Sesser
Franklin County

(G-18865)
C AND H PUBLISHING CO (PA)
Also Called: American Cooner
114 E Franklin St (62884-1844)
P.O. Box 777 (62884-0777)
PHONE.................618 625-2711
Terry Walker, *Owner*
EMP: 8 **EST:** 1952
SQ FT: 12,500
SALES (est): 728.9K **Privately Held**
WEB: www.huntinghoundsmen.com
SIC: 2741 Miscellaneous publishing

(G-18866)
SESSER CONCRETE PRODUCTS CO
910 S Cockrum St (62884-2028)
P.O. Box 100 (62884-0100)
PHONE.................618 625-2811
Michael K Thompson, *President*
Juanita Cook, *Vice Pres*
EMP: 14 **EST:** 1948
SALES (est): 1.8MM **Privately Held**
SIC: 3271 5032 Blocks, concrete or cinder: standard; brick, except refractory

Seward
Winnebago County

(G-18867)
EICKMANS PROCESSING CO INC
3226 S Pecatonica Rd (61077)
P.O. Box 118 (61077-0118)
PHONE.................815 247-8451
Michael P Eickman, *President*
Lori Eickman, *Corp Secy*
EMP: 27
SQ FT: 15,000
SALES (est): 3.4MM **Privately Held**
SIC: 2011 5421 5147 5812 Beef products from beef slaughtered on site; pork products from pork slaughtered on site; sausages from meat slaughtered on site; meat markets, including freezer provisioners; meats, fresh; caterers; storage, frozen or refrigerated goods; sausages & other prepared meats

GEOGRAPHIC SECTION

Shorewood - Will County (G-18893)

Seymour
Champaign County

(G-18868)
FIRST-LIGHT USA LLC
205 S Main St (61875-4806)
PHONE...................217 687-4048
Leslie Kirby, *Sales Mgr*
Todd Jones, *Marketing Staff*
Jeremy Ross, *Mng Member*
Chris Kutsor,
Jason Logsdon,
EMP: 10
SALES (est): 1.9MM **Privately Held**
SIC: 3648 Flashlights

(G-18869)
VALENT USA LLC
Also Called: Midwest Agracultural RES Ctr
1035 County Road 300 E (61875-9723)
PHONE...................816 206-3919
Jimmy Etheridge, *Area Mgr*
EMP: 15
SQ FT: 6,000 **Privately Held**
SIC: 2879 Agricultural chemicals
HQ: Valent U.S.A. Llc
1600 Riviera Ave Ste 200
Walnut Creek CA 94596
925 256-2700

Shannon
Carroll County

(G-18870)
L & J INDUSTRIAL STAPLES INC
15 W Market St (61078-9005)
P.O. Box 104 (61078-0104)
PHONE...................815 864-3337
Luther Revels, *President*
Lana Baker, *General Mgr*
Sue Revels, *Vice Pres*
▲ **EMP:** 8
SQ FT: 65,000
SALES: 1.2MM **Privately Held**
SIC: 3399 3315 Staples, nonferrous metal or wire; nails, steel: wire or cut

(G-18871)
MB MACHINE INC
10214 N Mount Vernon Rd (61078-9404)
PHONE...................815 864-3555
Michael Baker, *President*
EMP: 11
SQ FT: 10,000
SALES (est): 730K **Privately Held**
SIC: 3599 7692 3444 Machine shop, jobbing & repair; welding repair; sheet metalwork

(G-18872)
PROCESS SCREW PRODUCTS INC
10 N Shannon Rte (61078-9361)
P.O. Box 545 (61078-0545)
PHONE...................815 864-2220
Marilyn A Hammer, *President*
Marilyn Hammer, *President*
Joseph Hammer, *Vice Pres*
EMP: 25
SQ FT: 20,000
SALES (est): 4MM **Privately Held**
WEB: www.processscrewproducts.com
SIC: 3451 3462 3643 3568 Screw machine products; gears, forged steel; current-carrying wiring devices; power transmission equipment; machine tools, metal cutting type; valves & pipe fittings

(G-18873)
SAINT TECHNOLOGIES INC
10 N Locust St (61078-9009)
P.O. Box 66 (61078-0066)
PHONE...................815 864-3035
James F L Blair, *President*
Marilyn K Blair, *Corp Secy*
EMP: 4
SQ FT: 7,500
SALES (est): 496.3K **Privately Held**
WEB: www.sainttechnologies.net
SIC: 3452 Lock washers

(G-18874)
TEE LEE POPCORN INC
101 W Badger St (61078-9020)
P.O. Box 108 (61078-0108)
PHONE...................815 864-2363
James D Weaver, *President*
Marcos Perera, *Vice Pres*
Austin Weaver, *Vice Pres*
Carolyn L Weaver, *Vice Pres*
Ken Weaver, *Vice Pres*
▼ **EMP:** 20 **EST:** 1944
SQ FT: 25,000
SALES (est): 8.2MM **Privately Held**
SIC: 2099 5145 5046 2096 Popcorn, packaged: except already popped; popcorn & supplies; commercial equipment; potato chips & similar snacks

Shawneetown
Gallatin County

(G-18875)
JADER FUEL CO INC
Also Called: Downen Enterprises
117 S Edison St (62984-3138)
P.O. Box 520 (62984-0520)
PHONE...................618 269-3101
Robert Downen, *President*
Philip Downen, *Vice Pres*
William Downen, *Vice Pres*
Edward Downen, *Admin Sec*
C Donald Downen, *Asst Sec*
EMP: 8
SQ FT: 1,500
SALES: 1.2MM **Privately Held**
SIC: 1221 Strip mining, bituminous

Shelbyville
Shelby County

(G-18876)
BARNES MACHINE SHOP LLC
8 Boarman Dr (62565-9054)
PHONE...................217 774-5308
Paul Barnes, *President*
EMP: 7
SALES (est): 912.2K **Privately Held**
SIC: 3599 Machine shop, jobbing & repair

(G-18877)
BRAD MARTZ
Also Called: Mbo Painting
1250 State Highway 128 (62565-4461)
PHONE...................217 825-5855
Brad Martz, *Owner*
EMP: 3
SALES (est): 88.5K **Privately Held**
SIC: 3479 Painting, coating & hot dipping

(G-18878)
FOX REDI-MIX INC
870 County Highway 6 (62565-4136)
P.O. Box 558 (62565-0558)
PHONE...................217 774-2110
Shane Fox, *President*
Douglas Fox, *President*
Stephen Fox, *Corp Secy*
Stuart Fox, *Vice Pres*
EMP: 8
SALES (est): 1.4MM **Privately Held**
SIC: 3273 Ready-mixed concrete

(G-18879)
ICED
118 E Main St (62565-1654)
PHONE...................217 774-2247
Jodi Allen, *Owner*
EMP: 4 **EST:** 2012
SALES (est): 156.5K **Privately Held**
SIC: 2051 Bread, cake & related products

(G-18880)
IHI TURBO AMERICA CO (HQ)
1598 State Highway 16 (62565-4470)
Rural Route 36 (62565)
PHONE...................217 774-9571
Hiromu Furukawa, *President*
Michael Price, *Corp Secy*
Jennifer Briseno, *Buyer*
Matthew Rueff, *QC Mgr*
Devin Bauman, *Engineer*
▲ **EMP:** 75
SQ FT: 56,000
SALES (est): 24.4MM **Privately Held**
SIC: 3724 3999 Turbo-superchargers, aircraft; atomizers, toiletry

(G-18881)
MACARI SERVICE CENTER INC (PA)
Also Called: Macari Appliance Center
502 N Peter St Ste A (62565)
P.O. Box 64 (62565-0064)
PHONE...................217 774-4214
Joe Beck, *President*
Ron Saddoris, *Vice Pres*
EMP: 17
SQ FT: 12,000
SALES: 2MM **Privately Held**
WEB: www.macarisservice.com
SIC: 1711 3444 5722 Warm air heating & air conditioning contractor; ducts, sheet metal; electric household appliances; electric household appliances, major; gas household appliances

(G-18882)
P & H MANUFACTURING CO
604 S Lodge St (62565-1929)
P.O. Box 349 (62565-0349)
PHONE...................217 774-2123
Earl D Peifer, *President*
Earl A Holland, *Principal*
Charles D Peifer, *Principal*
Rob Quast, *Plant Mgr*
Clint Hagan, *Manager*
◆ **EMP:** 100
SQ FT: 250,000
SALES (est): 23MM **Privately Held**
WEB: www.phmfg.com
SIC: 3599 3523 Machine & other job shop work; farm machinery & equipment

(G-18883)
PRO-LUBE OF SHELBYVILLE INC
1715 W Main St (62565-4373)
PHONE...................217 774-4643
Rich Storm, *CEO*
David Ogden, *President*
Sherry Ogden, *Admin Sec*
EMP: 3
SALES (est): 259.5K **Privately Held**
SIC: 1389 Oil field services

(G-18884)
PROSSER CONSTRUCTION CO
1410 N 1500 East Rd (62565-4423)
P.O. Box 287 (62565-0287)
PHONE...................217 774-5032
David Cruitt, *President*
Charlie Adams, *Vice Pres*
Troy Wade, *Safety Mgr*
Ken Ozier, *Treasurer*
Vicky Redman, *Admin Sec*
EMP: 15
SQ FT: 3,500
SALES (est): 1.5MM **Privately Held**
SIC: 1611 1442 3272 2951 Highway & street paving contractor; gravel mining; concrete products; asphalt paving mixtures & blocks; concrete work

(G-18885)
REBER WELDING SERVICE
142 S Washington St (62565-2330)
PHONE...................217 774-3441
Rick D Reber, *Owner*
EMP: 3 **EST:** 1943
SQ FT: 5,000
SALES (est): 150K **Privately Held**
SIC: 7692 3548 3492 3441 Welding repair; welding apparatus; fluid power valves & hose fittings; fabricated structural metal

(G-18886)
SHELBY TOOL & DIE INC
813 W South 5th St (62565-1936)
P.O. Box 376 (62565-0376)
PHONE...................217 774-2189
Howard Ray Tull, *President*
EMP: 8 **EST:** 1960
SQ FT: 5,800
SALES: 400K **Privately Held**
SIC: 3544 3545 Special dies & tools; machine tool accessories

(G-18887)
STA-RITE GINNIE LOU INC
245 E South 1st St (62565-2332)
P.O. Box 435 (62565-0435)
PHONE...................217 774-3921
Noel Bolinger, *President*
▲ **EMP:** 10 **EST:** 1917
SQ FT: 18,000
SALES: 610K **Privately Held**
WEB: www.sta-riteginnielou.com
SIC: 3965 Hairpins, except rubber; hair curlers

(G-18888)
TONY WEISHAAR
Also Called: Tony's Welding & Repair Svc
Hwy 16 One 16th Mile E (62565)
PHONE...................217 774-2774
Tony Weishaar, *Owner*
EMP: 3
SALES (est): 206.6K **Privately Held**
SIC: 7692 Welding repair

Sheridan
Lasalle County

(G-18889)
HANSELS CUSTOM TECH INC
405 E Si Johnson Ave (60551)
P.O. Box 555 (60551-0555)
PHONE...................815 496-2345
Kevin Hansel, *President*
EMP: 6 **EST:** 1993
SALES: 635K **Privately Held**
SIC: 3544 Special dies & tools

(G-18890)
KPI MACHINING INC
225 W Plum St (60551)
P.O. Box 267 (60551-0267)
PHONE...................815 496-2246
Scott Carpenter, *President*
EMP: 8
SQ FT: 4,200
SALES (est): 305K **Privately Held**
SIC: 3541 Milling machines; turret lathes

Shirley
Mclean County

(G-18891)
FUNKS GROVE PURE MAPLE SYRUP
5257 Old Route 66 (61772-9601)
PHONE...................309 874-3360
Stephen Funk, *Owner*
EMP: 15
SALES (est): 797.2K **Privately Held**
SIC: 2099 Maple syrup

Shobonier
Fayette County

(G-18892)
DUTCH PRAIRIE CONVEYORS
844 N 1625 St (62885-4147)
PHONE...................618 349-6177
Harlan Weaver, *Owner*
EMP: 2
SALES: 600K **Privately Held**
SIC: 3523 Planting machines, agricultural

Shorewood
Will County

(G-18893)
BRAKUR CUSTOM CABINETRY INC
18656 S State Route 59 (60404-8625)
PHONE...................630 355-2244
Chad T Kurtz, *President*
Jim Sinadinos, *Human Res Mgr*
Dave Lynn, *Sales Mgr*
Mitch Kurtz, *Sales Staff*
Karen L Kurtz, *Admin Sec*

Shorewood - Will County (G-18894)

EMP: 130
SQ FT: 50,000
SALES (est): 20.6MM **Privately Held**
WEB: www.brakur.com
SIC: 2541 2434 Wood partitions & fixtures; wood kitchen cabinets

(G-18894)
BUTLER BROS STEEL RULE DIE CO
303 Amendodge Dr (60404-8200)
PHONE.....................815 630-4629
John Small, *Branch Mgr*
EMP: 3
SALES (corp-wide): 3MM **Privately Held**
WEB: www.butlerdie.com
SIC: 2675 Die-cut paper & board
PA: Butler Bros Steel Rule Die Co Inc
730 N 18th St
Saint Louis MO 63103
314 241-1540

(G-18895)
ETHAN COMPANY INCORPORATED
306 Harvard Ct (60404-9136)
PHONE.....................815 715-2283
William Long, *Principal*
Brian Long, *Vice Pres*
EMP: 3
SALES (est): 329.2K **Privately Held**
SIC: 2759 Commercial printing

(G-18896)
EXPRESS SIGNS & LIGHTING MAINT
212 Amendodge Dr (60404-9362)
PHONE.....................815 725-9080
Mary T Hartsell, *President*
Eddie B Hartsell, *Vice Pres*
EMP: 12
SQ FT: 5,400
SALES (est): 1.6MM **Privately Held**
SIC: 3993 1799 Electric signs; cable splicing service

(G-18897)
GRAPHIC PROMOTIONS INC
405 Earl Rd (60404-9402)
PHONE.....................815 726-3288
Stacey Sladek, *President*
Daryl Sladek, *Vice Pres*
EMP: 15
SQ FT: 20,000
SALES (est): 1MM **Privately Held**
SIC: 2752 Commercial printing, offset

(G-18898)
PAPER OR PLASTIC INC
850 Brookforest Ave F (60404-8515)
PHONE.....................815 582-3696
EMP: 3
SALES (est): 208.3K **Privately Held**
SIC: 3089 Plastics products

(G-18899)
PLASTIC FILM CORP AMERICA INC
007 Geneva St (60404)
PHONE.....................630 697-5635
EMP: 25
SALES (corp-wide): 5MM **Privately Held**
SIC: 3089 5162 Plastic processing; plastics sheets & rods
PA: Plastic Film Corporation Of America, Inc.
1011 State St Ste 140
Lemont IL 60439
630 887-0800

(G-18900)
PRAIRIE MATERIALS GROUP
19515 Ne Frontage Rd (60404-3567)
PHONE.....................815 207-6750
Bob Furlong, *General Mgr*
EMP: 4
SALES (est): 63K **Privately Held**
SIC: 3273 Ready-mixed concrete

(G-18901)
QUEST INTEGRITY
908 Geneva St (60404-9403)
PHONE.....................779 205-3068
EMP: 3 EST: 2015

SALES (est): 202.3K **Privately Held**
SIC: 3826 Analytical instruments

(G-18902)
RAPID FOODS INC
Also Called: Standard Provision Co
1007 Geneva St (60404-9409)
P.O. Box 307, Forest Park (60130-0307)
PHONE.....................708 366-0321
Joseph Stone, *Ch of Bd*
Michael Stone, *President*
Faith Stone, *Corp Secy*
EMP: 7
SQ FT: 1,300
SALES (est): 4.1MM **Privately Held**
WEB: www.rapidfoodsinc.com
SIC: 5147 2013 Meats, fresh; sausages & other prepared meats

Shumway
Effingham County

(G-18903)
KREMER PRECISION MACHINE INC
10748 E 1850th Ave (62461-2217)
PHONE.....................217 868-2627
Eugene J Kremer, *President*
Douglas Kremer, *Vice Pres*
Phyllis Kremer, *Vice Pres*
Pamela Kiefer, *Treasurer*
EMP: 17
SQ FT: 7,600
SALES (est): 2.6MM **Privately Held**
SIC: 3599 Machine shop, jobbing & repair

(G-18904)
MANUFCTRNG-RESOURCING INTL INC
5265 E 1800th Ave (62461-2018)
PHONE.....................217 821-3733
Sandy Cornett, *President*
▲ EMP: 10
SQ FT: 25,000
SALES (est): 2MM **Privately Held**
SIC: 3581 Mechanisms & parts for automatic vending machines

(G-18905)
METAL WORKS MACHINE INC
11100 E 1850th Ave (62461-2244)
PHONE.....................217 868-5111
Carol Levitt, *President*
Ed Levitt, *Admin Sec*
EMP: 4
SALES (est): 413.7K **Privately Held**
SIC: 3599 Machine shop, jobbing & repair

(G-18906)
SOUTHERN ILLINOIS MCHY CO INC
Also Called: Sim Products
6903 E 1600th Ave (62461-2343)
PHONE.....................217 868-5431
John A Newsome, *President*
John R Newsome, *Shareholder*
▲ EMP: 80
SQ FT: 50,000
SALES (est): 15.3MM **Privately Held**
SIC: 3555 Bookbinding machinery

Sigel
Shelby County

(G-18907)
SIGEL WELDING
103 S Main St (62462-1014)
PHONE.....................217 844-2412
Eric McWhorter, *Owner*
Kent Jansen, *Co-Owner*
EMP: 1
SALES (est): 250K **Privately Held**
SIC: 7692 Welding repair

Silvis
Rock Island County

(G-18908)
NATIONAL RAILWAY EQUIPMENT CO
300 9th St N (61282-1075)
PHONE.....................309 755-6800
Lorrie Winters, *Manager*
Gene Temkin, *Director*
Cynthia Martoccio, *Admin Sec*
EMP: 150
SALES (corp-wide): 314MM **Privately Held**
SIC: 3743 5088 Locomotives & parts; railroad equipment & supplies
PA: National Railway Equipment Co.
1100 Shawnee St
Mount Vernon IL 62864
618 242-6590

(G-18909)
RIVER CITY SIGN COMPANY INC
Also Called: Carol Douglas Company
915 1st Ave (61282-1046)
PHONE.....................309 796-3606
Carol Small, *President*
Douglas Small, *Vice Pres*
▲ EMP: 3
SQ FT: 4,000
SALES (est): 100K **Privately Held**
SIC: 3999 Wind chimes

Sims
Wayne County

(G-18910)
ROBERTSON REPAIR
Hwy 15 (62886)
PHONE.....................618 895-2593
Bill Robertson, *Owner*
EMP: 4
SALES (est): 243.9K **Privately Held**
SIC: 7692 Automotive welding

Skokie
Cook County

(G-18911)
A J CARBIDE GRINDING
8509 E Prairie Rd (60076-2322)
PHONE.....................847 675-5112
Arthur J Sala, *Owner*
EMP: 2
SALES (est): 500K **Privately Held**
SIC: 7389 3542 3544 Grinding, precision: commercial or industrial; machine tools, metal forming type; special dies, tools, jigs & fixtures

(G-18912)
ACE PCB DESIGN INC
5138 Conrad St (60077-2114)
PHONE.....................847 674-8745
John Callas, *President*
EMP: 3
SALES (est): 211.4K **Privately Held**
SIC: 3571 Electronic computers

(G-18913)
ALL CNC SOLUTIONS INC
7617 Parkside Ave (60077-2633)
PHONE.....................847 972-1139
Miroslav Kainovic, *President*
EMP: 5 EST: 2008
SALES (est): 658K **Privately Held**
SIC: 8711 3599 Machine tool design; machine & other job shop work

(G-18914)
ALL SIGNS INC
Also Called: Signarama Skokie
8088 Mccormick Blvd (60076-2919)
PHONE.....................847 324-5500
Sravan Ravi, *President*
EMP: 3
SALES (est): 102.9K **Privately Held**
SIC: 3993 Signs & advertising specialties

(G-18915)
ALL-VAC INDUSTRIES INC
7350 Central Park Ave (60076-4003)
PHONE.....................847 675-2290
Mitchell Stern, *President*
Joe Maggio, *Prdtn Mgr*
Harriet R Stern, *Treasurer*
Maureen Rottinger, *Officer*
▲ EMP: 10
SQ FT: 5,000
SALES (est): 2.1MM **Privately Held**
SIC: 3565 3086 3537 3444 Vacuum packaging machinery; cups & plates, foamed plastic; industrial trucks & tractors; sheet metalwork

(G-18916)
ALLIANCE INVESTMENT CORP
Also Called: Midland Printing
9150 Kenneth Ave (60076-1647)
PHONE.....................847 933-0400
Hossein Birjandi, *President*
EMP: 11
SQ FT: 3,000
SALES (est): 1MM **Privately Held**
SIC: 2752 Menus, lithographed

(G-18917)
AMERICAN ACRYLICS INC
8124 Central Park Ave (60076-2907)
PHONE.....................847 674-7800
James Scobie, *President*
EMP: 5
SALES (est): 657.7K **Privately Held**
SIC: 3089 Injection molding of plastics

(G-18918)
AMERICAN LOUVER COMPANY (PA)
Also Called: American Store Fixtures
7700 Austin Ave (60077-2603)
PHONE.....................847 470-0400
Geoffrey M Glass Jr, *President*
Glen Swazey, *Regional Mgr*
Lucy Polk, *CFO*
Kristine Hassmer, *Credit Mgr*
Roxanne Cordice, *Human Resources*
◆ EMP: 108
SQ FT: 55,000
SALES (est): 32.2MM **Privately Held**
WEB: www.americanlouver.com
SIC: 3083 Plastic finished products, laminated

(G-18919)
AMERICUT WIRE EDM INC
8045 Ridgeway Ave (60076-3408)
PHONE.....................847 675-1754
Nicola Babatchev, *President*
Nick Babatchev, *President*
EMP: 13
SALES: 950K **Privately Held**
WEB: www.americutedm.com
SIC: 3599 Machine shop, jobbing & repair

(G-18920)
AMMERAAL BELTECH INC (DH)
7501 Saint Louis Ave (60076-4033)
PHONE.....................847 673-6720
Prakash K Iyengar, *CEO*
Rod Parker, *District Mgr*
Michael Davison, *COO*
Dave Hill, *Opers Mgr*
Jeff Crum, *Traffic Mgr*
◆ EMP: 100 EST: 1913
SQ FT: 105,000
SALES (est): 46.8MM
SALES (corp-wide): 242.1K **Privately Held**
WEB: www.ammeraal-beltechusa.com
SIC: 3496 Miscellaneous fabricated wire products
HQ: Ammeraal Beltech Holding B.V.
Comeniusstraat 8
Alkmaar 1817
725 751-212

(G-18921)
APOLLO MACHINE & MANUFACTURING
7617 Parkside Ave (60077-2633)
PHONE.....................847 677-6444
Danicia Kaninovic, *President*
Danica Kaninovic, *President*
Danny Kainovic, *Treasurer*

EMP: 1
SQ FT: 5,000
SALES (est): 400K Privately Held
SIC: 3599 7692 3544 Machine shop, jobbing & repair; welding repair; special dies, tools, jigs & fixtures

(G-18922)
APR GRAPHICS INC
4825 Main St (60077-2508)
PHONE.................847 329-7800
Wayne Romano, *President*
Christine Romano, *Admin Sec*
EMP: 3
SQ FT: 1,200
SALES (est): 388.9K Privately Held
SIC: 2791 2796 Typesetting; platemaking services

(G-18923)
AR-EN PARTY PRINTERS INC
3416 Oakton St (60076-2951)
PHONE.................847 673-7390
Gary Morrison, *President*
▲ EMP: 28 EST: 1978
SQ FT: 9,500
SALES (est): 6.9MM Privately Held
WEB: www.ar-en.com
SIC: 2679 5199 Paper products, converted; party favors, balloons, hats, etc.

(G-18924)
ASTELLAS RES INST AMER LLC
8045 Lamon Ave (60077-5317)
PHONE.................847 933-7400
Toshio Goto, *President*
Kouichi Tamura, *Senior VP*
EMP: 18 EST: 2007
SALES (est): 3.4MM Privately Held
WEB: www.astellas.us
SIC: 2834 Pharmaceutical preparations
HQ: Astellas Pharma Us, Inc.
1 Astellas Way
Northbrook IL 60062

(G-18925)
ATA FINISHING CORP
8225 Kimball Ave (60076-2990)
PHONE.................847 677-8560
Ronald Anderson, *President*
Goldie Anderson, *Admin Sec*
EMP: 9
SQ FT: 10,000
SALES (est): 1MM Privately Held
WEB: www.atafinishing.com
SIC: 3471 2851 Finishing, metals or formed products; plating of metals or formed products; polishing, metals or formed products; paints & allied products

(G-18926)
AZUL 3D INC
8111 Saint Louis Ave # 2 (60076-2968)
PHONE.................321 277-7807
James Hedrick, *Principal*
Chad Mirkin, *Principal*
David Walker, *COO*
John Martin, *COO*
EMP: 14
SALES (est): 136.1K Privately Held
SIC: 5162 3087 3555 3552 Plastics products; custom compound purchased resins; printing trades machinery; textile machinery

(G-18927)
BAG TAGS INC
3415 Howard St Ste 101 (60076-4011)
PHONE.................847 983-4732
Lucy Doyle, *Branch Mgr*
EMP: 11
SALES (corp-wide): 2.8MM Privately Held
WEB: www.bagtagsinc.com
SIC: 2679 Tags, paper (unprinted): made from purchased paper
PA: Bag Tags, Inc.
1316 Sherman Ave Ste 215
Evanston IL 60201
847 424-1900

(G-18928)
BC INTERNATIONAL
4909 Old Orchard Ctr (60076-1439)
PHONE.................847 674-7384
Denny Hosch, *Principal*

EMP: 3
SIC: 3221 5084 Bottles for packing, bottling & canning: glass; food industry machinery

(G-18929)
BEST CUTTING DIE CO (PA)
8080 Mccormick Blvd (60076-2919)
PHONE.................847 675-5522
Edward J Porento Sr, *President*
John Scinteie, *General Mgr*
Gary Porento, *Principal*
Marion Porento, *Principal*
Robert Porento, *Principal*
▲ EMP: 110 EST: 1966
SQ FT: 60,000
SALES (est): 23.7MM Privately Held
WEB: www.bestcuttingdie.com
SIC: 3544 Paper cutting dies

(G-18930)
BOOMBOX BEVERAGE LLC
7415 Saint Louis Ave (60076-4031)
PHONE.................312 607-1038
Paul Seeman, *Mng Member*
EMP: 5
SALES (est): 500K Privately Held
SIC: 5149 5963 3999 Coffee & tea; beverage services, direct sales; manufacturing industries

(G-18931)
BP ELC MTRS PUMP & SVC INC
8135 Ridgeway Ave (60076-3352)
PHONE.................773 539-4343
Hasmij Papazion, *President*
Berg J Papazion, *Vice Pres*
EMP: 5
SQ FT: 4,200
SALES (est): 500K Privately Held
SIC: 7694 5999 5063 Electric motor repair; motors, electric; motors, electric

(G-18932)
BR CONCEPTS INTERNATIONAL INC
Also Called: BRC Manufacturing Co
7436 Kildare Ave (60076-3822)
PHONE.................847 674-9481
Naum Ligum, *President*
EMP: 5
SALES (est): 5MM Privately Held
SIC: 3443 Metal parts

(G-18933)
BRIAN ROBERT AWNING CO
8152 Lawndale Ave (60076-3322)
PHONE.................847 679-1140
Robert Lucius, *President*
Joan Lucius, *Admin Sec*
EMP: 5
SQ FT: 5,000
SALES (est): 369.9K Privately Held
SIC: 2394 Awnings, fabric: made from purchased materials

(G-18934)
BRIGHTON COLLECTIBLES LLC
4999 Old Orchard Ctr M17 (60077-1467)
PHONE.................847 674-6719
Jerry Kohl, *Branch Mgr*
EMP: 17
SALES (corp-wide): 251.5MM Privately Held
SIC: 3111 Accessory products, leather
PA: Brighton Collectibles, Llc
14022 Nelson Ave
City Of Industry CA 91746
626 961-9381

(G-18935)
C D T MANUFACTURING INC
8020 Monticello Ave (60076-3438)
PHONE.................847 679-2361
Dieter Tantius, *President*
EMP: 4
SQ FT: 2,200
SALES (est): 468.6K Privately Held
SIC: 3541 3678 Machine tools, metal cutting type; electronic connectors

(G-18936)
CAMPUS CARDBOARD
5115 Church St 104 (60077-1201)
P.O. Box 12, Wilmette (60091-0012)
PHONE.................847 251-2594
Matthew Pope, *President*
EMP: 3
SALES (est): 223K Privately Held
SIC: 2631 Cardboard

(G-18937)
CASTWELL PRODUCTS LLC
7800 Austin Ave (60077-2641)
PHONE.................847 966-5050
Charlie Hoffman, *President*
Lisa Archer, *Production*
Michael Jacob, *Buyer*
Ray Flynn, *Manager*
Mark Barasa, *Supervisor*
EMP: 250
SALES (est): 52.6MM Privately Held
SIC: 3321 Gray iron castings

(G-18938)
CENTRAL SHEET METAL PDTS INC
7251 Linder Ave (60077-3216)
PHONE.................773 583-2424
Sheldon Silverstein, *President*
Joel Silverstein, *Vice Pres*
Peter Silverstein, *Vice Pres*
Claire Silverstein, *Admin Sec*
EMP: 25
SQ FT: 18,000
SALES (est): 4.6MM Privately Held
WEB: www.centralsheet.com
SIC: 3444 2542 Sheet metal specialties, not stamped; casings, sheet metal; cabinets: show, display or storage: except wood

(G-18939)
CENTURY FASTENERS & MCH CO INC
Also Called: Gail Glasser Brickman
4901 Fairview Ln Ste 1 (60077-3523)
P.O. Box 681 (60076-0681)
PHONE.................773 463-3900
Gail Brickman, *CEO*
Randy Gibbs, *Sales Staff*
EMP: 12
SQ FT: 10,000
SALES: 900K Privately Held
SIC: 3452 3561 Nuts, metal; bolts, metal; screws, metal; pumps & pumping equipment

(G-18940)
CHEM TRADE GLOBAL
3832 Dobson St (60076-3717)
PHONE.................847 675-2682
Ellen Jesse, *President*
▲ EMP: 3
SALES: 1MM Privately Held
SIC: 2899 Chemical supplies for foundries

(G-18941)
CHICAGO JEWISH NEWS
4638 Church St (60076-1545)
PHONE.................847 966-0606
Joseph Aaron, *Owner*
Ann Yellon, *Manager*
EMP: 10
SQ FT: 1,900
SALES: 929K Privately Held
SIC: 2711 8661 Commercial printing & newspaper publishing combined; religious organizations

(G-18942)
CHOICE FURNISHINGS INC
7518 Saint Louis Ave # 1053 (60076-4002)
PHONE.................847 329-0004
Maurice Freedman, *President*
Judice Freedman, *Admin Sec*
▲ EMP: 10
SQ FT: 4,000
SALES (est): 1.1MM Privately Held
SIC: 2511 5021 Chairs, household, except upholstered: wood; chairs

(G-18943)
CKS SIGNS INC
Also Called: Fastsigns
3437 Dempster St (60076-2441)
PHONE.................847 423-3456
Kim Hackl, *Principal*
Craig Hackl, *Principal*
EMP: 3
SALES (est): 216.8K Privately Held
SIC: 3993 Signs & advertising specialties

(G-18944)
CLOZ COMPANIES INC (PA)
Also Called: Adco Amrcn Day Camp Outfitters
5550 Touhy Ave Ste 202 (60077-3254)
PHONE.................773 247-8879
Michael Cohen, *President*
Randall Siegel, *Senior VP*
EMP: 45
SQ FT: 22,000
SALES (est): 4.3MM Privately Held
SIC: 2329 2339 2369 2395 Men's & boys' sportswear & athletic clothing; women's & misses' outerwear; girls' & children's outerwear; embroidery & art needlework; screen printing; advertising specialties

(G-18945)
CO-FAIR CORPORATION
7301 Saint Louis Ave (60076-4029)
PHONE.................847 626-1500
Robert Kaplan, *President*
David Miller, *Natl Sales Mgr*
EMP: 20
SQ FT: 25,000
SALES (est): 4.9MM Privately Held
SIC: 5033 2952 5211 Roofing & siding materials; roofing materials; lumber products

(G-18946)
COFAIR PRODUCTS INC
7301 Saint Louis Ave (60076-4029)
PHONE.................847 626-1500
Robert Kaplan, *President*
EMP: 3
SALES (est): 2.1MM Privately Held
WEB: www.cofair.com
SIC: 5033 2952 1761 1751 Roofing & siding materials; roofing materials; roofing & gutter work; window & door installation & erection

(G-18947)
CUSTOM CUT EDM INC
5423 Fargo Ave (60077-3211)
PHONE.................847 647-9500
EMP: 4
SQ FT: 4,500
SALES: 702K Privately Held
SIC: 3599 Custom Machine Shop Edm

(G-18948)
DENOYER - GEPPERT SCIENCE CO
7514 Saint Louis Ave (60076-4034)
P.O. Box 1727 (60076-8727)
PHONE.................800 621-1014
Mary Andros, *President*
Mark Gilbert, *Vice Pres*
Yongjoon Lee, *Vice Pres*
Robert Ortegon, *Purch Mgr*
Tracy Albano, *Relations*
◆ EMP: 30
SQ FT: 17,000
SALES (est): 3.8MM Privately Held
SIC: 3999 Models, general, except toy

(G-18949)
EDEN FUELS LLC
Also Called: Eden's and Old Orchard's Shell
5025 Old Orchard Rd (60077-1019)
PHONE.................847 676-9470
Sherri L Maddox, *Principal*
EMP: 6
SALES (est): 726.5K Privately Held
SIC: 2869 7538 Fuels; general automotive repair shops

(G-18950)
ENGERT CO INC
8103 Monticello Ave (60076-3325)
PHONE.................847 673-1633
Mark Heller, *President*

Skokie - Cook County (G-18951)

Gary Heller, *Vice Pres*
▼ **EMP:** 25 **EST:** 1934
SALES (est): 3MM **Privately Held**
SIC: 5072 3429 Hardware; manufactured hardware (general)

(G-18951)
ENGILITY CORPORATION
5600 Old Orchard Rd Bsmt (60077-1051)
PHONE 847 583-1216
Anna Kakotariti, *Branch Mgr*
EMP: 5
SALES (corp-wide): 6.3B **Publicly Held**
WEB: www.engilitycorp.com
SIC: 3812 Inertial guidance systems; navigational systems & instruments
HQ: Engility Corporation
 35 New England Bus Ctr Dr
 Andover MA 01810
 703 633-8300

(G-18952)
ENVIROCOAT INC
7440 Saint Louis Ave (60076-4032)
PHONE 847 673-3649
Igor Murokh, *Principal*
EMP: 5
SALES (est): 502.5K **Privately Held**
SIC: 3471 3479 Finishing, metals or formed products; painting, coating & hot dipping

(G-18953)
EXPERCOLOR INC
Also Called: Triangle
3737 Chase Ave (60076-4008)
PHONE 773 465-3400
Harvey Saltzman, *President*
David Saltzman, *Vice Pres*
Mike Mueller, *Prdtn Mgr*
Allison Rickett, *Director*
Monica Grier, *Creative Dir*
EMP: 50 **EST:** 1954
SQ FT: 50,000
SALES (est): 3.5MM **Privately Held**
SIC: 2796 7336 Color separations for printing; commercial art & graphic design

(G-18954)
FEDERAL-MOGUL MOTORPARTS LLC
7450 Mccormick Blvd (60076-4046)
PHONE 847 674-7700
Kathy Loomis, *Senior Buyer*
Don Chelmecki, *Engineer*
Kevin Finkle, *Financial Analy*
Derek Data, *Manager*
EMP: 1094
SALES (corp-wide): 17.4B **Publicly Held**
WEB: www.buyfmgear.com
SIC: 3714 Motor vehicle parts & accessories
HQ: Federal-Mogul Motorparts Llc
 27300 W 11 Mile Rd
 Southfield MI 48034
 248 354-7700

(G-18955)
FLAHERTY INCORPORATED
9047 Terminal Ave (60077-1570)
PHONE 773 472-8456
Catherine Flaherty, *President*
EMP: 3
SQ FT: 15,000
SALES (est): 452.7K **Privately Held**
SIC: 2035 2099 Mustard, prepared (wet); food preparations

(G-18956)
FORMULATIONS INC
Also Called: Natural Formulations
8050 Ridgeway Ave (60076-3409)
PHONE 847 674-9141
William Schwaber, *President*
EMP: 5
SQ FT: 10,000
SALES (est): 1MM **Privately Held**
SIC: 2841 2842 2844 Soap & other detergents; ammonia, household; plating & polishing; toilet preparations

(G-18957)
FRESENIUS KABI USA LLC
The Illinois Scienc (60077)
PHONE 847 983-7100
Michael Awe, *QC Mgr*
Brian Hoffman, *Engineer*
Chris Bryant, *Branch Mgr*
EMP: 35
SALES (corp-wide): 39.1B **Privately Held**
WEB: www.fresenius-kabi.us
SIC: 2834 Pharmaceutical preparations
HQ: Fresenius Kabi Usa, Llc
 3 Corporate Dr Fl 3 # 3
 Lake Zurich IL 60047
 847 550-2300

(G-18958)
GAERTNER SCIENTIFIC CORP
3650 Jarvis Ave (60076-4018)
PHONE 847 673-5006
Rusty Kutko, *President*
Lucilla Abad, *Treasurer*
Wsewolod A Popov, *Admin Sec*
EMP: 22 **EST:** 1896
SQ FT: 20,000
SALES (est): 3.9MM **Privately Held**
SIC: 3827 3826 Optical test & inspection equipment; analytical instruments

(G-18959)
GANJI KLAMES
Also Called: Babylon Travel & Tour Service
4455 Oakton St (60076-3222)
PHONE 773 478-9000
Klames Ganji, *Owner*
EMP: 4
SQ FT: 1,000
SALES (est): 168.7K **Privately Held**
SIC: 2711 4724 Newspapers, publishing & printing; tourist agency arranging transport, lodging & car rental

(G-18960)
GRACE PRINTING AND MAILING
8130 Saint Louis Ave (60076-2925)
PHONE 847 423-2100
Joseph Regi, *Prdtn Mgr*
EMP: 22 **EST:** 2010
SALES (est): 3.4MM **Privately Held**
WEB: www.graceprinting.com
SIC: 2752 Commercial printing, offset

(G-18961)
GROVER WELDING COMPANY
9120 Terminal Ave (60077-1514)
PHONE 847 966-3119
Lawrence Grover, *President*
Linda Grover, *CFO*
EMP: 5 **EST:** 1934
SQ FT: 3,000
SALES (est): 738.7K **Privately Held**
WEB: www.groverwelding.com
SIC: 7692 5082 3441 Welding repair; general construction machinery & equipment; fabricated structural metal

(G-18962)
H L CLAUSING INC
8038 Monticello Ave (60076-3438)
PHONE 847 676-0330
Howard L Clausing, *President*
Hl Clausing, *President*
Patricia Clausing, *Train & Dev Mgr*
EMP: 6 **EST:** 1927
SQ FT: 5,500
SALES (est): 900K **Privately Held**
WEB: www.clausing.com
SIC: 3827 8711 8748 Mirrors, optical; engineering services; testing services

(G-18963)
HADCO TOOL CO LLC
8105 Monticello Ave (60076-3325)
PHONE 847 677-6263
Steve Salbeck, *President*
EMP: 4 **EST:** 1955
SQ FT: 3,500
SALES (est): 370K **Privately Held**
SIC: 3599 Machine shop, jobbing & repair

(G-18964)
HARIG MANUFACTURING CORP
5423 Fargo Ave (60077-3211)
PHONE 847 647-9500
Theodore H Eckert, *Ch of Bd*
Theodore M Eckert, *Vice Pres*
Kelly Payton, *Sales Staff*
▲ **EMP:** 26 **EST:** 1937
SQ FT: 55,000
SALES (est): 5.7MM **Privately Held**
WEB: www.metaldisintegrator.com
SIC: 3545 3544 3469 Tools & accessories for machine tools; die sets for metal stamping (presses); jigs & fixtures; stamping metal for the trade

(G-18965)
HARRIS SKOKIE
9731 Skokie Blvd (60077-1383)
PHONE 847 675-6300
David Langebach, *Principal*
EMP: 3
SALES (est): 196.6K **Privately Held**
SIC: 3944 Banks, toy

(G-18966)
HY SPRECKMAN & SONS INC
9725 Woods Dr Unit 1302 (60077-4455)
PHONE 312 236-2173
Hyman Spreckman, *President*
Jeffrey Spreckman, *Vice Pres*
Steven Spreckman, *Vice Pres*
Lorraine Spreckman, *Admin Sec*
▼ **EMP:** 10
SQ FT: 2,500
SALES (est): 1.2MM **Privately Held**
SIC: 3911 5094 Jewel settings & mountings, precious metal; diamonds (gems)

(G-18967)
HYDRO INK CORP
7331 Monticello Ave (60076-4024)
PHONE 847 674-0057
EMP: 5 **EST:** 1988
SQ FT: 5,000
SALES: 610K **Privately Held**
SIC: 3952 2893 Mfg Lead Pencils/Art Goods Mfg Printing Ink

(G-18968)
INDIA BULLETIN INC
4332 Emerson St (60076-1476)
PHONE 847 674-7941
Bharati Shah, *President*
Sagar Shah, *Manager*
EMP: 4
SALES (est): 16.5K **Privately Held**
SIC: 2711 Newspapers, publishing & printing

(G-18969)
INVENTIVE MFG INC
5423 Fargo Ave (60077-3211)
PHONE 847 647-9500
Theodore H Eckert Sr, *President*
Hilda Chammas, *Purch Mgr*
Theodore H Eckert Jr, *Admin Sec*
EMP: 10 **EST:** 1945
SQ FT: 10,000
SALES (est): 1.3MM **Privately Held**
WEB: www.inventivmfg.com
SIC: 3599 3544 Electrical discharge machining (EDM); machine shop, jobbing & repair; special dies, tools, jigs & fixtures

(G-18970)
JEWEL OSCO INC
Also Called: Jewel-Osco 3465
9449 Skokie Blvd (60077-1317)
PHONE 847 677-3331
John Colton, *Manager*
EMP: 152
SALES (corp-wide): 60.5B **Privately Held**
SIC: 5411 2052 2051 Supermarkets, chain; cookies & crackers; bread, cake & related products
HQ: Jewel Osco, Inc.
 150 E Pierce Rd Ste 200
 Itasca IL 60143
 630 948-6000

(G-18971)
KAFKO INTERNATIONAL LTD
3555 Howard St (60076-4052)
PHONE 847 763-0333
Nicholas Kafkis, *Chairman*
Bob Kafkis, *Vice Pres*
George Kafkis, *Vice Pres*
Rick Morgando, *Marketing Staff*
Agatha Kafkis, *Admin Sec*
◆ **EMP:** 35
SALES (est): 9.4MM **Privately Held**
SIC: 2819 2842 4783 Industrial inorganic chemicals; specialty cleaning, polishes & sanitation goods; packing goods for shipping

(G-18972)
KECKLEY MANUFACTURING COMPANY
3400 Cleveland St (60076-2916)
PHONE 847 674-8422
Philip K Miller, *President*
Donald S Miller, *Treasurer*
EMP: 50 **EST:** 1914
SQ FT: 40,000
SALES: 7.7MM
SALES (corp-wide): 12.2MM **Privately Held**
WEB: www.keckley.com
SIC: 3491 3494 Pressure valves & regulators, industrial; valves & pipe fittings
PA: O. C. Keckley Company
 3400 Cleveland St
 Skokie IL 60076
 847 674-8422

(G-18973)
KOEHLER BINDERY INC
4315 Main St (60076-2048)
PHONE 773 539-7979
Ronald Hackl, *Vice Pres*
Walter J Hackl II, *Treasurer*
EMP: 5
SALES (est): 563.9K **Privately Held**
WEB: www.familyhistorybinding.com
SIC: 2789 Binding only: books, pamphlets, magazines, etc.

(G-18974)
L L BEAN INC
4999 Old Orchard Ctr F18 (60077-1455)
PHONE 847 568-3600
EMP: 6
SALES (corp-wide): 897.1MM **Privately Held**
WEB: www.llbean.com
SIC: 3949 Sporting & athletic goods
PA: L. L. Bean, Inc.
 15 Casco St
 Freeport ME 04033
 207 552-2000

(G-18975)
LAMONT WELLS INDUSTRIAL
5215 Old Orchard Rd # 725 (60077-1022)
PHONE 804 299-2557
EMP: 3
SALES (est): 151.5K **Privately Held**
SIC: 2381 Gloves, work: woven or knit, made from purchased materials

(G-18976)
LANZATECH INC (HQ)
Also Called: Freedom Pines
8045 Lamon Ave Ste 400 (60077-5318)
PHONE 630 439-3050
Jennifer Holmgren, *CEO*
Dave Meyer, *Business Mgr*
Mark Burton, *Vice Pres*
Ken C Lai, *Vice Pres*
Ken Lai, *Vice Pres*
▲ **EMP:** 80
SQ FT: 1,500
SALES (est): 21.6MM **Privately Held**
SIC: 2869 Industrial organic chemicals

(G-18977)
LASER REPRODUCTIONS INC
Also Called: Care Creations
8228 Mccormick Blvd (60076-2921)
PHONE 847 410-0397
Cary Green, *President*
◆ **EMP:** 20
SQ FT: 30,000
SALES (est): 6.2MM **Privately Held**
SIC: 5084 3555 Printing trades machinery, equipment & supplies; printing trades machinery

(G-18978)
LBL LIGHTING LLC (PA)
7400 Linder Ave (60077-3219)
PHONE 708 755-2100
Joan M Stone, *Corp Secy*
Steve Sorenso, *Vice Pres*
Ronald Stone,

GEOGRAPHIC SECTION

Skokie - Cook County (G-19007)

▲ EMP: 12 EST: 1971
SQ FT: 7,000
SALES (est): 3.4MM Privately Held
SIC: 3648 5063 Lighting fixtures, except electric: residential; lighting fixtures

(G-18979)
LETTERING SPECIALISTS INC
8020 Lawndale Ave (60076-3436)
PHONE...................847 674-3414
Robert L Narens, *President*
Frank D Billeck, *Corp Secy*
EMP: 10
SQ FT: 5,000
SALES (est): 1.4MM Privately Held
SIC: 3993 Signs, not made in custom sign painting shops

(G-18980)
LITTLE JOURNEYS LIMITED
7914 Kildare Ave (60076-3518)
PHONE...................847 677-0350
David S Lee, *President*
Davids Lee, *President*
Ronanna Berk, *Vice Pres*
EMP: 2
SALES (est): 206.2K Privately Held
SIC: 2369 5023 2339 Girls' & children's outerwear; coats: girls', children's & infants'; decorative home furnishings & supplies; women's & misses' jackets & coats, except sportswear

(G-18981)
LUTAMAR ELECTRICAL ASSEMBLIES
8030 Ridgeway Ave (60076-3409)
PHONE...................847 679-5400
Ida Wilk, *President*
Carl J Wilk, *Vice Pres*
▲ EMP: 30 EST: 1947
SQ FT: 10,000
SALES (est): 3.2MM Privately Held
WEB: www.lutamar.com
SIC: 3644 3699 3643 Terminal boards; electrical equipment & supplies; current-carrying wiring devices

(G-18982)
MARFA CABINETS INC
3426 W Touhy Ave (60076-6217)
PHONE...................847 701-5558
EMP: 20
SALES (est): 69.2K Privately Held
SIC: 2434 Wood kitchen cabinets

(G-18983)
MARK COLLINS
Also Called: Sign-A-Rama
4443 Oakton St (60076-3222)
PHONE...................847 324-5500
Mark Collins, *President*
EMP: 3
SQ FT: 1,200
SALES (est): 240K Privately Held
SIC: 3993 Signs & advertising specialties

(G-18984)
MARMON GROUP LLC
5215 Old Orchard Rd # 725 (60077-1035)
PHONE...................847 647-8200
John D Nichols, *President*
EMP: 80
SALES (corp-wide): 327.2B Publicly Held
SIC: 3589 Water filters & softeners, household type
HQ: The Marmon Group Llc
181 W Madison St Ste 2600
Chicago IL 60602

(G-18985)
MATHEW LUCANTE VIOLINS LLC
4200 Enfield Ave (60076-1951)
PHONE...................773 320-2997
Rivera Jennifer Caraig, *Principal*
EMP: 3
SALES (est): 229.2K Privately Held
SIC: 3931 Violins & parts

(G-18986)
MAYA ROMANOFF CORPORATION (PA)
3435 Madison St (60076-2928)
PHONE...................773 465-6909
Maya Romanoff, *President*
David Berkowitz, *Exec VP*
Jennifer Block, *Vice Pres*
Mike Lassin, *Opers Staff*
Richard Haught, *Finance Asst*
▲ EMP: 50
SQ FT: 18,000
SALES (est): 6.8MM Privately Held
SIC: 2221 2211 Wall covering fabrics, manmade fiber & silk; upholstery, tapestry & wall coverings: cotton

(G-18987)
MDM COMMUNICATIONS INC
8737 Central Park Ave (60076-2304)
PHONE...................708 582-9667
Rick Arons, *Principal*
EMP: 3
SALES (est): 207.5K Privately Held
SIC: 2721 Trade journals: publishing only, not printed on site

(G-18988)
METRO TOOL COMPANY
8315 Ridgeway Ave (60076-3494)
PHONE...................847 673-6790
Ramandahi Patel, *President*
EMP: 3
SALES (est): 462K Privately Held
SIC: 3544 3542 Industrial molds; machine tools, metal forming type

(G-18989)
MICRO CRAFT MANUFACTURING CO
7248 Saint Louis Ave (60076-4028)
PHONE...................847 679-2022
Jewel Mc Wherter, *President*
Debra Mc Wherter, *Vice Pres*
EMP: 10
SQ FT: 5,000
SALES (est): 1.3MM Privately Held
SIC: 3451 Screw machine products

(G-18990)
MIDLAND MANUFACTURING CORP
7733 Gross Point Rd (60077-2615)
PHONE...................847 677-0333
Thomas Zant, *President*
Jim Desautels, *District Mgr*
Keith Simon, *District Mgr*
Kevin Cook, *Vice Pres*
Michael Majerle, *Maint Spvr*
▲ EMP: 120 EST: 1994
SQ FT: 100,000
SALES: 39.5MM
SALES (corp-wide): 7.1B Publicly Held
WEB: www.midlandmfg.net
SIC: 3494 3715 3713 3545 Valves & pipe fittings; truck trailers; barges, building & repairing; machine tool accessories; industrial valves
PA: Dover Corporation
3005 Highland Pkwy # 200
Downers Grove IL 60515
630 541-1540

(G-18991)
MIDWEST SHARED NEWSLETTER
8621 Gross Point Rd (60077-2152)
PHONE...................847 933-9498
Elliot Freeman, *President*
EMP: 3
SALES (est): 111.4K Privately Held
SIC: 2741 Miscellaneous publishing

(G-18992)
MODERN TRADE COMMUNICATIONS (PA)
Also Called: Metal Construction News
7836 Frontage Rd (60077-2637)
PHONE...................847 674-2200
John S Lawrence, *CEO*
John Lawrence, *President*
Blanca Arteaga, *Opers Mgr*
Quentin Brown, *Prdtn Mgr*
Tina Lawrence, *Treasurer*

EMP: 10
SALES (est): 1.3MM Privately Held
WEB: www.metalconstructionnews.com
SIC: 2721 2741 2752 Trade journals: publishing only, not printed on site; directories: publishing only, not printed on site; cards, lithographed

(G-18993)
MULLEN CIRCLE BRAND INC
3514 W Touhy Ave (60076-6218)
P.O. Box 8487, Northfield (60093-8487)
PHONE...................847 676-1880
Kenneth Reed, *President*
Shirley R Reed, *Vice Pres*
EMP: 10
SQ FT: 40,000
SALES (est): 1.9MM Privately Held
WEB: www.circlecut.com
SIC: 2992 Oils & greases, blending & compounding; rust arresting compounds, animal or vegetable oil base

(G-18994)
MULTIPLE METAL PRODUCTION
8030 Lawndale Ave (60076-3436)
PHONE...................847 679-1510
Joe Clouser, *Owner*
EMP: 4
SALES (est): 400K Privately Held
SIC: 3312 Tool & die steel

(G-18995)
NATIONWIDE NEWS MONITOR
9239 Kilpatrick Ave (60076-1530)
PHONE...................312 424-4224
EMP: 3
SALES (est): 127.1K Privately Held
SIC: 2711 Newspapers, publishing & printing

(G-18996)
NOBILITY CORPORATION
5404 Touhy Ave (60077-3232)
PHONE...................847 677-3204
Bruce E Creger, *Ch of Bd*
Richard F Wharton, *President*
▲ EMP: 30
SQ FT: 30,000
SALES (est): 3MM Privately Held
SIC: 3678 Electronic connectors

(G-18997)
O C KECKLEY COMPANY (PA)
3400 Cleveland St (60076-2900)
P.O. Box 67 (60076-0067)
PHONE...................847 674-8422
Ross Miller, *President*
Donald S Miller, *Corp Secy*
Keith Lankton, *Vice Pres*
Michael Frederichs, *Engineer*
Matt Grund, *Accounts Mgr*
▲ EMP: 50 EST: 1914
SQ FT: 45,000
SALES (est): 12.2MM Privately Held
WEB: www.keckley.com
SIC: 3625 5085 3491 3494 Relays & industrial controls; valves & fittings; pressure valves & regulators, industrial; valves & pipe fittings

(G-18998)
OCTURA MODELS INC
7351 Hamlin Ave (60076-3998)
PHONE...................847 674-7351
Thomas Perzentka, *President*
Ruth Perzentka, *Corp Secy*
EMP: 3 EST: 1954
SQ FT: 2,400
SALES (est): 325.8K Privately Held
SIC: 3944 Boat & ship models, toy & hobby

(G-18999)
ONEIMS PRINTING LLC
8833 Groil Pt Rd Ste 202 (60077)
PHONE...................773 297-2050
Solomon Thimothy, *Principal*
Tracey Zielezinski, *Editor*
Taylor Rowe, *Marketing Staff*
Phil Kim, *Graphic Designe*
EMP: 2
SALES (est): 291.2K Privately Held
WEB: www.oneims.com
SIC: 2752 Commercial printing, lithographic

(G-19000)
OPEN WATERS SEAFOOD COMPANY
5010 Howard St (60077-2829)
PHONE...................847 329-8585
Leo Dy, *President*
EMP: 5
SALES (est): 318.7K Privately Held
SIC: 2092 Seafoods, frozen: prepared

(G-19001)
OREI LLC
7440 Long Ave (60077-3214)
PHONE...................847 983-4761
Shethwala Fuzail, *Mng Member*
Mubashir Shethwala,
▲ EMP: 4
SQ FT: 10,000
SALES: 4MM Privately Held
SIC: 3651 3612 Household audio & video equipment; power transformers, electric

(G-19002)
P S GREETINGS INC
4901 Main St (60077-2515)
PHONE...................847 673-7255
Mark McCracken, *Branch Mgr*
EMP: 15
SALES (corp-wide): 48.2MM Privately Held
SIC: 2771 Greeting cards
PA: P. S. Greetings, Inc.
5730 N Tripp Ave
Chicago IL 60646
708 831-5340

(G-19003)
PATRIN PHARMA INC
7817 Babb Ave (60077-3636)
P.O. Box 1481 (60076-8481)
PHONE...................800 936-3088
Jay Trivedi, *President*
Smita Quinn, *Admin Sec*
EMP: 25
SALES (est): 3.7MM Privately Held
SIC: 2834 Pharmaceutical preparations

(G-19004)
PHENOME TECHNOLOGIES INC
7815 N St Louis Ave (60076)
PHONE...................847 962-1273
Michael J Wellems, *President*
Debbie A Masloskie, *Vice Pres*
EMP: 3
SALES: 350K Privately Held
SIC: 3841 Surgical & medical instruments

(G-19005)
PINOY MONTHLY
5323 Wright Ter (60077-2073)
PHONE...................847 329-1073
Mariano Santos, *Owner*
EMP: 3
SALES (est): 172.1K Privately Held
SIC: 2711 Newspapers, publishing & printing

(G-19006)
POLYERA CORPORATION
8025 Lamon Ave Ste 43 (60077-5319)
PHONE...................847 677-7517
Ed Zschau, *Ch of Bd*
Philippe Inagaki, *President*
Chung Chin Hsiao, *Senior VP*
Prakash Ramachandran, *Admin Sec*
EMP: 25
SQ FT: 10,000
SALES (est): 4.4MM Privately Held
SIC: 3679 Electronic circuits

(G-19007)
POWER GRAPHICS & PRINT INC
7345 Monticello Ave (60076-4024)
PHONE...................847 568-1808
Phat Chung, *President*
EMP: 7
SQ FT: 2,600
SALES (est): 674.2K Privately Held
WEB: www.printersskokie.com
SIC: 2752 Commercial printing, offset

Skokie - Cook County (G-19008)

(G-19008)
PR ORTHOTICS & OT
4711 Golf Rd Ste 1055 (60076-1272)
PHONE 224 470-8550
Patricia Rogel, *Principal*
EMP: 4
SALES (est): 309.6K **Privately Held**
SIC: 3842 Surgical appliances & supplies

(G-19009)
PRECISION MACHINING & TOOL CO
7341 Monticello Ave (60076-4024)
PHONE 847 674-7111
Alex Pagakis, *President*
EMP: 3
SALES (est): 140K **Privately Held**
SIC: 3599 Machine shop, jobbing & repair

(G-19010)
PRIKOS & BECKER LLC
8109 Lawndale Ave (60076-3321)
PHONE 847 675-3910
Max Wakeman, *President*
William R Becker,
Michael L George,
EMP: 55
SQ FT: 20,000
SALES (est): 10.2MM
SALES (corp-wide): 14.4B **Publicly Held**
SIC: 3469 Metal stampings
HQ: Consolidated Aerospace Manufacturing, Llc
  1425 S Acacia Ave
  Fullerton CA 92831
  714 989-2797

(G-19011)
PRINCESS FOODS INC
Also Called: Sangam
8145 Monticello Ave (60076-3325)
PHONE 847 933-1820
Babu Dalal, *President*
▲ **EMP:** 25
SQ FT: 2,500
SALES (est): 1.5MM **Privately Held**
SIC: 2096 2064 Potato chips & similar snacks; candy & other confectionery products

(G-19012)
PRINT XPRESS
8058 Lincoln Ave (60077-3613)
PHONE 847 677-5555
Sam Eckerling, *President*
Samuel Eckerling, *President*
EMP: 4
SQ FT: 2,000
SALES (est): 699.8K **Privately Held**
WEB: www.iprintxpress.com
SIC: 2752 2791 Commercial printing, offset; typesetting, computer controlled

(G-19013)
PROCRAFT ENGRAVING INC
8241 Christiana Ave (60076-2910)
PHONE 847 673-1500
Milan Milojevic, *President*
Kenneth Schutz, *Vice Pres*
EMP: 4
SQ FT: 2,100
SALES (est): 290K **Privately Held**
SIC: 3544 7389 Special dies & tools; engraving service

(G-19014)
PROFILE NETWORK INC
Also Called: Sports Profiles Plus
4709 Golf Rd Ste 807 (60076-1258)
PHONE 847 673-0592
Lisa Levine, *President*
Paula Blaine, *Vice Pres*
Randy Golden, *Director*
EMP: 25
SQ FT: 3,000
SALES (est): 1.6MM **Privately Held**
SIC: 7941 2721 Professional & semi-professional sports clubs; magazines: publishing only, not printed on site

(G-19015)
PROMARK ASSOCIATES INC
3856 Oakton St Ste 250 (60076-3454)
PHONE 847 676-1894
Jeffrey L Roseberry, *President*
Bernice Valantinas, *Corp Secy*
EMP: 5
SQ FT: 33,300
SALES (est): 800K **Privately Held**
SIC: 3564 8748 Air purification equipment; business consulting

(G-19016)
PROMPT MOTOR REWINDING SERVICE
7509 Keystone Ave (60076-3928)
PHONE 847 675-7155
Rick Joseph, *CEO*
EMP: 5
SALES (est): 257.6K **Privately Held**
SIC: 7694 Rewinding stators

(G-19017)
PROTECTION CONTROLS INC
Also Called: Protectofire
7317 Lawndale Ave (60076-4055)
P.O. Box 287 (60076-0287)
PHONE 773 763-3110
Bruce G Yates, *President*
Douglas H Yates, *Corp Secy*
DH Yates, *Opers Mgr*
Daryl Myrick, *Sales Engr*
James Yates, *Officer*
EMP: 30
SQ FT: 27,000
SALES (est): 5.4MM **Privately Held**
WEB: www.protectioncontrolsinc.com
SIC: 3613 3823 3699 3625 Control panels, electric; industrial instrmnts msrmnt display/control process variable; electrical equipment & supplies; relays & industrial controls

(G-19018)
PUBLISHERS ROW
Also Called: Varda Graphics
9001 Keating Ave (60076-1505)
PHONE 847 568-0593
Alexander Gendler, *Owner*
EMP: 11
SALES (est): 600.6K **Privately Held**
WEB: www.universaljewishencyclopedia.com
SIC: 2741 Miscellaneous publishing

(G-19019)
RAW THRILLS INC
5441 Fargo Ave (60077-3211)
PHONE 847 679-8373
Eugene Jarvis, *President*
Marc Marquez, *Principal*
Andrew Eloff, *Vice Pres*
Andrew Sundt, *Engineer*
Kevin Uskali, *Engineer*
◆ **EMP:** 60
SQ FT: 22,000
SALES (est): 81.5MM **Privately Held**
SIC: 3944 Video game machines, except coin-operated

(G-19020)
RAYES BOILER & WELDING LTD
8252 Christiana Ave (60076-2911)
PHONE 847 675-6655
Raman Rayes, *Owner*
EMP: 5
SALES (est): 751.6K **Privately Held**
SIC: 3443 7699 Fabricated plate work (boiler shop); boiler repair shop

(G-19021)
REMCO TECHNOLOGY INC
7438 Channel Rd (60076-4006)
PHONE 847 329-8090
Ben Boris Schwartz, *President*
Eugeane Rapoporg, *Vice Pres*
EMP: 12
SQ FT: 8,000
SALES (est): 1.1MM **Privately Held**
SIC: 3086 Insulation or cushioning material, foamed plastic

(G-19022)
REZNIK INSTRUMENT CO
7337 Lawndale Ave (60076-4021)
PHONE 847 673-3444
Ben Reznik, *President*
Edith Reznik, *Admin Sec*
EMP: 4
SQ FT: 5,600
SALES (est): 520.5K **Privately Held**
SIC: 3841 Surgical & medical instruments

(G-19023)
RIKEN CORPORATION OF AMERICA (HQ)
4709 Golf Rd Ste 807 (60076-1258)
PHONE 847 673-1400
Takuma Suzuki, *President*
Rick Okano, *President*
Tetsuya Okumura, *Corp Secy*
Alice Poulsen, *Engineer*
▲ **EMP:** 103
SALES (est): 9.8MM **Privately Held**
SIC: 3089 5013 3592 Molding primary plastic; injection molding of plastics; motor vehicle supplies & new parts; carburetors, pistons, rings, valves

(G-19024)
ROGERS METAL SERVICES INC
7330 Monticello Ave (60076-4025)
PHONE 847 679-4642
Jonathan Zimmerman, *President*
EMP: 30 **EST:** 1961
SQ FT: 5,600
SALES (est): 7.1MM **Privately Held**
SIC: 3398 Brazing (hardening) of metal

(G-19025)
RT ENTERPRISES INC
7540 Linder Ave (60077-3222)
PHONE 847 675-1444
William P Ryan, *President*
▲ **EMP:** 13
SQ FT: 12,500
SALES (est): 1.6MM **Privately Held**
SIC: 5085 3061 3053 Seals, industrial; mechanical rubber goods; gaskets, packing & sealing devices

(G-19026)
SAFCO LLC
7631 Austin Ave (60077-2602)
PHONE 847 677-3204
Michael Beatty, *VP Opers*
Keith Sher, *Controller*
John Gable, *Accounts Mgr*
Richard F Wharton,
▲ **EMP:** 23
SALES (est): 5.4MM **Privately Held**
SIC: 3643 Current-carrying wiring devices

(G-19027)
SCIENTFIC BNDERY PRDCTIONS INC
8052 Monticello Ave # 206 (60076-3438)
P.O. Box 377, Highland Park (60035-0377)
PHONE 847 329-0510
Diane R Czerwinski, *President*
EMP: 4
SALES (est): 623.7K **Privately Held**
SIC: 2789 Bookbinding & related work

(G-19028)
SETHNESS PRODUCTS COMPANY (HQ)
Also Called: Sethness Caramel Color
3422 W Touhy Ave Ste 1 (60076-6207)
P.O. Box 1014, Rahway NJ (07065-1014)
PHONE 847 329-2080
Henry B Sethness, *President*
Thomas Schufreider, *COO*
Brian Sethness, *Exec VP*
Valerie Oliver, *Export Mgr*
Regina Lehman, *Human Res Mgr*
◆ **EMP:** 12 **EST:** 1880
SQ FT: 15,000
SALES (est): 12MM
SALES (corp-wide): 2.3B **Privately Held**
WEB: www.sethness.com
SIC: 2087 Food colorings
PA: Roquette Freres
  1 Rue De La Haute Loge
  Lestrem 62136
  963 628-743

(G-19029)
SG2
5250 Old Orchard Rd # 700 (60077-4463)
PHONE 847 779-5500
Shelley Myers, *Owner*
Eric Louie, *Officer*
EMP: 2 **EST:** 2010
SALES (est): 209.7K **Privately Held**
WEB: www.sg2.com
SIC: 5085 3577 Textile printers' supplies; printers, computer

(G-19030)
SKOKIE MILLWORK INC
8108 Lawndale Ave (60076-3322)
PHONE 847 673-7868
Herman Grosse Jr, *President*
Jim Grosse, *Vice Pres*
James Grosse, *Treasurer*
Paul Grosse, *Admin Sec*
EMP: 6
SQ FT: 5,500
SALES (est): 1.3MM **Privately Held**
WEB: www.skokiemillwork.com
SIC: 2431 5211 Millwork; lumber products

(G-19031)
SNYDERS-LANCE INC
Also Called: Snyders Lance
7661 New Gross Point Rd (60077-2647)
PHONE 847 581-1818
Joe Doherty, *Sales Staff*
EMP: 5
SALES (corp-wide): 8.1B **Publicly Held**
WEB: www.snyderslance.com
SIC: 2052 Cookies
HQ: Snyder's-Lance, Inc.
  13515 Balntyn Corp Pl
  Charlotte NC 28277
  704 554-1421

(G-19032)
SONS ENTERPRISES
4826 Main St (60077-2512)
PHONE 847 677-4444
Chuck Kmieciak, *President*
EMP: 12
SQ FT: 2,900
SALES (est): 1.2MM **Privately Held**
SIC: 2791 2752 Typesetting; commercial printing, lithographic

(G-19033)
SPECIALTY SELECTED LTD
Also Called: Specially Selected
9111 Terminal Ave (60077-1570)
PHONE 847 967-1701
Susan Weingard, *President*
Sarah Goldman, *Vice Pres*
EMP: 3
SQ FT: 2,800
SALES: 150K **Privately Held**
SIC: 3231 Art glass: made from purchased glass

(G-19034)
SPEEDPRO NORTH SHORE
8246 Kimball Ave (60076-2918)
PHONE 847 983-0095
EMP: 4
SALES (est): 237.6K **Privately Held**
SIC: 3993 Signs & advertising specialties

(G-19035)
SPINBALL SPORTS LLC (PA)
Also Called: Spinball Sports Products
9725 Woods Dr Unit 1015 (60077-4453)
PHONE 314 503-3194
Steven Spotanski, *Vice Pres*
Thomas Hart, *Mng Member*
EMP: 1
SALES (est): 515.2K **Privately Held**
SIC: 3949 7389 Sporting & athletic goods;

(G-19036)
STAR MEDIA GROUP
Also Called: Chicago Jewish Star
8200 Niles Center Rd (60077)
PHONE 847 674-7827
Douglas Wertheimer, *President*
EMP: 4
SALES (est): 278.3K **Privately Held**
SIC: 2711 Newspapers: publishing only, not printed on site

(G-19037)
STRUCTUREPOINT LLC
5420 Old Orchard Rd (60077-1053)
PHONE 847 966-4357
Iyad M Alsamsam, *Mng Member*
EMP: 12

GEOGRAPHIC SECTION

Smithton - St. Clair County (G-19064)

SALES (est): 1.2MM Privately Held
SIC: 7371 8711 7372 Computer software development; civil engineering; structural engineering; publishers' computer software

(G-19038)
STUDIO TECHNOLOGIES INC
7440 Frontage Rd (60077-3212)
PHONE..............................847 676-9177
Gordon Kapes, *President*
Carrie Gage, *Comms Mgr*
Frank Cavoto, *Agent*
Ruth Farnham Kapes, *Admin Sec*
EMP: 15
SQ FT: 10,000
SALES (est): 3.2MM Privately Held
SIC: 3651 3663 Audio electronic systems; radio & TV communications equipment

(G-19039)
SUB-SURFACE SIGN CO LTD
Also Called: ACS Susico
7410 Niles Center Rd (60077-3230)
PHONE..............................847 675-6530
Harry Kreiter, *President*
▲ EMP: 20 EST: 1981
SQ FT: 4,000
SALES: 1.5MM Privately Held
WEB: www.acssusico.com
SIC: 3993 Signs, not made in custom sign painting shops

(G-19040)
SWAROVSKI US HOLDING LIMITED
4999 Old Orchard Ctr B22 (60077-1450)
PHONE..............................847 679-8670
Jonathan Generous, *Branch Mgr*
EMP: 5
SALES (corp-wide): 4.7B Privately Held
SIC: 3961 Costume jewelry
HQ: Swarovski U.S. Holding Limited
    1 Kenney Dr
    Cranston RI 02920

(G-19041)
SYMBOL TOOL INC
8106 Ridgeway Ave (60076-3318)
PHONE..............................847 674-1080
Alex Kogan, *President*
Elizabeth Kogan, *Vice Pres*
EMP: 8
SQ FT: 3,000
SALES (est): 1.2MM Privately Held
SIC: 3599 3714 Machine shop, jobbing & repair; motor vehicle parts & accessories

(G-19042)
TANAKA DENTAL ENTERPRISES INC
Also Called: Tanaka Dental Products Div
8001 Lincoln Ave Ste 201 (60077-3657)
PHONE..............................847 679-1610
Asami Tanaka, *President*
Benita Zarling, *Vice Pres*
Asako Tanaka, *Admin Sec*
EMP: 14
SQ FT: 5,000
SALES (est): 1.3MM Privately Held
SIC: 8072 3843 8249 8221 Dental laboratories; dental equipment & supplies; dental tools; medical training services; colleges universities & professional schools

(G-19043)
TEMPEL STEEL COMPANY
5215 Old Orchard Rd (60077-1035)
PHONE..............................847 966-9099
EMP: 4
SALES (corp-wide): 389MM Privately Held
SIC: 3469 Stamping metal for the trade
HQ: Tempel Steel Company
    5500 N Wolcott Ave
    Chicago IL 60640

(G-19044)
TEMPRO INTERNATIONAL CORP
8343 Niles Center Rd (60077-2626)
P.O. Box 242 (60076-0242)
PHONE..............................847 677-5370
Kevin C Wade, *President*
Debbie Wade, *Admin Sec*
▲ EMP: 8 EST: 1973

SQ FT: 5,000
SALES: 590K Privately Held
SIC: 3823 3567 3829 3822 Thermocouples, industrial process type; heating units & devices, industrial: electric; measuring & controlling devices; auto controls regulating residntl & coml environmt & applncs; semiconductors & related devices; electric housewares & fans

(G-19045)
TERA-PRINT LLC
8140 Mccormick Blvd # 13 (60076-2920)
PHONE..............................224 534-7543
Chad Mirkin, *Mng Member*
Andrey Idankin,
William Ben Mirkin,
EMP: 5 EST: 2015
SQ FT: 100
SALES: 399.8K Privately Held
SIC: 2752 Color lithography

(G-19046)
TOTAL GRAPHICS SERVICES INC
8343 Niles Center Rd (60077-2626)
P.O. Box 554 (60076-0554)
PHONE..............................847 675-0800
Mark Greenfield, *President*
EMP: 5
SALES (est): 795.8K Privately Held
SIC: 2752 Commercial printing, offset

(G-19047)
TRAVEL HAMMOCK INC
Also Called: Grand Trunk
8136 Monticello Ave (60076-3326)
PHONE..............................847 486-0005
Kevin M Kaiser, *President*
Douglas R Kaiser, *CFO*
▲ EMP: 5
SALES (est): 748.7K Privately Held
SIC: 2399 Hammocks, fabric: made from purchased materials

(G-19048)
TRIANGLE PRINTERS INC
3737 Chase Ave (60076-4008)
PHONE..............................847 675-3700
Harvey Saltzman, *President*
David Saltzman, *Vice Pres*
William Kirby, *Manager*
EMP: 47 EST: 1955
SQ FT: 50,000
SALES (est): 6.6MM Privately Held
WEB: www.triangleprinters.com
SIC: 2752 Color lithography

(G-19049)
UMF CORPORATION (PA)
Also Called: Perfectclean
4709 Golf Rd Ste 300a (60076-1233)
PHONE..............................847 920-0370
George Clarke, *CEO*
Red Degala, *Vice Pres*
◆ EMP: 14
SQ FT: 4,700
SALES: 5MM Privately Held
SIC: 2842 3589 5047 Specialty cleaning, polishes & sanitation goods; commercial cleaning equipment; hospital equipment & furniture

(G-19050)
URESIL LLC
5418 Touhy Ave (60077-3232)
PHONE..............................847 982-0200
Lev Melinyshyn, *Mng Member*
Jim Sarns, *Exec Dir*
Brenten Kinnison, *Director*
Gerard Boreger,
John Morrissey,
EMP: 39
SQ FT: 35,000
SALES (est): 8.8MM Privately Held
SIC: 3841 Surgical instruments & apparatus

(G-19051)
URWAY DESIGN AND MANUFACTURING
8101 Monticello Ave (60076-3325)
PHONE..............................847 674-7464
Mark Bogdan, *President*
EMP: 3
SQ FT: 2,800

SALES (est): 300K Privately Held
SIC: 3544 Special dies & tools

(G-19052)
VAC SERVE INC
4240 Oakton St (60076-3263)
PHONE..............................224 766-6445
Vanio Ivanov, *Manager*
EMP: 3
SALES (est): 170.4K Privately Held
SIC: 3821 Vacuum pumps, laboratory

(G-19053)
WAG INDUSTRIES INC
4117 Grove St (60076-1713)
PHONE..............................847 329-8932
Gail Gilbert, *President*
Doris Gilbert, *Admin Sec*
EMP: 10
SQ FT: 35,000
SALES (est): 663.8K Privately Held
SIC: 2599 5046 3713 3556 Bar furniture; commercial cooking & food service equipment; truck & bus bodies; food products machinery

(G-19054)
WAYNE ENGINEERING (PA)
8242 Christiana Ave (60076-2911)
PHONE..............................416 943-6271
Harry Wayne, *Owner*
Elaine Wayne, *Owner*
EMP: 1
SQ FT: 3,000
SALES (est): 250K Privately Held
SIC: 3827 Optical instruments & lenses

(G-19055)
WELLS LAMONT INDUST GROUP LLC
5215 Old Orchard Rd # 725 (60077-1035)
PHONE..............................800 247-3295
Trainer William, *Principal*
EMP: 1400
SALES (est): 54.7MM
SALES (corp-wide): 327.2B Publicly Held
SIC: 2381 Gloves, work: woven or knit, made from purchased materials
HQ: Marmon Industrial Llc
    181 W Madison St Fl 26
    Chicago IL 60602
    312 372-9500

(G-19056)
WM W NUGENT & CO INC
3440 Cleveland St (60076-2916)
P.O. Box 948 (60076-0948)
PHONE..............................847 673-8109
Brian Sabin, *President*
EMP: 35
SQ FT: 40,000
SALES (est): 9.9MM Privately Held
WEB: www.nugentfilters.com
SIC: 3569 Filters

(G-19057)
WOODWARD INC
7320 Linder Ave (60077-3217)
PHONE..............................847 673-8300
Mark Dietz, *Engineer*
Joel Hutchison, *Engineer*
Senad Jakupovic, *Engineer*
Ganga Jayaraman, *Engineer*
Mike Nielsen, *Engineer*
EMP: 14
SALES (corp-wide): 2.9B Publicly Held
SIC: 3625 3824 Industrial controls: push button, selector switches, pilot; mechanical & electromechanical counters & devices
PA: Woodward, Inc.
    1081 Woodward Way
    Fort Collins CO 80524
    970 482-5811

(G-19058)
WOODWARD CONTROLS INC (HQ)
7320 Linder Ave (60077-3217)
PHONE..............................847 673-8300
Thomas A Gendron, *CEO*
Jim Mueller, *Engineer*
Robert F Weber Jr, *CFO*
◆ EMP: 200
SQ FT: 70,000

SALES (est): 16.9MM
SALES (corp-wide): 2.9B Publicly Held
WEB: www.woodward.com
SIC: 3625 3643 3613 Industrial electrical relays & switches; switches, electric power; switches, electronic applications; solenoid switches (industrial controls); current-carrying wiring devices; switchgear & switchboard apparatus
PA: Woodward, Inc.
    1081 Woodward Way
    Fort Collins CO 80524
    970 482-5811

(G-19059)
WRAP & SEND SERVICES
Also Called: Gift Wrapping Center
4909 Old Orchard Ctr (60077-1439)
PHONE..............................847 329-2559
EMP: 16
SALES (est): 1.1MM Privately Held
SIC: 3086 Mfg Plastic Foam Products

(G-19060)
ZELDACO LTD (PA)
Also Called: Zelda's Sweet Shoppe
4113 Main St (60076-2753)
PHONE..............................847 674-0033
Linda Neiman, *President*
Daniel Neiman, *Opers Mgr*
Leah Neiman, *Manager*
EMP: 20
SQ FT: 3,500
SALES: 2MM Privately Held
SIC: 2064 5812 Chocolate candy, except solid chocolate; popcorn balls or other treated popcorn products; caterers

---
Sleepy Hollow
Kane County

(G-19061)
AMERICAN WOODWORKS
718 Hillcrest Dr (60118-1905)
PHONE..............................630 279-1629
Bob Mucha, *Owner*
EMP: 2
SALES: 450K Privately Held
SIC: 2431 Millwork

(G-19062)
SCIENTIFIC MANUFACTURING INC
209 Hilltop Ln (60118-1843)
PHONE..............................847 414-5658
Michael Harris, *Principal*
EMP: 3
SALES (est): 201.6K Privately Held
SIC: 3999 Manufacturing industries

Smithfield
Fulton County

(G-19063)
CORSAW HARDWOOD LUMBER INC
26015 N County Highway 2 (61477-9433)
PHONE..............................309 293-2055
Lyndell Corsaw, *President*
Marie Corsaw, *Corp Secy*
EMP: 14
SQ FT: 15,000
SALES (est): 2.5MM Privately Held
SIC: 2448 2421 2431 5211 Pallets, wood; sawmills & planing mills, general; millwork; lumber products; landscaping equipment; floor coverings

---
Smithton
St. Clair County

(G-19064)
GRAYS LASER & INSTRUMENT RPR
214 Suburban Dr (62285-3051)
PHONE..............................618 222-1791
Steve Gray, *Owner*

Smithton - St. Clair County (G-19065)

EMP: 3
SALES (est): 256.1K **Privately Held**
SIC: 3826 Laser scientific & engineering instruments

(G-19065)
HYDAC RUBBER MANUFACTURING
Also Called: Hy-Dac Rubber Mfg Co
301 S Main St (62285-1801)
P.O. Box 326 (62285-0326)
PHONE..................................618 233-2129
Jeanne E Brown, *President*
Pat Carr, *Vice Pres*
David Stellhorn, *Plant Mgr*
Kim Hobbs, *QC Mgr*
Julie Lentz, *Admin Sec*
EMP: 25
SQ FT: 20,000
SALES (est): 4.3MM **Privately Held**
SIC: 3069 Rolls, solid or covered rubber

(G-19066)
INDUSTRIAL ROLLER CO (PA)
301 S Main St (62285-1801)
PHONE..................................618 234-0740
George Linne, *President*
E A Karandjeff Jr, *Chairman*
Don Copple, *Sales Staff*
Richard Klaber, *Admin Sec*
EMP: 18
SQ FT: 20,000
SALES (est): 3.8MM **Privately Held**
WEB: www.industrialrollerco.com
SIC: 3069 3061 Roll coverings, rubber; mechanical rubber goods

(G-19067)
INDUSTRIAL ROLLER CO
211 N Smith St (62285-1523)
P.O. Box 329 (62285-0329)
PHONE..................................618 234-0740
EMP: 18
SALES (corp-wide): 2.6MM **Privately Held**
SIC: 3069 Mfg Fabricated Rubber Products
PA: Industrial Roller Co.
218 N Main St
Smithton IL 62285
618 234-0740

(G-19068)
PADDOCK INDUSTRIES INC
306 N Main St (62285-1514)
P.O. Box 906 (62285-0906)
PHONE..................................618 277-1580
Philip S Boekers, *President*
Julie M Boekers, *Vice Pres*
Virginia Collins, *Sales Staff*
EMP: 16
SQ FT: 12,000
SALES: 440K
SALES (corp-wide): 1MM **Privately Held**
WEB: www.paddock-inc.com
SIC: 3993 8661 3469 2396 Signs & advertising specialties; religious organizations; metal stampings; automotive & apparel trimmings
PA: Pantech Industries Inc
306 N Main St
Smithton IL
618 277-1680

Somonauk
Dekalb County

(G-19069)
COMDATA INC
239 W Lasalle St (60552-9766)
PHONE..................................630 847-6988
EMP: 4 **Publicly Held**
SIC: 7372 Prepackaged software
HQ: Comdata, Inc.
5301 Maryland Way
Brentwood TN 37027

(G-19070)
DURO CAST INC
145 E Market St (60552-3225)
P.O. Box 367 (60552-0367)
PHONE..................................815 498-2317
James C Schrader Jr, *President*

William Schrader, *Vice Pres*
EMP: 1
SALES (est): 4.4MM
SALES (corp-wide): 6.3MM **Privately Held**
SIC: 3363 Aluminum die-castings
PA: Precision Enterprises Foundry & Machine Inc.
1000 E Precision Dr
Somonauk IL 60552
815 797-1000

(G-19071)
PEDDLERS DEN INC
Also Called: Creative Design
119 W Market St (60552-9846)
P.O. Box 339 (60552-0339)
PHONE..................................815 498-3429
Tonya Weakley, *President*
EMP: 4
SQ FT: 1,000
SALES: 165K **Privately Held**
SIC: 2759 Commercial printing

(G-19072)
PRAIRIE MANUFACTURING INC
405 E Lafayette St Ste 1 (60552-9128)
P.O. Box 356 (60552-0356)
PHONE..................................815 498-1593
Darwin Classon, *Owner*
EMP: 4
SALES (est): 330.8K **Privately Held**
SIC: 3599 Machine shop, jobbing & repair

(G-19073)
PRECISION ENTPS FNDRY MCH INC (PA)
1000 E Precision Dr (60552)
PHONE..................................815 797-1000
James C Schrader Jr, *President*
William Schrader, *Vice Pres*
Lisa Garafolo, *Manager*
EMP: 5 EST: 1945
SALES (est): 6.3MM **Privately Held**
WEB: www.precision-enterprises.com
SIC: 3363 3542 3543 Aluminum die-castings; die casting machines; industrial patterns

(G-19074)
PRECISION ENTPS FNDRY MCH INC
Also Called: Amco Machines Division
900 E Precision Dr (60552)
P.O. Box 307 (60552-0307)
PHONE..................................815 498-2317
Bill Schrader, *Branch Mgr*
EMP: 30
SALES (corp-wide): 6.3MM **Privately Held**
SIC: 3363 3365 Aluminum die-castings; aluminum & aluminum-based alloy castings
PA: Precision Enterprises Foundry & Machine Inc.
1000 E Precision Dr
Somonauk IL 60552
815 797-1000

South Barrington
Lake County

(G-19075)
BINDERY & DISTRIBUTION SERVICE
9 Overbrook Rd (60010-9568)
PHONE..................................847 550-7000
Dennis D Uchimoto, *President*
EMP: 2
SALES (est): 223.7K **Privately Held**
SIC: 2789 7336 Bookbinding & repairing: trade, edition, library, etc.; graphic arts & related design

(G-19076)
LANCASTER TRADITIONS LLC
100 W Higgins Rd Unit E5 (60010-9416)
PHONE..................................847 428-5446
Debra Jenrette, *Owner*
EMP: 3
SALES (est): 120.2K **Privately Held**
WEB: www.annasheachocolates.com
SIC: 2099 Food preparations

(G-19077)
TEENFITNATION LLC
12 Westlake Dr (60010-5341)
PHONE..................................847 322-2953
SRI Ranjitha Yammanuru, *CEO*
Lalitha Gundlapalli, *President*
Rama Gundlapalli, *Vice Pres*
Rama Yammanuru, *Vice Pres*
Prafulla Srinivasan, *CFO*
EMP: 6
SALES (est): 264.5K **Privately Held**
SIC: 7372 Educational computer software; application computer software

(G-19078)
TEMCO JAPAN CO LTD
Also Called: Temco Communications
13 Chipping Campden Dr (60010-6121)
PHONE..................................847 359-3277
Sidric Nakajo, *Manager*
EMP: 3 **Privately Held**
SIC: 4899 3663 Communication signal enhancement network system; radio broadcasting & communications equipment
PA: Temco Japan Co., Ltd.
2-21-4, Honan
Suginami-Ku TKY 168-0

South Beloit
Winnebago County

(G-19079)
ALL METAL MACHINE
14305 Dorr Rd (61080-2571)
PHONE..................................815 389-0168
Lavern C Bumeister, *Owner*
EMP: 2
SALES: 200K **Privately Held**
SIC: 7692 Welding repair

(G-19080)
AMERICAN CONTROL ELEC LLC
Also Called: Minarik Drives
14300 De La Tour Dr (61080-3006)
P.O. Box 275 (61080-0275)
PHONE..................................815 624-6950
Dan Schnabel, *President*
Brandon Jones, *Engineer*
Richard Lopez, *Engineer*
Michael Viola, *Engineer*
Austin Burgener, *Design Engr*
EMP: 1
SQ FT: 35,000
SALES: 8MM
SALES (corp-wide): 18MM **Privately Held**
WEB: www.minarikdrives.com
SIC: 3625 Electric controls & control accessories, industrial
PA: Hti Technology And Industries, Inc.
315 Tech Park Dr Ste 100
La Vergne TN 37086
615 793-0495

(G-19081)
AMERICAN EXTRUSION INTL CORP (PA)
498 Prairie Hill Rd (61080-2563)
PHONE..................................815 624-6616
Richard J Warner, *President*
Mauriem Warner, *Corp Secy*
Micheal Lauric, *Engineer*
Henry Miller, *Engineer*
Peter Smith, *Human Res Mgr*
◆ EMP: 40
SQ FT: 64,000
SALES (est): 7.8MM **Privately Held**
SIC: 3599 Machine shop, jobbing & repair

(G-19082)
AXIS DISPLAY GROUP INC
8272 Douglas Ave (61080-9560)
PHONE..................................513 342-1884
Ellette Thomas, *CEO*
EMP: 5
SALES (est): 855K **Privately Held**
SIC: 2541 Wood partitions & fixtures

(G-19083)
BELOIT PATTERN WORKS
819 Ingersoll Pl (61080-1336)
PHONE..................................815 389-2578
Kenneth Hanson, *Partner*

Darleen Hanson, *Partner*
David Hanson, *General Mgr*
Robert Sherwood, *Engineer*
EMP: 15
SQ FT: 7,500
SALES (est): 2.7MM **Privately Held**
SIC: 3543 2431 Industrial patterns; millwork

(G-19084)
BELOIT TOOL INC (PA)
215 Elmwood Ave (61080-1900)
P.O. Box 116 (61080-0116)
PHONE..................................815 389-2300
G Curtis Lansbery, *President*
Roger K Taylor, *President*
B V Bowersock, *Senior VP*
Bernie Bowersock, *Senior VP*
Jim Hoyt, *Vice Pres*
EMP: 17
SQ FT: 33,000
SALES: 12MM **Privately Held**
SIC: 3545 Machine tool accessories

(G-19085)
BESLY CUTTING TOOLS INC
16200 Woodmint Ln (61080-9588)
PHONE..................................815 389-2231
Ho Keun Song, *President*
James Deeds, *Vice Pres*
Delaine Morga, *Cust Svc Dir*
Sherrie McKearn, *Sales Staff*
Ken Nelson, *Info Tech Mgr*
EMP: 17
SALES (est): 2.5MM **Privately Held**
SIC: 3545 Machine tool accessories

(G-19086)
CHALLENGER FABRICATORS INC
4095 Prairie Hill Rd (61080-2518)
PHONE..................................815 704-0077
Robert Rasmussen, *President*
Debbie Rasmussen, *Vice Pres*
EMP: 8
SALES (est): 400K **Privately Held**
SIC: 3441 Fabricated structural metal

(G-19087)
CLINKENBEARD & ASSOCIATES INC
810 Progressive Ln (61080-2625)
PHONE..................................815 226-0291
Matt Gustafson, *President*
Ronald Gustafson, *Vice Pres*
EMP: 23 EST: 1966
SQ FT: 13,400
SALES (est): 5MM **Privately Held**
WEB: www.clinkenbeard.com
SIC: 3599 3543 3599 Machine shop, jobbing & repair; industrial patterns; nonferrous foundries

(G-19088)
CUTTING EDGE WATER JET SERVICE
Also Called: Esc Integris
441 Clark St (61080-1355)
P.O. Box 7 (61080-0007)
PHONE..................................815 389-0100
Ron Fairchild, *Manager*
EMP: 3
SQ FT: 10,000
SALES (est): 90.7K **Privately Held**
SIC: 3599 Machine shop, jobbing & repair

(G-19089)
D C ESTATE WINERY
8925 Stateline Rd (61080-9574)
PHONE..................................815 218-0573
Heidi Wirth, *Owner*
Tia Lasswell, *Manager*
EMP: 4
SALES (est): 367.4K **Privately Held**
WEB: www.dcestatewinery.com
SIC: 2084 Wines

(G-19090)
FAPME
810 Progressive Ln (61080-2625)
PHONE..................................815 624-8538
EMP: 3
SALES (est): 208K **Privately Held**
SIC: 3089 Mfg Plastic Products

GEOGRAPHIC SECTION
South Beloit - Winnebago County

(G-19091)
FIRST AMRCN PLSTIC MLDING ENTP
810 Progressive Ln (61080-2625)
P.O. Box 620, Roscoe (61073-0620)
PHONE..............................815 624-8538
Bill Bartlett, *Partner*
Robert Deperro, *Partner*
Paul Petriekis, *Partner*
John Schwan, *Partner*
William Bartlett, *General Ptnr*
▲ **EMP:** 67
SQ FT: 39,000
SALES (est): 14.2MM **Privately Held**
SIC: 3089 Injection molding of plastics

(G-19092)
FIVES LANDIS CORP
Also Called: Gardner Abrasive Products
481 Gardner St (61080-1326)
PHONE..............................815 389-2251
Al Donahue, *Branch Mgr*
Allen Donahue, *Executive*
EMP: 100
SALES (corp-wide): 871.2K **Privately Held**
WEB: www.fivesgroup.com
SIC: 3291 Abrasive products
HQ: Fives Landis Corp.
  16778 Halfway Blvd
  Hagerstown MD 21740

(G-19093)
FORTERRA PRESSURE PIPE INC (PA)
4416 Prairie Hill Rd (61080-2545)
PHONE..............................815 389-4800
Mark Carpenter, *President*
Steven M Paul, *CFO*
▲ **EMP:** 46 **EST:** 2000
SQ FT: 20,000
SALES (est): 110.2MM **Privately Held**
SIC: 3272 3317 Pressure pipe, reinforced concrete; steel pipe & tubes

(G-19094)
GAYLEE CORPORATION SAWS
215 Elmwood Ave (61080-1900)
PHONE..............................586 803-1100
Roger K Taylor, *Principal*
EMP: 3
SALES (est): 204.9K **Privately Held**
WEB: www.globalspecialtysolutions.com
SIC: 3545 Machine tool accessories

(G-19095)
GOODYEAR TIRE & RUBBER COMPANY
16049 Willowbrook Rd (61080-9562)
PHONE..............................815 389-8222
EMP: 4
SALES (corp-wide): 14.7B **Publicly Held**
WEB: www.goodyear.com
SIC: 5531 3011 Automotive tires; inner tubes, all types
PA: The Goodyear Tire & Rubber Company
  200 E Innovation Way
  Akron OH 44316
  330 796-2121

(G-19096)
GREENBERG CASEWORK COMPANY INC
14328 Commercial Pkwy (61080-2623)
PHONE..............................815 624-0288
Troy Greenberg, *President*
Darius Evans, *Marketing Mgr*
EMP: 20
SQ FT: 18,000
SALES (est): 3.1MM **Privately Held**
SIC: 2541 1751 Store & office display cases & fixtures; cabinet & finish carpentry

(G-19097)
JAMCO PRODUCTS INC (HQ)
1 Jamco Ct (61080-2600)
P.O. Box 66 (61080-0066)
PHONE..............................815 624-0400
James Alexander, *CEO*
Dan Johnson, *President*
Dave Tanner, *Vice Pres*
EMP: 68
SQ FT: 50,000
SALES (est): 20.7MM
SALES (corp-wide): 515.7MM **Publicly Held**
WEB: www.jamcoproducts.com
SIC: 3312 5084 Blast furnaces & steel mills; industrial machinery & equipment
PA: Myers Industries, Inc.
  1293 S Main St
  Akron OH 44301
  330 253-5592

(G-19098)
MARLAND CLUTCH
449 Gardner St (61080-1326)
PHONE..............................800 216-3515
Myron Angel, *Principal*
EMP: 3
SALES (est): 164.1K
SALES (corp-wide): 1.8B **Publicly Held**
SIC: 3568 Clutches, except vehicular
PA: Altra Industrial Motion Corp.
  300 Granite St Ste 201
  Braintree MA 02184
  781 917-0600

(G-19099)
MATRIX INTERNATIONAL LTD
449 Gardner St (61080-1326)
PHONE..............................815 389-3771
R Burnett, *President*
EMP: 4
SALES (est): 284K
SALES (corp-wide): 1.8B **Publicly Held**
SIC: 3714 Clutches, motor vehicle
PA: Altra Industrial Motion Corp.
  300 Granite St Ste 201
  Braintree MA 02184
  781 917-0600

(G-19100)
MC CLEARY EQUIPMENT INC
239 Oak Grove Ave (61080-1936)
P.O. Box 187 (61080-0187)
PHONE..............................815 389-3053
Charles P Mc Cleary, *President*
EMP: 2
SQ FT: 36,000
SALES (est): 571.8K **Privately Held**
SIC: 3556 Food products machinery

(G-19101)
MCCLEARY INC (PA)
Also Called: Trans-Astro
239 Oak Grove Ave (61080-1936)
P.O. Box 187 (61080-0187)
PHONE..............................815 389-3053
Pat McCleary, *CEO*
Nancy Schilsky, *President*
Jerry Stokely, *President*
Jerry L Stokely, *President*
Leon Schwitters, *Prdtn Mgr*
EMP: 145
SQ FT: 80,000
SALES (est): 45.4MM **Privately Held**
WEB: www.axiumfoods.com
SIC: 2096 2064 Tortilla chips; popcorn balls or other treated popcorn products

(G-19102)
MEADOWELD MACHINE INC
530 Eastern Ave (61080-1924)
PHONE..............................815 623-3939
Casey Meadows, *President*
Terri Meadows, *Corp Secy*
Cassidy Meadows, *Vice Pres*
Jaime Wallace, *Treasurer*
EMP: 5
SQ FT: 10,600
SALES (est): 825K **Privately Held**
WEB: www.meadoweld.com
SIC: 5084 3541 7692 3743 Industrial machine parts; saws & sawing machines; welding repair; railroad equipment; metalworking machinery

(G-19103)
MID-STATES CONCRETE INDS LLC
500 S Park Ave 550 (61080-2099)
P.O. Box 58, Beloit WI (53512-0058)
PHONE..............................815 389-2277
Charles H Harker, *CEO*
Hagen Harker, *President*
Jeremy Olivotti, *Vice Pres*
Tracy Miller, *Safety Mgr*
Tim Kyser, *Foreman/Supr*
▲ **EMP:** 55 **EST:** 1946
SQ FT: 80,000
SALES (est): 22.5MM **Privately Held**
WEB: www.midstatesconcrete.com
SIC: 3272 8711 Concrete products, pre-cast; engineering services

(G-19104)
NATC LLC
215 Elmwood Ave (61080-1900)
PHONE..............................815 389-2300
G Curtis Lansbery, *President*
EMP: 12
SALES (est): 484K
SALES (corp-wide): 18.2MM **Privately Held**
SIC: 3545 Precision measuring tools
PA: Gws Tool Holdings, Llc
  595 County Road 448
  Tavares FL 32778
  352 343-8778

(G-19105)
NUTTALL GEAR LLC
449 Gardner St (61080-1326)
PHONE..............................815 389-6267
EMP: 7
SQ FT: 155,000
SALES (est): 1.2MM **Privately Held**
SIC: 3566 Speed changers, drives & gears

(G-19106)
PAPER MACHINE SERVICES INC
7283 Barngate Dr (61080-8027)
PHONE..............................608 365-8095
Duane Steinert, *President*
Cindy Steinert, *Vice Pres*
EMP: 5
SALES (est): 518.8K **Privately Held**
SIC: 2621 Paper mills

(G-19107)
PMP AMERICAS INC
16200 Woodmint Ln (61080-9588)
PHONE..............................815 633-9962
Robert Matuska, *President*
Linda Springer, *Engineer*
◆ **EMP:** 15
SQ FT: 6,000
SALES (est): 1.2MM **Privately Held**
SIC: 3499 Reels, cable: metal

(G-19108)
PRECISION QUINCY OVENS LLC
483 Gardner St (61080-1326)
PHONE..............................302 602-8738
Matthew Zakaras, *President*
EMP: 30
SALES (est): 4.3MM **Privately Held**
SIC: 3567 Industrial furnaces & ovens

(G-19109)
PRICE BROTHERS CO
4416 Prairie Hill Rd (61080-2545)
P.O. Box 67 (61080-0067)
PHONE..............................815 389-4800
James S Clift, *Ch of Bd*
EMP: 75
SALES (est): 4.6MM **Privately Held**
SIC: 3272 Prestressed concrete products

(G-19110)
QUAD INC (PA)
810 Progressive Ln (61080-2625)
PHONE..............................815 624-8538
William Bartlett, *President*
Robert Deperro, *President*
John H Schwan, *Admin Sec*
▲ **EMP:** 49 **EST:** 1993
SQ FT: 39,000
SALES (est): 11.7MM **Privately Held**
SIC: 3089 Injection molding of plastics

(G-19111)
RT BLACKHAWK MCH PDTS INC
956 Gardner St (61080-1402)
P.O. Box 55 (61080-0055)
PHONE..............................815 389-3632
Russell Tiritilli, *President*
Kay Tiritilli, *Corp Secy*
EMP: 7
SQ FT: 6,400
SALES (est): 550K **Privately Held**
SIC: 3599 3462 Machine shop, jobbing & repair; iron & steel forgings

(G-19112)
RUBY AUTOMATION LLC
14300 De La Tour Dr (61080-3006)
P.O. Box 265 (61080-0265)
PHONE..............................815 624-5959
John Hegel, *President*
Dan Schurman, *Marketing Staff*
Dave Witwer, *Manager*
EMP: 14
SALES (corp-wide): 735.6MM **Privately Held**
SIC: 3621 3823 3625 3566 Electric motor & generator auxillary parts; industrial instrmnts msrmnt display/control process variable; relays & industrial controls; speed changers, drives & gears
HQ: Ruby Automation, Llc
  1 Vision Way
  Bloomfield CT 06002
  860 687-5000

(G-19113)
S G ACQUISITION INC
14392 De La Tour Dr (61080-3006)
P.O. Box 894, Roscoe (61073-0894)
PHONE..............................815 624-6501
Bob Sealy, *President*
Tom Grossner, *Vice Pres*
EMP: 14
SQ FT: 4,500
SALES (est): 1.4MM **Privately Held**
SIC: 3556 3565 7699 Food products machinery; packaging machinery; industrial machinery & equipment repair

(G-19114)
SOUTHERN WISCONSIN METAL FABRC
4241 Prairie Hill Rd (61080-2548)
PHONE..............................815 389-3021
William G Leasure, *President*
EMP: 14
SALES (est): 1.9MM **Privately Held**
SIC: 3444 Sheet metalwork

(G-19115)
SUGAR RIVER MACHINE SHOP
667 Progressive Ln (61080-2615)
PHONE..............................815 624-0214
Diane Klingenmeyer, *President*
David J Klingenmeyer, *Principal*
Heath Alberts, *Opers Mgr*
Gary Naser, *Manager*
EMP: 21
SALES (est): 2.6MM **Privately Held**
SIC: 3599 3444 Machine shop, jobbing & repair; sheet metalwork

(G-19116)
TB WOODS INCORPORATED
449 Gardner St (61080-1326)
P.O. Box 381 (61080-0381)
PHONE..............................815 389-6600
Leah Lorenze, *Branch Mgr*
EMP: 70
SALES (corp-wide): 1.8B **Publicly Held**
WEB: www.tbwoods.com
SIC: 3568 Power transmission equipment
HQ: Tb Wood's Incorporated
  440 5th Ave
  Chambersburg PA 17201
  717 264-7161

(G-19117)
TREEHOUSE PRIVATE BRANDS INC
1450 Pate Plaza Dr (61080-1430)
PHONE..............................815 389-2745
Keith Simpson, *Finance Mgr*
Carol Amundson, *Executive*
EMP: 200
SALES (corp-wide): 4.2B **Publicly Held**
SIC: 2052 Cookies
HQ: Treehouse Private Brands, Inc.
  2021 Spring Rd Ste 600
  Oak Brook IL 60523

South Beloit - Winnebago County (G-19118)

(G-19118)
UNITED TOOL AND ENGINEERING CO
4095 Prairie Hill Rd (61080-2518)
PHONE 815 389-3021
Glen Leasure, *President*
Robert Rasmussen, *Vice Pres*
Kevin Wollslair, *Opers Mgr*
Melesia Boyer, *Sales Staff*
Megan Rozinsky, *Office Mgr*
EMP: 65 **EST:** 1956
SQ FT: 60,000
SALES (est): 13.2MM **Privately Held**
SIC: 3544 3469 3541 7692 Special dies & tools; metal stampings; milling machines; welding repair

(G-19119)
WALLACE INDUSTRIES INC
530 Eastern Ave (61080-1924)
PHONE 815 389-8999
Douglas Wallace, *President*
EMP: 5
SQ FT: 11,000
SALES (est): 360.3K **Privately Held**
SIC: 3743 Railroad equipment

(G-19120)
WALNUT CREEK HARDWOOD
Also Called: Laser Creations
851 Doner Dr (61080-2199)
PHONE 815 389-3317
Frank Long, *President*
Julie Long, *Vice Pres*
Lynn Fofler, *Admin Sec*
EMP: 7
SQ FT: 5,000
SALES (est): 630K **Privately Held**
SIC: 2435 3993 7389 5999 Panels, hardwood plywood; signs & advertising specialties; engraving service; trophies & plaques; taxidermist tools & equipment

(G-19121)
WARNER ELECTRIC LLC
Warner Linear
449 Gardner St (61080-1397)
PHONE 815 547-1106
Elaine Thomas, *Plant Mgr*
Chris Miller, *Design Engr*
EMP: 30
SALES (corp-wide): 1.8B **Publicly Held**
WEB: www.warnerelectric.com
SIC: 3625 Flow actuated electrical switches
HQ: Warner Electric Llc
   449 Gardner St
   South Beloit IL 61080
   815 389-4300

(G-19122)
WARNER ELECTRIC LLC (HQ)
Also Called: Warner Electric Indus Pdts
449 Gardner St (61080-1397)
PHONE 815 389-4300
Carl Brehm, *Business Mgr*
Christina Valentine, *Senior Buyer*
Adam Hallett, *Buyer*
George Gill, *Engineer*
Daniel Johnson, *Engineer*
▲ **EMP:** 230
SALES: 101.2MM
SALES (corp-wide): 1.8B **Publicly Held**
SIC: 3714 Clutches, motor vehicle
PA: Altra Industrial Motion Corp.
   300 Granite St Ste 201
   Braintree MA 02184
   781 917-0600

(G-19123)
WESTRAN THERMAL PROCESSING LLC
483 Gardner St (61080-1326)
PHONE 815 634-1001
Matthew Zakaras,
William Diemel,
EMP: 28
SQ FT: 45,000
SALES (est): 2.5MM **Privately Held**
SIC: 3567 Industrial furnaces & ovens

(G-19124)
WINNEBAGO FOUNDRY INC
132 Blackhawk Blvd (61080-1366)
P.O. Box 5 (61080-0005)
PHONE 815 389-3533
Gary Anderson, *President*
Jed Weldon, *Vice Pres*
Connie Corcoran, *Prdtn Mgr*
Rich Whippler, *Sales Mgr*
Tammy Severson, *Manager*
EMP: 74
SQ FT: 30,000
SALES (est): 14MM **Privately Held**
SIC: 3321 Gray iron castings; ductile iron castings

(G-19125)
WORLD CLASS TOOL & MACHINE
698 Quality Ln (61080-2608)
PHONE 815 962-2081
David Loveland, *President*
Shawn Sweeney, *Treasurer*
EMP: 8
SALES (est): 1.1MM **Privately Held**
SIC: 3599 Machine shop, jobbing & repair

(G-19126)
WORLD CONTRACT PACKAGERS INC
14392 De La Tour Dr (61080-3006)
PHONE 815 624-6501
Bob Seay, *President*
EMP: 6
SALES (est): 661.6K **Privately Held**
SIC: 2671 Plastic film, coated or laminated for packaging

(G-19127)
WORLD CUP PACKAGING INC
14392 De La Tour Dr (61080-3006)
P.O. Box 894, Roscoe (61073-0894)
PHONE 815 624-6501
Bob R Seay, *President*
Tom Grossner, *Vice Pres*
EMP: 8
SQ FT: 11,600
SALES (est): 1.4MM **Privately Held**
SIC: 3556 3565 7699 Food products machinery; packaging machinery; industrial machinery & equipment repair

South Elgin — Kane County

(G-19128)
ADVANCE PALLET INCORPORATED
600 Woodbury St (60177-1359)
PHONE 847 697-5700
Jerry Anderson, *President*
George Hanson, *Vice Pres*
Eric Girman, *Sales Staff*
EMP: 35
SQ FT: 22,000
SALES (est): 5.5MM **Privately Held**
SIC: 2448 Pallets, wood

(G-19129)
ADVANCED WEB TECHNOLOGIES LLC
393 Joseph Dr (60177-2268)
PHONE 847 985-3833
Tom Nelson, *Mng Member*
EMP: 40
SALES (corp-wide): 27.8MM **Privately Held**
SIC: 7379 2672 Computer related consulting services; coated & laminated paper
PA: Advanced Web Technologies, Llc
   600 Hoover St Ne Ste 500
   Minneapolis MN 55413
   612 706-3700

(G-19130)
AEROSOURCEX LLC
9 Cascade Ct (60177-3046)
PHONE 314 565-4026
Batool Ahmed, *Mng Member*
Sarwar Ahmed,
EMP: 10 **EST:** 2015
SQ FT: 30,000
SALES: 1.2MM **Privately Held**
SIC: 3365 Aerospace castings, aluminum

(G-19131)
ALLCOM PRODUCTS ILLINOIS LLC
695 Sundown Rd (60177-1145)
PHONE 847 468-8830
William R Kohl III,
EMP: 22
SQ FT: 9,000
SALES (est): 3.9MM **Privately Held**
SIC: 3663 Radio & TV communications equipment

(G-19132)
AM SWISS SCREW MCH PDTS INC
345 Industrial Dr (60177-1198)
PHONE 847 468-9300
Jim Brewer, *President*
Bill Leod, *Vice Pres*
Bill Mac Leod, *Vice Pres*
EMP: 15
SQ FT: 16,500
SALES (est): 1MM **Privately Held**
SIC: 3451 Screw machine products

(G-19133)
ARMIN MOLDING CORP
Also Called: Armin Industries
1500 N La Fox St (60177-1240)
PHONE 847 742-1864
Paul Stoll, *President*
Arthur C Stoll, *Chairman*
Kathy S Stoll, *Admin Sec*
EMP: 45
SQ FT: 72,000
SALES (est): 8.6MM **Privately Held**
SIC: 3089 Injection molding of plastics

(G-19134)
ARMIN TOOL AND MFG CO (PA)
1500 N Lafox St (60177)
PHONE 847 742-1864
Arthur C Stoll, *Ch of Bd*
Paul R Stoll, *President*
EMP: 82 **EST:** 1951
SQ FT: 102,000
SALES (est): 11.6MM **Privately Held**
WEB: www.armin-ind.com
SIC: 3544 Special dies, tools, jigs & fixtures

(G-19135)
BAUM HOLDINGS INC
506 Sundown Rd (60177-1146)
PHONE 847 488-0650
Simon Nussbaum,
EMP: 7
SALES (est): 604.7K **Privately Held**
SIC: 3993 7336 Electric signs; graphic arts & related design

(G-19136)
BECSIS LLC
2197 Brookwood Dr (60177-3235)
PHONE 630 400-6454
Michael Boruta, *Managing Prtnr*
Nicholas Boruta, *Managing Prtnr*
Jerome Nalywajko, *Managing Prtnr*
EMP: 4 **EST:** 2014
SALES (est): 249.9K **Privately Held**
SIC: 3621 Power generators

(G-19137)
BERNY METAL PRODUCTS INC
655 Sundown Rd (60177-1145)
PHONE 847 742-8500
Harold Reich, *President*
Lucille Reich, *Corp Secy*
Bill Reich, *Vice Pres*
Patrick Milet, *VP Sales*
EMP: 9
SQ FT: 20,000
SALES (est): 1.1MM **Privately Held**
SIC: 3469 Stamping metal for the trade

(G-19138)
BESTPROTO INC
1627 Louise Dr (60177-2242)
PHONE 224 387-3280
Gary Lynch, *President*
Robert Wettermann, *Chairman*
Garth Cates, *Business Mgr*
Garths Cates, *Treasurer*
EMP: 10
SALES: 1.5MM **Privately Held**
SIC: 3672 Circuit boards, television & radio printed

(G-19139)
C L GRAPHICS MARKETING INC
365 Industrial Dr (60177-1198)
PHONE 815 455-0900
Richard Schildgen, *President*
Dave Heiden, *Manager*
EMP: 20
SQ FT: 11,000
SALES (est): 3.8MM **Privately Held**
SIC: 2752 Commercial printing, offset

(G-19140)
CAT I MANUFACTURING INC
Also Called: Cat-I Glass
865 Commerce Dr (60177-2633)
P.O. Box 208 (60177-0208)
PHONE 847 931-8986
Robert Jaynes, *President*
Ryan O'Connell, *Engineer*
Meghan Dahl, *Manager*
▲ **EMP:** 170
SQ FT: 70,000
SALES (est): 25.1MM **Privately Held**
SIC: 3211 Flat glass

(G-19141)
CUSTOM ALUMINUM PRODUCTS INC (PA)
Also Called: Winco Finishing Div
414 Division St (60177-1196)
PHONE 847 717-5000
Steve Dillett, *CEO*
James J Castoro, *Ch of Bd*
Elizabeth Saldana, *Vice Pres*
Jeffrey Sawyers, *Plant Mgr*
Kyle Wille, *Prdtn Mgr*
▲ **EMP:** 370 **EST:** 1960
SQ FT: 380,000
SALES (est): 80.9MM **Privately Held**
WEB: www.custom-aluminum.com
SIC: 3354 3442 Aluminum extruded products; sash, door or window: metal; metal doors

(G-19142)
DATUM TOOL AND MFG INC
200 Kane St (60177-1516)
PHONE 847 742-4092
Michael Long, *President*
Georgeann Long, *Vice Pres*
EMP: 18
SQ FT: 11,000
SALES: 2MM **Privately Held**
SIC: 3599 Machine shop, jobbing & repair

(G-19143)
ELITE IMPRESSIONS & GRAPHICS
645 Stevenson Rd (60177-1134)
PHONE 847 695-3730
Barbara Mozina, *President*
Victor Meuraskas, *Manager*
EMP: 4
SQ FT: 50,000
SALES (est): 200K **Privately Held**
SIC: 2759 Imprinting

(G-19144)
EXTRACTOR CORPORATION
685 Martin Dr (60177-1171)
PHONE 847 742-3532
H Jon Hoffman, *President*
EMP: 16
SQ FT: 13,000
SALES (est): 3.9MM **Privately Held**
SIC: 3582 3634 Extractors, commercial laundry; electric housewares & fans

(G-19145)
FOX VALLEY PREGNANCY CENTER (PA)
101 E State St (60177-2048)
PHONE 847 697-0200
Christopher Hahn, *Principal*
EMP: 8
SALES: 289.6K **Privately Held**
SIC: 2835 Pregnancy test kits

▲ = Import ▼ = Export
◆ = Import/Export

GEOGRAPHIC SECTION

South Elgin - Kane County (G-19174)

(G-19146)
FOX VALLEY STAMPING COMPANY
385 Production Dr (60177-2636)
PHONE................847 741-2277
Doug Morrison, *President*
Cindy Morrison, *Treasurer*
Kim Niccolai, *Marketing Staff*
Constantine Constance, *Admin Sec*
EMP: 17 **EST:** 1965
SQ FT: 81,000
SALES (est): 3.2MM **Privately Held**
WEB: www.foxvalleystamping.com
SIC: 3469 Stamping metal for the trade

(G-19147)
GLOBETEC MIDWEST PARTNERS LLC
403 Joseph Dr (60177-2268)
PHONE................847 608-9300
Richard Nemeth,
Thomas M Hazelhurst,
Mark Sokniewicz,
EMP: 5
SALES (est): 540.6K **Privately Held**
WEB: www.g-tecmidwest.com
SIC: 3523 Farm machinery & equipment

(G-19148)
GRAPHIC INDUSTRIES INC
645 Stevenson Rd (60177-1134)
PHONE................847 357-9870
S Joseph Kukla III, *President*
Doug Leonard, *Vice Pres*
Joe Kukla, *Administration*
EMP: 24 **EST:** 2000
SQ FT: 25,000
SALES (est): 4.1MM **Privately Held**
SIC: 2754 2677 Commercial printing, gravure; envelopes

(G-19149)
GRAPHIC SCREEN FASHION LTD
Also Called: G S F
365 Woodbury St (60177-1367)
PHONE................847 695-5566
Rocky Binetti, *President*
Frank Binetti, *Vice Pres*
Bob Eisenach, *Manager*
EMP: 12
SQ FT: 7,500
SALES (est): 1MM **Privately Held**
SIC: 3552 Frames, doubling & twisting, textile machinery

(G-19150)
GREAT LAKES FINISHING EQP INC
842 Schneider Dr (60177-2641)
PHONE................708 345-5300
Tom Milo, *President*
Rick Nowak, *Treasurer*
EMP: 6
SQ FT: 6,000
SALES: 1.4MM **Privately Held**
SIC: 3471 Cleaning & descaling metal products; cleaning, polishing & finishing; finishing, metals or formed products; sand blasting of metal parts

(G-19151)
HERCL SIGNS & SERVICE INC
23 Barcroft Ct (60177-3056)
PHONE................847 471-4015
Timothy Hercl, *President*
Kiersty Hercl, *Vice Pres*
EMP: 3 **EST:** 2015
SALES (est): 98.8K **Privately Held**
SIC: 3993 1799 Signs & advertising specialties; sign installation & maintenance

(G-19152)
HOFFER PLASTICS CORPORATION
500 N Collins St (60177-1195)
PHONE................847 741-5740
William A Hoffer, *President*
Joel David, *Business Mgr*
Lee Fantone, *Business Mgr*
Jay Grizzle, *Business Mgr*
Marion Metz, *Business Mgr*
◆ **EMP:** 375 **EST:** 1953
SQ FT: 360,000
SALES (est): 110.4MM **Privately Held**
WEB: www.hofferplastics.com
SIC: 3089 Injection molding of plastics

(G-19153)
I F & G METAL CRAFT CO
405 Industrial Dr (60177-1188)
PHONE................847 488-0630
Ignacio Fernandez, *Owner*
EMP: 6
SALES (est): 750K **Privately Held**
SIC: 3444 Sheet metalwork

(G-19154)
IF WALLS COULD TALK
323 W Harvard Cir (60177-2735)
PHONE................847 219-5527
Victoria Kozlowski, *Owner*
EMP: 4
SALES (est): 197K **Privately Held**
SIC: 2851 Paints & allied products

(G-19155)
INTEGRATED PRINT GRAPHICS INC (PA)
Also Called: I P G
645 Stevenson Rd (60177-1134)
PHONE................847 695-6777
Gary Mozina, *President*
Frederick McGough, *COO*
John Brahm, *Exec VP*
John Petruso, *Plant Mgr*
Chris Mastny, *Purch Mgr*
EMP: 130 **EST:** 1970
SQ FT: 62,000
SALES (est): 34MM **Privately Held**
SIC: 2752 7331 2761 Business forms, lithographed; direct mail advertising services; manifold business forms

(G-19156)
INTEGRATED PRINT GRAPHICS INC
J. B. Vision Graphics
635 Stevenson Rd (60177-1134)
PHONE................847 888-2880
EMP: 130
SALES (corp-wide): 34MM **Privately Held**
SIC: 2752 Business forms, lithographed
PA: Integrated Print & Graphics, Inc.
645 Stevenson Rd
South Elgin IL 60177
847 695-6777

(G-19157)
INTERACTIVE INKS COATINGS CORP
1610 Shanahan Dr (60177-2277)
P.O. Box 158 (60177-0158)
PHONE................847 289-8710
Thomas Tinerella, *President*
Felicia Tinerella, *Corp Secy*
Bob Giancarlo, *Purchasing*
Tom Tinerella, *Research*
Sue Battalini, *Accountant*
EMP: 15
SQ FT: 10,000
SALES (est): 3.3MM **Privately Held**
WEB: www.interactiveinks.com
SIC: 2893 Printing ink

(G-19158)
J & J EXPRESS ENVELOPES INC
645 Stevenson Rd (60177-1134)
PHONE................847 253-7146
Jimmy Popovtschak, *President*
EMP: 8
SQ FT: 6,500
SALES (est): 760K **Privately Held**
SIC: 2759 Envelopes: printing

(G-19159)
KINETIC BEI LLC
2197 Brookwood Dr (60177-3235)
PHONE................847 888-8060
M Boruta J Jerovek, *Principal*
EMP: 10
SALES (est): 522.4K **Privately Held**
SIC: 3861 Developing machines & equipment, still or motion picture

(G-19160)
KLAPPERICH TOOL INC
857 Schneider Dr (60177-2639)
PHONE................847 608-8471
Paul Klapperich, *President*
EMP: 15 **EST:** 1998
SQ FT: 1,200
SALES (est): 2.5MM **Privately Held**
WEB: www.klapperichtool.com
SIC: 8711 3599 Mechanical engineering; machine shop, jobbing & repair

(G-19161)
KRIS DEE AND ASSOCIATES INC
Also Called: Krisdee
755 Schneider Dr (60177-1161)
PHONE................630 503-4093
Russell P Majewski, *President*
Donna Belback, *Director*
Jeffrey Majewski, *Admin Sec*
Steve Burback, *Maintence Staff*
▲ **EMP:** 70
SQ FT: 40,000
SALES (est): 17.5MM **Privately Held**
SIC: 3599 Machine shop, jobbing & repair

(G-19162)
LAFARGE AGGREGATES ILL INC (DH)
7n394 S Mclean Blvd (60177)
PHONE................847 742-6060
Nathan Creech, *General Mgr*
EMP: 6
SQ FT: 2,000
SALES (est): 8.8MM
SALES (corp-wide): 4.5B **Privately Held**
SIC: 1411 1442 Limestone, dimension-quarrying; common sand mining; gravel mining
HQ: Aggregate Industries Management, Inc.
8700 W Bryn Mawr Ave # 300
Chicago IL 60631
773 372-1000

(G-19163)
LAFARGE NORTH AMERICA INC
1310 Rt 31 (60177)
PHONE................847 742-6060
Nathan Creech, *Branch Mgr*
John Fay, *Manager*
EMP: 27
SALES (corp-wide): 4.5B **Privately Held**
SIC: 3241 Cement, hydraulic
HQ: Lafarge North America Inc.
8700 W Bryn Mawr Ave
Chicago IL 60631
773 372-1000

(G-19164)
LAFOX SCREW PRODUCTS INC
440 N Gilbert St (60177-1397)
PHONE................847 695-1732
Samuel Joy, *President*
Walter Kiel, *Vice Pres*
Kathy Joy, *Admin Sec*
EMP: 5
SQ FT: 7,500
SALES (est): 879.3K **Privately Held**
WEB: www.lafoxscrewproducts.com
SIC: 3451 Screw machine products

(G-19165)
LAKEVIEW PRCSION MACHINING INC
751 Schneider Dr (60177-1161)
PHONE................847 742-7170
Debra Sommers, *President*
Emily Sommers, *Accounting Mgr*
EMP: 15 **EST:** 1951
SQ FT: 18,000
SALES: 3.4MM **Privately Held**
WEB: www.lakeviewprecision.com
SIC: 3451 Screw machine products

(G-19166)
LANE TOOL & MFG CO INC
655 Sundown Rd (60177-1145)
PHONE................847 622-1506
Edward Arnieri, *Principal*
EMP: 30
SQ FT: 20,000
SALES (est): 5MM **Privately Held**
SIC: 3599 3544 3549 Machine shop, jobbing & repair; special dies, tools, jigs & fixtures; metalworking machinery

(G-19167)
MIDWEST SKYLITE COMPANY INC
1505 Gilpen Ave (60177-1211)
PHONE................847 214-9505
John F Harris, *President*
EMP: 20
SALES (est): 259.4K **Privately Held**
WEB: www.mwskylite.com
SIC: 3444 1761 Skylights, sheet metal; skylight installation

(G-19168)
MOLDING SERVICES GROUP INC
2051 N La Fox St Lowr 1 (60177-1205)
PHONE................847 931-1491
Vincent Occhipinti, *President*
EMP: 30
SQ FT: 45,000
SALES (est): 6MM **Privately Held**
SIC: 3089 Molding primary plastic; injection molding of plastics

(G-19169)
NEW IMAGE UPHOLSTERY
21 Cedar Ct (60177-2823)
PHONE................630 542-5560
Robert J Stahulak, *Principal*
EMP: 10
SALES (est): 612K **Privately Held**
SIC: 2512 Upholstered household furniture

(G-19170)
PERSONALIZED PRINTING MAILING
5 Lydia Ct (60124-8765)
PHONE................847 441-2955
EMP: 4 **EST:** 2014
SALES (est): 208.5K **Privately Held**
SIC: 2752 Commercial printing, offset

(G-19171)
RESIDNTIAL STL FABRICATORS INC
1555 Gilpen Ave (60177-1211)
PHONE................847 695-3400
James Czechowski, *President*
EMP: 42
SQ FT: 20,000
SALES (est): 7.3MM **Privately Held**
SIC: 3312 Structural shapes & pilings, steel

(G-19172)
RICHARDS FINE JEWELRY & DESIGN
Also Called: Richars's
321 Randall Rd (60177-2248)
PHONE................847 697-4053
Richard C Zimmerman, *President*
Richard Zimmerman, *President*
Renette Zimmerman, *Vice Pres*
EMP: 2
SALES (est): 257.3K **Privately Held**
SIC: 5944 3911 Jewelry, precious stones & precious metals; jewelry, precious metal

(G-19173)
SAKAMOTO KANAGATA USA INC
433 Joseph Dr (60177-2268)
PHONE................224 856-2008
Seiji Tanigaki, *President*
Gerhard Kelter Jr, *Admin Sec*
▲ **EMP:** 5
SALES (est): 775.1K **Privately Held**
SIC: 3089 Injection molding of plastics
HQ: Sakamotokanagatakosakusho, K.K.
3-30, Ikagamidorimachi
Hirakata OSK 573-0

(G-19174)
SHRECK KITCHENS
Also Called: Schreck Kitchens
260 Sundown Rd (60177-1100)
PHONE................847 695-4154
Tom Bowen, *President*
Tom Bowman, *Partner*

South Elgin - Kane County (G-19175)

Craig Bowman, *Partner*
Robert B Bowman, *Partner*
EMP: 6
SQ FT: 3,500
SALES (est): 468.6K **Privately Held**
WEB: www.schreckkitchens.com
SIC: 2434 Wood kitchen cabinets

(G-19175)
T & C GRAPHICS INC
Also Called: Singles Plus Printing
645 Stevenson Rd (60177-1134)
P.O. Box 249, Addison (60101-0249)
PHONE..................630 532-5050
Chris Mueller, *Principal*
EMP: 38
SQ FT: 12,800
SALES (est): 4.6MM **Privately Held**
SIC: 2752 Commercial printing, offset

(G-19176)
T-MOBILE USA INC
416 Randall Rd (60177-3325)
PHONE..................847 289-9988
Dan Georgen, *Owner*
EMP: 11
SALES (corp-wide): 45B **Publicly Held**
SIC: 4812 3663 Cellular telephone services; mobile communication equipment
HQ: T-Mobile Usa, Inc.
12920 Se 38th St
Bellevue WA 98006
425 378-4000

(G-19177)
TRI-PAR DIE AND MOLD CORP
670 Sundown Rd (60177-1144)
PHONE..................630 232-8800
William Plocinski, *Manager*
EMP: 26
SALES (corp-wide): 3MM **Privately Held**
SIC: 3544 3089 Special dies & tools; molding primary plastic
PA: Tri-Par Die And Mold Corporation
143 Roma Jean Pkwy
Streamwood IL

(G-19178)
TRIPLE EDGE MANUFACTURING INC
320 Production Dr (60177-2637)
PHONE..................847 468-9156
Kirk Johnson, *CEO*
Ann-Marie Johnson, *President*
Ewa Gubernat, *Vice Pres*
Krzysztof Gubernat, *Admin Sec*
EMP: 8 **EST:** 1999
SQ FT: 7,500
SALES: 1.2MM **Privately Held**
WEB: www.tripleedgemfg.com
SIC: 3599 Custom machinery

(G-19179)
WARNER OFFSET INC
640 Stevenson Rd (60177-1133)
PHONE..................847 695-9400
Mark J Warner, *President*
Richard W Doyle, *Vice Pres*
EMP: 32
SQ FT: 12,100
SALES (est): 4.2MM **Privately Held**
SIC: 2752 Commercial printing, offset

(G-19180)
WHITE JIG GRINDING
625 Martin Dr (60177-1171)
PHONE..................847 888-2260
William R White Jr, *President*
EMP: 2
SQ FT: 1,000
SALES (est): 202.8K **Privately Held**
SIC: 3599 Machine shop, jobbing & repair

(G-19181)
WIENMAR INC
Also Called: Marble Works
1601 N La Fox St (60177-1247)
PHONE..................847 742-9222
Thomas J Wienckowski Jr, *President*
Margaret Wienckowski, *Admin Sec*
EMP: 125
SQ FT: 45,000
SALES (est): 18.1MM **Privately Held**
SIC: 3281 1799 Household articles, except furniture: cut stone; counter top installation

(G-19182)
WINSLYN INDUSTRIES
777 W Thornwood Dr (60177-3735)
PHONE..................630 401-8051
William Stuedner, *President*
EMP: 6
SALES (est): 220.9K **Privately Held**
SIC: 2434 Wood kitchen cabinets

(G-19183)
WRT INC
400 Industrial Dr (60177-1182)
PHONE..................847 922-2235
Patrick Baudhuin, *President*
Norm Gehrke, *Vice Pres*
EMP: 3
SQ FT: 475
SALES (est): 470.3K **Privately Held**
SIC: 3441 Fabricated structural metal

(G-19184)
YORK SPRING CO
1551 N La Fox St (60177-1209)
P.O. Box 36 (60177-0036)
PHONE..................847 695-5978
James R York, *CEO*
Zelma York, *President*
Betty L York, *Exec VP*
Michael York, *Vice Pres*
Cindy Miller, *Manager*
EMP: 45 **EST:** 1956
SQ FT: 16,000
SALES (est): 6.7MM **Privately Held**
WEB: www.yorkspring.com
SIC: 3495 Wire springs

South Holland
Cook County

(G-19185)
3V PALLET
133 W 154th St (60473-1020)
PHONE..................708 620-7790
EMP: 4 **EST:** 2013
SALES (est): 356.6K **Privately Held**
WEB: www.3vpallet.com
SIC: 2448 Pallets, wood

(G-19186)
A J ADHESIVES INC
15461 La Salle St (60473-1220)
PHONE..................708 210-1111
Andy Schwartz, *CEO*
EMP: 4
SALES (est): 476.7K **Privately Held**
WEB: www.ajadhesives.com
SIC: 2891 Adhesives
PA: A. J. Adhesives, Inc.
4800 Miami St
Saint Louis MO 63116

(G-19187)
ABBOTTS MINUTE PRINTING INC
611 E 170th St (60473-3408)
PHONE..................708 339-6010
Linda Abbott, *President*
Michael Abbott, *Vice Pres*
EMP: 5
SQ FT: 2,000
SALES (est): 350K **Privately Held**
SIC: 2752 Commercial printing, offset

(G-19188)
AE2009 TECHNOLOGIES INC
Also Called: Ability Engineering
16140 Vincennes Ave (60473-1256)
PHONE..................708 331-0025
Eugene Botsoe, *President*
Joseph A Zawistowski, *Exec VP*
Sandra Morgan, *Treasurer*
Patricia D Zawistowski, *Admin Sec*
▲ **EMP:** 25
SQ FT: 40,000
SALES (est): 6.5MM **Privately Held**
WEB: www.abilityengineering.com
SIC: 3441 3443 Fabricated structural metal; fabricated plate work (boiler shop); reactor containment vessels, metal plate

(G-19189)
ALL-STEEL STRUCTURES INC
16301 Vincennes Ave (60473-2017)
PHONE..................708 210-1313
Theodore Bratsos, *President*
▲ **EMP:** 24
SQ FT: 22,500
SALES (est): 6MM **Privately Held**
SIC: 3993 3446 3449 1799 Signs, not made in custom sign painting shops; stairs, staircases, stair treads: prefabricated metal; miscellaneous metalwork; sign installation & maintenance; ornamental metal work

(G-19190)
ALLOCATOR LOGISTICS CO
22 W 154th St (60473-1013)
PHONE..................708 339-5678
Eunice L Larry, *Principal*
Kizzy Larry, *Principal*
EMP: 3
SALES (est): 110.8K **Privately Held**
SIC: 3613 Power circuit breakers; power switching equipment; control panels, electric

(G-19191)
AMERICAN CATHOLIC PRESS INC
Also Called: ACP PUBLICATIONS
16565 State St (60473-2025)
PHONE..................708 331-5485
Joseph Russo, *Treasurer*
Michael Gilligan, *Exec Dir*
Connor Loesch, *Admin Sec*
EMP: 10
SQ FT: 4,400
SALES: 180.7K **Privately Held**
SIC: 2721 2731 Magazines: publishing only, not printed on site; periodicals: publishing only; books: publishing only; book music: publishing only, not printed on site

(G-19192)
AMERICAN CLASSIC REBAR CORP
15810 Suntone Dr (60473-1238)
PHONE..................708 225-1010
Pete Pidrak, *Vice Pres*
EMP: 4
SALES (est): 400K **Privately Held**
SIC: 3449 Bars, concrete reinforcing: fabricated steel

(G-19193)
AMERICAN PIPING PRODUCTS INC
15801 Van Drunen Rd (60473-1245)
PHONE..................708 339-1753
Alfred Rheinnecker, *Branch Mgr*
EMP: 48 **Privately Held**
WEB: www.amerpipe.com
SIC: 3498 Fabricated pipe & fittings
PA: American Piping Products, Inc.
825 Mryvlle Ctr Dr Ste 31
Chesterfield MO 63017

(G-19194)
AMERICAN SHTMTL FABRICATORS
665 W Armory Dr (60473-2724)
PHONE..................708 877-7200
Dennis Debartolo, *President*
Frank Debartolo, *Vice Pres*
EMP: 11 **EST:** 2011
SALES: 2MM **Privately Held**
WEB: www.asmfabricators.com
SIC: 3444 Sheet metalwork

(G-19195)
ANIMATED MANUFACTURING COMPANY
106 W 154th St (60473-1015)
P.O. Box 448 (60473-0448)
PHONE..................708 333-6688
Allen White, *CEO*
Randy R Schafer, *President*
Pauline White, *Vice Pres*
EMP: 18 **EST:** 1953
SQ FT: 30,000
SALES: 3.3MM **Privately Held**
WEB: www.animatedmfgco.com
SIC: 3469 Stamping metal for the trade

(G-19196)
AQUAGREEN DISPOSITIONS LLC
1514 E 168th St (60473-2642)
PHONE..................708 606-0211
Ryan Cattoni, *Principal*
EMP: 2
SALES (est): 211.8K **Privately Held**
SIC: 3569 Cremating ovens

(G-19197)
ARMACELL LLC
16800 S Canal St (60473-2729)
PHONE..................708 596-9501
Denny Castello, *Manager*
Paul Scheiwe, *Manager*
EMP: 100 **Privately Held**
SIC: 3086 Insulation or cushioning material, foamed plastic
HQ: Armacell, Llc
55 Vilcom Center Dr # 200
Chapel Hill NC 27514

(G-19198)
ARMIL/CFS INC
15660 La Salle St (60473-1273)
P.O. Box 114 (60473-0114)
PHONE..................708 339-6810
Walter Parduhn, *President*
Joe Gall, *Finance Mgr*
Jeff Parduhn, *Manager*
◆ **EMP:** 30 **EST:** 1968
SQ FT: 20,000
SALES (est): 11.7MM **Privately Held**
WEB: www.armilcfs.com
SIC: 3567 5085 Heating units & devices, industrial: electric; refractory material

(G-19199)
BEDFORD RAKIM
17125 Evans Dr (60473-3475)
PHONE..................773 759-3947
Rakim Bedford, *Owner*
EMP: 4
SALES (est): 184K **Privately Held**
SIC: 3714 Transmissions, motor vehicle

(G-19200)
BENNU GROUP INC
Also Called: Ability Engineering Technology
16140 Vincennes Ave (60473-1256)
PHONE..................708 331-0025
Eugene Botsoe, *President*
Tim Niehof, *COO*
Michael Naurisak, *Engineer*
Joseph A Zawistowski, *CFO*
EMP: 19
SALES: 10MM **Privately Held**
SIC: 3443 Industrial vessels, tanks & containers; boilers: industrial, power, or marine

(G-19201)
BESSCO TUBE BENDING PIPE FABG
16000 Van Drunen Rd (60473-1242)
PHONE..................708 339-3977
Edward Eggebrecht, *Owner*
EMP: 3 **EST:** 2009
SALES (est): 45.4K **Privately Held**
SIC: 3498 Tube fabricating (contract bending & shaping)

(G-19202)
BROWN PACKING COMPANY INC
Also Called: Dutch Valley Veal
15801 Greenwood Rd (60473-1954)
PHONE..................708 849-7990
John A Oedzes, *President*
Bryan Scott, *COO*
Brian Oedzes, *Vice Pres*
EMP: 50 **EST:** 1944
SALES (est): 7.5MM **Privately Held**
WEB: www.dutchvalleyveal.com
SIC: 2011 2013 Veal from meat slaughtered on site; sausages & other prepared meats

(G-19203)
BUDDING POLISHING & MET FINSHG
130 E 168th St (60473-2836)
PHONE..................708 396-1166
Todd Kuipers, *Owner*

GEOGRAPHIC SECTION

South Holland - Cook County (G-19230)

Warren Kuipers, *Co-Owner*
EMP: 3
SQ FT: 3,300
SALES: 499K **Privately Held**
WEB: www.buddingpolishing.com
SIC: 3471 Finishing, metals or formed products; polishing, metals or formed products

(G-19204)
CARPENTERS MILLWORK CO
16046 Vandustrial Ln (60473-1255)
PHONE..................708 339-7707
Gary Smits, *President*
EMP: 10
SALES (est): 1.3MM
SALES (corp-wide): 1.3MM **Privately Held**
SIC: 2434 2431 2421 5031 Wood kitchen cabinets; millwork; sawmills & planing mills, general; doors & windows
PA: Carpenters Millwork Co (Inc)
224 W Stone Rd
Villa Park IL 60181
708 339-7707

(G-19205)
CHESTERFIELD AWNING CO INC (PA)
Also Called: Independent Awning Co
16999 Van Dam Rd (60473-2660)
PHONE..................708 596-4434
Howard B Ausema, *President*
David Ausema, *Vice Pres*
Jeremy Lopez, *Sales Staff*
Ed Ritzema, *Sales Associate*
Steve Agonis, *Manager*
EMP: 18
SQ FT: 10,000
SALES (est): 3.8MM **Privately Held**
WEB: www.chesterfieldawning.com
SIC: 2394 5999 3444 Awnings, fabric: made from purchased materials; awnings; sheet metalwork

(G-19206)
DAVID H VANDER PLOEG
Also Called: Rapid Printing Service
534 W 162nd St (60473-2011)
PHONE..................708 331-7700
David H Vander Ploeg, *Owner*
EMP: 6 EST: 1970
SQ FT: 5,000
SALES (est): 630.9K **Privately Held**
SIC: 2752 2791 2789 Commercial printing, offset; typesetting; bookbinding & related work

(G-19207)
DEBCOR INC
513 W Taft Dr (60473-2030)
PHONE..................708 333-2191
Doris Wilson, *President*
Howard Wilson, *Director*
EMP: 3
SQ FT: 1,100
SALES (est): 509.2K **Privately Held**
SIC: 5049 3443 2522 2521 School supplies; fabricated plate work (boiler shop); office furniture, except wood; wood office furniture; wood household furniture

(G-19208)
DOCTORS INTERIOR PLANTSCAPING
255 W Taft Dr (60473-2052)
PHONE..................708 333-3323
Cynthia Dorn, *President*
EMP: 5
SALES: 225K **Privately Held**
SIC: 2431 0782 Interior & ornamental woodwork & trim; lawn & garden services

(G-19209)
DOH SERVICES INC
16525 Van Dam Rd Ste 2 (60473-2652)
PHONE..................708 331-3811
Brian Tennis, *President*
Bill Kress, *Vice Pres*
John Dexter, *Admin Sec*
EMP: 4
SQ FT: 3,000
SALES: 510K **Privately Held**
SIC: 3281 5999 Monument or burial stone, cut & shaped; monuments & tombstones

(G-19210)
ENGINEERED FOAM SOLUTIONS INC
16000 Van Drunen Rd # 600 (60473-1242)
P.O. Box 699, Flossmoor (60422-0699)
PHONE..................708 769-4130
Keith Hasty, *President*
EMP: 5
SQ FT: 10,000
SALES (est): 461.3K **Privately Held**
SIC: 3086 Plastics foam products

(G-19211)
ESMA INC
450 Taft Dr Ste 101 (60473-2056)
P.O. Box 734 (60473-0734)
PHONE..................708 331-0456
Tim Beezhold, *President*
Paul Beezhold, *Vice Pres*
▲ EMP: 8
SQ FT: 5,000
SALES (est): 1.5MM **Privately Held**
SIC: 2819 3841 5169 Industrial inorganic chemicals; ultrasonic medical cleaning equipment; chemicals & allied products

(G-19212)
G F LTD
Also Called: Standard Wire & Steel Works
16255 Vincennes Ave (60473-1268)
P.O. Box 710 (60473-0710)
PHONE..................708 333-8300
Jess Sehgal, *President*
Jagdish S Sehgal, *President*
Ken Czaja, *Vice Pres*
▲ EMP: 25 EST: 1895
SQ FT: 30,000
SALES (est): 5.5MM **Privately Held**
WEB: www.standardwiresteel.com
SIC: 3496 Mesh, made from purchased wire

(G-19213)
GASKOA INC
16928 State St (60473-2841)
PHONE..................708 339-5000
Ed Gardiner, *Manager*
EMP: 38
SALES (corp-wide): 2MM **Privately Held**
SIC: 3053 3452 3499 Gaskets, all materials; washers, metal; shims, metal
PA: Gaskoa, Inc.
1001 Warrenville Rd # 500
Lisle IL

(G-19214)
GIBRALTAR CHEMICAL WORKS INC
114 E 168th St (60473-2836)
PHONE..................708 333-0600
James R Fencil, *President*
Joe Wolak, *Plant Engr*
Rebecca Mason, *Controller*
Joan Fencil, *Admin Sec*
▲ EMP: 19
SQ FT: 100,000
SALES (est): 6.3MM **Privately Held**
WEB: www.gibraltarchemical.com
SIC: 2851 Paints & paint additives

(G-19215)
GLOBAL WATER TECHNOLOGY INC
354 W Armory Dr (60473-2820)
PHONE..................708 349-9991
Maria Villarreal, *President*
Alex Wight, *Manager*
EMP: 26
SALES: 950K **Privately Held**
SIC: 8711 2869 2899 5169 Engineering services; industrial organic chemicals; antiscaling compounds, boiler; industrial chemicals; swimming pool & spa chemicals; air, water or soil test kits

(G-19216)
GRIER ABRASIVE CO INC
123 W Taft Dr (60473-2034)
PHONE..................708 333-6445
Chris Price, *General Mgr*
Virginia Yaksic, *Vice Pres*
Roberta Dubuc, *Vice Pres*
Sandra Mangel, *Admin Mgr*
Sandra Osborne, *Technology*
▲ EMP: 120
SALES (est): 16.9MM **Privately Held**
WEB: www.grierabrasive.com
SIC: 3291 7389 Wheels, abrasive;

(G-19217)
GRISWOLD MACHINE CO (PA)
241 W Taft Dr (60473-2036)
PHONE..................708 333-4258
Larry Griswold, *President*
EMP: 3
SALES (est): 306.3K **Privately Held**
SIC: 3599 Machine shop, jobbing & repair

(G-19218)
HADADY CORPORATION (PA)
510 W 172nd St (60473-2717)
PHONE..................219 322-7417
Jane Sullivan, *President*
Peter Lanman, *Vice Pres*
Eric Masnick, *Buyer*
Jason Songer, *Design Engr*
Roger Gordon, *CFO*
▲ EMP: 30
SALES (est): 24.8MM **Privately Held**
SIC: 3499 3743 3452 Machine bases, metal; locomotives & parts; pins

(G-19219)
HEMINGWAY CHIMNEY INC
16940 Vincennes Ave (60473-2807)
P.O. Box 922 (60473-0922)
PHONE..................708 333-0355
Scott Sievert, *President*
EMP: 7 EST: 2015
SQ FT: 12,000
SALES (est): 362.3K **Privately Held**
SIC: 1761 3444 Architectural sheet metal work; elbows, for air ducts, stovepipes, etc.: sheet metal; restaurant sheet metalwork

(G-19220)
HERSHEY CREAMERY COMPANY
601 W 167th St (60473-2703)
PHONE..................708 339-4656
Matt Kramer, *Manager*
EMP: 10
SALES (corp-wide): 128MM **Privately Held**
SIC: 2024 Ice cream, bulk
PA: Hershey Creamery Company
301 S Cameron St
Harrisburg PA 17101
717 238-8134

(G-19221)
HI TECH MACHINING & WELDING
16120 Vincennes Ave (60473-1256)
PHONE..................708 331-3608
Joe Olson, *Principal*
EMP: 7
SALES (est): 560K **Privately Held**
SIC: 3599 Machine shop, jobbing & repair

(G-19222)
HOLLAND PRINTING INC
922 E 162nd St (60473-2442)
PHONE..................708 596-9000
Mark Lareau, *President*
Mark La Reau, *Sales Mgr*
EMP: 11
SQ FT: 4,364
SALES: 980K **Privately Held**
WEB: www.hollandprinting.com
SIC: 2752 Commercial printing, offset

(G-19223)
HYSPAN PRECISION PRODUCTS INC
Also Called: Universal Metal Hose
17111 Wallace St (60473-2735)
PHONE..................773 277-0700
Patricia Johnson, *Office Mgr*
EMP: 32
SALES (corp-wide): 108.6MM **Privately Held**
SIC: 3568 3498 3429 3441 Ball joints, except aircraft & automotive; fabricated pipe & fittings; manufactured hardware (general); fabricated structural metal
PA: Hyspan Precision Products, Inc.
1685 Brandywine Ave
Chula Vista CA 91911
619 421-1355

(G-19224)
INDUSTRIAL SPECIALTY CHEM INC (DH)
Also Called: ISC Water Solutions
410 W 169th St (60473-2713)
PHONE..................708 339-1313
Christopher Dooley, *President*
EMP: 30
SQ FT: 24,000
SALES (est): 5.2MM **Privately Held**
SIC: 2899 3589 Chemical preparations; sewage & water treatment equipment
HQ: Industrial Water Treatment Solutions Corporation
16880 Lathrop Ave
Harvey IL
708 339-1313

(G-19225)
K H HUPPERT CO
16850 State St (60473-4800)
PHONE..................708 339-2020
Richard Farmer, *Principal*
EMP: 3
SALES (est): 180.9K **Privately Held**
SIC: 3567 Industrial furnaces & ovens

(G-19226)
KB PUBLISHING INC (PA)
Also Called: Park Press
924 E 162nd St (60473-2442)
PHONE..................708 331-6352
Daniell Kallemeyn, *President*
David Kallemeyn, *Vice Pres*
Arlo Kallemeyn, *Admin Sec*
EMP: 75
SQ FT: 6,000
SALES (est): 9.1MM **Privately Held**
WEB: www.parkpress.com
SIC: 2752 Commercial printing, offset

(G-19227)
KB PUBLISHING INC
930 E 162nd St (60473-2442)
PHONE..................708 331-6352
Arlo Kallemeyn, *Partner*
EMP: 25
SALES (corp-wide): 9.1MM **Privately Held**
SIC: 2752 Commercial printing, offset
PA: K.B. Publishing Inc.
924 E 162nd St
South Holland IL 60473
708 331-6352

(G-19228)
KRYGIER MACHINE COMPANY INC
15938 Suntone Dr (60473-1239)
PHONE..................708 331-5255
Larry Krygier, *President*
Thomas Haskins, *Research*
Debbie Haskins, *Manager*
Linda Lou Waterson, *Shareholder*
EMP: 7
SQ FT: 3,306
SALES (est): 902.5K **Privately Held**
SIC: 3599 Machine shop, jobbing & repair

(G-19229)
KUNZ INDUSTRIES INC
15800 Suntone Dr (60473-1238)
PHONE..................708 596-7717
Gordon Kunz Sr, *President*
Gordon Kunz Jr, *Treasurer*
EMP: 6
SQ FT: 5,500
SALES (est): 1MM **Privately Held**
SIC: 7699 2821 Wheel & caster repair; polyurethane resins

(G-19230)
LONG WOLF EXPRESS INC
16260 Louis Ave (60473-5201)
PHONE..................708 673-1583
Charles Gardner Jr, *CEO*
EMP: 4
SALES: 450K **Privately Held**
SIC: 3711 Truck tractors for highway use, assembly of

South Holland - Cook County

(G-19231)
MCKERNIN EXHIBITS INC
570 W Armory Dr (60473-2824)
PHONE..................................708 333-4500
Dan Mc Kernin, *President*
Tim Mc Kernin, *Treasurer*
Jim Mc Kernin, *Admin Sec*
EMP: 18
SQ FT: 40,000
SALES (est): 3MM **Privately Held**
SIC: 3993 Displays & cutouts, window & lobby

(G-19232)
MFW SERVICES INC
215 W 155th St (60473-1208)
P.O. Box 429, Worth (60482-0429)
PHONE..................................708 522-5879
David Clark, *President*
EMP: 3
SALES (est): 443.2K **Privately Held**
SIC: 3549 7692 Metalworking machinery; welding repair

(G-19233)
MOORKET INC
430 E 162nd St Ste 486 (60473-2258)
PHONE..................................888 275-0277
EMP: 3
SALES (est): 57.1K **Privately Held**
SIC: 2844 Hair preparations, including shampoos

(G-19234)
MSEED GROUP LLC
535 W Taft Dr (60473-2030)
PHONE..................................847 226-1147
Erica Douglas, *CEO*
Barry W Williams, *COO*
EMP: 5
SQ FT: 6,000
SALES (est): 341.5K **Privately Held**
SIC: 2844 Cosmetic preparations

(G-19235)
NIAGARA LASALLE CORPORATION
16655 S Canal St (60473-2726)
PHONE..................................708 596-2700
Mark Ruder, *Branch Mgr*
Roy Miller, *Maintence Staff*
Joe Rodriguez, *Maintence Staff*
EMP: 150
SALES (corp-wide): 506MM **Privately Held**
SIC: 3316 Bars, steel, cold finished, from purchased hot-rolled
HQ: Niagara Lasalle Corporation
1412 150th St
Hammond IN 46327
219 853-6000

(G-19236)
PALLETS INTERNATIONAL HOLDING
500 W Armory Dr (60473-2851)
PHONE..................................773 391-7223
Norman H Gordon, *Manager*
EMP: 4
SALES (est): 396K **Privately Held**
SIC: 2448 Pallets, wood & wood with metal

(G-19237)
PARK PRESS INC
930 E 162nd St (60473-2442)
PHONE..................................708 331-6352
Dam Kallemeyn, *President*
EMP: 15
SALES (est): 1MM **Privately Held**
SIC: 2752 Commercial printing, offset

(G-19238)
PASSION FRUIT DRINK INC
17335 Sterling Ct (60473-3779)
PHONE..................................708 769-4749
Grover Calvert, *President*
EMP: 4
SALES (est): 330K **Privately Held**
SIC: 2087 Beverage bases, concentrates, syrups, powders & mixes

(G-19239)
PEERLESS CHAIN COMPANY
Also Called: Letellier Material Hdlg Eqp
16650 State St (60473-2826)
PHONE..................................708 339-0545
Bob Dwyer, *Branch Mgr*
EMP: 35
SALES (corp-wide): 79MM **Privately Held**
SIC: 3536 Hoists
HQ: Peerless Chain Company
1416 E Sanborn St
Winona MN 55987
507 457-9100

(G-19240)
PERKINS ENTERPRISE INC
15518 S Park Ave (60473-1303)
PHONE..................................708 560-3837
Wayne Perkins, *President*
EMP: 5
SALES (est): 100K **Privately Held**
SIC: 3571 Electronic computers

(G-19241)
ROBERTS COLONIAL HOUSE INC
Also Called: Roberts Displays
15960 Suntone Dr (60473-1239)
P.O. Box 308 (60473-0308)
PHONE..................................708 331-6233
Floyd Hurley, *President*
Dolores Hurley, *Corp Secy*
▲ **EMP:** 15 **EST:** 1941
SQ FT: 8,000
SALES (est): 1.7MM **Privately Held**
WEB: www.robertsdisplays.com
SIC: 3999 Advertising display products

(G-19242)
S & J INDUSTRIAL SUPPLY CORP
16060 Suntone Dr (60473-1240)
PHONE..................................708 339-1708
Robert C Stuart, *President*
Cathy Popjevach, *Purchasing*
EMP: 17
SQ FT: 10,000
SALES (est): 7.2MM **Privately Held**
WEB: www.s-jindustrial.com
SIC: 5085 3545 3546 3425 Industrial supplies; machine tool accessories; power-driven handtools; saw blades & handsaws; abrasive products

(G-19243)
SAMBOR STONE LTD
15527 La Salle St (60473-1267)
PHONE..................................708 388-0804
Jonathon Sambor, *President*
EMP: 1
SALES (est): 200.7K **Privately Held**
SIC: 3281 Table tops, marble

(G-19244)
SHAMROCK MANUFACTURING CO INC
15920 Suntone Dr (60473-1239)
PHONE..................................708 331-7776
Robert Bacon, *President*
EMP: 5
SQ FT: 4,000
SALES (est): 320K **Privately Held**
SIC: 3441 3444 Fabricated structural metal; sheet metalwork

(G-19245)
SOUTH CHICAGO PACKING LLC (DH)
16250 Vincennes Ave (60473-1260)
PHONE..................................708 589-2400
Ron Miniat, *Ch of Bd*
David J Miniat, *President*
Tim Meyer, *Vice Pres*
Charles Nalon, *Vice Pres*
Shawna Lecuyer, *Admin Sec*
▼ **EMP:** 80
SQ FT: 92,000
SALES (est): 106.2MM
SALES (corp-wide): 397.8MM **Privately Held**
SIC: 2079 Compound shortenings

HQ: Miniat Holdings Llc
16250 Vincennes Ave
South Holland IL 60473
708 589-2400

(G-19246)
STEEL-GUARD SAFETY CORP
16520 Vincennes Ave (60473-2020)
PHONE..................................708 589-4588
Greg J Pretsch, *President*
Anita Miller, *Sales Staff*
▼ **EMP:** 8
SALES (est): 1.6MM **Privately Held**
SIC: 3625 3842 3442 5085 Noise control equipment; personal safety equipment; rolling doors for industrial buildings or warehouses, metal; industrial supplies; welding supplies; welding supplies

(G-19247)
SURGE CLUTCH & DRIVE LINE CO
16145 Thornton Blue Is (60473)
P.O. Box 100 (60473-0100)
PHONE..................................708 331-1352
Rhonda Jesernik, *President*
George Polmen, *Corp Secy*
EMP: 9
SQ FT: 11,000
SALES (est): 900K **Privately Held**
SIC: 3714 5013 3568 3566 Drive shafts, motor vehicle; clutches, motor vehicle; clutches; power transmission equipment; speed changers, drives & gears

(G-19248)
TECHNO - GRPHICS TRNSLTONS INC
Also Called: Electronic Technology Group
1451 E 168th St (60473-2641)
PHONE..................................708 331-3333
David L Bond, *President*
Rizza Antonov, *Human Resources*
Dan McFalls, *MIS Mgr*
Mary W Bond, *Admin Sec*
EMP: 25
SQ FT: 5,000
SALES (est): 2.5MM **Privately Held**
SIC: 2741 7389 7373 Technical manuals: publishing only, not printed on site; translation services; value-added resellers, computer systems

(G-19249)
THE CALUMET CARTON COMPANY (PA)
16920 State St (60473-2841)
P.O. Box 405 (60473-0405)
PHONE..................................708 331-7910
Albert Inwood, *Ch of Bd*
John A Inwood, *President*
Kenneth J Roush, *President*
John Inwood, *Vice Pres*
Don Wolski, *Purchasing*
▲ **EMP:** 90 **EST:** 1930
SQ FT: 110,000
SALES (est): 18.3MM **Privately Held**
WEB: www.calumetcarton.com
SIC: 2653 2677 2657 2631 Boxes, solid fiber: made from purchased materials; envelopes; folding paperboard boxes; paperboard mills

(G-19250)
YOURFEEL PRODUCTS CORP
505 W Taft Dr (60473-2030)
PHONE..................................708 596-2150
Robert E Dalton, *President*
EMP: 5
SALES (est): 727.2K **Privately Held**
SIC: 2851 Paints & allied products

South Jacksonville
Morgan County

(G-19251)
OUTBREAK DESIGNS
1458 S Main St (62650-3440)
PHONE..................................217 370-5418
Rick Rolson, *Owner*
EMP: 5 **EST:** 2017
SALES (est): 400K **Privately Held**
SIC: 2759 Screen printing

South Roxana
Madison County

(G-19252)
CORRECTIVE ASPHALT MTLS LLC
300 Daniel Boone Trl (62087-1594)
P.O. Box 87129 (62087-7129)
PHONE..................................618 254-3855
Tony Witte, *CEO*
Marc Taillon, *Vice Pres*
Byron Farrell, *QC Mgr*
Byron L Farrell, *Mng Member*
Jack Holleran, *Area Spvr*
EMP: 9 **EST:** 1975
SQ FT: 5,000
SALES: 1.5MM **Privately Held**
WEB: www.correctiveasphalt.com
SIC: 1611 2951 Highway & street paving contractor; asphalt & asphaltic paving mixtures (not from refineries)

(G-19253)
MIKES INC (PA)
109 Velma Ave (62087-1528)
P.O. Box 87069 (62087-7069)
PHONE..................................618 254-4491
Mike Marko Sr, *President*
Sharon Kessler, *Admin Sec*
▲ **EMP:** 51
SQ FT: 20,000
SALES (est): 19MM **Privately Held**
WEB: www.mikesinc.com
SIC: 3731 7538 5082 Shipbuilding & repairing; general automotive repair shops; construction & mining machinery

Sparland
Marshall County

(G-19254)
STEUBEN TOWNSHIP
374 County Road 850 E (61565-9393)
PHONE..................................309 208-7073
Josh Crobyn, *Commissioner*
EMP: 12
SALES (est): 840K **Privately Held**
SIC: 3531 Drags, road (construction & road maintenance equipment)

Sparta
Randolph County

(G-19255)
JMS METALS INC
1255 W Broadway St (62286-1659)
PHONE..................................618 443-1000
Joan Stork, *President*
Ron Stork, *Treasurer*
EMP: 5
SALES (est): 609.3K **Privately Held**
SIC: 3499 Machine bases, metal

(G-19256)
LEE GILSTER-MARY CORPORATION
403 E 4th St (62286-1886)
PHONE..................................618 443-5676
Steve Armstrong, *Manager*
EMP: 45
SALES (corp-wide): 1B **Privately Held**
SIC: 2098 2043 2099 2045 Macaroni products (e.g. alphabets, rings & shells), dry; cereal breakfast foods; popcorn, packaged: except already popped; blended flour: from purchased flour; plastic containers, except foam
HQ: Gilster-Mary Lee Corporation
1037 State St
Chester IL 62233
618 826-2361

GEOGRAPHIC SECTION

(G-19257)
MCCLATCHY NEWSPAPERS INC
Also Called: Plaindealer
116 W Main St (62286-2064)
P.O. Box 217 (62286-0217)
PHONE..................618 443-2145
Carol Mulholland, *General Mgr*
EMP: 16
SALES (corp-wide): 709.5MM **Publicly Held**
SIC: 2711 Newspapers: publishing only, not printed on site
HQ: Mcclatchy Newspapers, Inc.
2100 Q St
Sacramento CA 95816
916 321-1855

(G-19258)
NORVIDA USA INC
Also Called: Big T Graphics
310 S Vine St (62286-1832)
PHONE..................618 282-2992
Fax: 618 443-3437
EMP: 2
SALES (est): 200K **Privately Held**
SIC: 3861 Manufacturer Of Graphic Arts Proof Paper

(G-19259)
SIGN SOLUTIONS
1255 W Broadway St (62286-1659)
P.O. Box 271 (62286-0271)
PHONE..................618 443-6565
EMP: 2
SALES (est): 286K **Privately Held**
SIC: 3993 Mfg Signs/Advertising Specialties

(G-19260)
SPARTAN LIGHT METAL PDTS INC (PA)
510 E Mcclurken Ave (62286-1850)
PHONE..................618 443-4346
Donald A Jubel, *President*
Jeremy Long, *General Mgr*
Stephen Gordon, *Opers Mgr*
Stephen Rdon, *Opers Mgr*
Brian Smith, *Buyer*
◆ **EMP:** 25 **EST:** 1961
SQ FT: 132,000
SALES: 140MM **Privately Held**
WEB: www.spartanlmp.com
SIC: 3363 3364 3369 3365 Aluminum die-castings; magnesium & magnesium-base alloy die-castings; nonferrous foundries; aluminum foundries

(G-19261)
SPARTAN LIGHT METAL PDTS INC
405 E 4th St (62286)
PHONE..................618 443-4346
Ed Bean, *CFO*
EMP: 600
SALES (corp-wide): 140MM **Privately Held**
WEB: www.spartanlmp.com
SIC: 3363 3364 Aluminum die-castings; magnesium & magnesium-base alloy die-castings
PA: Spartan Light Metal Products, Inc.
510 E Mcclurken Ave
Sparta IL 62286
618 443-4346

Spring Grove
Mchenry County

(G-19262)
A PLUS APPAREL
9902 Fox Bluff Ln (60081-8829)
P.O. Box 205 (60081-0205)
PHONE..................815 675-2117
Cheryl Ready, *Owner*
EMP: 1
SALES: 200K **Privately Held**
SIC: 2395 Embroidery products, except schiffli machine

(G-19263)
ALL RITE SPRING CO
2200 Spring Ridge Dr (60081-8119)
PHONE..................815 675-1350
John Bilik, *President*
Bob Chapman, *QC Mgr*
Oliver Plunkett, *CFO*
Debbie Wiegman, *Accounting Mgr*
Kerry Manuel, *Manager*
▲ **EMP:** 55 **EST:** 1947
SQ FT: 32,000
SALES (est): 14.3MM **Privately Held**
WEB: www.allrite.com
SIC: 3493 3495 Steel springs, except wire; wire springs

(G-19264)
ALL RITE SPRING COMPANY
2302 Spring Ridge Dr (60081-8696)
PHONE..................815 675-1350
EMP: 10
SALES (est): 1.2MM **Privately Held**
SIC: 3495 Wire springs

(G-19265)
ASTRO-CRAFT INC
7509 Spring Grove Rd (60081-8916)
PHONE..................815 675-1500
Richard Dschida, *President*
Richard F Dschida, *President*
Edward Dschida, *Admin Sec*
EMP: 24 **EST:** 1966
SQ FT: 15,000
SALES: 3.4MM **Privately Held**
WEB: www.astrocraft.com
SIC: 3599 3451 Machine shop, jobbing & repair; screw machine products

(G-19266)
AUTONAMIC CORPORATION
7806 Industrial Dr (60081-8251)
P.O. Box 43 (60081-0043)
PHONE..................815 675-6300
Roger Dumke, *President*
EMP: 6 **EST:** 1965
SQ FT: 14,000
SALES (est): 1.1MM **Privately Held**
SIC: 3451 Screw machine products

(G-19267)
BAXTER HEALTHCARE CORPORATION
1606 Beech St (60081-8080)
PHONE..................847 948-3206
Martha Olson, *Principal*
EMP: 105
SALES (corp-wide): 11.3B **Publicly Held**
WEB: www.baxter.com
SIC: 3841 Surgical & medical instruments
HQ: Baxter Healthcare Corporation
1 Baxter Pkwy
Deerfield IL 60015
224 948-2000

(G-19268)
BLACK MOUNTAIN PRODUCTS INC
7705 Industrial Dr Ste B (60081-8359)
PHONE..................224 655-5955
Daniel Borak, *President*
Julie Weidener, *Principal*
Patricia Weidener, *Principal*
Richard Weidner, *Vice Pres*
Tom Wiznerowicz, *Sales Dir*
▲ **EMP:** 6
SALES (est): 1MM **Privately Held**
WEB: www.blackmountainproducts.com
SIC: 3499 Stabilizing bars (cargo), metal

(G-19269)
C R V ELECTRONICS CORP
2249 Pierce Dr (60081-9703)
PHONE..................815 675-6500
James Vyduna, *President*
Matthew W Krueger, *Vice Pres*
David Niehus, *Opers Mgr*
Jeanette Vyduna, *Treasurer*
Chris Strossner, *Sales Engr*
EMP: 60 **EST:** 1967
SQ FT: 16,000
SALES (est): 16.2MM **Privately Held**
WEB: www.crvelect.com
SIC: 3679 3496 3357 5063 Electronic circuits; miscellaneous fabricated wire products; nonferrous wiredrawing & insulating; electrical apparatus & equipment

(G-19270)
CLEAN HARBORS WICHITA LLC
2500 Westward Dr (60081-8828)
PHONE..................815 675-1272
EMP: 3 **Privately Held**
SIC: 2992 Oils & greases, blending & compounding
HQ: Clean Harbors Wichita, Llc
2824 N Ohio St
Wichita KS 67219
316 832-0151

(G-19271)
COILTECHNIC INC
2402 Spring Ridge Dr C (60081-8693)
PHONE..................815 675-9260
Rick Scott, *President*
Tim Scott, *Vice Pres*
EMP: 12
SQ FT: 5,400
SALES (est): 956K **Privately Held**
SIC: 3612 Transformers, except electric

(G-19272)
D & G WELDING SUPPLY COMPANY
7705 Industrial Dr Ste E (60081-8359)
PHONE..................815 675-9890
EMP: 2
SALES (est): 247K **Privately Held**
SIC: 3548 Welding apparatus

(G-19273)
DYNAMIC MACHINING INC
2304 Spring Ridge Dr C (60081-8646)
P.O. Box 467 (60081-0467)
PHONE..................815 675-3330
Leo Navoichick, *President*
EMP: 5
SALES (est): 810K **Privately Held**
SIC: 3599 Machine shop, jobbing & repair

(G-19274)
ELAS TEK MOLDING INC
Also Called: Elastek Molding
7517 Meyer Rd Ste 1 (60081-7805)
PHONE..................815 675-9012
Jayne Davis, *President*
EMP: 22
SQ FT: 9,000
SALES: 1MM **Privately Held**
SIC: 3089 3841 2822 Injection molded finished plastic products; surgical & medical instruments; synthetic rubber

(G-19275)
HAWTHORNE PRESS INC
208 Chateau Dr (60081-8928)
PHONE..................847 587-0582
EMP: 4
SALES (est): 270K **Privately Held**
SIC: 2752 2791 2789 Lithographic Commercial Printing Typesetting Services Bookbinding/Related Work

(G-19276)
INTERMATIC INCORPORATED (PA)
7777 Winn Rd (60081-9698)
PHONE..................815 675-7000
David Schroeder, *President*
Mary Prokulewicz, *President*
Rick Boutilier, *Principal*
Cindy Nichols, *Regional Mgr*
Mary Dembski, *District Mgr*
◆ **EMP:** 623
SQ FT: 357,000
SALES: 124.7MM **Privately Held**
WEB: www.intermaticstore.com
SIC: 3645 3612 Residential lighting fixtures; line voltage regulators

(G-19277)
INTERNATIONAL RD DYNAMICS CORP
2402 Spring Ridge Dr E (60081-8693)
PHONE..................815 675-1430
Randy Hanson, *President*
David Cortens, *CFO*
Vivien Varga, *Sales Staff*
Rino Quinones, *Supervisor*
EMP: 34
SQ FT: 5,000
SALES: 48.2MM
SALES (corp-wide): 113.8MM **Privately Held**
WEB: www.internationalroaddynamicsinc.com
SIC: 3596 Scales & balances, except laboratory
PA: International Road Dynamics Inc
702 43rd St E
Saskatoon SK S7K 3
306 653-6600

(G-19278)
JOHNSON CUSTOM CABINETS
7609 Blivin St (60081-9689)
PHONE..................815 675-9690
Edward Johnson, *Owner*
EMP: 2
SALES (est): 226.9K **Privately Held**
SIC: 2434 Wood kitchen cabinets

(G-19279)
KITCHEN KRAFTERS INC
7801 Industrial Dr Ste D (60081-8298)
PHONE..................815 675-6061
Jeff Johnson, *President*
Moira Johnson, *Admin Sec*
EMP: 6
SQ FT: 2,560
SALES: 460K **Privately Held**
SIC: 2541 1799 2434 Counter & sink tops; counter top installation; wood kitchen cabinets

(G-19280)
KNOLL STEEL INC
2851 N Us Highway 12 (60081-7808)
PHONE..................815 675-9400
Kenneth R Knoll, *President*
EMP: 16
SALES (est): 1.6MM **Privately Held**
SIC: 3441 Building components, structural steel

(G-19281)
KOSMOS TOOL INC
2727 N Us Highway 12 (60081-8699)
P.O. Box 279 (60081-0279)
PHONE..................815 675-2200
John Ferguson, *President*
Richard Sadowski, *Vice Pres*
EMP: 19
SQ FT: 20,000
SALES (est): 2.9MM **Privately Held**
SIC: 3544 3469 Special dies & tools; stamping metal for the trade

(G-19282)
KUNA CORP
Also Called: Netnotes
1512 Spring Ct (60081-7811)
PHONE..................815 675-0140
EMP: 6
SALES (est): 307.6K **Privately Held**
SIC: 3661 Mfg Telephone/Telegraph Apparatus

(G-19283)
MC SQUARED GROUP INC
7801 Industrial Dr Ste F (60081-8298)
PHONE..................815 322-2485
Jody McCrea, *President*
EMP: 1
SALES (est): 217K **Privately Held**
SIC: 5047 3841 Instruments, surgical & medical; surgical & medical instruments

(G-19284)
MIKE MEIER & SONS FENCE MFG
7501 Meyer Rd Ste 1 (60081-8600)
PHONE..................847 587-1111
Debbie Meier, *President*
Mike Meier, *Vice Pres*
EMP: 20
SQ FT: 6,000
SALES (est): 2.1MM **Privately Held**
SIC: 2499 3446 5211 Fencing, wood; fences or posts, ornamental iron or steel; fencing

(G-19285)
MINIC PRECISION INC
7706 Industrial Dr Ste K (60081-8278)
PHONE..................815 675-0451
Michael K Gajewski, *President*

Spring Grove - Mchenry County (G-19286)

EMP: 10
SQ FT: 3,000
SALES (est): 750K **Privately Held**
SIC: 3451 Screw machine products

(G-19286)
MODERN ABRASIVE CORP
2855 N Us Highway 12 (60081-7808)
P.O. Box 219 (60081-0219)
PHONE..................815 675-2352
Edward Prebe, *Ch of Bd*
Harvey B Nudelman, *President*
Harvey Nudelman, *President*
Mark Salmon, *Vice Pres*
Jerry Turner, *Vice Pres*
▲ EMP: 75 EST: 1959
SQ FT: 45,000
SALES (est): 13.3MM **Privately Held**
WEB: www.modernabrasive.com
SIC: 3291 Wheels, abrasive

(G-19287)
NATIONAL CAP AND SET SCREW CO
2991 N Us Highway 12 (60081-7809)
P.O. Box 280 (60081-0280)
PHONE..................815 675-2363
Peter C May, *President*
Teresa Twardy, *Corp Secy*
Timothy May, *Shareholder*
EMP: 14 EST: 1941
SQ FT: 15,588
SALES: 1MM **Privately Held**
WEB: www.natlcap.com
SIC: 3451 3452 5072 Screw machine products; screws, metal; bolts, nuts & screws

(G-19288)
NATIONAL EMERGENCY MED ID INC
100 Lincolnwood Ct (60081-8726)
PHONE..................847 366-1267
Melissa Wilhelm, *President*
EMP: 3
SQ FT: 1,100
SALES (est): 524.3K **Privately Held**
SIC: 5099 3089 7363 Safety equipment & supplies; identification cards, plastic; help supply services

(G-19289)
NORTHERN ORDINANCE CORPORATION
Also Called: Nordco
7806 Industrial Dr (60081-8251)
P.O. Box 194 (60081-0194)
PHONE..................815 675-6400
Roger N Dumke, *President*
Pat Browning, *Corp Secy*
EMP: 3
SQ FT: 300
SALES (est): 286.5K **Privately Held**
WEB: www.microest.com
SIC: 3423 3484 Mechanics' hand tools; guns (firearms) or gun parts, 30 mm. & below

(G-19290)
NOWFAB
6413 Johnsburg Rd (60081-9686)
PHONE..................815 675-2916
Steven Nowaczek, *President*
EMP: 2
SALES (est): 200K **Privately Held**
SIC: 3441 Fabricated structural metal

(G-19291)
OLSON MACHINING INC
1804 Holian Dr (60081-7904)
PHONE..................815 675-2900
John R Olson, *President*
Frank William Olson III, *Vice Pres*
Deborah G Olson, *Admin Sec*
EMP: 27
SQ FT: 13,000
SALES (est): 6.1MM **Privately Held**
SIC: 3599 Machine shop, jobbing & repair

(G-19292)
PATLIN ENTERPRISES INC
2907 N Us Highway 12 (60081-7809)
P.O. Box 98 (60081-0098)
PHONE..................815 675-6606
Thomas Fry, *President*

Patricia Fry, *Corp Secy*
EMP: 10
SQ FT: 18,000
SALES (est): 1.8MM **Privately Held**
SIC: 3599 Custom machinery

(G-19293)
PIMCO PLASTICS INC
7517 Meyer Rd (60081-7805)
P.O. Box 40 (60081-0040)
PHONE..................815 675-6464
Robert Schuehle, *President*
EMP: 4
SALES (est): 577.8K **Privately Held**
SIC: 3089 Injection molded finished plastic products

(G-19294)
PRECISION MOLDED CONCEPTS
Also Called: P M C
2402 Spring Ridge Dr C (60081-8693)
PHONE..................815 675-0060
Tim Scott, *President*
Richard Scott, *Vice Pres*
EMP: 12
SQ FT: 6,000
SALES (est): 1.2MM **Privately Held**
SIC: 3089 Injection molding of plastics

(G-19295)
PRO CIRCLE GOLF CENTERS INC
Also Called: Pro Circle Golf Driving Range
1810 N Us Highway 12 (60081-5700)
PHONE..................815 675-2747
Clarence W Shastal, *President*
Gary Shastal, *President*
Gary W Shastal, *Vice Pres*
Mildred C Shastal, *Treasurer*
EMP: 3 EST: 1965
SQ FT: 2,800
SALES (est): 408.2K **Privately Held**
SIC: 5941 7999 3949 Golf goods & equipment; golf driving range; miniature golf course operation; golf equipment

(G-19296)
QUEST MANUFACTURING INC
2503 Spring Ridge Dr (60081-7807)
P.O. Box 430 (60081-0430)
PHONE..................815 675-2442
John Lichter, *President*
EMP: 112
SQ FT: 40,000
SALES (est): 2MM **Privately Held**
SIC: 3443 Metal parts

(G-19297)
QUICKER ENGINEERING
7516 Buena Vis (60081-8925)
PHONE..................815 675-6516
Richard Derosa, *Owner*
EMP: 3
SALES (est): 170.7K **Privately Held**
SIC: 3944 Cars, play (children's vehicles)

(G-19298)
RAINBOW SIGNS
2404 Spring Ridge Dr A (60081-8692)
PHONE..................815 675-6750
Ronald Ottinger, *President*
EMP: 14
SQ FT: 6,000
SALES (est): 1.6MM **Privately Held**
SIC: 3993 Electric signs; neon signs

(G-19299)
RINGMASTER MFG
8001 Winn Rd (60081-9687)
P.O. Box 8 (60081-0008)
PHONE..................815 675-4230
Dave Hobbs, *Principal*
EMP: 4
SALES (est): 482.4K **Privately Held**
SIC: 3999 Manufacturing industries

(G-19300)
SCOT FORGE COMPANY (PA)
8001 Winn Rd (60081-9687)
PHONE..................815 675-1000
John L Cain, *President*
Michelle Riedel, *President*
Ronald E Hahn, *COO*
Perry Detlor, *Plant Mgr*

Sean Semler, *Opers Mgr*
◆ EMP: 325 EST: 1893
SQ FT: 375,000
SALES (est): 107MM **Privately Held**
WEB: www.scotforge.com
SIC: 3462 Aircraft forgings, ferrous

(G-19301)
SPORTDECALS INC
Also Called: Absolutely Custom
2504 Spring Ridge Dr (60081-8698)
PHONE..................800 435-6110
Christopher Gagnon, *President*
Michelle Schafer, *Sales Staff*
Amy Mitchell, *Manager*
Chris Ross, *Manager*
Lori Vetter, *Director*
EMP: 90 EST: 2015
SQ FT: 40,000
SALES (est): 6.6MM **Privately Held**
SIC: 2759 Decals: printing

(G-19302)
THREAD & GAGE CO INC
3000 N Us Highway 12 (60081-9362)
P.O. Box 6 (60081-0006)
PHONE..................815 675-2305
Deno A Buralli Jr, *President*
Joseph Buralli, *Vice Pres*
EMP: 2 EST: 1956
SQ FT: 28,000
SALES: 400K **Privately Held**
WEB: www.threadgageco.com
SIC: 3452 3545 3823 3541 Screws, metal; gauges (machine tool accessories); industrial instrmnts msrmnt display/control process variable; machine tools, metal cutting type; hand & edge tools

(G-19303)
THREE R PLASTICS INC
1801 Holian Dr (60081-7930)
PHONE..................815 675-0844
Michael Gore, *President*
Raymond Gore, *Vice Pres*
EMP: 15
SQ FT: 5,000
SALES (est): 3.3MM **Privately Held**
SIC: 3089 Injection molding of plastics

(G-19304)
TONERHEAD INC
Also Called: Laser Tek Industries
3106 N Us Highway 12 (60081-9362)
PHONE..................815 331-3200
Harold E Nicodem, *President*
▼ EMP: 41
SALES (est): 7MM **Privately Held**
SIC: 3955 Print cartridges for laser & other computer printers

(G-19305)
TRU-MACHINE CO INC
7502 Mayo Ct Unit 3 (60081-7905)
PHONE..................815 675-6735
Lou Sikora, *President*
Daintri Sikora, *Vice Pres*
EMP: 3
SQ FT: 10,000
SALES: 500K **Privately Held**
SIC: 3599 Machine shop, jobbing & repair

(G-19306)
US POST CO INC
2701 N Us Highway 12 A (60081-7815)
PHONE..................815 675-9313
Richard A Parent, *President*
EMP: 5
SQ FT: 500
SALES: 550K **Privately Held**
SIC: 3444 Mail (post office) collection or storage boxes, sheet metal

Spring Valley
Bureau County

(G-19307)
AQUA CONTROL INC
Also Called: Aci
6a Wolfer Industrial Park (61362-9504)
PHONE..................815 664-4900
Willis Dane, *President*

Robert Hurless, *Purchasing*
Steve Dacko, *Design Engr*
▲ EMP: 30
SQ FT: 35,000
SALES (est): 7.9MM **Privately Held**
SIC: 3561 3272 3523 Pumps & pumping equipment; fountains, concrete; farm machinery & equipment

(G-19308)
HONEYWELL INTERNATIONAL INC
410 Richard A Mautino Dr (61362-1140)
PHONE..................815 663-2011
Ralph Hill, *VP Human Res*
Amy Gustafson, *Advt Staff*
Charlie Hardin, *Branch Mgr*
Kent Barrow, *Manager*
Vicki Gensini, *IT/INT Sup*
EMP: 150
SALES (corp-wide): 36.7B **Publicly Held**
SIC: 3724 Aircraft engines & engine parts
PA: Honeywell International Inc.
    300 S Tryon St
    Charlotte NC 28202
    704 627-6200

(G-19309)
M BUCKMAN & SON CO
200 S Greenwood St (61362)
PHONE..................815 663-9411
George Buckman, *President*
EMP: 3
SQ FT: 1,500
SALES (est): 362.8K **Privately Held**
SIC: 5093 3341 Ferrous metal scrap & waste; secondary nonferrous metals

(G-19310)
MAUTINO DISTRIBUTING CO INC
501 W 1st St (61362-1204)
P.O. Box 190 (61362-0190)
PHONE..................815 664-4311
Mark Mautino, *President*
Anton F Mautino, *Admin Sec*
▲ EMP: 50
SQ FT: 36,000
SALES (est): 5.3MM **Privately Held**
SIC: 5963 2037 Bottled water delivery; fruit juices

(G-19311)
REGENEX CORP
1 Wolfer Industrial Park (61362-9601)
P.O. Box 169 (61362-0169)
PHONE..................815 663-2003
Daniel J Berent, *President*
Doug Woerner, *Plant Mgr*
EMP: 11
SALES (est): 1.1MM **Privately Held**
SIC: 2611 Pulp manufactured from waste or recycled paper

(G-19312)
RIVERFRONT MACHINE INC
6 Wolfer Industrial Park (61362-9702)
PHONE..................815 663-5000
John O Zurliene, *President*
EMP: 75
SQ FT: 90,000
SALES (est): 14.5MM **Privately Held**
SIC: 3469 Machine parts, stamped or pressed metal

Springfield
Sangamon County

(G-19313)
A & B PRINTING SERVICE INC
2122 N Republic St (62702-1851)
PHONE..................217 789-9034
Randy Bruso, *President*
Elmer Bruso, *Vice Pres*
EMP: 5
SQ FT: 2,000
SALES (est): 24.8K **Privately Held**
SIC: 2752 Commercial printing, offset

(G-19314)
ACE SIGN CO
2540 S 1st St (62704-4728)
PHONE..................217 522-8417
Dennis Bringuet, *President*

GEOGRAPHIC SECTION

Springfield - Sangamon County (G-19342)

Jo E Higgins, *General Mgr*
Brian Moulton, *General Mgr*
Ryan Williams, *Vice Pres*
Philip Mulford, *Accounts Mgr*
EMP: 23 **EST:** 1940
SALES (est): 2.8MM **Privately Held**
WEB: www.acesignco.com
SIC: 3993 Signs, not made in custom sign painting shops

(G-19315)
ACOUSTIC AVENUE INC
Also Called: Legacy Audio
3023 E Sangamon Ave (62702-1422)
PHONE.....................217 544-9810
William Dudleston, *President*
Doug Brown, *VP Sales*
Victoria Dudleston, *Marketing Mgr*
Debra Albright, *Admin Sec*
◆ **EMP:** 12
SALES (est): 2MM **Privately Held**
SIC: 3651 5064 5731 7622 Speaker systems; high fidelity equipment; radio, television & electronic stores; home entertainment repair services

(G-19316)
AFAR IMPORTS & INTERIORS INC (PA)
Also Called: Tuxhorn Drapery
3125 S Douglas Ave (62704-5813)
PHONE.....................217 744-3262
Tara McVary, *President*
EMP: 3
SQ FT: 1,200
SALES (est): 787.8K **Privately Held**
SIC: 5714 3499 5231 5713 Draperies; trophies, metal, except silver; ladders, portable: metal; wallpaper; floor covering stores; gifts & novelties; interior design services

(G-19317)
ALL AMERICAN READY MIX
2510 Richards Ln (62702)
PHONE.....................217 931-2344
Pat Mlangheim, *President*
EMP: 12
SALES (est): 1.4MM **Privately Held**
WEB: www.allamericanreadymix.com
SIC: 3273 Ready-mixed concrete

(G-19318)
ANDERSON LANETTE
1045 N Osburn Ave (62702-2419)
PHONE.....................217 284-6603
Lanette Anderson, *Owner*
EMP: 3
SALES: 20K **Privately Held**
SIC: 2844 Hair preparations, including shampoos

(G-19319)
APPROVED CONTACT LLC (PA)
1 The Elms (62712-8915)
PHONE.....................800 449-7137
Dana Sale,
Daron Worth,
EMP: 4
SALES (est): 509.5K **Privately Held**
WEB: www.approvedcontact.com
SIC: 7372 7389 Prepackaged software;

(G-19320)
ARNOLD MONUMENT CO INC (PA)
1621 Wabash Ave (62704-5310)
PHONE.....................217 546-2102
Thomas A Green Jr, *President*
Mary Green, *Corp Secy*
EMP: 7
SALES (est): 950.8K **Privately Held**
SIC: 5999 3471 3281 Monuments, finished to custom order; plating & polishing; cut stone & stone products

(G-19321)
ASSOCIATES ENGRAVING COMPANY
Also Called: Metal Decor
2601 Colt Rd (62707-9782)
P.O. Box 19452 (62794-9452)
PHONE.....................217 523-4565
Stephen Wells, *President*
Gary Hills, *Regional Mgr*

Tim Mattsson, *Purch Dir*
Kevin Dubois, *Buyer*
Diane Dolenc, *Treasurer*
▲ **EMP:** 80
SQ FT: 48,000
SALES (est): 10.4MM **Privately Held**
WEB: www.mddesigns.com
SIC: 2796 Engraving on copper, steel, wood or rubber; printing plates

(G-19322)
AWEM CORPORATION
1 W Old State Capitol Plz # 703 (62701-1200)
PHONE.....................217 670-1451
Andreas Knauer, *CEO*
EMP: 3
SALES (est): 215.2K **Privately Held**
WEB: www.awem.org
SIC: 3621 Windmills, electric generating

(G-19323)
AZTEC PRODUCTS
3321 Blueberry Ln (62711-8253)
PHONE.....................217 726-8631
Robert Lee Smith, *President*
Linda Mae Smith, *Admin Sec*
EMP: 6
SQ FT: 10,000
SALES (est): 99.4K **Privately Held**
SIC: 3069 3061 Molded rubber products; mechanical rubber goods

(G-19324)
BAILEY HARDWOODS INC
628 Kimble Ct (62703-4760)
PHONE.....................217 529-6800
Jennifer J Desart, *President*
EMP: 6
SQ FT: 6,500
SALES: 498.2K **Privately Held**
SIC: 5211 2431 3446 Millwork & lumber; staircases & stairs, wood; moldings, wood: unfinished & prefinished; architectural metalwork

(G-19325)
BI-PETRO INC (PA)
3150 Executive Park Dr (62703-4509)
P.O. Box 19246 (62794-9246)
PHONE.....................217 535-0181
Lawrence A Sweat, *CEO*
John F Homeier, *Ch of Bd*
Skippy G Homeier, *President*
Charlie Woods, *Corp Secy*
Bobby L Foreman, *Vice Pres*
EMP: 20
SQ FT: 10,000
SALES (est): 30.3MM **Privately Held**
SIC: 5171 1311 Petroleum terminals; crude petroleum production

(G-19326)
BILL WEEKS INC
Also Called: Weeks Seatcovers
229 N Grand Ave W (62702-2550)
PHONE.....................217 523-8735
Dorathy Weeks, *CEO*
Dorthory Weeks, *President*
Rodney Weeks, *President*
Delilah Weeks, *Admin Sec*
EMP: 4 **EST:** 1938
SQ FT: 9,600
SALES (est): 352.7K **Privately Held**
SIC: 7641 2399 2511 7532 Reupholstery; seat covers, automobile; wood household furniture; tops (canvas or plastic), installation or repair: automotive; motor vehicle parts & accessories

(G-19327)
BITSIO INC
920 S Spring St Ste 1200 (62704-2725)
PHONE.....................217 793-2827
Kalpana Krishnamurthi, *Mng Member*
EMP: 7
SALES: 923.2K **Privately Held**
WEB: www.bitsioinc.com
SIC: 7371 8243 7372 Computer software systems analysis & design, custom; computer software development & applications; computer software development; software programming applications; software training, computer; prepackaged software

(G-19328)
BOB FOLDER LURES CO
2071 Hazlett Rd (62707-2600)
PHONE.....................217 787-1116
Robert L Folder, *Owner*
Mary Folder, *Treasurer*
EMP: 10
SALES (est): 579.4K **Privately Held**
SIC: 3949 5091 Fishing tackle, general; flies, fishing; artificial; fishing tackle

(G-19329)
BRANDT CONSOLIDATED INC (PA)
Also Called: Agvision
2935 S Koke Mill Rd (62711-9651)
PHONE.....................217 547-5800
Glen A Brandt, *Ch of Bd*
Rick C Brandt, *President*
Bill Garver, *General Mgr*
Gregory Jackson, *Regional Mgr*
Dan Pinther, *Regional Mgr*
▼ **EMP:** 45
SQ FT: 25,000
SALES (est): 159MM **Privately Held**
WEB: www.brandt.co
SIC: 2875 5191 Fertilizers, mixing only; farm supplies

(G-19330)
BSN SPORTS LLC
510 E Apple Orchard Rd # 107 (62703-4017)
PHONE.....................217 788-0914
EMP: 6
SALES (corp-wide): 1.1B **Privately Held**
SIC: 3949 Sporting & athletic goods
HQ: Bsn Sports, Llc
14460 Varsity Brands Way
Farmers Branch TX 75244
972 484-9484

(G-19331)
BUNN-O-MATIC CORPORATION
1400 Stevenson Dr (62703-4291)
PHONE.....................217 529-6601
EMP: 4
SALES (corp-wide): 277.8MM **Privately Held**
SIC: 3589 Coffee brewing equipment
PA: Bunn-O-Matic Corporation
1400 Adlai Stevenson Dr
Springfield IL 62703
217 529-6601

(G-19332)
BUNN-O-MATIC CORPORATION
5020 Ash Grove Dr (62711-6329)
PHONE.....................562 926-0764
Scott Bennett, *Plant Mgr*
Steve Baker, *Sales Staff*
Shari Oroscio, *Manager*
Tony Eguia, *Manager*
Mark Ericsson, *Manager*
EMP: 27
SALES (corp-wide): 277.8MM **Privately Held**
SIC: 4225 2621 3634 General warehousing; filter paper; electric housewares & fans
PA: Bunn-O-Matic Corporation
1400 Adlai Stevenson Dr
Springfield IL 62703
217 529-6601

(G-19333)
BUNN-O-MATIC CORPORATION
825 S Airport Dr (62707-8486)
PHONE.....................217 528-8739
David Masterson, *Manager*
EMP: 9
SALES (corp-wide): 277.8MM **Privately Held**
SIC: 3589 Coffee brewing equipment
PA: Bunn-O-Matic Corporation
1400 Adlai Stevenson Dr
Springfield IL 62703
217 529-6601

(G-19334)
BUNN-O-MATIC CORPORATION
1500 Stevenson Dr (62703-4229)
PHONE.....................217 529-6601
EMP: 3

SALES (corp-wide): 277.8MM **Privately Held**
SIC: 3589 Asbestos removal equipment
PA: Bunn-O-Matic Corporation
1400 Adlai Stevenson Dr
Springfield IL 62703
217 529-6601

(G-19335)
CABINETLAND OF SPRINGFIELD
4340 N Peoria Rd (62702-1127)
PHONE.....................217 523-7253
Russ Hirschman, *Partner*
EMP: 6
SALES (est): 714.3K **Privately Held**
SIC: 2434 Wood kitchen cabinets

(G-19336)
CANE PLUS
2225 S Whittier Ave (62704-4651)
P.O. Box 9409 (62791-9409)
PHONE.....................217 522-4035
Ronald Earley, *President*
Maureen Earley, *Vice Pres*
Chris Redcliff, *Manager*
EMP: 4
SALES (est): 276.3K **Privately Held**
SIC: 3999 Canes & cane trimmings, except precious metal

(G-19337)
CANHAM GRAPHICS
4524 Industrial Ave (62703-5316)
P.O. Box 435, Pawnee (62558-0435)
PHONE.....................217 585-5085
Bill Canham, *Owner*
EMP: 3
SQ FT: 3,600
SALES (est): 180K **Privately Held**
SIC: 7532 3993 Truck painting & lettering; signs & advertising specialties

(G-19338)
CAPITOL CITY MACHINE
2840 Adlai Stevenson Dr B (62703-4482)
PHONE.....................217 529-0293
Tim Wilkerson, *Principal*
EMP: 2 **EST:** 2001
SALES (est): 257.6K **Privately Held**
SIC: 3599 Machine shop, jobbing & repair

(G-19339)
CAPITOL CITY TOOL & DESIGN
1330 Taylor Ave (62703-5638)
PHONE.....................217 544-9250
Michael Moe, *President*
EMP: 2 **EST:** 1951
SQ FT: 5,000
SALES (est): 250K **Privately Held**
SIC: 3544 Die sets for metal stamping (presses)

(G-19340)
CAPITOL READY-MIX INC (PA)
1900 E Mason St (62702-5812)
PHONE.....................217 528-1100
Lou Marcy, *President*
EMP: 25
SQ FT: 1,200
SALES (est): 2.9MM **Privately Held**
SIC: 3273 Ready-mixed concrete

(G-19341)
CAPITOL WOOD WORKS LLC
Also Called: Kwik-Wall Company
1010 E Edwards St (62703-1327)
PHONE.....................217 522-5553
Mike Etter, *Vice Pres*
Mike Hoyle, *CFO*
Cynthia Ingram, *Controller*
Mark Wilson, *Manager*
Tim Berry, *Info Tech Mgr*
▲ **EMP:** 75 **EST:** 1929
SQ FT: 75,000
SALES (est): 20.3MM **Privately Held**
WEB: www.kwik-wall.com
SIC: 2542 3446 2541 Partitions & fixtures, except wood; architectural metalwork; wood partitions & fixtures

(G-19342)
CAST INDUSTRIES INC
580 North St (62704-5801)
PHONE.....................217 522-8292
James Stevens, *President*

Springfield - Sangamon County (G-19343) — GEOGRAPHIC SECTION

Ron Stevens, *Vice Pres*
Sharon Stevens, *Treasurer*
EMP: 28
SQ FT: 4,500
SALES (est): 3.3MM **Privately Held**
SIC: 3949 Lures, fishing: artificial

(G-19343)
CDS OFFICE SYSTEMS INC (PA)
Also Called: Cds Office Technologies
612 S Dirksen Pkwy (62703-2183)
P.O. Box 3566 (62708-3566)
PHONE..................800 367-1508
Jerome L Watson, *President*
Markham F Watson, *President*
Russell Taylor, *Regional Mgr*
John Bolser, *Vice Pres*
Dan Matthews, *Vice Pres*
EMP: 83
SQ FT: 23,000
SALES (est): 43.8MM **Privately Held**
SIC: 5999 7629 7378 3861 Business machines & equipment; facsimile equipment; business machine repair, electric; computer maintenance & repair; photographic equipment & supplies; computer peripheral equipment; copying equipment

(G-19344)
CDS OFFICE SYSTEMS INC
Also Called: C D S Office Technologies
612 S Dirksen Pkwy (62703-2183)
PHONE..................630 305-9034
Richard Eden, *Manager*
EMP: 14
SALES (corp-wide): 43.8MM **Privately Held**
SIC: 5044 7629 5999 5943 Office equipment; business machine repair, electric; business machines & equipment; stationery stores; commercial printing, lithographic
PA: C.D.S. Office Systems Incorporated
612 S Dirksen Pkwy
Springfield IL 62703
800 367-1508

(G-19345)
CENTRAL ILL COMMUNICATIONS LLC
Also Called: Illinois Times
1240 S 6th St (62703-2408)
P.O. Box 5256 (62705-5256)
PHONE..................217 753-2226
Fletcher F Farrar Jr, *President*
EMP: 12 **EST:** 1997
SALES (est): 530K **Privately Held**
SIC: 7383 8661 2711 News reporting services for newspapers & periodicals; religious organizations; commercial printing & newspaper publishing combined

(G-19346)
CENTRAL ILLINOIS SIGN COMPANY
3040 E Linden Ave (62702-6018)
PHONE..................217 523-4740
Elloise Conaway, *President*
Fred Conaway, *Vice Pres*
EMP: 4
SQ FT: 5,000
SALES (est): 348.6K **Privately Held**
SIC: 3993 1721 7389 Electric signs; neon signs; letters for signs, metal; commercial painting; lettering & sign painting services

(G-19347)
CERTIFIED TANK & MFG LLC
2500 Richards Ln (62702-1124)
PHONE..................217 525-1433
William D Rohr, *President*
Max Bumgardner, *Administration*
Brent Brandvold,
EMP: 40
SQ FT: 50,000
SALES: 6MM **Privately Held**
SIC: 3443 Fabricated plate work (boiler shop)

(G-19348)
CHARLES C THOMAS PUBLISHER
2600 S 1st St (62704-4730)
PHONE..................217 789-8980
Cheryl Steelman, *Controller*
Darleen McCarty, *Admin Sec*
EMP: 9 **EST:** 1927
SQ FT: 50,000
SALES (est): 2MM **Privately Held**
WEB: www.ccthomas.com
SIC: 2731 2752 2732 Books: publishing only; commercial printing, lithographic; book printing

(G-19349)
CHGO DAILY LAW BULLETIN
401 S 2nd St (62701-1727)
PHONE..................217 525-6735
EMP: 3
SALES (est): 123.3K **Privately Held**
SIC: 2711 Newspapers-Publishing/Printing

(G-19350)
CHRISTIAN SPECIALIZED SERVICES
2312 S Wiggins Ave (62704-4373)
PHONE..................217 546-7338
Judy Noll, *Partner*
EMP: 3
SALES (est): 150K **Privately Held**
SIC: 8661 2741 Religious organizations; miscellaneous publishing

(G-19351)
CLEAR LAKE SAND & GRAVEL CO
2500 Shadow Chaser Dr (62711-7225)
PHONE..................217 725-6999
Ronald Drennan, *President*
David Drennan, *Vice Pres*
EMP: 10
SQ FT: 1,500
SALES (est): 900K **Privately Held**
SIC: 1442 Construction sand mining; gravel mining

(G-19352)
COCA-COLA REFRESHMENTS USA INC
3495 E Sangamon Ave (62707-9731)
PHONE..................217 544-4892
Jeff Ryan, *Branch Mgr*
EMP: 50
SALES (corp-wide): 37.2B **Publicly Held**
SIC: 2086 5182 Bottled & canned soft drinks; neutral spirits
HQ: Coca-Cola Refreshments Usa, Inc.
2500 Windy Ridge Pkwy Se
Atlanta GA 30339
770 989-3000

(G-19353)
CONNECTIONS
511 E Ash St (62703-3101)
PHONE..................217 553-7920
Marcella Little Brownlee, *Owner*
EMP: 10
SALES: 35K **Privately Held**
SIC: 3549 Assembly machines, including robotic

(G-19354)
CONTECH ENGNERED SOLUTIONS LLC
1110 Stevenson Dr (62703-4222)
PHONE..................217 529-5461
Dick Stultz, *Plant Engr*
Doug Bower, *Branch Mgr*
EMP: 50
SQ FT: 55,000 **Privately Held**
WEB: www.conteches.com
SIC: 3443 Fabricated plate work (boiler shop)
HQ: Contech Engineered Solutions Llc
9025 Centre Pointe Dr # 400
West Chester OH 45069
513 645-7000

(G-19355)
CRATE AND PALLET PACKG CO LLC
401 Colbrook Dr (62702-3370)
PHONE..................217 679-2681
Gerald Vondebur,
Maura McCormick,
EMP: 50 **EST:** 2008
SALES: 2.5MM **Privately Held**
WEB: www.crateandpallet.com
SIC: 2448 Pallets, wood

(G-19356)
CREASEY PRINTING SERVICES INC
1905 Morning Sun Ln (62711-5635)
PHONE..................217 787-1055
William Creasey, *CEO*
Kelli Lynch, *President*
Greg Lynch, *Corp Secy*
Suzy Creasey, *Exec VP*
Sydney Lynch, *Assistant*
EMP: 7
SALES (est): 919K **Privately Held**
SIC: 2741 2752 2732 Catalogs: publishing & printing; commercial printing, lithographic; book printing

(G-19357)
CUSTOM CHEMICAL INC
Also Called: Custom Chemical Engineering
4524 Industrial Ave (62703-5316)
P.O. Box 3191 (62708-3191)
PHONE..................217 529-0878
Jack D Fair, *President*
Virgene Fair, *Corp Secy*
Scott Fair, *Vice Pres*
EMP: 4
SQ FT: 7,000
SALES (est): 628.3K **Privately Held**
SIC: 2899 2851 2841 2869 Water treating compounds; paint removers; soap: granulated, liquid, cake, flaked or chip; industrial organic chemicals

(G-19358)
CUSTOM WOODWORK & INTERIORS (PA)
Also Called: Gary Bryan Kitchens & Bath
3208 S Douglas Ave (62704-5816)
PHONE..................217 546-0006
Michael P Bedolli, *President*
Doris Pierce, *Vice Pres*
Sharon Bedolli, *Treasurer*
EMP: 17 **EST:** 1976
SQ FT: 30,000
SALES (est): 4.3MM **Privately Held**
WEB: www.garybryankitchens.com
SIC: 5211 2541 2434 Lumber & other building materials; wood partitions & fixtures; vanities, bathroom: wood

(G-19359)
DAL ACRES WEST KENNEL
2508 W Jefferson St (62702-3405)
PHONE..................217 793-3647
Patricia Hudspeth, *President*
Kathy Knoles, *Owner*
EMP: 6
SALES (est): 452.1K **Privately Held**
SIC: 3999 Pet supplies

(G-19360)
DR PEPPER/7 UP BOTTLING GROUP
4600 Industrial Ave (62703-5318)
PHONE..................217 585-1496
Jamil Saba, *Principal*
EMP: 7
SALES (est): 538K **Privately Held**
SIC: 2086 Soft drinks: packaged in cans, bottles, etc.

(G-19361)
ELLIOT INST FOR SCIAL SCNCES R
Also Called: ACORN BOOK
524 E Lawrence Ave (62703-2319)
P.O. Box 194, Saint Peters MO (63376-0003)
PHONE..................217 525-8202
David C Reardon, *Exec Dir*
David Reardon, *Exec Dir*
EMP: 3
SALES: 105.1K **Privately Held**
WEB: www.afterabortion.org
SIC: 2731 2741 8733 Books: publishing only; pamphlets: publishing only, not printed on site; newsletter publishing; noncommercial research organizations

(G-19362)
EMBROIDEA CUSTOM EMBROIDERY
60 Providence Ln (62711-8024)
PHONE..................217 698-6422
Zileide Giddings, *Manager*
EMP: 3 **EST:** 2009
SALES (est): 194K **Privately Held**
WEB: www.embroidea.com
SIC: 2395 Embroidery & art needlework

(G-19363)
ENVIRNMNTAL CTRL SOLUTIONS INC (PA)
Also Called: Ecsi
2020 Timberbrook Dr (62702-4627)
PHONE..................217 793-8966
Steven Foster, *President*
Chris Benson, *Vice Pres*
EMP: 7
SQ FT: 5,000
SALES (est): 981.4K **Privately Held**
SIC: 3625 5063 Relays & industrial controls; motor controls, starters & relays: electric

(G-19364)
F J MURPHY & SON INC
1800 Factory St (62702-2820)
PHONE..................217 787-3477
Robert L Murphy, *Ch of Bd*
John M Pasko, *President*
Roger Marmor, *Senior VP*
Brian Sickinger, *Vice Pres*
EMP: 60 **EST:** 1956
SQ FT: 23,000
SALES (est): 8.9MM **Privately Held**
WEB: www.fjmurphy.com
SIC: 1711 3321 Plumbing contractors; warm air heating & air conditioning contractor; fire sprinkler system installation; gray & ductile iron foundries

(G-19365)
FARMER BROS CO
Also Called: Farmers Brothers Coffee
3430c Constitution Dr (62711-9402)
PHONE..................217 787-7565
Frank Carol, *Manager*
EMP: 8
SALES (corp-wide): 595.9MM **Publicly Held**
SIC: 2095 5149 Coffee roasting (except by wholesale grocers); coffee & tea
PA: Farmer Bros. Co.
1912 Farmer Brothers Dr
Northlake TX 76262
888 998-2468

(G-19366)
FERENBACH MARUCCO STODDARD
Also Called: MSF&w
3445 Liberty Dr (62704-6521)
PHONE..................217 698-3535
John Marucco, *President*
Darrel Stoddard, *Admin Sec*
Darrell Stoddard, *Admin Sec*
EMP: 39
SQ FT: 8,000
SALES: 4MM **Privately Held**
SIC: 7371 7372 Computer software systems analysis & design, custom; prepackaged software

(G-19367)
FINANCIAL AND PROFESSIONAL REG
Also Called: State Comptroller Print Shop
325 W Adams St Lbby (62704-7306)
PHONE..................217 782-2127
Rhonda Rathbone, *Branch Mgr*
EMP: 5 **Privately Held**
WEB: www.idfpr.com
SIC: 2752 9311 Commercial printing, lithographic; finance, taxation & monetary policy;
HQ: Illinois Department Of Financial And Professional Regulation
320 W Washington St Fl 3
Springfield IL 62701
217 785-0820

(G-19368)
FIRST ELECTRIC MOTOR SHOP INC
1130 W Reynolds St (62702-2311)
PHONE..................217 698-0672
Jack Burris Jr, *President*
Dave Burris, *Vice Pres*

GEOGRAPHIC SECTION
Springfield - Sangamon County (G-19396)

EMP: 4 **EST:** 1949
SQ FT: 4,600
SALES: 531K Privately Held
SIC: 7694 5999 Electric motor repair; motors, electric

(G-19369)
FIRST STEP WOMENS CENTER
104 E North Grand Ave A (62702-3693)
PHONE......................217 523-0100
Gregory Brewer, *Principal*
Debbie Shultz, *Principal*
EMP: 4
SALES: 288K Privately Held
WEB: www.firststepwomenscenter.org
SIC: 8011 2899 Primary care medical clinic;

(G-19370)
FREEMAN ENERGY CORPORATION (DH)
3008 Happy Landing Dr (62711-6259)
PHONE......................217 698-3949
Walter A Gregory, *President*
EMP: 10
SALES (est): 114.6MM
SALES (corp-wide): 39.3B Publicly Held
SIC: 1241 Coal mining services

(G-19371)
FREEMAN UNITED COAL MINING CO (DH)
4440 Ash Grove Dr Ste A (62711-6423)
PHONE......................217 698-3300
Walter Gregory, *President*
Victor Vencill, *Corp Secy*
Michael Caldwell, *Vice Pres*
EMP: 33
SQ FT: 10,000
SALES (est): 54.9MM
SALES (corp-wide): 39.3B Publicly Held
SIC: 1241 Coal mining exploration & test boring

(G-19372)
FRYE-WILLIAMSON PRESS INC
901 N Macarthur Blvd (62702-2307)
P.O. Box 1057 (62705-1057)
PHONE......................217 522-7744
Richard Lee Serena, *President*
Lynn Serena, *Vice Pres*
Steve Kesegi, *Executive*
AMI Teegarden, *Representative*
EMP: 29
SQ FT: 12,000
SALES (est): 5.6MM Privately Held
WEB: www.fryewilliamson.com
SIC: 2759 2752 Commercial printing; commercial printing, offset

(G-19373)
GATEHOUSE MEDIA LLC
State Journal-Register, The
1 Copley Plz (62701-1927)
PHONE......................217 788-1300
Patrick Coburn, *Principal*
EMP: 375
SQ FT: 80,000
SALES (corp-wide): 1.8B Publicly Held
SIC: 2711 2791 2752 Newspapers, publishing & printing; typesetting; commercial printing, lithographic
HQ: Gatehouse Media, Llc
175 Sullys Trl Fl 3
Pittsford NY 14534
585 598-0030

(G-19374)
GATEHUSE MDIA ILL HLDNGS II IN
Also Called: State Journal Register, The
1 Copley Plz (62701-1927)
PHONE......................217 788-1300
Patrick Coburn, *Principal*
Gary Schieffer, *Editor*
Daron Walker, *Editor*
Kristi Muller, *Opers Staff*
Suzanne Lair, *Asst Controller*
EMP: 375
SALES (est): 28.6MM
SALES (corp-wide): 1.8B Publicly Held
SIC: 2711 Commercial printing & newspaper publishing combined

PA: Gannett Co., Inc.
7950 Jones Branch Dr
Mc Lean VA 22102
703 854-6000

(G-19375)
GOLD STANDARD ENTERPRISES INC
Also Called: Binnys Beverage Depot
2490 Wabash Ave (62704-4201)
PHONE......................217 546-1633
EMP: 28
SALES (corp-wide): 66.4MM Privately Held
SIC: 5921 5149 2086 Liquor stores; beverages, except coffee & tea; bottled & canned soft drinks
PA: Gold Standard Enterprises, Inc.
5100 Dempster St
Skokie IL 60077
847 674-4200

(G-19376)
GONE FOR GOOD
101 N 16th St (62703-1101)
PHONE......................217 753-0414
Char Fanning, *Principal*
EMP: 3
SALES (est): 300.3K Privately Held
SIC: 3559 Tire shredding machinery

(G-19377)
HABEGGER CORPORATION
Also Called: Rsp
2900 Old Rochester Rd (62703-5659)
PHONE......................217 789-4328
Matt Cassidy, *Branch Mgr*
Doug Gholson, *Manager*
EMP: 3
SALES (corp-wide): 78.3MM Privately Held
SIC: 3585 Refrigeration & heating equipment
PA: The Habegger Corporation
4995 Winton Rd
Cincinnati OH 45232
513 853-6644

(G-19378)
HART - CLAYTON INC
2000 E Cornell Ave Ste 2 (62703-3396)
PHONE......................217 525-1610
George Hart, *President*
Lorraine Hart, *Corp Secy*
Benjamin Klaves, *Sales Dir*
EMP: 14
SQ FT: 17,000
SALES (est): 1.9MM Privately Held
SIC: 2448 Pallets, wood

(G-19379)
HEART 4 HEART INC (PA)
2924 N Dirksen Pkwy (62702-1434)
PHONE......................217 544-2699
Gerald Davis, *President*
Luann Davis, *Vice Pres*
EMP: 7
SQ FT: 4,000
SALES (est): 1.2MM Privately Held
WEB: www.heart4heart.com
SIC: 3842 Wheelchairs

(G-19380)
HEARTLAND COCA-COLA BTLG LLC
3495 E Sangamon Ave (62707-9731)
PHONE......................217 544-4891
Bradley Harden, *Manager*
EMP: 3090
SALES (corp-wide): 23.9B Privately Held
SIC: 5149 2086 Beverages, except coffee & tea; carbonated beverages, nonalcoholic; bottled & canned
PA: Heartland Coca-Cola Bottling Company Llc
9000 Marshall Dr
Lenexa KS

(G-19381)
HEARTLAND PUBLICATIONS INC
7900 Olde Carriage Way (62712-6829)
PHONE......................217 529-9506
Lynell Loftus, *Principal*
EMP: 2

SALES (est): 250.3K Privately Held
SIC: 2741 Miscellaneous publishing

(G-19382)
HORSE CREEK OUTFITTERS
600 S Dirksen Pkwy 600a (62703-2111)
PHONE......................217 544-2740
Mandy McCormick, *Owner*
EMP: 9
SQ FT: 4,000
SALES: 300K Privately Held
SIC: 5699 3144 Western apparel; boots, canvas or leather; women's

(G-19383)
HUNT CHARLES
3161 W White Oaks Dr (62704-7406)
PHONE......................217 793-5151
Hunt Charles, *Principal*
EMP: 3 **EST:** 2010
SALES (est): 161.8K Privately Held
WEB: www.charleshuntonline.com
SIC: 3519 Internal combustion engines

(G-19384)
ILL DEPT NATURAL RESOURCES
Land Reclaimation Div
1 Natural Resources Way # 100 (62702-1290)
PHONE......................217 782-4970
Don Pflederer, *Branch Mgr*
EMP: 16 Privately Held
SIC: 1411 9512 Dimension stone;
HQ: Illinois Department Of Natural Resources
1 Natural Resources Way # 100
Springfield IL 62702

(G-19385)
ILLINOIS ASSN CNTY OFFICIALS
Also Called: IACO
1417 James St (62703-5379)
P.O. Box 9296 (62791-9296)
PHONE......................217 585-9065
Scott Erickson, *President*
EMP: 17
SALES: 175.3K Privately Held
SIC: 8641 7372 Educator's association; application computer software

(G-19386)
ILLINOIS INST CNTNG LEGL ED
Also Called: IICLE
2395 W Jefferson St (62702-2209)
PHONE......................217 787-2080
Carole Chew, *Editor*
Angela Moody, *Publications*
Megan Smith, *Marketing Staff*
Chris Hull, *Manager*
Barton Lorimor, *Manager*
EMP: 49
SQ FT: 11,000
SALES: 3.6MM Privately Held
SIC: 8244 2731 Business & secretarial schools; book publishing

(G-19387)
ILLINOIS NEWSPAPER IN EDUCATN
1 Copley Plz (62701-1927)
P.O. Box 280, Arlington Heights (60006-0280)
PHONE......................847 427-4388
Susan Groves, *President*
Edith Weaver, *President*
EMP: 10
SALES (est): 380.2K Privately Held
SIC: 2711 Newspapers, publishing & printing

(G-19388)
IMCO PRECAST LLC
4390 Jeffory St (62703-5344)
PHONE......................217 742-5300
Dan Sheley, *Principal*
Patricia Sheley, *Mng Member*
EMP: 3
SALES: 130K Privately Held
SIC: 3272 Concrete products, precast

(G-19389)
INFORMATIVE SYSTEMS INC
Also Called: ISI Printing
5119 Old Route 36 (62707-3124)
P.O. Box 13347 (62791-3347)
PHONE......................217 523-8422
James A Palazzolo, *President*
Maryann Palazzolo, *Vice Pres*
EMP: 10
SQ FT: 12,000
SALES (est): 1.5MM Privately Held
SIC: 5112 2752 2791 Business forms; commercial printing, offset; typesetting

(G-19390)
ITG BRANDS LLC
900 Christopher Ln Ste 7 (62712-8707)
PHONE......................217 529-5746
Mary Kessler, *CEO*
EMP: 4
SALES (corp-wide): 40B Privately Held
SIC: 5194 2111 Cigars; cigarettes
HQ: Itg Brands, Llc
714 Green Valley Rd
Greensboro NC 27408
336 335-7000

(G-19391)
J & J ELECTRIC MOTOR REPAIR SP
2800 S 11th St (62703-4170)
PHONE......................217 529-0015
James W Riba, *President*
Sandra Riba, *Corp Secy*
Robin Riba, *Vice Pres*
EMP: 5
SQ FT: 2,880
SALES (est): 973.2K Privately Held
SIC: 7694 Electric motor repair

(G-19392)
J GOOCH & ASSOCIATES INC
Also Called: Gooch & Associates Printing
140 W Lenox Ave (62704-4713)
PHONE......................217 522-7575
James Feagans, *President*
Sherry Feagans, *Vice Pres*
EMP: 7
SQ FT: 5,800
SALES (est): 760K Privately Held
SIC: 2752 2761 Commercial printing, offset; manifold business forms

(G-19393)
JAVA EXPRESS
1827 N Peoria Rd (62702-2756)
PHONE......................217 525-2430
EMP: 9
SALES (est): 340K Privately Held
SIC: 2741 Misc Publishing

(G-19394)
JEFF E ALLEN
Also Called: Hammer Down Construction
1928 E Watch Ave (62702-3027)
PHONE......................217 801-6878
Jeff E Allen, *Owner*
EMP: 6
SALES: 150K Privately Held
SIC: 1389 Construction, repair & dismantling services

(G-19395)
JEFFERIES ORCHARD SAWMILL
1016 Jefferies Rd (62707-8578)
PHONE......................217 487-7582
Dale Jefferies, *Principal*
EMP: 5
SALES (est): 687.5K Privately Held
SIC: 2421 Sawmills & planing mills, general

(G-19396)
L P S EXPRESS INC
1620 S 5th St Ste A (62703-3174)
PHONE......................217 636-7683
Roger Krick, *President*
Roger Kreck, *President*
EMP: 5
SALES (est): 861.1K Privately Held
SIC: 2893 7378 Printing ink; computer peripheral equipment repair & maintenance

Springfield - Sangamon County (G-19397)

(G-19397)
LAKE AREA DISPOSAL SERVICE INC
Also Called: Lake Area Recycling Services
2742 S 6th St (62703-4070)
PHONE...................................217 522-9271
Donny Crenshaw, *Manager*
EMP: 20
SALES (corp-wide): 4.7MM **Privately Held**
WEB: www.lakeareadisposal.com
SIC: 4953 5093 3341 2611 Recycling, waste materials; metal scrap & waste materials; secondary nonferrous metals; pulp mills
PA: Lake Area Disposal Service, Inc.
2106 E Cornell Ave
Springfield IL 62703
217 522-9317

(G-19398)
LEGAL FILES SOFTWARE INC
801 S Durkin Dr Ste A (62704-6028)
PHONE...................................217 726-6000
John Kanoski, *CEO*
Ron Kanoski, *Chairman*
Hope Engelmann, *Project Mgr*
Amanda Schoon, *Project Mgr*
Shannon Hermes, *Bookkeeper*
EMP: 30 **EST:** 1990
SQ FT: 8,000
SALES (est): 3.6MM **Privately Held**
WEB: www.legalfiles.com
SIC: 7372 Business oriented computer software

(G-19399)
LOCAL 46 TRAINING PROGRAM TR
2888 E Cook St (62703-2167)
PHONE...................................217 528-4041
EMP: 7
SALES: 183.3K **Privately Held**
SIC: 1389 8631 Construction, repair & dismantling services; labor unions & similar labor organizations

(G-19400)
LONG ELEVATOR AND MCH CO INC (DH)
2908 Old Rochester Rd (62703-5659)
P.O. Box 500, Riverton (62561-0500)
PHONE...................................217 629-9648
Patrick Long, *President*
Warren Long Jr, *Treasurer*
Michael Long, *Admin Sec*
EMP: 60 **EST:** 1929
SQ FT: 48,000
SALES (est): 8.3MM
SALES (corp-wide): 11B **Privately Held**
SIC: 3534 7699 Elevators & equipment; elevators: inspection, service & repair
HQ: Kone Inc.
4225 Naperville Rd # 400
Lisle IL 60532
630 577-1650

(G-19401)
MAGROS PROCESSING
3150 Stanton St (62703-4318)
PHONE...................................217 438-2880
Tony Magro, *President*
EMP: 4
SALES (est): 438.5K **Privately Held**
SIC: 2011 Meat packing plants

(G-19402)
MANSEEMANWANT LLC
4055 W Jefferson St (62707-7705)
PHONE...................................217 610-8888
James Ellenberg,
EMP: 5
SALES (est): 155K **Privately Held**
SIC: 3944 5731 Electronic games & toys; radio, television & electronic stores

(G-19403)
MAXIM INC
2709 E Ash St (62703-5606)
PHONE...................................217 544-7015
Charles T Merrill, *President*
EMP: 13
SALES (est): 1.9MM **Privately Held**
SIC: 3711 3714 Automobile assembly, including specialty automobiles; motor vehicle parts & accessories

(G-19404)
MEL-O-CREAM DONUTS INTL INC
5456 International Pkwy (62711-7086)
PHONE...................................217 483-1825
David W Waltrip, *President*
Dan Alewelt, *Prdtn Mgr*
Tad Barrow, *Warehouse Mgr*
Jeff Alexander, *Purch Mgr*
Jim Eck, *Research*
EMP: 80 **EST:** 1932
SQ FT: 73,000
SALES (est): 19MM **Privately Held**
WEB: www.mel-o-cream.com
SIC: 2051 5142 5149 2053 Bread, cake & related products; bakery products, partially cooked (except frozen); doughnuts, except frozen; crullers, except frozen; bakery products, frozen; bakery products; doughnuts, frozen

(G-19405)
MERVIS INDUSTRIES INC
Also Called: Mervis Recycling
1100 S 9th St (62703-2523)
PHONE...................................217 753-1492
David Sample, *Branch Mgr*
EMP: 6
SALES (corp-wide): 161.2MM **Privately Held**
SIC: 4953 3341 5093 5051 Recycling, waste materials; secondary nonferrous metals; metal scrap & waste materials; steel
PA: Mervis Industries, Inc.
3295 E Main St Ste C
Danville IL 61834
217 442-5300

(G-19406)
MICHAEL P JONES
Also Called: Jones Watch and Jewelry Repair
3124 Montvale Dr Ste C (62704-6938)
PHONE...................................217 787-7457
Michael P Jones, *Owner*
EMP: 4
SQ FT: 1,100
SALES (est): 268.8K **Privately Held**
SIC: 7631 3911 Jewelry repair services; watch repair; jewel settings & mountings, precious metal

(G-19407)
MIDWEST FIBER SOLUTIONS
1600 Hunter Ridge Dr (62704-6580)
PHONE...................................217 971-7400
Robert Patterson, *Principal*
EMP: 3
SALES (est): 500.7K **Privately Held**
SIC: 3643 Current-carrying wiring devices

(G-19408)
MPC GLOBAL LLC
1800 E Adams St (62703-1127)
PHONE...................................816 399-4710
Manuel Pereira, *CEO*
James E Bauser, *Manager*
EMP: 8
SQ FT: 10,000
SALES (est): 2.2MM **Privately Held**
SIC: 3519 5082 Diesel, semi-diesel or duel-fuel engines, including marine; mining machinery & equipment, except petroleum

(G-19409)
MR AUTO ELECTRIC
2649 E Cook St (62703-1901)
PHONE...................................217 523-3659
Michael Atterberry, *Owner*
EMP: 4
SQ FT: 2,200
SALES: 250K **Privately Held**
SIC: 3714 7539 Motor vehicle electrical equipment; electrical services

(G-19410)
NAPIER MACHINE & WELDING INC
2519 South Grand Ave E (62703-5614)
P.O. Box 1239 (62705-1239)
PHONE...................................217 525-8740
Keith Napier, *President*
EMP: 2 **EST:** 1946
SQ FT: 6,000
SALES (est): 302.2K **Privately Held**
SIC: 3599 7692 7629 Machine shop, jobbing & repair; welding repair; electrical repair shops

(G-19411)
NIEMANN FOODS INC
Also Called: Cub Foods 83
3001 S Veterans Pkwy (62704-6405)
PHONE...................................217 793-4091
Rick Gardner, *Manager*
EMP: 250
SQ FT: 62,000
SALES (corp-wide): 79K **Privately Held**
SIC: 5411 5992 5812 2051 Supermarkets, chain; florists; eating places; bread, cake & related products
PA: Niemann Foods, Inc.
923 N 12th St
Quincy IL 62301
217 221-5600

(G-19412)
NPI HOLDING CORP (DH)
1500 Taylor Ave (62703-5663)
PHONE...................................217 391-1229
Darryl Rosser, *President*
EMP: 6
SALES (est): 93.1MM **Privately Held**
SIC: 3083 3089 5033 3444 Plastic finished products, laminated; extruded finished plastic products; fiberglass building materials; awnings, sheet metal; investment holding companies, except banks
HQ: Stabilit America, Inc.
285 Industrial Dr
Moscow TN 38057
901 877-3010

(G-19413)
NUDO PRODUCTS INC
2508 South Grand Ave E (62703-5613)
PHONE...................................217 528-5636
Patrick Eudo, *Vice Pres*
EMP: 125 **Privately Held**
WEB: www.nudo.com
SIC: 3083 Plastic finished products, laminated
HQ: Nudo Products, Inc.
1500 Taylor Ave
Springfield IL 62703
217 528-5636

(G-19414)
NUDO PRODUCTS INC (DH)
1500 Taylor Ave (62703-5663)
PHONE...................................217 528-5636
Darryl Rosser, *President*
Blake Ward, *Business Mgr*
Charles Pineau, *COO*
Mark Jutte, *Vice Pres*
George Drobnack, *Buyer*
▲ **EMP:** 183
SQ FT: 250,000
SALES (est): 92.4MM **Privately Held**
WEB: www.nudo.com
SIC: 3083 3089 5033 3444 Plastic finished products, laminated; extruded finished plastic products; fiberglass building materials; awnings, sheet metal
HQ: Npi Holding Corp.
1500 Taylor Ave
Springfield IL 62703
217 391-1229

(G-19415)
O-DONUTS INC (PA)
Also Called: Mel-O-Cream Donuts
227 E Laurel St (62704-3947)
PHONE...................................217 544-4644
Christopher K Weihmeir, *President*
Dennis Leland, *Sales Staff*
EMP: 12 **EST:** 1970
SALES (est): 3.3MM **Privately Held**
SIC: 5461 2051 Doughnuts; doughnuts, except frozen

(G-19416)
OCTAPHARMA PLASMA INC
1770 Wabash Ave (62704-5302)
PHONE...................................217 546-8605
Dallas York, *Branch Mgr*
Tiffany Barnes, *Asst Mgr*
Lance McNicoll, *Asst Mgr*
EMP: 3
SALES (corp-wide): 2B **Privately Held**
WEB: www.octapharma.se
SIC: 2836 Plasmas
HQ: Octapharma Nordic Ab
Elersvagen 40
Stockholm 112 5
850 126-565

(G-19417)
OGLESBY & OGLESBY GUNMAKERS
744 W Andrew Rd (62707-4626)
PHONE...................................217 487-7100
William D Oglesby, *President*
EMP: 7
SALES: 3MM **Privately Held**
SIC: 3484 7699 5941 Guns (firearms) or gun parts, 30 mm. & below; gun parts made to individual order; firearms

(G-19418)
ORATECH INC
4777 Alex Blvd (62711-6346)
PHONE...................................217 793-2735
Norman Ross, *President*
Lisa Barker, *Office Mgr*
EMP: 30
SQ FT: 2,000
SALES (est): 1.6MM **Privately Held**
WEB: www.oratechlabs.com
SIC: 8072 3843 Crown & bridge production; dental equipment & supplies

(G-19419)
PANHANDLE EASTRN PIPE LINE LP
1801 Business Park Dr (62703-5626)
PHONE...................................217 753-1108
Paul Degenhart, *Branch Mgr*
EMP: 34 **Publicly Held**
WEB: www.peplmessenger.energytransfer.com
SIC: 1389 Pipe testing, oil field service
HQ: Panhandle Eastern Pipe Line Company, Lp
8111 Westchester Dr # 600
Dallas TX 75225
214 981-0700

(G-19420)
PARKWAY PRINTERS
3755 N Dirksen Pkwy (62707-7612)
PHONE...................................217 525-2485
Charles Martin, *Owner*
EMP: 2
SALES (est): 218.4K **Privately Held**
SIC: 2752 Commercial printing, offset

(G-19421)
PAWNEE OIL CORPORATION
1204 N 5th St (62702-3818)
P.O. Box 1425 (62705-1425)
PHONE...................................217 522-5440
Frank Vala, *President*
Rosalie Mc Dermott, *Corp Secy*
EMP: 10
SQ FT: 2,400
SALES (est): 1.1MM **Privately Held**
SIC: 1311 Crude petroleum production

(G-19422)
PEASES INC (PA)
Also Called: Pease's Candy Shops
1701 S State St (62704-4011)
PHONE...................................217 523-3721
Robert M Flesher, *President*
Douglas Anderson, *Vice Pres*
EMP: 12 **EST:** 1930
SQ FT: 1,200
SALES (est): 2.9MM **Privately Held**
WEB: www.peasescandy.com
SIC: 5441 2064 Candy; nuts; candy & other confectionery products

GEOGRAPHIC SECTION
Springfield - Sangamon County (G-19451)

(G-19423)
PEASES INC
4753 Jeffory St (62703-5377)
PHONE..................217 529-2912
Fax: 217 391-0168
EMP: 15
SALES (corp-wide): 2.4MM **Privately Held**
SIC: 5441 2068 2066 2064 Ret Candy/Confectionery Mfg Roasted Nuts/Seeds Mfg Chocolate/Cocoa Prdt Mfg Candy/Confectionery
PA: Pease's, Inc.
1701 S State St
Springfield IL 62704
217 523-3721

(G-19424)
PERTEN INSTRUMENTS INC
3200 Robbins Rd Ste 100a (62704-6534)
P.O. Box 13424 (62791-3424)
PHONE..................217 585-9440
Gavin O'Reilly, *President*
EMP: 35
SQ FT: 10,000
SALES (est): 5.8MM
SALES (corp-wide): 355.8K **Privately Held**
SIC: 8734 3821 Testing laboratories; laboratory measuring apparatus
HQ: Perten Instruments Ab
Instrumentvagen 31
Hagersten 126 5
888 099-0

(G-19425)
PETERSBURG POWER WASHING INC
Also Called: Petersburg Painting & Pwr Wshg
829 S. 11th St (62703-1716)
PHONE..................217 415-9013
Donna Hillyer, *President*
Richard Hillyer, *Vice Pres*
EMP: 14
SALES: 100K **Privately Held**
SIC: 3479 7349 7389 Etching & engraving; building & office cleaning services; swimming pool & hot tub service & maintenance

(G-19426)
POOL CENTER INC
3740 Wabash Ave Ste C (62711-9622)
PHONE..................217 698-7665
Edward Osman, *President*
Diane Osman, *Admin Sec*
EMP: 2
SALES (est): 1MM **Privately Held**
SIC: 8748 1389 7389 Business consulting; construction, repair & dismantling services; swimming pool & hot tub service & maintenance

(G-19427)
PREMIUM PALLETS
2877 N Dirksen Pkwy (62702-1408)
PHONE..................217 974-0155
EMP: 4
SALES (est): 265.9K **Privately Held**
SIC: 2448 Pallets, wood

(G-19428)
PRESS FUEL
2501 Wabash Ave (62704-4276)
PHONE..................217 546-9606
Chris Homeier, *Principal*
EMP: 4
SALES (est): 156.1K **Privately Held**
WEB: www.freshfuel.la
SIC: 2741 Miscellaneous publishing

(G-19429)
PRIMO DESIGNS INC
2417 E North Grand Ave B (62702-4365)
PHONE..................217 523-6373
Leonard A Naumovich, *President*
Nick Naumovich, *Prdtn Mgr*
Paul Cumby, *Sales Staff*
Thomas Wayland, *Shareholder*
EMP: 10
SQ FT: 2,200
SALES (est): 278.8K **Privately Held**
SIC: 2759 Screen printing

(G-19430)
PT HOLDINGS INC (PA)
2 White Oak Rd (62711-9206)
PHONE..................217 691-1793
William Patrick Riters, *President*
Timothy M Lyons, *Admin Sec*
EMP: 8
SALES (est): 6.4MM **Privately Held**
SIC: 6719 3469 Personal holding companies, except banks; kitchen fixtures & equipment, porcelain enameled; kitchen fixtures & equipment: metal, except cast aluminum

(G-19431)
PURE SKIN LLC
27 Forest Rdg (62712-8910)
PHONE..................217 679-6267
Marivic Lohse, *Principal*
EMP: 7 EST: 2013
SALES (est): 699.6K **Privately Held**
SIC: 2657 1799 Paperboard backs for blister or skin packages; spa or hot tub installation or construction

(G-19432)
REFRESHMENT SERVICES INC
Also Called: Pepsico
1337 E Cook St (62703)
PHONE..................217 522-8841
Keith Creceoious, *Manager*
EMP: 50
SALES (corp-wide): 88.8MM **Privately Held**
SIC: 2086 Carbonated soft drinks, bottled & canned
PA: Refreshment Services, Inc.
1121 Locust St
Quincy IL 62301
217 223-8600

(G-19433)
RICHARDS & STEHMAN LLC
317 E Monroe St (62701-1408)
PHONE..................217 522-6801
Ann Burton,
Larry Burton,
Katherine L Dobron,
EMP: 3 EST: 1954
SQ FT: 1,500
SALES (est): 283.6K **Privately Held**
SIC: 3953 Marking devices

(G-19434)
RICHARDSON MANUFACTURING CO
2209 Old Jacksonville Rd (62704-2299)
PHONE..................217 546-2249
William L Richardson Jr, *President*
Michael Corry, *Business Mgr*
W L Richardson Jr, *Corp Secy*
Jeff Richardson, *Vice Pres*
Ian Richardson, *Project Mgr*
EMP: 100
SQ FT: 125,000
SALES (est): 22.4MM **Privately Held**
WEB: www.rmc-bigcnc.com
SIC: 3599 Machine shop, jobbing & repair

(G-19435)
ROLLING MEADOWS BREWERY LLC
1660 W Leland Ave (62704-3388)
PHONE..................217 725-2492
Caren C Trudeau, *Mng Member*
EMP: 3
SALES (est): 280K **Privately Held**
SIC: 2082 Brewers' grain

(G-19436)
RUDIN PRINTING COMPANY INC
927 E Jackson St (62701-1914)
PHONE..................217 528-5111
Carl P Rudin, *President*
Chris Rudin, *General Mgr*
EMP: 12
SQ FT: 4,000
SALES (est): 1.2MM **Privately Held**
WEB: www.rudinprinting.com
SIC: 2752 7334 2791 2789 Commercial printing, offset; photocopying & duplicating services; typesetting; bookbinding & related work

(G-19437)
RUYLE INCORPORATED
1325 Ne Bond St (62703)
PHONE..................309 674-6644
Chris Benson, *Vice Pres*
Kimberly Whitfield, *Admin Asst*
EMP: 50 EST: 2007
SALES (est): 3.5MM **Privately Held**
WEB: www.ruylecorp.com
SIC: 1711 5075 3585 Warm air heating & air conditioning contractor; air conditioning & ventilation equipment & supplies; refrigeration & heating equipment

(G-19438)
SAGA COMMUNICATIONS INC
Also Called: Illinois Radio Network
3501 E Sangamon Ave (62707-9777)
PHONE..................248 631-8099
Sharon Johnson, *Principal*
Dennis Mellott, *Branch Mgr*
EMP: 7 **Publicly Held**
SIC: 3663 Radio receiver networks
PA: Saga Communications, Inc.
73 Kercheval Ave
Grosse Pointe Farms MI 48236

(G-19439)
SARA LEE BAKING GROUP
6100 S 2nd St (62711-7405)
PHONE..................217 585-3462
EMP: 4
SALES (est): 219.9K **Privately Held**
SIC: 2051 Mfg Bread/Related Products

(G-19440)
SCUBA SPORTS INC
1609 S Macarthur Blvd (62704-3622)
PHONE..................217 787-3483
Jeff Unland, *President*
EMP: 4
SQ FT: 500
SALES (est): 411.1K **Privately Held**
WEB: www.scubasports.net
SIC: 5941 7999 3949 5091 Skin diving, scuba equipment & supplies; scuba & skin diving instruction; sporting & athletic goods; diving equipment & supplies

(G-19441)
SELVAGGIO ORNA & STRL STL INC
Also Called: Selvaggio Steel
1119 W Dorlan Ave (62702-2302)
PHONE..................217 528-4077
Mark Selvaggio, *President*
Tony Selvaggio, *Vice Pres*
Luke Lowe, *Project Mgr*
EMP: 24
SQ FT: 18,000
SALES (est): 8.2MM **Privately Held**
WEB: www.selvaggiosteel.com
SIC: 3441 3446 Fabricated structural metal; architectural metalwork

(G-19442)
SENIOR NEWS & TIME FOR ILL
1000 N 1st St (62702-2590)
P.O. Box 6366 (62708-6366)
PHONE..................217 528-1882
Loretta Prindle, *Principal*
EMP: 4
SALES (est): 219.9K **Privately Held**
SIC: 2711 Newspapers, publishing & printing

(G-19443)
SHINN ENTERPRISES
Also Called: Bad Boys Neons
3310 W Jefferson St (62707-9623)
PHONE..................217 698-3344
Rossetta Shinn, *President*
EMP: 8
SALES (est): 714.8K **Privately Held**
SIC: 2813 3993 Neon; neon signs

(G-19444)
SIGNKRAFT CO
1215 W Miller St (62702-3627)
PHONE..................217 787-7105
Cecil Hill, *Owner*
EMP: 3
SQ FT: 1,600
SALES (est): 220.8K **Privately Held**
SIC: 3993 5999 Signs & advertising specialties; banners, flags, decals & posters

(G-19445)
SIGNWORX SIGN & LIGHTING CO
1048 Francella Ct (62702-2331)
PHONE..................217 413-2532
Michael Gay, *President*
EMP: 4 EST: 2014
SALES (est): 125.8K **Privately Held**
SIC: 3993 Electric signs

(G-19446)
SIMPLEX INC (PA)
5300 Rising Moon Rd (62711-6228)
P.O. Box 7388 (62791-7388)
PHONE..................217 483-1600
Thomas Debrey, *President*
Jill Debrey, *COO*
Don Skowronski, *Opers Mgr*
Tressa Putnam, *Purch Agent*
Jon Thaxton, *Project Engr*
▼ EMP: 175 EST: 1931
SQ FT: 100,000
SALES (est): 25.9MM **Privately Held**
WEB: www.simplexdirect.com
SIC: 3613 3643 3625 3612 Generator control & metering panels; current-carrying wiring devices; relays & industrial controls; transformers, except electric; fabricated plate work (boiler shop)

(G-19447)
SKY SNACKS LLC
1129 Taintor Rd (62702-1760)
PHONE..................217 522-3345
Brad Turasky,
EMP: 12
SALES (est): 536.4K **Privately Held**
SIC: 3556 Meat, poultry & seafood processing machinery

(G-19448)
SNS PHARMA 427
1501 S Dirksen Pkwy (62703-2128)
PHONE..................217 527-8408
EMP: 4 EST: 2008
SALES (est): 277.8K **Privately Held**
SIC: 2834 Pharmaceutical preparations

(G-19449)
SOLOMON COLORS INC (PA)
4050 Color Plant Rd (62702-1060)
P.O. Box 8288 (62791-8288)
PHONE..................217 522-3112
Richard R Solomon, *President*
Charles Kreutzer, *Vice Pres*
Mark Nester, *Mfg Staff*
John Boxman, *Treasurer*
Victoria Franco, *Manager*
◆ EMP: 80
SQ FT: 150,000
SALES (est): 35.7MM **Privately Held**
WEB: www.solomoncolors.com
SIC: 2816 Inorganic pigments

(G-19450)
SOLUTION PRINTING INC
Also Called: Solution Printing & Signs
3135 S 14th St (62703-4128)
PHONE..................217 529-9700
Steve Shelton, *President*
Greg Shelton, *Manager*
Nick Gentry, *Graphic Designe*
EMP: 2
SALES (est): 436.5K **Privately Held**
SIC: 2752 Commercial printing, offset

(G-19451)
SPRINGFIELD COAL COMPANY LLC
3008 Happy Landing Dr (62711-6259)
P.O. Box 9320 (62791-9320)
PHONE..................217 698-3300
Michael Caldwell, *Vice Pres*
James Martin, *Technical Staff*
Brian Veldhuizen,
Tom Austin,
EMP: 29
SALES (est): 4.9MM **Privately Held**
SIC: 1241 Coal mining services

Springfield - Sangamon County (G-19452)

(G-19452)
SPRINGFIELD IRON & METAL CO
930 N Wolfe St (62702-4335)
PHONE..................217 544-7131
Russell Weller, *President*
EMP: 6 **EST:** 1956
SQ FT: 1,200
SALES (est): 778.8K **Privately Held**
SIC: 5093 3341 Automotive wrecking for scrap; secondary nonferrous metals

(G-19453)
SPRINGFIELD PEPSI-COLA BTLG CO (PA)
Also Called: Pepsico
2900 Singer Ave (62703-2135)
P.O. Box 4146 (62708-4146)
PHONE..................217 522-8841
John Faloon, *President*
Shawn Vecchie, *Vice Pres*
Patrick Beveridge, *Controller*
Shawn Faloon, *Human Resources*
Eileen White, *Info Tech Mgr*
EMP: 150
SQ FT: 4,000
SALES (est): 20.8MM **Privately Held**
SIC: 2086 Carbonated soft drinks, bottled & canned

(G-19454)
SPRINGFIELD PRINTING INC
Also Called: Byers Printing Company
3500 Constitution Dr (62711-7192)
P.O. Box 548 (62705-0548)
PHONE..................217 787-3500
Victor Krumm, *President*
EMP: 7
SALES (est): 1.2MM **Privately Held**
SIC: 2761 2789 2731 2752 Manifold business forms; bookbinding & related work; books: publishing & printing; commercial printing, lithographic

(G-19455)
SPRINGFIELD PUBLISHERS INC
Also Called: Springfield Business Journal
1118 W Laurel St (62704-3562)
PHONE..................217 726-6600
Brant W Mackey, *President*
Michelle Ownbey, *Publisher*
Patrick Yeagle, *Assoc Editor*
John Schilsky, *Admin Sec*
Scott Faingold, *Correspondent*
EMP: 5
SQ FT: 4,000
SALES (est): 339K **Privately Held**
SIC: 2711 Newspapers, publishing & printing

(G-19456)
SPRINGFIELD SALES ASSOC INC
3513 Tamarak Dr (62712-9102)
PHONE..................217 529-6987
Jack Milbourn, *President*
Howard Sutker, *President*
EMP: 4
SALES (est): 422.5K **Privately Held**
WEB: www.springfieldsalesassociates.com
SIC: 3143 3144 5661 Orthopedic shoes, men's; orthopedic shoes, women's; custom & orthopedic shoes

(G-19457)
SPRINGFIELD WELDING & AUTO BDY
Also Called: Springfield Auto Ctr Stor Pool
2720 Holmes Ave (62704-5110)
PHONE..................217 523-5365
James Paoli, *President*
Ronald Paoli, *President*
EMP: 22
SQ FT: 12,800
SALES: 1.2MM **Privately Held**
WEB: www.springfieldautobody.net
SIC: 7532 7539 7521 7692 Body shop, automotive; machine shop, automotive; automobile storage garage; automotive welding; general automotive repair shops

(G-19458)
STATE ATTORNEY APPELLATE
Also Called: Iepa Printing
1021 E North Grand Ave (62702-4059)
P.O. Box 19276 (62794-9276)
PHONE..................217 782-3397
Tamara Moore, *Sales Mgr*
Doug Scott, *Branch Mgr*
EMP: 7 **Privately Held**
SIC: 2752 9222 Commercial printing, lithographic; Attorney General's office
HQ: The State's Attorneys Appellate Prosecutor Illinois Office Of
725 S 2nd St
Springfield IL 62704

(G-19459)
STUDIO MOULDING
2650 Colt Rd (62707-8862)
PHONE..................217 523-2101
Karl Kienitz, *Branch Mgr*
EMP: 3 **Privately Held**
SIC: 3089 Molding primary plastic
PA: Studio Moulding
918 Avenue N
Grand Prairie TX 75050

(G-19460)
SUPERIOR HOME PRODUCTS INC
3000 Great Northern (62711-6097)
PHONE..................217 726-9300
Dan Ulrich, *Branch Mgr*
EMP: 7
SALES (corp-wide): 10MM **Privately Held**
SIC: 7389 3281 Advertising, promotional & trade show services; marble, building: cut & shaped
PA: Superior Home Products, Inc.
211 Edinger Rd
Wentzville MO
636 332-9040

(G-19461)
TAYLOR COMMUNICATIONS INC
450 S Durkin Dr Ste C (62704-7211)
P.O. Box 7319 (62791-7319)
PHONE..................217 793-1900
Mike Jastram, *Branch Mgr*
EMP: 4
SALES (corp-wide): 2.5B **Privately Held**
SIC: 2761 Manifold business forms
HQ: Taylor Communications, Inc.
1725 Roe Crest Dr
North Mankato MN 56003
866 541-0937

(G-19462)
TEEJET TECHNOLOGIES LLC (HQ)
1801 Business Park Dr (62703-5626)
PHONE..................630 665-5002
Pam Yasinski, *Purch Agent*
Duane Stewart, *VP Engrg*
Dennis Grim, *Design Engr*
Steve Stone, *Design Engr*
Duston Traylor, *Design Engr*
◆ **EMP:** 53
SQ FT: 21,000
SALES (est): 15.9MM
SALES (corp-wide): 320.3MM **Privately Held**
SIC: 3679 Electronic circuits
PA: Spraying Systems Co.
200 W North Ave
Glendale Heights IL 60139
630 665-5000

(G-19463)
TEMPLEGATE PUBLISHERS
302 E Adams St (62701-1403)
P.O. Box 5152 (62705-5152)
PHONE..................217 522-3353
Thomas Garvey, *Owner*
Nancy Wu, *Sales Staff*
EMP: 4 **EST:** 1947
SQ FT: 4,800
SALES: 500K **Privately Held**
WEB: www.templegate.com
SIC: 2731 8661 Books: publishing only; religious organizations

(G-19464)
THERMIONICS CORP (PA)
1214 Bunn Ave Ste 5 (62703-5339)
P.O. Box 2526, Sioux Falls SD (57101-2526)
PHONE..................800 800-5728
Gregg Harwood, *President*
▲ **EMP:** 14
SQ FT: 4,800
SALES: 2.5MM **Privately Held**
SIC: 3299 Ceramic fiber

(G-19465)
TMC SERVICES INC
920 S Spring St (62704-2725)
P.O. Box 113 (62705-0113)
PHONE..................217 528-2297
EMP: 5
SALES (est): 474.6K **Privately Held**
SIC: 2631 Paperboard mills

(G-19466)
TODD SCANLAN
Also Called: Woodhaven Woodworks
3112 Normandy Rd (62703-5875)
PHONE..................217 585-1717
Todd Scanlan, *Owner*
EMP: 7
SQ FT: 7,500
SALES: 400K **Privately Held**
SIC: 2499 Decorative wood & woodwork

(G-19467)
UPPER LIMITS MIDWEST INC
1205 S 2nd St Ste B (62704-3008)
PHONE..................217 679-4315
Matt Fortin, *President*
EMP: 5 **EST:** 2013
SALES: 100K **Privately Held**
SIC: 5159 3634 5047 3229 Tobacco distributors & products; vaporizers, electric: household; medical equipment & supplies; scientific glassware; medicinals & botanicals

(G-19468)
WYZZ INC
Also Called: W I C S
2680 E Cook St (62703-1902)
P.O. Box 3920 (62708-3920)
PHONE..................217 753-5620
Jack Connors, *President*
EMP: 60
SALES (corp-wide): 4.2B **Publicly Held**
SIC: 4833 2711 Television broadcasting stations; newspapers
HQ: Wyzz Inc
2714 E Lincoln St
Bloomington IL 61704
309 661-4343

(G-19469)
XTREM GRAPHIX SOLUTIONS INC
1620 S 5th St Ste A (62703-3174)
PHONE..................217 698-6424
Jeryn Meister, *President*
EMP: 4 **EST:** 2012
SALES (est): 528.5K **Privately Held**
SIC: 7336 3993 Graphic arts & related design; signs & advertising specialties

(G-19470)
Y T PACKING CO
Also Called: Turasky Meats
1129 Taintor Rd (62702-1760)
P.O. Box 57 (62705-0057)
PHONE..................217 522-3345
Joseph Turasky, *President*
EMP: 10 **EST:** 1949
SQ FT: 13,000
SALES: 2MM **Privately Held**
WEB: www.turaskymeats.com
SIC: 5147 5421 2013 2011 Meats, fresh; meat markets, including freezer provisioners; sausages & other prepared meats; meat packing plants

(G-19471)
ZIMMER SMITH & ASSOCIATES INC
120 E Scarritt St Ste A (62704-3015)
PHONE..................217 788-5800
Ronald Smith, *President*
EMP: 12
SALES (est): 628.9K **Privately Held**
SIC: 3841 Surgical & medical instruments

Stanford
Mclean County

(G-19472)
D N D COATING
313 W Main St (61774-7541)
P.O. Box 209 (61774-0209)
PHONE..................309 379-3021
Gerry Doehrmann, *Partner*
EMP: 8
SALES (est): 592.5K **Privately Held**
SIC: 3479 5014 Coating of metals with silicon; truck tires & tubes

(G-19473)
QUALITY METAL WORKS INC
Also Called: Speidel Applicators
200 School St (61774-7577)
P.O. Box 358 (61774-0358)
PHONE..................309 379-5311
Ronald Lubke, *President*
Linda Lubke, *Vice Pres*
EMP: 3
SQ FT: 14,000
SALES: 300K **Privately Held**
SIC: 3599 7692 3444 3523 Machine shop, jobbing & repair; welding repair; sheet metalwork; weeding machines, agricultural

Staunton
Macoupin County

(G-19474)
BOFA AMERICAS INC
303 S Madison St (62088-1929)
P.O. Box 235 (62088-0235)
PHONE..................618 205-5007
John Podwojski, *President*
◆ **EMP:** 7
SQ FT: 7,500
SALES (est): 1.8MM
SALES (corp-wide): 2.8B **Publicly Held**
WEB: www.bofaamericas.com
SIC: 3564 Air purification equipment
HQ: Bofa International Ltd.
21-22 Balena Close
Poole
120 269-9444

(G-19475)
BRIAN BEQUETTE CABINETRY
18630 White City Rd (62088-4012)
PHONE..................618 670-5427
Brian Bequette, *Principal*
EMP: 2
SALES (est): 221.6K **Privately Held**
WEB: www.brianbcabinetry.com
SIC: 2434 Wood kitchen cabinets

(G-19476)
C I F INDUSTRIES INC
20988 Old Route 66 (62088-4312)
PHONE..................618 635-2010
Rick C Clark, *President*
Lori Pope, *Mfg Staff*
Noel Malone, *Accountant*
EMP: 24
SALES: 4.4MM **Privately Held**
WEB: www.cifindustriesinc.com
SIC: 7692 5521 3713 Welding repair; trucks, tractors & trailers: used; dump truck bodies

(G-19477)
SANKS MACHINING INC
22991 Ruschaupt Rd (62088-4410)
PHONE..................618 635-8279
William Sanks, *President*
Janie Sanks, *Admin Sec*
EMP: 5
SQ FT: 2,400
SALES (est): 266.2K **Privately Held**
WEB: www.sanksmachining.com
SIC: 3599 Machine shop, jobbing & repair

GEOGRAPHIC SECTION

Sterling - Whiteside County (G-19503)

(G-19478)
SHALE LAKE LLC
Also Called: Winery At Shale Lake The
1499 Washington Ave (62088-3047)
PHONE....................618 637-2470
David Wesa, *Executive*
EMP: 4
SALES (est): 319K **Privately Held**
SIC: 2084 7032 0721 0752 Wine cellars, bonded: engaged in blending wines; recreational camps; orchard tree & vine services; animal boarding services; boarding services, horses: racing & non-racing

(G-19479)
STAR-TIMES PUBLISHING CO INC
Also Called: Staunton Star Times
108 W Main St (62088-1453)
P.O. Box 180 (62088-0180)
PHONE....................618 635-2000
Walter F Haase Jr, *President*
EMP: 8 **EST:** 1933
SQ FT: 3,000
SALES (est): 794K **Privately Held**
WEB: www.stauntonstartimes.com
SIC: 2711 2759 Newspapers: publishing only, not printed on site; commercial printing

Steeleville
Randolph County

(G-19480)
DORMAKABA USA INC
1003 W Broadway (62288-1311)
P.O. Box 8 (62288-0008)
PHONE....................618 965-3491
Carolyn Bollman, *Safety Mgr*
Steve Malone, *Branch Mgr*
Tom Bevis, *Manager*
EMP: 70
SALES (corp-wide): 2.7B **Privately Held**
SIC: 3429 Builders' hardware
HQ: Dormakaba Usa Inc.
  100 Dorma Dr
  Reamstown PA 17567
  717 336-3881

(G-19481)
LEE GILSTER-MARY CORPORATION
705 N Sparta St (62288-1547)
PHONE....................618 965-3426
Louis Oulvey, *Opers-Prdtn-Mfg*
EMP: 100
SALES (corp-wide): 1B **Privately Held**
SIC: 2045 2099 2098 2087 Prepared flour mixes & doughs; food preparations; macaroni & spaghetti; flavoring extracts & syrups; canned specialties
HQ: Gilster-Mary Lee Corporation
  1037 State St
  Chester IL 62233
  618 826-2361

(G-19482)
LEE GILSTER-MARY CORPORATION
10 Industrial Park (62288-1246)
PHONE....................618 965-3449
Louis Oulvey, *Superintendent*
EMP: 500
SALES (corp-wide): 1B **Privately Held**
SIC: 7389 2098 2063 2062 Packaging & labeling services; macaroni & spaghetti; beet sugar; cane sugar refining
HQ: Gilster-Mary Lee Corporation
  1037 State St
  Chester IL 62233
  618 826-2361

(G-19483)
MC CHEMICAL COMPANY
1208 N Cherry St (62288-1255)
P.O. Box 52 (62288-0052)
PHONE....................618 965-3668
Denny Fulkrod, *Branch Mgr*
EMP: 4
SALES (est): 299.9K
SALES (corp-wide): 4.9MM **Privately Held**
WEB: www.mcproducts.com
SIC: 2899 2296 Chemical preparations; tire cord & fabrics
PA: Mc Chemical Company
  720 South St
  Rockford IL 61102
  815 964-7687

(G-19484)
MEVERT AUTOMOTIVE INC
Also Called: Mevert Automotive & Welding
1014 W Broadway (62288-1312)
PHONE....................618 965-9609
Matthew Mevert, *President*
EMP: 2
SALES (est): 299.2K **Privately Held**
SIC: 7538 7692 1799 Engine repair; welding repair; welding on site

(G-19485)
VISION MACHINE & FABRICATION
1102 N Cherry St (62288-1254)
P.O. Box 66 (62288-0066)
PHONE....................618 965-3199
Ronald P Scherby, *President*
Wayne Heincke, *Vice Pres*
EMP: 7
SQ FT: 12,000
SALES: 1.3MM **Privately Held**
SIC: 3556 Food products machinery

Steger
Cook County

(G-19486)
1 FEDERAL SUPPLY SOURCE INC
30 E 34th St (60475-1759)
PHONE....................708 964-2222
Darnell Muhammad, *President*
EMP: 5
SQ FT: 1,800
SALES (est): 137.1K **Privately Held**
SIC: 5047 3841 3842 3821 Medical & hospital equipment; surgical & medical instruments; surgical appliances & supplies; incubators, laboratory; toiletries

(G-19487)
ALL-RIGHT SIGN INC
3628 Union Ave Ste 1 (60475-1787)
PHONE....................708 754-6366
Teresa Bowen, *President*
James M Bowen, *Vice Pres*
Brittany Bowen, *Admin Sec*
EMP: 12
SQ FT: 2,500
SALES (est): 550K **Privately Held**
SIC: 3993 1799 Signs, not made in custom sign painting shops; sign installation & maintenance

(G-19488)
ARCHER GENERAL CONTG & FABG
22498 Miller Rd (60475-5560)
P.O. Box 264 (60475-0264)
PHONE....................708 757-7902
Roger Buchler, *President*
Judy Buchler, *Treasurer*
Douglas R Buchler, *Admin Sec*
EMP: 6
SQ FT: 6,000
SALES: 390K **Privately Held**
SIC: 1731 3441 General electrical contractor; fabricated structural metal

(G-19489)
BUILDERS IRONWORKS INC
3242 Louis Sherman Dr (60475-1184)
PHONE....................708 754-4092
EMP: 6
SALES (corp-wide): 680.6K **Privately Held**
SIC: 3423 Mfg Hand/Edge Tools
PA: Builders Ironworks, Inc.
  399 Greenbriar Dr
  Crete IL 60417
  708 672-1047

(G-19490)
J D M COATINGS INC
3300 Louis Sherman Dr (60475-1187)
PHONE....................708 755-6300
Donald F Schultz, *President*
Janice Schultz, *Corp Secy*
Kenneth Latzky, *Vice Pres*
EMP: 6
SQ FT: 7,400
SALES (est): 363K **Privately Held**
SIC: 3399 Metal powders, pastes & flakes

(G-19491)
P & L TOOL & MANUFACTURING CO
3624 Union Ave (60475-1748)
PHONE....................708 754-4777
Louis Lucente, *President*
Paolo Pizzoferrato, *Vice Pres*
EMP: 4
SQ FT: 2,600
SALES (est): 350K **Privately Held**
SIC: 3544 Special dies & tools

(G-19492)
SPECIALTY CRATE FACTORY (PA)
3320 Louis Sherman Dr (60475-1187)
PHONE....................708 756-2100
K Michael Bless, *Owner*
EMP: 2
SQ FT: 1,800
SALES (est): 328.9K **Privately Held**
SIC: 2449 5031 Rectangular boxes & crates, wood; doors & windows

(G-19493)
STONECRAFT CAST STONE LLC
3025 Louis Sherman Dr (60475-1190)
P.O. Box 45 (60475-0045)
PHONE....................708 653-1477
EMP: 3
SALES (est): 320K **Privately Held**
SIC: 3272 Concrete products

(G-19494)
TROPHIES AND AWARDS PLUS
3344 Chicago Rd Ste 3 (60475-1233)
P.O. Box 69 (60475-0069)
PHONE....................708 754-7127
Priscilla Kidd, *Owner*
EMP: 3
SQ FT: 3,000
SALES (est): 150K **Privately Held**
SIC: 5999 3479 Trophies & plaques; engraving jewelry silverware, or metal

(G-19495)
UNION AVE AUTO INC
3236 Union Ave (60475-1257)
PHONE....................708 754-3899
Marlene Delisio, *President*
Dennis Delisio, *President*
EMP: 5 **EST:** 1937
SQ FT: 12,800
SALES (est): 390K **Privately Held**
SIC: 7538 7532 5511 3732 Engine repair; body shop, automotive; automobiles, new & used; boat building & repairing

(G-19496)
UNIVERSAL COATINGS INC
3001 Louis Sherman Dr (60475-1190)
PHONE....................708 756-7000
Sandra Casey, *President*
EMP: 2
SALES (est): 246K **Privately Held**
SIC: 3471 Finishing, metals or formed products

Sterling
Whiteside County

(G-19497)
ALTRAN MAGNETICS LLC
1741 Industrial Dr # 14 (61081-9290)
PHONE....................815 632-3150
Amer Jaber, *President*
Angela Magness, *Director*
EMP: 8
SALES (est): 444.7K **Privately Held**
SIC: 3559 5063 Electronic component making machinery; motors, electric

(G-19498)
ASTEC MOBILE SCREENS INC
2704 W Le Fevre Rd (61081-7703)
PHONE....................815 626-6374
Timothy Gonigam, *President*
David Osterhaus, *Controller*
Stephen Anderson, *Admin Sec*
◆ **EMP:** 116
SQ FT: 60,000
SALES (est): 45.3MM
SALES (corp-wide): 1.1B **Publicly Held**
SIC: 3535 Conveyors & conveying equipment
PA: Astec Industries, Inc.
  1725 Shepherd Rd
  Chattanooga TN 37421
  423 899-5898

(G-19499)
AZCON INC
101 Avenue K (61081-3229)
PHONE....................815 548-7000
Lance Caldwell, *Branch Mgr*
EMP: 16
SALES (corp-wide): 61.4MM **Privately Held**
SIC: 3533 3715 3823 3589 Water well drilling equipment; semitrailers for truck tractors; water quality monitoring & control systems; garbage disposers & compactors, commercial; ferrous metal scrap & waste; structural shapes, iron or steel
PA: Azcon, Inc.
  820 W Jackson Blvd # 425
  Chicago IL 60607
  312 559-3100

(G-19500)
B F SHAW PRINTING COMPANY
Also Called: Sauk Valley Newspaper
3200 E Lincolnway (61081-1773)
P.O. Box 498 (61081-0498)
PHONE....................815 625-3600
Thomas Shaw, *President*
EMP: 1
SALES (est): 810K
SALES (corp-wide): 73.4MM **Privately Held**
SIC: 2711 2752 Newspapers, publishing & printing; commercial printing, lithographic
PA: 'b. F. Shaw Printing Company, The'
  3200 E Lincolnway
  Sterling IL
  815 284-4000

(G-19501)
BOSTON LEATHER INC
1801 Eastwood Dr (61081-9234)
P.O. Box 1213 (61081-8213)
PHONE....................815 622-1635
Geri Valentino, *President*
Anthony E Valentino, *Vice Pres*
▲ **EMP:** 25 **EST:** 1938
SQ FT: 15,000
SALES (est): 3.8MM **Privately Held**
WEB: www.bostonleather.com
SIC: 3199 Leather garments; holsters, leather

(G-19502)
C W PUBLICATIONS INC
1705 37th Ave (61081-4231)
P.O. Box 744 (61081-0744)
PHONE....................800 554-5537
Charles Wilkinson, *President*
EMP: 1
SALES: 500K **Privately Held**
SIC: 5961 7372 7812 2741 Educational supplies & equipment, mail order; educational computer software; video tape production; miscellaneous publishing; book publishing

(G-19503)
DANA
2001 Eastwood Dr (61081-9234)
PHONE....................419 887-3000
EMP: 2
SALES (est): 345.6K **Privately Held**
SIC: 3714 Motor vehicle parts & accessories

Sterling - Whiteside County (G-19504)

(G-19504)
DANA DRIVESHAFT MFG LLC
Also Called: Dana Driveshaft Products
2001 Eastwood Dr (61081-9234)
PHONE...................815 626-6700
Doug Rader, *Sales Staff*
Kelvin Wright, *Manager*
Eric Staples, *Info Tech Mgr*
EMP: 48
SQ FT: 30,000 **Publicly Held**
SIC: 3714 Drive shafts, motor vehicle
HQ: Dana Driveshaft Manufacturing, Llc
3939 Technology Dr
Maumee OH 43537

(G-19505)
DK KNUTSEN
609 W 3rd St (61081-3358)
PHONE...................815 626-4388
Kraig Knutsen, *Owner*
EMP: 4 **EST:** 1989
SALES (est): 304.8K **Privately Held**
SIC: 2541 Counter & sink tops

(G-19506)
DURAGRIND INC
2910 W Le Fevre Rd (61081-9228)
PHONE...................815 625-6500
Kyle Young, *President*
EMP: 26
SALES (est): 4.8MM **Privately Held**
WEB: www.duragrind.com
SIC: 3599 Machine shop, jobbing & repair

(G-19507)
EIKENBERRY SHEET METAL WORKS
412 E 3rd St (61081-3702)
P.O. Box 354, Tampico (61283-0354)
PHONE...................815 625-0955
Norden Scalan, *President*
Ann Scalan, *Admin Sec*
EMP: 6
SQ FT: 1,500
SALES (est): 708.9K **Privately Held**
SIC: 1711 3444 Warm air heating & air conditioning contractor; ventilation & duct work contractor; sheet metalwork

(G-19508)
FRANTZ MANUFACTURING COMPANY (PA)
Also Called: Frantz Bearing Division
3201 W Lefevre Rd (61081)
P.O. Box 497 (61081-0497)
PHONE...................815 625-3333
El Froeliger, *Ch of Bd*
J M Gvozdjak, *President*
John Gvozdjak, *COO*
Denver Owen, *Plant Mgr*
Deborah Combs, *Purch Mgr*
◆ **EMP:** 5
SQ FT: 6,900
SALES (est): 53.8MM **Privately Held**
WEB: www.frantz-mfg.com
SIC: 3562 Roller bearings & parts; ball bearings & parts

(G-19509)
FRANTZ MANUFACTURING COMPANY
Also Called: Sterling Steel Ball
3809 W Lincoln Hwy (61081)
P.O. Box 497 (61081-0497)
PHONE...................815 625-7063
Kyle Dir, *Branch Mgr*
EMP: 54
SALES (corp-wide): 53.8MM **Privately Held**
SIC: 3562 5084 3624 Ball bearings & parts; industrial machinery & equipment; carbon & graphite products
PA: Frantz Manufacturing Company Inc
3201 W Lefevre Rd
Sterling IL 61081
815 625-3333

(G-19510)
FRANTZ MANUFACTURING COMPANY
Also Called: Bearing Division
3201 W Le Fevre Rd (61081-9230)
P.O. Box 497 (61081-0497)
PHONE...................815 564-0991
Carl Boehm, *Branch Mgr*
EMP: 95
SALES (corp-wide): 53.8MM **Privately Held**
SIC: 3535 3714 3568 Conveyors & conveying equipment; motor vehicle parts & accessories; power transmission equipment
PA: Frantz Manufacturing Company Inc
3201 W Lefevre Rd
Sterling IL 61081
815 625-3333

(G-19511)
GALLOWAY COMO PROCESSING
Also Called: Galloway Meats & Poultry
24578 Stone St (61081-8898)
P.O. Box 70, Galt (61037-0070)
PHONE...................815 626-0305
Darin Galloway, *Owner*
EMP: 2
SALES (est): 209.1K **Privately Held**
SIC: 2011 2015 Meat packing plants; poultry slaughtering & processing

(G-19512)
GENESIS DURAGRIND INC
2910 W Le Fevre Rd (61081-9228)
PHONE...................815 625-6500
Kyle Young, *President*
EMP: 8
SALES (est): 592.1K **Privately Held**
WEB: www.duragrind.com
SIC: 3541 Grinding machines, metalworking

(G-19513)
JJM PRINTING INC
311 1st Ave (61081-3601)
PHONE...................815 499-3067
EMP: 3
SALES (est): 228.1K **Privately Held**
SIC: 2752 Commercial printing, lithographic

(G-19514)
MAG MO SYSTEMS
Also Called: Megli Lawn Care
302 Wallace St (61081-3446)
P.O. Box 423 (61081-0423)
PHONE...................815 625-0125
EMP: 10
SALES: 400K **Privately Held**
SIC: 3524 Lawn & garden mowers & accessories

(G-19515)
MALLARD HANDLING SOLUTIONS LLC (PA)
Also Called: Mallard Manufacturing
101 Mallard Rd (61081-1217)
PHONE...................815 625-9491
Randy Miller, *Opers Mgr*
Al Wade, *Opers Mgr*
Jim Schultz, *Prdtn Mgr*
Scott Mascho, *Warehouse Mgr*
Scott Garriott, *Engineer*
▲ **EMP:** 34
SQ FT: 45,000
SALES (est): 7.7MM **Privately Held**
WEB: www.mallardmfg.com
SIC: 3535 Conveyors & conveying equipment

(G-19516)
MARVIN SCHUMAKER PLBG INC
25457 Front St (61081-8966)
PHONE...................815 626-8130
Caroline Schumaker, *President*
Dennis Schumaker, *Vice Pres*
David Schumaker, *Admin Sec*
EMP: 3 **EST:** 1945
SALES (est): 223.5K **Privately Held**
SIC: 1711 3585 Plumbing contractors; warm air heating & air conditioning contractor; refrigeration & heating equipment

(G-19517)
MCR TECHNOLOGIES GROUP INC
1704 Westwood Dr (61081-9294)
P.O. Box 1016 (61081-8016)
PHONE...................815 622-3181
Mark Humphreys, *President*
Carol Humphreys, *CFO*
Marvin Reyes, *Marketing Staff*
▲ **EMP:** 6 **EST:** 1998
SQ FT: 2,500
SALES (est): 1MM **Privately Held**
WEB: www.mcrtechnologiesgroup.com
SIC: 3535 5999 Conveyors & conveying equipment; alcoholic beverage making equipment & supplies

(G-19518)
MENK USA LLC
2207 Enterprise Dr (61081-8930)
PHONE...................815 626-9730
Karl Gross,
▲ **EMP:** 40
SQ FT: 52,000
SALES (est): 8.5MM
SALES (corp-wide): 38.4MM **Privately Held**
SIC: 3634 Radiators, electric
PA: Menk Apparatebau Gmbh
Fritz-Von-Opel-Str. 20
Bad Marienberg (Westerwald) 56470
266 162-10

(G-19519)
MICRON INDUSTRIES CORPORATION
Also Called: Micron Power
1801 Westwood Dr Ste 2 (61081-9221)
PHONE...................815 380-2222
Allen Wade, *Manager*
Raquel Martinez, *Prgrmr*
EMP: 89
SALES (corp-wide): 41.9MM **Privately Held**
SIC: 3612 Control transformers
PA: Micron Industries Corporation
1211 W 22nd St Ste 200
Oak Brook IL 60523
630 516-1222

(G-19520)
MMXIX CAPITAL INC
65 Carriage Hill Dr (61081-9629)
PHONE...................815 441-2647
Paul A Sandefer, *President*
▼ **EMP:** 70
SALES (est): 11.2MM **Privately Held**
SIC: 3993 Signs, not made in custom sign painting shops

(G-19521)
MOORE MACHINE WORKS
706 Gregden Shores Dr (61081-9602)
P.O. Box 719 (61081-0719)
PHONE...................815 625-0536
Evan Moore, *President*
John Moore, *Vice Pres*
Judy Moore, *Treasurer*
EMP: 5 **EST:** 1942
SQ FT: 15,000
SALES (est): 500K **Privately Held**
SIC: 3599 Machine shop, jobbing & repair

(G-19522)
NEW MILLENIUM DIRECTORIES (PA)
324 1st Ave (61081-3602)
PHONE...................815 626-5737
Terry Brininger, *President*
Terry Johnson, *Consultant*
Katrina Hicks, *Administration*
Chris Fudala, *Graphic Designe*
EMP: 22
SQ FT: 1,200
SALES: 1.5MM **Privately Held**
SIC: 2741 Telephone & other directory publishing

(G-19523)
P & P INDUSTRIES INC (PA)
2100 Enterprise Dr (61081-8929)
PHONE...................815 623-3297
Warren Pruis, *President*
Tony Nardi, *Vice Pres*
Marsha Pruis, *Vice Pres*
Brian Pruis, *Purch Mgr*
Marcia Pruis, *CFO*
EMP: 51
SQ FT: 50,000
SALES (est): 12.5MM **Privately Held**
SIC: 3089 Injection molding of plastics

(G-19524)
PINNEY PRINTING COMPANY
1991 Industrial Dr (61081-9064)
PHONE...................815 626-2727
Charles Arp, *President*
Dave Zimmerman, *Plant Mgr*
Julie Burken, *Sales Staff*
Dave Garriott, *Administration*
EMP: 16 **EST:** 1909
SQ FT: 15,000
SALES: 2.2MM **Privately Held**
WEB: www.pinney.com
SIC: 2752 2789 Commercial printing, offset; bookbinding & related work

(G-19525)
PRESCOTTS INC
Also Called: Prescott's TV & Appliance
1910 E 4th St (61081-3013)
PHONE...................815 626-2996
James L Prescott, *President*
Rick Renner, *Vice Pres*
EMP: 5 **EST:** 1955
SQ FT: 28,000
SALES (est): 876.1K **Privately Held**
SIC: 3651 Audio electronic systems

(G-19526)
QUALITY PLATING
406 Oak Ave (61081-1860)
PHONE...................815 626-5223
Gary Schultz, *Owner*
EMP: 3
SALES (est): 213.2K **Privately Held**
SIC: 3471 3751 Plating of metals or formed products; motorcycles, bicycles & parts

(G-19527)
QUALITY READY MIX CONCRETE CO
13134 Galt Rd (61081-8913)
PHONE...................815 625-0750
Roger Dykema, *Manager*
EMP: 8
SALES (corp-wide): 3.7MM **Privately Held**
SIC: 3273 Ready-mixed concrete
PA: Quality Ready Mix Concrete Co.
14849 Lyndon Rd
Morrison IL 61270
815 772-7181

(G-19528)
R & C AUTO SUPPLY CORP
Also Called: Ron's Automotive Machine Shop
2526 E Lincolnway (61081-3052)
PHONE...................815 625-4414
Ronald George, *President*
Carol George, *Treasurer*
EMP: 3
SQ FT: 4,000
SALES (est): 327.5K **Privately Held**
SIC: 7538 5531 3519 Engine rebuilding: automotive; automotive parts; internal combustion engines

(G-19529)
RONNIE P FABER
Also Called: Faber Builders Discount
2901 Polo Rd (61081-9724)
PHONE...................815 626-4561
Ronnie P Faber, *Owner*
EMP: 2
SALES: 200K **Privately Held**
SIC: 5211 2434 Home centers; wood kitchen cabinets

(G-19530)
ROTARY AIRLOCK LLC
301 W 3rd St L (61081-3411)
PHONE...................800 883-8955
Glen McClure,
EMP: 20
SQ FT: 25,000
SALES (est): 6.6MM **Privately Held**
SIC: 3443 Airlocks

(G-19531)
SAUK VALLEY COMMUNITY COLLEGE
601 W 13th St (61081-2215)
PHONE...................815 835-6321
Debi Hill, *Principal*
EMP: 3 **EST:** 2011

SALES (est): 126.2K **Privately Held**
WEB: www.svcc.edu
SIC: 2711 Newspapers, publishing & printing

(G-19532)
SAUK VALLEY GUNSMITHING ✪
710 4th Ave (61081-3728)
PHONE.................................815 441-0260
Cody Benson, *Principal*
EMP: 3 **EST:** 2019
SALES (est): 117.7K **Privately Held**
SIC: 2711 Newspapers, publishing & printing

(G-19533)
STEIN INC
Also Called: Stein Steel Mini Services
610 Wallace St (61081-3300)
P.O. Box 1206 (61081-8206)
PHONE.................................815 626-9355
Gary Grantham, *Branch Mgr*
EMP: 11
SALES (corp-wide): 83.5MM **Privately Held**
SIC: 3295 Minerals, ground or treated
PA: Stein, Inc.
1929 E Royalton Rd Ste C
Cleveland OH 44147
440-526-9301

(G-19534)
STERLING BOX COMPANY INC
Also Called: Sauk Valley Container Corp.
1980 Eastwood Dr (61081-9233)
PHONE.................................815 626-9657
Jake Amsbaugh, *President*
Lynn Hammer, *Vice Pres*
EMP: 15
SQ FT: 8,000
SALES (est): 3MM **Privately Held**
SIC: 2653 Boxes, corrugated: made from purchased materials

(G-19535)
STERLING STEEL COMPANY LLC
Also Called: Sterling Steel 0530
101 Avenue K (61081-3229)
PHONE.................................815 548-7000
Tom Vercillo, *Controller*
Joseph D Downes Jr, *Mng Member*
Shonna L Koch, *Mng Member*
Andrew R More, *Mng Member*
Kevin Mullen, *Manager*
◆ **EMP:** 260
SALES (est): 115.8MM
SALES (corp-wide): 4.7B **Publicly Held**
SIC: 3312 Rods, iron & steel: made in steel mills
PA: Leggett & Platt, Incorporated
1 Leggett Rd
Carthage MO 64836
417 358-8131

(G-19536)
STERLING SYSTEMS & CONTROLS
Also Called: Prater-Sterling
24711 Emerson Rd (61081-9171)
P.O. Box 418 (61081-0418)
PHONE.................................815 625-0852
Robert S Prater, *Chairman*
Don Goshert, *Vice Pres*
EMP: 18 **EST:** 1973
SQ FT: 12,000
SALES (est): 4.1MM
SALES (corp-wide): 28.1MM **Privately Held**
SIC: 3625 Relays & industrial controls
HQ: Prater Industries, Inc.
2 Sammons Ct
Bolingbrook IL 60440
630 679-3200

(G-19537)
STERLING VAULT COMPANY
Also Called: Wilbert Vault
2411 W Lincolnway (61081-8981)
PHONE.................................815 625-0077
Michael Banks, *President*
Kathy Banks, *Corp Secy*
EMP: 11
SQ FT: 13,500

SALES (est): 2MM **Privately Held**
WEB: www.sterlingwilbert.com
SIC: 3272 7261 Burial vaults, concrete or precast terrazzo; crematory

(G-19538)
TC ELECTRIC CONTROLS LLC
1741 Industrial Dr # 14 (61081-9290)
PHONE.................................815 213-7680
Amer M Jaber,
EMP: 4
SALES (corp-wide): 642.2K **Privately Held**
WEB: www.tcelectriccontrols.com
SIC: 3625 Relays & industrial controls
PA: Tc Electric Controls, Llc
1320 Tower Rd
Schaumburg IL 60173
815 213-7680

(G-19539)
UNITED CRAFTSMEN LTD
1500 W 4th St (61081-3121)
PHONE.................................815 626-7802
Douglas Grunnet, *President*
Patricia Grunnet, *Principal*
Paul Hackbarth, *Principal*
Kathy Sedig, *Bookkeeper*
EMP: 10
SQ FT: 13,000
SALES (est): 1.1MM **Privately Held**
SIC: 3599 3544 Machine shop, jobbing & repair; special dies, tools, jigs & fixtures

(G-19540)
WAHL CLIPPER CORPORATION (PA)
2900 Locust St (61081-9500)
P.O. Box 578 (61081-0578)
PHONE.................................815 625-6525
John Wahl, *CEO*
Gregory S Wahl, *President*
James O Wahl, *Exec VP*
Don Ouellette, *Vice Pres*
Brian Wahl, *Vice Pres*
◆ **EMP:** 720 **EST:** 1911
SQ FT: 380,000
SALES (est): 449.7MM **Privately Held**
WEB: www.wahl.com
SIC: 3999 Hair clippers for human use, hand & electric

(G-19541)
WAHL CLIPPER CORPORATION
2902 Locust St (61081)
PHONE.................................815 625-6525
Jerold I Horn, *Branch Mgr*
EMP: 10
SALES (corp-wide): 449.7MM **Privately Held**
SIC: 3999 Hair clippers for human use, hand & electric
PA: Wahl Clipper Corporation
2900 Locust St
Sterling IL 61081
815 625-6525

(G-19542)
WESTWOOD MACHINE & TOOL CO
Also Called: M SM
1703 Westwood Dr (61081-9296)
PHONE.................................815 626-5090
David Hurless, *President*
Jerry Crenshaw, *Treasurer*
Joseph Schneiderbauer, *Admin Sec*
EMP: 19 **EST:** 1977
SQ FT: 15,000
SALES: 2MM **Privately Held**
SIC: 3544 Special dies & tools

Stickney
Cook County

(G-19543)
M & A GROCERY
6719 Pershing Rd (60402-4069)
PHONE.................................708 749-9786
EMP: 3
SALES (est): 180K **Privately Held**
SIC: 3999 Mfg Misc Products

Stillman Valley
Ogle County

(G-19544)
ALLIED PRODUCTION DRILLING
5746 N Hales Corner Rd (61084-9721)
PHONE.................................815 969-0940
EMP: 10
SQ FT: 4,000
SALES: 620K **Privately Held**
SIC: 3469 Mfg Stamping Metal

(G-19545)
R C SALES & MANUFACTURING INC
5999 N Cox Rd (61084-9358)
PHONE.................................815 645-8898
Roger Carlson, *President*
Yvonne Raymond, *Corp Secy*
Brad Cain, *Vice Pres*
EMP: 8
SQ FT: 9,000
SALES: 500K **Privately Held**
SIC: 3089 3599 Plastic processing; machine shop, jobbing & repair

(G-19546)
STRAIT-O-FLEX
7372 Kishwaukee Rd (61084-9529)
PHONE.................................815 965-2625
Vicki Walker, *Principal*
EMP: 3
SALES (est): 188.9K **Privately Held**
WEB: www.straitoflex.com
SIC: 3498 Tube fabricating (contract bending & shaping)

(G-19547)
TOOLMASTERS LLC
Also Called: Small Tools Div
206 S Walnut St (61084-8917)
P.O. Box 115 (61084-0115)
PHONE.................................815 645-2224
EMP: 13
SALES (corp-wide): 2.5MM **Privately Held**
SIC: 3545 3546 Mfg Machine Tool Accessories Mfg Power-Driven Handtools
PA: Toolmasters Llc
1439 Railroad Ave Ste 1
Rockford IL 61109
815 968-0961

Stockton
Jo Daviess County

(G-19548)
BREWSTER CHEESE COMPANY
300 W Railroad Ave (61085-1545)
PHONE.................................815 947-3361
John Scott, *Principal*
Charles Loehr, *Plant Mgr*
Ronda Dower, *Manager*
EMP: 90
SALES (corp-wide): 139.5MM **Privately Held**
SIC: 2022 Natural cheese
PA: Brewster Cheese Company
800 Wabash Ave S
Brewster OH 44613
330 767-3492

(G-19549)
DURA OPERATING LLC
301 S Simmons St (61085-1513)
PHONE.................................815 947-3333
Mick Arand, *Plant Mgr*
Karl F Storrie, *Branch Mgr*
EMP: 125
SALES (corp-wide): 4.1B **Privately Held**
WEB: www.duraauto.com
SIC: 3089 3429 Injection molded finished plastic products; manufactured hardware (general)
HQ: Dura Operating, Llc
1780 Pond Run
Auburn Hills MI 48326

(G-19550)
STOCKTON STAINLESS INC
11434 E Willow Rd (61085-9539)
PHONE.................................815 947-2168
Amy McPeek, *Officer*
EMP: 28 **EST:** 2000
SALES (est): 2.1MM **Privately Held**
SIC: 7692 Automotive welding

Stone Park
Cook County

(G-19551)
AMERICAN WELDING & GAS INC
3900 W North Ave (60165-1036)
PHONE.................................630 527-2550
Ray Petty, *President*
Mark Stears, *Vice Pres*
EMP: 24
SALES (corp-wide): 202.6MM **Privately Held**
WEB: www.amwelding.com
SIC: 7692 5999 5169 5084 Welding repair; welding supplies; industrial gases; petroleum industry machinery
PA: American Welding & Gas, Inc.
4900 Falls Of Neuse Rd # 150
Raleigh NC 27609
918 573-2982

(G-19552)
ARCHITECTURAL WOOD EXPRESSIONS
3200 W Le Moyne Ave (60165-1009)
PHONE.................................708 731-2355
Adriatik Selfollari, *President*
EMP: 4
SALES (est): 611.1K **Privately Held**
SIC: 2431 Millwork; doors & door parts & trim, wood

(G-19553)
EES INC
4300 W North Ave (60165-1038)
PHONE.................................708 343-1800
Jacek Helenowski, *President*
Tim Green, *Info Tech Mgr*
EMP: 6 **EST:** 2012
SALES (est): 631.6K **Privately Held**
SIC: 5063 3621 3629 Generators; power transmission equipment, electric; generating apparatus & parts, electrical; electronic generation equipment

(G-19554)
ENGINE REBUILDERS & SUPPLY
4010 W North Ave (60165-1037)
PHONE.................................708 338-1113
Andy Frontzak, *President*
EMP: 4 **EST:** 1940
SQ FT: 5,000
SALES (est): 542K **Privately Held**
WEB: www.ersinc1.com
SIC: 7699 7538 3714 3621 Engine repair & replacement, non-automotive; engine rebuilding: automotive; motor vehicle parts & accessories; motors & generators

(G-19555)
FRA NO 3800 W DIVISION
3800 Division St (60165-1115)
PHONE.................................708 338-0690
Paul Basile, *Publisher*
EMP: 5
SALES (est): 307.9K **Privately Held**
SIC: 2711 Newspapers, publishing & printing

(G-19556)
LEE FOSS ELECTRIC MOTOR SVC
3418 W North Ave (60165-1043)
PHONE.................................708 681-5335
Charles Fossen, *President*
Terry Likens, *Corp Secy*
EMP: 3
SQ FT: 5,000
SALES: 600K **Privately Held**
SIC: 7694 Electric motor repair

Stonefort
Saline County

(G-19557)
CARDINAL ENTERPRISES
562 Ferrel Rd (62987-1205)
PHONE...................................618 994-4454
Steve Borntrater, *Partner*
EMP: 2
SALES (est): 221.9K **Privately Held**
SIC: 3448 Prefabricated metal buildings

Streamwood
Cook County

(G-19558)
A 1 TROPHIES AWARDS & ENGRV
Also Called: Allen Awards
1534 Brandy Pkwy (60107-1810)
PHONE...................................630 837-6000
Ray Begy, *President*
Susan Begy, *Vice Pres*
EMP: 4
SALES: 520K **Privately Held**
SIC: 5094 5999 3993 Trophies; trophies & plaques; signs & advertising specialties

(G-19559)
ADVANCED ASSEMBLY
703 Blue Ridge Dr (60107-4503)
PHONE...................................630 379-6158
Manu Patel, *Manager*
Ravi Patel, *Director*
EMP: 2
SALES: 300K **Privately Held**
SIC: 3449 Bars, concrete reinforcing: fabricated steel

(G-19560)
ALUMINUM COIL ANODIZING CORP (PA)
Also Called: A C A
501 E Lake St (60107-4100)
PHONE...................................630 837-4000
Gary Rusch, *President*
Gary Nesbit, *Business Mgr*
Kevin R Wasag, *Vice Pres*
Kevin Wasag, *Vice Pres*
Kevin R Wasag, *Vice Pres*
▲ **EMP:** 134 **EST:** 1960
SQ FT: 105,000
SALES (est): 37.3MM **Privately Held**
SIC: 3471 5051 Anodizing (plating) of metals or formed products; aluminum bars, rods, ingots, sheets, pipes, plates, etc.

(G-19561)
AMERICAN CONCORDE SYSTEMS
1548 Burgundy Pkwy (60107-1812)
P.O. Box 1011, Northbrook (60065-1011)
PHONE...................................773 342-9951
Paul Hansfield, *President*
Ron Kaplan, *General Mgr*
EMP: 15
SQ FT: 12,500
SALES (est): 1.5MM **Privately Held**
SIC: 3728 Aircraft parts & equipment

(G-19562)
ARTISAN GRAPHICS CO
1527 Burgundy Pkwy (60107-1811)
PHONE...................................847 841-9200
Ovi Condrea, *President*
Tony Doppke, *Manager*
EMP: 3 **EST:** 2009
SQ FT: 4,000
SALES: 120K **Privately Held**
SIC: 3993 Signs & advertising specialties

(G-19563)
ATHLETIC & SPORTS SEATING
676 Bonded Pkwy Ste L (60107-1815)
PHONE...................................630 837-5566
Daisy Gonzalez, *Principal*
EMP: 3
SALES (est): 226.6K **Privately Held**
WEB: www.athleticseating.com
SIC: 5712 5021 2511 Office furniture; household furniture; chairs, household, except upholstered: wood

(G-19564)
CAFFERO TOOL & MFG
Also Called: Jim's Plumbing
1537 Brandy Pkwy (60107-1809)
P.O. Box 288, Gilberts (60136-0288)
PHONE...................................224 293-2600
Paul Caffero, *CEO*
EMP: 75
SALES: 505K **Privately Held**
SIC: 3599 Machine shop, jobbing & repair

(G-19565)
CENTURION NON DESTRUCTIVE TSTG
Also Called: Centurion NDT
1400 Yorkshire Dr (60107-2272)
PHONE...................................630 736-5500
Kenneth F Strass Jr, *President*
Norma Strass, *Corp Secy*
EMP: 10
SQ FT: 5,000
SALES (est): 1.8MM **Privately Held**
SIC: 3825 8734 3829 Test equipment for electronic & electrical circuits; testing laboratories; measuring & controlling devices

(G-19566)
CONSOLIDATED CARQUEVILLE PRTG
1536 Bourbon Pkwy (60107-1808)
PHONE...................................630 246-6451
Philip Wicklander, *President*
Chuck McDermott, *Vice Pres*
Charlie Hummer, *Accounts Exec*
EMP: 110
SQ FT: 78,000
SALES (est): 23.9MM
SALES (corp-wide): 6.2B **Publicly Held**
SIC: 2752 Commercial printing, offset
HQ: Consolidated Graphics, Inc.
  5858 Westheimer Rd # 200
  Houston TX 77057
  713 787-0977

(G-19567)
CONTROLLED THERMAL PROCESSING (PA)
1521 Bourbon Pkwy (60107-1836)
PHONE...................................847 651-5511
Frederick Diekman, *President*
EMP: 3
SQ FT: 2,400
SALES (est): 500K **Privately Held**
SIC: 3823 3399 Thermal conductivity instruments, industrial process type; cryogenic treatment of metal

(G-19568)
COPY-MOR INC
Also Called: CMI
1536 Bourbon Pkwy (60107-1808)
PHONE...................................312 666-4000
David Steinberg, *President*
Quinn Tiritilli, *Production*
Sean Brennan, *Manager*
▲ **EMP:** 44
SALES (est): 14.4MM
SALES (corp-wide): 6.2B **Publicly Held**
SIC: 2752 2791 2789 Commercial printing, offset; typesetting; bookbinding & related work
HQ: Consolidated Graphics, Inc.
  5858 Westheimer Rd # 200
  Houston TX 77057
  713 787-0977

(G-19569)
CUSTOM FABRICATORS LLC (PA)
302 Roma Jean Pkwy (60107-2933)
PHONE...................................630 372-4399
Elias Villalpando, *Principal*
EMP: 13 **EST:** 2012
SALES (est): 2.6MM **Privately Held**
SIC: 3499 7692 7389 Fabricated metal products; welding repair; metal cutting services

(G-19570)
CUSTOM FABRICATORS LLC
106 Heine Dr (60107-1950)
PHONE...................................773 814-2757
Elias Villalpando, *Branch Mgr*
EMP: 14
SALES (corp-wide): 2.6MM **Privately Held**
SIC: 3441 Fabricated structural metal
PA: Custom Fabricators Llc
  302 Roma Jean Pkwy
  Streamwood IL 60107
  630 372-4399

(G-19571)
DSR SCREENPRINTING
676 Bonded Pkwy Ste L (60107-1815)
PHONE...................................630 855-2790
Wayne Sommers, *Owner*
EMP: 6
SALES (est): 825.7K **Privately Held**
WEB: www.dsrtshirts.com
SIC: 2752 Commercial printing, lithographic

(G-19572)
EMBEDDEDKITS
1025 Oakland Dr (60107-2106)
PHONE...................................847 401-7488
Silvano Romeo, *Owner*
EMP: 5
SALES (est): 497.3K **Privately Held**
SIC: 3544 Special dies & tools

(G-19573)
ENVELOPES ONLY INC
2000 S Park Ave (60107-2945)
PHONE...................................630 213-2500
Deborah L Craig, *President*
EMP: 23
SQ FT: 20,000
SALES (est): 4.6MM **Privately Held**
SIC: 2752 5112 Commercial printing, lithographic; envelopes

(G-19574)
FRESH EXPRESS INCORPORATED
1109 E Lake St (60107-4332)
PHONE...................................630 736-3900
Stuart Wilcox, *Principal*
Juan Ocampo, *Supervisor*
EMP: 46
SALES (corp-wide): 3B **Privately Held**
SIC: 0723 2099 Vegetable packing services; food preparations
HQ: Fresh Express Incorporated
  4757 The Grove Dr Ste 260
  Windermere FL 34786
  407 612-5000

(G-19575)
FRICKE DENTAL MANUFACTURING CO
165 Roma Jean Pkwy (60107-2962)
PHONE...................................630 540-1900
EMP: 6 **EST:** 1939
SQ FT: 7,500
SALES (est): 779.3K **Privately Held**
SIC: 3843 8021 Mfg Dental Equipment/Supplies Dentist's Office

(G-19576)
FURNACE FIXERS INC
308a Roma Jean Pkwy (60107-2933)
PHONE...................................630 736-0670
Duane Lamotte, *President*
Thomas Gogoel Jr, *President*
Leonard Gogoel, *Vice Pres*
EMP: 4
SQ FT: 5,000
SALES: 750K **Privately Held**
SIC: 3567 1711 Industrial furnaces & ovens; plumbing, heating, air-conditioning contractors

(G-19577)
HALLMARK INDUSTRIES INC
411 E North Ave (60107-2541)
PHONE...................................847 301-8050
Henry Huang, *President*
Jackie Wu, *Vice Pres*
▲ **EMP:** 10
SALES (est): 2MM **Privately Held**
SIC: 3621 5063 3545 Motors, electric; electrical apparatus & equipment; machine tool accessories

(G-19578)
J R MOLD INC
65 Sangra Ct (60107-2908)
PHONE...................................630 289-2192
Joseph M Raia, *President*
Patirica J Raia, *Corp Secy*
EMP: 5
SQ FT: 1,500
SALES (est): 450K **Privately Held**
WEB: www.sparxedm.com
SIC: 3544 Special dies & tools

(G-19579)
JB ENTERPRISES II INC (PA)
Also Called: Sealmaster Industries
375 Roma Jean Pkwy (60107-2932)
PHONE...................................630 372-8300
Michael J Bashir, *President*
Jonathan Bashir, *Vice Pres*
Irene Bashir, *Admin Sec*
EMP: 19
SQ FT: 4,250
SALES (est): 2.2MM **Privately Held**
SIC: 2951 Asphalt paving mixtures & blocks

(G-19580)
JC TOOL AND MOLD INC
1529 Burgundy Pkwy (60107-1811)
PHONE...................................630 483-2203
Jack J Coldsetti, *President*
EMP: 3
SALES (est): 314.9K **Privately Held**
SIC: 3544 Special dies & tools

(G-19581)
KOOL TECHNOLOGIES INC
Also Called: Alpine Refrigeration
714 Bonded Pkwy Ste A (60107-1803)
PHONE...................................630 483-2256
Kristine Schmitz, *President*
EMP: 4
SALES (est): 2MM **Privately Held**
SIC: 3585 1711 7623 Refrigeration & heating equipment; heating & air conditioning contractors; refrigeration service & repair

(G-19582)
KSO METALFAB INC
250 Roma Jean Pkwy (60107-2963)
PHONE...................................630 372-1200
Dora Kuzelka, *President*
Jeff T Nguyen, *Project Mgr*
Jeff Nguyen, *Project Mgr*
Virgilio Gamero, *Engineer*
Jack Cook, *Director*
EMP: 39
SQ FT: 34,000
SALES (est): 13.6MM **Privately Held**
SIC: 3441 Fabricated structural metal

(G-19583)
L I K INC
304 Roma Jean Pkwy (60107-2933)
PHONE...................................630 213-1282
Lisa Jurgens Carso, *President*
◆ **EMP:** 15
SQ FT: 14,000
SALES (est): 3.4MM **Privately Held**
SIC: 3679 Electronic circuits; harness assemblies for electronic use: wire or cable

(G-19584)
MENUS TO GO
676 Bonded Pkwy Ste A (60107-1815)
PHONE...................................630 483-0848
EMP: 2
SALES (est): 259.7K **Privately Held**
SIC: 2752 Lithographic Commercial Printing

(G-19585)
MEYER MATERIAL CO MERGER CORP
Also Called: Meyer Mtl Streamwood Yard 3
1021 Frances Dr (60107-2269)
PHONE...................................815 331-7200
Tony Grosso, *Manager*
EMP: 50

GEOGRAPHIC SECTION

Streator - Lasalle County (G-19614)

SALES (corp-wide): 4.5B *Privately Held*
SIC: 3273 Ready-mixed concrete
HQ: Meyer Material Company Llc
580 S Wolf Rd
Des Plaines IL 60016
815 331-7200

(G-19586)
MMM UNO CORP
142 Emerald Dr (60107-1282)
PHONE..............................773 577-7329
Ion Moraru, *President*
EMP: 5
SALES (est): 210.2K *Privately Held*
SIC: 3715 Truck trailers

(G-19587)
OMNITRONIX CORPORATION
349 Roma Jean Pkwy (60107-2932)
PHONE..............................630 837-1400
Allen M Ernst, *President*
Jason Ernst, *Vice Pres*
EMP: 18
SQ FT: 15,950
SALES (est): 3.4MM *Privately Held*
SIC: 3679 5065 Harness assemblies for electronic use; wire or cable; connectors, electronic

(G-19588)
PALLET SOLUTION
205 S Bartlett Rd (60107-1304)
PHONE..............................773 837-8677
Roberto De Lara, *Principal*
EMP: 4
SALES (est): 246.2K *Privately Held*
SIC: 2448 Pallets, wood

(G-19589)
PRIMO MICROPHONE INC ✪
2 Canterbury Ct (60107-1076)
PHONE..............................630 837-6119
EMP: 3 EST: 2019
SALES (est): 153.2K *Privately Held*
SIC: 3661 Telephone & telegraph apparatus

(G-19590)
PROGRESSIVE CONCEPTS
305 S Bartlett Rd Ste D (60107-2418)
PHONE..............................630 736-9822
Eric Hoppe, *Owner*
Sara Enriquez, *Sales Staff*
EMP: 2
SQ FT: 1,200
SALES (est): 226.9K *Privately Held*
SIC: 5731 3663 Radios, two-way, citizens' band, weather, short-wave, etc.; radio broadcasting & communications equipment

(G-19591)
PURE N NATURAL SYSTEMS INC
519 S Bartlett Rd (60107-1309)
P.O. Box 1137 (60107-8137)
PHONE..............................630 372-9681
Joseph A Roy Jr, *Principal*
Brenda Roy, *Vice Pres*
EMP: 10
SALES (est): 1MM *Privately Held*
SIC: 3585 3589 5075 Humidifiers & dehumidifiers; water filters & softeners, household type; air filters

(G-19592)
RANDOLPH PACKING CO
Also Called: Imperial Pizza
275 Roma Jean Pkwy (60107-2964)
PHONE..............................630 830-3100
A W Carmignani, *President*
Angelo B Carmignani, *Vice Pres*
Brooks Carmignani, *Vice Pres*
EMP: 100 EST: 1960
SQ FT: 50,000
SALES (est): 57.9MM *Privately Held*
WEB: www.randolphpacking.com
SIC: 5143 5149 7389 5142 Cheese; pizza supplies; packaging & labeling services; meat, frozen; packaged; sausages from purchased meat

(G-19593)
RETONDO ENTERPRISES INC
Also Called: Kut-Rite Tool Co.
1539 Brandy Pkwy (60107-1809)
PHONE..............................630 837-8130
Mark E Retondo, *President*
EMP: 4 EST: 1994
SALES (est): 291.2K *Privately Held*
SIC: 3545 Machine tool attachments & accessories

(G-19594)
SCIMITAR PROTOTYPING INC
1529 Bourbon Pkwy (60107-1836)
PHONE..............................630 483-3875
Stuart Garner, *President*
Jeffrey Garner, *Manager*
EMP: 3
SQ FT: 2,400
SALES (est): 583.2K *Privately Held*
SIC: 3089 Molding primary plastic

(G-19595)
SPARX EDM INC
65 Sangra Ct (60107-2908)
PHONE..............................847 722-7577
Joseph Raia, *President*
Laura Raia, *Admin Sec*
EMP: 7
SQ FT: 3,500
SALES (est): 600K *Privately Held*
SIC: 3089 5084 Injection molding of plastics; machinists' precision measuring tools

(G-19596)
STREAMWOOD PLATING CO
1545 Brandy Pkwy (60107-1809)
P.O. Box 569 (60107-0569)
PHONE..............................630 830-6363
Andy Patel, *President*
EMP: 9
SQ FT: 5,800
SALES (est): 1.1MM *Privately Held*
SIC: 3471 Plating of metals or formed products

(G-19597)
THREE CASTLE PRESS INC
213 Mayfield Dr (60107-1724)
PHONE..............................630 540-0120
EMP: 3 EST: 1969
SQ FT: 2,000
SALES (est): 220K *Privately Held*
SIC: 2759 2752 Commercial Printing Lithographic Commercial Printing

(G-19598)
TRELLBORG SLING SLTIONS US INC
Also Called: Trelleborg Slng Slns Strmwd
901 Phoenix Lake Ave (60107-2362)
PHONE..............................630 289-1500
Tom Zobitz, *General Mgr*
EMP: 99
SALES (corp-wide): 3.7B *Privately Held*
SIC: 3492 3053 Fluid power valves & hose fittings; gaskets, packing & sealing devices
HQ: Trelleborg Sealing Solutions Us, Inc.
2531 Bremer Rd
Fort Wayne IN 46803
260 749-9631

(G-19599)
TRIANGLE TECHNOLOGIES INC
687 Bonded Pkwy (60107-1840)
P.O. Box 8180, Bartlett (60103-8180)
PHONE..............................630 736-3318
Roger Mauer, *President*
▲ EMP: 5
SALES: 1MM *Privately Held*
SIC: 3565 8711 Packaging machinery; consulting engineer

(G-19600)
TVP COLOR GRAPHICS INC
230 Roma Jean Pkwy (60107-2963)
PHONE..............................630 837-3600
Uma Ravi, *President*
Bhaskar Ravi, *Vice Pres*
Chris Scheffki, *Prdtn Mgr*
Sudhir Ravi, *VP Mktg*
▲ EMP: 6
SALES (est): 930K *Privately Held*
SIC: 2752 7334 2732 Commercial printing, offset; photocopying & duplicating services; books: printing & binding

(G-19601)
VISOS MACHINE SHOP & MFG
686 Bonded Pkwy (60107-1839)
PHONE..............................630 372-3925
Darlene Viso, *President*
Nino Viso, *Vice Pres*
EMP: 2
SQ FT: 2,500
SALES (est): 242K *Privately Held*
SIC: 3599 Machine shop, jobbing & repair

(G-19602)
WET INTERNATIONAL INC
316 Roma Jean Pkwy (60107-2933)
PHONE..............................630 540-2113
Domingo Mesa, *President*
EMP: 29 EST: 1994
SALES (est): 6.6MM *Privately Held*
SIC: 2899 2841 2819 5169 Chemical preparations; soap & other detergents; charcoal (carbon), activated; chemicals & allied products; service establishment equipment; disinfecting services

(G-19603)
WET USA INC
Also Called: Water Environmental Tech
316 Roma Jean Pkwy (60107-2933)
PHONE..............................630 540-2113
Luz Uy, *President*
Domingo Mesa, *Vice Pres*
Jimmy Uy, *Consultant*
EMP: 7
SALES (est): 969.6K *Privately Held*
SIC: 8748 2899 Environmental consultant; chemical preparations

(G-19604)
WOODWORK APTS LLC
124 Linden Ave (60107-3161)
PHONE..............................224 595-9691
EMP: 4
SALES (est): 308.4K *Privately Held*
SIC: 2431 Millwork

Streator
Lasalle County

(G-19605)
BRAVE PRODUCTS INC
1705 N Shabbona St (61364-1301)
PHONE..............................815 672-0551
Paul Walker, *President*
EMP: 6 EST: 2001
SALES (est): 926.9K *Privately Held*
SIC: 3531 Log splitters

(G-19606)
CORAS WELDING SHOP INC
Also Called: Coras Trailer Manufacturing
1901 N Shabbona St (61364-1381)
P.O. Box 566 (61364-0566)
PHONE..............................815 672-7950
Luis Castaneda, *President*
Carlos Castaneda, *President*
Brian Heider, *Sales Staff*
▲ EMP: 8
SALES (est): 2.7MM *Privately Held*
SIC: 7692 Welding repair

(G-19607)
DOVIN MACHINE SHOP INC
521 Lundy St (61364-3013)
PHONE..............................815 672-5247
William Dovin Jr, *President*
EMP: 2
SALES (est): 265.9K *Privately Held*
SIC: 3599 Machine shop, jobbing & repair

(G-19608)
FLINK COMPANY (PA)
502 N Vermillion St (61364-2245)
PHONE..............................815 673-4321
Mike Supergan, *President*
Laura Webster, *Project Mgr*
Duane Kruger, *Opers Staff*
Karen Downey, *Human Res Mgr*
Michelle Wright, *Human Res Mgr*
EMP: 49 EST: 1929
SQ FT: 24,000
SALES (est): 10.7MM *Privately Held*
WEB: www.flinkco.com
SIC: 3531 Snow plow attachments; aggregate spreaders

(G-19609)
GUARDIAN ANGEL OUTREACH
111 Spring St (61364-3332)
PHONE..............................815 672-4567
Joyce Redfern, *Director*
EMP: 3 EST: 2008
SALES (est): 181.5K *Privately Held*
WEB: www.ccdop.org
SIC: 2835 Pregnancy test kits

(G-19610)
GUZZLER MANUFACTURING INC
1621 S Illinois St (61364-3945)
PHONE..............................815 672-3171
Bill Gass, *President*
Greg Grant, *Production*
Pamela Holmes, *Purchasing*
Sarah Studnicki, *QA Dir*
Doug Johnson, *QC Mgr*
EMP: 170
SALES (est): 29.8MM *Privately Held*
WEB: www.guzzler.com
SIC: 3559 3561 Automotive related machinery; industrial pumps & parts

(G-19611)
IMAGE PRINT INC (PA)
31070 N 600 East Rd (61364-8895)
PHONE..............................815 672-1068
David C Fitzsimmons, *President*
Thomas Fitzsimmons, *Vice Pres*
EMP: 5 EST: 1960
SQ FT: 5,000
SALES (est): 456.5K *Privately Held*
WEB: www.imageprintweb.com
SIC: 2752 2791 2789 Commercial printing, offset; typesetting; bookbinding & related work

(G-19612)
JOE HATZER & SON INC (PA)
Also Called: Hatzer Ready Mix
602 Lundy St (61364-3051)
PHONE..............................815 673-5571
Dennis Hatzer, *President*
Sandra Hatzer, *Corp Secy*
Jeff Hatzer, *Vice Pres*
EMP: 20
SQ FT: 7,500
SALES (est): 2.4MM *Privately Held*
WEB: www.joehatzerandson.com
SIC: 3273 1794 7353 Ready-mixed concrete; excavation work; cranes & aerial lift equipment, rental or leasing

(G-19613)
JOE HATZER & SON INC
Also Called: Hatzer Ready Mix
2515 1/2 N Bloomington St (61364)
PHONE..............................815 672-2161
Dennis Hatzer, *President*
EMP: 5
SALES (corp-wide): 2.4MM *Privately Held*
SIC: 3273 Ready-mixed concrete
PA: Joe Hatzer & Son, Inc.
602 Lundy St
Streator IL 61364
815 673-5571

(G-19614)
MID-AMERICA TRUCK CORPORATION
Also Called: U S Truck Body-Midwest
1807 N Bloomington St (61364-1317)
PHONE..............................815 672-3211
Paul Walker, *President*
James L Walker, *Vice Pres*
Chris Walker, *Admin Sec*
Thomas Walker, *Admin Sec*
EMP: 70
SQ FT: 48,000
SALES (est): 15.2MM
SALES (corp-wide): 83MM *Privately Held*
SIC: 3713 Van bodies
HQ: Streator Industrial Handling, Inc.
1705 N Shabbona St
Streator IL 61364
815 672-0551

Streator - Lasalle County (G-19615)

(G-19615)
MORTON BUILDINGS INC
1519 N Il Route 23 (61364-9393)
PHONE.................................630 904-1122
Fax: 630 904-1161
EMP: 13
SALES (corp-wide): 418.2MM **Privately Held**
SIC: 3448 1542 Mfg Prefabricated Metal Buildings Nonresidential Construction
PA: Morton Buildings, Inc.
   252 W Adams St
   Morton IL 61550
   309 263-7474

(G-19616)
MURRAY CABINETRY & TOPS INC
Also Called: Luxury Bath Systems
407 N Bloomington St (61364-2201)
PHONE.................................815 672-6992
Doug J Murray, *Owner*
Pauline Murray, *Principal*
EMP: 6
SQ FT: 20,000
SALES (est): 1MM **Privately Held**
WEB: www.mctluxbath.com
SIC: 2541 2542 2434 Counters or counter display cases, wood; office & store showcases & display fixtures; wood kitchen cabinets

(G-19617)
MUSHRO MACHINE & TOOL CO
819 E Bridge St (61364-3034)
P.O. Box 444 (61364-0444)
PHONE.................................815 672-5848
Chris Walker, *President*
Paul Walker, *Vice Pres*
Dan Kusch, *Treasurer*
Shirley Hammer, *Office Mgr*
EMP: 10 EST: 1975
SQ FT: 5,300
SALES (est): 825K
SALES (corp-wide): 83MM **Privately Held**
SIC: 3599 7692 3544 Machine shop, jobbing & repair; welding repair; special dies, tools, jigs & fixtures
HQ: Streator Industrial Handling, Inc.
   1705 N Shabbona St
   Streator IL 61364
   815 672-0551

(G-19618)
OI GLASS CONTAINERS OI G9
901 N Shabbona St (61364-2058)
PHONE.................................815 673-5120
Ken Sokol, *Plant Mgr*
▲ EMP: 2
SALES (est): 749.8K **Privately Held**
SIC: 3231 Products of purchased glass

(G-19619)
OWENS-BROCKWAY GLASS CONT INC
901 N Shabbona St (61364-2096)
PHONE.................................815 672-3141
Ken Sokol, *Systems Mgr*
EMP: 210
SALES (corp-wide): 6.6B **Publicly Held**
WEB: www.o-i.com
SIC: 3221 Packers' ware (containers), glass
HQ: Owens-Brockway Glass Container Inc.
   1 Michael Owens Way
   Perrysburg OH 43551

(G-19620)
PHOTO GRAPHIC DESIGN SERVICE
124 N Bloomington St (61364-2208)
PHONE.................................815 672-4417
James C Olmsted, *President*
Barbara Olmsted, *Vice Pres*
EMP: 4
SQ FT: 2,000
SALES (est): 340.9K **Privately Held**
SIC: 2752 2791 Commercial printing, offset; typesetting

(G-19621)
PMW HOLDINGS INC (PA)
1705 N Shabbona St (61364-1301)
PHONE.................................815 672-0551
Paul A Walker, *President*
EMP: 5
SALES (est): 83MM **Privately Held**
SIC: 3537 3714 Lift trucks, industrial: fork, platform, straddle, etc.; motor vehicle parts & accessories

(G-19622)
SIEMENS INDUSTRY INC
810 W Grant St (61364-1912)
PHONE.................................815 672-2653
Jeffery Cain, *Vice Pres*
Jeffrey Sousa, *Vice Pres*
Edwin Castaneda, *Project Mgr*
Adair Andrew, *Opers Mgr*
Peter Seitz, *Production*
EMP: 5
SALES (corp-wide): 96.9B **Privately Held**
WEB: www.new.siemens.com
SIC: 3589 Sewage & water treatment equipment
HQ: Siemens Industry, Inc.
   1000 Deerfield Pkwy
   Buffalo Grove IL 60089
   847 215-1000

(G-19623)
SOUTH POST LLC
104 E Livingston Rd (61364-3802)
PHONE.................................815 510-9395
Pflibsen R Brian, *Principal*
EMP: 4
SALES (est): 200.8K **Privately Held**
SIC: 2711 Newspapers, publishing & printing

(G-19624)
STERTIL ALM CORP
200 Benchmark Indus Dr (61364-9400)
PHONE.................................815 673-5546
Jan Bosch, *President*
Douglas F Grunnet, *Principal*
Allan Pavlick, *Vice Pres*
Allan Pavlik, *Vice Pres*
Ron Ansteth, *Site Mgr*
◆ EMP: 60 EST: 1982
SQ FT: 60,000
SALES (est): 18.2MM
SALES (corp-wide): 242.1K **Privately Held**
SIC: 3536 Hoists, cranes & monorails
HQ: Stertil Group B.V.
   Westkern 3
   Kootstertille 9288
   512 334-444

(G-19625)
STREATOR ASPHALT INC
1019 E Livingston Rd (61364-3928)
PHONE.................................815 672-8683
EMP: 8
SALES (corp-wide): 4.2MM **Privately Held**
SIC: 3531 2951 Mfg Construction Machinery Mfg Asphalt Mixtures/Blocks
HQ: Streator Asphalt, Inc
   104 S Park Rd
   Herscher IL 60941

(G-19626)
STREATOR INDUSTRIAL HDLG INC (HQ)
Also Called: Streator Dependable Mfg
1705 N Shabbona St (61364-1301)
PHONE.................................815 672-0551
Paul Walker, *President*
Chris G Walker, *Exec VP*
James Walker, *Vice Pres*
Jeremy Walker, *Vice Pres*
Thomas Walker, *Treasurer*
◆ EMP: 60 EST: 1945
SQ FT: 80,000
SALES (est): 83MM **Privately Held**
WEB: www.streatordependable.com
SIC: 3443 Industrial vessels, tanks & containers; bins, prefabricated metal plate
PA: Pmw Holdings, Inc.
   1705 N Shabbona St
   Streator IL 61364
   815 672-0551

(G-19627)
STREATOR MACHINE COMPANY
Also Called: Streator Machine Mfg Co
504 E Larue St (61364-2040)
PHONE.................................815 672-2436
Rody J Hays, *President*
Donna Hays, *Corp Secy*
Patricia Hays, *Vice Pres*
Arthur Hays, *Director*
EMP: 5 EST: 1924
SQ FT: 5,000
SALES (est): 611.4K **Privately Held**
WEB: www.streatordependable.com
SIC: 3599 Machine shop, jobbing & repair

(G-19628)
SUN TIMES NEWS AGENCY
56 Sunset Dr (61364-2623)
PHONE.................................815 672-1260
Michael Renner, *Principal*
EMP: 5
SALES (est): 139.5K **Privately Held**
SIC: 2711 7383 Newspapers, publishing & printing; news syndicates

(G-19629)
TELEWELD INC
502 N Vermillion St (61364-2256)
PHONE.................................815 672-4561
Mike Suergan, *President*
Duane Kruger, *Opers Staff*
Karen Downey, *Hum Res Coord*
Chad Wissen, *Sales Staff*
Charles F Marquis, *Shareholder*
EMP: 10 EST: 1957
SQ FT: 11,000
SALES (est): 2.3MM **Privately Held**
WEB: www.teleweld.com
SIC: 3743 3531 Railroad equipment, except locomotives; railway track equipment

(G-19630)
TIMES-PRESS PUBLISHING CO
115 Oak St (61364-2805)
PHONE.................................815 673-3771
Jean Alice Small, *Ch of Bd*
James Malley, *President*
EMP: 35
SQ FT: 10,000
SALES (est): 1.8MM
SALES (corp-wide): 131.4MM **Privately Held**
SIC: 2711 Commercial printing & newspaper publishing combined
HQ: Ottawa Publishing Co Inc
   110 W Jefferson St
   Ottawa IL 61350
   815 433-2000

(G-19631)
TRANSCO PRODUCTS INC
1215 E 12th St (61364-3967)
PHONE.................................312 427-2818
Edward Wolbert, *President*
Bruce Alpha, *Vice Pres*
Brian Condon, *Production*
Orie Barnes, *QC Mgr*
Steven Grieshaber, *Engineer*
▲ EMP: 77
SALES: 16.3MM
SALES (corp-wide): 96.7MM **Privately Held**
SIC: 3479 3296 Coating of metals & formed products; insulation: rock wool, slag & silica minerals
PA: Transco Inc.
   200 N La Salle St # 1550
   Chicago IL 60601
   312 896-8527

(G-19632)
VACTOR MANUFACTURING INC
1621 S Illinois St (61364-3945)
PHONE.................................815 672-3171
Samuel Miceli, *President*
Lloyd Hillyer, *Mfg Mgr*
Roy Snyder, *Safety Mgr*
Gerald Huddleston, *Mfg Staff*
Jerry Reihl, *Production*
◆ EMP: 1500
SQ FT: 109,488
SALES (est): 228.8MM
SALES (corp-wide): 1.2B **Publicly Held**
SIC: 3537 Industrial trucks & tractors
PA: Federal Signal Corporation
   1415 W 22nd St Ste 1100
   Oak Brook IL 60523
   630 954-2000

Stronghurst
Henderson County

(G-19633)
D C COOPER CORPORATION
Junction 116 & 94 (61480)
P.O. Box 210 (61480-0210)
PHONE.................................309 924-1941
Kim R Gullberg, *President*
EMP: 9
SQ FT: 12,500
SALES (est): 1.7MM **Privately Held**
WEB: www.dccoopertanks.com
SIC: 3443 Industrial vessels, tanks & containers; metal parts

(G-19634)
HENDERSON HANCOCK QUILL INC
Also Called: Henderson County Quill
102 N Broadway St (61480-5023)
P.O. Box 149 (61480-0149)
PHONE.................................309 924-1871
Dessa Roddeffer, *President*
Shirley Linder, *Editor*
EMP: 5
SALES (est): 221.5K **Privately Held**
SIC: 2711 Newspapers: publishing only, not printed on site

Sublette
Lee County

(G-19635)
COUNTRY VILLAGE MEATS
401 N Pennsylvania St (61367-9400)
PHONE.................................815 849-5532
Edward L Morrissey, *President*
EMP: 5
SALES (est): 427.2K **Privately Held**
SIC: 5421 2013 2011 Meat markets, including freezer provisioners; sausages & other prepared meats; meat packing plants

(G-19636)
ERBES ELECTRIC
409 W Main St (61367-9443)
P.O. Box 92 (61367-0092)
PHONE.................................815 849-5508
Douglas Erbes, *Owner*
EMP: 2
SALES (est): 250K **Privately Held**
SIC: 7694 1731 Electric motor repair; electrical work

Sugar Grove
Kane County

(G-19637)
AXIS DESIGN ARCHITECTUAL MLLWK
239 State Route 47 (60554-9423)
P.O. Box 154 (60554-0154)
PHONE.................................630 466-4549
Bear Wegener, *President*
Edward Wegener, *Treasurer*
EMP: 10
SQ FT: 3,300
SALES (est): 400K **Privately Held**
SIC: 2499 1751 Food handling & processing products, wood; cabinet & finish carpentry

(G-19638)
BETA PAK INC
1600 Beta Dr (60554-7901)
PHONE.................................708 466-7844
John Bensen, *President*
EMP: 10
SALES (est): 453.7K **Privately Held**
SIC: 2782 Looseleaf binders & devices

(G-19639)
CHICAGO JET GROUP LLC (PA)
43 W 522 Rr 30 (60554)
PHONE.................................630 466-3600

GEOGRAPHIC SECTION

Michael J Mitera, *Mng Member*
EMP: 20
SALES (est): 5.4MM Privately Held
SIC: 3519 Jet propulsion engines

(G-19640)
CMC ELECTRONICS AURORA LLC
84 N Dugan Rd (60554-9417)
PHONE.................630 556-9619
Greg Yeldon,
EMP: 100
SQ FT: 6,000
SALES (est): 15.5MM
SALES (corp-wide): 5.2B Publicly Held
SIC: 3728 Aircraft assemblies, subassemblies & parts
HQ: Esterline Technologies Corp
  1301 E 9th St Ste 3000
  Cleveland OH 44114
  425 453-9400

(G-19641)
CYLINDER SERVICES INC
629 N Heartland Dr (60554-9594)
PHONE.................630 466-9820
Art Gehrs, *President*
Michael Gehrs, *Vice Pres*
Holly Gehrs, *Admin Sec*
EMP: 5
SQ FT: 5,000
SALES (est): 636.9K Privately Held
SIC: 7699 7692 Hydraulic equipment repair; welding repair

(G-19642)
DEEP COAT LLC
550 N Heartland Dr (60554-9586)
PHONE.................630 466-1505
Rick Fellabaum, *Opers Dir*
Kim Thorson, *Engineer*
Kim M Thorson, *Mng Member*
Allyson Plonka, *Admin Asst*
EMP: 25 EST: 2008
SQ FT: 30,000
SALES (est): 3.2MM Privately Held
WEB: www.deepcoat.com
SIC: 3471 Plating of metals or formed products

(G-19643)
FALEX CORPORATION
Also Called: F L C
1020 Airpark Dr (60554-9452)
PHONE.................630 556-3679
Leslie R Heerdt, *Ch of Bd*
Tim Stola, *VP Mfg*
Eric Menzer, *Purchasing*
Michael Feltman, *Engineer*
Erin Kerr, *Engineer*
EMP: 48
SQ FT: 15,000
SALES (est): 9.5MM Privately Held
WEB: www.falex.com
SIC: 8742 3829 3825 Management consulting services; physical property testing equipment; instruments to measure electricity

(G-19644)
FINISHES UNLIMITED INC
Also Called: C C I
482 Wheeler Rd (60554-9749)
P.O. Box 69 (60554-0069)
PHONE.................630 466-4881
Kenneth W Burton, *President*
Peter Smelyansky, *Vice Pres*
John R Schwartz, *VP Mfg*
Jill Olson, *Treasurer*
EMP: 17
SQ FT: 20,000
SALES (est): 6.4MM Privately Held
SIC: 2851 Paints & paint additives; lacquers, varnishes, enamels & other coatings

(G-19645)
FRANKLIN AUTOMATION INC
1981 Bucktail Ln (60554-9609)
PHONE.................630 466-1900
Frank Kigyos Jr, *President*
Susan J Kigyos, *Vice Pres*
Norm Pierce, *Engineer*
Brian Buchberger, *Manager*
▲ **EMP:** 15
SQ FT: 10,000

SALES (est): 9MM Privately Held
SIC: 5084 3599 Conveyor systems; custom machinery

(G-19646)
HFR PRECISION MACHINING INC
1015 Airpark Dr (60554-9585)
PHONE.................630 556-4325
Leslie R Heerdt, *Ch of Bd*
Richard Tarbaz, *President*
Andrew R Faville, *COO*
▲ **EMP:** 50 EST: 1958
SQ FT: 50,000
SALES (est): 10.1MM Privately Held
WEB: www.hfrprecision.com
SIC: 3599 7692 Machine shop, jobbing & repair; grinding castings for the trade; welding repair

(G-19647)
HY-TEK MANUFACTURING CO INC
Also Called: HMC
1998 Bucktail Ln (60554-9609)
PHONE.................630 466-7664
John Bastian, *President*
John Jude, *Engineer*
Christopher Bastian, *VP Bus Dvlpt*
Mary Lake, *Accounting Mgr*
▲ **EMP:** 46
SQ FT: 45,000
SALES (est): 8.3MM Privately Held
SIC: 3599 Machine shop, jobbing & repair

(G-19648)
OSHKOSH/MCNLUS FNCL SVCS PRTNR
490 N Heartland Dr (60554-9321)
PHONE.................630 466-5100
Scott Whetvel, *Owner*
Joseph Kraft, *Manager*
EMP: 6
SALES (est): 496.7K
SALES (corp-wide): 1.2MM Privately Held
SIC: 3711 Motor vehicles & car bodies
PA: Oshkosh/Mcneilus Financial Services Partnership
  524 E Highway St
  Dodge Center MN 55927
  507 374-6321

(G-19649)
PLASTAK INC
44w40 Scott Rd (60554)
PHONE.................630 466-4100
Susan Slamans, *President*
Bruce Slamans, *General Mgr*
EMP: 8
SALES (est): 666.2K Privately Held
SIC: 3599 Machine shop, jobbing & repair

(G-19650)
PRODUCERS CHEMICAL COMPANY
1960 Bucktail Ln (60554-9609)
PHONE.................630 466-4584
Roger T Harris, *CEO*
Jeff Szklarek, *President*
Brian Shannon, *Vice Pres*
David Sweigert, *Vice Pres*
EMP: 24
SQ FT: 45,000
SALES (est): 22MM Privately Held
WEB: www.producerschemical.com
SIC: 5169 2899 Industrial chemicals; chemical preparations

(G-19651)
QUALIFIED INNOVATION INC
1016 Airpark Dr Ste B (60554-9847)
PHONE.................630 556-4136
Gary L Fuller, *President*
Sue Fuller, *Manager*
EMP: 10
SQ FT: 37,000
SALES (est): 2.5MM Privately Held
SIC: 2672 5113 Coated & laminated paper; industrial & personal service paper

(G-19652)
QUANTUM SIGN CORPORATION
693 N Heartland Dr (60554-9594)
PHONE.................630 466-0372

David Stover, *President*
Roger Perotti, *Vice Pres*
Adam Mozdzierz, *Foreman/Supr*
Mike Miller, *Project Engr*
Holly Mueller, *Human Res Mgr*
▲ **EMP:** 19
SQ FT: 12,000
SALES (est): 9.2MM Privately Held
WEB: www.quantumsigncorp.com
SIC: 5046 3993 Signs, electrical; signs & advertising specialties

(G-19653)
SCOT INDUSTRIES INC
1961 W Us Highway 30 (60554-9615)
P.O. Box 309 (60554-0309)
PHONE.................630 466-7591
Clint Mabey, *General Mgr*
Ray Folyer, *Plant Mgr*
Chris Rasmussen, *Production*
Christine Pritts, *Purch Agent*
Brian Ransom, *Buyer*
EMP: 58
SALES (corp-wide): 140.7MM Privately Held
WEB: www.scotindustries.com
SIC: 3599 5051 3498 3471 Machine shop, jobbing & repair; metals service centers & offices; fabricated pipe & fittings; plating & polishing
PA: Scot Industries, Inc.
  3756 Fm 250 N
  Lone Star TX 75668
  903 639-2551

(G-19654)
SELECTIVE LABEL & TABS INC
1962 Us Rte 30 (60554)
PHONE.................630 466-0091
Tom Kennedy, *President*
Ralph Chneider, *President*
Helen Hornung, *Principal*
Dale Klungland, *Vice Pres*
Miriam Kinzel, *Admin Sec*
EMP: 10
SQ FT: 10,000
SALES (est): 1.2MM Privately Held
SIC: 2759 Labels & seals: printing

(G-19655)
SELECTIVE LABEL & TABS INC
1962 W Us Highway 30 (60554-9621)
PHONE.................630 466-0091
Tom Kennedy, *President*
EMP: 7
SQ FT: 6,000
SALES (est): 1.1MM Privately Held
SIC: 2759 Commercial printing

(G-19656)
SIGN FX
769 N Heartland Dr Ste E (60554-9347)
PHONE.................630 466-7446
Marc E Ebert, *Principal*
EMP: 6
SALES (est): 1.1MM Privately Held
SIC: 3993 Signs & advertising specialties

(G-19657)
SUPERIOR METAL PRODUCTS INC
1993 Bucktail Ln (60554-9609)
PHONE.................630 466-1150
Brian Warren, *President*
Beth Warren, *Corp Secy*
Darrell Warren, *Vice Pres*
EMP: 14
SQ FT: 13,000
SALES (est): 2.9MM Privately Held
SIC: 3469 Stamping metal for the trade

(G-19658)
TUSKIN EQUIPMENT CORPORATION
483 N Heartland Dr Ste F (60554-8206)
PHONE.................630 466-5590
Kristine O'Dwyer, *President*
Jeffrey O'Dwyer, *Admin Sec*
EMP: 5
SQ FT: 7,000
SALES: 900K Privately Held
SIC: 3561 3559 Industrial pumps & parts; plastics working machinery

Sullivan
Moultrie County

(G-19659)
AGRI-FAB INC
701 W Eden St (61951-1728)
PHONE.................217 728-8388
John Benda, *President*
EMP: 5
SALES (corp-wide): 29.3MM Privately Held
SIC: 3469 Metal stampings
HQ: Agri-Fab, Inc.
  809 S Hamilton St
  Sullivan IL 61951
  217 728-8388

(G-19660)
B & B FABRICATIONS LLC
901 W Jefferson St (61951-1753)
PHONE.................217 620-3210
Michael Bernius, *President*
Joshua Bernius, *Vice Pres*
EMP: 2 EST: 2011
SQ FT: 12,000
SALES (est): 787.3K Privately Held
SIC: 3317 3441 Steel pipe & tubes; fabricated structural metal

(G-19661)
BEST NEWSPAPERS IN ILL INC
Also Called: News Progress
100 W Monroe St (61951-1427)
P.O. Box 290 (61951-0290)
PHONE.................217 728-7381
Robert Best, *President*
Kathy Best, *Vice Pres*
EMP: 8 EST: 1961
SQ FT: 4,800
SALES (est): 618.4K Privately Held
WEB: www.newsprogress.com
SIC: 2711 Commercial printing & newspaper publishing combined; job printing & newspaper publishing combined

(G-19662)
BRUDER TANK INC
901 W Jefferson St (61951-1753)
PHONE.................217 292-9058
Michael S Bernius, *President*
Joshua Bernius, *Mng Member*
EMP: 35 EST: 2014
SALES (est): 1.6MM Privately Held
WEB: www.brudertank.com
SIC: 3713 3312 3443 3795 Tank truck bodies; stainless steel; tanks for tank trucks, metal plate; tanks & tank components

(G-19663)
CARROLLS WELDING & FABRICATION
819 N Market St (61951-8802)
PHONE.................217 728-8720
John Carroll, *Owner*
EMP: 4 EST: 1991
SQ FT: 5,500
SALES (est): 254.2K Privately Held
SIC: 7692 Welding repair

(G-19664)
CENTRAL WOOD PRODUCTS INC
1809 Cr 1300e (61951-6532)
PHONE.................217 728-4412
Kenny Bontraaer, *President*
EMP: 20
SQ FT: 18,000
SALES (est): 3.2MM Privately Held
SIC: 2448 2449 2441 Pallets, wood; wood containers; nailed wood boxes & shook

(G-19665)
CIRCLE T MANUFACTURING LLC
1801a Cr 1300e (61951-6535)
PHONE.................217 728-4834
Clarence Otto,
EMP: 8

Sullivan - Moultrie County (G-19666) GEOGRAPHIC SECTION

SALES (est): 973.5K **Privately Held**
SIC: 3999 Barber & beauty shop equipment

(G-19666)
EVERLAST PORTABLE BUILDINGS
1565 Cr 1800n (61951-6576)
PHONE..................217 543-4080
Eldon Miller, *Owner*
EMP: 5
SQ FT: 3,200
SALES (est): 1MM **Privately Held**
SIC: 2452 Prefabricated wood buildings

(G-19667)
FAZE CHANGE PRODUX
Also Called: Econodome Kits
1331 Cr 1470e (61951-6862)
PHONE..................217 728-2184
Wil Fidroeff, *Owner*
EMP: 30
SQ FT: 3,000
SALES (est): 1.9MM **Privately Held**
SIC: 2452 Prefabricated wood buildings

(G-19668)
HYDRO-GEAR INC (DH)
1411 S Hamilton St (61951-2264)
PHONE..................217 728-2581
Ray Hauser, *President*
Gary Harvey, *Partner*
Jack Obiala, *Partner*
David Dunten, *Business Mgr*
Mike McCoy, *Vice Pres*
▲ EMP: 212
SQ FT: 80,000
SALES (est): 70.8MM
SALES (corp-wide): 250.7K **Privately Held**
SIC: 3594 Hydrostatic drives (transmissions)
HQ: Danfoss A/S
    Nordborgvej 81
    Nordborg 6430
    748 822-22

(G-19669)
ILLINOIS PRINTING SERVICES INC
800 S Patterson Rd (61951-8403)
P.O. Box 106 (61951-0106)
PHONE..................217 728-2786
Thomas M Bunfill, *President*
Chris Eckel, *Production*
Kelsey Binder, *Manager*
EMP: 6
SALES (est): 772.3K **Privately Held**
SIC: 2752 Commercial printing, offset

(G-19670)
MID-STATE TANK CO INC
1357 Johnson Creek Rd (61951)
P.O. Box 317 (61951-0317)
PHONE..................217 728-8383
Gery V Conlin, *President*
Elmer Gingrich, *Vice Pres*
Gene Good, *Vice Pres*
Jason Fleming, *QC Mgr*
Brian Kidd, *Engineer*
EMP: 88
SQ FT: 33,000
SALES (est): 39.6MM **Privately Held**
SIC: 3443 Tanks, standard or custom fabricated: metal plate

(G-19671)
MONARCH MFG CORP AMER
Hc 32 Box S (61951)
P.O. Box 653 (61951-0653)
PHONE..................217 728-2552
Donald Jesse, *President*
Pam Jesse, *Vice Pres*
Amy Graven, *Sales Mgr*
EMP: 32 EST: 1976
SQ FT: 16,000
SALES (est): 5.1MM **Privately Held**
WEB: www.monarchcabinetry.com
SIC: 2434 Wood kitchen cabinets

(G-19672)
MOULTRI CNTY HSTRCL/GNLGCL SCT
Also Called: Historcal Genealogical Soc Mou
117 E Harrison St (61951-2001)
P.O. Box 588 (61951-0588)
PHONE..................217 728-4085
Jenny Sutton, *President*
Mary L Storm, *Director*
EMP: 10
SALES (est): 267.7K **Privately Held**
SIC: 7299 7532 1711 3599 Genealogical investigation service; exterior repair services; boiler & furnace contractors; machine shop, jobbing & repair

(G-19673)
MOULTRIE COUNTY REDI-MIX CO
622 S Worth St (61951-2199)
PHONE..................217 728-2334
Roger Daily, *Owner*
Barb Daily, *Corp Secy*
David Daily, *Vice Pres*
EMP: 7
SALES (est): 1.4MM **Privately Held**
SIC: 3273 Ready-mixed concrete

(G-19674)
O K JOBBERS INC
Also Called: O.k Jobbers
215 S Hamilton St (61951-1951)
PHONE..................217 728-7378
Chad Dust, *CEO*
Ron Jenkins, *Manager*
Bill West, *Manager*
EMP: 5 EST: 1946
SQ FT: 12,000
SALES (est): 723.6K **Privately Held**
SIC: 5013 5531 3599 Automotive supplies & parts; automotive parts; automotive accessories; machine shop, jobbing & repair

(G-19675)
WIL SON PALLET
1858 Cr 1300e (61951-6533)
PHONE..................217 543-3555
Matt Schlabach, *Owner*
▲ EMP: 25
SQ FT: 18,000
SALES (est): 1.5MM **Privately Held**
SIC: 2449 2448 Rectangular boxes & crates, wood; pallets, wood

Summit Argo
Cook County

(G-19676)
ACH FOOD COMPANIES INC
Also Called: Best Foods Baking Group
6400 S Archer Rd (60501-1935)
P.O. Box 448 (60501-0448)
PHONE..................708 458-8690
Ronald Kuehn, *Branch Mgr*
EMP: 200
SALES (corp-wide): 20B **Privately Held**
SIC: 5149 2079 Groceries & related products; edible fats & oils
HQ: Ach Food Companies, Inc.
    1 Parkview Plz Ste 500
    Oakbrook Terrace IL 60181

(G-19677)
ACTION TURBINE REPAIR SVC INC
5120 W Lawndale Ave (60501-1075)
PHONE..................708 924-9601
Jozef Krezel, *President*
Charles Siebert, *Sales Staff*
EMP: 10
SALES (est): 2.2MM **Privately Held**
WEB: www.actiontrs.com
SIC: 3511 7699 Turbines & turbine generator sets; industrial machinery & equipment repair

(G-19678)
DYERS MACHINE SERVICE INC
Also Called: Dyer's Superchargers
7665 W 63rd St (60501-1811)
PHONE..................708 496-8100
Gary Dyer, *President*
Bill Dyer, *Vice Pres*
EMP: 6
SQ FT: 6,000
SALES (est): 260K **Privately Held**
SIC: 3599 7692 Machine shop, jobbing & repair; welding repair

(G-19679)
HERITAGE MEDIA SVCS CO OF ILL
Also Called: Des Plaines Valley News
7676 W 63rd St (60501-1812)
P.O. Box 348 (60501-0348)
PHONE..................708 594-9340
Bob Bong, *Principal*
EMP: 6
SQ FT: 3,000
SALES (est): 205K **Privately Held**
SIC: 2711 2791 Newspapers: publishing only, not printed on site; typesetting

(G-19680)
INGREDION INCORPORATED
6400 S Archer Rd (60501-1935)
PHONE..................708 728-3535
Jose Godina, *Manager*
EMP: 152
SALES (corp-wide): 6.2B **Publicly Held**
SIC: 2046 Wet corn milling
PA: Ingredion Incorporated
    5 Westbrook Corporate Ctr # 500
    Westchester IL 60154
    708 551-2600

(G-19681)
SAM SOLUTIONS INC
5120 S Lawndale Ave (60501)
PHONE..................708 594-0480
Renata Malecki, *President*
Joseph Malecki, *Admin Secy*
EMP: 5
SALES: 1MM **Privately Held**
SIC: 3599 Machine shop, jobbing & repair

(G-19682)
SUMMIT SHEET METAL SPECIALISTS
7325 W 59th St (60501-1419)
PHONE..................708 458-8622
Katheleen M Pavloski, *President*
EMP: 17
SQ FT: 3,600
SALES (est): 2MM **Privately Held**
SIC: 3444 Sheet metal specialties, not stamped

(G-19683)
SUMMIT WINDOW CO INC
7719 W 60th Pl Ste 6 (60501-1591)
PHONE..................708 594-3200
Alex Nitchoff, *President*
EMP: 6
SALES (est): 720K **Privately Held**
SIC: 3442 Window & door frames

(G-19684)
VONDRAK PUBLISHING CO INC
Also Called: Southwest Senior
7676 W 63rd St (60501-1812)
PHONE..................773 476-4800
James Von Drak, *President*
Rob Gusanders, *Vice Pres*
EMP: 35
SQ FT: 9,500
SALES (est): 2.2MM **Privately Held**
WEB: www.swnewsherald.com
SIC: 2711 7313 2741 Newspapers: publishing only, not printed on site; radio, television, publisher representatives; miscellaneous publishing

(G-19685)
WILLIMS-HYWARD INTL CTINGS INC (PA)
Also Called: Williams-Hayward Protective Co
7425 W 59th St (60501-1417)
PHONE..................708 563-5182
Wayne E Kurcz, *CEO*
Joseph F Kurcz, *President*
Jacqueline Frett, *Vice Pres*
Jacqueline Kurcz, *Vice Pres*
Edward J Kurcz, *CFO*
◆ EMP: 28 EST: 1920
SQ FT: 1,200
SALES (est): 9.7MM **Privately Held**
WEB: www.williams-hayward.com
SIC: 2851 Paints & paint additives

Sumner
Lawrence County

(G-19686)
FRANK E GALLOWAY
Also Called: Galloway Logging
4808 Moffett Ln (62466-4716)
PHONE..................618 948-2578
Frank Galloway, *Principal*
EMP: 3 EST: 2011
SALES (est): 274.9K **Privately Held**
SIC: 2411 Logging

(G-19687)
J B OIL FIELD CNSTR & SUP
218 E Sycamore St (62466-1076)
PHONE..................618 936-2350
Jerry Brian, *President*
Pamela K Brian, *Corp Secy*
EMP: 4
SALES (est): 270K **Privately Held**
SIC: 1389 Lease tanks, oil field: erecting, cleaning & repairing; oil & gas wells: building, repairing & dismantling

(G-19688)
SUMNER PRESS
216 S Christy Ave (62466-1142)
P.O. Box 126 (62466-0126)
PHONE..................618 936-2212
J C Cunningham, *President*
Jo Ann Dowty, *Editor*
Roscoe D Cunningham, *Admin Sec*
EMP: 4
SALES (est): 224.9K **Privately Held**
WEB: www.sumnerpress.com
SIC: 2711 Newspapers: publishing only, not printed on site

(G-19689)
YODERS PORTABLE BUILDINGS LLC (PA)
5425 Larkspur Rd (62466-4756)
PHONE..................618 936-2419
Wilhelm Marten, *Mng Member*
Joseph Marten,
EMP: 2
SQ FT: 280
SALES (est): 1.2MM **Privately Held**
SIC: 2452 Farm buildings, prefabricated or portable: wood

Swansea
St. Clair County

(G-19690)
CHARLES E MAHONEY COMPANY
Also Called: Mahoney Asphalt
209 Service St (62226-3944)
PHONE..................618 235-3355
Charles K Mahoney, *President*
Michael Mahoney, *Vice Pres*
Michael P Mahoney, *Treasurer*
EMP: 20
SQ FT: 5,000
SALES (est): 4.7MM **Privately Held**
WEB: www.mahoneyasphalt.com
SIC: 2951 1611 1771 Asphalt & asphaltic paving mixtures (not from refineries); highway & street paving contractor; concrete work

(G-19691)
CROWDSOURCE SOLUTIONS INC (PA)
33 Bronze Pointe Blvd (62226-8305)
PHONE..................855 276-9376
Stephanie Leffler, *CEO*
Ryan Noble, *President*
Kelly Stevens, *Vice Pres*
Steve Williams, *Vice Pres*
Aaron Eversgerd, *Opers Staff*
EMP: 6
SALES (est): 1.4MM **Privately Held**
SIC: 7372 Application computer software

GEOGRAPHIC SECTION

(G-19692)
GOODMAN MANUFACTURING CO LP
120 Corporate Dr (62226-2033)
PHONE.....................618 234-2781
Carolyn Kuhn, *Branch Mgr*
EMP: 5 **Privately Held**
SIC: 3585 Air conditioning units, complete: domestic or industrial
HQ: Goodman Manufacturing Company, Lp
5151 San Felipe St # 500
Houston TX 77056
713 861-2500

(G-19693)
METRO EAST MANUFACTURING
1120 N Illinois St (62226-4378)
P.O. Box 348, Belleville (62222-0348)
PHONE.....................618 233-0182
Jeffrey R Lutz, *President*
EMP: 12
SALES (corp-wide): 1.1MM **Privately Held**
SIC: 3599 Grinding castings for the trade
PA: Metro East Manufacturing
1150 N Illinois St
Swansea IL
618 233-0182

(G-19694)
QUAD COUNTY READY MIX SWANSEA
300 Old Fullerton Rd (62226-2906)
PHONE.....................618 257-9530
Kant Hustedde, *Manager*
EMP: 7 **EST:** 2001
SALES (est): 480.2K **Privately Held**
SIC: 3273 Ready-mixed concrete

(G-19695)
QUANTUM VISION CENTERS
3990 N Illinois St (62226-1919)
PHONE.....................618 656-7774
EMP: 5
SALES (est): 260.6K **Privately Held**
SIC: 3572 Computer storage devices

(G-19696)
RAUCKMAN HIGH VOLTAGE SALES
37 Ednick Dr (62226-1914)
PHONE.....................618 239-0399
James Rauckman, *Owner*
Jana Badgett, *Sales Staff*
Chris Boyle, *Sales Staff*
Laura Snodgrass, *Sales Staff*
EMP: 5
SALES (est): 457.8K **Privately Held**
SIC: 3613 Distribution boards, electric

(G-19697)
SAMTEK INTERNATIONAL INC
10 Emerald Ter Ste C (62226-2310)
PHONE.....................314 954-4005
Ameem Eajwa, *Manager*
EMP: 1 **EST:** 2009
SQ FT: 12,000
SALES: 500K **Privately Held**
SIC: 1389 Oil & gas wells: building, repairing & dismantling

(G-19698)
STEIBEL LICENSE SERVICE
2704 N Illinois St Ste D (62226-2313)
PHONE.....................618 233-7555
Susan Steibel, *Owner*
EMP: 4
SALES (est): 296.9K **Privately Held**
SIC: 3469 Automobile license tags, stamped metal

Sycamore
Dekalb County

(G-19699)
ADIENT US LLC
1701 Bethany Rd (60178-3104)
PHONE.....................815 895-2095
Andre Ware, *Manager*
EMP: 175
SQ FT: 75,000 **Privately Held**
SIC: 3714 Motor vehicle parts & accessories
HQ: Adient Us Llc
49200 Halyard Dr
Plymouth MI 48170
734 254-5000

(G-19700)
AMPLE SUPPLY COMPANY
Also Called: ASC Fasteners
1401 S Prairie Dr (60178-3225)
PHONE.....................815 895-3500
Michael J Larocco, *President*
Mary E Larocco, *Admin Sec*
◆ **EMP:** 20
SALES (est): 10.8MM **Privately Held**
WEB: www.amplesupply.com
SIC: 5085 3965 Staplers & tackers; fasteners

(G-19701)
AQUAVIVA WINERY (PA)
219 W State St (60178-1418)
PHONE.....................815 899-4444
Sergio Benavides, *Principal*
EMP: 7
SALES (est): 596.3K **Privately Held**
WEB: www.acquavivawinery.com
SIC: 2084 Wines

(G-19702)
AUTO METER PRODUCTS INC
413 W Elm St (60178-1796)
PHONE.....................815 895-8141
Jeff King, *President*
Mike Gathman, *COO*
Dean Panettieri, *Vice Pres*
Michael Quirk, *Purch Mgr*
Ron Bakkelund, *Senior Buyer*
▲ **EMP:** 186 **EST:** 1957
SQ FT: 5,000
SALES (est): 25.2MM
SALES (corp-wide): 30.7MM **Privately Held**
WEB: www.autometer.com
SIC: 3824 3825 3829 3823 Tachometer, centrifugal; speedometers; gauges for computing pressure temperature corrections; battery testers, electrical; measuring & controlling devices; industrial instrmnts msrmnt display/control process variable; motor vehicle parts & accessories; machine tool accessories
PA: Promus Equity Partners, Llc
156 N Jefferson St # 300
Chicago IL 60661
312 784-3990

(G-19703)
CUSTOM HARDWOODS LLC
446 Alden Dr (60178-8906)
PHONE.....................815 784-9974
Dale Mitchell,
EMP: 3 **EST:** 1996
SALES: 200K **Privately Held**
WEB: www.stairparts.net
SIC: 2431 Millwork

(G-19704)
D & D SUKACH INC
Also Called: D & D Jewelers
1733 Dekalb Ave (60178-2707)
PHONE.....................815 895-3377
Clyde Cooper, *President*
EMP: 5
SALES (est): 594.2K **Privately Held**
SIC: 3961 7631 Costume jewelry; watch, clock & jewelry repair

(G-19705)
DAWN EQUIPMENT COMPANY INC
370 N Cross St (60178-1230)
P.O. Box 497 (60178-0497)
PHONE.....................815 899-8000
James H Bassett, *President*
Joseph D Bassett, *President*
Margarett Bassett, *Corp Secy*
Jim Bassett, *Vice Pres*
Jeff Svendsen, *Sales Staff*
EMP: 17
SQ FT: 30,000
SALES (est): 6.9MM **Privately Held**
SIC: 3523 Farm machinery & equipment

(G-19706)
DER HOLTZMACHER LTD
Also Called: Der-Holtzmacher
1649 Afton Rd (60178-3253)
PHONE.....................815 895-4887
Michael Holtz, *President*
Barbara Holtz, *Admin Sec*
EMP: 6
SQ FT: 12,300
SALES (est): 790.7K **Privately Held**
SIC: 2431 2541 2517 2434 Interior or ornamental woodwork & trim; wood partitions & fixtures; home entertainment unit cabinets, wood; vanities, bathroom: wood

(G-19707)
DEVNET INCORPORATED
1709 Afton Rd (60178-3224)
PHONE.....................815 899-6850
Michael Gentry, *President*
Jason Crome, *Vice Pres*
Scott Lepenske, *Vice Pres*
Brandon McPherson, *Vice Pres*
Michael Sager, *Vice Pres*
EMP: 42
SQ FT: 8,000
SALES (est): 5.7MM **Privately Held**
SIC: 7372 Prepackaged software

(G-19708)
DOTY & SONS CONCRETE PRODUCTS
1275 E State St (60178-9578)
PHONE.....................815 895-2884
Calvin L Doty, *President*
Thomas C Doty, *Vice Pres*
Samuel J Doty, *Treasurer*
Helen C Doty, *Admin Sec*
EMP: 13
SQ FT: 17,000
SALES (est): 2.5MM **Privately Held**
WEB: www.dotyconcrete.com
SIC: 3272 Concrete products, precast

(G-19709)
E K KUHN INC
Also Called: Banner Up Signs
1170 E State St (60178-9576)
PHONE.....................815 899-9211
Ed Kuhn, *President*
Karen Kuhn, *Corp Secy*
EMP: 4
SQ FT: 3,000
SALES: 600K **Privately Held**
SIC: 3993 2759 7532 Signs, not made in custom sign painting shops; screen printing; truck painting & lettering

(G-19710)
ELMER L LARSON L C (PA)
21218 Airport Rd (60178-8215)
PHONE.....................815 895-4837
Chris Alessia, *Treasurer*
Randall Huffman, *Manager*
John S Larson,
Dan Larson, *Admin Sec*
Michael D Larson,
EMP: 14 **EST:** 1933
SQ FT: 1,600
SALES (est): 3.8MM **Privately Held**
SIC: 1442 1422 6552 Construction sand & gravel; crushed & broken limestone; subdividers & developers

(G-19711)
GENOA BUSINESS FORMS INC
445 Park Ave (60178-2100)
P.O. Box 450 (60178-0450)
PHONE.....................815 895-2800
David Paulson, *President*
Ernest Westlund, *Finance*
EMP: 49 **EST:** 1957
SQ FT: 38,000
SALES (est): 9.7MM **Privately Held**
WEB: www.genoabusforms.com
SIC: 2752 2761 Commercial printing, offset; business form & card printing, lithographic; manifold business forms

(G-19712)
HARDWOOD CONNECTION
1810 W State St (60178-8531)
PHONE.....................815 895-8733
Kenneth Burtch, *Owner*
EMP: 3
SQ FT: 9,500
SALES: 394.8K **Privately Held**
WEB: www.thehardwoodconnection.com
SIC: 2431 Millwork

(G-19713)
HEARTLAND INSPECTION COMPANY
Also Called: Play It Again Sports 11417
510 Nathan Lattin Ln (60178-8755)
PHONE.....................630 788-3607
Edward Saunders, *President*
EMP: 6
SQ FT: 3,612
SALES (est): 380K **Privately Held**
SIC: 3949 Sporting & athletic goods

(G-19714)
IDEAL INDUSTRIES INC (PA)
1375 Park Ave (60178-2429)
PHONE.....................815 895-5181
David W Juday, *Ch of Bd*
Jim James, *President*
Jeff Miller, *President*
Doug Sanford, *Senior VP*
Vicki Slomka, *Vice Pres*
◆ **EMP:** 250 **EST:** 1916
SQ FT: 60,000
SALES (est): 335.9MM **Privately Held**
WEB: www.idealindustries.com
SIC: 3825 3643 Electrical power measuring equipment; current-carrying wiring devices

(G-19715)
IDEAL INDUSTRIES INC
434 Borden Ave Dock14 (60178-2428)
PHONE.....................815 895-1108
Randy Thomson, *Branch Mgr*
EMP: 200
SALES (corp-wide): 335.9MM **Privately Held**
SIC: 3643 3825 3625 3545 Current-carrying wiring devices; electrical power measuring equipment; relays & industrial controls; machine tool accessories; abrasive products; hand & edge tools
PA: Ideal Industries, Inc.
1375 Park Ave
Sycamore IL 60178
815 895-5181

(G-19716)
IDEAL INDUSTRIES INC
1000 Park Ave (60178-2420)
PHONE.....................815 895-5181
David W Juday, *CEO*
EMP: 200
SQ FT: 87,000
SALES (corp-wide): 335.9MM **Privately Held**
SIC: 3643 Current-carrying wiring devices
PA: Ideal Industries, Inc.
1375 Park Ave
Sycamore IL 60178
815 895-5181

(G-19717)
INNOVATIVE GROWERS EQP INC
421 N California St (60178-1290)
P.O. Box 6295, Elgin (60121-6295)
PHONE.....................815 991-5010
Christopher Mayer, *President*
Bruce Zierk, *Principal*
◆ **EMP:** 40
SALES (est): 8.3MM **Privately Held**
SIC: 3523 Planting machines, agricultural

(G-19718)
J HOFFMAN LUMBER CO INC
1330 E State St (60178-9580)
PHONE.....................815 899-2260
Vickey Hoffman, *Principal*
EMP: 2
SALES (est): 302.6K **Privately Held**
SIC: 2431 Millwork

(G-19719)
JENSEN AND SON INC
353 N Maple St (60178-1436)
PHONE.....................815 895-3855
Daniel Jensen, *President*
Toni Jensen, *Corp Secy*
EMP: 7 **EST:** 1943
SQ FT: 5,000

Sycamore - Dekalb County (G-19720)

SALES (est): 846.4K **Privately Held**
WEB: www.jensensons.com
SIC: 3544 Special dies & tools

(G-19720)
K & S PRINTING SERVICES
510 N Main St Ste 1 (60178-1236)
PHONE 815 899-2923
Steve Caldwell, *Owner*
EMP: 1
SALES (est): 270K **Privately Held**
SIC: 2752 Commercial printing, offset

(G-19721)
LEDIL INC
228 W Page St Ste D (60178-1473)
PHONE 815 766-3204
Benjamin Sweadberg, *President*
Konstantinos Kyranas, *Sales Dir*
Lauri Haarala, *Regl Sales Mgr*
Kevin Vaughn, *Regl Sales Mgr*
Martin Lengwenus, *Sales Staff*
EMP: 10
SALES (est): 1.5MM
SALES (corp-wide): 2.6B **Privately Held**
SIC: 3646 Commercial indusl & institutional electric lighting fixtures
HQ: Ledil Oy
   Joensuunkatu 13
   Salo 24100
   401 764-406

(G-19722)
LEGACY VULCAN LLC
Midwest Division
12502 Lloyd Rd (60178-8118)
PHONE 815 895-6501
Dan Larson, *Manager*
EMP: 15 **Publicly Held**
SIC: 1442 Gravel mining
HQ: Legacy Vulcan, Llc
   1200 Urban Center Dr
   Vestavia AL 35242
   205 298-3000

(G-19723)
M & M WELDING INC
410 N Main St (60178-1216)
PHONE 815 895-3955
Greg Mathey, *President*
EMP: 2
SALES (est): 327K **Privately Held**
SIC: 7692 Welding repair

(G-19724)
MARK S MACHINE SHOP INC
416 N Main St (60178-1216)
PHONE 815 895-3955
Francis Mathey, *President*
EMP: 7
SQ FT: 4,800
SALES (est): 1.2MM **Privately Held**
SIC: 5012 7692 8999 Truck bodies; automotive welding; actuarial consultant

(G-19725)
NEWBY OIL COMPANY INC
Also Called: Newby, Wayne Nsp
2270 Oakland Dr (60178-3112)
PHONE 815 756-7688
Viola Newby, *President*
Wayne Newby, *President*
Dave Newby, *Vice Pres*
EMP: 8
SQ FT: 5,625
SALES (est): 2.6MM **Privately Held**
SIC: 5171 2842 5999 5091 Petroleum bulk stations; window cleaning preparations; swimming pool chemicals, equipment & supplies; swimming pools, equipment & supplies

(G-19726)
ODOM TOOL AND TECHNOLOGY INC
216 W Page St (60178-1439)
PHONE 815 895-8545
Jim W Odom, *President*
Ronda Odom, *Vice Pres*
EMP: 7
SQ FT: 10,000
SALES (est): 847.9K **Privately Held**
SIC: 3544 7692 Special dies & tools; welding repair

(G-19727)
ORORA PACKAGING SOLUTIONS
Also Called: Mpp Sycamore Div 6063
215 Fair St (60178-1644)
PHONE 815 895-2343
Dave Haish, *Design Engr*
Brian Sheehan, *Sales Staff*
Larry Kendzora, *Manager*
EMP: 54 **Privately Held**
SIC: 5113 2653 Paper & products, wrapping or coarse; boxes, corrugated: made from purchased materials
HQ: Orora Packaging Solutions
   6600 Valley View St
   Buena Park CA 90620
   714 562-6000

(G-19728)
PRATT-READ TOOLS LLC
1375 Park Ave (60178-2429)
P.O. Box 129 (60178-0129)
PHONE 815 895-1121
James Pfotenhauer,
▲ EMP: 4
SALES (est): 559.7K **Privately Held**
SIC: 3423 Screw drivers, pliers, chisels, etc. (hand tools)

(G-19729)
RICHARD A ANDERSON
Also Called: Anderson, Richard Shop
1653 W Motel Rd (60178)
PHONE 815 895-5627
Richard A Anderson, *Owner*
EMP: 7
SALES (est): 585.2K **Privately Held**
SIC: 3599 Machine shop, jobbing & repair

(G-19730)
SEYMOUR OF SYCAMORE INC (PA)
917 Crosby Ave (60178-1394)
PHONE 815 895-9101
Christopher Heatley, *President*
Michael Weiss, *Division Mgr*
Jon Larson, *Vice Pres*
Don Jankowski, *Plant Mgr*
Kristen Moser, *Production*
◆ EMP: 135 EST: 1949
SQ FT: 80,000
SALES (est): 33.8MM **Privately Held**
WEB: www.seymourpaint.com
SIC: 2851 2899 Paints: oil or alkyd vehicle or water thinned; enamels; lacquer: bases, dopes, thinner; coating, air curing; chemical preparations

(G-19731)
SK HAND TOOL LLC
1600 S Prairie Dr (60178-3203)
PHONE 815 895-7701
Claude Fuger, *CEO*
Cliff Rusnak, *Chairman*
Shiela Johnsen, *Vice Pres*
James Pfotenhauer, *Vice Pres*
Joe Saganowich, *Vice Pres*
EMP: 15
SALES (est): 4.3MM
SALES (corp-wide): 335.9MM **Privately Held**
SIC: 3423 Wrenches, hand tools; screw drivers, pliers, chisels, etc. (hand tools)
PA: Ideal Industries, Inc.
   1375 Park Ave
   Sycamore IL 60178
   815 895-5181

(G-19732)
SMART MOTION ROBOTICS INC
805 Thornwood Dr (60178-8881)
PHONE 815 895-8550
Scott Gilmore, *President*
Douglas Jones, *President*
Vickie Gilmore, *CFO*
Victoria L Gilmore, *CFO*
▼ EMP: 20
SQ FT: 35,000
SALES (est): 5.4MM **Privately Held**
SIC: 3535 4783 5084 Robotic conveyors; packing & crating; industrial machinery & equipment

(G-19733)
SUTER COMPANY INC
1015 Bethany Rd (60178-3066)
PHONE 815 895-9186
Brigitte Kramer, *Controller*
EMP: 150
SALES (corp-wide): 56.2MM **Privately Held**
SIC: 2099 Salads, fresh or refrigerated
PA: The Suter Company Inc
   258 May St
   Sycamore IL 60178
   815 895-9186

(G-19734)
TEL-COMM INCORPORATED
Also Called: Barrett Graphic Services
804 Coventry Cir S (60178-8945)
P.O. Box 502, Saint Charles (60174-0502)
PHONE 847 593-8480
Frank Barrett, *President*
Gina Barrett, *CFO*
EMP: 25
SQ FT: 6,000
SALES (est): 5.4MM **Privately Held**
WEB: www.barrettgraphics.com
SIC: 3555 Printing trade parts & attachments

(G-19735)
THOMPSON INDUSTRIES INC (PA)
1018 Crosby Ave (60178-1348)
P.O. Box 127 (60178-0127)
PHONE 815 899-6670
Tim Siegmeier, *Prdtn Mgr*
Edward Thompson Jr, *Shareholder*
EMP: 26 EST: 1973
SQ FT: 22,000
SALES (est): 4.2MM **Privately Held**
SIC: 3599 Machine shop, jobbing & repair

(G-19736)
TRAFFICGUARD INC
1730 Afton Rd Ste 1 (60178-3289)
P.O. Box 201, Geneva (60134-0201)
PHONE 877 727-7347
Mike Schram, *President*
EMP: 6
SQ FT: 5,000
SALES (est): 250.1K **Privately Held**
SIC: 3499 Barricades, metal

(G-19737)
TRENDY SCREENPRINTING
155 E Maplewood Dr (60178-1142)
PHONE 815 895-0081
Jerry Breiling, *Owner*
EMP: 3
SALES (est): 299.3K **Privately Held**
SIC: 2759 Screen printing

(G-19738)
UPSTAGING INC (PA)
821 Park Ave (60178-2419)
PHONE 815 899-9888
Robert Carone, *President*
Shawn Haynes, *General Mgr*
Ken Burns, *Chief*
Ed Duda, *Chief*
Mike Hosp, *Chief*
▼ EMP: 168 EST: 1972
SQ FT: 124,000
SALES (est): 27.7MM **Privately Held**
SIC: 7922 3537 Lighting, theatrical; trucks, tractors, loaders, carriers & similar equipment

(G-19739)
VISUAL PERSUASION INC
Also Called: Priority Promotions
337 E State St (60178-1513)
PHONE 815 899-6609
Patrick Marsden, *President*
Cindy Carlson, *Treasurer*
Josephine Kingsbury, *Marketing Mgr*
EMP: 10
SQ FT: 2,500
SALES (est): 764.2K **Privately Held**
SIC: 7389 2395 Embroidering of advertising on shirts, etc.; embroidery products, except schiffli machine

(G-19740)
VULCAN MATERIALS COMPANY
12502 Lloyd Rd (60178-8118)
PHONE 815 899-7204
Fax: 815 895-3883
EMP: 20
SALES (corp-wide): 3.4B **Publicly Held**
SIC: 1422 Crushed/Broken Limestone
PA: Vulcan Materials Company
   1200 Urban Center Dr
   Vestavia AL 35242
   205 298-3000

Tamaroa
Perry County

(G-19741)
BLUECHIP FABRICATION
25 N Chestnut St (62888-4529)
P.O. Box 69 (62888-0069)
PHONE 618 496-3569
Curtise Stube, *Owner*
EMP: 3
SQ FT: 5,250
SALES (est): 198.5K **Privately Held**
SIC: 3599 Machine shop, jobbing & repair

Tamms
Alexander County

(G-19742)
COVIA HOLDINGS CORPORATION
110 Railroad St (62988)
PHONE 618 747-2355
EMP: 3
SALES (corp-wide): 125.5MM **Publicly Held**
SIC: 1446 1499 1422 1459 Silica mining; quartz crystal (pure) mining; dolomite, crushed & broken-quarrying; nepheline syenite quarrying; steam railroads; construction sand & gravel
HQ: Covia Holdings Corporation
   3 Summit Park Dr Ste 700
   Independence OH 44131
   440 214-3284

(G-19743)
COVIA HOLDINGS CORPORATION
32079 State Highway 127 (62988-3011)
PHONE 618 747-2338
Al Jonier, *Branch Mgr*
EMP: 25
SQ FT: 25,000
SALES (corp-wide): 125.5MM **Publicly Held**
SIC: 1446 Silica mining
HQ: Covia Holdings Corporation
   3 Summit Park Dr Ste 700
   Independence OH 44131
   440 214-3284

Tampico
Whiteside County

(G-19744)
MIDWEST BIO MANUFACTURING DIV
310 2650 N Ave (61283-9017)
PHONE 815 542-6417
Edwin Blosser, *President*
Carey Richardson, *Principal*
Ernest Blosser, *Vice Pres*
EMP: 12
SALES (est): 1.1MM **Privately Held**
SIC: 2836 Biological products, except diagnostic

(G-19745)
MIDWEST BIO-SYSTEMS INC
28933 35 E St (61283-9003)
PHONE 815 438-7200
Edwin Blosser, *President*
Ernest Blosser, *Vice Pres*
Cary Richardson, *Sales Staff*

GEOGRAPHIC SECTION

Kelly Setchell, *Sales Staff*
Karla J Blosser, *Admin Sec*
◆ **EMP:** 11
SQ FT: 2,000
SALES: 3.5MM **Privately Held**
SIC: 3523 0711 Farm machinery & equipment; soil testing services

Taylor Ridge
Rock Island County

(G-19746)
MALLARDTONE GAME CALLS
10406 96th Street Ct W (61284-9419)
PHONE 309 798-2481
John Joseph Rasmussen, *Owner*
John Rasmussen, *Owner*
EMP: 3
SQ FT: 1,000
SALES (est): 250K **Privately Held**
SIC: 3949 Decoys, duck & other game birds

(G-19747)
QUAD CITY HOSE
9707 86th Street Ct W (61284-9248)
PHONE 563 386-8936
J Gary Zespy, *President*
EMP: 25
SQ FT: 21,500
SALES (est): 6.2MM **Privately Held**
SIC: 3492 3052 Hose & tube fittings & assemblies, hydraulic/pneumatic; rubber & plastics hose & beltings

Taylorville
Christian County

(G-19748)
AHLSTRM-MUNKSJO FILTRATION LLC
1200 E Elm St (62568-1642)
P.O. Box 680 (62568-0680)
PHONE 217 824-9611
John Flahive, *Manager*
EMP: 60
SALES (corp-wide): 3.2B **Privately Held**
WEB: www.ahlstrom.com
SIC: 2621 Filter paper
HQ: Ahlstrom-Munksjo Filtration Llc
215 Nebo Rd
Madisonville KY 42431
270 821-0140

(G-19749)
AQUA GOLF INC (PA)
6 Manor Ct (62568-8926)
P.O. Box 106 (62568-0106)
PHONE 217 824-2097
Deane Peabody, *President*
Pamela Peabody, *Corp Secy*
EMP: 6
SQ FT: 5,000
SALES (est): 1.5MM **Privately Held**
SIC: 3944 Games, toys & children's vehicles

(G-19750)
BIG M MANUFACTURING LLC
928 E 1090 North Rd (62568-8341)
PHONE 217 824-9372
Mel Repscher,
EMP: 5
SALES (est): 300K **Privately Held**
SIC: 3585 Heating equipment, complete

(G-19751)
BOTKIN LUMBER COMPANY INC
Also Called: Illinois Box & Pallet
201 S Baughman Rd (62568-9387)
PHONE 217 287-2127
Philip Kelmel, *Branch Mgr*
EMP: 20
SQ FT: 54,500

SALES (corp-wide): 18.3MM **Privately Held**
SIC: 2421 2448 2441 Lumber: rough, sawed or planed; pallets, wood; packing cases, wood: nailed or lock corner; shipping cases, wood: nailed or lock corner
PA: Botkin Lumber Company, Inc.
1901 Progress Dr
Farmington MO 63640
573 756-2400

(G-19752)
BREEZE PRINTING COMPANY (PA)
Also Called: Breeze-Courier
212 S Main St (62568-2219)
P.O. Box 440 (62568-0440)
PHONE 217 824-2233
Mary Lee Rasar, *President*
Mary Lee Lasswell, *President*
Wilda Cooper, *Vice Pres*
Owen Lasswels, *CFO*
J Robert Cooper, *Admin Sec*
EMP: 18
SQ FT: 20,000
SALES (est): 1.6MM **Privately Held**
WEB: www.breezecourier.com
SIC: 2711 7359 Job printing & newspaper publishing combined; equipment rental & leasing

(G-19753)
CHRISTIAN CNTY MNTAL HLTH ASSN (PA)
Also Called: Ccmha
707 Mcadam Dr (62568-2300)
P.O. Box 438 (62568-0438)
PHONE 217 824-9675
Brent De Michael, *President*
Tanya Hughs, *Purchasing*
EMP: 200
SALES (est): 7.3MM **Privately Held**
SIC: 2499 8621 Spools, wood; health association

(G-19754)
DESIGN CORRUGATING COMPANY
400 S Baughman Rd (62568-9378)
PHONE 314 821-4300
Barry W Mauer, *President*
Barry Mauer, *President*
Karen Izmirlian, *Vice Pres*
▲ **EMP:** 22
SALES (est): 4.1MM **Privately Held**
SIC: 3599 Machine shop, jobbing & repair

(G-19755)
DESIGN MANUFACTURING & EQP CO
400 S Baughman Rd (62568-9378)
PHONE 217 824-9219
Tony Elinger, *Manager*
EMP: 15
SALES (corp-wide): 1.7MM **Privately Held**
SIC: 3523 3316 Planting, haying, harvesting & processing machinery; cold finishing of steel shapes
PA: Design Manufacturing & Equipment Co Inc
5215 Northrup Ave
Saint Louis MO
314 771-0503

(G-19756)
DOMINO ENGINEERING CORP
208 S Spresser St (62568-9282)
P.O. Box 376 (62568-0376)
PHONE 217 824-9441
Lawrence Peterson, *President*
Alan J Peterson, *Treasurer*
EMP: 10
SALES (est): 500K **Privately Held**
SIC: 3625 Relays & industrial controls

(G-19757)
GSI GROUP LLC
2400 S Spresser St (62568-9227)
PHONE 217 287-6244
Brian Juberigan, *Engineer*
Brian Atwood, *Manager*
EMP: 120 **Publicly Held**
SIC: 3523 Crop storage bins

HQ: The Gsi Group Llc
1004 E Illinois St
Assumption IL 62510
217 226-4421

(G-19758)
LLA EXPLORATION INC
1747 N 800 East Rd (62568-7843)
PHONE 217 623-4096
Clifford Mansfield, *President*
EMP: 1
SALES: 700K **Privately Held**
SIC: 1382 Oil & gas exploration services

(G-19759)
MIDSTATE SALVAGE CORP
Also Called: Midstate Iron & Metals
1402 W South St (62568-9385)
PHONE 217 824-6047
William Neal Lebeter, *President*
Robin Vancil, *Admin Sec*
EMP: 7 **EST:** 1965
SQ FT: 1,000
SALES (est): 919.6K **Privately Held**
WEB: www.midstatesalvagecorp.com
SIC: 5093 3341 Ferrous metal scrap & waste; secondary nonferrous metals

(G-19760)
POGGENPOHL LLC
105 N Baughman Rd (62568-9304)
PHONE 217 824-2020
Russell Poggenpohl, *Partner*
EMP: 2
SALES (corp-wide): 2.8MM **Privately Held**
SIC: 1521 1542 3273 Single-family housing construction; commercial & office building contractors; ready-mixed concrete
PA: Poggenpohl, L.L.C.
31 Sparks St
Raymond IL 62560
217 229-3411

(G-19761)
RAMSEYS MACHINE CO
1333 N Webster St (62568-2729)
PHONE 217 824-2320
John Harris, *Owner*
EMP: 3
SALES (est): 276K **Privately Held**
SIC: 3536 7692 Hoists; welding repair

(G-19762)
SIEMENS INDUSTRY INC
1058 E Langleyville Rd (62568-7867)
P.O. Box 595 (62568-0595)
PHONE 217 824-6833
Norman Ramsey, *Manager*
EMP: 5
SALES (corp-wide): 96.9B **Privately Held**
SIC: 3625 Relays & industrial controls
HQ: Siemens Industry, Inc.
1000 Deerfield Pkwy
Buffalo Grove IL 60089
847 215-1000

(G-19763)
WATSON LLC
1900 S Spresser St (62568-9383)
PHONE 217 824-4440
Miles Feller, *Manager*
EMP: 25 **Privately Held**
SIC: 2045 2087 Prepared flour mixes & doughs; flavoring extracts & syrups
HQ: Watson Llc
301 Heffernan Dr
West Haven CT 06516
203 932-3000

Teutopolis
Effingham County

(G-19764)
BRUMLEVE INDUSTRIES INC
Also Called: Brumleve Canvas Products
1317 W Main St (62467-1215)
P.O. Box 279 (62467-0279)
PHONE 217 857-3777
Donald J Brumleve, *President*
Joan Brumleve, *Vice Pres*
EMP: 15

SALES (est): 5.6MM **Privately Held**
WEB: www.brumleveind.com
SIC: 5199 3792 2394 Canvas products; travel trailers & campers; canvas & related products

(G-19765)
C & H GRAVEL C INC
Also Called: C and H Gravel
14046 N 1600th St (62467-3427)
PHONE 217 857-3425
Paul Harmon, *Manager*
EMP: 6
SALES (corp-wide): 4.1MM **Privately Held**
SIC: 1442 4212 Gravel mining; local trucking, without storage
PA: C & H Gravel C Inc
1406 E Fayette Ave
Teutopolis IL
217 857-3425

(G-19766)
CASEY STONE CO
14046 N 1600th St (62467-3427)
PHONE 217 857-3425
Janice Heuerman, *President*
Becky Landers, *Admin Sec*
EMP: 8
SALES (est): 1.3MM **Privately Held**
SIC: 3272 Cast stone, concrete

(G-19767)
COMMUNITY SUPPORT SYSTEMS (PA)
618 W Main St (62467-1210)
PHONE 217 705-4300
Deb Parmenter, *Business Mgr*
Debra Parmenter, *Business Mgr*
Elaine Arnold, *Vice Pres*
Susan Williams, *Treasurer*
Andrew Kistler, *Exec Dir*
EMP: 75
SQ FT: 13,000
SALES (est): 7MM **Privately Held**
WEB: www.arc-css.org
SIC: 8331 8361 2448 2441 Sheltered workshop; home for the mentally retarded; wood pallets & skids; nailed wood boxes & shook

(G-19768)
D D SALES INC
Also Called: Dale's Diesel Service
1608 W Main St (62467-1283)
PHONE 217 857-3196
Dale Ruholl, *President*
Jason Ruholl, *Opers Dir*
EMP: 21 **EST:** 1986
SALES (est): 3.1MM **Privately Held**
SIC: 7538 3715 7532 General truck repair; truck trailers; top & body repair & paint shops

(G-19769)
FARMWELD INC
605 E Main St (62467-1357)
P.O. Box 520 (62467-0520)
PHONE 217 857-6423
Frank A Brummer, *President*
Lora K Runde, *Admin Sec*
▲ **EMP:** 30
SALES (est): 7.6MM **Privately Held**
SIC: 3523 3444 Farm machinery & equipment; sheet metalwork

(G-19770)
K & W AUTO ELECTRIC
103 N Automotive Dr (62467-1285)
PHONE 217 857-1717
Rick Kreke, *Partner*
Karl Wendt, *Partner*
EMP: 10
SQ FT: 7,200
SALES (est): 750K **Privately Held**
SIC: 3714 3694 3625 Motor vehicle engines & parts; engine electrical equipment; relays & industrial controls

(G-19771)
PERFORMANCE LAWN & POWER
1311 W Main St (62467-1215)
PHONE 217 857-3717
Thomas Mette, *Owner*
EMP: 2

Teutopolis - Effingham County (G-19772)

SALES (est): 220K **Privately Held**
SIC: 2431 5251 Millwork; tools, power

(G-19772)
SIEMER ENTERPRISES INC (PA)
Also Called: Mangelsdorf Seed Co
515 W Main St (62467-1209)
P.O. Box 580 (62467-0580)
PHONE..................................217 857-3171
Gwenn S Croft, *Corp Secy*
Dorothy Siemer, *Shareholder*
Michael Siemer, *Shareholder*
▲ EMP: 50
SQ FT: 105,000
SALES (est): 33.9MM **Privately Held**
SIC: 5191 2048 5083 Feed; bird food, prepared; lawn machinery & equipment; garden machinery & equipment

(G-19773)
STEVENS CABINETS INC (PA)
Also Called: Stevens Tot-Mate
704 W Main St (62467-1212)
PHONE..................................217 857-7100
Todd Wegman, *President*
Tom Wegman, *President*
Ed Wiessing, *Vice Pres*
Ryan Lee, *Safety Mgr*
Tom Hemmen, *Maint Spvr*
◆ EMP: 400 EST: 1967
SQ FT: 480,000
SALES (est): 120.4MM **Privately Held**
WEB: www.stevensind.com
SIC: 2531 2679 2511 Public building & related furniture; wallboard, decorated: made from purchased material; juvenile furniture: wood

(G-19774)
THREE-Z PRINTING CO (PA)
Also Called: Three Z Printing
902 W Main St (62467-1329)
P.O. Box 550 (62467-0550)
PHONE..................................217 857-3153
Dan Zerrusen, *President*
William Zerrusen, *Assistant VP*
Bill Zerrusen, *Vice Pres*
Bill Zerrusenis, *Vice Pres*
Tim Smith, *Safety Mgr*
EMP: 375 EST: 1977
SQ FT: 450,000
SALES (est): 139.1MM **Privately Held**
SIC: 2752 Commercial printing, offset

Thomasboro
Champaign County

(G-19775)
ALTAMONT CO
901 N Church St (61878-9700)
P.O. Box 309 (61878-0309)
PHONE..................................800 626-5774
Kenneth Enright, *President*
Denise Enright, *Admin Sec*
▲ EMP: 90
SQ FT: 45,000
SALES (est): 19.4MM **Privately Held**
SIC: 3089 3949 Handles, brush or tool: plastic; sporting & athletic goods

(G-19776)
MASTERS SHOP
Also Called: The Master's Shop
1621 County Road 2500 N (61878-9663)
PHONE..................................217 643-7826
John L Powell, *President*
EMP: 1
SALES (est): 300K **Privately Held**
SIC: 1751 2434 Finish & trim carpentry; wood kitchen cabinets

Thompsonville
Franklin County

(G-19777)
3ABN
6020 Green Meadow Rd (62890-2410)
P.O. Box 220, West Frankfort (62896-0220)
PHONE..................................618 627-4651
EMP: 3 EST: 2008

SALES (est): 150K **Privately Held**
SIC: 2836 Biological Products, Except Diagnostic

(G-19778)
KEYROCK ENERGY LLC
20227 Thorn Rd (62890-4408)
PHONE..................................618 982-9710
EMP: 40
SALES (corp-wide): 8MM **Privately Held**
SIC: 1241 Coal mining exploration & test boring
PA: Keyrock Energy Llc
106 Ferrell Ave Ste 5
Kingsport TN 37663
423 726-2070

(G-19779)
MCFARLAND WELDING AND MACHINE
4066 N Thompsonville Rd (62890-2601)
PHONE..................................618 627-2838
Jerome McFarland, *Owner*
EMP: 3
SQ FT: 4,000
SALES (est): 50K **Privately Held**
SIC: 7692 Welding repair

Thomson
Carroll County

(G-19780)
CARROLL COUNTY REVIEW
809 W Main St (61285-7776)
P.O. Box 369 (61285-0369)
PHONE..................................815 259-2131
Jonathan Whitney, *Owner*
EMP: 5
SQ FT: 4,200
SALES (est): 170K **Privately Held**
WEB: www.carrollcounty.com
SIC: 2711 Commercial printing & newspaper publishing combined

(G-19781)
CULTOR FOOD SCIENCE DANIS
10994 Three Mile Rd (61285-7633)
PHONE..................................815 259-3311
Sarah Rice, *Principal*
EMP: 3
SALES (est): 209.2K **Privately Held**
WEB: www.danisco.com
SIC: 2099 Food preparations

(G-19782)
DANISCO USA INC
10994 Three Mile Rd (61285-7633)
PHONE..................................815 259-3311
EMP: 3
SALES (est): 568.3K
SALES (corp-wide): 21.5B **Publicly Held**
WEB: www.danisco.com
SIC: 2099 Food preparations
HQ: E. I. Du Pont De Nemours And Company
974 Centre Rd Bldg 735
Wilmington DE 19805
302 485-3000

(G-19783)
E I DU PONT DE NEMOURS & CO
Also Called: Danisco Sweeteners
10994 Three Mile Rd (61285-7633)
PHONE..................................815 259-3311
Craig Myers, *Branch Mgr*
EMP: 70
SALES (corp-wide): 21.5B **Publicly Held**
SIC: 2099 Emulsifiers, food
HQ: E. I. Du Pont De Nemours And Company
974 Centre Rd Bldg 735
Wilmington DE 19805
302 485-3000

Thornton
Cook County

(G-19784)
A B C BLIND INC
108 S Julian St (60476-1230)
PHONE..................................708 877-7100
Katherine Snell, *President*
Harry Snells, *Vice Pres*
Audra Coniglio, *Admin Sec*
EMP: 3
SQ FT: 4,000
SALES (est): 250K **Privately Held**
SIC: 2591 2211 Window blinds; draperies & drapery fabrics, cotton

(G-19785)
BOEKELOO HEATING & SHEET METAL
601 N Williams St (60476-1097)
PHONE..................................708 877-6560
David Boekeloo, *President*
Dolores Boekeloo, *Corp Secy*
EMP: 6
SQ FT: 1,200
SALES (est): 750K **Privately Held**
SIC: 1711 1761 3444 Warm air heating & air conditioning contractor; siding contractor; sheet metalwork

(G-19786)
GALLAGHER ASPHALT CORPORATION (PA)
18100 Indiana Ave (60476-1276)
PHONE..................................708 877-7160
Charles J Gallagher, *President*
Carl A Erickson, *Superintendent*
Ben Morrow, *Superintendent*
Patrick Gallagher, *COO*
Dan Gallagher, *Vice Pres*
EMP: 40 EST: 1927
SQ FT: 3,000
SALES (est): 10.8MM **Privately Held**
WEB: www.gallagherasphalt.com
SIC: 1611 2951 Highway & street paving contractor; asphalt & asphaltic paving mixtures (not from refineries)

(G-19787)
GPL INDUSTRIES INCORPORATED
395 Armory Dr (60476-1046)
PHONE..................................708 877-8200
Leo Piekosz, *Principal*
EMP: 52
SQ FT: 60,000
SALES (est): 9.1MM **Privately Held**
SIC: 3599 Machine shop, jobbing & repair

(G-19788)
GROUP INDUSTRIES INC
Drum Parts Midwest Div
459 N Williams St (60476-1059)
PHONE..................................708 877-6200
Lane Zamin, *President*
Steve Zamin, *Vice Pres*
Terri Hebda, *Sales Staff*
EMP: 25
SQ FT: 26,000
SALES (corp-wide): 9.9MM **Privately Held**
SIC: 3442 3499 3462 3444 Moldings & trim, except automobile: metal; fire- or burglary-resistive products; iron & steel forgings; sheet metalwork; gray & ductile iron foundries
PA: Group Industries, Inc.
7580 Garfield Blvd
Cleveland OH 44125
216 271-0702

(G-19789)
INTEGRATED POWER SERVICES LLC
17001 Vincennes Rd (60476-1066)
PHONE..................................708 877-5310
Rich Harris, *Manager*
EMP: 50

SALES (corp-wide): 862.6MM **Privately Held**
SIC: 7629 7694 3621 Electrical repair shops; armature rewinding shops; motors & generators
HQ: Integrated Power Services Llc
3 Independence Pt Ste 100
Greenville SC 29615

(G-19790)
MATERIAL SERVICE CORPORATION
620 W 183rd St (60476-1026)
P.O. Box 179 (60476-0179)
PHONE..................................708 877-6540
Toby Breedlove, *Branch Mgr*
EMP: 80
SALES (corp-wide): 20.8B **Privately Held**
SIC: 3295 1422 Minerals, ground or treated; crushed & broken limestone
HQ: Material Service Corporation
2235 Entp Dr Ste 3504
Westchester IL 60154
708 731-2600

(G-19791)
VENTURA FOODS LLC
Also Called: Marie's Salad Dressings
201 Armory Dr (60476-1044)
PHONE..................................708 877-5150
Ray McCoy, *Branch Mgr*
EMP: 40 **Privately Held**
SIC: 2099 Food preparations
PA: Ventura Foods, Llc
40 Pointe Dr
Brea CA 92821

Tilden
Randolph County

(G-19792)
SOUTHERN ILL AUTO ELEC INC
Also Called: S I A Electronics
730 N Minnie Ave (62292-1101)
PHONE..................................618 587-3308
Scott A Bement, *President*
Linda Baker,
EMP: 12
SQ FT: 7,200
SALES (est): 1.9MM **Privately Held**
SIC: 3694 Automotive electrical equipment

Tilton
Vermilion County

(G-19793)
CARNAGHI TOWING & REPAIR INC
2000 Georgetown Rd (61833-8121)
PHONE..................................217 446-0333
Brian Carnaghi, *President*
Stephanie Carnaghi, *Vice Pres*
EMP: 12 EST: 1924
SQ FT: 3,500
SALES (est): 1.4MM **Privately Held**
WEB: www.towing-danville.com
SIC: 7549 5541 2097 7538 Towing service, automotive; filling stations, gasoline; manufactured ice; general automotive repair shops

(G-19794)
CITY OF DANVILLE
5 Southgate Ct (61833-8132)
PHONE..................................217 442-1564
Brenda Bostic, *Branch Mgr*
EMP: 6 **Privately Held**
SIC: 3469 Automobile license tags, stamped metal
PA: City Of Danville
17 W Main St
Danville IL 61832
217 431-2200

(G-19795)
CUSTOM SIGNS ON METAL LLC
Also Called: Photosteel
301 Mayfield St (61833-7460)
PHONE..................................217 443-5347
Don Davis,

Joe Davis,
EMP: 10
SQ FT: 14,000
SALES: 500K **Privately Held**
SIC: 3993 Signs, not made in custom sign painting shops

(G-19796)
RUMSHINE DISTILLING LLC
8 Hodge St (61832-7609)
PHONE....................217 446-6960
Ernie L Trinkle II, *Mng Member*
Tyler Langston, *Mng Member*
EMP: 3 **EST:** 2014
SALES (est): 172.7K **Privately Held**
SIC: 2085 5813 Distilled & blended liquors; cocktail lounge

Timewell
Brown County

(G-19797)
C & L TILING INC (PA)
Also Called: Timewell Drainage Pdts & Svcs
196 Us 24 1075n Ave (62375)
PHONE....................217 773-3357
Donald Colclasure, *President*
Tyler Edge, *Regional Mgr*
Steve Johnson, *Sales Staff*
Mike Loscheider, *Sales Staff*
Mark Wieland, *Sales Staff*
EMP: 80
SALES (est): 68.3MM **Privately Held**
WEB: www.timewellpipe.com
SIC: 1629 3259 Irrigation system construction; clay sewer & drainage pipe & tile

Tinley Park
Cook County

(G-19798)
AERO RUBBER COMPANY INC
8100 185th St (60487-9201)
PHONE....................800 662-1009
John A Kasman, *President*
◆ **EMP:** 45
SALES (est): 14.6MM **Privately Held**
SIC: 3069 Molded rubber products; sheets, hard rubber; tubing, rubber

(G-19799)
ALL-STYLE CUSTOM TOPS
5555 175th St (60477-3007)
PHONE....................708 532-6606
Tom Manzke, *Partner*
Ed Manzke, *Partner*
EMP: 3
SQ FT: 2,600
SALES (est): 393.2K **Privately Held**
SIC: 2541 Table or counter tops, plastic laminated

(G-19800)
ALLSTATES RUBBER & TOOL CORP
8201 183rd St Ste M (60487-9752)
PHONE....................708 342-1030
Mike Burke, *President*
Bill Burke, *Vice Pres*
William Burke, *Admin Sec*
▲ **EMP:** 10
SQ FT: 5,400
SALES (est): 1.9MM **Privately Held**
SIC: 5085 5084 2822 Rubber goods, mechanical; materials handling machinery; synthetic rubber

(G-19801)
ALLTEC GATES INC (PA)
15941 Harlem Ave Ste 325 (60477-1609)
PHONE....................708 301-9361
EMP: 3
SALES (est): 384.7K **Privately Held**
SIC: 3452 Gate hooks

(G-19802)
AMERICAN GRAPHIC SYSTEMS INC
7650 185th St Ste A (60477-6290)
PHONE....................708 614-7007
Timothy Vernon, *President*
Larry Baker, *VP Opers*
Nelson Patrick, *Sales Mgr*
Vicky Barr, *Data Proc Dir*
Joel Purpura, *Art Dir*
▲ **EMP:** 35
SQ FT: 50,000
SALES (est): 4MM **Privately Held**
SIC: 2396 2759 Printing & embossing on plastics fabric articles; letterpress & screen printing; decals: printing

(G-19803)
AMEX NOOTER LLC
18501 Maple Creek Dr # 900 (60477-6781)
PHONE....................708 429-8300
Bernie Wicklein, *President*
Greg Harper, *Senior VP*
Jim Stalley, *Safety Dir*
Ryan Winkelman, *Safety Mgr*
Dan Pullen, *Purch Mgr*
EMP: 10
SALES (est): 3.5MM
SALES (corp-wide): 590.6MM **Privately Held**
SIC: 1541 3443 3479 Industrial buildings & warehouses; tanks, standard or custom fabricated: metal plate; etching & engraving
HQ: Nooter Construction Company
1500 S 2nd St
Saint Louis MO 63104

(G-19804)
ANCHOR ABRASIVES COMPANY
7651 185th St (60477-6267)
PHONE....................708 444-4300
John C Shoemaker, *President*
Frank Shoemaker, *Vice Pres*
Penny Budz, *Purchasing*
Jeff Shoemaker, *Project Engr*
Carl Manchester, *Sales Staff*
EMP: 45
SALES (est): 12.5MM **Privately Held**
SIC: 3291 Abrasive products

(G-19805)
ANVIL INTERNATIONAL LLC
7979 183rd St Ste D (60477-5391)
PHONE....................708 534-1414
EMP: 11
SALES (corp-wide): 472.6MM **Privately Held**
SIC: 3498 Fabricated pipe & fittings
PA: Anvil International, Llc
160 Frenchtown Rd
North Kingstown RI 02852
401 558-2578

(G-19806)
ATLAS PUTTY PRODUCTS CO
8351 185th St (60487-9282)
PHONE....................708 429-5858
David Payton, *President*
Jackie Bueschel, *COO*
Matthew Payton, *COO*
Jack Payton, *Vice Pres*
Nancy Payton, *Vice Pres*
▲ **EMP:** 55 **EST:** 1947
SQ FT: 100,000
SALES (est): 20.4MM **Privately Held**
WEB: www.putty.com
SIC: 2851 4783 Putty, wood fillers & sealers; putty; wood fillers or sealers; packing & crating

(G-19807)
BELLMAN-MELCOR HOLDINGS INC
7575 183rd St (60477-6208)
PHONE....................708 532-5000
Steven Campbell, *President*
Joy Ausec, *Agent*
▲ **EMP:** 13
SALES (est): 2.1MM **Privately Held**
SIC: 2819 Alkali metals: lithium, cesium, francium, rubidium

(G-19808)
BENDA MANUFACTURING INC
18504 West Creek Dr Ste B (60477-6321)
PHONE....................708 633-4600
EMP: 5
SALES (est): 295.4K **Privately Held**
SIC: 3535 Conveyors & conveying equipment

(G-19809)
BENNETT TECHNOLOGIES INC
Also Called: Bti Dental
17049 Harlem Ave (60477-2739)
PHONE....................708 389-9501
William J Bennett, *CEO*
Paul Bennett, *President*
Lynn Bennett, *Admin Sec*
EMP: 10
SALES (est): 1.6MM **Privately Held**
SIC: 3843 8072 Dental equipment & supplies; crown & bridge production

(G-19810)
BEST-TRONICS MFG INC
18500 Graphic Ct (60477-6265)
PHONE....................708 802-9677
Stanley F Bartosz, *President*
Mary Patsy, *COO*
Kip Bartosz, *Vice Pres*
Janet Vecchi, *Admin Sec*
▲ **EMP:** 150
SQ FT: 21,000
SALES (est): 27.9MM **Privately Held**
SIC: 3661 Telephones & telephone apparatus; data sets, telephone or telegraph

(G-19811)
BIG TENT INC
Also Called: Amfotek
7700 185th St (60477-6770)
PHONE....................708 532-1222
Ellen Jordan Reidy, *President*
Ed Morgan, *Purch Mgr*
EMP: 42
SALES (est): 12.7MM **Privately Held**
SIC: 2087 Flavoring extracts & syrups

(G-19812)
BLACK BOX CORPORATION
9365 Windsor Pkwy (60487-7361)
PHONE....................312 656-8807
John Toops, *Branch Mgr*
EMP: 11 **Privately Held**
SIC: 3577 Computer peripheral equipment
HQ: Black Box Corporation
1000 Park Dr
Lawrence PA 15055
724 746-5500

(G-19813)
BROKERS PRINT MAIL RSOURCE INC
17732 Oak Park Ave (60477-3934)
PHONE....................708 532-9900
Thomas Lewis, *President*
EMP: 3 **EST:** 2010
SQ FT: 1,000
SALES: 2.5MM **Privately Held**
SIC: 2752 Commercial printing, lithographic

(G-19814)
BRYCO MACHINE INC
8059 185th St (60487-9200)
PHONE....................708 614-1900
Bryon Bettinardi, *President*
Angela Zehner, *Human Resources*
Dan Schultz, *Manager*
▲ **EMP:** 38
SQ FT: 25,000
SALES (est): 6.8MM **Privately Held**
SIC: 3599 Machine shop, jobbing & repair

(G-19815)
CABINET WHOLESALE SUPPLY INC
17532 Duvan Dr (60477-3631)
PHONE....................708 536-7090
John Limza, *President*
John Groff, *Sales Staff*
EMP: 20
SQ FT: 18,000
SALES (est): 437.3K **Privately Held**
SIC: 2434 Wood kitchen cabinets

(G-19816)
CORTUBE PRODUCTS CO
18500 Spring Creek Dr (60477-6237)
PHONE....................708 429-6700
Albert J Roth, *President*
Tom Roth, *Vice Pres*
▲ **EMP:** 8
SQ FT: 15,000
SALES (est): 760K **Privately Held**
SIC: 3498 5074 3083 Tube fabricating (contract bending & shaping); plumbing & hydronic heating supplies; laminated plastics plate & sheet

(G-19817)
CREATIVE CAKES LLC
16649 Oak Park Ave Ste F (60477-1843)
PHONE....................708 614-9755
Elizabeth Fahey,
Rebecca Palermo,
EMP: 22
SQ FT: 3,050
SALES (est): 1.3MM **Privately Held**
SIC: 2051 5812 Cakes, pies & pastries; caterers

(G-19818)
CREATIVE PERKY CUISINE LLC
6601 Martin France Cir (60477-6447)
PHONE....................312 870-0282
Shay Atkins, *Principal*
EMP: 5
SALES (est): 363.9K **Privately Held**
SIC: 3275 Gypsum products

(G-19819)
CROSSMARK PRINTING INC (PA)
18400 76th Ave Ste A (60477-6222)
PHONE....................708 532-8263
Martin F Ward, *President*
Nancy R Ward, *Admin Sec*
EMP: 14
SQ FT: 2,400
SALES (est): 1.9MM **Privately Held**
SIC: 2752 2796 2791 2789 Commercial printing, offset; platemaking services; typesetting; bookbinding & related work

(G-19820)
CYPRESS MULTIGRAPHICS LLC (PA)
Also Called: CM Associates
8500 185th St Ste A (60477-9346)
PHONE....................708 633-1166
Roger Szafranski,
EMP: 20
SQ FT: 13,000
SALES (est): 7.6MM **Privately Held**
SIC: 3993 2672 2752 Name plates: except engraved, etched, etc.: metal; signs, not made in custom sign painting shops; labels (unprinted), gummed: made from purchased materials; decals, lithographed

(G-19821)
D W RAM MANUFACTURING CO
18530 Spring Creek Dr # 1 (60477-6244)
PHONE....................708 633-7900
Douglas Murdaugh, *CEO*
Michael Kehrenbacher, *President*
EMP: 20
SQ FT: 30,000
SALES (est): 3.8MM **Privately Held**
SIC: 3663 3556 Radio & TV communications equipment; food products machinery

(G-19822)
ED CO
8304 Lilac Ln (60477-6574)
PHONE....................708 614-0695
EMP: 20
SALES (est): 1.3MM **Privately Held**
SIC: 3663 Mfg Radio/Tv Communication Equipment

(G-19823)
ELITE DIE & FINISHING INC
18650 Graphic Ct (60477-6254)
PHONE....................708 389-4848
Steve Stanek, *President*
EMP: 9

Tinley Park - Cook County (G-19824)

SALES: 500K **Privately Held**
SIC: **7383** 3544 2759 Press service; special dies, tools, jigs & fixtures; commercial printing

(G-19824)
EMERSON ELECTRIC CO
7650 185th St Ste D (60477-6290)
PHONE...................708 263-6100
EMP: 3
SALES (corp-wide): 18.3B **Publicly Held**
SIC: **3823** Industrial instrmnts msrmnt display/control process variable
PA: Emerson Electric Co.
8000 West Florissant Ave
Saint Louis MO 63136
314 553-2000

(G-19825)
EVEREADY WELDING SERVICE INC
18111 Harlem Ave (60477-3608)
PHONE...................708 532-2432
Robert Haavig Jr, *President*
Janet Haavig, *Vice Pres*
Robert Haavig Sr, *Treasurer*
EMP: 5
SALES (est): 670K **Privately Held**
SIC: **7692** Welding repair

(G-19826)
EYELATION INC
18501 Maple Creek Dr # 400 (60477-5122)
PHONE...................888 308-4703
Stacey Michel, *Accounts Mgr*
Bob Woods, *Accounts Mgr*
Lauren Gawron, *Software Dev*
Bradley Kirschner,
EMP: 12
SALES (est): 1.8MM **Privately Held**
WEB: www.en.eyelation.com
SIC: **5995** 7372 Optical goods stores; prepackaged software

(G-19827)
FIRST STRING ENTERPRISES INC (PA)
Also Called: Force Enterprises
18650 Graphic Ct (60477-6254)
PHONE...................708 614-1200
Ronald A Strenge, *President*
Joyce Strenge, *Admin Sec*
EMP: 20
SQ FT: 27,200
SALES (est): 3.2MM **Privately Held**
SIC: **2759** 2789 7331 Thermography; binding only: books, pamphlets, magazines, etc.; mailing service

(G-19828)
FOUR-TECH INDUSTRIES CO
18545 West Creek Dr (60477-6246)
PHONE...................708 444-8230
Dariusz Fudala, *President*
Matt Fudala, *Sales Mgr*
EMP: 6
SQ FT: 3,000
SALES (est): 1.2MM **Privately Held**
SIC: **3599** Machine shop, jobbing & repair

(G-19829)
FREDDIE BEAR SPORTS
Also Called: Freddie Bear Sports.com
17250 Oak Park Ave (60477-3402)
PHONE...................708 532-4133
Theodore Lutger, *Owner*
EMP: 12
SQ FT: 4,000
SALES (est): 880K **Privately Held**
WEB: www.freddiebearsports.com
SIC: **5941** 5961 2759 Archery supplies; hunting equipment; fishing equipment; clothing, mail order (except women's); advertising literature: printing

(G-19830)
GERBER MANUFACTURING (GM) LLC
Also Called: GM Lighting
18700 Ridgeland Ave (60477-4186)
PHONE...................708 478-0100
Ashley Gloster, *Vice Pres*
Steve Ceseretti, *Sales Staff*
Steve Cuttrell, *Sales Staff*
Richard Stellar, *Marketing Staff*
Dennis Ziegler, *Manager*
▲ EMP: 11
SALES: 2.2MM **Privately Held**
SIC: **3645** Residential lighting fixtures

(G-19831)
GIRLYGIRL
17037 Odell Ave (60477-2623)
PHONE...................708 633-7290
EMP: 3
SALES (est): 117.5K **Privately Held**
SIC: **2399** Mfg Fabricated Textile Products

(G-19832)
GLOBAL GENERAL CONTRACTORS LLC
9018 Walnut Ln (60487-5250)
PHONE...................708 663-0476
Bill Asmar,
Jose Morales,
EMP: 3
SALES (est): 183.5K **Privately Held**
SIC: **1521** 1522 1542 1389 Single-family housing construction; condominium construction; commercial & office building, new construction; construction, repair & dismantling services; building construction consultant

(G-19833)
GOODHEART-WILLCOX COMPANY INC (PA)
Also Called: Goodheart Wilcox Publisher
18604 West Creek Dr (60477-6243)
PHONE...................708 687-0315
John F Flanagan, *Ch of Bd*
Juliet Schreiner, *Editor*
Faith Zosky, *Editor*
Shannon Deprofio, *Vice Pres*
Todd J Scheffers, *Vice Pres*
EMP: 96 EST: 1972
SQ FT: 122,000
SALES (est): 19.3MM **Publicly Held**
WEB: www.g-w.com
SIC: **2731** Textbooks: publishing only, not printed on site

(G-19834)
GOPHERCENTRAL
7851 185th St Ste 106 (60477-6251)
PHONE...................708 478-4500
Jeanie Davis, *COO*
Tom Zegar, *Vice Pres*
Schoiber Rachael, *Opers Mgr*
Michele Chojnowski, *Manager*
Andrew Meyers, *Info Tech Mgr*
EMP: 4
SALES (est): 187.4K **Privately Held**
WEB: www.gophercentral.com
SIC: **2741** Miscellaneous publishing

(G-19835)
HARBOR TOOL MANUFACTURING CO
8300 185th St (60487-9275)
P.O. Box 43047, Chicago (60643-0002)
PHONE...................708 614-6400
Ernest Levine, *Principal*
Donat Czerny, *Engineer*
John Temple, *Engineer*
Charles Hinds, *Controller*
EMP: 21
SALES (est): 3.8MM **Privately Held**
SIC: **3599** Machine shop, jobbing & repair

(G-19836)
ILLIANA ORTHOPEDICS INC
17378 Overhill Ave (60477-3269)
PHONE...................708 532-0061
John Seibt Jr, *President*
Catherine Seibt, *Corp Secy*
EMP: 2
SQ FT: 1,200
SALES (est): 200K **Privately Held**
SIC: **3842** Limbs, artificial; braces, orthopedic

(G-19837)
ILLINOIS TOOL WORKS INC
Also Called: ITW Deltar Fuel Systems
8402 183rd St Ste D (60487-9285)
PHONE...................708 479-3346
EMP: 7

SALES (corp-wide): 14.1B **Publicly Held**
SIC: **3089** Injection molded finished plastic products
PA: Illinois Tool Works Inc.
155 Harlem Ave
Glenview IL 60025
847 724-7500

(G-19838)
ILLINOIS TOOL WORKS INC
Also Called: ITW Deltar Fuel Systems
8402 183rd St Ste D (60487-9285)
PHONE...................708 479-3346
EMP: 5
SALES (corp-wide): 14.3B **Publicly Held**
SIC: **3089** 3714 3544 Mfg Plastic Products Mfg Motor Vehicle Parts/Accessories Mfg Dies/Tools/Jigs/Fixtures
PA: Illinois Tool Works Inc.
155 Harlem Ave
Glenview IL 60025
847 724-7500

(G-19839)
IMAGE PACT PRINTING
18650 Graphic Ct (60477-6254)
PHONE...................708 460-6070
Bruce Nelson, *President*
Ronald S A Strenge, *Owner*
EMP: 20
SALES (est): 1.4MM **Privately Held**
SIC: **2752** Commercial printing, offset

(G-19840)
ITT WATER & WASTEWATER USA INC
8402 W 183 Th Ste A (60477)
PHONE...................708 342-0484
Michael Retter, *Branch Mgr*
EMP: 11 **Publicly Held**
SIC: **5084** 3561 3511 Industrial machinery & equipment; pumps & pumping equipment; turbines & turbine generator sets
HQ: Itt Water & Wastewater U.S.A., Inc.
1 Greenwich Pl Ste 2
Shelton CT 06484
262 548-8181

(G-19841)
J&E STORM SERVICES INC
17807 65th Ct (60477-4376)
PHONE...................630 401-3793
Anthony Jones, *President*
Dina Humbert, *Vice Pres*
EMP: 2
SQ FT: 1,000
SALES: 350K **Privately Held**
SIC: **2431** Storm windows, wood

(G-19842)
JR LIGHTING DESIGN INC
18464 West Creek Dr (60477-6273)
PHONE...................708 460-6319
Jason Reberski, *President*
Kevin Rosenhagen, *Opers Staff*
Denise Koziel, *CFO*
Cole Jurgens, *Department Mgr*
Denise Reberski, *Admin Sec*
EMP: 2
SALES (est): 300.1K **Privately Held**
SIC: **3648** Lighting fixtures, except electric: residential

(G-19843)
KVH INDUSTRIES INC
8412 185th St (60487-9237)
PHONE...................708 444-2800
Sid Bennett, *Vice Pres*
Mark Guthrie, *Vice Pres*
Jay Napoli, *Vice Pres*
Jeff Brunner, *VP Opers*
Al Nobis, *Opers Mgr*
EMP: 50
SALES (corp-wide): 170.7MM **Publicly Held**
WEB: www.kvh.com
SIC: **3812** 3663 Navigational systems & instruments; mobile communication equipment
PA: Kvh Industries, Inc.
50 Enterprise Ctr
Middletown RI 02842
401 847-3327

(G-19844)
LEESONS CAKES INC
6713 163rd Pl (60477-1717)
PHONE...................708 429-1330
Scott Leeson, *President*
Nancy Leeson, *Vice Pres*
EMP: 3
SALES (est): 50K **Privately Held**
SIC: **5149** 5461 2051 Bakery products; cakes; bread, cake & related products

(G-19845)
M C S INC
7230 171st St Unit 344 (60477-5613)
PHONE...................708 323-9233
Marcia Byrd,
EMP: 10
SALES (est): 308.4K **Privately Held**
SIC: **3471** Cleaning, polishing & finishing

(G-19846)
MULLARKEY ASSOCIATES INC
8141 185th St (60487-9202)
PHONE...................708 597-5555
Martin E Mullarkey Jr, *President*
Michael Mullarkey, *Vice Pres*
▲ EMP: 15
SQ FT: 21,800
SALES (est): 2.4MM **Privately Held**
SIC: **3589** 3949 Water purification equipment, household type; swimming pools, except plastic

(G-19847)
NELSON STUD WELDING INC
18601 Graphic Ct (60477-6262)
PHONE...................708 430-3770
Don Sues, *Manager*
EMP: 10
SALES (corp-wide): 14.4B **Publicly Held**
SIC: **7692** Welding repair
HQ: Nelson Stud Welding, Inc.
7900 W Ridge Rd
Elyria OH 44035
440 329-0400

(G-19848)
PANDUIT CORP (PA)
18900 Panduit Dr (60487-3600)
PHONE...................708 532-1800
Dennis Renaud, *CEO*
Andrew M Caveney, *Vice Pres*
Michael G Kenny, *Vice Pres*
Rina Lim, *Vice Pres*
Joanne Tyree, *Vice Pres*
◆ EMP: 1100 EST: 1953
SALES (est): 1.4B **Privately Held**
WEB: www.panduit.com
SIC: **3699** 3644 5063 Electrical equipment & supplies; electric conduits & fittings; electrical apparatus & equipment

(G-19849)
PROCESS PIPING INC
18005 Semmler Dr (60487-8617)
PHONE...................708 717-0513
Jenny Leblanc, *President*
EMP: 4
SALES (est): 530.3K **Privately Held**
SIC: **3494** Pipe fittings

(G-19850)
PROMO ANSWERS INC
15943 Blackwater Ct (60477-6758)
PHONE...................708 633-6653
EMP: 4
SALES (est): 349.8K **Privately Held**
SIC: **2752** Commercial printing, lithographic

(G-19851)
QBF GROUP INC
18650 Graphic Ct (60477-6254)
PHONE...................708 781-9580
Kenneth Larney Jr, *President*
Mary Lou Larney, *Admin Sec*
EMP: 9
SQ FT: 20,000
SALES (est): 1.5MM **Privately Held**
WEB: www.qbfgraphicsgroup.com
SIC: **2752** Commercial printing, offset

GEOGRAPHIC SECTION

(G-19852)
QUALITY INTGRTED SOLUTIONS INC
18521 Spring Creek Dr (60477-6202)
PHONE..................815 464-4772
Ted Kowalczyk, *President*
Mike Montvidas, *Opers Mgr*
EMP: 8
SALES (est): 1.2MM **Privately Held**
SIC: 1731 3699 5099 Closed circuit television installation; security devices; fire extinguishers

(G-19853)
RK MAINTENANCE INC
17310 Queen Elizabeth Ln (60477-7874)
PHONE..................708 429-2215
Ralph Kick, *President*
EMP: 2
SALES (est): 206.8K **Privately Held**
SIC: 7692 Welding repair

(G-19854)
ROBS AQUATICS
17135 Harlem Ave (60477-3369)
PHONE..................708 444-7627
EMP: 3
SALES (est): 229.7K **Privately Held**
SIC: 3999 Pet supplies

(G-19855)
SILK SCREEN EXPRESS INC
7611 185th St (60477-6267)
PHONE..................708 845-5600
Dawn Coleman, *President*
EMP: 15
SQ FT: 15,000
SALES (est): 3.4MM **Privately Held**
SIC: 2759 Screen printing

(G-19856)
SOUNDGROWLER BREWING COMPANY
8201 183rd St (60487-9248)
PHONE..................708 263-0083
Arturo Lamas, *President*
EMP: 3
SALES (est): 68.6K **Privately Held**
SIC: 2082 Beer (alcoholic beverage)

(G-19857)
SOUTHTOWN STAR NEWSPAPERS
18312 West Creek Dr (60477-6240)
PHONE..................708 633-4800
EMP: 4 EST: 2014
SALES (est): 25.1K **Privately Held**
WEB: www.southtownstar.com
SIC: 2711 Newspapers, publishing & printing

(G-19858)
STROMBERG ALLEN AND COMPANY
18504 West Creek Dr Ste A (60477-6321)
PHONE..................773 847-7131
G William Kruchko, *President*
Peter Kruchko, *CFO*
Paul Wirtz, *Marketing Staff*
Gloria Olbera, *Info Tech Mgr*
Mary K Skoning, *Admin Sec*
▲ EMP: 43
SQ FT: 80,000
SALES (est): 6.4MM **Privately Held**
WEB: www.strombergallen.com
SIC: 2752 2759 7389 Commercial printing, offset; letterpress printing; printers' services: folding, collating

(G-19859)
SURFACE SHIELDS INC (PA)
8451 183rd Pl (60487-9271)
PHONE..................708 226-9810
Kyle W Behringer, *President*
Caleb Nerstad, *Opers Mgr*
Pj McCain, *Sales Staff*
Tom Fergus, *Marketing Staff*
Trevor Stedronsky, *Marketing Staff*
◆ EMP: 40
SQ FT: 21,000
SALES (est): 11.4MM **Privately Held**
SIC: 3996 Hard surface floor coverings

(G-19860)
TOMANTRON INC
17942 66th Ave (60477-4133)
PHONE..................708 532-2456
Jiri Toman, *President*
EMP: 10
SALES (est): 840K **Privately Held**
SIC: 3823 3625 3577 Digital displays of process variables; relays & industrial controls; computer peripheral equipment

(G-19861)
TRANE US INC
18452 West Creek Dr (60477-6273)
PHONE..................708 532-8004
Manny Guerrero, *Branch Mgr*
EMP: 3 **Privately Held**
SIC: 3585 Refrigeration & heating equipment
HQ: Trane U.S. Inc.
3600 Pammel Creek Rd
La Crosse WI 54601
608 787-2000

(G-19862)
TYLKA PRINTING INC
18400 76th Ave Ste A (60477-6286)
PHONE..................773 767-3775
David Tylka, *President*
Linda Hlado, *Vice Pres*
EMP: 4
SALES: 800K **Privately Held**
SIC: 2752 Commercial printing, offset

(G-19863)
U G N INC (HQ)
Also Called: Ugn Automotive
18410 Crossing Dr Ste C (60487-6209)
PHONE..................773 437-2400
Peter Anthony, *President*
Donald Nelson, *COO*
Kevin Bohan, *Vice Pres*
Darrell Cook, *Vice Pres*
Esther Jones, *Vice Pres*
▲ EMP: 91
SQ FT: 28,000
SALES (est): 395.4MM
SALES (corp-wide): 2.3B **Privately Held**
SIC: 3714 Motor vehicle parts & accessories
PA: Autoneum Holding Ag
Schlosstalstrasse 43
Winterthur ZH
522 448-282

(G-19864)
U S RAILWAY SERVICES
8201 183rd St Ste C (60487-9208)
P.O. Box 1125 (60477-7925)
PHONE..................708 468-8343
James J Provencher, *Principal*
EMP: 5
SALES (est): 873.8K **Privately Held**
SIC: 4011 3531 Interurban railways; railway track equipment

(G-19865)
UP AT DAWN INC
18504 West Creek Dr (60477-6320)
PHONE..................773 457-3859
Phil Stevens, *President*
Katie Zmuda, *Principal*
EMP: 52
SALES (est): 88.8K **Privately Held**
SIC: 2051 Bread, cake & related products

(G-19866)
US MINERALS INC (PA)
18635 West Creek Dr Ste 2 (60477-6224)
P.O. Box 547, Anaconda MT (59711-0547)
PHONE..................708 623-1935
Michael Johnston, *President*
Jeffrey Fink, *Vice Pres*
Jason Vukas, *Vice Pres*
Clint Napton, *Plant Mgr*
David Feyma, *Engineer*
▲ EMP: 10
SALES (est): 34.3MM **Privately Held**
SIC: 3291 Abrasive products

(G-19867)
VITAL CARE REPS
18470 Thompson Ct Ste 1b (60477-6774)
PHONE..................708 342-2680
Sillisa Humphrey, *Human Resources*
EMP: 5

SALES (est): 512.8K **Privately Held**
SIC: 3841 Surgical & medical instruments

(G-19868)
WYMAN AND COMPANY
17324 Oak Park Ave (60477-3404)
PHONE..................708 532-9064
Kathy Wyman, *Owner*
EMP: 3
SALES (est): 130K **Privately Held**
SIC: 2499 Picture frame molding, finished

(G-19869)
X-CEL TECHNOLOGIES INC
7800 Graphic Dr (60477-6266)
PHONE..................708 802-7400
Robert J Bettinardi, *President*
Ann Bettinardi, *Admin Sec*
▲ EMP: 30
SQ FT: 30,000
SALES (est): 7MM **Privately Held**
SIC: 3599 Machine shop, jobbing & repair

(G-19870)
XTREME CYLINDERS LLC
7601 191st St (60487-9216)
PHONE..................877 219-9001
William J Nero, *Principal*
EMP: 2
SALES (est): 225.4K **Privately Held**
SIC: 3593 Fluid power cylinders, hydraulic or pneumatic

Tiskilwa
Bureau County

(G-19871)
BUREAU VALLEY CHIEF
108 W Main St (61368-9652)
P.O. Box 476 (61368-0476)
PHONE..................815 646-4731
John Murphy, *Owner*
Ginger Murphy, *Co-Owner*
EMP: 3
SQ FT: 1,790
SALES: 100K **Privately Held**
SIC: 2711 2752 5994 Newspapers: publishing only, not printed on site; commercial printing, offset; news dealers & newsstands

(G-19872)
CRESCENT RIDGE LLC
6250 1475 East St (61368-9305)
PHONE..................815 646-4119
Kathleen Esposito,
EMP: 2
SALES (est): 214.8K **Privately Held**
SIC: 3621 Windmills, electric generating

(G-19873)
HYDROTEC SYSTEMS COMPANY INC (PA)
Also Called: H2o Mobil
145 E Main St (61368-9659)
P.O. Box 61 (61368-0061)
PHONE..................815 624-6644
Warren Searles, *President*
Doreen Searles, *Treasurer*
EMP: 3
SQ FT: 15,000
SALES (est): 500K **Privately Held**
SIC: 3589 8742 Water treatment equipment, industrial; automation & robotics consultant

Toledo
Cumberland County

(G-19874)
BAG AND BARRIER CORPORATION
505 E Rte 121 (62468)
P.O. Box 129 (62468-0129)
PHONE..................217 849-3271
Timothy Olmstead, *President*
Sandy Olmstead, *Corp Secy*
EMP: 4 EST: 1951
SQ FT: 10,000

SALES (est): 349.9K **Privately Held**
SIC: 5632 2674 2673 Handbags; paper bags: made from purchased materials; bags: plastic, laminated & coated

(G-19875)
GENTRY SMALL ENGINE REPAIR
124 Court House Sq (62468)
P.O. Box 269 (62468-0269)
PHONE..................217 849-3378
Mike Gentry, *Partner*
Julie Gentry, *Partner*
EMP: 3
SALES (est): 250K **Privately Held**
SIC: 7699 5261 3546 Engine repair & replacement, non-automotive; lawn & garden equipment; saws & sawing equipment

(G-19876)
HIGH POINT RECOVERY COMPANY
603 County Road 500 E (62468-4042)
PHONE..................217 821-7777
Irvin Figgins Jr, *President*
EMP: 4
SALES (est): 295.1K **Privately Held**
SIC: 3531 Automobile wrecker hoists

(G-19877)
SCHROCK CUSTOM WOODWORKING
705 Industrial Dr (62468-4236)
P.O. Box 249 (62468-0249)
PHONE..................217 849-3375
Jeffrey Schrock, *President*
EMP: 6
SALES (est): 711.3K **Privately Held**
SIC: 2434 2541 Wood kitchen cabinets; store fixtures, wood

(G-19878)
SOUTH CENTRAL FS INC
708 S Meridian St (62468-1228)
PHONE..................217 849-2242
Bellmark Markwell, *Manager*
EMP: 10
SALES (corp-wide): 90.7MM **Privately Held**
SIC: 2875 5191 5172 5153 Fertilizers, mixing only; fertilizer & fertilizer materials; feed; seeds: field, garden & flower; petroleum brokers; grain elevators
HQ: South Central Fs, Inc.
405 S Banker St
Effingham IL 62401
217 342-9231

(G-19879)
TOLEDO DEMOCRAT
116 Court House Sq (62468)
P.O. Box 7 (62468-0007)
PHONE..................217 849-2000
Billie Chambers, *Partner*
Wes Chambers, *Partner*
EMP: 3 EST: 1926
SALES (est): 250.9K **Privately Held**
SIC: 2711 2791 2759 2752 Job printing & newspaper publishing combined; commercial printing & newspaper publishing combined; typesetting; commercial printing; commercial printing, lithographic

(G-19880)
TOLEDO MACHINE & WELDING INC
607 E Illinois Rt 121 (62468)
P.O. Box 84 (62468-0084)
PHONE..................217 849-2251
Chuck Pruemer, *President*
EMP: 3
SALES (est): 390.4K **Privately Held**
SIC: 7692 Welding repair

(G-19881)
TSC PYROFERRIC INTERNATIONAL (PA)
Also Called: TSC Ferrite International
507 E Madison (62468)
PHONE..................217 849-2230
Tim Smith, *President*
Tempel Smith, *Chairman*
▲ EMP: 110
SQ FT: 30,000

Toledo - Cumberland County (G-19882)

SALES (est): 9MM **Privately Held**
SIC: 3264 3356 Ferrite & ferrite parts; nickel & nickel alloy: rolling, drawing or extruding

(G-19882)
WARNER HARVEY LEE FARM INC
Also Called: Warner Farms
556 County Road 800 E (62468-4031)
PHONE.................................217 849-2548
Harvey Lee Warner, *Owner*
EMP: 3
SALES (est): 109.1K **Privately Held**
SIC: 2083 0191 Corn malt; general farms, primarily crop

Tolono
Champaign County

(G-19883)
ILLINOIS FOUNDATION SEEDS INC
1178 County Road 900 N (61880-9624)
PHONE.................................217 485-6420
Dave Deutscher, *Branch Mgr*
EMP: 14
SALES (corp-wide): 20MM **Privately Held**
SIC: 2068 5191 8731 0723 Seeds: dried, dehydrated, salted or roasted; seeds: field, garden & flower; commercial physical research; crop preparation services for market
PA: Illinois Foundation Seeds Inc
    1083 County Road 900 N
    Tolono IL
    217 485-6260

(G-19884)
SHADE SOLUTIONS INC
1102 County Road 900 N (61880-9624)
PHONE.................................217 239-0718
Kevin Yonce, *President*
EMP: 10
SALES (est): 793.3K **Privately Held**
SIC: 2394 1799 3444 7699 Awnings, fabric: made from purchased materials; awning installation; awnings & canopies; awnings, sheet metal; awning repair shop; awnings

Toluca
Marshall County

(G-19885)
AJINOMOTO FOODS NORTH AMER INC
110 N Main St (61369-9430)
PHONE.................................815 452-2559
Rick Alden, *Branch Mgr*
EMP: 12 **Privately Held**
SIC: 2038 Frozen specialties
HQ: Ajinomoto Foods North America, Inc.
    4200 Concours Ste 100
    Ontario CA 91764

(G-19886)
AJINOMOTO FOODS NORTH AMER INC
301 W 3rd St (61369-9686)
PHONE.................................815 452-2361
Rick Alden, *Partner*
Alex Stoeger, *General Mgr*
Frank Stoeger, *Plant Engr*
Paula Nenne, *Accountant*
William Deckelmann, *Manager*
EMP: 216 **Privately Held**
SIC: 2099 Food preparations
HQ: Ajinomoto Foods North America, Inc.
    4200 Concours Ste 100
    Ontario CA 91764

Tonica
Lasalle County

(G-19887)
BRIAN D OBERMILLER
Also Called: Obermiller Kustom Fabrication
124 S Peru St Louis (61370)
P.O. Box 221 (61370-0221)
PHONE.................................815 830-3100
Brian D Obermiller, *Owner*
EMP: 3
SALES: 250K **Privately Held**
SIC: 7692 Welding repair

(G-19888)
DAUBER COMPANY INC
577 N 18tth Rd Tth (61370)
PHONE.................................815 442-3569
Eric Dauber, *President*
Gayle Dauber, *Vice Pres*
Ken Miller, *Human Res Mgr*
Susan Sebben, *Clerk*
▲ EMP: 23
SQ FT: 1,800
SALES (est): 10.7MM **Privately Held**
SIC: 3674 2819 3295 Silicon wafers, chemically doped; industrial inorganic chemicals; minerals, ground or treated

(G-19889)
ILLINOIS VALLEY MINERALS LLC
575 N 18th Rd (61370-9423)
P.O. Box 376, Hennepin (61327-0376)
PHONE.................................815 442-8402
Eric E Dauber, *CEO*
Bill Johnson,
John Redshaw,
EMP: 7
SQ FT: 30,000
SALES (est): 630.3K **Privately Held**
SIC: 1481 Nonmetallic mineral services

Toulon
Stark County

(G-19890)
CITY OF TOULON
Also Called: Toulon City Water & Sew
120 N Franklin St (61483-5105)
PHONE.................................309 286-7073
R Shane Milroy, *Branch Mgr*
EMP: 6 **Privately Held**
SIC: 9111 3589 Executive offices, state & local; sewage & water treatment equipment
PA: City Of Toulon
    122 N Franklin St
    Toulon IL 61483
    309 286-5042

(G-19891)
STARK COUNTY COMMUNICATIONS
101 W Main St (61483-5229)
P.O. Box 240 (61483-0240)
PHONE.................................309 286-4444
Jim Nowlan, *President*
EMP: 6
SALES (est): 455K **Privately Held**
SIC: 2711 Newspapers: publishing only, not printed on site; newspapers, publishing & printing

Towanda
Mclean County

(G-19892)
ALEXANDER MANUFACTURING CO
114 N Lincoln St (61776-7619)
P.O. Box 169 (61776-0169)
PHONE.................................309 728-2224
Jeff Wilkerson, *Branch Mgr*
EMP: 75
SALES (corp-wide): 12MM **Privately Held**
SIC: 3993 3952 3951 Signs & advertising specialties; lead pencils & art goods; pens & mechanical pencils
PA: Alexander Manufacturing Company
    1283 Research Blvd
    Saint Louis MO 63132
    314 692-7030

(G-19893)
WINDY HILL WOODWORKING INC
4 Candle Ridge Rd (61776-7514)
PHONE.................................309 275-2415
Jayson Hines, *President*
Barbara Welch, *Vice Pres*
EMP: 3
SALES (est): 150K **Privately Held**
SIC: 2541 Cabinets, except refrigerated: show, display, etc.: wood

Tower Hill
Shelby County

(G-19894)
REALT IMAGES INC
Also Called: R I Plastics
172 Williamsburg Hl A (62571)
PHONE.................................217 567-3487
Alan L Thompson, *President*
Barry Thompson, *Vice Pres*
EMP: 9
SQ FT: 6,000
SALES (est): 300K **Privately Held**
SIC: 3081 3993 Plastic film & sheet; signs & advertising specialties

Tremont
Tazewell County

(G-19895)
CULLINAN & SONS INC (PA)
Also Called: Rowe Construction Div
121 W Park St (61568-7520)
P.O. Box 166 (61568-0166)
PHONE.................................309 925-2711
Michael N Cullinan, *Ch of Bd*
Stephen Cullinan, *Principal*
Elizabeth Mathers, *Principal*
Ronald L Olson, *Treasurer*
John G Moser, *Admin Sec*
EMP: 40 EST: 1914
SQ FT: 3,500
SALES (est): 14.7MM **Privately Held**
WEB: www.ucm.biz
SIC: 1611 2951 1752 1731 Surfacing & paving; asphalt paving mixtures & blocks; floor laying & floor work; electrical work; water, sewer & utility lines; construction sand & gravel

(G-19896)
G T SERVICES OF ILLINOIS INC
Also Called: Gt Business Services
22387 State Route 9 (61568-9102)
P.O. Box 1402 (61568-1402)
PHONE.................................309 925-5111
Greg Mills, *President*
Tami Mills, *Vice Pres*
Tammy Mills, *Vice Pres*
EMP: 6
SQ FT: 4,000
SALES (est): 322.1K **Privately Held**
SIC: 2752 7336 Commercial printing, lithographic; commercial art & graphic design

(G-19897)
K R J INC
Also Called: Litwiller Machine and Supply
101 S West St (61568)
P.O. Box 1404 (61568-1404)
PHONE.................................309 925-5123
Kenneth Ropp, *President*
Joyce Ropp, *Corp Secy*
EMP: 3
SALES (est): 309.6K **Privately Held**
SIC: 3599 1731 Machine shop, jobbing & repair; general electrical contractor

(G-19898)
MATHIS ENERGY LLC
701 E Pearl St (61568-7507)
P.O. Box 102 (61568-0102)
PHONE.................................309 925-3177
Danivan L Mathis,
EMP: 2
SALES (est): 223K **Privately Held**
WEB: www.mathisenergy.com
SIC: 3568 Couplings, shaft: rigid, flexible, universal joint, etc.

(G-19899)
TREKON COMPANY INC
115 E South St (61568-7919)
P.O. Box 1126 (61568-1126)
PHONE.................................309 925-7942
Steve Gunter, *President*
Greg Gunter, *Vice Pres*
Jim Lonergan, *Production*
Cynthia Springer, *Admin Sec*
EMP: 8
SQ FT: 30,000
SALES (est): 1.6MM **Privately Held**
SIC: 2677 Envelopes

(G-19900)
TREMONT KITCHEN TOPS INC
100 N West St (61568-7982)
P.O. Box 1402 (61568-1402)
PHONE.................................309 925-5736
Sheila Robbins, *President*
Jeff Graves, *Vice Pres*
EMP: 5
SALES (est): 292.8K **Privately Held**
SIC: 2434 Wood kitchen cabinets

(G-19901)
TREND SETTERS LTD
22500 State Route 9 (61568-9156)
PHONE.................................309 929-7012
Joeliyn Jablonski, *President*
EMP: 15 EST: 1989
SQ FT: 16,000
SALES: 1.2MM **Privately Held**
WEB: www.trendsettersltd.com
SIC: 3861 7384 Printing frames, photographic; photofinishing laboratory

Trenton
Clinton County

(G-19902)
COUNTY ASPHALT INC
427 S Madison St (62293-1143)
PHONE.................................618 224-9033
Dawn Gruender, *President*
Bart Gruender, *Treasurer*
EMP: 3
SALES (est): 234K **Privately Held**
SIC: 2951 Asphalt paving mixtures & blocks

(G-19903)
KMK METAL FABRICATORS INC
Also Called: K M K
408 E Broadway (62293-1608)
PHONE.................................618 224-2000
Kirk Kassel, *President*
Kraig Kassel, *Vice Pres*
David Mollett, *Vice Pres*
Darron Vandorn, *Plant Mgr*
Mike Wetzel, *Engineer*
EMP: 32
SQ FT: 100,000
SALES (est): 10.1MM **Privately Held**
WEB: www.kmkmetal.com
SIC: 3441 Fabricated structural metal

(G-19904)
KUNZ CARPENTRY (PA)
16 E Broadway (62293-1302)
PHONE.................................618 224-7892
Frank Kunz, *Owner*
EMP: 8
SQ FT: 700
SALES (est): 966.5K **Privately Held**
SIC: 5712 2511 2434 Cabinet work, custom; wood household furniture; vanities, bathroom: wood

GEOGRAPHIC SECTION

(G-19905)
TRENTON SUN
19 W Broadway (62293-1303)
P.O. Box 118 (62293-0118)
PHONE..................................618 224-9422
Michael Conley, *Owner*
Sybil Conley, *Co-Owner*
EMP: 6 **EST:** 1990
SQ FT: 3,000
SALES: 75K **Privately Held**
WEB: www.printingservicetrenton.com
SIC: 2791 2752 2711 5812 Typesetting; commercial printing, lithographic; commercial printing & newspaper publishing combined; coffee shop

Trivoli
Peoria County

(G-19906)
FRAME MATERIAL SUPPLY INC
Also Called: Fms
520 N Trivoli Rd (61569-9701)
P.O. Box 133 (61569-0133)
PHONE..................................309 362-2323
Bradley Stevens, *President*
Mary Stevens, *Admin Sec*
EMP: 2
SQ FT: 17,500
SALES (est): 409.8K **Privately Held**
SIC: 3547 Steel rolling machinery

(G-19907)
MIDLAND COAL COMPANY
2203 N Trivoli Rd (61569-9542)
PHONE..................................309 362-2795
Philip Christy, *Manager*
EMP: 1
SALES (est): 250K **Privately Held**
SIC: 0191 1031 0115 0116 General farms, primarily crop; lead & zinc ores; corn; soybeans

Trout Valley
Mchenry County

(G-19908)
POLITECH INC
108 Turkey Run Rd (60013-2455)
PHONE..................................847 516-2717
Peter Politeki, *President*
EMP: 5
SALES (est): 430K **Privately Held**
SIC: 7372 Prepackaged software

Troy
Madison County

(G-19909)
ABBEY PRODUCTS LLP
112 Willing Way (62294-1287)
PHONE..................................636 922-5577
EMP: 2
SALES (est): 238.6K **Privately Held**
SIC: 3652 5099 5113 7379 Mfg Recorded Record/Tape Whol Durable Goods Whol Indstl/Svc Paper Computer Related Svcs

(G-19910)
ADVANTEX INC OF ILLINOIS
326 Bargraves Blvd (62294-2304)
P.O. Box 67, Glen Carbon (62034-0067)
PHONE..................................618 505-0701
Gregory Byers, *President*
Nick Fadden, *Vice Pres*
▲ **EMP:** 100
SQ FT: 4,500
SALES (est): 11.3MM **Privately Held**
SIC: 2337 5131 Uniforms, except athletic: women's, misses' & juniors'; textiles, woven

(G-19911)
ADVANTEX INC
326 Bargraves Blvd (62294-2304)
PHONE..................................618 505-0701
Fax: 618 288-6431

EMP: 5
SALES (est): 569.5K **Privately Held**
SIC: 2299 Mfg Textile Goods

(G-19912)
CCO HOLDINGS LLC
523 Troy Plz (62294-1349)
PHONE..................................618 505-3505
EMP: 3
SALES (corp-wide): 45.7B **Publicly Held**
SIC: 5064 4841 3663 3651 Electrical appliances, television & radio; cable & other pay television services; radio & TV communications equipment; household audio & video equipment
HQ: Cco Holdings, Llc
400 Atlantic St
Stamford CT 06901
203 905-7801

(G-19913)
CUSTOM FOAM WORKS INC
31 Sequoia Dr (62294-3226)
PHONE..................................618 920-2810
Dane Tippett, *President*
EMP: 8
SALES (est): 591.7K **Privately Held**
SIC: 3086 Packaging & shipping materials, foamed plastic

(G-19914)
GATEWAY IMPRESSIONS
218 Edwardsville Rd (62294-1341)
PHONE..................................618 505-7544
Tyler Yager, *Principal*
Karla Merlak, *Administration*
EMP: 3
SALES (est): 258.2K **Privately Held**
WEB: www.gatewayimpressions.com
SIC: 2759 Screen printing

(G-19915)
HICKORY STREET CABINETS
208 S Hickory St (62294-1626)
PHONE..................................618 667-9676
Jon Dillard, *Owner*
Steve Hein, *Manager*
EMP: 2
SQ FT: 3,800
SALES: 350K **Privately Held**
SIC: 5712 2541 5211 2434 Cabinet work, custom; wood partitions & fixtures; cabinets, kitchen; wood kitchen cabinets

(G-19916)
JUST ANOTHER BUTTON
116 W Market St (62294-1412)
PHONE..................................618 667-8531
Cecile McPeak, *Partner*
Patti Connor, *Partner*
EMP: 13 **EST:** 1996
SALES (est): 1.6MM **Privately Held**
WEB: www.justanotherbuttoncompany.com
SIC: 3965 Buttons & parts

(G-19917)
NEWSPRINT INK INC
Also Called: Times-Tribune
507 Ohara Dr Ste 1 (62294-2348)
P.O. Box 68 (62294-0068)
PHONE..................................618 667-3111
EMP: 10
SALES (est): 464.7K **Privately Held**
SIC: 2711 Newspapers, publishing & printing

(G-19918)
QUAD-COUNTY READY MIX CORP
2458 Formosa Rd (62294-3177)
PHONE..................................618 288-4000
Eric Hollenkamp, *Branch Mgr*
EMP: 5
SALES (corp-wide): 16.1MM **Privately Held**
SIC: 3273 Ready-mixed concrete
PA: Quad-County Ready Mix Corp.
300 W 12th St
Okawville IL 62271
618 243-6430

(G-19919)
R L ALLEN INDUSTRIES
Also Called: National Peace Officers' Press
120 Collinsville Rd Ofc (62294-1396)
PHONE..................................618 667-2544

Terry Allen, *President*
Eva Allen, *Vice Pres*
EMP: 2
SQ FT: 8,000
SALES (est): 252.8K **Privately Held**
SIC: 2759 8399 3999 2741 Promotional printing; fund raising organization, non-fee basis; identification plates; miscellaneous publishing

Troy Grove
Lasalle County

(G-19920)
COVIA HOLDINGS CORPORATION
S Peru St (61372)
P.O. Box 110 (61372-0110)
PHONE..................................815 539-6734
Scott Atkins, *Opers-Prdtn-Mfg*
EMP: 5
SALES (corp-wide): 125.5MM **Publicly Held**
SIC: 1446 Silica sand mining
HQ: Covia Holdings Corporation
3 Summit Park Dr Ste 700
Independence OH 44131
440 214-3284

(G-19921)
FAIRMOUNT SANTROL INC
Also Called: Technisand
300 S Vermillion St (61372-1068)
P.O. Box 50 (61372-0050)
PHONE..................................815 538-2645
George Oak, *Branch Mgr*
EMP: 26
SALES (corp-wide): 125.5MM **Publicly Held**
SIC: 1442 Construction sand & gravel
HQ: Fairmount Santrol Inc.
3 Summit Park Dr Ste 700
Independence OH 44131
440 214-3200

Tuscola
Douglas County

(G-19922)
ALLOY TECH
608 E Pinzon St (61953-1952)
PHONE..................................217 253-3939
Ron D Clapp, *Owner*
EMP: 3 **EST:** 1968
SQ FT: 1,000
SALES (est): 200K **Privately Held**
SIC: 3714 Motor vehicle engines & parts

(G-19923)
BEAR CREEK TRUSS INC
615 N County Road 250 E (61953-7037)
PHONE..................................217 543-3329
EMP: 40
SQ FT: 8,640
SALES: 8.6MM **Privately Held**
WEB: www.bearcreektruss.com
SIC: 2439 Trusses, wooden roof

(G-19924)
CABOT CORPORATION
700 E Us Highway 36 (61953-7520)
PHONE..................................217 253-3370
Jeffry Mudd, *Research*
Colleen Creuz, *Engineer*
Bryan Pierce, *Engineer*
Cory Watkins, *Plant Engr*
Dean Nelson, *Project Engr*
EMP: 31
SALES (corp-wide): 3.3B **Publicly Held**
WEB: www.cabot-corp.com
SIC: 2819 Industrial inorganic chemicals
PA: Cabot Corporation
2 Seaport Ln Ste 1300
Boston MA 02210
617 345-0100

(G-19925)
CABOT CORPORATION
700 E Us Highway 36 (61953-7520)
P.O. Box 307, Waverly WV (26184)
PHONE..................................217 253-5752

Kevin Quinlan, *Human Res Mgr*
Raj Ahuja, *Manager*
EMP: 53
SALES (corp-wide): 3.3B **Publicly Held**
WEB: www.cabot-corp.com
SIC: 2895 3624 2899 Carbon black; carbon & graphite products; chemical preparations
PA: Cabot Corporation
2 Seaport Ln Ste 1300
Boston MA 02210
617 345-0100

(G-19926)
EQUISTAR CHEMICALS LP
625 E Us Highway 36 (61953-7507)
PHONE..................................217 253-3311
Mauren Radi, *Engineer*
Larry Noonan, *Persnl Mgr*
Bill Foot, *Manager*
EMP: 23
SALES (corp-wide): 39.1B **Privately Held**
SIC: 2869 Butadiene (industrial organic chemical)
HQ: Equistar Chemicals, Lp
1221 Mckinney St Ste 300
Houston TX 77010

(G-19927)
HASTINGS PRINTING
111 Sale St (61953)
PHONE..................................217 253-5086
Randy Hastings, *President*
Greg Hasting, *Owner*
EMP: 3
SALES (est): 218.5K **Privately Held**
SIC: 2759 Commercial printing

(G-19928)
HERSCHBERGER WINDOW INC
623 N County Road 250 E (61953-7037)
PHONE..................................217 543-2106
D L Herschberger, *President*
Darrell L Herschberger, *Owner*
EMP: 3
SQ FT: 2,500
SALES (est): 400K **Privately Held**
SIC: 3089 5031 Windows, plastic; metal doors, sash & trim

(G-19929)
PVH CORP
Also Called: Van Heusen
1011 E Southline Rd (61953)
PHONE..................................217 253-3398
Crystal Schrock, *Manager*
EMP: 10
SALES (corp-wide): 9.9B **Publicly Held**
SIC: 2321 Men's & boys' dress shirts
PA: Pvh Corp.
200 Madison Ave Bsmt 1
New York NY 10016
212 381-3500

(G-19930)
R & N COMPONENTS CO
261 E County Road 600 N (61953-7039)
PHONE..................................217 543-3495
Ruben Gingerich, *Owner*
EMP: 9
SALES (est): 1.3MM **Privately Held**
SIC: 2452 Panels & sections, prefabricated, wood

(G-19931)
TEWELL BROS MACHINE INC
300 N Parke St (61953-1408)
PHONE..................................217 253-6303
Thomas A Tewell, *President*
John P Tewell, *Admin Sec*
EMP: 11 **EST:** 2000
SALES (est): 4.5MM **Privately Held**
WEB: www.toolbros.com
SIC: 5084 7692 3537 3444 Metalworking tools (such as drills, taps, dies, files); welding repair; industrial trucks & tractors; sheet metalwork

(G-19932)
TUSCOLA JOURNAL INCORPORATED
Also Called: Tri County Journal
115 W Sale St (61953-1443)
P.O. Box 170 (61953-0170)
PHONE..................................217 253-5086
Beverly Hastings, *President*

Tuscola - Douglas County (G-19933)

Aaron Hastings, *Advt Staff*
EMP: 5
SALES: 170K **Privately Held**
SIC: 2711 Newspapers: publishing only, not printed on site

(G-19933)
TUSCOLA STONE COMPANY
1199 E Us Highway 36 (61953-8043)
P.O. Box 318 (61953-0318)
PHONE.................217 253-4705
Randy Reed, *Superintendent*
EMP: 15
SALES (corp-wide): 7.7MM **Privately Held**
SIC: 1422 5032 Agricultural limestone, ground; stone, crushed or broken
PA: Tuscola Stone Company
　　1250 Larkin Ave Ste 10
　　Elgin IL

(G-19934)
WENGER WOODCRAFT
676 N County Road 250 E (61953-7037)
PHONE.................217 578-3440
Steve Wenger, *Partner*
Keith Schmidt, *Partner*
Gregory Wenger, *Partner*
EMP: 4
SALES: 140K **Privately Held**
SIC: 2431 5211 1799 1751 Doors & door parts & trim, wood; cabinets, kitchen; kitchen & bathroom remodeling; cabinet & finish carpentry

Ullin
Pulaski County

(G-19935)
JACK SHEPARD LOGGING
14225 Shepard Ln (62992-3007)
PHONE.................618 845-3496
Jack Shepard, *Owner*
EMP: 5
SALES (est): 382K **Privately Held**
SIC: 2411 Logging camps & contractors

(G-19936)
RODNEY TITE WELDING
391 N Locust St (62992-1024)
PHONE.................618 845-9072
Rodney Tite, *Owner*
Lori Tite, *Co-Owner*
EMP: 5
SALES (est): 205.7K **Privately Held**
SIC: 7692 Welding repair

Union
Mchenry County

(G-19937)
BAGMAKERS INC
6606 S Union Rd (60180-9535)
P.O. Box 431 (60180-0431)
PHONE.................815 923-2247
Maribeth Sandford, *CEO*
Jeremy Bayness, *President*
Chuck Sandford, *President*
Sue Kennedy, *Regl Sales Mgr*
Nancy Bercovitz, *Regional*
◆ **EMP:** 400
SQ FT: 40,000
SALES (est): 125.5MM **Privately Held**
SIC: 2673 2674 Plastic bags: made from purchased materials; paper bags: made from purchased materials

(G-19938)
CENTRAL WIRE INC (HQ)
6509 Olson Rd (60180-9730)
P.O. Box 423 (60180-0423)
PHONE.................800 435-8317
Paul From, *CEO*
John Zaharek, *President*
Britnee Berman, *Marketing Staff*
Donald Hohnstine, *Admin Sec*
▲ **EMP:** 102
SALES (est): 26.3MM
SALES (corp-wide): 36.2MM **Privately Held**
SIC: 3315 3312 Wire & fabricated wire products; wire products, steel or iron
PA: Central Wire Industries Ltd
　　1 North St
　　Perth ON K7H 2
　　613 267-3752

(G-19939)
JAS EXPRESS INC
8307 Seeman Rd (60180-9531)
PHONE.................847 836-7984
Jaime Velazquez, *Principal*
EMP: 4
SALES (est): 362.4K **Privately Held**
SIC: 2741 Miscellaneous publishing

(G-19940)
JK CABINETS PLUS LLC
6614 S Union Rd (60180-9514)
PHONE.................952 237-1825
Erik J Halwix, *Principal*
EMP: 3 **EST:** 2014
SALES (est): 93.3K **Privately Held**
WEB: www.jkcabinetsplus.com
SIC: 2434 Wood kitchen cabinets

(G-19941)
NEW DIMENSIONS PRECISION MAC
6614 S Union Rd (60180-9514)
PHONE.................815 923-8300
Nancy Ann Halwix, *President*
Jeff Person, *QC Mgr*
Jeff Doud, *Engineer*
Bill Jones, *Data Proc Exec*
Brian Halwix, *Director*
EMP: 98
SQ FT: 117,000
SALES (est): 25.1MM **Privately Held**
SIC: 3599 Machine shop, jobbing & repair

(G-19942)
PRO FORM INDUSTRIES INC
17714 Jefferson St (60180-9536)
P.O. Box 24 (60180-0024)
PHONE.................815 923-2555
Michael Szczesny, *President*
EMP: 5
SALES: 500K **Privately Held**
SIC: 3069 Fabricated rubber products

Union Hill
Kankakee County

(G-19943)
VAN VOORST LUMBER COMPANY INC
1 Center St (60969-9800)
P.O. Box 35 (60969-0035)
PHONE.................815 426-2544
Hugh E Van Voorst, *President*
Leann R Anderson, *Admin Sec*
EMP: 36
SQ FT: 2,000
SALES (est): 6.6MM **Privately Held**
WEB: www.vanvoorstlumber.com
SIC: 2449 5211 Wood containers; lumber & other building materials

(G-19944)
VANFAB INC
1 Center St (60969-9800)
P.O. Box 15 (60969-0015)
PHONE.................815 426-2544
Hugh E Van Voorst, *President*
Grant Van Voorst, *Vice Pres*
Kyle Nelson, *Purchasing*
EMP: 20 **EST:** 1976
SQ FT: 20,000
SALES (est): 6.9MM **Privately Held**
WEB: www.vanfab.com
SIC: 3444 Casings, sheet metal

University Park
Will County

(G-19945)
ALTRA DIVISION 5 LLC
650 Central Ave (60484-3149)
PHONE.................708 534-1100
Jose Noriega,
EMP: 13
SALES (est): 516.2K **Privately Held**
SIC: 3441 Fabricated structural metal

(G-19946)
APPLIED SYSTEMS INC (PA)
Also Called: Ivans Insurance Solutions
200 Applied Pkwy (60484-4131)
PHONE.................708 534-5575
Taylor Rhodes, *CEO*
Christopher Peterlin, *Supervisor*
Frank Smith, *Supervisor*
EMP: 600
SQ FT: 160,723
SALES (est): 362MM **Privately Held**
SIC: 7371 6411 7372 Computer software development; insurance information & consulting services; business oriented computer software

(G-19947)
AVATAR CORPORATION
500 Central Ave (60484-3147)
PHONE.................708 534-5511
Michael L Shamie, *President*
Reece Dixon, *Production*
Vaccarro Lewis, *Production*
Michael Kline, *QC Dir*
Cabrina Cramer, *Sales Staff*
▲ **EMP:** 65
SQ FT: 125
SALES (est): 28.9MM **Privately Held**
SIC: 2843 2841 2079 2869 Surface active agents; soap & other detergents; edible fats & oils; industrial organic chemicals; lubricating oils & greases

(G-19948)
BC ASI CAPITAL II INC
200 Applied Pkwy (60484-4110)
PHONE.................708 534-5575
Bruce Cox, *Principal*
EMP: 622
SALES (est): 13.6MM **Privately Held**
SIC: 7371 5045 7378 8711 Computer software development; computers, peripherals & software; computer maintenance & repair; engineering services; prepackaged software

(G-19949)
BIMBA MANUFACTURING COMPANY (HQ)
25150 S Governors Hwy (60484-8895)
PHONE.................708 534-8544
Patrick J Ormsby, *CEO*
Jatin Rai, *QC Mgr*
Kristin Smith, *Cust Mgr*
▲ **EMP:** 325 **EST:** 1969
SQ FT: 150,000
SALES: 125.5MM
SALES (corp-wide): 2.4B **Privately Held**
WEB: www.bimba.com
SIC: 3593 Fluid power cylinders, hydraulic or pneumatic
PA: Imi Plc
　　4060 Lakeside
　　Birmingham W MIDLANDS B37 7
　　121 717-3700

(G-19950)
BRENNAN EQUIPMENT AND MFG INC
Also Called: Little Giant
730 Central Ave (60484-3138)
PHONE.................708 534-5500
Terry D Thomason, *President*
John Brennan, *President*
Terry Y Thomason, *General Mgr*
Vicki Duran, *Production*
Anthony Pripusich, *Engineer*
◆ **EMP:** 75 **EST:** 1954
SQ FT: 48,000
SALES (est): 45.9MM **Privately Held**
WEB: www.littlegiant-usa.com
SIC: 5084 3799 Materials handling machinery; pushcarts & wheelbarrows

(G-19951)
CLAWMOUNTS MFG INC
2595 Bond St (60484-3103)
PHONE.................708 525-7552
Steve Adams, *President*
EMP: 4
SALES: 270K **Privately Held**
WEB: www.clawmounts.com
SIC: 3312 Tool & die steel & alloys

(G-19952)
FEDERAL SIGNAL CORPORATION
Also Called: Federal Signal-Codespear
2645 Federal Signal Dr (60484-3195)
PHONE.................708 534-4756
Mark Reid, *Branch Mgr*
EMP: 20
SALES (corp-wide): 1.2B **Publicly Held**
WEB: www.federalsignal.com
SIC: 3711 Chassis, motor vehicle
PA: Federal Signal Corporation
　　1415 W 22nd St Ste 1100
　　Oak Brook IL 60523
　　630 954-2000

(G-19953)
FEDERAL SIGNAL CORPORATION
2645 Federal Signal Dr (60484-3195)
PHONE.................708 534-3400
EMP: 71
SALES (corp-wide): 1.2B **Publicly Held**
SIC: 3993 Signs & advertising specialties
PA: Federal Signal Corporation
　　1415 W 22nd St Ste 1100
　　Oak Brook IL 60523
　　630 954-2000

(G-19954)
FEDERAL SIGNAL CORPORATION
Also Called: Security Systems Group
2645 Federal Signal Dr (60484-3195)
PHONE.................708 534-3400
Ron Featherly, *Branch Mgr*
EMP: 25
SALES (corp-wide): 1.2B **Publicly Held**
SIC: 3711 Chassis, motor vehicle
PA: Federal Signal Corporation
　　1415 W 22nd St Ste 1100
　　Oak Brook IL 60523
　　630 954-2000

(G-19955)
FS DEPOT INC
2645 Federal Signal Dr (60484-3167)
PHONE.................847 468-2350
Daniel Schueller, *President*
Jennifer L Sherman, *Admin Sec*
◆ **EMP:** 3
SALES (est): 754.6K
SALES (corp-wide): 1.2B **Publicly Held**
WEB: www.federalsignal.com
SIC: 3711 Motor vehicles & car bodies
PA: Federal Signal Corporation
　　1415 W 22nd St Ste 1100
　　Oak Brook IL 60523
　　630 954-2000

(G-19956)
HIGH IMPACT FABRICATING LLC
1149 Central Ave (60484-3166)
PHONE.................708 235-8912
Elijah Kragulj,
EMP: 6
SALES (est): 512.8K **Privately Held**
SIC: 3714 Bumpers & bumperettes, motor vehicle

(G-19957)
M & R GRAPHICS INC
2401 Bond St (60484-3101)
PHONE.................708 534-6621
Ruth Moore, *President*
Keith Reimel, *Vice Pres*
Chris Moore, *Prdtn Mgr*
EMP: 16
SQ FT: 11,800

GEOGRAPHIC SECTION

Urbana - Champaign County (G-19982)

SALES (est): 2.7MM **Privately Held**
SIC: **2759** 2672 Labels & seals: printing; coated & laminated paper

(G-19958)
M LIZEN MANUFACTURING CO
Also Called: A A Coil Products
2625 Federal Signal Dr (60484-4104)
PHONE.....................................708 755-7213
Bradley K Lizen, *President*
EMP: 24
SQ FT: 30,000
SALES (est): 5.5MM **Privately Held**
WEB: www.mlizen.com
SIC: **3469** 3495 Stamping metal for the trade; wire springs

(G-19959)
MEAD FLUID DYNAMICS INC
25150 S Governors Hwy (60484-4435)
PHONE.....................................773 685-6800
Bill Gorski, *President*
▲ EMP: 50
SALES (est): 9MM
SALES (corp-wide): 2.4B **Privately Held**
SIC: **3492** 3593 3494 Control valves, fluid power: hydraulic & pneumatic; fluid power cylinders & actuators; valves & pipe fittings
HQ: Bimba Manufacturing Company Inc
25150 S Governors Hwy
University Park IL 60484
708 534-8544

(G-19960)
METALTEK FABRICATING INC
Also Called: Chicago Bullet Proof
2595 Bond St (60484-3103)
PHONE.....................................708 534-9102
Benedict Stohr, *President*
Maxwell Stohr, *Vice Pres*
George Boltz, *Admin Sec*
EMP: 17
SQ FT: 22,000
SALES: 2.5MM **Privately Held**
SIC: **3441** 1799 Fabricated structural metal; screening contractor: window, door, etc.

(G-19961)
MIDWEST CUSTOM CASE INC (PA)
Also Called: Midwest Store Fixtures
425 Crossing Dr Unit A (60484-4133)
PHONE.....................................708 672-2900
Karen A Papiese, *President*
Dave Graczyk, *Project Mgr*
Paul Murawski, *Project Mgr*
Frank Opiola, *Project Mgr*
Richard J Papiese, *CFO*
◆ EMP: 103
SQ FT: 500,000
SALES: 53.1MM **Privately Held**
WEB: www.mw-sf.com
SIC: **2542** Partitions & fixtures, except wood

(G-19962)
MILLER PRODUCTS INC
Also Called: M P I Labels Systems
825 Central Ave (60484-3141)
PHONE.....................................708 534-5111
John Holley, *Branch Mgr*
Scott Hanson, *Director*
EMP: 25
SALES (corp-wide): 39.9MM **Privately Held**
SIC: **2672** 2759 2671 Labels (unprinted), gummed: made from purchased materials; commercial printing; packaging paper & plastics film, coated & laminated
PA: Miller Products, Inc.
450 Courtney Rd
Sebring OH 44672
330 938-2134

(G-19963)
MRB ROOFING INC
1018 Samson Dr (60484-3253)
PHONE.....................................872 814-4390
Michael Bullock II, *President*
EMP: 8
SALES: 800K **Privately Held**
SIC: **2952** 7371 7389 Roofing materials; computer software development & applications

(G-19964)
POINT UNLIMITED ✪
594 Farmview Ct (60484-3332)
PHONE.....................................708 244-7730
Brian Pointer, *Representative*
EMP: 1 EST: 2019
SALES: 250K **Privately Held**
SIC: **3537** Trucks, tractors, loaders, carriers & similar equipment

(G-19965)
QH INC
Also Called: Supreme Hinge
2412 Bond St (60484-3102)
PHONE.....................................708 534-7801
Greg Grimler, *President*
George Boss, *Vice Pres*
EMP: 25
SQ FT: 15,000
SALES (est): 6.2MM **Privately Held**
SIC: **3442** Metal doors, sash & trim
PA: Supreme Hinge, Inc.
2412 Bond St
University Park IL 60484

(G-19966)
QUALITY HNGE A DIV SPREME HNGE
2412 Bond St (60484-3102)
PHONE.....................................708 534-7801
Greg Grimler, *Principal*
EMP: 28 EST: 2015
SALES (est): 1.5MM **Privately Held**
SIC: **3429** Manufactured hardware (general)

(G-19967)
SOLVAY USA INC
24601 Governors Hwy (60484-4127)
PHONE.....................................708 235-7200
Dave Hardin, *Branch Mgr*
EMP: 22
SALES (corp-wide): 13.8MM **Privately Held**
SIC: **2899** 2869 2821 Chemical preparations; fluorinated hydrocarbon gases; silicones; plastics materials & resins
HQ: Solvay Usa Inc.
504 Carnegie Ctr
Princeton NJ 08540
609 860-4000

(G-19968)
TINLEY ICE COMPANY
Also Called: Three Penguin Ice
450 Central Ave Ste A (60484-3160)
PHONE.....................................708 532-8777
Timothy Teehan, *President*
EMP: 38
SQ FT: 19,000
SALES: 3MM **Privately Held**
SIC: **2097** Manufactured ice

(G-19969)
TRICON WEAR SOLUTIONS LLC
2605 Federal Signal Dr (60484-4104)
PHONE.....................................708 235-4064
Dean Aring, *Manager*
EMP: 23
SALES (corp-wide): 201.2MM **Privately Held**
SIC: **5051** 3443 Steel; fabricated plate work (boiler shop)
HQ: Tricon Wear Solutions Llc
2700 5th Ave S
Irondale AL 35210
205 956-2567

(G-19970)
U S NAVAL INSTITUTE
2427 Bond St (60484-3177)
PHONE.....................................800 233-8764
Thomas Wilkerson, *Branch Mgr*
EMP: 4
SALES (corp-wide): 10.3MM **Privately Held**
SIC: **2731** Book publishing
PA: U S Naval Institute
291 Wood Rd Fl 2
Annapolis MD 21402
410 268-6110

(G-19971)
YOSHINO AMERICA CORPORATION
2500 Palmer Ave (60484-3164)
PHONE.....................................708 534-1141
Keiji Shimamoto, *President*
Shigeru Nakayama, *Admin Sec*
◆ EMP: 50
SQ FT: 200,000
SALES (est): 13.8MM **Privately Held**
SIC: **3089** Plastic containers, except foam
PA: Yoshino Kogyosho Co., Ltd.
3-2-6, Ojima
Koto-Ku TKY 136-0

Urbana
Champaign County

(G-19972)
APL ENGINEERED MATERIALS INC
2401 Willow Rd (61802-7332)
PHONE.....................................217 367-1340
Wayne Hellman, *Ch of Bd*
James Schoolenberg, *President*
Dianne Szydel, *President*
Sharon Fotzler, *Corp Secy*
Amy Patrick, *Admin Sec*
▲ EMP: 50
SQ FT: 120,000
SALES (est): 9.1MM **Privately Held**
SIC: **2899** Chemical preparations
PA: Apl Japan Co.,Ltd.
2-31-19, Shiba
Minato-Ku TKY 105-0

(G-19973)
BENDER MAT FCTRY FTON SLEPSHOP (PA)
Also Called: Benders Mat Fctry Sleep Shoppe
1206 N Cunningham Ave A (61802-1812)
PHONE.....................................217 328-1700
Thomas Bender, *President*
EMP: 8
SQ FT: 8,000
SALES (est): 718.8K **Privately Held**
SIC: **2515** 2511 Mattresses, innerspring or box spring; wood household furniture

(G-19974)
BIG R CAR WASH INC (PA)
501 E University Ave (61802-2059)
PHONE.....................................217 367-4958
Ivan Richardson, *President*
EMP: 2
SQ FT: 3,200
SALES (est): 329.7K **Privately Held**
SIC: **3589** Car washing machinery

(G-19975)
BIRKEYS FARM STORE INC
Also Called: Birkeys Construction Equipment
2202 S High Cross Rd (61802-9598)
PHONE.....................................217 337-1772
Jeffrey Hedge, *Branch Mgr*
EMP: 40
SALES (corp-wide): 248.8MM **Privately Held**
SIC: **5083** 7699 5511 5082 Farm implements; agricultural equipment repair services; automobiles, new & used; excavating machinery & equipment; farm supplies; farm machinery & equipment
PA: Birkey's Farm Store, Inc.
2102 W Park Ct
Champaign IL 61821
217 693-7200

(G-19976)
CENTRAL ILL FBRCATION WHSE INC
Also Called: Kurland Steel Company
510 E Main St (61802-2747)
P.O. Box 442 (61803-0442)
PHONE.....................................217 367-2323
Jeffry M Ping, *President*
Cathy Mitchell, *Principal*
Keith Wolfe, *Principal*
Albert L Mitchell, *CFO*
Zack Brown, *Technology*
EMP: 17
SQ FT: 13,000

SALES (est): 5.5MM **Privately Held**
WEB: www.kurlandsteel.com
SIC: **3441** 5051 Building components, structural steel; metals service centers & offices

(G-19977)
CHAMPAIGN CNTY TENT & AWNG CO
Also Called: Twin City Tent & Awning Co
308 E Anthony Dr (61802-7345)
P.O. Box 638 (61803-0638)
PHONE.....................................217 328-5749
Kevin Yonce, *CEO*
Byron Yonce, *President*
Wayne M Yonce, *President*
Ron Crick, *Vice Pres*
Wanda K Yonce, *Vice Pres*
EMP: 25 EST: 1929
SQ FT: 32,600
SALES (est): 4MM **Privately Held**
SIC: **2394** 7359 Awnings, fabric: made from purchased materials; equipment rental & leasing; tent & tarpaulin rental

(G-19978)
COCA-COLA REFRESHMENTS USA INC
2809 N Lincoln Ave (61802-7298)
PHONE.....................................217 367-1761
Brian Dodd, *General Mgr*
EMP: 28
SALES (corp-wide): 37.2B **Publicly Held**
SIC: **2086** Bottled & canned soft drinks
HQ: Coca-Cola Refreshments Usa, Inc.
2500 Windy Ridge Pkwy Se
Atlanta GA 30339
770 989-3000

(G-19979)
CONCRETE SUPPLY TOLONO INC
Also Called: Csi of Tolono
1466 County Road 1100 N (61802-7135)
PHONE.....................................217 485-3100
Kerrelton D Grove, *President*
Becky Grove, *Admin Sec*
EMP: 4
SALES (est): 514.7K **Privately Held**
SIC: **3273** Ready-mixed concrete

(G-19980)
COX ELECTRIC MOTOR SERVICE
1409 Triumph Dr (61802-9767)
PHONE.....................................217 344-2458
Melissa Brown, *President*
EMP: 6
SQ FT: 3,600
SALES: 761K **Privately Held**
SIC: **7629** 5063 7694 Electrical repair shops; motors, electric; armature rewinding shops

(G-19981)
EMULSICOAT INC (HQ)
705 E University Ave (61802-2031)
PHONE.....................................217 344-7775
Fred M Fehsenfeld Jr, *President*
Lewis L Davis, *Corp Secy*
Rick Beyers, *Vice Pres*
EMP: 11
SQ FT: 3,000
SALES (est): 1.3MM
SALES (corp-wide): 240.7MM **Privately Held**
SIC: **2891** 2951 2952 Adhesives; asphalt paving mixtures & blocks; coating compounds, tar
PA: Asphalt Materials, Inc.
5400 W 86th St
Indianapolis IN 46268
317 872-6010

(G-19982)
ENTIENCE
305 W Michigan Ave (61801-4945)
PHONE.....................................217 649-2590
Rhanor Gillette, *CEO*
Ekaterina Gribkova, *Co-Venturer*
Mikhail Voloshin, *Co-Venturer*
EMP: 3
SALES (est): 71.1K **Privately Held**
SIC: **7372** Application computer software

Urbana - Champaign County (G-19983)

(G-19983)
FLEX-N-GATE CORPORATION
502 E Anthony Dr (61802-7347)
PHONE......................217 255-5025
Suzi Puckett, *Manager*
Nick Wiegand, *Manager*
EMP: 504
SALES (corp-wide): 3.3B **Privately Held**
SIC: 3714 Motor vehicle parts & accessories
PA: Flex-N-Gate Llc
    1306 E University Ave
    Urbana IL 61802
    217 384-6600

(G-19984)
FLEX-N-GATE LLC (PA)
1306 E University Ave (61802-2093)
P.O. Box 727 (61803-0727)
PHONE......................217 384-6600
Shahid Khan, *President*
Paul Connolly, *General Mgr*
Bill Beistline, *Vice Pres*
Robert Kern, *Vice Pres*
Dave Kirkolis, *Vice Pres*
▲ EMP: 340
SQ FT: 75,000
SALES (est): 3.3B **Privately Held**
WEB: www.flex-n-gate.com
SIC: 3714 Bumpers & bumperettes, motor vehicle

(G-19985)
FLEX-N-GATE LLC
Also Called: Guardian West
601 Guardian Way (61802-2880)
P.O. Box 877 (61803-0877)
PHONE......................217 278-2400
Jack Antonini, *Branch Mgr*
EMP: 504
SALES (corp-wide): 3.3B **Privately Held**
SIC: 3714 Motor vehicle parts & accessories
PA: Flex-N-Gate Llc
    1306 E University Ave
    Urbana IL 61802
    217 384-6600

(G-19986)
FRASCA INTERNATIONAL INC (PA)
Also Called: Frasca Air Services
906 Airport Rd (61802-7375)
PHONE......................217 344-9200
Rudolf Frasca, *Ch of Bd*
John Frasca, *President*
Lucille Frasca, *Corp Secy*
Tom Silver, *Project Mgr*
Carm Dalton, *Mfg Staff*
▲ EMP: 190
SQ FT: 93,000
SALES (est): 58.2MM **Privately Held**
SIC: 3728 Aircraft training equipment

(G-19987)
HEARTLAND COCA-COLA BTLG LLC
2809 N Lincoln Ave (61802-7229)
PHONE......................217 367-1761
Ray Reddrick, *Vice Pres*
EMP: 3090
SALES (corp-wide): 23.9B **Privately Held**
SIC: 5149 2086 Beverages, except coffee & tea; carbonated beverages, nonalcoholic; bottled & canned
PA: Heartland Coca-Cola Bottling Company Llc
    9000 Marshall Dr
    Lenexa KS

(G-19988)
MID-AMERICA SAND & GRAVEL
Also Called: Billing Office
2906 N Oak St (61802-7203)
PHONE......................217 355-1307
Bill Booker, *Manager*
EMP: 9
SALES (corp-wide): 2MM **Privately Held**
SIC: 1442 Construction sand & gravel
PA: Mid-America Sand & Gravel
    250 County Rd 2050 N
    Mahomet IL 61853
    217 586-4536

(G-19989)
MWK RAIL LLC
3021 E Stillwater Lndg (61802-7277)
PHONE......................815 671-5217
Michael Wayne Kizior, *Mng Member*
◆ EMP: 1
SALES: 500K **Privately Held**
SIC: 3743 7389 Railroad equipment;

(G-19990)
NEWS-GAZETTE INC
Also Called: News Gazette
300 W Main St (61801-2624)
P.O. Box 6677 (61801)
PHONE......................217 351-5311
Amy Eckard, *Branch Mgr*
EMP: 10 **Privately Held**
SIC: 2711 Newspapers, publishing & printing
PA: The News-Gazette Inc
    15 E Main St
    Champaign IL 61820

(G-19991)
OSO TECHNOLOGIES INC
Also Called: Plantlink
722 W Killarney St (61801-1015)
PHONE......................844 777-2575
Mercedes Mane, *President*
EMP: 5
SALES (est): 237.9K
SALES (corp-wide): 3.1B **Publicly Held**
SIC: 3494 3825 Valves & pipe fittings; analog-digital converters, electronic instrumentation type
PA: The Scotts Miracle-Gro Company
    14111 Scottslawn Rd
    Marysville OH 43040
    937 644-0011

(G-19992)
PERSONIFY INC (PA)
Also Called: Nuvixa
208a W Main St (61801-2622)
PHONE......................217 840-2638
Sanjay Patel, *CEO*
EMP: 6
SALES (est): 1.3MM **Privately Held**
SIC: 7819 7372 Services allied to motion pictures; prepackaged software

(G-19993)
PLASTIC CONTAINER CORPORATION (PA)
Also Called: PCC
2508 N Oak St (61802-7207)
P.O. Box 438, Champaign (61824-0438)
PHONE......................217 352-2722
Ronald E Rhoades, *President*
Bob Turpin, *Plant Mgr*
Brett Penick, *CFO*
Spencer C Atkins, *Admin Sec*
▲ EMP: 100
SQ FT: 102,000
SALES (est): 32.4MM **Privately Held**
SIC: 3085 3089 3999 Plastics bottles; plastic containers, except foam; atomizers, toiletry

(G-19994)
POWER102JAMZ
202 S Broadway Ave # 203 (61801-3313)
PHONE......................312 912-2766
Erin Harris, *Owner*
EMP: 4
SALES (est): 92.1K **Privately Held**
SIC: 7389 7372 Radio broadcasting music checkers; application computer software

(G-19995)
PRIVATE STUDIOS
705 Western Ave (61801-3114)
PHONE......................217 367-3530
Jonathan Pines, *Owner*
EMP: 7
SQ FT: 6,500
SALES: 150K **Privately Held**
SIC: 3652 8742 Pre-recorded records & tapes; industrial & labor consulting services

(G-19996)
PROJECT TE INC
2209 E University Ave B (61802-2811)
PHONE......................217 344-9833
Maurice Mehling, *President*
EMP: 6
SQ FT: 1,400
SALES: 120K **Privately Held**
SIC: 2759 2395 Screen printing; embroidery products, except schiffli machine

(G-19997)
REDS MUFFLER SHOP
102 W University Ave (61801-1739)
PHONE......................217 344-1676
Wayne Shaw, *Owner*
EMP: 4
SQ FT: 3,000
SALES (est): 415K **Privately Held**
SIC: 3564 Exhaust fans: industrial or commercial

(G-19998)
RIGGS BEER COMPANY
1901 S High Cross Rd (61802-7843)
PHONE......................217 649-4286
Caroline Riggs, *Principal*
Matt Riggs, *Technical Staff*
EMP: 5
SALES (est): 329.3K **Privately Held**
WEB: www.riggsbeer.com
SIC: 2082 Beer (alcoholic beverage)

(G-19999)
ROBERT HIGGINS
Also Called: Super Phone Store
405 E Pennsylvania Ave (61801-5130)
PHONE......................217 337-0734
Robert Higgins, *CEO*
EMP: 90
SALES (est): 7.3MM **Privately Held**
SIC: 3625 Switches, electronic applications

(G-20000)
SERIONIX INC
730 W Killarney St (61801-1015)
PHONE......................651 503-3930
James Langer, *Principal*
EMP: 3
SALES (est): 278.4K **Privately Held**
SIC: 2821 Plastics materials & resins

(G-20001)
SOLO CUP OPERATING CORPORATION
1505 E Main St (61802-2834)
PHONE......................217 384-1800
Sue Sharp, *Human Resources*
Mike Oakley, *Branch Mgr*
Brent Kincheloe, *Manager*
EMP: 300
SALES (corp-wide): 965.8MM **Privately Held**
SIC: 3089 Plastic containers, except foam; cups, plastic, except foam; plates, plastic
HQ: Solo Cup Operating Corporation
    500 Hogsback Rd
    Mason MI 48854
    800 248-5960

(G-20002)
VENTURE PUBLISHING INC
1807 N Federal Dr (61801-1051)
PHONE......................217 359-5940
Frank Guadagnolo, *President*
Geoff Godbey, *Editor*
Kay Whiteside, *Manager*
EMP: 6
SALES: 540K **Privately Held**
SIC: 2731 Books: publishing only; textbooks: publishing only, not printed on site

(G-20003)
WINGFIELD MANUFACTURING LLC
5811 N High Cross Rd (61802-7814)
PHONE......................800 637-6712
Judith Cochran, *Principal*
EMP: 2
SALES (est): 205.5K **Privately Held**
WEB: www.americanharrow.com
SIC: 3999 Manufacturing industries

Ursa
Adams County

(G-20004)
KAYSER LURE CORP
107 Junction St (62376-1040)
P.O. Box 68 (62376-0068)
PHONE......................217 964-2110
Terry Kayser, *President*
Carol Virginia Kayser, *Vice Pres*
EMP: 6
SALES (est): 516.2K **Privately Held**
SIC: 3949 Lures, fishing: artificial; fishing tackle, general

Utica
Lasalle County

(G-20005)
AUGUSTHILL WINERY CO
106 Mill St (61373-9450)
PHONE......................815 667-5211
Nojo Sawin, *Manager*
Teri Venzel, *Executive*
EMP: 4
SALES (est): 323.4K **Privately Held**
SIC: 2084 Wines

(G-20006)
PQ CORPORATION
340 E Grove St (61373-9001)
P.O. Box 410 (61373-0410)
PHONE......................815 667-4241
Lloyd Koplin, *Opers Spvr*
Craig R Powers, *Opers-Prdtn-Mfg*
Pete Bray, *Purchasing*
Mark Vincent, *Marketing Mgr*
Stephen Halm, *Technician*
EMP: 45
SALES (corp-wide): 1.5B **Publicly Held**
WEB: www.pqcorp.com
SIC: 2819 2899 Industrial inorganic chemicals; chemical preparations
HQ: Pq Corporation
    300 Lindenwood Dr
    Malvern PA 19355
    610 651-4200

(G-20007)
UTICA STONE CO INC
773 N 27th Rd (61373)
PHONE......................815 667-4690
Toni Biagioni, *Manager*
EMP: 4
SALES (est): 167.3K **Privately Held**
SIC: 1422 Crushed & broken limestone

(G-20008)
UTICA TERMINAL INC
715 N 27th Rd (61373)
P.O. Box 1060, Jacksonville (62651-1060)
PHONE......................217 245-6181
James C Davidsmeyer, *President*
Greg Pennel, *Vice Pres*
Thomas Slayback, *Admin Sec*
P Devon Davidsmeyer,
EMP: 7
SQ FT: 3,000
SALES (est): 1.6MM
SALES (corp-wide): 36MM **Privately Held**
WEB: www.ircgrp.com
SIC: 2951 Asphalt & asphaltic paving mixtures (not from refineries)
PA: Illinois Road Contractors, Inc.
    520 N Webster Ave
    Jacksonville IL 62650
    217 245-6181

Valmeyer
Monroe County

(G-20009)
MAR GRAPHICS
523 S Meyer Ave (62295-3120)
PHONE......................618 935-2111
Richard D Roever, *President*
Audrey A Roever, *Corp Secy*

Bobbie Klinkhardt, *Vice Pres*
Scott Roever, *CFO*
Patrick Marshall, *Sales Staff*
EMP: 90 **EST:** 1961
SALES (est): 30.3MM **Privately Held**
WEB: www.margraphics.com
SIC: 2752 Commercial printing, offset

Vandalia
Fayette County

(G-20010)
DORAN OIL PROPERTIES
415 1/2 W Gallatin St (62471-2746)
P.O. Box 151 (62471-0151)
PHONE 618 283-2460
Dorothy Ann Jenkins, *Partner*
Ed Brown, *Partner*
EMP: 3
SALES (est): 230K **Privately Held**
SIC: 1311 0919 Crude petroleum production; whale oil production, crude

(G-20011)
FAYCO ENTERPRISES INC (PA)
1313 Sunset Dr (62471-3212)
P.O. Box 277 (62471-0277)
PHONE 618 283-0638
Vickie Depew, *Bookkeeper*
Patsy Challans, *Finance*
Tim Corbus, *Payroll Mgr*
Meta Fry, *Supervisor*
C Robert Lindberg, *Exec Dir*
EMP: 150
SQ FT: 25,000
SALES: 5.8MM **Privately Held**
SIC: 3951 Ball point pens & parts

(G-20012)
GSI GROUP LLC
Also Called: Grain Systems
110 S Coles St (62471-2520)
PHONE 618 283-9792
EMP: 60
SALES (corp-wide): 10.7B **Publicly Held**
SIC: 5083 3556 Whol Farm/Garden Machinery Mfg Food Products Machinery
HQ: The Gsi Group Llc
1004 E Illinois St
Assumption IL 62510
217 226-4421

(G-20013)
JENKINS DISPLAYS CO
Also Called: Jenkins Truck & Farm
1910 Hollow Dr (62471-3814)
PHONE 618 335-3874
Scott Jenkins, *President*
Stephanie Alexandropoulos, *Admin Sec*
EMP: 5 **EST:** 1935
SQ FT: 30,000
SALES (est): 1MM **Privately Held**
WEB: www.jenkinsdisplays.com
SIC: 3993 5999 0762 Electric signs; farm equipment & supplies; farm management services

(G-20014)
MEDLINE INDUSTRIES INC
1015 W Jefferson St (62471-1624)
PHONE 618 283-4036
EMP: 3
SALES (corp-wide): 7.4B **Privately Held**
SIC: 2391 Curtains & draperies
PA: Medline Industries, Inc.
3 Lakes Dr
Northfield IL 60093
847 949-5500

(G-20015)
MID-ILLINOIS CONCRETE INC
Also Called: Vandalia Ready-Mix
1021 Janette Dr (62471-3530)
PHONE 618 283-1600
Glenn Gelsinger, *Manager*
EMP: 14
SALES (corp-wide): 17.2MM **Privately Held**
WEB: www.mid-illinoisconcrete.com
SIC: 3272 3273 Concrete products, precast; ready-mixed concrete

PA: Mid-Illinois Concrete, Inc.
1805 S 4th St
Effingham IL
217 342-2498

(G-20016)
MIDWEST BLOW MOLDING LLC
1111 Imco Dr (62471-3522)
PHONE 618 283-9223
John F Romano, *CEO*
EMP: 1 **EST:** 2015
SALES (est): 265K
SALES (corp-wide): 31.4MM **Privately Held**
SIC: 3089 Molding primary plastic
PA: The Fountainhead Group Inc
23 Garden St
New York Mills NY 13417
315 736-0037

(G-20017)
OLD CAPITOL MONUMENT WORKS INC (PA)
627 S 6th St (62471-3016)
P.O. Box 27 (62471-0027)
PHONE 217 324-5673
Roy G Nichols, *President*
Lavonda L Nichols, *Vice Pres*
EMP: 5
SALES (est): 683.4K **Privately Held**
WEB: www.oldcapitolmonument.com
SIC: 3281 5999 Monuments, cut stone (not finishing or lettering only); monuments, finished to custom order

(G-20018)
P & G MACHINE & TOOL INC
Also Called: P & G Machine Shop
1910 Illini Ave (62471-3421)
PHONE 618 283-0273
Charles Philpot, *President*
Ramona Philpot, *Admin Sec*
EMP: 5 **EST:** 1963
SQ FT: 2,400
SALES (est): 699K **Privately Held**
SIC: 3599 7692 Machine shop, jobbing & repair; welding repair

(G-20019)
PRAIRIE PROFILE
1437 E 1050 Ave (62471-4110)
PHONE 618 846-2116
Jason Weaver, *Partner*
Marian Weaver, *Partner*
EMP: 4
SQ FT: 7,000
SALES (est): 213.1K **Privately Held**
SIC: 5191 3312 5999 Beekeeping supplies (non-durable); beehive coke oven products; alcoholic beverage making equipment & supplies

(G-20020)
PRO-FAB METALS INC
10949 Us 40 (62471)
PHONE 618 283-2986
Charles E Wagoner, *Owner*
EMP: 3 **EST:** 1996
SQ FT: 3,000
SALES (est): 366.5K **Privately Held**
SIC: 7692 3441 Welding repair; building components, structural steel

(G-20021)
PURINA ANIMAL NUTRITION LLC
Also Called: Land O'Lake Purina Seed
1500 Veterans Ave (62471-3315)
PHONE 618 283-2291
Brad Gottula, *Manager*
EMP: 7
SALES (corp-wide): 6B **Privately Held**
SIC: 2048 Prepared feeds
HQ: Purina Animal Nutrition Llc
100 Danforth Dr
Gray Summit MO 63039

(G-20022)
PURINA MILLS LLC
1500 Veterans Ave (62471-3315)
PHONE 618 283-2291
Calvin Scott, *Branch Mgr*
EMP: 26
SALES (corp-wide): 6B **Privately Held**
SIC: 2048 Prepared feeds

HQ: Purina Mills, Llc
555 Maryvle Univ Dr 200
Saint Louis MO 63141

(G-20023)
SHULMAN BROTHERS INC
101 S 4th St (62471-2809)
P.O. Box 99 (62471-0099)
PHONE 618 283-3253
Maurice Shulman, *CEO*
Todd Shulman, *Vice Pres*
EMP: 8 **EST:** 1938
SQ FT: 250
SALES (est): 871.7K **Privately Held**
SIC: 1311 Crude petroleum production

(G-20024)
SIGNATURE LABEL OF ILLINOIS
2025 N 8th St (62471-4003)
PHONE 618 283-5145
Jay Viery, *President*
Angelique Bohannon, *Purchasing*
EMP: 4
SALES (est): 772.5K **Privately Held**
SIC: 3552 2671 2396 2672 Silk screens for textile industry; packaging paper & plastics film, coated & laminated; automotive & apparel trimmings; coated & laminated paper

(G-20025)
SOUTH CENTRAL FS INC
10 Interstate Dr (62471-3432)
P.O. Box 363 (62471-0363)
PHONE 618 283-1557
John Wait, *Branch Mgr*
Amy Jackson, *Admin Asst*
EMP: 9
SALES (corp-wide): 90.7MM **Privately Held**
SIC: 5171 5191 2875 Petroleum bulk stations; farm supplies; fertilizers, mixing only
HQ: South Central Fs, Inc.
405 S Banker St
Effingham IL 62401
217 342-9231

(G-20026)
T C4 INC
1207 N Carlisle Rd (62471)
PHONE 618 335-3486
Tina Cook, *President*
Joseph Cook, *Vice Pres*
EMP: 15
SALES (est): 1MM **Privately Held**
SIC: 2048 Cereal-, grain-, & seed-based feeds

(G-20027)
VANDALIA ELECTRIC MTR SVC INC
561 Il 185 (62471-3449)
PHONE 618 283-0068
Kurt Kroll, *President*
EMP: 5
SQ FT: 4,800
SALES (est): 1.1MM **Privately Held**
WEB: www.vandaliaelectricmotorservice.com
SIC: 7694 5063 Electric motor repair; motors, electric

(G-20028)
VANDALIA SAND & GRAVEL INC
Rr 2 (62471-9802)
P.O. Box 391 (62471-0391)
PHONE 618 283-4029
Michael Themig, *President*
Debbie Themig, *Admin Sec*
EMP: 10
SALES (est): 745.3K **Privately Held**
SIC: 1442 Construction sand & gravel

(G-20029)
VANSEAL CORPORATION
815 Payne Dr (62471-4006)
PHONE 618 283-4700
Thomas E Gebhardt, *President*
Kathy Kidd, *Plant Mgr*
John Thompson, *Plant Mgr*
Roger Hill, *Engineer*
Scott Gehle, *Supervisor*
EMP: 100
SQ FT: 125,000

SALES: 11.5MM **Privately Held**
SIC: 3053 Gaskets, packing & sealing devices

(G-20030)
WEHRLE LUMBER CO INC
820 E 1900 Ave (62471-4555)
PHONE 618 283-4859
Ruth Duggins, *President*
Eric Wehrle, *Admin Sec*
EMP: 15
SQ FT: 18,000
SALES (est): 2.7MM **Privately Held**
SIC: 2653 Pallets, solid fiber: made from purchased materials

Varna
Marshall County

(G-20031)
BRIAN LINDSTROM
Also Called: Lindstrom Farm
2412 Wenona Rd (61375-9469)
PHONE 309 463-2388
Brian Lindstrom, *Owner*
EMP: 4
SALES (est): 161.7K **Privately Held**
SIC: 3523 Driers (farm): grain, hay & seed

(G-20032)
KOHNS ELECTRIC
1555 Key Ct S (61375-9405)
PHONE 309 463-2331
Jeffrey Akohn, *Principal*
EMP: 4 **EST:** 2010
SALES (est): 459.4K **Privately Held**
SIC: 3699 1731 Electrical equipment & supplies; electrical work

(G-20033)
MYERS INC
99999 Route 1 S (61375)
P.O. Box 197, Cooksville (61730-0197)
PHONE 309 725-3710
Fax: 309 725-3361
EMP: 3
SALES (est): 110K **Privately Held**
SIC: 2875 Mfg Fertilizers-Mix Only

Venedy
Washington County

(G-20034)
GATEWAY FS INC
18 N Mill Rd (62214-1222)
P.O. Box 525, Addieville (62214)
PHONE 618 824-6631
Ken Lintker, *Branch Mgr*
EMP: 6 **Privately Held**
SIC: 4221 2873 2874 Grain elevator, storage only; nitrogenous fertilizers; phosphatic fertilizers
PA: Gateway Fs, Inc.
221 E Pine St
Red Bud IL 62278

Venice
Madison County

(G-20035)
PALLET SALES AND RECYCLING
1200 Thistle St (62090)
PHONE 314 452-5175
Robert Immekus, *President*
EMP: 12
SALES (est): 446.8K **Privately Held**
SIC: 2448 Pallets, wood

(G-20036)
SHO PAK LLC
Also Called: Ics Saint Louis
1226 Bissell St (62090-1183)
PHONE 618 876-1597
EMP: 4
SALES: 1MM **Privately Held**
SIC: 2631 Paperboard Mill

Vermont
Fulton County

(G-20037)
MAHONEY FOUNDRIES INC
Vermont Foundry Co
29 N Main St (61484)
P.O. Box 290 (61484-0290)
PHONE................................309 784-2311
John Mahoney Jr, *Branch Mgr*
EMP: 40
SQ FT: 39,681
SALES (corp-wide): 20.1MM **Privately Held**
SIC: 3364 3363 3369 3366 Brass & bronze die-castings; aluminum die-castings; nonferrous foundries; copper foundries; secondary nonferrous metals; primary copper
PA: Mahoney Foundries Inc
209 W Ohio St
Kendallville IN 46755
260 347-1768

Vernon Hills
Lake County

(G-20038)
ABBVIE INC
75 N Fairway Dr (60061-1845)
PHONE................................847 367-7621
James Springer, *Program Mgr*
Leann Miller, *Manager*
Martin Babcock, *Systems Dir*
Jennifer Ross, *Technology*
Shelly Webb, *Executive*
EMP: 7
SALES (corp-wide): 33.2B **Publicly Held**
WEB: www.abbvie.com
SIC: 2834 Pharmaceutical preparations
PA: Abbvie Inc.
1 N Waukegan Rd
North Chicago IL 60064
847 932-7900

(G-20039)
AKORN INC
50 Lakeview Pkwy Ste 112 (60061-1578)
PHONE................................847 279-6166
Marilou Ferrara, *Research*
Saeed Khan, *Research*
Biswajit Pati, *Branch Mgr*
Andrew Martin, *Director*
Lana Vostrova, *Associate Dir*
EMP: 7
SALES (corp-wide): 682.4MM **Privately Held**
SIC: 2834 Pharmaceutical preparations
PA: Akorn, Inc.
1925 W Field Ct Ste 300
Lake Forest IL 60045
847 279-6100

(G-20040)
ALI GROUP NORTH AMERICA CORP (DH)
101 Corporate Woods Pkwy (60061-3109)
PHONE................................847 215-6565
Filipo Berti, *President*
Rob Geile, *Vice Pres*
Rob August, *VP Bus Dvlpt*
Glenda Buzhardt, *CFO*
Brad Willis, *CFO*
EMP: 122
SALES (est): 711.2MM
SALES (corp-wide): 2.6MM **Privately Held**
SIC: 3589 Cooking equipment, commercial
HQ: Ali Holding Srl
Via Piero Gobetti 2/A
Cernusco Sul Naviglio MI
029 219-9292

(G-20041)
ALTCO INC
Also Called: Illini Line, Ltd.
1000 Woodlands Pkwy (60061-3188)
PHONE................................847 549-0321
Neil Fine, *President*
Lois Fine, *Vice Pres*
Crissy Ocheltree, *Purch Mgr*
Sabrina Wilt, *Marketing Mgr*
Patricia Hones, *Office Mgr*
◆ **EMP:** 65 **EST:** 1951
SQ FT: 63,000
SALES (est): 7.9MM **Privately Held**
WEB: www.illiniline.com
SIC: 3993 5013 2759 Signs & advertising specialties; motor vehicle supplies & new parts; commercial printing
PA: Neil International, Inc.
1000 Woodlands Pkwy
Vernon Hills IL 60061

(G-20042)
ANYWAVE COMMUNICATION TECH INC
100 N Fairway Dr (60061-1859)
PHONE................................847 415-2258
Wenhua LI, *Ch of Bd*
Jingsong Xia, *President*
David Neff, *General Mgr*
Paul Dadian, *Sales Mgr*
Frank Massa, *Sales Mgr*
EMP: 11 **EST:** 2011
SALES (est): 1.6MM
SALES (corp-wide): 2.3MM **Privately Held**
SIC: 3663 Studio equipment, radio & television broadcasting
HQ: Anywave Communication Technologies Co., Ltd.
Room 401-01,03,05, Building 1,
No.900, Yishan Road, Xuhui Distri
Shanghai 20022
215 423-4031

(G-20043)
BAUERMEISTER INC
601 Corporate Woods Pkwy (60061-3111)
PHONE................................901 363-0921
Clare Gorman, *Principal*
Hermann Bauermeister, *Principal*
▲ **EMP:** 9 **EST:** 2007
SALES (est): 1.4MM **Privately Held**
WEB: www.bauermeisterusa.com
SIC: 3556 Grinders, commercial, food

(G-20044)
BAXTER HEALTHCARE CORPORATION
400 Lakeview Pkwy (60061-1843)
PHONE................................847 522-8600
Marcey Guralnick, *Principal*
EMP: 260
SALES (corp-wide): 11.3B **Publicly Held**
WEB: www.baxter.com
SIC: 2834 Pharmaceutical preparations
HQ: Baxter Healthcare Corporation
1 Baxter Pkwy
Deerfield IL 60015
224 948-2000

(G-20045)
BAXTER HEALTHCARE CORPORATION
440 N Fairway Dr (60061-1879)
PHONE................................847 367-2544
Robert L Parkinson, *CEO*
Mary Ramirez, *Chairman*
Tim Simmons, *Manager*
Steve Schofield, *Technology*
George Terada, *Technical Staff*
EMP: 250
SALES (corp-wide): 11.3B **Publicly Held**
SIC: 3841 Surgical & medical instruments
HQ: Baxter Healthcare Corporation
1 Baxter Pkwy
Deerfield IL 60015
224 948-2000

(G-20046)
BENCHMARC DISPLAY INCORPORATED (PA)
1001 Woodlands Pkwy (60061-3181)
PHONE................................847 541-2828
Robert Osmond, *President*
Lou Fanning, *President*
Nicole Rafferty, *General Mgr*
Martha Beck, *Project Mgr*
Isaac Callejas, *Prdtn Mgr*
◆ **EMP:** 30 **EST:** 1974
SQ FT: 32,000
SALES (est): 5.7MM **Privately Held**
SIC: 3993 Displays & cutouts, window & lobby

(G-20047)
BENDE INC
925 Corporate Woods Pkwy (60061-3159)
PHONE................................847 913-0304
Eniko B Suto, *President*
EMP: 8 **EST:** 1996
SALES (est): 1.1MM **Privately Held**
SIC: 2013 Sausages from purchased meat

(G-20048)
CHICAGO SIGN GROUP
305 Albert Dr (60061-1613)
PHONE................................847 899-9021
David E Bromley, *Principal*
▲ **EMP:** 8
SALES (est): 976K **Privately Held**
SIC: 3993 Electric signs

(G-20049)
DENNIS WRIGHT
229 Augusta Dr (60061-2033)
PHONE................................847 816-6110
EMP: 3
SALES (est): 254.4K **Privately Held**
SIC: 3577 Mfg Computer Peripheral Equipment

(G-20050)
ELORAC INC (PA)
100 N Fairway Dr Ste 134 (60061-1859)
PHONE................................847 362-8200
Joel E Bernstein, *President*
Scott B Phillips, *Senior VP*
Barry Hollingsworth, *CFO*
Christopher Gabanski, *Officer*
EMP: 10
SALES (est): 802.2K **Privately Held**
SIC: 2834 Pharmaceutical preparations

(G-20051)
EMBROIDERY EXPERTS INC
595 Lakeview Pkwy (60061-1827)
PHONE................................847 403-0200
Michael Schrimmer, *President*
Gary David, *Vice Pres*
EMP: 50
SALES (est): 1MM **Privately Held**
SIC: 2395 Embroidery products, except schiffli machine

(G-20052)
ENVIRO-CHEM INC
228 Alexandria Dr (60061-2048)
PHONE................................847 549-7797
Tom Conway, *Manager*
EMP: 3
SALES (est): 250.5K
SALES (corp-wide): 3.9MM **Privately Held**
SIC: 3341 Secondary precious metals
PA: Enviro-Chem, Inc.
21821 Industrial Blvd
Rogers MN 55374
763 428-4002

(G-20053)
FEDEX CORPORATION
281 W Townline Rd Ste 100 (60061-4334)
PHONE................................847 918-7730
Fax: 847 918-7247
EMP: 11
SALES (corp-wide): 47.4B **Publicly Held**
SIC: 7389 5099 2752 Business Services Whol Durable Goods Lithographic Commercial Printing
PA: Fedex Corporation
942 Shady Grove Rd S
Memphis TN 38120
901 818-7500

(G-20054)
FLAME GUARD USA LLC
Also Called: Fg Manufacturing
1000 Bttrfld Rd Ste 1029 (60061)
PHONE................................815 219-4074
Joseph Kuesis,
James Mackey,
EMP: 6
SQ FT: 5,000
SALES (est): 607.6K **Privately Held**
SIC: 3999 5099 5063 5087 Fire extinguishers, portable; fire extinguishers; fire alarm systems; firefighting equipment; sprinkler systems, fire: automatic

(G-20055)
GB MARKETING INC
200 N Fairway Dr Ste 202 (60061-1861)
PHONE................................847 367-0101
Thomas Gust, *President*
Gerard Gust, *Vice Pres*
EMP: 16 **EST:** 1981
SQ FT: 4,000
SALES (est): 2.3MM **Privately Held**
SIC: 3577 5064 Computer peripheral equipment; electrical entertainment equipment

(G-20056)
GHETZLER AERO-POWER CORP
26 Manchester Ln (60061-2312)
PHONE................................224 513-5636
Richard Ghetzler, *President*
Michael Mast, *Vice Pres*
EMP: 8
SQ FT: 12,200
SALES (est): 1.2MM **Privately Held**
SIC: 3621 8711 5049 Power generators; engineering services; engineers' equipment & supplies

(G-20057)
H & H GRAPHICS LLC
Also Called: Winning Promotions
450 Corporate Woods Pkwy (60061-4117)
PHONE................................847 383-6285
Dariusz Derri Celewicz, *Vice Pres*
John Lipkowski, *Vice Pres*
Michelle Leissner, *Mng Member*
▼ **EMP:** 20
SALES (est): 2.2MM **Privately Held**
SIC: 2759 Screen printing

(G-20058)
H & H GRAPHICS ILLINOIS INC
450 Corporate Woods Pkwy (60061-4117)
PHONE................................847 383-6285
Michelle Leissner, *President*
Dariusz D Celewicz, *Vice Pres*
Dariusz Celewicz, *VP Opers*
Larry Barela, *Plant Mgr*
John Lipkowski, *VP Sales*
EMP: 25
SQ FT: 50,000
SALES (est): 3.3MM **Privately Held**
WEB: www.hhgrfx.com
SIC: 2759 Screen printing

(G-20059)
HARMAN INTERNATIONAL INDS INC
702 N Deerpath Dr (60061-1802)
PHONE................................847 996-8118
Dinesh C Paliwal, *President*
EMP: 79 **Privately Held**
SIC: 5064 3651 Electrical entertainment equipment; household audio & video equipment
HQ: Harman International Industries Incorporated
400 Atlantic St Ste 15
Stamford CT 06901
203 328-3500

(G-20060)
HEATHROW SCIENTIFIC LLC
620 Lakeview Pkwy (60061-1828)
PHONE................................847 816-5070
Douglas C Reed, *President*
Barbara Hester, *Purchasing*
Alfredo Villanueva, *Regl Sales Mgr*
Alfonso Espinoza, *Sales Staff*
Magdalena Hernandez-Mccal, *Sales Staff*
▲ **EMP:** 15 **EST:** 1998
SALES: 3.4MM **Privately Held**
WEB: www.heathrowscientific.com
SIC: 3089 Plastic processing

(G-20061)
HOWLAN INC
880 Corporate Woods Pkwy (60061-3154)
P.O. Box 5981 (60061-5981)
PHONE................................847 478-1760
EMP: 4
SALES (est): 391K **Privately Held**
SIC: 2752 Commercial printing, lithographic

GEOGRAPHIC SECTION

(G-20062)
ILEESH PRODUCTS LLC
Also Called: Lilipi Brands
100 N Fairway Dr Ste 114 (60061-1859)
PHONE..................224 424-4682
Oleg Lee, *Mng Member*
▲ **EMP:** 10
SQ FT: 10,000
SALES: 1.3MM **Privately Held**
SIC: 2392 Cushions & pillows

(G-20063)
ILLINOIS TOOL WORKS INC
Also Called: ITW Paslode
888 Forest Edge Dr (60061-3105)
P.O. Box 8117 (60061-8117)
PHONE..................847 634-1900
EMP: 80
SALES (corp-wide): 14.3B **Publicly Held**
SIC: 3546 Mfg Power-Driven Handtools
PA: Illinois Tool Works Inc.
155 Harlem Ave
Glenview IL 60025
847 724-7500

(G-20064)
ILLINOIS TOOL WORKS INC
Also Called: ITW Paslode
888 Forest Edge Dr (60061-3105)
PHONE..................847 634-1900
EMP: 50
SALES (corp-wide): 14.3B **Publicly Held**
SIC: 3423 3546 Mfg Hand/Edge Tools Mfg Power-Driven Handtools
PA: Illinois Tool Works Inc.
155 Harlem Ave
Glenview IL 60025
847 724-7500

(G-20065)
ILLINOIS TOOL WORKS INC
ITW AMP
888 Forest Edge Dr (60061-3105)
PHONE..................847 821-2170
Tom Southall, *General Mgr*
Cali Davenport, *Sales Staff*
Susan Fenley, *Sales Staff*
Eric Fernandes, *Marketing Mgr*
Larry Moeller, *Manager*
EMP: 7
SALES (corp-wide): 14.1B **Publicly Held**
SIC: 3423 3315 3496 Hand & edge tools; nails, steel; wire or cut; staples, made from purchased wire
PA: Illinois Tool Works Inc.
155 Harlem Ave
Glenview IL 60025
847 724-7500

(G-20066)
INDEPENDENT EYEWEAR MFG LLC
Also Called: IEM
255 Corp Woods Pkwy (60061-3109)
PHONE..................847 537-0008
Jerry Wolowicz,
Jason Stanley,
EMP: 54
SALES (est): 1.9MM
SALES (corp-wide): 12.1MM **Privately Held**
SIC: 3851 Protective eyeware
PA: Europa Eye Wear Corp.
255 Corporate Woods Pkwy
Vernon Hills IL 60061
847 537-0008

(G-20067)
IO LIGHTING LLC
370 Corporate Woods Pkwy (60061-3107)
PHONE..................847 735-7000
Ann REO, *CEO*
▲ **EMP:** 29
SQ FT: 1,600
SALES (est): 3.8MM **Privately Held**
SIC: 3645 Residential lighting fixtures
HQ: Cooper Industries Unlimited Company
41 A B Drury Street
Dublin

(G-20068)
JOHNSON CONTROLS INC
859 W End Ct (60061-1361)
PHONE..................847 549-2350
EMP: 3 **Privately Held**
SIC: 2531 Seats, automobile

HQ: Johnson Controls, Inc.
5757 N Green Bay Ave
Milwaukee WI 53209
414 524-1200

(G-20069)
KANAFLEX CORPORATION ILLINOIS (DH)
800 Woodlands Pkwy (60061-3170)
PHONE..................847 634-6100
Shigeki Kanao, *President*
Tokiyoshi Kosaka, *Vice Pres*
▲ **EMP:** 5
SQ FT: 100,000
SALES (est): 1.7MM **Privately Held**
SIC: 3052 Heater hose, plastic; heater hose, rubber

(G-20070)
L S STARRETT CO
50 Lakeview Pkwy Ste 107 (60061-1578)
PHONE..................847 816-9999
Doug Starrett, *President*
EMP: 4
SALES (est): 296.9K **Privately Held**
SIC: 3545 Precision measuring tools

(G-20071)
LA FORCE INC
280 Corporate Woods Pkwy (60061-3171)
PHONE..................847 415-5107
Tom Van Ess, *Sales Staff*
John Knier, *Branch Mgr*
EMP: 25
SALES (corp-wide): 156.3MM **Privately Held**
SIC: 3442 Window & door frames
PA: La Force, Inc.
1060 W Mason St
Green Bay WI 54303
920 497-7100

(G-20072)
LEARNING RESOURCES INC (PA)
Also Called: Educational Insights
380 N Fairway Dr (60061-1836)
PHONE..................847 573-8400
Barb Plain, *Vice Pres*
Kim Radke, *Prdtn Mgr*
Jeff Belda, *Production*
Jeff Kelley, *Production*
Galina Shuster, *Controller*
◆ **EMP:** 100
SQ FT: 216,000
SALES (est): 30.6MM **Privately Held**
SIC: 3999 5092 Education aids, devices & supplies; educational toys

(G-20073)
LOOMCRAFT TEXTILE & SUPPLY CO
647 Lakeview Pkwy (60061-1829)
PHONE..................847 680-0000
Bob Meroney, *Manager*
EMP: 50
SQ FT: 728,000
SALES (corp-wide): 31.2MM **Privately Held**
WEB: www.thefabricoutlet.com
SIC: 5131 5714 5719 2221 Upholstery fabrics, woven; drapery & upholstery stores; upholstery materials; window furnishings; broadwoven fabric mills, man-made
PA: Loomcraft Textile & Supply Company
2801 Lawndale Dr
Greensboro NC 27408
336 282-1100

(G-20074)
MIRACLE SEALANTS COMPANY LLC
11 E Hawthorn Pkwy (60061-1402)
PHONE..................626 443-6433
Joseph Salvo, *Co-CEO*
Albert P Salvo, *Co-CEO*
Bruce Palmore, *CFO*
Bill Brown, *Asst Controller*
◆ **EMP:** 26
SALES: 26.8MM
SALES (corp-wide): 5.5B **Publicly Held**
SIC: 2899 2891 Chemical preparations; adhesives & sealants

HQ: Rust-Oleum Corporation
11 E Hawthorn Pkwy
Vernon Hills IL 60061
847 367-7700

(G-20075)
MITSUBISHI ELC AUTOMTN INC (DH)
Also Called: Meau
500 Corporate Woods Pkwy (60061-3108)
P.O. Box 52778 Eagle Way, Chicago (60678-0001)
PHONE..................847 478-2100
Toshio Kawai, *CEO*
Dan Delallo, *Business Mgr*
Steve Palmer, *Materials Mgr*
Theresa Osterhoff, *Export Mgr*
Veronica Pallach, *Export Mgr*
▲ **EMP:** 200
SQ FT: 228,000
SALES (est): 123.2MM **Privately Held**
SIC: 5511 3566 3612 3613 Automobiles, new & used; speed changers, drives & gears; transformers, except electric; switchgear & switchboard apparatus; auto controls regulating residntl & coml environmt & applncs; measuring & controlling devices
HQ: Mitsubishi Electric Us Holdings, Inc.
5900 Katella Ave Ste A
Cypress CA 90630
714 220-2500

(G-20076)
MOOR PRINTING SERVICES INC
Also Called: Media Services
438 Pine Lake Cir (60061-1202)
PHONE..................847 687-7287
Erich D Moor, *President*
EMP: 6
SALES (est): 71.1K **Privately Held**
SIC: 2759 Commercial printing

(G-20077)
NEIL ENTERPRISES INC
1000 Woodlands Pkwy (60061-3188)
PHONE..................847 549-7627
Neil Fine, *President*
Carol Jacobson, *Vice Pres*
Brian Garbutt, *Warehouse Mgr*
Janis Demars, *Purch Mgr*
Lisa Africk, *CFO*
◆ **EMP:** 100 **EST:** 1961
SQ FT: 63,000
SALES (est): 9.8MM **Privately Held**
WEB: www.neilenterprises.com
SIC: 3089 Injection molded finished plastic products
PA: Neil International, Inc.
1000 Woodlands Pkwy
Vernon Hills IL 60061

(G-20078)
NEIL INTERNATIONAL INC (PA)
1000 Woodlands Pkwy (60061-3188)
PHONE..................847 549-7627
Jerry Fine, *Ch of Bd*
Neil Fine, *President*
Lois Fine, *Admin Sec*
▲ **EMP:** 150
SQ FT: 63,000
SALES (est): 14.1MM **Privately Held**
SIC: 3089 3993 Injection molded finished plastic products; signs & advertising specialties

(G-20079)
OVN LLC
714 Grosse Pointe Cir (60061-3412)
PHONE..................646 204-6781
Oleh Holovatiuk, *President*
EMP: 5 **EST:** 2017
SALES (est): 197.6K **Privately Held**
SIC: 2711 Newspapers: publishing only, not printed on site

(G-20080)
P H C ENTERPRISES INC
Also Called: AlphaGraphics
222 Hawthorn Vlg Cmns (60061-1519)
PHONE..................847 816-7373
Patrick Canary, *President*
Barbara Canary, *Vice Pres*
Michael Zelmar, *Admin Sec*
EMP: 8
SQ FT: 2,000

SALES: 950K **Privately Held**
SIC: 2752 2791 2789 2759 Commercial printing, lithographic; typesetting; bookbinding & related work; commercial printing

(G-20081)
PACTRA CORP
2112 Beaver Creek Dr (60061-3813)
PHONE..................847 281-0308
Robert J Cheon, *Principal*
Robert Cheon, *Director*
EMP: 5 **EST:** 2010
SALES (est): 640.9K **Privately Held**
WEB: www.pactraco.com
SIC: 3612 5065 Transformers, except electric; electronic parts & equipment

(G-20082)
PARKER INTERNATIONAL PDTS INC
Also Called: Parker Metal
650 Forest Edge Dr (60061-4115)
PHONE..................815 524-5831
▲ **EMP:** 96 **EST:** 1969
SQ FT: 170,000
SALES (est): 8.4MM **Privately Held**
SIC: 3452 6512 8741 Mfg Bolts/Screws/Rivets Nonresdentl Bldg Operatr Management Services

(G-20083)
PRECISION RESOURCE INC
Also Called: Precision Resource Ill Div
700 Hickory Hill Dr (60061-3104)
PHONE..................847 383-1300
Sarah Wong, *Human Resources*
Curt Krueger, *Branch Mgr*
EMP: 120
SALES (corp-wide): 286.1MM **Privately Held**
WEB: www.precisionresource.com
SIC: 3469 3544 Stamping metal for the trade; special dies, tools, jigs & fixtures
PA: Precision Resource, Inc.
25 Forest Pkwy
Shelton CT 06484
203 925-0012

(G-20084)
RAINBOW MIDWEST INC
Also Called: Rainbow Play Systems Illinois
300 Corporate Woods Pkwy (60061-3107)
PHONE..................847 955-9300
Joanie Barrus, *Manager*
EMP: 4 **Privately Held**
SIC: 3949 5941 Playground equipment; playground equipment
PA: Rainbow Midwest Inc
900 W 80th St
Minneapolis MN 55420

(G-20085)
REMKE INDUSTRIES INC (PA)
730 Lakeview Pkwy (60061-1834)
PHONE..................847 541-3780
Thomas O'Gara, *CEO*
Mark Sweeney, *President*
Michael Zeddies, *Chairman*
Jim Alton, *Vice Pres*
Michael B Zeddies Jr, *Vice Pres*
▲ **EMP:** 55
SQ FT: 22,000
SALES: 17.6MM **Privately Held**
WEB: www.remke.com
SIC: 3643 Connectors & terminals for electrical devices

(G-20086)
RICHARD WOLF MED INSTRS CORP
353 Corporate Woods Pkwy (60061-3110)
PHONE..................847 913-1113
Juergen Pfab, *President*
Alfons Notheis, *President*
Wade Hatfield, *Regional Mgr*
Rick Jeffries, *Regional Mgr*
Siegfried Karst, *COO*
▼ **EMP:** 193
SQ FT: 165,000
SALES (est): 92.5MM
SALES (corp-wide): 177.9K **Privately Held**
SIC: 5047 3841 Medical equipment & supplies; surgical & medical instruments

Vernon Hills - Lake County (G-20087)   GEOGRAPHIC SECTION

HQ: Richard Wolf Gmbh
Pforzheimer Str. 32
Knittlingen 75438
704 335-0

(G-20087)
RUST-LEUM CON PRTCTION SYSTEMS
Also Called: CPS
11 E Hawthorn Pkwy (60061-1402)
P.O. Box 9545, Tulsa OK (74157-0545)
PHONE..................918 446-6399
Garrett Gifford, *General Mgr*
Garret Gifford, *General Mgr*
▼ EMP: 26
SALES (est): 8.1MM
SALES (corp-wide): 5.5B **Publicly Held**
SIC: 2851 Plastics base paints & varnishes
HQ: Rust-Oleum Corporation
11 E Hawthorn Pkwy
Vernon Hills IL 60061
847 367-7700

(G-20088)
RUST-OLEUM (CANADA) LTD
11 E Hawthorn Pkwy (60061-1402)
PHONE..................847 367-7700
Wilbert Bartelt Sr, *Vice Pres*
Mark Sadler, *Project Mgr*
Steve Gillmann, *VP Human Res*
EMP: 350 EST: 1970
SQ FT: 50,000
SALES (est): 24K
SALES (corp-wide): 5.5B **Publicly Held**
SIC: 2851 Paints & allied products
HQ: Rust-Oleum Corporation
11 E Hawthorn Pkwy
Vernon Hills IL 60061
847 367-7700

(G-20089)
RUST-OLEUM CORPORATION (HQ)
11 E Hawthorn Pkwy (60061-1499)
PHONE..................847 367-7700
Peter Jug, *Principal*
Tom Schweiger, *Principal*
Chris Holman, *Area Mgr*
Cindy Scariano, *Area Mgr*
Beth Wilson, *Area Mgr*
◆ EMP: 150 EST: 1932
SQ FT: 100,000
SALES (est): 619.3MM
SALES (corp-wide): 5.5B **Publicly Held**
WEB: www.rustoleum.com
SIC: 2891 2899 2816 2842 Adhesives & sealants; chemical preparations; inorganic pigments; specialty cleaning, polishes & sanitation goods; paints, waterproof
PA: Rpm International Inc.
2628 Pearl Rd
Medina OH 44256
330 273-5090

(G-20090)
SAB TOOL SUPPLY CO (PA)
Also Called: Yg-1 Tool USA
730 Corporate Woods Pkwy (60061-3153)
PHONE..................847 634-3700
Hokeun Song, *President*
▲ EMP: 5
SALES (est): 835.8K **Privately Held**
SIC: 5251 3423 Tools; hand & edge tools

(G-20091)
SANTAS BEST (PA)
100 N Fairway Dr Ste 120 (60061-1859)
PHONE..................847 459-3301
Edward H Ruff, *CEO*
Barry Hausauer, *COO*
EMP: 18
SQ FT: 14,000
SALES (est): 20.8MM **Privately Held**
SIC: 3699 3641 Christmas tree lighting sets, electric; electric lamps & parts for specialized applications

(G-20092)
SCOTSMAN GROUP INC (DH)
Also Called: Scotsman Ice Systems Division
101 Corporate Woods Pkwy (60061-3109)
PHONE..................847 215-4500
Mark McClanahan, *President*
EMP: 100
SQ FT: 36,000
SALES (est): 55.8MM
SALES (corp-wide): 2.6MM **Privately Held**
SIC: 3585 Ice making machinery
HQ: Scotsman Industries, Inc.
101 Corporate Woods Pkwy
Vernon Hills IL 60061
847 215-4500

(G-20093)
SCOTSMAN INDUSTRIES INC (DH)
Also Called: Scotsman of Los Angeles
101 Corporate Woods Pkwy (60061-3109)
PHONE..................847 215-4500
David McCulloch, *President*
◆ EMP: 65
SALES (est): 299.3MM
SALES (corp-wide): 2.6MM **Privately Held**
SIC: 3585 3632 Refrigeration equipment, complete; ice making machinery; ice boxes, industrial; cold drink dispensing equipment (not coin-operated); ice boxes, household: metal or wood; refrigerators, mechanical & absorption: household
HQ: Ali Holding Srl
Via Piero Gobetti 2/A
Cernusco Sul Naviglio MI
029 219-9292

(G-20094)
SEAT COVER PRO LLC
Also Called: 4knines
100 N Fairway Dr Ste 106 (60061-1859)
PHONE..................847 990-1506
Bruce Grieve, *Mng Member*
EMP: 3
SALES (corp-wide): 4MM **Privately Held**
SIC: 3199 2211 Dog furnishings: collars, leashes, muzzles, etc.: leather; seat cover cloth, automobile: cotton
PA: Seat Cover Pro, Llc
1820 N Glnvlle Dr Ste 124
Richardson TX 75081
847 990-1506

(G-20095)
SECURITY LOCKNUT LLC
999 Forest Edge Dr (60061-3106)
PHONE..................847 970-4050
Raymond Wiltgen, *CEO*
Jennifer Pucevich, *Office Admin*
◆ EMP: 22 EST: 1974
SALES (est): 4.1MM **Privately Held**
SIC: 3452 3451 Nuts, metal; bolts, metal; screw machine products

(G-20096)
SENNA DESIGN LLC
100 Corporate Woods Pkwy (60061-4127)
PHONE..................847 821-7877
EMP: 8
SQ FT: 20,000
SALES (est): 80.6K **Privately Held**
SIC: 3469 3264 Mfg Metal Stampings Mfg Porcelain Electrical Supplies

(G-20097)
SENSOR SYNERGY
200 N Fairway Dr Ste 198 (60061-1861)
P.O. Box 5019, Buffalo Grove (60089-5019)
PHONE..................847 353-8200
James Wiczer, *President*
Michael Wiczer, *Engineer*
Ralph Bergen, *Marketing Mgr*
EMP: 6
SALES (est): 540K **Privately Held**
WEB: www.sensorsynergy.com
SIC: 3823 Computer interface equipment for industrial process control

(G-20098)
SMITHS MEDICAL
330 Corporate Woods Pkwy (60061-3107)
PHONE..................847 383-1400
Dominick Arena, *Principal*
▲ EMP: 5
SALES (est): 445.8K **Privately Held**
SIC: 3841 Surgical & medical instruments

(G-20099)
SOLUTION DESIGNS INC
2042 Laurel Valley Dr (60061-4556)
PHONE..................847 680-7788
Patrick Marsek, *President*
Tracy Rieke, *Admin Sec*
EMP: 5
SALES (est): 604.5K **Privately Held**
SIC: 2873 Nitrogenous fertilizers

(G-20100)
STEAMGARD LLC
Also Called: Engineering Resources
730 Forest Edge Dr (60061-3172)
PHONE..................847 913-8400
C Stavropoulos, *Principal*
REA S Lorence, *Principal*
Nicholas Stavropoulos, *Principal*
Peter Kopsaftis, *Business Mgr*
Tom Marnane, *Vice Pres*
EMP: 30
SQ FT: 11,000
SALES (est): 6.8MM **Privately Held**
SIC: 3494 8711 Steam fittings & specialties; designing: ship, boat, machine & product

(G-20101)
SWAGGER FOODS CORPORATION
900 Corporate Woods Pkwy (60061-3155)
PHONE..................847 913-1200
Tai Ryang Shin, *President*
You Hyun Shin, *Admin Sec*
EMP: 20 EST: 1978
SQ FT: 41,500
SALES (est): 4.5MM **Privately Held**
SIC: 2099 Sauces: dry mixes; gravy mixes, dry; seasonings: dry mixes

(G-20102)
SWAROVSKI NORTH AMERICA LTD
116 Hawthorne Shopg Ctr (60061)
PHONE..................847 680-5150
Luz Osequera, *Branch Mgr*
EMP: 7
SALES (corp-wide): 4.7B **Privately Held**
WEB: www.swarovski.com
SIC: 3961 Costume jewelry
HQ: Swarovski North America Limited
1 Kenney Dr
Cranston RI 02920
401 463-6400

(G-20103)
TETRA PAK INC
600 Bunker Ct (60061-1847)
PHONE..................847 955-6000
Gustav Korsholm, *President*
Todd Hutson, *Managing Dir*
Paul Zhu, *Vice Pres*
Travis Coe, *Project Mgr*
Jeffrey Guardino, *Opers Staff*
EMP: 75 **Privately Held**
SIC: 2671 3565 5084 Paper coated or laminated for packaging; packaging machinery; hydraulic systems equipment & supplies
HQ: Tetra Pak Inc.
3300 Airport Rd
Denton TX 76207
940 565-8800

(G-20104)
TETRA PAK MATERIALS LP (DH)
101 Corporate Woods Pkwy (60061-3109)
PHONE..................847 955-6000
Uno Kjellberg, *President*
Rachel Wang, *Buyer*
Alexandru Ciungu, *Engineer*
Martin Johnsson, *Engineer*
Susan Hu, *Train & Dev Mgr*
◆ EMP: 66
SQ FT: 2,000
SALES (est): 115.5MM **Privately Held**
SIC: 3556 Food products machinery
HQ: Tetra Pak Inc.
3300 Airport Rd
Denton TX 76207
940 565-8800

(G-20105)
THERMOSOFT INTERNATIONAL CORP
701 Corporate Woods Pkwy (60061-3112)
PHONE..................847 279-3800
Eric Kochman, *President*
Russ Dunn, *Vice Pres*
Dmitry Kochman, *Vice Pres*
Mike Lavit, *Vice Pres*
Eugene Pavloutine, *Opers Mgr*
▲ EMP: 47
SQ FT: 15,000
SALES (est): 9MM **Privately Held**
WEB: www.thermosoftinternational.com
SIC: 3634 Heaters, tape; heating pads, electric

(G-20106)
THREE HANDS TECHNOLOGIES
462 Harrison Ct (60061-1369)
PHONE..................847 680-5358
Tom McGuigan, *President*
EMP: 3
SALES: 100K **Privately Held**
SIC: 3699 Electronic training devices

(G-20107)
TRI INDUSTRIES NFP
Also Called: Triumph Workplace Solutions
780 Corporate Woods Pkwy (60061-3153)
PHONE..................773 754-3100
Ann Curley, *Business Mgr*
Jay Burrell, *Vice Pres*
Ken Bell, *Exec Dir*
▲ EMP: 30
SQ FT: 15,000
SALES: 5.1MM **Privately Held**
SIC: 3861 Toners, prepared photographic (not made in chemical plants)

(G-20108)
VMA GROUP INC
13 Saint Clair Ln (60061-3225)
PHONE..................847 877-7039
Vadim Klugman, *Principal*
Annaleise Hollis, *Executive*
▲ EMP: 4
SALES (est): 320K **Privately Held**
SIC: 2084 Wines, brandy & brandy spirits

(G-20109)
WAGNER INTERNATIONAL LLC
Also Called: My Sports Warehouse
105 W Townline Rd Ste 160 (60061-1424)
PHONE..................224 619-9247
Jim Wagner, *Mng Member*
EMP: 1
SALES: 400K **Privately Held**
SIC: 7389 3949 2759 Embroidering of advertising on shirts, etc.; sporting & athletic goods; screen printing

(G-20110)
WESTERN ANALYTICAL PRODUCTS
625 Bunker Ct (60061-1830)
PHONE..................800 541-8421
EMP: 3
SALES (est): 201.1K **Privately Held**
SIC: 3826 Analytical instruments

(G-20111)
WINSTON PHARMACEUTICALS INC (HQ)
100 N Fairway Dr Ste 134 (60061-1859)
PHONE..................847 362-8200
Joel E Bernstein MD, *President*
Neal S Penneys MD, *Principal*
Robert A Yolles, *Principal*
Scott B Phillips MD, *Senior VP*
Scott Phillips, *Vice Pres*
EMP: 9
SQ FT: 7,300
SALES (est): 607.3K **Privately Held**
SIC: 2834 Pharmaceutical preparations

(G-20112)
WONDERLIC INC
400 Lakeview Pkwy Ste 200 (60061-1850)
PHONE..................847 680-4900
Charles F Wonderlic Jr, *CEO*
David Hammond, *President*
Richard E Wonderlic, *CFO*
EMP: 83
SQ FT: 24,193
SALES: 14.3MM
SALES (corp-wide): 12.8MM **Privately Held**
SIC: 2741 Miscellaneous publishing
PA: Wonderlic Holdings, Inc.
544 Lakeview Pkwy Ste 210
Vernon Hills IL 60061
877 605-9496

▲ = Import ▼ = Export ◆ = Import/Export

GEOGRAPHIC SECTION

Villa Park - Dupage County (G-20140)

(G-20113)
XOMI INSTRUMENTS CO LTD
1463 Pinehurst Dr (60061-1230)
PHONE.................847 660-4614
Jie Xie, *President*
EMP: 3
SALES (est): 70.8K **Privately Held**
SIC: 3669 Communications equipment

(G-20114)
ZF NORTH AMERICA INC
Also Called: ZF Services North America
777 Hickory Hill Dr (60061-3182)
PHONE.................847 478-6868
Timothy J Corcoran, *Vice Pres*
EMP: 200
SALES (corp-wide): 216.2K **Privately Held**
SIC: 3714 Motor vehicle parts & accessories
HQ: Zf North America, Inc.
15811 Centennial Dr 48
Northville MI 48168
734 416-6200

(G-20115)
ZF SERVICES LLC
Also Called: ZF Industries
777 Hickory Hill Dr (60061-3182)
PHONE.................847 478-6868
Stefan Sommer, *CEO*
Robert Marasco, *Transportation*
Terry Gregorin, *Engineer*
Tony Price, *Engineer*
Mark Thorpe, *Sales Staff*
◆ EMP: 320
SALES (est): 86.1MM
SALES (corp-wide): 216.2K **Privately Held**
SIC: 3714 Motor vehicle parts & accessories
HQ: Zf Friedrichshafen Ag
Lowentaler Str. 20
Friedrichshafen 88046
754 177-0

Verona
Grundy County

(G-20116)
CHICKS AND SALSA LLC
427 Smith St (60479-3120)
P.O. Box 58 (60479-0058)
PHONE.................815 735-6660
Amber N Button, *Principal*
EMP: 3
SALES (est): 112.6K **Privately Held**
SIC: 2099 Dips, except cheese & sour cream based

Vienna
Johnson County

(G-20117)
DRY SYSTEMS TECHNOLOGIES LLC
1430 Us Highway 45 N (62995-2675)
PHONE.................618 658-3000
Terry McDonald, *Branch Mgr*
EMP: 12
SALES (corp-wide): 14.2MM **Privately Held**
SIC: 3532 Mining machinery
HQ: Dry Systems Technologies Llc
10420 Rising Ct
Woodridge IL 60517
630 427-2051

(G-20118)
MATT SNELL AND SONS
4530 Mount Shelter Rd (62995-3119)
PHONE.................618 695-3555
EMP: 4
SALES (est): 193K **Privately Held**
SIC: 0191 3715 Business Services At Non-Commercial Site

(G-20119)
SHAWNEE WINERY
200 Commercial St (62995-1689)
PHONE.................618 658-8400
EMP: 5
SQ FT: 6,000
SALES (est): 340K **Privately Held**
SIC: 2084 Wine Manufacture

(G-20120)
W BOZARTH LOGGING
540 Hillside Ln (62995-2325)
PHONE.................618 658-4016
Wayne Bozart, *Owner*
EMP: 2
SALES (est): 266.1K **Privately Held**
SIC: 2411 Logging camps & contractors

Villa Grove
Douglas County

(G-20121)
AF ANTRONICS INC
2 N Main St (61956-1517)
PHONE.................217 328-0800
Fred Ore Jr, *President*
Alice Ore, *Admin Sec*
EMP: 3
SQ FT: 3,000
SALES (est): 429.5K **Privately Held**
WEB: www.afantronics.com
SIC: 3663 Antennas, transmitting & communications

(G-20122)
DEEM WOODWORKS
22 N Deer Lk (61956-9622)
PHONE.................217 832-9614
Charles Deem, *Owner*
EMP: 2
SALES: 250K **Privately Held**
SIC: 2431 Millwork

(G-20123)
HERMAN BADE & SONS
Also Called: Bade Herman & Son Trucking
608 N Henson Rd (61956-1643)
PHONE.................217 832-9444
Everett Bade, *Partner*
Phillip Bade, *Partner*
Stanley Bade, *Partner*
EMP: 3 EST: 1936
SALES (est): 210K **Privately Held**
SIC: 1771 5039 3273 Concrete work; mobile homes; ready-mixed concrete

(G-20124)
LAKE FABRICATION INC
4 S Sycamore St (61956-1533)
P.O. Box 136 (61956-0136)
PHONE.................217 832-2761
Pete Lake, *Owner*
Randy Lake, *Co-Owner*
EMP: 2
SQ FT: 20,000
SALES (est): 402K **Privately Held**
SIC: 3535 7699 7692 Belt conveyor systems, general industrial use; farm machinery repair; welding repair

(G-20125)
PAULS MACHINE & WELDING CORP (PA)
Also Called: Mordern Flow Equipment
650 N Sycamore St (61956-9772)
PHONE.................217 832-2541
Edward Cler, *President*
Keith Cler, *Corp Secy*
Thomas D Cler, *Vice Pres*
Tom Burton, *Engineer*
Jon Mc Nussen, *Manager*
▲ EMP: 78
SQ FT: 40,000
SALES (est): 16.8MM **Privately Held**
SIC: 7692 Welding repair

Villa Park
Dupage County

(G-20126)
A TO Z TOOL INC
400 W Saint Charles Rd # 1 (60181-2442)
PHONE.................630 787-0478
Fax: 630 279-4134
EMP: 9
SQ FT: 12,400
SALES: 600K **Privately Held**
SIC: 3423 Mfg Hand Tools

(G-20127)
ADDISON ENGRAVING INC
204 W Ridge Rd (60181-1515)
PHONE.................630 833-9123
Gerald D Dobey, *President*
Steven E Dobey, *Vice Pres*
EMP: 2 EST: 1960
SQ FT: 1,800
SALES (est): 201.9K **Privately Held**
WEB: www.addisonengraving.com
SIC: 3479 3993 Engraving jewelry silverware, or metal; name plates: engraved, etched, etc.; signs & advertising specialties

(G-20128)
ADVANCE PRESS SIGN INC
719 N Addison Rd (60181-1493)
PHONE.................630 833-1600
Geary Mallek, *President*
Mildred Mallek, *Vice Pres*
EMP: 4
SQ FT: 2,500
SALES (est): 250K **Privately Held**
SIC: 2759 3993 Screen printing; signs & advertising specialties

(G-20129)
AIR LAND AND SEA INTERIORS
Also Called: Riggs Brothers Auto Interiors
220 E Saint Charles Rd (60181-2433)
PHONE.................630 834-1717
William Keifer, *President*
Linda Keifer, *Admin Sec*
EMP: 4
SQ FT: 2,800
SALES (est): 160K **Privately Held**
SIC: 7641 3732 3728 3714 Reupholstery; boat building & repairing; aircraft parts & equipment; motor vehicle parts & accessories; canvas & related products

(G-20130)
ALL METAL RECYCLING COMPANY
409 N Addison Rd (60181-1950)
PHONE.................847 530-4825
Tom Mitchell, *Owner*
EMP: 4 EST: 2014
SALES (est): 196.6K **Privately Held**
SIC: 3559 3569 Recycling machinery; baling machines, for scrap metal, paper or similar material

(G-20131)
AMERICAN METAL INSTALLERS & FA
55 W Home Ave (60181-2566)
PHONE.................630 993-0812
Fax: 630 993-0890
EMP: 2
SQ FT: 9,200
SALES: 499K **Privately Held**
SIC: 1711 7692 3556 3444 Plumbing/Heat/Ac Contr Welding Repair Mfg Food Prdts Mach Mfg Sheet Metalwork

(G-20132)
BATTERIES PLUS 287
240 E Roosevelt Rd (60181-3500)
PHONE.................630 279-3478
Paul Bessey, *Principal*
EMP: 3
SALES (est): 299.8K **Privately Held**
SIC: 3691 5063 5531 Storage batteries; batteries; batteries, automotive & truck

(G-20133)
BEAR MTAL WLDG FABRICATION INC
111 W Home Ave (60181-2568)
PHONE.................630 261-9353
Dean Mormino, *President*
Melisa Mormino, *Corp Secy*
EMP: 6
SALES: 400K **Privately Held**
SIC: 7692 Welding repair

(G-20134)
BIEWER FABRICATING INC
208 W Stone Rd (60181-1518)
PHONE.................630 530-8922
Joe Biewer, *President*
Judy Biewer, *Vice Pres*
EMP: 7
SQ FT: 2,500
SALES: 1.1MM **Privately Held**
SIC: 3441 Fabricated structural metal

(G-20135)
BURDETT BURNER MFG INC
335 S Ardmore Ave (60181-2943)
PHONE.................630 617-5060
Thomas L Monick, *President*
EMP: 4
SALES (est): 523.3K **Privately Held**
SIC: 3567 3433 Fuel-fired furnaces & ovens; gas infrared heating units

(G-20136)
C KELLER MANUFACTURING INC
925 N Ellsworth Ave (60181-1107)
PHONE.................630 833-5593
Fred Keller, *CEO*
John Jacobi, *President*
Tony Marzovilla, *Vice Pres*
Dan Piorek, *Engineer*
Eric Keller, *Treasurer*
EMP: 40
SQ FT: 15,000
SALES (est): 8.3MM **Privately Held**
SIC: 3441 3469 7692 3444 Fabricated structural metal; stamping metal for the trade; welding repair; sheet metalwork

(G-20137)
CARPENTERS MILLWORK CO (PA)
224 W Stone Rd (60181-1518)
PHONE.................708 339-7707
Gary Smits, *President*
Deborah J Smits, *Corp Secy*
EMP: 10
SQ FT: 10,000
SALES (est): 1.3MM **Privately Held**
SIC: 2434 2431 2421 5031 Wood kitchen cabinets; millwork; sawmills & planing mills, general; doors & windows

(G-20138)
CASTLE CRAFT PRODUCTS INC
1133 N Ellsworth Ave (60181-1040)
PHONE.................630 279-7494
Gregory Venchus, *President*
Maryland Venchus, *CFO*
EMP: 12
SALES (est): 2.4MM **Privately Held**
SIC: 2541 2521 Store fixtures, wood; cabinets, office: wood

(G-20139)
COBALT TOOL & MANUFACTURING
131 W Home Ave (60181-2568)
PHONE.................630 530-8898
Fred J Hoyne Jr, *President*
Barbara Jeanne Hoyne, *Vice Pres*
EMP: 4
SQ FT: 1,200
SALES (est): 538.2K **Privately Held**
SIC: 3599 3825 Machine shop, jobbing & repair; instruments to measure electricity

(G-20140)
CONSTRCTION SLTONS CHICAGO INC
222 W Stone Rd (60181-1518)
PHONE.................630 834-1929
Frank Sullivan, *President*
Meg Sullivan, *Vice Pres*

Villa Park - Dupage County (G-20141)

EMP: 8
SQ FT: 7,000
SALES: 1.1MM **Privately Held**
WEB: www.reclaimedtable.com
SIC: 3553 Furniture makers' machinery, woodworking

(G-20141)
CONXALL CORPORATION
601 E Wildwood Ave (60181-2762)
PHONE 630 834-7504
Keith A Bandolik, *President*
Jeanne Mazurek, *General Mgr*
Michael Bingen, *Prdtn Mgr*
James Collado, *Engineer*
Dave Bandolik, *CFO*
EMP: 150
SQ FT: 33,500
SALES (est): 30.4MM **Publicly Held**
SIC: 3678 Electronic connectors
HQ: Switchcraft, Inc.
5555 N Elston Ave
Chicago IL 60630
773 792-2700

(G-20142)
COURTESY METAL POLISHING
735 N Addison Rd Ste B (60181-1469)
PHONE 630 832-1862
Juventino Dorado, *Owner*
EMP: 3
SQ FT: 2,500
SALES (est): 252.4K **Privately Held**
SIC: 3471 Buffing for the trade; polishing, metals or formed products

(G-20143)
CROWN BATTERY MANUFACTURING CO
1199 N Ellsworth Ave (60181-1040)
PHONE 630 530-8060
Peter Chavez, *Branch Mgr*
EMP: 6
SALES (corp-wide): 151.3MM **Privately Held**
SIC: 3691 Storage batteries
PA: Crown Battery Manufacturing Company
1445 Majestic Dr
Fremont OH 43420
419 334-7181

(G-20144)
DELTA ERECTORS INC
18w178 Buckingham Ln (60181-3820)
PHONE 708 267-9721
Thomas R Chambers, *President*
▲ **EMP:** 10
SALES (est): 520K **Privately Held**
SIC: 1791 3441 3449 7389 Building front installation metal; building components, structural steel; curtain walls for buildings, steel;

(G-20145)
E A A ENTERPRISES INC
Also Called: Sir Speedy Print Signs Mktg
250 E Saint Charles Rd (60181-2472)
PHONE 630 279-0150
Bill Schaub, *President*
Ann Schaub, *Vice Pres*
EMP: 6
SQ FT: 2,500
SALES (est): 1MM **Privately Held**
SIC: 2752 3993 Commercial printing, lithographic; signs & advertising specialties

(G-20146)
EMPIRE SCREW MANUFACTURING CO
747 N Yale Ave (60181-1679)
PHONE 630 833-7060
Peter Sparacio, *President*
Toni Sparacio, *Corp Secy*
Salvatore Sparacio, *Vice Pres*
EMP: 18 **EST:** 1944
SQ FT: 5,000
SALES (est): 998.2K **Privately Held**
WEB: www.empirescrew.com
SIC: 3451 Screw machine products

(G-20147)
FLORIDA METROLOGY LLC
Also Called: Acme Scale Systems
1100 N Villa Ave (60181-1054)
PHONE 630 833-3800
Ron Kupper, *Mng Member*
Jeff Michaels, *Manager*
EMP: 15
SALES (corp-wide): 4MM **Privately Held**
SIC: 5046 7699 7359 3821 Scales, except laboratory; scale repair service; equipment rental & leasing; calibration tapes for physical testing machines
HQ: Florida Metrology, Llc
645 Nw Entp Dr Ste 106
Port Saint Lucie FL 34986
772 212-7158

(G-20148)
GRAPHIC ARTS SERVICES INC (PA)
333 W Saint Charles Rd (60181-2451)
PHONE 630 629-7770
George Hoganson, *Ch of Bd*
Thomas Hoganson, *President*
Matt Hoganson, *Manager*
Albert Treado, *Technology*
Mary Hoganson, *Admin Sec*
EMP: 30
SQ FT: 8,500
SALES (est): 6MM **Privately Held**
SIC: 2752 Commercial printing, offset

(G-20149)
GRAPHIC CHEMICAL & INK CO
728 N Yale Ave (60181-1683)
P.O. Box 7027 (60181-7027)
PHONE 630 832-6004
Dean Clark, *Principal*
Sarah C Canniff, *Treasurer*
Elizabeth A Clark, *Admin Sec*
▲ **EMP:** 18 **EST:** 1920
SQ FT: 10,000
SALES (est): 2.9MM **Privately Held**
WEB: www.graphicchemical.com
SIC: 3952 2893 5111 Artists' materials, except pencils & leads; gravure ink; letterpress or offset ink; lithographic ink; fine paper

(G-20150)
HAIMER USA LLC
134 E Hill St (60181-1805)
PHONE 630 833-1500
Claudia Haimer, *CEO*
Brendt Holden, *President*
Jordan Tetzlaff, *Regional Mgr*
Steve Baier, *Vice Pres*
Robert Bied, *Vice Pres*
▲ **EMP:** 5
SALES (est): 1.3MM
SALES (corp-wide): 32.6MM **Privately Held**
SIC: 3545 Tool holders
PA: Haimer Gmbh
Weiherstr. 21
Hollenbach 86568
825 799-880

(G-20151)
J & L GEAR INCORPORATED
726 N Princeton Ave Ste C (60181-1657)
PHONE 630 832-1880
Joseph Lovecchio Jr, *President*
EMP: 10
SQ FT: 4,000
SALES (est): 1.3MM **Privately Held**
SIC: 3462 3541 Gears, forged steel; machine tools, metal cutting type

(G-20152)
JOHN TOBIN MILLWORK CO (PA)
231 W North Ave (60181-1160)
PHONE 630 832-3780
John B Tobin Jr, *President*
Julianne Driscoll, *Treasurer*
EMP: 8 **EST:** 1960
SQ FT: 3,400
SALES (est): 2.5MM **Privately Held**
SIC: 5211 2431 Millwork & lumber; door & window products; millwork; doors & door parts & trim, wood

(G-20153)
JOMAR ELECTRIC COIL MFG INC
218 W Stone Rd (60181-1518)
PHONE 630 279-1494
Joseph Petitto, *President*
Mary Petitto, *Admin Sec*
EMP: 4
SALES: 250K **Privately Held**
SIC: 3621 Motors & generators

(G-20154)
KABERT INDUSTRIES INC (PA)
321 W Saint Charles Rd (60181-2493)
P.O. Box 6270 (60181-5317)
PHONE 630 833-2115
Robert A Peacock, *President*
Elizabeth Peacock, *Corp Secy*
Karen Hartman, *Vice Pres*
Karl Hatman, *VP Sales*
▲ **EMP:** 123
SQ FT: 15,000
SALES (est): 13.5MM **Privately Held**
WEB: www.kabert.com
SIC: 2221 3369 Fiberglass fabrics; nonferrous foundries

(G-20155)
KENCOR STAIRS & WOODWORKING
311 W Stone Rd (60181-1521)
PHONE 630 279-8980
Tom Kennedy, *President*
EMP: 9 **EST:** 1962
SQ FT: 6,000
SALES (est): 1.6MM **Privately Held**
WEB: www.kencorstairs.com
SIC: 2431 3446 Staircases & stairs, wood; stair railings, wood; architectural metalwork

(G-20156)
KEPNER PRODUCTS COMPANY
995 N Ellsworth Ave (60181-1192)
PHONE 630 279-1550
Hugh G Kepner, *President*
Jim Warren, *Mfg Mgr*
Greg Lyon, *Facilities Mgr*
Bob Reese, *Purch Mgr*
Jan Paney, *QC Mgr*
EMP: 65 **EST:** 1948
SQ FT: 31,500
SALES (est): 13.9MM **Privately Held**
WEB: www.kepner.com
SIC: 3494 3492 Valves & pipe fittings; fluid power valves & hose fittings

(G-20157)
M-PRIME COMPANY
649 N Ardmore Ave (60181-1655)
P.O. Box 6240 (60181-5316)
PHONE 630 834-9400
John E Hadley, *President*
◆ **EMP:** 30 **EST:** 1964
SQ FT: 100,000
SALES (est): 5.7MM **Privately Held**
SIC: 3087 7389 4226 5162 Custom compound purchased resins; packaging & labeling services; special warehousing & storage; resins, synthetic

(G-20158)
MANUFACTURERS ALLIANCE CORP
Also Called: Productionpro
320 W Saint Charles Rd (60181-2403)
PHONE 847 696-1600
P Douglas Tello, *Principal*
Christopher Smith, *Info Tech Dir*
EMP: 10
SALES (est): 2MM **Privately Held**
SIC: 3552 Creels, textile machinery

(G-20159)
MASTER MANUFACTURING CO
747 N Yale Ave (60181-1679)
PHONE 630 833-7060
Peter Sparacio, *President*
Salvatore Sparacio, *Vice Pres*
Antoinette Sparacio, *Treasurer*
EMP: 10 **EST:** 1932
SQ FT: 5,000
SALES (est): 1.1MM **Privately Held**
SIC: 3563 3564 3549 Spraying outfits; metals, paints & chemicals (compressor); blowers & fans; metalworking machinery

(G-20160)
MOBIL TRAILER TRANSPORT INC
223 E Adele Ct (60181-1208)
PHONE 630 993-1200
Lois Pivar, *President*
EMP: 20
SALES (est): 36.6K **Privately Held**
SIC: 4213 2451 Mobile homes transport; mobile homes

(G-20161)
MORTGAGE MARKET INFO SVCS
53 E Saint Charles Rd (60181-2465)
PHONE 630 834-7555
EMP: 40
SQ FT: 2,500
SALES (est): 3.1MM **Privately Held**
SIC: 2759 Commercial Printing

(G-20162)
NIKRO INDUSTRIES INC
1115 N Ellsworth Ave (60181-1040)
PHONE 630 530-0558
James Nicholson, *President*
Roland Nicholson, *Admin Sec*
◆ **EMP:** 15
SQ FT: 7,000
SALES (est): 4.1MM **Privately Held**
SIC: 3589 Vacuum cleaners & sweepers, electric; industrial

(G-20163)
OLY OLA EDGING INC
Also Called: Olyola Etching
124 E Saint Charles Rd (60181-2414)
PHONE 630 833-3033
Sandra Hechler, *President*
Aymie Clayton, *Sales Mgr*
EMP: 10
SQ FT: 3,500
SALES (est): 4.2MM **Privately Held**
WEB: www.olyola.com
SIC: 5083 2821 Landscaping equipment; plastics materials & resins

(G-20164)
PEP INDUSTRIES INC
725 N Wisconsin Ave (60181-1506)
PHONE 630 833-0404
Phil Greco, *President*
Phyllis Greco, *Corp Secy*
Renee Greco, *Cust Svc Dir*
EMP: 12 **EST:** 1950
SQ FT: 13,000
SALES (est): 970K **Privately Held**
SIC: 2531 3446 3281 3444 Church furniture; ornamental metalwork; church furniture, cut stone; sheet metalwork

(G-20165)
PRECISION ENGINEERING & DEV CO
Also Called: Pedco
701 N Iowa Ave (60181-1592)
PHONE 630 834-5956
Dan Wagner, *President*
Carolyn Wagner, *Vice Pres*
Diane Wagner, *Vice Pres*
EMP: 20 **EST:** 1949
SQ FT: 5,500
SALES (est): 1.5MM **Privately Held**
SIC: 3544 3599 Jigs & fixtures; machine shop, jobbing & repair

(G-20166)
PROGRAF LLC
119 W Home Ave (60181-2568)
P.O. Box 398, Oregon (61061-0398)
PHONE 815 234-4848
Doug Calabro, *Principal*
EMP: 3
SQ FT: 3,000
SALES (est): 205.2K **Privately Held**
SIC: 3728 5084 Blades, aircraft propeller; metal or wood; printing trades machinery, equipment & supplies

(G-20167)
QC POWDER INC
226 E Sidney Ct (60181-1138)
PHONE 630 832-0606
Charles Stitzel, *President*
Paul Podedworny, *Admin Sec*
EMP: 45
SQ FT: 26,000
SALES (est): 4.9MM **Privately Held**
SIC: 3479 Painting, coating & hot dipping

GEOGRAPHIC SECTION

Virginia - Cass County (G-20193)

(G-20168)
REAL NEON INC
226 E Adele Ct (60181-1208)
PHONE..................630 543-0995
Jacek Menel, *President*
Malgorzata Kocylowska, *Admin Sec*
EMP: 10
SQ FT: 3,000
SALES (est): 1.2MM **Privately Held**
SIC: 3993 Neon signs

(G-20169)
RECLAIMEDTABLE.COM
222 W Stone Rd (60181-1518)
PHONE..................630 834-1929
Frank Sullivan, *Principal*
Meg Sullivan, *Mktg Dir*
EMP: 5
SALES (est): 400.5K **Privately Held**
WEB: www.reclaimedtable.com
SIC: 2431 Millwork

(G-20170)
SAICOR INC
708 N Princeton Ave (60181-1604)
PHONE..................630 530-0350
Idris Atcha, *President*
EMP: 7 EST: 1979
SQ FT: 3,000
SALES (est): 1.1MM **Privately Held**
WEB: www.saicorinc.com
SIC: 3569 Baling machines, for scrap metal, paper or similar material

(G-20171)
SCHMID TOOL & ENGINEERING CORP
930 N Villa Ave (60181-1140)
PHONE..................630 333-1733
Nancy Schmid, *President*
Heidi Schaefer, *Vice Pres*
Eric Schmid, *Vice Pres*
Alexander Arov, *Engineer*
EMP: 25 EST: 1946
SQ FT: 11,600
SALES: 40.5MM **Privately Held**
WEB: www.schmidtool.com
SIC: 3599 3549 3462 3452 Machine shop, jobbing & repair; metalworking machinery; iron & steel forgings; bolts, nuts, rivets & washers

(G-20172)
SIGN A RAMA INC
Also Called: Sign-A-Rama
100 E Roosevelt Rd Ste 34 (60181-3529)
PHONE..................630 359-5125
Steve Peterson, *Branch Mgr*
EMP: 5 **Privately Held**
SIC: 3993 Signs & advertising specialties
HQ: Sign A Rama Inc.
2121 Vista Pkwy
West Palm Beach FL 33411
561 640-5570

(G-20173)
SIR COOPER INC
203 W Saint Charles Rd (60181-2402)
PHONE..................630 279-0162
EMP: 6
SALES (est): 500K **Privately Held**
SIC: 2759 Commercial Printing

(G-20174)
SUBURBAN DRIVELINE INC
Also Called: Suburban Drive Line
747 W North Ave (60181-1322)
PHONE..................630 941-7101
Phil Floral, *President*
Rosemarie Floral, *Corp Secy*
EMP: 8
SQ FT: 3,000
SALES (est): 1.2MM **Privately Held**
SIC: 3714 5013 Drive shafts, motor vehicle; automotive supplies & parts

(G-20175)
UXM STUDIO INC
707 N Iowa Ave (60181-1510)
P.O. Box 13010, Chicago (60613-0010)
PHONE..................773 359-1333
Marc Cain, *President*
Scott Goldberg, *Treasurer*
Christopher Anderson, *Admin Sec*
EMP: 7 EST: 2015

SALES (est): 292.9K **Privately Held**
SIC: 7372 7371 Application computer software; custom computer programming services

(G-20176)
WHEATLAND CSTM CBNTRY WDWKG LL
228 W Ridge Rd (60181-1551)
PHONE..................630 359-8553
Brent M Hyland,
EMP: 5
SALES (est): 59.5K **Privately Held**
SIC: 2434 1751 Wood kitchen cabinets; cabinet & finish carpentry

(G-20177)
WRECK ROOM INC
207 W Saint Charles Rd (60181-2402)
PHONE..................630 530-2166
Don Murphy, *President*
EMP: 11
SQ FT: 10,000
SALES (est): 2MM **Privately Held**
SIC: 3061 7549 7532 5013 Automotive rubber goods (mechanical); emissions testing without repairs, automotive; inspection & diagnostic service, automotive; paint shop, automotive; body shop, automotive; body repair or paint shop supplies, automotive

Village of Lakewood
Mchenry County

(G-20178)
DVA MAYDAY CORPORATION
8108 Redtail Dr (60014-3324)
PHONE..................847 848-7555
Michael May, *President*
EMP: 1 EST: 2012
SQ FT: 1,500
SALES (est): 2MM **Privately Held**
SIC: 3646 3433 Commercial indusl & institutional electric lighting fixtures; solar heaters & collectors

(G-20179)
PERSPECTO MAP COMPANY INC
367 Cumberland Ln (60014-5507)
P.O. Box 1288, Crystal Lake (60039-1288)
PHONE..................815 356-1288
Teresa Conrad, *President*
EMP: 5
SQ FT: 500
SALES (est): 150K **Privately Held**
SIC: 2741 Atlas, map & guide publishing

Viola
Mercer County

(G-20180)
MIDWEST FIBRE PRODUCTS INC
2819 95th Ave (61486-9527)
P.O. Box 397 (61486-0397)
PHONE..................309 596-2955
Joseph Di Lulio, *President*
Joseph Di Iulio, *President*
Elizabeth Joan Di Iulio, *Corp Secy*
Pete Di Iulio, *Vice Pres*
Elizabeth Di Iulio, *Treasurer*
EMP: 35 EST: 1962
SQ FT: 44,000
SALES (est): 8.4MM **Privately Held**
WEB: www.midwestfibreproducts.com
SIC: 2653 3161 2657 Boxes, corrugated: made from purchased materials; boxes, solid fiber: made from purchased materials; luggage; folding paperboard boxes

(G-20181)
P R MANUFACTURING CO
2650 85th Ave (61486-9585)
P.O. Box 308 (61486-0308)
PHONE..................309 596-2986
Ron Mayne, *Owner*
Paul Tompkins, *Vice Pres*
EMP: 8 EST: 2011

SALES (est): 1.4MM **Privately Held**
SIC: 3599 Machine shop, jobbing & repair

(G-20182)
PAUL & RON MANUFACTURING INC
2650 85th Ave (61486-9585)
P.O. Box 308 (61486-0308)
PHONE..................309 596-2986
Ronald E Mayne, *President*
Paul Tompkins, *Vice Pres*
Sherri Crow, *Admin Sec*
EMP: 13
SALES (est): 1.7MM **Privately Held**
SIC: 3599 Machine shop, jobbing & repair

(G-20183)
VIOLA ICE CREAM SHOPPE
Also Called: Milkhouse Diner
1003 13th St (61486-9437)
PHONE..................309 596-2131
Cheryl Naynard, *President*
EMP: 9
SALES (est): 312.9K **Privately Held**
SIC: 2024 Ice cream & frozen desserts

Virden
Macoupin County

(G-20184)
FIVE STAR PRINTING INC
Also Called: Gold Market Publications
169 W Jackson St (62690-1269)
P.O. Box 440 (62690-0440)
PHONE..................217 965-3355
Martin Jones, *President*
Nathan Jones, *Vice Pres*
Norris Jones, *Vice Pres*
Chris Schmitt, *Treasurer*
Joe Michlich, *Admin Sec*
EMP: 9
SQ FT: 2,500
SALES (est): 680K **Privately Held**
SIC: 2752 Commercial printing, offset

(G-20185)
GOLD NUGGET PUBLICATIONS INC (PA)
Also Called: Virden Recorder
169 W Jackson St (62690-1269)
P.O. Box 440 (62690-0440)
PHONE..................217 965-3355
Dorothy A Jones, *Publisher*
Julie J Westerhausen, *Business Mgr*
Norris Jones, *Vice Pres*
Martin Jones, *Vice Pres*
Nathan Jones, *Vice Pres*
EMP: 30 EST: 1866
SQ FT: 4,000
SALES (est): 1.9MM **Privately Held**
WEB: www.gnnews.net
SIC: 2711 5943 Newspapers: publishing only, not printed on site; office forms & supplies

(G-20186)
INKORPORATED DESIGNS
423 N Springfield St (62690-1439)
PHONE..................217 965-4653
Rob Miller, *Owner*
EMP: 3
SALES (est): 228.2K **Privately Held**
SIC: 2759 Screen printing

(G-20187)
LUMBERYARD SUPPLIERS INC
Also Called: Truss Slater
700 S Springfield St (62690-1600)
PHONE..................217 965-4911
Cathy Slater, *Vice Pres*
Douglas Slater, *Manager*
EMP: 40
SALES (corp-wide): 64.4MM **Privately Held**
SIC: 2439 5211 2435 Trusses, except roof: laminated lumber; trusses, wooden roof; planing mill products & lumber; hardwood veneer & plywood
PA: Lumberyard Suppliers, Inc.
300 Pinecrest Dr
East Peoria IL 61611
309 694-4356

(G-20188)
MASTER ENGRAVING
246 E Dean St (62690-1402)
PHONE..................217 965-5885
Rick Roberts, *Owner*
EMP: 3 EST: 2000
SALES (est): 231.5K **Privately Held**
SIC: 2789 2759 Bookbinding & related work; invitation & stationery printing & engraving

(G-20189)
ROYER SYSTEMS INC
Also Called: Royell Communications
427 W Dean St (62690-1335)
PHONE..................217 965-3699
Joseph Royer, *President*
Debra Royer, *Vice Pres*
EMP: 6
SALES (est): 724.7K **Privately Held**
SIC: 3571 4813 Electronic computers;

Virgil
Kane County

(G-20190)
C S O CORP (PA)
Also Called: Sauber Mfg. Co.
10 N Sauber Rd (60151-1001)
PHONE..................630 365-6600
Charles J Sauber, *CEO*
▲ EMP: 85
SQ FT: 90,000
SALES (est): 37.3MM **Privately Held**
SIC: 5082 3531 3713 Construction & mining machinery; construction machinery attachments; truck bodies (motor vehicles)

(G-20191)
SAUBER MANUFACTURING COMPANY
10 N Sauber Rd (60151-1001)
PHONE..................630 365-6600
Charles J Sauber, *CEO*
Jim Sauber, *President*
Julio Ortega, *Engineer*
Eddy Quintero, *Project Leader*
Ted Smith, *Project Leader*
EMP: 85
SQ FT: 90,000
SALES (est): 13.5MM
SALES (corp-wide): 37.3MM **Privately Held**
WEB: www.saubermfg.com
SIC: 3531 3713 5082 Construction machinery attachments; truck bodies (motor vehicles); construction & mining machinery
PA: C S O, Corp.
10 N Sauber Rd
Virgil IL 60151
630 365-6600

Virginia
Cass County

(G-20192)
BPS FUELS INC
352 N Morgan St (62691-1373)
P.O. Box 1263, Bloomington (61702-1263)
PHONE..................217 452-7608
Lois Dotzert, *Manager*
EMP: 4 EST: 2010
SALES (est): 388.1K **Privately Held**
SIC: 2869 Fuels

(G-20193)
CASS MEATS
5815 Il Route 78 (62691-1398)
PHONE..................217 452-3072
Frank Bell, *Owner*
EMP: 4 EST: 1977
SQ FT: 2,000
SALES (est): 140K **Privately Held**
SIC: 0751 2011 5421 2013 Slaughtering: custom livestock services; meat packing plants; meat markets, including freezer provisioners; sausages & other prepared meats

Virginia - Cass County (G-20194) GEOGRAPHIC SECTION

(G-20194)
KATHYS KITCHEN LLC
201 N Pitt St (62691-1000)
PHONE..................217 452-3035
Daryl Keylor, *Owner*
Kathy Keylor, *Co-Owner*
EMP: 4
SALES: 105K **Privately Held**
SIC: **2035** Pickles, sauces & salad dressings

(G-20195)
PRECISION TANK & EQUIPMENT CO (PA)
3503 Conover Rd (62691-8013)
P.O. Box 20 (62691-0020)
PHONE..................217 452-7228
David Hemmimg, *CEO*
Ron Swearingen, *Vice Pres*
Paul Sabelhaus, *Plant Mgr*
Vernon E Ames, *Project Mgr*
Brent Hicks, *CFO*
▲ EMP: 80
SQ FT: 25,000
SALES (est): 25.4MM **Privately Held**
WEB: www.precisiontank.com
SIC: **3443** Fabricated plate work (boiler shop)

Volo
Lake County

(G-20196)
BIOGREEN ORGANICS INC
30937 N Gilmer Rd (60073-9525)
PHONE..................847 740-9637
Dan Neilson, *President*
EMP: 5
SALES (est): 740K **Privately Held**
SIC: **2875** 0782 2873 Fertilizers, mixing only; lawn care services; nitrogenous fertilizers

(G-20197)
CHICAGO SEA RAY INC
31535 N Us Highway 12 (60073-9773)
PHONE..................815 385-2720
Mike Pretasky Sr, *President*
Dennis Ellerbrock, *VP Opers*
▼ EMP: 33
SQ FT: 66,000
SALES (est): 4.8MM **Privately Held**
WEB: www.skipperbuds.com
SIC: **5551** 5941 5699 3732 Motor boat dealers; outboard motors; marine supplies; skiing equipment; sports apparel; boat building & repairing

(G-20198)
COMPOSITE CUTTER TECH INC
Also Called: C C T
31632 N Ellis Dr Unit 210 (60073-9673)
PHONE..................847 740-6875
Rachel Cuillo, *President*
Rachel Ciullo, *President*
EMP: 9
SALES (est): 1.2MM **Privately Held**
SIC: **3541** 3545 3451 Machine tools, metal cutting: exotic (explosive, etc.); cutting tools for machine tools; screw machine products

(G-20199)
J AND K MOLDING
31632 N Ellis Dr Unit 201 (60073-9672)
PHONE..................224 276-3355
EMP: 3
SALES (est): 295.8K **Privately Held**
SIC: **3089** Molding primary plastic

(G-20200)
KENNETH W TEMPLEMAN
382 Minuet Cir (60073-5917)
PHONE..................847 912-2740
Kenneth Templeman, *Principal*
EMP: 2
SALES (est): 217.1K **Privately Held**
SIC: **3499** 7692 7389 Fabricated metal products; welding repair;

(G-20201)
KOENEMANN SAUSAGE CO
27090 Volo Village Rd (60073-9669)
PHONE..................815 385-6260
William F Koenemann, *President*
Hilde M Koenemann, *Vice Pres*
Gerlinde M Koenemann, *Admin Sec*
EMP: 9
SQ FT: 20,000
SALES (est): 3.2MM **Privately Held**
WEB: www.koenemannsausage.com
SIC: **5141** 5411 2013 Groceries, general line; grocery stores, independent; sausages & other prepared meats

(G-20202)
LAKE ELECTRONICS INC
31632 N Ellis Dr Unit 203 (60073-9672)
PHONE..................847 201-1270
Pat Sahay, *President*
Jeff Wisniewski, *Vice Pres*
EMP: 15
SQ FT: 6,000
SALES (est): 2.8MM **Privately Held**
SIC: **3823** Computer interface equipment for industrial process control

(G-20203)
MARINE TECHNOLOGIES INC
Also Called: M T I Industries
31632 N Ellis Dr Unit 301 (60073-9673)
PHONE..................847 546-9001
Thomas Wisniewski, *President*
Sandra Wisniewski, *Corp Secy*
▲ EMP: 20
SQ FT: 8,000
SALES (est): 4.3MM **Privately Held**
SIC: **3669** 3812 Emergency alarms; burglar alarm apparatus, electric; smoke detectors; search & detection systems & instruments; detection apparatus: electronic/magnetic field, light/heat

(G-20204)
MOBOTREX INC
31632 N Ellis Dr Unit 305 (60073-9673)
PHONE..................847 546-1616
Paul Leddy, *Branch Mgr*
EMP: 4
SALES (corp-wide): 26.4MM **Privately Held**
SIC: **3669** Traffic signals, electric
PA: Mobotrex, Inc.
109 W 55th St
Davenport IA 52806
563 323-0009

(G-20205)
RCC CONVEYORS INC
31632 N Ellis Dr Unit 105 (60073-9672)
PHONE..................224 338-8841
Roland Malschafsky, *President*
EMP: 3
SALES (est): 189.6K **Privately Held**
WEB: www.rccc-usa.com
SIC: **3559** Automotive related machinery

(G-20206)
WOLD PRINTING SERVICES LTD
26639 W Commerce Dr # 402 (60073-9639)
PHONE..................847 546-3110
Terrill Wold, *President*
Cris Wold, *Vice Pres*
Tim Wold, *Vice Pres*
Scott Wold, *Manager*
Chris Wold, *Officer*
EMP: 8
SQ FT: 1,000
SALES: 1MM **Privately Held**
SIC: **2752** 2759 2732 Commercial printing, offset; commercial printing; book printing

Wadsworth
Lake County

(G-20207)
15679 WADSWORTH INC
15679 W Wadsworth Rd (60083-9125)
PHONE..................847 662-4561
EMP: 5 EST: 2004
SALES (est): 460K **Privately Held**
SIC: **1321** Natural Gas Liquids Production

(G-20208)
CENTURY KITCHEN & BATH INC
Also Called: Donato Remodeling
39133 N Us Highway 41 (60083-8915)
PHONE..................847 395-3418
Steven J Donato, *President*
EMP: 4
SALES (est): 498.2K **Privately Held**
SIC: **2434** Wood kitchen cabinets

(G-20209)
FERRITE INTERNATIONAL COMPANY
Also Called: TSC Ferrite International
39105 Magnetics Blvd (60083-8914)
P.O. Box 399 (60083-0399)
PHONE..................847 249-4900
Tempel Smith Jr, *President*
▲ EMP: 47
SALES (est): 8.3MM **Privately Held**
SIC: **3612** Specialty transformers

(G-20210)
LAKE COUNTY TOOL WORKS NORTH
15986 Hwy 173 (60083)
P.O. Box 280 (60083-0280)
PHONE..................847 662-4542
Peter Dodich, *President*
EMP: 4
SALES (est): 374.5K **Privately Held**
SIC: **8711** 3599 3544 Engineering services; machine shop, jobbing & repair; special dies, tools, jigs & fixtures

(G-20211)
PERSONALIZED PILLOWS CO
16783 W Old Orchard Dr (60083-9608)
PHONE..................847 226-7393
Ann-Marie Burke, *Owner*
EMP: 3
SALES (est): 100K **Privately Held**
SIC: **2392** Pillowcases: made from purchased materials

(G-20212)
R & L TRUCK SERVICE INC
39935 N Prairie View Dr (60083-9609)
PHONE..................847 489-7135
Ron Kelver, *President*
Laurie Kelver, *Manager*
EMP: 10
SALES (est): 1.5MM **Privately Held**
SIC: **3713** Truck & bus bodies

(G-20213)
ROYAL FABRICATORS INC
38360 N Cashmore Rd (60083-9718)
PHONE..................847 775-7466
Royal Rockow, *President*
Judy Rockow, *Corp Secy*
EMP: 17
SQ FT: 7,200
SALES (est): 2.1MM **Privately Held**
SIC: **2541** 2434 2542 2511 Counter & sink tops; cabinets, except refrigerated: show, display, etc.: wood; wood kitchen cabinets; partitions & fixtures, except wood; wood household furniture

(G-20214)
TSC INTERNATIONAL INC
Also Called: TSC Ferrite International
39105 Magnetics Blvd (60083-8914)
P.O. Box 399 (60083-0399)
PHONE..................847 249-4900
Tempel Smith, *President*
Tim Olrick, *Admin Sec*
EMP: 12
SALES (est): 2MM **Privately Held**
SIC: **3499** Magnetic shields, metal

(G-20215)
WEDGEWOOD
4555 W York House Rd (60083-9127)
PHONE..................847 672-4497
John Zaruk, *President*
EMP: 3
SALES (est): 60.7K **Privately Held**
WEB: www.wedgewoodweddings.com
SIC: **2499** Wood products

Walnut
Bureau County

(G-20216)
AVANTI FOODS COMPANY
Also Called: Gino's Pizza
109 Depot St (61376)
P.O. Box 457 (61376-0457)
PHONE..................815 379-2155
Anthony Zueger, *President*
Robert Linley, *Corp Secy*
EMP: 45 EST: 1955
SQ FT: 100,000
SALES (est): 7.6MM **Privately Held**
WEB: www.avantifoods.com
SIC: **2022** 2038 5149 Natural cheese; pizza, frozen; pizza supplies

(G-20217)
EBE INDUSTRIAL LLC
507 W North St (61376-9495)
P.O. Box 160 (61376-0160)
PHONE..................815 379-2400
Rick Omalley, *Engineer*
Tom Schuler, *CFO*
Mark Ebersole,
EMP: 15
SALES (est): 2.8MM **Privately Held**
SIC: **3542** Riveting machines

(G-20218)
GBH WALNUT INC (PA)
300 Wyanet Rd (61376)
P.O. Box 605 (61376-0605)
PHONE..................815 379-2151
Charles Gonigam, *President*
Gary L Erickson, *Vice Pres*
Ken Johnson, *Regl Sales Mgr*
Charles Gonigan, *Info Tech Mgr*
Roxanne J March, *Admin Sec*
EMP: 65
SALES (est): 10.7MM **Privately Held**
SIC: **2452** Prefabricated buildings, wood

(G-20219)
MAINSTREAM RENEWABLE POWER
108 Jackson St (61376-8922)
PHONE..................815 379-2784
EMP: 3
SALES (est): 118.7K **Privately Held**
SIC: **3511** Turbines & turbine generator sets

(G-20220)
TRICON INDS MFG & EQP SLS
Also Called: TCI Manufacturing & Eqp Sls
28524 1250 E St (61376)
P.O. Box 306 (61376-0306)
PHONE..................815 379-2090
Michael Maynard, *President*
Carolyn Thompson, *Admin Sec*
◆ EMP: 40
SQ FT: 26,000
SALES (est): 21.5MM **Privately Held**
WEB: www.tcimfg.com
SIC: **3535** Conveyors & conveying equipment

(G-20221)
WALNUT CUSTOM HOMES INC
300 Wyanet Rd (61376)
P.O. Box 605 (61376-0605)
PHONE..................815 379-2151
Gary Erickson, *VP Prdtn*
Sharon L Free, *Nurse*
EMP: 40
SALES (corp-wide): 10.7MM **Privately Held**
SIC: **3441** Building components, structural steel
PA: Gbh Walnut, Inc.
300 Wyanet Rd
Walnut IL 61376
815 379-2151

Walnut Hill
Marion County

(G-20222)
SCHWARTZ OILFIELD SERVICES (PA)
501 Schwartz Rd (62893-1039)
P.O. Box Ac, Centralia (62801-9163)
PHONE..............................618 532-0232
Tony Schwartz, *President*
EMP: 11
SQ FT: 8,000
SALES (est): 2MM **Privately Held**
SIC: 1389 Oil field services

Warren
Jo Daviess County

(G-20223)
HONEYWELL INTERNATIONAL INC
814 Anson St (61087-9751)
PHONE..............................815 745-2131
Don Munz, *Principal*
EMP: 200
SALES (corp-wide): 36.7B **Publicly Held**
WEB: www.honeywell.com
SIC: 3643 3575 Electric switches; computer terminals
PA: Honeywell International Inc.
 300 S Tryon St
 Charlotte NC 28202
 704 627-6200

(G-20224)
SFC OF ILLINOIS INC
400 S Railroad St (61087-9428)
PHONE..............................815 745-2100
EMP: 50 **EST:** 1932
SQ FT: 32,000
SALES (est): 7.9MM **Privately Held**
SIC: 3621 3825 3566 Mfg Motors/Generators Mfg Elec Measuring Instr Mfg Speed Changer/Drives

(G-20225)
STABLE BEGINNING CORPORATION
Also Called: Carter Motor Company
400 S Railroad St (61087-9428)
P.O. Box 647 (61087-0647)
PHONE..............................815 745-2100
Keith Geisler, *President*
Roxanne Geisler, *Vice Pres*
EMP: 25
SQ FT: 30,000
SALES (est): 1.4MM **Privately Held**
SIC: 3621 Electric motor & generator parts

Warrensburg
Macon County

(G-20226)
CROWN CORK & SEAL USA INC
970 W North St (62573-9700)
PHONE..............................217 672-3533
Jerry Nelson, *Manager*
EMP: 59
SALES (corp-wide): 11.6B **Publicly Held**
SIC: 3411 Metal cans
HQ: Crown Cork & Seal Usa, Inc.
 770 Township Line Rd # 100
 Yardley PA 19067
 215 698-5100

(G-20227)
PW SERVICES LLC
390 W North St (62573)
P.O. Box 260 (62573-0260)
PHONE..............................217 672-3225
Jeremy M Phillips, *Mng Member*
EMP: 7
SALES (est): 1.8MM **Privately Held**
WEB: www.pwservicesllc.com
SIC: 3443 5075 Heat exchangers, plate type; heat exchangers

Warrenville
Dupage County

(G-20228)
ACTION SCREEN PRINT INC
30 W 260 Bttrfeld Rd Ste (60555)
P.O. Box 827 (60555-0827)
PHONE..............................630 393-1990
Alan Arrighi, *President*
Dana Arrighi, *Vice Pres*
EMP: 11
SQ FT: 5,000
SALES (est): 1.1MM **Privately Held**
WEB: www.actionscreen.com
SIC: 2395 2396 Embroidery products, except schiffli machine; fabric printing & stamping

(G-20229)
ADVANCED BIONICS LLC
4520 Weaver Pkwy (60555-3914)
PHONE..............................708 946-3406
EMP: 3
SALES (est): 146.8K **Privately Held**
SIC: 3842 Surgical appliances & supplies

(G-20230)
AMETEK INC
Also Called: Ametek Power Instruments
27755 Diehl Rd Ste 300 (60555-4035)
PHONE..............................630 621-3121
Tony Ciampitti, *President*
Frank Kay, *Opers Mgr*
Sanjay Jivani, *Engineer*
Berny Pazos, *Engineer*
Ewa Hartsfield, *Manager*
EMP: 50
SALES: 2MM
SALES (corp-wide): 5.1B **Publicly Held**
SIC: 3823 Industrial instrmnts msrmnt display/control process variable
PA: Ametek, Inc.
 1100 Cassatt Rd
 Berwyn PA 19312
 610 647-2121

(G-20231)
ARROWHEAD BRICK PAVERS INC
30w218 Bttrfeld Rd Unit A (60555)
PHONE..............................630 393-1584
Michael Borsuk, *President*
Mark Dalki, *Vice Pres*
Jamie Mayorga, *Vice Pres*
EMP: 32
SQ FT: 5,000
SALES (est): 2.7MM **Privately Held**
SIC: 3251 Paving brick, clay

(G-20232)
BP AMERICA INC (HQ)
4101 Winfield Rd Ste 200 (60555-3523)
PHONE..............................630 420-5111
H Lamar McKay, *Ch of Bd*
Susan Dio, *President*
Orlando Alvarez, *Vice Pres*
Bradley Anderson, *Vice Pres*
James Cunningham, *Vice Pres*
◆ **EMP:** 2000
SALES (est): 19.8B
SALES (corp-wide): 278.4B **Privately Held**
WEB: www.bp.com
SIC: 2911 5171 4612 4613 Petroleum refining; petroleum bulk stations & terminals; crude petroleum pipelines; refined petroleum pipelines; deep sea domestic transportation of freight
PA: Bp P.L.C.
 1 St. James's Square
 London SW1Y
 207 496-4000

(G-20233)
CONLEY STEEL INC
3s710 Mignin Dr (60555-3515)
PHONE..............................630 393-1193
William Conley Sr, *Owner*
EMP: 2
SALES (est): 239.1K **Privately Held**
SIC: 3441 Fabricated structural metal

(G-20234)
DONNELLEY FINANCIAL LLC
Also Called: Donnelley Financial Solutions
4101 Winfield Rd (60555-3521)
PHONE..............................630 963-9494
EMP: 5
SALES (corp-wide): 874.7MM **Publicly Held**
SIC: 2752 Commercial printing, lithographic
HQ: Donnelley Financial, Llc
 35 W Wacker Dr
 Chicago IL 60601
 844 866-4337

(G-20235)
DRAGON DIE MOLD INC
30w250 Butterfield Rd # 311 (60555-1568)
PHONE..............................630 836-0699
Joe Kotvan, *President*
EMP: 4 **EST:** 1995
SALES (est): 446.7K **Privately Held**
SIC: 3544 Industrial molds

(G-20236)
FROMM AIRPAD INC
3s320 Rockwell St (60555-2919)
PHONE..............................630 393-9790
Eugene Gerhardstein, *President*
Frank Whitney, *Superintendent*
Olga K Gerhardstein, *Corp Secy*
Tom Gerhardstein, *Vice Pres*
▲ **EMP:** 10
SQ FT: 6,000
SALES (est): 2.8MM **Privately Held**
SIC: 5084 5199 3565 Packaging machinery & equipment; packaging materials; packaging machinery

(G-20237)
FUEL TECH INC (PA)
27601 Bella Vista Pkwy (60555-1617)
PHONE..............................630 845-4500
Vincent J Arnone, *Ch of Bd*
Brad Johnson, *Counsel*
William E Cummings Jr, *Senior VP*
Albert G Grigonis, *Senior VP*
James M Pach, *CFO*
◆ **EMP:** 116
SQ FT: 40,000
SALES: 30.4MM **Publicly Held**
WEB: www.ftek.com
SIC: 3564 3823 Air purification equipment; boiler controls: industrial, power & marine type

(G-20238)
HEICO HOLDING INC (PA)
27501 Bella Vista Pkwy (60555-1609)
PHONE..............................630 353-5100
Michael E Heisley, *President*
E A Roskovensky, *Exec VP*
Donna Petrusha, *Manager*
Stanley H Meadows, *Admin Sec*
Terence Rogers, *Admin Sec*
◆ **EMP:** 35 **EST:** 1937
SQ FT: 45,000
SALES (est): 1.2B **Privately Held**
WEB: www.heicocompanies.com
SIC: 3559 Automotive related machinery

(G-20239)
ISBIR BULK BAG USA LLC
27475 Ferry Rd (60555-3808)
PHONE..............................972 722-9200
Tuncer Ertoklar, *Exec Dir*
Kursat Saatci,
▲ **EMP:** 2
SALES: 5.1MM **Privately Held**
SIC: 5199 5999 2673 Packaging materials; packaging materials: boxes, padding, etc.; bags: plastic, laminated & coated
HQ: Isbir Sentetik Dokuma Sanayi Anonim Sirketi
 No:29 Cayirhisar Mahallesi
 Balikesir 10185

(G-20240)
KLEEN CUT TOOL INC
30w250 Bttrfeld Rd Unit 3 (60555)
PHONE..............................630 447-7020
Mark E Wujciga, *President*
EMP: 6 **EST:** 1961
SQ FT: 4,000
SALES (est): 800K **Privately Held**
SIC: 3544 3469 Special dies & tools; metal stampings

(G-20241)
KSM ELECTRONICS INC
Also Called: Ksm Electronics Midwest
27745 Diehl Rd (60555-3998)
PHONE..............................630 393-9310
Len Partyka, *Branch Mgr*
EMP: 200
SALES (corp-wide): 52.8MM **Privately Held**
SIC: 3629 3679 Static elimination equipment, industrial; harness assemblies for electronic use: wire or cable
PA: Ksm Electronics, Inc.
 5607 Hiatus Rd Ste 600
 Tamarac FL 33321
 954 642-7050

(G-20242)
M H ELECTRIC MOTOR & CTRL CORP
30w250 Calumet Ave W (60555-1516)
PHONE..............................630 393-3736
Michael Holz, *President*
Michael H Holz, *Vice Pres*
Phil Lafayette, *Prgrmr*
EMP: 6
SQ FT: 10,000
SALES (est): 941.8K **Privately Held**
SIC: 7694 5999 Electric motor repair; motors, electric

(G-20243)
OHMITE HOLDING LLC (HQ)
Also Called: Ohmite Manufacturing
27501 Bella Vista Pkwy (60555-1609)
PHONE..............................847 258-0300
Greg Pace, *President*
Derran Smith, *Vice Pres*
Bill McCormick, *Purch Mgr*
Jamie Savino, *Purchasing*
Alex Herrera, *Engineer*
▲ **EMP:** 30
SQ FT: 250,000
SALES (est): 87MM **Privately Held**
SIC: 3625 5065 Resistors & resistor units; rheostats; industrial electrical relays & switches; resistors, electronic; electronic parts

(G-20244)
PETTIBONE LLC (HQ)
Also Called: An Affliate of Heico Companies
27501 Bella Vista Pkwy (60555-1609)
PHONE..............................630 353-5000
Michael E Heisley Sr, *Ch of Bd*
El Roskovensky, *President*
Douglas J Johnson, *Vice Pres*
Dawn O'Connell, *Vice Pres*
Derran Smith, *Vice Pres*
◆ **EMP:** 16
SQ FT: 12,357
SALES (est): 492MM
SALES (corp-wide): 1.2B **Privately Held**
SIC: 3559 Automotive related machinery
PA: Heico Holding, Inc.
 27501 Bella Vista Pkwy
 Warrenville IL 60555
 630 353-5100

(G-20245)
PHONAK LLC (DH)
4520 Weaver Pkwy Ste 1 (60555-4027)
PHONE..............................630 821-5000
Mark A Sanger, *President*
Dipak Aher, *General Mgr*
William Lesiecki, *General Mgr*
Michael Jacobi, *Principal*
Tom Cardosi, *Regional Mgr*
▲ **EMP:** 600
SALES: 206.3MM
SALES (corp-wide): 2.7B **Privately Held**
SIC: 3842 5999 Hearing aids; hearing aids
HQ: Sonova Ag
 Laubisrutistrasse 28
 StAfa ZH 8712
 589 280-101

(G-20246)
PLYMOUTH TUBE COMPANY (PA)
29w 150 Warrenville Rd (60555)
PHONE..............................630 393-3550

Warrenville - Dupage County (G-20247)

Donald C Van Pelt Jr, *Ch of Bd*
Donald C Van Pelt Sr, *Ch of Bd*
David Crouch, *General Mgr*
Tom Centa, *Vice Pres*
Ajay Ramaswami, *Vice Pres*
◆ **EMP:** 50 **EST:** 1924
SQ FT: 10,000
SALES (est): 221.4MM **Privately Held**
WEB: www.plymouth.com
SIC: 3317 3354 Tubes, seamless steel; tubes, wrought: welded or lock joint; shapes, extruded aluminum; tube, extruded or drawn, aluminum

(G-20247)
PRECISE PRODUCTS INC
3s286 Talbot Ave (60555-1544)
P.O. Box 310 (60555-0310)
PHONE.................................630 393-9698
Ernest Tucker, *President*
Robert Goblet, *Vice Pres*
◆ **EMP:** 40 **EST:** 1966
SQ FT: 10,000
SALES (est): 8.9MM **Privately Held**
WEB: www.preciseproductsinc.com
SIC: 3451 Screw machine products

(G-20248)
PREMIUM TEST EQUIPMENT CORP
30 W 270 Butterfield (60555)
PHONE.................................630 400-2681
Jeffrey Newman, *President*
EMP: 3
SALES (est): 331.3K **Privately Held**
SIC: 3825 Test equipment for electronic & electric measurement

(G-20249)
PREZIOSIO LTD
Also Called: East Side Cafe
30 W 270 Butterfield Rd D (60555)
PHONE.................................630 393-0920
Anthony Preziosio, *President*
Julie Preziosio, *Vice Pres*
Peggy Preziosio, *Treasurer*
Fred J Preziosio, *Admin Sec*
EMP: 11
SALES (est): 1.7MM **Privately Held**
SIC: 2038 Pizza, frozen

(G-20250)
PROCESS TECHNOLOGIES GROUP
Also Called: PTG Impax
30w106 Butterfield Rd (60555-1563)
PHONE.................................630 393-4777
Jerrold McCabe, *President*
Jerrold Mc Cabe, *President*
Ed Evensen, *Vice Pres*
EMP: 8
SQ FT: 5,000
SALES (est): 300K **Privately Held**
SIC: 3625 5084 3823 Relays & industrial controls; instruments & control equipment; industrial instrmnts msrmnt display/control process variable

(G-20251)
R R DONNELLEY & SONS COMPANY
Also Called: R R Donnelley
4101 Winfield Rd Ste 100 (60555-3522)
PHONE.................................630 322-6268
Tom Carroll, *Officer*
EMP: 730
SALES (corp-wide): 6.2B **Publicly Held**
SIC: 2752 Commercial printing, lithographic
PA: R. R. Donnelley & Sons Company
35 W Wacker Dr
Chicago IL 60601
312 326-8000

(G-20252)
ROBAL COMPANY INC
Also Called: B & H Industries
30 W 250th Butterfield304 (60555)
PHONE.................................630 393-0777
Jim Hurckes, *Partner*
EMP: 10
SALES (est): 420.6K
SALES (corp-wide): 15MM **Privately Held**
SIC: 7334 2789 2759 Blueprinting service; bookbinding & related work; commercial printing
PA: Robal Company, Inc.
80 W Seegers Rd
Arlington Heights IL 60005
847 593-3161

(G-20253)
TEXAS INSTRUMENTS INCORPORATED
27715 Diehl Rd (60555-3998)
PHONE.................................630 836-2827
John Bonfitto, *Design Engr*
Steve Anderson, *Branch Mgr*
EMP: 100
SALES (corp-wide): 14.3B **Publicly Held**
SIC: 3613 Switches, electric power except snap, push button, etc.; regulators, power
PA: Texas Instruments Incorporated
12500 Ti Blvd
Dallas TX 75243
214 479-3773

(G-20254)
TOX- PRESSOTECHNIK LLC
4250 Weaver Pkwy (60555-3924)
PHONE.................................630 447-4600
EMP: 7
SALES (corp-wide): 30MM **Privately Held**
SIC: 7699 3542 3545 Repair Services Mfg Machine Tools- Forming Mfg Machine Tool Accessories
PA: Tox- Pressotechnik L.L.C.
4250 Weaver Pkwy
Warrenville IL 60555
630 447-4600

(G-20255)
TRU-COLOUR PRODUCTS LLC
27575 Ferry Rd Fl 2 (60555-3862)
PHONE.................................630 447-0559
Toby Meisenheimer, *CEO*
EMP: 5
SQ FT: 4,000
SALES (est): 303.8K **Privately Held**
SIC: 2211 Bandage cloths, cotton

(G-20256)
TWO BROTHERS BREWING COMPANY
30w315 Calumet Ave W (60555-1565)
PHONE.................................630 393-2337
Jason Ebel, *President*
Gabe Nanni, *General Mgr*
Jeremy Bigelow, *Regional Mgr*
James V Ebel II, *Vice Pres*
▲ **EMP:** 7 **EST:** 1996
SQ FT: 10,000
SALES (est): 2.6MM **Privately Held**
WEB: www.twobrothersbrewing.com
SIC: 5921 2095 5812 Wine & beer; roasted coffee; family restaurants

(G-20257)
WOODLAND FENCE FOREST PDTS INC
3 S 264 Hc 59 (60555)
PHONE.................................630 393-2220
Stewart Aschauer, *President*
Stuart Aschauer, *President*
EMP: 4
SQ FT: 1,200
SALES (est): 516K **Privately Held**
SIC: 5941 5211 1799 3949 Playground equipment; fencing; fence construction; sporting & athletic goods; miscellaneous fabricated wire products

Warsaw
Hancock County

(G-20258)
MIDWEST MKTG/PDCTN MFG CO
Also Called: Realty World
521 Main St (62379-1248)
PHONE.................................217 256-3414
Steven C Siegrist, *Owner*
James S Clinton, *Principal*
EMP: 1
SQ FT: 25,000
SALES (est): 206K **Privately Held**
SIC: 6531 2449 Real estate agent, residential; containers, plywood & veneer wood

(G-20259)
PRODUCTION MANUFACTURING
Also Called: Production Engineering
305 Main St (62379-1244)
PHONE.................................217 256-4211
Kenneth Jones, *Owner*
EMP: 3
SQ FT: 15,000
SALES: 200K **Privately Held**
SIC: 3599 2449 7692 3444 Machine shop, jobbing & repair; containers, plywood & veneer wood; welding repair; sheet metalwork; metal barrels, drums & pails

Wasco
Kane County

(G-20260)
ARGO MANUFACTURING CO
4n944 Old Lafox Rd (60183-8000)
P.O. Box 359 (60183-0359)
PHONE.................................630 377-1750
Ken Mitson, *President*
Darlene Mitson, *Corp Secy*
▲ **EMP:** 17 **EST:** 1952
SQ FT: 17,000
SALES (est): 3MM **Privately Held**
SIC: 3599 Custom machinery; machine shop, jobbing & repair

(G-20261)
PACE MACHINERY GROUP INC
4n944 Old Lafox Rd (60183-8000)
P.O. Box 359 (60183-0359)
PHONE.................................630 377-1750
Ken Mitson, *President*
Darlene Mitson, *Corp Secy*
▲ **EMP:** 15
SQ FT: 20,000
SALES (est): 3.2MM **Privately Held**
SIC: 3545 Tools & accessories for machine tools

Washburn
Marshall County

(G-20262)
ALVAR INC
112 State Route 89 (61570-9767)
PHONE.................................309 248-7523
Arthur F Lersch, *President*
Martha Kyle Allen, *Admin Sec*
▲ **EMP:** 15
SQ FT: 21,000
SALES (est): 5.1MM **Privately Held**
SIC: 2851 Varnishes; intaglio ink vehicle

(G-20263)
GREBNER MACHINE & TOOL INC
1866 County Road 00 N (61570-9792)
PHONE.................................309 248-7768
Alvin A Grebner, *President*
Mike Grebner, *Treasurer*
Beth Grebner, *Admin Sec*
EMP: 4
SQ FT: 4,000
SALES (est): 200K **Privately Held**
SIC: 3599 Machine shop, jobbing & repair

(G-20264)
K B METAL COMPANY
1172 County Road 2100 N (61570-9366)
PHONE.................................309 248-7355
Don Kennell, *Managing Prtnr*
Bill Kennell, *Partner*
Lawrence Kennell, *Partner*
Nancy Kennell, *Partner*
EMP: 4
SALES (est): 388.9K **Privately Held**
SIC: 3444 Housings for business machines, sheet metal

Washington
Tazewell County

(G-20265)
ALLIANCE WHEEL SERVICES LLC
302 W Holland St (61571-2515)
PHONE.................................309 444-4334
Kevin Deany,
Robert Coup,
EMP: 4
SALES (est): 1.1MM **Privately Held**
SIC: 3743 Railroad equipment

(G-20266)
BAKER AVENUE INVESTMENTS INC
Also Called: Lincoln Office
205 Eastgate Dr (61571-9238)
PHONE.................................309 427-2500
William E Pape, *President*
Jerry Sweet, *CFO*
EMP: 55 **EST:** 2005
SALES (est): 1.7MM **Privately Held**
SIC: 1799 7389 5021 2273 Home/office interiors finishing, furnishing & remodeling; office furniture installation; interior design services; office & public building furniture; carpets & rugs; office furniture, except wood; tables, office: except wood; panel systems & partitions, office: except wood; office cabinets & filing drawers: except wood; personal holding companies, except banks

(G-20267)
BTD MANUFACTURING INC
118 Muller Rd (61571-2343)
PHONE.................................309 444-1268
Paul Gintner, *President*
Vijay Maddineni, *Engineer*
EMP: 14 **Publicly Held**
SIC: 3441 Fabricated structural metal
HQ: Btd Manufacturing, Inc.
1111 13th Ave Se
Detroit Lakes MN 56501
218 847-4446

(G-20268)
CATERPILLAR INC
28194 Caterpillar Ln (61571-9600)
P.O. Box 1895, Peoria (61656-1895)
PHONE.................................309 578-2086
EMP: 355
SALES (corp-wide): 53.8B **Publicly Held**
SIC: 3531 Construction machinery
PA: Caterpillar Inc.
510 Lake Cook Rd Ste 100
Deerfield IL 60015
224 551-4000

(G-20269)
COMET SUPPLY INC
312 Muller Rd (61571-2347)
P.O. Box 98 (61571-0098)
PHONE.................................309 444-2712
Wayne Pruss, *President*
EMP: 6
SQ FT: 20,000
SALES (est): 1.4MM **Privately Held**
WEB: www.cometsupply.com
SIC: 2992 Oils & greases, blending & compounding

(G-20270)
IPLASTICS LLC (PA)
Also Called: Illinois Valley Plastics
300 N Cummings Ln (61571-2198)
PHONE.................................309 444-8884
Daryl R Lindemann, *CEO*
Tom Williams, *Vice Pres*
▲ **EMP:** 81 **EST:** 1953
SQ FT: 52,000
SALES (est): 22.4MM **Privately Held**
WEB: www.ivplastics.com
SIC: 3089 3544 Injection molding of plastics; industrial molds

GEOGRAPHIC SECTION

(G-20271)
IVP PLASTICS OF MISSOURI LLC
300 N Cummings Ln (61571-2198)
PHONE.....................309 444-8884
EMP: 13 EST: 2015
SALES (est): 2.4MM Privately Held
SIC: 3089 Injection molding of plastics

(G-20272)
JAMES RANDALL
201 Monroe St (61571-1465)
PHONE.....................309 444-8765
James Randall, *Owner*
Rebecca Randall, *Co-Owner*
EMP: 7
SALES (est): 470.4K Privately Held
SIC: 2395 4212 Trucking, for the trade; local trucking, without storage

(G-20273)
LINCOLN OFFICE LLC (PA)
205 Eastgate Dr (61571-9238)
PHONE.....................309 427-2500
Bob Domnick, *CEO*
Tim Kaiser, *CFO*
Donna Pritchard, *Administration*
Kim Wessel, *Representative*
EMP: 52
SQ FT: 35,000
SALES (est): 19MM Privately Held
WEB: www.lincolnoffice.com
SIC: 2522 5021 1799 Office furniture, except wood; tables, office: except wood; panel systems & partitions, office: except wood; office cabinets & filing drawers: except wood; office furniture; home/office interiors finishing, furnishing & remodeling; office furniture installation

(G-20274)
M4 STEEL LLC
1208 Dorchester Ct (61571-3605)
PHONE.....................309 222-6027
Frank Mendoza, *Mng Member*
EMP: 1
SALES: 300K Privately Held
SIC: 3443 7389 Boiler & boiler shop work;

(G-20275)
MAXHEIMER CONSTRUCTION INC
Also Called: Maxco Ready Mix
25130 Schuck Rd (61571-9789)
PHONE.....................309 444-4200
Steven Maxheimer, *President*
EMP: 4
SQ FT: 3,000
SALES (est): 529.9K Privately Held
SIC: 3273 Ready-mixed concrete

(G-20276)
PRAIRIELAND PRINTING
Also Called: Prairieland Printing Spp
1237 Peoria St (61571-2352)
PHONE.....................309 647-5425
Carol A Reed, *Owner*
David Reed, *Co-Owner*
EMP: 5
SALES (est): 436K Privately Held
WEB: www.prairielandprinting.com
SIC: 7334 2789 2752 Photocopying & duplicating services; bookbinding & related work; commercial printing, lithographic

(G-20277)
PRO-LINE WINNING WAYS & PENLAN
2095 Washington Rd (61571-2059)
PHONE.....................309 745-8530
Paige Hirstein, *Owner*
EMP: 2
SALES (est): 237.3K Privately Held
SIC: 2844 3944 Shampoos, rinses, conditioners: hair; games, toys & children's vehicles

(G-20278)
PUBPAL LLC
25130 Schuck Rd (61571-9789)
PHONE.....................309 222-5062
Michael Maxheimer,
Josh Jacob,
EMP: 4

SALES: 1K Privately Held
SIC: 7372 Prepackaged software

(G-20279)
RICH PRODUCTS CORPORATION
1902 Cobblestone (61571-3429)
PHONE.....................309 886-2465
Todd High, *Branch Mgr*
EMP: 750
SALES (corp-wide): 5B Privately Held
SIC: 2053 Frozen bakery products, except bread
PA: Rich Products Corporation
1 Robert Rich Way
Buffalo NY 14213
716 878-8000

(G-20280)
SERVICE AUTO SUPPLY
Also Called: U-Haul
101 N Wood St (61571-2577)
PHONE.....................309 444-9704
Bill Donnager, *President*
EMP: 12
SQ FT: 6,500
SALES (est): 1.3MM Privately Held
SIC: 5531 3599 5261 7513 Automobile & truck equipment & parts; machine shop, jobbing & repair; garden tractors & tillers; truck rental & leasing, no drivers

(G-20281)
TEAM WORKS BY HOLZHAUER INC
2168 Washington Rd (61571-1954)
PHONE.....................309 745-9924
Kathleen Holzhauer, *President*
Roger Holzhauer, *Vice Pres*
EMP: 5
SALES: 550K Privately Held
SIC: 2396 Screen printing on fabric articles

(G-20282)
WASHINGTON COURIER
Also Called: Courier Publishing Co
100 Ford Ln (61571-2668)
P.O. Box 349 (61571-0349)
PHONE.....................309 444-3139
Roger Lyle Hagel, *President*
Joi Hagel-Dearmond, *President*
EMP: 15
SQ FT: 4,000
SALES (est): 955.4K Privately Held
WEB: www.courierpapers.com
SIC: 2711 2759 Newspapers: publishing only, not printed on site; letterpress printing

(G-20283)
WASHINGTON WOODWORKING
1514 Willow Dr (61571-9345)
PHONE.....................309 339-0913
Thomas Stefani, *Principal*
EMP: 2 EST: 2011
SALES (est): 202.3K Privately Held
SIC: 2431 Millwork

(G-20284)
WICC LTD
119 Muller Rd (61571-2357)
P.O. Box 252 (61571-0252)
PHONE.....................309 444-4125
Terry Bierrie, *President*
Dennis Russman, *Engineer*
EMP: 61
SQ FT: 16,000
SALES (est): 11.3MM Privately Held
SIC: 3612 Power transformers, electric

(G-20285)
ZG3 SYSTEMS LLC
25232 Spring Creek Rd (61571-9724)
PHONE.....................309 745-3398
Richard E Brummett, *President*
Douglas A Rasmussen, *Vice Pres*
EMP: 3
SQ FT: 1,920
SALES (est): 2.3MM Privately Held
SIC: 3536 Hoists, cranes & monorails

Wataga
Knox County

(G-20286)
HUNTER LOGISTICS
280 Knox Road 2200 N (61488)
PHONE.....................309 299-7015
Melanie Smith, *Partner*
Jon Hengehold, *Partner*
EMP: 5
SALES: 290K Privately Held
SIC: 4731 4231 4512 4513 Freight transportation arrangement; freight forwarding; trucking terminal facilities; air transportation, scheduled; air courier services; truck trailers; trucking, except local

(G-20287)
WEST CENTRAL FS INC
Also Called: Spoon River F S
686 N Depot Rd (61488-9614)
PHONE.....................309 375-6904
Doug Long, *Manager*
EMP: 6
SALES (corp-wide): 81.2MM Privately Held
SIC: 2875 5261 1542 Fertilizers, mixing only; nurseries & garden centers; agricultural building contractors
PA: West Central Fs Inc
1445 Monmouth Blvd
Galesburg IL 61401
309 343-1600

Waterloo
Monroe County

(G-20288)
COLUMBIA QUARRY COMPANY
5440 Quarry Dr (62298-2838)
P.O. Box 58 (62298-0058)
PHONE.....................618 939-8833
Bill Groh, *Branch Mgr*
EMP: 27
SALES (corp-wide): 6.5MM Privately Held
SIC: 1422 Crushed & broken limestone
PA: Columbia Quarry Company
210 State Route 158
Columbia IL 62236
618 281-7631

(G-20289)
D E SIGNS & STORAGE LLC
Also Called: Dealers Edge
6167 State Route 3 (62298-3063)
PHONE.....................618 939-8050
Melinda L Sale,
EMP: 3
SQ FT: 24,000
SALES (est): 256.1K Privately Held
SIC: 4225 2752 3993 General warehousing & storage; business form & card printing, lithographic; signs & advertising specialties

(G-20290)
GATEWAY FBRCTION SOLUTIONS LLC
5819 Lrc Rd (62298-6557)
PHONE.....................618 612-3170
Michael Wiegand, *Mng Member*
EMP: 5
SALES: 500K Privately Held
SIC: 3498 3317 3471 Fabricated pipe & fittings: steel pipe & tubes; plating of metals or formed products
PA: Gateway Fabrication Solutions Mexico, S.A.P.I. De C.V.
Ing. Tomas Limon Gutierrez No. 123
Guadalajara JAL. 44940

(G-20291)
ITS SOLAR LLC
946 Park St Ste A (62298-1887)
PHONE.....................618 476-7678
Richard C Schmidt Jr, *President*
EMP: 40
SALES (est): 177.6K Privately Held
SIC: 3613 Control panels, electric

(G-20292)
MIDWEST BLOCK AND BRICK INC
8605 State Route 3 (62298-5505)
PHONE.....................618 939-7600
Mike Lloyd, *Manager*
EMP: 5
SALES (corp-wide): 59.8MM Privately Held
WEB: www.midwestblock.com
SIC: 3271 Blocks, concrete or cinder: standard
PA: Midwest Block And Brick, Inc.
2203 E Mccarty St
Jefferson City MO 65101
573 635-7119

(G-20293)
OMEGA PRODUCTS INC
502 Walnut St (62298-1467)
P.O. Box 122 (62298-0122)
PHONE.....................618 939-3445
William Ebeler, *President*
Jeanne Ebeler, *Admin Sec*
EMP: 7
SQ FT: 5,000
SALES (est): 1.1MM Privately Held
SIC: 3312 3444 Stainless steel; sheet metalwork; ventilators, sheet metal; hoods, range: sheet metal

(G-20294)
R & L BUSINESS FORMS INC
8603 Gilmore Lake Rd (62298)
P.O. Box 47 (62298-0047)
PHONE.....................618 939-6535
Larry E Menke, *President*
Robert W Menke, *Vice Pres*
EMP: 12
SQ FT: 10,860
SALES (est): 750K Privately Held
SIC: 2761 Unit sets (manifold business forms); continuous forms, office & business

(G-20295)
RAYS POWER WSHG SVC PEGGY RAY
318 Bradford Ln (62298-3250)
PHONE.....................618 939-6306
Ray Power, *Owner*
Peggy Power, *Co-Owner*
EMP: 5 EST: 2014
SALES: 50K Privately Held
SIC: 7542 3589 7389 Carwashes; floor washing & polishing machines, commercial;

(G-20296)
REPUBLIC TIMES LLC
205 W Mill St (62298-1235)
P.O. Box 147 (62298-0147)
PHONE.....................618 939-3814
Kermit Constantine, *Mng Member*
EMP: 8
SALES (est): 369.8K Privately Held
SIC: 2711 Newspapers: publishing only, not printed on site

Waterman
Dekalb County

(G-20297)
1803 CANDLES
360 E Lincoln Hwy (60556-9706)
P.O. Box 1168, Hinckley (60520-1168)
PHONE.....................815 264-3009
Darryl Beach, *Owner*
EMP: 3
SALES (est): 285.5K Privately Held
SIC: 3999 Candles

(G-20298)
KAUFFMAN POULTRY FARMS INC
Also Called: Ho-Ka Turkey Farm
8519 Leland Rd (60556-7069)
P.O. Box 205 (60556-0205)
PHONE.....................815 264-3470
Robert Kauffman, *President*
Jean L Clowers, *Corp Secy*
EMP: 13 EST: 1933

Waterman - Dekalb County (G-20299)

SQ FT: 6,000
SALES: 2.1MM **Privately Held**
WEB: www.hokaturkeys.com
SIC: **2015** 0115 Turkey processing & slaughtering; corn

(G-20299)
MONSANTO COMPANY
8350 Minnegan Rd (60556-7113)
PHONE..................................815 758-9293
John Robben, *Branch Mgr*
EMP: 70
SALES (corp-wide): 48.1B **Privately Held**
SIC: **2879** Agricultural chemicals
HQ: Monsanto Company
   800 N Lindbergh Blvd
   Saint Louis MO 63167
   314 694-1000

(G-20300)
PRODUCTION CUTTING SERVICES
9341 State Route 23 (60556-7163)
PHONE..................................815 264-3505
EMP: 52
SALES (corp-wide): 20MM **Privately Held**
WEB: www.productioncutting.com
SIC: **3312** Blast furnaces & steel mills
PA: Production Cutting Services, Inc
   1033 7th St
   East Moline IL 61244
   309 755-4601

(G-20301)
VISION PICKLING AND PROC INC
Also Called: Pickling Steel
9341 State Route 23 (60556-7163)
PHONE..................................815 264-7755
Steven F Whitney, *President*
EMP: 13
SQ FT: 240,000
SALES (est): 2.5MM **Privately Held**
SIC: **3547** 3471 Picklers & pickling lines (rolling mill equipment); plating & polishing

(G-20302)
WATERMAN WINERY & VINEYARDS
11582 Waterman Rd (60556-7194)
PHONE..................................815 264-3268
Terrie Tuntland, *President*
EMP: 4
SALES (est): 214.1K **Privately Held**
SIC: **2084** 5921 Wines; wine

(G-20303)
WILLIAM BADAL
Also Called: 5 B'S Catering Service
190 W Lincoln Hwy (60556-9730)
P.O. Box 365 (60556-0365)
PHONE..................................815 264-7752
William Badal, *Owner*
EMP: 3
SQ FT: 4,000
SALES (est): 66.5K **Privately Held**
WEB: www.5bscatering.com
SIC: **5812** 2013 Caterers; sausages & other prepared meats

Watseka
Iroquois County

(G-20304)
ALL AMERICAN ATHLETICS LTD
100 Laird Ln (60970-7561)
PHONE..................................815 432-8326
EMP: 3 EST: 2004
SALES (est): 170K **Privately Held**
SIC: **3949** Sporting Goods

(G-20305)
GRISWOLD FEED INC
450 S Cips St (60970-1565)
PHONE..................................815 432-2811
Gary Griswold, *President*
Margaret Griswold, *Treasurer*
EMP: 5
SQ FT: 2,000
SALES (est): 348.5K **Privately Held**
SIC: **2048** Livestock feeds

(G-20306)
HIPRO MANUFACTURING INC
1909 E 1800 N Rd (60970)
PHONE..................................815 432-5271
Clifford Stan, *President*
EMP: 20
SALES (est): 2.5MM **Privately Held**
SIC: **3523** 3524 Farm machinery & equipment; lawn & garden equipment

(G-20307)
I D TOOL SPECIALTY COMPANY
819 N Jefferson St (60970)
P.O. Box 131 (60970-0131)
PHONE..................................815 432-2007
Larry Parks, *President*
Mary Parks, *Manager*
EMP: 8
SQ FT: 6,000
SALES (est): 818.1K **Privately Held**
SIC: **1389** Well plugging & abandoning, oil & gas; servicing oil & gas wells

(G-20308)
JAY A MORRIS (PA)
Also Called: Jay Morris Trucking
2238 E Township Road 165 (60970-8731)
PHONE..................................815 432-6440
Jay Morris, *Owner*
EMP: 2
SALES (est): 4MM **Privately Held**
SIC: **2431** 4212 1794 Millwork; local trucking, without storage; excavation work

(G-20309)
LYON LLC
Also Called: Pride Metal
475 N Veterans Pkwy (60970-1839)
PHONE..................................815 432-4595
George McGeorge, *Manager*
EMP: 125
SALES (corp-wide): 114.1MM **Privately Held**
SIC: **2542** Partitions & fixtures, except wood
HQ: Lyon, Llc
   420 N Main St
   Montgomery IL 60538
   630 892-8941

(G-20310)
MASSEY GRAFIX
1637 E 1900 North Rd (60970-7901)
PHONE..................................815 644-4620
Craig Massey, *Owner*
Graig Massey, *Manager*
EMP: 4
SALES (est): 120K **Privately Held**
SIC: **3993** Signs & advertising specialties

(G-20311)
METAL MFG LLC
Also Called: Pride Metal Products
475 N Veterans Pkwy (60970-1839)
PHONE..................................815 432-4595
Darren Crook, *Opers Mgr*
EMP: 150
SALES (est): 7.3MM **Privately Held**
SIC: **3429** Metal fasteners

(G-20312)
MPD MEDICAL SYSTEMS INC
602 E Walnut St (60970-1459)
PHONE..................................815 477-0707
Thomas Parr, *President*
George Mede, *Vice Pres*
Roger Dittrich, *Treasurer*
▼EMP: 4
SALES (est): 597.2K **Privately Held**
SIC: **2599** Hospital furniture, except beds

(G-20313)
ORR RUDOLPH
Also Called: Orr Farms
2642 E 2300 North Rd (60970-6053)
PHONE..................................815 429-3996
Roger Orr, *Owner*
Patricia Orr, *Co-Owner*
EMP: 3 EST: 1956
SALES (est): 150K **Privately Held**
SIC: **0115** 1389 Corn; bailing, cleaning, swabbing & treating of wells

(G-20314)
PEOPLES COAL AND LUMBER CO (PA)
Also Called: Peoples Cmplete Buiding Centre
121 S 3rd St (60970-1665)
P.O. Box 70 (60970-0070)
PHONE..................................815 432-2456
Richard A Martin, *Ch of Bd*
Daniel Martin, *President*
Samuel Martin II, *Vice Pres*
EMP: 15
SQ FT: 8,000
SALES (est): 1.8MM **Privately Held**
WEB: www.peopleslbm.com
SIC: **5251** 3273 5211 Hardware; ready-mixed concrete; lumber & other building materials

(G-20315)
QSE INC (PA)
316 W Hickory St (60970-1236)
P.O. Box 360 (60970-0360)
PHONE..................................815 432-5281
Anthony J Imburgia, *President*
▲EMP: 20
SQ FT: 28,000
SALES (est): 10MM **Privately Held**
SIC: **3677** Electronic coils, transformers & other inductors

(G-20316)
STANDARD REGISTER INC
Also Called: Uarco
112 E Walnut St Ste B (60970-1381)
PHONE..................................815 432-4203
Fax: 815 432-5106
EMP: 16
SQ FT: 236,000
SALES (corp-wide): 3.8B **Privately Held**
SIC: **2761** Mfg Manifold Business Forms
HQ: Standard Register, Inc.
   600 Albany St
   Dayton OH
   937 221-1000

(G-20317)
STEEL SOLUTIONS USA
602 E Walnut St (60970-1459)
PHONE..................................815 432-4938
Steve Huggins, *Principal*
EMP: 9
SALES: 356.4K
SALES (corp-wide): 20.5MM **Privately Held**
SIC: **2522** Office furniture, except wood
PA: T & D Metal Products, Llc
   602 E Walnut St
   Watseka IL 60970
   815 432-4938

(G-20318)
T & D METAL PRODUCTS LLC (PA)
Also Called: T&D Trucking
602 E Walnut St (60970-1459)
PHONE..................................815 432-4938
Roger Dittrich, *Principal*
Tim Schwartz, *Plant Supt*
Steve Lambert, *Plant Mgr*
Russ Keath, *Engineer*
Trudy Lambert, *Human Res Mgr*
EMP: 9
SQ FT: 140,000
SALES (est): 20.5MM **Privately Held**
SIC: **2542** 3469 3799 Cabinets: show, display or storage: except wood; boxes: tool, lunch, mail, etc.: stamped metal; go-carts, except children's

(G-20319)
T & S BUSINESS GROUP LLC
Also Called: Petersen/Tru-Cut Automotive
602 E Walnut St (60970-1459)
PHONE..................................815 432-7084
Roger Pj Dittrich,
EMP: 10
SQ FT: 70,000
SALES: 4MM **Privately Held**
SIC: **3559** Automotive related machinery

(G-20320)
TIMES REPUBLIC (HQ)
Also Called: Twin States Publishing Co
1492 E Walnut St (60970-1806)
P.O. Box 250 (60970-0250)
PHONE..................................815 432-5227
Larry Perrotto, *President*
Joan Williams, *Vice Pres*
EMP: 50
SQ FT: 2,500
SALES (est): 11MM **Privately Held**
SIC: **2711** 2791 2759 2752 Newspapers: publishing only, not printed on site; typesetting; commercial printing; commercial printing, lithographic

(G-20321)
UNITED VALIDATION & COM
1728 E 1700 North Rd (60970-7636)
PHONE..................................815 953-6068
Raymond White, *President*
EMP: 1
SQ FT: 2,200
SALES: 500K **Privately Held**
SIC: **3559** Pharmaceutical machinery

Watson
Effingham County

(G-20322)
K & P WELDING
12374 E 550th Ave (62473-2238)
P.O. Box 38 (62473-0038)
PHONE..................................217 536-5245
Kenny Bergfeld, *Owner*
EMP: 2
SQ FT: 3,000
SALES (est): 250K **Privately Held**
SIC: **7692** Welding repair

Wauconda
Lake County

(G-20323)
A J WAGNER & SON
1120 N Rand Rd Frnt 1 (60084-1174)
PHONE..................................773 935-1414
Daniel A Wagner, *Vice Pres*
Albert J Wagner III, *Admin Sec*
EMP: 12
SQ FT: 8,000
SALES: 1MM **Privately Held**
WEB: www.wagnerandsons.org
SIC: **1761** 3444 Sheet metalwork; sheet metalwork

(G-20324)
A TO Z ENGRAVING CO INC
Also Called: A To Z Engrvg
1150 Brown St Ste G (60084-1154)
PHONE..................................847 526-7396
Joan Nelson, *President*
Gary Nelson, *Vice Pres*
EMP: 5 EST: 1954
SQ FT: 4,000
SALES (est): 682.4K **Privately Held**
SIC: **3089** 3993 3953 2789 Engraving of plastic; signs & advertising specialties; marking devices; bookbinding & related work

(G-20325)
ABLE BARMILLING & MFG CO INC
Also Called: Able Barmilling & Mfg Inc
1111 N Old Rand Rd (60084-1241)
PHONE..................................708 343-5666
Ronald Spears, *President*
Laura Spears, *Vice Pres*
Kristin Kaese, *Manager*
EMP: 10 EST: 1945
SQ FT: 21,000
SALES (est): 1.8MM **Privately Held**
WEB: www.ablebar.com
SIC: **3599** Machine shop, jobbing & repair

(G-20326)
ABOUT LEARNING INC
441 W Bonner Rd (60084-1184)
PHONE..................................847 487-1800

GEOGRAPHIC SECTION

Wauconda - Lake County (G-20355)

Michael Mc Carthy, *CEO*
Bernice Mc Carthy, *President*
EMP: 14
SQ FT: 5,000
SALES (est): 1.4MM **Privately Held**
SIC: 2741 5192 Technical manual & paper publishing; books

(G-20327) ACCU-GRIND MANUFACTURING INC
386 Hollow Hill Rd (60084-9762)
PHONE.................................847 526-2700
Henry Sauer Sr, *President*
EMP: 11
SQ FT: 4,300
SALES (est): 800K **Privately Held**
SIC: 3545 7389 Gauges (machine tool accessories); grinding, precision: commercial or industrial

(G-20328) ALLIANCE LASER SALES INC (PA)
275 Industrial Dr (60084-1078)
PHONE.................................847 487-1945
John P Demakis, *President*
Vincent G Sabella, *Vice Pres*
▲ **EMP:** 22
SALES (est): 2.8MM **Privately Held**
SIC: 3699 Laser welding, drilling & cutting equipment

(G-20329) ALLIANCE SPECIALTIES CORP
275 Industrial Dr (60084-1078)
PHONE.................................847 487-1945
Vincent G Sabella, *President*
John P De Makis, *Vice Pres*
Jessica Dean, *Manager*
Jim Grantland, *Technician*
Mike Zender, *Maintence Staff*
EMP: 12
SQ FT: 20,000
SALES (est): 1.8MM **Privately Held**
SIC: 3471 Finishing, metals or formed products; polishing, metals or formed products

(G-20330) AMERICAN CUSTOM WOODWORKING
1247 Karl Ct (60084-1098)
PHONE.................................847 526-5900
Thomas Peters, *President*
Pam Peters, *Corp Secy*
EMP: 10
SQ FT: 20,000
SALES: 1.5MM **Privately Held**
SIC: 2431 2434 Millwork; wood kitchen cabinets

(G-20331) AMKINE INC
Also Called: Regency Crystal
230 Industrial Dr (60084-1077)
PHONE.................................847 526-7088
Harshad Amin, *President*
Rita Amin, *Corp Secy*
▲ **EMP:** 10
SQ FT: 8,000
SALES (est): 811.2K **Privately Held**
SIC: 7389 3229 Engraving service; glassware, art or decorative

(G-20332) ART & SON SIGN INC
Also Called: Art & Son Design
1090 Brown St (60084-1106)
PHONE.................................847 526-7205
Thomas Holland, *President*
Douglas Holland, *Vice Pres*
Arthur T Holland, *Director*
Madeline Holland, *Director*
EMP: 10
SQ FT: 10,000
SALES (est): 639.8K **Privately Held**
SIC: 3993 Electric signs

(G-20333) ATHLETIC SPECIALTIES INC
1230 Karl Ct Unit A (60084-1170)
PHONE.................................847 487-7880
Scott Palmberg, *President*
▲ **EMP:** 9

SALES: 10MM **Privately Held**
SIC: 5091 3949 Athletic goods; sporting & athletic goods

(G-20334) BECKER JULES D WOOD PRODUCTS
25250 W Old Rand Rd (60084-2475)
PHONE.................................847 526-8002
Fax: 847 526-8002
EMP: 3 **EST:** 1960
SQ FT: 2,000
SALES (est): 210K **Privately Held**
SIC: 2434 2431 Cabinet Maker And Specialty Woodwork

(G-20335) BLANKE INDUSTRIES INCORPORATED
1099 Brown St Ste 103 (60084-3106)
PHONE.................................847 487-2780
John Blanke, *President*
EMP: 8
SQ FT: 1,000
SALES (est): 500K **Privately Held**
SIC: 3826 5531 Environmental testing equipment; automobile & truck equipment & parts

(G-20336) C D NELSON CONSULTING INC
Also Called: Nelson C D Mfg & Sup Co
27421 N Darrell Rd (60084-9792)
P.O. Box 726 (60084-0726)
PHONE.................................847 487-4870
Clinton D Nelson, *President*
▲ **EMP:** 4
SALES (est): 300.7K **Privately Held**
SIC: 3915 8742 Jewelers' materials & lapidary work; management consulting services

(G-20337) C M F ENTERPRISES INC
Also Called: Cover Connection
950 N Rand Rd Ste 113 (60084-1108)
PHONE.................................847 526-9499
Mary L Fisher, *President*
EMP: 10
SQ FT: 6,600
SALES (est): 1.8MM **Privately Held**
SIC: 3081 5045 7389 7336 Vinyl film & sheet; computer peripheral equipment; embroidering of advertising on shirts, etc.; silk screen design; advertising novelties

(G-20338) C N C HI-TECH INC
1150 Brown St Ste H (60084-1154)
PHONE.................................847 431-4335
EMP: 3 **EST:** 2017
SALES (est): 141K **Privately Held**
SIC: 3599 Machine shop, jobbing & repair

(G-20339) CAMPBELL INTERNATIONAL INC
Also Called: Campbell Cab
120 Kent Ave (60084-2441)
P.O. Box 875 (60084-0875)
PHONE.................................408 661-0794
James M Campbell III, *President*
EMP: 40 **EST:** 1946
SQ FT: 40,000
SALES (est): 631.3K **Privately Held**
WEB: www.campbellcab.com
SIC: 3713 3567 Truck cabs for motor vehicles; industrial furnaces & ovens

(G-20340) CORTEK ENDOSCOPY INC
206 Jamie Ln (60084)
PHONE.................................847 526-2266
Cornel Topala, *President*
EMP: 4
SALES (est): 435.8K **Privately Held**
WEB: www.cortek-endoscopy.com
SIC: 7699 3845 Optical instrument repair; endoscopic equipment, electromedical

(G-20341) DARD PRODUCTS INC
Also Called: Tag Master Line
1230 Karl Ct Unit A (60084-1170)
PHONE.................................847 328-5000

Cary J Shevin, *President*
Harriette Shevin, *CFO*
Pam Levy, *Admin Sec*
▲ **EMP:** 200 **EST:** 1946
SALES (est): 30MM **Privately Held**
WEB: www.dardproducts.com
SIC: 3993 7311 Signs & advertising specialties; advertising consultant

(G-20342) DOMENY TOOL & STAMPING COMPANY
354 Hollow Hill Rd (60084-3300)
PHONE.................................847 526-5700
Marge Domeny, *President*
Kristin Dummler, *Plant Mgr*
Anthony Ruiz, *Accounts Mgr*
▲ **EMP:** 19
SQ FT: 24,000
SALES (est): 2.5MM **Privately Held**
WEB: www.domenytool.com
SIC: 3469 3544 Machine parts, stamped or pressed metal; special dies & tools

(G-20343) DONS WELDING
552 S Rand Rd (60084-2321)
PHONE.................................847 526-1177
Don Schaal, *President*
Stan Schaal, *President*
EMP: 8
SQ FT: 6,400
SALES (est): 907.5K **Privately Held**
SIC: 7692 Welding repair

(G-20344) DU BRO PRODUCTS INC
Also Called: Pine Ridge Archery
480 W Bonner Rd (60084-1198)
P.O. Box 815 (60084-0815)
PHONE.................................847 526-2136
Jim Broberg, *President*
Terry Weiland, *Purch Agent*
Gayle Lundgren, *Treasurer*
Jerry Tepps, *Sales Staff*
Brian Bychowski, *Marketing Staff*
▲ **EMP:** 30
SQ FT: 40,000
SALES (est): 5.6MM **Privately Held**
WEB: www.dubro.com
SIC: 3944 3452 3429 Board games, puzzles & models, except electronic; craft & hobby kits & sets; airplane models, toy & hobby; railroad models: toy & hobby; bolts, nuts, rivets & washers; manufactured hardware (general)

(G-20345) DURO-CHROME INDUSTRIES INC
275 Indl Dr (60084)
PHONE.................................847 487-2900
Margoreto Garcia, *President*
Vince Sabella, *Corp Secy*
John Demakis, *Vice Pres*
EMP: 23
SQ FT: 10,000
SALES (est): 2.8MM **Privately Held**
SIC: 3471 Electroplating of metals or formed products

(G-20346) DYNAMIC PRECISION PRODUCTS
1280 Kyle Ct (60084-1076)
PHONE.................................847 526-2054
Eric B Rasmussen, *President*
Mark Rasmussen, *Treasurer*
EMP: 13
SQ FT: 7,200
SALES (est): 2MM **Privately Held**
SIC: 3599 Machine shop, jobbing & repair

(G-20347) EAW MACHINING
1205 Karl Ct (60084-1088)
PHONE.................................847 865-5162
Waldemar Padlo, *Principal*
EMP: 3
SALES (est): 356.9K **Privately Held**
SIC: 3599 Machine shop, jobbing & repair

(G-20348) ENZYMES INCORPORATED
1099 Brown St Ste 102 (60084-3106)
PHONE.................................847 487-5401
Susan Brandau, *CFO*
▼ **EMP:** 4
SQ FT: 2,300
SALES (est): 556.7K **Privately Held**
SIC: 2869 Enzymes

(G-20349) EXCALBUR PR-KEYED SHAFTING INC
1111 N Old Rand Rd (60084-1241)
PHONE.................................800 487-0514
Ronald A Spears, *President*
EMP: 15
SALES (est): 1.3MM **Privately Held**
SIC: 3568 Couplings, shaft: rigid, flexible, universal joint, etc.

(G-20350) EXTRUSION TOOLING TECHNOLOGY
Also Called: Etti
1000 N Rand Rd Ste 210 (60084-3104)
PHONE.................................847 526-1606
Wesley Scott, *President*
EMP: 7
SQ FT: 3,600
SALES (est): 1MM **Privately Held**
SIC: 3544 Special dies & tools; extrusion dies

(G-20351) FISH OVEN AND EQUIPMENT CORP
120 Kent Ave (60084-2441)
P.O. Box 875 (60084-0875)
PHONE.................................847 526-8686
James M Campbell III, *President*
Janice Campbell, *Vice Pres*
EMP: 40
SQ FT: 40,000
SALES (est): 7.8MM **Privately Held**
SIC: 3567 Industrial furnaces & ovens

(G-20352) FONTANA ASSOCIATES INC
Also Called: Breachers Tape
282 Jamie Ln (60084-1079)
PHONE.................................888 707-8273
Nicholas Caradonna Jr, *President*
EMP: 1
SALES: 500K **Privately Held**
SIC: 2891 5085 Adhesives & sealants; adhesives, tape & plasters

(G-20353) GEHRKE TECHNOLOGY GROUP INC (PA)
1050 N Rand Rd (60084-1165)
PHONE.................................847 498-7320
Greg Gehrke, *President*
Elizabeth Gehrke, *Admin Sec*
▲ **EMP:** 11
SALES (est): 5.6MM **Privately Held**
SIC: 4941 5074 3589 Water supply; water purification equipment; water treatment equipment, industrial

(G-20354) GOLDMAN PRODUCTS INC
Also Called: Goldman Dental
379 Hollow Hill Rd (60084-9794)
P.O. Box 101, Island Lake (60042-0101)
PHONE.................................847 526-1166
Edward Kwan Rim, *President*
Edward Rim, *Sales Executive*
Elizabeth Gaffney, *Marketing Staff*
Juliet Rim, *Admin Sec*
EMP: 29
SQ FT: 10,000
SALES: 3MM **Privately Held**
WEB: www.goldmandental.com
SIC: 3843 Dental equipment

(G-20355) HELIVALUES
Also Called: Offical Helicopter Blue Book
1001 N Old Rand Rd # 101 (60084-1288)
P.O. Box 275 (60084-0275)
PHONE.................................847 487-8258
Barry D Desfor, *Ch of Bd*
Sharon Desfor, *President*

Wauconda - Lake County (G-20356)

Sue Kandefer, *Vice Pres*
Jason Kmiecik, *Vice Pres*
Lindsay Higgins, *Marketing Staff*
EMP: 8
SQ FT: 5,200
SALES (est): 1.1MM **Privately Held**
SIC: 2731 3721 Books: publishing only; helicopters

(G-20356)
HM MANUFACTURING INC
1200 Henri Dr (60084-1000)
PHONE.................847 487-8700
Kenneth W Wolter, *President*
Mary E Devlin, *Admin Sec*
EMP: 10 **EST:** 1975
SQ FT: 10,000
SALES (est): 1.8MM **Privately Held**
WEB: www.hmmanufacturing.com
SIC: 3429 3714 3462 Pulleys metal; power transmission equipment, motor vehicle; iron & steel forgings

(G-20357)
HOLLAND DESIGN GROUP INC
1090 Brown St (60084-1106)
PHONE.................847 526-8848
Thomas Holland, *President*
Douglas Holland, *Corp Secy*
EMP: 10
SQ FT: 10,000
SALES (est): 820K **Privately Held**
SIC: 3993 1799 Signs & advertising specialties; sign installation & maintenance

(G-20358)
HORIZON MFG ENTPS INC
Also Called: Rack'ems
1230 Karl Ct Unit C (60084-1170)
P.O. Box 7174, Buffalo Grove (60089-7174)
PHONE.................847 438-0888
EMP: 5
SQ FT: 3,700
SALES (est): 1.5MM **Privately Held**
SIC: 2499 Mfg Wood Products

(G-20359)
ILLINOIS MOLD BUILDERS INC
Also Called: Dynasty Mold Builders
250 Jamie Ln (60084-1079)
PHONE.................847 526-0400
Paul Makray, *President*
John Schiller, *Project Mgr*
Don Nowack, *Department Mgr*
Nancy Harney, *Admin Sec*
EMP: 12
SQ FT: 12,500
SALES (est): 2.2MM **Privately Held**
WEB: www.dynastymold.com
SIC: 3544 Industrial molds

(G-20360)
ILLINOIS STERLING LTD
540 S Rand Rd (60084-2375)
PHONE.................847 526-5151
Barbara Herrmann, *President*
EMP: 4
SQ FT: 22,000
SALES (est): 350.2K **Privately Held**
SIC: 3711 Motor vehicles & car bodies

(G-20361)
INTECH INDUSTRIES INC
Also Called: Midwest Control
1101 Brown St (60084-1105)
P.O. Box 100 (60084-0100)
PHONE.................847 487-5599
Terrence Connolly, *President*
Veda Connolly, *Vice Pres*
Kristen Drexler, *Vice Pres*
▲ **EMP:** 11
SQ FT: 8,000
SALES: 3.5MM **Privately Held**
SIC: 3569 3822 3545 3494 Filters; gradual switches, pneumatic; machine tool accessories; valves & pipe fittings; gaskets, packing & sealing devices; fasteners, industrial: nuts, bolts, screws, etc.

(G-20362)
INTREPID MOLDING INC
285 Industrial Dr (60084-1078)
PHONE.................847 526-9477
Mike Durkin, *President*
John Webb, *Treasurer*
Shirley Durkin, *Admin Sec*
▲ **EMP:** 30
SQ FT: 15,000
SALES (est): 5.9MM **Privately Held**
SIC: 3089 Injection molding of plastics

(G-20363)
JANCO PROCESS CONTROLS INC
368 W Liberty St (60084-2493)
PHONE.................847 526-0800
James T Cheslock, *President*
EMP: 22
SALES (est): 4.5MM **Privately Held**
SIC: 3823 Industrial process control instruments

(G-20364)
JOHNSON BAG CO INC
1001 N Old Rand Rd 103a (60084-1288)
PHONE.................847 438-2424
Robert L Johnson, *President*
Doreen Johnson-Taylor, *Corp Secy*
Dan Johnson, *Vice Pres*
EMP: 10
SALES (est): 1.8MM **Privately Held**
WEB: www.johnsonbag.com
SIC: 3089 Plastic processing

(G-20365)
KELLERMANN MANUFACTURING INC
Also Called: Kellermann Manufacturing Co
1000 N Rand Rd Ste 224 (60084-3100)
PHONE.................847 526-7266
Robert M Kellermann, *President*
Robert Kellermann Jr, *Corp Secy*
EMP: 5
SALES (est): 443.8K **Privately Held**
SIC: 3366 Copper foundries

(G-20366)
KIPP MANUFACTURING COMPANY INC
375 Hollow Hill Rd (60084-9794)
P.O. Box 2603, Glenview (60025-6603)
PHONE.................630 768-9051
Ron Kinder, *President*
Mike Ravesloot, *Vice Pres*
Kristine J Christ, *Admin Sec*
▲ **EMP:** 10 **EST:** 1944
SQ FT: 15,000
SALES: 900K **Privately Held**
SIC: 3465 3542 3444 3089 Moldings or trim, automobile: stamped metal; brakes, metal forming; spouts, sheet metal; spouting, plastic & glass fiber reinforced; metal stampings; crowns & closures

(G-20367)
KOSTO FOOD PRODUCTS COMPANY
1325 N Old Rand Rd (60084-3302)
PHONE.................847 487-2600
Donald F Colby, *President*
EMP: 10
SQ FT: 12,000
SALES (est): 1.4MM **Privately Held**
SIC: 2087 2099 2035 Food colorings; emulsifiers, food; packaged combination products: pasta, rice & potato; pickles, sauces & salad dressings

(G-20368)
KREBS CUSTOM INC
Also Called: Krebs Custom Guns
1000 N Rand Rd Ste 106 (60084-3103)
PHONE.................847 487-7776
Mark Krebs, *President*
Virginia Krebs, *Vice Pres*
Brian Conrad, *Technology*
EMP: 7
SALES (est): 636.9K **Privately Held**
SIC: 7699 5099 3489 Gunsmith shop; machine guns; guns or gun parts, over 30 mm.

(G-20369)
LOGAN GRAPHIC PRODUCTS INC
1100 Brown St (60084-1192)
PHONE.................847 526-5515
Malcolm Logan, *CEO*
Curt Logan, *President*
Pat Dezina, *Materials Mgr*
Carlos Salvador, *Safety Mgr*
Pam Prosi, *Controller*
▲ **EMP:** 60 **EST:** 1971
SQ FT: 20,000
SALES (est): 11.3MM **Privately Held**
WEB: www.logangraphic.com
SIC: 3545 3496 3541 2631 Machine tool accessories; mats & matting; machine tools, metal cutting type; paperboard mills

(G-20370)
M M MARKETING
522 S Rand Rd (60084-2375)
PHONE.................815 459-7968
Greg Bruns, *Owner*
Jim Mc Neil, *Owner*
EMP: 4
SALES (est): 274.2K **Privately Held**
SIC: 2741 7336 2752 2791 Miscellaneous publishing; commercial art & graphic design; commercial printing, lithographic; typesetting; banners, flags, decals & posters

(G-20371)
MAG DADDY LLC
278 Jamie Ln (60084-1079)
PHONE.................847 719-5600
William R Smith,
Lori Perrault,
▲ **EMP:** 2 **EST:** 2011
SALES (est): 313.2K **Privately Held**
WEB: www.magdaddyusa.com
SIC: 3714 5531 Motor vehicle parts & accessories; automotive & home supply stores

(G-20372)
MARK INDUSTRIES
535 N Legion Ct (60084)
PHONE.................847 487-8670
Mark Schneider, *Owner*
EMP: 4
SALES (est): 395K **Privately Held**
SIC: 3844 5047 X-ray apparatus & tubes; hospital equipment & furniture

(G-20373)
MASTERCRAFT AUTO REBUILDING
265 Industrial Dr (60084-1078)
PHONE.................847 487-8787
Mike Delmedico II, *President*
EMP: 10
SQ FT: 12,500
SALES (est): 880.2K **Privately Held**
SIC: 3732 Boat building & repairing

(G-20374)
MATRIX INDUSTRIES INC (PA)
375 Hollow Hill Rd (60084-9794)
PHONE.................847 975-7701
EMP: 5 **EST:** 2011
SALES (est): 928.8K **Privately Held**
SIC: 3999 Manufacturing industries

(G-20375)
MECHANICAL POWER INC
135 Kerry Ln (60084-1134)
PHONE.................847 487-0070
Douglas Zwiener, *CEO*
Brent Lalonde, *President*
James Dorn, *Chairman*
♦ **EMP:** 20
SQ FT: 20,000
SALES (est): 5MM **Privately Held**
SIC: 3562 Ball bearings & parts

(G-20376)
MENGES ROLLER CO INC
260 Industrial Dr (60084-3215)
PHONE.................847 487-8877
Matthew Menges, *President*
Louis Menges, *Principal*
EMP: 27 **EST:** 1981
SQ FT: 20,000
SALES (est): 6.4MM
SALES (corp-wide): 2.9B **Privately Held**
WEB: www.mengesroller.com
SIC: 3069 5084 Roll coverings, rubber; printing trades machinery, equipment & supplies
HQ: Maxcess International Holding Corp.
222 W Memorial Rd
Oklahoma City OK 73114
405 755-1600

(G-20377)
MIK TOOL & DIE CO INC
1000 Brown St Ste 304 (60084-3111)
PHONE.................847 487-4311
Nick Vadina, *President*
Jelena Vadina, *Admin Sec*
EMP: 4
SQ FT: 2,800
SALES (est): 632.5K **Privately Held**
SIC: 3544 Special dies & tools; jigs & fixtures

(G-20378)
MORRIS MAGNETICS INC
1220 N Old Rand Rd (60084-1160)
PHONE.................847 487-0829
Elizabeth Morris, *President*
Michael Morris, *Vice Pres*
EMP: 30
SQ FT: 14,000
SALES (est): 3.3MM **Privately Held**
SIC: 3499 Magnets, permanent: metallic

(G-20379)
MUELLER DOOR COMPANY
27100 N Darrell Rd (60084-9756)
P.O. Box 69 (60084-0069)
PHONE.................815 385-8550
Duer L Miller, *Ch of Bd*
Suzanne Miller, *President*
Peter Miller, *CFO*
EMP: 48
SQ FT: 90,000
SALES (est): 6.8MM **Privately Held**
SIC: 3089 3442 Doors, folding: plastic or plastic coated fabric; metal doors, sash & trim

(G-20380)
MURPHYS PUB
110 Slocum Lake Rd (60084-1883)
PHONE.................847 526-1431
EMP: 4 **EST:** 1977
SQ FT: 2,000
SALES (est): 180K **Privately Held**
SIC: 5813 2261 Edrinking Place Cotton Finishing Plant

(G-20381)
NEX GEN MANUFACTURING INC
1055 N Old Rand Rd (60084-1239)
PHONE.................847 487-7077
John Fyock, *President*
Chai Fyock, *Vice Pres*
EMP: 7
SQ FT: 9,000
SALES (est): 998.2K **Privately Held**
WEB: www.nexgenmfg.com
SIC: 3599 Machine shop, jobbing & repair

(G-20382)
PHP RACENGINES INC
950 N Rand Rd Ste 107 (60084-1179)
PHONE.................847 526-9393
Barry Sale, *President*
Elizabeth Sale, *Admin Sec*
EMP: 3
SQ FT: 1,900
SALES (est): 200K **Privately Held**
SIC: 3714 Motor vehicle engines & parts

(G-20383)
POWERTECH SYSTEMS
2548 Bluewater Dr (60084-5024)
PHONE.................847 553-1867
Brett Bjorkquist, *Principal*
EMP: 2 **EST:** 2008
SALES (est): 265.6K **Privately Held**
SIC: 3699 Electrical equipment & supplies

(G-20384)
PROFESSIONAL SALES ASSOCIATES
Also Called: P S A
1000 Brown St Ste 303 (60084-3111)
PHONE.................847 487-1900
Bill Barber Jr, *President*
William Barber, *Director*
EMP: 4
SQ FT: 1,800
SALES (est): 340K **Privately Held**
SIC: 3953 5084 Marking devices; printing trades machinery, equipment & supplies

GEOGRAPHIC SECTION

Waukegan - Lake County (G-20411)

(G-20385)
PROGRSSIVE CMPONENTS INTL CORP (PA)
235 Industrial Dr (60084-1078)
PHONE.....................847 487-1000
Glenn Starkey, *President*
Michael Bolton, *CFO*
Rebecca Hamstra, *Sales Staff*
Donald R Starkey Jr, *Admin Sec*
▲ **EMP:** 55 **EST:** 1970
SQ FT: 15,000
SALES (est): 37.4MM **Privately Held**
SIC: 5084 3545 Tool & die makers' equipment; cutting tools for machine tools

(G-20386)
PROTECTIVE PRODUCTS INTL
140 Kerry Ln (60084-1116)
PHONE.....................847 526-1180
Alan Nishiguchi, *President*
◆ **EMP:** 6
SALES (est): 1MM **Privately Held**
SIC: 3081 5162 2891 2842 Plastic film & sheet; plastics film; adhesives & sealants; specialty cleaning, polishes & sanitation goods

(G-20387)
R/K INDUSTRIES INC
375 Hollow Hill Rd (60084-9794)
PHONE.....................847 526-2222
Ronald Kinder, *President*
Karen Kinder, *Admin Sec*
EMP: 10
SQ FT: 5,000
SALES (est): 2.4MM **Privately Held**
SIC: 5023 5192 3599 Kitchen tools & utensils; books, periodicals & newspapers; amusement park equipment

(G-20388)
RD HUSEMOLLER LTD
Also Called: Stera-Sheen
1255 Karl Ct (60084-1098)
PHONE.....................847 526-5505
Robert D Husemoller, *President*
Carolyn Husemoller, *Corp Secy*
Paul Huesmoller, *Exec VP*
▲ **EMP:** 12 **EST:** 1950
SALES (est): 3.3MM **Privately Held**
WEB: www.purdyproducts.com
SIC: 2842 Sanitation preparations

(G-20389)
ROBERT KELLERMAN & CO
1000 N Rand Rd Ste 224 (60084-3100)
PHONE.....................847 526-7266
Robert Kellerman, *Owner*
EMP: 3
SQ FT: 5,000
SALES (est): 75K **Privately Held**
SIC: 8721 3369 3365 Certified public accountant; nonferrous foundries; aluminum foundries

(G-20390)
SCHUBERT CONTROLS CORPORATION
1099 Brown St Ste 109 (60084-3106)
PHONE.....................847 526-8200
Gabor L Solymossy, *President*
Mary F Solymossy, *Admin Sec*
EMP: 6
SQ FT: 4,600
SALES (est): 810K **Privately Held**
SIC: 3613 Control panels, electric

(G-20391)
STICKON ADHESIVE INDS INC
Also Called: Stickon Packaging Systems
282 Jamie Ln (60084-1079)
PHONE.....................847 593-5959
Nicholas M Caradonna, *President*
EMP: 4
SALES (est): 6MM **Privately Held**
SIC: 5199 7699 5084 2295 Packaging materials; industrial equipment services; processing & packaging equipment; packaging machinery & equipment; coated fabrics, not rubberized; tape, varnished; plastic & other coated (except magnetic)

(G-20392)
STONECASTERS LLC
1250 Henri Dr (60084-1000)
PHONE.....................847 526-5200
Mario Chairez, *Production*
Dennis Prosperi, *Treasurer*
Jill Honold, *Controller*
Marjorie Giannosa, *Cust Mgr*
Frank Honold, *Mng Member*
▲ **EMP:** 57 **EST:** 2012
SQ FT: 145,000
SALES (est): 8.8MM **Privately Held**
SIC: 3281 Cut stone & stone products

(G-20393)
SUREBONDER ADHESIVES INC
355 Hollow Hill Rd (60084-9794)
PHONE.....................847 487-4583
Michael Kamins, *President*
Jeana Tyche,
EMP: 5
SALES (est): 509.4K **Privately Held**
WEB: www.surebonder.com
SIC: 2891 Adhesives

(G-20394)
SYNERGY FLAVORS INC (HQ)
1500 Synergy Dr (60084-1073)
PHONE.....................847 487-1011
Roderick Sowders, *President*
Johnny Pigg, *Regional Mgr*
Amy Loomis, *Business Mgr*
Jim Abraham, *Vice Pres*
Jeremy Macht, *Plant Mgr*
▲ **EMP:** 58
SQ FT: 40,000
SALES (est): 19.3MM **Privately Held**
SIC: 2087 Extracts, flavoring

(G-20395)
SYNERGY FLAVORS NY COMPANY LLC (DH)
Also Called: Vanlab
1500 Synergy Dr (60084-1073)
PHONE.....................585 232-6648
Robert Blassick,
Roderick Sowders,
▲ **EMP:** 30
SQ FT: 25,000
SALES (est): 4.1MM **Privately Held**
SIC: 2087 Extracts, flavoring; syrups, flavoring (except drink)
HQ: Synergy Flavors, Inc.
1500 Synergy Dr
Wauconda IL 60084
847 487-1011

(G-20396)
T J M & ASSOCIATES INC
Also Called: Reflections In Glass
1160 N Dato Ln (60084-1142)
PHONE.....................847 382-1993
Tim Meade, *President*
EMP: 7
SALES (est): 1.2MM **Privately Held**
SIC: 3431 5039 5231 1793 Shower stalls, metal; exterior flat glass; plate or window; glass, leaded or stained; glass & glazing work

(G-20397)
TAMARACK PRODUCTS INC
1071 N Old Rand Rd (60084-1239)
PHONE.....................847 526-9333
David Steidinger, *President*
Mark Steidinger, *Vice Pres*
Jayne Stork, *Controller*
Diane McNulty, *Sales Staff*
Scott Steidinger, *Technical Staff*
EMP: 24
SQ FT: 11,000
SALES: 3.1MM **Privately Held**
SIC: 3555 Printing trades machinery

(G-20398)
TENT MAKER INDUSTRIAL SUP INC
Also Called: T M I S
531 Brown St (60084-1261)
P.O. Box 151 (60084-0151)
PHONE.....................847 469-6070
David F Macphail, *President*
Virginia Macphail, *Vice Pres*
EMP: 4
SQ FT: 825
SALES (est): 1MM **Privately Held**
SIC: 5063 3599 Electrical apparatus & equipment; machine shop, jobbing & repair

(G-20399)
THREE STAR MFG CO INC
375 Hollow Hill Rd (60084-9794)
PHONE.....................847 526-2222
Ron Kinder, *President*
EMP: 9 **EST:** 1945
SQ FT: 26,800
SALES (est): 1.4MM **Privately Held**
SIC: 3544 3469 Special dies & tools; stamping metal for the trade

(G-20400)
UNITED INDUSTRIES ILLINOIS LTD
270 Jamie Ln (60084-1079)
PHONE.....................847 526-9485
Joel Aronson, *President*
EMP: 5
SALES (est): 855K **Privately Held**
SIC: 3441 Fabricated structural metal

(G-20401)
WAGNER PUMP & SUPPLY CO INC
809 Lake Shore Dr (60084-1529)
PHONE.....................847 526-8573
Bill Wagner, *Owner*
EMP: 4
SALES (est): 230.9K **Privately Held**
SIC: 5251 5084 5074 3561 Pumps & pumping equipment; pumps & pumping equipment; plumbing & hydronic heating supplies; pumps & pumping equipment

(G-20402)
WEEB ENTERPRISES LLC
770 Peninsula Dr (60084-1058)
P.O. Box 121 (60084-0121)
PHONE.....................815 861-2625
Chris Smith,
EMP: 2
SALES (est): 209.1K **Privately Held**
SIC: 8748 3842 Business consulting; personal safety equipment

(G-20403)
WIKOFF COLOR CORPORATION
240 Jamie Ln (60084-1079)
PHONE.....................847 487-2704
Jim Rickert, *Prdtn Mgr*
Bowman Shaw, *Manager*
EMP: 8
SALES (corp-wide): 175.5MM **Privately Held**
WEB: www.wikoff.com
SIC: 2893 5084 Printing ink; printing trades machinery, equipment & supplies
PA: Wikoff Color Corporation
1886 Merritt Rd
Fort Mill SC 29715
803 548-2210

Waukegan
Lake County

(G-20404)
A W RADTKE TOOL CORPORATION
111 E Greenwood Ave (60087)
P.O. Box 193 (60079-0193)
PHONE.....................847 662-7373
Arthur W Radtke, *President*
Nancy Radtke, *Vice Pres*
EMP: 3
SQ FT: 3,000
SALES: 250K **Privately Held**
SIC: 3599 3544 Machine shop, jobbing & repair; special dies, tools, jigs & fixtures

(G-20405)
AB SPECIALTY SILICONES LLC (PA)
Also Called: A B
3725 Hawthorne Ct (60087-3223)
PHONE.....................908 273-8015
Mac Penman, *Principal*
Angela Moses, *Research*
Robert Kemper, *CFO*
Kevin Leslie, *VP Sales*
Paul Duffy, *Accounts Mgr*
◆ **EMP:** 65
SALES (est): 18.4MM **Privately Held**
SIC: 2869 Silicones

(G-20406)
ABBOTT LABORATORIES
3561 Burwood Dr (60085-8320)
PHONE.....................847 938-3220
Asminda Bracamontes, *Accountant*
Doug Obizauf, *Branch Mgr*
EMP: 39
SALES (corp-wide): 31.9B **Publicly Held**
WEB: www.abbott.com
SIC: 2834 Pharmaceutical preparations
PA: Abbott Laboratories
100 Abbott Park Rd
Abbott Park IL 60064
224 667-6100

(G-20407)
ABBOTT LABORATORIES
3629 Burwood Dr (60085-9100)
PHONE.....................847 937-6100
Angel Gonzales, *Branch Mgr*
Jerry Luna, *Analyst*
EMP: 22
SALES (corp-wide): 31.9B **Publicly Held**
SIC: 2834 Pharmaceutical preparations
PA: Abbott Laboratories
100 Abbott Park Rd
Abbott Park IL 60064
224 667-6100

(G-20408)
ABBOTT LABORATORIES
1150 S Northpoint Blvd (60085-6763)
PHONE.....................847 937-6100
John Stansbury, *Manager*
EMP: 175
SALES (corp-wide): 31.9B **Publicly Held**
SIC: 2834 Pharmaceutical preparations
PA: Abbott Laboratories
100 Abbott Park Rd
Abbott Park IL 60064
224 667-6100

(G-20409)
ABBVIE INC
1150 S Northpoint Blvd (60085-6757)
PHONE.....................847 473-4787
Sheila Lockwood, *Manager*
Mahendran Ravichandran, *Manager*
Todd Turner, *Technician*
Paul Sonders, *Associate*
EMP: 50
SALES (corp-wide): 33.2B **Publicly Held**
SIC: 2834 Pharmaceutical preparations
PA: Abbvie Inc.
1 N Waukegan Rd
North Chicago IL 60064
847 932-7900

(G-20410)
AFX INC (PA)
Also Called: Afco Lite American Fluorescent
2345 Ernie Krueger Cir (60087-3225)
PHONE.....................847 249-5970
William R Solomon, *CEO*
Tim Tevyaw, *President*
Karin Koniarski, *Senior Buyer*
Paul Cuitino, *CFO*
Mark Dugan, *Human Res Dir*
◆ **EMP:** 150 **EST:** 1938
SQ FT: 95,000
SALES (est): 25.6MM **Privately Held**
WEB: www.americanfluorescent.com
SIC: 3645 3646 Residential lighting fixtures; commercial indusl & institutional electric lighting fixtures

(G-20411)
AKZO NOBEL COATINGS INC
Also Called: Akzo Nobel Aerospace Coatings
E Water St (60085)
PHONE.....................847 623-4200
Rod McQueen, *Branch Mgr*
Trish Lewis, *Manager*
EMP: 15
SALES (corp-wide): 10.2B **Privately Held**
SIC: 2851 Paints: oil or alkyd vehicle or water thinned

Waukegan - Lake County (G-20412)
GEOGRAPHIC SECTION

HQ: Akzo Nobel Coatings Inc.
8220 Mohawk Dr
Strongsville OH 44136
440 297-5100

(G-20412)
ALDON CO
3410 Sunset Ave (60087-3295)
P.O. Box 66973, Chicago (60666-0973)
PHONE.................................847 623-8800
Ralph V Switzer, *Ch of Bd*
Joseph R Ornig, *President*
Mike Lannan, *Vice Pres*
Kathy Christensen, *Buyer*
Jan Cardinali, *Marketing Staff*
▲ **EMP:** 19 **EST:** 1904
SQ FT: 13,000
SALES (est): 4.1MM **Privately Held**
WEB: www.aldonco.com
SIC: 3743 3536 3429 3423 Railroad equipment; hoists, cranes & monorails; manufactured hardware (general); hand & edge tools; blast furnaces & steel mills; wood pallets & skids

(G-20413)
ALLIE WOODWORKING
3035 Sunset Ave (60087-3437)
PHONE.................................847 244-1919
William Allie, *Owner*
EMP: 4
SALES (est): 233.3K **Privately Held**
SIC: 1751 2541 2511 2434 Cabinet & finish carpentry; wood partitions & fixtures; wood household furniture; wood kitchen cabinets; millwork

(G-20414)
AMERICAN OUTFITTERS LTD
3700 Sunset Ave (60087-3212)
PHONE.................................847 623-3959
Lawrence A Rettig, *President*
Gary N Rettig, *Corp Secy*
David Griffin, *Prdtn Mgr*
Mary Roegner, *Sales Staff*
Thomas Van, *Sales Staff*
EMP: 35 **EST:** 1975
SQ FT: 30,000
SALES (est): 5.7MM **Privately Held**
SIC: 7336 5699 5136 5137 Silk screen design; customized clothing & apparel; sportswear, men's & boys'; sportswear, women's & children's; screen printing

(G-20415)
AMERICAN PALLET CO INC
1105 Greenfield Ave (60085-7629)
PHONE.................................847 662-5525
Tammy Ash, *President*
EMP: 70
SQ FT: 10,000
SALES (est): 9.5MM **Privately Held**
SIC: 2448 Pallets, wood

(G-20416)
AMETEK INC
Also Called: Ametek Powervar
1450 S Lakeside Dr (60085-8301)
PHONE.................................847 596-7000
Doug Griffin, *Engineer*
Bessie Ippen, *Accounting Mgr*
EMP: 143
SALES (corp-wide): 5.1B **Publicly Held**
SIC: 3629 Electronic generation equipment
PA: Ametek, Inc.
1100 Cassatt Rd
Berwyn PA 19312
610 647-2121

(G-20417)
ARCOA GROUP INC (PA)
Also Called: Arcoa USA
3300 Washington St (60085-4716)
PHONE.................................847 693-7519
Cari Clark, *Business Mgr*
Jeff Datkuliak, *Vice Pres*
Terry Levy, *Vice Pres*
Brad Schmidt, *Safety Mgr*
Joe Clayton, *VP Business*
EMP: 31 **EST:** 2013
SALES (est): 15.3MM **Privately Held**
WEB: www.arcoausa.com
SIC: 3559 Recycling machinery

(G-20418)
ARMSTRONG AEROSPACE INC (HQ)
Also Called: Astronics Armstrong Aerospace
804 S Northpoint Blvd (60085-8211)
PHONE.................................847 244-4500
Robert Abbinante, *President*
Brian Roland, *Opers Staff*
Robert Louis, *Engineer*
Dominick Zaccaro, *Exec Dir*
Matt Wilfong, *Associate*
EMP: 100
SALES (est): 16.2MM
SALES (corp-wide): 772.7MM **Publicly Held**
SIC: 8711 3728 Consulting engineer; aircraft parts & equipment
PA: Astronics Corporation
130 Commerce Way
East Aurora NY 14052
716 805-1599

(G-20419)
ASTRONICS CNNCTVITY SYSTEMS CR (HQ)
Also Called: Astronics CSC
804 S Northpoint Blvd (60085-8211)
PHONE.................................847 821-3059
Peter J Gundermann, *President*
Michael Kuehn, *President*
Nick Cucci, *Principal*
Matthew Wilken, *CFO*
David Burney, *Admin Sec*
EMP: 12
SALES (est): 39MM
SALES (corp-wide): 772.7MM **Publicly Held**
SIC: 3647 3728 Aircraft lighting fixtures; aircraft parts & equipment
PA: Astronics Corporation
130 Commerce Way
East Aurora NY 14052
716 805-1599

(G-20420)
ATTURO TIRE CORP
3250 N Oak Grove Ave (60087-1825)
PHONE.................................855 632-8031
Michael Mathis, *President*
EMP: 4 **EST:** 2009
SALES (est): 156.2K **Privately Held**
SIC: 3011 Tires & inner tubes

(G-20421)
B W M GLOBAL
3740 Hawthorne Ct (60087-3222)
PHONE.................................847 785-1355
Brad Fish, *Owner*
Bradford Fish, *Partner*
▲ **EMP:** 8 **EST:** 2013
SALES (est): 1.1MM **Privately Held**
WEB: www.bwmglobal.com
SIC: 3993 Advertising novelties

(G-20422)
BAXTER HEALTHCARE CORPORATION
2105 S Waukegan Rd (60085-6737)
PHONE.................................847 578-4671
Chris Cooper, *Manager*
EMP: 30
SALES (corp-wide): 11.3B **Publicly Held**
SIC: 2835 2389 3842 5047 Blood derivative diagnostic agents; hospital gowns; surgical appliances & supplies; medical laboratory equipment; catheters
HQ: Baxter Healthcare Corporation
1 Baxter Pkwy
Deerfield IL 60015
224 948-2000

(G-20423)
BOWLERO CORP
385 Frederick Plz (60085)
PHONE.................................847 473-2600
EMP: 88
SALES (corp-wide): 280MM **Privately Held**
SIC: 3949 Sporting & athletic goods
PA: Bowlero Corp.
222 W 44th St
New York NY 10036
212 777-2214

(G-20424)
CARDINAL HEALTH INC
Also Called: Cardinal Medical Services
1500 S Waukegan Rd (60085-6728)
PHONE.................................847 578-4443
Paul Schranz, *Opers Mgr*
Sue Hufford, *Sales Staff*
Laura Korczynski, *Sales Staff*
Geoff Sobey, *Sales Staff*
James Gil, *Branch Mgr*
EMP: 400
SALES (corp-wide): 145.5B **Publicly Held**
SIC: 3841 5047 Surgical & medical instruments; medical & hospital equipment
PA: Cardinal Health, Inc.
7000 Cardinal Pl
Dublin OH 43017
614 757-5000

(G-20425)
CARDINAL HEALTH 200 LLC
1430 S Waukegan Rd (60085-6787)
PHONE.................................847 689-8410
Rick Epstein, *Vice Pres*
EMP: 44
SALES (corp-wide): 145.5B **Publicly Held**
SIC: 3841 Surgical & medical instruments
HQ: Cardinal Health 200, Llc
3651 Birchwood Dr
Waukegan IL 60085

(G-20426)
CASSINI CABINETRY
701 Belvidere Rd (60085-6309)
P.O. Box 9013 (60079-9013)
PHONE.................................847 244-9755
EMP: 3 **EST:** 2005
SALES (est): 180K **Privately Held**
SIC: 2434 Mfg Wood Kitchen Cabinets

(G-20427)
CHASSIS SERVICE UNLIMITED
2984 W Wadsworth Rd (60087-1253)
PHONE.................................847 336-2305
Jim Quinn, *Owner*
▼ **EMP:** 4
SQ FT: 5,000
SALES (est): 360.4K **Privately Held**
SIC: 3711 Automobile assembly, including specialty automobiles

(G-20428)
CIRCUIT WORKS CORPORATION (PA)
3135 N Oak Grove Ave (60087-1800)
PHONE.................................847 283-8600
Fred Wacker III, *Chairman*
Lisa Edwards, *Purch Mgr*
Marcy Ayala, *Buyer*
Carole Mulvaney, *Purchasing*
Daniel Guzman, *Engineer*
▲ **EMP:** 65
SQ FT: 57,000
SALES (est): 27.4MM **Privately Held**
SIC: 3672 Circuit boards, television & radio printed

(G-20429)
CNH INDUSTRIAL AMERICA LLC
2450 W Air Ln (60087-1480)
PHONE.................................847 263-5793
Matthew Cooth, *Manager*
EMP: 9
SALES (corp-wide): 28B **Privately Held**
SIC: 3523 Farm machinery & equipment
HQ: Cnh Industrial America Llc
700 State St
Racine WI 53404
262 636-6011

(G-20430)
CORNFIELDS LLC
3830 Sunset Ave (60087-3258)
PHONE.................................847 263-7000
Claire Cretors, *President*
Jeffrey M McMahon, *CFO*
◆ **EMP:** 120
SQ FT: 208,000
SALES (est): 43.1MM
SALES (corp-wide): 145.8MM **Privately Held**
WEB: www.cornfieldsinc.com
SIC: 2099 Popcorn, packaged; except already popped

PA: Eagle Family Foods Group Llc
1975 E 61st St
Cleveland OH 44103
330 382-3725

(G-20431)
COUNTER CRAFT INC
2113 Northwestern Ave (60087-4144)
PHONE.................................847 336-8205
Gregory Meyers, *President*
Scott Meyers, *Vice Pres*
EMP: 6
SQ FT: 1,800
SALES: 800K **Privately Held**
SIC: 2541 5712 2434 Counter & sink tops; custom made furniture, except cabinets; cabinet work, custom; wood kitchen cabinets

(G-20432)
D N WELDING & FABRICATING INC
3627 Washington St Bldg 5 (60085-4767)
PHONE.................................847 244-6410
Danny Darnell, *President*
Scott Nelson, *Vice Pres*
EMP: 4
SQ FT: 6,000
SALES (est): 410.4K **Privately Held**
SIC: 7692 Welding repair

(G-20433)
D-M-S HOLDINGS INC (HQ)
Also Called: Healthsmart International
1931 Norman Dr (60085-6715)
PHONE.................................515 327-6416
Bruce Dan, *President*
Dean Economos, *Analyst*
◆ **EMP:** 24 **EST:** 1995
SALES (est): 42.2MM
SALES (corp-wide): 150MM **Privately Held**
SIC: 5047 3841 Medical equipment & supplies; surgical & medical instruments
PA: Briggs Medical Service Company
4900 University Ave # 200
West Des Moines IA 50266
515 327-6400

(G-20434)
DAVID LINDERHOLM
Also Called: Edgetool Industrial Supplies
2210 Grand Ave Unit 2 (60085-3311)
PHONE.................................847 336-3755
David R Linderholm, *Owner*
EMP: 4
SQ FT: 1,500
SALES (est): 147.7K **Privately Held**
SIC: 7699 3545 5085 Knife, saw & tool sharpening & repair; machine tool accessories; industrial tools

(G-20435)
DERSE INC
3696 Burwood Dr (60085-8399)
PHONE.................................847 473-2149
Ken Aden-Buie, *General Mgr*
EMP: 85
SALES (corp-wide): 117.4MM **Privately Held**
SIC: 3993 Displays & cutouts, window & lobby
PA: Derse, Inc.
3800 W Canal St
Milwaukee WI 53208
414 257-2000

(G-20436)
DESIGN PHASE INC
1771 S Lakeside Dr (60085-8313)
PHONE.................................847 473-0077
Michael P Eckert, *President*
William B Brice, *Project Mgr*
Brian Korda, *Project Mgr*
David Pope, *Engineer*
John Skalski, *Engineer*
▲ **EMP:** 22
SQ FT: 65,000
SALES (est): 4.8MM **Privately Held**
SIC: 3993 7319 Displays & cutouts, window & lobby; display advertising service

(G-20437)
DEUBLIN COMPANY (PA)
2050 Norman Dr (60085-8270)
PHONE.................................847 689-8600

▲ = Import ▼ = Export
◆ = Import/Export

GEOGRAPHIC SECTION

Waukegan - Lake County (G-20464)

Donald Deubler, *Ch of Bd*
Ronald Kelner, *President*
Matt Bell, *District Mgr*
Dave Gardner, *District Mgr*
Dave Short, *Plant Mgr*
◆ **EMP:** 200 **EST:** 1945
SQ FT: 110,000
SALES (est): 149.2MM **Privately Held**
WEB: www.deublin.com
SIC: 3498 3492 3568 3494 Fabricated pipe & fittings; fluid power valves & hose fittings; power transmission equipment; valves & pipe fittings

(G-20438)
DIE CAST MACHINERY LLC
3246 W Monroe St (60085-3029)
PHONE 847 360-9170
Kaufman David, *Principal*
Cochran Steven, *Principal*
Steven Cochran, *COO*
David Kaufman, *Mng Member*
EMP: 10
SALES (est): 607.5K **Privately Held**
SIC: 3542 Die casting machines

(G-20439)
E2 MANUFACTURING GROUP LLC
3776 Hawthorne Ct (60087-3222)
PHONE 224 399-9608
James Martin, *
EMP: 3
SALES (est): 294.1K **Privately Held**
WEB: www.e2-mfg.com
SIC: 3999 Barber & beauty shop equipment

(G-20440)
EAGLE HIGH MAST LTG CO INC
1070a S Northpoint Blvd (60085-8213)
PHONE 847 473-3800
Fax: 847 473-3870
EMP: 7
SQ FT: 12,000
SALES (est): 680K **Privately Held**
SIC: 3648 5063 Mfg Lighting Equipment Whol Electrical Equip

(G-20441)
ECOLOGIC INDUSTRIES LLC
3742 Hawthorne Ct (60087-3222)
PHONE 847 234-5855
Dan Goldman, *
▲ **EMP:** 30
SALES (est): 5.5MM **Privately Held**
SIC: 3999 Chairs, hydraulic, barber & beauty shop

(G-20442)
F & R PLASTICS INC
642 Westmoreland Ave (60085-3447)
PHONE 847 336-1330
Frank Mlinar, *President*
Rosalie Mlinar, *Vice Pres*
EMP: 3
SQ FT: 3,000
SALES: 200K **Privately Held**
SIC: 3089 3544 Injection molding of plastics; special dies, tools, jigs & fixtures

(G-20443)
FERRO CORPORATION
1219 Glen Rock Ave (60085-6230)
PHONE 847 623-0370
Tracy Stahlkopf, *Manager*
EMP: 250
SALES (corp-wide): 1B **Publicly Held**
SIC: 3264 Porcelain electrical supplies
PA: Ferro Corporation
  6060 Parkland Blvd # 250
  Mayfield Heights OH 44124
  216 875-5600

(G-20444)
G-P MANUFACTURING CO INC
1535 S Lakeside Dr. (60085-8312)
PHONE 847 473-9001
Robert Price, *CEO*
Harold Price, *President*
Frances Price, *Admin Sec*
EMP: 40 **EST:** 1938
SQ FT: 50,000
SALES (est): 6.6MM **Privately Held**
SIC: 3081 3082 Packing materials, plastic sheet; rods, unsupported plastic; tubes, unsupported plastic

(G-20445)
GOLOSINAS EL CANTO
1115 Washington St (60085-5301)
PHONE 847 625-5103
Mark Amirez, *Owner*
EMP: 9
SALES (est): 749K **Privately Held**
SIC: 2051 Bread, cake & related products

(G-20446)
HFD MANUFACTURING INC
Also Called: Hfd Graphics Equipment
1813 W Glen Flora Ave (60085-1724)
PHONE 847 263-5050
William E Dziallo, *President*
EMP: 3
SALES (est): 280K **Privately Held**
SIC: 3554 3541 Paper industries machinery; machine tools, metal cutting type

(G-20447)
ILLINOIS CARBIDE TOOL CO INC (PA)
Also Called: Brake Drum Tool Co America Div
1322 Belvidere Rd (60085-6206)
PHONE 847 244-1110
John Mini, *President*
A G Mini, *Chairman*
Michael Mini, *Vice Pres*
EMP: 18 **EST:** 1959
SQ FT: 20,000
SALES (est): 4.6MM **Privately Held**
WEB: www.crobaltusa.com
SIC: 3545 Cutting tools for machine tools

(G-20448)
INKN TEES
2901 N Delany Rd Ste 105 (60087-1886)
PHONE 847 244-2266
Steven Stams, *Principal*
EMP: 3
SALES (est): 418.7K **Privately Held**
SIC: 2759 Screen printing

(G-20449)
INSTYPRINTS OF WAUKEGAN INC
Also Called: Insty-Prints
1711 Grand Ave Ste 1 (60085-3594)
PHONE 847 336-5599
James Bush, *President*
EMP: 4 **EST:** 1970
SQ FT: 2,000
SALES (est): 508.2K **Privately Held**
SIC: 2752 2796 2791 2789 Commercial printing, lithographic; platemaking services; typesetting; bookbinding & related work

(G-20450)
INTERNATIONAL PAINT LLC
Akzo Nobel Aerospace Coatings
1 E Water St (60085-5635)
PHONE 847 623-4200
Alan Gerling, *Engineer*
Kevin Fleetwood, *Branch Mgr*
Allan Donnellan, *Manager*
Andy Jameson, *Technical Staff*
EMP: 18
SALES (corp-wide): 10.2B **Privately Held**
SIC: 2851 Polyurethane coatings
HQ: International Paint Llc
  6001 Antoine Dr
  Houston TX 77091
  713 682-1711

(G-20451)
J D PLATING WORKS INC
1424 12th St (60085-7693)
PHONE 847 662-6484
John Dobnikar, *CEO*
Jose A Gonzales, *Vice Pres*
EMP: 2 **EST:** 1938
SQ FT: 4,000
SALES (est): 271K **Privately Held**
SIC: 3471 Plating of metals or formed products; polishing, metals or formed products

(G-20452)
JACOBSON ACQSTION HOLDINGS LLC
Also Called: S. I. Jacobson Mfg. Company
1414 Jacobson Dr (60085-7601)
PHONE 847 623-1414
Charles Gonzalez, *CEO*
Patricia Stemp, *Principal*
Terry Tank, *Design Engr*
Kathryn Wagner, *Human Res Mgr*
Joe Forsman, *Accounts Mgr*
▲ **EMP:** 225 **EST:** 1934
SQ FT: 87,500
SALES (est): 29MM **Privately Held**
WEB: www.sij.com
SIC: 2211 2673 3161 2782 Bags & bagging, cotton; plastic bags: made from purchased materials; briefcases; looseleaf binders & devices; signs & advertising specialties

(G-20453)
K O G MFG & BINDERY CORP
1813 W Glen Flora Ave (60085-1724)
PHONE 847 263-5050
Timothy W Arnold, *President*
EMP: 15
SQ FT: 20,000
SALES: 2MM **Privately Held**
SIC: 2789 Bookbinding & related work

(G-20454)
KAUFMAN-WORTHEN MACHINERY INC
2326 W Wadsworth Rd (60087-1244)
P.O. Box 7921, Gurnee (60031-7007)
PHONE 847 360-9170
David Kaufman, *President*
Rick Worthen, *Vice Pres*
EMP: 6
SALES (est): 490K **Privately Held**
SIC: 3542 Die casting machines

(G-20455)
KLEIN TOOLS INC
2920 W Aviation Dr (60087-1202)
PHONE 847 249-4930
Dave Swieczkowski, *Principal*
EMP: 3
SALES (est): 385.1K **Privately Held**
SIC: 3423 3199 Hand & edge tools; belting for machinery: solid, twisted, flat, etc.: leather

(G-20456)
KONNECTRONIX INC
2340 Ernie Krueger Cir (60087-3224)
PHONE 847 672-8685
Allison Burke, *President*
Gloria Burke, *Principal*
Denise Ogren, *Sales Staff*
Chris Hinojosa, *Director*
▲ **EMP:** 20
SALES: 14.2MM
SALES (corp-wide): 772.7MM **Publicly Held**
SIC: 3678 Electronic connectors
HQ: Astronics Connectivity Systems & Certification Corp.
  804 S Northpoint Blvd
  Waukegan IL 60085
  847 821-3059

(G-20457)
LAFARGE NORTH AMERICA INC
Also Called: Lafargeholcim
315 E Sea Horse Dr (60085-2144)
PHONE 847 244-3800
Larry Brewer, *Branch Mgr*
EMP: 11
SALES (corp-wide): 4.5B **Privately Held**
SIC: 3241 Cement, hydraulic
HQ: Lafarge North America Inc.
  8700 W Bryn Mawr Ave
  Chicago IL 60631
  773 372-1000

(G-20458)
LAKE COUNTY PRESS INC (PA)
98 Noll St (60085-3031)
P.O. Box 9209 (60079-9209)
PHONE 847 336-4333
Ralph L Johnson, *President*
Dan Smith, *President*
Jeannette C Zissis, *Counsel*
Peter Douglas, *Senior VP*
Lisa Arsenault, *Vice Pres*
EMP: 223
SQ FT: 79,500
SALES (est): 87MM **Privately Held**
SIC: 2791 7334 Typesetting; blueprinting service

(G-20459)
LIVINGSTON INNOVATIONS LLC
3242 W Monroe St (60085-3029)
PHONE 847 808-0900
Megan Millman, *Manager*
Troy Livingston, *Manager*
EMP: 4
SALES (est): 234.1K **Privately Held**
SIC: 3499 Wheels: wheelbarrow, stroller, etc.: disc, stamped metal; machine bases, metal

(G-20460)
LIVINGSTON PRODUCTS INC
3242 W Monroe St (60085-3029)
PHONE 847 808-0900
Troy W Livingston, *President*
Seren Livingston, *Vice Pres*
Daniel Livingston, *Plant Mgr*
EMP: 18
SQ FT: 15,000
SALES (est): 3.1MM **Privately Held**
SIC: 3599 8711 Custom machinery; mechanical engineering

(G-20461)
LMT ONSRUD LP
Also Called: Onsrud Cutter
1081 S Northpoint Blvd (60085-8215)
PHONE 847 362-1560
Leslie Banduch, *Partner*
Maulik Bhatt, *Engineer*
Bill Hallam, *VP Finance*
Bryan Cardinal, *Sales Staff*
Gail Hamilton, *Sales Staff*
▲ **EMP:** 107
SQ FT: 60,000
SALES (est): 31.3MM
SALES (corp-wide): 474MM **Privately Held**
SIC: 3423 3545 Hand & edge tools; machine tool accessories
HQ: Lmt Tool Systems Gmbh & Co. Kg
  Heidenheimer Str. 84
  Oberkochen 73447

(G-20462)
LMT USA INC
1081 S Northpoint Blvd (60085-8215)
PHONE 630 969-5412
EMP: 6
SALES (corp-wide): 402.9MM **Privately Held**
SIC: 5084 3545 3544 3444 Whol Industrial Machinery Mfg Machine Tool Accessories Special Dies Tools Die Sets Sheet Metalwork & Steel Foundaries
HQ: Lmt Usa, Inc.
  1081 S Northpoint Blvd
  Waukegan IL 60085
  630 969-5412

(G-20463)
LORDAHL MANUFACTURING CO (PA)
Also Called: Lordahl Engineering Co
1001 S Lewis Ave (60085-7665)
P.O. Box 5769, Buffalo Grove (60089-5769)
PHONE 847 244-0448
Var E Lordahl Sr, *President*
Frank O'Sullivan, *Vice Pres*
Tatyama Rivtis, *Controller*
Carol Lordahl, *Admin Sec*
▲ **EMP:** 30
SQ FT: 30,000
SALES (est): 7.6MM **Privately Held**
SIC: 3088 Plastics plumbing fixtures

(G-20464)
LTC HOLDINGS INC
Also Called: Laserage
3021 N Delany Rd (60087-1826)
PHONE 847 249-5900
Stephen L Capp, *CEO*
Joseph S Coel, *Vice Pres*
Michael W Wimmer, *CFO*
EMP: 125

Waukegan - Lake County (G-20465)

SQ FT: 34,000
SALES: 25MM
SALES (corp-wide): 5.1B **Publicly Held**
WEB: www.laserage.com
SIC: **3449** 3841 Curtain wall, metal; inhalation therapy equipment
PA: Ametek, Inc.
1100 Cassatt Rd
Berwyn PA 19312
610 647-2121

(G-20465)
MEDICAL RECORDS CO
Also Called: Computaforms
317 Stewart Ave (60085-2061)
PHONE..................847 662-6373
Thomas J Streit, *Owner*
Helen S Streit, *Co-Owner*
EMP: 5
SALES (est): 310K **Privately Held**
SIC: **5112** 2752 Business forms; commercial printing, lithographic

(G-20466)
MEDLINE INDUSTRIES INC
1170 S Northpoint Blvd (60085-6757)
PHONE..................847 949-5500
Bill Sanders, *President*
Jim O'Brian, *General Mgr*
Alyson Dega, *Purch Mgr*
Beth Marz, *Marketing Mgr*
Rita Taylor, *Manager*
EMP: 400
SALES (corp-wide): 7.4B **Privately Held**
SIC: **3842** 3841 Surgical appliances & supplies; surgical & medical instruments
PA: Medline Industries, Inc.
3 Lakes Dr
Northfield IL 60093
847 949-5500

(G-20467)
MERCHANTS METALS LLC
2800 Northwestern Ave (60087-5333)
PHONE..................847 249-4086
EMP: 6
SALES (corp-wide): 1.7B **Privately Held**
SIC: **3446** Mfg Architectural Metalwork
HQ: Merchants Metals Llc
900 Ashwood Pkwy Ste 600
Atlanta GA 30346
770 741-0300

(G-20468)
NEW NGC INC
515 E Sea Horse Dr (60085-2165)
PHONE..................847 623-8100
Gene Kropfelder, *Manager*
EMP: 92
SALES (corp-wide): 795.8MM **Privately Held**
SIC: **3275** Gypsum products
HQ: New Ngc, Inc.
2001 Rexford Rd
Charlotte NC 28211

(G-20469)
NORTH SHORE PRINTERS INC
535 S Sheridan Rd (60085-7553)
PHONE..................847 623-0037
Charlotte Wozniak, *President*
Amy Callahan, *Treasurer*
Michael Galbraith, *Admin Sec*
EMP: 13
SQ FT: 30,000
SALES (est): 1.7MM **Privately Held**
WEB: www.nsprinters.com
SIC: **2752** Commercial printing, offset

(G-20470)
NORTH SHORE WTR RCLAMATION DST
Dahringer Rd (60085)
PHONE..................847 623-6060
Eugene Lukasik, *Branch Mgr*
EMP: 30
SALES (corp-wide): 23.6MM **Privately Held**
SIC: **3589** Sewage treatment equipment
PA: North Shore Water Reclamation District
14770 W Wlliam Koepsel Dr
Gurnee IL 60031
847 623-6060

(G-20471)
NOSCO INC
651 S Mrtn Lther King Jr (60085-7500)
PHONE..................847 360-4874
Russ Haraf, *President*
Rick Potochnick, *Plant Mgr*
Dick Petkus, *Mfg Staff*
Mike Biesboer, *CFO*
Ernie Sio, *Controller*
EMP: 90
SALES (corp-wide): 314MM **Privately Held**
SIC: **2752** 2657 2672 2759 Commercial printing, lithographic; folding paperboard boxes; adhesive papers, labels or tapes: from purchased material; labels (unprinted); gummed: made from purchased materials; commercial printing; packaging paper & plastics film, coated & laminated
HQ: Nosco, Inc
2199 N Delany Rd
Gurnee IL 60031
847 336-4200

(G-20472)
OBROTHERS BAKERY INC
2820 Belvidere Rd (60085-6040)
PHONE..................847 249-0091
Ramiro Ortega, *President*
EMP: 7
SALES (est): 575.1K **Privately Held**
SIC: **2051** 5461 Bakery: wholesale or wholesale/retail combined; bakeries

(G-20473)
OCTANE MOTORSPORTS LLC
3056 Washington St 2b (60085-4844)
PHONE..................224 419-5460
Renee Goodwin, *Principal*
Nick Christodoulou, *Mfg Mgr*
EMP: 4
SALES (est): 234.3K **Privately Held**
SIC: **3599** 8711 7373 Machine & other job shop work; engineering services; computer-aided design (CAD) systems service; computer-aided manufacturing (CAM) systems service; computer-aided engineering (CAE) systems service

(G-20474)
OREILLY AUTOMOTIVE STORES INC
Also Called: Oreilly's Auto Parts
2507 Grand Ave (60085-3316)
PHONE..................847 360-0012
Ted Weiss, *Branch Mgr*
EMP: 4 **Publicly Held**
SIC: **7699** 7694 7538 5531 Engine repair & replacement, non-automotive; rebuilding motors, except automotive; engine repair; automotive parts
HQ: O'reilly Automotive Stores, Inc.
233 S Patterson Ave
Springfield MO 65802
417 862-2674

(G-20475)
PEER CHAIN COMPANY
2300 Norman Dr (60085-8207)
PHONE..................847 775-4600
Glenn Spungen, *President*
Jeremy Fogo, *Regional Mgr*
Kenneth W Spungen, *Vice Pres*
Eric MA, *Engineer*
Susan Simmermon, *Human Res Dir*
▲ EMP: 70
SALES (est): 17.8MM **Privately Held**
WEB: www.peerchain.com
SIC: **3568** 3462 8734 Power transmission equipment; iron & steel forgings; testing laboratories

(G-20476)
PFANSTIEHL INC
1219 Glen Rock Ave (60085-6230)
PHONE..................847 623-0370
Cindy Kerker, *President*
V J Comanita, *Vice Pres*
Edurdo Mar, *Director*
▲ EMP: 24 EST: 1997
SQ FT: 7,500
SALES (est): 19.4MM **Privately Held**
WEB: www.pfanstiehl.com
SIC: **2834** Pharmaceutical preparations

PA: Med Opportunity Partners, Llc
1 Roger Dr
Greenwich CT 06831

(G-20477)
PFANSTIEHL HOLDINGS INC
1219 Glen Rock Ave (60085-6230)
PHONE..................847 623-0370
EMP: 3
SALES (est): 81.8K **Privately Held**
SIC: **2834** Pharmaceutical preparations

(G-20478)
POLYMAX THRMPLSTC ELSTMERS LL
Also Called: Polymax Tpe
3210 N Oak Grove Ave (60087-1887)
PHONE..................847 316-9900
Yun Martin Lu, *CEO*
Xin Zhang, *Project Engr*
Tom Castile, *VP Sales*
Leanne Teplitz, *Manager*
Ron Sheu,
▲ EMP: 25 EST: 2013
SQ FT: 41,108
SALES (est): 792.7K **Privately Held**
SIC: **2822** 2821 Synthetic rubber; thermoplastic materials; elastomers, nonvulcanizable (plastics)

(G-20479)
POLYMER NATION LLC (PA)
405 N Oakwood Ave (60085-3006)
PHONE..................847 972-2157
Christopher O'Brien, *President*
Don Kessler, *CFO*
EMP: 1 EST: 2007
SALES (est): 8MM **Privately Held**
SIC: **2851** 1791 1752 1761 Paints & allied products; exterior wall system installation; access flooring system installation; ceilings, metal: erection & repair

(G-20480)
POWERVAR INC (HQ)
1450 S Lakeside Dr (60085-8301)
PHONE..................847 596-7000
George Ardolino, *President*
▲ EMP: 120
SQ FT: 50,000
SALES (est): 22.2MM
SALES (corp-wide): 5.1B **Publicly Held**
SIC: **3629** Electronic generation equipment
PA: Ametek, Inc.
1100 Cassatt Rd
Berwyn PA 19312
610 647-2121

(G-20481)
PRECISION LABORATORIES LLC
1429 S Shields Dr (60085-8310)
PHONE..................847 282-7228
Richard L Wohlner, *President*
Bo Barefoot, *District Mgr*
Larry Conkings, *District Mgr*
Tom Hogan, *District Mgr*
Erick Koskinen, *District Mgr*
▲ EMP: 35
SQ FT: 40,000
SALES (est): 21.7MM **Privately Held**
WEB: www.precisionlab.com
SIC: **2879** Agricultural chemicals

(G-20482)
PRISTINE WATER SOLUTIONS INC
1570 S Lakeside Dr (60085-8309)
P.O. Box 599, Peru (61354-0599)
PHONE..................847 689-1100
EMP: 11
SALES (est): 2MM
SALES (corp-wide): 417MM **Publicly Held**
SIC: **3589** Water Solution Treatment
HQ: Met-Pro Technologies Llc
460 E Swedesford Rd # 2030
Wayne PA 19087
215 717-7909

(G-20483)
PRONTO SIGNS AND ENGRAVING
2114 Grand Ave (60085-3416)
PHONE..................847 249-7874

Jim Cogan, *President*
EMP: 3
SALES (est): 254.2K **Privately Held**
WEB: www.prontosigns.net
SIC: **3993** Signs, not made in custom sign painting shops

(G-20484)
PROTOTYPE EQUIPMENT CORP
Also Called: Goodman Packaging Equipment
1081 S Northpoint Blvd (60085-8215)
PHONE..................847 596-9000
James A Goodman, *President*
Ann D Goodman, *Corp Secy*
William H Goodman, *Vice Pres*
David Marberger, *CFO*
EMP: 70
SQ FT: 67,500
SALES (est): 13.5MM **Privately Held**
SIC: **3565** Packaging machinery

(G-20485)
PURSUIT BEVERAGE COMPANY LLC
972 S Northpoint Blvd (60085-8212)
PHONE..................888 606-3353
Dominick Voso, *President*
Richard Atkinson, *Vice Pres*
EMP: 9
SALES (est): 1.4MM **Privately Held**
SIC: **2086** Bottled & canned soft drinks

(G-20486)
PYRAMID BOTTLING LLC
3500 Sunset Ave (60087-3204)
PHONE..................847 565-9412
James A Onan, *Manager*
EMP: 3
SALES (est): 91.3K **Privately Held**
SIC: **2086** Mineral water, carbonated: packaged in cans, bottles, etc.

(G-20487)
RAMPRO FACILITIES SVCS CORP
1701 Grand Ave (60085-3501)
PHONE..................224 639-6378
Rubullah Mahdee, *President*
EMP: 5 EST: 2016
SQ FT: 1,200
SALES: 300K **Privately Held**
SIC: **7349** 2899 7389 3639 Janitorial service, contract basis; fire extinguisher charges; fire extinguisher servicing; major kitchen appliances, except refrigerators & stoves; access flooring system installation

(G-20488)
RJW GRAPHICS INC
Also Called: Fastsigns
3420 Grand Ave (60085-2282)
PHONE..................847 336-4515
Sandra J Wagner, *Principal*
Bob Wagner, *Principal*
EMP: 5
SALES (est): 313.8K **Privately Held**
SIC: **3993** Signs & advertising specialties

(G-20489)
ROCK-TRED 2 LLC (PA)
Also Called: Ora Holdings
405 N Oakwood Ave (60085-3006)
PHONE..................888 762-5873
Chris O'Brien, *CEO*
Mark Moran, *President*
Erik Sebby, *General Mgr*
Michael Fugatt, *Regional Mgr*
Brian Wilson, *Plant Mgr*
EMP: 35 EST: 1939
SQ FT: 120,000
SALES (est): 8.1MM **Privately Held**
WEB: www.rocktred.com
SIC: **2842** 2851 Specialty cleaning, polishes & sanitation goods; polyurethane coatings

(G-20490)
RUBIS BAKERY INC
1703 Washington St (60085-5133)
P.O. Box 9148 (60079-9148)
PHONE..................847 623-4094
Hector Leal, *Principal*
Aurelia Leal, *Principal*
EMP: 7

GEOGRAPHIC SECTION

Waukegan - Lake County (G-20518)

SALES (est): 601.8K **Privately Held**
SIC: **2051** Bakery; wholesale or wholesale/retail combined

(G-20491)
SALUD NATURAL ENTREPRENEUR INC
Also Called: Salud Natural Entrepreneurs
1120 Glen Rock Ave (60085-5458)
PHONE..........................224 789-7400
Monica Velasquez, *General Mgr*
EMP: 26
SQ FT: 42,000 **Privately Held**
WEB: www.nopalinausa.com
SIC: **2023** Dietary supplements, dairy & non-dairy based
PA: Salud Natural Entrepreneur, Inc.
   1120 Glen Rock Ave
   Waukegan IL 60085

(G-20492)
SALUD NATURAL ENTREPRENEUR INC (PA)
Also Called: Nopalina
1120 Glen Rock Ave (60085-5458)
PHONE..........................224 789-7400
Hector Olivaa, *President*
Monica Velasquez, *General Mgr*
Sergio Oliva, *Vice Pres*
◆ EMP: 26
SQ FT: 50,000
SALES (est): 10MM **Privately Held**
SIC: **2023** 2041 Dietary supplements, dairy & non-dairy based; bran & middlings (except rice)

(G-20493)
SEASONAL DESIGNS INC (PA)
Also Called: Liberty Flags
1595 S Shields Dr (60085-8304)
PHONE..........................847 688-0280
John Cutler, *President*
Chris Machalski, *Finance Mgr*
▲ EMP: 45
SQ FT: 40,000
SALES (est): 32.9MM **Privately Held**
SIC: **5131** 2399 Flags & banners; flags, fabric

(G-20494)
SHATTUC CORD SPECIALTIES INC
2340 Ernie Krueger Cir (60087-3224)
PHONE..........................847 360-9500
John Runzel, *President*
John S Runzel, *President*
EMP: 14
SQ FT: 3,500
SALES (est): 3.4MM **Privately Held**
SIC: **3643** Connectors, electric cord

(G-20495)
SILGAN CONTAINERS MFG CORP
1301 W Dugdale Rd (60085-7225)
PHONE..........................847 336-0552
Bill Callale, *Manager*
EMP: 43 **Publicly Held**
SIC: **3411** Metal cans
HQ: Silgan Containers Manufacturing Corporation
   21600 Oxnard St Ste 1600
   Woodland Hills CA 91367

(G-20496)
SILGAN EQUIPMENT COMPANY
1301 W Dugdale Rd (60085-7225)
PHONE..........................847 336-0552
Arun Lamba, *General Mgr*
▲ EMP: 44
SALES (est): 7.1MM **Publicly Held**
SIC: **3411** 3086 Metal cans; packaging & shipping materials, foamed plastic
HQ: Silgan Containers Llc
   21600 Oxnard St Ste 1600
   Woodland Hills CA 91367
   818 710-3700

(G-20497)
SIX COLOR PRINT LLC (PA)
2233 Northwestern Ave B (60087-4150)
PHONE..........................847 336-3287
Zatz Steven G,
EMP: 13

SALES (est): 1.3MM **Privately Held**
WEB: www.sixcolorprint.com
SIC: **2752** Commercial printing, offset

(G-20498)
STEVENS INSTRUMENT COMPANY
111 W Greenwood Ave (60087-5134)
P.O. Box 193 (60079-0193)
PHONE..........................847 336-9375
Sharon Kordt, *President*
Jon Kordt, *Corp Secy*
EMP: 6 EST: 1971
SQ FT: 6,000
SALES (est): 638.1K **Privately Held**
SIC: **3825** 3829 Engine electrical test equipment; measuring & controlling devices

(G-20499)
STRADIS MEDICAL LLC
Also Called: Stradis Healthcare
3600 Burwood Dr (60085-8399)
PHONE..........................847 887-8400
EMP: 18
SALES (corp-wide): 10.8MM **Privately Held**
WEB: www.stradishealthcare.com
SIC: **3841** Surgical & medical instruments
PA: Stradis Medical, Llc
   3025 Northwoods Pkwy
   Peachtree Corners GA 30071
   770 962-2425

(G-20500)
TECHNIQUE ENG INC
968 S Northpoint Blvd (60085-8212)
PHONE..........................847 816-1870
Rudy Avramovich, *President*
EMP: 12
SALES (est): 1.6MM **Privately Held**
SIC: **2821** Plastics materials & resins

(G-20501)
TECHNIQUE ENGINEERING INC
968 S Northpoint Blvd (60085-8212)
PHONE..........................847 816-1870
Rudy Avramovich, *President*
EMP: 12
SQ FT: 20,000
SALES (est): 2.1MM **Privately Held**
SIC: **3544** 8711 Special dies, tools, jigs & fixtures; mechanical engineering

(G-20502)
TECNOVA ELECTRONICS INC
2383 N Delany Rd (60085-1836)
PHONE..........................847 336-6160
Terry Coleman Sr, *President*
Terry Coleman Jr, *Corp Secy*
▲ EMP: 90
SQ FT: 70,000
SALES (est): 27MM **Privately Held**
SIC: **3672** 8711 Printed circuit boards; engineering services

(G-20503)
THELEN SAND & GRAVEL INC
Also Called: Waukegan Ready Mix
1020 Elizabeth St (60085-7626)
P.O. Box 730, Spring Grove (60081-0730)
PHONE..........................847 662-0760
Christian Daman, *Opers Staff*
Frank Roznik, *Manager*
Bill Bolger, *Director*
EMP: 12
SALES (est): 382.9K
SALES (corp-wide): 30.7MM **Privately Held**
SIC: **1442** Construction sand & gravel
PA: Thelen Sand & Gravel, Inc.
   28955 W Il Route 173 # 1
   Antioch IL 60002
   847 838-8800

(G-20504)
THERMOFLEX CORP (PA)
1535 S Lakeside Dr (60085-8312)
PHONE..........................847 473-9001
Robert Price, *CEO*
Jacob Price, *Vice Pres*
Patrick Stanglewicz, *Production*
Teresa Lechuga, *Purchasing*
Mick Myers, *QC Mgr*
▼ EMP: 11
SQ FT: 228,000

SALES (est): 16.8MM **Privately Held**
SIC: **2821** Plastics materials & resins

(G-20505)
THERMOFLEX CORP
1817-1855 S Waukegan Rd (60085)
PHONE..........................847 473-9001
Eric Weitz, *CFO*
EMP: 3
SALES (corp-wide): 16.8MM **Privately Held**
SIC: **2821** Plastics materials & resins
PA: Thermoflex Corp.
   1535 S Lakeside Dr
   Waukegan IL 60085
   847 473-9001

(G-20506)
TKG SWEEPING & SERVICES LLC
345 N Lakewood Ave (60085-3049)
PHONE..........................847 505-1400
Brett Katz, *Mng Member*
Daniel Katz, *Mng Member*
Richard Katz, *Mng Member*
EMP: 3 EST: 2009
SALES (est): 551.6K **Privately Held**
SIC: **4959** 3589 Sweeping service: road, airport, parking lot, etc.; dirt sweeping units, industrial; carpet sweepers, except household electric vacuum sweepers

(G-20507)
TOLAR GROUP LLC
Also Called: Tolar Wstgate Fnrals Crmations
616 Washington St (60085-5421)
PHONE..........................847 662-8000
Eric Tolar,
EMP: 50
SQ FT: 3,500
SALES (est): 780.6K **Privately Held**
SIC: **0181** 3995 4212 5087 Florists' greens & flowers; burial caskets; delivery service, vehicular; cemetery & funeral directors' equipment & supplies; monuments & grave markers

(G-20508)
TOLERANCE MANUFACTURING INC
1435 10th St (60085-7605)
PHONE..........................847 244-8836
Barbara Furlan, *President*
Kenneth Furlan, *President*
EMP: 14 EST: 1967
SQ FT: 7,200
SALES (est): 1.8MM **Privately Held**
SIC: **3599** 3429 Machine shop, jobbing & repair; furniture hardware

(G-20509)
TONYS BAKERY
1117 Washington St (60085-5301)
PHONE..........................847 599-1590
Antonio Aricmedi, *Owner*
◆ EMP: 4
SALES (est): 207.5K **Privately Held**
SIC: **2051** Bakery; wholesale or wholesale/retail combined

(G-20510)
TRIAD CIRCUITS INC
3135 N Oak Grove Ave (60087-1800)
PHONE..........................847 283-8600
Shawn Bixler, *President*
EMP: 30
SQ FT: 25,900
SALES (est): 3.5MM **Privately Held**
SIC: **3672** Printed circuit boards

(G-20511)
TWISTSHAKE LLC
1070 S Northpoint Blvd (60085-8213)
PHONE..........................224 419-0086
Martin Astrom, *Mng Member*
EMP: 4
SQ FT: 20,000
SALES: 400K
SALES (corp-wide): 7.8MM **Privately Held**
WEB: www.twistshake.com
SIC: **3085** Plastics bottles
PA: Twistshake Of Sweden Ab
   Kopparbergsvagen 10
   Vasteras 722 1
   214 440-140

(G-20512)
UCC HOLDINGS CORPORATION (HQ)
2100 Norman Dr (60085-6752)
PHONE..........................847 473-5900
Andrew Warrington, *President*
Frederick K Schroeder, *Admin Sec*
EMP: 21
SALES (est): 158.3MM
SALES (corp-wide): 183.7MM **Privately Held**
SIC: **3443** 8711 Fabricated plate work (boiler shop); designing: ship, boat, machine & product

(G-20513)
UNITED CONVEYOR CORPORATION (DH)
2100 Norman Dr (60085-6753)
PHONE..........................847 473-5900
Douglas S Basler, *President*
Tony Piccolini, *District Mgr*
Mark Burns, *Vice Pres*
Mark A Burns, *Vice Pres*
Dan E Charhut, *Vice Pres*
◆ EMP: 250 EST: 1920
SQ FT: 100,000
SALES (est): 147.5MM
SALES (corp-wide): 183.7MM **Privately Held**
WEB: www.unitedconveyor.com
SIC: **3535** Conveyors & conveying equipment

(G-20514)
UNITED CONVEYOR SUPPLY COMPANY (DH)
2100 Norman Dr (60085-6752)
PHONE..........................847 672-5100
Douglas S Basler, *President*
Mark Springer, *CFO*
▲ EMP: 54
SQ FT: 100,000
SALES (est): 24.7MM
SALES (corp-wide): 183.7MM **Privately Held**
SIC: **3535** Conveyors & conveying equipment

(G-20515)
VG ATES AND WELDING
33 Le Baron St (60085-3047)
PHONE..........................847 263-4416
EMP: 8
SALES (est): 88.7K **Privately Held**
SIC: **7692** Welding repair

(G-20516)
WAUKEGAN STEEL LLC
1201 Belvidere Rd (60085-6203)
PHONE..........................847 662-2810
Wayne Griesbaum, *President*
Marie G Kropp, *Chairman*
Lee T Simmons, *Corp Secy*
Jini Grogan, *Manager*
EMP: 40
SQ FT: 67,000
SALES (est): 18.2MM
SALES (corp-wide): 824.7MM **Privately Held**
WEB: www.waukegansteel.com
SIC: **3441** 3446 Fabricated structural metal; ornamental metalwork
PA: National Material L.P.
   1965 Pratt Blvd
   Elk Grove Village IL 60007
   847 806-7200

(G-20517)
WELDING BY K &K LLC
54 Le Baron St (60085-3025)
PHONE..........................847 360-1190
Mike Knop, *Principal*
▲ EMP: 2
SALES (est): 285.8K **Privately Held**
SIC: **7692** Welding repair

(G-20518)
WESTROCK CP LLC
3145 Central Ave (60085-4865)
PHONE..........................847 625-8284
Isaac Lopez, *Manager*
EMP: 3

(PA)=Parent Co (HQ)=Headquarters (DH)=Div Headquarters
✪ = New Business established in last 2 years

Waukegan - Lake County (G-20519)

GEOGRAPHIC SECTION

SALES (corp-wide): 18.2B **Publicly Held**
SIC: 2621 2631 Paper mills; paperboard mills
HQ: Westrock Cp, Llc
1000 Abernathy Rd Ste 125
Atlanta GA 30328

(G-20519)
WOODLAND FOODS LTD (PA)
3751 Sunset Ave (60087-3213)
PHONE 847 625-8600
David Moore, *President*
Erin Evins, *Representative*
Marisol Gonzales, *Representative*
◆ **EMP:** 250
SQ FT: 130,000
SALES (est): 63.4MM **Privately Held**
SIC: 2034 5149 Dehydrated fruits, vegetables, soups; dried or canned foods

(G-20520)
YASKAWA AMERICA INC (HQ)
Also Called: Drives & Motion Division
2121 Norman Dr (60085-6751)
PHONE 847 887-7000
Gen Kudo, *CEO*
Michael Knapek, *President*
Nory Takada, *President*
Robert Richard, *Area Mgr*
Patty Chybowski, *Vice Pres*
◆ **EMP:** 200
SQ FT: 112,530
SALES (est): 762.3MM **Privately Held**
SIC: 3621 7694 5063 3566 Motors, electric; electric motor repair; motors, electric; speed changers, drives & gears; industrial instrmnts msrmnt display/control process variable; relays & industrial controls

(G-20521)
Z & L MACHINING INC (PA)
3140 Central Ave (60085-4864)
PHONE 847 623-9500
John E Lemm Jr, *President*
Paul Benz, *Vice Pres*
Amber Akers, *Purchasing*
John Lemm, *Controller*
Dave Fletcher, *Manager*
▼ **EMP:** 47
SQ FT: 50,000
SALES (est): 8.8MM **Privately Held**
SIC: 3599 Machine shop, jobbing & repair

(G-20522)
ZERO GROUND LLC
2340 Ernie Krueger Cir (60087-3224)
PHONE 847 360-9500
Mark Panko,
EMP: 11
SQ FT: 100,000
SALES: 5MM **Privately Held**
SIC: 3679 3317 Harness assemblies for electronic use; wire or cable; conduit: welded, lock joint or heavy riveted

Waverly
Morgan County

(G-20523)
WAVERLY JOURNAL
130 S Pearl St (62692-1166)
P.O. Box 78 (62692-0078)
PHONE 217 435-9221
Nancy Copelin, *President*
Julie Springer, *Vice Pres*
EMP: 3
SQ FT: 1,400
SALES (est): 203.1K **Privately Held**
SIC: 2711 Newspapers, publishing & printing

Wedron
Lasalle County

(G-20524)
FML TERMINAL LOGISTICS LLC
2069 N 3462 Rd (60557)
P.O. Box 119 (60557-0119)
PHONE 815 433-2449
EMP: 4

SALES (corp-wide): 125.5MM **Publicly Held**
SIC: 1442 Construction sand & gravel
HQ: Fml Terminal Logistics, Llc
3 Summit Park Dr Ste 700
Independence OH 44131
440 214-3200

(G-20525)
WEDRON SILICA COMPANY
3450 E 2056th Rd (60557-9900)
P.O. Box 119 (60557-0119)
PHONE 815 433-2449
Jenniffer Deckard, *President*
Charles Fowler, *President*
William Conway, *Chairman*
Joseph Fodo, *Vice Pres*
David Crandall, *Admin Sec*
EMP: 90
SQ FT: 4,500
SALES (est): 42.4MM
SALES (corp-wide): 125.5MM **Publicly Held**
SIC: 1446 Industrial sand
HQ: Covia Holdings Corporation
3 Summit Park Dr Ste 700
Independence OH 44131
440 214-3284

Wenona
Marshall County

(G-20526)
HEARTHSIDE FOOD SOLUTIONS LLC
Also Called: Oak State
775 State Route 251 (61377-7587)
PHONE 815 853-4348
EMP: 350 **Privately Held**
SIC: 2051 Bread, cake & related products
PA: Hearthside Food Solutions, Llc
3500 Lacey Rd Ste 300
Downers Grove IL 60515

(G-20527)
WENONA FOOD & FUEL
3075 Il Route 17 (61377-9662)
PHONE 815 853-4141
Rose Laus, *Principal*
EMP: 4
SALES (est): 364.5K **Privately Held**
WEB: www.cityofwenona.org
SIC: 2869 Fuels

West Chicago
Dupage County

(G-20528)
21 HOLDINGS LLC
501 Conde St (60185-3433)
PHONE 630 876-4886
Ken Wegner,
EMP: 4
SALES (est): 116.1K **Privately Held**
SIC: 2085 Distilled & blended liquors

(G-20529)
2M CONTROL SYSTEMS INC
245 W Roosevelt Rd Ste 86 (60185-4838)
PHONE 630 709-6225
Mariusz Smialek, *President*
▲ **EMP:** 5
SALES (est): 599.2K **Privately Held**
SIC: 3555 Printing trades machinery

(G-20530)
A J HORNE INC
893 Industrial Dr (60185-1833)
PHONE 630 231-8686
Paul Loomis, *President*
Rosemary Horne, *Vice Pres*
Deborah A Horne, *Treasurer*
Patrice Annerino, *Admin Sec*
EMP: 5 EST: 1946
SQ FT: 2,500
SALES: 260K **Privately Held**
WEB: www.ajhorneinc.com
SIC: 3599 3546 3452 Machine shop, jobbing & repair; power-driven handtools; bolts, nuts, rivets & washers

(G-20531)
ADVANCED ELECTRONICS INC
721 Winston St (60185-5121)
PHONE 630 293-3300
Prem Chaudhari, *President*
Nipul Patel, *Project Mgr*
Ramsi Chaudhari, *Admin Sec*
▲ **EMP:** 55
SQ FT: 25,000
SALES (est): 7.7MM **Privately Held**
SIC: 3672 Printed circuit boards

(G-20532)
AGCO CORPORATION
1160 Powis Rd (60185-1665)
PHONE 630 293-9905
Martin H Richenhagen, *CEO*
EMP: 9 **Publicly Held**
WEB: www.agcocorp.com
SIC: 3523 Farm machinery & equipment
PA: Agco Corporation
4205 River Green Pkwy
Duluth GA 30096

(G-20533)
AIRGAS USA LLC
1250 W Washington St (60185-2653)
PHONE 630 231-9260
Amy Huff, *President*
Doug Fish, *Principal*
Daniel Bartel, *Research*
EMP: 24
SALES (corp-wide): 129.8MM **Privately Held**
SIC: 2813 3548 5084 5169 Industrial gases; welding apparatus; welding machinery & equipment; chemicals & allied products
HQ: Airgas Usa, Llc
259 N Radnor Chester Rd
Radnor PA 19087
610 687-5253

(G-20534)
ALL RIGHT SALES INC
28w240 Trieste Ln (60185-1481)
PHONE 773 558-4800
Amratlal S Patel, *President*
Shalies Patel, *Vice Pres*
▲ **EMP:** 7
SQ FT: 25,000
SALES (est): 1.1MM **Privately Held**
SIC: 3499 5199 Picture frames, metal; variety store merchandise

(G-20535)
ALPHA COATING TECHNOLOGIES LLC
1725 Western Dr (60185-1880)
PHONE 630 268-8787
Muthiah Jeno,
Anita Jeno,
▲ **EMP:** 20
SALES (est): 4MM
SALES (corp-wide): 15.1B **Publicly Held**
SIC: 2851 Paints & paint additives
PA: Ppg Industries, Inc.
1 Ppg Pl
Pittsburgh PA 15272
412 434-3131

(G-20536)
ALTIUM PACKAGING
1300 Northwest Ave (60185-1628)
PHONE 630 231-7150
Mary Sniegowski, *Controller*
Sean Guinan, *Branch Mgr*
EMP: 115
SQ FT: 105,000
SALES (corp-wide): 14.9B **Publicly Held**
SIC: 3089 Plastic containers, except foam
HQ: Altium Packaging Llc
2500 Windy Ridge Pkwy Se # 1
Atlanta GA 30339
678 742-4600

(G-20537)
AMERICAN CONTROLS & AUTOMATION
897 Industrial Dr (60185-1833)
PHONE 630 293-8841
Paul Hoskins, *President*
Sang Cho, *Vice Pres*
EMP: 3
SQ FT: 2,500

SALES (est): 1.2MM **Privately Held**
SIC: 3625 3672 7373 Industrial electrical relays & switches; circuit boards, television & radio printed; systems software development services

(G-20538)
AMERICAN PARTSMITH INC
901 Atlantic Dr (60185-5100)
PHONE 630 520-0432
Bonita Schroeder, *Principal*
EMP: 3
SALES (est): 283K **Privately Held**
SIC: 3469 3429 3499 Metal stampings; manufactured hardware (general); magnetic shields, metal

(G-20539)
AMERICAN STANDARD CIRCUITS INC
Also Called: ASC
475 Industrial Dr (60185-1891)
PHONE 630 639-5444
Anaya Vardya, *CEO*
Francis Chackanad, *President*
Gordhan Patel, *Chairman*
Jay Hirpara, *Exec VP*
Jayanti Hirpara, *Vice Pres*
▲ **EMP:** 115
SQ FT: 52,000
SALES: 16.3MM **Privately Held**
SIC: 3672 Printed circuit boards

(G-20540)
ANCHOR BRAKE SHOE COMPANY LLC
1111 Harvester Rd (60185-1607)
PHONE 630 293-1110
EMP: 3
SALES (corp-wide): 711.6K **Privately Held**
SIC: 3321 Railroad car wheels & brake shoes, cast iron
HQ: Anchor Brake Shoe Company, Llc
1920 Downs Dr
West Chicago IL 60185

(G-20541)
ANCHOR BRAKE SHOE COMPANY LLC (DH)
1920 Downs Dr (60185-1808)
PHONE 630 293-1110
Richard A Mathes, *President*
Michael Hawthorne, *President*
Donald Popernick, *Corp Secy*
EMP: 11
SALES (est): 20MM
SALES (corp-wide): 711.6K **Privately Held**
SIC: 3321 3743 5088 Railroad car wheels & brake shoes, cast iron; railroad equipment; railroad equipment & supplies

(G-20542)
APOLLO SENSORS INC
778 W Hawthorne Ln (60185-1968)
PHONE 630 293-5820
Carry Mangrum, *President*
Vicki L McComb, *Vice Pres*
EMP: 12
SQ FT: 4,100
SALES (est): 700K **Privately Held**
SIC: 3829 Thermometers & temperature sensors

(G-20543)
ARCHITECTURAL CAST STON
2775 Norton Creek Dr (60185-6411)
PHONE 630 377-4800
Todd W Surta, *President*
Craig B Surta, *Admin Sec*
EMP: 50
SALES (est): 10MM **Privately Held**
SIC: 3272 5211 Concrete products, precast; masonry materials & supplies

(G-20544)
ARCHITECTURAL CAST STONE LLC
2775 Norton Creek Dr (60185-6411)
PHONE 630 377-4800
Todd Surta, *Principal*
Craig Surta, *Principal*
Lisa Meador, *Human Res Mgr*
Lisa Kral, *HR Admin*

▲ = Import ▼ = Export
◆ = Import/Export

GEOGRAPHIC SECTION
West Chicago - Dupage County (G-20573)

EMP: 2 EST: 2016
SALES (est): 452.1K **Privately Held**
SIC: 3272 Concrete products

(G-20545)
ASSURED WELDING SERVICE INC
975 Aster Ln (60185-1749)
PHONE..................................847 671-1414
EMP: 5
SALES (est): 418.9K **Privately Held**
SIC: 7692 Welding Repair

(G-20546)
ASTRO TOOL CO INC
1200 Atlantic Dr (60185-5171)
PHONE..................................630 876-3402
William Kleiner, *President*
Robert Klehr, *Vice Pres*
Mary Ann Smith, *Office Mgr*
Leslie Kleiner, *Admin Sec*
EMP: 9
SQ FT: 12,000
SALES (est): 920.7K **Privately Held**
SIC: 3544 Special dies & tools

(G-20547)
B N K INC
Also Called: Dunkin' Donuts
330 S Neltnor Blvd (60185-2928)
PHONE..................................630 231-5640
Danny Patel, *President*
EMP: 8
SALES (est): 410.2K **Privately Held**
SIC: 5461 2051 5812 Doughnuts; doughnuts, except frozen; ice cream stands or dairy bars

(G-20548)
BALL PUBLISHING
622 Town Rd (60185-2614)
P.O. Box 1660 (60186-1660)
PHONE..................................630 208-9080
Fax: 630 231-5254
◆ EMP: 13
SALES (est): 2.2MM **Privately Held**
SIC: 2741 Misc Publishing

(G-20549)
BARCO STAMPING CO (PA)
1095 Carolina Dr (60185-1799)
PHONE..................................630 293-5155
Thomas Mullally, *President*
Brad Weber, *Vice Pres*
Ronald Tampa, *Admin Sec*
▲ EMP: 45 EST: 1981
SQ FT: 3,500
SALES (est): 21.8MM **Privately Held**
SIC: 3469 3544 Stamping metal for the trade; die sets for metal stamping (presses)

(G-20550)
BATAVIA INSTANT PRINT
33w480 Fabyan Pkwy # 104 (60185-9611)
PHONE..................................630 262-0370
Brian R Pacetti, *President*
Bonny Pacetti, *Corp Secy*
Scot Brockner, *Vice Pres*
EMP: 8
SQ FT: 1,800
SALES (est): 800K **Privately Held**
SIC: 2759 2752 Ready prints; commercial printing, lithographic

(G-20551)
BERRIDGE MANUFACTURING COMPANY
1175 Carolina Dr (60185-1713)
PHONE..................................630 231-7495
Dan Mohs, *Manager*
EMP: 3
SALES (corp-wide): 59.5MM **Privately Held**
SIC: 3444 5033 Metal roofing & roof drainage equipment; roofing, siding & insulation
PA: Berridge Manufacturing Company, Inc
6515 Fratt Rd
San Antonio TX 78218
210 650-7056

(G-20552)
BLACHFORD INVESTMENTS INC
1400 Nuclear Dr (60185-1636)
PHONE..................................630 231-8300
M C Long, *President*
Mike Piehl, *Business Mgr*
Joe Borean, *Vice Pres*
Mike Cundari, *Vice Pres*
Steve Erickson, *Vice Pres*
◆ EMP: 107
SQ FT: 76,000
SALES (est): 23.2MM **Privately Held**
SIC: 3625 3086 2273 Noise control equipment; plastics foam products; carpets & rugs
PA: Blachford Enterprises, Inc.
1400 Nuclear Dr
West Chicago IL 60185

(G-20553)
BLACK MARKET PARTS INC
776 W Hawthorne Ln (60185-1968)
PHONE..................................630 562-9400
Dave Bauer, *President*
EMP: 4
SALES (est): 450K **Privately Held**
SIC: 3559 Ammunition & explosives, loading machinery

(G-20554)
BORNS PICTURE FRAMES
540 Belleview Ave (60185-2156)
PHONE..................................630 876-1709
Howard W Born, *President*
Erlaine Born, *Corp Secy*
EMP: 3 EST: 1954
SALES (est): 400K **Privately Held**
SIC: 2499 Picture & mirror frames, wood

(G-20555)
BRUCHER MACHINING INC
1030 Atlantic Dr (60185-5101)
PHONE..................................630 876-1661
Scott E Kuhar, *President*
Melanie A Kuhar, *Admin Sec*
EMP: 12
SQ FT: 7,300
SALES (est): 2.1MM **Privately Held**
SIC: 3599 Machine shop, jobbing & repair

(G-20556)
BULK MOLDING COMPOUNDS INC (DH)
1600 Powis Ct (60185-1016)
PHONE..................................630 377-1065
Mike Huff, *CEO*
Christopher Vaisvil, *President*
Francis Zappitelli, *Vice Pres*
Robert Zurek, *Vice Pres*
Rick Dettman, *CFO*
▲ EMP: 71
SQ FT: 80,000
SALES (est): 137.8MM
SALES (corp-wide): 39.1B **Privately Held**
SIC: 3087 Custom compound purchased resins
HQ: Citadel Plastics Holdings Inc
3637 Ridgewood Rd
Fairlawn OH 44333
330 666-3751

(G-20557)
CAMEO MOLD CORP
Also Called: Cameo Mold & Duplicating
1125 Carolina Dr (60185-1713)
PHONE..................................630 876-1340
David Salvesen, *President*
Kathy Heinze, *Office Mgr*
EMP: 15 EST: 1978
SQ FT: 7,000
SALES (est): 2.7MM **Privately Held**
SIC: 3544 Industrial molds

(G-20558)
CAMERON PRINTING INC
1275 W Roosevelt Rd # 119 (60185-4815)
PHONE..................................630 231-3301
Martin J Finlayson, *President*
EMP: 3
SQ FT: 2,500
SALES: 600K **Privately Held**
SIC: 2752 2791 2789 Commercial printing, offset; business form & card printing, lithographic; typesetting; bookbinding & related work

(G-20559)
CAREY COLOR INC
2500 Enterprise Cir # 100 (60185-9624)
PHONE..................................630 761-2605
Roger Dalberg, *General Mgr*
EMP: 3 EST: 2010
SALES (est): 213.7K **Privately Held**
WEB: www.careyweb.com
SIC: 2752 Commercial printing, lithographic

(G-20560)
CENTRAL INK CORPORATION (PA)
Also Called: Central Ink of Wisconsin Div
1100 Harvester Rd (60185-1608)
PHONE..................................630 231-6500
Richard Breen, *CEO*
Gregg Dahleen, *President*
Jeff Ryder, *Corp Secy*
Jim Donnelly, *Prdtn Mgr*
Tony Triner, *Opers Staff*
▲ EMP: 88
SQ FT: 108,000
SALES (est): 29.7MM **Privately Held**
SIC: 2893 Letterpress or offset ink

(G-20561)
CHIPS MANUFACTURING INC
741 Winston St (60185-5121)
PHONE..................................630 682-4477
James J Jett, *President*
Edward Stedman, *Corp Secy*
Peter Baumann, *Prdtn Mgr*
Roberto Piga, *Facilities Mgr*
Gail Shay, *QC Mgr*
EMP: 65
SQ FT: 45,000
SALES (est): 13.5MM **Privately Held**
SIC: 3599 Machine shop, jobbing & repair

(G-20562)
CLARIANT PLAS COATINGS USA LLC
625 Wegner Dr (60185-6011)
PHONE..................................630 562-9700
Bob Anderson, *Vice Pres*
Jennifer Riordan, *Sales Staff*
Ashley B Anderson, *Manager*
Chris Spencer, *Supervisor*
Thomas Toso, *Maintence Staff*
EMP: 100
SALES (corp-wide): 4.4B **Privately Held**
SIC: 2865 2851 Dyes & pigments; paints & allied products
HQ: Clariant Plastics & Coatings Usa Llc
85 Industrial Dr
Holden MA 01520
508 829-6321

(G-20563)
CLARIOS
Also Called: Johnson Controls
1800 W Hawthorne Ln E2 (60185-1860)
PHONE..................................630 562-4602
Jim Spade, *Manager*
EMP: 5 **Privately Held**
SIC: 3556 Meat, poultry & seafood processing machinery
HQ: Johnson Controls, Inc.
5757 N Green Bay Ave
Milwaukee WI 53209
414 524-1200

(G-20564)
CLOVER PLASTICS LLC
1145 Howard Dr (60185-1621)
PHONE..................................630 473-6488
Kevin McNulty,
EMP: 6
SQ FT: 29,000
SALES (est): 670K **Privately Held**
SIC: 3089 Air mattresses, plastic

(G-20565)
COBRA COAL INC
3n060 Powis Rd (60185-1017)
PHONE..................................630 560-1050
David Hansen, *President*
Kenneth Phlamm, *Vice Pres*
Chris Vargas, *CFO*
▼ EMP: 30
SALES (est): 1MM **Privately Held**
SIC: 1241 Coal mining services

(G-20566)
COMPONENT PRECAST SUPPLY INC
4n325 Powis Rd (60185-1002)
P.O. Box 553 (60186-0553)
PHONE..................................630 483-2900
John C Perritt, *President*
EMP: 6
SALES (est): 991.8K **Privately Held**
SIC: 3272 Precast terrazo or concrete products

(G-20567)
CONWED PLAS ACQUISITION V LLC
390 Wegner Dr Ste B (60185-2617)
P.O. Box 520 (60186-0520)
PHONE..................................630 293-3737
Mark Lewry, *President*
John Burke, *Executive*
EMP: 75
SALES (est): 10.1MM **Privately Held**
WEB: www.conwedplastics.com
SIC: 3089 Injection molding of plastics

(G-20568)
CTC MACHINE SERVICE INC
756 W Hawthorne Ln (60185-1968)
PHONE..................................630 876-5120
Robert A Berg, *President*
EMP: 7
SALES (est): 1MM **Privately Held**
WEB: www.ctcmachineservice.com
SIC: 3541 Machine tool replacement & repair parts, metal cutting types

(G-20569)
DELTA CIRCUITS INC
730 W Hawthorne Ln (60185-1968)
PHONE..................................630 876-0691
Mike Chaudhari, *President*
Mukesh Chaudhari, *President*
Kieren Mike, *Vice Pres*
EMP: 25
SQ FT: 46,000
SALES (est): 5.1MM **Privately Held**
SIC: 3672 3679 Circuit boards, television & radio printed; electronic circuits

(G-20570)
DF FAN SERVICES INC
495 Wegner Dr (60185-2675)
PHONE..................................630 876-1495
Douglas Gifford Jr, *President*
EMP: 10
SQ FT: 10,000
SALES (est): 900K **Privately Held**
SIC: 3564 5064 Blowers & fans; fans, household; electric

(G-20571)
DIPPIT INC
Also Called: Prolong Tool
1879 N Neltnor Blvd 326 (60185-5932)
PHONE..................................630 762-6500
Steve Joyaux, *President*
EMP: 2
SALES: 400K **Privately Held**
SIC: 3399 Cryogenic treatment of metal

(G-20572)
DML LLC
419 Colford Ave (60185-2818)
PHONE..................................630 231-8873
Micheal Jankovic, *Partner*
EMP: 3 EST: 1996
SALES (est): 181.4K **Privately Held**
SIC: 3589 Sewer cleaning equipment, power

(G-20573)
ENGINEERED SEC & SOUND INC
1275 W Roosevelt Rd # 110 (60185-4815)
PHONE..................................630 876-8853
Jack R Oulicky, *President*
Robert Stevenson, *Vice Pres*
Patrick Corso, *Treasurer*
Ronald Rocco, *Admin Sec*
EMP: 8

(PA)=Parent Co (HQ)=Headquarters (DH)=Div Headquarters
○ = New Business established in last 2 years

West Chicago - Dupage County (G-20574)

SALES: 1.2MM **Privately Held**
SIC: 3699 Security control equipment & systems

(G-20574)
ENVIRONMENTAL INKS & CODING (PA)
450 Wegner Dr (60185-2674)
PHONE.................................630 231-7313
EMP: 15
SALES (est): 1.1MM **Privately Held**
SIC: 2893 Mfg Printing Ink

(G-20575)
EVEREDE TOOL COMPANY LLC (HQ)
850 W Hawthorne Ln (60185-1998)
PHONE.................................623 414-4800
Rick McIntyre, *CEO*
▲ EMP: 52
SQ FT: 3,000
SALES (est): 8.8MM
SALES (corp-wide): 18.2MM **Privately Held**
SIC: 3545 3541 Cutting tools for machine tools; machine tools, metal cutting type
PA: Gws Tool Holdings, Llc
 595 County Road 448
 Tavares FL 32778
 352 343-8778

(G-20576)
EVEREDE TOOL COMPANY LLC
Everede Tool Company Div
850 W Hawthorne Ln (60185-1998)
PHONE.................................773 467-4200
Randy Rinehart, *Vice Pres*
Keith Browning, *Mfg Spvr*
John Husar, *Engineer*
Bret Tayne, *Manager*
EMP: 35
SALES (corp-wide): 18.2MM **Privately Held**
SIC: 3541 3545 Machine tools, metal cutting type; cutting tools for machine tools
HQ: Everede Tool Company, Llc
 850 W Hawthorne Ln
 West Chicago IL 60185

(G-20577)
EVO EXHIBITS LLC
399 Wegner Dr (60185-2673)
PHONE.................................630 520-0710
Kent Jean, *Principal*
Michael McCord, *Vice Pres*
Alex Deback, *Project Mgr*
Alyson Miller, *Project Mgr*
Cathie Stefanski, *Project Mgr*
EMP: 5
SALES (est): 1MM **Privately Held**
WEB: www.evoexhibits.com
SIC: 5999 5963 3999 8742 Banners; direct sales, telemarketing; preparation of slides & exhibits; marketing consulting services

(G-20578)
EVOLUTION SORBENT PRODUCTS LLC
1270 Nuclear Dr (60185-1632)
PHONE.................................630 293-8055
Bryan Sims,
EMP: 5 **Privately Held**
SIC: 2621 Absorbent paper
PA: Evolution Sorbent Products, Llc
 1149 Howard Dr
 West Chicago IL 60185

(G-20579)
EVOLUTION SORBENT PRODUCTS LLC (PA)
1149 Howard Dr (60185-1621)
PHONE.................................630 293-8055
Ron Bielski, *General Mgr*
Larry Wolf, *CFO*
Israel Ramirez, *Sales Staff*
Bryan Sims,
◆ EMP: 15
SQ FT: 40,000
SALES: 16.1MM **Privately Held**
SIC: 2621 Absorbent paper

(G-20580)
EXTRUDED SOLUTIONS INC
1185 W Hawthorne Ln (60185-1913)
PHONE.................................630 871-6450
Victor Battiato, *President*
Melissa Battiato, *Vice Pres*
Chris Caliva, *Manager*
Harold Hogarth, *Consultant*
▼ EMP: 8
SQ FT: 20,000
SALES (est): 1.1MM **Privately Held**
WEB: www.extrudedsolutions.com
SIC: 3089 Automotive parts, plastic

(G-20581)
EYES FORWARD INNOVATIONS CORP
1s735 Pamela Ct (60185-4412)
PHONE.................................281 755-5826
David H Smith, *President*
EMP: 5
SALES (est): 150.7K **Privately Held**
SIC: 3999 Manufacturing industries

(G-20582)
EZTECH MANUFACTURING INC
1200 Howard Dr (60185-1624)
PHONE.................................630 293-0010
Edwin T Smiling, *CEO*
EMP: 16
SQ FT: 20,000
SALES (est): 3.4MM **Privately Held**
SIC: 3699 3444 Electrical equipment & supplies; sheet metalwork

(G-20583)
FIRST LIGHT INC
Also Called: Fli Products
245 W Roosevelt Rd Ste 3 (60185-4838)
PHONE.................................630 520-0017
Kevin Cody, *President*
Jane Price, *Accounting Mgr*
EMP: 5
SALES (est): 1.5MM **Privately Held**
SIC: 5063 3646 Lighting fixtures, commercial & industrial; commercial indusl & institutional electric lighting fixtures

(G-20584)
FLI PRODUCTS LLC
245 W Roosevelt Rd Ste 3 (60185-4838)
PHONE.................................630 520-0017
Kevin Cody, *Principal*
EMP: 6 EST: 2013
SQ FT: 3,500
SALES (est): 617K **Privately Held**
SIC: 3646 3645 Commercial indusl & institutional electric lighting fixtures; desk lamps, commercial; desk lamps

(G-20585)
FLOLO CORPORATION (PA)
1400 Harvester Rd (60185-1614)
PHONE.................................630 595-1010
George Flolo, *President*
Norman Flolo, *Vice Pres*
Dennis Lamb, *Sales Staff*
Gary Gottsehalk, *Manager*
EMP: 44 EST: 1945
SQ FT: 42,000
SALES (est): 16.2MM **Privately Held**
WEB: www.flolo.com
SIC: 7694 5063 Electric motor repair; motors, electric

(G-20586)
FLOWSERVE CORPORATION
1400 Powis Ct (60185-6413)
PHONE.................................630 762-4100
Diana Moore, *Controller*
Mashall Heller, *Manager*
Gina Fleisher, *Manager*
Mike Smith, *Manager*
EMP: 30
SALES (corp-wide): 3.9B **Publicly Held**
SIC: 3561 Pumps & pumping equipment
PA: Flowserve Corporation
 5215 N Ocnnor Blvd Ste 23 Connor
 Irving TX 75039
 972 443-6500

(G-20587)
FORMING AMERICA LTD (PA)
1200 N Prince Crossing Rd (60185-1712)
PHONE.................................888 993-1304
James Langkamp, *President*
Joshua Jones, *Manager*
Anndrea Kuhn, *Manager*
EMP: 30
SALES (est): 8.3MM **Privately Held**
SIC: 5051 3444 Forms, concrete construction (steel); concrete forms, sheet metal

(G-20588)
GO STEADY LLC
505 Wegner Dr (60185-2626)
PHONE.................................630 293-3243
Leslie Doyle, *Opers Mgr*
Robert E Hendricks, *Mng Member*
EMP: 6
SQ FT: 600
SALES: 22.4K **Privately Held**
WEB: www.ordergosteady.com
SIC: 3842 3069 Crutches & walkers; canes, orthopedic; grips or handles, rubber

(G-20589)
GRAHAM PACKAGING CO EUROPE LLC
1760 W Hawthorne Ln (60185-1841)
PHONE.................................630 293-8616
Russell Killion, *VP Sales*
David Randall, *Manager*
EMP: 1000 **Publicly Held**
SIC: 3089 Plastic containers, except foam
HQ: Graham Packaging Company Europe Llc
 2401 Pleasant Valley Rd # 2
 York PA 17402

(G-20590)
GRAHAM PACKAGING CO EUROPE LLC
Also Called: Plant 4
1445 Northwest Ave (60185-1629)
PHONE.................................630 562-5912
Billy Williams, *President*
Alma Dela Cruz, *Human Res Dir*
EMP: 150 **Publicly Held**
SIC: 3089 Plastic containers, except foam
HQ: Graham Packaging Company Europe Llc
 2401 Pleasant Valley Rd # 2
 York PA 17402

(G-20591)
GRINDING SPECIALTY CO INC
1879 N Neltnor Blvd (60185-5932)
PHONE.................................847 724-6493
Rhuia Smith, *President*
Dale Elkins, *Vice Pres*
Patricia Derner, *Admin Sec*
EMP: 20 EST: 1983
SALES (est): 2MM **Privately Held**
SIC: 3544 Special dies, tools, jigs & fixtures

(G-20592)
HEALTHFUL HABITS LLC
245 W Roosevelt Rd # 143 (60185-4818)
PHONE.................................224 489-4256
David Phoi, *Mng Member*
Jeff Adezcko,
Gloria Athanis,
EMP: 3
SQ FT: 5,000
SALES: 100K **Privately Held**
SIC: 2064 Candy bars, including chocolate covered bars

(G-20593)
HOWLER FABRICATION & WLDG INC
Also Called: H F I
1100 Carolina Dr (60185-5126)
PHONE.................................630 293-9300
Walter L Howler, *CEO*
Ray Hussman, *Director*
▼ EMP: 30 EST: 1967
SQ FT: 48,000
SALES (est): 10.6MM **Privately Held**
SIC: 3444 Sheet metalwork

(G-20594)
INFINITI GOLF
245 W Roosevelt Rd Ste 9 (60185-4804)
PHONE.................................630 520-0626
Eric Yeh, *President*
Tom Michalowski, *Vice Pres*
▲ EMP: 2
SALES (est): 212.5K **Privately Held**
SIC: 3949 Golf equipment

(G-20595)
INHANCE TECHNOLOGIES LLC
829 W Hawthorne Ln (60185-1965)
PHONE.................................630 231-7515
Jinny Pool, *Branch Mgr*
EMP: 22
SALES (corp-wide): 14.7MM **Privately Held**
SIC: 3085 2851 Plastics bottles; paints & allied products
HQ: Inhance Technologies Llc
 16223 Park Row Ste 100
 Houston TX 77084
 800 929-1743

(G-20596)
INLAND FASTENER INC
750 W Hawthorne Ln (60185-1968)
PHONE.................................630 293-3800
James J Ricke, *President*
Tim Gardner, *Vice Pres*
Tracy Leonhard, *Vice Pres*
Carol Ricke, *Vice Pres*
Marge Sarna, *Sales Associate*
▲ EMP: 11 EST: 1959
SQ FT: 32,000
SALES (est): 2.8MM **Privately Held**
WEB: www.inlandfastener.com
SIC: 3452 3965 3429 Screws, metal; fasteners; manufactured hardware (general)

(G-20597)
INNOCOR INC
Also Called: Advance Ureathane
1700 Downs Dr Ste 200 (60185-1834)
PHONE.................................630 231-0622
Cristine Rush, *Branch Mgr*
EMP: 10 **Privately Held**
SIC: 2515 Mattresses & foundations
HQ: Innocor, Inc.
 200 Schulz Dr Ste 2
 Red Bank NJ 07701

(G-20598)
INNOCOR FOAM TECH W CHCAGO LLC
1750 Downs Dr (60185-1804)
PHONE.................................732 945-6222
Carol S Eicher, *CEO*
▲ EMP: 50
SALES (est): 4.8MM **Privately Held**
SIC: 3495 2392 2821 Wire springs; mattress pads; plastics materials & resins
HQ: Innocor Foam Technologies, Llc
 200 Schulz Dr Ste 2
 Red Bank NJ 07701

(G-20599)
INNOCOR FOAM TECHNOLOGIES LLC
1750 Downs Dr (60185-1804)
PHONE.................................630 293-0780
Kyle Schultz, *Plant Mgr*
Michael C Thompson, *Branch Mgr*
EMP: 16 **Privately Held**
SIC: 3086 Plastics foam products
HQ: Innocor Foam Technologies, Llc
 200 Schulz Dr Ste 2
 Red Bank NJ 07701

(G-20600)
INX INTERNATIONAL INK CO
1860 Western Dr (60185-1881)
PHONE.................................630 681-7200
Tom Jasinski, *Manager*
EMP: 35 **Privately Held**
SIC: 2893 2899 Printing ink; ink or writing fluids
HQ: Inx International Ink Co.
 150 N Martingale Rd # 700
 Schaumburg IL 60173
 630 382-1800

(G-20601)
INX INTERNATIONAL INK CO
1760 Western Dr (60185-1864)
PHONE.................................630 681-7100
Kotaro Moita, *Branch Mgr*
EMP: 50 **Privately Held**

GEOGRAPHIC SECTION

West Chicago - Dupage County (G-20629)

SIC: 8731 2893 2899 Commercial physical research; printing ink; ink or writing fluids
HQ: Inx International Ink Co.
150 N Martingale Rd # 700
Schaumburg IL 60173
630 382-1800

(G-20602)
J H H OF ILLINOIS INC
Also Called: Jamar Packaging
1331 Howard Dr (60185-1625)
PHONE.................................630 293-0739
Jeff H Heise, *President*
Dave Mayday, *Vice Pres*
EMP: 15 EST: 1979
SQ FT: 10,000
SALES (est): 4.7MM **Privately Held**
SIC: 2653 Boxes, corrugated: made from purchased materials

(G-20603)
JEL SERT CO (PA)
Also Called: J S
Conde St Rr 59 (60185)
PHONE.................................630 231-7590
Gary Ricco, *CEO*
Charles Wegner IV, *Ch of Bd*
Kenneth Wegner, *President*
Laurie Peard, *Counsel*
Lisa De Martini, *Asst Controller*
◆ EMP: 235
SQ FT: 400,000
SALES (est): 73.9MM **Privately Held**
WEB: www.jelsert.com
SIC: 2087 2024 2099 5499 Concentrates, flavoring (except drink); fruit pops, frozen; desserts, ready-to-mix; beverage stores; ice cream & ices

(G-20604)
JJC EPOXY INC
Also Called: Polygem
1105 Carolina Dr (60185-1713)
PHONE.................................630 231-5600
Anton J Schmid, *President*
Catherine Lay, *Corp Secy*
Juan Alvarado, *Vice Pres*
EMP: 5
SALES (est): 1.2MM **Privately Held**
SIC: 3479 Coating of metals & formed products

(G-20605)
JUNKER INC
391 Wegner Dr Ste A (60185-2695)
P.O. Box 645 (60186-0645)
PHONE.................................630 231-3770
Jason Drury, *CEO*
EMP: 9
SALES (est): 88.6K
SALES (corp-wide): 435.4K **Privately Held**
SIC: 3549 Metalworking machinery
HQ: Otto Junker Gesellschaft Mit Beschrankter Haftung
Jagerhausstr. 22
Simmerath 52152
247 360-10

(G-20606)
KOALA CABINETS
333 Charles Ct (60185-2604)
PHONE.................................630 818-1289
EMP: 6 EST: 2010
SALES (est): 535.5K **Privately Held**
SIC: 2434 Wood kitchen cabinets

(G-20607)
LIBBEY INC
1850 Blackhawk Dr (60185-1666)
PHONE.................................630 818-3400
Chris Fuentes, *Branch Mgr*
EMP: 963 **Privately Held**
SIC: 3229 Pressed & blown glass
PA: Libbey Inc.
300 Madison Ave
Toledo OH 43604

(G-20608)
LIPSCOMB ENGINEERING INC
1215 W Washington St (60185-2652)
PHONE.................................630 231-3833
Robert J Lipscomb, *President*
Mary Ellen Lipscomb, *Admin Secy*
EMP: 9 EST: 1978

SQ FT: 10,000
SALES (est): 1.6MM **Privately Held**
SIC: 7699 3549 Industrial machinery & equipment repair; metalworking machinery

(G-20609)
LUXON PRINTING INC
375 Wegner Dr (60185-2673)
PHONE.................................630 293-7710
John W Luxon, *President*
EMP: 15
SQ FT: 10,000
SALES (est): 900K **Privately Held**
SIC: 2752 Commercial printing, offset

(G-20610)
M S TOOL & ENGINEERING
Also Called: Ms Astral Tool
1200 Atlantic Dr (60185-5171)
PHONE.................................630 876-3437
Daniel Kruger, *President*
EMP: 11
SALES (est): 1.5MM **Privately Held**
SIC: 3544 Special dies & tools

(G-20611)
MANUFCTURE DSIGN INNVATION INC
Also Called: Mdi-Co
1760 Metoyer Ct Unit F (60185-6410)
PHONE.................................773 526-7773
Drew Johnson, *President*
Arne Toman, *Treasurer*
Marcin Musial, *Admin Sec*
EMP: 5 EST: 2014
SALES (est): 400K **Privately Held**
WEB: www.mdi-co.com
SIC: 7389 3544 Design services; industrial molds

(G-20612)
MAPEI CORPORATION
430 Industrial Dr (60185-1867)
PHONE.................................630 293-5800
EMP: 3
SALES (est): 229.4K **Privately Held**
SIC: 2891 Adhesives & sealants

(G-20613)
MAPEI CORPORATION
Also Called: North American Adhesives
530 Industrial Dr (60185-1828)
PHONE.................................630 293-5800
Jose Granillo, *Manager*
EMP: 100 **Privately Held**
SIC: 2891 2899 2821 Adhesives; chemical preparations; plastics materials & resins
HQ: Mapei Corporation
1144 E Newport Center Dr
Deerfield Beach FL 33442
954 246-8888

(G-20614)
MARCY LABORATORIES INC
4n215 Powis Rd (60185-1002)
PHONE.................................630 377-6655
Larry Murison, *President*
Merrily Murison, *Exec VP*
Larry Murison Jr, *Vice Pres*
▲ EMP: 35
SQ FT: 30,000
SALES (est): 7.1MM **Privately Held**
WEB: www.marcylaboratories.com
SIC: 2844 Cosmetic preparations

(G-20615)
MARS INCORPORATED
120 N Aurora St (60185-1957)
PHONE.................................630 293-9066
Judy Piszczek, *Branch Mgr*
▼ EMP: 4
SALES (corp-wide): 38.5B **Privately Held**
SIC: 2067 Chewing gum
PA: Mars, Incorporated
6885 Elm St Ste 1
Mc Lean VA 22101
703 821-4900

(G-20616)
MASONITE CORPORATION
1955 Powis Rd (60185-1002)
PHONE.................................630 584-6330
John Bott, *Director*
Jan Ettrich, *Director*

EMP: 96
SALES (corp-wide): 2.1B **Publicly Held**
SIC: 2431 3469 Doors, wood; doors & door parts & trim, wood; stamping metal for the trade
HQ: Masonite Corporation
201 N Franklin St Ste 300
Tampa FL 33602
813 877-2726

(G-20617)
MICROLITE CORPORATION (DH)
Also Called: Lighting Control Systems
1150 Powis Rd Ste 8 (60185-1664)
PHONE.................................630 876-0500
Darrell Chelcun, *Vice Pres*
EMP: 7
SALES (est): 2.4MM
SALES (corp-wide): 153.8MM **Privately Held**
SIC: 5063 3648 Lighting fixtures; area & sports luminaries
HQ: Musco Sports Lighting, Llc.
100 1st Ave W
Oskaloosa IA 52577
800 825-6030

(G-20618)
MIDWEST SAW INC
850 Meadowview Xing Ste 4 (60185-2577)
PHONE.................................630 293-4252
Joseph Denicolo, *President*
EMP: 7
SQ FT: 4,000
SALES (est): 979K **Privately Held**
SIC: 3425 7699 Saw blades for hand or power saws; knife, saw & tool sharpening & repair

(G-20619)
MINERAL MASTERS CORPORATION
130 W Grand Lake Blvd (60185-1937)
PHONE.................................630 293-7727
Andrew Bassi, *President*
Julie Spotts, *Exec VP*
Pamela Bassi, *Admin Sec*
▲ EMP: 15
SALES: 5MM **Privately Held**
SIC: 2899 5169 Chemical preparations; chemicals, industrial & heavy

(G-20620)
MOBILE PALLET SERVICE INC
1300 W Roosevelt Rd (60185-4828)
PHONE.................................630 231-6597
Nick Perez, *Manager*
EMP: 15 **Privately Held**
WEB: www.mobilepalletservice.com
SIC: 2448 Pallets, wood
PA: Mobile Pallet Service, Inc.
858 S Main St
Wayland MI 49348

(G-20621)
MONCO FABRICATORS INC
645 Joliet St (60185-3354)
PHONE.................................630 293-0063
Peter Verive, *President*
Dawn Verive, *Corp Secy*
Steve Verive, *Vice Pres*
EMP: 3
SQ FT: 1,500
SALES (est): 400K **Privately Held**
SIC: 3498 Fabricated pipe & fittings

(G-20622)
NISSAN
27w261 North Ave (60185-1533)
PHONE.................................630 957-4360
EMP: 3
SALES (est): 104.5K **Privately Held**
SIC: 5511 5012 3711 Automobiles, new & used; automobile auction; motor vehicles & car bodies

(G-20623)
NORDIC AUTO PLOW LLC
Also Called: Nordic Plow
771 W North Ave (60185-6202)
PHONE.................................815 353-8267
Richard Behan, *President*
EMP: 3

SALES (est): 250.8K **Privately Held**
WEB: www.nordicplow.com
SIC: 3531 5082 Snow plow attachments; blades for graders, scrapers, dozers & snow plows; blades for graders, scrapers, dozers & snow plows

(G-20624)
NORIX GROUP INC
1800 W Hawthorne Ln Ste N (60185-1863)
PHONE.................................630 231-1331
Richard B Karl, *CEO*
Scott C Karl, *President*
Heather L Karl, *Senior VP*
Bill Karl, *Vice Pres*
Julie Premer, *Buyer*
◆ EMP: 25
SQ FT: 45,000
SALES (est): 22.7MM **Privately Held**
SIC: 5021 2599 Office furniture; office & public building furniture; cafeteria furniture

(G-20625)
NORTHWESTERN FLAVORS LLC
120 N Aurora St (60185-1957)
PHONE.................................630 231-6111
R V Clark, *Engineer*
Don Dicking,
◆ EMP: 35
SQ FT: 79,000
SALES (est): 7.4MM
SALES (corp-wide): 38.5B **Privately Held**
SIC: 2087 Extracts, flavoring
HQ: Wm. Wrigley Jr. Company
930 W Evergreen Ave
Chicago IL 60642
312 280-4710

(G-20626)
OPTI-SAND INCORPORATED
31 W 037 North Ave (60185)
P.O. Box 565, Geneva (60134-0565)
PHONE.................................630 293-1245
Robert Kohnke, *President*
Bob Kohnke, *Marketing Mgr*
EMP: 6
SALES: 410K **Privately Held**
SIC: 1442 Sand mining

(G-20627)
OSI INDUSTRIES LLC
Also Called: OSI Group
711 Industrial Dr (60185-1831)
P.O. Box 338 (60186-0338)
PHONE.................................630 231-9090
Darren Lange, *Opers Mgr*
Adam Ponitz, *Production*
Samantha Teal, *QA Dir*
Melissa Torres, *Human Res Mgr*
Lisa Niemann, *Hum Res Coord*
EMP: 220 **Privately Held**
WEB: www.osigroup.com
SIC: 5147 2013 Meats & meat products; sausages & other prepared meats
HQ: Osi Industries, Llc.
1225 Corp Blvd Ste 105
Aurora IL 60505
630 851-6600

(G-20628)
PERFORMANCE BATTERY GROUP INC
870 W Hawthorne Ln Ste A (60185-1915)
P.O. Box 88803, Carol Stream (60188-0803)
PHONE.................................630 293-5505
Gordon Close, *President*
Arron Smith, *General Ptnr*
Robert Hawco, *Business Mgr*
William Isett, *Sales Mgr*
EMP: 9
SALES (est): 1.1MM **Privately Held**
WEB: www.performancebatterygroup.com
SIC: 3621 3691 Generators for storage battery chargers; storage batteries; lead acid batteries (storage batteries)

(G-20629)
PERFORMANCE MANUFACTURING
782 W Hawthorne Ln (60185-1968)
PHONE.................................630 231-8099
Francis Winslow, *Principal*
EMP: 3

(PA)=Parent Co (HQ)=Headquarters (DH)=Div Headquarters
✪ = New Business established in last 2 years

West Chicago - Dupage County (G-20630)

SALES (est): 209.7K **Privately Held**
WEB: www.amsperformance.com
SIC: **5013** 3999 3714 Automotive brakes; manufacturing industries; motor vehicle brake systems & parts

(G-20630)
POLARIS LASER LAMINATIONS LLC
2725 Norton Creek Dr B2 (60185-6411)
PHONE.................................630 444-0760
Joe Fela, *Vice Pres*
Lynn Girard,
Jozef Fela,
Toan Truong,
EMP: 31
SALES: 4.3MM **Privately Held**
SIC: **3399** 7389 3479 Laminating steel; metal cutting services; coating of metals & formed products

(G-20631)
POWERMASTER
Also Called: Powermaster Motorsports
1833 Downs Dr (60185-1805)
PHONE.................................630 957-4019
John Babcock, *President*
Betty Baldwin, *Controller*
EMP: 2
SALES (est): 263.9K **Privately Held**
SIC: **3694** Alternators, automotive

(G-20632)
PRESS A LIGHT CORPORATION
300 Industrial Dr (60185-1890)
PHONE.................................630 231-6566
▲ **EMP:** 15
SQ FT: 20,000
SALES (est): 2.3MM **Privately Held**
SIC: **3648** Mfg Lighting Equipment

(G-20633)
PRO-PAK INDUSTRIES INC
Also Called: Pro-Line Safety Products
1099 Atlantic Dr Ste 1 (60185-5173)
PHONE.................................630 876-1050
Darrell G Holmes, *President*
Bryan Holmes, *Vice Pres*
Cheryl Holmes, *Vice Pres*
Dan Mehrbrodt, *VP Sales*
Cheryl A Holmes, *Admin Sec*
▲ **EMP:** 15
SQ FT: 17,000
SALES (est): 3.4MM **Privately Held**
SIC: **3953** 2671 5063 2311 Marking devices; plastic film, coated or laminated for packaging; power wire & cable; coats, overcoats & vests

(G-20634)
QUANTUM PRECISION INC
385 Wegner Dr (60185-2673)
PHONE.................................630 692-1545
Zygmunt Soszko Jr, *President*
Rex Soszko, *Director*
EMP: 25
SQ FT: 10,000
SALES (est): 4.3MM **Privately Held**
SIC: **3599** 3451 Machine shop, jobbing & repair; screw machine products

(G-20635)
READY ACCESS INC
1815 Arthur Dr (60185-1601)
PHONE.................................800 621-5045
John R Radek Jr, *President*
Dan Radek, *Opers Staff*
Bob Mc Keever, *CFO*
Kelly McGoldrick, *Sales Staff*
Robert J McKeever, *Admin Sec*
▼ **EMP:** 32
SQ FT: 65,000
SALES (est): 7.1MM **Privately Held**
SIC: **3444** Restaurant sheet metalwork

(G-20636)
RICON COLORS INC
675 Wegner Dr (60185-6011)
PHONE.................................630 562-9000
Gerald P McDonald, *President*
Pete Patel, *Vice Pres*
EMP: 10

SALES (est): 1.2MM
SALES (corp-wide): 4.4B **Privately Held**
SIC: **3089** 5169 Thermoformed finished plastic products; synthetic resins, rubber & plastic materials
PA: Clariant Ag
  Rothausstrasse 61
  Muttenz BL 4132
  614 695-111

(G-20637)
RITE SYSTEMS EAST INC (DH)
625 Wegner Dr (60185-6011)
PHONE.................................630 293-9174
Manu Jogani, *President*
Drew Babcock, *Vice Pres*
Mary Beth McGee, *Opers Mgr*
▲ **EMP:** 40
SQ FT: 50,000
SALES (est): 4.5MM
SALES (corp-wide): 4.4B **Privately Held**
SIC: **2865** 5169 Color pigments, organic; synthetic resins, rubber & plastic materials
HQ: Clariant Corporation
  4000 Monroe Rd
  Charlotte NC 28205
  704 331-7000

(G-20638)
ROOSEVELT MOBILE
60 W Roosevelt Rd (60185-3928)
PHONE.................................630 293-7630
EMP: 3
SALES (est): 170K **Privately Held**
SIC: **1311** Crude Petroleum/Natural Gas Production

(G-20639)
ROYAL CORINTHIAN INC
603 Fenton Ln (60185-2671)
PHONE.................................630 876-8899
Paul Savenok, *President*
Peter Savenok, *Vice Pres*
EMP: 25
SALES (est): 4MM **Privately Held**
SIC: **3272** Concrete stuctural support & building material

(G-20640)
SELROK INC
1151 Atlantic Dr Ste 2 (60185-5166)
P.O. Box 48 (60186-0048)
PHONE.................................630 876-8322
Stephanie Barkley, *Owner*
Charles Barkley, *Vice Pres*
EMP: 5
SALES (est): 688.7K **Privately Held**
SIC: **3589** Floor washing & polishing machines, commercial

(G-20641)
SIEGWERK EIC LLC
Also Called: Environmental Inks & Coatings
450 Wegner Dr (60185-2674)
PHONE.................................800 728-8200
EMP: 12
SALES (corp-wide): 940.5K **Privately Held**
SIC: **2899** Ink or writing fluids
HQ: Siegwerk Eic Llc
  1 Quality Products Rd
  Morganton NC 28655
  800 368-4657

(G-20642)
SIGN A RAMA
Also Called: Sign-A-Rama
946 N Neltnor Blvd # 114 (60185-5959)
PHONE.................................630 293-7300
Don Infusino, *Owner*
EMP: 5
SALES (est): 415K **Privately Held**
WEB: www.signarama.com
SIC: **3993** 5999 5099 Signs & advertising specialties; banners, flags, decals & posters; signs, except electric

(G-20643)
SIMPSON STRONG-TIE COMPANY INC
Also Called: Simpson Anchor Systems
2505 Enterprise Cir (60185-9605)
PHONE.................................630 613-5100
Phillip T Kingsfather, *CEO*
Roger Dankel, *President*
Patricia Telle, *Purchasing*
Barclay Simpson, *Executive*
▲ **EMP:** 25
SALES (est): 7.2MM
SALES (corp-wide): 1.1B **Publicly Held**
SIC: **3462** 5072 3452 2891 Anchors, forged; builders' hardware; bolts, nuts, rivets & washers; adhesives & sealants
HQ: Simpson Strong-Tie Company Inc.
  5956 W Las Positas Blvd
  Pleasanton CA 94588
  925 560-9000

(G-20644)
SONOCO PRODUCTS COMPANY
1500 Powis Rd (60185-1646)
PHONE.................................630 231-1489
Telissa McElveen, *Controller*
Mark Whittingtonsteve Lutes, *Manager*
EMP: 80
SALES (corp-wide): 5.3B **Publicly Held**
SIC: **2655** 2653 2631 Fiber cans, drums & similar products; corrugated & solid fiber boxes; paperboard mills
PA: Sonoco Products Company
  1 N 2nd St
  Hartsville SC 29550
  843 383-7000

(G-20645)
SPECTRUM MACHINING CO
776 W Hawthorne Ln (60185-1968)
PHONE.................................630 562-9400
Dave Bauer, *President*
EMP: 40
SALES (est): 3.5MM **Privately Held**
SIC: **3599** Machine shop, jobbing & repair

(G-20646)
SPEED POWDER COATINGS INC
870 W Hawthorne Ln Ste C (60185-1915)
PHONE.................................630 549-0657
EMP: 2 **EST:** 2017
SALES (est): 237K **Privately Held**
SIC: **3479** Coating of metals & formed products

(G-20647)
SUBCO FOODS OF ILLINOIS INC (PA)
1150 Commerce Dr (60185-2680)
PHONE.................................630 231-0003
Masroor Khan, *President*
Joan McGrath, *Vice Pres*
Robert Humes, *QC Mgr*
Bob Dujka, *Finance*
Robert Dujka, *Human Res Dir*
▼ **EMP:** 100
SQ FT: 55,000
SALES (est): 20MM **Privately Held**
SIC: **2099** Food preparations

(G-20648)
SUN PATTERN & MODEL INC
505 Wegner Dr (60185-2626)
PHONE.................................630 293-3366
Dennis J Lee, *President*
Mary Lee, *Admin Sec*
EMP: 20
SQ FT: 25,000
SALES (est): 3.3MM **Privately Held**
SIC: **3543** 3999 3089 Industrial patterns; models, general, except toy; injection molded finished plastic products; injection molding of plastics

(G-20649)
TEMPRITE COMPANY
1555 W Hawthorne Ln 1e (60185-1809)
PHONE.................................630 293-5910
George Schmidt, *CEO*
Thomas Schmidt, *President*
John Canning, *Prdtn Mgr*
Bill Degraf, *Engineer*
Bob Brown, *Controller*
▲ **EMP:** 30
SQ FT: 12,000
SALES (est): 8MM **Privately Held**
SIC: **3822** 3443 Air conditioning & refrigeration controls; fabricated plate work (boiler shop)

(G-20650)
TEXTRON AVIATION INC
2700 Intl Dr Ste 304 (60185-1658)
PHONE.................................630 443-5080
EMP: 5
SALES (corp-wide): 13.7B **Publicly Held**
SIC: **3728** 3721 5599 Mfg Aircraft Parts/Equip Mfg Aircraft Ret Misc Vehicles
HQ: Textron Aviation Inc.
  1 Cessna Blvd
  Wichita KS 67215
  316 517-6000

(G-20651)
THERMAL-TECH SYSTEMS INC
1215 Atlantic Dr (60185-5165)
PHONE.................................630 639-5115
Monika Frary, *President*
EMP: 28
SQ FT: 25,000
SALES (est): 5.6MM **Privately Held**
SIC: **3089** 3545 Injection molding of plastics; machine tool accessories

(G-20652)
TOMENSON MACHINE WORKS INC
1150 Powis Rd (60185-1664)
PHONE.................................630 377-7670
Scott T Roake, *President*
Jerry Blake, *Admin Sec*
EMP: 60 **EST:** 1976
SALES (est): 8.9MM **Privately Held**
SIC: **3599** 3594 Machine shop, jobbing & repair; fluid power pumps & motors

(G-20653)
TORNADO INDUSTRIES LLC
333 Charles Ct Ste 109 (60185-2604)
PHONE.................................817 551-6507
▲ **EMP:** 53
SQ FT: 88,000
SALES (est): 10MM
SALES (corp-wide): 187.6MM **Privately Held**
WEB: www.tornadovac.com
SIC: **3589** Vacuum cleaners & sweepers, electric: industrial; floor washing & polishing machines, commercial; carpet sweepers, except household electric vacuum sweepers
PA: Tacony Corporation
  1760 Gilsinn Ln
  Fenton MO 63026
  636 349-3000

(G-20654)
TREUDT CORPORATION
Also Called: West Chicago Printing Company
131 Fremont St (60185-1924)
P.O. Box 1 (60186-0001)
PHONE.................................630 293-0500
W Bruce Treudt, *President*
Steve Treudt, *Vice Pres*
EMP: 9
SQ FT: 7,300
SALES (est): 1.3MM **Privately Held**
WEB: www.westchicagoprinting.com
SIC: **2752** Lithographing on metal; commercial printing, offset

(G-20655)
TURNER JCT PRTG & LITHO SVC
850 Meadowview Xing Ste 2 (60185-2576)
PHONE.................................630 293-1377
Craig A Bublitz, *President*
Scott Bublitz, *Vice Pres*
William S Bublitz, *Vice Pres*
Penny B Campbell, *Vice Pres*
Bonnie Bublitz, *Admin Sec*
EMP: 4
SQ FT: 2,500
SALES: 400K **Privately Held**
SIC: **2752** Lithographing on metal

(G-20656)
VATOR ACCESSORIES INC
1090 Atlantic Dr (60185-5101)
PHONE.................................630 876-8370
Lisa Grimes, *Principal*
◆ **EMP:** 2
SALES (est): 404.7K **Privately Held**
SIC: **3534** Elevators & equipment

(G-20657)
VEGA WAVE SYSTEMS INC
1275 W Roosevelt Rd # 104 (60185-4815)
PHONE.................................630 562-9433

Alan Sugg, *President*
Alan R Sugg, *President*
EMP: 4
SALES (est): 664.6K **Privately Held**
SIC: 3674 Semiconductors & related devices

(G-20658)
WES TECH PRINTING GRAPHIC
1555 W Hawthorne Ln (60185-1809)
PHONE..................................630 520-9041
Barbara Doyle, *Owner*
EMP: 4
SALES: 200K **Privately Held**
SIC: 2759 Commercial printing

(G-20659)
WISE PLASTICS TECHNOLOGIES INC
1601 W Hawthorne Ln (60185-1823)
PHONE..................................847 697-2840
Silvia Denninger, *Opers Staff*
EMP: 6
SALES (corp-wide): 36.8MM **Privately Held**
SIC: 3089 Injection molding of plastics
PA: Wise Plastics Technologies, Inc.
3810 Stern Ave
Saint Charles IL 60174
847 697-2840

West Dundee
Kane County

(G-20660)
144 INTERNATIONAL INC
740 S 8th St (60118-2102)
P.O. Box 178, Elgin (60121-0178)
PHONE..................................847 426-8881
David Perlman, *President*
Sandra Perlman, *Vice Pres*
EMP: 12
SQ FT: 1,200
SALES (est): 1.2MM **Privately Held**
SIC: 3915 Diamond cutting & polishing

(G-20661)
D & M PERLMAN FINE JEWELRY
740 S 8th St (60118-2102)
PHONE..................................847 426-8881
David Perlman,
EMP: 5
SQ FT: 7,500
SALES: 800K **Privately Held**
SIC: 5944 3911 Jewelry, precious stones & precious metals; jewelry, precious metal

(G-20662)
DIVERGENT ALLIANCE LLC
511 Eichler Dr (60118-2733)
PHONE..................................847 531-0559
Matthew Jay Moeller, *Mng Member*
EMP: 5 **EST:** 2017
SALES (est): 549.2K **Privately Held**
WEB: www.divergentalliance.com
SIC: 3629 Electrical industrial apparatus

(G-20663)
EMMETTS TAVERN & BREWING CO (PA)
128 W Main St (60118-2017)
PHONE..................................847 428-4500
Andrew Burns, *President*
Timothy Burns, *Vice Pres*
EMP: 45
SQ FT: 16,000
SALES (est): 3.2MM **Privately Held**
SIC: 5812 2082 5182 Chicken restaurant; beer (alcoholic beverage); wine & distilled beverages

(G-20664)
JEWEL OSCO INC
1250 W Main St (60118-1902)
PHONE..................................847 428-3547
Glenn Paulson, *Manager*
EMP: 125
SALES (corp-wide): 60.5B **Privately Held**
SIC: 5411 5421 2051 Supermarkets, chain; meat & fish markets; bread, cake & related products

HQ: Jewel Osco, Inc.
150 E Pierce Rd Ste 200
Itasca IL 60143
630 948-6000

(G-20665)
POLY-RESYN INC
518 Market Loop Ste A (60118-2182)
PHONE..................................847 428-4031
Robert Schreurs, *President*
Sharen J Schreurs, *Admin Sec*
Jeff Schreurs, *Administration*
EMP: 10 **EST:** 1976
SALES (est): 2MM **Privately Held**
SIC: 2821 Plastics materials & resins

(G-20666)
STITCH MAGIC USA INC
785 S 8th St (60118-2108)
PHONE..................................847 836-5000
Dan Denk, *Treasurer*
Larry Zenger, *Admin Sec*
EMP: 20
SQ FT: 2,800
SALES (est): 1.7MM **Privately Held**
SIC: 2395 Emblems, embroidered; embroidery products, except schiffli machine

(G-20667)
WATERS INDUSTRIES INC
Also Called: Panthervision
213 W Main St (60118-2018)
PHONE..................................847 783-5900
Michael A Waters, *President*
Betsy Grutzmacher, *Sales Staff*
Augie Hinnenkamp, *Sales Staff*
Chris Sourwine, *Sales Associate*
Chuck Freeman, *Director*
◆ **EMP:** 30
SQ FT: 2,000
SALES (est): 5.5MM **Privately Held**
SIC: 3641 3851 3648 2253 Electric lamps; eyeglasses, lenses & frames; protective eyewear; flashlights; hats & headwear, knit

West Frankfort
Franklin County

(G-20668)
BIT BROKERS INTERNATIONAL LTD
5568 Logan Rd (62896-4317)
P.O. Box 100, Logan (62856-0100)
PHONE..................................618 435-5811
Tim Thomas, *President*
Cliff Thomas, *Vice Pres*
Zach Peebels, *VP Mktg*
Annette Borgra, *Marketing Staff*
Alan Thomas, *Manager*
◆ **EMP:** 20 **EST:** 1988
SQ FT: 7,500
SALES: 7MM **Privately Held**
SIC: 5084 3423 Drilling bits; hammers (hand tools)

(G-20669)
BUDMARK OIL COMPANY INC
106 E Oak St (62896-2741)
PHONE..................................618 937-2495
Jim Dunston, *President*
Judy Dunston, *Corp Secy*
EMP: 9
SQ FT: 4,000
SALES: 500K **Privately Held**
SIC: 1311 Crude petroleum production

(G-20670)
DIXIE CREAM DONUT SHOP
510 W Main St (62896-2231)
PHONE..................................618 937-4866
Eugene Forgatch, *Owner*
EMP: 20 **EST:** 1955
SQ FT: 2,000
SALES (est): 772.1K **Privately Held**
SIC: 5461 2051 Doughnuts; charlotte russe, bakery product: except frozen

(G-20671)
FIELDERS CHOICE
25 Frankfort Dr (62896-1728)
PHONE..................................618 937-2294
Carl Harris, *Owner*

Ann Harris, *Partner*
Max Lude, *Partner*
Sharon Lude, *Partner*
◆ **EMP:** 6
SQ FT: 1,800
SALES: 200K **Privately Held**
SIC: 5611 5947 5999 5699 Clothing, sportswear, men's & boys'; hats, men's & boys'; trading cards: baseball or other sports, entertainment, etc.; trophies & plaques; sports apparel; embroidery & art needlework

(G-20672)
FREEDOM MATERIAL RESOURCES INC
1186 State Highway 37 (62896-5005)
P.O. Box 248 (62896-0248)
PHONE..................................618 937-6415
Robert Orr, *President*
EMP: 60
SALES (est): 10.6MM **Privately Held**
SIC: 3532 Mining machinery

(G-20673)
GATEHOUSE MEDIA LLC
Also Called: Daily American, The
111 S Emma St (62896-2729)
P.O. Box 219, Springfield (62705-0219)
PHONE..................................618 937-2850
Scott Carr, *General Mgr*
EMP: 40
SALES (corp-wide): 1.8B **Publicly Held**
SIC: 2711 Newspapers, publishing & printing
HQ: Gatehouse Media, Llc
175 Sullys Trl Fl 3
Pittsford NY 14534
585 598-0030

(G-20674)
KINSMAN ENTERPRISES INC
10804 Mark Twain Rd (62896-4105)
PHONE..................................618 932-3838
Ernest M Hanners, *President*
Judy Hanners, *Vice Pres*
Rick Hanners, *Vice Pres*
▲ **EMP:** 8
SQ FT: 4,000
SALES (est): 1MM **Privately Held**
SIC: 2599 3842 2531 Hospital furniture, except beds; surgical appliances & supplies; public building & related furniture

(G-20675)
LEISURE PROPERTIES LLC
Also Called: Crownline Boats
11884 Country Club Rd (62896-5064)
PHONE..................................618 937-6426
Scott Lahrman, *President*
Barb McCrary, *Buyer*
Anthony Zielinski, *Mng Member*
Dave Wilson,
Lisa Wilson,
▼ **EMP:** 550
SQ FT: 250,000
SALES (est): 163.6MM **Privately Held**
SIC: 3732 Boats, fiberglass: building & repairing

(G-20676)
LIBERTY GROUP PUBLISHING
111 S Emma St (62896-2729)
P.O. Box 617 (62896-0617)
PHONE..................................618 937-2850
Mary Mocaby, *Bookkeeper*
EMP: 5
SALES (corp-wide): 1.6MM **Privately Held**
SIC: 2711 Newspapers: publishing only, not printed on site
PA: Liberty Group Publishing
108 W 1st St
Geneseo IL 61254
309 944-1779

(G-20677)
LITTLE EGYPT GAS A & WLDG SUPS
Also Called: A A A Cylinder
10603 Bencie Ln (62896-4716)
PHONE..................................618 937-2271
Susan Collins, *President*
Bill Collins, *Vice Pres*
EMP: 3

SALES (est): 1MM **Privately Held**
SIC: 3714 5169 Cylinder heads, motor vehicle; oxygen

(G-20678)
MILES BROS
1000 S Jefferson St (62896-3313)
PHONE..................................618 937-4115
Lisa King, *Principal*
EMP: 2
SALES (est): 353.5K **Privately Held**
SIC: 3556 Meat processing machinery

(G-20679)
R&R RACING OF PALM BEACH INC
15942 Mine 25 Rd Ste 28 (62896-5327)
PHONE..................................618 937-6767
Brett Ray, *President*
Patty Ray, *Corp Secy*
EMP: 2
SALES (est): 238.2K **Privately Held**
SIC: 3365 Aluminum foundries

(G-20680)
RAYTECH MACHINING FABRICATION
10925 Mainline Rd (62896-4293)
PHONE..................................618 932-2511
Ray Measimer, *President*
EMP: 20
SQ FT: 19,000
SALES (est): 2.5MM **Privately Held**
SIC: 2821 Plasticizer/additive based plastic materials

(G-20681)
ROE MACHINE INC
12725 Union Rd (62896)
P.O. Box 531 (62896-0531)
PHONE..................................618 983-5524
Willard Strain, *CEO*
Jeff Kirby, *Principal*
Darla Strain, *Admin Sec*
EMP: 27
SQ FT: 8,000
SALES (est): 4.4MM **Privately Held**
SIC: 3599 3532 Machine shop, jobbing & repair; mining machinery

(G-20682)
SANDNER ELECTRIC CO INC
903 E Saint Louis St (62896-1448)
P.O. Box 158 (62896-0158)
PHONE..................................618 932-2179
Harold Chase, *President*
Charles Lintner Sr, *Vice Pres*
EMP: 5
SQ FT: 13,250
SALES (est): 330K **Privately Held**
SIC: 7694 5063 Electric motor repair; motors, electric

(G-20683)
SIMPLE SOLUTIONS
110 E Main St (62896-2430)
PHONE..................................618 932-6177
Tim Grigsby, *Owner*
EMP: 3
SQ FT: 2,000
SALES (est): 253.9K **Privately Held**
SIC: 2741 2752 Miscellaneous publishing; commercial printing, offset

(G-20684)
SPECIAL MINE SERVICES INC (PA)
11782 Country Club Rd (62896-5037)
P.O. Box 188 (62896-0188)
PHONE..................................618 932-2151
Dwayne Coffey, *President*
Steve Kissinger, *President*
EMP: 55
SQ FT: 33,000
SALES: 14MM **Privately Held**
SIC: 3643 5063 Connectors & terminals for electrical devices; electrical apparatus & equipment

(G-20685)
TWIN MILLS TIMBER & TIE CO INC
3268 State Highway 37 (62896-4291)
P.O. Box 34 (62896-0034)
PHONE..................................618 932-3662

West Peoria - Peoria County (G-20686)

Fred Wilson, *President*
Keith Wilson, *Admin Sec*
EMP: 22
SQ FT: 10,000
SALES (est): 4.4MM **Privately Held**
SIC: 3537 Platforms, stands, tables, pallets & similar equipment

West Peoria
Peoria County

(G-20686)
H&H CRUSHING INC
2401 W Rhodora Ave (61604-3826)
PHONE.................309 275-0643
EMP: 3
SALES (est): 183.8K **Privately Held**
SIC: 1422 Crushed/Broken Limestone

(G-20687)
KOENIG BODY & EQUIPMENT INC
2428 W Farmington Rd (61604-5099)
PHONE.................309 673-7435
Mark Koenig, *President*
EMP: 22
SQ FT: 2,800
SALES (est): 5MM **Privately Held**
WEB: www.koenigbody.com
SIC: 3711 5012 Snow plows (motor vehicles), assembly of; truck bodies

West Salem
Edwards County

(G-20688)
RODGERS BILL OIL MIN BITS SVC
Also Called: Bill Rodgers Drlg & Producing
20226 Wabash 20 Ave (62476-3012)
PHONE.................618 299-7771
Bill Rodgers, *Owner*
Jenny Rodgers, *Manager*
EMP: 4
SALES (est): 300K **Privately Held**
SIC: 5084 1381 1311 Drilling bits; drilling oil & gas wells; crude petroleum & natural gas

(G-20689)
WEST SALEM KNOX COUNTY HTCHY
Also Called: George's Farm Supply
615 W Church St (62476-1258)
PHONE.................618 456-3601
Dince Goodwin, *President*
EMP: 5
SALES (est): 73.2K **Privately Held**
SIC: 5999 2452 Feed & farm supply; artists' supplies & materials; fire extinguishers; farm & agricultural buildings, prefabricated wood

West Union
Clark County

(G-20690)
FORESTECH WOOD PRODUCTS
204 W Washington St (62477-1025)
PHONE.................217 279-3659
Steve Shawler, *Owner*
Corolyn Shawler, *Manager*
EMP: 4 **EST:** 1971
SALES (est): 250K **Privately Held**
SIC: 2421 Sawmills & planing mills, general

Westchester
Cook County

(G-20691)
ALISUN INC
Also Called: Alisun Business Printing
937 S Mannheim Rd Ste 2 (60154-2552)
PHONE.................708 571-3451
EMP: 6
SALES (est): 803.6K **Privately Held**
SIC: 2752 Commercial printing, offset

(G-20692)
BRAINLAB INC
5 Westbrook Corp Ctr (60154-5749)
PHONE.................800 784-7700
Stefan Vilsmeier, *CEO*
Sean Clark, *President*
Isabelle Doll, *General Mgr*
Chris Kemp, *Regional Mgr*
Sascha Elgas, *Business Mgr*
▲ **EMP:** 227 **EST:** 1998
SALES (est): 146.1MM
SALES (corp-wide): 314.6MM **Privately Held**
WEB: www.brainlab.com
SIC: 5047 3841 Medical equipment & supplies; surgical & medical instruments
PA: Brainlab Ag
  Olof-Palme-Str. 9
  Munchen 81829
  899 915-680

(G-20693)
CHIPITA AMERICA INC (DH)
1 Westbrook Corporate Ctr (60154-5701)
PHONE.................708 731-2434
George Chalkias, *CEO*
Antonios Pouftis, *CFO*
▲ **EMP:** 20
SQ FT: 3,000
SALES (est): 34.8MM
SALES (corp-wide): 183.7K **Privately Held**
WEB: www.chipita.us.com
SIC: 5461 2052 2096 5145 Bakeries; cookies & crackers; cookies; biscuits, dry; potato chips & similar snacks; confectionery; snack foods; groceries & related products; crackers, cookies & bakery products; cookies

(G-20694)
CML TECHNOLOGIES INC
10330 W Roosevelt Rd # 205 (60154-2564)
Fax: 708 540-1975
EMP: 3 **EST:** 1990
SALES (est): 331.9K **Privately Held**
SIC: 3661 Mfg Telephone/Telegraph Apparatus

(G-20695)
COMMSCOPE SOLUTIONS INTL INC (HQ)
4 Westbrook Corp Ctr (60154-5752)
PHONE.................828 324-2200
Marvin S Edwards, *CEO*
Beth Scholtes, *Vice Pres*
Barbara Ghini, *Export Mgr*
EMP: 4 **EST:** 2003
SALES (est): 29.2MM **Publicly Held**
SIC: 3663 Radio & TV communications equipment

(G-20696)
CROWN KANDY ENTERPRISE LTD
Also Called: Crown Kandy Publishing
1127 S Mannheim Rd # 313 (60154-2570)
PHONE.................708 580-6494
Latoya M White, *CEO*
Antonio Ward, *Business Mgr*
Shyreeta Benbow, *Vice Pres*
Tammarah Silmon, *CFO*
EMP: 10
SALES (est): 321.4K **Privately Held**
SIC: 2731 Books: publishing & printing

(G-20697)
ESSENTRA CORP (DH)
2 Westbrook Corp Ctr # 200 (60154-5718)
PHONE.................814 899-7671
Auste Graham, *Vice Pres*
Vanderlei Souza, *Director*
EMP: 1 **EST:** 1987
SALES (est): 118.5MM
SALES (corp-wide): 1.2B **Privately Held**
SIC: 3999 2621 7389 3089 Cigarette filters; cigarette paper; packaging & labeling services; injection molding of plastics; plastics products; sealing compounds for pipe threads or joints
HQ: Essentra Holdings Corp.
  2 Westbrook Corporate Ctr # 200
  Westchester IL 60154
  804 518-0322

(G-20698)
ESSENTRA HOLDINGS CORP (HQ)
2 Westbrook Corporate Ctr # 200 (60154-5718)
PHONE.................804 518-0322
◆ **EMP:** 8
SALES (est): 250.7MM
SALES (corp-wide): 1.2B **Privately Held**
SIC: 3081 3082 3999 3951 Unsupported plastics film & sheet; unsupported plastics profile shapes; cigarette filters; pens & mechanical pencils; cigarette tow, cellulosic fiber
PA: Essentra Plc
  Avebury House
  Milton Keynes BUCKS
  190 835-9100

(G-20699)
ESSENTRA PACKAGING US INC (DH)
2 Westbrook Corp Ctr (60154-5702)
PHONE.................704 418-8692
◆ **EMP:** 5
SALES (est): 236.8MM
SALES (corp-wide): 1.2B **Privately Held**
SIC: 2673 2621 2752 8741 Plastic bags: made from purchased materials; business form paper; commercial printing, lithographic; management services
HQ: Essentra International Llc
  2 Westbrook Corp Ctr
  Westchester IL 60154
  866 800-0775

(G-20700)
ILLINI PRECAST LLC
2255 Entp Dr Ste 5501 (60154)
PHONE.................708 562-7700
Craig Wagenbach, *Principal*
Ming King,
EMP: 14
SALES (est): 3.8MM **Privately Held**
SIC: 3272 Concrete products, precast; precast terrazo or concrete products

(G-20701)
INGREDION INCORPORATED (PA)
5 Westbrook Corporate Ctr # 500 (60154-5795)
PHONE.................708 551-2600
Gregory B Kenny, *Ch of Bd*
James P Zallie, *President*
Anthony P Delio, *Senior VP*
Larry Fernandes, *Senior VP*
Jose Bertoli, *Vice Pres*
EMP: 800 **EST:** 1906
SALES: 6.2B **Publicly Held**
WEB: www.ingredion.com
SIC: 2046 Corn & other vegetable starches; corn starch; potato starch

(G-20702)
KW PRECAST LLC (PA)
2255 Entp Dr Ste 1510 (60154)
PHONE.................708 562-7700
Raig R Wagenbach,
EMP: 16
SALES (est): 5.1MM **Privately Held**
SIC: 3272 4789 Concrete products, precast; pipeline terminal facilities, independently operated

(G-20703)
LITT ALUMINUM & SHTMTL CO
9825 W Roosevelt Rd (60154-2400)
PHONE.................708 366-4720
Erich W Little, *President*
EMP: 7 **EST:** 2003
SQ FT: 1,800
SALES (est): 600K **Privately Held**
WEB: www.littaluminum.com
SIC: 3444 Siding, sheet metal

(G-20704)
MATERIAL SERVICE CORPORATION
2235 Entp Dr Ste 3504 (60154)
PHONE.................708 447-1100
Don Stewart, *Principal*
EMP: 35
SALES (corp-wide): 20.8B **Privately Held**
WEB: www.reliablematerials.com
SIC: 3281 1442 Stone, quarrying & processing of own stone products; construction sand and gravel
HQ: Material Service Corporation
  2235 Entp Dr Ste 3504
  Westchester IL 60154
  708 731-2600

(G-20705)
MATERIAL SERVICE CORPORATION (DH)
Also Called: Hanson Material Service
2235 Entp Dr Ste 3504 (60154)
PHONE.................708 731-2600
Gerald Nagel, *President*
Dennis Dolan, *President*
Michael Stanczak, *President*
Walter Serwa, *CFO*
Karen Cox, *Manager*
EMP: 200
SQ FT: 80,000
SALES (est): 201.1MM
SALES (corp-wide): 20.8B **Privately Held**
SIC: 1422 1442 Crushed & broken limestone; construction sand mining; gravel mining
HQ: Hanson Aggregates Llc
  8505 Freport Pkwy Ste 500
  Irving TX 75063
  469 417-1200

(G-20706)
ORACLE SYSTEMS CORPORATION
3 Westbrook Corp Ctr # 900 (60154-5765)
PHONE.................708 409-7800
Diane Carlson, *Manager*
EMP: 70
SALES (corp-wide): 39.5B **Publicly Held**
SIC: 7372 Prepackaged software
HQ: Oracle Systems Corporation
  500 Oracle Pkwy
  Redwood City CA 94065

(G-20707)
P P GRAPHICS INC
Also Called: Minuteman Press
1939 S Mannheim Rd (60154-4322)
PHONE.................708 343-2530
Paul Gangi, *President*
Michele Caron, *Engineer*
EMP: 3
SQ FT: 1,200
SALES (est): 424.2K **Privately Held**
SIC: 2752 2791 2789 Commercial printing, lithographic; typesetting; bookbinding & related work

(G-20708)
PHOENIX TRUCKING INC
Also Called: Phoenix Pckg Mtrls/Phnix Plltt
3036 Downing Ave (60154-5123)
P.O. Box 7842 (60154-7842)
PHONE.................708 514-2094
Robert J Kucera, *President*
Pat Kucera, *Admin Sec*
EMP: 5
SALES (est): 330K **Privately Held**
SIC: 4213 3537 5031 Trucking, except local; industrial trucks & tractors; lumber, plywood & millwork

(G-20709)
RUTKE SIGNS INC
Also Called: Rutke Signs and Safety
1 Westbrook Corporate Ctr # 300 (60154-5701)
PHONE.................708 841-6464
Julia Rutke, *President*
Rob Rutke, *Vice Pres*
Robert Rutke Sr, *Vice Pres*
EMP: 3
SQ FT: 1,500

SALES: 500K **Privately Held**
SIC: 7389 3993 5999 Sign painting & lettering shop; signs & advertising specialties; safety supplies & equipment

(G-20710)
SHERWIN-WILLIAMS COMPANY
10551 W Cermak Rd (60154-5222)
PHONE.....................708 409-4728
EMP: 5
SALES (corp-wide): 17.9B **Publicly Held**
SIC: 5231 5198 2851 Paint; paints, varnishes & supplies; wood fillers or sealers
PA: The Sherwin-Williams Company
101 W Prospect Ave # 1020
Cleveland OH 44115
216 566-2000

(G-20711)
SLIPON NIPPLE COMPANY
10849 Kingston St (60154-5018)
PHONE.....................708 345-2525
Michael Farhi, *President*
Fred Castillo, *Vice Pres*
John Farhi, *Vice Pres*
EMP: 3
SALES (est): 153K **Privately Held**
SIC: 3069 Nipples, rubber

(G-20712)
SPARROW COFFEE ROASTERY
10330 W Roosevelt Rd # 200 (60154-2571)
PHONE.....................321 648-6415
EMP: 5
SALES (corp-wide): 1.5MM **Privately Held**
SIC: 2095 2099 Mfg Roasted Coffee Mfg Food Preparations
PA: Sparrow Coffee Roastery
1201 W Lake St Ste 2
Chicago IL

(G-20713)
SYNERGY MECHANICAL INC
9835 Derby Ln (60154-3707)
P.O. Box 765, Hillside (60162-0765)
PHONE.....................708 410-1004
Mike Descourouez, *President*
EMP: 5
SQ FT: 1,500
SALES (est): 487.1K **Privately Held**
WEB: www.synergymech.com
SIC: 1711 3444 Mechanical contractor; ducts, sheet metal

(G-20714)
TNP MACHINERY CO INC
9860 Derby Ln (60154-3746)
PHONE.....................708 344-7750
Nick Belcin, *President*
EMP: 6
SQ FT: 3,000
SALES (est): 750K **Privately Held**
SIC: 3599 Machine shop, jobbing & repair

(G-20715)
TROTTIE PUBLISHING GROUP INC
Also Called: West Suburban Journal News
9930 Derby Ln Ste 102 (60154-3770)
PHONE.....................708 344-5975
L Nicole Trottie, *Publisher*
EMP: 4 EST: 2011
SALES (est): 144K **Privately Held**
WEB: www.westsuburbanjournal.com
SIC: 2711 Newspapers, publishing & printing

(G-20716)
TY MILES INCORPORATED
9855 Derby Ln (60154-3792)
PHONE.....................708 344-5480
Steve Mueller, *President*
Raymond A Mueller, *Corp Secy*
Phil Klos, *Vice Pres*
Alex Lekakh, *Engineer*
Rick Shea, *Engineer*
EMP: 25
SQ FT: 18,000
SALES (est): 5.8MM **Privately Held**
WEB: www.tymiles.com
SIC: 3541 3549 Machine tools, metal cutting type; metalworking machinery

(G-20717)
USMSS INC
2428 Pinecrest Ln (60154-5944)
PHONE.....................708 409-9010
George Fleming, *Manager*
Bill Dow, *Exec Dir*
EMP: 2
SALES (est): 229.6K **Privately Held**
SIC: 2759 Screen printing

Western Springs
Cook County

(G-20718)
AALBORG COMPANY
4521 Harvey Ave (60558-1648)
PHONE.....................708 246-8858
James Larsen, *President*
Mary Larsen, *Admin Sec*
EMP: 3
SALES (est): 353.5K **Privately Held**
SIC: 3821 Ovens, laboratory

(G-20719)
CERTIFIED POLYMERS INC
4479 Lawn Ave (60558-2431)
P.O. Box 102 (60558-0102)
PHONE.....................630 515-0007
Gary C Kompare, *President*
EMP: 7
SALES (est): 1.8MM **Privately Held**
SIC: 5162 3089 Plastics resins; synthetic resin finished products

(G-20720)
DADO LIGHTING LLC
4700 Gilbert Ave 47-217 (60558-1753)
PHONE.....................877 323-6584
Dave Doubek, *Principal*
David Zilbro, *Vice Pres*
Dj Ziobro, *Vice Pres*
EMP: 6 EST: 2015
SQ FT: 5,000
SALES (est): 700K **Privately Held**
SIC: 3646 5063 Commercial indusl & institutional electric lighting fixtures; lighting fixtures

(G-20721)
DREHER ORTHOPEDIC INDUSTRIES (PA)
5129 Woodland Ave (60558-1831)
PHONE.....................708 848-4646
Peter Dreher Jr, *President*
EMP: 8
SQ FT: 2,000
SALES (est): 1.1MM **Privately Held**
SIC: 3842 Orthopedic appliances

(G-20722)
INITIALLY EWE
1058 Hillgrove Ave (60558-1420)
PHONE.....................708 246-7777
EMP: 3
SALES (est): 410.3K **Privately Held**
WEB: www.initiallyeweboutique.com
SIC: 3552 Knitting machines

(G-20723)
PROPELLER HR SOLUTIONS INC
5350 Wolf Rd (60558-1858)
PHONE.....................312 342-7355
Bill Blouin, *President*
EMP: 2
SALES (est): 209.2K **Privately Held**
SIC: 3366 Propellers

(G-20724)
RESEARCH DESIGN INC
3901 Clausen Ave (60558-1226)
PHONE.....................708 246-8166
Robert Genaze, *President*
EMP: 3
SALES (est): 397.3K **Privately Held**
SIC: 3842 5999 Prosthetic appliances; orthopedic & prosthesis applications

(G-20725)
RYLIN MEDIA LLC
5028 Lawn Ave (60558-1820)
PHONE.....................708 246-7599
Philip Saran, *Mng Member*
Roger D Herrin,
EMP: 5
SALES: 3MM **Privately Held**
SIC: 2721 Magazines: publishing & printing

(G-20726)
TAKE YOUR MARK SPORTS LLC
1010 Longmeadow Ln (60558-2108)
P.O. Box 626 (60558-0626)
PHONE.....................708 655-0525
Robert Craig, *Mng Member*
Therese Craig,
EMP: 2
SALES: 500K **Privately Held**
SIC: 3953 7389 Cancelling stamps, hand: rubber or metal;

Westmont
Dupage County

(G-20727)
AMER SURGICAL INSTRUMENTS INC
Also Called: Asico
26 Plaza Dr (60559-1130)
PHONE.....................630 986-8032
Ravi Nallakrishnan, *President*
Radah Nallakrishnan, *Vice Pres*
EMP: 15
SALES (est): 1.6MM **Privately Held**
SIC: 3841 Surgical & medical instruments

(G-20728)
AMERICAN COUPLINGS CO
40 Chestnut Ave (60559-1128)
PHONE.....................630 323-4442
Jim Jablonsky, *Manager*
▲ EMP: 2
SALES (est): 202.2K **Privately Held**
WEB: www.americancouplings.com
SIC: 3429 Clamps & couplings, hose

(G-20729)
ASICO LLC
26 Plaza Dr (60559-1130)
PHONE.....................630 986-8032
Volha Dziadyk, *Accountant*
Nupnau Kelsey, *Marketing Mgr*
Ramaa RAO, *Manager*
Putti Tiasuwan, *Manager*
Ravi Nallakrishnan,
EMP: 15
SQ FT: 7,000
SALES (est): 3MM **Privately Held**
SIC: 3851 5048 Ophthalmic goods; ophthalmic goods

(G-20730)
BROAD-OCEAN MOTOR LLC
910 Pasquinelli Dr (60559-5526)
PHONE.....................630 908-4720
Terry Zhang,
Chuping Lu,
Haiming Xu,
EMP: 20
SQ FT: 25,000
SALES (est): 3.2MM
SALES (corp-wide): 1.2B **Privately Held**
SIC: 3621 Motors, electric
HQ: Broad-Ocean Motor Ev Co., Ltd.
No.5, Yongfeng Road, Haidian District
Beijing 10009
105 871-1726

(G-20731)
CAMBRIDGE BUSINESS PUBLISHERS
102 Chestnut Ave (60559-1137)
PHONE.....................630 321-0173
Marnee Fieldman, *Vice Pres*
Kelly Budnik, *Accounts Mgr*
EMP: 7
SALES (est): 330.9K **Privately Held**
SIC: 2741 Miscellaneous publishing

(G-20732)
CLEAR SIGHT INC
220 Rosewood Ct (60559-1577)
PHONE.....................630 323-3590
Paul Osenkarski, *President*
EMP: 3
SALES (est): 206.5K **Privately Held**
SIC: 3851 Ophthalmic goods

(G-20733)
CONTEXT SOFTWARE SYSTEMS
601 Oakmont Ln Fl 2 (60559-5523)
PHONE.....................630 654-0291
EMP: 4
SALES (est): 261.4K **Privately Held**
SIC: 3572 Computer storage devices

(G-20734)
DATAIR EMPLOYEE BENEFT SYSTEMS
735 N Cass Ave (60559-1100)
PHONE.....................630 325-2600
Aaron Venouziou, *President*
Robin Snyder, *Sales Staff*
Ken Faikus, *Marketing Mgr*
EMP: 45
SQ FT: 15,600
SALES (est): 4.8MM **Privately Held**
SIC: 7372 8742 Business oriented computer software; management consulting services

(G-20735)
DENBUR INC (PA)
650 Blackhawk Dr (60559-9504)
P.O. Box 3473, Oak Brook (60522-3473)
PHONE.....................630 986-9667
Monica Maissami, *President*
EMP: 8
SQ FT: 4,500
SALES (est): 3.6MM **Privately Held**
SIC: 3843 Dental equipment & supplies

(G-20736)
DESIGN TECHNOLOGY INC
768 Burr Oak Dr (60559-1122)
PHONE.....................630 920-1300
Stephen O Myers, *President*
Marjorie K Newpher, *Vice Pres*
▲ EMP: 21 EST: 1978
SQ FT: 10,000
SALES: 2MM **Privately Held**
SIC: 3825 8711 Measuring instruments & meters, electric; mechanical engineering

(G-20737)
DESIGNA ACCESS CORPORATION (DH)
777 Oakmont Ln Ste 2000 (60559-5580)
PHONE.....................630 891-3105
Steve Gorski, *CEO*
Elliott Nemerson, *Regional Mgr*
Hans Michael Kraus, *Admin Sec*
EMP: 33
SQ FT: 1,000
SALES (est): 6.4MM
SALES (corp-wide): 1.1B **Privately Held**
SIC: 7372 Operating systems computer software
HQ: Designa Verkehrsleittechnik Gmbh
Faluner Weg 3
Kiel 24109
431 533-60

(G-20738)
DIXON BRASS
40 Chestnut Ave (60559-1128)
PHONE.....................630 323-3716
Richard L Goodall, *Owner*
▲ EMP: 25
SALES (est): 4.4MM
SALES (corp-wide): 279.8MM **Privately Held**
SIC: 3494 5085 Pipe fittings; industrial supplies
PA: Dvcc, Llc
800 High St
Chestertown MD 21620
410 778-2000

(G-20739)
DVCC INC
40 Chestnut Ave (60559-1128)
PHONE.....................630 323-3105
Richard L Goodall, *President*
EMP: 37
SALES (corp-wide): 279.8MM **Privately Held**
SIC: 3494 5085 Pipe fittings; industrial supplies

Westmont - Dupage County (G-20740)

PA: Dvcc, Llc
800 High St
Chestertown MD 21620
410 778-2000

(G-20740)
ELPRESS INC
900 Oakmont Ln Ste 207 (60559-5572)
PHONE.................................331 814-2910
Carsten Mathiesen, *CEO*
EMP: 5 **EST:** 2016
SALES: 3MM **Privately Held**
SIC: 3542 Crimping machinery, metal

(G-20741)
EMT INTERNATIONAL INC
760 Pasquinelli Dr # 300 (60559-1290)
PHONE.................................630 655-4145
Jim Driscoll, *Manager*
EMP: 3
SALES (est): 221K
SALES (corp-wide): 27.9MM **Privately Held**
SIC: 3555 3554 3544 5084 Printing trades machinery; paper industries machinery; punches, forming & stamping; printing trades machinery, equipment & supplies
PA: Emt International, Inc.
780 Centerline Dr
Hobart WI 54155
920 468-5475

(G-20742)
EZ BLINDS AND DRAPERY INC (PA)
Also Called: Eddie Z'S
550 Quail Ridge Dr (60559-6154)
PHONE.................................708 246-6600
James E Zakoor, *President*
Craig Duff, *President*
Mark Lokanc, *CFO*
Gabe Courey, *Admin Sec*
▲ **EMP:** 15
SQ FT: 528
SALES (est): 31.7MM **Privately Held**
SIC: 5023 2591 Window furnishings; window blinds

(G-20743)
GRETTA TRANSPORTATION INC
133 Hampton Ave (60559-8619)
PHONE.................................252 202-7714
EMP: 22
SALES (est): 8.5MM **Privately Held**
SIC: 3669 Transportation signaling devices

(G-20744)
HA-INTERNATIONAL LLC (DH)
Also Called: Ha International
630 Oakmont Ln (60559-5548)
PHONE.................................630 575-5700
Douglas Sanford, *President*
Michael Feehan, *Vice Pres*
Edward Brown, *Materials Mgr*
Nick Baker, *Buyer*
Daniel Mubima, *Research*
▲ **EMP:** 40
SQ FT: 22,000
SALES (est): 160.8MM
SALES (corp-wide): 250.7K **Privately Held**
WEB: www.ha-international.com
SIC: 2869 Industrial organic chemicals
HQ: Ha-Usa, Inc.
630 Oakmont Ln
Westmont IL 60559
630 575-5700

(G-20745)
HA-USA INC (DH)
Also Called: Delta-Ha, Inc.
630 Oakmont Ln (60559-5548)
PHONE.................................630 575-5700
Donald W Hansen, *Ch of Bd*
Richard Smith, *President*
Peter J Puccio, *CFO*
EMP: 8 **EST:** 1933
SQ FT: 45,000
SALES (est): 160.8MM
SALES (corp-wide): 250.7K **Privately Held**
WEB: www.ha-international.com
SIC: 2869 Industrial organic chemicals

HQ: HUttenes-Albertus Chemische Werke Gesellschaft Mit Beschrankter Haftung
Wiesenstr. 23
Dusseldorf 40549
211 508-70

(G-20746)
HANTEMP CORPORATION
Also Called: Hantemp Controls
33 Chestnut Ave (60559-1127)
PHONE.................................630 537-1049
Charles C Hansen, *Owner*
Bill Banks, *Mktg Dir*
EMP: 6
SQ FT: 8,000
SALES (est): 400K **Privately Held**
WEB: www.hantempcontrols.com
SIC: 3592 Valves

(G-20747)
HIGH SPEED WELDING INC
728 Vandustrial Dr Ste 5 (60559-2499)
PHONE.................................630 971-8929
Dennis Spal, *President*
EMP: 1
SQ FT: 1,350
SALES (est): 288K **Privately Held**
SIC: 7692 3711 Welding repair; automobile assembly, including specialty automobiles

(G-20748)
I HARDWARE DIRECT INC
642 Blackhawk Dr (60559-1116)
PHONE.................................708 325-0000
Tim Scalf, *President*
EMP: 3
SQ FT: 8,000
SALES: 700K **Privately Held**
SIC: 3429 Manufactured hardware (general)

(G-20749)
INTERVRSITY CHRSTN FLLWSHP/USA
Also Called: Intervarsity Press
430 Plaza Dr Frnt (60559-1247)
P.O. Box 1400, Downers Grove (60515-1426)
PHONE.................................630 734-4000
Jeff Crosby, *Publisher*
Bob Fryling, *Principal*
Mike Zeeman, *Opers Staff*
Bill Cochran, *Production*
Nadine Hunt, *Accountant*
EMP: 90
SALES (corp-wide): 119.4MM **Privately Held**
SIC: 2731 Books: publishing only
PA: Intervarsity Christian Fellowship/Usa
635 Science Dr
Madison WI 53711
608 274-9001

(G-20750)
JJM PRODUCTS LLC
1052 Zygmunt Cir (60559-2692)
PHONE.................................630 319-9325
Jeffery A Rozell, *Principal*
EMP: 4
SALES (est): 477.7K **Privately Held**
SIC: 2448 Pallets, wood

(G-20751)
KAYBEE ENGINEERING COMPANY INC
Also Called: Kaybee Engnrng
100 E Quincy St (60559-1823)
P.O. Box 316 (60559-0316)
PHONE.................................630 968-7100
Robert N Britz, *President*
EMP: 34
SQ FT: 4,400
SALES (est): 5.6MM **Privately Held**
SIC: 3699 3621 Electrical equipment & supplies; motors & generators

(G-20752)
KD STEEL INCORPORATED
420 N Park St (60559-1427)
PHONE.................................630 201-1619
David Wilson, *President*
EMP: 7

SALES: 700K **Privately Held**
SIC: 1791 3462 3441 Structural steel erection; iron & steel forgings; building components, structural steel

(G-20753)
KELEEN LEATHERS INC
1010 Executive Dr Ste 400 (60559-6156)
PHONE.................................630 590-5300
▼ **EMP:** 17
SALES (est): 1.6MM **Privately Held**
SIC: 5948 5199 2386 Ret Luggage/Leather Goods Whol Nondurable Goods Mfg Leather Clothing

(G-20754)
KMP PRODUCTS LLC
Also Called: Safe Pet Products
1060 Zygmunt Cir (60559-2692)
PHONE.................................630 956-0438
Heather L Hester, *Owner*
John L Hester,
▲ **EMP:** 2 **EST:** 2007
SQ FT: 1,600
SALES: 1MM **Privately Held**
WEB: www.safepetproducts.com
SIC: 3999 Pet supplies

(G-20755)
MAGNET-SCHULTZ AMER HOLDG LLC (HQ)
401 Plaza Dr (60559-1233)
PHONE.................................630 789-0600
Wolfgang Schultz,
Theodore Gault,
Greg Roskuszka,
David Stockwell,
EMP: 10
SALES (est): 21MM
SALES (corp-wide): 500.6MM **Privately Held**
SIC: 3451 3625 3599 Screw machine products; solenoid switches (industrial controls); brakes, electromagnetic; machine & other job shop work
PA: Magnet-Schultz Gmbh & Co. Kg
Allgauer Str. 30
Memmingen 87700
833 110-40

(G-20756)
MAGNET-SCHULTZ AMERICA INC
Also Called: MSA
401 Plaza Dr (60559-1233)
PHONE.................................630 789-0600
David L Stockwell, *President*
Albert Schultz, *Vice Pres*
Michael Schneider, *Facilities Mgr*
Ken McKendrick, *Production*
Dorothy Dziaba, *Purchasing*
▲ **EMP:** 85
SQ FT: 42,000
SALES (est): 21MM
SALES (corp-wide): 500.6MM **Privately Held**
SIC: 3451 3625 3599 Screw machine products; solenoid switches (industrial controls); brakes, electromagnetic; machine & other job shop work
HQ: Magnet-Schultz America Holding, Llc
401 Plaza Dr
Westmont IL 60559

(G-20757)
MANROLAND INC (DH)
Also Called: Manroland Websystems
800 E Oakhill Dr (60559-5587)
PHONE.................................630 920-2000
Michael Mugavero, *CEO*
Franz Von Frstenberg, *Managing Dir*
Chris Howes, *Assistant VP*
Brian Gott, *CFO*
Al Muccari, *Manager*
▲ **EMP:** 40
SQ FT: 120,000
SALES (est): 21.2MM
SALES (corp-wide): 907.4MM **Privately Held**
WEB: www.manroland.us.com
SIC: 3555 5084 Printing trades machinery; printing trades machinery, equipment & supplies

HQ: Manroland Sheetfed Gmbh
Muhlheimer Str. 341
Offenbach Am Main 63075
698 305-0

(G-20758)
MCCRONE ASSOCIATES INC
McCrone Microscopes & ACC
850 Pasquinelli Dr (60559-5594)
PHONE.................................630 887-7100
Jeffrey D McGinn, *President*
David Wiley, *President*
Charles Zona, *Principal*
EMP: 8
SALES (corp-wide): 7.7MM **Privately Held**
SIC: 3826 3827 Analytical instruments; microscopes, except electron, proton & corneal
HQ: Mccrone Associates, Inc.
850 Pasquinelli Dr
Westmont IL 60559
630 887-7100

(G-20759)
MIDCO EXPLORATION INC
414 Plaza Dr Ste 204 (60559-3507)
P.O. Box 1278 (60559-3878)
PHONE.................................630 655-2198
Kent Weltmer, *President*
Earl Joyce, *Vice Pres*
EMP: 3
SALES (est): 271.3K
SALES (corp-wide): 684.6K **Privately Held**
SIC: 1382 Oil & gas exploration services
PA: Midco Production Co Inc
414 Plaza Dr Ste 204
Westmont IL 60559
630 655-2198

(G-20760)
MIDCO PETROLEUM INC
336 S Cass Ave (60559-1932)
P.O. Box 1278 (60559-3878)
PHONE.................................630 655-2198
Kent H Weltmer, *President*
EMP: 3
SALES (est): 260.1K **Privately Held**
SIC: 1311 Crude petroleum production

(G-20761)
MIDCO PRODUCTION CO INC (PA)
414 Plaza Dr Ste 204 (60559-3507)
P.O. Box 1278 (60559-3878)
PHONE.................................630 655-2198
Kent H Weltmer, *President*
EMP: 4 **EST:** 1979
SALES (est): 684.6K **Privately Held**
SIC: 1311 Natural gas production

(G-20762)
MURPHYS SIGN STUDIO
29 E Chicago Ave (60559-1726)
PHONE.................................630 963-0677
Jim Wardle, *Owner*
EMP: 3
SALES (est): 286.6K **Privately Held**
SIC: 3993 Signs & advertising specialties

(G-20763)
OOSTMAN FABRICATING & WLDG INC
45 E Chicago Ave (60559-1726)
PHONE.................................630 241-1315
Norman J Oostman, *President*
Roseann J Oostman, *Admin Sec*
EMP: 11
SQ FT: 12,000
SALES (est): 1.9MM **Privately Held**
SIC: 3599 7692 3441 3544 Machine shop, jobbing & repair; welding repair; fabricated structural metal; special dies, tools, jigs & fixtures

(G-20764)
ORIGINAL SOFTWARE INC
1010 Executive Dr Ste 230 (60559-6137)
PHONE.................................630 413-5762
Colin Armitage, *CEO*
Christopher Armitage, *President*
George Wilson, *COO*
Richard Carbray, *Administration*
EMP: 40

GEOGRAPHIC SECTION

SALES (est): 3.1MM **Privately Held**
SIC: 7372 Prepackaged software

(G-20765)
POSITRON CORPORATION (PA)
530 Oakmont Ln (60559-3700)
PHONE.................317 576-0183
Joseph G Oliverio, *Ch of Bd*
Adel Abdullah, *President*
Aaron Hargrave, *Vice Pres*
Corey N Conn, *CFO*
EMP: 22
SQ FT: 2,000
SALES (est): 1.4MM **Publicly Held**
SIC: 3845 Position emission tomography (PET scanner)

(G-20766)
PPG INDUSTRIES INC
Also Called: PPG 9449
6136 S Cass Ave (60559-2623)
PHONE.................630 960-3600
Kevin Price, *Manager*
EMP: 3
SALES (corp-wide): 15.1B **Publicly Held**
SIC: 2851 Paints & allied products
PA: Ppg Industries, Inc.
1 Ppg Pl
Pittsburgh PA 15272
412 434-3131

(G-20767)
PRAIRIE ISLAND INC
325 Cromwell Ct (60559-2697)
PHONE.................630 395-9846
Biljana Zivanovic, *President*
EMP: 4
SALES (est): 373.2K **Privately Held**
SIC: 3743 Freight cars & equipment

(G-20768)
RAINBOW CLEANERS
836 E Ogden Ave (60559-1246)
PHONE.................630 789-6989
EMP: 3
SALES (est): 75K **Privately Held**
SIC: 2842 Dry Cleaning & Laundry

(G-20769)
REBCO MACHINE SPECIALTIES INC
138 E Quincy St (60559-1823)
PHONE.................630 852-3419
Audrey Busse, *CEO*
James E Bresnahan, *President*
EMP: 10
SQ FT: 12,000
SALES (est): 1.8MM **Privately Held**
SIC: 3599 Machine shop, jobbing & repair

(G-20770)
SAFEGUARD 201 CORP
Also Called: Safeguard Print & Promo
1129 Fairview Ave (60559-2709)
PHONE.................630 241-0370
Patrick Ryan, *President*
EMP: 6
SALES: 1MM **Privately Held**
SIC: 2752 Commercial printing, lithographic

(G-20771)
SANDLOCK SANDBOX LLC
1069 Zygmunt Cir (60559-2678)
PHONE.................630 963-9422
Chris Freres, *Principal*
▲ EMP: 4 EST: 2005
SQ FT: 2,000
SALES: 500K **Privately Held**
WEB: www.sandlock.com
SIC: 5941 2531 Playground equipment; school furniture

(G-20772)
SHEER GRAPHICS INC
47 Chestnut Ave (60559-1127)
PHONE.................630 654-4422
Nancy Sheers, *President*
Simon Sheers, *Treasurer*
EMP: 7 EST: 1972
SALES (est): 945.5K **Privately Held**
WEB: www.sheergraphics.com
SIC: 7334 2759 2752 2791 Photocopying & duplicating services; commercial printing; commercial printing, lithographic; typesetting; coated & laminated paper

(G-20773)
SONOCO DISPLAY & PACKAGING LLC
1111 Pasquinelli Dr # 600 (60559-1241)
PHONE.................630 789-1111
Jim Ghere, *Branch Mgr*
EMP: 11
SALES (corp-wide): 5.3B **Publicly Held**
SIC: 2653 Display items, corrugated: made from purchased materials
HQ: Sonoco Display & Packaging, Llc
555 Aureole St
Winston Salem NC 27107

(G-20774)
SURE-WAY DIE DESIGNS INC (PA)
Also Called: Sure-Way Products
414 Lindley Ave (60559-2225)
PHONE.................630 323-0370
Russell De Cicco, *President*
Debra Winkleman, *President*
Kenneth Sloup, *Admin Sec*
EMP: 18 EST: 1967
SALES (est): 2.7MM **Privately Held**
WEB: www.surewayproducts.com
SIC: 3469 3544 3542 Stamping metal for the trade; special dies, tools, jigs & fixtures; machine tools, metal forming type

(G-20775)
TEMPO ENTERPRISES INC
21 Fountainhead Dr # 201 (60559-2537)
PHONE.................331 903-2786
Milivoje Mijatovic, *President*
EMP: 2
SALES: 300K **Privately Held**
SIC: 3537 Trucks, tractors, loaders, carriers & similar equipment

(G-20776)
TESLA MOTORS
50 W Ogden Ave (60559-1345)
PHONE.................630 541-1214
EMP: 2
SALES (est): 204.9K **Privately Held**
SIC: 3711 Motor vehicles & car bodies

(G-20777)
TRADING SQUARE COMPANY INC
6434 S Cass Ave (60559-3209)
PHONE.................630 960-0606
May Tsui, *President*
▲ EMP: 4
SALES (est): 271.5K **Privately Held**
SIC: 2395 Emblems, embroidered; embroidery products, except schiffli machine

Westville
Vermilion County

(G-20778)
BETTER BUILT BUILDINGS
604 E Kelly Ave (61883-1026)
PHONE.................217 267-7824
Mark Lete, *Owner*
EMP: 6
SALES (est): 358.4K **Privately Held**
SIC: 2499 1542 Poles, wood; agricultural building contractors

(G-20779)
CREATIVE IRON
108 Westville Ln (61883-6032)
PHONE.................217 267-7797
Michael E Spisok, *Owner*
Maureen Spisok, *Co-Owner*
EMP: 2
SQ FT: 3,500
SALES (est): 212.1K **Privately Held**
SIC: 3446 3441 3366 3364 Architectural metalwork; fabricated structural metal; copper foundries; nonferrous die-castings except aluminum

(G-20780)
DYNACHEM INC
15662 E 980 North Rd (61883-6138)
P.O. Box 19, Georgetown (61846-0019)
PHONE.................217 662-2136
Keith Rife, *President*

Craig McCall, *Vice Pres*
Jerry Smith, *CFO*
Arman Melikyan, *Shareholder*
Patrick Stewart, *Shareholder*
▲ EMP: 60
SQ FT: 25,000
SALES (est): 29.4MM **Privately Held**
SIC: 2821 2869 Plastics materials & resins; industrial organic chemicals

(G-20781)
LUBE RITE
802 S State St (61883-1744)
PHONE.................217 267-7766
EMP: 5
SALES: 90K **Privately Held**
SIC: 2992 Mfg Lubricating Oils/Greases

(G-20782)
WESTVILLE READY MIX INC
1409 English St (61883-1821)
PHONE.................217 267-2082
Jenny Wiese, *President*
Keith Wiese, *Vice Pres*
EMP: 5
SALES (est): 800K **Privately Held**
SIC: 3273 Ready-mixed concrete

Wheaton
Dupage County

(G-20783)
A AND T LABS INCORPORATED
1926 Berkshire Pl (60189-8150)
P.O. Box 4884 (60189-4884)
PHONE.................630 668-8562
Reinhard Metz, *President*
Isola Metz, *Vice Pres*
EMP: 2
SALES (est): 207.1K **Privately Held**
SIC: 3651 5961 Electronic kits for home assembly: radio, TV, phonograph; electronic kits & parts, mail order

(G-20784)
ACME SCREW CO (PA)
1201 W Union Ave (60187-4869)
P.O. Box 906 (60187-0906)
PHONE.................630 665-2200
William J Roche, *Ch of Bd*
Christine M Roche, *President*
Cliff Hauger, *Vice Pres*
George Kalebich, *Vice Pres*
Steve Murray, *Vice Pres*
▲ EMP: 100 EST: 1948
SQ FT: 100,000
SALES (est): 22.9MM **Privately Held**
WEB: www.acmecompanies.com
SIC: 3452 Bolts, metal; screws, metal; rivets, metal

(G-20785)
ACRO TECH CORPORATION
1540 Spero Ct (60187-3768)
PHONE.................630 408-2248
Masaaki Ito, *President*
▲ EMP: 2
SALES (est): 4MM **Privately Held**
SIC: 3441 Fabricated structural metal

(G-20786)
ADM IMAGING INC
100 W Roosevelt Rd A1-20 (60187-5260)
PHONE.................630 834-7100
Sam Kancherlapalli, *President*
Arnand Kancherlapalli, *Vice Pres*
EMP: 4
SALES (est): 507.6K **Privately Held**
SIC: 3841 Surgical & medical instruments

(G-20787)
AIXACCT SYSTEMS INC
715 N Wheaton Ave (60187-4134)
PHONE.................952 303-4077
Andreas Roelofs, *President*
EMP: 2
SALES: 500K **Privately Held**
SIC: 3829 Measuring & controlling devices

(G-20788)
ARID TECHNOLOGIES INC
323 S Hale St (60187-5219)
PHONE.................630 681-8500

Tedmund Tiberi, *President*
Michael Heffernan, *Vice Pres*
Luke Howard, *Vice Pres*
Stephen Matus, *Engineer*
Mary Tiberi, *Admin Sec*
EMP: 20
SALES (est): 3.5MM **Privately Held**
SIC: 3533 Oil & gas field machinery

(G-20789)
AUTUMN WOODS LTD
112 N Main St (60187-5327)
PHONE.................630 868-3535
EMP: 9
SALES (corp-wide): 4.7MM **Privately Held**
SIC: 2434 Wood kitchen cabinets
PA: Autumn Woods Ltd
375 Gundersen Dr
Carol Stream IL 60188
630 668-2080

(G-20790)
BODYSMART USA INC
2077 W Roosevelt Rd (60187-6028)
P.O. Box 1432 (60187-1432)
PHONE.................630 682-9701
Shahzad Paul, *CEO*
EMP: 5
SQ FT: 5,000
SALES (est): 500K **Privately Held**
SIC: 3949 Sporting & athletic goods

(G-20791)
BUCKNER SAND CO
1500 N Main St 200 (60187-3584)
PHONE.................630 653-3700
Stephanie Chodera, *Principal*
EMP: 4
SALES (est): 290.6K **Privately Held**
SIC: 1442 Sand mining

(G-20792)
CALDWELL PLUMBING CO
821 Childs St (60187-4810)
PHONE.................630 588-8900
Nick Tenerelli, *President*
Todd Sanders, *Superintendent*
Mike Tenerelli, *Vice Pres*
EMP: 12
SQ FT: 5,000
SALES: 13MM **Privately Held**
SIC: 3432 4961 Plumbing fixture fittings & trim; air conditioning supply services

(G-20793)
CHASE CORPORATION
1800 S Naperville Rd (60189-8130)
PHONE.................630 752-3622
Brad Karkula, *Branch Mgr*
EMP: 11
SALES (corp-wide): 281.3MM **Publicly Held**
WEB: www.chasecorp.com
SIC: 3644 Noncurrent-carrying wiring services
PA: Chase Corporation
295 University Ave
Westwood MA 02090
781 332-0700

(G-20794)
CROSSCOM INC
528 W Roosevelt Rd Lla (60187-5092)
PHONE.................630 871-5500
Daniel B Lites, *President*
EMP: 14
SQ FT: 1,800
SALES: 6.5MM **Privately Held**
WEB: www.crosscominc.com
SIC: 7389 7299 2952 Telephone services; home improvement & renovation contractor agency; roofing materials

(G-20795)
DARK SPEED WORKS
122 N Wheaton Ave # 551 (60187-6557)
P.O. Box 551 (60187-0551)
PHONE.................312 772-3275
Greg Grunner, *Owner*
EMP: 5
SALES (est): 140K **Privately Held**
SIC: 3949 Sporting & athletic goods

Wheaton - Dupage County (G-20796)

(G-20796)
DIGITALDRIVE TECH
1601 E Prairie Ave (60187-3758)
PHONE....................................630 510-1580
Robert Anderson, *Owner*
Darcy Evon, *Co-Owner*
EMP: 4
SALES (est): 194.8K **Privately Held**
SIC: 3621 Motors, electric

(G-20797)
EMMETTS TAVERN & BREWING CO
Also Called: Emmett's Ale House
121 W Front St (60187-5108)
PHONE....................................630 480-7181
Allyssa Anderson, *Manager*
EMP: 9
SALES (corp-wide): 3.2MM **Privately Held**
SIC: 5812 2082 5182 Chicken restaurant; beer (alcoholic beverage); wine & distilled beverages
PA: Emmett's Tavern & Brewing Co.
128 W Main St
West Dundee IL 60118
847 428-4500

(G-20798)
EXPRESS DONUTS ENTERPRISE INC
Also Called: Dunkin' Donuts
15 Danada Sq E (60189-8484)
PHONE....................................630 510-9310
Manu Patel, *President*
EMP: 10
SALES (est): 354.4K **Privately Held**
SIC: 5461 5812 2051 Doughnuts; eating places; doughnuts, except frozen

(G-20799)
FLEMING MUSIC TECHNOLOGY CTR
Also Called: Jeremiah Fleming Music Sites
408 W Elm St (60189-6341)
PHONE....................................708 316-8662
Jeremiah Fleming, *President*
EMP: 6
SALES (est): 1.7K **Privately Held**
SIC: 2741 7929 7389 Music books: publishing & printing; musical entertainers;

(G-20800)
GILBERTS CRAFT SAUSAGES LLC
123 W Front St Ste 210 (60187-5105)
PHONE....................................630 923-8969
Eric Romberg, *Mng Member*
Christopher Salm, *Mng Member*
EMP: 2
SALES (est): 6.6MM **Privately Held**
SIC: 3556 Sausage stuffers

(G-20801)
GOOD NEWS PUBLISHERS (PA)
Also Called: Crossway Bibles, Nfp
1300 Crescent St (60187-5883)
PHONE....................................630 682-4300
Lane T Dennis, *President*
Clair Kassebaum, *Marketing Staff*
Colton Seager, *Marketing Staff*
Greg Bailey, *Director*
Stephen Kopalchick, *Director*
◆ **EMP:** 50 **EST:** 1938
SQ FT: 43,000
SALES (est): 20.3MM **Privately Held**
WEB: www.crossway.org
SIC: 2731 Pamphlets: publishing only, not printed on site; textbooks: publishing only, not printed on site

(G-20802)
HOLSTEIN GARAGE INC
309 W Front St (60187-5082)
PHONE....................................630 668-0328
Jeff Holstein, *President*
Mark Holstein, *Vice Pres*
EMP: 4 **EST:** 1906
SQ FT: 12,342
SALES (est): 777.5K **Privately Held**
WEB: www.holsteinsgarage.com
SIC: 7538 7692 General truck repair; automotive welding

(G-20803)
HOUSE ON THE HILL INC
2206 N Main St (60187-9140)
PHONE....................................630 279-4455
Constance Meisinger, *President*
Stephen Meisinger, *Vice Pres*
EMP: 3
SALES (est): 242.7K **Privately Held**
SIC: 2499 Bakers' equipment, wood

(G-20804)
HTS CHICAGO INC
107 W Willow Ave (60187-5236)
PHONE....................................630 352-3690
Derek Gordon, *President*
David Warner, *Vice Pres*
David Kviring, *CFO*
Choudhry Raza, *Controller*
Robert McCabe, *Director*
EMP: 7
SQ FT: 800
SALES (est): 4MM
SALES (corp-wide): 92MM **Privately Held**
SIC: 3567 Heating units & devices, industrial: electric
PA: Hts Engineering Ltd
115 Norfinch Dr
North York ON M3N 1
416 661-3400

(G-20805)
HYDROGEN EDUCATION COUNCIL
1115 Aurora Way (60187-6207)
PHONE....................................630 681-1732
Annie M Kane, *Director*
EMP: 3 **EST:** 2018
SALES (est): 123.2K **Privately Held**
SIC: 2813 Hydrogen

(G-20806)
INTERNTNAL AWKENING MINISTRIES
123 N Washington St (60187-5312)
P.O. Box 232 (60187-0232)
PHONE....................................630 653-8616
Richard Roberts, *President*
James Crain, *Treasurer*
Lowell Yoder, *Admin Sec*
EMP: 3
SALES (est): 50.5K **Privately Held**
SIC: 8661 2732 Miscellaneous denomination church; book printing

(G-20807)
KJELLBERG PRINTING
805 W Liberty Dr (60187-4844)
P.O. Box 725 (60187-0725)
PHONE....................................630 653-2244
William S Kjellberg Jr, *President*
Doris J Kjellberg, *Corp Secy*
Kevin J Kjellberg, *Vice Pres*
EMP: 12 **EST:** 1956
SALES (est): 1.5MM **Privately Held**
WEB: www.kjellbergprinting.com
SIC: 2759 2752 2732 Letterpress printing; commercial printing, lithographic; book printing

(G-20808)
KMF ENTERPRISES INC
Also Called: Towntees
20 Danada Sq W (60189-2000)
PHONE....................................630 858-2210
Kevin Fahey, *President*
EMP: 4
SALES (est): 478.6K **Privately Held**
SIC: 2759 Screen printing

(G-20809)
KNOWLEDGESHIFT INC
26w245 Grand Ave Ste 200 (60187-2967)
PHONE....................................630 221-8759
Nancy Monroe, *President*
Dennis Monroe, *Admin Sec*
EMP: 3
SQ FT: 300
SALES (est): 226K **Privately Held**
SIC: 7372 8742 Publishers' computer software; management consulting services

(G-20810)
LAKESHORE LACROSSE LLC
20 Danada Sq W Ste 289 (60189-2000)
PHONE....................................773 350-4356
Bridget Olp, *Owner*
Michelle Sebastian, *Co-Owner*
Gwen Tegart, *Controller*
EMP: 6 **EST:** 2004
SALES (est): 363.7K **Privately Held**
WEB: www.lakeshorelacrosse.com
SIC: 7032 3792 Sporting camps; travel trailers & campers

(G-20811)
LATTICE INCORPORATED
1751 S Nprvlle Rd Ste 100 (60189)
PHONE....................................630 949-3250
Peter Muzzy, *President*
Patrick Heniff, *VP Sales*
Parker Haney, *Accounts Exec*
Michael Roth, *Software Engr*
John Ericson, *Director*
EMP: 47
SALES (est): 4.1MM **Privately Held**
SIC: 7372 7371 Business oriented computer software; custom computer programming services

(G-20812)
LEE-WEL PRINTING CORPORATION
1554 S County Farm Rd (60189-7121)
PHONE....................................630 682-0935
Thomas A Welter, *President*
Gail Welter, *Vice Pres*
Rosemary Welter, *Treasurer*
EMP: 6
SQ FT: 15,000
SALES (est): 450K **Privately Held**
SIC: 2752 5199 2789 2759 Commercial printing, offset; advertising specialties; bookbinding & related work; commercial printing; die-cut paper & board; automotive & apparel trimmings

(G-20813)
NANO TECHNOLOGIES INC
Also Called: I T Audit Search
1765 Mustang Ct (60189-8483)
PHONE....................................630 517-8824
Ralph Dahm, *Principal*
EMP: 2
SALES (est): 288.9K **Privately Held**
SIC: 3571 Computers, digital, analog or hybrid

(G-20814)
ORINOCO SYSTEMS LLC (PA)
300 S Carlton Ave Ste 100 (60187-4830)
P.O. Box 1458 (60187-1458)
PHONE....................................630 510-0775
Diego Ferrer, *Mng Member*
EMP: 12
SQ FT: 596
SALES (est): 1.3MM **Privately Held**
SIC: 7371 7372 7373 Computer software systems analysis & design, custom; computer software development & applications; application computer software; educational computer software; systems software development services

(G-20815)
PRINTWISE INC
1670 Monticello Ct Unit E (60189-8235)
PHONE....................................630 833-2845
Darrell Davis, *President*
Marilyn Davis, *Vice Pres*
EMP: 3
SALES (est): 290.1K **Privately Held**
SIC: 2752 Commercial printing, lithographic

(G-20816)
PRO-TEK PRODUCTS INC
1755 S Nprvlle Rd Ste 100 (60189)
PHONE....................................630 293-5100
Paul Zalantis, *President*
Wayne Niemie, *Vice Pres*
EMP: 2
SQ FT: 700
SALES (est): 469.6K **Privately Held**
SIC: 2879 Agricultural chemicals

(G-20817)
R H JOHNSON OIL CO INC (PA)
Also Called: Johnson Oil Company
1017 Delles Rd (60189-6320)
P.O. Box 169 (60187-0169)
PHONE....................................630 668-3649
Herbert Johnson, *President*
Reynold Johnson, *Admin Sec*
EMP: 5
SALES: 1.5MM **Privately Held**
SIC: 5172 1311 Fuel oil; crude petroleum & natural gas production

(G-20818)
REGUNATHAN & ASSOC INC
1490 Jasper Dr (60189-8985)
PHONE....................................630 653-0387
Perialwar Regunathan, *President*
EMP: 3 **EST:** 1999
SALES (est): 200.9K **Privately Held**
SIC: 3589 8748 Water treatment equipment, industrial; business consulting

(G-20819)
RMH ENTERPRISES
611 Cadillac Dr (60187-3601)
PHONE....................................630 525-5552
Roger Herforth, *Owner*
EMP: 1
SALES (est): 650K **Privately Held**
SIC: 3599 Industrial machinery

(G-20820)
ROBIS ELECTIONS INC
1751 S Nprvlle Rd Ste 104 (60189)
P.O. Box 39 (60187-0039)
PHONE....................................630 752-0220
David M Davoust, *President*
Lisa Davoust, *Vice Pres*
Timothy Herman, *Vice Pres*
Daryl Lucas, *Vice Pres*
EMP: 18
SQ FT: 5,500
SALES (est): 753.7K **Privately Held**
SIC: 7372 Business oriented computer software

(G-20821)
RV6 PERFORMANCE
26w148 Waterbury Ct (60187-1306)
PHONE....................................630 346-7998
Richard Wong, *Owner*
▲ **EMP:** 2
SALES (est): 201.2K **Privately Held**
SIC: 3448 Prefabricated metal buildings

(G-20822)
S G NELSON & CO
209 N Hale St Ste 1 (60187-5100)
P.O. Box 121 (60187-0121)
PHONE....................................630 668-7900
Stephen G Nelson, *Owner*
EMP: 4
SQ FT: 4,000
SALES (est): 500K **Privately Held**
SIC: 3911 5094 3915 Jewel settings & mountings, precious metal; jewelry & precious stones; diamond cutting & polishing

(G-20823)
SERVETECH WATER SOLUTIONS INC
112 W Liberty Dr (60187-5123)
PHONE....................................630 784-9050
Bryan Block, *President*
EMP: 5
SALES (est): 673.2K **Privately Held**
SIC: 3589 5074 Water treatment equipment, industrial; water purification equipment

(G-20824)
SIGN AUTHORITY
901 W Liberty Dr A (60187-4846)
PHONE....................................630 462-9850
Richard Tampier, *President*
Leanne Tampier, *Vice Pres*
EMP: 3
SALES (est): 360.7K **Privately Held**
SIC: 3993 Signs & advertising specialties

(G-20825)
SOFTWAREIDM INC (PA)
213 W Wesley St Ste 200 (60187-5102)
PHONE....................................331 218-0001

Todd Mollerup, *Principal*
EMP: 8
SALES (est): 1.6MM **Privately Held**
SIC: 7372 Prepackaged software

(G-20826)
THEOSOPHICAL SOCIETY IN AMER (PA)
Also Called: THEOSOPHICAL PUBLISHING HOUSE
1926 N Main St (60187-3136)
P.O. Box 270 (60187-0270)
PHONE..................630 665-0130
Betty Bland, *President*
Tim Boyd, *President*
Ed Abdul, *Vice Pres*
August Hirt, *CFO*
Theresa Kennedy, *CFO*
▲ **EMP:** 44
SQ FT: 200,000
SALES: 2.2MM **Privately Held**
SIC: 8641 2721 2731 8661 Educator's association; periodicals; book publishing; non-church religious organizations

(G-20827)
THEOSOPHICAL SOCIETY IN AMER
Also Called: Theosphcal Pubg Hs/Quest Bk Sp
306 W Geneva Rd (60187-2421)
P.O. Box 270 (60187-0270)
PHONE..................630 665-0123
David Bland, *Branch Mgr*
Diana Cabigting, *Representative*
EMP: 15
SALES (corp-wide): 2.2MM **Privately Held**
SIC: 8641 2731 2721 8699 Educator's association; book publishing; periodicals; reading rooms & other cultural organizations
PA: Theosophical Society In America Inc
  1926 N Main St
  Wheaton IL 60187
  630 665-0130

(G-20828)
THIA & CO
519 W Front St (60187-4933)
PHONE..................630 510-9770
EMP: 3
SALES (est): 160K **Privately Held**
SIC: 5947 2759 Ret Gifts/Novelties Commercial Printing

(G-20829)
TOUCHSENSOR TECHNOLOGIES LLC
203 N Gables Blvd (60187-4818)
PHONE..................630 221-9000
Thomas Schreiber, *CEO*
Gregory Pardus, *Business Mgr*
Randy Hornig, *Engineer*
Patrick Rohlik, *Engineer*
Dave Gradl, *Senior Engr*
▲ **EMP:** 300
SQ FT: 25,000
SALES (est): 147.9MM
SALES (corp-wide): 1B **Publicly Held**
SIC: 5065 3674 Electronic parts & equipment; modules, solid state
PA: Methode Electronics, Inc
  8750 W Bryn Mawr Ave # 1000
  Chicago IL 60631
  708 867-6777

(G-20830)
UNI-BALL CORPORATION
400 S County Farm Rd # 300 (60187-4622)
PHONE..................310 505-5926
Benjamin F Gould, *Principal*
EMP: 7
SALES (est): 1MM **Privately Held**
SIC: 3951 Pens & mechanical pencils; ball point pens & parts
PA: Mitsubishi Pencil Co.,Ltd.
  5-23-37, Higashioi
  Shinagawa-Ku TKY 140-0

(G-20831)
WHEATON TROPHY & ENGRAVERS
107 W Front St Ste 3 (60187-5148)
PHONE..................630 682-4200
Fax: 630 682-0247
EMP: 2
SQ FT: 2,200
SALES: 280K **Privately Held**
SIC: 5999 3479 Ret Misc Merchandise Coating/Engraving Service

(G-20832)
WYCKOFF ADVERTISING INC
Also Called: Equipmentbag.com
1203 E Prairie Ave (60187-3717)
PHONE..................630 260-2525
Thomas Wyckoff, *President*
Ellen G Wyckoff, *Shareholder*
EMP: 2
SALES: 300K **Privately Held**
WEB: www.equipmentbag.com
SIC: 7311 7335 7336 2752 Advertising consultant; photographic studio, commercial; graphic arts & related design; commercial printing, lithographic

Wheeler
Jasper County

(G-20833)
TDW WELDING LLC (PA)
17515 N 400th St (62479-2102)
PHONE..................217 690-3521
EMP: 8
SALES (est): 353K **Privately Held**
SIC: 7692 Welding repair

Wheeling
Cook County

(G-20834)
10X MICROSTRUCTURES LLC
420 Harvester Ct (60090-4735)
PHONE..................847 215-7448
Scott Thielman, *President*
EMP: 2
SALES (est): 381.3K **Privately Held**
SIC: 3542 Electroforming machines

(G-20835)
A & M TOOL CO INC
5 W Waltz Dr (60090-6052)
PHONE..................847 215-8140
Dieter Ade, *President*
Reiner Mayer, *Corp Secy*
Alexander Mosenkis, *Plant Mgr*
EMP: 30
SQ FT: 20,270
SALES (est): 5.3MM **Privately Held**
SIC: 3599 Machine shop, jobbing & repair

(G-20836)
AARGUS INDUSTRIES INC
540 Allendale Dr Ste 100a (60090-2603)
PHONE..................847 325-4444
Jerome Starr, *President*
EMP: 7
SALES (est): 766.2K **Privately Held**
SIC: 2673 Plastic bags: made from purchased materials

(G-20837)
AARGUS PLASTICS INC
Also Called: Aargus Industries
540 Allendale Dr Ste 100a (60090-2603)
PHONE..................847 325-4444
Jerome Starr, *President*
Alfred Teo, *Chairman*
Scott Starr, *Vice Pres*
Bob Schlink, *Opers Mgr*
Michael Ferraro, *CFO*
▲ **EMP:** 110
SQ FT: 125,000
SALES (est): 46.3MM **Privately Held**
SIC: 2673 3081 Plastic & pliofilm bags; polyethylene film

(G-20838)
ABBOTT INTERFAST LLC
190 Abbott Dr Ste A (60090-5872)
PHONE..................847 459-6200
James Calabrese, *President*
Jim Sullivan, *District Mgr*
Bob Baer, *Vice Pres*
Robert Baer, *Vice Pres*
Alan Sherrill, *Plant Mgr*
▲ **EMP:** 75 **EST:** 1948
SQ FT: 100,000
SALES (est): 18MM **Privately Held**
WEB: www.abbott-interfast.com
SIC: 3451 3452 Screw machine products; bolts, nuts, rivets & washers

(G-20839)
ABSOLUTE TURN INC
1704 S Wolf Rd (60090-6517)
PHONE..................847 459-4629
Roy H Urban, *President*
Marie Urban, *Admin Sec*
EMP: 25
SQ FT: 8,000
SALES (est): 40MM **Privately Held**
SIC: 3599 Machine shop, jobbing & repair

(G-20840)
ACCU-FAB INCORPORATED
1550 Abbott Dr (60090-5820)
PHONE..................847 541-4230
Patrick M Erickson, *President*
Joleen Licari, *Purch Mgr*
Ken Larsen, *Engineer*
John Riportella, *Sales Staff*
◆ **EMP:** 40
SQ FT: 60,000
SALES (est): 12.8MM **Privately Held**
SIC: 3444 Sheet metalwork

(G-20841)
ADHESIVE COATING TECH INC
420 Northgate Pkwy (60090-2647)
PHONE..................847 215-8355
Dimitri Poulokefalos, *President*
▲ **EMP:** 11 **EST:** 2011
SQ FT: 60,000
SALES (est): 3.4MM **Privately Held**
SIC: 2891 Adhesives

(G-20842)
AGSCO CORPORATION (PA)
160 W Hintz Rd (60090-5755)
PHONE..................847 520-4455
Harvey R Plonsker, *President*
Edward M Plonsker, *Corp Secy*
Michael D Michaelis, *Vice Pres*
Michael Michaelis, *Vice Pres*
Julian Castro, *Plant Mgr*
◆ **EMP:** 33 **EST:** 1888
SQ FT: 60,000
SALES: 23.3MM **Privately Held**
WEB: www.agsco.com
SIC: 5085 3291 Abrasives; rouge, polishing: abrasive

(G-20843)
ALEXETER TECHNOLOGIES LLC (PA)
830 Seton Ct Ste 6 (60090-5772)
PHONE..................847 419-1507
James P Whelan PHD, *General Mgr*
Yvonne Gullbring, *Sales Staff*
Tom Fryzel, *Mktg Dir*
EMP: 11
SQ FT: 5,000
SALES: 1.5MM **Privately Held**
SIC: 3826 8111 Environmental testing equipment; legal services

(G-20844)
ALFA CONTROLS INC
311 Egidi Dr (60090-2653)
PHONE..................847 978-9245
Felix Gorfin, *President*
Ana Koreshkov, *Controller*
Alexandre Kolobaw, *Admin Sec*
◆ **EMP:** 5
SQ FT: 12,000
SALES (est): 1.1MM **Privately Held**
SIC: 3621 5084 Electric motor & generator parts; industrial machinery & equipment

(G-20845)
ALLTEMATED INC (PA)
541 Northgate Pkwy (60090-2663)
PHONE..................847 394-5800
Randall J Temple, *President*
Steve Hall, *Vice Pres*
Tom Rogers, *IT/INT Sup*
EMP: 55
SALES (est): 7.5MM **Privately Held**
SIC: 3661 7389 Telephone & telegraph apparatus; packaging & labeling services

(G-20846)
AMERICA PRINTING INC
716 Gregor Ln (60090-7302)
PHONE..................847 229-8358
William Schmitt, *President*
Linda Schmitt, *Vice Pres*
EMP: 5
SQ FT: 2,000
SALES: 500K **Privately Held**
SIC: 2752 Commercial printing, offset

(G-20847)
AMERICAN DRILLING INC
625 Glenn Ave (60090-6017)
PHONE..................847 850-5090
Jim Shanahan, *President*
Jim Shanahan Jr, *Vice Pres*
Tom Shanahan, *Treasurer*
EMP: 45
SQ FT: 19,200
SALES (est): 7.7MM **Privately Held**
SIC: 3599 Machine shop, jobbing & repair

(G-20848)
AMERIFLON LTD (PA)
930 Seton Ct (60090-5705)
PHONE..................847 541-6000
Alex Provenzano, *President*
George Bingham, *Treasurer*
EMP: 6
SQ FT: 12,000
SALES (est): 971.7K **Privately Held**
SIC: 3087 2992 2821 Custom compound purchased resins; lubricating oils & greases; plastics materials & resins

(G-20849)
ANDREW TECHNOLOGIES INC
305 Alderman Ave (60090-6505)
PHONE..................847 520-5770
Kathleen A Michals, *President*
David Michals, *Vice Pres*
Jason King, *Comptroller*
Tim Kostelancik, *Manager*
EMP: 30
SQ FT: 15,000
SALES (est): 6.4MM **Privately Held**
SIC: 3679 Electronic circuits

(G-20850)
ARTISTIC FRAMING INC (PA)
860 Chaddick Dr Ste F (60090-6462)
PHONE..................847 808-0200
Thomas M Wolk, *CEO*
Larry Thomas, *President*
Minda Smythe, *Vice Pres*
Cokkie West, *Vice Pres*
Zach Wolk, *Purch Agent*
EMP: 200
SQ FT: 80,000
SALES (est): 29.4MM **Privately Held**
SIC: 2499 3499 Picture frame molding, finished; picture frames, metal

(G-20851)
ARTTIG ART
100 Chaddick Dr (60090-6006)
PHONE..................847 804-8001
EMP: 3
SALES (est): 207.1K **Privately Held**
SIC: 3229 Art, decorative & novelty glassware

(G-20852)
ASTEROID PRECISION INC
1075 Chaddick Dr (60090-6401)
PHONE..................847 298-8109
Michael Vigue, *Partner*
John Pack, *Principal*
Alexia Vigue, *Principal*
Sandra Vigue, *Principal*
James Vigue, *Vice Pres*
EMP: 75
SQ FT: 22,000

Wheeling - Cook County (G-20853) — GEOGRAPHIC SECTION

SALES (est): 7.7MM **Privately Held**
SIC: 3599 Grinding castings for the trade; machine shop, jobbing & repair

(G-20853)
AVAILABLE SPRING AND MFG CO
350 Holbrook Dr (60090-5812)
P.O. Box 526 (60090-0526)
PHONE...................847 520-4854
J Matthew Eggemeyer, *President*
Wade S Keats, *Corp Secy*
Matthew M Keats, *Vice Pres*
EMP: 5 EST: 1971
SQ FT: 12,000
SALES (est): 437.8K **Privately Held**
SIC: 3495 3496 3469 Wire springs; miscellaneous fabricated wire products; metal stampings

(G-20854)
B A I PUBLISHERS
190 Abbott Dr Ste A (60090-5800)
PHONE...................847 537-1300
Richard Binder, *President*
EMP: 6
SALES (est): 320K **Privately Held**
WEB: www.nationwidedirectory.com
SIC: 2741 Directories: publishing only, not printed on site

(G-20855)
B M W INC
110 Carpenter Ave (60090-6008)
PHONE...................847 439-0095
Boris Raslin, *President*
Gary Iklov, *Vice Pres*
EMP: 25
SQ FT: 17,000
SALES (est): 4.6MM **Privately Held**
SIC: 3599 Machine shop, jobbing & repair

(G-20856)
BAHR TOOL & DIE CO
2201 Foster Ave (60090-6508)
PHONE...................847 392-4447
Heinz Bahr, *Owner*
EMP: 5 EST: 1977
SQ FT: 2,000
SALES (est): 641.8K **Privately Held**
SIC: 3599 Machine shop, jobbing & repair

(G-20857)
BEACON FAS & COMPONENTS INC
Also Called: Beacon Terminal Pin
198 Carpenter Ave (60090-6008)
PHONE...................847 541-0404
Robert Wegner, *President*
Gary Pavlik, *Vice Pres*
Jeff Ryan, *Plant Mgr*
Kameron Dorsey, *Natl Sales Mgr*
Samantha Lustig, *Sales Staff*
▲ EMP: 35
SQ FT: 35,000
SALES (est): 18.8MM **Privately Held**
SIC: 5072 3644 Bolts; nuts (hardware); rivets; screws; electric conduits & fittings

(G-20858)
BEYOND COMPONENTS WEST INC
505 Chaddick Dr (60090-6053)
PHONE...................847 465-0480
Brian Gabel, *Sales Associate*
Bronson Andrews, *Branch Mgr*
EMP: 3
SALES (corp-wide): 33.7MM **Privately Held**
SIC: 3629 Blasting machines, electrical
HQ: Beyond Components West, Inc
12110 Prichard Farm Rd
Maryland Heights MO 63043
314 344-0344

(G-20859)
BIO INDUSTRIES INC
540 Allendale Dr Ste B (60090-2603)
PHONE...................847 215-8999
Judy Hale, *Ch of Bd*
Gene Wisniewski, *President*
David Hale, *Corp Secy*
William Lavelle, *CFO*
EMP: 56
SQ FT: 35,000
SALES (est): 12.1MM **Privately Held**
SIC: 2673 4953 Plastic bags: made from purchased materials; recycling, waste materials

(G-20860)
BLOCK AND COMPANY INC (HQ)
Also Called: Block Midland Group
1111 Wheeling Rd (60090-5795)
PHONE...................847 537-7200
Jason Smith, *President*
Rob Silvester, *Managing Prtnr*
Philip Robins, *General Mgr*
Elaine Nissen, *Vice Pres*
Paul Sprecht, *Engineer*
◆ EMP: 159
SQ FT: 125,000
SALES: 100MM
SALES (corp-wide): 178.1MM **Privately Held**
WEB: www.blockandcompany.com
SIC: 3469 2761 2393 5049 Cash & stamp boxes, stamped metal; manifold business forms; textile bags; bank equipment & supplies; stationery & office supplies
PA: Speyside Equity Fund I Lp
430 E 86th St
New York NY 10028
212 994-0308

(G-20861)
BOB C BEVERAGES LLC
Also Called: Bob Chinn's Premium Beverages
419 Harvester Ct (60090-4734)
PHONE...................847 520-7582
EMP: 3
SQ FT: 800
SALES (est): 1MM **Privately Held**
SIC: 2082 Mfg Malt Beverages

(G-20862)
BONA FIDE CORP
100 Shepard Ave (60090-6022)
PHONE...................847 970-8693
Marcin Cartek, *President*
Gabriela Chrapek, *Admin Sec*
EMP: 5
SALES: 953.3K **Privately Held**
SIC: 3553 Cabinet makers' machinery

(G-20863)
BOOM COMPANY INC
Also Called: Slam Door Co
161 Wheeling Rd (60090-4807)
PHONE...................847 459-6199
John Posch, *President*
EMP: 3
SQ FT: 2,700
SALES (est): 400.4K **Privately Held**
SIC: 2431 7699 3442 3231 Windows & window parts & trim, wood; door & window repair; metal doors, sash & trim; products of purchased glass; screens, door & window

(G-20864)
BOWE BELL + HWELL SCANNERS LLC
760 S Wolf Rd (60090-6232)
PHONE...................847 675-7600
EMP: 50
SALES (est): 3.6MM
SALES (corp-wide): 1.5B **Publicly Held**
SIC: 3577 Mfg Computer Peripheral Equipment
PA: Eastman Kodak Company
343 State St
Rochester NY 14650
585 724-4000

(G-20865)
BOZKI INC
325 N Milwaukee Ave (60090-3071)
PHONE...................312 767-2122
EMP: 5
SALES (est): 272K **Privately Held**
SIC: 3679 Headphones, radio

(G-20866)
BRIDGESTONE COMPANY INC
41 Century Dr (60090-6051)
PHONE...................847 325-5172
Tim Iida, *President*
Christi Poulsen, *Accounts Exec*
Mary Shellenbrg, *Admin Sec*
◆ EMP: 30 EST: 1970
SQ FT: 17,000
SALES (est): 5.8MM **Privately Held**
SIC: 3451 Screw machine products

(G-20867)
C R PLASTICS INC
851 Seton Ct Ste 1c (60090-5764)
PHONE...................847 541-3601
▲ EMP: 8
SQ FT: 10,000
SALES (est): 1.6MM **Privately Held**
SIC: 3089 Mfg Plastic Products

(G-20868)
C&R SCRAP IRON & METAL
251 E Dundee Rd (60090-3072)
PHONE...................847 459-9815
Ronald Misson, *Owner*
EMP: 3
SALES (est): 200K **Privately Held**
SIC: 5093 3341 Metal scrap & waste materials; secondary nonferrous metals

(G-20869)
CAST FILMS INC
401 Chaddick Dr (60090-6066)
PHONE...................847 808-0363
Richard Witcraft, *President*
EMP: 19
SQ FT: 34,200
SALES (est): 3.3MM **Privately Held**
SIC: 3081 Plastic film & sheet

(G-20870)
CK GRINDING AND MACHINING INC
169 Wheeling Rd (60090-4807)
PHONE...................847 541-0960
Kazimierz Casey Kordek, *President*
Mariel Kordek, *Vice Pres*
EMP: 6
SQ FT: 3,000
SALES (est): 600K **Privately Held**
SIC: 3599 Machine shop, jobbing & repair

(G-20871)
CLOROX HIDDEN VALLEY MFG
1197 Willis Ave (60090-5816)
PHONE...................847 229-5500
James Zawacki, *Executive*
EMP: 15 EST: 2008
SALES (est): 2.8MM **Privately Held**
SIC: 5149 2842 Condiments; bleaches, household: dry or liquid

(G-20872)
CLOROX MANUFACTURING COMPANY
1197 Willis Ave (60090-5816)
PHONE...................847 229-5500
Tracy Strandberg, *Human Res Mgr*
Paul Unitas, *Manager*
EMP: 150
SQ FT: 68,000
SALES (corp-wide): 6.2B **Publicly Held**
SIC: 2842 2812 Specialty cleaning, polishes & sanitation goods; alkalies & chlorine
HQ: Clorox Manufacturing Company
1221 Broadway
Oakland CA 94612

(G-20873)
CLUB JEWELRY MANUFACTURING INC
137 N Milwaukee Ave (60090-3013)
PHONE...................847 541-0700
Alex Babitsky, *President*
Vladimir Shifrin, *Admin Sec*
EMP: 2
SALES (est): 202.9K **Privately Held**
SIC: 3911 Jewelry, precious metal

(G-20874)
COIN MACKE LAUNDRY
124b Messner Dr (60090-6434)
PHONE...................847 459-1109
EMP: 2
SALES (est): 203.7K **Privately Held**
SIC: 3633 Mfg Home Laundry Equipment

(G-20875)
CONTINENTAL SCREWS MCH PDTS
160 Abbott Dr (60090-5802)
PHONE...................847 459-7766
Martin Binder, *Ch of Bd*
Richard Binder, *President*
Jim Bubis, *Plant Mgr*
EMP: 45
SQ FT: 12,000
SALES (est): 6MM **Privately Held**
SIC: 3451 Screw machine products

(G-20876)
CREDIT CARD SYSTEMS INC
180 Shepard Ave (60090-6022)
PHONE...................847 459-8320
Peter A Lazzari, *President*
Rita Lazzari, *Vice Pres*
Phil Lazzari, *Prdtn Mgr*
Maribel Rodriguez, *Buyer*
Peter Lazzari, *Human Res Mgr*
EMP: 15
SQ FT: 12,000
SALES (est): 1.9MM **Privately Held**
SIC: 3083 3559 Plastic finished products, laminated; plastics working machinery

(G-20877)
CRESCENT CARDBOARD COMPANY LLC
100 W Willow Rd (60090-6587)
PHONE...................888 293-3956
C S Ozmun, *President*
Steven Kosmalski, *President*
Kevin McCarthy, *Vice Pres*
Jeremy Cooper, *Sales Mgr*
Potomac Corporation,
◆ EMP: 195
SALES (est): 49.1MM **Privately Held**
SIC: 2679 Paperboard products, converted
PA: Potomac Corporation
2063 Foster Ave
Wheeling IL 60090
847 259-0546

(G-20878)
DIAMOND DIE & BEVEL CUTNG LLC
2087 Foster Ave (60090-6520)
PHONE...................224 387-3200
C S Ozmun, *President*
Matthew Ozmun, *Vice Pres*
Scott Dvorak, *Sales Staff*
Terry Boffeli, *Admin Sec*
▲ EMP: 24
SALES (est): 3.9MM **Privately Held**
SIC: 3544 Special dies, tools, jigs & fixtures

(G-20879)
DISTINCTIVE FOODS LLC (PA)
Also Called: Pie Piper Products
654 Wheeling Rd (60090-5707)
PHONE...................847 459-3600
Mike Vovk, *Engineer*
Ron Buck, *CFO*
Andrew Holzman, *Sales Staff*
Josh Harris, *Mng Member*
▼ EMP: 100
SQ FT: 15,000
SALES (est): 25.1MM **Privately Held**
SIC: 2038 Frozen specialties

(G-20880)
DTK CONSTRUCTION INC
Also Called: Dtk Stone Works
296 W Palatine Rd (60090-5815)
P.O. Box 241, Morton Grove (60053-0241)
PHONE...................312 296-2762
Dimitre Koldanov, *President*
▲ EMP: 6
SQ FT: 10,000
SALES: 1.5MM **Privately Held**
SIC: 3281 Cut stone & stone products

(G-20881)
DURABLE INC (PA)
Also Called: Durable Packaging Intl
750 Northgate Pkwy (60090-2660)
PHONE...................847 541-4400
Scott Anders, *President*
Jessica Anders, *Natl Sales Mgr*
Gina Deutsch, *Natl Sales Mgr*
Kevin Hanus, *Manager*

▲ = Import ▼ = Export
◆ = Import/Export

GEOGRAPHIC SECTION

Wheeling - Cook County (G-20906)

Darren Anders, *Admin Sec*
▲ **EMP:** 750 **EST:** 1943
SQ FT: 400,000
SALES (est): 99MM **Privately Held**
WEB: www.durablepackaging.com
SIC: 3497 3354 Foil containers for bakery goods & frozen foods; aluminum extruded products

(G-20882)
DYNOMAX INC
230 W Palatine Rd (60090-5825)
PHONE 847 680-8833
EMP: 25
SALES (corp-wide): 109.3MM **Privately Held**
SIC: 3724 Aircraft engines & engine parts
PA: Dynomax, Inc.
   1535 Abbott Dr
   Wheeling IL 60090
   847 680-8833

(G-20883)
DYNOMAX INC (PA)
1535 Abbott Dr (60090-5821)
PHONE 847 680-8833
Richard Zic, *President*
Maura Zic, *Corp Secy*
Mark Zic, *Vice Pres*
Guerman Atanassov, *Engineer*
Trevor Bermingham, *Engineer*
▲ **EMP:** 275
SQ FT: 500,000
SALES (est): 109.3MM **Privately Held**
SIC: 3724 3545 3678 3599 Aircraft engines & engine parts; machine tool accessories; calipers & dividers; comparators (machinists' precision tools); electronic connectors; machine & other job shop work; plating & polishing

(G-20884)
EASTERN COMPANY
Illinois Lock Company
301 W Hintz Rd (60090-5754)
P.O. Box 9068 (60090-9068)
PHONE 847 537-1800
Brian Ott, *Plant Mgr*
Henry Royce, *Engineer*
Michael Misner, *Design Engr*
Mark Pekovitch, *Design Engr*
Thomas Butler, *Sales Staff*
EMP: 120
SQ FT: 45,000
SALES (corp-wide): 251.7MM **Publicly Held**
WEB: www.easterncompany.com
SIC: 3429 5099 Locks or lock sets; locks & lock sets
PA: The Eastern Company
   112 Bridge St
   Naugatuck CT 06770
   203 729-2255

(G-20885)
EBERLE MANUFACTURING COMPANY
230 Larkin Dr (60090-6456)
PHONE 847 215-0100
Robert Eberle, *President*
Dan Leisner, *General Mgr*
John Agazim, *COO*
Anna Eberle, *Treasurer*
EMP: 12 **EST:** 1953
SQ FT: 16,500
SALES: 830K **Privately Held**
WEB: www.eberlemfg.com
SIC: 3544 3569 Special dies & tools; assembly machines, non-metalworking

(G-20886)
EDGAR A WEBER & COMPANY
Also Called: Weber Flavors
549 Palwaukee Dr (60090-6049)
P.O. Box 546 (60090-0546)
PHONE 847 215-1980
William Igou, *President*
Andrew G Plennert, *President*
Tim Carter, *Vice Pres*
Alysen Terretta, *Vice Pres*
David Samuels, *Opers Staff*
◆ **EMP:** 20
SQ FT: 5,000
SALES (est): 6.8MM **Privately Held**
WEB: www.weberflavors.com
SIC: 2087 Extracts, flavoring

(G-20887)
EDGAR A WEBER & COMPANY
Also Called: Weber Flavors
549 Palwaukee Dr (60090-6049)
P.O. Box 546 (60090-0546)
PHONE 847 215-1980
EMP: 20 **EST:** 1995
SALES (est): 2.8MM **Privately Held**
SIC: 2087 Mfg Flavor Extracts/Syrup

(G-20888)
EJ CADY & COMPANY
Also Called: Caddy
135 Wheeling Rd (60090-4807)
PHONE 847 537-2239
Thomas D Chatterton, *President*
Bonnie Chatterton, *Corp Secy*
EMP: 4 **EST:** 1895
SQ FT: 3,000
SALES (est): 675.4K **Privately Held**
WEB: www.ejcady.com
SIC: 3829 5084 3826 3596 Testing equipment: abrasion, shearing strength, etc.; industrial machinery & equipment; analytical instruments; scales & balances, except laboratory; machine tool accessories

(G-20889)
ELENCO ELECTRONICS INC
150 Carpenter Ave (60090-6062)
PHONE 847 541-3800
James T Cecchin, *President*
Linda Kramer, *Corp Secy*
Gerald J Cecchin, *Vice Pres*
Marc Lehner, *Engineer*
Janes Smith, *Sales Staff*
◆ **EMP:** 39 **EST:** 1972
SQ FT: 56,000
SALES (est): 13.1MM **Privately Held**
SIC: 3825 5945 3699 3625 Oscillographs & oscilloscopes; power measuring equipment, electrical; hobby, toy & game shops; electrical equipment & supplies; relays & industrial controls; switchgear & switchboard apparatus

(G-20890)
ELGIN FASTENER GROUP LLC
288 Holbrook Dr (60090-5810)
PHONE 847 465-0048
Chris Peri, *CFO*
Brian Nadel, *Manager*
EMP: 500 **EST:** 2016
SALES (est): 30.6MM **Privately Held**
SIC: 3462 Machinery forgings, ferrous

(G-20891)
ENGIS CORPORATION (PA)
105 W Hintz Rd (60090-5769)
PHONE 847 808-9400
Sean Gilmore, *President*
Martin Steindler, *Chairman*
Kenneth Werner, *Vice Pres*
Dean Jensen, *Project Mgr*
Laurence Dillon, *Prdtn Mgr*
▲ **EMP:** 135 **EST:** 1938
SQ FT: 121,125
SALES (est): 39.7MM **Privately Held**
WEB: www.engis.com
SIC: 3541 3291 3545 3471 Machine tools, metal cutting type; diamond powder; machine tool accessories; plating & polishing

(G-20892)
EPAZZ INC (PA)
325 N Milwaukee Ave Ste G (60090-3071)
PHONE 312 955-8161
Shaun Passley, *Ch of Bd*
EMP: 8
SQ FT: 2,522
SALES (est): 1.6MM **Publicly Held**
SIC: 7372 Application computer software

(G-20893)
ERWIN WICZER INDUSTRIES INC
500 Harvester Ct Ste 8 (60090-4755)
PHONE 847 541-9556
Erwin Wiczer, *President*
EMP: 7
SQ FT: 2,500
SALES: 1MM **Privately Held**
SIC: 3429 Manufactured hardware (general)

(G-20894)
ETHNIC MEDIA LLC
704 S Milwaukee Ave (60090-6202)
PHONE 224 676-0778
Alexander Khodos,
EMP: 4
SALES (est): 354.7K **Privately Held**
SIC: 2711 Newspapers

(G-20895)
ETI SOLID STATE LIGHTING INC
720 Northgate Pkwy (60090-2660)
PHONE 855 384-7754
Eva Kim Yung Chan, *CEO*
Gary Van Winkle, *Vice Pres*
Suk Yee Leung, *CFO*
Caren Hagan, *Manager*
Yoel Lavenda, *Manager*
◆ **EMP:** 20
SALES: 18MM
SALES (corp-wide): 576.3MM **Privately Held**
SIC: 3646 5719 Commercial indusl & institutional electric lighting fixtures; lighting, lamps & accessories
PA: Elec-Tech International Co., Ltd.
   No. 1 Jinfeng Road, Tangjiawan Town, Xiangzhou District
   Zhuhai 51908
   756 339-0188

(G-20896)
EXACT TOOL COMPANY INC
2123 Foster Ave (60090-6506)
PHONE 847 632-1140
Renate Drost, *President*
Ray Drost, *Vice Pres*
EMP: 8 **EST:** 1969
SQ FT: 21,000
SALES (est): 1.2MM **Privately Held**
WEB: www.exacttool.com
SIC: 3544 Dies & die holders for metal cutting, forming, die casting; punches, forming & stamping

(G-20897)
FLP INDUSTRIES LLC
404 Mercantile Ct (60090-4738)
PHONE 847 215-8650
Hajime Furukawa,
EMP: 11
SALES (est): 1.3MM **Privately Held**
SIC: 3679 Harness assemblies for electronic use: wire or cable

(G-20898)
FLUID MANAGEMENT INC (HQ)
Also Called: FM
1023 Wheeling Rd (60090-5776)
PHONE 847 537-0880
Dennis Williams, *Ch of Bd*
Suzanne Burns, *President*
Jerry N Derck, *Vice Pres*
Douglas C Lennox, *Vice Pres*
Wayne P Sayatovic, *Vice Pres*
◆ **EMP:** 290
SQ FT: 147,000
SALES (est): 82.1MM
SALES (corp-wide): 2.4B **Publicly Held**
WEB: www.fluidman.com
SIC: 3559 Paint making machinery
PA: Idex Corporation
   1925 W Field Ct Ste 200
   Lake Forest IL 60045
   847 498-7070

(G-20899)
FLUID MNAGEMENT OPERATIONS LLC (HQ)
1023 Wheeling Rd (60090-5768)
PHONE 847 537-0880
Lawrence D Kingsley, *Ch of Bd*
▲ **EMP:** 5
SALES (est): 13.2MM
SALES (corp-wide): 2.4B **Publicly Held**
SIC: 3531 Mixers: ore, plaster, slag, sand, mortar, etc.
PA: Idex Corporation
   1925 W Field Ct Ste 200
   Lake Forest IL 60045
   847 498-7070

(G-20900)
FOUNTAIN TECHNOLOGIES LTD
423 Denniston Ct (60090-4730)
PHONE 847 537-3677
Robert Watson, *President*
Mark Saulka, *Principal*
Pat Saulka, *Vice Pres*
Justin Hauad, *Project Mgr*
Matt Saulka, *Manager*
EMP: 30
SALES: 4MM **Privately Held**
WEB: www.fountaintechnologies.com
SIC: 1799 3272 5145 Fountain installation; fountains, concrete; fountain supplies

(G-20901)
FRANKENSTITCH PROMOTIONS LLC
311 Egidi Dr (60090-2653)
PHONE 847 459-4840
Adam Frank, *Mng Member*
Howard N Frank,
EMP: 10
SQ FT: 15,000
SALES (est): 819.9K **Privately Held**
WEB: www.frankenstitch.net
SIC: 5099 2261 5046 2621 Signs, except electric; roller printing of cotton broadwoven fabrics; signs, electrical; printing paper; posters: publishing & printing; promotional printing, gravure

(G-20902)
FUN INCORPORATED
333 Alice St (60090-5805)
PHONE 773 745-3837
Graham R Putnam, *President*
Kathryn Andersen-Putnam, *Vice Pres*
Tracy O'Lear, *Office Mgr*
▲ **EMP:** 20 **EST:** 1941
SQ FT: 42,500
SALES (est): 3.2MM **Privately Held**
WEB: www.funinc.com
SIC: 3944 3993 Games, toys & children's vehicles; advertising novelties

(G-20903)
G & Z INDUSTRIES INC
541 Chaddick Dr (60090-6053)
PHONE 847 215-2300
David Gill, *President*
Wayne Schott, *Corp Secy*
Jesse Siwiec, *Vice Pres*
Ted Smoczynski, *Materials Mgr*
Dennis Monzel, *Opers Staff*
EMP: 48 **EST:** 1958
SQ FT: 19,000
SALES (est): 9.4MM **Privately Held**
WEB: www.gzind.com
SIC: 3599 Machine shop, jobbing & repair

(G-20904)
GEORGE INDUSTRIES LLC
Also Called: Numerical Precision
2200 Foster Ave (60090-6509)
PHONE 847 394-3610
Mike Hasley, *Branch Mgr*
EMP: 50
SALES (corp-wide): 16.8MM **Privately Held**
SIC: 3448 Prefabricated metal buildings
PA: George Industries Llc
   1 S Page Ave
   Endicott NY 13760
   607 748-3371

(G-20905)
H V MANUFACTURING VANGUAR
1197 Willis Ave (60090-5816)
PHONE 847 229-5502
Gerald Johnston, *CEO*
EMP: 3 **EST:** 2010
SALES (est): 285K **Privately Held**
SIC: 3999 Manufacturing industries

(G-20906)
HAGEN MANUFACTURING INC
318 Holbrook Dr (60090-5812)
PHONE 224 735-2099
Mark Hagen, *President*
EMP: 3 **EST:** 2011
SALES (est): 376K **Privately Held**
WEB: www.hagenmfg.com
SIC: 3999 Chairs, hydraulic, barber & beauty shop

Wheeling - Cook County (G-20907)

(G-20907)
HANDI-FOIL CORP (PA)
135 E Hintz Rd (60090-6059)
PHONE...................................847 520-1000
Norton Sarnoff, *President*
Brad Sarnoff, *Vice Pres*
Peter Perkins, *CFO*
David Sarnoff, *Admin Sec*
◆ **EMP:** 700
SQ FT: 650,000
SALES (est): 121.4MM **Privately Held**
SIC: 3497 Foil containers for bakery goods & frozen foods

(G-20908)
HFA INC
Also Called: Handi-Foil of America
135 E Hintz Rd (60090-6035)
PHONE...................................847 520-1000
Norton Sarnoff, *President*
Brad Sarnoff, *Vice Pres*
David Sarnoff, *Vice Pres*
Peter Perkins, *CFO*
◆ **EMP:** 700
SQ FT: 500,000
SALES (est): 228.8MM **Privately Held**
SIC: 3497 Foil containers for bakery goods & frozen foods

(G-20909)
HK WOODWORK
925 Seton Ct Ste 7 (60090-5771)
PHONE...................................773 964-2468
Jakub S Kosik, *Principal*
EMP: 2
SALES (est): 211.6K **Privately Held**
SIC: 2431 Millwork

(G-20910)
HOLDINGS LIQUIDATION INC
Also Called: Bowebellhowell
760 S Wolf Rd (60090-6232)
PHONE...................................312 541-9300
Leslie F Stern, *CEO*
Doug Hess, *District Mgr*
Larry Blue, *COO*
Hendrik Fischer, *Vice Pres*
Mark Van Gorp, *Vice Pres*
▲ **EMP:** 1710
SQ FT: 50,000
SALES (est): 217MM **Privately Held**
SIC: 3579 Mailing, letter handling & addressing machines; address labeling machines

(G-20911)
HOOKSET ENTERPRISES LLC
Also Called: Decoplate
1120 Larkin Dr Ste A (60090-6412)
PHONE...................................224 374-1935
William Rychel,
EMP: 10
SALES (est): 597K **Privately Held**
WEB: www.deco-plate.com
SIC: 3953 Screens, textile printing

(G-20912)
IAM ACQUISITION LLC
Also Called: Coregistics
230 W Palatine Rd (60090-5825)
PHONE...................................847 259-7800
Robert Jorgensen, *General Mgr*
Erin Hunt, *Branch Mgr*
EMP: 35 **Privately Held**
SIC: 2671 Plastic film, coated or laminated for packaging
PA: Iam Acquisition, Llc
    240 Northpoint Pkwy
    Acworth GA 30102

(G-20913)
ILMACHINE COMPANY INC
421 Harvester Ct (60090-4734)
PHONE...................................847 243-9900
Igor Levin, *President*
Demitrius Sokolsky, *Vice Pres*
EMP: 13
SQ FT: 11,000
SALES (est): 2.7MM **Privately Held**
SIC: 3444 7692 Sheet metal specialties, not stamped; welding repair

(G-20914)
IMPERIAL GLASS STRUCTURES CO
2120 Foster Ave (60090-6578)
PHONE...................................847 253-6150
Dieter Jankowski, *President*
Mike Malicki, *Vice Pres*
EMP: 15
SQ FT: 16,000
SALES (est): 3.5MM **Privately Held**
SIC: 3444 Skylights, sheet metal

(G-20915)
INDUSTRIAL MOTION CONTROL LLC (DH)
Also Called: De-Sta-Co Camco Products
1444 S Wolf Rd (60090-6514)
PHONE...................................847 459-5200
Ian Nilson, *CFO*
Lou Wozniak, *Director*
▲ **EMP:** 125
SQ FT: 100,000
SALES: 40MM
SALES (corp-wide): 7.1B **Publicly Held**
SIC: 3568 3535 3625 3566 Power transmission equipment; conveyors & conveying equipment; relays & industrial controls; speed changers, drives & gears
HQ: Dover Energy, Inc.
    691 N Squirrel Rd Ste 250
    Auburn Hills MI 48326
    248 836-6700

(G-20916)
INTERNATIONAL ELECTRO MAGNETIC
Also Called: Instrument Laboratories Div
1033 Noel Ave (60090-5813)
PHONE...................................847 358-4622
Anthony M Pretto, *President*
EMP: 5 **EST:** 1961
SQ FT: 5,000
SALES (est): 490K **Privately Held**
WEB: www.iemmag.com
SIC: 3825 Test equipment for electronic & electrical circuits

(G-20917)
IP MEDIA HOLDINGS
55 E Hintz Rd (60090-6043)
PHONE...................................847 714-1177
William Polich, *CEO*
Russell Chatskis, *President*
▲ **EMP:** 25
SALES (est): 4MM **Privately Held**
SIC: 3678 Electronic connectors

(G-20918)
JACOB HAY COMPANY
509 N Wolf Rd (60090-3027)
PHONE...................................847 215-8880
Dennis H Gardino, *President*
Christopher Gardino, *Treasurer*
EMP: 7 **EST:** 1935
SQ FT: 3,000
SALES (est): 1.8MM **Privately Held**
WEB: www.jacobhay.com
SIC: 5085 5169 2842 Industrial supplies; polishes; specialty cleaning, polishes & sanitation goods

(G-20919)
JEFFREY JAE INC
1125 Wheeling Rd (60090-5716)
PHONE...................................847 808-2002
Jeffery-Jae Bersch, *CEO*
EMP: 40
SQ FT: 25,000
SALES (corp-wide): 11MM **Privately Held**
SIC: 3452 Screws, metal
PA: Jae Jeffrey Inc
    907 E Brookwood Dr
    Arlington Heights IL

(G-20920)
JELCO INC
450 Wheeling Rd (60090-4742)
PHONE...................................847 459-5207
Edwin Elliott, *President*
Linda Elliott, *Treasurer*
Andy Kraus, *Accounting Mgr*
▲ **EMP:** 13
SQ FT: 21,000
SALES (est): 2.2MM **Privately Held**
SIC: 3161 Attache cases; briefcases; camera carrying bags; cases, carrying

(G-20921)
JOINTECHLABS INC
505 N Wolf Rd (60090-3027)
PHONE...................................773 954-1076
Nathan Katz, *CEO*
EMP: 3 **EST:** 2010
SALES (est): 237.9K **Privately Held**
SIC: 3841 8731 Medical instruments & equipment, blood & bone work; biotechnical research, commercial

(G-20922)
K&S INTERNATIONAL INC
760 Glenn Ave (60090-6020)
PHONE...................................847 229-0202
Kenneth B Glazer, *President*
Scott Glazer, *Vice Pres*
Christy Keller, *VP Sales*
◆ **EMP:** 8
SQ FT: 30,000
SALES (est): 1.6MM **Privately Held**
WEB: www.ksintl.com
SIC: 2421 Flooring (dressed lumber), softwood

(G-20923)
KEATS MANUFACTURING CO (PA)
350 Holbrook Dr (60090-5812)
P.O. Box 526 (60090-0526)
PHONE...................................847 520-1133
Wade Keats, *CEO*
Matt Eggemeyer, *COO*
Matthew Keats, *Vice Pres*
David Fink, *Materials Mgr*
Donald Klein, *Engineer*
▲ **EMP:** 100
SQ FT: 20,000
SALES (est): 17.6MM **Privately Held**
WEB: www.keatsmfg.com
SIC: 3496 3312 Clips & fasteners, made from purchased wire; tool & die steel

(G-20924)
KITAMURA MACHINERY USA INC (HQ)
78 Century Dr (60090-6050)
PHONE...................................847 520-7755
Koichiro Kitamura, *Ch of Bd*
Akihiro Aki Kitamura, *President*
Shozo Kitamura, *Treasurer*
Minoru Umeno, *Admin Sec*
◆ **EMP:** 13
SQ FT: 20,000
SALES (est): 4.3MM **Privately Held**
WEB: www.kitamura-machinery.com
SIC: 3545 Cutting tools for machine tools

(G-20925)
KIWI CODERS CORP
265 Messner Dr (60090-6495)
PHONE...................................847 541-4511
Allen Mc Kay, *President*
Brent Mc Kay, *Vice Pres*
Brent E Mc Kay, *Admin Sec*
EMP: 42
SQ FT: 55,000
SALES (est): 7.2MM **Privately Held**
WEB: www.kiwicoders.com
SIC: 3953 3555 Marking devices; printing trades machinery

(G-20926)
KLH PRINTING CORP
664 Wheeling Rd (60090-5707)
PHONE...................................847 459-0115
Kenneth Meyer, *President*
EMP: 4 **EST:** 1928
SQ FT: 2,800
SALES (est): 422.8K **Privately Held**
SIC: 2752 2791 2789 2759 Color lithography; typesetting; bookbinding & related work; letterpress printing

(G-20927)
KYOWA INDUSTRIAL CO LTD USA
711 Glenn Ave (60090-6019)
PHONE...................................847 459-3500
Tsuneo Matsui, *President*
Hideki Sakamoto, *Vice Pres*
▲ **EMP:** 15
SQ FT: 15,000
SALES (est): 3MM **Privately Held**
SIC: 3544 Special dies & tools
PA: Kyowa Industrial Co.,Ltd.
    29-1, Kamisugoro
    Sanjo NIG 955-0

(G-20928)
LAKE COUNTY C V JOINTS INC
Also Called: Lake Cook C V
133 Wheeling Rd (60090-4807)
PHONE...................................847 537-7588
Jerry Bullock, *President*
EMP: 3
SALES (est): 250K **Privately Held**
SIC: 3944 Trains & equipment, toy: electric & mechanical

(G-20929)
LANG DENTAL MFG CO INC
175 Messner Dr (60090-6433)
P.O. Box 969 (60090-0969)
PHONE...................................847 215-6622
David J Lang, *President*
Daniel Beck, *Exec VP*
Samuel Lang, *Mfg Staff*
Joanne Lang, *Director*
◆ **EMP:** 18
SQ FT: 21,000
SALES (est): 4.9MM **Privately Held**
WEB: www.langdental.com
SIC: 3843 Compounds, dental

(G-20930)
LEAD N GLASS TM
2039 Foster Ave Ste A (60090-6513)
PHONE...................................847 255-2074
James La Caeyse, *President*
Jarett La Caeyse, *President*
Todd La Caeyse, *Vice Pres*
Sharon La Caeyse, *Treasurer*
EMP: 11
SQ FT: 5,500
SALES (est): 970K **Privately Held**
SIC: 3231 5031 Decorated glassware: chipped, engraved, etched, etc.; kitchen cabinets

(G-20931)
LEROYS WELDING & FABG INC
363 Alice St (60090-5805)
PHONE...................................847 215-6151
Neil Rubly, *President*
Vince Centineo, *Vice Pres*
Tina Centineo, *Treasurer*
EMP: 10
SQ FT: 8,500
SALES (est): 1.7MM **Privately Held**
SIC: 7692 3441 Welding repair; fabricated structural metal

(G-20932)
LEWIS PAPER PLACE INC
220 E Marquardt Dr (60090-6430)
PHONE...................................847 808-1343
EMP: 2
SALES (est): 268.7K **Privately Held**
SIC: 5084 2679 5112 Industrial machinery & equipment; paper products, converted; office supplies

(G-20933)
LIVING ROYAL
500 Quail Hollow Dr (60090-2651)
PHONE...................................312 906-7600
EMP: 16
SALES (est): 1.1MM **Privately Held**
SIC: 2252 Mfg Hosiery

(G-20934)
LIVING ROYAL INC
333 W Hintz Rd (60090-5712)
PHONE...................................312 906-7600
Michael Elyash, *CEO*
Mariya Rakhman, *President*
EMP: 30
SALES (est): 165.4K **Privately Held**
SIC: 5961 2252 2389 Women's apparel, mail order; socks; apparel for handicapped

GEOGRAPHIC SECTION

Wheeling - Cook County (G-20965)

(G-20935)
MANAGED MARKETING INC
Also Called: Direct Envelope
2232 Foster Ave (60090-6509)
PHONE 847 279-8260
Suzan Edwards, *President*
Dirk Edwards, *Admin Sec*
EMP: 9
SQ FT: 15,000
SALES (est): 1.8MM **Privately Held**
SIC: 2677 2759 Envelopes; invitation & stationery printing & engraving

(G-20936)
MANAN MEDICAL PRODUCTS INC (DH)
Also Called: Argon Medical
241 W Palatine Rd (60090-5824)
PHONE 847 637-3333
George Leondis, *President*
Gary Price, *Safety Mgr*
Sharon McNally, *VP Finance*
Sharon C McNally, *Admin Sec*
▲ **EMP:** 75
SALES (est): 27MM
SALES (corp-wide): 240.9MM **Privately Held**
SIC: 3842 3841 Surgical appliances & supplies; surgical & medical instruments
HQ: Argon Medical Devices, Inc.
2600 Dallas Pkwy Ste 440
Frisco TX 75034
903 675-9321

(G-20937)
MANAN TOOL & MANUFACTURING
241 W Palatine Rd (60090-5824)
PHONE 847 637-3333
Werner Mittermeier, *Principal*
Manfred Mittermeier, *Principal*
EMP: 1112
SQ FT: 82,000
SALES (est): 109.3MM **Privately Held**
WEB: www.argonmedical.com
SIC: 3541 3841 Machine tools, metal cutting type; needles, suture

(G-20938)
MARATHON CUTTING DIE INC
2340 Foster Ave (60090-6511)
PHONE 847 398-5165
Michael Bauer, *President*
EMP: 22
SALES (est): 4.3MM **Privately Held**
SIC: 3544 Special dies & tools

(G-20939)
MATTS COOKIE COMPANY
482 N Milwaukee Ave (60090-3067)
PHONE 847 537-3888
Mike Halverson, *CEO*
EMP: 8
SALES: 193.5K **Privately Held**
SIC: 2052 Cookies

(G-20940)
MICROTECH MACHINE INC
222 Camp Mcdonald Rd (60090-6533)
PHONE 847 870-0707
Elizabeth Iwanicki, *President*
EMP: 20
SQ FT: 18,200
SALES (est): 3.8MM **Privately Held**
SIC: 3599 Machine shop, jobbing & repair

(G-20941)
MIDLAND PAPER COMPANY (PA)
Also Called: Midland Paper Packaging & Sups
101 E Palatine Rd (60090-6512)
PHONE 847 777-2700
Michael Graves, *CEO*
David Goldschmidt, *President*
Ralph Deletto, *CFO*
Derek Jordan, *Sales Staff*
Don Krihak, *Sales Staff*
◆ **EMP:** 180 **EST:** 1907
SQ FT: 140,000
SALES (est): 749.1MM **Privately Held**
WEB: www.midlandpaper.com
SIC: 5111 2621 Printing paper; packaging paper

(G-20942)
MOTR GRAFX LLC
225 Larkin Dr Ste 5 (60090-7209)
PHONE 847 600-5656
Lissette Hern, *Partner*
Paul Literno, *Partner*
Delia Saboya, *Partner*
EMP: 8 **EST:** 2011
SALES (est): 15MM **Privately Held**
SIC: 2752 2759 7336 Commercial printing, lithographic; promotional printing; commercial art & graphic design

(G-20943)
NETCOM INC
599 Wheeling Rd (60090-4743)
PHONE 847 537-6300
Bob Cantarutti, *CEO*
Evangelos Argoudelis, *Ch of Bd*
Soren Pihlman, *President*
John Victor, *Principal*
Wayne Roecer, *Vice Pres*
◆ **EMP:** 121
SALES (est): 35.3MM **Privately Held**
SIC: 3679 3677 Electronic crystals; oscillators; power supplies, all types: static; filtration devices, electronic

(G-20944)
NEWSPAPER 7 DAYS (PA)
704 S Milwaukee Ave (60090-6202)
PHONE 847 272-2212
Roman Poliroski, *Principal*
EMP: 3
SALES (est): 442.8K **Privately Held**
SIC: 2711 Newspapers, publishing & printing

(G-20945)
NORTH AMERICAN SIGNAL CO
605 Wheeling Rd (60090-5736)
PHONE 847 537-8888
William Neiman, *President*
Mary Hook, *Safety Dir*
Pat Wiber, *Sales Mgr*
Mike Maloney, *Sales Staff*
Scot Tennant, *Sales Staff*
◆ **EMP:** 50 **EST:** 1959
SQ FT: 45,000
SALES (est): 11.3MM **Privately Held**
WEB: www.nasig.com
SIC: 3648 3669 Lighting equipment; sirens, electric: vehicle, marine, industrial & air raid

(G-20946)
NORTHSTAR TRADING LLC
50 Messner Dr (60090-6448)
PHONE 630 312-8434
EMP: 20
SQ FT: 14,000
SALES (est): 4.6MM **Privately Held**
SIC: 3089 Plastic processing

(G-20947)
NU-PRO POLYMERS INC
555 Allendale Dr (60090-2638)
PHONE 224 676-1663
EMP: 5
SALES (est): 879.6K **Privately Held**
SIC: 2821 Plastics materials & resins

(G-20948)
NUMERIDEX INCORPORATED
632 Wheeling Rd (60090-5707)
PHONE 847 541-8840
Alberto Hoyos, *President*
Stephen Ryd, *Admin Sec*
EMP: 10
SQ FT: 9,000
SALES (est): 2.3MM **Privately Held**
WEB: www.numeridex.com
SIC: 5049 5063 3572 Drafting supplies; electrical apparatus & equipment; tape storage units, computer

(G-20949)
OMEX TECHNOLOGIES INC
300 E Marquardt Dr # 107 (60090-6425)
PHONE 847 850-5858
Alexander Zaltz, *President*
Jenny Zaltz, *Vice Pres*
EMP: 5
SQ FT: 2,000
SALES: 750K **Privately Held**
SIC: 3825 3845 3827 3577 Spectroscopic & other optical properties measuring equipment; electromedical equipment; optical instruments & lenses; computer peripheral equipment

(G-20950)
OMNI PUBLISHING CO
45 Versailles Ct (60090-6756)
PHONE 847 483-9668
Zenja Glass, *President*
EMP: 4
SALES (est): 246.9K **Privately Held**
SIC: 2741 Miscellaneous publishing

(G-20951)
ONLY 1 PRINTERS INC
Also Called: Only For One Printers
540 Allendale Dr Ste K (60090-2603)
PHONE 847 947-4119
Gen Young Kim, *Principal*
▲ **EMP:** 10
SALES (est): 1.2MM **Privately Held**
SIC: 2752 Commercial printing, offset

(G-20952)
ORANGE CRUSH LLC
571 Wheeling Rd (60090-4743)
PHONE 847 537-7900
Ray Pagnozvi, *Branch Mgr*
Mark Tubay, *Manager*
EMP: 5
SALES (est): 310.9K
SALES (corp-wide): 104.2MM **Privately Held**
WEB: www.orangecrushllc.com
SIC: 1795 2951 Concrete breaking for streets & highways; asphalt paving mixtures & blocks
PA: Orange Crush, L.L.C.
321 Center St
Hillside IL 60162
708 544-9440

(G-20953)
PACTIV LLC
777 Wheeling Rd (60090-5708)
PHONE 847 459-8049
H M Weil, *Owner*
EMP: 350 **Publicly Held**
SIC: 3089 Thermoformed finished plastic products
HQ: Pactiv Llc
1900 W Field Ct
Lake Forest IL 60045
847 482-2000

(G-20954)
PALWAUKEE PRINTING COMPANY
1684 S Wolf Rd (60090-6516)
PHONE 847 459-0240
Joe Ropski, *President*
EMP: 4
SQ FT: 4,200
SALES (est): 380K **Privately Held**
SIC: 2752 Commercial printing, offset

(G-20955)
PAMARCO GLOBAL GRAPHICS INC
171 E Marquardt Dr (60090-6427)
PHONE 847 459-6000
Jim Nicpon, *Branch Mgr*
EMP: 17 **Privately Held**
SIC: 3069 3555 2796 Rubber rolls & roll coverings; printing trades machinery; platemaking services
HQ: Pamarco Global Graphics, Inc.
235 E 11th Ave
Roselle NJ 07203
908 241-1200

(G-20956)
PAPER TUBE LLC
971 N Milwaukee Ave # 22 (60090-1893)
PHONE 847 477-0563
Agrawal Parag, *Principal*
EMP: 4 **EST:** 2016
SALES (est): 399.1K **Privately Held**
SIC: 2655 Fiber cans, drums & similar products

(G-20957)
PERMISSIONS GROUP INC
401 S Milwaukee Ave # 180 (60090-5079)
PHONE 847 635-6550
Sherry Hoesly, *President*
Katy Mulcrone, *Project Mgr*
EMP: 8
SALES (est): 927.5K **Privately Held**
SIC: 2731 Books: publishing only

(G-20958)
PETERSON INTL ENTP LTD
504 Glenn Ave (60090-6016)
P.O. Box 480573, Niles (60714-0541)
PHONE 847 541-3700
William Pfeifer, *President*
Larry Foiles, *Design Engr*
EMP: 12
SALES (est): 2.2MM **Privately Held**
SIC: 3651 Household audio & video equipment

(G-20959)
PHOENIX ART WOODWORKS
500 Harvester Ct Ste 7 (60090-4755)
PHONE 847 279-1576
Ilya Ustr, *Owner*
EMP: 2
SALES (est): 231.3K **Privately Held**
WEB: www.aphoenixartwoodworks.com
SIC: 2431 Millwork

(G-20960)
PLASTECH MOLDING INC
2222 Foster Ave (60090-6509)
PHONE 847 398-0355
Stephan Memmem, *Principal*
EMP: 7
SALES (est): 775.3K **Privately Held**
SIC: 3089 Injection molding of plastics

(G-20961)
PLAZA TOOL & MOLD CO
500 Harvester Ct Ste 2 (60090-4755)
PHONE 847 537-2320
Mark Plaza, *President*
Mike Plaza, *Vice Pres*
Ann Plaza, *Admin Sec*
EMP: 3
SALES (est): 450.4K **Privately Held**
SIC: 3544 Industrial molds; special dies & tools

(G-20962)
POTOMAC CORPORATION (PA)
Also Called: Crescent Cardboard Company
2063 Foster Ave (60090-6520)
PHONE 847 259-0546
C S Ozmun, *CEO*
Matt Ozmun, *Exec VP*
Dave Rodiek, *Safety Mgr*
Selim Alegoz, *Opers Staff*
Gary Szmurlo, *Purch Mgr*
◆ **EMP:** 200
SQ FT: 300,000
SALES (est): 49.1MM **Privately Held**
SIC: 2679 0212 2675 Paperboard products, converted; beef cattle except feedlots; die-cut paper & board

(G-20963)
PRECISION FINISHING SYSTEMS IN
682 Chaddick Dr (60090-6057)
PHONE 847 907-4266
EMP: 12 **EST:** 2014
SALES (est): 1.6MM **Privately Held**
WEB: www.precisionfsinc.com
SIC: 3471 Cleaning, polishing & finishing

(G-20964)
PRECISION MEDICAL MFG LLC
852 Seton Ct (60090-5703)
PHONE 847 229-1551
Jerry M Brown,
Janice Politef,
EMP: 19
SALES (est): 2.3MM **Privately Held**
SIC: 3841 Surgical & medical instruments

(G-20965)
PRECISION PAPER TUBE COMPANY (PA)
1033 Noel Ave (60090-5899)
PHONE 847 537-4250

Wheeling - Cook County (G-20966)

Rick L Hatton, *President*
Susan Hatton, *Admin Sec*
EMP: 220 **EST:** 1934
SQ FT: 100,000
SALES (est): 25.1MM **Privately Held**
WEB: www.pptube.com
SIC: 2655 Tubes, for chemical or electrical uses: paper or fiber

(G-20966)
PROSPECT GRINDING INCORPORATED
925 Seton Ct Ste 11 (60090-5771)
PHONE 847 229-9240
Carol Dyrkacz, *President*
Ralph Dyrkacz, *Vice Pres*
EMP: 4
SQ FT: 2,500
SALES (est): 400K **Privately Held**
SIC: 3599 7389 Machine shop, jobbing & repair; grinding, precision: commercial or industrial

(G-20967)
PROTOTYPE & PRODUCTION CO
546 Quail Hollow Dr (60090-2651)
PHONE 847 419-1553
Sam Bakaturski, *President*
Mike Bakaturski, *QC Mgr*
EMP: 20
SQ FT: 15,000
SALES (est): 2.2MM **Privately Held**
SIC: 3541 3549 3545 3544 Machine tool replacement & repair parts, metal cutting types; sawing & cutoff machines (metalworking machinery); metalworking machinery; machine tool accessories; special dies, tools, jigs & fixtures

(G-20968)
RAJNER QUALITY MACHINE WORKS
2092 Foster Ave (60090-6521)
PHONE 847 394-8999
Richard Rajner, *President*
Lucy Rajner, *Corp Secy*
Edward Rajner, *Vice Pres*
Mark Rajner, *Vice Pres*
EMP: 2
SALES (est): 288.8K **Privately Held**
SIC: 3599 3544 Machine shop, jobbing & repair; special dies, tools, jigs & fixtures

(G-20969)
RAND MANUFACTURING NETWORK INC
840 Tanglewood Dr (60090-5775)
P.O. Box 414, Prospect Heights (60070-0414)
PHONE 847 299-8884
Neal E Katz, *President*
EMP: 3
SQ FT: 700
SALES (est): 472K **Privately Held**
SIC: 3089 Hardware, plastic

(G-20970)
RCM INDUSTRIES INC
Also Called: Northern Prints
161 Carpenter Ave (60090-6007)
PHONE 847 455-1950
Robert Marconi, *Owner*
Samir Yousif, *Plant Mgr*
Jimmy Scatchell, *Purch Mgr*
Rigo Acosta, *Manager*
Wilfred Mendez, *Supervisor*
EMP: 170 **Privately Held**
SIC: 3363 3365 Aluminum die-castings; aluminum foundries
PA: R.C.M. Industries, Inc.
3021 Cullerton St
Franklin Park IL 60131

(G-20971)
READY 2 ROLL INC
96 Mchenry Rd (60090-2683)
PHONE 847 620-9768
EMP: 3
SALES (est): 205.6K **Privately Held**
SIC: 3273 Ready-mixed concrete

(G-20972)
REMKE PRINTING INC
225 Larkin Dr Ste 7 (60090-7209)
PHONE 847 520-7300
Karen Coli, *President*
Jim Coli, *Vice Pres*
EMP: 4
SALES (est): 691.5K **Privately Held**
WEB: www.remkeprinting.com
SIC: 2752 2791 2789 2759 Commercial printing, offset; typesetting; bookbinding & related work; commercial printing

(G-20973)
RESINITE CORPORATION
1033 Noel Ave (60090-5813)
PHONE 847 537-4250
Rick L Hatton, *President*
W A Bowers, *President*
R L Hatton, *President*
EMP: 150 **EST:** 1948
SQ FT: 100,000
SALES (est): 16MM
SALES (corp-wide): 25.1MM **Privately Held**
WEB: www.pptube.com
SIC: 3644 3555 3544 3082 Insulators & insulation materials, electrical; printing trades machinery; special dies, tools, jigs & fixtures; unsupported plastics profile shapes; fiber cans, drums & similar products
PA: Precision Paper Tube Company Inc
1033 Noel Ave
Wheeling IL 60090
847 537-4250

(G-20974)
RESOLUTE INDUSTRIAL LLC (PA)
298 Messner Dr (60090-6436)
PHONE 800 537-9675
Mike McGraw, *CEO*
Robert Russell,
▲ **EMP:** 70
SALES (est): 33MM **Privately Held**
SIC: 3563 7359 1711 Air & gas compressors including vacuum pumps; equipment rental & leasing; boiler & furnace contractors

(G-20975)
ROADEX CARRIERS INC
446 Irvine Ct (60090-5127)
PHONE 773 454-8772
Oksana Lopatkin, *President*
William Lopatkin, *Vice Pres*
EMP: 4
SALES (est): 467.2K **Privately Held**
SIC: 3715 Truck trailers

(G-20976)
RODIN ENTERPRISES INC
Also Called: Minuteman Press
544b W Dundee Rd (60090-2675)
PHONE 847 412-1370
Allan Rodin, *President*
Aviva Rodin, *Admin Sec*
EMP: 3
SQ FT: 2,000
SALES (est): 444.1K **Privately Held**
SIC: 2752 2791 2789 2759 Commercial printing, lithographic; typesetting; bookbinding & related work; commercial printing

(G-20977)
RT ASSOCIATES INC
385 Gilman Ave (60090-5807)
PHONE 847 577-0700
Robert Radzis, *President*
Alex Rosario, *Senior Mgr*
EMP: 63
SQ FT: 28,000
SALES (est): 10.7MM **Privately Held**
SIC: 2752 2791 2759 Commercial printing, lithographic; typesetting; commercial printing

(G-20978)
SATURN SIGN
240 Industrial Ln Ste 1 (60090-6388)
PHONE 847 520-9009
Michael Williams, *Owner*
EMP: 2
SALES: 200K **Privately Held**
SIC: 3993 Signs, not made in custom sign painting shops

(G-20979)
SEGERDAHL CORP (PA)
Also Called: Sg360
1351 Wheeling Rd (60090-5997)
PHONE 847 541-1080
John Wallace, *President*
Richard D Joutras, *Chairman*
Don Eldert, *Exec VP*
Jeff Reimers, *Exec VP*
Paul White, *Exec VP*
EMP: 190 **EST:** 1956
SQ FT: 246,000
SALES (est): 290.2MM **Privately Held**
WEB: www.sg360.com
SIC: 2752 Commercial printing, offset

(G-20980)
SEGERDAHL CORP
Also Called: Sg360
385 Gilman Ave (60090-5807)
PHONE 847 850-8811
Kirby Ashby, *General Mgr*
Shai Halivni, *Exec VP*
Anthony Ferruzza, *Vice Pres*
Philomena Perez-Vaughan, *Vice Pres*
Paul White, *Accounts Exec*
EMP: 100
SALES (corp-wide): 290.2MM **Privately Held**
SIC: 2752 Commercial printing, offset
PA: The Segerdahl Corp
1351 Wheeling Rd
Wheeling IL 60090
847 541-1080

(G-20981)
SEGERDAHL GRAPHICS INC
1351 Wheeling Rd (60090-5913)
PHONE 847 541-1080
Richard D Joutras, *President*
▲ **EMP:** 350
SQ FT: 108,000
SALES (est): 114.5MM
SALES (corp-wide): 290.2MM **Privately Held**
WEB: www.sg360.com
SIC: 2752 8742 Commercial printing, offset; marketing consulting services
PA: The Segerdahl Corp
1351 Wheeling Rd
Wheeling IL 60090
847 541-1080

(G-20982)
SHAPCO INC
Also Called: R V Designer Collections
602 Wheeling Rd (60090-5707)
PHONE 847 229-1439
David Shapiro, *President*
Catherine Huart, *Vice Pres*
EMP: 8
SALES (est): 660K **Privately Held**
SIC: 3429 5023 Manufactured hardware (general); window furnishings

(G-20983)
SHERWIN-WILLIAMS COMPANY
1191 Wheeling Rd (60090-5716)
PHONE 847 541-9000
Stuart Graff, *President*
David Lee, *Branch Mgr*
Jeff Rowe, *Manager*
EMP: 99
SALES (corp-wide): 17.9B **Publicly Held**
SIC: 2851 Paints & paint additives; lacquers, varnishes, enamels & other coatings; stains: varnish, oil or wax; putty, wood fillers & sealers
PA: The Sherwin-Williams Company
101 W Prospect Ave # 1020
Cleveland OH 44115
216 566-2000

(G-20984)
SHURE INCORPORATED
Also Called: Shure Elec of Ill Div Shure
995 Chaddick Dr (60090-6449)
PHONE 847 520-4404
Anita Tucker, *Manager*
EMP: 12
SALES (corp-wide): 354MM **Privately Held**
SIC: 3651 5099 Microphones; video & audio equipment
PA: Shure Incorporated
5800 W Touhy Ave
Niles IL 60714
847 600-2000

(G-20985)
SIELC TECHNOLOGIES CORPORATION
Also Called: Allsep Techonologies
804 Seton Ct (60090-5703)
PHONE 847 229-2629
Yury Zelechonok, *President*
Nikita Kazantsev, *Software Engr*
EMP: 2
SALES: 300K **Privately Held**
SIC: 3561 Pumps & pumping equipment

(G-20986)
SIGNS OF DISTINCTION INC
149 Wheeling Rd (60090-4807)
PHONE 847 520-0787
William McDonald, *President*
EMP: 7
SQ FT: 4,000
SALES (est): 863.7K **Privately Held**
SIC: 3993 Signs & advertising specialties

(G-20987)
SLIDE PRODUCTS INC
430 Wheeling Rd (60090-4742)
P.O. Box 156 (60090-0156)
PHONE 847 541-7220
James Harms, *President*
Erica Young, *Vice Pres*
Pat McCue, *Sales Mgr*
Lavonne Bernacke, *Data Proc Staff*
EMP: 18 **EST:** 1953
SQ FT: 17,000
SALES (est): 2.3MM **Privately Held**
WEB: www.slideproducts.com
SIC: 2813 Aerosols

(G-20988)
SNAP DIAGNOSTICS LLC
5210 Capitol Dr (60090-7901)
PHONE 847 777-0000
Gil Raviv,
Gabe Raviv,
EMP: 10
SQ FT: 5,000
SALES (est): 1.9MM **Privately Held**
SIC: 3845 Electromedical equipment

(G-20989)
STELOC FASTENER CO
160 Abbott Dr (60090-5802)
PHONE 847 459-6200
Richard M Binder, *President*
Martin R Binder, *Admin Sec*
EMP: 15 **EST:** 1962
SQ FT: 12,000
SALES (est): 1.7MM **Privately Held**
SIC: 3452 Bolts, nuts, rivets & washers

(G-20990)
STERLING BRANDS LLC
555 Allendale Dr (60090-2638)
PHONE 847 229-1600
Rick Renjilian, *President*
Albert Cheris,
Paul Moniuszko,
EMP: 22
SALES (est): 4.4MM **Privately Held**
SIC: 3357 Building wire & cable, nonferrous

(G-20991)
STIGLMEIER SAUSAGE CO INC
619 Chaddick Dr (60090-6053)
PHONE 847 537-9988
Gertrude Stiglmeier, *President*
John Stiglmeier, *Vice Pres*
Anton Stiglmeier, *Shareholder*
EMP: 12
SQ FT: 13,000
SALES (est): 2MM **Privately Held**
WEB: www.stiglmeier.com
SIC: 2013 2011 5147 Sausages from purchased meat; meat packing plants; meats & meat products

GEOGRAPHIC SECTION

White Hall - Greene County (G-21017)

(G-20992)
SUBURBAN MACHINE CORPORATION
512 Northgate Pkwy (60090-2664)
PHONE 847 808-9095
Dennis Salinas, *President*
Debi Salinas, *Office Mgr*
Daniel Salinas Jr, *Officer*
Baron Buehring, *Admin Sec*
EMP: 31 **EST:** 1975
SQ FT: 20,000
SALES (est): 6.4MM **Privately Held**
SIC: 3599 3565 Machine shop, jobbing & repair; packaging machinery

(G-20993)
SUBURBAN SURGICAL CO
275 12th St Ste A (60090-2798)
PHONE 847 537-9320
James M Pinkerman, *President*
Todd Pinkerman, *Principal*
Steve Dephillips, *Sales Staff*
Peter Gootrad, *Sales Executive*
Karen Pinkerman, *Admin Sec*
▼ **EMP:** 200 **EST:** 1943
SQ FT: 200,000
SALES (est): 47.2MM **Privately Held**
WEB: www.suburbansurgical.com
SIC: 3821 3914 Worktables, laboratory; trays, stainless steel

(G-20994)
SWAN ANALYTICAL USA INC
225 Larkin Dr Ste 4 (60090-7209)
PHONE 847 229-1290
Jeff Parke, *President*
Sam Bruketta, *Sales Staff*
▲ **EMP:** 12
SQ FT: 6,000
SALES: 3MM
SALES (corp-wide): 13.7MM **Privately Held**
SIC: 3826 Water testing apparatus
PA: Swan Analytische Instrumente Ag
Studbachstrasse 13
Hinwil ZH 8340
449 436-300

(G-20995)
SWISS PRECISION MACHINING INC
Also Called: S P M
634 Glenn Ave (60090-6018)
PHONE 847 647-7111
Michael W Haupers, *President*
Kathy H Haupers, *Corp Secy*
Joe Cece, *Opers Staff*
Bob Hahn, *Purch Agent*
Jennifer Haupers, *QC Mgr*
▲ **EMP:** 90
SQ FT: 35,000
SALES (est): 20.9MM **Privately Held**
SIC: 3599 Machine shop, jobbing & repair

(G-20996)
TAAP CORP
300 Holbrook Dr (60090-5812)
PHONE 224 676-0653
Seymour Ivice, *CEO*
Gary Ivice, *President*
Michael Seldin, *Purch Mgr*
Abe Freeman, *Shareholder*
Jerome Ivice, *Shareholder*
▲ **EMP:** 15
SQ FT: 11,200
SALES (est): 3.1MM **Privately Held**
SIC: 3714 Windshield wiper systems, motor vehicle

(G-20997)
TAUBENSEE STEEL & WIRE COMPANY (PA)
600 Diens Dr (60090-2686)
PHONE 847 459-5100
Casey Bouton, *President*
Vern Abel, *President*
Kent T Taubensee, *President*
Bruce Taubensee, *Senior VP*
Jill Taubensee Havey, *Vice Pres*
▲ **EMP:** 110 **EST:** 1946
SQ FT: 16,000
SALES (est): 60MM **Privately Held**
WEB: www.taubensee.com
SIC: 3315 3316 Wire, steel: insulated or armored; bars, steel, cold finished, from purchased hot-rolled

(G-20998)
TECHNATOOL INC
2222 Foster Ave (60090-6509)
P.O. Box 6179, Vernon Hills (60061-6179)
PHONE 847 398-0355
Frank Hauptmann, *President*
EMP: 8
SQ FT: 1,500
SALES: 1MM **Privately Held**
SIC: 3089 Injection molding of plastics

(G-20999)
TEX TREND INC
767 Kristy Ln (60090-5595)
PHONE 847 215-6796
Frank Dime, *Vice Pres*
Richard A Rosen, *Admin Sec*
EMP: 35
SQ FT: 38,000
SALES (est): 3.5MM **Privately Held**
SIC: 3089 2399 3296 Plastic processing; hand woven & crocheted products; mineral wool

(G-21000)
THERM-O-WEB INC
770 Glenn Ave (60090-6020)
PHONE 847 520-5200
Julia Sandvoss, *Director*
Kenneth B Glazer, *Admin Sec*
▲ **EMP:** 35
SQ FT: 35,000
SALES (est): 9MM **Privately Held**
SIC: 2891 Adhesives & sealants

(G-21001)
TRES JOLI DESIGNS LTD
634 Wheeling Rd (60090-5707)
PHONE 847 520-3903
Mary Conlon, *President*
EMP: 8
SALES (est): 885.9K **Privately Held**
SIC: 2391 5714 Curtains & draperies; draperies

(G-21002)
TRU-CUT TOOL & SUPPLY CO
1480 S Wolf Rd (60090-6514)
PHONE 708 396-1122
Greg Muntean, *President*
EMP: 18
SQ FT: 15,000
SALES (est): 1.3MM **Privately Held**
SIC: 3425 5084 Saw blades for hand or power saws; industrial machinery & equipment

(G-21003)
US TSUBAKI HOLDINGS INC (HQ)
Also Called: U.S.T.H.
301 E Marquardt Dr (60090-6497)
PHONE 847 459-9500
Tetsuya Yamamoto, *President*
Dan Butterfield, *President*
Craig Beasley, *General Mgr*
Joe Sanfillippo, *Business Mgr*
Thomas Barton, *Senior VP*
▲ **EMP:** 150
SQ FT: 115,000
SALES (est): 299.4MM **Privately Held**
SIC: 5085 3568 Power transmission equipment & apparatus; drives, chains & sprockets; sprockets (power transmission equipment)

(G-21004)
US TSUBAKI POWER TRANSM LLC (DH)
301 E Marquardt Dr (60090-6497)
PHONE 847 459-9500
Ted Palubinski, *Mfg Spvr*
Steven Turner, *QC Mgr*
Katie Blonn, *Accountant*
Erica Small, *Human Resources*
Camille Angluben, *Marketing Staff*
EMP: 209
SALES (est): 127MM **Privately Held**
SIC: 3568 5085 5063 3714 Drives, chains & sprockets; chain, power transmission; power transmission equipment & apparatus; chains, power transmission; power transmission equipment, electric; motor vehicle parts & accessories; iron & steel forgings; rolling mill rolls, cast steel
HQ: U.S. Tsubaki Holdings, Inc.
301 E Marquardt Dr
Wheeling IL 60090
847 459-9500

(G-21005)
USMEDEXPORT COMPANY
772 River Walk Dr (60090-6391)
PHONE 847 749-5520
Victor Beloff, *President*
EMP: 3
SALES (est): 140.6K **Privately Held**
SIC: 7372 Prepackaged software

(G-21006)
V & L ENTERPRISES INC
422 Mercantile Ct (60090-4738)
PHONE 847 541-1760
John Rozylowicz, *President*
Frank Bellgrav, *Treasurer*
EMP: 10 **EST:** 1951
SQ FT: 6,000
SALES (est): 1.5MM **Privately Held**
SIC: 3599 Machine shop, jobbing & repair

(G-21007)
V AND L RED DEVIL MFG CO
422 Mercantile Ct (60090-4738)
PHONE 847 215-1377
Steve Dzieglewicz, *President*
Ken Bruckner, *VP Mfg*
EMP: 20 **EST:** 1945
SQ FT: 15,000
SALES (est): 1.7MM **Privately Held**
WEB: www.vandl-reddevil.com
SIC: 3451 3452 3356 Screw machine products; bolts, nuts, rivets & washers; nonferrous rolling & drawing

(G-21008)
VAN METER GRAPHX INC
Also Called: Van Meter Mail
970 Seton Ct (60090-5705)
PHONE 847 465-0600
Bruce Van Meter, *President*
EMP: 4
SQ FT: 3,500
SALES (est): 483.5K **Privately Held**
SIC: 2741 7336 2752 7331 Catalogs: publishing only, not printed on site; graphic arts & related design; commercial printing, offset; mailing service

(G-21009)
VIANT WHEELING INC
140 E Hintz Rd (60090-6044)
PHONE 847 520-1553
EMP: 4
SALES (est): 265.5K
SALES (corp-wide): 368.7MM **Privately Held**
SIC: 3841 Surgical instruments & apparatus
PA: Viant Medical Holdings, Inc.
2 Hampshire St
Foxborough MA 02035
480 553-6400

(G-21010)
VICMA TOOL CO
505 Harvester Ct Ste J (60090-4754)
PHONE 847 541-0177
David Choma, *Owner*
EMP: 3
SQ FT: 3,600
SALES (est): 220K **Privately Held**
SIC: 3544 Industrial molds

(G-21011)
WALTZ BROTHERS INC
10 W Waltz Dr (60090-6052)
PHONE 847 520-1122
Larry Waltz, *President*
Larry D Waltz Jr, *Vice Pres*
Larry J Waltz, *Vice Pres*
▲ **EMP:** 47
SQ FT: 50,000
SALES (est): 10.6MM **Privately Held**
WEB: www.waltzbros.com
SIC: 3812 3714 Acceleration indicators & systems components, aerospace; motor vehicle body components & frame

(G-21012)
WESTERN INDUSTRIES INC (HQ)
1111 Wheeling Rd (60090-5763)
PHONE 920 261-0660
Tom Hall, *President*
Robert A Schneider, *Vice Pres*
Barry Trimble, *Engineer*
Laurie Mariano, *Accountant*
Betty Reyna, *Director*
▲ **EMP:** 200 **EST:** 1944
SALES (est): 275.6MM **Privately Held**
WEB: www.3dcartstores.com
SIC: 3443 3469 3089 3444 Fuel tanks (oil, gas, etc.): metal plate; stamping metal for the trade; injection molded finished plastic products; injection molding of plastics; sheet metalwork; sheet metalwork; automatic regulating & control valves

(G-21013)
WIELAND HOLDINGS INC (DH)
567 Northgate Pkwy (60090-2663)
PHONE 847 537-3990
Werner T Traa, *President*
Sebastian Koehler, *Admin Sec*
EMP: 1900
SALES (corp-wide): 4.8MM **Privately Held**
SIC: 6719 3341 3469 3351 Investment holding companies, except banks; copper smelting & refining (secondary); metal stampings; brass rolling & drawing
HQ: Wieland-Werke Ag
Graf-Arco-Str. 36
Ulm 89079
731 944-0

(G-21014)
WINDY CITY DISTILLING INC
Also Called: Oppidan Spirits
140 Shepard Ave Ste B (60090-6072)
PHONE 312 788-7503
Jeffrey Walsh, *President*
EMP: 6 **EST:** 2012
SALES (est): 598.6K **Privately Held**
SIC: 2085 Gin (alcoholic beverage); rye whiskey

(G-21015)
WOODBRIDGE INC
Also Called: Rv Designer Collection
602 Wheeling Rd (60090-5707)
PHONE 847 229-1741
David Shapiro, *President*
Barry Levy, *Principal*
Catherine Huart, *Vice Pres*
▲ **EMP:** 10
SQ FT: 5,000
SALES (est): 990K **Privately Held**
SIC: 2396 3714 3429 2591 Automotive & apparel trimmings; motor vehicle parts & accessories; manufactured hardware (general); drapery hardware & blinds & shades

(G-21016)
ZIC INCORPORATED (PA)
1535 Abbott Dr (60090-5821)
PHONE 847 680-8833
Richard Zic, *President*
EMP: 2
SALES (est): 419.6K **Privately Held**
SIC: 3679 3566 Electronic circuits; speed changers, drives & gears

---

White Hall
Greene County

(G-21017)
BALLARD BROS INC
Also Called: Ballard Bros Con Pdts & Excav
420 E Lincoln St (62092-1344)
P.O. Box 341 (62092-0341)
PHONE 217 374-2137
James H Ballard, *President*

Dan Ballard, *Vice Pres*
EMP: 10
SQ FT: 2,400
SALES: 689.3K **Privately Held**
SIC: 1794 3273 1611 Excavation & grading, building construction; ready-mixed concrete; concrete construction: roads, highways, sidewalks, etc.

(G-21018)
DRAKE ENVELOPE PRINTING CO
207 White St (62092-1263)
P.O. Box 219 (62092-0219)
PHONE...................................217 374-2772
James Evans, *President*
Beverly Evans, *Corp Secy*
EMP: 9
SQ FT: 4,000
SALES (est): 1.6MM **Privately Held**
SIC: 2759 2752 Commercial printing; commercial printing, lithographic

(G-21019)
JAGJITA CORP
654 N Main St (62092-1153)
PHONE...................................217 374-6016
Archita Patel, *Vice Pres*
EMP: 3
SALES (est): 263.3K **Privately Held**
SIC: 2869 Fuels

Whittington
Franklin County

(G-21020)
KNIFFEN BROTHERS SAWMILL
16794 Buxton Rd (62897-1102)
PHONE...................................618 629-2437
Terald Kniffen, *Owner*
EMP: 4
SALES: 200K **Privately Held**
SIC: 2421 Sawmills & planing mills, general

(G-21021)
PHEASANT HOLLOW WINERY INC
14931 State Highway 37 (62897-1208)
PHONE...................................618 629-2302
Bruce Morgenstern, *President*
EMP: 8
SALES (est): 776.4K **Privately Held**
SIC: 2084 Wines

Williamsville
Sangamon County

(G-21022)
ARCH COAL INC
5945 Lester Rd (62693-9205)
PHONE...................................217 566-3000
Roger Dennison, *President*
Terry Evoy, *Maintence Staff*
EMP: 11
SALES (corp-wide): 2.2B **Publicly Held**
SIC: 1221 Bituminous coal & lignite-surface mining
PA: Arch Resources, Inc.
1 Cityplace Dr Ste 300
Saint Louis MO 63141
314 994-2700

(G-21023)
ICG ILLINOIS LLC (DH)
Also Called: Aci Illinois, LLC
5945 Lester Rd (62693-9205)
PHONE...................................217 566-3000
Paul Lang, *Principal*
EMP: 10
SALES (est): 40.3MM
SALES (corp-wide): 2.2B **Publicly Held**
SIC: 1241 Coal mining services

Willow Hill
Jasper County

(G-21024)
KELLER GRAIN & LIVESTOCK INC
7031 N 1900th St (62480-2307)
PHONE...................................618 455-3634
Robert Keller, *President*
EMP: 4
SALES: 1.2MM **Privately Held**
SIC: 3523 Driers (farm): grain, hay & seed

Willow Springs
Cook County

(G-21025)
DATA COM PLD INC
153 Santa Fe Ln (60480-1624)
PHONE...................................708 267-5657
James McLamore, *President*
EMP: 2
SALES (est): 500K **Privately Held**
SIC: 2759 Business forms: printing

(G-21026)
ILLINOIS PALLETS INC
8075 Tec Air Ave (60480-1525)
PHONE...................................773 640-9228
Ranulfo Cardina, *President*
Silvia Salazar, *Administration*
EMP: 8
SALES (est): 926K **Privately Held**
SIC: 2448 Pallets, wood

(G-21027)
PRIME DEVICES CORPORATION
11450 German Church Rd (60480-1069)
P.O. Box 152, Morton Grove (60053-0152)
PHONE...................................847 729-2550
Charles Cohon, *President*
Rob Shirley, *Vice Pres*
Robert Shirley, *Manager*
EMP: 12
SALES (est): 1.6MM **Privately Held**
SIC: 3699 5084 Electrical equipment & supplies; industrial machinery & equipment

Willowbrook
Dupage County

(G-21028)
A-FLEX LABEL LLC
Also Called: Labeltape Group
655 Executive Dr (60527-5603)
PHONE...................................630 325-7265
Thomas Carroll,
EMP: 2 **EST:** 2012
SALES (est): 519.6K
SALES (corp-wide): 1.2MM **Privately Held**
SIC: 2759 Labels & seals: printing
PA: The Labeltape Group Inc
5100 Beltway Dr Se
Caledonia MI 49316
616 698-1830

(G-21029)
APPLIED TECH PUBLICATIONS INC
Also Called: Maintenance Tech Training
535 Plainfield Rd Ste A (60527-7608)
PHONE...................................847 382-8100
Arthur L Rice, *CEO*
Philip Saran, *Vice Pres*
Gregory Pietras, *Production*
Stephen Donohue, *Manager*
EMP: 15
SQ FT: 4,553
SALES (est): 3.3MM **Privately Held**
SIC: 2721 Magazines: publishing only, not printed on site

(G-21030)
B & H BIOTECHNOLOGIES LLC
6520 Chaucer Rd (60527-5405)
PHONE...................................630 915-3227
Jane Wang, *Owner*
EMP: 5
SALES (est): 393.2K **Privately Held**
SIC: 2834 Pharmaceutical preparations

(G-21031)
BEZARR
10s515 Ivy Ln (60527-7302)
PHONE...................................651 200-5641
Wayne Reed, *Ch of Bd*
EMP: 5
SALES (est): 51.9K **Privately Held**
SIC: 5735 7311 8999 5199 Records, audio discs & tapes; advertising agencies; advertising copy writing; advertising specialties; advertising display products; financial services

(G-21032)
BORSE INDUSTRIES INC
7409 S Quincy St (60527-5521)
PHONE...................................630 325-1210
Brian Beth, *Principal*
EMP: 8 **EST:** 2013
SALES (est): 803.2K **Privately Held**
SIC: 3999 Manufacturing industries

(G-21033)
CABINETRY SOLUTIONS IMPRVS LLC (PA)
6944 Kingery Hwy (60527-2201)
PHONE...................................630 333-9195
Raymond O'Gorman Jr,
Francis T Ciscato,
EMP: 3
SQ FT: 2,200
SALES: 1.4MM **Privately Held**
WEB: www.cabinetrysi.com
SIC: 2434 Wood kitchen cabinets

(G-21034)
CAPERS NORTH AMERICA LLC
632 Executive Dr (60527-5610)
PHONE...................................708 995-7500
Reed Konnerth, *CEO*
Vincent Goffette, *Director*
EMP: 10
SALES (est): 295.2K **Privately Held**
SIC: 7372 Prepackaged software

(G-21035)
CHICAGO DATA SOLUTIONS INC
146 Somerset Rd (60527-5429)
PHONE...................................847 370-4609
Xiaohua Ning, *Chief Engr*
EMP: 3 **EST:** 2013
SALES (est): 82.4K **Privately Held**
SIC: 7372 7371 Application computer software; business oriented computer software; educational computer software; computer software development

(G-21036)
CLOROX COMPANY
7201 S Adams St (60527-5570)
PHONE...................................510 271-7000
Bob Dorsey, *Systems Staff*
EMP: 36
SALES (corp-wide): 6.2B **Publicly Held**
SIC: 2842 3081 Laundry cleaning preparations; plastic film & sheet
PA: The Clorox Company
1221 Broadway Ste 1300
Oakland CA 94612
510 271-7000

(G-21037)
COMVIGO INC
410 Woodgate Ct (60527-5444)
PHONE...................................312 933-3385
James P Tanner, *President*
EMP: 1
SALES: 200K **Privately Held**
SIC: 7379 7372 Computer related consulting services; application computer software

(G-21038)
CORRECTIONAL TECHNOLOGIES INC
Also Called: Cortech USA
7530 Plaza Ct (60527-5611)
PHONE...................................630 455-0811
Joseph R Claffy, *President*
Patricia Miller, *CFO*
David Jennings, *Director*
EMP: 11
SQ FT: 10,000
SALES: 6.1MM **Privately Held**
SIC: 2531 Public building & related furniture

(G-21039)
CZECH AMERICAN TV HERALD
124 Sunset Ridge Rd (60527-8401)
P.O. Box 100001, Cape Coral FL (33910-0001)
PHONE...................................708 813-0028
Jan Honner, *Principal*
EMP: 3
SALES (est): 112.6K **Privately Held**
WEB: www.catvusa.com
SIC: 2711 Newspapers, publishing & printing

(G-21040)
D & D BUSINESS INC
Also Called: Ddi Printing
10s428 Carrington Cir (60527-6945)
PHONE...................................630 935-3522
Darmi Parikh, *President*
EMP: 5
SQ FT: 3,000
SALES: 490K **Privately Held**
SIC: 2752 Commercial printing, offset

(G-21041)
EJL CUSTOM GOLF CLUBS INC (PA)
825 75th St Ste F (60527-8428)
PHONE...................................630 654-8887
Everett J Lockenvitz, *President*
Josephine Lockenvitz, *Vice Pres*
EMP: 5
SALES: 950K **Privately Held**
SIC: 3949 5941 Golf equipment; shafts, golf club; golf goods & equipment

(G-21042)
EMPIRE CORP
6262 Kingery Hwy Ste 307 (60527-2987)
PHONE...................................630 887-8228
Tim Tsui, *President*
Helen Tsui, *Admin Sec*
EMP: 3
SQ FT: 700
SALES (est): 328.4K **Privately Held**
SIC: 3911 Jewelry, precious metal

(G-21043)
FLEETPRIDE INC
7630 S Madison St (60527-7545)
PHONE...................................630 455-6881
David Blitz, *President*
EMP: 10 **Privately Held**
SIC: 7549 7694 Automotive maintenance services; motor repair services
HQ: Fleetpride, Inc.
600 Las Colinas Blvd E # 400
Irving TX 75039
469 249-7500

(G-21044)
GENESIS LTG MANAGEMET SVCS
7320 S Mddson Ave Unit 10 (60527)
PHONE...................................630 986-3900
Chris Rimbos, *President*
Tim Rimbos, *Manager*
EMP: 10
SALES (est): 750K **Privately Held**
SIC: 3648 Lighting equipment

(G-21045)
GLOBAL MANUFACTURING
324 Central Ave (60527-6156)
PHONE...................................630 908-7633
Eugene Miron, *Owner*
Dorina Pop, *Info Tech Mgr*
EMP: 3
SALES: 500K **Privately Held**
SIC: 3699 Electrical equipment & supplies

GEOGRAPHIC SECTION

(G-21046)
HEAT SYSTEMS INSTRS SVC CO LLC
10s115 Clarendon Hills Rd (60527-6077)
PHONE..................................630 404-6884
Diane Galiniak,
EMP: 2
SALES (est): 600K **Privately Held**
SIC: 3567 7389 Industrial furnaces & ovens;

(G-21047)
ILF TECHNOLOGIES LLC
7001 S Adams St (60527-7592)
PHONE..................................630 789-9770
EMP: 6
SALES (est): 583.2K **Privately Held**
SIC: 2843 Manufacture Inline Finishing

(G-21048)
LA FORCE INC
7501 S Quincy St Ste 180 (60527-8508)
PHONE..................................630 325-1950
Daryl Linnert, *Branch Mgr*
EMP: 7
SALES (corp-wide): 156.3MM **Privately Held**
SIC: 5031 5072 3442 Doors; builders' hardware; window & door frames
PA: La Force, Inc.
1060 W Mason St
Green Bay WI 54303
920 497-7100

(G-21049)
MICHAEL WILTON CSTM HOMES INC
Also Called: All Suburban Generator
6458 Cambridge Rd (60527-5402)
PHONE..................................630 508-1200
Michael Wilton, *President*
EMP: 2
SALES (est): 202.7K **Privately Held**
SIC: 3511 Turbo-generators

(G-21050)
MIDTRONICS INC (PA)
7000 Monroe St (60527-5655)
PHONE..................................630 323-2800
Stephen J McShane, *President*
Mayur Patel, *Engineer*
▲ EMP: 100
SQ FT: 60,000
SALES (est): 20.2MM **Privately Held**
SIC: 7622 3825 3694 Radio repair shop; battery testers, electrical; meters: electric, pocket, portable, panelboard, etc.; automotive electrical equipment

(G-21051)
MIDWEST TUNGSTEN SERVICE INC
540 Executive Dr (60527-8449)
PHONE..................................630 325-1001
Joel R Stava, *President*
Blake Baron, *Program Mgr*
Kevin M Anetsberger, *Admin Sec*
▲ EMP: 30
SALES (est): 6.8MM **Privately Held**
SIC: 3496 Miscellaneous fabricated wire products

(G-21052)
MIWON NA
669 Executive Dr (60527-5603)
PHONE..................................630 568-5850
EMP: 3
SALES (est): 158.8K **Privately Held**
SIC: 2869 Industrial organic chemicals

(G-21053)
NATIONAL TEMP-TROL PRODUCTS
Also Called: National Window Shade Co
667 Executive Dr (60527-5603)
PHONE..................................630 920-1919
Berislav Dujlovich, *President*
Lisa Dujlovich, *Vice Pres*
EMP: 4 EST: 1973
SALES (est): 390K **Privately Held**
SIC: 2591 Window shades

(G-21054)
NOGI BRANDS LLC
6448 Cambridge Rd (60527-5402)
PHONE..................................312 371-7974
Paul Rashid, *Principal*
EMP: 3
SALES (est): 173.1K **Privately Held**
SIC: 2032 Canned specialties

(G-21055)
NYB PROCESS FANS INC (HQ)
Also Called: Mountain Highway Holdings
7660 S Quincy St (60527-5530)
PHONE..................................630 794-5700
Joseph A Centers, *President*
Adrianne Gabel, *Admin Sec*
EMP: 3
SQ FT: 15,000
SALES (est): 6.8MM
SALES (corp-wide): 117.7MM **Privately Held**
SIC: 3564 Ventilating fans: industrial or commercial; blowing fans: industrial or commercial
PA: The New York Blower Company
7660 S Quincy St
Willowbrook IL 60527
630 794-5700

(G-21056)
OEC GRAPHICS-CHICAGO LLC
7630 S Quincy St (60527-5526)
PHONE..................................630 455-6700
Brian Sokolowski, *Sales Staff*
Mark Jensen,
▲ EMP: 40
SQ FT: 18,000
SALES (est): 7.3MM
SALES (corp-wide): 68.5MM **Privately Held**
WEB: www.oecgraphics.com
SIC: 3555 2796 2759 Printing plates; platemaking services; commercial printing
PA: O E C Graphics, Inc.
555 W Waukau Ave
Oshkosh WI 54902
920 235-7770

(G-21057)
PREMIER TRAVEL MEDIA
621 Plainfield Rd Ste 406 (60527-5391)
PHONE..................................630 794-0696
Jeff Gayduk, *President*
Eric Moore, *Business Mgr*
Linda Ragusin, *Business Mgr*
Annie Gavin, *Sales Staff*
Harry Peck, *Marketing Staff*
EMP: 4
SALES (est): 333.3K **Privately Held**
SIC: 2741 Miscellaneous publishing

(G-21058)
REACT COMPUTER SERVICES INC
7654 Plaza Ct (60527-5607)
PHONE..................................630 323-6200
EMP: 60
SALES (est): 6.5MM **Privately Held**
SIC: 7622 7378 7371 Prepackaged software; computer maintenance & repair; custom computer programming services

(G-21059)
SCROLLEX CORPORATION
7888 S Quincy St (60527-5534)
PHONE..................................630 887-8817
EMP: 5
SQ FT: 6,000
SALES: 156.9K **Privately Held**
SIC: 3563 Mfg Air/Gas Compressors

(G-21060)
SHADOWTECH LABS INC
760 N Frontage Rd Ste 102 (60527-5656)
PHONE..................................630 413-4478
Michael Collins, *President*
Brian King, *Vice Pres*
David Nahlik, *Vice Pres*
Casey Walsh, *Vice Pres*
EMP: 4
SALES (est): 794K **Privately Held**
SIC: 3728 Military aircraft equipment & armament

(G-21061)
TPC METALS LLC (PA)
7000 S Adams St (60527-7564)
PHONE..................................330 479-9510
Marty Mezydlo, *General Mgr*
Mike Crisan, *Vice Pres*
Chris Culberson, *Manager*
EMP: 7
SALES (est): 2.5MM **Privately Held**
SIC: 3339 5094 Precious metals; precious stones & metals

(G-21062)
TPG PLASTICS LLC
7409 S Quincy St (60527-5521)
PHONE..................................630 828-2800
Pavel Smyshlyaev, *CFO*
Saquib Toor,
EMP: 4
SALES (est): 107.6K **Privately Held**
SIC: 3089 Blow molded finished plastic products

(G-21063)
TRANE US INC
Also Called: Chicago/West Michigan
7100 S Madison St (60527-5505)
PHONE..................................630 734-3200
Larry Devito, *Foreman/Supr*
Austin Fiegel, *Sales Engr*
Dick Kasperek, *Manager*
EMP: 195 **Privately Held**
SIC: 3585 Refrigeration & heating equipment
HQ: Trane U.S. Inc.
3600 Pammel Creek Rd
La Crosse WI 54601
608 787-2000

(G-21064)
TRIUMPH GROUP INC
621 Plainfield Rd Ste 309 (60527-8457)
PHONE..................................312 498-2516
Tasi Mitev, *Branch Mgr*
EMP: 4 **Publicly Held**
SIC: 3728 Aircraft body & wing assemblies & parts
PA: Triumph Group, Inc.
899 Cassatt Rd Ste 210
Berwyn PA 19312

(G-21065)
TRU FRAGRANCE & BEAUTY LLC
7725 S Quincy St (60527-5531)
PHONE..................................630 563-4110
Monte Henige, *CEO*
Melody Dworin, *President*
Reagan Heidelberg, *Vice Pres*
Ramiro Lopez, *Warehouse Mgr*
Stephanie Svaldi, *Production*
▲ EMP: 36 EST: 1969
SQ FT: 31,000
SALES (est): 9.8MM **Privately Held**
SIC: 2844 Perfumes & colognes

(G-21066)
UBIPASS INC
5931 Stewart Dr Apt 1021 (60527-3158)
PHONE..................................312 626-4624
Nasser Ghazi, *President*
Saarah Ghazi, *Principal*
Zoya Ghazi, *Principal*
EMP: 3 EST: 2015
SALES (est): 127.8K **Privately Held**
SIC: 7372 Application computer software

(G-21067)
WEDCO MOLDED PRODUCTS
7409 S Quincy St (60527-5521)
PHONE..................................630 455-6711
Brian Beth, *Principal*
EMP: 5
SALES (est): 305.9K **Privately Held**
SIC: 3089 Injection molded finished plastic products

Wilmette
Cook County

(G-21068)
AL BAR LABORATORIES INC
Also Called: Al Bar-Wilmette Platers
127 Green Bay Rd (60091-3398)
PHONE..................................847 251-1218
Robert M Mintz, *President*
Greg Bettenhausen, *Chief Mktg Ofcr*
EMP: 10 EST: 1937
SQ FT: 3,000
SALES (est): 1.6MM **Privately Held**
WEB: www.albarwilmette.com
SIC: 3471 5719 5944 Electroplating of metals or formed products; housewares; silverware

(G-21069)
BIERDEMAN BOX LLC
3445 Riverside Dr (60091-1061)
PHONE..................................847 256-0302
Herb Goldstein, *President*
Herbert Goldstein, *Vice Pres*
Sarell Albert, *Treasurer*
EMP: 45 EST: 1932
SQ FT: 58,000
SALES (est): 4.4MM **Privately Held**
SIC: 2652 Setup paperboard boxes

(G-21070)
BRANCH LINES LTD
1200 N Branch Rd (60091-1035)
PHONE..................................847 256-4294
EMP: 3
SALES (est): 160.9K **Privately Held**
SIC: 3944 Mfg Games/Toys

(G-21071)
BRANDT INTERIORS
803 Ridge Rd (60091-2445)
PHONE..................................847 251-3543
Linda Runnfeldt, *Partner*
Frank Runnfeldt, *Partner*
EMP: 3 EST: 1936
SQ FT: 1,000
SALES (est): 180K **Privately Held**
SIC: 7641 3842 Reupholstery; drapes, surgical (cotton)

(G-21072)
BREAKFAST FUEL LLC
1222 Washington Ct (60091-2615)
PHONE..................................847 251-3835
Genevieve Lennon, *Mng Member*
EMP: 6
SALES (est): 516.1K **Privately Held**
WEB: www.fuelwilmette.com
SIC: 2869 Fuels

(G-21073)
CHALLINOR WOOD PRODUCTS INC
1213 Wilmette Ave Ste 208 (60091-2566)
PHONE..................................847 256-8828
Mark A Challinor, *President*
Alice Challinor, *Treasurer*
▲ EMP: 3
SQ FT: 600
SALES (est): 557.5K **Privately Held**
SIC: 2435 7389 Hardwood veneer & plywood; log & lumber broker

(G-21074)
CONGRESS DRIVE INC
1189 Wilmette Ave (60091-2719)
PHONE..................................972 875-6060
Jerry Wheaton, *Principal*
Thomas Price, *Principal*
EMP: 42
SALES (est): 7.9MM **Privately Held**
SIC: 3364 3429 Zinc & zinc-base alloy die-castings; manufactured hardware (general)

(G-21075)
FLAT-TECH INC
3330 Old Glenview Rd # 14 (60091-2963)
PHONE..................................847 364-4333
Barry Mancell, *President*
EMP: 3
SQ FT: 2,650

Wilmette - Cook County (G-21076)

(G-21076)
HADLEY CAPITAL FUND II LP (PA)
1200 Central Ave Ste 300 (60091-2654)
PHONE..................847 906-5300
Scott Dickes, *Partner*
Clay Brock, *Partner*
Paul Wormley, *Partner*
EMP: 5
SALES: 62.8K **Privately Held**
SIC: **3448** 6799 Docks: prefabricated metal; investors

(G-21077)
HANIGS FOOTWEAR INC
1515 Sheridan Rd Ste 2 (60091-1825)
PHONE..................773 248-1977
EMP: 15
SALES (est): 136.7K **Privately Held**
SIC: **5661** 3131 Shoe stores; boot & shoe accessories

(G-21078)
HOMERS ICE CREAM INC
Also Called: Homers Rest & Ice Cream Parlor
1237 Green Bay Rd (60091-1699)
PHONE..................847 251-0477
Stephen G Poulos, *President*
Nick Poulos, *General Mgr*
John Poulos, *Corp Secy*
Dean Poulos, *Vice Pres*
EMP: 28 **EST**: 1925
SQ FT: 7,500
SALES (est): 3.7MM **Privately Held**
WEB: www.homersicecream.com
SIC: **2024** 5812 Ice cream, bulk; eating places

(G-21079)
INTERNATIONAL SOURCE SOLUTIONS
3229 Wilmette Ave (60091-2956)
PHONE..................847 251-8265
Yvette Stinehart, *Owner*
EMP: 2
SALES (est): 221.3K **Privately Held**
SIC: **3444** Sheet metal specialties, not stamped

(G-21080)
JAPAN ELECTRONIC MANUFACTURERS
Also Called: Jema
1000 Skokie Blvd Ste 120 (60091-1198)
PHONE..................972 735-0463
William Taki Jr, *Ch of Bd*
Peter Oyama, *President*
Judith Taki, *Corp Secy*
Jennifer Davis, *Representative*
▲ EMP: 10
SQ FT: 2,000
SALES (est): 1.3MM **Privately Held**
WEB: www.jema.com
SIC: **5065** 3651 Electronic parts; household audio & video equipment

(G-21081)
KENILWORTH PRESS INCORPORATED
1223 Green Bay Rd (60091-1643)
PHONE..................847 256-5210
Fax: 847 256-5279
EMP: 5
SQ FT: 3,000
SALES: 300K **Privately Held**
SIC: **2752** 2791 Lithographic Commercial Printing Typesetting Services

(G-21082)
KERRIGAN CORPORATION
811 Ridge Rd (60091-2445)
P.O. Box 314 (60091-0314)
PHONE..................847 251-8994
Jerome Kerrigan, *President*
Mike Kerrigan, *Vice Pres*
Alberto Flores, *Foreman/Supr*
Pat Kerrigen, *Admin Sec*
EMP: 4
SALES: 500K **Privately Held**
SIC: **3543** Industrial patterns

(G-21083)
KILLEEN CONFECTIONERY LLC (PA)
600 20th St (60091-2391)
PHONE..................312 804-0009
Liam Killeen,
EMP: 1
SALES (est): 15MM **Privately Held**
SIC: **2064** Candy & other confectionery products

(G-21084)
LIGHT WAVES LLC
1000 Skokie Blvd (60091-1161)
PHONE..................847 251-1622
Robert Russell,
EMP: 11
SQ FT: 2,800
SALES (est): 555.3K **Privately Held**
SIC: **3993** 7389 Signs & advertising specialties; engraving service

(G-21085)
LITURGICAL CONFERENCE
1125 Wilmette Ave (60091-2603)
P.O. Box 31, Evanston (60204-0031)
PHONE..................847 866-3875
E Byron Anderson, *President*
Marjorie Eckhardt, *President*
David Heetland, *Vice Pres*
Luis Rivera, *Med Doctor*
Barbara Adams, *Director*
EMP: 7 **EST**: 1940
SALES (est): 586.9K **Privately Held**
WEB: www.swlc.org
SIC: **2721** Periodicals

(G-21086)
LORTON GROUP LLC
940 Seneca Rd (60091-1225)
PHONE..................844 352-5089
Stephen Hatton,
Marc Hatton,
EMP: 5
SALES: 500K **Privately Held**
SIC: **2299** Textile goods

(G-21087)
MID CENTRAL PRINTING & MAILING
1211 Wilmette Ave (60091-2557)
PHONE..................847 251-4040
John Korzak Jr, *President*
Carrie Korzak, *Vice Pres*
Gretchen Korzak, *Vice Pres*
EMP: 11 **EST**: 1953
SQ FT: 4,500
SALES (est): 740K **Privately Held**
WEB: www.mcpm.com
SIC: **7331** 2752 2789 Mailing service; commercial printing, offset; bookbinding & related work

(G-21088)
MODULAR WOOD SYSTEMS INC
736 12th St Ste C (60091-2629)
PHONE..................847 251-6401
Robert Sobel, *President*
EMP: 2
SALES (est): 251.2K **Privately Held**
SIC: **3652** 2514 Pre-recorded records & tapes; cabinets, radio & television: metal

(G-21089)
MONOPAR THERAPEUTICS INC (PA)
1000 Skokie Blvd Ste 350 (60091-1146)
PHONE..................847 388-0349
Chandler D Robinson, *CEO*
Christopher M Starr, *Ch of Bd*
Andrew P Mazar, *Exec VP*
Kim R Tsuchimoto, *CFO*
Patrice Rioux, *Chief Mktg Ofcr*
EMP: 5
SQ FT: 1,202
SALES (est): 520.9K **Publicly Held**
SIC: **2834** Pharmaceutical preparations

(G-21090)
ORREN PICKELL BUILDERS INC
Also Called: Cabinetwerks
444 Skokie Blvd Ste 200 (60091-3074)
PHONE..................847 572-5200
Orren Pickell, *Owner*
Vince Janowski, *Superintendent*
EMP: 16
SALES (est): 1.7MM
SALES (corp-wide): 0 **Privately Held**
SIC: **2499** 5031 1751 Decorative wood & woodwork; kitchen cabinets; cabinet & finish carpentry
PA: Orren Pickell Builders, Incorporated
550 W Frontage Rd # 3800
Northfield IL 60093
847 572-5200

(G-21091)
REBEL BRANDS LLC
600 20th St (60091-2391)
PHONE..................312 804-0009
William Killeen, *CEO*
EMP: 1
SALES: 15MM **Privately Held**
SIC: **2064** 7389 Candy & other confectionery products
PA: Killeen Confectionery, Llc
600 20th St
Wilmette IL 60091
312 804-0009

(G-21092)
RESOLUTION SYSTEMS INC
1189 Wilmette Ave (60091-2719)
PHONE..................616 392-8001
EMP: 7
SQ FT: 8,000
SALES (est): 1.6MM **Privately Held**
SIC: **2833** Mfg Medicinal/Botanical Products

(G-21093)
SOURCENNEX INTERNATIONAL CO
825 Green Bay Rd Ste 240 (60091-2500)
PHONE..................847 251-5500
Dennis S Xie, *President*
▲ EMP: 5
SALES (est): 482.8K **Privately Held**
WEB: www.sourcennex.com
SIC: **3842** Welders' hoods

(G-21094)
TOP HAT COMPANY INC (PA)
2407 Birchwood Ln (60091-2349)
P.O. Box 66 (60091-0066)
PHONE..................847 256-6565
Marla Murray, *President*
EMP: 31
SALES (est): 4.4MM **Privately Held**
SIC: **2099** Sauces: gravy, dressing & dip mixes

Wilmington
Will County

(G-21095)
A & J SIGNS
2104 Woodview Dr (60481-1756)
PHONE..................815 476-0128
Jasson Robards, *Owner*
EMP: 10
SALES (est): 776.5K **Privately Held**
SIC: **3993** Signs, not made in custom sign painting shops

(G-21096)
ALLKUT TOOL INCORPORATED
601 Davy Ln (60481-9236)
P.O. Box 217 (60481-0217)
PHONE..................815 476-9656
Charles Nicholson, *President*
Diana Nicholson, *Treasurer*
EMP: 6
SALES (est): 1.1MM **Privately Held**
SIC: **3545** 7699 3425 Cutting tools for machine tools; tool repair services; saw blades & handsaws

(G-21097)
ED HILL S CUSTOM CANVAS
8655 E Mallard Ln (60481-9222)
PHONE..................815 476-5042
Edward Hill, *Principal*
EMP: 4
SALES (est): 275.6K **Privately Held**
SIC: **2394** Canvas & related products

(G-21098)
FREE PRESS NEWSPAPERS
Also Called: Free Press Advocate
111 S Water St (60481-1373)
P.O. Box 327 (60481-0327)
PHONE..................815 476-7966
Eric Fisher, *President*
Greg Fisher, *Manager*
EMP: 30 **EST**: 1975
SALES: 1,000K **Privately Held**
WEB: www.freepressnewspapers.com
SIC: **2711** Newspapers, publishing & printing

(G-21099)
G-W COMMUNICATIONS INC
Also Called: Wilmington Free Press
111 S Water St (60481-1373)
P.O. Box 327 (60481-0327)
PHONE..................815 476-7966
George Fisher, *President*
Janet A Fisher, *Treasurer*
EMP: 9
SQ FT: 3,000
SALES (est): 578.4K **Privately Held**
SIC: **2711** Newspapers: publishing only, not printed on site

(G-21100)
HAYNES-BENT INC
35179 S Old Chicago Rd (60481-9650)
PHONE..................630 845-3316
EMP: 12
SQ FT: 150
SALES (est): 1.1MM **Privately Held**
SIC: **3825** Mfg Electrical Measuring Instruments

(G-21101)
RS WOODWORKING
119 N Water St (60481-1229)
PHONE..................815 476-1818
Sam Madia, *President*
EMP: 3
SALES (est): 206.9K **Privately Held**
SIC: **2431** Millwork

(G-21102)
RWAY PLASTICS LTD
30650 S State Route 53 (60481-9010)
P.O. Box 215 (60481-0215)
PHONE..................815 476-5252
EMP: 15
SQ FT: 14,500
SALES: 1.5MM **Privately Held**
SIC: **3089** Mfg Plastic Injection Moldings

(G-21103)
S & S MAINTENANCE
1305 Widows Rd (60481-9389)
PHONE..................815 725-9263
Stacey Wolcott, *Owner*
EMP: 2
SALES (est): 200K **Privately Held**
SIC: **3531** Road construction & maintenance machinery

Winchester
Scott County

(G-21104)
CAMPBELL PUBLISHING INC
Also Called: Scott County Times
4 S Hill St (62694-1212)
P.O. Box 64 (62694-0064)
PHONE..................217 742-3313
James Bruce Campbell, *President*
EMP: 49 **EST**: 1962
SQ FT: 3,500
SALES (est): 1.6MM **Privately Held**
SIC: **2711** 2759 2752 Newspapers: publishing only, not printed on site; commercial printing; commercial printing, lithographic

(G-21105)
FOURELL CORP
410 E Jefferson St (62694-8034)
PHONE..................217 742-3186
John A Lashmett, *President*
EMP: 5

SALES (est): 257.8K
SALES (corp-wide): 1MM Privately Held
SIC: 2299 Felts & felt products; yarns & thread, made from non-fabric materials
PA: Fourell Corp
4645 N Magnolia Ave
Chicago IL
773 271-4776

(G-21106)
LASHCON INC
Also Called: 4l Waterjet
540 Coultas Rd (62694-9796)
P.O. Box 222 (62694-0222)
PHONE 217 742-3186
Dorothy Lashmett, *President*
EMP: 8
SALES (est): 1.6MM Privately Held
SIC: 3532 Mining machinery

Windsor
Shelby County

(G-21107)
QUALITY PALLETS INC
601 Kentucky Ave (61957-1655)
PHONE 217 459-2655
Cinda M Smith, *President*
Greg Smith, *Vice Pres*
EMP: 20
SQ FT: 9,500
SALES (est): 3.4MM Privately Held
SIC: 2448 3086 Pallets, wood; plastics foam products

Winfield
Dupage County

(G-21108)
BW INDUSTRIES
27w230 Beecher Ave Ste 1 (60190-1220)
PHONE 630 784-1020
Ken Le Beau, *Principal*
EMP: 8
SALES (est): 823.1K Privately Held
SIC: 3999 Manufacturing industries

(G-21109)
CLEAVENGER ASSOCIATES INC
27w474 Jewell Rd Ste 2w (60190-1225)
P.O. Box 295, Wayne (60184-0295)
PHONE 630 221-0007
Timothy Cleavenger, *President*
Barbara Keyes, *Admin Sec*
EMP: 2
SQ FT: 1,000
SALES (est): 323.4K Privately Held
SIC: 3569 5085 3229 7389 Gas producers, generators & other gas related equipment; valves & fittings; tubing, glass; interior decorating

(G-21110)
EDISON PALLET & WOOD PRODUCTS
371 County Farm Rd (60190)
P.O. Box 195 (60190-0195)
PHONE 630 653-3416
Chester L Edison, *Owner*
EMP: 2
SALES (est): 209.3K Privately Held
SIC: 2448 Pallets, wood

(G-21111)
JONES DESIGN GROUP LTD
27w230 Beecher Ave Ste 1 (60190-1220)
PHONE 630 462-9340
Ed Jones, *President*
EMP: 4
SALES (est): 470K Privately Held
SIC: 2434 1721 Wood kitchen cabinets; painting & paper hanging

(G-21112)
LOCALFIX SOLUTIONS LLC
26w194 Prestwick Ln (60190-2310)
PHONE 312 569-0619
Matthew Ruesch, *CEO*
EMP: 3

SALES (est): 158.6K Privately Held
SIC: 7372 7371 Business oriented computer software; computer software writing services; computer software development

(G-21113)
OSTROM & CO INC
Also Called: Ostrom Glass & Metal Works
28w600 Roosevelt Rd (60190-1515)
PHONE 503 281-6469
Chuck Toombs, *President*
▲ EMP: 13
SQ FT: 17,000
SALES (est): 1.2MM Privately Held
SIC: 3231 3479 Ornamental glass: cut, engraved or otherwise decorated; etching on metals

(G-21114)
PARADIGM DEVELOPMENT GROUP INC
27 W 230 Becher Ave Ste 2 (60190)
PHONE 847 545-9600
Steven Hund, *President*
Ken Zamecnik, *Vice Pres*
EMP: 18
SQ FT: 9,000
SALES (est): 1.5MM Privately Held
SIC: 3999 Models, general, except toy

(G-21115)
PINEHURST BUS SOLUTIONS CORP
26w362 Pinehurst Dr (60190-2329)
PHONE 630 842-6155
Peter Arnolds, *President*
EMP: 4
SALES: 100K Privately Held
SIC: 3571 3572 7373 7377 Electronic computers; computer storage devices; computer integrated systems design; computer rental & leasing; computer maintenance & repair; computer related maintenance services;

(G-21116)
S & R MONOGRAMMING INC
28w600 Roosevelt Rd (60190-1515)
PHONE 630 369-5468
Susan C Hallbauer, *President*
Richard D Hallbauer, *Admin Sec*
EMP: 2
SALES (est): 400K Privately Held
SIC: 5199 2395 Advertising specialties; pleating & stitching

(G-21117)
SAGE CLOVER
26w400 Torrey Pines Ct (60190-2354)
P.O. Box 288 (60190-0288)
PHONE 630 220-9600
Krishna Narsimhan, *Principal*
EMP: 2
SALES (est): 314.7K Privately Held
SIC: 5092 2531 Educational toys; school furniture

Winnebago
Winnebago County

(G-21118)
A BURST OF SUN INC
817 N Elida St (61088-8617)
PHONE 815 335-2331
Tiffany Whitehead, *President*
EMP: 3 EST: 1999
SQ FT: 2,100
SALES (est): 311.1K Privately Held
SIC: 3648 Sun tanning equipment, incl. tanning beds

(G-21119)
EQUISOFT INC
8176 W Oliver Rd (61088-8843)
PHONE 815 629-2789
Delvin Insko, *President*
Jaquline Santoro, *Corp Secy*
Kathryn Insko, *Admin Sec*
EMP: 3
SALES (est): 200K Privately Held
SIC: 7372 Prepackaged software

(G-21120)
I D ROCKFORD SHOP INC
105 N Pecatonica St (61088-9099)
PHONE 815 335-1150
Robert D Dowdakin, *President*
William J Dowdakin, *Treasurer*
Savannah Liston, *Consultant*
Tammi Cunningham, *Admin Sec*
Mark Dowdakin, *Admin Sec*
EMP: 8 EST: 1965
SQ FT: 10,500
SALES (est): 1.1MM Privately Held
WEB: www.rockford-id.com
SIC: 3599 3451 3423 3724 Machine shop, jobbing & repair; screw machine products; hand & edge tools; aircraft engines & engine parts

(G-21121)
TRU-CUT PRODUCTION INC
211 W Main St (61088-7722)
P.O. Box 631 (61088-0631)
PHONE 815 335-2215
Phil Whitehead, *President*
Wendell Whitehead, *Vice Pres*
Phil W Whitehead, *Manager*
EMP: 8 EST: 1996
SQ FT: 100,000
SALES (est): 750K Privately Held
SIC: 3599 Machine shop, jobbing & repair

(G-21122)
Z-TECH INC
1958 S Winnebago Rd (61088-9162)
PHONE 815 335-7395
Rebecca A Oakley, *President*
Myron Oakley, *Vice Pres*
EMP: 3
SQ FT: 3,000
SALES (est): 487.2K Privately Held
SIC: 3599 8711 3544 Custom machinery; mechanical engineering; electrical or electronic engineering; special dies, tools, jigs & fixtures

Winnetka
Cook County

(G-21123)
AL3 INC
170 Linden St (60093-3862)
PHONE 847 441-7888
James H Williamson, *President*
Janet Williamson, *Treasurer*
EMP: 5
SALES: 76.5K Privately Held
SIC: 3354 Aluminum extruded products

(G-21124)
ALLIANCE ENVELOPE & PRINT LLC
854 Prospect Ave (60093-1945)
PHONE 847 446-4079
Joseph Reinert, *Principal*
EMP: 2
SALES (est): 2MM Privately Held
SIC: 2759 Commercial printing

(G-21125)
APPSANITY ADVISORY LLC
335 Auburn Ave (60093-3603)
PHONE 847 638-1172
John S Ivers, *Mng Member*
EMP: 1
SALES (est): 400K Privately Held
SIC: 7372 Application computer software

(G-21126)
BELLOWS SHOPPE
1048 Gage St Ste 301 (60093-1703)
PHONE 847 446-5533
Steven Schmid, *Owner*
EMP: 6
SQ FT: 1,200
SALES (est): 549.2K Privately Held
SIC: 5719 7629 7699 3471 Lamps & lamp shades; lamp repair & mounting; metal reshaping & replating services; plating & polishing

(G-21127)
BLISS RING COMPANY INC
Also Called: Ring-O-Bliss
1095 Willow Rd (60093-3642)
PHONE 847 446-3440
Charles R Drucker II, *President*
Paul M Drucker, *Vice Pres*
Jean Drucker, *Admin Sec*
EMP: 17 EST: 1934
SALES (est): 1MM Privately Held
SIC: 3911 Rings, finger: precious metal

(G-21128)
ELN GROUP LLC
39 Longmeadow Rd (60093-3524)
PHONE 847 477-1496
Lenore McCarthy,
Nina Krasikoff,
Eric Ladewig,
Laurine Sargent,
EMP: 4
SALES (est): 282.7K Privately Held
SIC: 3842 Bandages & dressings

(G-21129)
ENZYME MECHANISMS CONFERENCE
755 Sheridan Rd (60093-2309)
PHONE 847 491-5653
Richard B Silverman, *Ch of Bd*
EMP: 3
SALES (est): 94.7K Privately Held
SIC: 2869 Enzymes

(G-21130)
HL METALS LLC
910 Spruce St (60093-2219)
PHONE 312 590-3360
Hui Lin Lim,
EMP: 1
SALES (est): 380.2K Privately Held
WEB: www.hlmetalsllc.com
SIC: 3449 7389 Miscellaneous metalwork;

(G-21131)
KASKEY KIDS INC
1485 Scott Ave (60093-1448)
PHONE 847 441-3092
Cristy Kaskey, *President*
Bruce Kaskey, *Admin Sec*
▲ EMP: 3
SALES (est): 410.8K Privately Held
SIC: 3944 Games, toys & children's vehicles

(G-21132)
MANCILLAS INTERNATIONAL LTD (PA)
Also Called: Mancillas Intl
47 Longmeadow Rd (60093-3524)
PHONE 847 441-7748
Marcial R Mancillas, *President*
Mary Louise Mancillas, *Admin Sec*
EMP: 15 EST: 1970
SQ FT: 20,000
SALES (est): 1.5MM Privately Held
SIC: 2311 Suits, men's & boys': made from purchased materials

(G-21133)
MEDICAL ADHERENCE TECH INC
825 Heather Ln (60093-1316)
PHONE 847 525-6300
Sanjay Mehrotra, *President*
EMP: 3
SALES (est): 117.4K Privately Held
SIC: 3841 Surgical & medical instruments

(G-21134)
NANEX LLC
818 Elm St Uppr 2 (60093-2224)
PHONE 847 501-4787
Eric S Hunsader, *Mng Member*
EMP: 3
SALES (est): 266.8K Privately Held
SIC: 7372 Business oriented computer software

(G-21135)
PHOEBE & FRANCES
566 Chestnut St (60093-2228)
PHONE 847 446-5480
Nina Busemi, *Partner*
Sarah Torenef, *Partner*

Winnetka - Cook County (G-21136)

EMP: 10
SALES (est): 941.7K **Privately Held**
SIC: 2389 Apparel & accessories

(G-21136)
SNOW & GRAHAM LLC
829 Foxdale Ave (60093-1909)
PHONE....................773 665-9000
Ebony Chafey,
EMP: 8
SALES (est): 1.2MM **Privately Held**
WEB: www.snowandgraham.com
SIC: 2621 Stationery, envelope & tablet papers

(G-21137)
WILLIAMSON J HUNTER & COMPANY
170 Linden St (60093-3862)
PHONE....................847 441-7888
James Williamson, *President*
EMP: 3
SALES: 300K **Privately Held**
SIC: 3731 Shipbuilding & repairing

(G-21138)
WINNETKA MEWS CONDOMINIUM ASSN
640 Winnetka Mews (60093-1966)
PHONE....................847 501-2770
Marlyn Strauss, *Principal*
EMP: 3
SALES (est): 229.2K **Privately Held**
SIC: 8641 3273 Condominium association; ready-mixed concrete

Winslow
Stephenson County

(G-21139)
MITEK CORPORATION
Also Called: Mtx/Oaktron
1 Mitek Plz (61089-9700)
PHONE....................608 328-5560
David Smythe, *Manager*
EMP: 110
SALES (corp-wide): 84.5MM **Privately Held**
SIC: 3651 Speaker systems
PA: Mitek Corporation
   4545 E Baseline Rd
   Phoenix AZ 85042
   602 438-4545

(G-21140)
MITEK CORPORATION
Also Called: Mtx
1 Mitek Plz (61089-9700)
P.O. Box 38 (61089-0038)
PHONE....................815 367-3000
Ric Joranlien, *QC Mgr*
Lloyd Ivey, *Branch Mgr*
Melissa Davis,
EMP: 130
SALES (corp-wide): 84.5MM **Privately Held**
SIC: 3651 Household audio equipment
PA: Mitek Corporation
   4545 E Baseline Rd
   Phoenix AZ 85042
   602 438-4545

Winthrop Harbor
Lake County

(G-21141)
MEYER ENGINEERING CO
1139 Lewis Ave (60096-1428)
PHONE....................847 746-1500
Martin H Meyer, *President*
Sandra L Meyer, *Admin Sec*
EMP: 7
SQ FT: 13,000
SALES (est): 2.1MM **Privately Held**
SIC: 3429 Marine hardware

(G-21142)
RD DAILY ENTERPRISES
Also Called: Daily Highway Express
911 Fulton Ave (60096-1725)
P.O. Box 146 (60096-0146)
PHONE....................847 872-7632
Roger Daily, *President*
EMP: 3
SALES (est): 253.5K **Privately Held**
SIC: 4212 2711 Local trucking, without storage; newspapers, publishing & printing

Wonder Lake
Mchenry County

(G-21143)
BAXTER HEALTHCARE CORPORATION
7621 Center Dr (60097-9261)
PHONE....................847 270-4757
Peter Simpson, *Branch Mgr*
EMP: 5
SALES (corp-wide): 11.3B **Publicly Held**
WEB: www.baxter.com
SIC: 3841 Surgical & medical instruments
HQ: Baxter Healthcare Corporation
   1 Baxter Pkwy
   Deerfield IL 60015
   224 948-2000

(G-21144)
D & H PRECISION TOOLING CO
7522 Barnard Mill Rd (60097-8132)
PHONE....................815 653-9611
David V Jones, *President*
EMP: 4 EST: 1968
SQ FT: 2,400
SALES (est): 200K **Privately Held**
SIC: 3599 7692 3544 Machine shop, jobbing & repair; welding repair; special dies, tools, jigs & fixtures

(G-21145)
MAY SAND AND GRAVEL INC
3013 Thompson Rd (60097-9494)
PHONE....................815 338-4761
Roger May, *Owner*
EMP: 3
SALES (est): 188.8K **Privately Held**
SIC: 1442 Construction sand & gravel

Wood Dale
Dupage County

(G-21146)
1776 FABRICATION LLC
735 N Edgewood Ave Ste J (60191-1261)
PHONE....................773 895-7590
Matt Lisnich, *Mng Member*
Peter Cison, *Mng Member*
EMP: 3
SALES: 150K **Privately Held**
SIC: 3499 Aerosol valves, metal

(G-21147)
AAR AIRCRAFT & ENG SLS & LSG
1100 N Wood Dale Rd (60191-1060)
PHONE....................630 227-2000
Timothy Romenesko, *President*
Ronald Fogleman, *Director*
▲ EMP: 6
SALES (est): 1.3MM
SALES (corp-wide): 2B **Publicly Held**
SIC: 3728 Aircraft parts & equipment
PA: Aar Corp.
   1100 N Wood Dale Rd
   Wood Dale IL 60191
   630 227-2000

(G-21148)
AAR ALLEN SERVICES INC (HQ)
1100 N Wood Dale Rd (60191-1060)
PHONE....................630 227-2410
David Storch, *CEO*
Timothy J Romenesko, *President*
Jack M Arehart, *Vice Pres*
Robert Regan, *Admin Sec*
▼ EMP: 72
SALES (est): 33.7MM
SALES (corp-wide): 2B **Publicly Held**
SIC: 3728 Aircraft parts & equipment
PA: Aar Corp.
   1100 N Wood Dale Rd
   Wood Dale IL 60191
   630 227-2000

(G-21149)
AAR CORP (PA)
Also Called: AAR Doing It Right
1100 N Wood Dale Rd (60191-1094)
PHONE....................630 227-2000
David P Storch, *Ch of Bd*
John M Holmes, *President*
Eloy Herrera, *Business Mgr*
Mike Carr, *Vice Pres*
Peter Chapman, *Vice Pres*
▲ EMP: 60 EST: 1951
SALES: 2B **Publicly Held**
WEB: www.aarcorp.com
SIC: 3724 4581 3537 5599 Aircraft engines & engine parts; aircraft maintenance & repair services; aircraft servicing & repairing; containers (metal); air cargo; aircraft, self-propelled; aircraft rental

(G-21150)
AAR GOVERNMENT SERVICES INC (HQ)
1100 N Wood Dale Rd (60191-1060)
PHONE....................630 227-2000
Nicholas Gross, *Principal*
John Holmes, *Principal*
David Lund, *Principal*
Robert Regan, *Principal*
David Storch, *Principal*
EMP: 38
SALES: 16.7MM
SALES (corp-wide): 2B **Publicly Held**
SIC: 3728 Aircraft parts & equipment
PA: Aar Corp.
   1100 N Wood Dale Rd
   Wood Dale IL 60191
   630 227-2000

(G-21151)
AAR SUPPLY CHAIN INC (HQ)
Also Called: AAR Defense Systems Logistics
1100 N Wood Dale Rd (60191-1060)
PHONE....................630 227-2000
David Storch, *CEO*
Timothy J Romenesko, *President*
Scot Cerka, *Vice Pres*
Peter Chapman, *Vice Pres*
Ed Dewaard, *Vice Pres*
▲ EMP: 95
SQ FT: 250,000
SALES (est): 256.7MM
SALES (corp-wide): 2B **Publicly Held**
SIC: 5088 3728 Aircraft & parts; aircraft parts & equipment
PA: Aar Corp.
   1100 N Wood Dale Rd
   Wood Dale IL 60191
   630 227-2000

(G-21152)
ABITZY INC
945 Sivert Dr (60191-1210)
PHONE....................847 659-9228
Maria Medema, *CEO*
EMP: 10 EST: 2013
SALES (est): 1.5MM **Privately Held**
SIC: 2541 Wood partitions & fixtures

(G-21153)
ACCURATE RIVET MANUFACTURING
343 Beinoris Dr (60191-1222)
P.O. Box 7050 (60191-7050)
PHONE....................630 766-3401
Joseph Losacco, *President*
Maria Losacco, *Corp Secy*
Joseph Losacco Jr, *Vice Pres*
EMP: 9
SQ FT: 7,000
SALES: 1.2MM **Privately Held**
WEB: www.accuraterivet.com
SIC: 3452 Rivets, metal

(G-21154)
ACD USA INC
1001 Mittel Dr (60191-1176)
PHONE....................929 428-1744
Andreas Zwissler, *Principal*
Joel Paritz, *Principal*
Henry Roske, *Principal*
Chris Gould, *Sales Staff*
EMP: 3
SALES (est): 289.8K **Privately Held**
SIC: 3714 Motor vehicle parts & accessories

(G-21155)
ADDVALUE2PRINT LLC
737 N Central Ave (60191-1240)
PHONE....................847 551-1570
Ivan Verheye, *Partner*
EMP: 4
SALES (est): 473K **Privately Held**
SIC: 2752 Commercial printing, offset

(G-21156)
AFFRI INC
850 Dillon Dr (60191-1269)
PHONE....................224 374-0931
Roberto Affri, *President*
EMP: 3
SQ FT: 1,000
SALES (est): 500K **Privately Held**
SIC: 3599 5013 Amusement park equipment; testing equipment, engine

(G-21157)
ALL AMERICAN NUT & CANDY CORP
255 Beinoris Dr (60191-1200)
PHONE....................630 595-6473
Isidor Budina, *CEO*
EMP: 18 EST: 2011
SALES: 1.5MM **Privately Held**
SIC: 2064 Fruit & fruit peel confections; nuts, candy covered

(G-21158)
ALLMETAL INC
377 Balm Ct (60191-1253)
PHONE....................630 350-2524
Randy King, *Manager*
EMP: 40
SALES (corp-wide): 78.4MM **Privately Held**
SIC: 3442 3444 Metal doors, sash & trim; sheet metalwork
PA: Allmetal, Inc.
   1 Pierce Pl Ste 295w
   Itasca IL 60143
   630 250-8090

(G-21159)
ALLSTATE METAL FABRICATORS INC
365 Beinoris Dr (60191-1222)
PHONE....................630 860-1500
Mike Mc Namara, *President*
Mike McNamara, *President*
Pat McNamara, *Vice Pres*
David McNamara, *Shareholder*
▼ EMP: 7
SQ FT: 10,600
SALES (est): 1.3MM **Privately Held**
WEB: www.allstatemetalfab.com
SIC: 3441 Fabricated structural metal

(G-21160)
AMAITIS AND ASSOCIATES INC (PA)
810 Lively Blvd (60191-1202)
PHONE....................847 428-1269
Edward J Amaitis Jr, *President*
Edward J Amaitis Sr, *Vice Pres*
Laurie Carbery, *Controller*
Jerry Amaitis, *Admin Sec*
EMP: 11
SQ FT: 10,000
SALES (est): 2.5MM **Privately Held**
WEB: www.amaitis.com
SIC: 7379 3572 Computer related consulting services; computer tape drives & components

(G-21161)
AMBIR TECHNOLOGY INC
Also Called: Document Capture Technologies
820 Sivert Dr (60191-2610)
PHONE....................630 530-5400
Michael O'Leary, *President*
Rolf Schmoldt, *Partner*
Randy Thompson, *Cust Mgr*
Mike Hansen, *CTO*

GEOGRAPHIC SECTION

Wood Dale - Dupage County (G-21188)

Mark Druziak, *Director*
▲ EMP: 8
SALES (est): 1.8MM **Privately Held**
SIC: 3577 Computer peripheral equipment

(G-21162)
AMERICAN BULLNOSE CO MIDW
640 Pond Dr Ste C (60191-1167)
PHONE..................................630 238-1300
Lou Harting, *Manager*
EMP: 6
SALES: 300K **Privately Held**
SIC: 3253 5032 Ceramic wall & floor tile; ceramic wall & floor tile

(G-21163)
AMERICAN DAWN INC
1269 N Wood Dale Rd (60191-1160)
PHONE..................................312 961-2909
Mike Greenburg, *Manager*
EMP: 6
SALES (corp-wide): 26MM **Privately Held**
SIC: 2299 5023 5131 2393 Linen fabrics; linens & towels; textiles, woven; cushions, except spring & carpet; purchased materials; pillows, bed: made from purchased materials
PA: American Dawn, Inc.
  401 W Artesia Blvd
  Compton CA 90220
  800 821-2221

(G-21164)
AMERICAN DIE SUPPLIES ACQUISIT
618 N Edgewood Ave (60191-2604)
PHONE..................................630 766-6226
Robert Jarka, *Manager*
▲ EMP: 2
SALES (est): 218.3K **Privately Held**
SIC: 3544 Dies & die holders for metal cutting, forming, die casting

(G-21165)
AMERIKEN DIE SUPPLY INC
618 N Edgewood Ave (60191-2604)
PHONE..................................630 766-6226
Dale Kengott, *President*
▲ EMP: 50 EST: 1953
SALES (est): 9MM **Privately Held**
WEB: www.ameriken.com
SIC: 3544 Dies & die holders for metal cutting, forming, die casting; special dies & tools

(G-21166)
ARO METAL STAMPING COMPANY INC
935 N Central Ave (60191-1218)
PHONE..................................630 351-7676
Tony Dupasquier, *President*
Anthony Dupasquier, *President*
Tracey Stanczyk, *Materials Mgr*
Frank Kraft, *Project Engr*
Connie Thomas, *CFO*
EMP: 25
SALES (est): 9MM **Privately Held**
WEB: www.arometal.com
SIC: 3599 3469 Machine shop, jobbing & repair; stamping metal for the trade

(G-21167)
BECKMAN COULTER INC
1500 N Mittel Blvd (60191-1072)
PHONE..................................800 526-3821
Paul Hodnick, *Manager*
EMP: 3
SALES (corp-wide): 17.9B **Publicly Held**
SIC: 3826 Analytical instruments
HQ: Beckman Coulter, Inc.
  250 S Kraemer Blvd
  Brea CA 92821
  714 993-5321

(G-21168)
BI-PHASE TECHNOLOGIES LLC
201 Mittel Dr (60191-1116)
PHONE..................................952 886-6450
Bryan White, *General Mgr*
Victor Van Dyke, *General Mgr*
▲ EMP: 13
SALES (est): 2.3MM
SALES (corp-wide): 22.9B **Privately Held**
WEB: www.bi-phase.com
SIC: 3714 7538 Fuel systems & parts, motor vehicle; general automotive repair shops
HQ: Power Solutions International, Inc.
  201 Mittel Dr
  Wood Dale IL 60191

(G-21169)
BITFORMS INC
Also Called: AlphaGraphics 468
165 Hansen Ct Ste 111e (60191-1144)
PHONE..................................630 595-6800
Jeff Bittner, *President*
Nicola Bittner, *Vice Pres*
Ronald Bittner, *Treasurer*
Bonnie Bittner, *Admin Sec*
EMP: 6
SQ FT: 3,100
SALES (est): 758K **Privately Held**
SIC: 2752 Commercial printing, lithographic

(G-21170)
BJ MOLD & DIE INC
780 Creel Dr Ste 1 (60191-2619)
PHONE..................................630 595-1797
Bogdan Janiszewski, *President*
EMP: 3
SALES (est): 477.4K **Privately Held**
SIC: 3089 Molding primary plastic; injection molding of plastics

(G-21171)
BOSWELL BUILDING CONTRS INC
Also Called: BBC
933 Dillon Dr (60191-1274)
PHONE..................................630 595-5027
Susan Boswell, *President*
EMP: 10
SALES (est): 2.1MM **Privately Held**
SIC: 3444 Sheet metalwork

(G-21172)
BRUNET SNOW SERVICE COMPANY
174 Hawthorne Ave (60191-1455)
PHONE..................................847 846-0037
Bobby Brunet, *President*
EMP: 4
SALES: 100K **Privately Held**
SIC: 3585 7389 Snowmaking machinery;

(G-21173)
C CRETORS & CO (PA)
176 Mittel Dr (60191-1119)
PHONE..................................847 616-6900
Charles D Cretors, *CEO*
Andrew Cretors, *President*
John Concannon, *Vice Pres*
Van Neathery, *Vice Pres*
Kevin Gorman, *Warehouse Mgr*
◆ EMP: 54 EST: 1885
SQ FT: 53,000
SALES (est): 32MM **Privately Held**
WEB: www.cretors.com
SIC: 3589 Popcorn machines, commercial

(G-21174)
CAL-TRONICS SYSTEMS INC
729 Creel Dr (60191-2609)
PHONE..................................630 350-0044
Salvatore J Caldrone, *President*
Joe Scianna, *Engineer*
Paul Sampson, *Admin Sec*
EMP: 36
SALES (est): 8.5MM **Privately Held**
SIC: 3679 Electronic circuits

(G-21175)
CHAMPION CONTAINER CORP
1455 N Michael Dr (60191-1015)
PHONE..................................630 530-1990
William Shanklin, *President*
Chris Borzello, *Sales Mgr*
Gerry Sliwicki, *Sales Staff*
Tom Zappa, *Sales Staff*
Paul Doyle, *Admin Sec*
EMP: 100 EST: 1975
SALES (est): 6.1MM **Privately Held**
WEB: www.champion-container.com
SIC: 2631 Container, packaging & boxboard

(G-21176)
CLASSIC PRTG THERMOGRAPHY INC
735 N Edgewood Ave Ste F (60191-1261)
PHONE..................................630 595-7765
Christopher Wilk, *President*
Adrian Wilk, *Vice Pres*
EMP: 4 EST: 1976
SQ FT: 2,000
SALES (est): 420K **Privately Held**
SIC: 2752 Commercial printing, offset

(G-21177)
CMETRIX INC
165 Mittel Dr (60191-1116)
PHONE..................................630 595-9800
Robert Mielcarski, *President*
Paul Machala, *Vice Pres*
EMP: 4
SALES (est): 1.8MM **Privately Held**
SIC: 3679 Electronic circuits

(G-21178)
COMPOSITE BEARINGS MFG
Also Called: MBC Cmpsite Bring Mnfactoring
720 N Edgewood Ave (60191-1249)
PHONE..................................630 595-8334
Luigi Mongodi, *President*
▲ EMP: 12
SQ FT: 5,000
SALES (est): 2.1MM **Privately Held**
SIC: 5085 3568 Bearings; bearings, plain

(G-21179)
D&W FINE PACK HOLDINGS LLC (HQ)
777 Mark St (60191-2802)
PHONE..................................847 378-1200
David H Randall, *President*
Matthew Bell, *Manager*
Roxanne Hale, *Manager*
Peggy Iacovoni, *Manager*
EMP: 1 EST: 2009
SQ FT: 530,000
SALES (est): 834MM
SALES (corp-wide): 614.5MM **Privately Held**
WEB: www.dwfinepack.com
SIC: 3089 Plastic kitchenware, tableware & houseware
PA: Mid Oaks Investments Llc
  750 W Lake Cook Rd # 460
  Buffalo Grove IL 60089
  847 215-3475

(G-21180)
D&W FINE PACK LLC
777 Mark St (60191-2802)
PHONE..................................215 362-1501
Dave Randall, *CEO*
Mike Horn, *Controller*
EMP: 321
SALES (corp-wide): 614.5MM **Privately Held**
SIC: 3089 Plastic processing
HQ: D&W Fine Pack Llc
  777 Mark St
  Wood Dale IL 60191

(G-21181)
DAMEN CARBIDE TOOL COMPANY INC
344 Beinoris Dr (60191-1223)
PHONE..................................630 766-7875
John Bachmeier, *President*
Nady Osmat, *COO*
Rita Olvera, *Vice Pres*
Jakob Bachmeier, *Treasurer*
▲ EMP: 25
SQ FT: 22,000
SALES (est): 8.8MM **Privately Held**
WEB: www.damencarbide.com
SIC: 3545 3546 Cutting tools for machine tools; power-driven handtools

(G-21182)
DRAPERYLAND INC
368 Georgetown Sq (60191-1832)
PHONE..................................630 521-1000
Tony Altabello, *President*
William Schachner, *President*
EMP: 10
SQ FT: 2,000
SALES (est): 660K **Privately Held**
SIC: 5714 7389 2591 2391 Draperies; interior designer; drapery hardware & blinds & shades; curtains & draperies

(G-21183)
EARTHWISE ENVIRONMENTAL INC
777 N Edgewood Ave (60191-1254)
PHONE..................................630 475-3070
Robert Miller, *President*
John Kentgen, *Sales Staff*
Mark Sylvester, *Director*
EMP: 9
SQ FT: 4,000
SALES (est): 2.1MM **Privately Held**
SIC: 3589 Water treatment equipment, industrial

(G-21184)
ECURRENT LLC
Also Called: Ecurrent Led
740 N Edgewood Ave (60191-1249)
PHONE..................................888 815-5786
William G Haberkorn, *Mng Member*
Thomas M Haberkorn,
Maria P Jara,
EMP: 3
SALES (est): 334.2K **Privately Held**
SIC: 3648 Outdoor lighting equipment

(G-21185)
EMR MANUFACTURING INC
Also Called: J. P. Bell Fabricating, Inc.
617 N Central Ave (60191-1452)
PHONE..................................630 766-3366
Nate Rupczynski, *President*
Ken Adamik, *Sales Mgr*
EMP: 23
SQ FT: 16,500
SALES (est): 4.9MM **Privately Held**
SIC: 3444 Sheet metal specialties, not stamped

(G-21186)
FABRICATING MACHINERY SALES
Also Called: Fabricating Machinery & Eqp
640 Pond Dr Ste A (60191-1167)
PHONE..................................630 350-2266
John Joseph Rinaldo, *President*
Donna Rinaldo, *Admin Sec*
EMP: 20
SQ FT: 10,000
SALES (est): 2.5MM **Privately Held**
SIC: 3444 3312 3544 3469 Sheet metalwork; tool & die steel; special dies, tools, jigs & fixtures; metal stampings

(G-21187)
FLOYD STEEL ERECTORS INC
310 Richert Rd (60191-1207)
PHONE..................................630 238-8383
Tim Flloyd, *President*
Tim Floyd, *President*
Kent Floyd, *Treasurer*
EMP: 17 EST: 1947
SQ FT: 13,500
SALES: 8.6MM **Privately Held**
WEB: www.floydcrane.com
SIC: 3441 7353 Fabricated structural metal; cranes & aerial lift equipment, rental or leasing

(G-21188)
FORBO SIEGLING LLC
Also Called: Siegling America
918 N Central Ave (60191-1216)
PHONE..................................630 595-4031
Nicholas Casali, *Sales Staff*
Susan Durango, *Branch Mgr*
EMP: 11
SALES (corp-wide): 1.2B **Privately Held**
SIC: 3535 3568 Belt conveyor systems, general industrial use; power transmission equipment
HQ: Forbo Siegling, Llc
  12201 Vanstory Dr
  Huntersville NC 28078
  704 948-0800

Wood Dale - Dupage County (G-21189)

(G-21189)
FOREST AWARDS & ENGRAVING
336 E Irving Park Rd (60191-1647)
PHONE..................630 595-2242
Gib F Beane, *President*
Barbara Beane, *Treasurer*
EMP: 3
SQ FT: 3,000
SALES (est): 346K **Privately Held**
SIC: 3479 2499 3993 Name plates: engraved, etched, etc.; decorative wood & woodwork; signs & advertising specialties

(G-21190)
FORMCO METAL PRODUCTS INC
556 Clayton Ct (60191-1115)
PHONE..................630 766-4441
Peter J Weiss, *President*
EMP: 25
SQ FT: 20,000
SALES (est): 5.8MM **Privately Held**
SIC: 3469 Stamping metal for the trade

(G-21191)
FREY WISS PRCSION MCHINING INC
384 Beinoris Dr (60191-1223)
PHONE..................630 595-9073
Adolf Frey, *Ch of Bd*
Ernie Pabon, *President*
Linda Rosenberg, *Purchasing*
Susan Ralph, *Executive*
EMP: 30
SQ FT: 10,046
SALES (est): 5.5MM **Privately Held**
SIC: 3599 Machine shop, jobbing & repair

(G-21192)
G & M DIE CASTING COMPANY INC
284 Richert Rd (60191-1206)
PHONE..................630 595-2340
Mark Hirsh, *President*
Clarissa M Fleps, *Admin Sec*
EMP: 80
SQ FT: 64,000
SALES (est): 16MM **Privately Held**
SIC: 3363 3544 Aluminum die-castings; special dies & tools

(G-21193)
GE HEALTHCARE INC
945 N Edgewood Ave Ste A1 (60191-1252)
PHONE..................630 595-6642
Otha Bright, *Manager*
EMP: 20
SALES (corp-wide): 95.2B **Publicly Held**
SIC: 2833 Medicinals & botanicals
HQ: Ge Healthcare Inc.
251 Locke Dr
Marlborough MA 01752
800 526-3593

(G-21194)
GLUETECH INC
701 Creel Dr (60191-2609)
PHONE..................847 455-2707
James Nierodzik, *President*
EMP: 10
SQ FT: 11,000
SALES (est): 1.6MM **Privately Held**
SIC: 2677 Envelopes

(G-21195)
GREG SCREW MACHINE PRODUCTS
647 N Central Ave Ste 103 (60191-1475)
PHONE..................630 694-8875
Greg Rapacz, *President*
Miroslaw Reusicki, *Vice Pres*
EMP: 2
SQ FT: 2,500
SALES (est): 319.2K **Privately Held**
SIC: 3451 Screw machine products

(G-21196)
HCF BUILDING CORPORATION
Also Called: Twin Plex Manufacturing
840 Lively Blvd (60191-1202)
PHONE..................630 595-2040
Ken Floyd, *President*
Steve Floyd, *Vice Pres*
EMP: 17
SQ FT: 60,000
SALES (est): 1MM **Privately Held**
SIC: 3469 Stamping metal for the trade

(G-21197)
HEIDOLPH NA LLC
Also Called: Heidolph North America
1235 N Mittel Blvd B (60191-1022)
PHONE..................224 265-9600
Nicole Kvasnicka, *Marketing Staff*
James Dawson, *Mng Member*
Deborah Zinsser-Krys,
EMP: 18 **EST:** 2008
SALES (est): 5.7MM **Privately Held**
WEB: www.heidolphna.com
SIC: 3564 3821 3561 Air cleaning systems; shakers & stirrers; pumps & pumping equipment

(G-21198)
HOSPITAL THERAPY PRODUCTS INC
757 N Central Ave (60191-1240)
PHONE..................630 766-7101
Timothy Roberts, *President*
▲ **EMP:** 18 **EST:** 1975
SQ FT: 5,000
SALES (est): 2.8MM **Privately Held**
SIC: 3841 Surgical & medical instruments

(G-21199)
I S C AMERICA INC (PA)
750 Creel Dr (60191-2608)
PHONE..................630 616-1331
Woo Chul, *CEO*
Suengyoon Han, *President*
▲ **EMP:** 5
SQ FT: 10,000
SALES (est): 1.6MM **Privately Held**
SIC: 2899 3555 2893 Ink or writing fluids; printing trades machinery; printing ink

(G-21200)
ICON METALCRAFT INC
940 Dillon Dr (60191-1233)
PHONE..................630 766-5600
Silvia McLain, *CEO*
Lorena Soto, *Opers Mgr*
Mark Wedick, *Purchasing*
Jeff Szemplinski, *QC Mgr*
Claudia Soto, *Human Res Mgr*
EMP: 105
SQ FT: 50,000
SALES (est): 24.3MM **Privately Held**
SIC: 3444 3544 Sheet metal specialties, not stamped; special dies & tools

(G-21201)
INNOVATIVE RACK & GEAR COMPANY
365 Balm Ct (60191-1253)
PHONE..................630 766-2652
Zenon Cichon, *President*
Jerry Cichon, *Vice Pres*
EMP: 14
SQ FT: 6,500
SALES (est): 3.3MM **Privately Held**
SIC: 3462 Gear & chain forgings

(G-21202)
INTELLIGENT SCM LLC
Also Called: Awa
1263 N Wood Dale Rd (60191-1160)
PHONE..................630 625-7229
Graham Burford, *CEO*
Peter Lamy, *President*
Jesse Maugle, *Vice Pres*
Regina March, *CFO*
Alex Knowles, *Director*
EMP: 3 **EST:** 2010
SALES (est): 99K **Privately Held**
WEB: www.intelligentscm.com
SIC: 3674 Microprocessors

(G-21203)
K R KOMAREK INC (DH)
548 Clayton Ct (60191-1115)
PHONE..................847 956-0060
Jan Pflugfelder, *President*
Thomas P Barnett, *Vice Pres*
Edward R Chapman, *Vice Pres*
Rocco Casamassimo, *Admin Sec*
◆ **EMP:** 29
SQ FT: 20,000
SALES (est): 13.8MM
SALES (corp-wide): 81.4MM **Privately Held**
WEB: www.komarek.com
SIC: 3542 3544 Industrial machinery & equipment; pressing machines
HQ: Koppern Equipment, Inc.
7930 W Kenton Cir Ste 305
Huntersville NC 28078
704 357-3322

(G-21204)
KKT CHILLERS INC
765 Dillon Dr (60191-1273)
PHONE..................847 734-1600
John Carmody, *President*
Erica Lazaridis, *Treasurer*
Dina Shamoon, *Admin Mgr*
Sarah Ames, *Admin Sec*
▲ **EMP:** 25 **EST:** 2007
SALES (est): 3.2MM
SALES (corp-wide): 2.5B **Privately Held**
WEB: www.kkt-chillers.com
SIC: 3585 Refrigeration & heating equipment
HQ: Ait-Deutschland Gmbh
Industriestr. 3
Kasendorf 95359
922 899-060

(G-21205)
KRYGIER DESIGN INC
635 Wheat Ln (60191-1128)
PHONE..................620 766-1001
Margaret Krygier, *President*
Kris Krygier, *Vice Pres*
EMP: 10
SQ FT: 5,000
SALES (est): 1.3MM **Privately Held**
WEB: www.krygierdesign.com
SIC: 3535 Unit handling conveying systems

(G-21206)
L A M INC DE
620 Wheat Ln Ste B (60191-1164)
PHONE..................630 860-9700
Lavern A Miller, *Ch of Bd*
Malinda Cochran, *President*
EMP: 8
SQ FT: 27,000
SALES (est): 832.2K **Privately Held**
SIC: 3826 3829 3821 3812 Analytical instruments; measuring & controlling devices; laboratory apparatus & furniture; search & navigation equipment; miscellaneous publishing

(G-21207)
LEAFFILTER NORTH LLC
587 N Edgewood Ave (60191-2600)
PHONE..................630 595-9605
Armando Garza, *Principal*
EMP: 53 **Privately Held**
WEB: www.leaffilter.com
SIC: 3569 Filters
PA: Leaffilter North Llc
1595 Georgetown Rd Ste G
Hudson OH 44236

(G-21208)
LTB GRAPHICS INC
749 N Edgewood Ave (60191-1254)
PHONE..................630 238-1754
Kenneth Kent, *President*
EMP: 3
SQ FT: 1,760
SALES (est): 140K **Privately Held**
SIC: 2759 Screen printing

(G-21209)
M & M TOOLING INC
395 E Potter St (60191-2133)
PHONE..................630 595-8834
Michael Mirante, *President*
EMP: 3
SALES (est): 427.7K **Privately Held**
SIC: 3541 Machine tool replacement & repair parts, metal cutting types

(G-21210)
MACLEAN SENIOR INDUSTRIES LLC
610 Pond Dr (60191-1111)
PHONE..................630 350-1600
Joe Francaviglia, *Mng Member*
◆ **EMP:** 1
SALES (est): 4.8MM
SALES (corp-wide): 1.2B **Privately Held**
SIC: 3643 3644 Ground clamps (electric wiring devices); pole line hardware
HQ: Maclean Power, L.L.C.
481 Munn Rd Ste 300
Fort Mill SC 29715

(G-21211)
MADDEN COMMUNICATIONS INC (PA)
901 Mittel Dr (60191-1118)
P.O. Box 1054, Park Ridge (60068-7054)
PHONE..................630 787-2200
James P Donahugh, *Ch of Bd*
Sean Madden, *President*
John McMahon, *COO*
Larry Gundrum, *Senior VP*
Ruben Gomez, *Vice Pres*
◆ **EMP:** 185
SQ FT: 251,000
SALES (est): 130.9MM **Privately Held**
SIC: 2752 Commercial printing, offset

(G-21212)
MAGNETIC COIL MANUFACTURING CO
325 Beinoris Dr Ste A (60191-2616)
PHONE..................630 787-1948
Joseph T Sommer Jr, *President*
Denna Myrda, *Office Mgr*
EMP: 25 **EST:** 1945
SQ FT: 12,500
SALES (est): 1.5MM **Privately Held**
WEB: www.magcoil.com
SIC: 3677 3621 3612 Coil windings, electronic; transformers power supply, electronic type; motors & generators; transformers, except electric

(G-21213)
MARITOOL INCORPORATED
242 Beinoris Dr (60191-1250)
PHONE..................888 352-7773
Frank Mari Jr, *Principal*
Tom Fetcho, *Vice Pres*
Agnieszka Mari, *Admin Sec*
EMP: 1
SALES (est): 268.5K **Privately Held**
WEB: www.maritool.com
SIC: 3599 Machine shop, jobbing & repair

(G-21214)
MATRIX PLASTIC PRODUCTS INC
Also Called: Matrix Tooling
949 Aec Dr (60191-1143)
PHONE..................630 595-6144
Paul Ziegenhorn, *President*
Andy Ziegenhorn, *COO*
Jim Ziegenhorn, *Vice Pres*
James Ziegenhorn, *VP Mfg*
John Sauber, *Project Mgr*
EMP: 85
SQ FT: 30,000
SALES (est): 20.3MM **Privately Held**
SIC: 3544 3089 Industrial molds; injection molding of plastics

(G-21215)
MET-PRO TECHNOLOGIES LLC
Flex Kleen Division of Met Pro
905 Sivert Dr (60191-1210)
PHONE..................630 775-0707
Fax: 630 295-9019
EMP: 35
SALES (corp-wide): 417MM **Publicly Held**
SIC: 3564 Mfg Blowers/Fans
HQ: Met-Pro Technologies Llc
460 E Swedesford Rd # 2030
Wayne PA 19087
215 717-7909

(G-21216)
MICH ENTERPRISES INC
Also Called: Earl Mich
720 Creel Dr (60191-2608)
PHONE..................630 616-9000
Ben Mich, *President*
Greg McKay, *Vice Pres*
Corey Hennings, *Info Tech Dir*
EMP: 15
SQ FT: 10,000

GEOGRAPHIC SECTION

Wood Dale - Dupage County (G-21244)

SALES (est): 4MM **Privately Held**
WEB: www.earlmich.com
SIC: **2675** 5085 3993 3953 Letters, cardboard, die-cut: from purchased materials; signmaker equipment & supplies; signs & advertising specialties; marking devices; commercial printing, lithographic; coated & laminated paper

(G-21217)
MOTOR CAPACITORS INC
335 Beinoris Dr (60191-1222)
PHONE.................................773 774-6666
Liam Doherty, *President*
Terry Noon, *President*
Jim Olson, *Manager*
Carolyn Noone, *Info Tech Mgr*
Carolyn Noon, *Admin Sec*
▲ EMP: 17
SQ FT: 15,000
SALES (est): 2.2MM **Privately Held**
SIC: **3629** 3675 Capacitors & condensers; electronic capacitors

(G-21218)
MT CASE COMPANY
569 N Edgewood Ave (60191-2600)
PHONE.................................630 227-1019
Mario Educate, *President*
Vickie Lenhart, *Vice Pres*
EMP: 17
SQ FT: 280
SALES (est): 850K **Privately Held**
WEB: www.mtcases.com
SIC: **2522** Filing boxes, cabinets & cases: except wood

(G-21219)
NATURAL DISTRIBUTION COMPANY
550 Clayton Ct (60191-1115)
PHONE.................................630 350-1700
Dennis P Ryan, *President*
EMP: 1
SALES (est): 472.4K **Privately Held**
SIC: **5149** 2037 Natural & organic foods; fruit juices

(G-21220)
NEMETH TOOL INC (PA)
143 Murray Dr (60191-2238)
PHONE.................................630 595-0409
John F Nemeth, *President*
Mary Ann Nemeth, *Admin Sec*
EMP: 1 EST: 1979
SALES (est): 476.5K **Privately Held**
SIC: **3544** Industrial molds

(G-21221)
NEP ELECTRONICS INC (PA)
805 Mittel Dr (60191-1118)
PHONE.................................630 595-8500
Thomas Lotus, *President*
Chris Corbet, *Warehouse Mgr*
Rocco Dote, *Purchasing*
Randy Westlake, *Engineer*
Karoline Korzeniowski, *Human Res Mgr*
▲ EMP: 106 EST: 1977
SQ FT: 35,000
SALES (est): 67.7MM **Privately Held**
SIC: **5065** 3679 3824 Electronic parts; harness assemblies for electronic use: wire or cable; electromechanical counters

(G-21222)
NGK SPARK PLUGS (USA) INC
Also Called: N G K Spark Plugs
850 Aec Dr (60191-1122)
PHONE.................................630 595-7894
Andre Zangara, *Sales/Mktg Mgr*
EMP: 26 **Privately Held**
SIC: **3714** Motor vehicle parts & accessories
HQ: Ngk Spark Plugs (U.S.A.), Inc.
46929 Magellan
Wixom MI 48393
248 926-6900

(G-21223)
NOVATRONIX INC
600 Wheat Ln (60191-1109)
PHONE.................................630 860-4300
Anthony Kenevan, *President*
Edward Kenevan, *Vice Pres*
Jim Groth, *Opers Staff*
Donna Ellinger, *Purch Mgr*

Ray Spence, *Electrical Engi*
▲ EMP: 45
SALES (est): 12.7MM **Privately Held**
SIC: **3672** 7629 Printed circuit boards; circuit board repair

(G-21224)
O ADJUST MATIC PUMP COMPANY
Also Called: Wood Dale Pipe & Supply Co
429 E Potter St (60191-2117)
P.O. Box 424 (60191-0424)
PHONE.................................630 766-1490
Joe Peters, *President*
EMP: 2
SQ FT: 10,000
SALES (est): 300K **Privately Held**
SIC: **3561** 5084 Pumps & pumping equipment; industrial machinery & equipment

(G-21225)
OCS AMERICA INC
945 Dillon Dr (60191-1274)
PHONE.................................630 595-0111
Kazuki Ishikawa, *Manager*
Carmelo Gonzalez, *Supervisor*
EMP: 25 **Privately Held**
SIC: **7389** 5192 2711 5994 Courier or messenger service; newspapers; newspapers: publishing only, not printed on site; newsstand; magazine stand
HQ: Ocs America Inc.
11100 Hindry Ave
Los Angeles CA 90045

(G-21226)
P & P ARTEC INC (DH)
Also Called: P & P Artec Handrail Div
700 Creel Dr (60191-2608)
PHONE.................................630 860-2990
Christian Potthoff-Sewing, *President*
▲ EMP: 19
SQ FT: 15,000
SALES (est): 3.7MM
SALES (corp-wide): 137.3K **Privately Held**
SIC: **3446** Ornamental metalwork
HQ: Poppe + Potthoff Gmbh
Dammstr. 17
Werther (Westf.) 33824
520 391-660

(G-21227)
PARAMOUNT LAMINATES INC
907 N Central Ave (60191-1218)
PHONE.................................630 594-1840
Paul Lee, *President*
Cindy Wong, *Vice Pres*
Cindy L Wong, *Admin Sec*
▲ EMP: 2
SALES (est): 387.1K **Privately Held**
SIC: **3672** Circuit boards, television & radio printed

(G-21228)
POWER SOLUTIONS INTL INC (HQ)
201 Mittel Dr (60191-1116)
PHONE.................................630 350-9400
John P Miller, *President*
Kelly Crosier, *Counsel*
Rick Nielsen, *Exec VP*
Kenneth Winemaster, *Exec VP*
Curtis Boyd, *Vice Pres*
▲ EMP: 170
SALES: 546MM
SALES (corp-wide): 22.9B **Privately Held**
SIC: **3511** 5084 Turbines & turbine generator sets; oil refining machinery, equipment & supplies
PA: Weichai Power Co., Ltd.
Jia No.197, Foshou E. Street, High-Tech Industrial Development Z
Weifang 26106
536 819-7787

(G-21229)
PRECISION INDUSTRIAL KNIFE
850 Dillon Dr (60191-1269)
PHONE.................................630 350-7898
Kenneth Machynia, *President*
EMP: 5
SQ FT: 8,000
SALES: 1.2MM **Privately Held**
SIC: **3423** Knives, agricultural or industrial

(G-21230)
PRECISION MACHINE PRODUCTS
655 N Central Ave Ste G (60191-1467)
PHONE.................................630 860-0861
Jan Glabus, *President*
EMP: 3
SQ FT: 2,300
SALES: 190K **Privately Held**
SIC: **3599** Machine shop, jobbing & repair

(G-21231)
PRIME LABEL & PACKAGING LLC
501 N Central Ave (60191-1473)
PHONE.................................630 227-1300
Kollman Kevin J,
EMP: 65
SQ FT: 57,600
SALES (est): 10MM **Privately Held**
WEB: www.primelabelpkg.com
SIC: **2759** 2671 Flexographic printing; packaging paper & plastics film, coated & laminated
PA: Prime Packaging, Llc
1000 Garey Dr
Yardley PA 19067

(G-21232)
PRINT & MAILING SOLUTIONS LLC
745 Dillon Dr (60191-1273)
PHONE.................................708 544-9400
James Hezinger,
EMP: 4
SALES (est): 276.9K
SALES (corp-wide): 518.4K **Privately Held**
SIC: **2752** Commercial printing, lithographic
PA: Print And Mailing Solutions Llc
1053 N Schmidt Rd
Romeoville IL 60446
708 544-9400

(G-21233)
QUALITY SURFACE MOUNT INC
965 Dillon Dr (60191-1274)
PHONE.................................630 350-8556
Steve Zielinski, *President*
Jack Kopis, *Vice Pres*
EMP: 20
SQ FT: 12,000
SALES (est): 5.2MM **Privately Held**
SIC: **3672** Circuit boards, television & radio printed

(G-21234)
REBA MACHINE CORP
767 N Edgewood Ave (60191-1254)
PHONE.................................630 595-1272
Mario Lew, *CEO*
EMP: 6 EST: 1998
SALES (est): 737.5K **Privately Held**
WEB: www.rebamachine.com
SIC: **3599** Machine shop, jobbing & repair

(G-21235)
RUBY INDUSTRIAL TECH LLC
827 N Central Ave (60191-1219)
PHONE.................................317 248-8355
Tim Sulikowski, *Branch Mgr*
EMP: 20
SALES (corp-wide): 735.6MM **Privately Held**
SIC: **3721** Helicopters
PA: Ruby Industrial Technologies, Llc
1 Vision Way
Bloomfield CT 06002
860 687-5000

(G-21236)
RUCO USA INC
915 N Central Ave (60191-1218)
PHONE.................................866 373-7912
▲ EMP: 22
SALES (est): 2.5MM **Privately Held**
SIC: **2759** Screen printing

(G-21237)
SA INDUSTRIES INC
756 N Edgewood Ave (60191-1249)
PHONE.................................847 730-4823
Arthur Szelag, *President*
EMP: 5

SALES: 250K **Privately Held**
SIC: **3553** Woodworking machinery

(G-21238)
SEA CONVERTING INC
895 Sivert Dr (60191-1208)
PHONE.................................630 694-9178
Paula Johnson, *President*
Jim Johnson, *Vice Pres*
EMP: 18
SQ FT: 18,000
SALES: 1MM **Privately Held**
SIC: **3353** Coils, sheet aluminum

(G-21239)
SEABEE SUPPLY CO
390 E Irving Park Rd (60191-1645)
PHONE.................................630 860-1293
Grace Jamrozik, *Owner*
EMP: 4
SALES: 75K **Privately Held**
SIC: **2679** Paper products, converted

(G-21240)
SETTIMA USA INC
1555 N Mittel Blvd Ste A (60191-1023)
PHONE.................................630 812-1433
Michael E Williams, *Principal*
EMP: 4 EST: 2015
SALES (est): 191.1K
SALES (corp-wide): 355.8K **Privately Held**
SIC: **3594** Pumps, hydraulic power transfer
HQ: Settima Meccanica Srl
Piazzale Luigi Cadorna 6
Milano MI 20123
052 336-5029

(G-21241)
SLOAN INDUSTRIES INC
1550 N Michael Dr (60191-1003)
PHONE.................................630 350-1614
Henry Slowinski, *President*
Adam Niedospial, *Vice Pres*
▲ EMP: 30
SQ FT: 24,000
SALES (est): 4.7MM **Privately Held**
SIC: **7699** 8711 3542 Industrial equipment services; machine tool design; machine tools, metal forming type

(G-21242)
STANDARD REFRIGERATION LLC
Also Called: Alfa Laval Standard
321 Foster Ave (60191-1432)
PHONE.................................608 855-5800
Richard Levin, *CEO*
▲ EMP: 100
SALES (est): 14.6MM
SALES (corp-wide): 66.9MM **Privately Held**
SIC: **3585** Refrigeration & heating equipment
PA: Multistack, Llc
1065 Maple Ave
Sparta WI 54656
608 366-2400

(G-21243)
STAR LITE MFG
735 N Edgewood Ave Ste C (60191-1261)
PHONE.................................630 595-8338
Chris Zinkiewicz, *Owner*
EMP: 8
SALES (est): 838.7K **Privately Held**
SIC: **3999** Manufacturing industries

(G-21244)
STRYKER CORPORATION
1360 N Wood Dale Rd Ste B (60191-1075)
PHONE.................................630 616-0606
Jim Liston, *Manager*
EMP: 8
SALES (corp-wide): 14.8B **Publicly Held**
WEB: www.stryker.com
SIC: **3841** Surgical instruments & apparatus
PA: Stryker Corporation
2825 Airview Blvd
Portage MI 49002
269 385-2600

Wood Dale - Dupage County (G-21245)

(G-21245)
T T T INC
387 Crestwood Rd (60191-2551)
P.O. Box 7080 (60191-7080)
PHONE..................................630 860-7499
Dennis F Sowa, *President*
EMP: 2
SALES (est): 5MM **Privately Held**
SIC: **3823** Industrial process measurement equipment

(G-21246)
TARGIN SIGN SYSTEMS INC
160 W Irving Park Rd (60191-1340)
PHONE..................................630 766-7667
Steve A Gruber, *President*
EMP: 7
SQ FT: 7,000
SALES (est): 713.3K **Privately Held**
SIC: **3993** 7336 Signs, not made in custom sign painting shops; electric signs; art design services; graphic arts & related design

(G-21247)
TECHNYMON TECHNOLOGY USA INC
730 N Edgewood Ave (60191-1249)
PHONE..................................630 787-0501
Luigi Mongodi, *President*
▲ EMP: 9
SQ FT: 10,000
SALES: 1.4MM **Privately Held**
SIC: **3568** Bearings, plain

(G-21248)
TEMPCO ELECTRIC HEATER CORP (PA)
607 N Central Ave (60191-1452)
PHONE..................................630 350-2252
Fermin Adames, *President*
William Kilberry, *Vice Pres*
Richard Sachs, *Vice Pres*
Abe Joseph, *VP Opers*
Andy Hagen, *Plant Mgr*
◆ EMP: 330
SQ FT: 130,000
SALES (est): 63.9MM **Privately Held**
SIC: **3567** 3369 3829 Heating units & devices, industrial: electric; castings, except die-castings, precision; thermocouples

(G-21249)
THERMAL INDUSTRIES INC
830 Sivert Dr (60191-2610)
PHONE..................................800 237-0560
Linda Cade, *Manager*
EMP: 20
SALES (corp-wide): 4.8B **Publicly Held**
SIC: **3442** 3081 Screens, window, metal; vinyl film & sheet
HQ: Thermal Industries, Inc.
 3700 Haney Ct
 Murrysville PA 15668
 724 325-6100

(G-21250)
TOPGOLF INTERNATIONAL INC
1001 N Prospect Ave (60191-1234)
PHONE..................................630 595-4653
Stefanie Mitchell, *Partner*
MO Yassin, *General Mgr*
Rodney Ferrell, *Vice Pres*
Drew Boatman, *Project Mgr*
Barry Callahan, *Project Mgr*
EMP: 5
SALES (corp-wide): 196.8MM **Privately Held**
SIC: **3949** Driving ranges, golf, electronic
PA: Topgolf International, Inc.
 8750 N Cntl Expy Ste 1200
 Dallas TX 75231
 214 377-0663

(G-21251)
TOYO INK INTERNATIONAL CORP (HQ)
1225 N Michael Dr (60191-1019)
PHONE..................................866 969-8696
Fusao Ito, *President*
Joe Sentendrey, *Exec VP*
Vipul Shah, *Vice Pres*
Rodrigo Denolan, *Research*
Sumathy Ganesh, *Research*
◆ EMP: 15
SALES (est): 82.1MM **Privately Held**
SIC: **2893** 5112 Printing ink; writing ink

(G-21252)
TROPAR TROPHY MANUFACTURING CO
839 N Central Ave (60191-1219)
PHONE..................................630 787-1900
Peter Ilaria, *Principal*
EMP: 20
SALES (corp-wide): 14.7MM **Privately Held**
SIC: **8742** 3999 Manufacturing management consultant; atomizers, toiletry
PA: Tropar Trophy Manufacturing Co. Inc
 5 Vreeland Rd
 Florham Park NJ 07932
 973 822-2400

(G-21253)
TRUSTY WARNS INC (PA)
229 N Central Ave (60191-1603)
PHONE..................................630 766-9015
Karl O Niedermeyer, *President*
Amy R Niedermeyer, *Vice Pres*
Sandy Niedermeyer, *Vice Pres*
EMP: 20 EST: 1948
SQ FT: 8,600
SALES (est): 4.2MM **Privately Held**
WEB: www.trustywarns.com
SIC: **3561** 3533 3523 Pumps & pumping equipment; oil & gas field machinery; farm machinery & equipment

(G-21254)
TWINPLEX MANUFACTURING CO
Also Called: Twinplex Stamping Company
840 Lively Blvd (60191-1202)
PHONE..................................630 595-2040
Kenneth Floyd, *President*
Steve Floyd, *Vice Pres*
Christine Shanahan, *Accountant*
EMP: 18 EST: 1940
SQ FT: 60,000
SALES: 4.3MM **Privately Held**
WEB: www.twinplex.com
SIC: **3469** Stamping metal for the trade

(G-21255)
VIDEOJET TECHNOLOGIES INC (HQ)
Also Called: Foba Pdts Aplicat Ctr Svc Ctr
1500 N Mittel Blvd (60191-1072)
PHONE..................................630 860-7300
Christopher Riley, *President*
Jackie Okwudi-Mcgee, *Principal*
Marco Sanchez, *Vice Pres*
Diana Yan, *Vice Pres*
David Hueneman, *Export Mgr*
◆ EMP: 650
SQ FT: 250,000
SALES (est): 630.8MM
SALES (corp-wide): 17.9B **Publicly Held**
SIC: **3699** Laser systems & equipment
PA: Danaher Corporation
 2200 Penn Ave Nw Ste 800w
 Washington DC 20037
 202 828-0850

(G-21256)
WATERS TECHNOLOGIES CORP
Also Called: Waters Associates
1360 N Wood Dale Rd Ste C (60191-1075)
PHONE..................................630 766-6249
Tim Willamson, *Branch Mgr*
EMP: 12 **Publicly Held**
SIC: **3826** Chromatographic equipment, laboratory type
HQ: Waters Technologies Corporation,
 34 Maple St
 Milford MA 01757
 508 478-2000

(G-21257)
WELD SEAM INC
Also Called: Weld-Seam
875 Lively Blvd (60191-1201)
PHONE..................................773 588-1012
Martin Bruner, *President*
Christine Bruner, *Vice Pres*
Robert Wolinski, *QC Mgr*
Bryan Bruner, *Manager*
EMP: 15
SQ FT: 10,000
SALES (est): 2.6MM **Privately Held**
SIC: **1799** 3449 Welding on site; miscellaneous metalwork

(G-21258)
WOODS MANUFACTURING CO INC
300 Beinoris Dr (60191-1223)
PHONE..................................630 595-6620
Michael Woods, *President*
Deborah Woods, *Admin Sec*
EMP: 4 EST: 1978
SQ FT: 3,000
SALES (est): 606.6K **Privately Held**
WEB: www.woodsmfg.com
SIC: **3053** 3492 Gaskets, all materials; fluid power valves & hose fittings

Wood River
Madison County

(G-21259)
AMERICLEAN INC
23 E Ferguson Ave (62095-1903)
P.O. Box 557 (62095-0557)
PHONE..................................314 741-8901
George R Adams, *President*
Carolyn Drake, *Corp Secy*
Robert D Drake Sr, *Vice Pres*
EMP: 12
SQ FT: 5,000
SALES (est): 2.2MM **Privately Held**
SIC: **2899** 3559 Chemical preparations; recycling machinery

(G-21260)
BUDGET SIGNS
Also Called: Budget Signs Trophies Plaques
333 E Edwardsville Rd (62095-1647)
PHONE..................................618 259-4460
Dan Jones, *Owner*
EMP: 10
SALES (est): 851K **Privately Held**
SIC: **3914** 3299 5099 5999 Trophies; plaques: clay, plaster or papier mache; signs, except electric; trophies & plaques; novelties; advertising novelties

(G-21261)
FIRST LOOK WHOLESALE LAB INC
90 Enviro Way (62095-1473)
PHONE..................................618 462-9042
Bob Jensen, *Manager*
Ronnie Jackson, *Director*
EMP: 5
SALES (est): 678.9K **Privately Held**
SIC: **3851** Ophthalmic goods

(G-21262)
GAMESTOP CORP
662 Wesley Dr (62095-1894)
PHONE..................................618 258-8611
Wendy Thurig, *Branch Mgr*
EMP: 4 **Publicly Held**
SIC: **5945** 3944 Hobby, toy & game shops; video game machines, except coin-operated
PA: Gamestop Corp.
 625 Westport Pkwy
 Grapevine TX 76051

(G-21263)
ICAN CLINIC LLC
Also Called: Alignlife
203 E Ferguson Ave (62095-2001)
PHONE..................................618 254-2273
Michael Harbison,
EMP: 3
SALES (est): 98.7K **Privately Held**
SIC: **6512** 1389 1771 Commercial & industrial building operation; excavating slush pits & cellars; stucco, gunite & grouting contractors

(G-21264)
INNOVATIVE MARINE SAFETY INC
35 W Ferguson Ave (62095-1905)
P.O. Box 346 (62095-0346)
PHONE..................................618 254-9470
Paul Dowdy, *President*
EMP: 3
SALES (est): 263.6K **Privately Held**
SIC: **3823** Boiler controls: industrial, power & marine type

(G-21265)
KIENSTRA-ILLINOIS LLC
201 W Ferguson Ave (62095-1408)
PHONE..................................618 251-6345
Jeanne Gent, *Principal*
Scott Mayberry, *Manager*
EMP: 13
SALES (est): 1.8MM **Privately Held**
SIC: **3273** Ready-mixed concrete

(G-21266)
PUMP HOUSE
1523 E Edwardsville Rd (62095-2295)
PHONE..................................618 216-2404
Gary Vollmer, *Owner*
EMP: 3
SALES (est): 363.1K **Privately Held**
SIC: **5084** 3561 Pumps & pumping equipment; pumps & pumping equipment

(G-21267)
SHELL OIL COMPANY
200 E Lorena Ave (62095-2020)
P.O. Box 76, Roxana (62084-0068)
PHONE..................................618 254-7371
E G Johnson, *Branch Mgr*
EMP: 140
SALES (corp-wide): 344.8B **Privately Held**
SIC: **2911** Gasoline
HQ: Shell Oil Company
 150 N Dairy Ashford Rd A
 Houston TX 77079
 713 241-6161

(G-21268)
WOOD RIVER PRINTING & PUBG CO
22 N 1st St (62095-2039)
P.O. Box 101 (62095-0101)
PHONE..................................618 254-3134
Bradney Racey, *President*
Vicki Truetzschler, *General Mgr*
Tony Hall, *CFO*
W Joseph Racey, *Admin Sec*
EMP: 9
SQ FT: 10,000
SALES (est): 1.7MM **Privately Held**
WEB: www.woodriverprinting.com
SIC: **2752** 2759 Commercial printing, offset; bookbinding & related work; commercial printing
PA: D E Asbury Inc
 1479 Keokuk St
 Hamilton IL 62341

Woodridge
Dupage County

(G-21269)
10G LLC
100 Morey Dr (60517-8135)
PHONE..................................630 754-2400
Paul Boast,
EMP: 15
SALES: 4.6MM
SALES (corp-wide): 53.8B **Publicly Held**
SIC: **3629** 3675 8711 3825 Electronic generation equipment; electronic capacitors; engineering services; engine electrical test equipment
PA: Caterpillar Inc.
 510 Lake Cook Rd Ste 100
 Deerfield IL 60015
 224 551-4000

(G-21270)
3VUE LLC
6440 Main St Ste 330 (60517-1290)
PHONE..................................630 796-7441
Aline Ceciliano, *Principal*
EMP: 5
SALES (est): 518.4K **Privately Held**
WEB: www.3vuellc.com
SIC: **7372** Prepackaged software

▲ = Import ▼ = Export
◆ = Import/Export

GEOGRAPHIC SECTION

Woodridge - Dupage County (G-21297)

(G-21271)
A CORPORATE PRINTING SERVICE
7705 Dalewood Pkwy (60517-2903)
PHONE...............630 515-0432
James Rennie, *Principal*
EMP: 10
SALES (est): 939.4K **Privately Held**
SIC: 2759 Commercial printing

(G-21272)
A-CREATIONS INC
8102 Lemont Rd Ste 1500 (60517-7776)
PHONE...............630 541-5801
Jim Earl, *President*
Denise Earle, *Manager*
EMP: 9
SALES (est): 1.1MM **Privately Held**
WEB: www.acreations.net
SIC: 2759 Screen printing

(G-21273)
AH TENSOR INTERNATIONAL LLC
10330 Argonne Woods Dr # 300 (60517-5088)
PHONE...............630 739-9600
Mattias Andersson, *CEO*
Michael Pavone, *COO*
▼ **EMP:** 40 **EST:** 2012
SALES (est): 5.6MM **Privately Held**
SIC: 2752 Commercial printing, offset
PA: Automation House Sweden Ab
Haggastrandsvagen 5
Kinna

(G-21274)
AMERICAN HOLIDAY LIGHTS INC
6813 Hobson Valley Dr # 102 (60517-1451)
PHONE...............630 769-9999
Jeff Krall, *President*
EMP: 2
SALES (est): 241.7K **Privately Held**
WEB: www.americanholidaylights.com
SIC: 3699 5063 Christmas tree lighting sets, electric; lighting fixtures

(G-21275)
APL LOGISTICS AMERICAS LTD
2649 Internationale Pkwy (60517-4803)
PHONE...............630 783-0200
Crystal Stram, *President*
▲ **EMP:** 18
SALES (est): 88.2MM **Privately Held**
SIC: 3531 Construction machinery
HQ: Apl Logistics Americas, Ltd
17600 N Perimeter Dr # 150
Scottsdale AZ 85255
602 586-4800

(G-21276)
ARTISAN ELEMENT
6128 Allan Dr (60517-1042)
PHONE...............630 229-5654
EMP: 4
SALES (est): 266.9K **Privately Held**
SIC: 2819 Elements

(G-21277)
AUTOMAX CORPORATION
1940 Intrntonale Pkwy # 550 (60517-3186)
PHONE...............630 972-1919
Frank L Gronowski, *President*
Raymond S Gronowski, *Vice Pres*
EMP: 8
SQ FT: 3,800
SALES (est): 580K **Privately Held**
SIC: 5084 3822 3561 Controlling instruments & accessories; materials handling machinery; auto controls regulating residntl & coml environmt & applncs; pumps & pumping equipment

(G-21278)
BARK PROJECT MANAGEMENT INC
7017 Roberts Dr (60517-1904)
PHONE...............630 964-5876
Robert S Kennard Sr, *President*
EMP: 3
SALES (est): 463.3K **Privately Held**
SIC: 2542 Office & store showcases & display fixtures

(G-21279)
BOLER COMPANY
Also Called: Hendrickson
800 S Frontage Rd (60517-4900)
PHONE...............630 910-2800
John Boler, *Branch Mgr*
EMP: 133
SALES (corp-wide): 980.2MM **Privately Held**
SIC: 3714 Motor vehicle parts & accessories
PA: The Boler Company
500 Park Blvd Ste 1010
Itasca IL 60143
630 773-9111

(G-21280)
CARGILL INCORPORATED
10420 Woodward Ave (60517-4934)
PHONE...............630 739-1746
EMP: 5
SALES (corp-wide): 113.4B **Privately Held**
SIC: 5153 2075 Grain & field beans; soybean oil, cake or meal
PA: Cargill, Incorporated
15407 Mcginty Rd W
Wayzata MN 55391
952 742-7575

(G-21281)
CARGILL MEAT SOLUTIONS CORP
Also Called: Cargill Food Distribution
10420 Woodward Ave (60517-4934)
PHONE...............630 739-1746
EMP: 182
SALES (corp-wide): 113.4B **Privately Held**
SIC: 2011 Meat packing plants
HQ: Cargill Meat Solutions Corp
151 N Main St Ste 900
Wichita KS 67202
316 291-2500

(G-21282)
CFPG LTD (DH)
Also Called: Gerber Plumbing Fixtures
2500 Intrntonale Pkwy (60517-4979)
PHONE...............630 679-1420
Frank Feraco, *President*
Ila J Lewis, *President*
James Schwartz, *Controller*
Jon Kinnas, *Accountant*
Bill Tipps, *Regl Sales Mgr*
▲ **EMP:** 129 **EST:** 1932
SQ FT: 20,000
SALES (est): 35.2MM **Privately Held**
WEB: www.gerberonline.com
SIC: 3261 3432 Plumbing fixtures, vitreous china; plumbers' brass goods: drain cocks, faucets, spigots, etc.
HQ: Globe Union Group Inc.
2500 Internationale Pkwy
Woodridge IL 60517
630 679-1420

(G-21283)
CHAMPION PACKAGING & DIST INC
2501 Internationale Pkwy (60517-4802)
PHONE...............630 972-0100
Thomas J Pecora, *CEO*
Heidi Miller, *Buyer*
Chad T Pecora, *Admin Sec*
EMP: 160
SALES (est): 80.8MM **Privately Held**
WEB: www.champakinc.com
SIC: 2842 2812 Ammonia, household; chlorine, compressed or liquefied

(G-21284)
CHICAGO BRICK OVEN LLC (PA)
1020 Davey Rd Ste 300 (60517-5161)
PHONE...............630 359-4793
William Pathen, *Vice Pres*
Carmen Parisi, *Mng Member*
▼ **EMP:** 4
SALES (est): 1.5MM **Privately Held**
WEB: www.chicagobrickoven.com
SIC: 3567 Industrial furnaces & ovens

(G-21285)
CLARKE EQUIPMENT COMPANY
2649 Internationale Pkwy (60517-4803)
PHONE...............701 241-8700
EMP: 3 **Privately Held**
SIC: 3531 Backhoes, tractors, cranes, plows & similar equipment
HQ: Clark Equipment Company
250 E Beaton Dr
West Fargo ND 58078
701 241-8700

(G-21286)
COLUMBUS MCKINNON CORPORATION
Also Called: Abel Howe Crane
10321 Werch Dr Ste 100 (60517-4812)
PHONE...............630 783-1195
Eric Bach, *Manager*
EMP: 40
SALES (corp-wide): 809.1MM **Publicly Held**
SIC: 3536 Hoists
PA: Columbus Mckinnon Corporation
205 Crosspoint Pkwy
Getzville NY 14068
716 689-5400

(G-21287)
CONTEGO DEFENSE GROUP
7546 Janes Ave (60517-2926)
PHONE...............630 532-1063
Jonathan Villanueva, *Principal*
EMP: 3 **EST:** 2017
SALES (est): 232.8K **Privately Held**
WEB: www.contegodefensegroup.com
SIC: 3812 Defense systems & equipment

(G-21288)
COOPERS HWK INTERMEDTE HOLDNG
9016 Murphy Rd Ste 200 (60517-1123)
PHONE...............708 215-5674
EMP: 13
SALES (corp-wide): 246.9MM **Privately Held**
SIC: 2084 Wines
PA: Cooper's Hawk Intermediate Holding, Llc
3500 Lacey Rd Ste 1000
Downers Grove IL 60515
708 839-2920

(G-21289)
CUPCAKE HOLDINGS LLC
2240 75th St (60517-2333)
PHONE...............800 794-5866
Jerry W Levin, *Mng Member*
EMP: 200
SALES (est): 15.5MM **Privately Held**
WEB: www.wilton.com
SIC: 5023 2731 2721 7812 Kitchenware; kitchen tools & utensils; frames & framing, picture & mirror; books: publishing only; periodicals: publishing only; video tape production; candy making goods & supplies

(G-21290)
CUPCAKEOLOGIST LLC
2124 Country Club Dr (60517-3031)
PHONE...............630 656-2272
Mikhail Milad, *Principal*
EMP: 4 **EST:** 2014
SALES (est): 312.4K **Privately Held**
WEB: www.cupcakeologist.us
SIC: 2051 Bread, cake & related products

(G-21291)
DANZE INC
2500 Internationale Pkwy (60517-4073)
PHONE...............630 754-0277
Michael Werner, *President*
Ron Cox, *Regl Sales Mgr*
Alyson Angotti, *Marketing Mgr*
Craig Holthus, *Director*
Robert Larson, *Director*
◆ **EMP:** 100 **EST:** 2002
SQ FT: 300,000
SALES (est): 20.9MM **Privately Held**
WEB: www.danze.com
SIC: 3088 Plastics plumbing fixtures
HQ: Globe Union Group Inc.
2500 Internationale Pkwy
Woodridge IL 60517
630 679-1420

(G-21292)
DARBE PRODUCTS COMPANY INC
2936 Two Paths Dr (60517-4511)
PHONE...............630 985-0769
Fax: 630 985-0777
EMP: 4
SALES (est): 150K **Privately Held**
SIC: 3496 5085 Mfg Miscellaneous Fabricated Wire Products & Whol Industrial Supplies

(G-21293)
DAVID MICHAEL PRODUCTIONS
1340 Internationale Pkwy # 100 (60517-5115)
PHONE...............630 972-9640
David Pollock, *President*
EMP: 10
SALES (est): 2.5MM **Privately Held**
WEB: www.davidmichaelproductions.com
SIC: 3648 Lighting equipment

(G-21294)
DOBER CHEMICAL CORP (PA)
Also Called: Dober Group
11230 Katherines Crossin (60517)
PHONE...............630 410-7300
John G Dobrez, *President*
Daniel Dobrez, *Exec VP*
Scott Dobrez, *Exec VP*
Scott Smith, *Senior VP*
Michael Engels, *Vice Pres*
◆ **EMP:** 140
SALES (est): 32.4MM **Privately Held**
WEB: www.dober.com
SIC: 2842 2899 Specialty cleaning, polishes & sanitation goods; water treating compounds

(G-21295)
DOMINOS PIZZA LLC
10410 Woodward Ave # 100 (60517-4934)
PHONE...............630 783-0738
Greg Higgins, *Manager*
EMP: 40
SALES (corp-wide): 3.6B **Publicly Held**
WEB: www.dominos.com
SIC: 5812 2045 Pizzeria, chain; prepared flour mixes & doughs
HQ: Domino's Pizza Llc
30 Frank Lloyd Wright Dr
Ann Arbor MI 48105
734 930-3030

(G-21296)
DRY SYSTEMS TECHNOLOGIES LLC (HQ)
10420 Rising Ct (60517-7789)
PHONE...............630 427-2051
Ronald D Eberhart, *Mng Member*
▲ **EMP:** 50
SALES (est): 5.2MM
SALES (corp-wide): 14.2MM **Privately Held**
SIC: 3532 Mining machinery
PA: Yorkshire Equity Llc
100 Fillmore St Ste 500
Denver CO 80206
303 385-8434

(G-21297)
ECP INCORPORATED
Also Called: Protector, The
11210 Katherines Xing # 100 (60517-4043)
P.O. Box 1098, Oak Brook (60522-1098)
PHONE...............630 754-4200
Larry Bettendorf, *President*
Tom Damato, *District Mgr*
Mike Feely, *Exec VP*
Ryan Gillespie, *Inv Control Mgr*
Dolores G Wojciechowicz, *Human Res Mgr*
EMP: 54
SQ FT: 136,000
SALES (est): 22.1MM **Privately Held**
SIC: 2842 2899 2841 5169 Specialty cleaning preparations; automobile polish; waxes for wood, leather & other materials; rust resisting compounds; soap & other detergents; rustproofing chemicals

Woodridge - Dupage County (G-21298)

(G-21298)
EGAN WAGNER CORPORATION
2929 Two Paths Dr (60517-4512)
PHONE..................................630 985-8007
Richard Wagner, *President*
Bonnie Egan, *Chairman*
EMP: 4
SALES (est): 450K **Privately Held**
SIC: 3694 Engine electrical equipment

(G-21299)
ELEVANCE RNEWABLE SCIENCES INC (PA)
2501 Davey Rd (60517-4957)
P.O. Box 1100, Bolingbrook (60440-8602)
PHONE..................................630 296-8880
K'Lynne Johnson, *CEO*
Mel Luetkens, *COO*
Del Craig, *Exec VP*
Andy Shafer, *Exec VP*
Jeffery Duncan, *Vice Pres*
▼ **EMP:** 139
SALES (est): 31.8MM **Privately Held**
SIC: 2869 Industrial organic chemicals

(G-21300)
ELGALABWATER LLC
5 Earl Ct Ste 100 (60517-7622)
PHONE..................................630 343-5251
Klaus Andersen, *Mng Member*
▲ **EMP:** 6
SALES (est): 570K **Privately Held**
SIC: 3542 Machine tools, metal forming type

(G-21301)
FLOWSERVE US INC
1020 Davey Rd Ste 100 (60517-5108)
PHONE..................................630 783-1468
Paula Wroda, *Sales Staff*
Michael Daugherty, *Marketing Staff*
John Stillane, *Manager*
EMP: 55
SALES (corp-wide): 3.9B **Publicly Held**
SIC: 3561 Pumps & pumping equipment
HQ: Flowserve Us Inc.
5215 N Oconnor Blvd Ste Connor
Irving TX 75039
972 443-6500

(G-21302)
FRI JADO INC
1401 Davey Rd Ste 100 (60517-4964)
PHONE..................................630 633-7944
Erik J Bos, *President*
Edwin Van Sprundel, *CFO*
Martin Pb Wawrzyniak, *Admin Sec*
▲ **EMP:** 8
SALES (est): 1.1MM
SALES (corp-wide): 242.1K **Privately Held**
SIC: 3221 Food containers, glass
HQ: Fri-Jado B.V.
Blauwhekken 2
Oud Gastel 4751
765 085-200

(G-21303)
GERBER PLUMBING FIXTURES LLC
2500 Intrntonale Pkwy (60517-4073)
PHONE..................................630 679-1420
Keith Yurco, *President*
Bryan Fiala, *Admin Sec*
▲ **EMP:** 53
SALES (est): 165MM **Privately Held**
SIC: 3261 Plumbing fixtures, vitreous china
HQ: Globe Union Group Inc.
2500 Internationale Pkwy
Woodridge IL 60517
630 679-1420

(G-21304)
GLOBE UNION GROUP INC (HQ)
2500 Internationale Pkwy (60517-5090)
PHONE..................................630 679-1420
Dennis Dugas, *Principal*
Joe Sell, *Vice Pres*
Keith Yurko, *Vice Pres*
Teresa Lin, *Sales Mgr*
Bridget Kenar, *Sales Staff*
◆ **EMP:** 100
SALES (est): 221.1MM **Privately Held**
SIC: 3261 3432 7699 Plumbing fixtures, vitreous china; plumbers' brass goods: drain cocks, faucets, spigots, etc.; general household repair services

(G-21305)
GOVQA INC
900 S Frontage Rd Ste 110 (60517-4902)
PHONE..................................630 985-1300
John Dilenschneider, *CEO*
Gregory Pengiel, *CTO*
Chris Woods, *Info Tech Dir*
Jennifer Snyder, *Officer*
Brandon Collie, *Executive*
EMP: 18
SALES (est): 108.2K **Privately Held**
SIC: 7372 Prepackaged software
PA: Webqa Incorporated
900 S Frontage Rd Ste 110
Woodridge IL 60517

(G-21306)
GRAHAM PACKAGING COMPANY LP
2400 Internationale Pkwy # 1 (60517-4977)
PHONE..................................630 739-9150
Paul Wu, *General Mgr*
Mark Schneider, *Director*
EMP: 50 **Publicly Held**
SIC: 3089 3085 Plastic containers, except foam; plastics bottles
HQ: Graham Packaging Company, L.P.
700 Indian Springs Dr # 100
Lancaster PA 17601
717 849-8500

(G-21307)
GREAT LAKES TOOL & MOLD INC
6817 Hobson Valley Dr # 116 (60517-1452)
PHONE..................................630 964-7121
Steve Creagan, *Owner*
EMP: 2
SQ FT: 2,100
SALES (est): 230K **Privately Held**
SIC: 3544 Industrial molds

(G-21308)
GYCOR INTERNATIONAL LTD
10216 Werch Dr Ste 108 (60517-5124)
PHONE..................................630 754-8070
David J Rogers, *President*
John Gyann, *President*
Karen Decaro, *Bookkeeper*
Ron Voelker, *Manager*
Francine Gyann, *Admin Sec*
EMP: 14
SQ FT: 12,000
SALES (est): 3.4MM **Privately Held**
SIC: 2819 2099 2087 Industrial inorganic chemicals; food preparations; flavoring extracts & syrups

(G-21309)
H C SCHAU & SON INC
10350 Argonne Dr Ste 400 (60517-4999)
PHONE..................................630 783-1000
Charles H Schau, *CEO*
Randall C Schau, *Vice Pres*
Fay Schau, *Admin Sec*
EMP: 200
SALES (est): 104.9MM **Privately Held**
WEB: www.hcschau.com
SIC: 5147 2099 Meats, fresh; food preparations
HQ: Clover Us Holdings, Llc
3333 Finley Rd Ste 800
Downers Grove IL 60515
630 967-3600

(G-21310)
HEARTHSIDE USA LLC
10350 Argonne Dr Ste 400 (60517-4999)
PHONE..................................630 783-1000
Woody McTootle, *Technology*
Harry Lys, *Admin Sec*
EMP: 10 **Privately Held**
WEB: www.hearthsidefoods.com
SIC: 2099 Food preparations
HQ: Hearthside Usa, Llc
3333 Finley Rd Ste 800
Downers Grove IL 60515
978 716-2530

(G-21311)
HENDRICKSON INTERNATIONAL CORP (HQ)
840 S Frontage Rd (60517-4900)
PHONE..................................630 874-9700
Gary Gerstenslager, *President*
◆ **EMP:** 30
SALES (est): 153.8MM
SALES (corp-wide): 980.2MM **Privately Held**
SIC: 3714 Motor vehicle parts & accessories
PA: The Boler Company
500 Park Blvd Ste 1010
Itasca IL 60143
630 773-9111

(G-21312)
HENDRICKSON USA LLC
Hendrickson Truck Commercial
800 S Frontage Rd (60517-4900)
PHONE..................................630 910-2800
James Burrier, *Regional Mgr*
Randy Couchman, *Materials Mgr*
Kevin Gordon, *Production*
Dave Rees, *Purchasing*
Gabe Anaya, *Engineer*
EMP: 20
SALES (corp-wide): 980.2MM **Privately Held**
SIC: 3714 Motor vehicle parts & accessories
HQ: Hendrickson Usa, L.L.C.
800 S Frontage Rd
Woodridge IL 60517

(G-21313)
HENDRICKSON USA LLC (HQ)
Also Called: Hendrickson Truck Suspension
800 S Frontage Rd (60517-4900)
PHONE..................................630 910-2844
Perry Bahr, *Vice Pres*
Mike Keeler, *Vice Pres*
David Willis, *Materials Mgr*
Mike Barker, *Maint Spvr*
Jeremy Piccuica, *Senior Buyer*
◆ **EMP:** 224
SALES (est): 660.9MM
SALES (corp-wide): 980.2MM **Privately Held**
SIC: 3714 Motor vehicle parts & accessories
PA: The Boler Company
500 Park Blvd Ste 1010
Itasca IL 60143
630 773-9111

(G-21314)
HOME RUN INN FROZEN FOODS CORP
1300 Internationale Pkwy (60517-4928)
PHONE..................................630 783-9696
Joseph Perrino, *President*
Marilyn Carlson, *President*
Lucretia Costello, *President*
Steven E Larek, *CFO*
John C Carlson, *Admin Sec*
EMP: 100
SQ FT: 44,000
SALES (est): 27MM **Privately Held**
SIC: 2038 Pizza, frozen

(G-21315)
INTELLIGRATED SYSTEMS INC
9014 Heritage Pkwy # 308 (60517-5078)
PHONE..................................630 985-4350
Paula Steffensmeier, *Manager*
EMP: 264
SALES (corp-wide): 36.7B **Publicly Held**
SIC: 3535 5084 7371 Conveyors & conveying equipment; industrial machinery & equipment; computer software development
HQ: Intelligrated Systems, Inc.
7901 Innovation Way
Mason OH 45040
866 936-7300

(G-21316)
INVENTUS POWER INC (HQ)
1200 Internationale Pkwy (60517-4975)
PHONE..................................630 410-7900
Patrick Trippel, *CEO*
Nuo MA, *Exec VP*
Michael Stuart, *Exec VP*
Ilyas Ayub, *Vice Pres*
Michelle Imhoff, *Vice Pres*
◆ **EMP:** 200
SALES (est): 1B **Privately Held**
SIC: 3629 3691 Battery chargers, rectifying or nonrotating; storage batteries
PA: Inventus Power Holdings, Inc.
1200 Internationale Pkwy
Woodridge IL 60517
630 410-7900

(G-21317)
INVENTUS POWER (ILLINOIS) LLC
1200 Internationale Pkwy (60517-4975)
PHONE..................................630 410-7900
Patrick Trippel, *President*
Derek Kane, *Vice Pres*
Anson Martin, *Vice Pres*
Nuo MA, *Vice Pres*
Michael Foy, *CFO*
▲ **EMP:** 140
SQ FT: 17,000
SALES (est): 34.8MM
SALES (corp-wide): 1B **Privately Held**
SIC: 3699 3621 3679 3537 Electrical equipment & supplies; electric motor & generator parts; armatures, industrial; coils, for electric motors or generators; electronic loads & power supplies; power supplies, all types: static; loading docks: portable, adjustable & hydraulic
HQ: Inventus Power, Inc.
1200 Internationale Pkwy
Woodridge IL 60517

(G-21318)
INVENTUS POWER HOLDINGS INC (PA)
Also Called: Iccn Holdings
1200 Internationale Pkwy (60517-4975)
PHONE..................................630 410-7900
Patrick Trippel, *CEO*
Pat Trippel, *CEO*
Doug Eaton, *Engineer*
Kelly Dobson, *Accountant*
EMP: 6
SALES (est): 1B **Privately Held**
SIC: 3691 Storage batteries

(G-21319)
KARA GRAPHICS INC
6823 Hobson Valley Dr # 201 (60517-5454)
PHONE..................................630 964-8122
Teri Reuter, *President*
Ken Reuter, *Vice Pres*
EMP: 7
SQ FT: 600
SALES (est): 1MM **Privately Held**
SIC: 2759 Business forms: printing

(G-21320)
MAGNUSON GROUP INC
1400 Internationale Pkwy (60517-4942)
PHONE..................................630 783-8100
Kelly Quackbush, *President*
Peter Magnuson, *Chairman*
◆ **EMP:** 15
SQ FT: 25,000
SALES (est): 2.6MM **Privately Held**
SIC: 2521 Wood office furniture

(G-21321)
MANROLAND GOSS WEB SYSTEMS INT (HQ)
9018 Heritage Pkwy # 1200 (60517-5041)
PHONE..................................630 796-7560
Richard Nichols, *CEO*
Jochen Meissner, *President*
◆ **EMP:** 21
SALES (est): 163.6MM **Privately Held**
SIC: 3555 5084 Printing presses; printing trades machinery, equipment & supplies

(G-21322)
MANUFACTURERS CUSTOM PRODUCTS
3510 Hobson Rd Ste 101c (60517-1440)
PHONE..................................630 988-5055
EMP: 3
SALES (est): 202K **Privately Held**
SIC: 3089 Injection molding of plastics

GEOGRAPHIC SECTION

Woodridge - Dupage County (G-21349)

(G-21323)
MICROSUN ELECTRONICS CORP
1200 Internationale Pkwy # 101 (60517-4976)
PHONE..................630 410-7900
Nancie Elshafei, *CEO*
EMP: 11 **EST:** 2011
SALES (est): 1.2MM Privately Held
SIC: 3672 Circuit boards, television & radio printed

(G-21324)
MONOLITHIC INDUSTRIES INC
7613 Woodridge Dr (60517-2813)
PHONE..................630 985-6009
Ken Earle, *President*
EMP: 3
SALES (est): 367.1K Privately Held
WEB: www.monolithicind.com
SIC: 3825 8748 Test equipment for electronic & electrical circuits; business consulting

(G-21325)
NAVITAS ELECTRONICS CORP
1200 Internationale Pkwy (60517-4975)
PHONE..................702 293-4670
Alan Elshafei, *President*
Ralph Kuprewicz, *General Mgr*
Mark Aramli, *Vice Pres*
Thomas Golab, *Vice Pres*
Michael Ciaccio, *Engineer*
EMP: 35
SQ FT: 22,000
SALES: 5MM Privately Held
SIC: 3679 Electronic circuits

(G-21326)
NAVITAS SYSTEMS LLC (HQ)
1200 Internationale Pkwy # 125 (60517-5042)
PHONE..................630 755-7920
Christopher E Pruitt, *President*
Les Alexander, *General Mgr*
Thomas Golab, *Vice Pres*
Tim Whalen, *Mfg Staff*
Michael Ciaccio, *Engineer*
▲ **EMP:** 10 **EST:** 2011
SQ FT: 14,000
SALES (est): 3.5MM
SALES (corp-wide): 2.8B Privately Held
SIC: 3691 Storage batteries
PA: East Penn Manufacturing Co.
102 Deka Rd
Lyon Station PA 19536
610 682-6361

(G-21327)
NIMLOK CO
9033 Murphy Rd (60517-1100)
PHONE..................855 764-6565
EMP: 3
SALES (est): 275K Privately Held
WEB: www.nimlok.com
SIC: 3993 Signs & advertising specialties

(G-21328)
ORBUS LLC (PA)
Also Called: Orbus Exhibit & Display Group
9033 Murphy Rd (60517-1100)
PHONE..................630 226-1155
Giles Douglas, *President*
Kate Kincaid, *Regional Mgr*
Jim Apostle, *Vice Pres*
Jaime Herand, *Vice Pres*
Aaron Kozar, *Vice Pres*
◆ **EMP:** 185 **EST:** 2001
SQ FT: 128,000
SALES (est): 39.5MM Privately Held
WEB: www.orbus.com
SIC: 3993 Signs & advertising specialties

(G-21329)
ORBUS HOLDINGS INC
Also Called: Orbus Trade Show
9033 Murphy Rd (60517-1100)
PHONE..................630 226-1155
Giles N Douglas, *President*
Tina Del Fiacco, *Regional Mgr*
James Apostle, *Vice Pres*
John Warman, *Vice Pres*
Matt Robinson, *Production*
EMP: 90 Privately Held

SIC: 6719 3999 Investment holding companies, except banks; advertising display products

(G-21330)
PALLADIUM ENERGY GROUP INC (DH)
1200 Internationale Pkwy # 101 (60517-4976)
PHONE..................630 410-7900
John J Gatti, *CEO*
Ken Tarbell, *President*
Dr Like Xie, *Vice Pres*
Mike Pomeroy, *CFO*
Robb Warwick, *Asst Treas*
▲ **EMP:** 29
SALES (est): 22.5MM
SALES (corp-wide): 1B Privately Held
SIC: 3691 Batteries, rechargeable

(G-21331)
PARKER-HANNIFIN CORPORATION
Integrated Elastomeric Sys
10625 Beaudin Blvd (60517-4993)
PHONE..................630 427-2020
Doug Vanlue, *Branch Mgr*
EMP: 160
SALES (corp-wide): 14.3B Publicly Held
SIC: 2822 Synthetic rubber
PA: Parker-Hannifin Corporation
6035 Parkland Blvd
Cleveland OH 44124
216 896-3000

(G-21332)
PMT NUCLEAR
9341 Adam Don Pkwy (60517-8140)
PHONE..................630 887-7700
Ben Campbell, *President*
EMP: 4
SALES (est): 169.2K Privately Held
SIC: 3443 Fabricated plate work (boiler shop)

(G-21333)
POWERS WOODWORKING
6804 Hobson Valley Dr # 117 (60517-1448)
PHONE..................630 663-9644
Michael Powers, *Principal*
EMP: 8
SALES (est): 742.2K Privately Held
SIC: 2499 Decorative wood & woodwork

(G-21334)
PRINTSMART PRINTING & GRAPHICS
3024 Hobson Rd (60517-1510)
PHONE..................630 434-2000
Michael Burke, *President*
Constance Burke, *Treasurer*
EMP: 4
SQ FT: 1,600
SALES (est): 469.4K Privately Held
SIC: 2752 Commercial printing, offset

(G-21335)
PRODUCEPRO INC (PA)
9014 Heritage Pkwy # 304 (60517-5078)
PHONE..................630 395-9700
David R Donat, *President*
Courtney Heim, *Marketing Staff*
Julie Schlosser, *Manager*
Jacob Dehart, *Software Dev*
David Tomecek, *Software Dev*
EMP: 3
SQ FT: 6,500
SALES (est): 6.1MM Privately Held
SIC: 7372 Application computer software

(G-21336)
RANCILIO NORTH AMERICA INC
11130 Katherines Xing (60517-5046)
PHONE..................630 427-1703
Glenn Surlet, *Admin Sec*
◆ **EMP:** 23 **EST:** 1999
SALES (est): 5.9MM Privately Held
WEB: www.ranciliogroupna.com
SIC: 3556 Roasting machinery: coffee, peanut, etc.

(G-21337)
ROBINSPORT LLC
2613 York Ct (60517-1609)
PHONE..................630 724-9280

Kreig Robinson,
EMP: 6
SALES (est): 461.3K Privately Held
SIC: 4212 3713 4789 Local trucking, without storage; truck cabs for motor vehicles; cargo loading & unloading services

(G-21338)
SAMUEL SON & CO (USA) INC (HQ)
Also Called: Samuel Packaging Systems Group
1401 Davey Rd Ste 300 (60517-4963)
PHONE..................630 783-8900
Mark C Samuel, *Ch of Bd*
Bobby Gosschalk, *General Mgr*
Joe Lux, *Regional Mgr*
Stacey Poltrok, *District Mgr*
Steve Swalm, *District Mgr*
◆ **EMP:** 60
SQ FT: 30,000
SALES (est): 241.9MM
SALES (corp-wide): 1.8B Privately Held
SIC: 3499 5085 Strapping, metal; industrial supplies
PA: Samuel, Son & Co., Limited
2360 Dixie Rd
Mississauga ON L4Y 1
905 279-5460

(G-21339)
SCHAU SOUTHEAST SUSHI INC
10350 Argonne Dr Ste 400 (60517-5114)
PHONE..................630 783-1000
EMP: 30
SALES (est): 800K Privately Held
SIC: 5147 5812 2099 Meats & meat products; eating places; food preparations

(G-21340)
SOLEO HEALTH INC
10210 Werch Dr Ste 202 (60517-4814)
PHONE..................630 478-8240
Kevin Witt, *Owner*
EMP: 9 Privately Held
SIC: 2834 5912 Druggists' preparations (pharmaceuticals); drug stores & proprietary stores
HQ: Soleo Health Inc.
950 Calcon Hook Rd Ste 19
Sharon Hill PA 19079
888 244-2340

(G-21341)
SPECTRUM TECHNOLOGIES INTL LTD
6368 Greene Rd (60517-1497)
PHONE..................630 961-5244
Kirk Kreutzig, *President*
EMP: 3
SALES (est): 369.8K Privately Held
SIC: 3443 Nuclear reactors, military or industrial

(G-21342)
SYMBRIA RX SERVICES LLC (PA)
Also Called: Friendly Remedies
7125 Janes Ave Ste 300 (60517-2304)
PHONE..................630 981-8000
Jill Krueger, *CEO*
Mary McVay, *Opers Staff*
Thomas Noesen Jr, *CFO*
Ruben Velez, *Mktg Coord*
Jay Mandra, *Director*
EMP: 50 **EST:** 1997
SALES (est): 12MM Privately Held
WEB: www.symbria.com
SIC: 2834 5122 Pharmaceutical preparations; pharmaceuticals

(G-21343)
TACKNOLOGIES
10720 Beaudin Blvd Ste A (60517-5121)
PHONE..................630 729-9900
Robert Listello, *Principal*
EMP: 3
SALES (est): 699.7K Privately Held
SIC: 3443 Liners/lining

(G-21344)
TELEDYNE DEFENSE ELEC LLC
Also Called: Teledyne Storm Microwave
10221 Werch Dr (60517-4973)
PHONE..................630 754-3300

Alex Villarreal, *Business Mgr*
Bob Barrath, *Engineer*
Tom Martin, *Engineer*
Hilary Rice, *Human Res Mgr*
Larry Lundgren, *Sales Staff*
EMP: 101
SALES (corp-wide): 3.1B Publicly Held
SIC: 3679 3357 Microwave components; coaxial cable, nonferrous
HQ: Teledyne Defense Electronics, Llc
1274 Terra Bella Ave
Mountain View CA 94043
650 691-9800

(G-21345)
WALTERSCHEID INC WOODRIDGE (DH)
2715 Davey Rd (60517-5064)
PHONE..................630 972-9300
Bryan Craig, *Managing Dir*
Hugo Perez, *Treasurer*
◆ **EMP:** 139
SQ FT: 75,000
SALES (est): 57.1MM
SALES (corp-wide): 242.1K Privately Held
SIC: 5083 3568 Agricultural machinery & equipment; power transmission equipment
HQ: Wpg Us Holdco Llc
330 N Wabash Ave Ste 3750
Chicago IL 60611
312 517-3750

(G-21346)
WEBQA INCORPORATED (PA)
900 S Frontage Rd Ste 110 (60517-4807)
PHONE..................630 985-1300
John Dilenschneider, *CEO*
Kim Sullivan, *Business Mgr*
Kevin Obrien, *Vice Pres*
Kent Hartsfield, *Sales Mgr*
Derek Ludwig, *Sales Engr*
EMP: 90
SALES (est): 12.6MM Privately Held
SIC: 7372 Application computer software

(G-21347)
WESTERN REMAC INC (PA)
Also Called: Wri
1740 Internationale Pkwy (60517-4994)
PHONE..................630 972-7770
Michael Conoscenti, *President*
Vicki Fiegl, *Vice Pres*
Jimmy Domschke, *Production*
Jill Longoria, *CFO*
Gregory Longoria, *Admin Sec*
EMP: 42
SQ FT: 44,000
SALES (est): 7.7MM Privately Held
SIC: 3993 3669 Signs, not made in custom sign painting shops; visual communication systems

(G-21348)
WILLOW RIDGE GLASS INC (PA)
8102 Lemont Rd Ste 100 (60517-7760)
PHONE..................630 910-8300
Glenn O James, *President*
Millicent James, *Corp Secy*
Mark Olin, *Vice Pres*
EMP: 12
SALES (est): 1.3MM Privately Held
SIC: 1793 3211 Glass & glazing work; tempered glass

(G-21349)
WILTON HOLDINGS INC
Also Called: Wilton Industries
2240 75th St (60517-2333)
PHONE..................630 963-7100
Steven Fraser, *CEO*
Deborah Bennett, *President*
Dan Kochenash, *COO*
Rodney Poole, *Senior VP*
Jason Riske, *Director*
▼ **EMP:** 2400
SALES (est): 221.8MM Privately Held
SIC: 5023 2731 2721 7812 Kitchenware; books: publishing only; periodicals: publishing only; video tape production; candy making goods & supplies

Woodridge - Dupage County (G-21350)

(G-21350)
YCL INTERNATIONAL INC
3118 Whispering Oaks Ln (60517-3757)
PHONE..................................630 873-0768
Chung LI, *President*
Yong Jiu Yang, *Admin Sec*
EMP: 50
SALES (est): 5.7MM **Privately Held**
SIC: 3714 8742 Motor vehicle parts & accessories; management consulting services

Woodson
Morgan County

(G-21351)
PERFECTION VAULT CO INC
403 N Ladue Rd (62695)
P.O. Box 155 (62695-0155)
PHONE..................................217 673-6111
EMP: 14
SALES (est): 1.3MM **Privately Held**
SIC: 3272 Mfg Burial Vaults & Septic Tanks

Woodstock
Mchenry County

(G-21352)
A & A MAGNETICS INC
520 Magnet Way (60098-9432)
P.O. Box 1427 (60098-1427)
PHONE..................................815 338-6054
Jeffrey Arnold, *President*
Gail Arnold, *Vice Pres*
EMP: 14
SQ FT: 20,000
SALES: 1.5MM **Privately Held**
SIC: 3542 Magnetic forming machines

(G-21353)
A HARTLETT & SONS INC
406 N Eastwood Dr (60098-3533)
PHONE..................................815 338-0109
Tom Hartlett, *President*
EMP: 2
SALES (est): 232.8K **Privately Held**
SIC: 3444 1711 Sheet metalwork; plumbing, heating, air-conditioning contractors

(G-21354)
ADVANCED MOLDING TECH INC
1425 Lake Ave (60098-7419)
PHONE..................................815 334-3600
Kevin Kelly, *President*
Michael J Kelly, *Chairman*
Kimberly F Kelly, *Admin Sec*
EMP: 80 EST: 1977
SQ FT: 60,000
SALES (est): 14.5MM
SALES (corp-wide): 89.4MM **Privately Held**
SIC: 3544 3089 Special dies, tools, jigs & fixtures; injection molded finished plastic products
HQ: Guardian Electric Manufacturing Co.
1425 Lake Ave
Woodstock IL 60098
815 334-3600

(G-21355)
ADVANTECH PLASTICS LLC
2500 S Eastwood Dr (60098-9112)
PHONE..................................815 338-8383
Albert Zoller, *Mng Member*
Jerry Cullger,
▲ EMP: 62
SQ FT: 26,000
SALES (est): 22.4MM **Privately Held**
WEB: www.advantechplastics.com
SIC: 3089 Injection molding of plastics
PA: Advan-Tech Industries, Inc.
540 Pine Ln
Lake Forest IL 60045

(G-21356)
ADVOCATIONS INC
17709 Collins Rd (60098-9241)
PHONE..................................815 568-7505
Dinnes Obraits, *Owner*
EMP: 4
SALES (est): 299.8K **Privately Held**
SIC: 3732 Boats, fiberglass: building & repairing

(G-21357)
AMERICAN AD BAG COMPANY INC
1510 Lamb Rd (60098-9688)
PHONE..................................815 338-0300
Virginia Semrow, *President*
Loriann Ochoa, *Director*
Lenore Maggs,
▲ EMP: 120
SALES (est): 16.7MM **Privately Held**
SIC: 2759 Bag, wrapper & seal printing & engraving; bags, plastic: printing

(G-21358)
AMERICAN PACKAGING MCHY INC
Also Called: A P M
2550 S Eastwood Dr (60098-9112)
PHONE..................................815 337-8580
Tadija Peric, *President*
Stefan Martelli, *Marketing Mgr*
Mato Zovkic, *Manager*
John A Cook, *Admin Sec*
EMP: 25
SQ FT: 10,000
SALES (est): 7.2MM **Privately Held**
SIC: 3565 Packaging machinery

(G-21359)
APT TOOL INC
1301 Cobblestone Way (60098-5202)
PHONE..................................815 337-0051
Guy Thompson, *President*
Anita Thompson, *Vice Pres*
EMP: 7
SQ FT: 3,600
SALES (est): 860.2K **Privately Held**
SIC: 3544 Forms (molds), for foundry & plastics working machinery

(G-21360)
ARNTZEN CORPORATION
14600 Washington St (60098-9308)
PHONE..................................815 334-0788
John Arntzen, *Branch Mgr*
Alex Arntzen, *Manager*
EMP: 20
SALES (corp-wide): 16.8MM **Privately Held**
WEB: www.arntzenrolling.com
SIC: 3317 5051 3498 3444 Steel pipe & tubes; steel; fabricated pipe & fittings; sheet metalwork; blast furnaces & steel mills
PA: Arntzen Corporation
1025 School St
Rockford IL 61101
815 964-9413

(G-21361)
ARROW ALUMINUM CASTINGS INC
2617 S Il Route 47 (60098-7557)
PHONE..................................815 338-4480
Denis J Moeller, *President*
Virginia Moeller, *Corp Secy*
EMP: 8
SQ FT: 7,000
SALES (est): 1.3MM **Privately Held**
WEB: www.arrowaluminum.net
SIC: 3363 3365 Aluminum die-castings; aluminum foundries

(G-21362)
B T M INDUSTRIES INC
604 Washington St (60098-2251)
PHONE..................................815 338-6464
Timothy Porter, *President*
▲ EMP: 9 EST: 1976
SQ FT: 14,000
SALES (est): 1.2MM **Privately Held**
WEB: www.btmindustries.com
SIC: 3599 Machine shop, jobbing & repair

(G-21363)
BERRY GLOBAL INC
1008 Courtaulds Dr (60098-7390)
PHONE..................................815 334-5225
Chris Luscavich, *Manager*
James Fabian, *Manager*
EMP: 127 **Publicly Held**
WEB: www.berryplastics.com
SIC: 3089 Plastic containers, except foam
HQ: Berry Global, Inc.
101 Oakley St
Evansville IN 47710

(G-21364)
BEST METAL CORPORATION
925 Dieckman St (60098-9262)
PHONE..................................815 337-0420
Craig Paul, *President*
Susan Paullin, *Admin Sec*
EMP: 29
SQ FT: 15,000
SALES (est): 5.9MM
SALES (corp-wide): 22.9MM **Privately Held**
SIC: 3411 Oil cans, metal
PA: Psm Industries, Inc.
14000 Avalon Blvd
Los Angeles CA 90061
888 663-8256

(G-21365)
BIGFOOT CONSTRUCTION EQP INC
1111 Broadway Ct (60098-3001)
PHONE..................................888 743-7320
William E Steiner, *President*
EMP: 4
SALES (est): 370.7K **Privately Held**
SIC: 3531 Construction machinery

(G-21366)
BOTTS WELDING AND TRCK SVC INC (PA)
335 N Eastwood Dr (60098-3504)
P.O. Box 430 (60098-0430)
PHONE..................................815 338-0594
Gordon R Botts, *President*
EMP: 40
SQ FT: 22,500
SALES (est): 8MM **Privately Held**
WEB: www.bottswelding.com
SIC: 5013 7539 7538 7692 Truck parts & accessories; frame repair shops, automotive; general truck repair; automotive welding

(G-21367)
BROCK EQUIPMENT COMPANY (PA)
1001 Rail Dr Unit 4 (60098-9411)
P.O. Box 218, Crystal Lake (60039-0218)
PHONE..................................815 459-4210
Marvin H Richer, *President*
Gail L Richer, *Treasurer*
John Dylik, *Marketing Mgr*
EMP: 20 EST: 1945
SALES (est): 1.3MM **Privately Held**
SIC: 3594 3563 3566 Pumps, hydraulic power transfer; air & gas compressors including vacuum pumps; speed changers, drives & gears

(G-21368)
BULL VALLEY HARDWOOD (PA)
18014 Collins Rd (60098-9243)
PHONE..................................815 701-9400
Daniel Deserto, *President*
Silvio Deserto, *Vice Pres*
EMP: 5 EST: 2015
SQ FT: 14,150
SALES: 1MM **Privately Held**
SIC: 2421 5031 5211 Sawmills & planing mills, general; lumber, plywood & millwork; millwork & lumber

(G-21369)
CABLE X-PERTS INC
721 Amsterdam St (60098-2306)
P.O. Box 193, Lincolnshire (60069-0193)
PHONE..................................800 828-3340
Sam Cosmano, *President*
EMP: 6
SALES (est): 774.6K **Privately Held**
SIC: 3357 Nonferrous wiredrawing & insulating

(G-21370)
CARL GORR PRINTING CO
Also Called: Gorr Communication Products
1002 Mchenry Ave (60098-3036)
P.O. Box 105, Cary (60013-0105)
PHONE..................................815 338-3191
Fred Gorr, *President*
David W Gorr, *Vice Pres*
Fredrica Brown, *Admin Sec*
EMP: 23
SQ FT: 15,000
SALES (est): 3.1MM **Privately Held**
SIC: 2759 3083 2396 Screen printing; laminated plastics plate & sheet; automotive & apparel trimmings

(G-21371)
CATALENT PHARMA SOLUTIONS LLC
2210 Lake Shore Dr (60098-6919)
PHONE..................................815 338-9500
EMP: 67 **Publicly Held**
WEB: www.catalent.com
SIC: 2834 Pharmaceutical preparations
HQ: Catalent Pharma Solutions, Llc
14 Schoolhouse Rd
Somerset NJ 08873

(G-21372)
CATALENT PHARMA SOLUTIONS INC
2210 Lake Shore Dr (60098-6919)
PHONE..................................815 338-9500
Mike Hitchingham, *Manager*
EMP: 200 **Publicly Held**
SIC: 2834 Pharmaceutical preparations
HQ: Catalent Pharma Solutions, Inc.
14 Schoolhouse Rd
Somerset NJ 08873

(G-21373)
CHARTER DURA-BAR INC (HQ)
Also Called: Dura-Bar Div
2100 W Lake Shore Dr (60098-7468)
P.O. Box 217, Mequon WI (53092-0217)
PHONE..................................815 338-3900
Thomas W Wells, *President*
Frank Abruzzo, *Vice Pres*
Arthur Berman, *Vice Pres*
Michael Hackworthy, *Vice Pres*
Timothy Heagney, *Vice Pres*
◆ EMP: 25 EST: 1946
SQ FT: 380,000
SALES (est): 95.8MM
SALES (corp-wide): 681.7MM **Privately Held**
WEB: www.wellsmanufacturing.com
SIC: 3321 5051 Gray iron castings; ductile iron castings; bars, metal
PA: Charter Manufacturing Company, Inc.
12121 Corporate Pkwy
Mequon WI 53092
262 243-4752

(G-21374)
CHARTER DURA-BAR INC
Also Called: Dura Bar Division
1800 W Lake Shore Dr (60098-7426)
PHONE..................................815 338-7800
Brian Schlump, *General Mgr*
Staral Ray, *Engineer*
Benz Spencer, *Senior Engr*
Bill Rorig, *Controller*
Lydia Pasieka, *Human Res Mgr*
EMP: 225
SQ FT: 325,000
SALES (corp-wide): 681.7MM **Privately Held**
SIC: 3321 8711 3441 3369 Gray iron castings; engineering services; fabricated structural metal; nonferrous foundries
HQ: Charter Dura-Bar, Inc.
2100 W Lake Shore Dr
Woodstock IL 60098
815 338-3900

(G-21375)
CONTEMPO INDUSTRIES INC
Also Called: Woodstock Gardens
455 Borden St (60098-2132)
PHONE..................................815 337-6267
EMP: 82
SQ FT: 42,000
SALES (est): 13.1MM **Privately Held**
SIC: 3524 Lawn & garden equipment

(G-21376)
COOL FLUIDICS INC
123 S Eastwood Dr Ste 145 (60098-3519)
PHONE..................................815 861-4063
Christina Coalson, *CEO*
EMP: 3

GEOGRAPHIC SECTION
Woodstock - Mchenry County (G-21402)

SALES (est): 229.2K **Privately Held**
SIC: 3561 Pumps & pumping equipment

(G-21377)
COPY EXPRESS INC
301 E Calhoun St Ste 2 (60098-4290)
PHONE..................815 338-7161
James A O'Leary, *President*
Vicki O'Leary, *Vice Pres*
Sheryl Dicicco, *Manager*
EMP: 10 EST: 1975
SQ FT: 7,000
SALES (est): 1.4MM **Privately Held**
WEB: www.copyexpressyes.com
SIC: 2752 7334 2791 Photo-offset printing; photocopying & duplicating services; typesetting

(G-21378)
CRESWELL WOODWORKING CA
911 Rail Dr Unit C (60098-9435)
PHONE..................847 381-9222
Mike Creswell, *Owner*
EMP: 3 EST: 2009
SALES (est): 337.1K **Privately Held**
SIC: 2431 Millwork

(G-21379)
CUSTOM TELEPHONE PRINTING CO
1002 Mchenry Ave (60098-3036)
PHONE..................815 338-0000
Dale Gibson, *President*
John Farella, *Admin Sec*
Tina Havis, *Representative*
EMP: 10
SALES (est): 1.3MM **Privately Held**
SIC: 2752 3993 2396 Commercial printing, offset; signs & advertising specialties; automotive & apparel trimmings

(G-21380)
DALE K BROWN
Also Called: Schmidt Printing
130 Wshngton St Unit Rear (60098)
PHONE..................815 338-0222
Dale K Brown, *Owner*
EMP: 3
SALES (est): 252.3K **Privately Held**
SIC: 2752 2759 2791 2789 Commercial printing, offset; letterpress printing; typesetting; bookbinding & related work

(G-21381)
DILARS EMBROIDERY & MONOGRAMS
1320 Zimmerman Rd (60098-7786)
PHONE..................815 338-6066
Larry Monaghan, *Owner*
Marlene Monaghan, *Bookkeeper*
EMP: 5
SALES: 160K **Privately Held**
SIC: 2395 Embroidery products, except schiffli machine

(G-21382)
DORDAN MANUFACTURING COMPANY
2025 Castle Rd (60098-9271)
PHONE..................815 334-0087
Daniel J Slavin, *CEO*
Alice Whatley, *Vice Pres*
Bob Cross, *Engineer*
Rod Russell, *Accounts Mgr*
Richard Partlow, *Accounts Exec*
EMP: 50
SALES (est): 10MM **Privately Held**
WEB: www.dordan.com
SIC: 3089 Injection molding of plastics

(G-21383)
DRAMATIC PUBLISHING COMPANY
311 Washington St (60098-3308)
P.O. Box 129 (60098-0129)
PHONE..................815 338-7170
Christopher Sergel Jr, *President*
William Flynn, *Principal*
Linda Habjan, *Editor*
Gayle Sergel, *Vice Pres*
Susan Sergel, *Vice Pres*
EMP: 19 EST: 1885
SQ FT: 10,000
SALES (est): 1.8MM **Privately Held**
WEB: www.dramaticpublishing.com
SIC: 2741 7922 Miscellaneous publishing; theatrical producers & services

(G-21384)
E3 ARTISAN INC
Also Called: Ethereal Confections
140 Cass St (60098-3254)
PHONE..................815 575-9315
Ervin Sara, *President*
Marisa Allen, *Sales Mgr*
Shawna Higgins, *Sales Mgr*
Paul Sigrist, *Sales Mgr*
Linda Mugdur, *Manager*
EMP: 20
SALES (est): 2.9MM **Privately Held**
SIC: 2099 Pasta, uncooked: packaged with other ingredients

(G-21385)
EMTECH MACHINING & GRINDING
911 Rail Dr (60098-9435)
P.O. Box 1810 (60098-1810)
PHONE..................815 338-1580
Charlotte Emricson, *President*
Shelly Eslick, *Exec VP*
EMP: 7
SQ FT: 38,000
SALES (est): 820K **Privately Held**
WEB: www.emtechmachining.com
SIC: 3599 3545 Machine shop, jobbing & repair; machine tool accessories

(G-21386)
EPS SOLUTIONS INCORPORATED
1525 W Lake Shore Dr (60098-6917)
PHONE..................815 206-0868
David H Hoffmann, *CEO*
Mark C Coleman, *President*
Jeffrey A Richardson, *President*
Christopher P Massey, *Principal*
Erik R Watts, *Principal*
EMP: 606 EST: 2004
SQ FT: 9,000
SALES (est): 141.5MM **Privately Held**
WEB: www.epssolutions.com
SIC: 2676 Towels, napkins & tissue paper products

(G-21387)
FLEX-WELD INC
Also Called: Keflex
1425 Lake Ave (60098-7419)
PHONE..................815 338-3662
Kevin G Kelly, *CEO*
Michael J Kelly, *Ch of Bd*
Karen Kelly Conway, *Admin Sec*
Kimberly F Kelly, *Admin Sec*
▲ EMP: 58
SQ FT: 100,000
SALES (est): 10.1MM **Privately Held**
SIC: 3599 3568 3643 3498 Bellows, industrial: metal; hose, flexible metallic; joints, swivel & universal, except aircraft & automotive; current-carrying wiring devices; fabricated pipe & fittings; fabricated structural metal

(G-21388)
FLOCON INC
11595 Mcconnell Rd (60098-7336)
PHONE..................815 527-7990
EMP: 3 EST: 2018
SALES (est): 140.6K **Privately Held**
SIC: 2752 Commercial printing, lithographic

(G-21389)
FOCUS HEALTH AND FITNESS LLC
123 S Eastwood Dr (60098-3519)
PHONE..................847 975-8687
Jennifer Robson,
EMP: 5
SALES: 60K **Privately Held**
SIC: 7991 7372 Physical fitness facilities; application computer software

(G-21390)
FOX TOOL & MANUFACTURING INC
900 Dieckman St (60098-9286)
P.O. Box 855 (60098-0855)
PHONE..................815 338-3046
Barry Glass, *President*
Bruce D Glass, *Vice Pres*
EMP: 18
SQ FT: 12,000
SALES (est): 3.4MM **Privately Held**
SIC: 3599 Machine shop, jobbing & repair

(G-21391)
GAMA ELECTRONICS INC
1240 Cobblestone Way (60098-5205)
PHONE..................815 356-9600
Carl Gerken, *Owner*
▲ EMP: 13
SQ FT: 6,000
SALES (est): 3MM **Privately Held**
SIC: 3565 8711 3844 Packaging machinery; engineering services; X-ray apparatus & tubes

(G-21392)
GUARDIAN CONSOLIDATED TECH INC (HQ)
1425 Lake Ave (60098-7419)
PHONE..................815 334-3600
Kevin Kelly, *President*
Michael J Kelly, *Chairman*
EMP: 4
SQ FT: 100,000
SALES (est): 75MM
SALES (corp-wide): 89.4MM **Privately Held**
SIC: 3625 Relays & industrial controls
PA: Kelco Industries, Inc.
1425 Lake Ave
Woodstock IL 60098
815 334-3600

(G-21393)
GUARDIAN ELECTRIC MFG CO (DH)
1425 Lake Ave (60098-7419)
PHONE..................815 334-3600
Kevin Kelly, *President*
Michael Kelly, *Chairman*
Dan Budaj, *Mfg Staff*
Laura Lucy, *Buyer*
Don Grandt, *Engineer*
▲ EMP: 80 EST: 1931
SQ FT: 100,000
SALES (est): 28.7MM
SALES (corp-wide): 89.4MM **Privately Held**
WEB: www.guardian-electric.com
SIC: 3679 3625 Solenoids for electronic applications; relays & industrial controls; relays, electric power; switches, electric power; solenoid switches (industrial controls)

(G-21394)
HAL MATHER & SONS INCORPORATED
Also Called: Mather Dataforms
11803 Highway 120 (60098-8516)
P.O. Box 1900 (60098-1900)
PHONE..................815 338-4000
Douglas L Mather, *President*
James R Mather, *Vice Pres*
EMP: 32 EST: 1934
SQ FT: 33,850
SALES (est): 4.4MM **Privately Held**
SIC: 2752 2759 Commercial printing, offset; letterpress printing

(G-21395)
IMAGO MANUFACTURING
321 Schryver Ave (60098-3960)
PHONE..................815 333-5272
Ryan Bankel, *Owner*
EMP: 1 EST: 2008
SALES (est): 227.1K **Privately Held**
WEB: www.imagomfg.com
SIC: 3541 Machine tool replacement & repair parts, metal cutting types

(G-21396)
INNOQUEST INC
910 Hobe Rd (60098-9010)
PHONE..................815 337-8555
William Hughes, *President*
▲ EMP: 6
SQ FT: 4,000
SALES: 700K **Privately Held**
SIC: 3829 Rain gauges

(G-21397)
KAM TOOL AND MOLD
1300 Cobblestone Way (60098-5201)
PHONE..................815 338-8360
Kurt W Johnson, *Owner*
EMP: 5
SQ FT: 3,750
SALES (est): 498.8K **Privately Held**
SIC: 3544 Special dies & tools

(G-21398)
KELCO INDUSTRIES INC (PA)
1425 Lake Ave (60098-7419)
PHONE..................815 334-3600
Michael J Kelly, *Ch of Bd*
Kevin G Kelly, *President*
Marietta Kelly, *Vice Pres*
▲ EMP: 6
SQ FT: 2,000
SALES (est): 89.4MM **Privately Held**
SIC: 3599 3069 3494 3585 Flexible metal hose, tubing & bellows; molded rubber products; valves & pipe fittings; expansion joints pipe; heating equipment, complete; air conditioning units, complete: domestic or industrial; industrial molds; relays, for electronic use; switches, electronic applications

(G-21399)
KHC CORPORATION
333 E Judd St (60098-3417)
PHONE..................815 337-7630
Sota Katahira, *CEO*
Shuichi Katahira, *President*
▲ EMP: 25
SQ FT: 10,000
SALES (est): 4.4MM **Privately Held**
SIC: 3493 Steel springs, except wire
PA: Keihin Hatsujyo Co., Ltd.
5-2931, Uragocho
Yokosuka KNG 237-0

(G-21400)
KNIGHT PLASTICS LLC
1008 Courtaulds Dr (60098-7390)
PHONE..................815 334-1240
Ira Boots, *President*
▲ EMP: 160
SALES (est): 14.3MM **Publicly Held**
SIC: 3089 Injection molded finished plastic products
HQ: Berry Global, Inc.
101 Oakley St
Evansville IN 47710

(G-21401)
KRAFT HEINZ FOODS COMPANY
Kraft Foods
1300 Claussen Dr (60098-2155)
PHONE..................815 338-7000
Gerry Lales, *Opers-Prdtn-Mfg*
EMP: 400
SQ FT: 132,000
SALES (corp-wide): 24.9B **Publicly Held**
SIC: 2035 2033 Pickles, vinegar; canned fruits & specialties
HQ: Kraft Heinz Foods Company
1 Ppg Pl Fl 34
Pittsburgh PA 15222
412 456-5700

(G-21402)
LAMKA ENTERPRISES INC
8700 Crystal Springs Rd (60098-8058)
PHONE..................630 659-5965
John Lamka, *President*
Cherisse Lamka, *Principal*
Kevin Hansen, *Sales Staff*
EMP: 4
SALES (est): 232.1K **Privately Held**
SIC: 1799 1542 1521 1541 Kitchen & bathroom remodeling; parking lot maintenance; commercial & office buildings, renovation & repair; single-family home remodeling, additions & repairs; renovation, remodeling & repairs: industrial buildings; remodeling, multi-family dwellings; farm & utility buildings

Woodstock - Mchenry County (G-21403)

(G-21403)
LANDAIRSEA SYSTEMS INC
2040 Dillard Ct (60098-6600)
PHONE..................847 462-8100
Robert Wagner, *President*
Lin Xu, *General Mgr*
Kris Husch, *VP Opers*
Kathy Karlak, *Bookkeeper*
Rob Phillips, *Software Engr*
▲ **EMP:** 15
SALES (est): 2.2MM **Privately Held**
WEB: www.landairsea.com
SIC: 3823 Transmitters of process variables, stand. signal conversion

(G-21404)
LAS SYSTEMS INC
2040 Dillard Ct (60098-6600)
PHONE..................847 462-8100
Robert Wagner, *President*
Teresa Wagner, *Manager*
Lin Xu, *Shareholder*
▲ **EMP:** 25
SQ FT: 3,000
SALES (est): 3.6MM **Privately Held**
WEB: www.landairsea.com
SIC: 3663 3625 Transmitter-receivers, radio; timing devices, electronic

(G-21405)
LESTER L BROSSARD CO
930 Dieckman St (60098-9286)
P.O. Box 708 (60098-0708)
PHONE..................815 338-7825
George L Brossard, *President*
Patricia Brossard, *Director*
▲ **EMP:** 10
SQ FT: 10,000
SALES (est): 1.4MM **Privately Held**
WEB: www.brossardmirrors.com
SIC: 3231 3842 Mirrored glass; surgical appliances & supplies

(G-21406)
LINDSAY METAL MADNESS INC
13706 Washington St (60098-9453)
PHONE..................815 568-4560
EMP: 2
SALES (est): 271.7K **Privately Held**
SIC: 5051 3399 3499 Metals service centers & offices; primary metal products; fabricated metal products

(G-21407)
LUSTER LEAF PRODUCTS INC (PA)
1961 Dillard Ct (60098-6601)
PHONE..................815 337-5560
Larry Holbein, *President*
Ryan Schoenberg, *Exec VP*
Natalie Heckmon, *Cust Svc Dir*
Margaret Godfrey, *Admin Sec*
▲ **EMP:** 13
SALES (est): 2.8MM **Privately Held**
WEB: www.lusterleaf.com
SIC: 2899 3829 3423 Soil testing kits; measuring & controlling devices; hand & edge tools

(G-21408)
MARKHAM INDUSTRY INC
Also Called: Sno-Belt Industries
2220 Tech Ct (60098-9200)
PHONE..................815 338-0116
R W Markham, *President*
Mary E Markham, *Admin Sec*
EMP: 7
SALES (est): 750K **Privately Held**
SIC: 3471 Finishing, metals or formed products; polishing, metals or formed products; buffing for the trade

(G-21409)
MATRIX IV INC
610 E Judd St (60098-3424)
PHONE..................815 338-4500
Patricia Miller, *President*
▲ **EMP:** 50
SQ FT: 76,000
SALES (est): 12.5MM **Privately Held**
SIC: 3089 8711 Molding primary plastic; engineering services

(G-21410)
MICHAEL CHRISTOPHER LTD
1007 Trakk Ln (60098-9488)
PHONE..................815 308-5018
Michael Amster, *President*
EMP: 8
SALES: 750K **Privately Held**
SIC: 2844 Perfumes & colognes

(G-21411)
MIGATRON CORPORATION
935 Dieckman St Ste A (60098-9203)
P.O. Box 1229 (60098-1229)
PHONE..................815 338-5800
Frank C Wroga Jr, *President*
William Richard Wroga, *Vice Pres*
Elizabeth A Wroga, *CFO*
Rebecca Moon, *Technology*
EMP: 20
SQ FT: 9,000
SALES (est): 3.4MM **Privately Held**
WEB: www.migatron.com
SIC: 3829 3699 Ultrasonic testing equipment; electrical equipment & supplies

(G-21412)
MILLER MIDWESTERN DIE CO
1076 Lake Ave (60098-7408)
PHONE..................815 338-6686
Thomas L Miller, *President*
Charles Ruth, *Admin Sec*
EMP: 6
SQ FT: 9,000
SALES: 900K **Privately Held**
SIC: 3544 Dies & die holders for metal cutting, forming, die casting

(G-21413)
MIX N MINGLE
124 Cass St Ste 2 (60098-3296)
PHONE..................815 308-5170
Nat Grindeland, *Principal*
EMP: 5
SALES (est): 344.6K **Privately Held**
WEB: www.mixinmingle.com
SIC: 3273 Ready-mixed concrete

(G-21414)
MP MANUFACTURING INC
13802 Washington St Ste B (60098-9489)
PHONE..................815 334-1112
Dale Hildebrand, *Principal*
EMP: 9
SALES (est): 921.1K **Privately Held**
SIC: 3999 Atomizers, toiletry

(G-21415)
MULTITECH INDUSTRIES
10603 Arabian Trl (60098-8494)
PHONE..................815 206-0015
Jeffery Mossman, *Principal*
Stephanie Falcone, *Accounts Mgr*
EMP: 2
SALES (est): 253.4K **Privately Held**
WEB: www.multitechind.com
SIC: 3312 3316 Primary finished or semi-finished shapes; cold finishing of steel shapes

(G-21416)
MURPHY USA INC
1265 Lake Ave (60098-7415)
PHONE..................815 337-2440
Tiffany Patton, *Owner*
EMP: 13 **Publicly Held**
WEB: www.murphyusa.com
SIC: 5541 1311 Filling stations, gasoline; crude petroleum & natural gas production
PA: Murphy Usa Inc.
200 E Peach St
El Dorado AR 71730

(G-21417)
ORTHO MOLECULAR PRODUCTS INC (PA)
1991 Duncan Pl (60098-7394)
PHONE..................815 337-0089
Gary Powers, *President*
Kristen Brokaw, *Sales Staff*
Jason Friedman, *Sales Staff*
Bushra Hassan, *Nutritionist*
Angela Lucterhand, *Manager*
▲ **EMP:** 25
SALES (est): 15MM **Privately Held**
SIC: 2834 Antiseptics, medicinal

(G-21418)
P B R W ENTERPRISES INC
Also Called: Software Maniacs
12201 Baker Ter (60098-8721)
P.O. Box 64, Sharpsburg MD (21782-0064)
PHONE..................815 337-5519
EMP: 4
SALES (est): 263.1K **Privately Held**
SIC: 7372 Prepackaged Software Services

(G-21419)
PACIFIC CUSTOM COMPONENTS CORP
10200 Us Highway 14 (60098-7365)
PHONE..................815 206-5450
James Gorman, *President*
Terry Neeley, *Exec VP*
▲ **EMP:** 15
SQ FT: 50,000
SALES: 6MM **Privately Held**
SIC: 3669 Emergency alarms; intercommunication systems, electric

(G-21420)
PARSONICS CORP
935 Dieckman St Ste A (60098-9203)
PHONE..................815 338-6509
Bill Rogan, *Principal*
EMP: 7
SALES (est): 950.4K **Privately Held**
WEB: www.parsonicscorp.com
SIC: 3829 Measuring & controlling devices

(G-21421)
PHOENIX WOODWORKING CORP
2000 Duncan Pl (60098-7311)
PHONE..................815 338-9338
Sandra Pierce, *President*
EMP: 20
SQ FT: 21,450
SALES (est): 2.7MM **Privately Held**
SIC: 2434 Wood kitchen cabinets

(G-21422)
POWERS PAINT SHOP INC
1065 Dieckman St (60098-9262)
PHONE..................815 338-3619
Daniel F Powers, *President*
Cindy Powers, *Corp Secy*
EMP: 4
SQ FT: 8,000
SALES (est): 547.2K **Privately Held**
SIC: 3479 3471 Coating of metals & formed products; painting of metal products; plating & polishing

(G-21423)
PRECISION VISION INC
1725 Kilkenny Ct (60098-7437)
PHONE..................815 223-2022
Ed Kopidlansky, *President*
Jessica Kopidlansky, *Sales Staff*
EMP: 7
SQ FT: 22,000
SALES (est): 1.2MM **Privately Held**
SIC: 3841 3827 Eye examining instruments & apparatus; optical instruments & lenses

(G-21424)
PREMIER WOODWORKING CONCEPTS
1016 Rail Dr (60098-9486)
PHONE..................815 334-0888
Dean Lukey, *Partner*
EMP: 7
SALES (est): 952.7K **Privately Held**
SIC: 2434 Wood kitchen cabinets

(G-21425)
PSM INDUSTRIES INC
Also Called: Bestmetal, A Division of PSM
925 Dieckman St (60098-9262)
PHONE..................815 337-8800
Sean Kenney, *Principal*
EMP: 29
SALES (corp-wide): 22.9MM **Privately Held**
SIC: 3499 Friction material, made from powdered metal
PA: Psm Industries, Inc.
14000 Avalon Blvd
Los Angeles CA 90061
888 663-8256

(G-21426)
QUAD/GRAPHICS INC
Also Called: Brown Printing
11595 Mcconnell Rd (60098-7336)
P.O. Box 1149 (60098-1149)
PHONE..................815 338-6750
Bill Gallagher, *Manager*
EMP: 600
SALES (corp-wide): 3.9B **Publicly Held**
SIC: 2721 2759 2752 Magazines: publishing only, not printed on site; commercial printing; commercial printing, lithographic
PA: Quad/Graphics Inc.
N61w23044 Harrys Way
Sussex WI 53089
414 566-6000

(G-21427)
R & B METAL PRODUCTS INC
801 Mchenry Ave (60098-3031)
PHONE..................815 338-1890
John Kise, *CEO*
Joseph Kelter, *Vice Pres*
EMP: 22
SQ FT: 23,000
SALES (est): 4MM **Privately Held**
WEB: www.rbmetalproducts.com
SIC: 3599 3446 3444 3443 Machine shop, jobbing & repair; architectural metalwork; sheet metalwork; fabricated plate work (boiler shop); fabricated structural metal

(G-21428)
R & S SCREEN PRINTING INC
739 Mchenry Ave (60098-3058)
PHONE..................815 337-3935
Tim Redden, *President*
Ryan Redden, *Vice Pres*
Nancy Redden, *Admin Sec*
EMP: 3
SALES (est): 250K **Privately Held**
SIC: 2759 Screen printing

(G-21429)
RANGER REDI-MIX & MTLS INC
1100 Borden Ln (60098-2320)
PHONE..................815 337-2662
Steve Gavers, *President*
Dan Gavers, *Vice Pres*
EMP: 4
SALES (est): 429.5K **Privately Held**
SIC: 3273 Ready-mixed concrete

(G-21430)
SAND SCULPTURE CO
327 S Jefferson St (60098-3909)
PHONE..................815 334-9101
Theodore Siebert, *Partner*
Laura Siebert, *Partner*
EMP: 4
SALES: 350K **Privately Held**
SIC: 3299 8412 Architectural sculptures: gypsum, clay, papier mache, etc.; museums & art galleries

(G-21431)
SERIEN MANUFACTURING INC
Also Called: L M J Tooling & Manufacturing
900 S Eastwood Dr (60098-4639)
P.O. Box 215 (60098-0215)
PHONE..................815 337-1447
Tracey A Odishoo, *President*
EMP: 5
SQ FT: 7,000
SALES: 400K **Privately Held**
SIC: 3541 Machine tools, metal cutting type

(G-21432)
SHANNON INDUSTRIAL CORPORATION (PA)
2041 Dillard Ct (60098-6600)
PHONE..................815 337-2349
Gerald W Grossi, *President*
Rich Campbell, *Sales Staff*
▲ **EMP:** 10
SQ FT: 65,000
SALES (est): 22.9MM **Privately Held**
SIC: 5162 3087 Plastics materials; custom compound purchased resins

GEOGRAPHIC SECTION

Wyoming - Stark County (G-21460)

(G-21433)
SHANNON INDUSTRIES INC
Also Called: Jones Products Co
114 S Shannon Dr (60098-9475)
PHONE..................................815 338-8960
Paul Fitzpatrick, *President*
EMP: 7
SQ FT: 5,000
SALES (est): 1MM **Privately Held**
WEB: www.shannonindustrial.com
SIC: 3089 Netting, plastic

(G-21434)
SHERWIN-WILLIAMS COMPANY
631 S Eastwood Dr (60098-4632)
PHONE..................................815 337-0942
EMP: 5
SALES (corp-wide): 17.9B **Publicly Held**
SIC: 5231 5198 2851 Paint; paints, varnishes & supplies; wood fillers or sealers
PA: The Sherwin-Williams Company
101 W Prospect Ave # 1020
Cleveland OH 44115
216 566-2000

(G-21435)
SILGAN PLASTICS LLC
1005 Courtaulds Dr (60098-7390)
PHONE..................................815 334-1200
James Hill, *Branch Mgr*
EMP: 230 **Publicly Held**
SIC: 3089 Plastic containers, except foam
HQ: Silgan Plastics Llc
14515 North Outer 40 Rd # 210
Chesterfield MO 63017
800 274-5426

(G-21436)
SUBURBAN SCREW MACHINE PDTS
16210 Us Highway 14 (60098-9477)
PHONE..................................815 337-0434
Russell Evertsen, *CEO*
Ella Evertsen, *Corp Secy*
Herbert Evertsen, *Vice Pres*
EMP: 6
SQ FT: 5,000
SALES (est): 332.7K **Privately Held**
SIC: 3451 Screw machine products

(G-21437)
SUPERIOR X RAY TUBE COMPANY
1220 Claussen Dr (60098-2139)
PHONE..................................815 338-4424
Mark McDonnell, *President*
Todd Carlson, *Engineer*
EMP: 9
SQ FT: 9,000
SALES (est): 1.2MM **Privately Held**
SIC: 3844 X-ray apparatus & tubes

(G-21438)
SWS INDUSTRIES INC
Also Called: McGill
280 Prairie Ridge Dr (60098-4183)
PHONE..................................904 482-0091
Wayne Schwartzman, *President*
Becki McDaniel, *Exec VP*
▲ EMP: 40
SQ FT: 57,000
SALES (est): 6.3MM **Privately Held**
WEB: www.mcgillinc.com
SIC: 3579 5044 5199 3544 Binding machines, plastic & adhesive; paper cutters, trimmers & punches; office equipment; art goods & supplies; special dies, tools, jigs & fixtures; heating equipment, except electric; hand & edge tools

(G-21439)
T & K TOOL & MANUFACTURING CO
2250 S Eastwood Dr (60098-4608)
P.O. Box 47 (60098-0047)
PHONE..................................815 338-0954
Robert Thurow, *President*
Erich Thurow, *Admin Sec*
Tom Landers, *Teacher*
EMP: 4 EST: 1944
SQ FT: 4,800
SALES (est): 275K **Privately Held**
WEB: www.stans.com
SIC: 3599 3544 3549 Machine shop, jobbing & repair; special dies, tools, jigs & fixtures; metalworking machinery

(G-21440)
T K O WATERPROOF COATING LLP
427 E Judd St (60098-3419)
PHONE..................................815 338-2006
EMP: 6
SALES (est): 884.8K **Privately Held**
SIC: 2899 Mfg Waterproof Roof Coatings

(G-21441)
TU-STAR MANUFACTURING CO INC
1200 Cobblestone Way (60098-5205)
PHONE..................................815 338-5760
Doyle E Green, *Owner*
EMP: 5
SQ FT: 3,000
SALES (est): 324.4K **Privately Held**
SIC: 3499 3469 3444 Machine bases, metal; metal stampings; sheet metalwork

(G-21442)
USA PRINTWORKS LLC
1525 W Lake Shore Dr (60098-6917)
PHONE..................................815 206-0854
Jeffrey Richardson, *CEO*
Tania Boon-Richardson, *Manager*
EMP: 40
SALES (est): 1.5MM **Privately Held**
SIC: 2759 Promotional printing

(G-21443)
VETERANS PARKING LOT MAINT
240 Mchenry Ave (60098-3452)
PHONE..................................815 245-7584
Mark Finn, *Principal*
EMP: 4
SALES: 100K **Privately Held**
SIC: 2951 Asphalt paving mixtures & blocks

(G-21444)
VG PALLET INC
320 E Church St (60098-3442)
PHONE..................................815 527-5344
Victor Gonzalez, *Manager*
EMP: 4
SALES (est): 468.1K **Privately Held**
SIC: 2448 Pallets, wood

(G-21445)
VORTEQ WOODSTOCK LLC
Also Called: P.V.S. Manufacturing Div
15920 Nelson Rd (60098-9526)
PHONE..................................815 338-6410
Jim Dockey, *CEO*
Richard Given, *Purch Agent*
EMP: 20
SQ FT: 36,000
SALES (est): 2.7MM
SALES (corp-wide): 45.7MM **Privately Held**
SIC: 3479 Coating of metals & formed products
PA: Vorteq Coil Finishers, Llc
930 Armour Rd
Oconomowoc WI 53066
262 567-1112

(G-21446)
WANDAS BAKERY LLC
4409 Greenwood Rd (60098-8656)
PHONE..................................815 900-6268
Sarah Ferris, *Manager*
EMP: 3
SALES: 50K **Privately Held**
SIC: 2052 Bakery products, dry

(G-21447)
WESTERN CONSOLIDATED TECH INC
1425 Lake Ave (60098-7419)
PHONE..................................815 334-3684
Chuck Shortridge, *Sales Staff*
EMP: 10
SALES (est): 2.1MM **Privately Held**
SIC: 3052 Rubber & plastics hose & beltings

(G-21448)
WILLIAM J KLINE & CO INC
425 Borden St (60098-2132)
PHONE..................................815 338-2055
Mark Emricson, *President*
Marilyn Kline, *Vice Pres*
Tami Emricson, *Treasurer*
EMP: 12
SQ FT: 5,500
SALES: 1.2MM **Privately Held**
SIC: 3544 Industrial molds

(G-21449)
WONDER TUCKY DISTILLERY & BTLG
315 E South St (60098-4219)
P.O. Box 2181, Loves Park (61130-0181)
PHONE..................................224 678-4396
EMP: 6
SALES (est): 336K **Privately Held**
SIC: 2086 Bottled & canned soft drinks

(G-21450)
WOODSTOCK INDEPENDENT
671 E Calhoun St (60098-4262)
PHONE..................................815 338-8040
Larry Lough, *Editor*
Kin Kubiak, *Manager*
EMP: 3
SALES (est): 69.2K **Privately Held**
SIC: 2711 Newspapers, publishing & printing

(G-21451)
ZOIA MONUMENT COMPANY
222 Washington St (60098-3307)
PHONE..................................815 338-0358
James Zoia, *President*
Shirley Zoia, *Corp Secy*
Anthony Zoia, *Manager*
EMP: 5
SQ FT: 5,000
SALES (est): 547.4K **Privately Held**
WEB: www.zoiamonumentcompany.com
SIC: 5999 3281 Monuments, finished to custom order; cut stone & stone products

Woosung
Ogle County

(G-21452)
MIDWEST CEMENT PRODUCTS INC
809 Central St (61091)
P.O. Box 92 (61091-0092)
PHONE..................................815 284-2342
Douglas Nielsen, *President*
Clarence D Nielsen, *Vice Pres*
EMP: 4 EST: 1922
SQ FT: 2,800
SALES (est): 663.6K **Privately Held**
WEB: www.midwestcement.com
SIC: 3272 3271 Concrete products; concrete block & brick

Worth
Cook County

(G-21453)
ACCURATE ELC MTR & PUMP CO
6955 W 111th St (60482-1824)
PHONE..................................708 448-2792
Patrick Macias, *President*
Mark Stabosz, *Vice Pres*
EMP: 3
SQ FT: 5,000
SALES: 2MM **Privately Held**
WEB: www.allelectricmotor.com
SIC: 5999 7694 7699 5063 Motors, electric; electric motor repair; pumps & pumping equipment repair; motors, electric
PA: All Electric Motor Repair & Service, Inc.
6726 S Ashland Ave
Chicago IL 60636
773 925-2404

(G-21454)
AUTO HEAD AND ENGINE EXCHANGE
Also Called: Worth Auto Parts
6603 W 111th St (60482-1909)
PHONE..................................708 448-8762
Anthony Uzzardo, *President*
Alfred Uzzardo, *Corp Secy*
Theresa Uzzardo, *Manager*
EMP: 3
SQ FT: 6,500
SALES (est): 300K **Privately Held**
SIC: 3599 Machine & other job shop work

(G-21455)
BEST ADVERTISING SPC & PRTG
11437 S Natoma Ave (60482-2131)
PHONE..................................708 448-1110
Jerry Janicki, *Owner*
EMP: 4
SQ FT: 1,000
SALES (est): 80K **Privately Held**
SIC: 2752 5947 3993 Commercial printing, offset; gift, novelty & souvenir shop; signs & advertising specialties

(G-21456)
TIMES ENERGY
11241 S Natoma Ave (60482-1903)
PHONE..................................773 444-9282
Aamer Alobaidi, *Business Mgr*
EMP: 2
SALES (est): 157K **Privately Held**
SIC: 1382 5983 Oil & gas exploration services; fuel oil dealers

Wyoming
Stark County

(G-21457)
ALDRICO INC
Also Called: Aldrich Company
341 E Williams St (61491-1505)
P.O. Box 97 (61491-0097)
PHONE..................................309 695-2311
Susan Howard, *President*
Amy Hillan, *Vice Pres*
EMP: 22
SQ FT: 65,000
SALES: 3.7MM **Privately Held**
SIC: 3433 Heating equipment, except electric

(G-21458)
CARDINAL CATTLE
Rr 2 Box 181 (61491)
PHONE..................................309 479-1302
Jack Riley, *Owner*
EMP: 3
SALES (est): 86.6K **Privately Held**
WEB: www.cardinalcattlecompany.com
SIC: 0212 3523 Beef cattle except feedlots; cattle feeding, handling & watering equipment

(G-21459)
FMC CORPORATION
Hwy 17 E (61491)
P.O. Box 180 (61491-0180)
PHONE..................................309 695-2571
Bryan Westerby, *Manager*
EMP: 20
SALES (corp-wide): 4.6B **Publicly Held**
WEB: www.fmc.com
SIC: 2812 Alkalies & chlorine
PA: Fmc Corporation
2929 Walnut St
Philadelphia PA 19104
215 299-6000

(G-21460)
FMC CORPORATION
Hwy 17 (61491)
P.O. Box 180 (61491-0180)
PHONE..................................309 695-2571
EMP: 25
SALES (corp-wide): 4.6B **Publicly Held**
SIC: 2879 Agricultural chemicals; insecticides, agricultural or household; pesticides, agricultural or household; agricultural disinfectants

Wyoming - Stark County (G-21461)

PA: Fmc Corporation
2929 Walnut St
Philadelphia PA 19104
215 299-6000

(G-21461)
QUALITY CABLE & COMPONENTS INC
109 N Madison Ave (61491-1425)
P.O. Box 88 (61491-0088)
PHONE.................309 695-3435
Cindy M Brittingham, *Owner*
EMP: 35
SQ FT: 10,000
SALES (est): 6.3MM **Privately Held**
SIC: 3679 5063 Harness assemblies for electronic use; wire or cable; wire & cable

(G-21462)
STAHL LUMBER COMPANY (PA)
Also Called: Stahl Ready Mix Concrete
117 S Galena Ave (61491-1407)
P.O. Box 10 (61491-0010)
PHONE.................309 695-4331
James I Stahl, *Ch of Bd*
Joanne K Holman, *Corp Secy*
EMP: 14 EST: 1933
SQ FT: 3,000
SALES (est): 2.3MM **Privately Held**
SIC: 3273 1521 5211 Ready-mixed concrete; single-family housing construction; lumber & other building materials

(G-21463)
STAHL LUMBER COMPANY
Also Called: Stahl Ready Concrete
117 S Galena Ave (61491-1407)
P.O. Box 10 (61491-0010)
PHONE.................309 385-2552
James Stahl, *Manager*
EMP: 10
SALES (est): 534.3K
SALES (corp-wide): 2.3MM **Privately Held**
SIC: 3273 Ready-mixed concrete
PA: Stahl Lumber Company
117 S Galena Ave
Wyoming IL 61491
309 695-4331

(G-21464)
YER KILN ME LLC
108 N 7th St (61491-4406)
PHONE.................309 606-9007
Cox Nicole, *Principal*
EMP: 3 EST: 2015
SALES (est): 155.2K **Privately Held**
SIC: 3559 Kilns

Xenia
Clay County

(G-21465)
ALVIN F LAMBRIGHT
209 County Road 1715 N (62899-4245)
PHONE.................618 835-2050
Alvin F Lambright, *Principal*
EMP: 3
SALES (est): 150.8K **Privately Held**
SIC: 3442 Metal doors, sash & trim

(G-21466)
BASELINE SERVICES INC
1360 Ironwood Rd (62899-2220)
PHONE.................618 678-2753
Chad S Williams, *President*
Elizabeth A Williams, *Admin Sec*
EMP: 6 EST: 2009
SALES (est): 940.7K **Privately Held**
SIC: 1389 Oil field services

(G-21467)
BRENDA MILLER
Also Called: M & W Curios
130 Old Highway 50 (62899-2291)
PHONE.................618 678-2639
Brenda Miller, *Owner*
EMP: 6
SALES (est): 467.9K **Privately Held**
WEB: www.mandwcurios.com
SIC: 3231 Glass sheet, bent: made from purchased glass

(G-21468)
M D HARMON INC (PA)
752 Jupiter Dr (62899)
P.O. Box 196 (62899-0196)
PHONE.................618 662-8925
Martin Harmon, *President*
Ryan Harmon, *Admin Sec*
EMP: 11
SQ FT: 22,000
SALES: 800K **Privately Held**
SIC: 2421 0212 Sawmills & planing mills, general; beef cattle except feedlots

(G-21469)
XENIA MFG INC (PA)
1507 Church St (62899-1283)
P.O. Box 237 (62899-0237)
PHONE.................618 678-2218
Paul Andrew Knapp, *President*
Rick L Forth, *Corp Secy*
Charles Knapp, *Vice Pres*
Ed Knapp, *Vice Pres*
EMP: 140
SQ FT: 40,000
SALES: 22MM **Privately Held**
SIC: 3694 Harness wiring sets, internal combustion engines

Yates City
Knox County

(G-21470)
BURT COYOTE CO
104 N Union St (61572-7521)
P.O. Box 165 (61572-0165)
PHONE.................309 358-1602
Curtis Price, *President*
Ivan Price, *Vice Pres*
Melissa Swindler, *Admin Sec*
EMP: 14
SQ FT: 1,232
SALES (est): 1.8MM **Privately Held**
SIC: 3949 Archery equipment, general

Yorkville
Kendall County

(G-21471)
ALPHA PRECISION INC
9750 Rte 126 (60560)
PHONE.................630 553-7331
Kevin W Brolsma, *President*
EMP: 19 EST: 1965
SQ FT: 10,000
SALES (est): 2.3MM **Privately Held**
WEB: www.alphaprecision.com
SIC: 3229 Pressed & blown glass

(G-21472)
ANDREW TOSCHAK
1025 Mchugh Rd (60560-1228)
PHONE.................630 553-3434
Andrew Toschak, *President*
EMP: 3
SALES (est): 212K **Privately Held**
SIC: 3599 Machine shop, jobbing & repair

(G-21473)
AURORA SPCLTY TXTLES GROUP INC
2705 N Bridge St (60560-9256)
P.O. Box 70, Aurora (60507-0070)
PHONE.................800 864-0303
Marcia Ayala, *President*
John Ricci, *VP Finance*
Douglas C Miller, *Admin Sec*
▼ **EMP:** 85
SALES (est): 36.1MM
SALES (corp-wide): 379.3MM **Privately Held**
SIC: 2261 2231 Finishing plants, cotton; broadwoven fabric mills, wool
PA: Meridian Industries, Inc.
735 N Water St Ste 630
Milwaukee WI 53202
414 224-0610

(G-21474)
CABINET STILES INC
1165 N Bridge St (60560-1114)
PHONE.................630 553-8639
Brad Warsman, *CEO*
EMP: 3
SALES (est): 155.6K **Privately Held**
SIC: 2434 Wood kitchen cabinets

(G-21475)
CHARTNET TECHNOLOGIES INC
220 Garden St (60560-8921)
P.O. Box 285, Hudson OH (44236-0285)
PHONE.................630 385-4100
Lee Tkachuk, *CEO*
Thomas Trainor, *CFO*
EMP: 11
SALES (est): 300K **Privately Held**
SIC: 7372 Business oriented computer software

(G-21476)
D AND K PLASTICS
2127 State Route 47 (60560-4521)
P.O. Box 668 (60560-0668)
PHONE.................712 723-5372
Cheri Little, *Owner*
EMP: 4
SQ FT: 3,800
SALES (est): 337.1K **Privately Held**
SIC: 3599 5162 Machine shop, jobbing & repair; plastics sheets & rods

(G-21477)
DANKO INDUSTRIES
181 Wolf St Unit C (60560-1955)
PHONE.................630 882-6070
Ernest Brain, *Owner*
EMP: 6
SALES (est): 626.3K **Privately Held**
SIC: 2842 Specialty cleaning, polishes & sanitation goods

(G-21478)
DEKALB BLOWER INC
319 E Van Emmon St (60560-2097)
P.O. Box 516 (60560-0516)
PHONE.................630 553-8831
Eric Johansen, *President*
Chester F Johansen, *Principal*
EMP: 13
SALES (est): 3.2MM **Privately Held**
SIC: 3564 Dust or fume collecting equipment, industrial

(G-21479)
DEVICE TECHNOLOGIES INC
1211 Badger St Ste H (60560-1785)
PHONE.................630 553-7178
Richard Kunzelman, *President*
Susan Kunzelman, *Treasurer*
EMP: 3
SQ FT: 4,000
SALES (est): 500K **Privately Held**
SIC: 7389 3599 7692 Design, commercial & industrial; machine shop, jobbing & repair; welding repair

(G-21480)
DEYCO INC
Also Called: Meryll 200000 Mile Check
102 Beaver St (60560-1703)
PHONE.................630 553-5666
Terry Young, *President*
EMP: 8
SALES (est): 309.9K **Privately Held**
SIC: 7539 3535 8711 2399 Automotive repair shops; unit handling conveying systems; engineering services; seat belts, automobile & aircraft

(G-21481)
EDWARD J WARREN JR
Also Called: Tdr Transport
2921 Alden Ave (60560-4698)
PHONE.................630 882-8817
Edward J Warren Jr, *Principal*
EMP: 4
SALES (est): 365.9K **Privately Held**
SIC: 3537 7389 Trucks: freight, baggage, etc.: industrial, except mining;

(G-21482)
FLURRY INDUSTRIES INC
2002 Prairie Rose Ln (60560-1912)
PHONE.................630 882-8361
Christopher Maury, *President*
EMP: 5
SALES (est): 420.4K **Privately Held**
SIC: 3999 Manufacturing industries

(G-21483)
FOX VALLEY SANDBLASTING INC
1211 Badger St (60560-1783)
P.O. Box 63 (60560-0063)
PHONE.................630 553-6050
James Schwebke, *President*
Andrea Schwebke, *Admin Sec*
EMP: 2
SALES (est): 408.2K **Privately Held**
SIC: 1799 3471 Sandblasting of building exteriors; plating & polishing

(G-21484)
GANNETT STLLITE INFO NTWRK LLC
Also Called: USA Today
136 Bertram Dr Unit C (60560-3216)
PHONE.................630 629-1280
Douglas McCorkindale, *CEO*
EMP: 117
SALES (corp-wide): 1.8B **Publicly Held**
WEB: www.gannett.com
SIC: 2711 Newspapers, publishing & printing
HQ: Gannett Satellite Information Network, Llc
7950 Jones Branch Dr
Mc Lean VA 22102
703 854-6000

(G-21485)
GERARD MITCHELL COMPANY LLC
Also Called: Bridge Street Foods
291 Walsh Cir (60560-9198)
PHONE.................708 205-0828
Gerard Mitchell, *Mng Member*
EMP: 5
SQ FT: 500
SALES: 50K **Privately Held**
SIC: 2099 Pasta, uncooked: packaged with other ingredients

(G-21486)
GR8 SEAS HOLDINGS INC
803 N Bridge St Ste A (60560-2156)
PHONE.................630 862-5099
Bob Jeter, *President*
EMP: 5
SALES (est): 218.4K **Privately Held**
SIC: 3565 Bottling machinery: filling, capping, labeling

(G-21487)
H E ASSOCIATES INC
201 Beaver St (60560-1706)
PHONE.................630 553-6382
Harvey A Knell, *President*
Margaret Knell, *Corp Secy*
EMP: 15
SALES (est): 2.2MM **Privately Held**
SIC: 3089 3645 3423 Planters, plastic; residential lighting fixtures; hand & edge tools

(G-21488)
HARRIS CONTAINER CORP
113 Riverside Dr (60560-9471)
P.O. Box 1000 (60560-0816)
PHONE.................630 553-0027
Robert J Harris Jr, *President*
EMP: 3
SALES: 1.4MM **Privately Held**
SIC: 2653 Boxes, corrugated: made from purchased materials

(G-21489)
KENDALL COUNTY RECORD (PA)
109 W Veterans Pkwy (60560-1905)
PHONE.................630 553-7034
Jeff Farren, *President*
Kathleen Farren, *Principal*
EMP: 21 EST: 1864
SQ FT: 5,000

GEOGRAPHIC SECTION

Zion - Lake County (G-21518)

SALES (est): 1.3MM **Privately Held**
SIC: 2711 Newspapers, publishing & printing

(G-21490)
KENDALL PRINTING CO
948 N Bridge St (60560-1109)
PHONE..................................630 553-9200
Annette Powell, *Owner*
EMP: 3
SQ FT: 1,000
SALES (est): 324.7K **Privately Held**
SIC: 2752 2791 2789 Commercial printing, offset; typesetting; bookbinding & related work

(G-21491)
LAMBERT PRINT SOURCE LLC
Also Called: PRINTING
301 Walsh Cir (60560-9134)
PHONE..................................630 708-0505
Jason Lambert, *President*
EMP: 2
SALES: 546.6K **Privately Held**
SIC: 7336 2621 2759 2752 Commercial art & graphic design; printing paper; screen printing; flexographic printing; commercial printing, offset; signs & advertising specialties

(G-21492)
LUXE CLASSIC KITCHENS & INTERI
135 E Van Emmon St Ste 1 (60560-1581)
PHONE..................................630 774-9337
Tommy Okapal, *President*
EMP: 2
SALES (est): 374.3K **Privately Held**
SIC: 2434 Wood kitchen cabinets

(G-21493)
MCKILLIP INDUSTRIES INC (PA)
Also Called: Usa/Docufinish
207 Beaver St (60560-1706)
PHONE..................................815 439-1050
John McKillip MBA, *CEO*
Jason Lambert, *Vice Pres*
Robert Szablewski, *Admin Sec*
EMP: 39
SQ FT: 50,000
SALES (est): 6.3MM **Privately Held**
SIC: 2759 Screen printing

(G-21494)
OLIVE LECLAIRE OIL CO
1524 Coral Dr (60560-3060)
PHONE..................................888 255-1867
EMP: 3
SALES (est): 121.6K **Privately Held**
SIC: 2079 Olive oil

(G-21495)
OMALLEY WELDING AND FABG
1209 Badger St (60560-1702)
PHONE..................................630 553-1604
Mark O'Malley, *President*
EMP: 3
SQ FT: 6,500
SALES (est): 607.5K **Privately Held**
SIC: 3441 Fabricated structural metal

(G-21496)
P M MFG SERVICES INC
9626 Lisbon Rd (60560-9338)
PHONE..................................630 553-6924
Dawn E Mulligan, *President*
Paul Mulligan, *Vice Pres*
EMP: 3
SQ FT: 2,400
SALES (est): 200K **Privately Held**
SIC: 3599 3357 Machine shop, jobbing & repair; nonferrous wiredrawing & insulating

(G-21497)
POXYPROS INC
4657 Plymouth Ave (60560-6033)
PHONE..................................630 675-5924
John Spencer, *President*
EMP: 4
SALES (est): 181.6K **Privately Held**
SIC: 2891 Epoxy adhesives

(G-21498)
PREMIUM PRODUCTS INC
207 Wolf St (60560-1739)
P.O. Box 9335, Naperville (60567-0335)
PHONE..................................630 553-6160
D G Dhake, *President*
EMP: 12
SQ FT: 25,000
SALES: 7MM **Privately Held**
SIC: 2851 Paints & allied products

(G-21499)
PRIMEDIA SOURCE LLC
627 White Oak Way (60560-9581)
PHONE..................................630 553-8451
Jennifer Cherney, *President*
EMP: 1
SALES (est): 259.5K **Privately Held**
SIC: 5112 2672 5085 5113 Office supplies; adhesive papers, labels or tapes: from purchased material; industrial supplies; shipping supplies; labels & seals: printing; flexographic printing

(G-21500)
RIGHT RAIL LLC
99 Wooden Bridge Dr (60560-9708)
PHONE..................................630 882-9335
David Katz, *Principal*
EMP: 5 EST: 2014
SALES (est): 426.1K **Privately Held**
WEB: www.rightrailllc.com
SIC: 3743 Railroad equipment

(G-21501)
STRAUSBRGER ASSOC SLS MKTG INC
Also Called: Jns Glass & Coatings
701 Teri Ln (60560-2202)
PHONE..................................630 768-6179
Nate Strausberger, *President*
EMP: 6
SALES: 4MM **Privately Held**
SIC: 3827 Optical instruments & lenses

(G-21502)
TIEM ENGINEERING CORPORATION
202 Beaver St (60560-1705)
P.O. Box 790 (60560-0790)
PHONE..................................630 553-7484
John Lovetere, *President*
Philip D Lovetere, *Corp Secy*
David Lovetere, *Vice Pres*
Lori Eallonardo, *Info Tech Mgr*
Marianne Linebaugh, *Shareholder*
▲ EMP: 10 EST: 1972
SQ FT: 20,000
SALES (est): 934.5K **Privately Held**
SIC: 4783 2759 Packing goods for shipping; labels & seals: printing

(G-21503)
TITAN INJECTION PARTS & SVC
Also Called: Tips
204 Beaver St (60560-1994)
PHONE..................................630 882-8455
Jaime Torres, *President*
Ricardo Valle, *Vice Pres*
Gordy Wilson, *VP Sales*
EMP: 5
SALES (est): 1.2MM **Privately Held**
SIC: 3556 Smokers, food processing equipment

(G-21504)
VALLEY RUN STONE INC
6369 Whitetail Ridge Ct (60560-3239)
PHONE..................................630 553-7974
Maryl Betzwiser, *President*
Grant Avery, *Owner*
David Avery, *Vice Pres*
Mike Avery, *Vice Pres*
EMP: 20
SALES (est): 1.7MM **Privately Held**
SIC: 1442 Gravel & pebble mining

(G-21505)
WATER PRODUCTS COMPANY ILL INC
Cascade Water Works
1213 Badger St (60560-1702)
PHONE..................................630 553-0840
Sam Eskew, *Branch Mgr*
EMP: 20

SALES (corp-wide): 15.4MM **Privately Held**
SIC: 3569 Filters & strainers, pipeline
PA: Water Products Company Of Illinois, Inc.
3255 E New York St
Aurora IL 60504
630 898-6100

(G-21506)
WISE CONSTRUCTION SERVICES
1107 S Bridge St Ste E (60560-1747)
PHONE..................................630 553-6350
Joseph Wisniewski, *President*
Beverly Weeks, *Manager*
EMP: 3
SALES (est): 308.1K **Privately Held**
WEB: www.wiseconstruction.net
SIC: 5719 3292 Wicker, rattan or reed home furnishings; wick, asbestos

(G-21507)
WRIGLEY MANUFACTURING CO LLC
Also Called: Wrigley's
2800 State Route 47 (60560-9441)
PHONE..................................630 553-4800
Lupe Alvarez, *Manager*
Doug Tozier, *Manager*
EMP: 400
SALES (corp-wide): 38.5B **Privately Held**
SIC: 2067 2064 Chewing gum; candy & other confectionery products
HQ: Wrigley Manufacturing Company Llc
410 N Michigan Ave
Chicago IL 60611
312 644-2121

Zion
Lake County

(G-21508)
ANDERSSON TOOL & DIE LLP
1717 Kenosha Rd (60099-9342)
PHONE..................................847 746-8866
Rolf A Andersson, *Partner*
George Andersson, *Partner*
EMP: 12
SQ FT: 6,000
SALES (est): 79.8K **Privately Held**
SIC: 3599 3544 Machine shop, jobbing & repair; special dies, tools, jigs & fixtures

(G-21509)
ATLANTIC ENGINEERING
42008 N Delany Rd (60099-9661)
PHONE..................................847 782-1762
Henry Scheffner, *Owner*
EMP: 2
SQ FT: 3,500
SALES (est): 200K **Privately Held**
SIC: 3469 3544 Stamping metal for the trade; special dies, tools, jigs & fixtures

(G-21510)
CORAL CHEMICAL COMPANY
1915 Industrial Ave (60099-1435)
PHONE..................................847 246-6666
Joseph D Pemberton, *Principal*
EMP: 40
SALES (corp-wide): 18.4MM **Privately Held**
SIC: 2842 2812 Cleaning or polishing preparations; alkalies & chlorine
PA: Coral Chemical Company
1915 Indusrial Ave
Zion IL 60099
847 246-6666

(G-21511)
D & M TOOL LLC
2013 Horizon Ct (60099-1488)
PHONE..................................847 731-3600
Dave Velcover, *Owner*
EMP: 4
SQ FT: 3,750
SALES: 400K **Privately Held**
SIC: 3599 3544 Machine shop, jobbing & repair; special dies, tools, jigs & fixtures

(G-21512)
DYNACOIL INC
2000 Lewis Ave (60099-1546)
PHONE..................................847 731-3300
Tony Devito, *President*
Peter Dosedla, *Vice Pres*
Brian Swanson, *Project Mgr*
Perry Villani, *Project Mgr*
Ken Hotchkiss, *Materials Mgr*
EMP: 45
SQ FT: 35,000
SALES (est): 13MM **Privately Held**
SIC: 3444 Sheet metalwork

(G-21513)
ERA TOOL AND MANUFACTURING CO
3200 16th St (60099-1416)
PHONE..................................847 298-6333
Rosa Molina, *Ch of Bd*
Robert J Lonze, *President*
Howard Jack, *Vice Pres*
EMP: 40 EST: 1937
SQ FT: 20,000
SALES (est): 7.2MM **Privately Held**
SIC: 3469 3544 Stamping metal for the trade; die sets for metal stamping (presses)

(G-21514)
FEDERAL EQUIPMENT & SVCS INC
3200 16th St (60099-1416)
PHONE..................................847 731-9002
Rosa Molina, *President*
▲ EMP: 10
SQ FT: 10,000
SALES (est): 1.6MM **Privately Held**
SIC: 5198 3363 Paints, varnishes & supplies; aluminum die-castings

(G-21515)
GRAPHIC PARTNERS INC
Also Called: GP
4300 Il Route 173 (60099-4089)
PHONE..................................847 872-9445
Arthur Larsen, *President*
Kirk Larsen, *Vice Pres*
Keith Love, *Vice Pres*
Daniel Sikora, *Admin Sec*
EMP: 50
SQ FT: 26,000
SALES (est): 1.9MM **Privately Held**
SIC: 2752 Commercial printing, offset; advertising posters, lithographed; post cards, picture: lithographed

(G-21516)
H A FRIEND & COMPANY INC (PA)
1535 Lewis Ave (60099-1493)
PHONE..................................847 746-1248
Richard W Friend Sr, *Ch of Bd*
Randy Friend, *President*
Richard Friend Jr, *Vice Pres*
EMP: 50
SQ FT: 40,000
SALES (est): 5MM **Privately Held**
WEB: www.friendsstationery.com
SIC: 2759 5112 5021 5044 Embossing on paper; office supplies; office furniture; office equipment

(G-21517)
HIGHLAND PARK MECHANICAL INC
3204 16th St (60099-1416)
P.O. Box 607, Highland Park (60035-0607)
PHONE..................................847 269-3863
Tabitha Haggie, *President*
D Patrick Haggie, *Vice Pres*
EMP: 5
SQ FT: 5,000
SALES (est): 594.9K **Privately Held**
SIC: 1711 1761 3585 Warm air heating & air conditioning contractor; ventilation & duct work contractor; sheet metalwork; heating equipment, complete

(G-21518)
JOSEPH KRISTAN
Also Called: J & J Powder Coating
2805 Ebenezer Ave (60099-2753)
PHONE..................................847 731-3131
Joseph Kristan, *Owner*

Zion - Lake County (G-21519)

EMP: 3
SALES (est): 204.4K **Privately Held**
SIC: **3479** Coating of metals & formed products

(G-21519)
JSQ INC
2817 Ezra Ave (60099-2523)
PHONE.................................847 731-8800
Eugene Mauser, *President*
EMP: 4
SALES: 400K **Privately Held**
SIC: **1389** Construction, repair & dismantling services

(G-21520)
MC KINNEY STEEL & SALES INC
813 29th St (60099-3263)
PHONE.................................847 746-3344
Ryan Rodbro, *President*
Debra Rodbro, *Admin Sec*
EMP: 20
SQ FT: 20,000
SALES (est): 5.3MM **Privately Held**
SIC: **3441** Building components, structural steel

(G-21521)
NORTHPOINT HEATING & AIR COND
1101 Shiloh Blvd Rear 2 (60099-2602)
P.O. Box 303, Winthrop Harbor (60096-0303)
PHONE.................................847 731-1067
Paul Sheppard, *Owner*
EMP: 4
SALES (est): 284.7K **Privately Held**
WEB: www.northpointheating.com
SIC: **3567** Industrial furnaces & ovens

(G-21522)
OLIVE TREE FOODS INC
2439 Galilee Ave (60099-2908)
PHONE.................................847 872-2762
Craig Peterson, *Principal*
EMP: 4
SALES (est): 352.5K **Privately Held**
SIC: **3421** Table & food cutlery, including butchers'

(G-21523)
ONCQUEST
Also Called: Oncquest Pharma
43323 N Oak Crest Ln (60099-9413)
PHONE.................................847 682-4703
Richard J Pariza, *Principal*
Kathryn Pariza, *Principal*
EMP: 5
SALES (est): 310.5K **Privately Held**
SIC: **2834** Pharmaceutical preparations

(G-21524)
PARAMOUNT SINTERED PDTS LLP
1717 Kenosha Rd (60099-9342)
PHONE.................................847 746-8866
George Anderson, *Partner*
Rolf Andersson, *Partner*
David Johnson, *Partner*
EMP: 5
SQ FT: 7,000
SALES (est): 474.9K **Privately Held**
SIC: **3599** Machine shop, jobbing & repair

(G-21525)
PHILMAR LLC (PA)
Also Called: Colorful Fire
2502 Deborah Ave (60099-2708)
P.O. Box 633 (60099-0633)
PHONE.................................847 282-0204
Karen Diamond,
Fred Martin,
Gus Phillips,
▲ EMP: 9
SALES (est): 2.2MM **Privately Held**
SIC: **2899** Flares, fireworks & similar preparations

(G-21526)
S & G IRON WORKS
2173 Galilee Ave (60099-2226)
PHONE.................................224 789-7178
Stephan Sarver, *Owner*
EMP: 4
SQ FT: 3,200
SALES (est): 503.4K **Privately Held**
SIC: **3446** Stairs, staircases, stair treads: prefabricated metal

(G-21527)
UNITED COMMUNICATIONS CORP
2711 Sheridan Rd Ste 202 (60099-2650)
PHONE.................................847 746-1515
EMP: 118
SALES (corp-wide): 64.2MM **Privately Held**
SIC: **2711** Newspapers-Publishing/Printing
PA: United Communications Corporation
    5800 7th Ave
    Kenosha WI 53140
    262 657-1000

(G-21528)
UNITED COMMUNICATIONS CORP
Bargineer
2711 Shrridon Rd Unit 202 (60099)
P.O. Box 111 (60099-0111)
PHONE.................................847 746-4700
EMP: 20
SALES (corp-wide): 73.4MM **Privately Held**
SIC: **2711** Newspaper
PA: United Communications Corporation
    5800 7th Ave
    Kenosha WI 53140
    262 657-1000

(G-21529)
WAUKEGAN ARCHITECTURAL INC
3505 16th St (60099-1421)
PHONE.................................847 746-9077
Michael Maglio, *President*
▲ EMP: 8
SQ FT: 8,000
SALES (est): 1.3MM **Privately Held**
WEB: www.mausoleumbronze.com
SIC: **3446 3444 3442 3341** Ornamental metalwork; sheet metalwork; metal doors, sash & trim; secondary nonferrous metals

(G-21530)
WHITESIDE DRAPERY FABRICATORS
2701 Deborah Ave Ste A (60099-2793)
PHONE.................................847 746-5300
Bryan Mueller, *President*
Jon Whiteside, *Corp Secy*
EMP: 17
SQ FT: 15,000
SALES (est): 1.6MM **Privately Held**
SIC: **2391** Draperies, plastic & textile: from purchased materials

SIC INDEX

Standard Industrial Classification Alphabetical Index

SIC NO PRODUCT

A

3291 Abrasive Prdts
2891 Adhesives & Sealants
3563 Air & Gas Compressors
3585 Air Conditioning & Heating Eqpt
3721 Aircraft
3724 Aircraft Engines & Engine Parts
3728 Aircraft Parts & Eqpt, NEC
2812 Alkalies & Chlorine
3363 Aluminum Die Castings
3354 Aluminum Extruded Prdts
3365 Aluminum Foundries
3355 Aluminum Rolling & Drawing, NEC
3353 Aluminum Sheet, Plate & Foil
3483 Ammunition, Large
3826 Analytical Instruments
2077 Animal, Marine Fats & Oils
1231 Anthracite Mining
2389 Apparel & Accessories, NEC
3446 Architectural & Ornamental Metal Work
7694 Armature Rewinding Shops
3292 Asbestos products
2952 Asphalt Felts & Coatings
3822 Automatic Temperature Controls
3581 Automatic Vending Machines
3465 Automotive Stampings
2396 Automotive Trimmings, Apparel Findings, Related Prdts

B

2673 Bags: Plastics, Laminated & Coated
2674 Bags: Uncoated Paper & Multiwall
3562 Ball & Roller Bearings
2836 Biological Prdts, Exc Diagnostic Substances
1221 Bituminous Coal & Lignite: Surface Mining
1222 Bituminous Coal: Underground Mining
2782 Blankbooks & Looseleaf Binders
3312 Blast Furnaces, Coke Ovens, Steel & Rolling Mills
3564 Blowers & Fans
3732 Boat Building & Repairing
3452 Bolts, Nuts, Screws, Rivets & Washers
2732 Book Printing, Not Publishing
2789 Bookbinding
2731 Books: Publishing & Printing
3131 Boot & Shoe Cut Stock & Findings
2342 Brassieres, Girdles & Garments
2051 Bread, Bakery Prdts Exc Cookies & Crackers
3251 Brick & Structural Clay Tile
3991 Brooms & Brushes
3995 Burial Caskets
2021 Butter

C

3578 Calculating & Accounting Eqpt
2064 Candy & Confectionery Prdts
2033 Canned Fruits, Vegetables & Preserves
2032 Canned Specialties
2394 Canvas Prdts
3624 Carbon & Graphite Prdts
2895 Carbon Black
3955 Carbon Paper & Inked Ribbons
3592 Carburetors, Pistons, Rings & Valves
2273 Carpets & Rugs
2823 Cellulosic Man-Made Fibers
3241 Cement, Hydraulic
3253 Ceramic Tile
2043 Cereal Breakfast Foods
2022 Cheese
1479 Chemical & Fertilizer Mining
2899 Chemical Preparations, NEC
2067 Chewing Gum
2361 Children's & Infants' Dresses & Blouses
3261 China Plumbing Fixtures & Fittings
3262 China, Table & Kitchen Articles
2066 Chocolate & Cocoa Prdts
2111 Cigarettes
2257 Circular Knit Fabric Mills
3255 Clay Refractories
1459 Clay, Ceramic & Refractory Minerals, NEC
1241 Coal Mining Svcs
3479 Coating & Engraving, NEC
2095 Coffee
3316 Cold Rolled Steel Sheet, Strip & Bars
3582 Commercial Laundry, Dry Clean & Pressing Mchs

2759 Commercial Printing
2754 Commercial Printing: Gravure
2752 Commercial Printing: Lithographic
3646 Commercial, Indl & Institutional Lighting Fixtures
3669 Communications Eqpt, NEC
3577 Computer Peripheral Eqpt, NEC
3572 Computer Storage Devices
3575 Computer Terminals
3271 Concrete Block & Brick
3272 Concrete Prdts
3531 Construction Machinery & Eqpt
1442 Construction Sand & Gravel
2679 Converted Paper Prdts, NEC
3535 Conveyors & Eqpt
2052 Cookies & Crackers
3366 Copper Foundries
1021 Copper Ores
2298 Cordage & Twine
2653 Corrugated & Solid Fiber Boxes
3961 Costume Jewelry & Novelties
2261 Cotton Fabric Finishers
2211 Cotton, Woven Fabric
2074 Cottonseed Oil Mills
3466 Crowns & Closures
1311 Crude Petroleum & Natural Gas
1423 Crushed & Broken Granite
1422 Crushed & Broken Limestone
1429 Crushed & Broken Stone, NEC
3643 Current-Carrying Wiring Devices
2391 Curtains & Draperies
3087 Custom Compounding Of Purchased Plastic Resins
3281 Cut Stone Prdts
3421 Cutlery
2865 Cyclic-Crudes, Intermediates, Dyes & Org Pigments

D

3843 Dental Eqpt & Splys
2835 Diagnostic Substances
2675 Die-Cut Paper & Board
3544 Dies, Tools, Jigs, Fixtures & Indl Molds
1411 Dimension Stone
2047 Dog & Cat Food
3942 Dolls & Stuffed Toys
2591 Drapery Hardware, Window Blinds & Shades
2381 Dress & Work Gloves
2034 Dried Fruits, Vegetables & Soup
1381 Drilling Oil & Gas Wells

E

3263 Earthenware, Whiteware, Table & Kitchen Articles
3634 Electric Household Appliances
3641 Electric Lamps
3694 Electrical Eqpt For Internal Combustion Engines
3629 Electrical Indl Apparatus, NEC
3699 Electrical Machinery, Eqpt & Splys, NEC
3845 Electromedical & Electrotherapeutic Apparatus
3313 Electrometallurgical Prdts
3675 Electronic Capacitors
3677 Electronic Coils & Transformers
3679 Electronic Components, NEC
3571 Electronic Computers
3678 Electronic Connectors
3676 Electronic Resistors
3471 Electroplating, Plating, Polishing, Anodizing & Coloring
3534 Elevators & Moving Stairways
3431 Enameled Iron & Metal Sanitary Ware
2677 Envelopes
2892 Explosives

F

2241 Fabric Mills, Cotton, Wool, Silk & Man-Made
3499 Fabricated Metal Prdts, NEC
3498 Fabricated Pipe & Pipe Fittings
3443 Fabricated Plate Work
3069 Fabricated Rubber Prdts, NEC
3441 Fabricated Structural Steel
2399 Fabricated Textile Prdts, NEC
2295 Fabrics Coated Not Rubberized
2297 Fabrics, Nonwoven
3523 Farm Machinery & Eqpt
3965 Fasteners, Buttons, Needles & Pins
2875 Fertilizers, Mixing Only
2655 Fiber Cans, Tubes & Drums
2091 Fish & Seafoods, Canned & Cured

2092 Fish & Seafoods, Fresh & Frozen
3211 Flat Glass
2087 Flavoring Extracts & Syrups
2045 Flour, Blended & Prepared
2041 Flour, Grain Milling
3824 Fluid Meters & Counters
3593 Fluid Power Cylinders & Actuators
3594 Fluid Power Pumps & Motors
3492 Fluid Power Valves & Hose Fittings
2657 Folding Paperboard Boxes
3556 Food Prdts Machinery
2099 Food Preparations, NEC
3149 Footwear, NEC
2053 Frozen Bakery Prdts
2037 Frozen Fruits, Juices & Vegetables
2038 Frozen Specialties
2599 Furniture & Fixtures, NEC

G

3944 Games, Toys & Children's Vehicles
3524 Garden, Lawn Tractors & Eqpt
3053 Gaskets, Packing & Sealing Devices
2369 Girls' & Infants' Outerwear, NEC
3221 Glass Containers
3231 Glass Prdts Made Of Purchased Glass
1041 Gold Ores
3321 Gray Iron Foundries
2771 Greeting Card Publishing
3769 Guided Missile/Space Vehicle Parts & Eqpt, NEC
3764 Guided Missile/Space Vehicle Propulsion Units & parts
3761 Guided Missiles & Space Vehicles
2861 Gum & Wood Chemicals
3275 Gypsum Prdts

H

3423 Hand & Edge Tools
3425 Hand Saws & Saw Blades
3429 Hardware, NEC
2426 Hardwood Dimension & Flooring Mills
2435 Hardwood Veneer & Plywood
2353 Hats, Caps & Millinery
3433 Heating Eqpt
3536 Hoists, Cranes & Monorails
2252 Hosiery, Except Women's
2251 Hosiery, Women's Full & Knee Length
2392 House furnishings: Textile
3639 Household Appliances, NEC
3651 Household Audio & Video Eqpt
3631 Household Cooking Eqpt
2519 Household Furniture, NEC
3633 Household Laundry Eqpt
3632 Household Refrigerators & Freezers
3635 Household Vacuum Cleaners

I

2097 Ice
2024 Ice Cream
2819 Indl Inorganic Chemicals, NEC
3823 Indl Instruments For Meas, Display & Control
3569 Indl Machinery & Eqpt, NEC
3567 Indl Process Furnaces & Ovens
3537 Indl Trucks, Tractors, Trailers & Stackers
2813 Industrial Gases
2869 Industrial Organic Chemicals, NEC
3543 Industrial Patterns
1446 Industrial Sand
3491 Industrial Valves
2816 Inorganic Pigments
3825 Instrs For Measuring & Testing Electricity
3519 Internal Combustion Engines, NEC
3462 Iron & Steel Forgings
1011 Iron Ores

J

3915 Jewelers Findings & Lapidary Work
3911 Jewelry: Precious Metal

K

1455 Kaolin & Ball Clay
2253 Knit Outerwear Mills
2254 Knit Underwear Mills
2259 Knitting Mills, NEC

L

3821 Laboratory Apparatus & Furniture

SIC INDEX

SIC NO	PRODUCT
1031	Lead & Zinc Ores
3952	Lead Pencils, Crayons & Artist's Mtrls
2386	Leather & Sheep Lined Clothing
3151	Leather Gloves & Mittens
3199	Leather Goods, NEC
3111	Leather Tanning & Finishing
3648	Lighting Eqpt, NEC
3274	Lime
3996	Linoleum & Hard Surface Floor Coverings, NEC
2085	Liquors, Distilled, Rectified & Blended
2411	Logging
2992	Lubricating Oils & Greases
3161	Luggage

M

SIC NO	PRODUCT
2098	Macaroni, Spaghetti & Noodles
3545	Machine Tool Access
3541	Machine Tools: Cutting
3542	Machine Tools: Forming
3599	Machinery & Eqpt, Indl & Commercial, NEC
3322	Malleable Iron Foundries
2083	Malt
2082	Malt Beverages
2761	Manifold Business Forms
3999	Manufacturing Industries, NEC
3953	Marking Devices
2515	Mattresses & Bedsprings
3829	Measuring & Controlling Devices, NEC
3586	Measuring & Dispensing Pumps
2011	Meat Packing Plants
3568	Mechanical Power Transmission Eqpt, NEC
2833	Medicinal Chemicals & Botanical Prdts
2329	Men's & Boys' Clothing, NEC
2323	Men's & Boys' Neckwear
2325	Men's & Boys' Separate Trousers & Casual Slacks
2321	Men's & Boys' Shirts
2311	Men's & Boys' Suits, Coats & Overcoats
2326	Men's & Boys' Work Clothing
3143	Men's Footwear, Exc Athletic
3412	Metal Barrels, Drums, Kegs & Pails
3411	Metal Cans
3442	Metal Doors, Sash, Frames, Molding & Trim
3497	Metal Foil & Leaf
3398	Metal Heat Treating
2514	Metal Household Furniture
1081	Metal Mining Svcs
1099	Metal Ores, NEC
3469	Metal Stampings, NEC
3549	Metalworking Machinery, NEC
2026	Milk
2023	Milk, Condensed & Evaporated
2431	Millwork
3296	Mineral Wool
3295	Minerals & Earths: Ground Or Treated
3532	Mining Machinery & Eqpt
3496	Misc Fabricated Wire Prdts
2741	Misc Publishing
3449	Misc Structural Metal Work
1499	Miscellaneous Nonmetallic Mining
2451	Mobile Homes
3061	Molded, Extruded & Lathe-Cut Rubber Mechanical Goods
3716	Motor Homes
3714	Motor Vehicle Parts & Access
3711	Motor Vehicles & Car Bodies
3751	Motorcycles, Bicycles & Parts
3621	Motors & Generators
3931	Musical Instruments

N

SIC NO	PRODUCT
1321	Natural Gas Liquids
2711	Newspapers: Publishing & Printing
2873	Nitrogenous Fertilizers
3297	Nonclay Refractories
3644	Noncurrent-Carrying Wiring Devices
3364	Nonferrous Die Castings, Exc Aluminum
3463	Nonferrous Forgings
3369	Nonferrous Foundries: Castings, NEC
3357	Nonferrous Wire Drawing
3299	Nonmetallic Mineral Prdts, NEC
1481	Nonmetallic Minerals Svcs, Except Fuels

O

SIC NO	PRODUCT
2522	Office Furniture, Except Wood
3579	Office Machines, NEC
1382	Oil & Gas Field Exploration Svcs
1389	Oil & Gas Field Svcs, NEC
3533	Oil Field Machinery & Eqpt
3851	Ophthalmic Goods
3827	Optical Instruments
3489	Ordnance & Access, NEC
3842	Orthopedic, Prosthetic & Surgical Appliances/Splys

P

SIC NO	PRODUCT
3565	Packaging Machinery
2851	Paints, Varnishes, Lacquers, Enamels
2671	Paper Coating & Laminating for Packaging
2672	Paper Coating & Laminating, Exc for Packaging
3554	Paper Inds Machinery
2621	Paper Mills
2631	Paperboard Mills
2542	Partitions & Fixtures, Except Wood
2951	Paving Mixtures & Blocks
3951	Pens & Mechanical Pencils
2844	Perfumes, Cosmetics & Toilet Preparations
2721	Periodicals: Publishing & Printing
3172	Personal Leather Goods
2879	Pesticides & Agricultural Chemicals, NEC
2911	Petroleum Refining
2834	Pharmaceuticals
3652	Phonograph Records & Magnetic Tape
1475	Phosphate Rock
2874	Phosphatic Fertilizers
3861	Photographic Eqpt & Splys
2035	Pickled Fruits, Vegetables, Sauces & Dressings
3085	Plastic Bottles
3086	Plastic Foam Prdts
3083	Plastic Laminated Plate & Sheet
3084	Plastic Pipe
3088	Plastic Plumbing Fixtures
3089	Plastic Prdts
3082	Plastic Unsupported Profile Shapes
3081	Plastic Unsupported Sheet & Film
2821	Plastics, Mtrls & Nonvulcanizable Elastomers
2796	Platemaking & Related Svcs
2395	Pleating & Stitching For The Trade
3432	Plumbing Fixture Fittings & Trim, Brass
3264	Porcelain Electrical Splys
1474	Potash, Soda & Borate Minerals
2096	Potato Chips & Similar Prdts
3269	Pottery Prdts, NEC
2015	Poultry Slaughtering, Dressing & Processing
3546	Power Hand Tools
3612	Power, Distribution & Specialty Transformers
3448	Prefabricated Metal Buildings & Cmpnts
2452	Prefabricated Wood Buildings & Cmpnts
7372	Prepackaged Software
2048	Prepared Feeds For Animals & Fowls
3229	Pressed & Blown Glassware, NEC
3692	Primary Batteries: Dry & Wet
3399	Primary Metal Prdts, NEC
3339	Primary Nonferrous Metals, NEC
3334	Primary Production Of Aluminum
3331	Primary Smelting & Refining Of Copper
3672	Printed Circuit Boards
2893	Printing Ink
3555	Printing Trades Machinery & Eqpt
2999	Products Of Petroleum & Coal, NEC
2531	Public Building & Related Furniture
2611	Pulp Mills
3561	Pumps & Pumping Eqpt

R

SIC NO	PRODUCT
3663	Radio & T V Communications, Systs & Eqpt, Broadcast/Studio
3671	Radio & T V Receiving Electron Tubes
3743	Railroad Eqpt
3273	Ready-Mixed Concrete
2493	Reconstituted Wood Prdts
3695	Recording Media
3625	Relays & Indl Controls
3645	Residential Lighting Fixtures
2044	Rice Milling
2384	Robes & Dressing Gowns
3547	Rolling Mill Machinery & Eqpt
3351	Rolling, Drawing & Extruding Of Copper
3356	Rolling, Drawing-Extruding Of Nonferrous Metals
3021	Rubber & Plastic Footwear
3052	Rubber & Plastic Hose & Belting

S

SIC NO	PRODUCT
2068	Salted & Roasted Nuts & Seeds
2656	Sanitary Food Containers
2676	Sanitary Paper Prdts
2013	Sausages & Meat Prdts
2421	Saw & Planing Mills
3596	Scales & Balances, Exc Laboratory
2397	Schiffli Machine Embroideries
3451	Screw Machine Prdts
3812	Search, Detection, Navigation & Guidance Systs & Instrs
3341	Secondary Smelting & Refining Of Nonferrous Metals
3674	Semiconductors
3589	Service Ind Machines, NEC
2652	Set-Up Paperboard Boxes
3444	Sheet Metal Work
3731	Shipbuilding & Repairing
2079	Shortening, Oils & Margarine
3993	Signs & Advertising Displays
2262	Silk & Man-Made Fabric Finishers
2221	Silk & Man-Made Fiber
1044	Silver Ores
3914	Silverware, Plated & Stainless Steel Ware
3484	Small Arms
3482	Small Arms Ammunition
2841	Soap & Detergents
2086	Soft Drinks
2436	Softwood Veneer & Plywood
2075	Soybean Oil Mills
2842	Spec Cleaning, Polishing & Sanitation Preparations
3559	Special Ind Machinery, NEC
2429	Special Prdt Sawmills, NEC
3566	Speed Changers, Drives & Gears
3949	Sporting & Athletic Goods, NEC
2678	Stationery Prdts
3511	Steam, Gas & Hydraulic Turbines & Engines
3325	Steel Foundries, NEC
3324	Steel Investment Foundries
3317	Steel Pipe & Tubes
3493	Steel Springs, Except Wire
3315	Steel Wire Drawing & Nails & Spikes
3691	Storage Batteries
3259	Structural Clay Prdts, NEC
2439	Structural Wood Members, NEC
2063	Sugar, Beet
2061	Sugar, Cane
2062	Sugar, Cane Refining
2843	Surface Active & Finishing Agents, Sulfonated Oils
3841	Surgical & Medical Instrs & Apparatus
3613	Switchgear & Switchboard Apparatus
2824	Synthetic Organic Fibers, Exc Cellulosic
2822	Synthetic Rubber (Vulcanizable Elastomers)

T

SIC NO	PRODUCT
3795	Tanks & Tank Components
3661	Telephone & Telegraph Apparatus
2393	Textile Bags
2269	Textile Finishers, NEC
2299	Textile Goods, NEC
3552	Textile Machinery
2284	Thread Mills
2296	Tire Cord & Fabric
3011	Tires & Inner Tubes
2131	Tobacco, Chewing & Snuff
3799	Transportation Eqpt, NEC
3792	Travel Trailers & Campers
3713	Truck & Bus Bodies
3715	Truck Trailers
2791	Typesetting

U

SIC NO	PRODUCT
1094	Uranium, Radium & Vanadium Ores

V

SIC NO	PRODUCT
3494	Valves & Pipe Fittings, NEC
2076	Vegetable Oil Mills
3647	Vehicular Lighting Eqpt

W

SIC NO	PRODUCT
3873	Watch & Clock Devices & Parts
2385	Waterproof Outerwear
3548	Welding Apparatus
7692	Welding Repair
2046	Wet Corn Milling
2084	Wine & Brandy
3495	Wire Springs
2331	Women's & Misses' Blouses
2335	Women's & Misses' Dresses
2339	Women's & Misses' Outerwear, NEC
2337	Women's & Misses' Suits, Coats & Skirts
3144	Women's Footwear, Exc Athletic
2341	Women's, Misses' & Children's Underwear & Nightwear
2441	Wood Boxes
2449	Wood Containers, NEC
2511	Wood Household Furniture
2512	Wood Household Furniture, Upholstered
2434	Wood Kitchen Cabinets
2521	Wood Office Furniture
2448	Wood Pallets & Skids
2499	Wood Prdts, NEC
2491	Wood Preserving

SIC INDEX

SIC NO	PRODUCT
2517	Wood T V, Radio, Phono & Sewing Cabinets
2541	Wood, Office & Store Fixtures
3553	Woodworking Machinery
2231	Wool, Woven Fabric

X

SIC NO	PRODUCT
3844	X-ray Apparatus & Tubes

SIC INDEX

Standard Industrial Classification Numerical Index

SIC NO	PRODUCT

10 metal mining
1011 Iron Ores
1021 Copper Ores
1031 Lead & Zinc Ores
1041 Gold Ores
1044 Silver Ores
1081 Metal Mining Svcs
1094 Uranium, Radium & Vanadium Ores
1099 Metal Ores, NEC

12 coal mining
1221 Bituminous Coal & Lignite: Surface Mining
1222 Bituminous Coal: Underground Mining
1231 Anthracite Mining
1241 Coal Mining Svcs

13 oil and gas extraction
1311 Crude Petroleum & Natural Gas
1321 Natural Gas Liquids
1381 Drilling Oil & Gas Wells
1382 Oil & Gas Field Exploration Svcs
1389 Oil & Gas Field Svcs, NEC

14 mining and quarrying of nonmetallic minerals, except fuels
1411 Dimension Stone
1422 Crushed & Broken Limestone
1423 Crushed & Broken Granite
1429 Crushed & Broken Stone, NEC
1442 Construction Sand & Gravel
1446 Industrial Sand
1455 Kaolin & Ball Clay
1459 Clay, Ceramic & Refractory Minerals, NEC
1474 Potash, Soda & Borate Minerals
1475 Phosphate Rock
1479 Chemical & Fertilizer Mining
1481 Nonmetallic Minerals Svcs, Except Fuels
1499 Miscellaneous Nonmetallic Mining

20 food and kindred products
2011 Meat Packing Plants
2013 Sausages & Meat Prdts
2015 Poultry Slaughtering, Dressing & Processing
2021 Butter
2022 Cheese
2023 Milk, Condensed & Evaporated
2024 Ice Cream
2026 Milk
2032 Canned Specialties
2033 Canned Fruits, Vegetables & Preserves
2034 Dried Fruits, Vegetables & Soup
2035 Pickled Fruits, Vegetables, Sauces & Dressings
2037 Frozen Fruits, Juices & Vegetables
2038 Frozen Specialties
2041 Flour, Grain Milling
2043 Cereal Breakfast Foods
2044 Rice Milling
2045 Flour, Blended & Prepared
2046 Wet Corn Milling
2047 Dog & Cat Food
2048 Prepared Feeds For Animals & Fowls
2051 Bread, Bakery Prdts Exc Cookies & Crackers
2052 Cookies & Crackers
2053 Frozen Bakery Prdts
2061 Sugar, Cane
2062 Sugar, Cane Refining
2063 Sugar, Beet
2064 Candy & Confectionery Prdts
2066 Chocolate & Cocoa Prdts
2067 Chewing Gum
2068 Salted & Roasted Nuts & Seeds
2074 Cottonseed Oil Mills
2075 Soybean Oil Mills
2076 Vegetable Oil Mills
2077 Animal, Marine Fats & Oils
2079 Shortening, Oils & Margarine
2082 Malt Beverages
2083 Malt
2084 Wine & Brandy
2085 Liquors, Distilled, Rectified & Blended
2086 Soft Drinks
2087 Flavoring Extracts & Syrups
2091 Fish & Seafoods, Canned & Cured
2092 Fish & Seafoods, Fresh & Frozen
2095 Coffee
2096 Potato Chips & Similar Prdts
2097 Ice
2098 Macaroni, Spaghetti & Noodles
2099 Food Preparations, NEC

21 tobacco products
2111 Cigarettes
2131 Tobacco, Chewing & Snuff

22 textile mill products
2211 Cotton, Woven Fabric
2221 Silk & Man-Made Fiber
2231 Wool, Woven Fabric
2241 Fabric Mills, Cotton, Wool, Silk & Man-Made
2251 Hosiery, Women's Full & Knee Length
2252 Hosiery, Except Women's
2253 Knit Outerwear Mills
2254 Knit Underwear Mills
2257 Circular Knit Fabric Mills
2259 Knitting Mills, NEC
2261 Cotton Fabric Finishers
2262 Silk & Man-Made Fabric Finishers
2269 Textile Finishers, NEC
2273 Carpets & Rugs
2284 Thread Mills
2295 Fabrics Coated Not Rubberized
2296 Tire Cord & Fabric
2297 Fabrics, Nonwoven
2298 Cordage & Twine
2299 Textile Goods, NEC

23 apparel and other finished products made from fabrics and similar material
2311 Men's & Boys' Suits, Coats & Overcoats
2321 Men's & Boys' Shirts
2323 Men's & Boys' Neckwear
2325 Men's & Boys' Separate Trousers & Casual Slacks
2326 Men's & Boys' Work Clothing
2329 Men's & Boys' Clothing, NEC
2331 Women's & Misses' Blouses
2335 Women's & Misses' Dresses
2337 Women's & Misses' Suits, Coats & Skirts
2339 Women's & Misses' Outerwear, NEC
2341 Women's, Misses' & Children's Underwear & Nightwear
2342 Brassieres, Girdles & Garments
2353 Hats, Caps & Millinery
2361 Children's & Infants' Dresses & Blouses
2369 Girls' & Infants' Outerwear, NEC
2381 Dress & Work Gloves
2384 Robes & Dressing Gowns
2385 Waterproof Outerwear
2386 Leather & Sheep Lined Clothing
2389 Apparel & Accessories, NEC
2391 Curtains & Draperies
2392 House furnishings: Textile
2393 Textile Bags
2394 Canvas Prdts
2395 Pleating & Stitching For The Trade
2396 Automotive Trimmings, Apparel Findings, Related Prdts
2397 Schiffli Machine Embroideries
2399 Fabricated Textile Prdts, NEC

24 lumber and wood products, except furniture
2411 Logging
2421 Saw & Planing Mills
2426 Hardwood Dimension & Flooring Mills
2429 Special Prdt Sawmills, NEC
2431 Millwork
2434 Wood Kitchen Cabinets
2435 Hardwood Veneer & Plywood
2436 Softwood Veneer & Plywood
2439 Structural Wood Members, NEC
2441 Wood Boxes
2448 Wood Pallets & Skids
2449 Wood Containers, NEC
2451 Mobile Homes
2452 Prefabricated Wood Buildings & Cmpnts
2491 Wood Preserving
2493 Reconstituted Wood Prdts
2499 Wood Prdts, NEC

25 furniture and fixtures
2511 Wood Household Furniture
2512 Wood Household Furniture, Upholstered
2514 Metal Household Furniture
2515 Mattresses & Bedsprings
2517 Wood T V, Radio, Phono & Sewing Cabinets
2519 Household Furniture, NEC
2521 Wood Office Furniture
2522 Office Furniture, Except Wood
2531 Public Building & Related Furniture
2541 Wood, Office & Store Fixtures
2542 Partitions & Fixtures, Except Wood
2591 Drapery Hardware, Window Blinds & Shades
2599 Furniture & Fixtures, NEC

26 paper and allied products
2611 Pulp Mills
2621 Paper Mills
2631 Paperboard Mills
2652 Set-Up Paperboard Boxes
2653 Corrugated & Solid Fiber Boxes
2655 Fiber Cans, Tubes & Drums
2656 Sanitary Food Containers
2657 Folding Paperboard Boxes
2671 Paper Coating & Laminating for Packaging
2672 Paper Coating & Laminating, Exc for Packaging
2673 Bags: Plastics, Laminated & Coated
2674 Bags: Uncoated Paper & Multiwall
2675 Die-Cut Paper & Board
2676 Sanitary Paper Prdts
2677 Envelopes
2678 Stationery Prdts
2679 Converted Paper Prdts, NEC

27 printing, publishing, and allied industries
2711 Newspapers: Publishing & Printing
2721 Periodicals: Publishing & Printing
2731 Books: Publishing & Printing
2732 Book Printing, Not Publishing
2741 Misc Publishing
2752 Commercial Printing: Lithographic
2754 Commercial Printing: Gravure
2759 Commercial Printing
2761 Manifold Business Forms
2771 Greeting Card Publishing
2782 Blankbooks & Looseleaf Binders
2789 Bookbinding
2791 Typesetting
2796 Platemaking & Related Svcs

28 chemicals and allied products
2812 Alkalies & Chlorine
2813 Industrial Gases
2816 Inorganic Pigments
2819 Indl Inorganic Chemicals, NEC
2821 Plastics, Mtrls & Nonvulcanizable Elastomers
2822 Synthetic Rubber (Vulcanizable Elastomers)
2823 Cellulosic Man-Made Fibers
2824 Synthetic Organic Fibers, Exc Cellulosic
2833 Medicinal Chemicals & Botanical Prdts
2834 Pharmaceuticals
2835 Diagnostic Substances
2836 Biological Prdts, Exc Diagnostic Substances
2841 Soap & Detergents
2842 Spec Cleaning, Polishing & Sanitation Preparations
2843 Surface Active & Finishing Agents, Sulfonated Oils
2844 Perfumes, Cosmetics & Toilet Preparations
2851 Paints, Varnishes, Lacquers, Enamels
2861 Gum & Wood Chemicals
2865 Cyclic-Crudes, Intermediates, Dyes & Org Pigments
2869 Industrial Organic Chemicals, NEC
2873 Nitrogenous Fertilizers
2874 Phosphatic Fertilizers
2875 Fertilizers, Mixing Only
2879 Pesticides & Agricultural Chemicals, NEC
2891 Adhesives & Sealants
2892 Explosives
2893 Printing Ink
2895 Carbon Black
2899 Chemical Preparations, NEC

29 petroleum refining and related industries
2911 Petroleum Refining

SIC INDEX

SIC NO	PRODUCT
2951	Paving Mixtures & Blocks
2952	Asphalt Felts & Coatings
2992	Lubricating Oils & Greases
2999	Products Of Petroleum & Coal, NEC

30 rubber and miscellaneous plastics products

- 3011 Tires & Inner Tubes
- 3021 Rubber & Plastic Footwear
- 3052 Rubber & Plastic Hose & Belting
- 3053 Gaskets, Packing & Sealing Devices
- 3061 Molded, Extruded & Lathe-Cut Rubber Mechanical Goods
- 3069 Fabricated Rubber Prdts, NEC
- 3081 Plastic Unsupported Sheet & Film
- 3082 Plastic Unsupported Profile Shapes
- 3083 Plastic Laminated Plate & Sheet
- 3084 Plastic Pipe
- 3085 Plastic Bottles
- 3086 Plastic Foam Prdts
- 3087 Custom Compounding Of Purchased Plastic Resins
- 3088 Plastic Plumbing Fixtures
- 3089 Plastic Prdts

31 leather and leather products

- 3111 Leather Tanning & Finishing
- 3131 Boot & Shoe Cut Stock & Findings
- 3143 Men's Footwear, Exc Athletic
- 3144 Women's Footwear, Exc Athletic
- 3149 Footwear, NEC
- 3151 Leather Gloves & Mittens
- 3161 Luggage
- 3172 Personal Leather Goods
- 3199 Leather Goods, NEC

32 stone, clay, glass, and concrete products

- 3211 Flat Glass
- 3221 Glass Containers
- 3229 Pressed & Blown Glassware, NEC
- 3231 Glass Prdts Made Of Purchased Glass
- 3241 Cement, Hydraulic
- 3251 Brick & Structural Clay Tile
- 3253 Ceramic Tile
- 3255 Clay Refractories
- 3259 Structural Clay Prdts, NEC
- 3261 China Plumbing Fixtures & Fittings
- 3262 China, Table & Kitchen Articles
- 3263 Earthenware, Whiteware, Table & Kitchen Articles
- 3264 Porcelain Electrical Splys
- 3269 Pottery Prdts, NEC
- 3271 Concrete Block & Brick
- 3272 Concrete Prdts
- 3273 Ready-Mixed Concrete
- 3274 Lime
- 3275 Gypsum Prdts
- 3281 Cut Stone Prdts
- 3291 Abrasive Prdts
- 3292 Asbestos products
- 3295 Minerals & Earths: Ground Or Treated
- 3296 Mineral Wool
- 3297 Nonclay Refractories
- 3299 Nonmetallic Mineral Prdts, NEC

33 primary metal industries

- 3312 Blast Furnaces, Coke Ovens, Steel & Rolling Mills
- 3313 Electrometallurgical Prdts
- 3315 Steel Wire Drawing & Nails & Spikes
- 3316 Cold Rolled Steel Sheet, Strip & Bars
- 3317 Steel Pipe & Tubes
- 3321 Gray Iron Foundries
- 3322 Malleable Iron Foundries
- 3324 Steel Investment Foundries
- 3325 Steel Foundries, NEC
- 3331 Primary Smelting & Refining Of Copper
- 3334 Primary Production Of Aluminum
- 3339 Primary Nonferrous Metals, NEC
- 3341 Secondary Smelting & Refining Of Nonferrous Metals
- 3351 Rolling, Drawing & Extruding Of Copper
- 3353 Aluminum Sheet, Plate & Foil
- 3354 Aluminum Extruded Prdts
- 3355 Aluminum Rolling & Drawing, NEC
- 3356 Rolling, Drawing-Extruding Of Nonferrous Metals
- 3357 Nonferrous Wire Drawing
- 3363 Aluminum Die Castings
- 3364 Nonferrous Die Castings, Exc Aluminum
- 3365 Aluminum Foundries
- 3366 Copper Foundries
- 3369 Nonferrous Foundries: Castings, NEC
- 3398 Metal Heat Treating
- 3399 Primary Metal Prdts, NEC

34 fabricated metal products, except machinery and transportation equipment

- 3411 Metal Cans
- 3412 Metal Barrels, Drums, Kegs & Pails
- 3421 Cutlery
- 3423 Hand & Edge Tools
- 3425 Hand Saws & Saw Blades
- 3429 Hardware, NEC
- 3431 Enameled Iron & Metal Sanitary Ware
- 3432 Plumbing Fixture Fittings & Trim, Brass
- 3433 Heating Eqpt
- 3441 Fabricated Structural Steel
- 3442 Metal Doors, Sash, Frames, Molding & Trim
- 3443 Fabricated Plate Work
- 3444 Sheet Metal Work
- 3446 Architectural & Ornamental Metal Work
- 3448 Prefabricated Metal Buildings & Cmpnts
- 3449 Misc Structural Metal Work
- 3451 Screw Machine Prdts
- 3452 Bolts, Nuts, Screws, Rivets & Washers
- 3462 Iron & Steel Forgings
- 3463 Nonferrous Forgings
- 3465 Automotive Stampings
- 3466 Crowns & Closures
- 3469 Metal Stampings, NEC
- 3471 Electroplating, Plating, Polishing, Anodizing & Coloring
- 3479 Coating & Engraving, NEC
- 3482 Small Arms Ammunition
- 3483 Ammunition, Large
- 3484 Small Arms
- 3489 Ordnance & Access, NEC
- 3491 Industrial Valves
- 3492 Fluid Power Valves & Hose Fittings
- 3493 Steel Springs, Except Wire
- 3494 Valves & Pipe Fittings, NEC
- 3495 Wire Springs
- 3496 Misc Fabricated Wire Prdts
- 3497 Metal Foil & Leaf
- 3498 Fabricated Pipe & Pipe Fittings
- 3499 Fabricated Metal Prdts, NEC

35 industrial and commercial machinery and computer equipment

- 3511 Steam, Gas & Hydraulic Turbines & Engines
- 3519 Internal Combustion Engines, NEC
- 3523 Farm Machinery & Eqpt
- 3524 Garden, Lawn Tractors & Eqpt
- 3531 Construction Machinery & Eqpt
- 3532 Mining Machinery & Eqpt
- 3533 Oil Field Machinery & Eqpt
- 3534 Elevators & Moving Stairways
- 3535 Conveyors & Eqpt
- 3536 Hoists, Cranes & Monorails
- 3537 Indl Trucks, Tractors, Trailers & Stackers
- 3541 Machine Tools: Cutting
- 3542 Machine Tools: Forming
- 3543 Industrial Patterns
- 3544 Dies, Tools, Jigs, Fixtures & Indl Molds
- 3545 Machine Tool Access
- 3546 Power Hand Tools
- 3547 Rolling Mill Machinery & Eqpt
- 3548 Welding Apparatus
- 3549 Metalworking Machinery, NEC
- 3552 Textile Machinery
- 3553 Woodworking Machinery
- 3554 Paper Inds Machinery
- 3555 Printing Trades Machinery & Eqpt
- 3556 Food Prdts Machinery
- 3559 Special Ind Machinery, NEC
- 3561 Pumps & Pumping Eqpt
- 3562 Ball & Roller Bearings
- 3563 Air & Gas Compressors
- 3564 Blowers & Fans
- 3565 Packaging Machinery
- 3566 Speed Changers, Drives & Gears
- 3567 Indl Process Furnaces & Ovens
- 3568 Mechanical Power Transmission Eqpt, NEC
- 3569 Indl Machinery & Eqpt, NEC
- 3571 Electronic Computers
- 3572 Computer Storage Devices
- 3575 Computer Terminals
- 3577 Computer Peripheral Eqpt, NEC
- 3578 Calculating & Accounting Eqpt
- 3579 Office Machines, NEC
- 3581 Automatic Vending Machines
- 3582 Commercial Laundry, Dry Clean & Pressing Mchs
- 3585 Air Conditioning & Heating Eqpt
- 3586 Measuring & Dispensing Pumps
- 3589 Service Ind Machines, NEC
- 3592 Carburetors, Pistons, Rings & Valves
- 3593 Fluid Power Cylinders & Actuators
- 3594 Fluid Power Pumps & Motors
- 3596 Scales & Balances, Exc Laboratory
- 3599 Machinery & Eqpt, Indl & Commercial, NEC

36 electronic and other electrical equipment and components, except computer

- 3612 Power, Distribution & Specialty Transformers
- 3613 Switchgear & Switchboard Apparatus
- 3621 Motors & Generators
- 3624 Carbon & Graphite Prdts
- 3625 Relays & Indl Controls
- 3629 Electrical Indl Apparatus, NEC
- 3631 Household Cooking Eqpt
- 3632 Household Refrigerators & Freezers
- 3633 Household Laundry Eqpt
- 3634 Electric Household Appliances
- 3635 Household Vacuum Cleaners
- 3639 Household Appliances, NEC
- 3641 Electric Lamps
- 3643 Current-Carrying Wiring Devices
- 3644 Noncurrent-Carrying Wiring Devices
- 3645 Residential Lighting Fixtures
- 3646 Commercial, Indl & Institutional Lighting Fixtures
- 3647 Vehicular Lighting Eqpt
- 3648 Lighting Eqpt, NEC
- 3651 Household Audio & Video Eqpt
- 3652 Phonograph Records & Magnetic Tape
- 3661 Telephone & Telegraph Apparatus
- 3663 Radio & T V Communications, Systs & Eqpt, Broadcast/Studio
- 3669 Communications Eqpt, NEC
- 3671 Radio & T V Receiving Electron Tubes
- 3672 Printed Circuit Boards
- 3674 Semiconductors
- 3675 Electronic Capacitors
- 3676 Electronic Resistors
- 3677 Electronic Coils & Transformers
- 3678 Electronic Connectors
- 3679 Electronic Components, NEC
- 3691 Storage Batteries
- 3692 Primary Batteries: Dry & Wet
- 3694 Electrical Eqpt For Internal Combustion Engines
- 3695 Recording Media
- 3699 Electrical Machinery, Eqpt & Splys, NEC

37 transportation equipment

- 3711 Motor Vehicles & Car Bodies
- 3713 Truck & Bus Bodies
- 3714 Motor Vehicle Parts & Access
- 3715 Truck Trailers
- 3716 Motor Homes
- 3721 Aircraft
- 3724 Aircraft Engines & Engine Parts
- 3728 Aircraft Parts & Eqpt, NEC
- 3731 Shipbuilding & Repairing
- 3732 Boat Building & Repairing
- 3743 Railroad Eqpt
- 3751 Motorcycles, Bicycles & Parts
- 3761 Guided Missiles & Space Vehicles
- 3764 Guided Missile/Space Vehicle Propulsion Units & parts
- 3769 Guided Missile/Space Vehicle Parts & Eqpt, NEC
- 3792 Travel Trailers & Campers
- 3795 Tanks & Tank Components
- 3799 Transportation Eqpt, NEC

38 measuring, analyzing and controlling instruments; photographic, medical an

- 3812 Search, Detection, Navigation & Guidance Systs & Instrs
- 3821 Laboratory Apparatus & Furniture
- 3822 Automatic Temperature Controls
- 3823 Indl Instruments For Meas, Display & Control
- 3824 Fluid Meters & Counters
- 3825 Instrs For Measuring & Testing Electricity
- 3826 Analytical Instruments
- 3827 Optical Instruments
- 3829 Measuring & Controlling Devices, NEC
- 3841 Surgical & Medical Instrs & Apparatus
- 3842 Orthopedic, Prosthetic & Surgical Appliances/Splys
- 3843 Dental Eqpt & Splys
- 3844 X-ray Apparatus & Tubes
- 3845 Electromedical & Electrotherapeutic Apparatus
- 3851 Ophthalmic Goods
- 3861 Photographic Eqpt & Splys
- 3873 Watch & Clock Devices & Parts

39 miscellaneous manufacturing industries

- 3911 Jewelry: Precious Metal
- 3914 Silverware, Plated & Stainless Steel Ware

SIC INDEX

SIC NO	PRODUCT
3915	Jewelers Findings & Lapidary Work
3931	Musical Instruments
3942	Dolls & Stuffed Toys
3944	Games, Toys & Children's Vehicles
3949	Sporting & Athletic Goods, NEC
3951	Pens & Mechanical Pencils
3952	Lead Pencils, Crayons & Artist's Mtrls
3953	Marking Devices
3955	Carbon Paper & Inked Ribbons
3961	Costume Jewelry & Novelties
3965	Fasteners, Buttons, Needles & Pins
3991	Brooms & Brushes
3993	Signs & Advertising Displays
3995	Burial Caskets
3996	Linoleum & Hard Surface Floor Coverings, NEC
3999	Manufacturing Industries, NEC

73 business services

7372 Prepackaged Software

76 miscellaneous repair services

7692 Welding Repair

7694 Armature Rewinding Shops

SIC SECTION

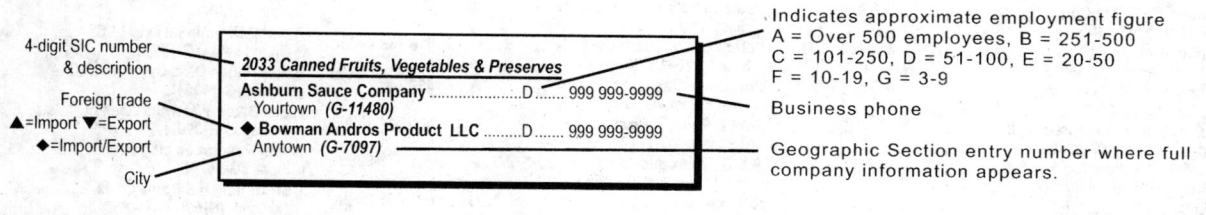

4-digit SIC number & description
Foreign trade
▲=Import ▼=Export
◆=Import/Export
City

Indicates approximate employment figure
A = Over 500 employees, B = 251-500
C = 101-250, D = 51-100, E = 20-50
F = 10-19, G = 3-9
Business phone
Geographic Section entry number where full company information appears.

See footnotes for symbols and codes identification.
- The SIC codes in this section are from the latest Standard Industrial Classification manual published by the U.S. Government's Office of Management and Budget. For more information regarding SICs, see the Explanatory Notes.
- Companies may be listed under multiple classifications.

10 METAL MINING

1011 Iron Ores
Global Technologies I LLC .... D 312 255-8350
  Chicago (G-4699)
Idlr USA Inc .... G 630 375-0101
  Aurora (G-980)
Q Lotus Holdings Inc .... G 312 379-1800
  Chicago (G-5921)
▲ Regal Converting Co Inc .... F 630 257-3581
  Lockport (G-13021)

1021 Copper Ores
▲ Ventec USA LLC .... G 847 621-2261
  Elk Grove Village (G-9301)

1031 Lead & Zinc Ores
◆ Big River Zinc Corporation .... G 618 274-5000
  Sauget (G-18389)
Ebers Drilling Co .... G 618 826-5398
  Chester (G-3454)
Midland Coal Company .... G 309 362-2795
  Trivoli (G-19907)

1041 Gold Ores
Billy Cash For Gold Inc .... G 773 905-2447
  Melrose Park (G-13831)
Coeur Mining Inc .... D 312 489-5800
  Chicago (G-4194)
Global Technologies I LLC .... D 312 255-8350
  Chicago (G-4699)

1044 Silver Ores
▼ Callahan Mining Corporation .... D 312 489-5800
  Chicago (G-4006)
Coeur Mining Inc .... D 312 489-5800
  Chicago (G-4194)
Coeur Rochester Inc .... G 312 661-2436
  Chicago (G-4195)

1081 Metal Mining Svcs
Ave Inc .... G 815 727-0153
  Joliet (G-11825)
Caterpillar Inc .... A 309 675-6223
  Mossville (G-14458)
Caterpillar Inc .... B 309 494-0858
  Aurora (G-1071)
Coeur Capital Inc .... G 312 489-5800
  Chicago (G-4193)
Mab Equipment Company .... G 630 551-4017
  Oswego (G-16012)
Regal Johnson Co .... G 630 885-0688
  Bolingbrook (G-2232)
SF Contracting LLC .... E 618 926-1477
  Raleigh (G-16963)
Trane Technologies Company LLC .... E 630 530-3800
  Elmhurst (G-9436)

1094 Uranium, Radium & Vanadium Ores
Phosphate Resource Ptrs .... A 847 739-1200
  Lake Forest (G-12290)

1099 Metal Ores, NEC
Alpha Consultings .... G 773 251-0053
  Chicago (G-3628)

12 COAL MINING

1221 Bituminous Coal & Lignite: Surface Mining
Alpha Natural Resources Inc .... C 618 298-2394
  Keensburg (G-12012)
Arch Coal Inc .... F 217 566-3000
  Williamsville (G-21022)
▲ Hillsboro Energy LLC .... G 217 532-7310
  Hillsboro (G-11315)
Hnrc Dissolution Co .... C 618 758-4501
  Coulterville (G-7032)
Illinois Fuel Company LLC .... D 618 275-4486
  Herod (G-11170)
▲ Interminal Services .... E 773 978-8129
  Chicago (G-4950)
Jader Fuel Co Inc .... G 618 269-3101
  Shawneetown (G-18875)
Keller Group Inc .... B 847 446-7550
  Northfield (G-15520)
Peabody Coal Company .... C 618 758-2395
  Coulterville (G-7033)
Peabody Coulterville Min LLC .... G 618 758-3597
  Coulterville (G-7034)
Peabody Energy Corporation .... G 314 342-3400
  Equality (G-9470)
Peabody Midwest Mining LLC .... C 618 276-5006
  Equality (G-9471)
Standard Laboratories Inc .... E 618 539-5836
  Freeburg (G-10095)
▲ Sun Coke International Inc .... D 630 824-1000
  Lisle (G-12944)
▲ White County Coal LLC .... D 618 382-4651
  Carmi (G-2919)

1222 Bituminous Coal: Underground Mining
Alpha Natural Resources Inc .... C 618 298-2394
  Keensburg (G-12012)
▲ American Coal Company .... G 618 268-6311
  Galatia (G-10161)
Exxon Mobil Corporation .... B 217 854-3291
  Carlinville (G-2875)
Gateway North Mine .... G 618 758-1515
  Coulterville (G-7031)
Illinois Fuel Company LLC .... D 618 275-4486
  Herod (G-11170)
Jewell Resources Corporation .... G 276 935-8810
  Lisle (G-12903)
Keller Group Inc .... B 847 446-7550
  Northfield (G-15520)
Knight Hawk Coal LLC .... G 618 426-3662
  Percy (G-16559)
Mid-America Carbonates LLC .... D 618 944-6171
  Cave In Rock (G-3220)
▲ Sun Coke International Inc .... D 630 824-1000
  Lisle (G-12944)

1231 Anthracite Mining
Fabick Mining LLC .... F 618 982-9000
  Norris City (G-15249)

1241 Coal Mining Svcs
▼ Cobra Coal Inc .... E 630 560-1050
  West Chicago (G-20565)
Exxon Mobil Corporation .... B 217 854-3291
  Carlinville (G-2875)
Fjcj LLC .... F 618 785-2217
  Baldwin (G-1184)

Freeman Energy Corporation .... F 217 698-3949
  Springfield (G-19370)
Freeman United Coal Mining Co .... C 217 627-2161
  Girard (G-10381)
Freeman United Coal Mining Co .... E 217 698-3300
  Springfield (G-19371)
Hamilton County Coal LLC .... B 618 648-2603
  Dahlgren (G-7307)
Icg Illinois .... E 217 947-2332
  Elkhart (G-9318)
Icg Illinois LLC .... F 217 566-3000
  Williamsville (G-21023)
Keyrock Energy LLC .... E 618 982-9710
  Thompsonville (G-19778)
Knight Hawk Coal LLC .... G 618 426-3662
  Percy (G-16559)
Knight Hawk Coal LLC .... C 618 497-2768
  Cutler (G-7304)
Mach Mining LLC .... G 618 983-3020
  Marion (G-13520)
Macoupin Energy LLC .... F 217 854-3291
  Carlinville (G-2880)
Macoupin Energy LLC .... G 217 854-3291
  Carlinville (G-2881)
Seneca Rebuild LLC .... F 618 435-9445
  Macedonia (G-13317)
Springfield Coal Company LLC .... E 217 698-3300
  Springfield (G-19451)
Suncoke Energy Inc .... C 630 824-1000
  Lisle (G-12945)
Surface Mining Reclamation Off .... E 618 463-6460
  Alton (G-573)
▲ White Oak Resources LLC .... A 618 643-5500
  Dahlgren (G-7310)
Wildcat Hills .... G 618 273-8600
  Eldorado (G-8486)

13 OIL AND GAS EXTRACTION

1311 Crude Petroleum & Natural Gas
Ashley Oil Co .... G 217 932-2112
  Casey (G-3198)
B Quad Oil Inc .... G 618 656-4419
  Edwardsville (G-8347)
Bam Operating Inc .... G 254 629-8561
  Evanston (G-9497)
Basin Transports .... G 618 829-3323
  Saint Elmo (G-18305)
Basnett Investments .... G 618 842-4040
  Fairfield (G-9619)
Belden Enterprises LP .... F 618 829-3274
  Saint Elmo (G-18306)
Bell Brothers .... G 618 544-2157
  Robinson (G-17107)
Bi-Petro Inc .... E 217 535-0181
  Springfield (G-19325)
Booth Resources Inc .... G 618 662-4955
  Flora (G-9676)
BP Products North America Inc .... G 630 420-4300
  Naperville (G-14783)
Brehm Oil Inc .... F 618 242-4620
  Mount Vernon (G-14600)
Brookstone Resources Inc .... G 618 382-2893
  Carmi (G-2900)
Bruce McCullough .... G 217 773-3130
  Mount Sterling (G-14589)
Budmark Oil Company Inc .... G 618 937-2495
  West Frankfort (G-20669)
Carter Anna Brooks LLC .... G 618 382-3939
  Carmi (G-2903)

13 OIL AND GAS EXTRACTION

Citation Oil & Gas Corp ....G....... 618 676-1044
  Clay City (G-6904)
Citation Oil & Gas Corp ....E....... 618 966-2101
  Crossville (G-7150)
Collins Brothers Oil Corp ....G....... 618 244-1093
  Mount Vernon (G-14602)
Concord Well Service Inc ....G....... 618 395-4405
  Olney (G-15858)
▲ Continental Resources III Inc ....E....... 618 242-1717
  Mount Vernon (G-14603)
D & Z Exploration Inc ....G....... 618 829-3274
  Saint Elmo (G-18307)
D Little Drilling ....G....... 618 943-3721
  Saint Francisville (G-18313)
Deep Rock Energy Corporation ....F....... 618 548-2779
  Salem (G-18335)
Doran Oil Properties ....G....... 618 283-2460
  Vandalia (G-20010)
Drig Corporation ....D....... 312 265-1509
  Rosemont (G-18020)
Duncan Oil Company Inc ....G....... 618 548-2923
  Salem (G-18336)
Ensource Inc ....G....... 312 912-1048
  Chicago (G-4513)
Evans Talaiha ....G....... 618 327-8200
  Nashville (G-14996)
Finks Oil Co Inc ....G....... 618 548-5757
  Salem (G-18339)
Friend Oil Co ....G....... 618 842-9161
  Fairfield (G-9624)
Gas Depot Inc ....G....... 847 581-0303
  Morton Grove (G-14409)
Glover Oil Field Service Inc ....F....... 618 395-3624
  Olney (G-15863)
Gulf Coast Exploration Inc ....G....... 847 226-4654
  Highland Park (G-11268)
Herman L Loeb LLC ....E....... 618 943-2227
  Lawrenceville (G-12535)
Hocking Oil Company Inc ....G....... 618 263-3258
  Mount Carmel (G-14472)
Howard Energy Corporation ....G....... 618 263-3000
  Mount Carmel (G-14473)
J W Rudy Co Inc ....F....... 618 676-1616
  Clay City (G-6906)
Jarvis Drilling Co ....G....... 217 422-3120
  Decatur (G-7511)
Jbl - Alton ....G....... 618 466-0411
  Alton (G-561)
Jim Haley Oil Production Co ....F....... 618 382-7338
  Carmi (G-2907)
Kerogen Resources Inc ....G....... 618 382-3114
  Carmi (G-2908)
L & J Producers Inc ....G....... 217 932-5639
  Casey (G-3204)
La Quinta Gas Pipeline Company .....G....... 217 430-6781
  Quincy (G-16906)
Lakeshore Operating LLC ....E....... 844 557-4763
  Chicago (G-5165)
Lampley Oil Inc ....G....... 618 439-6288
  Benton (G-1931)
Lawrence Oil Company Inc ....G....... 618 262-4138
  Mount Carmel (G-14477)
Midco Petroleum Inc ....G....... 630 655-2198
  Westmont (G-20760)
Midco Production Co Inc ....G....... 630 655-2198
  Westmont (G-20761)
Midwest Oil LLC ....G....... 309 456-3663
  Good Hope (G-10670)
Mitchco Farms LLC ....F....... 618 382-5032
  Carmi (G-2911)
MRC Global (us) Inc ....F....... 314 231-3400
  Granite City (G-10727)
Murphy USA Inc ....G....... 815 463-9965
  New Lenox (G-15044)
Murphy USA Inc ....G....... 815 337-2440
  Woodstock (G-21416)
Murphy USA Inc ....F....... 815 936-6144
  Kankakee (G-11992)
Natural Gas Pipeline Amer LLC ....E....... 618 495-2211
  Centralia (G-3240)
Natural Gas Pipeline Amer LLC ....F....... 815 426-2151
  Herscher (G-11185)
Natural Gas Pipeline Amer LLC ....E....... 618 829-3224
  Saint Elmo (G-18310)
New Triangle Oil Company ....G....... 618 262-4131
  Mount Carmel (G-14483)
Oelze Equipment Company LLC ....E....... 618 327-4474
  Nashville (G-15006)
Oq 168 NM Propco LLC ....G....... 312 542-6116
  Chicago (G-5687)

Pawnee Oil Corporation ....F....... 217 522-5440
  Springfield (G-19421)
Petco Petroleum Corporation ....G....... 630 654-1740
  Hinsdale (G-11372)
Petron Oil Production Inc ....F....... 618 783-4486
  Newton (G-15090)
Phosphate Resource Ptrs ....A....... 847 739-1200
  Lake Forest (G-12290)
Pool & Pool Oil Productions ....G....... 618 544-7590
  Robinson (G-17122)
R & D Oil Producers 217 773-9299
  Mount Sterling (G-14592)
R H Johnson Oil Co Inc ....G....... 630 668-3649
  Wheaton (G-20817)
Republic Oil Co Inc ....G....... 618 842-7591
  Fairfield (G-9635)
River City Oil LLC ....G....... 309 693-2249
  Peoria (G-16510)
Robinson Production Inc ....G....... 618 842-6111
  Fairfield (G-9636)
Rodgers Bill Oil Min Bits Svc ....G....... 618 299-7771
  West Salem (G-20688)
Ronnie Joe Graham ....G....... 618 548-5544
  Salem (G-18355)
Roosevelt Mobile ....G....... 630 293-7630
  West Chicago (G-20638)
Ross Oil Co Inc ....G....... 618 592-3808
  Oblong (G-15828)
Shawnee Exploration Partners ....G....... 618 382-3223
  Carmi (G-2915)
Shulman Brothers Inc ....G....... 618 283-3253
  Vandalia (G-20023)
Smoco Inc ....G....... 618 662-6458
  Flora (G-9693)
Southern Triangle Oil Company ....F....... 618 262-4131
  Mount Carmel (G-14486)
Spartan Petroleum Company ....G....... 618 262-4197
  Mount Carmel (G-14487)
St Pierre Oil Company Inc ....G....... 618 783-4441
  Newton (G-15093)
Star Energy Corp Inc ....G....... 618 584-3631
  Flat Rock (G-9674)
Steven A Zanetis ....G....... 618 393-2176
  Olney (G-15889)
Team Energy LLC ....F....... 618 943-1010
  Bridgeport (G-2316)
Tri Family Oil Co ....G....... 618 654-1137
  Highland (G-11243)
Tri-State Producing Developing ....G....... 618 393-2176
  Olney (G-15890)
Trojan Oil Inc ....G....... 618 754-3474
  Newton (G-15095)
Tussey G K Oil Explrtn & Prdc ....G....... 618 948-2871
  Saint Francisville (G-18315)
Two Rivers Oil & Gas Co Inc ....G....... 217 773-3356
  Mount Sterling (G-14594)
UOP LLC ....D....... 708 442-7400
  Mc Cook (G-13704)
▲ Warren Oil MGT Co IL LLC ....G....... 618 997-5951
  Marion (G-13542)
Western Oil & Gas Dev Co ....F....... 618 544-8646
  Robinson (G-17128)
White Land & Mineral Inc ....G....... 618 262-5102
  Mount Carmel (G-14492)
William R Becker ....F....... 618 378-3337
  Norris City (G-15252)
Wood Energy Inc ....G....... 618 244-1590
  Mount Vernon (G-14644)
Yockey Oil Incorporated ....G....... 618 393-6236
  Olney (G-15895)
Zanetis Oil Company 618 262-4593
  Mount Carmel (G-14493)

1321 Natural Gas Liquids

15679 Wadsworth Inc ....G....... 847 662-4561
  Wadsworth (G-20207)
▲ Aux Sable Liquid Products LP .....E....... 815 941-5800
  Morris (G-14292)
Aux Sable Midstream LLC ....E....... 815 941-5800
  Morris (G-14293)
C4 Petrolum Transport Inc ....G....... 815 690-0356
  Romeoville (G-17802)
Dcc Propane LLC ....G....... 217 395-2648
  Roberts (G-17105)
Enterprise Products Company ....G....... 708 534-6266
  Monee (G-14197)
Ferrellgas LP ....G....... 815 877-7333
  Machesney Park (G-13342)
FMC Technologies Inc ....G....... 312 803-4321
  Chicago (G-4612)

1381 Drilling Oil & Gas Wells

A and P Directional Drlg LLC ....G....... 708 715-1192
  Alsip (G-407)
A and P Directional Drlg LLC ....G....... 708 715-1192
  Orland Park (G-15932)
Baker Hghes Olfld Oprtions LLC ......F....... 618 393-2919
  Olney (G-15854)
Black Bison Water Services LLC .....E....... 630 272-5935
  Chicago (G-3907)
Booth Resources Inc 618 662-4955
  Flora (G-9676)
C&R Directional Boring ....G....... 630 458-0055
  Addison (G-60)
Coursons Coring & Drilling 618 349-8765
  Saint Peter (G-18323)
Crystal Precision Drilling 815 633-5460
  Loves Park (G-13199)
Dee Drilling Co ....E....... 618 262-4136
  Mount Carmel (G-14470)
Drig Corporation ....D....... 312 265-1509
  Rosemont (G-18020)
Ebers Drilling Co ....G....... 618 826-5398
  Chester (G-3454)
Evergreen Energy LLC ....G....... 618 384-9295
  Carmi (G-2905)
Five P Drilling Inc ....E....... 618 943-9771
  Bridgeport (G-2313)
Glover Oil Field Service Inc ....F....... 618 395-3624
  Olney (G-15863)
J H Robison & Associates Ltd ....G....... 847 559-9662
  Northbrook (G-15408)
Jackson Oil Corporation ....G....... 618 263-6521
  Mount Carmel (G-14475)
Jerry D Graham Oil ....G....... 618 548-5540
  Salem (G-18344)
Kapp Company LLC ....G....... 618 676-1000
  Olney (G-15868)
Kincaid Oil Producers Inc ....G....... 618 686-3084
  Louisville (G-13179)
Kinoco Inc ....G....... 618 378-3802
  Norris City (G-15250)
Marion Oelze ....G....... 618 327-9224
  Nashville (G-15001)
Mashburn Well Drilling ....G....... 217 794-3728
  Maroa (G-13553)
Mid-America Underground LLC .....E....... 630 443-9999
  Aurora (G-1134)
Murvin & Meier Oil Co ....G....... 847 277-8380
  Barrington (G-1231)
Paragon Oil Company Inc ....G....... 618 244-5541
  Mount Vernon (G-14632)
Quality Drilling Service LLP ....G....... 937 663-4715
  Alton (G-568)
Raimonde Drilling Corp ....F....... 630 458-0590
  Addison (G-265)
Rays Electrical Service LLC ....G....... 847 214-2944
  Elgin (G-8715)
Reef Development Inc ....F....... 618 842-7711
  Fairfield (G-9634)
Rodgers Bill Oil Min Bits Svc ....G....... 618 299-7771
  West Salem (G-20688)
Royal Drilling & Producing ....G....... 618 966-2221
  Crossville (G-7151)
Runyon Oil Production Inc ....G....... 618 395-8510
  Olney (G-15887)
Southern Triangle Oil Company ....F....... 618 262-4131
  Mount Carmel (G-14486)
Spartan Petroleum Company ....G....... 618 262-4197
  Mount Carmel (G-14487)
Ta Oil Field Service Inc ....G....... 618 249-9001
  Richview (G-17034)
TCI Companies Inc ....E....... 309 965-2057
  Goodfield (G-10677)
Tussey G K Oil Explrtn & Prdc ....G....... 618 948-2871
  Saint Francisville (G-18315)

1382 Oil & Gas Field Exploration Svcs

Angel Rose Energy LLC 618 392-3700
  Olney (G-15853)
Baker Hghes Olfld Oprtions LLC ......F....... 618 393-2919
  Olney (G-15854)
Bell Brothers 618 544-2157
  Robinson (G-17107)
Benchmark Properties Ltd 618 395-7023
  Olney (G-15855)
Citation Oil & Gas Corp ....F....... 618 548-2331
  Odin (G-15834)
Crawford County Oil LLC 618 544-3493
  Robinson (G-17109)

Digital H2o Inc....F....847 456-8424
Chicago (G-4360)
Drig Corporation....D....312 265-1509
Rosemont (G-18020)
Energy Group Inc....E....847 836-2000
Dundee (G-8127)
Howard Energy Corporation....G....618 263-3000
Mount Carmel (G-14473)
Ion Inc....G....224 875-1313
Lincolnshire (G-12775)
J H Robison & Associates Ltd....G....847 559-9662
Northbrook (G-15408)
L C Neelydrilling Inc....G....618 544-2726
Robinson (G-17118)
Lla Exploration Inc....G....217 623-4096
Taylorville (G-19758)
Map Oil Co Inc....G....618 375-7616
Grayville (G-10813)
Martin Exploration Mgt Co....G....708 385-6500
Alsip (G-472)
Mid States Salvage....G....618 842-6741
Fairfield (G-9632)
Midco Exploration Inc....G....630 655-2198
Westmont (G-20759)
Midwest Oil Co Inc....G....847 928-9999
Schiller Park (G-18826)
Mohican Petroleum Inc....G....312 782-6385
Chicago (G-5485)
Moran Properties Inc....G....312 440-1962
Chicago (G-5498)
Murphy USA Inc....G....630 801-4950
Montgomery (G-14264)
Murvin & Meir Oil Co....G....618 395-4405
Olney (G-15876)
Murvin Oil Company....E....618 393-2124
Olney (G-15877)
Northern Illinois Gas Company....E....630 983-8676
Kankakee (G-11993)
Northern Illinois Gas Company....F....217 357-3105
Carthage (G-3141)
Northern Illinois Gas Company....C....630 983-8676
Crystal Lake (G-7240)
Northern Illinois Gas Company....D....815 433-3850
Ottawa (G-16065)
Northern Illinois Gas Company....C....815 693-3907
Joliet (G-11908)
Northern Illinois Gas Company....F....815 223-8097
Mendota (G-13951)
Ofgd Inc....G....708 283-7101
Olympia Fields (G-15897)
Oil and Gas Discoverer LLC....F....847 877-1257
Highland Park (G-11289)
Stevenson Oil Inc....G....773 237-6185
Chicago (G-6247)
Stewart Producers Inc....G....618 244-3754
Mount Vernon (G-14640)
Strata Exploration Inc....G....618 842-2610
Fairfield (G-9637)
Tenexco Inc....G....708 771-7870
Oakbrook Terrace (G-15816)
Third Day Oil & Gas LLC....G....618 553-5538
Oblong (G-15831)
Times Energy....G....773 444-9282
Worth (G-21456)
Woodrow Todd....G....618 838-9105
Flora (G-9697)

1389 Oil & Gas Field Svcs, NEC

1 Heavy Equipment Loading Inc....F....773 581-7374
Bedford Park (G-1451)
Abner Trucking Co Inc....G....618 676-1301
Clay City (G-6902)
Abundance House Treasure Nfp....G....312 788-4316
Chicago (G-3511)
Advanced Lubrication Inc....G....815 932-3288
Kankakee (G-11957)
Air Pure LLC....G....815 275-8990
Freeport (G-10098)
ANR Pipeline Company....G....309 667-2158
New Windsor (G-15071)
Armstrong Tool LLC....G....618 382-4184
Carmi (G-2899)
Atk Services Inc....G....618 726-5114
O Fallon (G-15568)
Aurel Construction LLC....G....312 998-5000
Chicago (G-3773)
B & B Equipment....F....217 562-2511
Assumption (G-888)
B & B Tank Truck Construction....F....618 378-3337
Norris City (G-15246)
Baker Hghes Olfld Oprtions LLC....F....618 393-2919
Olney (G-15854)
Baker Petrolite LLC....F....618 966-3688
Crossville (G-7149)
Bangert Casing Pulling Corp....G....618 676-1411
Clay City (G-6903)
Baseline Services Inc....G....618 678-2753
Xenia (G-21466)
Blue Yonder Inc....G....630 701-1492
Naperville (G-14781)
Buckeye Partners LP....G....217 342-2336
Effingham (G-8390)
Campbell Energy LLC....G....618 382-3939
Carmi (G-2901)
Cdg Operations LLC....G....618 943-8700
Bridgeport (G-2311)
Clinton Oil Corp....G....815 356-1124
Crystal Lake (G-7183)
Concord Oil & Gas Corporation....E....618 393-2124
Olney (G-15857)
Construction Contg Svcs Inc....F....219 779-0900
Lansing (G-12489)
Craftwood Inc....E....630 758-1740
Elmhurst (G-9354)
Creed Group LLC....G....708 261-8387
Matteson (G-13621)
Cross Oil & Well Service Inc....F....618 592-4609
Oblong (G-15825)
▲ Crystatech Inc....F....847 768-0500
Des Plaines (G-7752)
D Kersey Construction Co....G....847 919-4980
Northbrook (G-15371)
De Vries International Inc....E....773 248-6695
Chicago (G-4327)
Deep Rock Energy Corporation....E....618 548-2779
Kinmundy (G-12058)
Duncan Oil Company Inc....G....618 548-2923
Salem (G-18336)
East St Louis Trml & Stor Co....E....618 271-2185
East Saint Louis (G-8306)
Evergreen Marathon....G....708 636-5700
Evergreen Park (G-9594)
Fairfield Acid and Frac Co....F....618 842-9186
Fairfield (G-9622)
Fedder Oil Co Inc....G....618 344-0050
Collinsville (G-6960)
Feller Oilfield Service Inc....F....618 267-5650
Saint Elmo (G-18308)
Finite Resources Ltd....G....618 252-3733
Harrisburg (G-11023)
First American Restoration Inc....F....800 209-3609
Harwood Heights (G-11105)
Foltz Welding Ltd....C....618 432-7777
Patoka (G-16303)
Franklin Well Services Inc....D....812 494-2800
Lawrenceville (G-12532)
Gain Wireline Services Inc....G....618 842-2914
Fairfield (G-9625)
Gcpro LLC....E....773 764-2776
Lombard (G-13082)
Gholson Pump & Repairs Co....G....618 382-4730
Carmi (G-2906)
Global General Contractors LLC....G....708 663-0476
Tinley Park (G-19832)
Glover Oil Field Service Inc....F....618 395-3624
Olney (G-15863)
Gunner Energy Corporation....G....618 237-2829
Mount Vernon (G-14612)
Haggard Well Services Inc....G....618 262-5060
Mount Carmel (G-14471)
Harold L Ray Truck & Trctr Svc....F....618 673-2701
Cisne (G-6893)
Harris Drilling Fluids Inc....G....618 395-7395
Olney (G-15864)
Howard Energy Corporation....G....618 263-3000
Mount Carmel (G-14473)
I D Tool Specialty Company....G....815 432-2007
Watseka (G-20307)
Ican Clinic LLC....G....618 254-2273
Wood River (G-21263)
Invenergy Investment Company L....G....312 224-1400
Chicago (G-4962)
J B Oil Field Cnstr & Sup....G....618 936-2350
Sumner (G-19687)
Ja-T & Associates Inc....F....773 744-2094
Chicago (G-4996)
Jeff E Allen....G....217 801-6878
Springfield (G-19394)
Jsq Inc....G....847 731-8800
Zion (G-21519)
Kincaid Oil Producers Inc....G....618 686-3084
Louisville (G-13179)
Ktm Lab Service Co Inc....G....708 351-6780
Schaumburg (G-18593)
Les Wilson Inc....C....618 382-4667
Carmi (G-2909)
Local 46 Training Program Tr....G....217 528-4041
Springfield (G-19399)
Luxury Upgrade Inc....G....773 875-8018
Arlington Heights (G-773)
M & I Acid Company Inc....G....618 676-1638
Clay City (G-6907)
M & L Well Service Inc....E....618 393-7144
Olney (G-15870)
M & L Well Service Inc....G....618 395-4538
Olney (G-15871)
M & S Oil Well Cementing Co....G....618 262-7962
Mount Carmel (G-14478)
Mac Construction....E....618 541-4092
Millstadt (G-14050)
Macon Gc LLC....D....309 897-8216
Bradford (G-2275)
Matrix North Amercn Cnstr Inc....G....312 754-6605
Chicago (G-5366)
McLean Subsurface Utility....G....336 988-2520
Decatur (G-7521)
McNdt Pipeline Ltd....F....815 467-5200
Channahon (G-3388)
Mdm Construction Supply LLC....G....815 847-7340
Rockford (G-17512)
Mid-States Services LLC....F....618 842-4726
Fairfield (G-9633)
Miller Testing Service....E....618 262-5911
Mount Carmel (G-14479)
Mitchco Farms LLC....F....618 382-5032
Carmi (G-2911)
Oelze Equipment Company LLC....E....618 327-9111
Nashville (G-15006)
Orr Rudolph....G....815 429-3996
Watseka (G-20313)
P J Repair Service Inc....F....618 548-5690
Salem (G-18349)
Panhandle Eastrn Pipe Line LP....E....217 753-1108
Springfield (G-19419)
Pinnacle Exploration Corp....G....618 395-8100
Olney (G-15883)
Platt G Mostardi....F....630 993-2100
Hoffman Estates (G-11443)
Pool Center Inc....G....217 698-7665
Springfield (G-19426)
Precision Plugging and Sls Inc....F....618 395-8510
Olney (G-15884)
Pro-Lube of Shelbyville Inc....G....217 774-4643
Shelbyville (G-18883)
Protus Construction....G....773 405-9999
Chicago (G-5907)
Purified Lubricants Inc....E....708 478-3500
Mokena (G-14111)
R Energy LLC....G....618 382-7313
Carmi (G-2913)
Roark Oil Field Services Inc....G....618 382-4703
Carmi (G-2914)
Runyon Oil Tools Inc....G....618 395-5045
Olney (G-15888)
Samtek International Inc....G....314 954-4005
Swansea (G-19697)
Schwartz Oilfield Services....F....618 532-0232
Walnut Hill (G-20222)
Seek Design....G....312 804-6629
Evanston (G-9574)
Seip Service & Supply Inc....F....618 532-1923
Centralia (G-3250)
Sids Well Service....G....618 375-5411
Grayville (G-10815)
Sims Company Inc....G....618 665-3901
Louisville (G-13180)
Stages Construction Inc....G....773 619-2977
Glenview (G-10624)
T & T Complete Construction....F....312 929-5352
Chicago (G-6305)
Ta Oil Field Service Inc....G....618 249-9001
Richview (G-17034)
Tdw Services Inc....F....815 407-0675
Romeoville (G-17880)
Team Energy LLC....F....618 943-1010
Bridgeport (G-2316)
Toppert Jetting Service Inc....G....309 755-2240
East Moline (G-8244)
Tri Kote Inc....G....618 262-4156
Mount Carmel (G-14489)

S I C

Employee Codes: A=Over 500 employees, B=251-500
C=101-250, D=51-100, E=20-50, F=10-19, G=3-9
2020 Harris Illinois
Industrial Directory
809

Tri State Acid Co Inc..................G 618 676-1111
Clay City *(G-6908)*
United Oil Co..................G 309 378-3049
Downs *(G-8114)*
Warren Service Company..................G 618 384-2117
Carmi *(G-2918)*
Water & Gas Technologies..................G 708 829-3254
Palos Park *(G-16217)*
Wayne County Well Surveys Inc..................F 618 842-9116
Fairfield *(G-9641)*
Wilpro..................G 618 382-4667
Carmi *(G-2920)*

14 MINING AND QUARRYING OF NONMETALLIC MINERALS, EXCEPT FUELS

1411 Dimension Stone

Anna Quarries Inc..................E 618 833-5121
Anna *(G-581)*
▲ **Architectural Limestone Inc**..................F 847 623-0100
Gurnee *(G-10861)*
Blue Pearl Stone Tech LLC..................G 708 698-5700
La Grange *(G-12073)*
Columbia Quarry Company..................E 618 281-7631
Columbia *(G-6987)*
Gary Galassi and Sons Inc..................E 815 886-3906
Romeoville *(G-17827)*
Ill Dept Natural Resources..................F 217 782-4970
Springfield *(G-19384)*
JKS Ventures Inc..................F 708 345-9344
Melrose Park *(G-13886)*
Joliet Sand and Gravel Company..................D 815 741-2090
Rockdale *(G-17262)*
Lafarge Aggregates Ill Inc..................G 847 742-6060
South Elgin *(G-19162)*
Lafarge Aggregates Ill Inc..................G 630 365-3600
Elburn *(G-8457)*
Material Service Corporation..................D 708 485-8211
Mc Cook *(G-13696)*
Nokomis Quarry Company..................F 217 563-2011
Nokomis *(G-15196)*
Pana Limestone Company..................G 217 562-4231
Pana *(G-16219)*
Picture Stone Inc..................G 773 875-5021
Mount Prospect *(G-14562)*
Red Hill Lava Products Inc..................G 800 528-2765
Rock Island *(G-17240)*
Stolle Casper Quar & Contg Co..................E 618 337-5212
Dupo *(G-8146)*
Tri-State Cut Stone Co..................E 815 469-7550
Frankfort *(G-9845)*
▲ **Wendell Adams**..................E 217 345-9587
Charleston *(G-3416)*

1422 Crushed & Broken Limestone

Anna Quarries Inc..................E 618 833-5121
Anna *(G-581)*
Argyle Cut Stone Co..................E 847 456-6210
Des Plaines *(G-7733)*
Calhoun Quarry Incorporated..................F 618 396-2229
Batchtown *(G-1442)*
Calhoun Quarry Incorporated..................G 618 576-9223
Hardin *(G-11016)*
Callender Construction Co Inc..................F 217 285-2161
Pittsfield *(G-16630)*
Central Limestone Company Inc..................F 815 736-6341
Morris *(G-14298)*
Central Stone Company..................G 217 335-2615
Barry *(G-1248)*
Central Stone Company..................F 309 776-3900
Colchester *(G-6946)*
Central Stone Company..................G 217 327-4300
Chambersburg *(G-3259)*
Central Stone Company..................F 217 723-4410
Pittsfield *(G-16632)*
Central Stone Company..................F 217 224-7330
Quincy *(G-16870)*
Charleston Stone Company..................E 217 345-6292
Ashmore *(G-886)*
Civil Constructors Inc..................G 815 858-2691
Elizabeth *(G-8786)*
Collinson Stone Co..................F 309 787-7983
Milan *(G-14004)*
Columbia Quarry Company..................E 618 939-8833
Waterloo *(G-20288)*
Conmat Inc..................G 815 238-3885
Galena *(G-10167)*
Conmat Inc..................E 815 235-2200
Freeport *(G-10104)*
Covia Holdings Corporation..................G 618 747-2355
Tamms *(G-19742)*
Elmer L Larson L C..................F 815 895-4837
Sycamore *(G-19710)*
Elmhurst-Chicago Stone Company..................E 630 983-6410
Bolingbrook *(G-2173)*
Gray Quarries Inc..................F 217 847-2712
Hamilton *(G-10955)*
H&H Crushing Inc..................G 309 275-0643
West Peoria *(G-20686)*
Hastie Min & Trckg Ltd Partnr..................E 618 289-4536
Cave In Rock *(G-3219)*
Huyear Trucking Inc..................G 217 854-3551
Carlinville *(G-2876)*
Iola Quarry Inc..................F 217 682-3865
Mode *(G-14067)*
Kimmaterials Inc..................G 618 466-0352
Godfrey *(G-10655)*
Lee Quarry Inc..................G 815 547-7141
Kirkland *(G-12063)*
Legacy Vulcan LLC..................G 217 963-2196
Decatur *(G-7516)*
Legacy Vulcan LLC..................G 847 578-9622
Lake Bluff *(G-12192)*
Legacy Vulcan LLC..................F 630 904-1110
Plainfield *(G-16683)*
Legacy Vulcan LLC..................E 815 468-8141
Manteno *(G-13450)*
Macklin Inc..................F 815 562-4803
Rochelle *(G-17147)*
Martha Lacey..................G 217 723-4380
Pearl *(G-16318)*
Material Service Corporation..................C 708 731-2600
Westchester *(G-20705)*
Material Service Corporation..................E 217 563-2531
Nokomis *(G-15194)*
Material Service Corporation..................E 217 732-2117
Athens *(G-897)*
Material Service Corporation..................D 708 877-6540
Thornton *(G-19790)*
Meyer Material Co Merger Corp..................D 815 943-2605
Harvard *(G-11060)*
Mid-America Carbonates LLC..................G 217 222-3500
Quincy *(G-16913)*
Mill Creek Mining Inc..................G 309 787-1414
Milan *(G-14017)*
Mining International LLC..................E 815 722-0900
Joliet *(G-11906)*
Nokomis Quarry Company..................F 217 563-2011
Nokomis *(G-15196)*
Omni Materials Inc..................E 618 262-5118
Mount Carmel *(G-14484)*
Quality Lime Company..................F 217 826-2343
Marshall *(G-13577)*
R L ONeal & Sons Inc..................F 309 458-3350
Plymouth *(G-16750)*
Renner Quarries Ltd..................G 815 288-6699
Dixon *(G-7910)*
Riverstone Group Inc..................G 309 462-3003
Saint Augustine *(G-18139)*
Riverstone Group Inc..................F 309 933-1123
Cleveland *(G-6912)*
Riverstone Group Inc..................E 309 787-3141
Milan *(G-14026)*
Savanna Quarry Inc..................G 815 273-4208
Savanna *(G-18411)*
Shawnee Stone LLC..................F 618 548-1585
Salem *(G-18359)*
Shawnee Stone LLC..................G 618 833-2323
Anna *(G-588)*
Southern Illinois Stone Co..................E 618 995-2392
Buncombe *(G-2630)*
Southern Illinois Stone Co..................F 573 334-5261
Buncombe *(G-2629)*
Southfield Corporation..................E 815 842-2333
Pontiac *(G-16780)*
Southfield Corporation..................F 815 468-8700
Manteno *(G-13457)*
St Marys Cement..................G 773 995-5100
Chicago *(G-6224)*
Stolle Casper Quar & Contg Co..................E 618 337-5212
Dupo *(G-8146)*
Tower Rock Stone Company..................F 618 281-4106
Columbia *(G-6994)*
Tri-State Cut Stone Co..................E 815 469-7550
Frankfort *(G-9845)*
Tuscola Stone Company..................F 217 253-4705
Tuscola *(G-19933)*
Utica Stone Co Inc..................G 815 667-4690
Utica *(G-20007)*
Valley View Industries Inc..................E 815 358-2236
Cornell *(G-7014)*
Vulcan Construction Mtls LLC..................E 630 955-8500
Naperville *(G-14943)*
Vulcan Materials Company..................E 815 899-7204
Sycamore *(G-19740)*
William Charles Cnstr Co LLC..................G 815 654-4720
Belvidere *(G-1711)*

1423 Crushed & Broken Granite

Martin Marietta Materials Inc..................F 618 285-6267
Golconda *(G-10667)*
Pacific Granites Inc..................G 312 835-7777
Chicago *(G-5738)*

1429 Crushed & Broken Stone, NEC

Gateway Crushing & Screening..................E 618 337-1954
East Saint Louis *(G-8309)*
Mid Illinois Quarry Company..................G 217 932-2611
Casey *(G-3206)*
Monmouth Stone Co..................F 309 734-7951
Monmouth *(G-14224)*

1442 Construction Sand & Gravel

A E Frasz Inc..................F 630 232-6223
Elburn *(G-8440)*
Aggregate Materials Company..................G 815 747-2430
East Dubuque *(G-8174)*
Allendale Gravel Co Inc..................F 618 263-3521
Allendale *(G-402)*
Amigoni Construction..................G 309 923-3701
Roanoke *(G-17098)*
Beverly Materials LLC..................G 847 695-9300
Hoffman Estates *(G-11407)*
Bluemastiff Group LLC..................G 708 704-3529
Chicago *(G-3916)*
Buckner Sand Co..................G 630 653-3700
Wheaton *(G-20791)*
C & H Gravel C Inc..................G 217 857-3425
Teutopolis *(G-19765)*
Carlyle Sand & Gravel Ltd..................G 618 594-8263
Carlyle *(G-2889)*
Clear Lake Sand & Gravel Co..................F 217 725-6999
Springfield *(G-19351)*
Consolidated Materials Inc..................G 815 568-1538
Marengo *(G-13482)*
Consolidated Materials Inc..................F 847 658-4342
Crystal Lake *(G-7185)*
Contractors Ready-Mix Inc..................G 217 482-5530
Mason City *(G-13610)*
County Materials Corp..................E 217 352-4181
Champaign *(G-3283)*
Covia Holdings Corporation..................G 618 747-2355
Tamms *(G-19742)*
Cullinan & Sons Inc..................E 309 925-2711
Tremont *(G-19895)*
Edge Capital Group Inc..................F 773 295-4774
Chicago *(G-4451)*
Edk Construction Inc..................G 630 853-3484
Darien *(G-7406)*
Elmer L Larson L C..................F 815 895-4837
Sycamore *(G-19710)*
Elmhurst-Chicago Stone Company..................E 630 832-4000
Elmhurst *(G-9360)*
Elmhurst-Chicago Stone Company..................F 630 557-2446
Kaneville *(G-11954)*
Elmhurst-Chicago Stone Company..................E 630 983-6410
Bolingbrook *(G-2173)*
Empire Acoustical Systems Inc..................E 815 261-0072
Princeton *(G-16807)*
Fairmount Santrol Inc..................F 815 587-4410
Ottawa *(G-16052)*
Fairmount Santrol Inc..................E 815 538-2645
Troy Grove *(G-19921)*
FML Terminal Logistics LLC..................G 815 433-2449
Wedron *(G-20524)*
Galena Road Gravel Inc..................E 309 274-6388
Chillicothe *(G-6817)*
Gregory Gravel Co..................G 618 943-2796
Lawrenceville *(G-12533)*
H & H Services Inc..................F 618 633-2837
Hamel *(G-10949)*
H & H Stone LLC..................G 815 782-5700
Bolingbrook *(G-2182)*
Hastie Min & Trckg Ltd Partnr..................E 618 289-4536
Cave In Rock *(G-3219)*
Jackson County Sand & Grav Co..................G 618 763-4711
Gorham *(G-10682)*

SIC SECTION

20 FOOD AND KINDRED PRODUCTS

Joliet Sand and Gravel Company ....D 815 741-2090
  Rockdale (G-17262)
Lafarge Aggregates III Inc ....G 847 742-6060
  South Elgin (G-19162)
Lafarge Aggregates III Inc ....G 630 365-3600
  Elburn (G-8457)
Lafarge Aux Sable LLC ....G 815 941-1423
  Morris (G-14309)
◆ Lafarge North America Inc ....C 773 372-1000
  Chicago (G-5156)
Lake County Grading Co LLC ....D 847 362-2590
  Libertyville (G-12665)
Legacy Vulcan LLC ....E 815 468-8141
  Manteno (G-13450)
Legacy Vulcan LLC ....E 815 937-7928
  Kankakee (G-11989)
Legacy Vulcan LLC ....E 217 498-7263
  Rochester (G-17168)
Legacy Vulcan LLC ....F 815 895-6501
  Sycamore (G-19722)
Legacy Vulcan LLC ....G 217 963-2196
  Harristown (G-11032)
Lt Construction ....G 815 243-6807
  Rockford (G-17498)
Material Service Corporation ....E 815 942-1830
  Romeoville (G-17847)
Material Service Corporation ....E 815 838-3420
  Romeoville (G-17848)
Material Service Corporation ....E 847 658-4559
  Algonquin (G-380)
Material Service Corporation ....E 708 447-1100
  Westchester (G-20704)
Material Service Corporation ....C 708 731-2600
  Westchester (G-20705)
Material Service Corporation ....E 815 838-2400
  Romeoville (G-17846)
May Sand and Gravel Inc ....G 815 338-4761
  Wonder Lake (G-21145)
Mel Price Company Inc ....F 217 442-9092
  Danville (G-7364)
Menoni & Mocogni Inc ....F 847 432-0850
  Highland Park (G-11283)
Mertel Gravel Company Inc ....F 815 223-0468
  Peru (G-16581)
Mid-America Sand & Gravel ....G 217 586-4536
  Mahomet (G-13426)
Mid-America Sand & Gravel ....G 217 355-1307
  Urbana (G-19988)
Newton Ready Mix Inc ....F 618 783-8611
  Newton (G-15088)
Opti-Sand Incorporated ....G 630 293-1245
  West Chicago (G-20626)
Otter Creek Sand & Gravel ....F 309 759-4293
  Havana (G-11119)
Pdss Construction ....F 847 980-6090
  Morton Grove (G-14431)
Pekin Sand and Gravel LLC ....G 309 347-8917
  Pekin (G-16353)
Petersen Sand & Gravel Inc ....F 815 344-1060
  Lakemoor (G-12473)
Plote Construction Inc ....E 847 695-0422
  Hoffman Estates (G-11444)
Plote Construction Inc ....D 847 695-9300
  Hoffman Estates (G-11445)
Plote Inc ....D 847 695-9467
  Hoffman Estates (G-11446)
Prosser Construction Co ....F 217 774-5032
  Shelbyville (G-18884)
Quality Sand Company Inc ....G 618 346-1070
  Collinsville (G-6973)
Randy Wright & Son Cnstr ....G 217 478-4171
  Alexander (G-363)
Reliable Sand and Gravel Co ....G 815 385-5020
  McHenry (G-13787)
Riverstone Group Inc ....G 309 787-1415
  Rock Island (G-17243)
Rock River Ready Mix Inc ....G 815 288-2260
  Dixon (G-7911)
Rock River Ready Mix Inc ....G 815 438-2510
  Rock Falls (G-17194)
Rockford Blacktop Cnstr Co ....D 815 654-4700
  Rockford (G-17586)
Rockford Sand & Gravel Co ....E 815 654-4700
  Loves Park (G-13258)
Rogers Ready Mix & Mtls Inc ....F 815 389-2223
  Roscoe (G-17927)
Rogers Ready Mix & Mtls Inc ....D 815 234-8212
  Byron (G-2757)
Rogers Redi-Mix Inc ....F 618 282-3844
  Ruma (G-18106)

Sand Valley Sand & Gravel Inc ....F 217 446-4210
  Danville (G-7380)
Sangamon Valley Sand & Gravel ....G 217 498-7189
  Rochester (G-17171)
Seneca Sand & Gravel LLC ....G 630 746-9183
  Seneca (G-18862)
Southfield Corporation ....G 217 379-3606
  Paxton (G-16316)
Southfield Corporation ....E 309 676-0576
  Peoria (G-16527)
Stokes Sand & Gravel Inc ....G 815 489-0680
  Batavia (G-1420)
Super Aggregates Inc ....E 815 385-8000
  McHenry (G-13800)
Thelen Sand & Gravel Inc ....D 847 838-8800
  Antioch (G-636)
Thelen Sand & Gravel Inc ....F 847 662-0760
  Waukegan (G-20503)
Tri-Con Materials Inc ....E 815 872-3206
  Princeton (G-16824)
Valley Run Stone Inc ....E 630 553-7974
  Yorkville (G-21504)
Vandalia Sand & Gravel Inc ....F 618 283-4029
  Vandalia (G-20028)
Voss Sandworks Inc ....G 815 795-9366
  Morris (G-14339)
Voss Sandworks West Inc ....G 815 474-4042
  La Salle (G-12124)
Wayland Ready Mix Concrete Svc ....F 309 833-2064
  Galesburg (G-10222)

1446 Industrial Sand

Clifford W Estes Co Inc ....F 815 433-0944
  Ottawa (G-16047)
Covia Holdings Corporation ....G 618 747-2355
  Tamms (G-19742)
Covia Holdings Corporation ....D 815 732-2121
  Oregon (G-15916)
Covia Holdings Corporation ....G 815 539-6734
  Troy Grove (G-19920)
Covia Holdings Corporation ....E 618 747-2338
  Tamms (G-19743)
Covia Holdings Corporation 203 966-8880
  Ottawa (G-16049)
Fairmount Santrol Inc ....F 815 433-2449
  Ottawa (G-16051)
Fjcj LLC ....F 618 785-2217
  Baldwin (G-1184)
Husar Abatement Ltd ....F 847 349-9105
  Franklin Park (G-9960)
Snyder Industries Inc ....D 630 773-9510
  Bensenville (G-1895)
Spectron Manufacturing ....G 720 879-7605
  Bloomingdale (G-2015)
U S Silica Company ....G 800 635-7263
  Ottawa (G-16082)
Unimin Lime Corporation ....F 203 966-8880
  Ottawa (G-16083)
Wedron Silica Company ....F 815 433-2449
  Wedron (G-20525)

1455 Kaolin & Ball Clay

Huber Carbonates LLC ....F 217 224-8737
  Quincy (G-16893)

1459 Clay, Ceramic & Refractory Minerals, NEC

◆ Amcol International Corp ....E 847 851-1500
  Hoffman Estates (G-11405)
American Colloid Company ....E 618 452-8143
  Granite City (G-10694)
American Colloid Company ....F 304 882-2123
  Elgin (G-8506)
▼ American Colloid Company ....F 800 527-9948
  Arlington Heights (G-690)
American Colloid Company ....F 815 547-5369
  Belvidere (G-1648)
◆ American Colloid Company ....E 847 851-1700
  Hoffman Estates (G-11406)
Carpentersville Quarry Inc ....F 847 836-1550
  Carpentersville (G-3096)
Covia Holdings Corporation ....G 618 747-2355
  Tamms (G-19742)
Entec Polymers LLC ....G 866 598-8941
  Plainfield (G-16660)
Oil-Dri Corporation America ....D 618 745-6881
  Mounds (G-14463)
Oil-Dri Corporation America ....B 312 321-1516
  Chicago (G-5667)

◆ Profile Products LLC ....E 847 215-1144
  Buffalo Grove (G-2590)

1474 Potash, Soda & Borate Minerals

◆ Pcs Phosphate Company Inc ....D 847 849-4200
  Northbrook (G-15457)
◆ US Borax Inc ....C 773 270-6500
  Chicago (G-6499)

1475 Phosphate Rock

◆ Pcs Phosphate Company Inc ....D 847 849-4200
  Northbrook (G-15457)
Phosphate Resource Ptrs ....A 847 739-1200
  Lake Forest (G-12290)

1479 Chemical & Fertilizer Mining

Chicago Salt Company Inc ....G 708 906-4718
  River Grove (G-17058)
Hastie Min & Trckg Ltd Partnr ....E 618 289-4536
  Cave In Rock (G-3219)
◆ Morton Salt Inc ....C 312 807-2000
  Chicago (G-5501)

1481 Nonmetallic Minerals Svcs, Except Fuels

Harsco Corporation ....G 309 347-1962
  Pekin (G-16337)
Hastie Mining & Trucking ....G 618 285-3600
  Rosiclare (G-18063)
Illinois Valley Minerals LLC ....G 815 442-8402
  Tonica (G-19889)
Natural Resources Ill Dept ....E 618 439-4320
  Benton (G-1933)
Pennasis Group LLC ....G 630 699-8390
  North Aurora (G-15268)
Raimonde Drilling Corp ....F 630 458-0590
  Addison (G-265)
Vigo Coal Operating Co Inc ....G 618 262-7022
  Mount Carmel (G-14490)

1499 Miscellaneous Nonmetallic Mining

Covia Holdings Corporation ....G 618 747-2355
  Tamms (G-19742)
Diamond Icic Corporation ....E 309 269-8652
  Rock Island (G-17218)
Markman Peat Corp ....E 815 772-4014
  Morrison (G-14345)
Professional Gem Sciences Inc ....G 312 920-1541
  Chicago (G-5897)

20 FOOD AND KINDRED PRODUCTS

2011 Meat Packing Plants

Allens Farm Quality Meats ....G 217 896-2532
  Homer (G-11474)
Amelio Bros Meats ....G 708 300-2920
  Richton Park (G-17027)
▼ Amity Packing Company Inc ....C 312 942-0270
  Chicago (G-3680)
Aurora Packing Company Inc ....C 630 897-0551
  North Aurora (G-15255)
Bar-B-Que Industries Inc ....F 773 227-5400
  Chicago (G-3829)
▲ Belmont Sausage Company ....E 847 357-1515
  Elk Grove Village (G-8864)
Best Chicago Meat Company LLC ....F 773 523-8161
  Chicago (G-3870)
Brown Packing Company Inc ....E 708 849-7990
  South Holland (G-19202)
▲ Bruss Company ....E 773 282-2900
  Chicago (G-3969)
Bushnell Locker Service ....G 309 772-2783
  Bushnell (G-2739)
Butterball LLC ....B 800 575-3365
  Montgomery (G-14237)
Calihan Pork Processors Inc ....D 309 674-9175
  Peoria (G-16396)
Cargill Meat Solutions Corp ....C 630 739-1746
  Woodridge (G-21281)
Cass Meats ....G 217 452-3072
  Virginia (G-20193)
Chenoa Locker Inc ....G 815 945-7323
  Chenoa (G-3432)
Cherry Meat Packers Inc ....E 773 927-1200
  Chicago (G-4083)
Chicago Meat Authority Inc ....B 773 254-3811
  Chicago (G-4113)

Employee Codes: A=Over 500 employees, B=251-500
C=101-250, D=51-100, E=20-50, F=10-19, G=3-9

20 FOOD AND KINDRED PRODUCTS SIC SECTION

Chicago Premier Meats Inc..........G....... 773 847-5400
Chicago *(G-4124)*

▼ City Foods Inc..........C....... 773 523-1566
Chicago *(G-4155)*

Consumers Packing Co Inc..........D....... 708 344-0047
Melrose Park *(G-13844)*

Country Village Meats..........G....... 815 849-5532
Sublette *(G-19635)*

Dawn Food Products Inc..........C....... 815 933-0600
Bradley *(G-2280)*

Deer Processing..........F....... 309 799-5994
Coal Valley *(G-6935)*

Earlville Cold Stor Lckr LLC..........G....... 815 246-9469
Earlville *(G-8160)*

Ed Kabrick Beef Inc..........G....... 217 656-3263
Plainville *(G-16729)*

Edgar County Locker Service..........G....... 217 466-5000
Paris *(G-16229)*

Eickmans Processing Co Inc..........E....... 815 247-8451
Seward *(G-18867)*

Eureka Locker Inc..........F....... 309 467-2731
Eureka *(G-9482)*

Fabbri Sausage Manufacturing..........E....... 312 829-6363
Chicago *(G-4554)*

Farmers Packing Inc..........F....... 618 445-3822
Albion *(G-350)*

Farmington Locker/Ice Plant Co..........G....... 309 245-4621
Farmington *(G-9661)*

Galloway Como Processing..........G....... 815 626-0305
Sterling *(G-19511)*

God Family Country LLC..........F....... 217 285-6487
Pittsfield *(G-16634)*

Golden Locker Inc..........G....... 217 696-4456
Camp Point *(G-2811)*

Graized LLC..........G....... 815 615-1012
Moweaqua *(G-14651)*

Grant Park Packing Company Inc..........E....... 312 421-4096
Franklin Park *(G-9952)*

▼ Great Lakes Packing Co Intl..........G....... 773 927-6660
Chicago *(G-4737)*

◆ Grecian Delight Foods Inc..........C....... 847 364-1010
Elk Grove Village *(G-9022)*

Gurman Food Co..........F....... 847 837-1100
Mundelein *(G-14693)*

Halsted Packing House Co..........G....... 312 421-5147
Chicago *(G-4774)*

Hansen Packing Co..........G....... 618 498-3714
Jerseyville *(G-11792)*

Hartrich Meats Inc..........G....... 618 455-3172
Sainte Marie *(G-18326)*

Heinkels Packing Company Inc..........E....... 217 428-4401
Decatur *(G-7501)*

Honey Foods Inc..........G....... 847 989-8186
Franklin Park *(G-9957)*

J Brodie Meat Products Inc..........F....... 309 342-1500
Galesburg *(G-10202)*

Jancorp LLC..........G....... 217 892-4830
Rantoul *(G-16977)*

Jbs USA Food Company..........E....... 217 323-6200
Beardstown *(G-1447)*

▼ John Hofmeister & Son Inc..........D....... 773 847-0700
Chicago *(G-5041)*

Johnsons Processing Plant..........G....... 815 684-5183
Chadwick *(G-3258)*

Jones Packing Co..........G....... 815 943-4488
Harvard *(G-11058)*

▼ Kelly Corned Beef Co Chicago..........E....... 773 588-2882
Chicago *(G-5092)*

Korte Meat Processors Inc..........G....... 618 654-3813
Highland *(G-11230)*

▲ Kuna Meat Company Inc..........C....... 618 286-4000
Dupo *(G-8139)*

Lake Pacific Partners LLC..........B....... 312 578-1110
Chicago *(G-5161)*

Lena AJS Maid Meats..........F....... 815 369-4522
Lena *(G-12602)*

Magros Processing..........G....... 217 438-2880
Springfield *(G-19401)*

Main Street Market Roscoe Inc..........G....... 815 623-6328
Roscoe *(G-17915)*

Mangold Networks..........G....... 224 402-0068
Elgin *(G-8648)*

▼ Meats By Linz Inc..........E....... 708 862-0830
Calumet City *(G-2783)*

Momence Packing Co..........B....... 815 472-6485
Momence *(G-14188)*

Morris Meat Packing Co Inc..........G....... 708 865-8566
Maywood *(G-13673)*

Moweaqua Packing Plant..........G....... 217 768-4714
Moweaqua *(G-14652)*

National Beef Packing Co LLC..........G....... 312 332-6166
Chicago *(G-5544)*

Nea Agora Packing Co..........G....... 312 421-5130
Chicago *(G-5560)*

New SBL Inc..........E....... 773 376-8280
Chicago *(G-5578)*

Oriental Kitchen Corporation..........F....... 312 738-2850
Chicago *(G-5698)*

Paris Frozen Foods Inc..........G....... 217 532-3822
Hillsboro *(G-11318)*

Park Packing Company Inc..........E....... 773 254-0100
Chicago *(G-5764)*

Paxton Packing LLC..........F....... 623 707-5604
Paxton *(G-16312)*

Peer Foods Inc..........F....... 773 927-1440
Chicago *(G-5781)*

Peoria Packing Ltd..........F....... 312 226-2600
Chicago *(G-5787)*

Peoria Packing Ltd..........F....... 815 465-9824
Grant Park *(G-10750)*

Plumrose Usa Inc..........G....... 732 253-5257
Chicago *(G-5823)*

▲ Plumrose Usa Inc..........E....... 800 526-4909
Downers Grove *(G-8077)*

Raber Packing Company..........E....... 309 673-0721
Peoria *(G-16507)*

Reasons Inc..........G....... 309 537-3424
Buffalo Prairie *(G-2626)*

Rochelle Foods LLC..........A....... 815 562-4141
Rochelle *(G-17155)*

Rose Packing Co Inc..........G....... 708 458-9300
Chicago *(G-6061)*

Rose Packing Company Inc..........A....... 708 458-9300
Chicago *(G-6062)*

Rose Packing Company Inc..........F....... 708 458-9300
Chicago *(G-6063)*

Ryan Meat Company..........G....... 773 783-3840
Evergreen Park *(G-9599)*

Saratoga Specialties Co Inc..........G....... 630 833-3810
Elmhurst *(G-9424)*

Skyline Provisions Inc..........F....... 708 331-1982
Harvey *(G-11095)*

Smithfeld Pckged Mats Sls Corp..........F....... 757 365-3541
Lisle *(G-12938)*

Smithfield Packaged Meats Corp..........C....... 630 993-8763
Bolingbrook *(G-2243)*

Smithfield Packaged Meats Corp..........G....... 815 747-8809
East Dubuque *(G-8183)*

Smithfield Packaged Meats Corp..........A....... 309 734-5353
Monmouth *(G-14227)*

Smithfield Packaged Meats Corp..........E....... 630 281-5224
Lisle *(G-12939)*

Sommers Fare LLC..........E....... 877 377-9797
Mundelein *(G-14737)*

Specialty Foods Group LLC..........C....... 773 378-1300
Chicago *(G-6213)*

Specialty Foods Group LLC..........G....... 630 599-5900
Lombard *(G-13132)*

Spectrum Preferred Meats Inc..........D....... 815 946-3816
Mount Morris *(G-14502)*

Steinbach Provision Company..........G....... 773 538-1511
Chicago *(G-6238)*

Stewart Brothers Packing Co..........G....... 217 422-7741
Decatur *(G-7551)*

Stiglmeier Sausage Co Inc..........F....... 847 537-9988
Wheeling *(G-20991)*

T & J Meatpacking Inc..........D....... 708 758-6748
Chicago Heights *(G-6778)*

◆ Teys (usa) Inc..........G....... 312 492-7163
Chicago *(G-6356)*

Tomcyndi Inc..........E....... 773 847-5400
Chicago *(G-6389)*

Tyson..........F....... 773 282-2900
Chicago *(G-6451)*

Tyson Fresh Meats Inc..........C....... 309 658-3377
Hillsdale *(G-11323)*

Tyson Fresh Meats Inc..........F....... 309 965-2565
Goodfield *(G-10678)*

Tyson Fresh Meats Inc..........F....... 847 836-5550
Elgin *(G-8764)*

Valley Meats LLC..........E....... 309 799-7341
Coal Valley *(G-6939)*

Victor Food Products..........G....... 773 478-9529
Chicago *(G-6544)*

Wichita Packing Co..........E....... 312 421-0606
Chicago *(G-6622)*

Y T Packing Co..........F....... 217 522-3345
Springfield *(G-19470)*

Zabiha Halal Mt Processors Inc..........G....... 630 620-5000
Addison *(G-340)*

2013 Sausages & Meat Prdts

A New Dairy Company..........E....... 312 421-1234
Chicago *(G-3489)*

Allens Farm Quality Meats..........G....... 217 896-2532
Homer *(G-11474)*

Amylu Foods LLC..........E....... 312 829-2250
Chicago *(G-3689)*

▲ Andys Deli and Mikolajczyk..........E....... 773 722-1000
Chicago *(G-3694)*

Another Chance Community Dev..........E....... 773 998-1641
Chicago *(G-3702)*

Arts Tamales..........G....... 309 367-2850
Metamora *(G-13958)*

Atlantic Beverage Company Inc..........G....... 847 412-6200
Northbrook *(G-15342)*

B B M Packing Co Inc..........G....... 312 243-1061
Chicago *(G-3807)*

Ba Le Meat Processing & Whl Co..........F....... 773 506-2499
Chicago *(G-3810)*

Bar-B-Que Industries Inc..........F....... 773 227-5400
Chicago *(G-3829)*

Barbecue Select Inc..........F....... 773 847-0230
Chicago *(G-3830)*

▲ Belmont Sausage Company..........E....... 847 357-1515
Elk Grove Village *(G-8864)*

Bende Inc..........G....... 847 913-0304
Vernon Hills *(G-20047)*

▲ Bkbg Enterprises Inc..........D....... 847 228-7070
Carol Stream *(G-2947)*

Bob Evans Farms Inc..........D....... 309 932-2194
Galva *(G-10229)*

Bobak Sausage Company..........E....... 773 735-5334
Chicago *(G-3922)*

Branding Iron Holdings Inc..........G....... 618 337-8400
Sauget *(G-18390)*

▲ Bridgford Foods Corporation..........B....... 312 733-0300
Chicago *(G-3958)*

Brown Packing Company Inc..........E....... 708 849-7990
South Holland *(G-19202)*

▲ Bruss Company..........E....... 773 282-2900
Chicago *(G-3969)*

C & F Packing Co Inc..........C....... 847 245-2000
Lake Villa *(G-12348)*

Carl Buddig and Company..........E....... 708 798-0900
Homewood *(G-11489)*

Carroll County Locker..........G....... 815 493-2370
Lanark *(G-12478)*

Cass Meats..........G....... 217 452-3072
Virginia *(G-20193)*

Charles Autin Limited..........D....... 312 432-0888
Chicago *(G-4072)*

Cherry Meat Packers Inc..........E....... 773 927-1200
Chicago *(G-4083)*

Chicago Local Foods LLC..........E....... 312 432-6575
Chicago *(G-4111)*

Columbus Meats Inc..........G....... 312 829-2480
Chicago *(G-4207)*

Conagra Brands Inc..........C....... 312 549-5000
Chicago *(G-4212)*

Conagra Brands Inc..........C....... 630 857-1000
Naperville *(G-14803)*

Consumers Packing Co Inc..........D....... 708 344-0047
Melrose Park *(G-13844)*

Country Village Meats..........G....... 815 849-5532
Sublette *(G-19635)*

Crawford Sausage Co Inc..........E....... 773 277-3095
Chicago *(G-4260)*

Crown Corned Beef and Foods..........G....... 312 738-0099
Chicago *(G-4277)*

Dabecca Natural Foods Inc..........C....... 773 291-1428
Chicago *(G-4304)*

Danielson Food Products Inc..........E....... 773 285-2111
Chicago *(G-4314)*

Dawn Food Products Inc..........C....... 815 933-0600
Bradley *(G-2280)*

Dons Meat Market..........G....... 309 968-6026
Manito *(G-13438)*

Dreymiller & Kray Inc..........G....... 847 683-2271
Hampshire *(G-10969)*

Earlville Cold Stor Lckr LLC..........G....... 815 246-9469
Earlville *(G-8160)*

Ed Kabrick Beef Inc..........G....... 217 656-3263
Plainville *(G-16729)*

Edgar County Locker Service..........G....... 217 466-5000
Paris *(G-16229)*

Eickmans Processing Co Inc..........E....... 815 247-8451
Seward *(G-18867)*

Elburn Market Inc..........E....... 630 365-6461
Elburn *(G-8451)*

Emmel Inc ....G....... 847 254-5178
Lake In The Hills *(G-12334)*
Eureka Locker Inc ....F 309 467-2731
Eureka *(G-9482)*
Fabbri Sausage Manufacturing ....E 312 829-6363
Chicago *(G-4554)*
▼ Farmington Foods Inc ....C....... 708 771-3600
Forest Park *(G-9714)*
Farmington Locker/Ice Plant Co..................G....... 309 245-4621
Farmington *(G-9661)*
Food Purveyors Logistics..................F 630 229-6168
Naperville *(G-14829)*
Freedom Sausage Inc..................F 815 792-8276
Earlville *(G-8161)*
George Nottoli & Sons Inc ....G....... 773 589-1010
Chicago *(G-4683)*
Givaudan Flavors Corporation ....C....... 630 682-5600
Carol Stream *(G-2992)*
Glenmark Industries Ltd..................C....... 773 927-4800
Chicago *(G-4694)*
Golden Locker Inc..................G....... 217 696-4456
Camp Point *(G-2811)*
◆ Grecian Delight Foods Inc..................C....... 847 364-1010
Elk Grove Village *(G-9022)*
Greenleaf Foods Spc..................E 800 268-3708
Elmhurst *(G-9369)*
▲ Greenridge Farm Inc..................E 847 434-1803
Elk Grove Village *(G-9024)*
Gridley Meat Products LLC..................G....... 309 747-2120
Gridley *(G-10844)*
H & B Hams ....G....... 618 372-8690
Brighton *(G-2400)*
Halsted Packing House Co ....G....... 312 421-5147
Chicago *(G-4774)*
Hansen Packing Co ....G....... 618 498-3714
Jerseyville *(G-11792)*
Hartrich Meats Inc..................G....... 618 455-3172
Sainte Marie *(G-18326)*
▼ Hillshire Brands Company ....B 312 614-6000
Chicago *(G-4820)*
Hillshire Brands Company..................A 312 614-6000
Chicago *(G-4821)*
Hillshire Brands Company..................B 800 727-2533
Rochelle *(G-17144)*
Hillshire Brands Company..................G....... 888 317-5867
Chicago *(G-4822)*
Hillshire Brands Company..................E 312 614-6000
Downers Grove *(G-8022)*
Hillshire Brands Company..................G....... 847 310-9400
Schaumburg *(G-18549)*
Hillshire Brands Company..................F 630 991-5100
Downers Grove *(G-8023)*
Holten Meat Inc ....D....... 618 337-8400
Sauget *(G-18394)*
Houser Meats ....G....... 217 322-4994
Rushville *(G-18110)*
▲ Ifa International Inc..................F 847 566-0008
Mundelein *(G-14698)*
J Brodie Meat Products Inc..................F 309 342-1500
Galesburg *(G-10202)*
Jackson & Partners LLC ....G....... 630 219-1598
Naperville *(G-14853)*
John J Moesle Whl Meats Inc ....F 773 847-4900
Chicago *(G-5042)*
Johnsons Processing Plant..................G....... 815 684-5183
Chadwick *(G-3258)*
Jones Packing Co..................G....... 815 943-4488
Harvard *(G-11058)*
Koenemann Sausage Co..................G....... 815 385-6260
Volo *(G-20201)*
Korte Meat Processors Inc..................G....... 618 654-3813
Highland *(G-11230)*
Kraft Foods Asia PCF Svcs LLC..................G....... 847 943-4000
Deerfield *(G-7627)*
▼ Kronos Foods Corp ....B 224 353-5400
Glendale Heights *(G-10465)*
Lake Pacific Partners LLC..................B....... 312 578-1110
Chicago *(G-5161)*
▲ Land OFrost Inc ....C....... 708 474-7100
Lansing *(G-12502)*
Lena AJS Maid Meats ....F 815 369-4522
Lena *(G-12602)*
M E F Corp..................F 815 965-8604
Rockford *(G-17501)*
Makowskis Real Sausage Co..................E 312 842-5330
Chicago *(G-5321)*
▼ Meats By Linz Inc..................E 708 862-0830
Calumet City *(G-2783)*
Mistica Foods LLC..................C....... 630 543-5409
Addison *(G-219)*

Momence Packing Co..................B 815 472-6485
Momence *(G-14188)*
Mondelez International Inc..................G....... 815 710-2114
Morris *(G-14316)*
◆ Mondelez International Inc ....A 847 943-4000
Chicago *(G-5490)*
Morris Meat Packing Co Inc..................G....... 708 865-8566
Maywood *(G-13673)*
Moweaqua Packing Plant..................G....... 217 768-4714
Moweaqua *(G-14652)*
Nea Agora Packing Co ....G....... 312 421-5130
Chicago *(G-5560)*
New Specialty Products Inc..................E 773 847-0230
Chicago *(G-5579)*
O Chilli Frozen Foods Inc..................E 847 562-1991
Northbrook *(G-15442)*
▼ Ogden Foods LLC..................E 773 277-8207
Chicago *(G-5660)*
Ogden Foods LLC..................G....... 773 801-0125
Chicago *(G-5661)*
Old Fashioned Meat Co Inc..................G....... 312 421-4555
Chicago *(G-5668)*
▲ On-Cor Frozen Foods LLC ....E 630 851-6600
Aurora *(G-1142)*
Oriental Kitchen Corporation..................F 312 738-2850
Chicago *(G-5698)*
Oscars Foods Inc..................G....... 773 622-6822
Chicago *(G-5708)*
OSI Industries LLC..................C....... 630 231-9090
West Chicago *(G-20627)*
OSI Industries LLC..................B 773 847-2000
Chicago *(G-5710)*
▲ OSI International Foods Ltd..................D....... 630 851-6600
Aurora *(G-1005)*
Papa Charlies Inc..................E 773 522-7900
Chicago *(G-5752)*
Park Packing Company Inc..................E 773 254-0100
Chicago *(G-5764)*
Pcj II Inc ....E 312 829-2250
Chicago *(G-5773)*
▲ Plumrose Usa Inc..................E 800 526-4909
Downers Grove *(G-8077)*
Polancics Meats & Tenderloins ....G....... 815 433-0324
Ottawa *(G-16073)*
Portillos Food Service Inc..................E 630 620-0460
Addison *(G-247)*
Powers John..................G....... 309 742-8929
Elmwood *(G-9449)*
R&R Meat Co ....G....... 270 898-6296
Metropolis *(G-13976)*
Randolph Packing Co..................D....... 630 830-3100
Streamwood *(G-19592)*
Rapid Foods Inc..................G....... 708 366-0321
Shorewood *(G-18902)*
Roca Inc..................F 312 421-2345
Chicago *(G-6047)*
Rochelle Foods LLC ....A....... 815 562-4141
Rochelle *(G-17155)*
Roma Packing Co ....G....... 773 927-7371
Chicago *(G-6055)*
Rose Packing Company Inc..................A 708 458-9300
Chicago *(G-6062)*
Russo Wholesale Meat Inc..................G....... 708 385-0500
Alsip *(G-507)*
Ryan Meat Company..................G....... 773 783-3840
Evergreen Park *(G-9599)*
Salatas Smoked Meats ....G....... 224 433-1205
McHenry *(G-13790)*
Seifferts Locker & Meat Proc ....F 618 594-3921
Carlyle *(G-2895)*
Smithfield Packaged Meats Corp ....A 309 734-5353
Monmouth *(G-14227)*
Smolich Brothers Sausage Inc ....G....... 815 727-2144
Joliet *(G-11931)*
Sparrer Sausage Company Inc..................C....... 773 762-3334
Chicago *(G-6208)*
Specialty Foods Group LLC..................G....... 630 599-5900
Lombard *(G-13132)*
Specialty Foods Group LLC..................C....... 773 378-1300
Chicago *(G-6213)*
▲ Stampede Meat Inc ....A 773 376-4300
Bridgeview *(G-2389)*
Steinbach Provision Company ....G....... 773 538-1511
Chicago *(G-6238)*
Stiglmeier Sausage Co Inc..................F 847 537-9988
Wheeling *(G-20991)*
T & J Meatpacking Inc ....D....... 708 758-6748
Chicago Heights *(G-6778)*
Tandem Usa LLC..................G....... 224 653-8840
Schaumburg *(G-18739)*

Think Jerky LLC..................G....... 917 623-1989
Chicago *(G-6364)*
Tomcyndi Inc..................E 773 847-5400
Chicago *(G-6389)*
▼ Trim-Rite Food Corporation ....C....... 847 649-3400
Carpentersville *(G-3121)*
Tyson Foods..................C....... 312 614-6000
Chicago *(G-6452)*
Tyson Fresh Meats Inc ....F 847 836-5550
Elgin *(G-8764)*
V A M D Inc ....G....... 773 631-8400
Chicago *(G-6512)*
▼ Van Hessen USA Inc ....E 773 376-9200
Chicago *(G-6519)*
Vhrk Food Inc..................G....... 630 640-6525
Chicago *(G-6541)*
▼ Vienna Beef Ltd..................E 773 278-7800
Chicago *(G-6548)*
Vienna Beef Ltd..................F 800 366-3647
Chicago *(G-6549)*
Viscofan Usa Inc ....D....... 217 444-8000
Danville *(G-7392)*
West Loop Salumi Co..................G....... 312 255-7004
Chicago *(G-6604)*
William Badal..................G....... 815 264-7752
Waterman *(G-20303)*
Wurst Kitchen Inc ....G....... 630 898-9242
Aurora *(G-1171)*
Y T Packing Co..................F 217 522-3345
Springfield *(G-19470)*

2015 Poultry Slaughtering, Dressing & Processing

2000plus Groups Inc..................G....... 630 528-3220
Oak Brook *(G-15587)*
2000plus Groups Inc..................C....... 800 939-6268
Chicago *(G-3463)*
Aspen Foods Inc..................C....... 312 829-7282
Park Ridge *(G-16268)*
Central Illinois Poultry Proc..................F 217 543-2937
Arthur *(G-845)*
Charles Autin Limited..................D....... 312 432-0888
Chicago *(G-4072)*
▲ Eggology Inc ....F 818 610-2222
Pearl City *(G-16319)*
Galloway Como Processing..................G....... 815 626-0305
Sterling *(G-19511)*
Gift Check Program 2013 Inc..................G....... 630 986-5081
Downers Grove *(G-8011)*
Grant Park Packing Company Inc ....E 312 421-4096
Franklin Park *(G-9952)*
Handcut Foods LLC..................D....... 312 239-0381
Chicago *(G-4776)*
Hillshire Brands Company..................E 312 614-6000
Downers Grove *(G-8022)*
Jcg Industries Inc ....C....... 312 829-7282
Park Ridge *(G-16286)*
Kauffman Poultry Farms Inc ....F 815 264-3470
Waterman *(G-20298)*
Koch Meat Co Inc..................B 847 384-5940
Chicago *(G-5113)*
▼ Koch Poultry..................G....... 847 455-0902
Franklin Park *(G-9977)*
Lean Protein Team LLC ....G....... 440 525-1532
Chicago *(G-5191)*
Love ME Tenders LLC ....G....... 773 502-8000
Highland Park *(G-11282)*
Midwest Poultry Services LP ....D....... 217 386-2313
Loda *(G-13030)*
Nduja Artisans Co ....G....... 312 550-6991
Chicago *(G-5559)*
New Specialty Products Inc..................E 773 847-0230
Chicago *(G-5579)*
Tru-Native Enterprises..................G....... 630 409-3258
Addison *(G-317)*
Tyson Foods Inc..................F 309 658-2291
Hillsdale *(G-11322)*
Tyson Foods Inc..................F 773 650-4000
Chicago *(G-6453)*
West Liberty Foods LLC..................B 603 679-2300
Bolingbrook *(G-2253)*

2021 Butter

Danish Maid Butter Company..................F 773 731-8787
Chicago *(G-4315)*
◆ Hoogwegt US Inc..................D....... 847 918-8787
Lake Forest *(G-12254)*
Madison Farms Butter Company..................E 217 854-2547
Carlinville *(G-2882)*

S I C

20 FOOD AND KINDRED PRODUCTS

Old Heritage Creamery LLC .... G 217 268-4355
  Arcola *(G-661)*

2022 Cheese

Arthur Schuman Inc .... E 847 851-8500
  Elgin *(G-8514)*
▲ Arthur Schuman Midwest LLC ....D 847 851-8500
  Elgin *(G-8515)*
Avanti Foods Company .... E 815 379-2155
  Walnut *(G-20216)*
Bel Americas Inc .... G 646 454-8220
  Chicago *(G-3859)*
◆ Bel Brands Usa Inc .... E 312 462-1500
  Chicago *(G-3860)*
Berner Food & Beverage LLC ......B 815 563-4222
  Dakota *(G-7311)*
Berner Food & Beverage LLC ......E 815 865-5136
  Rock City *(G-17174)*
Brewster Cheese Company ....D 815 947-3361
  Stockton *(G-19548)*
Carl Buddig and Company ....E 708 798-0900
  Homewood *(G-11489)*
▲ Cheese Merchants America LLC ...B 630 221-0580
  Bartlett *(G-1272)*
▲ Churny Company Inc ....B 847 646-5500
  Chicago *(G-4148)*
◆ Conagra Dairy Foods Company ..B 630 848-0975
  Chicago *(G-4213)*
El Encanto Products Inc ....F 773 940-1807
  Chicago *(G-4464)*
Handcut Foods LLC ....D 312 239-0381
  Chicago *(G-4776)*
◆ Hoogwegt US Inc ....D 847 918-8787
  Lake Forest *(G-12254)*
▲ Kolb-Lena Inc ....D 815 369-4577
  Lena *(G-12600)*
Kraft Foods Asia PCF Svcs LLC ...G 847 943-4000
  Deerfield *(G-7627)*
Kraft Heinz Company ....C 847 646-2000
  Chicago *(G-5129)*
Kraft Heinz Foods Company ....G 412 456-5700
  Chicago *(G-5130)*
Kraft Heinz Foods Company ....C 847 646-2000
  Northfield *(G-15521)*
Kraft Heinz Foods Company ....D 217 378-1900
  Champaign *(G-3315)*
La Hispamex Food Products Inc ...G 708 780-1808
  Chicago *(G-5147)*
Mancuso Cheese Company ....F 815 722-2475
  Joliet *(G-11897)*
Marcoot Jersey Creamery LLC ....F 618 664-1110
  Greenville *(G-10837)*
▲ Mondelez Global LLC ....C 847 943-4000
  Deerfield *(G-7637)*
Mondelez International Inc ....G 815 710-2114
  Morris *(G-14316)*
◆ Mondelez International Inc ....A 847 943-4000
  Chicago *(G-5490)*
Nuestro Queso LLC ....C 815 443-2100
  Kent *(G-12018)*
Nuestro Queso LLC ....E 224 366-4320
  Chicago *(G-5641)*
Prairie Pure Cheese ....G 815 568-5000
  Marengo *(G-13493)*
▲ Saputo Cheese USA Inc ....D 847 267-1100
  Lincolnshire *(G-12794)*
Saputo Inc ....E 715 755-3485
  Lincolnshire *(G-12795)*
Savencia Cheese USA LLC ....G 815 369-4577
  Lena *(G-12608)*
Two Tribes LLC ....G 847 272-7711
  Glenview *(G-10634)*
V & V Supremo Foods Inc ....C 312 733-5652
  Chicago *(G-6511)*
▲ V Formusa Co ....F 224 938-9360
  Des Plaines *(G-7863)*
We Love Soy Inc ....G 630 629-9667
  Addison *(G-332)*
Wengers Springbrook Cheese Inc ...F 815 865-5855
  Davis *(G-7420)*
Wiscon Corp ....E 708 450-0074
  Melrose Park *(G-13930)*
◆ Wiscon Corp ....E 708 450-0074
  Melrose Park *(G-13929)*

2023 Milk, Condensed & Evaporated

Abbott Laboratories ....E 800 551-5838
  Chicago *(G-3504)*
▲ Abbott Laboratories ....A 224 667-6100
  Abbott Park *(G-1)*

Abbott Laboratories ....A 847 932-7900
  North Chicago *(G-15293)*
Armada Nutrition LLC ....G 931 451-7808
  Carol Stream *(G-2940)*
Bay Valley Foods LLC ....D 815 239-2631
  Pecatonica *(G-16321)*
Corefx Ingredients LLC ....F 773 271-2663
  Orangeville *(G-15908)*
Deja Investments Inc ....D 630 408-9222
  Bolingbrook *(G-2168)*
Erie Group International Inc ....D 309 659-2233
  Rochelle *(G-17139)*
◆ Fonterra (usa) Inc ....D 847 928-1600
  Chicago *(G-4616)*
Health King Enterprise Inc ....G 312 567-9978
  Chicago *(G-4791)*
Healthy Body LLC ....G 208 409-6602
  Ottawa *(G-16054)*
◆ Hoogwegt US Inc ....D 847 918-8787
  Lake Forest *(G-12254)*
▲ Lifeway Foods Inc ....C 847 967-1010
  Morton Grove *(G-14420)*
Liqua Fit Inc ....D 630 965-8067
  Grayslake *(G-10787)*
Mead Johnson Nutrition Company ...C 312 466-5800
  Chicago *(G-5379)*
Meadowvale Inc ....E 630 553-0202
  Sandwich *(G-18377)*
◆ Milk Products Holdings N Amer ...E 847 928-1600
  Rosemont *(G-18036)*
MSI Green Inc ....G 312 421-6550
  Chicago *(G-5519)*
Nestle Usa Inc ....C 309 263-2651
  Morton *(G-14374)*
Nestle Usa Inc ....C 217 243-9175
  Jacksonville *(G-11778)*
Nestle Usa Inc ....C 815 754-2550
  Dekalb *(G-7694)*
Nestle Usa Inc ....C 309 829-1031
  Bloomington *(G-2083)*
Rich Products Corporation ....D 847 581-1749
  Niles *(G-15165)*
Saasoom LLC ....G 630 561-7300
  Saint Charles *(G-18263)*
Salud Natural Entrepreneur Inc .....E 224 789-7400
  Waukegan *(G-20491)*
◆ Salud Natural Entrepreneur Inc ...E 224 789-7400
  Waukegan *(G-20492)*
Santa Cruz Holdings LLC ....G 217 821-0304
  Effingham *(G-8424)*
◆ Treehouse Foods Inc ....C 708 483-1300
  Oak Brook *(G-15665)*
Vital Proteins LLC ....E 224 544-9110
  Chicago *(G-6562)*

2024 Ice Cream

A&W Stone Masonry LLC ....G 618 499-7239
  Harrisburg *(G-11019)*
Al Gelato Chicago LLC ....G 847 455-5355
  Franklin Park *(G-9864)*
Amani Froyo LLC ....G 941 744-1111
  Oakbrook Terrace *(G-15782)*
Baldwin Richardson Foods Co .....G 815 464-9994
  Oakbrook Terrace *(G-15787)*
Creamery Inc ....G 708 479-5706
  Mokena *(G-14077)*
Deja Investments Inc ....D 630 408-9222
  Bolingbrook *(G-2168)*
Delicious Treats LLC ....G 618 410-6722
  East Saint Louis *(G-8303)*
Dianas Bananas Inc ....F 773 638-6800
  Chicago *(G-4353)*
Five Star Desserts and Foods ......G 773 375-5100
  Chicago *(G-4599)*
Gayety Candy Co Inc ....E 708 418-0062
  Lansing *(G-12494)*
Genes Ice Cream Inc ....G 309 846-5925
  Bloomington *(G-2051)*
Gregs Frozen Custard Company ...G 847 837-4175
  Mundelein *(G-14692)*
Gyood ....G 773 360-8810
  Chicago *(G-4754)*
Hershey Creamery Company ....F 708 339-4656
  South Holland *(G-19220)*
Homers Ice Cream Inc ....E 847 251-0477
  Wilmette *(G-21078)*
Icream Group LLC ....G 773 342-2834
  Chicago *(G-4873)*
◆ Jel Sert Co ....C 630 231-7590
  West Chicago *(G-20603)*

Kent Precision Foods Group Inc ...E 630 226-0071
  Bolingbrook *(G-2201)*
Lezza Spumoni and Desserts Inc ...E 708 547-5969
  Bellwood *(G-1631)*
Los Mangos ....G 773 542-1522
  Chicago *(G-5262)*
Los Mangos ....G 815 630-2611
  Crest Hill *(G-7091)*
ME and Gia Inc ....G 708 583-1111
  Elmwood Park *(G-9454)*
Mitchlls Cndies Ice Creams Inc ....F 708 799-3835
  Homewood *(G-11501)*
Muller-Pinehurst Dairy Inc ....C 815 968-0441
  Rockford *(G-17533)*
Neveria Michoacana LLC ....G 630 783-3518
  Bolingbrook *(G-2220)*
▲ Paleteria Azteca Inc ....G 773 277-1423
  Chicago *(G-5746)*
Paleteria Carrucel ....G 773 310-5749
  Chicago *(G-5747)*
Paleteria El Sabor ....G 312 243-2308
  Chicago *(G-5748)*
Paleteria El Sabor De Michoacn ...G 773 376-3880
  Chicago *(G-5749)*
▲ Profile Food Ingredients LLC ......E 847 622-1700
  Elgin *(G-8697)*
Richards Sper Prmium Ice Cream ...F 773 614-8999
  Chicago *(G-6026)*
Roesers Bakery ....E 773 489-6900
  Chicago *(G-6050)*
Sisler Dairy Products Company ....G 815 376-2913
  Ohio *(G-15845)*
Union Foods Inc ....G 201 327-2828
  Chicago *(G-6465)*
Viola Ice Cream Shoppe ....G 309 596-2131
  Viola *(G-20183)*
We Love Soy Inc ....G 630 629-9667
  Addison *(G-332)*

2026 Milk

Bay Valley Foods LLC ....D 815 239-2631
  Pecatonica *(G-16321)*
Berner Food & Beverage LLC ......B 815 563-4222
  Dakota *(G-7311)*
Berner Food & Beverage LLC ......E 815 865-5136
  Rock City *(G-17174)*
Chester Dairy Company Inc ....F 618 826-2394
  Chester *(G-3452)*
Chester Dairy Company Inc ....G 618 826-2395
  Chester *(G-3453)*
Dean Dairy Fluid LLC ....D 815 490-5578
  Rockford *(G-17371)*
Dean Dairy Fluid LLC ....G 815 943-7375
  Harvard *(G-11052)*
Dean Dairy Fluid LLC ....G 847 669-5508
  Huntley *(G-11534)*
Dean Dairy Fluid LLC ....G 217 428-6726
  Decatur *(G-7483)*
Dean Dairy Ice Cream LLC ....G 815 544-2105
  Belvidere *(G-1665)*
Dean Dairy Ice Cream LLC ....G 937 323-5777
  Franklin Park *(G-9927)*
Dean Dairy Ice Cream LLC ....E 630 879-0800
  Batavia *(G-1372)*
Dean Food Products Company .....E 847 678-1680
  Franklin Park *(G-9928)*
Deja Investments Inc ....D 630 408-9222
  Bolingbrook *(G-2168)*
Douglas Graybill ....G 815 218-1749
  Freeport *(G-10106)*
East Side Jersey Dairy Inc ....E 217 854-2547
  Carlinville *(G-2873)*
East Side Jersey Dairy Inc ....G 662 289-3344
  Edwardsville *(G-8358)*
Erie Group International Inc ....D 309 659-2233
  Rochelle *(G-17139)*
◆ Gametime Snacks LLC ....E 309 517-6342
  Milan *(G-14011)*
Kraft Heinz Foods Company ....D 217 378-1900
  Champaign *(G-3315)*
▲ Lifeway Foods Inc ....C 847 967-1010
  Morton Grove *(G-14420)*
Lulus Real Froyo ....G 630 299-3854
  Aurora *(G-999)*
Maple Hill Creamery LLC ....E 518 758-7777
  Deerfield *(G-7635)*
Midwest Ice Cream Company LLC ...F 815 544-2105
  Belvidere *(G-1687)*
Muller-Pinehurst Dairy Inc ....C 815 968-0441
  Rockford *(G-17533)*

SIC SECTION

20 FOOD AND KINDRED PRODUCTS

Oberweis Dairy Inc ....F 847 368-9060
  Arlington Heights (G-782)
Oberweis Dairy Inc ....E 630 906-6455
  Oswego (G-16017)
Oberweis Dairy Inc ....E 708 660-1350
  Oak Park (G-15767)
Oberweis Dairy Inc ....F 630 782-0141
  Elmhurst (G-9407)
Oberweis Dairy Inc ....F 847 290-9222
  Rolling Meadows (G-17757)
Oberweis Dairy Inc ....E 630 801-6100
  Glen Ellyn (G-10415)
Prairie Farms Dairy Inc ....G 618 451-5600
  Granite City (G-10730)
Prairie Farms Dairy Inc ....E 618 457-4167
  Carbondale (G-2854)
Rich Products Corporation ....D 847 581-1749
  Niles (G-15165)
▲ Socius Ingredients LLC ....F 847 440-0156
  Evanston (G-9575)

2032 Canned Specialties

AA Superb Food Corporation ....E 773 927-3233
  Chicago (G-3497)
▲ Alm Distributors LLC ....G 708 865-8000
  Melrose Park (G-13823)
Archer-Daniels-Midland Company ..E 309 772-2141
  Bushnell (G-2737)
Castro Foods Wholesale Inc ....E 773 869-0641
  Chicago (G-4038)
Earthgrains ....G 630 859-8782
  North Aurora (G-15259)
▲ Essen Nutrition Corporation ......E 630 739-6700
  Romeoville (G-17817)
Henkel Consumer Goods Inc ....C 630 892-4381
  Montgomery (G-14246)
▲ Hop Kee Incorporated ....E 312 791-9111
  Chicago (G-4839)
Kraft Heinz Foods Company ....G 412 456-5700
  Chicago (G-5130)
Kraft Heinz Foods Company ....C 847 291-3900
  Northbrook (G-15415)
Lee Gilster-Mary Corporation ....D 618 965-3426
  Steeleville (G-19481)
▲ Lightlife Foods Inc ....C 413 774-9000
  Elmhurst (G-9392)
Lpz Inc ....G 773 579-6120
  Chicago (G-5271)
▲ Lynfred Winery Inc ....E 630 529-9463
  Roselle (G-17965)
McShares Inc ....E 217 762-2561
  Monticello (G-14281)
Mexico Enterprise Corporation ....G 920 568-8900
  Chicago (G-5415)
Nogi Brands LLC ....G 312 371-7974
  Willowbrook (G-21054)
Nurture Life Inc ....E 312 517-1888
  Chicago (G-5642)
Ole Mexican Foods Inc ....E 708 458-3296
  Bedford Park (G-1487)
Pastorelli Food Products Inc ....G 312 455-1006
  Chicago (G-5770)
◆ Quay Corporation Inc ....F 847 676-4233
  Lincolnwood (G-12836)
Sofrito Foods LLC ....G 224 535-9252
  North Aurora (G-15275)
Supalicious Soups Inc ....G 708 491-9738
  Chicago (G-6279)
Supreme Tamale Co ....G 773 622-3777
  Elk Grove Village (G-9261)
Tom Tom Tamales Mfg Co Inc ....F 773 523-9675
  Chicago (G-6387)
◆ Treehouse Foods Inc ....C 708 483-1300
  Oak Brook (G-15665)
▲ Vanee Foods Company ....D 708 449-7300
  Berkeley (G-1945)

2033 Canned Fruits, Vegetables & Preserves

▲ 78 Brand Co ....G 312 344-1602
  Chicago (G-3479)
Andrias Food Group Inc ....G 618 632-3118
  O Fallon (G-15566)
Andrias Food Group Inc ....E 618 632-4866
  O Fallon (G-15565)
Bear-Stewart Corporation ....E 773 276-0400
  Chicago (G-3854)
Berner Food & Beverage LLC ....B 815 563-4222
  Dakota (G-7311)
Campbell Soup Company ....G 618 548-3001
  Salem (G-18333)

Campbell Soup Company ....C 630 241-6200
  Downers Grove (G-7964)
Clearly Kosher Foods ....F 630 546-2052
  Aurora (G-1076)
Del Monte Foods Inc ....G 309 968-7033
  Manito (G-13437)
Dingo Inc ....G 217 868-5615
  Effingham (G-8395)
Fast Technologies Corp ....G 815 234-4744
  Oregon (G-15920)
Florida Fruit Juices Inc ....E 773 586-6200
  Chicago (G-4611)
Fresh Factory ....E 630 580-9038
  Carol Stream (G-2988)
General Mills Inc ....G 815 544-7399
  Belvidere (G-1671)
Ginas Jams ....G 773 622-1051
  Chicago (G-4692)
H J M P Corp ....C 708 345-5370
  Melrose Park (G-13877)
Here Holdings LLC ....G 563 723-1008
  Carol Stream (G-2997)
Hooray Puree Inc ....G 312 515-0266
  Park Ridge (G-16284)
Iya Foods LLC ....G 630 854-7107
  North Aurora (G-15264)
◆ Juice Tyme Inc ....F 773 579-1291
  Chicago (G-5058)
Key Colony Inc ....G 630 783-8572
  Lemont (G-12568)
Korinek & Co Inc ....G 708 652-2870
  Cicero (G-6860)
Kraft Heinz Foods Company ....C 847 291-3900
  Northbrook (G-15415)
Kraft Heinz Foods Company ....C 847 646-3690
  Glenview (G-10581)
Kraft Heinz Foods Company ....E 630 505-0170
  Lisle (G-12907)
Kraft Heinz Foods Company ....B 815 338-7000
  Woodstock (G-21401)
Kraft Heinz Receivables LLC ....C 847 646-2000
  Glenview (G-5131)
Kuntry Kettle ....G 618 426-1600
  Ava (G-1173)
La Tropicana Inc ....G 773 476-1107
  Chicago (G-5150)
▼ Lawrence Foods Inc ....C 847 437-2400
  Elk Grove Village (G-9088)
Legacy Foods Mfg LLC ....F 847 595-9106
  Elk Grove Village (G-9091)
▲ Lynfred Winery Inc ....E 630 529-9463
  Roselle (G-17965)
Mancuso Cheese Company ....F 815 722-2475
  Joliet (G-11897)
Margies Brands Inc ....G 773 643-1417
  Chicago (G-5332)
Millers Country Crafts Inc ....G 618 426-3108
  Ava (G-1175)
MSI Green Inc ....G 312 421-6550
  Chicago (G-5519)
Mullen Foods LLC ....G 773 716-9001
  Chicago (G-5522)
Mullins Food Products Inc ....B 708 344-3224
  Broadview (G-2455)
Nation Pizza Products LP ....A 847 397-3320
  Schaumburg (G-18644)
Odwalla Inc ....E 773 687-8667
  Chicago (G-5656)
Pappone Inc ....G 630 234-4738
  Chicago (G-5754)
Pastorelli Food Products Inc ....G 312 455-1006
  Chicago (G-5770)
Planks Apple Butter ....G 217 268-4933
  Arcola (G-662)
▼ R&B Foods Inc ....G 847 590-0059
  Mount Prospect (G-14564)
Rana Meal Solutions LLC ....E 630 581-4100
  Bartlett (G-1303)
▲ Rana Meal Solutions LLC ....B 630 581-4100
  Oak Brook (G-15659)
Russo Wholesale Meat Inc ....G 708 385-0500
  Alsip (G-507)
Seneca Foods Corporation ....E 309 385-4301
  Princeville (G-16829)
Seneca Foods Corporation ....D 309 545-2233
  Manito (G-13439)
Simply Salsa LLC ....G 815 514-3993
  Homer Glen (G-11486)
◆ Sokol and Company ....D 708 482-8250
  Countryside (G-7071)

Split Nutrition LLC ....G 855 775-4801
  Chicago (G-6217)
Stable Foods Inc ....F 773 793-2547
  Chicago (G-6225)
Stewart Ingridents Systems Inc .....F 312 254-3539
  Chicago (G-6248)
◆ Treehouse Foods Inc ....C 708 483-1300
  Oak Brook (G-15665)
▲ V Formusa Co ....F 224 938-9360
  Des Plaines (G-7863)
▲ Vegetable Juices Inc ....D 708 924-9500
  Bedford Park (G-1509)
Wisconsin Wilderness Food Pdts ..G 847 735-8661
  Lake Forest (G-12323)

2034 Dried Fruits, Vegetables & Soup

Ali VS Kitchen LLC ....G 312 852-5090
  Chicago (G-3606)
Bernard Food Industries Inc ....D 847 869-5222
  Evanston (G-9499)
Biovie Inc ....G 978 998-4756
  Chicago (G-3898)
Bran-Zan Holdings LLC ....F 847 342-0000
  Arlington Heights (G-708)
Chef Lmt Foods LLC ....E 847 279-6490
  Arlington Heights (G-714)
Custom Culinary Inc ....D 630 928-4898
  Lombard (G-13061)
Grandma Mauds Inc ....G 773 493-5353
  Chicago (G-4723)
▼ Graziano TI Inc ....E 847 741-1900
  Elgin (G-8600)
Handcut Foods LLC ....G 312 239-0381
  Chicago (G-4776)
◆ Hot Mexican Peppers Inc ....G 773 843-9774
  Chicago (G-4847)
◆ Karlin Foods Corp ....F 847 441-8330
  Northfield (G-15519)
Kent Precision Foods Group Inc ....E 630 226-0071
  Bolingbrook (G-2201)
Kent Precision Foods Group Inc ....F 630 226-0071
  Bolingbrook (G-2202)
▲ Lightlife Foods Inc ....C 413 774-9000
  Elmhurst (G-9392)
Noon Hour Food Products Inc ....E 312 382-1177
  Chicago (G-5612)
Pknd Llc ....G 773 491-0070
  Chicago (G-5816)
◆ R J Van Drunen & Sons Inc ....G 815 472-3100
  Momence (G-14191)
R J Van Drunen & Sons Inc ....E 830 422-2167
  Momence (G-14192)
R J Van Drunen & Sons Inc ....D 815 472-3211
  Momence (G-14193)
Red Rumi LLC ....G 847 757-8433
  Algonquin (G-387)
Sono Italiano Corporation ....G 817 472-8903
  Manteno (G-13456)
Swiss Products LP ....E 773 394-6480
  Chicago (G-6297)
TEC Foods Inc ....E 800 315-8002
  Chicago (G-6333)
▲ Vanee Foods Company ....D 708 449-7300
  Berkeley (G-1945)
◆ Woodland Foods Ltd ....C 847 625-8600
  Waukegan (G-20519)

2035 Pickled Fruits, Vegetables, Sauces & Dressings

Andrias Food Group Inc ....G 618 632-3118
  O Fallon (G-15566)
Andrias Food Group Inc ....E 618 632-4866
  O Fallon (G-15565)
Arts Tamales ....G 309 367-2850
  Metamora (G-13958)
Boetje Foods Inc ....G 309 788-4352
  Rock Island (G-17208)
Cains Foods Inc ....D 978 772-0300
  Oak Brook (G-15604)
▼ Earthgrains Refrigertd Dough P ..A 630 455-5200
  Downers Grove (G-7996)
▲ Essen Nutrition Corporation ......E 630 739-6700
  Romeoville (G-17817)
Fgfi LLC ....E 708 598-0909
  Countryside (G-7052)
Flaherty Incorporated ....G 773 472-8456
  Skokie (G-18955)
Foods & Things Inc ....G 618 526-4478
  Breese (G-2303)

Employee Codes: A=Over 500 employees, B=251-500
C=101-250, D=51-100, E=20-50, F=10-19, G=3-9

20 FOOD AND KINDRED PRODUCTS SIC SECTION

Fournie Farms Inc E 618 344-8527
Collinsville *(G-6961)*

▲ **Hop Kee Incorporated** E 312 791-9111
Chicago *(G-4839)*

Kathys Kitchen LLC G 217 452-3035
Virginia *(G-20194)*

Kent Precision Foods Group Inc F 630 226-0071
Bolingbrook *(G-2202)*

Kosto Food Products Company F 847 487-2600
Wauconda *(G-20367)*

Kraft Foods Asia PCF Svcs LLC G 847 943-4000
Deerfield *(G-7627)*

Kraft Heinz Company C 847 646-2000
Chicago *(G-5129)*

Kraft Heinz Foods Company B 815 338-7000
Woodstock *(G-21401)*

Kraft Heinz Foods Company D 217 378-1900
Champaign *(G-3315)*

Legacy Foods Mfg LLC F 847 595-9106
Elk Grove Village *(G-9091)*

◆ **Mizkan America Inc** E 847 590-0059
Mount Prospect *(G-14547)*

◆ **Mondelez International Inc** A 847 943-4000
Chicago *(G-5490)*

Mullins Food Products Inc B 708 344-3224
Broadview *(G-2455)*

New Specialty Products Inc E 773 847-0230
Chicago *(G-5579)*

North Star Pickle LLC F 847 970-5555
Lake Zurich *(G-12439)*

▲ **Pastafresh Co** G 773 745-5888
Chicago *(G-5769)*

Plochman Inc E 815 468-3434
Manteno *(G-13454)*

Simply Salsa LLC G 815 514-3993
Homer Glen *(G-11486)*

◆ **Treehouse Foods Inc** C 708 483-1300
Oak Brook *(G-15665)*

Treehouse Private Brands Inc F 630 455-5265
Downers Grove *(G-8102)*

◆ **Treehouse Private Brands Inc** C 314 877-7300
Oak Brook *(G-15666)*

▲ **V Formusa Co** F 224 938-9360
Des Plaines *(G-7863)*

▼ **Vienna Beef Ltd** E 773 278-7800
Chicago *(G-6548)*

Wisconsin Wilderness Food Pdts G 847 735-8661
Lake Forest *(G-12323)*

2037 Frozen Fruits, Juices & Vegetables

Citrus Systems G 608 271-3000
Downers Grove *(G-7971)*

Dulce Vida Juice Bar LLC G 224 236-5045
Hanover Park *(G-11002)*

Fresh Factory E 630 580-9038
Carol Stream *(G-2988)*

General Mills Inc E 815 544-7399
Belvidere *(G-1671)*

▲ **Greenwood Associates Inc** F 847 579-5500
Niles *(G-15127)*

H J M P Corp C 708 345-5370
Melrose Park *(G-13877)*

Here Holdings LLC G 563 723-1008
Carol Stream *(G-2997)*

J J Mata Inc G 773 750-0643
Chicago *(G-4991)*

◆ **Juice Tyme Inc** F 773 579-1291
Chicago *(G-5058)*

Key Colony Inc G 630 783-8572
Lemont *(G-12568)*

Kraft Heinz Foods Company C 847 291-3900
Northbrook *(G-15415)*

Lawlor Marketing G 847 357-1080
Arlington Heights *(G-767)*

Lx/Jt Intermediate Holdings G 773 369-2652
Chicago *(G-5291)*

▲ **Mautino Distributing Co Inc** E 815 664-4311
Spring Valley *(G-19310)*

◆ **McCain Foods Usa Inc** B 630 955-0400
Oakbrook Terrace *(G-15807)*

McCain Foods Usa Inc B 920 563-6625
Oakbrook Terrace *(G-15808)*

▼ **McCain Usa Inc** C 800 938-7799
Oakbrook Terrace *(G-15809)*

Natural Distribution Company G 630 350-1700
Wood Dale *(G-21219)*

NGL Crude Logistics LLC F 618 274-4306
Sauget *(G-18396)*

Premier Beverage Solutions LLC G 309 369-7117
East Peoria *(G-8284)*

R J Van Drunen & Sons Inc D 815 472-3211
Momence *(G-14193)*

◆ **R J Van Drunen & Sons Inc** D 815 472-3100
Momence *(G-14191)*

R J Van Drunen & Sons Inc E 830 422-2167
Momence *(G-14192)*

Shady Creek Vineyard Inc G 847 275-7979
Palatine *(G-16157)*

2038 Frozen Specialties

A New Dairy Company E 312 421-1234
Chicago *(G-3489)*

Afs Classico LLC E 309 786-8833
Rock Island *(G-17200)*

Ajinomoto Foods North Amer Inc F 815 452-2559
Toluca *(G-19885)*

Aryzta LLC C 815 306-7171
Romeoville *(G-17796)*

Avanti Foods Company E 815 379-2155
Walnut *(G-20216)*

Balton Corporation F 773 933-7927
Chicago *(G-3822)*

▲ **Biagios Gourmet Foods Inc** E 708 867-4641
Chicago *(G-3880)*

Campbell Soup Company G 618 548-3001
Salem *(G-18333)*

Campbell Soup Company C 630 241-6200
Downers Grove *(G-7964)*

Champion Foods LLC G 815 648-2725
Hebron *(G-11140)*

Chateau Food Products Inc F 708 863-4207
Chicago *(G-4079)*

Conagra Brands Inc C 312 549-5000
Chicago *(G-4212)*

Conagra Brands Inc C 630 857-1000
Naperville *(G-14803)*

▲ **Danziger Kosher Catering Inc** E 847 982-1818
Chicago *(G-4316)*

▼ **Distinctive Foods LLC** D 847 459-3600
Wheeling *(G-20879)*

Distinctive Foods LLC E 847 459-3600
Bensenville *(G-1787)*

Doreens Pizza Inc F 708 862-7499
Calumet City *(G-2775)*

General Mills Inc E 815 544-7399
Belvidere *(G-1671)*

General Mills Green Giant G 815 547-5311
Belvidere *(G-1672)*

Givaudan Flavors Corporation C 630 682-5600
Carol Stream *(G-2992)*

Globus Food Products LLC G 847 378-8221
Elk Grove Village *(G-9018)*

▲ **Gonnella Baking Co** D 312 733-2020
Schaumburg *(G-18538)*

▼ **Hearthside Food Solutions LLC** E 630 967-3600
Downers Grove *(G-8019)*

▲ **Heartland Harvest Inc** G 815 932-2100
Kankakee *(G-11975)*

Herman Seekamp Inc C 630 628-6555
Addison *(G-149)*

Home Run Inn Frozen Foods Corp D 630 783-9696
Woodridge *(G-21314)*

▲ **Italia Foods Inc** E 847 397-4479
Schaumburg *(G-18573)*

Kraft Heinz Foods Company C 847 291-3900
Northbrook *(G-15415)*

Lezza Spumoni and Desserts Inc E 708 547-5969
Bellwood *(G-1631)*

Little Lady Foods Inc C 847 806-1440
Elk Grove Village *(G-9096)*

Lucrezia LLC G 630 263-0088
Naperville *(G-14866)*

Luvo Usa LLC E 847 485-8595
Schaumburg *(G-18613)*

Luvo Usa LLC E 847 485-8595
Schaumburg *(G-18614)*

McCain Foods Usa Inc B 920 563-6625
Oakbrook Terrace *(G-15808)*

▼ **McCain Usa Inc** C 800 938-7799
Oakbrook Terrace *(G-15809)*

Mondelez Intl Holdings LLC F 800 572-3847
Deerfield *(G-7638)*

Nation Pizza Products LP A 847 397-3320
Schaumburg *(G-18644)*

▼ **Nestle Pizza Company Inc** E 847 646-2000
Glenview *(G-10593)*

Nestle Prepared Foods Company B 630 671-3721
Glendale Heights *(G-10478)*

O Chilli Frozen Foods Inc E 847 562-1991
Northbrook *(G-15442)*

▲ **On-Cor Frozen Foods LLC** E 630 851-6600
Aurora *(G-1142)*

Open Kitchens Inc E 312 666-5334
Chicago *(G-5681)*

◆ **Paani Foods Inc** F 312 420-4624
Chicago *(G-5734)*

Pinnacle Foods Group LLC C 731 343-4995
Centralia *(G-3244)*

Pinnacle Foods Group LLC B 618 829-3275
Saint Elmo *(G-18311)*

Preziosio Ltd F 630 393-0920
Warrenville *(G-20249)*

RCM Smith Inc F 309 786-8833
Rock Island *(G-17239)*

Reggios Pizza Inc D 773 933-7927
Chicago *(G-6004)*

Smh2 Manufacturing LLC G 773 793-6643
Chicago *(G-6191)*

Supreme Tamale Co G 773 622-3777
Elk Grove Village *(G-9261)*

Teresa Foods Inc F 708 258-6200
Peotone *(G-16558)*

WEI-Chuan USA Inc F 708 352-8886
Hodgkins *(G-11401)*

2041 Flour, Grain Milling

ADM Grain Company E 217 424-5200
Decatur *(G-7432)*

▲ **Agritech Worldwide Inc** F 847 549-6002
Mundelein *(G-14660)*

American Milling Company F 309 347-6888
Pekin *(G-16323)*

Archer-Daniels-Midland Company G 217 764-3345
Macon *(G-13404)*

Archer-Daniels-Midland Company D 217 424-5882
Decatur *(G-7441)*

Archer-Daniels-Midland Company G 217 451-8909
Decatur *(G-7442)*

Archer-Daniels-Midland Company G 618 238-4800
Edgewood *(G-8334)*

Archer-Daniels-Midland Company G 217 424-5236
Decatur *(G-7443)*

Archer-Daniels-Midland Company C 309 673-7828
Peoria *(G-16385)*

Archer-Daniels-Midland Company G 815 428-7513
Martinton *(G-13589)*

Archer-Daniels-Midland Company G 217 419-5100
Champaign *(G-3267)*

Archer-Daniels-Midland Company B 800 257-5743
Decatur *(G-7444)*

Archer-Daniels-Midland Company G 618 483-6171
Altamont *(G-530)*

Archer-Daniels-Midland Company E 309 772-2141
Bushnell *(G-2737)*

Archer-Daniels-Midland Company E 309 699-9581
Creve Coeur *(G-7148)*

Archer-Daniels-Midland Company G 815 384-4011
Rochelle *(G-17132)*

Archer-Daniels-Midland Company G 815 857-2058
Amboy *(G-579)*

Archer-Daniels-Midland Company G 217 676-3811
Mount Auburn *(G-14464)*

Archer-Daniels-Midland Company G 217 424-5806
Decatur *(G-7445)*

Archer-Daniels-Midland Company F 217 451-4460
Decatur *(G-7446)*

Archer-Daniels-Midland Company E 217 424-5413
Decatur *(G-7447)*

Archer-Daniels-Midland Company G 217 228-0805
Quincy *(G-16855)*

Archer-Daniels-Midland Company D 217 424-5200
Decatur *(G-7448)*

Archer-Daniels-Midland Company G 217 754-3300
Meredosia *(G-13955)*

Archer-Daniels-Midland Company G 815 538-3771
Mendota *(G-13936)*

Archer-Daniels-Midland Company C 217 424-5200
Decatur *(G-7449)*

Archer-Daniels-Midland Company E 217 424-5830
Decatur *(G-7450)*

Archer-Daniels-Midland Company D 217 451-8169
Decatur *(G-7451)*

Archer-Daniels-Midland Company G 815 539-6219
Mendota *(G-13937)*

Archer-Daniels-Midland Company G 815 692-2324
Fairbury *(G-9603)*

Archer-Daniels-Midland Company F 815 223-7907
Peru *(G-16566)*

Archer-Daniels-Midland Company E 217 424-5660
Decatur *(G-7452)*

SIC SECTION   20 FOOD AND KINDRED PRODUCTS

Archer-Daniels-Midland Company ....E 217 424-5858
Decatur *(G-7453)*
Archer-Daniels-Midland Company ....G 217 887-2514
Hume *(G-11526)*
Archer-Daniels-Midland Company ....E 217 224-1800
Quincy *(G-16856)*
Archer-Daniels-Midland Company ....F 815 459-1600
Crystal Lake *(G-7162)*
▼ Archer-Daniels-Midland Company ...G 217 429-3054
Decatur *(G-7454)*
Archer-Daniels-Midland Company ....D 217 424-5785
Decatur *(G-7455)*
Archer-Daniels-Midland Company ....E 217 224-1800
Quincy *(G-16857)*
Archer-Daniels-Midland Company ....G 618 432-7194
Patoka *(G-16302)*
Archer-Daniels-Midland Company ....F 217 451-4481
Decatur *(G-7456)*
Archer-Daniels-Midland Company ....B 217 451-6528
Decatur *(G-7457)*
Archer-Daniels-Midland Company ....G 217 423-2788
Decatur *(G-7458)*
Archer-Daniels-Midland Company ....D 217 224-1875
Quincy *(G-16858)*
Archer-Daniels-Midland Company ....D 217 424-5200
Decatur *(G-7459)*
Archer-Daniels-Midland Company ....F 217 424-5669
Decatur *(G-7460)*
◆ Archer-Daniels-Midland Company ...A 312 634-8100
Chicago *(G-3728)*
Ardent Mills LLC ....E 618 826-2371
Chester *(G-3449)*
Balton Corporation ....F 773 933-7927
Chicago *(G-3822)*
Bio Fuels By American Farmers ....F 561 859-6251
Benton *(G-1921)*
▼ Cargill Dry Corn Ingrdents Inc ....G 217 465-5331
Paris *(G-16226)*
▼ Dix-Mcguire Commodities - LLC ....G 847 496-5320
Palatine *(G-16112)*
▼ Earthgrains Refrigertd Dough P ....A 630 455-5200
Downers Grove *(G-7996)*
General Mills Inc ....E 309 342-9165
Galesburg *(G-10197)*
Hayden Mills Inc ....E 618 962-3136
Omaha *(G-15900)*
▲ J R Short Milling Company ....C 800 544-8734
Kankakee *(G-11979)*
J R Short Milling Company ....C 815 937-2633
Kankakee *(G-11980)*
Kws Cereals Usa LLC ....G 815 200-2666
Champaign *(G-3316)*
▲ LLC Urban Farmer ....D 815 468-7200
Manteno *(G-13451)*
McShares Inc ....E 217 762-2561
Monticello *(G-14281)*
Mennel Milling Co ....F 217 999-2161
Mount Olive *(G-14506)*
Natures American Co ....G 630 246-4274
Chicago *(G-5553)*
Nauvoo Mill & Bakery ....G 217 453-6734
Nauvoo *(G-15014)*
▼ New Alliance Production LLC ....E 309 928-3123
Farmer City *(G-9656)*
Pillsbury Company LLC ....G 847 541-8888
Buffalo Grove *(G-2586)*
Problend-Eurogerm LLC ....G 847 221-5004
Rolling Meadows *(G-17767)*
Quaker Oats Company ....A 217 443-4995
Danville *(G-7375)*
Ron & Pats Pizza Shack ....G 847 395-5005
Antioch *(G-633)*
Roquette America Inc ....F 630 232-2157
Geneva *(G-10304)*
◆ Salud Natural Entrepreneur Inc ....E 224 789-7400
Waukegan *(G-20492)*
▲ Sunrise Distributors Inc ....G 630 400-8786
Elk Grove Village *(G-9259)*
TEC Foods Inc ....E 800 315-8002
Chicago *(G-6333)*
Temperance Beer Company LLC ....G 847 864-1000
Evanston *(G-9583)*
▼ U S Soy LLC ....F 217 235-1020
Mattoon *(G-13655)*

2043 Cereal Breakfast Foods

▲ Clover US Holdings LLC ....D 630 967-3600
Downers Grove *(G-7975)*
General Mills Inc ....D 630 844-1125
Montgomery *(G-14244)*
General Mills Inc ....B 630 231-1140
Calumet City *(G-2778)*
General Mills Operations LLC ....G 630 844-1125
Montgomery *(G-14245)*
◆ Gilster-Mary Lee Corporation ....A 618 826-2361
Chester *(G-3456)*
▼ Hearthside Food Solutions LLC ....E 630 967-3600
Downers Grove *(G-8019)*
Kellogg Company ....B 773 254-0900
Chicago *(G-5090)*
Kellogg Company ....F 217 258-3251
Mattoon *(G-13640)*
Kellogg Company ....G 773 995-7200
Chicago *(G-5091)*
Kraft Foods Asia PCF Svcs LLC ....G 847 943-4000
Deerfield *(G-7627)*
Kraft Heinz Company ....C 847 646-2000
Chicago *(G-5129)*
Kws Cereals Usa LLC ....G 815 200-2666
Champaign *(G-3316)*
Lee Gilster-Mary Corporation ....E 618 826-2361
Chester *(G-3457)*
Lee Gilster-Mary Corporation ....E 618 443-5676
Sparta *(G-19256)*
◆ Mary Lee Packaging Corporation ....E 618 826-2361
Chester *(G-3458)*
Mondelez Global LLC ....B 630 369-1909
Naperville *(G-14874)*
Mondelez International Inc ....G 815 710-2114
Morris *(G-14316)*
◆ Mondelez International Inc ....A 847 943-4000
Chicago *(G-5490)*
◆ Quaker Oats Company ....A 312 821-1000
Chicago *(G-5927)*
Quaker Oats Company ....A 217 443-4995
Danville *(G-7375)*
Quaker Oats Europe Inc ....G 312 821-1000
Chicago *(G-5928)*
Ralston Food Sales Inc ....G 314 877-7000
Oak Brook *(G-15658)*
Treehouse Private Brands Inc ....F 630 455-5265
Downers Grove *(G-8102)*
◆ Treehouse Private Brands Inc ....C 314 877-7300
Oak Brook *(G-15666)*

2044 Rice Milling

Grandma Mauds Inc ....G 773 493-5353
Chicago *(G-4723)*
◆ International Golden Foods Inc ....F 630 860-5552
Bensenville *(G-1823)*

2045 Flour, Blended & Prepared

Arro Corporation ....E 708 352-7412
Hodgkins *(G-11385)*
Arro Corporation ....C 708 352-8200
Hodgkins *(G-11384)*
Arro Corporation ....G 773 978-1251
Chicago *(G-3733)*
Bear-Stewart Corporation ....E 773 276-0400
Chicago *(G-3854)*
Brolite Products Incorporated ....E 630 830-0340
Bartlett *(G-1270)*
Continental Mills Inc ....F 800 426-0955
Chicago *(G-4229)*
Continental Mills Inc ....C 217 540-4000
Effingham *(G-8392)*
Dawn Food Products Inc ....E 815 468-6286
Manteno *(G-13446)*
Diversfied Ill Green Works LLC ....D 773 544-7777
Chicago *(G-4369)*
Dominos Pizza LLC ....G 630 783-0738
Woodridge *(G-21295)*
▲ Dunbar Systems Inc ....E 630 257-2900
Lemont *(G-12563)*
Fleetchem LLC ....F 708 957-5311
Flossmoor *(G-9698)*
◆ Gilster-Mary Lee Corporation ....A 618 826-2361
Chester *(G-3456)*
Inside Beverages ....C 847 438-1338
Lake Zurich *(G-12423)*
▲ Joshi Brothers Inc ....E 847 895-0200
Schaumburg *(G-18578)*
Kerry Inc ....D 708 450-3260
Melrose Park *(G-13888)*
Lee Gilster-Mary Corporation ....D 618 965-3426
Steeleville *(G-19481)*
Lee Gilster-Mary Corporation ....E 618 826-2361
Chester *(G-3457)*
Lee Gilster-Mary Corporation ....E 618 443-5676
Sparta *(G-19256)*
Lee Gilster-Mary Corporation ....D 815 472-6456
Momence *(G-14186)*
Loders Croklaan BV ....C 815 730-5200
Channahon *(G-3386)*
Nation Pizza Products LP ....A 847 397-3320
Schaumburg *(G-18644)*
Parke & Son Inc ....G 217 875-0572
Decatur *(G-7535)*
◆ Quaker Oats Company ....A 312 821-1000
Chicago *(G-5927)*
Quaker Oats Europe Inc ....G 312 821-1000
Chicago *(G-5928)*
Russo Wholesale Meat Inc ....G 708 385-0500
Alsip *(G-507)*
Watson Foods Co Inc ....D 847 245-8404
Lindenhurst *(G-12855)*
Watson LLC ....E 217 824-4440
Taylorville *(G-19763)*

2046 Wet Corn Milling

ADM Holdings LLC ....G 217 422-7281
Decatur *(G-7433)*
ADM Holdings LLC ....G 312 634-8100
Chicago *(G-3548)*
◆ ADM Holdings LLC ....G 217 424-5200
Decatur *(G-7434)*
▼ Archer-Daniels-Midland Company ...A 312 634-8100
Chicago *(G-3728)*
Bio Fuels By American Farmers ....F 561 859-6251
Benton *(G-1921)*
Cargill Incorporated ....E 630 505-7788
Chicago *(G-4031)*
Enjoy Life Natural Brands LLC ....E 773 632-2163
Chicago *(G-4511)*
Gro Alliance LLC ....G 217 792-3355
Mount Pulaski *(G-14587)*
Ingredion Incorporated ....A 708 551-2600
Westchester *(G-20701)*
Ingredion Incorporated ....D 309 550-9136
Mapleton *(G-13473)*
Ingredion Incorporated ....G 708 551-2600
Chicago *(G-4923)*
Ingredion Incorporated ....C 708 728-3535
Summit Argo *(G-19680)*
Ingredion Incorporated ....C 708 563-2400
Argo *(G-673)*
Ktm Industries Inc ....G 217 224-5861
Quincy *(G-16905)*
Lee Gilster-Mary Corporation ....D 815 472-6456
Momence *(G-14186)*
Mgp Ingredients Illinois Inc ....C 309 353-3990
Pekin *(G-16345)*
Mgpi Processing Inc ....C 309 353-3990
Pekin *(G-16346)*
◆ Tate & Lyle Americas LLC ....C 217 421-3268
Decatur *(G-7557)*
Tate Lyle Ingrdnts Amricas LLC ....F 847 396-7500
Hoffman Estates *(G-11467)*
◆ Tate Lyle Ingrdnts Amricas LLC ....A 217 423-4411
Decatur *(G-7558)*
Tate Lyle Ingrdnts Amricas LLC ....G 309 473-2721
Heyworth *(G-11191)*

2047 Dog & Cat Food

Denta Treet LLC ....G 618 384-1028
Mount Vernon *(G-14609)*
Dr & Dr Property Leasing LLC ....G 309 965-3200
Goodfield *(G-10674)*
◆ Evangers Dog and Cat Fd Co Inc ....E 847 537-0102
Markham *(G-13548)*
Kraft Heinz Foods Company ....C 847 291-3900
Northbrook *(G-15415)*
Lincoln Bark LLC ....C 800 428-4027
Chicago *(G-5224)*
Midwestern Pet Foods Inc ....E 309 734-3121
Monmouth *(G-14223)*
Nutripack LLC ....C 847 537-0102
Markham *(G-13549)*
Papmpered Pups ....G 815 782-8383
Joliet *(G-11912)*
Pet Celebrations Inc ....G 630 832-6549
Elmhurst *(G-9410)*
◆ Pet-Ag Inc ....E 847 683-2288
Hampshire *(G-10983)*
Phelps Industries LLC ....E 815 397-0236
Rockford *(G-17553)*
Yotta Pet Products Inc ....F 217 466-4777
Paris *(G-16247)*

Employee Codes: A=Over 500 employees, B=251-500
C=101-250, D=51-100, E=20-50, F=10-19, G=3-9

20 FOOD AND KINDRED PRODUCTS
SIC SECTION

2048 Prepared Feeds For Animals & Fowls

▲ **Agresearch Inc** ....F 815 726-0410
Joliet *(G-11818)*
▲ **Alfa-Pet Inc** ....E 314 865-0400
Godfrey *(G-10648)*
▲ **All-Feed Proc & Packg Inc** ....F 309 629-0001
Alpha *(G-405)*
All-Feed Proc & Packg Inc ....G 309 932-3119
Galva *(G-10226)*
Altair Corporation ....E 847 634-9540
Lincolnshire *(G-12744)*
Aqua-Tech Co ....G 847 383-7075
Elgin *(G-8513)*
Archer-Daniels-Midland Company ....E 217 222-7100
Quincy *(G-16854)*
Archer-Daniels-Midland Company ....E 217 342-3986
Effingham *(G-8385)*
Archer-Daniels-Midland Company ....G 618 432-7194
Patoka *(G-16302)*
Ardent Mills LLC ....E 618 826-2371
Chester *(G-3449)*
B B Milling Co Inc ....G 217 376-3131
Emden *(G-9466)*
B&A Livestock Feed Company LLC ....G 618 245-6422
Farina *(G-9650)*
Bill Chandler Farms ....G 618 752-7551
Noble *(G-15188)*
Cargill Incorporated ....F 618 662-8070
Flora *(G-9677)*
Cargill Incorporated ....G 309 587-8111
New Boston *(G-15026)*
▼ **Cargill Dry Corn Ingrdents Inc** ....G 217 465-5331
Paris *(G-16226)*
Chatham Corporation ....F 847 634-5506
Lincolnshire *(G-12749)*
Cloverleaf Feed Co Inc ....G 217 589-5010
Roodhouse *(G-17892)*
Darling Ingredients Inc ....E 708 388-3223
Blue Island *(G-2117)*
Darling Ingredients Inc ....E 309 476-8111
Lynn Center *(G-13289)*
▼ **Dawes LLC** ....F 847 577-2020
Arlington Heights *(G-726)*
Dr & Dr Property Leasing LLC ....G 309 965-3200
Goodfield *(G-10674)*
Effingham Equity ....F 217 268-5128
Arcola *(G-648)*
Fish King Inc ....G 773 736-4974
Chicago *(G-4595)*
◆ **Furst-Mcness Company** ....D 800 435-5100
Freeport *(G-10112)*
Garver Feeds ....E 217 422-2201
Decatur *(G-7496)*
Grain Densification Intl LLC ....G 618 823-5122
Granite City *(G-10711)*
Griswold Feed Inc ....G 815 432-2811
Watseka *(G-20305)*
Helfter Enterprises Inc ....F 309 522-5505
Osco *(G-15988)*
▲ **Herris Group LLC** ....G 630 908-7393
Orland Park *(G-15959)*
Hueber LLC ....G 815 625-4546
Rock Falls *(G-17185)*
Hueber LLC ....F 815 393-4879
Creston *(G-7102)*
K-Pro US LLC ....G 872 529-5776
O Fallon *(G-15576)*
Kent Nutrition Group Inc ....F 815 874-2411
Rockford *(G-17483)*
Kent Nutrition Group Inc ....F 217 323-1216
Beardstown *(G-1448)*
Lafeber Distribution LLC ....G 630 524-4845
Cornell *(G-7013)*
Lebanon Seaboard Corporation ....E 217 446-0983
Danville *(G-7358)*
Liberty Feed Mill ....F 217 645-3441
Liberty *(G-12623)*
Lockport Fish Pantry ....G 815 588-3543
Lockport *(G-13007)*
Lokman Enterprises Inc ....G 773 654-0525
Chicago *(G-5252)*
M & W Feed Service ....G 815 858-2412
Elizabeth *(G-8787)*
Mendota Agri-Products Inc ....E 815 539-5633
Mendota *(G-13946)*
Mgp Ingredients Illinois Inc ....C 309 353-3990
Pekin *(G-16345)*
Mont Eagle Products Inc ....G 618 455-3344
Sainte Marie *(G-18327)*
▼ **Morgan Robt Inc** ....E 217 466-4777
Paris *(G-16235)*
◆ **Nutriad Inc** ....E 847 214-4860
Hampshire *(G-10981)*
Oceanic Food Express Inc ....G 847 480-7217
Northbrook *(G-15443)*
Pcs Phosphate Company Inc ....E 815 795-5111
Marseilles *(G-13563)*
◆ **Pet-Ag Inc** ....E 847 683-2288
Hampshire *(G-10983)*
Petdine LLC ....G 815 770-0342
Harvard *(G-11062)*
Prince Agri Products Inc ....G 217 222-8854
Quincy *(G-16924)*
Prince Agri Products Inc ....E 217 222-8854
Quincy *(G-16925)*
Procal Inc ....G 847 219-7257
Palatine *(G-16151)*
Purina Animal Nutrition LLC ....G 618 283-2291
Vandalia *(G-20021)*
Purina Animal Nutrition LLC ....E 618 478-5555
Nashville *(G-15007)*
Purina Mills LLC ....E 618 283-2291
Vandalia *(G-20022)*
Quality Liquid Feeds Inc ....F 815 224-1553
La Salle *(G-12120)*
Quincy Farm Products LLC ....F 217 214-1905
Quincy *(G-16931)*
Rare Birds Inc ....G 847 259-7286
Arlington Heights *(G-796)*
Reconserve of Illinois Inc ....E 708 354-4641
Hodgkins *(G-11394)*
▲ **Sem Minerals LP** ....D 217 224-8766
Quincy *(G-16944)*
▲ **Siemer Enterprises Inc** ....E 217 857-3171
Teutopolis *(G-19772)*
T C4 Inc ....F 618 335-3486
Vandalia *(G-20026)*
Tate Lyle Ingrdnts Amricas LLC ....G 309 473-2721
Heyworth *(G-11191)*
Transagra International Inc ....G 312 856-1010
Chicago *(G-6407)*
Trouw Nutrition Usa LLC ....G 618 654-2070
Highland *(G-11244)*
◆ **Trouw Nutrition Usa LLC** ....E 618 654-2070
Highland *(G-11245)*
Trouw Nutrition Usa LLC ....E 618 654-2070
Highland *(G-11246)*
Trouw Nutrition Usa LLC ....E 618 654-2070
Highland *(G-11247)*
United Animal Health Inc ....E 309 747-2196
Gridley *(G-10848)*
Veal Tech Inc ....G 630 554-0410
Oswego *(G-16030)*
Wagners LLC ....E 815 889-4101
Milford *(G-14037)*
Western Yeast Company Inc ....E 309 274-3160
Chillicothe *(G-6823)*
Westway Feed Products LLC ....F 309 654-2211
Cordova *(G-7011)*
Zoetis LLC ....D 708 757-2592
Chicago Heights *(G-6787)*

2051 Bread, Bakery Prdts Exc Cookies & Crackers

Ace Bakeries ....F 312 225-4973
Chicago *(G-3521)*
American Kitchen Delights Inc ....D 708 210-3200
Harvey *(G-11073)*
Amling Donuts Inc ....E 847 426-5327
Carpentersville *(G-3093)*
Anns Bakery Inc ....G 773 384-5562
Chicago *(G-3700)*
Aryzta LLC ....G 708 757-4671
Chicago Heights *(G-6731)*
Athenian Foods Co ....F 708 343-6700
Melrose Park *(G-13827)*
Auntie Mmmms ....G 217 509-6012
Camp Point *(G-2809)*
B N K Inc ....G 630 231-5640
West Chicago *(G-20547)*
Bear-Stewart Corporation ....E 773 276-0400
Chicago *(G-3854)*
▼ **Bimbo Bakehouse LLC** ....E 800 550-6810
Chicago *(G-3889)*
Bimbo Bakeries Usa Inc ....G 630 469-4579
Glendale Heights *(G-10438)*
Bimbo Bakeries Usa Inc ....E 773 254-3578
Chicago *(G-3890)*
Bimbo Bakeries Usa Inc ....D 815 626-6797
Rock Falls *(G-17177)*
Bimbo Bakeries Usa Inc ....B 217 235-3181
Mattoon *(G-13631)*
Bimbo Bakeries Usa Inc ....E 309 797-4968
Moline *(G-14134)*
Bimbo Qsr Chicago LLC ....F 773 376-4444
Chicago *(G-3891)*
◆ **Bimbo Qsr Us LLC** ....C 740 450-3869
Chicago *(G-3892)*
Bion Dillos Baking Co ....E 773 921-8282
Chicago *(G-3896)*
Bodines Baking Company ....G 217 853-7707
Decatur *(G-7465)*
Bullards Bakery ....G 618 842-6666
Fairfield *(G-9620)*
Butera Finer Foods Inc ....D 708 456-5939
Norridge *(G-15231)*
C & C Bakery Inc ....G 773 276-4233
Chicago *(G-3991)*
Callies Cuties Inc ....G 815 566-6885
Plainfield *(G-16646)*
Campbell Soup Company ....G 618 548-3001
Salem *(G-18333)*
Campbell Soup Company ....C 630 241-6200
Downers Grove *(G-7964)*
Casa Nostra Bakery Co Inc ....F 847 455-5175
Franklin Park *(G-9899)*
Cathys Sweet Creations ....G 815 886-6769
Plainfield *(G-16648)*
Cbc Restaurant Corp ....D 773 463-0665
Chicago *(G-4046)*
Charles Cicero Fingerhut ....F 708 652-3643
Chicago *(G-4073)*
Charleston County Market ....D 217 345-7031
Charleston *(G-3399)*
Chateau Food Products Inc ....F 708 863-4207
Chicago *(G-4079)*
Chicago Baking Company ....A 630 684-2335
Darien *(G-7404)*
Chicago Bread Company ....F 630 620-1849
Addison *(G-69)*
Chicago Pastry Inc ....C 630 972-0404
Bolingbrook *(G-2156)*
Chicago Pastry Inc ....D 630 529-6161
Bloomingdale *(G-1985)*
Christys Kitchen ....G 815 735-6791
La Salle *(G-12107)*
Cositas Cupcakes & More ....G 773 992-7088
Chicago *(G-4244)*
Creative Cakes LLC ....E 708 614-9755
Tinley Park *(G-19817)*
Cub Foods Inc ....C 309 689-0140
Peoria *(G-16428)*
Cupcakeologist LLC ....G 630 656-2272
Woodridge *(G-21290)*
DAmatos Bakery Inc ....G 312 733-6219
Chicago *(G-4309)*
Dessertwerks Inc ....G 847 487-8239
Libertyville *(G-12647)*
Dimples Donuts ....G 630 406-0303
Batavia *(G-1373)*
Dinkels Bakery Inc ....E 773 281-7300
Chicago *(G-4362)*
Distinctive Foods LLC ....E 847 459-3600
Bensenville *(G-1787)*
Dixie Cream Donut Shop ....E 618 937-4866
West Frankfort *(G-20670)*
Dominicks Finer Foods Inc ....D 630 584-1750
Saint Charles *(G-18185)*
Dominos Pastries Inc ....G 773 889-3549
Hickory Hills *(G-11195)*
Donchef Inc ....G 224 619-2223
Chicago *(G-4381)*
Doughnut Boy ....E 773 463-6328
Lincolnshire *(G-12760)*
Dunajec Bakery & Deli ....F 773 585-9611
Bridgeview *(G-2341)*
▲ **Dunbar Systems Inc** ....F 630 257-2900
Lemont *(G-12563)*
Dunkin Donuts ....E 708 460-3088
Orland Park *(G-15954)*
▼ **Earthgrains Refrigertd Dough P** ....A 630 455-5200
Downers Grove *(G-7996)*
El Moro De Letran Churros & Ba ....F 312 733-3173
Chicago *(G-4465)*
Enjoy Life Natural Brands LLC ....E 773 632-2163
Chicago *(G-4511)*
Entrust Services LLC ....G 630 699-9132
Naperville *(G-14825)*

SIC SECTION
20 FOOD AND KINDRED PRODUCTS

Express Donuts Enterprise Inc.............F 630 510-9310
Wheaton *(G-20798)*
Father Marcellos & Son..........................C....... 312 654-2565
Chicago *(G-4567)*
Faustos Bakery.......................................G....... 847 255-9049
Arlington Heights *(G-735)*
Flowers Foods Inc.................................F 618 286-3300
Dupo *(G-8137)*
Flowers Foods Inc.................................F 217 347-2308
Effingham *(G-8400)*
Folsoms Bakery Inc...............................F 815 622-7870
Rock Falls *(G-17181)*
Fortuna Baking Company.......................G....... 630 681-3000
Carol Stream *(G-2987)*
G & K Baking LLC..................................G....... 708 741-7260
Hickory Hills *(G-11196)*
Gadgetworld Enterprises Inc.................G....... 773 703-0796
Chicago *(G-4655)*
Gold Standard Baking Inc......................C....... 773 523-2333
Chicago *(G-4712)*
Golosinas El Canto.................................G....... 847 625-5103
Waukegan *(G-20445)*
▲ **Gonnella Baking Co**............................D....... 312 733-2020
Schaumburg *(G-18538)*
Gonnella Baking Co................................D....... 312 733-2020
Schaumburg *(G-18539)*
Gonnella Baking Co................................D....... 630 820-3433
Aurora *(G-974)*
Gonnella Frozen Products LLC...............C....... 847 884-8829
Schaumburg *(G-18540)*
Gordon Hann...E 630 761-1835
Batavia *(G-1381)*
Gourmet Frog Pastry Shop......................G....... 847 433-7038
Highland Park *(G-11266)*
◆ **Grecian Delight Foods Inc**...................C....... 847 364-1010
Elk Grove Village *(G-9022)*
Harners Bakery Restaurant......................D....... 630 892-5545
North Aurora *(G-15263)*
Hearthside Food Solutions LLC..............B 815 853-4348
Wenona *(G-20526)*
Herbs Bakery Inc....................................F 847 741-0249
Elgin *(G-8614)*
Herman Seekamp Inc...............................C....... 630 628-6555
Addison *(G-149)*
Hermanitas Cupcakes..............................G....... 708 620-9396
Calumet City *(G-2781)*
Highland Baking Company Inc.................A....... 847 677-2789
Northbrook *(G-15400)*
▼ **Hillshire Brands Company**.....................B 312 614-6000
Chicago *(G-4820)*
Homer Vintage Bakery..............................G....... 217 896-2538
Homer *(G-11476)*
Honey Fluff Doughnuts............................G....... 708 579-1826
Countryside *(G-7058)*
Hostess Brands LLC.................................D....... 773 745-9800
Chicago *(G-4844)*
Iced..G....... 217 774-2247
Shelbyville *(G-18879)*
Illinois Baking...G....... 773 995-7200
Chicago *(G-4888)*
J & J Snack Foods Corp............................C....... 708 377-0400
Alsip *(G-460)*
Jay Elka..F 847 540-7776
Lake Zurich *(G-12426)*
Jewel Osco Inc...C....... 773 728-7730
Chicago *(G-5026)*
Jewel Osco Inc...C....... 773 784-1922
Chicago *(G-5027)*
Jewel Osco Inc...C....... 708 352-0120
Countryside *(G-7061)*
Jewel Osco Inc...D....... 630 859-1212
Aurora *(G-1118)*
Jewel Osco Inc...C....... 847 677-3331
Skokie *(G-18970)*
Jewel Osco Inc...C....... 630 584-4594
Saint Charles *(G-18218)*
Jewel Osco Inc...C....... 847 428-3547
West Dundee *(G-20664)*
Jewel Osco Inc...C....... 630 355-2172
Naperville *(G-14854)*
Jewel Osco Inc...D....... 630 226-1892
Bolingbrook *(G-2198)*
Jewel Osco Inc...C....... 847 296-7786
Des Plaines *(G-7791)*
Jewel Osco Inc...C....... 815 464-5352
Frankfort *(G-9810)*
Jr Bakery...E 773 465-6733
Chicago *(G-5055)*
Kellogg Company.......................................C....... 630 941-0300
Elmhurst *(G-9387)*

Kerry Inc...G....... 847 595-1003
Elk Grove Village *(G-9076)*
Kerry Ingredients & Flavours....................F 847 595-1003
Elk Grove Village *(G-9077)*
Korinek & Co Inc..G....... 708 652-2870
Cicero *(G-6860)*
Kroger Co..C....... 309 694-6298
East Peoria *(G-8275)*
Kroger Co..C....... 815 332-7267
Rockford *(G-17485)*
La Dolce Bella Cupcakes............................G....... 847 987-3738
Lockport *(G-13005)*
La Luc Bakery Inc...G....... 847 740-0303
Round Lake *(G-18079)*
Labaquette Kedzie Inc.................................G....... 773 925-0455
Chicago *(G-5151)*
Le Petit Pain Holdings LLC.........................G....... 312 981-3770
Chicago *(G-5189)*
Leas Baking Company LLC..........................G....... 708 710-3404
Homer Glen *(G-11483)*
Leesons Cakes Inc..G....... 708 429-1330
Tinley Park *(G-19844)*
Leos Sweet Sensations Inc..........................D....... 773 237-1200
Chicago *(G-5207)*
Lewis Brothers Bakeries Inc........................E 708 531-6435
Melrose Park *(G-13890)*
Liborio Baking Co Inc...................................G....... 708 452-7222
River Grove *(G-17061)*
Linx Enterprises LLC....................................G....... 224 409-2206
Chicago *(G-5232)*
Lucksfood...G....... 773 878-7778
Chicago *(G-5277)*
Maiers Bakery...G....... 847 967-8042
Morton Grove *(G-14424)*
Mandys Soul Food Kitchen LLC...................F 630 485-7291
Bolingbrook *(G-2209)*
Mangel and Co..F 847 634-0730
Long Grove *(G-13162)*
Marias Bakery Inc...G....... 847 266-0811
Highwood *(G-11309)*
Mariegold Bake Shoppe..................................G....... 773 561-1978
Chicago *(G-5335)*
Marzeya Bakery Inc..G....... 773 374-7855
Chicago *(G-5357)*
Mel-O-Cream Donuts Intl Inc.........................D....... 217 483-1825
Springfield *(G-19404)*
Melinda I Rhodes...G....... 815 569-2789
Capron *(G-2836)*
Michele Baking Company................................F 847 451-9481
Franklin Park *(G-9996)*
Milano Bakery Inc..E 815 727-2253
Joliet *(G-11905)*
Molino Baking Co...G....... 708 385-6616
Blue Island *(G-2131)*
More Cupcakes LLC...G....... 312 951-0001
Chicago *(G-5499)*
Morningfields...G....... 847 309-8460
Park Ridge *(G-16288)*
◆ **Nablus Sweets Inc**..E 708 529-3911
Bridgeview *(G-2367)*
Nak Won Korean Bakery..................................G....... 773 588-8769
Chicago *(G-5538)*
National Biscuit Company................................G....... 773 925-0654
Chicago *(G-5545)*
Nauvoo Mill & Bakery.......................................G....... 217 453-6734
Nauvoo *(G-15014)*
New Chicago Wholesale Bky Inc.....................E 847 981-1600
Elk Grove Village *(G-9146)*
Niemann Foods Inc...C....... 217 222-0190
Quincy *(G-16918)*
Niemann Foods Inc...C....... 217 793-4091
Springfield *(G-19411)*
O-Donuts Inc..F 217 544-4644
Springfield *(G-19415)*
OBrothers Bakery Inc..G....... 847 249-0091
Waukegan *(G-20472)*
Original Ferrara Inc..F 312 666-2200
Chicago *(G-5700)*
Orland Park Bakery Ltd.....................................E 708 349-8516
Orland Park *(G-15973)*
Perfect Desserts LLC..E 630 579-6100
Aurora *(G-1007)*
Pin Hsiao & Associates LLC...............................E 206 818-0155
Flossmoor *(G-9700)*
▲ **Profile Food Ingredients LLC**..........................E 847 622-1700
Elgin *(G-8697)*
Rain Creek Baking Corp.......................................G....... 559 347-9960
Glendale Heights *(G-10487)*
Riverside Bake Shop...E 815 385-0044
McHenry *(G-13788)*

Roesers Bakery...E 773 489-6900
Chicago *(G-6050)*
Rolfs Patisserie Inc...C....... 847 675-6565
Lincolnwood *(G-12840)*
Roma Bakeries Inc..F 815 964-6737
Rockford *(G-17614)*
Royal Oak Farm Inc...F 815 648-4141
Harvard *(G-11066)*
Rubis Bakery Inc...G....... 847 623-4094
Waukegan *(G-20490)*
Sara Lee Baking Group..G....... 217 585-3462
Springfield *(G-19439)*
Say Cheese Cake..G....... 618 532-6001
Centralia *(G-3249)*
Schnuck Markets Inc..C....... 618 466-0825
Godfrey *(G-10663)*
▲ **Schulze and Burch Biscuit Co**..............................B 773 927-6622
Chicago *(G-6115)*
Schulze and Burch Biscuit Co...................................G....... 708 354-7050
Hodgkins *(G-11395)*
Sprinkles Confetti...G....... 815 304-5974
Kankakee *(G-12006)*
Sugar Monkey Cupcakes Inc......................................G....... 630 527-1869
Naperville *(G-14989)*
Sunset Food Mart Inc...C....... 847 234-0854
Lake Forest *(G-12307)*
Superior Baking Stone Inc..G....... 815 726-4610
Joliet *(G-11935)*
Sustainable Innovations Inc...G....... 815 713-1637
Rockford *(G-17650)*
Sweet Annies Bakery Inc..F 708 297-7066
Flossmoor *(G-9704)*
Swirlcup..G....... 847 229-2200
Lincolnshire *(G-12796)*
Tags Bakery Inc...E 847 328-1200
Evanston *(G-9582)*
Tahini Empire Inc...G....... 773 742-2382
Chicago *(G-6310)*
Tam Tav Bakery Inc..E 773 764-8877
Chicago *(G-6316)*
Tarte Cupcakery Company..G....... 312 898-2103
Lansing *(G-12521)*
▲ **Todays Temptations Inc**...F 773 385-5355
Chicago *(G-6383)*
◆ **Tonys Bakery**..G....... 847 599-1590
Waukegan *(G-20509)*
Tortilleria Atotonilco Inc...E 773 523-0800
Chicago *(G-6398)*
Two Wild Seeds Baking Company...G....... 630 797-5350
Saint Charles *(G-18293)*
Up At Dawn Inc...D....... 773 457-3859
Tinley Park *(G-19865)*
Verzenay LLC...G....... 817 875-0699
Elk Grove Village *(G-9303)*
Walter & Kathy Anczerewicz..G....... 708 448-3676
Palos Heights *(G-16194)*
Walter Lagestee Inc...C....... 708 957-2974
Homewood *(G-11504)*
◆ **Wilton Brands LLC**...B 630 963-7100
Naperville *(G-14948)*
Zb Importing Inc..E 708 222-8330
Chicago *(G-6709)*
◆ **Zb Importing Inc**..D....... 708 222-8330
Cicero *(G-6890)*

2052 Cookies & Crackers

Aryzta LLC..D....... 312 836-2300
Chicago *(G-3745)*
▲ **Baily International Inc**...D....... 618 451-8878
Granite City *(G-10699)*
Blissful Brownies Inc...G....... 541 308-0226
Lake Forest *(G-12231)*
Campbell Soup Company..G....... 618 548-3001
Salem *(G-18333)*
Campbell Soup Company..C....... 630 241-6200
Downers Grove *(G-7964)*
Carols Cookies Inc..G....... 847 831-4500
Northbrook *(G-15353)*
Casa Nostra Bakery Co Inc...F 847 455-5175
Franklin Park *(G-9899)*
Charleston County Market...D....... 217 345-7031
Charleston *(G-3399)*
Chicago Pastry Inc...D....... 630 529-6161
Bloomingdale *(G-1985)*
▲ **Chipita America Inc**..E 708 731-2434
Westchester *(G-20693)*
Christian Wolf Inc..G....... 618 667-9522
Bartelso *(G-1252)*
Comwell..D....... 618 282-6233
Red Bud *(G-16991)*

SIC

Employee Codes: A=Over 500 employees, B=251-500
C=101-250, D=51-100, E=20-50, F=10-19, G=3-9
2020 Harris Illinois
Industrial Directory
819

20 FOOD AND KINDRED PRODUCTS SIC SECTION

Cookie Kingdom Inc ....D 815 883-3331
Oglesby *(G-15840)*
DAmatos Bakery Inc ....G 312 733-6219
Chicago *(G-4309)*
Dinkels Bakery Inc ....E 773 281-7300
Chicago *(G-4362)*
F C L Kelloggs ....G 815 467-8198
Minooka *(G-14060)*
▲ **Fortella Company Inc** ....G 312 567-9000
Chicago *(G-4622)*
Griffin Industries LLC ....G 815 357-8200
Seneca *(G-18858)*
Herman Seekamp Inc ....C 630 628-6555
Addison *(G-149)*
Hometown Food Company ....F 312 500-7710
Chicago *(G-4835)*
▲ **Hop Kee Incorporated** ....E 312 791-9111
Chicago *(G-4839)*
Jewel Osco Inc ....C 847 677-3331
Skokie *(G-18970)*
Jewel Osco Inc ....C 630 355-2172
Naperville *(G-14854)*
Jr Bakery ....E 773 465-6733
Chicago *(G-5055)*
Katys LLC ....G 708 522-9814
Oak Park *(G-15760)*
Keebler Foods Company ....E 630 833-2900
Elmhurst *(G-9386)*
Kellogg Company ....C 630 941-0300
Elmhurst *(G-9387)*
Kroger Co ....C 815 332-7267
Rockford *(G-17485)*
Lofthouse Bakery Products Inc ....G 630 455-5229
Downers Grove *(G-8047)*
Maiers Bakery ....G 847 967-8042
Morton Grove *(G-14424)*
Matts Cookie Company ....G 847 537-3888
Wheeling *(G-20939)*
▲ **Mondelez Global LLC** ....C 847 943-4000
Deerfield *(G-7637)*
Mondelez Global LLC ....B 630 369-1909
Naperville *(G-14874)*
Paleo Prime LLC ....G 312 659-6596
Chicago *(G-5745)*
Pepperidge Farm Incorporated ....G 708 478-7450
Mokena *(G-14106)*
Pepperidge Farm Incorporated ....G 630 241-6372
Downers Grove *(G-8072)*
Pures Food Specialties LLC ....E 708 344-8884
Broadview *(G-2461)*
◆ **Quaker Oats Company** ....A 312 821-1000
Chicago *(G-5927)*
Roma Bakeries Inc ....F 815 964-6737
Rockford *(G-17614)*
▲ **Schulze and Burch Biscuit Co** ....B 773 927-6622
Chicago *(G-6115)*
Snyders-Lance Inc ....G 847 581-1818
Skokie *(G-19031)*
Sustainable Innovations Inc ....G 815 713-1637
Rockford *(G-17650)*
Tags Bakery Inc ....E 847 328-1200
Evanston *(G-9582)*
Th Foods Inc ....G 702 565-2816
Loves Park *(G-13273)*
Treehouse Private Brands Inc ....C 815 389-2745
South Beloit *(G-19117)*
Treehouse Private Brands Inc ....F 630 455-5265
Downers Grove *(G-8102)*
◆ **Treehouse Private Brands Inc** ....C 314 877-7300
Oak Brook *(G-15666)*
Walter Lagestee Inc ....C 708 957-2974
Homewood *(G-11504)*
Wandas Bakery LLC ....G 815 900-6268
Woodstock *(G-21446)*
Wex Distributors Inc ....G 847 691-5823
Antioch *(G-643)*

2053 Frozen Bakery Prdts

Bear-Stewart Corporation ....E 773 276-0400
Chicago *(G-3854)*
Cake Factory ....G 708 897-0872
Alsip *(G-425)*
▼ **Earthgrains Refrigertd Dough P** ....A 630 455-5200
Downers Grove *(G-7996)*
▼ **Elis Cheesecake Company** ....C 773 205-3800
Chicago *(G-4485)*
Forno Palese Baking Company ....F 630 595-5502
Bartlett *(G-1281)*
Griffin Industries LLC ....G 815 357-8200
Seneca *(G-18858)*
Herman Seekamp Inc ....C 630 628-6555
Addison *(G-149)*
▼ **Hillshire Brands Company** ....B 312 614-6000
Chicago *(G-4820)*
Hostess Brands LLC ....D 773 745-9800
Chicago *(G-4844)*
Kimmykakes Co ....G 312 927-3933
Chicago *(G-5104)*
Le Chocolat Du Bouchard LLC ....G 630 355-5720
Naperville *(G-14861)*
Mel-O-Cream Donuts Intl Inc ....D 217 483-1825
Springfield *(G-19404)*
Pepperidge Farm Incorporated ....G 708 478-7450
Mokena *(G-14106)*
Pepperidge Farm Incorporated ....G 630 241-6372
Downers Grove *(G-8072)*
Quality Bakeries LLC ....F 630 553-7377
Saint Charles *(G-18255)*
Rich Products Corporation ....A 815 729-4509
Crest Hill *(G-7096)*
Rich Products Corporation ....A 309 886-2465
Washington *(G-20279)*
Solublend Technologies LLC ....G 815 534-5778
Frankfort *(G-9839)*
Sweet Creation By Sheila ....G 708 754-7938
Glenwood *(G-10645)*
▼ **Vienna Beef Ltd** ....E 773 278-7800
Chicago *(G-6548)*
Wilseys Handmade Sweets LLC ....G 314 504-0851
Edwardsville *(G-8380)*

2061 Sugar, Cane

Nablus Sweets Inc ....E 708 205-6534
Chicago *(G-5534)*
Westway Feed Products LLC ....F 309 654-2211
Cordova *(G-7011)*

2062 Sugar, Cane Refining

Atlas Trade Solutions LLC ....G 618 954-6119
Belleville *(G-1531)*
Domino Foods Inc ....E 773 254-8282
Chicago *(G-4379)*
Lee Gilster-Mary Corporation ....B 618 965-3449
Steeleville *(G-19482)*
▲ **Necta Sweet Inc** ....E 847 215-9955
Buffalo Grove *(G-2579)*
▲ **Pullman Sugar LLC** ....E 773 260-9180
Chicago *(G-5913)*

2063 Sugar, Beet

Atlas Trade Solutions LLC ....G 618 954-6119
Belleville *(G-1531)*
Jo Snow Inc ....G 773 732-3045
Chicago *(G-5033)*
Lee Gilster-Mary Corporation ....B 618 965-3449
Steeleville *(G-19482)*
Merisant Us Inc ....C 815 929-2700
Chicago *(G-5399)*
Sweet Specialty Solutions LLC ....E 630 739-9151
Lemont *(G-12592)*

2064 Candy & Confectionery Prdts

▲ **Affy Tapple LLC** ....E 773 338-1100
Niles *(G-15100)*
All American Nut & Candy Corp ....F 630 595-6473
Wood Dale *(G-21157)*
American Convenience Inc ....F 815 344-6040
McHenry *(G-13718)*
Amy Wertheim ....G 309 830-4361
Atlanta *(G-904)*
Andersons Candy Shop Inc ....F 815 678-6000
Richmond *(G-17009)*
Arndts Stores Inc ....G 618 783-2511
Newton *(G-15080)*
Baldi Candy Co ....E 773 267-5770
Chicago *(G-3818)*
Baldi Candy Co ....D 773 267-5770
Chicago *(G-3819)*
Belgian Chocolatier Piron Inc ....G 847 864-5504
Evanston *(G-9498)*
Bobbie Haycraft ....G 217 856-2194
Humboldt *(G-11522)*
Cambridge Brands Mfg Inc ....G 773 838-3400
Chicago *(G-4010)*
▲ **Capol LLC** ....G 224 545-5095
Deerfield *(G-7599)*
Cellas Confections Inc ....D 773 838-3400
Chicago *(G-4053)*
CGC Corporation ....D 773 838-3400
Chicago *(G-4066)*
Chocolate Potpourri Ltd ....F 847 729-8878
Glenview *(G-10535)*
▼ **Colleens Confection** ....G 630 653-2231
Carol Stream *(G-2964)*
▲ **Das Foods LLC** ....G 224 715-9289
Chicago *(G-4320)*
Deli Star Ventures Inc ....F 618 233-0400
Belleville *(G-1544)*
◆ **Doumak Inc** ....G 800 323-0318
Bensenville *(G-1788)*
Doumak Inc ....D 847 981-2180
Elk Grove Village *(G-8953)*
▲ **Element Bars Inc** ....E 888 411-3536
Chicago *(G-4480)*
Fannie May Cnfctons Brands Inc ....F 330 494-0833
Chicago *(G-4558)*
Fattah Trading Company Inc ....G 773 227-2525
Chicago *(G-4568)*
◆ **Ferrara Candy Company** ....B 708 366-0500
Chicago *(G-4582)*
Ferrara Candy Company ....G 800 323-1768
Itasca *(G-11655)*
Ferrara Candy Company ....B 630 366-0500
Forest Park *(G-9715)*
Ferrara Candy Company ....F 630 378-4197
Bolingbrook *(G-2177)*
Ferrara Candy Company ....C 507 452-3433
Chicago *(G-4583)*
Ferrara Candy Company ....F 708 432-4407
Bellwood *(G-1624)*
Ferrara Candy Company ....B 708 488-1892
Forest Park *(G-9716)*
Galenas Kandy Kitchen ....G 815 777-0241
Galena *(G-10171)*
Goelitz Confectionery Company ....C 847 689-2225
North Chicago *(G-15313)*
▼ **Graziano Tl Inc** ....E 847 741-1900
Elgin *(G-8600)*
Healthful Habits LLC ....G 224 489-4256
West Chicago *(G-20592)*
Hershey Company ....A 618 544-3111
Robinson *(G-17116)*
Hollingworth Candies Inc ....E 815 838-2275
Lockport *(G-13000)*
▲ **Imaginings 3 Inc** ....E 847 647-1370
Niles *(G-15131)*
Jelly Belly Candy Company ....C 847 689-2225
North Chicago *(G-15315)*
Jessis Hideout ....G 618 343-4346
Caseyville *(G-3215)*
◆ **John B Sanfilippo & Son Inc** ....C 847 289-1800
Elgin *(G-8632)*
Killeen Confectionery LLC ....G 312 804-0009
Wilmette *(G-21083)*
▲ **Long Grove Confectionery Co** ....E 847 459-3100
Buffalo Grove *(G-2565)*
Mars Chocolate North Amer LLC ....A 662 335-8000
Chicago *(G-5347)*
Mars Chocolate North Amer LLC ....C 630 850-9898
Burr Ridge *(G-2699)*
Mars Snackfood US ....F 773 637-0659
Chicago *(G-5348)*
McCleary Inc ....C 815 389-3053
South Beloit *(G-19101)*
▲ **Mederer Group** ....G 630 860-4587
Des Plaines *(G-7801)*
Mexicandy Distributor Inc ....G 773 847-0024
Chicago *(G-5414)*
Mondelez Global LLC ....C 815 877-8081
Loves Park *(G-13238)*
Morkes Inc ....F 847 359-3511
Palatine *(G-16141)*
MSI Green Inc ....G 312 421-6550
Chicago *(G-5519)*
Nature S American Co ....G 630 246-4776
Lombard *(G-13107)*
Nestle Chclat Cnfctons A Div N ....G 847 957-7850
Franklin Park *(G-10008)*
Nestle Usa Inc ....C 630 773-2090
Itasca *(G-11711)*
Nestle Usa Inc ....D 847 957-7850
Franklin Park *(G-10009)*
▲ **Office Snax Inc** ....G 630 789-1783
Oak Brook *(G-15652)*
Opalek Frontier Inc ....G 312 733-2700
Chicago *(G-5679)*
Orbit Room ....G 773 588-8540
Chicago *(G-5694)*

SIC SECTION

20 FOOD AND KINDRED PRODUCTS

Peases Inc	F	217 523-3721	Springfield *(G-19422)*
Peases Inc	F	217 529-2912	Springfield *(G-19423)*
▲ Primrose Candy Co	C	800 268-9522	Chicago *(G-5875)*
▲ Princess Foods Inc	E	847 933-1820	Skokie *(G-19011)*
▲ Profile Food Ingredients LLC	E	847 622-1700	Elgin *(G-8697)*
◆ Quaker Oats Company	A	312 821-1000	Chicago *(G-5927)*
Rebel Brands LLC	G	312 804-0009	Wilmette *(G-21091)*
▲ Ruckers Mkin Batch Candies Inc	E	618 945-7778	Bridgeport *(G-2314)*
Ruckers Wholesale & Service Co	C	618 945-2411	Bridgeport *(G-2315)*
Samad General Services Inc	G	773 593-3332	Addison *(G-280)*
Taylors Candy Inc	E	708 371-0332	Alsip *(G-515)*
Toffee Time	G	309 788-2466	Rock Island *(G-17251)*
Tootsie Roll Company Inc	A	773 838-3400	Chicago *(G-6391)*
▲ Tootsie Roll Industries Inc	A	773 838-3400	Chicago *(G-6392)*
Tootsie Roll Industries LLC	G	773 245-4202	Chicago *(G-6393)*
◆ Tootsie Roll Worldwide Ltd	G	773 838-3400	Chicago *(G-6394)*
Tri International Co	A	773 838-3400	Chicago *(G-6417)*
Tri Sales Co	F	773 838-3400	Chicago *(G-6418)*
Tri Sales Co	F	773 838-3400	Chicago *(G-6419)*
Tri Sales Co	F	773 838-3400	Chicago *(G-6420)*
▼ Tri Sales Co	G	773 838-3400	Chicago *(G-6421)*
We Love Soy Inc	G	630 629-9667	Addison *(G-332)*
White Stokes Company Inc	E	773 254-5000	Lincolnwood *(G-12851)*
▼ Wm Wrigley Jr Company	B	312 280-4710	Chicago *(G-6654)*
Wm Wrigley Jr Company	A	312 644-2121	Chicago *(G-6656)*
Wrigley Manufacturing Co LLC	B	630 553-4800	Yorkville *(G-21507)*
◆ Zb Importing Inc	D	708 222-8330	Cicero *(G-6890)*
Zb Importing Inc	E	708 222-8330	Chicago *(G-6709)*
Zeldaco Ltd	E	847 674-0033	Skokie *(G-19060)*

2066 Chocolate & Cocoa Prdts

American Convenience Inc	F	815 344-6040	McHenry *(G-13718)*
Andersons Candy Shop Inc	F	815 678-6000	Richmond *(G-17009)*
Barry Callebaut USA LLC	G	312 496-7300	Chicago *(G-3839)*
◆ Barry Callebaut USA LLC	B	312 496-7300	Chicago *(G-3840)*
Barry Callebaut USA LLC	G	312 496-7372	Robinson *(G-17106)*
Belgian Chocolatier Piron Inc	G	847 864-5504	Evanston *(G-9498)*
Blommer Chocolate Company	F	800 621-1606	Chicago *(G-3911)*
Chocolate Potpourri Ltd	F	847 729-8878	Glenview *(G-10535)*
◆ Compact Industries Inc	C	630 513-9600	Saint Charles *(G-18173)*
Cora Lee Candies Inc	F	847 724-2754	Glenview *(G-10538)*
Dekalb Confectionary Inc	E	815 758-5990	Dekalb *(G-7676)*
Galenas Kandy Kitchen	G	815 777-0241	Galena *(G-10171)*
Gayety Candy Co Inc	E	708 418-0062	Lansing *(G-12494)*
Godiva Chocolatier Inc	E	630 820-5842	Aurora *(G-973)*
Hershey Company	G	800 468-1714	Deerfield *(G-7614)*
Hershey Company	A	618 544-3111	Robinson *(G-17116)*
Inside Beverages	C	847 438-1338	Lake Zurich *(G-12423)*
◆ John B Sanfilippo & Son Inc	C	847 289-1800	Elgin *(G-8632)*
▲ Kruger North America Inc	F	708 851-3670	Oak Park *(G-15761)*
Mars Chocolate North Amer LLC	C	630 850-9898	Burr Ridge *(G-2699)*
Mars Chocolate North Amer LLC	A	662 335-8000	Chicago *(G-5347)*
▲ Mondelez Global LLC	C	847 943-4000	Deerfield *(G-7637)*
Morkes Inc	F	847 359-3511	Palatine *(G-16141)*
Peases Inc	F	217 529-2912	Springfield *(G-19423)*
▲ Vosges Ltd	D	773 388-5560	Chicago *(G-6570)*
▲ Worlds Finest Chocolate Inc	B	773 847-4600	Chicago *(G-6677)*

2067 Chewing Gum

Ford Gum & Machine Company Inc	F	847 955-0003	Buffalo Grove *(G-2540)*
▼ Mars Incorporated	G	630 293-9066	West Chicago *(G-20615)*
Mid Pack	G	773 626-3500	Chicago *(G-5427)*
▲ Mondelez Global LLC	C	847 943-4000	Deerfield *(G-7637)*
Wm Wrigley Jr Company	C	312 644-2121	Romeoville *(G-17889)*
Wm Wrigley Jr Company	E	312 205-2300	Chicago *(G-6655)*
▼ Wm Wrigley Jr Company	B	312 280-4710	Chicago *(G-6654)*
Wm Wrigley Jr Company	A	312 644-2121	Chicago *(G-6656)*
▲ Wrigley Manufacturing Co LLC	A	312 644-2121	Chicago *(G-6686)*
Wrigley Manufacturing Co LLC	B	630 553-4800	Yorkville *(G-21507)*
Wrigley Manufacturing Co LLC	A	312 644-2121	Chicago *(G-6687)*
▼ Wrigley Sales Company LLC	F	312 644-2121	Chicago *(G-6688)*

2068 Salted & Roasted Nuts & Seeds

▲ Anton-Argires Inc	G	708 388-6250	Alsip *(G-416)*
Arthur/Busse Properties Inc	F	847 289-1800	Elk Grove Village *(G-8840)*
▼ Graziano Tl Inc	E	847 741-1900	Elgin *(G-8600)*
Illinois Foundation Seeds Inc	F	217 485-6420	Tolono *(G-19883)*
◆ John B Sanfilippo & Son Inc	C	847 289-1800	Elgin *(G-8632)*
John B Sanfilippo & Son Inc	C	847 690-8432	Elgin *(G-8633)*
Peases Inc	F	217 529-2912	Springfield *(G-19423)*
▲ Sesame Solutions LLC	E	630 427-3400	Bolingbrook *(G-2237)*
Specialty Nut & Bky Sup Co Inc	G	630 268-8500	Addison *(G-294)*
Treehouse Private Brands Inc	F	630 455-5265	Downers Grove *(G-8102)*
◆ Treehouse Private Brands Inc	C	314 877-7300	Oak Brook *(G-15666)*

2074 Cottonseed Oil Mills

Archer-Daniels-Midland Company	G	815 539-6219	Mendota *(G-13937)*
◆ Archer-Daniels-Midland Company	A	312 634-8100	Chicago *(G-3728)*
Lee Gilster-Mary Corporation	C	618 533-4808	Centralia *(G-3237)*
Maxs One Stop	G	618 235-4005	Belleville *(G-1572)*
O-Liminator LLC	G	630 400-0373	Saint Charles *(G-18235)*

2075 Soybean Oil Mills

Archer-Daniels-Midland Company	G	815 539-6219	Mendota *(G-13937)*
Archer-Daniels-Midland Company	E	217 424-5858	Decatur *(G-7453)*
◆ Archer-Daniels-Midland Company	A	312 634-8100	Chicago *(G-3728)*
Archer-Daniels-Midland Company	E	217 224-1800	Quincy *(G-16856)*
Bunge North America Foundation	C	217 784-8261	Gibson City *(G-10335)*
Cargill Incorporated	E	309 827-7100	Bloomington *(G-2031)*
Cargill Incorporated	G	815 942-0932	Morris *(G-14296)*
Cargill Incorporated	G	630 739-1746	Woodridge *(G-21280)*
Cherith Agro Inc	G	847 258-3865	Elk Grove Village *(G-8890)*
▲ Clarkson Soy Products LLC	G	217 763-9511	Cerro Gordo *(G-3256)*
Devansoy Inc	G	712 792-9665	Rock City *(G-17175)*
▲ Incobrasa Industries Ltd	C	815 265-4803	Gilman *(G-10380)*
Pioneer Hi-Bred Intl Inc	F	309 962-2931	Saint Joseph *(G-18318)*
Solae	G	217 784-2085	Gibson City *(G-10346)*
Solae LLC	C	217 784-8261	Gibson City *(G-10347)*
Syngenta Seeds LLC	E	309 478-3686	Pekin *(G-16363)*

2076 Vegetable Oil Mills

Abitec Corporation	E	217 465-8577	Paris *(G-16223)*
Bio Fuels By American Farmers	F	561 859-6251	Benton *(G-1921)*
Dawn Food Products Inc	C	815 933-0600	Bradley *(G-2280)*

2077 Animal, Marine Fats & Oils

Abitec Corporation	E	217 465-8577	Paris *(G-16223)*
Ace Grease Service Inc	G	618 781-1207	Millstadt *(G-14041)*
Ace Grease Service Inc	G	618 337-0974	Millstadt *(G-14042)*
Chaos Ai Art LLC	G	847 274-9158	Chicago *(G-4070)*
Darling Ingredients Inc	E	773 376-5550	Chicago *(G-4319)*
Darling Ingredients Inc	E	618 271-8190	National Stock Yards *(G-15012)*
Darling Ingredients Inc	E	217 482-3261	Mason City *(G-13611)*
Darling Ingredients Inc	E	309 476-8111	Lynn Center *(G-13289)*
K-Pro US LLC	G	872 529-5776	O Fallon *(G-15576)*
Kostelac Grease Service Inc	E	314 436-7166	Belleville *(G-1566)*
McShares Inc	E	217 762-2561	Monticello *(G-14281)*
Mendota Agri-Products Inc	E	815 539-5633	Mendota *(G-13946)*
▲ Micro Surface Corporation	F	815 942-4221	Morris *(G-14312)*
Millstadt Rendering Company	E	618 538-5312	Belleville *(G-1578)*
MW Hopkins & Sons Inc	G	847 458-1010	Lake In The Hills *(G-12341)*
Schnowske & Sons Trucking Inc	G	309 937-3323	Cambridge *(G-2807)*
▲ Sdr Corp	G	773 638-1800	Chicago *(G-6123)*
South Chicago Packing LLC	D	708 589-2400	Chicago *(G-6206)*
Sustainable Sourcing LLC	F	815 714-8055	Mokena *(G-14120)*

2079 Shortening, Oils & Margarine

Ach Food Companies Inc	C	866 386-8282	Oakbrook Terrace *(G-15780)*
◆ Ach Food Companies Inc	C	866 386-8282	Oakbrook Terrace *(G-15781)*
Ach Food Companies Inc	C	708 458-8690	Summit Argo *(G-19676)*
All Fresh Food Products	G	847 864-5030	Evanston *(G-9491)*
Allfresh Food Products Inc	F	847 869-3100	Evanston *(G-9492)*

SIC

Employee Codes: A=Over 500 employees, B=251-500
C=101-250, D=51-100, E=20-50, F=10-19, G=3-9

2020 Harris Illinois
Industrial Directory

821

20 FOOD AND KINDRED PRODUCTS

SIC SECTION

Company	Code	Phone
Archer-Daniels-Midland Company Quincy (G-16856)	E	217 224-1800
▲ Avatar Corporation University Park (G-19947)	D	708 534-5511
Cargill Incorporated Chicago (G-4030)	F	773 375-7255
▼ Cfc Inc Des Plaines (G-7743)	D	847 257-8920
Darling Ingredients Inc Mason City (G-13611)	E	217 482-3261
Dawn Food Products Inc Bradley (G-2280)	C	815 933-0600
Fgfi LLC Countryside (G-7052)	E	708 598-0909
Loders Croklaan BV Channahon (G-3386)	C	815 730-5200
▲ Loders Croklaan Usa LLC Channahon (G-3387)	C	815 730-5200
Mahoney Environmental Inc Joliet (G-11896)	E	815 730-2087
Midwest Processing Company Decatur (G-7525)	D	217 424-5200
Old Town Oil Evanston Evanston (G-9562)	G	312 787-9595
Olivaceto La Grange (G-12084)	G	708 639-4408
Olive and Vinnies Glen Ellyn (G-10416)	G	630 534-6457
Olive Leclaire Oil Co Yorkville (G-21494)	G	888 255-1867
Olive Oil Market Place Godfrey (G-10659)	G	618 304-3769
Olive Oil Marketplace Inc Alton (G-567)	G	618 304-3769
Olive Oil Store Inc Geneva (G-10297)	F	630 262-0210
Olive Oils & More LLC Edwardsville (G-8373)	G	618 656-4645
Pastorelli Food Products Inc Chicago (G-5770)	G	312 455-1006
▼ South Chicago Packing LLC South Holland (G-19245)	D	708 589-2400
South Chicago Packing LLC Chicago (G-6206)	D	708 589-2400
Stratas Foods LLC Decatur (G-7552)	E	217 424-5660
▲ V Formusa Co Des Plaines (G-7863)	F	224 938-9360

2082 Malt Beverages

Company	Code	Phone
Abbey Ridge LLC Pomona (G-16762)	G	618 713-2537
Aero Alehouse LLC Loves Park (G-13183)	G	815 977-5602
Alao Temitope Collinsville (G-6953)	F	331 454-3333
Aldi Inc Machesney Park (G-13326)	F	815 877-0861
Ale Syndicate Brewers LLC Chicago (G-3600)	G	773 340-2337
Anheuser-Busch LLC Lisle (G-12865)	C	630 512-9002
Apple Rush Company Glenview (G-10527)	G	847 730-5324
Bent River Brewing Co Moline (G-14133)	F	309 797-2722
Blue Island Beer Co Blue Island (G-2111)	G	708 954-8085
Bob C Beverages LLC Wheeling (G-20861)	G	847 520-7582
Breakroom Brewery Chicago (G-3949)	G	773 564-9534
Burrell Beverage Co Chicago (G-3977)	E	708 581-6953
Carlyle Brewing Co Rockford (G-17336)	G	815 963-2739
Church Street Brewing Co LLC Itasca (G-11636)	F	630 438-5725
Cicerone Certification Program Chicago (G-4150)	G	773 549-4800
Colleagues of Beer Inc Grayslake (G-10762)	G	847 727-3318
Common Culture Brewing Co Evanston (G-9506)	F	847 584-2337
Crazy Llama Brewing Co LLC Roscoe (G-17901)	G	779 200-1878
Crystal Lake Beer Company Crystal Lake (G-7187)	F	779 220-9288
▲ Dept 28 Inc Schaumburg (G-18505)	G	847 285-1343
Dj Liquors Inc Davis Junction (G-7421)	G	815 645-1145
Dovetail Brewery Inc Chicago (G-4392)	E	773 683-1414
Drewrys Brewing Company McHenry (G-13738)	G	815 385-9115
Emmetts Tavern & Brewing Co Downers Grove (G-8000)	G	630 434-8500
Emmetts Tavern & Brewing Co Wheaton (G-20797)	G	630 480-7181
Emmetts Tavern & Brewing Co Palatine (G-16115)	F	847 359-1533
Emmetts Tavern & Brewing Co West Dundee (G-20663)	G	847 428-4500
Excel Bottling Co Breese (G-2302)	G	618 526-7159
Finchs Beer Company LLC Chicago (G-4588)	G	312 929-4773
Ginger Windmill Brew LLC Geneva (G-10274)	G	630 677-2850
Gmb Partners LLC Chicago (G-4703)	E	773 248-4038
Gnome Brew LLC Chicago (G-4707)	G	773 961-7750
Goose Holdings Inc Chicago (G-4718)	G	312 226-1119
Great Revivalist Brewing LLC Geneseo (G-10243)	F	309 944-5466
Haymarket Brewing Company LLC Chicago (G-4789)	G	312 638-0700
Hop Brewery LLC Christopher (G-6825)	G	866 724-4677
Lagunitas Brewing Company Chicago (G-5159)	C	773 522-1308
Libertyville Brewing Company Libertyville (G-12668)	D	847 362-6688
Lil Beaver Brewery LLC Bloomington (G-2071)	F	309 808-2590
Maverick Ales & Lagers LLC Chicago (G-5368)	G	408 605-1508
Metropolitan Brewing LLC Chicago (G-5413)	G	773 474-6893
◆ Molson Coors Bev Co USA LLC Chicago (G-5488)	A	312 496-2700
Only Child Brewing Company LLC Gurnee (G-10909)	G	847 877-9822
Pac Partners LLC Chicago (G-5735)	G	773 315-0828
Rebellion Brew Haus Moline (G-14172)	G	309 524-5219
Riggs Beer Company Urbana (G-19998)	G	217 649-4286
Rolling Meadows Brewery LLC Springfield (G-19435)	G	217 725-2492
Soundgrowler Brewing Company Tinley Park (G-19856)	G	708 263-0083
St Nicholas Brewing Co Du Quoin (G-8124)	G	618 790-9212
Tenth and Blake Beer Company Chicago (G-6351)	G	312 496-2759
▲ Wirtz Beverage Illinois LLC Cicero (G-6888)	C	847 228-9000

2083 Malt

Company	Code	Phone
Archer-Daniels-Midland Company Decatur (G-7448)	D	217 424-5200
◆ Archer-Daniels-Midland Company Chicago (G-3728)	A	312 634-8100
◆ Muntons Malted Ingredients Inc Lombard (G-13105)	G	630 812-1600
Warner Harvey Lee Farm Inc Toledo (G-19882)	G	217 849-2548

2084 Wine & Brandy

Company	Code	Phone
Acquaviva Winery LLC Maple Park (G-13459)	G	630 365-0333
Aeries Riverview Winery Inc Grafton (G-10683)	G	618 786-7477
Alto Vineyards Limited Alto Pass (G-538)	F	618 893-4898
Aquaviva Winery Sycamore (G-19701)	G	815 899-4444
▲ August Hill Winery Peru (G-16567)	G	815 224-8199
Augusthill Winery Co Utica (G-20005)	G	815 667-5211
Barrington Cardinal Whse LLC Barrington (G-1213)	G	847 387-3676
Baxter Vineyards Nauvoo (G-15013)	G	217 453-2528
Bella Terra Winery LLC Creal Springs (G-7080)	F	618 658-8882
Benessere Vineyard Inc Oak Brook (G-15596)	G	708 560-9840
Beverage Art Inc Chicago (G-3875)	G	773 881-9463
Blue Sky Vineyard Makanda (G-13427)	G	618 995-9463
Bluffs Vineyard & Winery L L C Murphysboro (G-14751)	G	618 763-4447
Bonanno Vintners LLC Chicago (G-3933)	G	773 477-8351
Broken Earth Winery Long Grove (G-13158)	F	847 383-5052
Cellar LLC Carterville (G-3131)	G	618 956-9900
Coopers Hawk Intrmdate Hldg LL Downers Grove (G-7981)	C	708 839-2920
Coopers Hawk Intrmdate Hldg LL Countryside (G-7048)	F	708 215-5674
▲ Coopers Hawk Production LLC Countryside (G-7049)	G	708 839-2920
Coopers Hawk Winery Saint Charles (G-18175)	F	630 940-1000
Coopers Hwk Intermedte Holdng Woodridge (G-21288)	F	708 215-5674
Copper Dock Pocahontas (G-16751)	G	618 669-2675
D C Estate Winery South Beloit (G-19089)	G	815 218-0573
▲ De Vine Distributors LLC Chicago (G-4326)	G	773 248-7005
Diageo Plainfield (G-16655)	F	815 267-4499
Diageo North America Inc Plainfield (G-16656)	E	815 267-4400
Distillery Wine & Allied Pekin (G-16329)	G	309 347-1444
▲ Dlux Brand LLC Lombard (G-13069)	G	630 215-5557
DVine Wine Crafters LLC Algonquin (G-372)	G	847 658-4900
Famous Fossil Vinyard & Winery Freeport (G-10107)	G	815 563-4665
Fox Valley Winery Inc Oswego (G-16005)	G	630 554-0404
Galena Cellars Winery Galena (G-10169)	E	815 777-3330
Galena Cellars Winery Galena (G-10170)	G	815 777-3429
Glunz Fmly Winery Cellars Inc Grayslake (G-10777)	E	847 548-9463
Grafton Winery Inc Grafton (G-10684)	F	618 786-3001
Hedman Orchard and Vineyard Alto Pass (G-539)	G	618 893-4923
Hidden Lake Winery Ltd Aviston (G-1179)	E	618 228-9111
Hogg Hollow Winery LLC Golconda (G-10665)	G	618 695-9463
Katy Lynn Winery LLC Carbondale (G-2848)	G	618 964-1818
Kickapoo Creek Winery Edwards (G-8338)	G	309 495-9463
Klehm Family Winery LLC Hampshire (G-10975)	G	847 609-9997
Lake Hill Winery Inc Carthage (G-3137)	G	217 357-2675
Lau Nae Winery Inc Red Bud (G-16997)	G	618 282-9463
Lavender Crest Winery Colona (G-6975)	E	309 949-2565
Lincoln Heritage Winery LLC Cobden (G-6942)	G	618 833-3783
▲ Lynfred Winery Inc Roselle (G-17965)	E	630 529-9463
Main Street Market Roscoe Inc Roscoe (G-17915)	G	815 623-6328
Mark Anthony Brewing Inc Chicago (G-5339)	G	312 202-3700
▲ Mary McHelle Winery Vinyrd LLC Carrollton (G-3127)	F	217 942-6250
Old Mill Vineyard LLC Metamora (G-13965)	G	309 258-9954
Pheasant Hollow Winery Inc Whittington (G-21021)	G	618 629-2302
Pomona Winery Pomona (G-16764)	G	618 893-2623
Pour It Again Sam Inc Lynwood (G-13297)	G	708 474-1744

SIC SECTION

20 FOOD AND KINDRED PRODUCTS

Prairie State Winery ....G....... 815 784-4540
Genoa *(G-10322)*

Prp Wine International Inc ....F....... 630 995-4500
Naperville *(G-14903)*

Rapid Displays Inc ....G....... 773 884-0900
Chicago *(G-5972)*

Rapid Displays Inc ....D....... 773 927-1500
Chicago *(G-5973)*

Red Bud Winery Inc ....G....... 618 282-9463
Ruma *(G-18105)*

Rhine Hall ....G....... 312 243-4313
Chicago *(G-6023)*

Robert Boldrey ....G....... 618 592-4892
Oblong *(G-15827)*

Sensus LLC ....G....... 312 379-9463
Chicago *(G-6136)*

Shale Lake LLC ....G....... 618 637-2470
Staunton *(G-19478)*

Shawnee Grapevines LLC ....G....... 618 893-9463
Cobden *(G-6943)*

Shawnee Winery ....G....... 618 658-8400
Vienna *(G-20119)*

Southern Ill Wine Trail Nfp ....G....... 618 695-9463
Golconda *(G-10668)*

◆ Terlato Wine Group Ltd ....E....... 847 604-8900
Lake Bluff *(G-12210)*

Terraneo Merchants Inc ....G....... 312 753-9134
Lincolnwood *(G-12845)*

Tuscan Hills Winery LLC ....G....... 217 347-9463
Effingham *(G-8427)*

Valentino Vineyards Inc ....G....... 847 634-2831
Long Grove *(G-13173)*

Village Vintner Winery Brewry ....G....... 847 658-4900
Algonquin *(G-392)*

Vins & Vignobles LLC ....G....... 312 375-7656
Mount Prospect *(G-14581)*

▲ Vma Group Inc ....G....... 847 877-7039
Vernon Hills *(G-20108)*

Walnut St Winery Plus Saunas ....G....... 217 498-9800
Rochester *(G-17173)*

Waterman Winery & Vineyards ....G....... 815 264-3268
Waterman *(G-20302)*

Weingarten LLC ....G....... 618 973-1879
Belleville *(G-1610)*

Willetts Winery & Cellar ....G....... 309 968-7070
Manito *(G-13441)*

Winery West of Wise ....G....... 217 632-6003
Petersburg *(G-16605)*

Wyldewood Cellars 2 LLC ....G....... 217 469-9463
Saint Joseph *(G-18321)*

2085 Liquors, Distilled, Rectified & Blended

21 Holdings LLC ....G....... 630 876-4886
West Chicago *(G-20528)*

▲ 773 LLC ....G....... 312 707-8780
Chicago *(G-3477)*

773 LLC ....G....... 312 707-8780
Chicago *(G-3478)*

Angels Share Brands LLC ....G....... 312 494-1100
Chicago *(G-3697)*

▲ Apostrophe Brands ....F....... 312 832-0300
Chicago *(G-3713)*

Barnstormer Distilleries ....G....... 314 397-1100
Rockford *(G-17313)*

Barrel ....G....... 312 754-0156
Chicago *(G-3836)*

Bartesian Corp ....G....... 847 302-4467
Chicago *(G-3844)*

◆ Beam Global Spirits & Wine LLC ....C....... 847 948-8888
Chicago *(G-3851)*

◆ Beam Suntory Inc ....C....... 312 964-6999
Chicago *(G-3852)*

Black Band LLC ....G....... 309 208-0323
Peoria *(G-16393)*

▲ Blaum Brothers Distilling Co ....F....... 815 777-1000
Galena *(G-10164)*

▲ Callison Distributing LLC ....D....... 618 277-4300
Belleville *(G-1537)*

Cliffords Pub Inc ....G....... 847 259-3000
Palatine *(G-16100)*

Copper Fiddle Distilery ....G....... 847 847-7613
Lake Zurich *(G-12397)*

Crystal Rain Distillery I ....G....... 224 508-9361
Lake Forest *(G-12242)*

Diageo North America Inc ....E....... 815 267-4400
Plainfield *(G-16656)*

Distillery Geeks Inc ....G....... 630 240-7259
Chicago *(G-4368)*

Dtrs Enterprises Inc ....G....... 630 296-6890
Bolingbrook *(G-2170)*

Fire & Ice Imports LLC ....G....... 310 871-1695
Morris *(G-14305)*

▲ Future Brands LLC ....C....... 847 444-1880
Chicago *(G-4645)*

Glunz Fmly Winery Cellars Inc ....E....... 847 548-9463
Grayslake *(G-10777)*

Heaven Hill Distillery Inc ....G....... 773 564-9791
Chicago *(G-4796)*

◆ Jim Beam Brands Co ....B....... 847 948-8903
Deerfield *(G-7620)*

JK Williams Distilling LLC ....G....... 309 839-0591
East Peoria *(G-8272)*

Kats Meow ....G....... 815 747-2113
East Dubuque *(G-8177)*

Kindred Spirits Distillery ....G....... 815 910-7116
Mendota *(G-13944)*

◆ Kothe Distilling Tech Inc ....G....... 312 878-7766
Chicago *(G-5125)*

▲ Koval Inc ....F....... 312 878-7988
Chicago *(G-5126)*

▲ Koval Inc ....F....... 773 944-0089
Chicago *(G-5127)*

Let There Be Distillers LLC ....G....... 217 741-0392
Chicago *(G-5209)*

Makers Mark Distillery Inc ....G....... 312 964-6999
Chicago *(G-5320)*

Mega Equipment Inc ....G....... 309 764-5310
Moline *(G-14160)*

Mgp Ingredients Illinois Inc ....C....... 309 353-3990
Pekin *(G-16345)*

Mgpi Processing Inc ....C....... 309 353-3990
Pekin *(G-16346)*

Mid-Oak Distillery Inc ....F....... 708 926-9131
Posen *(G-16797)*

Most Enterprise Inc ....D....... 800 792-4669
Chicago *(G-5504)*

North Shore Distillery LLC ....G....... 847 574-2499
Libertyville *(G-12689)*

Podhalanska LLC ....G....... 630 247-9256
Lemont *(G-12584)*

▲ Premiere Distillery LLC ....G....... 847 662-4444
Gurnee *(G-10915)*

Rumshine Distilling LLC ....G....... 217 446-6960
Tilton *(G-19796)*

▲ Sazerac North America Inc ....E....... 502 423-5225
Chicago *(G-6108)*

Skeptic Distillery Co ....G....... 708 223-8286
Melrose Park *(G-13915)*

Sun Beam Logistics Inc ....G....... 847 454-5884
Chicago *(G-6267)*

Tailwinds Distillery ....G....... 630 746-7526
Plainfield *(G-16721)*

Tiller Farms Holdings LLC ....G....... 224 572-7814
Beach Park *(G-1444)*

Two Eagles Distillery Llc ....G....... 773 450-7575
Mount Prospect *(G-14577)*

Vincit Omnia LLC ....G....... 773 631-4020
Chicago *(G-6553)*

Whiskey Acres Distilling Co ....F....... 815 739-8711
Dekalb *(G-7714)*

Windy City Distilling Inc ....G....... 312 788-7503
Wheeling *(G-21014)*

2086 Soft Drinks

AD Huesing Corporation ....E....... 309 788-5652
Rock Island *(G-17199)*

American Bottling Company ....E....... 217 356-0577
Champaign *(G-3264)*

American Bottling Company ....B....... 708 947-5000
Northlake *(G-15540)*

American Bottling Company ....E....... 815 877-7777
Loves Park *(G-13188)*

American Bottling Company ....E....... 309 693-2777
Edwards *(G-8336)*

Amwell ....F....... 630 898-6900
Aurora *(G-1051)*

Arbor Private Inv Co LLC ....G....... 312 981-3770
Chicago *(G-3718)*

▲ Balon International Corp ....E....... 773 379-7779
Chicago *(G-3821)*

Beastman Tea LLC ....G....... 636 362-4594
Edwardsville *(G-8350)*

Berner Food & Beverage LLC ....B....... 815 563-4222
Dakota *(G-7311)*

Brewers Bottlers & Bev Corp ....G....... 773 262-9711
Chicago *(G-3952)*

Central State Coca-Cola Peru ....G....... 815 220-3100
Peru *(G-16572)*

Chicago Bottling Industries ....G....... 847 885-8093
Hoffman Estates *(G-11413)*

Clearly Kosher Foods ....F....... 630 546-2052
Aurora *(G-1076)*

▲ Clover Club Bottling Co Inc ....F....... 773 261-7100
Chicago *(G-4180)*

Coca Cola ....G....... 630 588-8786
Carol Stream *(G-2963)*

Coca Cola Bottling Compan ....G....... 847 227-6766
Rosemont *(G-18006)*

Coca Cola Fleet Service ....G....... 847 600-2279
Niles *(G-15111)*

Coca-Cola Btlg Wisconsin Del ....B....... 847 647-0200
Niles *(G-15112)*

Coca-Cola Company ....D....... 847 647-0200
Niles *(G-15113)*

Coca-Cola Refreshments USA Inc ....C....... 630 513-5247
Saint Charles *(G-18171)*

Coca-Cola Refreshments USA Inc ....G....... 217 348-1001
Charleston *(G-3400)*

Coca-Cola Refreshments USA Inc ....C....... 708 597-6700
Alsip *(G-433)*

Coca-Cola Refreshments USA Inc ....D....... 847 647-0200
Niles *(G-15114)*

Coca-Cola Refreshments USA Inc ....D....... 708 597-4700
Chicago *(G-4188)*

Coca-Cola Refreshments USA Inc ....D....... 309 697-8600
Bartonville *(G-1329)*

Coca-Cola Refreshments USA Inc ....E....... 217 544-4892
Springfield *(G-19352)*

Coca-Cola Refreshments USA Inc ....E....... 217 367-1761
Urbana *(G-19978)*

Coca-Cola Refreshments USA Inc ....C....... 813 298-1000
Rosemont *(G-18007)*

Coca-Cola Refreshments USA Inc ....C....... 618 542-2101
Du Quoin *(G-8117)*

Containers Inc ....G....... 708 442-2000
Lyons *(G-13306)*

Crisp Container Corporation ....D....... 618 998-0400
Marion *(G-13508)*

Decatur Bottling Co ....D....... 217 429-5415
Decatur *(G-7485)*

Dr Pepper/7 Up Bottling Group ....G....... 217 585-1496
Springfield *(G-19360)*

Ds Services of America Inc ....C....... 773 586-8600
Chicago *(G-4399)*

Ds Services of America Inc ....F....... 800 322-6272
Rockford *(G-17386)*

Ds Services of America Inc ....E....... 815 469-7100
Frankfort *(G-9787)*

E & J Gallo Winery ....E....... 630 505-4000
Lisle *(G-12886)*

Egg Cream America Inc ....G....... 847 559-2700
Northbrook *(G-15381)*

▼ Emmert John ....F....... 773 292-6580
Chicago *(G-4499)*

▲ Essen Nutrition Corporation ....E....... 630 739-6700
Romeoville *(G-17817)*

Excel Bottling Co ....E....... 618 526-7159
Breese *(G-2302)*

Fast Forward Energy Inc ....G....... 312 860-0978
Chicago *(G-4562)*

Florida Fruit Juices Inc ....E....... 773 586-6200
Chicago *(G-4611)*

Flowers Distributing Inc ....E....... 618 255-1021
East Alton *(G-8165)*

▼ Gatorade Company ....A....... 312 821-1000
Chicago *(G-4662)*

Gold Standard Enterprises Inc ....E....... 217 546-1633
Springfield *(G-19375)*

Great Lakes Coca-Cola Dist LLC ....D....... 847 227-6500
Rosemont *(G-18025)*

Heartland Coca-Cola Btlg LLC ....A....... 217 544-4891
Springfield *(G-19380)*

Heartland Coca-Cola Btlg LLC ....A....... 217 223-3336
Quincy *(G-16890)*

Heartland Coca-Cola Btlg LLC ....A....... 217 367-1761
Urbana *(G-19987)*

Heartland Coca-Cola Btlg LLC ....A....... 309 697-8600
Bartonville *(G-1332)*

Heartland Coca-Cola Btlg LLC ....A....... 217 348-1001
Charleston *(G-3403)*

Henderson Water District ....G....... 618 498-6418
Jerseyville *(G-11793)*

▲ Hinckley & Schmitt Inc ....A....... 773 586-8600
Chicago *(G-4823)*

Home Juice Corp ....G....... 708 345-5370
Melrose Park *(G-13880)*

Iberia Foods Corp ....G....... 847 678-2200
Bensenville *(G-1821)*

Kalena LLC ....G....... 773 598-0033
Chicago *(G-5078)*

Employee Codes: A=Over 500 employees, B=251-500
C=101-250, D=51-100, E=20-50, F=10-19, G=3-9

2020 Harris Illinois
Industrial Directory

823

20 FOOD AND KINDRED PRODUCTS

Keurig Dr Pepper Inc ....D...... 708 947-5000
  Northlake (G-15549)
Keurig Dr Pepper Inc ....G...... 815 877-7777
  Loves Park (G-13228)
Key Colony Inc ....G...... 630 783-8572
  Lemont (G-12568)
Komodo Brands LLC ....G...... 312 788-2730
  Chicago (G-5121)
Lee Gilster-Mary Corporation .....D...... 815 472-6456
  Momence (G-14186)
Lifeway Kefir Shop LLC ....E...... 847 967-1010
  Morton Grove (G-14421)
P-Americas LLC ....E...... 217 446-0123
  Danville (G-7371)
P-Americas LLC ....D...... 847 437-1520
  Elk Grove Village (G-9167)
P-Americas LLC ....B...... 773 893-2300
  Chicago (G-5731)
P-Americas LLC ....D...... 815 939-3123
  Kankakee (G-11996)
P-Americas LLC ....C...... 309 266-2400
  Morton (G-14375)
P-Americas LLC ....D...... 312 821-2266
  Chicago (G-5732)
P-Americas LLC ....C...... 773 624-8013
  Chicago (G-5733)
Pepsi Cola Gen Bttlers of Lima ......G...... 847 253-1000
  Rolling Meadows (G-17760)
Pepsi Mid America ....G...... 217 826-8118
  Marshall (G-13576)
Pepsi Midamerica Co ....A...... 618 997-1377
  Marion (G-13525)
Pepsi Midamerica Co ....B...... 618 242-6285
  Mount Vernon (G-14634)
Pepsi-Cola Chmpgn Urbana Btlr ...D...... 217 352-4126
  Champaign (G-3330)
Pepsi-Cola Metro Btlg Co Inc ....D...... 847 598-3000
  Chicago (G-5788)
Pepsico ....F...... 217 443-8607
  Danville (G-7373)
Pepsico Inc ....D...... 312 821-1000
  Chicago (G-5789)
Pepsico Inc ....B...... 847 767-2026
  Barrington (G-1234)
Pespico ....G...... 708 625-3450
  Bridgeview (G-2374)
Powercoco LLC ....G...... 614 323-5890
  Chicago (G-5848)
Protein2o Inc ....E...... 646 919-5320
  Elk Grove Village (G-9199)
Pure Flo Bottling Inc ....G...... 815 963-4797
  Rockford (G-17562)
Pursuit Beverage Company LLC ....G...... 888 606-3353
  Waukegan (G-20485)
Pyramid Bottling LLC ....G...... 847 565-9412
  Waukegan (G-20486)
◆ Quaker Oats Company ....A...... 312 821-1000
  Chicago (G-5927)
Quaker Oats Company ....C...... 708 458-7090
  Bridgeview (G-2376)
Quincy Pepsi-Cola Bottling Co ......F...... 309 833-4263
  Macomb (G-13399)
Quincy Pepsi-Cola Bottling Co ......D...... 217 223-8600
  Quincy (G-16934)
Refreshment Services Inc ....F...... 217 223-8600
  Quincy (G-16939)
Refreshment Services Inc ....E...... 217 522-8841
  Springfield (G-19432)
Refreshment Services Inc ....E...... 217 429-5415
  Decatur (G-7541)
◆ Reyes Holdings LLC ....E...... 847 227-6500
  Rosemont (G-18048)
Rockys Beverages LLC ....F...... 312 561-3182
  Glenview (G-10613)
Rorke & Riley Specialty B ....G...... 773 929-2522
  Chicago (G-6060)
Royal Crown Tresses LLC ....G...... 773 967-8409
  Lynwood (G-13299)
Sirius Performance Company LLC G...... 312 909-0775
  Glenview (G-10622)
Springfield Pepsi-Cola Btlg Co ....C...... 217 522-8841
  Springfield (G-19453)
Team Sider Inc ....G...... 847 767-0107
  Highland Park (G-11303)
Tst/Impreso Inc ....G...... 630 775-9555
  Addison (G-320)
◆ Vision Wholesale Corp ....G...... 708 496-6015
  Chicago (G-6558)
▲ West Water Inc ....G...... 312 326-7480
  Chicago (G-6606)

Win Soon Chicago Inc ....C...... 630 585-7090
  Oswego (G-16032)
Wis - Pak Inc ....D...... 217 224-6800
  Quincy (G-16958)
Wonder Tucky Distillery & Btlg ......C...... 224 678-4396
  Woodstock (G-21449)

2087 Flavoring Extracts & Syrups

A Barr Ftn Beverage Sls & Svc ......D...... 708 442-2000
  Lemont (G-12550)
Abelei Inc ....F...... 630 859-1410
  North Aurora (G-15253)
Amt Group LLC ....D...... 847 324-4411
  Niles (G-15103)
▼ Beverage Flavors Intl LLC ....F...... 773 248-3860
  Chicago (G-3876)
Big Tent Inc ....E...... 708 532-1222
  Tinley Park (G-19811)
▲ Capol LLC ....G...... 224 545-5095
  Deerfield (G-7599)
Caravan Ingredients Inc ....D...... 708 849-8590
  Dolton (G-7935)
Coca-Cola Refreshments USA Inc C...... 618 542-2101
  Du Quoin (G-8117)
◆ Compact Industries Inc ....C...... 630 513-9600
  Saint Charles (G-18173)
Containers Inc ....G...... 708 442-2000
  Lyons (G-13306)
Culinary Co-Pack Incorporated .....E...... 847 451-1551
  Franklin Park (G-9921)
Custom Culinary Inc ....D...... 630 299-0500
  Oswego (G-16000)
Dawn Food Products Inc ....C...... 815 933-0600
  Bradley (G-2280)
Dennco Inc ....G...... 708 862-0070
  Burnham (G-2645)
◆ Edgar A Weber & Company ....E...... 847 215-1980
  Wheeling (G-20886)
Edgar A Weber & Company ....E...... 847 215-1980
  Wheeling (G-20887)
◆ Edlong Corporation ....D...... 847 439-9230
  Elk Grove Village (G-8969)
◆ Equi-Chem International Inc .....F...... 630 784-0432
  Carol Stream (G-2979)
FBC Industries Inc ....E...... 847 839-0880
  Rochelle (G-17140)
Flavor Concepts Inc ....F...... 630 520-9060
  Addison (G-123)
Flavor Savor Inc ....E...... 630 868-0350
  Carol Stream (G-2985)
◆ Flavorchem Corporation ....D...... 630 932-8100
  Downers Grove (G-8004)
Flavorfocus LLC ....F...... 630 520-9060
  Addison (G-124)
Fona International Inc ....E...... 630 578-8600
  Batavia (G-1380)
Fona International Inc ....G...... 630 578-8600
  Saint Charles (G-18200)
▲ Fona International Inc ....E...... 630 578-8600
  Geneva (G-10269)
Fona Uk Ltd ....C...... 331 442-5779
  Geneva (G-10270)
Gycor International Ltd ....F...... 630 754-8070
  Woodridge (G-21308)
H B Taylor Co ....E...... 773 254-4805
  Chicago (G-4758)
Inside Beverages ....C...... 847 438-1338
  Lake Zurich (G-12423)
Insight Beverages Inc ....E...... 847 438-1598
  Lake Zurich (G-12424)
◆ Insight Beverages Inc ....E...... 847 438-1598
  Lake Zurich (G-12425)
Institutional Foods Packing Co .....E...... 847 904-5250
  Glenview (G-10569)
Interntnal Ingredient Mall LLC ......G...... 630 462-1414
  Geneva (G-10285)
◆ Jel Sert Co ....G...... 630 231-7590
  West Chicago (G-20603)
Jo Snow Inc ....C...... 773 732-3045
  Chicago (G-5033)
Key Colony Inc ....G...... 630 783-8572
  Lemont (G-12568)
Kosto Food Products Company ....F...... 847 487-2600
  Wauconda (G-20367)
Kraft Foods Asia PCF Svcs LLC ...G...... 847 943-4000
  Deerfield (G-7627)
Kraft Heinz Company ....F...... 847 646-2000
  Chicago (G-5129)
▲ Kruger North America Inc ....F...... 708 851-3670
  Oak Park (G-15761)

Lansing Wings Inc ....G...... 708 895-3300
  Lansing (G-12504)
Lee Gilster-Mary Corporation ....D...... 618 965-3426
  Steeleville (G-19481)
▲ Mondelez Global LLC ....C...... 847 943-4000
  Deerfield (G-7637)
◆ Mondelez International Inc ......A...... 847 943-4000
  Chicago (G-5490)
▲ Necta Sweet Inc ....E...... 847 215-9955
  Buffalo Grove (G-2579)
▲ Neiman Bros Co Inc ....E...... 773 463-3000
  Chicago (G-5564)
NFC Company Inc ....G...... 773 472-6468
  Chicago (G-5594)
◆ Northwestern Flavors LLC ....E...... 630 231-6111
  West Chicago (G-20625)
Passion Fruit Drink Inc ....G...... 708 769-4749
  South Holland (G-19238)
Pepsico Inc ....D...... 312 821-1000
  Chicago (G-5789)
Ra Energy Drink Inc ....G...... 773 503-8574
  Chicago (G-5956)
▲ Royal Foods & Flavors Inc ....F...... 847 595-9166
  Elk Grove Village (G-9222)
Sensient Flavors ....C...... 847 645-7002
  Hoffman Estates (G-11456)
◆ Sensient Flavors LLC ....B...... 317 243-3521
  Hoffman Estates (G-11457)
Sensient Flavors LLC ....F...... 815 857-3691
  Amboy (G-580)
Sensient Technologies Corp ....E...... 708 481-0910
  Matteson (G-13628)
◆ Sethness Products Company ....F...... 847 329-2080
  Skokie (G-19028)
▲ Silesia Flavors Inc ....E...... 847 645-0270
  Hoffman Estates (G-11459)
◆ Stepan Company ....B...... 847 446-7500
  Northfield (G-15531)
Sterling Extract Company Inc ....E...... 847 451-9728
  Franklin Park (G-10053)
▲ Synergy Flavors Inc ....D...... 847 487-1011
  Wauconda (G-20394)
▲ Synergy Flavors NY Company LLC E 585 232-6648
  Wauconda (G-20395)
Tampico Beverages Inc ....F...... 773 296-0190
  Chicago (G-6318)
◆ Tampico Beverages Inc ....E...... 773 296-0190
  Chicago (G-6319)
▼ Tone Products Inc ....E...... 708 681-3660
  Melrose Park (G-13923)
◆ Treehouse Foods Inc ....C...... 708 483-1300
  Oak Brook (G-15665)
Ur Inc ....G...... 630 450-5279
  Batavia (G-1437)
Watson LLC ....E...... 217 824-4440
  Taylorville (G-19763)
White Stokes Company Inc ....E...... 773 254-5000
  Lincolnwood (G-12851)
▼ Wm Wrigley Jr Company ....B...... 312 280-4710
  Chicago (G-6654)
Wm Wrigley Jr Company ....A...... 312 644-2121
  Chicago (G-6656)

2091 Fish & Seafoods, Canned & Cured

F&A Specialty Foods Inc ....G...... 312 887-1344
  Chicago (G-4553)
Kraft Heinz Foods Company ....C...... 847 291-3900
  Northbrook (G-15415)
◆ Sokol and Company ....D...... 708 482-8250
  Countryside (G-7071)
◆ Vita Food Products Inc ....D...... 312 738-4500
  Chicago (G-6560)

2092 Fish & Seafoods, Fresh & Frozen

Betty Watters ....G...... 618 232-1150
  Hamburg (G-10948)
Dar Enterprises Inc ....G...... 815 961-8748
  Rockford (G-17367)
Ethos Seafood Group LLC ....D...... 312 858-3474
  Hodgkins (G-11388)
King Midas Seafood Entps Inc ......E...... 847 566-2192
  Mundelein (G-14707)
Open Waters Seafood Company ....E...... 847 329-8585
  Skokie (G-19000)
Orin Briant Inc ....G...... 779 206-2800
  New Lenox (G-15048)
Rich Products Corporation ....D...... 847 581-1749
  Niles (G-15165)
Sudpack USA Inc ....E...... 630 258-4015
  Naperville (G-14921)

SIC SECTION
20 FOOD AND KINDRED PRODUCTS

▲ Vanee Foods Company ....D....... 708 449-7300
   Berkeley *(G-1945)*
Wisepak Foods LLC ....E....... 773 772-0072
   Chicago *(G-6650)*

2095 Coffee

Art House Coffee LLC......................G....... 618 659-0571
   Edwardsville *(G-8345)*
Back of Yards Coffee LLC ....G....... 773 475-6381
   Chicago *(G-3812)*
Bamenda Coffee Company Inc ....G....... 214 566-8175
   Chicago *(G-3823)*
Berner Food & Beverage LLC ....B....... 815 563-4222
   Dakota *(G-7311)*
Big Shoulders Coffee Works ....G....... 312 888-3042
   Chicago *(G-3882)*
Coffee Brewmasters Usa LLC ....F....... 773 294-9665
   Buffalo Grove *(G-2526)*
◆ Compact Industries Inc..................C....... 630 513-9600
   Saint Charles *(G-18173)*
Cup O Joe Coffee LLC.....................G....... 877 828-7656
   Chicago *(G-4284)*
Farmer Bros Co ....G....... 217 787-7565
   Springfield *(G-19365)*
Hillshire Brands Company ....C....... 847 956-7575
   Elk Grove Village *(G-9035)*
◆ Insight Beverages Inc....................E....... 847 438-1598
   Lake Zurich *(G-12425)*
Javamania Coffee Roastery Inc.........G....... 815 885-4661
   Loves Park *(G-13223)*
Kraft Foods Asia PCF Svcs LLC ....G....... 847 943-4000
   Deerfield *(G-7627)*
Kraft Heinz Company ....C....... 847 646-2000
   Chicago *(G-5129)*
Limitless Coffee LLC ....E....... 630 779-3778
   Chicago *(G-5223)*
Manhattan Island ....G....... 312 762-5152
   Chicago *(G-5326)*
Mondelez International Inc................G....... 815 710-2114
   Morris *(G-14316)*
◆ Mondelez International Inc ....A....... 847 943-4000
   Chicago *(G-5490)*
▲ Napco Inc ....E....... 630 406-1100
   Batavia *(G-1397)*
Sparrow Coffee Roastery ....G....... 321 648-6415
   Westchester *(G-20712)*
Stewarts Prvate Blend Fods Inc ....E....... 773 489-2500
   Carol Stream *(G-3077)*
Trade-Mark Coffee Corporation ....F....... 847 382-4200
   North Barrington *(G-15289)*
▲ Two Brothers Brewing Company.....G....... 630 393-2337
   Warrenville *(G-20256)*
Wolfart Maciej ....G....... 312 248-3575
   Chicago *(G-6663)*

2096 Potato Chips & Similar Prdts

Altona Co ....G....... 815 232-7819
   Freeport *(G-10099)*
Aunt Ems Gourmet Popcorn Inc ....F....... 309 447-6612
   Deer Creek *(G-7571)*
▲ Azteca Foods Inc.........................C....... 708 563-6600
   Chicago *(G-3802)*
Benestar Brands LLC.......................G....... 773 254-7400
   Chicago *(G-3868)*
Campbell Soup Company ....G....... 618 548-3001
   Salem *(G-18333)*
Campbell Soup Company ....C....... 630 241-6200
   Downers Grove *(G-7964)*
▲ Chipita America Inc.....................E....... 708 731-2434
   Westchester *(G-20693)*
Chips Aleeces Pita ....G....... 309 699-8859
   East Peoria *(G-8260)*
Creekstone Kettle Works Ltd ....F....... 217 246-5355
   Raymond *(G-16988)*
Donkey Brands LLC ....F....... 630 251-2007
   Carol Stream *(G-2977)*
El Popocatapetl Industries Inc..........F....... 773 843-0888
   Chicago *(G-4466)*
El-Ranchero Food Products ....F....... 773 843-0430
   Chicago *(G-4473)*
▲ El-Ranchero Food Products ....E....... 773 847-9167
   Chicago *(G-4474)*
Evans Food Group Ltd ....G....... 773 254-7400
   Chicago *(G-4536)*
◆ Evans Foods Inc ....D....... 773 254-7400
   Chicago *(G-4537)*
Frito-Lay North America Inc............C....... 217 532-5040
   Hillsboro *(G-11311)*
Great American Popcorn Company ...G....... 815 777-4116
   Galena *(G-10173)*

Hello Delicious Brands LLC..............F....... 844 845-4544
   Northbrook *(G-15399)*
◆ John B Sanfilippo & Son Inc ....C....... 847 289-1800
   Elgin *(G-8632)*
Masa Uno Inc..................................G....... 708 749-4866
   Berwyn *(G-1956)*
McCleary Inc ....C....... 815 389-3053
   South Beloit *(G-19101)*
Mozaics LLC ....G....... 614 306-1881
   Chicago *(G-5513)*
Mrs Fishers Inc...............................F....... 815 964-9114
   Rockford *(G-17532)*
Ole Saltys of Rockford Inc ....G....... 815 637-2447
   Rockford *(G-17543)*
Ole Saltys of Rockford Inc ....G....... 815 637-2447
   Loves Park *(G-13241)*
Pepsico Inc ....D....... 312 821-1000
   Chicago *(G-5789)*
Prairieland Food Products Co ....G....... 708 396-8826
   Alsip *(G-496)*
▲ Princess Foods Inc ....E....... 847 933-1820
   Skokie *(G-19011)*
◆ Quality Snack Foods Inc ....D....... 708 377-7120
   Alsip *(G-499)*
R and B Distributors Inc..................G....... 815 433-6843
   Ottawa *(G-16074)*
Revolution Companies Inc...............G....... 800 826-4083
   Chicago *(G-6019)*
Safe Fair Food Company LLC ....F....... 904 930-4277
   Chicago *(G-6088)*
Scotts Popcorn LLC ....G....... 773 608-9625
   Chicago *(G-6121)*
Select Snacks Company Inc ....D....... 773 933-2167
   Chicago *(G-6133)*
Snak-King Corp...............................C....... 815 232-6700
   Freeport *(G-10142)*
▼ Tee Lee Popcorn Inc ....E....... 815 864-2363
   Shannon *(G-18874)*
▲ Thanasi Foods LLC......................E....... 720 570-1065
   Chicago *(G-6359)*
Tpf Liquidation Co ....D....... 847 362-0028
   Lake Forest *(G-12315)*
Utz Quality Foods LLC....................D....... 309 245-2191
   Farmington *(G-9664)*
Utz Quality Foods LLC....................E....... 309 772-2798
   Bushnell *(G-2747)*
Wisconsin Wilderness Food Pdts .....G....... 847 735-8661
   Lake Forest *(G-12323)*

2097 Ice

Carnaghi Towing & Repair Inc ....F....... 217 446-0333
   Tilton *(G-19793)*
Collinsville Ice & Fuel Co ....F....... 618 344-3272
   Collinsville *(G-6955)*
Four Seasons Ace Hardware ....G....... 618 439-2101
   Benton *(G-1925)*
Home City Ice ....F....... 773 622-9400
   Chicago *(G-4833)*
Interntnal Ice Bgging Systems ....G....... 312 633-4000
   Glencoe *(G-10431)*
Just Ice Inc ....G....... 773 301-7323
   Chicago *(G-5062)*
Muller-Pinehurst Dairy Inc ....C....... 815 968-0441
   Rockford *(G-17533)*
Pro Rep Sale IL ....F....... 847 382-1592
   Barrington *(G-1238)*
Sisler Dairy Products Company ....G....... 815 376-2913
   Ohio *(G-15845)*
Sislers Ice Inc.................................E....... 815 756-6903
   Dekalb *(G-7701)*
Tinley Ice Company ....E....... 708 532-8777
   University Park *(G-19968)*

2098 Macaroni, Spaghetti & Noodles

Baily International Inc.....................D....... 773 927-3233
   Chicago *(G-3816)*
Burgess & Burgess Inc ....G....... 847 855-1048
   Gurnee *(G-10863)*
General Mills Inc ....B....... 630 231-1140
   Calumet City *(G-2778)*
◆ Gilster-Mary Lee Corporation ....A....... 618 826-2361
   Chester *(G-3456)*
Golden Grain Company ....G....... 708 458-7020
   Bridgeview *(G-2351)*
Kraft Heinz Foods Company ....G....... 217 378-1900
   Champaign *(G-3315)*
Lee Gilster-Mary Corporation ....G....... 618 826-2361
   Chester *(G-3457)*
Lee Gilster-Mary Corporation ....G....... 618 443-5676
   Sparta *(G-19256)*

Lee Gilster-Mary Corporation ....D....... 815 472-6456
   Momence *(G-14186)*
Lee Gilster-Mary Corporation ....B....... 618 965-3449
   Steeleville *(G-19482)*
Lee Gilster-Mary Corporation ....G....... 618 965-3426
   Steeleville *(G-19481)*
◆ Mary Lee Packaging Corporation ..E....... 618 826-2361
   Chester *(G-3458)*
Noodle Party ....G....... 773 205-0505
   Chicago *(G-5610)*
▲ Pastafresh Co ....G....... 773 745-5888
   Chicago *(G-5769)*
Tank Noodle Inc..............................G....... 773 878-2253
   Chicago *(G-6323)*
Trinity Services Inc ....G....... 815 485-5612
   New Lenox *(G-15066)*
Zapp Noodle ....G....... 618 979-8863
   O Fallon *(G-15586)*

2099 Food Preparations, NEC

A-Z Sales Inc ....G....... 630 334-2869
   Chicago *(G-3495)*
Abelei Inc ....F....... 630 859-1410
   North Aurora *(G-15253)*
◆ Ach Food Companies Inc ....C....... 866 386-8282
   Oakbrook Terrace *(G-15781)*
▲ Agritech Worldwide Inc ....E....... 847 549-6002
   Mundelein *(G-14660)*
Ajinomoto Foods North Amer Inc.....C....... 815 452-2361
   Toluca *(G-19886)*
Alexia Foods ....G....... 312 374-3449
   Chicago *(G-3605)*
Altona Co ....G....... 815 232-7819
   Freeport *(G-10099)*
American Kitchen Delights Inc ....D....... 708 210-3200
   Harvey *(G-11073)*
American Tristar Inc ....G....... 630 262-5500
   Geneva *(G-10252)*
Archer-Daniels-Midland Company ....E....... 309 772-2141
   Bushnell *(G-2737)*
Arts Tamales ....G....... 309 367-2850
   Metamora *(G-13958)*
Athenian Foods Co ....F....... 708 343-6700
   Melrose Park *(G-13827)*
Avani Spices LLC ....G....... 847 532-1075
   Algonquin *(G-366)*
▲ Azteca Foods Inc.........................C....... 708 563-6600
   Chicago *(G-3802)*
◆ Barilla America Inc ....D....... 515 956-4400
   Northbrook *(G-15345)*
Bay Valley Foods LLC ....D....... 773 927-7700
   Chicago *(G-3847)*
Bear-Stewart Corporation ....E....... 773 276-0400
   Chicago *(G-3854)*
Bellisario Holdings LLC ....G....... 847 867-2960
   Park Ridge *(G-16270)*
Bernard Food Industries Inc ....D....... 847 869-5222
   Evanston *(G-9499)*
Briannas Pancake Cafe ....G....... 630 365-4770
   Elburn *(G-8447)*
Cahokia Rice ....G....... 618 661-1060
   Mc Clure *(G-13686)*
Calma Optima Foods ....G....... 847 962-8329
   Franklin Park *(G-9897)*
Canadian Harvest LP ....F....... 309 343-7808
   Galesburg *(G-10187)*
Canyon Foods Inc ....G....... 773 890-9888
   Chicago *(G-4016)*
Caravan Ingredients Inc ....D....... 708 849-8590
   Dolton *(G-7935)*
Castro Foods Wholesale Inc ....E....... 773 869-0641
   Chicago *(G-4038)*
▼ Cfc Inc ....D....... 847 257-8920
   Des Plaines *(G-7743)*
Char Crust Co Inc ....G....... 773 528-0600
   Chicago *(G-4071)*
Chateau Food Products Inc ....F....... 708 863-4207
   Chicago *(G-4079)*
Chicago Coml & Consmr Brands .....G....... 773 484-5771
   Chicago *(G-4097)*
Chicago Coml Consmr Brands LLC ..G....... 773 488-2639
   Chicago *(G-4098)*
Chicago Oriental Cnstr Inc ....G....... 312 733-9633
   Chicago *(G-4120)*
Chicks and Salsa LLC ....G....... 815 735-6660
   Verona *(G-20116)*
Christian Wolf Inc ....G....... 618 667-9522
   Bartelso *(G-1252)*
Cindys Pocket Kitchen ....G....... 815 388-8385
   Harvard *(G-11050)*

Employee Codes: A=Over 500 employees, B=251-500
C=101-250, D=51-100, E=20-50, F=10-19, G=3-9

2020 Harris Illinois
Industrial Directory

20 FOOD AND KINDRED PRODUCTS

Clown Global Brands LLC .... G 847 564-5950
  Northbrook (G-15362)
Combined Technologies Inc .... G 847 968-4855
  Libertyville (G-12645)
Conagra Brands Inc .... C 312 549-5000
  Chicago (G-4212)
Conagra Brands Inc .... C 630 857-1000
  Naperville (G-14803)
Consumer Vinegar and Spice .... G 708 354-1144
  La Grange (G-12076)
◆ Cornfields LLC .... C 847 263-7000
  Waukegan (G-20430)
Creative Contract Packg LLC .... D 630 851-6226
  Aurora (G-944)
Culinary Co-Pack Inc .... G 847 451-1551
  Franklin Park (G-9920)
Culinary Co-Pack Incorporated .... E 847 451-1551
  Franklin Park (G-9921)
Cultor Food Science Danis .... G 815 259-3311
  Thomson (G-19781)
Custom Culinary Inc .... D 630 928-4898
  Lombard (G-13061)
Custom Culinary Inc .... G 630 299-0500
  Oswego (G-16000)
◆ Custom Menu Insights LLC .... G 312 237-3860
  Chicago (G-4290)
▲ Damron Corporation .... E 773 265-2724
  Chicago (G-4310)
Danisco USA Inc .... G 815 259-3311
  Thomson (G-19782)
Deja Investments Inc .... D 630 408-9222
  Bolingbrook (G-2168)
Deliteful Taste Foods Inc .... G 708 251-5121
  Lansing (G-12490)
Dell Cove Spice Co .... G 312 339-8389
  Chicago (G-4333)
Delobian Foods .... G 773 564-0913
  Chicago (G-4335)
Dennco Inc .... G 708 862-0070
  Burnham (G-2645)
Dominique Graves .... G 773 368-5289
  Broadview (G-2430)
Domino Foods Inc .... F 773 646-2203
  Chicago (G-4380)
Dutch American Foods .... G 708 304-2648
  Crete (G-7139)
E I Du Pont De Nemours & Co .... D 815 259-3311
  Thomson (G-19783)
E3 Artisan Inc .... E 815 575-9315
  Woodstock (G-21384)
▼ Ebro Foods Inc .... D 773 696-0150
  Chicago (G-4443)
Eckert Orchards Inc .... C 618 233-0513
  Belleville (G-1549)
El Popocatapetl Industries Inc .... E 312 421-6143
  Chicago (G-4467)
El Tradicional .... G 773 925-0335
  Chicago (G-4469)
El Valle Florido .... G 630 898-0689
  Aurora (G-1087)
▲ El-Milagro Inc .... B 773 579-6120
  Chicago (G-4470)
El-Milagro Inc .... G 773 650-1614
  Chicago (G-4471)
El-Milagro Inc .... E 773 299-1216
  Chicago (G-4472)
▲ El-Ranchero Food Products .... E 773 847-9167
  Chicago (G-4474)
◆ Equi-Chem International Inc .... F 630 784-0432
  Carol Stream (G-2979)
▲ Essen Nutrition Corporation .... E 630 739-6700
  Romeoville (G-17817)
Euphoria Catering and Events .... G 630 301-4369
  Aurora (G-1092)
Famar Flavor LLC .... G 708 926-2951
  Crestwood (G-7117)
▲ Far East Food Inc .... G 312 733-1688
  Chicago (G-4560)
Father and Son Commercial .... G 773 424-3301
  Chicago (G-4566)
▲ FBC Industries Inc .... G 847 241-6143
  Schaumburg (G-18526)
FBC Industries Inc .... G 847 839-0880
  Rochelle (G-17140)
Fibergel Technologies Inc .... G 847 549-6002
  Mundelein (G-14688)
Flaherty Incorporated .... G 773 472-8456
  Skokie (G-18955)
Fleischmanns Vinegar Co Inc .... F 773 523-2817
  (G-4602)

Food Service .... D 815 933-0725
  Kankakee (G-11972)
Fresh Express Incorporated .... E 630 736-3900
  Streamwood (G-19574)
Fresh Factory .... E 630 580-9038
  Carol Stream (G-2988)
Frito-Lay North America Inc .... F 815 468-3940
  Manteno (G-13448)
Frito-Lay North America Inc .... C 708 331-7200
  Oak Forest (G-15679)
Fruit Fancy .... E 708 724-2613
  Chicago (G-4638)
Funks Grove Pure Maple Syrup .... F 309 874-3360
  Shirley (G-18891)
Futters Nut Butters .... G 847 540-0565
  Hoffman Estates (G-11426)
General Mills Inc .... B 630 231-1140
  Calumet City (G-2778)
Georgies Greek Tasty Food Inc .... G 773 987-1298
  Chicago (G-4685)
Gerard Mitchell Company LLC .... G 708 205-0828
  Yorkville (G-21485)
◆ Gilster-Mary Lee Corporation .... A 618 826-2361
  Chester (G-3456)
Givaudan Flavors Corporation .... G 630 682-5600
  Carol Stream (G-2992)
▲ Gonnella Baking Co .... D 312 733-2020
  Schaumburg (G-18538)
Good Foods Inc .... F 773 260-9110
  Chicago (G-4715)
Good World Noodle Inc .... G 312 326-0441
  Chicago (G-4716)
Gotham Greens Pullman LLC .... E 779 379-0307
  Chicago (G-4719)
▲ Gourmet Gorilla Inc .... C 877 219-3663
  Chicago (G-4720)
Granadino Food Services Corp .... G 708 717-2930
  Bridgeview (G-2352)
Grantco Inc .... G 941 567-9259
  Mundelein (G-14691)
Great American Popcorn Company .... G 815 777-4116
  Galena (G-10173)
◆ Grecian Delight Foods Inc .... E 847 364-1010
  Elk Grove Village (G-9022)
◆ Griffith Foods Group Inc .... F 708 371-0900
  Alsip (G-451)
▲ Griffith Foods Inc .... B 708 371-0900
  Alsip (G-452)
Griffith Foods Inc .... E 773 523-7509
  Chicago (G-4743)
Griffith Foods Worldwide Inc .... G 708 371-0900
  Alsip (G-4443)
Gycor International Ltd .... F 630 754-8070
  Woodridge (G-21308)
H C Schau & Son Inc .... G 630 783-1000
  Woodridge (G-21309)
Hearthside Usa LLC .... F 630 783-1000
  Woodridge (G-21310)
▲ Hearthside Usa LLC .... B 978 716-2530
  Downers Grove (G-8020)
Hensaal Management Group Inc .... E 312 624-8133
  Chicago (G-4804)
Here Holdings LLC .... E 563 723-1008
  Carol Stream (G-2997)
Herman Seekamp Inc .... C 630 628-6555
  Addison (G-149)
Hogback Haven Maple Farm .... E 815 291-9440
  Orangeville (G-15909)
Holcomb Hollow .... G 847 837-9123
  Mundelein (G-14697)
Holton Food Products Company .... F 708 352-5599
  La Grange (G-12078)
Home Style .... G 847 455-5000
  Franklin Park (G-9956)
▲ Hop Kee Incorporated .... G 312 791-9111
  Chicago (G-4839)
Ingredients Golden Hill .... G 773 852-5112
  Chicago (G-4922)
◆ Insight Beverages Inc .... E 847 438-1598
  Lake Zurich (G-12425)
▲ Italia Foods Inc .... E 847 397-4479
  Schaumburg (G-18573)
▲ Ixtapa Foods .... G 773 788-9701
  Chicago (G-4980)
◆ Jbc Holding Co .... G 217 347-7701
  Effingham (G-8404)
◆ Jel Sert Co .... G 630 231-7590
  West Chicago (G-20603)
John B Sanfilippo & Son Inc .... C 847 690-8432
  Elgin (G-8633)

◆ John B Sanfilippo & Son Inc .... C 847 289-1800
  Elgin (G-8632)
Johnny Vans Smokehouse .... G 773 750-1589
  Chicago (G-5045)
Josephs Food Products Co Inc .... G 708 338-4090
  Broadview (G-2446)
JRS J Rettenmaier and Soh .... G 309 343-7808
  Galesburg (G-10203)
K M J Enterprises Inc .... E 847 688-1200
  Gurnee (G-10892)
Kanbo International (us) Inc .... G 630 873-6320
  Lisle (G-12905)
Kent Precision Foods Group Inc .... F 630 226-0071
  Bolingbrook (G-2202)
Kerry Inc .... D 708 450-3260
  Melrose Park (G-13888)
Kosto Food Products Company .... F 847 487-2600
  Wauconda (G-20367)
Kraft Heinz Foods Company .... G 630 907-2590
  Aurora (G-1121)
Kraft Heinz Foods Company .... C 847 646-2000
  Glenview (G-10582)
Kraft Heinz Foods Company .... B 618 451-4820
  Granite City (G-10718)
Kraft Heinz Foods Company .... G 217 378-1900
  Champaign (G-3315)
▲ Kruger North America Inc .... F 708 851-3670
  Oak Park (G-15761)
La Criolla Inc .... E 312 243-8882
  Alsip (G-468)
La Espanola Food Dist Corp .... F 312 733-0775
  Chicago (G-5146)
La Mexicana Tortilleria Inc .... E 773 247-5443
  Chicago (G-5148)
Lancaster Traditions LLC .... G 847 428-5446
  South Barrington (G-19076)
▲ Land OFrost Inc .... C 708 474-7100
  Lansing (G-12502)
Laredo Foods Inc .... E 773 762-1500
  Chicago (G-5177)
▼ Lawrence Foods Inc .... C 847 437-2400
  Elk Grove Village (G-9088)
Lcv Company .... G 309 738-6452
  East Moline (G-8232)
Lee Gilster-Mary Corporation .... D 618 965-3426
  Steeleville (G-19481)
Lee Gilster-Mary Corporation .... G 618 826-2361
  Chester (G-3457)
Lee Gilster-Mary Corporation .... E 618 443-5676
  Sparta (G-19256)
Lee Gilster-Mary Corporation .... D 815 472-6456
  Momence (G-14186)
Legacy Foods Mfg LLC .... G 224 639-5297
  Elk Grove Village (G-9090)
▲ Leos Gluten Free LLC .... G 847 233-9211
  Franklin Park (G-9981)
Liborio Baking Co Inc .... G 708 452-7222
  River Grove (G-17061)
▲ Lightlife Foods Inc .... C 413 774-9000
  Elmhurst (G-9392)
Little Lady Foods Inc .... C 847 806-1440
  Elk Grove Village (G-9096)
Los Gamas Inc .... G 872 829-3514
  Chicago (G-5261)
Ludis Foods Adams Inc .... C 312 939-2877
  Chicago (G-5278)
Mangel and Co .... F 847 634-0730
  Long Grove (G-13162)
Mangel and Co .... E 847 459-3100
  Buffalo Grove (G-2567)
Mareta Ravioli Inc .... F 815 856-2621
  Leonore (G-12612)
Margies Brands Inc .... E 773 643-1417
  Chicago (G-5332)
◆ Mary Lee Packaging Corporation .... E 618 826-2361
  Chester (G-3458)
◆ Mizkan America Inc .... E 847 590-0059
  Mount Prospect (G-14547)
◆ Mizkan America Holdings Inc .... G 847 590-0059
  Mount Prospect (G-14548)
Monterey Mushrooms Inc .... G 815 875-4436
  Princeton (G-16815)
Munoz Flour Tortilleria Inc .... F 773 523-1837
  Chicago (G-5525)
My Own Meals Inc .... G 773 378-6505
  Chicago (G-5530)
▼ My Own Meals Inc .... G 847 948-1118
  Deerfield (G-7639)
Nanas Kitchen Inc .... G 815 363-8500
  Johnsburg (G-11808)

National Vinegar Co ... F ... 618 395-1011
Olney *(G-15878)*
▲ **Necta Sweet Inc** ... E ... 847 215-9955
Buffalo Grove *(G-2579)*
▲ **Neiman Bros Co Inc** ... E ... 773 463-3000
Chicago *(G-5564)*
Nepaley LLC ... G ... 224 420-2310
Chicago *(G-5571)*
New Taste Good Noodle Inc ... G ... 312 842-8980
Chicago *(G-5582)*
◆ **Newly Weds Foods Inc** ... A ... 773 489-7000
Chicago *(G-5584)*
Newly Weds Foods Inc ... D ... 773 628-6900
Chicago *(G-5585)*
Newly Weds Foods Inc ... B ... 773 489-7000
Chicago *(G-5586)*
Ninos LLC ... E ... 708 932-5555
Bloomingdale *(G-2002)*
No Denial Foods ... G ... 312 890-5267
Chicago *(G-5606)*
Noodles Factory LLC ... G ... 312 842-6500
Chicago *(G-5611)*
Nutrivo LLC ... E ... 630 270-1700
Aurora *(G-1140)*
O Chilli Frozen Foods Inc ... E ... 847 562-1991
Northbrook *(G-15442)*
Oakland Noodle Company ... G ... 217 346-2322
Oakland *(G-15819)*
▲ **On-Cor Frozen Foods LLC** ... E ... 630 851-6600
Aurora *(G-1142)*
Open Kitchens Inc ... C ... 312 666-5334
Chicago *(G-5680)*
Open Kitchens Inc ... E ... 312 666-5334
Chicago *(G-5681)*
◆ **OSI Group LLC** ... D ... 630 851-6600
Aurora *(G-1143)*
◆ **OSI Industries LLC** ... D ... 630 851-6600
Aurora *(G-1144)*
OSI Industries LLC ... G ... 773 650-4000
Chicago *(G-5709)*
Papys Foods Inc ... E ... 815 385-3313
McHenry *(G-13776)*
▲ **Pastafresh Co** ... G ... 773 745-5888
Chicago *(G-5769)*
Pastorelli Food Products Inc ... G ... 312 455-1006
Chicago *(G-5770)*
Peanut Butter Partners LLC ... G ... 847 489-5322
Glen Ellyn *(G-10418)*
Pennant Foods ... G ... 708 752-8730
Alsip *(G-489)*
Pepperidge Farm Incorporated ... G ... 708 478-7450
Mokena *(G-14106)*
Pepperidge Farm Incorporated ... G ... 630 241-6372
Downers Grove *(G-8072)*
▲ **Perfect Pasta Inc** ... G ... 630 543-8300
Addison *(G-237)*
Pickles Sorrel Inc ... F ... 773 379-4748
Chicago *(G-5806)*
PO Food Specialists Ltd ... G ... 847 517-8315
Hoffman Estates *(G-11448)*
Pop Box LLC ... F ... 630 509-2281
Chicago *(G-5841)*
Pop Brands LLC ... G ... 630 205-7146
Chicago *(G-5842)*
Positive Mama Enterprises LLC ... G ... 618 508-1995
Flora *(G-9689)*
Pregel America ... G ... 847 258-3725
Elk Grove Village *(G-9194)*
◆ **Prinova Solutions LLC** ... E ... 630 868-0300
Carol Stream *(G-3053)*
Proven Partners Group LLC ... D ... 847 488-1230
Elgin *(G-8702)*
Purac America Inc ... G ... 847 634-6330
Lincolnshire *(G-12793)*
Quaker Oats Company ... A ... 217 443-4995
Danville *(G-7375)*
◆ **Quaker Oats Company** ... A ... 312 821-1000
Chicago *(G-5927)*
R J Van Drunen & Sons Inc ... D ... 815 472-3211
Momence *(G-14193)*
◆ **R J Van Drunen & Sons Inc** ... D ... 815 472-3100
Momence *(G-14191)*
R J Van Drunen & Sons Inc ... E ... 830 422-2167
Momence *(G-14192)*
Rawnature5 LLC ... F ... 312 800-3239
Chicago *(G-5977)*
Raymundos Food Group LLC ... C ... 708 344-8400
Bedford Park *(G-1497)*
Real Taste Noodles Mfg Inc ... G ... 312 738-1893
Chicago *(G-5984)*
◆ **Regal Health Foods Intl Inc** ... E ... 773 252-1044
Chicago *(G-6000)*
Relish Labs LLC ... G ... 872 225-2433
Chicago *(G-6012)*
Republic of Tea Inc ... G ... 618 478-5520
Nashville *(G-15009)*
Revolution Brands LLC ... G ... 847 902-3320
Huntley *(G-11563)*
Roma Bakeries Inc ... F ... 815 964-6737
Rockford *(G-17614)*
Romaine Empire Inc ... D ... 312 229-0099
Chicago *(G-6056)*
▲ **Royal Foods & Flavors Inc** ... F ... 847 595-9166
Elk Grove Village *(G-9222)*
Rt Wholesale ... D ... 847 678-3663
Schiller Park *(G-18841)*
Ryans Rub LLC ... G ... 773 573-8939
Aledo *(G-360)*
S&J Food Management Corp ... G ... 630 323-9296
Hinsdale *(G-11376)*
Sabinas Food Products Inc ... E ... 312 738-2412
Chicago *(G-6087)*
Salsa Verde Batavia Inc ... G ... 630 425-3521
Batavia *(G-1412)*
Schau Southeast Sushi Inc ... E ... 630 783-1000
Woodridge *(G-21339)*
▲ **Schulze and Burch Biscuit Co** ... B ... 773 927-6622
Chicago *(G-6115)*
▲ **Sdr Corp** ... G ... 773 638-1800
Chicago *(G-6123)*
Sensient Technologies Corp ... E ... 708 481-0910
Matteson *(G-13628)*
Sentry Seasonings Inc ... E ... 630 530-5370
Elmhurst *(G-9426)*
Simple Mills Inc ... E ... 312 600-6196
Chicago *(G-6174)*
Snak-King Corp ... C ... 815 232-6700
Freeport *(G-10142)*
◆ **Sokol and Company** ... D ... 708 482-8250
Countryside *(G-7071)*
◆ **Solae** ... F ... 217 784-8261
Gibson City *(G-10345)*
Solo Foods ... G ... 800 328-7656
Countryside *(G-7072)*
Sono Italiano Corporation ... G ... 817 472-8903
Manteno *(G-13456)*
Sotiros Foods Inc ... G ... 708 371-0002
Alsip *(G-511)*
Sparrow Coffee Roastery ... G ... 321 648-6415
Westchester *(G-20712)*
Stepan Specialty Products LLC ... G ... 847 446-7500
Northfield *(G-15532)*
Stewarts Prvate Blend Fods Inc ... E ... 773 489-2500
Carol Stream *(G-3077)*
▼ **Subco Foods of Illinois Inc** ... D ... 630 231-0003
West Chicago *(G-20647)*
Sunny Day Distributing Inc ... G ... 630 779-8466
Cortland *(G-7027)*
Sunny Enterprises Inc ... F ... 847 219-1045
Chicago *(G-6274)*
Suter Company Inc ... C ... 815 895-9186
Sycamore *(G-19733)*
Swagger Foods Corporation ... E ... 847 913-1200
Vernon Hills *(G-20101)*
▼ **Sweet Solutions LLC** ... G ... 630 364-2843
Plainfield *(G-16720)*
Sweetener Supply Corporation ... F ... 708 484-3455
Berwyn *(G-1961)*
Swiss Products LP ... E ... 773 394-6480
Chicago *(G-6297)*
Tara International LP ... D ... 708 354-7050
Hodgkins *(G-11398)*
Taylor Farms Illinois Inc ... B ... 312 432-6800
Chicago *(G-6331)*
Teasdale Foods Inc ... D ... 217 283-7771
Hoopeston *(G-11514)*
▼ **Tee Lee Popcorn Inc** ... E ... 815 864-2363
Shannon *(G-18874)*
Teresa Foods Inc ... F ... 708 258-6200
Peotone *(G-16558)*
▲ **Th Foods Inc** ... C ... 800 896-2396
Loves Park *(G-13274)*
Thomas Proestler ... G ... 630 971-0185
Lisle *(G-12951)*
Top Hat Company Inc ... E ... 847 256-6565
Wilmette *(G-21094)*
Tpf Liquidation Co ... D ... 847 362-0028
Lake Forest *(G-12315)*
Triple Sticks Foods LLC ... D ... 800 468-3354
Belleville *(G-1602)*
▲ **Troverco Inc** ... E ... 800 468-3354
Belleville *(G-1603)*
▲ **United Food Ingredients Inc** ... G ... 630 655-9494
Burr Ridge *(G-2729)*
▲ **Urban Accents Incorporated** ... G ... 773 528-9515
Chicago *(G-6494)*
▲ **USspice Mill Inc** ... F ... 773 378-6800
Chicago *(G-6507)*
▲ **Vanee Foods Company** ... D ... 708 449-7300
Berkeley *(G-1945)*
Ventura Foods LLC ... E ... 708 877-5150
Thornton *(G-19791)*
▲ **Wah King Noodle Co Inc** ... F ... 323 268-0222
Chicago *(G-6584)*
Whitney Foods Inc ... F ... 773 842-8511
Glencoe *(G-10434)*
Windward Brands LLC ... G ... 224 432-5704
Glenview *(G-10637)*
Wisconsin Wilderness Food Pdts ... G ... 847 735-8661
Lake Forest *(G-12323)*
▲ **Xena International Inc** ... D ... 630 587-2734
Polo *(G-16759)*
▲ **YMC Corp** ... F ... 312 842-4900
Chicago *(G-6702)*
▲ **Ys Health Corporation** ... F ... 847 391-9122
Mount Prospect *(G-14585)*
▲ **Zaibak Bros** ... E ... 312 564-5800
Chicago *(G-6706)*
Zenb US Inc ... G ... 312 581-6574
Chicago *(G-6715)*
Zuchem Inc ... G ... 312 997-2150
Chicago *(G-6726)*

21 TOBACCO PRODUCTS

2111 Cigarettes

8 Electronic Cigarette Inc ... G ... 630 708-6803
Saint Charles *(G-18140)*
Cigtechs ... F ... 630 855-6513
Roselle *(G-17945)*
Itg Brands LLC ... G ... 217 529-5746
Springfield *(G-19390)*
Philip Morris USA Inc ... D ... 847 605-9595
Schaumburg *(G-18673)*
Royal Smoke Shop ... G ... 815 539-3499
Mendota *(G-13954)*

2131 Tobacco, Chewing & Snuff

Diamond Wholesale Group Inc ... G ... 708 529-7495
Bridgeview *(G-2340)*
Having A Good Time ... G ... 847 330-8460
Schaumburg *(G-18543)*
◆ **Inter-Continental Trdg USA Inc** ... D ... 847 640-1777
Mount Prospect *(G-14537)*
Paralleldirect LLC ... G ... 847 748-2025
Lincolnshire *(G-12791)*
Paramount Plastics LLC ... D ... 815 834-4100
Chicago *(G-5761)*
Republic Group Inc ... G ... 800 288-8888
Glenview *(G-10612)*
▲ **Top Tobacco LP** ... G ... 847 832-9700
Glenview *(G-10633)*
Ugly Hookah Tobacco Inc ... G ... 708 724-9621
Oak Lawn *(G-15737)*
US Smokeless Tob Mfg Co LLC ... F ... 804 274-2000
Franklin Park *(G-10070)*
Ust Inc ... G ... 847 957-5104
Franklin Park *(G-10071)*

22 TEXTILE MILL PRODUCTS

2211 Cotton, Woven Fabric

A B C Blind Inc ... G ... 708 877-7100
Thornton *(G-19784)*
Akr Industries Inc ... G ... 732 998-5662
Peoria *(G-16379)*
Alpha Bedding LLC ... F ... 847 550-5110
Lake Zurich *(G-12383)*
Anees Upholstery ... G ... 312 243-2919
Chicago *(G-3695)*
Annas Draperies & Associates ... G ... 773 282-1365
Chicago *(G-3699)*
Barrett NJide Yvonne ... F ... 312 701-3962
Chicago *(G-3838)*
Chicor Inc ... G ... 630 953-6154
Oak Brook *(G-15609)*
City Living Design Inc ... G ... 312 335-0711
Chicago *(G-4156)*

SIC

Employee Codes: A=Over 500 employees, B=251-500
C=101-250, D=51-100, E=20-50, F=10-19, G=3-9

2020 Harris Illinois
Industrial Directory

827

22 TEXTILE MILL PRODUCTS

▲ Dec Art Designs Inc ....G....... 312 329-0553
  Northbrook (G-15374)
DLS Custom Embroidery Inc ....E....... 847 593-5957
  Elk Grove Village (G-8952)
Dpe Incorporated ....G....... 773 306-0105
  Chicago (G-4394)
Drapery Room Inc ....F....... 708 301-3374
  Homer Glen (G-11478)
F & L Drapery Inc ....G....... 815 932-8997
  Saint Anne (G-18134)
Fresco Plaster Finishes Inc ....G....... 847 277-1484
  Barrington (G-1219)
Haakes Awning ....G....... 618 529-4808
  Carbondale (G-2844)
Hygienic Fabrics & Filters Inc ....G....... 815 493-2502
  Lanark (G-12482)
▲ Jacobson Acqstion Holdings LLC.......C....... 847 623-1414
  Waukegan (G-20452)
Kempco Window Treatments Inc ....E....... 708 754-4484
  Chicago Heights (G-6755)
Lingle Design Group Inc ....E....... 815 369-9155
  Lena (G-12605)
▲ Maya Romanoff Corporation ....E....... 773 465-6909
  Skokie (G-18986)
▲ Moss Holding Company ....C....... 847 238-4200
  Elk Grove Village (G-9132)
Netranix Enterprise ....E....... 630 312-8141
  Bolingbrook (G-2219)
Robert Harlan Ernst ....G....... 217 627-3401
  Girard (G-10385)
▲ Rubin Manufacturing Inc ....B....... 312 942-1111
  Chicago (G-6077)
Sea-Rich Corp ....G....... 773 261-6633
  Chicago (G-6124)
Seat Cover Pro LLC ....G....... 847 990-1506
  Vernon Hills (G-20094)
Toco ....G....... 618 257-8626
  Belleville (G-1600)
Tru-Colour Products LLC ....G....... 630 447-0559
  Warrenville (G-20255)
▲ Veltex Corporation ....E....... 312 235-4014
  Chicago (G-6530)

2221 Silk & Man-Made Fiber

Accu-Wright Fiberglass Inc ....G....... 618 337-3318
  East Saint Louis (G-8295)
Aim LLC ....E....... 727 544-3000
  Alsip (G-413)
◆ BP Amoco Chemical Company ....B....... 630 420-5111
  Naperville (G-14782)
▲ Dyne Inc ....G....... 815 521-1111
  Minooka (G-14058)
Fiberglass Solutions Corp ....G....... 630 458-0756
  Addison (G-121)
▲ Fiberteq LLC ....D....... 217 431-2111
  Danville (G-7333)
Haakes Awning ....G....... 618 529-4808
  Carbondale (G-2844)
▲ Henry-Lee & Company LLC ....F....... 312 242-2501
  Highland Park (G-11270)
Jalaa Fiberglass Inc ....G....... 217 923-3433
  Greenup (G-10821)
▲ Kabert Industries Inc ....C....... 630 833-2115
  Villa Park (G-20154)
▲ Kobawala Poly-Pack Inc ....G....... 312 664-3810
  Naperville (G-14859)
Lift-All Company Inc ....E....... 800 909-1964
  Itasca (G-11692)
Loomcraft Textile & Supply Co ....E....... 847 680-0000
  Vernon Hills (G-20073)
Mahans Fiberglass ....G....... 309 562-7349
  Easton (G-8330)
▲ Maya Romanoff Corporation ....E....... 773 465-6909
  Skokie (G-18986)
MHS Ltd ....F....... 773 736-3333
  Chicago (G-5419)
▲ Neptune USA Inc ....G....... 847 987-3804
  Schaumburg (G-18647)
Next Gen Manufacturing Inc ....G....... 847 289-8444
  Elgin (G-8670)
Ogden Top & Trim Shop Inc ....G....... 708 484-5422
  Berwyn (G-1958)
Robert Harlan Ernst ....G....... 217 627-3401
  Girard (G-10385)
Sea-Rich Corp ....G....... 773 261-6633
  Chicago (G-6124)
Srm Industries Inc ....G....... 847 735-0077
  Lake Forest (G-12306)
Upholstered Walls By Anne Mari ....G....... 847 202-0642
  Palatine (G-16169)

2231 Wool, Woven Fabric

▼ Aurora Spclty Txtles Group Inc ....D....... 800 864-0303
  Yorkville (G-21473)
EW Bredemeier and Co ....F....... 773 237-1600
  Chicago (G-4542)
▲ Modern Specialties Company ....G....... 312 648-5800
  Chicago (G-5481)
Salt Creek Alpacas Inc ....G....... 309 530-7904
  Farmer City (G-9657)
Without A Trace Weaver Inc ....F....... 773 588-4922
  Chicago (G-6652)

2241 Fabric Mills, Cotton, Wool, Silk & Man-Made

Adhes Tape Technology Inc ....G....... 847 496-7949
  Arlington Heights (G-683)
Chase Corporation ....E....... 847 866-8500
  Evanston (G-9503)
▲ F Hyman & Co ....G....... 312 664-3810
  Chicago (G-4549)
Grant Technologies LLC ....G....... 847 370-9306
  Chicago (G-4725)
Harbor Village LLC ....G....... 773 338-2222
  Chicago (G-4779)
Lea & Sachs Inc ....F....... 847 296-8000
  Des Plaines (G-7796)
Phoenix Graphix ....G....... 618 531-3664
  Pinckneyville (G-16618)
Shoelace Inc ....G....... 847 854-2500
  Kildeer (G-12053)
Shoelace Inc ....G....... 847 854-2500
  Crystal Lake (G-7265)
▲ Technical Sealants Inc ....F....... 815 777-9797
  Galena (G-10179)
UNI-Label and Tag Corporation ....E....... 847 956-8900
  Elk Grove Village (G-9294)
Voss Belting & Specialty Co ....E....... 847 673-8900
  Lincolnwood (G-12873)
W & W Associates Inc ....G....... 847 719-1760
  Lake Zurich (G-12469)

2251 Hosiery, Women's Full & Knee Length

◆ Bee Sales Company ....D....... 847 600-4400
  Niles (G-15106)
Felice Hosiery Co Inc ....G....... 312 922-3710
  Chicago (G-4578)

2252 Hosiery, Except Women's

◆ Bee Sales Company ....D....... 847 600-4400
  Niles (G-15106)
Emeelys Socks and More ....G....... 847 529-3026
  Chicago (G-4493)
Felice Hosiery Co Inc ....G....... 312 922-3710
  Chicago (G-4578)
Felice Hosiery Company Inc ....E....... 312 922-3710
  Chicago (G-4579)
Living Royal ....F....... 312 906-7600
  Wheeling (G-20933)
Living Royal Inc ....E....... 312 906-7600
  Wheeling (G-20934)
Midwest Socks LLC ....G....... 773 283-3952
  Chicago (G-5447)
Quincy Socks House ....G....... 217 506-6106
  Quincy (G-16935)
Sock Obsessed ....G....... 847 920-4834
  Chicago (G-6196)
Soy City Sock Co Inc ....G....... 217 762-2157
  Monticello (G-14287)
Zzzsock LLC ....G....... 224 330-7364
  Mount Prospect (G-14586)

2253 Knit Outerwear Mills

A&B Apparel ....G....... 815 962-5070
  Rockford (G-17281)
Bird Dog Bay Inc ....G....... 312 631-3108
  Chicago (G-3899)
Chicago Knitting Mills ....G....... 773 463-1464
  Northbrook (G-15358)
Creative Clothing Created 4 U ....G....... 847 543-0051
  Grayslake (G-10764)
Csi Chicago Inc ....G....... 773 665-2226
  Chicago (G-4280)
Derbyteescom ....G....... 309 264-1033
  Henry (G-11162)
Five Brother Inc ....G....... 309 663-6323
  Bloomington (G-2043)
Heartfelt Gifts Inc ....G....... 309 852-2296
  Kewanee (G-12039)
M & G Simplicitees ....G....... 224 372-7426
  Lake Villa (G-12359)
Main Street Records ....G....... 618 244-2737
  Mount Vernon (G-14623)
Mr T Shirt and Dollar Plus ....G....... 708 596-9150
  Harvey (G-11093)
▲ NRR Corp ....F....... 630 915-8388
  Oak Brook (G-15651)
Russell Brands LLC ....D....... 309 454-6737
  Normal (G-15223)
Sue Peterson ....G....... 847 730-3035
  Glenview (G-10628)
The Lifeguard Store Inc ....G....... 630 548-5500
  Naperville (G-14932)
◆ Waters Industries Inc ....E....... 847 783-5900
  West Dundee (G-20667)

2254 Knit Underwear Mills

▲ Top Ace Inc ....G....... 847 581-0550
  Morton Grove (G-14445)

2257 Circular Knit Fabric Mills

Chicago Knitting Mills ....G....... 773 463-1464
  Northbrook (G-15358)

2259 Knitting Mills, NEC

AR Impex Inc ....G....... 404 649-4581
  Bolingbrook (G-2148)
Intelex Usa LLC ....G....... 844 927-6437
  East Dundee (G-8202)
◆ Omar Medical Supplies Inc ....F....... 708 922-4276
  Chicago (G-5673)
▲ Tiger Accessory Group LLC ....F....... 847 821-9630
  Long Grove (G-13171)

2261 Cotton Fabric Finishers

▼ Aurora Spclty Txtles Group Inc ....D....... 800 864-0303
  Yorkville (G-21473)
B and A Screen Printing ....G....... 217 762-2632
  Monticello (G-14277)
Charles H Luck Envelope Inc ....F....... 847 451-1500
  Franklin Park (G-9903)
Frankenstitch Promotions LLC ....F....... 847 459-4840
  Wheeling (G-20901)
Grey Shirt Guys LLC ....G....... 800 787-4478
  Mascoutah (G-13597)
Holy Cow Sports Incorporated ....F....... 630 852-9001
  Downers Grove (G-8025)
Meridian Industries Inc ....G....... 630 892-7651
  Aurora (G-1131)
Murphys Pub ....G....... 847 526-1431
  Wauconda (G-20380)
Player Sports Ltd ....G....... 773 764-4111
  Chicago (G-5822)
Proell Inc ....G....... 630 587-2300
  Saint Charles (G-18251)
Saati Americas Corporation ....F....... 847 296-5090
  Mount Prospect (G-14568)
Top Notch Silk Screening ....G....... 773 847-6335
  Chicago (G-6395)
Toyota Tsusho America Inc ....D....... 847 439-8500
  Elk Grove Village (G-9281)

2262 Silk & Man-Made Fabric Finishers

David H Pool ....G....... 847 695-5007
  Elgin (G-8563)
Image Plus Inc ....G....... 630 852-4920
  Downers Grove (G-8028)
Insignia Design Ltd ....G....... 301 254-9221
  Rolling Meadows (G-17741)
Jdl Graphics Inc ....G....... 815 694-2979
  Clifton (G-6915)
Peacock Printing Inc ....G....... 618 242-3157
  Mount Vernon (G-14633)
Saati Americas Corporation ....F....... 847 296-5090
  Mount Prospect (G-14568)
Starline Designs ....G....... 773 683-7506
  Chicago (G-6234)
Ultimate Distributing Inc ....G....... 847 566-2250
  Mundelein (G-14745)

2269 Textile Finishers, NEC

Chicago Dye Works ....G....... 847 931-7968
  Elgin (G-8538)
Fas-Trak Industries Inc ....G....... 708 570-0650
  Monee (G-14199)
Mount Vernon Mills ....G....... 618 882-6300
  Highland (G-11233)

▲ Sato Lbling Solutions Amer Inc..............D....... 630 771-4200
  Romeoville (G-17874)

2273 Carpets & Rugs

Aspen Carpet Designs............................G....... 815 483-8501
  Mokena (G-14073)
Baker Avenue Investments Inc................D....... 309 427-2500
  Washington (G-20266)
◆ Blachford Investments Inc....................C....... 630 231-8300
  West Chicago (G-20552)
Ds Production LLC................................G....... 708 873-3142
  Orland Park (G-15953)
▲ Eagle Carpet Services Ltd......................G....... 956 971-8560
  Addison (G-109)
East West Martial Arts Sups....................G....... 773 878-7711
  Chicago (G-4434)
Edward Fields Incorporated...................G....... 312 644-0400
  Chicago (G-4461)
Interfaceflor LLC....................................E....... 312 836-3389
  Chicago (G-4945)
Interfaceflor LLC....................................F....... 312 822-9640
  Chicago (G-4946)
L & L Flooring Inc..................................E....... 773 935-9314
  Chicago (G-5140)
Lessy Messy LLC..................................F....... 708 790-7589
  Naperville (G-14977)
▼ March Industries Inc.............................F....... 224 654-6500
  Hampshire (G-10978)
Milliken & Company...............................F....... 800 241-4826
  Chicago (G-5460)
Minasian Rug Corporation.....................G....... 847 864-1010
  Evanston (G-9553)
Mohawk Industries Inc..........................D....... 630 972-8000
  Bolingbrook (G-2215)
▲ Organic Looms Inc..............................G....... 312 832-0900
  Chicago (G-5697)
Protect Assoc..G....... 847 446-8664
  Northbrook (G-15469)
Shaw Industries Group Inc....................G....... 312 467-1331
  Chicago (G-6149)
Shiir LLC...F....... 312 828-0400
  Chicago (G-6153)
Skandia Inc..D....... 800 945-7435
  Davis Junction (G-7427)

2284 Thread Mills

▲ Advent Tool & Mfg Inc.........................F....... 847 395-9707
  Antioch (G-594)
Greco Graphics Inc...............................G....... 217 483-2877
  Glenarm (G-10425)
Machine Tool Acc & Mfg Co..................G....... 773 489-0903
  Chicago (G-5309)
Team Print Inc......................................F....... 815 933-5111
  Bourbonnais (G-2269)

2295 Fabrics Coated Not Rubberized

Ace Anodizing Impregnating Inc...........D....... 708 547-6680
  Hillside (G-11324)
▲ Advanced Flxble Composites Inc........D....... 847 658-3938
  Lake In The Hills (G-12327)
Allerton Charter Coach..........................G....... 217 344-2600
  Champaign (G-3261)
Brasel Products Inc..............................G....... 630 879-3759
  Batavia (G-1360)
J M Fabricating Inc...............................G....... 815 359-2024
  Harmon (G-11018)
▲ JAm International Co Ltd....................G....... 847 827-6391
  Riverwoods (G-17094)
Jessup Manufacturing Company...........E....... 847 362-0961
  Lake Bluff (G-12190)
Lanmar Inc..G....... 800 233-5520
  Northbrook (G-15418)
Metal Impregnating Corp......................G....... 630 543-3443
  Addison (G-198)
Phoenix Leather Goods LLC................G....... 815 676-6712
  Bolingbrook (G-2227)
Stickon Adhesive Inds Inc....................G....... 847 593-5959
  Wauconda (G-20391)
▲ Technical Sealants Inc........................F....... 815 777-9797
  Galena (G-10179)
Vacumet Corp..F....... 708 562-7290
  Northlake (G-15564)
▲ Wisdom Adhesives LLC.......................E....... 847 841-7002
  Elgin (G-8783)

2296 Tire Cord & Fabric

▲ Advanced Flxble Composites Inc........D....... 847 658-3938
  Lake In The Hills (G-12327)

Mc Chemical Company..........................G....... 618 965-3668
  Steeleville (G-19483)

2297 Fabrics, Nonwoven

Cowtan and Tout Inc.............................F....... 312 644-0717
  Chicago (G-4251)
◆ Fibertex Nonwovens LLC....................A....... 815 349-3200
  Ingleside (G-11581)
Fin North America Holding Inc..............D....... 815 349-3219
  Ingleside (G-11582)
▲ Midwest Nonwovens LLC....................E....... 618 337-9662
  Sauget (G-18395)
Smart-Fab Inc.......................................G....... 855 276-2783
  Buffalo Grove (G-2607)
Windwrap LLC.......................................G....... 773 594-1724
  Chicago (G-6639)

2298 Cordage & Twine

All Gear Inc..G....... 847 564-9016
  Northbrook (G-15335)
All Line Inc...G....... 630 820-1800
  Naperville (G-14955)
Calvert Systems....................................G....... 309 523-3262
  Port Byron (G-16786)
Clark Wire & Cable Co Inc...................F....... 847 949-9944
  Mundelein (G-14678)
CT Group Inc..G....... 708 466-8277
  Glen Ellyn (G-10399)
▲ Erin Rope Corporation........................F....... 708 377-1084
  Blue Island (G-2122)
◆ Lehigh Consumer Products LLC........C....... 630 851-7330
  Aurora (G-997)
MHS Ltd...G....... 773 736-3333
  Chicago (G-5419)
▲ Mighty Hook Inc.................................E....... 773 378-1909
  Chicago (G-5453)
Nichols Net & Twine Inc.......................G....... 618 797-0211
  Granite City (G-10728)
Obies Tackle Co Inc.............................G....... 618 234-5638
  Belleville (G-1581)
Turf Inc...G....... 630 365-3903
  Elburn (G-8478)
◆ Unicord Corporation............................E....... 708 385-7999
  Calumet Park (G-2800)

2299 Textile Goods, NEC

Advantex Inc...G....... 618 505-0701
  Troy (G-19911)
American Dawn Inc...............................G....... 312 961-2909
  Wood Dale (G-21163)
C B E Inc..G....... 630 571-2610
  Oak Brook (G-15603)
◆ Cellusuede Products Inc....................E....... 815 964-8619
  Rockford (G-17342)
Deelone Distributing Inc.......................G....... 309 788-1444
  Rock Island (G-17215)
Federal Prison Industries.....................F....... 618 664-6361
  Greenville (G-10834)
Federal Prison Industries.....................C....... 309 346-8588
  Pekin (G-16333)
Filter Technology Inc............................E....... 773 523-7200
  Bedford Park (G-1467)
Fourell Corp..G....... 217 742-3186
  Winchester (G-21105)
Gilday Services.....................................G....... 847 395-0853
  Antioch (G-613)
Glenraven Inc.......................................G....... 847 515-1321
  Huntley (G-11537)
Hugo Boss Usa Inc..............................F....... 847 517-1461
  Schaumburg (G-18552)
Lorton Group LLC.................................G....... 844 352-5089
  Wilmette (G-21086)
Novipax LLC..F....... 630 686-2735
  Oak Brook (G-15649)
Superior Felt & Filtration LLC...............E....... 815 331-6382
  Ingleside (G-11590)
Superior Health Linens LLC..................D....... 630 593-5091
  Batavia (G-1423)
Sustainable Innovations Inc................G....... 815 713-1637
  Rockford (G-17650)
◆ Tex Tana Inc......................................G....... 773 561-9270
  Chicago (G-6355)

23 APPAREL AND OTHER FINISHED PRODUCTS MADE FROM FABRICS AND SIMILAR MATERIAL

2311 Men's & Boys' Suits, Coats & Overcoats

▲ Demoulin Brothers & Company...........C....... 618 664-2000
  Greenville (G-10832)
J G Uniforms Inc..................................G....... 773 545-4644
  Chicago (G-4990)
Mancillas International Ltd...................F....... 847 441-7748
  Winnetka (G-21132)
Oxxford Clothes Xx Inc........................C....... 312 829-3600
  Chicago (G-5723)
▲ Pro-Pak Industries Inc.......................F....... 630 876-1050
  West Chicago (G-20633)
Signature Design & Tailoring................F....... 773 375-4915
  Chicago (G-6168)
Vertex International Inc........................G....... 312 242-1864
  Oak Brook (G-15669)
▲ W Diamond Group Corporation...........A....... 646 647-2790
  Des Plaines (G-7866)

2321 Men's & Boys' Shirts

Drywear Apparel LLC............................G....... 847 687-8540
  Kildeer (G-12046)
Perry Ellis International Inc..................G....... 847 678-7108
  Rosemont (G-18040)
Pvh Corp..F....... 217 253-3398
  Tuscola (G-19929)
Riddle McIntyre Inc..............................G....... 312 782-3317
  Chicago (G-6030)
Salmons and Brown..............................G....... 312 929-6756
  Chicago (G-6095)

2323 Men's & Boys' Neckwear

Amazing Mascots..................................G....... 727 475-0255
  Chicago (G-3643)
Backyard Bucket Co..............................G....... 773 771-0743
  Chicago (G-3813)
▲ Corporate Textiles Inc........................G....... 847 433-4111
  Lincolnwood (G-12815)
Jerjerb LLC...G....... 917 415-3319
  Chicago (G-5020)
Shertwinz Inc..G....... 630 886-5681
  Naperville (G-14914)
Trafalgar Company LLC........................G....... 847 292-8300
  Rosemont (G-18054)

2325 Men's & Boys' Separate Trousers & Casual Slacks

Guess Inc...E....... 312 440-9592
  Chicago (G-4749)
▲ Kanan Fashions Inc............................E....... 630 240-1234
  Oak Brook (G-15629)
Levi Strauss & Co.................................F....... 773 486-3900
  Chicago (G-5211)
Levi Strauss & Co.................................G....... 847 619-0655
  Schaumburg (G-18605)
Oxxford Clothes Xx Inc........................C....... 312 829-3600
  Chicago (G-5723)

2326 Men's & Boys' Work Clothing

Advance Uniform Company...................F....... 312 922-1797
  Chicago (G-3559)
Ai Ind...E....... 773 265-6640
  Chicago (G-3586)
◆ Apparel Works Intl LLC......................G....... 847 778-9559
  Lake Bluff (G-12171)
Atlas Uniform Company........................G....... 312 492-8527
  Chicago (G-3769)
▲ Choi Brands Inc.................................C....... 773 489-2800
  Chicago (G-4142)
Cintas Corporation................................D....... 708 563-2626
  Chicago (G-4151)
▲ Demoulin Brothers & Company..........C....... 618 664-2000
  Greenville (G-10832)
False Hope Brand Co............................G....... 312 265-1364
  Chicago (G-4556)
▲ High Performance Entp Inc................E....... 773 283-1778
  Chicago (G-4816)
Hot Topic Inc...G....... 708 453-1216
  Norridge (G-15236)
▲ Iguanamed LLC..................................G....... 312 546-4182
  Chicago (G-4881)
◆ Magid Glove Safety Mfg Co LLC.........B....... 773 384-2070
  Romeoville (G-17844)

23 APPAREL AND OTHER FINISHED PRODUCTS MADE FROM FABRICS AND SIMILAR MATERIAL

Mennon Rbr & Safety Pdts Inc .... G 847 678-8250
  Schiller Park (G-18823)
Mighty Mites Awards and Sons .... G 847 297-0035
  Des Plaines (G-7802)
Most Enterprise Inc .... D 800 792-4669
  Chicago (G-5504)
Rubin Nsa Bros LLC .... G 312 942-1111
  Chicago (G-6078)
Silk Road Logistics Co .... G 773 432-5619
  Mount Prospect (G-14570)
Standard Safety Equipment Co .... E 815 363-8565
  McHenry (G-13795)
◆ Universal Overall Company .... E 312 226-3336
  Chicago (G-6482)
◆ V-Tex Inc .... E 847 325-4140
  Buffalo Grove (G-2615)
Woolenwear Co .... F 847 520-9243
  Prospect Heights (G-16848)

2329 Men's & Boys' Clothing, NEC

Athletic Sewing Mfg Co .... E 773 589-0361
  Chicago (G-3759)
Athllete LLC .... F 773 829-3752
  Bolingbrook (G-2151)
BMW Sportswear Inc .... G 773 265-0110
  Chicago (G-3921)
▲ Choi Brands Inc .... C 773 489-2800
  Chicago (G-4142)
Cloz Companies Inc .... E 773 247-8879
  Skokie (G-18944)
Curt Smith Sporting Goods Inc .... E 618 233-5177
  Belleville (G-1541)
Da Closet .... G 708 206-1414
  Country Club Hills (G-7038)
▼ Dnepr Techologies Inc .... F 773 603-3360
  Chicago (G-4374)
Exclusive Pro Sports Ltd .... E 815 877-8585
  Rockford (G-17409)
Express LLC .... E 708 453-0566
  Norridge (G-15234)
Foot Locker Retail Inc .... G 630 678-0155
  Lombard (G-13078)
Forever Fly LLC .... G 312 981-9161
  Chicago (G-4619)
H & H Fabric Cutters .... G 773 772-1904
  Chicago (G-4757)
Lloyd M Hughes Enterprises Inc .... G 773 363-6331
  Chicago (G-5245)
Miglio Di Mario Uomo Inc .... G 312 391-0831
  Chicago (G-5454)
Moxie Apparel LLC .... G 312 243-9040
  Chicago (G-5512)
Pro-AM Team Sports LLC .... F 708 995-1511
  Mokena (G-14110)
Sansabelt .... G 312 357-5119
  Chicago (G-6101)
Tfo Group LLC .... G 608 469-7519
  Chicago (G-6358)
Vertex International Inc .... G 312 242-1864
  Oak Brook (G-15669)
◆ Vista Outdoor Inc .... G 309 693-2746
  Rantoul (G-16985)

2331 Women's & Misses' Blouses

◆ Apparel Works Intl LLC .... G 847 778-9559
  Lake Bluff (G-12171)
Forever Fly LLC .... G 312 981-9161
  Chicago (G-4619)
Joriki LLC .... G 312 848-1136
  Chicago (G-5050)
Rubin Nsa Bros LLC .... G 312 942-1111
  Chicago (G-6078)
▲ Yolanda Lorente Ltd .... E 773 334-4536
  Chicago (G-6703)

2335 Women's & Misses' Dresses

▲ Alyce Designs Inc .... E 847 966-6933
  Morton Grove (G-14389)
Caroline Rose Inc .... G 708 386-1011
  Oak Park (G-15748)
Casa Di Castronovo Inc .... G 815 962-4731
  Rockford (G-17338)
Doris Bridal Boutique .... G 847 433-2575
  Highwood (G-11306)
G-III Apparel Group Ltd .... C 630 236-8900
  Aurora (G-966)
Halanick Enterprises Inc .... G 708 403-3334
  Orland Park (G-15958)
Igar Bridal Inc .... G 224 318-2337
  Arlington Heights (G-754)

Jane Stodden Bridals .... G 815 223-2091
  La Salle (G-12116)
Runway Liquidation LLC .... G 574 247-1500
  Northbrook (G-15476)
Salmons and Brown .... G 312 929-6756
  Chicago (G-6095)
▲ Yolanda Lorente Ltd .... E 773 334-4536
  Chicago (G-6703)

2337 Women's & Misses' Suits, Coats & Skirts

Advance Uniform Company .... F 312 922-1797
  Chicago (G-3559)
▲ Advantex Inc of Illinois .... D 618 505-0701
  Troy (G-19910)
Atlas Uniform Company .... G 312 492-8527
  Chicago (G-3769)
▲ Choi Brands Inc .... C 773 489-2800
  Chicago (G-4142)
Cintas Corporation .... D 708 563-2626
  Chicago (G-4151)
Cintas Corporation No 2 .... G 708 424-4747
  Oak Lawn (G-15709)
▲ Demoulin Brothers & Company ...... C 618 664-2000
  Greenville (G-10832)
Fashahnn Corporation .... G 773 994-3132
  Chicago (G-4561)
▲ Iguanamed LLC .... G 312 546-4182
  Chicago (G-4881)
Mademoiselle Inc .... F 773 394-4555
  Chicago (G-5311)
Tfo Group LLC .... G 608 469-7519
  Chicago (G-6358)
▲ Yolanda Lorente Ltd .... E 773 334-4536
  Chicago (G-6703)

2339 Women's & Misses' Outerwear, NEC

Anart Inc .... E 708 447-0225
  Riverside (G-17080)
Athllete LLC .... F 773 829-3752
  Bolingbrook (G-2151)
Caroline Rose Inc .... G 708 386-1011
  Oak Park (G-15748)
Chicago Knitting Mills .... G 773 463-1464
  Northbrook (G-15358)
▲ Choi Brands Inc .... C 773 489-2800
  Chicago (G-4142)
Cintas Corporation .... D 708 563-2626
  Chicago (G-4151)
Cloz Companies Inc .... E 773 247-8879
  Skokie (G-18944)
▲ Daniel Bruce LLC .... F 917 583-1538
  Palatine (G-16108)
▲ Demoulin Brothers & Company ...... C 618 664-2000
  Greenville (G-10832)
Doughman Don & Assoc .... G 312 321-1011
  Chicago (G-4389)
Exclusive Pro Sports Ltd .... E 815 877-8585
  Rockford (G-17409)
Fashahnn Corporation .... G 773 994-3132
  Chicago (G-4561)
▲ Gennco International Inc .... F 847 541-3333
  Northbrook (G-15393)
Golda Inc .... C 217 895-3602
  Neoga (G-15017)
James Rosenbaum Co .... G 847 859-7660
  Evanston (G-9541)
Jenny Capp Co .... F 773 217-0057
  Chicago (G-5018)
▲ Laqueus Inc .... F 773 508-1993
  Chicago (G-5176)
Leg Up LLC .... G 312 282-2725
  Chicago (G-5196)
Levi Strauss & Co .... F 773 486-3900
  Chicago (G-5211)
Libaerty LLC .... G 312 330-2767
  Chicago (G-5216)
Little Journeys Limited .... G 847 677-0350
  Skokie (G-18980)
Mademoiselle Inc .... F 773 394-4555
  Chicago (G-5311)
Marena Marena Two Inc .... G 773 327-0619
  Chicago (G-5331)
Paul Sisti .... G 773 472-5615
  Chicago (G-5772)
Pola Company .... G 847 470-1182
  Niles (G-15160)
▲ Srh Holdings Inc .... G 847 583-2295
  Niles (G-15175)

Trim Suits By Show-Off Inc .... G 630 894-0100
  Roselle (G-17994)
Woolenwear Co .... F 847 520-9243
  Prospect Heights (G-16848)
▲ Yolanda Lorente Ltd .... E 773 334-4536
  Chicago (G-6703)

2341 Women's, Misses' & Children's Underwear & Nightwear

Aurora Narinder .... G 773 275-2100
  Chicago (G-3774)
Kai Lee Couture Inc .... G 773 426-1668
  Chicago (G-5075)
Victorias Secret Stores LLC .... G 312 583-0488
  Chicago (G-6547)

2342 Brassieres, Girdles & Garments

Golda Inc .... C 217 895-3602
  Neoga (G-15017)

2353 Hats, Caps & Millinery

Amenities Home Design .... G 312 421-2450
  Chicago (G-3645)
◆ American Needle Inc .... E 847 215-0011
  Buffalo Grove (G-2511)
◆ Bee Sales Company .... D 847 600-4400
  Niles (G-15106)
Cap Factory .... F 618 273-9662
  Eldorado (G-8480)
Federal Prison Industries .... C 309 346-8588
  Pekin (G-16333)
Hats For You .... G 773 481-1611
  Chicago (G-4785)
Jenny Capp Co .... F 773 217-0057
  Chicago (G-5018)
Lids Corporation .... G 708 873-9606
  Orland Park (G-15965)
Mademoiselle Inc .... F 773 394-4555
  Chicago (G-5311)
Midway Cap Company .... E 773 384-0911
  Chicago (G-5436)
Midway Cap Company .... E 773 384-0911
  Chicago (G-5437)
Miglio Di Mario Uomo Inc .... G 312 391-0831
  Chicago (G-5454)
New ERA Cap Co Inc .... B 504 581-2445
  Chicago (G-5577)

2361 Children's & Infants' Dresses & Blouses

Dino Design Incorporated .... G 773 763-4223
  Morton Grove (G-14400)

2369 Girls' & Infants' Outerwear, NEC

◆ Bee Sales Company .... D 847 600-4400
  Niles (G-15106)
Cloz Companies Inc .... E 773 247-8879
  Skokie (G-18944)
Laurenceleste Inc .... G 708 383-3432
  Oak Park (G-15762)
Little Journeys Limited .... G 847 677-0350
  Skokie (G-18980)
▼ Slick Sugar Inc .... G 815 782-7101
  Plainfield (G-16714)
Trim Suits By Show-Off Inc .... G 630 894-0100
  Roselle (G-17994)

2381 Dress & Work Gloves

▲ Boss Holdings Inc .... D 309 852-2131
  Kewanee (G-12023)
◆ Boss Manufacturing Company .... E 309 852-2131
  Kewanee (G-12024)
▲ Boss Manufacturing Holdings .... F 309 852-2781
  Kewanee (G-12025)
▲ Illinois Glove Company .... G 847 291-1700
  Northbrook (G-15402)
Klein Tools Inc .... D 847 228-6999
  Elk Grove Village (G-9078)
Klein Tools Inc .... E 847 821-5500
  Lincolnshire (G-12779)
▲ Kunz Glove Co Inc .... G 312 733-8780
  Chicago (G-5136)
Lamont Wells Industrial .... G 804 299-2557
  Skokie (G-18975)
◆ Magid Glove Safety Mfg Co LLC .... B 773 384-2070
  Romeoville (G-17844)
Magid Glove Safety Mfg Co LLC .... B 773 384-2070
  Chicago (G-5316)

SIC SECTION
23 APPAREL AND OTHER FINISHED PRODUCTS MADE FROM FABRICS AND SIMILAR MATERIAL

Nationwide Glove Co Inc .... D 618 252-7192
  Harrisburg *(G-11027)*
PW Masonry Inc .... G 847 573-0510
  Libertyville *(G-12699)*
Wells Lamont Indust Group LLC ...... A 800 247-3295
  Skokie *(G-19055)*

2384 Robes & Dressing Gowns
Halanick Enterprises Inc .... E 708 403-3334
  Orland Park *(G-15958)*
Herff Jones LLC .... C 317 612-3705
  Hillside *(G-11341)*
Maries Custom Made Choir Robes ... G 773 826-1214
  Chicago *(G-5336)*
◆ Universal Mfg Corporation .... C 630 613-7340
  Oakbrook Terrace *(G-15817)*

2385 Waterproof Outerwear
▲ Boss Holdings Inc .... D 309 852-2131
  Kewanee *(G-12023)*
▲ Boss Manufacturing Holdings .... F 309 852-2781
  Kewanee *(G-12025)*
▲ Petra Manufacturing Co .... D 773 622-1475
  Chicago *(G-5797)*
Polyconversions Inc .... E 217 893-3330
  Champaign *(G-3335)*

2386 Leather & Sheep Lined Clothing
▼ Keleen Leathers Inc .... F 630 590-5300
  Westmont *(G-20753)*

2389 Apparel & Accessories, NEC
Allen Larson .... G 773 454-2210
  Chicago *(G-3614)*
▲ American Church Supply .... G 847 464-4140
  Saint Charles *(G-18145)*
Andrea and ME and ME Too .... G 708 955-3850
  Matteson *(G-13618)*
Andy Dallas & Co .... F 217 351-5974
  Champaign *(G-3265)*
Anntaylor Retail Inc .... G 309 693-2762
  Peoria *(G-16383)*
Baxter Healthcare Corporation .... E 847 578-4671
  Waukegan *(G-20422)*
Browns Global Exchange .... D 708 345-0955
  Maywood *(G-13664)*
Cayenne Couture Atelier .... G 773 408-4664
  Chicago *(G-4045)*
Custom & Hard To Find Wigs .... F 773 777-0222
  Chicago *(G-4288)*
▲ Daniel Bruce LLC .... F 917 583-1538
  Palatine *(G-16108)*
▲ Demoulin Brothers & Company ...... C 618 664-2000
  Greenville *(G-10832)*
Facemakers Inc .... F 815 273-3944
  Savanna *(G-18405)*
Facemakers Inc .... E 815 273-3944
  Savanna *(G-18406)*
Four Star Denim and AP LLC .... F 847 707-6365
  Chicago *(G-4626)*
▲ Gennco International Inc .... F 847 541-3333
  Northbrook *(G-15393)*
Herff Jones LLC .... C 217 268-4543
  Arcola *(G-651)*
Herff Jones LLC .... C 317 612-3705
  Hillside *(G-11341)*
▲ Jero Medical Eqp & Sups Inc .... E 773 305-4193
  Chicago *(G-5022)*
K&G Mens Company Inc .... G 708 349-2579
  Orland Park *(G-15963)*
◆ Learning Curve International .... E 630 573-7200
  Oak Brook *(G-15632)*
Living Royal Inc .... E 312 906-7600
  Wheeling *(G-20934)*
Luna Medical Inc .... F 800 380-4339
  Chicago *(G-5286)*
Midwest Pub Safety Outfitters .... F 866 985-0013
  Poplar Grove *(G-16782)*
New York & Company Inc .... F 630 232-7693
  Geneva *(G-10293)*
New York & Company Inc .... F 630 783-2910
  Bolingbrook *(G-2221)*
Nu-Life Inc of Illinois .... G 618 943-4500
  Lawrenceville *(G-12536)*
Orr Marketing Corp .... F 847 401-5171
  Elgin *(G-8680)*
Phoebe & Frances .... F 847 446-5480
  Winnetka *(G-21135)*

Pollack Service .... D 773 528-8096
  Chicago *(G-5833)*
Roq Innovation LLC .... G 917 770-2403
  Chicago *(G-6059)*
Sieden Sticker USA Ltd .... G 312 280-7711
  Chicago *(G-6163)*
Sunglass Otftters By Snglass H .... G 847 645-0476
  Hoffman Estates *(G-11465)*
▲ Sunnywood Incorporated .... G 815 675-9777
  McHenry *(G-13799)*
Taitt Burial Garments .... F 773 483-7424
  Chicago *(G-6312)*
▲ Zagone Studios LLC .... G 773 509-0610
  Melrose Park *(G-13932)*

2391 Curtains & Draperies
A B Kelly Inc .... G 847 639-1022
  Cary *(G-3142)*
A D Specialty Sewing .... G 847 639-0390
  Fox River Grove *(G-9756)*
Aracon Drpery Vntian Blind Ltd .... G 773 252-1281
  Chicago *(G-3717)*
Baker Drapery Corporation .... G 309 691-3295
  Dunlap *(G-8132)*
Berg Industries Inc .... F 815 874-1588
  Rockford *(G-17318)*
Dezign Sewing Inc .... G 773 549-4336
  Chicago *(G-4349)*
Dons Drapery Service .... G 815 385-4759
  McHenry *(G-13737)*
Drapery Room Inc .... F 708 301-3374
  Homer Glen *(G-11478)*
Draperyland Inc .... G 630 521-1000
  Wood Dale *(G-21182)*
Drexel House of Drapes Inc .... G 618 624-5415
  Belleville *(G-1547)*
E J Self Furniture .... G 847 394-0899
  Arlington Heights *(G-731)*
Interior Fashions Contract .... G 847 358-6050
  Palatine *(G-16131)*
Logoskirt Corporation .... F 773 584-7300
  Chicago *(G-5251)*
Medline Industries Inc .... G 618 283-4036
  Vandalia *(G-20014)*
North-West Drapery Service .... G 773 282-7117
  Chicago *(G-5622)*
Robert Harlan Ernst .... G 217 627-3401
  Girard *(G-10385)*
Roberts Draperies Center Inc .... G 847 255-4040
  Mount Prospect *(G-14567)*
Shade Aire Company .... G 815 623-7597
  Roscoe *(G-17933)*
Shade Brookline Co .... F 773 274-5513
  Chicago *(G-6145)*
Slagel Drapery Service .... G 815 692-3834
  Fairbury *(G-9613)*
Tailored Inc .... G 708 387-9854
  Brookfield *(G-2493)*
Tazewell Floor Covering Inc .... F 309 266-6371
  Morton *(G-14386)*
Tenggren-Mehl Co Inc .... G 773 763-3290
  Chicago *(G-6349)*
Tres Joli Designs Ltd .... G 847 520-3903
  Wheeling *(G-21001)*
Unitex Industries Inc .... E 708 524-0664
  Oak Park *(G-15777)*
Whiteside Drapery Fabricators .... F 847 746-5300
  Zion *(G-21530)*
Zirlin Interiors Inc .... F 773 334-5530
  Chicago *(G-6720)*

2392 House furnishings: Textile
A D Specialty Sewing .... G 847 639-0390
  Fox River Grove *(G-9756)*
American Dawn Inc .... G 312 961-2909
  Wood Dale *(G-21163)*
Ameriguard Corporation .... G 630 986-1900
  Burr Ridge *(G-2652)*
Ameritex Industries Inc .... F 217 324-4044
  Litchfield *(G-12960)*
▲ Bean Products Inc .... E 312 666-3600
  Chicago *(G-3853)*
Caroline Cole Inc .... G 618 233-0600
  Belleville *(G-1538)*
▼ Cotton Goods Manufacturing Co .... F 773 265-0088
  Chicago *(G-4247)*
▲ Don Leventhal Group LLC .... E 618 783-4424
  Newton *(G-15082)*
Eastern Accents Inc .... C 773 604-7300
  Chicago *(G-4435)*

Encompass Group LLC .... E 847 680-3388
  Mundelein *(G-14686)*
Envision Unlimited .... C 773 651-1100
  Chicago *(G-4521)*
▲ FHP-Berner USA LP .... E 630 270-1400
  Aurora *(G-961)*
▲ Freudenberg Household Pdts LP ... C 630 270-1400
  Aurora *(G-964)*
▲ Ileesh Products LLC .... F 224 424-4682
  Vernon Hills *(G-20062)*
▲ Innocor Foam Tech W Chcago LLC .. E .. 732 945-6222
  West Chicago *(G-20598)*
Interior Fashions Contract .... G 847 358-6050
  Palatine *(G-16131)*
L & W Bedding Inc .... G 309 762-6019
  Moline *(G-14155)*
◆ Libman Company .... C 217 268-4200
  Arcola *(G-655)*
Logoskirt Corporation .... C 773 584-7300
  Chicago *(G-5251)*
My Konjac Sponge Inc .... F 630 345-3653
  North Barrington *(G-15288)*
Personalized Pillows Co .... G 847 226-7393
  Wadsworth *(G-20211)*
Peterson Dermond Design LLC .... G 414 383-5029
  Evanston *(G-9565)*
Piccolino Inc .... G 708 259-2072
  Hinsdale *(G-11373)*
Pyar & Co LLC .... G 312 451-5073
  Chicago *(G-5920)*
◆ Qst Industries Inc .... E 312 930-9400
  Chicago *(G-5923)*
Quiltmaster Inc .... E 847 426-6741
  Carpentersville *(G-3117)*
Rome Metal Mfg Inc .... F 773 287-1755
  Chicago *(G-6057)*
Shiir LLC .... F 312 828-0400
  Chicago *(G-6153)*
Slagel Drapery Service .... G 815 692-3834
  Fairbury *(G-9613)*
Superior Table Pad Co .... F 773 248-7232
  Chicago *(G-6284)*
Tailored Inc .... G 708 387-9854
  Brookfield *(G-2493)*
Trotta Enterprises Inc .... D 312 829-7084
  Chicago *(G-6433)*
Unitex Industries Inc .... E 708 524-0664
  Oak Park *(G-15777)*
Van Stockum Kristine .... G 847 914-0015
  Deerfield *(G-7656)*

2393 Textile Bags
▲ ABG Bag Inc .... F 815 963-9525
  Rockford *(G-17286)*
Advance Tools LLC .... G 630 337-5904
  Glenview *(G-10520)*
Ajr Enterprises Inc .... C 630 377-8886
  Saint Charles *(G-18143)*
▼ Amcraft Manufacturing Inc .... F 847 439-4565
  Elk Grove Village *(G-8821)*
American Dawn Inc .... G 312 961-2909
  Wood Dale *(G-21163)*
▲ Bearse Manufacturing Co .... D 773 235-8710
  Chicago *(G-3857)*
◆ Block and Company Inc .... C 847 537-7200
  Wheeling *(G-20860)*
▲ Hunter-Nusport Inc .... G 815 254-7520
  Plainfield *(G-16674)*
▲ J Design Works Inc .... G 847 812-0891
  Bolingbrook *(G-2196)*
Jarries Shoe Bags .... G 773 379-4044
  Chicago *(G-5008)*
Keeper Thermal Bag Co Inc .... G 630 213-0125
  Bartlett *(G-1292)*
Midwest Linen Recovery LLC .... F 217 675-2766
  Franklin *(G-9856)*
Mondi Bags Usa LLC .... C 502 361-1371
  Romeoville *(G-17856)*
▲ Omg Handbags LLC .... G 847 337-9499
  Chicago *(G-5675)*
Sea-Rich Corp .... F 773 261-6633
  Chicago *(G-6124)*

2394 Canvas Prdts
A B Kelly Inc .... G 847 639-1022
  Cary *(G-3142)*
Acme Awning Co .... G 847 446-0153
  Highland Park *(G-11251)*
Air Land and Sea Interiors .... G 630 834-1717
  Villa Park *(G-20129)*

23 APPAREL AND OTHER FINISHED PRODUCTS MADE FROM FABRICS AND SIMILAR MATERIAL SIC SECTION

Albax Inc .... E 630 758-1072
Elmhurst *(G-9323)*

◆ **Americana Building Pdts Inc** .... D 618 548-2800
Salem *(G-18328)*

▲ **Awnings By Zip-Dee Inc** .... E 847 640-0460
Elk Grove Village *(G-8851)*

Berg Industries Inc .... F 815 874-1588
Rockford *(G-17318)*

Blake Co Inc .... G 815 962-3852
Rockford *(G-17325)*

Bloomington Tent & Awning Inc .... G 309 828-3411
Bloomington *(G-2027)*

Brian Robert Awning Co .... G 847 679-1140
Skokie *(G-18933)*

Brumleve Industries Inc .... F 217 857-3777
Teutopolis *(G-19764)*

Champaign Cnty Tent & Awng Co .... E 217 328-5749
Urbana *(G-19977)*

Chesterfield Awning Co Inc .... F 708 596-4434
South Holland *(G-19205)*

Chicago Dropcloth Tarpaulin Co .... E 773 588-3123
Chicago *(G-4100)*

Creative Covers Inc .... G 708 233-6880
Bridgeview *(G-2338)*

Custom Canvas LLC .... G 847 587-0225
Ingleside *(G-11580)*

Eclipse Awnings Inc .... F 708 636-3160
Evergreen Park *(G-9593)*

Ed Hill S Custom Canvas .... G 815 476-5042
Wilmington *(G-21097)*

Environetics Inc .... F 815 838-8331
Lockport *(G-12993)*

Evanston Awning Company .... G 847 864-4520
Evanston *(G-9515)*

Flex-O-Glass Inc .... C 773 261-5200
Chicago *(G-4605)*

Haakes Awning .... G 618 529-4808
Carbondale *(G-2844)*

Hunzinger Williams Inc .... F 847 381-1878
Lake Barrington *(G-12151)*

Jelinek & Sons Inc .... G 630 355-3474
Plainfield *(G-16676)*

Johnson Seat & Canvas Shop .... G 815 756-2037
Cortland *(G-7021)*

Kankakee Tent & Awning Co .... G 815 932-8000
Kankakee *(G-11986)*

Kastelic Canvas Inc .... G 815 436-8160
Plainfield *(G-16679)*

▲ **M Mauritzon & Company Inc** .... E 773 235-6000
Chicago *(G-5303)*

◆ **M Putterman & Co LLC** .... D 773 927-4120
Chicago *(G-5304)*

Material Control Inc .... F 630 892-4274
Batavia *(G-1393)*

Midwest Awnings Inc .... G 309 762-3339
Cameron *(G-2808)*

Mpc Containment Systems LLC .... D 773 927-4121
Chicago *(G-5515)*

Mpc Group LLC .... C 773 927-4120
Chicago *(G-5517)*

Nieman & Considine Inc .... F 312 326-1053
Chicago *(G-5600)*

North Sails Group LLC .... G 773 489-1308
Chicago *(G-5621)*

Nuyen Awning Co .... G 630 892-3995
Aurora *(G-1141)*

Ogden Top & Trim Shop Inc .... G 708 484-5422
Berwyn *(G-1958)*

Ottos Canvas Shop .... G 217 543-3307
Arthur *(G-875)*

Polyair Inter Pack Inc .... D 773 995-1818
Chicago *(G-5838)*

Rehabilitation and Vocational .... E 618 833-5344
Anna *(G-587)*

▼ **Seamcraft International LLC** .... E 773 281-5150
Chicago *(G-6126)*

Shade Solutions Inc .... F 217 239-0718
Tolono *(G-19884)*

Shading Solutions Group Inc .... G 630 444-2102
Geneva *(G-10305)*

Shelter Systems .... G 773 281-9270
Chicago *(G-6151)*

Sleep6 LLC .... G 844 375-3376
Chicago *(G-6186)*

Stritzel Awnng Svc/Aurra Tent .... E 630 420-2000
Plainfield *(G-16718)*

Tarps Manufacturing Inc .... F 217 245-6181
Meredosia *(G-13957)*

Thatcher Oaks Inc .... E 630 833-5700
Elmhurst *(G-9435)*

Traube Canvas Products Inc .... F 618 281-0696
Dupo *(G-8147)*

Tri City Canvas Products Inc .... F 618 797-1662
Granite City *(G-10746)*

Tri Vantage LLC .... F 630 530-5333
Elmhurst *(G-9438)*

United Canvas Inc .... E 847 395-1470
Antioch *(G-641)*

2395 Pleating & Stitching For The Trade

A B S Embroidery Inc .... G 708 597-7785
Alsip *(G-408)*

A Plus Apparel .... G 815 675-2117
Spring Grove *(G-19262)*

Acme Button & Buttonhole Co .... G 773 907-8400
Chicago *(G-3526)*

Action Screen Print Inc .... F 630 393-1990
Warrenville *(G-20228)*

Advanced Flexible Mtls LLC .... F 312 961-9231
Chicago *(G-3564)*

All In Stitches .... G 309 944-4084
Geneseo *(G-10238)*

All Stars -N- Stitches Inc .... G 618 435-5555
Benton *(G-1918)*

Allstar Embroidery .... G 847 913-1133
Buffalo Grove *(G-2509)*

Alternative TS .... G 618 257-0230
Belleville *(G-1529)*

Ameri-Tex .... G 847 247-0777
Mundelein *(G-14663)*

Art-Flo Shirt & Lettering Co .... E 708 656-5422
Chicago *(G-3738)*

Artistic Embroidery Creations .... G 815 385-8854
McHenry *(G-13721)*

ASap Specialties Inc Del .... G 847 223-7699
Grayslake *(G-10759)*

Athletic Outfitters Inc .... G 815 942-6696
Morris *(G-14291)*

Award Emblem Mfg Co Inc .... F 630 739-0800
Bolingbrook *(G-2153)*

B & B Custom TS & Gifts .... G 618 463-0443
Alton *(G-544)*

B JS Printables .... G 618 656-8625
Edwardsville *(G-8346)*

Barnes & Noble College .... E 309 677-2320
Peoria *(G-16390)*

Bee Designs Embroidery & Scree .... G 815 393-4593
Esmond *(G-9475)*

Bullseye Imprinting & EMB .... G 630 834-8175
Elmhurst *(G-9339)*

C & C Embroidery Inc .... G 815 777-6167
Galena *(G-10165)*

C & C Sport Stop .... G 618 632-7812
O Fallon *(G-15569)*

Camilles of Canton Inc .... G 309 647-7403
Canton *(G-2822)*

Chicago Knitting Mills .... G 773 463-1464
Northbrook *(G-15358)*

◆ **Chicago Printing and EMB Inc** .... F 630 628-1777
Addison *(G-71)*

Classic Embroidery Inc .... F 708 485-7034
Chicago *(G-4168)*

Cloz Companies Inc .... E 773 247-8879
Skokie *(G-18944)*

Cq Industries Inc .... G 630 530-0177
Elmhurst *(G-9353)*

Creative Clothing Created 4 U .... G 847 543-0051
Grayslake *(G-10764)*

Cubby Hole of Carlinville Inc .... F 217 854-8511
Carlinville *(G-2872)*

Custom Enterprises .... G 618 439-6626
Benton *(G-1923)*

Custom Monogramming .... G 815 625-9044
Rock Falls *(G-17180)*

D & D Embroidery .... G 309 266-7092
Morton *(G-14357)*

▲ **D & J International Inc** .... F 847 966-9260
Niles *(G-15115)*

Dabel Incorporated .... G 217 398-3389
Champaign *(G-3284)*

Design Loft Imaging Inc .... G 847 439-2486
Elk Grove Village *(G-8946)*

Digistitch Embroidery & Design .... G 773 229-8630
Chicago *(G-4357)*

Dilars Embroidery & Monograms .... G 815 338-6066
Woodstock *(G-21381)*

Donghia Showrooms Inc .... G 312 822-0766
Chicago *(G-4383)*

Doras Spinning Wheel Inc .... G 618 466-1900
Alton *(G-553)*

Dpe Incorporated .... G 773 306-0105
Chicago *(G-4394)*

Elegant Embroidery Inc .... G 847 540-8003
Lake Zurich *(G-12407)*

Embroid ME .... G 847 272-9000
Northbrook *(G-15384)*

Embroidea Custom Embroidery .... G 217 698-6422
Springfield *(G-19362)*

Embroidery Experts Inc .... E 847 403-0200
Vernon Hills *(G-20051)*

Embroidery Services Inc .... G 847 588-2660
Niles *(G-15120)*

Embroidme .... G 847 301-1010
Lake Villa *(G-12349)*

Ensign Emblem Ltd .... D 217 877-8224
Decatur *(G-7493)*

Essential Creat Chicago Inc .... G 773 238-1700
Chicago *(G-4533)*

Expressions By Christine Inc .... F 217 223-2750
Quincy *(G-16881)*

Fast Lane Threads Custom EMB .... G 815 544-9898
Belvidere *(G-1667)*

Femina Sport Inc .... G 630 271-1876
Downers Grove *(G-8002)*

◆ **Fielders Choice** .... G 618 937-2294
West Frankfort *(G-20671)*

First Impression .... G 815 883-3357
Oglesby *(G-15841)*

Fitness Wear Inc .... G 847 486-1704
Glenview *(G-10546)*

G & M Embroidery .... G 708 636-7005
Chicago Ridge *(G-6795)*

G and D Enterprises Inc .... E 847 981-8661
Arlington Heights *(G-739)*

Harlan Vance Company .... F 309 888-4804
Normal *(G-15205)*

▲ **Hermans Inc** .... E 309 206-4892
Rock Island *(G-17222)*

Hyperstitch .... F 815 568-0590
Marengo *(G-13485)*

I D Togs .... G 618 235-1538
Belleville *(G-1556)*

Illinois Embroidery Service .... G 618 526-8006
Breese *(G-2304)*

Image Plus Inc .... G 630 852-4920
Downers Grove *(G-8028)*

Incredible Threads LLC .... G 847 970-0183
Elgin *(G-8624)*

Initial Choice .... F 847 234-5884
Lake Forest *(G-12267)*

J C Embroidery & Screen Print .... G 630 595-4670
Bensenville *(G-1827)*

James Randall .... G 309 444-8765
Washington *(G-20272)*

Johnos Inc .... G 630 897-6929
Aurora *(G-1119)*

Keneal Industries Inc .... F 815 886-1300
Romeoville *(G-17837)*

Midwest Stitch .... G 815 394-1516
Rockford *(G-17528)*

Midwest Swiss Embroideries Co .... E 773 631-7120
Chicago *(G-5448)*

Minerva Sportswear Inc .... F 309 661-2387
Bloomington *(G-2080)*

Minor League Inc .... G 618 548-8040
Salem *(G-18347)*

Mt Greenwood Embroidery .... G 773 779-5798
Chicago *(G-5521)*

Need To Know Inc .... G 309 691-3877
Peoria *(G-16484)*

Nelson Enterprises Inc .... G 815 633-1100
Roscoe *(G-17920)*

Personalized Threads .... G 815 431-1815
Ottawa *(G-16071)*

Pictures & More .... G 618 662-4572
Flora *(G-9688)*

Project Te Inc .... G 217 344-9833
Urbana *(G-19996)*

Quiltmaster Inc .... E 847 426-6741
Carpentersville *(G-3117)*

Reel Mate Mfg Co .... G 708 423-8005
Oak Lawn *(G-15734)*

Rock Tops Inc .... G 708 672-1450
Crete *(G-7144)*

Ronald J Nixon .... G 708 748-8130
Park Forest *(G-16259)*

S & R Monogramming Inc .... G 630 369-5468
Winfield *(G-21116)*

Sango Embroidery .... G 773 582-4354
Chicago *(G-6100)*

832
2020 Harris Illinois
Industrial Directory

SIC SECTION — 23 APPAREL AND OTHER FINISHED PRODUCTS MADE FROM FABRICS AND SIMILAR MATERIAL

Second Chance Inc ....F 630 904-5955
  Naperville (G-14986)
Select Screen Prints & EMB ....F 309 829-6511
  Bloomington (G-2093)
Senn Enterprises Inc ....G 309 673-4384
  Peoria (G-16520)
Senn Enterprises Inc ....F 309 637-1147
  Peoria (G-16519)
Sg Screen Graphics Inc ....G 309 699-8513
  Pekin (G-16360)
Signature of Chicago Inc ....G 630 271-1876
  Downers Grove (G-8095)
Stans Sportsworld Inc ....G 217 359-8474
  Champaign (G-3355)
Star Silkscreen Design Inc ....G 217 877-0804
  Decatur (G-7550)
Stitch By Stitch Incorporated ....G 847 541-2543
  Prospect Heights (G-16846)
Stitch Magic Usa Inc ....E 847 836-5000
  West Dundee (G-20666)
Stitchables Embroidery ....G 217 322-3000
  Rushville (G-18113)
Stitched Conversation ....G 312 966-1146
  Oak Park (G-15775)
Stitchin Image ....G 815 578-9890
  Richmond (G-17024)
T Graphics ....G 618 592-4145
  Oblong (G-15830)
T J Marche Ltd ....G 618 445-2314
  Albion (G-353)
Time Embroidery ....G 847 364-4371
  Elk Grove Village (G-9274)
Town Hall Sports Inc ....F 618 235-9881
  Belleville (G-1601)
▲ Trading Square Company Inc ....G 630 960-0606
  Westmont (G-20777)
Triangle Screen Print Inc ....F 847 678-9200
  Franklin Park (G-10066)
Trimark Screen Printing Inc ....G 630 629-2823
  Lombard (G-13146)
Tryad Specialties Inc ....F 630 549-0079
  Saint Charles (G-18292)
Twin Towers Marketing ....G 815 544-5554
  Belvidere (G-1706)
U Keep US In Stitches ....G 847 427-8127
  Mount Prospect (G-14578)
U R On It ....G 847 382-0182
  Lake Barrington (G-12167)
Ultimate Distributing Inc ....G 847 566-2250
  Mundelein (G-14745)
USA Embroidery ....G 309 692-1391
  Peoria (G-16543)
Visual Persuasion Inc ....F 815 899-6609
  Sycamore (G-19739)
Waist Up Imprntd Sprtswear LLC ...G 847 963-1400
  Palatine (G-16171)
Waldos Sports Corner Inc ....G 309 688-2425
  Peoria (G-16545)
Wellspring Investments LLC ....G 773 736-1213
  Chicago (G-6602)
Welsh Industries Ltd ....E 815 756-1111
  Dekalb (G-7712)
▲ Wilton Ww Co ....E 615 501-3000
  Naperville (G-14950)
Winning Stitch ....G 217 348-8279
  Charleston (G-3417)
Winning Streak Inc ....D 618 277-8191
  Dupo (G-8150)
Woolenwear Co ....F 847 520-9243
  Prospect Heights (G-16848)

2396 Automotive Trimmings, Apparel Findings, Related Prdts

A & R Screening LLC ....F 708 598-2480
  Crestwood (G-7103)
Action Screen Print Inc ....F 630 393-1990
  Warrenville (G-20228)
◆ Adolph Kiefer & Associates LLC ..D 309 451-5858
  Bloomington (G-2021)
Alternative TS ....G 618 257-0230
  Belleville (G-1529)
Ambrit Inc ....G 847 593-3301
  Elk Grove Village (G-8820)
American Enlightenment LLC ....G 773 687-8996
  Chicago (G-3652)
▲ American Graphic Systems Inc ...E 708 614-7007
  Tinley Park (G-19802)
American Name Plate & Metal De ..E 773 376-1400
  Chicago (G-3663)

Angels Heavenly Funeral Home ....G 773 239-8700
  Chicago (G-3696)
Arbetman & Associates ....G 708 386-8586
  Oak Park (G-15745)
Art Newvo Incorporated ....G 847 838-0304
  Antioch (G-600)
Art-Flo Shirt & Lettering Co ....E 708 656-5422
  Chicago (G-3738)
Ashland Screening Corporation ....E 708 758-8800
  Chicago Heights (G-6732)
Authority Screenprint & EMB ....G 630 236-0289
  Plainfield (G-16643)
B & B Custom TS & Gifts ....G 618 463-0443
  Alton (G-544)
B and A Screen Printing ....G 217 762-2632
  Monticello (G-14277)
B JS Printables ....G 618 656-8625
  Edwardsville (G-8346)
Bailleu & Bailleu Printing Inc ....G 309 852-2517
  Kewanee (G-12021)
Bobbi Screen Printing ....G 773 847-8200
  Chicago (G-3923)
Bow Brothers Co Inc ....G 217 359-0555
  Champaign (G-3272)
Breedlove Sporting Goods Inc ....F 309 852-2434
  Kewanee (G-12028)
Breedlove Sporting Goods Inc ....G 309 852-2434
  Kewanee (G-12029)
C & C Sport Stop ....G 618 632-7812
  O Fallon (G-15569)
Carl Gorr Printing Co ....E 815 338-3191
  Woodstock (G-21370)
Color Tone Printing ....G 708 385-1442
  Blue Island (G-2114)
Creative Clothing Created 4 U ....G 847 543-0051
  Grayslake (G-10764)
Cubby Hole of Carlinville Inc ....F 217 854-8511
  Carlinville (G-2872)
Custom Enterprises ....G 618 439-6626
  Benton (G-1923)
Custom Monogramming ....G 815 625-9044
  Rock Falls (G-17180)
Custom Telephone Printing Co ....F 815 338-0000
  Woodstock (G-21379)
Custom Towels Inc ....G 618 539-5005
  Freeburg (G-10088)
Custom Trophies ....G 217 422-3353
  Decatur (G-7480)
Dabel Incorporated ....G 217 398-3389
  Champaign (G-3284)
Darnall Printing ....G 309 827-7212
  Bloomington (G-2039)
Desk & Door Nameplate Company ..F 815 806-8670
  Frankfort (G-9785)
Diamond Teez & More LLC ....G 618 579-9876
  Alton (G-552)
▲ Diemasters Manufacturing Inc ....C 847 640-9900
  Elk Grove Village (G-8950)
DMarv Design Specialty Prtrs ....G 708 389-4420
  Blue Island (G-2118)
Earl Ad Inc ....G 312 666-7106
  Chicago (G-4431)
Enterprise Signs Inc ....G 708 691-1273
  Blue Island (G-2121)
▲ Excel Screen Prtg & EMB Inc .....D 847 801-5200
  Schiller Park (G-18808)
Fantastic Lettering Inc ....G 773 685-7650
  Chicago (G-4559)
Fast Lane Threads Custom EMB .....G 815 544-9898
  Belvidere (G-1667)
Fitness Wear Inc ....G 847 486-1704
  Glenview (G-10546)
Fresh Concept Enterprises Inc ....G 815 254-7295
  Plainfield (G-16667)
G and D Enterprises Inc ....E 847 981-8661
  Arlington Heights (G-739)
Gabriel Enterprises ....G 773 342-8705
  Chicago (G-4654)
Gcg Corp ....G 847 298-2285
  Glenview (G-10548)
George Lauterer Corporation ....E 312 913-1881
  Chicago (G-4682)
Go Van Goghs Tee Shirt ....G 309 342-1112
  Galesburg (G-10198)
Good Impressions Inc ....G 847 831-4317
  Highland Park (G-11265)
Graphic Screen Printing Inc ....G 708 429-3330
  Orland Park (G-15957)
Hamsher Lakeside Funerals ....G 847 587-2100
  Fox Lake (G-9747)

Hazen Display Corporation ....E 815 248-2925
  Davis (G-7418)
Hole In The Wall Screen Arts ....G 217 243-9100
  Jacksonville (G-11767)
Ikan Creations LLC ....G 312 204-7333
  Chicago (G-4884)
Image Plus Inc ....G 630 852-4920
  Downers Grove (G-8028)
J & D Instant Signs ....G 847 965-2800
  Morton Grove (G-14414)
Johnson Rolan Co Inc ....G 309 674-9671
  Peoria (G-16464)
K and A Graphics Inc ....G 847 244-2345
  Gurnee (G-10890)
Lee-Wel Printing Corporation ....G 630 682-0935
  Wheaton (G-20812)
Linda Levinson Designs Inc ....G 312 951-6943
  Chicago (G-5226)
Lloyd Midwest Graphics ....G 815 282-8828
  Machesney Park (G-13357)
Lochman Ref Silk Screen Co ....F 847 475-6266
  Evanston (G-9547)
Locker Room Screen Printing ....G 630 759-2533
  Bolingbrook (G-2206)
M Wells Printing Co ....G 312 455-0400
  Chicago (G-5305)
Marketing Card Technology LLC ....D 630 985-7900
  Downers Grove (G-8052)
Maxs Screen Machine Inc ....G 773 878-4949
  Chicago (G-5370)
Mer-Pla Inc ....F 847 530-9798
  Chicago (G-5393)
Mexacali Silkscreen Inc ....G 630 628-9313
  Addison (G-201)
Midwest Stitch ....G 815 394-1516
  Rockford (G-17528)
Mighty Mites Awards and Sons ....G 847 297-0035
  Des Plaines (G-7802)
Minerva Sportswear Inc ....F 309 661-2387
  Bloomington (G-2080)
Navitor Inc ....B 800 323-0253
  Harwood Heights (G-11106)
Need To Know Inc ....G 309 691-3877
  Peoria (G-16484)
Nu-Art Printing ....G 618 533-9971
  Centralia (G-3242)
Offworld Designs ....G 815 786-7080
  Sandwich (G-18378)
Olympic Trophy and Awards Co ......F 773 631-9500
  Chicago (G-5672)
Paddock Industries Inc ....F 618 277-1580
  Smithton (G-19068)
Papyrus Press Inc ....F 773 342-0700
  Chicago (G-5755)
▲ Petra Manufacturing Co ....D 773 622-1475
  Chicago (G-5797)
Plastics Printing Group Inc ....F 773 473-4481
  Chicago (G-5820)
Precision Screen Specialties ....G 630 220-1361
  Saint Charles (G-18250)
Pressd Apparel LLC ....G 312 767-1877
  Chicago (G-5868)
Priority Print ....G 708 485-7080
  Brookfield (G-2491)
◆ Qst Industries Inc ....E 312 930-9400
  Chicago (G-5923)
Qst Industries Inc ....D 312 930-9400
  Chicago (G-5924)
Quality Spraying Screen Prtg ....E 630 584-8324
  Saint Charles (G-18256)
R J S Silk Screening Co ....G 708 974-3009
  Palos Hills (G-16206)
R R Donnelley & Sons Company .....D 630 762-7600
  Saint Charles (G-18258)
Rainbow Art Inc ....F 312 421-5600
  Chicago (G-5965)
▲ Rebel Screeners Inc ....D 312 525-2670
  Chicago (G-5988)
◆ Rico Industries Inc ....D 312 427-0313
  Niles (G-15166)
Ronald J Nixon ....G 708 748-8130
  Park Forest (G-16259)
Scheiwes Print Shop ....G 815 683-2398
  Crescent City (G-7082)
Screen Machine Incorporated ....G 847 439-2233
  Elk Grove Village (G-9234)
Select Screen Prints & EMB ....F 309 829-6511
  Bloomington (G-2093)
Sg Screen Graphics Inc ....G 309 699-8513
  Pekin (G-16360)

23 APPAREL AND OTHER FINISHED PRODUCTS MADE FROM FABRICS AND SIMILAR MATERIAL | SIC SECTION

▼ **Shree Mahavir Inc** G 312 408-1080
Chicago *(G-6159)*

Signature Label of Illinois G 618 283-5145
Vandalia *(G-20024)*

Signature Screen Printing Corp G 773 866-0070
Chicago *(G-6169)*

Signcraft Screenprint Inc C 815 777-3030
Galena *(G-10178)*

Signs In Dundee Inc G 847 742-9530
Elgin *(G-8731)*

Sport Connection G 630 980-1787
Roselle *(G-17990)*

Stans Sportsworld Inc G 217 359-8474
Champaign *(G-3355)*

Star Silkscreen Design Inc G 217 877-0804
Decatur *(G-7550)*

▲ **Stellar Recognition Inc** D 773 282-8060
Chicago *(G-6243)*

▲ **Stevens Sign Co Inc** G 708 562-4888
Northlake *(G-15560)*

Super Sublimation LLC G 309 256-0184
Morton *(G-14384)*

Team Works By Holzhauer Inc G 309 745-9924
Washington *(G-20281)*

Teds Shirt Shack Inc G 217 224-9705
Quincy *(G-16946)*

Think Ink Inc G 815 459-4565
Crystal Lake *(G-7282)*

Toni Federici F 618 244-4842
Mount Vernon *(G-14642)*

Top Notch Silk Screening G 773 847-6335
Chicago *(G-6395)*

Triangle Screen Print Inc F 847 678-9200
Franklin Park *(G-10066)*

Trimark Screen Printing Inc G 630 629-2823
Lombard *(G-13146)*

Ultimate Distributing Inc G 847 566-2250
Mundelein *(G-14745)*

▲ **Unique Assembly & Decorating** E 630 241-4300
Downers Grove *(G-8103)*

▲ **Wagner Zip-Change Inc** E 708 681-4100
Melrose Park *(G-13926)*

Waldos Sports Corner Inc G 309 688-2425
Peoria *(G-16545)*

Weiskamp Screen Printing G 217 398-8428
Champaign *(G-3370)*

Wellspring Investments LLC G 773 736-1213
Chicago *(G-6602)*

Windy City Silkscreening Inc E 312 842-0030
Chicago *(G-6644)*

Winning Stitch G 217 348-8279
Charleston *(G-3417)*

▲ **Woodbridge Inc** F 847 229-1741
Wheeling *(G-21015)*

2397 Schiffli Machine Embroideries

Midwest Swiss Embroideries Co E 773 631-7120
Chicago *(G-5448)*

2399 Fabricated Textile Prdts, NEC

Action Advertising Inc G 312 791-0660
Chicago *(G-3534)*

▲ **AWego Enterprises Inc** G 815 765-1957
Belvidere *(G-1651)*

Bill Weeks Inc G 217 523-8735
Springfield *(G-19326)*

Decal Solutions Unlimited Inc G 847 590-5405
Arlington Heights *(G-727)*

Deyco Inc G 630 553-5666
Yorkville *(G-21480)*

▲ **Duo North America** G 312 421-7755
Chicago *(G-4406)*

Duracrest Fabrics G 847 350-0030
Elk Grove Village *(G-8959)*

▲ **Fabric Images Inc** D 847 488-9877
Elgin *(G-8583)*

George Lauterer Corporation E 312 913-1881
Chicago *(G-4682)*

Girlygirl G 708 633-7290
Tinley Park *(G-19831)*

Heiman Sign Studio G 815 397-6909
Rockford *(G-17447)*

Hooker Custom Harness Inc G 815 233-5478
Freeport *(G-10119)*

▲ **J C Schultz Enterprises Inc** D 800 323-9127
Batavia *(G-1388)*

▲ **Moss Holding Company** C 847 238-4200
Elk Grove Village *(G-9132)*

N Henry & Son Inc D 847 870-0797
Itasca *(G-11706)*

Precise Digital Printing Inc E 847 593-2645
Bensenville *(G-1871)*

Rock Tops Inc G 708 672-1450
Crete *(G-7144)*

Romel Press Inc G 708 343-6090
Melrose Park *(G-13909)*

▼ **Seamcraft International LLC** E 773 281-5150
Chicago *(G-6126)*

▲ **Seasonal Designs Inc** E 847 688-0280
Waukegan *(G-20493)*

Signcraft Screenprint Inc C 815 777-3030
Galena *(G-10178)*

Tex Trend Inc E 847 215-6796
Wheeling *(G-20999)*

▲ **Travel Hammock Inc** G 847 486-0005
Skokie *(G-19047)*

Vel-Tye LLC G 757 518-5400
Plainfield *(G-16725)*

W G N Flag & Decorating Co F 773 768-8076
Chicago *(G-6573)*

24 LUMBER AND WOOD PRODUCTS, EXCEPT FURNITURE

2411 Logging

Beeman & Sons Inc F 217 232-4268
Martinsville *(G-13581)*

Big Creek Forestry & Logging L G 217 822-8282
Marshall *(G-13565)*

Bourrette Logging G 815 591-3761
Hanover *(G-10995)*

Brian Kinney G 309 206-4219
Rock Island *(G-17209)*

Christiansen Sawmill and Log G 815 315-7520
Caledonia *(G-2769)*

Cnv Enterprises Inc G 815 405-6762
Plainfield *(G-16653)*

Dust Logging LLC G 217 844-2305
Effingham *(G-8396)*

Ericson S Log & Lumber Co G 309 667-2147
New Windsor *(G-15073)*

Frank E Galloway G 618 948-2578
Sumner *(G-19686)*

G & C Enterprises Inc G 618 747-2272
Jonesboro *(G-11946)*

Heartland Hardwoods Inc E 217 844-3312
Effingham *(G-8402)*

Illiana Real Log Homes Inc G 815 471-4004
Milford *(G-14035)*

Jack Shepard Logging G 618 845-3496
Ullin *(G-19935)*

K D Custom Sawing Logging G 309 231-4805
Green Valley *(G-10817)*

Kelly & Son Forestry & Log LLC G 815 275-6877
Crystal Lake *(G-7216)*

Larry Musgrave Logging G 618 842-6386
Fairfield *(G-9630)*

Loneoak Timber & Veneere Co G 618 426-3065
Ava *(G-1174)*

Lonnie Hickam G 618 893-4223
Pomona *(G-16763)*

Lte-Little Timber Enterprises G 224 321-0361
Lake Villa *(G-12358)*

Poignant Logging G 309 246-5647
Lacon *(G-12133)*

Powell Tree Care Inc G 847 364-1181
Elk Grove Village *(G-9186)*

S Carpenter Logging G 618 548-6187
Salem *(G-18356)*

Tallwood G 815 786-8186
Plano *(G-16744)*

W Bozarth Logging G 618 658-4016
Vienna *(G-20120)*

Warrior Logging & Perforagine G 618 662-7373
Flora *(G-9695)*

Warrior Well Services Inc G 618 662-7710
Flora *(G-9696)*

2421 Saw & Planing Mills

Alstat Wood Products F 618 684-5167
Murphysboro *(G-14750)*

Autumn Mill G 217 795-3399
Argenta *(G-671)*

Bach Timber & Pallet Inc G 815 885-3774
Caledonia *(G-2768)*

Backyard Creations G 217 836-5678
Petersburg *(G-16600)*

Bailey Business Group G 618 548-3566
Salem *(G-18330)*

Boise Cascade Company E 618 491-7030
Granite City *(G-10700)*

Bond Brothers Hardwoods G 618 272-4811
Ridgway *(G-17035)*

Botkin Lumber Company Inc E 217 287-2127
Taylorville *(G-19751)*

Boyd Sawmill G 618 735-2056
Dix *(G-7881)*

Bull Valley Hardwood G 815 701-9400
Woodstock *(G-21368)*

Bull Valley Hardwood G 815 701-9400
Crystal Lake *(G-7174)*

Cairo Dry Kilns Inc E 618 734-1039
Cairo *(G-2766)*

Carpenters Millwork Co F 708 339-7707
South Holland *(G-19204)*

Carpenters Millwork Co F 708 339-7707
Villa Park *(G-20137)*

Charles Horn Lumber Company F 773 847-7397
Cicero *(G-6832)*

Charles K Eichen G 217 854-9751
Carlinville *(G-2871)*

Christiansen Sawmill and Log G 815 315-7520
Caledonia *(G-2769)*

Clarence Hancock Sawmill Inc G 618 854-2232
Noble *(G-15189)*

Corsaw Hardwood Lumber Inc F 309 293-2055
Smithfield *(G-19063)*

Crooked Trails Sawmill G 618 244-1547
Opdyke *(G-15904)*

Darrell Fickas G 618 599-3632
Mount Vernon *(G-14605)*

Deborah Zeitler Associates Inc G 312 527-3733
Chicago *(G-4328)*

E-Z Tree Recycling Inc G 773 493-8600
Chicago *(G-4428)*

Eichen Lumber Co Inc G 217 854-9751
Carlinville *(G-2874)*

Ericson S Log & Lumber Co G 309 667-2147
New Windsor *(G-15073)*

Farrow Lumber Co G 618 734-0255
Cairo *(G-2767)*

Five Star Pallets Inc G 847 613-8488
McHenry *(G-13744)*

Forestech Wood Products G 217 279-3659
West Union *(G-20690)*

Francis L Morris G 618 676-1724
Clay City *(G-6905)*

Fraser Millwork Inc G 708 447-3262
Lyons *(G-13309)*

G L Beaumont Lumber Company F 618 423-2323
Ramsey *(G-16964)*

Goodale Corporation G 312 421-9663
Chicago *(G-4717)*

Goodman Sawmill G 309 547-3597
Lewistown *(G-12615)*

▲ **Griffard & Associates LLC** G 217 316-1732
Quincy *(G-16887)*

Heartland Hardwoods Inc E 217 844-3312
Effingham *(G-8402)*

IMC Outdoor Living G 314 373-1171
Godfrey *(G-10653)*

Intelligent Flrg Systems LLC G 630 587-1800
Saint Charles *(G-18214)*

J M Lustig Custom Cabinets Co F 217 342-6661
Effingham *(G-8403)*

Jefferies Orchard Sawmill G 217 487-7582
Springfield *(G-19395)*

Jht Robertson Lumber Inc G 618 842-2004
Fairfield *(G-9628)*

◆ **K&S International Inc** G 847 229-0202
Wheeling *(G-20922)*

Kirkland Sawmill Inc G 815 522-6150
Kirkland *(G-12062)*

Kniffen Brothers Sawmill G 618 629-2437
Whittington *(G-21020)*

Koppers Industries Inc E 309 343-5157
Galesburg *(G-10206)*

▲ **Lamboo Inc** E 866 966-2999
Litchfield *(G-12970)*

Larry Musgrave Logging G 618 842-6386
Fairfield *(G-9630)*

Liese Lumber Co Inc G 618 234-0105
Belleville *(G-1568)*

M D Harmon Inc F 618 662-8925
Xenia *(G-21468)*

Marvin Suckow G 618 483-5570
Mason *(G-13608)*

◆ **Mechanics Planing Mill Inc** E 618 288-3000
Glen Carbon *(G-10390)*

Mesic Vale LLC F 309 335-8521
Galesburg *(G-10209)*

Mulvain Woodworks G 815 248-2305
Durand *(G-8154)*

Old School Timber Works Co G 847 918-8626
Libertyville *(G-12692)*

Oltenia Inc G 773 987-2888
Norridge *(G-15242)*

Paulette Colson F 618 372-8888
Medora *(G-13815)*

Png Transport LLC G 312 218-8116
Chicago *(G-5827)*

▲ **Red River Lumber Inc** D 708 388-1818
Blue Island *(G-2135)*

Rjt Wood Services G 815 858-2081
Galena *(G-10177)*

Sawmill Construction Inc G 815 937-0037
Bourbonnais *(G-2268)*

Schrocks Sawmill G 217 268-3632
Arcola *(G-665)*

Simonton Hardwood Lumber LLC F 618 594-2132
Carlyle *(G-2896)*

Southeast Wood Treating Inc F 815 562-5007
Rochelle *(G-17160)*

▲ **Towerleaf LLC** G 847 985-1937
Schaumburg *(G-18750)*

Tree-O Lumber Inc E 618 357-2576
Pinckneyville *(G-16620)*

Triezenberg Millwork Co G 708 489-9062
Crestwood *(G-7132)*

Tronox Incorporated E 203 705-3704
Madison *(G-13418)*

Twin City Wood Recycling Corp G 309 827-9663
Bloomington *(G-2106)*

Weatherguard Buildings G 217 894-6213
Clayton *(G-6911)*

Westrock Cp LLC G 630 655-6951
Burr Ridge *(G-2733)*

Westrock Cp LLC D 312 346-6600
Chicago *(G-6611)*

Willenborg Hardwood Inds Inc F 217 844-2082
Effingham *(G-8431)*

Willowbrook Sawmill G 618 592-3806
Oblong *(G-15832)*

Woodcraft Enterprises Inc G 815 485-2787
New Lenox *(G-15070)*

Wooded Wonderland G 815 777-1223
Galena *(G-10182)*

2426 Hardwood Dimension & Flooring Mills

Art Jewel Enterprises Ltd F 630 260-0400
Carol Stream *(G-2941)*

Bond Brothers Hardwoods G 618 272-4811
Ridgway *(G-17035)*

Boyd Sawmill G 618 735-2056
Dix *(G-7881)*

▲ **Builders Warehouse Inc** G 309 672-1760
Peoria *(G-16395)*

Central Illinois Hardwood G 309 352-2363
Green Valley *(G-10816)*

Christiansen Sawmill and Log G 815 315-7520
Caledonia *(G-2769)*

◆ **Connor Sports Flooring LLC** D 847 290-9020
Bensenville *(G-1775)*

Eichen Lumber Co Inc G 217 854-9751
Carlinville *(G-2874)*

Enterprise Pallet Inc F 815 928-8546
Bourbonnais *(G-2260)*

Ericson S Log & Lumber Co G 309 667-2147
New Windsor *(G-15073)*

Flooring Warehouse Direct Inc G 815 730-6767
Homer Glen *(G-11479)*

G L Beaumont Lumber Company F 618 423-2323
Ramsey *(G-16964)*

Grads Inc G 847 426-3904
East Dundee *(G-8198)*

Greatlkes Archtctral Mllwrks L E 312 829-7110
Chicago *(G-4739)*

▲ **Hakwood Inc** G 630 219-3388
Naperville *(G-14971)*

Hardwood Lumber Products Co G 309 538-4411
Kilbourne *(G-12044)*

Heartland Hardwoods Inc E 217 844-3312
Effingham *(G-8402)*

Historic Timber & Plank Inc E 618 372-4546
Brighton *(G-2401)*

Knapp Industrial Wood F 815 657-8854
Forrest *(G-9734)*

Moultrie County Hardwoods LLC G 217 543-2643
Arthur *(G-870)*

New Line Hardwoods Inc D 309 657-7621
Beardstown *(G-1449)*

▲ **Red River Lumber Inc** D 708 388-1818
Blue Island *(G-2135)*

Redbox Workshop Ltd E 773 478-7077
Chicago *(G-5993)*

▲ **Ridgefield Industries Co LLC** E 800 569-0316
Crystal Lake *(G-7256)*

Riverside Custom Woodworking G 815 589-3608
Fulton *(G-10157)*

Scv Floorsmith G 661 476-5034
Hoffman Estates *(G-11455)*

Second City Flooring LLC G 973 262-3272
Chicago *(G-6127)*

▲ **Signature Innovations LLC** G 847 758-9600
Elk Grove Village *(G-9241)*

Simonton Hardwood Lumber LLC F 618 594-2132
Carlyle *(G-2896)*

T J P Investments Inc G 309 673-8383
Peoria *(G-16534)*

Tree-O Lumber Inc E 618 357-2576
Pinckneyville *(G-16620)*

Unity Hardwoods LLC F 708 701-2943
Chicago *(G-6479)*

Vlasici Hardwood Floors Co G 815 505-4308
Romeoville *(G-17885)*

Woodcraft Enterprises Inc G 815 485-2787
New Lenox *(G-15070)*

Wooded Wonderland G 815 777-1223
Galena *(G-10182)*

Woodmac Industries Inc F 708 755-3545
S Chicago Hts *(G-18130)*

▲ **Woodworkers Shop Inc** E 309 347-5111
Pekin *(G-16371)*

Woodx Lumber Inc G 331 979-2171
Elmhurst *(G-9447)*

2429 Special Prdt Sawmills, NEC

◆ **Iko Midwest Inc** E 815 936-9600
Chicago *(G-4885)*

Upcycle Products Inc G 815 383-6220
Minooka *(G-14066)*

2431 Millwork

A & M Wood Products Inc G 630 323-2555
Burr Ridge *(G-2647)*

A and J Development Plus LLC G 630 470-9539
Plainfield *(G-16639)*

A-Squared Woodworking Inc G 773 742-7234
Bridgeview *(G-2318)*

Ability Cabinet Co Inc G 847 678-6678
Franklin Park *(G-9859)*

Absolute Windows Inc E 708 599-9191
Oak Lawn *(G-15693)*

Accurate Cstm Sash Mllwk Corp G 708 423-0423
Oak Lawn *(G-15694)*

Adel Woodworks G 815 886-9006
Romeoville *(G-17787)*

Agusta Mill Works G 309 787-4616
Milan *(G-13999)*

All American Wood Register Co F 815 356-1000
Crystal Lake *(G-7155)*

Alliance Door and Hardware LLC G 630 451-7070
Hillside *(G-11326)*

Allie Woodworking G 847 244-1919
Waukegan *(G-20413)*

Allied Garage Door Inc E 630 279-0795
Addison *(G-27)*

American Custom Woodworking F 847 526-5900
Wauconda *(G-20330)*

American Woodworks G 630 279-1629
Sleepy Hollow *(G-19061)*

▲ **Ameriscan Designs Inc** D 773 542-1291
Chicago *(G-3677)*

Amron Stair Works Inc F 847 426-4800
Gilberts *(G-10350)*

Architectual Woodworking G 847 259-3331
Prospect Heights *(G-16835)*

Architectural Mall Inc G 630 543-5253
Carol Stream *(G-2939)*

Architectural Wdwkg Design Inc G 630 810-1604
Downers Grove *(G-7954)*

Architectural Wood Expressions G 708 731-2355
Stone Park *(G-19552)*

Artisan Millwork LLC G 847 417-5236
Saint Charles *(G-18150)*

Aspen Shutters Inc G 847 979-0166
Schaumburg *(G-18446)*

Back Forty WD Works & Nurs LLC G 618 898-1241
Johnsonville *(G-11811)*

Bailey Hardwoods Inc G 217 529-6800
Springfield *(G-19324)*

Baker Elements Inc G 630 660-8100
Oak Park *(G-15746)*

Becker Jules D Wood Products G 847 526-8002
Wauconda *(G-20334)*

Beloit Pattern Works F 815 389-2578
South Beloit *(G-19083)*

Benchmark Cabinets & Mllwk Inc E 309 697-5855
Peoria *(G-16391)*

▼ **Bernhard Woodwork Ltd** D 847 291-1040
Northbrook *(G-15348)*

Blue Chip Construction Inc F 630 208-5254
Geneva *(G-10255)*

Blueberry Woodworking Inc G 773 230-7179
Franklin Park *(G-9890)*

Bond Brothers Hardwoods G 618 272-4811
Ridgway *(G-17035)*

Boom Company Inc G 847 459-6199
Wheeling *(G-20863)*

Botti Studio of Architectural E 847 869-5933
Glenview *(G-10532)*

▲ **Brown Wood Products Company** F 847 673-4780
Lincolnwood *(G-12814)*

Brown Woodworking G 815 477-8333
Crystal Lake *(G-7172)*

Byttow Enterprises Inc G 708 372-4450
Lansing *(G-12486)*

C A Larson & Son Inc E 847 717-6010
Maple Park *(G-13461)*

C and S Carpentry LLC G 224 523-8064
Elgin *(G-8527)*

CA Custom Woodworking G 630 201-6154
Newark *(G-15074)*

Cabinets Doors and More LLC G 847 395-6334
Antioch *(G-607)*

Cain Millwork Inc D 815 561-9700
Rochelle *(G-17134)*

Carpenters Millwork Co F 708 339-7707
South Holland *(G-19204)*

Carpenters Millwork Co F 708 339-7707
Villa Park *(G-20137)*

Central Wood LLC G 217 543-2662
Arcola *(G-646)*

Cervantes/Salgado LLC G 630 806-4864
Montgomery *(G-14239)*

Chicago School Woodworking LLC G 773 275-1170
Chicago *(G-4128)*

Christos Woodworking G 708 975-5045
Alsip *(G-431)*

City Screen Inc G 773 588-5642
Chicago *(G-4161)*

▲ **Classic Woodwork Inc** G 815 356-9000
Crystal Lake *(G-7182)*

Clopay Building Pdts Co Inc G 708 346-0901
Chicago Ridge *(G-6791)*

CM Woodwords Inc G 847 945-7689
Deerfield *(G-7604)*

Cmp Millwork Co G 630 832-6462
Elmhurst *(G-9348)*

Contract Industries Inc E 708 458-8150
Bedford Park *(G-1464)*

Cooper Lake Millworks Inc G 217 847-2681
Hamilton *(G-10951)*

Corsaw Hardwood Lumber Inc F 309 293-2055
Smithfield *(G-19063)*

Craiger Inc G 815 479-9660
Crystal Lake *(G-7186)*

Crea and Crea G 630 292-5625
Bartlett *(G-1273)*

Creative Millwork LLC E 630 762-0002
Saint Charles *(G-18178)*

Creswell Woodworking CA G 847 381-9222
Woodstock *(G-21378)*

Curtis Woodworking Inc G 815 544-3543
Belvidere *(G-1664)*

Custom Crafted Door Inc F 309 527-5075
El Paso *(G-8435)*

Custom Hardwoods LLC G 815 784-9974
Sycamore *(G-19703)*

Custom Railz & Stairz Inc G 773 592-7210
Chicago *(G-4291)*

Custom Window Accents F 815 943-7651
Harvard *(G-11051)*

Custom Wood Creations G 618 346-2208
Collinsville *(G-6956)*

Dandurand Custom Woodworking G 708 489-6440
Posen *(G-16793)*

▲ **Daniel M Powers & Assoc Ltd** D 630 685-8400
Bolingbrook *(G-2166)*

Decorators Supply Corporation ....E 773 847-6300
Chicago *(G-4330)*
Decore-Ative Specialties ....B 630 947-6294
Cary *(G-3155)*
Deem Woodworks ....G....... 217 832-9614
Villa Grove *(G-20122)*
▲ **Del Great Frame Up Systems Inc** .....E 847 808-1955
Franklin Park *(G-9929)*
Demeter Millwork LLC ....F 312 224-4440
Chicago *(G-4338)*
Der Holtzmacher Ltd ....G....... 815 895-4887
Sycamore *(G-19706)*
Designed Stairs Inc ....E 815 786-2021
Sandwich *(G-18367)*
DLM Manufacturing Inc ....F 815 964-3800
Rockford *(G-17382)*
Doctors Interior Plantscaping ....G....... 708 333-3323
South Holland *(G-19208)*
Douglas County Mil Moldings ....G....... 217 268-4689
Arcola *(G-647)*
Duhack Lehn & Associates Inc ....G....... 815 777-3460
Galena *(G-10168)*
Dunigan Custom Woodworking ....G....... 708 351-5213
Homewood *(G-11491)*
Eiesland Builders Inc ....E 847 998-1731
Glenview *(G-10544)*
Elite Custom Woodworking ....G....... 630 888-4322
Batavia *(G-1376)*
European Wood Works Inc ....G....... 773 662-6607
Carol Stream *(G-2982)*
Extreme Woodworking Inc ....G....... 224 338-8179
Round Lake *(G-18074)*
Four Acre Wood Products ....F 217 543-2971
Arthur *(G-858)*
Fraser Millwork Inc ....G....... 708 447-3262
Lyons *(G-13309)*
G & M Woodworking Inc ....G....... 708 425-4013
Oak Lawn *(G-15717)*
Gavin Woodworking Inc ....G....... 815 786-2242
Sandwich *(G-18371)*
Gc Custom Woodworking LLC ....G....... 847 724-7292
Glenview *(G-10547)*
Geo J Rothan Co ....E 309 674-5189
Peoria *(G-16445)*
George Drowne Cabinet Sand ....G....... 847 234-1487
Lake Bluff *(G-12183)*
George Pagels Company ....G....... 708 478-7036
Mokena *(G-14087)*
Gingerich Custom Woodworking ....F 217 578-3491
Arthur *(G-860)*
Glass & Wood Work Inc ....G....... 708 945-9558
Bridgeview *(G-2350)*
Glendale Woodworking ....G....... 630 545-1520
Glendale Heights *(G-10453)*
Gmk Finishing ....G....... 630 837-0568
Bartlett *(G-1284)*
Grays Cabinet Co ....G....... 618 948-2211
Saint Francisville *(G-18314)*
Greatlkes Archtctral Mllwrks L ....E 312 829-7110
Chicago *(G-4739)*
H & M Woodworks ....G....... 608 289-3141
Hamilton *(G-10957)*
Hardwood Connection ....G....... 815 895-8733
Sycamore *(G-19712)*
Harold Prefinished Wood Inc ....F 618 548-1414
Salem *(G-18342)*
Heartland Hardwoods Inc ....E 217 844-3312
Effingham *(G-8402)*
Heritage Moulding Inc ....G....... 630 961-0001
Plainfield *(G-16672)*
Herner-Geissler Wdwkg Corp ....D....... 312 226-3400
Chicago *(G-4809)*
Hill Design Products Inc ....F 815 344-3333
McHenry *(G-13748)*
Historic Timber & Plank Inc ....E 618 372-4546
Brighton *(G-2401)*
HK Woodwork ....G....... 773 964-2468
Wheeling *(G-20909)*
Hogan Woodwork Inc ....G....... 708 354-4525
Countryside *(G-7056)*
Hpmillwork LLC ....G....... 630 220-4387
Northbrook *(G-15401)*
Hylan Design Ltd ....G....... 312 243-7341
Chicago *(G-4863)*
Ideal Cabinet Solutions Inc ....G....... 618 514-7087
Alhambra *(G-401)*
Imperial Store Fixtures Inc ....G....... 773 348-1137
Chicago *(G-4901)*
Imperial Woodworking Entps Inc ....E 847 358-6920
Palatine *(G-16128)*

J Hoffman Lumber Co Inc ....G....... 815 899-2260
Sycamore *(G-19718)*
J K Custom Countertops ....G....... 630 495-2324
Lombard *(G-13088)*
J R Husar Inc ....F 312 243-7888
Chicago *(G-4994)*
J&E Storm Services Inc ....G....... 630 401-3793
Tinley Park *(G-19841)*
Janik Custom Millwork Inc ....G....... 708 482-4844
Hodgkins *(G-11390)*
Jay A Morris ....G....... 815 432-6440
Watseka *(G-20308)*
Jeld-Wen Inc ....D....... 217 893-4444
Rantoul *(G-16978)*
Jelinek & Sons Inc ....G....... 630 355-3474
Plainfield *(G-16676)*
Jj Wood Working ....G....... 708 426-6854
Bridgeview *(G-2359)*
Jlm Woodworking ....G....... 309 275-8259
Normal *(G-15206)*
John Tobin Millwork Co ....G....... 630 832-3780
Villa Park *(G-20152)*
Kabinet Kraft ....F 618 395-1047
Olney *(G-15867)*
◆ **Kempner Company Inc** ....F 312 733-1606
Chicago *(G-5095)*
Kencor Stairs & Woodworking ....G....... 630 279-8980
Villa Park *(G-20155)*
Kep Woodworking ....G....... 847 480-9545
Newark *(G-15077)*
Knotty By Nature ....G....... 618 610-2481
Grafton *(G-10685)*
L Surges Custom Woodwork ....G....... 815 774-9663
Joliet *(G-11892)*
Lake Shore Stair Co Inc ....E 815 363-7777
Ingleside *(G-11586)*
Lake Shore Stair Co Inc ....E 847 362-3262
Libertyville *(G-12666)*
Landquist & Son Inc ....E 847 674-6600
Mokena *(G-14094)*
Lyko Woodworking & Cnstr ....G....... 773 583-4561
Chicago *(G-5292)*
M & R Custom Millwork Inc ....G....... 815 547-8549
Belvidere *(G-1682)*
Majestic Archtctural Wdwrk Inc ....G....... 708 240-8484
Bellwood *(G-1632)*
Masonite Corporation ....D....... 630 584-6330
West Chicago *(G-20616)*
Master Cabinets ....G....... 847 639-1323
Cary *(G-3178)*
May Wood Industries Inc ....F 708 489-1515
Alsip *(G-475)*
Menard Inc ....C 815 474-6767
Plano *(G-16734)*
Menard Inc ....D....... 708 346-9144
Evergreen Park *(G-9597)*
Menard Inc ....D....... 715 876-5911
Plano *(G-16735)*
Merkel Woodworking Inc ....F 630 458-0700
Addison *(G-197)*
Metal Products Sales Corp ....G....... 708 301-6844
Lockport *(G-13013)*
▲ **Metrie** ....E 815 717-2660
New Lenox *(G-15042)*
Micanan Systems Inc ....G....... 630 501-1909
Addison *(G-204)*
▲ **Middletons Mouldings Inc** ....D....... 517 278-6610
Schaumburg *(G-18629)*
Midwest Architectural Millwork ....G....... 847 621-2013
Elk Grove Village *(G-9126)*
Midwest Woodcrafters Inc ....G....... 630 665-0901
Carol Stream *(G-3031)*
Midwestern Wood Products Co ....G....... 309 266-9771
Morton *(G-14366)*
Minimill Technologies Inc ....G....... 315 857-7107
Chicago *(G-5465)*
▲ **Monda Window & Door Corp** ....E 773 254-8888
Chicago *(G-5489)*
▲ **Motion Access LLC** ....E 847 357-8832
Elk Grove Village *(G-9134)*
Mulvain Woodworks ....G....... 815 248-2305
Durand *(G-8154)*
Navillus Woodworks LLC ....G....... 312 375-2680
Chicago *(G-5556)*
Neisewander Enterprises Inc ....A 815 288-1431
Dixon *(G-7904)*
Nelson Door Co ....G....... 217 543-3489
Arthur *(G-871)*
Oetee LLC ....G....... 630 373-4671
Chicago *(G-5657)*

Olivet Woodworking ....G....... 773 505-5225
Lake Zurich *(G-12441)*
Omega Moulding North Amer Inc ....G....... 630 509-2397
Elk Grove Village *(G-9162)*
Onsite Woodwork Corporation ....C 815 633-6400
Loves Park *(G-13242)*
Original Shutter Man ....G....... 773 966-7160
Chicago *(G-5701)*
Orstrom Woodworking Ltd ....G....... 847 697-1163
Elgin *(G-8681)*
Osmer Woodworking Inc ....G....... 815 973-5809
Dixon *(G-7905)*
Overhead Door Corporation ....G....... 630 775-9118
Itasca *(G-11715)*
Paragon Mill & Casework Inc ....F 815 388-7453
Crystal Lake *(G-7243)*
Parenti & Raffaelli Ltd ....C 847 253-5550
Mount Prospect *(G-14558)*
Parenti and Raffaelli Ltd ....G....... 847 204-8116
Mount Prospect *(G-14559)*
Performance Lawn & Power ....G....... 217 857-3717
Teutopolis *(G-19771)*
Peters Construction ....G....... 773 489-5555
Chicago *(G-5794)*
Phoenix Art Woodworks ....G....... 847 279-1576
Wheeling *(G-20959)*
Pinnacle Wood Products Inc ....G....... 815 385-0792
McHenry *(G-13778)*
Pio Woodworking Inc ....G....... 630 628-6900
Addison *(G-240)*
Prairie Woodworks Inc ....G....... 309 378-2418
Downs *(G-8112)*
Pro Woodworking ....G....... 708 508-5948
Bedford Park *(G-1495)*
R W G Manufacturing Inc ....G....... 708 755-8035
S Chicago Hts *(G-18127)*
Ramar Industries Inc ....G....... 847 451-0445
Franklin Park *(G-10032)*
◆ **Raynor Mfg Co** ....A 815 288-1431
Dixon *(G-7908)*
Reclaimedtablecom ....G....... 630 834-1929
Villa Park *(G-20169)*
Rhyme or Reason Woodworking ....G....... 217 678-8301
Bement *(G-1715)*
Richard King and Sons ....G....... 815 654-0226
Loves Park *(G-13253)*
▲ **River City Millwork Inc** ....D....... 800 892-9297
Rockford *(G-17573)*
Riverside Custom Woodworking ....G....... 815 589-3608
Fulton *(G-10157)*
Roseland II LLC ....G....... 708 479-5010
Orland Park *(G-15976)*
ROW Window Company ....G....... 815 725-5491
Plainfield *(G-16712)*
Rs Woodworking ....G....... 815 476-1818
Wilmington *(G-21101)*
Sandwich Millworks Inc ....G....... 815 786-2700
Sandwich *(G-18384)*
Sauder Industries Limited ....E 815 717-2660
New Lenox *(G-15057)*
Scheffler Custom Woodworking ....G....... 815 284-6564
Dixon *(G-7915)*
Skokie Millwork Inc ....G....... 847 673-7868
Skokie *(G-19030)*
Sleepy Woodworks ....G....... 773 779-2990
Chicago *(G-6188)*
Spec Built ....G....... 312 623-5533
Palos Park *(G-16215)*
Stairsland ....G....... 708 853-9593
Lyons *(G-13314)*
Stancy Woodworking Co Inc ....F 847 526-0252
Island Lake *(G-11611)*
Star Moulding & Trim Company ....E 708 458-1040
Bedford Park *(G-1506)*
Step One Stairworks Inc ....F 815 286-7464
Hinckley *(G-11359)*
Stine Woodworking LLC ....G....... 618 885-2229
Dow *(G-7947)*
Stovers Fine Woodworking Inc ....G....... 630 557-0072
Maple Park *(G-13466)*
Sugarcreek Woodworking ....G....... 618 584-3817
Flat Rock *(G-9675)*
Torblo Inc ....G....... 815 941-2684
Morris *(G-14333)*
Tree-O Lumber Inc ....E 618 357-2576
Pinckneyville *(G-16620)*
Tri State Aluminum Products ....F 815 877-6081
Loves Park *(G-13277)*
Triezenberg Millwork Co ....G....... 708 489-9062
Crestwood *(G-7132)*

SIC SECTION 24 LUMBER AND WOOD PRODUCTS, EXCEPT FURNITURE

Ultimate Millwork Inc ....G.... 773 343-3070
Elk Grove Village *(G-9291)*
Unimode Inc ....G.... 773 343-6754
Burr Ridge *(G-2728)*
Vas Design Inc ....G.... 773 794-1368
Chicago *(G-6524)*
Vermilion Millworks LLC ....F.... 217 446-8443
Danville *(G-7390)*
Vista Woodworking ....G.... 815 922-2297
Joliet *(G-11942)*
Wagners Custom Wood Design ....G.... 847 487-2788
Island Lake *(G-11613)*
Washington Woodworking ....G.... 309 339-0913
Washington *(G-20283)*
Wenger Woodcraft ....G.... 217 578-3440
Tuscola *(G-19934)*
West Zwick Corp ....G.... 217 222-0228
Quincy *(G-16955)*
Wiegmann Woodworking ....F.... 618 248-1300
Damiansville *(G-7316)*
Wilderness Woodworks LLC ....G.... 815 210-3751
Custer Park *(G-7303)*
Willard R Schorck ....F.... 217 543-2160
Arthur *(G-882)*
Wm Huber Cabinet Works ....E.... 773 235-7660
Chicago *(G-6653)*
▲ Wood Creations Incorporated ....G.... 773 772-1375
Chicago *(G-6665)*
Wood Creations Incorporated ....G.... 773 772-1375
Chicago *(G-6666)*
Woodcraft Enterprises Inc ....G.... 815 485-2787
New Lenox *(G-15070)*
Wooden World of Richmond Inc ....G.... 815 405-4503
Richmond *(G-17026)*
Woodlogic Custom Millwork Inc ....E.... 847 640-4500
Elk Grove Village *(G-9311)*
Woodwork Apts LLC ....G.... 224 595-9691
Streamwood *(G-19604)*
Woodwork Refined Corporation ....G.... 708 385-7255
Alsip *(G-525)*
Woodwrights Shoppe Inc ....G.... 309 360-6603
Metamora *(G-13970)*

2434 Wood Kitchen Cabinets

360 Cabinetry Inc ....G.... 630 879-0701
Batavia *(G-1338)*
A & A Cabinet Creations Inc ....F.... 630 350-1560
Bensenville *(G-1720)*
Aba Custom Woodworking ....G.... 815 356-9663
Crystal Lake *(G-7153)*
Ability Cabinet Co Inc ....G.... 847 678-6678
Franklin Park *(G-9859)*
Action Cabinet Sales Inc ....G.... 847 717-0011
Elgin *(G-8494)*
ADM Custome Cabinet Chicago ....G.... 773 688-5379
Chicago *(G-3547)*
▲ Advanced Cabinets Corp ....G.... 847 928-0001
Franklin Park *(G-9860)*
Aji Custom Cabinets ....G.... 847 312-7847
McHenry *(G-13716)*
Allie Woodworking ....G.... 847 244-1919
Waukegan *(G-20413)*
Alm Fine Cabinetry Inc ....G.... 815 562-6667
Rochelle *(G-17131)*
Amberleaf Cabinetry Inc ....F.... 773 247-8282
Chicago *(G-3644)*
American Custom Woodworking ....F.... 847 526-5900
Wauconda *(G-20330)*
▲ Ameriscan Designs Inc ....D.... 773 542-1291
Chicago *(G-3677)*
Anderson & Marter Cabinets ....G.... 630 406-9840
Batavia *(G-1349)*
Architctlly Designed Cabinetry ....G.... 618 248-5931
Albers *(G-343)*
Aurora Line ....G.... 847 670-1600
Arlington Heights *(G-698)*
Autumn Woods Ltd ....G.... 630 868-3535
Wheaton *(G-20789)*
Autumn Woods Ltd ....E.... 630 668-2080
Carol Stream *(G-2943)*
B & B Formica Appliers Inc ....F.... 773 804-1015
Chicago *(G-3804)*
Becker Jules D Wood Products ....G.... 847 526-8002
Wauconda *(G-20334)*
Bell Cabinet & Millwork Co ....G.... 708 425-1200
Palos Hills *(G-16196)*
Benchmark Cabinets & Mllwk Inc ....E.... 309 697-5855
Peoria *(G-16391)*
Birom Cabinetry LLC ....G.... 312 286-7132
Burr Ridge *(G-2657)*
Bolhuis Woodworking Co ....G.... 708 333-5100
Manhattan *(G-13431)*
Brakur Custom Cabinetry Inc ....C.... 630 355-2244
Shorewood *(G-18893)*
Brian Bequette Cabinetry ....G.... 618 670-5427
Staunton *(G-19475)*
Bridgeview Custom Kit Cabinets ....F.... 708 598-1221
Bridgeview *(G-2330)*
Brighton Cabinetry Inc ....F.... 217 235-1978
Mattoon *(G-13633)*
Brighton Cabinetry Inc ....E.... 217 895-3000
Neoga *(G-15016)*
Brown Woodworking ....G.... 815 477-8333
Crystal Lake *(G-7172)*
Byttow Enterprises Inc ....G.... 708 372-4450
Lansing *(G-12486)*
C-V Cstom Cntrtops Cbinets Inc ....F.... 708 388-5066
Blue Island *(G-2113)*
Cabinet Creations Plus ....F.... 847 245-3800
Mundelein *(G-14670)*
Cabinet Stiles Inc ....G.... 630 553-8639
Yorkville *(G-21474)*
Cabinet Wholesale Supply Inc ....G.... 708 536-7090
Tinley Park *(G-19815)*
Cabinetland of Springfield ....G.... 217 523-7253
Springfield *(G-19335)*
Cabinetry Solutions Imprvs LLC ....G.... 630 333-9195
Willowbrook *(G-21033)*
▲ Cabinets & Granite Direct LLC ....F.... 630 588-8886
Carol Stream *(G-2952)*
Cabinets By Custom Craft Inc ....G.... 815 637-4001
Roscoe *(G-17900)*
Cabinets City ....G.... 847 440-3371
Mount Prospect *(G-14518)*
Cabinets Doors and More LLC ....G.... 847 395-6334
Antioch *(G-607)*
Carpenters Millwork Co ....F.... 708 339-7707
South Holland *(G-19204)*
Carpenters Millwork Co ....F.... 708 339-7707
Villa Park *(G-20137)*
Cassini Cabinetry ....G.... 847 244-9755
Waukegan *(G-20426)*
CCC Chicago Cabinet Center LLC ....F.... 855 508-5525
Elk Grove Village *(G-8883)*
Century Kitchen & Bath Inc ....G.... 847 395-3418
Wadsworth *(G-20208)*
▲ Charles N Benner Inc ....E.... 312 829-4300
Chicago *(G-4075)*
Chicago Cabinet & Fixture Co ....G.... 630 616-8071
Bensenville *(G-1768)*
Chicago Cabinet Co ....G.... 708 429-5100
New Lenox *(G-15027)*
Choice Cabinet Chicago ....G.... 630 599-1099
Glendale Heights *(G-10443)*
Complex Woodwork Inc ....G.... 630 651-3637
Joliet *(G-11846)*
Con-Temp Cabinets Inc ....F.... 630 892-7300
North Aurora *(G-15257)*
Contract Industries Inc ....E.... 708 458-8150
Bedford Park *(G-1464)*
Cooper Lake Millworks Inc ....G.... 217 847-2681
Hamilton *(G-10951)*
Counter Craft Inc ....G.... 847 336-8205
Waukegan *(G-20431)*
Creative Cabinets Countertops ....F.... 217 446-6406
Danville *(G-7327)*
▲ Creative Designs Kitc ....E.... 773 327-8400
Chicago *(G-4261)*
Crestwood Custom Cabinets ....G.... 708 385-3167
Crestwood *(G-7115)*
Crj Cabinets ....G.... 331 303-0326
Chicago *(G-4271)*
Crooked Oak LLC ....G.... 708 344-6955
Broadview *(G-2428)*
Crown Coverings Inc ....E.... 630 546-2959
Roselle *(G-17949)*
Crown Custom Cabinetry Inc ....G.... 815 942-0432
Morris *(G-14300)*
Custom Cabinet Refacers Inc ....G.... 847 695-8800
Elgin *(G-8559)*
Custom Wood Designs Inc ....G.... 708 799-3439
Crestwood *(G-7116)*
Custom Woodwork & Interiors ....F.... 217 546-0006
Springfield *(G-19358)*
Cws Cabinets ....G.... 847 258-4468
Elk Grove Village *(G-8929)*
▲ Daniel M Powers & Assoc Ltd ....D.... 630 685-8400
Bolingbrook *(G-2166)*
Der Holtzmacher Ltd ....G.... 815 895-4887
Sycamore *(G-19706)*
Design Woodworks ....G.... 847 566-6603
Mundelein *(G-14682)*
Designers Point Inc ....G.... 224 578-7043
Rolling Meadows *(G-17726)*
Deuce Development Corp ....G.... 309 353-6324
Pekin *(G-16328)*
Dicks Custom Cabinet Shop ....G.... 815 358-2663
Cornell *(G-7012)*
Donald Kranz ....G.... 847 428-1616
Carpentersville *(G-3101)*
Dpcac LLC ....F.... 630 741-7900
Itasca *(G-11644)*
Dvoraks Creations Inc ....G.... 815 838-2214
Lockport *(G-12991)*
Eddie Gapastione ....G.... 708 430-3881
Bridgeview *(G-2344)*
Edgars Custom Cabinets ....G.... 847 928-0922
Franklin Park *(G-9937)*
Edward Hull Cabinet Shop ....G.... 217 864-3011
Mount Zion *(G-14645)*
Elkay Manufacturing Company ....G.... 800 223-5529
Downers Grove *(G-7999)*
En Pointe Cabinetry LLC ....G.... 847 787-0777
Elk Grove Village *(G-8977)*
Encon Environmental Concepts ....F.... 630 543-1583
Addison *(G-115)*
Euro-Tech Cabinetry Rmdlg Corp ....G.... 815 254-3876
Plainfield *(G-16661)*
F & B Woodworking Inc ....G.... 217 543-2531
Arthur *(G-857)*
Forest City Counter Tops Inc ....F.... 815 633-8602
Loves Park *(G-13212)*
Four Acre Wood Products ....F.... 217 543-2971
Arthur *(G-858)*
Fra-Milco Cabinets Co Inc ....G....
Frankfort *(G-9795)*
Fraser Millwork Inc ....G.... 708 447-3262
Lyons *(G-13309)*
Garver Inc ....G.... 217 932-2441
Casey *(G-3201)*
Geneva Cabinet Gallery ....G.... 630 232-9500
Geneva *(G-10271)*
Glenview Custom Cabinets Inc ....G.... 847 345-5754
Glenview *(G-10551)*
Gold Seal Cabinets Countertops ....E.... 630 906-0366
Aurora *(G-1104)*
Grays Cabinet Co ....G.... 618 948-2211
Saint Francisville *(G-18314)*
Hansen Custom Cabinet Inc ....G.... 847 356-1100
Lake Villa *(G-12353)*
Hci Cabinetry and Design Inc ....G.... 630 584-0266
Addison *(G-148)*
Helmuth Custom Kitchens LLC ....E.... 217 543-3588
Arthur *(G-862)*
Hester Cabinets & Millwork ....G.... 815 634-4555
Coal City *(G-6933)*
Hickory Street Cabinets ....G.... 618 667-9676
Troy *(G-19915)*
Hidalgo Fine Cabinetry ....G.... 630 753-9323
Naperville *(G-14972)*
Hylan Design Ltd ....G.... 312 243-7341
Chicago *(G-4863)*
I Kustom Cabinets Inc ....G.... 773 343-6858
Highwood *(G-11307)*
Ideal Cabinet Solutions Inc ....G.... 618 514-7087
Alhambra *(G-401)*
▲ J & K Cabinetry Inc ....G.... 847 758-7808
Elk Grove Village *(G-9062)*
J & M Custom Cabinets ....G.... 217 677-2229
La Place *(G-12099)*
J K Custom Countertops ....G.... 630 495-2324
Lombard *(G-13088)*
J M Lustig Custom Cabinets Co ....F.... 217 342-6661
Effingham *(G-8403)*
Janik Custom Millwork Inc ....G.... 708 482-4844
Hodgkins *(G-11390)*
Jk Cabinets Plus LLC ....G.... 952 237-1825
Union *(G-19940)*
Johnson Custom Cabinets ....G.... 815 675-9690
Spring Grove *(G-19278)*
Joliet Cabinet Company Inc ....E.... 815 727-4096
Lockport *(G-13003)*
Jones Design Group Ltd ....G.... 630 462-9340
Winfield *(G-21111)*
Juniors Custom Cabinets ....G.... 773 495-6962
Chicago *(G-5059)*
Kabinet Kraft ....F.... 618 395-1047
Olney *(G-15867)*
Kanneberg Custom Kitchens Inc ....G.... 815 654-1110
Machesney Park *(G-13353)*

SIC

Employee Codes: A=Over 500 employees, B=251-500
C=101-250, D=51-100, E=20-50, F=10-19, G=3-9
2020 Harris Illinois
Industrial Directory
837

24 LUMBER AND WOOD PRODUCTS, EXCEPT FURNITURE

Kaufmans Custom Cabinets ....F........ 217 268-4330
  Arcola *(G-653)*
◆ Kempner Company Inc ....F........ 312 733-1606
  Chicago *(G-5095)*
Kit Artisan Cab Refinishers ....G........ 630 922-9714
  Plainfield *(G-16680)*
Kitchen & Bath Cabinet Company ......G........ 217 352-1900
  Champaign *(G-3314)*
Kitchen Krafters Inc ....G........ 815 675-6061
  Spring Grove *(G-19279)*
Km Cabinet Supply ....G........ 312 927-8860
  Evergreen Park *(G-9596)*
Koala Cabinets ....G........ 630 818-1289
  West Chicago *(G-20606)*
Kowal Custom Cabinet & Furn ....G........ 708 597-3367
  Blue Island *(G-2129)*
Krafty Kabinets ....G........ 815 369-5250
  Lena *(G-12601)*
Kuche Fine Cabinetry ....G........ 217 342-2244
  Effingham *(G-8406)*
Kunz Carpentry ....G........ 618 224-7892
  Trenton *(G-19904)*
L2 Supply DBA Ica Cab Supp Ly ......G........ 773 382-8037
  Chicago *(G-5145)*
▲ Lacava LLC ....E........ 773 637-9600
  Chicago *(G-5154)*
Lamico Designers Deerfield Inc ......G........ 847 465-8850
  Highland Park *(G-11279)*
Living Laminates Inc ....G........ 847 741-2004
  Maple Park *(G-13464)*
Luxe Classic Kitchens & Interi ....G........ 630 774-9337
  Yorkville *(G-21492)*
Lyko Woodworking & Cnstr ....G........ 773 583-4561
  Chicago *(G-5292)*
M & R Custom Millwork Inc ....G........ 815 547-8549
  Belvidere *(G-1682)*
Marfa Cabinets Inc ....E........ 847 701-5558
  Skokie *(G-18982)*
Markham Cabinet Works Inc ....G........ 708 687-3074
  Midlothian *(G-13993)*
Markus Cabinet Manufacturing ....E........ 618 228-7376
  Aviston *(G-1181)*
Masco Corporation ....D........ 847 303-3088
  Schaumburg *(G-18621)*
Master Cabinets ....G........ 847 639-1323
  Cary *(G-3178)*
Masterbrand Cabinets Inc ....B........ 217 543-3311
  Arthur *(G-867)*
Masterbrand Cabinets Inc ....G........ 217 543-3466
  Arthur *(G-868)*
Masterbrand Cabinets Inc ....G........ 503 241-4964
  Arthur *(G-869)*
Masterpiece Cabinetry Design ....G........ 217 258-6880
  Mattoon *(G-13644)*
Masters Shop ....G........ 217 643-7826
  Thomasboro *(G-19776)*
Mc Laminated Cabinets ....G........ 773 301-0393
  Franklin Park *(G-9987)*
Metro Cabinet Refinishers ....G........ 217 498-7174
  Rochester *(G-17169)*
Mettes Cabinet Corner Inc ....F........ 217 342-9552
  Effingham *(G-8410)*
Mica Furniture Mfg Inc ....G........ 708 430-1150
  Addison *(G-203)*
▲ Middletons Mouldings Inc ....D........ 517 278-6610
  Schaumburg *(G-18629)*
Midwest Woodcrafters Inc ....G........ 630 665-0901
  Carol Stream *(G-3031)*
Millcraft ....G........ 618 426-9819
  Campbell Hill *(G-2817)*
Mirek Cabinets ....G........ 630 350-8336
  Franklin Park *(G-10001)*
Monarch Mfg Corp Amer ....G........ 217 728-2552
  Sullivan *(G-19671)*
Mueller Custom Cabinetry Inc ....G........ 815 448-5448
  Mazon *(G-13683)*
Multiplex Display Fixture Co ....E........ 800 325-3350
  Dupo *(G-8141)*
Murray Cabinetry & Tops Inc ....G........ 815 672-6992
  Streator *(G-19616)*
Murray Custom Cabinetry ....G........ 309 966-0624
  Peoria *(G-16481)*
Natl Ktchn and Bath Cabinetry ....G........ 815 733-8888
  Romeoville *(G-17860)*
Neumann Custom Woodworking ....G........ 847 979-3199
  Arlington Heights *(G-781)*
New Style Cabinets Inc ....G........ 773 622-3114
  Chicago *(G-5581)*
New Vision Cstm Cabinets Mllwk ....G........ 847 265-2723
  Lake Villa *(G-12362)*

Northstar Custom Cabinetry ....G........ 708 597-2099
  Posen *(G-16799)*
Northwest Marble Products ....E........ 630 860-2288
  Hoffman Estates *(G-11473)*
OGorman Son Carpentry Contrs ....E........ 815 485-8997
  New Lenox *(G-15045)*
Okaw Valley Woodworking LLC ......F........ 217 543-5180
  Arthur *(G-874)*
Orchard Hill Cabinetry Inc ....E........ 312 829-4300
  Chicago *(G-5695)*
◆ Pace Industries Inc ....C........ 312 226-5500
  Chicago *(G-5737)*
Parenti & Raffaelli Ltd ....G........ 847 253-5550
  Mount Prospect *(G-14558)*
Peaceful Valley Cabinetry ....G........ 618 584-3615
  Flat Rock *(G-9672)*
▲ Pentwater Furnishing Inc ....F........ 630 984-4703
  Lombard *(G-13119)*
Perkins Construction ....G........ 815 233-9655
  Freeport *(G-10132)*
Phoenix Woodworking Corp ....E........ 815 338-9338
  Woodstock *(G-21421)*
Pintas Cultured Marble ....G........ 708 385-3360
  Alsip *(G-492)*
Plain & Posh LLC ....G........ 630 960-0048
  Darien *(G-7411)*
Planks Cabinet Shop Inc ....G........ 217 543-2687
  Arthur *(G-876)*
Prairie Woodworks Inc ....G........ 309 378-2418
  Downs *(G-8112)*
Premier Woodworking Concepts ....G........ 815 334-0888
  Woodstock *(G-21424)*
Pro Cabinets Inc ....G........ 618 993-0008
  Marion *(G-13531)*
Quality Finishing Service Inc ....G........ 847 616-0336
  Elk Grove Village *(G-9204)*
R & R Custom Cabinet Making ......G........ 847 358-6188
  Palatine *(G-16152)*
Rapp Cabinets & Woodworks Inc ....F........ 618 736-2955
  Dahlgren *(G-7309)*
Rawson Custom Woodworks LLC ..G........ 815 332-9222
  Cherry Valley *(G-3445)*
Raymond Earl Fine Woodworking ..G........ 309 565-7661
  Hanna City *(G-10994)*
Regency Custom Woodworking ......F........ 815 689-2117
  Cullom *(G-7300)*
Richard King and Sons ....G........ 815 654-0226
  Loves Park *(G-13253)*
Richard Schrock ....G........ 217 543-3111
  Arthur *(G-878)*
Riverbend Kitchen & Mllwk LLC ......G........ 618 462-8955
  Alton *(G-569)*
Riverside Custom Woodworking ......G........ 815 589-3608
  Fulton *(G-10157)*
▲ Riverton Cabinet Company ....G........ 815 462-5300
  New Lenox *(G-15056)*
Roeckers Inc ....G........ 309 693-2929
  Peoria *(G-16513)*
▲ Rogan Granitindustrie Inc ....G........ 708 758-0050
  Lynwood *(G-13298)*
Romar Cabinet & Top Co Inc ....D........ 815 467-4452
  Channahon *(G-3392)*
Roncin Custom Design ....G........ 847 669-0260
  Huntley *(G-11565)*
Ronnie P Faber ....G........ 815 626-4561
  Sterling *(G-19529)*
Royal Fabricators Inc ....F........ 847 775-7466
  Wadsworth *(G-20213)*
Santelli Custom Cabinetry ....G........ 708 771-3884
  River Forest *(G-17055)*
Schrock Custom Woodworking ......G........ 217 849-3375
  Toledo *(G-19877)*
Schrocks Woodworking ....G........ 217 578-3259
  Arthur *(G-879)*
Seigles Cabinet Center LLC ....G........ 224 535-7034
  Elgin *(G-8726)*
Seneca Custom Cabinetry ....G........ 815 357-1322
  Seneca *(G-18861)*
Shews Custom Woodworking ....G........ 217 737-5543
  Lincoln *(G-12738)*
Shreck Kitchens ....G........ 847 695-4154
  South Elgin *(G-19174)*
Silver Bell Cnstr & Furn Inc ....G........ 773 578-9450
  Chicago *(G-6171)*
Sleeping Bear Inc ....G........ 630 541-7220
  Lisle *(G-12937)*
Snaidero USA ....G........ 312 644-6662
  Chicago *(G-6194)*
Specialized Woodwork Inc ....G........ 630 627-0450
  Lombard *(G-13131)*

Stancy Woodworking Co Inc ....F........ 847 526-0252
  Island Lake *(G-11611)*
Steve Janik Cabinetry LLC ....G........ 630 553-8383
  Aurora *(G-1157)*
Stonetree Fabrication Inc ....E........ 618 332-1700
  East Saint Louis *(G-8325)*
Stylish Kit Bath Cabinets Corp ....G........ 773 525-8667
  Chicago *(G-6260)*
Superior Cabinet Company ....G........ 708 658-6613
  Bridgeview *(G-2391)*
Superior Cabinet Supply Inc ....G........ 815 464-2700
  Frankfort *(G-9841)*
T and T Cabinet Co ....G........ 815 245-6322
  McHenry *(G-13804)*
▲ T2 Cabinets Inc ....F........ 312 593-1507
  Chicago *(G-6308)*
Thoennes & Thoennes Inc ....G........ 309 663-4053
  Bloomington *(G-2101)*
Timberland Custom Cab & Tops ....G........ 815 722-0825
  Joliet *(G-11936)*
Tremont Kitchen Tops Inc ....G........ 309 925-5736
  Tremont *(G-19900)*
Tri Star Cabinet & Top Co Inc ....D........ 815 485-2564
  New Lenox *(G-15065)*
True Woods Cabinetry Inc ....G........ 847 550-1860
  Lake Zurich *(G-12466)*
Val Custom Cabinets & Flrg Inc ......G........ 708 790-8373
  Bensenville *(G-1907)*
Vanities Inc ....G........ 847 483-0240
  Arlington Heights *(G-825)*
Vida Cabinets Inc ....G........ 847 258-4468
  Elk Grove Village *(G-9304)*
Viking Metal Cabinet Co LLC ....D........ 800 776-7767
  Montgomery *(G-14273)*
Viking Metal Cabinet Company ......G........ 630 863-7234
  Montgomery *(G-14274)*
Wheatland Cstm Cbntry Wdwkg LL ..G........ 630 359-8553
  Villa Park *(G-20176)*
Wheaton Cabinetry ....G........ 815 729-1085
  Lockport *(G-13027)*
Wilcor Solid Surface Inc ....F........ 888 956-1001
  Elk Grove Village *(G-9309)*
Wills Milling and Hardwood Inc ......E........ 217 854-9056
  Carlinville *(G-2884)*
Winslyn Industries ....G........ 630 401-8051
  South Elgin *(G-19182)*
Wolf Cabinetry & Ganite ....G........ 847 358-9922
  Palatine *(G-16176)*
Wolters Custom Cabinets LLC ....G........ 618 282-3158
  Evansville *(G-9591)*
Wood Shop ....G........ 773 994-6666
  Chicago *(G-6667)*
Wood Specialties Incorporated ......F........ 217 678-8420
  Bement *(G-1716)*
Woodcraft Enterprises Inc ....G........ 815 485-2787
  New Lenox *(G-15070)*
Woodhill Cabinetry Design Inc ....G........ 815 431-0545
  Ottawa *(G-16086)*
Woodstreet Cabinet ....G........ 708 995-6077
  Mokena *(G-14128)*
Woodways Industries LLC ....E........ 616 956-3070
  Chicago *(G-6668)*
Your Custom Cabinetry Corp ....G........ 773 290-7247
  Melrose Park *(G-13931)*

2435 Hardwood Veneer & Plywood

▲ Aircraft Plywood Mfg Inc ....G........ 618 654-6740
  Highland *(G-11204)*
Best Veneer Company LLC ....F........ 630 541-8312
  Burr Ridge *(G-2655)*
▲ Challinor Wood Products Inc ......G........ 847 256-8828
  Wilmette *(G-21073)*
Chalon Wood Products Inc ....G........ 630 243-9793
  Lemont *(G-12560)*
Klaman Hardwood ....G........ 217 972-7888
  Decatur *(G-7514)*
L Land Hardwoods ....G........ 708 496-9000
  Bedford Park *(G-1478)*
Lumberyard Suppliers Inc ....E........ 217 965-4911
  Virden *(G-20187)*
R S Bacon Veneer Company ....G........ 331 777-4762
  Lisle *(G-12933)*
◆ R S Bacon Veneer Company ......C........ 630 323-1414
  Lisle *(G-12932)*
R-Squared Construction Inc ....G........ 815 232-7433
  Freeport *(G-10135)*
▲ Red River Lumber Inc ....D........ 708 388-1818
  Blue Island *(G-2135)*
Walnut Creek Hardwood ....G........ 815 389-3317
  South Beloit *(G-19120)*

SIC SECTION 24 LUMBER AND WOOD PRODUCTS, EXCEPT FURNITURE

Westrock Cp LLC .... D 312 346-6600
Chicago *(G-6611)*
Woodcraft Enterprises Inc .... G 815 485-2787
New Lenox *(G-15070)*

2436 Softwood Veneer & Plywood

Best Veneer Company LLC .... F 630 541-8312
Burr Ridge *(G-2655)*
Westrock Cp LLC .... D 312 346-6600
Chicago *(G-6611)*

2439 Structural Wood Members, NEC

Alexander Lumber Co .... G 815 754-1000
Cortland *(G-7016)*
Anderson Truss Company .... G 618 982-9228
Pittsburg *(G-16626)*
Atlas Building Components Inc .... E 618 639-0222
Jerseyville *(G-11787)*
Atlas Components Inc .... E 815 332-4904
Cherry Valley *(G-3437)*
Bear Creek Truss Inc .... E 217 543-3329
Tuscola *(G-19923)*
Central Illinois Truss .... F 309 447-6644
Deer Creek *(G-7572)*
Central Illinois Truss .... G 309 266-8787
Morton *(G-14356)*
Central Wood LLC .... G 217 543-2662
Arcola *(G-646)*
◆ **Connor Sports Flooring LLC** .... D 847 290-9020
Bensenville *(G-1775)*
Cooper Lake Millworks Inc .... G 217 847-2681
Hamilton *(G-10951)*
F5d Inc .... G 815 953-9183
Herscher *(G-11183)*
Jesse B Holt Inc .... D 618 783-3075
Newton *(G-15086)*
Lamboo Technologies LLC .... G 866 966-2999
Litchfield *(G-12971)*
Lumberyard Suppliers Inc .... E 217 965-4911
Virden *(G-20187)*
Okaw Truss Inc .... B 217 543-3371
Arthur *(G-873)*
Rehkemper & Sons Inc .... E 618 526-2269
Breese *(G-2307)*
Southern Truss Inc .... E 618 252-8144
Harrisburg *(G-11029)*
Strat-O-Span Buildings Inc .... G 618 526-4566
Breese *(G-2308)*
Triumph Truss & Steel Company .... F 815 522-6000
Elgin *(G-8762)*
Truss Components Inc .... F 800 678-7877
Columbia *(G-6995)*
WW Timbers Inc .... G 708 423-9112
Chicago Ridge *(G-6811)*

2441 Wood Boxes

Arrowtech Pallet & Crating .... D 815 547-9300
Belvidere *(G-1650)*
Botkin Lumber Company Inc .... E 217 287-2127
Taylorville *(G-19751)*
◆ **BP Shipping** .... F 630 393-1032
Naperville *(G-14784)*
Central Wood Products Inc .... E 217 728-4412
Sullivan *(G-19664)*
Chicago Export Packing Co .... E 773 247-8911
Chicago *(G-4102)*
Chrometec LLC .... G 630 792-8777
Lombard *(G-13053)*
Community Support Systems .... D 217 705-4300
Teutopolis *(G-19767)*
D/C Export & Domestic Pkg Inc .... E 847 593-4200
Elk Grove Village *(G-8935)*
Dexton Enterprises .... G 309 788-1881
Rock Island *(G-17217)*
Du-Call Miller Plastics Inc .... F 630 964-6020
Elburn *(G-8450)*
Elm Street Industries Inc .... F 309 854-7000
Kewanee *(G-12032)*
Export Packaging Co Inc .... A 309 756-4288
Milan *(G-14010)*
▲ **Extreme Tools Inc** .... G 630 202-8324
Naperville *(G-14826)*
Fca LLC .... E 309 949-3999
Coal Valley *(G-6936)*
Fca LLC .... E 309 385-2588
Princeville *(G-16827)*
Jordan Paper Box Company .... F 773 287-5362
Chicago *(G-5048)*
Kccdd Inc .... D 309 344-2030
Galesburg *(G-10205)*
Kunde Woodwork Inc .... G 847 669-2030
Huntley *(G-11549)*
Nefab Packaging N Centl LLC .... C 630 451-5314
Hanover Park *(G-11010)*
▲ **Ockerlund Industries Inc** .... E 630 620-1269
Addison *(G-230)*
▲ **Pak Source Inc** .... E 309 786-7374
Rock Island *(G-17231)*
Pierce Packaging Co .... F 815 636-5650
Loves Park *(G-13245)*
Pierce Packaging Co .... G 815 636-5656
Peoria *(G-16497)*
Pierce Packaging Co .... F 815 636-5656
Loves Park *(G-13246)*
◆ **Pregis LLC** .... D 847 597-2200
Deerfield *(G-7644)*
R & H Products Inc .... G 815 744-4110
Rockdale *(G-17270)*
Specialty Box Corp .... F 630 897-7278
North Aurora *(G-15277)*
Trade Industries .... E 618 643-4321
Mc Leansboro *(G-13709)*
Wesling Products Inc .... G 773 533-2850
Chicago *(G-6603)*

2448 Wood Pallets & Skids

355 Pallet Service .... G 773 431-6688
Addison *(G-12)*
3v Pallet .... G 708 620-7790
South Holland *(G-19185)*
3v Pallet .... G 708 333-1113
Lansing *(G-12483)*
815 Pallets Inc .... E 815 678-0012
Richmond *(G-17006)*
A & F Pallet Service Inc .... F 773 767-9500
Chicago *(G-3482)*
AA Pallet Inc .... E 773 536-3699
Chicago *(G-3496)*
ADP Pallet Inc .... F 773 638-3800
Chicago *(G-3551)*
Advance Pallet Incorporated .... E 847 697-5700
South Elgin *(G-19128)*
AGCO Recycling LLC .... F 217 224-9048
Quincy *(G-16851)*
▲ **Aldon Co** .... F 847 623-8800
Waukegan *(G-20412)*
All Pallet Service .... G 618 451-7545
Granite City *(G-10693)*
American Pallet Co Inc .... D 847 662-5525
Waukegan *(G-20415)*
American Pallet Industries Inc .... F 815 678-0680
Richmond *(G-17008)*
Amerigreen Pallets .... G 309 698-3463
East Peoria *(G-8250)*
Arrows Up Inc .... G 847 305-2550
Arlington Heights *(G-696)*
Arrowtech Pallet & Crating .... D 815 547-9300
Belvidere *(G-1650)*
ASAP Pallets Inc .... F 630 350-7689
Franklin Park *(G-9875)*
ASAP Pallets Inc .... G 630 917-0180
Bellwood *(G-1614)*
Ash Pallet Management Inc .... D 847 473-5700
Antioch *(G-601)*
Bach Timber & Pallet Inc .... G 815 885-3774
Caledonia *(G-2768)*
Best Pallet Company LLC .... F 815 637-1500
Loves Park *(G-13194)*
Best Pallet Company LLC .... F 312 242-4009
Chicago *(G-3873)*
Blue Comet Transport Inc .... G 773 617-9512
Chicago *(G-3913)*
Botkin Lumber Company Inc .... E 217 287-2127
Taylorville *(G-19751)*
Brothers Pallets Co .... G 773 306-2695
Chicago *(G-3966)*
Buckeye Diamond Logistics Inc .... G 630 236-1174
Aurora *(G-928)*
Caisson Inc .... E 815 547-5925
Belvidere *(G-1658)*
Cardinal Pallet Co .... E 773 725-5387
Chicago *(G-4026)*
Central States Pallets .... G 217 494-2710
Chatham *(G-3418)*
Central Wood Products Inc .... E 217 728-4412
Sullivan *(G-19664)*
Champion Wood Pallets Inc .... G 630 801-8036
Aurora *(G-1072)*
Chicago Heights Pallets Co .... F 708 757-7641
Chicago Heights *(G-6741)*
Chicago Pallet Service Inc .... E 847 439-8754
Elk Grove Village *(G-8892)*
Chicago Pallet Service II Inc .... E 847 439-8330
Elk Grove Village *(G-8893)*
▲ **Cimc Leasing Usa Inc** .... G 630 785-6875
Oakbrook Terrace *(G-15793)*
City Wide Pallet .... G 773 891-2561
Chicago *(G-4163)*
Cole Pallet Services Corp .... E 815 758-3226
Dekalb *(G-7668)*
Commercial Pallet Inc .... E 312 226-6699
Chicago *(G-4209)*
Community Support Systems .... D 217 705-4300
Teutopolis *(G-19767)*
Comwell .... D 618 282-6233
Red Bud *(G-16991)*
Corr-Pak Corporation .... E 708 442-7806
Mc Cook *(G-13690)*
Corsaw Hardwood Lumber Inc .... F 309 293-2055
Smithfield *(G-19063)*
Craft Pallet Inc .... G 618 437-5382
INA *(G-11575)*
Crate and Pallet Packg Co LLC .... E 217 679-2681
Springfield *(G-19355)*
Crossroad Crating & Pallet .... G 815 657-8409
Forrest *(G-9732)*
Crystal Lake Pallets .... G 815 526-3637
Crystal Lake *(G-7188)*
D & G Pallet Service Inc .... F 773 265-8470
Chicago *(G-4296)*
D and D Pallets .... F 630 800-1102
Aurora *(G-1082)*
◆ **Darios Pallets Corp** .... E 312 421-3413
Chicago *(G-4318)*
Dexton Enterprises .... G 309 788-1881
Rock Island *(G-17217)*
Dg Wood Processing .... F 217 543-2128
Arthur *(G-852)*
Diaz Pallets II Corporation .... G 630 340-3736
Aurora *(G-1085)*
Direct Pallet Inc .... E 847 697-1019
Elgin *(G-8566)*
Dixon Pallet Service .... G 773 238-9569
Chicago *(G-4370)*
Eam Pallets .... G 708 333-0596
Harvey *(G-11082)*
Earthwise Recycled Pallet .... G 618 286-6015
Dupo *(G-8136)*
Edgar Pallets .... G 773 454-8919
Chicago *(G-4450)*
Edison Pallet & Wood Products .... G 630 653-3416
Winfield *(G-21110)*
Eds Pallet Service .... F 618 248-5386
Albers *(G-344)*
Enterprise Pallet Inc .... F 815 928-8546
Bourbonnais *(G-2260)*
▼ **Equustock LLC** .... F 866 962-4686
Loves Park *(G-13210)*
Export Packaging Co Inc .... A 309 756-4288
Milan *(G-14010)*
F and L Pallets Inc .... G 773 364-0798
Chicago *(G-4547)*
Fca LLC .... E 309 385-2588
Princeville *(G-16827)*
Fca LLC .... E 309 792-3444
Moline *(G-14145)*
Four Season Pallets Inc .... G 708 940-5545
Harvey *(G-11085)*
Fulton County Rehabilitation .... E 309 647-6510
Canton *(G-2826)*
G & S Pallets .... G 630 574-2741
Oak Brook *(G-15623)*
General Pallet .... G 773 660-8550
Chicago *(G-4676)*
Georgetown Wood and Pallet Co .... E 217 662-2563
Georgetown *(G-10327)*
Glitter Your Pallet .... G 708 516-8494
Homer Glen *(G-11482)*
▲ **Graphic Pallet & Transport** .... E 630 904-4951
Plainfield *(G-16669)*
Great Lakes Lbr & Pallet Inc .... G 773 243-6839
Chicago *(G-4736)*
Great Lakes Lumber and Pallet .... G 773 243-6839
Park Ridge *(G-16282)*
Gueros Pallets Inc .... G 312 523-5561
Chicago *(G-4748)*
Hammer Enterprises Inc .... F 217 662-8225
Georgetown *(G-10328)*
Hardwood Lumber Products Co .... G 309 538-4411
Kilbourne *(G-12044)*

SIC

Hart - Clayton Inc ....F 217 525-1610
Springfield *(G-19378)*

Harvey Pallets Inc ....C 708 293-1831
Blue Island *(G-2125)*

Hill Top Pallet ....G 618 426-9810
Ava *(G-1172)*

HMM Pallets Inc ....G 773 927-3448
Chicago Heights *(G-6749)*

Hope Pallet Inc ....G 815 412-4606
Rockdale *(G-17259)*

Ht Lumber & Crates Inc ....F 847 683-0200
Hampshire *(G-10973)*

Ifco ....G 630 226-0650
Bolingbrook *(G-2188)*

Illinois Pallets Inc ....G 773 640-9228
Willow Springs *(G-21026)*

Industrial Pallets LLC ....G 708 351-8783
Glendale Heights *(G-10461)*

J & J Quality Pallets Inc ....G 618 262-6426
Mount Carmel *(G-14474)*

J&A Pallets Service Inc ....F 708 333-6601
Chicago Heights *(G-6751)*

Jjm Products LLC ....G 630 319-9325
Westmont *(G-20750)*

Jose Pallets ....G 773 376-8320
Chicago *(G-5052)*

Joseph B Krisher ....G 618 677-2016
Mascoutah *(G-13600)*

Kccdd Inc ....D 309 344-2030
Galesburg *(G-10205)*

Kirk Wood Products Inc ....E 309 829-6661
Bloomington *(G-2068)*

Kirkwood Crates LLC ....G 651 373-5945
Kirkwood *(G-12067)*

Kryder Wood Products LLC ....F 815 494-1208
Rockford *(G-17486)*

Lake Street Pallets ....G 773 889-2266
Chicago *(G-5162)*

Lakeland Pallets Inc ....G 616 949-9515
Geneva *(G-10288)*

Los Primos Pallets Inc ....G 773 418-3584
Chicago *(G-5263)*

Lottus Inc ....G 847 691-9464
Glenview *(G-10585)*

M & M Paltech Inc ....D 630 350-7890
Belvidere *(G-1681)*

M and M Pallet Inc ....G 708 272-4447
Blue Island *(G-2130)*

Malvaes Solutions Incorporated ....G 773 823-1034
Chicago *(G-5324)*

McKean Pallet Co ....G 309 246-7543
Lacon *(G-12130)*

Mental Health Ctrs Centl Ill ....D 217 735-1413
Lincoln *(G-12735)*

Midland Wood Products ....G 618 344-5640
Collinsville *(G-6970)*

Mills Pallet ....F 773 533-6458
Chicago *(G-5462)*

Millwood Inc ....F 708 343-7341
Melrose Park *(G-13893)*

Mobile Pallet Service Inc ....F 630 231-6597
West Chicago *(G-20620)*

Momence Pallet Corporation ....E 815 472-6451
Momence *(G-14189)*

Morris Pallet Skids Inc ....G 618 786-2241
Dow *(G-7946)*

Muro Pallets Corp ....G 773 640-8606
Chicago *(G-5527)*

Murrihy Pallet Co ....E 615 370-7000
Chicago *(G-5528)*

Nefab Packaging N Centl LLC ....C 630 451-5314
Hanover Park *(G-11010)*

Newport Pallet ....G 217 662-6577
Georgetown *(G-10329)*

Northern Illinois Pallet Inc ....G 815 236-9242
Fox Lake *(G-9749)*

Northern Pallet and Supply Co ....G 847 716-1400
Northfield *(G-15524)*

Northwest Pallet Services LLC ....A 815 544-6001
Belvidere *(G-1691)*

▼ **One Way Solutions LLC** ....G 847 446-0872
Northfield *(G-15526)*

▲ **Pak Source Inc** ....E 309 786-7374
Rock Island *(G-17231)*

Pallet Sales and Recycling ....F 314 452-5175
Venice *(G-20035)*

Pallet Services Inc ....G 630 860-9233
Bensenville *(G-1866)*

Pallet Solution ....G 773 837-8677
Streamwood *(G-19588)*

Pallet Solution Inc ....E 618 445-2316
Albion *(G-351)*

Pallet Wrapz ....F 847 729-5850
Glenview *(G-10597)*

Pallet Wrapz Inc ....G 847 729-5850
Glenview *(G-10598)*

Palletmaxx Inc ....G 708 385-9595
Crestwood *(G-7124)*

Pallets International Holding ....G 773 391-7223
South Holland *(G-19236)*

Pallets Plus Inc ....G 847 318-1853
Park Ridge *(G-16291)*

Peco Pallet ....G 773 646-0976
Chicago *(G-5779)*

Piece Works Specialists Inc ....F 309 266-7016
Morton *(G-14378)*

Premium Pallets ....G 217 974-0155
Springfield *(G-19427)*

▲ **Prime Wood Craft Inc** ....E 216 738-2222
Schaumburg *(G-18683)*

Prime Wood Craft Inc ....G 716 803-3425
Schaumburg *(G-18684)*

Quality Pallets Inc ....E 217 459-2655
Windsor *(G-21107)*

R & H Products Inc ....G 815 744-4110
Rockdale *(G-17270)*

R & R Services Illinois Inc ....G 217 424-2602
Decatur *(G-7538)*

R K J Pallets Inc ....F 708 493-0701
Bellwood *(G-1636)*

R&M Pallets ....G 773 317-0574
Crest Hill *(G-7093)*

Raildecks Intermodal ....G 630 442-7676
Downers Grove *(G-8086)*

Rapid Pallets Inc ....F 708 259-4016
Chicago *(G-5974)*

Rapid Pallets Inc ....E 708 424-2306
Bridgeview *(G-2378)*

Rbj Inc ....F 309 344-5066
Galesburg *(G-10217)*

Robbins Resource MGT Inc ....E 309 734-8817
Monmouth *(G-14226)*

Rock Valley Pallet Company ....G 815 654-4850
Machesney Park *(G-13369)*

Rose Pallet LLC ....G 708 333-3000
Bridgeview *(G-2384)*

Round Lake Pallets Inc ....G 847 637-6162
Round Lake *(G-18081)*

RPI Business Co Inc ....G 773 254-7095
Chicago *(G-6070)*

S & S Pallet Corp ....E 618 219-3218
Granite City *(G-10735)*

Schroeders Pallet Service Inc ....F 708 371-9046
Blue Island *(G-2139)*

Service Pallet LLC ....G 708 458-9100
North Aurora *(G-15274)*

Simonton Hardwood Lumber LLC ....F 618 594-2132
Carlyle *(G-2896)*

Singleton Pallets Co ....G 708 687-7006
Oak Forest *(G-15688)*

◆ **Sterling Site Access Sol** ....C 708 388-2223
Phoenix *(G-16609)*

Steve Forrest ....F 815 765-9040
Poplar Grove *(G-16784)*

Timber Creek Pallets ....G 217 268-3062
Arcola *(G-668)*

Timberline Pallet & Skid Inc ....F 309 752-1770
East Moline *(G-8243)*

Trade Industries ....E 618 643-4321
Mc Leansboro *(G-13709)*

Try Our Pallets Inc ....G 708 343-0166
Maywood *(G-13679)*

Twin City Wood Recycling Corp ....G 309 827-9663
Bloomington *(G-2106)*

Universal Pallet Inc ....G 815 928-8546
Bradley *(G-2295)*

US Pallett Supply Inc ....E 618 243-6449
Okawville *(G-15848)*

Vg Pallet Inc ....G 815 527-5344
Woodstock *(G-21444)*

Walnut Grove Packaging ....G 217 268-5112
Arcola *(G-669)*

▲ **Wil Son Pallet** ....E 217 543-3555
Sullivan *(G-19675)*

Workshop Ltd Inc ....G 708 458-3222
Bedford Park *(G-1514)*

2449 Wood Containers, NEC

A & M Wood Products Inc ....G 630 323-2555
Burr Ridge *(G-2647)*

▲ **Aetna Plywood Inc** ....D 708 343-1515
Maywood *(G-13658)*

Caisson Inc ....E 815 547-5925
Belvidere *(G-1658)*

Central Wood Products Inc ....E 217 728-4412
Sullivan *(G-19664)*

Chicago Crate Inc ....G 708 380-4716
Downers Grove *(G-7969)*

Chicago Floral Planters Inc ....G 708 423-2754
Chicago Ridge *(G-6790)*

Cole Pallet Services Corp ....E 815 758-3226
Dekalb *(G-7668)*

D/C Export & Domestic Pkg Inc ....E 847 593-4200
Elk Grove Village *(G-8935)*

Elm Street Industries Inc ....F 309 854-7000
Kewanee *(G-12032)*

Heritage Structures Inc ....F 618 895-8028
Mc Leansboro *(G-13706)*

Induspac Rtp Inc ....E 919 484-9484
Bridgeview *(G-2358)*

Midwest Mktg/Pdctn Mfg Co ....G 217 256-3414
Warsaw *(G-20258)*

Nefab Packaging N Centl LLC ....C 630 451-5314
Hanover Park *(G-11010)*

Polamer Inc ....G 773 774-3600
Chicago *(G-5832)*

Production Manufacturing ....G 217 256-4211
Warsaw *(G-20259)*

R & H Products Inc ....G 815 744-4110
Rockdale *(G-17270)*

Specialty Crate Factory ....G 708 756-2100
Steger *(G-19492)*

▼ **T2 Site Amenities Incorporated** ....G 847 579-9003
Highland Park *(G-11302)*

Van Voorst Lumber Company Inc ....E 815 426-2544
Union Hill *(G-19943)*

Wesling Products Inc ....G 773 533-2850
Chicago *(G-6603)*

▲ **Wil Son Pallet** ....E 217 543-3555
Sullivan *(G-19675)*

2451 Mobile Homes

Carlin Mfg A Div Grs Holdg LLC ....E 559 276-0123
Naperville *(G-14789)*

Gerald Graff ....E 312 343-2612
Lincolnwood *(G-12822)*

Mobil Trailer Transport Inc ....E 630 993-1200
Villa Park *(G-20160)*

Shur Co of Illinois ....G 217 877-8277
Decatur *(G-7546)*

Skender Construction LLC ....D 312 781-0265
Chicago *(G-6179)*

Skiman Sales Inc ....G 847 888-8200
Elgin *(G-8737)*

Southmoor Estates Inc ....G 815 756-1299
Dekalb *(G-7705)*

Superior Mobile Home Service ....G 708 672-7799
Crete *(G-7146)*

2452 Prefabricated Wood Buildings & Cmpnts

Alply Insulated Panels LLC ....G 217 324-6700
Litchfield *(G-12959)*

Ashton Diversified Enterprises ....G 630 739-0981
Lemont *(G-12554)*

▼ **Bitter End Yacht Club Intl** ....F 312 506-6205
Chicago *(G-3902)*

Coach House Inc ....E 217 543-3761
Arthur *(G-847)*

Cook Sales Inc ....E 618 893-2114
Cobden *(G-6941)*

Csi Manufacturing Inc ....E 309 937-2653
Cambridge *(G-2804)*

Dave White ....G 618 898-1130
Cisne *(G-6892)*

Everlast Portable Buildings ....G 217 543-4080
Sullivan *(G-19666)*

Faze Change Produx ....E 217 728-2184
Sullivan *(G-19667)*

Frederking Construction Co ....G 618 483-5031
Altamont *(G-532)*

Gbh Walnut Inc ....D 815 379-2151
Walnut *(G-20218)*

Greenfield Contractors LLC ....D 309 385-1859
Princeville *(G-16828)*

Grs Holding LLC ....F 630 355-1660
Naperville *(G-14838)*

Homeway Homes Inc ....D 309 965-2312
Deer Creek *(G-7575)*

24 LUMBER AND WOOD PRODUCTS, EXCEPT FURNITURE

Jack Bartlett ....G....... 217 659-3575
  Dallas City *(G-7314)*
Kitchens To Go LLC ....E....... 630 364-3083
  Naperville *(G-14858)*
Lester Building Systems LLC ....E....... 217 364-8664
  Charleston *(G-3406)*
McDonnell Components Inc ....D....... 815 547-9555
  Belvidere *(G-1685)*
Omni-Tech Systems Inc ....E....... 309 962-2281
  Le Roy *(G-12540)*
Otten Construction Co Inc ....G....... 618 768-4310
  Addieville *(G-11)*
R & N Components Co ....G....... 217 543-3495
  Tuscola *(G-19930)*
Schrocks Wood Shop ....G....... 217 773-3842
  Mount Sterling *(G-14593)*
Snagamon Valley Log Builders ....G....... 217 632-7609
  Petersburg *(G-16604)*
Steel Span Inc ....F....... 815 943-9071
  Harvard *(G-11068)*
Strat-O-Span Buildings Inc ....G....... 618 526-4566
  Breese *(G-2308)*
Tuff Shed Inc ....F....... 847 704-1147
  Palatine *(G-16167)*
West Salem Knox County Htchy ......G....... 618 456-3601
  West Salem *(G-20689)*
Yoders Portable Buildings LLC ....G....... 618 936-2419
  Sumner *(G-19689)*
Z-Modular LLC ....E....... 312 275-1600
  Chicago *(G-6705)*

2491 Wood Preserving

Brd Development Group LLC ....F....... 312 912-7110
  Chicago *(G-3947)*
Chicago Flameproof WD Spc Corp ..E....... 630 859-0009
  Montgomery *(G-14240)*
John A Biewer Lumber Company .....F....... 815 357-6792
  Seneca *(G-18859)*
Koppers Industries Inc ....E....... 309 343-5157
  Galesburg *(G-10206)*
Midwest Intgrted Companies LLC ...C....... 847 426-6354
  Gilberts *(G-10361)*
Northern Illinois Lumber Spc ....E....... 630 859-3226
  Montgomery *(G-14265)*
Northwest Snow Timber Svc Ltd .....G....... 847 778-4998
  Lombard *(G-13109)*
Nu Again ....F....... 630 564-5590
  Bartlett *(G-1299)*
▲ Red River Lumber Inc ....D....... 708 388-1818
  Blue Island *(G-2135)*
Southeast Wood Treating Inc ....F....... 815 562-5007
  Rochelle *(G-17160)*
Tronox Incorporated ....E....... 203 705-3704
  Madison *(G-13418)*
Willard Miller ....G....... 618 252-4407
  Carrier Mills *(G-3125)*

2493 Reconstituted Wood Prdts

Blue Ridge Fiberboard 800 233-8721
  Hampshire *(G-10965)*
Claridge Products and Eqp Inc ....G....... 847 991-8822
  Elgin *(G-8543)*
Craftmaster Manufacturing Inc ....A....... 800 405-2233
  Chicago *(G-4256)*
Jeld-Wen Inc ....C....... 312 544-5041
  Chicago *(G-5014)*
▲ Vecchio Manufacturing of Ill ....F....... 847 742-8429
  Elgin *(G-8773)*

2499 Wood Prdts, NEC

▲ A & M Products Company ....G....... 815 875-2667
  Princeton *(G-16803)*
Aba Custom Woodworking ....G....... 815 356-9663
  Crystal Lake *(G-7153)*
All American Wood Register Co ......F....... 815 356-1000
  Crystal Lake *(G-7155)*
▲ Aph Custom Wood & Metal Pdts 708 410-1274
  Broadview *(G-2417)*
Artistic Framing Inc ....C....... 847 808-0200
  Wheeling *(G-20850)*
Axis Design Architectual Mllwk ....F....... 630 466-4549
  Sugar Grove *(G-19637)*
Barsanti Woodwork Corporation .....E....... 773 284-6888
  Chicago *(G-3842)*
Bergeron Group Inc ....E....... 815 741-1635
  Joliet *(G-11830)*
Better Built Buildings ....G....... 217 267-7824
  Westville *(G-20778)*
Borns Picture Frames ....G....... 630 876-1709
  West Chicago *(G-20554)*

Bravura Moulding Company ....G....... 262 633-1882
  Lake Bluff *(G-12175)*
▲ Brown Wood Products Company ..F....... 847 673-4780
  Lincolnwood *(G-12814)*
Brown Woodworking ....G....... 815 477-8333
  Crystal Lake *(G-7172)*
Christian Cnty Mntal Hlth Assn 217 824-9675
  Taylorville *(G-19753)*
Cma Inc ....E....... 847 848-0674
  Joliet *(G-11841)*
Cma Inc ....D....... 630 551-3100
  Oswego *(G-15996)*
Colbert Custom Framing Inc ....F....... 630 717-1448
  Naperville *(G-14802)*
Country Stone Inc ....E....... 309 787-1744
  Milan *(G-14005)*
Crown Brands LLC ....E....... 224 513-2917
  Lincolnshire *(G-12757)*
Curtis Woodworking Inc ....G....... 815 544-3543
  Belvidere *(G-1664)*
Custom Framework Inc ....G....... 618 401-8494
  Edwardsville *(G-8354)*
Danlee Wood Products Inc ....G....... 815 938-9016
  Forreston *(G-9739)*
Delleman Associates & Corp ....G....... 708 345-9520
  Maywood *(G-13668)*
Dusty Lane Wood Products ....G....... 618 426-9045
  Campbell Hill *(G-2815)*
E-Z Tree Recycling Inc ....G....... 773 493-8600
  Chicago *(G-4428)*
▲ Edgewater Products Company Inc ....F....... 708 345-9200
  Melrose Park *(G-13860)*
Elegant Concepts Ltd ....G....... 708 456-9590
  Elmwood Park *(G-9451)*
▼ Equustock LLC ....F....... 866 962-4686
  Loves Park *(G-13210)*
▲ Excel Group Holdings Inc ....G....... 630 773-1815
  Itasca *(G-11653)*
Forest Awards & Engraving ....G....... 630 595-2242
  Wood Dale *(G-21189)*
Frame Game ....G....... 573 754-2385
  Pleasant Hill *(G-16748)*
Frame House Inc ....G....... 708 383-1616
  Oak Park *(G-15753)*
Frame Mart Inc ....G....... 309 452-0658
  Normal *(G-15203)*
▲ Frank A Edmunds & Co Inc ....F....... 773 586-2772
  Chicago *(G-4629)*
Fredericks Frame Studio Inc ....F....... 312 243-2950
  Chicago *(G-4632)*
Gavin Woodworking Inc ....G....... 815 786-2242
  Sandwich *(G-18371)*
Golden Valley Hardscapes LLC ....G....... 309 654-2261
  Cordova *(G-7007)*
Greencycle of Indiana Inc ....G....... 847 441-6606
  Northfield *(G-15515)*
Haight Company ....E....... 224 407-0763
  Elgin *(G-8603)*
Haleys Corker Inc ....G....... 708 228-1427
  River Forest *(G-17052)*
Herschberger Wood Working ....G....... 217 543-4075
  Arthur *(G-863)*
Hexacomb Corporation ....G....... 847 955-7984
  Buffalo Grove *(G-2546)*
Horizon Mfg Entps Inc ....G....... 847 438-0888
  Wauconda *(G-20358)*
House of Color ....F....... 708 352-3222
  Countryside *(G-7059)*
House On The Hill Inc ....G....... 630 279-4455
  Wheaton *(G-20803)*
Illinois Tool Works Inc ....F....... 708 720-7070
  Frankfort *(G-9806)*
Illinois Wood Fiber Products ....G....... 847 836-6176
  Carpentersville *(G-3105)*
Iloilo Custom Framing ....G....... 773 334-2844
  Chicago *(G-4893)*
Iron Castle Inc ....G....... 773 890-0575
  Chicago *(G-4969)*
Jack Ruch Quality Homes Inc ....G....... 309 663-6595
  Bloomington *(G-2063)*
Jacobs Reproduction ....G....... 618 374-2198
  Elsah *(G-9458)*
John Joda Post 54 ....G....... 815 692-3222
  Fairbury *(G-9610)*
Jones Wood Products ....G....... 618 826-2682
  Rockwood *(G-17706)*
Joseph Woodworking Corporation ..G....... 847 233-9766
  Schiller Park *(G-18816)*
Kaufman Woodworking ....G....... 217 543-3607
  Arthur *(G-864)*

Kaufmans Custom Cabinets ....F....... 217 268-4330
  Arcola *(G-653)*
Kohout Woodwork Inc ....G....... 630 628-6257
  Addison *(G-174)*
Larson-Juhl US LLC ....E....... 630 307-9700
  Roselle *(G-17963)*
Lee Armand & Co Ltd ....E....... 312 455-1200
  Chicago *(G-5194)*
Liftseat Corporation ....E....... 630 424-2840
  Oak Brook *(G-15636)*
Little Creek Woodworking ....G....... 217 543-2815
  Arthur *(G-866)*
M & R Custom Millwork Inc ....G....... 815 547-8549
  Belvidere *(G-1682)*
Magick Woods Inc ....G....... 630 229-0121
  Aurora *(G-1126)*
Mc Mechanical Contractors Inc ......G....... 708 460-0075
  Orland Park *(G-15967)*
▲ Melyx Inc ....F....... 309 654-2551
  Cordova *(G-7010)*
Mercurys Green LLC ....E....... 708 865-9134
  Franklin Park *(G-9993)*
Mhwp ....G....... 618 228-7600
  Aviston *(G-1182)*
Michels Frame Shop ....G....... 847 647-7366
  Niles *(G-15145)*
Midwest Lifting Products Inc ....G....... 214 356-7102
  Granite City *(G-10724)*
Mike Meier & Sons Fence Mfg ....G....... 847 587-1111
  Spring Grove *(G-19284)*
▲ New Century Picture Corp ....E....... 773 638-8888
  Chicago *(G-5575)*
Northwest Frame Company Inc ......G....... 847 359-0987
  Palatine *(G-16144)*
◆ Nu-Dell Manufacturing Co Inc ......F....... 847 803-4500
  Chicago *(G-5637)*
Orren Pickell Builders Inc ....E....... 847 572-5200
  Wilmette *(G-21090)*
Oso900 Nfp ....E....... 312 206-4219
  Chicago *(G-5711)*
Pearl Design Group LLC ....E....... 630 295-8401
  Bloomingdale *(G-2009)*
Picture Frame Fulfillment LLC ....D....... 708 483-8537
  Franklin Park *(G-10017)*
Powers Woodworking ....G....... 630 663-9644
  Woodridge *(G-21333)*
Premium Wood Products Inc ....E....... 815 787-3669
  Dekalb *(G-7698)*
Quality Plus ....F....... 618 779-4931
  Litchfield *(G-12974)*
R Maderite Inc ....G....... 773 235-1515
  Chicago *(G-5947)*
◆ R S Bacon Veneer Company ....C....... 630 323-1414
  Lisle *(G-12932)*
Rainbow Farms Enterprises Inc ......G....... 708 534-1070
  Monee *(G-14206)*
Reynolds Holdings Inc ....G....... 630 739-0110
  Romeoville *(G-17869)*
Roselle Custom Woodwork LLC .....G....... 630 980-5655
  Roselle *(G-17980)*
Rosewood Custom Framing LLC ....G....... 217 430-7669
  Quincy *(G-16943)*
RR Mulch and Soil LLC ....G....... 708 596-7200
  Markham *(G-13551)*
◆ Sarj USA Inc ....E....... 708 865-9134
  Franklin Park *(G-10043)*
Shawcraft Sign Co ....G....... 815 282-4105
  Machesney Park *(G-13374)*
Silver Line ....G....... 708 832-9100
  Calumet City *(G-2791)*
Smoke Rite Wood Products ....G....... 708 485-8910
  Brookfield *(G-2492)*
Springfield Woodworks ....G....... 217 483-7234
  Chatham *(G-3424)*
Stancy Woodworking Co Inc ....F....... 847 526-0252
  Island Lake *(G-11611)*
Star Cabinetry ....G....... 773 725-4651
  Chicago *(G-6233)*
Supreme Frame & Moulding Co ......F....... 312 930-9056
  Chicago *(G-6286)*
Tender Loving Care Inds Inc ....D....... 847 891-0230
  Elgin *(G-8753)*
Tepromark International Inc ....G....... 847 329-7881
  Chicago *(G-6352)*
Todd Scanlan ....G....... 217 585-1717
  Springfield *(G-19466)*
▲ Vaughan & Bushnell Mfg Co ....F....... 815 648-2446
  Hebron *(G-11153)*
Villa Foods LLC ....G....... 815 721-1136
  Rockford *(G-17675)*

24 LUMBER AND WOOD PRODUCTS, EXCEPT FURNITURE

Company	Code	Phone
Wedgewood — Wadsworth (G-20215)	G	847 672-4497
Wensco Michigan Corporation — Addison (G-334)	F	630 333-4440
Werner Co — Crystal Lake (G-7294)	E	815 459-6020
Windy City Fine Framing LLC — Chicago (G-6641)	E	312 455-1213
Wood Shop — Chicago (G-6667)	G	773 994-6666
Woodmac Industries Inc — S Chicago Hts (G-18130)	F	708 755-3545
Woodwind Specialists — Decatur (G-7570)	G	217 423-4122
Wyman and Company — Tinley Park (G-19868)	G	708 532-9064

25 FURNITURE AND FIXTURES

2511 Wood Household Furniture

Company	Code	Phone
A Closet Wholesaler — Chicago (G-3486)	F	312 654-1400
AB&d Custom Furniture Inc — Homewood (G-11487)	E	708 922-9061
Aba Custom Woodworking — Crystal Lake (G-7153)	G	815 356-9663
Allie Woodworking — Waukegan (G-20413)	G	847 244-1919
▲ Amtab Manufacturing Corp — Bensenville (G-1746)	D	630 301-7600
Athletic & Sports Seating — Streamwood (G-19563)	G	630 837-5566
Bell Cabinet & Millwork Co — Palos Hills (G-16196)	G	708 425-1200
Bender Mat Fctry Fton Slepshop — Urbana (G-19973)	G	217 328-1700
Bill Weeks Inc — Springfield (G-19326)	G	217 523-8735
Broome & Greene Online LLC — Chicago (G-3964)	G	312 584-1580
Butcher Block Furn By Oneill — Chicago (G-3986)	G	312 666-9144
Cabinets Doors and More LLC — Antioch (G-607)	G	847 395-6334
Carson Properties Inc — Elmhurst (G-9341)	E	630 832-3322
Chicago Booth Mfg Inc — Chicago (G-4093)	F	773 378-8400
Chicago Honeymooners LLC — Chicago (G-4106)	G	312 399-5699
◆ Chicago Wicker & Trading Co — Alsip (G-429)	E	708 563-2890
Chicagoland Closets LLC — Aurora (G-1075)	E	630 906-0000
Chicagos Finest Ironworks — Lansing (G-12488)	G	708 895-4484
▲ Choice Furnishings Inc — Skokie (G-18942)	G	847 329-0004
▲ Churchill Cabinet Company — Cicero (G-6833)	E	708 780-0070
City Living Design Inc — Chicago (G-4156)	G	312 335-0711
Columbia Woodworks Corporation — Addison (G-77)	F	202 526-2387
Comwell — Red Bud (G-16991)	D	618 282-6233
Country Workshop — Arthur (G-849)	G	217 543-4094
Creative Wood Concepts Inc — Chicago (G-4268)	G	773 384-9960
Custom Designs By Georgio — Franklin Park (G-9922)	F	847 233-0410
Custom Window Accents — Harvard (G-11051)	G	815 943-7651
Custom Wood Designs Inc — Crestwood (G-7116)	G	708 799-3439
▲ D D G Inc — Northbrook (G-15370)	G	847 412-0277
Debcor Inc — South Holland (G-19207)	G	708 333-2191
Dendro Co — Lakemoor (G-12471)	G	312 772-6836
Dicks Custom Cabinet Shop — Cornell (G-7012)	G	815 358-2663
Diebolds Cabinet Shop — Chicago (G-4356)	G	773 772-3076
Douglas County Wood Products — Arthur (G-854)	G	217 543-2888
E J Self Furniture — Arlington Heights (G-731)	G	847 394-0899
Eddie Gapastione — Bridgeview (G-2344)	G	708 430-3881
Five Star Industries Inc — Du Quoin (G-8120)	D	618 542-4880
Fredman Bros Furniture Co Inc — Peoria (G-16441)	E	309 674-2011
Gavin Woodworking Inc — Sandwich (G-18371)	G	815 786-2242
Great Spirit Hardwoods LLC — East Dundee (G-8199)	G	224 801-1969
Green Gables Country Store — Bradford (G-2273)	D	309 897-7160
Guess Whackit & Hope Inc — Chicago (G-4750)	G	773 342-4273
Hanley Design Inc — Peoria (G-16452)	G	309 682-9665
Hylan Design Ltd — Chicago (G-4863)	G	312 243-7341
Imperial Kitchens & Bath Inc — Brookfield (G-2486)	F	708 485-0020
Innovative Fix Solutions LLC — Rockford (G-17466)	D	815 395-8500
Innovative Mktg Solutions Inc — Schaumburg (G-18561)	F	630 227-4300
International Wood Design Inc — Chicago (G-4956)	G	773 227-9270
J M Lustig Custom Cabinets Co — Effingham (G-8403)	F	217 342-6661
◆ Jbc Holding Co — Effingham (G-8404)	G	217 347-7701
Joliet Cabinet Company Inc — Lockport (G-13003)	E	815 727-4096
Kaufmans Custom Cabinets — Arcola (G-653)	F	217 268-4330
Kinser Woodworks — Makanda (G-13428)	G	618 549-4540
Kowal Custom Cabinet & Furn — Blue Island (G-2129)	G	708 597-3367
Kunz Carpentry — Trenton (G-19904)	G	618 224-7892
Laverns Wood Items — Arcola (G-654)	G	217 268-4544
Legacy Woodwork Inc — Franklin Park (G-9980)	G	847 451-7602
Leggett & Platt Incorporated — North Aurora (G-15267)	G	630 801-0609
M Inc — Chicago (G-5301)	G	312 853-0152
Mamagreen LLC — Chicago (G-5325)	G	312 953-3557
Master Cabinets — Cary (G-3178)	G	847 639-1323
Mastercraft Furn Rfnishing Inc — Chicago (G-5361)	F	773 722-5730
Meier Granite Company — Franklin Park (G-9989)	G	847 678-7300
Mica Furniture Mfg Inc — Addison (G-203)	G	708 430-1150
Mobilia Inc — Bellwood (G-1634)	E	708 865-0700
Morningside Woodcraft — Arcola (G-659)	G	217 268-4313
Muhs Funiture Manufacturing — Noble (G-15190)	G	618 723-2590
O & I Woodworking — Arthur (G-872)	G	217 543-3155
Okaw Valley Woodworking LLC — Arthur (G-874)	F	217 543-5180
ONeill Products Inc — Chicago (G-5678)	G	312 243-3413
Patio Plus — Ottawa (G-16070)	G	815 433-2399
▲ Philip Reinisch Company — Naperville (G-14899)	F	312 644-6776
Planks Cabinet Shop Inc — Arthur (G-876)	G	217 543-2687
Prairie Woodworks Inc — Downs (G-8112)	G	309 378-2418
R Maderite Inc — North Chicago (G-15320)	G	847 785-0875
Riverside Custom Woodworking — Fulton (G-10157)	G	815 589-3608
Roncin Custom Design — Huntley (G-11565)	G	847 669-0260
Rooms Redux Chicago Inc — Chicago (G-6058)	F	312 835-1192
Rose Custom Cabinets Inc — Mundelein (G-14732)	E	847 816-4800
Royal Fabricators Inc — Wadsworth (G-20213)	F	847 775-7466
Shews Custom Woodworking — Lincoln (G-12738)	G	217 737-5543
▲ Signature Innovations LLC — Elk Grove Village (G-9241)	G	847 758-9600
Silver Bell Cnstr & Furn Inc — Chicago (G-6171)	G	773 578-9450
Specialized Woodwork Inc — Lombard (G-13131)	G	630 627-0450
Spirit Concepts Inc — Crestwood (G-7128)	G	708 388-4500
Stancy Woodworking Co Inc — Island Lake (G-11611)	F	847 526-0252
◆ Stevens Cabinets Inc — Teutopolis (G-19773)	B	217 857-7100
Suburban Laminating Inc — Melrose Park (G-13918)	G	708 389-6106
Tender Loving Care Inds Inc — Elgin (G-8753)	D	847 891-0230
▲ Trendler Inc — Chicago (G-6416)	G	773 284-6600
United Woodworking Inc — Schaumburg (G-18767)	E	847 352-3066
▲ Urban Home Furniture & ACC Inc — Batavia (G-1438)	E	630 761-3200
▼ Urban Wood Goods Ltd — Gurnee (G-10941)	F	248 310-7668
Verlo Mattress of Lake Geneva — Crystal Lake (G-7289)	G	815 455-2570
◆ Waco Manufacturing Co Inc — Chicago (G-6582)	F	312 733-0054
What We Make Inc — Algonquin (G-396)	G	331 442-4830
Whitacres Country Oaks Shop — Hudson (G-11521)	F	309 726-1305
▲ Wicks Organ Company — Highland (G-11249)	E	618 654-2191
Wolfart Maciej — Chicago (G-6663)	G	312 248-3575
Woodcraft Enterprises Inc — New Lenox (G-15070)	G	815 485-2787
Wooden World of Richmond Inc — Richmond (G-17026)	G	815 405-4503
Zakrose Inc — Chicago (G-6707)	G	847 372-7309

2512 Wood Household Furniture, Upholstered

Company	Code	Phone
Addison Interiors Company — Addison (G-20)	G	630 628-1345
Brusic-Rose Inc — Bedford Park (G-1460)	E	708 458-9900
Coles Appliance & Furn Co — Chicago (G-4199)	G	773 525-1797
E J Self Furniture — Arlington Heights (G-731)	G	847 394-0899
E M C Industry — Arthur (G-855)	G	217 543-2894
◆ Groupe Lacasse LLC — Chicago (G-4745)	C	312 670-9100
New Image Upholstery — South Elgin (G-19169)	F	630 542-5560
Patrick Cabinetry Inc — Bloomingdale (G-2007)	G	630 307-9333
Scibor Upholstering & Gallery — Chicago (G-6117)	G	708 671-9700
▲ Sherwood Industries Inc — Niles (G-15170)	F	847 626-0300
Shoppe De Lee Inc — Elk Grove Village (G-9237)	G	847 350-0580
▲ Trp Acquisition Corp — Lombard (G-13147)	G	630 261-2380
Vintage Modern Collection Inc — Chicago (G-6554)	G	312 774-8424
Vinyl Life North — North Aurora (G-15281)	G	630 906-9686

2514 Metal Household Furniture

Company	Code	Phone
▲ Chicago American Mfg LLC — Chicago (G-4088)	C	773 376-0100
Chicagos Finest Ironworks — Lansing (G-12488)	G	708 895-4484
Dixline Corporation — Galva (G-10230)	F	309 932-2011
Dpcac LLC — Itasca (G-11644)	F	630 741-7900
Durable Design Products Inc — River Forest (G-17051)	G	708 707-1147
▲ Duracare Seating Company Inc — Chicago (G-4409)	F	888 592-1102

European Ornamental Iron Works.........G....... 630 705-9300
Addison (G-117)
▲ Metal Box International LLC ....C....... 847 455-8500
Franklin Park (G-9994)
Modular Wood Systems Inc..................G....... 847 251-6401
Wilmette (G-21088)
◆ Pace Industries Inc...........................C....... 312 226-5500
Chicago (G-5737)
Richardson Ironworks LLC..................G....... 217 359-3333
Champaign (G-3342)
▲ Smart Solar Inc...............................F....... 813 343-5770
Libertyville (G-12708)
Tesko Welding & Mfg Co......................D....... 708 452-0045
Norridge (G-15244)
US Foods Culinary Eqp Sups LLC........G....... 847 720-8000
Rosemont (G-18057)
Viking Metal Cabinet Co LLC................D....... 800 776-7767
Montgomery (G-14273)
Viking Metal Cabinet Company............D....... 630 863-7234
Montgomery (G-14274)

2515 Mattresses & Bedsprings

▲ Bedding Group Inc.........................D....... 309 788-0401
Rock Island (G-17204)
Bender Mat Fctry Fton Slepshop..........G....... 217 328-1700
Urbana (G-19973)
Ceragem 26th St....................................G....... 773 277-0672
Chicago (G-4064)
Corsicana Bedding LLC.......................G....... 708 331-9000
Aurora (G-1080)
Fredman Bros Furniture Co Inc.............E....... 309 674-2011
Peoria (G-16441)
Homwarehouse.......................................G....... 224 500-3367
Des Plaines (G-7777)
▲ Hospitology Products LLC...............G....... 630 359-5075
Addison (G-153)
Innocor Inc...F....... 630 231-0622
West Chicago (G-20597)
◆ Kolcraft Enterprises Inc...................D....... 312 361-6315
Chicago (G-5119)
L A Bedding Corp..................................G....... 773 715-9641
Chicago (G-5141)
Leggett & Platt Incorporated................D....... 773 907-0261
Chicago (G-5198)
Leggett & Platt Incorporated................F....... 630 851-0101
Aurora (G-996)
Leggett & Platt Incorporated................D....... 815 233-0022
Freeport (G-10124)
Leggett & Platt Incorporated.................E....... 312 529-2053
Chicago (G-5199)
Leggett & Platt Incorporated.................E....... 630 801-0609
North Aurora (G-15267)
Leggett & Platt Incorporated.................G....... 800 699-0607
Chicago (G-5200)
Made Rite Bedding Company...............F....... 847 349-5886
Franklin Park (G-9983)
My Bed Inc...F....... 800 326-9233
Lockport (G-13015)
Pace Foundation....................................E....... 309 691-3553
Peoria (G-16490)
Piersons Mattress Inc............................G....... 309 637-8455
Peoria (G-16498)
◆ Quality Sleep Shop Inc....................G....... 708 246-2224
La Grange Highlands (G-12093)
Robin Hood Mat & Quilting Corp..........G....... 312 953-2960
Chicago (G-6045)
Royal Bedding Company Inc................D....... 847 645-0200
Hoffman Estates (G-11451)
Sealy Mattress Company......................C....... 630 879-8011
Batavia (G-1415)
▲ Shevick Sales Corp..........................G....... 312 487-2865
Niles (G-15171)
Ther A Pedic Midwest Inc......................G....... 309 788-0401
Rock Island (G-17249)
Verlo Mat of Skokie-Evanston...............G....... 847 966-9988
Morton Grove (G-14446)
Verlo Mattress of Lake Geneva.............G....... 815 455-2570
Crystal Lake (G-7289)
Wicoff Inc...G....... 618 988-8888
Herrin (G-11182)

2517 Wood T V, Radio, Phono & Sewing Cabinets

Anderson & Marter Cabinets.................G....... 630 406-9840
Batavia (G-1349)
Cabinets By Custom Craft Inc...............G....... 815 637-4001
Roscoe (G-17900)
Cooper Lake Millworks Inc.....................G....... 217 847-2681
Hamilton (G-10951)
Creative Wood Concepts Inc.................G....... 773 384-9960
Chicago (G-4268)
Crestwood Custom Cabinets................G....... 708 385-3167
Crestwood (G-7115)
Der Holtzmacher Ltd.............................G....... 815 895-4887
Sycamore (G-19706)
Eddie Gapastione...................................G....... 708 430-3881
Bridgeview (G-2344)
Elm Street Industries Inc.......................F....... 309 854-7000
Kewanee (G-12032)
Grays Cabinet Co...................................G....... 618 948-2211
Saint Francisville (G-18314)
HI Tech...G....... 708 957-4210
Homewood (G-11496)
Midwest Woodcrafters Inc.....................G....... 630 665-0901
Carol Stream (G-3031)
Roncin Custom Design..........................G....... 847 669-0260
Huntley (G-11565)
Silver Bell Cnstr & Furn Inc...................G....... 773 578-9450
Chicago (G-6171)
Spirit Concepts Inc.................................G....... 708 388-4500
Crestwood (G-7128)
Timberside Woodworking......................G....... 217 578-3201
Arthur (G-880)
Woodhill Cabinetry Design Inc..............G....... 815 431-0545
Ottawa (G-16086)
▲ Zenith Electronics Corporation........E....... 847 941-8000
Lincolnshire (G-12806)

2519 Household Furniture, NEC

Albert Vivo Upholstery Co Inc...............G....... 312 226-7779
Burr Ridge (G-2651)
Bradley Terrace Inc................................G....... 773 775-6579
Chicago (G-3941)
Gensler Gardens Inc..............................F....... 815 874-9634
Davis Junction (G-7424)
Glass Artistry..G....... 847 998-5800
Northbrook (G-15394)
▼ House of Rattan Inc..........................E....... 630 627-8160
Lombard (G-13086)
Kozaczka Inc..G....... 224 435-6180
Arlington Heights (G-766)
▲ Ligo Products Inc..............................E....... 708 478-1800
Mokena (G-14096)
Mitchel Home..G....... 773 205-9902
Chicago (G-5469)
Patio Plus..G....... 815 433-2399
Ottawa (G-16070)
Petro Enterprises Inc.............................G....... 708 425-1551
Chicago Ridge (G-6806)
Rustic Woodcrafts..................................G....... 618 584-3912
Flat Rock (G-9673)
▲ Standard Container Co of Edgar......E....... 847 438-1510
Lake Zurich (G-12460)
◆ Suncast Corporation.........................A....... 630 879-2050
Batavia (G-1422)
▲ Thomas Monahan Company............F....... 217 268-5771
Arcola (G-667)
▲ Zenith Electronics Corporation........E....... 847 941-8000
Lincolnshire (G-12806)

2521 Wood Office Furniture

AB&d Custom Furniture Inc...................E....... 708 922-9061
Homewood (G-11487)
Aba Custom Woodworking....................G....... 815 356-9663
Crystal Lake (G-7153)
Accurate Custom Cabinets Inc.............E....... 630 458-0460
Addison (G-15)
Almacen Inc..G....... 847 934-7955
Inverness (G-11593)
▲ Amtab Manufacturing Corp...............D....... 630 301-7600
Bensenville (G-1746)
B & B Formica Appliers Inc...................F....... 773 804-1015
Chicago (G-3804)
◆ Bretford Manufacturing Inc..............B....... 847 678-2545
Franklin Park (G-9892)
C-V Cstom Cntrtops Cbinets Inc..........F....... 708 388-5066
Blue Island (G-2113)
Cabinet Gallery LLC..............................G....... 618 882-4801
Highland (G-11207)
Castle Craft Products Inc......................F....... 630 279-7494
Villa Park (G-20138)
Cmp Millwork Co....................................G....... 630 832-6462
Elmhurst (G-9348)
Complete Custom Woodworks..............G....... 309 644-1911
Coal Valley (G-6934)
Crestwood Custom Cabinets................G....... 708 385-3167
Crestwood (G-7115)
▲ Daniel M Powers & Assoc Ltd..........D....... 630 685-8400
Bolingbrook (G-2166)
Debcor Inc..G....... 708 333-2191
South Holland (G-19207)
Dendro Co...G....... 312 772-6836
Lakemoor (G-12471)
Diebolds Cabinet Shop..........................G....... 773 772-3076
Chicago (G-4356)
▲ Dirtt Envmtl Solutions Inc................C....... 312 245-2870
Chicago (G-4364)
Djr Inc..F....... 773 581-5204
Chicago (G-4372)
Donald Kranz..G....... 847 428-1616
Carpentersville (G-3101)
Eddie Gapastione...................................G....... 708 430-3881
Bridgeview (G-2344)
Gianni Incorporated...............................D....... 708 863-6696
Cicero (G-6849)
Global Industries Inc..............................F....... 630 681-2818
Glendale Heights (G-10454)
Grays Cabinet Co...................................G....... 618 948-2211
Saint Francisville (G-18314)
◆ Groupe Lacasse LLC........................C....... 312 670-9100
Chicago (G-4745)
Ideal Cabinet Solutions Inc....................G....... 618 514-7087
Alhambra (G-401)
Innovant Inc..D....... 646 368-6254
Chicago (G-4930)
Interstuhl USA Inc..................................G....... 312 385-0240
Chicago (G-4959)
J K Custom Countertops........................G....... 630 495-2324
Lombard (G-13088)
J M Lustig Custom Cabinets Co...........F....... 217 342-6661
Effingham (G-8403)
Knoll Inc..E....... 312 454-6920
Chicago (G-5112)
▲ Lacava LLC.......................................E....... 773 637-9600
Chicago (G-5154)
◆ Magnuson Group Inc.......................F....... 630 783-8100
Woodridge (G-21320)
Marcy Enterprises Inc............................G....... 708 352-7220
La Grange Park (G-12098)
Marvel Group Inc....................................C....... 773 523-4804
Chicago (G-5354)
Mastercraft Furn Rfnishing Inc..............F....... 773 722-5730
Chicago (G-5361)
◆ Mayline Investments Inc..................G....... 847 948-9340
Northbrook (G-15428)
▼ Mlp Seating Corp.............................E....... 847 956-1700
Rockdale (G-17269)
Mobilia Inc...E....... 708 865-0700
Bellwood (G-1634)
◆ Nova Solutions Inc...........................E....... 217 342-7070
Effingham (G-8416)
Office Furniture Parts LLC.....................G....... 708 546-5841
Forest Park (G-9723)
Pio Woodworking Inc.............................G....... 630 628-6900
Addison (G-240)
Regency Custom Woodworking............F....... 815 689-2117
Cullom (G-7300)
Rieke Office Interiors Inc.......................D....... 847 622-9711
Elgin (G-8720)
Roevolution 226 LLC.............................G....... 773 658-4022
Riverwoods (G-17095)
S & J Woodproducts...............................G....... 815 973-1970
Rockford (G-17618)
Stay Straight Manufacturing..................G....... 312 226-2137
Chicago (G-6236)
Steelcase Inc..F....... 312 321-3720
Chicago (G-6237)
▲ Systems Unlimited Inc......................C....... 630 285-0010
Itasca (G-11743)
Wm Huber Cabinet Works......................E....... 773 235-7660
Chicago (G-6653)
Woodhill Cabinetry Design Inc..............G....... 815 431-0545
Ottawa (G-16086)

2522 Office Furniture, Except Wood

Accurate Custom Cabinets Inc.............E....... 630 458-0460
Addison (G-15)
Almacen Inc..G....... 847 934-7955
Inverness (G-11593)
▲ Amtab Manufacturing Corp...............D....... 630 301-7600
Bensenville (G-1746)
Baker Avenue Investments Inc.............D....... 309 427-2500
Washington (G-20266)
◆ Bretford Manufacturing Inc..............B....... 847 678-2545
Franklin Park (G-9892)
C-V Cstom Cntrtops Cbinets Inc..........F....... 708 388-5066
Blue Island (G-2113)
Capitol Carton Company........................E....... 312 563-9690
Chicago (G-4017)

S
I
C

Central Radiator Cabinet Co ....G 773 539-1700
Lena *(G-12599)*
Debcor Inc ....G 708 333-2191
South Holland *(G-19207)*
▲ Dirtt Envmtl Solutions Inc ....C 312 245-2870
Chicago *(G-4364)*
Durable Design Products Inc ....G 708 707-1147
River Forest *(G-17051)*
◆ Edsal Manufacturing Co LLC ....A 773 475-3000
Chicago *(G-4454)*
Edsal Manufacturing Co LLC ....C 773 475-3165
Chicago *(G-4455)*
Edsal Manufacturing Co LLC ....C 773 475-3013
Chicago *(G-4456)*
Fanmar Inc ....E 847 621-2010
Elk Grove Village *(G-8995)*
◆ Groupe Lacasse LLC ....C 312 670-9100
Chicago *(G-4745)*
Hanley Design Inc ....G 309 682-9665
Peoria *(G-16452)*
▲ Iceberg Enterprises LLC ....F 847 685-9500
Des Plaines *(G-7782)*
▲ IMS Engineered Products LLC ....C 847 391-8100
Des Plaines *(G-7787)*
J & E Seating LLC ....E 847 956-1700
Rockdale *(G-17260)*
Kimball Office Inc ....F 800 349-9827
Chicago *(G-5102)*
L & D Group Inc ....B 630 892-8941
Montgomery *(G-14252)*
Lincoln Office LLC ....D 309 427-2500
Washington *(G-20273)*
Marvel Group Inc ....C 773 523-4804
Chicago *(G-5354)*
▲ Marvel Group Inc ....C 773 523-4804
Chicago *(G-5355)*
Marvel Group Inc ....F 773 523-4804
Chicago *(G-5356)*
◆ Mayline Investments Inc ....G 847 948-9340
Northbrook *(G-15428)*
▲ Metal Box International LLC ....C 847 455-8500
Franklin Park *(G-9994)*
▼ Mlp Seating Corp ....E 847 956-1700
Rockdale *(G-17269)*
MT Case Company ....F 630 227-1019
Wood Dale *(G-21218)*
Niedermaier Inc ....D 312 492-9400
Chicago *(G-5599)*
▲ Ortho Seating LLC ....F 773 276-3539
Chicago *(G-5706)*
▲ Paoli Inc ....G 312 644-5509
Chicago *(G-5751)*
▲ Pointe International Company ....F 847 550-7001
Lake Barrington *(G-12164)*
▲ Richardson Seating Corporation ....E 312 829-4040
Chicago *(G-6027)*
Rome Metal Mfg Inc ....G 773 287-1755
Chicago *(G-6057)*
◆ Rwi Manufacturing Inc ....C 800 277-1699
Aurora *(G-1151)*
Steel Solutions USA ....G 815 432-4938
Watseka *(G-20317)*
Steelcase Inc ....F 312 321-3720
Chicago *(G-6237)*
T J Van Der Bosch & Associates ....E 815 344-3210
McHenry *(G-13805)*
▼ T2 Site Amenities Incorporated ....G 847 579-9003
Highland Park *(G-11302)*
Viking Metal Cabinet Co LLC ....D 800 776-7767
Montgomery *(G-14273)*
Viking Metal Cabinet Company ....D 630 863-7234
Montgomery *(G-14274)*
◆ Waco Manufacturing Co Inc ....F 312 733-0054
Chicago *(G-6582)*

2531 Public Building & Related Furniture

Abundant Living Christian Ctr ....G 708 896-6181
Dolton *(G-7928)*
Atwood-Hamlin Mfg Co Inc ....F 815 678-7291
Richmond *(G-17010)*
B/E Aerospace Inc ....C 561 791-5000
Hanover Park *(G-11000)*
◆ Belson Outdoors LLC ....E 630 897-8489
Naperville *(G-14778)*
Center-111 W Burnham Wash LLC ....E 312 368-5320
Chicago *(G-4055)*
▲ Chicago American Mfg LLC ....C 773 376-0100
Chicago *(G-4088)*
Chicago Booth Mfg Inc ....F 773 378-8400
Chicago *(G-4093)*
Claridge Products ....G 847 991-8822
Elgin *(G-8542)*
Claridge Products and Eqp Inc ....G 847 991-8822
Elgin *(G-8543)*
Clarios ....C 815 288-3859
Dixon *(G-7893)*
Clarios ....E 309 427-2800
East Peoria *(G-8261)*
Clarios ....D 630 573-0897
Oak Brook *(G-15611)*
Clarios ....G 331 212-3800
Aurora *(G-940)*
Clarios ....D 630 279-0050
Elmhurst *(G-9347)*
Clarios ....G 630 351-9407
Bloomingdale *(G-1986)*
Clarios ....F 630 871-7700
Carol Stream *(G-2961)*
Correctional Technologies Inc ....F 630 455-0811
Willowbrook *(G-21038)*
Fbsa LLC ....G 773 524-2440
Chicago *(G-4570)*
▲ Fortune Brands Home & SEC Inc ....D 847 484-4400
Deerfield *(G-7610)*
▲ Freedman Seating Company ....C 773 524-3255
Chicago *(G-4633)*
Hanley Design Inc ....G 309 682-9665
Peoria *(G-16452)*
Harrier Interior Products ....G 847 934-1310
Palatine *(G-16122)*
Ill Dept Natural Resources ....G 217 498-9208
Rochester *(G-17167)*
Inter Swiss Ltd ....F 773 379-0400
Chicago *(G-4943)*
Irwin Seating Company ....C 618 483-6157
Altamont *(G-534)*
▲ Irwin Telescopic Seating Co ....C 618 483-6157
Altamont *(G-535)*
J C Decaux New York Inc ....E 312 456-2999
Chicago *(G-4989)*
James Howard Co ....G 815 497-2831
Compton *(G-6996)*
Jcdecaux Chicago LLC ....E 312 456-2999
Chicago *(G-5013)*
Johnson Controls Inc ....G 847 549-2350
Vernon Hills *(G-20068)*
Johnson Controls Inc ....E 847 364-1500
Arlington Heights *(G-762)*
▲ Kinsman Enterprises Inc ....G 618 932-3838
West Frankfort *(G-20674)*
Mfp Holding Co ....G 312 666-3366
Chicago *(G-5418)*
◆ Nu-Dell Manufacturing Co Inc ....F 847 803-4500
Chicago *(G-5637)*
Partners Resource Inc ....G 630 620-9161
Glen Ellyn *(G-10417)*
Patio Plus ....G 815 433-2399
Ottawa *(G-16070)*
Pep Industries Inc ....F 630 833-0404
Villa Park *(G-20164)*
▲ Pointe International Company ....F 847 550-7001
Lake Barrington *(G-12164)*
Redbox Workshop Ltd ....E 773 478-7077
Chicago *(G-5993)*
Roberts & Downey Chapel Eqp ....G 217 795-2391
Argenta *(G-672)*
Sage Clover ....G 630 220-9600
Winfield *(G-21117)*
▲ Sandlock Sandbox LLC ....G 630 963-9422
Westmont *(G-20771)*
▲ Sedia Systems Inc ....G 312 212-8010
Chicago *(G-6129)*
Serious Energy Inc ....E 312 515-4606
Chicago *(G-6137)*
◆ Stevens Cabinets Inc ....B 217 857-7100
Teutopolis *(G-19773)*
▼ T2 Site Amenities Incorporated ....G 847 579-9003
Highland Park *(G-11302)*
▲ Tao Trading Corporation ....G 773 764-6542
Chicago *(G-6326)*
◆ The United Group Inc ....E 847 816-7100
Lake Forest *(G-12314)*
▲ Vecchio Manufacturing of Ill ....F 847 742-8429
Elgin *(G-8773)*
◆ Waco Manufacturing Co Inc ....F 312 733-0054
Chicago *(G-6582)*
Wise Co Inc ....G 618 594-4091
Carlyle *(G-2898)*
Yanfeng US Automotive ....A 779 552-7300
Belvidere *(G-1712)*

2541 Wood, Office & Store Fixtures

AB&d Custom Furniture Inc ....E 708 922-9061
Homewood *(G-11487)*
Ability Cabinet Co Inc ....G 847 678-6678
Franklin Park *(G-9859)*
Abitzy Inc ....F 847 659-9228
Wood Dale *(G-21152)*
Action Cabinet Sales Inc ....G 847 717-0011
Elgin *(G-8494)*
Akrylix Inc ....F 773 869-9005
Frankfort *(G-9764)*
All Stone Inc ....G 815 529-1754
Romeoville *(G-17790)*
All-Style Custom Tops ....G 708 532-6606
Tinley Park *(G-19799)*
Allie Woodworking ....G 847 244-1919
Waukegan *(G-20413)*
Anderson & Marter Cabinets ....G 630 406-9840
Batavia *(G-1349)*
Axis Display Group Inc ....G 513 342-1884
South Beloit *(G-19082)*
B & B Formica Appliers Inc ....F 773 804-1015
Chicago *(G-3804)*
▲ Bards Products Inc ....E 800 323-5499
Mundelein *(G-14665)*
▼ Bernhard Woodwork Ltd ....D 847 291-1040
Northbrook *(G-15348)*
Bolhuis Woodworking Co ....G 708 333-5100
Manhattan *(G-13431)*
Brakur Custom Cabinetry Inc ....C 630 355-2244
Shorewood *(G-18893)*
Brothers Leal LLC ....G 708 385-4400
Alsip *(G-424)*
C-V Cstom Cntrtops Cbinets Inc ....F 708 388-5066
Blue Island *(G-2113)*
Cabinets By Custom Craft Inc ....G 815 637-4001
Roscoe *(G-17900)*
▲ Capitol Wood Works LLC ....D 217 522-5553
Springfield *(G-19341)*
Castle Craft Products Inc ....F 630 279-7494
Villa Park *(G-20138)*
Chicago Booth Mfg Inc ....F 773 378-8400
Chicago *(G-4093)*
▲ Churchill Cabinet Company ....E 708 780-0070
Cicero *(G-6833)*
Clover Custom Counters Inc ....G 708 598-8912
Bridgeview *(G-2336)*
◆ Colony Display LLC ....E 847 426-5300
Elgin *(G-8545)*
Con-Temp Cabinets Inc ....F 630 892-7300
North Aurora *(G-15257)*
Contempo Marble & Granite Inc ....G 312 455-0022
Chicago *(G-4225)*
▲ Continental Marketing Inc ....F 773 467-8300
Chicago *(G-4227)*
Contract Industries Inc ....E 708 458-8150
Bedford Park *(G-1464)*
Cooper Lake Millworks Inc ....G 217 847-2681
Hamilton *(G-10951)*
Coordinated Kitchen Dev Inc ....G 847 847-7692
Lake Zurich *(G-12396)*
Counter Craft Inc ....G 847 336-8205
Waukegan *(G-20431)*
Countertop Creations ....F 618 736-2700
Dahlgren *(G-7306)*
Crown Coverings Inc ....E 630 546-2959
Roselle *(G-17949)*
Custom Window Accents ....F 815 943-7651
Harvard *(G-11051)*
Custom Woodwork & Interiors ....F 217 546-0006
Springfield *(G-19358)*
Cut - To - Size Technology Inc ....E 630 543-8328
Addison *(G-85)*
▲ Daniel M Powers & Assoc Ltd ....D 630 685-8400
Bolingbrook *(G-2166)*
Der Holtzmacher Ltd ....G 815 895-4887
Sycamore *(G-19706)*
Design Woodworks ....G 847 566-6603
Mundelein *(G-14682)*
DK Knutsen ....G 815 626-4388
Sterling *(G-19505)*
Dpcac LLC ....F 630 741-7900
Itasca *(G-11644)*
▲ Dunhill Corp ....F 815 806-8600
Frankfort *(G-9788)*
▲ Duo Usa Incorporated ....G 312 421-7755
Chicago *(G-4407)*
Durable Design Products Inc ....G 708 707-1147
River Forest *(G-17051)*

Eddie Gapastione....G....... 708 430-3881
Bridgeview (G-2344)
Election Works....G....... 630 232-4030
Geneva (G-10268)
Forest City Counter Tops Inc....F....... 815 633-8602
Loves Park (G-13212)
Fra-Milco Cabinets Co Inc....G .....
Frankfort (G-9795)
Gerali Custom Design Inc....D....... 847 760-0500
Elgin (G-8593)
Glenview Custom Cabinets Inc....G....... 847 345-5754
Glenview (G-10551)
Graniteworks....G....... 815 288-3350
Dixon (G-7901)
Greenberg Casework Company Inc....E....... 815 624-0288
South Beloit (G-19096)
Hallmark Cabinet Company....D....... 708 757-7807
Minooka (G-14061)
Hanley Design Inc....G....... 309 682-9665
Peoria (G-16452)
Hansen Custom Cabinet Inc....G....... 847 356-1100
Lake Villa (G-12353)
Harts Top and Cabinet Shop....G....... 708 957-4666
Country Club Hills (G-7040)
Hickory Street Cabinets....G....... 618 667-9676
Troy (G-19915)
Hire-Nelson Company Inc....E....... 630 543-9400
Addison (G-150)
Hylan Design Ltd....G....... 312 243-7341
Chicago (G-4863)
Imperial Kitchens & Bath Inc....F....... 708 485-0020
Brookfield (G-2486)
▲ Imperial Woodworking Company....D....... 847 221-2107
Palatine (G-16127)
J K Custom Countertops....G....... 630 495-2324
Lombard (G-13088)
Janik Custom Millwork Inc....G....... 708 482-4844
Hodgkins (G-11390)
◆ Jbc Holding Co....G....... 217 347-7701
Effingham (G-8404)
John F Mate Co....G....... 847 381-8131
Lake Barrington (G-12154)
Kabinet Kraft....F....... 618 395-1047
Olney (G-15867)
Kewaunee Scientific Corp....G....... 847 675-7744
Highland Park (G-11278)
Kitchen Krafters Inc....G....... 815 675-6061
Spring Grove (G-19279)
▲ Laminated Components Inc....E....... 815 648-4811
Hebron (G-11146)
Laminated Designs Countertops....G....... 815 877-7222
Machesney Park (G-13356)
M & R Custom Millwork Inc....G....... 815 547-8549
Belvidere (G-1682)
Marcy Enterprises Inc....G....... 708 352-7220
La Grange Park (G-12098)
Markham Cabinet Works Inc....G....... 708 687-3074
Midlothian (G-13993)
Marmon Retail Technologies Co....F....... 312 332-0317
Chicago (G-5346)
◆ Marv-O-Lus Manufacturing Co....F....... 773 826-1717
Chicago (G-5353)
Maxwell Counters Inc....E....... 309 928-2848
Farmer City (G-9655)
Meier Granite Company....G....... 847 678-7300
Franklin Park (G-9989)
Midwest Display & Mfg Inc....G....... 815 962-2199
Rockford (G-17526)
Miller Manufacturing Co Inc....D....... 636 343-5700
Dupo (G-8140)
▲ Morgan Li LLC....E....... 708 758-5300
Chicago Heights (G-6761)
▲ Moss Holding Company....C....... 847 238-4200
Elk Grove Village (G-9132)
Multiplex Display Fixture Co....E....... 800 325-3350
Dupo (G-8141)
Murray Cabinetry & Tops Inc....G....... 815 672-6992
Streator (G-19616)
Nelson - Harkins Inds Inc....E....... 773 478-6243
Lake Bluff (G-12199)
▲ New Age Surfaces LLC....G....... 630 226-0011
Romeoville (G-17861)
Northwest Marble Products....E....... 630 860-2288
Hoffman Estates (G-11473)
OGorman Son Carpentry Contrs....E....... 815 485-8997
New Lenox (G-15045)
Olsen Woodwork Co....G....... 847 865-5054
Island Lake (G-11610)
Omni Craft Inc....G....... 815 838-1285
Lockport (G-13017)
Pac Team US Productions LLC....G....... 773 360-8960
Chicago (G-5736)
Perfection Custom Closets & Co....F....... 847 647-6461
Niles (G-15156)
Prestige Distribution Inc....G....... 847 480-7667
Northbrook (G-15465)
Proto Productions Inc....E....... 630 628-6626
Addison (G-257)
Quantum Storage Systems....G....... 630 274-6610
Elk Grove Village (G-9206)
R & R Custom Cabinet Making....G....... 847 358-6188
Palatine (G-16152)
▲ Randal Wood Displays Inc....D....... 630 761-0400
Batavia (G-1409)
Rapp Cabinets & Woodworks Inc....F....... 618 736-2955
Dahlgren (G-7309)
Rays Countertop Shop Inc....F....... 217 483-2514
Glenarm (G-10427)
Redbox Workshop Ltd....E....... 773 478-7077
Chicago (G-5993)
Regency Custom Woodworking....F....... 815 689-2117
Cullom (G-7300)
Roncin Custom Design....G....... 847 669-0260
Huntley (G-11565)
Royal Fabricators Inc....F....... 847 775-7466
Wadsworth (G-20213)
Schrock Custom Woodworking....G....... 217 849-3375
Toledo (G-19877)
Shelving and Bath Unlimited....G....... 815 378-3328
Cherry Valley (G-3446)
Specialized Woodwork Inc....G....... 630 627-0450
Lombard (G-13131)
Stone Fabricators Company....G....... 847 788-8296
Arlington Heights (G-813)
Suburban Fabricators Inc....G....... 847 729-0866
Glenview (G-10627)
Suburban Fix & Installation....G....... 847 823-4047
Park Ridge (G-16298)
Suburban Laminating Inc....G....... 708 389-6106
Melrose Park (G-13918)
Surface Solutions Illinois Inc....G....... 708 571-3449
Mokena (G-14119)
Swan Surfaces LLC....C....... 618 532-5673
Centralia (G-3252)
Unistrut International Corp....D....... 630 773-3460
Addison (G-323)
Valley Custom Woodwork Inc....E....... 815 544-3939
Belvidere (G-1707)
Wilcor Solid Surface Inc....F....... 888 956-1001
Elk Grove Village (G-9309)
Wilson Kitchens Inc....D....... 618 253-7449
Harrisburg (G-11031)
Wind Point Partners Vi LP....G....... 312 255-4800
Chicago (G-6638)
Windy Hill Woodworking Inc....G....... 309 275-2415
Towanda (G-19893)
Woodhill Cabinetry Design Inc....G....... 815 431-0545
Ottawa (G-16086)
Woodworking Unlimited Inc....F....... 630 469-7023
Carol Stream (G-3089)
Ww Displays Inc....F....... 847 566-6979
Mundelein (G-14747)

2542 Partitions & Fixtures, Except Wood

◆ 555 International Inc....D....... 773 869-0555
Chicago (G-3476)
▲ Acco Brands Inc....A....... 847 541-9500
Lake Zurich (G-12373)
▲ Accurate Partitions Corp....G....... 708 442-6801
Burr Ridge (G-2649)
Acrylic Service Inc....G....... 630 543-0336
Addison (G-18)
Advert Display Products Inc....G....... 815 513-5432
Morris (G-14290)
◆ Alessco Inc....F....... 773 327-7919
Chicago (G-3602)
Apex Wire Products Company Inc....F....... 847 671-1830
Franklin Park (G-9871)
Armbrust Paper Tubes Inc....E....... 773 586-3232
Chicago (G-3730)
Art Wire Works Inc....F....... 708 458-3993
Bedford Park (G-1457)
Astoria Wire Products Inc....D....... 708 496-9950
Bedford Park (G-1459)
B-O-F Corporation....E....... 630 585-0020
Aurora (G-921)
Bar Stool Depotcom....G....... 815 727-7294
Joliet (G-11827)
Bark Project Management Inc....G....... 630 964-5876
Woodridge (G-21278)
Bel Mar Wire Products Inc....F....... 773 342-3800
Chicago (G-3861)
Bilt-Rite Metal Products Inc....E....... 815 495-2211
Leland (G-12547)
Bunzl Retail LLC....F....... 847 733-1469
Morton Grove (G-14392)
C-V Cstom Cntrtops Cbinets Inc....F....... 708 388-5066
Blue Island (G-2113)
Cameo Container Corporation....C....... 773 254-1030
Chicago (G-4011)
Capitol Carton Company....E....... 312 563-9690
Chicago (G-4017)
▲ Capitol Wood Works LLC....D....... 217 522-5553
Springfield (G-19341)
◆ Carl Stahl Decrcabl Innovtns I....F....... 312 474-1100
Burr Ridge (G-2660)
Central Sheet Metal Pdts Inc....E....... 773 583-2424
Skokie (G-18938)
▲ Chicago American Mfg LLC....C....... 773 376-0100
Chicago (G-4088)
◆ Colony Display LLC....E....... 847 426-5300
Elgin (G-8545)
Consolidated Displays Co Inc....G....... 630 851-8666
Oswego (G-15998)
Creative Metal Products....F....... 773 638-3200
Chicago (G-4264)
◆ Crown Metal Manufacturing Co....C....... 630 279-9800
Elmhurst (G-9355)
DAmico Associates Inc....G....... 847 291-7446
Northbrook (G-15373)
▲ Diversified Metal Products Inc....E....... 847 753-9595
Northbrook (G-15377)
Easyshow LLC....G....... 847 480-7177
Northbrook (G-15378)
Echelon Capital LLC....G....... 312 263-0263
Chicago (G-4445)
◆ Edsal Manufacturing Co LLC....A....... 773 475-3000
Chicago (G-4454)
Edsal Manufacturing Co LLC....C....... 773 475-3165
Chicago (G-4455)
Edsal Manufacturing Co LLC....C....... 773 475-3013
Chicago (G-4456)
Enclosures Inc....G....... 847 678-2020
Schiller Park (G-18803)
▲ Fixture Hardware Co....E....... 773 777-6100
Melrose Park (G-13867)
Fleetwood Fixtures....G....... 773 271-3390
Chicago (G-4601)
Forest City Counter Tops Inc....F....... 815 633-8602
Loves Park (G-13212)
Gerali Custom Design Inc....D....... 847 760-0500
Elgin (G-8593)
Harder Signs Inc....F....... 815 874-7777
Rockford (G-17443)
▲ HMC Holdings LLC....F....... 800 874-6625
Buffalo Grove (G-2547)
Igd Display LLC....F....... 630 916-0700
Downers Grove (G-8027)
Illinois Rack Enterprises Inc....E....... 815 385-5750
Lakemoor (G-12472)
Imperial Store Fixtures Inc....G....... 773 348-1137
Chicago (G-4901)
▲ IMS Engineered Products LLC....C....... 847 391-8100
Des Plaines (G-7787)
▼ Industrial Enclosure Corp....E....... 630 898-7499
Aurora (G-1111)
Innovative Mktg Solutions Inc....F....... 630 227-4300
Schaumburg (G-18561)
Inter-Market Inc....G....... 847 729-5330
Glenview (G-10570)
Interlake Mecalux Inc....C....... 815 844-7191
Pontiac (G-16772)
◆ Interlake Mecalux Inc....B....... 708 344-9999
Melrose Park (G-13883)
▲ Inventive Display Group LLC....F....... 847 588-1100
Niles (G-15134)
▲ Iretired LLC....E....... 630 285-9500
Itasca (G-11678)
Ivan Carlson Associates Inc....E....... 312 829-4616
Chicago (G-4979)
◆ Jbc Holding Co....G....... 217 347-7701
Effingham (G-8404)
Jet Rack Corp....E....... 773 586-2150
Chicago (G-5025)
John H Best & Sons Inc....E....... 309 932-2124
Galva (G-10234)
Kewaunee Scientific Corp....G....... 847 675-7744
Highland Park (G-11278)
Keystone Display Inc....D....... 815 648-2456
Hebron (G-11144)

S I C

Employee Codes: A=Over 500 employees, B=251-500
C=101-250, D=51-100, E=20-50, F=10-19, G=3-9
2020 Harris Illinois
Industrial Directory
845

25 FURNITURE AND FIXTURES

Klein Tools Inc .... D 847 228-6999
  Elk Grove Village *(G-9078)*
Klein Tools Inc .... E 847 821-5500
  Lincolnshire *(G-12779)*
L & D Group Inc .... B 630 892-8941
  Montgomery *(G-14252)*
Liam Brex .... G 630 848-0222
  Naperville *(G-14862)*
LL Display Group Ltd .... E 847 982-0231
  Chicago *(G-5244)*
▲ Lyon LLC .... C 630 892-8941
  Montgomery *(G-14258)*
Lyon LLC .... C 815 432-4595
  Watseka *(G-20309)*
Lyon LLC .... G 217 465-6321
  Paris *(G-16232)*
Lyon Workspace Products Inc .... G 630 892-8941
  Montgomery *(G-14259)*
Marmon Retail Technologies Co .... F 312 332-0317
  Chicago *(G-5346)*
◆ Marv-O-Lus Manufacturing Co ... F 773 826-1717
  Chicago *(G-5353)*
▲ Material Control Systems Inc .... D 309 523-3774
  East Moline *(G-8233)*
Material Control Systems Inc .... G 309 654-9031
  Cordova *(G-7009)*
▲ Metal Box International LLC ...... C 847 455-8500
  Franklin Park *(G-9994)*
▲ Middletons Mouldings Inc .... D 517 278-6610
  Schaumburg *(G-18629)*
◆ Midwest Custom Case Inc .... C 708 672-2900
  University Park *(G-19961)*
Multiplex Display Fixture Co .... E 800 325-3350
  Dupo *(G-8141)*
Murray Cabinetry & Tops Inc .... G 815 672-6992
  Streator *(G-19616)*
Nycor Products Inc .... G 815 727-9883
  Joliet *(G-11910)*
Proto Productions Inc .... E 630 628-6626
  Addison *(G-257)*
R B White Inc .... E 309 452-5816
  Normal *(G-15220)*
Rack Builders Inc .... G 217 214-9482
  Quincy *(G-16937)*
◆ REB Steel Equipment Corp .... E 773 252-0400
  Chicago *(G-5987)*
Rome Metal Mfg Inc .... G 773 287-1755
  Chicago *(G-6057)*
▲ Room Dividers Now LLC .... G 847 224-7900
  Barrington *(G-1242)*
Royal Fabricators Inc .... F 847 775-7466
  Wadsworth *(G-20213)*
RTC Industries Inc .... D 847 640-2400
  Chicago *(G-6075)*
Rwi Holdings Inc .... F 630 897-6951
  Aurora *(G-1150)*
Ryan Metal Products Inc .... E 815 936-0700
  Kankakee *(G-12000)*
▼ Schaumburg Specialties Co .... G 847 451-0070
  Schaumburg *(G-18706)*
▲ Southern Imperial Inc .... C 815 877-7041
  Rockford *(G-17637)*
T & D Metal Products LLC .... C 815 432-4938
  Watseka *(G-20318)*
Tesko Welding & Mfg Co .... D 708 452-0045
  Norridge *(G-15244)*
West Zwick Corp .... G 217 222-0228
  Quincy *(G-16955)*
Wilson Kitchens Inc .... D 618 253-7449
  Harrisburg *(G-11031)*
Wind Point Partners Vi LP .... G 312 255-4800
  Chicago *(G-6638)*
▲ Wiremasters Incorporated .... E 773 254-3700
  Chicago *(G-6649)*
Wm F Meyer Co .... E 773 772-7272
  Aurora *(G-1038)*
◆ Workspace Lyon Products LLC .. B 630 892-8941
  Montgomery *(G-14276)*
Ww Displays Inc .... F 847 566-6979
  Mundelein *(G-14747)*
▲ Yetter Manufacturing Company .. D 309 776-3222
  Colchester *(G-6948)*

2591 Drapery Hardware, Window Blinds & Shades

▲ 21st Century Us-Sino Services ... G 312 808-9328
  Chicago *(G-3464)*
9161 Corporation .... G 847 470-8828
  Niles *(G-15097)*
A B C Blind Inc .... G 708 877-7100
  Thornton *(G-19784)*
Aracon Drpery Vntian Blind Ltd .... G 773 252-1281
  Chicago *(G-3717)*
Baker Drapery Corporation .... G 309 691-3295
  Dunlap *(G-8132)*
Bills Shade & Blind Service .... G 773 493-5000
  Chicago *(G-3888)*
Carol Andrzejewski .... G 630 369-9711
  Naperville *(G-14790)*
Chicago Blind Company .... G 815 553-5525
  Joliet *(G-11839)*
Chicago Shade Makers Inc .... G 708 597-5590
  Alsip *(G-428)*
Custom Window Accents .... F 815 943-7651
  Harvard *(G-11051)*
Dezign Sewing Inc .... G 773 549-4336
  Chicago *(G-4349)*
Dons Drapery Service .... G 815 385-4759
  McHenry *(G-13737)*
Draperyland Inc .... G 630 521-1000
  Wood Dale *(G-21182)*
▲ EZ Blinds and Drapery Inc .... G 708 246-6600
  Westmont *(G-20742)*
◆ Fixture Hardware Co .... G 773 777-6100
  Melrose Park *(G-13867)*
Hansens Mfrs Win Coverings .... E 815 935-0010
  Bradley *(G-2284)*
House of Atlas LLC .... G 847 491-1800
  Evanston *(G-9536)*
J & J Inc of Illinois .... F 217 306-0787
  Greenview *(G-10823)*
Jack Beall Vertical Service In .... G 847 426-7958
  Abingdon *(G-10)*
Levolor Inc .... G 800 346-3278
  Oak Brook *(G-15633)*
Logoskirt Corporation .... F 773 584-7300
  Chicago *(G-5251)*
National Temp-Trol Products .... G 630 920-1919
  Willowbrook *(G-21053)*
◆ Newell Operating Company .... C 815 235-4171
  Freeport *(G-10129)*
Offsprings Inc .... G 773 525-1800
  Chicago *(G-5659)*
Ottos Drapery Service Inc .... G 773 777-7755
  Chicago *(G-5713)*
Regent Window Fashions LLC ...... G 773 871-6400
  Chicago *(G-6003)*
Roberts Draperies Center Inc .... G 847 255-4040
  Mount Prospect *(G-14567)*
Shade Aire Company .... G 815 623-7597
  Roscoe *(G-17933)*
Shade Brookline Co .... F 773 274-5513
  Chicago *(G-6145)*
UNI-Glide Corp .... G 773 235-2100
  Chicago *(G-6462)*
Unitex Industries Inc .... G 708 524-0664
  Oak Park *(G-15777)*
Vertical Tower Partner .... G 217 819-3040
  Champaign *(G-3364)*
▲ Woodbridge Inc .... F 847 229-1741
  Wheeling *(G-21015)*
Zirlin Interiors Inc .... E 773 334-5530
  Chicago *(G-6720)*
Znl Corporation .... G 815 654-0870
  Loves Park *(G-13284)*

2599 Furniture & Fixtures, NEC

3-Switch LLC .... G 217 721-4546
  Chicago *(G-3466)*
▲ Aero Products Holdings Inc ...... E 847 485-3200
  Schaumburg *(G-18429)*
▲ Akerue Industries LLC .... E 847 395-3300
  Antioch *(G-597)*
▲ Aline International LLC .... F 708 478-2471
  Mokena *(G-14069)*
◆ American Metalcraft Inc .... D 800 333-9133
  Franklin Park *(G-9866)*
Anderson & Marter Cabinets .... G 630 406-9840
  Batavia *(G-1349)*
Baker Elements Inc .... G 630 660-8100
  Oak Park *(G-15746)*
Be McGonagle Inc .... G 847 394-0413
  Arlington Heights *(G-704)*
Buhlwork Design Guild .... G 630 325-5340
  Oak Brook *(G-15601)*
Campeche Restaurant Inc .... G 815 776-9950
  Galena *(G-10166)*
Chicago Booth Mfg Inc .... F 773 378-8400
  Chicago *(G-4093)*
Classic Remix .... G 312 915-0521
  Chicago *(G-4170)*
▲ Co-Rect Products Inc .... E 763 542-9200
  Lincolnshire *(G-12751)*
Concord Cabinets Inc .... F 217 894-6507
  Clayton *(G-6909)*
Contract Industries Inc .... E 708 458-8150
  Bedford Park *(G-1464)*
Custom Wood & Laminate Ltd ...... G 815 727-4168
  Joliet *(G-11850)*
Display Plan Lpdg .... E 773 525-3787
  Chicago *(G-4366)*
E-J Industries Inc .... D 312 226-5023
  Chicago *(G-4427)*
◆ Edsal Manufacturing Co LLC ..... A 773 475-3000
  Chicago *(G-4454)*
Edsal Manufacturing Co LLC .... C 773 475-3165
  Chicago *(G-4455)*
Edsal Manufacturing Co LLC .... C 773 475-3013
  Chicago *(G-4456)*
◆ Euromarket Designs Inc .... A 847 272-2888
  Northbrook *(G-15386)*
▲ Fortune Brands Home & SEC Inc .. D 847 484-4400
  Deerfield *(G-7610)*
Glenview Custom Cabinets Inc .... G 847 345-5754
  Glenview *(G-10551)*
Haute Diggity Dawgs .... G 773 801-0195
  Chicago *(G-4786)*
Hylan Design Ltd .... G 312 243-7341
  Chicago *(G-4863)*
Jackhammer .... G 773 743-5772
  Chicago *(G-4997)*
Jeleniz .... G 217 235-6789
  Mattoon *(G-13639)*
Joe Anthony & Associates .... G 708 935-0804
  Richton Park *(G-17029)*
K K O Inc .... G 815 569-2324
  Capron *(G-2833)*
Kci Satellite .... G 800 664-2602
  Pittsfield *(G-16635)*
Kewaunee Scientific Corp .... G 847 675-7744
  Highland Park *(G-11278)*
▲ Kinsman Enterprises Inc .... G 618 932-3838
  West Frankfort *(G-20674)*
▲ Kreg Medical Inc .... E 312 829-8904
  Melrose Park *(G-13889)*
L & D Group Inc .... B 630 892-8941
  Montgomery *(G-14252)*
Lacava .... G 773 637-9600
  Chicago *(G-5153)*
Lena Mercantile .... F 815 369-9955
  Lena *(G-12603)*
M L Rongo Inc .... E 630 540-1120
  Bartlett *(G-1294)*
Marks Custom Seating .... G 630 980-8270
  Roselle *(G-17968)*
Mizrahi Grill .... F 847 831-1400
  Highland Park *(G-11284)*
Montauk Chicago Inc .... G 312 951-5688
  Chicago *(G-5493)*
▼ Mpd Medical Systems Inc .... G 815 477-0707
  Watseka *(G-20312)*
Muffys Inc .... G 815 433-6839
  Ottawa *(G-16063)*
◆ Norix Group Inc .... E 630 231-1331
  West Chicago *(G-20624)*
Perfection Custom Closets & Co .. F 847 647-6461
  Niles *(G-15156)*
Pollard Bros Mfg Co .... F 773 763-6868
  Chicago *(G-5834)*
Powerhouse Ent Inc .... G 312 877-4303
  Chicago *(G-5849)*
Precision Service .... G 618 345-2047
  Collinsville *(G-6972)*
▲ Railcraft Nexim Design .... G 309 937-2360
  Cambridge *(G-2806)*
Route 45 Wayside .... G 217 867-2000
  Pesotum *(G-16599)*
S L Fixtures Inc .... G 217 423-9907
  Decatur *(G-7545)*
Soni Mohnish .... G 312 473-7669
  Des Plaines *(G-7848)*
Sport Incentives Inc .... F 847 427-8650
  Elk Grove Village *(G-9250)*
Tads .... G 815 654-3500
  Loves Park *(G-13269)*
▼ Urban Wood Goods Ltd .... F 248 310-7668
  Gurnee *(G-10941)*
Vault Furniture Inc .... G 734 323-4166
  Chicago *(G-6525)*

Vinyl Life North .... G 630 906-9686
North Aurora *(G-15281)*
◆ Waco Manufacturing Co Inc .... F 312 733-0054
Chicago *(G-6582)*
Wag Industries Inc .... F 847 329-8932
Skokie *(G-19053)*
X Hale .... G 847 884-6250
Harwood Heights *(G-11113)*

26 PAPER AND ALLIED PRODUCTS

2611 Pulp Mills

Better Earth LLC .... G 844 243-6333
Chicago *(G-3874)*
Better Earth Premium Compost .... G 309 697-0963
Peoria *(G-16392)*
BFI Waste Systems N Amer Inc .... E 847 429-7370
Elgin *(G-8521)*
Buster Services Inc .... E 773 247-2070
Chicago *(G-3983)*
C & M Recycling Inc .... E 847 578-1066
North Chicago *(G-15308)*
Cicero Iron Metal & Paper Inc .... G 708 863-8601
Cicero *(G-6834)*
Coyote Transportation Inc .... G 630 204-5729
Bensenville *(G-1779)*
International Paper Company .... E 630 250-1300
Itasca *(G-11677)*
International Paper Company .... C 217 735-1221
Lincoln *(G-12731)*
J & I Resources LLC .... E 773 436-4028
Chicago *(G-4983)*
Kaskaskia Mechanical Insul Co .... G 618 768-4526
Mascoutah *(G-13601)*
Lake Area Disposal Service Inc .... E 217 522-9271
Springfield *(G-19397)*
M J Kull LLC .... G 217 246-5952
Lerna *(G-12614)*
ND Fairmont LLC .... G 937 328-3870
Oakbrook Terrace *(G-15810)*
Ohio Pulp Mills Inc .... F 312 337-7822
Chicago *(G-5665)*
Paper Moon Recycling Inc .... G 847 548-8875
Grayslake *(G-10795)*
◆ Profile Products LLC .... E 847 215-1144
Buffalo Grove *(G-2590)*
R & J Trucking and Recycl Inc .... F 708 563-2600
Chicago *(G-5943)*
Regenex Corp .... F 815 663-2003
Spring Valley *(G-19311)*
Tradebe Environmental Svcs LLC .... G 219 354-2452
Oak Brook *(G-15664)*
Tri State Recycling Service .... E 708 865-9939
Northlake *(G-15562)*
Westrock Cp LLC .... D 312 346-6600
Chicago *(G-6611)*
Weyerhaeuser Company .... D 630 778-7070
Naperville *(G-14947)*

2621 Paper Mills

Advantage Printing Inc .... G 630 627-7468
Lombard *(G-13036)*
Ahlstrm-Munksjo Filtration LLC .... D 217 824-9611
Taylorville *(G-19748)*
AIM Distribution Inc .... F 815 986-2770
Rockford *(G-17298)*
Alsip Minimill LLC .... F 708 625-0098
Alsip *(G-414)*
◆ Amcor Flexibles LLC .... C 224 313-7000
Buffalo Grove *(G-2510)*
▲ Amic Global Inc .... G 847 600-3590
Buffalo Grove *(G-2512)*
Ashleys Inc .... G 630 794-0804
Hinsdale *(G-11362)*
◆ Boise White Paper LLC .... F 847 482-3000
Lake Forest *(G-12232)*
Boise White Paper LLC .... F 208 805-1424
Lake Forest *(G-12233)*
Brahman Spirit Tribe .... F 773 957-2828
Chicago *(G-3942)*
Brothers Decorating .... G 815 648-2214
Hebron *(G-11139)*
Bunn-O-Matic Corporation .... E 562 926-0764
Springfield *(G-19332)*
Cellmark Inc .... G 630 775-9500
Bloomingdale *(G-1984)*
Chartwell Studio Inc .... G 847 868-8674
Chicago *(G-4077)*
▲ Colorkraft Roll Products Inc .... E 217 382-4967
Martinsville *(G-13582)*
Cowtan and Tout Inc .... F 312 644-0717
Chicago *(G-4251)*
▲ Danco Converting .... G 630 949-8112
Carol Stream *(G-2972)*
Deines-Nitz Solutions LLC .... E 309 658-9985
Erie *(G-9472)*
Dude Products Inc .... G 800 898-7304
Chicago *(G-4401)*
Essentra Corp .... G 814 899-7671
Westchester *(G-20697)*
◆ Essentra Packaging US Inc .... G 704 418-8692
Westchester *(G-20699)*
Evolution Sorbent Products LLC .... G 630 293-8055
West Chicago *(G-20578)*
◆ Evolution Sorbent Products LLC .... F 630 293-8055
West Chicago *(G-20579)*
Frankenstitch Promotions LLC .... F 847 459-4840
Wheeling *(G-20901)*
Georgia-Pacific LLC .... F 815 423-9990
Elwood *(G-9463)*
Hollingsworth & Vose Company .... G 847 222-9228
Arlington Heights *(G-750)*
Illinois Tool Works Inc .... G 847 657-4639
Glenview *(G-10561)*
Inservio3 LLC .... G 310 343-3486
Chicago *(G-4934)*
International Paper Company .... F 618 233-5460
Belleville *(G-1558)*
International Paper Company .... C 815 398-2100
Rockford *(G-17469)*
International Paper Company .... F 630 449-7200
Aurora *(G-985)*
International Paper Company .... F 630 653-3500
Carol Stream *(G-3005)*
International Paper Company .... E 847 390-1300
Des Plaines *(G-7788)*
International Paper Company .... C 847 228-7227
Elk Grove Village *(G-9057)*
International Paper Company .... C 630 585-3400
Aurora *(G-987)*
International Paper Company .... E 630 250-1300
Itasca *(G-11677)*
International Paper Company .... C 217 735-1221
Lincoln *(G-12731)*
IVEX Specialty Paper LLC .... E 309 686-3830
Peoria *(G-16461)*
K C Printing Services Inc .... F 847 382-8822
Lake Barrington *(G-12156)*
▼ Kapstone Kraft Paper Corp .... F 252 533-6000
Northbrook *(G-15411)*
▲ Kdm Enterprises LLC .... E 877 591-9768
Carpentersville *(G-3106)*
Kimberly-Clark Corporation .... D 312 371-5166
Deerfield *(G-7626)*
Kimberly-Clark Corporation .... C 815 886-7872
Romeoville *(G-17838)*
Kimberly-Clark Corporation .... G 847 885-1050
Chicago *(G-5103)*
Kimberly-Clark Corporation .... E 708 409-8500
Northlake *(G-15550)*
Lambert Print Source Llc .... G 630 708-0505
Yorkville *(G-21491)*
Lsc Communications Inc .... C 773 272-9200
Chicago *(G-5272)*
Lsc Communications Mm LLC .... F 815 844-1819
Chicago *(G-5273)*
Lsc Communications Us LLC .... B 844 572-5720
Chicago *(G-5274)*
Master Mechanic Mfg Inc .... G 847 573-3812
Mundelein *(G-14714)*
▲ Matt Pak Inc .... D 847 451-4018
Franklin Park *(G-9985)*
Meyer Enterprises LLC .... G 309 698-0062
East Peoria *(G-8278)*
◆ Midland Paper Company .... C 847 777-2700
Wheeling *(G-20941)*
▲ Midwest Converting Inc .... D 708 924-1510
Bedford Park *(G-1483)*
Mii Inc .... F 630 879-3000
Batavia *(G-1395)*
◆ ND Paper Inc .... G 513 200-0908
Oakbrook Terrace *(G-15811)*
ND Paper LLC .... F 937 528-3870
Oakbrook Terrace *(G-15812)*
Packaging Corporation America .... G 224 404-6616
Elk Grove Village *(G-9168)*
Pactiv Intl Holdings Inc .... G 847 482-2000
Lake Forest *(G-12278)*
Pactiv LLC .... C 217 479-1144
Jacksonville *(G-11779)*
Paper Investments LLC .... G 309 686-3830
Peoria *(G-16491)*
Paper Machine Services Inc .... G 608 365-8095
South Beloit *(G-19106)*
Paper Spot .... G 815 464-8533
Frankfort *(G-9820)*
Pen At Hand .... G 847 498-9174
Northbrook *(G-15458)*
Pontiac Recyclers Inc .... G 815 844-6419
Pontiac *(G-16777)*
Proofing Technologies Ltd .... G 847 222-7100
Rolling Meadows *(G-17768)*
Ripa LLC .... G 708 938-1600
Broadview *(G-2464)*
Roll Source Paper .... G 630 875-0308
Itasca *(G-11728)*
▲ S and K Packaging Incorporated .... G 563 582-8895
East Dubuque *(G-8181)*
◆ Simu Ltd .... F 708 688-2200
Mc Cook *(G-13701)*
Snow & Graham LLC .... G 773 665-9000
Winnetka *(G-21136)*
Stergo Roofing .... E 312 640-9008
Mount Prospect *(G-14572)*
Ted Muller .... G 312 435-0978
Chicago *(G-6336)*
▲ Transpac Usa Inc .... G 847 605-1616
Schaumburg *(G-18752)*
Tst/Impreso Inc .... G 630 775-9555
Addison *(G-320)*
▲ Upm-Kymmene Inc .... D 630 922-2500
Naperville *(G-14938)*
Voyager Enterprise Inc .... G 815 436-2431
Plainfield *(G-16727)*
W/S Packaging Group Inc .... G 847 658-7363
Algonquin *(G-393)*
Westrock Cp LLC .... G 847 625-8284
Waukegan *(G-20518)*
Westrock Cp LLC .... D 312 346-6600
Chicago *(G-6611)*
Westrock Rkt LLC .... A 312 346-6600
Chicago *(G-6614)*
Weyerhaeuser Company .... G 815 987-0395
Rockford *(G-17682)*

2631 Paperboard Mills

Accord Packaging LLC .... E 708 272-3050
Alsip *(G-411)*
Armbrust Paper Tubes Inc .... E 773 586-3232
Chicago *(G-3730)*
▲ Barrington Packaging Systems .... G 847 382-8063
Barrington *(G-1215)*
Campus Cardboard .... G 847 373-7673
Northbrook *(G-15351)*
Campus Cardboard .... G 847 251-2594
Skokie *(G-18936)*
Capitol Carton Company .... E 312 563-9690
Chicago *(G-4017)*
Caraustar Industries Inc .... E 773 308-7622
Chicago *(G-4022)*
Champion Container Corp .... D 630 530-1990
Wood Dale *(G-21175)*
Combined Technologies Inc .... G 847 968-4855
Libertyville *(G-12645)*
Gpi Midwest LLC .... E 847 741-0247
Elgin *(G-8599)*
Grafcor Packaging Inc .... F 815 639-2380
Loves Park *(G-13215)*
Grafcor Packaging Inc .... F 815 963-1300
Rockford *(G-17434)*
Graphic Packaging Corporation .... C 847 451-7400
Franklin Park *(G-9953)*
Graphic Packaging Intl LLC .... B 630 260-6500
Carol Stream *(G-2993)*
Graphic Packaging Intl LLC .... C 630 260-6500
Carol Stream *(G-2994)*
Igd Display LLC .... F 630 916-0700
Downers Grove *(G-8027)*
International Paper Company .... C 217 735-1221
Lincoln *(G-12731)*
Jsc Products Inc .... G 847 290-9520
Elk Grove Village *(G-9071)*
▲ Logan Graphic Products Inc .... D 847 526-5515
Wauconda *(G-20369)*
▲ Mac American Corporation .... G 847 277-9450
Barrington *(G-1226)*
Midwest Cortland Inc .... E 847 671-0376
Addison *(G-209)*
▲ Nefab Inc .... G 705 748-4888
Chicago *(G-5562)*

Ox Paperboard LLC E 309 346-4118
Pekin *(G-16348)*

◆ **Packaging Corporation America** C 847 482-3000
Lake Forest *(G-12277)*

PCA Central Cal Corrugated LLC G 847 482-3000
Lake Forest *(G-12283)*

Pekin Paperboard Company LP E 309 346-4118
Pekin *(G-16352)*

Pulver Inc E 847 734-9000
Elk Grove Village *(G-9202)*

▼ **Rjg Enterprises Ltd** G 847 752-2065
Grayslake *(G-10798)*

RTS Packaging LLC C 708 338-2800
Hillside *(G-11355)*

Sho Pak LLC G 618 876-1597
Venice *(G-20036)*

Signode Industrial Group LLC E 815 939-0033
Kankakee *(G-12003)*

Sonoco Products Company D 630 231-1489
West Chicago *(G-20644)*

Sonoco Prtective Solutions Inc D 847 398-0110
Arlington Heights *(G-811)*

Stevenson Paper Co Inc G 630 879-5000
Batavia *(G-1419)*

Tegrant Corporation D 630 879-0121
Batavia *(G-1428)*

▲ **The Calumet Carton Company** D 708 331-7910
South Holland *(G-19249)*

TMC Services Inc G 217 528-2297
Springfield *(G-19465)*

◆ **Transcontinental Holding Corp** G 773 877-3300
Chicago *(G-6410)*

Unofficial Cardboard Inc G 224 565-5391
Deerfield *(G-7655)*

UPS Store G 312 372-2727
Chicago *(G-6491)*

Westrock Converting LLC E 630 783-6700
Bolingbrook *(G-2254)*

Westrock Cp LLC D 630 443-3538
Saint Charles *(G-18299)*

Westrock Cp LLC G 773 254-1030
Chicago *(G-6610)*

Westrock Cp LLC E 630 924-0104
Bartlett *(G-1260)*

Westrock Cp LLC D 312 346-6600
Chicago *(G-6611)*

Westrock Cp LLC G 847 625-8284
Waukegan *(G-20518)*

Westrock Cp LLC D 708 458-5288
Bedford Park *(G-1513)*

Westrock Cp LLC C 309 342-0121
Galesburg *(G-10224)*

Westrock CP LLC G 773 264-3516
Chicago *(G-6612)*

Westrock Mwv LLC C 773 221-9015
Chicago *(G-6613)*

Westrock Mwv LLC E 217 442-2247
Danville *(G-7397)*

Westrock Mwv LLC C 630 289-8537
Bartlett *(G-1323)*

Westrock Rkt LLC A 312 346-6600
Chicago *(G-6614)*

2652 Set-Up Paperboard Boxes

Armbrust Paper Tubes Inc E 773 586-3232
Chicago *(G-3730)*

Bierdeman Box LLC E 847 256-0302
Wilmette *(G-21069)*

▲ **Colbert Packaging Corporation** C 847 367-5990
Lake Forest *(G-12238)*

▲ **Elegant Acquisition LLC** D 708 652-3400
Cicero *(G-6845)*

International Paper Company E 708 728-1000
Bedford Park *(G-1473)*

Jordan Paper Box Company F 773 287-5362
Chicago *(G-5048)*

Master Paper Box Company Inc C 773 927-0252
Chicago *(G-5358)*

Racine Paper Box Manufacturing E 773 227-3900
Chicago *(G-5958)*

Reddi-Pac Inc F 847 657-5222
Glenview *(G-10609)*

2653 Corrugated & Solid Fiber Boxes

A Trustworthy Sup Source Inc G 773 480-0255
Chicago *(G-3492)*

Akers Packaging Service Inc D 773 731-2900
Chicago *(G-3594)*

Akers Packaging Solutions Inc E 217 468-2396
Oreana *(G-15910)*

All-Pak Manufacturing Corp D 630 851-5859
Aurora *(G-1046)*

Alois Box Co Inc E 708 681-4090
Melrose Park *(G-13824)*

American Boxboard LLC E 708 924-9810
Batavia *(G-1348)*

Ameriguard Corporation G 630 986-1900
Burr Ridge *(G-2652)*

APAC Unlimited Inc G 847 441-4282
Northfield *(G-15505)*

Armbrust Paper Tubes Inc E 773 586-3232
Chicago *(G-3730)*

Batavia Container Inc C 630 879-2100
Batavia *(G-1355)*

Blackhawk Corrugated LLC E 844 270-2296
Carol Stream *(G-2948)*

Blackhawk Courtyards LLC G 416 298-8101
Carol Stream *(G-2949)*

Box Manufacturing Inc G 309 637-6228
Peoria *(G-16394)*

Box USA G 708 562-6000
Northlake *(G-15543)*

Cameo Container Corporation C 773 254-1030
Chicago *(G-4011)*

Cano Container Corporation E 630 585-7500
Aurora *(G-934)*

Capitol Carton Company E 312 563-9690
Chicago *(G-4017)*

Capitol Carton Company E 312 491-2220
Chicago *(G-4018)*

Cascades Plastics Inc E 450 469-3389
Aurora *(G-935)*

Combined Technologies Inc G 847 968-4855
Libertyville *(G-12645)*

Compak Inc E 815 399-2699
Machesney Park *(G-13335)*

Corr-Pak Corporation E 708 442-7806
Mc Cook *(G-13690)*

Corrugated Solutions LLC G 847 220-8348
Lake Forest *(G-12241)*

▲ **Corrugated Supplies Co LLC** E 708 458-5525
Bedford Park *(G-1465)*

Cross Container Corporation E 847 844-3200
Carpentersville *(G-3099)*

Custom Boxes Inc F 630 364-3944
Bolingbrook *(G-2162)*

D/C Export & Domestic Pkg Inc E 847 593-4200
Elk Grove Village *(G-8935)*

DDN Industries Inc G 847 885-8595
Hoffman Estates *(G-11417)*

Dexton Enterprises G 309 788-1881
Rock Island *(G-17217)*

Elm Street Industries Inc F 309 854-7000
Kewanee *(G-12032)*

Fca LLC E 309 949-3999
Coal Valley *(G-6936)*

Forest Packaging Corporation E 847 981-7000
Elk Grove Village *(G-9003)*

Georg-Pcific Corrugated IV LLC C 630 896-3610
Aurora *(G-967)*

Georgia-Pacific LLC C 217 999-2511
Mount Olive *(G-14503)*

Glass Haus G 815 459-5849
McHenry *(G-13746)*

Grafcor Packaging Inc F 815 639-2380
Loves Park *(G-13215)*

Graphic Packaging Intl LLC B 630 260-6500
Carol Stream *(G-2993)*

Green Bay Packaging Inc E 847 455-2553
Downers Grove *(G-8014)*

Greif Inc D 217 468-2396
Oreana *(G-15911)*

H Field & Sons Inc F 847 434-0970
Arlington Heights *(G-745)*

Harris Container Corp G 630 553-0027
Yorkville *(G-21488)*

Heritage Packaging LLC E 217 735-4406
Lincoln *(G-12730)*

▲ **Ideal Box Co** C 708 594-3100
Chicago *(G-4875)*

Illinois Valley Container Inc E 815 223-7200
Peru *(G-16578)*

Inglese Box Co Ltd E 847 669-1700
Huntley *(G-11543)*

International Paper Company C 708 728-8200
Chicago *(G-4954)*

International Paper Company C 630 896-2061
Montgomery *(G-14251)*

International Paper Company D 708 562-6000
Northlake *(G-15548)*

International Paper Company C 217 735-1221
Lincoln *(G-12731)*

International Paper Company C 630 585-3300
Aurora *(G-986)*

J H H of Illinois Inc F 630 293-0739
West Chicago *(G-20602)*

J Wallace & Associates Inc G 630 960-4221
Downers Grove *(G-8033)*

▼ **John J Monaco Products Co Inc** E 708 344-3333
Melrose Park *(G-13887)*

Jordan Paper Box Company F 773 287-5362
Chicago *(G-5048)*

Kindlon Enterprises Inc G 708 367-4000
Aurora *(G-994)*

Kodiak LLC E 248 545-7520
Chicago *(G-5115)*

Kodiak LLC E 773 284-9975
Chicago *(G-5116)*

Liberty Diversified Intl Inc E 217 935-8361
Clinton *(G-6925)*

Liberty Diversified Intl Inc C 309 787-6161
Rock Island *(G-17227)*

M and M Box Partition Co E 773 276-8400
Chicago *(G-5298)*

Menasha Corp G 630 679-8000
Bolingbrook *(G-2210)*

Menasha Packaging Company LLC G 630 263-4547
Champaign *(G-3320)*

Menasha Packaging Company LLC C 773 227-6000
Chicago *(G-5391)*

Menasha Packaging Company LLC B 312 880-4620
Chicago *(G-5392)*

Menasha Packaging Company LLC F 618 931-7805
Edwardsville *(G-8369)*

Menasha Packaging Company LLC C 630 236-4011
Aurora *(G-1130)*

Menasha Packaging Company LLC C 708 552-8946
Bridgeview *(G-2362)*

Menasha Packaging Company LLC C 618 501-6040
Edwardsville *(G-8370)*

Menasha Packaging Company LLC C 708 482-7619
Bolingbrook *(G-2211)*

Menasha Packaging Company LLC G 773 489-8332
Northbrook *(G-15432)*

Menasha Packaging Company LLC G 708 552-8946
Bridgeview *(G-2363)*

Menasha Packaging Company LLC C 312 880-4631
Bolingbrook *(G-2212)*

Menasha Packaging Company LLC B 630 391-1741
Minooka *(G-14062)*

Menasha Packaging Company LLC B 708 853-5450
Alsip *(G-476)*

Menasha Packaging Company LLC B 309 787-1747
Rock Island *(G-17229)*

Midwest Fibre Products Inc E 309 596-2955
Viola *(G-20180)*

Midwest Packaging & Cont Inc D 815 633-6800
Machesney Park *(G-13361)*

▲ **Murnane Specialties Inc** E 708 449-1200
Northlake *(G-15553)*

Murnane Specialties Inc F 708 449-1200
Geneva *(G-10291)*

▲ **Nation Inc** E 847 844-7300
Carpentersville *(G-3109)*

▲ **Ockerlund Industries Inc** E 630 620-1269
Addison *(G-230)*

Orora North America D 630 613-2600
Lombard *(G-13114)*

Orora Packaging Solutions D 815 895-2343
Sycamore *(G-19727)*

Packaging Corporation America F 847 388-6000
Mundelein *(G-14722)*

Packaging Corporation America D 708 821-1600
Chicago *(G-5739)*

Packaging Corporation America G 773 378-8700
Chicago *(G-5740)*

Packaging Corporation America D 708 594-5260
Bedford Park *(G-1489)*

Packaging Corporation America G 618 662-6700
Flora *(G-9687)*

◆ **Packaging Corporation America** C 847 482-3000
Lake Forest *(G-12277)*

Packaging Design Corporation E 630 323-1354
Burr Ridge *(G-2712)*

▲ **Pak Source Inc** E 309 786-7374
Rock Island *(G-17231)*

▲ **Patti Group Incorporated** F 630 243-6320
Lemont *(G-12579)*

PCA Central Cal Corrugated LLC G 847 482-3000
Lake Forest *(G-12283)*

◆ PCA Corrugated and Display LLC ....A....... 847 482-3000
Lake Forest *(G-12284)*
PCA International Inc ....G....... 847 482-3000
Lake Forest *(G-12285)*
Precision Die Cutting & Finish ....G....... 773 252-5625
Chicago *(G-5856)*
Pry-Bar Company ....F....... 815 436-3383
Joliet *(G-11918)*
▲ Reliable Container Inc ....E....... 630 543-6131
Addison *(G-269)*
Rex Carton Company Inc ....E....... 773 581-4115
Bridgeview *(G-2382)*
Royal Box Group LLC ....C....... 708 656-2020
Cicero *(G-6871)*
Royal Box Group LLC ....E....... 630 543-4464
Addison *(G-277)*
Royal Box Group LLC ....F....... 708 222-4650
Cicero *(G-6872)*
Rudd Container Corporation ....D....... 773 847-7600
Chicago *(G-6079)*
Ruscorr LLC ....G....... 708 458-5525
Bedford Park *(G-1500)*
SCI Box LLC ....E....... 618 244-7244
Mount Vernon *(G-14637)*
Simon Box Mfg Co ....G....... 815 722-6661
Lockport *(G-13023)*
Sisco Corporation ....E....... 618 327-3066
Nashville *(G-15010)*
Sonoco Display & Packaging LLC ....F....... 630 789-1111
Westmont *(G-20773)*
Sonoco Products Company ....D....... 630 231-1489
West Chicago *(G-20644)*
Specialty Box Corp ....F....... 630 897-7278
North Aurora *(G-15277)*
Stand Fast Group LLC ....D....... 630 600-0900
Carol Stream *(G-3075)*
Sterling Box Company Inc ....F....... 815 626-9657
Sterling *(G-19534)*
Stitch TEC Co Inc ....G....... 618 327-8054
Nashville *(G-15011)*
▲ Strive Converting Corporation ....C....... 773 227-6000
Chicago *(G-6254)*
Sun Container Inc ....G....... 417 681-0503
Mount Vernon *(G-14641)*
▲ The Calumet Carton Company ....D....... 708 331-7910
South Holland *(G-19249)*
Thomas Glenn Holdings LLC ....E....... 630 916-8090
Lombard *(G-13144)*
Tri-City Corrugated Inc ....F....... 630 372-6200
Bartlett *(G-1317)*
United Container Corporation ....E....... 773 342-2200
Chicago *(G-6471)*
Vangard Distribution Inc ....G....... 708 484-9895
Berwyn *(G-1962)*
▲ Vangard Distribution Inc ....G....... 708 588-8400
Brookfield *(G-2497)*
Wabash Container Corporation ....E....... 618 263-3586
Mount Carmel *(G-14491)*
Wehrle Lumber Co Inc ....F....... 618 283-4859
Vandalia *(G-20030)*
Welch Packaging Group Inc ....E....... 815 547-1505
Belvidere *(G-1710)*
Westrock Container LLC ....D....... 847 239-8800
Northbrook *(G-15501)*
Westrock Converting LLC ....E....... 618 709-5284
Edwardsville *(G-8379)*
Westrock Cp LLC ....C....... 309 342-0121
Galesburg *(G-10224)*
Westrock Cp LLC ....C....... 847 689-4200
North Chicago *(G-15324)*
Westrock Cp LLC ....C....... 618 654-2141
Highland *(G-11248)*
Westrock Cp LLC ....D....... 708 458-8100
Bridgeview *(G-2399)*
Westrock Cp LLC ....D....... 630 384-5200
Carol Stream *(G-3087)*
Westrock Cp LLC ....D....... 708 458-5288
Bedford Park *(G-1513)*
Westrock Rkt LLC ....E....... 815 756-8913
Dekalb *(G-7713)*
Westrock Rkt LLC ....E....... 630 325-9670
Burr Ridge *(G-2734)*
Westrock Rkt LLC ....C....... 630 429-2400
Aurora *(G-1170)*
Westrock Rkt LLC ....A....... 312 346-6600
Chicago *(G-6614)*
Weyerhaeuser Company ....C....... 847 439-1111
Elk Grove Village *(G-9307)*
York Corrugated Container Corp ....D....... 630 260-2900
Glendale Heights *(G-10516)*

2655 Fiber Cans, Tubes & Drums

Advantage Structures LLC ....G....... 773 734-9305
Chicago *(G-3570)*
Armbrust Paper Tubes Inc ....E....... 773 586-3232
Chicago *(G-3730)*
Capitol Carton Company ....E....... 312 563-9690
Chicago *(G-4017)*
Caraustar Industrial and Con ....D....... 217 323-5225
Beardstown *(G-1446)*
▲ Chicago Mailing Tube Company ....E....... 312 243-6050
Chicago *(G-4112)*
Fibre Drum Company ....E....... 815 933-3222
Kankakee *(G-11971)*
G T Express Ltd ....G....... 708 338-0303
River Grove *(G-17060)*
Greif Inc ....E....... 708 371-4777
Alsip *(G-450)*
Greif Inc ....E....... 630 753-1859
Naperville *(G-14836)*
Greif Inc ....E....... 630 961-1842
Naperville *(G-14837)*
Illiana Cores Inc ....E....... 618 586-9800
Palestine *(G-16178)*
Paper Tube LLC ....G....... 847 477-0563
Wheeling *(G-20956)*
Polynt Composites II LLC ....G....... 847 428-2657
Carpentersville *(G-3113)*
Precision Paper Tube Company ....C....... 847 537-4250
Wheeling *(G-20965)*
Resinite Corporation ....C....... 847 537-4250
Wheeling *(G-20973)*
▲ Rolled Edge Inc ....E....... 773 283-9500
Chicago *(G-6054)*
Sonoco Products Company ....D....... 630 231-1489
West Chicago *(G-20644)*
Staffco Inc ....G....... 309 688-3223
Peoria *(G-16528)*
TJ Assemblies Inc ....E....... 847 671-0060
Bensenville *(G-1902)*

2656 Sanitary Food Containers

▲ Best Diamond Plastics LLC ....F....... 773 336-3485
Chicago *(G-3871)*
Box Form Inc ....E....... 773 927-8808
Chicago *(G-3938)*
▼ Earthgrains Refrigertd Dough P ....A....... 630 455-5200
Downers Grove *(G-7996)*
International Paper Company ....C....... 217 735-1221
Lincoln *(G-12731)*
Pactiv LLC ....C....... 219 924-4120
Lake Forest *(G-12280)*
Pactiv LLC ....C....... 630 262-6335
Saint Charles *(G-18241)*

2657 Folding Paperboard Boxes

Accord Carton Co ....C....... 708 272-3050
Alsip *(G-410)*
Americraft Carton ....G....... 630 225-7311
Oak Brook *(G-15593)*
Arbor Private Inv Co LLC ....G....... 312 981-3770
Chicago *(G-3718)*
Box Form Inc ....E....... 773 927-8808
Chicago *(G-3938)*
Capitol Carton Company ....E....... 312 563-9690
Chicago *(G-4017)*
▲ Colbert Packaging Corporation ....C....... 847 367-5990
Lake Forest *(G-12238)*
Combined Technologies Inc ....G....... 847 968-4855
Libertyville *(G-12645)*
Gpi Midwest LLC ....E....... 847 741-0247
Elgin *(G-8599)*
Graphic Packaging Intl LLC ....D....... 618 533-2721
Centralia *(G-3233)*
Graphic Packaging Intl LLC ....B....... 630 260-6500
Carol Stream *(G-2993)*
H Field & Sons Inc ....F....... 847 434-0970
Arlington Heights *(G-745)*
Impac Group Inc ....A....... 708 344-9100
Melrose Park *(G-13881)*
Jordan Paper Box Company ....F....... 773 287-5362
Chicago *(G-5048)*
▲ Knight Paper Box Company ....D....... 773 585-2035
Bridgeview *(G-2360)*
▲ Lbp Manufacturing LLC ....B....... 800 545-6200
Cicero *(G-6863)*
Master Paper Box Company Inc ....C....... 773 927-0252
Chicago *(G-5358)*
▲ MB Box Inc ....G....... 815 589-3043
Fulton *(G-10155)*

Midwest Fibre Products Inc ....E....... 309 596-2955
Viola *(G-20180)*
▲ Nosco Inc ....B....... 847 336-4200
Gurnee *(G-10904)*
Nosco Inc ....D....... 847 360-4874
Waukegan *(G-20471)*
▲ P S Greetings Inc ....C....... 708 831-5340
Chicago *(G-5729)*
Pactiv LLC ....C....... 630 262-6335
Saint Charles *(G-18241)*
▲ Plasticrest Products Inc ....F....... 773 826-2163
Chicago *(G-5818)*
Pure Skin LLC ....G....... 217 679-6267
Springfield *(G-19431)*
Racine Paper Box Manufacturing ....E....... 773 227-3900
Chicago *(G-5958)*
Rex Carton Company Inc ....E....... 773 581-4115
Bridgeview *(G-2382)*
Specialty Box Corp ....F....... 630 897-7278
North Aurora *(G-15277)*
▲ The Calumet Carton Company ....D....... 708 331-7910
South Holland *(G-19249)*
United Press Inc ....F....... 847 482-0597
Lincolnshire *(G-12799)*
Westrock Cp LLC ....C....... 309 342-0121
Galesburg *(G-10224)*

2671 Paper Coating & Laminating for Packaging

Acorn Diversified Inc ....F....... 708 478-1051
Orland Park *(G-15933)*
Allegra Print & Imaging Inc ....G....... 847 697-1434
Elgin *(G-8502)*
◆ Amcor Flexibles LLC ....C....... 224 313-7000
Buffalo Grove *(G-2510)*
American Graphics Network Inc ....F....... 847 729-7220
Glenview *(G-10522)*
American Name Plate & Metal De ....E....... 773 376-1400
Chicago *(G-3663)*
Ampac Flexicon LLC ....E....... 630 439-3160
Hanover Park *(G-10998)*
Ampac Flexicon LLC ....G....... 952 541-0730
Hanover Park *(G-10999)*
▲ Ampac Flexicon LLC ....D....... 847 639-3530
Cary *(G-3147)*
Applied Products Inc ....E....... 815 633-3825
Machesney Park *(G-13327)*
Arbor Private Inv Co LLC ....G....... 312 981-3770
Chicago *(G-3718)*
Arcadia Press Inc ....F....... 847 451-6390
Franklin Park *(G-9872)*
Avery Dnnson Ret Info Svcs LLC ....G....... 626 304-2000
Chicago *(G-3787)*
AZ Plastics Inc ....G....... 773 679-0988
Chicago *(G-3798)*
AZ Plastics Inc ....E....... 773 679-0988
Chicago *(G-3799)*
B & B Printing Company ....G....... 217 285-6072
Pittsfield *(G-16628)*
◆ Bagcraftpapercon I LLC ....C....... 620 856-2800
Chicago *(G-3814)*
Bagcraftpapercon II LLC ....A....... 773 843-8000
Chicago *(G-3815)*
▲ Bema Inc ....D....... 630 279-7800
Elmhurst *(G-9331)*
Bucktown Polymers ....G....... 312 436-1460
Chicago *(G-3971)*
Burgopak Limited ....E....... 312 255-0827
Chicago *(G-3976)*
▲ Daubert Cromwell LLC ....E....... 708 293-7750
Alsip *(G-439)*
Deco Adhesive Pdts 1985 Ltd ....E....... 847 472-2100
Elk Grove Village *(G-8941)*
Dresbach Distributing Co ....G....... 815 223-0116
Peru *(G-16574)*
Elite Extrusion Technology Inc ....G....... 630 485-2020
Saint Charles *(G-18195)*
Ennis Inc ....E....... 815 875-2000
Princeton *(G-16808)*
Farm Plastic Supply Inc ....G....... 312 625-1024
Itasca *(G-11654)*
Fisher Container Holdings LLC ....G....... 847 541-0000
Buffalo Grove *(G-2537)*
Flex-O-Glass Inc ....E....... 815 288-1424
Dixon *(G-7899)*
▲ General Packaging Products Inc ....D....... 312 226-5611
Chicago *(G-4675)*
▲ H S Crocker Company Inc ....D....... 847 669-3600
Huntley *(G-11538)*

S I C

Hanlon Group Ltd G 773 525-3666
Chicago *(G-4778)*
Hexacomb Corporation G 847 955-7984
Buffalo Grove *(G-2546)*
Iam Acquisition LLC E 847 259-7800
Wheeling *(G-20912)*
Illinois Tag Co E 773 626-0542
Carol Stream *(G-3001)*
Label Graphics Co Inc F 815 648-2478
Hebron *(G-11145)*
▲ Labels & Specialty Pdts LLC E 630 513-8060
Saint Charles *(G-18223)*
Labels Unlimited Incorporated E 773 523-7500
Chicago *(G-5152)*
Lasons Label Co G 773 775-2606
Chicago *(G-5179)*
MEI LLC G 630 285-1505
Itasca *(G-11699)*
Midwest Lminating Coatings Inc E 708 653-9500
Alsip *(G-478)*
Miller Products Inc E 708 534-5111
University Park *(G-19962)*
Miracle Press Company F 773 722-6176
Chicago *(G-5467)*
▲ Morcor Industries Inc G 224 293-2000
Elgin *(G-8664)*
Multi Packaging Solutions Inc G 773 283-9500
Chicago *(G-5523)*
▲ Nation Inc E 847 844-7300
Carpentersville *(G-3109)*
No Surrender Inc F 773 929-7920
Chicago *(G-5607)*
Noor International Inc G 847 985-2300
Bartlett *(G-1256)*
Nosco Inc D 847 360-4874
Waukegan *(G-20471)*
Odra Inc G 847 249-2910
Gurnee *(G-10906)*
Pdoc LLC C 773 843-8000
Chicago *(G-5774)*
Pelican Holdco LLC F 847 597-2200
Deerfield *(G-7642)*
Perryco Inc F 815 436-2431
Plainfield *(G-16701)*
▲ Petra Manufacturing Co D 773 622-1475
Chicago *(G-5797)*
Phoenix Converting Inc D 630 258-1500
Itasca *(G-11718)*
Photo Techniques Corp E 630 690-9360
Carol Stream *(G-3046)*
▼ Pioneer Labels Inc C 618 546-5418
Robinson *(G-17121)*
Polyair Inter Pack Inc D 773 995-1818
Chicago *(G-5838)*
▲ Ppc Flexible Packaging LLC C 847 541-0000
Buffalo Grove *(G-2588)*
Preferred Printing Service G 312 421-2343
Chicago *(G-5861)*
Pregis Innovative Packg LLC E 847 597-2200
Deerfield *(G-7643)*
Pregis LLC A 847 597-2200
Deerfield *(G-7645)*
Prime Label & Packaging LLC D 630 227-1300
Wood Dale *(G-21231)*
Prime Label Group LLC G 773 630-8793
Batavia *(G-1405)*
Printpack Inc C 847 888-7150
Elgin *(G-8696)*
▲ Pro-Pak Industries Inc F 630 876-1050
West Chicago *(G-20633)*
Quality Bags Inc F 630 543-9800
Addison *(G-260)*
R R Donnelley & Sons Company D 630 762-7600
Saint Charles *(G-18258)*
▲ Rapak LLC C 630 296-2000
Romeoville *(G-17868)*
RTC Industries Inc D 847 640-2400
Chicago *(G-6075)*
▲ Selig Sealing Products Inc G 815 785-2100
Forrest *(G-9737)*
▲ Seshin USA Inc G 847 550-5556
Lake Zurich *(G-12456)*
Signature Label of Illinois G 618 283-5145
Vandalia *(G-20024)*
▲ Signode Industrial Group LLC E 847 724-7500
Glenview *(G-10618)*
Signode Industrial Group LLC E 847 724-6100
Glenview *(G-10620)*
Signode Intl Holdings LLC F 800 648-8864
Glenview *(G-10621)*
◆ Stepac USA Corporation G 630 296-2000
Romeoville *(G-17877)*
Stephen Fossler Company D 847 635-7200
Des Plaines *(G-7852)*
Tetra Pak Inc D 847 955-6000
Vernon Hills *(G-20103)*
TLC Dental Care LLC G 425 442-9000
Elgin *(G-8755)*
Triumph Packaging Georgia LLC E 312 251-9600
Lake Forest *(G-12316)*
Triumph Packaging Group E 312 251-9600
Lake Forest *(G-12317)*
UNI-Label and Tag Corporation E 847 956-8900
Elk Grove Village *(G-9294)*
Waxstar Inc G 708 755-3530
S Chicago Hts *(G-18129)*
◆ Westrock Cnsmr Packg Group LLC A 804 444-1000
Melrose Park *(G-13928)*
◆ Winpak Portion Packaging Inc D 708 753-5700
Sauk Village *(G-18401)*
World Contract Packagers Inc G 815 624-6501
South Beloit *(G-19126)*
▲ Xshredders Inc D 847 205-1875
Northbrook *(G-15503)*

2672 Paper Coating & Laminating, Exc for Packaging

Acco Brands Corporation A 847 541-9500
Lake Zurich *(G-12374)*
Acco Brands International Inc G 847 541-9500
Lake Zurich *(G-12375)*
Advanced Web Technologies LLC E 847 985-3833
South Elgin *(G-19129)*
American Name Plate & Metal De E 773 376-1400
Chicago *(G-3663)*
Arcadia Press Inc F 847 451-6390
Franklin Park *(G-9872)*
Avery Dennison Corporation C 847 824-7450
Mount Prospect *(G-14513)*
Avery Dennison Corporation D 877 214-0909
Niles *(G-15104)*
Avery Dennison Rfid Company F 626 304-2000
Chicago *(G-3786)*
Basswood Associates Inc F 312 240-9400
Chicago *(G-3845)*
Bisco Intl Inc G 708 544-6308
Hillside *(G-11331)*
Brasel Products Inc G 630 879-3759
Batavia *(G-1360)*
▲ Budnick Converting Inc C 618 281-8090
Columbia *(G-6986)*
◆ Channeled Resources Inc E 312 733-4200
Chicago *(G-4069)*
Chase Corporation E 847 866-8500
Evanston *(G-9503)*
Citadel Specialty Products Inc G 630 820-4134
Aurora *(G-939)*
Classique Signs & Engrv Inc G 217 228-7446
Quincy *(G-16872)*
Condor Labels Inc G 708 429-0707
Palos Park *(G-16209)*
▲ Continental Datalabel Inc C 847 742-1600
Elgin *(G-8552)*
Cushing and Company E 312 266-8228
Chicago *(G-4287)*
Cypress Multigraphics LLC E 708 633-1166
Tinley Park *(G-19820)*
Daubert Vci Inc F 630 203-6800
Burr Ridge *(G-2668)*
Fedex Office & Print Svcs Inc F 847 329-9464
Lincolnwood *(G-12819)*
Fedex Office & Print Svcs Inc E 309 685-4093
Peoria *(G-16437)*
Gallas Label & Decal F 773 775-1000
Chicago *(G-4656)*
General Laminating Company G 847 639-8770
Cary *(G-3164)*
▲ H S Crocker Company Inc D 847 669-3600
Huntley *(G-11538)*
◆ Highland Supply Corporation B 618 654-2161
Highland *(G-11224)*
◆ Holden Industries Inc F 847 940-1500
Deerfield *(G-7616)*
▲ Hollymatic Corporation D 708 579-3700
Countryside *(G-7057)*
Hugh Courtright & Co Ltd F 708 534-8400
Monee *(G-14202)*
Identco International Corp D 815 385-0011
Ingleside *(G-11584)*
Intertape Polymer Corp D 618 549-2131
Carbondale *(G-2847)*
J & D Instant Signs G 847 965-2800
Morton Grove *(G-14414)*
Keneal Industries Inc F 815 886-1300
Romeoville *(G-17837)*
Knight Prtg & Litho Svc Ltd G 847 487-7700
Island Lake *(G-11609)*
L & S Label Printing Inc G 815 964-6753
Cherry Valley *(G-3443)*
Label Graphics Co Inc F 815 648-2478
Hebron *(G-11145)*
Label Tek Inc F 630 820-8499
Aurora *(G-995)*
Labels Unlimited Incorporated E 773 523-7500
Chicago *(G-5152)*
Lasons Label Co G 773 775-2606
Chicago *(G-5179)*
Line Craft Inc F 630 932-1182
Lombard *(G-13095)*
M & R Graphics Inc F 708 534-6621
University Park *(G-19957)*
Mich Enterprises Inc F 630 616-9000
Wood Dale *(G-21216)*
Midwest Lminating Coatings Inc E 708 653-9500
Alsip *(G-478)*
Miller Products Inc E 708 534-5111
University Park *(G-19962)*
National Data-Label Corp E 630 616-9595
Bensenville *(G-1856)*
Navitor Inc B 800 323-0253
Harwood Heights *(G-11106)*
Noor International Inc G 847 985-2300
Bartlett *(G-1256)*
Nosco Inc D 847 360-4874
Waukegan *(G-20471)*
▼ Pioneer Labels Inc C 618 546-5418
Robinson *(G-17121)*
▲ Plitek LLC D 847 827-6680
Des Plaines *(G-7827)*
Prairie State Graphics Inc D 847 801-3100
Franklin Park *(G-10022)*
▲ Prairie State Impressions LLC D 847 801-3100
Franklin Park *(G-10023)*
Preferred Printing Service G 312 421-2343
Chicago *(G-5861)*
Primedia Source LLC G 630 553-8451
Yorkville *(G-21499)*
Print-O-Tape Inc E 847 362-1476
Mundelein *(G-14729)*
Printing Etc Inc G 815 562-6151
Rochelle *(G-17152)*
Pro Patch Systems Inc G 847 356-8100
Lake Villa *(G-12364)*
Protex Products LLC G 312 292-1310
Chicago *(G-5906)*
Punch Products Manufacturing E 773 533-2800
Chicago *(G-5915)*
Qualified Innovation Inc F 630 556-4136
Sugar Grove *(G-19651)*
▲ Rjm Manufacturing Inc D 215 736-3644
Carbondale *(G-2856)*
Service Packaging Design Inc G 847 966-6592
Morton Grove *(G-14440)*
Sheer Graphics Inc G 630 654-4422
Westmont *(G-20772)*
Signature Label of Illinois G 618 283-5145
Vandalia *(G-20024)*
Signcraft Screenprint Inc C 815 777-3030
Galena *(G-10178)*
Specialty Tape & Label Co Inc E 708 863-3800
Lyons *(G-13313)*
Stephen Fossler Company D 847 635-7200
Des Plaines *(G-7852)*
▲ Strata-Tac Inc F 630 879-9388
Saint Charles *(G-18279)*
▲ Tek Pak Inc D 630 406-0560
Batavia *(G-1429)*
Upm Raflatac Inc C 815 285-6100
Dixon *(G-7924)*
Voss Belting & Specialty Co E 847 673-8900
Lincolnwood *(G-12849)*
◆ Weber Marking Systems Inc B 847 364-8500
Arlington Heights *(G-831)*
William Holloway Ltd G 847 866-9520
Evanston *(G-9588)*
▲ Zebra Technologies Corporation B 847 634-6700
Lincolnshire *(G-12804)*
▲ Zih Corp G 847 634-6700
Lincolnshire *(G-12807)*

SIC SECTION

26 PAPER AND ALLIED PRODUCTS

2673 Bags: Plastics, Laminated & Coated

Aargus Industries Inc ..... G ..... 847 325-4444 Wheeling *(G-20836)*
▲ Aargus Plastics Inc ..... C ..... 847 325-4444 Wheeling *(G-20837)*
▲ ABG Bag Inc ..... F ..... 815 963-9525 Rockford *(G-17286)*
Advanced Custom Shapes ..... F ..... 618 684-2222 Murphysboro *(G-14749)*
Bag and Barrier Corporation ..... G ..... 217 849-3271 Toledo *(G-19874)*
◆ Bagcraftpapercon I LLC ..... C ..... 620 856-2800 Chicago *(G-3814)*
◆ Bagmakers Inc ..... B ..... 815 923-2247 Union *(G-19937)*
Bio Industries Inc ..... D ..... 847 215-8999 Wheeling *(G-20859)*
Closet Concept ..... G ..... 217 375-4214 Milford *(G-14033)*
▲ Colonial Bag Corporation ..... D ..... 630 690-3999 Carol Stream *(G-2965)*
▲ Diamond Cellophane Pdts Inc ..... E ..... 847 418-3000 Northbrook *(G-15375)*
Drumheller Bag Corporation ..... D ..... 309 676-1006 Peoria *(G-16431)*
Duro Bag Manufacturing Company ..... D ..... 708 385-8674 Alsip *(G-443)*
▲ E-Z Products Inc ..... F ..... 847 551-9199 Gilberts *(G-10354)*
▲ Engineered Materials Inc ..... G ..... 847 821-8280 Buffalo Grove *(G-2534)*
Envision Inc ..... G ..... 847 735-0789 Lake Forest *(G-12246)*
◆ Essentra Packaging US Inc ..... G ..... 704 418-8692 Westchester *(G-20699)*
◆ Fischer Paper Products Inc ..... D ..... 847 395-6060 Antioch *(G-611)*
Fisher Container Holdings LLC ..... G ..... 847 541-0000 Buffalo Grove *(G-2537)*
Flex-O-Glass Inc ..... C ..... 773 261-5200 Chicago *(G-4605)*
◆ Foodhandler Inc ..... F ..... 866 931-3613 Elk Grove Village *(G-9002)*
◆ Highland Supply Corporation ..... B ..... 618 654-2161 Highland *(G-11224)*
▲ Isbir Bulk Bag Usa LLC ..... G ..... 972 722-9200 Warrenville *(G-20239)*
▲ Jacobson Acqstion Holdings LLC ..... C ..... 847 623-1414 Waukegan *(G-20452)*
▲ Kam Group Inc ..... F ..... 630 679-9668 Bolingbrook *(G-2200)*
Kapak Company LLC ..... G ..... 952 541-0730 Hanover Park *(G-11008)*
Keenpac LLC ..... F ..... 845 291-8680 Morton Grove *(G-14417)*
▲ Keenpac LLC ..... G ..... 845 291-8680 Morton Grove *(G-14418)*
Kleer Pak Mfg Co Inc ..... E ..... 630 543-0208 Addison *(G-171)*
▲ Laminet Cover Company ..... E ..... 773 622-6700 Chicago *(G-5171)*
Morris Packaging LLC ..... G ..... 309 663-9100 Bloomington *(G-2081)*
Natural Packaging Inc ..... G ..... 708 246-3420 La Grange *(G-12083)*
P-S Business Acquisition Inc ..... G ..... 616 887-8837 Carol Stream *(G-3044)*
Pactiv Intl Holdings Inc ..... G ..... 847 482-2000 Lake Forest *(G-12278)*
Pactiv LLC ..... C ..... 708 924-2402 Bridgeview *(G-2372)*
Pactiv LLC ..... C ..... 815 469-2112 Frankfort *(G-9819)*
Pactiv LLC ..... C ..... 217 479-1144 Jacksonville *(G-11779)*
◆ Pactiv LLC ..... A ..... 847 482-2000 Lake Forest *(G-12279)*
▲ Pak Source Inc ..... E ..... 309 786-7374 Rock Island *(G-17231)*
Peelmaster Packaging Corp ..... E ..... 847 966-6161 Niles *(G-15155)*
Plastics D-E-F ..... G ..... 312 226-4337 Chicago *(G-5819)*
◆ Pliant LLC ..... A ..... 812 424-2904 Rolling Meadows *(G-17761)*
Poly Plastics Films Corp ..... G ..... 815 636-0821 Machesney Park *(G-13365)*
Polytech Inc ..... G ..... 806 338-2008 Chicago *(G-5840)*
▲ Ppc Flexible Packaging LLC ..... C ..... 847 541-0000 Buffalo Grove *(G-2588)*
Pregis LLC ..... A ..... 847 597-2200 Deerfield *(G-7645)*
Pride Packaging LLC ..... G ..... 309 663-9100 Bloomington *(G-2086)*
Printpack Inc ..... C ..... 847 888-7150 Elgin *(G-8696)*
▲ Procon Pacific LLC ..... F ..... 630 575-0551 Lombard *(G-13122)*
Quality Bags Inc ..... F ..... 630 543-9800 Addison *(G-260)*
R Popernik Co Inc ..... F ..... 773 434-4300 Chicago *(G-5949)*
▲ Recycling Solutions Inc ..... E ..... 773 617-6955 Chicago *(G-5992)*
◆ Renew Packaging LLC ..... G ..... 312 421-6699 Chicago *(G-6014)*
Reynolds Consumer Products Inc ..... A ..... 800 879-5067 Lake Forest *(G-12296)*
Silgan Plastics LLC ..... D ..... 618 662-4471 Flora *(G-9692)*
◆ Transcontinental Holding Corp ..... G ..... 773 877-3300 Chicago *(G-6410)*
Transcontinental Tech LLC ..... G ..... 877 447-3539 Chicago *(G-6411)*
Vej Holdings LLC ..... G ..... 630 219-1598 Naperville *(G-14940)*
▼ Vilutis and Co Inc ..... E ..... 815 469-2116 Frankfort *(G-9849)*
Waxstar Inc ..... G ..... 708 755-3530 S Chicago Hts *(G-18129)*
Windy Polymers Inc ..... G ..... 630 272-7453 Saint Charles *(G-18300)*

2674 Bags: Uncoated Paper & Multiwall

Bag and Barrier Corporation ..... G ..... 217 849-3271 Toledo *(G-19874)*
◆ Bagcraftpapercon I LLC ..... C ..... 620 856-2800 Chicago *(G-3814)*
◆ Bagmakers Inc ..... B ..... 815 923-2247 Union *(G-19937)*
Duro Bag Manufacturing Company ..... D ..... 708 385-8674 Alsip *(G-443)*
◆ Fischer Paper Products Inc ..... D ..... 847 395-6060 Antioch *(G-611)*
Gateway Packaging Company LLC ..... G ..... 618 451-0010 Granite City *(G-10709)*
Graphic Packaging Intl LLC ..... C ..... 630 260-6500 Carol Stream *(G-2994)*
Langston Bag of Peoria LLC ..... D ..... 309 676-1006 Peoria *(G-16468)*
▲ Lexington Leather Goods Co ..... F ..... 773 287-5500 Chicago *(G-5213)*
◆ Mondi Romeoville Inc ..... D ..... 630 378-9886 Romeoville *(G-17857)*
Morris Packaging LLC ..... G ..... 309 663-9100 Bloomington *(G-2081)*
Pride Packaging LLC ..... G ..... 309 663-9100 Bloomington *(G-2086)*
Proampac Pg Borrower LLC ..... B ..... 618 451-0010 Granite City *(G-10733)*
▲ Recycling Solutions Inc ..... E ..... 773 617-6955 Chicago *(G-5992)*
▲ Studley Products Inc ..... C ..... 309 663-2313 Bloomington *(G-2097)*
Waxstar Inc ..... G ..... 708 755-3530 S Chicago Hts *(G-18129)*
Westrock Rkt LLC ..... A ..... 312 346-6600 Chicago *(G-6614)*

2675 Die-Cut Paper & Board

11th Street Express Prtg Inc ..... F ..... 815 968-0208 Rockford *(G-17275)*
◆ Acco Brands USA LLC ..... B ..... 800 222-6462 Lake Zurich *(G-12376)*
Acco Brands USA LLC ..... D ..... 847 272-3700 Lincolnshire *(G-12741)*
▲ Ade Inc ..... E ..... 773 646-3400 Chicago *(G-3541)*
Andrews Converting LLC ..... E ..... 708 352-2555 La Grange *(G-12072)*
Animated Advg Techniques Inc ..... G ..... 312 372-4694 Chicago *(G-3698)*
Anselmo Die and Index Co Inc ..... F ..... 847 397-1200 Schaumburg *(G-18440)*
B Allan Graphics Inc ..... F ..... 708 396-1704 Alsip *(G-420)*
Business Forms Finishing Svc ..... G ..... 773 229-0230 Chicago *(G-3979)*
Butler Bros Steel Rule Die Co ..... G ..... 815 630-4629 Shorewood *(G-18894)*
Capital Prtg & Die Cutng Inc ..... G ..... 630 896-5520 Aurora *(G-1069)*
Carson Printing Inc ..... G ..... 847 836-0900 East Dundee *(G-8189)*
Creative Label Inc ..... D ..... 847 956-6960 Elk Grove Village *(G-8919)*
Deco Adhesive Pdts 1985 Ltd ..... E ..... 847 472-2100 Elk Grove Village *(G-8941)*
Delta Press Inc ..... E ..... 847 671-3200 Palatine *(G-16111)*
Diecrafters Inc ..... E ..... 708 656-3336 Cicero *(G-6841)*
Global Abrasive Products Inc ..... E ..... 630 543-9466 Addison *(G-142)*
Gpi Midwest LLC ..... E ..... 847 741-0247 Elgin *(G-8599)*
▲ Graphic Arts Finishing Company ..... D ..... 708 345-8484 Melrose Park *(G-13875)*
Impression Printing ..... F ..... 708 614-8660 Oak Forest *(G-15682)*
Intra-Cut Die Cutting Inc ..... F ..... 773 775-6228 Chicago *(G-4960)*
Lee-Wel Printing Corporation ..... G ..... 630 682-0935 Wheaton *(G-20812)*
M S A Printing Co ..... G ..... 847 593-5699 Elk Grove Village *(G-9103)*
M Wells Printing Co ..... G ..... 312 455-0400 Chicago *(G-5305)*
McGrath Press Inc ..... E ..... 815 356-5246 Crystal Lake *(G-7224)*
Mich Enterprises Inc ..... F ..... 630 616-9000 Wood Dale *(G-21216)*
Midwest Cortland Inc ..... E ..... 847 671-0376 Addison *(G-209)*
Midwest Index Inc ..... D ..... 847 995-8425 Addison *(G-210)*
▼ Murnane Packaging Corporation ..... E ..... 708 449-1200 Northlake *(G-15552)*
Plastics Printing Group Inc ..... F ..... 773 473-4481 Chicago *(G-5820)*
PMC Converting Corp ..... G ..... 773 481-2269 Chicago *(G-5825)*
◆ Potomac Corporation ..... C ..... 847 259-0546 Wheeling *(G-20962)*
Precision Die Cutting & Finish ..... G ..... 773 252-5625 Chicago *(G-5856)*
Pry-Bar Company ..... F ..... 815 436-3383 Joliet *(G-11918)*
Racine Paper Box Manufacturing ..... E ..... 773 227-3900 Chicago *(G-5958)*
▲ Rapid Displays Inc ..... C ..... 773 927-5000 Chicago *(G-5971)*
Review Printing Co Inc ..... G ..... 309 788-7094 Rock Island *(G-17241)*
Rhopac Fabricated Products LLC ..... E ..... 847 362-3300 Libertyville *(G-12702)*
Rohrer Corporation ..... D ..... 847 961-5920 Huntley *(G-11564)*
Ross-Gage Inc ..... E ..... 708 347-3659 Homewood *(G-11502)*
RTS Packaging LLC ..... C ..... 708 338-2800 Hillside *(G-11355)*
Sales Midwest Prtg & Packg Inc ..... G ..... 309 764-5544 Moline *(G-14175)*
Sign Centre ..... G ..... 847 595-7300 Elk Grove Village *(G-9239)*
Stevenson Paper Co Inc ..... G ..... 630 879-5000 Batavia *(G-1419)*
Village Press Inc ..... G ..... 847 362-1856 Libertyville *(G-12724)*
▲ Warwick Publishing Company ..... D ..... 630 584-3871 Saint Charles *(G-18296)*
◆ Weber Marking Systems Inc ..... B ..... 847 364-8500 Arlington Heights *(G-831)*
▲ Young Shin USA Limited ..... G ..... 847 598-3611 Schaumburg *(G-18779)*

2676 Sanitary Paper Prdts

Barrington Company ..... G ..... 815 933-3233 Bradley *(G-2276)*
Dude Products Inc ..... G ..... 800 898-7304 Chicago *(G-4401)*
EPS Solutions Incorporated ..... A ..... 815 206-0868 Woodstock *(G-21386)*
Evergreen Manufacturing Inc ..... E ..... 217 382-5108 Martinsville *(G-13584)*
Johnson & Johnson ..... G ..... 847 640-5400 Elk Grove Village *(G-9069)*

SIC

26 PAPER AND ALLIED PRODUCTS

Kimberly-Clark Corporation ....D....... 312 371-5166
  Deerfield (G-7626)
Kimberly-Clark Corporation ....C....... 815 886-7872
  Romeoville (G-17838)
Kimberly-Clark Corporation ....G....... 847 885-1050
  Chicago (G-5103)
Kimberly-Clark Corporation ....E....... 708 409-8500
  Northlake (G-15550)
Procter & Gamble Co ....G....... 847 936-4621
  North Chicago (G-15319)
Procter & Gamble Company ....G....... 847 375-5400
  Chicago (G-5892)
Sonoco Prtective Solutions Inc ....E....... 708 946-3244
  Beecher (G-1521)
Wells Janitorial Service Inc ....G....... 872 226-9983
  Chicago (G-6600)

2677 Envelopes

American Graphics Network Inc............F....... 847 729-7220
  Glenview (G-10522)
Diamond Envelope Corporation ....D....... 630 499-2800
  Aurora (G-951)
▲ Federal Envelope Company ....D....... 630 595-2000
  Bensenville (G-1799)
Forest Envelope Company ....E....... 630 515-1200
  Bolingbrook (G-2178)
Gaw-Ohara Envelope Co ....E....... 773 638-1200
  Chicago (G-4664)
Gluetech Inc ....F....... 847 455-2707
  Wood Dale (G-21194)
Graphic Industries Inc ....E....... 847 357-9870
  South Elgin (G-19148)
Managed Marketing Inc ....G....... 847 279-8260
  Wheeling (G-20935)
Office Express Inc ....G....... 888 526-8438
  Evanston (G-9560)
Overt Press Inc ....E....... 773 284-0909
  Chicago (G-5718)
Roodhouse Envelope Co ....D....... 217 589-4321
  Roodhouse (G-17894)
▲ The Calumet Carton Company ....D....... 708 331-7910
  South Holland (G-19249)
Trekon Company Inc ....G....... 309 925-7942
  Tremont (G-19899)
Unique Envelope Corporation ....E....... 773 586-0330
  Chicago (G-6468)

2678 Stationery Prdts

Assemble and Mail Group Inc ....G....... 309 473-2006
  Heyworth (G-11189)
▲ Carl Manufacturing USA Inc ....F....... 847 884-2842
  Itasca (G-11635)
Chicago Contract Bridge Assn ....G....... 630 355-5560
  Naperville (G-14797)
Coudal Partners Inc ....G....... 312 243-1107
  Chicago (G-4248)
Discount Computer Supply Inc ....G....... 847 883-8743
  Buffalo Grove (G-2533)
Dove Foundation ....G....... 312 217-3683
  Chicago (G-4390)
▲ House of Doolittle Ltd ....E....... 847 228-9591
  Arlington Heights (G-751)
▲ Mudlark Papers Inc ....E....... 630 717-7616
  Naperville (G-14876)

2679 Converted Paper Prdts, NEC

All Weather Products Co LLC ....F....... 847 981-0386
  Elk Grove Village (G-8814)
Ameri Label Company ....F....... 847 895-8000
  Bartlett (G-1253)
▲ Ar-En Party Printers Inc ....F....... 847 673-7390
  Skokie (G-18923)
Bag Tags Inc ....F....... 847 983-4732
  Skokie (G-18927)
Corydon Converting Company Inc ....F....... 630 898-9896
  Naperville (G-14809)
◆ Corydon Converting Company Inc ....E....... 630 983-1900
  Aurora (G-1081)
◆ Crescent Cardboard Company LLC ..C....... 888 293-3956
  Wheeling (G-20877)
Deco Adhesive Pdts 1985 Ltd ....E....... 847 472-2100
  Elk Grove Village (G-8941)
Dietzgen Corporation ....F....... 217 348-8111
  Charleston (G-3401)
Diversfied Lbling Slutions Inc ....C....... 630 625-1225
  Itasca (G-11643)
Found Inc ....G....... 773 279-3000
  Chicago (G-4624)
Franch & Sons Trnsp Inc ....G....... 630 392-3307
  Addison (G-129)

General Laminating Company ....G....... 847 639-8770
  Cary (G-3164)
Gro-Mar Industries Inc ....F....... 708 343-5901
  Melrose Park (G-13876)
Hospital Hlth Care Systems Inc ....E....... 708 863-3400
  Lyons (G-13311)
I M M Inc ....F....... 773 767-3700
  Chicago (G-4866)
Identco West LLC ....G....... 815 385-0011
  Ingleside (G-11585)
Identi-Graphics Inc ....E....... 630 801-4845
  Montgomery (G-14250)
Illinois Tag Co ....E....... 773 626-0542
  Carol Stream (G-3001)
▲ Integrated Label Corporation ....F....... 815 874-2500
  Rockford (G-17467)
K & N Laboratories Inc ....F....... 708 482-3240
  La Grange (G-12081)
Lewis Paper Place Inc ....G....... 847 808-1343
  Wheeling (G-20932)
Linn West Paper Company ....G....... 773 561-3839
  Chicago (G-5231)
Loyola Paper Company ....G....... 847 956-7770
  Elk Grove Village (G-9098)
Lucky Games Inc ....F....... 773 549-9051
  Northbrook (G-15422)
▼ Midland Davis Corporation ....D....... 309 277-1617
  Moline (G-14161)
Mitchell Black LLC ....F....... 312 667-4477
  Chicago (G-5470)
▲ Mudlark Papers Inc ....E....... 630 717-7616
  Naperville (G-14876)
Norwood Industries Inc ....F....... 773 788-1508
  Chicago (G-5629)
Oce-Van Der Grinten NV ....E....... 217 348-8111
  Charleston (G-3408)
Oei Products Inc ....G....... 630 377-1121
  Bartlett (G-1300)
▲ Pap-R Products Company ....D....... 800 637-4937
  Martinsville (G-13587)
◆ Potomac Corporation ....C....... 847 259-0546
  Wheeling (G-20962)
Precision Press & Label Inc ....G....... 630 625-1225
  Itasca (G-11722)
Proampac Pg Borrower LLC ....B....... 618 451-0010
  Granite City (G-10733)
Protex Products LLC ....G....... 312 292-1310
  Chicago (G-5906)
Quality Paper Inc ....F....... 847 258-3999
  Elk Grove Village (G-9205)
RTS Packaging LLC ....C....... 708 338-2800
  Hillside (G-11355)
Schwab Paper Products Company ....E....... 815 372-2233
  Romeoville (G-17875)
Seabee Supply Co ....G....... 630 860-1293
  Wood Dale (G-21239)
Service Packaging Design Inc ....G....... 847 966-6592
  Morton Grove (G-14440)
Signode Industrial Group LLC ....E....... 815 939-0033
  Kankakee (G-12003)
Signode Industrial Group LLC ....E....... 708 371-9050
  Blue Island (G-2140)
◆ Stanford Products LLC ....E....... 618 548-2600
  Salem (G-18361)
◆ Stevens Cabinets Inc ....B....... 217 857-7100
  Teutopolis (G-19773)
Tag Diamond & Label ....E....... 630 844-9395
  Aurora (G-1159)
▲ Tercor Inc ....G....... 773 549-8303
  Chicago (G-6353)
Terrapin Xpress Inc ....G....... 866 823-7323
  Palos Heights (G-16193)
Trade Label & Decal ....G....... 630 773-0447
  Itasca (G-11747)
▼ Tricel Corporation ....F....... 847 336-1321
  Gurnee (G-10938)
Trimaco LLC ....E....... 919 674-3476
  Elk Grove Village (G-9286)
▲ Wexford Home Corp ....G....... 847 922-5738
  Northbrook (G-15502)
▲ Xertrex International Inc ....E....... 630 773-4020
  Itasca (G-11755)
▲ Zebra Technologies Corporation .....B....... 847 634-6700
  Lincolnshire (G-12804)

27 PRINTING, PUBLISHING, AND ALLIED INDUSTRIES

2711 Newspapers: Publishing & Printing

22nd Century Media ....G....... 847 272-4565
  Northbrook (G-15328)
22nd Century Media ....E....... 708 326-9170
  Orland Park (G-15931)
Ada Holding Company Inc ....F....... 312 440-2897
  Chicago (G-3537)
Advantage News ....G....... 618 463-0612
  Alton (G-541)
Advocate ....G....... 815 694-2122
  Clifton (G-6913)
Agri-News Publications Inc ....D....... 815 223-2558
  La Salle (G-12100)
All Star Publishing ....G....... 630 428-1515
  Naperville (G-14772)
Altamont News ....G....... 618 483-6176
  Altamont (G-529)
Always Faitfhul Dog Traning ....G....... 630 696-2572
  Saint Charles (G-18144)
Amboy News ....G....... 815 857-2311
  Amboy (G-578)
Americn Foreign Lang Newspaper ....E....... 312 368-4815
  Chicago (G-3676)
Arcola Record Herald ....G....... 217 268-4950
  Arcola (G-645)
Arthur Graphic Clarion ....G....... 217 543-2151
  Arthur (G-842)
Augusta Eagle ....G....... 217 392-2715
  Augusta (G-909)
B F Shaw Printing Company ....G....... 815 625-3600
  Sterling (G-19500)
Baier Publishing Company ....G....... 815 457-2245
  Cissna Park (G-6895)
Bar Code Dr Inc ....G....... 815 547-1001
  Cherry Valley (G-3438)
Bar Stool Depotcom ....G....... 815 727-7294
  Joliet (G-11827)
Beacon Solutions Inc ....F....... 303 513-0469
  Chicago (G-3850)
Beardstown Newspapers Inc ....G....... 217 323-1010
  Beardstown (G-1445)
Belair Hd Studios LLC ....E....... 312 254-5188
  Chicago (G-3863)
Belleville News Democrat ....C....... 618 239-2552
  Belleville (G-1533)
Belvidere Daily Republican Co ....E....... 815 547-0084
  Belvidere (G-1655)
Benton Evening News Co ....G....... 618 438-5611
  Benton (G-1919)
Benton Gazette ....G....... 618 438-6397
  Benton (G-1920)
Best Newspapers In Ill Inc ....G....... 217 728-7381
  Sullivan (G-19661)
Better News Papers Inc ....G....... 618 566-8282
  Mascoutah (G-13593)
Better News Papers Inc ....G....... 618 483-6176
  Altamont (G-531)
Blue Island Sun ....G....... 708 388-9033
  Blue Island (G-2112)
Bond & Fayette County Shopper ....G....... 618 664-4566
  Greenville (G-10827)
Bond Broadcasting Inc ....F....... 618 664-3300
  Greenville (G-10828)
Boone County Shopper Inc ....F....... 815 544-2166
  Belvidere (G-1656)
▼ Breese Publishing Co Inc ....G....... 618 526-7211
  Breese (G-2299)
Breeze Printing Company ....F....... 217 824-2233
  Taylorville (G-19752)
Bulletin ....G....... 618 553-9764
  Oblong (G-15824)
Bunker Hill Publication ....G....... 618 585-4411
  Bunker Hill (G-2633)
Bureau Valley Chief ....G....... 815 646-4731
  Tiskilwa (G-19871)
C & C Publications ....G....... 815 723-0325
  Joliet (G-11836)
Cambridge Chronicle ....G....... 309 937-3303
  Cambridge (G-2802)
Campbell Publishing Co Inc ....F....... 618 498-1234
  Jerseyville (G-11788)
Campbell Publishing Co Inc ....G....... 217 285-2345
  Pittsfield (G-16631)
Campbell Publishing Inc ....E....... 217 742-3313
  Winchester (G-21104)

27 PRINTING, PUBLISHING, AND ALLIED INDUSTRIES

Company	Code	Phone
Carbondale Night Life, Carbondale (G-2839)	F	618 549-2799
Carmi Times, Carmi (G-2902)	F	618 382-4176
Carroll County Review, Thomson (G-19780)	G	815 259-2131
Carterville Courier, Carterville (G-3130)	G	618 985-6187
Catholic Press Assn of The US, Chicago (G-4043)	G	312 380-6789
Central Ill Communications LLC, Springfield (G-19345)	F	217 753-2226
Central Illinois Newspapers, Clinton (G-6920)	G	217 935-3171
Central Newspaper Incorporated, Naperville (G-14795)	G	630 416-4191
Centralia Morning Sentinel, Centralia (G-3224)	D	618 532-5601
Centralia Press Ltd, Centralia (G-3225)	D	618 532-5604
Centralia Press Ltd, Mount Vernon (G-14601)	F	618 246-2000
Chgo Daily Law Bulletin, Springfield (G-19349)	G	217 525-6735
Chicago, Arlington Heights (G-715)	G	847 437-7700
▲ Chicago Chinese Times, Naperville (G-14796)	G	630 717-4567
Chicago Citizen Newsppr Group, Chicago (G-4096)	F	773 783-1251
Chicago Crusader News Group, Chicago (G-4099)	G	773 752-2500
Chicago Group Acquisition LLC, Chicago (G-4105)	G	312 755-0720
Chicago Jewish News, Skokie (G-18941)	F	847 966-0606
Chicago Sun-Times Features Inc, Chicago (G-4131)	A	312 321-3000
Chicago Tribune Company, Chicago (G-4133)	A	312 222-3232
▲ Chicago Tribune Company LLC, Chicago (G-4134)	A	312 222-3232
Chicago Weekly, Chicago (G-4136)	G	773 702-7718
▲ China Journal Inc, Chicago (G-4140)	G	312 326-3228
Chinese American News, Chicago (G-4141)	G	312 225-5600
Chronicle Newspapers Inc, Geneva (G-10259)	G	630 845-5247
Clinton Journal, Bloomington (G-2032)	G	309 242-3900
Cnhi LLC, Effingham (G-8391)	F	217 774-2161
Cnlc-Stc Inc, Chicago (G-4186)	A	312 321-3000
Coal City Courant, Coal City (G-6930)	G	815 634-0315
Crain Communications Inc, Chicago (G-4259)	C	312 649-5200
Czech American TV Herald, Willowbrook (G-21039)	G	708 813-0028
Daily Dollar Savings LLC, Morton Grove (G-14398)	G	860 883-0351
Daily Egyptian Siu Newspaper, Carbondale (G-2840)	D	618 536-3311
Daily Fastner, Palatine (G-16107)	G	847 907-9830
Daily General LLC, Chicago (G-4305)	G	217 273-0719
Daily Kratom, Joliet (G-11851)	G	815 768-7104
Daily Lawrenceville Record, Lawrenceville (G-12529)	F	618 943-2331
Daily Lawrenceville Record, Lawrenceville (G-12530)	G	618 544-2101
Daily Money Matters LLC, Glenview (G-10541)	G	847 729-8393
Daily News Condominium Assn, Chicago (G-4306)	E	312 492-8526
Daily News Tribune Inc, La Salle (G-12210)	C	815 223-2558
Daily Robinson News Inc, Robinson (G-17211)	E	618 544-2101
Daily Whale, Chicago (G-4307)	G	312 787-5204
Dancyn Recovery Systems, Bloomington (G-2038)	G	309 829-5450
Danny Fender, Louisville (G-13178)	G	618 665-3135
De Boer & Associates, Bolingbrook (G-2167)	G	630 972-1600
Debbie Harshman, Barry (G-1249)	G	217 335-2112
Delavan Times, Delavan (G-7715)	G	309 244-7111
Democrat Company Corp, Carthage (G-3135)	G	217 357-2149
Democrat Message, Mount Sterling (G-14591)	G	217 773-3371
Dennis Kellogg Ofc, Chicago (G-4339)	G	773 588-3421
Des Plaines Journal Inc, Des Plaines (G-7755)	D	847 299-5511
Desi Talk LLC, Chicago (G-4345)	G	212 675-7515
District 97, Oak Park (G-15750)	G	708 289-7064
Dixon Telegraph, Dixon (G-7897)	G	815 284-2224
Dmi Information Process Center, Chicago (G-4373)	E	773 378-2644
Dow Jones & Company Inc, Highland (G-11214)	G	618 651-2300
Dow Jones & Company Inc, Chicago (G-4393)	D	312 580-1023
E & L Communication, Chicago (G-4420)	G	773 890-1656
E & R Media LLC, Du Quoin (G-8119)	F	618 790-9376
Ea Mackay Enterprises Inc, Lombard (G-13070)	E	630 627-7010
Eagle Publications Inc, Fairview Heights (G-9645)	E	618 345-5400
East Central Communications Co, Rantoul (G-16975)	E	217 892-9613
Edwardsville Publishing Co, Edwardsville (G-8361)	D	618 656-4700
Effingham Ttplis News Rport In, Effingham (G-8399)	G	217 342-5583
Eisenhower High School - Blue, Blue Island (G-2120)	G	708 385-6815
El Dia Newspaper, Berwyn (G-1952)	G	708 956-7282
El Paso Journal, El Paso (G-8437)	G	309 527-8595
El Sol Dechicago Newspaper, Chicago (G-4468)	G	773 235-7655
Elise S Allen, Peoria (G-16434)	G	309 673-2613
Elliott Publishing Inc, Liberty (G-12622)	G	217 645-3033
Elliott Publishing Inc, Camp Point (G-2810)	G	217 593-6515
Ethnic Media LLC, Wheeling (G-20894)	G	224 676-0778
Examiner Publications Inc, Bartlett (G-1279)	G	630 830-4145
Experimental Aircraft Examiner, Cary (G-3158)	G	847 226-0777
Farina News, Farina (G-9652)	G	618 245-6216
Farm Week, Bloomington (G-2042)	E	309 557-3140
Final Call Inc, Chicago (G-4587)	D	773 602-1230
Food Service Publishing Co, Des Plaines (G-7772)	F	847 699-3300
Forrest Consulting, Glen Ellyn (G-10403)	G	630 730-9619
Fox Valley Labor News Inc, Aurora (G-1099)	G	630 897-4022
Fox Valley Park District, Aurora (G-1100)	D	630 892-1550
Fra No 3800 W Division, Stone Park (G-19555)	G	708 338-0690
Free Press Newspapers, Wilmington (G-21098)	E	815 476-7966
Freeburg Printing & Publishing, Freeburg (G-10089)	G	618 539-3320
Friends Pyramid State Park Inc, Pinckneyville (G-16615)	F	618 318-3992
G-W Communications Inc, Wilmington (G-21099)	G	815 476-7966
Galesburg Register-Mail, Galesburg (G-10193)	C	309 343-7181
Ganji Klames, Skokie (G-18959)	G	773 478-9000
Gannett Stllite Info Ntwrk LLC, Yorkville (G-21484)	C	630 629-1280
Gannett Stllite Info Ntwrk LLC, Hoffman Estates (G-11427)	D	847 839-1700
Gatehouse Media LLC, Kewanee (G-12035)	F	309 852-2181
Gatehouse Media LLC, Newton (G-15083)	G	618 783-2324
Gatehouse Media LLC, Springfield (G-19373)	B	217 788-1300
Gatehouse Media LLC, Olney (G-15862)	E	618 393-2931
Gatehouse Media LLC, West Frankfort (G-20673)	E	618 937-2850
Gatehouse Media LLC, Oakbrook Terrace (G-15799)	D	585 598-0030
Gatehouse Media LLC, Pontiac (G-16771)	E	815 842-1153
Gatehouse Media LLC, Harrisburg (G-11024)	E	618 253-7146
Gatehouse Media - Wstn Ill Div, Galesburg (G-10195)	G	309 299-6135
Gatehouse Media Ill Holdings, Peoria (G-16442)	G	585 598-0030
Gatehuse Mdia Ill Hldngs II In, Springfield (G-19374)	B	217 788-1300
Gazette, Galena (G-10172)	E	815 777-0105
Gazette Democrat, Anna (G-583)	E	618 833-2150
Gazette Printing Co, Glasford (G-10387)	G	309 389-2811
Gazette-Democrat, Anna (G-584)	E	618 833-2158
▲ Geomentum Inc, Downers Grove (G-8007)	B	630 729-7500
Geomentum Inc, Downers Grove (G-8008)	G	630 729-7500
German American Nat Congress, Chicago (G-4688)	F	773 561-9181
Gilman Star Inc, Gilman (G-10378)	G	815 265-7332
Gmd Mobile Pressure Wshg Svcs, Chicago (G-4704)	G	773 826-1903
Gold Nugget Publications Inc, Virden (G-20185)	E	217 965-3355
Golda House, Chicago (G-4713)	G	773 927-0140
Golden Prairie News, Assumption (G-889)	G	217 226-3721
Golf Gazette, Lockport (G-12997)	G	815 838-0184
Greene Jersey Shoppers, Carrollton (G-3126)	G	217 942-3626
Greenville Advocate Inc, Greenville (G-10835)	G	618 664-3144
Hancock County Shopper, Hamilton (G-10959)	G	217 847-6628
Hardschellreport, Evanston (G-9531)	G	773 972-2500
Hearst Communications Inc, Bloomington (G-2056)	C	309 829-9000
Hearst Corporation, Alton (G-558)	G	618 463-2500
Hearst Corporation, Jacksonville (G-11766)	G	217 245-6121
Heartland News, Humboldt (G-11523)	G	217 856-2332
Henderson Hancock Quill Inc, Stronghurst (G-19634)	G	309 924-1871
Henry News Republican, Henry (G-11166)	G	309 364-3250
Herald Mount Olive, Mount Olive (G-14504)	G	217 999-3941
Herald Newspapers Inc, Chicago (G-4806)	E	773 643-8533
Herald Publications, Mascoutah (G-13599)	F	618 566-8282
Herald Whig Quincy, Quincy (G-16891)	G	217 222-7600
Heritage Media Svcs Co of Ill, Summit Argo (G-19679)	G	708 594-9340
HI India, Chicago (G-4813)	G	773 552-6083
Highland News Leader, Highland (G-11220)	G	618 654-2366
Hillsboro Journal Inc, Hillsboro (G-11316)	E	217 532-3933
Horizon Publications Inc, Marion (G-13515)	C	618 993-1711
Horizon Publications (2003), Marion (G-13516)	G	618 993-1711

Employee Codes: A=Over 500 employees, B=251-500, C=101-250, D=51-100, E=20-50, F=10-19, G=3-9

27 PRINTING, PUBLISHING, AND ALLIED INDUSTRIES

Hpc of Pennsylvania Inc .... D 618 993-1711
  Marion (G-13517)
Illini Media Co .... B 217 337-8300
  Champaign (G-3306)
Illinois Newspaper In Educatn .... F 847 427-4388
  Springfield (G-19387)
Illinois Valley Press East .... G 217 586-2512
  Mahomet (G-13424)
Independent News .... G 217 662-6001
  Danville (G-7350)
India Bulletin Inc .... G 847 674-7941
  Skokie (G-18968)
India Tribune Ltd Corporation .... F 773 588-5077
  Chicago (G-4905)
Indiana Agri-News Inc .... G 317 726-5391
  La Salle (G-12114)
Inn Intl Newspaper Network .... G 309 764-5314
  Moline (G-14150)
International News .... G 773 283-8323
  Chicago (G-4953)
John Dagys Media LLC .... G 708 373-0180
  Palos Park (G-16212)
Joliet Herald Newspaper .... E 815 280-4100
  Joliet (G-11886)
▲ Joong-Ang Daily News .... E 847 228-7200
  Rolling Meadows (G-17743)
Journal News .... G 217 532-3933
  Hillsboro (G-11317)
Journal News .... G 217 324-6604
  Litchfield (G-12968)
Journal of Banking and Fin .... G 618 203-9074
  Glen Carbon (G-10389)
Journal Standard .... G 815 232-1171
  Freeport (G-10122)
Jury Verdict Reporter .... G 312 644-7800
  Chicago (G-5061)
Kaages News Service .... G 847 529-7199
  Chicago (G-5073)
Kaneland Publications Inc .... F 630 365-6446
  Saint Charles (G-18220)
Kankakee Daily Journal Co LLC ..... C 815 937-3300
  Kankakee (G-11985)
Kathleen A Badasch .... G 618 462-5881
  Alton (G-562)
Kendall County Record .... E 630 553-7034
  Yorkville (G-21489)
Kerala Express Newspaper .... G 773 465-5359
  Chicago (G-5096)
KK Stevens Publishing Co .... E 309 329-2151
  Astoria (G-893)
Knockout LLC Evanston .... G 224 714-3007
  Evanston (G-9544)
▲ Korea Times .... D 847 626-0388
  Glenview (G-10579)
Korea Times Chicago Inc .... E 847 626-0388
  Glenview (G-10580)
Korea Tribune Inc .... G 847 956-9101
  Mount Prospect (G-14543)
▲ Korean Media Group LLC .... F 847 391-4112
  Northbrook (G-15414)
La Raza Chicago Inc .... G 312 870-7000
  Chicago (G-5149)
Lacon Home Journal .... G 309 246-2865
  Lacon (G-12128)
Lambda Publications Inc .... F 773 871-7610
  Chicago (G-5169)
Launch Press .... G 773 669-8372
  Lombard (G-13094)
Lawndale Press Inc .... F 708 656-6900
  Cicero (G-6862)
Lee Enterprises Incorporated .... F 309 829-9000
  Bloomington (G-2070)
Lee Enterprises Incorporated .... G 309 743-0800
  Moline (G-14158)
Lee Enterprises Incorporated .... G 618 998-8499
  Marion (G-13519)
Lee Enterprises Incorporated .... C 217 421-6920
  Decatur (G-7515)
Lee Enterprises Incorporated .... C 618 529-5454
  Carbondale (G-2849)
Leroy E Ritzert .... G 815 737-8210
  Capron (G-2835)
Liberty Group Publishing .... F 309 944-1779
  Geneseo (G-10245)
Liberty Group Publishing .... G 618 937-2850
  West Frankfort (G-20676)
Liberty Group Publishing .... G 309 937-3303
  Cambridge (G-2805)
Liberty Suburban Chicago .... G 630 368-1100
  Oak Brook (G-15635)
Lincolndailynewscom .... G 217 732-7443
  Lincoln (G-12734)
Litchfield News Herald Inc .... F 217 324-2121
  Litchfield (G-12972)
Lithuanian Catholic Press .... E 773 585-9500
  Chicago (G-5236)
Live Daily LLC .... G 312 286-6706
  Chicago (G-5241)
Long View Publishing Co Inc .... F 773 446-9920
  Chicago (G-5255)
Los Angles Tmes Cmmnctions LLC ... G 312 467-4670
  Chicago (G-5260)
Macoupin County Enquirer Inc ...... E 217 854-2534
  Carlinville (G-2879)
Mahoney Publishing Inc .... G 815 369-5384
  Lena (G-12606)
Marengo Union Times .... G 815 568-5400
  Marengo (G-13490)
Marion Star .... G 618 997-7827
  Marion (G-13521)
Marshall County Publishing Co ..... G 309 246-2865
  Lacon (G-12129)
Martin Publishing Co .... G 309 647-9501
  Canton (G-2828)
Martin Publishing Co .... E 309 543-2000
  Havana (G-11116)
Martin Publishing Co .... G 309 647-9501
  Canton (G-2829)
Mason City Banner Times .... F 217 482-3276
  Mason City (G-13612)
McClatchy Newspapers Inc .... B 618 239-2624
  Belleville (G-1574)
McClatchy Newspapers Inc .... D 618 654-2366
  Highland (G-11231)
McClatchy Newspapers Inc .... F 618 443-2145
  Sparta (G-19257)
McDonough County Shopper Inc ... G 309 833-2114
  Macomb (G-13393)
McDonough Democrat Inc .... F 309 772-2129
  Bushnell (G-2744)
Mendota Reporter .... F 815 539-9396
  Mendota (G-13948)
Messenger .... G 618 235-9601
  Belleville (G-1576)
Military Medical News .... E 312 368-4860
  Chicago (G-5457)
Mirror-Democrat .... G 815 244-2411
  Mount Carroll (G-14496)
Monitor Newspaper Inc .... G 618 271-0468
  East Saint Louis (G-8315)
Morris Publishing Company .... G 815 942-3221
  Morris (G-14317)
Mt Carmel Register Co Inc .... E 618 262-5144
  Mount Carmel (G-14481)
Nadig Newspapers Inc .... F 773 286-6100
  Chicago (G-5537)
Naperville Hanna Andersson .... G 331 250-7100
  Naperville (G-14880)
Nashville News .... F 618 327-3411
  Nashville (G-15005)
Nationwide News Monitor .... G 312 424-4224
  Skokie (G-18995)
New City Communications .... E 312 243-8786
  Chicago (G-5576)
News & Letters .... G 312 663-0839
  Chicago (G-5587)
News Media Corporation .... E 815 562-2061
  Rochelle (G-17150)
News-Gazette Inc .... G 217 373-7450
  Champaign (G-3325)
News-Gazette Inc .... E 217 351-5300
  Champaign (G-3326)
News-Gazette Inc .... G 217 351-8128
  Champaign (G-3327)
News-Gazette Inc .... G 217 384-2302
  Champaign (G-3328)
News-Gazette Inc .... F 217 351-5311
  Urbana (G-19990)
News-Gazette Inc .... B 217 351-5252
  Champaign (G-3329)
News-Gazette Inc .... G 217 762-2511
  Monticello (G-14282)
News-Gazette Inc .... F 217 443-8484
  Danville (G-7369)
Newser LLC .... F 312 284-2300
  Chicago (G-5588)
Newspaper 7 Days .... G 847 272-2212
  Wheeling (G-20944)
Newspaper Holding Inc .... G 618 643-2387
  Mc Leansboro (G-13707)
Newspaper Holding Inc .... E 217 446-1000
  Danville (G-7370)
Newspaper Holding Inc .... D 217 347-7151
  Effingham (G-8415)
Newspaper National Network .... G 312 644-1142
  Chicago (G-5589)
Newspaper Solutions Inc .... F 773 930-3404
  Chicago (G-5590)
Newsprint Ink Inc .... F 618 667-3111
  Troy (G-19917)
Nicado Publishing Company Inc ... G 312 593-2557
  Chicago (G-5595)
Normalite Newspaper .... F 309 454-5476
  Normal (G-15213)
North County News Inc .... G 618 282-3803
  Red Bud (G-16998)
Northwestern Illinois Farmer .... G 815 369-2811
  Lena (G-12607)
Nowuba LLC .... G 801 510-8086
  Fox Lake (G-9751)
Nuevos Semana Newspaper .... G 847 991-3939
  Palatine (G-16145)
Ocs America Inc .... E 630 595-0111
  Wood Dale (G-21225)
Ogle County Life .... G 815 732-2156
  Oregon (G-15925)
Okawville Times .... G 618 243-5563
  Okawville (G-15846)
Old Gary Inc .... F 219 648-3000
  Chicago (G-5669)
Osborne Publications Inc .... G 217 422-9702
  Decatur (G-7534)
Ottawa Publishing Co Inc .... C 815 433-2000
  Ottawa (G-16068)
Ottawa Publishing Co Inc .... F 815 434-3330
  Ottawa (G-16069)
Ovn LLC .... G 646 204-6781
  Vernon Hills (G-20079)
Paddock Publications Inc .... B 847 427-4300
  Arlington Heights (G-786)
Paddock Publications Inc .... C 847 608-2700
  Elgin (G-8683)
Paddock Publications Inc .... G 847 427-5545
  Schaumburg (G-18662)
Paddock Publications Inc .... E 847 680-5800
  Libertyville (G-12693)
Pakistan News .... G 773 271-6400
  Chicago (G-5744)
Pana News Inc .... E 217 562-2111
  Pana (G-16221)
Pantagraph Publishing Co .... G 309 451-0006
  Normal (G-15216)
Pantagraph Publishing Co .... F 309 829-9000
  Bloomington (G-2085)
Paper .... E 815 584-1901
  Dwight (G-8157)
Peg N Reds .... G 618 586-2015
  New Lenox (G-15049)
People & Places Newspaper .... F 847 804-6985
  Schiller Park (G-18831)
Peoria Journal Star Credit Un ...... G 309 686-3191
  Peoria (G-16492)
▲ Peoria Journal Star Inc .... C 309 686-3000
  Peoria (G-16493)
Peoria Post Inc .... F 309 688-3628
  Peoria (G-16495)
Perryco Inc .... E 303 652-8282
  Downers Grove (G-8074)
Perryco Inc .... F 815 436-2431
  Plainfield (G-16701)
Perryco Inc .... G 217 322-3321
  Rushville (G-18112)
Petersburg Observer Co Inc .... G 217 632-2236
  Petersburg (G-16603)
Pike County Express .... F 217 285-5415
  Pittsfield (G-16638)
Pilot Club of Moline .... F 309 792-4102
  Moline (G-14166)
Pinoy Monthly .... G 847 329-1073
  Skokie (G-19005)
Pioneer Newspapers Inc .... G 847 486-0600
  Chicago (G-5809)
Pioneer Newspapers Inc .... G 708 383-3200
  Oak Park (G-15768)
Pioneer Newspapers Inc .... E 630 887-0600
  Hinsdale (G-11374)
Porterville Recorder Inc .... G 559 784-5000
  Marion (G-13528)
Progress Reporter Inc .... G 815 472-2000
  Momence (G-14190)

SIC SECTION

27 PRINTING, PUBLISHING, AND ALLIED INDUSTRIES

Publishing Properties LLC G 312 321-2299
Chicago *(G-5912)*
Puro Futbol Newspaper G 847 858-7493
Gurnee *(G-10919)*
Quad City Clown Troupe Inc G 309 788-1278
Rock Island *(G-17235)*
Quincy Herald-Whig LLC F 217 223-5100
Quincy *(G-16933)*
Rachel Switall Mag Group Nfp G 773 344-7123
Chicago *(G-5957)*
Randolph County Herald Tribune F 618 826-2385
Chester *(G-3460)*
Rankin Publishing Inc F 217 268-4959
Arcola *(G-664)*
Rantoul Youth Wrestling G 217 377-9523
Rantoul *(G-16982)*
RCP Publications Inc G 773 227-4066
Chicago *(G-5979)*
Rd Daily Enterprises G 847 872-7632
Winthrop Harbor *(G-21142)*
Real Times II LLC G 312 225-2400
Chicago *(G-5985)*
Realclearpolitics F 773 255-5846
Chicago *(G-5986)*
Record Inc G 312 985-7270
Chicago *(G-5989)*
Redwood Landings LLC G 312 508-4953
Chicago *(G-5995)*
Refined Haystack Inc G 773 627-3534
Chicago *(G-5998)*
Reflejos Publications LLC E 847 806-1111
Arlington Heights *(G-797)*
Register Publishing Co E 618 253-7146
Harrisburg *(G-11028)*
Reporter Inc E 217 932-5211
Casey *(G-3208)*
Republic Times LLC G 618 939-3814
Waterloo *(G-20296)*
Review G 309 659-2761
Erie *(G-9474)*
Review G 618 997-2222
Marion *(G-13533)*
Robert McCormick Tribune Lbrry G 847 619-7980
Schaumburg *(G-18698)*
Rochelle Newspapers Inc E 815 562-4171
Rochelle *(G-17156)*
Rochelle Newspapers Inc E 815 562-4171
Rochelle *(G-17157)*
Rock River Times F 815 964-9767
Rockford *(G-17582)*
Rock Valley Publishing LLC E 815 467-6397
Loves Park *(G-13255)*
Rock Valley Publishing LLC G 815 234-4821
Byron *(G-2756)*
Rock Valley Publishing LLC F 815 654-4854
Durand *(G-8155)*
Rockford Newspapers Inc B 815 987-1200
Rockford *(G-17600)*
Rodney J Gieseke G 630 830-7063
Bartlett *(G-1305)*
Russell Publications Inc E 708 258-3473
Peotone *(G-16557)*
S & R Media LLC F 618 375-7502
Grayville *(G-10814)*
Salem Times-Commoner Inc E 618 548-3330
Salem *(G-18358)*
Sauk Valley Community College G 815 835-6321
Sterling *(G-19531)*
Sauk Valley Gunsmithing G 815 441-0260
Sterling *(G-19532)*
Sauk Valley Printing G 815 284-2222
Dixon *(G-7914)*
Savanna Times Journal G 815 273-2277
Savanna *(G-18412)*
Schaumburg Review F 847 998-3400
Chicago *(G-6110)*
Senior News & Time For Ill G 217 528-1882
Springfield *(G-19442)*
Shaw Suburban Media Group Inc C 815 459-4040
Crystal Lake *(G-7264)*
Shoppers Guide G 815 369-4112
Lena *(G-12609)*
Slack Publications G 217 268-4950
Arcola *(G-666)*
Small Newspaper Group C 815 937-3300
Kankakee *(G-12004)*
Small Nwsppr Group Shred Svcs G 309 764-4344
East Moline *(G-8241)*
Small Nwsppr Group Shred Svcs G 309 757-8377
East Moline *(G-8242)*
South County Publications F 217 438-6155
Auburn *(G-907)*
South Post LLC G 815 510-9395
Streator *(G-19623)*
Southland Voice E 708 214-8582
Crete *(G-7145)*
Southtown Star Newspapers G 708 633-4800
Tinley Park *(G-19857)*
Southwest Messenger Press Inc E 708 388-2425
Midlothian *(G-13996)*
Springfield Publishers Inc G 217 726-6600
Springfield *(G-19455)*
Stadium G 312 455-2582
Chicago *(G-6226)*
Star Media Group G 847 674-7827
Skokie *(G-19036)*
Star-Times Publishing Co Inc G 618 635-2000
Staunton *(G-19479)*
Stark County Communications G 309 286-4444
Toulon *(G-19891)*
Steven Brownstein G 847 909-6677
Morton Grove *(G-14442)*
Stm Reader LLC G 312 222-6920
Chicago *(G-6249)*
Streetwise F 773 334-6600
Chicago *(G-6252)*
Strohm Newspapers Inc G 217 826-3600
Marshall *(G-13578)*
Students Publishing Company In G 847 491-7206
Evanston *(G-9579)*
Success Journal Corp G 847 583-9000
Morton Grove *(G-14444)*
Sumner Press G 618 936-2212
Sumner *(G-19688)*
Sun Times News Agency G 815 672-1260
Streator *(G-19628)*
Sun-Times Media LLC F 312 222-6920
Chicago *(G-6270)*
Sun-Times Media Group Inc D 312 321-3000
Chicago *(G-6271)*
Sun-Times Media Holdings LLC E 312 321-2299
Chicago *(G-6272)*
Sv Family Evanston LLC G 773 420-6767
Evanston *(G-9581)*
T R Communications Inc F 773 238-3366
Chicago *(G-6307)*
Tegna Inc C 847 490-6657
Hoffman Estates *(G-11468)*
Teleguia Inc E 708 656-6675
Cicero *(G-6880)*
The b F Shaw Printing Co E 815 875-4461
Princeton *(G-16823)*
The b F Shaw Printing Co G 815 732-6166
Oregon *(G-15928)*
The Times G 815 433-2000
Ottawa *(G-16081)*
Times Record Company E 309 582-5112
Aledo *(G-362)*
Times Republic E 815 432-5227
Watseka *(G-20320)*
Times Republic G 217 283-5111
Hoopeston *(G-11515)*
Times-Press Publishing Co E 815 673-3771
Streator *(G-19630)*
Tini Martini G 773 269-2900
Chicago *(G-6381)*
Todays Advantage Inc F 618 463-0612
Alton *(G-574)*
Toledo Democrat G 217 849-2000
Toledo *(G-19879)*
Trenton Sun G 618 224-9422
Trenton *(G-19905)*
Tribune Publishing Company C 312 222-9100
Chicago *(G-6423)*
Tribune Publishing Company LLC E 312 222-9100
Chicago *(G-6424)*
Tribune Publishing Company LLC D 312 832-6711
Chicago *(G-6425)*
Trottie Publishing Group Inc G 708 344-5975
Westchester *(G-20715)*
Trx Pubco LLC G 312 222-9100
Chicago *(G-6442)*
Tuscola Journal Incorporated G 217 253-5086
Tuscola *(G-19932)*
Union Banner Publishing Ltd G 618 594-3131
Carlyle *(G-2897)*
United Communications Corp C 847 746-1515
Zion *(G-21527)*
United Communications Corp E 847 746-4700
Zion *(G-21528)*
Urdu Times G 773 274-3100
Chicago *(G-6496)*
US Oil Morris IL G 815 513-3496
Morris *(G-14337)*
Vernon Township Offices E 847 634-4600
Buffalo Grove *(G-2617)*
Village of Mt Zion G 217 864-4212
Mount Zion *(G-14650)*
Villagers Voice G 618 378-3094
Norris City *(G-15251)*
Vital Times G 847 675-2577
Lincolnwood *(G-12848)*
Voice G 630 966-8642
Aurora *(G-1167)*
Vondrak Publishing Co Inc E 773 476-4800
Summit Argo *(G-19684)*
W G N Radio Mass Calling G 312 591-7200
Chicago *(G-6574)*
Want ADS of Champaign Inc G 217 356-4804
Champaign *(G-3368)*
Waseet America G 708 430-1950
Bedford Park *(G-1511)*
Washington Courier F 309 444-3139
Washington *(G-20282)*
Waverly Journal G 217 435-9221
Waverly *(G-20523)*
Wayne County Press Inc E 618 842-2662
Fairfield *(G-9640)*
Wednesday Journal Inc D 708 386-5555
Chicago *(G-6597)*
Weekly Journals G 815 459-4040
Crystal Lake *(G-7293)*
Weekly Visitor G 815 845-2328
Scales Mound *(G-18422)*
West Suburban Journal G 708 344-5975
Bloomingdale *(G-2020)*
Wheels & Deals G 217 423-6333
Decatur *(G-7569)*
Willis Publishing F 618 497-8272
Percy *(G-16561)*
Wns Publications Inc E 815 772-7244
Morrison *(G-14349)*
Wnta Studio Line G 815 874-7861
Rockford *(G-17689)*
Woodstock Independent G 815 338-8040
Woodstock *(G-21450)*
World Journal LLC F 312 842-8005
Chicago *(G-6674)*
World Journal LLC F 312 842-8080
Chicago *(G-6675)*
Wrapports LLC F 312 321-3000
Chicago *(G-6683)*
Wyzz Inc D 217 753-5620
Springfield *(G-19468)*
Zweibel Worldwide Productions F 312 751-0503
Chicago *(G-6727)*

2721 Periodicals: Publishing & Printing

3 Point Ink LLC G 618 664-1550
Greenville *(G-10825)*
Aais Services Corporation E 630 681-8347
Lisle *(G-12856)*
Aais Services Corporation G 630 457-3263
Lisle *(G-12857)*
Aana Publishing Inc G 847 692-7050
Park Ridge *(G-16262)*
Abc Inc E 312 980-1000
Chicago *(G-3506)*
Ada Holding Company Inc F 312 440-2897
Chicago *(G-3537)*
Alali Enterprises Inc G 630 827-9231
Carol Stream *(G-2930)*
Allen Entertainment Management E 630 752-0903
Carol Stream *(G-2931)*
Allured Publishing Corporation E 630 653-2155
Carol Stream *(G-2932)*
American Assn Endodontists E 312 266-7255
Chicago *(G-3648)*
American Assn Nurosurgeons Inc E 847 378-0500
Rolling Meadows *(G-17710)*
American Bar Association A 312 988-5000
Chicago *(G-3650)*
American Catholic Press Inc F 708 331-5485
South Holland *(G-19191)*
American City Bus Journals Inc G 312 873-2200
Chicago *(G-3651)*
American Cllege Chest Physcans D 224 521-9800
Glenview *(G-10521)*
American Custom Publishing G 847 816-8660
Libertyville *(G-12628)*

SIC

27 PRINTING, PUBLISHING, AND ALLIED INDUSTRIES

American Hosp Assn Svcs Del .... E 312 422-2000
  Chicago *(G-3654)*
American Inquiry LLC .... G 312 922-1910
  Chicago *(G-3655)*
American Library Association .... E 312 280-5718
  Chicago *(G-3657)*
American Medical Association .... A 312 464-5000
  Chicago *(G-3660)*
American Soc HM Inspectors Inc ...... F 847 759-2820
  Des Plaines *(G-7728)*
American Soc Plastic Surgeons .... D 847 228-9900
  Arlington Heights *(G-691)*
American Trade Magazines LLC ...... G 312 497-7707
  Chicago *(G-3671)*
Anderson House Foundation .... G 630 461-7254
  Glen Ellyn *(G-10395)*
Andover Junction Publications 815 538-3060
  Mendota *(G-13935)*
Antigua Casa Sherry-Brener .... G 773 737-1711
  Joliet *(G-11824)*
API Publishing Services LLC .... E 312 644-6610
  Chicago *(G-3711)*
Applied Tech Publications Inc .... F 847 382-8100
  Willowbrook *(G-21029)*
Area Marketing Inc .... G 815 806-8844
  Frankfort *(G-9768)*
Art In Print Review 773 697-9478
  Chicago *(G-3735)*
Associated Equipment Distrs .... E 630 574-0650
  Schaumburg *(G-18447)*
▲ Associated Publications Inc .... F 312 266-8680
  Chicago *(G-3752)*
Association Management Center ...... D 847 375-4700
  Chicago *(G-3753)*
At Home Magazine .... G 217 351-5282
  Champaign *(G-3268)*
Banner Publications .... G 309 338-3294
  Cuba *(G-7297)*
Baptist General Conference .... D 800 323-4215
  Arlington Heights *(G-703)*
Barks Publications Inc .... F 312 321-9440
  Chicago *(G-3834)*
Be Group Inc .... G 312 436-0301
  Chicago *(G-3848)*
Bhs Media LLC .... E 312 701-0000
  Chicago *(G-3879)*
▲ Bible Truth Publishers Inc .... G 630 543-1441
  Addison *(G-49)*
BNP Media Inc .... C 847 205-5660
  Deerfield *(G-7598)*
Bowtie Inc .... G 630 515-9493
  Lombard *(G-13048)*
Business Insurance .... F 877 812-1587
  Chicago *(G-3980)*
C2 Publishing Inc .... F 630 834-4994
  Hillside *(G-11332)*
Caduceus Communications Inc 773 549-4800
  Chicago *(G-4001)*
CAM Systems 800 208-3244
  Chicago *(G-4009)*
Cap Today .... F 847 832-7377
  Northfield *(G-15510)*
Care Education Group Inc .... G 708 361-4110
  Palos Park *(G-16208)*
▲ CCH Incorporated .... A 847 267-7000
  Riverwoods *(G-17090)*
Central Illinois Bus Publs Inc 309 683-3060
  Peoria *(G-16416)*
▲ Central Illinois Homes Guide 309 688-6419
  Peoria *(G-16417)*
Challenge Publications L T D .... G 309 421-0392
  Macomb *(G-13388)*
Chambers Marketing Options 847 584-2626
  Elk Grove Village *(G-8888)*
Chas Levy Circulating Co .... G 630 353-2500
  Lisle *(G-12876)*
Chester White Swine Rcord Assn 309 691-0151
  Peoria *(G-16421)*
CHI Home Improvement Mag Inc ...... G 630 801-7788
  Aurora *(G-1073)*
Chicago Agent Magazine .... G 773 296-6001
  Chicago *(G-4086)*
Chicago and Suburbs .... G 773 306-3787
  Chicago *(G-4089)*
Chicago Boating Publications .... G 312 266-8400
  Chicago *(G-4092)*
Chicago Sports Media Inc .... G 847 676-1900
  Niles *(G-15109)*
▲ Christian Century .... F 312 263-7510
  Chicago *(G-4144)*

Christianity Today Intl .... C 630 260-6200
  Carol Stream *(G-2959)*
Church of Brethren Inc .... D 847 742-5100
  Elgin *(G-8539)*
Code Black LLC .... G 773 493-4500
  Chicago *(G-4191)*
College Bound Publications .... G 773 262-5810
  Chicago *(G-4201)*
Community Magazine Group .... G 312 880-0370
  Chicago *(G-4210)*
Concierge Preferred .... G 312 360-1770
  Chicago *(G-4215)*
Construction Bus Media LLC .... G 847 359-6493
  Palatine *(G-16105)*
Cook Communications Minis .... D 847 741-5168
  Elgin *(G-8556)*
Cook Communications Ministries ...... C 847 741-0800
  Elgin *(G-8557)*
Corbett Accel Healthcare Grp C .... C 312 475-2505
  Chicago *(G-4234)*
Cornerstone Communications .... E 773 989-2087
  Chicago *(G-4236)*
Cosmopolitan Foot Care .... G 312 984-5111
  Chicago *(G-4246)*
Country Journal Publishing Co .... F 217 877-9660
  Decatur *(G-7477)*
▲ Crain Communications Inc .... E 312 649-5200
  Chicago *(G-4258)*
Crain Communications Inc .... C 312 649-5200
  Chicago *(G-4259)*
CSP Information Group Inc .... E 630 574-5075
  Oak Brook *(G-15614)*
Cube Tomato Inc .... G 224 653-2655
  Schaumburg *(G-18499)*
Cupcake Holdings LLC .... C 800 794-5866
  Woodridge *(G-21289)*
◆ Dadant & Sons Inc .... D 217 847-3324
  Hamilton *(G-10954)*
Damien Corporation .... G 630 369-3549
  Naperville *(G-14814)*
Dobinski Marketing .... G 773 248-5880
  Chicago *(G-4376)*
Dorenfest Group Ltd .... D 312 464-3000
  Chicago *(G-4385)*
Dow Jones & Company Inc .... D 312 580-1023
  Chicago *(G-4393)*
Eagle Forum .... G 618 462-5415
  Alton *(G-554)*
Earl G Graves Pubg Co Inc .... G 312 274-0682
  Chicago *(G-4432)*
Ensembleiq Inc .... G 847 438-7357
  Kildeer *(G-12047)*
Entrepreneur Media Inc .... G 312 923-0818
  Chicago *(G-4516)*
ESP Properties LLC .... E 312 725-5100
  Chicago *(G-4531)*
Evang Lthn Ch Dr Mrtn Luth KG .... F 773 380-2540
  Chicago *(G-4535)*
Evanston Woman Magazine .... G 847 722-5654
  Evanston *(G-9517)*
Express Publishing Inc .... G 773 725-6218
  Chicago *(G-4545)*
Fabricators & Mfrs Assn Intl .... E 815 399-8700
  Elgin *(G-8584)*
Fanning Communications Inc .... G 708 293-1430
  Crestwood *(G-7118)*
Filmfax Magazine Inc .... G 847 866-7155
  Evanston *(G-9520)*
Financial Publishing Svcs Co .... F 847 501-4120
  Northfield *(G-15513)*
Fma Communicatons Inc .... D 815 227-8284
  Elgin *(G-8589)*
Food Service Publishing Co .... F 847 699-3300
  Des Plaines *(G-7772)*
Frank R Walker Company .... G 630 613-9312
  Lombard *(G-13079)*
Futures Magazine Inc .... G 312 846-4600
  Chicago *(G-4646)*
Gail McGrath & Associates Inc .... F 847 770-4620
  Northbrook *(G-15392)*
▲ Gary Grimm & Associates Inc ...... G 217 357-3401
  Carthage *(G-3136)*
Gazette .... E 815 777-0105
  Galena *(G-10172)*
Gemworld International Inc .... G 847 657-0555
  Glenview *(G-10549)*
Genesis Comics Group .... G 312 544-7473
  Chicago *(G-4680)*
Global Telephony Magazine .... E 312 840-8405
  Chicago *(G-4700)*

Good Sam Enterprises LLC .... E 847 229-6720
  Lincolnshire *(G-12767)*
Grandstand Publishing LLC .... G 847 491-6440
  Gurnee *(G-10883)*
Half Price Bks Rec Mgzines Inc .... E 847 588-2286
  Niles *(G-15128)*
Halper Publishing Company .... G 847 542-9793
  Evanston *(G-9530)*
Healthleaders Inc .... E 312 932-0848
  Chicago *(G-4793)*
Hearst Corporation .... E 312 984-5100
  Chicago *(G-4795)*
HH Backer Associates Inc .... F 312 578-1818
  Chicago *(G-4812)*
Highpoint Publishing Inc .... G 928 717-0100
  O Fallon *(G-15573)*
Home School Enrichment Inc .... G 309 347-1392
  Pekin *(G-16338)*
Homewood-Flossmoor Chronicle ...... G 630 728-2661
  Homewood *(G-11497)*
Homnay Magazine .... G 773 334-6655
  Chicago *(G-4836)*
Hotel Amerika .... G 219 508-9418
  Chicago *(G-4848)*
Hw Holdco LLC .... D 773 824-2400
  Rosemont *(G-18026)*
Icd Publications Inc .... G 847 913-8295
  Lincolnshire *(G-12773)*
Icon Acquisition Holdings LP .... G 312 751-8000
  Chicago *(G-4872)*
◆ Ideal Media LLC .... D 312 456-2822
  Chicago *(G-4876)*
Illini Media Co .... B 217 337-8300
  Champaign *(G-3306)*
Imagination Publishing LLC .... E 312 887-1000
  Chicago *(G-4894)*
India Tribune Ltd Corporation .... F 773 588-5077
  Chicago *(G-4905)*
Industrial Market Place .... E 847 676-1900
  Niles *(G-15133)*
Informa Business Media Inc .... D 312 595-1080
  Chicago *(G-4915)*
Informa Media Inc .... F 212 204-4200
  Chicago *(G-4916)*
Ink Spots Prtg & Meida Design .... G 708 754-1300
  Homewood *(G-11498)*
Inside Council .... F 312 654-3500
  Chicago *(G-4935)*
Inside Track Trading .... G 630 585-9218
  Aurora *(G-984)*
Institute For Public Affairs .... F 773 772-0100
  Chicago *(G-4938)*
Instrumentalists Inc .... F 847 446-5000
  Northbrook *(G-15406)*
International College Surgeons .... G 312 642-6502
  Chicago *(G-4952)*
Irish Dancing Magazine .... G 630 279-7521
  Elmhurst *(G-9381)*
▼ J S Paluch Co Inc .... C 847 678-9300
  Franklin Park *(G-9969)*
Jinny Corp .... G 773 588-7200
  Chicago *(G-5031)*
John C Grafft .... F 847 842-9200
  Lake Barrington *(G-12153)*
Johnson Press America Inc .... E 815 844-5161
  Pontiac *(G-16773)*
Keystone Printing & Publishing .... G 815 678-2591
  Richmond *(G-17016)*
Kiss ME Comix .... G 773 982-8334
  Chicago *(G-5107)*
▲ Korea Times .... D 847 626-0388
  Glenview *(G-10579)*
Lakeland Boating Magazine .... G 312 276-0610
  Evanston *(G-9546)*
Lakeside Publishing Co LLC .... G 847 491-6440
  Gurnee *(G-10894)*
Lambda Publications Inc .... F 773 871-7610
  Chicago *(G-5169)*
Lawrence Rgan Cmmnications Inc .... G 312 960-4100
  Chicago *(G-5184)*
Lightworks Communcation Inc .... G 847 966-1110
  Morton Grove *(G-14422)*
Lithuanian Catholic Press .... G 773 585-9500
  Chicago *(G-5236)*
Lithuanian Press Inc .... G 773 776-3399
  Chicago *(G-5237)*
Liturgical Conference .... G 847 866-3875
  Wilmette *(G-21085)*
Lsc Communications Inc .... C 773 272-9200
  Chicago *(G-5272)*

SIC SECTION
27 PRINTING, PUBLISHING, AND ALLIED INDUSTRIES

Lsc Communications Mm LLC ....F 815 844-1819
  Chicago (G-5273)
Lsc Communications Us LLC ....A 815 844-5181
  Pontiac (G-16774)
Lsc Communications Us LLC ....B 844 572-5720
  Chicago (G-5274)
Luby Publishing Inc ....F 312 341-1110
  Chicago (G-5276)
M & B Supply Inc ....F 309 944-3206
  Geneseo (G-10246)
M I T Financial Group Inc ....E 847 205-3000
  Northbrook (G-15425)
Magazine Plus ....G 773 281-4106
  Chicago (G-5314)
Maher Publications Inc ....F 630 941-2030
  Elmhurst (G-9398)
Mariah Media Inc ....G 312 222-1100
  Chicago (G-5334)
▲ Marketing & Technology Group ....E 312 266-3311
  Chicago (G-5340)
Mdm Communications Inc ....G 708 582-9667
  Skokie (G-18987)
Mediatec Publishing Inc ....E 312 676-9900
  Chicago (G-5386)
Mediatec Publishing Inc ....G 510 834-0100
  Chicago (G-5387)
Medical Liability Monitor Inc ....G 312 944-7900
  Elmwood Park (G-9455)
Medtext Inc ....G 630 325-3277
  Burr Ridge (G-2702)
Meredith Corp ....D 312 580-1623
  Chicago (G-5395)
Metal Center News ....F 630 571-1067
  Oak Brook (G-15643)
Metro Printing & Pubg Inc ....F 618 476-9587
  Millstadt (G-14052)
Midwest Outdoors Ltd ....E 630 887-7722
  Burr Ridge (G-2704)
Midwestern Family Magazine LLC ....G 309 303-7309
  Peoria (G-16477)
Modern Luxury Media LLC ....E 312 274-2500
  Chicago (G-5479)
Modern Trade Communications ....F 847 674-2200
  Skokie (G-18992)
Monitor Publishing Inc ....G 773 205-0303
  Chicago (G-5491)
Moody Bible Inst of Chicago ....E 312 329-2102
  Chicago (G-5496)
MTS Publishing Co ....F 630 955-9750
  Lisle (G-12916)
Narda Inc ....F 312 648-2300
  Chicago (G-5540)
National Association Realtors ....C 800 874-6500
  Chicago (G-5543)
National Bus Trader Inc ....F 815 946-2341
  Polo (G-16757)
National Publishing Company ....F 630 837-2044
  Norridge (G-15241)
National Safety Council ....B 630 285-1121
  Itasca (G-11707)
National Sporting Goods Assn ....F 847 296-6742
  Downers Grove (G-8063)
New Life Printing & Publishing ....G 847 658-4111
  Algonquin (G-382)
Northern Illinois Real Estate ....G 630 257-2480
  Lemont (G-12573)
Northwest Publishing LLC ....F 312 329-0600
  Chicago (G-5624)
One Accord Unity Nfp ....G 630 649-0793
  Bolingbrook (G-2223)
Outdoor Notebook Publishing ....F 630 257-6534
  Lemont (G-12575)
P&L Group Ltd of Illinois ....F 833 362-2100
  Chicago (G-5730)
Packaging World ....G 305 448-6875
  Chicago (G-5741)
Parade Publications Inc ....F 312 661-1620
  Chicago (G-5756)
Pierce Crandell & Co Inc ....G 847 549-6015
  Libertyville (G-12696)
Pitchfork Media Inc ....E 773 395-5937
  Chicago (G-5812)
Poetry Foundation ....E 312 787-7070
  Chicago (G-5830)
Practical Communications Inc ....E 773 754-3250
  Schaumburg (G-18681)
Profile Network Inc ....E 847 673-0592
  Skokie (G-19014)
Progressive Publications Inc ....G 847 697-9181
  Elgin (G-8699)

◆ Publications International Ltd ....B 847 676-3470
  Morton Grove (G-14434)
▼ Putman Media Inc ....D 630 467-1301
  Schaumburg (G-18689)
Quad/Graphics Inc ....A 815 338-6750
  Woodstock (G-21426)
R L D Communications Inc ....F 312 338-7007
  Chicago (G-5946)
Randall Publications ....F 847 437-6604
  Elk Grove Village (G-9213)
Randall Publishing Inc ....F 847 437-6604
  Elk Grove Village (G-9214)
Rankin Publishing Inc ....F 217 268-4959
  Arcola (G-664)
Rbp Services ....F 206 238-3526
  Morris (G-14324)
RCP Publications Inc ....G 773 227-4066
  Chicago (G-5979)
Real Estate News Corp ....G 773 866-9900
  Chicago (G-5983)
Reelchicagocom Enterprises Inc ....G 312 274-9980
  Chicago (G-5997)
Reilly Communication Group ....F 630 756-1225
  Arlington Heights (G-799)
Relx Inc ....F 937 247-3469
  Chicago (G-6013)
Relx Inc ....E 309 689-1000
  Peoria (G-16509)
Rochelle Newspapers Inc ....G 815 562-4171
  Rochelle (G-17156)
Rookie LLC ....G 708 278-1628
  Oak Park (G-15770)
Royal Publishing Inc ....G 309 829-6191
  Normal (G-15222)
RSM International ....D 312 634-3400
  Chicago (G-6074)
Rylin Media LLC ....G 708 246-7599
  Western Springs (G-20725)
S R Bastien Co ....F 847 858-1175
  Evanston (G-9573)
Sagamore Publishing LLC ....F 217 359-5940
  Champaign (G-3345)
Sanderson and Associates ....F 312 829-4350
  Chicago (G-6099)
◆ Scranton Glltte Cmmnctions Inc ....D 847 391-1000
  Arlington Heights (G-805)
SGC Horizon LLC ....F 847 391-1000
  Arlington Heights (G-808)
Sherman Media Company Inc ....G 312 335-1962
  Lake Forest (G-12302)
Silent W Communications Inc ....G 630 479-7950
  Montgomery (G-14270)
Specialty Publishing Company ....E 630 933-0844
  Carol Stream (G-3072)
Sports Illustrated For Kids ....G 312 321-7828
  Chicago (G-6219)
Stagnito Partners LLC ....E 224 632-8200
  Chicago (G-6227)
Surplus Record LLC ....F 312 372-9077
  Chicago (G-6290)
Tails Inc ....F 773 564-9300
  Chicago (G-6311)
▲ Talcott Communications Corp ....E 312 849-2220
  Chicago (G-6313)
▲ Techgraphic Solutions Inc ....F 309 693-9400
  Peoria (G-16536)
Tegna Inc ....C 847 490-6657
  Hoffman Estates (G-11468)
▲ Theosophical Society In Amer ....E 630 665-0130
  Wheaton (G-20826)
Theosophical Society In Amer ....F 630 665-0123
  Wheaton (G-20827)
Thg International Publishing ....E 312 540-3000
  Chicago (G-6363)
This Week In Chicago Inc ....G 312 943-0838
  Chicago (G-6367)
TI Gotham Inc ....F 312 321-7833
  Chicago (G-6376)
Tmb Publishing Inc ....G 847 564-1127
  Niles (G-15181)
Transportation Eqp Advisors ....D 847 318-7575
  Rosemont (G-18055)
Tribune Publishing Company LLC ....D 312 832-6711
  Chicago (G-6425)
Trmg LLP ....F 847 441-4122
  Northfield (G-15535)
Trusted Media Brands Inc ....F 312 540-0035
  Chicago (G-6439)
Tube & Pipe Association Intl ....D 815 399-8700
  Elgin (G-8763)

University of Chicago ....B 773 702-1722
  Chicago (G-6485)
US Catholic Magazine ....G 312 236-7782
  Chicago (G-6500)
Utility Business Media Inc ....F 815 459-1796
  Crystal Lake (G-7287)
Verone Publishing Inc ....G 773 866-0811
  Chicago (G-6537)
Vertical Web Media LLC ....E 312 362-0076
  Chicago (G-6539)
Walnecks Inc ....G 630 985-2097
  Downers Grove (G-8106)
Watt Publishing Co ....E 815 966-5400
  Rockford (G-17678)
Willis Stein & Partners Manage ....F 312 422-2400
  Chicago (G-6632)
▼ Wilton Holdings Inc ....A 630 963-7100
  Woodridge (G-21349)
▼ Wilton Industries Inc ....B 630 963-7100
  Naperville (G-14949)
Wilton Industries Inc ....F 815 834-9390
  Romeoville (G-17888)
Winsight LLC ....C 312 876-0004
  Chicago (G-6646)
◆ Wolters Kluwer US Inc ....E 847 580-5000
  Riverwoods (G-17097)

2731 Books: Publishing & Printing

3b Media Inc ....F 312 563-9363
  Chicago (G-3467)
A Trustworthy Sup Source Inc ....G 773 480-0255
  Chicago (G-3492)
Acta Publications ....G 773 989-3036
  Chicago (G-3533)
Advantage Press Inc ....G 630 960-5305
  Lisle (G-12858)
Adventures Unlimited ....G 815 253-6390
  Kempton (G-12013)
African-American Images Inc ....F 708 672-4909
  Crete (G-7134)
▲ Agate Publishing Inc ....G 847 475-4457
  Evanston (G-9488)
AJS Publications ....G 847 526-5027
  Island Lake (G-11604)
▲ Albert Whitman & Company ....E 847 232-2800
  Park Ridge (G-16266)
▼ Allegro Publishing Inc ....G 847 565-9083
  Chicago (G-3613)
American Association of Indivi ....E 312 280-0170
  Chicago (G-3649)
American Bar Association ....A 312 988-5000
  Chicago (G-3650)
American Catholic Press Inc ....F 708 331-5485
  South Holland (G-19191)
American Hosp Assn Svcs Del ....E 312 422-2000
  Chicago (G-3654)
◆ American Labelmark Company ....C 773 478-0900
  Chicago (G-3656)
American Supply Association ....F 630 467-0000
  Itasca (G-11622)
Anonymous Press Inc ....G 509 779-4094
  Chicago (G-3701)
Antigua Casa Sherry-Brener ....G 773 737-1711
  Joliet (G-11824)
▲ Art Media Resources Inc ....G 312 663-5351
  Chicago (G-3736)
Arthur Coyle Press ....G 773 465-8418
  Chicago (G-3739)
Arvamont ....G 630 926-2468
  Hinsdale (G-11361)
Audio Tech Bus Bk Summaries ....G 630 734-0500
  Oak Brook (G-15595)
Baptist General Conference ....D 800 323-4215
  Arlington Heights (G-703)
Barks Publications Inc ....F 312 321-9440
  Chicago (G-3834)
Bendinger Bruce Crtve Comm In ....G 773 871-1179
  Chicago (G-3866)
Bestwords Org Corp ....F 618 939-4324
  Columbia (G-6985)
Blooming Color Inc ....D 630 705-9200
  Lombard (G-13047)
▲ Bolchazy-Carducci Publishers ....F 847 526-4344
  Mundelein (G-14668)
Bookends Publishing ....G 312 988-1500
  Chicago (G-3934)
Brainworx Studio ....F 773 743-8200
  Chicago (G-3944)
Broken Oar Inc ....G 847 639-9468
  Port Barrington (G-16785)

Employee Codes: A=Over 500 employees, B=251-500
C=101-250, D=51-100, E=20-50, F=10-19, G=3-9

Brown & Miller Literary Assoc ......G 312 922-3063
Chicago *(G-3967)*
C W Publications Inc ......G 800 554-5537
Sterling *(G-19502)*
▲ **Carus Publishing Company** ......G 603 924-7209
Chicago *(G-4033)*
Carus Publishing Company ......F 312 701-1720
Chicago *(G-4034)*
Castlegate Publishers Inc ......G 847 382-6420
Barrington *(G-1216)*
Catalyst Chicago ......G 312 427-4830
Chicago *(G-4040)*
Caxton Club ......G 312 266-8825
Chicago *(G-4044)*
▲ **CCH Incorporated** ......A 847 267-7000
Riverwoods *(G-17090)*
Charles C Thomas Publisher ......G 217 789-8980
Springfield *(G-19348)*
▲ **Chicago Review Press Inc** ......E 312 337-0747
Chicago *(G-4126)*
Christian National Womans ......G 847 864-1396
Evanston *(G-9505)*
▲ **Christianica Center** ......G 847 657-3818
Glenview *(G-10536)*
City of Chicago ......G 773 581-8000
Chicago *(G-4158)*
Coaching For Excellence LLC ......F 708 957-6047
Country Club Hills *(G-7036)*
Computer Industry Almanac Inc ......G 847 758-1926
Arlington Heights *(G-718)*
▲ **Continental Sales Inc** ......G 847 381-6530
Barrington *(G-1218)*
Contractors Register Inc ......F 630 519-3480
Lombard *(G-13058)*
Cook Communications Minis ......D 847 741-5168
Elgin *(G-8556)*
Cook Communications Ministries ......C 847 741-0800
Elgin *(G-8557)*
Cornerstone Community Outreach ......F 773 506-4904
Chicago *(G-4237)*
Creative Curricula Inc ......G 815 363-9419
McHenry *(G-13732)*
Crown Kandy Enterprise Ltd ......F 708 580-6494
Westchester *(G-20696)*
▲ **Crystal Productions Co** ......F 847 657-8144
Northbrook *(G-15369)*
Cupcake Holdings LLC ......C 800 794-5866
Woodridge *(G-21289)*
Curbside Splendor ......G 224 515-6512
Chicago *(G-4285)*
Damien Corporation ......G 630 369-3549
Naperville *(G-14814)*
Dasher Dependable Reindeer LLC ......G 630 513-7737
Saint Charles *(G-18179)*
Do You See What I See Entertai ......G 773 612-1269
Chicago *(G-4375)*
Doxa Enterprises LLC ......G 618 515-4470
East Saint Louis *(G-8305)*
Eagle Forum ......G 618 462-5415
Alton *(G-554)*
Ebonyenergy Publishing Inc Nfp ......G 773 851-5159
Chicago *(G-4442)*
Ebooks2go ......G 847 598-1145
Schaumburg *(G-18513)*
Elliot Inst For Scial Scnces R ......G 217 525-8202
Springfield *(G-19361)*
Empowered Press LLC ......G 630 400-3127
Oswego *(G-16003)*
▲ **Encyclopaedia Britannica Inc** ......C 312 347-7000
Chicago *(G-4505)*
Final Call Inc ......D 773 602-1230
Chicago *(G-4587)*
Foundation Lithuanian Minor ......G 630 969-1316
Downers Grove *(G-8005)*
Frank R Walker Company ......G 630 613-9312
Lombard *(G-13079)*
▲ **Gary Grimm & Associates Inc** ......G 217 357-3401
Carthage *(G-3136)*
◆ **Good News Publishers** ......E 630 682-4300
Wheaton *(G-20801)*
Goodheart-Willcox Company Inc ......D 708 687-0315
Tinley Park *(G-19833)*
Gordon Burke John Publisher ......G 847 866-8625
Evanston *(G-9526)*
Gorman & Associates ......G 309 691-9087
Peoria *(G-16446)*
◆ **Grace and Truth** ......G 217 442-1120
Danville *(G-7340)*
Graphic Score Book Co Inc ......G 847 823-7382
Park Ridge *(G-16281)*
▲ **Great Books Foundation** ......E 312 332-5870
Chicago *(G-4732)*
Greek Art Printing & Pubg Co ......G 847 724-8860
Glenview *(G-10553)*
Green Around Sills LLC ......G 847 868-8957
Evanston *(G-9527)*
H G Acquisition Corp ......G 630 382-1000
Burr Ridge *(G-2679)*
Helivalues ......G 847 487-8258
Wauconda *(G-20355)*
Highlight of Chicago Bress ......G 773 944-0085
Chicago *(G-4818)*
Hmh Sports LLC ......G 773 330-3789
Evanston *(G-9532)*
Holder Publishing Corporation ......G 309 828-7533
Bloomington *(G-2058)*
Hope Publishing Company ......F 630 665-3200
Carol Stream *(G-2999)*
◆ **Houghton Mifflin Harcourt** ......E 928 467-9599
Geneva *(G-10275)*
Houghton Mifflin Harcourt Co ......G 630 467-6049
Itasca *(G-11666)*
Houghton Mifflin Harcourt Co ......G 303 504-9312
Geneva *(G-10276)*
Houghton Mifflin Harcourt Co ......G 800 225-5425
Evanston *(G-9533)*
Houghton Mifflin Harcourt Pubg ......C 630 208-5704
Geneva *(G-10277)*
Houghton Mifflin Harcourt Pubg ......B 630 467-6095
Itasca *(G-11667)*
Houghton Mifflin Harcourt Pubg ......B 847 869-2300
Evanston *(G-9534)*
Houghton Mifflin Harcourt Pubg ......B 708 869-2300
Evanston *(G-9535)*
How To Be Good For Santa Inc ......G 281 961-4002
North Barrington *(G-15285)*
Human Factor RES Group Inc ......G 618 476-3200
Millstadt *(G-14047)*
IB Source Inc ......G 312 698-7062
Chicago *(G-4869)*
Illinois Inst Cntng Legl Ed ......E 217 787-2080
Springfield *(G-19386)*
Information Usa Inc ......G 312 943-6288
Chicago *(G-4919)*
Intervrsity Chrstn Fllwshp/Usa ......D 630 734-4000
Westmont *(G-20749)*
▼ **J S Paluch Co Inc** ......C 847 678-9300
Franklin Park *(G-9969)*
◆ **Kidsbooks LLC** ......F 773 509-0707
Chicago *(G-5101)*
Kishknows Inc ......G 708 252-3648
Richton Park *(G-17030)*
Koza ......G 773 646-0958
Chicago *(G-5128)*
Linmore Publishing Co ......G 847 382-7606
Barrington *(G-1224)*
Literacy Resources LLC ......G 708 366-5947
Oak Park *(G-15763)*
LMS Innovations Inc ......G 312 613-2345
Chicago *(G-5247)*
Manufctrers Clring Hse Ill Inc ......G 773 545-6300
Chicago *(G-5327)*
Marantha Wrld Rvval Ministries ......G 773 384-7717
Chicago *(G-5328)*
Marytown ......E 847 367-7800
Libertyville *(G-12673)*
Media Associates Intl Inc ......F 630 260-9063
Carol Stream *(G-3022)*
Medical Memories LLC ......G 847 478-0078
Buffalo Grove *(G-2571)*
Michael A Greenberg MD Ltd ......F 847 364-4717
Elk Grove Village *(G-9122)*
◆ **Midpoint Trade Books Inc** ......F 212 727-0190
Chicago *(G-5435)*
Midwest Theological Forum Inc ......G 630 739-9750
Downers Grove *(G-8057)*
Monitor Publishing Inc ......G 773 205-0303
Chicago *(G-5491)*
Moody Bible Inst of Chicago ......E 312 329-2102
Chicago *(G-5496)*
◆ **Moody Bible Inst of Chicago** ......A 312 329-4000
Chicago *(G-5495)*
Motamed Medical Publishing Co ......G 773 761-6667
Chicago *(G-5505)*
Movie Facts Inc ......E 847 299-9700
Des Plaines *(G-7807)*
Multi Packaging Solutions Inc ......G 773 283-9500
Chicago *(G-5523)*
National Bus Trader Inc ......F 815 946-2341
Polo *(G-16757)*
National School Services Inc ......E 847 438-3859
Long Grove *(G-13167)*
Nature House Inc ......D 217 833-2393
Griggsville *(G-10850)*
Need To Know Inc ......G 309 691-3877
Peoria *(G-16484)*
Nexus Supply Consortium Inc ......G 630 649-2868
Bolingbrook *(G-2222)*
Oasis Audio LLC ......G 630 668-5367
Carol Stream *(G-3042)*
Oasis International Limited ......G 630 326-0045
Geneva *(G-10295)*
Ohrvall Media LLC ......G 630 378-9738
Plainfield *(G-16698)*
Pamacheyon Publishing Inc ......G 815 395-0101
Rockford *(G-17547)*
Permissions Group Inc ......G 847 635-6550
Wheeling *(G-20957)*
Perry Johnson Inc ......F 847 635-0010
Rosemont *(G-18041)*
▲ **Phoenix Intl Publications Inc** ......B 877 277-9441
Chicago *(G-5803)*
Pieces of Learning Inc ......G 618 964-9426
Marion *(G-13526)*
▲ **Pivot Point Usa Inc** ......C 800 886-4247
Chicago *(G-5814)*
Poetry Center ......G 312 899-1229
Chicago *(G-5829)*
Polonia Book Store Inc ......G 773 481-6968
Chicago *(G-5835)*
Practice Management Info Corp ......E 800 633-7467
Downers Grove *(G-8081)*
Press Syndication Group LLC ......G 646 325-3221
Chicago *(G-5867)*
◆ **Preston Industries Inc** ......C 847 647-0611
Niles *(G-15162)*
Psytec Inc ......G 815 758-1415
Dekalb *(G-7699)*
◆ **Publications International Ltd** ......B 847 676-3470
Morton Grove *(G-14434)*
▼ **Putman Media Inc** ......D 630 467-1301
Schaumburg *(G-18689)*
Raven Tree Press LLC ......G 800 323-8270
Crystal Lake *(G-7253)*
Research Press Company Inc ......F 217 352-3273
Champaign *(G-3341)*
Respect Incorporated ......G 815 806-1907
Manhattan *(G-13435)*
Rite-TEC Communications ......G 815 459-7712
Crystal Lake *(G-7258)*
Riverside Assessments LLC ......G 800 767-8420
Itasca *(G-11725)*
Rohrer Graphic Arts Inc ......F 630 832-3434
Elmhurst *(G-9419)*
Rookie LLC ......G 708 278-1628
Oak Park *(G-15770)*
Royal Publishing Inc ......G 309 343-4007
Galesburg *(G-10219)*
Royal Publishing Inc ......G 815 220-0400
Peru *(G-16592)*
S R Bastien Co ......F 847 858-1175
Evanston *(G-9573)*
Sagamore Publishing LLC ......F 217 359-5940
Champaign *(G-3345)*
Scholastic Inc ......E 630 443-8197
Saint Charles *(G-18267)*
Scholastic Inc ......E 630 671-0601
Roselle *(G-17984)*
◆ **Shure Products Inc** ......F 773 227-1001
Chicago *(G-6162)*
◆ **Sourcebooks Llc** ......D 630 961-3900
Naperville *(G-14918)*
Springfield Printing Inc ......G 217 787-3500
Springfield *(G-19454)*
Sterling Books Limited ......G 630 325-3853
Hinsdale *(G-11380)*
Students Publishing Company In ......G 847 491-7206
Evanston *(G-9579)*
Success Publishing Group Inc ......F 708 565-2681
Chicago *(G-6262)*
Surrey Books Inc ......G 847 475-4457
Evanston *(G-9580)*
Taylor & Francis Group LLC ......G 630 482-9886
Batavia *(G-1424)*
Taylor Enterprises Inc ......G 847 367-1032
Libertyville *(G-12715)*
Templegate Publishers ......G 217 522-3353
Springfield *(G-19463)*
Theosophical Society In Amer ......F 630 665-0123
Wheaton *(G-20827)*

27 PRINTING, PUBLISHING, AND ALLIED INDUSTRIES

▲ Theosophical Society In Amer ..... E 630 665-0130
  Wheaton *(G-20826)*
Thg International Publishing ..... E 312 540-3000
  Chicago *(G-6363)*
Third Wrld Press Fundation Inc ..... F 773 651-0700
  Chicago *(G-6366)*
Thomson Reuters Corporation ..... D 312 288-4654
  Chicago *(G-6369)*
Trade Print Inc ..... G 773 625-0792
  Chicago *(G-6402)*
Triumph Books LLC ..... G 800 888-4741
  Chicago *(G-6431)*
◆ Triumph Books Corp ..... E 312 337-0747
  Chicago *(G-6432)*
Twain Media Mark Publishing ..... G 217 223-7008
  Quincy *(G-16953)*
U S Naval Institute ..... G 800 233-8764
  University Park *(G-19970)*
University of Chicago ..... B 773 702-1722
  Chicago *(G-6485)*
Urantia Corp ..... F 773 248-6616
  Chicago *(G-6492)*
Urantia Foundation ..... E 773 525-3319
  Chicago *(G-6493)*
Venture Publishing Inc ..... G 217 359-5940
  Urbana *(G-20002)*
West Publishing Corporation ..... D 312 894-1690
  Chicago *(G-6605)*
▼ Wilton Holdings Inc ..... A 630 963-7100
  Woodridge *(G-21349)*
◆ Wilton Industries Inc ..... B 630 963-7100
  Naperville *(G-14949)*
Wilton Industries Inc ..... F 815 834-9390
  Romeoville *(G-17888)*
Windsong Press Ltd ..... G 847 223-4586
  Grayslake *(G-10806)*
Windy City Publishers LLC ..... G 847 925-9434
  Palatine *(G-16175)*
◆ Wolters Kluwer US Inc ..... E 847 580-5000
  Riverwoods *(G-17097)*
▲ World Book Inc ..... E 312 729-5800
  Chicago *(G-6671)*

2732 Book Printing, Not Publishing

Advocate Print Shop ..... E 847 390-3594
  Mount Prospect *(G-14510)*
Andover Junction Publications ..... G 815 538-3060
  Mendota *(G-13935)*
Award/Visionps Inc ..... G 331 318-7800
  Chicago *(G-3791)*
Baker & Taylor LLC ..... B 815 802-2444
  Momence *(G-14183)*
Beslow Associates Inc ..... G 847 559-2703
  Northbrook *(G-15349)*
Bible Students Publications ..... G 630 595-0984
  Bensenville *(G-1753)*
Bostic Publishing Company ..... G 773 551-7065
  Chicago *(G-3937)*
Charles C Thomas Publisher ..... G 217 789-8980
  Springfield *(G-19348)*
Cook Communications Ministries ..... C 847 741-0800
  Elgin *(G-8557)*
Creasey Printing Services Inc ..... G 217 787-1055
  Springfield *(G-19356)*
Finishing Group ..... G 847 884-4890
  Schaumburg *(G-18528)*
Greek Art Printing & Pubg Co ..... G 847 724-8860
  Glenview *(G-10553)*
Hopper Graphics Inc ..... G 708 489-0459
  Palos Heights *(G-16189)*
In-Print Graphics Inc ..... E 708 396-1010
  Oak Forest *(G-15683)*
Ink Spots Prtg & Meida Design ..... G 708 754-1300
  Homewood *(G-11498)*
Interntnal Awakening Ministries ..... G 630 653-8616
  Wheaton *(G-20806)*
Johnson Press America Inc ..... E 815 844-5161
  Pontiac *(G-16773)*
Kellogg Printing Co ..... F 309 734-8388
  Monmouth *(G-14220)*
Kjellberg Printing ..... F 630 653-2244
  Wheaton *(G-20807)*
KK Stevens Publishing Co ..... G 309 329-2151
  Astoria *(G-893)*
Lsc Communications Inc ..... C 773 272-9200
  Chicago *(G-5272)*
Lsc Communications Inc ..... G 217 258-2832
  Mattoon *(G-13641)*
Lsc Communications Mm LLC ..... F 815 844-1819
  Chicago *(G-5273)*

Lsc Communications Us LLC ..... B 844 572-5720
  Chicago *(G-5274)*
Lsc Communications Us LLC ..... G 217 235-0561
  Mattoon *(G-13642)*
Marty Gannon ..... G 847 895-1059
  Schaumburg *(G-18620)*
Pantagraph Printing and Sty Co ..... F 309 829-1071
  Bloomington *(G-2084)*
Printers Row Press Inc ..... E 312 427-7150
  Chicago *(G-5879)*
Quad/Graphics Inc ..... A 815 734-4121
  Mount Morris *(G-14500)*
R R Donnelley & Sons Company ..... B 630 588-5000
  Lisle *(G-12931)*
R R Donnelley & Sons Company ..... C 312 326-8000
  Chicago *(G-5950)*
R R Donnelley & Sons Company ..... G 815 844-5181
  Pontiac *(G-16779)*
R R Donnelley & Sons Company ..... A 815 584-2770
  Dwight *(G-8158)*
Roger Fritz & Associates Inc ..... G 630 355-2614
  Naperville *(G-14911)*
RR Donnelley & Sons Company ..... C 312 236-8000
  Chicago *(G-6071)*
Rsn Mailing ..... G 314 724-3364
  Collinsville *(G-6974)*
Sandes Quynetta ..... G 815 275-4876
  Freeport *(G-10140)*
▲ Tvp Color Graphics Inc ..... G 630 837-3600
  Streamwood *(G-19600)*
University of Chicago ..... E 773 702-7000
  Chicago *(G-6486)*
Vision Intgrted Grphics Group ..... C 331 318-7800
  Bolingbrook *(G-2251)*
Wctu Press ..... G 847 864-1396
  Evanston *(G-9587)*
Wold Printing Services Ltd ..... G 847 546-3110
  Volo *(G-20206)*

2741 Misc Publishing

◆ 24land Express Inc ..... G 630 766-2424
  Elk Grove Village *(G-8789)*
2bald Inc ..... G 815 403-8870
  Johnsburg *(G-11800)*
About Learning Inc ..... F 847 487-1800
  Wauconda *(G-20326)*
Aerodine Magazine ..... G 847 358-4355
  Inverness *(G-11592)*
Affectionately Yours Ent ..... G 708 275-6333
  Matteson *(G-13616)*
Aj Auto ..... G 847 678-8200
  Schiller Park *(G-18783)*
AJS Ministry ..... G 773 403-4166
  Matteson *(G-13617)*
Allured Publishing Corporation ..... E 630 653-2155
  Carol Stream *(G-2932)*
Am-Don Partnership ..... G 217 355-7750
  Champaign *(G-3263)*
American Custom Publishing ..... G 847 816-8660
  Libertyville *(G-12628)*
Anash Educational Institute ..... G 773 338-7704
  Chicago *(G-3690)*
Angle Press Inc ..... G 847 439-6388
  Rolling Meadows *(G-17711)*
Arcsec Digital LLC ..... G 312 324-4794
  Lake Forest *(G-12225)*
Art In Print Review ..... G 773 697-9478
  Chicago *(G-3735)*
Arthur Coyle Press ..... G 773 465-8418
  Chicago *(G-3739)*
AT&T Corp ..... C 630 693-5000
  Lombard *(G-13041)*
AT&T Teleholdings Inc ..... F 800 288-2020
  Chicago *(G-3756)*
▲ Avenir Publishing Inc ..... E 872 228-2830
  Chicago *(G-3784)*
Avondale Adventures ..... G 773 588-5761
  Chicago *(G-3789)*
Award/Visionps Inc ..... G 331 318-7800
  Chicago *(G-3791)*
B A I Publishers ..... G 847 537-1300
  Wheeling *(G-20854)*
Baka Vitaliy ..... G 773 370-5522
  Chicago *(G-3817)*
◆ Ball Publishing ..... F 630 208-9080
  West Chicago *(G-20548)*
Ballotready Inc ..... G 301 706-0708
  Chicago *(G-3820)*
Band of Shoppers Inc ..... G 312 857-4250
  Chicago *(G-3824)*

◆ Bass-Mollett Publishers Inc ..... D 618 664-3141
  Greenville *(G-10826)*
Beardstown Newspapers Inc ..... G 217 323-1010
  Beardstown *(G-1445)*
Bendinger Bruce Crtve Comm In ..... G 773 871-1179
  Chicago *(G-3866)*
Beyond Limits Media Group LLC ..... G 773 948-9296
  Chicago *(G-3878)*
Bishop Engineering Company ..... F 630 305-9538
  Lisle *(G-12872)*
Biz 3 Publicity ..... G 773 342-3331
  Chicago *(G-3903)*
Boone County Shopper Inc ..... F 815 544-2166
  Belvidere *(G-1656)*
Brilliant Color Corp ..... G 847 367-3300
  Libertyville *(G-12640)*
Bureau of National Affairs Inc ..... G 773 775-8801
  Chicago *(G-3975)*
Businessmine LLC ..... G 630 541-8480
  Lombard *(G-13049)*
C and H Publishing Co ..... G 618 625-2711
  Sesser *(G-18865)*
C W Publications Inc ..... G 800 554-5537
  Sterling *(G-19502)*
Cab Communications Inc ..... G 847 963-8740
  Palatine *(G-16097)*
Cade Communications Inc ..... G 773 477-7184
  Chicago *(G-4000)*
Cambridge Business Publishers ..... G 630 321-0173
  Westmont *(G-20731)*
Cammun LLC ..... G 312 628-1201
  Chicago *(G-4013)*
Canright & Paule Inc ..... G 888 202-3894
  Chicago *(G-4015)*
Catalog Designers Inc ..... G 847 228-0025
  Elk Grove Village *(G-8881)*
Ceg Subsidiary LLC ..... G 618 262-8666
  Mount Carmel *(G-14468)*
▲ Central Illinois Homes Guide ..... G 309 688-6419
  Peoria *(G-16417)*
▲ Chase Group LLC ..... F 847 564-2000
  Northbrook *(G-15355)*
Chesley Limited ..... G 847 562-9292
  Northbrook *(G-15356)*
Chicago Sports Media Inc ..... G 847 676-1900
  Niles *(G-15109)*
Christian Specialized Services ..... G 217 546-7338
  Springfield *(G-19350)*
Cision US Inc ..... C 312 922-2400
  Chicago *(G-4154)*
City Press Juice & Bottle ..... G 773 360-7226
  Chicago *(G-4160)*
Common Ground Publishing LLC ..... E 217 721-6839
  Champaign *(G-3281)*
Communications Resource Inc ..... G 630 860-1661
  Schaumburg *(G-18482)*
Consumerbase LLC ..... C 312 600-8000
  Chicago *(G-4224)*
Cottage Door Press LLC ..... F 224 228-6000
  Rolling Meadows *(G-17724)*
Creasey Printing Services Inc ..... G 217 787-1055
  Springfield *(G-19356)*
Creative Directory Inc ..... G 773 427-7777
  Chicago *(G-4262)*
Creative Ideas Inc ..... G 217 245-1378
  Jacksonville *(G-11763)*
Cross Express Company ..... G 847 439-7457
  Elk Grove Village *(G-8922)*
Crystal L Smith ..... G 773 817-2797
  Evanston *(G-9507)*
Custom Design Services & Assoc ..... F 815 226-9747
  Rockford *(G-17362)*
Damien Corporation ..... G 630 369-3549
  Naperville *(G-14814)*
Debbie Harshman ..... G 217 335-2112
  Barry *(G-1249)*
Delair Publishing Company Inc ..... C 708 345-7000
  Melrose Park *(G-13847)*
Deshamusic Inc ..... G 818 257-2716
  Chicago *(G-4344)*
▲ Devils Due Publishing ..... G 773 412-6427
  Chicago *(G-4348)*
Dino Publishing LLC ..... G 312 822-9266
  Chicago *(G-4363)*
Doody Enterprises Inc ..... G 312 239-6226
  Oak Park *(G-15751)*
Dramatic Publishing Company ..... F 815 338-7170
  Woodstock *(G-21383)*
Ea Mackay Enterprises Inc ..... E 630 627-7010
  Lombard *(G-13070)*

Eagle Publications Inc.....E..... 618 345-5400
Fairview Heights *(G-9645)*
Earthcomber LLC.....F..... 708 366-1600
Oak Park *(G-15752)*
Edge Communication.....G..... 708 749-7818
Berwyn *(G-1951)*
Element Collection.....G..... 217 898-5175
Allerton *(G-403)*
Elliot Inst For Scial Scnces R.....G..... 217 525-8202
Springfield *(G-19361)*
Elliott Jsj & Associates Inc.....G..... 847 242-0412
Glencoe *(G-10429)*
Exclusive Publications Inc.....G..... 847 963-0400
Hoffman Estates *(G-11421)*
F M Aquisition Corp.....G..... 773 728-8351
Chicago *(G-4551)*
Farm Week.....E..... 309 557-3140
Bloomington *(G-2042)*
Financial Publishing Svcs Co.....F..... 847 501-4120
Northfield *(G-15513)*
Fire House Press.....G..... 217 864-2864
Decatur *(G-7494)*
Fisher Printing Inc.....C..... 708 598-1500
Bridgeview *(G-2346)*
Fleming Music Technology Ctr.....G..... 708 316-8662
Wheaton *(G-20799)*
Food Service Publishing Co.....G..... 847 699-3300
Park Ridge *(G-16276)*
Food Service Publishing Co.....F..... 847 699-3300
Des Plaines *(G-7772)*
Foodservice Database Co Inc.....F..... 773 745-9400
Chicago *(G-4617)*
Frank R Walker Company.....G..... 630 613-9312
Lombard *(G-13079)*
Frankenstitch Promotions LLC.....F..... 847 459-4840
Wheeling *(G-20901)*
Fresh Facs.....G..... 618 357-9697
Pinckneyville *(G-16614)*
Fully Equipped Inc.....G..... 312 978-9936
Chicago *(G-4641)*
Funny Valentine Press Inc.....G..... 773 769-6552
Chicago *(G-4643)*
▲ G I A Publications Inc.....E..... 708 496-3800
Chicago *(G-4650)*
▲ G R Leonard & Co Inc.....E..... 847 797-8101
Arlington Heights *(G-740)*
Gantec Pubg Solutions LLC.....F..... 847 598-1144
Schaumburg *(G-18534)*
Gatehouse Media III Holdings.....G..... 585 598-0030
Peoria *(G-16442)*
Glorius Renditions.....G..... 815 315-0177
Leaf River *(G-12542)*
Gophercentral.....G..... 708 478-4500
Tinley Park *(G-19834)*
Graphic Communicators Inc.....G..... 708 385-7550
Palos Heights *(G-16186)*
Graphic Press.....G..... 312 909-6100
Chicago *(G-4727)*
Halper Publishing Company.....G..... 847 542-9793
Evanston *(G-9530)*
Hancock County Shopper.....G..... 217 847-6628
Hamilton *(G-10959)*
Haute Noir Media Group Inc.....G..... 312 869-4526
Chicago *(G-4787)*
Havas Barn.....G..... 312 640-6800
Chicago *(G-4788)*
Health Administration Press.....D..... 312 424-2800
Chicago *(G-4790)*
Heartland Publications Inc.....G..... 217 529-9506
Springfield *(G-19381)*
Heritage Products Corporation.....G..... 847 419-8835
Buffalo Grove *(G-2545)*
Hermitage Group Inc.....E..... 773 561-3773
Chicago *(G-4808)*
Hill Reporter LLC.....G..... 309 532-4794
El Paso *(G-8438)*
Holder Publishing Corporation.....G..... 309 828-7533
Bloomington *(G-2058)*
Holsolutions Inc.....G..... 888 847-5467
Frankfort *(G-9801)*
Holt Publications Inc.....G..... 618 654-6206
Highland *(G-11226)*
Hope Publishing Company.....F..... 630 665-3200
Carol Stream *(G-2999)*
How To Be Good For Santa Inc.....G..... 281 961-4002
North Barrington *(G-15285)*
HP Interactive Inc.....G..... 773 681-4440
Chicago *(G-4855)*
Hunting Network LLC.....G..... 847 659-8200
Huntley *(G-11540)*
▲ I P G Warehouse Ltd.....E..... 773 722-5527
Chicago *(G-4867)*
Illini Media Co.....B..... 217 337-8300
Champaign *(G-3306)*
Imagination Publishing LLC.....E..... 312 887-1000
Chicago *(G-4894)*
Imedia Network Inc.....G..... 847 331-1774
Chicago *(G-4896)*
Inter-State Studio & Pubg Co.....E..... 815 874-0342
Rockford *(G-17468)*
J C Communications Company.....G..... 312 236-5122
Chicago *(G-4988)*
▼ J S Paluch Co Inc.....C..... 847 678-9300
Franklin Park *(G-9969)*
Janelle Publications Inc.....G..... 815 756-2300
Dekalb *(G-7686)*
JAS Express Inc.....G..... 847 836-7984
Union *(G-19939)*
Java Express.....G..... 217 525-2430
Springfield *(G-19393)*
John C Grafft.....F..... 847 842-9200
Lake Barrington *(G-12153)*
▲ Joong-Ang Daily News.....E..... 847 228-7200
Rolling Meadows *(G-17743)*
Kae Dj Publishing.....G..... 773 233-2609
Chicago *(G-5074)*
Kaelco Entrmt Holdings Inc.....G..... 217 600-7815
Champaign *(G-3312)*
Keane Gillette Publishing LLC.....G..... 630 279-7521
Elmhurst *(G-9385)*
Knighthouse Media Inc.....C..... 312 676-1100
Chicago *(G-5110)*
L A M Inc De.....G..... 630 860-9700
Wood Dale *(G-21206)*
L C Inn Partners.....F..... 309 743-0800
Moline *(G-14156)*
Labelquest Inc.....E..... 630 833-9400
Elmhurst *(G-9390)*
Lampe Publications.....G..... 309 741-9790
Elmwood *(G-9448)*
Law Bulletin Publishing Co.....C..... 312 644-2763
Chicago *(G-5182)*
Law Bulletin Publishing Co.....F..... 847 883-9100
Buffalo Grove *(G-2560)*
Liberty Group Publishing.....F..... 309 944-1779
Geneseo *(G-10245)*
Line of Advance Nfp.....G..... 312 768-0043
Chicago *(G-5227)*
LMS Innovations Inc.....G..... 312 613-2345
Chicago *(G-5247)*
Loyalty Publishing Inc.....E..... 309 693-0840
Bartonville *(G-1334)*
Loyola Press.....E..... 800 621-1008
Chicago *(G-5269)*
Luby Publishing Inc.....F..... 312 341-1110
Chicago *(G-5276)*
Luna Azul Communications Inc.....E..... 773 616-0007
Deerfield *(G-7630)*
Lyre Glass Press LLC.....G..... 847 834-9643
Glenview *(G-10586)*
M & G Graphics Inc.....E..... 773 247-1596
Chicago *(G-5295)*
M M Marketing.....G..... 815 459-7968
Wauconda *(G-20370)*
Manufacturers News Inc.....D..... 847 864-7000
Evanston *(G-9549)*
Marshall Pubg & Promotions.....G..... 224 238-3530
Barrington *(G-1227)*
Mcllvaine Co.....E..... 847 784-0012
Northfield *(G-15522)*
▲ McX Press.....G..... 630 784-4325
Bloomingdale *(G-2000)*
Mediatec Publishing Inc.....E..... 312 676-9900
Chicago *(G-5386)*
Mendota Reporter.....F..... 815 539-9396
Mendota *(G-13948)*
Merit Emplyment Asssment Svcs.....G..... 815 320-3680
New Lenox *(G-15041)*
Midwest Shared Newsletter.....G..... 847 933-9498
Skokie *(G-18991)*
Mindseye.....G..... 618 394-6444
Belleville *(G-1579)*
Modern Trade Communications.....F..... 847 674-2200
Skokie *(G-18992)*
Motorsports Publications House.....G..... 630 699-7629
Plainfield *(G-16692)*
Multi Print and Digital LLC.....G..... 630 985-2600
Darien *(G-7410)*
Nas Media Group Inc.....G..... 312 371-7499
Olympia Fields *(G-15896)*
New Millenium Directories.....E..... 815 626-5737
Sterling *(G-19522)*
▲ New Wave Express Inc.....G..... 630 238-3129
Bensenville *(G-1857)*
Nice Card Company.....G..... 773 467-8450
Park Ridge *(G-16290)*
North American Press Inc.....G..... 847 515-3882
Huntley *(G-11556)*
Northern Illinois University.....F..... 815 753-1826
Dekalb *(G-7695)*
▲ Norwood House Press Inc.....G..... 866 565-2900
Chicago *(G-5628)*
▼ Oag Aviation Worldwide LLC.....G..... 630 515-5300
Lisle *(G-12923)*
Odx Media LLC.....G..... 847 868-0548
Evanston *(G-9559)*
Olney Daily Mail.....E..... 618 393-2931
Olney *(G-15880)*
Omegacom Inc.....G..... 773 750-4621
Chicago *(G-5674)*
Omni Publishing Co.....G..... 847 483-9668
Wheeling *(G-20950)*
Paddock Publications Inc.....E..... 847 680-5800
Libertyville *(G-12693)*
Palm International Inc.....G..... 630 357-1437
Naperville *(G-14892)*
Pam Printers and Publs Inc.....F..... 217 222-4030
Quincy *(G-16922)*
Panache Editions Ltd.....G..... 847 921-8574
Glencoe *(G-10433)*
Paperworks.....G..... 630 969-3218
Downers Grove *(G-8069)*
Peoria Post Inc.....F..... 309 688-3628
Peoria *(G-16495)*
Perq/Hci LLC.....D..... 847 268-1600
Rosemont *(G-18039)*
Perspecto Map Company Inc.....G..... 815 356-1288
Village of Lakewood *(G-20179)*
Phoenix Press Inc.....G..... 630 833-2281
Addison *(G-239)*
▲ Phoenix Tree Publishing Inc.....G..... 773 251-0309
Chicago *(G-5804)*
Pierce Crandell & Co Inc.....G..... 847 549-6015
Libertyville *(G-12696)*
Popsugar Inc.....G..... 312 595-0533
Chicago *(G-5843)*
Preferred Bus Publications Inc.....G..... 815 717-6399
New Lenox *(G-15051)*
Premier Travel Media.....G..... 630 794-0696
Willowbrook *(G-21057)*
Prereo LLC.....G..... 800 555-1055
Chicago *(G-5866)*
Press Dough Inc.....G..... 630 243-6900
Lemont *(G-12585)*
Press Fuel.....G..... 217 546-9606
Springfield *(G-19428)*
Press On Inc.....G..... 630 628-1630
Addison *(G-254)*
Prime Publishing LLC.....E..... 847 205-9375
Northbrook *(G-15466)*
Publishers Row.....F..... 847 568-0593
Skokie *(G-19018)*
Qt Info Systems Inc.....F..... 800 240-8761
Chicago *(G-5925)*
R L Allen Industries.....G..... 618 667-2544
Troy *(G-19919)*
R R Donnelley & Sons Company.....C..... 847 393-3000
Libertyville *(G-12700)*
R R Donnelley & Sons Company.....A..... 815 584-2770
Dwight *(G-8158)*
▲ Rand McNally & Company.....B..... 847 329-8100
Chicago *(G-5968)*
Rand McNally International Co.....C..... 847 329-8100
Chicago *(G-5969)*
Rapid Circular Press Inc.....F..... 312 421-5611
Chicago *(G-5970)*
READ Worldwide LLC.....G..... 312 301-6276
Chicago *(G-5982)*
Redshelf Inc.....F..... 312 878-8586
Chicago *(G-5994)*
Reid Communications Inc.....E..... 847 741-9700
Elgin *(G-8717)*
Rickard Publishing.....F..... 217 482-3276
Mason City *(G-13613)*
◆ Rm Acquisition LLC.....C..... 847 329-8100
Chicago *(G-6039)*
Robert-Leslie Publishing LLC.....G..... 773 935-8358
Chicago *(G-6043)*
Rockford Map Publishers Inc.....F..... 815 708-6324
Rockford *(G-17599)*

SIC SECTION

27 PRINTING, PUBLISHING, AND ALLIED INDUSTRIES

Roger Fritz & Associates Inc ....G....... 630 355-2614
  Naperville *(G-14911)*
Royal Publishing Inc ....F....... 309 797-6630
  Moline *(G-14174)*
RR Donnelley Logistics SE ....F....... 630 672-2500
  Roselle *(G-17981)*
Rs Ductless Technical Support ....G....... 815 223-7949
  La Salle *(G-12122)*
Ryan Partnership LLC ....F....... 312 343-2611
  Chicago *(G-6080)*
Scars Publications ....G....... 847 281-9070
  Gurnee *(G-10925)*
Scholastic Testing Service ....F....... 630 766-7150
  Bensenville *(G-1891)*
Schumaker Publications Inc ....G....... 309 365-7105
  Lexington *(G-12621)*
Serbian Yellow Pages Inc ....F....... 847 588-0555
  Niles *(G-15169)*
Shoppers Weekly Inc ....F....... 618 533-7283
  Centralia *(G-3251)*
Sim Partners ....E....... 800 260-3380
  Chicago *(G-6172)*
Simon Global Services LLC ....G....... 773 334-7794
  Chicago *(G-6173)*
Simple Solutions ....G....... 618 932-6177
  West Frankfort *(G-20683)*
Sony/Atv Music Publishing LLC ....E....... 630 739-8129
  Bolingbrook *(G-2245)*
Spudnik Press Cooperative ....F....... 312 563-0302
  Chicago *(G-6222)*
St Johns United Church Christ ....G....... 847 491-6686
  Evanston *(G-9578)*
Starlight Express Coaches Inc ....G....... 708 388-3365
  Crestwood *(G-7129)*
▲ Sunrise Hitek Service Inc ....E....... 773 792-8880
  Chicago *(G-6277)*
Syndigo LLC ....C....... 309 690-5231
  Peoria *(G-16532)*
T R Communications Inc ....F....... 773 238-3366
  Chicago *(G-6307)*
Techno - Grphics Trnsltons Inc ....E....... 708 331-3333
  South Holland *(G-19248)*
Tele Guia Spanish TV Guide ....E....... 708 656-9800
  Cicero *(G-6879)*
Thomas Publishing Printing Div ....G....... 618 351-6655
  Carbondale *(G-2862)*
Thrice Publishing Nfp ....G....... 630 776-0478
  Roselle *(G-17993)*
Tighe Publishing Services Inc ....F....... 773 281-9100
  Chicago *(G-6378)*
Totalworks Inc ....E....... 773 489-4313
  Chicago *(G-6399)*
Translucent Publishing Corp ....F....... 312 447-5450
  Chicago *(G-6413)*
Trend Publishing Inc ....E....... 312 654-2300
  Chicago *(G-6415)*
TWT Marketing Inc ....G....... 773 274-4470
  Chicago *(G-6449)*
U S Free Press LLC ....G....... 319 524-3802
  Hamilton *(G-10961)*
Van Meter Graphx Inc ....G....... 847 465-0600
  Wheeling *(G-21008)*
Varsity Publications Inc ....G....... 309 353-4570
  Pekin *(G-16367)*
Vision Intgrted Grphics Group ....C....... 331 318-7800
  Bolingbrook *(G-2251)*
Vondrak Publishing Co Inc ....E....... 773 476-4800
  Summit Argo *(G-19684)*
Vortex Media Group Inc ....G....... 630 717-9541
  Naperville *(G-14942)*
W-F Professional Assoc Inc ....G....... 847 945-8050
  Deerfield *(G-7659)*
Wabash Publishing Co Inc ....G....... 312 939-5900
  Chicago *(G-6581)*
Want ADS of Champaign Inc ....G....... 217 356-4804
  Champaign *(G-3368)*
We Do Tech Americas Inc ....G....... 630 217-8723
  Lisle *(G-12957)*
Where 2 Get It LLC ....F....... 224 232-5550
  Arlington Heights *(G-832)*
Wireless Express Inc Central ....G....... 309 689-9933
  Peoria *(G-16547)*
Wolfsword Press ....G....... 773 403-1144
  Chicago *(G-6664)*
◆ Wolters Kluwer US Inc ....E....... 847 580-5000
  Riverwoods *(G-17097)*
Wonderlic Inc ....D....... 847 680-4900
  Vernon Hills *(G-20112)*
Wordspace Press Limited ....G....... 773 292-0292
  Chicago *(G-6669)*

World Book Encyclopedia Del ....C....... 312 729-5800
  Chicago *(G-6670)*
▲ World Book Inc ....E....... 312 729-5800
  Chicago *(G-6671)*
World Library Publications ....C....... 847 678-9300
  Franklin Park *(G-10087)*
Worlds Printing & Spc Co Ltd ....G....... 312 565-1401
  Chicago *(G-6678)*
▲ Zaptel Corporation ....G....... 847 386-8050
  Elk Grove Village *(G-9317)*

2752 Commercial Printing: Lithographic

11th Street Express Prtg Inc ....F....... 815 968-0208
  Rockford *(G-17275)*
360 Digital Print Inc ....G....... 630 682-3601
  Carol Stream *(G-2921)*
3d Printer Experience LLC ....G....... 312 896-3399
  Chicago *(G-3468)*
510 Holdings Company LLC ....F....... 618 659-8600
  Edwardsville *(G-8343)*
A & B Printing Service Inc ....G....... 217 789-9034
  Springfield *(G-19313)*
A A Swift Print Inc ....G....... 847 301-1122
  Schaumburg *(G-18424)*
A-Reliable Printing ....G....... 630 790-2525
  Glen Ellyn *(G-10392)*
Abbotts Minute Printing Inc ....G....... 708 339-6010
  South Holland *(G-19187)*
▲ ABC Business Forms Inc ....F....... 773 774-8282
  Chicago *(G-3507)*
Able Printing Service Inc ....G....... 708 788-7115
  Berwyn *(G-1947)*
▼ ABS Graphics Inc ....C....... 630 495-2400
  Itasca *(G-11615)*
Accurate Business Controls Inc ....G....... 815 633-5500
  Machesney Park *(G-13323)*
▲ Accurate Printing Inc ....G....... 708 824-0058
  Midlothian *(G-13989)*
▲ Ace Graphics Inc ....E....... 630 357-2244
  Naperville *(G-14764)*
Active Graphics Inc ....E....... 708 656-8900
  Cicero *(G-6827)*
Ad Works Inc ....G....... 217 342-9688
  Effingham *(G-8382)*
Adams Printing Co ....G....... 618 529-2396
  Carbondale *(G-2838)*
Adcraft Printers Inc ....F....... 815 932-6432
  Kankakee *(G-11956)*
Addvalue2print LLC ....G....... 847 551-1570
  Wood Dale *(G-21155)*
Adrenaline Prints ....G....... 618 277-9600
  Belleville *(G-1528)*
Advance Quick Print ....G....... 708 848-2200
  Oak Park *(G-15741)*
Advantage Printing Inc ....G....... 630 627-7468
  Lombard *(G-13036)*
Advocate ....G....... 815 694-2122
  Clifton *(G-6913)*
▼ Ah Tensor International LLC ....E....... 630 739-9600
  Woodridge *(G-21273)*
Aires Press Inc ....G....... 847 698-6813
  Park Ridge *(G-16265)*
Ajs Premier Printing Inc ....G....... 847 838-6350
  Antioch *(G-596)*
Alisun Inc ....G....... 708 571-3451
  Westchester *(G-20691)*
All Printing & Graphics Inc ....G....... 773 553-3049
  Chicago *(G-3611)*
All Printing & Graphics Inc ....F....... 708 450-1512
  Broadview *(G-2415)*
All-Ways Quick Print ....G....... 708 403-8422
  Orland Park *(G-15938)*
Allegra Network LLC ....G....... 331 253-2775
  Romeoville *(G-17791)*
Allegra Network LLC ....G....... 630 801-9335
  Aurora *(G-1047)*
Allegra Print & Imaging ....F....... 630 963-9100
  Lisle *(G-12860)*
Allegra Print & Imaging Inc ....G....... 847 697-1434
  Elgin *(G-8502)*
Alliance Creative Group Inc ....E....... 847 885-1800
  East Dundee *(G-8187)*
Alliance Graphics ....G....... 312 280-8000
  Chicago *(G-3617)*
Alliance Investment Corp ....F....... 847 933-0400
  Skokie *(G-18916)*
Alliance Printing Inc ....G....... 630 613-9529
  Addison *(G-26)*
▲ Allied Graphics Inc ....G....... 847 419-8730
  Buffalo Grove *(G-2508)*

Allied Printing Inc ....G....... 773 334-5200
  Chicago *(G-3619)*
Allprint Graphics Inc ....G....... 847 519-9898
  Schaumburg *(G-18433)*
Allprint Inc ....G....... 847 726-0658
  Hawthorn Woods *(G-11121)*
Alphadigital Inc ....G....... 708 482-4488
  La Grange *(G-12071)*
AlphaGraphics Printshops ....G....... 630 964-9600
  Lisle *(G-12861)*
Alwan Printing Inc ....F....... 708 598-9600
  Bridgeview *(G-2321)*
Amboy News ....G....... 815 857-2311
  Amboy *(G-578)*
America Printing Inc ....G....... 847 229-8358
  Wheeling *(G-20846)*
American Inks and Coatings Co ....G....... 630 226-0994
  Romeoville *(G-17793)*
◆ American Labelmark Company ....C....... 773 478-0900
  Chicago *(G-3656)*
American Litho Incorporated ....A....... 630 682-0600
  Carol Stream *(G-2934)*
▲ American Litho Incorporated ....B....... 630 462-1700
  Carol Stream *(G-2935)*
American Slide-Chart Co ....D....... 630 665-3333
  Carol Stream *(G-2937)*
Amric Resources ....G....... 309 664-0391
  Bloomington *(G-2024)*
Anikam Inc ....G....... 708 385-0200
  Alsip *(G-415)*
Apple Graphics Inc ....G....... 630 389-2222
  Batavia *(G-1350)*
Apple Press Inc ....G....... 815 224-1451
  Peru *(G-16565)*
Apprize Promotional Pdts Inc ....G....... 630 468-2043
  Oakbrook Terrace *(G-15786)*
Arbor Printing & Graphics Inc ....G....... 630 969-2277
  Lisle *(G-12867)*
Arbor Private Inv Co LLC ....G....... 312 981-3770
  Chicago *(G-3718)*
Arby Graphic Service Inc ....F....... 847 763-0900
  Glencoe *(G-10428)*
Arch Printing Inc ....G....... 630 966-0235
  Aurora *(G-1053)*
Arla Graphics Inc ....G....... 847 470-0005
  Deerfield *(G-7586)*
Art Newvo Incorporated ....G....... 847 838-0304
  Antioch *(G-600)*
Art-Craft Printers ....G....... 847 455-2201
  Franklin Park *(G-9874)*
Arthur Graphic Clarion ....G....... 217 543-2151
  Arthur *(G-842)*
Arthur R Baker Inc ....G....... 708 301-4828
  Homer Glen *(G-11477)*
Artpol Printing Inc ....G....... 773 622-0498
  Chicago *(G-3742)*
Aspen Printing Services LLC ....G....... 630 357-3203
  Naperville *(G-14775)*
Associated Printers Inc ....G....... 847 548-8929
  Antioch *(G-602)*
Astro Printing Inc ....G....... 773 436-0500
  Chicago *(G-3754)*
▲ Athena Design Group Inc ....E....... 312 733-2828
  Chicago *(G-3758)*
Atlantis Entp Investments Inc ....G....... 432 237-0404
  Chicago *(G-3761)*
Aurora Fastprint Inc ....G....... 630 896-5980
  Aurora *(G-1059)*
Automated Forms & Graphics Inc ....G....... 630 887-9811
  Lockport *(G-12982)*
Available Business Group Inc ....D....... 773 247-4141
  Chicago *(G-3781)*
Avid of Illinois Inc ....F....... 847 698-2775
  Saint Charles *(G-18152)*
Award/Visionps Inc ....G....... 331 318-7800
  Chicago *(G-3791)*
Azusa Inc ....G....... 618 244-6591
  Mount Vernon *(G-14597)*
B & B Printing Company ....G....... 217 285-6072
  Pittsfield *(G-16628)*
B Allan Graphics Inc ....F....... 708 396-1704
  Alsip *(G-420)*
B F Shaw Printing Company ....G....... 815 625-3600
  Sterling *(G-19500)*
B P I Printing & Duplicating ....F....... 773 327-7300
  Chicago *(G-3808)*
B P I Printing & Duplicating ....G....... 773 822-0111
  Bannockburn *(G-1191)*
Babak Inc ....G....... 312 419-8686
  Oak Forest *(G-15672)*

Employee Codes: A=Over 500 employees, B=251-500
C=101-250, D=51-100, E=20-50, F=10-19, G=3-9

27 PRINTING, PUBLISHING, AND ALLIED INDUSTRIES SIC SECTION

Bach & Associates G 618 277-1652
Belleville *(G-1532)*

Bailleu & Bailleu Printing Inc G 309 852-2517
Kewanee *(G-12021)*

Bally Foil Graphics Inc G 847 427-1509
Elk Grove Village *(G-8857)*

Balsley Printing Inc F 815 624-7515
Rockton *(G-17692)*

Balsley Printing Inc F 815 624-7515
Rockton *(G-17693)*

Bardash & Bukowski Inc G 312 829-2080
Chicago *(G-3831)*

Barnaby Inc F 815 895-6555
Aurora *(G-1061)*

Barrel Maker Printing G 773 490-3065
Chicago *(G-3837)*

Bass Company LLC G 618 526-7211
Breese *(G-2297)*

Basswood Associates Inc F 312 240-9400
Chicago *(G-3845)*

Bat Business Services Inc G 630 801-9335
Aurora *(G-1062)*

Batavia Instant Print G 630 262-0370
West Chicago *(G-20550)*

Beans Printing Inc G 217 223-5555
Quincy *(G-16861)*

Beardsley Printery Inc G 309 788-4041
Rock Island *(G-17203)*

▲ Bell Litho Inc D 847 952-3300
Elk Grove Village *(G-8862)*

Bell Litho Inc G 847 290-9300
Elk Grove Village *(G-8863)*

Belmonte Printing Co G 847 352-8841
Schaumburg *(G-18458)*

Belrock Printing Inc G 815 547-1096
Belvidere *(G-1652)*

Benton Evening News Co G 618 438-5611
Benton *(G-1919)*

Benzinger Printing G 815 784-6560
Genoa *(G-10315)*

Berland Printing Inc E 773 702-1999
Bannockburn *(G-1196)*

Best Advertising Spc & Prtg G 708 448-1110
Worth *(G-21455)*

Best In Printing Inc G 630 833-7366
Elmhurst *(G-9332)*

Bfc Forms Service Inc C 630 879-9240
Batavia *(G-1358)*

Bfc Print G 630 879-9240
Batavia *(G-1359)*

Biller Press & Manufacturing G 847 395-4111
Antioch *(G-604)*

Bitforms Inc G 630 595-6800
Wood Dale *(G-21169)*

Blooming Color Inc D 630 705-9200
Lombard *(G-13047)*

Bloomington Offset Process Inc D 309 662-3395
Bloomington *(G-2026)*

Blue Island Newspaper Prtg Inc D 708 333-1006
Harvey *(G-11079)*

Bluegrass Enterprises LLC G 630 544-3781
Saint Charles *(G-18158)*

Bmt Prnting Crtgraph Espclists G 773 646-4700
Chicago *(G-3920)*

Bond Brothers & Co F 708 442-5510
Lyons *(G-13303)*

Bopi G 312 320-1109
Bloomington *(G-2028)*

Branstiter Printing Co G 217 245-6533
Jacksonville *(G-11760)*

Breaker Press Co Inc G 773 927-1666
Chicago *(G-3948)*

▼ Breese Publishing Co Inc G 618 526-7211
Breese *(G-2299)*

Bridge Printing & Promotional F 847 776-0200
Roselle *(G-17941)*

Bridge Printing & Promotional F 312 929-1456
Chicago *(G-3954)*

Brilliant Color Corp G 847 367-3300
Libertyville *(G-12640)*

Brokers Print Mail Rsource Inc G 708 532-9900
Tinley Park *(G-19813)*

Bros Lithographing Company G 312 666-0919
Chicago *(G-3965)*

Budget Printing Center G 618 655-1636
Edwardsville *(G-8351)*

Buhl Press E 708 449-8989
Berkeley *(G-1939)*

Bureau Valley Chief G 815 646-4731
Tiskilwa *(G-19871)*

Burstan Inc G 847 787-0380
Elk Grove Village *(G-8874)*

Business Card Systems Inc F 815 877-0990
Machesney Park *(G-13331)*

Business Cards Tomorrow F 815 877-0990
Machesney Park *(G-13332)*

Button Man Printing Inc G 630 549-0438
Saint Charles *(G-18160)*

C & L Printing Company F 312 235-0380
Chicago *(G-3993)*

C E Dienberg Printing Company G 708 848-4406
Oak Park *(G-15747)*

C F C Interantional G 708 753-0679
Chicago Heights *(G-6737)*

C L Graphics Marketing Inc E 815 455-0900
South Elgin *(G-19139)*

C M J Associates Inc G 708 636-2995
Oak Lawn *(G-15705)*

C2 Imaging LLC E 847 439-7834
Elk Grove Village *(G-8876)*

Cadore-Miller Printing Inc F 708 430-7091
Hickory Hills *(G-11194)*

▲ Caldwell Letter Service Inc E 773 847-0708
Orland Park *(G-15943)*

Cambrdg Printing Corp G 630 510-2100
Carol Stream *(G-2954)*

Cameron Printing Inc G 630 231-3301
West Chicago *(G-20558)*

Campbell Publishing Inc E 217 742-3313
Winchester *(G-21104)*

Cannon Ball Marketing Inc G 630 971-2127
Lisle *(G-12875)*

Capital Prtg & Die Cutng Inc G 630 896-5520
Aurora *(G-1069)*

Capitol Impressions Inc E 309 633-1400
Peoria *(G-16397)*

Card Prsnlzation Solutions LLC E 630 543-2630
Glendale Heights *(G-10441)*

Cardinal Colorprint Prtg Corp E 630 467-1000
Itasca *(G-11634)*

Carey Color Inc G 630 761-2605
West Chicago *(G-20559)*

Carson Printing Inc G 847 836-0900
East Dundee *(G-8189)*

Carter Printing Co Inc G 217 227-4464
Farmersville *(G-9659)*

Catalina Graphics Inc G 773 973-7780
Chicago *(G-4039)*

Cavco Printers G 618 988-8011
Energy *(G-9467)*

CCL Label (chicago) Inc E 630 406-9991
Batavia *(G-1363)*

▲ CDI Corp E 773 205-2960
Chicago *(G-4049)*

CDs Office Systems Inc F 630 305-9034
Springfield *(G-19344)*

Central Illinois Newspapers G 217 935-3171
Clinton *(G-6920)*

Central Printers & Graphics G 773 586-3711
Bedford Park *(G-1462)*

Century Printing G 618 632-2486
O Fallon *(G-15570)*

Cenveo Worldwide Limited D 636 240-5817
Chicago *(G-4063)*

Challenge Printers G 773 252-0212
Chicago *(G-4067)*

Charles C Thomas Publisher G 217 789-8980
Springfield *(G-19348)*

Charles Chauncey Wells Inc G 708 524-0695
Oak Park *(G-15749)*

Cherokee Printing & Svcs Inc G 847 566-6116
Mundelein *(G-14676)*

CHI-Town Printing Inc G 773 577-2500
Chicago *(G-4085)*

Chicago Mltlingua Graphics Inc F 847 386-7187
Northfield *(G-15512)*

Chicago Press Corporation E 773 276-1500
Elk Grove Village *(G-8894)*

Chicago Print Group Inc G 312 251-1962
Calumet Park *(G-2795)*

Chicago Printers Guild G 303 819-6197
Chicago *(G-4125)*

Chicago Sun-Times Features Inc A 312 321-3000
Chicago *(G-4131)*

Child Evngelism Fellowship Inc E 630 983-7708
Naperville *(G-14799)*

Christopher R Cline Prtg Ltd F 847 981-0500
Elk Grove Village *(G-8897)*

Christopher Wagner G 630 205-9200
Oswego *(G-15995)*

Chromatech Printing Inc F 847 699-0333
Des Plaines *(G-7746)*

Cifuentes Luis & Nicole Inc G 847 490-3660
Schaumburg *(G-18477)*

Clark Printing & Marketing G 217 363-5300
Champaign *(G-3280)*

Classic Color Inc C 708 484-0000
Broadview *(G-2427)*

Classic Printery Inc G 847 546-6555
Hainesville *(G-10946)*

Classic Printing Co Inc G 217 428-1733
Decatur *(G-7475)*

Classic Prtg Thermography Inc G 630 595-7765
Wood Dale *(G-21176)*

Clear Print Inc G 815 795-6225
Ottawa *(G-16046)*

Clementi Printing Inc G 773 622-0795
Chicago *(G-4177)*

Cliffe Printing Company G 708 345-1665
Maywood *(G-13667)*

Clyde Printing Company F 773 847-5900
Chicago *(G-4184)*

Cmb Printing Inc F 630 323-1110
Burr Ridge *(G-2663)*

Color Communications LLC G 312 223-0204
Chicago *(G-4204)*

Color Tone Printing G 708 385-1442
Blue Island *(G-2114)*

Colvin Printing G 708 331-4580
Blue Island *(G-2115)*

Comet Conection Inc G 312 243-5400
Alsip *(G-434)*

Commercial Copy Printing Ctr F 847 981-8590
Elk Grove Village *(G-8903)*

Commercial Prtg of Rockford G 815 965-4759
Rockford *(G-17355)*

Communication Technologies Inc E 630 384-0900
Glendale Heights *(G-10444)*

Component Sales Incorporated F 630 543-9666
Addison *(G-78)*

Concept Printers G 708 481-2430
Chicago Heights *(G-6744)*

Concord Printing Inc G 847 734-1616
Elk Grove Village *(G-8908)*

Concorde Prtg Dgtal Imging Inc G 312 552-3006
Chicago *(G-4216)*

Consolidated Carqueville Prtg C 630 246-6451
Streamwood *(G-19566)*

Consolidated Printing Co Inc F 773 631-2800
Elk Grove Village *(G-8909)*

Consulate General Lithuania G 312 397-0382
Chicago *(G-4223)*

▲ Continental Web Press Inc C 630 773-1903
Itasca *(G-11639)*

▲ Continental Web Press KY Inc D 630 773-1903
Itasca *(G-11640)*

Cook JV Printing F 708 799-0007
Country Club Hills *(G-7037)*

Copies Overnight Inc E 630 690-2000
Carol Stream *(G-2966)*

Copy Express Inc F 815 338-7161
Woodstock *(G-21377)*

Copy Mat Printing G 309 452-1392
Bloomington *(G-2033)*

▲ Copy-Mor Inc E 312 666-4000
Streamwood *(G-19568)*

▲ Copyco Printing Inc E 847 824-4400
Rosemont *(G-18008)*

Corporate Business Card Ltd E 847 455-5760
Franklin Park *(G-9915)*

Corporate Graphics America Inc F 773 481-2100
Chicago *(G-4239)*

Corporate Print Source Inc G 847 724-1150
Glenview *(G-10539)*

Corporation Supply Co Inc E 312 726-3375
Chicago *(G-4241)*

Corps Levl Ventures Inc F 312 846-1441
Chicago *(G-4242)*

Corwin Printing G 618 263-3936
Mount Carmel *(G-14469)*

Cpg Printing & Graphics G 309 820-1392
Bloomington *(G-2034)*

Cpr Printing Inc F 630 377-8420
Geneva *(G-10263)*

Craftsmen Printing G 217 283-9574
Hoopeston *(G-11506)*

Creasey Printing Services Inc G 217 787-1055
Springfield *(G-19356)*

Creative Graphic Arts Inc G 847 498-2678
Northbrook *(G-15368)*

SIC SECTION
27 PRINTING, PUBLISHING, AND ALLIED INDUSTRIES

Creative Lithocraft Inc .....F 847 352-7002
  Schaumburg (G-18493)
Creative Prtg & Smart Ideas .....G 773 481-6522
  Chicago (G-4265)
Crli Acceptance Corp .....G 847 940-1500
  Deerfield (G-7606)
Crossmark Printing Inc .....F 708 532-8263
  Tinley Park (G-19819)
Crosswind Printing .....G 847 356-1009
  Lindenhurst (G-12853)
Crown Publications Inc .....G 217 893-4856
  Rantoul (G-16973)
Curtis 1000 Inc .....C 309 663-0325
  Bloomington (G-2036)
Custom Calendar Corp .....G 708 547-6191
  Lombard (G-13060)
Custom Telephone Printing Co .....F 815 338-0000
  Woodstock (G-21379)
Cynlar Inc .....G 630 820-2200
  Aurora (G-949)
Cypress Multigraphics LLC .....E 708 633-1166
  Tinley Park (G-19820)
D & D Business Inc .....G 630 935-3522
  Willowbrook (G-21040)
D & D Printing Inc .....G 708 425-2080
  Oak Lawn (G-15712)
D & R Press .....G 708 452-0500
  Elmwood Park (G-9450)
D E Asbury Inc .....F 217 222-0617
  Hamilton (G-10953)
D E Signs & Storage LLC .....G 618 939-8050
  Waterloo (G-20289)
D G Brandt Inc .....G 815 942-4064
  Morris (G-14301)
D L V Printing Service Inc .....F 773 626-1661
  Chicago (G-4301)
Dale K Brown .....G 815 338-0222
  Woodstock (G-21380)
Dallas Corporation .....F 630 322-8000
  Downers Grove (G-7983)
Damy Corp .....F 847 233-0515
  Schiller Park (G-18798)
Dandelion Distributors Inc .....G 815 675-9800
  Grayslake (G-10766)
Dans Printing & Off Sups Inc .....F 708 687-3055
  Oak Forest (G-15674)
Dark Matter Printing .....G 217 791-4059
  Decatur (G-7482)
Darnall Printing .....G 309 827-7212
  Bloomington (G-2039)
David H Vander Ploeg .....G 708 331-7700
  South Holland (G-19206)
Daxam Inc .....F 847 214-1733
  Elgin (G-8564)
DE Asbury Inc .....E 217 222-0617
  Quincy (G-16876)
Deadline Prtg Clor Copying LLC .....G 847 437-9000
  Elk Grove Village (G-8940)
Dean Printing Systems .....G 847 526-9545
  Fox Lake (G-9745)
Debbie Harshman .....G 217 335-2112
  Barry (G-1249)
Decatur Blue Print Company .....G 217 423-7589
  Decatur (G-7484)
▲ Deluxe Johnson .....C 847 635-7200
  Des Plaines (G-7754)
Deluxe Printing .....G 312 225-0061
  Chicago (G-4337)
Denor Graphics Inc .....F 847 364-1130
  Elk Grove Village (G-8944)
Des Plaines Journal Inc .....D 847 299-5511
  Des Plaines (G-7755)
Des Plaines Printing LLC .....F 847 465-3300
  Buffalo Grove (G-2532)
Design Graphics Inc .....G 815 462-3323
  Frankfort (G-9783)
Design On Time .....G 815 464-5750
  Frankfort (G-9784)
Designation Inc .....F 847 367-9100
  Mundelein (G-14683)
Dg Digital Printing .....G 815 961-0000
  Rockford (G-17374)
Di Stefani T Shirt Printing .....F 618 282-2380
  Red Bud (G-16992)
Di-Carr Printing Company .....G 708 863-0069
  Cicero (G-6840)
Diamond Envelope Corporation .....D 630 499-2800
  Aurora (G-951)
Diamond Graphics of Berwyn .....G 708 749-2500
  Berwyn (G-1950)

Diamond Web Printing LLC .....F 630 663-0351
  Downers Grove (G-7987)
Diaz Printing .....G 773 887-3366
  Chicago (G-4354)
Dicianni Graphics Incorporated .....F 630 833-5100
  Addison (G-91)
Digital Printing & Total Graph .....G 630 627-7400
  Lombard (G-13067)
Diversified Print Group .....G 630 893-8920
  Bloomingdale (G-1989)
Dixon Direct LLC .....F 815 284-2211
  Dixon (G-7896)
Dixon Graphics Incorporated .....G 217 351-6100
  Champaign (G-3285)
Dla Document Services .....F 618 256-4686
  Scott Air Force Base (G-18857)
DMarv Design Specialty Prtrs .....G 708 389-4420
  Blue Island (G-2118)
▲ Donnelley Financial LLC .....B 844 866-4337
  Chicago (G-4384)
Donnelley Financial LLC .....G 630 963-9494
  Warrenville (G-20234)
Donnells Printing & Off Pdts .....G 815 842-6541
  Pontiac (G-16768)
Dos Bro Corp .....G 773 334-1919
  Chicago (G-4386)
DOT Sharper Printing Inc .....G 847 581-9033
  Morton Grove (G-14401)
Double Image Press Inc .....F 630 893-6777
  Glendale Heights (G-10447)
Doubletake Marketing Inc .....G 845 598-3175
  Evanston (G-9511)
Douglas Press Inc .....C 800 323-0705
  Bellwood (G-1622)
Dps Digital Print Svc .....G 847 836-7734
  East Dundee (G-8192)
Drake Envelope Printing Co .....G 217 374-2772
  White Hall (G-21018)
Dreamwrks Grphic Cmmnctons LLC .....D 847 679-6710
  Glenview (G-10543)
Dsr Screenprinting .....G 630 855-2790
  Streamwood (G-19571)
Dun-Wel Lithograph Co Inc .....G 773 327-8811
  Chicago (G-4404)
Duo Graphics .....G 847 228-7080
  Elk Grove Village (G-8956)
Dupli Group Inc .....F 773 549-5285
  Chicago (G-4408)
Dynagraphics Incorporated .....E 217 876-9950
  Decatur (G-7492)
E & H Graphic Service Inc .....G 708 748-5656
  Matteson (G-13623)
E A A Enterprises Inc .....G 630 279-0150
  Villa Park (G-20145)
E&D Printing Services Inc .....G 815 609-8222
  Plainfield (G-16658)
E-Intrctve Mktg Solutions Inc .....G 312 241-1692
  Bridgeview (G-2342)
Eagle Printing Company .....G 309 762-0771
  Moline (G-14141)
East Central Communications Co .....E 217 892-9613
  Rantoul (G-16975)
Ed Garvey and Company .....D 847 647-1900
  Niles (G-15117)
Edwardsville Publishing Co .....D 618 656-4700
  Edwardsville (G-8361)
Einstein Crest .....G 847 965-7791
  Niles (G-15119)
Elgin Instant Print .....G 847 931-9006
  Elgin (G-8575)
Elise S Allen .....G 309 673-2613
  Peoria (G-16434)
Elliott Publishing Inc .....G 217 645-3033
  Liberty (G-12622)
Ennis Inc .....E 815 875-2000
  Princeton (G-16808)
Envelopes Only Inc .....E 630 213-2500
  Streamwood (G-19573)
◆ Essentra Packaging US Inc .....G 704 418-8692
  Westchester (G-20699)
Eugene Ewbank .....G 630 705-0400
  Oswego (G-16004)
▲ Evanston Graphic Imaging Inc .....G 847 869-7446
  Evanston (G-9516)
Excel Forms Inc .....G 630 801-1936
  Aurora (G-1094)
Expri Publishing & Printing .....G 773 274-5955
  Chicago (G-4546)
F Weber Printing Co Inc .....G 815 468-6152
  Manteno (G-13447)

Faith Printing .....G 217 675-2191
  Franklin (G-9855)
Falcon Press Inc .....G 815 455-9099
  Crystal Lake (G-7197)
Far West Print Solutions LLC .....G 630 879-9500
  North Aurora (G-15260)
Fast Print Shop .....G 618 997-1976
  Marion (G-13510)
Fast Printing of Joliet Inc .....G 815 723-0080
  Joliet (G-11864)
Fastway Printing Inc .....G 847 882-0950
  Schaumburg (G-18525)
Faulstich Printing Company Inc .....G 217 442-4994
  Danville (G-7332)
FCL Graphics Inc .....C 708 867-5500
  Harwood Heights (G-11104)
Fedex Corporation .....F 847 918-7730
  Vernon Hills (G-20053)
Fedex Office & Print Svcs Inc .....F 312 341-9644
  Chicago (G-4573)
Fedex Office & Print Svcs Inc .....F 312 755-0325
  Chicago (G-4574)
Fedex Office & Print Svcs Inc .....F 312 595-0768
  Chicago (G-4575)
Fedex Office & Print Svcs Inc .....F 312 663-1149
  Chicago (G-4576)
Fedex Office & Print Svcs Inc .....F 630 894-1800
  Bloomingdale (G-1995)
Fernwood Printers Ltd .....G 630 964-9449
  Oak Forest (G-15678)
▲ Fgs Inc .....F 312 421-3060
  Chicago (G-4584)
Fgs-IL LLC .....C 630 375-8500
  Aurora (G-960)
Fidelity Bindery Company .....E 708 343-6833
  Broadview (G-2435)
Fidelity Print Cmmncations LLC .....E 708 343-6833
  Broadview (G-2436)
Financial and Professional Reg .....G 217 782-2127
  Springfield (G-19367)
Fine Line Printing .....G 773 582-9709
  Chicago (G-4590)
Fisher Printing Inc .....C 708 598-1500
  Bridgeview (G-2346)
Fisheye Services Incorporated .....G 773 942-6314
  Chicago (G-4598)
Five Star Printing Inc .....G 217 965-3355
  Virden (G-20184)
FL 1 .....F 847 956-9400
  Elk Grove Village (G-8999)
Flash Printing Inc .....G 847 288-9101
  Franklin Park (G-9944)
Fleetwood Press Inc .....G 708 485-6811
  Brookfield (G-2483)
Flocon Inc .....G 815 527-7990
  Woodstock (G-21388)
▲ Flow-Eze Company .....F 815 965-1062
  Rockford (G-17416)
Flyerinc Corporation .....G 630 655-3400
  Oak Brook (G-15622)
FM Graphic Impressions Inc .....G 630 897-8788
  Aurora (G-1097)
Forcerl .....G 847 432-7588
  Highland Park (G-11263)
Forest Printing Co .....F 708 366-5100
  Forest Park (G-9718)
Forms Design Plus Coleman Prtg .....G 309 685-6000
  Peoria (G-16439)
Forms Press Inc .....G 815 455-4466
  Crystal Lake (G-7200)
Fortman & Associates Ltd .....F 847 524-0741
  Elk Grove Village (G-9005)
Foundry Printers Row Crossfit .....G 312 566-7201
  Chicago (G-4625)
Franks Dgtal Prtg Off Sups Inc .....G 630 892-2511
  Aurora (G-1101)
French Studio Ltd .....G 618 942-5328
  Herrin (G-11171)
Frye-Williamson Press Inc .....E 217 522-7744
  Springfield (G-19372)
Full Court Press Inc .....G 773 779-1135
  Chicago (G-4639)
Full Line Printing Inc .....G 312 642-8080
  Chicago (G-4640)
G & G Studios /Broadway Prtg .....G 815 933-8181
  Bradley (G-2282)
G F Printing .....G 618 797-0576
  Granite City (G-10708)
G T Services of Illionois Inc .....G 309 925-5111
  Tremont (G-19896)

Employee Codes: A=Over 500 employees, B=251-500
C=101-250, D=51-100, E=20-50, F=10-19, G=3-9

27 PRINTING, PUBLISHING, AND ALLIED INDUSTRIES SIC SECTION

Galesburg Register-Mail ... C ... 309 343-7181
Galesburg *(G-10193)*

Gallas Label & Decal ... F ... 773 775-1000
Chicago *(G-4656)*

Gamma Alpha Visual Communicatn ... G ... 847 956-0633
Park Ridge *(G-16279)*

Gannon Graphics ... G ... 847 895-1043
Schaumburg *(G-18533)*

Gatehouse Media LLC ... B ... 217 788-1300
Springfield *(G-19373)*

Gazette Printing Co ... G ... 309 389-2811
Glasford *(G-10387)*

Gemini Digital Inc ... G ... 630 894-9430
Roselle *(G-17954)*

General Converting Inc ... D ... 630 378-9800
Bolingbrook *(G-2179)*

Genoa Business Forms Inc ... E ... 815 895-2800
Sycamore *(G-19711)*

George Press Inc ... G ... 217 324-2242
Litchfield *(G-12964)*

George Vaggelatos ... G ... 847 361-3880
Itasca *(G-11661)*

Gerard Printing Company ... G ... 847 437-6442
Elk Grove Village *(G-9013)*

Gh Printing Co Inc ... G ... 630 663-0351
Downers Grove *(G-8009)*

Gh Printing Co Inc ... E ... 630 960-4115
Downers Grove *(G-8010)*

Gnk Technologies Inc ... G ... 847 382-1185
Barrington *(G-1220)*

Golden Prairie News ... G ... 217 226-3721
Assumption *(G-889)*

Good News Printing ... G ... 708 389-1127
Palos Heights *(G-16185)*

Goose Printing Co ... G ... 847 673-1414
Evanston *(G-9525)*

Gossett Printing Inc ... G ... 618 548-2583
Salem *(G-18341)*

Grace Enterprises Inc ... G ... 847 423-2100
Chicago *(G-4721)*

Grace Printing and Mailing ... E ... 847 423-2100
Skokie *(G-18960)*

Graf Ink Printing Inc ... G ... 618 273-4231
Harrisburg *(G-11025)*

Grand Forms & Systems Inc ... F ... 847 259-4600
Arlington Heights *(G-744)*

Grand Printing & Graphics Inc ... F ... 312 218-6780
Chicago *(G-4722)*

Granja & Sons Printing ... F ... 773 762-3840
Chicago *(G-4724)*

Graphic Arts Services Inc ... E ... 630 629-7770
Villa Park *(G-20148)*

Graphic Arts Studio Inc ... E ... 847 381-1105
Barrington *(G-1221)*

Graphic Image Corporation ... F ... 312 829-7800
Orland Park *(G-15956)*

Graphic Packaging Corporation ... C ... 847 451-7400
Franklin Park *(G-9953)*

Graphic Partners Inc ... E ... 847 872-9445
Zion *(G-21515)*

Graphic Promotions Inc ... F ... 815 726-3288
Shorewood *(G-18897)*

Graphic Source Group Inc ... G ... 847 854-2670
Lake In The Hills *(G-12336)*

Graphicmark Inc ... G ... 708 293-1200
Alsip *(G-448)*

Graphics 2000 Inc ... F ... 630 920-0022
Burr Ridge *(G-2676)*

Graphics 255 LLC ... F ... 312 266-9266
Chicago *(G-4728)*

Graphics Group LLC ... D ... 708 867-5500
Chicago *(G-4729)*

Grasso Graphics Inc ... G ... 708 489-2060
Alsip *(G-449)*

Great Impressions Inc ... G ... 847 367-6725
Libertyville *(G-12655)*

Greek Art Printing & Pubg Co ... G ... 847 724-8860
Glenview *(G-10553)*

Grovak Instant Printing Co ... G ... 847 675-2414
Mount Prospect *(G-14532)*

Grphic Richards Communications ... F ... 708 547-6000
Bellwood *(G-1626)*

Hafner Printing Co Inc ... F ... 312 362-0120
Chicago *(G-4767)*

▲ **Hako Minuteman Inc** ... G ... 630 627-6900
Addison *(G-144)*

Hal Mather & Sons Incorporated ... E ... 815 338-4000
Woodstock *(G-21394)*

Hammond Printing ... G ... 847 724-1539
Glenview *(G-10555)*

Hansen Printing Co Inc ... E ... 708 599-1500
Bridgeview *(G-2353)*

Hard Reset Printing Inc ... G ... 773 850-9277
Joliet *(G-11874)*

Harlan Vance Company ... F ... 309 888-4804
Normal *(G-15205)*

Harrison Martha Print Studio ... G ... 949 290-8630
Crystal Lake *(G-7205)*

Harry Otto Printing Company ... F ... 630 365-6111
Elburn *(G-8455)*

Hawthorne Press ... G ... 708 652-9000
Cicero *(G-6852)*

Hawthorne Press Inc ... G ... 847 587-0582
Spring Grove *(G-19275)*

Heart Printing Inc ... G ... 847 259-2100
Arlington Heights *(G-748)*

Heavenly Enterprises ... G ... 773 783-2981
Hickory Hills *(G-11197)*

Hempel Group Inc ... G ... 630 389-2222
Batavia *(G-1383)*

Henderson Family ... G ... 309 236-6783
Aledo *(G-357)*

Henry Printing Inc ... G ... 618 529-3040
Carbondale *(G-2845)*

Heritage Press Inc ... G ... 847 362-9699
Libertyville *(G-12657)*

Heritage Printing ... G ... 815 537-2372
Prophetstown *(G-16832)*

Hermitage Group Inc ... E ... 773 561-3773
Chicago *(G-4808)*

◆ **Hertzberg Ernst & Sons** ... E ... 773 525-3518
Chicago *(G-4810)*

Higgins Quick Print ... G ... 847 635-7700
Des Plaines *(G-7776)*

Highland Printers ... G ... 618 654-5880
Highland *(G-11221)*

Hillsboro Journal Inc ... E ... 217 532-3933
Hillsboro *(G-11316)*

◆ **Holden Industries Inc** ... F ... 847 940-1500
Deerfield *(G-7616)*

Holland Printing Inc ... F ... 708 596-9000
South Holland *(G-19222)*

▲ **House of Doolittle Ltd** ... E ... 847 228-9591
Arlington Heights *(G-751)*

House of Graphics ... E ... 630 682-0810
Carol Stream *(G-3000)*

Howard Custom Transfers Inc ... E ... 847 695-8195
Elgin *(G-8616)*

Howard Press Printing Inc ... G ... 708 345-7437
Northlake *(G-15547)*

Howlan Inc ... G ... 847 478-1760
Vernon Hills *(G-20061)*

Hq Printers Inc ... G ... 312 782-2020
Chicago *(G-4857)*

Hts Hancock Transcriptions Svc ... E ... 217 379-9241
Paxton *(G-16308)*

Hub Printing Company Inc ... F ... 815 562-7057
Rochelle *(G-17145)*

Huetone Imprints Inc ... G ... 630 694-9610
Elk Grove Village *(G-9038)*

Hunt Enterprises Inc ... G ... 708 354-8464
Oak Forest *(G-15681)*

Huston-Patterson Corporation ... D ... 217 429-5161
Decatur *(G-7503)*

Ideal Advertising & Printing ... F ... 815 965-1713
Rockford *(G-17456)*

Illiana Financial Inc ... F ... 630 941-3838
Elmhurst *(G-9375)*

Illini Digital Printing Co ... G ... 618 271-6622
East Saint Louis *(G-8311)*

Illinois Office Sup Elect Prtg ... E ... 815 434-0186
Ottawa *(G-16056)*

Illinois Printing Services Inc ... G ... 217 728-2786
Sullivan *(G-19669)*

Image Pact Printing ... E ... 708 460-6070
Tinley Park *(G-19839)*

Image Print Inc ... G ... 815 672-1068
Streator *(G-19611)*

Impact Prtrs & Lithographers ... E ... 847 981-9676
Elk Grove Village *(G-9048)*

Impossible Objects Inc ... F ... 847 400-9582
Northbrook *(G-15404)*

Impress Printing & Design Inc ... G ... 815 730-9440
Joliet *(G-11879)*

Impression Printing ... F ... 708 614-8660
Oak Forest *(G-15682)*

Impressions Count Printing ... F ... 847 395-2445
Antioch *(G-616)*

In Color Graphics Coml Prtg ... F ... 847 697-0003
Elgin *(G-8623)*

In-Print Graphics Inc ... E ... 708 396-1010
Oak Forest *(G-15683)*

Informative Systems Inc ... F ... 217 523-8422
Springfield *(G-19389)*

Ink Enterprises Inc ... G ... 815 547-5515
Belvidere *(G-1679)*

Ink Spot Printing ... G ... 773 528-0288
Chicago *(G-4926)*

Ink Spot Silk Screen ... G ... 847 724-6234
Glenview *(G-10567)*

Ink Spots Prtg & Meida Design ... G ... 708 754-1300
Homewood *(G-11498)*

Ink Well ... G ... 618 398-1427
Fairview Heights *(G-9647)*

Ink Well Printing & Design Ltd ... G ... 847 923-8060
Schaumburg *(G-18559)*

Inky Printers ... G ... 815 235-3700
Freeport *(G-10120)*

Innerworkings Inc ... D ... 312 642-3700
Chicago *(G-4927)*

Innova Print Fulfillment Inc ... G ... 630 845-3215
Geneva *(G-10282)*

Innovtive Design Graphics Corp ... G ... 847 475-7772
Evanston *(G-9540)*

Insty Prints Palatine Inc ... F ... 847 963-0000
Palatine *(G-16129)*

Instyprints of Waukegan Inc ... G ... 847 336-5599
Waukegan *(G-20449)*

Integra Graphics and Forms Inc ... F ... 708 385-0950
Crestwood *(G-7120)*

Integra Print & Data Services ... G ... 708 337-6265
Libertyville *(G-12663)*

Integrated Graphics Inc ... E ... 630 482-6100
Batavia *(G-1387)*

Integrated Print Graphics Inc ... C ... 847 695-6777
South Elgin *(G-19155)*

Integrated Print Graphics Inc ... C ... 847 888-2880
South Elgin *(G-19156)*

Integrity Prtg McHy Svcs LLC ... G ... 847 834-9484
Hoffman Estates *(G-11431)*

Intel Printing Inc ... G ... 708 343-1144
Broadview *(G-2444)*

Inter Solutions Co ... G ... 773 657-4437
Chicago *(G-4942)*

International Graphics & Assoc ... F ... 630 584-2248
Saint Charles *(G-18215)*

Intersports Screen Printing ... G ... 773 489-7383
Chicago *(G-4957)*

Irving Press Inc ... E ... 847 595-6650
Elk Grove Village *(G-9061)*

J & J Mr Quick Print Inc ... G ... 773 767-7776
Chicago *(G-4984)*

J and K Printing ... G ... 708 229-9558
Oak Lawn *(G-15721)*

J D Graphic Co Inc ... E ... 847 364-4000
Elk Grove Village *(G-9063)*

J Gooch & Associates Inc ... G ... 217 522-7575
Springfield *(G-19392)*

▲ **J J Collins Sons Inc** ... F ... 630 960-2525
Downers Grove *(G-8032)*

J J Collins Sons Inc ... D ... 217 345-7606
Charleston *(G-3405)*

J K Printing & Mailing Inc ... G ... 847 432-7717
Highland Park *(G-11276)*

J M Printers Inc ... F ... 815 727-1579
Crest Hill *(G-7087)*

J Oshana & Son Printing ... G ... 773 283-8311
Chicago *(G-4992)*

J S Printing Inc ... G ... 847 678-6300
Franklin Park *(G-9970)*

Jade Screen Printing ... G ... 618 463-2325
Alton *(G-560)*

Jamali Kopy Kat Printing Inc ... G ... 708 544-6164
Bellwood *(G-1629)*

James Ray Monroe Corporation ... F ... 618 532-4575
Centralia *(G-3236)*

▲ **James W Smith Printing Company** ... E ... 847 244-6486
Gurnee *(G-10888)*

Jamether Incorporated ... G ... 815 444-9971
Crystal Lake *(G-7211)*

Jans Graphics Inc ... F ... 312 644-4700
Chicago *(G-5006)*

Janssen Avenue Boys Inc ... G ... 630 627-0202
North Aurora *(G-15265)*

Jarr Printing Co ... F ... 815 363-5435
McHenry *(G-13750)*

Jay Printing ... G ... 847 934-6103
Palatine *(G-16133)*

Jds Printing Inc ... G ... 630 208-1195
Glendale Heights *(G-10463)*

27 PRINTING, PUBLISHING, AND ALLIED INDUSTRIES

Jeannie Wagner ....G....... 815 477-2700
  Crystal Lake (G-7212)
Jem Associates Ltd ....G....... 847 808-8377
  Chicago (G-5016)
Jjm Printing Inc ....G....... 815 499-3067
  Sterling (G-19513)
▲ JL Clark LLC ....C....... 815 961-5609
  Rockford (G-17476)
Joes Printing ....G....... 773 545-6063
  Chicago (G-5034)
▲ John S Swift Company Inc ....E....... 847 465-3300
  Buffalo Grove (G-2552)
Johns-Byrne Company ....D....... 847 583-3100
  Niles (G-15137)
Johnsbyrne Graphic Tech Corp ....G....... 847 583-3100
  Niles (G-15138)
Johnson Press America Inc ....E....... 815 844-5161
  Pontiac (G-16773)
Johnson Printing ....G....... 630 595-8815
  Bensenville (G-1833)
Johnsons Screen Printing ....G....... 630 262-8210
  Geneva (G-10287)
Josco Inc ....G....... 708 867-7189
  Chicago (G-5051)
Josephs Printing Service ....G....... 847 724-4429
  Glenview (G-10576)
Jost & Kiefer Printing Company ....E....... 217 222-5145
  Quincy (G-16897)
Jph Enterprises Inc ....G....... 847 390-0900
  Des Plaines (G-7792)
Jsn Printing Inc ....G....... 815 582-4014
  Joliet (G-11888)
Jsolo Corp ....G....... 847 964-9188
  Deerfield (G-7624)
July 25th Corporation ....F....... 309 664-6444
  Bloomington (G-2064)
Juskie Printing Corp ....G....... 630 663-8833
  Downers Grove (G-8035)
K & J Phillips Corporation ....G....... 630 355-0660
  Naperville (G-14856)
K & M Printing Company Inc ....D....... 847 884-1100
  Schaumburg (G-18584)
K & S Printing Services ....G....... 815 899-2923
  Sycamore (G-19720)
K Chae Corp ....G....... 847 763-0077
  Lincolnwood (G-12826)
KB Publishing Inc ....D....... 708 331-6352
  South Holland (G-19226)
KB Publishing Inc ....E....... 708 331-6352
  South Holland (G-19227)
Keane Inc ....F....... 847 952-9700
  Mount Prospect (G-14541)
Kellogg Printing Co ....F....... 309 734-8388
  Monmouth (G-14220)
Kelly Printing Co Inc ....E....... 217 443-1792
  Danville (G-7355)
Kelvyn Press Inc ....D....... 708 343-0448
  Broadview (G-2448)
Kelvyn Press Inc ....E....... 630 585-8160
  Aurora (G-991)
Kendall Printing Co ....G....... 630 553-9200
  Yorkville (G-21490)
Keneal Industries Inc ....F....... 815 886-1300
  Romeoville (G-17837)
Kenilworth Press Incorporated ....G....... 847 256-5210
  Wilmette (G-21081)
Kens Quick Print Inc ....F....... 847 831-4410
  Highland Park (G-11277)
Kestler Digital Printing Inc ....F....... 773 581-5918
  Chicago (G-5098)
Kevin Kewney ....G....... 217 228-7444
  Quincy (G-16899)
Key Printing ....G....... 815 933-1800
  Kankakee (G-11987)
Keystone Printing & Publishing ....G....... 815 678-2591
  Richmond (G-17016)
Keystone Printing Services ....G....... 773 622-7210
  Chicago (G-5099)
Kingery Printing Company ....C....... 217 347-5151
  Effingham (G-8405)
Kingsbury Enterprises Inc ....G....... 708 535-7590
  Oak Forest (G-15685)
Kjellberg Printing ....F....... 630 653-2244
  Wheaton (G-20807)
KK Stevens Publishing Co ....E....... 309 329-2151
  Astoria (G-893)
Klein Printing Inc ....G....... 773 235-2121
  Chicago (G-5108)
Klh Printing Corp ....G....... 847 459-0115
  Wheeling (G-20926)

Km Press Incorporated ....G....... 618 277-1222
  Belleville (G-1564)
Knight Prtg & Litho Svc Ltd ....G....... 847 487-7700
  Island Lake (G-11609)
Kon Printing Inc ....G....... 630 879-2211
  Batavia (G-1390)
Kram Digital Solutions Inc ....G....... 312 222-0431
  Glenview (G-10583)
Krueger International Inc ....F....... 312 467-6850
  Chicago (G-5134)
Kwik Print Inc ....G....... 630 773-3225
  Itasca (G-11689)
L & S Label Printing Inc ....G....... 815 964-6753
  Cherry Valley (G-3443)
L P M Inc ....G....... 847 866-9777
  Evanston (G-9545)
Labels Unlimited Incorporated ....E....... 773 523-7500
  Chicago (G-5152)
Lakes Reg Prtg & Graphics LLC ....G....... 847 838-5838
  Antioch (G-620)
▼ Lakeside Lithography LLC ....E....... 312 243-3001
  Chicago (G-5166)
Lambert Print Source Llc ....G....... 630 708-0505
  Yorkville (G-21491)
Lans Printing Inc ....G....... 708 895-6226
  Lynwood (G-13295)
Lazare Printing Co Inc ....G....... 773 871-2500
  Chicago (G-5187)
Lee Enterprises Incorporated ....C....... 618 529-5454
  Carbondale (G-2849)
Lee-Wel Printing Corporation ....G....... 630 682-0935
  Wheaton (G-20812)
Legend Promotions ....G....... 847 438-3528
  Lake Zurich (G-12428)
Leonard A Unes Printing Co ....G....... 309 674-4942
  Peoria (G-16469)
Leonard Emerson ....G....... 217 628-3441
  Divernon (G-7880)
Less Cost Copy Center Inc ....G....... 618 345-3121
  Collinsville (G-6965)
Lincoln Printers Inc ....G....... 217 732-3121
  Lincoln (G-12733)
Lincoln Square Printing ....G....... 773 334-9030
  Chicago (G-5225)
Lincolnshire Printing Inc ....G....... 815 578-0740
  McHenry (G-13759)
Lith Liqure ....G....... 847 458-5180
  Lake In The Hills (G-12339)
Litho Type LLC ....E....... 708 895-3720
  Lansing (G-12506)
Lithographic Industries Inc ....E....... 773 921-7955
  Broadview (G-2450)
Lithotype Company Inc ....F....... 630 771-1920
  Bolingbrook (G-2205)
Lithuanian Catholic Press ....E....... 773 585-9500
  Chicago (G-5236)
Little Village Printing Inc ....G....... 708 749-4414
  Berwyn (G-1955)
Lloyd Midwest Graphics ....G....... 815 282-8828
  Machesney Park (G-13357)
Lsc Communications Us LLC ....C....... 217 235-0561
  Mattoon (G-13642)
▲ Lsk Import ....G....... 847 342-8447
  Chicago (G-5275)
Lucmia Enterprises Inc ....G....... 800 785-3157
  River Grove (G-17062)
▲ Luke Graphics Inc ....F....... 773 775-6733
  Chicago (G-5279)
Lure Group LLC ....G....... 630 222-6515
  Bolingbrook (G-2207)
Lutheran General Printing Svcs ....G....... 847 298-8040
  Mount Prospect (G-14544)
Luxon Printing Inc ....F....... 630 293-7710
  West Chicago (G-20609)
Lyle James ....G....... 217 675-2191
  Jacksonville (G-11774)
Lynns Printing Co ....G....... 618 465-7701
  Alton (G-564)
M & R Printing Inc ....G....... 847 398-2500
  Rolling Meadows (G-17749)
M C F Printing Company ....G....... 630 279-0301
  Elmhurst (G-9396)
M L S Printing Co Inc ....G....... 847 948-9102
  Deerfield (G-7633)
M M Marketing ....G....... 815 459-7968
  Wauconda (G-20370)
M O W Printing Inc ....F....... 618 345-5525
  Collinsville (G-6967)
M S A Printing Co ....G....... 847 593-5699
  Elk Grove Village (G-9103)

M Wells Printing Co ....G....... 312 455-0400
  Chicago (G-5305)
M13 Inc ....E....... 847 310-1913
  Schaumburg (G-18617)
Mac Graphics Group Inc ....G....... 630 620-7200
  Oakbrook Terrace (G-15806)
Macoupin County Enquirer Inc ....E....... 217 854-2534
  Carlinville (G-2879)
◆ Madden Communications Inc ....C....... 630 787-2200
  Wood Dale (G-21211)
Madden Communications Inc ....E....... 630 784-4325
  Bloomingdale (G-1998)
Makkah Printing ....G....... 630 980-2315
  Glendale Heights (G-10472)
Mall Graphic Inc ....F....... 847 668-7600
  Huntley (G-11554)
Mallof Abruzino Nash Mktg Inc ....E....... 630 929-5200
  Carol Stream (G-3020)
Mar Graphics ....D....... 618 935-2111
  Valmeyer (G-20009)
Marc Business Forms Inc ....F....... 847 568-9200
  Lincolnwood (G-12829)
Marcus Press ....G....... 630 351-1857
  Bloomingdale (G-1999)
Marjo Graphics Inc ....G....... 847 367-1305
  Libertyville (G-12672)
Mark Twain Press Inc ....G....... 847 255-2700
  Mundelein (G-14713)
Marking Specialists/Poly ....F....... 847 793-8100
  Buffalo Grove (G-2568)
Marnic Inc ....G....... 309 343-1418
  Galesburg (G-10208)
Marquardt Printing Company ....E....... 630 887-8500
  Burr Ridge (G-2698)
Martinez Printing LLC ....G....... 773 732-8108
  Chicago (G-5350)
Marty Gannon ....E....... 847 895-1059
  Schaumburg (G-18620)
Mason City Banner Times ....F....... 217 482-3276
  Mason City (G-13612)
Master Graphics LLC ....D....... 815 562-5800
  Rochelle (G-17149)
Mattoon Printing Center ....G....... 217 234-3100
  Mattoon (G-13646)
Maximum Prtg & Graphics Inc ....F....... 630 737-0270
  Downers Grove (G-8053)
Mc Adams Multigraphics Inc ....G....... 630 990-1707
  Oak Brook (G-15641)
McGrath Press Inc ....G....... 815 356-5246
  Crystal Lake (G-7224)
McHenry Printing Services ....G....... 815 385-7600
  McHenry (G-13765)
McIntyre & Associates ....G....... 847 639-8050
  Fox Lake (G-9748)
Meck Print ....G....... 708 358-0600
  Oak Park (G-15764)
Media Unlimited Inc ....G....... 630 527-0900
  Naperville (G-14867)
Medical Records Co ....G....... 847 662-6373
  Waukegan (G-20465)
Mencarini Enterprises Inc ....F....... 815 398-9565
  Rockford (G-17516)
Menus To Go ....G....... 630 483-0848
  Streamwood (G-19584)
▲ Merrill Fine Arts Engrv Inc ....D....... 312 786-6300
  Chicago (G-5401)
Merritt & Edwards Corporation ....F....... 309 828-4741
  Bloomington (G-2075)
Metro Printing & Pubg Inc ....F....... 618 476-9587
  Millstadt (G-14052)
Metropolitan Graphic Arts Inc ....E....... 847 566-9502
  Gurnee (G-10896)
Metropolitan Printers ....G....... 309 694-1114
  East Peoria (G-8277)
▲ Meyercord Revenue Inc ....E....... 630 682-6200
  Carol Stream (G-3026)
MGA Innovation Inc ....G....... 847 672-9947
  Gurnee (G-10897)
Mgsolutions Inc ....G....... 630 530-2005
  Elmhurst (G-9401)
Mi-Te Fast Printers Inc ....G....... 312 236-3278
  Glencoe (G-10432)
Mi-Te Fast Printers Inc ....G....... 312 236-8352
  Chicago (G-5421)
Mich Enterprises Inc ....F....... 630 616-9000
  Wood Dale (G-21216)
Michael Burza ....G....... 815 909-0233
  Cortland (G-7024)
▲ Microdynamics Corporation ....C....... 630 276-0527
  Naperville (G-14870)

Employee Codes: A=Over 500 employees, B=251-500
C=101-250, D=51-100, E=20-50, F=10-19, G=3-9

2020 Harris Illinois Industrial Directory

Microprint Inc G 630 969-1710
Romeoville *(G-17852)*
Mid Central Printing & Mailing F 847 251-4040
Wilmette *(G-21087)*
Mid City Printing Service G 773 777-5400
Chicago *(G-5426)*
Mid-Central Business Forms G 309 692-9090
Peoria *(G-16474)*
MidAmerican Prtg Systems Inc E 312 663-4720
Schiller Park *(G-18824)*
Midwest Graphic Industries F 630 509-2972
Bensenville *(G-1853)*
Midwest Outdoors Ltd E 630 887-7722
Burr Ridge *(G-2704)*
Midwest Sign & Lighting Inc G 708 365-5555
Country Club Hills *(G-7042)*
Minute Man Press G 847 839-9600
Hoffman Estates *(G-11436)*
Minuteman Press G 708 524-4940
Oak Park *(G-15765)*
Minuteman Press G 708 598-4915
Hickory Hills *(G-11200)*
Minuteman Press G 630 584-7383
Naperville *(G-14872)*
Minuteman Press Inc G 847 577-2411
Arlington Heights *(G-776)*
Minuteman Press Intl Inc G 630 574-0090
Oak Brook *(G-15646)*
Minuteman Press Morton Grove G 847 470-0212
Morton Grove *(G-14429)*
Minuteman Press of Countryside G 708 354-2190
Countryside *(G-7064)*
Minuteman Press of Frankfort G 779 254-2912
Frankfort *(G-9817)*
Minuteman Press of Lansing G 708 895-0505
Lansing *(G-12509)*
Minuteman Press of Rockford G 815 633-2992
Loves Park *(G-13237)*
Minuteman Press of Waukegan G 847 244-6288
Gurnee *(G-10900)*
Miracle Press Company F 773 722-6176
Chicago *(G-5467)*
Mission Press Inc G 312 455-9501
Franklin Park *(G-10002)*
Mittera Illinois LLC D 708 449-8989
Berkeley *(G-1942)*
MJM Graphics G 847 234-1802
Lake Forest *(G-12274)*
Mmpcu Limited G 217 355-0500
Champaign *(G-3324)*
Modern Media Services F 847 548-0408
Grayslake *(G-10790)*
Modern Printing of Quincy F 217 223-1063
Quincy *(G-16917)*
Modern Trade Communications F 847 674-2200
Skokie *(G-18992)*
Moran Graphics Inc E 312 226-3900
Chicago *(G-5497)*
Mormor Incorporated G 630 268-0050
Lombard *(G-13104)*
▲ **Morton Suggestion Company LLC** G 847 255-4770
Mount Prospect *(G-14549)*
Motr Grafx LLC G 847 600-5656
Wheeling *(G-20942)*
▲ **Mountain Graphix LLC** F 630 681-8300
Carol Stream *(G-3033)*
▲ **MPS Chicago Inc** C 630 932-9000
Downers Grove *(G-8062)*
Msf Graphics Inc G 847 446-6900
Des Plaines *(G-7808)*
Mt Carmel Register Co Inc E 618 262-5144
Mount Carmel *(G-14481)*
Multicopy Corp G 847 446-7015
Grayslake *(G-10792)*
Murray Printing Service Inc G 847 310-8959
Schaumburg *(G-18642)*
N Bujarski Inc G 847 884-1600
Schaumburg *(G-18643)*
N P D Inc G 708 424-6788
Oak Lawn *(G-15729)*
Naco Printing Co Inc G 618 664-0423
Greenville *(G-10839)*
Nameonanythingcom LLC G 630 545-2642
Glen Ellyn *(G-10414)*
Nancy J Perkins G 815 748-7121
Dekalb *(G-7691)*
Nature House Inc D 217 833-2393
Griggsville *(G-10850)*
Need To Know Inc G 309 691-3877
Peoria *(G-16484)*
Negs & Litho Inc G 847 647-7770
Chicago *(G-5563)*
Network Printing Inc G 847 566-4146
Mundelein *(G-14720)*
New City Communications E 312 243-8786
Chicago *(G-5576)*
New Life Printing & Publishing G 847 658-4111
Algonquin *(G-382)*
New Vision Print & Marketing G 630 406-0509
Naperville *(G-14882)*
Newsweb Corporation E 773 975-5727
Chicago *(G-5591)*
▲ **NGS Printing Inc** E 847 741-4411
Elgin *(G-8672)*
▲ **Nissha Si-Cal Technologies Inc** E 508 898-1800
Burr Ridge *(G-2710)*
▲ **Nissha Usa Inc** E 847 413-2665
Schaumburg *(G-18650)*
Nite Owl Prints LLC G 630 541-6273
Downers Grove *(G-8066)*
Noniprint G 773 366-2846
Chicago *(G-5609)*
North County News Inc G 618 282-3803
Red Bud *(G-16998)*
North Shore Printers Inc F 847 623-0037
Waukegan *(G-20469)*
Northstar Group Inc F 847 726-0880
Lake Zurich *(G-12440)*
Northwest Graphics Inc G 815 544-3676
Cherry Valley *(G-3444)*
Northwest Premier Printing G 773 736-1882
Chicago *(G-5623)*
Northwest Printing Inc G 815 943-7977
Harvard *(G-11061)*
Nosco Inc E 847 336-4200
Gurnee *(G-10903)*
Nosco Bridgeview Inc D 773 585-2035
Bridgeview *(G-2369)*
▲ **Nosco Inc** B 847 336-4200
Gurnee *(G-10904)*
Nosco Inc D 847 360-4874
Waukegan *(G-20471)*
Nova Printing and Litho Co F 773 486-8500
Mount Prospect *(G-14552)*
Novak Business Forms Inc E 630 932-9850
Lombard *(G-13110)*
Nowuba LLC - Investio Print G 833 669-8221
Fox Lake *(G-9750)*
Npn360 E 847 215-7300
Bannockburn *(G-1205)*
Nu-Art Printing G 618 533-9971
Centralia *(G-3242)*
Off The Press LLC G 815 436-9612
Plainfield *(G-16697)*
Officers Printing Inc G 847 480-4663
Northbrook *(G-15444)*
Ogden Minuteman Inc G 773 542-6917
Chicago *(G-5662)*
Ogden Offset Printers Inc G 773 284-7797
Chicago *(G-5663)*
Olde Print Shoppe Inc G 618 395-3833
Olney *(G-15879)*
▲ **Omega Printing Inc** E 630 595-6344
Bensenville *(G-1861)*
Omega Royal Graphics Inc F 847 952-8000
Elk Grove Village *(G-9163)*
On Time Envelopes & Printing G 630 682-0466
Carol Stream *(G-3043)*
On Time Printing and Finishing G 708 544-4500
Hillside *(G-11351)*
Oneims Printing LLC G 773 297-2050
Skokie *(G-18999)*
Onetouchpoint Mtn States LLC G 303 227-1400
Oak Brook *(G-15653)*
▲ **Only 1 Printers Inc** F 847 947-4119
Wheeling *(G-20951)*
Oriole Enterprises Inc G 773 589-9696
Chicago *(G-5702)*
Orion Star Corp F 847 776-2300
Palatine *(G-16147)*
Oswego Vinyl G 331 725-4801
Oswego *(G-16019)*
Ottawa Publishing Co Inc C 815 433-2000
Ottawa *(G-16068)*
Overt Press Inc E 773 284-0909
Chicago *(G-5718)*
▼ **P & P Press Inc** E 309 691-8511
Peoria *(G-16488)*
P & S Cochran Printers Inc E 309 691-6668
Peoria *(G-16489)*
P F Pettibone & Co G 815 344-7811
Crystal Lake *(G-7242)*
P H C Enterprises Inc G 847 816-7373
Vernon Hills *(G-20080)*
P P Graphics Inc G 708 343-2530
Westchester *(G-20707)*
Paap Printing G 217 345-6878
Charleston *(G-3409)*
Pace Print Plus G 847 381-1720
Barrington *(G-1233)*
Palwaukee Printing Company G 847 459-0240
Wheeling *(G-20954)*
Pamco Printed Tape Label Inc C 847 803-2200
Des Plaines *(G-7817)*
Pana News Inc F 217 562-2111
Pana *(G-16221)*
Pantagraph Printing and Sty Co F 309 829-1071
Bloomington *(G-2084)*
▲ **Pap-R Products Company** D 800 637-4937
Martinsville *(G-13587)*
Pap-R-Tainer LLC G 217 382-4141
Martinsville *(G-13588)*
Papiros Graphics G 773 581-3000
Chicago *(G-5753)*
Papyrus Press Inc F 773 342-0700
Chicago *(G-5755)*
Paragon Print & Mail Prod Inc G 630 671-2222
Bloomingdale *(G-2006)*
Park Press Inc F 708 331-6352
South Holland *(G-19237)*
▲ **Park Printing Inc** G 708 430-4878
Palos Hills *(G-16203)*
Parkway Printers G 217 525-2485
Springfield *(G-19420)*
Parrot Press G 773 376-6333
Chicago *(G-5768)*
Patrick Impressions LLC G 630 257-9336
Lemont *(G-12578)*
Patterson Promotions & Prtg G 708 430-0224
Bridgeview *(G-2373)*
Patton Printing and Graphics G 217 347-0220
Effingham *(G-8417)*
Paul D Burton G 309 467-2613
Eureka *(G-9484)*
Paulson Press Inc E 847 290-0080
Elk Grove Village *(G-9170)*
Peacock Printing Inc G 618 242-3157
Mount Vernon *(G-14633)*
Peak Printing G 309 652-3655
Blandinsville *(G-1972)*
▲ **Perfect Plastic Printing Corp** C 630 584-1600
Saint Charles *(G-18242)*
Perfect Plastic Printing Corp D 630 584-1600
Saint Charles *(G-18243)*
Performance Mailing & Prtg Inc G 847 549-0500
Libertyville *(G-12694)*
Perma Graphics Printers G 815 485-6955
New Lenox *(G-15050)*
Perryco Inc F 815 436-2431
Plainfield *(G-16701)*
Personalized Printing Mailing G 847 441-2955
South Elgin *(G-19170)*
Petersburg Observer Co Inc G 217 632-2236
Petersburg *(G-16603)*
Phoenix Business Solutions LLC E 708 388-1330
Alsip *(G-491)*
Phoenix Press Inc G 630 833-2281
Addison *(G-239)*
Photo Graphic Design Service G 815 672-4417
Streator *(G-19620)*
▼ **Physicians Record Co Inc** D 800 323-9268
Berwyn *(G-1960)*
Pinney Printing Company F 815 626-2727
Sterling *(G-19524)*
Pioneer Printing Service Inc G 312 337-4283
Chicago *(G-5810)*
PIP Printing Inc G 815 464-0075
Frankfort *(G-9822)*
Platts Printing Company G 309 228-1069
Farmington *(G-9663)*
Plum Grove Printers Inc E 847 882-4020
Hoffman Estates *(G-11447)*
Poets Study Inc G 773 286-1355
Chicago *(G-5831)*
Poll Enterprises Inc F 708 756-1120
Chicago Heights *(G-6764)*
Polpress Inc G 773 792-1200
Chicago *(G-5836)*
Power Graphics & Print Inc G 847 568-1808
Skokie *(G-19007)*

Prairieland Printing....G.... 309 647-5425
Washington *(G-20276)*
Precision Dialogue Direct Inc....D.... 773 237-2264
Chicago *(G-5855)*
Precision Press & Label Inc....G.... 630 625-1225
Itasca *(G-11722)*
Precision Printing Inc....G.... 630 317-7004
Downers Grove *(G-8084)*
Precision Printing Inc....G.... 630 737-0075
Lombard *(G-13121)*
Precision Reproductions Inc....F.... 847 724-0182
Glenview *(G-10602)*
Preferred Press Inc....G.... 630 980-9799
Glendale Heights *(G-10484)*
Preferred Printing & Graphics....G.... 708 547-6880
Berkeley *(G-1944)*
Preferred Printing Service....G.... 312 421-2343
Chicago *(G-5861)*
Premier Printing and Packg Inc....G.... 847 970-9434
Rolling Meadows *(G-17766)*
Premier Printing Illinois Inc....D.... 217 359-2219
Champaign *(G-3339)*
▲ **Press America Inc**....E.... 847 228-0333
Elk Grove Village *(G-9195)*
Press Proof Printing....G.... 847 466-7156
Carpentersville *(G-3115)*
Press Tech Inc....F.... 847 824-4485
Des Plaines *(G-7832)*
Pride In Graphics Inc....F.... 312 427-2000
Chicago *(G-5872)*
Print & Design Services LLC....G.... 847 317-9001
Bannockburn *(G-1206)*
Print & Mailing Solutions LLC....G.... 708 544-9400
Romeoville *(G-17867)*
Print & Mailing Solutions LLC....G.... 708 544-9400
Wood Dale *(G-21232)*
Print and Mktg Solutions Group....E.... 847 498-9640
Chicago *(G-5876)*
Print Butler Inc....F.... 312 296-2804
Grayslake *(G-10796)*
Print Management Group Inc....G.... 847 671-0900
Schiller Park *(G-18837)*
Print Ninja LLC....G.... 877 396-4652
Evanston *(G-9569)*
Print Service & Dist Assn Psda....G.... 312 321-5120
Chicago *(G-5877)*
Print Shop....G.... 815 786-8278
Sandwich *(G-18381)*
Print Source For Business Inc....G.... 847 356-0190
Lake Villa *(G-12363)*
Print Tech Inc....F.... 847 949-5400
Mundelein *(G-14728)*
Print Turnaround Inc....F.... 847 228-1762
Arlington Heights *(G-791)*
Print Xpress....G.... 847 677-5555
Skokie *(G-19012)*
Printcrazy LLC....G.... 630 573-1020
Chicago Heights *(G-6765)*
Printed Impressions Inc....G.... 773 604-8585
Oakbrook Terrace *(G-15813)*
Printed Word Inc....G.... 847 328-1511
Evanston *(G-9570)*
Printers Ink of Paris Inc....G.... 217 463-2552
Paris *(G-16240)*
Printers Mark....G.... 309 732-1174
Rock Island *(G-17234)*
Printers Row Loft....G.... 312 431-1019
Chicago *(G-5878)*
Printers Row Press Inc....E.... 312 427-7150
Chicago *(G-5879)*
Printers Square Condo Assn....G.... 312 765-8794
Chicago *(G-5880)*
Printforce Inc....G.... 618 395-7746
Olney *(G-15885)*
Printing Inc....D.... 316 265-1201
Chicago *(G-5881)*
Printing Arts Cmmnications LLC....E.... 708 938-1600
Broadview *(G-2460)*
Printing By Joseph....G.... 708 479-2669
Mokena *(G-14109)*
Printing Craftsmen of Joliet....G.... 815 254-3982
Joliet *(G-11917)*
Printing Craftsmen of Pontiac....G.... 815 844-7118
Pontiac *(G-16778)*
Printing Dimensions....G.... 847 439-7521
Arlington Heights *(G-792)*
Printing Etc Inc....G.... 815 562-6151
Rochelle *(G-17152)*
Printing Impression Direc....G.... 815 385-6688
Lakemoor *(G-12476)*
Printing On Ashland Inc....G.... 773 488-4707
Chicago *(G-5883)*
Printing Plant....G.... 618 529-3115
Carbondale *(G-2855)*
Printing Plus....G.... 708 301-3900
Lockport *(G-13019)*
Printing Plus of Roselle Inc....G.... 630 893-0410
Roselle *(G-17974)*
Printing Shop....G.... 847 998-6330
Glenview *(G-10603)*
Printing Source Inc....G.... 773 588-2930
Morton Grove *(G-14433)*
Printing Works Inc....G.... 847 860-1920
Elk Grove Village *(G-9198)*
Printing You Can Trust....G.... 224 676-0482
Deerfield *(G-7646)*
Printmeisters Inc....G.... 708 474-8400
Lansing *(G-12512)*
Printsmart Printing & Graphics....G.... 630 434-2000
Woodridge *(G-21334)*
Printsource Plus Inc....G.... 708 389-6252
Blue Island *(G-2134)*
Printwise Inc....G.... 630 833-2845
Wheaton *(G-20815)*
Priority One Printing and Mail....G.... 217 224-8008
Quincy *(G-16928)*
Priority Print....G.... 708 485-7080
Brookfield *(G-2491)*
Priority Printing....G.... 773 889-6021
Chicago *(G-5884)*
Prism Commercial Printing Ctrs....G.... 773 735-5400
Chicago *(G-5885)*
Pro Graphics Ink....G.... 309 647-2526
Canton *(G-2831)*
Pro-Type Printing Inc....G.... 217 379-4715
Paxton *(G-16315)*
Production Press Inc....E.... 217 243-3353
Jacksonville *(G-11781)*
▲ **Professional Graphics Inc**....E.... 815 226-9422
Rockford *(G-17561)*
Professnal Mling Prtg Svcs Inc....F.... 630 510-1000
Carol Stream *(G-3054)*
Proform....G.... 309 676-2535
Peoria *(G-16503)*
Proforma....G.... 815 534-5461
Frankfort *(G-9828)*
Proforma Awards Print & Promot....G.... 630 897-9848
Oswego *(G-16021)*
Proforma Business Builders....G.... 309 692-6390
Peoria *(G-16504)*
Proforma Quality Business Svcs....G.... 847 356-1959
Gurnee *(G-10916)*
Progress Printing Corporation....E.... 773 927-0123
Chicago *(G-5898)*
Progressive Systems Netwrk Inc....G.... 312 382-8383
Chicago *(G-5902)*
Promo Answers Inc....G.... 708 633-6653
Tinley Park *(G-19850)*
Promo Corp....G.... 773 217-7666
Arlington Heights *(G-793)*
▼ **Promoframes LLC**....G.... 866 566-7224
Schaumburg *(G-18685)*
Provena Enterprises Inc....E.... 708 478-3230
Kankakee *(G-11997)*
QBF Group Inc....G.... 708 781-9580
Tinley Park *(G-19851)*
Qg LLC....B.... 217 347-7721
Effingham *(G-8419)*
◆ **Qst Industries Inc**....E.... 312 930-9400
Chicago *(G-5923)*
Quad City Press....F.... 309 764-8142
Moline *(G-14170)*
Quad/Graphics Inc....F.... 217 347-7721
Effingham *(G-8421)*
Quad/Graphics Inc....A.... 815 734-4121
Mount Morris *(G-14500)*
Quad/Graphics Inc....A.... 815 338-6750
Woodstock *(G-21426)*
Quality Blue & Offset Printing....G.... 630 759-8035
Bolingbrook *(G-2231)*
Quality Quickprint Inc....F.... 815 439-3430
Joliet *(G-11920)*
Quality Quickprint Inc....G.... 815 723-0941
Lemont *(G-12586)*
Quality Quickprint Inc....F.... 815 838-1784
Lockport *(G-13020)*
Quantum Color Graphics LLC....C.... 847 967-3600
Morton Grove *(G-14435)*
Quick Print Shoppe....G.... 309 694-1204
East Peoria *(G-8285)*
Quickprinters....G.... 309 833-5250
Macomb *(G-13398)*
Quik Impressions Group Inc....E.... 630 495-7845
Addison *(G-262)*
Quinn Print Inc....G.... 847 823-9100
Park Ridge *(G-16293)*
▲ **R & R Creative Graphics Inc**....G.... 630 208-4724
Geneva *(G-10301)*
R N R Photographers Inc....G.... 708 453-1868
River Grove *(G-17066)*
R R Donnelley & Sons Company....C.... 630 377-2586
Saint Charles *(G-18257)*
R R Donnelley & Sons Company....C.... 217 935-2113
Clinton *(G-6928)*
R R Donnelley & Sons Company....A.... 815 584-2770
Dwight *(G-8158)*
R R Donnelley & Sons Company....A.... 815 844-5181
Pontiac *(G-16779)*
R R Donnelley & Sons Company....A.... 630 322-6268
Warrenville *(G-20251)*
R R Donnelley & Sons Company....D.... 630 762-7600
Saint Charles *(G-18258)*
R R Donnelley & Sons Company....C.... 312 326-8000
Chicago *(G-5950)*
R T P Inc....G.... 312 664-6150
Chicago *(G-5954)*
Rainbow Manufacturing Inc....E.... 847 824-9600
Mundelein *(G-14731)*
Rapid Circular Press Inc....F.... 312 421-5611
Chicago *(G-5970)*
Rapid Copy & Duplicating Co....G.... 312 733-3353
Melrose Park *(G-13906)*
Rapid Print....G.... 309 673-0826
Peoria *(G-16508)*
Rayco Printing Services Inc....G.... 773 545-4545
Chicago *(G-5978)*
Reesha Printing Inc....G.... 708 233-6677
Bridgeview *(G-2381)*
Reign Print Solutions Inc....G.... 847 590-7091
Arlington Heights *(G-798)*
Rektrix....G.... 773 475-7926
Chicago *(G-6006)*
Reliable Mail Services Inc....F.... 847 677-6245
Glenview *(G-10611)*
Reliance Graphics Inc....G.... 847 593-6688
Arlington Heights *(G-800)*
Remke Printing Inc....G.... 847 520-7300
Wheeling *(G-20972)*
Repro-Graphics Inc....D.... 847 439-1775
Elk Grove Village *(G-9217)*
Review Graphics Inc....G.... 815 623-2570
Roscoe *(G-17925)*
Review Printing Co Inc....G.... 309 788-7094
Rock Island *(G-17241)*
▲ **Ribbon Print Company**....G.... 847 421-8208
Highland Park *(G-11294)*
Richardson & Edwards Inc....E.... 630 543-1818
Oak Brook *(G-15660)*
Rick Styfer....G.... 630 734-3244
Burr Ridge *(G-2717)*
Rightway Printing Inc....F.... 630 790-0444
Glendale Heights *(G-10488)*
River Bend Printing....G.... 217 324-6056
Litchfield *(G-12975)*
Riverside Graphics Corporation....G.... 312 372-3766
Chicago *(G-6037)*
Riverview Printing Inc....G.... 815 987-1425
Rockford *(G-17575)*
Ro-Web Inc....G.... 309 688-2155
Peoria *(G-16512)*
Rockford Newspapers Inc....B.... 815 987-1200
Rockford *(G-17600)*
Rodin Enterprises Inc....G.... 847 412-1370
Wheeling *(G-20976)*
Rohner Letterpress Inc....F.... 773 248-0800
Chicago *(G-6052)*
Rohrer Graphic Arts Inc....F.... 630 832-3434
Elmhurst *(G-9419)*
Rohrer Litho Inc....G.... 630 833-6610
Elmhurst *(G-9420)*
Romel Press Inc....G.... 708 343-6090
Melrose Park *(G-13909)*
Rose Business Forms & Printing....G.... 618 533-3032
Centralia *(G-3248)*
Roskuszka & Sons Inc....F.... 630 851-3400
Aurora *(G-1149)*
RR Donnelley Printing Co LP....A.... 217 235-0561
Mattoon *(G-13653)*
▲ **RR Donnelley Printing Co LP**....G.... 312 326-8000
Chicago *(G-6072)*

S I C

Employee Codes: A=Over 500 employees, B=251-500
C=101-250, D=51-100, E=20-50, F=10-19, G=3-9
2020 Harris Illinois
Industrial Directory
867

27 PRINTING, PUBLISHING, AND ALLIED INDUSTRIES SIC SECTION

Rrr Graphics & Film Corp......G...... 708 478-4573
Mokena *(G-14114)*
Rt Associates Inc......D...... 847 577-0700
Wheeling *(G-20977)*
Rudin Printing Company Inc......F...... 217 528-5111
Springfield *(G-19436)*
Rush Impressions Inc......G...... 847 671-0622
Schiller Park *(G-18842)*
Rush Order Signs & Prtg LLC......G...... 630 687-7874
Addison *(G-278)*
Rush Printing On Oak......G...... 815 344-8880
McHenry *(G-13789)*
Rusty & Angela Buzzard......G...... 217 342-9841
Effingham *(G-8423)*
Rutledge Printing Co......F...... 708 479-8282
Orland Park *(G-15977)*
S G C M Corp......G...... 630 953-2428
Oakbrook Terrace *(G-15815)*
S G S Inc......G...... 708 544-6061
Downers Grove *(G-8088)*
Safeguard 201 Corp......G...... 630 241-0370
Westmont *(G-20770)*
Saints Volo & Olha Uk Cath Par......G...... 312 829-5209
Chicago *(G-6091)*
Salem Times-Commoner Inc......E...... 618 548-3330
Salem *(G-18358)*
Sales Midwest Prtg & Packg Inc......G...... 309 764-5544
Moline *(G-14175)*
Salsedo Press Inc......F...... 773 533-9900
Chicago *(G-6096)*
Samecwei Inc......G...... 630 897-7888
Aurora *(G-1153)*
Save On Printing Inc......G...... 847 922-7855
Elk Grove Village *(G-9231)*
Savino Enterprises......G...... 708 385-5277
Blue Island *(G-2138)*
Scheiwes Print Shop......G...... 815 683-2398
Crescent City *(G-7082)*
Schiele Graphics Inc......D...... 847 434-5455
Elk Grove Village *(G-9233)*
Schneider Graphics Inc......E...... 847 550-4310
Lake Zurich *(G-12454)*
Schommer Inc......G...... 815 344-1404
McHenry *(G-13791)*
Schwartzkopf Printing Inc......F...... 618 463-0747
Alton *(G-571)*
Schwebel Printing......G...... 618 684-3911
Murphysboro *(G-14759)*
Screen Machine Incorporated......G...... 847 439-2233
Elk Grove Village *(G-9234)*
Screen Print Plus Inc......G...... 630 236-0260
Naperville *(G-14985)*
Second City Prints......G...... 630 504-2423
Batavia *(G-1416)*
Segerdahl Corp......C...... 847 541-1080
Wheeling *(G-20979)*
Segerdahl Corp......D...... 630 754-7104
Bolingbrook *(G-2235)*
Segerdahl Corp......D...... 847 850-8811
Wheeling *(G-20980)*
▲ Segerdahl Graphics Inc......B...... 847 541-1080
Wheeling *(G-20981)*
Selnar Inc......G...... 309 699-3977
East Peoria *(G-8290)*
Semper Fl Printing LLC......G...... 847 640-7737
Arlington Heights *(G-807)*
Service Packaging Design Inc......G...... 847 966-6592
Morton Grove *(G-14440)*
Service Printing Corporation......G...... 847 669-9620
Huntley *(G-11566)*
Sg Screen Graphics Inc......G...... 309 699-8513
Pekin *(G-16360)*
Sg360 A Segerdahl Company......F...... 847 465-3368
Broadview *(G-2468)*
Shanin Company......D...... 847 676-1200
Lincolnwood *(G-12843)*
Shawver Press Inc......G...... 815 772-4700
Morrison *(G-14348)*
Sheer Graphics Inc......G...... 630 654-4422
Westmont *(G-20772)*
Shoreline Graphics Inc......G...... 847 587-4804
Ingleside *(G-11589)*
▼ Shree Mahavir Inc......G...... 312 408-1080
Chicago *(G-6159)*
Shree Printing Corp......G...... 773 267-9500
Chicago *(G-6160)*
Sigley Printing & Off Sup Co......G...... 618 997-5304
Marion *(G-13535)*
Sigma Graphics Inc......F...... 815 433-1000
Ottawa *(G-16078)*
Signcraft Screenprint Inc......C...... 815 777-3030
Galena *(G-10178)*
Signs In Dundee Inc......G...... 847 742-9530
Elgin *(G-8731)*
Signs Today Inc......G...... 847 934-9777
Palatine *(G-16158)*
Simple Canvas Prints LLC......G...... 800 900-4244
Des Plaines *(G-7845)*
Simple Solutions......G...... 618 932-6177
West Frankfort *(G-20683)*
Sir Speedy Printing......G...... 312 337-0774
Chicago *(G-6177)*
Sir Speedy Printing Cntr 6129......G...... 708 349-7789
Orland Park *(G-15979)*
Six Color Print LLC......F...... 847 336-3287
Waukegan *(G-20497)*
Sleepeck Printing Company......C...... 708 544-8900
Chicago *(G-6187)*
Small Newspaper Group......C...... 815 937-3300
Kankakee *(G-12004)*
Small Nwsppr Group Shred Svcs......G...... 309 764-4344
East Moline *(G-8241)*
Smart Office Services Inc......G...... 773 227-1121
Chicago *(G-6190)*
Snow Printing LLC......G...... 618 233-0712
Belleville *(G-1596)*
Solid Impressions Inc......G...... 630 543-7300
Carol Stream *(G-3070)*
Solution 3 Graphics Inc......F...... 773 233-3600
Chicago *(G-6199)*
Solution Printing Inc......G...... 217 529-9700
Springfield *(G-19450)*
Sommers & Fahrenbach Inc......F...... 773 478-3033
Chicago *(G-6201)*
Sons Enterprises......F...... 847 677-4444
Skokie *(G-19032)*
Southwest Printing Co......G...... 708 389-0800
Alsip *(G-512)*
SPD Press Prtg Solutions LLC......G...... 773 299-1700
Chicago *(G-6211)*
Specialty Printing Midwest......G...... 618 799-8472
Roxana *(G-18102)*
▲ Specialty Promotions Inc......C...... 847 588-2580
Niles *(G-15174)*
Speedys Quick Print......G...... 217 431-0510
Danville *(G-7381)*
Spell It With Color Inc......G...... 630 961-5617
Naperville *(G-14919)*
Sphere Inc......G...... 847 566-4800
Mundelein *(G-14738)*
Splat Creative Inc......G...... 708 567-8412
Chicago *(G-6216)*
Springfield Printing Inc......G...... 217 787-3500
Springfield *(G-19454)*
Sprinter Coml Print Label Corp......G...... 630 460-3492
Naperville *(G-14988)*
State Attorney Appellate......G...... 217 782-3397
Springfield *(G-19458)*
Stationery Print Shop Inc......G...... 214 256-3583
Buffalo Grove *(G-2610)*
Stecker Graphics Inc......G...... 309 786-4973
Rock Island *(G-17246)*
Steiner Impressions Inc......G...... 815 633-4135
Loves Park *(G-13266)*
Stellato Printing Inc......G...... 815 280-5664
Crest Hill *(G-7097)*
Steve Bortman......G...... 708 442-1669
Lyons *(G-13315)*
Steve O Inc......G...... 847 473-4466
North Chicago *(G-15321)*
Stevens Group LLC......E...... 331 209-2100
Elmhurst *(G-9431)*
Strathmore Company......E...... 630 232-9677
Geneva *(G-10309)*
▲ Stromberg Allen and Company......E...... 773 847-7131
Tinley Park *(G-19858)*
Studio 88 Creative Design LLC......G...... 312 288-3955
Chicago *(G-6257)*
Suncraft Technologies Inc......C...... 630 369-7900
Naperville *(G-14922)*
Sung Ji USA Inc......F...... 847 956-9400
Elk Grove Village *(G-9258)*
▲ Sunrise Hitek Group LLC......E...... 773 792-8880
Chicago *(G-6276)*
▲ Sunrise Hitek Service Inc......E...... 773 792-8880
Chicago *(G-6277)*
Sunrise Printing Inc......F...... 847 928-1800
Schiller Park *(G-18846)*
Superior Print Services Inc......G...... 630 257-7012
Lemont *(G-12591)*
Swift Impressions Inc......G...... 312 372-0002
Chicago *(G-6296)*
Swifty Print......G...... 630 584-9063
Saint Charles *(G-18283)*
T & C Graphics Inc......E...... 630 532-5050
South Elgin *(G-19175)*
T C W F Inc......E...... 630 369-1360
Naperville *(G-14925)*
T F N W Inc......G...... 630 584-7383
Naperville *(G-14926)*
Tampico Press......G...... 312 243-5448
Chicago *(G-6320)*
Tampoprint Mid-West Corp......G...... 312 971-7715
Chicago *(G-6321)*
Tangent Screen Print Inc......F...... 773 342-1223
Evergreen Park *(G-9601)*
Taykit Inc......E...... 847 888-1150
Elgin *(G-8745)*
Taylor Communication......C...... 309 664-0444
Bloomington *(G-2100)*
Team Cncept Prtg Thrmgrphy Inc......E...... 630 653-8326
Carol Stream *(G-3079)*
Techprint Inc......F...... 847 616-0109
Elk Grove Village *(G-9269)*
Tele Print......G...... 630 941-7877
Elmhurst *(G-9434)*
Temper Enterprises Inc......G...... 815 553-0374
Crest Hill *(G-7098)*
Tera-Print LLC......G...... 224 534-7543
Skokie *(G-19045)*
The b F Shaw Printing Co......E...... 815 875-4461
Princeton *(G-16823)*
▼ The Web Cmmnications Group Inc......G...... 630 467-0900
Itasca *(G-11746)*
Thiessen Communications Inc......E...... 847 884-0980
Schaumburg *(G-18746)*
Thomas Printing & Sty Co......G...... 618 435-2801
Benton *(G-1937)*
Thomas Tees Inc......G...... 217 488-2288
New Berlin *(G-15025)*
Three Angels Printing Svcs Inc......F...... 630 333-4305
Addison *(G-308)*
Three Castle Press Inc......G...... 630 540-0120
Streamwood *(G-19597)*
Three-Z Printing Co......B...... 217 857-3153
Teutopolis *(G-19774)*
Thrift n Swift......G...... 847 455-1350
Palatine *(G-16164)*
Times Record Company......E...... 309 582-5112
Aledo *(G-362)*
Times Republic......E...... 815 432-5227
Watseka *(G-20320)*
Tlm Enterprises Inc......G...... 815 284-5040
Dixon *(G-7923)*
TOA Resource......G...... 312 317-3957
Glen Ellyn *(G-10422)*
Toledo Democrat......G...... 217 849-2000
Toledo *(G-19879)*
Topweb LLC......E...... 773 975-0400
Chicago *(G-6396)*
Total Graphics Services Inc......G...... 847 675-0800
Skokie *(G-19046)*
Total Print Solutions Inc......G...... 630 494-0160
Bloomingdale *(G-2018)*
Tower Printing & Design......G...... 630 495-1976
Lombard *(G-13145)*
▲ TPS Enterprises Inc......E...... 618 783-2978
Newton *(G-15094)*
Trade Print Inc......G...... 773 625-0792
Chicago *(G-6402)*
Trafficcom......G...... 773 997-8351
Chicago *(G-6405)*
Tree Towns Reprographics Inc......F...... 630 832-0209
Elmhurst *(G-9437)*
Trenton Sun......G...... 618 224-9422
Trenton *(G-19905)*
Treudt Corporation......G...... 630 293-0500
West Chicago *(G-20654)*
Tri-Tower Printing Inc......G...... 847 640-6633
Rolling Meadows *(G-17782)*
Triangle Printers Inc......E...... 847 675-3700
Skokie *(G-19048)*
Tru Line Lithographing Inc......E...... 262 554-7300
Niles *(G-15183)*
Trump Printing Inc......F...... 217 429-9001
Decatur *(G-7563)*
Turner Jct Prtg & Litho Svc......G...... 630 293-1377
West Chicago *(G-20655)*
▲ Tvp Color Graphics Inc......G...... 630 837-3600
Streamwood *(G-19600)*

Two JS Copies Now Inc ..... G 847 292-2679
Chicago *(G-6447)*

Tylka Printing Inc ..... G 773 767-3775
Tinley Park *(G-19862)*

Unique Prtrs Lithographers Inc ..... D 708 656-8900
Cicero *(G-6883)*

Unique/Active LLC ..... E 708 656-8900
Cicero *(G-6884)*

United General Graphics LLC ..... F 262 657-5054
Niles *(G-15185)*

▲ **United Graphics Llc** ..... C 217 235-7161
Mattoon *(G-13656)*

United Letter Service Inc ..... F 312 408-2404
Elk Grove Village *(G-9297)*

United Lithograph Inc ..... G 847 803-1700
Des Plaines *(G-7861)*

United Press Inc ..... F 847 482-0597
Lincolnshire *(G-12799)*

United Printers Inc ..... G 773 376-1955
Chicago *(G-6473)*

University of Illinois ..... E 217 333-9350
Champaign *(G-3361)*

Unlimited Graphix Inc ..... E 630 759-0007
Lockport *(G-13026)*

Up North Printing Inc ..... G 630 584-8675
Addison *(G-324)*

Upmerch LLC ..... G 847 674-8601
Lincolnwood *(G-12847)*

Urban Imaging Group Inc ..... G 773 961-7500
Chicago *(G-6495)*

V C P Inc ..... E 847 658-5090
Algonquin *(G-391)*

Valee Inc ..... G 847 364-6464
Elk Grove Village *(G-9300)*

Valid Usa Inc ..... G 630 852-8200
Lisle *(G-12955)*

Van Meter Graphx Inc ..... G 847 465-0600
Wheeling *(G-21008)*

Venus Printing Inc ..... G 847 985-7510
Schaumburg *(G-18770)*

Versa Press Inc ..... C 309 822-0260
East Peoria *(G-8294)*

Veterans Print Management ..... G 630 816-0853
Palos Park *(G-16216)*

Vigil Printing Inc ..... G 773 794-8808
Chicago *(G-6550)*

Viking Printing & Copying Inc ..... G 312 341-0985
Chicago *(G-6551)*

Viking Prtg Graphic Forms Inc ..... F 630 521-0150
Bensenville *(G-1909)*

Village Press Inc ..... G 847 362-1856
Libertyville *(G-12724)*

Vis-O-Graphic Inc ..... E 630 590-6100
Addison *(G-331)*

Vision Intgrted Grphics Group ..... E 312 373-6300
Chicago *(G-6557)*

Vision Intgrted Grphics Group ..... C 331 318-7800
Bolingbrook *(G-2251)*

Voris Communication Co Inc ..... C 630 898-4268
Berkeley *(G-1946)*

W B Mason Co Inc ..... E 888 926-2766
Carol Stream *(G-3085)*

W R S Inc ..... G 630 279-0400
Elmhurst *(G-9443)*

W W Barthel & Co ..... G 847 392-5643
Arlington Heights *(G-830)*

Wagner John ..... G 847 564-0017
Northbrook *(G-15498)*

Warehouse Direct Inc ..... C 847 952-1925
Des Plaines *(G-7867)*

Warner Offset Inc ..... E 847 695-9400
South Elgin *(G-19179)*

▲ **Warwick Publishing Company** ..... D 630 584-3871
Saint Charles *(G-18296)*

Washburn Graficolor Inc ..... G 630 596-0880
Naperville *(G-14944)*

Wayne Printing Company ..... E 309 691-2496
Edwards *(G-8341)*

Wayne Printing Company ..... E 309 691-2496
Edwards *(G-8342)*

We-B-Print Inc ..... G 309 353-8801
Pekin *(G-16368)*

Weakley Printing & Sign Shop ..... G 847 473-4466
North Chicago *(G-15323)*

Weary & Baity Inc ..... G 312 943-6197
Chicago *(G-6594)*

Webb-Mason Inc ..... F 630 428-5838
Naperville *(G-14945)*

Weber Press Inc ..... G 773 561-9815
Chicago *(G-6596)*

West Vly Graphics & Print Inc ..... G 630 377-7575
Saint Charles *(G-18298)*

Westrock Mwv LLC ..... E 217 442-2247
Danville *(G-7397)*

Whipples Printing Press Inc ..... G 309 787-3538
Milan *(G-14031)*

White Graphics Inc ..... F 630 791-0232
Downers Grove *(G-8109)*

Willert Company ..... G 630 860-1620
Franklin Park *(G-10086)*

William Holloway Ltd ..... G 847 866-9520
Evanston *(G-9588)*

Willis Publishing ..... F 618 497-8272
Percy *(G-16561)*

Wold Printing Services Ltd ..... G 847 546-3110
Volo *(G-20206)*

Wood River Printing & Pubg Co ..... G 618 254-3134
Wood River *(G-21268)*

Woogl Corporation ..... E 847 806-1160
Elk Grove Village *(G-9312)*

Wortman Printing Company Inc ..... G 217 347-3775
Effingham *(G-8432)*

Wyckoff Advertising Inc ..... G 630 260-2525
Wheaton *(G-20832)*

Yes Print Management Inc ..... G 312 226-4444
Chicago *(G-6698)*

Yorke Printe Shoppe Inc ..... E 630 627-4960
Lombard *(G-13156)*

Z Print Inc ..... G 773 685-4878
Chicago *(G-6704)*

2754 Commercial Printing: Gravure

◆ **American Labelmark Company** ..... C 773 478-0900
Chicago *(G-3656)*

Arcadia Press Inc ..... F 847 451-6390
Franklin Park *(G-9872)*

C2 Imaging LLC ..... E 312 238-3800
Chicago *(G-3996)*

Chicago Producers Inc ..... F 312 226-6900
Forest Park *(G-9709)*

Cook Communications Minis ..... D 847 741-5168
Elgin *(G-8556)*

Cucchi-BLT America Inc ..... G 224 829-1400
Lake In The Hills *(G-12331)*

Diversfied Lbling Slutions Inc ..... C 630 625-1225
Itasca *(G-11643)*

Donnells Printing & Off Pdts ..... G 815 842-6541
Pontiac *(G-16768)*

Field Holdings LLC ..... D 847 509-2250
Northbrook *(G-15388)*

Frankenstitch Promotions LLC ..... F 847 459-4840
Wheeling *(G-20901)*

▲ **General Packaging Products Inc** ..... D 312 226-5611
Chicago *(G-4675)*

Graphic Industries Inc ..... E 847 357-9870
South Elgin *(G-19148)*

Illinois Tool Works Inc ..... D 630 752-4000
Carol Stream *(G-3002)*

Integrated Media Inc ..... F 217 854-6260
Carlinville *(G-2877)*

International Graphics & Assoc ..... F 630 584-2248
Saint Charles *(G-18215)*

Kl Watch Service Inc ..... G 847 368-8780
Bartlett *(G-1293)*

Label Tek Inc ..... F 630 820-8499
Aurora *(G-995)*

Lsc Communications Us LLC ..... C 217 235-0561
Mattoon *(G-13642)*

Marketing Card Technology LLC ..... D 630 985-7900
Downers Grove *(G-8052)*

National Gift Card Corp ..... E 815 477-4288
Crystal Lake *(G-7236)*

Pingotopia Inc ..... F 847 503-9333
Northbrook *(G-15459)*

▼ **Pioneer Labels Inc** ..... C 618 546-5418
Robinson *(G-17121)*

Precision Dialogue Inc ..... C 773 237-2264
Chicago *(G-5854)*

Proforma-Ppg Inc ..... G 847 429-9349
Elgin *(G-8698)*

Qg LLC ..... D 217 347-7721
Effingham *(G-8420)*

Quad/Graphics Inc ..... A 815 734-4121
Mount Morris *(G-14500)*

R R Donnelley & Sons Company ..... G 309 808-3018
Normal *(G-15221)*

R R Donnelley & Sons Company ..... E 847 622-1026
Elgin *(G-8714)*

R R Donnelley & Sons Company ..... B 630 588-5000
Lisle *(G-12931)*

R R Donnelley & Sons Company ..... C 312 326-8000
Chicago *(G-5950)*

Rogers Loose Leaf Co ..... F 312 226-1947
Glenview *(G-10614)*

RR Donnelley & Sons Company ..... C 312 236-8000
Chicago *(G-6071)*

RR Donnelley Printing Co LP ..... A 217 235-0561
Mattoon *(G-13653)*

▲ **RR Donnelley Printing Co LP** ..... G 312 326-8000
Chicago *(G-6072)*

Standard Register Inc ..... F 630 467-8300
Itasca *(G-11740)*

Tst/Impreso Inc ..... G 630 775-9555
Addison *(G-320)*

Unique Envelope Corporation ..... E 773 586-0330
Chicago *(G-6468)*

White Graphics Printing Svcs ..... G 630 629-9300
Downers Grove *(G-8110)*

Xpress Printing & Copying Co ..... G 630 980-9600
Roselle *(G-17997)*

2759 Commercial Printing

3rd Coast Imaging Inc ..... G 312 322-3111
Chicago *(G-3470)*

A & R Screening LLC ..... F 708 598-2480
Crestwood *(G-7103)*

A Corporate Printing Service ..... F 630 515-0432
Woodridge *(G-21271)*

A-Creations Inc ..... G 630 541-5801
Woodridge *(G-21272)*

A-Flex Label LLC ..... G 630 325-7265
Willowbrook *(G-21028)*

Aaction Printing ..... G 951 788-5111
Pittsfield *(G-16627)*

Abbey Copying Support Svcs Inc ..... G 618 466-3300
Godfrey *(G-10647)*

Abbott Label Inc ..... E 630 773-3614
Itasca *(G-11614)*

ABC Imaging of Washington ..... E 312 253-0040
Chicago *(G-3508)*

▼ **ABS Graphics Inc** ..... C 630 495-2400
Itasca *(G-11615)*

Accord Carton Co ..... C 708 272-3050
Alsip *(G-410)*

Ace Printing Co ..... G 618 259-2711
East Alton *(G-8162)*

Acj Partners LLC ..... G 630 745-1335
Chicago *(G-3524)*

Active Graphics Inc ..... E 708 656-8900
Cicero *(G-6827)*

Ad Images ..... G 847 956-1887
Hoffman Estates *(G-11403)*

Ad Works Inc ..... G 217 342-9688
Effingham *(G-8382)*

Advance Press Sign Inc ..... G 630 833-1600
Villa Park *(G-20128)*

▲ **Aim Screen Printing Supply LLC** ..... G 630 357-4293
Naperville *(G-14954)*

Ajs Premier Printing Inc ..... G 847 838-6350
Antioch *(G-596)*

All She Wrote ..... F 773 529-0100
Chicago *(G-3612)*

All Stars -N- Stitches Inc ..... G 618 435-5555
Benton *(G-1918)*

Allan Brooks & Associates Inc ..... F 847 537-7500
Lake Villa *(G-12345)*

Allegra Marketing Print Mail ..... G 630 790-0444
Schaumburg *(G-18431)*

Alliance Envelope & Print LLC ..... G 847 446-4079
Winnetka *(G-21124)*

▲ **Allied Graphics Inc** ..... G 847 419-8830
Buffalo Grove *(G-2508)*

Allprint Graphics Inc ..... G 847 519-9898
Schaumburg *(G-18433)*

Aloha Document Services Inc ..... E 312 542-1300
Chicago *(G-3626)*

Alphabet Shop Inc ..... E 847 888-3150
Elgin *(G-8505)*

Alta Vista Solutions Inc ..... F 312 473-3050
Chicago *(G-3634)*

◆ **Altco Inc** ..... D 847 549-0321
Vernon Hills *(G-20041)*

▲ **American Ad Bag Company Inc** ..... C 815 338-0300
Woodstock *(G-21357)*

American Bell Screen Prtg Co ..... G 815 623-5522
Roscoe *(G-17899)*

▲ **American Graphic Systems Inc** ..... E 708 614-7007
Tinley Park *(G-19802)*

American Graphics Network Inc ..... F 847 729-7220
Glenview *(G-10522)*

Employee Codes: A=Over 500 employees, B=251-500
C=101-250, D=51-100, E=20-50, F=10-19, G=3-9

2020 Harris Illinois
Industrial Directory

869

27 PRINTING, PUBLISHING, AND ALLIED INDUSTRIES

Company	Class	Phone
American Label Company, Schaumburg (G-18437)	G	630 830-4444
American Litho Incorporated, Carol Stream (G-2934)	A	630 682-0600
American Outfitters Ltd, Waukegan (G-20414)	E	847 623-3959
▲ American Sportswear Inc, Aurora (G-1049)	G	630 859-8998
Americas Community Bankers, Chicago (G-3675)	E	312 644-3100
Amy Schutt, Carrier Mills (G-3123)	G	618 994-7405
Apple Press Inc, Peru (G-16565)	G	815 224-1451
Arcadia Press Inc, Franklin Park (G-9872)	F	847 451-6390
Arch Printing, North Aurora (G-15254)	G	630 896-6610
Arena Sports Usa Inc, McHenry (G-13720)	F	847 809-7268
Arjay Instant Printing, Mundelein (G-14664)	G	847 438-9059
Art-Craft Printers, Franklin Park (G-9874)	G	847 455-2201
Art-Flo Shirt & Lettering Co, Chicago (G-3738)	E	708 656-5422
▼ Artisan Handprints Inc, Chicago (G-3740)	G	773 725-1799
Artistry Engraving & Embossing, Chicago (G-3741)	G	773 775-4888
Artline Screen Printing Inc, Rockford (G-17308)	G	815 963-8125
Artwear, Belleville (G-1530)	G	618 234-5522
Ashland Screening Corporation, Chicago Heights (G-6732)	E	708 758-8800
Associated Design Inc, Palos Hills (G-16195)	F	708 974-9100
AT&I Resources LLC, Addison (G-42)	G	918 925-0154
Athletic Image, Effingham (G-8386)	G	217 347-7377
Augusta Label Corp, Burr Ridge (G-2653)	G	630 537-1961
Authority Screenprint & EMB, Plainfield (G-16643)	G	630 236-0289
Available Business Group Inc, Chicago (G-3781)	D	773 247-4141
Award/Visionps Inc, Chicago (G-3791)	G	331 318-7800
B & B Printing Company, Pittsfield (G-16628)	G	217 285-6072
B Allan Graphics Inc, Alsip (G-420)	F	708 396-1704
B Creative Screen Print Co, Frankfort (G-9769)	G	815 806-3037
B D Enterprises, Alton (G-545)	G	618 462-5861
Babbletees, Chicago (G-3811)	G	815 780-1953
◆ Bagcraftpapercon I LLC, Chicago (G-3814)	C	620 856-2800
Bailleu & Bailleu Printing Inc, Kewanee (G-12021)	G	309 852-2517
Baker La Russo, Naperville (G-14776)	G	630 788-5108
Bally Foil Graphics Inc, Elk Grove Village (G-8857)	G	847 427-1509
Bar Code Graphics Inc, Chicago (G-3827)	F	312 664-0700
Barnaby Inc, Aurora (G-1061)	F	815 895-6555
◆ Bass-Mollett Publishers Inc, Greenville (G-10826)	D	618 664-3141
Batavia Instant Print, West Chicago (G-20550)	G	630 262-0370
Bee Designs Embroidery & Scree, Esmond (G-9475)	G	815 393-4593
Belboz Corp, Dolton (G-7933)	G	708 856-6099
Bellen Container Corporation, Elgin (G-8520)	E	847 741-5600
Belmonte Printing Co, Schaumburg (G-18458)	G	847 352-8841
Benzinger Printing, Genoa (G-10315)	G	815 784-6560
Bes Designs & Associates Inc, Danville (G-7323)	G	217 443-4619
Beslow Associates Inc, Northbrook (G-15349)	G	847 559-2703
Biller Press & Manufacturing, Antioch (G-604)	G	847 395-4111
Bizbash Media Inc, Chicago (G-3904)	G	312 436-2525
Blazing Color Inc, Chester (G-3450)	G	618 826-3001
Blooming Color Inc, Lombard (G-13047)	D	630 705-9200
Bobs Tshirt Store, Mascoutah (G-13594)	G	618 567-1730
Bond Brothers & Co, Lyons (G-13303)	F	708 442-5510
Boree Unlimited LLC, Chicago (G-3935)	G	773 498-6591
Branstiter Printing Co, Jacksonville (G-11760)	G	217 245-6533
Brooke Graphics LLC, Elk Grove Village (G-8870)	E	847 593-1300
▼ BT Steelle Investments Inc, Highland (G-11206)	G	618 410-0534
Bunzl Retail Services LLC, Morton Grove (G-14393)	E	847 966-2550
Business Cards Etc, Morton Grove (G-14394)	G	847 470-8848
Business Cards Tomorrow, Machesney Park (G-13332)	F	815 877-0990
C & E Specialties Inc, Rockford (G-17332)	E	815 229-9230
C E Dienberg Printing Company, Oak Park (G-15747)	G	708 848-4406
C F C Interantional, Chicago Heights (G-6737)	G	708 753-0679
C2 Imaging LLC, Chicago (G-3996)	E	312 238-3800
Calmark Group LLC, Bedford Park (G-1461)	G	708 728-0101
Campbell Publishing Inc, Winchester (G-21104)	E	217 742-3313
Campus Sportswear Incorporated, Champaign (G-3274)	F	217 344-0944
Cannon Ball Marketing Inc, Lisle (G-12875)	G	630 971-2127
Capital Prtg & Die Cutng Inc, Aurora (G-1069)	G	630 896-5520
Capitol Impressions Inc, Peoria (G-16397)	G	309 633-1400
Cara ANAM Enterprises Inc, Saint Charles (G-18163)	G	630 587-8700
Card Prsnlzation Solutions LLC, Glendale Heights (G-10441)	E	630 543-2630
Carl Gorr Printing Co, Woodstock (G-21370)	E	815 338-3191
Carson Printing Inc, East Dundee (G-8189)	G	847 836-0900
Carter Printing Co Inc, Farmersville (G-9659)	G	217 227-4464
Castle-Printech Inc, Dekalb (G-7667)	G	815 758-5484
Catalog Designers Inc, Elk Grove Village (G-8881)	G	847 228-0025
Cavco Printers, Energy (G-4067)	G	618 988-8011
CDs Office Systems Inc, Champaign (G-3278)	F	217 351-5046
Central Decal Company Inc, Burr Ridge (G-2661)	D	630 325-9892
Central IL Business Magazine, Champaign (G-3279)	G	217 351-5281
Century Printing, O Fallon (G-15570)	G	618 632-2486
Challenge Printers, Chicago (G-4067)	G	773 252-0212
Cherry Street Printing & Award, Harrisburg (G-11021)	G	618 252-6814
Chicago Envelope Inc, Carol Stream (G-2957)	E	630 668-0400
Chicago Print Partners LLC, Addison (G-70)	F	312 525-2015
◆ Chicago Printing and EMB Inc, Addison (G-71)	F	630 628-1777
Chii Clothing Company, Chicago (G-4139)	E	312 243-8304
Churchill Wilmslow Corporation, Chicago (G-4147)	G	312 759-8911
Cifuentes Luis & Nicole Inc, Schaumburg (G-18477)	G	847 490-3660
Cityblue Technologies LLC, Peoria (G-16423)	F	309 550-5000
Classic Screen Printing Inc, Forest Park (G-9711)	G	708 771-9355
Classique Signs & Engrv Inc, Quincy (G-16872)	G	217 228-7446
Cliffe Printing Company, Maywood (G-13667)	G	708 345-1665
Cloz Companies Inc, Skokie (G-18944)	E	773 247-8879
Clyde Printing Company, Chicago (G-4184)	F	773 847-5900
Color Communications LLC, Chicago (G-4203)	G	773 638-1400
Color Tone Printing, Blue Island (G-2114)	G	708 385-1442
Color4, Libertyville (G-12644)	F	847 996-6880
Colvin Printing, Blue Island (G-2115)	G	708 331-4580
Com-Graphics Inc, Chicago (G-4208)	D	312 226-0900
Concept One Design Inc, Naperville (G-14804)	F	708 807-3111
Condor Labels Inc, Palos Park (G-16209)	G	708 429-0707
Connies Home Health Care, Park Forest (G-16253)	G	708 790-4000
Continent Corp, Bolingbrook (G-2158)	G	773 733-1584
Corporate Business Card Ltd, Franklin Park (G-9915)	G	847 455-5760
Corporation Supply Co Inc, Chicago (G-4241)	E	312 726-3375
Corwin Printing, Mount Carmel (G-14469)	G	618 263-3936
Craftsmen Printing, Hoopeston (G-11506)	G	217 283-9574
Creative Lithocraft Inc, Schaumburg (G-18493)	F	847 352-7002
Creative Pig Minds Designwear, Rockford (G-17360)	G	815 968-7447
Crest Greetings Inc, Chicago (G-4269)	F	708 210-0800
Crossmark Printing Inc, Chicago Heights (G-6745)	G	708 754-4000
Crown Publications Inc, Rantoul (G-16973)	G	217 893-4856
▲ CTI/Usa Inc, Carol Stream (G-2969)	F	847 258-1000
Custom Graphics Inc, Bartonville (G-1330)	E	309 633-0850
Custom Screen Printing, Arthur (G-850)	G	217 543-3691
D & R Press, Elmwood Park (G-9450)	G	708 452-0500
D G Brandt Inc, Morris (G-14301)	E	847 942-4064
D G Printing Inc, Hawthorn Woods (G-11122)	G	847 397-7779
D L V Printing Service Inc, Chicago (G-4301)	F	773 626-1661
Dale K Brown, Woodstock (G-21380)	G	815 338-0222
Dans Printing & Off Sups Inc, Oak Forest (G-15674)	G	708 687-3055
▲ Darwill Inc, Hillside (G-11335)	C	708 449-7770
Data Com PLD Inc, Willow Springs (G-21025)	G	708 267-5657
Datasite Global Corporation, Chicago (G-4321)	C	312 263-3524
Decal Solutions Unlimited Inc, Arlington Heights (G-727)	G	847 590-5405
▲ Decal Works LLC, Kingston (G-12055)	E	815 784-4000
Decorative Industries Inc, Chicago (G-4329)	G	773 229-0015
Delta Label Inc, Belleville (G-1545)	G	618 233-8984
Deluxe Corporation, Des Plaines (G-7753)	C	847 635-7200
Deluxe Printing, Chicago (G-4337)	G	312 225-0061
Den Graphix Inc, Le Roy (G-12539)	F	309 962-2000
Design Graphics Inc, Frankfort (G-9783)	G	815 462-3323
Diamond Screen Process Inc, Elk Grove Village (G-8948)	G	847 439-6200
Diamond Web Printing LLC, Downers Grove (G-7987)	F	630 663-0351
Digital Hub LLC, Berkeley (G-1940)	E	312 943-6161

27 PRINTING, PUBLISHING, AND ALLIED INDUSTRIES

Digital Prtg & Total Graphics ....G....... 630 627-7400
  Lombard (G-13068)
Display Link Inc ....G....... 815 968-0778
  Rockford (G-17380)
Dixon Graphics Incorporated ....G....... 217 351-6100
  Champaign (G-3285)
DMarv Design Specialty Prtrs ....G....... 708 389-4420
  Blue Island (G-2118)
Document Publishing Group ....E....... 847 783-0670
  Elgin (G-8567)
Dolls Lettering Inc ....G....... 815 467-8000
  Minooka (G-14057)
Domino Amjet Inc ....E....... 847 662-3148
  Gurnee (G-10869)
Donald J Leventhal ....G....... 309 662-8080
  Bloomington (G-2040)
Donnells Printing & Off Pdts ....G....... 815 842-6541
  Pontiac (G-16768)
Dpe Incorporated ....G....... 773 306-0105
  Chicago (G-4394)
Drake Envelope Printing Co ....G....... 217 374-2772
  White Hall (G-21018)
Duckys Formal Wear Inc ....G....... 309 342-5914
  Galesburg (G-10191)
Duo Graphics ....G....... 847 228-7080
  Elk Grove Village (G-8956)
E & H Graphic Service Inc ....G....... 708 748-5656
  Matteson (G-13623)
E K Kuhn Inc ....G....... 815 899-9211
  Sycamore (G-19709)
Eagle Express Mail LLC ....G....... 618 377-6245
  Bethalto (G-1964)
Eagle Screen Print Inds Inc ....F....... 708 579-0454
  Countryside (G-7051)
Earl Ad Inc ....G....... 312 666-7106
  Chicago (G-4431)
Edv Dstrict 7 Clringhouse Vine ....G....... 312 380-1349
  Chicago (G-4459)
Edwards Creative Services LLC ......F....... 309 756-0199
  Milan (G-14007)
Elegant Embroidery Inc ....G....... 847 540-8003
  Lake Zurich (G-12407)
Elite Die & Finishing Inc ....G....... 708 389-4848
  Tinley Park (G-19823)
Elite Impressions & Graphics ....G....... 847 695-3730
  South Elgin (G-19143)
Elliott Publishing Inc ....G....... 217 645-3033
  Liberty (G-12622)
Embroid ME ....G....... 815 485-4155
  New Lenox (G-15033)
▲ Emsur USA LLC ....E....... 847 367-8787
  Elk Grove Village (G-8976)
Energy Tees ....G....... 708 771-0000
  Forest Park (G-9713)
Envision Graphics LLC ....D....... 630 825-1200
  Bloomingdale (G-1993)
Eternal Quality Group ....G....... 309 799-3800
  Milan (G-14009)
Ethan Company Incorporated ....G....... 815 715-2283
  Shorewood (G-18895)
Etlon Enterprises ....G....... 847 258-5265
  Elk Grove Village (G-8983)
Eugene Ewbank ....G....... 630 705-0400
  Oswego (G-16004)
▲ Evanston Graphic Imaging Inc ....G....... 847 869-7446
  Evanston (G-9516)
Excel Glass Inc ....G....... 847 801-5200
  Schiller Park (G-18807)
F & S Engraving Inc ....E....... 847 870-8400
  Mount Prospect (G-14527)
F Weber Printing Co Inc ....G....... 815 468-6152
  Manteno (G-13447)
F-C Enterprises Inc ....G....... 815 254-7295
  Plainfield (G-16663)
Falcon Press Inc ....G....... 815 455-9099
  Crystal Lake (G-7197)
Fantastic Lettering Inc ....G....... 773 685-7650
  Chicago (G-4559)
Fast Print Shop ....G....... 618 997-1976
  Marion (G-13510)
Father & Daughters Printing ....G....... 708 749-8286
  Berwyn (G-1953)
Faulstich Printing Company Inc .....G....... 217 442-4994
  Danville (G-7332)
Fedex Ground Package Sys Inc ......G....... 800 463-3339
  Glendale Heights (G-10450)
Fedex Office & Print Svcs Inc ....G....... 630 759-5784
  Bolingbrook (G-2176)
Fedex Office & Print Svcs Inc ....G....... 847 670-7283
  Mount Prospect (G-14528)

Fedex Office & Print Svcs Inc ....E....... 217 355-3400
  Champaign (G-3292)
Fedex Office & Print Svcs Inc ....E....... 309 685-4093
  Peoria (G-16437)
Fedex Office & Print Svcs Inc ....E....... 708 452-0149
  Elmwood Park (G-9452)
Fedex Office & Print Svcs Inc ....F....... 312 670-4460
  Chicago (G-4577)
▲ Fgs Inc ....F....... 312 421-3060
  Chicago (G-4584)
Financial Graphic Services Inc ....D....... 708 343-0448
  Broadview (G-2437)
Fine Arts Engraving Co ....G....... 800 688-4400
  Chicago (G-4589)
Fine Line Printing ....G....... 773 582-9709
  Chicago (G-4590)
First Impression ....G....... 815 883-3357
  Oglesby (G-15841)
First Impression of Chicago ....G....... 773 224-3434
  Chicago (G-4594)
First String Enterprises Inc ....E....... 708 614-1200
  Tinley Park (G-19827)
Fisheye Services Incorporated ....G....... 773 942-6314
  Chicago (G-4598)
Fleetwood Press Inc ....G....... 708 485-6811
  Brookfield (G-2483)
Flexografix Inc ....F....... 630 350-0100
  Carol Stream (G-2986)
▲ Flow-Eze Company ....G....... 815 965-1062
  Rockford (G-17416)
FM Graphic Impressions Inc ....E....... 630 897-8788
  Aurora (G-1097)
Forest Envelope Company ....G....... 630 515-1200
  Bolingbrook (G-2178)
Fort Dearborn Company ....C....... 773 774-4321
  Niles (G-15121)
Forte Print Corporation ....G....... 773 391-0105
  Chicago (G-4621)
Freddie Bear Sports ....F....... 708 532-4133
  Tinley Park (G-19829)
Freeburg Printing & Publishing ......G....... 618 539-3320
  Freeburg (G-10089)
Freeport Press Inc ....G....... 815 232-1181
  Freeport (G-10111)
Fresh Concept Enterprises Inc ....G....... 815 254-7295
  Plainfield (G-16667)
Frye-Williamson Press Inc ....E....... 217 522-7744
  Springfield (G-19372)
G and D Enterprises Inc ....E....... 847 981-8661
  Arlington Heights (G-739)
G F Printing ....G....... 618 797-0576
  Granite City (G-10708)
G Force Labels & Printing Inc ....G....... 630 552-8911
  Plano (G-16733)
G Y Industries LLC ....G....... 708 210-0800
  Chicago (G-4651)
Gallas Label & Decal ....G....... 773 775-1000
  Chicago (G-4656)
Galleon Industries Inc ....G....... 708 478-5444
  Joliet (G-11867)
Gallimore Industries Inc ....F....... 847 356-3331
  Lake Villa (G-12352)
Game Day Incentives Inc ....G....... 630 854-0581
  Naperville (G-14967)
Gateway Impressions ....F....... 618 505-7544
  Troy (G-19914)
▲ General Packaging Products Inc ..D....... 312 226-5611
  Chicago (G-4675)
George Press Inc ....G....... 217 324-2242
  Litchfield (G-12964)
Gfx International LLC ....C....... 847 543-7179
  Grayslake (G-10774)
Golden Prairie News ....G....... 217 226-3721
  Assumption (G-889)
Golf Tee Printers Inc ....G....... 973 328-4008
  Schaumburg (G-18537)
Good Impressions Inc ....G....... 847 831-4317
  Highland Park (G-11265)
Grand Forms & Systems Inc ....F....... 847 259-4600
  Arlington Heights (G-744)
Granja & Sons Printing ....F....... 773 762-3840
  Chicago (G-4724)
Graphic Press Inc ....G....... 847 272-6000
  Morton Grove (G-14410)
Graphic Screen Printing Inc ....G....... 708 429-3330
  Orland Park (G-15957)
Graphics Group LLC ....D....... 708 867-5500
  Chicago (G-4729)
Great Display Company Llc ....F....... 309 821-1037
  Bloomington (G-2052)

Great Guy Inc ....G....... 312 203-9872
  Medinah (G-13813)
Greco Graphics Inc ....G....... 217 483-2877
  Glenarm (G-10425)
Greek Art Printing & Pubg Co ....G....... 847 724-8860
  Glenview (G-10553)
Griffin John ....G....... 708 301-2316
  Lockport (G-12999)
▲ Gsipc LLC ....G....... 630 325-8181
  Burr Ridge (G-2678)
▼ H & H Graphics LLC ....E....... 847 383-6285
  Vernon Hills (G-20057)
H & H Graphics Illinois Inc ....G....... 847 383-6285
  Vernon Hills (G-20058)
H & H Printing ....G....... 847 866-9520
  Evanston (G-9529)
H A Friend & Company Inc ....E....... 847 746-1248
  Zion (G-21516)
Hafner Printing Co Inc ....F....... 312 362-0120
  Chicago (G-4767)
Hairy Ant Inc ....G....... 630 338-7194
  Saint Charles (G-18205)
Hal Mather & Sons Incorporated ....E....... 815 338-4000
  Woodstock (G-21394)
Harry Otto Printing Company ....F....... 630 365-6111
  Elburn (G-8455)
Hastings Printing ....G....... 217 253-5086
  Tuscola (G-19927)
Hawthorne Press ....G....... 708 652-9000
  Cicero (G-6852)
Hazen Display Corporation ....E....... 815 248-2925
  Davis (G-7418)
Healthcare Labels Inc ....F....... 847 382-3993
  North Barrington (G-15284)
Heart Printing Inc ....G....... 847 259-2100
  Arlington Heights (G-748)
Heartland Labels Inc ....E....... 217 826-8324
  Marshall (G-13572)
Henry News Republican ....G....... 309 364-3250
  Henry (G-11166)
Hermitage Group Inc ....E....... 773 561-3773
  Chicago (G-4808)
High-5 Printwear Inc ....G....... 847 818-0081
  Arlington Heights (G-749)
Highland Journal Printing Inc ....G....... 618 654-4131
  Highland (G-11217)
Hillsboro Journal Inc ....E....... 217 532-3933
  Hillsboro (G-11316)
Hole In The Wall Screen Arts ....G....... 217 243-9100
  Jacksonville (G-11767)
Hopper Graphics Inc ....G....... 708 489-0459
  Palos Heights (G-16189)
Howard Press Printing Inc ....G....... 708 345-7437
  Northlake (G-15547)
Hub Printing Company Inc ....F....... 815 562-7057
  Rochelle (G-17145)
ID Label Inc ....E....... 847 265-1200
  Lake Villa (G-12355)
Ideal Advertising & Printing ....F....... 815 965-1713
  Rockford (G-17456)
Identi-Graphics Inc ....E....... 630 801-4845
  Montgomery (G-14250)
Iemco Corporation ....G....... 773 728-4400
  Chicago (G-4878)
Illinois Office Sup Elect Prtg ....E....... 815 434-0186
  Ottawa (G-16056)
Illinois Tag Co ....E....... 773 626-0542
  Carol Stream (G-3001)
Image Plus Inc ....G....... 630 852-4920
  Downers Grove (G-8028)
Impression Printing ....F....... 708 614-8660
  Oak Forest (G-15682)
Impressive Impressions ....G....... 312 432-0501
  Chicago (G-4902)
Impro International Inc ....G....... 847 398-3870
  Arlington Heights (G-757)
Imtran Industries Inc ....D....... 630 752-4000
  Carol Stream (G-3004)
In Color Graphics Coml Prtg ....F....... 847 697-0003
  Elgin (G-8623)
Independent Shoppers ....G....... 309 647-5200
  Lewistown (G-12616)
Ink Spots Prtg & Meida Design ....G....... 708 754-1300
  Homewood (G-11498)
Ink Your Wear Inc ....G....... 708 329-4444
  Riverside (G-17085)
Inkn Tees ....G....... 847 244-2266
  Waukegan (G-20448)
Inkorporated Designs ....G....... 217 965-4653
  Virden (G-20186)

Employee Codes: A=Over 500 employees, B=251-500
C=101-250, D=51-100, E=20-50, F=10-19, G=3-9

27 PRINTING, PUBLISHING, AND ALLIED INDUSTRIES

Integra Graphics and Forms Inc ....F 708 385-0950
 Crestwood *(G-7120)*
Invitation Creations Inc ....G 847 432-4441
 Highland Park *(G-11274)*
J & J Express Envelopes Inc ....G 847 253-7146
 South Elgin *(G-19158)*
J & J Silk Screening ....G 773 838-9000
 Chicago *(G-4985)*
J S Printing Inc ....G 847 678-6300
 Franklin Park *(G-9970)*
Jdl Graphics ....G 815 401-1120
 Saint Anne *(G-18135)*
JLJ Corp ....G 847 726-9795
 Lake Zurich *(G-12427)*
Joes Printing ....G 773 545-6063
 Chicago *(G-5034)*
Johnson Printing ....G 630 595-8815
 Bensenville *(G-1833)*
Joliet Pattern Works Inc ....D 815 726-5373
 Crest Hill *(G-7088)*
◆ Jordan Industries Inc ....F 847 945-5591
 Deerfield *(G-7621)*
Jph Enterprises Inc ....G 847 390-0900
 Des Plaines *(G-7792)*
K and A Graphics Inc ....G 847 244-2345
 Gurnee *(G-10890)*
Kara Graphics Inc ....G 630 964-8122
 Woodridge *(G-21319)*
Kellogg Printing Co ....F 309 734-8388
 Monmouth *(G-14220)*
Kelly Printing Co Inc ....E 217 443-1792
 Danville *(G-7355)*
Keneal Industries Inc ....F 815 886-1300
 Romeoville *(G-17837)*
Kens Quick Print Inc ....F 847 831-4410
 Highland Park *(G-11277)*
Kevin Kewney ....G 217 228-7444
 Quincy *(G-16899)*
Kevron Printing & Design Inc ....G 708 229-7725
 Hickory Hills *(G-11199)*
Kjellberg Printing ....F 630 653-2244
 Wheaton *(G-20807)*
Klein Printing Inc ....G 773 235-2121
 Chicago *(G-5108)*
Klh Printing Corp ....G 847 459-0115
 Wheeling *(G-20926)*
Kmf Enterprises Inc ....G 630 858-2210
 Wheaton *(G-20808)*
Knight Prtg & Litho Svc Ltd ....G 847 487-7700
 Island Lake *(G-11609)*
Kon Printing Inc ....G 630 879-2211
 Batavia *(G-1390)*
▲ Korea Times ....D 847 626-0388
 Glenview *(G-10579)*
Kwik Print Inc ....G 630 773-3225
 Itasca *(G-11689)*
Label Design ....G 815 462-4949
 Mokena *(G-14093)*
Label Printers LP ....D 630 897-6970
 Aurora *(G-1122)*
Label Tek Inc ....F 630 820-8499
 Aurora *(G-995)*
▲ Labels & Specialty Pdts LLC ....E 630 513-8060
 Saint Charles *(G-18223)*
Labels Unlimited Incorporated ....E 773 523-7500
 Chicago *(G-5152)*
Lambert Print Source Llc ....G 630 708-0505
 Yorkville *(G-21491)*
Landmarx Screen Printing ....F 217 223-4601
 Quincy *(G-16907)*
Laninver USA Inc ....G 847 367-8787
 Elk Grove Village *(G-9084)*
Lans Printing Inc ....G 708 895-6226
 Lynwood *(G-13295)*
▲ Larry & Myra Stone ....G 847 433-0540
 Highland Park *(G-11280)*
Larsen Envelope Co Inc ....E 847 952-9020
 Elk Grove Village *(G-9085)*
◆ Laserskotch Ltd ....F 630 243-6360
 Romeoville *(G-17840)*
Lasons Label Co ....G 773 775-2606
 Chicago *(G-5179)*
Laughing Dog Graphics ....G 309 392-3330
 Minier *(G-14054)*
Lazare Printing Co Inc ....G 773 871-2500
 Chicago *(G-5187)*
Lee-Wel Printing Corporation ....G 630 682-0935
 Wheaton *(G-20812)*
Legacy Prints ....G 815 946-9112
 Polo *(G-16756)*

Legend Promotions ....G 847 438-3528
 Lake Zurich *(G-12428)*
Liberty Group Publishing ....G 309 937-3303
 Cambridge *(G-2805)*
Lighthouse Marketing Services ....G 630 482-9900
 Elburn *(G-8458)*
Lighthouse Printing Inc ....G 708 479-7776
 New Lenox *(G-15039)*
Lincolnshire Printing Inc ....G 815 578-0740
 McHenry *(G-13759)*
Lithuanian Catholic Press ....E 773 585-9500
 Chicago *(G-5236)*
Little Shop of Papers Ltd ....G 847 382-7733
 Barrington *(G-1225)*
Lloyd Midwest Graphics ....G 815 282-8828
 Machesney Park *(G-13357)*
Locker Room Screen Printing ....G 630 759-2533
 Bolingbrook *(G-2206)*
Logo Wear Unlimited Inc ....G 309 367-2333
 Metamora *(G-13962)*
Logo Works ....G 815 942-4700
 Morris *(G-14310)*
Lsc Communications Us LLC ....C 217 235-0561
 Mattoon *(G-13642)*
Ltb Graphics Inc ....G 630 238-1754
 Wood Dale *(G-21208)*
M & G Graphics Inc ....E 773 247-1596
 Chicago *(G-5295)*
M & R Graphics Inc ....F 708 534-6621
 University Park *(G-19957)*
M L S Printing Co Inc ....G 847 948-8902
 Deerfield *(G-7633)*
M S A Printing Co ....G 847 593-5699
 Elk Grove Village *(G-9103)*
M Wells Printing Co ....G 312 455-0400
 Chicago *(G-5305)*
Mac Graphics Group Inc ....G 630 620-7200
 Oakbrook Terrace *(G-15806)*
Macoupin County Enquirer Inc ....E 217 854-2534
 Carlinville *(G-2879)*
Managed Marketing Inc ....G 847 279-8260
 Wheeling *(G-20935)*
Maro Carton Inc ....G 708 649-9982
 Bellwood *(G-1633)*
Martin Stees LLC ....G 630 664-6273
 Aurora *(G-1127)*
Mason City Banner Times ....F 217 482-3276
 Mason City *(G-13612)*
Master Engraving ....G 217 965-5885
 Virden *(G-20188)*
▲ Master Marketing Intl Inc ....E 630 653-5525
 Carol Stream *(G-3021)*
Master Tape Printers Inc ....E 773 283-8273
 Chicago *(G-5360)*
Mattoon Printing Center ....G 217 234-3100
 Mattoon *(G-13646)*
Mbh Promotions Inc ....G 847 634-2411
 Buffalo Grove *(G-2570)*
Mc Adams Multigraphics Inc ....G 630 990-1707
 Oak Brook *(G-15641)*
◆ McCracken Label Co ....E 773 581-8860
 Chicago *(G-5375)*
McGrath Press Inc ....G 815 356-5246
 Crystal Lake *(G-7224)*
McHenry Printing Services ....G 815 385-7600
 McHenry *(G-13765)*
McKillip Industries Inc ....E 815 439-1050
 Yorkville *(G-21493)*
McKnights Long Term Care News ....G 847 559-2884
 Northbrook *(G-15429)*
Melon Ink Screen Print ....G 847 726-0003
 Lake Zurich *(G-12431)*
Meltdown Creative Works Inc ....G 309 310-1978
 Bloomington *(G-2074)*
Merrill Corporation ....C 312 386-2200
 Chicago *(G-5400)*
▲ Merrill Fine Arts Engrv Inc ....D 312 786-6300
 Chicago *(G-5401)*
Meto-Grafics Inc ....F 847 639-0044
 Crystal Lake *(G-7226)*
Mexacali Silkscreen Inc ....G 630 628-9313
 Addison *(G-201)*
Mi-Te Fast Printers Inc ....G 312 236-3278
 Glencoe *(G-10432)*
▲ Microdynamics Corporation ....C 630 276-0527
 Naperville *(G-14870)*
Mid City Printing Service ....G 773 777-5400
 Chicago *(G-5426)*
Mid State Graphics ....G 309 772-3843
 Bushnell *(G-2745)*

MidAmerican Prtg Systems Inc ....E 312 663-4720
 Schiller Park *(G-18824)*
Midwest Gold Stampers Inc ....F 773 775-5253
 Chicago *(G-5442)*
Midwest Labels and Decals Inc ....G 630 543-7556
 Addison *(G-211)*
Midwest Silkscreening Inc ....G 217 892-9596
 Rantoul *(G-16980)*
Miller Products Inc ....E 708 534-5111
 University Park *(G-19962)*
Minerva Sportswear Inc ....F 309 661-2387
 Bloomington *(G-2080)*
Minuteman Press ....G 630 584-7383
 Naperville *(G-14872)*
Minuteman Press Inc ....G 847 577-2411
 Arlington Heights *(G-776)*
MJM Graphics ....G 847 234-1802
 Lake Forest *(G-12274)*
Mjt Design and Prtg Entps Inc ....G 708 240-4323
 Hillside *(G-11348)*
Modern Methods Creative Inc ....G 309 263-4100
 Morton *(G-14368)*
Modern Printing of Quincy ....F 217 223-1063
 Quincy *(G-16917)*
Moor Printing Services Inc ....G 847 687-7287
 Vernon Hills *(G-20076)*
Mortgage Market Info Svcs ....E 630 834-7555
 Villa Park *(G-20161)*
Mosaic Label & Print LLC ....G 847 904-1375
 Glenview *(G-10591)*
Moss Inc ....G 800 341-1557
 Elk Grove Village *(G-9133)*
Moss Inc ....D 800 341-1557
 Chicago *(G-5503)*
Motr Grafx LLC ....G 847 600-5656
 Wheeling *(G-20942)*
MPS Chicago Inc ....E 630 932-5583
 Bolingbrook *(G-2217)*
Msf Graphics Inc ....G 847 446-6900
 Des Plaines *(G-7808)*
Muir Omni Graphics Inc ....E 309 673-7034
 Peoria *(G-16480)*
Multi Packaging Solutions Inc ....G 773 283-9500
 Chicago *(G-5523)*
National Data Svcs Chicago Inc ....C 630 597-9100
 Carol Stream *(G-3038)*
National Data-Label Corp ....E 630 616-9595
 Bensenville *(G-1856)*
▲ NBC Meshtec Americas Inc ....E 630 293-5454
 Batavia *(G-1398)*
Nbs Systems Inc ....E 217 999-3472
 Mount Olive *(G-14507)*
New Image Designs ....G 217 498-9830
 Rochester *(G-17170)*
Newport Printing Services Inc ....G 847 632-1000
 Schaumburg *(G-18648)*
Next Gerneration ....F 630 261-1477
 Lombard *(G-13108)*
▲ Nissha Usa Inc ....E 847 413-2665
 Schaumburg *(G-18650)*
Noor International Inc ....G 847 985-2300
 Bartlett *(G-1256)*
Northwest Premier Printing ....G 773 736-1882
 Chicago *(G-5623)*
Northwestern Illinois Farmer ....G 815 369-2811
 Lena *(G-12607)*
Norway Press Inc ....G 773 846-9422
 Chicago *(G-5627)*
Nosco Inc ....D 847 360-4874
 Waukegan *(G-20471)*
Nu-Art Printing ....G 618 533-9971
 Centralia *(G-3242)*
▲ Oec Graphics-Chicago LLC ....E 630 455-6700
 Willowbrook *(G-21056)*
OfficeMax North America Inc ....E 815 748-3007
 Dekalb *(G-7696)*
Offworld Designs ....G 815 786-7080
 Sandwich *(G-18378)*
Olde Print Shoppe Inc ....E 618 395-3833
 Olney *(G-15879)*
Olympic Trophy and Awards Co ....F 773 631-9500
 Chicago *(G-5672)*
Orland Sports Ltd ....G 773 685-3711
 Chicago *(G-5703)*
Orora Visual TX LLC ....E 414 423-2200
 Niles *(G-15154)*
Osborne Publications Inc ....G 217 422-9702
 Decatur *(G-7534)*
Ottawa Publishing Co Inc ....F 815 434-3330
 Ottawa *(G-16069)*

Outbreak Designs G 217 370-5418 — South Jacksonville *(G-19251)*
Overt Press Inc E 773 284-0909 — Chicago *(G-5718)*
▲ P & L Mark-It Inc E 630 879-7590 — Batavia *(G-1402)*
P H C Enterprises Inc G 847 816-7373 — Vernon Hills *(G-20080)*
Pamco Printed Tape Label Inc C 847 803-2200 — Des Plaines *(G-7817)*
Pana News Inc F 217 562-2111 — Pana *(G-16221)*
Pantagraph Printing and Sty Co F 309 829-1071 — Bloomington *(G-2084)*
Panther Products G 618 664-1071 — Greenville *(G-10841)*
Papyrus Press Inc F 773 342-0700 — Chicago *(G-5755)*
Parker Systems Inc G 847 726-8600 — Kildeer *(G-12051)*
Patrick Impressions LLC G 630 257-9336 — Lemont *(G-12578)*
Paul D Burton G 309 467-2613 — Eureka *(G-9484)*
Pcbl Retail Holdings LLC G 610 761-4838 — Northbrook *(G-15452)*
Peacock Printing Inc G 618 242-3157 — Mount Vernon *(G-14633)*
Peddlers Den Inc G 815 498-3429 — Somonauk *(G-19071)*
Pelegan Inc G 708 442-9797 — Riverside *(G-17088)*
Perryco Inc F 815 436-2431 — Plainfield *(G-16701)*
Pete Aj Co G 217 825-5822 — Gillespie *(G-10376)*
Petersburg Observer Co Inc G 217 632-2236 — Petersburg *(G-16603)*
PHI Group Inc C 847 824-5610 — Mount Prospect *(G-14561)*
Phoenix Graphics Inc G 847 699-9520 — Des Plaines *(G-7823)*
Phoenix Marketing Services F 630 616-8000 — Mundelein *(G-14726)*
Photo Techniques Corp E 630 690-9360 — Carol Stream *(G-3046)*
▼ Physicians Record Co Inc D 800 323-9268 — Berwyn *(G-1960)*
Pioneer Forms Inc G 773 539-8587 — Glenview *(G-10599)*
Pioneer Printing Service Inc G 312 337-4283 — Chicago *(G-5810)*
Plastics Printing Group Inc F 773 473-4481 — Chicago *(G-5820)*
▲ Platform Technologies G 847 357-0435 — Des Plaines *(G-7825)*
Platts Printing Company G 309 228-1069 — Farmington *(G-9663)*
Poets Study Inc G 773 286-1355 — Chicago *(G-5831)*
Pontiac Engraving G 630 834-4424 — Bensenville *(G-1870)*
Positive Impressions G 618 438-7030 — Benton *(G-1935)*
Precision Screen Specialties G 630 220-1361 — Saint Charles *(G-18250)*
Preferred Printing Service G 312 421-2343 — Chicago *(G-5861)*
Premier Printing & Promotions F 815 282-3890 — Machesney Park *(G-13367)*
Premier Printing Illinois Inc D 217 359-2219 — Champaign *(G-3339)*
Prime Label & Packaging LLC D 630 227-1300 — Wood Dale *(G-21231)*
Primedia Source LLC G 630 553-8451 — Yorkville *(G-21499)*
Primo Designs Inc F 217 523-6373 — Springfield *(G-19429)*
Print Management Partners Inc E 847 699-2999 — Des Plaines *(G-7833)*
Print Shop of Morris G 815 710-5030 — Morris *(G-14322)*
Printer Connection G 217 268-3252 — Arcola *(G-663)*
Printforce Inc G 618 395-7746 — Olney *(G-15885)*
Printing Craftsmen of Joliet G 815 254-3982 — Joliet *(G-11917)*
Printing Craftsmen of Pontiac G 815 844-7118 — Pontiac *(G-16778)*
Printing Gallery Inc G 773 525-7102 — Chicago *(G-5882)*
Printing System G 630 339-5900 — Glendale Heights *(G-10485)*
Printmeisters Inc G 708 474-8400 — Lansing *(G-12512)*
Printsource Plus Inc G 708 389-6252 — Blue Island *(G-2134)*
Printworld G 815 544-1000 — Belvidere *(G-1696)*
Priority Print G 708 485-7080 — Brookfield *(G-2491)*
Prismatec Inc G 847 562-9022 — Northbrook *(G-15467)*
▲ Pro Tuff Decal Inc E 815 356-9160 — Crystal Lake *(G-7249)*
Productive Portable Disp Inc G 630 458-9100 — Bensenville *(G-1873)*
Proell Inc G 630 587-2300 — Saint Charles *(G-18251)*
Progress Printing Corporation E 773 927-0123 — Chicago *(G-5898)*
Project Te Inc G 217 344-9833 — Urbana *(G-19996)*
Promark Advertising Specialtie G 618 483-6025 — Altamont *(G-536)*
Pryde Graphics Plus G 630 882-5103 — Plano *(G-16743)*
Publishers Graphics LLC E 630 221-1850 — Carol Stream *(G-3055)*
Qg LLC D 217 347-7721 — Effingham *(G-8420)*
Quad/Graphics Inc A 815 338-6750 — Woodstock *(G-21426)*
Quad/Graphics Inc A 815 734-4121 — Mount Morris *(G-14500)*
Quality Bags Inc F 630 543-9800 — Addison *(G-260)*
Quality Blue & Offset Printing G 630 759-8035 — Bolingbrook *(G-2231)*
Quickprinters G 309 833-5250 — Macomb *(G-13398)*
R & S Screen Printing Inc G 815 337-3935 — Woodstock *(G-21428)*
R L Allen Industries G 618 667-2544 — Troy *(G-19919)*
R N R Photographers Inc G 708 453-1868 — River Grove *(G-17066)*
R Popernik Co Inc F 773 434-4300 — Chicago *(G-5949)*
R R Donnelley & Sons Company C 312 326-8000 — Chicago *(G-5950)*
R R Donnelley & Sons Company E 217 258-2675 — Mattoon *(G-13652)*
R R Donnelley & Sons Company E 847 622-1026 — Elgin *(G-8714)*
R R Donnelley & Sons Company A 815 584-2770 — Dwight *(G-8158)*
R R Donnelley & Sons Company B 630 588-5000 — Lisle *(G-12931)*
Rainbow Art Inc F 312 421-5600 — Chicago *(G-5965)*
Rapid Circular Press Inc F 312 421-5611 — Chicago *(G-5970)*
Ready Inc F 630 501-1352 — Elmhurst *(G-9416)*
Redeen Engraving Inc G 847 593-6500 — Elk Grove Village *(G-9216)*
Reid Communications Inc E 847 741-9700 — Elgin *(G-8717)*
Remke Printing Inc G 847 520-7300 — Wheeling *(G-20972)*
▲ Renishaw Inc D 847 286-9953 — Dundee *(G-8131)*
Response Graphics & EMB LLC G 630 364-1471 — Plainfield *(G-16710)*
Review Printing Co Inc G 309 788-7094 — Rock Island *(G-17241)*
Rick Styfer G 630 734-3244 — Burr Ridge *(G-2717)*
Ripa LLC G 708 938-1600 — Broadview *(G-2464)*
Robal Company Inc F 630 393-0777 — Warrenville *(G-20252)*
Rodin Enterprises Inc G 847 412-1370 — Wheeling *(G-20976)*
▲ Roeda Signs Inc E 708 333-3021 — Chicago Heights *(G-6772)*
Rohner Engraving Inc G 773 244-8343 — Chicago *(G-6051)*
Rose Business Forms & Printing G 618 533-3032 — Centralia *(G-3248)*
Roshan Ag Inc G 773 267-1635 — Chicago *(G-6064)*
Rowboat Creative LLC F 773 675-2628 — Chicago *(G-6067)*
Royal Envelope Corporation D 773 376-1212 — Chicago *(G-6069)*
RR Donnelley & Sons Company C 312 236-8000 — Chicago *(G-6071)*
RR Donnelley Logistics SE F 630 672-2500 — Roselle *(G-17981)*
Rsn Mailing G 314 724-3364 — Collinsville *(G-6974)*
Rt Associates Inc D 847 577-0700 — Wheeling *(G-20977)*
▲ Ruco USA Inc E 866 373-7912 — Wood Dale *(G-21236)*
Rusty & Angela Buzzard G 217 342-9841 — Effingham *(G-8423)*
Rv Enterprises Ltd F 847 509-8710 — Niles *(G-15168)*
S & K Label Co G 630 307-2577 — Bloomingdale *(G-2012)*
S V C Printing Co G 773 286-2219 — Chicago *(G-6086)*
Samecwei Inc G 630 897-7888 — Aurora *(G-1153)*
Sass-N-Class Inc G 630 655-2420 — Hinsdale *(G-11377)*
▲ Sato Lbling Solutions Amer Inc F 630 771-4200 — Romeoville *(G-17873)*
▲ Sato Lbling Solutions Amer Inc D 630 771-4200 — Romeoville *(G-17874)*
Scheiwes Print Shop G 815 683-2398 — Crescent City *(G-7082)*
Schultz Brothers Inc G 630 458-1437 — Addison *(G-282)*
Schwebel Printing G 618 684-3911 — Murphysboro *(G-14759)*
Scorpion Graphics Inc F 773 927-3203 — Chicago *(G-6119)*
Scribes Inc G 630 654-3800 — Burr Ridge *(G-2718)*
Sebis Direct Inc E 312 243-9300 — Bedford Park *(G-1504)*
▲ Selah USA Inc G 847 758-0702 — Elk Grove Village *(G-9235)*
Select Screen Prints & EMB F 309 829-6511 — Bloomington *(G-2093)*
Selective Label & Tabs Inc F 630 466-0091 — Sugar Grove *(G-19654)*
Selective Label & Tabs Inc G 630 466-0091 — Sugar Grove *(G-19655)*
Self Pro Motions LLC G 847 749-6077 — Chicago *(G-6134)*
Sentro Printing Equip N Movers G 779 423-0255 — Rockton *(G-17701)*
Sepire LLC E 312 965-2500 — Burr Ridge *(G-2719)*
Seritex Inc G 201 755-3002 — Addison *(G-285)*
Service Envelope Corporation E 847 559-0004 — Northbrook *(G-15480)*
Sew Wright Embroidery Inc G 309 691-5780 — Peoria *(G-16521)*
Sg Screen Graphics Inc G 309 699-8513 — Pekin *(G-16360)*
Shamrock Scientific E 800 323-0249 — Bellwood *(G-1638)*
Shanin Company D 847 676-1200 — Lincolnwood *(G-12843)*
Sharprint Slkscrn & Grphcs D 877 649-2554 — Chicago *(G-6148)*
Shawver Press Inc G 815 772-4700 — Morrison *(G-14348)*
Sheer Graphics Inc G 630 654-4422 — Westmont *(G-20772)*
Shirt Off My Back Cstm Tees MO G 331 999-2399 — Montgomery *(G-14269)*
Shirt Printing 4u Inc G 708 588-8272 — Countryside *(G-7069)*
Shirt Tales G 309 582-5566 — Aledo *(G-361)*
Shirts Galore & More G 618 797-9801 — Granite City *(G-10736)*
▼ Shree Mahavir Inc G 312 408-1080 — Chicago *(G-6159)*
Sigley Printing & Off Sup Co G 618 997-5304 — Marion *(G-13535)*

SIC

Employee Codes: A=Over 500 employees, B=251-500
C=101-250, D=51-100, E=20-50, F=10-19, G=3-9

2020 Harris Illinois
Industrial Directory

873

Signs In Dundee Inc.....G.....847 742-9530
Elgin *(G-8731)*
Silk Screen Express Inc.....F.....708 845-5600
Tinley Park *(G-19855)*
Silkworm Inc.....D.....618 687-4077
Murphysboro *(G-14760)*
◆ **Simu Ltd**.....F.....708 688-2200
Mc Cook *(G-13701)*
Sir Cooper Inc.....G.....630 279-0162
Villa Park *(G-20173)*
Skyline.....G.....312 300-4700
Mc Cook *(G-13702)*
Skyline Printing Sales.....G.....847 412-1931
Northbrook *(G-15481)*
Southwest Printing Co.....G.....708 389-0800
Alsip *(G-512)*
Spectrum Media Inc.....G.....217 234-2044
Mattoon *(G-13654)*
Speedpro Imaging.....G.....847 856-8220
Gurnee *(G-10929)*
Spirit Warrior Inc.....G.....708 614-0020
Orland Park *(G-15983)*
Sportdecals Inc.....D.....800 435-6110
Spring Grove *(G-19301)*
Sports All Sorts AP & Design.....G.....815 756-9910
Dekalb *(G-7706)*
Sports Designs & Graphics.....E.....217 342-2777
Effingham *(G-8426)*
Sports Recreation and AP Inc.....G.....815 962-7767
Rockford *(G-17642)*
Spotlight Graphic Solutions.....G.....847 944-9600
Schaumburg *(G-18725)*
Squeegee Brothers Inc.....F.....630 510-9152
Carol Stream *(G-3073)*
▲ **Ssn LLC**.....G.....815 978-8729
Byron *(G-2759)*
Star-Times Publishing Co Inc.....G.....618 635-2000
Staunton *(G-19479)*
▲ **Stellar Recognition Inc**.....D.....773 282-8060
Chicago *(G-6243)*
Stellato Printing Inc.....F.....815 280-5664
Joliet *(G-11933)*
Stephen Fossler Company.....D.....847 635-7200
Des Plaines *(G-7852)*
Strathmore Press.....E.....513 483-3600
Saint Charles *(G-18280)*
▲ **Stromberg Allen and Company**.....E.....773 847-7131
Tinley Park *(G-19858)*
Sunburst Sportswear Inc.....F.....630 717-8680
Glendale Heights *(G-10505)*
▲ **Sunny Direct LLC**.....G.....630 795-0800
Naperville *(G-14924)*
▲ **Sunrise Hitek Service Inc**.....E.....773 792-8880
Chicago *(G-6277)*
Swifty Print.....G.....630 584-9063
Saint Charles *(G-18283)*
Systematics Screen Printing.....F.....630 521-1123
Itasca *(G-11742)*
T F N W Inc.....G.....630 584-7383
Naperville *(G-14926)*
T Graphics.....G.....618 592-4145
Oblong *(G-15830)*
T Shirtz Etc Inc.....G.....815 962-5194
Rockford *(G-17651)*
Tailored Printing Inc.....G.....217 498-1057
Rochester *(G-17172)*
Tampico Press.....G.....312 243-5448
Chicago *(G-6320)*
Taylor Communication.....C.....309 664-0444
Bloomington *(G-2100)*
Te Shurt Shop Inc.....F.....217 344-1226
Champaign *(G-3357)*
Team Cncept Prtg Thrmgrphy Inc.....E.....630 653-8326
Carol Stream *(G-3079)*
Team Impressions Inc.....E.....847 357-9270
Elk Grove Village *(G-9266)*
Tease.....G.....630 960-4950
Downers Grove *(G-8100)*
Technicraft Supply Co.....G.....309 495-5245
Peoria *(G-16537)*
Techprint Inc.....F.....847 616-0109
Elk Grove Village *(G-9269)*
Teds Shirt Shack Inc.....G.....217 224-9705
Quincy *(G-16946)*
Tees and Things.....G.....708 351-8584
Chicago *(G-6337)*
Tees Ink.....G.....815 462-7300
New Lenox *(G-15064)*
Teestyler Inc.....G.....630 484-3104
Plainfield *(G-16722)*
Temper Enterprises Inc.....G.....815 553-0374
Crest Hill *(G-7098)*
The b F Shaw Printing Co.....E.....815 875-4461
Princeton *(G-16823)*
Thermo-Graphic LLC.....E.....630 350-2226
Bensenville *(G-1901)*
Thia & Co.....G.....630 510-9770
Wheaton *(G-20828)*
Think Ink Inc.....G.....815 459-4565
Crystal Lake *(G-7282)*
Thomas Printing & Sty Co.....G.....618 435-2801
Benton *(G-1937)*
Thomas Publishing Printing Div.....G.....618 351-6655
Carbondale *(G-2862)*
Three Castle Press Inc.....G.....630 540-0120
Streamwood *(G-19597)*
▲ **Tiem Engineering Corporation**.....F.....630 553-7484
Yorkville *(G-21502)*
Time Out Chicago Partners Lllp.....F.....312 924-9555
Chicago *(G-6379)*
Times Republic.....E.....815 432-5227
Watseka *(G-20320)*
Toledo Democrat.....G.....217 849-2000
Toledo *(G-19879)*
Toms Signs.....G.....630 377-8525
Saint Charles *(G-18290)*
Town Square Publications LLC.....G.....847 427-4633
Arlington Heights *(G-820)*
Tree Towns Reprographics Inc.....F.....630 832-0209
Elmhurst *(G-9437)*
Trendy Screenprinting.....G.....815 895-0081
Sycamore *(G-19737)*
Tri Star Plowing.....G.....847 584-5070
Schaumburg *(G-18755)*
Tri-City Sports Inc.....G.....217 224-2489
Quincy *(G-16951)*
Tri-Tower Printing Inc.....G.....847 640-6633
Rolling Meadows *(G-17782)*
Triangle Screen Print Inc.....F.....847 678-9200
Franklin Park *(G-10066)*
Trimark Screen Printing Inc.....G.....630 629-2823
Lombard *(G-13146)*
Tru Line Lithographing Inc.....E.....262 554-7300
Niles *(G-15183)*
Tst/Impreso Inc.....G.....630 775-9555
Addison *(G-320)*
Ultimate Distributing Inc.....G.....847 566-2250
Mundelein *(G-14745)*
UNI-Label and Tag Corporation.....E.....847 956-8900
Elk Grove Village *(G-9294)*
▲ **Unique Assembly & Decorating**.....E.....630 241-4300
Downers Grove *(G-8103)*
Unique Envelope Corporation.....E.....773 586-0330
Chicago *(G-6468)*
Uniquee Tees Inc.....G.....309 839-0280
Peoria *(G-16540)*
United Engravers Inc.....E.....847 301-3740
Schaumburg *(G-18765)*
Universal Digital Printing.....G.....708 389-0133
Midlothian *(G-13998)*
UPS Authorized Retailer.....G.....708 354-8772
La Grange *(G-12090)*
USA Printworks LLC.....E.....815 206-0854
Woodstock *(G-21442)*
Usmss Inc.....G.....708 409-9010
Westchester *(G-20717)*
Valee Inc.....G.....847 364-6464
Elk Grove Village *(G-9300)*
Valid Secure Solutions LLC.....F.....260 633-0728
Lisle *(G-12954)*
Var Graphics.....G.....708 456-2028
Elmwood Park *(G-9457)*
Victor Envelope Mfg Corp.....C.....630 616-2750
Bensenville *(G-1908)*
Village Press Inc.....G.....847 362-1856
Libertyville *(G-12724)*
Vision Intgrted Grphics Group.....C.....331 318-7800
Bolingbrook *(G-2251)*
Vr Printing Co Inc.....G.....630 980-2315
Glendale Heights *(G-10514)*
W W Barthel & Co.....G.....847 392-5643
Arlington Heights *(G-830)*
Wagner John.....G.....847 564-0017
Northbrook *(G-15498)*
Wagner International LLC.....G.....224 619-9247
Vernon Hills *(G-20109)*
Waist Up Imprntd Sprtswear LLC.....G.....847 963-1400
Palatine *(G-16171)*
Warehouse Direct Inc.....C.....847 952-1925
Des Plaines *(G-7867)*
Washington Courier.....F.....309 444-3139
Washington *(G-20282)*
Wave Graphics Inc.....G.....217 234-8100
Mattoon *(G-13657)*
Weakley Printing & Sign Shop.....G.....847 473-4466
North Chicago *(G-15323)*
Webe Ink.....G.....618 498-7620
Jerseyville *(G-11799)*
Weber Press Inc.....G.....773 561-9815
Chicago *(G-6596)*
Weiskamp Screen Printing.....G.....217 398-8428
Champaign *(G-3370)*
Wes Tech Printing Graphic.....G.....630 520-9041
West Chicago *(G-20658)*
White Graphics Printing Svcs.....G.....630 629-9300
Downers Grove *(G-8110)*
Wide Image Incorporated.....G.....773 279-9183
Schaumburg *(G-18773)*
William Holloway Ltd.....G.....847 866-9520
Evanston *(G-9588)*
Winnetka Sign Co Inc.....G.....847 473-9378
North Chicago *(G-15325)*
Winning Streak Inc.....D.....618 277-8191
Dupo *(G-8150)*
Wold Printing Services Ltd.....G.....847 546-3110
Volo *(G-20206)*
Wolfam Holdings Corporation.....G.....312 407-0100
Chicago *(G-6662)*
◆ **Wolters Kluwer US Inc**.....E.....847 580-5000
Riverwoods *(G-17097)*
Wood River Printing & Pubg Co.....G.....618 254-3134
Wood River *(G-21268)*
Woolenwear Co.....F.....847 520-9243
Prospect Heights *(G-16848)*
Workshop.....E.....815 777-2211
Galena *(G-10183)*
Wortman Printing Company Inc.....G.....217 347-3775
Effingham *(G-8432)*
Xtreme Dzignz.....G.....309 633-9311
Bartonville *(G-1337)*
Your Images Group Inc.....G.....847 437-6688
Schaumburg *(G-18780)*
Your Logo Here.....G.....708 258-6666
Frankfort *(G-9853)*
Zell Co.....G.....312 226-9191
Chicago *(G-6714)*
Zorch International Inc.....E.....312 751-8010
Chicago *(G-6723)*

2761 Manifold Business Forms

Acco Brands Corporation.....A.....847 541-9500
Lake Zurich *(G-12374)*
Acco Brands International Inc.....G.....847 541-9500
Lake Zurich *(G-12375)*
◆ **Acco Brands USA LLC**.....B.....800 222-6462
Lake Zurich *(G-12376)*
Acco Brands USA LLC.....D.....847 272-3700
Lincolnshire *(G-12741)*
American Graphics Network Inc.....F.....847 729-7220
Glenview *(G-10522)*
Azusa Inc.....G.....618 244-6591
Mount Vernon *(G-14597)*
B & B Printing Company.....G.....217 285-6072
Pittsfield *(G-16628)*
◆ **Block and Company Inc**.....C.....847 537-7200
Wheeling *(G-20860)*
Certified Business Forms Inc.....G.....773 286-8194
Chicago *(G-4065)*
Ennis Inc.....E.....815 875-2000
Princeton *(G-16808)*
Fast Print Shop.....G.....618 997-1976
Marion *(G-13510)*
Frank R Walker Company.....G.....630 613-9312
Lombard *(G-13079)*
Gem Acquisition Company Inc.....F.....773 735-3300
Chicago *(G-4667)*
Genoa Business Forms Inc.....E.....815 895-2800
Sycamore *(G-19711)*
Grand Forms & Systems Inc.....F.....847 259-4600
Arlington Heights *(G-744)*
Integrated Print Graphics Inc.....C.....847 695-6777
South Elgin *(G-19155)*
J Gooch & Associates Inc.....G.....217 522-7575
Springfield *(G-19392)*
Kellogg Printing Co.....F.....309 734-8388
Monmouth *(G-14220)*
Keneal Industries Inc.....F.....815 886-1300
Romeoville *(G-17837)*
M L S Printing Co Inc.....G.....847 948-8902
Deerfield *(G-7633)*

M Wells Printing Co ....G.... 312 455-0400
Chicago *(G-5305)*
Marc Business Forms Inc ....F.... 847 568-9200
Lincolnwood *(G-12829)*
Midwest Graphic Industries ....F.... 630 509-2972
Bensenville *(G-1853)*
Multi Packaging Solutions Inc ....G.... 773 283-9500
Chicago *(G-5523)*
N Bujarski Inc ....G.... 847 884-1600
Schaumburg *(G-18643)*
Nbs Systems Inc ....E.... 217 999-3472
Mount Olive *(G-14507)*
Novak Business Forms Inc ....E.... 630 932-9850
Lombard *(G-13110)*
▲ **Perftech Inc** ....E.... 630 554-0010
North Aurora *(G-15270)*
▼ **Physicians Record Co Inc** ....D.... 800 323-9268
Berwyn *(G-1960)*
Proform ....G.... 309 676-2535
Peoria *(G-16503)*
R & L Business Forms Inc ....F.... 618 939-6535
Waterloo *(G-20294)*
R R Donnelley & Sons Company ....D.... 847 593-1200
Elk Grove Village *(G-9210)*
R R Donnelley & Sons Company ....G.... 847 956-4187
Elk Grove Village *(G-9211)*
R R Donnelley & Sons Company ....C.... 217 935-2113
Clinton *(G-6928)*
Shanin Company ....D.... 847 676-1200
Lincolnwood *(G-12843)*
Springfield Printing Inc ....G.... 217 787-3500
Springfield *(G-19454)*
Standard Register Inc ....F.... 815 432-4203
Watseka *(G-20316)*
Taylor Communications Inc ....G.... 309 693-3700
Peoria *(G-16535)*
Taylor Communications Inc ....G.... 217 793-1900
Springfield *(G-19461)*
Taylor Communications Inc ....G.... 708 560-7600
Oak Forest *(G-15691)*
Taylor Communications Inc ....G.... 630 368-0336
Oak Brook *(G-15663)*

2771 Greeting Card Publishing

Advantage Printing Inc ....G.... 630 627-7468
Lombard *(G-13036)*
Alex Smart Inc ....G.... 773 244-9275
Chicago *(G-3604)*
Cardthartic LLC ....F.... 217 239-5895
Champaign *(G-3275)*
Cook Communications Ministries ....C.... 847 741-0800
Elgin *(G-8557)*
Crest Greetings Inc ....F.... 708 210-0800
Chicago *(G-4269)*
▲ **Ggc Corp** ....D.... 847 671-6500
Schiller Park *(G-18810)*
Gram Colossal Inc ....G.... 847 223-5757
Grayslake *(G-10778)*
▲ **Gue Liquidation Delivery Inc** ....G.... 630 719-7800
Downers Grove *(G-8015)*
Harry Otto Printing Company ....F.... 630 365-6111
Elburn *(G-8455)*
K Chae Corp ....F.... 847 763-0077
Lincolnwood *(G-12826)*
Karen Young ....F.... 312 202-0142
Chicago *(G-5081)*
▲ **P S Greetings Inc** ....C.... 708 831-5340
Chicago *(G-5729)*
P S Greetings Inc ....F.... 847 673-7255
Skokie *(G-19002)*
▲ **Recycled Paper Greetings Inc** ....E.... 773 348-6410
Chicago *(G-5991)*
▲ **Salamander Studios Chicago Inc** ....F.... 773 379-2211
Chicago *(G-6092)*
Tukaiz LLC ....F.... 847 288-4804
Franklin Park *(G-10068)*
United Press Inc ....F.... 847 482-0597
Lincolnshire *(G-12799)*

2782 Blankbooks & Looseleaf Binders

Acco Brands Corporation ....A.... 847 541-9500
Lake Zurich *(G-12374)*
Acco Brands International Inc ....G.... 847 541-9500
Lake Zurich *(G-12375)*
Acco Europe Fin Holdings LLC ....G.... 800 222-6462
Lake Zurich *(G-12377)*
Acco Intl Holdings Inc ....G.... 800 222-6462
Lake Zurich *(G-12378)*
Americas Community Bankers ....E.... 312 644-3100
Chicago *(G-3675)*
Assemble and Mail Group Inc ....G.... 309 473-2006
Heyworth *(G-11189)*
Beta Pak Inc ....F.... 708 466-7844
Sugar Grove *(G-19638)*
Bindery Maintenance Services ....G.... 618 945-7480
Bridgeport *(G-2309)*
▲ **Bound + D Termined Inc** ....G.... 847 696-1501
Park Ridge *(G-16271)*
▲ **Carousel Checks Inc** ....F.... 708 613-2452
Palos Hills *(G-16197)*
Chartwell Studio Inc ....G.... 847 868-8674
Chicago *(G-4077)*
Counter Cft Svc Systems & Pdts ....G.... 630 629-7336
Lombard *(G-13059)*
Deluxe Corporation ....C.... 847 635-7200
Des Plaines *(G-7753)*
Funeral Register Books Inc ....F.... 217 627-3235
Girard *(G-10382)*
General Loose Leaf Bindery Inc ....E.... 847 244-9700
Chicago *(G-4672)*
▲ **General Products** ....E.... 773 463-2424
Chicago *(G-4678)*
George S Music Room ....G.... 773 767-4676
Chicago *(G-4684)*
Got 2b Scrappin ....G.... 217 347-3600
Effingham *(G-8401)*
Harris Bmo Bank National Assn ....E.... 815 886-1900
Romeoville *(G-17830)*
Heart & Soul Memories Inc ....G.... 847 478-1931
Buffalo Grove *(G-2544)*
▲ **Howard Medical Company** ....G.... 773 278-1440
Chicago *(G-4850)*
J-Industries Inc ....F.... 815 654-0055
Loves Park *(G-13220)*
▲ **Jacobson Acqstion Holdings LLC** ....C.... 847 623-1414
Waukegan *(G-20452)*
K & L Looseleaf Products Inc ....D.... 847 357-9733
Elk Grove Village *(G-9072)*
▲ **Multi Swatch Corporation** ....D.... 708 344-9440
Broadview *(G-2456)*
Polyvinyl Record Co ....G.... 217 403-1752
Champaign *(G-3336)*
Post Press Production Inc ....F.... 630 860-9833
Elk Grove Village *(G-9185)*
Protek Inc ....G.... 888 536-5466
Saint Charles *(G-18252)*
◆ **Simu Ltd** ....F.... 708 688-2200
Mc Cook *(G-13701)*
Tower Plastics Mfg Inc ....G.... 847 788-1700
Burr Ridge *(G-2723)*
Zookbinders Inc ....D.... 847 272-5745
Deerfield *(G-7663)*

2789 Bookbinding

11th Street Express Prtg Inc ....F.... 815 968-0208
Rockford *(G-17275)*
A A Swift Print Inc ....G.... 847 301-1122
Schaumburg *(G-18424)*
A To Z Engraving Co Inc ....G.... 847 526-7396
Wauconda *(G-20324)*
▼ **ABS Graphics Inc** ....C.... 630 495-2400
Itasca *(G-11615)*
Accord Carton Co ....C.... 708 272-3050
Alsip *(G-410)*
Adams Printing Co ....G.... 618 529-2396
Carbondale *(G-2838)*
Adcraft Printers Inc ....F.... 815 932-6432
Kankakee *(G-11956)*
All Printing & Graphics Inc ....F.... 708 450-1512
Broadview *(G-2415)*
All-Ways Quick Print ....G.... 708 403-8422
Orland Park *(G-15938)*
Allegra Network LLC ....G.... 630 801-9335
Aurora *(G-1047)*
Allegra Print & Imaging Inc ....G.... 847 697-1434
Elgin *(G-8502)*
Alphadigital Inc ....G.... 708 482-4488
La Grange *(G-12071)*
AlphaGraphics Printshops ....G.... 630 964-9600
Lisle *(G-12861)*
American Litho Incorporated ....A.... 630 682-0600
Carol Stream *(G-2934)*
Apple Graphics Inc ....G.... 630 389-2222
Batavia *(G-1350)*
Apple Press Inc ....G.... 815 224-1451
Peru *(G-16565)*
Arch Printing Inc ....G.... 630 966-0235
Aurora *(G-1053)*
Art Bookbinders of America ....E.... 312 226-4100
Chicago *(G-3734)*
Avid of Illinois Inc ....F.... 847 698-2775
Saint Charles *(G-18152)*
B & B Printing Company ....G.... 217 285-6072
Pittsfield *(G-16628)*
B J Plastic Molding Co ....E.... 630 766-3200
Franklin Park *(G-9882)*
Bailleu & Bailleu Printing Inc ....G.... 309 852-2517
Kewanee *(G-12021)*
Barnaby Inc ....F.... 815 895-6555
Aurora *(G-1061)*
Bb Services LLC ....G.... 630 941-8122
Elmhurst *(G-9328)*
▲ **Bell Litho Inc** ....D.... 847 952-3300
Elk Grove Village *(G-8862)*
Benzinger Printing ....G.... 815 784-6560
Genoa *(G-10315)*
Biller Press & Manufacturing ....G.... 847 395-4111
Antioch *(G-604)*
Bindery & Distribution Service ....G.... 847 550-7000
South Barrington *(G-19075)*
Branstiter Printing Co ....G.... 217 245-6533
Jacksonville *(G-11760)*
Business Forms Finishing Svc ....G.... 773 229-0230
Chicago *(G-3979)*
Cadore-Miller Printing Inc ....F.... 708 430-7091
Hickory Hills *(G-11194)*
Cameron Printing Inc ....G.... 630 231-3301
West Chicago *(G-20558)*
Cannon Ball Marketing Inc ....G.... 630 971-2127
Lisle *(G-12875)*
Capitol Impressions Inc ....E.... 309 633-1400
Peoria *(G-16397)*
Cardinal Colorprint Prtg Corp ....E.... 630 467-1000
Itasca *(G-11634)*
Carter Printing Co Inc ....G.... 217 227-4464
Farmersville *(G-9659)*
Century Printing ....G.... 618 632-2486
O Fallon *(G-15570)*
Challenge Printers ....G.... 773 252-0212
Chicago *(G-4067)*
Christopher R Cline Prtg Ltd ....F.... 847 981-0500
Elk Grove Village *(G-8897)*
Cifuentes Luis & Nicole Inc ....G.... 847 490-3660
Schaumburg *(G-18477)*
Cmb Printing Inc ....F.... 630 323-1110
Burr Ridge *(G-2663)*
Commercial Copy Printing Ctr ....F.... 847 981-8590
Elk Grove Village *(G-8903)*
Continental Bindery Corp ....D.... 847 439-6811
Elk Grove Village *(G-8910)*
Copy Mat Printing ....G.... 309 452-1392
Bloomington *(G-2033)*
Copy Service Inc ....G.... 815 758-1151
Dekalb *(G-7670)*
▲ **Copy-Mor Inc** ....E.... 312 666-4000
Streamwood *(G-19568)*
Cpr Printing Inc ....F.... 630 377-8420
Geneva *(G-10263)*
Craftsmen Printing ....G.... 217 283-9574
Hoopeston *(G-11506)*
Creative Label Inc ....D.... 847 956-6960
Elk Grove Village *(G-8919)*
Crossmark Printing Inc ....F.... 708 532-8263
Tinley Park *(G-19819)*
D E Asbury Inc ....F.... 217 222-0617
Hamilton *(G-10953)*
D G Brandt Inc ....G.... 815 942-4064
Morris *(G-14301)*
D L V Printing Service Inc ....F.... 773 626-1661
Chicago *(G-4301)*
Dale K Brown ....G.... 815 338-0222
Woodstock *(G-21380)*
Darnall Printing ....G.... 309 827-7212
Bloomington *(G-2039)*
▲ **Darwill Inc** ....C.... 708 449-7770
Hillside *(G-11335)*
David H Vander Ploeg ....G.... 708 331-7700
South Holland *(G-19206)*
DE Asbury Inc ....E.... 217 222-0617
Quincy *(G-16876)*
Deadline Prtg Clor Copying LLC ....G.... 847 437-9000
Elk Grove Village *(G-8940)*
▲ **Deluxe Johnson** ....C.... 847 635-7200
Des Plaines *(G-7754)*
Denor Graphics Inc ....F.... 847 364-1130
Elk Grove Village *(G-8944)*
Design Graphics Inc ....G.... 815 462-3323
Frankfort *(G-9783)*
Diamond Graphics of Berwyn ....G.... 708 749-2500
Berwyn *(G-1950)*

S I C

Employee Codes: A=Over 500 employees, B=251-500
C=101-250, D=51-100, E=20-50, F=10-19, G=3-9
2020 Harris Illinois
Industrial Directory
875

27 PRINTING, PUBLISHING, AND ALLIED INDUSTRIES

DMarv Design Specialty Prtrs .... G 708 389-4420
  Blue Island *(G-2118)*
Donnells Printing & Off Pdts .... G 815 842-6541
  Pontiac *(G-16768)*
E & H Graphic Service Inc .... G 708 748-5656
  Matteson *(G-13623)*
Einstein Crest .... G 847 965-7791
  Niles *(G-15119)*
Elgin Instant Print .... G 847 931-9006
  Elgin *(G-8575)*
Elliott Publishing Inc .... G 217 645-3033
  Liberty *(G-12622)*
Excellent Bindery Inc .... E 630 766-9050
  Bensenville *(G-1798)*
F Weber Printing Co Inc .... G 815 468-6152
  Manteno *(G-13447)*
Fast Printing of Joliet Inc .... G 815 723-0080
  Joliet *(G-11864)*
Fastway Printing Inc .... G 847 882-0950
  Schaumburg *(G-18525)*
Fedex Office & Print Svcs Inc .... E 217 355-3400
  Champaign *(G-3292)*
Fedex Office & Print Svcs Inc .... F 847 475-8650
  Evanston *(G-9519)*
Fedex Office & Print Svcs Inc .... F 815 229-0033
  Rockford *(G-17412)*
Fedex Office & Print Svcs Inc .... G 847 329-9464
  Lincolnwood *(G-12819)*
Fedex Office & Print Svcs Inc .... G 847 729-3030
  Glenview *(G-10545)*
Fedex Office & Print Svcs Inc .... E 309 685-4093
  Peoria *(G-16437)*
Fedex Office & Print Svcs Inc .... G 847 459-8008
  Buffalo Grove *(G-2536)*
Fedex Office & Print Svcs Inc .... E 708 452-0149
  Elmwood Park *(G-9452)*
Fedex Office & Print Svcs Inc .... G 847 823-9360
  Park Ridge *(G-16274)*
Fedex Office & Print Svcs Inc .... E 630 894-1800
  Bloomingdale *(G-1995)*
Fedex Office & Print Svcs Inc .... E 847 670-4100
  Arlington Heights *(G-736)*
Fedex Office & Print Svcs Inc .... F 312 670-4460
  Chicago *(G-4577)*
Fernwood Printers Ltd .... G 630 964-9449
  Oak Forest *(G-15678)*
Fidelity Bindery Company .... E 708 343-6833
  Broadview *(G-2435)*
First Impression of Chicago .... G 773 224-3434
  Chicago *(G-4594)*
First String Enterprises Inc .... E 708 614-1200
  Tinley Park *(G-19827)*
Fisheye Services Incorporated .... G 773 942-6314
  Chicago *(G-4598)*
Flash Printing Inc .... G 847 288-9101
  Franklin Park *(G-9944)*
Fleetwood Press Inc .... G 708 485-6811
  Brookfield *(G-2483)*
FM Graphic Impressions Inc .... E 630 897-8788
  Aurora *(G-1097)*
Forman Co Inc .... G 309 734-3413
  Monmouth *(G-14217)*
Forms Design Plus Coleman Prtg .... G 309 685-6000
  Peoria *(G-16439)*
French Studio Ltd .... G 618 942-5328
  Herrin *(G-11171)*
G F Printing .... G 618 797-0576
  Granite City *(G-10708)*
Gamma Alpha Visual Communicatn .... G 847 956-0633
  Park Ridge *(G-16279)*
Gossett Printing Inc .... G 618 548-2583
  Salem *(G-18341)*
Graphic Arts Bindery LLC .... D 708 416-4290
  Rochelle *(G-17143)*
Graphics Group LLC .... D 708 867-5500
  Chicago *(G-4729)*
Grasso Graphics Inc .... G 708 489-2060
  Alsip *(G-449)*
Group O Inc .... E 309 736-8100
  Milan *(G-14015)*
Grovak Instant Printing Co .... G 847 675-2414
  Mount Prospect *(G-14532)*
Harris Bookbinding LLC .... E 773 287-9414
  Downers Grove *(G-8016)*
Harry Otto Printing Company .... F 630 365-6111
  Elburn *(G-8455)*
Hawthorne Press .... G 708 652-9000
  Cicero *(G-6852)*
Hawthorne Press Inc .... G 847 587-0582
  Spring Grove *(G-19275)*

Heart Printing Inc .... G 847 259-2100
  Arlington Heights *(G-748)*
Heritage Press Inc .... G 847 362-9699
  Libertyville *(G-12657)*
Highland Printers .... G 618 654-5880
  Highland *(G-11221)*
Homan Bindery .... E 773 276-1500
  Chicago *(G-4832)*
Hopkins Printing & Envelope Co .... F 630 543-8227
  Addison *(G-152)*
House of Graphics .... E 630 682-0810
  Carol Stream *(G-3000)*
Hq Printers Inc .... G 312 782-2020
  Chicago *(G-4857)*
Hub Printing Company Inc .... F 815 562-7057
  Rochelle *(G-17145)*
Ideal Advertising & Printing .... F 815 965-1713
  Rockford *(G-17456)*
Illinois Office Sup Elect Prtg .... E 815 434-0186
  Ottawa *(G-16056)*
Illinois Tool Works Inc .... E 708 720-0300
  Frankfort *(G-9807)*
Image Print Inc .... G 815 672-1068
  Streator *(G-19611)*
Impression Printing .... F 708 614-8660
  Oak Forest *(G-15682)*
In-Print Graphics Inc .... G 708 396-1010
  Oak Forest *(G-15683)*
Ink Well Printing & Design Ltd .... G 847 923-8060
  Schaumburg *(G-18559)*
Instant Collating Service Inc .... F 312 243-4703
  Chicago *(G-4937)*
Insty Prints Palatine Inc .... F 847 963-0000
  Palatine *(G-16129)*
Instyprints of Waukegan Inc .... G 847 336-5599
  Waukegan *(G-20449)*
Integra Graphics and Forms Inc .... F 708 385-0950
  Crestwood *(G-7120)*
International Graphics & Assoc .... F 630 584-2248
  Saint Charles *(G-18215)*
J & J Mr Quick Print Inc .... G 773 767-7776
  Chicago *(G-4984)*
J D Graphic Co Inc .... E 847 364-4000
  Elk Grove Village *(G-9063)*
J R Finishers Inc .... D 847 301-2556
  Schaumburg *(G-18574)*
Jay Printing .... G 847 934-6103
  Palatine *(G-16133)*
Jeannie Wagner .... G 815 477-2700
  Crystal Lake *(G-7212)*
Joes Printing .... G 773 545-6063
  Chicago *(G-5034)*
Johns-Byrne Company .... D 847 583-3100
  Niles *(G-15137)*
Johnson Press America Inc .... E 815 844-5161
  Pontiac *(G-16773)*
Josco Inc .... G 708 867-7189
  Chicago *(G-5051)*
Jph Enterprises Inc .... G 847 390-0900
  Des Plaines *(G-7792)*
Juskie Printing Corp .... G 630 663-8833
  Downers Grove *(G-8035)*
K & M Printing Company Inc .... D 847 884-1100
  Schaumburg *(G-18584)*
K O G Mfg & Bindery Corp .... F 847 263-5050
  Waukegan *(G-20453)*
Kelly Printing Co Inc .... E 217 443-1792
  Danville *(G-7355)*
Kendall Printing Co .... G 630 553-9200
  Yorkville *(G-21490)*
Kens Quick Print Inc .... F 847 831-4410
  Highland Park *(G-11277)*
Kevin Kewney .... G 217 228-7444
  Quincy *(G-16899)*
Key Printing .... G 815 933-1800
  Kankakee *(G-11987)*
Klein Printing Inc .... G 773 235-2121
  Chicago *(G-5108)*
Klh Printing Corp .... G 847 459-0115
  Wheeling *(G-20926)*
Koehler Bindery Inc .... G 773 539-7979
  Skokie *(G-18973)*
Kwik Print Inc .... G 630 773-3225
  Itasca *(G-11689)*
LAC Enterprises Inc .... G 815 455-5044
  Crystal Lake *(G-7219)*
Lans Printing Inc .... G 708 895-6226
  Lynwood *(G-13295)*
Lasons Label Co .... G 773 775-2606
  Chicago *(G-5179)*

Lee-Wel Printing Corporation .... G 630 682-0935
  Wheaton *(G-20812)*
Leonard Emerson .... G 217 628-3441
  Divernon *(G-7880)*
Lynns Printing Co .... G 618 465-7701
  Alton *(G-564)*
M & G Graphics Inc .... E 773 247-1596
  Chicago *(G-5295)*
M O W Printing Inc .... F 618 345-5525
  Collinsville *(G-6967)*
Macoupin County Enquirer Inc .... E 217 854-2534
  Carlinville *(G-2879)*
Mall Graphic Inc .... F 847 668-7600
  Huntley *(G-11554)*
Marcus Press .... G 630 351-1857
  Bloomingdale *(G-1999)*
Mark Twain Press Inc .... G 847 255-2700
  Mundelein *(G-14713)*
Marquardt Printing Company .... E 630 887-8500
  Burr Ridge *(G-2698)*
Mason City Banner Times .... F 217 482-3276
  Mason City *(G-13612)*
Master Engraving .... G 217 965-5885
  Virden *(G-20188)*
Mattoon Printing Center .... G 217 234-3100
  Mattoon *(G-13646)*
McGrath Press Inc .... E 815 356-5246
  Crystal Lake *(G-7224)*
McHenry Printing Services .... G 815 385-7600
  McHenry *(G-13765)*
Mencarini Enterprises Inc .... F 815 398-9565
  Rockford *(G-17516)*
Merritt & Edwards Corporation .... F 309 828-4741
  Bloomington *(G-2075)*
Metro Printing & Pubg Inc .... F 618 476-9587
  Millstadt *(G-14052)*
Mid Central Printing & Mailing .... F 847 251-4040
  Wilmette *(G-21087)*
Mid City Printing Service .... G 773 777-5400
  Chicago *(G-5426)*
Midwest Gold Stampers Inc .... F 773 775-5253
  Chicago *(G-5442)*
Minuteman Press Inc .... G 847 577-2411
  Arlington Heights *(G-776)*
Minuteman Press Morton Grove .... G 847 470-0212
  Morton Grove *(G-14429)*
Minuteman Press of Rockford .... G 815 633-2992
  Loves Park *(G-13237)*
Modern Printing of Quincy .... F 217 223-1063
  Quincy *(G-16917)*
Mormor Incorporated .... G 630 268-0050
  Lombard *(G-13104)*
Msf Graphics Inc .... G 847 446-6900
  Des Plaines *(G-7808)*
Multicopy Corp .... G 847 446-7015
  Grayslake *(G-10792)*
N Bujarski Inc .... G 847 884-1600
  Schaumburg *(G-18643)*
N P D Inc .... G 708 424-6788
  Oak Lawn *(G-15729)*
National Binding Sups Eqp Inc .... G 630 801-7600
  Geneva *(G-10292)*
New Life Printing & Publishing .... G 847 658-4111
  Algonquin *(G-382)*
Northwest Premier Printing .... G 773 736-1882
  Chicago *(G-5623)*
Northwest Printing Inc .... G 815 943-7977
  Harvard *(G-11061)*
Nu-Art Printing .... G 618 533-9971
  Centralia *(G-3242)*
Off The Press LLC .... G 815 436-9612
  Plainfield *(G-16697)*
Ogden Offset Printers Inc .... G 773 284-7797
  Chicago *(G-5663)*
Olde Print Shoppe Inc .... G 618 395-3833
  Olney *(G-15879)*
Olympic Bindery Inc .... D 847 577-8132
  Arlington Heights *(G-785)*
On Time Printing and Finishing .... G 708 544-4500
  Hillside *(G-11351)*
P & S Cochran Printers Inc .... E 309 691-6668
  Peoria *(G-16489)*
P H C Enterprises Inc .... G 847 816-7373
  Vernon Hills *(G-20080)*
P P Graphics Inc .... G 708 343-2530
  Westchester *(G-20707)*
Parrot Press .... G 773 376-6333
  Chicago *(G-5768)*
Patrick Impressions LLC .... G 630 257-9336
  Lemont *(G-12578)*

Patton Printing and Graphics ....G 217 347-0220
Effingham *(G-8417)*
Perma Graphics Printers ....G 815 485-6955
New Lenox *(G-15050)*
Perryco Inc ....F 815 436-2431
Plainfield *(G-16701)*
Phoenix Binding Corp ....D 847 981-1111
Itasca *(G-11717)*
Pinney Printing Company ....F 815 626-2727
Sterling *(G-19524)*
PIP Printing Inc ....G 815 464-0075
Frankfort *(G-9822)*
Prairieland Printing ....G 309 647-5425
Washington *(G-20276)*
Precision Die Cutting & Finish ....G 773 252-5625
Chicago *(G-5856)*
Preferred Printing Service ....G 312 421-2343
Chicago *(G-5861)*
Print & Design Services LLC ....G 847 317-9001
Bannockburn *(G-1206)*
Print Turnaround Inc ....F 847 228-1762
Arlington Heights *(G-791)*
Printed Word Inc ....G 847 328-1511
Evanston *(G-9570)*
Printing Inc ....D 316 265-1201
Chicago *(G-5881)*
Printing By Joseph ....G 708 479-2669
Mokena *(G-14109)*
Printing Craftsmen of Joliet ....G 815 254-3982
Joliet *(G-11917)*
Printing Etc Inc ....G 815 562-6151
Rochelle *(G-17152)*
Printing Plus ....G 708 301-3900
Lockport *(G-13019)*
Printing Plus of Roselle Inc ....G 630 893-0410
Roselle *(G-17974)*
Printing Shop ....G 847 998-6330
Glenview *(G-10603)*
Printing Source Inc ....G 773 588-2930
Morton Grove *(G-14433)*
Printmeisters Inc ....G 708 474-8400
Lansing *(G-12512)*
Printsource Plus Inc ....G 708 389-6252
Blue Island *(G-2134)*
Pro-Type Printing Inc ....G 217 379-4715
Paxton *(G-16315)*
Progress Printing Corporation ....E 773 927-0123
Chicago *(G-5898)*
Quad City Press ....F 309 764-8142
Moline *(G-14170)*
Quad/Graphics Inc ....A 815 734-4121
Mount Morris *(G-14500)*
Quality Quickprint Inc ....F 815 439-3430
Joliet *(G-11920)*
Quality Quickprint Inc ....F 815 838-1784
Lockport *(G-13020)*
Quickprinters ....G 309 833-5250
Macomb *(G-13398)*
Quinn Print Inc ....G 847 823-9100
Park Ridge *(G-16293)*
R & R Bindery Service Inc ....C 217 627-2143
Girard *(G-10384)*
R R Donnelley & Sons Company ....A 815 584-2770
Dwight *(G-8158)*
R R Donnelley & Sons Company ....A 815 844-5181
Pontiac *(G-16779)*
Rapid Print ....G 309 673-0826
Peoria *(G-16508)*
Remke Printing Inc ....G 847 520-7300
Wheeling *(G-20972)*
Reprographics ....G 815 477-1018
Crystal Lake *(G-7254)*
Review Printing Co Inc ....G 309 788-7094
Rock Island *(G-17241)*
Rickard Circular Folding Co ....D 312 243-6300
Chicago *(G-6028)*
Ricter Corporation ....F 708 344-3300
Buffalo Grove *(G-2593)*
Rightway Printing Inc ....F 630 790-0444
Glendale Heights *(G-10488)*
River Bend Printing ....G 217 324-6056
Litchfield *(G-12975)*
Rkf Enterprises ....G 773 723-7038
Chicago *(G-6038)*
Ro-Web Inc ....G 309 688-2155
Peoria *(G-16512)*
Robal Company Inc ....F 630 393-0777
Warrenville *(G-20252)*
Rodin Enterprises Inc ....G 847 412-1370
Wheeling *(G-20976)*
Rohrer Litho Inc ....G 630 833-6610
Elmhurst *(G-9420)*
Rose Business Forms & Printing ....G 618 533-3032
Centralia *(G-3248)*
Rrr Graphics & Film Corp ....G 708 478-4573
Mokena *(G-14114)*
Rudin Printing Company Inc ....F 217 528-5111
Springfield *(G-19436)*
Rusty & Angela Buzzard ....G 217 342-9841
Effingham *(G-8423)*
S B Liquidating Company ....D 847 758-9500
Elk Grove Village *(G-9225)*
Salem Times-Commoner Inc ....E 618 548-3330
Salem *(G-18358)*
Samecwei Inc ....G 630 897-7888
Aurora *(G-1153)*
Scheiwes Print Shop ....G 815 683-2398
Crescent City *(G-7082)*
Schommer Inc ....G 815 344-1404
McHenry *(G-13791)*
Schwebel Printing ....G 618 684-3911
Murphysboro *(G-14759)*
Scientfic Bndery Prdctions Inc ....G 847 329-0510
Skokie *(G-19027)*
Service Printing Corporation ....G 847 669-9620
Huntley *(G-11566)*
Shawver Press Inc ....G 815 772-4700
Morrison *(G-14348)*
Shoreline Graphics Inc ....G 847 587-4804
Ingleside *(G-11589)*
▼ **Shree Mahavir Inc** ....G 312 408-1080
Chicago *(G-6159)*
Shree Printing Corp ....G 773 267-9500
Chicago *(G-6160)*
Sigley Printing & Off Sup Co ....G 618 997-5304
Marion *(G-13535)*
Sir Speedy Printing ....G 312 337-0774
Chicago *(G-6177)*
Sommers & Fahrenbach Inc ....F 773 478-3033
Chicago *(G-6201)*
Speedys Quick Print ....G 217 431-0510
Danville *(G-7381)*
Springfield Printing Inc ....G 217 787-3500
Springfield *(G-19454)*
Stearns Printing of Charleston ....G 217 345-7518
Charleston *(G-3414)*
Steve Bortman ....G 708 442-1669
Lyons *(G-13315)*
Swifty Print ....G 630 584-9063
Saint Charles *(G-18283)*
T F N W Inc ....G 630 584-7383
Naperville *(G-14926)*
Techprint Inc ....F 847 616-0109
Elk Grove Village *(G-9269)*
The b F Shaw Printing Co ....E 815 875-4461
Princeton *(G-16823)*
Thomas Printing & Sty Co ....G 618 435-2801
Benton *(G-1937)*
Tower Printing & Design ....G 630 495-1976
Lombard *(G-13145)*
Tree Towns Reprographics Inc ....F 630 832-0209
Elmhurst *(G-9437)*
Tri-Tower Printing Inc ....G 847 640-6633
Rolling Meadows *(G-17782)*
Tru Line Lithographing Inc ....E 262 554-7300
Niles *(G-15183)*
Trump Printing Inc ....F 217 429-9001
Decatur *(G-7563)*
▲ **United Bindery Service** ....E 312 243-0240
Chicago *(G-6470)*
United Lithograph Inc ....G 847 803-1700
Des Plaines *(G-7861)*
Viking Printing & Copying Inc ....G 312 341-0985
Chicago *(G-6551)*
Voris Communication Co Inc ....C 630 898-4268
Berkeley *(G-1946)*
Wagner John ....G 847 564-0017
Northbrook *(G-15498)*
We-B-Print Inc ....G 309 353-8801
Pekin *(G-16368)*
Weakley Printing & Sign Shop ....G 847 473-4466
North Chicago *(G-15323)*
West Vly Graphics & Print Inc ....G 630 377-7575
Saint Charles *(G-18298)*
William Holloway Ltd ....G 847 866-9520
Evanston *(G-9588)*
Wood River Printing & Pubg Co ....G 618 254-3134
Wood River *(G-21268)*
Woogl Corporation ....E 847 806-1160
Elk Grove Village *(G-9312)*
Wortman Printing Company Inc ....G 217 347-3775
Effingham *(G-8432)*

2791 Typesetting

11th Street Express Prtg Inc ....F 815 968-0208
Rockford *(G-17275)*
A To Z Type & Graphic Inc ....G 312 587-1887
Chicago *(G-3491)*
Adcraft Printers Inc ....F 815 932-6432
Kankakee *(G-11956)*
All-Ways Quick Print ....G 708 403-8422
Orland Park *(G-15938)*
Allegra Print & Imaging Inc ....G 847 697-1434
Elgin *(G-8502)*
Alphadigital Inc ....G 708 482-4488
La Grange *(G-12071)*
AlphaGraphics Printshops ....G 630 964-9600
Lisle *(G-12861)*
Amboy News ....G 815 857-2311
Amboy *(G-578)*
American Graphics Network Inc ....F 847 729-7220
Glenview *(G-10522)*
Apple Graphics Inc ....G 630 389-2222
Batavia *(G-1350)*
Apple Press Inc ....G 815 224-1451
Peru *(G-16565)*
Apr Graphics Inc ....G 847 329-7800
Skokie *(G-18922)*
Arby Graphic Service Inc ....F 847 763-0900
Glencoe *(G-10428)*
Arcadia Press Inc ....F 847 451-6390
Franklin Park *(G-9872)*
Arch Printing Inc ....G 630 966-0235
Aurora *(G-1053)*
Artistry Engraving & Embossing ....G 773 775-4888
Chicago *(G-3741)*
Avid of Illinois Inc ....F 847 698-2775
Saint Charles *(G-18152)*
Azusa Inc ....G 618 244-6591
Mount Vernon *(G-14597)*
B & B Printing Company ....G 217 285-6072
Pittsfield *(G-16628)*
B Allan Graphics Inc ....F 708 396-1704
Alsip *(G-420)*
Babak Inc ....G 312 419-8686
Oak Forest *(G-15672)*
Bailleu & Bailleu Printing Inc ....G 309 852-2517
Kewanee *(G-12021)*
Bally Foil Graphics Inc ....G 847 427-1509
Elk Grove Village *(G-8857)*
Banner Publications ....G 309 338-3294
Cuba *(G-7297)*
Barnaby Inc ....F 815 895-6555
Aurora *(G-1061)*
Baseline Graphics Inc ....G 630 964-9566
Downers Grove *(G-7958)*
Belmonte Printing Co ....G 847 352-8841
Schaumburg *(G-18458)*
Benzinger Printing ....G 815 784-6560
Genoa *(G-10315)*
Beslow Associates Inc ....G 847 559-2703
Northbrook *(G-15349)*
Biller Press & Manufacturing ....G 847 395-4111
Antioch *(G-604)*
Blazing Color Inc ....G 618 826-3001
Chester *(G-3450)*
Bond Brothers & Co ....F 708 442-5510
Lyons *(G-13303)*
Branstiter Printing Co ....G 217 245-6533
Jacksonville *(G-11760)*
Breaker Press Co Inc ....G 773 927-1666
Chicago *(G-3948)*
Budget Printing Center ....G 618 655-1636
Edwardsville *(G-8351)*
Cameron Printing Inc ....G 630 231-3301
West Chicago *(G-20558)*
Cardinal Colorprint Prtg Corp ....E 630 467-1000
Itasca *(G-11634)*
Carson Printing Inc ....G 847 836-0900
East Dundee *(G-8189)*
Carter Printing Co Inc ....G 217 227-4464
Farmersville *(G-9659)*
Century Printing ....G 618 632-2486
O Fallon *(G-15570)*
Challenge Printers ....G 773 252-0212
Chicago *(G-4067)*
Chicago Citizen Newsppr Group ....F 773 783-1251
Chicago *(G-4096)*
Chicago Mltlingua Graphics Inc ....F 847 386-7187
Northfield *(G-15512)*

Employee Codes: A=Over 500 employees, B=251-500
C=101-250, D=51-100, E=20-50, F=10-19, G=3-9

2020 Harris Illinois
Industrial Directory

877

Christopher R Cline Prtg Ltd.................F....... 847 981-0500
Elk Grove Village *(G-8897)*
Cifuentes Luis & Nicole Inc....................G....... 847 490-3660
Schaumburg *(G-18477)*
Clementi Printing Inc.............................G....... 773 622-0795
Chicago *(G-4177)*
Clyde Printing Company.........................F....... 773 847-5900
Chicago *(G-4184)*
Cmb Printing Inc...................................F....... 630 323-1110
Burr Ridge *(G-2663)*
Color Smiths Inc....................................E....... 708 562-0061
Elmhurst *(G-9349)*
Commercial Copy Printing Ctr...............F....... 847 981-8590
Elk Grove Village *(G-8903)*
Communications Resource Inc...........G....... 630 860-1661
Schaumburg *(G-18482)*
Composition One Inc..............................E....... 630 588-1900
Roselle *(G-17946)*
Copy Express Inc....................................F....... 815 338-7161
Woodstock *(G-21377)*
Copy Mat Printing...................................G....... 309 452-1392
Bloomington *(G-2033)*
Copy Service Inc......................................G....... 815 758-1151
Dekalb *(G-7670)*
▲ **Copy-Mor Inc**.......................................E....... 312 666-4000
Streamwood *(G-19568)*
Copyset Shop Inc....................................G....... 847 768-2679
Des Plaines *(G-7751)*
Corwin Printing..G....... 618 263-3936
Mount Carmel *(G-14469)*
Cpr Printing Inc.......................................F....... 630 377-8420
Geneva *(G-10263)*
Craftsmen Printing...................................G....... 217 283-9574
Hoopeston *(G-11506)*
Creative Image Inc..................................G....... 708 647-2860
Hazel Crest *(G-11128)*
Crossmark Printing Inc..........................F....... 708 532-8263
Tinley Park *(G-19819)*
Crosstech Communications Inc.............E....... 312 382-0111
Chicago *(G-4273)*
Custom Direct Inc....................................F....... 630 529-1936
Roselle *(G-17950)*
D E Asbury Inc...F....... 217 222-0617
Hamilton *(G-10953)*
D L V Printing Service Inc......................F....... 773 626-1661
Chicago *(G-4301)*
Dale K Brown..G....... 815 338-0222
Woodstock *(G-21380)*
Darnall Printing..G....... 309 827-7212
Bloomington *(G-2039)*
David H Vander Ploeg..............................G....... 708 331-7700
South Holland *(G-19206)*
DE Asbury Inc...E....... 217 222-0617
Quincy *(G-16876)*
▲ **Deluxe Johnson**....................................C....... 847 635-7200
Des Plaines *(G-7754)*
Denor Graphics Inc..................................F....... 847 364-1130
Elk Grove Village *(G-8944)*
Des Plaines Journal Inc...........................D....... 847 299-5511
Des Plaines *(G-7755)*
Design Graphics Inc.................................G....... 815 462-3323
Frankfort *(G-9783)*
Diamond Graphics of Berwyn.................G....... 708 749-2500
Berwyn *(G-1950)*
Donnas House of Type Inc.......................G....... 217 522-5050
Athens *(G-896)*
Donnells Printing & Off Pdts..................G....... 815 842-6541
Pontiac *(G-16768)*
Dupli Group Inc..F....... 773 549-5285
Chicago *(G-4408)*
E & H Graphic Service Inc.......................G....... 708 748-5656
Matteson *(G-13623)*
Early Bird Advertising Inc.......................G....... 847 253-1423
Prospect Heights *(G-16839)*
Edwardsville Publishing Co....................D....... 618 656-4700
Edwardsville *(G-8361)*
Einstein Crest...G....... 847 965-7791
Niles *(G-15119)*
Elgin Instant Print....................................G....... 847 931-9006
Elgin *(G-8575)*
Everything Xclusive..................................G....... 309 370-7450
Peoria *(G-16436)*
F Weber Printing Co Inc...........................G....... 815 468-6152
Manteno *(G-13447)*
Fedex Office & Print Svcs Inc..................F....... 847 475-8650
Evanston *(G-9519)*
Fedex Office & Print Svcs Inc..................F....... 815 229-0033
Rockford *(G-17412)*
Fedex Office & Print Svcs Inc..................F....... 847 329-9464
Lincolnwood *(G-12819)*
Fedex Office & Print Svcs Inc..................E....... 847 729-3030
Glenview *(G-10545)*
Fedex Office & Print Svcs Inc..................G....... 847 459-8008
Buffalo Grove *(G-2536)*
Fedex Office & Print Svcs Inc..................E....... 708 452-0149
Elmwood Park *(G-9452)*
Fedex Office & Print Svcs Inc..................G....... 847 823-9360
Park Ridge *(G-16274)*
Fedex Office & Print Svcs Inc..................F....... 630 894-1800
Bloomingdale *(G-1995)*
Fedex Office & Print Svcs Inc..................F....... 312 670-4460
Chicago *(G-4577)*
Fedex Office & Print Svcs Inc..................E....... 309 685-4093
Peoria *(G-16437)*
Fine Line Printing.....................................G....... 773 582-9709
Chicago *(G-4590)*
First Impression of Chicago.....................G....... 773 224-3434
Chicago *(G-4594)*
Fisheye Services Incorporated...............G....... 773 942-6314
Chicago *(G-4598)*
Flash Printing Inc.....................................G....... 847 288-9101
Franklin Park *(G-9944)*
Fleetwood Press Inc.................................G....... 708 485-6811
Brookfield *(G-2483)*
FM Graphic Impressions Inc....................E....... 630 897-8788
Aurora *(G-1097)*
French Studio Ltd.....................................G....... 618 942-5328
Herrin *(G-11171)*
G F Printing...G....... 618 797-0576
Granite City *(G-10708)*
Gamma Alpha Visual Communicatn.......G....... 847 956-0633
Park Ridge *(G-16279)*
Gatehouse Media LLC..............................B....... 217 788-1300
Springfield *(G-19373)*
Gazette Printing Co..................................G....... 309 389-2811
Glasford *(G-10387)*
Gorman & Associates..............................G....... 309 691-9087
Peoria *(G-16446)*
Gossett Printing Inc..................................G....... 618 548-2583
Salem *(G-18341)*
Graphic Image Corporation.....................F....... 312 829-7800
Orland Park *(G-15956)*
Graphics Group LLC.................................D....... 708 867-5500
Chicago *(G-4729)*
Grasso Graphics Inc.................................G....... 708 489-2060
Alsip *(G-449)*
▲ **Gsipc LLC**..D....... 630 325-8181
Burr Ridge *(G-2678)*
Hawthorne Press Inc................................G....... 847 587-0582
Spring Grove *(G-19275)*
Heart Printing Inc.....................................G....... 847 259-2100
Arlington Heights *(G-748)*
Henderson Co Inc......................................F....... 773 628-7216
Chicago *(G-4800)*
Heritage Media Svcs Co of Ill...................G....... 708 594-9340
Summit Argo *(G-19679)*
Heritage Press Inc.....................................G....... 847 362-9699
Libertyville *(G-12657)*
Heritage Printing.......................................G....... 815 537-2372
Prophetstown *(G-16832)*
Highland Printers......................................G....... 618 654-5880
Highland *(G-11221)*
House of Graphics.....................................E....... 630 682-0810
Carol Stream *(G-3000)*
Hq Printers Inc..G....... 312 782-2020
Chicago *(G-4857)*
Hub Printing Company Inc.......................F....... 815 562-7057
Rochelle *(G-17145)*
Huston-Patterson Corporation................D....... 217 429-5161
Decatur *(G-7503)*
Ideal Advertising & Printing....................F....... 815 965-1713
Rockford *(G-17456)*
Illinois Office Sup Elect Prtg....................E....... 815 434-0186
Ottawa *(G-16056)*
Image Print Inc..G....... 815 672-1068
Streator *(G-19611)*
Informative Systems Inc............................F....... 217 523-8422
Springfield *(G-19389)*
Ink Spot Printing..G....... 773 528-0288
Chicago *(G-4926)*
Inky Printers...G....... 815 235-3700
Freeport *(G-10120)*
Innovtive Design Graphics Corp...............G....... 847 475-7772
Evanston *(G-9540)*
Insty Prints Palatine Inc...........................F....... 847 963-0000
Palatine *(G-16129)*
Instyprints of Waukegan Inc....................G....... 847 336-5599
Waukegan *(G-20449)*
International Graphics & Assoc...............F....... 630 584-2248
Saint Charles *(G-18215)*
J & J Mr Quick Print Inc...........................G....... 773 767-7776
Chicago *(G-4984)*
J Oshana & Son Printing...........................G....... 773 283-8311
Chicago *(G-4992)*
J P Printing Inc..G....... 773 626-5222
Chicago *(G-4993)*
James Ray Monroe Corporation...............F....... 618 532-4575
Centralia *(G-3236)*
Jay Printing..G....... 847 934-6103
Palatine *(G-16133)*
JD Pro Productions Inc.............................G....... 708 485-2126
Brookfield *(G-2487)*
Jds Printing Inc..G....... 630 208-1195
Glendale Heights *(G-10463)*
Jeannie Wagner..G....... 815 477-2700
Crystal Lake *(G-7212)*
Johns-Byrne Company................................D....... 847 583-3100
Niles *(G-15137)*
Johnson Press America Inc......................E....... 815 844-5161
Pontiac *(G-16773)*
Josco Inc...G....... 708 867-7189
Chicago *(G-5051)*
Josephs Printing Service...........................G....... 847 724-4429
Glenview *(G-10576)*
Jph Enterprises Inc....................................G....... 847 390-0900
Des Plaines *(G-7792)*
July 25th Corporation................................F....... 309 664-6444
Bloomington *(G-2064)*
Just Your Type Inc......................................G....... 847 864-8890
Evanston *(G-9543)*
K & M Printing Company Inc.....................D....... 847 884-1100
Schaumburg *(G-18584)*
Kelly Printing Co Inc..................................E....... 217 443-1792
Danville *(G-7355)*
Kendall Printing Co....................................G....... 630 553-9200
Yorkville *(G-21490)*
Kenilworth Press Incorporated................G....... 847 256-5210
Wilmette *(G-21081)*
Kens Quick Print Inc..................................F....... 847 831-4410
Highland Park *(G-11277)*
Kevin Kewney...G....... 217 228-7444
Quincy *(G-16899)*
KK Stevens Publishing Co..........................E....... 309 329-2151
Astoria *(G-893)*
Klein Printing Inc..G....... 773 235-2121
Chicago *(G-5108)*
Klh Printing Corp..G....... 847 459-0115
Wheeling *(G-20926)*
▲ **Korea Times**...D....... 847 626-0388
Glenview *(G-10579)*
LAC Enterprises Inc....................................G....... 815 455-5044
Crystal Lake *(G-7219)*
Lake County Press Inc................................C....... 847 336-4333
Waukegan *(G-20458)*
Lans Printing Inc...G....... 708 895-6226
Lynwood *(G-13295)*
Laser Expressions Ltd.................................G....... 847 419-9600
Buffalo Grove *(G-2559)*
Legend Promotions.....................................G....... 847 438-3528
Lake Zurich *(G-12428)*
Leonard Emerson..G....... 217 628-3441
Divernon *(G-7880)*
Lithuanian Catholic Press...........................E....... 773 585-9500
Chicago *(G-5236)*
Lloyd Midwest Graphics..............................G....... 815 282-8828
Machesney Park *(G-13357)*
Lynns Printing Co...G....... 618 465-7701
Alton *(G-564)*
M & R Printing Inc.......................................G....... 847 398-2500
Rolling Meadows *(G-17749)*
M M Marketing..G....... 815 459-7968
Wauconda *(G-20370)*
M O W Printing Inc.......................................F....... 618 345-5525
Collinsville *(G-6967)*
Macoupin County Enquirer Inc...................E....... 217 854-2534
Carlinville *(G-2879)*
Marcus Press...G....... 630 351-1857
Bloomingdale *(G-1999)*
Mark Twain Press Inc...................................G....... 847 255-2700
Mundelein *(G-14713)*
Mason City Banner Times.............................F....... 217 482-3276
Mason City *(G-13612)*
Mattoon Printing Center..............................G....... 217 234-3100
Mattoon *(G-13646)*
Mc Adams Multigraphics Inc.......................G....... 630 990-1707
Oak Brook *(G-15641)*
McGrath Press Inc..E....... 815 356-5246
Crystal Lake *(G-7224)*
McHenry Printing Services..........................G....... 815 385-7600
McHenry *(G-13765)*

Mencarini Enterprises Inc.....F....815 398-9565
Rockford *(G-17516)*
Metro Printing & Pubg Inc.....F....618 476-9587
Millstadt *(G-14052)*
Metropolitan Graphic Arts Inc.....E....847 566-9502
Gurnee *(G-10896)*
Mid City Printing Service.....G....773 777-5400
Chicago *(G-5426)*
Midwest Outdoors Ltd.....E....630 887-7722
Burr Ridge *(G-2704)*
Minuteman Press.....G....630 584-7383
Naperville *(G-14872)*
Minuteman Press of Rockford.....G....815 633-2992
Loves Park *(G-13237)*
Minuteman Press of Waukegan.....G....847 244-6288
Gurnee *(G-10900)*
Mormor Incorporated.....G....630 268-0050
Lombard *(G-13104)*
Multicopy Corp.....G....847 446-7015
Grayslake *(G-10792)*
N & M Type & Design.....G....630 834-3696
Elmhurst *(G-9404)*
N Bujarski Inc.....G....847 884-1600
Schaumburg *(G-18643)*
N P D Inc.....G....708 424-6788
Oak Lawn *(G-15729)*
Negs & Litho Inc.....G....847 647-7770
Chicago *(G-5563)*
New City Communications.....E....312 243-8786
Chicago *(G-5576)*
New Life Printing & Publishing.....G....847 658-4111
Algonquin *(G-382)*
Northwest Premier Printing.....G....773 736-1882
Chicago *(G-5623)*
Northwest Printing Inc.....G....815 943-7977
Harvard *(G-11061)*
Nu-Art Printing.....G....618 533-9971
Centralia *(G-3242)*
Off The Press LLC.....G....815 436-9612
Plainfield *(G-16697)*
Okawville Times.....G....618 243-5563
Okawville *(G-15846)*
Olde Print Shoppe Inc.....G....618 395-3833
Olney *(G-15879)*
Omni Craft Inc.....G....815 838-1285
Lockport *(G-13017)*
On Time Printing and Finishing.....G....708 544-4500
Hillside *(G-11351)*
Osborne Publications Inc.....G....217 422-9702
Decatur *(G-7534)*
P & S Cochran Printers Inc.....E....309 691-6668
Peoria *(G-16489)*
P H C Enterprises Inc.....G....847 816-7373
Vernon Hills *(G-20080)*
P P Graphics Inc.....G....708 343-2530
Westchester *(G-20707)*
Papyrus Press Inc.....F....773 342-0700
Chicago *(G-5755)*
▲ **Park Printing Inc**.....G....708 430-4878
Palos Hills *(G-16203)*
Patrick Impressions LLC.....G....630 257-9336
Lemont *(G-12578)*
Patton Printing and Graphics.....G....217 347-0220
Effingham *(G-8417)*
Perma Graphics Printers.....G....815 485-6955
New Lenox *(G-15050)*
Perryco Inc.....F....815 436-2431
Plainfield *(G-16701)*
Photo Graphic Design Service.....G....815 672-4417
Streator *(G-19620)*
PIP Printing Inc.....G....815 464-0075
Frankfort *(G-9822)*
Poets Study Inc.....G....773 286-1355
Chicago *(G-5831)*
Preferred Printing Service.....G....312 421-2343
Chicago *(G-5861)*
Prime Market Targeting Inc.....E....815 469-4555
Frankfort *(G-9826)*
Print & Design Services LLC.....G....847 317-9001
Bannockburn *(G-1206)*
Print Turnaround Inc.....F....847 228-1762
Arlington Heights *(G-791)*
Print Xpress.....G....847 677-5555
Skokie *(G-19012)*
Printed Impressions Inc.....G....773 604-8585
Oakbrook Terrace *(G-15813)*
Printed Word Inc.....G....847 328-1511
Evanston *(G-9570)*
Printing Inc.....D....316 265-1201
Chicago *(G-5881)*
Printing By Joseph.....G....708 479-2669
Mokena *(G-14109)*
Printing Craftsmen of Joliet.....G....815 254-3982
Joliet *(G-11917)*
Printing Etc Inc.....G....815 562-6151
Rochelle *(G-17152)*
Printing Plus of Roselle Inc.....G....630 893-0410
Roselle *(G-17974)*
Printing Source Inc.....G....773 588-2930
Morton Grove *(G-14433)*
Printmeisters Inc.....G....708 474-8400
Lansing *(G-12512)*
Printsource Plus Inc.....G....708 389-6252
Blue Island *(G-2134)*
Pro-Type Printing Inc.....G....217 379-4715
Paxton *(G-16315)*
Progress Printing Corporation.....E....773 927-0123
Chicago *(G-5898)*
Quad City Press.....F....309 764-8142
Moline *(G-14170)*
Quality Quickprint Inc.....F....815 439-3430
Joliet *(G-11920)*
Quality Quickprint Inc.....F....815 838-1784
Lockport *(G-13020)*
Quickprinters.....G....309 833-5250
Macomb *(G-13398)*
Quinn Print Inc.....G....847 823-9100
Park Ridge *(G-16293)*
R N R Photographers Inc.....G....708 453-1868
River Grove *(G-17066)*
Rapid Circular Press Inc.....F....312 421-5611
Chicago *(G-5970)*
Remke Printing Inc.....G....847 520-7300
Wheeling *(G-20972)*
Reprographics.....G....815 477-1018
Crystal Lake *(G-7254)*
Review Graphics Inc.....G....815 623-2570
Roscoe *(G-17925)*
Review Printing Co Inc.....G....309 788-7094
Rock Island *(G-17241)*
Rightway Printing Inc.....F....630 790-0444
Glendale Heights *(G-10488)*
Rite-TEC Communications.....G....815 459-7712
Crystal Lake *(G-7258)*
River Bend Printing.....G....217 324-6056
Litchfield *(G-12975)*
Ro-Web Inc.....G....309 688-2155
Peoria *(G-16512)*
Rodin Enterprises Inc.....G....847 412-1370
Wheeling *(G-20976)*
Rohrer Graphic Arts Inc.....F....630 832-3434
Elmhurst *(G-9419)*
Rohrer Litho Inc.....G....630 833-6610
Elmhurst *(G-9420)*
Rose Business Forms & Printing.....G....618 533-3032
Centralia *(G-3248)*
Rrr Graphics & Film Corp.....G....708 478-4573
Mokena *(G-14114)*
Rt Associates Inc.....D....847 577-0700
Wheeling *(G-20977)*
Rudin Printing Company Inc.....F....217 528-5111
Springfield *(G-19436)*
Rusty & Angela Buzzard.....G....217 342-9841
Effingham *(G-8423)*
Salem Times-Commoner Inc.....E....618 548-3330
Salem *(G-18358)*
Samecwei Inc.....G....630 897-7888
Aurora *(G-1153)*
Schiele Graphics Inc.....D....847 434-5455
Elk Grove Village *(G-9233)*
Schommer Inc.....G....815 344-1404
McHenry *(G-13791)*
Schwebel Printing.....G....618 684-3911
Murphysboro *(G-14759)*
Shawver Press Inc.....G....815 772-4700
Morrison *(G-14348)*
Sheer Graphics Inc.....G....630 654-4422
Westmont *(G-20772)*
Shoreline Graphics Inc.....G....847 587-4804
Ingleside *(G-11589)*
▼ **Shree Mahavir Inc**.....G....312 408-1080
Chicago *(G-6159)*
Shree Printing Corp.....G....773 267-9500
Chicago *(G-6160)*
Sigley Printing & Off Sup Co.....G....618 997-5304
Marion *(G-13535)*
Sir Speedy Printing.....G....312 337-0774
Chicago *(G-6177)*
Small Newspaper Group.....C....815 937-3300
Kankakee *(G-12004)*
Solid Impressions Inc.....G....630 543-7300
Carol Stream *(G-3070)*
Sommers & Fahrenbach Inc.....F....773 478-3033
Chicago *(G-6201)*
Sons Enterprises.....F....847 677-4444
Skokie *(G-19032)*
Speedys Quick Print.....G....217 431-0510
Danville *(G-7381)*
Stearns Printing of Charleston.....G....217 345-7518
Charleston *(G-3414)*
Steve Bortman.....G....708 442-1669
Lyons *(G-13315)*
Swifty Print.....G....630 584-9063
Saint Charles *(G-18283)*
T F N W Inc.....G....630 584-7383
Naperville *(G-14926)*
T R Communications Inc.....F....773 238-3366
Chicago *(G-6307)*
The b F Shaw Printing Co.....E....815 875-4461
Princeton *(G-16823)*
Times Record Company.....E....309 582-5112
Aledo *(G-362)*
Times Republic.....E....815 432-5227
Watseka *(G-20320)*
Tlm Enterprises Inc.....G....815 284-5040
Dixon *(G-7923)*
Toledo Democrat.....G....217 849-2000
Toledo *(G-19879)*
Tower Printing & Design.....G....630 495-1976
Lombard *(G-13145)*
Trenton Sun.....G....618 224-9422
Trenton *(G-19905)*
Tri-Tower Printing Inc.....G....847 640-6633
Rolling Meadows *(G-17782)*
Tru Line Lithographing Inc.....E....262 554-7300
Niles *(G-15183)*
Trump Printing Inc.....F....217 429-9001
Decatur *(G-7563)*
United Lithograph Inc.....G....847 803-1700
Des Plaines *(G-7861)*
V C P Inc.....E....847 658-5090
Algonquin *(G-391)*
Valee Inc.....G....847 364-6464
Elk Grove Village *(G-9300)*
Viking Printing & Copying Inc.....G....312 341-0985
Chicago *(G-6551)*
Village Typographers Inc.....G....618 235-6756
Belleville *(G-1607)*
Voris Communication Co Inc.....C....630 898-4268
Berkeley *(G-1946)*
W R Typesetting Co.....F....847 966-8327
Morton Grove *(G-14447)*
Wagner John.....G....847 564-0017
Northbrook *(G-15498)*
Washburn Graficolor Inc.....G....630 596-0880
Naperville *(G-14944)*
Weakley Printing & Sign Shop.....G....847 473-4466
North Chicago *(G-15323)*
Weber Press Inc.....G....773 561-9815
Chicago *(G-6596)*
Westrock Mwv LLC.....E....217 442-2247
Danville *(G-7397)*
Woogl Corporation.....E....847 806-1160
Elk Grove Village *(G-9312)*
World Journal LLC.....F....312 842-8005
Chicago *(G-6674)*
Wortman Printing Company Inc.....G....217 347-3775
Effingham *(G-8432)*

2796 Platemaking & Related Svcs

Apr Graphics Inc.....G....847 329-7800
Skokie *(G-18922)*
▲ **Associates Engraving Company**.....D....217 523-4565
Springfield *(G-19321)*
Autotype Americas Incorporated.....G....847 818-8262
Rolling Meadows *(G-17715)*
B Allan Graphics Inc.....F....708 396-1704
Alsip *(G-420)*
Banner Moulded Products.....E....708 452-0033
River Grove *(G-17057)*
Blooming Color Inc.....D....630 705-9200
Lombard *(G-13047)*
Brilliant Color Corp.....G....847 367-3300
Libertyville *(G-12640)*
C F C Interantional.....G....708 753-0679
Chicago Heights *(G-6737)*
Cardinal Colorprint Prtg Corp.....E....630 467-1000
Itasca *(G-11634)*
Carson Printing Inc.....G....847 836-0900
East Dundee *(G-8189)*

S I C

Employee Codes: A=Over 500 employees, B=251-500
C=101-250, D=51-100, E=20-50, F=10-19, G=3-9
2020 Harris Illinois
Industrial Directory
879

Chicago Prepress Color Inc..................G....... 708 385-3465
Midlothian *(G-13990)*
▲ **Chromium Industries Inc**..................E....... 773 287-3716
Chicago *(G-4145)*
Clodfelter Engraving Inc..................G....... 314 968-8418
Alton *(G-547)*
Color Smiths Inc..................E....... 708 562-0061
Elmhurst *(G-9349)*
Commercial Copy Printing Ctr..................F....... 847 981-8590
Elk Grove Village *(G-8903)*
Cpr Printing Inc..................F....... 630 377-8420
Geneva *(G-10263)*
Creative Label Inc..................D....... 847 956-6960
Elk Grove Village *(G-8919)*
Crossmark Printing Inc..................F....... 708 532-8263
Tinley Park *(G-19819)*
Crosstech Communications Inc..................E....... 312 382-0111
Chicago *(G-4273)*
Delta Press Inc..................E....... 847 671-3200
Palatine *(G-16111)*
Dupli Group Inc..................F....... 773 549-5285
Chicago *(G-4408)*
E C Schultz & Co Inc..................F....... 847 640-1190
Elk Grove Village *(G-8963)*
Eugene Ewbank..................G....... 630 705-0400
Oswego *(G-16004)*
Excel Color Corporation..................G....... 847 734-1270
Elk Grove Village *(G-8985)*
Expercolor Inc..................E....... 773 465-3400
Skokie *(G-18953)*
Graphic Arts Studio Inc..................E....... 847 381-1105
Barrington *(G-1221)*
Graphic Engravers Inc..................E....... 630 595-0400
Bensenville *(G-1816)*
Graphic Image Corporation..................F....... 312 829-7800
Orland Park *(G-15956)*
Henderson Co Inc..................F....... 773 628-7216
Chicago *(G-4800)*
Hurst Chemical Company..................G....... 815 964-0451
Rockford *(G-17454)*
Iemco Corporation..................G....... 773 728-4400
Chicago *(G-4878)*
Impression Printing..................F....... 708 614-8660
Oak Forest *(G-15682)*
Instyprints of Waukegan Inc..................G....... 847 336-5599
Waukegan *(G-20449)*
J D Graphic Co Inc..................E....... 847 364-4000
Elk Grove Village *(G-9063)*
Jph Enterprises Inc..................G....... 847 390-0900
Des Plaines *(G-7792)*
Lasons Label Co..................G....... 773 775-2606
Chicago *(G-5179)*
Lincoln Electric Company..................F....... 630 783-3600
Bolingbrook *(G-2204)*
Lloyd Midwest Graphics..................G....... 815 282-8828
Machesney Park *(G-13357)*
Luttrell Engraving Inc..................E....... 708 489-3800
Alsip *(G-470)*
M & G Graphics Inc..................E....... 773 247-1596
Chicago *(G-5295)*
M L S Printing Co Inc..................G....... 847 948-8902
Deerfield *(G-7633)*
M S A Printing Co..................G....... 847 593-5699
Elk Grove Village *(G-9103)*
Marcus Press..................G....... 630 351-1857
Bloomingdale *(G-1999)*
Motherboard Gifts & More LLC..................G....... 847 550-2222
Lake Zurich *(G-12436)*
Multicopy Corp..................G....... 847 446-7015
Grayslake *(G-10792)*
N Bujarski Inc..................G....... 847 884-1600
Schaumburg *(G-18643)*
Naco Printing Co Inc..................G....... 618 664-0423
Greenville *(G-10839)*
▲ **Oec Graphics-Chicago LLC**..................E....... 630 455-6700
Willowbrook *(G-21056)*
Pamarco Global Graphics Inc..................E....... 630 879-7300
Batavia *(G-1403)*
Pamarco Global Graphics Inc..................F....... 847 459-6000
Wheeling *(G-20955)*
Panda Marketing Group Inc..................E....... 847 383-5270
Chicago *(G-5750)*
Pontiac Engraving..................G....... 630 834-4424
Bensenville *(G-1870)*
Precision Die Cutting & Finish..................G....... 773 252-5625
Chicago *(G-5856)*
Prime Market Targeting Inc..................E....... 815 469-4555
Frankfort *(G-9826)*
Printing Inc..................D....... 316 265-1201
Chicago *(G-5881)*
Priority Printing..................G....... 773 889-6021
Chicago *(G-5884)*
Rohrer Graphic Arts Inc..................F....... 630 832-3434
Elmhurst *(G-9419)*
Rohrer Litho Inc..................G....... 630 833-6610
Elmhurst *(G-9420)*
Rotation Dynamics Corporation..................E....... 630 769-9700
Chicago *(G-6065)*
Rotation Dynamics Corporation..................D....... 773 247-5600
Chicago *(G-6066)*
Servi-Sure Corporation..................E....... 773 271-5900
Chicago *(G-6140)*
Sharper Image Engravers Inc..................E....... 630 403-1600
Lombard *(G-13129)*
Southern Graphic Systems LLC..................E....... 847 695-9515
Rosemont *(G-18050)*
▲ **Sunrise Hitek Service Inc**..................E....... 773 792-8880
Chicago *(G-6277)*
The b F Shaw Printing Co..................E....... 815 875-4461
Princeton *(G-16823)*
Tru Line Lithographing Inc..................E....... 262 554-7300
Niles *(G-15183)*
Village Press Inc..................G....... 847 362-1856
Libertyville *(G-12724)*
Voss Pattern Works Inc..................G....... 618 233-4242
Belleville *(G-1609)*
West Vly Graphics & Print Inc..................G....... 630 377-7575
Saint Charles *(G-18298)*
Woogl Corporation..................E....... 847 806-1160
Elk Grove Village *(G-9312)*

28 CHEMICALS AND ALLIED PRODUCTS

2812 Alkalies & Chlorine

Arkema Inc..................C....... 708 396-3001
Alsip *(G-417)*
Arkema Inc..................C....... 708 385-2188
Alsip *(G-418)*
▲ **Aspen API Inc**..................F....... 847 635-0985
Des Plaines *(G-7734)*
Champion Packaging & Dist Inc..................C....... 630 972-0100
Woodridge *(G-21283)*
Clorox Manufacturing Company..................C....... 847 229-5500
Wheeling *(G-20872)*
Coral Chemical Company..................E....... 847 246-6666
Zion *(G-21510)*
FMC Corporation..................E....... 309 695-2571
Wyoming *(G-21459)*
KA Steel Chemicals Inc..................E....... 630 257-3900
Downers Grove *(G-8037)*
Occidental Chemical Corp..................F....... 618 482-6346
Sauget *(G-18397)*
Olin Chlor Alkali Pdts Vinyls..................G....... 844 238-3445
Downers Grove *(G-8068)*

2813 Industrial Gases

Air Liquide America LP..................G....... 815 747-6803
East Dubuque *(G-8175)*
Air Products and Chemicals Inc..................E....... 618 452-5335
Granite City *(G-10691)*
Air Products and Chemicals Inc..................E....... 815 223-2924
La Salle *(G-12101)*
Air Products and Chemicals Inc..................D....... 618 451-0577
Granite City *(G-10692)*
Air Products and Chemicals Inc..................E....... 815 423-5032
Channahon *(G-3373)*
Airgas Inc..................F....... 773 785-3000
Chicago *(G-3588)*
Airgas Usa LLC..................E....... 630 231-9260
West Chicago *(G-20533)*
Airgas Usa LLC..................E....... 708 354-0813
Countryside *(G-7043)*
Airgas Usa LLC..................G....... 618 439-7207
Benton *(G-1917)*
Amer Nitrogen Co..................G....... 847 681-1068
Highland Park *(G-11253)*
AmeriGas..................D....... 708 544-1131
Hillside *(G-11328)*
Boc Global Helium Inc..................C....... 630 897-1900
Montgomery *(G-14235)*
Brewer Company..................F....... 708 339-9000
Harvey *(G-11080)*
◆ **Chase Products Co**..................D....... 708 865-1000
Broadview *(G-2425)*
Chicago Neon and Sign LLC..................G....... 708 255-5284
Brookfield *(G-2480)*
Claire-Sprayway Inc..................D....... 630 628-3000
Downers Grove *(G-7973)*
Continental Carbonic Pdts Inc..................E....... 217 428-2068
Decatur *(G-7476)*
Continental Carbonic Pdts Inc..................E....... 309 346-7515
Pekin *(G-16326)*
▲ **Custom Blending & Pckaging of**..................F....... 618 286-1140
Dupo *(G-8135)*
◆ **Diversified CPC Intl Inc**..................E....... 815 424-2000
Channahon *(G-3380)*
Dixie Carbonic Inc..................D....... 217 428-2068
Decatur *(G-7490)*
Everbrite LLC..................G....... 618 242-0645
Mount Vernon *(G-14610)*
Gano Welding Supplies Inc..................F....... 217 345-3777
Charleston *(G-3402)*
Hands To Work Railroading..................G....... 708 489-9776
Alsip *(G-454)*
Hydrogen Education Council..................G....... 630 681-1732
Wheaton *(G-20805)*
◆ **Ilmo Products Company**..................E....... 217 245-2183
Jacksonville *(G-11770)*
Industrial Gas Products Inc..................G....... 618 337-1030
East Saint Louis *(G-8312)*
K-G Spray-Pak Inc..................G....... 630 543-7600
Downers Grove *(G-8036)*
Linde Gas North America LLC..................F....... 630 857-6460
Broadview *(G-2449)*
Linde Gas North America LLC..................F....... 630 257-3108
Lockport *(G-13006)*
Maccarb Inc..................G....... 877 427-2499
Elgin *(G-8645)*
Matheson Tri-Gas Inc..................E....... 815 727-2202
Joliet *(G-11899)*
Matheson Tri-Gas Inc..................F....... 309 697-1933
Mapleton *(G-13476)*
Medicate Dme Inc..................F....... 618 874-3000
East Saint Louis *(G-8314)*
Messer LLC..................E....... 309 353-9717
Pekin *(G-16344)*
Messer LLC..................E....... 630 515-2576
Naperville *(G-14869)*
Messer LLC..................E....... 618 251-5217
Hartford *(G-11035)*
Messer LLC..................F....... 630 690-3010
Carol Stream *(G-3024)*
Messer North America Inc..................G....... 630 897-1900
Montgomery *(G-14262)*
Messer North America Inc..................E....... 630 257-3612
Lockport *(G-13012)*
Neon Nights Dj Svc..................G....... 309 820-9000
Bloomington *(G-2082)*
Neon Street Productions..................G....... 217 304-4514
Danville *(G-7368)*
Nitrogen Labs Inc..................G....... 312 504-8134
Chicago *(G-5605)*
Plz Aeroscience Corporation..................E....... 630 628-3000
Downers Grove *(G-8078)*
Praxair Inc..................E....... 847 428-3405
Gilberts *(G-10365)*
Praxair Inc..................G....... 708 728-9353
Chicago *(G-5853)*
Praxair Inc..................F....... 309 347-5575
Pekin *(G-16356)*
Praxair Distribution Inc..................E....... 314 664-7900
Cahokia *(G-2763)*
Quality Neon Service..................G....... 847 299-2969
Des Plaines *(G-7834)*
Shinn Enterprises..................G....... 217 698-3344
Springfield *(G-19443)*
Slide Products Inc..................F....... 847 541-7220
Wheeling *(G-20987)*
Technical Propellants Inc..................F....... 815 942-2900
Morris *(G-14332)*
▼ **Weldstar Company**..................E....... 630 859-3100
Aurora *(G-1169)*

2816 Inorganic Pigments

Accel Corporation..................E....... 630 579-6961
Batavia *(G-1340)*
◆ **American Chemet Corporation**..................F....... 847 948-0800
Deerfield *(G-7585)*
▲ **Cathay Industries (usa) Inc**..................G....... 219 531-5359
Bartlett *(G-1271)*
▲ **Chroma Color Corporation**..................C....... 877 385-8777
McHenry *(G-13726)*
▲ **Chromium Industries Inc**..................E....... 773 287-3716
Chicago *(G-4145)*
Colors For Plastics Inc..................D....... 847 437-0033
Elk Grove Village *(G-8901)*
▲ **Fortune International Tech LLC**..................G....... 847 429-9791
Hoffman Estates *(G-11425)*

Kasha Industries Inc E 618 375-2511
Grayville *(G-10811)*
Kasha Industries Inc F 618 375-2511
Grayville *(G-10812)*
▲ **Plastics Color Corp Illinois** D 708 868-3800
Calumet City *(G-2787)*
Polyone Corporation D 847 364-0011
Elk Grove Village *(G-9183)*
Prince Minerals LLC G 646 747-4222
Quincy *(G-16926)*
Prince Minerals LLC G 646 747-4200
Quincy *(G-16927)*
◆ **Rust-Oleum Corporation** C 847 367-7700
Vernon Hills *(G-20089)*
▲ **Scientific Colors Inc** C 815 741-1391
Rockdale *(G-17273)*
◆ **Solomon Colors Inc** D 217 522-3112
Springfield *(G-19449)*
◆ **Southern Color Company Inc** G 770 386-4766
East Saint Louis *(G-8323)*
Toyal America Inc G 630 505-2160
Naperville *(G-14935)*
◆ **Toyal America Inc** D 630 505-2160
Lockport *(G-13025)*
Versatile Materials Inc G 773 924-3700
Chicago *(G-6538)*

2819 Indl Inorganic Chemicals, NEC

51 Elements G 847 712-5550
Buffalo Grove *(G-2503)*
▲ **Acl Inc** F 773 285-0295
Chicago *(G-3525)*
Advanced Diamond Tech Inc E 815 293-0900
Northbrook *(G-15332)*
Alltech Associates Inc D 773 261-2252
Chicago *(G-3624)*
Amcol International G 847 392-4673
Arlington Heights *(G-689)*
◆ **American Chemet Corporation** F 847 948-0800
Deerfield *(G-7585)*
Americo Chemical Products Inc E 630 588-0830
Carol Stream *(G-2938)*
Amnetic LLC G 877 877-3678
Des Plaines *(G-7730)*
Aquion Partners Ltd Partnr G 847 437-9400
Elk Grove Village *(G-8836)*
Arcturus Performance Pdts LLC G 630 204-0211
Saint Charles *(G-18147)*
Artisan Element G 630 229-5654
Woodridge *(G-21276)*
Batavia Bio Processing Limited G 630 761-1180
Batavia *(G-1354)*
▲ **Bellman-Melcor Holdings Inc** F 708 532-5000
Tinley Park *(G-19807)*
◆ **Big River Zinc Corporation** G 618 274-5000
Sauget *(G-18389)*
Boyer Corporation G 708 352-2553
La Grange *(G-12074)*
◆ **BP Amoco Chemical Company** B 630 420-5111
Naperville *(G-14782)*
Brainerd Chemical Midwest LLC G 918 622-1214
Danville *(G-7325)*
Bullen Midwest Inc E 773 785-2300
Chicago *(G-3973)*
C & S Chemicals Inc G 815 722-6671
Joliet *(G-11837)*
Cabot Corporation E 217 253-3370
Tuscola *(G-19924)*
Cabot McRlectronics Globl Corp G 630 375-6631
Aurora *(G-930)*
◆ **Cabot Microelectronics Corp** D 630 375-6631
Aurora *(G-931)*
Cabot Microelectronics Corp C 630 375-6631
Aurora *(G-933)*
Campbell Camie Inc E 314 968-3222
Downers Grove *(G-7963)*
Campbell Science Corp F 815 962-7415
Rockford *(G-17333)*
Carus Corporation D 815 223-1565
La Salle *(G-12105)*
Carus Group Inc D 815 223-1500
Peru *(G-16570)*
◆ **Carus LLC** D 815 223-1500
Peru *(G-16571)*
Carus LLC C 815 223-1500
La Salle *(G-12106)*
◆ **Catalytic Products Intl Inc** E 847 438-0334
Lake Zurich *(G-12390)*
▲ **Cater Chemical Co** G 630 980-2300
Roselle *(G-17943)*

Chemtech Services Inc F 815 838-4800
Lockport *(G-12986)*
Chemtrade Chemicals US LLC E 618 274-4363
East Saint Louis *(G-8301)*
Chemtrade Logistics (us) Inc G 704 369-2496
Chicago *(G-4082)*
Chicago Salt Company Inc G 708 906-4718
River Grove *(G-17058)*
Circle Systems Inc F 815 286-3271
Hinckley *(G-11357)*
Condy Holdings LLC G 815 223-1500
Peru *(G-16573)*
Covachem LLC G 779 500-0918
Rockford *(G-17359)*
Cs Elements LLC G 219 508-9270
Chicago *(G-4279)*
▲ **Dauber Company Inc** E 815 442-3569
Tonica *(G-19888)*
Delta Products Group Inc F 630 357-5544
Aurora *(G-1084)*
Dfg Mercury Corp G 847 869-7800
Evanston *(G-9510)*
Dow Chemical Company E 847 439-2240
Elk Grove Village *(G-8954)*
Dow Chemical Company C 815 653-2411
Ringwood *(G-17042)*
Dow Chemical Company D 815 933-8900
Kankakee *(G-11966)*
▲ **DSM Desotech Inc** C 847 697-0400
Elgin *(G-8570)*
E I Du Pont De Nemours & Co E 847 965-6580
Morton Grove *(G-14402)*
E I Du Pont De Nemours & Co G 815 562-7570
Rochelle *(G-17137)*
Element Events LLC G 630 717-2800
Naperville *(G-14822)*
Elemental Art Jewelry G 773 844-4812
Chicago *(G-4481)*
Elements Group G 312 664-2252
Chicago *(G-4482)*
Emco Chemical Distributors Inc C 262 427-0400
North Chicago *(G-15310)*
Entrust Services LLC G 630 699-9132
Naperville *(G-14825)*
▲ **Esma Inc** G 708 331-0456
South Holland *(G-19211)*
First Element Solutions G 847 691-8381
Mount Prospect *(G-14529)*
Frank Miller & Sons Inc E 708 201-7200
Mokena *(G-14083)*
Fusion Chemical Corporation G 847 656-5285
Park Ridge *(G-16278)*
Gcp Applied Technologies F 708 728-2420
Chicago *(G-4665)*
Gcp Applied Technologies Inc C 617 876-1400
Bannockburn *(G-1202)*
Gmm Holdings LLC F 312 255-9830
Chicago *(G-4706)*
Gycor International Ltd F 630 754-8070
Woodridge *(G-21308)*
Hallstar Company E 901 948-8663
Chicago *(G-4771)*
Helena Agri-Enterprises LLC F 217 382-4241
Martinsville *(G-13585)*
Helena Agri-Enterprises LLC G 217 234-2726
Mattoon *(G-13636)*
Honeywell International Inc B 618 524-2111
Metropolis *(G-13972)*
Hussain Shaheen G 630 405-8009
Bolingbrook *(G-2187)*
▲ **Hydrox Chemical Company Inc** D 847 468-9400
Elgin *(G-8618)*
Illinois Capacitor Inc B 847 675-1760
Des Plaines *(G-7783)*
Incon Industries Inc G 630 728-4014
Saint Charles *(G-18211)*
Incon Processing LLC E 630 305-8556
Batavia *(G-1385)*
Innophos Inc C 708 757-6111
Chicago Heights *(G-6750)*
Innophos Inc G 773 468-2300
Chicago *(G-4929)*
◆ **Interra Global Corporation** F 847 292-8600
Park Ridge *(G-16285)*
J B Watts Company Inc G 773 643-1855
Chicago *(G-4987)*
J Stilling Enterprises Inc G 630 584-5050
Saint Charles *(G-18217)*
JM Huber Corporation E 217 224-1100
Quincy *(G-16895)*

JM Huber Corporation D 217 224-1123
Quincy *(G-16896)*
◆ **Kafko International Ltd** E 847 763-0333
Skokie *(G-18971)*
Klean-Ko Inc D 630 620-1860
Lombard *(G-13092)*
Konzen Chemicals Inc F 708 878-7636
Matteson *(G-13626)*
Lonza LLC D 309 697-7200
Mapleton *(G-13475)*
▲ **Maclee Chemical Company Inc** G 847 480-0953
Northbrook *(G-15426)*
Magrabar LLC F 847 965-7550
Morton Grove *(G-14423)*
▼ **March Industries Inc** F 224 654-6500
Hampshire *(G-10978)*
McClendon Holdings LLC G 773 251-2314
Chicago *(G-5373)*
McShares Inc E 217 762-2561
Monticello *(G-14281)*
Merichem Chem Rfinery Svcs LLC C 847 285-3850
Schaumburg *(G-18628)*
Metal Finishing Research Corp F 773 373-0800
Chicago *(G-5404)*
Milliken & Company D 864 473-1601
Chicago *(G-5461)*
Minus Nine Technologies G 224 399-9393
Gurnee *(G-10899)*
Murdock Company Inc G 847 566-0050
Mundelein *(G-14719)*
▲ **Nanochem Solutions Inc** F 708 563-9200
Naperville *(G-14878)*
Nanochem Solutions Inc F 815 224-8480
Peru *(G-16583)*
National Interchem LLC G 708 597-7777
Blue Island *(G-2133)*
▲ **Nikkin Flux Corp** G 618 656-2125
Edwardsville *(G-8372)*
▲ **NNt Enterprises Incorporated** E 630 875-9600
Itasca *(G-11712)*
Nouryon Chemicals LLC C 312 544-7000
Chicago *(G-5630)*
Nouryon USA LLC F 312 544-7000
Chicago *(G-5633)*
Occidental Chemical Corp G 630 505-3242
Lisle *(G-12924)*
Orica USA Inc E 815 357-8711
Morris *(G-14320)*
◆ **Pcs Phosphate Company Inc** D 847 849-4200
Northbrook *(G-15457)*
Perkinelmer Hlth Sciences Inc C 630 969-6000
Downers Grove *(G-8073)*
Pharmasyn Inc G 847 752-8405
Libertyville *(G-12695)*
Phosphate Resource Ptrs A 847 739-1200
Lake Forest *(G-12290)*
▲ **Plaze Inc** C 630 628-4240
Downers Grove *(G-8076)*
▼ **Potash Corp Ssktchewan Fla Inc** C 847 849-4200
Northbrook *(G-15461)*
Powerlab Inc F 815 273-7718
Savanna *(G-18410)*
PQ Corporation E 815 667-4241
Utica *(G-20006)*
PQ Corporation F 847 662-8566
Gurnee *(G-10914)*
Pure Element G 309 269-7823
Moline *(G-14168)*
PVS Chemical Solutions Inc E 773 933-8800
Chicago *(G-5919)*
Radco Industries Inc E 630 232-7966
Batavia *(G-1408)*
Reagent Chemical & RES Inc G 618 271-8140
East Saint Louis *(G-8319)*
▲ **Reliance Specialty Pdts Inc** F 847 640-8923
Carol Stream *(G-3059)*
▲ **Remuriate LLC** G 815 220-5050
La Salle *(G-12121)*
Rhone-Poulenc Basic Chem Co G 708 757-6111
Chicago Heights *(G-6769)*
▲ **Rockform Tooling & Machinery** E 770 345-4624
Rockford *(G-17610)*
▲ **Rohm and Haas Company** F 815 728-4602
Ringwood *(G-17047)*
Sanford Chemical Co Inc F 847 437-3530
Elk Grove Village *(G-9229)*
◆ **Scholle Ipn Corporation** F 708 562-7290
Northlake *(G-15558)*
Schwanog LLC F 847 289-1055
Elgin *(G-8724)*

S I C

28 CHEMICALS AND ALLIED PRODUCTS SIC SECTION

Solvay Chemicals Inc...E... 618 274-0755
East Saint Louis *(G-8322)*
Solvay Finance (america) LLC...F... 713 525-6000
Chicago *(G-6200)*
Solvay USA Inc...E... 708 441-6041
Chicago Heights *(G-6775)*
Solvay USA Inc...E... 708 371-2000
Blue Island *(G-2141)*
Spartan Flame Retardants Inc...F... 815 459-8500
Crystal Lake *(G-7267)*
Stellar Manufacturing Company...D... 618 823-3761
Cahokia *(G-2764)*
Tally Metals Holdings LLC...G... 773 264-5900
Chicago *(G-6315)*
Toyal America Inc...G... 630 505-2160
Naperville *(G-14935)*
Tr Chem Solutions LLC...G... 262 865-7228
Gurnee *(G-10937)*
Trico Technologies Inc...G... 847 662-9224
Gurnee *(G-10939)*
Uncommon Elements LLC...G... 847 414-0708
Oakwood Hills *(G-15823)*
Universal Chem & Coatings Inc...E... 847 297-2001
Elk Grove Village *(G-9299)*
◆ **Universal Cat LLC**...E... 708 753-8070
S Chicago Hts *(G-18128)*
UOP LLC...C... 708 442-3681
Chicago *(G-6488)*
UOP LLC...C... 847 391-2540
Des Plaines *(G-7862)*
UOP LLC...D... 708 442-7400
Mc Cook *(G-13704)*
◆ **US Borax Inc**...C... 773 270-6500
Chicago *(G-6499)*
US Silica Holdings Inc...C... 312 589-7539
Chicago *(G-6503)*
US Silica Holdings Inc...F... 312 291-4400
Chicago *(G-6504)*
US Silica Holdings Inc...F... 815 667-7085
Ottawa *(G-16084)*
Vacumet Corp...F... 708 562-7290
Northlake *(G-15564)*
◆ **Velsicol Chemical LLC**...G... 847 813-7888
Rosemont *(G-18060)*
Vernon Micheal...G... 217 735-4005
Lincoln *(G-12739)*
Vertex Chemical Corporation...F... 618 286-5207
Dupo *(G-8149)*
W R Grace & Co...C... 773 838-3200
Chicago *(G-6575)*
W R Grace & Co-Conn...F... 708 458-9700
Chicago *(G-6577)*
Wet International Inc...E... 630 540-2113
Streamwood *(G-19602)*
Xena International Inc...E... 815 946-2626
Polo *(G-16760)*
▲ **Xingfa USA Corporation**...F... 630 305-9097
Schaumburg *(G-18777)*

2821 Plastics, Mtrls & Nonvulcanizable Elastomers

Aabbitt Adhesives Inc...D... 773 227-2700
Chicago *(G-3499)*
Acomtech Mold Inc...G... 847 741-3537
Elgin *(G-8493)*
▲ **Ade Inc**...E... 773 646-3400
Chicago *(G-3541)*
Advanced Polymer Alloys LLC...G... 847 836-8119
Carpentersville *(G-3091)*
▲ **Advanced Prototype Molding**...G... 847 202-4200
Palatine *(G-16090)*
Akrylix Inc...F... 773 869-9005
Frankfort *(G-9764)*
◆ **Akshar Plastic Inc**...E... 815 635-3536
Bloomington *(G-2022)*
Akzo Nobel Coatings Inc...E... 630 792-1619
Lombard *(G-13038)*
◆ **Amcol Hlth Buty Solutions Inc**...F... 847 851-1300
Hoffman Estates *(G-11404)*
◆ **Amcor Flexibles LLC**...C... 224 313-7000
Buffalo Grove *(G-2510)*
Americas Styrenics LLC...D... 815 418-6403
Channahon *(G-3374)*
Ameriflon Ltd...G... 847 541-6000
Wheeling *(G-20848)*
Amsty...G... 815 418-6430
Channahon *(G-3375)*
▲ **Atlas Fibre Company**...D... 847 674-1234
Northbrook *(G-15343)*
Atsp Innovations Inc...G... 217 778-4400
Champaign *(G-3269)*
BASF Corporation...B... 815 932-6751
Kankakee *(G-11959)*
◆ **BP Amoco Chemical Company**...B... 630 420-5111
Naperville *(G-14782)*
Brinkman Company Inc...G... 630 595-3640
Bensenville *(G-1757)*
Camryn Industries LLC...C... 815 544-1900
Belvidere *(G-1660)*
Carver Plastic Products Inc...G... 708 588-0081
La Grange *(G-12075)*
Coda Resources Ltd...F... 718 649-1666
Chicago *(G-4190)*
Cope Plastics Inc...G... 309 787-4465
East Peoria *(G-8263)*
Corro-Shield International Inc...F... 847 298-7770
Elk Grove Village *(G-8916)*
▲ **Crown Premiums Inc**...F... 815 469-8789
Frankfort *(G-9781)*
Custom Films Inc...F... 217 826-2326
Marshall *(G-13569)*
▼ **De Enterprises Inc**...F... 708 345-8088
Broadview *(G-2429)*
Dip Seal Plastics Inc...G... 815 398-3533
Rockford *(G-17379)*
Dow Chemical Company...C... 815 423-5921
Channahon *(G-3381)*
Dow Chemical Company...E... 847 439-2240
Elk Grove Village *(G-8954)*
Dow Chemical Company...C... 815 653-2411
Ringwood *(G-17042)*
Dow Chemical Company...D... 815 933-8900
Kankakee *(G-11966)*
Drum Manufacturing...F... 217 923-5625
Greenup *(G-10819)*
▲ **DSM Desotech Inc**...C... 847 697-0400
Elgin *(G-8570)*
▲ **Dynachem Inc**...D... 217 662-2136
Westville *(G-20780)*
Eastman Chemical Company...F... 618 482-6409
Sauget *(G-18393)*
Ecologic LLC...F... 630 869-0495
Oakbrook Terrace *(G-15797)*
▲ **Elevator Cable & Supply Co**...E... 708 338-9700
Broadview *(G-2433)*
Emerald Performance Mtls LLC...E... 309 364-2311
Henry *(G-11164)*
Ems Acrylics & Silk Screener...F... 773 777-5656
Chicago *(G-4502)*
Evergreen Scale Models Inc...F... 224 567-8099
Des Plaines *(G-7761)*
Excelsior Inc...E... 815 987-2900
Rockford *(G-17407)*
F5d Inc...G... 815 953-9183
Herscher *(G-11183)*
▲ **Fabritek LLC**...G... 630 983-0211
Naperville *(G-14827)*
▲ **Fitz Chem LLC**...E... 630 467-8383
Itasca *(G-11658)*
Flex-O-Glass Inc...E... 815 288-1424
Dixon *(G-7899)*
Flint Hills Resources LP...G... 815 224-5232
Peru *(G-16576)*
Gallagher Corporation...D... 847 249-3440
Gurnee *(G-10881)*
Hanlon Group Ltd...G... 773 525-3666
Chicago *(G-4778)*
Hexion Inc...E... 708 728-8834
Bedford Park *(G-1472)*
Huntsman Expndable Polymers Lc...C... 815 224-5463
Peru *(G-16577)*
Huntsman International LLC...D... 815 653-1500
Ringwood *(G-17044)*
ID Additives Inc...G... 708 588-0081
La Grange *(G-12079)*
Ineos Americas LLC...G... 630 857-7463
Naperville *(G-14845)*
Ineos Americas LLC...G... 630 857-7000
Lisle *(G-12900)*
Ineos Styrolution America LLC...G... 815 423-5541
Channahon *(G-3385)*
◆ **Ineos Styrolution America LLC**...C... 630 820-9500
Aurora *(G-982)*
▲ **Innocor Foam Tech W Chcago LLC**...E... 732 945-6222
West Chicago *(G-20598)*
▲ **Innovative Hess Products LLC**...B... 847 676-3260
Mount Prospect *(G-14535)*
Italmatch Sc LLC...G... 708 929-9657
Bedford Park *(G-1474)*
J L M Plastics Corporation...F... 815 722-0066
Joliet *(G-11884)*
J6 Polymers LLC...G... 815 517-1179
Genoa *(G-10319)*
Jakes World Design...G... 217 348-3043
Lerna *(G-12613)*
Jasch North America Company...G... 815 282-4463
Loves Park *(G-13222)*
▲ **Kastalon Inc**...D... 708 389-2210
Alsip *(G-463)*
Kns Companies Inc...E... 630 665-9010
Carol Stream *(G-3013)*
▲ **Ko-Polymer Inc**...F... 847 742-7700
Elgin *(G-8638)*
Kunz Industries Inc...G... 708 596-7717
South Holland *(G-19229)*
Lanxess Solutions US Inc...F... 309 633-9480
Mapleton *(G-13474)*
Lyondell Chemical Company...B... 815 942-7011
Morris *(G-14311)*
Lyondllbsell Advnced Plymers I...E... 847 426-3350
Carpentersville *(G-3107)*
Mapei Corporation...D... 630 293-5800
West Chicago *(G-20613)*
Maxwell Counters Inc...E... 309 928-2848
Farmer City *(G-9655)*
Mega Polymers Inc...F... 815 230-0092
Romeoville *(G-17849)*
Midwest Innovative Pdts LLC...E... 888 945-4545
Joliet *(G-11903)*
▲ **Miner Elastomer Products Corp**...E... 630 232-3000
Geneva *(G-10290)*
Minova USA Inc...D... 618 993-2611
Marion *(G-13522)*
Mossan Inc...G... 857 247-4122
Schaumburg *(G-18633)*
◆ **MRC Polymers Inc**...D... 773 890-9000
Chicago *(G-5518)*
▼ **Nanocor LLC**...E... 847 851-1900
Hoffman Estates *(G-11438)*
◆ **National Casein Co**...D... 773 846-7300
Burr Ridge *(G-2707)*
Natural Polymers LLC...G... 888 563-3111
Cortland *(G-7025)*
Nova Chemicals Inc...D... 815 224-1525
Peru *(G-16586)*
Novipax LLC...F... 630 686-2735
Oak Brook *(G-15649)*
Nu-Pro Polymers Inc...G... 224 676-1663
Wheeling *(G-20947)*
Oly Ola Edging Inc...F... 630 833-3033
Villa Park *(G-20163)*
Owens Corning Sales LLC...D... 815 226-4627
Rockford *(G-17545)*
P M S Consolidated...G... 847 364-0011
Elk Grove Village *(G-9166)*
Pcc Inc...G... 708 868-3800
Calumet City *(G-2785)*
Pintas Cultured Marble...E... 708 385-3360
Alsip *(G-492)*
Plastics Color & Compounding...D... 708 868-3800
Calumet City *(G-2786)*
▲ **Poly Compounding LLC**...G... 847 488-0683
Elgin *(G-8691)*
Poly-Resyn Inc...F... 847 428-4031
West Dundee *(G-20665)*
Polybilt Body Company LLC...G... 708 345-8050
Itasca *(G-11721)*
Polycast...F... 815 648-4438
Hebron *(G-11148)*
Polyconversions Inc...E... 217 893-3330
Champaign *(G-3335)*
◆ **Polyform Products Company**...E... 847 427-0020
Elk Grove Village *(G-9182)*
▲ **Polymax Thrmplstic Elstmers LL**...E... 847 316-9900
Waukegan *(G-20478)*
Polynt Composites USA Inc...G... 815 942-4600
Morris *(G-14321)*
▲ **Polynt Composites USA Inc**...C... 847 428-2657
Carpentersville *(G-3114)*
Polyone Corporation...D... 815 385-8500
McHenry *(G-13782)*
Polyone Corporation...F... 815 385-8500
Mchenry *(G-13783)*
Polyone Corporation...C... 309 364-2154
Henry *(G-11168)*
Polyone Corporation...D... 630 972-0505
Romeoville *(G-17865)*
▲ **Polyurethane Products Corp**...E... 630 543-6700
Addison *(G-245)*

SIC SECTION
28 CHEMICALS AND ALLIED PRODUCTS

PPG Architectural Finishes Inc ......B 217 584-1323
Meredosia *(G-13956)*
Quantum Polymers Inc ......G 630 834-8427
Elmhurst *(G-9413)*
R T P Company ......G 618 286-6100
Dupo *(G-8143)*
Ravago Americas LLC ......E 815 609-4800
Plainfield *(G-16709)*
Raytech Machining Fabrication ......E 618 932-2511
West Frankfort *(G-20680)*
Recycled Vinyls LLC ......E 847 624-1880
Lake Forest *(G-12294)*
▲ **Recycling Solutions Inc** ......E 773 617-6955
Chicago *(G-5992)*
Reichhold Industries Inc ......E 815 942-4600
Morris *(G-14325)*
Reichhold Industries Inc ......E 919 990-7500
Carpentersville *(G-3118)*
Resin Exchange Inc ......E 630 628-7266
Addison *(G-271)*
Resin8 Inc ......G 773 551-3633
Elmhurst *(G-9418)*
Rhopac Fabricated Products LLC ......E 847 362-3300
Libertyville *(G-12702)*
Sabic Innovative Plas US LLC ......B 815 434-7000
Ottawa *(G-16075)*
▼ **Savannah Industries Inc** ......G 773 927-3484
Chicago *(G-6107)*
◆ **Scholle Ipn Corporation** ......F 708 562-7290
Northlake *(G-15558)*
Sejasmi Corp ......G 586 725-5300
Des Plaines *(G-7841)*
◆ **Senior Holdings Inc** ......D 630 837-1811
Bartlett *(G-1309)*
Serionix Inc ......G 651 503-3930
Urbana *(G-20000)*
▲ **Sherman Plastics Corp** ......E 630 369-6170
Naperville *(G-14913)*
Snyder Industries Inc ......D 630 773-9510
Bensenville *(G-1895)*
Solvay USA Inc ......E 708 235-7200
University Park *(G-19967)*
Spherotech Inc ......E 847 680-8922
Lake Forest *(G-12304)*
Standard Rubber Products Co ......E 847 593-5630
Elk Grove Village *(G-9252)*
Star Thermoplastic Alloys and ......E 708 343-1100
Broadview *(G-2469)*
Star Thermoplastic Alloys and ......F 708 343-1100
Broadview *(G-2470)*
▲ **Stellar Performance Mfg LLC** ......E 312 951-2311
Chicago *(G-6242)*
◆ **Stepan Company** ......B 847 446-7500
Northfield *(G-15531)*
Stepan Company ......B 847 446-7500
Elwood *(G-9464)*
Sunemco Technologies Inc ......G 630 369-8947
Naperville *(G-14923)*
▲ **Tangent Technologies LLC** ......C 630 264-1110
Aurora *(G-1160)*
Targun Plastic Co ......G 847 509-9355
Northbrook *(G-15491)*
Techmer Pm LLC ......F 630 579-6961
Batavia *(G-1427)*
Technique Eng Inc ......F 847 816-1870
Waukegan *(G-20500)*
▲ **Texxon Plastics Corporation** ......G 630 369-6850
Naperville *(G-14930)*
▼ **Thermoflex Corp** ......F 847 473-9001
Waukegan *(G-20504)*
Thermoflex Corp ......G 847 473-9001
Waukegan *(G-20505)*
Total Plastics Inc ......F 847 593-5000
Elk Grove Village *(G-9278)*
Underground Devices Inc ......F 847 205-9000
Northbrook *(G-15495)*
United Gilsonite Labs Inc ......E 217 243-7878
Jacksonville *(G-11784)*
Vacumet Corp ......F 708 562-7290
Northlake *(G-15564)*
Voss Belting & Specialty Co ......E 847 673-8900
Lincolnwood *(G-12849)*
Wilcor Solid Surface Inc ......F 888 956-1001
Elk Grove Village *(G-9309)*
Yankee Mold Inc ......G 815 986-1776
Machesney Park *(G-13384)*

2822 Synthetic Rubber (Vulcanizable Elastomers)

▲ **Advanced Prototype Molding** ......G 847 202-4200
Palatine *(G-16090)*
▲ **Allstates Rubber & Tool Corp** ......F 708 342-1030
Tinley Park *(G-19800)*
Bamberger Polymers Inc ......F 630 773-8626
Itasca *(G-11624)*
Crown Polymers LLC ......G 847 683-0800
Hampshire *(G-10968)*
Crown Polymers Corporation ......F 847 659-0300
Huntley *(G-11532)*
▼ **Custom Seal & Rubber Products** ......G 888 356-2966
Mount Morris *(G-14499)*
Elas Tek Molding Inc ......E 815 675-9012
Spring Grove *(G-19274)*
Everon Polymers LLC ......G 815 681-8800
Joliet *(G-11863)*
Excelsior Inc ......E 815 987-2900
Rockford *(G-17407)*
Hallstar Company ......D 708 594-5947
Bedford Park *(G-1470)*
Honeywell Safety Pdts USA Inc ......C 630 343-3731
Bolingbrook *(G-2185)*
Liberty Chemical Corp ......G 773 657-1282
Elk Grove Village *(G-9094)*
Mexichem Specialty Resins Inc ......F 309 364-2154
Henry *(G-11167)*
▲ **Modern Silicone Tech Inc** ......F 727 507-9800
Lincolnshire *(G-12785)*
Moriteq Rubber Co ......F 847 734-0970
Arlington Heights *(G-778)*
◆ **Morton Salt Inc** ......C 312 807-2000
Chicago *(G-5501)*
Nauvoo Products Inc ......F 217 453-2817
Nauvoo *(G-15015)*
Parker-Hannifin Corporation ......C 630 427-2020
Woodridge *(G-21331)*
Plastic Specialties & Tech Inc ......G 847 781-2414
Schaumburg *(G-18675)*
▲ **Polymax Thrmplstic Elstmers LL** ......E 847 316-9900
Waukegan *(G-20478)*
Star Thermoplastic Alloys and ......F 708 343-1100
Broadview *(G-2470)*
T9 Group LLC ......G 847 912-8862
Hawthorn Woods *(G-11126)*
◆ **Tradex International Inc** ......D 216 651-4788
Elwood *(G-9465)*
Vibracoustic Usa Inc ......E 618 382-5891
Carmi *(G-2916)*
Voss Belting & Specialty Co ......E 847 673-8900
Lincolnwood *(G-12849)*
▲ **Weiler Rubber Technologies LLC** ......G 773 826-8900
Chicago *(G-6598)*

2823 Cellulosic Man-Made Fibers

◆ **Essentra Holdings Corp** ......G 804 518-0322
Westchester *(G-20698)*
Higgins Bros Inc ......F 773 523-0124
Chicago *(G-4815)*

2824 Synthetic Organic Fibers, Exc Cellulosic

Acrylic Design Works Inc ......F 773 843-1300
Chicago *(G-3532)*
Fairfield Processing Corp ......E 618 452-8404
Granite City *(G-10706)*
Gig Karasek LLC ......F 630 549-0394
Saint Charles *(G-18204)*
Magnetic Occasions & More Inc ......G 815 462-4141
New Lenox *(G-15040)*
◆ **RITA Corporation** ......E 815 337-2500
Crystal Lake *(G-7257)*
Vinylworks Inc ......G 815 477-9680
Crystal Lake *(G-7290)*

2833 Medicinal Chemicals & Botanical Prdts

▲ **Animal Center International** ......G 217 214-0536
Quincy *(G-16853)*
Ataraxia LLC ......E 618 446-3219
Albion *(G-346)*
▲ **Bean Products Inc** ......E 312 666-3600
Chicago *(G-3853)*
Biomerieux Inc ......F 630 600-5516
Lombard *(G-13045)*
Biomerieux Inc ......E 630 628-6055
Lombard *(G-13046)*
Bright Brain ......F 844 272-4645
Bloomingdale *(G-1982)*
▲ **Chemblend of America LLC** ......F 630 521-1600
Bensenville *(G-1767)*
▲ **Chemsci Technologies Inc** ......G 815 608-9135
Belvidere *(G-1662)*
Covachem LLC ......G 779 500-0918
Rockford *(G-17359)*
◆ **Daito Pharmaceuticals Amer Inc** ......G 847 205-0800
Northbrook *(G-15372)*
▼ **Dawes LLC** ......F 847 577-2020
Arlington Heights *(G-726)*
Dottikon Es America Inc ......G 215 295-2295
Chicago *(G-4387)*
Frontida Biopharm Inc ......G 215 620-3527
Aurora *(G-965)*
▲ **GE Healthcare Holdings Inc** ......A 847 398-8400
Arlington Heights *(G-741)*
GE Healthcare Inc ......E 630 595-6642
Wood Dale *(G-21193)*
Glanbia Performance Ntrtn Inc ......E 630 256-7445
Aurora *(G-969)*
Glanbia Performance Ntrtn Inc ......F 630 236-0097
Aurora *(G-970)*
Glanbia Performance Ntrtn Inc ......D 800 336-2183
Aurora *(G-971)*
◆ **Glanbia Prfmce Ntrtn NA Inc** ......C 630 236-0097
Downers Grove *(G-8012)*
Green Thumb Industries Inc ......F 312 471-6720
Chicago *(G-4740)*
Gti Rock Island LLC ......F 312 664-5050
Chicago *(G-4746)*
Janssen Pharmaceuticals Inc ......F 312 750-0507
Chicago *(G-5007)*
Jewel Osco Inc ......C 847 882-6477
Hoffman Estates *(G-11432)*
Lonza LLC ......D 309 697-7200
Mapleton *(G-13475)*
Natures Healing Remedies Inc ......F 773 589-9996
Chicago *(G-5554)*
Nutritional Institute LLC ......G 847 223-7676
Grayslake *(G-10794)*
Oil-Dri Corporation America ......D 312 321-1515
Chicago *(G-5666)*
Orchard Products Inc ......G 847 818-6760
Mount Prospect *(G-14556)*
Organnica Inc ......G 312 925-7272
Berwyn *(G-1959)*
Resolution Systems Inc ......G 616 392-8001
Wilmette *(G-21092)*
◆ **RITA Corporation** ......E 815 337-2500
Crystal Lake *(G-7257)*
UOP LLC ......D 708 442-7400
Mc Cook *(G-13704)*
Vidasym Inc ......G 847 549-3357
Libertyville *(G-12723)*
▲ **Ys Health Corporation** ......F 847 391-9122
Mount Prospect *(G-14585)*
Zoetis LLC ......D 708 757-2592
Chicago Heights *(G-6787)*

2834 Pharmaceuticals

A-S Medication Solutions LLC ......D 847 680-3515
Libertyville *(G-12624)*
◆ **Aardvark Pharma LLC** ......E 630 248-2380
Oakbrook Terrace *(G-15779)*
▲ **Abbott Health Products Inc** ......D 847 937-6100
North Chicago *(G-15290)*
Abbott Laboratories ......A 224 330-0271
Libertyville *(G-12625)*
Abbott Laboratories ......A 847 937-2210
Chicago *(G-3503)*
Abbott Laboratories ......E 847 938-3220
Waukegan *(G-20406)*
Abbott Laboratories ......A 847 735-0573
Mettawa *(G-13977)*
Abbott Laboratories ......A 847 937-6100
North Chicago *(G-15291)*
Abbott Laboratories ......E 847 937-6100
Waukegan *(G-20407)*
Abbott Laboratories ......G 224 361-7129
Elk Grove Village *(G-8793)*
Abbott Laboratories ......D 847 938-4196
North Chicago *(G-15292)*
Abbott Laboratories ......A 847 932-7900
North Chicago *(G-15293)*
Abbott Laboratories ......A 847 935-8130
Gurnee *(G-10852)*
Abbott Laboratories ......F 312 944-0660
Bannockburn *(G-1188)*

S I C

Employee Codes: A=Over 500 employees, B=251-500
C=101-250, D=51-100, E=20-50, F=10-19, G=3-9
2020 Harris Illinois
Industrial Directory
883

Abbott Laboratories A 847 937-6100 Des Plaines ***(G-7718)***
Abbott Laboratories F 847 855-9217 Gurnee ***(G-10853)***
Abbott Laboratories G 847 937-6100 North Chicago ***(G-15294)***
Abbott Laboratories C 847 937-6100 Waukegan ***(G-20408)***
Abbott Laboratories G 800 551-5838 Lake Forest ***(G-12218)***
▲ **Abbott Laboratories** A 224 667-6100 Abbott Park ***(G-1)***
◆ **Abbott Laboratories Inc** C 224 668-2076 Abbott Park ***(G-2)***
Abbott Laboratories Intl Co F 847 937-6100 North Chicago ***(G-15295)***
◆ **Abbott Laboratories PCF Ltd** F 847 937-6100 North Chicago ***(G-15296)***
Abbott Laboratories Svcs Corp G 708 937-6100 North Chicago ***(G-15297)***
Abbott Labs Hlth Care Tr G 224 667-6100 Abbott Park ***(G-3)***
Abbott Nutrition Mfg Inc G 614 624-6083 Abbott Park ***(G-4)***
Abbott Point of Care Inc C 847 937-6100 Abbott Park ***(G-5)***
▲ **Abbott Products Inc** B 847 937-6100 Abbott Park ***(G-6)***
Abbott Universal LLC G 224 667-6100 Abbott Park ***(G-7)***
Abbott-Abbvie Multiple Employe G 847 473-2053 North Chicago ***(G-15298)***
Abbvie G 847 946-8753 Mundelein ***(G-14658)***
Abbvie G 847 548-1016 Grayslake ***(G-10758)***
Abbvie Endocrinology Inc F 888 857-0668 North Chicago ***(G-15299)***
Abbvie Holdings Inc D 847 937-7632 Abbott Park ***(G-8)***
Abbvie Inc G 847 367-7621 Vernon Hills ***(G-20038)***
Abbvie Inc D 847 937-4566 Abbott Park ***(G-9)***
◆ **Abbvie Inc** C 847 932-7900 North Chicago ***(G-15300)***
Abbvie Inc D 847 932-7900 North Chicago ***(G-15301)***
Abbvie Inc E 847 473-4787 Waukegan ***(G-20409)***
Abbvie Inc G 847 938-2042 North Chicago ***(G-15302)***
Abbvie Respiratory LLC G 847 937-6100 North Chicago ***(G-15303)***
▲ **Abbvie US LLC** G 800 255-5162 North Chicago ***(G-15304)***
Abraxis Bioscience LLC G 310 437-7715 Elk Grove Village ***(G-8797)***
Abraxis Bioscience LLC G 310 883-1300 Melrose Park ***(G-13819)***
Accelerated Pharma Inc G 773 517-0789 Burr Ridge ***(G-2648)***
Access Medical Supply Inc G 847 891-6210 Schaumburg ***(G-18425)***
Acura Pharmaceuticals Inc F 847 705-7709 Palatine ***(G-16089)***
Adello Biologics LLC G 312 620-1500 Chicago ***(G-3542)***
Aechem Scientific Corporation G 630 364-5106 Naperville ***(G-14768)***
Aeropharm Technology LLC G 847 937-6100 North Chicago ***(G-15306)***
Aidarex Pharmaceuticals LLC G 800 657-4724 Libertyville ***(G-12626)***
Ajinomoto Food Ingredients LLC G 773 714-1436 Itasca ***(G-11617)***
Akorn Inc F 847 625-1100 Gurnee ***(G-10857)***
◆ **Akorn Inc** C 847 279-6100 Lake Forest ***(G-12222)***
Akorn Inc C 217 428-1100 Decatur ***(G-7437)***
Akorn Inc C 217 423-9715 Decatur ***(G-7438)***
Akorn Inc G 847 279-6166 Vernon Hills ***(G-20039)***
Akorn Pharmaceuticals G 800 932-5676 Lake Forest ***(G-12223)***
Allergan Inc G 714 246-4500 Gurnee ***(G-10858)***
Altathera Pharmaceuticals LLC F 312 445-8900 Chicago ***(G-3635)***
Alva/MCO Phrmcal Companies Inc E 847 663-0700 Niles ***(G-15101)***
▲ **Am2pat Inc** G 847 726-9443 Chicago ***(G-3641)***
American Phrm Partners Inc F 847 969-2700 Schaumburg ***(G-18438)***
Amphix Bio Inc G 720 840-7327 Chicago ***(G-3684)***
▲ **Anritsu Infivis Inc** E 847 419-9729 Elk Grove Village ***(G-8834)***
App Pharmaceuticals Inc G 847 969-2700 Schaumburg ***(G-18442)***
Apser Laboratory Inc D 630 543-3333 Addison ***(G-36)***
Archer-Daniels-Midland Company D 217 424-5200 Decatur ***(G-7459)***
Ashland ABC Choice Inc G 773 488-7800 Chicago ***(G-3748)***
▲ **Aspen API Inc** F 847 635-0985 Des Plaines ***(G-7734)***
Assertio Holdings Inc B 224 419-7106 Lake Forest ***(G-12227)***
Assertio Therapeutics Inc D 224 419-7106 Lake Forest ***(G-12228)***
Astellas Pharma Global Dev Inc C 224 205-8800 Northbrook ***(G-15337)***
Astellas Pharma Inc E 800 695-4321 Northbrook ***(G-15338)***
▲ **Astellas Pharma Us Inc** B 800 888-7704 Northbrook ***(G-15339)***
Astellas RES Inst Amer LLC F 847 933-7400 Skokie ***(G-18924)***
Astellas Scntfic Med Affirs In C 224 205-5452 Northbrook ***(G-15340)***
Astellas US Holding Inc E 224 205-8800 Northbrook ***(G-15341)***
Astellas US LLC C 800 888-7704 Deerfield ***(G-7587)***
Astellas US Technologies Inc B 847 317-8800 Deerfield ***(G-7588)***
Athenex Pharmaceutical Div LLC F 847 922-8041 Schaumburg ***(G-18448)***
Avexis G 847 964-9948 Deerfield ***(G-7589)***
Avocet Polymer Tech Inc G 773 523-2872 Chicago ***(G-3788)***
B & H Biotechnologies LLC G 630 915-3227 Willowbrook ***(G-21030)***
▼ **Baxalta Export Corporation** C 224 948-2000 Bannockburn ***(G-1193)***
Baxalta Incorporated C 224 940-2000 Bannockburn ***(G-1194)***
Baxalta US Inc D 847 948-2000 Round Lake ***(G-18068)***
Baxalta World Trade LLC G 224 940-2000 Bannockburn ***(G-1195)***
Baxalta Worldwide LLC C 224 948-2000 Deerfield ***(G-7590)***
▼ **Baxter Global Holdings II Inc** E 224 948-1812 Deerfield ***(G-7591)***
Baxter Healthcare Corporation B 847 522-8600 Vernon Hills ***(G-20044)***
Baxter Healthcare Corporation A 224 270-6300 Round Lake ***(G-18071)***
Baxter International Inc A 224 948-2000 Deerfield ***(G-7595)***
Baxter World Trade Corporation F 224 948-2000 Deerfield ***(G-7596)***
Bayer Corporation G 847 725-6320 Elk Grove Village ***(G-8858)***
Bella Pharmaceuticals Inc G 847 722-1692 Glenview ***(G-10529)***
Bimeda Animal Health Inc G 630 928-0361 Oakbrook Terrace ***(G-15788)***
Bio Ascend LLC G 888 476-9129 Chicago ***(G-3893)***
Bio-Bridge Science Inc E 630 328-0213 Oakbrook Terrace ***(G-15789)***
Biolife Plasma LLC F 224 940-7611 Bannockburn ***(G-1197)***
Black Start Labs Inc G 630 444-1800 Saint Charles ***(G-18157)***
Blistex Global Inc G 630 571-2870 Oak Brook ***(G-15597)***
◆ **Blistex Inc** C 630 571-2870 Oak Brook ***(G-15598)***
Blistex Inc G 630 571-2870 Oak Brook ***(G-15599)***
BMC 1092 Inc E 708 544-2200 Broadview ***(G-2421)***
Brian K Wattleworth G 847 356-2103 Lake Villa ***(G-12346)***
Bridgeport Pharmacy Inc G 312 791-9000 Chicago ***(G-3956)***
Capstone Dev Svcs Co LLC G 847 999-0131 Rosemont ***(G-18002)***
Capstone Therapeutics Corp G 602 286-5520 Alsip ***(G-426)***
Catalent Pharma Solutions LLC D 815 338-9500 Woodstock ***(G-21371)***
Catalent Pharma Solutions Inc C 815 338-9500 Woodstock ***(G-21372)***
Celerity Pharmaceuticals LLC G 847 999-0131 Rosemont ***(G-18003)***
Celgene Corporation F 908 673-9000 Melrose Park ***(G-13840)***
Cg Nutritionals Inc G 224 667-6100 North Chicago ***(G-15309)***
Chem Rx - Chicago LLC G 708 449-7600 Hillside ***(G-11333)***
Chicago Dscovery Solutions LLC G 815 609-2071 Plainfield ***(G-16650)***
Clarus Therapeutics Inc G 847 562-4300 Northbrook ***(G-15361)***
Coretechs Corp F 847 295-3720 Lake Forest ***(G-12240)***
Cour Pharmaceuticals Dev G 773 621-3241 Northbrook ***(G-15367)***
Curatek Pharmaceuticals LLC G 702 215-5700 Elk Grove Village ***(G-8924)***
◆ **Daito Pharmaceuticals Amer Inc** G 847 205-0800 Northbrook ***(G-15372)***
▲ **Daniels Sharpsmart Inc** E 312 546-8900 Chicago ***(G-4313)***
Denovx LLC G 910 333-6689 Chicago ***(G-4340)***
▲ **Dental Technologies Inc** D 847 677-5500 Lincolnwood ***(G-12816)***
Dr Earles LLC G 312 225-7200 Chicago ***(G-4395)***
East West Intergrated Therapys G 815 788-0574 Crystal Lake ***(G-7195)***
Elim Pdtric Phrmaceuticals Inc G 412 266-5968 Rolling Meadows ***(G-17729)***
Elim Pdtric Phrmaceuticals Inc E 412 266-5968 Schaumburg ***(G-18517)***
Elim Pdtric Phrmaceuticals Inc G 412 266-5968 Rolling Meadows ***(G-17730)***
Elorac Inc F 847 362-8200 Vernon Hills ***(G-20050)***
Emalex Biosciences LLC G 847 715-0577 Northbrook ***(G-15383)***
Espee Biopharma & Finechem LLC G 224 355-5950 Schaumburg ***(G-18520)***
▲ **Espee Biopharma & Finechem LLC** G 888 851-6667 Schaumburg ***(G-18521)***
Eton Pharmaceuticals Inc F 847 787-7361 Deer Park ***(G-7581)***
◆ **First Priority Inc** D 847 531-1215 Elgin ***(G-8587)***
Frazier Management LLC G 815 484-8900 Rockford ***(G-17423)***
◆ **Fresenius Kabi LLC** D 847 550-2300 Lake Zurich ***(G-12413)***
Fresenius Kabi LLC E 630 350-7150 Bensenville ***(G-1805)***
Fresenius Kabi Pharm G 847 550-2300 Lake Zurich ***(G-12414)***
Fresenius Kabi Usa Inc C 708 410-4761 Melrose Park ***(G-13870)***
Fresenius Kabi Usa Inc C 708 345-6170 Melrose Park ***(G-13871)***
Fresenius Kabi Usa Inc B 708 450-7500 Melrose Park ***(G-13869)***
▲ **Fresenius Kabi Usa LLC** A 847 550-2300 Lake Zurich ***(G-12415)***
Fresenius Kabi Usa LLC E 847 983-7100 Skokie ***(G-18957)***
Fresenius Kabi Usa LLC E 847 550-2300 Lake Zurich ***(G-12416)***
GE Healthcare Inc D 774 249-6290 Arlington Heights ***(G-742)***
Genentech Inc G 650 225-1045 Libertyville ***(G-12653)***
Global Medical Services LLC G 847 460-8086 Plainfield ***(G-16668)***
Global Pharma Device Solutions G 708 212-5801 Chicago ***(G-4698)***

▼ **Globepharm Inc** ..... G ..... 224 904-3352 Northbrook *(G-15395)*
Healthy Life Nutraceutics Inc ..... G ..... 201 253-9053 Deerfield *(G-7613)*
Hepalink USA Inc ..... G ..... 630 206-1788 Chicago *(G-4805)*
Horizon Medicines LLC ..... C ..... 224 383-3110 Lake Forest *(G-12255)*
Horizon Pharma Inc ..... C ..... 224 383-3000 Lake Forest *(G-12256)*
Horizon Phrma Rheumatology LLC ..... F ..... 224 383-3000 Lake Forest *(G-12257)*
Horizon Therapeutics Usa Inc ..... E ..... 224 383-3000 Deerfield *(G-7617)*
Horizon Therapeutics Usa Inc ..... F ..... 312 332-1401 Chicago *(G-4842)*
▲ **Horizon Therapeutics Usa Inc** ..... E ..... 224 383-3000 Lake Forest *(G-12258)*
Hospira Inc ..... C ..... 224 212-6244 Lake Forest *(G-12260)*
◆ **Hospira Inc** ..... A ..... 224 212-2000 Lake Forest *(G-12259)*
Hot Shots Nm LLC ..... G ..... 815 484-0500 Rockford *(G-17453)*
▲ **Hydrox Chemical Company Inc** ..... D ..... 847 468-9400 Elgin *(G-8618)*
Hznp Usa Inc ..... F ..... 224 383-3000 Lake Forest *(G-12263)*
Illinois Tool Works Inc ..... E ..... 847 593-8811 Elk Grove Village *(G-9042)*
Inheris Biopharma Inc ..... D ..... 415 482-5652 Chicago *(G-4924)*
International Drug Dev Cons ..... G ..... 847 634-9586 Long Grove *(G-13160)*
Iria Pharma Inc ..... G ..... 217 979-1417 Champaign *(G-3309)*
Iterative Therapeutics Inc ..... G ..... 773 455-7203 Chicago *(G-4976)*
Iterum Therapeutics US Limited ..... G ..... 312 763-3975 Chicago *(G-4977)*
Jdp Therapeutics LLC ..... G ..... 847 739-0490 Deerfield *(G-7619)*
Johnson & Johnson ..... D ..... 815 282-5671 Loves Park *(G-13226)*
Johnson Matthey Inc ..... E ..... 630 268-6300 Oakbrook Terrace *(G-15804)*
Joseph B Pigato MD Ltd ..... G ..... 815 937-2122 Kankakee *(G-11983)*
Kashiv Biosciences LLC ..... G ..... 908 895-1576 Chicago *(G-5084)*
Kastle Therapeutics LLC ..... G ..... 312 883-5695 Chicago *(G-5085)*
Lodaat LLC ..... E ..... 630 248-2380 Oak Brook *(G-15637)*
Lodaat LLC ..... D ..... 630 852-7544 Downers Grove *(G-8046)*
▲ **Lundbeck LLC** ..... C ..... 847 282-1000 Deerfield *(G-7631)*
Lundbeck Pharmaceuticals LLC ..... A ..... 847 282-1000 Deerfield *(G-7632)*
Mab Pharmacy Inc ..... G ..... 773 342-5878 Chicago *(G-5308)*
Mar Cor Purification Inc ..... G ..... 630 435-1017 Downers Grove *(G-8051)*
Mead Johnson Nutrition Company ..... C ..... 312 466-5800 Chicago *(G-5379)*
▲ **Medefil Inc** ..... D ..... 630 682-4600 Glendale Heights *(G-10474)*
Medexus Pharma Inc ..... G ..... 312 854-0500 Chicago *(G-5382)*
Medicate Pharmacy Inc ..... G ..... 618 482-2002 Cahokia *(G-2762)*
Meitheal Pharmaceuticals Inc ..... G ..... 773 951-6542 Chicago *(G-5389)*
Melinta Subsidiary Corp ..... E ..... 203 624-5606 Lincolnshire *(G-12783)*
Melinta Subsidiary Corp ..... F ..... 203 624-5606 Lincolnshire *(G-12784)*
Meridian Healthcare ..... G ..... 815 633-5326 Rockford *(G-17517)*
Meridian Laboratories Inc ..... G ..... 847 808-0081 Buffalo Grove *(G-2572)*
▲ **Mgp Holding Corp** ..... B ..... 847 967-5600 Morton Grove *(G-14428)*
Midwest Biofluids Inc ..... G ..... 630 790-9708 Glen Ellyn *(G-10413)*
Midwest Research Labs LLC ..... G ..... 847 283-9176 Lake Forest *(G-12273)*
Miller Pharmacal Group Inc ..... G ..... 800 323-2935 Carol Stream *(G-3032)*
Monopar Therapeutics Inc ..... G ..... 847 388-0349 Wilmette *(G-21089)*
▲ **Morton Grove Phrmceuticals Inc** ..... B ..... 847 967-5600 Morton Grove *(G-14430)*
Mylan Inc ..... G ..... 217 424-8400 Decatur *(G-7532)*
Mylan Institutional LLC ..... E ..... 724 514-1800 Rockford *(G-17534)*
Nantpharma LLC ..... C ..... 847 243-1200 Elk Grove Village *(G-9143)*
Naurex Inc ..... G ..... 847 871-0377 Evanston *(G-9557)*
Neurotherapeutics Pharma Inc ..... G ..... 773 444-4180 Chicago *(G-5573)*
Nexus Pharmaceuticals Inc ..... D ..... 847 996-3790 Lincolnshire *(G-12786)*
Nourishlife LLC ..... G ..... 847 234-2334 Lake Bluff *(G-12202)*
Novalex Therapeutics Inc ..... G ..... 630 750-9334 Elburn *(G-8465)*
Novum Pharma LLC ..... F ..... 877 404-4724 Chicago *(G-5634)*
Now Health Group Inc ..... G ..... 888 669-3663 Roselle *(G-17972)*
◆ **Now Health Group Inc** ..... A ..... 888 669-3663 Bloomingdale *(G-2004)*
Now Health Group Inc ..... A ..... 630 545-9098 Bloomingdale *(G-2005)*
Ocularis Pharma ..... G ..... 708 712-6263 Riverside *(G-17087)*
Oncquest ..... G ..... 847 682-4703 Zion *(G-21523)*
Organics LLC ..... G ..... 847 897-6000 Northbrook *(G-15448)*
▲ **Ortho Molecular Products Inc** ..... E ..... 815 337-0089 Woodstock *(G-21417)*
Owp Pharmaceuticals Inc ..... F ..... 331 871-7424 Naperville *(G-14890)*
Oxalo Therapeutics Inc ..... G ..... 530 848-3499 Chicago *(G-5722)*
Pal Midwest Ltd ..... G ..... 815 965-2981 Rockford *(G-17546)*
Patel Dishaben ..... G ..... 312 880-8746 Schaumburg *(G-18669)*
Patrin Pharma Inc ..... E ..... 800 936-3088 Skokie *(G-19003)*
▲ **Pfanstiehl Inc** ..... E ..... 847 623-0370 Waukegan *(G-20476)*
Pfanstiehl Holdings Inc ..... G ..... 847 623-0370 Waukegan *(G-20477)*
Pfizer Inc ..... C ..... 630 634-3704 Itasca *(G-11716)*
Pfizer Inc ..... G ..... 847 778-9237 Chicago *(G-5800)*
Pfizer Inc ..... G ..... 224 212-3129 Lake Forest *(G-12287)*
▲ **Pharma Logistics** ..... D ..... 847 388-3104 Mundelein *(G-14725)*
Pharma Nature ..... G ..... 224 659-0906 Des Plaines *(G-7822)*
Pharmaceutical Labs and Cons I ..... G ..... 630 359-3831 Addison *(G-238)*
Pharmanutrients Inc ..... G ..... 847 234-2334 Lake Bluff *(G-12205)*
Pharmazz Inc ..... G ..... 630 780-6087 Naperville *(G-14898)*
Pharmdium Hlthcare Hldings Inc ..... G ..... 800 523-7749 Lake Forest *(G-12288)*
Pharmedium Healthcare Corp ..... E ..... 847 457-2300 Lake Forest *(G-12289)*
Phathom Pharmaceuticals Inc ..... F ..... 650 325-5156 Buffalo Grove *(G-2584)*
Powbab Inc ..... G ..... 630 481-6140 Oak Brook *(G-15656)*
Power Partners LLC ..... G ..... 773 465-8688 Chicago *(G-5847)*
Prestige Brands Inc ..... G ..... 224 235-4049 Northbrook *(G-15464)*
Protide Pharmaceuticals Inc ..... G ..... 847 726-3100 Lake Zurich *(G-12446)*
Ravens Wood Pharmacy ..... G ..... 708 667-0525 Chicago *(G-5976)*
Renaissance SSP Holdings Inc ..... G ..... 210 476-8194 Lake Forest *(G-12295)*
▲ **Respa Pharmaceuticals Inc** ..... E ..... 630 543-3333 Addison *(G-272)*
Riverside Medi-Center Inc ..... G ..... 815 932-6632 Kankakee *(G-11999)*
Rls USA Inc ..... A ..... 865 548-1449 Arlington Heights *(G-801)*
◆ **Roundtble Hlthcare Partners LP** ..... E ..... 847 739-3200 Lake Forest *(G-12299)*
Sagent Logistics LP ..... F ..... 847 908-1600 Schaumburg *(G-18700)*
Sagent Pharmaceuticals Inc ..... C ..... 847 908-1600 Schaumburg *(G-18701)*
▲ **Sagent Pharmaceuticals Inc** ..... D ..... 847 908-1600 Schaumburg *(G-18702)*
SC Holdings LLC ..... B ..... 217 821-0304 Effingham *(G-8425)*
Senior Care Pharmacy LLC ..... G ..... 847 579-0093 Highland Park *(G-11297)*
Sfc Chemicals Ltd ..... G ..... 847 221-2152 Chicago *(G-6144)*
Shaars International Inc ..... G ..... 815 315-0717 Rockford *(G-17627)*
Shire Pharmaceuticals LLC ..... E ..... 224 940-2000 Bannockburn *(G-1207)*
Siemens Med Solutions USA Inc ..... F ..... 847 793-4429 Buffalo Grove *(G-2603)*
Sns Pharma 427 ..... G ..... 217 527-8408 Springfield *(G-19448)*
Soleo Health Inc ..... G ..... 630 478-8240 Woodridge *(G-21340)*
Specgx LLC ..... E ..... 618 664-2111 Greenville *(G-10842)*
Sterling Phrm Svcs LLC ..... F ..... 618 286-4116 East Carondelet *(G-8173)*
Sterling Phrm Svcs LLC ..... G ..... 618 286-6060 Dupo *(G-8145)*
Strategic Applications Inc ..... G ..... 847 680-9385 Lake Villa *(G-12368)*
◆ **Sukgyung At Inc** ..... G ..... 847 298-6570 Des Plaines *(G-7853)*
▲ **Sunstar Pharmaceutical Inc** ..... D ..... 773 777-4000 Elgin *(G-8742)*
Superior Biologics Il Inc ..... G ..... 847 469-2400 Schaumburg *(G-18731)*
Sustainable Innovations Inc ..... G ..... 815 713-1637 Rockford *(G-17650)*
Symbria Rx Services LLC ..... E ..... 630 981-8000 Woodridge *(G-21342)*
Synergy Advnced Phrmctcals Inc ..... B ..... 212 297-0020 Chicago *(G-6302)*
Takeda ..... G ..... 847 902-0659 Hawthorn Woods *(G-11127)*
Takeda Pharmaceuticals USA Inc ..... G ..... 847 315-9228 Bannockburn *(G-1209)*
Takeda Phrmaceuticals Intl Inc ..... A ..... 224 554-6500 Bannockburn *(G-1210)*
Taylor Pharmacal Co ..... G ..... 217 423-9715 Decatur *(G-7559)*
Temprian Therapeutics Inc ..... G ..... 513 374-1180 Chicago *(G-6346)*
Therapeutic Skin Care ..... G ..... 630 244-1833 Lombard *(G-13143)*
Topical Pharmaceuticals Inc ..... F ..... 630 396-3970 Addison *(G-313)*
Topical Pharmaceuticals Inc ..... G ..... 630 396-3970 Addison *(G-314)*
Trudeau Approved Products Inc ..... G ..... 312 924-7230 Hinsdale *(G-11382)*
Tulip Tree Gardens Co ..... G ..... 708 612-7094 Beecher *(G-1522)*
Unichem International Inc ..... E ..... 630 302-1469 Huntley *(G-11571)*
Url Pharmpro LLC ..... G ..... 630 888-3820 Aurora *(G-1030)*
Vetter CM USA LLC ..... G ..... 847 813-5895 Des Plaines *(G-7864)*
Vital Proteins LLC ..... C ..... 224 544-9110 Chicago *(G-6561)*
VPI Holdings Corp ..... G ..... 770 499-8100 Lake Forest *(G-12321)*
Wellness Center Usa Inc ..... F ..... 847 925-1885 Hoffman Estates *(G-11471)*
▼ **Winlind Skincare LLC** ..... G ..... 630 789-9408 Burr Ridge *(G-2736)*
Winston Pharmaceuticals Inc ..... G ..... 847 362-8200 Vernon Hills *(G-20111)*
Wockhardt Holding Corp ..... B ..... 847 967-5600 Morton Grove *(G-14449)*
Xellia Pharaceuticals Inc ..... E ..... 847 986-7980 Grayslake *(G-10807)*
Xellia Pharmaceuticals USA LLC ..... C ..... 847 947-0254 Buffalo Grove *(G-2623)*
Xeris Pharmaceuticals Inc ..... E ..... 844 445-5704 Chicago *(G-6693)*
▲ **Xttrium Laboratories Inc** ..... D ..... 773 268-5800 Mount Prospect *(G-14584)*

Employee Codes: A=Over 500 employees, B=251-500
C=101-250, D=51-100, E=20-50, F=10-19, G=3-9

2020 Harris Illinois
Industrial Directory

885

28 CHEMICALS AND ALLIED PRODUCTS

Yeager JI & Associates Inc ....G...... 847 283-9162
  Lake Forest (G-12324)
Zedpharma ....G...... 847 295-1950
  Lake Forest (G-12325)
Zoetis LLC ....D...... 708 757-2592
  Chicago Heights (G-6787)

2835 Diagnostic Substances

3primedx Inc ....G...... 312 621-0643
  Chicago (G-3469)
▲ Abbott Laboratories ....A...... 224 667-6100
  Abbott Park (G-1)
Abbott Laboratories ....G...... 800 551-5838
  Lake Forest (G-12218)
Abbott Laboratories ....A...... 847 932-7900
  North Chicago (G-15293)
Abbott Molecular Inc ....G...... 224 361-7800
  Des Plaines (G-7719)
▲ Abbott Molecular Inc ....D...... 224 361-7800
  Des Plaines (G-7720)
Aid For Women Northern Lk Cnty ....F...... 847 249-2700
  Gurnee (G-10855)
Amoco Technology Company ....C...... 312 861-6000
  Chicago (G-3682)
Ancillary Genomic Systems LLC ....G...... 765 714-3799
  Chicago (G-3692)
▼ Baxalta Export Corporation ....C...... 224 948-2000
  Bannockburn (G-1193)
Baxalta US Inc ....F...... 312 648-2244
  Chicago (G-3846)
Baxalta World Trade LLC ....G...... 224 940-2000
  Bannockburn (G-1195)
Baxalta Worldwide LLC ....C...... 224 948-2000
  Deerfield (G-7590)
Baxter Healthcare Corporation ....E...... 847 578-4671
  Waukegan (G-20422)
Baxter International Inc ....A...... 224 948-2000
  Deerfield (G-7595)
Bioanalytics Inc ....G...... 217 649-6820
  Monticello (G-14278)
Bion Enterprises Ltd ....E...... 847 544-5044
  Des Plaines (G-7740)
Cairo Diagnostic Center ....F...... 618 734-1500
  Cairo (G-2765)
Cooper Equipment Company Inc ....G...... 708 367-1291
  Crete (G-7137)
Fisher Scientific Company LLC ....G...... 800 528-0494
  Chicago (G-4597)
Fox Valley Pregnancy Center ....G...... 847 697-0200
  South Elgin (G-19145)
▲ GE Healthcare Holdings Inc ....A...... 847 398-8400
  Arlington Heights (G-741)
Glucosentient Inc ....G...... 217 487-4087
  Champaign (G-3297)
Guardian Angel Outreach ....G...... 815 672-4567
  Streator (G-19609)
Innovative Molecular Diagnosti ....G...... 630 845-8246
  Geneva (G-10283)
Muhammad Sotavia ....G...... 708 966-2262
  Orland Park (G-15970)
Ohmx Corporation ....F...... 847 491-8500
  Evanston (G-9561)
Ortho-Clinical Diagnostics Inc. ....G...... 618 281-3882
  Columbia (G-6993)
Petnet Solutions Inc ....G...... 847 297-3721
  Des Plaines (G-7819)
Polaris Genomics Corporation ....G...... 773 547-2350
  Mount Prospect (G-14563)
Prenosis Inc ....G...... 949 246-3113
  Chicago (G-5865)
Pyramid Sciences Inc ....G...... 630 974-6110
  Burr Ridge (G-2715)
▲ Scientific Device Lab Inc ....E...... 847 803-9495
  Des Plaines (G-7839)
Soul Training Program Inc ....G...... 312 725-9768
  Chicago (G-6205)
▲ Sysmex Reagents America Inc ....E...... 847 996-4500
  Mundelein (G-14741)
Voyant Diagnostics Inc ....G...... 630 456-6340
  Chicago (G-6571)

2836 Biological Prdts, Exc Diagnostic Substances

3abn ....G...... 618 627-4651
  Thompsonville (G-19777)
◆ Abbvie Inc ....C...... 847 932-7900
  North Chicago (G-15300)
▲ Abbvie US LLC ....G...... 800 255-5162
  North Chicago (G-15304)

Amphix Bio Inc ....G...... 720 840-7327
  Chicago (G-3684)
▲ Aspen API Inc ....F...... 847 635-0985
  Des Plaines (G-7734)
Avexis Inc ....C...... 847 572-8280
  Bannockburn (G-1190)
Avexis Inc ....C...... 847 572-8280
  Libertyville (G-12633)
Avexis Inc ....E...... 847 572-8280
  Libertyville (G-12634)
Baxter Healthcare Corporation ....C...... 800 422-9837
  Deerfield (G-7592)
Bioaffinity Inc ....G...... 815 988-5077
  Rockford (G-17324)
Biologos Inc ....G...... 630 801-4740
  Montgomery (G-14234)
Bn National Trail ....G...... 618 783-8709
  Newton (G-15081)
C & S Chemicals Inc ....G...... 815 722-6671
  Joliet (G-11837)
Cislak Manufacturing Inc ....E...... 847 647-1819
  Niles (G-15110)
Csl Behring LLC ....B...... 815 932-6773
  Bradley (G-2279)
Csl Plasma Inc ....E...... 708 343-8845
  Melrose Park (G-13845)
Culture Media Supplies Inc ....G...... 630 499-5000
  Oswego (G-15999)
Grifols Shared Svcs N Amer Inc ....F...... 309 827-3031
  Bloomington (G-2053)
Kinesis Vaccines LLC ....G...... 847 543-7725
  Grayslake (G-10786)
Laboratory Media Corporation ....F...... 630 897-8000
  Montgomery (G-14254)
Midwest Bio Manufacturing Div ....F...... 815 542-6417
  Tampico (G-19744)
Northern Ill Blood Bnk Inc ....F...... 815 965-8751
  Rockford (G-17538)
Octapharma Plasma Inc ....G...... 708 409-0900
  Northlake (G-15554)
Octapharma Plasma Inc ....G...... 217 546-8605
  Springfield (G-19416)
Proteintech Group Inc ....E...... 312 455-8498
  Rosemont (G-18045)
Ptm Biolabs Inc ....G...... 312 802-6843
  Chicago (G-5911)
Quorum Labs LLC ....G...... 618 525-5600
  Eldorado (G-8482)
Roy Winnett ....G...... 309 367-4867
  Metamora (G-13967)
Splash Dog Therapy Inc ....G...... 847 296-4007
  Des Plaines (G-7850)
Vectorbuilder Inc ....F...... 510 552-3632
  Chicago (G-6529)
▼ W-R Industries Inc ....G...... 312 733-5200
  Bellwood (G-1642)
▼ West Laboratories Inc ....E...... 815 935-1630
  Kankakee (G-12011)

2841 Soap & Detergents

A & H Manufacturing Inc ....F...... 630 543-5900
  Addison (G-13)
Aerosols Danville Inc ....G...... 773 816-5132
  Chicago (G-3574)
▲ Aerosols Danville Inc ....B...... 217 442-1400
  Danville (G-7318)
Afton Chemical Corporation ....B...... 618 583-1000
  East Saint Louis (G-8296)
AM Harper Products Inc ....F...... 312 767-8283
  Chicago (G-3640)
Ashley Lauren ....G...... 847 733-9470
  Evanston (G-9496)
◆ Atm America Corp ....E...... 800 298-0030
  Chicago (G-3770)
▲ Avatar Corporation ....D...... 708 534-5511
  University Park (G-19947)
◆ Blachford Corporation ....E...... 815 464-2100
  Frankfort (G-9773)
▲ Black Swan Manufacturing Co ....F...... 773 227-3700
  Chicago (G-3908)
Blast Products Inc ....G...... 618 452-4700
  Madison (G-13406)
Blew Chemical Company ....G...... 708 448-5780
  Palos Heights (G-16181)
Bullen Midwest Inc ....E...... 773 785-2300
  Chicago (G-3973)
▲ Cater Chemical Co ....G...... 630 980-2300
  Roselle (G-17943)
▲ Cedar Concepts Corporation ......G...... 773 890-5790
  Chicago (G-4050)

Chemstation Chicago LLC ....E...... 630 279-2857
  Elmhurst (G-9344)
◆ Chemtool Incorporated ....C...... 815 957-4140
  Rockton (G-17694)
Chemtool Incorporated ....D...... 815 459-1250
  Crystal Lake (G-7180)
◆ Combe Laboratories Inc ....C...... 217 893-4490
  Rantoul (G-16971)
Consolidated Chem Works Ltd ....E...... 312 226-6150
  Chicago (G-4222)
▲ Custom Blending & Pckaging of ..F...... 618 286-1140
  Dupo (G-8135)
Custom Chemical Inc ....C...... 217 529-0878
  Springfield (G-19357)
▲ Cygnus Corporation ....D...... 773 785-2845
  Chicago (G-4294)
Dairy Dynamics LLC ....F...... 847 758-7300
  Elk Grove Village (G-8936)
Damco Products Inc ....G...... 618 452-4700
  Madison (G-13407)
Ecolab Inc ....G...... 708 496-5378
  Palos Heights (G-16183)
Ecp Incorporated ....D...... 630 754-4200
  Woodridge (G-21297)
First Ayd Corporation ....G...... 847 622-0001
  Elgin (G-8586)
Floor-Chem Inc ....G...... 630 789-2152
  Romeoville (G-17824)
Formulations Inc ....G...... 847 674-9141
  Skokie (G-18956)
Gea Farm Technologies Inc ....E...... 630 369-8100
  Romeoville (G-17828)
◆ Gea Farm Technologies Inc ....C...... 630 548-8200
  Naperville (G-14833)
Getex Corporation ....G...... 630 993-1300
  Aurora (G-968)
Henkel Consumer Goods Inc ....D...... 847 426-4552
  Chicago (G-4801)
Henkel Consumer Goods Inc ....C...... 630 892-4381
  Montgomery (G-14246)
▼ Interflo Industries Inc ....G...... 847 228-0606
  Elk Grove Village (G-9056)
Karimi Saifuddin ....G...... 630 943-8808
  Plainfield (G-16678)
Korex Chicago LLC ....E...... 708 458-4890
  Chicago (G-5124)
Marietta Corporation ....C...... 773 816-5137
  Chicago (G-5337)
Nader Wholesale Grocers Inc ....F...... 773 582-1000
  Chicago (G-5536)
▼ Nataz Specialty Coatings Inc ......F...... 773 247-7030
  Chicago (G-5542)
People Against Dirty Mfg Pbc ....D...... 415 568-4600
  Chicago (G-5785)
PLC Corp ....G...... 847 247-1900
  Lake Bluff (G-12206)
Procter & Gamble Company ....G...... 847 375-5400
  Chicago (G-5892)
▼ Progressive Solutions Corp ....G...... 847 639-7272
  Algonquin (G-384)
Rock River Blending ....G...... 815 968-7860
  Rockford (G-17581)
Sanford Chemical Co Inc ....F...... 847 437-3530
  Elk Grove Village (G-9229)
Scott Sawvel ....G...... 815 543-4136
  Roscoe (G-17932)
Standard Indus & Auto Eqp Inc ....E...... 630 289-9500
  Hanover Park (G-11014)
Sweet Thyme Soaps ....G...... 708 848-0234
  Oak Park (G-15776)
Tri Sect Corporation ....F...... 847 524-1119
  Schaumburg (G-18754)
Unichem Corporation ....E...... 773 376-8872
  Chicago (G-6463)
▲ Vantage Oleochemicals Inc ....C...... 773 376-9000
  Chicago (G-6522)
◆ Venus Laboratories Inc ....E...... 630 595-1900
  Addison (G-328)
▲ Vvf Illinois Services LLC ....B...... 630 892-4381
  Montgomery (G-14275)
Westfalia-Surge Inc ....G...... 630 759-7346
  Romeoville (G-17887)
Wet International Inc ....E...... 630 540-2113
  Streamwood (G-19602)

2842 Spec Cleaning, Polishing & Sanitation Preparations

▲ 300 Below Inc ....G...... 217 423-3070
  Decatur (G-7431)

A J Funk & Co ... G ... 847 741-6760
Elgin *(G-8489)*
▲ Acl Inc ... F ... 773 285-0295
Chicago *(G-3525)*
Advanage Diversified Pdts Inc ... F ... 708 331-8390
Harvey *(G-11069)*
▲ Aerosols Danville Inc ... B ... 217 442-1400
Danville *(G-7318)*
Anytime Window Cleaning Inc ... G ... 773 235-5677
Chicago *(G-3709)*
Apco Enterprises Inc ... G ... 708 430-7333
Bridgeview *(G-2324)*
◆ Apex Engineering Products Corp ... F ... 630 820-8888
Aurora *(G-912)*
◆ Atm America Corp ... E ... 800 298-0030
Chicago *(G-3770)*
Bass Brother Incorporated ... G ... 800 252-1114
Des Plaines *(G-7736)*
Blue Light Inc ... E ... 630 400-4539
Lisle *(G-12873)*
Boyer Corporation ... G ... 708 352-2553
La Grange *(G-12074)*
Brite Site Supply Inc ... G ... 773 772-7300
Chicago *(G-3959)*
Bullen Midwest Inc ... E ... 773 785-2300
Chicago *(G-3973)*
Bumper Scuffs ... G ... 847 489-7926
Lake Villa *(G-12347)*
Calumet Refining LLC ... F ... 708 832-2463
Burnham *(G-2644)*
▲ Cater Chemical Co ... G ... 630 980-2300
Roselle *(G-17943)*
Champion Packaging & Dist Inc ... C ... 630 972-0100
Woodridge *(G-21283)*
Chemical Specialties Mfg Corp ... G ... 309 697-5400
Mapleton *(G-13469)*
Chemix Corp ... F ... 708 754-2150
Glenwood *(G-10639)*
◆ Chemtool Incorporated ... C ... 815 957-4140
Rockton *(G-17694)*
Chemtool Incorporated ... D ... 815 459-1250
Crystal Lake *(G-7180)*
Circle K Industries Inc ... F ... 847 949-0363
Mundelein *(G-14677)*
City of Chicago ... E ... 312 744-0940
Chicago *(G-4157)*
City of Chicago ... E ... 312 746-6583
Chicago *(G-4159)*
▼ Claire-Sprayway Inc ... E ... 630 628-3000
Downers Grove *(G-7972)*
Claire-Sprayway Inc ... D ... 630 628-3000
Downers Grove *(G-7973)*
CLC Lubricants Company ... E ... 630 232-7900
Geneva *(G-10261)*
Clifton Chemical Company ... F ... 815 697-2343
Chebanse *(G-3429)*
Clorox Company ... E ... 510 271-7000
Willowbrook *(G-21036)*
Clorox Hidden Valley Mfg ... F ... 847 229-5500
Wheeling *(G-20871)*
Clorox Manufacturing Company ... C ... 847 229-5500
Wheeling *(G-20872)*
Colorex Chemical Co Inc ... G ... 630 238-3124
Bensenville *(G-1774)*
▲ Concept Laboratories Inc ... D ... 773 395-7300
Chicago *(G-4214)*
Consolidated Chem Works Ltd ... E ... 312 226-6150
Chicago *(G-4222)*
Coral Chemical Company ... E ... 847 246-6666
Zion *(G-21510)*
Creative Metal Products ... F ... 773 638-3200
Chicago *(G-4264)*
Damco Products Inc ... G ... 618 452-4700
Madison *(G-13407)*
Danko Industries ... G ... 630 882-6070
Yorkville *(G-21477)*
Detrex Corporation ... G ... 708 345-3806
Melrose Park *(G-13849)*
◆ Dober Chemical Corp ... C ... 630 410-7300
Woodridge *(G-21294)*
Doris Company ... G ... 224 302-5605
Round Lake Park *(G-18096)*
▼ Dura Wax Company ... F ... 815 385-5000
McHenry *(G-13739)*
Duraclean International Inc ... F ... 847 704-7100
Arlington Heights *(G-730)*
Ecolab Inc ... E ... 815 389-3441
Roscoe *(G-17905)*
Ecolab Inc ... E ... 815 729-7334
Joliet *(G-11857)*
Ecolab Inc ... G ... 847 350-2229
Elk Grove Village *(G-8967)*
Ecolab Inc ... E ... 847 350-2229
Elk Grove Village *(G-8968)*
Ecp Incorporated ... D ... 630 754-4200
Woodridge *(G-21297)*
▲ Elco Laboratories Inc ... D ... 708 534-3000
Coal City *(G-6932)*
First Ayd Corporation ... D ... 847 622-0001
Elgin *(G-8586)*
Floor-Chem Inc ... G ... 630 789-2152
Romeoville *(G-17824)*
Fola Community Action Services ... F ... 773 487-4310
Chicago *(G-4615)*
Formulations Inc ... G ... 847 674-9141
Skokie *(G-18956)*
▲ Fox Valley Chemical Company ... G ... 815 653-2660
Ringwood *(G-17043)*
Frank Miller & Sons Inc ... E ... 708 201-7200
Mokena *(G-14083)*
Gea Farm Technologies Inc ... E ... 630 369-8100
Romeoville *(G-17828)*
◆ Gea Farm Technologies Inc ... C ... 630 548-8200
Naperville *(G-14833)*
Getex Corporation ... G ... 630 993-1300
Aurora *(G-968)*
Gfl Environmental Svcs USA Inc ... E ... 866 579-6900
Mokena *(G-14088)*
Henkel Consumer Goods Inc ... C ... 630 892-4381
Montgomery *(G-14246)*
Houghton International Inc ... F ... 610 666-4000
Chicago *(G-4849)*
Hurst Chemical Company ... G ... 815 964-0451
Rockford *(G-17454)*
▼ Imagination Products Corp ... E ... 309 274-6223
Chillicothe *(G-6818)*
▼ Interflo Industries Inc ... G ... 847 228-0606
Elk Grove Village *(G-9056)*
Jacob Hay Company ... G ... 847 215-8880
Wheeling *(G-20918)*
Jaffee Investment Partnr LP ... C ... 312 321-1515
Chicago *(G-4999)*
K-Technology Inc ... G ... 708 458-4890
Chicago *(G-5072)*
◆ Kafko International Ltd ... E ... 847 763-0333
Skokie *(G-18971)*
Kik International Inc ... F ... 905 660-0444
Carol Stream *(G-3010)*
Kocour Co ... E ... 773 847-1111
Chicago *(G-5114)*
Korex Chicago LLC ... E ... 708 458-4890
Chicago *(G-5124)*
▼ Lundmark Inc ... F ... 630 628-1199
Addison *(G-186)*
Mackenzie Johnson ... G ... 630 244-2367
Maywood *(G-13672)*
◆ Minuteman International Inc ... C ... 630 627-6900
Pingree Grove *(G-16622)*
Newby Oil Company Inc ... G ... 815 756-7688
Sycamore *(G-19725)*
▲ Odorite International Inc ... F ... 816 920-5000
Saint Charles *(G-18236)*
Odors Away LLC ... G ... 888 235-7559
Elgin *(G-8676)*
Oil-Dri Corporation America ... D ... 312 321-1515
Chicago *(G-5666)*
Oil-Dri Corporation America ... D ... 618 745-6881
Mounds *(G-14463)*
◆ Penray Companies Inc ... D ... 800 323-6329
Downers Grove *(G-8071)*
Pete Frcano Sons Cstm HM Bldrs ... F ... 847 258-4626
Elk Grove Village *(G-9175)*
PLC Corp ... G ... 847 247-1900
Lake Bluff *(G-12206)*
Premium Oil Company ... F ... 815 963-3800
Rockford *(G-17559)*
Princeton Sealing Wax Co ... G ... 815 875-1943
Princeton *(G-16821)*
Procter & Gamble Company ... G ... 847 375-5400
Chicago *(G-5892)*
◆ Protective Products Intl ... G ... 847 526-1180
Wauconda *(G-20386)*
R E Z Packaging Inc ... G ... 773 247-0800
Chicago *(G-5945)*
R R Street & Co Inc ... E ... 773 247-1190
Chicago *(G-5951)*
R R Street & Co Inc ... E ... 630 416-4244
Naperville *(G-14905)*
R R Street & Co Inc ... F ... 773 254-1277
Chicago *(G-5952)*
Rainbow Cleaners ... G ... 630 789-6989
Westmont *(G-20768)*
▲ Rd Husemoller Ltd ... F ... 847 526-5505
Wauconda *(G-20388)*
Reed-Union Corporation ... F ... 312 644-3200
Chicago *(G-5996)*
Rochester Midland Corporation ... E ... 630 896-8543
Montgomery *(G-14267)*
Rock-Tred 2 LLC ... E ... 888 762-5873
Waukegan *(G-20489)*
◆ Rust-Oleum Corporation ... C ... 847 367-7700
Vernon Hills *(G-20089)*
◆ Rycoline Products LLC ... C ... 773 775-6755
Chicago *(G-6081)*
S C Johnson & Son Inc ... C ... 312 702-3100
Chicago *(G-6085)*
▲ Sandstrom Products Company ... E ... 309 523-2121
Port Byron *(G-16787)*
Sandstrom Products Company ... F ... 309 523-2121
Port Byron *(G-16788)*
Science Solutions LLC ... G ... 773 261-1197
Chicago *(G-6118)*
Scs Company ... E ... 708 269-2094
Crestwood *(G-7126)*
Sneaky Clean LLC ... G ... 312 550-9654
Downers Grove *(G-8097)*
Stellar Blending & Packaging ... F ... 314 520-7318
Dupo *(G-8144)*
Teitelbaum Brothers Inc ... G ... 847 729-3490
Glenview *(G-10630)*
▲ Tiger Accessory Group LLC ... F ... 847 821-9630
Long Grove *(G-13171)*
◆ Treatment Products Ltd ... E ... 773 626-8888
Chicago *(G-6414)*
Tri Sect Corporation ... F ... 847 524-1119
Schaumburg *(G-18754)*
Umf Corporation ... G ... 224 251-7822
Niles *(G-15184)*
◆ Umf Corporation ... F ... 847 920-0370
Skokie *(G-19049)*
◆ United Laboratories Inc ... D ... 630 377-0900
Saint Charles *(G-18295)*
Vanguard Chemical Corporation ... F ... 312 751-0717
Chicago *(G-6520)*
◆ Venus Laboratories Inc ... E ... 630 595-1900
Addison *(G-328)*
Voodoo Ride LLC ... G ... 312 944-0465
Chicago *(G-6569)*
Zoes Mfgco LLC ... F ... 312 666-4018
Chicago *(G-6722)*

2843 Surface Active & Finishing Agents, Sulfonated Oils

▲ Aerosols Danville Inc ... B ... 217 442-1400
Danville *(G-7318)*
▲ Avatar Corporation ... D ... 708 534-5511
University Park *(G-19947)*
▲ Cedar Concepts Corporation ... E ... 773 890-5790
Chicago *(G-4050)*
▲ Custom Blending & Pckaging of ... F ... 618 286-1140
Dupo *(G-8135)*
Griffin Industries LLC ... G ... 815 357-8200
Seneca *(G-18858)*
Houghton International Inc ... F ... 610 666-4000
Chicago *(G-4849)*
Ilf Technologies LLC ... G ... 630 789-9770
Willowbrook *(G-21047)*
▲ ISachs Sons Inc ... F ... 312 733-2815
Chicago *(G-4971)*
▲ Ivanhoe Industries Inc ... E ... 847 872-3311
Mundelein *(G-14702)*
Sadelco USA Corp ... G ... 847 781-8844
Hoffman Estates *(G-11454)*
Sanford Chemical Co Inc ... F ... 847 437-3530
Elk Grove Village *(G-9229)*
Solvay USA Inc ... E ... 708 371-2000
Blue Island *(G-2141)*
◆ Stepan Company ... B ... 847 446-7500
Northfield *(G-15531)*
Sun Ag Inc ... G ... 815 689-2144
Cullom *(G-7302)*
Union Drainage District ... G ... 618 445-2843
Mount Erie *(G-14498)*
Vantage Specialties Inc ... F ... 773 579-5842
Gurnee *(G-10942)*
Vantage Specialties Inc ... G ... 847 244-3410
Chicago *(G-6523)*

SIC

2844 Perfumes, Cosmetics & Toilet Preparations

4 Elements Company ... G ... 773 236-2284
Mundelein *(G-14655)*

A & H Manufacturing Inc ... F ... 630 543-5900
Addison *(G-13)*

A&B Apparel ... G ... 815 962-5070
Rockford *(G-17281)*

Abyss Salon Inc ... G ... 312 880-0263
Chicago *(G-3512)*

Aerosols Danville Inc ... G ... 773 816-5132
Chicago *(G-3574)*

▲ Aerosols Danville Inc ... B ... 217 442-1400
Danville *(G-7318)*

Affirmed LLC ... G ... 847 550-0170
Lake Zurich *(G-12381)*

All Dental ... G ... 708 749-0277
Berwyn *(G-1948)*

Amedico Laboratories LLC ... G ... 347 857-7546
Oakbrook Terrace *(G-15783)*

Anderson Lanette ... G ... 217 284-6603
Springfield *(G-19318)*

Art of Shaving - Fl LLC ... G ... 630 495-7316
Lombard *(G-13040)*

Art of Shaving - Fl LLC ... G ... 312 527-1604
Chicago *(G-3737)*

Art of Shaving - Fl LLC ... G ... 630 684-0277
Oak Brook *(G-15594)*

◆ Atm America Corp ... E ... 800 298-0030
Chicago *(G-3770)*

◆ Avlon Industries Inc ... D ... 708 344-0709
Melrose Park *(G-13829)*

Be Products Inc ... G ... 312 201-9669
Chicago *(G-3849)*

Bearmoon LLC ... G ... 815 312-2327
Oregon *(G-15912)*

Belle-Aire Fragrances Inc ... E ... 847 816-3500
Mundelein *(G-14666)*

Bethany Pharmacol Co Inc ... G ... 217 665-3395
Bethany *(G-1967)*

◆ Biocare Labs Inc ... G ... 708 496-8657
Posen *(G-16791)*

Bioelements Inc ... F ... 773 525-3509
Chicago *(G-3895)*

Body Wipe Corporation ... G ... 847 687-9321
Mundelein *(G-14667)*

▲ Cedar Concepts Corporation ... E ... 773 890-5790
Chicago *(G-4050)*

▲ Chemquest International Inc ... E ... 630 628-1900
Addison *(G-68)*

Clintex Laboratories Inc ... E ... 773 493-9777
Chicago *(G-4179)*

Collagen Usa Inc ... G ... 708 716-0251
Chicago *(G-4200)*

◆ Combe Laboratories Inc ... C ... 217 893-4490
Rantoul *(G-16971)*

Common Scents Mom ... G ... 309 389-3216
Mapleton *(G-13471)*

▲ Concept Laboratories Inc ... D ... 773 395-7300
Chicago *(G-4214)*

Conopco Inc ... C ... 773 916-4400
Chicago *(G-4220)*

Curlmix Inc ... G ... 773 234-6891
Chicago *(G-4286)*

D-Orum Corporation ... F ... 773 567-2064
Chicago *(G-4302)*

▲ Delta Laboratories Inc ... G ... 630 351-1798
Elk Grove Village *(G-8942)*

Deputante Inc ... G ... 773 545-9531
Chicago *(G-4342)*

Desforte LLC ... G ... 224 301-5364
Chicago *(G-4343)*

Dzro-Bans International Inc ... G ... 779 324-2740
Homewood *(G-11492)*

◆ Ecoco Inc ... E ... 773 745-7700
Chicago *(G-4448)*

▲ Eggology Inc ... F ... 818 610-2222
Pearl City *(G-16319)*

Emlin Cosmetics Inc ... D ... 630 860-5773
Bensenville *(G-1796)*

Essential Laser and Skin Inst ... G ... 815 381-7005
Rockford *(G-17401)*

Fareva Morton Grove Inc ... G ... 847 966-0200
Morton Grove *(G-14406)*

Formulations Inc ... G ... 847 674-9141
Skokie *(G-18956)*

Garcoa Inc ... B ... 708 905-5118
Brookfield *(G-2484)*

◆ Geka Manufacturing Corporation ... E ... 224 238-5080
Elgin *(G-8592)*

Gillette Company ... D ... 847 689-3111
North Chicago *(G-15312)*

Givaudan Fragrances Corp ... G ... 847 735-0221
Lake Forest *(G-12250)*

H N C Products Inc ... E ... 309 319-2151
Bloomington *(G-2055)*

Handcrafted By Jackie Turbot ... G ... 815 708-7200
Roscoe *(G-17909)*

Healing Scents ... G ... 815 874-0924
Rockford *(G-17446)*

Henkel Consumer Goods Inc ... C ... 630 892-4381
Montgomery *(G-14246)*

Holland Specialty Co ... E ... 309 697-9262
Peoria *(G-16453)*

▲ Hydrox Chemical Company Inc ... D ... 847 468-9400
Elgin *(G-8618)*

Inkjet Inc ... G ... 800 280-3245
Hoffman Estates *(G-11429)*

▲ Jindilli Beverages LLC ... G ... 630 581-5697
Burr Ridge *(G-2692)*

Kellyjo Makes Scents ... G ... 618 281-4241
Columbia *(G-6990)*

▲ Lab TEC Cosmt By Marzena Inc ... F ... 630 396-3970
Addison *(G-178)*

Labtec Cosmetics ... G ... 630 359-4569
Addison *(G-179)*

Lasner Bros Inc ... G ... 773 935-7383
Chicago *(G-5178)*

◆ Luster Products Inc ... B ... 773 579-1800
Chicago *(G-5287)*

Luxis International Inc ... G ... 800 240-1473
Dekalb *(G-7689)*

Luxurious Lathers Ltd ... G ... 844 877-7627
Hinsdale *(G-11369)*

▲ Marcy Laboratories Inc ... E ... 630 377-6655
West Chicago *(G-20614)*

Market Ready Inc ... G ... 847 689-1000
Round Lake Park *(G-18097)*

Maynard Inc ... G ... 773 235-5225
Chicago *(G-5371)*

Michael Christopher Ltd ... G ... 815 308-5018
Woodstock *(G-21410)*

Moorket Inc ... G ... 888 275-0277
South Holland *(G-19233)*

Moz Nutraceuticals LLC ... E ... 314 315-2541
Mount Vernon *(G-14627)*

Mseed Group LLC ... G ... 847 226-1147
South Holland *(G-19234)*

◆ Namaste Laboratories LLC ... D ... 708 824-1393
Chicago *(G-5539)*

▲ Natural Beginnings ... G ... 773 457-0509
Plainfield *(G-16693)*

New Usn Chicago LLC ... D ... 847 635-6772
Mount Prospect *(G-14551)*

Oak Court Creations ... G ... 815 467-7676
Minooka *(G-14065)*

Paket Corporation ... E ... 773 221-7300
Chicago *(G-5743)*

Pal Midwest Ltd ... G ... 815 965-2981
Rockford *(G-17546)*

Pearl Bath Bombs Inc ... F ... 312 661-2881
Chicago *(G-5777)*

Pivotal Production LLC ... G ... 773 726-7706
Chicago *(G-5815)*

Prevention Health Sciences Inc ... G ... 618 252-6922
Raleigh *(G-16962)*

Princeton Chemicals Inc ... G ... 847 975-6210
Highland Park *(G-11292)*

Pro-Line Winning Ways & Penlan ... G ... 309 745-8530
Washington *(G-20277)*

Procter & Gamble Company ... G ... 847 375-5400
Chicago *(G-5892)*

Proximity Capital Partners LLC ... F ... 773 628-7751
Chicago *(G-5909)*

▼ Raani Corporation ... C ... 708 496-1035
Bedford Park *(G-1496)*

Revlon Inc ... G ... 847 240-1558
Schaumburg *(G-18696)*

◆ RITA Corporation ... E ... 815 337-2500
Crystal Lake *(G-7257)*

◆ Rna Corporation ... D ... 708 597-7777
Blue Island *(G-2137)*

S C Johnson & Son Inc ... C ... 312 702-3100
Chicago *(G-6085)*

Safe Effective Alternatives ... F ... 618 236-2727
Belleville *(G-1595)*

San Telmo Ltd ... G ... 847 842-9115
Barrington *(G-1243)*

Schmit Laboratories Inc ... E ... 773 476-0072
Glendale Heights *(G-10491)*

▲ Sigan America LLC ... D ... 815 431-9830
Ottawa *(G-16076)*

Sigan America Holdings LLC ... G ... 815 431-9830
Ottawa *(G-16077)*

◆ Skyline Beauty Supply Inc ... F ... 773 275-6003
Franklin Park *(G-10047)*

Smile Aromatics Inc ... E ... 847 759-0350
Des Plaines *(G-7847)*

Spike Nanotech Inc ... G ... 847 504-6273
Matteson *(G-13629)*

Summit Laboratories Inc ... E ... 708 333-2995
Harvey *(G-11097)*

◆ Sunstar Americas Inc ... B ... 847 794-4157
Schaumburg *(G-18730)*

▲ Sunstar Pharmaceutical Inc ... D ... 773 777-4000
Elgin *(G-8742)*

Suretint Technologies LLC ... G ... 847 509-3625
Mount Prospect *(G-14574)*

Takasago Intl Corp USA ... G ... 815 479-5030
Crystal Lake *(G-7275)*

Tiege Hanley LLC ... G ... 312 953-4131
Chicago *(G-6377)*

Transom Symphony Opco LLC ... C ... 203 951-1919
Rantoul *(G-16984)*

▲ Tru Fragrance & Beauty LLC ... E ... 630 563-4110
Willowbrook *(G-21065)*

True Royalty Scents ... G ... 309 992-0688
Peoria *(G-16539)*

Trumans Brands LLC ... F ... 224 302-5605
Round Lake Park *(G-18099)*

Vee Pak LLC ... D ... 708 482-8881
Hodgkins *(G-11399)*

Vee Pak LLC ... E ... 708 482-8881
Countryside *(G-7076)*

Voyant Beauty LLC ... G ... 708 482-8881
Hodgkins *(G-11400)*

VPI Holding Company LLC ... G ... 312 255-4800
Chicago *(G-6572)*

▲ W-R Industries Inc ... G ... 312 733-5200
Bellwood *(G-1642)*

Walgreen Asia Services Sarl ... G ... 847 527-4341
Northbrook *(G-15499)*

Zotos International Inc ... C ... 847 390-0984
Rosemont *(G-18061)*

2851 Paints, Varnishes, Lacquers, Enamels

3d Printer Experience LLC ... G ... 312 896-3399
Chicago *(G-3468)*

▲ Accurate Color Compounding Inc ... E ... 630 978-1227
Aurora *(G-1041)*

Acm Inc ... G ... 847 473-1991
North Chicago *(G-15305)*

Agi Corp ... F ... 815 708-0502
Loves Park *(G-13184)*

Akzo Nobel Coatings Inc ... E ... 630 792-1619
Lombard *(G-13038)*

Akzo Nobel Coatings Inc ... F ... 847 623-4200
Waukegan *(G-20411)*

Akzo Nobel Coatings Inc ... F ... 312 544-7057
Chicago *(G-3595)*

Alliance Industries Inc ... F ... 847 288-9090
Broadview *(G-2416)*

▲ Alpha Coating Technologies LLC ... E ... 630 268-8787
West Chicago *(G-20535)*

▲ Alvar Inc ... F ... 309 248-7523
Washburn *(G-20262)*

▲ American Powder Coatings Inc ... E ... 630 762-0100
Saint Charles *(G-18146)*

Ata Finishing Corp ... G ... 847 677-8560
Skokie *(G-18925)*

▲ Atlas Putty Products Co ... D ... 708 429-5858
Tinley Park *(G-19806)*

Automatic Anodizing Corp ... E ... 773 478-3304
Chicago *(G-3777)*

Autonomic Materials Inc ... F ... 217 863-2023
Champaign *(G-3270)*

Basement Dewatering Systems ... F ... 309 647-0331
Canton *(G-2821)*

Behr Process Corporation ... D ... 630 289-6247
Bartlett *(G-1269)*

Behr Process Corporation ... D ... 708 753-0136
Chicago Heights *(G-6734)*

Behr Process Corporation ... D ... 708 753-1820
Lynwood *(G-13292)*

Behr Process Corporation ... C ... 708 757-6350
Chicago Heights *(G-6735)*

Belzona Gateway Inc ... G ... 888 774-2984
Caseyville *(G-3210)*

▲ Black Swan Manufacturing Co ... F ... 773 227-3700
Chicago *(G-3908)*

SIC SECTION
28 CHEMICALS AND ALLIED PRODUCTS

Company	Code	Phone
Carbit Corporation — Chicago (G-4023)	D	312 280-2300
Chase Corporation — Evanston (G-9503)	E	847 866-8500
◆ Chase Products Co — Broadview (G-2425)	D	708 865-1000
Chemix Corp — Glenwood (G-10639)	F	708 754-2150
Chicago Aerosol LLC — Bridgeview (G-2333)	D	708 598-7100
▲ Chromium Industries Inc — Chicago (G-4145)	E	773 287-3716
CIS Systems Inc — Glenview (G-10537)	G	847 827-0747
Clariant Plas Coatings USA LLC — West Chicago (G-20562)	D	630 562-9700
▲ Coatings International Inc — Franklin Park (G-9912)	E	847 455-1400
Continental Supply Co — Palos Heights (G-16182)	G	708 448-2728
Contract Transportation Sys Co — Effingham (G-8393)	C	217 342-5757
Creekside Exterior Solutions — Mulberry Grove (G-14653)	G	618 326-7654
Custom Chemical Inc — Springfield (G-19357)	E	217 529-0878
D and R Tech — Schaumburg (G-18503)	G	224 353-6693
Dip Seal Plastics Inc — Rockford (G-17379)	G	815 398-3533
▲ DSM Desotech Inc — Elgin (G-8570)	C	847 697-0400
Dunamis International — Chicago (G-4405)	G	773 504-5733
Dyco-TEC Products Ltd — Bartlett (G-1275)	G	630 837-6410
Endura Paint Chicago — Joliet (G-11861)	G	815 630-5083
F H Leinweber Co Inc — Chicago (G-4548)	E	773 568-7722
▲ Federated Paint Mfg Co — Chicago (G-4572)	F	708 345-4848
Finishes Unlimited Inc — Sugar Grove (G-19644)	F	630 466-4881
Finishing Company — Addison (G-122)	C	630 559-0808
▼ G J Nikolas & Co Inc — Bellwood (G-1625)	E	708 544-0320
▲ Gibraltar Chemical Works Inc — South Holland (G-19214)	F	708 333-0600
Hallstar Company — Bedford Park (G-1470)	D	708 594-5947
Hentzen Coatings Inc — Batavia (G-1384)	E	414 353-4200
I Pulloma Paints — Carpentersville (G-3104)	F	847 426-4140
If Walls Could Talk — South Elgin (G-19154)	G	847 219-5527
Inhance Technologies LLC — West Chicago (G-20595)	E	630 231-7515
International Paint LLC — Waukegan (G-20450)	F	847 623-4200
Jet Rack Corp — Chicago (G-5025)	E	773 586-2150
Jfb Hart Coatings Inc — Downers Grove (G-8034)	F	630 783-1917
▲ JR Edwrds Brshes Rollers Inc — Kankakee (G-11984)	E	815 933-3742
Kns Companies Inc — Carol Stream (G-3013)	E	630 665-9010
▲ Lawter Inc — Chicago (G-5185)	E	312 662-5700
◆ Magnum International Inc — Lansing (G-12507)	G	708 889-9999
Master Builders LLC — Gurnee (G-10895)	E	847 249-4080
Mate Technologies Inc — Elgin (G-8652)	F	847 289-1010
Metro Paint Supplies — Midlothian (G-13994)	G	708 385-7701
▲ Mid-Amrica Prtctive Ctings Inc — Addison (G-208)	G	630 628-4501
Midwest Ground Effects — Plainfield (G-16688)	G	708 516-5874
Miller Purcell Co Inc — New Lenox (G-15043)	G	815 485-2142
Mla Franklin Park Inc — Franklin Park (G-10003)	F	847 451-0279
◆ Morton Salt Inc — Chicago (G-5501)	C	312 807-2000
▼ Nataz Specialty Coatings Inc — Chicago (G-5542)	F	773 247-7030
▲ National Coatings Inc — Galesburg (G-10213)	E	309 342-4184
▲ Nb Coatings Inc — Lansing (G-12510)	C	800 323-3224
Neverstrip LLC — Hinsdale (G-11370)	G	708 588-9707
Nfca — Hillside (G-11350)	G	708 236-3411
Nu-Puttie Corporation — Maywood (G-13676)	E	708 681-1040
Owens Corning Sales LLC — Argo (G-675)	E	708 594-6935
◆ Penray Companies Inc — Downers Grove (G-8071)	C	800 323-6329
Petrochem Inc — Saint Charles (G-18245)	G	630 513-6350
▲ Plastics Color Corp Illinois — Calumet City (G-2787)	D	708 868-3800
Pmc Inc — Calumet City (G-2788)	F	708 868-3800
Polymer Nation LLC — Waukegan (G-20479)	G	847 972-2157
Polyone Corporation — Elk Grove Village (G-9183)	G	847 364-0011
Polyone Corporation — Romeoville (G-17865)	D	630 972-0505
Porcelain Enamel Finishers — Chicago (G-5845)	E	312 808-1560
PPG Architectural Finishes Inc — Peoria (G-16500)	G	309 673-3761
PPG Industries Inc — Gurnee (G-10913)	G	847 244-3410
PPG Industries Inc — Alsip (G-495)	G	708 597-7044
PPG Industries Inc — Elgin (G-8693)	E	847 742-3340
PPG Industries Inc — O Fallon (G-15582)	G	618 206-2250
PPG Industries Inc — Chicago (G-5851)	E	312 666-2277
PPG Industries Inc — Westmont (G-20766)	G	630 960-3600
PPG Vpn — Aurora (G-1145)	G	630 907-8910
Premium Products Inc — Yorkville (G-21498)	F	630 553-6160
Prescription Plus Ltd — Lebanon (G-12546)	F	618 537-6202
Quality Coating Co — Princeton (G-16822)	F	815 875-3228
R C Industries Inc — Chicago (G-5944)	F	773 378-1118
Rdl Marketing Inc — Chicago (G-5980)	F	773 254-7600
Reichhold Industries Inc — Morris (G-14325)	E	815 942-4600
Rock-Tred 2 LLC — Waukegan (G-20489)	E	888 762-5873
▼ Rust-Leum Con Prtction Systems — Vernon Hills (G-20087)	E	918 446-6399
Rust-Oleum (canada) Ltd — Vernon Hills (G-20088)	G	847 367-7700
Rust-Oleum Corporation — Rockford (G-17617)	D	815 967-4258
◆ Rust-Oleum Corporation — Vernon Hills (G-20089)	C	847 367-7700
▲ Sandstrom Products Company — Port Byron (G-16787)	F	309 523-2121
Sandstrom Products Company — Port Byron (G-16788)	F	309 523-2121
Sarco Putty Company — Chicago (G-6104)	G	773 735-5577
Sectional Snow Plow — Bradley (G-2291)	F	815 932-7569
◆ Seymour of Sycamore Inc — Sycamore (G-19730)	C	815 895-9101
Sherwin-Williams Company — Wheeling (G-20983)	D	847 541-9000
Sherwin-Williams Company — Rockford (G-17630)	E	815 987-3700
Sherwin-Williams Company — Savoy (G-18416)	G	217 359-4934
Sherwin-Williams Company — Elmhurst (G-9427)	G	630 834-1470
Sherwin-Williams Company — Flora (G-9691)	C	618 662-4415
Sherwin-Williams Company — Libertyville (G-12706)	G	847 573-0240
Sherwin-Williams Company — Woodstock (G-21434)	G	815 337-0942
Sherwin-Williams Company — Long Grove (G-13170)	G	847 478-0677
Sherwin-Williams Company — Westchester (G-20710)	G	708 409-4728
Sherwin-Williams Company — Romeoville (G-17876)	G	815 254-3559
Sherwin-Williams Company — Chicago (G-6152)	D	773 821-3027
Snow Command Incorporated — Flossmoor (G-9701)	G	708 991-7004
Snow Control Inc — Orland Park (G-15980)	G	708 670-6269
Tamms Industries Inc — Kirkland (G-12066)	D	815 522-3394
Taylor Coating Sales Inc — Brookfield (G-2494)	G	708 387-0305
Taylor Consultants Inc — Brookfield (G-2495)	G	708 387-0305
Tennant Company — Chicago (G-6350)	E	773 376-7132
▲ Testor Corporation — Rockford (G-17656)	D	815 962-6654
Tms Manufacturing Co — Alsip (G-516)	E	847 353-8000
Tru Serv Corp — Chicago (G-6435)	F	773 695-5674
True Value Company LLC — Cary (G-3196)	E	847 639-5383
◆ True Value Company LLC — Chicago (G-6437)	B	773 695-5000
U S Colors & Coatings Inc — Batavia (G-1435)	G	630 879-8898
United Gilsonite Labs Inc — Jacksonville (G-11784)	E	217 243-7878
▼ Universal Chem & Coatings Inc — Elgin (G-8769)	E	847 931-1700
Universal Chem & Coatings Inc — Elk Grove Village (G-9299)	E	847 297-2001
V J Dolan & Company Inc — Chicago (G-6514)	F	773 237-0100
Valspar — East Moline (G-8245)	G	309 743-7133
Vanex Inc — Mount Vernon (G-14643)	F	618 244-1413
▲ Voges Inc — Belleville (G-1608)	D	618 233-2760
▲ We Are Done LLC — Bridgeview (G-2398)	E	708 598-7100
◆ Willims-Hyward Intl Ctings Inc — Summit Argo (G-19685)	F	708 563-5182
Willims-Hyward Intl Ctings Inc — Argo (G-678)	F	708 458-0015
Yourfeel Products Corp — South Holland (G-19250)	F	708 596-2150

2861 Gum & Wood Chemicals

Company	Code	Phone
Bradley Smoker USA Inc — Galesburg (G-10186)	F	309 343-1124
Ryano Resins Inc — Aurora (G-1015)	G	630 621-5677

2865 Cyclic-Crudes, Intermediates, Dyes & Org Pigments

Company	Code	Phone
Apex Colors — Chicago (G-3710)	G	219 764-3301
◆ BP Amoco Chemical Company — Naperville (G-14782)	B	630 420-5111
▲ Chroma Color Corporation — McHenry (G-13726)	C	877 385-8777
Clariant Plas Coatings USA LLC — West Chicago (G-20562)	D	630 562-9700
Colors For Plastics Inc — Elk Grove Village (G-8901)	E	847 437-0033
Discount Computer Supply Inc — Buffalo Grove (G-2533)	G	847 883-8743
▲ General Press Colors Ltd — Chicago (G-4677)	E	630 543-7878
HI Tech Colorants — Saint Charles (G-18206)	E	630 762-0368
Koppers Industries Inc — Cicero (G-6859)	E	708 656-5900
Miller Purcell Co Inc — New Lenox (G-15043)	G	815 485-2142
▲ Nb Coatings Inc — Lansing (G-12510)	C	800 323-3224
Polyone Corporation — Elk Grove Village (G-9183)	D	847 364-0011

Employee Codes: A=Over 500 employees, B=251-500
C=101-250, D=51-100, E=20-50, F=10-19, G=3-9

28 CHEMICALS AND ALLIED PRODUCTS

Polyone Corporation ....D....... 630 972-0505
  Romeoville (G-17865)
▲ Rite Systems East Inc ....E....... 630 293-9174
  West Chicago (G-20637)
S C Johnson & Son Inc ....C....... 312 702-3100
  Chicago (G-6085)
▲ Scientific Colors Inc 815 741-1391
  Rockdale (G-17273)
Scientific Colors Inc ....C....... 815 744-5650
  Rockdale (G-17274)
◆ Southern Color Company Inc ....G....... 770 386-4766
  East Saint Louis (G-8323)
Stepan Company ....B....... 847 446-7500
  Elwood (G-9464)
◆ Stepan Company ....B....... 847 446-7500
  Northfield (G-15531)
U S Colors & Coatings Inc ....G....... 630 879-8898
  Batavia (G-1435)

2869 Industrial Organic Chemicals, NEC

◆ AB Specialty Silicones LLC ....D....... 908 273-8015
  Waukegan (G-20405)
Adkins Energy LLC ....E....... 815 369-9173
  Lena (G-12597)
Afs Inc ....F....... 847 437-2345
  Arlington Heights (G-684)
Afton Chemical Corporation ....B....... 618 583-1000
  East Saint Louis (G-8296)
AMP Americas LLC ....E....... 312 300-6700
  Chicago (G-3683)
▲ Amtex Chemicals LLC ....G....... 630 268-0085
  Lombard (G-13039)
Arvens Technology Inc ....G....... 650 776-5443
  Peoria (G-16387)
▲ Aspen API Inc ....F....... 847 635-0985
  Des Plaines (G-7734)
▼ AST Industries Inc ....F....... 847 455-2300
  Franklin Park (G-9878)
▼ Atmosphere Global LLC ....G....... 630 660-2833
  Chicago (G-3772)
Austins Saloon & Eatery ....G....... 847 549-1972
  Libertyville (G-12632)
▲ Avatar Corporation ....D....... 708 534-5511
  University Park (G-19947)
Aventine Rnwble Enrgy Hldngs L ...E....... 309 347-9200
  Pekin (G-16324)
Bala & Anula Fuels Inc ....G....... 630 766-1807
  Bensenville (G-1751)
BASF Corporation ....B....... 815 932-6751
  Kankakee (G-11959)
◆ Bell Flavors & Fragrances Inc ....C....... 847 291-8300
  Northbrook (G-15346)
Bell Flavors & Fragrances Inc ....G....... 847 291-8300
  Northbrook (G-15347)
Belle-Aire Fragrances Inc ....E....... 847 816-3500
  Mundelein (G-14666)
Big River Prairie Gold LLC ....G....... 319 753-1100
  Galva (G-10227)
Big River Resources Galva LLC .....C....... 309 932-2033
  Galva (G-10228)
Big Rver Rsrces W Brlngton LLC ...G....... 309 734-8423
  Monmouth (G-13413)
◆ BP Amoco Chemical Company ....B....... 630 420-5111
  Naperville (G-14782)
Bps Fuels Inc ....G....... 217 452-7608
  Virginia (G-20192)
Breakfast Fuel LLC ....G....... 847 251-3835
  Wilmette (G-21072)
Bullen Midwest Inc ....E....... 773 785-2300
  Chicago (G-3973)
▲ C U Plastic LLC ....G....... 888 957-9993
  Rochelle (G-17133)
Campbell Camie Inc ....G....... 314 968-3222
  Downers Grove (G-7963)
▲ Cedar Concepts Corporation ....E....... 773 890-5790
  Chicago (G-4050)
Center Ethanol Company LLC ....E....... 618 875-3008
  Sauget (G-18391)
Cheers Food and Fuel 240 ....G....... 618 995-9153
  Goreville (G-10679)
Cheers Food Fuel ....G....... 618 827-4836
  Dongola (G-7942)
Chem Free Solutions ....G....... 630 541-7931
  Darien (G-7403)
Chemtura Corporation 309 633-9480
  Mapleton (G-13470)
Chrisman Fuel ....G....... 217 463-3400
  Paris (G-16227)
Clean Motion Inc ....F....... 607 323-1778
  (G-4173)

Cooper Oil Co ....G....... 708 349-2893
  Orland Park (G-15949)
Covachem LLC ....F....... 815 714-8421
  Loves Park (G-13197)
Custom Chemical Inc 217 529-0878
  Springfield (G-19357)
Dow Chemical Company ....E....... 708 396-3009
  Alsip (G-442)
Dubois Chemicals Group Inc ....E....... 708 458-2000
  Chicago (G-4400)
▲ Dynachem Inc ....D....... 217 662-2136
  Westville (G-20780)
Ecolocap Solutions Inc ....G....... 312 585-6670
  Morton Grove (G-14403)
Eden Fuels LLC ....G....... 847 676-9470
  Skokie (G-18949)
▼ Elevance Rnewable Sciences Inc ..C....... 630 296-8880
  Woodridge (G-21299)
Emerald Biofuels LLC ....G....... 847 420-0898
  Chicago (G-4494)
Emerald One LLC ....G....... 601 529-6793
  Chicago (G-4496)
Entrust Services LLC ....G....... 630 699-9132
  Naperville (G-14825)
Enzyme Mechanisms Conference ...G....... 847 491-5653
  Winnetka (G-21129)
▼ Enzymes Incorporated ....G....... 847 487-5401
  Wauconda (G-20348)
Equa Star Chemical Corp ....G....... 815 942-7011
  Morris (G-14303)
Equistar Chemicals LP ....E....... 217 253-3311
  Tuscola (G-19926)
Ethyl Corp ....G....... 618 583-1292
  East Saint Louis (G-8307)
Evonik Corporation ....C....... 309 697-6220
  Mapleton (G-13472)
Evonik Corporation ....G....... 630 230-0176
  Burr Ridge (G-2673)
Executive Performance Fuel LLC ...G....... 847 364-1933
  Elk Grove Village (G-8991)
FBC Industries Inc ....G....... 847 839-0880
  Rochelle (G-17140)
Fci Flavors ....G....... 630 373-1707
  Addison (G-119)
Franmar Chemical ....G....... 309 829-5952
  Bloomington (G-2045)
Freedom Fuel & Food Inc ....G....... 773 233-5350
  Chicago (G-4634)
Friends Fuel ....G....... 773 434-9387
  Chicago (G-4637)
▲ Frigid Fluid Company ....E....... 708 836-1215
  Melrose Park (G-13872)
Gateway Fuels Inc ....G....... 618 248-5000
  Albers (G-345)
Givaudan Flavors Corporation ....C....... 847 608-6200
  Elgin (G-8595)
Givaudan Fragrances Corp ....G....... 847 645-7000
  Elgin (G-8596)
Global Water Technology Inc ....E....... 708 349-9991
  South Holland (G-19215)
Green Plains Partners LP ....F....... 618 451-4420
  Madison (G-13413)
H&Z Fuel & Food Inc ....G....... 815 399-9108
  Rockford (G-17438)
▲ Ha-International LLC ....E....... 630 575-5700
  Westmont (G-20744)
Ha-International LLC ....E....... 815 732-3898
  Oregon (G-15922)
Ha-Usa Inc ....G....... 630 575-5700
  Westmont (G-20745)
Hallstar ....G....... 330 945-5292
  Bedford Park (G-1469)
Hallstar Company ....E....... 901 948-8663
  Chicago (G-4771)
◆ Hallstar Company ....C....... 312 554-7400
  Chicago (G-4772)
Hallstar Company ....D....... 708 594-5947
  Bedford Park (G-1470)
Hallstar Services Corp ....C....... 312 554-7400
  Chicago (G-4773)
Harvey Fuels ....G....... 708 339-0777
  Harvey (G-11088)
Havanah Fuel ....G....... 309 543-2211
  Havana (G-11114)
Honeywell International Inc ....B....... 618 524-2111
  Metropolis (G-13972)
Horizon Fuel Cell Americas ....G....... 312 316-8050
  Chicago (G-4841)
Houghton International Inc ....F....... 610 666-4000
  Chicago (G-4849)

Hucks Food Fuel ....F....... 618 286-5111
  Dupo (G-8138)
Hudson Technologies Inc ....E....... 217 373-1414
  Champaign (G-3304)
Hurst Chemical Company ....G....... 815 964-0451
  Rockford (G-17454)
▲ Hydrox Chemical Company Inc ...D....... 847 468-9400
  Elgin (G-8618)
◆ ICP Industrial Inc ....E....... 630 227-1692
  Itasca (G-11668)
Illini Fs Inc 217 442-4737
  Potomac (G-16802)
Illinois Corn Processing LLC ....D....... 309 353-3990
  Pekin (G-16339)
▼ Illinois River Energy LLC ....G....... 815 561-0650
  Rochelle (G-17146)
▼ Indorama Ventures Oxide & Glyl ..E....... 800 365-0794
  Riverwoods (G-17092)
Ineos Joliet LLC ....C....... 815 467-3200
  Channahon (G-3384)
Jada Specialties Inc ....G....... 847 272-7799
  Northbrook (G-15409)
Jagjita Corp ....G....... 217 374-6016
  White Hall (G-21019)
K&H Fuel ....G....... 815 405-4364
  Frankfort (G-9811)
Koppers Industries Inc ....E....... 708 656-5900
  Cicero (G-6859)
L & W Fuels ....G....... 815 848-8360
  Fairbury (G-9611)
Lakeview Energy LLC ....E....... 312 386-5897
  Lakeview (G-5167)
▲ Lanzatech Inc ....D....... 630 439-3050
  Skokie (G-18976)
Liquid Resin International ....E....... 618 392-3590
  Olney (G-15869)
Lonza LLC ....D....... 309 697-7200
  Mapleton (G-13475)
Lyondell Chemical Company ....B....... 815 942-7011
  Morris (G-14311)
▼ March Industries Inc ....F....... 224 654-6500
  Hampshire (G-10978)
◆ Marquis Energy LLC ....D....... 815 925-7300
  Hennepin (G-11158)
Marquis Marine Inc ....G....... 815 925-9125
  Hennepin (G-11159)
◆ Merisant Company ....F....... 312 840-6000
  Chicago (G-5396)
▲ Merisant Foreign Holdings I ....F....... 312 840-6000
  Chicago (G-5397)
◆ Merisant Us Inc ....B....... 312 840-6000
  Chicago (G-5398)
Merisant Us Inc ....C....... 815 929-2700
  Chicago (G-5399)
Mgp Ingredients Illinois Inc ....C....... 309 353-3990
  Pekin (G-16345)
Mgpi Processing Inc ....C....... 309 353-3990
  Pekin (G-16346)
Midtown Fuels 217 347-7191
  Effingham (G-8411)
Miwon NA ....G....... 630 568-5850
  Willowbrook (G-21052)
National Interchem LLC ....G....... 708 597-7777
  Blue Island (G-2133)
Natures Appeal Mfg Corp ....G....... 630 880-6222
  Addison (G-227)
Natures Sources LLC ....G....... 847 663-9168
  Niles (G-15151)
▲ Necta Sweet Inc ....E....... 847 215-9955
  Buffalo Grove (G-2579)
Nikli Fuels Inc 309 363-2425
  Pekin (G-16347)
▲ Nouryon Functional Chem LLC ...D....... 312 544-7000
  Chicago (G-5631)
▲ Nufarm Americas Inc ....D....... 708 377-1330
  Alsip (G-485)
▲ Nutrasweet Company ....G....... 312 873-5000
  Chicago (G-5643)
One Earth Energy LLC ....E....... 217 784-5321
  Gibson City (G-10341)
Pacific Ethanol Canton LLC ....G....... 309 347-9200
  Pekin (G-16349)
Pacific Ethanol Pekin LLC ....C....... 309 347-9200
  Pekin (G-16350)
Patriot Renewable Fuels LLC ....D....... 309 935-5700
  Annawan (G-592)
◆ Penray Companies Inc ....D....... 800 323-6329
  Downers Grove (G-8071)
◆ Pmp Fermentation Products Inc ...E....... 309 637-0400
  Peoria (G-16499)

SIC SECTION

28 CHEMICALS AND ALLIED PRODUCTS

Company	Code	Phone
Polyenviro Labs Inc — Mokena (G-14108)	G	708 489-0195
◆ Prinova Solutions LLC — Carol Stream (G-3053)	E	630 868-0300
Pro Fuel Nine Inc — Oquawka (G-15907)	G	309 867-3375
▲ Purecircle USA Inc — Oak Brook (G-15657)	E	866 960-8242
PVS Chemical Solutions Inc — Chicago (G-5919)	F	773 933-8800
R & P Fuels — Hoffman Estates (G-11449)	G	630 855-2358
▲ Rahn USA Corp — Aurora (G-1012)	E	630 851-4220
Reg Seneca LLC — Seneca (G-18860)	E	888 734-8686
▲ RHO Chemical Company Inc — Joliet (G-11926)	F	815 727-4791
▲ RJ Distributing Co — East Peoria (G-8287)	E	309 685-2794
Rs Fuels Inc — Chicago (G-6073)	F	773 205-9833
Rsb Fuels Inc — Mount Olive (G-14508)	G	217 999-4409
▲ RTD Hallstar Inc — Chicago (G-6076)	C	908 852-6128
Saint Mary Fuel Company — Chicago (G-6090)	G	773 918-1681
▲ SB Boron Corporation — Bellwood (G-1637)	G	708 547-9002
Solutia Inc — Sauget (G-18399)	A	618 482-6536
Solvay Chemicals Inc — East Saint Louis (G-8322)	E	618 274-0755
Solvay USA Inc — Blue Island (G-2141)	E	708 371-2000
Solvay USA Inc — University Park (G-19967)	E	708 235-7200
Standard Rubber Products Co — Elk Grove Village (G-9252)	E	847 593-5630
Stateline Renewable Fuels LLC — Buffalo Grove (G-2609)	G	608 931-4634
Stepan Company — Elwood (G-9464)	B	847 446-7500
Swissport Fueling Incorpo — Chicago (G-6298)	G	773 203-5419
Tate Lyle Ingrdnts Amricas LLC — Heyworth (G-11191)	G	309 473-2721
◆ Tempil Inc — Elk Grove Village (G-9270)	E	908 757-8300
Uberlube Inc — Evanston (G-9586)	G	847 644-4230
Union Carbide Corporation — Alsip (G-519)	D	708 396-3000
Uzhavoor Fuels Inc — Dixon (G-7925)	G	630 401-6173
Vantage Corn Processors LLC — Decatur (G-7566)	B	217 424-5200
▲ Vantage Oleochemicals Inc — Chicago (G-6522)	C	773 376-9000
▲ Vantage Specialties Inc — Gurnee (G-10943)	D	773 376-9000
Vertec Biosolvents Inc — Downers Grove (G-8104)	G	630 960-0600
Wenona Food & Fuel — Wenona (G-20527)	G	815 853-4141
West Fuels Inc — Forest Park (G-9729)	G	708 488-8880
Wieman Fuels LP Gas Company — Belleville (G-1612)	G	618 632-4015
World Fuel Services Inc — Chicago (G-6673)	F	305 428-8000
Xena International Inc — Polo (G-16760)	E	815 946-2626

2873 Nitrogenous Fertilizers

Company	Code	Phone
Amsoil Inc — Bensenville (G-1745)	G	630 595-8385
Biogreen Organics Inc — Volo (G-20196)	G	847 740-9637
◆ CF Industries Inc — Deerfield (G-7601)	B	847 405-2400
CF Industries Holdings Inc — Deerfield (G-7602)	D	847 405-2400
◆ CF Industries Nitrogen LLC — Deerfield (G-7603)	B	847 405-2400
Clean Hrbors Es Indus Svcs Inc — Cicero (G-6836)	F	708 652-0575
Cronus Chemicals LLC — Chicago (G-4272)	G	312 863-8538
E N P Inc — Mendota (G-13940)	G	800 255-4906
E N P Inc — Mendota (G-13941)	G	815 539-7471
▲ East Dbque Ntrgn Frtlizers LLC — East Dubuque (G-8176)	C	815 747-3101
Farmers Manufacturing Company — Dorsey (G-7944)	G	618 377-6237
Gateway Fs Inc — Venedy (G-20034)	G	618 824-6631
Gold Star Fs Inc — Erie (G-9473)	G	309 659-2801
Harbach Gillan & Nixon Inc — Clinton (G-6922)	F	217 935-8378
Harbach Gillan & Nixon Inc — Maroa (G-13552)	G	217 794-5117
Hyponex Corporation — Morrison (G-14343)	E	815 772-2167
Michel Fertilizer & Equipment — Mount Vernon (G-14624)	G	618 242-6000
◆ Pcs Nitrogen Inc — Northbrook (G-15453)	D	847 849-4200
Pcs Nitrogen Fertilizer LP — Northbrook (G-15454)	F	847 849-4200
Pcs Nitrogen Trinidad Corp — Northbrook (G-15455)	G	847 849-4200
▲ Pcs Ntrgen Frtlzer Oprtons Inc — Northbrook (G-15456)	D	847 849-4200
▼ Potash Corp Ssktchewan Fla Inc — Northbrook (G-15461)	C	847 849-4200
Rentech Development Corp — East Dubuque (G-8179)	C	815 747-3101
Rentech Energy Midwest Corp — East Dubuque (G-8180)	C	815 747-3101
Scotts Company LLC — Channahon (G-3393)	E	815 467-1605
Scotts Company LLC — Buffalo Grove (G-2597)	E	847 777-0700
Solution Designs Inc — Vernon Hills (G-20099)	G	847 680-7788
Sun Ag Inc — Hudson (G-11520)	G	309 726-1331
Sunrise AG Service Company — Kilbourne (G-12045)	G	309 538-4287
▲ Terra Nitrogen Company LP — Deerfield (G-7652)	G	847 405-2400
Terra Nitrogen GP Inc — Deerfield (G-7653)	G	847 405-2400
Tri-County Chemical Inc — Eldorado (G-8485)	F	618 273-2071
Unity Envirotech Illinois LLC — Henry (G-11169)	E	309 364-2361

2874 Phosphatic Fertilizers

Company	Code	Phone
◆ CF Industries Inc — Deerfield (G-7601)	B	847 405-2400
CF Industries Holdings Inc — Deerfield (G-7602)	D	847 405-2400
◆ CF Industries Nitrogen LLC — Deerfield (G-7603)	B	847 405-2400
Gateway Fs Inc — Venedy (G-20034)	G	618 824-6631
Innophos Inc — Chicago (G-4929)	G	773 468-2300
Innophos Inc — Chicago Heights (G-6750)	C	708 757-6111
Occidental Chemical Corp — Chicago (G-5651)	F	773 284-0079
◆ Pcs Nitrogen Inc — Northbrook (G-15453)	D	847 849-4200
◆ Pcs Phosphate Company Inc — Northbrook (G-15457)	D	847 849-4200
Phosphate Resource Ptrs — Lake Forest (G-12290)	A	847 739-1200
▼ Potash Corp Ssktchewan Fla Inc — Northbrook (G-15461)	C	847 849-4200
Sun Ag Inc — Hudson (G-11520)	G	309 726-1331
Trainor AG Products LLC — Anna (G-589)	G	618 614-5770

2875 Fertilizers, Mixing Only

Company	Code	Phone
Allerton Supply Company — Homer (G-11475)	F	217 896-2522
Anp Inc — Moline (G-14132)	G	309 757-0372
Archer-Daniels-Midland Company — Altamont (G-530)	G	618 483-6171
Better Earth Premium Compost — Peoria (G-16392)	G	309 697-0963
Biogreen Organics Inc — Volo (G-20196)	G	847 740-9637
▼ Brandt Consolidated Inc — Springfield (G-19329)	E	217 547-5800
Brandt Consolidated Inc — Farmer City (G-9654)	G	217 626-1123
Brandt Consolidated Inc — Lexington (G-12618)	G	309 365-7201
Brandt Consolidated Inc — Auburn (G-906)	F	217 438-6158
Country Stone Inc — Milan (G-14005)	E	309 787-1744
E N P Inc — Mendota (G-13941)	G	815 539-7471
E N P Inc — Mendota (G-13940)	G	800 255-4906
Earnest Earth Agriculture Inc — Lynn Center (G-13290)	G	217 766-4401
Enp Investments LLC — Mendota (G-13942)	G	815 539-7471
Evergreen Fs Inc — Cullom (G-7298)	G	815 934-5422
F S Gateway Inc — Fults (G-10160)	G	618 458-6588
Green Earth Technologies Inc — Palatine (G-16120)	G	847 991-0436
Green Organics Inc — Carol Stream (G-2995)	F	630 871-0108
Harbach Gillan & Nixon Inc — Clinton (G-6922)	F	217 935-8378
Hayden Mills Inc — Omaha (G-15900)	E	618 962-3136
Hyponex Corporation — Morrison (G-14343)	E	815 772-2167
Kreider Services Incorporated — Dixon (G-7903)	D	815 288-6691
Lebanon Seaboard Corporation — Danville (G-7358)	E	217 446-0983
Midwest Intgrted Companies LLC — Gilberts (G-10361)	C	847 426-6354
Miller Fertilizer Inc — Casey (G-3207)	G	217 382-4241
Millers Fertilizer & Feed — Cowden (G-7079)	F	217 783-6321
Myers Inc — Varna (G-20033)	G	309 725-3710
Piatt County Service Co — Bement (G-1714)	G	217 678-5511
Piatt County Service Co — Mansfield (G-13442)	G	217 489-2411
Prairieland Fs Inc — Astoria (G-895)	G	309 329-2162
Randolph Agricultural Services — Heyworth (G-11190)	G	309 473-3256
South Central Fs Inc — Toledo (G-19878)	F	217 849-2242
South Central Fs Inc — Vandalia (G-20025)	G	618 283-1557
Van Diest Supply Company — Freeport (G-10149)	G	815 232-6053
Veteran Greens LLC — Chicago (G-6540)	G	773 599-9689
Wabash Valley Service Co — Olney (G-15893)	F	618 393-2971
West Central Fs Inc — Wataga (G-20287)	G	309 375-6904

2879 Pesticides & Agricultural Chemicals, NEC

Company	Code	Phone
Agriscience Inc — Peoria (G-16377)	G	212 365-4214
Agrochem Inc — Northbrook (G-15334)	F	847 564-1304
Agrofresh Inc — Chicago (G-3583)	C	267 317-9135
◆ Alpha AG Inc — Pleasant Plains (G-16749)	G	217 546-2724
◆ Chase Products Co — Broadview (G-2425)	D	708 865-1000
Claire-Sprayway Inc — Downers Grove (G-7973)	D	630 628-3000
Clarke Aquatic Services Inc — Saint Charles (G-18167)	D	630 894-2000
Clarke Group Inc — Saint Charles (G-18168)	C	630 894-2000
◆ Clarke Mosquito Ctrl Pdts Inc — Saint Charles (G-18169)	C	630 894-2000
Dow Agrosciences LLC — Pontiac (G-16769)	G	815 844-3128

Employee Codes: A=Over 500 employees, B=251-500, C=101-250, D=51-100, E=20-50, F=10-19, G=3-9

28 CHEMICALS AND ALLIED PRODUCTS

Du Pont Delaware Inc ....G....... 630 285-2700
  Itasca (G-11645)
E I Du Pont De Nemours & Co ....E....... 309 527-5115
  El Paso (G-8436)
E N P Inc ....G....... 800 255-4906
  Mendota (G-13940)
Farmers Manufacturing Company ....G....... 618 377-6237
  Dorsey (G-7944)
FMC Corporation ....E....... 309 695-2571
  Wyoming (G-21460)
Frank Miller & Sons Inc ....E....... 708 201-7200
  Mokena (G-14083)
Gdm Seeds Inc ....F....... 317 752-6783
  Gibson City (G-10338)
Harbach Nixon & Willson Inc ....G....... 217 935-8378
  Clinton (G-6923)
▲ Isky North America Inc ....G....... 937 641-1368
  Chicago (G-4972)
Maplehurst Farms Inc ....F....... 815 562-8723
  Rochelle (G-17148)
Monsanto Company ....D....... 618 249-6150
  Centralia (G-3239)
Monsanto Company ....G....... 815 758-9293
  Waterman (G-20299)
Nufarm Americas Inc ....D....... 708 756-2010
  Chicago Heights (G-6762)
▲ Nufarm Americas Inc ....G....... 708 377-1330
  Alsip (G-485)
Nuseed Americas Inc ....G....... 800 345-3330
  Alsip (G-487)
Pfizer Inc ....D....... 847 639-3020
  Cary (G-3182)
▲ Precision Laboratories LLC ....G....... 847 282-7228
  Waukegan (G-20481)
Pro-Tek Products Inc ....G....... 630 293-5100
  Wheaton (G-20816)
Rdl Marketing Inc ....G....... 773 254-7600
  Chicago (G-5980)
S C Johnson & Son Inc ....C....... 312 702-3100
  Chicago (G-6074)
Sanford Chemical Co Inc ....F....... 847 437-3530
  Elk Grove Village (G-9229)
▲ Sem Minerals LP ....D....... 217 224-8766
  Quincy (G-16944)
Smithereen Company ....D....... 800 340-1888
  Niles (G-15172)
Smithereen Company Del ....G....... 847 675-0010
  Niles (G-15173)
Soil Chemical Corporation ....G....... 714 761-3292
  Decatur (G-7547)
Trainor AG Products LLC ....G....... 618 614-5770
  Anna (G-589)
◆ Valent Biosciences LLC ....G....... 800 323-9597
  Libertyville (G-12722)
Valent USA LLC ....F....... 816 206-3919
  Seymour (G-18869)
Van Diest Supply Company ....G....... 815 232-6053
  Freeport (G-10149)

2891 Adhesives & Sealants

A J Adhesives Inc ....G....... 708 210-1111
  South Holland (G-19186)
A2 Creative Inc ....G....... 855 344-5667
  Edwardsville (G-8344)
Aabbitt Adhesives Inc ....D....... 773 227-2700
  Chicago (G-3499)
Aabbitt Adhesives Inc ....E....... 773 723-6780
  Chicago (G-3500)
◆ Adco Global Inc ....G....... 847 282-3485
  Lincolnshire (G-12742)
▲ Adhesive Coating Tech Inc ....F....... 847 215-8355
  Wheeling (G-20841)
All Weather Courts Inc ....G....... 217 364-4546
  Dawson (G-7428)
Alliance Industries Inc ....F....... 847 288-9090
  Broadview (G-2416)
▼ AST Industries Inc ....G....... 847 455-2300
  Franklin Park (G-9878)
▲ Black Swan Manufacturing Co ....G....... 773 227-3700
  Chicago (G-3908)
Bradley Adhsive Applctions Inc ......C....... 630 443-8424
  Saint Charles (G-18159)
Brown Packaging LLC ....F....... 224 415-3182
  Elk Grove Village (G-8871)
Campbell Camie Inc ....E....... 314 968-3222
  Downers Grove (G-7963)
Chase Corporation ....G....... 847 866-8500
  Evanston (G-9503)
Chicago Adhesive Products ....G....... 630 978-7766
  Aurora (G-937)

▲ Chromium Industries Inc ....E....... 773 287-3716
  Chicago (G-4145)
Cohera Medical Inc ....G....... 602 418-8788
  Chicago (G-4196)
◆ D & K Group Inc ....G....... 847 956-0160
  Elk Grove Village (G-8931)
D & K International Inc ....G....... 847 956-0160
  Elk Grove Village (G-8932)
◆ Daubert Industries Inc ....F....... 630 203-6800
  Burr Ridge (G-2667)
Dental Sealants & More ....G....... 309 692-6435
  Peoria (G-16429)
Dip Seal Plastics Inc ....G....... 815 398-3533
  Rockford (G-17379)
▲ Eco-Pur Solutions LLC ....G....... 630 917-8789
  Chicago (G-4446)
Eco-Pur Solutions LLC ....G....... 630 226-2300
  Romeoville (G-17815)
▼ Emecole Inc ....F....... 815 372-2493
  Romeoville (G-17816)
Emulsicoat Inc ....F....... 217 344-7775
  Urbana (G-19981)
Essentra Corp ....G....... 814 899-7671
  Westchester (G-20697)
F H Leinweber Co Inc ....E....... 708 424-7000
  Oak Lawn (G-15715)
F H Leinweber Co Inc ....E....... 773 568-7722
  Chicago (G-4548)
◆ Fitz Chem LLC ....G....... 630 467-8383
  Itasca (G-11658)
Fontana Associates Inc ....G....... 888 707-8273
  Wauconda (G-20352)
▼ G J Nikolas & Co Inc ....E....... 708 544-0320
  Bellwood (G-1625)
Gardner Asphalt Corporation ....G....... 800 237-1155
  Chicago (G-4659)
Glue Inc ....G....... 312 451-4018
  Chicago (G-4702)
Green Products LLC ....F....... 815 407-0900
  Romeoville (G-17829)
HB Fuller Adhesives LLC ....E....... 815 357-6726
  Morris (G-14307)
◆ HB Fuller Cnstr Pdts Inc ....C....... 630 978-7766
  Aurora (G-978)
Henkel US Operations Corp ....D....... 847 468-9200
  Elgin (G-8613)
◆ Highland Supply Corporation ....B....... 618 654-2161
  Highland (G-11224)
◆ ICP Industrial Inc ....E....... 630 227-1692
  Itasca (G-11668)
Illinois Tool Works Inc ....B....... 847 724-7500
  Glenview (G-10560)
Illinois Tool Works Inc ....C....... 630 372-2150
  Bartlett (G-1288)
Illinois Tool Works Inc ....C....... 847 783-5500
  Elgin (G-8621)
ITW Dynatec ....G....... 847 657-4830
  Glenview (G-10573)
J & J Industries Inc ....G....... 630 595-8878
  Mount Prospect (G-14538)
JW Sealants Inc ....G....... 630 398-1010
  Bartlett (G-1291)
◆ La-Co Industries Inc ....C....... 847 956-7600
  Elk Grove Village (G-9082)
▲ Lectro Stik Corp ....E....... 630 894-1355
  Glendale Heights (G-10466)
▲ Lintec of America Inc ....G....... 847 229-0547
  Schaumburg (G-18608)
Liquitube Industries LLC ....F....... 618 985-4445
  Herrin (G-11174)
▲ Mafomsic Incorporated ....F....... 630 279-2005
  Elmhurst (G-9397)
Mapei Corporation ....G....... 630 293-5800
  West Chicago (G-20612)
Mapei Corporation ....D....... 630 293-5800
  West Chicago (G-20613)
Maximum Sealants LLC ....G....... 815 985-7183
  Rockford (G-17510)
Miller Purcell Co Inc ....G....... 815 485-2142
  New Lenox (G-15043)
◆ Miracle Sealants Company LLC ......E....... 626 443-6433
  Vernon Hills (G-20074)
Morton Intl Inc Adhsves Spclty ......G....... 815 653-2042
  Ringwood (G-17045)
◆ Morton Salt Inc ....C....... 312 807-2000
  Chicago (G-5501)
▼ Nataz Specialty Coatings Inc ......F....... 773 247-7030
  Chicago (G-5542)
◆ National Casein Co ....D....... 773 846-7300
  Burr Ridge (G-2707)

▲ National Casein Company ....D....... 773 846-7300
  Burr Ridge (G-2708)
◆ National Casein New Jersey Inc ....E....... 773 846-7300
  Burr Ridge (G-2709)
ND Industries Inc ....E....... 847 498-3600
  Northbrook (G-15440)
Nolan Sealants Inc ....G....... 630 774-5713
  Bloomingdale (G-2003)
North Shore Consultants Inc ....E....... 847 290-1599
  Elk Grove Village (G-9153)
Nu-Puttie Corporation ....E....... 708 681-1040
  Maywood (G-13676)
◆ Opticote Inc ....E....... 847 678-8900
  Franklin Park (G-10012)
Owens Corning Sales LLC ....E....... 708 594-6935
  Argo (G-675)
Pierce & Stevens Chemical ....G....... 630 653-3800
  Carol Stream (G-3047)
Porcelain Enamel Finishers ....G....... 312 808-1560
  Chicago (G-5845)
Poxypros Inc ....G....... 630 675-5924
  Yorkville (G-21497)
PPG Architectural Finishes Inc ......B....... 217 584-1323
  Meredosia (G-13956)
Prime Blend LLC ....F....... 866 217-3732
  Elk Grove Village (G-9196)
Princeton Sealing Wax Co ....G....... 815 875-1943
  Princeton (G-16821)
◆ Protective Products Intl ....G....... 847 526-1180
  Wauconda (G-20386)
Quality Sealants Inc ....G....... 815 342-0409
  Roselle (G-17976)
▲ Remet Corporation ....E....... 480 766-3464
  Palatine (G-16153)
Rhopac Fabricated Products LLC ......E....... 847 362-3300
  Libertyville (G-12702)
Right/Pointe LLC ....D....... 815 754-5700
  Dekalb (G-7700)
RM Lucas Co ....E....... 773 523-4300
  Chicago (G-6040)
▼ RM Lucas Co ....E....... 773 523-4300
  Alsip (G-504)
▲ Roanoke Companies Group Inc ....G....... 630 375-0324
  Aurora (G-1014)
Roman Holdings Corporation ....D....... 708 891-0770
  Calumet City (G-2789)
◆ Roman Products LLC ....E....... 708 891-0770
  Calumet City (G-2790)
Royal Adhesives & Sealants LLC ......G....... 815 464-5606
  Frankfort (G-9833)
Royal Adhesives and Sealants ....G....... 815 464-3310
  Frankfort (G-9834)
◆ Rust-Oleum Corporation ....C....... 847 367-7700
  Vernon Hills (G-20089)
Rust-Oleum Corporation ....G....... 815 967-4258
  Rockford (G-17617)
Saf-T-Lok International Corp ....E....... 630 495-2001
  Lombard (G-13127)
▲ Sandstrom Products Company ....E....... 309 523-2121
  Port Byron (G-16787)
Sandstrom Products Company ....F....... 309 523-2121
  Port Byron (G-16788)
Sanford Chemical Co Inc ....F....... 847 437-3530
  Elk Grove Village (G-9229)
Sarco Putty Company ....G....... 773 735-5577
  Chicago (G-6104)
Sigma Coatings Inc ....G....... 630 628-5305
  Addison (G-289)
Sika Corporation ....G....... 815 431-1080
  Ottawa (G-16079)
▲ Simpson Strong-Tie Company Inc ....E....... 630 613-5100
  West Chicago (G-20643)
Ski Seal Coating Inc ....G....... 708 246-5656
  Countryside (G-7070)
▲ Spartan Products Inc ....F....... 815 459-8500
  Crystal Lake (G-7268)
◆ Specialty Cnstr Brands Inc ....F....... 630 851-0782
  Aurora (G-1019)
Spl-Usa LLC ....G....... 312 807-2000
  Chicago (G-6215)
Strytech Adhesives ....G....... 847 509-7566
  Northbrook (G-15489)
Surebond Inc ....E....... 630 762-0606
  Saint Charles (G-18282)
Surebonder Adhesives Inc ....G....... 847 487-4583
  Wauconda (G-20393)
Surebonder Com Inc ....G....... 847 270-0254
  Grayslake (G-10801)
◆ Tape Case Ltd ....E....... 847 299-7880
  Elk Grove Village (G-9265)

SIC SECTION

28 CHEMICALS AND ALLIED PRODUCTS

▲ Testor Corporation....D....815 962-6654
Rockford (G-17656)
▲ Therm-O-Web Inc....E....847 520-5200
Wheeling (G-21000)
◆ Tsv Adhesive Systems Inc....E....815 464-5606
Frankfort (G-9847)
United Adhesives Inc....G....224 436-0077
Buffalo Grove (G-2614)
United Gilsonite Labs Inc....E....217 243-7878
Jacksonville (G-11784)
▼ Universal Chem & Coatings Inc....E....847 931-1700
Elgin (G-8769)
Universal Chem & Coatings Inc....E....847 297-2001
Elk Grove Village (G-9299)
US Adhesives....G....312 829-7438
Chicago (G-6497)
Versatile Materials Inc....G....773 924-3700
Chicago (G-6538)
Vibracoustic Usa Inc....E....618 382-5891
Carmi (G-2916)
W R Grace & Co-Conn....F....708 458-9700
Chicago (G-6577)
Wisdom Adhesives LLC....G....847 841-7002
Elgin (G-8784)
▲ Wisdom Adhesives LLC....E....847 841-7002
Elgin (G-8783)
WW Henry Company LP....D....815 933-8059
Bourbonnais (G-2272)

2892 Explosives

Buckley Powder Co....G....217 285-5531
Pittsfield (G-16629)
Dyno Nobel Inc....E....217 285-5531
Detroit (G-7872)
Evenson Explosives LLC....E....815 942-5800
Morris (G-14304)
General Dynamics Ordnance....C....618 985-8211
Marion (G-13512)
Hanley Industries Inc....D....618 465-8892
Alton (G-557)
Orica USA Inc....E....815 357-8711
Morris (G-14320)

2893 Printing Ink

▲ ABM Marking Ltd....F....618 277-3773
Belleville (G-1526)
Actega North America Inc....G....847 690-9310
Elk Grove Village (G-8805)
▲ Alden & Ott Printing Inks Co....D....847 956-6830
Arlington Heights (G-686)
Alden & Ott Printing Inks Co....F....847 364-6817
Mount Prospect (G-14511)
Buzz Sales Company Inc....G....815 459-1170
Crystal Lake (G-7175)
▲ Central Ink Corporation....D....630 231-6500
West Chicago (G-20560)
CIS Systems Inc....G....847 827-0747
Glenview (G-10537)
Cudner & OConnor Co....F....773 826-0200
Chicago (G-4283)
Domino Holdings Inc....D....847 244-2501
Gurnee (G-10871)
Dots UT Inc....G....217 390-3286
Champaign (G-3286)
Dynamic Colors Inc....G....847 721-8834
Evanston (G-9512)
Environmental Inks & Coding....F....630 231-7313
West Chicago (G-20574)
▲ Environmental Specialties Inc....G....630 860-7070
Itasca (G-11651)
Flint Group US LLC....E....630 526-9903
Batavia (G-1379)
Flint Group US LLC....F....920 725-0101
Romeoville (G-17823)
Flint Group US LLC....F....618 349-8384
Saint Peter (G-18324)
▲ Graphic Chemical & Ink Co....F....630 832-6004
Villa Park (G-20149)
Hostmann Steinberg Inc....F....502 968-5961
Kankakee (G-11976)
◆ Hubergroup Usa Inc....D....815 929-9293
Rolling Meadows (G-17737)
Hurst Chemical Company....G....815 964-0451
Rockford (G-17454)
Hydro Ink Corp....G....847 674-0057
Skokie (G-18967)
▲ I C T W Ink....G....630 893-4658
Roselle (G-17957)
▲ I Q Infinity LLC....G....773 651-2556
Chicago (G-4868)
▲ I S C America Inc....G....630 616-1331
Wood Dale (G-21199)
▲ Ink Solutions LLC....F....847 593-5200
Elk Grove Village (G-9052)
Ink Systems Inc....G....847 427-2200
Elk Grove Village (G-9053)
Interactive Inks Coatings Corp....F....847 289-8710
South Elgin (G-19157)
◆ INX Digital International Co....F....630 382-1800
Schaumburg (G-18567)
INX Group....G....847 441-0600
Elk Grove Village (G-9060)
INX Group Ltd....G....708 799-1993
Homewood (G-11499)
◆ INX Group Ltd....G....630 382-1800
Schaumburg (G-18568)
◆ INX International Ink Co....D....630 382-1800
Schaumburg (G-18569)
INX International Ink Co....F....708 799-1993
Homewood (G-11500)
INX International Ink Co....E....630 681-7200
West Chicago (G-20600)
INX International Ink Co....E....708 496-3600
Chicago (G-4966)
INX International Ink Co....E....800 233-4657
Schaumburg (G-18570)
INX International Ink Co....E....630 382-1800
Chicago (G-4967)
INX International Ink Co....F....630 382-1800
Schaumburg (G-18571)
INX International Ink Co....E....630 681-7100
West Chicago (G-20601)
▼ Kolorcure Corporation....F....630 879-9050
Batavia (G-1389)
L P S Express Inc....G....217 636-7683
Springfield (G-19396)
Laser Technology Group Inc....G....847 524-4088
Elk Grove Village (G-9087)
▲ Midwest Ink Co....E....708 345-7177
Broadview (G-2451)
Paper Graphics Inc....G....847 276-2727
Lincolnshire (G-12790)
Precision Ink Corporation....F....847 952-1500
Elk Grove Village (G-9191)
▲ Process Supply Company Inc....G....312 943-8338
Chicago (G-5890)
◆ R A Kerley Ink Engineers Inc....E....708 344-1295
Broadview (G-2462)
Scientific Colors Inc....C....815 744-5650
Rockdale (G-17274)
Springbox Inc....G....708 921-9944
Flossmoor (G-9702)
Sun Chemical Corporation....C....708 562-0550
Northlake (G-15561)
Sun Chemical Corporation....D....815 939-0136
Kankakee (G-12009)
◆ Sun Graphic Inc....D....773 775-6755
Chicago (G-6269)
◆ Thrall Enterprises Inc....F....312 621-8200
Chicago (G-6372)
Toyo Ink International Corp....F....630 930-5100
Addison (G-316)
◆ Toyo Ink International Corp....F....866 969-8696
Wood Dale (G-21251)
U S Colors & Coatings Inc....G....630 879-8898
Batavia (G-1435)
Wikoff Color Corporation....G....847 487-2704
Wauconda (G-20403)

2895 Carbon Black

Cabot Corporation....D....217 253-5752
Tuscola (G-19925)

2899 Chemical Preparations, NEC

▲ 300 Below Inc....G....217 423-3070
Decatur (G-7431)
▲ ABM Marking Ltd....F....618 277-3773
Belleville (G-1526)
Accusol Incorporated....G....773 283-4686
Oak Lawn (G-15696)
Advantech Limited....G....815 289-7678
Aurora (G-1043)
Afton Chemical Corporation....E....708 728-1546
Bedford Park (G-1454)
Afton Chemical Corporation....B....618 583-1000
East Saint Louis (G-8296)
Alloy Chrome Inc....G....847 678-2880
Schiller Park (G-18784)
▲ American Chemical & Eqp Inc....G....815 675-9199
Northlake (G-15541)
American Colloid Company....E....618 452-8143
Granite City (G-10694)
American Colloid Company....F....304 882-2123
Elgin (G-8506)
◆ American Colloid Company....E....847 851-1700
Hoffman Estates (G-11406)
◆ American Metal Chemical Corp....E....773 254-1818
Chicago (G-3661)
American Technologies Inc....E....630 548-8150
Naperville (G-14773)
Americlean Inc....F....314 741-8901
Wood River (G-21259)
◆ Apex Engineering Products Corp....F....630 820-8888
Aurora (G-912)
▲ APL Engineered Materials Inc....E....217 367-1340
Urbana (G-19972)
Arbor Products....G....847 653-6210
Park Ridge (G-16267)
Arch Chemicals Inc....G....630 365-1720
Elburn (G-8444)
BASF Corporation....B....815 932-6751
Kankakee (G-11959)
▲ Bird-X Inc....E....312 226-2473
Elmhurst (G-9334)
▲ Black Swan Manufacturing Co....F....773 227-3700
Chicago (G-3908)
▲ Bmi Products Northern Ill Inc....E....847 395-7110
Antioch (G-605)
Bonsal American Inc....D....847 678-6220
Franklin Park (G-9891)
Brite Site Supply Inc....G....773 772-7300
Chicago (G-3959)
Bromine Systems Inc....G....331 209-9881
Addison (G-55)
◆ Butterfield Color Inc....E....630 906-1980
Aurora (G-1067)
Buzz Sales Company Inc....G....815 459-1170
Crystal Lake (G-7175)
C & S Chemicals Inc....G....815 722-6671
Joliet (G-11837)
Cabot Corporation....D....217 253-5752
Tuscola (G-19925)
Campbell Camie Inc....E....314 968-3222
Downers Grove (G-7963)
Carbon Clean Solutions USA Inc....G....872 206-0197
Chicago (G-4024)
◆ Castrol Industrial N Amer Inc....C....877 641-1600
Naperville (G-14792)
▲ Cater Chemical Co....G....630 980-2300
Roselle (G-17943)
◆ CCI Manufacturing IL Corp....E....630 739-0606
Lemont (G-12559)
CD Magic Inc....G....708 582-3496
Roselle (G-17944)
Championx LLC....G....618 740-1279
Salem (G-18334)
▲ Chem Trade Global....G....847 675-2682
Skokie (G-18940)
Chemical Processing & Acc....G....847 793-2387
Lincolnshire (G-12750)
Chemix Corp....F....708 754-2150
Glenwood (G-10639)
◆ Chemtool Incorporated....C....815 957-4140
Rockton (G-17694)
Chemtool Incorporated....D....815 459-1250
Crystal Lake (G-7180)
Chicago Ink & Research Co Inc....G....847 395-1078
Antioch (G-608)
Circle Systems Inc....F....815 286-3271
Hinckley (G-11357)
Claire-Sprayway Inc....D....630 628-3000
Downers Grove (G-7973)
CLC Lubricants Company....E....630 232-7900
Geneva (G-10261)
◆ Colloid Envmtl Tech Co LLC....C....847 851-1500
Hoffman Estates (G-11415)
Custom Chemical Inc....G....217 529-0878
Springfield (G-19357)
◆ Daubert Industries Inc....F....630 203-6800
Burr Ridge (G-2667)
Dayton Superior Corporation....C....815 936-3300
Kankakee (G-11964)
▼ De Enterprises Inc....F....708 345-8088
Broadview (G-2429)
Debourg Corp....G....815 338-7852
Bull Valley (G-2627)
◆ Dober Chemical Corp....C....630 410-7300
Woodridge (G-21294)
Domino Amjet Inc....E....847 662-3148
Gurnee (G-10869)

SIC

Employee Codes: A=Over 500 employees, B=251-500
C=101-250, D=51-100, E=20-50, F=10-19, G=3-9

2020 Harris Illinois
Industrial Directory

893

◆ **Domino Amjet Inc** ....D 847 244-2501
Gurnee *(G-10870)*
Ecp Incorporated ....D 630 754-4200
Woodridge *(G-21297)*
Emerald Polymer Additives LLC ....D 309 364-2311
Henry *(G-11165)*
Enterprise Oil Co ....E 312 487-2025
Chicago *(G-4514)*
▼ **Enviro Tech International Inc** ....G 708 343-6641
Melrose Park *(G-13865)*
▲ **Environmental Specialties Inc** ....G 630 860-7070
Itasca *(G-11651)*
Euclid Chemical Company ....F 815 522-2308
Kirkland *(G-12060)*
First Step Womens Center ....G 217 523-0100
Springfield *(G-19369)*
Flint Group US LLC ....F 920 725-0101
Romeoville *(G-17823)*
▲ **Fragrance Island Inc** ....G 773 488-2700
Chicago *(G-4628)*
Frank Miller & Sons Inc ....E 708 201-7200
Mokena *(G-14083)*
◆ **Fuchs Corporation** ....G 800 323-7755
Harvey *(G-11086)*
Garratt-Callahan Company ....G 630 543-4411
Addison *(G-135)*
▲ **Gelita USA Chicago** ....F 708 891-8400
Calumet City *(G-2776)*
Gelita USA Inc ....G 708 891-8400
Calumet City *(G-2777)*
Getex Corporation ....G 630 993-1300
Aurora *(G-968)*
Gillette Company ....D 847 689-3111
North Chicago *(G-15312)*
Girard Chemical Company ....G 630 293-5886
Bensenville *(G-1811)*
Global Water Technology Inc ....E 708 349-9991
South Holland *(G-19215)*
Graphic Sciences Inc ....G 630 226-0994
Bolingbrook *(G-2180)*
H-O-H Water Technology Inc ....E 847 358-7400
Palatine *(G-16121)*
Hallstar Company ....E 901 948-8663
Chicago *(G-4771)*
Hawkins Inc ....G 708 258-3797
Peotone *(G-16553)*
Helix Re Inc ....D 415 254-2724
Chicago *(G-4799)*
Henkel Technology Corporation ....G 708 924-9582
Chicago *(G-4802)*
HIG Chemicals Holdings ....C 773 376-9000
Chicago *(G-4814)*
◆ **Holland LP** ....C 708 672-2300
Crete *(G-7140)*
Houghton International Inc ....F 610 666-4000
Chicago *(G-4849)*
▲ **I S C America Inc** ....G 630 616-1331
Wood Dale *(G-21199)*
I W M Corporation ....G 847 695-0700
Elgin *(G-8619)*
Illinois Oil Products Inc ....F 309 788-1896
Rock Island *(G-17224)*
Illinois Tool Works Inc ....E 847 350-0193
Elk Grove Village *(G-9043)*
▲ **In3gredients Inc** ....G 312 577-4275
Chicago *(G-4904)*
Indorama Vntres USA Hldings LP ....G 847 943-3100
Riverwoods *(G-17093)*
Industrial Specialty Chem Inc ....E 708 339-1313
South Holland *(G-19224)*
Industrial Waste Elimination ....F 312 498-0880
Peoria *(G-16459)*
◆ **Interra Global Corporation** ....F 847 292-8600
Park Ridge *(G-16285)*
INX International Ink Co ....E 630 681-7200
West Chicago *(G-20600)*
INX International Ink Co ....F 630 382-1800
Schaumburg *(G-18571)*
INX International Ink Co ....E 630 681-7100
West Chicago *(G-20601)*
ITW Fluids North America ....G 630 384-0146
Carol Stream *(G-3008)*
▲ **Ivanhoe Industries Inc** ....E 847 872-3311
Mundelein *(G-14702)*
◆ **Jackson Marking Products Co** ....F 618 242-7901
Mount Vernon *(G-14617)*
Jamaica Pyrotechnics ....G 217 649-2902
Philo *(G-16606)*
JM Huber Corporation ....E 217 224-1100
Quincy *(G-16895)*
▲ **Johnny Rckets Firewrks Display** ....G 847 501-1270
Chicago *(G-5044)*
K+s Montana Holdings LLC ....G 312 807-2000
Chicago *(G-5069)*
K+s Salt LLC ....G 844 789-3991
Chicago *(G-5070)*
Klein Tools Inc ....D 847 228-6999
Elk Grove Village *(G-9078)*
Klein Tools Inc ....E 847 821-5500
Lincolnshire *(G-12779)*
Kop-Coat Inc ....F 847 272-2278
Buffalo Grove *(G-2557)*
◆ **La-Co Industries Inc** ....C 847 956-7600
Elk Grove Village *(G-9082)*
▲ **Lawter Inc** ....E 312 662-5700
Chicago *(G-5185)*
Litho Research Incorporated ....G 630 860-7070
Itasca *(G-11695)*
Lumina Inc ....G 312 829-8970
Chicago *(G-5283)*
▲ **Luster Leaf Products Inc** ....F 815 337-5560
Woodstock *(G-21407)*
◆ **M R O Solutions LLC** ....E 847 588-2480
Niles *(G-15143)*
Magnetic Inspection Lab Inc ....D 847 437-4488
Elk Grove Village *(G-9106)*
Mapei Corporation ....D 630 293-5800
West Chicago *(G-20613)*
Master Builders LLC ....G 847 249-4080
Gurnee *(G-10895)*
Mc Chemical Company ....G 618 965-3668
Steeleville *(G-19483)*
Mc Chemical Company ....E 815 964-7687
Rockford *(G-17511)*
Metal Finishing Research Corp ....F 773 373-0800
Chicago *(G-5404)*
▲ **Micro Surface Corporation** ....F 815 942-4221
Morris *(G-14312)*
▲ **Mid America Intl Inc** ....G 847 635-8303
Glenview *(G-10589)*
Miller Purcell Co Inc ....G 815 485-2142
New Lenox *(G-15043)*
▲ **Mineral Masters Corporation** ....F 630 293-7727
West Chicago *(G-20619)*
◆ **Miracle Sealants Company LLC** ....E 626 443-6433
Vernon Hills *(G-20074)*
▲ **Modern Printing Colors Inc** ....F 708 681-5678
Broadview *(G-2453)*
◆ **Morton Salt Inc** ....C 312 807-2000
Chicago *(G-5501)*
◆ **Nalco Holding Company** ....E 630 305-1000
Naperville *(G-14877)*
▼ **Nataz Specialty Coatings Inc** ....F 773 247-7030
Chicago *(G-5542)*
▼ **Nouryon Surface Chemistry LLC** ....E 312 544-7000
Chicago *(G-5632)*
Ochem Inc ....G 847 403-7044
Des Plaines *(G-7814)*
Ochem Inc ....F 847 403-7044
Chicago *(G-5654)*
Opsdirt LLC ....G 773 412-1179
Chicago *(G-5684)*
Opw Fueling Components Inc ....G 708 485-4200
Hodgkins *(G-11393)*
◆ **Penray Companies Inc** ....D 800 323-6329
Downers Grove *(G-8071)*
▲ **Philmar LLC** ....G 847 282-0204
Zion *(G-21525)*
▲ **Philos Technologies Inc** ....G 630 945-2933
Buffalo Grove *(G-2585)*
Phoenix Inks and Coatings LLC ....F 630 972-2500
Lemont *(G-12582)*
Planet Earth Antifreeze Inc ....G 815 282-2463
Loves Park *(G-13247)*
▲ **Plating International Inc** ....F 847 451-2101
Franklin Park *(G-10020)*
Polyenviro Labs Inc ....G 708 489-0195
Mokena *(G-14108)*
PQ Corporation ....E 815 667-4241
Utica *(G-20006)*
Prestone Products Corporation ....D 708 371-3000
Alsip *(G-497)*
▼ **Prestone Products Corporation** ....C 888 282-8960
Rosemont *(G-18043)*
Pro TEC Metal Finishing Corp ....G 773 384-7853
Chicago *(G-5888)*
Producers Chemical Company ....E 630 466-4584
Sugar Grove *(G-19650)*
▼ **Progressive Solutions Corp** ....G 847 639-7272
Algonquin *(G-384)*
PVS Chemical Solutions Inc ....E 773 933-8800
Chicago *(G-5919)*
▲ **Qualitek International Inc** ....E 630 628-8083
Addison *(G-259)*
Rampro Facilities Svcs Corp ....G 224 639-6378
Waukegan *(G-20487)*
Rda Inc ....F 815 427-8444
Saint Anne *(G-18137)*
Right/Pointe LLC ....D 815 754-5700
Dekalb *(G-7700)*
Rockford Chemical Co ....G 815 544-3476
Belvidere *(G-1700)*
▲ **RPS Products Inc** ....E 847 683-3400
Hampshire *(G-10986)*
◆ **Rust-Oleum Corporation** ....C 847 367-7700
Vernon Hills *(G-20089)*
◆ **Rycoline Products LLC** ....C 773 775-6755
Chicago *(G-6081)*
Samuel Rowell ....G 618 942-6970
Herrin *(G-11178)*
▼ **Sanchem Inc** ....E 312 733-6100
Chicago *(G-6098)*
Sanford Chemical Co Inc ....F 847 437-3530
Elk Grove Village *(G-9229)*
◆ **Seymour of Sycamore Inc** ....C 815 895-9101
Sycamore *(G-19730)*
Siegwerk Eic LLC ....F 800 728-8200
West Chicago *(G-20641)*
Sika Corporation ....G 815 431-1080
Ottawa *(G-16079)*
Solazyme ....G 309 258-5695
Peoria *(G-16525)*
Solvay Chemicals Inc ....E 618 274-0755
East Saint Louis *(G-8322)*
Solvay USA Inc ....E 708 235-7200
University Park *(G-19967)*
▲ **Specco Industries Inc** ....F 630 257-5060
Kankakee *(G-12005)*
◆ **Specialty Cnstr Brands Inc** ....F 630 851-0782
Aurora *(G-1019)*
▲ **Stutz Company** ....F 773 287-1068
Chicago *(G-6259)*
Suez Wts Usa Inc ....E 630 543-8480
Addison *(G-297)*
Sun Chemical Corporation ....C 630 513-5348
Saint Charles *(G-18281)*
Super-Dri Corp ....G 708 599-8700
Bridgeview *(G-2390)*
Swanson Water Treatment Inc ....G 847 680-1113
Libertyville *(G-12712)*
T D J Group Inc ....G 847 639-1113
Cary *(G-3193)*
T K O Waterproof Coating LLP ....G 815 338-2006
Woodstock *(G-21440)*
Tamms Industries Inc ....D 815 522-3394
Kirkland *(G-12066)*
Technic Inc ....G 773 262-2662
Arlington Heights *(G-817)*
Technical Ordnance Inc ....C 630 969-0620
Downers Grove *(G-8101)*
Technisand Inc ....G 815 433-2449
Ottawa *(G-16080)*
Ted Muller ....G 312 435-0978
Chicago *(G-6336)*
Tower Oil & Technology Co ....E 773 927-6161
Chicago *(G-6401)*
Trane Technologies Company LLC ....E 704 655-4000
Chicago *(G-6406)*
United Gilsonite Labs Inc ....E 217 243-7878
Jacksonville *(G-11784)*
Varn International Inc ....E 630 406-6501
Batavia *(G-1440)*
Vyse Gelatin LLC ....E 847 678-4780
Schiller Park *(G-18852)*
W R Grace & Co ....F 708 458-9700
Chicago *(G-6576)*
W R Grace & Co-Conn ....F 708 458-9700
Chicago *(G-6577)*
Wenesco Inc ....F 773 283-3004
Addison *(G-333)*
Wet International Inc ....E 630 540-2113
Streamwood *(G-19602)*
Wet USA Inc ....G 630 540-2113
Streamwood *(G-19603)*
Winn Star Inc ....G 618 964-1811
Carbondale *(G-2865)*
▼ **Wm Wrigley Jr Company** ....B 312 280-4710
Chicago *(G-6654)*
Wm Wrigley Jr Company ....A 312 644-2121
Chicago *(G-6656)*

29 PETROLEUM REFINING AND RELATED INDUSTRIES

2911 Petroleum Refining

Company	Code	Phone
4200 Kirchoff Corp	G	773 551-1541
Rolling Meadows (G-17707)		
Airgas Inc	F	773 785-3000
Chicago (G-3588)		
Blackhawk Biofuels LLC	E	217 431-6600
Freeport (G-10103)		
◆ BP America Inc	A	630 420-5111
Warrenville (G-20232)		
BP Products North America Inc	D	312 594-7689
Chicago (G-3939)		
Caibros Americas LLC	G	312 593-3128
Highland Park (G-11256)		
Cartel Holdings Inc	G	815 334-0250
Harvard (G-11049)		
Citation Oil & Gas Corp	E	618 966-2101
Crossville (G-7150)		
Citgo Petroleum Corporation	G	847 818-1800
Downers Grove (G-7970)		
CP Diesel Inc	G	815 979-9600
Cissna Park (G-6896)		
Drig Corporation	D	312 265-1509
Rosemont (G-18020)		
Equilon Enterprises LLC	F	312 733-1849
Chicago (G-4523)		
Esi Fuel & Energy Group LLC	G	716 465-4289
Collinsville (G-6959)		
ET Products LLC	G	800 325-5746
Burr Ridge (G-2671)		
Exxonmobil Pipeline Company	F	815 423-5571
Elwood (G-9462)		
Indilab Inc	E	847 928-1050
Franklin Park (G-9962)		
Koppers Industries Inc	E	708 656-5900
Cicero (G-6859)		
Lamson Oil Company	G	815 226-8090
Rockford (G-17490)		
Lub-Tek Petroleum Products	G	815 741-0414
Joliet (G-11895)		
Matheson Tri-Gas Inc	E	815 727-2202
Joliet (G-11899)		
Murphy USA Inc	G	847 245-3283
Round Lake Beach (G-18091)		
Murphy USA Inc	G	815 356-7633
Crystal Lake (G-7235)		
North American Refining Co	G	708 762-5117
Mc Cook (G-13697)		
Oxbow Carbon LLC	E	630 257-7751
Lemont (G-12576)		
Oxbow Midwest Calcining LLC	D	630 257-7751
Lemont (G-12577)		
▲ Patriot Fuels Biodiesel LLC	F	309 935-5700
Annawan (G-591)		
Pdv Midwest Refining LLC	A	630 257-7761
Lemont (G-12581)		
Power Lube LLC	G	847 806-7022
Elk Grove Village (G-9187)		
Premcor Incorporated	G	618 254-7301
Hartford (G-11037)		
Raymond D Wright	G	618 783-2206
Newton (G-15091)		
Seneca Petroleum Co Inc	E	708 396-1100
Crestwood (G-7127)		
Shell Oil Company	C	618 254-7371
Wood River (G-21267)		
South West Oil Inc	F	815 416-0400
Morris (G-14327)		
Southern Illinois Power Coop	G	618 995-2371
Buncombe (G-2628)		
◆ Suma America Inc	G	847 427-7880
Glenview (G-10629)		
Synsel Energy Inc	G	630 516-1284
Elmhurst (G-9432)		
Tatty Stick LLC	G	815 905-1023
Essex (G-9476)		
▲ W R B Refinery LLC	E	618 255-2345
Roxana (G-18104)		

2951 Paving Mixtures & Blocks

Company	Code	Phone
Advanced Asphalt Co	E	815 872-9911
Princeton (G-16804)		
Allied Asphalt Paving Co Inc	E	630 289-6080
Elgin (G-8503)		
Ambraw Asphalt Materials Inc	E	618 943-4716
Lawrenceville (G-12526)		
Arrow Road Construction Co	C	847 437-0700
Elk Grove Village (G-8839)		
Asphalt Mtls DBA Hritg Asp LLC	G	773 735-2233
Cicero (G-6830)		
Asphalt Products Inc	E	618 943-4716
Lawrenceville (G-12527)		
Bonsal American Inc	G	847 678-6220
Franklin Park (G-9891)		
Byron Blacktop Inc	G	815 234-2225
Byron (G-2751)		
Certified Asphalt Paving	G	847 441-5000
Northfield (G-15511)		
Cgk Enterprises Inc	G	847 888-1362
Elgin (G-8535)		
Charles E Mahoney Company	E	618 235-3355
Swansea (G-19690)		
Chicago Baking Company	A	630 684-2335
Darien (G-7404)		
Christ Bros Products LLC	G	618 537-6174
Lebanon (G-12543)		
Clean Sweep Environmental Inc	G	630 879-8750
Batavia (G-1367)		
Consolidated Paving Inc	G	309 693-3505
Peoria (G-16427)		
Cope & Sons Asphalt	G	618 462-2207
Alton (G-548)		
Corrective Asphalt Mtls LLC	G	618 254-3855
South Roxana (G-19252)		
County Asphalt Inc	G	618 224-9033
Trenton (G-19902)		
Crowley-Sheppard Asphalt Inc	F	708 499-2900
Chicago Ridge (G-6793)		
Cullinan & Sons Inc	E	309 925-2711
Tremont (G-19895)		
Curran Contracting Company	G	815 455-5100
Crystal Lake (G-7189)		
Curran Contracting Company	G	815 758-8113
Dekalb (G-7671)		
Dicks Asphalt Service	G	815 932-7157
Kankakee (G-11965)		
Don Anderson Co	G	618 495-2511
Hoffman (G-11402)		
Dougherty E J Oil & Stone Sup	G	618 271-4414
East Saint Louis (G-8304)		
Emulsicoat Inc	F	217 344-7775
Urbana (G-19981)		
Emulsions Inc	G	618 943-2615
Lawrenceville (G-12531)		
ET Simonds Materials Company	E	618 457-8191
Carbondale (G-2842)		
Frank S Johnson & Company Inc	G	847 492-1660
Evanston (G-9522)		
Freesen Inc	E	309 827-4554
Bloomington (G-2046)		
Fuller Asphalt & Landscape	G	618 797-1169
Granite City (G-10707)		
G & S Asphalt Inc	F	217 826-2421
Marshall (G-13571)		
Gallagher Asphalt Corporation	E	708 877-7160
Thornton (G-19786)		
Gardner Asphalt Corporation	G	800 237-1155
Chicago (G-4659)		
General Contractor Inc	G	618 533-5213
Sandoval (G-18364)		
Geneva Construction Company	G	630 892-6536
North Aurora (G-15261)		
Geske and Sons Inc	G	815 459-2407
Crystal Lake (G-7203)		
Geske and Sons Inc	G	815 459-2407
Crystal Lake (G-7202)		
Gorman Brothers Ready Mix Inc	F	618 498-2173
Jerseyville (G-11791)		
Hardscape Outpost LLC	G	630 551-6105
North Aurora (G-15262)		
Hassebrock Asphalt Sealing	E	618 566-7214
Mascoutah (G-13598)		
Hillyer Inc	G	309 837-6434
Macomb (G-13392)		
Illinois Road Contractors Inc	G	217 245-6181
Jacksonville (G-11769)		
Illinois Valley Paving Co Inc	F	217 422-1010
Elwin (G-9459)		
Jax Asphalt Company Inc	F	618 244-0500
Mount Vernon (G-14618)		
JB Enterprises II Inc	F	630 372-8300
Streamwood (G-19579)		
◆ Lafarge North America Inc	C	773 372-1000
Chicago (G-5156)		
Louis Marsch Inc	E	217 526-3723
Morrisonville (G-14351)		
Marathon Petroleum Company LP	G	618 829-3288
Saint Elmo (G-18309)		
Orange Crush LLC	C	708 544-9440
Hillside (G-11352)		
Orange Crush LLC	G	847 428-6176
East Dundee (G-8207)		
Orange Crush LLC	G	630 739-5560
Romeoville (G-17862)		
Orange Crush LLC	G	847 537-7900
Wheeling (G-20952)		
Owens Corning Sales LLC	E	708 594-6935
Argo (G-675)		
Peter Baker & Son Co	D	847 362-3663
Lake Bluff (G-12204)		
Plote Construction Inc	G	847 695-9300
Hoffman Estates (G-11445)		
Plote Inc	G	847 695-9467
Hoffman Estates (G-11446)		
Pothole Pros	G	847 815-5789
Elgin (G-8692)		
Prosser Construction Co	F	217 774-5032
Shelbyville (G-18884)		
Quikrete Companies LLC	G	309 346-1184
Pekin (G-16357)		
Reliable Asphalt Corporation	E	773 254-1121
Chicago (G-6009)		
Rock Road Companies Inc	E	815 874-2441
Rockford (G-17583)		
Rockford Blacktop Cnstr Co	D	815 654-4700
Rockford (G-17586)		
Sandeno Inc	E	815 730-9415
Rockdale (G-17272)		
Savanna Quarry Inc	G	815 273-4208
Savanna (G-18411)		
Schulze & Schulze Inc	E	618 687-1106
Murphysboro (G-14758)		
Sealmaster Inc	E	847 480-7325
Northbrook (G-15478)		
Sealmaster/Alsip	G	708 489-0900
Alsip (G-509)		
Seneca Petroleum Co Inc	E	630 257-2268
Lemont (G-12589)		
Sherwin Industries Inc	E	815 234-8007
Byron (G-2758)		
▲ Srj Inc	F	630 351-0639
Schaumburg (G-18726)		
St Clair Tennis Club LLC	E	618 632-1400
O Fallon (G-15584)		
Streator Asphalt Inc	G	815 672-8683
Streator (G-19625)		
Terry Terri Mulgrew	G	815 747-6248
East Dubuque (G-8185)		
Thorworks Industries Inc	G	815 969-0664
Rockford (G-17662)		
Utica Terminal Inc	G	217 245-6181
Utica (G-20008)		
Veterans Parking Lot Maint	G	815 245-7584
Woodstock (G-21443)		

2952 Asphalt Felts & Coatings

Company	Code	Phone
Allied Asphalt Paving Co Inc	E	630 289-6080
Elgin (G-8503)		
American Asp Surfc Recycl Inc	F	708 448-9540
Orland Park (G-15939)		
American Grinders Inc	G	815 943-4902
Harvard (G-11045)		
Atlas Roofing Corporation	E	309 752-7121
East Moline (G-8222)		
Black Rock Milling and Pav Co	F	847 952-0700
Arlington Heights (G-706)		
Bonsal American Inc	D	847 678-6220
Franklin Park (G-9891)		
Brewer Company	F	708 339-9000
Harvey (G-11080)		
Carlisle Syn TEC Inc	F	618 664-4540
Greenville (G-10829)		
Co-Fair Corporation	G	847 626-1500
Skokie (G-18945)		
Cofair Products Inc	G	847 626-1500
Skokie (G-18946)		
Cornerstone Building Products	G	217 543-2829
Arthur (G-848)		
Crosscom Inc	F	630 871-5500
Wheaton (G-20794)		
Crown Coatings Company	F	630 365-9925
Elburn (G-8448)		
Decatur Ras LLC	G	217 433-2794
Decatur (G-7489)		

Zeller + Gmelin Corporation .....G..... 630 443-8800
Saint Charles (G-18304)

Employee Codes: A=Over 500 employees, B=251-500
C=101-250, D=51-100, E=20-50, F=10-19, G=3-9

▲ **Deks North America Inc**.....G..... 312 219-2110
Chicago *(G-4331)*
Don Anderson Co.....G..... 618 495-2511
Hoffman *(G-11402)*
Emulsicoat Inc.....F..... 217 344-7775
Urbana *(G-19981)*
Gardner Asphalt Corporation.....E..... 800 237-1155
Chicago *(G-4659)*
▼ **Green Roof Solutions Inc**.....G..... 847 297-7936
Glenview *(G-10554)*
Harsco Corporation.....F..... 217 237-4335
Pawnee *(G-16304)*
Jax Asphalt Company Inc.....F..... 618 244-0500
Mount Vernon *(G-14618)*
Jesus People USA Full Gos.....G..... 773 989-2083
Chicago *(G-5023)*
▲ **Jura Films North America LLC**.....G..... 630 261-1226
Addison *(G-161)*
Karnak Midwest LLC.....F..... 708 338-3388
Broadview *(G-2447)*
Lakefront Roofing Supply.....E..... 773 509-0400
Chicago *(G-5163)*
Lifetime Rooftile Company.....G..... 630 355-7922
Naperville *(G-14863)*
Miller Purcell Co Inc.....G..... 815 485-2142
New Lenox *(G-15043)*
Mrb Roofing Inc.....G..... 872 814-4430
University Park *(G-19963)*
▼ **Nataz Specialty Coatings Inc**.....F..... 773 247-7030
Chicago *(G-5542)*
Nu-Puttie Corporation.....E..... 708 681-1040
Maywood *(G-13676)*
Omnimax International Inc.....E..... 309 747-2937
Gridley *(G-10846)*
Owens Corning Sales LLC.....B..... 708 594-6911
Argo *(G-674)*
Owens Corning Sales LLC.....E..... 708 594-6935
Argo *(G-675)*
Perdue Pavement Solutions Inc.....F..... 309 698-9440
East Peoria *(G-8283)*
Plote Inc.....D..... 847 695-9467
Hoffman Estates *(G-11446)*
Pure Asphalt Company.....F..... 773 247-7030
Chicago *(G-5916)*
▼ **RM Lucas Co**.....E..... 773 523-4300
Alsip *(G-504)*
▲ **Sales Stretcher Enterprises**.....F..... 815 223-9681
Peru *(G-16593)*
Sheet Metal Supply Ltd.....G..... 847 478-8500
Grayslake *(G-10799)*
St Louis Flexicore Inc.....F..... 618 531-8691
East Saint Louis *(G-8324)*
Ted Muller.....G..... 312 435-0978
Chicago *(G-6336)*
TMJ Architectural LLC.....G..... 815 388-7820
Crystal Lake *(G-7283)*
Vada LLC.....F..... 407 572-4979
Olney *(G-15892)*

2992 Lubricating Oils & Greases

Ameriflon Ltd.....G..... 847 541-6000
Wheeling *(G-20848)*
Amsoil Inc.....G..... 630 595-8385
Bensenville *(G-1745)*
◆ **Atm America Corp**.....E..... 800 298-0030
Chicago *(G-3770)*
▲ **Avatar Corporation**.....D..... 708 534-5511
University Park *(G-19947)*
Bioblend Lubricants Intl.....G..... 630 227-1800
Joliet *(G-11832)*
Boyer Corporation.....G..... 708 352-2553
La Grange *(G-12074)*
Calumet Refining LLC.....F..... 708 832-2463
Burnham *(G-2644)*
CAM Tek Lubricants Inc.....G..... 708 477-3000
Orland Park *(G-15945)*
Campbell Camie Inc.....E..... 314 968-3222
Downers Grove *(G-7963)*
Cargill Incorporated.....F..... 773 374-3808
Chicago *(G-4029)*
Cargill Incorporated.....F..... 773 375-7255
Chicago *(G-4030)*
Cartel Holdings Inc.....G..... 815 334-0250
Harvard *(G-11049)*
◆ **Castrol Industrial N Amer Inc**.....C..... 877 641-1600
Naperville *(G-14792)*
Chemix Corp.....F..... 708 754-2150
Glenwood *(G-10639)*
▲ **Chemtool Inc**.....F..... 815 459-1250
Crystal Lake *(G-7179)*
Chemtool Incorporated.....G..... 815 389-0250
Rockton *(G-17695)*
◆ **Chemtool Incorporated**.....C..... 815 957-4140
Rockton *(G-17694)*
Chemtool Incorporated.....D..... 815 459-1250
Crystal Lake *(G-7180)*
Claire-Sprayway Inc.....D..... 630 628-3000
Downers Grove *(G-7973)*
CLC Lubricants Company.....E..... 630 232-7900
Geneva *(G-10261)*
Clean Harbors Wichita LLC.....G..... 815 675-1272
Spring Grove *(G-19270)*
Comet Supply Inc.....G..... 309 444-2712
Washington *(G-20269)*
Darling Ingredients Inc.....E..... 217 482-3261
Mason City *(G-13611)*
Ecli Products LLC.....E..... 630 449-5000
Aurora *(G-955)*
Enterprise Oil Co.....E..... 312 487-2025
Chicago *(G-4514)*
Famous Lubricants Inc.....G..... 773 268-2555
Chicago *(G-4557)*
Filter Kleen Inc.....G..... 708 447-4666
Lyons *(G-13308)*
◆ **Fuchs Corporation**.....G..... 800 323-7755
Harvey *(G-11086)*
Gtx Inc.....G..... 847 699-7421
Des Plaines *(G-7775)*
Harris Lubricants.....G..... 708 849-1935
Dolton *(G-7936)*
Havoline Xpress Lube LLC.....G..... 847 221-5724
Palatine *(G-16123)*
High Performance Lubr LLC.....F..... 815 468-3535
Manteno *(G-13449)*
Houghton International Inc.....F..... 610 666-4000
Chicago *(G-4849)*
Huels Oil Company.....F..... 877 338-6277
Carlyle *(G-2890)*
▲ **Ideas Inc**.....G..... 630 620-2010
Lombard *(G-13087)*
Ideas Inc.....G..... 708 596-1055
Harvey *(G-11090)*
▲ **Illini Coolant Management Corp**.....G..... 847 966-1079
Morton Grove *(G-14412)*
Illinois Oil Products Inc.....F..... 309 788-1896
Rock Island *(G-17224)*
Italmatch Sc LLC.....G..... 708 929-9657
Bedford Park *(G-1474)*
▲ **Jx Nippon Oil & Energy Lubrica**.....F..... 847 413-2188
Schaumburg *(G-18582)*
◆ **Jx Nippon Oil & Energy USA Inc**.....E..... 847 413-2188
Schaumburg *(G-18583)*
K & J Synthetic Lubricants.....G..... 630 628-1011
Addison *(G-164)*
Konzen Chemicals Inc.....F..... 708 878-7636
Matteson *(G-13626)*
Kostelac Grease Service Inc.....E..... 314 436-7166
Belleville *(G-1566)*
Loves Travel Stops.....E..... 618 931-1575
Granite City *(G-10720)*
Lsp Industries Inc.....F..... 815 226-8090
Rockford *(G-17497)*
Lub-Tek Petroleum Products.....G..... 815 741-0414
Joliet *(G-11895)*
Lube Rite.....G..... 217 267-7766
Westville *(G-20781)*
Marathon Petroleum Company LP.....A..... 618 544-2121
Robinson *(G-17119)*
Midwest Recycling Co.....E..... 815 744-4922
Rockdale *(G-17268)*
Mistic Metal Mover Inc.....G..... 815 875-1371
Princeton *(G-16814)*
Motor Oil Inc.....F..... 847 956-7550
Elk Grove Village *(G-9135)*
Mullen Circle Brand Inc.....F..... 847 676-1880
Skokie *(G-18993)*
◆ **Nalco Holding Company**.....E..... 630 305-1000
Naperville *(G-14877)*
▼ **Nanolube Inc**.....G..... 630 706-1250
Lombard *(G-13106)*
Olympic Petroleum Corporation.....G..... 847 995-0996
Schaumburg *(G-18657)*
◆ **Olympic Petroleum Corporation**.....D..... 708 876-7900
Cicero *(G-6868)*
Pdv Midwest Refining LLC.....A..... 630 257-7761
Lemont *(G-12581)*
Perkins Products Inc.....E..... 708 458-2000
Bedford Park *(G-1491)*
Polyenviro Labs Inc.....G..... 708 489-0195
Mokena *(G-14108)*
Premium Oil Company.....F..... 815 963-3800
Rockford *(G-17559)*
Rilco Fluid Care Inc.....E..... 309 788-1854
Rock Island *(G-17242)*
Rock Valley Oil & Chemical Co.....D..... 815 654-2400
Loves Park *(G-13254)*
Rs Used Oil Services Inc.....G..... 618 781-1717
Roxana *(G-18101)*
Safety-Kleen Systems Inc.....G..... 618 875-8050
East Saint Louis *(G-8321)*
Sandstrom Products Company.....F..... 309 523-2121
Port Byron *(G-16788)*
▲ **Shima American Corporation**.....F..... 630 760-4330
Itasca *(G-11732)*
Spartacus Group Inc.....F..... 815 637-1574
Machesney Park *(G-13375)*
Superior Graphite Co.....E..... 708 458-0006
Chicago *(G-6281)*
Tower Oil & Technology Co.....E..... 773 927-6161
Chicago *(G-6401)*
Truckers Oil Pros Inc.....F..... 773 523-8990
Chicago *(G-6436)*
▲ **Uberlube Inc**.....G..... 847 372-3127
Evanston *(G-9585)*
William Ingram.....G..... 217 442-5075
Danville *(G-7398)*

2999 Products Of Petroleum & Coal, NEC

Chemalloy Company LLC.....E..... 847 696-2400
Rosemont *(G-18004)*

30 RUBBER AND MISCELLANEOUS PLASTICS PRODUCTS

3011 Tires & Inner Tubes

◆ **American Tire Distributors**.....G..... 708 680-5150
La Grange Highlands *(G-12091)*
Ameroc Export Inc.....G..... 818 961-6169
Glenview *(G-10523)*
Atturo Tire Corp.....G..... 855 632-8031
Waukegan *(G-20420)*
Best Designs Inc.....F..... 618 985-4445
Carterville *(G-3129)*
Bridgestone Americas.....E..... 309 452-4411
Normal *(G-15200)*
C&C Sealants.....F..... 708 717-0686
Elgin *(G-8528)*
Continental Tire Americas LLC.....D..... 618 242-7100
Mount Vernon *(G-14604)*
Continental Tire Americas LLC.....G..... 618 246-2585
Mascoutah *(G-13596)*
Dealer Tire LLC.....G..... 847 671-0683
Franklin Park *(G-9926)*
Dyneer Corporation.....B..... 217 228-6011
Quincy *(G-16877)*
Goodyear Tire & Rubber Company.....G..... 815 389-8222
South Beloit *(G-19095)*
Jireh Inc.....F..... 217 335-3276
Barry *(G-1251)*
Joseph Coppolino.....G..... 773 735-8647
Chicago *(G-5054)*
Kraly Tire Repair Materials.....G..... 708 863-5981
Cicero *(G-6861)*
Liberty Tire Recycling LLC.....G..... 773 871-6360
Chicago *(G-5218)*
Nova Lines Inc.....G..... 773 322-6262
River Grove *(G-17064)*
▲ **Otr Wheel Engineering Inc**.....E..... 217 223-7705
Quincy *(G-16920)*
▲ **Stop & Go International Inc**.....G..... 815 455-9080
Crystal Lake *(G-7269)*
Tbc Corporation.....G..... 630 428-2233
Naperville *(G-14927)*
Tbc Retail Group Inc.....G..... 630 692-0232
Montgomery *(G-14271)*
Titan International Inc.....C..... 217 228-6011
Quincy *(G-16948)*
Titan Tire Corporation.....B..... 217 228-6011
Quincy *(G-16949)*
Titan Tyre Corporation.....G..... 217 228-6011
Freeport *(G-10146)*

3021 Rubber & Plastic Footwear

◆ **Boss Manufacturing Company**.....E..... 309 852-2131
Kewanee *(G-12024)*
Crocs Inc.....F..... 630 820-3572
Aurora *(G-945)*
Honeywell Safety Pdts USA Inc.....C..... 309 786-7741
Rock Island *(G-17223)*

▲ **Leos Dancewear Inc** .... D 773 889-7700
River Forest *(G-17053)*
Nike Inc .... E 773 846-5460
Chicago *(G-5602)*
Plastic Specialists America .... G 847 406-7547
Gurnee *(G-10912)*
Polyconversions Inc .... E 217 893-3330
Champaign *(G-3335)*
Standard Safety Equipment Co .... E 815 363-8565
McHenry *(G-13795)*
Vans Inc .... F 718 349-2311
Chicago *(G-6521)*

3052 Rubber & Plastic Hose & Belting

6965 North Hamlin LLC .... G 847 673-8900
Lincolnwood *(G-12809)*
◆ **Bando Usa Inc** .... E 630 773-6600
Itasca *(G-11625)*
▲ **Behabelt USA** .... G 630 521-9835
Addison *(G-46)*
Bristol Hose & Fitting Inc .... E 708 492-3456
Melrose Park *(G-13837)*
Bristol Transport Inc .... E 708 343-6411
Melrose Park *(G-13838)*
Caterpillar Inc .... A 309 578-2473
Mossville *(G-14456)*
Chemi-Flex LLC .... E 630 627-9650
Lombard *(G-13051)*
Flexicraft Industries Inc .... F 312 229-7550
Chicago *(G-4609)*
▲ **Flexicraft Industries Inc** .... E 312 738-3588
Chicago *(G-4610)*
Gates Corporation .... C 309 343-7171
Galesburg *(G-10196)*
Geib Industries Inc .... E 847 455-4550
Bensenville *(G-1809)*
Gusco Silicone Rbr & Svcs LLC .... F 773 770-5008
Aurora *(G-1106)*
Industrial Rubber & Sup Entp .... G 217 429-3747
Decatur *(G-7507)*
▲ **Kanaflex Corporation Illinois** .... G 847 634-6100
Vernon Hills *(G-20069)*
Kemper Industries .... G 217 826-5712
Marshall *(G-13573)*
◆ **Kuriyama of America Inc** .... D 847 755-0360
Schaumburg *(G-18594)*
Lanmar Inc .... G 800 233-5520
Northbrook *(G-15418)*
▲ **Megadyne America LLC** .... E 630 752-0600
Carol Stream *(G-3023)*
Pix North America Inc .... F 855 800-0720
Danville *(G-7374)*
▲ **Power Port Products Inc** .... E 630 628-9102
Addison *(G-248)*
Quad City Hose .... E 563 386-8936
Taylor Ridge *(G-19747)*
Royal Brass Inc .... G 618 439-6341
Benton *(G-1936)*
▲ **Srj Inc** .... F 630 351-0639
Schaumburg *(G-18726)*
◆ **Suncast Corporation** .... A 630 879-2050
Batavia *(G-1422)*
▲ **Tigerflex Corporation** .... A 847 439-1766
Elk Grove Village *(G-9273)*
Voss Belting & Specialty Co .... E 847 673-8900
Lincolnwood *(G-12849)*
Western Consolidated Tech Inc .... F 815 334-3684
Woodstock *(G-21447)*

3053 Gaskets, Packing & Sealing Devices

▲ **Advantage Seal Inc** .... F 630 226-0200
Bolingbrook *(G-2147)*
All American Washer Werks Inc .... E 847 566-9091
Mundelein *(G-14661)*
All Products Gasket .... G 877 255-8700
Romeoville *(G-17789)*
All-State Industries Inc .... D 847 350-0460
Elk Grove Village *(G-8815)*
▲ **American Gasket Tech Inc** .... D 630 543-1510
Addison *(G-33)*
Better Gaskets Inc .... G 847 276-7635
Ingleside *(G-11579)*
▲ **Black Swan Manufacturing Co** .... F 773 227-3700
Chicago *(G-3908)*
Cal-Ill Gasket Co .... F 773 287-9605
Chicago *(G-4002)*
▲ **CFC International Corporation** .... C 708 323-4131
Chicago Heights *(G-6740)*
Chambers Gasket & Mfg Co .... E 773 626-8800
Chicago *(G-4068)*
Dana Sealing Manufacturing LLC .... B 618 544-8651
Robinson *(G-17113)*
Dike-O-Seal Incorporated .... F 773 254-3224
Chicago *(G-4361)*
Excelsior Inc .... G 815 987-2900
Rockford *(G-17408)*
Excelsior Inc .... E 815 987-2900
Rockford *(G-17407)*
Federal-Mogul Motorparts LLC .... E 248 354-7700
Berwyn *(G-1954)*
Flatout Group Llc .... G 847 837-9200
Mundelein *(G-14689)*
Flowserve US Inc .... E 630 655-5700
Burr Ridge *(G-2674)*
▲ **Fluid-Aire Dynamics Inc** .... E 847 678-8388
Schaumburg *(G-18530)*
▲ **Gasket & Seal Fabricators Inc** .... E 314 241-3673
East Saint Louis *(G-8308)*
Gaskoa Inc .... E 708 339-5000
South Holland *(G-19213)*
Hennig Gasket & Seals Inc .... G 312 243-8270
Chicago *(G-4803)*
Honeywell Safety Pdts USA Inc .... C 630 343-3731
Bolingbrook *(G-2185)*
Illinois Tool Works Inc .... C 708 325-2300
Bridgeview *(G-2356)*
Ilpea Industries Inc .... D 309 343-3332
Galesburg *(G-10201)*
Innovative Automation .... G 708 418-8720
Lansing *(G-12499)*
Inpro/Seal LLC .... C 309 787-8940
Rock Island *(G-17225)*
▲ **Intech Industries Inc** .... F 847 487-5599
Wauconda *(G-20361)*
J & J Industries Inc .... G 630 595-8878
Mount Prospect *(G-14538)*
▲ **James Walker Mfg Co** .... E 708 754-4020
Glenwood *(G-10641)*
◆ **John Crane Inc** .... A 312 605-7800
Chicago *(G-5039)*
John Crane Inc .... G 630 410-4444
Bolingbrook *(G-2199)*
John Crane Inc .... G 847 967-2400
Morton Grove *(G-14415)*
▲ **Jsn Inc** .... E 708 410-1800
Maywood *(G-13670)*
L A D Specialties .... G 708 430-1588
Oak Lawn *(G-15724)*
M Cor Inc .... F 630 860-1150
Bensenville *(G-1846)*
McAllister Equipment Co .... E 217 789-0351
Lincolnshire *(G-12782)*
Midwest Sealing Products Inc .... E 847 459-2202
Buffalo Grove *(G-2575)*
▲ **Modern Silicone Tech Inc** .... F 727 507-9800
Lincolnshire *(G-12785)*
Plastic Specialties & Tech Inc .... G 847 781-2414
Schaumburg *(G-18675)*
▲ **Plitek LLC** .... D 847 827-6680
Des Plaines *(G-7827)*
▲ **Pres-On Corporation** .... E 630 628-2255
Bolingbrook *(G-2229)*
Punch Products Manufacturing .... E 773 533-2800
Chicago *(G-5915)*
◆ **Qcc LLC** .... C 708 867-5400
Harwood Heights *(G-11107)*
Rhopac Fabricated Products LLC .... E 847 362-3300
Libertyville *(G-12702)*
Right Lane Industries LLC .... G 857 869-4132
Chicago *(G-6031)*
▲ **Rt Enterprises Inc** .... F 847 675-1444
Skokie *(G-19025)*
Rutgers Enterprises Inc .... G 847 674-7666
Lincolnwood *(G-12841)*
Seals & Components Inc .... G 708 895-5222
Lansing *(G-12514)*
Sealtec .... F 630 692-0633
Montgomery *(G-14268)*
Secon Rubber and Plastics Inc .... E 618 282-7700
Red Bud *(G-17001)*
SKF USA Inc .... D 847 742-0700
Elgin *(G-8734)*
SKF USA Inc .... D 847 742-0700
Elgin *(G-8736)*
SKF USA Inc .... D 847 742-0700
Elgin *(G-8735)*
Southland Industries Inc .... E 757 543-5701
Bannockburn *(G-1208)*
Standard Rubber Products Co .... E 847 593-5630
Elk Grove Village *(G-9252)*
Supreme Felt & Abrasives Inc .... E 708 344-0134
Cicero *(G-6878)*
Technetics Group LLC .... G 708 887-6080
Harwood Heights *(G-11111)*
Trellborg Sling Sltions US Inc .... D 630 289-1500
Streamwood *(G-19598)*
▲ **Triseal Corporation** .... E 815 648-2473
Hebron *(G-11151)*
▲ **Union Street Tin Co** .... G 312 379-8200
Park Ridge *(G-16300)*
▲ **United Gasket Corporation** .... D 708 656-3700
Cicero *(G-6885)*
Vangard Distribution Inc .... G 708 484-9895
Berwyn *(G-1962)*
▲ **Vangard Distribution Inc** .... G 708 588-8400
Brookfield *(G-2497)*
Vanseal Corporation .... D 618 283-4700
Vandalia *(G-20029)*
Vibracoustic Usa Inc .... C 618 382-2318
Carmi *(G-2917)*
Winner Cutting & Stamping Co .... F 630 963-1800
Downers Grove *(G-8111)*
Woods Manufacturing Co Inc .... G 630 595-6620
Wood Dale *(G-21258)*

3061 Molded, Extruded & Lathe-Cut Rubber Mechanical Goods

Adora Bella Medspa LLC .... G 779 206-8331
Chicago *(G-3550)*
All-State Industries Inc .... D 847 350-0460
Elk Grove Village *(G-8815)*
Andrews Automotive Company .... F 773 768-1122
Chicago *(G-3693)*
Aztec Products .... G 217 726-8631
Springfield *(G-19323)*
Calumet Rubber Corp .... G 773 536-6350
Chicago *(G-4008)*
▼ **Custom Seal & Rubber Products** .... G 888 356-2966
Mount Morris *(G-14499)*
Elk Grove Rubber & Plastic Co .... F 630 543-5656
Addison *(G-113)*
Excelsior Inc .... E 815 987-2900
Rockford *(G-17407)*
◆ **Fairchild Industries Inc** .... E 847 550-9580
Lake Zurich *(G-12409)*
Finzer Roller Inc .... E 410 939-1850
Des Plaines *(G-7769)*
Finzer Roller Inc .... E 812 829-1455
Des Plaines *(G-7771)*
▲ **Fmi LLC** .... D 847 350-1535
Lincolnshire *(G-12765)*
GC Laser Systems Inc .... G 844 532-1064
Forest Park *(G-9719)*
Industrial Roller Co .... F 618 234-0740
Smithton *(G-19066)*
▲ **James Walker Mfg Co** .... E 708 754-4020
Glenwood *(G-10641)*
▲ **Kokoku Rubber Inc** .... G 847 517-6770
Schaumburg *(G-18589)*
Louis J Hansen Enterprises Inc .... F 630 956-3765
Aurora *(G-1124)*
◆ **Mac Lean-Fogg Company** .... D 847 566-0010
Mundelein *(G-14710)*
▲ **Modern Silicone Tech Inc** .... F 727 507-9800
Lincolnshire *(G-12785)*
Nilan/Primarc Tool & Mold Inc .... F 847 885-2300
Hoffman Estates *(G-11439)*
Rotation Dynamics Corporation .... D 773 247-5600
Chicago *(G-6066)*
▲ **Rt Enterprises Inc** .... F 847 675-1444
Skokie *(G-19025)*
Sage Products LLC .... G 815 455-4700
Crystal Lake *(G-7260)*
Sanyo Seiki America Corp .... F 630 876-8270
Addison *(G-281)*
Smart Solutions Inc .... G 630 775-1517
Itasca *(G-11734)*
Standard Rubber Products Co .... E 847 593-5630
Elk Grove Village *(G-9252)*
Systems By Lar Inc .... G 815 694-3141
Clifton *(G-6916)*
Vibracoustic Usa Inc .... E 618 382-5891
Carmi *(G-2916)*
Vibracoustic Usa Inc .... C 618 382-2318
Carmi *(G-2917)*
Weiland Fast Trac Inc .... G 847 438-7996
Long Grove *(G-13174)*
Wreck Room Inc .... F 630 530-2166
Villa Park *(G-20177)*

SIC

3069 Fabricated Rubber Prdts, NEC

▲ **A Lakin & Sons Inc**....E.... 773 871-6360
Montgomery *(G-14229)*
A R B C Inc....F.... 815 777-6006
Galena *(G-10163)*
▲ **Accurate Products Incorporated**....E.... 773 878-2200
Chicago *(G-3520)*
Adhes Tape Technology Inc....G.... 847 496-7949
Arlington Heights *(G-683)*
◆ **Aero Rubber Company Inc**....E.... 800 662-1009
Tinley Park *(G-19798)*
◆ **Alessco Inc**....F.... 773 327-7919
Chicago *(G-3602)*
American Rubber Mfg Inc....G.... 331 551-9600
Bensenville *(G-1743)*
Arizon Strctures Worldwide LLC....E.... 618 451-7250
Granite City *(G-10697)*
Aztec Products....G.... 217 726-8631
Springfield *(G-19323)*
Barriersafe Solutions Intl Inc....C.... 866 931-3613
Lake Forest *(G-12230)*
◆ **Bls Enterprises Inc**....F.... 630 766-1300
Bensenville *(G-1754)*
Boss Balloon Company Inc....G.... 309 852-2131
Kewanee *(G-12022)*
▲ **Boss Holdings Inc**....D.... 309 852-2131
Kewanee *(G-12023)*
▲ **Bows Arts Inc**....F.... 847 501-3161
Glenview *(G-10533)*
Caroline Cole Inc....F.... 618 233-0600
Belleville *(G-1538)*
▲ **CTI Industries Corporation**....C.... 847 382-1000
Lake Barrington *(G-12146)*
CTI Industries Corporation....D.... 800 284-5605
Lake Zurich *(G-12400)*
▲ **Custom Product Innovations**....G.... 618 628-0111
Lebanon *(G-12545)*
▼ **Custom Seal & Rubber Products**....G.... 888 356-2966
Mount Morris *(G-14499)*
Davis Athletic Equipment Co....F.... 708 563-9006
Bedford Park *(G-1466)*
Day International Group Inc....D.... 630 406-6501
Batavia *(G-1371)*
Dennis Carnes....G.... 618 244-1770
Mount Vernon *(G-14608)*
◆ **Duraco Specialty Tapes LLC**....D.... 866 800-0775
Forest Park *(G-9712)*
Dyneer Corporation....B.... 217 228-6011
Quincy *(G-16877)*
Eco-Smart Flooring Company....G.... 847 404-5032
Chicago *(G-4447)*
▲ **Edgewater Products Company Inc**....F.... 708 345-9200
Melrose Park *(G-13860)*
◆ **Enesco LLC**....B.... 630 875-5300
Itasca *(G-11650)*
Excelsior Inc....E.... 815 987-2900
Rockford *(G-17407)*
◆ **Fenwal Inc**....B.... 800 333-6925
Lake Zurich *(G-12411)*
Finzer Holding LLC....G.... 847 390-6200
Des Plaines *(G-7768)*
Finzer Roller Inc....E.... 410 939-1850
Des Plaines *(G-7769)*
◆ **Finzer Roller Inc**....E.... 847 390-6200
Des Plaines *(G-7770)*
Finzer Roller Inc....E.... 812 829-1455
Des Plaines *(G-7771)*
▲ **Flexan LLC**....C.... 224 543-0003
Lincolnshire *(G-12764)*
Go Steady LLC....G.... 630 293-3243
West Chicago *(G-20588)*
Gusco Silicone Rbr & Svcs LLC....F.... 773 770-5008
Aurora *(G-1106)*
Honeywell Safety Pdts USA Inc....C.... 630 343-3731
Bolingbrook *(G-2185)*
Hst Materials Inc....F.... 847 640-1803
Elk Grove Village *(G-9037)*
Hydac Rubber Manufacturing....E.... 618 233-2129
Smithton *(G-19065)*
Industrial Roller Co....F.... 618 234-0740
Smithton *(G-19066)*
Industrial Roller Co....F.... 618 234-0740
Smithton *(G-19067)*
James Ray Monroe Corporation....F.... 618 532-4575
Centralia *(G-3236)*
Jessup Manufacturing Company....E.... 847 362-0961
Lake Bluff *(G-12190)*
▼ **Jvi Inc**....E.... 847 675-1560
Lincolnwood *(G-12825)*
▲ **Kelco Industries Inc**....G.... 815 334-3600
Woodstock *(G-21398)*
Lakin General Corporation....D.... 773 871-6360
Montgomery *(G-14255)*
Ljm Equipment Co....G.... 847 291-0162
Northbrook *(G-15420)*
Lochman Ref Silk Screen Co....F.... 847 475-6266
Evanston *(G-9547)*
▲ **Loop Attachment Co**....G.... 847 922-0642
Chicago *(G-5256)*
▼ **March Industries Inc**....F.... 224 654-6500
Hampshire *(G-10978)*
Menges Roller Co Inc....E.... 847 487-8877
Wauconda *(G-20376)*
Midwest Sealing Products Inc....E.... 847 459-2202
Buffalo Grove *(G-2575)*
▲ **Monogram Creative Group Inc**....G.... 312 802-1433
Glenview *(G-10590)*
Moon Jump Inc....G.... 630 983-0953
Addison *(G-222)*
Morrow Shoe and Boot Inc....G.... 217 342-6833
Effingham *(G-8413)*
Omni Products Inc....E.... 815 344-3100
McHenry *(G-13773)*
Pamarco Global Graphics Inc....F.... 847 459-6000
Wheeling *(G-20955)*
Polyonics Rubber Co....G.... 815 765-2033
Poplar Grove *(G-16783)*
Praire State Floor Covering....G.... 309 253-5982
Pekin *(G-16355)*
Prestige Motor Works Inc....G.... 630 780-6439
Naperville *(G-14983)*
Pro Form Industries Inc....G.... 815 923-2555
Union *(G-19942)*
Rahco Rubber Inc....D.... 847 298-4200
Des Plaines *(G-7835)*
▲ **RDF Inc**....F.... 618 273-4141
Eldorado *(G-8483)*
Rehling & Associates Inc....G.... 630 941-3560
Elmhurst *(G-9417)*
Reilly Foam Corp....E.... 630 392-2680
Naperville *(G-14908)*
Right Lane Industries LLC....G.... 857 869-4132
Chicago *(G-6031)*
Roho Inc....C.... 618 234-4899
Belleville *(G-1593)*
Rotation Dynamics Corporation....E.... 630 679-7053
Romeoville *(G-17871)*
Rutgers Enterprises Inc....G.... 847 674-7666
Lincolnwood *(G-12841)*
▲ **Safersonic Us Inc**....G.... 847 274-1534
Highland Park *(G-11296)*
▲ **Shepard Medical Products Inc**....G.... 630 539-7790
Roselle *(G-17988)*
Shore Capital Partners LLC....E.... 312 348-7580
Chicago *(G-6157)*
Singer Equities Inc....F.... 815 874-5364
Rockford *(G-17632)*
Slipon Nipple Company....G.... 708 345-2525
Westchester *(G-20711)*
Smith Industrial Rubber & Plas....F.... 815 874-5364
Rockford *(G-17636)*
Southland Industries Inc....E.... 757 543-5701
Bannockburn *(G-1208)*
◆ **Sponge-Cushion Inc**....D.... 815 942-2300
Morris *(G-14328)*
Standard Rubber Products Co....E.... 847 593-5630
Elk Grove Village *(G-9252)*
Superior Bumpers Inc....G.... 630 932-4910
Lombard *(G-13136)*
▲ **Superior Mfg Group - Europe**....G.... 708 458-4600
Chicago *(G-6283)*
▲ **Team Products Inc**....F.... 815 244-6100
Mount Carroll *(G-14497)*
Tholeo Design Inc....G.... 630 325-3792
Clarendon Hills *(G-6901)*
Tools Aviation LLC....G.... 630 377-7260
Oswego *(G-16028)*
Traeyne Corporation....G.... 309 936-7878
Atkinson *(G-903)*
Verona Rubber Works Inc....F.... 815 673-2929
Blackstone *(G-1971)*
Voss Belting & Specialty Co....E.... 847 673-8900
Lincolnwood *(G-12849)*
Weiland Fast Trac Inc....G.... 847 438-7996
Long Grove *(G-13174)*
Winfield Technology Inc....F.... 630 584-0475
Saint Charles *(G-18301)*

3081 Plastic Unsupported Sheet & Film

A B Kelly Inc....G.... 847 639-1022
Cary *(G-3142)*
▲ **Aargus Plastics Inc**....C.... 847 325-4444
Wheeling *(G-20837)*
Abbott Plastics & Supply Co....E.... 815 874-8500
Rockford *(G-17285)*
Alpha Industries MGT Inc....D.... 773 359-8000
Chicago *(G-3629)*
◆ **Amcor Flexibles LLC**....C.... 224 313-7000
Buffalo Grove *(G-2510)*
Avery Dennison Corporation....D.... 877 214-0909
Niles *(G-15104)*
Berry Global Inc....C.... 847 884-1200
Schaumburg *(G-18461)*
Berry Global Inc....G.... 630 375-0358
Aurora *(G-923)*
Berry Global Films LLC....D.... 708 239-4619
Alsip *(G-423)*
Bio Star Films LLC....G.... 773 254-5959
Chicago *(G-3894)*
C M F Enterprises Inc....F.... 847 526-9499
Wauconda *(G-20337)*
Cadillac Products Packaging Co....C.... 217 463-1444
Paris *(G-16225)*
Cast Films Inc....F.... 847 808-0363
Wheeling *(G-20869)*
Catalina Coating & Plas Inc....F.... 847 806-1340
Elk Grove Village *(G-8880)*
CFC International Inc....G.... 708 891-3456
Chicago Heights *(G-6739)*
▲ **CFC International Corporation**....C.... 708 323-4131
Chicago Heights *(G-6740)*
▲ **Clear Focus Imaging Inc**....E.... 707 544-7990
Franklin Park *(G-9910)*
Clear Pack Company....C.... 847 957-6282
Franklin Park *(G-9911)*
Clorox Company....E.... 510 271-7000
Willowbrook *(G-21036)*
▲ **Co-Ordinated Packaging Inc**....F.... 847 559-8877
Bensenville *(G-1772)*
▲ **Cosmo Films Inc**....E.... 317 790-9547
Addison *(G-82)*
Custom Films Inc....F.... 217 826-2326
Marshall *(G-13569)*
Custom Plastics of Peoria....G.... 309 697-2888
Bartonville *(G-1331)*
▲ **E-Z Products Inc**....F.... 847 551-9199
Gilberts *(G-10354)*
Environetics Inc....F.... 815 838-8331
Lockport *(G-12993)*
◆ **Essentra Holdings Corp**....G.... 804 518-0322
Westchester *(G-20698)*
◆ **Exclusively Expo**....D.... 630 378-4600
Romeoville *(G-17818)*
Fisher Container Holdings LLC....G.... 847 541-0000
Buffalo Grove *(G-2537)*
Flex-O-Glass Inc....C.... 773 261-5200
Chicago *(G-4605)*
Flex-O-Glass Inc....G.... 773 379-7878
Chicago *(G-4606)*
Flex-O-Glass Inc....E.... 815 288-1424
Dixon *(G-7899)*
G-P Manufacturing Co Inc....E.... 847 473-9001
Waukegan *(G-20444)*
H H Interantional Inc....G.... 847 697-7805
Elgin *(G-8602)*
▲ **Highland Mfg & Sls Co**....D.... 618 654-2161
Highland *(G-11219)*
◆ **Highland Supply Corporation**....B.... 618 654-2161
Highland *(G-11224)*
Huntsman Expndable Polymers Lc....C.... 815 224-5463
Peru *(G-16577)*
Jordan Specialty Plastics Inc....G.... 847 945-5591
Deerfield *(G-7622)*
Kns Companies Inc....E.... 630 665-9010
Carol Stream *(G-3013)*
Kw Plastics....F.... 708 757-5140
Chicago *(G-5138)*
Letters Unlimited Inc....G.... 847 891-7811
Schaumburg *(G-18604)*
◆ **Midwest Canvas Corp**....C.... 773 287-4400
Chicago *(G-5440)*
Midwest Lminating Coatings Inc....E.... 708 653-9500
Alsip *(G-478)*
Midwest Marketing Distrs Inc....G.... 309 663-6972
Bloomington *(G-2078)*
▲ **Midwest Marketing Distrs Inc**....F.... 309 688-8858
Peoria *(G-16476)*

SIC SECTION 30 RUBBER AND MISCELLANEOUS PLASTICS PRODUCTS

▲ Minigrip Inc....D.... 845 680-2710
Ottawa (G-16061)
▲ Morton Group Ltd....G.... 847 831-2766
Highland Park (G-11286)
▲ Neptune USA Inc....G.... 847 987-3804
Schaumburg (G-18647)
Orbis Rpm LLC....F.... 217 876-8655
Decatur (G-7533)
Orbis Rpm LLC....F.... 312 343-4902
Chicago (G-5693)
Perfect Circle Projectiles LLC....F.... 847 367-8960
Lake Forest (G-12286)
◆ Pliant LLC....A.... 812 424-2904
Rolling Meadows (G-17761)
Pliant Corp International....G.... 847 969-3300
Rolling Meadows (G-17762)
Pliant Investment Inc....G.... 847 969-3300
Schaumburg (G-18677)
Pliant Solutions Corporation....E.... 847 969-3300
Schaumburg (G-18678)
▲ Poli-Film America Inc....D.... 847 453-8104
Hampshire (G-10984)
Poly Films Inc....G.... 708 547-7963
Hillside (G-11353)
Polyair Inter Pack Inc....D.... 773 995-1818
Chicago (G-5838)
▲ Ppc Flexible Packaging LLC....C.... 847 541-0000
Buffalo Grove (G-2588)
Printpack Inc....C.... 847 888-7150
Elgin (G-8696)
◆ Protective Products Intl....G.... 847 526-1180
Wauconda (G-20386)
Realt Images Inc....G.... 217 567-3487
Tower Hill (G-19894)
Reynolds Food Packaging LLC....C.... 847 482-3500
Lake Forest (G-12298)
Right Lane Industries LLC....G.... 857 869-4132
Chicago (G-6031)
Sandee Manufacturing Co....E.... 847 671-1335
Franklin Park (G-10042)
◆ Scholle Ipn Corporation....F.... 708 562-7290
Northlake (G-15558)
Senoplast USA....G.... 630 898-0731
Aurora (G-1016)
Signode Industrial Group LLC....E.... 800 628-6787
Glenview (G-10619)
Sisco Corporation....E.... 618 327-3066
Nashville (G-15010)
Sonoco Products Company....C.... 847 957-6282
Franklin Park (G-10049)
◆ Sun Process Converting Inc....D.... 847 593-0447
Mount Prospect (G-14573)
▲ Tee Group Films Inc....D.... 815 894-2331
Ladd (G-12134)
Thermal Industries Inc....E.... 800 237-0560
Wood Dale (G-21249)
◆ Tradex International Inc....D.... 216 651-4788
Elwood (G-9465)
▲ Transcenda Inc....E.... 847 705-6670
Palatine (G-16166)
◆ Transcendia Inc....C.... 847 678-1800
Franklin Park (G-10063)
◆ Transcontinental Multifilm Inc....D.... 847 695-7600
Elgin (G-8757)
Transcontinental Multifilm Inc....G.... 847 695-7600
Elgin (G-8758)
▼ Transworld Plastic Films Inc....F.... 815 561-7117
Rochelle (G-17162)
Tredegar Film Products Corp....C.... 847 438-2111
Lake Zurich (G-12465)
Unique Blister Company....F.... 630 289-1232
Bartlett (G-1319)
Vacumet Corp....F.... 708 562-7290
Northlake (G-15564)
W R Grace & Co....C.... 773 838-3200
Chicago (G-6575)

3082 Plastic Unsupported Profile Shapes

Abbott Plastics & Supply Co....E.... 815 874-8500
Rockford (G-17285)
▲ Advanced Plastic Corp....D.... 847 674-2070
Lincolnwood (G-12812)
▲ Atlas Fibre Company....D.... 847 674-1234
Northbrook (G-15343)
Custom Films Inc....F.... 217 826-2326
Marshall (G-13569)
Custom Plastics of Peoria....G.... 309 697-2888
Bartonville (G-1331)
◆ Engineered Plastic Systems LLC....F.... 800 480-2327
Elgin (G-8580)
◆ Essentra Holdings Corp....G.... 804 518-0322
Westchester (G-20698)
Flex-O-Glass Inc....C.... 773 261-5200
Chicago (G-4605)
Flex-O-Glass Inc....G.... 773 379-7878
Chicago (G-4606)
Flex-O-Glass Inc....E.... 815 288-1424
Dixon (G-7899)
G-P Manufacturing Co Inc....E.... 847 473-9001
Waukegan (G-20444)
Resinite Corporation....C.... 847 537-4250
Wheeling (G-20973)
Sandee Manufacturing Co....E.... 847 671-1335
Franklin Park (G-10042)
Shape Master Inc....G.... 217 469-7027
Saint Joseph (G-18320)
Sonoco Plastics Inc....F.... 630 628-5859
Addison (G-292)
Streamwood Plastics Ltd....G.... 847 895-9190
Schaumburg (G-18728)

3083 Plastic Laminated Plate & Sheet

Acco Brands Corporation....A.... 847 541-9500
Lake Zurich (G-12374)
Acco Brands International Inc....G.... 847 541-9500
Lake Zurich (G-12375)
◆ American Louver Company....C.... 847 470-0400
Skokie (G-18918)
American Name Plate & Metal De....E.... 773 376-1400
Chicago (G-3663)
▲ Amerisan Designs Inc....D.... 773 542-1291
Chicago (G-3677)
▲ Atlas Fibre Company....D.... 847 674-1234
Northbrook (G-15343)
B & B Formica Appliers Inc....F.... 773 804-1015
Chicago (G-3804)
Blaige....G.... 312 337-5200
Chicago (G-3909)
▲ C Line Products Inc....D.... 847 827-6661
Mount Prospect (G-14517)
▲ Card Dynamix LLC....C.... 630 685-4060
Romeoville (G-17803)
Carl Gorr Printing Co....E.... 815 338-3191
Woodstock (G-21370)
Catalina Coating & Plas Inc....F.... 847 806-1340
Elk Grove Village (G-8880)
CFC International Inc....G.... 708 891-3456
Chicago Heights (G-6739)
Coilform Company....E.... 630 232-8000
Geneva (G-10262)
▲ Cortube Products Co....G.... 708 429-6700
Tinley Park (G-19816)
Credit Card Systems Inc....F.... 847 459-8320
Wheeling (G-20876)
Custom Films Inc....F.... 217 826-2326
Marshall (G-13569)
Custom Plastics of Peoria....G.... 309 697-2888
Bartonville (G-1331)
Dana Plastic Container Corp....E.... 630 529-7878
Schaumburg (G-18504)
Designed Plastics Inc....E.... 630 694-7300
Bensenville (G-1786)
▲ Diamond Cellophane Pdts Inc....E.... 847 418-3000
Northbrook (G-15375)
E-Jay Plastics Co....F.... 630 543-4000
Addison (G-108)
Field Ventures LLC....D.... 847 509-2250
Northbrook (G-15389)
Glazed Structures Inc....F.... 847 223-4560
Grayslake (G-10776)
Idemia America Corp....D.... 630 551-0792
Naperville (G-14844)
James Injection Molding Co....E.... 847 564-3820
Northbrook (G-15410)
John Maneely Company....C.... 773 254-0617
Chicago (G-5043)
▲ Lakone Company....D.... 630 892-4251
Montgomery (G-14256)
◆ Lamin-Art LLC....F.... 800 323-7624
Schaumburg (G-18598)
▲ Mak Design Group Incorporated....G.... 847 682-4504
Countryside (G-7063)
Npi Holding Corp....G.... 217 391-1229
Springfield (G-19412)
Nudo Products Inc....C.... 217 528-5636
Springfield (G-19413)
▲ Nudo Products Inc....C.... 217 528-5636
Springfield (G-19414)
Nypro Hanover Park....G.... 630 868-3517
Roselle (G-17973)
◆ Olon Industries Inc (us)....E.... 630 232-4705
Geneva (G-10298)
Photo Techniques Corp....E.... 630 690-9360
Carol Stream (G-3046)
Pioneer Plastics Inc....C.... 309 365-2951
Lexington (G-12620)
Pro Glass Corporation....G.... 630 553-3141
Bristol (G-2409)
R & R Custom Cabinet Making....G.... 847 358-6188
Palatine (G-16152)
Rainbow Colors Inc....F.... 847 640-7700
Elk Grove Village (G-9212)
Suburban Laminating Inc....G.... 708 389-6106
Melrose Park (G-13918)
◆ Sun Process Converting Inc....D.... 847 593-0447
Mount Prospect (G-14573)
Technologies Dvlpmnt....G.... 815 943-9922
Crystal Lake (G-7278)
Transcendia Inc....E.... 847 678-1800
Franklin Park (G-10064)
Unique Designs....G.... 309 454-1226
Normal (G-15227)
Upm Raflatac Inc....C.... 815 285-6100
Dixon (G-7924)
▲ Vecchio Manufacturing of Ill....F.... 847 742-8429
Elgin (G-8773)

3084 Plastic Pipe

Advanced Drainage Systems Inc....F.... 815 539-2160
Mendota (G-13933)
Atkore Rmcp Inc....G.... 708 339-1610
Harvey (G-11077)
Blackburn Sampling Inc....G.... 309 342-8429
Galesburg (G-10185)
Eastern Illinois Clay Company....F.... 815 427-8144
Saint Anne (G-18133)
Fusibond Piping Systems Inc....F.... 630 969-4488
Downers Grove (G-8006)
▲ General Products International....G.... 847 458-6357
Lake In The Hills (G-12335)
Nt Liquidating Inc....E.... 815 726-3351
Joliet (G-11909)

3085 Plastic Bottles

Alpha Packaging Minnesota Inc....G.... 507 454-3830
Chicago (G-3630)
Astro Plastic Containers Inc....F.... 708 458-7100
Bolingbrook (G-2150)
Container Specialties Inc....E.... 708 615-1400
Franklin Park (G-9914)
▲ Dana Plastic Container Corp....G.... 847 670-0650
Arlington Heights (G-725)
Dana Plastic Container Corp....E.... 630 529-7878
Schaumburg (G-18504)
Graham Packaging Company LP....E.... 630 739-9150
Woodridge (G-21306)
▲ Illinois Bottle Mfg Co....D.... 847 595-9000
Elk Grove Village (G-9040)
Inhance Technologies LLC....E.... 630 231-7515
West Chicago (G-20595)
Isovac Products LLC....G.... 630 679-1740
Romeoville (G-17834)
Logoplaste Chicago LLC....G.... 815 230-6961
Plainfield (G-16684)
Logoplaste Fort Worth LLC....G.... 815 230-6961
Plainfield (G-16685)
Logoplaste Racine LLC....G.... 815 230-6961
Plainfield (G-16686)
▲ Logoplaste Usa Inc....D.... 815 230-6961
Plainfield (G-16687)
Oak Hill Brands Corp....G.... 630 922-5010
Lombard (G-13111)
Phoenix Unlimited Ltd....G.... 847 515-1263
Huntley (G-11559)
▲ Plastic Container Corporation....D.... 217 352-2722
Urbana (G-19993)
Plastipak Packaging Inc....B.... 217 398-1832
Champaign (G-3334)
Plastipak Packaging Inc....C.... 708 385-0721
Alsip (G-493)
Pretium Packaging LLC....D.... 815 224-2633
Peru (G-16590)
Pvc Container Corporation....C.... 217 463-6600
Paris (G-16241)
Ring Container Tech LLC....E.... 217 875-5084
Decatur (G-7542)
Ring Container Tech LLC....E.... 815 229-9110
Rockford (G-17572)
Ringwood Containers LP....E.... 815 939-7270
Kankakee (G-11998)

S I C

Employee Codes: A=Over 500 employees, B=251-500
C=101-250, D=51-100, E=20-50, F=10-19, G=3-9

Silgan Plastics LLC....D....618 662-4471
Flora (G-9692)
Twistshake LLC....G....224 419-0086
Waukegan (G-20511)
Whitney Products Inc....F....847 966-6161
Niles (G-15187)

3086 Plastic Foam Prdts

▲ Ade Inc....E....773 646-3400
Chicago (G-3541)
All Foam Products....G....847 913-9341
Buffalo Grove (G-2507)
▲ All-Vac Industries Inc....F....847 675-2290
Skokie (G-18915)
Armacell LLC....D....708 596-9501
South Holland (G-19197)
Atlas Roofing Corporation....E....309 752-7121
East Moline (G-8222)
◆ Blachford Investments Inc....C....630 231-8300
West Chicago (G-20552)
Carlisle Construction Mtls LLC....D....847 671-2516
Franklin Park (G-9898)
▲ Co-Ordinated Packaging Inc....F....847 559-8877
Bensenville (G-1772)
Cushioneer Inc....D....815 748-5505
Dekalb (G-7673)
Custom Foam Works Inc....G....618 920-2810
Troy (G-19913)
Dart Container Corp Illinois....C....630 896-4631
North Aurora (G-15258)
Dart Container Corp Illinois....G....800 367-2877
Lincolnshire (G-12758)
Dow Chemical Company....C....815 423-5921
Channahon (G-3381)
◆ Duraco Specialty Tapes LLC....D....866 800-0775
Forest Park (G-9712)
Eagle Panel System Inc....G....618 326-7132
Mulberry Grove (G-14654)
▲ Elongated Plastics Inc....G....224 456-0559
Northbrook (G-15382)
Engineered Foam Solutions Inc....G....708 769-4130
South Holland (G-19210)
Epe Industries Usa Inc....F....800 315-0336
Elk Grove Village (G-8980)
Excelsior Inc....E....815 987-2900
Rockford (G-17407)
▲ Free-Flow Packaging Intl Inc....E....650 261-5300
Deerfield (G-7611)
Free-Flow Packaging Intl Inc....D....708 589-6500
Homewood (G-11494)
Grafcor Packaging Inc....F....815 963-1300
Rockford (G-17434)
Illinois Tool Works Inc....E....217 345-2166
Itasca (G-11673)
Innocor Foam Technologies LLC....F....630 293-0780
West Chicago (G-20599)
▲ K & S Service & Rental Corp....F....630 279-4292
Elmhurst (G-9384)
Layer Saver LLC....G....630 325-7287
Burr Ridge (G-2696)
Mailbox Plus....G....847 577-1737
Mount Prospect (G-14545)
Meadoworks LLC....F....847 640-8580
Schaumburg (G-18625)
Midpoint Packaging LLC....G....630 613-9922
Downers Grove (G-8056)
Minnesota Diversified Pdts Inc....E....815 539-3106
Mendota (G-13950)
Owens Corning Sales LLC....D....815 226-4627
Rockford (G-17545)
Polar Tech Industries Inc....E....815 784-9000
Genoa (G-10321)
Polyair Inter Pack Inc....D....773 995-1818
Chicago (G-5838)
▲ Positive Packaging Inc....G....708 560-3028
Rolling Meadows (G-17763)
Pregis LLC....A....847 597-2200
Deerfield (G-7645)
▲ Pres-On Corporation....E....630 628-2255
Bolingbrook (G-2229)
Punch Products Manufacturing....E....773 533-2800
Chicago (G-5915)
Quality Pallets Inc....E....217 459-2655
Windsor (G-21107)
Remco Technology Inc....F....847 329-8090
Skokie (G-19021)
Republic Systems Inc....G....773 233-6530
Chicago (G-6016)
Sales Midwest Prtg & Packg Inc....G....309 764-5544
Moline (G-14175)
Sealed Air Corporation....D....708 352-8700
Hodgkins (G-11396)
▲ Silgan Equipment Company....E....847 336-0552
Waukegan (G-20496)
Sonoco Display & Packaging LLC....D....630 972-1990
Bolingbrook (G-2244)
Sonoco Protective Solutions....E....847 398-0110
Arlington Heights (G-810)
Sonoco Prtective Solutions Inc....F....717 757-2683
Chicago (G-6202)
▲ Tek Pak Inc....D....630 406-0560
Batavia (G-1429)
◆ Thermos LLC....D....847 439-7821
Schaumburg (G-18745)
◆ Tkk USA Inc....C....847 439-7821
Rolling Meadows (G-17780)
Tri Pro Graphics LLC....G....309 664-5875
Bloomington (G-2104)
▼ Volflex Inc....E....708 478-1117
Mokena (G-14127)
W R Grace & Co-Conn....F....708 458-9700
Chicago (G-6577)
◆ Wave Pads LLC....G....224 444-9283
Plainfield (G-16728)
Wrap & Send Services....F....847 329-2559
Skokie (G-19059)
Wrapping Inc....G....773 871-2898
Chicago (G-6682)

3087 Custom Compounding Of Purchased Plastic Resins

Aabbitt Adhesives Inc....D....773 227-2700
Chicago (G-3499)
Ameriflon Ltd....G....847 541-6000
Wheeling (G-20848)
Antek Madison Plastics USA Ltd....F....773 933-0900
Chicago (G-3705)
Azul 3d Inc....F....321 277-7807
Skokie (G-18926)
Bach Plastic Works Inc....G....847 680-4342
Libertyville (G-12635)
▲ Bulk Molding Compounds Inc....D....630 377-1065
West Chicago (G-20556)
Enbarr LLC....G....630 217-2101
Bartlett (G-1278)
Lyondell Chemical Company....B....815 942-7011
Morris (G-14311)
◆ M-Prime Company....E....630 834-9400
Villa Park (G-20157)
Mervis Industries Inc....C....217 442-5300
Danville (G-7365)
Parker-Hannifin Corporation....D....847 836-6859
Elgin (G-8685)
Polyone Corporation....D....630 972-0505
Romeoville (G-17865)
Polyone Corporation....D....815 385-8500
McHenry (G-13782)
Polyone Corporation....F....815 385-8500
Mchenry (G-13783)
▲ Shannon Industrial Corporation....F....815 337-2349
Woodstock (G-21432)
Standard Rubber Products Co....E....847 593-5630
Elk Grove Village (G-9252)
Ticona Technical Polymers....G....847 949-1444
Mundelein (G-14744)

3088 Plastic Plumbing Fixtures

Bathwraps....E....630 227-1737
Roselle (G-17939)
BCI Acrylic Inc....E....847 963-8827
Libertyville (G-12636)
Carstin Brands Inc....D....217 543-3331
Arthur (G-844)
◆ Danze Inc....D....630 754-0277
Woodridge (G-21291)
G K L Corporation....D....815 886-5900
Romeoville (G-17826)
Industrial Fiberglass Inc....F....708 681-2707
Melrose Park (G-13882)
Jalaa Fiberglass Inc....G....217 923-3433
Greenup (G-10821)
▲ Lordahl Manufacturing Co....E....847 244-0448
Waukegan (G-20463)
Northwest Marble Products....E....630 860-2288
Hoffman Estates (G-11473)
Pure Processing LLC....G....877 718-6868
Carol Stream (G-3056)
Staffco Inc....G....309 688-3223
Peoria (G-16528)
Swan Surfaces LLC....C....618 532-5673
Centralia (G-3252)
T J Van Der Bosch & Associates....E....815 344-3210
McHenry (G-13805)

3089 Plastic Prdts

A P L Plastics....G....773 265-1370
Chicago (G-3490)
A To Z Engraving Co Inc....G....847 526-7396
Wauconda (G-20324)
A W Enterprises Inc....E....708 458-8989
Bedford Park (G-1452)
AAA Trash....G....618 775-1365
Odin (G-15833)
Abbacus Injection Molding Inc....E....815 637-9222
Machesney Park (G-13322)
Abbott Plastics & Supply Co....E....815 874-8500
Rockford (G-17285)
Aberdeen Technologies Inc....F....630 665-8590
Carol Stream (G-2923)
Able American Plastics Inc....F....815 678-4646
Richmond (G-17007)
◆ Acco Brands USA LLC....B....800 222-6462
Lake Zurich (G-12376)
Acco Brands USA LLC....D....847 272-3700
Lincolnshire (G-12741)
Accubow LLC....G....815 250-0607
Peru (G-16563)
▼ Ace Plastic Inc....F....815 635-3737
Chatsworth (G-3425)
Acme Awning Co Inc....G....847 446-0153
Lake Zurich (G-12379)
Acrylic Service Inc....G....630 543-0336
Addison (G-18)
Acrylic Ventures Inc....F....847 901-4440
Glenview (G-10517)
▲ Adams Apple Distributing LP....E....847 832-9900
Glenview (G-10518)
▲ Admo Inc....D....847 741-5777
Elgin (G-8495)
Advance Plastic Corp....F....773 637-5922
Chicago (G-3556)
Advanced Molding Tech Inc....D....815 334-3600
Woodstock (G-21354)
▲ Advanced Prototype Molding....G....847 202-4200
Palatine (G-16090)
▲ Advanced Window Corp....E....773 379-3500
Chicago (G-3568)
▲ Advangene Consumables Inc....G....847 295-2539
Lake Bluff (G-12168)
▲ Advantech Plastics LLC....D....815 338-8383
Woodstock (G-21355)
Advert Display Products Inc....G....815 513-5432
Morris (G-14290)
AEP Inc....G....618 466-7668
Alton (G-542)
▲ AGS Technology Inc....E....847 534-6600
Batavia (G-1344)
Akrylix Inc....F....773 869-9005
Frankfort (G-9764)
Algus Packaging Inc....D....815 756-1881
Dekalb (G-7665)
All Rite Industries Inc....E....847 540-0300
Lake Zurich (G-12382)
All Star Injection Molders Inc....G....630 978-4046
Naperville (G-14956)
◆ All West Plastics Inc....D....847 395-8830
Antioch (G-598)
Alliance Plastics....G....888 643-1432
Bensenville (G-1735)
◆ Allmetal Inc....D....630 250-8090
Itasca (G-11619)
Allmetal Inc....F....630 766-1407
Bensenville (G-1737)
Alltech Plastics Inc....G....847 352-2309
Schaumburg (G-18434)
Alpha Acrylic Design....G....847 818-8178
Arlington Heights (G-687)
▼ Alpha Omega Plastics Company....D....847 956-8777
Elk Grove Village (G-8817)
Alpha Star Tool and Mold Inc....F....815 455-2802
Crystal Lake (G-7156)
▲ Altamont Co....D....800 626-5774
Thomasboro (G-19775)
Altium Packaging....C....815 943-7828
Harvard (G-11042)
Altium Packaging....C....630 231-7150
West Chicago (G-20536)
Amcor Phrm Packg USA LLC....C....847 298-5626
Des Plaines (G-7726)

SIC SECTION | 30 RUBBER AND MISCELLANEOUS PLASTICS PRODUCTS

Amcor Rigid Packaging Usa LLC ... E ... 630 628-5859
Addison *(G-29)*
Amcor Rigid Packaging Usa LLC ... D ... 630 773-3235
Itasca *(G-11621)*
American Acrylics Inc ... G ... 847 674-7800
Skokie *(G-18917)*
◆ American Flange & Mfg Co Inc ... E ... 630 665-7900
Carol Stream *(G-2933)*
▲ American Gasket Tech Inc ... D ... 630 543-1510
Addison *(G-33)*
American Molding Tech Inc ... E ... 847 437-6900
Elk Grove Village *(G-8824)*
Amtec Molded Products Inc ... E ... 815 226-0187
Elgin *(G-8510)*
Andrews Automotive Company ... F ... 773 768-1122
Chicago *(G-3693)*
▲ Anfinsen Plastic Moulding Inc ... E ... 630 554-4100
Oswego *(G-15992)*
APAC II LLC ... G ... 618 426-1338
Campbell Hill *(G-2813)*
▲ Apollo Plastics Corporation ... D ... 773 282-9222
Chicago *(G-3712)*
Applied Arts & Sciences Inc ... G ... 407 288-8228
Mokena *(G-14072)*
Applied Polymer System Inc ... G ... 847 301-1712
Schaumburg *(G-18443)*
Aptargroup Inc ... G ... 847 816-9400
Libertyville *(G-12629)*
◆ Aptargroup Inc ... C ... 815 477-0424
Crystal Lake *(G-7160)*
Aptargroup Inc ... E ... 847 462-3900
McHenry *(G-13719)*
Aptargroup International LLC ... G ... 815 477-0424
Crystal Lake *(G-7161)*
Armbrust Paper Tubes Inc ... E ... 773 586-3232
Chicago *(G-3730)*
Armin Molding Corp ... E ... 847 742-1864
South Elgin *(G-19133)*
Arnel Industries Inc ... E ... 630 543-6500
Addison *(G-39)*
Aztec Plastic Company ... E ... 312 733-0900
Chicago *(G-3801)*
B & M Plastic Inc ... F ... 847 258-4437
Franklin Park *(G-9880)*
B J Plastic Molding Co ... E ... 630 766-3200
Franklin Park *(G-9882)*
B J Plastic Molding Co ... E ... 630 766-8750
Bensenville *(G-1750)*
▲ Bankier Companies Inc ... E ... 847 647-6565
Niles *(G-15105)*
Bannon Enterprises Inc ... G ... 847 529-9265
Geneva *(G-10254)*
▲ Baps Investors Group LLC ... E ... 847 818-8444
Rolling Meadows *(G-17718)*
▲ Bay Plastics ... F ... 847 299-2045
Des Plaines *(G-7737)*
Bee Boat Co Inc ... G ... 217 379-2605
Paxton *(G-16307)*
Berry Global Inc ... C ... 815 334-5225
Woodstock *(G-21363)*
Berry Global Inc ... C ... 847 884-1200
Schaumburg *(G-18461)*
Berry Global Inc ... C ... 847 541-7900
Buffalo Grove *(G-2515)*
Berry Global Inc ... G ... 630 375-0358
Aurora *(G-923)*
Berry Global Inc ... E ... 630 896-6200
Aurora *(G-1065)*
BJ Mold & Die Inc ... G ... 630 595-1797
Wood Dale *(G-21170)*
Blackfriars Corp ... G ... 818 597-3754
Northbrook *(G-15350)*
◆ Blackhawk Molding Co Inc ... C ... 630 628-6218
Addison *(G-51)*
Blackhawk Molding Co Inc ... F ... 630 543-3900
Addison *(G-52)*
▲ Bli Legacy Inc ... E ... 847 428-6059
Carpentersville *(G-3095)*
Boe Intermediate Holding Corp ... B ... 773 890-3300
Chicago *(G-3924)*
▲ Boss Manufacturing Holdings ... F ... 309 852-2781
Kewanee *(G-12025)*
▲ Box Enclsres Assembly Svcs Inc ... G ... 847 932-4700
Libertyville *(G-12639)*
Bway Corporation ... C ... 847 956-0750
Elk Grove Village *(G-8875)*
Bway Corporation ... C ... 773 254-8700
Chicago *(G-3987)*
▲ C Line Products Inc ... D ... 847 827-6661
Mount Prospect *(G-14517)*

▲ C R Plastics Inc ... G ... 847 541-3601
Wheeling *(G-20867)*
Cal-III Gasket Co ... F ... 773 287-9605
Chicago *(G-4002)*
Camis Mold & Tool Co ... G ... 847 593-6620
Elk Grove Village *(G-8878)*
▲ Capsonic Group LLC ... B ... 847 888-7264
Elgin *(G-8531)*
Cell Parts Manufacturing Co ... G ... 847 669-9690
Huntley *(G-11530)*
▲ Centech Plastics Inc ... C ... 847 364-4433
Elk Grove Village *(G-8884)*
Central Molded Products LLC ... F ... 773 622-4000
Chicago *(G-4057)*
Centro Inc ... G ... 309 751-9700
East Moline *(G-8224)*
Century Mold & Tool Co ... E ... 847 364-5858
Elk Grove Village *(G-8886)*
Certified Polymers Inc ... G ... 630 515-0007
Western Springs *(G-20719)*
▲ Chatham Plastics Inc ... G ... 217 483-1481
Chatham *(G-3419)*
Chem-Tainer Industries Inc ... G ... 630 932-7778
Lombard *(G-13050)*
▲ Chemtech Plastics Inc ... D ... 630 503-6000
Elgin *(G-8537)*
Chicago Molding Outlet ... G ... 773 471-6870
Chicago *(G-4118)*
Chicago Plastic Systems Inc ... E ... 815 455-4599
Crystal Lake *(G-7181)*
▲ Chroma Color Corporation ... C ... 877 385-8777
McHenry *(G-13726)*
Cicero Plastic Products Inc ... E ... 815 886-9522
Romeoville *(G-17808)*
Cim-Tech Plastics Inc ... F ... 847 350-0900
Elk Grove Village *(G-8898)*
▲ Circle Caster Engineering Co ... G ... 847 455-2206
Franklin Park *(G-9908)*
Cjt Automotive Inc ... G ... 847 671-0800
Rosemont *(G-18005)*
▲ Classic Fasteners LLC ... G ... 630 605-0195
Saint Charles *(G-18170)*
Classic Midwest Die Mold Inc ... F ... 773 227-8000
Chicago *(G-4169)*
Classic Molding Co Inc ... D ... 847 671-7888
Schiller Park *(G-18794)*
Clear Pack Company ... C ... 847 957-6282
Franklin Park *(G-9911)*
Clover Plastics LLC ... G ... 630 473-6488
West Chicago *(G-20564)*
◆ Cmt International Inc ... G ... 618 549-1829
Murphysboro *(G-14754)*
▲ Commercial Plastics Company ... C ... 847 566-1700
Mundelein *(G-14679)*
▲ Component Plastics Inc ... D ... 847 695-9200
Elgin *(G-8546)*
Computhink Inc ... E ... 630 705-9050
Lombard *(G-13057)*
Condor Tool & Manufacturing ... F ... 630 628-8200
Addison *(G-81)*
◆ Consolidated Foam Inc ... F ... 847 850-5011
Buffalo Grove *(G-2528)*
▼ Continental Window and GL Corp ... E ... 773 794-1600
Chicago *(G-4231)*
Conwed Plas Acquisition V LLC ... D ... 630 293-3737
West Chicago *(G-20567)*
Corplex Usa LLC ... E ... 630 755-3132
Romeoville *(G-17811)*
Cortina Companies Inc ... E ... 847 455-2800
Franklin Park *(G-9916)*
▲ Cortina Tool & Molding Co ... C ... 847 455-2800
Franklin Park *(G-9917)*
▲ Cosmos Plastics Company ... E ... 847 451-1307
Franklin Park *(G-9918)*
Cpg International LLC ... D ... 570 558-8000
Chicago *(G-4252)*
Cpg Newco LLC ... A ... 877 275-2935
Chicago *(G-4253)*
◆ Crane Composites Inc ... B ... 815 467-8600
Channahon *(G-3376)*
Crane Composites Inc ... D ... 630 378-9580
Bolingbrook *(G-2159)*
Crane Composites Inc ... C ... 815 467-1437
Channahon *(G-3377)*
Creative Concepts Fabrication ... F ... 630 940-0500
Saint Charles *(G-18177)*
Creative Conveniences By K&E ... G ... 847 975-8526
Lake Zurich *(G-12399)*
Crestwood Industries Inc ... F ... 847 680-9088
Mundelein *(G-14681)*

▲ Crystal Die and Mold Inc ... E ... 847 658-6535
Rolling Meadows *(G-17725)*
▲ CTI Industries Corporation ... C ... 847 382-1000
Lake Barrington *(G-12146)*
CTI Industries Corporation ... D ... 800 284-5605
Lake Zurich *(G-12400)*
CTS Automotive LLC ... E ... 815 385-9480
McHenry *(G-13734)*
◆ CTS Automotive LLC ... C ... 630 577-8800
Lisle *(G-12880)*
Custom Blow Molding ... G ... 630 820-9700
Aurora *(G-947)*
Custom Coating Innovations Inc ... F ... 618 808-0500
Lebanon *(G-12544)*
Custom Films Inc ... F ... 217 826-2326
Marshall *(G-13569)*
▲ Custom Plastics Inc ... C ... 847 439-6770
Elk Grove Village *(G-8926)*
Custom Plastics Inc ... F ... 847 439-6770
Elk Grove Village *(G-8927)*
Cutn Edge Cstm Fabrication LLC ... G ... 779 774-4991
Machesney Park *(G-13339)*
D & D Manufacturing ... G ... 815 339-9100
Hennepin *(G-11157)*
▲ D & J Plastics Inc ... G ... 847 534-0601
Roselle *(G-17951)*
D & M Custom Injection M ... D ... 847 683-2054
Burlington *(G-2640)*
D and S Molding & Dctg Inc ... G ... 815 399-2734
Rockford *(G-17366)*
D&W Fine Pack Holdings LLC ... G ... 847 378-1200
Wood Dale *(G-21179)*
D&W Fine Pack LLC ... G ... 800 323-0422
Lake Zurich *(G-12401)*
D&W Fine Pack LLC ... B ... 215 362-1501
Wood Dale *(G-21180)*
▲ Damron Corporation ... E ... 773 265-2724
Chicago *(G-4310)*
▲ Davies Molding LLC ... C ... 630 510-8188
Carol Stream *(G-2974)*
Dayton Superior Corporation ... C ... 815 936-3300
Kankakee *(G-11964)*
Designed Plastics Inc ... E ... 630 694-7300
Bensenville *(G-1786)*
▲ Deslauriers Inc ... E ... 708 544-4455
La Grange Park *(G-12095)*
Dice Mold & Engineering Inc ... E ... 630 773-3595
Itasca *(G-11642)*
Dike-O-Seal Incorporated ... F ... 773 254-3224
Chicago *(G-4361)*
▲ Dimension Molding Corporation ... E ... 630 628-0777
Addison *(G-94)*
Dirk Vander Noot ... G ... 224 558-1878
Prospect Heights *(G-16838)*
◆ Dometic Corporation ... A ... 847 447-7190
Rosemont *(G-18019)*
Dordan Manufacturing Company ... E ... 815 334-0087
Woodstock *(G-21382)*
Dove Products Inc ... E ... 815 727-4683
Lockport *(G-12989)*
DRG Molding & Pad Printing Inc ... F ... 847 223-3398
Round Lake Beach *(G-18088)*
Drp Solutions Inc ... G ... 815 782-2014
Plainfield *(G-16657)*
Drummond Industries Inc ... E ... 773 637-1264
Bensenville *(G-1790)*
Dss Rapak Inc ... G ... 630 296-2000
Romeoville *(G-17814)*
▲ Dti Molding Technologies Inc ... D ... 630 543-3600
Addison *(G-101)*
Du-Call Miller Plastics Inc ... F ... 630 964-6020
Elburn *(G-8450)*
Dukane Ias LLC ... E ... 630 797-4900
Saint Charles *(G-18191)*
Dunham Designs Inc ... G ... 815 462-0100
New Lenox *(G-15031)*
Dura Operating LLC ... C ... 815 947-3333
Stockton *(G-19549)*
Duratech Corporation ... G ... 618 533-8891
Centralia *(G-3229)*
▲ E A M & J Inc ... E ... 847 622-9200
Lake Bluff *(G-12180)*
E & C Custom Plastic Inc ... E ... 630 543-3325
Addison *(G-106)*
E & T Plastic Mfg Co Inc ... F ... 630 628-9048
Addison *(G-107)*
E-Jay Plastics Co ... F ... 630 543-4000
Addison *(G-108)*
E-Z Rotational Molder Inc ... G ... 847 806-1327
Elk Grove Village *(G-8966)*

SIC

Employee Codes: A=Over 500 employees, B=251-500
C=101-250, D=51-100, E=20-50, F=10-19, G=3-9
2020 Harris Illinois
Industrial Directory
901

30 RUBBER AND MISCELLANEOUS PLASTICS PRODUCTS SIC SECTION

Eagle Plastics & Supply Inc....G....708 331-6232
Chicago *(G-4430)*

Eco-Tech Plastics LLC....E....262 539-3811
Northbrook *(G-15380)*

Elas Tek Molding Inc....E....815 675-9012
Spring Grove *(G-19274)*

▲ Electroform Company....E....815 633-1113
Machesney Park *(G-13341)*

Elgin Die Mold Co....D....847 464-0140
Pingree Grove *(G-16621)*

▲ Elgin Molded Plastics Inc....D....847 931-2455
Elgin *(G-8576)*

▲ EMC Innovations Inc....G....815 741-2546
Joliet *(G-11860)*

Ems Acrylics & Silk Screener....F....773 777-5656
Chicago *(G-4502)*

◆ Energy Absorption Systems Inc....E....312 467-6750
Chicago *(G-4506)*

Engineered Plastic Pdts Corp....E....847 952-8400
Mount Prospect *(G-14526)*

Enginred Molding Solutions Inc....E....815 363-9600
McHenry *(G-13741)*

Entrigue Designs....G....708 647-6159
Homewood *(G-11493)*

Epp Composites Inc....G....847 612-3495
Bloomingdale *(G-1994)*

Essentra Corp....G....814 899-7671
Westchester *(G-20697)*

Evans Tool & Manufacturing....G....630 897-8656
Aurora *(G-1093)*

▼ Extruded Solutions Inc....G....630 871-6450
West Chicago *(G-20580)*

F & R Plastics Inc....G....847 336-1330
Waukegan *(G-20442)*

▲ Fabrik Industries Inc....B....815 385-9480
McHenry *(G-13743)*

Fapme....G....815 624-8538
South Beloit *(G-19090)*

Fasteners For Retail Inc....C....847 296-5511
Des Plaines *(G-7764)*

Fiberbasin Inc....F....630 978-0705
Aurora *(G-1095)*

Fiberglass Innovations LLC....F....815 962-9338
Rockford *(G-17413)*

Fiberglass Innovations LLC....G....815 962-3727
Rockford *(G-17414)*

◆ Filtertek Inc....B....815 648-2410
Hebron *(G-11143)*

▲ First Amrcn Plstic Mlding Entp....D....815 624-8538
South Beloit *(G-19091)*

Flex-N-Gate Corporation....G....217 442-4018
Danville *(G-7335)*

Flexan LLC....F....773 685-6446
Chicago *(G-4607)*

Flextronics Intl USA Inc....D....847 383-1529
Buffalo Grove *(G-2538)*

Flotek Inc....G....815 943-6816
Harvard *(G-11055)*

▲ Flow-Eze Company....F....815 965-1062
Rockford *(G-17416)*

Foreman Tool & Mold Corp....E....630 377-6389
Saint Charles *(G-18201)*

Foreman Tool and Mold....G....630 377-6389
Saint Charles *(G-18202)*

Foremost Plastic Pdts Co Inc....E....708 452-5300
Elmwood Park *(G-9453)*

▲ Form Plastics Company....D....630 443-1400
Saint Charles *(G-18203)*

Formco Plastics Inc....F....630 860-7998
Bensenville *(G-1801)*

Forreston Tool Inc....F....815 938-3626
Forreston *(G-9740)*

Four Seasons Gutter Prote....G....309 694-4565
East Peoria *(G-8268)*

▲ Four Star Tool Inc....D....224 735-2419
Rolling Meadows *(G-17733)*

▲ Fox Valley Molding Inc....C....630 552-3176
Plano *(G-16731)*

Fox Valley Windows LLC....G....630 210-6400
Aurora *(G-963)*

Frederics Frame Studio Inc....F....312 243-2950
Chicago *(G-4632)*

▲ Fuji Yusoki Kogyo Co Ltd....G....425 522-0722
Elk Grove Village *(G-9007)*

Furnel Inc....E....630 543-0885
Addison *(G-130)*

GAim Plastics Incorporated....F....630 350-9500
Bensenville *(G-1806)*

Gayton Group Inc....G....847 233-0509
Schiller Park *(G-18809)*

◆ Gilster-Mary Lee Corporation....A....618 826-2361
Chester *(G-3456)*

Glasstek Inc....G....630 978-9897
Naperville *(G-14969)*

Glo-Mold Inc....F....847 671-1762
Schiller Park *(G-18811)*

▲ Global Contract Mfg Inc....G....312 432-6200
Chicago *(G-4695)*

Global Packaging Dev LLC....F....847 209-3270
Chicago *(G-4697)*

▲ Gmt Inc....E....847 697-8161
Elgin *(G-8597)*

Goodco Products LLC....G....630 258-6384
Countryside *(G-7055)*

▲ Gord Industrial Plastics Inc....F....815 786-9494
Sandwich *(G-18372)*

Graham Packaging Co Europe LLC....A....630 293-8616
West Chicago *(G-20589)*

Graham Packaging Co Europe LLC....C....630 562-5912
West Chicago *(G-20590)*

Graham Packaging Company LP....E....630 739-9150
Woodridge *(G-21306)*

Greenwood Inc....E....217 431-6034
Danville *(G-7342)*

▲ Greenwood Inc....F....800 798-4900
Danville *(G-7341)*

Greif Inc....E....815 838-7210
Lockport *(G-12998)*

Greif Inc....E....815 935-7575
Bradley *(G-2283)*

H E Associates Inc....F....630 553-6382
Yorkville *(G-21487)*

H&K Perforating LLC....E....773 626-1800
Chicago *(G-4762)*

Han-Win Products Inc....E....630 897-1591
Aurora *(G-1107)*

▲ Hansen Plastics Corp....D....847 741-4510
Elgin *(G-8604)*

Hansen Plastics Corp....G....847 741-4510
Elgin *(G-8605)*

Hardwood Line Manufacturing Co....E....773 463-2600
Chicago *(G-4780)*

Hawk Molding Inc....G....224 523-2888
Harvard *(G-11056)*

Hazen Display Corporation....E....815 248-2925
Davis *(G-7418)*

▲ Hbp Inc....D....815 235-3000
Freeport *(G-10114)*

▲ Heathrow Scientific LLC....F....847 816-5070
Vernon Hills *(G-20060)*

Hemmerle Jr Irvin....G....630 334-4392
Naperville *(G-14841)*

Heritage Products Corporation....G....847 419-8835
Buffalo Grove *(G-2545)*

Herschberger Window Inc....G....217 543-2106
Tuscola *(G-19928)*

Hi-Tech Polymers Inc....F....815 282-2272
Loves Park *(G-13216)*

HK Paper (usa) Inc....G....847 969-9600
Schaumburg *(G-18550)*

▲ Hmt Manufacturing Inc....E....847 473-2310
North Chicago *(G-15314)*

◆ Hoffer Plastics Corporation....B....847 741-5740
South Elgin *(G-19152)*

◆ Home Pdts Intl - N Amer Inc....B....773 890-1010
Chicago *(G-4834)*

Hpi North America Inc....G....773 890-8927
Chicago *(G-4856)*

Husky Injection Molding....F....708 479-9049
Mokena *(G-14089)*

I TW Deltar Insert Molded Pdts....G....847 593-8811
Elk Grove Village *(G-9039)*

ICI Fiberite....G....708 403-3788
Orland Park *(G-15960)*

Id3 Inc....F....847 734-9781
Arlington Heights *(G-753)*

Idemia America Corp....D....630 551-0792
Naperville *(G-14844)*

Identatronics Inc....E....847 437-2654
Crystal Lake *(G-7208)*

▲ Identification Products Mfg Co....G....847 367-6452
Lake Forest *(G-12264)*

▲ Illinois Bottle Mfg Co....D....847 595-9000
Elk Grove Village *(G-9040)*

Illinois Electro Deburring Co....F....847 678-5010
Franklin Park *(G-9961)*

Illinois Tool Works Inc....B....847 724-7500
Glenview *(G-10560)*

Illinois Tool Works Inc....C....630 372-2150
Bartlett *(G-1288)*

Illinois Tool Works Inc....E....630 773-9300
Itasca *(G-11671)*

Illinois Tool Works Inc....D....708 720-0300
Frankfort *(G-9804)*

Illinois Tool Works Inc....C....708 720-2600
Frankfort *(G-9805)*

Illinois Tool Works Inc....D....630 787-3298
Elk Grove Village *(G-9041)*

Illinois Tool Works Inc....C....630 315-2150
Carol Stream *(G-3003)*

Illinois Tool Works Inc....G....708 479-3346
Tinley Park *(G-19837)*

Illinois Tool Works Inc....D....217 345-2166
Charleston *(G-3404)*

Illinois Tool Works Inc....D....708 720-7800
Richton Park *(G-17028)*

Illinois Tool Works Inc....C....847 299-2222
Des Plaines *(G-7785)*

Illinois Tool Works Inc....C....708 479-7200
Mokena *(G-14091)*

Illinois Tool Works Inc....B....847 724-6100
Glenview *(G-10563)*

Illinois Tool Works Inc....C....847 783-5500
Elgin *(G-8621)*

Illinois Tool Works Inc....C....815 448-7300
Mazon *(G-13681)*

Illinois Tool Works Inc....D....847 724-7500
Buffalo Grove *(G-2549)*

Illinois Tool Works Inc....G....708 479-3346
Tinley Park *(G-19838)*

Illinois Tool Works Inc....D....847 657-4022
Glenview *(G-10565)*

Illinois Tool Works Inc....B....630 595-3500
Roselle *(G-17958)*

Ilpea Industries Inc....D....309 343-3332
Galesburg *(G-10201)*

Indiana Precision Inc....F....765 361-0247
Danville *(G-7351)*

▲ Inland Plastics Inc....G....815 933-3500
Kankakee *(G-11977)*

▲ Innovative Components Inc....E....847 885-9050
Schaumburg *(G-18560)*

Innovative Plastech Inc....D....630 232-1808
Batavia *(G-1386)*

Inplex Custom Extruders LLC....D....847 827-7046
Naperville *(G-14849)*

◆ Insertech LLC....D....847 516-6184
Cary *(G-3171)*

Insertech International Inc....E....847 416-6184
Cary *(G-3172)*

Intec-Mexico LLC....B....847 358-0088
Palatine *(G-16130)*

Intergrted Thrmforming Systems....F....630 906-6895
Aurora *(G-1113)*

Intermolding Technology LLC....F....847 376-8517
Schaumburg *(G-18564)*

International Automotive Compo....B....815 544-2102
Belvidere *(G-1680)*

International Mold & Prod LLC....G....313 617-5251
Grayslake *(G-10783)*

▲ Intrepid Molding Inc....E....847 526-9477
Wauconda *(G-20362)*

▲ Iplastics LLC....D....309 444-8884
Washington *(G-20270)*

▲ Ironwood Industries Inc....D....847 362-8681
Libertyville *(G-12664)*

Isovac Products LLC....G....630 679-1740
Romeoville *(G-17834)*

▲ Itasca Plastics Inc....E....630 443-4446
Saint Charles *(G-18216)*

ITW Covid Security Group Inc....F....847 724-7500
Glenview *(G-10572)*

ITW International Holdings LLC....F....847 724-7500
Glenview *(G-10575)*

Ivp Plastics of Missouri LLC....F....309 444-8884
Washington *(G-20271)*

J and K Molding....G....224 276-3355
Volo *(G-20199)*

J C Products Inc....G....847 208-9616
Algonquin *(G-375)*

Jalaa Fiberglass Inc....G....217 923-3433
Greenup *(G-10821)*

James Injection Molding Co....E....847 564-3820
Northbrook *(G-15410)*

▼ Janler Corporation....E....773 774-0166
Chicago *(G-5005)*

Jay Cee Plastic Fabricators....F....773 276-1920
Chicago *(G-5012)*

Jdi Mold and Tool LLC....F....815 759-5646
Johnsburg *(G-11806)*

SIC SECTION
30 RUBBER AND MISCELLANEOUS PLASTICS PRODUCTS

▲ **Jessup Manufacturing Company** .....D....... 815 385-6650
Mchenry *(G-13753)*

▲ **Jigsaw Solutions Inc** .....G....... 630 926-1948
Romeoville *(G-17835)*

JL Clark LLC .....G....... 815 961-5677
Rockford *(G-17475)*

▲ **JL Clark LLC** .....C....... 815 961-5609
Rockford *(G-17476)*

Jodi Maurer .....G....... 847 961-5347
Lake In The Hills *(G-12337)*

John Thomas Inc .....E....... 815 288-2343
Dixon *(G-7902)*

Johnson Bag Co Inc .....F....... 847 438-2424
Wauconda *(G-20364)*

◆ **Jordan Industries Inc** .....F....... 847 945-5591
Deerfield *(G-7621)*

Jordan Specialty Plastics Inc .....G....... 847 945-5591
Deerfield *(G-7622)*

Jtec Industries Inc .....E....... 309 698-9301
East Peoria *(G-8273)*

K & S Manufacturing Co Inc .....F....... 815 232-7519
Freeport *(G-10123)*

K B Tool Inc .....G....... 630 595-4340
Bensenville *(G-1835)*

K H M Plastics Inc .....E....... 847 249-4910
Gurnee *(G-10891)*

▲ **Kalle USA Inc** .....G....... 847 775-0781
Gurnee *(G-10893)*

Kay Manufacturing Company LLC .....C....... 708 862-6800
Calumet City *(G-2782)*

Kevs Kans Inc .....G....... 309 303-3999
Roanoke *(G-17102)*

▲ **Ki Industries Inc** .....E....... 708 449-1990
Berkeley *(G-1941)*

▲ **Kipp Manufacturing Company Inc** .....F....... 630 768-9051
Wauconda *(G-20366)*

Kitchen Supply Wholesale .....G....... 224 603-1208
Antioch *(G-618)*

Klein Plastics Company LLC .....D....... 616 863-9900
Lincolnshire *(G-12777)*

▲ **Knight Plastics LLC** .....C....... 815 334-1240
Woodstock *(G-21400)*

Kunverji Enterprise Corp .....F....... 847 683-2954
Burlington *(G-2641)*

◆ **L & P Guarding LLC** .....C....... 708 325-0400
Bedford Park *(G-1477)*

L C Mold Inc .....E....... 847 593-5004
Rolling Meadows *(G-17746)*

L&P Plastics .....G....... 618 594-3692
Carlyle *(G-2892)*

Lake Pacific Partners LLC .....B....... 312 578-1110
Chicago *(G-5161)*

▲ **Lakone Company** .....D....... 630 892-4251
Montgomery *(G-14256)*

Laminarp .....E....... 847 884-9298
Schaumburg *(G-18599)*

▲ **Leapfrog Product Dev LLC** .....F....... 312 229-0089
Chicago *(G-5192)*

Lee Gilster-Mary Corporation .....G....... 618 826-2361
Chester *(G-3457)*

Lee Gilster-Mary Corporation .....E....... 618 443-5676
Sparta *(G-19256)*

Lee Gilster-Mary Corporation .....D....... 815 472-6456
Momence *(G-14186)*

Legacy Plastics Inc .....G....... 815 226-3013
Rockford *(G-17493)*

Lens Lenticlear Lenticular .....F....... 630 467-0900
Elk Grove Village *(G-9093)*

Leroys Plastic Co Inc .....F....... 630 898-7006
Aurora *(G-1123)*

▲ **Lewis Acquisition Corp** .....D....... 773 486-5660
Addison *(G-183)*

▲ **Limitless Innovations Inc** .....E....... 855 843-4828
McHenry *(G-13758)*

Lincoln Generating Fcilty LLC .....G....... 815 478-3799
Manhattan *(G-13433)*

Loop Automotive LLC .....E....... 847 912-9090
Chicago *(G-5257)*

Lordahl Manufacturing Co .....D....... 847 244-0448
Long Grove *(G-13161)*

◆ **M Putterman & Co LLC** .....D....... 773 927-4120
Chicago *(G-5304)*

◆ **Mac Lean-Fogg Company** .....D....... 847 566-0010
Mundelein *(G-14710)*

Mac Plastics Manufacturing Inc .....E....... 618 392-3010
Olney *(G-15872)*

Magenta LLC .....D....... 773 777-5050
Lockport *(G-13010)*

Magna Exteriors America Inc .....D....... 779 552-7400
Belvidere *(G-1683)*

Mako Mold Corporation .....G....... 630 377-9010
Saint Charles *(G-18229)*

▲ **Makray Manufacturing Company** .....E....... 708 456-7100
Norridge *(G-15240)*

Makray Manufacturing Company .....D....... 847 260-5408
Schiller Park *(G-18819)*

Manufacturers Custom Products .....G....... 630 988-5055
Woodridge *(G-21322)*

▲ **Marathon Manufacturing Inc** .....E....... 630 543-6262
Addison *(G-192)*

▲ **Mark Power International** .....F....... 815 877-5984
Machesney Park *(G-13358)*

Martinez Management Inc .....G....... 847 822-7202
Algonquin *(G-379)*

◆ **Mary Lee Packaging Corporation** .....E....... 618 826-2361
Chester *(G-3458)*

▲ **Master Molded Products LLC** .....C....... 847 695-9700
Elgin *(G-8651)*

▼ **Mastermolding Inc** .....E....... 815 741-1230
Joliet *(G-11898)*

Mat Capital LLC .....G....... 847 821-9630
Long Grove *(G-13163)*

Mate Technologies Inc .....F....... 847 289-1010
Elgin *(G-8652)*

Material Control Inc .....F....... 630 892-4274
Batavia *(G-1393)*

▲ **Matrix IV Inc** .....E....... 815 338-4500
Woodstock *(G-21409)*

Matrix Plastic Products Inc .....D....... 630 595-6144
Wood Dale *(G-21214)*

Mauser Pckg Sltons Intrmdate I .....G....... 770 645-4800
Oak Brook *(G-15640)*

Maxon Plastics Inc .....G....... 630 761-3667
Batavia *(G-1394)*

MCS Midwest LLC .....G....... 314 398-8107
Granite City *(G-10723)*

MCS Midwest LLC .....G....... 630 393-7402
Aurora *(G-1129)*

Medplast Group Inc .....B....... 630 706-5500
Oak Brook *(G-15642)*

▲ **Mega Corporation** .....E....... 847 985-1900
Schaumburg *(G-18626)*

▲ **Mercury Plastics Inc** .....E....... 888 884-1864
Chicago *(G-5394)*

Met Plastics .....G....... 847 228-5070
Elk Grove Village *(G-9115)*

Met2plastic LLC .....E....... 847 228-5070
Elk Grove Village *(G-9116)*

Mgs Group North America Inc .....D....... 847 371-1158
Libertyville *(G-12679)*

Mgs Mfg Group Inc .....E....... 847 968-4335
Libertyville *(G-12680)*

Micron Mold & Mfg Inc .....G....... 630 871-9531
Carol Stream *(G-3028)*

Microthincom Inc .....F....... 630 543-0501
Bensenville *(G-1851)*

Mid Oaks Investments LLC .....G....... 847 215-3475
Buffalo Grove *(G-2573)*

Mid-America Plastic Company .....E....... 815 938-3110
Forreston *(G-9741)*

Midland Plastics Inc .....E....... 262 938-7000
Roselle *(G-17970)*

Midwest Blow Molding LLC .....G....... 618 283-9223
Vandalia *(G-20016)*

◆ **Midwest Canvas Corp** .....C....... 773 287-4400
Chicago *(G-5440)*

Midwest Molding Inc .....D....... 224 208-1110
Bartlett *(G-1298)*

▲ **Midwest Molding Solutions** .....F....... 309 663-7374
Bloomington *(G-2079)*

Midwest Plastic Products .....G....... 630 262-1095
Addison *(G-213)*

Midwest Plastics Services Inc .....G....... 630 551-4921
Oswego *(G-16014)*

Midwest Tropical Entps Inc .....E....... 847 679-6666
Lincolnwood *(G-12831)*

◆ **Mold-Rite Plastics LLC** .....C....... 518 561-1812
Chicago *(G-5487)*

Molded Displays .....G....... 773 892-4098
Highland Park *(G-11285)*

Molding Services Group Inc .....E....... 847 931-1491
South Elgin *(G-19168)*

▲ **Molding Services Illinois Inc** .....E....... 618 395-3888
Olney *(G-15874)*

Molding Systems Engrg Corp .....E....... 618 395-3888
Olney *(G-15875)*

Moldtronics Inc .....E....... 630 968-7000
Downers Grove *(G-8058)*

▲ **Molor Products Company** .....F....... 630 375-5999
Oswego *(G-16015)*

▲ **Monahan Filaments LLC** .....D....... 217 268-4957
Arcola *(G-657)*

▲ **Monda Window & Door Corp** .....E....... 773 254-8888
Chicago *(G-5489)*

Mpc Group LLC .....C....... 773 927-4120
Chicago *(G-5517)*

◆ **MPD Inc** .....E....... 847 489-7705
Libertyville *(G-12686)*

▲ **Mpr Plastics Inc** .....E....... 847 468-9950
Elgin *(G-8666)*

Mueller Door Company .....E....... 815 385-8550
Wauconda *(G-20379)*

Multi Packaging Solutions Inc .....G....... 773 283-9500
Chicago *(G-5523)*

Mvs Molding Inc .....G....... 847 740-7700
Round Lake *(G-18080)*

National Emergency Med ID Inc .....G....... 847 366-1267
Spring Grove *(G-19288)*

Navitor Inc .....B....... 800 323-0253
Harwood Heights *(G-11106)*

◆ **Neil Enterprises Inc** .....D....... 847 549-7627
Vernon Hills *(G-20077)*

▲ **Neil International Inc** .....C....... 847 549-7627
Vernon Hills *(G-20078)*

Neomek Incorporated .....F....... 630 879-5400
Batavia *(G-1399)*

Newell Brands Inc .....D....... 815 266-0066
Freeport *(G-10128)*

◆ **Newell Operating Company** .....C....... 815 235-4171
Freeport *(G-10129)*

Newovo Plastics LLC .....G....... 224 535-8183
Elgin *(G-8669)*

Nissei America Inc .....G....... 847 228-5000
Elk Grove Village *(G-9149)*

North America Packaging Corp .....C....... 630 845-8726
Peotone *(G-16555)*

◆ **North America Packaging Corp** .....E....... 630 203-4100
Oak Brook *(G-15648)*

▲ **North American Fund III LP** .....G....... 312 332-4950
Chicago *(G-5619)*

▲ **Northern Precision Plastic Inc** .....E....... 815 544-8099
Belvidere *(G-1690)*

Northstar Trading LLC .....E....... 630 312-8434
Wheeling *(G-20946)*

Northwestern Cup & Logo Inc .....G....... 773 874-8000
Chicago *(G-5625)*

Npi Holding Corp .....G....... 217 391-1229
Springfield *(G-19412)*

◆ **Nu-Dell Manufacturing Co Inc** .....F....... 847 803-4500
Chicago *(G-5637)*

▲ **Nudo Products Inc** .....C....... 217 528-5636
Springfield *(G-19414)*

Nypro Inc .....E....... 630 671-2000
Hanover Park *(G-11011)*

Nypromold Inc .....C....... 847 855-2200
Gurnee *(G-10905)*

▲ **Oak Technical LLC** .....G....... 931 455-7011
Matteson *(G-13627)*

Odra Inc .....G....... 847 249-2910
Gurnee *(G-10906)*

Olcott Plastics Inc .....D....... 630 584-0555
Saint Charles *(G-18237)*

Owen Plastics LLC .....E....... 847 683-2054
Burlington *(G-2642)*

P & P Industries Inc .....D....... 815 623-3297
Sterling *(G-19523)*

Pactiv Intl Holdings Inc .....G....... 847 482-2000
Lake Forest *(G-12278)*

Pactiv LLC .....B....... 847 459-8049
Wheeling *(G-20953)*

Pactiv LLC .....C....... 708 496-2900
Bedford Park *(G-1490)*

Pactiv LLC .....F....... 708 496-2900
Chicago *(G-5742)*

◆ **Pactiv LLC** .....A....... 847 482-2000
Lake Forest *(G-12279)*

Pactiv LLC .....C....... 815 469-2112
Frankfort *(G-9819)*

Pactiv LLC .....C....... 217 479-1144
Jacksonville *(G-11779)*

Paper or Plastic Inc .....G....... 815 582-3696
Shorewood *(G-18898)*

Paragon Manufacturing Inc .....D....... 708 345-1717
Melrose Park *(G-13902)*

Paramount Plastics Inc .....D....... 815 834-4100
Chicago *(G-5760)*

Parting Line Tool Inc .....F....... 847 669-0331
Huntley *(G-11558)*

Peacock Colors Company Inc .....E....... 630 628-1960
Addison *(G-234)*

SIC

Employee Codes: A=Over 500 employees, B=251-500
C=101-250, D=51-100, E=20-50, F=10-19, G=3-9

2020 Harris Illinois
Industrial Directory

903

Peeps Inc ... G ... 708 935-4201
Palos Hills *(G-16204)*
▲ Perfect Plastic Printing Corp ... C ... 630 584-1600
Saint Charles *(G-18242)*
Perfect Shutters Inc ... E ... 815 648-2401
Hebron *(G-11147)*
Peritus Plastics LLC ... E ... 815 448-2005
Mazon *(G-13684)*
◆ Petrochem Corp ... G ... 431 205-8122
Chicago *(G-5799)*
▲ Pexco LLC ... C ... 847 296-5511
Des Plaines *(G-7820)*
▲ Phoenix Electric Mfg Co ... E ... 773 477-8855
Chicago *(G-5802)*
Piasa Plastics Inc ... G ... 618 372-7516
Brighton *(G-2403)*
Pimco Plastics Inc ... G ... 815 675-6464
Spring Grove *(G-19293)*
Plano Holding LLC ... F ... 630 552-3111
Plano *(G-16739)*
Plano Metal Specialties Inc ... F ... 630 552-8510
Plano *(G-16740)*
◆ Plano Molding Company LLC ... G ... 630 552-3111
Plano *(G-16741)*
Plano Molding Company LLC ... C ... 630 552-9557
Sandwich *(G-18379)*
Plano Molding Company LLC ... C ... 815 538-3111
Mendota *(G-13952)*
Plano Molding Company LLC ... C ... 815 786-3331
Sandwich *(G-18380)*
Planos Past Inc ... G ... 630 552-9119
Plano *(G-16742)*
◆ Plaspros Inc ... C ... 815 430-2300
McHenry *(G-13779)*
Plaspros Inc ... G ... 847 639-6492
Cary *(G-3183)*
Plastech Inc ... F ... 630 595-7222
Bensenville *(G-1868)*
Plastech Molding Inc ... G ... 847 398-0355
Wheeling *(G-20960)*
▲ Plastic Container Corporation ... D ... 217 352-2722
Urbana *(G-19993)*
Plastic Designs Inc ... E ... 217 379-9214
Paxton *(G-16314)*
◆ Plastic Film Corp America Inc ... F ... 630 887-0800
Lemont *(G-12583)*
Plastic Film Corp America Inc ... E ... 630 697-5635
Shorewood *(G-18899)*
▲ Plastic Parts Intl Inc ... E ... 815 637-9222
Machesney Park *(G-13364)*
Plastic Products Company Inc ... C ... 309 762-6532
Moline *(G-14167)*
Plastic Services Group ... G ... 847 368-1444
Arlington Heights *(G-788)*
▲ Plasticrest Products Inc ... F ... 773 826-2163
Chicago *(G-5818)*
Plastics ... G ... 847 931-9391
Elgin *(G-8689)*
Plasticworks Inc ... F ... 630 543-1750
Addison *(G-242)*
Plastipak Packaging Inc ... B ... 217 398-1832
Champaign *(G-3334)*
Plastipak Packaging Inc ... C ... 708 385-0721
Alsip *(G-493)*
Plastival Inc ... B ... 847 931-4771
Elgin *(G-8690)*
Plastruct Inc ... D ... 626 912-7017
Des Plaines *(G-7824)*
▲ Platt Luggage Inc ... D ... 773 838-2000
Chicago *(G-5821)*
◆ Pliant LLC ... A ... 812 424-2904
Rolling Meadows *(G-17761)*
▲ Plitek LLC ... D ... 847 827-6680
Des Plaines *(G-7827)*
▲ Plustech Inc ... G ... 847 490-8130
Schaumburg *(G-18679)*
Pnc Inc ... D ... 815 946-2328
Polo *(G-16758)*
Polar Tech Industries Inc ... E ... 815 784-9000
Genoa *(G-10321)*
Polyair Corporation ... G ... 773 253-1220
Chicago *(G-5837)*
Polydesigns Ltd ... G ... 847 433-9920
Highland Park *(G-11291)*
Polytec Plastics Inc ... E ... 630 584-8282
Saint Charles *(G-18246)*
Polytech Industries Inc ... E ... 630 443-6030
Saint Charles *(G-18247)*
Portola Packaging LLC ... E ... 630 515-8383
Downers Grove *(G-8079)*
Powerpath Microproducts Inc ... G ... 847 827-6330
Des Plaines *(G-7828)*
Precision Container Inc ... G ... 618 548-2830
Salem *(G-18351)*
Precision Molded Concepts ... F ... 815 675-0060
Spring Grove *(G-19294)*
Precision Plastic Products ... G ... 217 784-4920
Gibson City *(G-10342)*
Prestige Motor Works Inc ... G ... 630 780-6439
Naperville *(G-14983)*
Pretium Packaging LLC ... D ... 815 224-2633
Peru *(G-16590)*
▲ Prismier LLC ... E ... 630 592-4515
Bolingbrook *(G-2230)*
Process Systems Inc ... G ... 217 563-2872
Nokomis *(G-15197)*
Profile Plastics Inc ... D ... 847 604-5100
Lake Bluff *(G-12207)*
Prommar Plastics Inc ... G ... 815 770-0555
Harvard *(G-11065)*
Psa Equity LLC ... C ... 847 478-6000
Buffalo Grove *(G-2591)*
Pylon Plastics Inc ... G ... 630 968-6374
Lisle *(G-12930)*
Q C H Incorporated ... D ... 630 820-5550
Oswego *(G-16022)*
Qp Holdings LLC ... G ... 847 695-9700
Elgin *(G-8705)*
▲ Quad Inc ... E ... 815 624-8538
South Beloit *(G-19110)*
◆ Qualitas Manufacturing Inc ... D ... 630 529-7111
Itasca *(G-11723)*
Quality Custom Closets ... G ... 773 307-1105
Glenview *(G-10605)*
Quality Plastic Products Inc ... G ... 630 766-7593
Bensenville *(G-1879)*
◆ Quixote Corporation ... E ... 312 705-8400
Chicago *(G-5939)*
Quixote Transportation Safety ... D ... 312 467-6750
Chicago *(G-5940)*
◆ R and R Brokerage Co ... C ... 847 438-4600
Lake Zurich *(G-12448)*
R C Sales & Manufacturing Inc ... G ... 815 645-8898
Stillman Valley *(G-19545)*
R N I Industries Inc ... E ... 630 860-9147
Bensenville *(G-1881)*
Rackow Polymers Corporation ... E ... 630 766-3982
Bensenville *(G-1882)*
Railshop Inc ... G ... 847 816-0925
Libertyville *(G-12701)*
Ram Plastic Corp ... G ... 847 669-8003
Rockford *(G-17565)*
Rand Manufacturing Network Inc ... G ... 847 299-8884
Wheeling *(G-20969)*
▲ Ravenscroft Inc ... G ... 630 513-9911
Saint Charles *(G-18259)*
Really Useful Boxes Inc ... F ... 847 238-0444
Bloomingdale *(G-2011)*
Rensel-Chicago Inc ... E ... 773 235-2100
Chicago *(G-6015)*
Resins Inc ... G ... 847 884-0025
Hoffman Estates *(G-11450)*
Resource Plastics Inc ... D ... 708 389-3558
Alsip *(G-503)*
▲ Reum Corporation ... C ... 847 625-7386
Chicago *(G-6018)*
▲ Revcor Inc ... B ... 847 428-4411
Carpentersville *(G-3119)*
Rf Plastics Co ... G ... 630 628-6033
Addison *(G-273)*
Ricon Colors Inc ... F ... 630 562-9000
West Chicago *(G-20636)*
Right Lane Industries LLC ... G ... 857 869-4132
Chicago *(G-6031)*
▲ Riken Corporation of America ... C ... 847 673-1400
Skokie *(G-19023)*
Ring Container Tech LLC ... E ... 217 875-5084
Decatur *(G-7542)*
Rockford Molded Products Inc ... D ... 815 637-0585
Loves Park *(G-13257)*
Rohrer Corporation ... D ... 847 961-5920
Huntley *(G-11564)*
▲ Ropak Central Inc ... D ... 847 956-0750
Elk Grove Village *(G-9221)*
RPI Extrusion Co ... G ... 708 389-2584
Alsip *(G-506)*
▲ RPS Products Inc ... E ... 847 683-3400
Hampshire *(G-10986)*
Russell Stanley Midwest Inc ... G ... 630 739-7700
Bolingbrook *(G-2233)*
Rust-Oleum Corporation ... D ... 815 967-4258
Rockford *(G-17617)*
Rway Plastics Ltd ... F ... 815 476-5252
Wilmington *(G-21102)*
Rx Vials USA ... G ... 630 378-4417
Romeoville *(G-17872)*
▲ S4 Industries Inc ... F ... 224 699-9674
East Dundee *(G-8210)*
Safe-T-Quip Corporation ... F ... 773 235-2100
Chicago *(G-6089)*
Safeway Products Inc ... F ... 815 226-8322
Rockford *(G-17620)*
▲ Sakamoto Kanagata Usa Inc ... G ... 224 856-2008
South Elgin *(G-19173)*
Sandee Manufacturing Co ... E ... 847 671-1335
Franklin Park *(G-10042)*
◆ Sap Acquisition Co LLC ... E ... 847 229-1600
Buffalo Grove *(G-2594)*
◆ Scholle Ipn Corporation ... F ... 708 562-7290
Northlake *(G-15558)*
Scholle Packaging Inc ... G ... 708 273-3792
Northlake *(G-15559)*
Scimitar Prototyping Inc ... G ... 630 483-3875
Streamwood *(G-19594)*
Seals & Components Inc ... G ... 708 895-5222
Lansing *(G-12514)*
Seaquist Closures LLC ... G ... 262 363-7191
Crystal Lake *(G-7262)*
Security Molding Inc ... F ... 630 543-8607
Addison *(G-283)*
▲ Sek Corporation ... E ... 630 762-0606
Saint Charles *(G-18268)*
Selig S LLC ... G ... 815 785-2100
Forrest *(G-9735)*
Selig Sealing Holdings Inc ... F ... 815 785-2100
Forrest *(G-9736)*
Shamrock Plastics Inc ... E ... 309 243-7723
Peoria *(G-16522)*
Shannon Industries Inc ... G ... 815 338-8960
Woodstock *(G-21433)*
Shape Master Inc ... G ... 217 582-2638
Ogden *(G-15838)*
Sherwood Tool Inc ... F ... 815 648-1463
Hebron *(G-11149)*
Sikora Precision Inc ... G ... 847 468-0900
Elgin *(G-8732)*
Silgan Plastics LLC ... D ... 618 662-4471
Flora *(G-9692)*
Silgan Plastics LLC ... C ... 815 334-1200
Woodstock *(G-21435)*
Silver Line Building Pdts LLC ... B ... 708 474-9100
Lansing *(G-12516)*
Simonton Building Products Inc ... B ... 217 466-2851
Paris *(G-16244)*
Simplomatic Manufacturing Co ... E ... 773 342-7757
Elgin *(G-8733)*
Smt LLC Group ... E ... 630 961-3000
Naperville *(G-14915)*
Sno Gem Inc ... F ... 888 766-4367
McHenry *(G-13792)*
Snyder Industries Inc ... D ... 630 773-9510
Bensenville *(G-1895)*
Solo Cup Operating Corporation ... B ... 217 384-1800
Urbana *(G-20001)*
Solo Cup Operating Corporation ... C ... 773 767-3300
Chicago *(G-6197)*
Sonoco Products Company ... C ... 847 957-6282
Franklin Park *(G-10049)*
Sparx EDM Inc ... G ... 847 722-7577
Streamwood *(G-19595)*
Specialized Woodwork Inc ... G ... 630 627-0450
Lombard *(G-13131)*
Spinner Medical Products Inc ... B ... 312 944-8700
Chicago *(G-6214)*
▲ Spintex Inc ... G ... 847 608-5411
Elgin *(G-8738)*
Spirit Foodservice Inc ... C ... 214 634-1393
Lake Forest *(G-12305)*
Spraytech LLC ... G ... 847 973-9432
Fox Lake *(G-9755)*
Springfield Plastics Inc ... E ... 217 438-6167
Auburn *(G-908)*
Stanger Tool & Mold Inc ... G ... 847 426-5826
Belvidere *(G-1702)*
▲ Star Die Molding Inc ... D ... 847 766-7952
Elk Grove Village *(G-9255)*
Stellar Plastics Corporation ... D ... 630 443-1200
Saint Charles *(G-18277)*
Steven Plastics Inc ... E ... 847 885-2300
Hoffman Estates *(G-11463)*

SIC SECTION

Studio Moulding................................G....... 217 523-2101
  Springfield *(G-19459)*
Sullivan Tool and Repair Inc ....G....... 224 856-5867
  Elgin *(G-8741)*
▲ Summit Plastics Inc ....G....... 815 578-8700
  McHenry *(G-13797)*
Summit Polymers Inc ....G....... 269 532-1900
  Chicago *(G-6266)*
Sun Dome Inc ....F....... 773 890-5350
  Chicago *(G-6268)*
Sun Pattern & Model Inc ....E....... 630 293-3366
  West Chicago *(G-20648)*
Survyvn Ltd ....G....... 847 977-8665
  Ringwood *(G-17048)*
T C I Vacuum Forming Company.........E....... 847 622-9100
  Elgin *(G-8744)*
T L Swint Industries Inc ....G....... 847 358-3834
  Inverness *(G-11598)*
▼ T2 Site Amenities Incorporated ......G....... 847 579-9003
  Highland Park *(G-11302)*
Target Plastics Tech Corp ....D....... 630 545-1776
  Glendale Heights *(G-10510)*
Team Technologies Inc ....F....... 630 406-0678
  Batavia *(G-1425)*
Team Technologies Inc ....D....... 630 937-0380
  Batavia *(G-1426)*
Technatool Inc ....G....... 847 398-0355
  Wheeling *(G-20998)*
◆ Technipaq Inc ....C....... 815 477-1800
  Crystal Lake *(G-7277)*
Techny Plastics Corp ....E....... 847 498-2212
  Northbrook *(G-15493)*
Teepak Usa LLC ....G....... 217 446-6460
  Danville *(G-7382)*
Tegrant Alloyd Brands Inc ....B....... 815 756-8451
  Dekalb *(G-7708)*
Tek Pak Inc ....G....... 331 901-5570
  Saint Charles *(G-18287)*
Tekni-Plex Inc ....E....... 217 935-8311
  Clinton *(G-6929)*
Tempco Products Co ....D....... 618 544-3175
  Robinson *(G-17127)*
▲ Tenex Corporation ....E....... 847 504-0400
  Chicago *(G-6348)*
▲ Testor Corporation ....D....... 815 962-6654
  Rockford *(G-17656)*
Tex Trend Inc ....E....... 847 215-6796
  Wheeling *(G-20999)*
▲ The Intec Group Inc ....C....... 847 358-0088
  Palatine *(G-16162)*
Thermal-Tech Systems Inc ....E....... 630 639-5115
  West Chicago *(G-20651)*
▼ Thermform Engineered Qulty LLC...D....... 847 669-5291
  Huntley *(G-11568)*
Thermo-Graphic LLC ....E....... 630 350-2226
  Bensenville *(G-1901)*
Thoroughbred Plastics LLC ....G....... 815 985-5116
  Rockford *(G-17661)*
Three R Plastics Inc..........................F....... 815 675-0844
  Spring Grove *(G-19303)*
Three R Plastics Inc ....G....... 847 740-2845
  Round Lake *(G-18084)*
Thurow Tool Works Inc ....G....... 630 377-6403
  Saint Charles *(G-18288)*
Ticona Technical Polymers ....G....... 847 949-1444
  Mundelein *(G-14744)*
Time Rec Pubg Bbby Mrtin Prdct .....G....... 618 996-3803
  Marion *(G-13540)*
▲ Tmf Plastic Solutions LLC ....D....... 630 552-7575
  Plano *(G-16745)*
▲ Tmf Polymer Solutions Inc ....G....... 630 552-7575
  Plano *(G-16746)*
Tpg Plastics LLC ....G....... 630 828-2800
  Willowbrook *(G-21062)*
◆ Tradex International Inc ....D....... 216 651-4788
  Elwood *(G-9465)*
Transparent Container Co Inc ....D....... 630 543-1818
  Bensenville *(G-1903)*
Tredegar Film Products Corp ....C....... 847 438-2111
  Lake Zurich *(G-12465)*
Trellborg Sling Sltions US Inc ....F....... 630 539-5500
  Schaumburg *(G-18753)*
Trend Technologies LLC ....C....... 847 640-2382
  Elk Grove Village *(G-9282)*
Tri Guards Inc ....F....... 847 537-8444
  Elk Grove Village *(G-9283)*
Tri Par Die Mold................................G....... 847 515-3801
  Huntley *(G-11570)*
Tri-Par Die and Mold Corp ....E....... 630 232-8800
  South Elgin *(G-19177)*

Tri-Tech Molding ....G....... 847 263-7769
  Lake Villa *(G-12370)*
▲ Trident Manufacturing Inc ....E....... 847 464-0140
  Pingree Grove *(G-16624)*
▲ Trim-Tex Inc ....D....... 847 679-3000
  Lincolnwood *(G-12846)*
True Line Mold and Engrg Corp ....E....... 815 648-2739
  Hebron *(G-11152)*
Tsk Mnufacturing Solutions LLC ....G....... 847 450-4099
  Algonquin *(G-390)*
◆ Tuf-Tite Inc ....F....... 847 550-1011
  Lake Zurich *(G-12467)*
▲ Ucal Holdings Inc ....D....... 847 695-8030
  Elgin *(G-8765)*
▲ Ucal Systems Inc ....G....... 847 695-8030
  Elgin *(G-8767)*
Uniphase Inc ....E....... 630 584-4747
  Saint Charles *(G-18294)*
▲ Unique Assembly & Decorating .....E....... 630 241-4300
  Downers Grove *(G-8103)*
Universal Hovercraft Amer Inc ....F....... 815 963-1200
  Rockford *(G-17673)*
Urban Services of America ....G....... 847 278-3210
  Schaumburg *(G-18768)*
Urpoint LLC ....G....... 773 919-9002
  Homewood *(G-11503)*
◆ US Acrylic LLC ....D....... 847 837-4800
  Libertyville *(G-12720)*
Uwd Inc ....F....... 815 316-3080
  Roscoe *(G-17937)*
Vac-Matic Corporation ....G....... 630 543-4518
  Addison *(G-326)*
Van Norman Molding Company LLC...E....... 708 430-4343
  Oak Lawn *(G-15739)*
◆ Vector USA Inc ....F....... 800 929-4516
  Oak Brook *(G-15668)*
Veejay Plastics Inc ....F....... 847 683-2954
  Burlington *(G-2643)*
Vega Molded Products Inc ....G....... 847 428-7761
  Gilberts *(G-10374)*
Viscofan Usa Inc ....D....... 217 444-8000
  Danville *(G-7392)*
◆ Vision Wholesale Corp ....G....... 708 496-6015
  Chicago *(G-6558)*
◆ Viskase Companies Inc ....D....... 630 874-0700
  Lombard *(G-13151)*
▼ Viskase Corporation ....D....... 630 874-0700
  Lombard *(G-13152)*
▲ W M Plastics Inc ....D....... 815 578-8888
  McHenry *(G-13808)*
Wedco Molded Products ....G....... 630 455-6711
  Willowbrook *(G-21067)*
Werner Co ....E....... 815 459-6020
  Crystal Lake *(G-7294)*
Wesdar Technologies Inc ....G....... 630 761-0965
  Aurora *(G-1034)*
West Chicago Plastics Corp ....G....... 708 582-4014
  Bellwood *(G-1643)*
▲ Western Industries Inc ....C....... 920 261-0660
  Wheeling *(G-21012)*
◆ Wind Point Partners LP ....F....... 312 255-4800
  Chicago *(G-6637)*
▲ Winzeler Inc ....E....... 708 867-7971
  Harwood Heights *(G-11112)*
▲ Wise Plastics Technologies Inc ....C....... 847 697-2840
  Saint Charles *(G-18302)*
Wise Plastics Technologies Inc ....G....... 847 697-2840
  West Chicago *(G-20659)*
Woodland Engineering Company ......G....... 847 362-0110
  Lake Bluff *(G-12217)*
▼ Woodland Plastics Corp ....G....... 630 543-1144
  Addison *(G-336)*
Woojin Plaimm Inc ....F....... 708 606-5536
  Mount Prospect *(G-14583)*
▲ Xcell International Corp ....D....... 630 323-0107
  Lemont *(G-12596)*
Yankee Mold Inc ....G....... 815 986-1776
  Machesney Park *(G-13384)*
◆ Yoshino America Corporation ....E....... 708 534-1141
  University Park *(G-19971)*
◆ Zeller Plastik Usa Inc ....G....... 847 247-7900
  Libertyville *(G-12727)*
Zender Enterprises Ltd ....G....... 773 282-2293
  Chicago *(G-6716)*

31 LEATHER AND LEATHER PRODUCTS

3111 Leather Tanning & Finishing

Brighton Collectibles LLC ....F....... 847 674-6719
  Skokie *(G-18934)*
Darling Ingredients Inc ....E....... 618 271-8190
  National Stock Yards *(G-15012)*
▲ Horween Leather Company ....C....... 773 772-2026
  Chicago *(G-4843)*
Tannery Row LLC ....G....... 847 840-7647
  Chicago *(G-6324)*
Tyson Fresh Meats Inc ....F....... 847 836-5550
  Elgin *(G-8764)*
United Rawhide Mfg Co ....G....... 847 692-2791
  Park Ridge *(G-16301)*
Zoes Mfgco LLC ....F....... 312 666-4018
  Chicago *(G-6722)*

3131 Boot & Shoe Cut Stock & Findings

Counter ....G....... 312 666-5335
  Chicago *(G-4249)*
Counter-Intelligence ....G....... 708 974-3326
  Palos Hills *(G-16198)*
Curt Herrmann Construction Inc ......G....... 815 748-0531
  Dekalb *(G-7672)*
D R Walters ....G....... 618 926-6337
  Norris City *(G-15248)*
Fifth Quarter ....G....... 618 346-6659
  Saint Jacob *(G-18316)*
Hanigs Footwear Inc ....F....... 773 248-1977
  Wilmette *(G-21077)*
Painted Quarter Ridge ....G....... 618 534-9734
  Ava *(G-1176)*
Quarters Concessions Inc ....G....... 847 343-4864
  Carpentersville *(G-3116)*
Rays Countertop Shop Inc ....F....... 217 483-2514
  Glenarm *(G-10427)*
Red Wing ....G....... 217 655-2772
  Danville *(G-7378)*
Upper Urban Green Prprty Maint .....F....... 312 218-5903
  Chicago *(G-6489)*

3143 Men's Footwear, Exc Athletic

Barrett NJide Yvonne ....F....... 312 701-3962
  Chicago *(G-3838)*
▲ Leos Dancewear Inc ....D....... 773 889-7700
  River Forest *(G-17053)*
London Shoe Shop & Western Wr ...G....... 618 345-9570
  Collinsville *(G-6966)*
Springfield Sales Assoc Inc ....G....... 217 529-6987
  Springfield *(G-19456)*

3144 Women's Footwear, Exc Athletic

Horse Creek Outfitters ....G....... 217 544-2740
  Springfield *(G-19382)*
▲ Leos Dancewear Inc ....D....... 773 889-7700
  River Forest *(G-17053)*
Springfield Sales Assoc Inc ....G....... 217 529-6987
  Springfield *(G-19456)*

3149 Footwear, NEC

Patricia Jenkins ....G....... 224 436-7547
  Lake Forest *(G-12282)*

3151 Leather Gloves & Mittens

▲ Boss Holdings Inc ....D....... 309 852-2131
  Kewanee *(G-12023)*
▲ Boss Manufacturing Holdings ......F....... 309 852-2781
  Kewanee *(G-12025)*
▲ Kunz Glove Co Inc ....E....... 312 733-8780
  Chicago *(G-5136)*
◆ Magid Glove Safety Mfg Co LLC ...B....... 773 384-2070
  Romeoville *(G-17844)*
Magid Glove Safety Mfg Co LLC ......B....... 773 384-2070
  Chicago *(G-5316)*
Nationwide Glove Co Inc ....D....... 618 252-7192
  Harrisburg *(G-11027)*
Neckbone Skunks Logistics & Te .....F....... 312 218-0281
  Chicago *(G-5561)*

3161 Luggage

A W Enterprises Inc ....E....... 708 458-8989
  Bedford Park *(G-1452)*
Art Jewel Enterprises Ltd ....F....... 630 260-0400
  Carol Stream *(G-2941)*

31 LEATHER AND LEATHER PRODUCTS

Custom Case Co Inc ....E 773 585-1164
  Chicago (G-4289)
Du-Call Miller Plastics Inc ....F 630 964-6020
  Elburn (G-8450)
Hartmann ....G 618 684-6814
  Murphysboro (G-14755)
Ips & Luggage Co Inc ....G 630 894-2414
  Roselle (G-17960)
J-Industries Inc ....F 815 654-0055
  Loves Park (G-13220)
▲ Jacobson Acqstion Holdings LLC ...C 847 623-1414
  Waukegan (G-20452)
▲ Jelco Inc ....F 847 459-5207
  Wheeling (G-20920)
▲ Kingport Industries LLC ....G 847 480-5745
  Northbrook (G-15412)
▲ LC Industries Inc ....E 312 455-0500
  Elk Grove Village (G-9089)
▲ McKlein Company LLC ....F 773 235-0600
  Chicago (G-5378)
Mechanical Music Corp ....F 847 398-5444
  Arlington Heights (G-775)
Midwest Fibre Products Inc ....E 309 596-2955
  Viola (G-20180)
Plano Molding Company LLC ....C 815 786-3331
  Sandwich (G-18380)
▲ Platt Luggage Inc ....D 773 838-2000
  Chicago (G-5821)
▼ Seamcraft International LLC ....E 773 281-5150
  Chicago (G-6126)
Service & Manufacturing Corp ....E 773 287-5500
  Chicago (G-6141)
Sultry Satchels Inc ....G 312 810-1081
  Chicago (G-6264)
◆ Travel Caddy Inc ....E 847 621-7000
  Franklin Park (G-10065)

3172 Personal Leather Goods

A W Enterprises Inc ....E 708 458-8989
  Bedford Park (G-1452)
Curv Group LLC ....E 847 636-0101
  Elk Grove Village (G-8925)
▲ Elegant Acquisition LLC ....D 708 652-3400
  Cicero (G-6845)
◆ Hertzberg Ernst & Sons ....E 773 525-3518
  Chicago (G-4810)
J-Industries Inc ....F 815 654-0055
  Loves Park (G-13220)
◆ Plasticrest Products Inc ....F 773 826-2163
  Chicago (G-5818)
◆ Randa Accessories Lea Gds LLC ..D 847 292-8300
  Rosemont (G-18046)
◆ Rico Industries Inc ....D 312 427-0313
  Niles (G-15166)
SRS Global Ret Solutions LLC ....G 773 888-3094
  Evanston (G-9577)
Tia Tynette Designs Inc ....G 219 440-2859
  Olympia Fields (G-15899)
◆ World Richman Mfg Corp ....F 847 468-8898
  Elgin (G-8785)

3199 Leather Goods, NEC

▲ Boston Leather Inc ....E 815 622-1635
  Sterling (G-19501)
Cocajo Blades & Leather ....G 217 370-6634
  Franklin (G-9854)
◆ Hertzberg Ernst & Sons ....E 773 525-3518
  Chicago (G-4810)
◆ Klein Tools Inc ....B 847 821-5500
  Lincolnshire (G-12778)
Klein Tools Inc ....G 847 249-4930
  Waukegan (G-20455)
Klein Tools Inc ....D 847 228-6999
  Elk Grove Village (G-9078)
Klein Tools Inc ....E 847 821-5500
  Lincolnshire (G-12779)
Mast Harness Shop ....E 217 543-3463
  Campbell Hill (G-2816)
Pegai LLC ....G 312 799-0417
  Chicago (G-5783)
Seat Cover Pro LLC ....G 847 990-1506
  Vernon Hills (G-20094)
Spirit Industries Inc ....E 217 285-4500
  Griggsville (G-10851)

32 STONE, CLAY, GLASS, AND CONCRETE PRODUCTS

3211 Flat Glass

▲ Cat I Manufacturing Inc ....C 847 931-8986
  South Elgin (G-19140)
▲ Chicago Tempered Glass Inc ....F 773 583-2300
  Chicago (G-4132)
Day Star Systems LLC ....G 618 426-1868
  Campbell Hill (G-2814)
Duo Plex Glass Ltd 708 532-4422
  Palos Hills (G-16200)
Energy-Glazed Systems Inc 847 223-4500
  Grayslake (G-10769)
Engineered Glass Products LLC ....E 773 843-1964
  Chicago (G-4507)
▲ Euroview Enterprises LLC ....E 630 227-3300
  Elmhurst (G-9364)
Fuyao Glass Illinois Inc 217 864-2392
  Decatur (G-7495)
Glazed Structures Inc ....F 847 223-4560
  Grayslake (G-10776)
Great Lakes GL & Mirror Corp 847 647-1036
  Niles (G-15126)
Higgins Glass Studio LLC 708 447-2787
  Riverside (G-17084)
Lang Exterior Inc ....D 773 737-4500
  Chicago (G-5175)
Marsco Glass Products LLC ....D 312 326-4710
  Chicago (G-5349)
Montrose Glass & Mirror Corp ....G 773 478-6433
  Chicago (G-5494)
Pilkington North America Inc ....C 815 433-0932
  Ottawa (G-16072)
Pontiac Recyclers Inc ....G 815 844-6419
  Pontiac (G-16777)
Thermal Ceramics Inc ....E 217 627-2101
  Girard (G-10386)
Timeless Reflections ....G 815 663-8148
  Bureau (G-2639)
◆ Tru Vue Inc ....C 708 485-5080
  Countryside (G-7075)
Willow Ridge Glass Inc ....F 630 910-8300
  Woodridge (G-21348)

3221 Glass Containers

Alexander Technique ....G 847 337-7926
  Evanston (G-9490)
Amcor Phrm Packg USA LLC 847 298-5626
  Des Plaines (G-7726)
Ardagh Glass Inc ....G 847 869-7248
  Evanston (G-9495)
Ardagh Glass Inc ....D 708 849-4010
  Dolton (G-7929)
Ball Foster Glass Container ....G 708 849-1500
  Dolton (G-7932)
Bc International ....G 847 674-7384
  Skokie (G-18928)
◆ Enviro-Safe Refrigerants Inc ....E 309 346-1110
  Pekin (G-16331)
▲ Fri Jado Inc ....G 630 633-7944
  Woodridge (G-21302)
Gerresheimer Glass Inc ....C 708 843-4246
  Chicago Heights (G-6747)
Glass Haus 815 459-5849
  McHenry (G-13746)
Kavalierglass North Amer Inc ....F 847 364-7303
  Elk Grove Village (G-9075)
Libation Container Inc 312 636-7206
  Chicago (G-5217)
Owens-Brockway Glass Cont Inc ....C 815 672-3141
  Streator (G-19619)
Teamdance Illinois 815 463-9044
  Geneva (G-10310)
Wis - Pak Inc ....D 217 224-6800
  Quincy (G-16958)

3229 Pressed & Blown Glassware, NEC

Advanced Fiber Products LLC ....G 847 768-9001
  Des Plaines (G-7724)
Alpha Precision Inc ....F 630 553-7331
  Yorkville (G-21471)
Altamira Art Glass ....G 708 848-3799
  Oak Park (G-15744)
▲ Amkine Inc ....F 847 526-7088
  Wauconda (G-20331)
Arttig Art ....G 847 804-8001
  Wheeling (G-20851)
Barcor Inc ....F 847 940-0750
  Bannockburn (G-1192)
Cleavenger Associates Inc ....G 630 221-0007
  Winfield (G-21109)
◆ Corelle Brands Holdings Inc ....D 847 233-8600
  Rosemont (G-18009)
◆ Corelle Brands LLC ....C 847 233-8600
  Rosemont (G-18010)
Elite Fiber Optics LLC ....E 630 225-9454
  Franklin Park (G-9938)
▲ Finer Line Inc ....F 847 884-1611
  Itasca (G-11657)
▲ For Our Generation Inc ....G 312 282-1257
  Deerfield (G-6209)
▲ Harris Potteries LP ....G 847 564-5544
  Northbrook (G-15397)
▲ Hunter Mfg LLP ....D 859 254-7573
  Lake Forest (G-12262)
Industrial Fiberglass Inc ....F 708 681-2707
  Melrose Park (G-13882)
James R Wilbat Glass Studio ....G 847 940-0015
  Deerfield (G-7618)
Lang Exterior Inc ....D 773 737-4500
  Chicago (G-5175)
Libation Container Inc ....G 312 636-7206
  Chicago (G-5217)
Libbey Inc ....A 630 818-3400
  West Chicago (G-20607)
Lotton Art Glass Co ....G 708 672-1400
  Crete (G-7141)
Mattarusky Inc 630 469-4125
  Glen Ellyn (G-10412)
Montclare Scientific Glass ....G 847 255-6870
  Arlington Heights (G-777)
Neolight Labs LLC ....G 312 242-1773
  Ingleside (G-11588)
▲ Nippon Electric Glass Amer Inc ....G 630 285-8500
  Schaumburg (G-18649)
Norman P Moeller ....G 847 991-3933
  Lake Barrington (G-12162)
OBrien Scntfc GL Blowing LLC ....G 217 762-3636
  Monticello (G-14283)
Prairie Fire Glass Inc ....G 217 762-3332
  Monticello (G-14284)
Punch Products Manufacturing ....E 773 533-2800
  Chicago (G-5915)
Quality Coating Co ....F 815 875-3228
  Princeton (G-16822)
Roth Metal Fabricators Corp ....G 708 371-8300
  Alsip (G-505)
▲ Tadd LLC ....F 847 380-3540
  Cary (G-3194)
Thermal Ceramics Inc ....E 217 627-2101
  Girard (G-10386)
Upper Limits Midwest Inc ....G 217 679-4315
  Springfield (G-19467)

3231 Glass Prdts Made Of Purchased Glass

▼ Art Crystal II Enterprises Inc ....F 630 739-0222
  Lyons (G-13301)
▲ Bards Products Inc 800 323-5499
  Mundelein (G-14665)
Bertco Enterprises Inc ....G 618 234-9283
  Belleville (G-1535)
Besco Awards & Embroidery ....E 847 395-4862
  Antioch (G-603)
Biomerieux Inc ....E 630 628-6055
  Lombard (G-13046)
Boom Company Inc ....G 847 459-6199
  Wheeling (G-20863)
Botti Studio of Architectural ....E 847 869-5933
  Glenview (G-10532)
Brenda Miller ....G 618 678-2639
  Xenia (G-21467)
Central Illinois Glass & 309 367-4242
  Metamora (G-13960)
Ceramic Designs Unlimited 708 758-0690
  Chicago Heights (G-6738)
Circle Studio Stained Glass ....G 847 432-7249
  Highland Park (G-11258)
Circle Studio Stained Glass ....G 773 588-4848
  Chicago (G-4152)
Clear View Industries Inc ....G 815 267-3593
  Plainfield (G-16652)
Colorsmith Stained GL Studio ....G 708 447-8763
  Riverside (G-17083)
▲ Cristaux Inc ....G 312 778-8800
  Elk Grove Village (G-8921)
Crystal Cave ....F 847 251-1160
  Glenview (G-10540)

SIC SECTION
32 STONE, CLAY, GLASS, AND CONCRETE PRODUCTS

Doralco Inc ....E.... 708 388-9324
Alsip *(G-441)*
Duo Plex Glass Ltd ....G.... 708 532-4422
Palos Hills *(G-16200)*
Enameled Steel and Sign Co ....E.... 773 481-2270
Chicago *(G-4504)*
Engineered Glass Products LLC ....C.... 312 326-4710
Chicago *(G-4508)*
Engineered Glass Products LLC ....E.... 773 843-1964
Chicago *(G-4507)*
G & R Stained Glass ....G.... 847 455-7026
Franklin Park *(G-9948)*
Gerresheimer Glass Inc ....C.... 708 843-4246
Chicago Heights *(G-6747)*
Glass America Midwest LLC ....G.... 877 743-7237
Elmhurst *(G-9366)*
Glass Dimensions Inc ....F.... 708 410-2305
Melrose Park *(G-13874)*
Glass Fx ....G.... 217 359-0048
Champaign *(G-3295)*
Glass Haus ....G.... 815 459-5849
McHenry *(G-13746)*
Glazed Structures Inc ....F.... 847 223-4560
Grayslake *(G-10776)*
▲ Howw Manufacturing Company Inc ....E.... 847 382-4380
Lake Barrington *(G-12150)*
Illinois Valley Glass & Mirror ....F.... 309 682-6603
Peoria *(G-16457)*
J K Custom Countertops ....G.... 630 495-2324
Lombard *(G-13088)*
Lead n Glass Tm ....F.... 847 255-2074
Wheeling *(G-20930)*
Legend Dynamix Inc ....G.... 847 789-7007
Antioch *(G-622)*
▲ Lester L Brossard Co ....F.... 815 338-7825
Woodstock *(G-21405)*
Lotton Art Glass Co ....G.... 708 672-1400
Crete *(G-7141)*
Marsco Glass Products LLC ....D.... 312 326-4710
Chicago *(G-5349)*
Martin Glass Company ....F.... 618 277-1946
Belleville *(G-1571)*
Metal Products Sales Corp ....G.... 708 301-6844
Lockport *(G-13013)*
Midwest Tropical Entps Inc ....E.... 847 679-6666
Lincolnwood *(G-12831)*
▲ Monogram of Evanston Inc ....G.... 847 864-8100
Evanston *(G-9555)*
Montclare Scientific Glass ....G.... 847 255-6870
Arlington Heights *(G-777)*
Montrose Glass & Mirror Corp ....G.... 773 478-6433
Chicago *(G-5494)*
Mth Enterprises LLC ....D.... 708 498-1100
Hillside *(G-11349)*
▲ New Century Picture Corp ....E.... 773 638-8888
Chicago *(G-5575)*
Nexus Corporation ....E.... 217 303-5544
Pana *(G-16218)*
Norman P Moeller ....G.... 847 991-3933
Lake Barrington *(G-12162)*
OBrien Scntfic GL Blowing LLC ....G.... 217 762-3636
Monticello *(G-14283)*
▲ Oi Glass Containers Oi G9 ....G.... 815 673-5120
Streator *(G-19618)*
Oldcastle Buildingenvelope Inc ....G.... 773 523-8400
Chicago *(G-5671)*
Oldcastle Buildingenvelope Inc ....E.... 630 250-7270
Elk Grove Village *(G-9161)*
Ornament Shop Co Inc ....D.... 847 559-8844
Northbrook *(G-15449)*
▲ Ostrom & Co Inc ....F.... 503 281-6469
Winfield *(G-21113)*
Pilkington North America Inc ....C.... 815 433-0932
Ottawa *(G-16072)*
Precision Screen Specialties ....G.... 630 220-1361
Saint Charles *(G-18250)*
Pro Glass Corporation ....G.... 630 553-3141
Bristol *(G-2409)*
Pure 111 ....G.... 618 558-7888
Caseyville *(G-3218)*
▲ River City Millwork Inc ....D.... 800 892-9297
Rockford *(G-17573)*
Roscoe Glass Co ....G.... 815 623-6268
Roscoe *(G-17928)*
S P Industries Inc ....E.... 847 228-2851
Elk Grove Village *(G-9226)*
◆ Sarj USA Inc ....E.... 708 865-9134
Franklin Park *(G-10043)*
▲ See All Industries Inc ....F.... 773 927-3232
Chicago *(G-6130)*
Shoreline Glass Co Inc ....E.... 312 829-9500
Hillside *(G-11356)*
◆ Skyline Design Inc ....D.... 773 278-4660
Chicago *(G-6184)*
▲ Slee Corporation ....E.... 773 777-2444
Itasca *(G-11733)*
Specialty Selected Ltd ....G.... 847 967-1701
Skokie *(G-19033)*
Stained Glass of Peoria ....G.... 309 674-7929
Peoria *(G-16529)*
State Street Jewelers Inc ....F.... 630 232-2085
Geneva *(G-10307)*
Supertek Scientific LLC ....G.... 630 345-3450
Addison *(G-300)*
Sure Plus Manufacturing Co ....D.... 708 756-3100
Chicago Heights *(G-6777)*
▼ Tafco Corporation ....E.... 847 678-8425
Melrose Park *(G-13921)*
Tiffany Stained Glass Ltd ....G.... 312 642-0680
Forest Park *(G-9726)*
Tonjon Company ....F.... 630 208-1173
Geneva *(G-10312)*
▲ Torstenson Glass Co ....E.... 773 525-0435
Chicago *(G-6397)*
▲ Tuminello Enterprises Inc ....G.... 815 416-1007
Morris *(G-14334)*
Tuminello Enterprizes Inc ....G.... 815 416-1007
Morris *(G-14335)*
Will Hamms Stained Glass ....F.... 847 255-2230
Arlington Heights *(G-833)*

3241 Cement, Hydraulic

Bonsal American Inc ....D.... 847 678-6220
Franklin Park *(G-9891)*
Buzzi Unicem USA Inc ....E.... 815 768-3660
Joliet *(G-11835)*
Buzzi Unicem USA Inc ....G.... 610 882-5000
Rock Island *(G-17210)*
Coal City Redi-Mix Co Inc ....F.... 815 634-4455
Coal City *(G-6931)*
◆ Holcim (us) Inc ....D.... 773 372-1000
Chicago *(G-4827)*
Holcim Participations US Inc ....G.... 773 372-1000
Chicago *(G-4828)*
▲ Illinois Cement Company LLC ....C.... 815 224-2112
La Salle *(G-12113)*
▲ Lafarge Building Materials Inc ....D.... 678 746-2000
Chicago *(G-5155)*
Lafarge North America Inc ....E.... 630 892-1616
North Aurora *(G-15266)*
Lafarge North America Inc ....E.... 847 742-6060
South Elgin *(G-19163)*
Lafarge North America Inc ....E.... 815 741-2090
Rockdale *(G-17264)*
Lafarge North America Inc ....E.... 773 372-1000
Golconda *(G-10666)*
Lafarge North America Inc ....C.... 618 543-7541
Grand Chain *(G-10687)*
Lafarge North America Inc ....F.... 847 244-3800
Waukegan *(G-20457)*
Lafarge North America Inc ....E.... 773 372-1000
Chicago *(G-5157)*
Lafarge North America Inc ....G.... 773 646-5228
Chicago *(G-5158)*
◆ Lafarge North America Inc ....C.... 773 372-1000
Chicago *(G-5156)*
Lone Star Industries Inc ....G.... 815 883-3173
Oglesby *(G-15843)*
Promiz LLC ....G.... 618 533-3950
Centralia *(G-3246)*
Red-E-Mix Transportation LLC ....E.... 618 654-2166
Highland *(G-11238)*
Skyway Cement Company LLC ....E.... 800 643-1808
Chicago *(G-6185)*
Southfield Corporation ....C.... 815 284-3357
Dixon *(G-7918)*
Sport Redi-Mix LLC ....E.... 217 355-4222
Champaign *(G-3352)*
St Marys Cement Inc (us) ....E.... 313 842-4600
Dixon *(G-7920)*

3251 Brick & Structural Clay Tile

Arrowhead Brick Pavers Inc ....E.... 630 393-1584
Warrenville *(G-20231)*
Building Products Corp ....E.... 618 233-4427
Belleville *(G-1536)*
Complete Lawn and Snow Service ....F.... 847 776-7287
Palatine *(G-16102)*
Northshore Gardens Ltd ....G.... 847 672-4391
North Chicago *(G-15318)*
Rapid Landscaping Inc ....G.... 815 740-1000
Crest Hill *(G-7095)*
Richards Brick Company ....D.... 618 656-0230
Edwardsville *(G-8374)*
Selee Corporation ....E.... 847 428-4455
Gilberts *(G-10371)*

3253 Ceramic Tile

American Bullnose Co Midw ....G.... 630 238-1300
Wood Dale *(G-21162)*
◆ Curran Group Inc ....D.... 815 455-5100
Crystal Lake *(G-7190)*
◆ M H Detrick Company ....E.... 708 479-5085
Frankfort *(G-9814)*
Meier Granite Company ....G.... 847 678-7300
Franklin Park *(G-9989)*
Mosaicos Inc ....G.... 773 777-8453
Chicago *(G-5502)*
Pilla Exec Inc ....G.... 312 882-8263
Chicago *(G-5807)*
Southland Painting ....G.... 833 724-6803
Park Forest *(G-16260)*

3255 Clay Refractories

▲ Bmi Products Northern Ill Inc ....E.... 847 395-7110
Antioch *(G-605)*
Cimentos N Votorantim Amer Inc ....G.... 708 458-0400
Bridgeview *(G-2335)*
Great Lakes Clay & Supply Inc ....G.... 224 535-8127
Elgin *(G-8601)*
Harbisonwalker Intl Inc ....G.... 708 474-5350
Calumet City *(G-2779)*
▲ Holland Manufacturing Corp ....E.... 708 849-1000
Dolton *(G-7937)*
Thermal Ceramics Inc ....E.... 217 627-2101
Girard *(G-10386)*
V J Mattson Company ....D.... 708 479-1990
New Lenox *(G-15067)*

3259 Structural Clay Prdts, NEC

C & L Tiling Inc ....D.... 217 773-3357
Timewell *(G-19797)*
◆ Colloid Envmtl Tech Co LLC ....C.... 847 851-1500
Hoffman Estates *(G-11415)*
Coon Run Drainage & Levee Dst ....G.... 217 248-5511
Arenzville *(G-670)*

3261 China Plumbing Fixtures & Fittings

▲ BBC Innovation Corporation ....E.... 847 458-2334
Crystal Lake *(G-7168)*
▲ Cfpg Ltd ....C.... 630 679-1420
Woodridge *(G-21282)*
Coronado Conservation Inc ....G.... 301 512-4671
Chicago *(G-4238)*
Elkay Manufacturing Company ....B.... 708 681-1880
Broadview *(G-2434)*
▲ Gerber Plumbing Fixtures LLC ....D.... 630 679-1420
Woodridge *(G-21303)*
◆ Globe Union Group Inc ....D.... 630 679-1420
Woodridge *(G-21304)*
Kohler Co ....D.... 847 734-1777
Huntley *(G-11548)*
▲ Lacava LLC ....E.... 773 637-9600
Chicago *(G-5154)*
Sterline Manufacturing Corp ....E.... 847 244-1234
Gurnee *(G-10931)*
Swan Surfaces LLC ....C.... 618 532-5673
Centralia *(G-3252)*
▲ Wells Sinkware Corp ....G.... 312 850-3466
Chicago *(G-6601)*
Wonder Kids Inc ....G.... 773 437-8025
Evanston *(G-9589)*

3262 China, Table & Kitchen Articles

Cornerstone Fdsrvice Group Inc ....G.... 630 527-8600
Naperville *(G-14808)*
▲ Edwin M Knowles China Company ....F.... 847 581-8354
Niles *(G-15118)*

3263 Earthenware, Whiteware, Table & Kitchen Articles

Antioch Fine Arts Foundation ....G.... 847 838-2274
Antioch *(G-599)*

3264 Porcelain Electrical Splys

Arnold Magnetic Tech Corp ....E.... 815 568-2000
Marengo *(G-13480)*

Dpcac LLC F 630 741-7900
Itasca *(G-11644)*
Ferro Corporation C 847 623-0370
Waukegan *(G-20443)*
Johnson Sign Co G 847 678-2092
Franklin Park *(G-9975)*
Porcelain Enamel Finishers G 312 808-1560
Chicago *(G-5845)*
Senna Design LLC G 847 821-7877
Vernon Hills *(G-20096)*
▲ TSC Pyroferric International C 217 849-2230
Toledo *(G-19881)*
▲ Voges Inc D 618 233-2760
Belleville *(G-1608)*

3269 Pottery Prdts, NEC

▲ BSC Imports Incorporated G 773 844-4788
Chicago *(G-3970)*
C & L Manufacturing Entps G 618 465-7623
Alton *(G-546)*
In The Attic Inc G 847 949-5077
Mundelein *(G-14699)*
Ipsen Inc E 815 239-2385
Pecatonica *(G-16322)*
Spouts of Water Inc G 303 570-5104
Des Plaines *(G-7851)*
Ws Incorporated of Manmouth F 309 734-2161
Monmouth *(G-14228)*

3271 Concrete Block & Brick

Artistries By Tommy Musto Inc G 630 674-8667
Bloomingdale *(G-1977)*
Beelman Ready-Mix Inc G 618 247-3866
Sandoval *(G-18362)*
Bricks Inc F 773 523-5718
Chicago *(G-3953)*
Bricks Inc G 630 897-6926
Aurora *(G-1066)*
Building Products Corp E 618 233-4427
Belleville *(G-1536)*
Contractors Ready-Mix Inc G 217 482-5530
Mason City *(G-13610)*
County Materials Corp E 217 352-4181
Champaign *(G-3283)*
Elston Materials LLC G 773 235-3100
Chicago *(G-4490)*
Glen-Gery Corporation D 815 795-6911
Marseilles *(G-13555)*
Hamilton Concrete Products Co G 217 847-3118
Hamilton *(G-10958)*
Harvey Cement Products Inc F 708 333-1900
Harvey *(G-11087)*
▼ Kalb Corporation F 309 483-3600
Oneida *(G-15903)*
▲ Lafarge Building Materials Inc D 678 746-2000
Chicago *(G-5155)*
◆ Lafarge North America Inc C 773 372-1000
Chicago *(G-5156)*
Lion Concrete Products Inc G 630 892-7304
Montgomery *(G-14257)*
M & M Exposed Aggregate Co G 847 551-1818
Carpentersville *(G-3108)*
Macomb Concrete Products Inc G 309 772-3826
Bushnell *(G-2743)*
Max-Block Development LLC G 773 220-6214
Chicago *(G-5369)*
Mef Construction Inc G 847 741-8601
Elgin *(G-8655)*
Meno Stone Co Inc E 630 257-9220
Lemont *(G-12571)*
Midwest Block and Brick Inc G 618 939-7600
Waterloo *(G-20292)*
Midwest Cement Products Inc G 815 284-2342
Woosung *(G-21452)*
Midwest Water Group Inc E 866 526-6558
Crystal Lake *(G-7230)*
Monmouth Ready Mix Corp G 309 734-3211
Galesburg *(G-10212)*
New Panel Brick Company of Ill G 847 696-1686
Niles *(G-15152)*
Northfield Block Company G 708 458-8130
Berwyn *(G-1957)*
Paveloc Industries Inc F 815 568-4700
Marengo *(G-13492)*
Quikrete Companies LLC F 309 346-1184
Pekin *(G-16357)*
R & D Concrete Products Inc E 309 787-0264
Rock Island *(G-17237)*
Rockford Cement Products Co F 815 965-0537
Rockford *(G-17591)*
RR Mulch and Soil LLC G 708 596-7200
Markham *(G-13551)*
Scotts Exterior Maintenance Co G 309 660-3380
Bloomington *(G-2092)*
Sesser Concrete Products Co F 618 625-2811
Sesser *(G-18866)*
Southfield Corporation F 217 875-5455
Decatur *(G-7548)*
Southfield Corporation E 708 458-0400
Oak Lawn *(G-15735)*
Swansea Building Products Inc F 618 874-6282
East Saint Louis *(G-8326)*
Techo-Bloc Midwest Corp F 877 832-4625
Rock Island *(G-17248)*
Terrell Materials Corporation E 847 635-8530
Rosemont *(G-18053)*
Tison & Hall Concrete Products F 618 253-7808
Harrisburg *(G-11030)*
Valley View Industries Hc Inc E 800 323-9369
Crestwood *(G-7133)*

3272 Concrete Prdts

A&J Paving Inc G 773 889-9133
Chicago *(G-3493)*
Abel Vault & Monument Co Inc G 309 647-0105
Canton *(G-2820)*
Aimee M Ford G 630 308-9785
Aurora *(G-1044)*
American Cast Stone G 630 291-0250
Lemont *(G-12552)*
American Wilbert Vault Corp F 773 238-2746
Chicago *(G-3674)*
American Wilbert Vault Corp E 708 366-3210
Hillside *(G-11327)*
American Wilbert Vault Corp G 847 824-4415
Des Plaines *(G-7729)*
American Wilbert Vault Corp G 847 741-3089
Elgin *(G-8509)*
▲ Aqua Control Inc E 815 664-4900
Spring Valley *(G-19307)*
Architectural Cast Ston E 630 377-4800
West Chicago *(G-20543)*
Architectural Cast Stone LLC G 630 377-4800
West Chicago *(G-20544)*
Atmi Dynacore LLC D 815 838-9492
Aurora *(G-1056)*
Atmi Precast Inc E 630 897-0577
Aurora *(G-1057)*
Atmi Precast Inc E 630 897-0577
Aurora *(G-1058)*
Avan Precast Concrete Pdts Inc F 708 757-6200
Lynwood *(G-13291)*
B A Precast Inc G 309 645-0639
Ellisville *(G-9320)*
Bernard Cffey Vtrans Fundation G 630 687-0033
Naperville *(G-14779)*
Blue Pearl Stone Tech LLC G 708 698-5700
La Grange *(G-12073)*
Bobs Market & Greenhouse G 217 442-8155
Danville *(G-7324)*
Bonsal American Inc D 847 678-6220
Franklin Park *(G-9891)*
Bricks Inc G 630 897-6926
Aurora *(G-1066)*
C L Vault & Safe Srv G 708 237-0039
Oak Lawn *(G-15704)*
Casey Stone Co G 217 857-3425
Teutopolis *(G-19766)*
Christopher Concrete Products G 618 724-2951
Buckner *(G-2499)*
Classic Metal Vaults G 217 826-6302
Marshall *(G-13567)*
Classical Statuary & Decor G 815 462-3408
New Lenox *(G-15028)*
Clay Vollmar Products Co F 773 774-1234
Chicago *(G-4172)*
Clay Vollmar Products Co G 847 540-5850
Lake Zurich *(G-12394)*
Cline Concrete Products F 217 283-5012
Hoopeston *(G-11505)*
Component Precast Supply Inc G 630 483-2900
West Chicago *(G-20566)*
Concrete Products G 815 339-6395
Granville *(G-10754)*
Concrete Specialities Co Inc E 847 608-1200
Elgin *(G-8549)*
▼ Concrete Specialties Co E 847 608-1200
Elgin *(G-8550)*
▼ Connelly-Gpm Inc E 773 247-7231
Chicago *(G-4219)*
Contractors Ready-Mix Inc F 217 735-2565
Lincoln *(G-12728)*
Cortelyou Excavating G 309 772-2922
Bushnell *(G-2741)*
County Materials Corp E 217 352-4181
Champaign *(G-3283)*
Cpg International LLC D 570 558-8000
Chicago *(G-4252)*
Creative Inds Terrazzo Pdts G 773 235-9088
Chicago *(G-4263)*
Custom Stone Works Inc E 815 748-2109
Cortland *(G-7018)*
Details Etc F 708 932-5543
Mokena *(G-14078)*
Doric Products Inc D 217 826-6302
Marshall *(G-13570)*
Doty & Sons Concrete Products F 815 895-2884
Sycamore *(G-19708)*
Eagle Burial Vault G 815 722-8660
Frankfort *(G-9791)*
Eagle Stone and Brick Inc G 618 282-6722
Red Bud *(G-16993)*
▼ Ed Bell Investments Inc G 618 345-0799
Belleville *(G-1550)*
Electric Conduit Cnstr Co C 630 293-4474
Elburn *(G-8453)*
Elite Monument Co G 217 532-6080
Hillsboro *(G-11310)*
Elmhurst-Chicago Stone Company F 630 557-2446
Kaneville *(G-11954)*
Elmhurst-Chicago Stone Company E 630 832-4000
Elmhurst *(G-9360)*
Elmhurst-Chicago Stone Company E 630 983-6410
Bolingbrook *(G-2173)*
Elmos Tombstone Service G 773 643-0200
Chicago *(G-4488)*
Englewood Co Op G 773 873-1201
Chicago *(G-4510)*
Euro Marble Supply Ltd F 847 233-0700
Schiller Park *(G-18806)*
Evergreen Tank Solutions Inc G 708 235-0487
Monee *(G-14198)*
F H Leinweber Co Inc E 773 568-7722
Chicago *(G-4548)*
Farmington Wilbert Vault Corp F 309 245-2133
Farmington *(G-9662)*
Ferber George & Sons G 217 733-2184
Fairmount *(G-9643)*
Fire Orb LLC G 847 454-9198
Prospect Heights *(G-16840)*
Fischer Stone & Materials LLC G 815 233-3232
Freeport *(G-10108)*
Forrest Redi-Mix Inc G 815 657-8241
Forrest *(G-9733)*
Forsyth Brothers Concrete Pdts G 217 548-2770
Fithian *(G-9669)*
▲ Forterra Pressure Pipe Inc E 815 389-4800
South Beloit *(G-19093)*
Fountain Technologies Ltd E 847 537-3677
Wheeling *(G-20900)*
G P Concrete & Iron Works G 815 842-2270
Pontiac *(G-16770)*
Gary & Larry Brown Trucking G 618 268-6377
Raleigh *(G-16961)*
Graber Concrete Pipe Company E 630 894-5950
Bloomingdale *(G-1996)*
Great Lakes Envmtl Mar Del G 312 332-3377
Chicago *(G-4734)*
Great Lakes Lifting G 815 931-4825
Country Club Hills *(G-7039)*
Hahn Industries G 815 689-2133
Cullom *(G-7299)*
Hallen Burial Vault Inc G 815 544-6138
Belvidere *(G-1676)*
Hamel Tire and Concrete Pdts G 618 633-2405
Hamel *(G-10950)*
Hamilton Concrete Products Co G 217 847-3118
Hamilton *(G-10958)*
Hanson Aggregates East LLC E 815 398-2300
Rockford *(G-17442)*
Hardin Ready Mix Inc F 618 576-9313
Hardin *(G-11017)*
Hinckley Concrete Products Co G 815 286-3235
Hinckley *(G-11358)*
◆ Holcim (us) Inc D 773 372-1000
Chicago *(G-4827)*
Holcim Participations US Inc G 773 372-1000
Chicago *(G-4828)*
Hulse Excavating G 815 796-4106
Flanagan *(G-9670)*

Illini Precast G 815 795-6161
Marseilles *(G-13557)*

Illini Precast LLC F 708 562-7700
Westchester *(G-20700)*

Imco Precast LLC G 217 742-5300
Springfield *(G-19388)*

Impact Polymer LLC G 847 441-2394
Northfield *(G-15517)*

J E Tomes & Associates Inc F 708 653-5100
Blue Island *(G-2127)*

J P Vincent & Sons Inc G 815 777-2365
Galena *(G-10175)*

Jet Precast & Redimix Inc G 618 632-3594
O Fallon *(G-15575)*

Jgr Commercial Solutions Inc G 847 669-7010
Huntley *(G-11545)*

Kelley Vault Co Inc F 217 355-5551
Champaign *(G-3313)*

Kieft Bros Inc E 630 832-8090
Elmhurst *(G-9388)*

Kienstra Pipe & Precast LLC E 618 482-3283
Madison *(G-13416)*

Kingspan Light & Air LLC G 847 816-1060
Lake Forest *(G-12268)*

Kohnens Concrete Products Inc E 618 277-2120
Germantown *(G-10330)*

Kowalski Memorials Inc G 630 462-7226
Carol Stream *(G-3014)*

Kw Precast LLC F 708 562-7700
Westchester *(G-20702)*

◆ **Lafarge North America Inc** C 773 372-1000
Chicago *(G-5156)*

Legacy Vulcan LLC G 773 890-2360
Chicago *(G-5197)*

Leonards Unit Step Co G 815 744-1263
Rockdale *(G-17265)*

Leonards Unit Step of Moline G 309 792-9641
Colona *(G-6976)*

Libertyville Monuments G 641 295-3506
Libertyville *(G-12669)*

Lifetime Rooftile Company G 630 355-7922
Naperville *(G-14863)*

Lion Concrete Products Inc G 630 892-7304
Montgomery *(G-14257)*

Lombard Archtctral Prcast Pdts E 708 389-1060
Chicago *(G-5253)*

Lombard Investment Company D 708 389-1060
Alsip *(G-469)*

M & M Exposed Aggregate Co G 847 551-1818
Carpentersville *(G-3108)*

Macomb Concrete Products Inc G 309 772-3826
Bushnell *(G-2743)*

Mariachi Monumental De Mexico G 520 878-8688
Chicago *(G-5333)*

Material Service Corporation E 815 838-2400
Romeoville *(G-17846)*

McCann Concrete Products Inc E 618 377-3888
Dorsey *(G-7945)*

Merz Vault Company Inc E 618 548-2859
Salem *(G-18345)*

Meyer Material Co Merger Corp D 815 943-2605
Harvard *(G-11060)*

Mid-Illinois Concrete Inc G 217 382-6650
Martinsville *(G-13586)*

Mid-Illinois Concrete Inc G 618 664-1340
Greenville *(G-10838)*

Mid-Illinois Concrete Inc F 618 283-1600
Vandalia *(G-20015)*

Mid-Illinois Concrete Inc E 217 235-5858
Mattoon *(G-13650)*

▲ **Mid-States Concrete Inds LLC** D 815 389-2277
South Beloit *(G-19103)*

Midwest Cement Products Inc G 815 284-2342
Woosung *(G-21452)*

Midwest Perma-Column Inc G 309 589-7949
Edwards *(G-8339)*

MK Tile Ink G 773 964-8905
Chicago *(G-5474)*

Monumental Art Works G 708 389-3038
Blue Island *(G-2132)*

National Concrete Pipe Co E 630 766-3600
Franklin Park *(G-10006)*

North Star Stone Inc G 847 996-6850
Libertyville *(G-12691)*

Northern Illinois Wilbert Vlt G 815 544-3355
Belvidere *(G-1689)*

◆ **Northfield Block Company** C 847 816-9000
Mundelein *(G-14721)*

Northfield Block Company E 815 941-4100
Morris *(G-14319)*

Northfield Block Company G 708 458-8130
Berwyn *(G-1957)*

Nt Liquidating Inc E 815 726-3351
Joliet *(G-11909)*

Oakwood Memorial Park Inc G 815 433-0313
Ottawa *(G-16066)*

▲ **Orlandi Statuary Company** D 773 489-0303
Chicago *(G-5704)*

Ozinga Concrete Products Inc E 847 426-0920
Elgin *(G-8682)*

Ozinga Ready Mix Concrete Inc E 708 326-4200
Mokena *(G-14103)*

Peoria Wilbert Vault Co Inc F 309 383-2882
Metamora *(G-13966)*

Perfection Vault Co Inc F 217 673-6111
Woodson *(G-21351)*

Peter Baker & Son Co D 847 362-3663
Lake Bluff *(G-12204)*

Price Brothers Co D 815 389-4800
South Beloit *(G-19109)*

Prosser Construction Co F 217 774-5032
Shelbyville *(G-18884)*

Quad Cities Concrete Pdts LLC G 309 787-4919
Milan *(G-14021)*

Quick Building Systems Inc G 708 598-6733
Palos Hills *(G-16205)*

Quikrete Companies LLC F 309 346-1184
Pekin *(G-16357)*

Rex Vault Co F 618 783-2416
Newton *(G-15092)*

Rochelle Vault Co G 815 562-6484
Rochelle *(G-17158)*

Rockford Cement Products Co F 815 965-0537
Rockford *(G-17591)*

Rockford Sewer Co Inc G 815 877-9060
Loves Park *(G-13259)*

Royal Corinthian Inc E 630 876-8899
West Chicago *(G-20639)*

Schmalz Precast Concrete Mfg G 815 747-3939
East Dubuque *(G-8182)*

Skelcher Concrete Products G 618 457-2930
Carbondale *(G-2859)*

Slavish Inc G 309 754-8233
Matherville *(G-13615)*

Southern Ill Wilbert Vlt Co F 618 942-5845
Herrin *(G-11180)*

Southern Illinois Redimix Inc F 618 993-3600
Marion *(G-13539)*

Southern Illinois Stone Co F 573 334-5261
Buncombe *(G-2629)*

Southern Illinois Vault Co Inc G 270 554-4436
Herrin *(G-11181)*

Southfield Corporation F 217 875-5455
Decatur *(G-7548)*

Spacil Construction Co G 708 448-3809
Palos Heights *(G-16192)*

Spence Monuments Co G 217 348-5992
Charleston *(G-3413)*

St Louis Flexicore Inc F 618 531-8691
East Saint Louis *(G-8324)*

Sterling Vault Company F 815 625-0077
Sterling *(G-19537)*

Stockdale Block Systems LLC G 815 416-1030
Morris *(G-14329)*

Stone Installation & Maint Inc G 630 545-2326
Glendale Heights *(G-10503)*

Stonecraft Cast Stone LLC G 708 653-1477
Steger *(G-19493)*

Tagitsold Inc G 630 724-1800
Darien *(G-7412)*

Tanya Shipley G 708 476-0433
Mokena *(G-14121)*

Taurus Safety Products Inc G 630 620-7940
Lombard *(G-13140)*

Terrell Materials Corporation E 847 635-8530
Rosemont *(G-18053)*

Tickle Asphalt Co Ltd G 309 787-1308
Milan *(G-14029)*

Unique Concrete Concepts Inc F 618 466-0700
Jerseyville *(G-11797)*

US Fireplace Products Inc G 888 290-8181
Lake Bluff *(G-12211)*

Utility Concrete Products LLC E 815 416-1000
Morris *(G-14338)*

V & N Concrete Products Inc F 815 293-0315
Romeoville *(G-17884)*

▲ **Van-Packer Co** E 309 895-2311
Buda *(G-2500)*

Vcna Prairie Inc A 312 733-0094
Chicago *(G-6527)*

Vcna Prairie Indiana Inc E 708 458-0400
Bridgeview *(G-2396)*

Vitelli Concrete Products Inc G 708 754-5846
Chicago Heights *(G-6785)*

▲ **Welch Bros Inc** C 847 741-6134
Elgin *(G-8779)*

Welch Bros Inc G 815 547-3000
Belvidere *(G-1709)*

White Star Silo G 618 523-4735
Germantown *(G-10332)*

Wilbert Quincy Vault Co G 217 224-8557
Quincy *(G-16956)*

Wilbert Vault Company F 309 787-5281
Milan *(G-14032)*

Wolfe Burial Vault Co Inc G 815 697-2012
Chebanse *(G-3431)*

3273 Ready-Mixed Concrete

A & L Construction Inc E 708 343-1660
Melrose Park *(G-13816)*

Advanced On-Site Concrete Inc E 773 622-7836
Chicago *(G-3566)*

▲ **Aggregate Industries MGT Inc** G 773 372-1000
Chicago *(G-3581)*

All American Ready Mix F 217 931-2344
Springfield *(G-19317)*

Atlas Ready Mix Inc G 618 271-0774
East Saint Louis *(G-8297)*

Aztec Material Service Corp D 773 521-0909
Chicago *(G-3800)*

Ballard Bros Inc F 217 374-2137
White Hall *(G-21017)*

Barnett Redi-Mix Inc G 618 276-4298
Junction *(G-11948)*

Bee Line Service Inc G 815 233-1812
Freeport *(G-10102)*

Beelman Ready-Mix Inc G 618 357-6120
Pinckneyville *(G-16611)*

Beelman Ready-Mix Inc E 618 646-5300
East Saint Louis *(G-8299)*

Beelman Ready-Mix Inc G 618 244-9600
Mount Vernon *(G-14598)*

Beelman Ready-Mix Inc G 618 247-3866
Sandoval *(G-18362)*

Beelman Ready-Mix Inc G 618 478-2044
Nashville *(G-14995)*

Beelman Ready-Mix Inc F 618 526-0260
Breese *(G-2298)*

Biochemical Lab G 708 447-3923
Riverside *(G-17082)*

Bleigh Construction Company G 217 222-5005
Quincy *(G-16866)*

Blomberg Bros Inc F 618 245-6321
Farina *(G-9651)*

▲ **Bmi Products Northern Ill Inc** E 847 395-7110
Antioch *(G-605)*

Bob Barnett Redi-Mix Inc E 618 252-3581
Harrisburg *(G-11020)*

Breckenridge Material Company E 618 398-4141
Caseyville *(G-3211)*

Builders Ready-Mix Co E 847 866-6300
Evanston *(G-9501)*

Canton Redi-Mix Inc F 309 668-2261
Canton *(G-2823)*

Canton Redi-Mix Inc E 309 647-0019
Canton *(G-2824)*

Capitol Ready-Mix Inc E 217 528-1100
Springfield *(G-19340)*

Cemex Cement Inc G 773 995-5100
Chicago *(G-4054)*

Charleston Concrete Supply Co F 217 345-6404
Charleston *(G-3398)*

Chris Dj Mix LLC G 312 725-3838
Chicago *(G-4143)*

Clinard Ready Mix Inc E 217 773-3965
Mount Sterling *(G-14590)*

Clinton County Materials Corp F 618 533-4252
Centralia *(G-3226)*

Coal City Redi-Mix Co Inc F 815 634-4455
Coal City *(G-6931)*

Community Rady Mix of Pttsfeld G 217 285-5548
Pittsfield *(G-16633)*

Community Readymix Inc E 217 245-6668
Jacksonville *(G-11762)*

Concrete 1 Inc G 630 357-1329
Naperville *(G-14805)*

Concrete Supply LLC G 618 646-5300
East Saint Louis *(G-8302)*

Concrete Supply Tolono Inc G 217 485-3100
Urbana *(G-19979)*

S I C

Employee Codes: A=Over 500 employees, B=251-500
C=101-250, D=51-100, E=20-50, F=10-19, G=3-9

2020 Harris Illinois
Industrial Directory

909

Condominiums Northbrook Cort 1 ... G ... 847 498-1640
Lincolnshire *(G-12754)*
Continental Materials Corp ... F ... 312 541-7200
Chicago *(G-4228)*
Contractors Concrete ... G ... 217 826-2290
Marshall *(G-13568)*
Contractors Concrete Inc ... E ... 217 342-2299
Effingham *(G-8394)*
Contractors Ready-Mix Inc ... G ... 217 482-5530
Mason City *(G-13610)*
Contractors Ready-Mix Inc ... F ... 217 735-2565
Lincoln *(G-12728)*
Country Stone Inc ... E ... 309 787-1744
Milan *(G-14005)*
County Materials Corp ... E ... 217 352-4181
Champaign *(G-3283)*
Curry Ready Mix of Petersburg ... G ... 217 632-2516
Petersburg *(G-16601)*
Curry Ready-Mix of Decatur ... F ... 217 428-7177
Decatur *(G-7479)*
David Yates ... G ... 618 656-7879
Edwardsville *(G-8356)*
Diamond Ready Mix Inc ... F ... 630 355-5414
Naperville *(G-14815)*
Edwards Acquisition Corp ... F ... 309 944-2117
Geneseo *(G-10241)*
Edwards County Concrete LL ... G ... 618 445-2711
Harrisburg *(G-11022)*
Edwards County Concrete LLC ... G ... 618 445-2711
Albion *(G-349)*
Elmhurst-Chicago Stone Company ... E ... 630 832-4000
Elmhurst *(G-9360)*
Elmhurst-Chicago Stone Company ... E ... 630 983-6410
Bolingbrook *(G-2173)*
Fairfield Ready Mix Inc ... G ... 618 842-9462
Fairfield *(G-9623)*
Fehrenbacher Ready-Mix Inc ... G ... 618 395-2306
Olney *(G-15860)*
Ferber George & Sons ... G ... 217 733-2184
Fairmount *(G-9643)*
Fishstone Studio Inc ... G ... 815 276-0299
Crystal Lake *(G-7199)*
Flora Ready Mix Inc ... G ... 618 662-4818
Flora *(G-9681)*
Fnh Ready Mix Inc ... F ... 815 235-1400
Freeport *(G-10109)*
Forrest Redi-Mix Inc ... G ... 815 657-8241
Forrest *(G-9733)*
Fox Redi-Mix Inc ... G ... 217 774-2110
Shelbyville *(G-18878)*
Franklin Park Building Mtls ... G ... 847 455-3985
Franklin Park *(G-9945)*
Fuller Brothers Ready Mix ... G ... 217 532-2422
Hillsboro *(G-11312)*
Gary & Larry Brown Trucking ... G ... 618 268-6377
Raleigh *(G-16961)*
Goreville Concrete Inc ... E ... 618 995-2670
Goreville *(G-10681)*
Gorman Brothers Ready Mix Inc ... F ... 618 498-2173
Jerseyville *(G-11791)*
Great River Ready Mix Inc ... F ... 217 847-3515
Hamilton *(G-10956)*
Grohne Concrete Products Co ... G ... 217 877-4197
Decatur *(G-7498)*
H J Mohr & Sons Company ... F ... 708 366-0338
Oak Park *(G-15756)*
Hardin Ready Mix Inc ... F ... 618 576-9313
Hardin *(G-11017)*
Herman Bade & Sons ... G ... 217 832-9444
Villa Grove *(G-20123)*
Illini Concrete Inc ... F ... 618 235-4141
Belleville *(G-1557)*
Illini Concrete Inc ... G ... 618 398-4141
Caseyville *(G-3214)*
Illini Ready Mix Inc ... G ... 618 833-7321
Anna *(G-585)*
Illini Ready Mix Inc ... G ... 618 734-0287
Carbondale *(G-2846)*
J W Ossola Company Inc ... G ... 815 339-6112
Granville *(G-10755)*
J&J Ready Mix Inc ... G ... 309 676-0579
East Peoria *(G-8271)*
Jerry Berry Contracting Co ... G ... 618 594-3339
Carlyle *(G-2891)*
Joe Hatzer & Son Inc ... E ... 815 673-5571
Streator *(G-19612)*
Joe Hatzer & Son Inc ... G ... 815 672-2161
Streator *(G-19613)*
JW Ossola Co Inc ... G ... 815 339-6113
Granville *(G-10756)*

Kendall County Concrete Inc ... E ... 630 851-9197
Aurora *(G-992)*
Kienstra-Illinois LLC ... F ... 618 251-6345
Wood River *(G-21265)*
▲ **Lafarge Building Materials Inc** ... D ... 678 746-2000
Chicago *(G-5155)*
◆ **Lafarge North America Inc** ... C ... 773 372-1000
Chicago *(G-5156)*
Lahood Construction Inc ... E ... 309 699-5080
East Peoria *(G-8276)*
Langheim Ready Mix Inc ... G ... 217 625-2351
Girard *(G-10383)*
Legacy Vulcan LLC ... E ... 847 437-4181
Elk Grove Village *(G-9092)*
Legacy Vulcan LLC ... F ... 217 932-2611
Casey *(G-3205)*
Legacy Vulcan LLC ... F ... 815 726-6900
Joliet *(G-11894)*
Legacy Vulcan LLC ... F ... 630 739-0182
Romeoville *(G-17841)*
Legacy Vulcan LLC ... D ... 708 485-6602
Mc Cook *(G-13695)*
Legacy Vulcan LLC ... E ... 815 436-3535
Plainfield *(G-16682)*
Material Service Corporation ... E ... 815 838-2400
Romeoville *(G-17846)*
Max Miller ... F ... 708 758-7760
S Chicago Hts *(G-18124)*
Maxheimer Construction Inc ... G ... 309 444-4200
Washington *(G-20275)*
McLean County Asphalt Co ... D ... 309 827-6115
Bloomington *(G-2072)*
Menoni & Mocogni Inc ... F ... 847 432-0850
Highland Park *(G-11283)*
Mertel Gravel Company Inc ... F ... 815 223-0468
Peru *(G-16581)*
Metropolis Ready Mix Inc ... E ... 618 524-8221
Metropolis *(G-13974)*
Meyer Material Co Merger Corp ... F ... 847 658-7811
Algonquin *(G-381)*
Meyer Material Co Merger Corp ... E ... 847 824-4111
Elburn *(G-8460)*
Meyer Material Co Merger Corp ... E ... 815 331-7200
Streamwood *(G-19585)*
Meyer Material Co Merger Corp ... E ... 847 689-9200
Lake Bluff *(G-12196)*
Meyer Material Co Merger Corp ... D ... 815 943-2605
Harvard *(G-11060)*
Mid-Illinois Concrete Inc ... E ... 217 235-5858
Mattoon *(G-13650)*
Mid-Illinois Concrete Inc ... G ... 217 345-6404
Charleston *(G-3407)*
Mid-Illinois Concrete Inc ... G ... 217 382-6650
Martinsville *(G-13586)*
Mid-Illinois Concrete Inc ... G ... 618 664-1340
Greenville *(G-10838)*
Mid-Illinois Concrete Inc ... F ... 618 283-1600
Vandalia *(G-20015)*
Mindful Mix ... G ... 847 284-4404
Lake Zurich *(G-12434)*
Mix N Mingle ... G ... 815 308-5170
Woodstock *(G-21413)*
Moeller Ready Mix Inc ... F ... 217 243-7471
Jacksonville *(G-11776)*
Moline Consumers Co ... F ... 309 757-8289
Moline *(G-14162)*
Monmouth Ready Mix Corp ... G ... 309 734-3211
Galesburg *(G-10212)*
Moultrie County Redi-Mix Co ... G ... 217 728-2334
Sullivan *(G-19673)*
Mt Crmel Stblzation Group Inc ... E ... 618 262-5118
Mount Carmel *(G-14482)*
Myers Concrete & Construction ... G ... 815 732-2591
Oregon *(G-15924)*
Narvick Bros Lumber Co Inc ... E ... 815 521-1173
Minooka *(G-14064)*
Narvick Bros Lumber Co Inc ... E ... 815 942-1173
Morris *(G-14318)*
Newton Ready Mix Inc ... F ... 618 783-8611
Newton *(G-15088)*
ODaniel Trucking Co ... D ... 618 382-5371
Carmi *(G-2912)*
Odum Concrete Products Inc ... G ... 618 942-4572
Herrin *(G-11175)*
Odum Concrete Products Inc ... E ... 618 993-6211
Marion *(G-13523)*
Oldcastle Materials Inc ... F ... 309 627-2111
Monmouth *(G-14225)*
Oremus Materials LLC ... G ... 520 820-2265
Burr Ridge *(G-2711)*

Ozinga Bros Inc ... E ... 708 326-4200
Mokena *(G-14100)*
Ozinga Bros Inc ... E ... 815 568-2589
Marengo *(G-13491)*
Ozinga Bros Inc ... E ... 847 783-6500
Lake Bluff *(G-12203)*
Ozinga Bros Inc ... D ... 847 768-1697
Des Plaines *(G-7816)*
Ozinga Bros Inc ... E ... 847 783-6500
Algonquin *(G-383)*
Ozinga Bros Inc ... D ... 708 326-4200
Chicago Heights *(G-6763)*
Ozinga Bros Inc ... D ... 312 432-5700
Evanston *(G-9564)*
Ozinga Bros Inc ... D ... 815 332-8198
Belvidere *(G-1693)*
Ozinga Chicago Ready Mix Con ... E ... 708 479-9050
Alsip *(G-488)*
Ozinga Chicago Ready Mix Con ... E ... 312 432-5700
Chicago *(G-5724)*
Ozinga Chicago Ready Mix Con ... E ... 773 862-2817
Chicago *(G-5725)*
Ozinga Chicago Ready Mix Con ... E ... 847 447-0353
Chicago *(G-5726)*
Ozinga Concrete Products Inc ... G ... 708 479-9050
Hampshire *(G-10982)*
Ozinga Indiana Rdymx Con Inc ... G ... 708 479-9050
Mokena *(G-14101)*
Ozinga Materials Inc ... C ... 309 364-3401
Mokena *(G-14102)*
Ozinga Ready Mix Concrete Inc ... E ... 800 786-6382
Chicago *(G-5727)*
Ozinga Ready Mix Concrete Inc ... E ... 708 326-4200
Mokena *(G-14103)*
Ozinga S Subn Rdymx Con Inc ... F ... 708 479-3080
Mokena *(G-14104)*
Ozinga S Subn Rdymx Con Inc ... D ... 708 326-4201
Mokena *(G-14105)*
Paxton Ready Mix Inc ... G ... 217 379-2303
Paxton *(G-16313)*
Pbi Redi Mix & Trucking ... E ... 217 562-3717
Pana *(G-16222)*
Peoples Coal and Lumber Co ... F ... 815 432-2456
Watseka *(G-20314)*
Pike County Concrete Inc ... G ... 217 285-5548
Pittsfield *(G-16637)*
Poggenpohl LLC ... G ... 217 229-3411
Raymond *(G-16990)*
Poggenpohl LLC ... G ... 217 824-2020
Taylorville *(G-19760)*
Point Ready Mix LLC ... G ... 815 578-9100
McHenry *(G-13781)*
Prairie Central Ready Mix ... G ... 217 877-5210
Decatur *(G-7537)*
Prairie Group Management LLC ... D ... 708 458-0400
Bridgeview *(G-2375)*
Prairie Material ... F ... 708 458-0400
Bedford Park *(G-1493)*
Prairie Materials Group ... G ... 815 207-6750
Shorewood *(G-18900)*
Princeton Ready-Mix Inc ... F ... 815 875-3359
Princeton *(G-16820)*
Quad County Ready Mix Swansea ... G ... 618 257-9530
Swansea *(G-19694)*
Quad-County Ready Mix Corp ... F ... 618 243-6430
Okawville *(G-15847)*
Quad-County Ready Mix Corp ... F ... 618 588-4656
New Baden *(G-15022)*
Quad-County Ready Mix Corp ... G ... 618 526-7130
Breese *(G-2306)*
Quad-County Ready Mix Corp ... E ... 618 244-6973
Mount Vernon *(G-14635)*
Quad-County Ready Mix Corp ... G ... 618 288-4000
Troy *(G-19918)*
Quad-County Ready Mix Corp ... F ... 618 327-3748
Nashville *(G-15008)*
Quad-County Ready Mix Corp ... F ... 618 594-2732
Carlyle *(G-2894)*
Quad-County Ready Mix Corp ... G ... 618 548-2477
Salem *(G-18353)*
Quad-County Ready Mix Corp ... G ... 618 295-3000
Marissa *(G-13544)*
Quality Ready Mix Concrete Co ... G ... 815 589-2013
Fulton *(G-10156)*
Quality Ready Mix Concrete Co ... F ... 815 772-7181
Morrison *(G-14347)*
Quality Ready Mix Concrete Co ... G ... 815 625-0750
Sterling *(G-19527)*
Quality Ready Mix Concrete Co ... G ... 815 288-6416
Dixon *(G-7907)*

SIC SECTION — 32 STONE, CLAY, GLASS, AND CONCRETE PRODUCTS

R & L Ready Mix Inc .... F 618 544-7514
  Robinson (G-17123)
Ranger Redi-Mix & Mtls Inc .... G 815 337-2662
  Woodstock (G-21429)
Rapco Ltd .... G 618 249-6614
  Richview (G-17033)
Ready 2 Roll Inc .... G 847 620-9768
  Wheeling (G-20971)
Ready Mix Solutions LLC .... G 618 889-6188
  Marion (G-13532)
Red-E-Mix LLC .... D 618 654-2166
  Highland (G-11237)
Regional Ready Mix LLC .... F 815 562-1901
  Rochelle (G-17154)
Riber Construction Inc .... F 815 584-3337
  Dwight (G-8159)
River Redi Mix Inc .... G 815 795-2025
  Marseilles (G-13564)
Riverstone Group Inc .... G 309 757-8297
  Moline (G-14173)
Riverstone Group Inc .... F 309 788-9543
  Rock Island (G-17244)
Roanoke Concrete Products Co .... G 309 885-0250
  Pekin (G-16359)
Roanoke Concrete Products Co .... F 309 698-7882
  East Peoria (G-8288)
Rock River Ready Mix Inc .... G 815 625-1139
  Dixon (G-7912)
Rock River Ready-Mix .... E 815 288-2269
  Dixon (G-7913)
Rogers Ready Mix & Mtls Inc .... D 815 234-8212
  Byron (G-2757)
Rogers Ready Mix & Mtls Inc .... G 815 234-8044
  Oregon (G-15926)
Rogers Ready Mix & Mtls Inc .... E 815 874-6626
  Rockford (G-17613)
Rogers Ready Mix & Mtls Inc .... F 815 389-2223
  Roscoe (G-17927)
Rogers Redi-Mix Inc .... F 618 282-3844
  Ruma (G-18106)
Schirz Concrete Products Inc .... F 217 368-2153
  Greenfield (G-10818)
Silver Bros Inc .... F 217 283-7751
  Hoopeston (G-11513)
Southern Illinois Redimix Inc .... F 618 993-3600
  Marion (G-13539)
Southfield Corporation .... D 708 563-4056
  Addison (G-293)
Southfield Corporation .... D 309 676-6121
  Morton (G-14382)
Southfield Corporation .... C 815 284-3357
  Dixon (G-7918)
Southfield Corporation .... F 217 877-5210
  Decatur (G-7549)
Southfield Corporation .... D 708 458-0400
  Bridgeview (G-2388)
Southfield Corporation .... E 309 829-1087
  Bloomington (G-2096)
Southfield Corporation .... G 309 676-0576
  Peoria (G-16527)
Southfield Corporation .... E 708 458-0400
  Oak Lawn (G-15735)
Sport Redi-Mix LLC .... E 217 892-4222
  Rantoul (G-16983)
Stahl Lumber Company .... F 309 695-4331
  Wyoming (G-21462)
Stahl Lumber Company .... F 309 385-2552
  Wyoming (G-21463)
Staley Concrete Co .... E 217 356-9533
  Champaign (G-3353)
Sterling-Rock Falls Ready Mix .... F 815 288-3135
  Dixon (G-7921)
Super Mix Inc .... D 815 578-9100
  McHenry (G-13801)
Super Mix of Wisconsin Inc .... G 262 859-9000
  McHenry (G-13802)
Super Mix of Wisconsin Inc .... G 815 578-9100
  McHenry (G-13803)
T H Davidson & Co Inc .... E 815 464-2000
  Oak Forest (G-15690)
T H Davidson & Co Inc .... G 815 941-0280
  Morris (G-14331)
Thelen Sand & Gravel Inc .... D 847 838-8800
  Antioch (G-636)
Tri County Concrete .... G 309 222-4000
  Peoria (G-16538)
Tri-City Ready-Mix .... G 618 439-2071
  Benton (G-1938)
Tri-County Concrete Inc .... G 815 786-2179
  Sandwich (G-18385)

Triangle Concrete Co Inc .... G 309 853-4334
  Kewanee (G-12042)
United Ready Mix Inc .... E 309 676-3287
  Peoria (G-16541)
Upchurch Ready Mix Concrete .... G 618 235-6222
  Belleville (G-1605)
Upchurch Ready Mix Concrete .... G 618 286-4808
  Dupo (G-8148)
Upland Concrete .... G 224 699-9909
  East Dundee (G-8214)
Valley Concrete Inc .... G 815 725-2422
  Joliet (G-11940)
Vcna Praire Yard 1033 .... G 708 458-0400
  Chicago (G-6526)
Vcna Prairie LLC .... A 708 458-0400
  Bridgeview (G-2394)
Vcna Prairie Illinois Inc .... F 217 398-4346
  Champaign (G-3363)
Vcna Prairie Illinois Inc .... G 708 458-0400
  Bridgeview (G-2395)
Via Galante Cement Con In .... G 773 589-9893
  Chicago (G-6542)
Vulcan Materials Company .... F 847 695-0057
  Bartlett (G-1322)
Wayland Ready Mix Concrete Svc ... F 309 833-2064
  Galesburg (G-10222)
Welsch Ready Mix Inc .... G 815 524-1850
  Bolingbrook (G-2252)
Westmore Supply Co .... F 630 627-0278
  Lombard (G-13154)
Westville Ready Mix Inc .... G 217 267-2082
  Westville (G-20782)
Winnetka Mews Condominium Assn ... G 847 501-2770
  Winnetka (G-21138)

3274 Lime

▲ Lafarge Building Materials Inc .... D 678 746-2000
  Chicago (G-5155)
Mineral Products Inc .... G 618 433-3150
  Harrisburg (G-11026)

3275 Gypsum Prdts

Continental Studios Inc .... E 773 542-0309
  Chicago (G-4230)
Creative Perky Cuisine LLC .... G 312 870-0282
  Tinley Park (G-19818)
Ken Matthews & Associates Inc .... G 630 628-6470
  Addison (G-167)
New Ngc Inc .... D 847 623-8100
  Waukegan (G-20468)
Owens Corning Sales LLC .... D 815 226-4627
  Rockford (G-17545)
Patrick Industries Inc .... E 630 595-0595
  Franklin Park (G-10015)
◆ United States Gypsum Company .... B 312 606-4000
  Chicago (G-6478)
USG Corporation .... F 847 970-5200
  Libertyville (G-12721)
USG Corporation .... B 312 436-4000
  Chicago (G-6506)

3281 Cut Stone Prdts

AA Rigoni Brothers Inc .... E 815 838-9770
  Lockport (G-12980)
Acme Marble Co Inc .... G 630 964-7162
  Darien (G-7399)
All Saints Monument Co Inc .... G 847 824-1248
  Des Plaines (G-7725)
American Marble & Granite Inc .... G 815 741-1710
  Crest Hill (G-7083)
American Monument Co .... G 618 993-8968
  Marion (G-13503)
Argyle Cut Stone Co .... E 847 456-6210
  Des Plaines (G-7733)
Arnold Monument Co Inc .... G 217 546-2102
  Springfield (G-19320)
▲ Atelier Jvnce Stncarving Tiles .... G 312 492-7922
  Chicago (G-3757)
Beutel Corporation .... G 309 786-8134
  Rock Island (G-17207)
▲ Bevel Granite Company Inc .... D 708 371-4191
  Indian Head Park (G-11576)
Botti Studio of Architectural .... E 847 869-5933
  Glenview (G-10532)
Brombereks Flagstone Co Inc .... G 630 257-0686
  Lemont (G-12557)
Carrera Stone Systems of Chica .... E 847 566-2277
  Mundelein (G-14673)
Cline Concrete Products .... F 217 283-5012
  Hoopeston (G-11505)

Clugston Tibbitts Funeral Home .... G 309 833-2188
  Macomb (G-13389)
▲ Condor Granites Intl Inc .... G 847 635-7214
  Elgin (G-8551)
Contempo Marble & Granite Inc ...... G 312 455-0022
  Chicago (G-4225)
Contemporary Marble Inc .... G 618 281-6200
  Columbia (G-6989)
Contractors Ready-Mix Inc .... G 217 482-5530
  Mason City (G-13610)
Country Stone Inc .... E 309 787-1744
  Milan (G-14005)
Creative Inds Terrazzo Pdts .... G 773 235-9088
  Chicago (G-4263)
Custom Stone Wrks Acqstion Inc ..... G 630 669-1119
  Cortland (G-7019)
Czarnik Memorials Inc .... G 708 458-4443
  Justice (G-11951)
D & H Granite and Marble Sup .... E 773 869-9988
  Chicago (G-4297)
Daprato Rigali Studios Inc .... E 773 763-5511
  Chicago (G-4317)
Doh Services Inc .... F 708 331-3811
  South Holland (G-19209)
▲ Dtk Construction Inc .... G 312 296-2762
  Wheeling (G-20880)
Earth Stone Products III Inc .... G 847 671-3000
  Schiller Park (G-18801)
Effingham Monument Co Inc .... G 217 857-6085
  Effingham (G-8397)
Ford Marble and Tile Inc .... F 618 475-2987
  New Athens (G-15019)
Gallasi Cut Stone & Marble LLC .... E 708 479-9494
  Mokena (G-14086)
Galloy and Van Etten Inc .... E 773 928-4800
  Chicago (G-4657)
Gast Monuments Inc .... G 773 262-2400
  Chicago (G-4660)
Granite Mountain Inc .... G 708 774-1442
  New Lenox (G-15036)
Hollywood Traders LLC .... G 630 943-6461
  Lombard (G-13085)
▲ House Granite & Marble Corp .... G 847 928-1111
  Schiller Park (G-18814)
J W Reynolds Monument Co Inc .... G 618 833-6014
  Anna (G-586)
Jacksonville Monument Co .... G 217 245-2514
  Jacksonville (G-11772)
Keepes Funeral Home Inc .... F 618 262-5200
  Mount Carmel (G-14476)
King & Sons Monuments .... G 815 786-6321
  Sandwich (G-18376)
Knauer Industries Ltd .... E 815 725-0246
  Joliet (G-11891)
Lansing Cut Stone Co .... F 708 474-7515
  Lansing (G-12503)
Liberty Limestone Inc .... E 815 385-5011
  McHenry (G-13757)
Luxury MBL & Gran Design Inc .... G 773 656-2125
  Chicago (G-5288)
Machine & Design .... G 630 858-6416
  Glen Ellyn (G-10411)
▲ Marble Emporium Inc .... E 847 205-4000
  Northbrook (G-15427)
Material Service Corporation .... E 847 658-4559
  Algonquin (G-380)
Material Service Corporation .... E 708 447-1100
  Westchester (G-20704)
Material Service Corporation .... E 217 732-2117
  Athens (G-897)
Meier Granite Company .... G 847 678-7300
  Franklin Park (G-9989)
Mendota Monument Co .... G 815 539-7276
  Mendota (G-13947)
Meno Stone Co Inc .... E 630 257-9220
  Lemont (G-12571)
Midwest Stone Sales Inc .... F 815 254-6600
  Plainfield (G-16691)
Monumental Art Works .... G 708 389-3038
  Blue Island (G-2132)
Moore Memorials .... F 708 636-6532
  Chicago Ridge (G-6804)
Nashville Memorial Co .... G 618 327-8492
  Nashville (G-15004)
Natural Stone Inc .... G 847 735-1129
  Lake Bluff (G-12198)
Newton Ready Mix Inc .... F 618 783-8611
  Newton (G-15088)
Northwest Products .... G 630 860-2288
  Bensenville (G-1859)

Employee Codes: A=Over 500 employees, B=251-500
C=101-250, D=51-100, E=20-50, F=10-19, G=3-9

32 STONE, CLAY, GLASS, AND CONCRETE PRODUCTS

◆ Nu-Dell Manufacturing Co Inc .... F 847 803-4500
  Chicago *(G-5637)*
Old Capitol Monument Works Inc ...... G 217 324-5673
  Vandalia *(G-20017)*
Pana Monument Co .... G 217 562-5121
  Pana *(G-16220)*
Patterson Products .... G 618 723-2688
  Noble *(G-15191)*
Pep Industries Inc .... F 630 833-0404
  Villa Park *(G-20164)*
Peter Troost Monument Co .... G 773 585-0242
  Justice *(G-11953)*
Pintas Cultured Marble .... E 708 385-3360
  Alsip *(G-492)*
Pontiac Granite Company Inc .... F 815 842-1384
  Pontiac *(G-16776)*
Regal Cut Stone LLC .... F 773 826-8796
  Chicago *(G-5999)*
Rogan Granitindustrie Inc .... G 708 758-0050
  Indian Head Park *(G-11577)*
▲ Rogan Granitindustrie Inc .... G 708 758-0050
  Lynwood *(G-13298)*
Sambor Stone Ltd .... G 708 388-0804
  South Holland *(G-19243)*
Spence Monuments Co .... G 217 348-5992
  Charleston *(G-3413)*
St Charles Memorial Works Inc .... G 630 584-0183
  Saint Charles *(G-18275)*
▲ Standard Marble & Granite .... F 773 533-0450
  Chicago *(G-6229)*
Stone Center Inc .... G 630 971-2060
  Lisle *(G-12943)*
Stone Design Inc .... F 630 790-5715
  Glendale Heights *(G-10501)*
▲ Stone Design Inc .... E 630 790-5715
  Glendale Heights *(G-10502)*
▲ Stonecasters LLC .... D 847 526-5200
  Wauconda *(G-20392)*
▲ Stonecrafters Inc .... G 815 363-8730
  Lakemoor *(G-12477)*
Stylenquaza LLC .... G 847 981-0191
  Elk Grove Village *(G-9257)*
Superior Home Products Inc .... G 217 726-9300
  Springfield *(G-19460)*
Tisch Monuments Inc .... G 618 233-3017
  Belleville *(G-1599)*
Tri-State Cut Stone Co .... G 815 469-7550
  Frankfort *(G-9845)*
▲ Unilock .... C 262 742-3890
  Aurora *(G-1164)*
▲ Unilock Chicago Inc .... D 630 892-9191
  Aurora *(G-1165)*
United Granite & Marble .... G 815 582-3345
  Joliet *(G-11938)*
▲ Vecchio Manufacturing of Ill .... F 847 742-8429
  Elgin *(G-8773)*
Venetian Monument Company .... F 312 829-9622
  Chicago *(G-6531)*
Wasowski Jacek .... G 847 693-1878
  Palatine *(G-16172)*
▲ Weiss Monument Works Inc .... G 618 398-1811
  Belleville *(G-1611)*
▲ Wendell Adams .... E 217 345-9587
  Charleston *(G-3416)*
Wienmar Inc .... G 847 742-9222
  South Elgin *(G-19181)*
Wilson & Wilson Monument Co .... F 618 775-6488
  Odin *(G-15836)*
World Granite Inc .... G 815 288-3350
  Dixon *(G-7926)*
Worldwide Tiles Ltd Inc .... G 708 389-2992
  Alsip *(G-526)*
Zoia Monument Company .... G 815 338-0358
  Woodstock *(G-21451)*

3291 Abrasive Prdts

A Wheels Inc .... G 847 699-7000
  Des Plaines *(G-7717)*
▲ Abrasic 90 Inc .... E 847 647-5994
  Niles *(G-15098)*
Abrasive .... G 630 893-7800
  Bloomingdale *(G-1973)*
Abrasive Rubber Wheel Co .... F 847 587-0900
  Fox Lake *(G-9743)*
Abrasive Technology Inc .... E 847 888-7100
  Elgin *(G-8490)*
Abrasive-Form LLC .... C 630 220-3437
  Bloomingdale *(G-1974)*
◆ Agsco Corporation .... G 847 520-4455
  Wheeling *(G-20842)*

Anchor Abrasives Company .... E 708 444-4300
  Tinley Park *(G-19804)*
Avec Inc .... G 815 577-3122
  Aurora *(G-917)*
C M C Industries Inc .... E 630 377-0530
  Saint Charles *(G-18161)*
Carbco Manufacturing Inc .... F 630 377-1410
  Saint Charles *(G-18164)*
Diagrind Inc .... F 708 460-4333
  Orland Park *(G-15951)*
▼ Dura Wax Company .... F 815 385-5000
  McHenry *(G-13739)*
▲ Engis Corporation .... C 847 808-9400
  Wheeling *(G-20891)*
Fives Landis Corp .... D 815 389-2251
  South Beloit *(G-19092)*
▲ Global Material Tech Inc .... C 847 495-4700
  Buffalo Grove *(G-2542)*
Global Material Tech Inc .... C 773 247-6000
  Chicago *(G-4696)*
▲ Grier Abrasive Co Inc .... C 708 333-6445
  South Holland *(G-19216)*
Harsco Corporation .... F 217 237-4335
  Pawnee *(G-16304)*
Hayes Abrasives Inc .... F 217 532-6850
  Hillsboro *(G-11313)*
Higman LLC .... C 618 785-2545
  Baldwin *(G-1185)*
Ideal Industries Inc .... C 815 895-1108
  Sycamore *(G-19715)*
K & K Abrasives & Supplies .... E 773 582-9500
  Chicago *(G-5063)*
Meinhardt Diamond Tool Co .... G 773 267-3260
  Chicago *(G-5388)*
▲ Modern Abrasive Corp .... D 815 675-2352
  Spring Grove *(G-19286)*
Oswego Diamond .... G 630 636-9617
  Oswego *(G-16018)*
◆ Radiac Abrasives Inc .... C 618 548-4200
  Salem *(G-18354)*
Radiac Abrasives Inc .... E 630 898-0315
  Oswego *(G-16024)*
▲ Rh Preyda Company .... F 212 880-1477
  Chicago *(G-6022)*
▲ Rock Solid Imports LLC .... C 331 472-4522
  Naperville *(G-14910)*
S & J Industrial Supply Corp .... E 708 339-1708
  South Holland *(G-19242)*
Saint-Gobain Abrasives Inc .... C 630 238-3300
  Carol Stream *(G-3062)*
Saint-Gobain Abrasives Inc .... C 630 868-8060
  Carol Stream *(G-3063)*
▲ Sand-Rite Manufacturing Co .... G 312 997-2200
  Melrose Park *(G-13912)*
▲ Sandtech Inc .... F 847 470-9595
  Morton Grove *(G-14439)*
▲ SBS Steel Belt Systems USA Inc . F 847 841-3300
  Gilberts *(G-10369)*
Schram Enterprises Inc .... E 708 345-2252
  Melrose Park *(G-13914)*
◆ Severstal US Holdings II Inc .... E 708 756-0400
  Hinsdale *(G-11379)*
Superior Joining Tech Inc .... E 815 282-7581
  Machesney Park *(G-13376)*
Tyrolit Limited .... G 618 548-8314
  Oswego *(G-16029)*
▲ Uk Abrasives Inc .... E 847 291-3566
  Northbrook *(G-15494)*
Ultramatic Equipment Co .... E 630 543-4565
  Addison *(G-322)*
▲ US Minerals Inc .... F 708 623-1935
  Tinley Park *(G-19866)*
US Minerals Inc .... F 618 785-2217
  Baldwin *(G-1187)*
US Minerals Inc .... F 217 534-2370
  Coffeen *(G-6945)*
◆ Washington Mills Hennepin Inc .... D 815 925-7302
  Hennepin *(G-11160)*
Weld Cote Metals .... G 888 258-0121
  Niles *(G-15186)*

3292 Asbestos products

Asbestos Control & Envmtl Svc .... F 630 690-0189
  Eola *(G-9469)*
Celtic Environmental .... G 708 442-5823
  Chicago Ridge *(G-6789)*
Wise Construction Services .... G 630 553-6350
  Yorkville *(G-21506)*

3295 Minerals & Earths: Ground Or Treated

▲ Aero Industries Inc .... F 800 747-3553
  Harvard *(G-11041)*
Beelman Slag Sales .... B 618 452-8120
  Madison *(G-13405)*
▲ Dauber Company Inc .... E 815 442-3569
  Tonica *(G-19888)*
Fairmont Central LLC .... E 815 433-2449
  Ottawa *(G-16050)*
Harsco Corporation .... F 217 237-4335
  Pawnee *(G-16304)*
Imerys Refractory Mnrl USA Inc ...... E 618 285-6558
  Rosiclare *(G-18064)*
Jaffee Investment Partnr LP .... C 312 321-1515
  Chicago *(G-4999)*
Jmjocs Inc .... G 708 769-7981
  Chicago Ridge *(G-6800)*
John Crane Inc .... E 815 459-0420
  Crystal Lake *(G-7214)*
Material Service Corporation .... D 708 877-6540
  Thornton *(G-19790)*
McGill Asphalt Construction Co .... G 708 924-1755
  Chicago *(G-5376)*
▲ Mid River Minerals Inc .... G 815 941-7524
  Morris *(G-14313)*
Mineral Products Inc .... B 618 433-3150
  Harrisburg *(G-11026)*
Minerals Technologies Inc .... F 847 851-1500
  Hoffman Estates *(G-11435)*
Oil-Dri Corporation America .... D 618 745-6881
  Mounds *(G-14463)*
Oil-Dri Corporation America .... B 312 321-1516
  Chicago *(G-5667)*
Oil-Dri Corporation America .... D 312 321-1515
  Chicago *(G-5666)*
Phoenix Services LLC .... G 708 849-3527
  Riverdale *(G-17074)*
◆ Polyform Products Company .... E 847 427-0020
  Elk Grove Village *(G-9182)*
▼ Prince Minerals Inc .... F 618 285-6558
  Rosiclare *(G-18065)*
▲ Sem Minerals LP .... D 217 224-8766
  Quincy *(G-16944)*
Stein Inc .... F 815 626-9355
  Sterling *(G-19533)*
◆ Superior Graphite Co .... E 312 559-2999
  Chicago *(G-6280)*
Superior Graphite Co .... E 708 458-0006
  Chicago *(G-6281)*
Superior Graphite Co .... G 773 890-4100
  Chicago *(G-6282)*
Tms International LLC .... D 618 451-7840
  Granite City *(G-10742)*
Tms International LLC .... G 815 939-9460
  Bourbonnais *(G-2271)*

3296 Mineral Wool

Atlas Roofing Corporation .... E 309 752-7121
  East Moline *(G-8222)*
J & J Industries Inc .... E 630 595-8878
  Mount Prospect *(G-14538)*
Johns Manville Corporation .... C 815 744-1545
  Rockdale *(G-17261)*
Owens Corning Sales LLC .... B 708 594-6911
  Argo *(G-674)*
Owens-Corning Fiberglass Tech ...... G 708 563-9091
  Argo *(G-676)*
Safe-T-Quip Corporation .... F 773 235-2100
  Chicago *(G-6089)*
◆ Silbrico Corporation .... D 708 354-3350
  Hodgkins *(G-11397)*
Tex Trend Inc .... E 847 215-6796
  Wheeling *(G-20999)*
▲ Transco Products Inc .... D 312 427-2818
  Streator *(G-19631)*
USG Corporation .... F 847 970-5200
  Libertyville *(G-12721)*
USG Corporation .... B 312 436-4000
  Chicago *(G-6506)*

3297 Nonclay Refractories

Advanced Refr Instllation Tech .... F 847 741-3105
  Elgin *(G-8497)*
Gardner Asphalt Corporation .... E 800 237-1155
  Chicago *(G-4659)*
Ipsen Inc .... E 815 239-2385
  Pecatonica *(G-16322)*
◆ M H Detrick Company .... F 708 479-5085
  Frankfort *(G-9814)*

Magneco Inc ....D 630 543-6660
Addison (G-188)
Magneco Inc ....G 630 543-6660
Addison (G-189)
Miller Purcell Co Inc ....G 815 485-2142
New Lenox (G-15043)
▲ Ossola Industrials Inc ....F 618 451-2621
Granite City (G-10729)
▼ Plibrico Company LLC ....F 312 337-9000
Northbrook (G-15460)
▲ Vesuvius Crucible Company ....G 217 351-5000
Champaign (G-3365)
Vesuvius U S A Corporation ....D 708 757-7880
Chicago Heights (G-6784)
Vesuvius U S A Corporation ....C 217 897-1145
Fisher (G-9668)
Vesuvius U S A Corporation ....C 217 345-7044
Charleston (G-3415)
◆ Vesuvius U S A Corporation ....C 217 351-5000
Champaign (G-3366)

3299 Nonmetallic Mineral Prdts, NEC

Budget Signs ....F 618 259-4460
Wood River (G-21260)
Continental Studios Inc ....E 773 542-0309
Chicago (G-4230)
Daprato Rigali Studios Inc ....E 773 763-5511
Chicago (G-4317)
Decorators Supply Corporation ....E 773 847-6300
Chicago (G-4330)
Depth Action Marketing Group ....G 847 475-7122
Evanston (G-9509)
Espe Manufacturing Co ....F 847 678-8950
Schiller Park (G-18805)
▲ Ghp Group Inc ....E 847 324-5900
Niles (G-15125)
GL Downs Inc ....G 618 993-9777
Marion (G-13513)
Image Systems Bus Slutions LLC ....E 847 378-8249
Elk Grove Village (G-9046)
Lakefront Sculpture Exhibit ....G 312 719-0207
Chicago (G-5164)
Nanophase Technologies Corp ....F 630 771-6747
Burr Ridge (G-2706)
Nanophase Technologies Corp ....D 630 771-6700
Romeoville (G-17859)
▲ Orlandi Statuary Company ....D 773 489-0303
Chicago (G-5704)
Pillar Enterprises Inc ....G 630 966-2566
North Aurora (G-15271)
Quality Molding Products LLC ....G 224 286-4555
Gurnee (G-10921)
Sand Sculpture Co ....G 815 334-9101
Woodstock (G-21430)
Thermal Ceramics Inc ....E 217 627-2101
Girard (G-10386)
▲ Thermionics Corp ....F 800 800-5728
Springfield (G-19464)

33 PRIMARY METAL INDUSTRIES

3312 Blast Furnaces, Coke Ovens, Steel & Rolling Mills

5h Consulting & Design LLC ....E 618 317-5822
Ellis Grove (G-9319)
A & A Steel Fabricating Co ....F 708 389-4499
Posen (G-16789)
◆ A Finkl & Sons Co ....B 773 975-2510
Chicago (G-3488)
AC Americos ....F 312 366-2943
Chicago (G-3513)
Accurate Metals Illinois LLC ....F 815 966-6320
Rockford (G-17293)
Adams Elevator Equipment Co ....E 847 581-2900
Chicago (G-3538)
▼ Advance Steel Services Inc ....G 773 619-2977
Chicago (G-3558)
Advantage Tool and Mold Inc ....G 847 301-9020
Elk Grove Village (G-8811)
AK Steel Corporation ....B 815 267-3838
Plainfield (G-16640)
▲ Aldon Co ....F 847 623-8800
Waukegan (G-20412)
Alter Trading Corporation ....F 309 828-6084
Bloomington (G-2023)
◆ Arcelormittal Intl Amer LLC ....D 312 899-3400
Chicago (G-3719)
Arcelormittal USA Inc ....G 312 899-3500
Chicago (G-3721)
◆ Arcelormittal USA LLC ....B 312 346-0300
Chicago (G-3723)
Archer Metal & Paper Co ....F 773 585-3030
Chicago (G-3726)
Arntzen Corporation ....E 815 334-0788
Woodstock (G-21360)
ATI Flat Rlled Pdts Hldngs LLC ....F 708 974-8801
Bridgeview (G-2326)
Automation Design & Mfg Inc ....G 630 896-4206
Aurora (G-1060)
Bar Processing Corporation ....E 708 757-4570
Chicago Heights (G-6733)
Beh IL Corp ....G 630 616-1850
Hinsdale (G-11363)
◆ Bevstream Corp ....G 630 761-0060
Batavia (G-1357)
Bluestone Specialty Chem LLC ....F 815 727-3010
Joliet (G-11833)
Bruder Tank Inc ....E 217 292-9058
Sullivan (G-19662)
C & F Forge Company ....E 847 455-6609
Franklin Park (G-9895)
Cambridge Pattern Works ....G 309 937-5370
Cambridge (G-2803)
Caster Warehouse Inc ....F 847 836-5712
Carpentersville (G-3097)
▲ Central Wire Inc ....C 800 435-8317
Union (G-19938)
▲ CFC Wire Forms Inc ....E 630 879-7575
Batavia (G-1364)
Chicago Metal Fabricators Inc ....D 773 523-5755
Chicago (G-4114)
Chicago Pipe Bending & Coil Co ....F 773 379-1918
Chicago (G-4122)
▲ Chromium Industries Inc ....E 773 287-3716
Chicago (G-4145)
▼ CHS Acquisition Corp ....C 708 756-5648
Chicago Heights (G-6743)
Clawmounts Mfg Inc ....G 708 525-7552
University Park (G-19951)
Cobraa Inc ....G 618 228-7380
Aviston (G-1178)
Combined Metals Holding Inc ....C 708 547-8800
Bellwood (G-1619)
Commercial Metals Company ....G 815 928-9600
Kankakee (G-11961)
Commercial Stainless Svcs Inc ....F 847 349-1560
Elk Grove Village (G-8906)
▼ Connelly-Gpm Inc ....E 773 247-7231
Chicago (G-4219)
◆ Consolidated Mill Supply Inc ....G 847 706-6715
Palatine (G-16104)
Contour Tool Works Inc ....G 847 947-4700
Palatine (G-16106)
Covey Machine Inc ....F 773 650-1530
Chicago (G-4250)
▼ Craftsman Custom Metals LLC ....D 847 655-0040
Schiller Park (G-18797)
▲ D R Sperry & Co ....D 630 892-4361
Aurora (G-1083)
Economy Iron Inc ....F 708 343-1777
Melrose Park (G-13859)
Elg Metals Inc ....E 773 374-1500
Chicago (G-4484)
Ergoseal Inc ....G 630 462-9370
Carol Stream (G-2980)
◆ Evraz Inc NA ....D 312 533-3555
Chicago (G-4541)
Fabricating Machinery Sales ....E 630 350-2266
Wood Dale (G-21186)
▲ Feralloy Corporation ....E 503 286-8869
Chicago (G-4580)
Finkl Steel - Houston LLC ....F 773 975-2540
Chicago (G-4593)
Forza Customs ....G 708 474-6625
Lansing (G-12493)
▲ Fox Valley Iron & Metal Corp ....F 630 897-5907
Aurora (G-1098)
Franks Maintenance & Engrg ....G 847 475-1003
Evanston (G-9523)
▲ General Products International ....G 847 458-6357
Lake In The Hills (G-12335)
Gerald R Page Corporation ....F 847 398-5575
Prospect Heights (G-16842)
Gerdau Ameristeel US Inc ....G 800 237-0230
Chicago (G-4687)
Grab Brothers Ir Works Co Corp ....F 847 288-1055
Franklin Park (G-9951)
▲ Guardian Construction Pdts Inc ....E 630 820-8899
Naperville (G-14970)
Heidtman Steel Products Inc ....D 618 451-0052
Granite City (G-10714)
HI Tek Tool & Machining Inc ....G 847 836-6422
Algonquin (G-373)
Highland Southern Wire Inc ....G 618 654-2161
Highland (G-11222)
Hoosier Stamping & Mfg Corp ....G 812 426-2778
Grayville (G-10809)
▲ Illinois Engineered Pdts Inc ....E 312 850-3710
Chicago (G-4889)
Illinois Weld & Machine Inc ....F 309 565-0533
Hanna City (G-10992)
Industrial Pipe and Supply Co ....E 708 652-7511
Chicago (G-4909)
Jacobs Boiler & Mech Inds Inc ....E 773 385-9900
Chicago (G-4998)
Jamco Products Inc ....D 815 624-0400
South Beloit (G-19097)
Joe Zsido Sales & Design Inc ....E 618 435-2605
Benton (G-1929)
John Maneely Company ....C 773 254-0617
Chicago (G-5043)
▲ Keats Manufacturing Co ....D 847 520-1133
Wheeling (G-20923)
Keystone Consolidated Inds Inc ....E 309 697-7020
Peoria (G-16466)
Keystone Consolidated Inds Inc ....E 708 753-1200
Chicago Heights (G-6757)
Korhumel Inc ....G 847 330-0335
Schaumburg (G-18590)
Kusmierek Industries Inc ....G 708 258-3100
Peotone (G-16554)
Lawndale Forging & Tool Works ....G 773 277-2800
Chicago (G-5183)
Lexington Steel Corporation ....D 708 594-9200
Bedford Park (G-1480)
Marias Chicken ATI Atihan ....G 847 699-3113
Niles (G-15144)
Marqutte Stl Sup Fbrcation Inc ....F 815 433-0178
Ottawa (G-16060)
Matcon Manufacturing Inc ....E 309 755-1020
Cordova (G-7008)
Mc Chemical Company ....E 815 964-7687
Rockford (G-17511)
Metal-Matic Inc ....C 708 594-7553
Bedford Park (G-1481)
Mexinox USA Inc ....D 224 533-6700
Bannockburn (G-1203)
Middletown Coke Company LLC ....G 630 284-1755
Lisle (G-12910)
Midwest Wheel Covers Inc ....G 847 609-9980
Barrington (G-1228)
▲ Mittal Steel USA Inc ....F 312 899-3440
Chicago (G-5472)
Modern Tube LLC ....G 877 848-3300
Bloomingdale (G-2001)
Mt Tool and Manufacturing Inc ....G 847 985-6211
Schaumburg (G-18640)
Multiple Metal Production ....G 847 679-1510
Skokie (G-18994)
Multiplex Industries Inc ....G 630 906-9780
Montgomery (G-14263)
Multitech Industries ....G 815 206-0015
Woodstock (G-21415)
Nacme Steel Processing LLC ....G 847 806-7226
Elk Grove Village (G-9142)
Nacme Steel Processing LLC ....D 847 806-7200
Chicago (G-5535)
National Material LP ....E 773 646-6300
Chicago (G-5547)
National Material Processing ....G 773 646-6300
Chicago (G-5548)
▲ Nelsen Steel and Wire LP ....D 847 671-9700
Franklin Park (G-10007)
▲ New C F & I Inc ....A 312 533-3555
Chicago (G-5574)
Nucor Corporation ....G 630 887-1400
Hinsdale (G-11371)
▲ Nucor Steel Kankakee Inc ....B 815 937-3131
Bourbonnais (G-2266)
▲ O & K American Corp ....D 773 767-2500
Chicago (G-5644)
O & W Wire Co Inc ....F 773 776-5919
Chicago (G-5645)
Offko Tool Inc ....G 815 933-9474
Kankakee (G-11994)
Olympic Steel Inc ....E 847 584-4000
Schaumburg (G-18658)
Omega Products Inc ....G 618 939-3445
Waterloo (G-20293)

S I C

P B A Corp F 312 666-7370
Chicago *(G-5728)*

Paragon Spring Company E 773 489-6300
Chicago *(G-5759)*

Penn Aluminum Intl LLC C 618 684-2146
Murphysboro *(G-14756)*

Phillips & Johnston Inc F 815 778-3355
Lyndon *(G-13287)*

Prairie Profile G 618 846-2116
Vandalia *(G-20019)*

Precise Stamping Inc E 630 897-6477
North Aurora *(G-15272)*

Princeton Flighting Corp F 815 872-0945
Princeton *(G-16819)*

▲ Processed Steel Company B 815 459-2400
Crystal Lake *(G-7251)*

Production Cutting Services D 815 264-3505
Waterman *(G-20300)*

Progress Rail Services Corp E 309 963-4425
Danvers *(G-7317)*

Ptc Group Holdings Corp D 708 757-4747
Chicago Heights *(G-6766)*

Ptc Tubular Products LLC C 815 692-4900
Fairbury *(G-9612)*

R & E Quality Mfg Co G 773 286-6846
Chicago *(G-5942)*

R M Tool & Manufacturing Co G 847 888-0433
Elgin *(G-8713)*

◆ Raco Steel Company E 708 339-2958
Markham *(G-13550)*

Rain Cii Carbon LLC E 618 544-2193
Robinson *(G-17124)*

Residential Steel Services G 309 448-2900
Congerville *(G-7002)*

Residntial Stl Fabricators Inc E 847 695-3400
South Elgin *(G-19171)*

Revere Metals LLC G 708 995-6131
Mokena *(G-14112)*

▲ Rmi Inc F 708 756-5640
Chicago Heights *(G-6770)*

S 4 Global Inc G 708 325-1236
Bedford Park *(G-1501)*

SE Steel Inc G 847 350-9618
Antioch *(G-634)*

Seraph Industries LLC G 815 222-9686
Caledonia *(G-2771)*

Service Sheet Metal Works Inc F 773 229-0031
Chicago *(G-6143)*

Shapiro Bros of Illinois Inc E 618 244-3168
Mount Vernon *(G-14638)*

▲ Southern Steel and Wire Inc G 618 654-2161
Highland *(G-11240)*

▲ Ssab Sales Inc F 630 810-4800
Lisle *(G-12941)*

Ssab Texas Inc G 630 810-4800
Lisle *(G-12942)*

St Louis Scrap Trading LLC G 618 307-9002
Edwardsville *(G-8376)*

Steel Fabrication and Welding G 773 343-0731
Cicero *(G-6876)*

◆ Steel Whse Quad Cities LLC E 309 756-1089
Rock Island *(G-17247)*

Stein Inc D 618 452-0836
Granite City *(G-10739)*

◆ Sterling Steel Company LLC B 815 548-7000
Sterling *(G-19535)*

Strictly Stainless Inc G 847 885-2890
Hoffman Estates *(G-11464)*

▲ Sun Coke International Inc D 630 824-1000
Lisle *(G-12944)*

Sun Steel Trading LLC G 614 439-3390
Rosemont *(G-18052)*

Suncoke Energy Inc C 630 824-1000
Lisle *(G-12945)*

Suncoke Energy Partners LP G 630 824-1000
Lisle *(G-12946)*

Suncoke Technology and Dev LLC G 630 824-1000
Lisle *(G-12947)*

Superior Piling Inc G 708 496-1196
Bridgeview *(G-2392)*

Tdy Industries LLC D 847 564-0700
Northbrook *(G-15492)*

Titan International Inc C 217 228-6011
Quincy *(G-16948)*

Tj Tool Inc F 630 543-3595
Bloomingdale *(G-2017)*

Tj Wire Forming Inc G 630 628-9209
Addison *(G-310)*

Tms International LLC G 815 939-1178
Bourbonnais *(G-2270)*

Tms International LLC G 618 451-9526
Granite City *(G-10743)*

Tomko Machine Works Inc G 630 244-0902
Lemont *(G-12593)*

▲ Tritech International LLC G 847 888-0333
Elgin *(G-8761)*

▲ TSA Processing Chicago Inc G 630 860-5900
Bensenville *(G-1904)*

United States Steel Corp D 618 451-3456
Granite City *(G-10748)*

United Toolers of Illinois F 779 423-0548
Loves Park *(G-13279)*

Valbruna Stainless Inc F 630 871-5524
Carol Stream *(G-3083)*

Venus Processing & Storage D 847 455-0496
Franklin Park *(G-10077)*

Voestalpine Nortrak Inc D 708 753-2125
Chicago Heights *(G-6786)*

Waters Wire EDM Service G 630 640-3534
Downers Grove *(G-8107)*

Westwood Lands Inc G 618 877-4990
Madison *(G-13419)*

Wheel Worx North LLC G 309 346-3535
Pekin *(G-16369)*

Works In Progress Foundation G 847 997-8338
Lake Villa *(G-12372)*

3313 Electrometallurgical Prdts

Hickman Williams & Company F 630 574-2150
Palos Heights *(G-16188)*

Masters & Alloy LLC G 312 582-1880
Alsip *(G-473)*

◆ Miller and Company LLC E 847 696-2400
Rosemont *(G-18037)*

Prince Minerals LLC G 646 747-4222
Quincy *(G-16926)*

Prince Minerals LLC G 646 747-4200
Quincy *(G-16927)*

Tempel Holdings Inc F 847 244-5330
Old Mill Creek *(G-15849)*

◆ Tempel Holdings Inc A 773 250-8000
Chicago *(G-6343)*

3315 Steel Wire Drawing & Nails & Spikes

Accurate Wire Strip Frming Inc F 630 260-1000
Carol Stream *(G-2924)*

Ace Custom Upholstery & Rod Sp G 618 842-2913
Fairfield *(G-9616)*

Aif Inc E 630 495-0077
Addison *(G-24)*

Allform Manufacturing Co G 847 680-0144
Libertyville *(G-12627)*

Apex Wire Products Company Inc F 847 671-1830
Franklin Park *(G-9871)*

Arcelormittal South Chicago G 312 899-3300
Chicago *(G-3720)*

Aspen Guard LLC G 708 325-0400
Bedford Park *(G-1458)*

◆ Atlantis Products Inc G 630 971-9680
Bolingbrook *(G-2152)*

Berens Inc G 815 935-3237
Saint Anne *(G-18132)*

Blue Ridge Forge Inc G 309 274-5377
Chillicothe *(G-6814)*

C & L Manufacturing Entps G 618 465-7623
Alton *(G-546)*

▲ Central Wire Inc C 800 435-8317
Union *(G-19938)*

City Ornamental Iron Works G 847 888-8898
Elgin *(G-8541)*

Combined Metals Chicago LLC F 847 683-0500
Hampshire *(G-10967)*

Dayton Superior Corporation E 219 476-4106
Kankakee *(G-11962)*

Dayton Superior Corporation C 815 936-3300
Kankakee *(G-11964)*

E H Baare Corporation C 618 546-1575
Robinson *(G-17114)*

Estad Stamping & Mfg Co E 217 442-4600
Danville *(G-7331)*

▲ Excel Specialty Corp E 773 262-7575
Lake Forest *(G-12248)*

Fairbanks Wire Corporation G 847 683-2600
Hampshire *(G-10972)*

Gerdau Ameristeel US Inc G 800 237-0230
Chicago *(G-4687)*

▲ Hamalot Inc E 847 944-1500
Schaumburg *(G-18542)*

◆ Heico Companies LLC F 312 419-8220
Chicago *(G-4798)*

Highland Wire Inc F 618 654-2161
Highland *(G-11225)*

Hohmann & Barnard Illinois LLC E 773 586-6700
Chicago Ridge *(G-6798)*

▲ Ifastgroupe Usa LLC G 450 658-7148
Downers Grove *(G-8026)*

▲ Illinois Engineered Pdts Inc E 312 850-3710
Chicago *(G-4889)*

Illinois Tool Works Inc G 847 821-2170
Vernon Hills *(G-20065)*

▲ ITW Bldg Components Group G 847 634-1900
Glenview *(G-10571)*

▲ Krueger and Company E 630 833-5650
Elmhurst *(G-9389)*

▲ L & J Industrial Staples Inc G 815 864-3337
Shannon *(G-18870)*

Major Wire Incorporated F 708 457-0121
Norridge *(G-15239)*

Mapes & Sprowl Steel LLC G 800 777-1025
Elk Grove Village *(G-9110)*

Master-Halco Inc E 618 395-4365
Olney *(G-15873)*

Mfr Manufacturing Corp Inc G 815 552-3333
Aurora *(G-1133)*

National Material Company LLC E 847 806-7200
Elk Grove Village *(G-9144)*

▲ Pneu Fast Company F 847 866-8787
Evanston *(G-9568)*

▲ Powernail Company E 800 323-1653
Lake Zurich *(G-12445)*

▲ Raajrtna Stinless Wire USA Inc F 847 923-8000
Schaumburg *(G-18695)*

Reino Tool & Manufacturing Co F 773 588-5800
Chicago *(G-6005)*

▲ Rockford Rigging Inc F 309 263-0566
Roscoe *(G-17926)*

Southwire Company LLC D 618 662-8341
Flora *(G-9694)*

Stephens Pipe & Steel LLC E 800 451-2612
North Aurora *(G-15278)*

▲ Taubensee Steel & Wire Company C 847 459-5100
Wheeling *(G-20997)*

The Parts House G 309 343-0146
Galesburg *(G-10221)*

▲ Vision Sales Incorporated G 630 483-1900
Bartlett *(G-1321)*

▲ W H Maze Company C 815 223-1742
Peru *(G-16596)*

W H Maze Company D 815 223-8290
Peru *(G-16597)*

W R Pabich Mfg Co Inc F 773 486-4141
Chicago *(G-6578)*

William Dach F 815 962-3455
Rockford *(G-17685)*

Wiretech Inc G 815 986-9614
Rockford *(G-17688)*

3316 Cold Rolled Steel Sheet, Strip & Bars

A & A Steel Fabricating Co F 708 389-4499
Posen *(G-16789)*

Arcelormittal Hennepin LLC C 815 925-2311
Hennepin *(G-11156)*

▲ Arcelormittal Riverdale LLC B 708 849-8803
Riverdale *(G-17067)*

◆ Arcelormittal USA LLC B 312 346-0300
Chicago *(G-3723)*

Bonell Manufacturing Company E 708 849-1770
Riverdale *(G-17069)*

Chase Fasteners Inc E 708 345-0335
Melrose Park *(G-13841)*

Combined Metals Chicago LLC F 847 683-0500
Hampshire *(G-10967)*

▲ Corey Steel Company C 708 735-8000
Cicero *(G-6837)*

Design Manufacturing & Eqp Co F 217 824-9219
Taylorville *(G-19755)*

Expandable Habitats G 815 624-6784
Rockton *(G-17697)*

Gartech Manufacturing Co E 217 324-6527
Litchfield *(G-12963)*

Geocyn Company Inc E 331 213-2851
Naperville *(G-14835)*

Harris Steel Company D 708 656-5500
Cicero *(G-6851)*

▲ Krueger and Company E 630 833-5650
Elmhurst *(G-9389)*

▲ Lapham-Hickey Steel Corp C 708 496-6111
Bedford Park *(G-1479)*

Madison Inds Holdings LLC G 312 277-0156
Chicago *(G-5313)*

Mid-State Industries Oper Inc ....E.... 217 268-3900 — Arcola *(G-656)*

Multiplex Industries Inc ....G.... 630 906-9780 — Montgomery *(G-14263)*

Multitech Industries ....G.... 815 206-0015 — Woodstock *(G-21415)*

New Process Steel LP ....D.... 708 389-3380 — Alsip *(G-484)*

Niagara Lasalle Corporation ....C.... 708 596-2700 — South Holland *(G-19235)*

Phillip C Cowen ....E.... 630 208-1848 — Geneva *(G-10299)*

Ptc Group Holdings Corp ....D.... 708 757-4747 — Chicago Heights *(G-6766)*

Rockford Secondary Co ....G.... 815 398-0401 — Rockford *(G-17605)*

Sandvik Inc ....D.... 847 519-1737 — Schaumburg *(G-18703)*

▲ Screws Industries Inc ....D.... 630 539-9200 — Glendale Heights *(G-10493)*

Skach Manufacturing Co Inc ....E.... 847 395-3560 — Antioch *(G-635)*

Soudan Metals Company Inc ....C.... 773 548-7600 — Chicago *(G-6204)*

▲ Taubensee Steel & Wire Company ....C.... 847 459-5100 — Wheeling *(G-20997)*

◆ Tempel Holdings Inc ....A.... 773 250-8000 — Chicago *(G-6343)*

Tinsley Steel Inc ....G.... 618 656-5231 — Edwardsville *(G-8378)*

▲ Worth Steel and Machine Co ....E.... 708 388-6300 — Alsip *(G-527)*

3317 Steel Pipe & Tubes

Addison Precision Tech LLC ....G.... 773 626-4747 — Chicago *(G-3540)*

▲ Advanced Valve Tech LLC ....E.... 847 364-3700 — Elk Grove Village *(G-8810)*

◆ Allied Tube & Conduit Corp ....A.... 708 339-1610 — Harvey *(G-11071)*

▲ American Diesel Tube Corp ....F.... 630 628-1830 — Addison *(G-32)*

Arcelrmttal N Amer Hldings LLC ....A.... 312 899-3400 — Chicago *(G-3724)*

Arntzen Corporation ....E.... 815 334-0788 — Woodstock *(G-21360)*

▲ Atkore International Inc ....E.... 708 339-1610 — Harvey *(G-11074)*

◆ Atlas Holding Inc ....F.... 773 646-4500 — Chicago *(G-3763)*

▲ Atlas Tube (chicago) LLC ....D.... 312 275-1672 — Chicago *(G-3768)*

B & B Fabrications LLC ....G.... 217 620-3210 — Sullivan *(G-19660)*

◆ Basor Electric Inc ....G.... 618 476-6300 — Millstadt *(G-14043)*

Basor Electric Inc ....G.... 618 476-6300 — Millstadt *(G-14044)*

Bull Moose Tube Company ....D.... 708 757-7700 — Chicago Heights *(G-6736)*

Chicago Tube and Iron Company ....E.... 815 834-2500 — Romeoville *(G-17807)*

Coda Resources Ltd ....F.... 718 649-1666 — Chicago *(G-4189)*

◆ CSM Tube Usa Inc ....G.... 847 640-6447 — Elk Grove Village *(G-8923)*

▲ D D G Inc ....G.... 847 412-0277 — Northbrook *(G-15370)*

▲ Durabilt Dyvex Inc ....F.... 708 397-4673 — Broadview *(G-2432)*

E & H Tubing Inc ....F.... 773 522-3100 — Chicago *(G-4419)*

Epix Tube Co Inc ....E.... 630 844-0960 — Aurora *(G-1090)*

◆ Evraz Inc NA ....D.... 312 533-3555 — Chicago *(G-4541)*

▲ Forterra Pressure Pipe Inc ....E.... 815 389-4800 — South Beloit *(G-19093)*

Gateway Fbrction Solutions LLC ....G.... 618 612-3170 — Waterloo *(G-20290)*

▲ Gerlin Inc ....G.... 630 653-5232 — Carol Stream *(G-2991)*

Hanna Steel Corporation ....C.... 309 478-3800 — Pekin *(G-16336)*

Harris William & Company Inc ....E.... 312 621-0590 — Chicago *(G-4782)*

Illinois Meter Inc ....G.... 618 438-6039 — Benton *(G-1927)*

Illinois Ni Cast LLC ....G.... 217 398-3200 — Champaign *(G-3307)*

John Maneely Company ....C.... 773 254-0617 — Chicago *(G-5043)*

Kroh-Wagner Inc ....E.... 773 252-2031 — Chicago *(G-5133)*

Kuhn Special Steel N Amer Inc ....G.... 262 788-9358 — Chicago *(G-5135)*

▲ Lapham-Hickey Steel Corp ....C.... 708 496-6111 — Bedford Park *(G-1479)*

▲ Leading Edge Group Inc ....C.... 815 316-3500 — Rockford *(G-17492)*

Legacy International Assoc LLC ....G.... 847 823-1602 — Park Ridge *(G-16287)*

Lex Holding Co ....G.... 708 594-9200 — Oak Brook *(G-15634)*

M C Steel Inc ....E.... 847 350-9618 — Antioch *(G-623)*

Maruichi Leavitt Pipe Tube LLC ....G.... 800 532-8488 — Chicago *(G-5351)*

◆ Maruichi Leavitt Pipe Tube LLC ....C.... 773 239-7700 — Chicago *(G-5352)*

Metal-Matic Inc ....C.... 708 594-7553 — Bedford Park *(G-1481)*

▲ National Metalwares LP ....C.... 630 892-9000 — Aurora *(G-1139)*

Nelson Global Products Inc ....F.... 309 263-8914 — Morton *(G-14373)*

◆ Nucor Tubular Products Inc ....D.... 708 496-0380 — Chicago *(G-5639)*

Nucor Tubular Products Inc ....D.... 815 795-4400 — Marseilles *(G-13561)*

◆ Plymouth Tube Company ....E.... 630 393-3550 — Warrenville *(G-20246)*

Plymouth Tube Company ....D.... 773 489-0226 — Chicago *(G-5824)*

Ptc Group Holdings Corp ....D.... 708 757-4747 — Chicago Heights *(G-6766)*

Ptc Tubular Products LLC ....C.... 815 692-4900 — Fairbury *(G-9612)*

▲ Roll McHning Tech Slutions Inc ....E.... 815 372-9100 — Romeoville *(G-17870)*

Steel Tube Institute N Amer ....G.... 847 461-1701 — Glenview *(G-10625)*

▲ Structural Steel Systems Limi ....F.... 815 937-3800 — Bradley *(G-2293)*

United Flexible Inc ....F.... 815 886-1140 — Romeoville *(G-17882)*

Whi Capital Partners ....G.... 312 621-0590 — Chicago *(G-6615)*

Zapp Tooling Alloys Inc ....G.... 847 599-0351 — Gurnee *(G-10945)*

Zekelman Industries Inc ....G.... 773 646-4500 — Chicago *(G-6712)*

▲ Zekelman Industries Inc ....E.... 312 275-1600 — Chicago *(G-6713)*

Zero Ground LLC ....F.... 847 360-9500 — Waukegan *(G-20522)*

3321 Gray Iron Foundries

▲ American Electronic Pdts Inc ....F.... 630 889-9977 — Oak Brook *(G-15592)*

◆ Amsted Industries Incorporated ....B.... 312 645-1700 — Chicago *(G-3685)*

Anchor Brake Shoe Company LLC ....G.... 630 293-1110 — West Chicago *(G-20540)*

Anchor Brake Shoe Company LLC ....F.... 630 293-1110 — West Chicago *(G-20541)*

Branchfield Casting Inc ....G.... 309 932-2278 — Matherville *(G-13614)*

Burgess-Norton Mfg Co Inc ....E.... 630 232-4100 — Geneva *(G-10257)*

Castwell Products LLC ....C.... 847 966-5050 — Skokie *(G-18937)*

◆ Charter Dura-Bar Inc ....E.... 815 338-3900 — Woodstock *(G-21373)*

Charter Dura-Bar Inc ....C.... 815 338-7800 — Woodstock *(G-21374)*

Decatur Foundry Inc ....D.... 217 429-5261 — Decatur *(G-7486)*

Demco Products Inc ....F.... 708 636-6240 — Oak Lawn *(G-15713)*

E H Baare Corporation ....C.... 618 546-1575 — Robinson *(G-17114)*

E Rowe Foundry & Machine Co ....D.... 217 382-4135 — Martinsville *(G-13583)*

Ej Pierogi ....F.... 773 318-3383 — Elk Grove Village *(G-8970)*

Ej Usa Inc ....F.... 815 740-1640 — New Lenox *(G-15032)*

F J Murphy & Son Inc ....D.... 217 787-3477 — Springfield *(G-19364)*

Fast Pipe Lining Inc ....G.... 815 712-8646 — La Salle *(G-12111)*

Group Industries Inc ....E.... 708 877-6200 — Thornton *(G-19788)*

Illini Foundry Co Inc ....G.... 309 697-3142 — Peoria *(G-16456)*

Johnston & Jennings Inc ....G.... 708 757-5375 — Chicago Heights *(G-6754)*

Kettler Casting Co Inc ....E.... 618 234-5303 — Belleville *(G-1562)*

Lemfco Inc ....E.... 815 777-0242 — Galena *(G-10176)*

◆ M H Detrick Company ....E.... 708 479-5085 — Frankfort *(G-9814)*

Meta TEC of Illinois Inc ....D.... 309 246-2960 — Lacon *(G-12132)*

Ptc Tubular Products LLC ....C.... 815 692-4900 — Fairbury *(G-9612)*

Reynolds Manufacturing Company ....E.... 309 787-8600 — Milan *(G-14025)*

▼ Rj Link International Inc ....F.... 815 874-8110 — Rockford *(G-17576)*

Russell Enterprises Inc ....B.... 847 692-6050 — Park Ridge *(G-16295)*

◆ Standard Car Truck Company ....E.... 847 692-6050 — Rosemont *(G-18051)*

State Line Foundries Inc ....D.... 815 389-3921 — Roscoe *(G-17934)*

▲ Sunrise Distributors Inc ....G.... 630 400-8786 — Elk Grove Village *(G-9259)*

Tmb Industries Inc ....A.... 312 280-2565 — Chicago *(G-6382)*

USP Holdings Inc ....A.... 847 604-6100 — Rosemont *(G-18058)*

Waupaca Foundry Inc ....C.... 217 347-0600 — Effingham *(G-8430)*

Westwick Foundry Ltd ....E.... 815 777-0815 — Galena *(G-10181)*

Winnebago Foundry Inc ....D.... 815 389-3533 — South Beloit *(G-19124)*

3322 Malleable Iron Foundries

Advanced Pattern Works LLC ....G.... 618 346-9039 — Collinsville *(G-6952)*

Du Page Precision Products Co ....D.... 630 849-2940 — Aurora *(G-954)*

◆ M H Detrick Company ....E.... 708 479-5085 — Frankfort *(G-9814)*

Wirco Inc ....D.... 217 398-3200 — Champaign *(G-3371)*

3324 Steel Investment Foundries

Barber Steel Foundry Corp ....F.... 231 894-1830 — Rosemont *(G-18000)*

3325 Steel Foundries, NEC

Alloys Tech Inc ....G.... 708 248-5041 — S Chicago Hts *(G-18116)*

Allquip Co Inc ....G.... 309 944-6153 — Geneseo *(G-10239)*

Ameri Rolls and Guides ....G.... 815 588-0486 — Lockport *(G-12981)*

Amsted Industries Incorporated ....G.... 312 819-1181 — Chicago *(G-3687)*

◆ Amsted Industries Incorporated ....B.... 312 645-1700 — Chicago *(G-3685)*

Arcelormittal USA LLC ....C.... 312 899-3400 — Chicago *(G-3722)*

◆ Arcelormittal USA LLC ....B.... 312 346-0300 — Chicago *(G-3723)*

Branchfield Casting Inc ....G.... 309 932-2278 — Matherville *(G-13614)*

Colson Group Holdings LLC ....E.... 630 613-2941 — Oakbrook Terrace *(G-15795)*

Combined Metals Holding Inc ....C.... 708 547-8800 — Bellwood *(G-1619)*

Componenta USA LLC ....G.... 309 691-7000 — Peoria *(G-16426)*

Dee Erectors Inc ....G.... 630 327-1185 — Downers Grove *(G-7985)*

Devco Casting ....G.... 312 456-0076 — Chicago *(G-4347)*

Du Page Precision Products Co ....D.... 630 849-2940 — Aurora *(G-954)*

E H Baare Corporation ....C.... 618 546-1575 — Robinson *(G-17114)*

◆ Evraz Inc NA ....D.... 312 533-3555 — Chicago *(G-4541)*

G S Foundry Mfg ....G.... 618 282-4114 — Red Bud *(G-16995)*

SIC

33 PRIMARY METAL INDUSTRIES

Illinois Ni Cast LLC .... G 217 398-3200
　Champaign *(G-3307)*
Lmt Usa Inc .... G 630 969-5412
　Waukegan *(G-20462)*
▲ Metal Resources Intl LLC .... F 847 806-7200
　Elk Grove Village *(G-9119)*
Monett Metals Inc .... G 773 478-8888
　Niles *(G-15148)*
Nisshin Holding Inc .... G 847 290-5100
　Chicago *(G-5604)*
Scot Forge Company .... D 847 678-6000
　Franklin Park *(G-10045)*
▲ T & H Lemont Inc .... D 708 482-1800
　Countryside *(G-7074)*
Universal Electric Foundry Inc ..... E 312 421-7233
　Chicago *(G-6480)*
US Tsubaki Power Transm LLC ... C 847 459-9500
　Wheeling *(G-21004)*

3331 Primary Smelting & Refining Of Copper

Atlas Trade Solutions LLC .... G 618 954-6119
　Belleville *(G-1531)*
▲ Bryan Metals LLC .... G 419 636-4571
　East Alton *(G-8163)*
◆ Cerro Flow Products LLC .... C 618 337-6000
　Sauget *(G-18392)*
Mahoney Foundries Inc .... E 309 784-2311
　Vermont *(G-20037)*
Spot Welding Products Inc .... F 630 238-0880
　Franklin Park *(G-10051)*

3334 Primary Production Of Aluminum

Huml Industries Inc .... G 847 426-8061
　Gilberts *(G-10358)*
New Century Performance Inc ..... G 618 466-6383
　Godfrey *(G-10658)*
Penn Aluminum Intl LLC .... C 618 684-2146
　Murphysboro *(G-14756)*

3339 Primary Nonferrous Metals, NEC

AG Medical Systems Inc .... F 847 458-3100
　Lake In The Hills *(G-12328)*
◆ Big River Zinc Corporation .... G 618 274-5000
　Sauget *(G-18389)*
Horizon Metals Inc .... E 773 478-8888
　Niles *(G-15129)*
Materion Brush Inc .... F 630 832-9650
　Elmhurst *(G-9400)*
Mayco Manufacturing LLC .... E 618 451-4400
　Granite City *(G-10721)*
Powerlab Inc .... F 815 273-7718
　Savanna *(G-18410)*
RE Met Corp .... G 312 733-6700
　Chicago *(G-5981)*
▲ Rockford Rigging Inc .... F 309 263-0566
　Roscoe *(G-17926)*
▲ Sipi Metals Corp .... C 773 276-0070
　Chicago *(G-6176)*
Sunshine Metals Inc .... G 304 422-0090
　Northbrook *(G-15490)*
Tanaka Kikinzoku Intl Amer Inc .... G 224 653-8309
　Schaumburg *(G-18737)*
Tanaka Kknzoku Intrnational Kk ... G 224 653-8309
　Schaumburg *(G-18738)*
TPC Metals LLC .... G 330 479-9510
　Willowbrook *(G-21061)*

3341 Secondary Smelting & Refining Of Non-ferrous Metals

Abco Metals Corporations .... F 773 881-1504
　Chicago *(G-3509)*
▲ Allied Metal Co .... E 312 225-2800
　Chicago *(G-3618)*
Alter Trading Corporation .... F 309 697-6161
　Bartonville *(G-1327)*
Alter Trading Corporation .... F 217 223-0156
　Quincy *(G-16852)*
Archer Metal & Paper Co .... F 773 585-3030
　Chicago *(G-3726)*
Belson Steel Center Scrap Inc .... E 815 932-7416
　Bourbonnais *(G-2256)*
BFI Waste Systems N Amer Inc .. E 847 429-7370
　Elgin *(G-8521)*
◆ Big River Zinc Corporation .... G 618 274-5000
　Sauget *(G-18389)*
Borders Metals Recovery .... G 217 586-2501
　Mahomet *(G-13422)*
Branchfield Casting Inc .... G 309 932-2278
　Matherville *(G-13614)*

C & M Recycling Inc .... E 847 578-1066
　North Chicago *(G-15308)*
C&R Scrap Iron & Metal .... G 847 459-9815
　Wheeling *(G-20868)*
Cicero Iron Metal & Paper Inc ...... G 708 863-8601
　Cicero *(G-6834)*
▲ D R Sperry & Co .... D 630 892-4361
　Aurora *(G-1083)*
Dels Metal Co .... F 309 788-1993
　Rock Island *(G-17216)*
Elg Metals Inc .... G 773 374-1500
　Chicago *(G-4484)*
Enviro-Chem Inc .... G 847 549-7797
　Vernon Hills *(G-20052)*
▲ Fox Valley Iron & Metal Corp ...... F 630 897-5907
　Aurora *(G-1098)*
Galva Iron and Metal Co Inc .... E 309 932-3450
　Galva *(G-10232)*
Global Brass and Copper Inc ...... G 502 873-3000
　East Alton *(G-8166)*
Global Brass Cop Holdings Inc ... G 847 240-4700
　Schaumburg *(G-18535)*
GM Scrap Metals .... G 618 259-8570
　Cottage Hills *(G-7028)*
▼ H Kramer & Co .... C 312 226-6600
　Chicago *(G-4759)*
▲ International Proc Co Amer .... E 847 437-8400
　Elk Grove Village *(G-9058)*
Lake Area Disposal Service Inc ... E 217 522-9271
　Springfield *(G-19397)*
Lemont Scrap Processing .... G 630 257-6532
　Lemont *(G-12569)*
M Buckman & Son Co .... G 815 663-9411
　Spring Valley *(G-19309)*
Mahoney Foundries Inc .... E 309 784-2311
　Vermont *(G-20037)*
Mervis Industries Inc .... F 217 235-5575
　Mattoon *(G-13648)*
Mervis Industries Inc .... E 217 753-1492
　Springfield *(G-19405)*
Metal Management Inc .... G 773 721-1100
　Chicago *(G-5405)*
Metal Management Inc .... E 773 489-1800
　Chicago *(G-5406)*
▼ Midland Davis Corporation .... D 309 277-1617
　Moline *(G-14161)*
Midstate Salvage Corp .... G 217 824-6047
　Taylorville *(G-19759)*
▼ Midwest Fiber Inc Decatur .... E 217 424-9460
　Decatur *(G-7524)*
National Material Company LLC .. G 773 468-2800
　Chicago *(G-5546)*
National Material Company LLC .. E 847 806-7200
　Elk Grove Village *(G-9144)*
Pontiac Recyclers Inc .... G 815 844-6419
　Pontiac *(G-16777)*
Precious Metal Ref Svcs Inc .... E 847 756-2700
　Barrington *(G-1237)*
Real Alloy Recycling LLC .... G 708 757-8900
　Chicago Heights *(G-6768)*
Rondout Iron & Metal Co Inc .... G 847 362-2750
　Lake Bluff *(G-12208)*
S & S Metal Recyclers Inc .... F 630 844-3344
　Aurora *(G-1152)*
Serlin Iron & Metal Co Inc .... E 773 227-3826
　Chicago *(G-6138)*
Shapiro Bros of Illinois Inc .... E 618 244-3168
　Mount Vernon *(G-14638)*
▲ Sipi Metals Corp .... C 773 276-0070
　Chicago *(G-6176)*
Springfield Iron & Metal Co .... G 217 544-7131
　Springfield *(G-19452)*
Sunshine Metals Inc .... G 304 422-0090
　Northbrook *(G-15490)*
T & C Metal Co .... G 815 459-4445
　Crystal Lake *(G-7274)*
Tms International LLC .... G 815 939-9460
　Bourbonnais *(G-2271)*
Top Metal Buyers Inc .... F 314 421-2721
　East Saint Louis *(G-8327)*
Tower Metal Products LP .... G 847 806-7200
　Elk Grove Village *(G-9280)*
Trialco Inc .... E 708 757-4200
　Chicago Heights *(G-6781)*
▲ Waukegan Architectural Inc ...... G 847 746-9077
　Zion *(G-21529)*
Weco Trading Inc .... F 847 615-1020
　Lake Bluff *(G-12215)*
Wieland Holdings Inc .... A 847 537-3990
　Wheeling *(G-21013)*

3351 Rolling, Drawing & Extruding Of Copper

American Bare Conductor Inc ..... E 815 224-3422
　La Salle *(G-12102)*
Aurubis Buffalo Inc .... G 630 980-8400
　Bloomingdale *(G-1978)*
▲ Bryan Metals LLC .... G 419 636-4571
　East Alton *(G-8163)*
◆ Cerro Flow Products LLC .... C 618 337-6000
　Sauget *(G-18392)*
▲ Chicago Hardware and Fix Co ... C 847 455-6609
　Franklin Park *(G-9905)*
Demco Products Inc .... F 708 636-6240
　Oak Lawn *(G-15713)*
▲ Empire Bronze Corp .... F 630 916-9722
　Lombard *(G-13073)*
Ems Industrial and Service Co .... E 815 678-2700
　Richmond *(G-17012)*
Fairbanks Wire Corporation .... G 847 683-2600
　Hampshire *(G-10972)*
Global Brass and Copper Inc ...... G 502 873-3000
　East Alton *(G-8166)*
Global Brass Cop Holdings Inc ... G 847 240-4700
　Schaumburg *(G-18535)*
▲ Industrial Wire Cable II Corp ..... F 847 726-8910
　Lake Zurich *(G-12422)*
Kroh-Wagner Inc .... E 773 252-2031
　Chicago *(G-5133)*
◆ Marmon Holdings Inc .... D 312 372-9500
　Chicago *(G-5343)*
▲ Midwest Model Aircraft Co .... F 773 229-0740
　Chicago *(G-5446)*
▲ Nehring Electrical Works Co ...... C 815 756-2741
　Dekalb *(G-7693)*
Olin Corporation .... G 618 258-2245
　Brighton *(G-2402)*
Technetics Group LLC .... C 708 887-6080
　Harwood Heights *(G-11111)*
Universal Electric Foundry Inc .... E 312 421-7233
　Chicago *(G-6480)*
Wieland Holdings Inc .... A 847 537-3990
　Wheeling *(G-21013)*
Wieland Rolled Pdts N Amer LLC .. G 630 260-0802
　Chicago *(G-6623)*

3353 Aluminum Sheet, Plate & Foil

Arconic Corporation .... D 217 431-3800
　Danville *(G-7321)*
▲ Climco Coils Company .... C 815 772-3717
　Morrison *(G-14342)*
Comet Roll & Machine Company .. E 630 268-1407
　Saint Charles *(G-18172)*
Howmet Aerospace Inc .... C 773 581-7200
　Chicago *(G-4852)*
Howmet Aerospace Inc .... C 217 324-4469
　Litchfield *(G-12965)*
Howmet Aerospace Inc .... C 309 674-0065
　Peoria *(G-16454)*
J-TEC Metal Products Inc .... F 630 875-1300
　Itasca *(G-11679)*
Kibar Americas Inc .... C 312 285-2553
　Chicago *(G-5100)*
◆ Mandel Metals Inc .... C 847 455-6606
　Franklin Park *(G-9984)*
Midwest Lminating Coatings Inc ... E 708 653-9500
　Alsip *(G-478)*
▲ Monda Window & Door Corp ..... E 773 254-8888
　Chicago *(G-5489)*
Nichols Aluminum LLC .... C 847 634-3150
　Lincolnshire *(G-12787)*
Pactiv LLC .... G 847 482-2000
　Lake Forest *(G-12281)*
Pechiney Cast Plate .... C 847 299-0220
　Chicago *(G-5778)*
Quanex Homeshield LLC .... F 815 635-3171
　Chatsworth *(G-3428)*
Reynolds Consumer Products LLC .. E 217 479-1126
　Jacksonville *(G-11782)*
Reynolds Consumer Products LLC .. G 217 479-1466
　Jacksonville *(G-11783)*
▼ Reynolds Consumer Products LLC .. B 847 482-3500
　Lake Forest *(G-12297)*
Reynolds Food Packaging .... F 815 465-2115
　Grant Park *(G-10751)*
Sea Converting Inc .... G 630 694-9178
　Wood Dale *(G-21238)*
Security Metal Products Inc .... G 815 933-3307
　Bradley *(G-2292)*
Tim Snyder .... G 309 657-4764
　Manito *(G-13440)*

SIC SECTION
33 PRIMARY METAL INDUSTRIES

Werner Co ....A 847 455-8001
Itasca *(G-11754)*

3354 Aluminum Extruded Prdts

Afco Industries Inc ....G 618 742-6469
Olmsted *(G-15850)*

Al3 Inc ....G 847 441-7888
Winnetka *(G-21123)*

American Alum Extrusion Co LLC ....C 815 525-3100
Roscoe *(G-17898)*

Central Tool Specialities Co ....G 630 543-6351
Addison *(G-66)*

▲ Century Aluminum Company ....C 312 696-3101
Chicago *(G-4059)*

Crown Cork & Seal Usa Inc ....C 815 933-9351
Bradley *(G-2278)*

Custom Aluminum Products Inc ....D 847 717-5000
Genoa *(G-10316)*

▲ Custom Aluminum Products Inc ....B 847 717-5000
South Elgin *(G-19141)*

▲ Durable Inc ....A 847 541-4400
Wheeling *(G-20881)*

Efco Corporation ....E 630 378-4720
Bolingbrook *(G-2171)*

F K Pattern & Foundry Company ....G 847 578-5260
North Chicago *(G-15311)*

▲ Hydro Extrusion Usa LLC ....C 877 710-7272
Rosemont *(G-18027)*

Imageworks Manufacturing Inc ....E 708 503-1122
Park Forest *(G-16255)*

JM Circle Enterprise Inc ....G 708 946-3333
Beecher *(G-1517)*

▲ Maytec Inc ....G 847 429-0321
Dundee *(G-8128)*

Metal Impact LLC ....D 847 718-0192
Elk Grove Village *(G-9117)*

Metal Impact South LLC ....F 847 718-9300
Elk Grove Village *(G-9118)*

▲ Midwest Model Aircraft Co ....F 773 229-0740
Chicago *(G-5446)*

▲ Monda Window & Door Corp ....E 773 254-8888
Chicago *(G-5489)*

Nichols Aluminum LLC ....C 847 634-3150
Lincolnshire *(G-12787)*

◆ Peerless America Incorporated ....C 217 342-0400
Effingham *(G-8418)*

Penn Aluminum Intl LLC ....C 618 684-2146
Murphysboro *(G-14756)*

◆ Plymouth Tube Company ....E 630 393-3550
Warrenville *(G-20246)*

Plymouth Tube Company ....D 773 489-0226
Chicago *(G-5824)*

Rotation Dynamics Corporation ....E 630 769-9700
Chicago *(G-6065)*

Sapa Extrusions North Amer LLC ....G 877 922-7272
Rosemont *(G-18049)*

Signa Group Inc ....G 847 386-7639
Northfield *(G-15529)*

Sno Gem Inc ....F 888 766-4367
McHenry *(G-13792)*

▲ Sternberg Lanterns Inc ....C 847 588-3400
Roselle *(G-17991)*

T A U Inc ....G 708 841-5757
Dolton *(G-7940)*

Werner Co ....A 847 455-8001
Itasca *(G-11754)*

William Dach ....F 815 962-3455
Rockford *(G-17685)*

3355 Aluminum Rolling & Drawing, NEC

▲ Conex Cable LLC ....E 800 877-8089
Dekalb *(G-7669)*

Corus America Inc ....E 847 585-2599
Schaumburg *(G-18491)*

▲ Lapham-Hickey Steel Corp ....C 708 496-6111
Bedford Park *(G-1479)*

Meyer Metal Systems Inc ....F 847 468-0500
Elgin *(G-8659)*

Msystems Group LLC ....G 630 567-3930
Saint Charles *(G-18233)*

▲ Nehring Electrical Works Co ....C 815 756-2741
Dekalb *(G-7693)*

Plastic Power Extrusions Corp ....E 847 233-9901
Schiller Park *(G-18832)*

Southwire Company LLC ....D 618 662-8341
Flora *(G-9694)*

Viakable Manufacturing LLC ....G 815 615-8355
La Salle *(G-12123)*

Werner Co ....E 815 459-6020
Crystal Lake *(G-7294)*

3356 Rolling, Drawing-Extruding Of Nonferrous Metals

Alloy Rod Products Inc ....G 815 562-8200
Aurora *(G-1048)*

Alloy Rod Products Inc ....F 815 562-8200
Rochelle *(G-17130)*

Alpha Assembly Solutions Inc ....C 847 426-4241
Elgin *(G-8504)*

▲ American/Jebco Corporation ....C 847 455-3150
Cicero *(G-6829)*

◆ Arcelormittal USA LLC ....B 312 346-0300
Chicago *(G-3723)*

AWI / Titanium ....G 708 263-9970
Oak Forest *(G-15671)*

◆ Big River Zinc Corporation ....G 618 274-5000
Sauget *(G-18389)*

Chicago Magnesium ....G 708 926-9531
Dixmoor *(G-7883)*

Continuous Cast Alloys LLC ....F 815 562-8200
Rochelle *(G-17136)*

◆ Cooper B-Line Inc ....A 618 654-2184
Highland *(G-11210)*

Daniel J Nickel & Assocs PC ....G 312 345-1850
Chicago *(G-4312)*

Dj Titanium ....G 312 823-2963
Chicago *(G-4371)*

Double Nickel Holdings LLC ....G 618 476-3200
Millstadt *(G-14046)*

Dupage Products Group ....D 630 969-7200
Downers Grove *(G-7993)*

◆ Elektron N Magnesium Amer Inc ....D 618 452-5190
Madison *(G-13410)*

Elgiloy Specialty Metals ....G 847 683-0500
Hampshire *(G-10971)*

Guardian Rollform LLC ....D 847 382-8074
Lake Barrington *(G-12148)*

Hadley Gear Manufacturing Co ....F 773 722-1030
Chicago *(G-4765)*

Horizon Metals Inc ....E 773 478-8888
Niles *(G-15129)*

IL International LLC ....G 773 276-0070
Chicago *(G-4886)*

Indium Corporation of America ....G 847 439-9134
Elk Grove Village *(G-9049)*

Kester LLC ....G 630 616-6882
Itasca *(G-11683)*

◆ Kester LLC ....D 630 616-4000
Itasca *(G-11684)*

Lawrence Brand Shot ....G 618 798-6112
Granite City *(G-10719)*

◆ Mat Holdings Inc ....D 847 821-9630
Long Grove *(G-13165)*

▲ Mayco-Granite City Inc ....E 618 451-4400
Granite City *(G-10722)*

◆ Midland Industries Inc ....E 312 664-7300
Chicago *(G-5434)*

Nickel Putter ....G 312 337-7888
Chicago *(G-5598)*

Nickels Electric ....G 309 676-1350
Peoria *(G-16486)*

Nickels Quarters LLC ....G 630 514-5779
Downers Grove *(G-8065)*

Nuclear Power Outfitters LLC ....F 630 963-0320
Lisle *(G-12922)*

Pat 24 Inc ....G 708 336-8671
Burbank *(G-2637)*

Suburban Industries Inc ....F 630 766-3773
Franklin Park *(G-10055)*

Tin Man Heating & Cooling Inc ....E 630 267-3232
Aurora *(G-1162)*

Tin Maung ....G 217 233-1405
Decatur *(G-7561)*

Tin Tree Gifts ....G 630 935-8086
Aurora *(G-1024)*

Tinsley Steel Inc ....G 618 656-5231
Edwardsville *(G-8378)*

Titanium Insulation Inc ....G 708 932-5927
Midlothian *(G-13997)*

Townley Engrg & Mfg Co Inc ....F 618 273-8271
Eldorado *(G-8484)*

▲ TSC Pyroferric International ....C 217 849-2230
Toledo *(G-19881)*

V and L Red Devil Mfg Co ....E 847 215-1377
Wheeling *(G-21007)*

▲ Wagner Zip-Change Inc ....E 708 681-4100
Melrose Park *(G-13926)*

Wooden Nickel Pub and Grill ....G 618 288-2141
Glen Carbon *(G-10391)*

3357 Nonferrous Wire Drawing

All Line Inc ....G 630 820-1800
Naperville *(G-14955)*

▲ Amerline Enterprises Co Inc ....E 847 671-6554
Schiller Park *(G-18786)*

Andrew Corporation ....E 779 435-6000
Joliet *(G-11822)*

Andrew New Zealand Inc ....E 708 873-3507
Orland Park *(G-15940)*

▲ ARI Industries Inc ....D 630 953-9100
Addison *(G-38)*

▲ Axon Cable Inc ....F 847 230-7813
Schaumburg *(G-18454)*

▲ Belford Electronics Inc ....E 630 705-3020
Addison *(G-47)*

C & L Manufacturing Entps ....G 618 465-7623
Alton *(G-546)*

C R V Electronics Corp ....D 815 675-6500
Spring Grove *(G-19269)*

Cable X-Perts Inc ....G 800 828-3340
Woodstock *(G-21369)*

▲ Central Rubber Company ....E 815 544-2191
Belvidere *(G-1661)*

Charles Industries LLC ....D 217 826-2318
Marshall *(G-13566)*

Chase Security Systems Inc ....G 773 594-1919
Chicago *(G-4078)*

▲ Chicago Car Seal Company ....G 773 278-9400
Chicago *(G-4095)*

Circom Inc ....E 630 595-4460
Bensenville *(G-1770)*

Coleman Cable LLC ....D 847 672-2300
Lincolnshire *(G-12753)*

◆ Coleman Cable LLC ....D 847 672-2300
Lincolnshire *(G-12752)*

Commscope Technologies LLC ....B 779 435-6000
Joliet *(G-11845)*

Data Cable Technologies Inc ....F 630 226-5600
Romeoville *(G-17812)*

▲ Emerge Technology Group LLC ....G 224 603-2161
Lake Villa *(G-12350)*

▲ Erin Rope Corporation ....F 708 377-1084
Blue Island *(G-2122)*

Essex Group Inc ....D 630 628-7841
Addison *(G-116)*

▲ Excel Specialty Corp ....E 773 262-7575
Lake Forest *(G-12248)*

General Cable Industries Inc ....C 618 542-4761
Du Quoin *(G-8122)*

▲ Gepco International Inc ....E 847 795-9555
Des Plaines *(G-7773)*

▲ Heil Sound Ltd ....F 618 257-3000
Fairview Heights *(G-9646)*

▲ Industrial Wire & Cable Corp ....E 847 726-8910
Lake Zurich *(G-12421)*

▲ Industrial Wire Cable II Corp ....F 847 726-8910
Lake Zurich *(G-12422)*

Lake Copper Conductors LLC ....G 847 378-7006
Bensenville *(G-1841)*

Live Wire & Cable Co ....G 847 577-5483
Arlington Heights *(G-770)*

Major Wire Incorporated ....F 708 457-0121
Norridge *(G-15239)*

Methode Development Co ....D 708 867-6777
Chicago *(G-5408)*

◆ Molex LLC ....A 630 969-4550
Lisle *(G-12911)*

Molex LLC ....G 630 527-4363
Bolingbrook *(G-2216)*

Molex LLC ....F 630 512-8787
Downers Grove *(G-8059)*

▲ Molex International Inc ....F 630 969-4550
Lisle *(G-12914)*

▲ Molex Premise Networks Inc ....A 866 733-6659
Lisle *(G-12915)*

P M Mfg Services Inc ....G 630 553-6924
Yorkville *(G-21496)*

▲ Pro Intercom LLC ....G 815 680-5205
Crystal Lake *(G-7247)*

Ruckus Wireless Inc ....E 630 281-3000
Lisle *(G-12935)*

SITech Inc ....F 630 761-3640
Batavia *(G-1417)*

Sterling Brands LLC ....E 847 229-1600
Wheeling *(G-20990)*

Teledyne Defense Elec LLC ....C 630 754-3300
Woodridge *(G-21344)*

Unified Wire and Cable Company ....E 815 748-4876
Dekalb *(G-7710)*

S I C

Employee Codes: A=Over 500 employees, B=251-500
C=101-250, D=51-100, E=20-50, F=10-19, G=3-9
2020 Harris Illinois
Industrial Directory
917

33 PRIMARY METAL INDUSTRIES

United Universal Inds Inc .... E 815 727-4445
  Joliet (G-11939)
▲ Woodhead Industries LLC .... B 847 353-2500
  Lincolnshire (G-12802)

3363 Aluminum Die Castings

Able Die Casting Corporation .... D 847 678-1991
  Schiller Park (G-18781)
▲ Acme Alliance LLC .... E 847 272-9520
  Northbrook (G-15330)
▲ Acme Die Casting LLC .... G 847 272-9520
  Northbrook (G-15331)
▲ Aluminum Castings Corporation .... E 309 343-8910
  Galesburg (G-10184)
▲ American Electronic Pdts Inc .... F 630 889-9977
  Oak Brook (G-15592)
Arrow Aluminum Castings Inc .... G 815 338-4480
  Woodstock (G-21361)
Belden Energy Solutions Inc .... G 800 235-3361
  Elmhurst (G-9330)
Branatt Enterprises LLC .... G 630 632-3532
  Byron (G-2750)
Burgess-Norton Mfg Co Inc .... E 630 232-4100
  Geneva (G-10257)
▲ Cast Aluminum Solutions LLC .... D 630 482-5325
  Batavia (G-1362)
▲ Cast Products Inc .... C 708 457-1500
  Norridge (G-15232)
◆ Chicago White Metal Cast Inc .... C 630 595-4424
  Bensenville (G-1769)
Craft Die Casting Corporation .... E 773 237-9710
  Chicago (G-4254)
▲ Crown Premiums Inc .... F 815 469-8789
  Frankfort (G-9781)
Curto-Lignier Foundries Co .... E 708 345-2250
  Melrose Park (G-13846)
Dart Castings Inc .... E 708 388-4914
  Alsip (G-438)
Dixline Corporation .... F 309 932-2011
  Galva (G-10230)
Dixline Corporation .... D 309 932-2011
  Galva (G-10231)
Duro Cast Inc .... G 815 498-2317
  Somonauk (G-19070)
Dynacast LLC .... C 847 608-2200
  Elgin (G-8572)
▲ Federal Equipment & Svcs Inc .... F 847 731-9002
  Zion (G-21514)
G & M Die Casting Company Inc .... D 630 595-2340
  Wood Dale (G-21192)
G & W Electric Company .... E 708 388-6363
  Blue Island (G-2123)
Lovejoy Industries Inc .... G 859 873-6828
  Northbrook (G-15421)
Mahoney Foundries Inc .... E 309 784-2311
  Vermont (G-20037)
▲ Mattoon Precision Mfg .... C 217 235-6000
  Mattoon (G-13645)
▲ Monnex International Inc .... E 847 850-5263
  Buffalo Grove (G-2576)
OFallon Pressure Cast Co .... G 618 632-8694
  O Fallon (G-15581)
Precision Entps Fndry Mch Inc .... G 815 797-1000
  Somonauk (G-19073)
Precision Entps Fndry Mch Inc .... E 815 498-2317
  Somonauk (G-19074)
▲ Prismier LLC .... E 630 592-4515
  Bolingbrook (G-2230)
▲ RCM Industries Inc .... C 847 455-1950
  Franklin Park (G-10033)
RCM Industries Inc .... C 847 455-1950
  Wheeling (G-20970)
Rockbridge Casting Inc .... G 618 753-3188
  Rockbridge (G-17255)
Soldy Manufacturing Inc .... D 847 671-3396
  Schiller Park (G-18844)
◆ Spartan Light Metal Pdts Inc .... E 618 443-4346
  Sparta (G-19260)
Spartan Light Metal Pdts Inc .... A 618 443-4346
  Sparta (G-19261)
Tompkins Aluminum Foundry Inc .... G 815 438-5578
  Rock Falls (G-17197)

3364 Nonferrous Die Castings, Exc Aluminum

Accucast Inc .... G 815 394-1875
  Rockford (G-17292)
▲ Acme Die Casting LLC .... G 847 272-9520
  Northbrook (G-15331)
▲ Allied Die Casting Corporation .... E 815 385-9330
  McHenry (G-13717)
Amcast Inc .... F 630 766-7450
  Bensenville (G-1741)
▲ American Cast Products Inc .... F 708 895-5152
  Lansing (G-12484)
Chicago Die Casting Mfg Co .... E 847 671-5010
  Franklin Park (G-9904)
◆ Chicago White Metal Cast Inc .... C 630 595-4424
  Bensenville (G-1769)
Condor Tool & Manufacturing .... F 630 628-8200
  Addison (G-81)
Congress Drive Inc .... E 972 875-6060
  Wilmette (G-21074)
Creative Iron 217 267-7797
  Westville (G-20779)
Curto-Lignier Foundries Co .... E 708 345-2250
  Melrose Park (G-13846)
Dart Castings Inc .... E 708 388-4914
  Alsip (G-438)
Direct Aerosystems Inc .... F 630 509-2141
  Aurora (G-952)
Dynacast LLC .... C 847 608-2200
  Elgin (G-8572)
G & W Electric Company .... E 708 388-6363
  Blue Island (G-2123)
Hub Manufacturing Company Inc .... E 773 252-1373
  Chicago (G-4859)
Lovejoy Industries Inc .... G 859 873-6828
  Northbrook (G-15421)
Mahoney Foundries Inc .... E 309 784-2311
  Vermont (G-20037)
Mumford Metal Casting LLC .... C 708 345-0400
  Bannockburn (G-1204)
Quality Die Casting Co .... F 847 214-8840
  Elgin (G-8707)
▲ Quality Metal Finishing Co .... C 815 234-2711
  Byron (G-2755)
Rockbridge Casting Inc .... G 618 753-3188
  Rockbridge (G-17255)
Serv-All Die & Tool Company .... G 815 459-2900
  Crystal Lake (G-7263)
Soldy Manufacturing Inc .... D 847 671-3396
  Schiller Park (G-18844)
◆ Spartan Light Metal Pdts Inc .... E 618 443-4346
  Sparta (G-19260)
Spartan Light Metal Pdts Inc .... A 618 443-4346
  Sparta (G-19261)
▲ Taurus Die Casting LLC .... F 815 316-6160
  Rockford (G-17654)
TI Squared Technologies Inc .... E 541 367-2929
  Schaumburg (G-18748)
Universal Die Cast Corporation .... G 815 633-1702
  Machesney Park (G-13381)
Vogel/Hill Corporation .... E 773 235-6916
  Chicago (G-6567)

3365 Aluminum Foundries

Able Die Casting Corporation .... D 847 678-1991
  Schiller Park (G-18781)
▲ Acme Die Casting LLC .... G 847 272-9520
  Northbrook (G-15331)
Aerosourcex LLC .... F 314 565-4026
  South Elgin (G-19130)
▲ Alcast Company .... D 309 691-5513
  Peoria (G-16380)
Alcast Company .... E 309 691-5513
  Peoria (G-16381)
Alcast Company .... F 309 691-5513
  Peoria (G-16382)
Altman & Koehler Foundry .... G 773 373-7737
  Chicago (G-3636)
Altman Pattern and Foundry Co .... F 773 586-9100
  Chicago (G-3637)
Amcast Inc .... F 630 766-7450
  Bensenville (G-1741)
Arrow Aluminum Castings Inc .... G 815 338-4480
  Woodstock (G-21361)
Atherton Foundry Products Inc .... G 708 849-4615
  Riverdale (G-17068)
Batavia Foundry and Machine Co .... G 630 879-1319
  Batavia (G-1356)
Becks Light Gauge Aluminum Co .... F 847 290-9990
  Elk Grove Village (G-8861)
Bio Services Inc .... G 630 808-2125
  Hillside (G-11330)
Cast Technologies Inc .... C 309 676-1715
  Peoria (G-16398)
Ceratizit Chicago Holding Inc .... F 847 923-8400
  Schaumburg (G-18469)
Chester Brass and Aluminum .... F 618 826-2391
  Chester (G-3451)
Curto-Lignier Foundries Co .... E 708 345-2250
  Melrose Park (G-13846)
▲ D R Sperry & Co .... D 630 892-4361
  Aurora (G-1083)
Du Page Precision Products Co .... D 630 849-2940
  Aurora (G-954)
Dynacast LLC .... C 847 608-2200
  Elgin (G-8572)
Illini Foundry Co Inc .... G 309 697-3142
  Peoria (G-16456)
Jsp Mold LLC .... G 815 225-7110
  Milledgeville (G-14039)
▲ Kabat American Inc .... G 870 739-1430
  Saint Charles (G-18219)
Kz Manufacturing Co .... G 708 937-8097
  Mc Cook (G-13694)
Levelor Corporation .... G 815 233-8684
  Freeport (G-10126)
Louis Meskan Brass Foundry Inc .... C 773 237-7662
  Chicago (G-5267)
Marble Machine Inc .... G 217 442-0746
  Danville (G-7362)
Martin Tool Works Inc .... F 847 923-8400
  Schaumburg (G-18619)
Master Foundry Inc .... F 217 223-7396
  Quincy (G-16911)
Nelson - Harkins Inds Inc .... E 773 478-6243
  Lake Bluff (G-12199)
◆ Newell Operating Company .... G 815 235-4171
  Freeport (G-10129)
Nexus Industries Corp .... G 708 673-9289
  Melrose Park (G-13898)
Olson Aluminum Castings Ltd .... E 815 229-3292
  Rockford (G-17544)
Precision Entps Fndry Mch Inc .... E 815 498-2317
  Somonauk (G-19074)
Quincy Foundry & Pattern Co .... G 217 222-0718
  Quincy (G-16932)
R&R Racing of Palm Beach Inc .... F 618 937-6767
  West Frankfort (G-20679)
RCM Industries Inc .... C 847 455-1950
  Wheeling (G-20970)
Reynolds Manufacturing Company .... E 309 787-8600
  Milan (G-14025)
Robert Kellerman & Co .... F 847 526-7266
  Wauconda (G-20389)
Rockford Foundries Inc .... F 815 965-7243
  Rockford (G-17594)
▲ Rome Industries Inc .... G 309 691-7120
  Peoria (G-16517)
Sonoco Prtective Solutions Inc .... E 815 787-5244
  Dekalb (G-7703)
◆ Spartan Light Metal Pdts Inc .... E 618 443-4346
  Sparta (G-19260)
Tazewell Machine Works Inc .... C 309 347-3181
  Pekin (G-16365)
Tompkins Aluminum Foundry Inc .... G 815 438-5578
  Rock Falls (G-17197)
Tricast/Presfore Corporation .... G 815 459-1820
  Crystal Lake (G-7285)
Trio Foundry Inc .... E 815 786-6616
  Sandwich (G-18386)
Trio Foundry Inc 630 892-1676
  Montgomery (G-14272)
Universal Electric Foundry Inc .... E 312 421-7233
  Chicago (G-6480)
Wagner Brass Foundry Inc .... G 773 276-7907
  Chicago (G-6583)

3366 Copper Foundries

AJ Oster LLC .... C 630 260-1040
  Carol Stream (G-2929)
Altman Pattern and Foundry Co .... F 773 586-9100
  Chicago (G-3637)
Alu-Bra Foundry Inc .... D 630 766-3112
  Bensenville (G-1740)
Amcast Inc .... F 630 766-7450
  Bensenville (G-1741)
American Bare Conductor Inc .... E 815 224-3422
  La Salle (G-12102)
Atherton Foundry Products Inc .... G 708 849-4615
  Riverdale (G-17068)
◆ Aurora Metals Division LLC .... C 630 844-4900
  Montgomery (G-14231)
▲ Bearing Sales Corporation .... E 773 282-8686
  Chicago (G-3855)
Calumet Brass Foundry Inc .... F 708 849-3040
  Dolton (G-7934)

Cast Technologies Inc .... C 309 676-1715
Peoria *(G-16398)*
Chester Brass and Aluminum .... F 618 826-2391
Chester *(G-3451)*
Chicago Alum Castings Co Inc .... G 773 762-3009
Chicago *(G-4087)*
Covey Machine Inc .... F 773 650-1530
Chicago *(G-4250)*
Creative Iron .... G 217 267-7797
Westville *(G-20779)*
Excel Foundry & Machine Inc .... G 309 347-6155
Pekin *(G-16332)*
F Kreutzer & Co .... G 773 826-5767
Chicago *(G-4550)*
Fiberlink LLC .... G 312 951-8500
Chicago *(G-4585)*
▲ **General Products International** .... G 847 458-6357
Lake In The Hills *(G-12335)*
Illini Foundry Co Inc .... G 309 697-3142
Peoria *(G-16456)*
Imperial Punch & Manufacturing .... F 815 226-8200
Rockford *(G-17457)*
▲ **Intermet Metals Services Inc** .... E 847 605-1300
Schaumburg *(G-18563)*
Kellermann Manufacturing Inc .... G 847 526-7266
Wauconda *(G-20365)*
Louis Meskan Aluminum & Brass .... G 773 637-8236
Chicago *(G-5266)*
Louis Meskan Brass Foundry Inc .... C 773 237-7662
Chicago *(G-5267)*
Mahoney Foundries Inc .... E 309 784-2311
Vermont *(G-20037)*
Petro Prop Inc .... G 630 910-4738
Downers Grove *(G-8075)*
Propeller Hr Solutions Inc .... G 312 342-7355
Western Springs *(G-20723)*
Reynolds Manufacturing Company .... E 309 787-8600
Milan *(G-14025)*
Rockford Foundries Inc .... F 815 965-7243
Rockford *(G-17594)*
Spot Welding Products Inc .... F 630 238-0880
Franklin Park *(G-10051)*
Tilton Pattern Works Inc .... F 217 442-1502
Danville *(G-7388)*
Tricast/Presfore Corporation .... G 815 459-1820
Crystal Lake *(G-7285)*
Trio Foundry Inc .... E 630 892-1676
Montgomery *(G-14272)*
Universal Electric Foundry Inc .... E 312 421-7233
Chicago *(G-6480)*
Wagner Brass Foundry Inc .... G 773 276-7907
Chicago *(G-6583)*

3369 Nonferrous Foundries: Castings, NEC

Able Die Casting Corporation .... D 847 678-1991
Schiller Park *(G-18781)*
▲ **Accurate Parts Mfg Co** .... E 630 616-4125
Bensenville *(G-1724)*
▲ **Acme Die Casting LLC** .... G 847 272-9520
Northbrook *(G-15331)*
Altman & Koehler Foundry .... G 773 373-7737
Chicago *(G-3636)*
Amcast Inc .... F 630 766-7450
Bensenville *(G-1741)*
Avan Tool & Die Co Inc .... F 773 287-1670
Chicago *(G-3782)*
◆ **Big River Zinc Corporation** .... G 618 274-5000
Sauget *(G-18389)*
Cast Glassworks .... G 847 831-0222
Highland Park *(G-11257)*
Cast Technologies Inc .... G 309 674-1402
Peoria *(G-16399)*
Charter Dura-Bar Inc .... C 815 338-7800
Woodstock *(G-21374)*
Clark Tashaunda .... G 708 247-8274
Calumet Park *(G-2796)*
Clinkenbeard & Associates Inc .... E 815 226-0291
South Beloit *(G-19087)*
Curto-Ligonier Foundries Co .... E 708 345-2250
Melrose Park *(G-13846)*
Darda Enterprises Inc .... F 847 270-0410
Palatine *(G-16109)*
Dmk Specialties .... G 815 919-7282
Lockport *(G-12987)*
Du Page Precision Products Co .... D 630 849-2940
Aurora *(G-954)*
Dynacast LLC .... C 847 608-2200
Elgin *(G-8572)*
G & W Electric Company .... E 708 388-6363
Blue Island *(G-2123)*
Illini Foundry Co Inc .... G 309 697-3142
Peoria *(G-16456)*
Impro Industries Usa Inc .... G 630 759-0280
Bolingbrook *(G-2191)*
Ipsen Inc .... E 815 239-2385
Pecatonica *(G-16322)*
▲ **Kabert Industries Inc** .... C 630 833-2115
Villa Park *(G-20154)*
Kettler Casting Co Inc .... E 618 234-5303
Belleville *(G-1562)*
Knock On Metal Inc .... G 312 372-4569
Chicago *(G-5111)*
Lemfco Inc .... E 815 777-0242
Galena *(G-10176)*
Libco Industries Inc .... F 815 623-7677
Roscoe *(G-17912)*
Mahoney Foundries Inc .... E 309 784-2311
Vermont *(G-20037)*
Marble Machine Inc .... G 217 442-0746
Danville *(G-7362)*
Master Foundry Inc .... F 217 223-7396
Quincy *(G-16911)*
Mumford Metal Casting LLC .... G 312 733-2600
Chicago *(G-5524)*
Quincy Foundry & Pattern Co .... G 217 222-0718
Quincy *(G-16932)*
Reynolds Manufacturing Company .... E 309 787-8600
Milan *(G-14025)*
Robert Kellerman & Co .... G 847 526-7266
Wauconda *(G-20389)*
Rockbridge Casting Inc .... G 618 753-3188
Rockbridge *(G-17255)*
Rockford Foundries Inc .... F 815 965-7243
Rockford *(G-17594)*
Sarcol .... G 773 533-3000
Chicago *(G-6105)*
◆ **Spartan Light Metal Pdts Inc** .... E 618 443-4346
Sparta *(G-19260)*
◆ **Tempco Electric Heater Corp** .... B 630 350-2252
Wood Dale *(G-21248)*
Tompkins Aluminum Foundry Inc .... G 815 438-5578
Rock Falls *(G-17197)*
Tricast/Presfore Corporation .... G 815 459-1820
Crystal Lake *(G-7285)*
Trio Foundry Inc .... E 815 786-6616
Sandwich *(G-18386)*
Trio Foundry Inc .... E 630 892-1676
Montgomery *(G-14272)*
Universal Electric Foundry Inc .... E 312 421-7233
Chicago *(G-6480)*
Wagner Brass Foundry Inc .... G 773 276-7907
Chicago *(G-6583)*
Wishzing .... E 217 413-8469
Dalton City *(G-7315)*

3398 Metal Heat Treating

▲ **300 Below Inc** .... G 217 423-3070
Decatur *(G-7431)*
Ace Sandblast Company .... F 773 777-6654
Chicago *(G-3523)*
Advanced Heat Treating Inc .... E 815 877-8593
Loves Park *(G-13182)*
Advanced Thermal Processing .... G 630 595-9000
Bensenville *(G-1732)*
▲ **Arrow Gear Company** .... B 630 969-7640
Downers Grove *(G-7955)*
▲ **Axletech International** .... D 773 264-1234
Chicago *(G-3795)*
Beechner Heat Treating Co Inc .... G 815 397-4314
Rockford *(G-17317)*
Bodycote Thermal Proc Inc .... D 708 236-5360
Melrose Park *(G-13832)*
Bodycote Thermal Proc Inc .... G 630 221-0385
Glendale Heights *(G-10439)*
Bonell Manufacturing Company .... E 708 849-1770
Riverdale *(G-17069)*
Bulaw Welding & Engineering Co .... D 630 228-8300
Itasca *(G-11632)*
Bwt LLC .... E 708 410-8000
Northlake *(G-15544)*
Bwt LLC .... E 630 210-4577
Rockford *(G-17331)*
CB Machine & Tool Corp .... G 847 288-1807
Franklin Park *(G-9901)*
Certified Heat Treating Co .... F 309 693-7711
Peoria *(G-16419)*
Chem-Plate Industries Inc .... E 708 345-3588
Maywood *(G-13665)*
Chem-Plate Industries Inc .... D 847 640-1600
Elk Grove Village *(G-8889)*
▲ **Cooley Wire Products Mfg Co** .... E 847 678-8585
Schiller Park *(G-18796)*
Curtis Metal Finishing Company .... F 815 282-1433
Machesney Park *(G-13337)*
Diamond Heat Treat Inc .... E 815 873-1348
Rockford *(G-17377)*
Eklund Metal Treating Inc .... E 815 877-7436
Loves Park *(G-13209)*
F P M LLC .... C 847 228-2525
Elk Grove Village *(G-8993)*
F P M LLC .... D 815 332-4961
Cherry Valley *(G-3440)*
Fpm Heat Treating .... F 815 332-4961
Cherry Valley *(G-3441)*
General Surface Hardening Inc .... E 312 226-5472
Chicago *(G-4679)*
Golfers Family Corporation .... E 815 968-0094
Rockford *(G-17431)*
▲ **Horizon Steel Treating Inc** .... D 847 639-4030
Cary *(G-3167)*
Hudapack Mtal Treating Ill Inc .... E 630 793-1916
Glendale Heights *(G-10457)*
Induction Heat Treating Corp .... E 815 477-7788
Crystal Lake *(G-7210)*
▲ **International Proc Co Amer** .... E 847 437-8400
Elk Grove Village *(G-9058)*
K V F Company .... E 847 437-5100
Elk Grove Village *(G-9073)*
K V F Company .... F 847 437-5019
Elk Grove Village *(G-9074)*
▲ **Lapham-Hickey Steel Corp** .... C 708 496-6111
Bedford Park *(G-1479)*
Metal Improvement Company LLC .... E 630 543-4950
Addison *(G-199)*
Metal Improvement Company LLC .... E 630 620-6808
Lombard *(G-13100)*
Metals Technology Corporation .... C 630 221-2500
Carol Stream *(G-3025)*
Metform LLC .... E 815 273-0230
Savanna *(G-18408)*
Morgan Ohare Inc .... D 630 543-6780
Addison *(G-223)*
Mp Steel Chicago LLC .... E 773 242-0853
Chicago *(G-5514)*
Nitrex Inc .... E 630 851-5880
Aurora *(G-1003)*
Precision Chrome Inc .... E 847 587-1515
Fox Lake *(G-9753)*
Precision Metal Technologies .... F 847 228-6630
Rolling Meadows *(G-17765)*
Progressive Steel Treating Inc .... E 815 877-2571
Loves Park *(G-13251)*
R-M Industries Inc .... F 630 543-3071
Addison *(G-264)*
Riverdale Pltg Heat Trting LLC .... E 708 849-2050
Riverdale *(G-17076)*
Rockford Heat Treaters Inc .... E 815 874-0089
Rockford *(G-17595)*
Rogers Metal Services Inc .... E 847 679-4642
Skokie *(G-19024)*
▼ **Salman Metal** .... G 630 359-5110
Elmhurst *(G-9421)*
Scientific Metal Treating Co .... E 630 582-0071
Roselle *(G-17985)*
Standard Heat Treating LLC .... E 773 242-0853
Cicero *(G-6875)*
Standard Heat Treating Co Inc .... D 708 447-7504
Chicago *(G-6228)*
Superheat Fgh Services Inc .... G 708 478-0205
New Lenox *(G-15060)*
Superheat Fgh Services Inc .... G 708 478-0205
New Lenox *(G-15061)*
▼ **Tc Industries Inc** .... C 815 459-2401
Crystal Lake *(G-7276)*
◆ **Tempel Holdings Inc** .... A 773 250-8000
Chicago *(G-6343)*
Terra Cotta Holdings Co .... E 815 459-2400
Crystal Lake *(G-7281)*
Tri-City Heat Treat Co Inc .... D 309 786-2689
Rock Island *(G-17252)*
Wec Welding and Machining LLC .... G 847 680-8100
Lake Bluff *(G-12214)*

3399 Primary Metal Prdts, NEC

A2 Sales LLC .... D 708 924-1200
Bedford Park *(G-1453)*
◆ **American Metal Fibers Inc** .... E 847 295-8166
Lake Bluff *(G-12170)*
▲ **Bearing Sales Corporation** .... E 773 282-8686
Chicago *(G-3855)*

S I C

Employee Codes: A=Over 500 employees, B=251-500
C=101-250, D=51-100, E=20-50, F=10-19, G=3-9
2020 Harris Illinois
Industrial Directory
919

33 PRIMARY METAL INDUSTRIES

▲ Burgess-Norton Mfg Co Inc .... B 630 232-4100
   Geneva *(G-10256)*
▼ Connelly-Gpm Inc .... E 773 247-7231
   Chicago *(G-4219)*
Controlled Thermal Processing ...... G 847 651-5500
   Streamwood *(G-19567)*
Dippit Inc .... G 630 762-6500
   West Chicago *(G-20571)*
Direct Selling Strategies .... G 847 993-3188
   Rosemont *(G-18018)*
Dva Metal Fabrication Inc .... G 224 577-8217
   Elk Grove Village *(G-8961)*
▲ Ecf Holdings LLC .... G 224 723-5524
   Northbrook *(G-15379)*
Filter Technology Inc .... E 773 523-7200
   Bedford Park *(G-1467)*
Finish Line USA Inc .... F 847 608-7800
   Elgin *(G-8585)*
Forge Resources Group LLC .... C 815 758-6400
   Dekalb *(G-7679)*
Forge Resources Group LLC .... C 815 758-6400
   Dekalb *(G-7680)*
Forge Resources Group LLC .... F 815 758-6400
   Dekalb *(G-7681)*
Gemco .... G 217 446-7900
   Danville *(G-7339)*
Hall Fabrication Inc .... G 217 322-2212
   Rushville *(G-18109)*
Hilti Inc .... F 847 364-9818
   Elmhurst *(G-9372)*
J D M Coatings Inc .... G 708 755-6300
   Steger *(G-19490)*
▲ L & J Industrial Staples Inc .... G 815 864-3337
   Shannon *(G-18870)*
Lamination Specialties LLC .... G 773 254-7500
   Chicago *(G-5170)*
Lamination Specialties LLC .... E 312 243-2181
   Oak Brook *(G-15631)*
Lindsay Metal Madness Inc .... G 815 568-4560
   Woodstock *(G-21406)*
Midwest Finishers Pwdrctng .... G 217 536-9098
   Effingham *(G-8412)*
MSC Pre Finish Metals Egv Inc ..... G 847 439-2210
   Elk Grove Village *(G-9137)*
Mt Vernon Iron Works LLC .... G 618 244-2313
   Mount Vernon *(G-14628)*
Mueller Company Plant 4 .... G 217 425-7424
   Decatur *(G-7529)*
Nanophase Technologies Corp ..... D 630 771-6700
   Romeoville *(G-17859)*
Nanophase Technologies Corp ..... F 630 771-6747
   Burr Ridge *(G-2706)*
National Material Company LLC .. E 847 806-7200
   Elk Grove Village *(G-9144)*
Orion Metals Co .... G 847 412-9532
   Glenview *(G-10596)*
Phillip C Cowen .... E 630 208-1848
   Geneva *(G-10299)*
Polaris Laser Laminations LLC .... E 630 444-0760
   West Chicago *(G-20630)*
Senju Comtek Corp. .... G 847 549-5690
   Mundelein *(G-14735)*
Stein Inc .... D 618 452-0836
   Granite City *(G-10739)*
▲ Topy Precision Mfg Inc .... D 847 228-5902
   Elk Grove Village *(G-9277)*
Toyal America Inc .... G 630 505-2160
   Naperville *(G-14935)*
◆ Toyal America Inc .... D 630 505-2160
   Lockport *(G-13025)*
Winning Colors .... G 815 462-4810
   Manhattan *(G-13436)*

34 FABRICATED METAL PRODUCTS, EXCEPT MACHINERY AND TRANSPORTATION EQUIPMENT

3411 Metal Cans

All Container Inc .... G 847 677-2100
   Lincolnwood *(G-12813)*
Amcor Rigid Plastics Usa LLC ..... F 630 406-3500
   Batavia *(G-1347)*
Best Metal Corporation .... G 815 337-0420
   Woodstock *(G-21364)*
Boe Intermediate Holding Corp .... B 773 890-3300
   Chicago *(G-3924)*
Brockway Standard Inc .... G 773 893-2100
   Chicago *(G-3962)*
Bway Corporation .... C 773 254-8700
   Chicago *(G-3987)*
Bway Corporation .... C 847 956-0750
   Elk Grove Village *(G-8875)*
▲ Central Can Company Inc .... C 773 254-8700
   Chicago *(G-4056)*
Cooler Concepts Inc .... G 815 462-3866
   New Lenox *(G-15029)*
Creative Metal Products .... F 773 638-3200
   Chicago *(G-4264)*
Crown Cork & Seal Usa Inc .... C 708 239-5555
   Alsip *(G-435)*
Crown Cork & Seal Usa Inc .... C 815 933-9351
   Bradley *(G-2278)*
Crown Cork & Seal Usa Inc .... C 708 239-5000
   Alsip *(G-436)*
Crown Cork & Seal Usa Inc .... F 708 385-8670
   Alsip *(G-437)*
Crown Cork & Seal Usa Inc .... D 217 672-3533
   Warrensburg *(G-20226)*
Crown Cork & Seal Usa Inc .... C 217 872-6100
   Decatur *(G-7478)*
Crown Cork & Seal Usa Inc .... E 630 851-7774
   Aurora *(G-946)*
D & B Fabricators & Distrs .... F 630 325-3811
   Lemont *(G-12562)*
▲ Ds Containers Inc .... C 630 406-9600
   Batavia *(G-1375)*
Ideal Fabricators Inc .... F 217 999-7017
   Mount Olive *(G-14505)*
▲ Ignite Usa LLC .... E 312 432-6223
   Chicago *(G-4880)*
Jamiel Inc .... C 217 423-1000
   Decatur *(G-7510)*
▲ JL Clark LLC .... C 815 961-5609
   Rockford *(G-17476)*
Jlo Metal Products Co A Corp ..... D 773 889-6242
   Chicago *(G-5032)*
Justrite Manufacturing Co LLC ... C 800 798-9250
   Deerfield *(G-7625)*
Kraft Heinz Company .... C 847 646-2000
   Chicago *(G-5129)*
Mauser Pckg Sltons Intrmdate I .. G 770 645-4800
   Oak Brook *(G-15640)*
▲ Metraflex Company .... D 312 738-3800
   Chicago *(G-5411)*
Mt Containers Inc .... G 708 458-9420
   Chicago *(G-5520)*
North America Packaging Corp .... F 847 979-1625
   Elk Grove Village *(G-9151)*
◆ Shenglong Intl Group Corp .... C 312 388-2345
   Glenview *(G-10615)*
Silgan Containers LLC .... D 815 562-1250
   Rochelle *(G-17159)*
Silgan Containers Mfg Corp .... C 217 283-5501
   Hoopeston *(G-11512)*
Silgan Containers Mfg Corp .... E 847 336-0552
   Waukegan *(G-20495)*
▲ Silgan Equipment Company ..... E 847 336-0552
   Waukegan *(G-20496)*
Silgan White Cap Americas LLC . F 630 515-8383
   Downers Grove *(G-8096)*
Silgan White Cap LLC .... C 217 398-1600
   Champaign *(G-3347)*
Spiked .... G 469 235-8103
   Evanston *(G-9576)*
Staffco Inc .... G 309 688-3223
   Peoria *(G-16528)*
Willow Farm Product Inc .... G 630 395-9246
   Darien *(G-7414)*

3412 Metal Barrels, Drums, Kegs & Pails

Arrows Up Inc .... G 847 305-2550
   Arlington Heights *(G-696)*
▲ Central Can Company Inc .... C 773 254-8700
   Chicago *(G-4056)*
Cleveland Steel Container Corp .. E 708 258-0700
   Peotone *(G-16552)*
D & B Fabricators & Distrs .... F 630 325-3811
   Lemont *(G-12562)*
Grafcor Packaging Inc .... F 815 639-2380
   Loves Park *(G-13215)*
Greif Inc .... E 815 935-7575
   Bradley *(G-2283)*
Higgins Bros Inc .... F 773 523-0124
   Chicago *(G-4815)*
Liberty Diversified Intl Inc .... E 217 935-8361
   Clinton *(G-6925)*
Mauser Usa LLC .... F 773 261-2332
   Chicago *(G-5367)*

SIC SECTION

Meyer Steel Drum Inc .... E 773 522-3030
   Chicago *(G-5416)*
▲ Meyer Steel Drum Inc .... C 773 376-8376
   Chicago *(G-5417)*
Mobile Mini Inc .... E 708 297-2004
   Calumet Park *(G-2799)*
Production Manufacturing .... G 217 256-4211
   Warsaw *(G-20259)*
Staffco Inc .... G 309 688-3223
   Peoria *(G-16528)*
◆ Van Leer Containers Inc .... C 708 371-4777
   Alsip *(G-520)*
Westrock Cp LLC .... C 847 689-4200
   North Chicago *(G-15324)*
Woods Equipment Company .... D 815 732-2141
   Oregon *(G-15929)*
▼ Zorin Material Handling Co .... C 773 342-3818
   Chicago *(G-6724)*

3421 Cutlery

Alps Group Inc .... G 815 469-3800
   Frankfort *(G-9765)*
Alps Group Inc .... G 815 469-3800
   Chicago *(G-3632)*
Art Jewel Enterprises Ltd .... F 630 260-0400
   Carol Stream *(G-2941)*
Art of Shaving - Fl LLC .... G 630 495-7316
   Lombard *(G-13040)*
Art of Shaving - Fl LLC .... G 312 527-1604
   Chicago *(G-3737)*
Art of Shaving - Fl LLC .... G 630 684-0277
   Oak Brook *(G-15594)*
Bmac Usa Inc .... G 630 279-5500
   Oak Brook *(G-15600)*
Bubble Bubble Inc .... G 815 455-2366
   Crystal Lake *(G-7173)*
Burrito Beach LLC .... F 312 861-1986
   Chicago *(G-3978)*
Custom Cutting Tools Inc .... G 815 986-0320
   Loves Park *(G-13200)*
Edgewell Per Care Brands LLC ... B 708 544-5550
   Melrose Park *(G-13861)*
◆ Estwing Manufacturing Co Inc . B 815 397-9521
   Rockford *(G-17402)*
Gillette Company .... D 847 689-3111
   North Chicago *(G-15312)*
Goodco Products LLC .... G 630 258-6384
   Countryside *(G-7055)*
Harris Precision Tools Inc .... G 708 422-5808
   Chicago Ridge *(G-6797)*
Irwin Industrial Tool Company ..... G 815 235-4171
   Freeport *(G-10121)*
Joseph Taylor Inc .... G 309 762-5323
   Moline *(G-14153)*
Kernel Kutter Inc .... G 815 877-1515
   Machesney Park *(G-13354)*
La Autentica Michoacana Never . G 630 516-1888
   Addison *(G-177)*
Lulus .... G 773 865-8978
   Chicago *(G-5280)*
Mega Manufacturing Inc .... G 620 663-1127
   Rockford *(G-17515)*
▲ Modern Specialties Company .. G 312 648-5800
   Chicago *(G-5481)*
Moes River North LLC .... G 312 245-2000
   Chicago *(G-5484)*
Olive Tree Foods Inc .... G 847 872-2762
   Zion *(G-21522)*
Ovs LLC .... G 312 428-3548
   Chicago *(G-5720)*
Pactiv LLC .... C 708 496-2900
   Bedford Park *(G-1490)*
Pactiv LLC .... F 708 496-2900
   Chicago *(G-5742)*
Procter & Gamble Company .... C 847 375-5400
   Chicago *(G-5892)*
River Bend Wild Game & Sausage G 217 688-3337
   Saint Joseph *(G-18319)*
Seadog .... G 773 235-8100
   Chicago *(G-6125)*
Solo Cup Operating Corporation . C 773 767-3300
   Chicago *(G-6197)*
▲ Speco Inc .... G 847 678-4240
   Schiller Park *(G-18845)*
Summervlle Consulting Svcs LLC G 618 547-7142
   Alma *(G-404)*
▲ Superior Knife Inc .... E 847 982-2280
   Niles *(G-15177)*
Tarrerias-Bonjean USA Inc .... G 216 217-1726
   Chicago *(G-6328)*

SIC SECTION
34 FABRICATED METAL PRODUCTS, EXCEPT MACHINERY AND TRANSPORTATION EQUIPMENT

▲ Wallace/Haskin Corp....G.... 630 789-2882
Downers Grove (G-8105)
◆ Whitney Roper LLC....D.... 815 962-3011
Rockford (G-17683)
▲ Whitney Roper Rockford Inc....D.... 815 962-3011
Rockford (G-17684)
Wings of Roselle LLC....G.... 630 529-5700
Roselle (G-17995)

3423 Hand & Edge Tools

A To Z Tool Inc....G.... 630 787-0478
Villa Park (G-20126)
Adel Tool Co LLP....G.... 708 867-8530
Park Ridge (G-16263)
◆ Adjustable Clamp Company....C.... 312 666-0640
Chicago (G-3546)
▲ Advance Equipment Mfg Co....F.... 773 287-8220
Chicago (G-3555)
▲ Ajax Tool Works Inc....D.... 847 455-5420
Franklin Park (G-9862)
▲ Aldon Co....F.... 847 623-8800
Waukegan (G-20412)
Atlas Die LLC....D.... 630 351-5140
Glendale Heights (G-10436)
▲ Beno J Gundlach Company....E.... 618 233-1781
Belleville (G-1534)
◆ Bit Brokers International Ltd....E.... 618 435-5811
West Frankfort (G-20668)
Brian Burcar....G.... 815 856-2271
Leonore (G-12611)
Builders Ironworks Inc....G.... 708 754-4092
Steger (G-19489)
C K North America Inc....F.... 815 524-4246
Romeoville (G-17800)
Chicago Grinding & Machine Co....E.... 708 343-4399
Melrose Park (G-13843)
Custom Cutting Tools Inc....G.... 815 986-0320
Loves Park (G-13200)
◆ Dasco Pro Inc....D.... 815 962-3727
Rockford (G-17368)
Dobratz Sales Company Inc....G.... 224 569-3081
Lake In The Hills (G-12332)
Doerock Inc....G.... 217 543-2101
Arthur (G-853)
▲ Durabilt Dyvex Inc....F.... 708 397-4673
Broadview (G-2432)
E J Welch Co Inc....F.... 847 238-0100
Elk Grove Village (G-8964)
Ergo-Help Inc....G.... 847 593-0722
Fox River Grove (G-9757)
◆ Estwing Manufacturing Co Inc....B.... 815 397-9521
Rockford (G-17402)
Fitzpatrick Bros Inc....G.... 217 592-3500
Quincy (G-16882)
▲ Gaither Tool Co....G.... 217 245-0545
Jacksonville (G-11765)
▲ Galaxy Industries Inc....D.... 847 639-8580
Cary (G-3162)
Gartech Manufacturing Co....E.... 217 324-6527
Litchfield (G-12963)
Gaunt Industries Inc....G.... 847 671-0776
Franklin Park (G-9949)
Greenfield Products LLC....E.... 708 596-5200
Hazel Crest (G-11129)
H E Associates Inc....F.... 630 553-6382
Yorkville (G-21487)
H R Slater Co Inc....F.... 312 666-1855
Chicago (G-4760)
H&H Die Manufacturing Inc....G.... 708 479-6267
Frankfort (G-9799)
▲ Hand Tool America....G.... 847 947-2866
Buffalo Grove (G-2543)
Hydra Fold Auger Inc....G.... 217 379-2614
Loda (G-13028)
Hyponex Corporation....E.... 815 772-2167
Morrison (G-14343)
I D Rockford Shop Inc....G.... 815 335-1150
Winnebago (G-21120)
Ideal Industries Inc....C.... 815 895-1108
Sycamore (G-19715)
Illinois Tool Works Inc....E.... 847 634-1900
Vernon Hills (G-20064)
Illinois Tool Works Inc....G.... 847 821-2170
Vernon Hills (G-20065)
Illinois Tool Works Inc....E.... 563 422-5686
Glenview (G-10564)
▼ Ironwood Manufacturing Inc....G.... 630 969-1100
Naperville (G-14975)
Irwin Industrial Tool Company....C.... 815 235-4171
Freeport (G-10121)
K-C Tool Co....G.... 630 983-5960
Naperville (G-14857)
◆ Klein Tools Inc....B.... 847 821-5500
Lincolnshire (G-12778)
Klein Tools Inc....G.... 847 249-4930
Waukegan (G-20455)
Klein Tools Inc....D.... 847 228-6999
Elk Grove Village (G-9078)
Klein Tools Inc....E.... 847 821-5500
Lincolnshire (G-12779)
Lawndale Forging & Tool Works....G.... 773 277-2800
Chicago (G-5183)
Line Group Inc....E.... 847 593-6810
Arlington Heights (G-769)
▲ Link Tools Intl (usa) Inc....G.... 773 549-3000
Chicago (G-5229)
▲ Lmt Onsrud LP....C.... 847 362-1560
Waukegan (G-20461)
Lorette Dies Inc....G.... 630 279-9682
Elmhurst (G-9393)
Lsp Industries Inc....F.... 815 226-8090
Rockford (G-17497)
▲ Luster Leaf Products Inc....F.... 815 337-5560
Woodstock (G-21407)
M E Barber Co Inc....G.... 217 428-4591
Decatur (G-7518)
◆ Marmon Holdings Inc....D.... 312 372-9500
Chicago (G-5343)
▲ Modern Specialties Company....G.... 312 648-5800
Chicago (G-5481)
Nextstep Commercial Products....G.... 217 379-2377
Paxton (G-16310)
Northern Ordinance Corporation....G.... 815 675-6400
Spring Grove (G-19289)
P K Neuses Incorporated....G.... 847 253-6555
Rolling Meadows (G-17758)
▲ Patterson Avenue Tool Company....G.... 847 949-8100
Long Grove (G-13169)
Perkins Manufacturing Co....E.... 708 482-9500
Bolingbrook (G-2226)
▲ Power House Tool Inc....E.... 815 727-6301
Joliet (G-11915)
Power Planter Inc....G.... 217 379-2614
Loda (G-13031)
▲ Pratt-Read Tools LLC....G.... 815 895-1121
Sycamore (G-19728)
Precision Industrial Knife....G.... 630 350-7898
Wood Dale (G-21229)
Precision Instruments Inc....D.... 847 824-4194
Des Plaines (G-7830)
◆ Precision Products Inc....C.... 217 735-1590
Lincoln (G-12737)
Precision Tool....F.... 815 464-2428
Frankfort (G-9824)
▲ Proton Multimedia Inc....G.... 847 531-8664
Elgin (G-8701)
▲ Pullr Holding Company LLC....E.... 224 366-2500
Schaumburg (G-18688)
Ravco Incorporated....G.... 815 725-9095
Joliet (G-11923)
Remark Technologies Inc....G.... 815 985-2972
Rockford (G-17571)
▲ Rhino Tool Company....F.... 309 853-5555
Kewanee (G-12040)
▲ Rieco-Titan Products Inc....E.... 815 464-7400
Frankfort (G-9831)
◆ Rothenberger USA LLC....D.... 800 545-7698
Loves Park (G-13260)
▲ Ryeson Corporation....D.... 847 455-8677
Carol Stream (G-3061)
S & G Step Tool Inc....G.... 773 992-0808
Chicago (G-6084)
▲ Sab Tool Supply Co....G.... 847 634-3700
Vernon Hills (G-20090)
Sk Hand Tool LLC....F.... 815 895-7701
Sycamore (G-19731)
Stark Tools and Supply Inc....G.... 847 772-8974
Elk Grove Village (G-9256)
Stuhr Manufacturing Co....F.... 815 398-2460
Rockford (G-17648)
▲ Sws Industries Inc....E.... 904 482-0091
Woodstock (G-21438)
Thread & Gage Co Inc....G.... 815 675-2305
Spring Grove (G-19302)
Toby Small Engine Repair....G.... 708 699-6021
Richton Park (G-17031)
◆ Tuxco Corporation....F.... 847 244-2220
Gurnee (G-10940)
▲ Vaughan & Bushnell Mfg Co....F.... 815 648-2446
Hebron (G-11153)
Vaughan & Bushnell Mfg Co....C.... 309 772-2131
Bushnell (G-2748)
Wenco Manufacturing Co Inc....E.... 630 377-7474
Elgin (G-8781)
◆ Whitney Roper LLC....D.... 815 962-3011
Rockford (G-17683)
▲ Whitney Roper Rockford Inc....D.... 815 962-3011
Rockford (G-17684)
Woodland Engineering Company....G.... 847 362-0110
Lake Bluff (G-12217)
Zim Manufacturing Co....E.... 773 622-2500
Des Plaines (G-7870)

3425 Hand Saws & Saw Blades

Allkut Tool Incorporated....G.... 815 476-9656
Wilmington (G-21096)
▲ Amv International Inc....F.... 815 282-9990
Loves Park (G-13189)
◆ Contour Saws Inc....E.... 800 259-6834
Des Plaines (G-7749)
Contour Saws Inc....D.... 800 259-6834
Des Plaines (G-7750)
Custom Blades & Tools Inc....G.... 630 860-7650
Bensenville (G-1782)
◆ Estwing Manufacturing Co Inc....B.... 815 397-9521
Rockford (G-17402)
Jaeger Saw and Cutter Inc....G.... 815 963-0313
Rockford (G-17472)
Midwest Saw Inc....G.... 630 293-4252
West Chicago (G-20618)
Milwaukee Electric Tool Corp....B.... 847 588-3356
Niles (G-15147)
R & S Cutterhead Mfg Co....F.... 815 678-2611
Richmond (G-17020)
▲ Roentgen USA LLC....G.... 847 787-0135
Schiller Park (G-18840)
S & J Industrial Supply Corp....F.... 708 339-1708
South Holland (G-19242)
Saws International Inc....E.... 815 397-0985
Machesney Park (G-13373)
Saws Unlimited Inc....G.... 847 640-7450
Elk Grove Village (G-9232)
Tru-Cut Tool & Supply Co....F.... 708 396-1122
Wheeling (G-21002)
Unicut Corporation....G.... 773 525-4210
Chicago (G-6464)
▲ Wallace/Haskin Corp....G.... 630 789-2882
Downers Grove (G-8105)
▲ Wikus Saw Technology Corp....E.... 630 766-0960
Addison (G-335)

3429 Hardware, NEC

9161 Corporation....G.... 847 470-8828
Niles (G-15097)
A Ashland Lock Company....F.... 773 348-5106
Chicago (G-3485)
Aco Inc....E.... 773 774-5200
Chicago (G-3529)
◆ Adjustable Clamp Company....C.... 312 666-0640
Chicago (G-3546)
Advanced Custom Metals Inc....G.... 847 803-2090
Des Plaines (G-7723)
▼ Advanced Machine & Engrg Co....C.... 815 962-6076
Rockford (G-17296)
▲ Afc Cable Systems Inc....B.... 508 998-1131
Harvey (G-11070)
Agena Manufacturing Co....E.... 630 668-5086
Carol Stream (G-2928)
Alan Manufacturing Corp....G.... 815 568-6836
Marengo (G-13478)
▲ Aldon Co....F.... 847 623-8800
Waukegan (G-20412)
Allegion S&S Holding Co Inc....C.... 815 875-3311
Princeton (G-16805)
Allquip Co Inc....G.... 309 944-6153
Geneseo (G-10239)
▲ American Couplings Co....G.... 630 323-4442
Westmont (G-20728)
American Partsmith Inc....G.... 630 520-0432
West Chicago (G-20538)
▲ Amos Industries Inc....F.... 630 393-0606
Aurora (G-911)
Ashland Door Solutions LLC....G.... 773 348-5106
Elk Grove Village (G-8842)
Avoca Ridge Ltd....G.... 815 692-4772
Fairbury (G-9604)
Baker Drapery Corporation....G.... 309 691-3295
Dunlap (G-8132)
▲ Baron Manufacturing Co LLC....E.... 630 628-9110
Itasca (G-11626)

SIC

34 FABRICATED METAL PRODUCTS, EXCEPT MACHINERY AND TRANSPORTATION EQUIPMENT SIC SECTION

▲ **Bella Architectural Products**.............G....... 708 339-4782
Harvey *(G-11078)*
Berens Inc.............G....... 815 932-0913
Kankakee *(G-11960)*
Braun Manufacturing Co Inc.............E....... 847 635-2050
Mount Prospect *(G-14514)*
Buildingpoint Midwest LLC.............G....... 855 332-7527
Plainfield *(G-16645)*
▼ **Capital Rubber Corporation**.............F....... 630 595-6644
Bensenville *(G-1762)*
Caterpillar Inc.............A....... 309 578-2473
Mossville *(G-14456)*
Chas O Larson Co.............E....... 815 625-0503
Rock Falls *(G-17179)*
▲ **Chicago Car Seal Company**.............G....... 773 278-9400
Chicago *(G-4095)*
▲ **Chicago Hardware and Fix Co**.............C....... 847 455-6609
Franklin Park *(G-9905)*
Civiq Smartscapes LLC.............G....... 312 300-4776
Chicago *(G-4165)*
Cleats Mfg Inc.............F....... 773 521-0300
Chicago *(G-4175)*
Compx International Inc.............G....... 847 234-1864
Lake Bluff *(G-12176)*
▲ **Compx Security Products Inc**.............D....... 847 234-1864
Grayslake *(G-10763)*
Congress Drive Inc.............E....... 972 875-6060
Wilmette *(G-21074)*
◆ **Cooper B-Line Inc**.............A....... 618 654-2184
Highland *(G-11210)*
Crosby Group LLC.............G....... 708 333-3005
Harvey *(G-11081)*
Custom Stainless Steel Inc.............F....... 618 435-2605
Benton *(G-1924)*
Del Storm Products Inc.............F....... 217 446-3377
Danville *(G-7330)*
Dixline Corporation.............D....... 309 932-2011
Galva *(G-10231)*
Dixline Corporation.............F....... 309 932-2011
Galva *(G-10230)*
Dormakaba USA Inc.............D....... 618 965-3491
Steeleville *(G-19480)*
▲ **Du Bro Products Inc**.............E....... 847 526-2136
Wauconda *(G-20344)*
Dumore Supplies Inc.............F....... 312 949-6260
Chicago *(G-4403)*
Dura Operating LLC.............C....... 815 947-3333
Stockton *(G-19549)*
▲ **Durabilt Dyvex Inc**.............F....... 708 397-4673
Broadview *(G-2432)*
Eastern Company.............C....... 847 537-1800
Wheeling *(G-20884)*
▼ **Engert Co Inc**.............E....... 847 673-1633
Skokie *(G-18950)*
Erwin Wiczer Industries Inc.............G....... 847 541-9556
Wheeling *(G-20893)*
Estad Stamping & Mfg Co.............E....... 217 442-4600
Danville *(G-7331)*
◆ **Estwing Manufacturing Co Inc**.............B....... 815 397-9521
Rockford *(G-17402)*
Fenix Manufacturing LLC.............G....... 815 208-0755
Fulton *(G-10151)*
Focus Marketing Group Inc.............G....... 815 363-2525
Johnsburg *(G-11803)*
▲ **Fort Lock Corporation**.............E....... 708 456-1100
Grayslake *(G-10773)*
▲ **Fortune Brands Home & SEC Inc**.............D....... 847 484-4400
Deerfield *(G-7610)*
Geib Industries Inc.............E....... 847 455-4550
Bensenville *(G-1809)*
General Machinery & Mfg Co.............F....... 773 235-3700
Chicago *(G-4674)*
Graber Building Sup & Hdwr Inc.............G....... 217 268-3014
Arcola *(G-650)*
Grand Specialties Co.............F....... 630 629-8000
Oak Brook *(G-15625)*
Haddock Tool & Manufacturing.............G....... 815 786-2739
Sandwich *(G-18373)*
▲ **Heckmann Building Products Inc**.............E....... 708 865-2403
Melrose Park *(G-13879)*
Hendrickson International Corp.............C....... 815 727-4031
Joliet *(G-11876)*
HM Manufacturing Inc.............F....... 847 487-8700
Wauconda *(G-20356)*
Honeywell Safety Pdts USA Inc.............C....... 630 343-3731
Bolingbrook *(G-2185)*
Hunter-Stevens Company Inc.............F....... 847 671-5014
Franklin Park *(G-9959)*
◆ **Hymans Auto Supply Co**.............E....... 773 978-8221
Chicago *(G-4864)*
Hyspan Precision Products Inc.............E....... 773 277-0700
South Holland *(G-19223)*
I Hardware Direct Inc.............G....... 708 325-0000
Westmont *(G-20748)*
Illinois Fibre Specialty Co.............E....... 773 376-1122
Chicago *(G-4890)*
Illinois Tool Works Inc.............E....... 708 681-3891
Broadview *(G-2442)*
Industrial Rubber & Sup Entp.............G....... 217 429-3747
Decatur *(G-7507)*
▲ **Inland Fastener Inc**.............F....... 630 293-3800
West Chicago *(G-20596)*
Innerweld Cover Co.............F....... 847 497-3009
Mundelein *(G-14701)*
▲ **Innovative Components Inc**.............E....... 847 885-9050
Schaumburg *(G-18560)*
Jerome Remien Corporation.............F....... 847 806-0888
Elk Grove Village *(G-9067)*
Kemper Industries.............G....... 217 826-5712
Marshall *(G-13573)*
Kwikset Corporation.............G....... 630 577-0500
Lisle *(G-12908)*
L & M Hardware Ltd.............G....... 630 493-1026
Burr Ridge *(G-2694)*
Max Fire Training Inc.............F....... 618 210-2079
Godfrey *(G-10656)*
Metal Mfg LLC.............C....... 815 432-4595
Watseka *(G-20311)*
Meyer Engineering Co.............G....... 847 746-1500
Winthrop Harbor *(G-21141)*
MHS Ltd.............F....... 773 736-3333
Chicago *(G-5419)*
Miwa Lock Co.............G....... 630 365-4261
Elburn *(G-8462)*
MJT Incorporated.............G....... 708 597-0059
Alsip *(G-480)*
Nagel-Chase Inc.............G....... 847 336-4494
Gurnee *(G-10902)*
Neisewander Enterprises Inc.............A....... 815 288-1431
Dixon *(G-7904)*
Norforge and Machining Inc.............D....... 309 772-3124
Macomb *(G-13394)*
Nova Wildcat Amerock LLC.............F....... 815 266-6416
Freeport *(G-10131)*
▲ **OBerry Enterprises Inc**.............G....... 815 728-9480
Ringwood *(G-17046)*
Oso900 Nfp.............G....... 312 206-4219
Chicago *(G-5711)*
◆ **Peerless Industries Inc**.............C....... 630 375-5100
Aurora *(G-1006)*
◆ **Plews Inc**.............C....... 815 288-3344
Dixon *(G-7906)*
Practechal Marketing.............G....... 847 486-8600
Glenview *(G-10600)*
▲ **Prater Industries Inc**.............D....... 630 679-3200
Bolingbrook *(G-2228)*
◆ **Precision Brand Products Inc**.............E....... 630 969-7200
Downers Grove *(G-8082)*
Quality Hnge A Div Spreme Hnge.............E....... 708 534-7801
University Park *(G-19966)*
▲ **Reichel Hardware Company Inc**.............G....... 630 762-7394
Saint Charles *(G-18261)*
Reliable Machine Company.............E....... 815 968-8803
Rockford *(G-17570)*
▲ **Remin Laboratories Inc**.............D....... 815 723-1940
Joliet *(G-11924)*
▲ **Rifast Systems LLC**.............E....... 847 933-8330
Lincolnwood *(G-12839)*
Rockford Process Control LLC.............C....... 815 966-2000
Rockford *(G-17602)*
Royal Brass Inc.............G....... 618 439-6341
Benton *(G-1936)*
Royal Kit Bthroom Cabinets Inc.............F....... 847 588-0011
Niles *(G-15167)*
▲ **RPC Legacy Inc**.............D....... 815 966-2000
Rockford *(G-17616)*
S & D Products Inc.............E....... 630 372-2325
Bartlett *(G-1306)*
▼ **S & S Hinge Company**.............E....... 630 582-9500
Bloomingdale *(G-2013)*
S L Fixtures Inc.............G....... 217 423-9907
Decatur *(G-7545)*
Seamless Gutter Corp.............E....... 630 495-9800
Lombard *(G-13128)*
Shapco Inc.............G....... 847 229-1439
Wheeling *(G-20982)*
SPEP Acquisition Corp.............G....... 310 608-0693
Bolingbrook *(G-2246)*
Standard Truck Parts Inc.............G....... 815 726-4486
Joliet *(G-11932)*
Stanley Black & Decker Inc.............G....... 630 724-3632
Downers Grove *(G-8099)*
▲ **Strut & Supply Inc**.............G....... 847 756-4337
Lake Barrington *(G-12166)*
▲ **Stucchi Usa Inc**.............F....... 847 956-9720
Romeoville *(G-17878)*
▲ **Sweet Manufacturing Corp**.............E....... 847 546-5575
Chicago *(G-6294)*
▲ **Termax LLC**.............C....... 847 519-1500
Lake Zurich *(G-12463)*
Termax LLC.............G....... 847 519-1500
Lake Zurich *(G-12464)*
◆ **Thermos LLC**.............D....... 847 439-7821
Schaumburg *(G-18745)*
◆ **Tkk USA Inc**.............C....... 847 439-7821
Rolling Meadows *(G-17780)*
Tolerance Manufacturing Inc.............F....... 847 244-8836
Waukegan *(G-20508)*
Treetop Marketing Inc.............G....... 877 249-0479
Batavia *(G-1433)*
U S Tool & Manufacturing Co.............E....... 630 953-1000
Addison *(G-321)*
▲ **Unistrut International Corp**.............C....... 800 882-5543
Harvey *(G-11099)*
◆ **United Steel & Fasteners Inc**.............E....... 630 250-0900
Itasca *(G-11750)*
Value Engineered Products.............E....... 708 867-6777
Rolling Meadows *(G-17784)*
Van Craft Industry of Del Edel.............G....... 708 430-6670
Oak Lawn *(G-15738)*
Venturedyne Ltd.............E....... 708 597-7550
Chicago *(G-6535)*
Whiting Partners LLC.............G....... 773 978-8221
Chicago *(G-6620)*
◆ **William Dudek Manufacturing Co**.............E....... 773 622-2727
Chicago *(G-6629)*
Wind Point Partners Vi LP.............G....... 312 255-4800
Chicago *(G-6638)*
▲ **Woodbridge Inc**.............F....... 847 229-1741
Wheeling *(G-21015)*
Wozniak Industries Inc.............C....... 708 458-1220
Bedford Park *(G-1515)*
Zirlin Interiors Inc.............E....... 773 334-5530
Chicago *(G-6720)*
Zsi-Foster Inc.............G....... 800 323-7053
Chicago *(G-6725)*

3431 Enameled Iron & Metal Sanitary Ware

Byelkaycom Sales Inc.............G....... 630 574-8484
Oak Brook *(G-15602)*
Elkay Manufacturing Company.............B....... 708 681-1880
Broadview *(G-2434)*
Elkay Manufacturing Company.............G....... 800 223-5529
Downers Grove *(G-7999)*
Elkay Manufacturing Company.............B....... 815 273-7001
Savanna *(G-18404)*
Kohler Co.............G....... 920 457-4441
Chicago *(G-5118)*
Kohler Co.............E....... 630 323-7674
Burr Ridge *(G-2693)*
Kohler Co.............E....... 847 635-8071
Glenview *(G-10578)*
Kohler Co.............D....... 847 734-1777
Huntley *(G-11548)*
▲ **Lenova Inc**.............G....... 312 733-1098
Hillside *(G-11346)*
▲ **Mej 1933 Inc**.............C....... 847 678-5151
Franklin Park *(G-9990)*
Swan Surfaces LLC.............C....... 618 532-5673
Centralia *(G-3252)*
T J M & Associates Inc.............G....... 847 382-1993
Wauconda *(G-20396)*
▲ **Wedi Corp**.............E....... 847 357-9815
Batavia *(G-1441)*

3432 Plumbing Fixture Fittings & Trim, Brass

▲ **Anderson Copper & Brass Co LLC**.............E....... 708 535-9030
Frankfort *(G-9767)*
▲ **Black Swan Manufacturing Co**.............F....... 773 227-3700
Chicago *(G-3908)*
Caldwell Plumbing Co.............F....... 630 588-8900
Wheaton *(G-20792)*
▲ **Cfpg Ltd**.............C....... 630 679-1420
Woodridge *(G-21282)*
▲ **Couplings Company Inc**.............F....... 847 634-8990
Lincolnshire *(G-12755)*
▲ **Deks North America Inc**.............G....... 312 219-2110
Chicago *(G-4331)*
Elkay Manufacturing Company.............E....... 630 377-0150
Saint Charles *(G-18196)*

34 FABRICATED METAL PRODUCTS, EXCEPT MACHINERY AND TRANSPORTATION EQUIPMENT

Elkay Manufacturing Company .... B 708 681-1880
  Broadview (G-2434)
Elkay Manufacturing Company .... G 800 223-5529
  Downers Grove (G-7999)
G B Holdings Inc .... C 773 265-3000
  Chicago (G-4648)
◆ Globe Union Group Inc .... D 630 679-1420
  Woodridge (G-21304)
▲ Guardian Equipment Inc .... E 312 447-8100
  Chicago (G-4747)
▲ Homewerks Worldwide LLC .... E 224 543-1529
  Lake Bluff (G-12288)
▲ Hydrology Inc .... G 312 832-9000
  Chicago (G-4862)
Iodon Inc .... G 708 799-4062
  Country Club Hills (G-7041)
Isenberg Bath Corporation .... G 972 510-5916
  Bensenville (G-1826)
▲ Ki Industries Inc .... E 708 449-1990
  Berkeley (G-1941)
Kieft Bros Inc .... E 630 832-8090
  Elmhurst (G-9388)
Kohler Co .... D 847 734-1777
  Huntley (G-11548)
▲ Lacava LLC .... E 773 637-9600
  Chicago (G-5154)
Lavell General Handyman Svcs .... G 773 691-3101
  Chicago (G-5181)
Leyden Lawn Sprinklers .... E 630 665-5520
  Glen Ellyn (G-10409)
▲ Mifab Inc .... E 773 341-3030
  Chicago (G-5452)
▲ PSI Systems North America Inc .... G 630 830-9435
  Bartlett (G-1302)
Royale Innovation Group Ltd .... G 312 339-1406
  Itasca (G-11729)
Schulhof Company .... F 773 348-1123
  Richmond (G-17022)
Sergio Barajas .... G 708 238-7614
  La Grange (G-12089)
◆ Sloan Valve Company .... D 847 671-4300
  Franklin Park (G-10048)
Sterline Manufacturing Corp .... E 847 244-1234
  Gurnee (G-10931)
▲ Stz Industries LLC .... E 773 265-3000
  Chicago (G-6261)
◆ Suncast Corporation .... A 630 879-2050
  Batavia (G-1422)
◆ Water Saver Faucet Co .... C 312 666-5500
  Chicago (G-6588)
▲ White Racker Co Inc .... G 847 758-1640
  Elk Grove Village (G-9308)

3433 Heating Eqpt

Aldrico Inc .... E 309 695-2311
  Wyoming (G-21457)
All American Wood Register Co .... F 815 356-1000
  Crystal Lake (G-7155)
American Fuel Economy Inc .... G 815 433-3226
  Ottawa (G-16037)
▲ BP Solar International Inc .... A 301 698-4200
  Naperville (G-14785)
Burdett Burner Mfg Inc .... G 630 617-5060
  Villa Park (G-20135)
Cruise Boiler and Repr Co Inc .... F 630 279-7111
  Elmhurst (G-9356)
DS Air & Heating Inc .... G 773 826-7411
  Chicago (G-4398)
Dva Mayday Corporation .... G 847 848-7555
  Village of Lakewood (G-20178)
▲ Easy Heat Inc .... E 847 268-6000
  Rosemont (G-18022)
◆ Eclipse Inc .... D 815 877-3031
  Rockford (G-17388)
▲ Eclipse Combustion Inc .... C 815 877-3031
  Rockford (G-17389)
▲ Empire Comfort Systems Inc .... C 618 233-7420
  Belleville (G-1551)
Filtran Holdings LLC .... G 847 635-6670
  Des Plaines (G-7766)
◆ Filtran LLC .... C 847 635-6670
  Des Plaines (G-7767)
Goose Island Mfg & Supply Corp .... G 708 343-4225
  Lansing (G-12495)
▼ Grieve Corporation .... D 847 546-8225
  Round Lake (G-18078)
Hardy Radiator Repair .... F 217 223-8320
  Quincy (G-16889)
Industries Publication Inc .... G 630 357-5269
  Lisle (G-12899)

Ipsen Inc .... E 815 239-2385
  Pecatonica (G-16322)
▲ Midco International Inc .... E 773 604-8700
  Chicago (G-5433)
Polyair Inter Pack Inc .... D 773 995-1818
  Chicago (G-5838)
R & D Electronics Inc .... G 847 583-9080
  Niles (G-15163)
▲ Spirotherm Inc .... G 630 307-2662
  Glendale Heights (G-10497)
▲ Sws Industries Inc .... E 904 482-0091
  Woodstock (G-21438)
Tri-State Food Equipment .... G 217 228-1550
  Quincy (G-16952)

3441 Fabricated Structural Steel

555 Design Fabrication MGT Inc .... G 773 869-0555
  Chicago (G-3473)
A & A Steel Fabricating Co .... F 708 389-4499
  Posen (G-16789)
A & B Metal Polishing Inc .... F 773 847-1077
  Chicago (G-3480)
A & S Steel Specialties Inc .... E 815 838-8188
  Lockport (G-12979)
A Lucas & Sons .... E 309 673-8547
  Peoria (G-16372)
AAA Galvanizing - Joliet Inc .... E 815 284-5001
  Dixon (G-7887)
Aak Mechanical Inc .... D 217 935-8501
  Clinton (G-6917)
Ablaze Welding & Fabricating .... G 815 965-0046
  Rockford (G-17287)
Accurate Fabricators Inc .... E 618 451-1886
  Granite City (G-10689)
Accurate Metal Fabricating LLC .... D 773 235-0400
  Chicago (G-3518)
Ace Metal Crafts Company .... C 847 455-1010
  Bensenville (G-1726)
▲ Acro Tech Corporation .... E 630 408-2248
  Wheaton (G-20785)
Adams Steel Service Inc .... E 815 385-9100
  McHenry (G-13715)
Addison Steel Inc .... E 847 998-9445
  Glenview (G-10519)
Adermanns Welding & Mch & Co .... G 217 342-3234
  Effingham (G-8383)
Advance Iron Works Inc .... F 708 798-3540
  East Hazel Crest (G-8216)
Advanced Custom Metals Inc .... G 847 803-2090
  Des Plaines (G-7723)
Advanced Steel Fabrication .... G 847 956-6565
  Elk Grove Village (G-8809)
▲ Ae2009 Technologies Inc .... E 708 331-0025
  South Holland (G-19188)
Aetna Engineering Works Inc .... E 773 785-0489
  Chicago (G-3577)
Affton Fabg & Wldg Co Inc .... E 314 781-4100
  Sauget (G-18388)
Alfredos Iron Works Inc .... F 815 748-1177
  Cortland (G-7017)
▲ All Metal Solutions Inc .... G 312 483-4178
  Chicago (G-3610)
Alloy Specialties Inc .... E 815 586-4728
  Blackstone (G-1970)
Allquip Co Inc .... G 309 944-6153
  Geneseo (G-10239)
▼ Allstate Metal Fabricators Inc .... G 630 860-1500
  Wood Dale (G-21159)
Alton Sheet Metal Corp .... F 618 462-0609
  Alton (G-543)
Altra Division 5 Llc .... F 708 534-1100
  University Park (G-19945)
American Piping Group Inc .... D 815 772-7470
  Morrison (G-14340)
American Steel Services Inc .... F 815 774-0677
  Joliet (G-11820)
Anamet Inc .... G 217 234-8844
  Glen Ellyn (G-10394)
Anchor Welding & Fabrication .... E 815 937-1640
  Aroma Park (G-839)
Andersen Machine & Welding Inc .... G 815 232-4664
  Freeport (G-10101)
Andscot Co Inc .... E 847 455-5800
  Franklin Park (G-9870)
Archer General Contg & Fabg .... G 708 757-7902
  Steger (G-19488)
Architectural Metals LLC .... F 815 654-2370
  Loves Park (G-13191)
Arcorp Structures LLC .... E 773 791-1648
  Riverside (G-17081)

Arcosa Wind Towers Inc .... F 217 935-7900
  Clinton (G-6918)
Area Fabricators .... G 217 455-3426
  Coatsburg (G-6940)
Arlington Strl Stl Co Inc .... E 847 577-2200
  Arlington Heights (G-695)
Armor Contract Mfg Inc .... E 847 981-9800
  Elk Grove Village (G-8838)
Arnette Pattern Co Inc .... E 618 451-7700
  Granite City (G-10698)
AS Fabricating Inc .... E 618 242-7438
  Mount Vernon (G-14596)
▲ Aspen Industries Inc .... F 630 238-0611
  Bensenville (G-1748)
Atkore International Group Inc .... A 708 339-1610
  Harvey (G-11075)
Atkore Intl Holdings Inc .... G 708 225-2051
  Harvey (G-11076)
B & B Fabrications LLC .... G 217 620-3210
  Sullivan (G-19660)
Bending Specialists LLC .... E 815 726-6281
  Lockport (G-12983)
Bi State Steel Co .... G 309 755-0668
  East Moline (G-8223)
Biewer Fabricating Inc .... G 630 530-8922
  Villa Park (G-20134)
Binzel Industries LLC .... G 847 506-0003
  Lockport (G-12984)
Birdco Fabricators Inc .... E 217 408-8744
  Jacksonville (G-11758)
Birdsell Machine & Orna Inc .... G 217 243-5849
  Jacksonville (G-11759)
BJs Welding Services Etc Co .... G 773 964-5836
  Chicago (G-3905)
BR Machine Inc .... F 815 434-0427
  Ottawa (G-16042)
Bridge City Mechanical Inc .... F 309 944-4873
  Geneseo (G-10240)
Bridgeport Steel Sales Inc .... E 312 326-4800
  Chicago (G-3957)
Btd Manufacturing Inc .... F 309 444-1268
  Washington (G-20267)
Byus Steel Inc .... E 630 879-2200
  Batavia (G-1361)
C Keller Manufacturing Inc .... E 630 833-5593
  Villa Park (G-20136)
Canam Steel Corporation .... G 815 224-9588
  Peru (G-16569)
▲ Catapult Global LLC .... F 847 364-8149
  Elk Grove Village (G-8882)
Cem LLC .... D 708 333-3761
  Barrington (G-1217)
Central Ill Fbrcation Whse Inc .... F 217 367-2323
  Urbana (G-19976)
Central Illinois Steel Company .... E 217 854-3251
  Carlinville (G-2869)
▼ Central Steel Fabricators .... E 708 652-2037
  Broadview (G-2424)
Cervones Welding Service Inc .... G 847 985-6865
  Schaumburg (G-18471)
CFS Crtive Fbrction Sltons LLC .... G 309 264-3946
  Peoria (G-16420)
Challenger Fabricators Inc .... G 815 704-0077
  South Beloit (G-19086)
Charter Dura-Bar Inc .... E 815 338-7800
  Woodstock (G-21374)
Chicago Grinding & Machine Co .... E 708 343-4399
  Melrose Park (G-13843)
Chicago Metal Fabricators Inc .... D 773 523-5755
  Chicago (G-4114)
◆ Chicago Metal Rolled Pdts Co .... D 773 523-5757
  Chicago (G-4115)
Chicagoland Metal Fabricators .... G 847 260-5320
  Franklin Park (G-9906)
Circle Metal Specialties Inc .... E 708 597-1700
  Alsip (G-432)
CJ Drilling Inc .... D 847 669-8000
  Dundee (G-8126)
Clarkwestern Dietrich Building .... E 815 561-2360
  Rochelle (G-17135)
Cokel Dj Welding Bay & Muffler .... G 309 385-4567
  Princeville (G-16825)
Comet Fabricating & Welding Co .... E 815 229-0468
  Rockford (G-17354)
Commercial Fabricators Inc .... E 708 594-1199
  Bridgeview (G-2337)
Commercial Metals Company .... G 815 928-9600
  Kankakee (G-11961)
Conley Steel Inc .... E 630 393-1193
  Warrenville (G-20233)

Employee Codes: A=Over 500 employees, B=251-500
C=101-250, D=51-100, E=20-50, F=10-19, G=3-9

◆ **Cooper B-Line Inc** ....A.... 618 654-2184
Highland *(G-11210)*
Corsetti Structural Steel Inc ....E.... 815 726-0186
Joliet *(G-11848)*
Covey Machine Inc ....F.... 773 650-1530
Chicago *(G-4250)*
Creative Iron ....G.... 217 267-7797
Westville *(G-20779)*
Crest Metal Craft Inc ....G.... 773 978-0950
Chicago *(G-4270)*
Custom Fabricators LLC ....F.... 773 814-2757
Streamwood *(G-19570)*
Custom Fbrication Coatings Inc ....D.... 618 452-9540
Granite City *(G-10701)*
Custom Feeder Co of Rockford ....E.... 815 654-2444
Loves Park *(G-13201)*
Cyclops Welding Co ....G.... 815 223-0685
La Salle *(G-12109)*
D & M Welding Inc ....G.... 708 233-6080
Bridgeview *(G-2339)*
D L Austin Steel Supply Corp ....G.... 618 345-7200
Collinsville *(G-6957)*
D5 Design Met Fabrication LLC ....G.... 773 770-4705
Chicago *(G-4303)*
David Architectural Metals Inc ....E.... 773 376-3200
Chicago *(G-4323)*
Dayton Superior Corporation ....D.... 815 936-3300
Kankakee *(G-11963)*
Delta Erectors Inc ....F.... 708 267-9721
Villa Park *(G-20144)*
▲ **Delta Structures Inc** ....F.... 630 694-8700
Lombard *(G-13064)*
▲ **Dicke Tool Company** ....D.... 630 969-0050
Downers Grove *(G-7988)*
Dietrich Industries Inc ....E.... 815 207-0110
Joliet *(G-11855)*
▲ **DSI Spaceframes Inc** ....E.... 630 607-0045
Addison *(G-99)*
◆ **E B Inc** ....F.... 815 758-6646
De Kalb *(G-7429)*
▲ **East Moline Sheet Metal Co** ....G.... 309 755-1422
Moline *(G-14142)*
EC Harms Met Fabricators Inc ....F.... 309 385-2132
Princeville *(G-16826)*
Ed Stan Fabricating Co ....G.... 708 863-7668
Chicago *(G-4449)*
▲ **Ekstrom Carlson Fabg Co Inc** ....G.... 815 226-1511
Rockford *(G-17392)*
Emco Metals LLC ....F.... 312 925-1553
Cicero *(G-6846)*
Engineered Iron Works Inc ....F.... 773 887-5701
Chicago *(G-4509)*
▲ **Ermak Usa Inc** ....F.... 847 640-7765
Des Plaines *(G-7760)*
Esi Steel & Fabrication ....F.... 618 548-3017
Salem *(G-18338)*
European Ornamental Iron Works ....G.... 630 705-9300
Addison *(G-117)*
▲ **Ex-Cell Kaiser LLC** ....E.... 847 451-0451
Franklin Park *(G-9941)*
Exo Fabrication Inc ....G.... 630 501-1136
Addison *(G-118)*
F Kreutzer & Co ....G.... 773 826-5767
Chicago *(G-4550)*
F Vogelmann and Company ....F.... 815 469-2285
Frankfort *(G-9793)*
Fabco Enterprises Inc ....G.... 708 333-4644
Harvey *(G-11084)*
Fabricated Metal Systems Inc ....G.... 815 886-6200
Romeoville *(G-17821)*
Fabricating & Welding Corp ....E.... 773 928-2050
Chicago *(G-4555)*
Fanmar Inc ....E.... 847 621-2010
Elk Grove Village *(G-8995)*
Fbs Group Inc ....F.... 773 229-8675
Chicago *(G-4569)*
Fehring Ornamental Iron Works ....G.... 217 483-6727
Rochester *(G-17166)*
First Stage Fabrication Inc ....G.... 618 282-8320
Red Bud *(G-16994)*
▲ **Flex-Weld Inc** ....D.... 815 334-3662
Woodstock *(G-21387)*
Floyd Steel Erectors Inc ....F.... 630 238-8383
Wood Dale *(G-21187)*
Funk Linko Group Inc ....G.... 708 757-7421
Monee *(G-14200)*
Fusion Fabrication ....G.... 815 214-9148
Lockport *(G-12994)*
▼ **G & F Manufacturing Co Inc** ....E.... 708 424-4170
Oak Lawn *(G-15716)*
G & M Fabricating Inc ....G.... 815 282-1744
Roscoe *(G-17907)*
Gallon Industries Inc ....E.... 630 628-1020
Addison *(G-134)*
Garbe Iron Works Inc ....E.... 630 897-5100
Aurora *(G-1102)*
Gemini Steel Inc ....G.... 815 472-4462
Momence *(G-14185)*
Gerdau Ameristeel US Inc ....E.... 815 547-0400
Belvidere *(G-1673)*
Gma Inc ....G.... 630 595-1255
Bensenville *(G-1812)*
Go To Steel Inc ....G.... 773 814-3017
Norridge *(G-15235)*
Gooder-Henrichsen Company Inc ....D.... 708 757-5030
Chicago Heights *(G-6748)*
Great Lakes Precision Tube Inc ....E.... 630 859-8940
Aurora *(G-1105)*
Great Lakes Stair & Steel Inc ....G.... 708 430-2323
Chicago Ridge *(G-6796)*
Greg Lambert Construction ....E.... 815 468-7361
Bourbonnais *(G-2261)*
Gremp Steel Co ....E.... 708 389-7393
Posen *(G-16795)*
Grimm Metal Fabricators Inc ....E.... 630 792-1710
Lombard *(G-13083)*
Grover Welding Company ....G.... 847 966-3119
Skokie *(G-18961)*
Gsi Group LLC ....C.... 217 463-1612
Paris *(G-16230)*
H & S Mechanical Inc ....D.... 309 696-7066
Peoria *(G-16448)*
H3 Group LLC ....F.... 309 222-6027
Peoria *(G-16450)*
Hamilton Fbrcation Stl Sup Inc ....G.... 618 466-0012
Godfrey *(G-10652)*
Harmony Metal Fabrication Inc ....E.... 847 426-8900
Gilberts *(G-10356)*
Heartland Fabrication LLC ....G.... 309 448-2644
Congerville *(G-6999)*
◆ **Holden Industries Inc** ....F.... 847 940-1500
Deerfield *(G-7616)*
Huntley & Associates Inc ....G.... 224 381-8500
Lake Zurich *(G-12420)*
Hyspan Precision Products Inc ....E.... 773 277-0700
South Holland *(G-19223)*
Ideal Fabricators Inc ....F.... 217 999-7017
Mount Olive *(G-14505)*
▲ **Igm Solutions Inc** ....E.... 847 918-1790
Libertyville *(G-12661)*
Industrial Mint Wldg Machining ....D.... 773 376-6526
Chicago *(G-4908)*
▲ **Industrial Steel Cnstr Inc** ....C.... 630 232-7473
Geneva *(G-10280)*
▲ **Integrated Mfg Tech LLC** ....E.... 618 282-8306
Red Bud *(G-16996)*
Ireco LLC ....F.... 630 741-0155
Elmhurst *(G-9380)*
ITW Blding Cmponents Group Inc ....E.... 217 324-0303
Litchfield *(G-12967)*
J & G Fabricating Inc ....G.... 708 385-9147
Blue Island *(G-2126)*
J B Metal Works Inc ....G.... 847 824-4253
Des Plaines *(G-7790)*
J H Botts LLC ....E.... 815 726-5885
Joliet *(G-11883)*
J&A Mtchell Stl Fbricators Inc ....G.... 815 939-2144
Kankakee *(G-11981)*
Jalor Company ....G.... 847 202-1172
Elgin *(G-8631)*
▲ **James Walker Mfg Co** ....E.... 708 754-4020
Glenwood *(G-10641)*
Jameson Steel Fabrication Inc ....G.... 217 354-2205
Oakwood *(G-15820)*
Jarvis Welding Co ....G.... 309 647-0033
Canton *(G-2827)*
Jay RS Steel & Welding Inc ....G.... 847 949-9353
Mundelein *(G-14703)*
JB & S Machining ....G.... 815 258-4007
Bourbonnais *(G-2263)*
Jet Industries Inc ....E.... 773 586-8900
Chicago *(G-5024)*
Jhelsa Metal Polsg Fabrication ....G.... 773 385-6628
Chicago *(G-5029)*
K & K Iron Works LLC ....G.... 773 619-6899
Chicago *(G-5064)*
K & K Iron Works LLC ....D.... 708 924-0000
Mc Cook *(G-13693)*
K Three Welding Service Inc ....G.... 708 563-2911
Chicago *(G-5067)*
K-Met Industries Inc ....F.... 708 534-3300
Monee *(G-14203)*
Kd Steel Incorporated ....G.... 630 201-1619
Westmont *(G-20752)*
Kelco Construction Inc ....G.... 773 853-2974
Chicago *(G-5089)*
Kemper Industries ....G.... 217 826-5712
Marshall *(G-13573)*
Keystone Bar Products Inc ....E.... 708 753-1200
Chicago Heights *(G-6756)*
Kim Gough ....G.... 309 734-3511
Monmouth *(G-14221)*
King Metal Co ....G.... 708 388-3845
Alsip *(G-464)*
Kingery Steel Fabricators Inc ....E.... 708 474-6665
Lansing *(G-12501)*
Kmk Metal Fabricators Inc ....E.... 618 224-2000
Trenton *(G-19903)*
Knoll Steel Inc ....F.... 815 675-9400
Spring Grove *(G-19280)*
Kroh-Wagner Inc ....E.... 773 252-2031
Chicago *(G-5133)*
Ksem Inc ....G.... 618 656-5388
Edwardsville *(G-8367)*
Kso Metalfab Inc ....E.... 630 372-1200
Streamwood *(G-19582)*
Kure Steel Inc ....G.... 815 836-8027
Lockport *(G-13004)*
Laser Plus Technologies LLC ....G.... 847 787-9017
Elk Grove Village *(G-9086)*
Laystrom Manufacturing Co ....D.... 773 342-4800
Chicago *(G-5186)*
Leroys Welding & Fabg Inc ....F.... 847 215-6151
Wheeling *(G-20931)*
Lesker Company Inc ....E.... 708 343-2277
Bensenville *(G-1843)*
▼ **Liberty Machinery Company** ....F.... 847 276-2761
Lincolnshire *(G-12781)*
Lichtnwald - Johnston Ir Works ....E.... 847 966-1100
Morton Grove *(G-14419)*
Lickenbrock & Sons Inc ....G.... 618 632-4977
O Fallon *(G-15578)*
Linear Kinetics Inc ....G.... 630 365-0075
Maple Park *(G-13463)*
▲ **Littell International Inc** ....E.... 630 622-4950
Schaumburg *(G-18610)*
Lizotte Sheet Metal Inc ....G.... 618 656-3066
Edwardsville *(G-8368)*
Lockport Steel Fabricators LLC ....D.... 815 726-6281
Lockport *(G-13008)*
Loeffel Steel Products Inc ....E.... 847 382-6770
Lake Barrington *(G-12158)*
LPI Worldwide Inc ....G.... 773 826-8600
Chicago *(G-5270)*
Mace Iron Works Inc ....E.... 708 479-2456
Frankfort *(G-9815)*
Mapes & Sprowl LLC ....G.... 847 364-0055
Elk Grove Village *(G-9109)*
Marco Lighting Components Inc ....F.... 312 829-6900
Chicago *(G-5330)*
Marqutte Stl Sup Fbrcation Inc ....F.... 815 433-0178
Ottawa *(G-16060)*
Martin Steel Fabrication Inc ....G.... 618 410-7066
Mascoutah *(G-13602)*
▲ **Matcor Mtal Fbrication Ill Inc** ....E.... 309 263-1707
Morton *(G-14365)*
Max Fire Training Inc ....F.... 618 210-2079
Godfrey *(G-10656)*
Mc Kinney Steel & Sales Inc ....E.... 847 746-3344
Zion *(G-21520)*
McCloud Mtlwrks Indus Svcs Inc ....G.... 618 713-2318
Chester *(G-3459)*
McLaughlin Body Co ....C.... 309 736-6105
East Moline *(G-8234)*
▲ **McLaughlin Body Co** ....D.... 309 762-7755
Moline *(G-14159)*
Mdt Customs LLC ....G.... 573 316-5995
Mc Clure *(G-13687)*
Mechanical Indus Stl Svcs Inc ....E.... 815 521-1725
Channahon *(G-3389)*
Meno Stone Co Inc ....E.... 630 257-9220
Lemont *(G-12571)*
Metal Tech Inc ....E.... 630 529-7400
Roselle *(G-17969)*
Metals & Metals LLC ....G.... 630 866-4200
Bolingbrook *(G-2213)*
Metaltek Fabricating Inc ....F.... 708 534-9102
University Park *(G-19960)*
▲ **Metamora Industries LLC** ....E.... 309 367-2368
Metamora *(G-13964)*

▲ Metraflex Company D 312 738-3800
Chicago (G-5411)
Michelmann Steel Cnstr Co E 217 222-0555
Quincy (G-16912)
Midwest Metals Inc G 618 295-3444
Marissa (G-13543)
Miller Fabrication LLC D 307 358-4777
Chicago (G-5458)
Mj Snyder Ironworks Inc G 217 826-6440
Marshall (G-13575)
Mobile Mini Inc E 708 297-2004
Calumet Park (G-2799)
Mold Shields Inc G 708 983-5931
Oak Forest (G-15686)
Moline Welding Inc F 309 756-0643
Milan (G-14018)
Montefusco Hvac Inc G 309 691-7400
Peoria (G-16479)
Morey Industries Inc C 708 343-3220
Broadview (G-2454)
Morris Construction Inc E 618 544-8504
Robinson (G-17120)
▲ Morton Industries LLC A 309 263-2590
Morton (G-14371)
Mutual Svcs Highland Pk Inc F 847 432-3815
Highland Park (G-11287)
◆ National Cycle Inc C 708 343-0400
Maywood (G-13674)
National Machine Repair Inc F 708 672-7711
Crete (G-7142)
Neiweem Industries Inc G 847 487-1239
Oakwood Hills (G-15821)
New Metal Fabrication Corp E 618 532-9000
Centralia (G-3241)
Newman Welding & Machine Shop G 618 435-5591
Benton (G-1934)
Next Level Metal G 636 627-9497
Baldwin (G-1186)
Nicks Metal Fabg & Sons F 708 485-1170
Brookfield (G-2489)
Nnm Manufacturing LLC E 815 436-9201
Plainfield (G-16696)
North Chicago Iron Works Inc E 847 689-2000
North Chicago (G-15317)
Nowfab G 815 675-2916
Spring Grove (G-19290)
OBrien Architectural Mtls Inc F 773 868-1065
Chicago (G-5650)
Okaw Truss Inc B 217 543-3371
Arthur (G-873)
Old Style Iron Works Inc G 773 265-5787
Chicago (G-5670)
Olympic Steel Inc E 847 584-4000
Schaumburg (G-18658)
OMalley Welding and Fabg G 630 553-1604
Yorkville (G-21495)
▲ Onkens Incorporated F 309 562-7477
Easton (G-8331)
Oostman Fabricating & Wldg Inc F 630 241-1315
Westmont (G-20763)
▲ Orsolinis Welding & Fabg F 773 722-9855
Chicago (G-5705)
Paco Corporation F 708 430-2424
Bridgeview (G-2371)
▲ Pallet Repair Systems Inc F 217 291-0009
Jacksonville (G-11780)
Parkway Metal Products Inc D 847 789-4000
Des Plaines (G-7818)
Patrick Holdings Inc F 815 874-5300
Rockford (G-17549)
Paul Wever Construction Eqp Co F 309 965-2005
Goodfield (G-10676)
Performance Industries Inc E 972 393-6881
Carpentersville (G-3111)
Phoenix Fabrication & Sup Inc G 708 754-5901
Peotone (G-16556)
Phoenix Welding Co Inc F 630 616-1700
Franklin Park (G-10016)
Pittsfield Mch Tl & Wldg Co G 217 656-4000
Payson (G-16317)
Pools Welding Inc G 309 787-2083
Milan (G-14020)
▲ Premier Fabrication LLC C 309 448-2338
Congerville (G-7000)
Pro-Fab Inc E 309 263-8454
Morton (G-14379)
Pro-Fab Metals Inc G 618 283-2986
Vandalia (G-20020)
Pro-Tech Metal Specialties Inc E 630 279-7094
Elmhurst (G-9412)
Pro-Tran Inc G 217 348-9353
Charleston (G-3410)
Professional Metal Works LLC F 618 539-2214
Freeburg (G-10092)
R & B Metal Products Inc E 815 338-1890
Woodstock (G-21427)
R C Industrial Inc G 309 230-4631
Milan (G-14023)
Rail Exchange Inc E 708 757-3317
Chicago Heights (G-6767)
Reber Welding Service G 217 774-3441
Shelbyville (G-18885)
Rex Worldwide Ltd G 630 384-9361
Naperville (G-14909)
▲ Ri-Del Mfg Inc D 312 829-8720
Chicago (G-6024)
Ricar Industries Inc G 847 914-9083
Northbrook (G-15473)
▼ Rohn Products LLC D 309 697-4400
Peoria (G-16515)
Rohn Products LLC E 309 566-3000
Peoria (G-16516)
▼ Romero Steel Company Inc E 708 216-0001
Melrose Park (G-13910)
Roth Metal Fabricators Corp G 708 371-8300
Alsip (G-505)
Rrb Fabrication Inc F 815 977-5603
Loves Park (G-13261)
S & S Welding & Fabrication G 847 742-7344
Elgin (G-8722)
Selvaggio Orna & Strl Stl Inc E 217 528-4077
Springfield (G-19441)
◆ Senior Operations LLC B 630 372-3500
Bartlett (G-1311)
Shamrock Manufacturing Co Inc G 708 331-7776
South Holland (G-19244)
Sheas Iron Works Inc E 847 356-2922
Lake Villa (G-12367)
Sheet Metal Supply Ltd G 847 478-8500
Grayslake (G-10799)
Shew Brothers Inc G 618 997-4414
Marion (G-13534)
Silver Machine Shop Inc G 217 359-5717
Champaign (G-3348)
Simion Fabrication Inc G 618 724-7331
Christopher (G-6826)
Sivco Welding Company G 309 944-5171
Geneseo (G-10247)
▼ Skyjack Equipment Inc E 630 797-3299
Saint Charles (G-18270)
Smf Inc C 309 432-2586
Minonk (G-14055)
Smith Brothers Fabricating G 618 498-5612
Jerseyville (G-11796)
SNC Solutions Inc E 217 784-5212
Gibson City (G-10344)
Solid Metal Group Inc G 708 757-7421
Chicago Heights (G-6774)
South Subn Wldg & Fabg Co Inc G 708 385-7160
Posen (G-16801)
Spectracrafts Ltd G 847 824-4117
Lombard (G-13133)
Spg International LLC F 815 233-0022
Freeport (G-10143)
Spider Company Inc D 815 961-8200
Rockford (G-17640)
Stairs and Rails Inc G 708 216-0078
Melrose Park (G-13916)
Standard Sheet Metal Works Inc E 309 633-2300
Peoria (G-16530)
Steel Construction Svcs Inc G 815 678-7509
Richmond (G-17023)
Steel Management Inc G 630 397-5083
Geneva (G-10308)
Steel Span Inc F 815 943-9071
Harvard (G-11068)
Steelfab Inc E 815 935-6540
Kankakee (G-12008)
Stevenson Fabrication Svcs Inc G 815 468-7941
Manteno (G-13458)
Strat-O-Span Buildings Inc G 618 526-4566
Breese (G-2308)
Structural Design Corp G 847 816-3816
Libertyville (G-12710)
Sturdee Metal Products Inc G 773 523-3074
New Lenox (G-15059)
Sturdi Iron Inc G 815 464-1173
Frankfort (G-9840)
Summit Metal Products Inc G 630 879-7008
Batavia (G-1421)
▲ Sundstrom Pressed Steel Co E 773 721-2237
Chicago (G-6273)
Superior Joining Tech Inc E 815 282-7581
Machesney Park (G-13376)
Superior Metalcraft Inc F 708 418-8940
Lansing (G-12520)
Sycamore Welding & Fabg Co G 815 784-2557
Genoa (G-10325)
Taylor Off Road Racing G 815 544-4500
Belvidere (G-1703)
Testa Steel Constructors Inc F 815 729-4777
Channahon (G-3395)
Tgm Fabricating Inc G 708 533-0857
Chicago Heights (G-6780)
Thybar Corporation E 630 543-5300
Addison (G-309)
Tinsley Steel Inc G 618 656-5231
Edwardsville (G-8378)
Titan Industries Inc G 309 440-1010
Deer Creek (G-7576)
▼ Tower Works Inc F 630 557-2221
Maple Park (G-13467)
Transco Inc C 419 562-1031
Chicago (G-6408)
Tri-Cunty Wldg Fabrication LLC E 217 543-3304
Arthur (G-881)
Trifab Inc G 847 838-2083
Antioch (G-640)
Triton Industries Inc C 773 384-3700
Chicago (G-6430)
Ultra Stamping & Assembly Inc E 815 874-9888
Rockford (G-17670)
▲ Unistrut International Corp C 800 882-5543
Harvey (G-11099)
Unistrut International Corp D 630 773-3460
Addison (G-323)
United Industries Illinois Ltd G 847 526-9485
Wauconda (G-20400)
United Steel Perforating/ARC E 630 942-7300
Glendale Heights (G-10513)
◆ United Tactical Systems LLC E 260 478-2500
Lake Forest (G-12320)
US Fabg & Mine Svcs Inc G 618 983-7850
Johnston City (G-11815)
V A Robinson Ltd G 773 205-4364
Chicago (G-6513)
Valmont Industries Inc D 773 625-0354
Franklin Park (G-10073)
Van Pelt Corporation E 313 365-3600
East Moline (G-8246)
Vent Products Co Inc E 773 521-1900
Chicago (G-6532)
Veritas Steel LLC C 630 423-8708
Lisle (G-12956)
▲ Voges Inc D 618 233-2760
Belleville (G-1608)
Walnut Custom Homes Inc E 815 379-2151
Walnut (G-20221)
Walters Metal Fabrication Inc D 618 931-5551
Granite City (G-10749)
Waukegan Steel LLC E 847 662-2810
Waukegan (G-20516)
WEb Production & Fabg Inc F 312 733-6800
Chicago (G-6595)
Wehrli Custom Fabrication F 630 277-8239
Dekalb (G-7711)
Weld-Rite Service Inc E 708 458-6000
Bedford Park (G-1512)
Westmont Metal Mfg LLC F 708 343-0214
Broadview (G-2474)
Wherry Machine & Welding Inc G 309 828-5423
Bloomington (G-2107)
◆ Whiting Corporation C 800 861-5744
Monee (G-14212)
Willow Farm Products Inc G 630 430-7491
Lemont (G-12595)
Wilmouth Machine Works Inc G 618 372-3189
Brighton (G-2405)
Wrt Inc G 847 922-2235
South Elgin (G-19183)
Wsw Industrial Maintenance F 773 721-0675
Chicago (G-6689)
Youngberg Industries Inc D 815 544-2177
Belvidere (G-1713)

3442 Metal Doors, Sash, Frames, Molding & Trim

555 International Inc E 773 847-1400
Chicago (G-3474)

Employee Codes: A=Over 500 employees, B=251-500
C=101-250, D=51-100, E=20-50, F=10-19, G=3-9
2020 Harris Illinois
Industrial Directory
925

A-Ok Inc ... E ... 815 943-7431
Harvard *(G-11039)*
▲ Advantage Manufacturing Inc ... F ... 773 626-2200
Chicago *(G-3569)*
Alliance Door and Hardware LLC ... G ... 630 451-7070
Hillside *(G-11326)*
Allied Garage Door Inc ... E ... 630 279-0795
Addison *(G-27)*
Allmetal Inc ... E ... 630 766-8500
Bensenville *(G-1736)*
Allmetal Inc ... F ... 630 766-1407
Bensenville *(G-1737)*
Allmetal Inc ... E ... 630 350-2524
Wood Dale *(G-21158)*
▲ Aluminite of Paris ... G ... 217 463-2233
Paris *(G-16224)*
Alvin F Lambright ... G ... 618 835-2050
Xenia *(G-21465)*
Anchor Welding & Fabrication ... G ... 815 937-1640
Aroma Park *(G-839)*
Assa Abloy Entrance Systems US ... F ... 847 228-5600
Elk Grove Village *(G-8843)*
Assa Abloy Pry ... G ... 630 682-8800
Carol Stream *(G-2942)*
Barneys Aluminum Specialties ... G ... 815 723-5341
Joliet *(G-11828)*
Boom Company Inc ... G ... 847 459-6199
Wheeling *(G-20863)*
Builders Chicago Corporation ... D ... 224 654-2122
Rosemont *(G-18001)*
C B M Plastics Inc ... F ... 217 543-3870
Arthur *(G-843)*
◆ Centor North America Inc ... E ... 630 957-1000
Aurora *(G-936)*
Charles Sheridan and Sons ... G ... 847 903-7209
Evanston *(G-9502)*
◆ CHi Doors Holdings Inc ... G ... 217 543-2135
Arthur *(G-846)*
Chicago Iron Works Corporation ... F ... 312 829-1062
Chicago *(G-4108)*
Chicagone Developers Inc ... E ... 773 783-2105
Chicago *(G-4137)*
City Screen Inc ... G ... 773 588-5642
Chicago *(G-4161)*
Climate Guard Design ... G ... 773 873-0000
Chicago *(G-4178)*
Continental Window South Inc ... F ... 773 767-1300
Chicago *(G-4232)*
Custom Aluminum Products Inc ... D ... 847 717-5000
Genoa *(G-10316)*
▲ Custom Aluminum Products Inc ... B ... 847 717-5000
South Elgin *(G-19141)*
Defender Steel Door & Window ... E ... 708 780-7320
Cicero *(G-6839)*
▲ Del Great Frame Up Systems Inc ... E ... 847 808-1955
Franklin Park *(G-9929)*
Del Storm Products Inc ... F ... 217 446-3377
Danville *(G-7330)*
Dorbin Metal Strip Mfg Co ... F ... 708 656-2333
Cicero *(G-6842)*
Dormakaba USA Inc ... D ... 847 295-2700
Lake Bluff *(G-12178)*
Efco Corporation ... E ... 630 378-4720
Bolingbrook *(G-2171)*
▲ Entrematic HPD North Amer Inc ... D ... 847 562-4910
Mundelein *(G-14687)*
Erect-A-Tube Inc ... E ... 815 943-4091
Harvard *(G-11054)*
Eric Harr ... E ... 618 538-7889
East Carondelet *(G-8172)*
Fix It Fast Ltd ... F ... 708 401-8320
Midlothian *(G-13991)*
G P Concrete & Iron Works ... G ... 815 842-2270
Pontiac *(G-16770)*
Group Industries Inc ... E ... 708 877-6200
Thornton *(G-19788)*
▲ Hormann LLC ... C ... 630 859-3000
Montgomery *(G-14248)*
Huntley & Associates Inc ... G ... 224 381-8500
Lake Zurich *(G-12420)*
Imageworks Manufacturing Inc ... E ... 708 503-1122
Park Forest *(G-16255)*
Insulators Supply Inc ... G ... 847 394-2836
Prospect Heights *(G-16843)*
Kawneer Company Inc ... D ... 815 224-2708
Peru *(G-16579)*
Kramer Window Co ... G ... 708 343-4780
Maywood *(G-13671)*
Kroh-Wagner Inc ... E ... 773 252-2031
Chicago *(G-5133)*
La Force Inc ... G ... 630 325-1950
Willowbrook *(G-21048)*
La Force Inc ... E ... 847 415-5107
Vernon Hills *(G-20071)*
Lang Exterior Inc ... D ... 773 737-4500
Chicago *(G-5175)*
Logan Square Aluminum Sup Inc ... D ... 847 985-1700
Schaumburg *(G-18611)*
Logan Square Aluminum Sup Inc ... F ... 847 676-4767
Lincolnwood *(G-12828)*
Logan Square Aluminum Sup Inc ... C ... 773 278-3600
Chicago *(G-5249)*
◆ Mechanics Planing Mill Inc ... E ... 618 288-3000
Glen Carbon *(G-10390)*
Metal Products Sales Corp ... G ... 708 301-6844
Lockport *(G-13013)*
Michelmann Steel Cnstr Co ... E ... 217 222-0555
Quincy *(G-16912)*
▲ Middletons Mouldings Inc ... D ... 517 278-6610
Schaumburg *(G-18629)*
Midway Industries Inc ... C ... 708 594-2600
Chicago *(G-5438)*
Midwest Screens LLC ... G ... 847 557-5015
Antioch *(G-626)*
Mold Seekers ... G ... 847 650-8025
Grayslake *(G-10791)*
Moldtronics Inc ... E ... 630 968-7000
Downers Grove *(G-8058)*
Mueller Door Company ... E ... 815 385-8550
Wauconda *(G-20379)*
Neisewander Enterprises Inc ... A ... 815 288-1431
Dixon *(G-7904)*
Nelson Sash Systems Inc ... G ... 708 385-5815
Alsip *(G-483)*
Overhead Door Corporation ... G ... 630 775-9118
Itasca *(G-11715)*
Power-Sonic Corporation ... G ... 309 752-7750
East Moline *(G-8236)*
Protective Door Industries ... G ... 773 375-0300
Harvey *(G-11094)*
Qh Inc ... E ... 708 534-7801
University Park *(G-19965)*
◆ Qualitas Manufacturing Inc ... D ... 630 529-7111
Itasca *(G-11723)*
Quanex Screens LLC ... G ... 217 463-2233
Paris *(G-16242)*
◆ Raynor Mfg Co ... A ... 815 288-1431
Dixon *(G-7908)*
▲ River City Millwork Inc ... D ... 800 892-9297
Rockford *(G-17573)*
Ryans Glass & Metal Inc ... G ... 708 430-7790
Bridgeview *(G-2385)*
Salem Building Materials Inc ... G ... 618 548-3221
Salem *(G-18357)*
Security Holdings LLC ... G ... 309 856-6000
Kewanee *(G-12041)*
Security Metal Products Corp ... G ... 630 965-6355
Hampshire *(G-10987)*
Sheraton Road Lumber ... F ... 309 691-0858
Peoria *(G-16523)*
Shoreline Glass Co Inc ... E ... 312 829-9500
Hillside *(G-11356)*
Shutter Bag USA ... G ... 618 967-6247
Carbondale *(G-2858)*
Shutterbooth Specl Evnts By La ... G ... 618 973-1894
Granite City *(G-10738)*
Shutterview ... G ... 618 244-0656
Mount Vernon *(G-14639)*
Silver Line Building Pdts LLC ... B ... 708 474-9100
Lansing *(G-12516)*
▼ Steel-Guard Safety Corp ... G ... 708 589-4588
South Holland *(G-19246)*
Steele & Loeber Lumber ... G ... 708 544-8383
Bellwood *(G-1640)*
Summit Window Co Inc ... G ... 708 594-3200
Summit Argo *(G-19683)*
Supreme Frame & Moulding Co ... F ... 312 930-9056
Chicago *(G-6286)*
▼ Tafco Corporation ... E ... 847 678-8425
Melrose Park *(G-13921)*
Tempco Products Co ... D ... 618 544-3175
Robinson *(G-17127)*
Thermal Industries Inc ... E ... 800 237-0560
Wood Dale *(G-21249)*
Tri State Aluminum Products ... F ... 815 877-6081
Loves Park *(G-13277)*
Vent Products Co Inc ... E ... 773 521-1900
Chicago *(G-6532)*
▲ Waukegan Architectural Inc ... G ... 847 746-9077
Zion *(G-21529)*
Westinghouse A Brake Tech Corp ... C ... 847 777-6400
Buffalo Grove *(G-2622)*
YKK AP America Inc ... F ... 630 582-9602
Roselle *(G-17998)*

3443 Fabricated Plate Work

A & A Steel Fabricating Co ... F ... 708 389-4499
Posen *(G-16789)*
Abbey Metal Services Inc ... F ... 773 568-0330
Chicago *(G-3502)*
Ablaze Welding & Fabricating ... G ... 815 965-0046
Rockford *(G-17287)*
▲ Ae2009 Technologies Inc ... E ... 708 331-0025
South Holland *(G-19188)*
Allquip Co Inc ... G ... 309 944-6153
Geneseo *(G-10239)*
Alum-I-Tank Inc ... F ... 800 652-6630
Harvard *(G-11043)*
Alum-I-Tank Inc ... E ... 815 943-6649
Harvard *(G-11044)*
Amag Manufacturing Inc ... G ... 773 667-5184
Chicago *(G-3642)*
Ameralloy Steel Corporation ... E ... 847 967-0600
Morton Grove *(G-14390)*
American Chute Systems Inc ... G ... 815 723-7632
Joliet *(G-11819)*
Ameropan Oil Corp ... F ... 773 847-4400
Chicago *(G-3678)*
Amex Nooter LLC ... F ... 708 429-8300
Tinley Park *(G-19803)*
◆ Amsted Industries Incorporated ... B ... 312 645-1700
Chicago *(G-3685)*
Amsted Industries Incorporated ... F ... 312 645-1700
Chicago *(G-3686)*
Anchor Welding & Fabrication ... G ... 815 937-1640
Aroma Park *(G-839)*
Arthur Custom Tank LLC ... G ... 217 543-4022
Arthur *(G-841)*
AS Fabricating Inc ... G ... 618 242-7438
Mount Vernon *(G-14596)*
Asco LP ... F ... 630 789-2082
Arlington Heights *(G-697)*
Atlas Boiler & Welding Company ... G ... 815 963-3360
Elgin *(G-8517)*
▲ Atlas Tool & Die Works Inc ... D ... 708 442-1661
Lyons *(G-13302)*
Barker Metalcraft Inc ... G ... 773 588-9300
Chicago *(G-3833)*
Beaver Creek Enterprises Inc ... F ... 815 723-9455
Joliet *(G-11829)*
Befco Manufacturing Co Inc ... F ... 708 424-4170
Oak Lawn *(G-15702)*
Bennu Group Inc ... F ... 708 331-0025
South Holland *(G-19200)*
BR Concepts International Inc ... G ... 847 674-9481
Skokie *(G-18932)*
BR Machine Inc ... F ... 815 434-0427
Ottawa *(G-16042)*
Brenner Tank Services LLC ... G ... 773 468-6390
Chicago *(G-3950)*
Bruder Tank Inc ... E ... 217 292-9058
Sullivan *(G-19662)*
▲ Burns Machine Company ... E ... 815 434-1660
Ottawa *(G-16045)*
C J Holdings Inc ... G ... 309 274-3141
Chillicothe *(G-6815)*
▲ Cablofil Inc ... B ... 618 566-3230
Mascoutah *(G-13595)*
Cadillac Tank Met Fbrctors Inc ... E ... 630 543-2600
Addison *(G-62)*
Captain Hook Inc ... G ... 309 565-7676
Hanna City *(G-10991)*
CB&i LLC ... G ... 815 936-5440
Bourbonnais *(G-2258)*
CB&i Tyler LLC ... G ... 281 774-2200
Plainfield *(G-16649)*
Central Manufacturing Company ... G ... 309 387-6591
East Peoria *(G-8259)*
Certified Tank & Mfg LLC ... E ... 217 525-1433
Springfield *(G-19347)*
Chadwick Manufacturing Ltd ... G ... 815 684-5152
Chadwick *(G-3257)*
Cheap Dumpster For Rent ... G ... 773 770-4334
Chicago *(G-4080)*
Chicago Tank Lining Sales ... G ... 847 328-0500
Evanston *(G-9504)*
Colfax Welding & Fabricating ... G ... 847 359-4433
Palatine *(G-16101)*
Columbia Chutes LLC ... G ... 847 520-5989
Rockdale *(G-17257)*

▲ **Component Parts Company**.......G....... 815 477-2323
Crystal Lake *(G-7184)*
Contech Engnered Solutions LLC.......E....... 217 529-5461
Springfield *(G-19354)*
Contech Engnered Solutions LLC.......G....... 630 573-1110
Oak Brook *(G-15613)*
◆ **Cooper B-Line Inc**.......A....... 618 654-2184
Highland *(G-11210)*
Corrugated Converting Eqp.......F....... 618 532-2138
Centralia *(G-3227)*
Cyclops Welding Co.......G....... 815 223-0685
La Salle *(G-12109)*
D & D Manufacturing.......G....... 815 339-9100
Hennepin *(G-11157)*
D & K Tanks.......G....... 618 553-3186
Robinson *(G-17110)*
D & P Construction Co Inc.......E....... 773 714-9330
Chicago *(G-4299)*
D C Cooper Corporation.......G....... 309 924-1941
Stronghurst *(G-19633)*
Debcor Inc.......G....... 708 333-2191
South Holland *(G-19207)*
Diesel Radiator Co.......D....... 708 865-7299
Melrose Park *(G-13852)*
Dip Seal Plastics Inc.......G....... 815 398-3533
Rockford *(G-17379)*
◆ **Dometic Corporation**.......A....... 847 447-7190
Rosemont *(G-18019)*
Dumpster Dave LLC.......G....... 618 475-3835
Lenzburg *(G-12610)*
E H Baare Corporation.......C....... 618 546-1575
Robinson *(G-17114)*
Eastland Fabrication LLC.......G....... 815 493-8399
Lanark *(G-12479)*
◆ **Eclipse Inc**.......D....... 815 877-3031
Rockford *(G-17388)*
Ed Stan Fabricating Co.......G....... 708 863-7668
Chicago *(G-4449)*
Edmik Inc.......E....... 847 263-0460
Gurnee *(G-10874)*
◆ **Eirich Machines Inc**.......D....... 847 336-2444
Gurnee *(G-10875)*
▲ **Ekstrom Carlson Fabg Co Inc**.......G....... 815 226-1511
Rockford *(G-17392)*
Elite Fabrication Inc.......G....... 773 274-4474
Chicago *(G-4486)*
Elkay Manufacturing Company.......B....... 815 273-7001
Savanna *(G-18404)*
Energy Solutions Inc.......G....... 618 465-5404
Alton *(G-556)*
Erq Systems Inc.......E....... 815 469-1072
Chicago *(G-4527)*
Evapco Inc.......E....... 410 756-2600
Chicago *(G-4538)*
Evapco Inc.......C....... 217 923-3431
Greenup *(G-10820)*
Fabricated Products Co Inc.......F....... 630 898-6460
Aurora *(G-959)*
▲ **Fabtek Aero Ltd**.......F....... 630 552-3622
Sandwich *(G-18369)*
Faspro Technologies Inc.......C....... 847 392-9500
Arlington Heights *(G-734)*
G & M Fabricating Inc.......G....... 815 282-1744
Roscoe *(G-17907)*
▲ **G E Mathis Company**.......D....... 773 586-3800
Chicago *(G-4649)*
▲ **G K Enterprises Inc**.......G....... 708 587-2150
Monee *(G-14201)*
Gateway Fabricators Inc.......G....... 618 271-5700
East Saint Louis *(G-8310)*
▼ **Gpe Controls Inc**.......F....... 708 236-6000
Hillside *(G-11340)*
▼ **H A Phillips & Co**.......E....... 630 377-0050
Dekalb *(G-7683)*
▲ **Hoerbiger-Origa Corporation**.......D....... 800 283-1377
Glendale Heights *(G-10456)*
▲ **Howe Corporation**.......E....... 773 235-0200
Chicago *(G-4851)*
Hudson Boiler & Tank Company.......F....... 312 666-4780
Lockport *(G-13001)*
Ideal Fabricators Inc.......F....... 217 999-7017
Mount Olive *(G-14505)*
▼ **Ifh Group Inc**.......D....... 800 435-7003
Rock Falls *(G-17187)*
Ifh Group Inc.......G....... 815 380-2367
Galt *(G-10225)*
Illinois Oil Marketing Eqp Inc.......E....... 309 347-1819
Pekin *(G-16340)*
Illinois Oil Marketing Eqp Inc.......F....... 217 935-5107
Clinton *(G-6924)*

Illinois Rack Enterprises Inc.......E....... 815 385-5750
Lakemoor *(G-12472)*
Illinois Tool Works Inc.......C....... 708 325-2300
Bridgeview *(G-2356)*
Imbert Construction Inds Inc.......G....... 847 588-3170
Niles *(G-15132)*
Imperial Steel Tank.......G....... 773 779-4284
Chicago *(G-4900)*
ITW Blding Cmponents Group Inc.......E....... 217 324-0303
Litchfield *(G-12967)*
J & G Fabricating Inc.......G....... 708 385-9147
Blue Island *(G-2126)*
J B Metal Works Inc.......G....... 847 824-4253
Des Plaines *(G-7790)*
J H Botts LLC.......E....... 815 726-5885
Joliet *(G-11883)*
Jet Rack Corp.......E....... 773 586-2150
Chicago *(G-5025)*
Jiffy Metal Products Inc.......G....... 773 626-8090
Chicago *(G-5030)*
JM Industries LLC.......E....... 708 849-4700
Riverdale *(G-17072)*
Jodi Maurer.......G....... 847 961-5347
Lake In The Hills *(G-12337)*
JT Cullen Co Inc.......D....... 815 589-2412
Fulton *(G-10154)*
Kohnens Concrete Products Inc.......E....... 618 277-2120
Germantown *(G-10330)*
Lake Process Systems Inc.......E....... 847 381-7663
Lake Barrington *(G-12157)*
Lawndale Forging & Tool Works.......G....... 773 277-2800
Chicago *(G-5183)*
Lewis Process Systems Inc.......F....... 630 510-8200
Carol Stream *(G-3018)*
Lizotte Sheet Metal Inc.......G....... 618 656-3066
Edwardsville *(G-8368)*
◆ **Lmt Inc**.......F....... 217 568-8265
Galva *(G-10235)*
Luebbers Welding & Mfg Inc.......F....... 618 594-2489
Carlyle *(G-2893)*
M4 Steel LLC.......G....... 309 222-6027
Washington *(G-20274)*
Maccarb Inc.......G....... 877 427-2499
Elgin *(G-8645)*
Mach Mechanical Group LLC.......G....... 630 674-6224
Naperville *(G-14978)*
Madison Inds Holdings LLC.......G....... 312 277-0156
Chicago *(G-5313)*
Manchester Tank & Equipment Co.......E....... 217 224-7600
Quincy *(G-16909)*
Matrix Service Inc.......F....... 618 466-4862
Alton *(G-566)*
Melters and More.......G....... 815 419-2043
Chenoa *(G-3433)*
Mendota Welding & Mfg.......G....... 815 539-6944
Mendota *(G-13949)*
Mfi Industries Inc.......F....... 708 841-0727
Riverdale *(G-17073)*
Mid-State Tank Co Inc.......D....... 217 728-8383
Sullivan *(G-19670)*
Midwest Hydra-Line Inc.......G....... 309 674-6570
Peoria *(G-16475)*
Midwest Hydra-Line Inc.......F....... 309 342-6171
Galesburg *(G-10211)*
Midwest Imperial Steel.......F....... 815 469-1072
Oak Lawn *(G-15728)*
Mj Snyder Ironworks Inc.......G....... 217 826-6440
Marshall *(G-13575)*
Montefusco Hvac Inc.......G....... 309 691-7400
Peoria *(G-16479)*
Mpc Containment Systems LLC.......G....... 773 927-4120
Chicago *(G-5516)*
Mt Carmel Machine Shop Inc.......F....... 618 262-4591
Mount Carmel *(G-14480)*
Murdock Company Inc.......G....... 847 566-0050
Mundelein *(G-14719)*
Nalco Wtr Prtrtment Sltons LLC.......G....... 708 754-2550
Glenwood *(G-10644)*
Newman Welding & Machine Shop.......G....... 618 435-5591
Benton *(G-1934)*
Nuair Filter Company LLC.......G....... 309 888-4331
Normal *(G-15214)*
Paul D Stark & Associates.......F....... 630 964-7111
Downers Grove *(G-8070)*
◆ **Peerless America Incorporated**.......C....... 217 342-0400
Effingham *(G-8418)*
Petro Chem Echer Erhardt LLC.......G....... 773 847-7535
Chicago *(G-5798)*
Pmt Nuclear.......G....... 630 887-7700
Woodridge *(G-21332)*

Pools Welding Inc.......G....... 309 787-2083
Milan *(G-14020)*
Powerone Corp.......G....... 630 443-6500
Saint Charles *(G-18248)*
Precision Ibc Inc.......F....... 708 396-0750
Crestwood *(G-7125)*
▲ **Precision Tank & Equipment Co**.......D....... 217 452-7228
Virginia *(G-20195)*
Precision Tank & Equipment Co.......F....... 217 636-7023
Athens *(G-900)*
Pro-Tran Inc.......G....... 217 348-9353
Charleston *(G-3410)*
▼ **Pryco Inc**.......E....... 217 364-4467
Mechanicsburg *(G-13811)*
▲ **Pureline Treatment Systems LLC**.......C....... 847 963-8465
Bensenville *(G-1877)*
Pw Services LLC.......G....... 217 672-3225
Warrensburg *(G-20227)*
Quest Manufacturing Inc.......C....... 815 675-2442
Spring Grove *(G-19296)*
R & B Metal Products Inc.......E....... 815 338-1890
Woodstock *(G-21427)*
R L Hoener Co.......E....... 217 223-2190
Quincy *(G-16936)*
R-M Industries Inc.......F....... 630 543-3071
Addison *(G-264)*
Rayes Boiler & Welding Ltd.......G....... 847 675-6655
Skokie *(G-19020)*
▲ **Realwheels Corporation**.......E....... 847 662-7722
Gurnee *(G-10923)*
Reino Tool & Manufacturing Co.......F....... 773 588-5800
Chicago *(G-6005)*
▲ **Resist-A-Line Industries Inc**.......G....... 815 650-3177
Joliet *(G-11925)*
Rmb Engineered Products Inc.......G....... 847 382-0100
Barrington *(G-1240)*
Rockford Air Devices Inc.......F....... 815 654-3330
Machesney Park *(G-13370)*
Rode Welding Inc.......E....... 847 439-0910
Elk Grove Village *(G-9219)*
Rome Metal Mfg Inc.......G....... 773 287-1755
Chicago *(G-6057)*
Roney Machine Works Inc.......E....... 618 462-4113
Alton *(G-570)*
Ross and White Company.......F....... 847 516-3900
Cary *(G-3187)*
Rotary Airlock LLC.......E....... 800 883-8955
Sterling *(G-19530)*
Roth Metal Fabricators Corp.......G....... 708 371-8300
Alsip *(G-505)*
Ryan Manufacturing Inc.......G....... 815 695-5310
Newark *(G-15078)*
▲ **S+s Inspection Inc**.......G....... 770 493-9332
Bartlett *(G-1307)*
Sendra Service Corp.......G....... 815 462-0061
New Lenox *(G-15058)*
Shew Brothers Inc.......G....... 618 997-4414
Marion *(G-13534)*
▼ **Simplex Inc**.......C....... 217 483-1600
Springfield *(G-19446)*
South Subn Wldg & Fabg Co Inc.......G....... 708 385-7160
Posen *(G-16801)*
Spectrum Technologies Intl Ltd.......G....... 630 961-5244
Woodridge *(G-21341)*
SPX Corporation.......C....... 847 593-8855
Elk Grove Village *(G-9251)*
SPX Corporation.......B....... 815 874-5556
Rockford *(G-17643)*
Squibb Tank Company.......F....... 618 548-0141
Salem *(G-18360)*
Staffco Inc.......G....... 309 688-3223
Peoria *(G-16528)*
Starfire Industries LLC.......E....... 217 721-4165
Champaign *(G-3356)*
◆ **Streator Industrial Hdlg Inc**.......D....... 815 672-0551
Streator *(G-19626)*
Tacknologies.......G....... 630 729-9900
Woodridge *(G-21343)*
Tank Wind-Down Corp.......D....... 815 756-1551
Dekalb *(G-7707)*
Tech-Weld Inc.......F....... 630 365-3000
Elburn *(G-8474)*
▲ **Temprite Company**.......E....... 630 293-5910
West Chicago *(G-20649)*
Tinsley Steel Inc.......G....... 618 656-5231
Edwardsville *(G-8378)*
Titan US LLC.......G....... 331 212-5953
Aurora *(G-1026)*
▲ **Tranter Phe Inc**.......F....... 217 227-3470
Farmersville *(G-9660)*

Employee Codes: A=Over 500 employees, B=251-500
C=101-250, D=51-100, E=20-50, F=10-19, G=3-9
2020 Harris Illinois
Industrial Directory
927

Tri-State Disposal Inc E 708 388-9910
Riverdale *(G-17077)*

Tricon Wear Solutions LLC E 708 235-4064
University Park *(G-19969)*

Ucc Holdings Corporation E 847 473-5900
Waukegan *(G-20512)*

Unistrut International Corp D 630 773-3460
Addison *(G-323)*

▲ Vapor Corporation B 847 777-6400
Buffalo Grove *(G-2616)*

▲ Vapor Power International LLC D 630 694-5500
Franklin Park *(G-10075)*

Wb Tray LLC G 618 918-3821
Centralia *(G-3254)*

Wcr Inc E 309 697-0389
Peoria *(G-16546)*

▲ Western Industries Inc C 920 261-0660
Wheeling *(G-21012)*

◆ Whiting Corporation C 800 861-5744
Monee *(G-14212)*

Wilkos Industries G 563 249-6691
Savanna *(G-18413)*

WW Engineering Company LLC F 773 376-9494
Chicago *(G-6690)*

▲ Yinlun Usa Inc G 309 291-0843
Morton *(G-14387)*

3444 Sheet Metal Work

555 International Inc E 773 847-1400
Chicago *(G-3474)*

A & A Steel Fabricating Co F 708 389-4499
Posen *(G-16789)*

A D Skylights Inc G 847 854-2900
Algonquin *(G-365)*

A Hartlett & Sons Inc G 815 338-0109
Woodstock *(G-21353)*

A J Wagner & Son F 773 935-1414
Wauconda *(G-20323)*

A&S Machining & Welding Inc E 708 442-4544
Mc Cook *(G-13689)*

▲ Abbott Scott Manufacturing Co E 773 342-7200
Chicago *(G-3505)*

Ablaze Welding & Fabricating G 815 965-0046
Rockford *(G-17287)*

◆ Accu-Fab Incorporated E 847 541-4230
Wheeling *(G-20840)*

Ace Metal Spinning Inc F 708 389-5635
Alsip *(G-412)*

Advance Awnair Corp F 708 422-2730
Orland Park *(G-15934)*

Advanced Custom Metals Inc G 847 803-2090
Des Plaines *(G-7723)*

Aero Metals Alliance Inc F 225 236-1441
Northbrook *(G-15333)*

Aetna Engineering Works Inc E 773 785-0489
Chicago *(G-3577)*

▲ Afc Cable Systems Inc B 508 998-1131
Harvey *(G-11070)*

Agena Manufacturing Co E 630 668-5086
Carol Stream *(G-2928)*

Air Caddy G 708 383-5541
Oak Park *(G-15743)*

Air Flow Company Inc F 630 628-1138
Addison *(G-25)*

Air Vent Inc G 309 692-6969
Peoria *(G-16378)*

Air-Duct Manufacturing Inc G 630 620-9866
Aurora *(G-1045)*

All Seasons Heating & AC G 217 429-2022
Decatur *(G-7440)*

▲ All-Vac Industries Inc F 847 675-2290
Skokie *(G-18915)*

Allmetal Inc E 630 350-2524
Wood Dale *(G-21158)*

Alloy Welding Corp E 708 345-6756
Melrose Park *(G-13822)*

Allquip Co Inc G 309 944-6153
Geneseo *(G-10239)*

American Chute Systems Inc G 815 723-7632
Joliet *(G-11819)*

American Fuel Economy Inc G 815 433-3226
Ottawa *(G-16037)*

American Home Aluminium Co G 773 925-9442
Calumet Park *(G-2794)*

American Louver Company G 800 772-0355
Des Plaines *(G-7727)*

American Metal Installers & FA G 630 993-0812
Villa Park *(G-20131)*

American Shtmtl Fabricators F 708 877-7200
South Holland *(G-19194)*

◆ Americana Building Pdts Inc D 618 548-2800
Salem *(G-18328)*

Anchor Welding & Fabrication G 815 937-1640
Aroma Park *(G-839)*

Angle Metal Manufacturing Co G 847 437-8666
Elk Grove Village *(G-8831)*

Anytime Heating & AC F 630 851-6696
Naperville *(G-14959)*

Aquarius Metal Products Inc F 847 659-9266
Huntley *(G-11528)*

Arntzen Corporation E 815 334-0788
Woodstock *(G-21360)*

Arrow Sheet Metal Company E 815 455-2019
Crystal Lake *(G-7164)*

Art Wire Works Inc F 708 458-3993
Bedford Park *(G-1457)*

AS Fabricating Inc G 618 242-7438
Mount Vernon *(G-14596)*

Astoria Wire Products Inc D 708 496-9950
Bedford Park *(G-1459)*

Avenue Metal Manufacturing Co F 312 243-3483
Chicago *(G-3785)*

Awnings Over Chicagoland Inc G 847 233-0310
Franklin Park *(G-9879)*

B & D Independence Inc E 618 262-7117
Mount Carmel *(G-14465)*

B & J Wire Inc E 877 787-9473
Chicago *(G-3805)*

Barker Metalcraft Inc G 773 588-9300
Chicago *(G-3833)*

Bartec Orb Inc E 773 927-8600
Chicago *(G-3843)*

Belvin J & F Sheet Metal Co G 312 666-5222
Chicago *(G-3865)*

Berridge Manufacturing Company G 630 231-7495
West Chicago *(G-20551)*

Beverly Shear Mfg Corporation G 773 233-2063
Chicago *(G-3877)*

Bill West Enterprises Inc G 217 886-2591
Jacksonville *(G-11757)*

Bilt-Rite Metal Products Inc E 815 495-2211
Leland *(G-12547)*

Boekeloo Heating & Sheet Metal G 708 877-6560
Thornton *(G-19785)*

Boswell Building Contrs Inc F 630 595-5027
Wood Dale *(G-21171)*

Brex-Arlington Incorporated F 847 255-6284
Mount Prospect *(G-14515)*

Brian Burcar G 815 856-2271
Leonore *(G-12611)*

▲ Busatis Inc G 630 844-9803
Montgomery *(G-14236)*

Buww Coverings Incorporated E 815 394-1985
Rockford *(G-17330)*

C J Holdings Inc G 309 274-3141
Chillicothe *(G-6815)*

C Keller Manufacturing Inc E 630 833-5593
Villa Park *(G-20136)*

Carroll Distrg & Cnstr Sup Inc G 815 464-0100
Frankfort *(G-9778)*

Carroll Distrg & Cnstr Sup Inc G 630 892-4855
Aurora *(G-1070)*

Carroll Distrg & Cnstr Sup Inc G 630 243-0272
Lemont *(G-12558)*

Carroll Distrg & Cnstr Sup Inc G 815 941-1548
Morris *(G-14297)*

Carroll Distrg & Cnstr Sup Inc G 309 449-6044
Hopedale *(G-11516)*

Carroll Distrg & Cnstr Sup Inc F 630 369-6520
Naperville *(G-14791)*

Carroll International Corp C 630 983-5979
Lake Forest *(G-12236)*

Castle Metal Products Corp G 847 806-4540
Glendale Heights *(G-10442)*

▲ CCS Contractor Eqp & Sup Inc E 630 393-9020
Naperville *(G-14793)*

Central Radiator Cabinet Co G 773 539-1700
Lena *(G-12599)*

Central Sheet Metal Pdts Inc E 773 583-2424
Skokie *(G-18938)*

Cgi Automated Mfg Inc E 815 221-5300
Romeoville *(G-17805)*

Charles Atwater Assoc Inc G 815 678-4813
Richmond *(G-17011)*

Charles Industries LLC D 217 893-8335
Rantoul *(G-16970)*

Chesterfield Awning Co Inc F 708 596-4434
South Holland *(G-19205)*

◆ Chicago Metal Rolled Pdts Co D 773 523-5757
Chicago *(G-4115)*

▲ Chicago Metal Supply Inc G 773 417-7439
Chicago *(G-4116)*

Chicago Mtal Sup Fbrcation Inc F 773 227-6200
Chicago *(G-4119)*

Chicagoland Metal Fabricators G 847 260-5320
Franklin Park *(G-9906)*

▲ Chris Industries Inc E 847 729-9292
Northbrook *(G-15359)*

Christensen Precision Products G 630 543-6525
Addison *(G-72)*

City Screen Inc G 773 588-5642
Chicago *(G-4161)*

Classic Sheet Metal Inc E 630 694-0300
Addison *(G-73)*

Cleats Mfg Inc F 773 521-0300
Chicago *(G-4175)*

▲ Cobra Metal Works Inc C 847 214-8400
Elgin *(G-8544)*

Colfax Welding & Fabricating G 847 359-4433
Palatine *(G-16101)*

Comet Roll & Machine Company E 630 268-1407
Saint Charles *(G-18172)*

Control Equipment Company Inc F 847 891-7500
Schaumburg *(G-18487)*

◆ Cooper B-Line Inc A 618 654-2184
Highland *(G-11210)*

Corrpak Inc G 618 758-2755
Coulterville *(G-7030)*

Corrugated Metals Inc F 815 323-1310
Belvidere *(G-1663)*

▼ Craftsman Custom Metals LLC D 847 655-0040
Schiller Park *(G-18797)*

Crawford Heating & Cooling Co D 309 788-4573
Rock Island *(G-17211)*

Crown Concepts Corporation E 815 941-1081
Morris *(G-14299)*

Custom Copper Hoods Inc G 224 577-9000
Libertyville *(G-12646)*

Custom Fabrications Inc G 847 531-5912
Elgin *(G-8560)*

Cyclops Welding Co G 815 223-0685
La Salle *(G-12109)*

D & J Metalcraft Company Inc F 773 878-6446
Chicago *(G-4298)*

D & R Autochuck Inc E 815 394-1744
Rockford *(G-17364)*

D L Sheet Metal G 708 599-5538
Palos Hills *(G-16199)*

D W Terry Welding Company G 618 433-9722
Alton *(G-551)*

Dadant & Sons Inc F 217 852-3324
Dallas City *(G-7313)*

Daniel & Sons Mech Contrs Inc F 618 997-2822
Marion *(G-13509)*

Daniel Mfg Inc F 309 963-4227
Carlock *(G-2886)*

Daves Welding Service Inc G 630 655-3224
Darien *(G-7405)*

◆ Dayton Superior Corporation B 847 391-4700
Elk Grove Village *(G-8939)*

Delaney Sheet Metal Co G 847 991-9579
Palatine *(G-16110)*

Demco Inc F 708 345-4822
Melrose Park *(G-13848)*

Depue Mechanical Inc E 815 447-2267
Depue *(G-7716)*

▲ Diemasters Manufacturing Inc C 847 640-9900
Elk Grove Village *(G-8950)*

◆ Dometic Corporation A 847 447-7190
Rosemont *(G-18019)*

Duratrack Inc E 847 806-0202
Elk Grove Village *(G-8960)*

Duroweld Company Inc E 847 680-3064
Lake Bluff *(G-12179)*

Dynacoil Inc E 847 731-3300
Zion *(G-21512)*

E-M Metal Fabricator G 847 593-9970
Elk Grove Village *(G-8965)*

Eclipse Awnings Inc F 708 636-3160
Evergreen Park *(G-9593)*

Ed Stan Fabricating Co G 708 863-7668
Chicago *(G-4449)*

Eikenberry Sheet Metal Works G 815 625-0955
Sterling *(G-19507)*

▲ Ekstrom Carlson Fabg Co Inc G 815 226-1511
Rockford *(G-17392)*

▲ Elite Manufacturing Tech Inc C 630 351-5757
Bloomingdale *(G-1991)*

Elk Grove Custom Sheet Metal F 847 352-2845
Elk Grove Village *(G-8972)*

Emerald Machine Inc ....G 773 924-3659
Chicago (G-4495)
EMR Manufacturing Inc ....E 630 766-3366
Wood Dale (G-21185)
Enterprise AC & Htg Co ....G 708 430-2212
Chicago Ridge (G-6794)
Epic Metals Corporation ....G 847 803-6411
Des Plaines (G-7759)
Esi Steel & Fabrication ....F 618 548-3017
Salem (G-18338)
Estes Laser & Mfg Inc ....F 847 301-8231
Schaumburg (G-18523)
Evans Heating and Air Inc ....G 217 483-8440
Chatham (G-3420)
Expanded Metal Products Corp ....F 773 735-4500
Chicago (G-4544)
Exton Corp ....C 847 391-8100
Des Plaines (G-7763)
▲ Ezee Roll Manufacturing Co ....G 217 339-2279
Hoopeston (G-11508)
Eztech Manufacturing Inc ....F 630 293-0010
West Chicago (G-20582)
F Kreutzer & Co ....G 773 826-5767
Chicago (G-4550)
F Vogelmann and Company ....F 815 469-2285
Frankfort (G-9793)
Fab Werks Inc ....E 815 724-0317
Crest Hill (G-7086)
Fabricating Machinery Sales ....E 630 350-2266
Wood Dale (G-21186)
Fanmar Inc ....E 847 621-2010
Elk Grove Village (G-8995)
▲ Farmweld Inc ....E 217 857-6423
Teutopolis (G-19769)
Fbs Group Inc ....F 773 229-8675
Chicago (G-4569)
▲ Feralloy Corporation ....E 503 286-8869
Chicago (G-4580)
Floline Archtctral Systems LLC ....F 630 922-0550
Plainfield (G-16666)
Forming America Ltd ....E 888 993-1304
West Chicago (G-20587)
Fulton Metal Works Inc ....G 217 476-8223
Ashland (G-884)
G & M Fabricating Inc ....G 815 282-1744
Roscoe (G-17907)
G Branch Corp ....D 630 458-1909
Addison (G-131)
Gcb Metal Building Systems LLC ....G 224 268-3792
Elgin (G-8591)
General Machinery & Mfg Co ....F 773 235-3700
Chicago (G-4674)
▲ Genesis Inc ....D 630 351-4400
Roselle (G-17955)
Gengler-Lowney Laser Works ....F 630 801-4840
Aurora (G-1103)
Gerdau Ameristeel US Inc ....E 815 547-0400
Belvidere (G-1673)
Glazed Structures Inc ....F 847 223-4560
Grayslake (G-10776)
GLC Industries Inc ....E 630 628-5870
Addison (G-141)
Gma Inc ....G 630 595-1255
Bensenville (G-1812)
Goose Island Mfg & Supply Corp ....G 708 343-4225
Lansing (G-12495)
Grimm Metal Fabricators Inc ....E 630 792-1710
Lombard (G-13083)
GROsse&sons Htg &SHeet Met Inc ....G 708 447-8397
Lyons (G-13310)
Group Industries Inc ....E 708 877-6200
Thornton (G-19788)
Heartland Fabrication LLC ....G 309 448-2644
Congerville (G-6999)
▲ Helander Metal Spinning Co ....E 630 268-9292
Lombard (G-13084)
Hemingway Chimney Inc ....G 708 333-0355
South Holland (G-19219)
Hendrick Metal Products LLC ....D 847 742-7002
Elgin (G-8612)
Hennessy Sheet Metal ....G 708 754-6342
S Chicago Hts (G-18121)
▲ Hennig Inc ....G 815 636-9900
Machesney Park (G-13347)
Heritage Sheet Metal Inc ....G 847 724-8449
Glenview (G-10557)
Highland Mch & Screw Pdts Co ....D 618 654-2103
Highland (G-11218)
Hogg Welding Inc ....G 708 339-0033
Harvey (G-11089)

Hohlfider A H Shtmtl Htg Coolg ....G 815 965-9134
Rockford (G-17451)
▲ Hontech International Corp ....F 847 364-9800
Elk Grove Village (G-9036)
Hot Food Boxes Inc ....E 773 533-5912
Chicago (G-4846)
◆ Hovi Industries Incorporated ....E 815 512-7500
Bolingbrook (G-2186)
▼ Howler Fabrication & Wldg Inc ....E 630 293-9300
West Chicago (G-20593)
Hpl Stampings Inc ....E 847 540-1400
Lake Zurich (G-12419)
I F & G Metal Craft Co ....G 847 488-0630
South Elgin (G-19153)
Ibbotson Heating Co ....E 847 253-0866
Arlington Heights (G-752)
Icon Metalcraft Inc ....C 630 766-5600
Wood Dale (G-21200)
Illinois Valley Glass & Mirror ....F 309 682-6603
Peoria (G-16457)
ILmachine Company Inc ....F 847 243-9900
Wheeling (G-20913)
Imh Fabrication Inc ....F 815 537-2381
Prophetstown (G-16833)
Imperial Glass Structures Co ....F 847 253-6150
Wheeling (G-20914)
Imperial Mfg Group Inc ....F 618 465-3133
Alton (G-559)
▼ IMS Companies LLC ....D 847 391-8100
Des Plaines (G-7786)
▲ IMS Engineered Products LLC ....C 847 391-8100
Des Plaines (G-7787)
Innotech Manufacturing LLC ....E 618 244-6261
Mount Vernon (G-14616)
International Source Solutions ....G 847 251-8265
Wilmette (G-21079)
Ironform Holdings Co ....B 312 374-4810
Chicago (G-4970)
J & G Fabricating Inc ....G 708 385-9147
Blue Island (G-2126)
▲ J & I Son Tool Company Inc ....G 847 455-4200
Franklin Park (G-9967)
J & M Fab Metals Inc ....G 815 758-0354
Marengo (G-13486)
J F Schroeder Company Inc ....E 847 357-8600
Arlington Heights (G-759)
J K Manufacturing Co ....D 708 563-2500
Bedford Park (G-1475)
J Mac Metals Inc ....G 309 932-3001
Galva (G-10233)
J-TEC Metal Products Inc ....F 630 875-1300
Itasca (G-11679)
JB Metalfab Mfg Inc ....G 630 422-7420
Bensenville (G-1828)
John J Rickhoff Shtmtl Co Inc ....F 708 331-2970
Phoenix (G-16608)
Joiner Sheet Metal & Roofg Inc ....G 618 664-9488
Highland (G-11229)
JT Cullen Co Inc ....D 815 589-2412
Fulton (G-10154)
K & K Tool & Die Inc ....F 309 829-4479
Bloomington (G-2065)
K B Metal Company ....G 309 248-7355
Washburn (G-20264)
K Three Welding Service Inc ....G 708 563-2911
Chicago (G-5067)
Kcp Metal Fabrications Inc ....E 773 775-0318
Chicago (G-5088)
Keil-Forness Comfort Systems ....G 618 233-3039
Belleville (G-1560)
Kelley Construction Inc ....B 217 422-1800
Decatur (G-7513)
Kemper Industries ....G 217 826-5712
Marshall (G-13573)
Key West Metal Industries Inc ....C 708 371-1470
Crestwood (G-7121)
Kier Mfg Co ....G 630 953-9500
Addison (G-170)
Kim Gough ....G 309 734-3511
Monmouth (G-14221)
▲ Kipp Manufacturing Company Inc ....F 630 768-9051
Wauconda (G-20366)
Kirby Sheet Metal Works Inc ....E 773 247-6477
Chicago (G-5106)
Kormex Metal Craft Inc ....E 630 953-8856
Lombard (G-13093)
Kroh-Wagner Inc ....E 773 252-2031
Chicago (G-5133)
L M Sheet Metal Inc ....E 815 654-1837
Loves Park (G-13230)

L R Gregory and Son Inc ....E 847 247-0216
Lake Bluff (G-12191)
L/J Fabricators Inc ....E 815 397-9099
Rockford (G-17489)
Lake Iron Inc ....G 708 870-0546
Chicago (G-5160)
Lakefront Roofing Supply ....E 773 509-0400
Chicago (G-5163)
Lamco Slings & Rigging Inc ....E 309 764-7400
Moline (G-14157)
Laser Center Corporation ....E 630 523-1600
Schaumburg (G-18601)
Laystrom Manufacturing Co ....D 773 342-4800
Chicago (G-5186)
Lemanski Heating & AC ....G 815 232-4519
Freeport (G-10125)
Lewis Process Systems Inc ....F 630 510-8200
Carol Stream (G-3018)
Licon Inc ....G 618 485-2222
Ashley (G-885)
▲ Lindemann Chimney Service Inc ....F 847 918-7994
Lake Bluff (G-12193)
Litt Aluminium & Shtmtl Co ....G 708 366-4720
Westchester (G-20703)
Lizotte Sheet Metal Inc ....G 618 656-3066
Edwardsville (G-8368)
Lmt Usa Inc ....G 630 969-5412
Waukegan (G-20462)
Logan Square Aluminum Sup Inc ....D 847 985-1700
Schaumburg (G-18611)
Luebbers Welding & Mfg Inc ....F 618 594-2489
Carlyle (G-2893)
Mac Ster Inc ....G 847 359-3640
Palatine (G-16137)
Mac-Ster Inc ....F 847 830-7013
Addison (G-187)
Macari Service Center Inc ....F 217 774-4214
Shelbyville (G-18881)
Marcres Manufacturing Inc ....E 847 439-1808
Mount Prospect (G-14546)
MB Machine Inc ....F 815 864-3555
Shannon (G-18871)
▼ Mech-Tronics Corporation ....D 708 344-9823
Melrose Park (G-13891)
Meco Company LLC ....E 217 465-5620
Paris (G-16234)
Mendota Welding & Mfg ....G 815 539-6944
Mendota (G-13949)
Merz Air Conditioning and Htg ....E 217 342-2323
Effingham (G-8409)
▲ Metal Box International LLC ....C 847 455-8500
Franklin Park (G-9994)
Metal Culverts Inc ....E 309 543-2271
Havana (G-11117)
Metal Sales Manufacturing Corp ....E 309 787-1200
Rock Island (G-17230)
Metal Spinners Inc ....E 815 625-0390
Rock Falls (G-17189)
Metal Strip Buiding Products ....G 847 742-8500
Itasca (G-11700)
Metal-Rite Inc ....F 708 656-3832
Cicero (G-6866)
▲ Metals and Services Inc ....D 630 627-2900
Addison (G-200)
Midwest Awnings Inc ....G 309 762-3339
Cameron (G-2808)
Midwest Manufacturing & Distrg ....F 773 866-1010
Chicago (G-5443)
Midwest Skylite Company Inc ....E 847 214-9505
South Elgin (G-19167)
Midwest Skylite Service Inc ....G 847 214-9505
Schaumburg (G-18630)
▲ Mj Celco International LLC ....E 847 671-1900
Schiller Park (G-18827)
Mj Snyder Ironworks Inc ....G 217 826-6440
Marshall (G-13575)
Montana Metal Products LLC ....C 847 803-6600
Des Plaines (G-7803)
Montefusco Hvac Inc ....G 309 691-7400
Peoria (G-16479)
Mrt Sureway Inc ....D 847 801-3010
Franklin Park (G-10004)
Mucci Kirkpatrick Sheet Metal ....G 815 433-3350
Ottawa (G-16062)
National Metal Works Inc ....G 815 282-5533
Loves Park (G-13239)
Nature House Inc ....D 217 833-2393
Griggsville (G-10850)
Nelson Manufacturing Co Inc ....F 815 229-0161
Rockford (G-17537)

SIC

Employee Codes: A=Over 500 employees, B=251-500
C=101-250, D=51-100, E=20-50, F=10-19, G=3-9
2020 Harris Illinois
Industrial Directory
929

34 FABRICATED METAL PRODUCTS, EXCEPT MACHINERY AND TRANSPORTATION EQUIPMENT

Neomek Incorporated .... F 630 879-5400
  Batavia (G-1399)
Nesterowicz & Associates Inc .... G 815 522-4469
  Kirkland (G-12064)
North American Enclosures Inc .... G 630 290-7911
  Naperville (G-14887)
North Shore Truck & Equipment ...... F 847 887-0200
  Lake Bluff (G-12201)
▲ Northstar Industries Inc .... C 630 446-7800
  Glendale Heights (G-10480)
▼ Nova Metals Inc .... F 630 690-4300
  Carol Stream (G-3040)
Npi Holding Corp .... G 217 391-1229
  Springfield (G-19412)
▲ Nu-Way Industries Inc .... C 847 298-7710
  Des Plaines (G-7812)
▲ Nudo Products Inc .... G 217 528-5636
  Springfield (G-19414)
Odin Fabrication Inc .... G 630 365-2475
  Elburn (G-8466)
Odin Industries Inc .... F 630 365-2475
  Elburn (G-8467)
Olympia Manufacturing Inc .... G 309 387-2633
  East Peoria (G-8280)
Omega Products Inc .... G 618 939-3445
  Waterloo (G-20293)
Omnimax International Inc .... E 309 747-2937
  Gridley (G-10846)
Omnimax International Inc .... F 770 449-7066
  Bedford Park (G-1488)
Parker Fabrication Inc .... E 309 266-8413
  Morton (G-14376)
Pate Company Inc .... E 630 705-1920
  Lombard (G-13118)
Pep Industries Inc .... F 630 833-0404
  Villa Park (G-20164)
Peter Lehman Inc .... G 847 395-7997
  Antioch (G-630)
Peter Perella & Co .... F 815 727-4526
  Joliet (G-11913)
◆ Petersen Aluminum Corporation ... D 847 228-7150
  Elk Grove Village (G-9176)
Pittsfield Mch Tl & Wldg Co .... G 217 656-4000
  Payson (G-16317)
Pools Welding Inc .... E 309 787-2083
  Milan (G-14020)
Powdered Metal Tech LLC .... G 630 852-0500
  Downers Grove (G-8080)
Precision Metal Products Inc .... F 630 458-0100
  Addison (G-251)
Premier Manufacturing Corp .... F 847 640-6644
  Addison (G-253)
Prince Fabricators Inc .... E 630 588-0088
  Carol Stream (G-3051)
▲ Prismier LLC .... E 630 592-4515
  Bolingbrook (G-2230)
Pro-Bilt Buildings LLC .... F 217 532-9331
  Hillsboro (G-11319)
Pro-Tech Metal Specialties Inc .... E 630 279-7094
  Elmhurst (G-9412)
Pro-Tran Inc .... E 217 348-9353
  Charleston (G-3410)
Production Fabg & Stamping Inc .... F 708 755-5468
  S Chicago Hts (G-18126)
Production Manufacturing .... G 217 256-4211
  Warsaw (G-20259)
Progressive Sheet Metal Inc .... G 773 376-1155
  Chicago (G-5901)
▲ Pyramid Manufacturing Corp .... D 630 443-0141
  Saint Charles (G-18254)
Quad-Metal Inc .... F 630 953-0907
  Addison (G-258)
Quality Fabricators Inc .... D 630 543-0540
  Addison (G-261)
Quality Metal Works Inc .... G 309 379-5311
  Stanford (G-19473)
Quanex Homeshield LLC .... G 815 635-3171
  Chatsworth (G-3427)
Quicksilver Mechanical Inc .... G 847 577-1564
  Arlington Heights (G-794)
R & B Metal Products Inc .... E 815 338-1890
  Woodstock (G-21427)
R B Hayward Company .... G 847 671-0400
  Schiller Park (G-18838)
R B White Inc .... E 309 452-5816
  Normal (G-15220)
R P Solutions LLC .... G 773 971-1363
  Chicago (G-5948)
R&R Rf Inc .... G 847 669-3720
  Rock Falls (G-17192)

▼ Ready Access Inc .... E 800 621-5045
  West Chicago (G-20635)
Rebel Inc .... E 618 235-0582
  Belleville (G-1588)
Reliable Autotech Usa LLC .... G 815 945-7838
  Chenoa (G-3434)
▲ Remin Laboratories Inc .... D 815 723-1940
  Joliet (G-11924)
Rettick Enterprises Inc .... G 309 275-4967
  Bloomington (G-2088)
Rijon Manufacturing Company .... G 708 388-2295
  Blue Island (G-2136)
▲ Rogers Precision Machining .... F 815 233-0065
  Freeport (G-10138)
Rollex Corporation .... C 847 437-3000
  Elk Grove Village (G-9220)
Rome Metal Mfg Inc .... G 773 287-1755
  Chicago (G-6057)
Roth Metal Fabricators Corp .... G 708 371-8300
  Alsip (G-505)
▲ RPS Engineering Inc .... F 847 931-1950
  Elgin (G-8721)
Ruyle Mechanical Services Inc ...... D 309 674-6644
  Peoria (G-16518)
S & S Heating & Sheet Metal .... G 815 933-1993
  Bradley (G-2290)
S & S Welding & Fabrication .... G 847 742-7344
  Elgin (G-8722)
Safe-Air of Illinois Inc .... E 708 652-9100
  Cicero (G-6873)
Schubert Environmental Eqp Inc .... F 630 307-9400
  Glendale Heights (G-10492)
Seamless Gutter Corp .... E 630 495-9800
  Lombard (G-13128)
Serra Laser Precision LLC .... D 847 367-0282
  Libertyville (G-12705)
Service Metal Enterprises .... G 630 628-1444
  Addison (G-286)
Service Sheet Metal Works Inc ...... F 773 229-0031
  Chicago (G-6143)
Shade Solutions Inc .... F 217 239-0718
  Tolono (G-19884)
Shademaker Products Corp .... G 773 955-0998
  Chicago (G-6146)
Shamrock Manufacturing Co Inc .... G 708 331-7776
  South Holland (G-19244)
Shannon & Sons Welding .... G 630 898-7778
  Aurora (G-1155)
Sheas Iron Works Inc .... E 847 356-2922
  Lake Villa (G-12367)
Sheet Metal Connectors Inc .... F 815 874-4600
  Rockford (G-17629)
Sheet Metal Supply Ltd .... G 847 478-8500
  Grayslake (G-10799)
Sheet Metal Werks Inc .... D 847 827-4700
  Arlington Heights (G-809)
Shew Brothers Inc .... G 618 997-4414
  Marion (G-13534)
Silgan White Cap Americas LLC .... F 630 515-8383
  Downers Grove (G-8096)
Silver Machine Shop Inc .... G 217 359-5717
  Champaign (G-3348)
Skol Mfg Co .... E 773 878-5959
  Chicago (G-6181)
Smid Heating & Air .... G 815 467-0362
  Channahon (G-3394)
South Subn Wldg & Fabg Co Inc .... G 708 385-7160
  Posen (G-16801)
Southern Wisconsin Metal Fabrc .... F 815 389-3021
  South Beloit (G-19114)
Southwick Machine & Design Co ... G 309 949-2868
  Colona (G-6980)
Spartan Sheet Metal Inc .... G 773 895-7266
  Chicago (G-6210)
▲ Spiral-Helix Inc .... F 224 659-7870
  Bensenville (G-1897)
▲ Stainless Specialties Inc .... G 618 654-7723
  Pocahontas (G-16754)
▲ Star Forge Inc .... D 815 235-7750
  Freeport (G-10144)
Starmont Manufacturing Co .... G 815 939-1041
  Kankakee (G-12007)
Steel Services Enterprises .... E 708 259-1181
  Lansing (G-12519)
Steel Span Inc .... F 815 943-9071
  Harvard (G-11068)
Stueclken Manufacturing Co .... G 847 678-5130
  Franklin Park (G-10054)
Sturdee Metal Products Inc .... G 773 523-3074
  New Lenox (G-15059)

Suburban Welding & Steel LLC ..... F 847 678-1264
  Franklin Park (G-10057)
Sudholt Sheet Metal Inc .... G 618 228-7351
  Aviston (G-1183)
Sugar River Machine Shop .... E 815 624-0214
  South Beloit (G-19115)
Summit Sheet Metal Specialists .... F 708 458-8622
  Summit Argo (G-19682)
Superior Joining Tech Inc .... E 815 282-7581
  Machesney Park (G-13376)
Synergy Mechanical Inc .... G 708 410-1004
  Westchester (G-20713)
T & L Sheet Metal Inc .... F 630 628-7960
  Addison (G-302)
T/J Fabricators Inc .... D 630 543-2293
  Addison (G-303)
Tandem Industries Inc .... G 630 761-6615
  Saint Charles (G-18285)
▲ Tassos Metal Inc .... E 630 953-1333
  Lombard (G-13139)
Tcr Systems LLC .... D 217 877-5622
  Decatur (G-7560)
Tella Tool & Mfg Co .... C 630 495-0545
  Lombard (G-13142)
Temp Excel Properties LLC .... E 847 844-3845
  Elgin (G-8750)
Tesler Company of Illinois Inc .... G 773 522-4400
  Franklin Park (G-10060)
Tewell Bros Machine Inc .... F 217 253-6303
  Tuscola (G-19931)
Thomas Engineering Inc .... E 815 398-0280
  Rockford (G-17659)
Thybar Corporation .... E 630 543-5300
  Addison (G-309)
Tin Mans Garage Inc .... G 630 262-0752
  Elburn (G-8477)
Tinsley Steel Inc .... G 618 656-5231
  Edwardsville (G-8378)
Titan Metals Inc .... E 630 752-9700
  Glendale Heights (G-10512)
Tlk Industries Inc .... D 847 359-3200
  East Dundee (G-8212)
Tri City Sheet Metal .... G 630 232-4255
  Geneva (G-10313)
Tri State Aluminum Products .... E 815 877-6081
  Loves Park (G-13277)
Tru-Way Inc .... E 708 562-3690
  Northlake (G-15563)
Tu-Star Manufacturing Co Inc .... G 815 338-5760
  Woodstock (G-21441)
Two J S Sheet Metal Works Inc ..... G 773 436-9424
  Chicago (G-6446)
Ultratech Inc .... E 630 539-3578
  Bloomingdale (G-2019)
Unifab Mfg Inc .... G 630 682-8970
  Carol Stream (G-3082)
Unistrut International Corp .... G 630 773-3460
  Addison (G-323)
United Canvas Inc .... E 847 395-1470
  Antioch (G-641)
United Skys LLC .... F 847 546-7776
  Chicago (G-6474)
US Post Co Inc .... G 815 675-9313
  Spring Grove (G-19306)
Vanfab Inc .... G 815 426-2544
  Union Hill (G-19944)
Vent Products Co Inc .... E 773 521-1900
  Chicago (G-6532)
Venus Processing & Storage .... D 847 455-0496
  Franklin Park (G-10077)
Viking Metal Cabinet Co LLC .... D 800 776-7767
  Montgomery (G-14273)
Viking Metal Cabinet Company ..... D 630 863-7234
  Montgomery (G-14274)
Vorteq Coil Finishers LLC .... E 847 455-7200
  Franklin Park (G-10080)
W L Engler Distributing Inc .... G 630 898-5400
  Aurora (G-1032)
▲ Wagner Zip-Change Inc .... E 708 681-4100
  Melrose Park (G-13926)
▲ Waukegan Architectural Inc .... G 847 746-9077
  Zion (G-21529)
Welding Specialties .... G 708 798-5388
  East Hazel Crest (G-8219)
▲ Western Industries Inc .... C 920 261-0660
  Wheeling (G-21012)
White Sheet Metal .... G 217 465-3195
  Paris (G-16246)
◆ William Dudek Manufacturing Co .. E 773 622-2727
  Chicago (G-6629)

Wiltek Inc ....G.... 630 922-9200
Naperville *(G-14992)*
Wirfs Industries Inc ....F.... 815 344-0635
McHenry *(G-13809)*
Woodlawn Engineering Co Inc ....E.... 630 543-3550
Addison *(G-337)*
◆ **Wozniak Industries Inc** ....G.... 630 954-3400
Schaumburg *(G-18776)*
Wright Metals Inc ....G.... 847 267-1212
Bannockburn *(G-1212)*

3446 Architectural & Ornamental Metal Work

555 International Inc ....E.... 773 847-1400
Chicago *(G-3474)*
A Touch of Beauty Inc ....G.... 708 387-0360
Brookfield *(G-2477)*
▲ **Accurate Partitions Corp** ....G.... 708 442-6801
Burr Ridge *(G-2649)*
Aetna Engineering Works Inc ....E.... 773 785-0489
Chicago *(G-3577)*
Affton Fabg & Wldg Co Inc ....E.... 314 781-4100
Sauget *(G-18388)*
Aj Welding Services ....G.... 708 843-2701
Chicago *(G-3592)*
Alfredos Iron Works Inc ....E.... 815 748-1177
Cortland *(G-7017)*
▲ **All-Steel Structures Inc** ....E.... 708 210-1313
South Holland *(G-19189)*
Amron Stair Works Inc ....F.... 847 426-4800
Gilberts *(G-10350)*
Anchor Welding & Fabrication ....G.... 815 937-1640
Aroma Park *(G-839)*
Armstrong World Industries Inc ....E.... 847 362-8720
Libertyville *(G-12631)*
AS Fabricating Inc ....G.... 618 242-7438
Mount Vernon *(G-14596)*
Atkore International Group Inc ....A.... 708 339-1610
Harvey *(G-11075)*
Atkore Intl Holdings Inc ....G.... 708 225-2051
Harvey *(G-11076)*
◆ **Atlantis Products Inc** ....G.... 630 971-9680
Bolingbrook *(G-2152)*
Bailey Hardwoods Inc ....G.... 217 529-6800
Springfield *(G-19324)*
Barker Metalcraft Inc ....G.... 773 588-9300
Chicago *(G-3833)*
Birdsell Machine & Orna Inc ....G.... 217 243-5849
Jacksonville *(G-11759)*
Botti Studio of Architectural ....E.... 847 869-5933
Glenview *(G-10532)*
Brian Hobbs ....G.... 618 758-1303
Coulterville *(G-7029)*
Builders Ironworks Inc ....G.... 708 672-1047
Crete *(G-7135)*
▲ **Capitol Wood Works LLC** ....D.... 217 522-5553
Springfield *(G-19341)*
▲ **CCL Construction Inc** ....G.... 219 237-2911
Homewood *(G-11490)*
Chase Security Systems Inc ....G.... 773 594-1919
Chicago *(G-4078)*
Chicago Iron Works Corporation ....F.... 312 829-1062
Chicago *(G-4108)*
◆ **Chicago Metal Rolled Pdts Co** ....D.... 773 523-5757
Chicago *(G-4115)*
Chicago Ornamental Iron Inc ....E.... 773 321-9635
Chicago *(G-4121)*
Chicagos Finest Iron Works ....F.... 773 646-4484
Chicago *(G-4138)*
Chicagos Finest Ironworks ....G.... 708 895-4484
Lansing *(G-12488)*
Christopher Glass & Aluminum ....D.... 312 256-8500
Elmhurst *(G-9346)*
City Ornamental Iron Works ....G.... 847 888-8898
Elgin *(G-8541)*
City Screen Inc ....G.... 773 588-5642
Chicago *(G-4161)*
Cooper B-Line Inc ....C.... 618 357-5353
Pinckneyville *(G-16612)*
Creative Iron ....G.... 217 267-7797
Westville *(G-20779)*
Creative Panel Systems Inc ....G.... 630 625-5002
Itasca *(G-11641)*
Crosstree Inc ....G.... 773 227-1234
Chicago *(G-4274)*
Custom Railz & Stairs Inc ....G.... 773 592-7210
Oak Lawn *(G-15710)*
D5 Design Met Fabrication LLC ....G.... 773 770-4705
Chicago *(G-4303)*
Daves Welding Service Inc ....G.... 630 655-3224
Darien *(G-7405)*
Designed Eqp Acquisition Corp ....E.... 847 647-5000
Elk Grove Village *(G-8947)*
▲ **DSI Spaceframes Inc** ....E.... 630 607-0045
Addison *(G-99)*
Economy Iron Inc ....F.... 708 343-1777
Melrose Park *(G-13859)*
Ed Stan Fabricating Co ....G.... 708 863-7668
Chicago *(G-4449)*
▲ **Empire Bronze Corp** ....F.... 630 916-9722
Lombard *(G-13073)*
European Ornamental Iron Works ....G.... 630 705-9300
Addison *(G-117)*
Fariss John ....G.... 815 433-3803
Moline *(G-14144)*
Fastrack Stairs & Rails Ltd ....G.... 847 531-6252
Dekalb *(G-7677)*
Fbs Group Inc ....F.... 773 229-8675
Chicago *(G-4569)*
Fehring Ornamental Iron Works ....G.... 217 483-6727
Rochester *(G-17166)*
◆ **First Alert Inc** ....C.... 630 499-3295
Aurora *(G-962)*
Fusion Gates LLC ....G.... 618 650-9170
Edwardsville *(G-8364)*
G & M Fabricating Inc ....G.... 815 282-1744
Roscoe *(G-17907)*
G P Concrete & Iron Works ....G.... 815 842-2270
Pontiac *(G-16770)*
Gemini Steel Inc ....G.... 815 472-4462
Momence *(G-14185)*
Gilco Real Estate Company ....E.... 847 298-1717
Des Plaines *(G-7774)*
Goose Island Mfg & Supply Corp ....G.... 708 343-4225
Lansing *(G-12495)*
Greene Welding & Hardware Inc ....E.... 217 375-4244
East Lynn *(G-8220)*
▼ **Gs Metals Corp** ....C.... 618 357-5353
Pinckneyville *(G-16617)*
Harris Steel Ulc ....D.... 815 932-1200
Bourbonnais *(G-2262)*
Hart & Cooley Inc ....C.... 630 665-5549
Carol Stream *(G-2996)*
Ibarra Group LLC ....G.... 773 650-0503
Chicago *(G-4870)*
Industrial Fence Inc ....D.... 773 521-9900
Chicago *(G-4906)*
Iron & Wire LLC ....G.... 773 255-2672
Chicago *(G-4968)*
Iron Castle Inc ....F.... 773 890-0575
Chicago *(G-4969)*
ITW Blding Cmponents Group Inc ....E.... 217 324-0303
Litchfield *(G-12967)*
J B Metal Works Inc ....G.... 847 824-4253
Des Plaines *(G-7790)*
▲ **J C Schultz Enterprises Inc** ....D.... 800 323-9127
Batavia *(G-1388)*
J H Botts LLC ....E.... 815 726-5885
Joliet *(G-11883)*
Jack Rush Quality Homes Inc ....G.... 309 663-6595
Bloomington *(G-2063)*
John F Mate Co ....G.... 847 381-8131
Lake Barrington *(G-12154)*
K & K Iron Works LLC ....D.... 708 924-0000
Mc Cook *(G-13693)*
K D Iron Works ....G.... 847 991-3039
Palatine *(G-16134)*
K Three Welding Service Inc ....G.... 708 563-2911
Chicago *(G-5067)*
Kelley Ornamental Iron LLC ....E.... 309 697-9870
East Peoria *(G-8274)*
Kelley Ornamental Iron LLC ....F.... 309 820-7540
Bloomington *(G-2067)*
Kencor Stairs & Woodworking ....G.... 630 279-8980
Villa Park *(G-20155)*
▲ **Ki Industries Inc** ....E.... 708 449-1990
Berkeley *(G-1941)*
King Metal Co ....G.... 708 388-3845
Alsip *(G-464)*
Krum Kreations ....G.... 815 772-8296
Morrison *(G-14344)*
Lamonica Ornamental Iron Works ....G.... 773 638-6633
Chicago *(G-5172)*
Lawndale Forging & Tool Works ....G.... 773 277-2800
Chicago *(G-5183)*
Leggs Manufacturing ....G.... 618 842-9847
Fairfield *(G-9631)*
Legna Iron Works Inc ....E.... 630 894-8056
Roselle *(G-17964)*
Leonards Unit Step Co ....G.... 815 744-1263
Rockdale *(G-17265)*
Leonards Unit Step of Moline ....G.... 309 792-9641
Colona *(G-6976)*
Lickenbrock & Sons Inc ....G.... 618 632-4977
O Fallon *(G-15578)*
Lizotte Sheet Metal Inc ....G.... 618 656-3066
Edwardsville *(G-8368)*
▲ **M & D Industries Inc** ....E.... 847 362-8720
Libertyville *(G-12671)*
Mechanical Indus Stl Svcs Inc ....E.... 815 521-1725
Channahon *(G-3389)*
Merchants Metals LLC ....G.... 847 249-4086
Waukegan *(G-20467)*
Metal Edge Inc ....F.... 708 756-4696
Romeoville *(G-17850)*
Midwest Cage Company ....G.... 815 806-0005
Frankfort *(G-9816)*
Midwest Stair Parts ....G.... 630 723-3991
Naperville *(G-14979)*
Mike Meier & Sons Fence Mfg ....E.... 847 587-1111
Spring Grove *(G-19284)*
Milk Design Company ....G.... 312 563-6455
Posen *(G-16798)*
Millers Eureka Inc ....F.... 312 666-9383
Chicago *(G-5459)*
Mj Snyder Ironworks Inc ....G.... 217 826-6440
Marshall *(G-13575)*
Montefusco Hvac Inc ....G.... 309 691-7400
Peoria *(G-16479)*
Mueller Ornamental Iron Works ....F.... 847 758-9941
Elk Grove Village *(G-9140)*
Neiweem Industries Inc ....G.... 847 487-1239
Oakwood Hills *(G-15821)*
Nelson - Harkins Inds Inc ....E.... 773 478-6243
Lake Bluff *(G-12199)*
Nicks Metal Fabg & Sons ....F.... 708 485-1170
Brookfield *(G-2489)*
North Chicago Iron Works Inc ....E.... 847 689-2000
North Chicago *(G-15317)*
Old Style Iron Works Inc ....G.... 773 265-5787
Chicago *(G-5670)*
Oldcastle Infrastructure Inc ....F.... 309 661-4608
Normal *(G-15215)*
Ornamental Iron Shop ....G.... 618 281-6072
Columbia *(G-6992)*
▲ **Orsolinis Welding & Fabg** ....F.... 773 722-9855
Chicago *(G-5705)*
Otis Elevator Company ....D.... 312 454-1616
Chicago *(G-5712)*
P & M Ornamental Ir Works Inc ....F.... 708 267-2868
Melrose Park *(G-13901)*
▲ **P & P Artec Inc** ....F.... 630 860-2990
Wood Dale *(G-21226)*
Paco Corporation ....F.... 708 430-2424
Bridgeview *(G-2371)*
Patrick Holdings Inc ....F.... 815 874-5300
Rockford *(G-17549)*
Paul D Metal Products Inc ....D.... 773 847-1400
Chicago *(G-5771)*
Pep Industries Inc ....F.... 630 833-0404
Villa Park *(G-20164)*
Quality Iron Works Inc ....F.... 630 766-0885
Bensenville *(G-1878)*
R & B Metal Products Inc ....E.... 815 338-1890
Woodstock *(G-21427)*
R & I Ornamental Iron Inc ....E.... 847 836-6934
Gilberts *(G-10366)*
Roxul USA Inc ....A.... 800 323-7164
Chicago *(G-6068)*
Royal Stairs Co ....G.... 847 685-9448
Park Ridge *(G-16294)*
S & G Iron Works ....G.... 224 789-7178
Zion *(G-21526)*
Selco Industries ....G.... 708 499-1060
Chicago Ridge *(G-6810)*
Selvaggio Orna & Strl Stl Inc ....E.... 217 528-4077
Springfield *(G-19441)*
Sheas Iron Works Inc ....E.... 847 356-2922
Lake Villa *(G-12367)*
Sno Gem Inc ....F.... 888 766-4367
McHenry *(G-13792)*
South Subn Wldg & Fabg Co Inc ....G.... 708 385-7160
Posen *(G-16801)*
Steel Construction Svcs Inc ....G.... 815 678-7509
Richmond *(G-17023)*
Stevenson Fabrication Svcs Inc ....G.... 815 468-7941
Manteno *(G-13458)*
Summit Architectural Mtls LLC ....F.... 815 934-3484
Chicago *(G-6265)*
▲ **Tim Detwiler Enterprises Inc** ....G.... 815 758-9950
Dekalb *(G-7709)*

Employee Codes: A=Over 500 employees, B=251-500
C=101-250, D=51-100, E=20-50, F=10-19, G=3-9
2020 Harris Illinois
Industrial Directory
931

Tinsley Steel Inc..........G....... 618 656-5231
Edwardsville *(G-8378)*
Tuschall Engineering Co Inc..........E....... 630 655-9100
Burr Ridge *(G-2726)*
▲ **Unistrut International Corp**..........C....... 800 882-5543
Harvey *(G-11099)*
United Fence Co Inc..........G....... 773 924-0773
Chicago *(G-6472)*
▲ **Vector Custom Fabricating Inc**..........F....... 312 421-5161
Chicago *(G-6528)*
W G N Flag & Decorating Co..........F....... 773 768-8076
Chicago *(G-6573)*
▲ **Waukegan Architectural Inc**..........G....... 847 746-9077
Zion *(G-21529)*
Waukegan Steel LLC..........E....... 847 662-2810
Waukegan *(G-20516)*
WEb Production & Fabg Inc..........F....... 312 733-6800
Chicago *(G-6595)*
Werner Co..........A....... 847 455-8001
Itasca *(G-11754)*
Werner Co..........E....... 815 459-6020
Crystal Lake *(G-7294)*
Western Architectural Iron Co..........E....... 773 463-1500
Chicago *(G-6607)*
Wilson Railing & Metal Fabg Co..........G....... 847 662-1747
Park City *(G-16248)*
Winters Welding Inc..........G....... 773 860-7735
Chicago *(G-6648)*

3448 Prefabricated Metal Buildings & Cmpnts

Alvarez & Marsal Inc..........E....... 312 601-4220
Chicago *(G-3639)*
American Buildings Company..........C....... 309 527-5420
El Paso *(G-8433)*
American Deck & Sunroom C..........G....... 217 586-4840
Mahomet *(G-13421)*
American Steel Carports Inc..........F....... 800 487-4010
Kewanee *(G-12020)*
◆ **Americana Building Pdts Inc**..........D....... 618 548-2800
Salem *(G-18328)*
◆ **Arrow Shed LLC**..........E....... 618 526-4546
Breese *(G-2296)*
Associated Group Holdings LLC..........G....... 312 662-5488
Chicago *(G-3751)*
Atkore International Group Inc..........A....... 708 339-1610
Harvey *(G-11075)*
Atkore Intl Holdings Inc..........G....... 708 225-2051
Harvey *(G-11076)*
Beh IL Sub LLC..........G....... 630 616-1850
Hinsdale *(G-11364)*
Cardinal Enterprises..........G....... 618 994-4454
Stonefort *(G-19557)*
Chicago Enclosures..........G....... 708 344-6600
Melrose Park *(G-13842)*
Chicago Panel & Truss Inc..........E....... 630 870-1300
Aurora *(G-1074)*
Chicago Steel Inc..........E....... 800 344-3032
Chicago *(G-4130)*
▼ **Craig Industries Inc**..........D....... 217 228-2421
Quincy *(G-16873)*
D & D Construction Co LLC..........G....... 217 852-6631
Dallas City *(G-7312)*
Dspc Company..........E....... 815 997-1116
Rockford *(G-17387)*
Eagle Companies Inc..........F....... 309 686-9054
Chillicothe *(G-6816)*
▼ **Elfi LLC**..........E....... 815 439-1833
Chicago *(G-4483)*
Esi Steel & Fabrication..........F....... 618 548-3017
Salem *(G-18338)*
Fehring Ornamental Iron Works..........G....... 217 483-6727
Rochester *(G-17166)*
George Industries LLC..........E....... 847 394-3610
Wheeling *(G-20904)*
Hadley Capital Fund II LP..........G....... 847 906-5300
Wilmette *(G-21076)*
◆ **Heico Companies LLC**..........F....... 312 419-8220
Chicago *(G-4798)*
Illinois Green Cnstr Inc..........F....... 847 975-2312
Chicago *(G-4891)*
◆ **Interntional Grnhse Contrs Inc**..........E....... 217 443-0600
Danville *(G-7352)*
Jack Walters & Sons Corp..........E....... 618 842-2642
Fairfield *(G-9627)*
K & K Storage Barns LLC..........F....... 618 927-0533
Ewing *(G-9602)*
Lamka Enterprises Inc..........G....... 630 659-5965
Woodstock *(G-21402)*
McElroy Metal Mill Inc..........E....... 217 935-9421
Clinton *(G-6927)*
Minority Auto Hdlg Specialists..........F....... 708 757-8758
Chicago Heights *(G-6759)*
Mobile Mini Inc..........E....... 708 297-2004
Calumet Park *(G-2799)*
Morton Buildings Inc..........G....... 217 357-3713
Carthage *(G-3140)*
Morton Buildings Inc..........F....... 630 904-1122
Streator *(G-19615)*
Morton Buildings Inc..........F....... 309 936-7282
Atkinson *(G-902)*
Morton Buildings Inc..........F....... 309 263-3652
Morton *(G-14370)*
Nexus Corporation..........E....... 217 303-5544
Pana *(G-16218)*
Optimal Construction Svcs Inc..........G....... 630 365-5050
Elburn *(G-8468)*
Rampnow LLC..........G....... 630 892-7267
Montgomery *(G-14266)*
▲ **Rv6 Performance**..........G....... 630 346-7998
Wheaton *(G-20821)*
▼ **Safety Storage Inc**..........D....... 217 345-4422
Charleston *(G-3412)*
Signa Development Group Inc..........G....... 773 418-4506
Norridge *(G-15243)*
Singer Safety Company..........F....... 773 235-2100
Chicago *(G-6175)*
Steel Span Inc..........F....... 815 943-9071
Harvard *(G-11068)*
Strat-O-Span Buildings Inc..........G....... 618 526-4566
Breese *(G-2308)*
Super Target Systems LLC..........G....... 800 556-3162
Aurora *(G-1158)*
Tandem Industries Inc..........G....... 630 761-6615
Saint Charles *(G-18285)*
Tank Wind-Down Corp..........D....... 815 756-1551
Dekalb *(G-7707)*
▲ **Unistrut International Corp**..........C....... 800 882-5543
Harvey *(G-11099)*
US Aluminium IL..........G....... 708 458-9070
Chicago *(G-6498)*
White Star Silo..........G....... 618 523-4735
Germantown *(G-10332)*

3449 Misc Structural Metal Work

A & S Steel Specialties Inc..........E....... 815 838-8188
Lockport *(G-12979)*
Advanced Assembly..........G....... 630 379-6158
Streamwood *(G-19559)*
Affton Fabg & Wldg Co Inc..........E....... 314 781-4100
Sauget *(G-18388)*
▲ **All-Steel Structures Inc**..........E....... 708 210-1313
South Holland *(G-19189)*
American Classic Rebar Corp..........G....... 708 225-1010
South Holland *(G-19192)*
American Steel Fabricators Inc..........F....... 847 807-4200
Melrose Park *(G-13825)*
Bergst Special Tools Inc..........G....... 630 543-1020
Addison *(G-48)*
Bohler..........G....... 630 883-3000
Elgin *(G-8522)*
◆ **Chicago Metal Rolled Pdts Co**..........D....... 773 523-5757
Chicago *(G-4115)*
Chicago Ornamental Iron Inc..........E....... 773 321-9635
Chicago *(G-4121)*
▲ **Crown Premiums Inc**..........F....... 815 469-8789
Frankfort *(G-9781)*
Dayton Superior Corporation..........D....... 815 936-3300
Kankakee *(G-11963)*
Delta Erectors Inc..........F....... 708 267-9721
Villa Park *(G-20144)*
Dixline Corporation..........D....... 309 932-2011
Galva *(G-10231)*
Dixline Corporation..........F....... 309 932-2011
Galva *(G-10230)*
Duroweld Company Inc..........E....... 847 680-3064
Lake Bluff *(G-12179)*
▼ **Elfi LLC**..........E....... 815 439-1833
Chicago *(G-4483)*
Expanded Metal Products Corp..........F....... 773 735-4500
Chicago *(G-4544)*
Fabco Enterprises Inc..........G....... 708 333-4644
Harvey *(G-11084)*
Gerdau Ameristeel US Inc..........G....... 800 237-0230
Chicago *(G-4687)*
Gerdau Ameristeel US Inc..........E....... 815 547-0400
Belvidere *(G-1673)*
Glass Management Services Inc..........G....... 312 462-3257
Chicago *(G-4693)*
Gmh Metal Fabrication Inc..........G....... 309 253-6429
East Peoria *(G-8269)*
Harmon Inc..........E....... 630 759-8060
Bolingbrook *(G-2183)*
HI Metals LLC..........G....... 312 590-3360
Winnetka *(G-21130)*
J and D Installers Inc..........G....... 847 288-0783
Franklin Park *(G-9968)*
JC Metalcrafters Inc..........G....... 815 942-9891
Morris *(G-14308)*
Kroh-Wagner Inc..........E....... 773 252-2031
Chicago *(G-5133)*
Ltc Holdings Inc..........C....... 847 249-5900
Waukegan *(G-20464)*
MBI Tools LLC..........G....... 815 844-0937
Pontiac *(G-16775)*
Metal Strip Buiding Products..........G....... 847 742-8500
Itasca *(G-11700)*
▲ **Metalex LLC**..........C....... 847 362-5400
Libertyville *(G-12678)*
▲ **Metals and Services Inc**..........D....... 630 627-2900
Addison *(G-200)*
MMC Precision Holdings Corp..........A....... 309 266-7176
Morton *(G-14367)*
▲ **Nucor Steel Kankakee Inc**..........B....... 815 937-3131
Bourbonnais *(G-2266)*
Olin Engineered Systems Inc..........G....... 618 258-2874
East Alton *(G-8169)*
▲ **PNa Construction Tech Inc**..........F....... 770 668-9500
Itasca *(G-11720)*
Rode Welding Inc..........E....... 847 439-0910
Elk Grove Village *(G-9219)*
Sitexpedite LLC..........E....... 847 245-2185
Lindenhurst *(G-12854)*
Steel Fabricating Inc..........F....... 815 977-5355
Rockford *(G-17645)*
Steel Rebar Manufacturing LLC..........G....... 618 920-2748
Centreville *(G-3255)*
Thirteen Rf Inc..........E....... 618 687-1313
Murphysboro *(G-14761)*
Trinity Machined Products Inc..........E....... 630 876-6992
Aurora *(G-1028)*
Van Pelt Corporation..........E....... 313 365-3600
East Moline *(G-8246)*
▲ **Vermilion Steel Fabrication**..........G....... 217 442-5300
Danville *(G-7391)*
Weld Seam Inc..........F....... 773 588-1012
Wood Dale *(G-21257)*

3451 Screw Machine Prdts

A E Micek Engineering Corp..........E....... 847 455-8181
Franklin Park *(G-9857)*
Abbco Inc..........E....... 630 595-7115
Bensenville *(G-1722)*
▲ **Abbott Interfast LLC**..........D....... 847 459-6200
Wheeling *(G-20838)*
▲ **Abbott Scott Manufacturing Co**..........E....... 773 342-7200
Chicago *(G-3505)*
▲ **Ability Fasteners Inc**..........F....... 847 593-4230
Elk Grove Village *(G-8795)*
Accumation Inc..........F....... 815 455-6250
Crystal Lake *(G-7154)*
Acme Screw Co..........F....... 815 332-7548
Cherry Valley *(G-3436)*
Afco Products Incorporated..........E....... 847 299-1055
Lake Zurich *(G-12380)*
▲ **Afi Industries Inc**..........E....... 630 462-0400
Carol Stream *(G-2927)*
Alert Screw Products Corp..........G....... 847 587-1360
Fox Lake *(G-9744)*
Alpha Swiss Industries Inc..........G....... 815 455-3031
Crystal Lake *(G-7157)*
AM Swiss Screw Mch Pdts Inc..........F....... 847 468-9300
South Elgin *(G-19132)*
American Machine Pdts & Svcs..........G....... 708 743-9088
Mokena *(G-14071)*
American Screw Machine Co..........G....... 847 455-4308
Franklin Park *(G-9868)*
▲ **American/Jebco Corporation**..........C....... 847 455-3150
Cicero *(G-6829)*
Ampex Screw Mfg Inc..........G....... 847 228-1202
Arlington Heights *(G-692)*
Archer Engineering Company..........G....... 773 247-3501
Darien *(G-7402)*
Astro-Craft Inc..........E....... 815 675-1500
Spring Grove *(G-19265)*
▲ **Automatic Precision Inc**..........E....... 708 867-1116
Chicago *(G-3778)*
Automatic Swiss Corporation..........E....... 630 543-3888
Addison *(G-43)*

SIC SECTION — 34 FABRICATED METAL PRODUCTS, EXCEPT MACHINERY AND TRANSPORTATION EQUIPMENT

Automation Systems Inc ..... E 847 671-9515
  Melrose Park (G-13828)
Autonamic Corporation ..... G 815 675-6300
  Spring Grove (G-19266)
Autonetics Inc ..... F 847 426-8525
  Carpentersville (G-3094)
Avan Tool & Die Co Inc ..... F 773 287-1670
  Chicago (G-3782)
Avanti Engineering Inc ..... F 630 260-1333
  Glendale Heights (G-10437)
B Radtke and Sons Inc ..... G 847 546-3999
  Round Lake Park (G-18095)
Bal-Craft Screw Machine Co ..... G 847 398-7688
  Elk Grove Village (G-8855)
Bare Metals Inc ..... G 773 583-1100
  Chicago (G-3832)
Begoun Inc ..... G 630 617-0200
  Elmhurst (G-9329)
Bensenville Screw Products ..... G 630 860-5222
  Bensenville (G-1752)
Bradley Machining Inc ..... F 630 543-2875
  Addison (G-53)
◆ Bridgestone Company Inc ..... E 847 325-5172
  Wheeling (G-20866)
Calcon Machine Inc ..... G 815 495-9227
  Leland (G-12548)
Calumet Screw Machine Products ..... D 708 479-1660
  Mokena (G-14074)
Camco Manufacturing Inc ..... F 708 597-4288
  Crestwood (G-7108)
Camcraft Inc ..... C 630 582-6001
  Hanover Park (G-11001)
Central Autmtc Screw Pdts Inc ..... G 630 766-7966
  Bensenville (G-1764)
Century Automatics LLC ..... G 847 515-1188
  Huntley (G-11531)
Charter Precision LLC ..... D 847 214-8400
  Elgin (G-8536)
Chase Fasteners Inc ..... E 708 345-0335
  Melrose Park (G-13841)
▼ Chicago Rivet & Machine Co ..... D 630 357-8500
  Naperville (G-14798)
Composite Cutter Tech Inc ..... G 847 740-6875
  Volo (G-20198)
Continental Midland ..... G 708 441-1000
  Calumet Park (G-2797)
Continental Screws Mch Pdts ..... E 847 459-7766
  Wheeling (G-20875)
Contour Screw Products Inc ..... F 847 357-1190
  Arlington Heights (G-719)
CP Screw Machine Products ..... F 630 766-2313
  Bensenville (G-1780)
Demco Products Inc ..... F 708 636-6240
  Oak Lawn (G-15713)
▲ Devon Precision Machine Pdts ..... F 847 233-9700
  Franklin Park (G-9932)
Dune Manufacturing Company ..... F 708 681-2905
  Melrose Park (G-13854)
▲ E J Basler Co ..... D 847 678-8880
  Schiller Park (G-18800)
Ella Engineering Incorporated ..... G 847 354-4767
  Elk Grove Village (G-8974)
Empire Screw Manufacturing Co ..... F 630 833-7060
  Villa Park (G-20146)
Engineered Plastic Pdts Corp ..... E 847 952-8400
  Mount Prospect (G-14526)
F and F Screw Products ..... G 815 968-7330
  Rockford (G-17411)
▲ Flexicraft Industries Inc ..... E 312 738-3588
  Chicago (G-4610)
Formar Inc ..... F 630 543-1151
  Addison (G-128)
Forster Tool & Mfg Co Inc ..... E 630 616-8177
  Bensenville (G-1802)
Francis Screw Products Co Inc ..... G 847 647-9462
  Niles (G-15122)
Franklin Screw Products Inc ..... G 815 784-8500
  Genoa (G-10317)
Fsp LLC ..... G 773 992-2600
  Gurnee (G-10880)
G & E Automatic ..... G 815 654-7766
  Machesney Park (G-13345)
Gage Manufacturing Inc ..... F 847 228-7300
  Elk Grove Village (G-9009)
General Engineering Works ..... E 630 543-8000
  Addison (G-136)
Greg Screw Machine Products ..... G 630 694-8875
  Wood Dale (G-21195)
H & M Thread Rolling Co Inc ..... G 847 451-1570
  Franklin Park (G-9955)

Hi-Tech Welding Services Inc ..... G 630 595-8160
  Bensenville (G-1819)
Highland Mch & Screw Pdts Co ..... D 618 654-2103
  Highland (G-11218)
Highland Metal Inc ..... E 708 544-6641
  Hillside (G-11342)
I D Rockford Shop Inc ..... G 815 335-1150
  Winnebago (G-21120)
Illinois Tool Works Inc ..... G 815 654-1510
  Machesney Park (G-13348)
Illinois Tool Works Inc ..... G 847 741-7900
  Elgin (G-8620)
▲ J N R Custo-Matic Screw Inc ..... G 630 260-1333
  Glendale Heights (G-10462)
JB Mfg & Screw Machine ..... G 630 850-6978
  Burr Ridge (G-2691)
JB Mfg & Screw Machine PR ..... G 847 451-0892
  Franklin Park (G-9973)
Jedi Corporation ..... G 815 344-5334
  McHenry (G-13752)
Jim Sterner Machines ..... G 815 962-8983
  Rockford (G-17474)
Kenent Screw Machine Products ..... F 815 624-7216
  Rockton (G-17699)
L & W Tool & Screw Mch Pdts ..... E 847 238-1212
  Itasca (G-11690)
L D Redmer Screw Pdts Inc ..... G 630 787-0504
  Bensenville (G-1838)
Lab Ten LLC ..... G 815 877-1410
  Machesney Park (G-13355)
Lafox Screw Products Inc ..... G 847 695-1732
  South Elgin (G-19164)
Lakeside Screw Products Inc ..... G 630 495-1606
  Addison (G-181)
Lakeview Prcsion Machining Inc ..... F 847 742-7170
  South Elgin (G-19165)
Lawrence Screw Products Inc ..... G 217 735-1230
  Lincoln (G-12732)
Lombard Swiss Screw Company ..... G 630 576-5096
  Addison (G-185)
Lsl Precision Machining Inc ..... G 815 633-4701
  Loves Park (G-13234)
◆ Mac Lean-Fogg Company ..... G 847 566-0010
  Mundelein (G-14710)
Magnet-Schultz Amer Holdg LLC ..... F 630 789-0600
  Westmont (G-20755)
▲ Magnet-Schultz America Inc ..... G 630 789-0600
  Westmont (G-20756)
Magnus Screw Products Co ..... G 773 889-2344
  Chicago (G-5318)
Makerite Mfg Co Inc ..... E 815 389-3902
  Roscoe (G-17916)
Masters Yates Inc ..... G 815 227-9585
  Rockford (G-17509)
McHenry Screw Products Inc ..... G 815 344-4638
  McHenry (G-13766)
Meaden Precision ..... G 630 655-0888
  Burr Ridge (G-2700)
▲ Meaden Precision Machined Pdts ..... G 630 655-0888
  Burr Ridge (G-2701)
Meador Industries Inc ..... E 847 671-5042
  Franklin Park (G-9988)
▲ Metomic Corporation ..... E 773 247-4716
  Chicago (G-5410)
Micro Craft Manufacturing Co ..... F 847 679-2022
  Skokie (G-18889)
Micro Screw Machine Co Inc ..... G 815 397-2115
  Rockford (G-17522)
Midway Machine Products & Svcs ..... G 847 860-8180
  Elk Grove Village (G-9125)
Minic Precision Inc ..... F 815 675-0451
  Spring Grove (G-19285)
▲ Monnex International Inc ..... E 847 850-5263
  Buffalo Grove (G-2576)
▲ Multitech Cold Forming LLC ..... E 630 949-8200
  Carol Stream (G-3034)
Multitech Swiss Machining LLC ..... G 260 894-4180
  Carol Stream (G-3037)
National Cap and Set Screw Co ..... F 815 675-2363
  Spring Grove (G-19287)
◆ National Cycle Inc ..... C 708 343-0400
  Maywood (G-13674)
Nelson & Lavold Manufacturing ..... G 312 943-6300
  Chicago (G-5565)
Nu-Metal Products Inc ..... F 815 459-2075
  Crystal Lake (G-7241)
Nyclo Screw Machine Pdts Inc ..... F 815 229-7900
  Rockford (G-17540)
Oberg Medical Products Co LLC ..... E 847 965-3030
  Niles (G-15153)

Panek Precision Products Co ..... C 847 291-9755
  Northbrook (G-15451)
Pioneer Service Inc ..... E 630 628-0249
  Addison (G-241)
◆ Precise Products Inc ..... E 630 393-9698
  Warrenville (G-20247)
▲ Precision McHned Cmponents Inc ..... E 630 759-5555
  Romeoville (G-17866)
Precision Screw Machining Co ..... F 773 205-4280
  Chicago (G-5859)
▲ Precision Steel Warehouse Inc ..... C 800 323-0740
  Franklin Park (G-10026)
Precision-Tek Mfg Inc ..... E 847 364-7800
  Arlington Heights (G-789)
Preferred Fasteners Inc ..... G 630 510-0200
  Carol Stream (G-3048)
Princeton Industrial Pdts Inc ..... E 847 839-8500
  Elgin (G-8695)
Process Screw Products Inc ..... E 815 864-2220
  Shannon (G-18872)
Progressive Turnings Inc ..... F 630 898-3072
  Aurora (G-1146)
◆ Qcc LLC ..... C 708 867-5400
  Harwood Heights (G-11107)
Quality Control Corp ..... E 708 887-6239
  Harwood Heights (G-11109)
Quantum Precision Inc ..... E 630 692-1545
  West Chicago (G-20634)
R & N Machine Co ..... G 708 841-5555
  Riverdale (G-17075)
R B Evans Co ..... G 630 365-3554
  Elburn (G-8471)
Reino Tool & Manufacturing Co ..... F 773 588-5800
  Chicago (G-6005)
RF Mau Co ..... F 847 329-9731
  Lincolnwood (G-12838)
Roberts Swiss Inc ..... E 630 467-9100
  Itasca (G-11726)
▲ S & W Manufacturing Co Inc ..... G 630 595-5044
  Bensenville (G-1888)
Saturn Manufacturing Company ..... G 630 860-8474
  Bensenville (G-1889)
Screw Machine Engrg Co Inc ..... E 773 631-7600
  Chicago (G-6122)
▲ Screws Industries Inc ..... D 630 539-9200
  Glendale Heights (G-10493)
◆ Security Locknut LLC ..... E 847 970-4050
  Vernon Hills (G-20095)
Special Fastener Operations ..... G 815 544-6449
  Belvidere (G-1701)
▲ Specialty Screw Corporation ..... C 815 969-4100
  Rockford (G-17638)
St Charles Screw Products Inc ..... G 815 943-8060
  Harvard (G-11067)
Suburban Screw Machine Pdts ..... G 815 337-0434
  Woodstock (G-21436)
Supreme Manufacturing Company ..... E 847 297-8212
  Des Plaines (G-7854)
Supreme Screw Products ..... E 708 579-3500
  Countryside (G-7073)
Swebco Mfg Inc ..... E 815 636-7160
  Machesney Park (G-13377)
Swiss Automation Inc ..... D 847 381-4405
  Barrington (G-1246)
Swisstronics Corp ..... G 708 403-8877
  Orland Park (G-15986)
Tanko Scrw Prd Corp ..... G 708 418-0300
  Chicago Heights (G-6779)
Toledo Screw Machine Products ..... G 815 877-8213
  Rockford (G-17664)
Tri-Part Screw Products Inc ..... E 815 654-7311
  Machesney Park (G-13380)
Turnco Inc ..... F 708 756-6565
  Chicago Heights (G-6782)
Ty Precision Automatics Inc ..... F 815 963-9668
  Rockford (G-17669)
Ucal Systems Inc ..... D 847 695-8030
  Elgin (G-8766)
V and L Red Devil Mfg Co ..... E 847 215-1377
  Wheeling (G-21007)
Vandeventer Mfg Co Inc ..... E 630 879-2511
  Batavia (G-1439)
Vanguard Tool & Engineering Co ..... E 847 981-9595
  Mount Prospect (G-14580)
Vek Screw Machine Products ..... G 630 543-5557
  Addison (G-327)
Weber Metal Products Inc ..... F 815 844-3169
  Chenoa (G-3435)
Wenlyn Screw Company Inc ..... G 630 766-0050
  Bensenville (G-1911)

Employee Codes: A=Over 500 employees, B=251-500
C=101-250, D=51-100, E=20-50, F=10-19, G=3-9

34 FABRICATED METAL PRODUCTS, EXCEPT MACHINERY AND TRANSPORTATION EQUIPMENT SIC SECTION

Wilmette Screw Products ....G.... 773 725-2626
Chicago *(G-6634)*

Wilson Mfg Screw Mch Pdts ....F.... 815 964-8724
Rockford *(G-17686)*

3452 Bolts, Nuts, Screws, Rivets & Washers

A J Horne Inc ....G.... 630 231-8686
West Chicago *(G-20530)*

A J Kay Co ....F.... 224 475-0370
Mundelein *(G-14657)*

▲ Abbott Interfast LLC ....D.... 847 459-6200
Wheeling *(G-20838)*

▲ Ability Fasteners Inc ....F.... 847 593-4230
Elk Grove Village *(G-8795)*

Accurate Rivet Manufacturing ....G.... 630 766-3401
Wood Dale *(G-21153)*

▲ Acme Screw Co ....D.... 630 665-2200
Wheaton *(G-20784)*

▼ Advanced Machine & Engrg Co ....C.... 815 962-6076
Rockford *(G-17296)*

▲ Afi Industries Inc ....E.... 630 462-0400
Carol Stream *(G-2927)*

Agrati - Park Forest LLC ....C.... 708 228-5193
Park Forest *(G-16251)*

Agrati USA Corp ....B.... 708 228-5193
Park Forest *(G-16252)*

Alan Manufacturing Corp ....G.... 815 568-6836
Marengo *(G-13478)*

All American Washer Werks Inc ....E.... 847 566-9091
Mundelein *(G-14661)*

Allied Rivet Inc ....F.... 630 208-0120
Geneva *(G-10251)*

▲ Allstar Fasteners Inc ....E.... 847 640-7827
Elk Grove Village *(G-8816)*

Alltec Gates Inc ....G.... 708 301-9361
Tinley Park *(G-19801)*

Amber Engineering and Mfg Co ....D.... 847 595-6966
Elk Grove Village *(G-8819)*

▲ American/Jebco Corporation ....C.... 847 455-3150
Cicero *(G-6829)*

Ampex Screw Mfg Inc ....G.... 847 228-1202
Arlington Heights *(G-692)*

▲ Archer Screw Products Inc ....D.... 847 451-1150
Franklin Park *(G-9873)*

Arrow Pin and Products Inc ....F.... 708 755-7575
S Chicago Hts *(G-18117)*

Aspen Manufacturing Company ....G.... 630 495-0922
Addison *(G-41)*

▲ Aztech Engineering Inc ....E.... 630 236-3200
Aurora *(G-918)*

BBC Fasteners Inc ....E.... 708 597-9100
Alsip *(G-421)*

Big Bolt LLC ....C.... 630 539-9400
Bloomingdale *(G-1981)*

Bolt & Hide Co ....G.... 773 231-2002
Chicago *(G-3932)*

▲ Brynolf Manufacturing Inc ....E.... 815 873-8878
Rockford *(G-17329)*

▲ Burgess-Norton Mfg Co Inc ....B.... 630 232-4100
Geneva *(G-10256)*

Burgess-Norton Mfg Co Inc ....E.... 630 232-4100
Geneva *(G-10257)*

Camcar LLC ....E.... 815 544-7574
Belvidere *(G-1659)*

Century Fasteners & Mch Co Inc ....F.... 773 463-3900
Skokie *(G-18939)*

Chas O Larson Co ....E.... 815 625-0503
Rock Falls *(G-17179)*

Chase Fasteners Inc ....E.... 708 345-0335
Melrose Park *(G-13841)*

▲ Chicago Hardware and Fix Co ....C.... 847 455-6609
Franklin Park *(G-9905)*

▼ Chicago Rivet & Machine Co ....D.... 630 357-8500
Naperville *(G-14798)*

▲ Classic Fasteners LLC ....G.... 630 605-0195
Saint Charles *(G-18170)*

Contmid Inc ....G.... 708 747-1200
Park Forest *(G-16254)*

◆ Cooper B-Line Inc ....A.... 618 654-2184
Highland *(G-11210)*

Dayton Superior Corporation ....E.... 219 476-4106
Kankakee *(G-11962)*

Dayton Superior Corporation ....C.... 815 936-3300
Kankakee *(G-11964)*

▲ Dml Distribution Inc ....F.... 630 839-9041
Schaumburg *(G-18509)*

▲ Du Bro Products Inc ....E.... 847 526-2136
Wauconda *(G-20344)*

▲ Elite Fasteners Inc ....E.... 815 397-8848
Rockford *(G-17395)*

▲ Fastron Co ....E.... 630 766-5000
Melrose Park *(G-13866)*

Folkerts Manufacturing Inc ....G.... 815 968-7426
Rockford *(G-17417)*

Forest City Industry Inc ....F.... 815 877-4084
Loves Park *(G-13213)*

Formed Fastener Mfg Inc ....E.... 708 496-1219
Bridgeview *(G-2348)*

Freedom Fastener Inc ....G.... 847 891-3686
Bensenville *(G-1804)*

Freeway-Rockford Inc ....E.... 815 397-6425
Rockford *(G-17425)*

G-Fast Distribution Inc ....G.... 847 926-0722
Highland Park *(G-11264)*

Gaskoa Inc ....E.... 708 339-5000
South Holland *(G-19213)*

▲ Gateway Screw & Rivet Inc ....E.... 630 539-2232
Glendale Heights *(G-10452)*

Geocyn Company Inc ....E.... 331 213-2851
Naperville *(G-14835)*

Global Fastener Engrg Inc ....F.... 847 929-9563
Lake Zurich *(G-12417)*

▲ Great Lakes Washer Company ....F.... 630 887-7447
Burr Ridge *(G-2677)*

▲ Hadady Corporation ....E.... 219 322-7417
South Holland *(G-19218)*

Haddock Tool & Manufacturing ....G.... 815 786-2739
Sandwich *(G-18373)*

Hadley Gear Manufacturing Co ....F.... 773 722-1030
Chicago *(G-4765)*

Hill Holdings Inc ....E.... 815 625-6600
Rock Falls *(G-17183)*

Hunter-Stevens Company Inc ....F.... 847 671-5014
Franklin Park *(G-9959)*

Illinois Tool Works Inc ....C.... 630 595-3500
Itasca *(G-11672)*

Illinois Tool Works Inc ....E.... 847 741-7900
Elgin *(G-8620)*

Illinois Tool Works Inc ....F.... 708 681-3891
Broadview *(G-2443)*

Illinois Tool Works Inc ....F.... 815 654-1510
Machesney Park *(G-13349)*

Illinois Tool Works Inc ....C.... 847 766-9000
Elk Grove Village *(G-9044)*

▲ Inland Fastener Inc ....F.... 630 293-3800
West Chicago *(G-20596)*

J H Botts LLC ....E.... 815 726-5885
Joliet *(G-11883)*

Jeffrey Jae Inc ....E.... 847 808-2002
Wheeling *(G-20919)*

Jupiter Industries Inc ....G.... 847 925-5120
Schaumburg *(G-18580)*

Kdk Upset Forging Co ....E.... 708 388-8770
Blue Island *(G-2128)*

Kile Machine & Tool Inc ....G.... 217 446-8616
Danville *(G-7357)*

Klinck Inc ....E.... 815 397-3306
Rockford *(G-17484)*

▲ Komar Screw Corp ....E.... 847 965-9090
Niles *(G-15139)*

L & M Screw Machine Products ....F.... 630 801-0455
Montgomery *(G-14253)*

Laundry Services Company ....G.... 630 327-9329
Downers Grove *(G-8042)*

Lawndale Forging & Tool Works ....G.... 773 277-2800
Chicago *(G-5183)*

◆ Lehigh Consumer Products LLC ....C.... 630 851-7330
Aurora *(G-997)*

▲ Locknut Technology Inc ....F.... 630 628-5330
Addison *(G-184)*

▲ Lre Products Inc ....E.... 630 238-8321
Bensenville *(G-1845)*

◆ Mac Lean-Fogg Company ....D.... 847 566-0010
Mundelein *(G-14710)*

Machine Tool Acc & Mfg Co ....G.... 773 489-0903
Chicago *(G-5309)*

▲ Maclen-Fogg Cmpnent Sltons LLC ....E.... 248 853-2525
Mundelein *(G-14711)*

Marengo Tool & Die Works Inc ....E.... 815 568-7411
Marengo *(G-13489)*

▲ Marmon Group LLC ....G.... 312 372-9500
Chicago *(G-5342)*

Matthew Warren Inc ....E.... 847 364-5000
Elk Grove Village *(G-9113)*

Matthew Warren Inc ....G.... 630 860-7766
Bensenville *(G-1848)*

Maxi-Vac Inc ....G.... 630 620-6669
Elgin *(G-8653)*

Metform LLC ....E.... 815 273-2201
Mount Carroll *(G-14495)*

Metform LLC ....C.... 815 273-2201
Savanna *(G-18407)*

Metform LLC ....E.... 815 273-0230
Savanna *(G-18408)*

▲ Mighty Hook Inc ....E.... 773 378-1909
Chicago *(G-5453)*

MNP Precision Parts LLC ....C.... 815 391-5256
Rockford *(G-17530)*

▲ Multitech Cold Forming LLC ....E.... 630 949-8200
Carol Stream *(G-3034)*

National Cap and Set Screw Co ....F.... 815 675-2363
Spring Grove *(G-19287)*

ND Industries Inc ....E.... 847 498-3600
Northbrook *(G-15440)*

Nekg Holdings Inc ....G.... 815 383-1379
Channahon *(G-3391)*

Nylok LLC ....D.... 847 674-9680
Lincolnwood *(G-12834)*

▲ Optimas Oe Solutions LLC ....G.... 224 999-1000
Glenview *(G-10595)*

▲ Parker International Pdts Inc ....D.... 815 524-5831
Vernon Hills *(G-20082)*

Pearson Fastener Corporation ....F.... 815 397-4460
Rockford *(G-17550)*

Pin Up Tattoo ....G.... 815 477-7515
Crystal Lake *(G-7244)*

Pins & Needles Consingment ....G.... 217 299-7365
Pawnee *(G-16305)*

Pontiac Engraving ....G.... 630 834-4424
Bensenville *(G-1870)*

▲ Prairie State Screw & Bolt Co ....F.... 847 858-9551
Northbrook *(G-15463)*

R & N Machine Co ....F.... 708 841-5555
Riverdale *(G-17075)*

Reino Tool & Manufacturing Co ....F.... 773 588-5800
Chicago *(G-6005)*

Ring Screw LLC ....G.... 815 544-7574
Belvidere *(G-1699)*

Roberts Swiss Inc ....E.... 630 467-9100
Itasca *(G-11726)*

Rockford Ball Screw Company ....D.... 815 961-7700
Rockford *(G-17585)*

Rockford Bolt & Steel Co ....E.... 815 968-0514
Rockford *(G-17587)*

Saint Technologies Inc ....G.... 815 864-3035
Shannon *(G-18873)*

Sanco Industries Inc ....F.... 847 243-8675
Kildeer *(G-12052)*

Schmid Tool & Engineering Corp ....E.... 630 333-1733
Villa Park *(G-20171)*

▲ Screws Industries Inc ....D.... 630 539-9200
Glendale Heights *(G-10493)*

◆ Security Locknut LLC ....E.... 847 970-4050
Vernon Hills *(G-20095)*

Semblex Corporation ....E.... 630 833-2880
Elmhurst *(G-9425)*

▲ Set Screw & Mfg Co ....E.... 847 717-3700
Elgin *(G-8727)*

▲ Si Enterprises Inc ....G.... 630 539-9200
Glendale Heights *(G-10494)*

▲ Simpson Strong-Tie Company Inc ....E.... 630 613-5100
West Chicago *(G-20643)*

Skach Manufacturing Co Inc ....E.... 847 395-3560
Antioch *(G-635)*

▲ Slidematic Industries Inc ....C.... 815 986-0500
Rockford *(G-17634)*

▲ Slidemtic Prcsion Cmpnents Inc ....C.... 815 986-0500
Rockford *(G-17635)*

◆ Slsb LLC ....D.... 618 219-4115
Madison *(G-13417)*

Southern Imperial Inc ....G.... 815 877-7041
Loves Park *(G-13265)*

Stelfast Inc ....F.... 847 783-0161
Elgin *(G-8740)*

Steloc Fastener Co ....F.... 847 459-6200
Wheeling *(G-20989)*

Suburban Industries Inc ....F.... 630 766-3773
Franklin Park *(G-10055)*

Thread & Gage Co Inc ....G.... 815 675-2305
Spring Grove *(G-19302)*

Tour Industries Inc ....E.... 847 854-9400
Lake In The Hills *(G-12344)*

▲ Unytite Inc ....C.... 815 224-2221
Peru *(G-16595)*

V and L Red Devil Mfg Co ....E.... 847 215-1377
Wheeling *(G-21007)*

Valley Fastener Group LLC ....E.... 630 548-5679
Naperville *(G-14939)*

Valley Fastener Group LLC ....F.... 708 343-2496
Melrose Park *(G-13924)*

SIC SECTION 34 FABRICATED METAL PRODUCTS, EXCEPT MACHINERY AND TRANSPORTATION EQUIPMENT

Venturedyne Ltd....E.... 708 597-7550
Chicago *(G-6535)*
Wenco Manufacturing Co Inc....E.... 630 377-7474
Elgin *(G-8781)*
Wenlyn Screw Company Inc....G.... 630 766-0050
Bensenville *(G-1911)*
Willie Washer Mfg Co....C.... 847 956-1344
Elk Grove Village *(G-9310)*

3462 Iron & Steel Forgings

Allied Gear Co....G.... 773 287-8742
River Forest *(G-17049)*
Anchor-Harvey Components LLC....D.... 815 233-3833
Freeport *(G-10100)*
Andrew McDonald....G.... 618 867-2323
De Soto *(G-7430)*
Anvil Acquisition Corp....F.... 309 365-8270
Lexington *(G-12617)*
▲ **Arrow Gear Company**....B.... 630 969-7640
Downers Grove *(G-7955)*
As 1902 LLC....D.... 773 287-0874
Chicago *(G-3746)*
C & F Forge Company....E.... 847 455-6609
Franklin Park *(G-9895)*
Carmona Gear Cutting....G.... 815 963-8236
Rockford *(G-17337)*
Chicago Clamp Company....G.... 708 343-8311
Broadview *(G-2426)*
▲ **Chicago Hardware and Fix Co**....C.... 847 455-6609
Franklin Park *(G-9905)*
Clark Gear Works Inc....G.... 630 561-2320
Carol Stream *(G-2962)*
Cleveland Hdwr & Forging Co....D.... 630 896-9850
Aurora *(G-1077)*
▲ **Core Pipe Products Inc**....C.... 630 690-7000
Carol Stream *(G-2967)*
Cornell Forge Company....D.... 708 458-1582
Chicago *(G-4235)*
▲ **Crown Industrial**....G.... 607 745-8709
Dixon *(G-7894)*
Danfoss Power Solutions US Co....C.... 815 233-4200
Freeport *(G-10105)*
Dayton Superior Corporation....C.... 815 936-3300
Kankakee *(G-11964)*
Deer Creek Flange Pipe Co Inc....G.... 309 447-6981
Deer Creek *(G-7574)*
Dss Inc....G.... 630 587-1169
Saint Charles *(G-18187)*
E M Glabus Co Inc....F.... 630 766-3027
Bensenville *(G-1792)*
Eduardo Enterprises Inc....G.... 708 599-9700
Bridgeview *(G-2345)*
Elgin Fastener Group LLC....B.... 847 465-0048
Wheeling *(G-20890)*
Emco Gears Inc....E.... 847 220-4327
Elk Grove Village *(G-8975)*
▲ **Excel Gear Inc**....E.... 815 623-3414
Roscoe *(G-17906)*
Finkl Steel - Houston LLC....F.... 773 975-2540
Chicago *(G-4593)*
Forge Group Dekalb LLC....D.... 815 756-3538
Dekalb *(G-7678)*
Forge Resources Group LLC....F.... 815 758-6400
Dekalb *(G-7681)*
Forgings & Stampings Inc....E.... 815 962-5597
Rockford *(G-17421)*
Gear & Repair....G.... 708 387-0144
Brookfield *(G-2485)*
General Forging Die Co Inc....E.... 815 874-4224
Rockford *(G-17428)*
Great Lakes Forge Company....G.... 773 277-2800
Chicago *(G-4735)*
Group Industries Inc....E.... 708 877-6200
Thornton *(G-19788)*
Hadley Gear Manufacturing Co....F.... 773 722-1030
Chicago *(G-4765)*
HM Manufacturing Inc....F.... 847 487-8700
Wauconda *(G-20356)*
I Forge Company LLC....G.... 815 535-0600
Rock Falls *(G-17186)*
Illinois Expedited Express Inc....E.... 217 926-2171
Lansing *(G-12498)*
Innovative Rack & Gear Company....F.... 630 766-2652
Wood Dale *(G-21201)*
J & L Gear Incorporated....F.... 630 832-1880
Villa Park *(G-20151)*
Jernberg Industries LLC....C.... 773 268-3004
Chicago *(G-5021)*
Jernberg Industries LLC....C.... 630 972-7000
Bolingbrook *(G-2197)*
Kd Steel Incorporated....G.... 630 201-1619
Westmont *(G-20752)*
Kdk Upset Forging Co....E.... 708 388-8770
Blue Island *(G-2128)*
Keller Group Inc....B.... 847 446-7550
Northfield *(G-15520)*
Ken Elliott Co....G.... 618 466-8200
Godfrey *(G-10654)*
Kz Manufacturing Co....G.... 708 937-8097
Mc Cook *(G-13694)*
Lawndale Forging & Tool Works....G.... 773 277-2800
Chicago *(G-5183)*
◆ **Lehigh Consumer Products LLC**....C.... 630 851-7330
Aurora *(G-997)*
Liberty Spclty Stels Amer Inc....G.... 847 521-6464
Schaumburg *(G-18606)*
Loch Precision Technologies....G.... 847 438-1400
Lake Zurich *(G-12429)*
Machine Tool Acc & Mfg Co....G.... 773 489-0903
Chicago *(G-5309)*
Malca-Amit North America Inc....G.... 312 346-1507
Chicago *(G-5322)*
Metform LLC....C.... 815 273-2201
Savanna *(G-18407)*
▲ **Metform LLC**....G.... 847 566-0010
Mundelein *(G-14717)*
Metform LLC....E.... 815 273-0230
Savanna *(G-18408)*
Midwest Brass Forging Co....E.... 847 678-7023
Franklin Park *(G-9998)*
Mitsutoyo-Kiko USA Inc....G.... 847 981-5200
Rolling Meadows *(G-17751)*
Modern Gear & Machine Inc....F.... 630 350-9173
Bensenville *(G-1854)*
▲ **Moline Forge Inc**....D.... 309 762-5506
Moline *(G-14163)*
Norforge and Machining Inc....D.... 309 772-3124
Macomb *(G-13394)*
▲ **Park-Hio Frged McHned Pdts LLC**....D.... 708 652-6691
Chicago *(G-5765)*
▲ **Peer Chain Company**....D.... 847 775-4600
Waukegan *(G-20475)*
Phoenix Trading Chicago Inc....G.... 847 304-5181
Lake Barrington *(G-12163)*
◆ **Prime Stainless Products LLC**....G.... 847 678-0800
Schiller Park *(G-18836)*
Process Screw Products Inc....E.... 815 864-2220
Shannon *(G-18872)*
Productigear Inc....E.... 773 847-4505
Chicago *(G-5893)*
Products In Motion Inc....G.... 815 213-7251
Rock Falls *(G-17191)*
Rail Exchange Inc....E.... 708 757-3317
Chicago Heights *(G-6767)*
Raycar Gear & Machine Company....E.... 815 874-3948
Rockford *(G-17566)*
Reag Inc....G.... 708 344-0875
Bridgeview *(G-2379)*
▼ **Rj Link International Inc**....F.... 815 874-8110
Rockford *(G-17576)*
Rkfd LLC Grua....G.... 815 414-2392
Rockford *(G-17577)*
Rkfd LLC Grua....G.... 815 414-2392
Rockford *(G-17578)*
Rockford Drop Forge Company....D.... 815 963-9611
Rockford *(G-17592)*
Rockford Jobbing Service Inc....G.... 815 398-8661
Rockford *(G-17596)*
RT Blackhawk Mch Pdts Inc....G.... 815 389-3632
South Beloit *(G-19111)*
Sbic America Inc....G.... 847 303-5430
Schaumburg *(G-18704)*
▲ **Schafer Gear Works Roscoe LLC**....C.... 815 874-4327
Roscoe *(G-17931)*
Schmid Tool & Engineering Corp....E.... 630 333-1733
Villa Park *(G-20171)*
◆ **Scot Forge Company**....B.... 815 675-1000
Spring Grove *(G-19300)*
Scot Forge Company....D.... 847 678-6000
Franklin Park *(G-10045)*
▲ **Simpson Strong-Tie Company Inc**....E.... 630 613-5100
West Chicago *(G-20643)*
▲ **Star Forge Inc**....D.... 815 235-7750
Freeport *(G-10144)*
Sumitomo Machinery Corp Amer....E.... 630 752-0200
Glendale Heights *(G-10504)*
◆ **Thyssenkrupp Crankshaft Co LLC**....C.... 217 431-0060
Danville *(G-7383)*
Thyssenkrupp Crankshaft Co LLC....C.... 217 444-5400
Danville *(G-7384)*
Thyssenkrupp Crankshaft Co LLC....C.... 217 444-5500
Danville *(G-7385)*
◆ **Timken Drives LLC**....D.... 815 589-2211
Fulton *(G-10158)*
Timken Drives LLC....G.... 312 274-9710
Chicago *(G-6380)*
Timken Gears & Services Inc....F.... 708 720-9400
Mokena *(G-14122)*
Tomko Machine Works Inc....G.... 630 244-0902
Lemont *(G-12593)*
US Tsubaki Power Transm LLC....C.... 847 459-9500
Wheeling *(G-21004)*
Welch Steel Products Inc....F.... 847 741-2623
Elgin *(G-8780)*
▲ **Weldbend Corporation**....C.... 708 594-1700
Argo *(G-677)*
Wozniak Industries Inc....C.... 708 458-1220
Bedford Park *(G-1515)*
◆ **Wozniak Industries Inc**....G.... 630 954-3400
Schaumburg *(G-18776)*

3463 Nonferrous Forgings

Acme Screw Co....F.... 815 332-7548
Cherry Valley *(G-3436)*
Burgess-Norton Mfg Co Inc....E.... 630 232-4100
Geneva *(G-10257)*
Genacc LLC....G.... 309 253-9034
Peoria *(G-16444)*
Jernberg Industries LLC....C.... 773 268-3004
Chicago *(G-5021)*
Voss Engineering Inc....E.... 847 673-8900
Lincolnwood *(G-12850)*

3465 Automotive Stampings

Amis Inc....G.... 708 598-9700
Bridgeview *(G-2323)*
Borgwarner Inc....C.... 815 288-1462
Dixon *(G-7892)*
Borgwarner Transm Systems Inc....A.... 708 547-2600
Bellwood *(G-1618)*
Bosch Auto Svc Solutions Inc....F.... 815 407-3900
Romeoville *(G-17799)*
Clay Cnty Rhbilitation Ctr Inc....F.... 618 662-6607
Flora *(G-9678)*
Ford Motor Company....A.... 708 757-5700
Ford Heights *(G-9706)*
G & M Manufacturing Corp....E.... 815 455-1900
Crystal Lake *(G-7201)*
Gs Custom Works Inc....G.... 815 233-4724
Freeport *(G-10113)*
Illinois Tool Works Inc....G.... 708 720-3541
Frankfort *(G-9808)*
Inland Tool Company....E.... 217 792-3206
Mount Pulaski *(G-14588)*
ITW Dynatec....G.... 847 657-4830
Glenview *(G-10573)*
Jahm Inc....F.... 847 647-7650
Niles *(G-15135)*
▲ **Kipp Manufacturing Company Inc**....F.... 630 768-9051
Wauconda *(G-20366)*
Laystrom Manufacturing Co....D.... 773 342-4800
Chicago *(G-5186)*
◆ **Marmon Industries LLC**....G.... 312 372-9500
Chicago *(G-5345)*
▲ **Mercury Products Corp**....C.... 847 524-4400
Schaumburg *(G-18627)*
Mmma....F.... 309 888-8765
Normal *(G-15211)*
MNP Precision Parts LLC....C.... 815 391-5256
Rockford *(G-17530)*
▲ **Perfection Spring Stmping Corp**....D.... 847 437-3900
Mount Prospect *(G-14560)*
▲ **Plastic Technologies Inc**....E.... 847 841-8610
Elgin *(G-8688)*
Rhino Pros....G.... 815 235-7767
Freeport *(G-10137)*
T R Z Motorsports Inc....G.... 815 806-0838
Frankfort *(G-9843)*
▲ **Taurus Die Casting LLC**....F.... 815 316-6160
Rockford *(G-17654)*
▲ **Topy Precision Mfg Inc**....D.... 847 228-5902
Elk Grove Village *(G-9277)*
Tower Atmtive Oprtons USA I LL....B.... 773 646-6550
Chicago *(G-6400)*
Troy Design & Manufacturing Co....G.... 312 692-9706
Chicago *(G-6434)*
Tsm Inc....G.... 815 544-5012
Belvidere *(G-1705)*
Waupaca Foundry Inc....C.... 217 347-0600
Effingham *(G-8430)*

S I C

Employee Codes: A=Over 500 employees, B=251-500
C=101-250, D=51-100, E=20-50, F=10-19, G=3-9
2020 Harris Illinois
Industrial Directory
935

34 FABRICATED METAL PRODUCTS, EXCEPT MACHINERY AND TRANSPORTATION EQUIPMENT

3466 Crowns & Closures

Alcon Tool & Mfg Co Inc .... F 773 545-8742
  Chicago (G-3598)
◆ Amcor Flexibles LLC .... C 224 313-7000
  Buffalo Grove (G-2510)
Kile Machine & Tool Inc .... G 217 446-8616
  Danville (G-7357)
▲ Kipp Manufacturing Company Inc .... F 630 768-9051
  Wauconda (G-20366)
Precise Technology .... G 847 459-1001
  Buffalo Grove (G-2589)
Product Service Craft Inc .... F 630 964-5160
  Downers Grove (G-8085)
▲ Sorini Manufacturing Corp .... E 773 247-5858
  Chicago (G-6203)
▲ Walter H Jelly & Co Inc .... G 847 455-4235
  Franklin Park (G-10082)

3469 Metal Stampings, NEC

10 4 Irp Inc .... G 708 485-1040
  Brookfield (G-2476)
Aable License Consultants .... F 708 836-1235
  Broadview (G-2411)
▲ Abbott Scott Manufacturing Co .... E 773 342-7200
  Chicago (G-3505)
▲ Ability Metal Company .... E 847 437-7040
  Elk Grove Village (G-8796)
Accurate Perforating Co Inc .... D 773 254-3232
  Chicago (G-3519)
Accurate Wire Strip Frming Inc .... F 630 260-1000
  Carol Stream (G-2924)
Ace Metal Spinning Inc .... F 708 389-5635
  Alsip (G-412)
Ace Plating Company .... E 773 927-2711
  Chicago (G-3522)
▲ Acme Spinning Company Inc .... F 773 927-2711
  Chicago (G-3528)
Action Tool & Mfg Inc .... E 815 874-5775
  Rockford (G-17294)
Ada Metal Products Inc .... E 847 673-1190
  Lincolnwood (G-12811)
Advanced Custom Metals Inc .... G 847 803-2090
  Des Plaines (G-7723)
Agri-Fab Inc .... G 217 728-8388
  Sullivan (G-19659)
▼ Alagor Industries Incorporated .... D 630 766-2910
  Bensenville (G-1734)
Alan Manufacturing Corp .... G 815 568-6836
  Marengo (G-13478)
Alcon Tool & Mfg Co Inc .... F 773 545-8742
  Chicago (G-3598)
All American Spring Stamping .... G 847 928-9468
  Franklin Park (G-9865)
All American Washer Werks Inc .... E 847 566-9091
  Mundelein (G-14661)
Allied Production Drilling .... F 815 969-0940
  Stillman Valley (G-19544)
▲ Alpha Products Inc .... E 708 594-3883
  Bedford Park (G-1455)
American Industrial Company .... F 847 855-9200
  Gurnee (G-10859)
American Partsmith Inc .... G 630 520-0432
  West Chicago (G-20538)
Amity Die and Stamping Co .... E 847 680-6600
  Lake Forest (G-12224)
Ammentorp Tool Company Inc .... G 847 671-9290
  Franklin Park (G-9869)
Angle Tool Company .... E 847 593-7572
  Elk Grove Village (G-8832)
Animated Manufacturing Company .... F 708 333-6688
  South Holland (G-19195)
Apex Wire Products Company Inc .... F 847 671-1830
  Franklin Park (G-9871)
Archer Manufacturing Corp .... E 773 585-7181
  Chicago (G-3725)
◆ Ark Technologies Inc .... D 630 377-8855
  Saint Charles (G-18149)
Aro Metal Stamping Company Inc .... E 630 351-7676
  Wood Dale (G-21166)
Ascent Mfg Co .... E 847 806-6600
  Elk Grove Village (G-8841)
◆ Ask Products Inc .... D 630 896-4056
  Aurora (G-1054)
Astoria Wire Products Inc .... D 708 496-9950
  Bedford Park (G-1459)
Atlantic Engineering .... G 847 782-1762
  Zion (G-21509)
▲ Atlas Tool & Die Works Inc .... D 708 442-1661
  Lyons (G-13259)

Austin Tool & Die Co .... D 847 509-5800
  Northbrook (G-15344)
Available Spring and Mfg Co .... G 847 520-4854
  Wheeling (G-20853)
B & D Murray Manufacturing Co .... G 815 568-6176
  Marengo (G-13481)
B Radtke and Sons Inc .... G 847 546-3999
  Round Lake Park (G-18095)
▲ Barco Stamping Co .... E 630 293-5155
  West Chicago (G-20549)
Barrington Automation Ltd .... E 847 458-0900
  Lake In The Hills (G-12329)
Bel-Air Manufacturing Inc .... E 773 276-7550
  Chicago (G-3862)
◆ Bellota Agrsltions Tls USA LLC ..... E 309 787-2491
  Rock Island (G-17205)
Berny Metal Products Inc .... E 847 742-8500
  South Elgin (G-19137)
▲ Bi-Link Metal Specialties Inc .... C 630 858-5900
  Bloomingdale (G-1980)
▲ Big 3 Precision Products Inc .... C 618 533-3251
  Centralia (G-3222)
Bilt-Rite Metal Products Inc .... E 815 495-2211
  Leland (G-12547)
Bingamn-Prcsion Mtal Spnning C .... E 847 392-5620
  Rolling Meadows (G-17719)
◆ Block and Company Inc .... C 847 537-7200
  Wheeling (G-20860)
Blue Chip Mfg LLC .... G 630 553-6321
  Oswego (G-15993)
Bomel Tool Manufacturing Co .... C 708 343-3663
  Broadview (G-2422)
Borgwarner Transm Systems Inc .... A 708 547-2600
  Bellwood (G-1618)
Braun Manufacturing Co Inc .... E 847 635-2050
  Mount Prospect (G-14514)
Briergate Tool & Engrg Co .... F 630 766-7050
  Bensenville (G-1756)
▲ Buhrke Industries LLC .... B 847 981-7550
  Arlington Heights (G-711)
Burnex Corporation .... E 815 728-1317
  Ringwood (G-17040)
C & C Can Co Inc .... G 312 421-2372
  Chicago (G-3992)
▲ C & J Metal Products Inc .... F 847 455-0766
  Franklin Park (G-9896)
C E R Machining & Tooling Ltd .... E 708 442-9614
  Lyons (G-13305)
C J Holdings Inc .... G 309 274-3141
  Chillicothe (G-6815)
C Keller Manufacturing Inc .... E 630 833-5593
  Villa Park (G-20136)
Cac Corporation .... E 630 221-5200
  Carol Stream (G-2953)
Cardinal Engineering Inc .... G 309 342-7474
  Galesburg (G-10188)
Carlson Capitol Mfg Co .... F 815 398-3110
  Rockford (G-17335)
Celco Tool & Engineering Inc .... F 847 671-2520
  Schiller Park (G-18792)
Central Radiator Cabinet Co .... G 773 539-1700
  Lena (G-12599)
Central Tool Specialities Inc .... G 630 543-6351
  Addison (G-66)
Century Metal Spinning Co Inc .... E 630 595-3900
  Bensenville (G-1765)
▲ Chicago Car Seal Company .... G 773 278-9400
  Chicago (G-4095)
▲ Chicago Cutting Die Co .... D 847 509-5800
  Northbrook (G-15357)
Chicago Metal Fabricators Inc .... D 773 523-5755
  Chicago (G-4114)
Cicero Plastic Products Inc .... E 815 886-9522
  Romeoville (G-17808)
City of Danville .... G 217 442-1564
  Tilton (G-19794)
Coda Resources Ltd .... F 718 649-1666
  Chicago (G-4190)
Columbia Metal Spinning Co .... D 773 685-2800
  Chicago (G-4206)
◆ Columbian Home Products LLC .... C 847 307-8600
  North Barrington (G-15282)
Component Tool & Mfg Co .... F 708 672-7505
  Crete (G-7136)
◆ Corelle Brands Holdings Inc .... D 847 233-8600
  Rosemont (G-18009)
◆ Cosmos Manufacturing Inc .... F 708 756-1400
  S Chicago Hts (G-18119)
Craft Metal Spinning Co .... F 773 685-4700
  Chicago (G-4255)

▼ Craftsman Custom Metals LLC ..... D 847 655-0040
  Schiller Park (G-18797)
Creative Metal Products .... F 773 638-3200
  Chicago (G-4264)
Crown Brands LLC .... E 224 513-2917
  Lincolnshire (G-12757)
Crystal Precision Drilling .... G 815 633-5460
  Loves Park (G-13199)
Cs Legacy Corp .... E 847 741-3101
  Elgin (G-8558)
CSI Cutting Specialist Inc .... D 731 352-5351
  Edwardsville (G-8353)
D & B Fabricators & Distrs .... F 630 325-3811
  Lemont (G-12562)
D & J Machine Shop Inc .... G 815 472-6057
  Momence (G-14184)
Dadum Inc .... G 847 541-7851
  Buffalo Grove (G-2530)
Delta Metal Products Co .... G 773 745-9220
  Chicago (G-4336)
Desk & Door Nameplate Company ... F 815 806-8670
  Frankfort (G-9785)
Dial Tool Industries Inc .... D 630 543-3600
  Addison (G-87)
▲ Diemasters Manufacturing Inc ...... C 847 640-9900
  Elk Grove Village (G-8950)
Dixline Corporation .... E 309 932-2011
  Galva (G-10230)
Dixline Corporation .... D 309 932-2011
  Galva (G-10231)
Dkb Partners Inc .... G 618 632-6718
  O Fallon (G-15572)
▲ Domeny Tool & Stamping Company F 847 526-5700
  Wauconda (G-20342)
Dovee Manufacturing Inc .... F 847 437-8122
  Elgin (G-8569)
▲ Dudek & Bock Spring Mfg Co .... C 773 379-4100
  Chicago (G-4402)
E H Baare Corporation .... E 618 546-1575
  Robinson (G-17114)
Ed Stan Fabricating Co .... G 708 863-7668
  Chicago (G-4449)
▲ Elburn Metal Stamping Inc .... E 630 365-2500
  Elburn (G-8452)
Ems Industrial and Service Co .... E 815 678-2700
  Richmond (G-17012)
▲ Entropy Cab Solutions Inc USA .... F 630 834-3872
  Elmhurst (G-9362)
Equinox Group Inc .... G 312 226-7002
  Chicago (G-4524)
▼ Equipto Electronics Corp .... E 630 897-4691
  Aurora (G-1091)
ERA Tool and Manufacturing Co .... E 847 298-6333
  Zion (G-21513)
Erickson Tool & Machine Co .... G 815 397-2653
  Rockford (G-17400)
▲ Erva Tool & Die Company .... G 773 533-7806
  Chicago (G-4528)
Estad Stamping & Mfg Co .... E 217 442-4600
  Danville (G-7331)
Exclusive Stone .... G 847 593-6963
  Elk Grove Village (G-8989)
Exton Corp .... C 847 391-8100
  Des Plaines (G-7763)
Fabricating Machinery Sales .... E 630 350-2266
  Wood Dale (G-21186)
Fabricators Unlimited Inc .... E 847 223-7986
  Grayslake (G-10772)
Fanmar Inc .... E 847 621-2010
  Elk Grove Village (G-8995)
▲ FIC America Corp .... A 630 871-7609
  Carol Stream (G-2984)
Force Manufacturing Inc .... E 847 265-6500
  Lake Villa (G-12351)
Ford Motor Company .... A 708 757-5700
  Ford Heights (G-9706)
Form-All Spring Stamping Inc .... E 630 595-8833
  Bensenville (G-1800)
Formco Metal Products Inc .... E 630 766-4441
  Wood Dale (G-21190)
Forster Tool & Mfg Co Inc .... E 630 616-8177
  Bensenville (G-1802)
▲ Fortune Brands Home & SEC Inc .. D 847 484-4400
  Deerfield (G-7610)
Fountain Products Inc .... G 630 991-7237
  Elgin (G-8590)
▲ Four Star Tool Inc .... D 224 735-2419
  Rolling Meadows (G-17733)
Fox Valley Stamping Company .... F 847 741-2277
  South Elgin (G-19146)

Fulton Corporation D 815 589-3211
Fulton *(G-10152)*

G & M Manufacturing Corp E 815 455-1900
Crystal Lake *(G-7201)*

G & M Metal Fabricators Inc D 847 678-6501
Franklin Park *(G-9947)*

G T L Technologies Inc G 630 469-9818
Glendale Heights *(G-10451)*

Gem Equipment & Mfg LLC E 309 923-7312
Roanoke *(G-17101)*

General Machinery & Mfg Co F 773 235-3700
Chicago *(G-4674)*

▲ **Gilbert Spring Corporation** E 773 486-6030
Chicago *(G-4691)*

Global Brass and Copper Inc G 502 873-3000
East Alton *(G-8166)*

Global Brass Cop Holdings Inc E 847 240-4700
Schaumburg *(G-18535)*

Graphic Parts Intl Inc F 773 725-4900
Chicago *(G-4726)*

H&K Perforating LLC E 773 626-1800
Chicago *(G-4762)*

Haddock Tool & Manufacturing G 815 786-2739
Sandwich *(G-18373)*

▲ **Harig Manufacturing Corp** E 847 647-9500
Skokie *(G-18964)*

Harrington King Prforating Inc C 773 626-1800
Chicago *(G-4781)*

Hcf Building Corporation F 630 595-2040
Wood Dale *(G-21196)*

Headly Manufacturing Co D 708 338-0800
Broadview *(G-2440)*

Headly Manufacturing Co D 708 338-0800
Broadview *(G-2441)*

Highland Southern Wire Inc G 618 654-2161
Highland *(G-11222)*

▲ **HMC Holdings LLC** F 800 874-6625
Buffalo Grove *(G-2547)*

Hoosier Stamping & Mfg Corp E 618 375-2057
Grayville *(G-10810)*

Hpl Stampings Inc E 847 540-1400
Lake Zurich *(G-12419)*

Hub Manufacturing Company Inc E 773 252-1373
Chicago *(G-4859)*

Hudson Tool & Die Co F 847 678-8710
Franklin Park *(G-9958)*

I C Universal Inc G 630 766-1169
Bensenville *(G-1820)*

▲ **Icon Power Roller Inc** E 630 545-2345
Marseilles *(G-13556)*

Illinois Tool Works Inc F 708 681-3891
Broadview *(G-2443)*

Illinois Tool Works Inc C 847 299-2222
Des Plaines *(G-7785)*

Imh Fabrication Inc F 815 537-2381
Prophetstown *(G-16833)*

▼ **IMS Companies LLC** D 847 391-8100
Des Plaines *(G-7786)*

▲ **IMS Engineered Products LLC** C 847 391-8100
Des Plaines *(G-7787)*

IMS Olson LLC D 630 969-9400
Downers Grove *(G-8030)*

▼ **Industrial Enclosure Corp** E 630 898-7499
Aurora *(G-1111)*

Industrial Park Machine & Tool F 708 754-7080
S Chicago Hts *(G-18122)*

Inland Tool Company E 217 792-3206
Mount Pulaski *(G-14588)*

Integrity Manufacturing Inc G 815 514-8230
Romeoville *(G-17832)*

▼ **Integrity Metals LLC** E 630 963-4126
Romeoville *(G-17833)*

International Spring Company D 847 470-8170
Morton Grove *(G-14413)*

▼ **Interplex Daystar Inc** D 847 455-2424
Franklin Park *(G-9966)*

Ironform Holdings Co B 312 374-4810
Chicago *(G-4970)*

J F Schroeder Company Inc E 847 357-8600
Arlington Heights *(G-759)*

J-TEC Metal Products Inc F 630 875-1300
Itasca *(G-11679)*

Jahm Inc F 847 647-7650
Niles *(G-15135)*

Jason Incorporated C 630 627-7000
Addison *(G-158)*

▲ **JD Norman Industries Inc** D 630 458-3700
Addison *(G-159)*

Jenco Metal Products Inc F 847 956-0550
Mount Prospect *(G-14539)*

Jiffy Metal Products Inc G 773 626-8090
Chicago *(G-5030)*

Jlo Metal Products Co A Corp D 773 889-6242
Chicago *(G-5032)*

Johnson Tool Company G 708 453-8600
Huntley *(G-11547)*

▲ **Jsn Inc** E 708 410-1800
Maywood *(G-13670)*

Kaiser Mfg Co C 773 235-4705
Chicago *(G-5076)*

Kaman Tool Corporation G 708 652-9023
Cicero *(G-6858)*

Kaskaskia Tool and Machine Inc E 618 475-3301
New Athens *(G-15020)*

Kay Manufacturing Company LLC C 708 862-6800
Calumet City *(G-2782)*

◆ **Kenmode Tool and Engrg Inc** C 847 658-5041
Algonquin *(G-376)*

Kensen Tool & Die Inc F 847 455-0150
Franklin Park *(G-9976)*

Kernel Kutter Inc G 815 877-1515
Machesney Park *(G-13354)*

Kier Mfg Co G 630 953-9500
Addison *(G-170)*

▲ **Kipp Manufacturing Company Inc** F 630 768-9051
Wauconda *(G-20366)*

Kleen Cut Tool Inc G 630 447-7020
Warrenville *(G-20240)*

Klein Tools Inc D 847 228-6999
Elk Grove Village *(G-9078)*

Klein Tools Inc E 847 821-5500
Lincolnshire *(G-12779)*

Klinck Inc E 815 397-3306
Rockford *(G-17484)*

Knapheide Manufacturing Co E 217 223-1848
Quincy *(G-16902)*

Kosmos Tool Inc F 815 675-2200
Spring Grove *(G-19281)*

Kr Machine G 815 248-2250
Durand *(G-8153)*

Kz Manufacturing Co G 708 937-8097
Mc Cook *(G-13694)*

▲ **Lakeview Metals Inc** D 847 838-9800
Antioch *(G-621)*

▲ **Larsen Manufacturing LLC** C 847 970-9600
Mundelein *(G-14709)*

Laystrom Manufacturing Co D 773 342-4800
Chicago *(G-5186)*

Lew-El Tool & Manufacturing Co F 773 804-1133
Chicago *(G-5212)*

Lewis Spring and Mfg Company D 847 588-7030
Niles *(G-15140)*

Line Group Inc E 847 593-6810
Arlington Heights *(G-769)*

Lorbern Mfg Inc E 847 301-8600
Schaumburg *(G-18612)*

▲ **Lsa United Inc** C 773 476-7439
Lombard *(G-13098)*

▲ **M J Celco Inc** D 847 671-1900
Schiller Park *(G-18818)*

M Lizen Manufacturing Co E 708 755-7213
University Park *(G-19958)*

M Ward Manufacturing Co Inc E 847 864-4786
Evanston *(G-9548)*

Macon Resources Inc C 217 875-1910
Decatur *(G-7520)*

Major Die & Engineering Co F 630 773-3444
Itasca *(G-11696)*

Manor Tool and Mfg Co D 847 678-2020
Schiller Park *(G-18820)*

Marengo Tool & Die Works Inc E 815 568-7411
Marengo *(G-13489)*

Mark Development Corporation C 815 339-2226
Mark *(G-13545)*

Marlboro Wire Ltd E 217 224-7989
Quincy *(G-16910)*

Masonite Corporation D 630 584-6330
West Chicago *(G-20616)*

Mayfair Metal Spinning Co Inc G 847 358-7450
Palatine *(G-16139)*

Mengarelli Enterprises Inc D 847 272-6980
Northbrook *(G-15433)*

▲ **Mercury Products Corp** C 847 524-4400
Schaumburg *(G-18627)*

▲ **Meridian Parts Inc** G 630 718-1995
Naperville *(G-14868)*

Metal Spinners Inc E 815 625-0390
Rock Falls *(G-17189)*

▲ **Metalex LLC** C 847 362-5400
Libertyville *(G-12678)*

▲ **Metalstamp Inc** E 815 467-7800
Minooka *(G-14063)*

Micromatic Spring Stamping Inc E 630 607-0141
Addison *(G-207)*

Mid-West Spring & Stamping Inc G 630 739-3800
Romeoville *(G-17853)*

Midland Stamping and Fabg Corp D 847 678-7573
Schiller Park *(G-18825)*

Midwest Nameplate Corp G 708 614-0606
Orland Park *(G-15968)*

Milans Machining & Mfg Co Inc D 708 780-6600
Cicero *(G-6867)*

Millenia Metals LLC D 630 458-0401
Itasca *(G-11703)*

▲ **Millenia Products Group Inc** C 630 458-0401
Itasca *(G-11704)*

Mint Masters Inc E 847 451-1133
Franklin Park *(G-10000)*

Mity Inc G 630 365-5030
Elburn *(G-8461)*

▲ **Mj Celco International LLC** E 847 671-1900
Schiller Park *(G-18827)*

MNP Precision Parts LLC C 815 391-5256
Rockford *(G-17530)*

Modineer P-K Tool LLC E 773 235-4700
Chicago *(G-5483)*

Moline Welding Inc F 309 756-0643
Milan *(G-14018)*

Mueller Mfg Corp E 847 640-1666
Elk Grove Village *(G-9139)*

My-Lin Manufacturing Co Inc E 630 897-4100
Aurora *(G-1137)*

Natura Products Inc F 847 509-5835
Northbrook *(G-15439)*

Navitor Inc B 800 323-0253
Harwood Heights *(G-11106)*

Nelson Manufacturing Co Inc F 815 229-0161
Rockford *(G-17537)*

New Dimension Models G 815 935-1001
Aroma Park *(G-840)*

Newko Tool & Engineering Co E 847 359-1670
Palatine *(G-16142)*

North Star Stamping & Tool Inc F 847 658-9400
Lake In The Hills *(G-12342)*

▲ **Northfield Holdings LLC** E 847 755-0700
Schaumburg *(G-18652)*

▲ **Nu-Way Industries Inc** C 847 298-7710
Des Plaines *(G-7812)*

Octavia Tool & Gage Company G 847 913-9233
Elk Grove Village *(G-9159)*

Odm Tool & Mfg Co Inc D 708 485-6130
Hodgkins *(G-11391)*

Offko Tool Inc G 815 933-9474
Kankakee *(G-11994)*

OHare Spring Company Inc E 847 298-1360
Elk Grove Village *(G-9160)*

Olson Metal Products LLC F 847 981-7550
Arlington Heights *(G-784)*

▲ **Omiotek Coil Spring Co** D 630 495-4056
Lombard *(G-13113)*

P T L Manufacturing Inc E 618 277-6789
Belleville *(G-1582)*

Paddock Industries Inc F 618 277-1580
Smithton *(G-19068)*

Paragon Spring Company E 773 489-6300
Chicago *(G-5759)*

Paris Metal Products LLC D 217 465-6321
Paris *(G-16239)*

Park Manufacturing Corp Inc F 708 345-6090
Melrose Park *(G-13903)*

Parkway Metal Products Inc D 847 789-4000
Des Plaines *(G-7818)*

Patko Tool & Manufacturing G 630 616-8802
Bensenville *(G-1867)*

PDQ Tool & Stamping Co E 708 841-3000
Dolton *(G-7938)*

Pecora Tool Service Inc G 847 524-1275
Schaumburg *(G-18672)*

▲ **Perfection Spring Stmping Corp** D 847 437-3900
Mount Prospect *(G-14560)*

▲ **Performance Stamping Co Inc** E 847 426-2233
Carpentersville *(G-3112)*

Plano Molding Company LLC C 815 538-3111
Mendota *(G-13952)*

▲ **Plasticrest Products Inc** F 773 826-2163
Chicago *(G-5818)*

Porcelain Enamel Finishers G 312 808-1560
Chicago *(G-5845)*

Precise Stamping Inc E 630 897-6477
North Aurora *(G-15272)*

SIC

Employee Codes: A=Over 500 employees, B=251-500
C=101-250, D=51-100, E=20-50, F=10-19, G=3-9
2020 Harris Illinois
Industrial Directory
937

34 FABRICATED METAL PRODUCTS, EXCEPT MACHINERY AND TRANSPORTATION EQUIPMENT

Precision Forming Stamping Co ....E...... 773 489-6868
Chicago (G-5857)
Precision Metal Spinning Corp ....E...... 847 392-5672
Rolling Meadows (G-17764)
Precision Metal Technologies ....F...... 847 228-6630
Rolling Meadows (G-17765)
Precision Resource Inc ....C...... 847 383-1300
Vernon Hills (G-20083)
▲ Precision Stamping Pdts Inc ....E...... 847 678-0800
Schiller Park (G-18835)
Premier Metal Works Inc ....G...... 312 226-7414
Chicago (G-5863)
Prikos & Becker LLC ....D...... 847 675-3910
Skokie (G-19010)
▲ Principal Manufacturing Corp ....B...... 708 865-7500
Broadview (G-2459)
▲ Prismier LLC ....E...... 630 592-4515
Bolingbrook (G-2230)
Pro Machining Inc ....F...... 815 633-4140
Loves Park (G-13250)
Pro-Tech Metal Specialties Inc ....E...... 630 279-7094
Elmhurst (G-9412)
Production Fabg & Stamping Inc ....F...... 708 755-5468
S Chicago Hts (G-18126)
Production Stampings Inc ....G...... 815 495-2800
Leland (G-12549)
Pt Holdings Inc ....G...... 217 691-1793
Springfield (G-19430)
R B White Inc ....E...... 309 452-5816
Normal (G-15220)
R C Coil Spring Mfg Co Inc ....E...... 630 790-3500
Glendale Heights (G-10486)
R Hansel & Son Inc ....G...... 815 784-5500
Genoa (G-10323)
R Z Tool Inc ....F...... 847 647-2350
Niles (G-15164)
Radiad Manufacturing ....G...... 847 678-5808
Franklin Park (G-10031)
Rail Exchange Inc ....E...... 708 757-3317
Chicago Heights (G-6767)
Rapid Wash Group Ltd ....G...... 847 376-8442
Des Plaines (G-7836)
▲ Realwheels Corporation ....G...... 847 662-7722
Gurnee (G-10923)
Reliable Die Service Inc ....F...... 708 458-5155
Bedford Park (G-1498)
Reliable Machine Company ....E...... 815 968-8803
Rockford (G-17570)
Reliable Metal Stamping Co Inc ....F...... 773 625-1177
Franklin Park (G-10034)
Reliance Tool & Mfg Co ....E...... 847 695-1235
Elgin (G-8718)
Relyon Metal Products Co ....G...... 847 679-1510
Elgin (G-8719)
▲ Ri-Del Mfg Inc ....D...... 312 829-8720
Chicago (G-6024)
▲ Rich Industries Inc ....E...... 630 766-9150
Bensenville (G-1884)
Rijon Manufacturing Company ....G...... 708 388-2295
Blue Island (G-2136)
◆ Rittal North America LLC ....A...... 847 240-4600
Schaumburg (G-18697)
Riverfront Machine Inc ....D...... 815 663-5000
Spring Valley (G-19312)
▲ Rj Stuckel Co Inc ....E...... 800 789-7220
Elk Grove Village (G-9218)
Rockford Toolcraft Inc ....C...... 815 398-5507
Rockford (G-17608)
Rockford Toolcraft Inc ....E...... 815 398-5507
Rockford (G-17609)
▲ Rockwell Metal Products Inc ....G...... 773 762-7030
Chicago (G-6048)
Roesch Acquisitions LLC ....D...... 618 233-2760
Belleville (G-1590)
Roth Metal Fabricators Corp ....G...... 708 371-8300
Alsip (G-505)
▲ Royal Die & Stamping Co Inc ....C...... 630 766-2685
Carol Stream (G-3060)
Runge Enterprises Inc ....G...... 630 365-2000
Elburn (G-8472)
Rursch Specialties Inc ....G...... 309 795-1502
Reynolds (G-17005)
▲ S & W Manufacturing Co Inc ....E...... 630 595-5044
Bensenville (G-1888)
S&L Tool Company Inc ....G...... 847 455-5550
Franklin Park (G-10039)
▲ Sealco Industries Inc ....E...... 847 741-3101
Elgin (G-8725)
Secretary of State Illinois ....G...... 217 466-5220
Paris (G-16243)

Secretary of State Illinois ....G...... 708 388-9199
Midlothian (G-13995)
Senna Design LLC ....G...... 847 821-7877
Vernon Hills (G-20096)
Service Sheet Metal Works Inc ....F...... 773 229-0031
Chicago (G-6143)
Service Stampings of IL Inc ....E...... 630 894-7880
Roselle (G-17987)
Sharp Metal Products ....E...... 847 439-5393
Elk Grove Village (G-9236)
Simplomatic Manufacturing Co ....E...... 773 342-7757
Elgin (G-8733)
Skill-Di Inc ....F...... 708 544-6080
Bellwood (G-1639)
Slidematic Products Co ....E...... 773 545-4213
Chicago (G-6189)
Spannagel Tool & Die ....E...... 630 969-7575
Downers Grove (G-8098)
Spectracrafts Ltd ....E...... 847 824-4117
Lombard (G-13133)
St Charles Stamping Inc ....F...... 630 584-2029
Saint Charles (G-18276)
▲ Stanley Spring & Stamping Corp ....D...... 773 777-2600
Chicago (G-6230)
Stanron Corporation ....D...... 773 777-2600
Chicago (G-6231)
Starmont Manufacturing Co ....G...... 815 939-1041
Kankakee (G-12007)
Starmont Manufacturing Co ....E...... 708 758-2525
Chicago Heights (G-6776)
Steibel License Service ....E...... 618 233-7555
Swansea (G-19698)
Stuecklen Manufacturing Co ....E...... 847 678-5130
Franklin Park (G-10054)
Stumpfoll Tool & Mfg ....E...... 312 733-2632
Chicago (G-6258)
Style Rite Restaurant Eqp Co ....G...... 630 628-0940
Addison (G-296)
Suburban Metalcraft Inc ....E...... 847 678-7550
Franklin Park (G-10056)
Superior Metal Products Inc ....F...... 630 466-1150
Sugar Grove (G-19657)
Sure-Way Die Designs Inc ....F...... 630 323-0370
Westmont (G-20774)
▲ Sweet Manufacturing Corp ....E...... 847 546-5575
Chicago (G-6294)
Syr-Tech Perforating Co ....E...... 630 942-7300
Glendale Heights (G-10508)
T & D Metal Products LLC ....E...... 815 432-4938
Watseka (G-20318)
T A U Inc ....E...... 708 841-5757
Dolton (G-7940)
T H K Holdings of America LLC ....G...... 847 310-1111
Schaumburg (G-18735)
Ta Delaware Inc ....E...... 773 646-6550
Chicago (G-6309)
Tarney Inc ....E...... 773 235-0331
Chicago (G-6327)
Tauber Brothers Tool & Die Co ....E...... 708 867-9100
Chicago (G-6330)
Technical Metals Inc ....D...... 815 692-4643
Fairbury (G-9614)
Tellenar Inc ....F...... 815 356-8044
Crystal Lake (G-7280)
◆ Tempel Holdings Inc ....A...... 773 250-8000
Chicago (G-6343)
Tempel Holdings Inc ....A...... 773 250-8000
Chicago (G-6344)
Tempel Steel Company ....E...... 847 966-9099
Skokie (G-19043)
Tempel Steel Company ....G...... 773 250-8000
Chicago (G-6345)
Three Star Mfg Co Inc ....G...... 847 526-2222
Wauconda (G-20399)
Thryselius Stamping Inc ....G...... 630 232-0795
Geneva (G-10311)
Tj Wire Forming Inc ....G...... 630 628-9209
Addison (G-310)
▲ Tlk Tool & Stamping Inc ....G...... 224 293-6941
East Dundee (G-8213)
Tool Automation Enterprises ....G...... 708 799-6847
East Hazel Crest (G-8218)
Trinity Machined Products Inc ....E...... 630 876-6992
Aurora (G-1028)
Trio Wire Products Inc ....E...... 815 469-2148
Frankfort (G-9846)
Triton Industries Inc ....C...... 773 384-3700
Chicago (G-6430)
Tro Manufacturing Company Inc ....E...... 847 455-3765
Franklin Park (G-10067)

Tru-Way Inc ....E...... 708 562-3690
Northlake (G-15563)
Tryson Metal Stampg & Mfg Inc ....E...... 630 458-0591
Addison (G-319)
Tu-Star Manufacturing Co Inc ....G...... 815 338-5760
Woodstock (G-21441)
Tvh Parts Co ....E...... 847 223-1000
Grayslake (G-10803)
Twinplex Manufacturing Co ....F...... 630 595-2040
Wood Dale (G-21254)
▲ Ucal Holdings Inc ....D...... 847 695-8030
Elgin (G-8765)
▲ Ucal Systems Inc ....C...... 847 695-8030
Elgin (G-8767)
Ultra Stamping & Assembly Inc ....E...... 815 874-9888
Rockford (G-17670)
Unified Tool Die & Mfg Co Inc ....F...... 847 678-3773
Schiller Park (G-18848)
United Tool and Engineering Co ....G...... 815 389-3021
South Beloit (G-19118)
Vanart Engineering Company ....E...... 847 678-6255
Franklin Park (G-10074)
▲ Vindee Industries Inc ....G...... 815 469-3300
Frankfort (G-9850)
Voco Tool & Mfg Inc ....G...... 708 771-3800
Forest Park (G-9728)
▲ Voges Inc ....D...... 618 233-2760
Belleville (G-1608)
Voges Inc ....G...... 618 233-2760
Evansville (G-9590)
Wardzala Industries Inc ....F...... 847 288-9909
Franklin Park (G-10083)
Wauconda Tool & Engrg LLC ....D...... 847 658-4588
Algonquin (G-394)
Wenco Manufacturing Co Inc ....E...... 630 377-7474
Elgin (G-8781)
▲ Western Industries Inc ....C...... 920 261-0660
Wheeling (G-21012)
Wieland Holdings Inc ....A...... 847 537-3990
Wheeling (G-21013)
◆ William Dudek Manufacturing Co ....E...... 773 622-2727
Chicago (G-6629)
Willie Washer Mfg Co ....C...... 847 956-1344
Elk Grove Village (G-9310)
Wireformers Inc ....E...... 847 718-1920
Mount Prospect (G-14582)
World Washer & Stamping Inc ....F...... 630 543-6749
Addison (G-338)
Wozniak Industries Inc ....C...... 630 820-4052
Aurora (G-1040)
◆ Wozniak Industries Inc ....G...... 630 954-3400
Schaumburg (G-18776)
ZF Active Safety & Elec US LLC ....B...... 217 826-3011
Marshall (G-13580)

3471 Electroplating, Plating, Polishing, Anodizing & Coloring

A & B Metal Polishing Inc ....F...... 773 847-1077
Chicago (G-3480)
A & J Finishers ....G...... 847 352-5408
Schaumburg (G-18423)
A and R Custom Chrome ....G...... 708 728-1005
Chicago (G-3484)
AAA Mold Finishers Inc ....G...... 773 775-3977
Chicago (G-3498)
AAM-Ro Corporation ....F...... 708 343-5543
Broadview (G-2412)
Aaro Roller Corp ....G...... 815 398-7655
Rockford (G-17283)
Able Electropolishing Co Inc ....D...... 773 277-1600
Chicago (G-3510)
Accent Metal Finishing Inc ....F...... 847 678-7420
Schiller Park (G-18782)
Accurate Metal Finishing Co ....G...... 847 428-7705
Gilberts (G-10349)
Ace Anodizing Impregnating Inc ....D...... 708 547-6680
Hillside (G-11324)
Ace Metal Refinishers Inc ....G...... 800 323-7147
Oak Brook (G-15588)
▲ Ace Metal Refinishers Inc ....G...... 630 778-9200
Lombard (G-13034)
Ace Plating Company ....G...... 773 927-2711
Chicago (G-3522)
Advanced Galvanics ....G...... 630 422-5157
Bensenville (G-1730)
Advanced Graphics Tech Inc ....C...... 817 481-8561
Romeoville (G-17788)
Aerospace Metals LLC ....G...... 888 600-7811
Sauget (G-18387)

SIC SECTION 34 FABRICATED METAL PRODUCTS, EXCEPT MACHINERY AND TRANSPORTATION EQUIPMENT

Aggresive Motor Sports ....G.... 630 761-1550
Batavia ***(G-1342)***
Al Bar Laboratories Inc ....F.... 847 251-1218
Wilmette ***(G-21068)***
All-Brite Anodizing Co Inc ....E.... 708 562-0502
Northlake ***(G-15539)***
Alliance Specialties Corp ....F.... 847 487-1945
Wauconda ***(G-20329)***
Alloy Chrome Inc ....G.... 847 678-2880
Schiller Park ***(G-18784)***
▲ **Aluminum Coil Anodizing Corp** ....C.... 630 837-4000
Streamwood ***(G-19560)***
▲ **American Plating & Mfg Co** ....F.... 773 890-4907
Chicago ***(G-3664)***
Ameriplate Inc ....E.... 815 744-8585
Joliet ***(G-11821)***
Anodizing Specialists Ltd ....G.... 847 437-9495
Elk Grove Village ***(G-8833)***
Archer Tinning & Re-Tinning Co ....F.... 773 927-7240
Chicago ***(G-3727)***
▲ **Arlington Plating Company** ....C.... 847 359-1490
Palatine ***(G-16094)***
Arnold Monument Co Inc ....G.... 217 546-2102
Springfield ***(G-19320)***
Ata Finishing Corp ....G.... 847 677-8560
Skokie ***(G-18925)***
Automatic Anodizing Corp ....E.... 773 478-3304
Chicago ***(G-3777)***
B & T Polishing Co ....E.... 847 658-6415
Chicago ***(G-3806)***
Bales Mold Service Inc ....E.... 630 852-4665
Downers Grove ***(G-7957)***
Bar Processing Corporation ....E.... 708 757-4570
Chicago Heights ***(G-6733)***
Baroque Silversmith Inc ....G.... 312 357-2813
Chicago ***(G-3835)***
Barron Metal Finishing LLC ....F.... 815 962-8053
Rockford ***(G-17314)***
Bellows Shoppe ....G.... 847 446-5533
Winnetka ***(G-21126)***
Bellwood Industries Inc ....G.... 773 522-1002
Chicago ***(G-3864)***
Belmont Plating Works Inc ....C.... 847 678-0200
Franklin Park ***(G-9885)***
Berge Plating Works Inc ....G.... 309 788-2831
Rock Island ***(G-17206)***
Brite One Inc ....G.... 708 481-8005
Matteson ***(G-13620)***
Buchtel Metal Finishing Corp ....F.... 847 427-8704
Elk Grove Village ***(G-8872)***
Budding Polishing & Met Finshg ....G.... 708 396-1166
South Holland ***(G-19203)***
California Technical Pltg Corp ....E.... 818 365-8205
Chicago ***(G-4005)***
▲ **Capron Mfg Co** ....D.... 815 569-2301
Capron ***(G-2832)***
Cardinal Plating Solutions Inc ....G.... 309 582-6215
Aledo ***(G-355)***
Cardon Mold Finishing Inc ....G.... 630 543-5431
Addison ***(G-63)***
Castle Metal Finishing Corp ....F.... 847 678-6041
Schiller Park ***(G-18791)***
Celinco Inc ....G.... 815 964-2256
Rockford ***(G-17341)***
Chem Processing Inc ....D.... 815 874-8118
Rockford ***(G-17346)***
Chem Processing Inc ....F.... 815 965-1037
Rockford ***(G-17347)***
Chem-Plate Industries Inc ....E.... 708 345-3588
Maywood ***(G-13665)***
Chem-Plate Industries Inc ....D.... 847 640-1600
Elk Grove Village ***(G-8889)***
Chemix Corp ....F.... 708 754-2150
Glenwood ***(G-10639)***
Chemtool Incorporated ....D.... 815 459-1250
Crystal Lake ***(G-7180)***
Chicago Anodizing Company ....D.... 773 533-3737
Chicago ***(G-4090)***
Chris Plating Inc ....E.... 847 729-9271
Northbrook ***(G-15360)***
▲ **Chromium Industries Inc** ....E.... 773 287-3716
Chicago ***(G-4145)***
Chromium Industries LLC ....E.... 773 287-3716
Chicago ***(G-4146)***
Chromold Plating Inc ....G.... 815 344-8644
McHenry ***(G-13727)***
Circle Studio Stained Glass ....G.... 847 432-7249
Highland Park ***(G-11258)***
Circle Studio Stained Glass ....G.... 773 588-4848
Chicago ***(G-4152)***
Ciske & Dresch ....G.... 630 251-9200
Batavia ***(G-1366)***
Classic Metal Company Inc ....G.... 815 252-0104
Mendota ***(G-13939)***
Clybourn 1200 ....G.... 312 477-7442
Chicago ***(G-4182)***
Clybourn Metal Finishing Co ....E.... 773 525-8162
Chicago ***(G-4183)***
Cmp Associates Inc ....F.... 847 956-1313
Elk Grove Village ***(G-8900)***
Coating Specialty Inc ....G.... 708 754-3311
S Chicago Hts ***(G-18118)***
Cody Metal Finishing Inc ....F.... 773 252-2026
Chicago ***(G-4192)***
Comwell ....D.... 618 282-6233
Red Bud ***(G-16991)***
▲ **Cooley Wire Products Mfg Co** ....E.... 847 678-8585
Schiller Park ***(G-18796)***
Cornerstone Polishing Company ....G.... 618 777-2754
Ozark ***(G-16087)***
Courtesy Metal Polishing ....G.... 630 832-1862
Villa Park ***(G-20142)***
Craftsman Pltg & Tinning Corp ....E.... 773 477-1040
Chicago ***(G-4257)***
Curtis Metal Finishing Company ....D.... 815 633-6693
Machesney Park ***(G-13338)***
Custom Chrome & Polishing ....G.... 618 885-9499
Jerseyville ***(G-11789)***
Custom Hard Chrome Service Co ....G.... 847 759-1420
Rosemont ***(G-18015)***
D & N Deburring Co Inc ....G.... 847 451-7702
Franklin Park ***(G-9924)***
De Kalb Plating Co Inc ....G.... 815 756-6112
Dekalb ***(G-7675)***
Deal Mold Polishing Inc ....G.... 815 363-8200
Crystal Lake ***(G-7192)***
Decatur Plating & Mfg Co ....F.... 217 422-8514
Decatur ***(G-7488)***
Deep Coat LLC ....E.... 630 466-1505
Sugar Grove ***(G-19642)***
Delta Secondary Inc ....E.... 630 766-1180
Bensenville ***(G-1785)***
Diamond Plating Company Inc ....E.... 618 451-7740
Madison ***(G-13408)***
▲ **Diamond Spray Painting Inc** ....G.... 630 513-5600
Saint Charles ***(G-18183)***
Dixline Corporation ....D.... 309 932-2011
Galva ***(G-10231)***
Dixline Corporation ....F.... 309 932-2011
Galva ***(G-10230)***
Dover Industrial Chrome Inc ....G.... 773 478-2022
Chicago ***(G-4391)***
Duro-Chrome Industries Inc ....E.... 847 487-2900
Wauconda ***(G-20345)***
Duroweld Company Inc ....E.... 847 680-3064
Lake Bluff ***(G-12179)***
Durr - All Corporation ....G.... 815 943-1032
Harvard ***(G-11053)***
Dyna-Burr Chicago Inc ....F.... 708 250-6744
Northlake ***(G-15546)***
▲ **Dynomax Inc** ....B.... 847 680-8833
Wheeling ***(G-20883)***
E and J Polishing and Buffing ....G.... 773 569-0661
Chicago ***(G-4422)***
▲ **Eifeler Coatings Tech Inc** ....E.... 630 587-1220
Saint Charles ***(G-18194)***
Ej Somerville Plating Co ....G.... 708 345-5100
Melrose Park ***(G-13862)***
Electro-Max Inc ....D.... 847 683-4100
Hampshire ***(G-10970)***
Electronic Plating Co ....E.... 708 652-8100
Cicero ***(G-6844)***
Ellwood Group Inc ....F.... 815 725-9030
Joliet ***(G-11859)***
Empire Hard Chrome Inc ....B.... 773 762-3156
Chicago ***(G-4500)***
Empire Hard Chrome Inc ....C.... 312 226-7548
Chicago ***(G-4501)***
▲ **En-Chro Plating Inc** ....E.... 708 450-1250
Melrose Park ***(G-13864)***
Enameled Steel and Sign Co ....E.... 773 481-2270
Chicago ***(G-4504)***
▲ **Engis Corporation** ....C.... 847 808-9400
Wheeling ***(G-20891)***
Envirocoat Inc ....G.... 847 673-3649
Skokie ***(G-18952)***
Expert Metal Finishing Inc ....F.... 708 583-2550
River Grove ***(G-17059)***
▲ **Feralloy Corporation** ....E.... 503 286-8869
Chicago ***(G-4580)***
Finished Metals Incorporated ....F.... 773 229-1600
Chicago ***(G-4591)***
Finishing Company ....C.... 630 559-0808
Addison ***(G-122)***
Finishing Touch Inc ....F.... 773 774-7349
Chicago ***(G-4592)***
Floor-Chem Inc ....G.... 630 789-2152
Romeoville ***(G-17824)***
Forest Plating Co ....G.... 708 366-2071
Forest Park ***(G-9717)***
Formulations Inc ....G.... 847 674-9141
Skokie ***(G-18956)***
Fox Valley Sandblasting Inc ....G.... 630 553-6050
Yorkville ***(G-21483)***
▲ **G L Tool and Manufacturing Co** ....F.... 630 628-1992
Addison ***(G-132)***
Gateway Fbrction Solutions LLC ....G.... 618 612-3170
Waterloo ***(G-20290)***
Gatto Industrial Platers Inc ....C.... 773 287-0100
Chicago ***(G-4663)***
GC Laser Systems Inc ....G.... 844 532-1064
Forest Park ***(G-9719)***
General Plating Co Inc ....G.... 630 543-0088
Addison ***(G-138)***
Glass Fx ....G.... 217 359-0048
Champaign ***(G-3295)***
Great Lakes Finishing Eqp Inc ....G.... 708 345-5300
South Elgin ***(G-19150)***
Griffin Plating Co Inc ....G.... 773 342-5181
Chicago ***(G-4742)***
Grove Plating Company Inc ....F.... 847 639-7651
Fox River Grove ***(G-9759)***
Gyro Processing Inc ....E.... 800 491-0733
Chicago ***(G-4755)***
Hausner Hard - Chrome Inc ....E.... 847 439-6010
Elk Grove Village ***(G-9029)***
HBm Electro Chemical Company ....G.... 708 895-7710
Lansing ***(G-12497)***
Heidtman Steel Products Inc ....D.... 618 451-0052
Granite City ***(G-10714)***
Illinois Electro Deburring Co ....F.... 847 678-5010
Franklin Park ***(G-9961)***
Imperial Plating Company Ill ....E.... 773 586-3500
Chicago ***(G-4899)***
Industrial Hard Chrome Ltd ....C.... 630 208-7000
Geneva ***(G-10279)***
International Plating Svc LLC ....F.... 619 734-2335
Franklin Park ***(G-9965)***
▲ **International Proc Co Amer** ....E.... 847 437-8400
Elk Grove Village ***(G-9058)***
International Silver Plating ....G.... 847 835-0705
Glencoe ***(G-10430)***
Interntional Metal Finshg Svcs ....G.... 815 234-5254
Byron ***(G-2754)***
Irmko Tool Works Inc ....E.... 630 350-7550
Bensenville ***(G-1825)***
▲ **J & M Plating Inc** ....C.... 815 964-4975
Rockford ***(G-17471)***
J D Plating Works Inc ....G.... 847 662-6484
Waukegan ***(G-20451)***
James Precious Metals Plating ....F.... 773 774-8700
Chicago ***(G-5003)***
▼ **Jensen Plating Works Inc** ....E.... 773 252-7733
Chicago ***(G-5019)***
Jvk Precision Hard Chrome Inc ....G.... 630 628-0810
Addison ***(G-162)***
K & P Industries Inc ....G.... 630 628-6676
Addison ***(G-165)***
K V F Company ....E.... 847 437-5100
Elk Grove Village ***(G-9073)***
K V F Company ....F.... 847 437-5019
Elk Grove Village ***(G-9074)***
K&J Finishing Inc ....F.... 815 965-9655
Rockford ***(G-17478)***
Koderhandt Inc ....G.... 618 233-4808
Belleville ***(G-1565)***
Krel Laboratories Inc ....F.... 773 826-4487
Chicago ***(G-5132)***
▲ **Krueger and Company** ....E.... 630 833-5650
Elmhurst ***(G-9389)***
Lee Quigley Company ....G.... 708 563-1600
Chicago ***(G-5195)***
M & B Services Ltd Inc ....F.... 217 463-2162
Paris ***(G-16233)***
M C S Inc ....F.... 708 323-9233
Tinley Park ***(G-19845)***
Magnetic Inspection Lab Inc ....D.... 847 437-4488
Elk Grove Village ***(G-9106)***
▲ **Main Steel Polishing Co Inc** ....E.... 847 916-1220
Elk Grove Village ***(G-9107)***

S I C

Employee Codes: A=Over 500 employees, B=251-500
C=101-250, D=51-100, E=20-50, F=10-19, G=3-9
2020 Harris Illinois
Industrial Directory
939

Manner Plating Inc.....G..... 815 877-7791
Loves Park *(G-13235)*
Marjan Inc.....G..... 630 906-0053
Montgomery *(G-14261)*
Markham Industry Inc.....G..... 815 338-0116
Woodstock *(G-21408)*
Master Polishing & Buffing.....G..... 773 731-3883
Chicago *(G-5359)*
Masters Plating Co Inc.....G..... 815 226-8846
Rockford *(G-17508)*
Meminger Metal Finishing Inc.....F..... 309 582-3363
Aledo *(G-358)*
Metal Arts Finishing Inc.....E..... 630 892-6744
Aurora *(G-1132)*
Metal Finishing Pros Corp.....G..... 630 883-8339
Elgin *(G-8657)*
Metal Images Inc.....G..... 847 488-9877
Elgin *(G-8658)*
Metco Treating and Dev Co.....D..... 773 277-1600
Chicago *(G-5407)*
Meto-Grafics Inc.....F..... 847 639-0044
Crystal Lake *(G-7226)*
Metokote Corporation.....E..... 815 223-1190
Peru *(G-16582)*
Mexicali Hard Chrome Corp.....E..... 630 543-0646
Addison *(G-202)*
▲ **Micro Surface Corporation**.....F..... 815 942-4221
Morris *(G-14312)*
Midwest Galvanizing Inc.....F..... 773 434-2682
Chicago *(G-5441)*
Midwest Metal Finishing Inc.....G..... 773 521-0700
Chicago *(G-5445)*
Midwest Power Equipment.....G..... 815 669-6331
Joliet *(G-11904)*
▲ **Midwestern Rust Proof Inc**.....D..... 773 725-6636
Chicago *(G-5451)*
Mikes Anodizing Co.....E..... 773 722-5778
Chicago *(G-5456)*
▲ **Modern Plating Corporation**.....D..... 815 235-1790
Freeport *(G-10127)*
Morgan Ohare Inc.....D..... 630 543-6780
Addison *(G-223)*
MSC Pre Finish Metals Egv Inc.....C..... 847 439-2210
Elk Grove Village *(G-9137)*
Nb Finishing Inc.....F..... 847 364-7500
Melrose Park *(G-13897)*
Neiland Custom Products.....G..... 815 825-2233
Malta *(G-13430)*
Nobert Plating Co.....G..... 312 421-4040
Chicago *(G-5608)*
North American EN Inc.....F..... 847 952-3680
Elk Grove Village *(G-9152)*
▲ **Nova-Chrome Inc**.....F..... 847 455-8200
Franklin Park *(G-10010)*
▲ **Oerlikon Blzers Cating USA Inc**.....F..... 847 619-5541
Schaumburg *(G-18656)*
Omega Plating Inc.....F..... 708 389-5410
Crestwood *(G-7123)*
P B A Corp.....F..... 312 666-7370
Chicago *(G-5728)*
Paradigm Coatings LLC.....G..... 847 961-6466
Huntley *(G-11557)*
Pariso Inc.....F..... 773 889-4383
Chicago *(G-5763)*
Perfection Plating Inc.....D..... 847 593-6506
Elk Grove Village *(G-9172)*
Perfection Plating Inc.....D..... 847 593-6506
Elk Grove Village *(G-9173)*
Performance Auto Salon Inc.....E..... 815 468-6882
Manteno *(G-13453)*
Performance Finishes Powder.....G..... 309 631-0664
Rock Island *(G-17232)*
Petersen Finishing Corporation.....G..... 847 228-7150
Elk Grove Village *(G-9177)*
Plano Metal Specialties Inc.....F..... 630 552-8510
Plano *(G-16740)*
▲ **Plating International Inc**.....F..... 847 451-2101
Franklin Park *(G-10020)*
Polyenviro Labs Inc.....G..... 708 489-0195
Mokena *(G-14108)*
Possehl Connector Svcs SC Inc.....E..... 803 366-8316
Elk Grove Village *(G-9184)*
Powers Paint Shop Inc.....G..... 815 338-3619
Woodstock *(G-21422)*
▲ **Precise Finishing Co Inc**.....E..... 847 451-2077
Franklin Park *(G-10024)*
Precision Chrome Inc.....E..... 847 587-1515
Fox Lake *(G-9753)*
Precision Finishing Systems In.....F..... 847 907-4266
Wheeling *(G-20963)*
Precision Metal Crafts Inc.....G..... 815 254-2306
Plainfield *(G-16705)*
Precision Plating of Quincy.....G..... 217 223-6590
Quincy *(G-16923)*
Pro TEC Metal Finishing Corp.....G..... 773 384-7853
Chicago *(G-5888)*
Production Chemical Co Inc.....E..... 847 455-8450
Franklin Park *(G-10027)*
Quality Plating.....G..... 815 626-5223
Sterling *(G-19526)*
R C Industries Inc.....F..... 773 378-1118
Chicago *(G-5944)*
R&R Research Co.....G..... 847 345-5051
Mount Prospect *(G-14565)*
Rainbow Art Inc.....F..... 312 421-5600
Chicago *(G-5965)*
Redi-Strip Company Inc.....G..... 630 529-2442
Roselle *(G-17978)*
Reliable Plating Corporation.....D..... 312 421-4747
Chicago *(G-6010)*
Riverdale Pltg Heat Trting LLC.....E..... 708 849-2050
Riverdale *(G-17076)*
Rockford Metal Polishing Co.....G..... 815 282-4448
Loves Park *(G-13256)*
Saporito Finishing Co.....D..... 708 222-5300
Cicero *(G-6874)*
Saporito Finishing Co.....E..... 708 222-5300
Chicago *(G-6103)*
Scot Industries Inc.....D..... 630 466-7591
Sugar Grove *(G-19653)*
Selective Plating Inc.....E..... 630 543-1380
Addison *(G-284)*
Skilled Plating Corp.....G..... 773 227-0262
Chicago *(G-6180)*
South Holland Met Finshg Inc.....D..... 708 235-0842
Monee *(G-14209)*
Southern Plating Inc.....G..... 618 983-6350
Johnston City *(G-11814)*
Specialty Pntg Soda Blastg Inc.....G..... 815 577-0006
Plainfield *(G-16716)*
Spider Company Inc.....D..... 815 961-8200
Rockford *(G-17641)*
Sterling Plating Inc.....E..... 708 867-6587
Harwood Heights *(G-11110)*
Streamwood Plating Co.....G..... 630 830-6363
Streamwood *(G-19596)*
Stripmasters Services Inc.....G..... 217 429-0904
Decatur *(G-7553)*
Superior Metal Finishing.....F..... 815 282-8888
Loves Park *(G-13268)*
Surcom Industries Inc.....G..... 773 378-0736
Chicago *(G-6287)*
Sure Shine Polishing.....G..... 217 853-4888
Decatur *(G-7554)*
Surface Manufacturing Company.....F..... 815 569-2362
Capron *(G-2837)*
▲ **Swd Inc**.....D..... 630 543-3003
Addison *(G-301)*
T M T Industries Inc.....E..... 815 562-0111
Rochelle *(G-17161)*
TFC Group LLC.....D..... 630 559-0808
Addison *(G-306)*
Thomson Steel Polishing Corp.....G..... 773 586-2345
Chicago *(G-6370)*
Three JS Industries Inc.....F..... 847 640-6080
Elk Grove Village *(G-9271)*
Transcend Corp.....G..... 847 395-6630
Antioch *(G-638)*
Tri-Fin LLC.....E..... 630 467-0991
Elk Grove Village *(G-9284)*
Tru Coat Plating and Finishing.....F..... 708 544-3940
Bellwood *(G-1641)*
Twr Service Corporation.....F..... 847 923-0692
Schaumburg *(G-18761)*
Ultra Polishing.....G..... 224 769-7140
Elgin *(G-8768)*
Ultra Polishing Inc.....E..... 630 635-2926
Schaumburg *(G-18762)*
Unitech Industries Inc.....F..... 847 357-8800
Elk Grove Village *(G-9295)*
Universal Coatings Inc.....G..... 708 756-7000
Steger *(G-19496)*
Universal-Spc Inc.....G..... 847 742-4400
Elgin *(G-8770)*
US Chrome Corp Illinois.....E..... 815 544-3487
Kingston *(G-12057)*
US Plating Co Inc.....F..... 773 522-7300
Chicago *(G-6502)*
V and L Polishing Co.....G..... 630 543-5999
Addison *(G-325)*
V P Anodizing Inc.....G..... 773 622-9100
Chicago *(G-6515)*
Victoria Metal Processor Inc.....G..... 773 633-7497
Chicago *(G-6546)*
Vision Pickling and Proc Inc.....F..... 815 264-7755
Waterman *(G-20301)*
W D Mold Finishing Inc.....G..... 847 678-8449
Schiller Park *(G-18853)*
Wear-Cote International Inc.....E..... 309 793-1250
Rock Island *(G-17254)*
West Town Plating Inc.....E..... 708 652-1600
Cicero *(G-6887)*
▲ **White Racker Co Inc**.....G..... 847 758-1640
Elk Grove Village *(G-9308)*
Wood Graphics Inc.....F..... 704 872-5798
Romeoville *(G-17890)*
Xd Industries Inc.....F..... 630 766-2843
Bensenville *(G-1916)*

3479 Coating & Engraving, NEC

AAA Galvanizing - Joliet Inc.....E..... 815 284-5001
Dixon *(G-7887)*
▲ **AAA Galvanizing - Joliet Inc**.....D..... 815 723-5000
Joliet *(G-11816)*
▲ **AAA Galvanizing - Peoria Inc**.....E..... 309 697-4100
Peoria *(G-16373)*
ABC Coating Company III Inc.....E..... 708 258-9633
Manteno *(G-13443)*
Accent Metal Finishing Inc.....F..... 847 678-7420
Schiller Park *(G-18782)*
Accurate Finishers.....G..... 630 543-8575
Addison *(G-16)*
Accurate Metallizing Inc.....G..... 708 424-7747
Oak Lawn *(G-15695)*
Ace Engraving & Specialties Co.....G..... 815 759-2093
McHenry *(G-13714)*
Addison Engraving Inc.....G..... 630 833-9123
Villa Park *(G-20127)*
Advance Enameling Co.....E..... 773 737-7356
Chicago *(G-3554)*
Advanced Graphics Tech Inc.....C..... 817 481-8561
Romeoville *(G-17788)*
Aggressive Motorsports Inc.....G..... 847 846-7488
Batavia *(G-1343)*
All City Brick Staining LLC.....G..... 312 459-8937
Chicago *(G-3608)*
Ambrotos Inc.....G..... 815 355-8217
Crystal Lake *(G-7159)*
Americana Powder Finishing LLC.....D..... 618 548-2800
Salem *(G-18329)*
Amex Nooter LLC.....F..... 708 429-8300
Tinley Park *(G-19803)*
Aqua Coat Inc.....G..... 815 209-0808
Elgin *(G-8512)*
Armoloy of Illinois Inc.....E..... 815 758-6657
Dekalb *(G-7666)*
Bertco Enterprises Inc.....G..... 618 234-9283
Belleville *(G-1535)*
Bfw Coating.....G..... 847 639-2155
Cary *(G-3150)*
Bishops Engrv & Trophy Svc Inc.....G..... 773 777-5014
Chicago *(G-3901)*
BL Downey Company LLC.....D..... 708 345-8000
Broadview *(G-2420)*
Blue Brothers Coatings.....G..... 847 265-5400
Round Lake Beach *(G-18087)*
Brad Martz.....G..... 217 825-5855
Shelbyville *(G-18877)*
Britt Industries Inc.....E..... 847 640-1177
Arlington Heights *(G-710)*
Casting Impregnators Inc.....F..... 847 455-1000
Franklin Park *(G-9900)*
Cavero Coatings Company LLC.....G..... 630 616-2868
Bensenville *(G-1763)*
Chem Processing Inc.....F..... 815 965-1037
Rockford *(G-17347)*
Chem Processing Inc.....D..... 815 874-8118
Rockford *(G-17346)*
Chicago Tank Lining Sales.....G..... 847 328-0500
Evanston *(G-9504)*
Clad-Rex Steel LLC.....E..... 847 455-7373
Franklin Park *(G-9909)*
Coating Methods Incorporated.....F..... 847 428-8800
Carpentersville *(G-3098)*
▲ **Comet Die & Engraving Company**.....D..... 630 833-5600
Elmhurst *(G-9350)*
Commercial Finishes Co Ltd.....E..... 847 981-9222
Elk Grove Village *(G-8904)*
Core Finishing Inc.....E..... 630 521-9635
Bensenville *(G-1776)*

SIC SECTION 34 FABRICATED METAL PRODUCTS, EXCEPT MACHINERY AND TRANSPORTATION EQUIPMENT

Creative Powder Coating Inc ....G.... 815 260-3124
Crest Hill *(G-7085)*

Crown Trophy ....G.... 309 699-1766
East Peoria *(G-8264)*

Curtis Metal Finishing Company ....D.... 815 633-6693
Machesney Park *(G-13338)*

Czarnik Precision Grinding Mch ....G.... 708 229-9639
Oak Lawn *(G-15711)*

D N D Coating ....G.... 309 379-3021
Stanford *(G-19472)*

▲ **Diamond Spray Painting Inc** ....G.... 630 513-5600
Saint Charles *(G-18183)*

Dover Industrial Chrome Inc ....G.... 773 478-2022
Chicago *(G-4391)*

▼ **Downey Investments Inc** ....B.... 708 345-8000
Broadview *(G-2431)*

Drs Electrostatic Painting ....G.... 708 681-5535
Bellwood *(G-1623)*

◆ **Dt Metronic Inc** ....G.... 224 567-8414
Des Plaines *(G-7757)*

Durable Longlasting ....E.... 847 350-0113
Elk Grove Village *(G-8957)*

Durable Engravers Inc ....E.... 630 766-6420
Franklin Park *(G-9934)*

E & R Powder Coatings Inc ....E.... 773 523-9510
Chicago *(G-4421)*

Ecosystem Protective Coatings ....G.... 815 725-6343
Joliet *(G-11858)*

Enameled Steel and Sign Co ....E.... 773 481-2270
Chicago *(G-4504)*

Envirocoat Inc ....G.... 847 673-3649
Skokie *(G-18952)*

Epscca ....E.... 815 568-3020
Marengo *(G-13484)*

Etch-Tech Inc ....G.... 630 833-4234
Elmhurst *(G-9363)*

Faspro Technologies Inc ....F.... 847 364-9999
Elk Grove Village *(G-8996)*

▲ **Finer Line Inc** ....F.... 847 884-1611
Itasca *(G-11657)*

Finishing Company ....C.... 630 559-0808
Addison *(G-122)*

Forest Awards & Engraving ....G.... 630 595-2242
Wood Dale *(G-21189)*

Fresh Look & Sons ....G.... 815 325-9692
Morris *(G-14306)*

Group O Inc ....B.... 309 736-8311
Milan *(G-14014)*

Hoeing Die & Mold Engraving ....G.... 630 543-0006
Addison *(G-151)*

◆ **ICP Industrial Inc** ....E.... 630 227-1692
Itasca *(G-11668)*

ICP Industries LLC ....E.... 888 672-2123
Itasca *(G-11669)*

Iemco Corporation ....G.... 773 728-4400
Chicago *(G-4878)*

Industrial Cstm Pwdr Cting Inc ....F.... 217 423-4272
Decatur *(G-7506)*

Industrial Finishing Inc ....F.... 847 451-4230
Franklin Park *(G-9963)*

J and J Prfmce Powdr Coating ....G.... 309 376-4340
Carlock *(G-2887)*

Jet Finishers Inc ....D.... 847 718-0501
Addison *(G-160)*

Jet Rack Corp ....E.... 773 586-2150
Chicago *(G-5025)*

Jjc Epoxy Inc ....G.... 630 231-5600
West Chicago *(G-20604)*

Johnos Inc ....G.... 630 897-6929
Aurora *(G-1119)*

Joseph Kristan ....G.... 847 731-3131
Zion *(G-21518)*

Kobac ....G.... 847 520-6000
Buffalo Grove *(G-2553)*

Kobelco Advnced Cting Amer Inc ....A.... 847 520-6000
Buffalo Grove *(G-2554)*

▲ **Krueger and Company** ....E.... 630 833-5650
Elmhurst *(G-9389)*

Kvf-Quad Corporation ....E.... 563 529-1916
East Moline *(G-8231)*

Legend Dynamix Inc ....G.... 847 789-7007
Antioch *(G-622)*

Lifetime Creations ....G.... 708 895-2770
Lansing *(G-12505)*

Lo-Ko Performance Coatings ....G.... 708 424-7863
Oak Lawn *(G-15726)*

Long Construction Services ....G.... 217 443-2876
Danville *(G-7360)*

M J Burton Engraving Co ....G.... 217 223-7273
Quincy *(G-16908)*

▲ **Marie Gere Corporation** ....C.... 847 540-1154
Lake Zurich *(G-12430)*

Material Sciences Corporation ....E.... 847 439-2210
Elk Grove Village *(G-9112)*

Metal Impregnating Corp ....G.... 630 543-3443
Addison *(G-198)*

Metal Prep Services Inc ....G.... 815 874-7631
Rockford *(G-17519)*

Meto-Grafics Inc ....F.... 847 639-0044
Crystal Lake *(G-7226)*

Metokote Corporation ....E.... 815 223-1190
Peru *(G-16582)*

Micron Metal Finishing LLC ....G.... 708 599-0055
Bridgeview *(G-2364)*

Midwest Coatings Inc ....G.... 815 717-8914
Bolingbrook *(G-2214)*

Midwest Galvanizing Inc ....F.... 773 434-2682
Chicago *(G-5441)*

Midwest Metal Coatings LLC ....E.... 618 451-2971
Granite City *(G-10725)*

Midwest Nameplate Corp ....G.... 708 614-0606
Orland Park *(G-15968)*

Mobile Air Inc ....F.... 847 755-0586
Glendale Heights *(G-10476)*

▲ **Monogram of Evanston Inc** ....G.... 847 864-8100
Evanston *(G-9555)*

MSC Pre Finish Metals Egv Inc ....C.... 847 439-2210
Elk Grove Village *(G-9137)*

Nameplate Robinson & Precision ....G.... 847 678-2255
Franklin Park *(G-10005)*

National Rubber Stamp Co Inc ....G.... 773 281-6522
Chicago *(G-5552)*

Neiland Custom Products ....G.... 815 825-2233
Malta *(G-13430)*

New Process Steel LP ....D.... 708 389-3380
Alsip *(G-484)*

Nickel Composite Coatings Inc ....E.... 708 563-2780
Chicago *(G-5597)*

Oerlikon Blzers Cating USA Inc ....F.... 630 208-0958
Geneva *(G-10296)*

▲ **Oerlikon Blzers Cating USA Inc** ....F.... 847 619-5541
Schaumburg *(G-18656)*

Oerlikon Blzers Cating USA Inc ....E.... 847 695-5200
Elgin *(G-8677)*

Omega Plating Inc ....F.... 708 389-5410
Crestwood *(G-7123)*

▲ **Ostrom & Co Inc** ....F.... 503 281-6469
Winfield *(G-21113)*

Palapa Coatings Inc ....G.... 847 628-6360
Elgin *(G-8684)*

Paradigm Coatings LLC ....G.... 847 961-6466
Huntley *(G-11557)*

Petersburg Power Washing Inc ....F.... 217 415-9013
Springfield *(G-19425)*

Photo Techniques Corp ....E.... 630 690-9360
Carol Stream *(G-3046)*

Pioneer Powder Coatings LLC ....E.... 847 671-1100
Franklin Park *(G-10019)*

Polaris Laser Laminations LLC ....E.... 630 444-0760
West Chicago *(G-20630)*

Porcelain Enamel Finishers ....G.... 312 808-1560
Chicago *(G-5845)*

Powder Coating Specialists ....G.... 708 387-8000
Brookfield *(G-2490)*

Powers Paint Shop Inc ....G.... 815 338-3619
Woodstock *(G-21422)*

▲ **Pre Fnish Mtals Mrrisville Inc** ....D.... 847 439-2211
Elk Grove Village *(G-9188)*

Precoat Metals Corp ....D.... 618 451-0909
Granite City *(G-10731)*

Production Chemical Co Inc ....E.... 847 455-8450
Franklin Park *(G-10027)*

Progressive Coating Corp ....F.... 773 261-8900
Chicago *(G-5900)*

Protective Coatings & Waterpro ....G.... 708 403-7650
Orland Park *(G-15975)*

▲ **Qc Finishers Inc** ....E.... 847 678-2660
Franklin Park *(G-10028)*

Qc Powder Inc ....E.... 630 832-0606
Villa Park *(G-20167)*

Quality Coating Co ....F.... 815 875-3228
Princeton *(G-16822)*

R & B Powder Coatings Inc ....E.... 773 247-8300
Chicago *(G-5941)*

▲ **R & O Specialties Incorporated** ....D.... 309 736-8660
Milan *(G-14022)*

Rainbow Art Inc ....F.... 312 421-5600
Chicago *(G-5965)*

Rebechini Studio Inc ....F.... 847 437-9030
Elk Grove Village *(G-9215)*

Reliable Autotech Usa LLC ....G.... 815 945-7838
Chenoa *(G-3434)*

Reliable Galvanizing Company ....E.... 773 651-2500
Northbrook *(G-15472)*

Ro Pal Grinding Inc ....F.... 815 964-5894
Rockford *(G-17580)*

S & B Finishing Co Inc ....D.... 773 533-0033
Chicago *(G-6082)*

Safeway Services Rockford Inc ....E.... 815 986-1504
Rockford *(G-17621)*

Sc2 Inc ....G.... 309 677-5980
East Peoria *(G-8289)*

SKW Industries LLC ....F.... 773 261-8900
Chicago *(G-6182)*

Specialty Pntg Soda Blastg Inc ....G.... 815 577-0006
Plainfield *(G-16716)*

Speed Powder Coatings Inc ....G.... 630 549-0657
West Chicago *(G-20646)*

Star Su Fellows Cutter LLC ....D.... 847 649-1450
Hoffman Estates *(G-11462)*

Stripmasters Illinois Inc ....G.... 618 452-1060
Granite City *(G-10740)*

Sub Source Inc ....E.... 815 968-7800
Rockford *(G-17649)*

Superior Coatings Illinois LLC ....F.... 309 367-9625
Metamora *(G-13969)*

Surface Solutions Group LLC ....D.... 773 427-2084
Chicago *(G-6288)*

▲ **Sycamore Precision** ....D.... 815 784-5151
Genoa *(G-10324)*

Thomson Steel Polishing Corp ....G.... 773 586-2345
Chicago *(G-6370)*

◆ **Tiger Drylac USA Inc** ....F.... 630 587-2918
Saint Charles *(G-18289)*

▲ **Transco Products Inc** ....D.... 312 427-2818
Streator *(G-19631)*

Trophies and Awards Plus ....G.... 708 754-7127
Steger *(G-19494)*

Tru-Tone Finishing Inc ....E.... 630 543-5520
Addison *(G-318)*

Valmont Coatings Inc ....G.... 847 455-0884
Franklin Park *(G-10072)*

Viking Awards Inc ....G.... 630 833-1733
Elmhurst *(G-9441)*

▲ **Voges Inc** ....D.... 618 233-2760
Belleville *(G-1608)*

Vorteq Woodstock LLC ....E.... 815 338-6410
Woodstock *(G-21445)*

Wear-Cote International Inc ....E.... 309 793-1250
Rock Island *(G-17254)*

Wheaton Trophy & Engravers ....G.... 630 682-4200
Wheaton *(G-20831)*

Willis Stein & Partners Manage ....F.... 312 422-2400
Chicago *(G-6632)*

Zegers Inc ....F.... 708 474-7700
Lansing *(G-12525)*

3482 Small Arms Ammunition

A & S Arms Inc ....G.... 224 267-5670
Antioch *(G-593)*

▲ **Bison Aerospace and Def LLC** ....G.... 618 795-2678
Savanna *(G-18403)*

Dan Moy ....G.... 217 243-2572
Jacksonville *(G-11764)*

RR Defense Systems Inc ....F.... 773 529-6007
Elk Grove Village *(G-9223)*

Vista Outdoor Inc ....D.... 217 893-7254
Rantoul *(G-16986)*

3483 Ammunition, Large

General Dynamics Corporation ....E.... 618 993-9207
Marion *(G-13511)*

General Dynamics Ordnance ....C.... 618 985-8211
Marion *(G-13512)*

3484 Small Arms

A & S Arms Inc ....G.... 224 267-5670
Antioch *(G-593)*

Art Jewel Enterprises Ltd ....F.... 630 260-0400
Carol Stream *(G-2941)*

▲ **Bison Aerospace and Def LLC** ....G.... 618 795-2678
Savanna *(G-18403)*

D S Arms Incorporated ....E.... 847 277-7258
Lake Barrington *(G-12147)*

Devil Dog Arms Inc ....G.... 847 790-4004
Lake Zurich *(G-12402)*

Double Nickel LLC ....G.... 618 476-3200
Millstadt *(G-14045)*

Fim Engineering LLC ....G.... 773 880-8841
Milford *(G-14034)*

S
I
C

Employee Codes: A=Over 500 employees, B=251-500
C=101-250, D=51-100, E=20-50, F=10-19, G=3-9

2020 Harris Illinois
Industrial Directory

941

34 FABRICATED METAL PRODUCTS, EXCEPT MACHINERY AND TRANSPORTATION EQUIPMENT

Gregory Martin ....G...... 815 265-4527
 Gilman (G-10379)
Manticore Arms Inc ....G...... 630 715-0334
 Elburn (G-8459)
▲ Nelson-Whittaker Ltd ....E...... 815 459-6000
 Crystal Lake (G-7237)
Northern Ordinance Corporation ......G...... 815 675-6400
 Spring Grove (G-19289)
Oglesby & Oglesby Gunmakers ....G...... 217 487-7100
 Springfield (G-19417)
Olin Corporation ....C...... 618 258-2000
 East Alton (G-8168)
Phalanx Training Inc ....G...... 847 859-9156
 Evanston (G-9566)
Pro Tech Engineering ....G...... 309 475-2502
 Saybrook (G-18419)
▼ Rock River Arms Inc ....D...... 309 792-5780
 Colona (G-6979)
RR Defense Systems Inc ....F...... 773 529-6007
 Elk Grove Village (G-9223)
▲ Springfield Inc ....C...... 309 944-5631
 Geneseo (G-10248)

3489 Ordnance & Access, NEC

Devil Dog Arms Inc ....G...... 847 790-4004
 Lake Zurich (G-12402)
General Dynamics Ordnance ....C...... 618 985-8211
 Marion (G-13512)
Krebs Custom Inc ....G...... 847 487-7776
 Wauconda (G-20368)
◆ United Tactical Systems LLC ....E...... 260 478-2500
 Lake Forest (G-12320)

3491 Industrial Valves

Advanced Valve Tech LLC ....E...... 877 489-4909
 Blue Island (G-2110)
Aptargroup Inc ....B...... 847 639-2124
 Cary (G-3148)
▲ Aquatrol Inc ....F...... 630 365-2363
 Elburn (G-8443)
Chicago Valves & Controls LLC .....G...... 312 637-3551
 Elk Grove Village (G-8895)
◆ Corken Inc ....D...... 405 946-5576
 Lake Bluff (G-12177)
Cyrus Shank Company ....F...... 331 212-5488
 Aurora (G-950)
Cyrus Shank Company ....G...... 708 652-2700
 Cicero (G-6838)
Deltrol Corp ....C...... 708 547-0500
 Bellwood (G-1621)
Dresser LLC ....D...... 847 437-5940
 Elk Grove Village (G-8955)
Emerson Automation Solutions ....G...... 309 946-5205
 Geneseo (G-10242)
▲ Emerson Process Management ....D...... 708 535-5120
 Oak Forest (G-15677)
Engineered Fluid Inc ....C...... 618 533-1351
 Centralia (G-3230)
Ergo-Tech Incorporated ....G...... 630 773-2222
 Itasca (G-11652)
Evsco Inc ....F...... 847 362-7068
 McHenry (G-13742)
Flexicraft Industries Inc ....E...... 312 428-4750
 Chicago (G-4608)
▲ Flexicraft Industries Inc ....E...... 312 738-3588
 Chicago (G-4610)
▲ Flocon Inc ....E...... 815 444-1500
 Cary (G-3159)
General Assembly & Mfg Corp ....E...... 847 516-6462
 Cary (G-3163)
▼ Gpe Controls Inc ....F...... 708 236-6000
 Hillside (G-11340)
▼ H A Phillips & Co ....F...... 630 377-0050
 Dekalb (G-7683)
▲ Henry Pratt Company LLC ....C...... 630 844-4000
 Aurora (G-1108)
Henry Pratt Company LLC ....G...... 620 208-8100
 Decatur (G-7502)
▲ Henry Technologies Inc ....G...... 217 483-2406
 Chatham (G-3421)
▲ Homewerks Worldwide LLC ....G...... 224 543-1529
 Lake Bluff (G-12188)
▲ Honeywell Analytics Inc ....E...... 847 955-8200
 Lincolnshire (G-12770)
Hydra-Stop LLC ....E...... 708 389-5111
 Burr Ridge (G-2684)
Keckley Manufacturing Company .....E...... 847 674-8422
 Skokie (G-18972)
L & J Holding Company Ltd ....D...... 708 236-6000
 Hillside (G-11345)

▲ Lilly Industries Inc ....F...... 630 773-2222
 Itasca (G-11694)
▲ Midland Manufacturing Corp ....C...... 847 677-0333
 Skokie (G-18990)
Midwest Innovative Tech Inc ....G...... 618 740-0074
 Salem (G-18346)
Midwest Water Group Inc ....E...... 866 526-6558
 Crystal Lake (G-7230)
Mueller Service Co LLC ....E...... 217 423-4471
 Decatur (G-7530)
▲ O C Keckley Company ....E...... 847 674-8422
 Skokie (G-18997)
Parker-Hannifin Corporation ....E...... 708 681-6300
 Broadview (G-2457)
Pioneer Pump and Packing Inc .....F...... 217 791-5293
 Decatur (G-7536)
▲ Pressure Specialist Inc ....E...... 815 477-0007
 Crystal Lake (G-7246)
Rebuilders Enterprises Inc ....G...... 708 430-0030
 Bridgeview (G-2380)
▲ Rhino Tool Company ....F...... 309 853-5555
 Kewanee (G-12040)
Schrader-Bridgeport Intl Inc ....G...... 815 288-3344
 Dixon (G-7916)
SMC Corporation of America ....E...... 630 449-0600
 Aurora (G-1017)
Spirax Sarco Inc ....F...... 630 493-4525
 Lisle (G-12940)
Strahman Valves Inc ....G...... 630 208-9343
 Lafox (G-12139)
▲ Sycamore Precision ....D...... 815 784-5151
 Genoa (G-10324)
USP Holdings Inc ....A...... 847 604-6100
 Rosemont (G-18058)
▲ Val-Matic Valve and Mfg Corp .....C...... 630 941-7600
 Elmhurst (G-9440)
Vonberg Valve Inc ....E...... 847 259-3800
 Rolling Meadows (G-17785)
▲ Western Industries Inc ....G...... 920 261-0660
 Wheeling (G-21012)

3492 Fluid Power Valves & Hose Fittings

A Len Radiator Shoppe Inc ....G...... 630 852-5445
 Downers Grove (G-7948)
All Type Hydraulics Corp ....G...... 618 585-4844
 Bunker Hill (G-2632)
Bristol Hose & Fitting Inc ....E...... 708 492-3456
 Melrose Park (G-13837)
Bristol Transport Inc ....E...... 708 343-6411
 Melrose Park (G-13838)
▲ Ckd USA Corporation ....E...... 847 368-0539
 Schaumburg (G-18478)
Crane Nuclear Inc ....G...... 630 226-4900
 Bolingbrook (G-2160)
▲ Delta Power Company ....D...... 815 397-6628
 Rockford (G-17372)
Deltrol Corp ....C...... 708 547-0500
 Bellwood (G-1621)
◆ Deublin Company ....C...... 847 689-8600
 Waukegan (G-20437)
▲ Flexitech Inc ....C...... 309 665-0658
 Bloomington (G-2044)
Flow Valves International LLC ....G...... 847 866-1188
 Evanston (G-9521)
Fluid Logic Inc ....G...... 847 459-2202
 Buffalo Grove (G-2539)
Hurst Manufacturing Co Inc ....F...... 309 756-9960
 Milan (G-14016)
Hydac Technology Corp ....E...... 630 545-0800
 Glendale Heights (G-10458)
▲ Hydraforce Inc ....A...... 847 793-2300
 Lincolnshire (G-12772)
J C Hose & Tube Inc ....G...... 630 543-4747
 Addison (G-157)
▲ James Walker Mfg Co ....E...... 708 754-4020
 Glenwood (G-10641)
Kepner Products Company ....D...... 630 279-1550
 Villa Park (G-20156)
Kocsis Technologies Inc ....F...... 708 597-4177
 Alsip (G-466)
Kocsis Technologies Inc ....E...... 708 597-4177
 Alsip (G-467)
Lsl Precision Machining Inc ....G...... 815 633-4701
 Loves Park (G-13234)
◆ Mac Lean-Fogg Company ....D...... 847 566-0010
 Mundelein (G-14710)
▲ Marmon Industrial LLC ....G...... 312 372-9500
 Chicago (G-5344)
MEA Inc ....E...... 847 766-9040
 Elk Grove Village (G-9114)

▲ Mead Fluid Dynamics Inc ....E...... 773 685-6800
 University Park (G-19959)
▲ Megadyne America LLC ....E...... 630 752-0600
 Carol Stream (G-3023)
Midwest Hose & Fittings Inc ....G...... 815 578-9040
 Johnsburg (G-11807)
Mj Works Hose & Fitting LLC ....G...... 708 995-5723
 Mokena (G-14098)
◆ Nagano International Corp ....E...... 847 537-0011
 Buffalo Grove (G-2578)
Nanco Sales Co Inc ....G...... 630 892-9820
 Aurora (G-1138)
▲ Plews Inc ....C...... 815 288-3344
 Dixon (G-7906)
Quad City Hose ....E...... 563 386-8936
 Taylor Ridge (G-19747)
Reber Welding Service ....E...... 217 774-3441
 Shelbyville (G-18885)
▲ Rehobot Inc ....E...... 815 385-7777
 McHenry (G-13786)
◆ Robertshaw Controls Company ....C...... 630 260-3400
 Itasca (G-11727)
Rotary Ram Inc ....E...... 618 466-2651
 Godfrey (G-10662)
Royal Brass Inc ....E...... 618 439-6341
 Benton (G-1936)
Seals & Components Inc ....G...... 708 895-5222
 Lansing (G-12514)
SMC Corporation of America ....E...... 630 449-0600
 Aurora (G-1017)
Standard Truck Parts Inc ....G...... 815 726-4486
 Joliet (G-11932)
T & T Distribution Inc ....G...... 815 223-0715
 Peru (G-16594)
Trellborg Sling Sltions US Inc ....D...... 630 289-1500
 Streamwood (G-19598)
Vonberg Valve Inc ....E...... 847 259-3800
 Rolling Meadows (G-17785)
Vrg Controls LLC ....G...... 844 356-9874
 Lake Zurich (G-12468)
▲ Wandfluh of America Inc ....F...... 847 566-5700
 Mundelein (G-14746)
Woods Manufacturing Co Inc ....G...... 630 595-6620
 Wood Dale (G-21258)

3493 Steel Springs, Except Wire

A J Kay Co ....E...... 224 475-0370
 Mundelein (G-14657)
▲ Alco Spring Industries Inc ....D...... 708 755-0438
 Chicago Heights (G-6730)
▲ All Rite Spring Co ....D...... 815 675-1350
 Spring Grove (G-19263)
◆ Boler Company ....F...... 630 773-9111
 Itasca (G-11628)
Burnex Corporation ....E...... 815 728-1317
 Ringwood (G-17040)
▲ Capitol Coil Inc ....F...... 847 891-1390
 Schaumburg (G-18467)
Casey Spring Co Inc ....F...... 708 867-8949
 Park Ridge (G-16272)
▲ Dudek & Bock Spring Mfg Co .....C...... 773 379-4100
 Chicago (G-4402)
▲ Gilbert Spring Corporation ....C...... 773 486-6030
 Chicago (G-4691)
High-Life Products Inc ....G...... 847 991-9449
 Palatine (G-16124)
Highland Spring & Specialty ....E...... 618 654-3831
 Highland (G-11223)
Johnson Tool Company ....G...... 708 453-8600
 Huntley (G-11547)
Kdk Upset Forging Co ....E...... 708 388-8770
 Blue Island (G-2128)
▲ Khc Corporation ....E...... 815 337-7630
 Woodstock (G-21399)
Lew-El Tool & Manufacturing Co .....F...... 773 804-1133
 Chicago (G-5212)
Lewis Spring and Mfg Company ......D...... 847 588-7030
 Niles (G-15140)
Matthew Warren Inc ....E...... 847 349-5760
 Rosemont (G-18035)
Mid-West Spring & Stamping Inc ....G...... 630 739-3800
 Romeoville (G-17854)
Mid-West Spring & Stamping Inc ....G...... 630 739-3800
 Romeoville (G-17853)
Mid-West Spring Mfg Co ....C...... 630 739-3800
 Romeoville (G-17855)
Mw Industries Inc ....D...... 773 539-5600
 Bensenville (G-1855)
▲ Omiotek Coil Spring Co ....D...... 630 495-4056
 Lombard (G-13113)

Paragon Spring Company ....E 773 489-6300
Chicago *(G-5759)*
Park Manufacturing Corp Inc ....F 708 345-6090
Melrose Park *(G-13903)*
R & G Spring Co Inc ....G 847 228-5640
Elk Grove Village *(G-9208)*
▲ **Smalley Steel Ring Co** ....C 847 537-7600
Lake Zurich *(G-12458)*
Spirolox Inc ....B 847 719-5900
Lake Zurich *(G-12459)*
Spring R-R Corporation ....E 630 543-7445
Addison *(G-295)*
Spring Specialist Corporation ....G 815 562-7991
Kings *(G-12054)*
▲ **Stanley Spring & Stamping Corp** ....D 773 777-2600
Chicago *(G-6230)*
United Spring & Manufacturing ....E 773 384-8464
Chicago *(G-6475)*
◆ **William Dudek Manufacturing Co** ....E 773 622-2727
Chicago *(G-6629)*

3494 Valves & Pipe Fittings, NEC

ADS LLC ....D 256 430-3366
Burr Ridge *(G-2650)*
Advanced Plbg & Pipe Fitting ....G 618 554-2677
Newton *(G-15079)*
▲ **Aquatrol Inc** ....F 630 365-2363
Elburn *(G-8443)*
Arnel Industries Inc ....E 630 543-6500
Addison *(G-39)*
B&B Machining Incorporated ....F 630 898-3009
Aurora *(G-920)*
Barrington Automation Ltd ....E 847 458-0900
Lake In The Hills *(G-12329)*
Bi-Torq Valve Automation Inc ....G 630 208-9343
Lafox *(G-12135)*
Catching Hydraulics Co Ltd ....E 708 344-2334
Melrose Park *(G-13839)*
Caterpillar Inc ....B 815 729-5511
Joliet *(G-11838)*
Chicago Pipe Bending & Coil Co ....F 773 379-1918
Chicago *(G-4122)*
Control Equipment Company Inc ....F 847 891-7500
Schaumburg *(G-18487)*
▲ **Couplings Company Inc** ....F 847 634-8990
Lincolnshire *(G-12755)*
Deltrol Corp ....C 708 547-0500
Bellwood *(G-1621)*
◆ **Deublin Company** ....C 847 689-8600
Waukegan *(G-20437)*
▲ **Dixon Brass** ....E 630 323-3716
Westmont *(G-20738)*
Dooley Brothers Plumbing & Htg ....G 309 852-2720
Kewanee *(G-12031)*
Dresser LLC ....D 847 437-5940
Elk Grove Village *(G-8955)*
Dvcc Inc ....E 630 323-3105
Westmont *(G-20739)*
◆ **Eclipse Inc** ....D 815 877-3031
Rockford *(G-17388)*
▲ **Emerson Process Management** ....D 708 535-5120
Oak Forest *(G-15677)*
Evsco Inc ....F 847 362-7068
McHenry *(G-13742)*
▲ **Flender Corporation** ....C 847 931-1990
Elgin *(G-8588)*
Flexicraft Industries Inc ....F 312 428-4750
Chicago *(G-4608)*
Flexicraft Industries Inc ....F 312 229-7550
Chicago *(G-4609)*
▲ **Flexicraft Industries Inc** ....E 312 738-3588
Chicago *(G-4610)*
Groovjoint LLC ....G 312 803-2627
Chicago *(G-4744)*
▲ **Henry Technologies Inc** ....G 217 483-2406
Chatham *(G-3421)*
Hoosier Stamping & Mfg Corp ....E 618 375-2057
Grayville *(G-10810)*
▲ **Intech Industries Inc** ....F 847 487-5599
Wauconda *(G-20361)*
▲ **J/B Industries Inc** ....D 630 851-9444
Aurora *(G-1115)*
Keckley Manufacturing Company ....E 847 674-8422
Skokie *(G-18972)*
▲ **Kelco Industries Inc** ....G 815 334-3600
Woodstock *(G-21398)*
Kepner Products Company ....D 630 279-1550
Villa Park *(G-20156)*
Key West Metal Industries Inc ....C 708 371-1470
Crestwood *(G-7121)*
Lewis Process Systems Inc ....F 630 510-8200
Carol Stream *(G-3018)*
▲ **Lilly Industries Inc** ....F 630 773-2222
Itasca *(G-11694)*
M CA Chicago ....G 312 384-1220
Burr Ridge *(G-2697)*
▲ **Mead Fluid Dynamics Inc** ....E 773 685-6800
University Park *(G-19959)*
Mechanical Engineering Pdts ....G 312 421-3375
Chicago *(G-5380)*
▲ **Metraflex Company** ....D 312 738-3800
Chicago *(G-5411)*
▲ **Midland Manufacturing Corp** ....C 847 677-0333
Skokie *(G-18990)*
Mity Inc ....G 630 365-5030
Elburn *(G-8461)*
Newman-Green Inc ....D 630 543-6500
Addison *(G-228)*
▲ **O C Keckley Company** ....E 847 674-8422
Skokie *(G-18997)*
Oso Technologies Inc ....G 844 777-2575
Urbana *(G-19991)*
Pokorney Manufacturing Co ....G 630 458-0406
Addison *(G-244)*
Pro-Quip Incorporated ....F 708 352-5732
La Grange *(G-12087)*
Process Piping Inc ....G 708 717-0513
Tinley Park *(G-19849)*
Process Screw Products Inc ....E 815 864-2220
Shannon *(G-18872)*
RF Mau Co ....F 847 329-9731
Lincolnwood *(G-12838)*
◆ **Sloan Valve Company** ....D 847 671-4300
Franklin Park *(G-10048)*
Smith Cooper International Inc ....D 847 595-7572
Elk Grove Village *(G-9244)*
Solomon Plumbing ....G 847 498-6388
Glenview *(G-10623)*
Spirax Sarco Inc ....F 630 493-4525
Lisle *(G-12940)*
Spreader Inc ....G 217 568-7219
Gifford *(G-10348)*
SPX Flow US LLC ....G 815 874-5556
Rockford *(G-17644)*
Steamgard LLC ....E 847 913-8400
Vernon Hills *(G-20100)*
Strahman Valves Inc ....E 630 208-9343
Lafox *(G-12139)*
Victaulic Company ....B 630 585-2919
Aurora *(G-1031)*
Vonberg Valve Inc ....E 847 259-3800
Rolling Meadows *(G-17785)*
▲ **Wrap-On Company LLC** ....E 708 496-2150
Alsip *(G-528)*

3495 Wire Springs

A J Kay Co ....F 224 475-0370
Mundelein *(G-14657)*
All American Spring Stamping ....G 847 928-9468
Franklin Park *(G-9865)*
▲ **All Rite Spring Co** ....D 815 675-1350
Spring Grove *(G-19263)*
All Rite Spring Company ....F 815 675-1350
Spring Grove *(G-19264)*
◆ **Ark Technologies Inc** ....D 630 377-8855
Saint Charles *(G-18149)*
Ascent Mfg Co ....E 847 806-6600
Elk Grove Village *(G-8841)*
Available Spring and Mfg Co ....G 847 520-4854
Wheeling *(G-20853)*
▲ **Capitol Coil Inc** ....F 847 891-1390
Schaumburg *(G-18467)*
Century Spring Corporation ....G 800 237-5225
Chicago *(G-4062)*
▲ **CFC Wire Forms Inc** ....E 630 879-7575
Batavia *(G-1364)*
▲ **Classic Products Inc** ....E 815 344-0051
McHenry *(G-13728)*
David V Michals ....D 847 671-6767
Schiller Park *(G-18799)*
Form-All Spring Stamping Inc ....E 630 595-8833
Bensenville *(G-1800)*
▲ **Gerb Vibration Control Systems** ....G 630 724-1660
Lisle *(G-12895)*
Highland Spring & Specialty ....F 618 654-3831
Highland *(G-11223)*
▲ **Innocor Foam Tech W Chcago LLC** ..E 732 945-6222
West Chicago *(G-20598)*
International Spring Company ....D 847 470-8170
Morton Grove *(G-14413)*
Jackson Spring & Mfg Co ....D 847 952-8850
Elk Grove Village *(G-9065)*
▲ **JD Norman Industries Inc** ....D 630 458-3700
Addison *(G-159)*
Johnson Tool Company ....G 708 453-8600
Huntley *(G-11547)*
Kaylen Industries Inc ....D 847 671-6767
Schiller Park *(G-18817)*
Lew-El Tool & Manufacturing Co ....F 773 804-1133
Chicago *(G-5212)*
Lewis Spring and Mfg Company ....D 847 588-7030
Niles *(G-15140)*
M Lizen Manufacturing Co ....E 708 755-7213
University Park *(G-19958)*
Majestic Spring Inc ....F 847 593-8887
Elk Grove Village *(G-9108)*
Master Spring & Wire Form Co ....E 708 453-2570
Itasca *(G-11698)*
Matthew Warren Inc ....G 847 671-6767
Schiller Park *(G-18821)*
Micromatic Spring Stamping Inc ....E 630 607-0141
Addison *(G-207)*
Mid-West Spring & Stamping Inc ....G 630 739-3800
Romeoville *(G-17853)*
Mid-West Spring & Stamping Inc ....G 630 739-3800
Romeoville *(G-17854)*
Mid-West Spring Mfg Co ....C 630 739-3800
Romeoville *(G-17855)*
Mw Industries Inc ....D 773 539-5600
Bensenville *(G-1855)*
OHare Spring Company Inc ....E 847 298-1360
Elk Grove Village *(G-9160)*
Ohare Spring Company Inc ....G 847 298-1360
Des Plaines *(G-7815)*
Paragon Spring Company ....E 773 489-6300
Chicago *(G-5759)*
Patrick Manufacturing Inc ....E 847 697-5920
Elgin *(G-8686)*
▲ **Perfection Spring Stmping Corp** ....D 847 437-3900
Mount Prospect *(G-14560)*
R & G Spring Co Inc ....G 847 228-5640
Elk Grove Village *(G-9208)*
R C Coil Spring Mfg Co Inc ....E 630 790-3500
Glendale Heights *(G-10486)*
R G Spring Company Inc ....G 847 695-2986
Elgin *(G-8712)*
Riverside Spring Company ....G 815 963-3334
Rockford *(G-17574)*
Sanco Industries Inc ....F 847 243-8675
Kildeer *(G-12052)*
▲ **Schaff International LLC** ....E 847 438-4560
Lake Zurich *(G-12453)*
▲ **Smalley Steel Ring Co** ....C 847 537-7600
Lake Zurich *(G-12458)*
▲ **Solar Spring Company** ....C 847 437-7838
Elk Grove Village *(G-9245)*
Spirolox Inc ....B 847 719-5900
Lake Zurich *(G-12459)*
Spring Specialist Corporation ....G 815 562-7991
Kings *(G-12054)*
▲ **Stanley Spring & Stamping Corp** ....D 773 777-2600
Chicago *(G-6230)*
Sterling Spring LLC ....D 773 582-6464
Chicago *(G-6245)*
Sterling Spring LLC ....E 773 777-4647
Bedford Park *(G-1507)*
▲ **Taycorp Inc** ....E 708 629-0921
Alsip *(G-514)*
United Spring & Manufacturing ....E 773 384-8464
Chicago *(G-6475)*
White Eagle Spring & ....F 773 384-4455
Chicago *(G-6618)*
Willdon Corp ....E 773 276-7080
Chicago *(G-6628)*
York Spring Co ....E 847 695-5978
South Elgin *(G-19184)*

3496 Misc Fabricated Wire Prdts

A J Kay Co ....F 224 475-0370
Mundelein *(G-14657)*
◆ **Acco Brands USA LLC** ....B 800 222-6462
Lake Zurich *(G-12376)*
Acco Brands USA LLC ....D 847 272-3700
Lincolnshire *(G-12741)*
Accurate Wire Strip Frming Inc ....F 630 260-1000
Carol Stream *(G-2924)*
▲ **Acme Wire Products LLC** ....E 708 345-4430
Broadview *(G-2413)*
▼ **Acorn Wire and Iron Works LLC** ....E 312 243-6414
Chicago *(G-3530)*

S I C

Employee Codes: A=Over 500 employees, B=251-500
C=101-250, D=51-100, E=20-50, F=10-19, G=3-9
2020 Harris Illinois
Industrial Directory
943

34 FABRICATED METAL PRODUCTS, EXCEPT MACHINERY AND TRANSPORTATION EQUIPMENT

Action Electric Sales Co Inc ....D....... 773 539-1800
Chicago (G-3535)
▲ Advantage Components Inc............E....... 815 725-8644
Joliet (G-11817)
Agena Manufacturing Co ....E....... 630 668-5086
Carol Stream (G-2928)
▼ Alagor Industries Incorporated ....D....... 630 766-2910
Bensenville (G-1734)
Alecto Industries Inc...........................E....... 708 344-1488
Maywood (G-13659)
Allform Manufacturing Co ....G....... 847 680-0144
Libertyville (G-12627)
▲ Alloy Sling Chains Inc ....D....... 708 647-4900
East Hazel Crest (G-8217)
▲ Altak Inc ....D....... 630 622-0300
Bloomingdale (G-1975)
Amag Manufacturing Inc ....G....... 773 667-5184
Chicago (G-3642)
Ameriguard Corporation ....G....... 630 986-1900
Burr Ridge (G-2652)
◆ Ammeraal Beltech Inc ....D....... 847 673-6720
Skokie (G-18920)
Amsysco Inc ....E....... 630 296-8383
Romeoville (G-17794)
Androck Hardware Corporation ....F....... 815 229-1144
Rockford (G-17305)
Apex Wire Products Company Inc ....F....... 847 671-1830
Franklin Park (G-9871)
▲ Archer Wire International Corp ....C....... 708 563-1700
Bedford Park (G-1456)
Armstrong/Alar Inc ....G....... 847 808-8885
Prospect Heights (G-16836)
Art Wire Works Inc ....F....... 708 458-3993
Bedford Park (G-1457)
Ascent Mfg Co ....E....... 847 806-6600
Elk Grove Village (G-8841)
Astoria Wire Products Inc ....D....... 708 496-9950
Bedford Park (G-1459)
Atkore International Group Inc ....A....... 708 339-1610
Harvey (G-11075)
Atkore Intl Holdings Inc ....G....... 708 225-2051
Harvey (G-11076)
Available Spring and Mfg Co ....E....... 847 520-4854
Wheeling (G-20853)
B & J Wire Inc ....E....... 877 787-9473
Chicago (G-3805)
Bel Mar Wire Products Inc ....F....... 773 342-3800
Chicago (G-3861)
Bergeron Group Inc ....E....... 815 741-1635
Joliet (G-11830)
Bristar ....G....... 847 678-5000
Franklin Park (G-9893)
Burnex Corporation ....E....... 815 728-1317
Ringwood (G-17040)
▲ C & J Metal Products Inc ....F....... 847 455-0766
Franklin Park (G-9896)
C R V Electronics Corp.......................D....... 815 675-6500
Spring Grove (G-19269)
Cal-Ill Gasket Co ....F....... 773 287-9605
Chicago (G-4002)
▲ Capitol Coil Inc ....F....... 847 891-1390
Schaumburg (G-18467)
Casey Spring Co Inc ....F....... 708 867-8949
Park Ridge (G-16272)
Cda Industries Inc ....G....... 630 357-7654
Naperville (G-14794)
▲ CFC Wire Forms Inc ....G....... 630 879-7575
Batavia (G-1364)
Chas O Larson Co ....E....... 815 625-0503
Rock Falls (G-17179)
▲ Chicago Car Seal Company ....G....... 773 278-9400
Chicago (G-4095)
▲ Chicago Hardware and Fix Co ....G....... 847 455-6609
Franklin Park (G-9905)
Chicagos Finest Ironworks ....G....... 708 895-4484
Lansing (G-12488)
Circle K Industries Inc ....F....... 847 949-0363
Mundelein (G-14677)
City Screen Inc ....G....... 773 588-5642
Chicago (G-4161)
Contractors Ready-Mix Inc ....G....... 217 482-5530
Mason City (G-13610)
▲ Cooley Wire Products Mfg Co ....F....... 847 678-8585
Schiller Park (G-18796)
Cutting Edge Industries Inc ....G....... 847 678-1777
Franklin Park (G-9923)
D & S Wire Inc ....F....... 847 766-5520
Elk Grove Village (G-8934)
Darbe Products Company Inc ....G....... 630 985-0769
Woodridge (G-21292)

Dayton Superior Corporation ....C....... 815 936-3300
Kankakee (G-11964)
Dove Industries Inc ....F....... 618 234-4509
Belleville (G-1546)
◆ Dudek & Bock Spring Mfg Co ....C....... 773 379-4100
Chicago (G-4402)
▲ Durabilt Dyvex Inc ....F....... 708 397-4673
Broadview (G-2432)
E H Baare Corporation ....C....... 618 546-1575
Robinson (G-17114)
Economy Iron Inc ....F....... 708 343-1777
Melrose Park (G-13859)
Elite Wireworks Corporation ....F....... 630 837-9100
Bartlett (G-1277)
European Ornamental Iron Works.........G....... 630 705-9300
Addison (G-117)
Expandable Habitats ....G....... 815 624-6784
Rockton (G-17697)
Fbs Group Inc ....F....... 773 229-8675
Chicago (G-4569)
▲ Fixture Displays ....G....... 630 296-4190
Downers Grove (G-8003)
Fortune Rope & Metal Co Inc ....G....... 630 787-9715
Bensenville (G-1803)
Franklin Display Group Inc ....G....... 815 544-5300
Belvidere (G-1669)
Franklin Wire Works Inc ....G....... 815 544-6676
Belvidere (G-1670)
▲ G F Ltd ....E....... 708 333-8300
South Holland (G-19212)
Gall Machine Co ....F....... 708 352-2800
Countryside (G-7054)
Guide Line Industries Inc ....E....... 815 777-3722
Scales Mound (G-18420)
▲ Hamalot Inc ....E....... 847 944-1500
Schaumburg (G-18542)
Highland Southern Wire Inc ....G....... 618 654-2161
Highland (G-11222)
Hohmann & Barnard Illinois LLC..........E....... 773 586-6700
Chicago Ridge (G-6798)
Hohmann & Barnard Inc ....G....... 773 586-6700
Chicago Ridge (G-6799)
Hudson Tool & Die Co ....F....... 847 678-8710
Franklin Park (G-9958)
Illinois Tool Works Inc ....G....... 847 821-2170
Vernon Hills (G-20065)
▲ Industrial Wire & Cable Corp ....E....... 847 726-8910
Lake Zurich (G-12421)
Innovation Specialists Inc ....E....... 815 372-9001
New Lenox (G-15037)
Innovative Fix Solutions LLC ....F....... 815 395-8500
Rockford (G-17465)
Jason Incorporated............................C....... 630 627-7000
Addison (G-158)
▲ JD Norman Industries Inc ....D....... 630 458-3700
Addison (G-159)
Jenco Metal Products Inc ....F....... 847 956-0550
Mount Prospect (G-14539)
John Sakash Company Inc ....E....... 630 833-3940
Elmhurst (G-9383)
Johnson Tool Company ....G....... 708 453-8600
Huntley (G-11547)
▲ Jsn Inc ....E....... 708 410-1800
Maywood (G-13670)
▲ Keats Manufacturing Co..................D....... 847 520-1133
Wheeling (G-20923)
Keystone Consolidated Inds Inc ....E....... 309 697-7020
Peoria (G-16466)
Klimp Industries Inc ....G....... 630 682-0752
Carol Stream (G-3011)
Klimp Industries Inc ....G....... 630 790-0600
Carol Stream (G-3012)
◆ L & P Guarding LLC ....F....... 708 325-0400
Bedford Park (G-1477)
▲ Lake Cable LLC ....C....... 888 518-8086
Bensenville (G-1840)
Lamco Slings & Rigging Inc ....E....... 309 764-7400
Moline (G-14157)
Lee Jensen Sales Co Inc ....E....... 815 459-0929
Crystal Lake (G-7220)
▲ Letraw Manufacturing LLC.............G....... 815 987-9670
Rockford (G-17496)
Lew-El Tool & Manufacturing Co ....F....... 773 804-1133
Chicago (G-5212)
Lewis Spring and Mfg Company ....D....... 847 588-7030
Niles (G-15140)
Lift-All Company Inc ....E....... 800 909-1964
Itasca (G-11692)
Lift-All Company Inc ....E....... 630 534-6860
Glendale Heights (G-10468)

▲ Logan Graphic Products Inc............D....... 847 526-5515
Wauconda (G-20369)
▲ Manufasteners House Iq Inc ....G....... 847 705-6538
Palatine (G-16138)
Marcal Rope & Rigging Inc ....E....... 618 462-0172
Alton (G-565)
Marlboro Wire Ltd ....E....... 217 224-7989
Quincy (G-16910)
Master Spring & Wire Form Co ....E....... 708 453-2570
Itasca (G-11698)
Master-Halco Inc ....E....... 618 395-4365
Olney (G-15873)
▲ Mazel & Co Inc ....F....... 773 533-1600
Chicago (G-5372)
MHS Ltd ....F....... 773 736-3333
Chicago (G-5419)
Mid-States Wire Proc Corp ....F....... 773 379-3775
Chicago (G-5431)
▲ Midwest Tungsten Service Inc ....E....... 630 325-1001
Willowbrook (G-21051)
Midwest Wire Works LLC ....F....... 815 874-1701
Rockford (G-17529)
▲ Minerallac Company ....E....... 630 543-7080
Hampshire (G-10979)
Moffat Wire & Display Inc ....F....... 630 458-8560
Addison (G-221)
▲ Nixalite of America Inc ....F....... 309 755-8771
East Moline (G-8235)
Nvent Electric Public Ltd Co ....G....... 618 918-3821
Centralia (G-3243)
OHare Spring Company Inc ....E....... 847 298-1360
Elk Grove Village (G-9160)
Paragon Spring Company ....E....... 773 489-6300
Chicago (G-5759)
Park Manufacturing Corp Inc ....F....... 708 345-6090
Melrose Park (G-13903)
Partex Marking Systems Inc ....G....... 630 516-0400
Lombard (G-13117)
▲ Perfection Spring Stmping Corp .....D....... 847 437-3900
Mount Prospect (G-14560)
Precision Forming Stamping Co ....E....... 773 489-6868
Chicago (G-5857)
▲ Precision Steel Warehouse Inc ....C....... 800 323-0740
Franklin Park (G-10026)
▲ Precitec Corporation ....D....... 847 949-2800
Mundelein (G-14727)
Rapid Wire Forms Inc ....E....... 773 586-6600
Chicago (G-5975)
Reino Tool & Manufacturing Co ....F....... 773 588-5800
Chicago (G-6005)
▲ Remin Laboratories Inc ....D....... 815 723-1940
Joliet (G-11924)
Riverside Spring Company ....G....... 815 963-3334
Rockford (G-17574)
▲ Rockford Rigging Inc ....F....... 309 263-0566
Roscoe (G-17926)
Sanco Industries Inc ....F....... 847 243-8675
Kildeer (G-12052)
▲ Schaff International LLC ....E....... 847 438-4560
Lake Zurich (G-12453)
Simonton Hardwood Lumber LLC........F....... 618 594-2132
Carlyle (G-2896)
▲ Solar Spring Company ....C....... 847 437-7838
Elk Grove Village (G-9245)
▲ Southern Steel and Wire Inc ....G....... 618 654-2161
Highland (G-11240)
Spring Specialist Corporation ....E....... 815 562-7991
Kings (G-12054)
Sterling Wire Products Inc ....E....... 815 625-3015
Rock Falls (G-17196)
The Parts House ....G....... 309 343-0146
Galesburg (G-10221)
Trio Wire Products Inc ....E....... 815 469-2148
Frankfort (G-9846)
◆ Tru Vue Inc ....C....... 708 485-5080
Countryside (G-7075)
▲ Unistrut International Corp ....C....... 800 882-5543
Harvey (G-11099)
Wardzala Industries Inc ....F....... 847 288-9909
Franklin Park (G-10083)
White Eagle Spring & ....F....... 773 384-4455
Chicago (G-6618)
Will Don Corp ....F....... 773 276-7081
Chicago (G-6627)
Willdon Corp ....F....... 773 276-7080
Chicago (G-6628)
William Dach ....F....... 815 962-3455
Rockford (G-17685)
◆ William Dudek Manufacturing Co ...E....... 773 622-2727
Chicago (G-6629)

34 FABRICATED METAL PRODUCTS, EXCEPT MACHINERY AND TRANSPORTATION EQUIPMENT

Wirco Inc ....D...... 217 398-3200
  Champaign (G-3371)
Wire Mesh LLC ....G...... 815 579-8597
  Oglesby (G-15844)
Wireformers Inc ....E...... 847 718-1920
  Mount Prospect (G-14582)
▲ Wiremasters Incorporated ....E...... 773 254-3700
  Chicago (G-6649)
Woodland Fence Forest Pdts Inc ....G...... 630 393-2220
  Warrenville (G-20257)

3497 Metal Foil & Leaf

◆ Bagcraftpapercon I LLC ....C...... 620 856-2800
  Chicago (G-3814)
D W Machine Products Inc ....G...... 618 654-2161
  Highland (G-11212)
▲ Durable Inc ....A...... 847 541-4400
  Wheeling (G-20881)
◆ Handi-Foil Corp ....A...... 847 520-1000
  Wheeling (G-20907)
◆ Hfa Inc ....A...... 847 520-1000
  Wheeling (G-20908)
◆ Highland Supply Corporation ....B...... 618 654-2161
  Highland (G-11224)
Intellisource Inc ....E...... 847 426-7400
  Elgin (G-8629)
Kurz Transfer Products LP ....E...... 847 228-0001
  Elk Grove Village (G-9080)
Pactiv LLC ....E...... 847 482-2000
  Lake Forest (G-12281)
Pactiv LLC ....C...... 217 479-1144
  Jacksonville (G-11779)
◆ Q Sales & Leasing LLC ....F...... 708 331-0094
  Hazel Crest (G-11136)
◆ R and R Brokerage Co ....C...... 847 438-4600
  Lake Zurich (G-12448)
▲ Tinscape LLC ....G...... 630 236-7236
  Aurora (G-1025)
Winpak Heat Seal Corp ....D...... 309 477-6600
  Pekin (G-16370)

3498 Fabricated Pipe & Pipe Fittings

Acrofab ....G...... 630 350-7941
  Bensenville (G-1727)
ADS LLC ....D...... 256 430-3366
  Burr Ridge (G-2650)
▲ Alconix Usa Inc ....G...... 847 717-7407
  Elk Grove Village (G-8813)
Alert Tubing Fabricators Inc ....G...... 815 633-5065
  Loves Park (G-13186)
▲ American Diesel Tube Corp ....F...... 630 628-1830
  Addison (G-32)
American Piping Group Inc ....D...... 815 772-7470
  Morrison (G-14340)
American Piping Products Inc ....E...... 708 339-1753
  South Holland (G-19193)
▲ Anamet Electrical Inc ....C...... 217 234-8844
  Mattoon (G-13630)
Anvil International LLC ....F...... 708 534-1414
  Tinley Park (G-19805)
Anvil International Inc ....E...... 603 418-2800
  Chicago (G-3708)
Arntzen Corporation ....E...... 815 334-0788
  Woodstock (G-21360)
Art Wire Works Inc ....F...... 708 458-3993
  Bedford Park (G-1457)
Bessco Tube Bending Pipe Fabg ....G...... 708 339-3977
  South Holland (G-19201)
Boyce Industries Inc ....F...... 708 345-0455
  Melrose Park (G-13836)
Cain Tubular Products Inc ....G...... 630 584-5330
  Saint Charles (G-18162)
◆ Cerro Flow Products LLC ....C...... 618 337-6000
  Sauget (G-18392)
Chicago Metal Fabricators Inc ....D...... 773 523-5755
  Chicago (G-4114)
◆ Chicago Metal Rolled Pdts Co ....D...... 773 523-5757
  Chicago (G-4115)
Chicago Pipe Bending & Coil Co ....F...... 773 379-1918
  Chicago (G-4122)
Chicago Tube and Iron Company ......E...... 815 834-2500
  Romeoville (G-17807)
Chicago Tube and Iron Company ......E...... 309 787-4947
  Milan (G-14203)
▲ Cortube Products Co ....G...... 708 429-6700
  Tinley Park (G-19816)
▲ D & W Mfg Co Inc ....F...... 773 533-1542
  Chicago (G-4300)
◆ Deublin Company ....C...... 847 689-8600
  Waukegan (G-20437)
Dove Steel Inc ....F...... 815 588-3772
  Lockport (G-12990)
▲ Duraflex Inc ....F...... 847 462-1007
  Cary (G-3156)
E H Wachs ....G...... 815 943-4785
  Lincolnshire (G-12761)
◆ Flex-Weld Inc ....D...... 815 334-3662
  Woodstock (G-21387)
▲ Flexicraft Industries Inc ....E...... 312 738-3588
  Chicago (G-4610)
Flexicraft Industries Inc ....F...... 312 428-4750
  Chicago (G-4608)
Fulton Metal Works Inc ....G...... 217 476-8223
  Ashland (G-884)
Gateway Fbrction Solutions LLC ....E...... 618 612-3170
  Waterloo (G-20290)
Geib Industries Inc ....G...... 847 455-4550
  Bensenville (G-1809)
▲ Gerlin Inc ....G...... 630 653-5232
  Carol Stream (G-2991)
Global Maintenance LLC ....E...... 270 933-1281
  Metropolis (G-13971)
▲ Howe Corporation ....E...... 773 235-0200
  Chicago (G-4851)
Hub Manufacturing Company Inc ....G...... 773 252-1373
  Chicago (G-4859)
Hyspan Precision Products Inc ....E...... 773 277-0700
  South Holland (G-19223)
Icon Mech Cnstr & Engrg LLC ....E...... 618 452-0035
  Granite City (G-10716)
Illco Inc ....G...... 815 725-9100
  Joliet (G-11878)
Industrial Pipe and Supply Co ....E...... 708 652-7511
  Chicago (G-4909)
▲ Integrated Mfg Tech LLC ....E...... 618 282-8306
  Red Bud (G-16996)
James L Tracey Co ....G...... 630 907-8999
  Aurora (G-1117)
John Maneely Company ....F...... 773 254-0617
  Chicago (G-5043)
Key West Metal Industries Inc ....C...... 708 371-1470
  Crestwood (G-7121)
Lafox Manufacturing Corp ....G...... 630 232-0266
  Lafox (G-12136)
▲ Leading Edge Group Inc ....E...... 815 316-3500
  Rockford (G-17492)
Machine Tool Acc & Mfg Co ....G...... 773 489-0903
  Chicago (G-5309)
▲ Manufactured Specialties Inc ....F...... 630 444-1992
  Saint Charles (G-18230)
▲ Metamora Industries LLC ....E...... 309 367-2368
  Metamora (G-13964)
Monco Fabricators Inc ....G...... 630 293-0063
  West Chicago (G-20621)
Morris Construction Inc ....E...... 618 544-8504
  Robinson (G-17120)
▲ National Metalwares LP ....C...... 630 892-9000
  Aurora (G-1139)
Parker Fabrication Inc ....E...... 309 698-8080
  East Peoria (G-8282)
Parker Fabrication Inc ....E...... 309 266-8413
  Morton (G-14376)
◆ Peerless America Incorporated ....C...... 217 342-0400
  Effingham (G-8418)
Pekay Machine & Engrg Co Inc ....F...... 312 829-5530
  Chicago (G-5784)
◆ Perma-Pipe Inc ....F...... 847 966-1000
  Niles (G-15157)
Permalert Envmtl Spcialty Pdts ....F...... 847 966-2190
  Niles (G-15159)
Ptc Tubular Products LLC ....F...... 815 692-4900
  Fairbury (G-9612)
▲ Rovanco Piping Systems Inc ....D...... 815 741-6700
  Joliet (G-11928)
Scot Industries Inc ....D...... 630 466-7591
  Sugar Grove (G-19653)
Service Sheet Metal Works Inc ....F...... 773 229-0031
  Chicago (G-6143)
Sharlen Electric Co ....E...... 773 721-0700
  Chicago (G-6147)
Shew Brothers Inc ....F...... 618 997-4414
  Marion (G-13534)
Solid Metal Group Inc ....F...... 708 757-7421
  Chicago Heights (G-6774)
Strait-O-Flex ....F...... 815 965-2625
  Stillman Valley (G-19546)
Supplied Indus Solutions Inc ....F...... 618 452-8151
  Granite City (G-10741)
Tech-Weld Inc ....F...... 630 365-3000
  Elburn (G-8474)
Tesko Welding & Mfg Co ....D...... 708 452-0045
  Norridge (G-15244)
▲ Vindee Industries Inc ....E...... 815 469-3300
  Frankfort (G-9850)
Weatherford International LLC ....E...... 309 342-5154
  Galesburg (G-10223)
◆ Zeman Mfg Co ....E...... 630 960-2300
  Lisle (G-12958)

3499 Fabricated Metal Prdts, NEC

1776 Fabrication LLC ....G...... 773 895-7590
  Wood Dale (G-21146)
A - Square Manufacturing Inc ....E...... 800 628-6720
  Chicago (G-3483)
Abct Corporation ....G...... 773 427-1010
  Lincolnwood (G-12810)
▲ About Face Designs Inc ....E...... 847 914-9040
  Highland Park (G-11250)
Adk Products Inc ....G...... 847 710-0021
  Elk Grove Village (G-8808)
Afar Imports & Interiors Inc ....G...... 217 744-3262
  Springfield (G-19316)
▲ All Right Sales Inc ....G...... 773 558-4800
  West Chicago (G-20534)
All Star Custom Awards ....G...... 630 428-1515
  Naperville (G-14771)
American Machine ....E...... 815 539-6558
  Mendota (G-13934)
American Metal Mfg Inc ....G...... 847 651-6097
  Chicago (G-3662)
American Partsmith Inc ....G...... 630 520-0432
  West Chicago (G-20538)
American Trophy & Award Co Inc .....G...... 312 939-3252
  Chicago (G-3672)
Aptargroup Inc ....B...... 847 639-2124
  Cary (G-3148)
Aptargroup Inc ....E...... 847 816-9400
  Libertyville (G-12629)
◆ Aptargroup Inc ....C...... 815 477-0424
  Crystal Lake (G-7160)
Artistic Framing Inc ....C...... 847 808-0200
  Wheeling (G-20850)
Avondale Adventures ....G...... 773 588-5761
  Chicago (G-3789)
Avondale Customs Inc ....G...... 773 680-4631
  Chicago (G-3790)
Awards and More Inc ....G...... 773 581-7771
  Chicago (G-3792)
▲ Black Mountain Products Inc ....G...... 224 655-5955
  Spring Grove (G-19268)
Bronze Memorial Inc ....G...... 773 276-7972
  Chicago (G-3963)
Builders Chicago Corporation ....D...... 224 654-2122
  Rosemont (G-18001)
Cardinal Engineering Inc ....G...... 309 342-7474
  Galesburg (G-10188)
Chadwick Manufacturing Ltd ....G...... 815 684-5152
  Chadwick (G-3257)
Custom Fabricators LLC ....F...... 630 372-4399
  Streamwood (G-19569)
▲ Durabilt Dyvex Inc ....F...... 708 397-4673
  Broadview (G-2432)
Dva Metal Fabrication Inc ....G...... 224 577-8217
  Mundelein (G-14684)
◆ Energy Absorption Systems Inc ......E...... 312 467-6750
  Chicago (G-4506)
F5d Inc ....G...... 815 953-9183
  Herscher (G-11183)
◆ First Alert Inc ....E...... 630 499-3295
  Aurora (G-962)
Flexicraft Industries Inc ....F...... 312 428-4750
  Chicago (G-4608)
Flexicraft Industries Inc ....F...... 312 229-7550
  Chicago (G-4609)
▲ Flexicraft Industries Inc ....E...... 312 738-3588
  Chicago (G-4610)
Forge Group Star LLC ....E...... 815 758-6400
  Freeport (G-10110)
Fotofab LLC ....F...... 773 463-6211
  Chicago (G-4623)
Framery ....G...... 618 656-5749
  Edwardsville (G-8363)
Frederics Frame Studio Inc ....F...... 312 243-2950
  Chicago (G-4632)
G & M Fabricating Inc ....G...... 815 282-1744
  Roscoe (G-17907)
G & M Metal Fabricators Inc ....D...... 847 678-6501
  Franklin Park (G-9947)
Gaskoa Inc ....E...... 708 339-5000
  South Holland (G-19213)

Employee Codes: A=Over 500 employees, B=251-500
C=101-250, D=51-100, E=20-50, F=10-19, G=3-9

34 FABRICATED METAL PRODUCTS, EXCEPT MACHINERY AND TRANSPORTATION EQUIPMENT

▲ Gpi Manufacturing Inc .... E 847 615-8900
  Lake Bluff **(G-12184)**
Group Industries Inc .... E 708 877-6200
  Thornton **(G-19788)**
▲ Hadady Corporation .... E 219 322-7417
  South Holland **(G-19218)**
◆ Home Pdts Intl - N Amer Inc .... B 773 890-1010
  Chicago **(G-4834)**
Illinois Tool Works Inc .... C 708 458-7320
  Bridgeview **(G-2357)**
Illinois Tool Works Inc .... E 847 215-8925
  Buffalo Grove **(G-2548)**
Illinois Tool Works Inc .... B 847 724-7500
  Glenview **(G-10560)**
Illinois Tool Works Inc .... C 630 372-2150
  Bartlett **(G-1288)**
Illinois Tool Works Inc .... C 847 783-5500
  Elgin **(G-8621)**
Infrastructure Def Tech LLC .... G 800 379-1822
  Belvidere **(G-1678)**
Innerweld Cover Co .... F 847 497-3009
  Mundelein **(G-14701)**
Jerome Remien Corporation .... F 847 806-0888
  Elk Grove Village **(G-9067)**
▲ JL Clark LLC .... C 815 961-5609
  Rockford **(G-17476)**
JMS Metals Inc .... G 618 443-1000
  Sparta **(G-19255)**
John Thomas Inc .... E 815 288-2343
  Dixon **(G-7902)**
Kenneth W Templeman .... G 847 912-2740
  Volo **(G-20200)**
◆ Knaack LLC .... D 815 459-6020
  Crystal Lake **(G-7217)**
Laird Technologies Inc .... C 847 839-6000
  Schaumburg **(G-18597)**
Lake Iron Inc .... G 708 870-0546
  Chicago **(G-5160)**
▲ Lechler Inc .... D 630 377-6611
  Saint Charles **(G-18225)**
Lindsay Metal Madness Inc .... G 815 568-4560
  Woodstock **(G-21406)**
Livingston Innovations LLC .... G 847 808-0900
  Waukegan **(G-20459)**
Louisville Ladder Inc .... G 309 692-1895
  Peoria **(G-16470)**
Lynda Hervas .... G 847 985-1690
  Schaumburg **(G-18615)**
Macholl Metal Fabrication .... G 815 597-1908
  Garden Prairie **(G-10237)**
Mc Metals & Fabricating Inc .... G 847 961-5242
  Huntley **(G-11555)**
▲ McLean Manufacturing Company .... G 847 277-9912
  Lake Barrington **(G-12160)**
Metal Strip Buiding Products .... G 847 742-8500
  Itasca **(G-11700)**
Midland Stamping and Fabg Corp .... D 847 678-7573
  Schiller Park **(G-18825)**
Mighty Mites Awards and Sons .... G 847 297-0035
  Des Plaines **(G-7802)**
▲ Millenia Products Group Inc .... C 630 458-0401
  Itasca **(G-11704)**
Morris Magnetics Inc .... G 847 487-0829
  Wauconda **(G-20378)**
▲ MPS Chicago Inc .... C 630 932-9000
  Downers Grove **(G-8062)**
Nafisco Inc .... F 815 372-3300
  Romeoville **(G-17858)**
Newman-Green Inc .... D 630 543-6500
  Addison **(G-228)**
Noise Barriers LLC .... E 847 843-0500
  Libertyville **(G-12688)**
▲ North American Safety Pdts Inc .... G 815 469-1144
  Mokena **(G-14099)**
Ojedas Welding Co .... G 708 595-3799
  Maywood **(G-13677)**
Olympic Trophy and Awards Co .... F 773 631-9500
  Chicago **(G-5672)**
Orient Machining & Welding Inc .... E 708 371-3500
  Dixmoor **(G-7886)**
▲ Planter Inc .... D 773 637-7777
  Chicago **(G-5817)**
◆ Pmp Americas Inc .... F 815 633-9962
  South Beloit **(G-19107)**
◆ Precision Brand Products Inc .... E 630 969-7200
  Downers Grove **(G-8082)**
▲ Precision Steel Warehouse Inc .... C 800 323-0740
  Franklin Park **(G-10026)**
Product Service Craft Inc .... F 630 964-5160
  Downers Grove **(G-8085)**

Progressive Bronze Works Inc .... E 773 463-5500
  Chicago **(G-5899)**
Promus Equity Partners LLC .... F 312 784-3990
  Chicago **(G-5903)**
PSM Industries Inc .... E 815 337-8800
  Woodstock **(G-21425)**
Quinceaneraboutiquecom Inc .... G 779 324-5468
  Frankfort **(G-9830)**
Quixote Transportation Safety .... D 312 467-6750
  Chicago **(G-5940)**
▲ R S Owens & Co Inc .... B 773 282-6000
  Chicago **(G-5953)**
Renner & Co .... F 847 639-4900
  Cary **(G-3185)**
Robin L Barnhouse .... G 309 737-5431
  Joy **(G-11947)**
Roll Roll Met Fabricators Inc .... E 773 434-1315
  Chicago **(G-6053)**
◆ Samuel Son & Co (usa) Inc .... C 630 783-8900
  Woodridge **(G-21338)**
Signode Midwest Steel .... G 847 657-5385
  Bridgeview **(G-2386)**
Solid Metal Group Inc .... G 708 757-7421
  Chicago Heights **(G-6774)**
◆ Spraying Systems Co .... A 630 665-5000
  Glendale Heights **(G-10498)**
Spraying Systems Co .... G 630 665-5001
  Aurora **(G-1020)**
◆ Spraying Systems Midwest Inc .... G 630 665-5000
  Glendale Heights **(G-10499)**
Star Freeport Company LLC .... E 815 758-6400
  Freeport **(G-10145)**
Supreme Frame & Moulding Co .... F 312 930-9056
  Chicago **(G-6286)**
▲ Talaris Inc .... C 630 577-1000
  Lisle **(G-12948)**
▼ Tc Industries Inc .... C 815 459-2401
  Crystal Lake **(G-7276)**
Terra Cotta Holdings Co .... G 815 459-2400
  Crystal Lake **(G-7281)**
Trafficguard Inc .... G 877 727-7347
  Sycamore **(G-19736)**
▲ Trendler Inc .... B 773 284-6600
  Chicago **(G-6416)**
TSC International Inc .... F 847 249-4900
  Wadsworth **(G-20214)**
Tu-Star Manufacturing Co Inc .... G 815 338-5760
  Woodstock **(G-21441)**
Tvh Parts Co .... F 847 223-1000
  Grayslake **(G-10803)**
Two Four Seven Metal Laser .... G 847 250-5199
  Itasca **(G-11749)**
Variable Operations Tech Inc .... G 815 479-8528
  Crystal Lake **(G-7288)**
Viking Metal Cabinet Co LLC .... D 800 776-7767
  Montgomery **(G-14273)**
Viking Metal Cabinet Company .... D 630 863-7234
  Montgomery **(G-14274)**
Voss Pattern Works Inc .... G 618 233-4242
  Belleville **(G-1609)**
▲ Vulcan Ladder Usa LLC .... E 847 526-6321
  Crystal Lake **(G-7292)**
◆ Webster-Hoff Corporation .... D 630 858-8030
  Glendale Heights **(G-10515)**
▼ Welding Company of America .... E 630 806-2000
  Aurora **(G-1168)**
Werner Co .... E 815 459-6020
  Crystal Lake **(G-7294)**
▲ Wiremasters Incorporated .... E 773 254-3700
  Chicago **(G-6649)**
Zenith Fabricating Company .... E 773 622-2601
  Chicago **(G-6717)**

35 INDUSTRIAL AND COMMERCIAL MACHINERY AND COMPUTER EQUIPMENT

3511 Steam, Gas & Hydraulic Turbines & Engines

▲ A P S Gas Turbine Inc .... G 708 262-2939
  Alsip **(G-409)**
Abb Inc .... F 630 759-7428
  Bolingbrook **(G-2145)**
Acciona Windpower N Amer LLC .... G 319 643-9463
  Chicago **(G-3515)**
Action Turbine Repair Svc Inc .... F 708 924-9601
  Summit Argo **(G-19677)**

▲ Alin Machining Company Inc .... C 708 681-1043
  Melrose Park **(G-13821)**
Alturdyne Power Systems LLC .... G 619 440-5531
  Chicago **(G-3638)**
Angel Wind Energy Inc .... G 815 471-2020
  Onarga **(G-15901)**
▲ Area Diesel Service Inc .... E 217 854-2641
  Carlinville **(G-2867)**
B N Blance Enrgy Solutions LLC .... E 847 287-7466
  Palatine **(G-16096)**
Broadwind Energy Inc .... E 708 780-4800
  Cicero **(G-6831)**
Catching Hydraulics Co Ltd .... E 708 344-2334
  Melrose Park **(G-13839)**
Caterpillar Inc .... A 309 578-1615
  Mossville **(G-14459)**
Caterpillar Inc .... B 309 675-6590
  Peoria **(G-16411)**
Caterpillar Inc .... G 309 578-2185
  Mossville **(G-14452)**
▲ Caterpillar Inc .... A 224 551-4000
  Deerfield **(G-7600)**
Caterpillar Inc .... D 309 578-6118
  Mossville **(G-14453)**
Caterpillar Inc .... B 888 614-4328
  Peoria **(G-16407)**
Energy Parts Solutions Inc .... F 224 653-9412
  Schaumburg **(G-18518)**
Gds Enterprises .... G 217 543-3681
  Arthur **(G-859)**
Invenergy .... G 815 795-4964
  Marseilles **(G-13558)**
ITT Water & Wastewater USA Inc .... F 708 342-0484
  Tinley Park **(G-19840)**
Kliux Energies Intl Inc .... E 312 985-7717
  Chicago **(G-5109)**
◆ Laser Technologies Inc .... C 630 761-1200
  Naperville **(G-14860)**
Mainstream Renewable Power .... G 815 379-2784
  Walnut **(G-20219)**
Marty Lundeen .... G 630 250-8917
  Itasca **(G-11697)**
Michael Wilton Cstm Homes Inc .... G 630 508-1200
  Willowbrook **(G-21049)**
Nooter/Eriksen Inc .... G 636 651-1028
  Columbia **(G-6991)**
◆ Nordex Usa Inc .... D 312 386-4100
  Chicago **(G-5614)**
Pietro Carnaghi USA Inc .... G 779 368-0564
  Rockford **(G-17554)**
Pne Usa Inc .... G 773 329-3705
  Chicago **(G-5826)**
Power Plant Repair Svcs LLC .... D 708 345-8600
  Oswego **(G-16020)**
▲ Power Solutions Intl Inc .... G 630 350-9400
  Wood Dale **(G-21228)**
Rebuilders Enterprises Inc .... G 708 430-0030
  Bridgeview **(G-2380)**
Rockwind Venture Partners LLC .... G 630 881-6664
  Rockford **(G-17612)**
Siemens Energy Inc .... C 618 357-6360
  Pinckneyville **(G-16619)**
Solar Turbines Incorporated .... E 630 527-1700
  Naperville **(G-14916)**
▲ Sur-Fit Corporation .... E 815 301-5815
  Crystal Lake **(G-7272)**
Suzlon Wind Energy Corporation .... G 773 328-5077
  Elgin **(G-8743)**
▼ Union Iron Inc .... E 217 429-5148
  Decatur **(G-7564)**
University of Chicago .... F 773 702-9780
  Chicago **(G-6487)**
Xylem Lnc .... G 847 966-3700
  Morton Grove **(G-14451)**

3519 Internal Combustion Engines, NEC

American Speed Enterprises .... G 309 764-3601
  Moline **(G-14131)**
B & M Automotive .... G 309 637-4977
  Peoria **(G-16389)**
Boley Tool & Machine Works Inc .... C 309 694-2722
  East Peoria **(G-8254)**
◆ Brunswick Corporation .... B 847 735-4700
  Mettawa **(G-13979)**
Brunswick International Ltd .... E 847 735-4700
  Mettawa **(G-13980)**
C & M Engineering .... G 815 932-3388
  Bourbonnais **(G-2257)**
Caterpillar Gb LLC .... G 309 675-1000
  Peoria **(G-16403)**

Caterpillar Inc ....A.... 309 578-1615
Mossville (G-14459)
Caterpillar Inc ....B.... 309 675-6590
Peoria (G-16411)
Caterpillar Inc ....G.... 309 578-2185
Mossville (G-14452)
▲ Caterpillar Inc ....A.... 224 551-4000
Deerfield (G-7600)
Caterpillar Inc ....D.... 309 578-6118
Mossville (G-14453)
Caterpillar Inc ....B.... 888 614-4328
Peoria (G-16407)
Chicago Jet Group LLC ....E.... 630 466-3600
Sugar Grove (G-19639)
▲ Concentric Itasca Inc ....D.... 630 773-3355
Itasca (G-11638)
Cummins - Allison Corp ....D.... 847 299-9550
Mount Prospect (G-14521)
Cummins - Allison Corp ....C.... 847 299-9550
Mount Prospect (G-14522)
Cummins - Allison Corp ....F.... 630 833-2285
Elmhurst (G-9357)
Cummins Crosspoint LLC ....G.... 309 452-4454
Normal (G-15201)
Cummins Dist Holdco Inc ....E.... 309 787-4300
Rock Island (G-17213)
Cummins Inc ....E.... 309 787-4300
Rock Island (G-17214)
Cummins Npower LLC ....E.... 708 579-9222
Hodgkins (G-11387)
◆ Cummins-Allison Corp ....B.... 800 786-5528
Mount Prospect (G-14523)
Cummins-American Corp ....G.... 847 299-9550
Mount Prospect (G-14524)
◆ Diesel Radiator Co ....C.... 800 345-9244
Melrose Park (G-13851)
Diesel Radiator Co ....D.... 708 865-7299
Melrose Park (G-13852)
Engine Efficiency Systems LLC ....F.... 630 590-5241
Burr Ridge (G-2670)
◆ Heavy Quip Incorporated ....F.... 312 368-7997
Chicago (G-4797)
Honeywell International Inc ....A.... 847 391-2000
Des Plaines (G-7780)
Hunt Charles ....G.... 217 793-5151
Springfield (G-19383)
Jasiek Motor Rebuilding Inc ....G.... 815 883-3678
Oglesby (G-15842)
JDM Engines Chicago LLC ....G.... 214 235-5071
Elk Grove Village (G-9066)
L S Diesel Repair Inc ....G.... 217 283-5537
Hoopeston (G-11510)
Lv Ventures Inc ....G.... 312 993-1800
Chicago (G-5289)
Mpc Global LLC ....G.... 816 399-4710
Springfield (G-19408)
Navistar Inc ....B.... 317 352-4500
Melrose Park (G-13894)
◆ Navistar Inc ....C.... 331 332-5000
Lisle (G-12917)
◆ Navistar International Corp ....A.... 331 332-5000
Lisle (G-12921)
Nelson Enterprises Inc ....G.... 815 633-1100
Roscoe (G-17920)
Npt Automotive Machine Shop ....G.... 618 233-1344
Belleville (G-1580)
Performance Diesel Service ....G.... 217 375-4429
Hoopeston (G-11511)
◆ Perkins Engines Inc ....E.... 309 578-7364
Mossville (G-14461)
Precision Engine Rbldrs Inc ....G.... 815 254-2333
Plainfield (G-16704)
◆ Progress Rail Locomotive Inc ....A.... 800 255-5355
Mc Cook (G-13699)
Progress Rail Locomotive Inc ....F.... 708 387-5510
Mc Cook (G-13700)
R & C Auto Supply Corp ....G.... 815 625-4414
Sterling (G-19528)
Speed Tech Technology Inc ....G.... 847 516-2001
Cary (G-3191)
▲ Tpr America Inc ....G.... 847 446-5336
Schaumburg (G-18751)
◆ Unicarriers Americas Corp ....G.... 800 871-5438
Marengo (G-13496)
Waymore Power Co Inc ....F.... 618 729-3876
Piasa (G-16610)
Wuebbels Repair & Sales LLC ....G.... 618 648-2227
Mc Leansboro (G-13710)

3523 Farm Machinery & Eqpt

360 Yield Center LLC ....E.... 309 263-4360
Morton (G-14352)
◆ A P Livestock Division G S I ....G.... 217 226-4449
Assumption (G-887)
AGCO Corporation ....G.... 630 293-9905
West Chicago (G-20532)
AGCO Corporation ....E.... 630 406-3248
Batavia (G-1341)
Agri-Fab Inc ....F.... 217 875-7051
Decatur (G-7435)
Alvarez & Marsal Inc ....E.... 312 601-4220
Chicago (G-3639)
▲ Aqua Control Inc ....E.... 815 664-4900
Spring Valley (G-19307)
Arrows Up Inc ....G.... 847 305-2550
Arlington Heights (G-696)
▲ Avant Tecno USA Inc ....F.... 847 380-1308
Arlington Heights (G-700)
B J Fehr Machine Co ....G.... 309 923-8691
Roanoke (G-17099)
B T Brown Manufacturing ....G.... 815 947-3633
Kent (G-12017)
◆ Bellota Agrsltions Tls USA LLC ....E.... 309 787-2491
Rock Island (G-17205)
Bill Peterson ....G.... 815 378-8633
Harvard (G-11048)
Birkeys Farm Store Inc ....E.... 217 337-1772
Urbana (G-19975)
Blue Ridge Land and Cattle ....G.... 217 762-9652
Monticello (G-14279)
Brian Burcar ....G.... 815 856-2271
Leonore (G-12611)
Brian Lindstrom ....G.... 309 463-2388
Varna (G-20031)
▲ Bushnell Illinois Tank Co ....D.... 309 772-3106
Bushnell (G-2738)
▲ Calmer Corn Heads Inc ....E.... 309 629-9000
Lynn Center (G-13288)
Cardinal Cattle ....G.... 309 479-1302
Wyoming (G-21458)
▼ Caterpillar Brazil LLC ....A.... 309 675-1000
Peoria (G-16400)
Christopher Concrete Products ....G.... 618 724-2951
Buckner (G-2499)
Circle K Industries Inc ....F.... 847 949-0363
Mundelein (G-14677)
Cline Concrete Products ....F.... 217 283-5012
Hoopeston (G-11505)
Cnh America LLC ....F.... 309 965-2217
Goodfield (G-10671)
Cnh Industrial America LLC ....G.... 847 263-5793
Waukegan (G-20429)
Cnh Industrial America LLC ....E.... 309 965-2233
Goodfield (G-10672)
Cnh Industrial America LLC ....C.... 309 965-2217
Goodfield (G-10673)
Cnh Industrial America LLC ....C.... 630 887-2233
Burr Ridge (G-2664)
Cnh Industrial Capitl Amer LLC ....E.... 630 887-2233
Burr Ridge (G-2665)
Coyote Transportation Inc ....G.... 630 204-5729
Bensenville (G-1779)
Crane Quality Equipment LLC ....G.... 815 258-5375
Clifton (G-6914)
Custom Millers Supply Inc ....G.... 309 734-6312
Monmouth (G-14216)
Cutting Specialists Inc ....E.... 731 352-5351
Edwardsville (G-8355)
D & B Fabricators & Distrs ....F.... 630 325-3811
Lemont (G-12562)
D M Manufacturing 2 Inc ....G.... 618 455-3550
Sainte Marie (G-18325)
David Taylor ....E.... 217 222-6480
Quincy (G-16875)
Davidson Grain Incorporated ....E.... 815 384-3208
Creston (G-7101)
Davis Welding & Manfctg Inc ....F.... 217 784-5480
Gibson City (G-10336)
Dawn Equipment Company Inc ....F.... 815 899-8000
Sycamore (G-19705)
Deere & Company ....D.... 309 765-8275
Moline (G-14139)
Deere & Company ....A.... 309 765-8000
Moline (G-14138)
Demuth Steel Products Inc ....F.... 815 997-1116
Rockford (G-17373)
Design Manufacturing & Eqp Co ....F.... 217 824-9219
Taylorville (G-19755)
Dsi Inc ....G.... 309 965-5110
Goodfield (G-10675)
Dspc Company ....E.... 815 997-1116
Rockford (G-17387)
Dura Feed Inc ....G.... 815 395-1115
Loves Park (G-13208)
Dutch Prairie Conveyors ....G.... 618 349-6177
Shobonier (G-18892)
▲ E Z Trail Inc ....E.... 217 543-3471
Arthur (G-856)
Ecoturf Midwest Inc ....G.... 630 350-9500
Bensenville (G-1793)
▲ Farmweld Inc ....E.... 217 857-6423
Teutopolis (G-19769)
▲ Fehr Cab Interiors ....G.... 815 692-3355
Fairbury (G-9607)
◆ Gea Farm Technologies Inc ....C.... 630 548-8200
Naperville (G-14833)
Gem Equipment & Mfg LLC ....F.... 309 923-7312
Roanoke (G-17100)
Genwoods Holdco LLC ....A.... 815 732-2141
Oregon (G-15921)
Globetec Midwest Partners LLC ....G.... 847 608-9300
South Elgin (G-19147)
Grain Systems Inc ....G.... 888 474-2467
Assumption (G-890)
Gsi Group LLC ....G.... 217 226-4421
Assumption (G-891)
Gsi Group LLC ....C.... 217 287-6244
Taylorville (G-19757)
▼ Gsi Holdings Corp ....G.... 217 226-4421
Assumption (G-892)
H W Hostetler & Sons ....G.... 815 438-7816
Deer Grove (G-7577)
◆ Hcc Inc ....C.... 815 539-9371
Mendota (G-13943)
Hipro Manufacturing Inc ....E.... 815 432-5271
Watseka (G-20306)
Hoyer Outdoor Equipment Inc ....F.... 618 564-2080
Brookport (G-2498)
Hypermax Engineering Inc ....F.... 847 428-5655
Gilberts (G-10359)
Ideal Turf Inc ....G.... 309 691-3362
Peoria (G-16455)
◆ Innovative Growers Eqp Inc ....E.... 815 991-5010
Sycamore (G-19717)
J & J Equipment Inc ....G.... 309 449-5442
Hopedale (G-11517)
Jdis Dealers ....F.... 309 765-8000
East Moline (G-8230)
John Deere AG Holdings Inc ....G.... 309 765-8000
Moline (G-14152)
▲ John Rietveld Farms LLC ....E.... 815 936-9800
Bourbonnais (G-2264)
JWT Farms Inc ....G.... 618 664-3429
Pocahontas (G-16753)
Keller Grain & Livestock Inc ....G.... 618 455-3634
Willow Hill (G-21024)
King Systems Inc ....G.... 309 879-2668
Dahinda (G-7305)
◆ Kongskilde Industries Inc ....F.... 309 452-3300
Normal (G-15207)
Korhumel Inc ....G.... 847 330-0335
Schaumburg (G-18590)
Ksem Inc ....G.... 618 656-5388
Edwardsville (G-8367)
Ksi Conveyor Inc ....D.... 815 457-2403
Cissna Park (G-6897)
Kuchar Combine Performance ....G.... 217 854-9838
Carlinville (G-2878)
▼ Kunz Engineering Inc ....G.... 815 539-6954
Mendota (G-13945)
Lakeview Energy LLC ....E.... 312 386-5897
Chicago (G-5167)
Lawrence Allen ....G.... 618 786-3794
Grafton (G-10686)
Licon Inc ....G.... 618 485-2222
Ashley (G-885)
◆ Lmt Inc ....F.... 217 568-8265
Galva (G-10235)
▲ Malthandlingcom LLC ....G.... 773 888-7718
Chicago (G-5323)
Manitou Americas Inc ....G.... 262 334-9461
Belvidere (G-1684)
Mathews Company ....D.... 815 459-2210
Crystal Lake (G-7223)
▲ McLaughlin Body Co ....D.... 309 762-7755
Moline (G-14159)
Mega Equipment Inc ....G.... 309 764-5310
Moline (G-14160)

S I C

Employee Codes: A=Over 500 employees, B=251-500
C=101-250, D=51-100, E=20-50, F=10-19, G=3-9
2020 Harris Illinois
Industrial Directory
947

Meinhart Grain Farm Inc......G...... 217 683-2692
Montrose *(G-14289)*
Meteer Inc......G...... 217 636-7280
Athens *(G-898)*
◆ **Midwest Bio-Systems Inc**......F...... 815 438-7200
Tampico *(G-19745)*
Midwest Sport Turf Systems LLC......F...... 630 923-8342
Plainfield *(G-16690)*
MTS Jerseyville Inc......G...... 618 639-2583
Jerseyville *(G-11794)*
Newton Implement Partnership......E...... 618 783-8716
Newton *(G-15087)*
Niffty AG Inc......G...... 309 343-7447
Galesburg *(G-10214)*
▲ **Ogden Metalworks Inc**......F...... 217 582-2552
Ogden *(G-15837)*
Outdoor Space LLC......E...... 773 857-5296
Chicago *(G-5715)*
◆ **P & H Manufacturing Co**......D...... 217 774-2123
Shelbyville *(G-18882)*
Prairie Land Mllwrght Svcs Inc......F...... 815 538-3085
Mendota *(G-13953)*
▲ **Prater Industries Inc**......D...... 630 679-3200
Bolingbrook *(G-2228)*
Quality Metal Works Inc......G...... 309 379-5311
Stanford *(G-19473)*
Quality Trucking Inc......G...... 309 949-2021
Colona *(G-6977)*
R K Products Inc......G...... 309 792-1927
East Moline *(G-8239)*
R Lamar Academy Inc......G...... 309 712-8100
Peoria *(G-16506)*
R-Tech Feeders Inc......E...... 815 874-2990
Rockford *(G-17564)*
Rhinoag Inc......E...... 217 784-4261
Gibson City *(G-10343)*
Robert Swaar......G...... 217 968-2232
Greenview *(G-10824)*
Rudy Brenneman......G...... 618 317-2329
Percy *(G-16560)*
S & P Farms......G...... 309 772-3936
Bushnell *(G-2746)*
▼ **Seedburo Equipment Company**......F...... 312 738-3700
Des Plaines *(G-7840)*
◆ **Shoup Manufacturing Co Inc**......E...... 815 933-4439
Kankakee *(G-12001)*
Sopher Design & Manufacturing......G...... 309 699-6419
East Peoria *(G-8291)*
◆ **Speeco Incorporated**......C...... 303 279-5544
Oregon *(G-15927)*
Spreader Inc......G...... 217 568-7219
Gifford *(G-10348)*
▲ **Star Forge Inc**......D...... 815 235-7750
Freeport *(G-10144)*
Stephens Pipe & Steel LLC......E...... 800 451-2612
North Aurora *(G-15278)*
Straightline AG Inc......G...... 217 963-1270
Harristown *(G-11033)*
Tank Wind-Down Corp......D...... 815 756-1551
Dekalb *(G-7707)*
Tft Inc......G...... 309 531-2012
Colfax *(G-6951)*
Trusty Warns Inc......E...... 630 766-9015
Wood Dale *(G-21253)*
▼ **Union Iron Inc**......E...... 217 429-5148
Decatur *(G-7564)*
▲ **W A Rice Seed Company**......G...... 618 498-5538
Jerseyville *(G-11798)*
Weaver Equipment LLC......G...... 618 833-5521
Buncombe *(G-2631)*
Wernze Farms Inc......G...... 618 569-4820
Annapolis *(G-590)*
Western Ill Agri-Systems Inc......G...... 217 746-2144
Burnside *(G-2646)*
▲ **Whalen Manufacturing Company**......G...... 309 836-1438
Macomb *(G-13402)*
Woods Equipment Company......D...... 815 732-2141
Rockford *(G-17690)*
▼ **Yargus Manufacturing Inc**......E...... 217 826-6352
Marshall *(G-13579)*
▲ **Yetter Manufacturing Company**......D...... 309 776-3222
Colchester *(G-6948)*
Yoder John......G...... 217 676-3430
Blue Mound *(G-2142)*

3524 Garden, Lawn Tractors & Eqpt

▼ **Alpha Omega Profile Extrusion**......F...... 847 956-8777
Elk Grove Village *(G-8818)*
▲ **Amerisun Inc**......F...... 800 791-9458
Itasca *(G-11623)*
▲ **Avant Tecno USA Inc**......F...... 847 380-1308
Arlington Heights *(G-700)*
Beall Manufacturing Inc......E...... 618 307-9589
Edwardsville *(G-8349)*
Contempo Industries Inc......D...... 815 337-6267
Woodstock *(G-21375)*
Cutting Specialists Inc......E...... 731 352-5351
Edwardsville *(G-8355)*
David Taylor......E...... 217 222-6480
Quincy *(G-16875)*
Deere & Company......A...... 309 765-8000
Moline *(G-14138)*
◆ **Echo Incorporated**......A...... 847 540-8400
Lake Zurich *(G-12404)*
Echo Incorporated......E...... 847 540-3500
Lake Zurich *(G-12405)*
Grower Equipment & Supply Co......F...... 847 223-3100
Hainesville *(G-10947)*
Hevco Industries......G...... 708 344-1342
Aurora *(G-1109)*
Hipro Manufacturing Inc......E...... 815 432-5271
Watseka *(G-20306)*
Hyponex Corporation......E...... 815 772-2167
Morrison *(G-14343)*
◆ **Jeffs Small Engine Inc**......G...... 630 904-6840
Plainfield *(G-16675)*
John Deere AG Holdings Inc......G...... 309 765-8000
Moline *(G-14152)*
Lutz Corp......G...... 800 203-7740
Normal *(G-15208)*
M Martinez Inc......G...... 847 740-6364
Round Lake Heights *(G-18094)*
Mag MO Systems......F...... 815 625-0125
Sterling *(G-19514)*
◆ **Mat Holdings Inc**......D...... 847 821-9630
Long Grove *(G-13165)*
Oldcastle Lawn & Garden Inc......E...... 618 274-1222
East Saint Louis *(G-8317)*
◆ **Precision Products Inc**......C...... 217 735-1590
Lincoln *(G-12737)*
Randys Exper-Clean......G...... 217 423-1975
Decatur *(G-7539)*
Ryan Manufacturing Inc......G...... 815 695-5310
Newark *(G-15078)*
Sawier......E...... 630 297-8588
Downers Grove *(G-8090)*
◆ **Tuthill Corporation**......E...... 630 382-4900
Burr Ridge *(G-2727)*
Up-N-Runnin LLC......G...... 217 413-6293
Decatur *(G-7565)*
Valley View Industries Hc Inc......E...... 800 323-9369
Crestwood *(G-7133)*
▲ **Vaughan & Bushnell Mfg Co**......F...... 815 648-2446
Hebron *(G-11153)*
▼ **Yanmar (usa) Inc**......G...... 847 541-1900
Buffalo Grove *(G-2624)*

3531 Construction Machinery & Eqpt

Allegion S&S Holding Co Inc......C...... 815 875-3311
Princeton *(G-16805)*
Anchor Mechanical Inc......G...... 312 492-6994
Chicago *(G-3691)*
▲ **APL Logistics Americas Ltd**......F...... 630 783-0200
Woodridge *(G-21275)*
Associated Professionals......G...... 847 931-0095
Elgin *(G-8516)*
▲ **Avant Tecno USA Inc**......F...... 847 380-1308
Arlington Heights *(G-700)*
Avanti Motor Carriers Inc......G...... 630 313-9160
Naperville *(G-14960)*
Baird Inc......G...... 217 526-3407
Morrisonville *(G-14350)*
Bergstrom Elctrfied Systems LL......G...... 815 874-7821
Rockford *(G-17320)*
◆ **Bergstrom Inc**......B...... 815 874-7821
Rockford *(G-17321)*
▲ **Bergstrom Parts LLC**......G...... 815 874-7821
Rockford *(G-17323)*
Bigfoot Construction Eqp Inc......G...... 888 743-7320
Woodstock *(G-21365)*
Black Lab LLC......G...... 440 285-3189
Serena *(G-18863)*
Blount International Inc......G...... 800 319-6637
Oregon *(G-15914)*
Bonnell Industries Inc......D...... 815 284-3819
Dixon *(G-7890)*
Brave Products Inc......G...... 815 672-0551
Streator *(G-19605)*
Brunner & Lay Inc......C...... 847 678-3232
Bensenville *(G-1758)*
▲ **C S O Corp**......D...... 630 365-6600
Virgil *(G-20190)*
▲ **Caterpillar Forest Pdts Inc**......E...... 309 675-1000
Peoria *(G-16401)*
Caterpillar Foundation......G...... 309 675-4232
Peoria *(G-16402)*
Caterpillar Global Mining LLC......E...... 618 378-3441
Norris City *(G-15247)*
Caterpillar Inc......G...... 309 578-2185
Mossville *(G-14452)*
Caterpillar Inc......B...... 309 675-1000
East Peoria *(G-8255)*
▲ **Caterpillar Inc**......A...... 224 551-4000
Deerfield *(G-7600)*
Caterpillar Inc......B...... 815 729-5511
Joliet *(G-11838)*
Caterpillar Inc......B...... 309 675-1000
Peoria *(G-16404)*
Caterpillar Inc......D...... 309 675-2545
East Peoria *(G-8249)*
Caterpillar Inc......B...... 309 675-1000
East Peoria *(G-8256)*
Caterpillar Inc......D...... 309 578-6118
Mossville *(G-14453)*
Caterpillar Inc......E...... 309 675-5681
Peoria *(G-16405)*
Caterpillar Inc......B...... 217 475-4355
Decatur *(G-7472)*
Caterpillar Inc......A...... 309 633-8788
Mapleton *(G-13468)*
Caterpillar Inc......B...... 309 578-2086
Washington *(G-20268)*
Caterpillar Inc......F...... 309 675-8327
Edwards *(G-8337)*
Caterpillar Inc......D...... 304 327-7793
Morton *(G-14355)*
Caterpillar Inc......B...... 217 424-1809
Decatur *(G-7473)*
Caterpillar Inc......B...... 309 266-4294
Mossville *(G-14454)*
Caterpillar Inc......B...... 903 712-4505
Mossville *(G-14455)*
Caterpillar Inc......D...... 309 495-9216
East Peoria *(G-8257)*
Caterpillar Inc......F...... 309 578-4643
Peoria *(G-16406)*
Caterpillar Inc......B...... 888 614-4328
Peoria *(G-16407)*
Caterpillar Inc......G...... 309 675-1000
Peoria *(G-16408)*
Caterpillar Inc......G...... 217 475-4322
Decatur *(G-7474)*
Caterpillar Inc......A...... 309 578-2473
Mossville *(G-14456)*
Caterpillar Inc......B...... 309 675-1000
Mossville *(G-14457)*
Caterpillar Inc......E...... 309 675-3183
East Peoria *(G-8258)*
Caterpillar Inc......E...... 309 675-1000
Peoria *(G-16409)*
Caterpillar Inc......B...... 309 675-1000
Peoria *(G-16410)*
Caterpillar Inc......B...... 217 255-8500
Champaign *(G-3276)*
Caterpillar Inc......A...... 630 859-5000
Montgomery *(G-14238)*
Caterpillar Inc......A...... 217 475-4000
Decatur *(G-7471)*
Caterpillar Inc......A...... 309 578-1615
Mossville *(G-14459)*
Caterpillar Inc......B...... 309 675-6590
Peoria *(G-16411)*
▲ **Caterpillar Intl Lsg LLC**......G...... 309 675-1000
Peoria *(G-16412)*
▲ **Caterpillar Luxembourg LLC**......G...... 309 675-1000
Peoria *(G-16413)*
Caterpillar Power Systems Inc......G...... 309 675-1000
Peoria *(G-16414)*
Caterpillar World Trading Corp......E...... 309 675-1000
Peoria *(G-16415)*
Central Township Road & Bridge......G...... 618 704-5517
Greenville *(G-10830)*
Chicago Materials Corporation......E...... 630 257-5600
Lemont *(G-12561)*
Clarke Equipment Company......G...... 701 241-8700
Woodridge *(G-21285)*
▼ **CPM Co Inc**......E...... 815 385-7700
McHenry *(G-13731)*
▲ **CTS Advanced Materials LLC**......E...... 630 577-8800
Lisle *(G-12879)*

SIC SECTION

35 INDUSTRIAL AND COMMERCIAL MACHINERY AND COMPUTER EQUIPMENT

D & B Fabricators & Distrs.................F...... 630 325-3811
  Lemont (G-12562)
Deere & Company.............................A...... 309 765-8000
  Moline (G-14138)
Division 5 Metals Inc........................G...... 815 901-5001
  Kirkland (G-12059)
Domor Equipment LLC.....................E...... 309 467-3483
  Eureka (G-9481)
Dover Europe Inc.............................G...... 630 541-1540
  Downers Grove (G-7991)
Dun-Rite Tool & Machine Co..............E...... 815 758-5464
  Cortland (G-7020)
ED Etnyre & Co................................B...... 815 732-2116
  Oregon (G-15917)
◆ Eirich Machines Inc.......................D...... 847 336-2444
  Gurnee (G-10875)
◆ Etnyre International Ltd................B...... 815 732-2116
  Oregon (G-15918)
Flink Company..................................E...... 815 673-4321
  Streator (G-19608)
◆ Flsmidth Pekin LLC......................D...... 309 347-3031
  Pekin (G-16335)
▲ Fluid Mnagement Operations LLC....G...... 847 537-0880
  Wheeling (G-20899)
Gemtar Inc..G...... 618 548-1353
  Salem (G-18340)
Genesis III Inc..................................E...... 815 537-7900
  Prophetstown (G-16831)
◆ Global Track Property USA Inc......G...... 630 213-6863
  Bartlett (G-1283)
Harig Products Inc...........................F...... 847 695-1000
  Elgin (G-8607)
◆ Heico Companies LLC..................F...... 312 419-8220
  Chicago (G-4798)
Henderson Products Inc...................F...... 847 836-4996
  Gilberts (G-10357)
High Point Recovery Company..........G...... 217 821-7777
  Toledo (G-19876)
Illinois Tool Works Inc......................F...... 847 918-6473
  Libertyville (G-12662)
Imh Fabrication Inc..........................F...... 815 537-2381
  Prophetstown (G-16833)
Interstate Mechanical Inc.................G...... 312 961-9291
  Chicago (G-4958)
Jcb Inc...G...... 912 704-2995
  Aurora (G-990)
John Deere AG Holdings Inc............G...... 309 765-8000
  Moline (G-14152)
Jordan Services...............................G...... 630 416-6701
  Lisle (G-12904)
Jrb Attachments LLC.......................G...... 319 378-3696
  Oak Brook (G-15628)
Koflo Corporation.............................F...... 847 516-3700
  Cary (G-3174)
◆ Komatsu America Corp................B...... 847 437-5800
  Chicago (G-5120)
◆ Kress Corporation........................D...... 309 446-3395
  Brimfield (G-2406)
Kvd Enterprises LLC........................G...... 618 726-5114
  O Fallon (G-15577)
▼ Skyjack Equipment Inc..................E...... 630 797-3299
  Saint Charles (G-18270)
L & N Structures Inc........................E...... 815 426-2164
  Herscher (G-11184)
Lamination Specialties LLC..............E...... 312 243-2181
  Oak Brook (G-15631)
◆ Lanco International Inc.................B...... 708 596-5200
  Hazel Crest (G-11131)
Lanigan Holdings LLC......................F...... 708 596-5200
  Hazel Crest (G-11132)
◆ Lmt Inc..F...... 217 568-8265
  Galva (G-10235)
▲ Machine Solution Providers Inc.....D...... 630 717-7040
  Downers Grove (G-8049)
Manitou Americas Inc......................G...... 262 334-9461
  Belvidere (G-1684)
▼ Marine Acquisition Corp................A...... 217 324-9400
  Litchfield (G-12973)
Mega Equipment Inc........................G...... 309 764-5310
  Moline (G-14160)
Metrom Rail LLC..............................E...... 855 943-8726
  Crystal Lake (G-7227)
Mfs Holdings LLC............................E...... 815 385-7700
  McHenry (G-13769)
◆ Mi-Jack Products Inc...................B...... 708 596-5200
  Hazel Crest (G-11133)
Midwest Cnstr Svcs Inc Peoria.........F...... 309 697-1000
  Bartonville (G-1335)
Midwest Mixing Inc..........................G...... 708 422-8100
  Chicago Ridge (G-6803)
Millstadt Township............................G...... 618 476-3592
  Millstadt (G-14053)

Mineral Products Inc........................G...... 618 433-3150
  Harrisburg (G-11026)
Mj Snyder Ironworks Inc..................G...... 217 826-6440
  Marshall (G-13575)
Mjmc Inc..G...... 708 596-5200
  Hazel Crest (G-11135)
Multi-State Indus Contrs Inc.............G...... 217 423-4100
  Decatur (G-7531)
▲ National Tractor Parts Inc............G...... 630 552-4235
  Plano (G-16736)
Nordic Auto Plow LLC......................G...... 815 353-8267
  West Chicago (G-20623)
North Point Investments Inc.............G...... 312 977-4386
  Chicago (G-5620)
Omg Inc...E...... 413 789-0252
  Addison (G-232)
Ovis Loader Attachments Inc...........G...... 618 203-2757
  Carbondale (G-2853)
▲ Paladin Brands International H......G...... 319 378-3696
  Oak Brook (G-15655)
Paul Wever Construction Eqp Co......F...... 309 965-2005
  Goodfield (G-10676)
Paver Protector Inc..........................G...... 630 488-0069
  Gilberts (G-10364)
Peter Baker & Son Co......................G...... 815 344-1640
  Mc Henry (G-13705)
Pilot Township Road District.............G...... 815 426-6221
  Herscher (G-11186)
Podrez Enterprise LLC.....................G...... 815 353-5893
  Lakemoor (G-12474)
Prella Technologies Inc...................G...... 630 400-0626
  Huntley (G-11560)
Prime Group Inc...............................G...... 312 922-3883
  Chicago (G-5874)
▲ Rdi Group Inc..............................C...... 630 773-4900
  Itasca (G-11724)
Reload Sales Inc..............................G...... 618 588-2866
  New Baden (G-15023)
▲ Rhino Tool Company...................G...... 309 853-5555
  Kewanee (G-12040)
▲ Ringwood Company.....................D...... 708 458-6000
  Bedford Park (G-1499)
Roadsafe Traffic Systems Inc...........G...... 217 629-7139
  Riverton (G-17089)
Robbins Construction Sup LLC.........G...... 708 574-5944
  Hazel Crest (G-11137)
Rockford Rigging Inc........................G...... 309 263-0566
  Morton (G-14381)
Runge Equipment Inc.......................G...... 618 322-5628
  Mason (G-13609)
S & S Maintenance..........................G...... 815 725-9263
  Wilmington (G-21103)
S&S Recovery..................................G...... 217 538-2206
  Fillmore (G-9665)
Sauber Manufacturing Company......D...... 630 365-6600
  Virgil (G-20191)
Sebens Backhoe Service Inc...........G...... 217 762-7365
  Monticello (G-14286)
▼ Skyjack Equipment Inc..................E...... 630 797-3299
  Saint Charles (G-18270)
Skyjack Inc......................................G...... 630 262-0005
  Saint Charles (G-18271)
▲ Soosan USA Inc..........................G...... 224 653-8916
  Schaumburg (G-18715)
◆ Speeco Incorporated....................C...... 303 279-5544
  Oregon (G-15927)
Spreader Inc....................................G...... 217 568-7219
  Gifford (G-10348)
Steuben Township............................F...... 309 208-7073
  Sparland (G-19254)
Streator Asphalt Inc.........................G...... 815 426-2164
  Herscher (G-11187)
Streator Asphalt Inc.........................G...... 815 672-8683
  Streator (G-19625)
T J S Equipment Inc........................G...... 618 656-8046
  Edwardsville (G-8377)
Technical Services Intl Inc................G...... 708 596-5200
  Hazel Crest (G-11138)
Teleweld Inc....................................G...... 815 672-4561
  Streator (G-19629)
Terramac LLC..................................G...... 630 365-4800
  Elburn (G-8475)
Tim Wallace Ldscp Sup Co Inc........F...... 630 759-6813
  Bolingbrook (G-2250)
▲ Track Works LLC........................G...... 618 781-2375
  Highland (G-11242)
Tsm North America Inc....................G...... 815 372-1600
  Schaumburg (G-18760)
U S Railway Services.......................G...... 708 468-8343
  Tinley Park (G-19864)

Uesco Industries Inc........................G...... 708 385-7700
  Alsip (G-517)
▲ US Shredder Castings Group Inc....G...... 309 359-3151
  Peoria (G-16542)
▲ USA Hoist Company Inc...............E...... 815 740-1890
  Crest Hill (G-7100)
USA Star Group of Company............G...... 773 456-6677
  Chicago (G-6505)
▼ W N G S Inc.................................G...... 847 451-1224
  Franklin Park (G-10081)
W R Grace & Co-Conn.....................F...... 708 458-9700
  Chicago (G-6577)
Walter Payton Power Eqp LLC..........E...... 708 656-7700
  Riverdale (G-17079)
Wehrli Equipment Co Inc..................F...... 630 717-4150
  Naperville (G-14946)
West Side Tractor Sales Co..............E...... 815 961-3160
  Rockford (G-17680)
Wille Bros Co...................................G...... 708 535-4101
  Monee (G-14213)
Woods Equipment Company.............D...... 815 732-2141
  Oregon (G-15929)

3532 Mining Machinery & Eqpt

▲ American Equipment & Mch Inc....D...... 618 533-3857
  Centralia (G-3221)
Braden Rock Bit...............................G...... 618 435-4519
  Benton (G-1922)
Carroll International Corp.................C...... 630 983-5979
  Lake Forest (G-12236)
Caterpillar Globl Min Amer LLC.........D...... 618 982-9000
  Carrier Mills (G-3124)
◆ Centrifugal Services Inc...............D...... 618 268-4850
  Raleigh (G-16959)
◆ Diager USA Inc............................G...... 630 762-8443
  Saint Charles (G-18182)
▼ Drumbeaters of America Inc.........F...... 630 365-5527
  Elburn (G-8449)
▲ Dry Systems Technologies LLC....G...... 630 427-2051
  Woodridge (G-21296)
Dry Systems Technologies LLC.......F...... 618 658-3000
  Vienna (G-20117)
Elgin Equipment Group LLC............G...... 630 434-7200
  Downers Grove (G-7997)
◆ Elgin National Industries Inc........F...... 630 434-7200
  Downers Grove (G-7998)
Elgin National Industries Inc............D...... 314 776-2848
  Raleigh (G-16960)
▲ Fibro Inc.....................................F...... 815 229-1300
  Rockford (G-17415)
Fox International Corp.....................F...... 773 465-3634
  Chicago (G-4627)
Freedom Material Resources Inc......D...... 618 937-6415
  West Frankfort (G-20672)
G&D Integrated Services Inc...........E...... 309 284-6700
  Morton (G-14362)
GE Fairchild Mining Equipment........D...... 618 559-3216
  Du Quoin (G-8121)
▲ Gundlach Equipment Corporation....D...... 618 233-7208
  Belleville (G-1554)
Hydra Fold Auger Inc.......................G...... 217 379-2614
  Loda (G-13028)
◆ Komatsu America Corp................B...... 847 437-5800
  Chicago (G-5120)
Lashcon Inc.....................................G...... 217 742-3186
  Winchester (G-21106)
Logan Actuator Co...........................G...... 815 943-9500
  Harvard (G-11059)
◆ Martin Engineering Company.......C...... 309 852-2384
  Neponset (G-15018)
Midwest Machine Tool Inc...............G...... 815 427-8665
  Saint Anne (G-18136)
O-Cedar Commercial........................G...... 217 379-2377
  Paxton (G-16311)
Profile Screens Incorporated............G...... 309 543-2082
  Havana (G-11120)
Roe Machine Inc..............................E...... 618 983-5524
  West Frankfort (G-20681)
▲ Sollami Company.........................E...... 618 988-1521
  Herrin (G-11179)
Terrasource Global Corporation........D...... 618 641-6985
  Belleville (G-1597)
Townley Engrg & Mfg Co Inc...........F...... 618 273-8271
  Eldorado (G-8484)
Viking Mining LLC............................E...... 314 932-6140
  Macedonia (G-13318)

3533 Oil Field Machinery & Eqpt

▲ Alin Machining Company Inc.......C...... 708 681-1043
  Melrose Park (G-13821)

35 INDUSTRIAL AND COMMERCIAL MACHINERY AND COMPUTER EQUIPMENT

Arid Technologies Inc .... E 630 681-8500
  Wheaton (G-20788)
Azcon Inc .... F 815 548-7000
  Sterling (G-19499)
Bartec Orb Inc .... E 773 927-8600
  Chicago (G-3843)
Big Als Machines Inc .... G 618 963-2619
  Enfield (G-9468)
David L Kaufman .... F 217 543-4190
  Arthur (G-851)
◆ Dover Corporation .... C 630 541-1540
  Downers Grove (G-7989)
Gemtar Inc .... G 618 548-1353
  Salem (G-18340)
H & H Drilling Co .... G 618 529-3697
  Carbondale (G-2843)
▼ Hutchens-Bit Service Inc .... F 618 439-9485
  Benton (G-1926)
Innerweld Cover Co .... F 847 497-3009
  Mundelein (G-14701)
▲ Maass - Midwest Mfg Inc ...... E 847 669-5135
  Huntley (G-11553)
Mueller Co LLC .... E 217 423-4471
  Decatur (G-7528)
Oil Filter Recyclers Inc .... E 309 329-2131
  Astoria (G-894)
Pro Energy Trade Inc .... E 312 961-6404
  Chicago (G-5887)
Robit Inc. .... G 708 667-7892
  Chicago (G-6046)
Royal Brass Inc .... G 618 439-6341
  Benton (G-1936)
Squibb Tank Company .... F 618 548-0141
  Salem (G-18360)
Trusty Warns Inc .... E 630 766-9015
  Wood Dale (G-21253)
U O P Equitec Services Inc ...... A 847 391-2000
  Des Plaines (G-7860)

3534 Elevators & Moving Stairways

Adams Elevator Equipment Co .... E 847 581-2900
  Chicago (G-3538)
Bcr Elevators Incorporated .... F 219 689-5951
  Frankfort (G-9770)
CJ Anderson & Company .... E 708 867-4002
  Harwood Heights (G-11102)
Colley Elevator Company .... E 630 766-7230
  Bensenville (G-1773)
▼ D A Matot Inc .... D 708 547-1888
  Bellwood (G-1620)
Dover Europe Inc .... G 630 541-1540
  Downers Grove (G-7991)
▲ Elevator Cable & Supply Co .... E 708 338-9700
  Broadview (G-2433)
Fixture Company .... G 847 214-3100
  Chicago (G-4600)
▲ Formula Systems North America .... G 847 350-0655
  Elk Grove Village (G-9004)
Harris Companies Inc .... F 217 578-2231
  Atwood (G-905)
Hml Elevators Inc .... G 757 822-8285
  Chicago (G-4825)
◆ Hollister-Whitney Elev Co LLC .... B 217 222-0466
  Quincy (G-16892)
Integrated Display Systems Inc .... F 708 298-9661
  Cicero (G-6856)
Kafka Manufacturing Co .... E 708 771-0970
  Forest Park (G-9721)
▲ Kone Elevator .... E 309 764-6771
  Moline (G-14154)
◆ Kone Inc .... A 630 577-1650
  Lisle (G-12906)
Kone Inc. .... C 309 945-4961
  Coal Valley (G-6937)
Lifts of Illinois Inc .... G 309 923-7450
  Roanoke (G-17103)
Long Elevator and Mch Co Inc .... D 217 629-9648
  Springfield (G-19400)
▲ Mid-American Elevator Co Inc .... C 773 486-6900
  Chicago (G-5428)
Mid-American Elevator Co Inc .... E 815 740-1204
  Joliet (G-11902)
Mitsubishi Electric Us Inc .... E 708 354-2900
  Countryside (G-7065)
North Shore Stairs .... G 847 295-7906
  Lake Bluff (G-12200)
Otis Elevator Company .... E 312 454-1616
  Chicago (G-5712)
Otis Elevator Company .... F 618 529-3411
  Carbondale (G-2852)

Raytheon Technologies Corp ...... B 815 226-6000
  Rockford (G-17567)
◆ Vator Accessories Inc .... G 630 876-8370
  West Chicago (G-20656)

3535 Conveyors & Eqpt

Acro Magnetics Inc .... G 815 943-5018
  Harvard (G-11040)
Align Production Systems LLC .... E 217 423-6001
  Decatur (G-7439)
◆ Astec Mobile Screens Inc ..... C 815 626-6374
  Sterling (G-19498)
Atbc LLC .... E 847 648-2822
  Park Ridge (G-16269)
Automated Material Hdlg Svcs .... G 630 947-7605
  Batavia (G-1352)
Automatic Feeder Company Inc .... F 847 534-2300
  Schaumburg (G-18449)
Avasarala Inc .... E 847 969-0630
  Palatine (G-16095)
Bankmark Inc .... F 847 683-9834
  Hampshire (G-10963)
Barrington Automation Ltd ...... E 847 458-0900
  Lake In The Hills (G-12329)
◆ Barry-Whmller Cont Systems Inc .... C 630 759-6800
  Romeoville (G-17798)
Benda Manufacturing Inc .... G 708 633-4600
  Tinley Park (G-19808)
◆ Bettendorf Stanford Inc .... D 618 548-3555
  Salem (G-18331)
▼ Birnberg Machinery Inc .... E 847 673-5242
  Deerfield (G-7597)
Bost Corporation .... E 708 344-7023
  Maywood (G-13663)
Canconex Inc .... F 847 458-9955
  Algonquin (G-368)
Central Manufacturing Company .... E 309 387-6591
  East Peoria (G-8259)
Chicago Can Conveyor Corp .... G 708 430-0988
  Bridgeview (G-2334)
Chicago Chain and Transm Co .... E 630 482-9000
  Countryside (G-7046)
Cmd Conveyor Inc .... E 708 237-0996
  Chicago Ridge (G-6792)
Complete Conveying Svcs LLC .... G 815 695-5176
  Newark (G-15075)
Confab Systems Inc .... E 708 388-4103
  Posen (G-16792)
Container Hdlg Systems Corp .... E 708 482-9900
  Countryside (G-7047)
Container Service Group Inc .... F 815 744-8693
  Rockdale (G-17258)
Conveyor Specialties Inc .... E 815 727-7638
  Joliet (G-11847)
Conveyor Systems & Engineering .... G 847 593-2900
  Arlington Heights (G-720)
Conveyors Plus Inc .... G 708 361-1512
  Orland Park (G-15948)
▲ Dabrico Inc .... E 815 939-0580
  Bourbonnais (G-2259)
Dematic Corp .... F 630 852-9200
  Lisle (G-12885)
Deyco Inc .... G 630 553-5666
  Yorkville (G-21480)
Diversatech Metalfab LLC ...... E 309 747-4159
  Gridley (G-10843)
Diversified Fleet MGT Inc .... E 815 578-1051
  McHenry (G-13736)
Dspc Company .... E 815 997-1116
  Rockford (G-17387)
Duravant .... G 630 635-3910
  Downers Grove (G-7994)
◆ Duravant LLC .... F 630 635-3910
  Downers Grove (G-7995)
Eaglestone Inc .... F 630 587-1115
  Saint Charles (G-18192)
◆ Ehs Solutions LLC .... E 309 282-9121
  Peoria (G-16433)
◆ Eirich Machines Inc .... D 847 336-2444
  Gurnee (G-10875)
Engineered Plumbing Spc LLC .... E 630 682-1555
  Joliet (G-11862)
Engineering Products Company .... G 815 436-9055
  Plainfield (G-16659)
Erect - O -Veyor Corporation .... F 630 766-1200
  Franklin Park (G-9939)
▲ Ewab Engineering Inc .... E 847 247-0015
  Libertyville (G-12649)
Forbo Siegling LLC .... F 630 595-4031
  Wood Dale (G-21188)

◆ Forte Automation Systems Inc .... E 815 316-6247
  Machesney Park (G-13344)
Frantz Manufacturing Company .... D 815 564-0991
  Sterling (G-19510)
GE Fairchild Mining Equipment .... D 618 559-3216
  Du Quoin (G-8121)
GMI Packaging Co .... E 734 972-7389
  Chicago (G-4705)
Gsi Group LLC .... C 217 463-1612
  Paris (G-16230)
Icon Co .... G 630 545-2345
  Glen Ellyn (G-10405)
Illinois Conveyor Service Inc .... G 630 469-1300
  Glen Ellyn (G-10406)
▼ Industrial Kinetics Inc .... G 630 655-0300
  Downers Grove (G-8031)
▲ Industrial Motion Control LLC .... C 847 459-5200
  Wheeling (G-20915)
Intelligrated Systems Inc .... B 630 985-4350
  Woodridge (G-21315)
International Conveyors Amer .... G 630 549-4007
  Geneva (G-10284)
J W Todd Co .... G 630 406-5715
  Aurora (G-1114)
Joy Global Underground Min LLC .... E 618 242-3650
  Mount Vernon (G-14619)
K Transco Inc .... G 630 881-5411
  Lemont (G-12567)
Kamflex Conveyor Corporation .... G 630 682-1555
  Joliet (G-11889)
Kelly Systems Inc .... E 312 733-3224
  Chicago (G-5093)
Kimco USA Inc .... F 800 788-1133
  Marshall (G-13574)
◆ Kongskilde Industries Inc ..... F 309 452-3300
  Normal (G-15207)
Krygier Design Inc .... F 620 766-1001
  Wood Dale (G-21205)
▲ L M C Inc .... G 815 758-3514
  Dekalb (G-7687)
Lake Fabrication Inc .... G 217 832-2761
  Villa Grove (G-20124)
Logicon Group LLC .... G 618 558-7757
  Millstadt (G-14049)
Loop Belt Industries Inc .... G 630 469-1300
  Glen Ellyn (G-10410)
▲ Mallard Handling Solutions LLC .... E 815 625-9491
  Sterling (G-19515)
Matrix Design LLC .... D 847 841-8260
  Bartlett (G-1296)
▲ MCR Technologies Group Inc .... G 815 622-3181
  Sterling (G-19517)
Mid States Corporation .... E 708 754-1760
  S Chicago Hts (G-18125)
▲ Mid-American Elevator Co Inc .... C 773 486-6900
  Chicago (G-5428)
Mid-American Elevator Co Inc .... E 815 740-1204
  Joliet (G-11902)
Midstates Rail LLC .... F 708 758-7245
  Chicago Heights (G-6758)
Morrison Timing Screw Company .... D 708 756-6660
  Glenwood (G-10643)
Payson Casters Inc .... C 847 336-5033
  Gurnee (G-10910)
Pre Pack Machinery Inc .... G 217 352-1010
  Champaign (G-3338)
Precision Conveyor and Erct Co .... F 779 324-5269
  Frankfort (G-9823)
Return On Inv Systems Inc .... E 847 726-0081
  Lake Zurich (G-12449)
Roll-A-Way Conveyors Inc ..... F 847 336-5033
  Gurnee (G-10924)
◆ Rotec Industries Inc .... D 630 279-3300
  Hampshire (G-10985)
▲ RPS Engineering Inc .... F 847 931-1950
  Elgin (G-8721)
◆ Rwi Manufacturing Inc .... G 800 277-1699
  Aurora (G-1151)
SA Nat Industrial Cnstr Co Inc .... E 618 246-9402
  Mount Vernon (G-14636)
▲ Sardee Industries Inc .... G 630 824-4200
  Lisle (G-12936)
▲ SBS Steel Belt Systems USA Inc .... F 847 841-3300
  Gilberts (G-10369)
▼ Smart Motion Robotics Inc .... E 815 895-8550
  Sycamore (G-19732)
Special Tool Engineering Co .... F 773 767-6690
  Chicago (G-6212)
Superior Industries Inc .... F 309 346-1742
  Pekin (G-16362)

Tracoinsa USA......G...... 309 287-7046
Gridley *(G-10847)*
Translogic Corporation......F...... 847 392-3700
Rolling Meadows *(G-17781)*
◆ **Tricon Inds Mfg & Eqp Sls**......E...... 815 379-2090
Walnut *(G-20220)*
◆ **United Conveyor Corporation**......C...... 847 473-5900
Waukegan *(G-20513)*
▲ **United Conveyor Supply Company**..D...... 847 672-5100
Waukegan *(G-20514)*
United Systems Incorporated......F...... 708 479-1450
Mokena *(G-14125)*
US Conveyor Tech Mfg Inc......E...... 309 359-4088
Mackinaw *(G-13386)*
◆ **US Conveyor Technologies**......F...... 309 359-4088
Mackinaw *(G-13387)*
V & C Converters......G...... 708 251-5635
Lansing *(G-12523)*
Wes-Tech Automtn Solutions LLC......D...... 847 541-5070
Buffalo Grove *(G-2621)*
▲ **William W Meyer and Sons**......D...... 847 918-0111
Libertyville *(G-12726)*
▲ **Witron Intgrated Logistics Inc**......C...... 847 398-6130
Arlington Heights *(G-835)*

3536 Hoists, Cranes & Monorails

▲ **Aldon Co**......F...... 847 623-8800
Waukegan *(G-20412)*
Bucket Mart Inc......G...... 813 390-8626
Marion *(G-13506)*
Columbus McKinnon Corporation......C...... 800 548-2930
Eureka *(G-9478)*
Columbus McKinnon Corporation......E...... 630 783-1195
Woodridge *(G-21286)*
Crane Equipment & Services Inc......E...... 309 467-6262
Eureka *(G-9479)*
▲ **G K Enterprises Inc**......G...... 708 587-2150
Monee *(G-14201)*
Gemtar Inc......G...... 618 548-1353
Salem *(G-18340)*
▲ **Gh Cranes Corporation**......G...... 815 277-5328
Frankfort *(G-9797)*
H & B Machine Corporation......G...... 312 829-4850
Chicago *(G-4756)*
Handling Systems Intl Inc......E...... 708 352-1213
Mc Cook *(G-13692)*
Hyster Co......G...... 217 443-7000
Danville *(G-7347)*
◆ **Lanco International Inc**......B...... 708 596-5200
Hazel Crest *(G-11131)*
Logan Actuator Co......G...... 815 943-9500
Harvard *(G-11059)*
▲ **Manitex International Inc**......E...... 708 430-7500
Bridgeview *(G-2361)*
▲ **Matcon Usa Inc**......F...... 856 256-1330
Elmhurst *(G-9399)*
Peerless Chain Company......E...... 708 339-0545
South Holland *(G-19239)*
Ramseys Machine Co......G...... 217 824-2320
Taylorville *(G-19761)*
Sievert Electric Svc & Sls Co......D...... 708 771-1600
Forest Park *(G-9724)*
◆ **Stertil Alm Corp**......D...... 815 673-5546
Streator *(G-19624)*
◆ **Uesco Industries Inc**......E...... 800 325-8372
Alsip *(G-518)*
Uesco Industries Inc......G...... 708 385-7700
Alsip *(G-517)*
▲ **Vector Engineering & Mfg Corp**......E...... 708 474-3900
Lansing *(G-12524)*
Vm Hoist Crane......G...... 708 771-1600
Forest Park *(G-9727)*
◆ **Whiting Corporation**......C...... 800 861-5744
Monee *(G-14212)*
WW Engineering Company LLC......F...... 773 376-9494
Chicago *(G-6690)*
Zg3 Systems LLC......G...... 309 745-3398
Washington *(G-20285)*

3537 Indl Trucks, Tractors, Trailers & Stackers

A1 Skilled Staffing......E...... 309 281-1400
East Moline *(G-8221)*
▲ **AAR Corp**......D...... 630 227-2000
Wood Dale *(G-21149)*
Aidar Express Inc......G...... 773 757-3447
Chicago *(G-3587)*
Align Production Systems LLC......E...... 217 423-6001
Decatur *(G-7439)*
▲ **All-Vac Industries Inc**......F...... 847 675-2290
Skokie *(G-18915)*
Always There Express Corp......E...... 773 931-3744
Romeoville *(G-17792)*
◆ **Anthony Liftgates Inc**......C...... 815 842-3383
Pontiac *(G-16765)*
As Lawn & Land LLC......G...... 309 246-5012
Lacon *(G-12125)*
▲ **Avant Tecno USA Inc**......F...... 847 380-1308
Arlington Heights *(G-700)*
▲ **Big Lift LLC**......E...... 630 916-2600
Lombard *(G-13042)*
Blue Nile Trucking LLC......G...... 618 215-1077
East Saint Louis *(G-8300)*
Bo Inc......F...... 312 459-0013
Countryside *(G-7045)*
▲ **Bolzoni Auramo Inc**......E...... 708 957-8809
Homewood *(G-11488)*
C C P Express Inc......G...... 773 315-0317
Berwyn *(G-1949)*
Caldwell & Moten LLC......G...... 773 619-2584
Chicago *(G-4003)*
Candriene Logistics LLC......G...... 312 260-0740
Chicago *(G-4014)*
Caples-El Transport Inc......G...... 708 300-2727
Calumet City *(G-2772)*
Caterpillar Inc......A...... 630 859-5000
Montgomery *(G-14238)*
Centralia Machine & Fab Inc......G...... 618 533-9010
Centralia *(G-3223)*
CF Solutions Co......G...... 630 413-9058
Schaumburg *(G-18472)*
Chevron Commercial Inc......G...... 618 654-5555
Highland *(G-11209)*
Chicago Pallet Service Inc......E...... 847 439-8330
Maywood *(G-13666)*
Clark Caster Co......G...... 708 366-1913
Forest Park *(G-9710)*
Conveyors Plus Inc......G...... 708 361-1512
Orland Park *(G-15948)*
Crown Equipment Corporation......C...... 847 397-1900
Schaumburg *(G-18497)*
Crown Equipment Corporation......C...... 815 773-0022
Joliet *(G-11849)*
Crown Equipment Corporation......F...... 309 663-9200
Bloomington *(G-2035)*
Cwh LLC......G...... 847 489-7907
Buffalo Grove *(G-2529)*
▲ **Dfk America Inc**......G...... 630 324-6793
Downers Grove *(G-7986)*
Dicom Transportation Group LP......G...... 312 255-4800
Chicago *(G-4355)*
ED Etnyre & Co......B...... 815 732-2116
Oregon *(G-15917)*
Edward J Warren Jr......G...... 630 882-8817
Yorkville *(G-21481)*
◆ **Elgin Sweeper Company**......B...... 847 741-5370
Elgin *(G-8577)*
▲ **Ezee Roll Manufacturing Co**......G...... 217 339-2279
Hoopeston *(G-11508)*
F and S Enterprises Plainfield......G...... 815 439-9655
Plainfield *(G-16662)*
▼ **Forklift Firm LLC**......G...... 708 770-7207
Homer Glen *(G-11480)*
▲ **Freight Car Services Inc**......B...... 217 443-4106
Danville *(G-7336)*
Furdge Trucking Inc......G...... 773 800-5431
Chicago *(G-4644)*
Goldmax Carrier Inc......G...... 773 366-1718
Elk Grove Village *(G-9019)*
Grand Specialties Co......F...... 630 629-8000
Oak Brook *(G-15625)*
Grant J Grapperhaus......G...... 618 410-4428
Highland *(G-11216)*
Green Valley Mfg Ill Inc......E...... 217 864-4125
Mount Zion *(G-14647)*
H & B Machine Corporation......G...... 312 829-4850
Chicago *(G-4756)*
H R Slater Co Inc......F...... 312 666-1855
Chicago *(G-4760)*
Handling Systems Intl Inc......E...... 708 352-1213
Mc Cook *(G-13692)*
Henderson Products Inc......G...... 847 515-3482
Huntley *(G-11539)*
◆ **Holland Applied Technologies**......E...... 630 325-5130
Burr Ridge *(G-2683)*
Hyster-Yale Group Inc......E...... 217 443-7416
Danville *(G-7348)*
◆ **Illinois Lift Equipment Inc**......E...... 888 745-0577
Cary *(G-3169)*
Interstate Cargo Inc......E...... 630 701-7744
Bolingbrook *(G-2194)*
▲ **Inventus Power (illinois) LLC**......C...... 630 410-7900
Woodridge *(G-21317)*
It Transportation Company......F...... 773 383-5073
Chicago *(G-4975)*
J W Todd Co......G...... 630 406-5715
Aurora *(G-1114)*
Jcb Inc......G...... 912 704-2995
Aurora *(G-990)*
John Bean Technologies Corp......D...... 312 861-5900
Chicago *(G-5036)*
Jsc Freight Solutions LLC......G...... 708 731-0448
Joliet *(G-11887)*
KG Lift Inc......G...... 815 908-1855
Addison *(G-168)*
▲ **Komatsu Forklift USA LLC**......E...... 847 437-5800
Rolling Meadows *(G-17744)*
Kta Trucking Services Inc......G...... 224 788-8312
Antioch *(G-619)*
◆ **Lanco International Inc**......B...... 708 596-5200
Hazel Crest *(G-11131)*
Lexpress Inc......G...... 773 517-7095
Prospect Heights *(G-16844)*
Lion Trans Group Inc......G...... 970 402-8073
Rolling Meadows *(G-17748)*
▲ **Littell LLC**......E...... 630 916-6662
Schaumburg *(G-18609)*
Loso Trucking Inc......G...... 312 601-2231
Chicago *(G-5264)*
M&J Hauling Inc......G...... 312 342-6596
Chicago *(G-5306)*
Majesty Cases Inc......E...... 847 546-2558
Ingleside *(G-11587)*
▲ **Manitex International Inc**......E...... 708 430-7500
Bridgeview *(G-2361)*
Marcells Pallet Inc......G...... 773 265-1200
Chicago *(G-5329)*
Marvel Industries Incorporated......G...... 847 325-2930
Buffalo Grove *(G-2569)*
Mh Equipment Company......D...... 217 443-7210
Danville *(G-7366)*
MHS Ltd......F...... 773 736-3333
Chicago *(G-5419)*
Midaco Corporation......E...... 847 593-8420
Elk Grove Village *(G-9123)*
New Cie Inc......E...... 815 224-1511
Peru *(G-16584)*
Phoenix Trucking Inc......G...... 708 514-2094
Westchester *(G-20708)*
Platinum Inc......G...... 815 385-0910
McHenry *(G-13780)*
Pmw Holdings Inc......G...... 815 672-0551
Streator *(G-19621)*
Point Unlimited......G...... 708 244-7730
University Park *(G-19964)*
Pools Welding Inc......G...... 309 787-2083
Milan *(G-14020)*
Premier Cdl Training Svcs LLC......G...... 618 797-1725
Granite City *(G-10732)*
Pwf......G...... 815 967-0218
Rockford *(G-17563)*
▲ **Sardee Industries Inc**......G...... 630 824-4200
Lisle *(G-12936)*
Scott Janczak......G...... 773 545-7233
Chicago *(G-6120)*
Specialized Liftruck Svcs LLC......F...... 708 552-2705
Bedford Park *(G-1505)*
STI Holdings Inc......F...... 630 789-2713
Burr Ridge *(G-2722)*
Superior Truck Dock Services......G...... 630 978-1697
Aurora *(G-1021)*
Synergy Power Group LLC......E...... 618 247-3200
Sandoval *(G-18365)*
Systems Equipment Services......G...... 708 535-1273
Oak Forest *(G-15689)*
T & E Enterprises Herscher Inc......F...... 815 426-2761
Herscher *(G-11188)*
Tarnow Logistics Inc......G...... 773 844-3203
Melrose Park *(G-13922)*
Tdr Express Inc......G...... 224 805-0070
Chicago *(G-6332)*
Tempo Enterprises Inc......G...... 331 903-2786
Westmont *(G-20775)*
Tewell Bros Machine Inc......F...... 217 253-6303
Tuscola *(G-19931)*
Tomahawk AG & Industrial LLC......E...... 309 275-2874
Heyworth *(G-11192)*
Transfer Logistics Inc......G...... 773 646-0529
Chicago *(G-6412)*

Employee Codes: A=Over 500 employees, B=251-500
C=101-250, D=51-100, E=20-50, F=10-19, G=3-9
2020 Harris Illinois
Industrial Directory
951

35 INDUSTRIAL AND COMMERCIAL MACHINERY AND COMPUTER EQUIPMENT

Tri County Lift Trucks Inc ....G....... 847 838-0183
  Antioch (G-639)
Triple B Manufacturing Co Inc ....G....... 618 566-2888
  Mascoutah (G-13607)
Trx Express Inc ....G....... 815 582-3792
  Crest Hill (G-7099)
Tvh Parts Co ....E....... 847 223-1000
  Grayslake (G-10803)
Twin Mills Timber & Tie Co Inc ....G....... 618 932-3662
  West Frankfort (G-20685)
Universal Feeder Inc ....G....... 815 633-0752
  Machesney Park (G-13382)
▼ Upstaging Inc ....C....... 815 899-9888
  Sycamore (G-19738)
◆ Vactor Manufacturing Inc ....A....... 815 672-3171
  Streator (G-19632)
Wastequip Saint Louis ....E....... 216 292-0625
  East Saint Louis (G-8329)
▲ William W Meyer and Sons ....D....... 847 918-0111
  Libertyville (G-12726)
Yusraa Inc ....G....... 312 608-1916
  Dolton (G-7941)

3541 Machine Tools: Cutting

◆ 1883 Properties Inc ....D....... 847 537-8800
  Lincolnshire (G-12740)
A&W Tool Inc ....G....... 815 653-1700
  Ringwood (G-17037)
Abbco Inc ....E....... 630 595-7115
  Bensenville (G-1722)
Above & Beyond Black Oxiding ....G....... 708 345-7100
  Melrose Park (G-13818)
Accelrted Mch Design Engrg LLC .....E....... 815 316-6381
  Rockford (G-17290)
Accu-Cut Dmnd Bore Szing Syste .....F....... 708 457-8800
  Norridge (G-15229)
ADS LLC ....D....... 256 430-3366
  Burr Ridge (G-2650)
▼ Advanced Machine & Engrg Co ....C....... 815 962-6076
  Rockford (G-17296)
Air Mite Devices Inc ....E....... 224 338-0071
  Round Lake (G-18067)
Alliance Tool & Manufacturing ....F....... 708 345-5444
  Maywood (G-13660)
▼ American Machine Tools Inc ....G....... 773 775-6285
  Chicago (G-3658)
Atometric Inc ....G....... 815 505-2582
  Loves Park (G-13192)
Automatic Production Eqp Inc ....G....... 847 439-1448
  Elk Grove Village (G-8848)
B & B Machine Inc ....G....... 309 786-3279
  Rock Island (G-17202)
◆ Bavius Technologie Inc ....G....... 847 844-3300
  East Dundee (G-8188)
Belcar Products Inc ....G....... 630 462-1950
  Carol Stream (G-2946)
Belden Machine Corporation ....F....... 708 344-4600
  Broadview (G-2419)
▲ Bertsche Engineering Corp ....F....... 847 537-8757
  Buffalo Grove (G-2516)
Beverly Shear Mfg Corporation ....G....... 773 233-2063
  Chicago (G-3877)
Bilz Tool Company ....F....... 630 495-3996
  Lombard (G-13044)
Blackhawk Industrial Dist Inc ....F....... 773 736-9600
  Carol Stream (G-2950)
Bos Machine Tool Services Inc ....F....... 309 658-2223
  Hillsdale (G-11321)
Bourn & Bourn Inc ....C....... 815 965-4013
  Rockford (G-17327)
▲ Bourn & Koch Inc ....D....... 815 965-4013
  Rockford (G-17328)
Bury Industrial Service LLC ....G....... 847 235-2053
  Lake Forest (G-12235)
◆ Bystronic Inc ....C....... 847 214-0300
  Hoffman Estates (G-11410)
C D T Manufacturing Inc ....G....... 847 679-2361
  Skokie (G-18935)
Cavallo Tool Service Inc ....G....... 630 620-4445
  Addison (G-64)
Cdv Corp ....F....... 815 397-3903
  Rockford (G-17339)
Ceratizit Chicago Holding Inc ....C....... 847 923-8400
  Schaumburg (G-18469)
▲ Ceratizit Chicago Inc ....C....... 847 923-8400
  Schaumburg (G-18470)
Chad Mazeika ....G....... 815 298-8118
  Rockford (G-17343)
Chicago Grinding & Machine Co ....E....... 708 343-4399
  Melrose Park (G-13843)

Circle Cutting Tools Inc ....G....... 815 398-4153
  Rockford (G-17350)
Composite Cutter Tech Inc ....G....... 847 740-6875
  Volo (G-20198)
Condor Machine Tool ....G....... 773 767-5985
  Chicago (G-4217)
Crw Finishing Inc ....E....... 630 495-4994
  Addison (G-84)
Ctc Machine Service Inc ....G....... 630 876-5120
  West Chicago (G-20568)
▲ CTS Advanced Materials LLC .....E....... 630 577-8800
  Lisle (G-12879)
Custom Cutting Tools Inc ....G....... 815 986-0320
  Loves Park (G-13200)
Custom Tool Inc ....F....... 217 465-8538
  Paris (G-16228)
Cutting Tool Innovations Inc ....G....... 630 766-4839
  Bensenville (G-1784)
▲ Dainichi Machinery Inc ....G....... 630 681-1572
  Carol Stream (G-2970)
▲ Daito USA Inc ....G....... 847 437-6788
  Elk Grove Village (G-8937)
Dearborn Tool & Mfg Inc ....G....... 630 655-1260
  Burr Ridge (G-2669)
Delco West LLC ....G....... 309 799-7543
  Milan (G-14006)
Diamond Blast Corporation ....F....... 708 681-2640
  Melrose Park (G-13850)
Diamond Edge Manufacturing ....G....... 630 458-1630
  Addison (G-88)
▲ Dmg Charlotte LLC ....F....... 704 583-1193
  Hoffman Estates (G-11418)
▲ Dmg Mori Usa Inc ....D....... 847 593-5400
  Hoffman Estates (G-11419)
Dynamic Automation Inc ....G....... 312 782-8555
  Lincolnwood (G-12817)
E H Wachs ....G....... 815 943-4785
  Lincolnshire (G-12762)
▲ Edmpartscom Inc ....G....... 630 427-1603
  Lombard (G-13072)
▲ Electron Beam Technologies Inc .C....... 815 935-2211
  Kankakee (G-11967)
Emhart Teknologies LLC ....F....... 877 364-2781
  Chicago (G-4498)
Endofix Ltd ....G....... 708 715-3472
  Brookfield (G-2482)
◆ Engineered Abrasives Inc ....E....... 662 582-4143
  Alsip (G-445)
Engineered Mills Inc ....G....... 847 548-0044
  Grayslake (G-10770)
▲ Engis Corporation ....C....... 847 808-9400
  Wheeling (G-20891)
Everede Tool Company LLC ....F....... 773 467-4200
  West Chicago (G-20576)
▲ Everede Tool Company LLC ....D....... 623 414-4800
  West Chicago (G-20575)
▲ Express Cutting Tools Inc ....G....... 815 964-0410
  Rockford (G-17410)
Extrude Hone LLC ....E....... 847 669-5355
  Huntley (G-11536)
Flat-Tech Inc ....F....... 847 364-4333
  Wilmette (G-21075)
Folkerts Manufacturing Inc ....G....... 815 968-7426
  Rockford (G-17417)
Form Relief Tool Co Inc ....G....... 815 393-4263
  Davis Junction (G-7423)
Genesis Duragrind Inc ....G....... 815 625-6500
  Sterling (G-19512)
Giant Finishing Inc ....G....... 708 343-6900
  Addison (G-140)
Glaser USA Inc ....G....... 847 362-7878
  Lake Forest (G-12251)
◆ Graff-Pinkert & Co ....F....... 708 535-2200
  Oak Forest (G-15680)
◆ Greenlee Tools Inc ....C....... 800 435-0786
  Rockford (G-17435)
▲ Hardinge Grinding Group Inc .....E....... 847 888-0148
  Elgin (G-8606)
Harris Precision Tools Inc ....G....... 708 422-5808
  Chicago Ridge (G-6797)
Hartland Cutting Tools Inc ....F....... 847 639-9400
  Cary (G-3166)
Hausermann Abrading Process Co ..G....... 630 543-6688
  Addison (G-146)
Hfd Manufacturing Inc ....F....... 847 263-5050
  Waukegan (G-20446)
Hobsource ....G....... 847 229-9120
  Mount Prospect (G-14533)
▲ Hoffman J&M Farm Holdings Inc .D....... 847 671-6280
  Schiller Park (G-18813)

◆ Holden Industries Inc ....F....... 847 940-1500
  Deerfield (G-7616)
Hottinger Bldwn Msrements Inc ......E....... 217 328-5359
  Champaign (G-3303)
Huml Industries Inc ....G....... 847 426-8061
  Gilberts (G-10358)
Ibanum Manufacturing LLC ....G....... 815 262-5373
  Rockford (G-17455)
Illinois Broaching Company ....E....... 847 678-3080
  Schiller Park (G-18815)
Illinois Electro Deburring Co ....G....... 847 678-5010
  Franklin Park (G-9961)
Imago Manufacturing ....G....... 815 333-5272
  Woodstock (G-21395)
◆ Ingersoll Machine Tools Inc ....C....... 815 987-6000
  Rockford (G-17462)
▲ Ingersoll Prod Systems LLC ....D....... 815 637-8500
  Rockford (G-17463)
Inland Broaching and TI Co LLC ......G....... 847 233-0033
  Elgin (G-8626)
It For Whats Inc ....G....... 847 949-6522
  Hawthorn Woods (G-11124)
J & L Gear Incorporated ....F....... 630 832-1880
  Villa Park (G-20151)
J Francis & Assoc ....G....... 309 697-5931
  Bartonville (G-1333)
▲ J Schneerberger Corp ....G....... 847 888-3498
  Elgin (G-8630)
Jakes McHning Rbilding Svc Inc .....G....... 630 892-3291
  Aurora (G-1116)
John Crane Inc ....E....... 815 459-0420
  Crystal Lake (G-7214)
Jtekt Toyoda Americas Corp ....G....... 847 253-0340
  Arlington Heights (G-763)
▲ Jtekt Toyoda Americas Corp ......C....... 847 253-0340
  Arlington Heights (G-764)
▲ Kiene Diesel Accessories Inc .....E....... 630 543-7170
  Addison (G-169)
Kmp Tool Grinding Inc ....G....... 847 205-9640
  Northbrook (G-15413)
Kpi Machining Inc ....G....... 815 496-2246
  Sheridan (G-18890)
◆ Laser Technologies Inc ....C....... 630 761-1200
  Naperville (G-14860)
▲ Lc Holdings of Delaware Inc ....E....... 847 940-3550
  Deerfield (G-7629)
▲ Logan Graphic Products Inc ....D....... 847 526-5515
  Wauconda (G-20369)
M & M Tooling Inc ....G....... 630 595-8834
  Wood Dale (G-21209)
Machine Medics LLC ....G....... 309 633-5454
  Peoria (G-20891)
Machine Technology Inc ....F....... 815 795-6818
  Marseilles (G-13560)
▼ Magnetrol International Inc ....E....... 630 723-6600
  Aurora (G-1001)
Manan Tool & Manufacturing ....A....... 847 637-3333
  Wheeling (G-20937)
Master Machine Group Inc ....G....... 847 472-9940
  Elgin (G-8650)
Meadoweld Machine Inc ....G....... 815 623-3939
  South Beloit (G-19102)
Micro Lapping & Grinding Co ....E....... 847 455-5446
  Franklin Park (G-9997)
Mid-West Millwork Wholesale ....G....... 618 407-5940
  Mascoutah (G-13603)
Midwest Machine Tool Inc ....G....... 815 427-8665
  Saint Anne (G-18136)
Midwest Turned Products LLC ....E....... 847 551-4482
  Gilberts (G-10362)
▲ Miyano Machinery USA Inc ....E....... 630 766-4141
  Elk Grove Village (G-9128)
Modern Gear & Machine Inc ....F....... 630 350-9173
  Bensenville (G-1854)
▲ Modern Specialties Company ....G....... 312 648-5800
  Chicago (G-5481)
N W Horizontal Boring ....G....... 618 566-9117
  Mascoutah (G-13605)
▲ Nicholas Machine & Tool Inc ......G....... 847 298-2035
  Rosemont (G-18038)
▲ NNt Enterprises Incorporated ....E....... 630 875-9600
  Itasca (G-11712)
On Site Repair Services Inc ....F....... 815 223-4058
  La Salle (G-12119)
OSG Power Tools Inc ....C....... 630 561-4008
  Bensenville (G-1863)
◆ Peddinghaus Corporation ....C....... 815 937-3800
  Bradley (G-2288)
Pietro Carnaghi USA Inc ....G....... 779 368-0564
  Rockford (G-17554)

SIC SECTION
35 INDUSTRIAL AND COMMERCIAL MACHINERY AND COMPUTER EQUIPMENT

Pioneer Service Inc ... E ... 630 628-0249
Addison *(G-241)*
Ppt Industrial Machines Inc ... E ... 800 851-3586
Mount Carmel *(G-14485)*
▲ Prater Industries Inc ... D ... 630 679-3200
Bolingbrook *(G-2228)*
▲ Precise Lapping Grinding Corp ... F ... 708 615-0240
Melrose Park *(G-13904)*
Precision Chrome Inc ... E ... 847 587-1515
Fox Lake *(G-9753)*
Precision Ctng Tls Svc Mfg Inc ... G ... 847 901-6800
Glenview *(G-10601)*
▲ Precision McHned Cmponents Inc ... E ... 630 759-5555
Romeoville *(G-17866)*
Precision Tool & Die Company ... F ... 217 864-3371
Mount Zion *(G-14649)*
Process Screw Products Inc ... E ... 815 864-2220
Shannon *(G-18872)*
▲ Prosco Inc ... G ... 847 336-1323
Gurnee *(G-10917)*
Prototype & Production Co ... E ... 847 419-1553
Wheeling *(G-20967)*
R B Evans Co ... G ... 630 365-3554
Elburn *(G-8471)*
Rabbit Tool USA Inc ... F ... 309 793-4375
Rock Island *(G-17238)*
Radiac Abrasives Inc ... E ... 630 898-0315
Oswego *(G-16024)*
Ramco Group LLC ... F ... 847 639-9899
Crystal Lake *(G-7252)*
Rdh Inc of Rockford ... F ... 815 874-9421
Rockford *(G-17568)*
Redin Parts Inc ... G ... 815 398-1010
Rockford *(G-17569)*
Regal Beloit Corporation ... C ... 844 527-8392
Roscoe *(G-17923)*
Reliance Tool & Mfg Co ... E ... 847 695-1235
Elgin *(G-8718)*
Reliance Tool & Mfg Co ... G ... 847 455-4350
Franklin Park *(G-10035)*
Robbins Hdd LLC ... F ... 847 955-0050
Lake Zurich *(G-12451)*
◆ Robert Bosch LLC ... B ... 917 421-7209
Broadview *(G-2466)*
Roberts Swiss Inc ... E ... 630 467-9100
Itasca *(G-11726)*
Rockford Broach Inc ... F ... 815 484-0409
Rockford *(G-17588)*
Rodifer Enterprises Inc ... G ... 815 678-0100
Richmond *(G-17021)*
Roll Rite Inc ... G ... 815 645-8600
Davis Junction *(G-7426)*
Rsvp Tooling Inc ... G ... 815 725-3310
Joliet *(G-11929)*
Sacco-Camex Inc ... G ... 630 595-8090
Franklin Park *(G-10040)*
Schram Enterprises Inc ... E ... 708 345-2252
Melrose Park *(G-13914)*
Serien Manufacturing Inc ... G ... 815 337-1447
Woodstock *(G-21431)*
Service Machine Jobs ... G ... 815 986-3033
Rockford *(G-17626)*
Specialty Enterprises Inc ... G ... 630 595-7808
Franklin Park *(G-10050)*
Spectrum Metals Inc ... F ... 847 969-0887
Schaumburg *(G-18722)*
Spencer and Krahn Mch Tl Sls ... G ... 815 282-3300
Rockford *(G-17639)*
Star Su Fellows Cutter LLC ... D ... 847 649-1450
Hoffman Estates *(G-11462)*
▲ Sterling Gear Inc ... F ... 815 438-4327
Deer Grove *(G-7578)*
Stuhr Manufacturing Co ... F ... 815 398-2460
Rockford *(G-17648)*
Swisstronics Corp ... G ... 708 403-8877
Orland Park *(G-15986)*
Synax Inc ... F ... 224 352-2927
Buffalo Grove *(G-2612)*
T&J Turning Inc ... G ... 309 738-8762
Colona *(G-6981)*
Tauber Brothers Tool & Die Co ... E ... 708 867-9100
Chicago *(G-6330)*
Thread & Gage Co Inc ... G ... 815 675-2305
Spring Grove *(G-19302)*
Tiger Tool Inc ... G ... 888 551-4490
Glendale Heights *(G-10511)*
Tooling Solutions Inc ... G ... 847 472-9940
Elgin *(G-8756)*
Tools For Industry Inc ... G ... 847 658-0455
Algonquin *(G-388)*
Total Tooling Technology Inc ... F ... 847 437-5135
Elk Grove Village *(G-9279)*
◆ TT Technologies Inc ... D ... 630 851-8200
Aurora *(G-1029)*
Tvo Acquisition Corporation ... E ... 708 656-4240
Cicero *(G-6882)*
Ty Miles Incorporated ... E ... 708 344-5480
Westchester *(G-20716)*
Ultramatic Equipment Co ... E ... 630 543-4565
Addison *(G-322)*
United Tool and Engineering Co ... D ... 815 389-3021
South Beloit *(G-19118)*
Universal Broaching Inc ... F ... 847 228-1440
Elk Grove Village *(G-9298)*
Variable Operations Tech Inc ... E ... 815 479-8528
Crystal Lake *(G-7288)*
Vaughn & Sons Machine Shop ... G ... 618 842-9048
Fairfield *(G-9639)*
Versatility Tl Works Mfg Inc ... F ... 708 389-8909
Alsip *(G-522)*
Walega Precision Company Inc ... G ... 630 682-5000
Carol Stream *(G-3086)*
Walter Tool & Mfg Inc ... F ... 847 697-7230
Elgin *(G-8774)*
▲ We Innovex Inc ... G ... 847 291-3553
Northbrook *(G-15500)*
Wec Welding and Machining LLC ... G ... 847 680-8100
Lake Bluff *(G-12214)*
West Precision Tool Inc ... F ... 630 766-8304
Bensenville *(G-1912)*
Western Applied Robotics Corp ... G ... 815 735-6476
Frankfort *(G-9852)*

3542 Machine Tools: Forming

10x Microstructures LLC ... G ... 847 215-7448
Wheeling *(G-20834)*
A & A Magnetics Inc ... F ... 815 338-6054
Woodstock *(G-21352)*
A J Carbide Grinding ... G ... 847 675-5112
Skokie *(G-18911)*
Accurate Spring Tech Inc ... F ... 815 344-3333
McHenry *(G-13713)*
▲ Advanced Prototype Molding ... G ... 847 202-4200
Palatine *(G-16090)*
▲ Ajax Tool Works Inc ... D ... 847 455-5420
Franklin Park *(G-9862)*
Alan Manufacturing Corp ... G ... 815 568-6836
Marengo *(G-13478)*
Alco Manufacturing Corp LLC ... F ... 815 708-5540
Machesney Park *(G-13325)*
▲ Altman Manufacturing Co Inc ... F ... 630 963-0031
Lisle *(G-12862)*
▼ American Machine Tools Inc ... G ... 773 775-6285
Chicago *(G-3658)*
Best Brake Die Inc ... G ... 708 388-1896
Crestwood *(G-7107)*
Bohl Machine & Tool Company ... G ... 309 799-5122
Milan *(G-14001)*
Bourn & Bourn Inc ... C ... 815 965-4013
Rockford *(G-17327)*
▲ Ceg Subsidiary LLC ... D ... 618 262-8666
Mount Carmel *(G-14467)*
Centric Mfg Solutions Inc ... G ... 815 315-9258
Chicago *(G-4058)*
▼ Chicago Rivet & Machine Co ... D ... 630 357-8500
Naperville *(G-14798)*
Chisholm-Boyd & White ... G ... 708 597-7550
Alsip *(G-430)*
▲ Cloos Robotic Welding Inc ... F ... 847 923-9988
Schaumburg *(G-18479)*
▼ Crd Enterprises Inc ... G ... 847 438-4299
Lake Zurich *(G-12398)*
Cutting Edge Industries Inc ... G ... 847 678-1777
Franklin Park *(G-9923)*
▲ D R Sperry & Co ... D ... 630 892-4361
Aurora *(G-1083)*
Die Cast Machinery LLC ... F ... 847 360-9170
Waukegan *(G-20438)*
DJB Corporation ... G ... 815 469-7533
Frankfort *(G-9786)*
Dover Europe Inc ... G ... 630 541-1540
Downers Grove *(G-7991)*
Ebe Industrial LLC ... F ... 815 379-2400
Walnut *(G-20217)*
▲ Elgalabwater LLC ... G ... 630 343-5251
Woodridge *(G-21300)*
Elpress Inc ... G ... 331 814-2910
Westmont *(G-20740)*
Epcor Industrial Inc ... G ... 847 545-9212
Elk Grove Village *(G-8979)*
First Header Die Inc ... E ... 815 282-5161
Machesney Park *(G-13343)*
▲ Formtek Inc ... F ... 630 285-1500
Lisle *(G-12891)*
▲ Geo T Schmidt Inc ... D ... 847 647-7117
Niles *(G-15124)*
Giant Globes Inc ... G ... 773 772-2917
Chicago *(G-4689)*
▲ Hersheys Metal Meister LLC ... E ... 217 234-4700
Claremont *(G-6898)*
Hurst Manufacturing Co Inc ... F ... 309 756-9960
Milan *(G-14016)*
Illinois Tool Works Inc ... C ... 630 595-3500
Itasca *(G-11672)*
Infinity Metal Spinning Inc ... G ... 773 731-4467
Chicago *(G-4913)*
Ingenious Concepts Inc ... G ... 630 539-8059
Medinah *(G-13814)*
Innovate Technologies Inc ... G ... 630 587-4220
Saint Charles *(G-18212)*
▼ Integral Automation Inc ... F ... 630 654-4300
Burr Ridge *(G-2688)*
Ives-Way Products Inc ... G ... 847 740-0658
Round Lake Beach *(G-18090)*
John J Rickhoff Shtmtl Co Inc ... F ... 708 331-2970
Phoenix *(G-16608)*
K & S Precision Metals Co ... G ... 773 586-8503
Chicago *(G-5065)*
◆ K R Komarek Inc ... E ... 847 956-0060
Wood Dale *(G-21203)*
Kaufman-Worthen Machinery Inc ... G ... 847 360-9170
Waukegan *(G-20454)*
▲ Kipp Manufacturing Company Inc ... F ... 630 768-9051
Wauconda *(G-20366)*
▲ Komori America Corporation ... D ... 847 806-9000
Rolling Meadows *(G-17745)*
▲ Kwalyti Tling McHy Rblding Inc ... F ... 630 761-8040
Batavia *(G-1391)*
Kwik Mark Inc ... G ... 815 363-8268
McHenry *(G-13755)*
▼ Kwm Gutterman Inc ... E ... 815 725-9205
Rockdale *(G-17263)*
▲ L M C Inc ... G ... 815 758-3514
Dekalb *(G-7687)*
Lens Lenticlear Lenticular ... F ... 630 467-0900
Elk Grove Village *(G-9093)*
▲ Littell International Inc ... E ... 630 622-4950
Schaumburg *(G-18610)*
Lotus Creative Innovations LLC ... G ... 815 440-8999
Compton *(G-6997)*
▲ Madison Capital Partners Corp ... G ... 312 277-0323
Chicago *(G-5312)*
▼ Marsh Shipping Supply Co LLC ... F ... 618 343-1006
Collinsville *(G-6969)*
MB Corp & Associates ... F ... 847 214-8843
Elgin *(G-8654)*
▲ Mechanical Tool & Engrg Co ... C ... 815 397-4701
Rockford *(G-17513)*
Metro Tool Company ... G ... 847 673-6790
Skokie *(G-18988)*
Mgb Engineering Company ... E ... 847 956-7444
Elk Grove Village *(G-9121)*
Mikes Machinery Rebuilders ... G ... 630 543-6400
Addison *(G-215)*
Mzm Manufacturing Inc ... G ... 815 624-8666
Roscoe *(G-17919)*
New Lenox Machine Co Inc ... F ... 815 584-4866
Dwight *(G-8156)*
Nor Service Inc ... E ... 815 232-8379
Freeport *(G-10130)*
Park Engineering Inc ... E ... 847 455-1424
Franklin Park *(G-10013)*
▲ Petrak Industries Incorporated ... E ... 815 483-2290
Joliet *(G-11914)*
Ppt Industrial Machines Inc ... E ... 800 851-3586
Mount Carmel *(G-14485)*
Precision Entps Fndry Mch Inc ... G ... 815 797-1000
Somonauk *(G-19073)*
Precision Header Tooling Inc ... F ... 815 874-9116
Rockford *(G-17557)*
Precision Service Mtr Inc ... F ... 630 628-9900
Addison *(G-252)*
Presses Inc ... E ... 708 496-7450
Bedford Park *(G-1494)*
Punch Products Manufacturing ... E ... 773 533-2800
Chicago *(G-5915)*
R-K Press Brake Dies Inc ... F ... 708 371-1756
Chicago *(G-5955)*
Rae Products and Chem Corp ... G ... 708 396-1984
Alsip *(G-501)*

S I C

Employee Codes: A=Over 500 employees, B=251-500
C=101-250, D=51-100, E=20-50, F=10-19, G=3-9
2020 Harris Illinois
Industrial Directory
953

35 INDUSTRIAL AND COMMERCIAL MACHINERY AND COMPUTER EQUIPMENT

Rams Sheet Metal Equipment Inc ....G...... 224 788-9900
Antioch *(G-632)*
Right Lane Industries LLC ....G...... 857 869-4132
Chicago *(G-6031)*
Riteway Brake Dies Inc ....F...... 708 430-0795
Bridgeview *(G-2383)*
Rock Valley Die Sinking Inc ....G...... 815 874-8560
Rockford *(G-17584)*
Roll Rite Inc ....G...... 815 645-8600
Davis Junction *(G-7426)*
Rsvp Tooling Inc ....G...... 815 725-3310
Joliet *(G-11929)*
Service Machine Jobs ....G...... 815 986-3033
Rockford *(G-17626)*
▲ **Sloan Industries Inc** ....E...... 630 350-1614
Wood Dale *(G-21241)*
Straightline Erectors Inc ....G...... 708 430-5426
Oak Lawn *(G-15736)*
Sure-Way Die Designs Inc ....F...... 630 323-0370
Westmont *(G-20774)*
▲ **Tek-Cast Inc** ....D...... 630 422-1458
Elgin *(G-8748)*
Tox- Pressotechnik LLC ....G...... 630 447-4600
Warrenville *(G-20254)*
▲ **Uniflex of America LLC** ....G...... 847 519-1100
Schaumburg *(G-18764)*
Venturedyne Ltd ....E...... 708 597-7550
Chicago *(G-6535)*
Versatech Inc ....C...... 217 342-3500
Effingham *(G-8428)*
Visimark Inc ....F...... 866 344-7721
Franklin Park *(G-10079)*
Wardzala Industries Inc ....F...... 847 288-9909
Franklin Park *(G-10083)*
◆ **Whitney Roper LLC** ....D...... 815 962-3011
Rockford *(G-17683)*
▲ **Whitney Roper Rockford Inc** ....D...... 815 962-3011
Rockford *(G-17684)*
Williams White & Company ....C...... 309 797-7650
Moline *(G-14181)*
▲ **Winchester Interconnect Rugged** ....G...... 708 594-5890
Broadview *(G-2475)*

3543 Industrial Patterns

Advanced Pattern Works LLC ....G...... 618 346-9039
Collinsville *(G-6952)*
Alang Pattern Inc ....G...... 773 722-9481
Cicero *(G-6828)*
Arnette Pattern Co Inc ....E...... 618 451-7700
Granite City *(G-10698)*
Beloit Pattern Works ....F...... 815 389-2578
South Beloit *(G-19083)*
Cambridge Pattern Works ....G...... 309 937-5370
Cambridge *(G-2803)*
Capital Pttern Model Works Inc ....G...... 630 469-8200
Glendale Heights *(G-10440)*
Carroll Industrial Molds Inc ....F...... 815 225-7250
Milledgeville *(G-14038)*
Chem-Cast Ltd ....C...... 217 443-5532
Danville *(G-7326)*
Clinkenbeard & Associates Inc ....E...... 815 226-0291
South Beloit *(G-19087)*
Cores For You Inc ....E...... 217 847-3233
Hamilton *(G-10952)*
Curto-Ligonier Foundries Co ....E...... 708 345-2250
Melrose Park *(G-13846)*
Jls Industries Inc ....G...... 630 261-9445
Lombard *(G-13090)*
Johnson Pattern & Mch Works ....E...... 815 433-2775
Ottawa *(G-16057)*
Jsp Mold LLC ....G...... 815 225-7110
Milledgeville *(G-14039)*
Kerrigan Corporation ....G...... 847 251-8994
Wilmette *(G-21082)*
Koswell Pattern Works Inc ....G...... 708 757-5225
Lynwood *(G-13294)*
Master Foundry Inc ....F...... 217 223-7396
Quincy *(G-16911)*
Microtek Pattern Inc ....G...... 217 428-0433
Decatur *(G-7522)*
Midstate Core Co ....E...... 217 429-2673
Decatur *(G-7523)*
Midwest Patterns Inc ....C...... 217 228-6900
Quincy *(G-16914)*
Modern Pattern Works Inc ....G...... 309 676-2157
Peoria *(G-16478)*
N & S Pattern Co ....G...... 815 874-6166
Rockford *(G-17535)*
Olson Aluminum Castings Ltd ....E...... 815 229-3292
Rockford *(G-17544)*

P & H Pattern Inc ....G...... 815 795-2449
Marseilles *(G-13562)*
Park Products Inc ....G...... 630 543-2474
Addison *(G-233)*
Precision Entps Fndry Mch Inc ....G...... 815 797-1000
Somonauk *(G-19073)*
Precision Foundry Tooling Ltd ....F...... 217 847-3233
Hamilton *(G-10960)*
Prs Inc ....G...... 630 620-7259
Lombard *(G-13123)*
Quincy Foundry & Pattern Co 217 222-0718
Quincy *(G-16932)*
R & C Pattern Works Inc ....G...... 708 331-1882
Monee *(G-14204)*
R C Castings Inc ....G...... 708 331-1882
Monee *(G-14205)*
Rockbridge Casting Inc ....G...... 618 753-3188
Rockbridge *(G-17255)*
Spectron Manufacturing ....G...... 720 879-7605
Bloomingdale *(G-2015)*
Sun Pattern & Model Inc ....E...... 630 293-3366
West Chicago *(G-20648)*
Tilton Pattern Works Inc ....F...... 217 442-1502
Danville *(G-7388)*
Voss Pattern Works Inc ....G...... 618 233-4242
Belleville *(G-1609)*

3544 Dies, Tools, Jigs, Fixtures & Indl Molds

3d Industries Inc ....E...... 630 616-8702
Bensenville *(G-1719)*
A & B Machine Shop ....G...... 815 397-0495
Rockford *(G-17279)*
A & C Mold Company Inc ....E...... 630 587-0177
Saint Charles *(G-18141)*
A J Carbide Grinding ....G...... 847 675-5112
Skokie *(G-18911)*
A K Tool & Manufacturing Inc ....G...... 630 889-9220
Lombard *(G-13033)*
A M Tool & Die ....E...... 847 398-7530
Rolling Meadows *(G-17708)*
A R Tech & Tool Inc ....G...... 708 599-5745
Bridgeview *(G-2317)*
A W Radtke Tool Corporation ....G...... 847 662-7373
Waukegan *(G-20404)*
A&S Machining & Welding Inc ....E...... 708 442-4544
Mc Cook *(G-13689)*
▲ **A-1 Tool Corporation** ....D...... 708 345-5000
Melrose Park *(G-13817)*
A-B Die Mold Inc ....G...... 847 658-1199
Bartlett *(G-1261)*
AAA Cnc Manufacturing Corp ....G...... 708 288-2678
Crestwood *(G-7104)*
Aberdeen Technologies Inc ....F...... 630 665-8590
Carol Stream *(G-2923)*
ABS Tool & Machine Inc ....G...... 815 968-4630
Rockford *(G-17288)*
Accu Cast 2 Inc 423 622-4344
Elgin *(G-8491)*
Accurate Die Cutting Inc ....E...... 847 437-7215
Elk Grove Village *(G-8800)*
Accurate Grinding Co Inc ....G...... 708 371-1887
Posen *(G-16790)*
Ace Plating Company ....E...... 773 927-2711
Chicago *(G-3522)*
Acomtech Mold Inc ....G...... 847 741-3537
Elgin *(G-8493)*
Action Tool & Mfg Inc ....E...... 815 874-5775
Rockford *(G-17294)*
▲ **Admo Inc** ....G...... 847 741-5777
Elgin *(G-8495)*
Advanced Digital & Mold Inc ....G...... 630 595-8242
Bensenville *(G-1729)*
Advanced Molding Tech Inc ....D...... 815 334-3600
Woodstock *(G-21354)*
▲ **Airo Tool & Manufacturing Inc** ......F...... 815 547-7588
Belvidere *(G-1647)*
Alcon Tool & Mfg Co Inc ....G...... 773 545-8742
Chicago *(G-3598)*
Allstar Tool & Molds Inc ....G...... 630 766-0162
Bensenville *(G-1739)*
Alm Positioners Inc ....G...... 309 787-6200
Rock Island *(G-17201)*
Alpha Products Inc ....G...... 708 387-1580
Brookfield *(G-2478)*
Alpha Star Tool and Mold Inc ....F...... 815 455-2802
Crystal Lake *(G-7156)*
▲ **Altman Manufacturing Co Inc** ....F...... 630 963-0031
Lisle *(G-12862)*
▲ **American Die Supplies Acquisit** ......G...... 630 766-6226
Wood Dale *(G-21164)*

▼ **American Engraving Inc** ....G...... 630 543-2525
Bensenville *(G-1742)*
American Total Engine Co ....E...... 847 623-2737
Ingleside *(G-11578)*
▲ **Ameriken Die Supply Inc** ....E...... 630 766-6226
Wood Dale *(G-21165)*
Amity Die and Stamping Co ....E...... 847 680-6600
Lake Forest *(G-12224)*
Ammentorp Tool Company Inc ....G...... 847 671-9290
Franklin Park *(G-9869)*
Amtech Inc ....F...... 815 962-0500
Rockford *(G-17303)*
Andersson Tool & Die LLP ....F...... 847 746-8866
Zion *(G-21508)*
Angle Tool Company ....G...... 847 593-7572
Elk Grove Village *(G-8832)*
▲ **Apex Tool Works Inc** ....E...... 847 394-5810
Rolling Meadows *(G-17712)*
Apollo Machine & Manufacturing ......G...... 847 677-6444
Skokie *(G-18921)*
APT Tool Inc ....G...... 815 337-0051
Woodstock *(G-21359)*
ARC Industries Inc ....E...... 847 303-5005
Schaumburg *(G-18444)*
Armin Tool and Mfg Co ....D...... 847 742-1864
South Elgin *(G-19134)*
Arrow Engineering Inc ....E...... 815 397-0862
Rockford *(G-17307)*
Assurance Clg Restoration LLC ....F...... 630 444-3600
Saint Charles *(G-18151)*
Astro Tool Co Inc ....G...... 630 876-3402
West Chicago *(G-20546)*
Atlantic Engineering ....E...... 847 782-1762
Zion *(G-21509)*
Atlas Die LLC ....D...... 630 351-5140
Glendale Heights *(G-10436)*
▲ **Atlas Tool & Die Works Inc** ....D...... 708 442-1661
Lyons *(G-13302)*
Atomic Engineering Co ....F...... 847 228-1387
Elk Grove Village *(G-8846)*
Austin Tool & Die Co ....D...... 847 509-5800
Northbrook *(G-15344)*
Automation Design & Mfg Inc ....G...... 630 896-4206
Aurora *(G-1060)*
Avan Tool & Die Co Inc ....F...... 773 287-1670
Chicago *(G-3782)*
Azimuth Cnc Inc ....F...... 815 399-4433
Rockford *(G-17310)*
B & B Tool Co ....G...... 815 229-5792
Rockford *(G-17311)*
B & D Murray Manufacturing Co ......G...... 815 568-6176
Marengo *(G-13481)*
B A Die Mold Inc ....F...... 630 978-4747
Aurora *(G-919)*
B C Die & Mold Inc ....G...... 630 543-5090
Addison *(G-44)*
B L I Tool & Die Inc ....G...... 217 434-9106
Fowler *(G-9742)*
B Radtke and Sons Inc ....E...... 847 546-3999
Round Lake Park *(G-18095)*
B&H Machine Inc ....F...... 618 281-3737
Columbia *(G-6984)*
Banner Moulded Products ....E...... 708 452-0033
River Grove *(G-17057)*
▲ **Barco Stamping Co** ....E...... 630 293-5155
West Chicago *(G-20549)*
Bear Machine Tool & Die Inc ....G...... 815 932-4204
Bradley *(G-2277)*
Bel-Air Manufacturing Inc ....F...... 773 276-7550
Chicago *(G-3862)*
Bennett Metal Products Inc ....D...... 618 244-1911
Mount Vernon *(G-14599)*
Bergst Special Tools Inc ....G...... 630 543-1020
Addison *(G-48)*
▲ **Best Cutting Die Co** ....C...... 847 675-5522
Skokie *(G-18929)*
Best Metal Extrusions Inc ....E...... 847 981-0797
Elk Grove Village *(G-8865)*
Bg Die Mold Inc ....G...... 847 961-5861
Huntley *(G-11529)*
▲ **Bi-Link Metal Specialties Inc** ....C...... 630 858-5900
Bloomingdale *(G-1980)*
▲ **Big 3 Precision Products Inc** ....F...... 618 533-3251
Centralia *(G-3222)*
Binder Tool Inc ....G...... 847 678-4222
Franklin Park *(G-9887)*
▲ **Bluco Corporation** ....F...... 630 637-1820
Naperville *(G-14780)*
Bohl Machine & Tool Company ....G...... 309 799-5122
Milan *(G-14001)*

SIC SECTION
35 INDUSTRIAL AND COMMERCIAL MACHINERY AND COMPUTER EQUIPMENT

Bomel Tool Manufacturing Co ... C ... 708 343-3663
Broadview ***(G-2422)***
Briergate Tool & Engrg Co ... F ... 630 766-7050
Bensenville ***(G-1756)***
Bronson & Bratton Inc ... C ... 630 986-1815
Burr Ridge ***(G-2658)***
BT & E Co ... G ... 815 544-6431
Belvidere ***(G-1657)***
Burdzy Tool & Die Co ... F ... 847 671-6666
Schiller Park ***(G-18790)***
Burns Machine Company ... E ... 815 434-3131
Ottawa ***(G-16044)***
C & S Steel Rule Die Co Inc ... G ... 773 254-4027
Chicago ***(G-3994)***
C Tri Co ... E ... 309 467-4715
Eureka ***(G-9477)***
Cabot McRlectronics Polsg Corp ... E ... 630 543-6682
Addison ***(G-61)***
Cac Corporation ... E ... 630 221-5200
Carol Stream ***(G-2953)***
Cameo Mold Corp ... F ... 630 876-1340
West Chicago ***(G-20557)***
▲ Canny Tool & Mold Corporation ... G ... 847 548-1573
Grayslake ***(G-10760)***
Capitol City Tool & Design ... G ... 217 544-9250
Springfield ***(G-19339)***
Cardon Mold Finishing Inc ... G ... 630 543-5431
Addison ***(G-63)***
Carroll Industrial Molds Inc ... F ... 815 225-7250
Milledgeville ***(G-14038)***
CB Machine & Tool Corp ... G ... 847 288-1807
Franklin Park ***(G-9901)***
Cdv Corp ... F ... 815 397-3903
Rockford ***(G-17339)***
Center Tool Company ... G ... 847 683-7559
Hampshire ***(G-10966)***
Central Tool Specialities Co ... G ... 630 543-6351
Addison ***(G-66)***
Century Mold & Tool Co ... E ... 847 364-5858
Elk Grove Village ***(G-8886)***
CGR Technologies Inc ... E ... 847 934-7622
Palatine ***(G-16099)***
Challenge Tool Co ... G ... 847 640-8085
Elk Grove Village ***(G-8887)***
◆ Chase Products Co ... D ... 708 865-1000
Broadview ***(G-2425)***
Chelar Tool & Die Inc ... D ... 618 234-6550
Belleville ***(G-1539)***
Chem-Cast Ltd ... C ... 217 443-5532
Danville ***(G-7326)***
▲ Chicago Cutting Die Co ... D ... 847 509-5800
Northbrook ***(G-15357)***
▲ Chicago Heights Star Tool and ... F ... 708 758-2525
Chicago Heights ***(G-6742)***
Chicago Mold Engrg Co Inc ... D ... 630 584-1311
Saint Charles ***(G-18165)***
Chicago Quadrill Co ... G ... 847 824-4196
Des Plaines ***(G-7745)***
Chicago Roll Co Inc ... E ... 630 627-8888
Lombard ***(G-13052)***
Cll Engineering LLC ... G ... 630 628-8393
Addison ***(G-74)***
▲ Comet Die & Engraving Company ... D ... 630 833-5600
Elmhurst ***(G-9350)***
Complete Mold Polishing Inc ... G ... 630 406-7668
Batavia ***(G-1368)***
Component Tool & Mfg Co ... F ... 708 672-5505
Crete ***(G-7136)***
Comtec Industries Ltd ... G ... 630 759-9000
Bolingbrook ***(G-2157)***
Condor Tool & Manufacturing ... F ... 630 628-8200
Addison ***(G-81)***
Conform Industries Inc ... F ... 630 285-0272
Schaumburg ***(G-18484)***
▲ Converting Technology Inc ... D ... 847 290-0590
Elk Grove Village ***(G-8912)***
▲ Correct Tool Inc ... F ... 630 595-6055
Bensenville ***(G-1777)***
Corrugated Converting Eqp ... F ... 618 532-2138
Centralia ***(G-3227)***
County Tool & Die ... G ... 217 324-6527
Litchfield ***(G-12962)***
Craftsman Tool & Mold Co ... E ... 630 851-8700
Aurora ***(G-942)***
▲ Crystal Die and Mold Inc ... E ... 847 658-6535
Rolling Meadows ***(G-17725)***
Custom Cuttingedge Tool Inc ... G ... 847 622-0457
Batavia ***(G-1370)***
Custom Mold Services Inc ... F ... 847 364-6589
Mount Prospect ***(G-14525)***
Custom Tool Inc ... F ... 217 465-8538
Paris ***(G-16228)***
Cutting Edge Industries Inc ... G ... 847 678-1777
Franklin Park ***(G-9923)***
D & D Manufacturing Inc ... G ... 888 300-6869
Bolingbrook ***(G-2163)***
D & D Tooling and Mfg Inc ... D ... 888 300-6869
Bolingbrook ***(G-2164)***
D & D Tooling Inc ... C ... 630 759-0015
Bolingbrook ***(G-2165)***
D & H Precision Tooling Co ... G ... 815 653-9611
Wonder Lake ***(G-21144)***
D & J Machine Shop Inc ... G ... 815 472-6057
Momence ***(G-14184)***
D & M Tool Llc ... G ... 847 731-3600
Zion ***(G-21511)***
D C T/Precision LLC ... F ... 217 475-0141
Decatur ***(G-7481)***
▲ D E Specialty Tool & Mfg Inc ... E ... 847 678-0004
Franklin Park ***(G-9925)***
D M C Mold & Tool Corp ... G ... 847 639-3098
Cary ***(G-3152)***
D S Precision Tool Company ... G ... 630 627-0696
Downers Grove ***(G-7982)***
Dadum Inc ... G ... 847 541-7851
Buffalo Grove ***(G-2530)***
Dagger Tool Co Inc ... G ... 630 279-5050
Addison ***(G-86)***
Daley Automation LLC ... G ... 630 384-9900
Naperville ***(G-14812)***
Dangios Fine Art Inc ... G ... 773 533-3000
Chicago ***(G-4311)***
Davis Machine Company Inc ... G ... 815 723-9121
Joliet ***(G-11854)***
Davitz Mold Co Inc ... G ... 847 426-4848
East Dundee ***(G-8191)***
Dax Steel Rule Dies Inc ... G ... 708 448-4436
Orland Park ***(G-15950)***
Dearborn Tool & Mfg Inc ... E ... 630 655-1260
Burr Ridge ***(G-2669)***
Dec Tool Corp ... E ... 630 513-9883
Saint Charles ***(G-18181)***
Decore Tool & Mfg Inc ... F ... 630 681-9760
Carol Stream ***(G-2975)***
Design Systems Inc ... E ... 309 263-7706
Morton ***(G-14358)***
Dial Tool Industries Inc ... D ... 630 543-3600
Addison ***(G-87)***
▲ Diamond Die & Bevel Cutng LLC ... E ... 224 387-3200
Wheeling ***(G-20878)***
Diamond Tool & Mold Inc ... G ... 630 543-7011
Addison ***(G-90)***
Dice Mold & Engineering Inc ... E ... 630 773-3595
Itasca ***(G-11642)***
Die Cut Group Inc ... F ... 630 629-9211
Lombard ***(G-13065)***
Die Darrell ... G ... 309 282-9112
Eureka ***(G-9480)***
Die Mold Jig Grinding & Mfg ... G ... 847 228-1444
Elk Grove Village ***(G-8949)***
Die Pros Inc ... G ... 630 543-2025
Addison ***(G-93)***
Die Specialty Co ... G ... 312 303-5738
La Grange Park ***(G-12096)***
Die World Steel Rule Dies ... G ... 815 399-8675
Rockford ***(G-17378)***
▲ Diemasters Manufacturing Inc ... C ... 847 640-9900
Elk Grove Village ***(G-8950)***
▲ Diemold Service Company ... F ... 847 885-6007
Elk Grove Village ***(G-8951)***
Dies Plus Inc ... F ... 630 285-1065
Carpentersville ***(G-3100)***
Dike-O-Seal Incorporated ... F ... 773 254-3224
Chicago ***(G-4361)***
Dkb Partners Inc ... G ... 618 632-6718
O Fallon ***(G-15572)***
Dms Inc ... F ... 847 726-2828
Lake Zurich ***(G-12403)***
Do-Rite Die & Engineering Co ... F ... 708 754-4355
S Chicago Hts ***(G-18120)***
▲ Domeny Tool & Stamping Company F ... 847 526-5700
Wauconda ***(G-20342)***
Dooling Machine Products Inc ... G ... 618 254-0724
Hartford ***(G-11034)***
Doral Inc ... G ... 630 543-5523
Addison ***(G-96)***
Double M Machine Inc ... F ... 815 692-4676
Fairbury ***(G-9605)***
Dovee Manufacturing Inc ... F ... 847 437-8122
Elgin ***(G-8569)***
Dragon Die Mold Inc ... G ... 630 836-0699
Warrenville ***(G-20235)***
Durabuilt Die Corp ... G ... 847 437-2086
Elk Grove Village ***(G-8958)***
E C Schultz & Co Inc ... F ... 847 640-1190
Elk Grove Village ***(G-8963)***
E-Lite Tool & Mfg Co ... E ... 618 236-1580
Belleville ***(G-1548)***
East Side Tool & Die Co Inc ... F ... 618 397-1633
Caseyville ***(G-3212)***
East West Martial Arts Sups ... G ... 773 878-7711
Chicago ***(G-4434)***
Eberle Manufacturing Company ... F ... 847 215-0100
Wheeling ***(G-20885)***
EDM Products LLC ... G ... 630 785-2554
Elmhurst ***(G-9358)***
▼ Ehrhardt Tool & Machine LLC ... C ... 314 436-6900
Granite City ***(G-10704)***
Elba Tool Co Inc ... F ... 847 895-4100
Bloomingdale ***(G-1990)***
Elite Die & Finishing Inc ... G ... 708 389-4848
Tinley Park ***(G-19823)***
Elm Tool and Manufacturing Co ... G ... 847 455-6805
Melrose Park ***(G-13863)***
Embeddedkits ... G ... 847 401-7488
Streamwood ***(G-19572)***
Emerson Industries LLC ... F ... 630 279-0920
Itasca ***(G-11649)***
Emt International Inc ... G ... 630 655-4145
Westmont ***(G-20741)***
Engineering Design & Dev ... E ... 309 266-6298
Morton ***(G-14359)***
ERA Tool and Manufacturing Co ... E ... 847 298-6333
Zion ***(G-21513)***
Erickson Tool & Machine Co ... G ... 815 397-2653
Rockford ***(G-17400)***
▲ Erowa Technology Inc ... F ... 847 290-0295
Arlington Heights ***(G-733)***
▲ Erva Tool & Die Company ... G ... 773 533-7806
Chicago ***(G-4528)***
Etch-Tech Inc ... G ... 630 833-4234
Elmhurst ***(G-9363)***
Ever Ready Pin & Manufacturing ... D ... 815 874-4949
Rockford ***(G-17403)***
▲ Ewikon Molding Tech Inc ... G ... 815 874-7270
Rockford ***(G-17405)***
Exact Tool Company Inc ... G ... 847 632-1140
Wheeling ***(G-20896)***
Extrusion Tooling Technology ... G ... 847 526-1606
Wauconda ***(G-20350)***
F & R Plastics Inc ... G ... 847 336-1330
Waukegan ***(G-20442)***
F & S Engraving Inc ... E ... 847 870-8400
Mount Prospect ***(G-14527)***
Fabricating Machinery Sales ... E ... 630 350-2266
Wood Dale ***(G-21186)***
▲ Fabrik Industries Inc ... B ... 815 385-9480
McHenry ***(G-13743)***
◆ Federal Signal Corporation ... D ... 630 954-2000
Oak Brook ***(G-15618)***
▲ Fidelity Tool & Mold Ltd ... F ... 630 879-2300
Batavia ***(G-1377)***
First Header Die Inc ... E ... 815 282-5161
Machesney Park ***(G-13343)***
Flores Precision Products ... G ... 630 264-2222
Aurora ***(G-1096)***
Ford Tool & Machining Inc ... D ... 815 633-5727
Loves Park ***(G-13211)***
Forster Products Inc ... E ... 815 493-6360
Lanark ***(G-12481)***
Forster Tool & Mfg Co Inc ... E ... 630 616-8177
Bensenville ***(G-1802)***
▼ Fosbinder Fabrication Inc ... E ... 309 764-0913
Moline ***(G-14146)***
Frankfort Machine & Tools Inc ... G ... 815 469-9902
Frankfort ***(G-9796)***
Furnel Inc ... E ... 630 543-0885
Addison ***(G-130)***
Future Tool Inc ... F ... 815 395-0012
Rockford ***(G-17426)***
▲ G & J Hall Tools Inc ... G ... 314 968-5040
Lombard ***(G-13081)***
G & M Die Casting Company Inc ... D ... 630 595-2340
Wood Dale ***(G-21192)***
Gage Grinding Company Inc ... F ... 847 639-3888
Cary ***(G-3161)***
Gage Tool & Manufacturing Inc ... G ... 847 640-1069
Elk Grove Village ***(G-9010)***
Galaxy Precision Mfg Inc ... F ... 847 238-9066
Elk Grove Village ***(G-9011)***

S
I
C

Employee Codes: A=Over 500 employees, B=251-500
C=101-250, D=51-100, E=20-50, F=10-19, G=3-9
2020 Harris Illinois
Industrial Directory
955

35 INDUSTRIAL AND COMMERCIAL MACHINERY AND COMPUTER EQUIPMENT

Gemini Tool & Manufacturing ....F 847 678-5000
Franklin Park (G-9950)
General Forging Die Co Inc 815 874-4224
Rockford (G-17428)
General Machinery & Mfg Co ....F 773 235-3700
Chicago (G-4674)
Genesis Mold Corp ....G 847 573-9431
Libertyville (G-12654)
▲ Geo T Schmidt Inc ....D 847 647-7117
Niles (G-15124)
George Hansen & Co Inc ....F 630 628-8700
Addison (G-139)
Gerhard Designing & Mfg Inc 708 599-4664
Bridgeview (G-2349)
Glenwood Tool & Mold Inc ....F 630 289-3400
Bartlett (G-1282)
Global Tool & Die Inc ....G 847 956-1200
Elk Grove Village (G-9016)
Great Lakes Tool & Mold Inc ....G 630 964-7121
Woodridge (G-21307)
Grinding Specialty Co Inc ....E 847 724-6493
West Chicago (G-20591)
Grove Plastic Inc ....F 847 678-8244
Franklin Park (G-9954)
H & B Quality Tooling Inc 217 223-2387
Quincy (G-16888)
H & R Tool & Machine Co ....G 618 344-7683
Caseyville (G-3213)
H B Products Incorporated ....G 773 735-0936
Palos Park (G-16211)
H&H Die Manufacturing Inc ....G 708 479-6267
Frankfort (G-9799)
Haaker Mold Co Inc ....G 847 253-8103
Arlington Heights (G-746)
Hansels Custom Tech Inc ....G 815 496-2345
Sheridan (G-18889)
Harbor Manufacturing Inc ....D 708 543-1740
Frankfort (G-9800)
▲ Harig Manufacturing Corp ....E 847 647-9500
Skokie (G-18964)
Hatcher Associates Inc ....F 773 252-2171
Chicago (G-4784)
Hattan Tool Company 708 597-9308
Alsip (G-455)
Header Die and Tool Inc ....D 815 397-0123
Rockford (G-17445)
Headly Manufacturing Co ....D 708 338-0800
Broadview (G-2441)
Headly Manufacturing Co ....D 708 338-0800
Broadview (G-2440)
Heat Seal Tooling Corporation ....G 815 626-6009
Rock Falls (G-17182)
Helm Tool Company Incorporated ...E 847 952-9528
Elk Grove Village (G-9033)
Henning Machine & Die Works ....G 217 286-3393
Henning (G-11161)
Heritage Mold Incorporated ....F 815 397-1117
Rockford (G-17448)
HI Prcision Tl Makers McHy Inc ....G 630 694-0200
Bensenville (G-1818)
Hill Engineering Inc ....E 630 315-5070
Carol Stream (G-2998)
Hoffman Tool Inc 815 692-4643
Fairbury (G-9608)
Icon Metalcraft Inc ....C 630 766-5600
Wood Dale (G-21200)
Idea Tool & Manufacturing Co ....D 312 476-1080
Chicago (G-4874)
Iemco Corporation ....G 773 728-4400
Chicago (G-4878)
Illinois Mold Builders Inc ....F 847 526-0400
Wauconda (G-20359)
Illinois Tool Works Inc ....C 708 479-7200
Mokena (G-14091)
Illinois Tool Works Inc ....G 708 479-3346
Tinley Park (G-19838)
Imperial Punch & Manufacturing .....F 815 226-8200
Rockford (G-17457)
IMS Olson LLC ....D 630 969-9400
Downers Grove (G-8030)
Inc Midwest Die Mold ....G 224 353-6417
Schaumburg (G-18557)
Indiana Precision Inc ....F 765 361-0247
Danville (G-7351)
Industrial Modern Pattern ....G 847 296-4930
Elk Grove Village (G-9050)
Industrial Molded Products ....G 847 358-2160
Mundelein (G-14700)
▲ Industrial Molds Inc ....D 815 397-2971
Rockford (G-17459)

Industrial Park Machine & Tool ....F 708 754-7080
S Chicago Hts (G-18122)
Inland Tool Company 217 792-3206
Mount Pulaski (G-14588)
International Cutting Die Inc ....E 708 343-3333
Melrose Park (G-13884)
Inventive Mfg Inc ....F 847 647-9500
Skokie (G-18969)
▲ Iplastics LLC 309 444-8884
Washington (G-20270)
▲ J & J Carbide & Tool Inc 708 489-0300
Alsip (G-459)
J F Schroeder Company Inc 847 357-8600
Arlington Heights (G-759)
J H Benedict Co Inc ....D 309 694-3111
East Peoria (G-8270)
J R Mold Inc ....G 630 289-2192
Streamwood (G-19578)
Jamco Tool & Cams Inc ....F 847 678-0280
Franklin Park (G-9972)
▼ Janler Corporation ....E 773 774-0166
Chicago (G-5005)
Jasco Tool & Manufacturing 815 271-5158
McHenry (G-13751)
Jbw Machining Inc 847 451-0276
Franklin Park (G-9974)
JC Automation Inc 309 270-7000
Rock Island (G-17226)
JC Tool and Mold Inc ....G 630 483-2203
Streamwood (G-19580)
JC Tooling Company Inc ....F 618 327-9379
Nashville (G-14998)
Jenco Metal Products Inc 847 956-0550
Mount Prospect (G-14539)
Jensen and Son Inc ....G 815 895-3855
Sycamore (G-19719)
JM Tool & Die LLC ....G 630 616-7776
Bensenville (G-1832)
Johnson Steel Rule & Die ....G 708 547-1726
Bellwood (G-1630)
Johnson Steel Rule Die Co ....F 773 921-4334
Chicago (G-5046)
Jsp Mold LLC ....G 815 225-7110
Milledgeville (G-14039)
K & B Machining ....G 847 663-9534
Morton Grove (G-14416)
K & H Tool Co ....G 630 766-4588
Bensenville (G-1834)
K B Tool Inc ....G 630 595-4340
Bensenville (G-1835)
K P Enterprises Inc ....G 630 509-2174
Bensenville (G-1836)
Kam Tool and Mold ....G 815 338-8360
Woodstock (G-21397)
Kaskaskia Tool and Machine Inc ....E 618 475-3301
New Athens (G-15020)
Kazmier Tooling Inc ....G 773 586-0300
Chicago (G-5087)
▲ Kelco Industries Inc ....G 815 334-3600
Woodstock (G-21398)
◆ Kenmode Tool and Engrg Inc ....C 847 658-5041
Algonquin (G-376)
Kensen Tool & Die Inc ....F 847 455-0150
Franklin Park (G-9976)
Ki Machine Tools & Productions ......G 815 484-9216
Loves Park (G-13229)
Kleen Cut Tool Inc ....G 630 447-7020
Warrenville (G-20240)
▲ Knight Tool Works Inc ....F 847 678-1237
Elgin (G-8637)
Kosmos Tool Inc ....F 815 675-2200
Spring Grove (G-19281)
Koson Tool Inc ....G 815 277-2107
Frankfort (G-9813)
Kreis Tool & Mfg Co Inc ....E 847 289-3700
Elgin (G-8639)
▲ Kyowa Industrial Co Ltd USA 847 459-3500
Wheeling (G-20927)
L & M Tool & Die Co Inc ....G 847 364-9760
Elk Grove Village (G-9081)
L C Mold Inc ....E 847 593-5004
Rolling Meadows (G-17746)
L T L Co ....F 815 874-0913
Rockford (G-17488)
L-V Industries Inc ....F 630 595-9251
Bensenville (G-1839)
Lah Inc ....G 815 282-4939
Loves Park (G-13231)
Lake County Tool Works North ....G 847 662-4542
Wadsworth (G-20210)

Lane Tool & Mfg Co Inc ....E 847 622-1506
South Elgin (G-19166)
Laystrom Manufacturing Co 773 342-4800
Chicago (G-5186)
Lehman Fast Tech ....G 847 742-5202
Elgin (G-8641)
Lenhardt Tool and Die Company ......D 618 462-1075
Alton (G-563)
Lens Lenticlear Lenticular ....F 630 467-0900
Elk Grove Village (G-9093)
Lew-El Tool & Manufacturing Co .....F 773 804-1133
Chicago (G-5212)
Libco Industries Inc 815 623-7677
Roscoe (G-17912)
Line Group Inc 847 593-6810
Arlington Heights (G-769)
Lion Tool & Die Co ....F 847 658-8898
Algonquin (G-377)
Lmt Usa Inc ....G 630 969-5412
Waukegan (G-20462)
Lorette Dies Inc ....G 630 279-9682
Elmhurst (G-9393)
Lovejoy Industries Inc 859 873-6828
Northbrook (G-15421)
Lv Ventures Inc ....F 312 993-1800
Chicago (G-5289)
Lv Ventures Inc ....E 312 993-1758
Chicago (G-5290)
M S Tool & Engineering ....F 630 876-3437
West Chicago (G-20610)
M Ward Manufacturing Co Inc ....E 847 864-4786
Evanston (G-9548)
M-1 Tool Works Inc ....E 815 344-1275
McHenry (G-13761)
Magic Mold Removal ....G 630 486-0912
Aurora (G-1125)
Major Die & Engineering Co ....F 630 773-3444
Itasca (G-11696)
▲ Makray Manufacturing Company ..E 708 456-7100
Norridge (G-15240)
Manor Tool and Mfg Co ....D 847 678-2020
Schiller Park (G-18820)
Manufcture Design Innvation Inc ....G 773 526-7773
West Chicago (G-20611)
Marathon Cutting Die Inc 847 398-5165
Wheeling (G-20938)
Marengo Tool & Die Works Inc ....E 815 568-7411
Marengo (G-13489)
Marshall Mold Inc ....G 630 582-1800
Glendale Heights (G-10473)
Master Tech Tool Inc ....G 815 363-4001
McHenry (G-13764)
Matrix Plastic Products Inc ....D 630 595-6144
Wood Dale (G-21214)
Mbs Manufacturing ....G 630 227-0300
Franklin Park (G-9986)
McCurdy Tool & Machining Co ....D 815 765-2117
Caledonia (G-2770)
Melrose Mold & Machine Co Inc ......G 847 233-9970
Franklin Park (G-9991)
▲ Mennies Machine Company ....C 815 339-2226
Mark (G-13546)
Met Plastics ....G 847 228-5070
Elk Grove Village (G-9115)
Meta-Meg Tool Corporation ....G 847 742-3600
Elgin (G-8656)
Method Molds Inc ....G 815 877-0191
Loves Park (G-13236)
Metro Tool Company ....F 847 673-6790
Skokie (G-18988)
Micro Mold Corporation ....G 630 628-0777
Addison (G-206)
Micro Punch & Die Co ....F 815 874-5544
Rockford (G-17521)
Micron Engineering Co ....G 815 455-2888
Crystal Lake (G-7228)
Mid-City Die & Mold Corp ....G 773 278-4844
Chicago (G-5430)
Mid-States Forging Die-Tool ....G 815 226-2313
Rockford (G-17524)
Midwest Machine Tool Inc ....G 815 427-8665
Saint Anne (G-18136)
Midwest Press Brake Dies Inc ....F 708 598-3860
Bridgeview (G-2366)
Mik Tool & Die Co Inc ....G 847 487-4311
Wauconda (G-20377)
Milans Machining & Mfg Co Inc ....D 708 780-6600
Cicero (G-6867)
Millennium Mold & Tool ....G 847 438-5600
Lake Zurich (G-12433)

35 INDUSTRIAL AND COMMERCIAL MACHINERY AND COMPUTER EQUIPMENT

Company	Code	Phone
Miller Midwestern Die Co — Woodstock (G-21412)	G	815 338-6686
Mold Express Inc — Chicago (G-5486)	G	773 766-0874
Monarch Manufacturing — Lombard (G-13103)	G	630 519-4580
Monarch Tool & Die Co — Elmhurst (G-9403)	E	630 530-8886
Mp Mold Inc — Addison (G-224)	G	630 613-8086
Mt Vernon Mold Works Inc — Mount Vernon (G-14629)	E	618 242-6040
Mushro Machine & Tool Co — Streator (G-19617)	F	815 672-5848
National Component Sales Inc — Arlington Heights (G-780)	F	847 439-0333
Natura Products Inc — Northbrook (G-15439)	F	847 509-5835
Nemeth Tool Inc — Wood Dale (G-21220)	G	630 595-0409
Newko Tool & Engineering Co — Palatine (G-16142)	E	847 359-1670
▲ Nicholas Machine & Tool Inc — Rosemont (G-18038)	G	847 298-2035
North America O M C G Inc — Bensenville (G-1858)	G	630 860-1016
Northern Illinois Mold Corp — Dundee (G-8130)	F	847 669-2100
Octavia Tool & Gage Company — Elk Grove Village (G-9159)	G	847 913-9233
Odm Tool & Mfg Co Inc — Hodgkins (G-11391)	D	708 485-6130
Odom Tool and Technology Inc — Sycamore (G-19726)	G	815 895-8545
Ontario Die USA — Batavia (G-1401)	F	630 761-6562
Oostman Fabricating & Wldg Inc — Westmont (G-20763)	F	630 241-1315
P & L Tool & Manufacturing Co — Steger (G-19491)	G	708 754-4777
Panzer Tool Corp — Lombard (G-13116)	G	630 519-5214
Park Products Inc — Addison (G-233)	G	630 543-2474
Parker Tool & Die Co — Mundelein (G-14723)	G	847 566-2229
Parting Line Tool Inc — Huntley (G-11558)	F	847 669-0331
Partners Manufacturing Inc — Schaumburg (G-18668)	E	847 352-1080
PDQ Tool & Stamping Co — Dolton (G-7938)	E	708 841-3000
Pecora Tool & Die Co Inc — Schaumburg (G-18671)	G	847 524-1275
Pelco Tool & Mold Inc — Glendale Heights (G-10483)	E	630 871-4410
Perfect Mold Inc — Addison (G-236)	G	630 785-6105
Performance Design Inc — Lake Zurich (G-12443)	G	847 719-1535
▲ Performance Stamping Co Inc — Carpentersville (G-3112)	E	847 426-2233
▲ Phoenix Tool Corp — Elk Grove Village (G-9178)	F	847 956-1886
Plastic Products Company Inc — Moline (G-14167)	C	309 762-6532
Plaza Tool & Mold Co — Wheeling (G-20961)	G	847 537-2320
▲ PM Mold Company — Schaumburg (G-18680)	G	847 923-5400
Pontiac Engraving — Bensenville (G-1870)	G	630 834-4424
▲ Power House Tool Inc — Joliet (G-11915)	E	815 727-6301
Precise Rotary Die Inc — Schiller Park (G-18834)	E	847 678-0001
Precision Engineering & Dev Co — Villa Park (G-20165)	E	630 834-5956
Precision Header Tooling Inc — Rockford (G-17557)	F	815 874-9116
Precision Process Corp — Elk Grove Village (G-9192)	E	847 640-9820
Precision Resource Inc — Vernon Hills (G-20083)	C	847 383-1300
Precision Tool & Die Company — Mount Zion (G-14649)	F	217 864-3471
Pro Built Tool & Mold Inc — Plainfield (G-16707)	G	815 436-9088
Pro-Mold Incorporated — Roselle (G-17975)	D	630 893-3594
Pro-Tech Metal Specialties Inc — Elmhurst (G-9412)	E	630 279-7094
Procraft Engraving Inc — Skokie (G-19013)	G	847 673-1500
Production Fabg & Stamping Inc — S Chicago Hts (G-18126)	F	708 755-5468
Prototype & Production Co — Wheeling (G-20967)	E	847 419-1553
Ps3 Tool Mold & Assembly LLC — Saint Charles (G-18253)	D	630 802-9462
Quad City Engineering Company — East Moline (G-8238)	E	309 755-9762
Qualitek Manufacturing Inc — Gurnee (G-10920)	E	847 336-7570
Quality Tool & Machine Inc — Chicago (G-5931)	G	773 721-8655
R & R Machining Inc — Benld (G-1718)	G	217 835-4579
R M Tool & Manufacturing Co — Elgin (G-8713)	G	847 888-0433
R-K Press Brake Dies Inc — Chicago (G-5955)	F	708 371-1756
◆ Raco Steel Company — Markham (G-13550)	E	708 339-2958
Radius Machine & Tool Inc — Gurnee (G-10922)	F	847 662-7690
Rajner Quality Machine Works — Wheeling (G-20968)	G	847 394-8999
Ralph Cody Gravrok — Addison (G-266)	G	630 628-9570
▲ RAO Design International Inc — Morton Grove (G-14437)	G	847 671-6182
Rapid Manufacturing Inc — Algonquin (G-386)	G	847 458-0888
Ravco Incorporated — Joliet (G-11923)	G	815 725-9095
Ray Tool & Engineering Inc — Saint Charles (G-18260)	E	630 587-0000
Redeen Engraving Inc — Elk Grove Village (G-9216)	G	847 593-6500
Reliable Die Service Inc — Bedford Park (G-1498)	F	708 458-5155
Relyon Metal Products Co — Elgin (G-8719)	G	847 679-1510
Republic Drill — Melrose Park (G-13908)	F	708 865-7666
Resinite Corporation — Wheeling (G-20973)	C	847 537-4250
Reynolds Manufacturing Company — Milan (G-14025)	E	309 787-8600
Rijon Manufacturing Company — Blue Island (G-2136)	F	708 388-2295
Risk Never Die Inc — Chicago (G-6035)	G	708 240-4194
▲ Rj Stuckel Co Inc — Elk Grove Village (G-9218)	G	800 789-7220
Rock Valley Die Sinking Inc — Rockford (G-17584)	F	815 874-8560
Rockford Carbide Die & Tool — Rockford (G-17590)	G	815 394-0645
Rockford Tool and Mfg Co — Rockford (G-17607)	F	815 398-5876
Rockford Toolcraft Inc — Rockford (G-17608)	G	815 398-5507
Rockford Toolcraft Inc — Rockford (G-17609)	G	815 398-5507
Rogus Tool Inc — Des Plaines (G-7838)	G	847 824-5939
Roscoe Tool & Manufacturing — Roscoe (G-17929)	E	815 633-8808
Roto-Die Company Inc — Lombard (G-13125)	G	630 932-8605
▲ Royal Die & Stamping Co Inc — Carol Stream (G-3060)	C	630 766-2685
Schwarz Bros Manufacturing Co — Galesburg (G-10220)	G	309 342-5814
Select Tool & Die Inc — Bartlett (G-1308)	G	630 372-0300
Select Tool & Die Inc — Roselle (G-17986)	G	630 980-8458
Serv-All Die & Tool Company — Crystal Lake (G-7263)	D	815 459-2900
Service Machine Jobs — Rockford (G-17626)	G	815 986-3033
Shelby Tool & Die Inc — Shelbyville (G-18886)	G	217 774-2189
Shup Tool & Machine Co — Granite City (G-10737)	E	618 931-2596
Sieber Tooling Solutions Inc — Carol Stream (G-3069)	G	630 462-9370
Sierra Manufacturing Corp — Addison (G-288)	G	630 458-8830
Soldy Manufacturing Inc — Schiller Park (G-18844)	D	847 671-3396
Sonoco Prtective Solutions Inc — Dekalb (G-7703)	E	815 787-5244
Sopher Design & Manufacturing — East Peoria (G-8291)	G	309 699-6419
Southern Mold Finishing Inc — Johnston City (G-11813)	F	618 983-5049
▲ Southern Steel and Wire Inc — Highland (G-11240)	G	618 654-2161
Spannagel Tool & Die — Downers Grove (G-8098)	E	630 969-7575
Special Fastener Operations — Belvidere (G-1701)	G	815 544-6449
Specific Press Brake Dies Inc — Mokena (G-14116)	F	708 478-1776
▲ Speco Inc — Schiller Park (G-18845)	G	847 678-4240
Spectron Manufacturing — Bloomingdale (G-2015)	G	720 879-7605
Standard Machine & Tool Corp — Moline (G-14179)	F	309 762-6431
Standex International Corp — Carol Stream (G-3076)	E	630 588-0400
Stanick Tool Manufacturing Co — Lake Zurich (G-12461)	G	847 726-7090
▲ Star Die Molding Inc — Elk Grove Village (G-9255)	D	847 766-7952
Sterling Die Inc — Glendale Heights (G-10500)	G	216 267-1300
Sterling Tool & Manufacturing — Barrington (G-1245)	G	847 304-1800
Stumpfoll Tool & Mfg — Chicago (G-6258)	G	312 733-2632
Summit Tooling Inc — McHenry (G-13798)	F	815 385-7500
Sure-Way Die Designs Inc — Westmont (G-20774)	G	630 323-0370
Surfacetec Corp — Franklin Park (G-10058)	F	630 521-0001
▲ Suruga USA Corp — Schaumburg (G-18732)	E	630 628-0989
▲ Sws Industries Inc — Woodstock (G-21438)	E	904 482-0091
Synergetic Holdings LLC — Peoria (G-16533)	F	309 673-2437
▲ T & H Lemont Inc — Countryside (G-7074)	D	708 482-1800
T & K Tool & Manufacturing Co — Woodstock (G-21439)	G	815 338-0954
T M T Industries Inc — Rochelle (G-17161)	E	815 562-0111
Tapco USA Inc — Loves Park (G-13271)	G	815 877-4039
Tauber Brothers Tool & Die Co — Chicago (G-6330)	E	708 867-9100
Taylor Design Inc — Roscoe (G-17936)	G	815 389-3991
Technical Tool Enterprise — Addison (G-304)	G	630 893-3390
Technique Engineering Inc — Waukegan (G-20501)	F	847 816-1870
Tella Tool & Mfg Co — Lombard (G-13142)	C	630 495-0545
Three Star Mfg Co Inc — Wauconda (G-20399)	G	847 526-2222
Titan Tool Company Inc — Franklin Park (G-10061)	G	847 671-0045
Top Notch Tool & Supply Inc — Cherry Valley (G-3447)	G	815 633-6295
Tower Tool & Engineering Inc — Machesney Park (G-13378)	F	815 654-1115
Treasure Keeper Inc — Batavia (G-1432)	G	630 761-1500
Trend Technologies LLC — Elk Grove Village (G-9282)	C	847 640-2382
Tri-Par Die and Mold Corp — South Elgin (G-19177)	E	630 232-8800
Tri-Star Engineering Inc — Elk Grove Village (G-9285)	E	847 595-3377
Tri-State Tool & Design Inc — Camp Point (G-2812)	G	217 696-2477
▲ Triangle Dies and Supplies Inc — Batavia (G-1474)	D	630 454-3200
Triumph Twist Drill Co Inc — Crystal Lake (G-7286)	B	815 459-6250
Turbo Tool & Mold Co — Broadview (G-2473)	G	708 615-1730

Employee Codes: A=Over 500 employees, B=251-500
C=101-250, D=51-100, E=20-50, F=10-19, G=3-9

35 INDUSTRIAL AND COMMERCIAL MACHINERY AND COMPUTER EQUIPMENT SIC SECTION

Ultra Polishing Inc ....E 630 635-2926
Schaumburg *(G-18762)*
Ultra Specialty Holdings Inc ....E 847 437-8110
Elk Grove Village *(G-9293)*
Ultra-Metric Tool Co ....F 773 281-4200
Chicago *(G-6459)*
Unified Tool Die & Mfg Co Inc ....F 847 678-3773
Schiller Park *(G-18848)*
United Craftsmen Ltd ....F 815 626-7802
Sterling *(G-19539)*
United Skilled Inc ....G 815 874-9696
Rockford *(G-17671)*
United Tool and Engineering Co ....D 815 389-3021
South Beloit *(G-19118)*
Urway Design and Manufacturing ....G 847 674-7464
Skokie *(G-19051)*
Vanart Engineering Company ....E 847 678-6255
Franklin Park *(G-10074)*
Vega Molded Products Inc ....G 847 428-7761
Gilberts *(G-10374)*
▲ **Vhd Inc** ....E 815 544-2169
Belvidere *(G-1708)*
Vicma Tool Co ....G 847 541-0177
Wheeling *(G-21010)*
Voco Tool & Mfg Inc ....G 708 771-3800
Forest Park *(G-9728)*
▲ **Voestlpine Precision Strip LLC** ....D 847 227-5272
Elk Grove Village *(G-9306)*
Voss Pattern Works Inc ....G 618 233-4242
Belleville *(G-1609)*
▲ **Wagner Midwest Die Supply Inc** ....G 630 782-6230
Elmhurst *(G-9444)*
Walern Form Grinding Inc ....G 815 874-7000
Rockford *(G-17676)*
Wand Enterprises Inc ....F 847 433-0231
Highland Park *(G-11304)*
Wand Tool Enterprise ....G 847 433-0231
Highland Park *(G-11305)*
Wapro Inc ....G 888 927-8677
Chicago *(G-6586)*
Wardzala Industries Inc ....F 847 288-9909
Franklin Park *(G-10083)*
Wauconda Tool & Engrg LLC ....D 847 658-4588
Algonquin *(G-394)*
West End Tool & Die Inc ....G 815 462-3040
New Lenox *(G-15068)*
Westwood Machine & Tool Co ....F 815 626-5090
Sterling *(G-19542)*
◆ **Whitney Roper LLC** ....D 815 962-3011
Rockford *(G-17683)*
▲ **Whitney Roper Rockford Inc** ....D 815 962-3011
Rockford *(G-17684)*
William J Kline & Co Inc ....F 815 338-2055
Woodstock *(G-21448)*
Windy City Cutting Die Inc ....E 630 521-9410
Bensenville *(G-1913)*
Wirco Inc ....D 217 398-3200
Champaign *(G-3371)*
Wireformers Inc ....E 847 718-1920
Mount Prospect *(G-14582)*
Wisniwski Rchard Stl Rule Dies ....G 773 282-1144
Chicago *(G-6651)*
Witte Kendel Die & Mold ....G 815 233-9270
Freeport *(G-10150)*
WJ Die Mold Inc ....F 847 895-6561
Schaumburg *(G-18775)*
World Wide Rotary Die ....G 630 521-9410
Bensenville *(G-1915)*
Wright Tool & Die Inc ....F 815 669-2020
McHenry *(G-13810)*
Z-Tech Inc ....G 815 335-7395
Winnebago *(G-21122)*
Zender Enterprises Ltd ....G 773 282-2293
Chicago *(G-6716)*

3545 Machine Tool Access

▲ **2I Technologies LLC** ....G 312 526-3900
Chicago *(G-3465)*
A J Manufacturing Co Inc ....G 630 832-2828
Elmhurst *(G-9321)*
A R Tech & Tool Inc ....G 708 599-5745
Bridgeview *(G-2317)*
A&W Tool Inc ....G 815 653-1700
Ringwood *(G-17037)*
Abbco Inc ....E 630 595-7115
Bensenville *(G-1722)*
Accu-Cut Diamond Tool Company ....F 708 457-8800
Norridge *(G-15228)*
Accu-Grind Manufacturing Inc ....F 847 526-2700
Wauconda *(G-20327)*
▼ **Acme Industrial Company** ....C 847 428-3911
Carpentersville *(G-3090)*
Active Grinding & Mfg Co ....F 708 344-0510
Broadview *(G-2414)*
◆ **Adjustable Clamp Company** ....C 312 666-0640
Chicago *(G-3546)*
ADS LLC ....D 256 430-3366
Burr Ridge *(G-2650)*
Advanced Machine Co Inc ....G 773 545-9790
Chicago *(G-3565)*
▲ **Advent Tool & Mfg Inc** ....F 847 395-9707
Antioch *(G-594)*
Advent Tool and Mfg ....G 847 395-9707
Antioch *(G-595)*
▲ **Air Gage Company** ....C 847 695-0911
Elgin *(G-8500)*
Alcon Tool & Mfg Co Inc ....F 773 545-8742
Chicago *(G-3598)*
Alfa Mfg Industries Inc ....E 847 470-9595
Morton Grove *(G-14388)*
Alliance Tool & Manufacturing ....F 708 345-5444
Maywood *(G-13660)*
Allkut Tool Incorporated ....G 815 476-9656
Wilmington *(G-21096)*
Alpha Swiss Industries Inc ....G 815 455-3031
Crystal Lake *(G-7157)*
▼ **American Machine Tools Inc** ....G 773 775-6285
Chicago *(G-3658)*
Ammentorp Tool Company Inc ....G 847 671-9290
Franklin Park *(G-9869)*
Apergy Energy Automation LLC ....E 630 541-1540
Downers Grove *(G-7952)*
Arrow Engineering Inc ....E 815 397-0862
Rockford *(G-17307)*
Assurance Technologies Inc ....F 630 550-5000
Bartlett *(G-1265)*
◆ **Atm America Corp** ....E 800 298-0030
Chicago *(G-3770)*
▲ **Auto Meter Products Inc** ....C 815 895-8141
Sycamore *(G-19702)*
Autocut Machine Company Inc ....G 815 436-1900
Elwood *(G-9460)*
▲ **Automatic Precision Inc** ....E 708 867-1116
Chicago *(G-3778)*
Balanstar Corporation ....F 773 261-5034
Elk Grove Village *(G-8856)*
Barcor Inc ....F 847 940-0750
Bannockburn *(G-1192)*
Belcar Products Inc ....G 630 462-1950
Carol Stream *(G-2946)*
◆ **Belden Tools Inc** ....E 708 344-4600
Hillside *(G-11329)*
Beloit Tool Inc ....F 815 389-2300
South Beloit *(G-19084)*
▲ **Bertsche Engineering Corp** ....F 847 537-8757
Buffalo Grove *(G-2516)*
Besly Cutting Tools Inc ....F 815 389-2231
South Beloit *(G-19085)*
Big Kser Precision Tooling Inc ....E 847 228-7660
Hoffman Estates *(G-11409)*
Blackhawk Industrial Dist Inc ....F 773 736-9600
Carol Stream *(G-2950)*
Bourn & Bourn Inc ....C 815 965-4013
Rockford *(G-17327)*
Bradley Machining Inc ....F 630 543-2875
Addison *(G-53)*
Brunner & Lay Inc ....C 847 678-3232
Bensenville *(G-1758)*
Burnex Corporation ....E 815 728-1317
Ringwood *(G-17040)*
C & C Tooling Inc ....F 630 543-5523
Addison *(G-57)*
Carbco Manufacturing Inc ....F 630 377-1410
Saint Charles *(G-18164)*
Celinco Inc ....G 815 964-2256
Rockford *(G-17340)*
Center Tool Company ....G 847 683-7559
Hampshire *(G-10966)*
◆ **Champion Chisel Works Inc** ....F 815 535-0647
Rock Falls *(G-17178)*
▲ **Chicago Hardware and Fix Co** ....C 847 455-6609
Franklin Park *(G-9905)*
Chicago Quadrill Co ....G 847 824-4196
Des Plaines *(G-7745)*
Circle Cutting Tools Inc ....G 815 398-4153
Rockford *(G-17350)*
▲ **Cjt Koolcarb Inc** ....C 630 690-5933
Carol Stream *(G-2960)*
▲ **Comet Tool Inc** ....E 847 956-0126
Elk Grove Village *(G-8902)*
Composite Cutter Tech Inc ....G 847 740-6875
Volo *(G-20198)*
Con Form Industry Inc ....F 847 278-1143
Schaumburg *(G-18483)*
Coordinate Machine Company ....E 630 894-9880
Roselle *(G-17947)*
Craftstech Inc ....E 847 758-3100
Elk Grove Village *(G-8918)*
Crippa Usa LLC ....G 630 659-7720
Geneva *(G-10264)*
Custom Cutting Tools Inc ....G 815 986-0320
Loves Park *(G-13200)*
Custom Feeder Co of Rockford ....E 815 654-2444
Loves Park *(G-13201)*
Custom Tool Inc ....F 217 465-8538
Paris *(G-16228)*
D & R Autochuck Inc ....E 815 394-1744
Rockford *(G-17364)*
D & R Ekstrom Carlson Co ....G 815 394-1744
Rockford *(G-17365)*
▲ **Damen Carbide Tool Company Inc** ....E 630 766-7875
Wood Dale *(G-21181)*
David Linderholm ....G 847 336-3755
Waukegan *(G-20434)*
Delco West LLC ....G 309 799-7543
Milan *(G-14006)*
Design Systems Inc ....E 309 263-7706
Morton *(G-14358)*
Die Specialty Co ....G 312 303-5738
La Grange Park *(G-12096)*
▲ **Dmg Mori Usa Inc** ....D 847 593-5400
Hoffman Estates *(G-11419)*
◆ **Dormer Pramet LLC** ....C 800 877-3745
Elgin *(G-8568)*
Dundick Corporation ....E 708 656-6363
Cicero *(G-6843)*
Dynacut Industries Inc ....E 630 462-1900
Carol Stream *(G-2978)*
▲ **Dynomax Inc** ....B 847 680-8833
Wheeling *(G-20883)*
Edmik Inc ....E 847 263-0460
Gurnee *(G-10874)*
EJ Cady & Company ....G 847 537-2239
Wheeling *(G-20888)*
Electro-Matic Products Co ....F 773 235-4010
Chicago *(G-4477)*
Emtech Machining & Grinding ....G 815 338-1580
Woodstock *(G-21385)*
Engineering Products Company ....G 815 436-9055
Plainfield *(G-16659)*
▲ **Engis Corporation** ....C 847 808-9400
Wheeling *(G-20891)*
◆ **Estwing Manufacturing Co Inc** ....B 815 397-9521
Rockford *(G-17402)*
▲ **Everede Tool Company LLC** ....D 623 414-4800
West Chicago *(G-20575)*
Everede Tool Company LLC ....E 773 467-4200
West Chicago *(G-20576)*
◆ **Federal Signal Corporation** ....D 630 954-2000
Oak Brook *(G-15618)*
Forster Products Inc ....E 815 493-6360
Lanark *(G-12481)*
Fox Machine & Tool Inc ....G 847 357-1845
Elk Grove Village *(G-9006)*
Fulton Corporation ....D 815 589-3211
Fulton *(G-10152)*
G & S Manufacturing Inc ....F 847 674-7666
Bannockburn *(G-1201)*
Gage Assembly Co ....D 847 679-5180
Lincolnwood *(G-12820)*
▲ **Galaxy Industries Inc** ....D 847 639-8580
Cary *(G-3162)*
▲ **Galaxy Sourcing Inc** ....G 630 532-5003
Addison *(G-133)*
▲ **Gator Products Inc** ....G 847 836-0581
Gilberts *(G-10355)*
Gaylee Corporation Saws ....G 586 803-1100
South Beloit *(G-19094)*
General Cutng Tl Svc & Mfg Inc ....F 847 677-8770
Lincolnwood *(G-12821)*
Glen Products ....G 847 998-1361
Glenview *(G-10550)*
Greenlee Diamond Tool Co ....E 866 451-3316
Elk Grove Village *(G-9023)*
Grove Industrial ....G 815 385-4800
Johnsburg *(G-11804)*
Guide Line Industries Inc ....F 815 777-3722
Scales Mound *(G-18420)*
H R Slater Co Inc ....F 312 666-1855
Chicago *(G-4760)*

SIC SECTION 35 INDUSTRIAL AND COMMERCIAL MACHINERY AND COMPUTER EQUIPMENT

▲ **Haimer Usa LLC** G 630 833-1500
Villa Park *(G-20150)*
▲ **Hallmark Industries Inc** F 847 301-8050
Streamwood *(G-19577)*
▲ **Harig Manufacturing Corp** E 847 647-9500
Skokie *(G-18964)*
Harris Precision Tools Inc G 708 422-5808
Chicago Ridge *(G-6797)*
Hartland Cutting Tools Inc F 847 639-9400
Cary *(G-3166)*
▲ **Heidenhain Holding Inc** G 716 661-1700
Schaumburg *(G-18546)*
▲ **Henry Technologies Inc** G 217 483-2406
Chatham *(G-3421)*
Hg-Farley Holdings LLC F 815 874-1400
Rockford *(G-17449)*
▲ **Hg-Farley Laserlab USA Inc** G 815 874-1400
Rockford *(G-17450)*
Hilti Inc F 847 364-9818
Elmhurst *(G-9372)*
◆ **Holden Industries Inc** F 847 940-1500
Deerfield *(G-7616)*
Ideal Industries Inc C 815 895-1108
Sycamore *(G-19715)*
Illinois Broaching Company E 847 678-3080
Schiller Park *(G-18815)*
Illinois Carbide Tool Co Inc F 847 244-1110
Waukegan *(G-20447)*
Imprex International Inc G 847 364-4930
Arlington Heights *(G-756)*
▲ **Industrial Diamond Products** E 847 272-7840
Northbrook *(G-15405)*
Industrial Instrument Svc Corp G 773 581-3355
Chicago *(G-4907)*
▲ **Infinity Tool Mfg LLC** G 618 439-4042
Benton *(G-1928)*
▲ **Ingersoll Cutting Tool Company** B 815 387-6600
Rockford *(G-17461)*
◆ **Ingersoll Machine Tools Inc** C 815 987-6000
Rockford *(G-17462)*
Inland Tool Company E 217 792-3206
Mount Pulaski *(G-14588)*
▲ **Intech Industries Inc** F 847 487-5599
Wauconda *(G-20361)*
Irwin Industrial Tool Company C 815 235-4171
Freeport *(G-10121)*
Ivan Schwenker G 630 543-7798
Addison *(G-156)*
▲ **J & J Carbide & Tool Inc** E 708 489-0300
Alsip *(G-459)*
J H Benedict Co Inc D 309 694-3111
East Peoria *(G-8270)*
Jamco Tool & Cams Inc F 847 678-0280
Franklin Park *(G-9972)*
▲ **Jerhen Industries Inc** D 815 397-0400
Rockford *(G-17473)*
Johnson Pattern & Mch Works E 815 433-2775
Ottawa *(G-16057)*
▲ **Jrm International Inc** G 815 282-9330
Loves Park *(G-13227)*
Jupiter Machine Tool Inc G 309 297-1920
Galesburg *(G-10204)*
K Systems Corporation G 708 449-0400
Hillside *(G-11343)*
K-C Tool Co G 630 983-5960
Naperville *(G-14857)*
Kaydon Acquisition Xii Inc E 217 443-3592
Danville *(G-7354)*
Kennametal Inc F 309 578-1888
Mossville *(G-14460)*
Kenyeri Consulting LLC G 630 920-3497
Downers Grove *(G-8039)*
Keonix Corporation G 847 259-9430
Arlington Heights *(G-765)*
▲ **Keson Industries Inc** E 630 820-4200
Aurora *(G-993)*
Kile Machine & Tool Inc G 217 446-8616
Danville *(G-7357)*
▲ **Kitagawa Usa Inc** E 847 310-8198
Schaumburg *(G-18587)*
▲ **Kitagawa-Northtech Inc** E 847 310-8787
Schaumburg *(G-18588)*
◆ **Kitamura Machinery USA Inc** F 847 520-7755
Wheeling *(G-20924)*
Kmp Tool Grinding Inc G 847 205-9640
Northbrook *(G-15413)*
L & M Screw Machine Products F 630 801-0455
Montgomery *(G-14253)*
L S Starrett Co G 847 816-9999
Vernon Hills *(G-20070)*

▲ **LFA Industries Inc** G 630 762-7391
Saint Charles *(G-18227)*
▲ **Lmt Onsrud LP** C 847 362-1560
Waukegan *(G-20461)*
Lmt Usa Inc G 630 969-5412
Waukegan *(G-20462)*
Logan Actuator Co G 815 943-9500
Harvard *(G-11059)*
▲ **Logan Graphic Products Inc** D 847 526-5515
Wauconda *(G-20369)*
Machine Tool Acc & Mfg Co G 773 489-0903
Chicago *(G-5309)*
Matheu Tool Works Inc G 773 327-9274
Chicago *(G-5365)*
Meinhardt Diamond Tool Co G 773 267-3260
Chicago *(G-5388)*
Method Molds Inc G 815 877-0191
Loves Park *(G-13236)*
Metrom LLC (not Llc) G 847 847-7233
Lake Zurich *(G-12432)*
Mid-West Feeder Inc E 815 544-2994
Belvidere *(G-1686)*
▲ **Midland Manufacturing Corp** C 847 677-0333
Skokie *(G-18990)*
Midstates Cutting Tools Inc E 630 595-0700
Bensenville *(G-1852)*
Midwest Machine Tool Inc G 815 427-8665
Saint Anne *(G-18136)*
▲ **Mincon Inc** E 618 435-3404
Benton *(G-1932)*
Mitsubishi Materials USA Corp F 847 519-1601
Schaumburg *(G-18632)*
Miyanohitec Machinery Inc G 847 382-2794
Barrington *(G-1230)*
Modineer P-K Tool LLC E 773 235-4700
Chicago *(G-5483)*
Moldtronics Inc E 630 968-7000
Downers Grove *(G-8058)*
Natc LLC F 815 389-2300
South Beloit *(G-19104)*
National Bushing & Mfg G 847 847-1553
Lake Zurich *(G-12438)*
◆ **New World Products Inc** G 630 690-5625
Carol Stream *(G-3039)*
▲ **NNt Enterprises Incorporated** E 630 875-9600
Itasca *(G-11712)*
▼ **Obsidian Mfg Inds Inc** F 815 962-8700
Rockford *(G-17542)*
OSG Usa Inc E 800 837-2223
Saint Charles *(G-18239)*
OSG Usa Inc C 630 274-2100
Bensenville *(G-1864)*
P K Neuses Incorporated G 847 253-6555
Rolling Meadows *(G-17758)*
▲ **Pace Machinery Group Inc** F 630 377-1750
Wasco *(G-20261)*
Park Products Inc G 630 543-2474
Addison *(G-233)*
PDQ Machine Inc G 815 282-7575
Machesney Park *(G-13363)*
▲ **Pfeifer Industries LLC** G 630 596-9000
Naperville *(G-14897)*
Pixel Pushers Incorporated G 847 550-6560
Lake Zurich *(G-12444)*
Pontiac Engraving G 630 834-4424
Bensenville *(G-1870)*
Porcelain Enamel Finishers G 312 808-1560
Chicago *(G-5845)*
◆ **Precision Brand Products Inc** E 630 969-7200
Downers Grove *(G-8082)*
◆ **Precision Gage Company** F 630 655-2121
Burr Ridge *(G-2714)*
Precision Header Tooling Inc F 815 874-9116
Rockford *(G-17557)*
Precision Masters Inc E 815 397-3894
Rockford *(G-17558)*
Precision Tool & Die Company F 217 864-3371
Mount Zion *(G-14649)*
▲ **Progrssive Cmponents Intl Corp** D 847 487-1000
Wauconda *(G-20385)*
▼ **Proto-Cutter Inc** F 815 232-2300
Freeport *(G-10134)*
Prototype & Production Co E 847 419-1553
Wheeling *(G-20967)*
Quality Tech Tool Inc E 847 690-9643
Bensenville *(G-1880)*
Rdh Inc of Rockford F 815 874-9421
Rockford *(G-17568)*
Regal Beloit Corporation C 844 527-8392
Roscoe *(G-17923)*

▲ **Regal Cutting Tools Inc** C 815 389-3461
Roscoe *(G-17924)*
▲ **Reichel Hardware Company Inc** G 630 762-7394
Saint Charles *(G-18261)*
Reino Tool & Manufacturing Co F 773 588-5800
Chicago *(G-6005)*
Retondo Enterprises Inc G 630 837-8130
Streamwood *(G-19593)*
Rockford Jobbing Service Inc G 815 398-8661
Rockford *(G-17596)*
Rockform Tooling & Machinery G 815 398-7650
Rockford *(G-17611)*
▲ **Roll McHning Tech Slutions Inc** E 815 372-9100
Romeoville *(G-17870)*
Roll Rite Inc G 815 645-8600
Davis Junction *(G-7426)*
Roscoe Tool & Manufacturing E 815 633-8808
Roscoe *(G-17929)*
Rsvp Tooling Inc G 815 725-3310
Joliet *(G-11929)*
▲ **Ryeson Corporation** D 847 455-8677
Carol Stream *(G-3061)*
S & J Industrial Supply Corp F 708 339-1708
South Holland *(G-19242)*
▲ **S & W Manufacturing Co Inc** E 630 595-5044
Bensenville *(G-1888)*
S Vs Industries Inc G 630 408-1083
Hoffman Estates *(G-11453)*
Sacco-Camex Inc G 630 595-8090
Franklin Park *(G-10040)*
Saint-Gobain Abrasives Inc C 630 868-8060
Carol Stream *(G-3063)*
▲ **Sandtech Inc** F 847 470-9595
Morton Grove *(G-14439)*
Schaefer Technologies LLC G 630 406-9377
Batavia *(G-1413)*
▲ **Sensible Products Inc** G 773 774-7400
Chicago *(G-6135)*
▲ **Shape-Master Tool Co** E 815 522-6186
Kirkland *(G-12065)*
Shelby Tool & Die Inc G 217 774-2189
Shelbyville *(G-18886)*
▲ **Sollami Company** E 618 988-1521
Herrin *(G-11179)*
▲ **Spie Tool Co** E 847 891-6556
Schaumburg *(G-18724)*
Star Su Fellows Cutter LLC D 847 649-1450
Hoffman Estates *(G-11462)*
Stuhr Manufacturing Co F 815 398-2460
Rockford *(G-17648)*
▲ **SWB Inc** G 847 438-1800
Lake Zurich *(G-12462)*
Tag Sales Co Inc G 630 990-3434
Hinsdale *(G-11381)*
Tag Tool Services Incorporated E 309 694-2400
East Peoria *(G-8292)*
Tapco Cutting Tools Inc G 815 877-4039
Loves Park *(G-13270)*
Tapco USA Inc G 815 877-4039
Loves Park *(G-13271)*
Team Cnc Inc G 630 377-2723
Saint Charles *(G-18286)*
Technical Tool Enterprise G 630 893-3390
Addison *(G-304)*
Thermal-Tech Systems Inc E 630 639-5115
West Chicago *(G-20651)*
Thermoplastec Inc F 815 873-9288
Rockford *(G-17658)*
▲ **Thomas Packaging LLC** F 847 392-1652
Rolling Meadows *(G-17779)*
Thomas-Zientz Group Inc G 847 395-2363
Antioch *(G-637)*
Thread & Gage Co Inc G 815 675-2305
Spring Grove *(G-19302)*
Tool Engrg Consulting Mfg LLC G 815 316-2304
Rockford *(G-17666)*
Toolmasters LLC E 815 968-0961
Rockford *(G-17667)*
Toolmasters LLC F 815 645-2224
Stillman Valley *(G-19547)*
Top Notch Tool & Supply Inc G 815 633-6295
Cherry Valley *(G-3447)*
▲ **Tornos Technologies US Corp** G 630 812-2040
Des Plaines *(G-7857)*
Tox- Pressotechnik LLC G 630 447-4600
Warrenville *(G-20254)*
Tri-Star Engineering Inc E 847 595-3377
Elk Grove Village *(G-9285)*
Triad Cutting Tools Svc & Mfg G 847 352-0459
Schaumburg *(G-18756)*

SIC

Employee Codes: A=Over 500 employees, B=251-500
C=101-250, D=51-100, E=20-50, F=10-19, G=3-9

2020 Harris Illinois
Industrial Directory

959

Triumph Twist Drill Co Inc ....B 815 459-6250
Crystal Lake *(G-7286)*
▲ **Tru-Cut Inc** ....D 847 639-2090
Cary *(G-3195)*
Universal Broaching Inc ....F 847 228-1440
Elk Grove Village *(G-9298)*
Universal Feeder Inc ....G 815 633-0752
Machesney Park *(G-13382)*
Vanguard Tool & Engineering Co ....E 847 981-9595
Mount Prospect *(G-14580)*
▲ **Vhd Inc** ....E 815 544-2169
Belvidere *(G-1708)*
Wenco Manufacturing Co Inc ....E 630 377-7474
Elgin *(G-8781)*
West Precision Tool Inc ....F 630 766-8304
Bensenville *(G-1912)*
Willow Farm Products Inc ....G 630 430-7491
Lemont *(G-12595)*
Wozniak Industries Inc ....C 708 458-1220
Bedford Park *(G-1515)*
Wunderlich Diamond Tool Corp ....F 847 437-9904
Elk Grove Village *(G-9314)*
Yana House ....G 773 874-7120
Chicago *(G-6697)*
Z-Patch Inc ....E 618 529-2431
Carbondale *(G-2866)*

3546 Power Hand Tools

A J Horne Inc ....G 630 231-8686
West Chicago *(G-20530)*
▲ **Ajax Tool Works Inc** ....D 847 455-5420
Franklin Park *(G-9862)*
Allegion S&S Holding Co Inc ....C 815 875-3311
Princeton *(G-16805)*
Ally Global Corporation ....G 773 822-3373
Chicago *(G-3625)*
Black & Decker Corporation ....F 630 521-1097
Addison *(G-50)*
Brunner & Lay Inc ....C 847 678-3232
Bensenville *(G-1758)*
◆ **Champion Chisel Works Inc** ....F 815 535-0647
Rock Falls *(G-17178)*
Chicago Quadrill Co ....G 847 824-4196
Des Plaines *(G-7745)*
Custom Cutting Tools Inc ....G 815 986-0320
Loves Park *(G-13200)*
▲ **Damen Carbide Tool Company Inc** ....E 630 766-7875
Wood Dale *(G-21181)*
Decatur Custom Tool Inc ....G 618 244-4078
Mount Vernon *(G-14606)*
Ed Hartwig Trucking & Excvtg ....G 309 364-3672
Henry *(G-11163)*
◆ **Estwing Manufacturing Co Inc** ....B 815 397-9521
Rockford *(G-17402)*
Federal Prison Industries ....C 309 346-8588
Pekin *(G-16333)*
▲ **Gator Products Inc** ....G 847 836-0581
Gilberts *(G-10355)*
Gentry Small Engine Repair ....G 217 849-3378
Toledo *(G-19875)*
Gibson Insurance Inc ....G 217 864-4877
Mount Zion *(G-14646)*
◆ **Greenlee Tools Inc** ....C 800 435-0786
Rockford *(G-17435)*
Groff Testing Corporation ....G 815 939-1153
Kankakee *(G-11974)*
Harris Precision Tools Inc ....G 708 422-5808
Chicago Ridge *(G-6797)*
Hopkins Saws & Karts Inc ....G 618 756-2778
Belle Rive *(G-1525)*
I T W Ramset ....G 630 825-7900
Glendale Heights *(G-10459)*
Illinois Tool Works Inc ....D 847 634-1900
Vernon Hills *(G-20063)*
Illinois Tool Works Inc ....E 847 634-1900
Vernon Hills *(G-20064)*
Industrial Instrument Svc Corp ....G 773 581-3355
Chicago *(G-4907)*
Ivan Schwenker ....G 630 543-7798
Addison *(G-156)*
K-C Tool Co ....G 630 983-5960
Naperville *(G-14857)*
Kaser Power Equipment Inc ....G 309 289-2176
Knoxville *(G-12068)*
Kevins Small Engine Repair ....G 309 897-2026
Bradford *(G-2274)*
▲ **Link Tools Intl (usa) Inc** ....G 773 549-3000
Chicago *(G-5229)*
Michaels Equipment Co ....G 618 524-8560
Metropolis *(G-13975)*
Milwaukee Electric Tool Corp ....B 847 588-3356
Niles *(G-15147)*
National Detroit Inc ....E 815 877-4041
Rockford *(G-17536)*
▲ **NNt Enterprises Incorporated** ....E 630 875-9600
Itasca *(G-11712)*
Outdoor Power Inc ....F 217 228-9890
Quincy *(G-16921)*
Owen Walker ....G 217 285-4012
Pittsfield *(G-16636)*
Peoria Midwest Equipment Inc ....G 309 454-6800
Normal *(G-15217)*
Pgi Mfg LLC ....G 815 398-0313
Rockford *(G-17551)*
▲ **Powernail Company** ....E 800 323-1653
Lake Zurich *(G-12445)*
R & S Cutterhead Mfg Co ....F 815 678-2611
Richmond *(G-17020)*
Ralph Cody Gravrok ....G 630 628-9570
Addison *(G-266)*
Rdh Inc of Rockford ....F 815 874-9421
Rockford *(G-17568)*
▲ **Rhino Tool Company** ....F 309 853-5555
Kewanee *(G-12040)*
◆ **Robert Bosch Tool Corporation** ....A 224 232-2000
Mount Prospect *(G-14566)*
▲ **Rockford Commercial Whse Inc** ....G 815 623-8400
Machesney Park *(G-13371)*
S & J Industrial Supply Corp ....F 708 339-1708
South Holland *(G-19242)*
Saws Unlimited Inc ....G 847 640-7450
Elk Grove Village *(G-9232)*
Sierra Manufacturing Corp ....G 630 458-8830
Addison *(G-288)*
▲ **Sollami Company** ....E 618 988-1521
Herrin *(G-11179)*
Stange Industrial Group ....G 847 640-8470
Elk Grove Village *(G-9253)*
Suhner Manufacturing Inc ....G 847 308-8900
Buffalo Grove *(G-2611)*
◆ **T & T Carbide Inc** ....G 618 439-7253
Logan *(G-13032)*
Tapco USA Inc ....G 815 877-4039
Loves Park *(G-13271)*
Technical Tool Enterprise ....G 630 893-3390
Addison *(G-304)*
Toolmasters LLC ....F 815 645-2224
Stillman Valley *(G-19547)*
Total Tooling Technology Inc ....F 847 437-5135
Elk Grove Village *(G-9279)*
Triumph Twist Drill Co Inc ....B 815 459-6250
Crystal Lake *(G-7286)*
▲ **Tru-Cut Inc** ....D 847 639-2090
Cary *(G-3195)*
Unicut Corporation ....G 773 525-4210
Chicago *(G-6464)*
▲ **Wallace/Haskin Corp** ....G 630 789-2882
Downers Grove *(G-8105)*
Welliver & Sons Inc ....E 815 874-2400
Rockford *(G-17679)*
◆ **Whitney Roper LLC** ....D 815 962-3011
Rockford *(G-17683)*
▲ **Whitney Roper Rockford Inc** ....D 815 962-3011
Rockford *(G-17684)*
Wodack Electric Tool Corp ....F 773 287-9866
Chicago *(G-6661)*

3547 Rolling Mill Machinery & Eqpt

Bonell Manufacturing Company ....E 708 849-1770
Riverdale *(G-17069)*
Chicago Roll Co Inc ....E 630 627-8888
Lombard *(G-13052)*
Combined Metals Chicago LLC ....F 847 683-0500
Hampshire *(G-10967)*
▲ **Fkm Usa LLC** ....F 815 469-2473
Frankfort *(G-9794)*
Frame Material Supply Inc ....G 309 362-2323
Trivoli *(G-19906)*
Lb Metals LLC ....C 708 331-2600
Harvey *(G-11091)*
▲ **Leading Edge Group Inc** ....C 815 316-3500
Rockford *(G-17492)*
▲ **Littell LLC** ....E 630 916-6662
Schaumburg *(G-18609)*
Nor Service Inc ....E 815 232-8379
Freeport *(G-10130)*
▲ **Nucor Steel Kankakee Inc** ....B 815 937-3131
Bourbonnais *(G-2266)*
Vision Pickling and Proc Inc ....F 815 264-7755
Waterman *(G-20301)*
▲ **Worth Steel and Machine Co** ....E 708 388-6300
Alsip *(G-527)*

3548 Welding Apparatus

Adams Steel Service Inc ....E 815 385-9100
McHenry *(G-13715)*
Airgas Inc ....F 773 785-3000
Chicago *(G-3588)*
Airgas Usa LLC ....E 630 231-9260
West Chicago *(G-20533)*
▲ **American Vacuum Company** ....G 847 674-8383
Niles *(G-15102)*
Associate General Labs Inc ....G 847 678-2717
Franklin Park *(G-9877)*
◆ **Automation International Inc** ....D 217 446-9500
Danville *(G-7322)*
D & G Welding Supply Company ....G 815 675-9890
Spring Grove *(G-19272)*
▲ **Electron Beam Technologies Inc** ....C 815 935-2211
Kankakee *(G-11967)*
▲ **Ezee Roll Manufacturing Co** ....G 217 339-2279
Hoopeston *(G-11508)*
Fanuc America Corporation ....E 847 898-5000
Hoffman Estates *(G-11423)*
Globaltech International LLC ....G 630 327-6909
Aurora *(G-972)*
Industrial Welder Rebuilders ....G 708 371-5688
Alsip *(G-457)*
Kriese Mfg ....G 815 748-2683
Cortland *(G-7023)*
Linz Electric Inc ....F 847 595-1473
Northbrook *(G-15419)*
▲ **Littell International Inc** ....E 630 622-4950
Schaumburg *(G-18610)*
Micro Products Company ....G 309 697-1216
Peoria *(G-16473)*
Reber Welding Service ....G 217 774-3441
Shelbyville *(G-18885)*
▲ **Sommer Products Company Inc** ....D 309 697-1216
Peoria *(G-16526)*
Spot Welding Products Inc ....F 630 238-0880
Franklin Park *(G-10051)*
Wenesco Inc ....F 773 283-3004
Addison *(G-333)*

3549 Metalworking Machinery, NEC

Accelrted Mch Design Engrg LLC ....E 815 316-6381
Rockford *(G-17290)*
Active Automation Inc ....F 847 427-8100
Elk Grove Village *(G-8806)*
Advanced Robotics Research ....G 630 544-0040
Naperville *(G-14766)*
Advantage Machining Inc ....E 630 897-1220
Aurora *(G-1042)*
Amber Engineering and Mfg Co ....D 847 595-6966
Elk Grove Village *(G-8819)*
▲ **Arcam Cad To Metal Inc** ....G 630 357-5700
Naperville *(G-14774)*
Art Technologies Inc ....G 773 557-3896
Bensenville *(G-1747)*
◆ **Ats Sortimat USA LLC** ....D 847 925-1234
Rolling Meadows *(G-17713)*
Automation Systems Inc ....E 847 671-9515
Melrose Park *(G-13828)*
Bartell Corporation ....G 847 854-3232
Algonquin *(G-367)*
◆ **Bavius Technologie Inc** ....G 847 844-3300
East Dundee *(G-8188)*
Bear Machine Tool & Die Inc ....G 815 932-4204
Bradley *(G-2277)*
Beverly Shear Mfg Corporation ....G 773 233-2063
Chicago *(G-3877)*
◆ **Black Bros Co** ....D 815 539-7451
Mendota *(G-13938)*
◆ **Braner Usa Inc** ....E 847 671-6210
Schiller Park *(G-18789)*
Burns Machine Company ....E 815 434-3131
Ottawa *(G-16044)*
▲ **C B Ferrari Incorporated** ....G 847 756-4100
Lake Barrington *(G-12143)*
C E R Machining & Tooling Ltd ....G 708 442-9614
Lyons *(G-13305)*
Connections ....F 217 553-7920
Springfield *(G-19353)*
▲ **Crl Industries Inc** ....G 847 940-3550
Deerfield *(G-7605)*
▲ **Custom Assembly Solutions Inc** ....F 847 224-5800
Schaumburg *(G-18501)*
Darda Enterprises Inc ....F 847 270-0410
Palatine *(G-16109)*

◆ **Deluxe Stitcher Company Inc**..........D....... 847 455-4400
Franklin Park *(G-9931)*
▲ **Dmtg North America LLC**..........G....... 815 637-8500
Rockford *(G-17383)*
Dooling Machine Products Inc..........G....... 618 254-0724
Hartford *(G-11034)*
▲ **Drawing Technology Inc**..........G....... 815 877-5133
Rockford *(G-17385)*
◆ **Engineered Abrasives Inc**..........E....... 662 582-4143
Alsip *(G-445)*
Falcon Technologies Inc..........G....... 847 550-1866
Lake Zurich *(G-12410)*
Gerhard Designing & Mfg Inc..........E....... 708 599-4664
Bridgeview *(G-2349)*
GMC Technologies Inc..........G....... 847 426-8618
East Dundee *(G-8197)*
◆ **Greenlee Tools Inc**..........C....... 800 435-0786
Rockford *(G-17435)*
Hansel Walter J & Assoc Inc..........G....... 815 678-6065
Richmond *(G-17014)*
Hilscher North America Inc..........F....... 630 505-5301
Lisle *(G-12898)*
Illinois Tool Works Inc..........D....... 618 997-1716
Marion *(G-13518)*
▲ **International Technologies Inc**..........G....... 847 301-9005
Schaumburg *(G-18565)*
Jardis Industries Inc..........F....... 630 773-5600
Itasca *(G-11681)*
▲ **Jerhen Industries Inc**..........D....... 815 397-0400
Rockford *(G-17473)*
Junker Inc..........G....... 630 231-3770
West Chicago *(G-20605)*
Kormex Metal Craft Inc..........E....... 630 953-8856
Lombard *(G-13093)*
Lane Tool & Mfg Co Inc..........E....... 847 622-1506
South Elgin *(G-19166)*
▲ **Lc Holdings of Delaware Inc**..........G....... 847 940-3550
Deerfield *(G-7629)*
Leggett & Platt Incorporated..........D....... 847 768-6139
Des Plaines *(G-7798)*
Lipscomb Engineering Inc..........G....... 630 231-3833
West Chicago *(G-20608)*
▲ **Littell LLC**..........E....... 630 916-6662
Schaumburg *(G-18609)*
▲ **Littell International Inc**..........E....... 630 622-4950
Schaumburg *(G-18610)*
▲ **Magnum Steel Works Inc**..........D....... 618 244-5190
Mount Vernon *(G-14622)*
Master Machine Craft Inc..........G....... 815 874-3078
Rockford *(G-17507)*
Master Manufacturing Co..........F....... 630 833-7060
Villa Park *(G-20159)*
Meadoweld Machine Inc..........G....... 815 623-3939
South Beloit *(G-19102)*
Medford Aero Arms LLC..........G....... 773 961-7686
Chicago *(G-5383)*
Mfw Services Inc..........G....... 708 522-5879
South Holland *(G-19232)*
Modineer P-K Tool LLC..........E....... 773 235-4700
Chicago *(G-5483)*
Navillus Woodworks LLC..........G....... 312 375-2680
Chicago *(G-5556)*
North America O M C G Inc..........G....... 630 860-1016
Bensenville *(G-1858)*
▲ **Omiotek Coil Spring Co**..........D....... 630 495-4056
Lombard *(G-13113)*
Performance Design Inc..........G....... 847 719-1535
Lake Zurich *(G-12443)*
Precision Tool & Die Company..........F....... 217 864-3371
Mount Zion *(G-14649)*
Prototype & Production Co..........E....... 847 419-1553
Wheeling *(G-20967)*
Qc Service Associates Inc..........E....... 309 755-6785
East Moline *(G-8237)*
▼ **R+d Custom Automation Inc**..........E....... 847 395-3330
Lake Villa *(G-12365)*
▼ **Red Bud Industries Inc**..........C....... 618 282-3801
Red Bud *(G-17000)*
Remington Industries Inc..........F....... 815 385-1987
Johnsburg *(G-11809)*
Robert Brysiewicz Incorporated..........G....... 630 289-0903
Bartlett *(G-1304)*
Rockford Systems LLC..........D....... 815 874-7891
Rockford *(G-17606)*
Schmid Tool & Engineering Corp..........E....... 630 333-1733
Villa Park *(G-20171)*
Sigmatron International Inc..........G....... 847 586-5200
Elgin *(G-8730)*
▲ **Sigmatron International Inc**..........G....... 847 956-8000
Elk Grove Village *(G-9238)*
◆ **Sortimat Technology LP**..........D....... 847 925-1234
Rolling Meadows *(G-17776)*
T & K Tool & Manufacturing Co..........G....... 815 338-0954
Woodstock *(G-21439)*
Tellenar Inc..........F....... 815 356-8044
Crystal Lake *(G-7280)*
Titan Tool Company Inc..........G....... 847 671-0045
Franklin Park *(G-10061)*
Tool Rite Industries Inc..........G....... 630 406-6161
Batavia *(G-1431)*
Ty Miles Incorporated..........E....... 708 344-5480
Westchester *(G-20716)*
Ultramatic Equipment Co..........E....... 630 543-4565
Addison *(G-322)*
Variable Operations Tech Inc..........E....... 815 479-8528
Crystal Lake *(G-7288)*
▲ **Vindee Industries Inc**..........E....... 815 469-3300
Frankfort *(G-9850)*
Wes-Tech Automtn Solutions LLC..........D....... 847 541-5070
Buffalo Grove *(G-2621)*

3552 Textile Machinery

Azul 3d Inc..........F....... 321 277-7807
Skokie *(G-18926)*
Barudan America Inc..........G....... 815 227-1359
Rockford *(G-17315)*
▼ **Birnberg Machinery Inc**..........G....... 847 673-5242
Deerfield *(G-7597)*
Cargill Incorporated..........F....... 217 872-7653
Decatur *(G-7469)*
David H Pool..........G....... 847 695-5007
Elgin *(G-8563)*
Forest Lee LLC..........G....... 312 379-0032
Chicago *(G-4618)*
◆ **Forte Automation Systems Inc**..........E....... 815 316-6247
Machesney Park *(G-13344)*
Graphic Screen Fashion Ltd..........F....... 847 695-5566
South Elgin *(G-19149)*
Initial Impressions Inc..........G....... 630 208-9399
Geneva *(G-10281)*
Initially Ewe..........G....... 708 246-7777
Western Springs *(G-20722)*
Innovo Corp..........F....... 847 616-0063
Elk Grove Village *(G-9054)*
Intecells Inc..........G....... 586 612-9811
Elgin *(G-8627)*
Lmk Technologies LLC..........D....... 815 433-1275
Ottawa *(G-16059)*
▲ **M & R Printing Equipment Inc**..........B....... 630 858-6101
Roselle *(G-17966)*
▲ **M&R Holdings Inc**..........C....... 630 858-6101
Roselle *(G-17967)*
Manufacturers Alliance Corp..........F....... 847 696-1600
Villa Park *(G-20158)*
Modern Graphic Systems Inc..........G....... 773 476-6898
Chicago *(G-5477)*
Natural Fiber Welding Inc..........G....... 309 685-3591
Peoria *(G-16482)*
On Time Decorations Inc..........F....... 708 357-6072
Cicero *(G-6869)*
Peerless..........G....... 773 294-2667
Chicago *(G-5782)*
Signature Label of Illinois..........G....... 618 283-5145
Vandalia *(G-20024)*
Summit Graphics Inc..........F....... 309 799-5100
Moline *(G-14180)*

3553 Woodworking Machinery

◆ **Black Bros Co**..........D....... 815 539-7451
Mendota *(G-13938)*
Bona Fide Corp..........G....... 847 970-8693
Wheeling *(G-20862)*
Bw Exhibits..........G....... 847 697-9224
Gilberts *(G-10352)*
Coalesse..........F....... 312 622-6269
Chicago *(G-4187)*
Constrction Sltons Chicago Inc..........G....... 630 834-1929
Villa Park *(G-20140)*
▲ **Crl Industries Inc**..........G....... 847 940-3550
Deerfield *(G-7605)*
Doll Furniture Co Inc..........G....... 309 452-2606
Normal *(G-15202)*
Elliott Aviation Arcft Sls Inc..........G....... 309 799-3183
Milan *(G-14008)*
▲ **Lc Holdings of Delaware Inc**..........G....... 847 940-3550
Deerfield *(G-7629)*
Little Creek Woodworking..........G....... 217 543-2815
Arthur *(G-866)*
Prairie State Machine LLC..........G....... 217 543-3768
Arthur *(G-877)*
SA Industries Inc..........G....... 847 730-4823
Wood Dale *(G-21237)*
▲ **Sand-Rite Manufacturing Co**..........G....... 312 997-2200
Melrose Park *(G-13912)*
Total Tooling Technology Inc..........F....... 847 437-5135
Elk Grove Village *(G-9279)*
White Oak Technology..........G....... 309 228-4201
Germantown Hills *(G-10334)*
Yazdan Essie..........G....... 847 675-7916
Lincolnwood *(G-12852)*

3554 Paper Inds Machinery

▼ **Birnberg Machinery Inc**..........G....... 847 673-5242
Deerfield *(G-7597)*
◆ **Black Bros Co**..........D....... 815 539-7451
Mendota *(G-13938)*
British Converting Solutions..........G....... 630 219-1906
Elmhurst *(G-9337)*
Emt International Inc..........G....... 630 655-4145
Westmont *(G-20741)*
▲ **Finishers Exchange**..........G....... 847 462-0533
Fox River Grove *(G-9758)*
Gt Flow Technology Inc..........G....... 815 636-9982
Roscoe *(G-17908)*
Guerrero Industries LLC..........G....... 773 968-8648
Palos Heights *(G-16187)*
Hfd Manufacturing Inc..........G....... 847 263-5050
Waukegan *(G-20446)*
◆ **Keene Technology Inc**..........D....... 815 624-8989
Machesney Park *(G-13320)*
Midwest Gold Stampers Inc..........F....... 773 775-5253
Chicago *(G-5442)*
▲ **Platit Inc**..........G....... 847 680-5270
Libertyville *(G-12697)*
Quality Converting Inc..........G....... 847 669-9094
Huntley *(G-11561)*
▲ **Quipp Inc**..........F....... 305 623-8700
Glenview *(G-10606)*
▲ **Ringwood Company**..........D....... 708 458-6000
Bedford Park *(G-1499)*
▲ **Rosenthal Manufacturing Co Inc**..........E....... 847 714-0404
Northbrook *(G-15475)*
Ultra Packaging Inc..........G....... 630 595-9820
Bensenville *(G-1905)*
▲ **United Gasket Corporation**..........D....... 708 656-3700
Cicero *(G-6885)*

3555 Printing Trades Machinery & Eqpt

▲ **2m Control Systems Inc**..........G....... 630 709-6225
West Chicago *(G-20529)*
4l Technologies Inc..........A....... 815 431-8100
Ottawa *(G-16035)*
▲ **A-Korn Roller Inc**..........D....... 773 254-5700
Chicago *(G-3494)*
Aaxis Engravers Inc..........G....... 224 629-4045
Bensenville *(G-1721)*
Accu-Chem Industries Inc..........G....... 708 344-0900
Melrose Park *(G-13820)*
▲ **Advance World Trade Inc**..........D....... 773 777-7100
Chicago *(G-3561)*
Altair Corporation..........E....... 847 634-9540
Lincolnshire *(G-12744)*
▲ **Anderson & Vreeland-Illinois**..........F....... 847 255-2110
Arlington Heights *(G-693)*
Azul 3d Inc..........F....... 321 277-7807
Skokie *(G-18926)*
▲ **Baldwin OXY-Dry Corporation**..........D....... 630 595-3651
Addison *(G-45)*
Baldwin Technology Company Inc..........C....... 618 842-2664
Fairfield *(G-9618)*
Baldwin Technology Company Inc..........C....... 618 842-2664
Arlington Heights *(G-702)*
Banner Moulded Products..........E....... 708 452-0033
River Grove *(G-17057)*
Bisco Intl Inc..........G....... 708 544-6308
Hillside *(G-11331)*
Brahman Spirit Tribe..........F....... 773 957-2828
Chicago *(G-3942)*
▼ **Bst North America Inc**..........E....... 630 833-9900
Elmhurst *(G-9338)*
C & C Printing Controls Inc..........G....... 630 810-0484
Downers Grove *(G-7961)*
C CN Chicago Corp..........G....... 847 671-3319
Addison *(G-58)*
▲ **Central Graphics Corp**..........F....... 630 759-1696
Romeoville *(G-17804)*
Certus Industries N Amer LLC..........G....... 847 217-2537
Crystal Lake *(G-7178)*
Chatham Corporation..........F....... 847 634-5506
Lincolnshire *(G-12749)*

Employee Codes: A=Over 500 employees, B=251-500
C=101-250, D=51-100, E=20-50, F=10-19, G=3-9
2020 Harris Illinois
Industrial Directory
961

SIC

Cleveland Folder Service G 847 782-5850
Gurnee (G-10864)
Color Smiths Inc E 708 562-0061
Elmhurst (G-9349)
Container Graphics Corp E 847 584-0299
Schaumburg (G-18486)
Cy-Tec Inc G 815 756-8416
Dekalb (G-7674)
▲ D & K Custom Machine Design E 847 956-4757
Elk Grove Village (G-8930)
◆ D & K Group Inc E 847 956-0160
Elk Grove Village (G-8931)
Distribution Enterprises Inc F 847 582-9276
Lake Forest (G-12243)
Dms Inc F 847 726-2828
Lake Zurich (G-12403)
◆ Domino Amjet Inc D 847 244-2501
Gurnee (G-10870)
Ebway Industries Inc E 630 860-5959
Itasca (G-11646)
Emt International Inc G 630 655-4145
Westmont (G-20741)
▲ Environmental Specialties Inc G 630 860-7070
Itasca (G-11651)
◆ Global Web Systems Inc F 630 782-9690
Elk Grove Village (G-9017)
◆ Graphic Innovators Inc E 847 718-1516
Elk Grove Village (G-9021)
H R Slater Co Inc F 312 666-1855
Chicago (G-4760)
▲ I S C America Inc G 630 616-1331
Wood Dale (G-21199)
Ilf Technologies LLC F 630 759-1776
Cicero (G-6854)
Imtran Industries Inc D 630 752-4000
Carol Stream (G-3004)
Intersol Industries Inc F 630 238-0385
Bensenville (G-1824)
▲ Jardis Industries Inc E 630 860-5959
Itasca (G-11680)
Kiwi Coders Corp E 847 541-4511
Wheeling (G-20925)
◆ Klai-Co Idntification Pdts Inc E 847 573-0375
Lake Forest (G-12270)
▲ Komori America Corporation D 847 806-9000
Rolling Meadows (G-17745)
◆ Laser Reproductions Inc E 847 410-0397
Skokie (G-18977)
Luttrell Engraving Inc E 708 489-3800
Alsip (G-470)
▲ M & R Printing Equipment Inc B 630 858-6101
Roselle (G-17966)
◆ Manroland Goss Web Systems Int E 630 796-7560
Woodridge (G-21321)
▲ Manroland Inc E 630 920-2000
Westmont (G-20757)
◆ Martin Automatic Inc C 815 654-4800
Rockford (G-17505)
Midwest Index Inc D 847 995-8425
Addison (G-210)
Milans Machining & Mfg Co Inc D 708 780-6600
Cicero (G-6867)
Mmpcu Limited G 217 355-0500
Champaign (G-3324)
Nama Graphics E LLC G 262 966-3853
Homer Glen (G-11484)
▲ Oec Graphics-Chicago LLC E 630 455-6700
Willowbrook (G-21056)
Ortman-Mccain Co G 312 666-2244
Bellwood (G-1635)
Pamarco Global Graphics Inc E 630 879-7300
Batavia (G-1403)
Pamarco Global Graphics Inc F 847 459-6000
Wheeling (G-20955)
Paw Office Machines Inc G 815 363-9780
McHenry (G-13777)
Plate and Pre-Press Management G 847 352-0462
Schaumburg (G-18676)
Polyurthane Engrg Tchnques Inc E 847 362-1820
Lake Forest (G-12292)
Precision Screen Specialties G 630 220-1361
Saint Charles (G-18250)
Premium Converting LLC G 708 510-1842
Chicago (G-5864)
Resinite Corporation C 847 537-4250
Wheeling (G-20973)
Rotation Dynamics Corporation D 773 247-5600
Chicago (G-6066)
◆ Rycoline Products LLC C 773 775-6755
Chicago (G-6081)

Saati Americas Corporation F 847 296-5090
Mount Prospect (G-14568)
Schlesinger Machinery Inc G 630 766-4074
Bensenville (G-1890)
Sharper Image Engravers Inc E 630 403-1600
Lombard (G-13129)
▲ Smart Inc G 847 464-4160
Hampshire (G-10988)
Sommers & Fahrenbach Inc F 773 478-3033
Chicago (G-6201)
Sopher Design & Manufacturing G 309 699-6419
East Peoria (G-8291)
▲ Southern Illinois McHy Co Inc D 217 868-5431
Shumway (G-18906)
Special Tool Engineering Co F 773 767-6690
Chicago (G-6212)
Stolp Gore Company G 630 904-5180
Plainfield (G-16717)
Tamarack Products Inc E 847 526-9333
Wauconda (G-20397)
▲ Technotrans America Inc E 847 227-9200
Mount Prospect (G-14575)
Tel-Comm Incorporated E 847 593-8480
Sycamore (G-19734)
◆ Thermal Care Inc C 847 966-2260
Niles (G-15180)
Vm Electronics LLC G 847 663-9310
Chicago (G-6565)
◆ Weber Marking Systems Inc B 847 364-8500
Arlington Heights (G-831)
▲ Western Printing Machinery Co E 847 678-1740
Schiller Park (G-18854)
Western Printing Machinery Co E 847 678-1740
Schiller Park (G-18855)
Wpc Machinery Corp E 630 231-7721
Arlington Heights (G-836)
Zebra Outlet F 312 416-1518
Chicago (G-6710)

3556 Food Prdts Machinery

American Metal Installers & FA G 630 993-0812
Villa Park (G-20131)
Angel Equipment LLC G 847 730-3938
Glenview (G-10524)
Bakery McHy & Fabrication LLC G 815 224-1306
Peru (G-16568)
▲ Bauermeister Inc G 901 363-0921
Vernon Hills (G-20043)
Bbq Smokewagon Inc G 309 271-7002
East Peoria (G-8252)
▼ Beacon Inc F 708 544-9900
Alsip (G-422)
▲ Bettendorf Stanford Inc D 618 548-3555
Salem (G-18331)
Cartpac Inc E 630 283-8979
Carol Stream (G-2956)
Clarios G 630 562-4602
West Chicago (G-20563)
▲ CMC America Corporation F 815 726-4337
Joliet (G-11842)
◆ Cobatco Inc F 309 676-2663
Peoria (G-16425)
Colborne Acquisition Co LLC E 847 371-0101
Lake Forest (G-12239)
Comtec Industries Ltd G 630 759-9000
Bolingbrook (G-2157)
◆ Cornelius Inc B 630 539-6850
Glendale Heights (G-10445)
Cornelius Renew Inc F 309 734-9505
Monmouth (G-14215)
Corrigan Corporation America F 800 462-6478
Gurnee (G-10866)
Cozzini LLC C 773 478-9700
Elk Grove Village (G-8917)
Crm North America LLC G 708 603-3475
Franklin Park (G-9919)
Custom Systems Inc G 314 355-4575
Granite City (G-10702)
◆ Cvp Systems LLC D 630 852-1190
Elgin (G-8561)
D W Ram Manufacturing Co E 708 633-7900
Tinley Park (G-19821)
Dons Meat Market G 309 968-6026
Manito (G-13438)
▲ Dontech Industries Inc F 847 428-8222
Gilberts (G-10353)
◆ Dover Prtg Identification Inc D 630 541-1540
Downers Grove (G-7992)
▲ E-Quip Manufacturing Co E 815 464-0053
Frankfort (G-9790)

◆ Eirich Machines Inc D 847 336-2444
Gurnee (G-10875)
Entech Fabrications Inc G 708 597-5568
Posen (G-16794)
F & S Engraving Inc E 847 870-8400
Mount Prospect (G-14527)
Felste Co Inc G 217 283-4884
Hoopeston (G-11509)
◆ Food Equipment Technologies Co C 847 719-3000
Lake Zurich (G-12412)
Formax Inc E 708 479-3000
Mokena (G-14082)
▲ G K Enterprises Inc G 708 587-2150
Monee (G-14201)
Gilberts Craft Sausages LLC G 630 923-8969
Wheaton (G-20800)
Gold Medal Products Co G 630 860-2525
Bensenville (G-1814)
Gregor Jonsson Associates Inc E 847 247-4200
Lake Forest (G-12253)
Gsi Group LLC D 618 283-9792
Vandalia (G-20012)
◆ HC Duke & Son LLC C 309 755-4553
East Moline (G-8228)
Heat and Control Inc A 847 381-0290
Inverness (G-11601)
Heat and Control Inc D 309 342-5518
Galesburg (G-10200)
▲ Hollymatic Corporation D 708 579-3700
Countryside (G-7057)
◆ Home Fires Inc G 815 967-4100
Rockford (G-17452)
Hot Food Boxes Inc E 773 533-5912
Chicago (G-4846)
Houpt Revolving Cutters Inc G 618 395-1913
Olney (G-15865)
▲ IMI McR Inc E 309 734-6282
Monmouth (G-14218)
Institutional Equipment Inc E 630 771-0990
Bolingbrook (G-2192)
Ives Way Products Inc G 847 223-1020
Grayslake (G-10784)
John Bean Technologies Corp G 845 340-9727
Chicago (G-5035)
John Bean Technologies Corp D 312 861-5900
Chicago (G-5036)
Keating of Chicago Inc E 815 569-2324
Capron (G-2834)
Kitchy Koo Gourmet Co G 708 499-5236
Oak Lawn (G-15723)
◆ Marshall Middleby Inc C 847 741-3300
Elgin (G-8649)
Mc Cleary Equipment Inc G 815 389-3053
South Beloit (G-19100)
Middleby Corporation E 847 741-3300
Elgin (G-8660)
Middleby Corporation E 847 741-3300
Elgin (G-8661)
◆ Middleby Worldwide Inc G 847 741-3300
Elgin (G-8663)
Miles Bros G 618 937-4115
West Frankfort (G-20678)
Modern Process Equipment Inc E 773 254-3929
Chicago (G-5480)
Mww Food Processing USA LLC G 773 478-9700
Elk Grove Village (G-9141)
◆ Naegele Inc G 708 388-7766
Alsip (G-482)
▲ Nimco Corporation D 815 459-4200
Crystal Lake (G-7239)
▼ Optimal Automatics Co G 847 439-9110
Elk Grove Village (G-9165)
▲ Practical Baker Inc G 815 943-6040
Harvard (G-11063)
▲ Prater Industries Inc D 630 679-3200
Bolingbrook (G-2228)
Pre Pack Machinery Inc G 217 352-1010
Champaign (G-3338)
Precision Service G 618 345-2047
Collinsville (G-6972)
◆ Primedge Inc C 224 265-6600
Elk Grove Village (G-9197)
▲ R S Cryo Equipment Inc G 815 468-6115
Manteno (G-13455)
◆ Rancilio North America Inc E 630 427-1703
Woodridge (G-21336)
◆ Rantoul Foods LLC B 217 892-4178
Rantoul (G-16981)
▲ Rational Cooking Systems Inc D 224 366-3500
Rolling Meadows (G-17769)

Rodger Howard ... G ... 773 481-6990
Chicago *(G-6049)*

S G Acquisition Inc ... F ... 815 624-6501
South Beloit *(G-19113)*

▼ **Savage Bros Company** ... D ... 847 981-3000
Elk Grove Village *(G-9230)*

Sky Snacks LLC ... F ... 217 522-3345
Springfield *(G-19447)*

▲ **Sojuz Ent** ... G ... 847 215-9400
Bensenville *(G-1896)*

▲ **Speco Inc** ... E ... 847 678-4240
Schiller Park *(G-18845)*

Stephen Paoli Mfg Corp ... F ... 815 965-0621
Rockford *(G-17646)*

▲ **Taylor Co Asuess Taylor** ... G ... 815 624-8333
Rockton *(G-17702)*

◆ **Taylor Coml Foodservice Inc** ... F ... 815 624-8333
Rockton *(G-17703)*

Taylor Coml Foodservice Inc ... A ... 815 624-8333
Rockton *(G-17704)*

TEC Systems Inc ... F ... 815 722-2800
New Lenox *(G-15062)*

Terrace Holding Company ... A ... 708 652-5600
Cicero *(G-6881)*

◆ **Tetra Pak Materials LP** ... D ... 847 955-6000
Vernon Hills *(G-20104)*

Titan Injection Parts & Svc ... G ... 630 882-8455
Yorkville *(G-21503)*

Tyson Fresh Meats Inc ... F ... 847 836-5550
Elgin *(G-8764)*

▼ **Vilutis and Co Inc** ... E ... 815 469-2116
Frankfort *(G-9849)*

Vision Machine & Fabrication ... G ... 618 965-3199
Steeleville *(G-19485)*

Wag Industries Inc ... F ... 847 329-8932
Skokie *(G-19053)*

▲ **Wallace/Haskin Corp** ... G ... 630 789-2882
Downers Grove *(G-8105)*

▲ **Weidenmiller Co** ... F ... 630 250-2500
Itasca *(G-11753)*

Wemco Inc ... F ... 708 388-1980
Alsip *(G-524)*

Whiner Brewery LLC ... G ... 312 810-2271
Chicago *(G-6616)*

World Cup Packaging Inc ... G ... 815 624-6501
South Beloit *(G-19127)*

3559 Special Ind Machinery, NEC

Accelrted Mch Design Engrg LLC ... E ... 815 316-6381
Rockford *(G-17290)*

Ace Machine & Tool Inc ... G ... 815 793-5077
Cortland *(G-7015)*

Acro Magnetics Inc ... G ... 815 943-5018
Harvard *(G-11040)*

All Metal Recycling Company ... G ... 847 530-4825
Villa Park *(G-20130)*

Altran Magnetics LLC ... G ... 815 632-3150
Sterling *(G-19497)*

◆ **American Industrial Direct LLC** ... E ... 800 382-1200
Elgin *(G-8507)*

American Metal Coil Works Inc ... G ... 708 562-2645
Northlake *(G-15542)*

Americhem Systems Inc ... E ... 630 495-9300
Aurora *(G-1050)*

Americlean Inc ... F ... 314 741-8901
Wood River *(G-21259)*

▼ **Amiberica Inc** ... E ... 773 247-3600
Chicago *(G-3679)*

Arcoa Group Inc ... E ... 847 693-7519
Waukegan *(G-20417)*

Art Technologies Inc ... G ... 773 557-3896
Bensenville *(G-1747)*

Asahi Kasei Bioprocess Inc ... E ... 847 834-0800
Glenview *(G-10528)*

Asta Service Inc ... G ... 630 271-0960
Lisle *(G-12869)*

Atlas Maintenance Service Inc ... G ... 773 486-3386
Chicago *(G-3764)*

Automation Specialist Svcs LLC ... F ... 847 792-1692
Hampshire *(G-10962)*

Bailey Business Group ... G ... 618 548-3566
Salem *(G-18330)*

◆ **Black Bros Co** ... D ... 815 539-7451
Mendota *(G-13938)*

Black Market Parts Inc ... G ... 630 562-9400
West Chicago *(G-20553)*

Borgwarner Inc ... F ... 708 731-4540
Melrose Park *(G-13833)*

Brown Metal Products Ltd ... G ... 309 936-7384
Atkinson *(G-901)*

◆ **Bystronic Inc** ... C ... 847 214-0300
Hoffman Estates *(G-11410)*

Bystronic Mfg Americas LLC ... G ... 847 214-0300
Hoffman Estates *(G-11411)*

Carlson Sti Inc ... G ... 630 232-2460
Elgin *(G-8533)*

▲ **Carlson Tool & Machine Company** ... F ... 630 232-2460
Elgin *(G-8534)*

Chatham Corporation ... F ... 847 634-5506
Lincolnshire *(G-12749)*

Chemtech Services Inc ... F ... 815 838-4800
Lockport *(G-12986)*

▲ **CIC North America Inc** ... F ... 847 873-0860
Rolling Meadows *(G-17721)*

Credit Card Systems Inc ... F ... 847 459-8320
Wheeling *(G-20876)*

Crw Finishing Inc ... E ... 630 495-4994
Addison *(G-84)*

Cryogenic Systems Equipment ... E ... 708 385-4216
Blue Island *(G-2116)*

Cumberland Engrg Entps Inc ... B ... 314 727-5550
Schaumburg *(G-18500)*

▲ **D R Sperry & Co** ... D ... 630 892-4361
Aurora *(G-1083)*

Desco Inc ... G ... 847 439-2130
Elk Grove Village *(G-8945)*

▲ **Disa Holding Corp** ... G ... 630 820-3000
Oswego *(G-16002)*

◆ **Duravant LLC** ... F ... 630 635-3910
Downers Grove *(G-7995)*

▼ **Effective Energy Assoc LLC** ... G ... 815 248-9280
Davis *(G-7417)*

◆ **Eirich Machines Inc** ... D ... 847 336-2444
Gurnee *(G-10875)*

▲ **Engineering Finshg Systems LLC** ... F ... 815 893-6090
Elmhurst *(G-9361)*

ER&r Inc ... G ... 847 791-5671
Northbrook *(G-15385)*

▲ **Etel Inc** ... G ... 847 519-3380
Schaumburg *(G-18524)*

▲ **Ewikon Molding Tech Inc** ... G ... 815 874-7270
Rockford *(G-17405)*

Fanuc America Corporation ... E ... 847 898-5000
Hoffman Estates *(G-11423)*

Fast Radius Inc ... E ... 866 222-5458
Chicago *(G-4563)*

◆ **Federal Signal Corporation** ... D ... 630 954-2000
Oak Brook *(G-15618)*

Felix Partners LLC ... G ... 847 648-8449
Rolling Meadows *(G-17732)*

◆ **Fluid Management Inc** ... B ... 847 537-0880
Wheeling *(G-20898)*

Fortune Metal Midwest LLC ... E ... 630 778-7776
Sandwich *(G-18370)*

▲ **G K Enterprises Inc** ... G ... 708 587-2150
Monee *(G-14201)*

Gone For Good ... G ... 217 753-0414
Springfield *(G-19376)*

▲ **Graymills Corporation** ... D ... 773 477-4100
Broadview *(G-2439)*

Guzzler Manufacturing Inc ... C ... 815 672-3171
Streator *(G-19610)*

▲ **Hackett Precision Company Inc** ... E ... 615 227-3136
Chicago *(G-4764)*

Hardwood Line Manufacturing Co ... E ... 773 463-2600
Chicago *(G-4780)*

Harris Metals & Recycling ... G ... 217 235-1808
Mattoon *(G-13635)*

Haussermann Usa LLC ... G ... 847 272-9850
Northbrook *(G-15398)*

◆ **Heico Holding Inc** ... E ... 630 353-5100
Warrenville *(G-20238)*

▲ **Hmt Manufacturing Inc** ... E ... 847 473-2310
North Chicago *(G-15314)*

◆ **Hunter Foundry Machinery Corp** ... D ... 847 397-5110
Schaumburg *(G-18553)*

▲ **I T R Inc** ... E ... 217 245-4478
Jacksonville *(G-11768)*

Industrial Phrm Resources Inc ... F ... 630 823-4700
Bartlett *(G-1290)*

◆ **Innovtive Prcess Applctons LLC** ... G ... 708 844-6100
Crestwood *(G-7119)*

International Molding Mch Co ... G ... 708 354-1380
La Grange Park *(G-12097)*

▲ **Kirby Lester LLC** ... D ... 847 984-3377
Lake Forest *(G-12269)*

Koflo Corporation ... F ... 847 516-3700
Cary *(G-3174)*

Kps Capital Partners LP ... B ... 630 972-7000
Bolingbrook *(G-2203)*

▼ **Kuusakoski Philadelphia LLC** ... D ... 215 533-8323
Plainfield *(G-16681)*

Leonard Associates Inc ... E ... 815 226-9609
Rockford *(G-17494)*

Maac Machinery Co Inc ... E ... 630 665-1700
Carol Stream *(G-3019)*

▲ **Mamata Enterprises Inc** ... G ... 941 205-0227
Montgomery *(G-14260)*

Masterfeed Corporation ... G ... 630 879-1133
Batavia *(G-1392)*

▲ **McLaughlin Body Co** ... D ... 309 762-7755
Moline *(G-14159)*

Meminger Metal Finishing Inc ... F ... 309 582-3363
Aledo *(G-358)*

Mgb Engineering Company ... E ... 847 956-7444
Elk Grove Village *(G-9121)*

Midwest Innovations Inc ... G ... 815 578-1401
McHenry *(G-13770)*

Midwest Mixing Inc ... G ... 708 422-8100
Chicago Ridge *(G-6803)*

Morrell Incorporated ... F ... 630 858-4600
Glendale Heights *(G-10477)*

▲ **Multitech Industries Inc** ... E ... 630 784-9200
Carol Stream *(G-3035)*

▲ **Multitech McHned Cmponents LLC** ... E ... 630 949-8200
Carol Stream *(G-3036)*

Nal Worldwide Holdings Inc ... B ... 630 261-3100
Addison *(G-226)*

Ozonology Inc ... G ... 847 998-8808
Northfield *(G-15527)*

Parking Systems Inc ... G ... 847 891-3819
Schaumburg *(G-18666)*

Pekay Machine & Engrg Co Inc ... F ... 312 829-5530
Chicago *(G-5784)*

◆ **Pettibone LLC** ... F ... 630 353-5000
Warrenville *(G-20244)*

▲ **Pollmann North America Inc** ... E ... 815 834-1122
Romeoville *(G-17864)*

▲ **Prater Industries Inc** ... D ... 630 679-3200
Bolingbrook *(G-2228)*

Precisepower LLC ... E ... 847 908-5400
Schaumburg *(G-18682)*

Prinsco Inc ... E ... 815 635-3131
Chatsworth *(G-3426)*

Pro Tools & Equipment Inc ... G ... 847 838-6666
Antioch *(G-631)*

Quality Fastener Products Inc ... G ... 224 330-3162
Elgin *(G-8708)*

R & G Machine Shop Inc ... F ... 217 342-6622
Effingham *(G-8422)*

▲ **RAO Design International Inc** ... G ... 847 671-6182
Morton Grove *(G-14437)*

Rapid Electroplating Process ... G ... 708 344-2504
Melrose Park *(G-13907)*

Rapid Line Industries Inc ... F ... 815 727-4362
Joliet *(G-11922)*

Rcc Conveyors Inc ... G ... 224 338-8841
Volo *(G-20205)*

Renu Electronics Private Ltd ... G ... 630 879-8412
Batavia *(G-1410)*

Rex Morioka ... G ... 847 651-9400
Schiller Park *(G-18839)*

ROC Industries Inc ... G ... 618 277-6044
Belleville *(G-1589)*

Saint-Gobain Abrasives Inc ... C ... 630 868-8060
Carol Stream *(G-3063)*

▲ **SBE Varvit Usa LLC** ... G ... 331 205-7000
Aurora *(G-1154)*

Six Oaks Company ... G ... 312 343-4037
Chicago *(G-6178)*

SMC Corporation of America ... E ... 630 449-0600
Aurora *(G-1017)*

SMS Group Inc ... G ... 708 479-1333
Mokena *(G-14115)*

Spectral Dynamics Inc ... E ... 630 595-4288
Itasca *(G-11738)*

Spf Supplies Inc ... G ... 847 454-9081
Elk Grove Village *(G-9249)*

Srmd Solutions LLC ... G ... 217 925-5773
Dieterich *(G-7879)*

▲ **Sterling Systems Sales Corp** ... G ... 630 584-3580
Saint Charles *(G-18278)*

▲ **Stutz Company** ... F ... 773 287-1068
Chicago *(G-6259)*

▲ **Substrate Technology Inc** ... F ... 815 941-4800
Morris *(G-14330)*

T & S Business Group LLC ... F ... 815 432-7084
Watseka *(G-20319)*

▲ **Tek Pak Inc** ... D ... 630 406-0560
Batavia *(G-1429)*

Employee Codes: A=Over 500 employees, B=251-500
C=101-250, D=51-100, E=20-50, F=10-19, G=3-9

2020 Harris Illinois
Industrial Directory

963

35 INDUSTRIAL AND COMMERCIAL MACHINERY AND COMPUTER EQUIPMENT SIC SECTION

▲ Therma-Kleen Inc.....G..... 630 718-0212
Plainfield (G-16723)
◆ Thomas Engineering Inc.....D..... 847 358-5800
Hoffman Estates (G-11469)
Thomas Engineering Inc.....E..... 815 398-0280
Rockford (G-17659)
Top Brass Inc.....G..... 719 539-7242
Granite City (G-10744)
Top Brass LLC.....F..... 800 836-4683
Granite City (G-10745)
Tuskin Equipment Corporation.....G..... 630 466-5590
Sugar Grove (G-19658)
Ultramatic Equipment Co.....E..... 630 543-4565
Addison (G-322)
▲ Union Special LLC.....C..... 847 669-5101
Huntley (G-11572)
United Validation & Com.....G..... 815 953-6068
Watseka (G-20321)
Unitel Technologies Inc.....F..... 847 297-2265
Mount Prospect (G-14579)
Vacudyne Incorporated.....E..... 708 757-5200
Chicago Heights (G-6783)
◆ Vst America Inc.....G..... 847 952-3800
Arlington Heights (G-829)
Waupaca Foundry Inc.....C..... 217 347-0600
Effingham (G-8430)
WEI TO Associates Inc.....G..... 708 747-6660
Park Forest (G-16261)
Yer Kiln Me LLC.....G..... 309 606-9007
Wyoming (G-21464)

3561 Pumps & Pumping Eqpt

A-L-L Equipment Company.....G..... 815 877-7000
Loves Park (G-13181)
▲ Action Pump Co.....F..... 847 516-3636
Cary (G-3144)
Advanced Seal Technology Inc.....E..... 815 861-4010
Ringwood (G-17038)
Allegion S&S Holding Co Inc.....C..... 815 875-3311
Princeton (G-16805)
Apergy Energy Automation LLC.....E..... 630 541-1540
Downers Grove (G-7952)
Aptargroup Inc.....B..... 847 639-2124
Cary (G-3148)
▲ Aqua Control Inc.....E..... 815 664-4900
Spring Valley (G-19307)
Automax Corporation.....G..... 630 972-1919
Woodridge (G-21277)
▲ Basement Flood Protector Inc.....F..... 847 438-6770
Lake Zurich (G-12387)
Canada Organization & Dev LLC.....G..... 630 743-2563
Downers Grove (G-7965)
Century Fasteners & Mch Co Inc.....F..... 773 463-3900
Skokie (G-18939)
Cool Fluidics Inc.....G..... 815 861-4063
Woodstock (G-21376)
◆ Corken Inc.....D..... 405 946-5576
Lake Bluff (G-12177)
▲ CTS Advanced Materials LLC.....E..... 630 577-8800
Lisle (G-12879)
Davis Welding & Manfctg Inc.....F..... 217 784-5480
Gibson City (G-10336)
Dover Pmps Prcess Sltons Sgmen.....E..... 630 487-2240
Oakbrook Terrace (G-15796)
◆ Emco Wheaton Usa Inc.....E..... 217 222-5400
Quincy (G-16879)
Engineered Fluid Inc.....C..... 618 533-1351
Centralia (G-3230)
Engineered Fluid Inc.....D..... 618 533-1351
Centralia (G-3231)
▲ Ergoseal Inc.....E..... 630 462-9600
Carol Stream (G-2981)
◆ Evac North America Inc.....E..... 815 654-8300
Cherry Valley (G-3439)
FH Ayer Manufacturing Co.....E..... 708 755-0550
Chicago Heights (G-6746)
Flow Control US Holding Corp.....F..... 630 307-3000
Hanover Park (G-11005)
Flowserve Corporation.....E..... 630 762-4100
West Chicago (G-20586)
Flowserve Corporation.....E..... 630 543-4240
Addison (G-126)
Flowserve Corporation.....E..... 630 435-9596
Lombard (G-13076)
Flowserve US Inc.....D..... 630 783-1468
Woodridge (G-21301)
Fluid Handling LLC.....B..... 773 267-1600
Morton Grove (G-14408)
Fna Ip Holdings Inc.....D..... 847 348-1500
Elk Grove Village (G-9001)
▲ Fura Inc.....G..... 847 451-0000
Franklin Park (G-9946)
Gardner Denver Inc.....E..... 800 231-3628
Quincy (G-16885)
▲ Gas Compression Systems Inc.....F..... 630 766-6049
Bensenville (G-1807)
Georgetown Waste Water.....G..... 217 662-2525
Georgetown (G-10326)
Goulds Pumps LLC.....F..... 708 563-1220
Bedford Park (G-1468)
▲ Graymills Corporation.....D..... 773 477-4100
Broadview (G-2439)
Grundfos CBS Inc.....F..... 331 401-0057
Aurora (G-975)
▲ Grundfos Water Utility Inc.....D..... 630 236-5500
Aurora (G-976)
Guzzler Manufacturing Inc.....C..... 815 672-3171
Streator (G-19610)
Heidolph NA LLC.....F..... 224 265-9600
Wood Dale (G-21197)
Hidrostal LLC.....F..... 630 240-6271
Aurora (G-979)
Idex Corporation.....C..... 847 498-7070
Lake Forest (G-12265)
Inman Electric Motors Inc.....E..... 815 223-2288
La Salle (G-12115)
ITT Water & Wastewater USA Inc.....F..... 708 342-0484
Tinley Park (G-19840)
Jn Pump Holdings Inc.....F..... 708 754-2940
Chicago Heights (G-6753)
▲ Johnson Pumps America Inc.....E..... 847 671-7867
Rockford (G-17477)
▲ Lubeq Corporation.....F..... 847 931-1020
Elgin (G-8642)
▲ March Manufacturing Inc.....D..... 847 729-5300
Glenview (G-10587)
Mechanical Engineering Pdts.....G..... 312 421-3375
Chicago (G-5380)
▲ Metropolitan Industries Inc.....C..... 815 886-9200
Romeoville (G-17851)
Midwest Fuel Injction Svc Corp.....F..... 847 991-7867
Palatine (G-16140)
Murdock Company Inc.....G..... 847 566-0050
Mundelein (G-14719)
▲ Nexpump Inc.....G..... 630 365-4639
Elburn (G-8464)
O Adjust Matic Pump Company.....G..... 630 766-1490
Wood Dale (G-21224)
▲ Omni Pump Repairs Inc.....F..... 847 451-0000
Franklin Park (G-10011)
Park Engineering Inc.....E..... 847 455-1424
Franklin Park (G-10013)
Pentair Flow Technologies LLC.....C..... 630 859-7000
North Aurora (G-15269)
Pokorney Manufacturing Co.....G..... 630 458-0406
Addison (G-244)
Pump House.....G..... 618 216-2404
Wood River (G-21266)
R S Corcoran Co.....E..... 815 485-2156
New Lenox (G-15054)
Roth Pump Company.....E..... 309 787-1791
Milan (G-14027)
Roy E Roth Company.....G..... 309 787-1791
Milan (G-14028)
Rrp Enterprises Inc.....G..... 847 455-5674
Franklin Park (G-10038)
Ruthman Pump and Engineering.....G..... 708 754-2940
Chicago Heights (G-6773)
▲ S C C Pumps Inc.....G..... 847 593-8495
Arlington Heights (G-803)
S-P-D Incorporated.....G..... 847 882-9820
Palatine (G-16156)
Sielc Technologies Corporation.....G..... 847 229-2629
Wheeling (G-20985)
Spirax Sarco Inc.....F..... 630 493-4525
Lisle (G-12940)
Sulzer Pump Services (us) Inc.....F..... 815 600-7355
Joliet (G-11934)
▲ Swaby Manufacturing Company.....G..... 773 626-1400
Chicago (G-6292)
Tacmina USA Corporation.....G..... 312 810-8128
Schaumburg (G-18736)
Thomas Pump Company.....F..... 630 851-9393
Aurora (G-1023)
Townley Engrg & Mfg Co Inc.....F..... 618 273-8271
Eldorado (G-8484)
Tramco Pump Co.....E..... 312 243-5800
Romeoville (G-17881)
Trane Technologies Company LLC.....E..... 704 655-4000
Chicago (G-6406)
Trd Manufacturing Inc.....E..... 815 654-7775
Machesney Park (G-13379)
Trusty Warns Inc.....E..... 630 766-9015
Wood Dale (G-21253)
Tuskin Equipment Corporation.....G..... 630 466-5590
Sugar Grove (G-19658)
◆ Tuthill Corporation.....E..... 630 382-4900
Burr Ridge (G-2727)
Unique Indoor Comfort.....F..... 847 362-1910
Libertyville (G-12719)
W S Darley & Co.....F..... 630 735-3500
Itasca (G-11752)
Wagner Pump & Supply Co Inc.....G..... 847 526-8573
Wauconda (G-20401)
Xylem Inc.....D..... 847 966-3700
Morton Grove (G-14450)
◆ Yamada America Inc.....E..... 847 228-9063
Arlington Heights (G-838)

3562 Ball & Roller Bearings

Allegion S&S Holding Co Inc.....C..... 815 875-3311
Princeton (G-16805)
◆ American NTN Bearing Mfg Corp.....B..... 847 741-4545
Elgin (G-8508)
American NTN Bearing Mfg Corp.....E..... 847 671-5450
Schiller Park (G-18785)
Bearings Manufacturing Company.....F..... 773 583-6703
Chicago (G-3856)
Beauticontrol.....G..... 217 223-0382
Quincy (G-16862)
Caster Warehouse Inc.....F..... 847 836-5712
Carpentersville (G-3097)
▲ Ccty USA Bearing Co.....G..... 847 540-8196
Lake Zurich (G-12391)
Ewellix USA LLC.....G..... 618 392-3647
Olney (G-15859)
◆ Frantz Manufacturing Company.....G..... 815 625-3333
Sterling (G-19508)
Frantz Manufacturing Company.....D..... 815 625-7063
Sterling (G-19509)
▲ HRB America Corporation.....G..... 630 513-1800
Saint Charles (G-18208)
◆ Mechanical Power Inc.....E..... 847 487-0070
Wauconda (G-20375)
NTN Bearing Corporation.....G..... 847 298-7500
Macomb (G-13395)
▼ NTN USA Corporation.....C..... 847 298-4652
Mount Prospect (G-14554)
NTN-Bower Corporation.....G..... 309 833-4541
Macomb (G-13396)
◆ NTN-Bower Corporation.....G..... 309 837-0440
Macomb (G-13397)
▲ Pacific Bearing Corp.....C..... 815 389-5600
Roscoe (G-17921)
▲ Pan Pac International Inc.....G..... 847 222-9077
Arlington Heights (G-787)
Precision Plastic Ball Co.....G..... 847 678-2255
Franklin Park (G-10025)
Roberts Swiss Inc.....E..... 630 467-9100
Itasca (G-11726)
SKF USA Inc.....D..... 847 742-0700
Elgin (G-8735)
SKF USA Inc.....D..... 847 742-0700
Elgin (G-8736)
▲ Thomson Industries Inc.....A..... 815 568-4309
Marengo (G-13495)
Timken Company.....C..... 630 679-6756
Naperville (G-14990)

3563 Air & Gas Compressors

Agro-Chem Inc.....F..... 309 475-8311
Saybrook (G-18418)
Allegion S&S Holding Co Inc.....C..... 815 875-3311
Princeton (G-16805)
Atlas Copco Compressors LLC.....F..... 847 640-6067
Elk Grove Village (G-8845)
Atlas Copco Compressors LLC.....F..... 281 590-7500
Chicago (G-3762)
Bridgeport Air Comprsr & Tl Co.....G..... 618 945-7163
Bridgeport (G-2310)
Brock Equipment Company.....E..... 815 459-4210
Woodstock (G-21367)
Buell Manufacturing Company.....G..... 708 447-6320
Lyons (G-13304)
Compressed Air Advisors Inc.....G..... 877 247-2381
Hillside (G-11334)
◆ Corken Inc.....D..... 405 946-5576
Lake Bluff (G-12177)
◆ Cvp Systems LLC.....D..... 630 852-1190
Elgin (G-8561)

Demarco Industrial Vacuum Corp.........G....... 815 344-2222
Crystal Lake *(G-7194)*
▲ **Fluid-Aire Dynamics Inc**..................E....... 847 678-8388
Schaumburg *(G-18530)*
Fna Ip Holdings Inc..............................D....... 847 348-1500
Elk Grove Village *(G-9001)*
▲ **G H Meiser & Co**................................E....... 708 388-7867
Mokena *(G-14085)*
Gardner Denver Inc...............................D....... 217 222-5400
Quincy *(G-16884)*
Gardner Denver Inc...............................D....... 815 875-3321
Princeton *(G-16810)*
Gardner Denver Nash LLC......................F....... 331 457-5377
Naperville *(G-14968)*
◆ **Harris Equipment Corporation**..........E....... 708 343-0866
Melrose Park *(G-13878)*
▲ **Howe Corporation**..............................E....... 773 235-0200
Chicago *(G-4851)*
Idex Corporation....................................C....... 847 498-7070
Lake Forest *(G-12265)*
▲ **J/B Industries Inc**...............................D....... 630 851-9444
Aurora *(G-1115)*
Master Manufacturing Co........................F....... 630 833-7060
Villa Park *(G-20159)*
◆ **Mat Holdings Inc**.................................D....... 847 821-9630
Long Grove *(G-13165)*
◆ **Mat Industries LLC**.............................G....... 847 821-9630
Long Grove *(G-13166)*
Nordson Corporation..............................E....... 815 784-5025
Genoa *(G-10320)*
◆ **Ohio Medical LLC**...............................D....... 847 855-0500
Gurnee *(G-10907)*
Ortman-Mccain Co...................................G....... 312 666-2244
Bellwood *(G-1635)*
Rebuilders Enterprises Inc.....................G....... 708 430-0030
Bridgeview *(G-2380)*
▲ **Resolute Industrial LLC**......................D....... 800 537-9675
Wheeling *(G-20974)*
Rietschle Inc...G....... 410 712-4100
Quincy *(G-16941)*
Rpk Technologies Inc..............................G....... 630 595-0911
Bensenville *(G-1885)*
Ryan Manufacturing Inc..........................G....... 815 695-5310
Newark *(G-15078)*
Scrollex Corporation...............................G....... 630 887-8817
Willowbrook *(G-21059)*
Standard Car Truck Company.................D....... 630 860-5511
Bensenville *(G-1899)*
▲ **Standard Lifts & Equipment Inc**.........G....... 414 444-1000
Hanover Park *(G-11015)*
Technology Assistance USA LLC...........G....... 773 671-6712
Chicago *(G-6334)*
Thomas Gardner Denver Inc....................E....... 217 222-5400
Quincy *(G-16947)*
Trane Technologies Company LLC.......E....... 704 655-4000
Chicago *(G-6406)*
▲ **William W Meyer and Sons**...............D....... 847 918-0111
Libertyville *(G-12726)*

3564 Blowers & Fans

Aen Industries Inc...................................F....... 708 758-3000
Chicago Heights *(G-6728)*
Air Source Corp.......................................G....... 630 355-7655
Geneva *(G-10249)*
Air-Drive Inc...E....... 847 625-0226
Lake Forest *(G-12221)*
Altair Corporation....................................E....... 847 634-9540
Lincolnshire *(G-12744)*
American Air Filter Co Inc......................D....... 502 637-0011
Chicago *(G-3647)*
Architectural Fan Coil Inc......................G....... 312 399-1203
Chicago *(G-3729)*
Bact Process Systems Inc.......................G....... 847 577-0950
Arlington Heights *(G-701)*
Basement Dewatering Systems..............F....... 309 647-0331
Canton *(G-2821)*
Bce-USA LLC...G....... 815 556-8037
Franklin Park *(G-9884)*
Bee Clean Specialties LLC.....................F....... 847 451-0844
Schaumburg *(G-18457)*
Bisco Enterprise Inc................................F....... 630 628-1831
Schaumburg *(G-18463)*
Blowers LLC..E....... 708 594-1800
Elmhurst *(G-9336)*
◆ **Bofa Americas Inc**...............................G....... 618 205-5007
Staunton *(G-19474)*
Bost Corporation......................................E....... 708 344-7023
Maywood *(G-13663)*
Bost Corporation......................................F....... 708 450-9234
Melrose Park *(G-13835)*
C P Environmental Inc.............................F....... 630 759-8866
Romeoville *(G-17801)*
Calutech Inc..G....... 708 614-0228
Orland Park *(G-15944)*
Camfil USA Inc...D....... 815 459-6600
Crystal Lake *(G-7177)*
Car - Mon Products Inc............................E....... 847 695-9000
Elgin *(G-8532)*
◆ **Catalytic Products Intl Inc**..................E....... 847 438-0334
Lake Zurich *(G-12390)*
Chatham Corporation...............................F....... 847 634-5506
Lincolnshire *(G-12749)*
Chicago Plastic Systems Inc..................E....... 815 455-4599
Crystal Lake *(G-7181)*
Clark Filter Inc..E....... 216 896-3000
Chicago *(G-4167)*
▲ **Clean and Science USA Co Ltd**...........G....... 847 461-9292
Rolling Meadows *(G-17722)*
Communication Coil Inc...........................D....... 847 671-1333
Schiller Park *(G-18795)*
◆ **Conservation Technology Ltd**.............D....... 847 559-5500
Northbrook *(G-15366)*
Custom Systems Inc.................................G....... 314 355-4575
Granite City *(G-10702)*
Dekalb Blower Inc.....................................F....... 630 553-8831
Yorkville *(G-21478)*
Df Fan Services Inc..................................F....... 630 876-1495
West Chicago *(G-20570)*
Donaldson Company Inc..........................E....... 815 288-3374
Dixon *(G-7898)*
Durable Manufacturing Company............F....... 630 766-0398
Bensenville *(G-1791)*
Dust Patrol Inc...G....... 309 676-1161
Peoria *(G-16432)*
Dustcatchers Inc.......................................G....... 773 768-1440
Chicago *(G-4414)*
◆ **Eclipse Inc**..D....... 815 877-3031
Rockford *(G-17388)*
Filter Friend Z Inc.......................................G....... 847 824-4049
Des Plaines *(G-7765)*
◆ **Filtertek Inc**...B....... 815 648-2410
Hebron *(G-11143)*
▲ **Filtration Group Corporation**................D....... 512 593-7999
Oak Brook *(G-15619)*
Filtration Group LLC..................................E....... 815 726-4600
Joliet *(G-11865)*
Flsmidth Inc...G....... 309 347-3031
Pekin *(G-16334)*
▼ **Frequency Devices Inc**..........................F....... 815 434-7800
Ottawa *(G-16053)*
◆ **Fuel Tech Inc**...C....... 630 845-4500
Warrenville *(G-20237)*
G T C Industries Inc...................................G....... 708 369-9815
Naperville *(G-14832)*
GAG Industries Inc.....................................E....... 847 616-8710
Elk Grove Village *(G-9008)*
Gardner Denver Inc....................................D....... 770 632-5000
Quincy *(G-16883)*
Goose Island Mfg & Supply Corp..........G....... 708 343-4225
Lansing *(G-12495)*
H D A Fans Inc..G....... 630 627-2087
Elk Grove Village *(G-9025)*
Heidolph NA LLC..F....... 224 265-9600
Wood Dale *(G-21197)*
Henderson Engineering Co Inc................G....... 815 786-9471
Sandwich *(G-18374)*
▲ **Henry Technologies Inc**.........................G....... 217 483-2406
Chatham *(G-3421)*
▲ **Hydrosil International Ltd**....................G....... 847 741-1600
East Dundee *(G-8201)*
▲ **Illinois Blower Inc**..................................D....... 847 639-5500
Cary *(G-3168)*
Industrial Fiberglass Inc............................F....... 708 681-2707
Melrose Park *(G-13882)*
International Filter Mfg Corp....................F....... 217 324-2303
Litchfield *(G-12966)*
Jacobs Boiler & Mech Inds Inc...............E....... 773 385-9900
Chicago *(G-4998)*
Jan-Air Inc...E....... 815 678-4516
Richmond *(G-17015)*
Kap Holdings LLC.......................................F....... 708 948-0226
Oak Park *(G-15759)*
Keating of Chicago Inc..............................E....... 815 569-2324
Capron *(G-2834)*
Lilly Air Systems Co Inc.............................F....... 630 773-2225
Itasca *(G-11693)*
Mason Engineering & Designing............E....... 630 595-5000
Inverness *(G-11602)*
Master Manufacturing Co..........................F....... 630 833-7060
Villa Park *(G-20159)*
Met-Pro Technologies LLC........................E....... 630 775-0707
Wood Dale *(G-21215)*
Midwest Air Pro Inc....................................G....... 773 622-4566
Chicago *(G-5439)*
Mity Inc..G....... 630 365-5030
Elburn *(G-8461)*
Murdock Company Inc...............................G....... 847 566-0050
Mundelein *(G-14719)*
New York Blower Company.......................D....... 217 347-3233
Effingham *(G-8414)*
Nordic A Filtration N Amer Inc.................G....... 331 457-5289
Naperville *(G-14886)*
Nyb Process Fans Inc................................G....... 630 794-5700
Willowbrook *(G-21055)*
Paul D Stark & Associates........................F....... 630 964-7111
Downers Grove *(G-8070)*
◆ **Perma-Pipe Intl Holdings Inc**...............E....... 847 966-1000
Niles *(G-15158)*
▲ **Permatron Corporation**..........................E....... 847 434-1421
Elk Grove Village *(G-9174)*
Petairapy LLC..G....... 630 377-0348
Saint Charles *(G-18244)*
Promark Associates Inc.............................G....... 847 676-1894
Skokie *(G-19015)*
Quality Cleaning Fluids Inc.......................G....... 847 451-1190
Franklin Park *(G-10029)*
Reds Muffler Shop......................................G....... 217 344-1676
Urbana *(G-19997)*
▲ **Revcor Inc**..B....... 847 428-4411
Carpentersville *(G-3119)*
Robko Flock Coating Company................G....... 847 272-6202
Northbrook *(G-15474)*
▲ **Robuschi Usa Inc**...................................G....... 704 424-1018
Quincy *(G-16942)*
Rv Air Inc...G....... 309 657-4300
Addison *(G-279)*
▲ **Sanders Inc**..E....... 815 634-4611
Morris *(G-14326)*
Schubert Environmental Eqp Inc.............F....... 630 307-9400
Glendale Heights *(G-10492)*
Scott Industrial Blower Co.........................F....... 847 426-8800
Gilberts *(G-10370)*
▲ **Smith Filter Corporation**........................E....... 309 764-8324
Moline *(G-14178)*
▲ **Solberg International Ltd**......................G....... 630 616-4400
Itasca *(G-11735)*
◆ **Solberg Mfg Inc**......................................D....... 630 616-4400
Itasca *(G-11736)*
Solberg Mfg Inc..E....... 630 773-1363
Itasca *(G-11737)*
▲ **Storms Industries Inc**..............................E....... 312 243-7480
Chicago *(G-6251)*
Tdc Filter...F....... 503 521-9988
Bolingbrook *(G-2247)*
Tri-Dim Filter Corporation...........................E....... 847 695-5822
Elgin *(G-8759)*
Turbo Dry LLC..G....... 847 702-4430
Palatine *(G-16168)*
Universal Air Filter Company....................E....... 618 271-7300
East Saint Louis *(G-8328)*
Vent Products Co Inc...................................E....... 773 521-1900
Chicago *(G-6532)*
▲ **William W Meyer and Sons**....................D....... 847 918-0111
Libertyville *(G-12726)*

3565 Packaging Machinery

Algus Packaging Inc.....................................D....... 815 756-1881
Dekalb *(G-7665)*
▲ **All-Vac Industries Inc**...............................F....... 847 675-2290
Skokie *(G-18915)*
Alps..G....... 847 437-0665
Arlington Heights *(G-688)*
American Packaging McHy Inc..................E....... 815 337-8580
Woodstock *(G-21358)*
◆ **Arpac LLC**...C....... 847 678-9034
Schiller Park *(G-18787)*
◆ **Ats Sortimat USA LLC**..............................D....... 847 925-1234
Rolling Meadows *(G-17713)*
Automtic Lquid Pckg Sltons LLC...............E....... 847 372-3336
Arlington Heights *(G-699)*
▲ **Barrington Packaging Systems**...............G....... 847 382-8063
Barrington *(G-1215)*
Base 2 Marketing and Supply......................G....... 847 516-0012
Cary *(G-3149)*
Bevwrap LLC..G....... 773 580-5434
Elk Grove Village *(G-8866)*
▼ **Birnberg Machinery Inc**...........................G....... 847 673-5242
Deerfield *(G-7597)*
Bms Manufacturing Company Inc...............E....... 309 787-3158
Milan *(G-14000)*

S I C

◆ **Bprex Healthcare Packaging Inc** D 800 537-0178 Buffalo Grove ***(G-2519)***
Burghof Engineering & Mfg Co E 847 634-0737 Lincolnshire ***(G-12747)***
C N C Central Inc G 630 595-1453 Bensenville ***(G-1760)***
▲ **Cama USA Inc** G 847 607-8797 Buffalo Grove ***(G-2523)***
Cartpac Inc E 630 283-8979 Carol Stream ***(G-2956)***
Combined Technologies Inc G 847 968-4855 Libertyville ***(G-12645)***
Competitive Edge Opportunities G 815 981-4060 Island Lake ***(G-11605)***
◆ **Cvp Systems LLC** D 630 852-1190 Elgin ***(G-8561)***
David S Smith Hldings Amer Inc F 630 296-2000 Romeoville ***(G-17813)***
▲ **Diamond Machine Werks Inc** E 847 437-0665 Arlington Heights ***(G-728)***
Dover Europe Inc G 630 541-1540 Downers Grove ***(G-7991)***
◆ **Dover Prtg Identification Inc** D 630 541-1540 Downers Grove ***(G-7992)***
Dromont Corporation G 404 615-2336 Palatine ***(G-16114)***
Duravant G 630 635-3910 Downers Grove ***(G-7994)***
◆ **Duravant LLC** F 630 635-3910 Downers Grove ***(G-7995)***
Econopin G 708 599-5002 Bridgeview ***(G-2343)***
▼ **Eoe Inc** F 847 550-1665 Lake Zurich ***(G-12408)***
Fgwa G 630 759-6800 Romeoville ***(G-17822)***
▲ **Fromm Airpad Inc** F 630 393-9790 Warrenville ***(G-20236)***
▲ **Fuji Impulse American Corp** G 847 236-9190 Deerfield ***(G-7612)***
▲ **Gama Electronics Inc** F 815 356-9600 Woodstock ***(G-21391)***
Gr8 Seas Holdings Inc G 630 862-5099 Yorkville ***(G-21486)***
Hearthside USA B 630 845-9400 Bolingbrook ***(G-2184)***
Henkelman Inc G 331 979-2013 Elmhurst ***(G-9371)***
Illinois Tool Works Inc E 847 215-8925 Buffalo Grove ***(G-2548)***
Illinois Tool Works Inc E 217 345-2166 Itasca ***(G-11673)***
Illinois Tool Works Inc D 618 997-1716 Marion ***(G-13518)***
Illinois Tool Works Inc E 708 720-0300 Frankfort ***(G-9807)***
◆ **Integrated Packg & Fastener** D 847 439-5730 Elk Grove Village ***(G-9055)***
Jescorp Inc D 847 378-1200 Elk Grove Village ***(G-9068)***
John R Nalbach Engrg Co Inc E 708 579-9100 Countryside ***(G-7062)***
Jon Cagle G 618 559-3578 Carterville ***(G-3132)***
Libco Industries Inc F 815 623-7677 Roscoe ***(G-17912)***
▲ **Mamata Enterprises Inc** G 941 205-0227 Montgomery ***(G-14260)***
▼ **Marsh Shipping Supply Co LLC** F 618 343-1006 Collinsville ***(G-6969)***
◆ **Martin Automatic Inc** C 815 654-4800 Rockford ***(G-17505)***
MB Corp & Associates F 847 214-8843 Elgin ***(G-8654)***
◆ **Mc Brady Engineering Inc** F 815 744-8900 Rockdale ***(G-17267)***
Middleby Packg Solutions LLC E 847 741-3500 Elgin ***(G-8662)***
Midwest Fillers G 309 567-2957 Havana ***(G-11118)***
Midwest Mobile Canning LLC G 815 861-4515 Crystal Lake ***(G-7229)***
Mii Inc F 630 879-3000 Batavia ***(G-1395)***
Mssc LLC G 618 343-1006 Collinsville ***(G-6971)***
Nafm Llc G 513 504-4333 Libertyville ***(G-12687)***
Nortech Packaging LLC D 847 884-1805 Schaumburg ***(G-18651)***
Oden Corp G 630 416-4543 Naperville ***(G-14888)***
Park Lawn Association Inc F 708 425-7377 Oak Lawn ***(G-15731)***
Pioneer Container McHy Inc G 618 533-7833 Centralia ***(G-3245)***
PMI Cartoning Inc D 847 437-1427 Elk Grove Village ***(G-9181)***
◆ **Point Five Packaging LLC** G 847 531-4787 Schiller Park ***(G-18833)***
Pre Pack Machinery Inc G 217 352-1010 Champaign ***(G-3338)***
Prototype Equipment Corp D 847 596-9000 Waukegan ***(G-20484)***
Purchasing Services Ltd Inc E 618 566-8100 Mascoutah ***(G-13606)***
Q Products G 815 498-6356 Sandwich ***(G-18382)***
R P Grollman Co Inc G 847 607-0294 Highland Park ***(G-11293)***
◆ **Robert Bosch LLC** B 917 421-7209 Broadview ***(G-2466)***
Robert L Murphy G 708 424-0277 Evergreen Park ***(G-9598)***
Robey Packaging Eqp & Svc G 708 758-8250 Chicago Heights ***(G-6771)***
Rollstock Inc G 708 579-3700 Countryside ***(G-7068)***
▲ **Rosenthal Manufacturing Co Inc** E 847 714-0404 Northbrook ***(G-15475)***
S G Acquisition Inc F 815 624-6501 South Beloit ***(G-19113)***
▲ **Sardee Industries Inc** G 630 824-4200 Lisle ***(G-12936)***
▲ **Serac Inc** E 630 510-9343 Carol Stream ***(G-3068)***
Signode F 800 228-4744 Glenview ***(G-10616)***
Signode Industrial Group LLC E 800 862-7997 Glenview ***(G-10617)***
Signode Industrial Group LLC E 815 939-6192 Kankakee ***(G-12002)***
Signode Industrial Group LLC E 800 628-6787 Glenview ***(G-10619)***
Signode Supply Corporation C 708 458-7320 Bridgeview ***(G-2387)***
▲ **Sjd Direct Midwest LLC** G 618 931-2151 Edwardsville ***(G-8375)***
Small Different Better Inc G 224 302-5163 Round Lake Park ***(G-18098)***
Suburban Machine Corporation E 847 808-9095 Wheeling ***(G-20992)***
▼ **Sun Centre Usa Inc** F 224 699-9058 Crystal Lake ***(G-7271)***
▲ **Taisei Lamick USA Inc** F 847 258-3283 Elk Grove Village ***(G-9264)***
Taurus 80 LLC G 704 927-2793 Rockford ***(G-17653)***
Tegrant Alloyd Brands Inc B 815 756-8451 Dekalb ***(G-7708)***
Terco Inc E 630 894-8828 Bloomingdale ***(G-2016)***
Tetra Pak Inc D 847 955-6000 Vernon Hills ***(G-20103)***
Tishma Technology LLC F 847 884-1805 Schaumburg ***(G-18749)***
▲ **Triangle Technologies Inc** G 630 736-3318 Streamwood ***(G-19599)***
Ultra Packaging Inc G 630 595-9820 Bensenville ***(G-1905)***
Unique Blister Company F 630 289-1232 Bartlett ***(G-1319)***
Weigh Right Automatic Scale Co G 815 726-4626 Joliet ***(G-11944)***
▲ **Weiler Engineering Inc** D 847 697-4900 Elgin ***(G-8778)***
◆ **Winpak Portion Packaging Inc** D 708 753-5700 Sauk Village ***(G-18401)***
World Cup Packaging Inc G 815 624-6501 South Beloit ***(G-19127)***
◆ **Z Automation Company** E 847 483-0120 Mundelein ***(G-14748)***
Zitropack Ltd F 630 543-1016 Addison ***(G-341)***

3566 Speed Changers, Drives & Gears

Afton Chemical Corporation B 618 583-1000 East Saint Louis ***(G-8296)***
Allied Gear Co G 773 287-8742 River Forest ***(G-17049)***
American Gear Inc F 815 537-5111 Prophetstown ***(G-16830)***
Amk Automation Corp G 804 348-2125 Carpentersville ***(G-3092)***
▲ **Arrow Gear Company** B 630 969-7640 Downers Grove ***(G-7955)***
Brock Equipment Company E 815 459-4210 Woodstock ***(G-21367)***
▲ **Diequa Corporation** E 630 980-1133 Bloomingdale ***(G-1988)***
Dynamic Manufacturing Inc E 708 343-8753 Melrose Park ***(G-13857)***
Dynamic Powertrain Reman LLC F 708 343-5444 Melrose Park ***(G-13858)***
Engelhardt Gear Co E 847 766-7070 Elk Grove Village ***(G-8978)***
Fact NA LLC G 847 421-1125 Hoffman Estates ***(G-11422)***
Gam Enterprises Inc E 847 649-2500 Mount Prospect ***(G-14530)***
Hadley Gear Manufacturing Co F 773 722-1030 Chicago ***(G-4765)***
▲ **Industrial Motion Control LLC** C 847 459-5200 Wheeling ***(G-20915)***
▲ **Ll Gear Inc** G 630 226-1688 Romeoville ***(G-17843)***
Martin Sprocket & Gear Inc F 847 298-8844 Des Plaines ***(G-7800)***
Midwest Converters Inc F 815 229-9808 Rockford ***(G-17525)***
▲ **Mitsubishi Elc Automtn Inc** C 847 478-2100 Vernon Hills ***(G-20075)***
▲ **Nidec-Shimpo America Corp** E 630 924-7138 Glendale Heights ***(G-10479)***
Nuttall Gear LLC G 815 389-6267 South Beloit ***(G-19105)***
▲ **Omni Gear and Machine Corp** F 815 723-4327 Joliet ***(G-11911)***
▲ **Overton Chicago Gear Corp** D 773 638-0508 Chicago ***(G-5719)***
Productigear Inc E 773 847-4505 Chicago ***(G-5893)***
Prophet Gear Co E 815 537-2002 Prophetstown ***(G-16834)***
Quad Plus LLC E 815 740-0860 Joliet ***(G-11919)***
Raycar Gear & Machine Company E 815 874-3948 Rockford ***(G-17566)***
▲ **Reliance Gear Corporation** D 630 543-6640 Addison ***(G-270)***
▲ **Rhino Tool Company** F 309 853-5555 Kewanee ***(G-12040)***
▼ **Rj Link International Inc** F 815 874-8110 Rockford ***(G-17576)***
Rockford Jobbing Service Inc G 815 398-8661 Rockford ***(G-17596)***
Ruby Automation LLC F 815 624-5959 South Beloit ***(G-19112)***
Sfc of Illinois Inc E 815 745-2100 Warren ***(G-20224)***
Sumitomo Machinery Corp Amer E 630 752-0200 Glendale Heights ***(G-10504)***
Surge Clutch & Drive Line Co G 708 331-1352 South Holland ***(G-19247)***
Weldon Corporation E 708 343-4700 Maywood ***(G-13680)***
▲ **Wittenstein Inc** E 630 540-5300 Bartlett ***(G-1325)***
◆ **Yaskawa America Inc** C 847 887-7000 Waukegan ***(G-20520)***
Zic Incorporated G 847 680-8833 Wheeling ***(G-21016)***

3567 Indl Process Furnaces & Ovens

▼ **Amiberica Inc** E 773 247-3600 Chicago ***(G-3679)***
Anderson Msnry Refr Specialists G 847 540-8885 Lake Zurich ***(G-12384)***
◆ **Armil/Cfs Inc** E 708 339-6810 South Holland ***(G-19198)***
Burdett Burner Mfg Inc G 630 617-5060 Villa Park ***(G-20135)***
Calco Controls Inc F 847 639-3858 Crystal Lake ***(G-7176)***
Campbell International Inc E 408 661-0794 Wauconda ***(G-20339)***
◆ **Catalytic Products Intl Inc** E 847 438-0334 Lake Zurich ***(G-12390)***
▼ **Chicago Brick Oven LLC** G 630 359-4793 Woodridge ***(G-21284)***

Dane Industries LLC .... D 815 234-2811
Byron *(G-2752)*
Delta-Therm Corporation .... F 847 526-2407
Crystal Lake *(G-7193)*
Diablo Furnaces LLC .... F 815 636-7502
Machesney Park *(G-13340)*
▲ Durex International Corp .... B 847 639-5600
Cary *(G-3157)*
◆ Elastec Inc .... C 618 382-2525
Carmi *(G-2904)*
Elgin National Industries Inc .... D 314 776-2848
Raleigh *(G-16960)*
Enders Process Equipment Corp .... G 630 469-3787
Glendale Heights *(G-10449)*
Fish Oven and Equipment Corp .... E 847 526-8686
Wauconda *(G-20351)*
Furnace Fixers Inc .... G 630 736-0670
Streamwood *(G-19576)*
G & M Fabricating Inc .... G 815 282-1744
Roscoe *(G-17907)*
▼ Grieve Corporation .... D 847 546-8225
Round Lake *(G-18078)*
Heat Systems Instrs Svc Co LLC .... G 630 404-6884
Willowbrook *(G-21046)*
Henderson Engineering Co Inc .... G 815 786-9471
Sandwich *(G-18374)*
▲ Henry Technologies Inc .... G 217 483-2406
Chatham *(G-3421)*
Hts Chicago Inc .... G 630 352-3690
Wheaton *(G-20804)*
IDI Fabrication Inc .... F 630 783-2246
Lemont *(G-12566)*
Infratrol LLC .... E 779 475-3098
Byron *(G-2753)*
◆ Ipsen Inc .... C 815 332-4941
Cherry Valley *(G-3442)*
Ipsen Inc .... E 815 239-2385
Pecatonica *(G-16322)*
▲ J N Machinery Corp .... G 224 699-9161
East Dundee *(G-8203)*
K H Huppert Co .... G 708 339-2020
South Holland *(G-19225)*
Lv Ventures Inc .... E 312 993-1758
Chicago *(G-5290)*
◆ M H Detrick Company .... E 708 479-5085
Frankfort *(G-9814)*
◆ Magneco/Metrel Inc .... E 630 543-6660
Addison *(G-190)*
Maintenance Inc .... G 708 598-1390
La Grange *(G-12082)*
▼ McEnglevan Indus Frnc Mfg Inc .... G 217 446-0941
Danville *(G-7363)*
▲ Midco International Inc .... E 773 604-8700
Chicago *(G-5433)*
Moffitt Co .... G 847 678-5450
Schiller Park *(G-18828)*
Northpoint Heating & Air Cond .... G 847 731-1067
Zion *(G-21521)*
▼ Oakley Industrial McHy Inc .... E 847 966-0052
Elk Grove Village *(G-9157)*
Paul D Stark & Associates .... F 630 964-7111
Downers Grove *(G-8070)*
Pioneer Express .... G 217 236-3022
Perry *(G-16562)*
Precision Chrome Inc .... E 847 587-1515
Fox Lake *(G-9753)*
Precision Quincy Ovens LLC .... E 302 602-8738
South Beloit *(G-19108)*
Quincy Lab Inc .... E 773 622-2428
Chicago *(G-5938)*
◆ Tempco Electric Heater Corp .... B 630 350-2252
Wood Dale *(G-21248)*
▲ Tempro International Corp .... G 847 677-5370
Skokie *(G-19044)*
Thermal Solutions Inc .... G 217 352-7019
Savoy *(G-18417)*
Titanium Inc .... G 847 691-5446
Grayslake *(G-10802)*
Tks Control Systems Inc .... F 630 554-3020
Oswego *(G-16027)*
Uic Inc .... G 815 744-4477
Joliet *(G-11937)*
Westran Thermal Processing LLC .... E 815 634-1001
South Beloit *(G-19123)*
◆ Zeman Mfg Co .... E 630 960-2300
Lisle *(G-12958)*

3568 Mechanical Power Transmission Eqpt, NEC

Active Tool and Machine Inc .... F 708 599-0022
Oak Lawn *(G-15697)*
Allied Gear Co .... G 773 287-8742
River Forest *(G-17049)*
Allied-Locke Industries Inc .... E 800 435-7752
Dixon *(G-7888)*
▲ Arrow Gear Company .... B 630 969-7640
Downers Grove *(G-7955)*
◆ Aurora Bearing Company .... B 630 897-8941
Montgomery *(G-14230)*
▲ Bearing Sales Corporation .... E 773 282-8686
Chicago *(G-3855)*
Bearings Manufacturing Company .... F 773 583-6703
Chicago *(G-3856)*
Borgwarner Transm Systems Inc .... A 708 547-2600
Bellwood *(G-1618)*
Chicago Die Casting Mfg Co .... E 847 671-5010
Franklin Park *(G-9904)*
▲ Cobalt Chains Inc .... F 309 698-9250
East Peoria *(G-8262)*
▲ Composite Bearings Mfg .... F 630 595-8334
Wood Dale *(G-21178)*
◆ Deublin Company .... C 847 689-8600
Waukegan *(G-20437)*
Dyneer Corporation .... B 217 228-6011
Quincy *(G-16877)*
▲ E N M Company .... D 773 775-8400
Chicago *(G-4425)*
Excalbur Pr-Keyed Shafting Inc .... F 800 487-0514
Wauconda *(G-20349)*
Federal-Mogul Motorparts LLC .... C 773 478-0404
Chicago *(G-4571)*
▲ Flex-Weld Inc .... D 815 334-3662
Woodstock *(G-21387)*
Forbo Siegling LLC .... F 630 595-4031
Wood Dale *(G-21188)*
Force America Inc .... F 815 730-3600
Joliet *(G-11866)*
Frantz Manufacturing Company .... D 815 564-0991
Sterling *(G-19510)*
▲ Galaxy Sourcing Inc .... G 630 532-5003
Addison *(G-133)*
Grayslake Feed Sales Inc .... G 847 223-4855
Grayslake *(G-10779)*
Hadley Gear Manufacturing Co .... F 773 722-1030
Chicago *(G-4765)*
Hyspan Precision Products Inc .... E 773 277-0700
South Holland *(G-19223)*
▼ Illinois Pulley & Gear Inc .... G 847 407-9595
Schaumburg *(G-18556)*
▲ Industrial Motion Control LLC .... C 847 459-5200
Wheeling *(G-20915)*
Innovative Mag Drive LLC .... G 630 543-4240
Chicago *(G-4931)*
Innovative Mag-Drive LLC .... F 630 543-4240
Addison *(G-155)*
Isostatic Industries Inc .... E 773 286-3444
Chicago *(G-4973)*
J T C Inc .... F 773 292-9262
Chicago *(G-4995)*
▲ Kgbal Manufacturing LLC .... G 312 841-3545
Carol Stream *(G-3009)*
La Salle Co Esda .... G 815 433-5622
Ottawa *(G-16058)*
◆ Lovejoy Inc .... C 630 852-0500
Downers Grove *(G-8048)*
Lv Ventures Inc .... G 312 993-1800
Chicago *(G-5289)*
Marland Clutch .... G 800 216-3515
South Beloit *(G-19098)*
Martin Sprocket & Gear Inc .... F 847 298-8844
Des Plaines *(G-7800)*
Mathis Energy LLC .... G 309 925-3177
Tremont *(G-19898)*
Metal Ceramics Inc .... G 847 678-2293
Franklin Park *(G-9995)*
Nagel-Chase Inc .... G 847 336-4494
Gurnee *(G-10902)*
Naylor Automotive Engrg Co Inc .... F 773 582-6900
Chicago *(G-5558)*
▼ NTN USA Corporation .... C 847 298-4652
Mount Prospect *(G-14554)*
▲ Peer Chain Company .... D 847 775-4600
Waukegan *(G-20475)*
Process Screw Products Inc .... E 815 864-2220
Shannon *(G-18872)*
Productigear Inc .... E 773 847-4505
Chicago *(G-5893)*
Prophet Gear Co .... E 815 537-2002
Prophetstown *(G-16834)*
Raycar Gear & Machine Company .... E 815 874-3948
Rockford *(G-17566)*
▲ Reliance Gear Corporation .... D 630 543-6640
Addison *(G-270)*
Rexnord Industries LLC .... D 630 969-1770
Downers Grove *(G-8087)*
Rimtec Corporation .... F 630 628-0036
Addison *(G-275)*
▲ Ringspann Corporation .... F 847 678-3581
Franklin Park *(G-10036)*
Rockford Jobbing Service Inc .... G 815 398-8661
Rockford *(G-17596)*
S&R Precision Machine LLC .... F 815 469-6544
Frankfort *(G-9835)*
SKF USA Inc .... D 847 742-0700
Elgin *(G-8736)*
Surge Clutch & Drive Line Co .... G 708 331-1352
South Holland *(G-19247)*
Tb Woods Incorporated .... D 815 389-6600
South Beloit *(G-19116)*
▲ Technymon Technology USA Inc .... G 630 787-0501
Wood Dale *(G-21247)*
▲ Thk America Inc .... C 847 310-1111
Schaumburg *(G-18747)*
▲ US Tsubaki Holdings Inc .... C 847 459-9500
Wheeling *(G-21003)*
US Tsubaki Power Transm LLC .... C 847 459-9500
Wheeling *(G-21004)*
◆ Walterscheid Inc Woodridge .... C 630 972-9300
Woodridge *(G-21345)*
Worldwide Trans and Diff Corp .... G 773 930-3447
Chicago *(G-6679)*
Wpg US Holdco LLC .... B 312 517-3750
Chicago *(G-6681)*
Wrench .... G 773 609-1698
Chicago *(G-6684)*

3569 Indl Machinery & Eqpt, NEC

Aberdon Enterprises .... F 847 228-1300
Elk Grove Village *(G-8794)*
Accelrted Mch Design Engrg LLC .... E 815 316-6381
Rockford *(G-17290)*
All Metal Recycling Company .... G 847 530-4825
Villa Park *(G-20130)*
▲ Amkus Inc .... E 630 515-1800
Downers Grove *(G-7951)*
Apf US Inc .... G 217 304-0027
Danville *(G-7320)*
Aquagreen Dispositions LLC .... G 708 606-0211
Monee *(G-14196)*
Aquagreen Dispositions LLC .... G 708 606-0211
South Holland *(G-19196)*
▲ Arrow Pneumatics Inc .... D 708 343-6177
Broadview *(G-2418)*
Atlas Material Tstg Tech LLC .... E 773 327-4520
Chicago *(G-3767)*
▲ Atlas Material Tstg Tech LLC .... C 773 327-4520
Mount Prospect *(G-14512)*
◆ Ats Sortimat USA LLC .... D 847 925-1234
Rolling Meadows *(G-17713)*
Automatic Feeder Company Inc .... F 847 534-2300
Schaumburg *(G-18449)*
Automation Systems Inc .... E 847 671-9515
Melrose Park *(G-13828)*
Averus Usa Inc .... D 800 913-7034
Elgin *(G-8518)*
Barrington Automation Ltd .... E 847 458-0900
Lake In The Hills *(G-12329)*
Boley Tool & Machine Works Inc .... C 309 694-2722
East Peoria *(G-8254)*
Bowl Doctors Inc .... G 815 282-6009
Machesney Park *(G-13330)*
Camfil USA Inc .... D 815 459-6600
Crystal Lake *(G-7177)*
Centec Automation Inc .... G 847 791-9430
Palatine *(G-16098)*
Central Hydraulics Inc .... G 309 527-5238
El Paso *(G-8434)*
Century Filter Products Inc .... G 773 477-1790
Chicago *(G-4060)*
Citizenprime LLC .... G 708 995-1241
Mokena *(G-14075)*
▲ Classic Fasteners LLC .... G 630 605-0195
Saint Charles *(G-18170)*
Cleavenger Associates Inc .... G 630 221-0007
Winfield *(G-21109)*
▲ Component Products Inc .... E 847 301-1000
Elmhurst *(G-9352)*

S I C

35 INDUSTRIAL AND COMMERCIAL MACHINERY AND COMPUTER EQUIPMENT SIC SECTION

Concep Machine Co Inc E 847 498-9740
Northbrook *(G-15364)*

Concept and Design Services G 847 259-1675
Mount Prospect *(G-14519)*

▼ Csiteq LLC F 312 265-1509
Rosemont *(G-18011)*

▲ CTS Advanced Materials LLC E 630 577-8800
Lisle *(G-12879)*

▲ Custom Filter LLC D 630 906-2100
Aurora *(G-948)*

▲ Diamond Machine Werks Inc E 847 437-0665
Arlington Heights *(G-728)*

▲ Disa Holding Corp G 630 820-3000
Oswego *(G-16002)*

Doms Incorporated E 847 838-6723
Antioch *(G-610)*

Dtc Products Inc G 630 513-3323
Saint Charles *(G-18188)*

DTS America Inc G 847 783-0401
East Dundee *(G-8193)*

Eberle Manufacturing Company F 847 215-0100
Wheeling *(G-20885)*

Egd Manufacturing Inc G 815 964-2900
Rockford *(G-17391)*

Evac Systems Fire & Rescue F 309 764-7812
Moline *(G-14143)*

Evoqua Water Technologies LLC G 618 451-1205
Granite City *(G-10705)*

Fanuc America Corporation E 847 898-5000
Hoffman Estates *(G-11423)*

Fill-Weigh Inc G 815 254-4704
Plainfield *(G-16665)*

Filter Monkey LLC G 630 773-4402
Itasca *(G-11656)*

Filter Renew Tecnologies G 815 344-2200
McCullom Lake *(G-13711)*

Filters To You G 815 939-0700
Bradley *(G-2281)*

Fire Systems Holdings Inc F 708 333-4130
Mokena *(G-14081)*

Flame Guard Usa LLC G 815 219-4074
Vernon Hills *(G-20054)*

▲ Flow Pro Products Inc F 815 836-1900
Romeoville *(G-17825)*

▲ Fryer To Fuel Inc G 309 654-2875
Cordova *(G-7006)*

G & W Technical Corporation G 847 487-0990
Island Lake *(G-11607)*

G&K-Vijuk Intern Corp G 630 530-2203
Elmhurst *(G-9365)*

Gaunt Industries Inc G 847 671-0776
Franklin Park *(G-9949)*

Gutter Masters G 309 686-1234
Peoria *(G-16447)*

H2o Filter Inc G 630 963-3303
Lisle *(G-12896)*

◆ Helix International Inc G 847 709-0666
Itasca *(G-11663)*

Higman LLC G 618 785-2545
Baldwin *(G-1185)*

ICC Intrntonal Celsius Concept G 773 993-4405
Cicero *(G-6853)*

Illinois Tool Works Inc F 708 720-0300
Frankfort *(G-9803)*

Ima Automation Usa Inc D 815 885-8800
Loves Park *(G-13217)*

Industrial Filter Pump Mfg Co G 708 656-7800
Cicero *(G-6855)*

Industrial Pipe and Supply Co E 708 652-7511
Chicago *(G-4909)*

▲ Inlet & Pipe Protection Inc G 630 355-3288
Naperville *(G-14974)*

Innovative Industrial Svcs LLC F 309 527-2035
El Paso *(G-8439)*

▲ Intech Industries Inc F 847 487-5599
Wauconda *(G-20361)*

LDI Industries Inc D 847 669-7510
Huntley *(G-11550)*

Leading Americas Inc G 815 568-2199
Hampshire *(G-10976)*

Leaffilter North LLC D 630 595-9605
Wood Dale *(G-21207)*

Ll Chou Metals Inc G 312 451-4834
Chicago *(G-5215)*

Linear Kinetics Inc G 630 365-0075
Maple Park *(G-13463)*

Lsp Industries Inc F 815 226-8090
Rockford *(G-17497)*

▼ Micron Filter Cartridges Corp G 630 337-3877
Elmhurst *(G-9402)*

Mity Inc G 630 365-5030
Elburn *(G-8461)*

▼ Norman Filter Company LLC D 708 233-5521
Bridgeview *(G-2368)*

▲ Nsk-America Corporation F 847 843-7664
Hoffman Estates *(G-11440)*

Numerical Control Incorporated G 708 389-8140
Alsip *(G-486)*

Online Inc F 815 363-8008
McHenry *(G-13774)*

PAcrimson Fire Risk Svcs Inc G 630 424-3400
Lombard *(G-13115)*

▲ Paratech Incorporated D 815 469-3911
Frankfort *(G-9821)*

◆ Perma-Pipe Intl Holdings Inc E 847 966-1000
Niles *(G-15158)*

Pro Techmation Inc G 815 459-5909
Crystal Lake *(G-7248)*

Profile Screens Incorporated G 309 543-2082
Havana *(G-11120)*

Progressive Recovery Inc D 618 286-5000
Dupo *(G-8142)*

▲ Pulsarlube USA Inc G 847 593-5300
Elk Grove Village *(G-9201)*

Quality Cleaning Fluids Inc G 847 451-1190
Franklin Park *(G-10029)*

Rainmaker G 847 998-0838
Glenview *(G-10608)*

▲ Rehobot Inc G 815 385-7777
McHenry *(G-13786)*

Robko Flock Coating Company G 847 272-6202
Northbrook *(G-15474)*

Roodhouse Fire Protection Dst E 217 589-5134
Roodhouse *(G-17895)*

Rotospray Mfg Inc G 708 478-3307
Mokena *(G-14113)*

Saicor Inc G 630 530-0350
Villa Park *(G-20170)*

Smb Toolroom Inc G 309 353-7396
Pekin *(G-16361)*

Smith Power Transmission Co G 773 526-5512
Chicago *(G-6193)*

Standard Indus & Auto Eqp Inc E 630 289-9500
Hanover Park *(G-11014)*

State Line International Inc G 708 251-5772
Lansing *(G-12518)*

Superheat Fgh Services Inc F 618 251-9450
Roxana *(G-18103)*

Systems Piping G 847 948-1373
Deerfield *(G-7651)*

Tampotech Decorating Inc G 847 515-2968
Huntley *(G-11567)*

Technics Fabrication Inc F 630 938-4709
Bolingbrook *(G-2249)*

▲ Tomermo Inc E 815 229-5077
Rockford *(G-17665)*

Tri-Dim Filter Corporation E 847 695-5822
Elgin *(G-8759)*

Trueline Inc E 309 378-2571
Downs *(G-8113)*

U S Filter Products G 618 451-1205
Granite City *(G-10747)*

U S Filters G 815 932-8154
Bradley *(G-2294)*

United States Filter/Iwt G 815 877-3041
Rockford *(G-17672)*

Walach Manufacturing Co Inc F 773 836-2060
Chicago *(G-6585)*

Water Products Company Ill Inc E 630 553-0840
Yorkville *(G-21505)*

Western Slate Company D 847 683-4400
Hampshire *(G-10990)*

Wm W Nugent & Co Inc E 847 673-8109
Skokie *(G-19056)*

3571 Electronic Computers

Accelerated Assemblies Inc E 630 616-6680
Elk Grove Village *(G-8798)*

Ace Pcb Design Inc G 847 674-8745
Skokie *(G-18912)*

Alegria Company C 608 726-2336
Chicago *(G-3601)*

Antares Computer Systems Inc G 773 783-8855
Chicago *(G-3704)*

Atmark Trading Inc E 312 933-7907
Chicago *(G-3771)*

Bondfire LLC G 630 742-8022
Oswego *(G-15994)*

Derbytech Inc E 309 755-2662
East Moline *(G-8225)*

◆ Emac Inc E 618 529-4525
Carbondale *(G-2841)*

Fourier Systems Inc G 708 478-5333
Homer Glen *(G-11481)*

General Dynmics Mssion Systems C 703 876-3000
Chicago *(G-4670)*

George Press Inc G 217 324-2242
Litchfield *(G-12964)*

Gld Industries Inc G 217 390-9594
Champaign *(G-3296)*

High Power Inc F 773 581-7650
Chicago *(G-4817)*

Hp Inc B 650 857-1501
Chicago *(G-4853)*

Hp Inc D 309 664-4000
Bloomington *(G-2060)*

Hp Inc C 650 857-1501
Schaumburg *(G-18551)*

Hp Inc E 650 857-1501
Chicago *(G-4854)*

ICC Intrntonal Celsius Concept G 773 993-4405
Cicero *(G-6853)*

Integrity Technologies LLC G 850 240-6089
Elgin *(G-8628)*

Interntional Cmpt Concepts Inc E 847 808-7789
Northbrook *(G-15407)*

Inverom Corporation G 630 568-5609
Burr Ridge *(G-2690)*

Jets Computing Inc G 618 585-6676
Bunker Hill *(G-2634)*

Js Poole Inc F 847 241-8441
Chicago *(G-5057)*

Koi Computers Inc G 630 627-8811
Downers Grove *(G-8040)*

Konica Minolta G 630 893-8238
Roselle *(G-17962)*

Konica Mnlta Bus Sltons USA In E 309 671-1360
Peoria *(G-16467)*

Monroe Associates Inc G 217 665-3898
Bethany *(G-1968)*

Motorola Solutions Inc C 847 576-8600
Schaumburg *(G-18637)*

Motorola Solutions Inc G 847 341-3485
Oak Brook *(G-15647)*

Nano Technologies Inc G 630 517-8824
Wheaton *(G-20813)*

National Micro Systems Inc G 312 566-0414
Chicago *(G-5549)*

Nazdar Sourceone G 800 677-4657
Countryside *(G-7066)*

Northrop Grumman Systems Corp A 847 259-9600
Rolling Meadows *(G-17755)*

Officenation Inc E 847 504-3000
Northfield *(G-15525)*

Ogwuru Uzoaku G 312 286-5593
Chicago *(G-5664)*

Perkins Enterprise Inc G 708 560-3837
South Holland *(G-19240)*

Pinehurst Bus Solutions Corp G 630 842-6155
Winfield *(G-21115)*

Pro-Parts G 773 595-5966
Chicago *(G-5889)*

Rico Computers Enterprises Inc F 708 594-7426
Chicago *(G-6029)*

RMC Imaging Inc G 815 885-4521
Rockford *(G-17579)*

Royer Systems Inc G 217 965-3699
Virden *(G-20189)*

Tech Global Inc G 224 623-2000
Elgin *(G-8747)*

Texmac Inc G 630 244-4702
Mundelein *(G-14743)*

Toggle Inc G 323 882-6339
Chicago *(G-6384)*

W S C Inc G 312 372-1121
Chicago *(G-6579)*

3572 Computer Storage Devices

10th Magnitude LLC E 224 628-9047
Chicago *(G-3461)*

Ally Global Corporation G 773 822-3373
Chicago *(G-3625)*

Amaitis and Associates Inc F 847 428-1269
Wood Dale *(G-21160)*

Atmark Trading Inc E 312 933-7907
Chicago *(G-3771)*

▲ Ckd USA Corporation E 847 368-0539
Schaumburg *(G-18478)*

Context Software Systems G 630 654-0291
Westmont *(G-20733)*

Das Brothers LLC .... G 925 980-6180
Frankfort *(G-9782)*
▲ **Dickson/Unigage Inc** .... E 630 543-3747
Addison *(G-92)*
E Mc .... G 217 228-1280
Quincy *(G-16878)*
▲ **E N M Company** .... D 773 775-8400
Chicago *(G-4425)*
EMC Corporation .... E 312 577-0026
Chicago *(G-4491)*
EMC Corporation .... G 312 577-0026
Chicago *(G-4492)*
EMC Fire Inc .... G 480 225-5498
Channahon *(G-3382)*
File System Labs LLC .... F 617 431-4313
Northbrook *(G-15390)*
Guidance Software Inc .... G 847 994-7324
Chicago *(G-4751)*
Illinoi Eye Surgns/Quantm Visn .... G 618 315-6560
Mount Vernon *(G-14615)*
International Bus Mchs Corp .... C 312 423-6640
Chicago *(G-4951)*
Interntional Cmpt Concepts Inc .... E 847 808-7789
Northbrook *(G-15407)*
Numeridex Incorporated .... F 847 541-8840
Wheeling *(G-20948)*
Omobono Inc .... G 312 523-2179
Chicago *(G-5677)*
Pinehurst Bus Solutions Corp .... G 630 842-6155
Winfield *(G-21115)*
Quantum Corporation .... D 312 372-2857
Chicago *(G-5933)*
Quantum Healing .... G 217 414-2412
Mechanicsburg *(G-13812)*
Quantum Marketing LLC .... G 630 257-7012
Lemont *(G-12587)*
Quantum Vision Centers .... G 618 656-7774
Swansea *(G-19695)*
Western Digital Tech Inc .... G 949 672-7000
Chicago *(G-6608)*
Wevaultcom LLC .... G 877 938-2858
Crystal Lake *(G-7295)*
Xlogotech Inc .... G 888 244-5152
Palatine *(G-16177)*

3575 Computer Terminals

Art Cnc Machining LLC .... G 708 907-3090
Bridgeview *(G-2325)*
Blue Gem Computers Inc .... G 708 562-5524
Morris *(G-14295)*
Charles Industries LLC .... D 217 932-5292
Casey *(G-3200)*
◆ **Grayhill Inc** .... B 708 354-1040
La Grange *(G-12077)*
Grayhill Inc .... G 708 482-1411
Mc Cook *(G-13691)*
Honeywell International Inc .... C 815 745-2131
Warren *(G-20223)*
▲ **Kristel Limited Partnership** .... D 630 443-1290
Saint Charles *(G-18222)*
Lightfoot Technologies Inc .... G 331 302-1297
Naperville *(G-14864)*
Mimo Display LLC .... G 855 937-6466
Libertyville *(G-12681)*
◆ **Nec Display Solutions Amer Inc** .... C 630 467-3000
Downers Grove *(G-8064)*
T 26 Inc .... G 773 862-1201
Chicago *(G-6306)*
Teledyne Lecroy Inc .... E 847 888-0450
Elgin *(G-8749)*

3577 Computer Peripheral Eqpt, NEC

Adazon Inc .... G 847 235-2700
Lake Forest *(G-12220)*
▲ **Ambir Technology Inc** .... G 630 530-5400
Wood Dale *(G-21161)*
American Digital Corporation .... E 847 637-4300
Elk Grove Village *(G-8823)*
Andrew New Zealand Inc .... E 708 873-3507
Orland Park *(G-15940)*
Antares Computer Systems Inc .... G 773 783-8855
Chicago *(G-3704)*
Applus Technologies Inc .... E 312 661-1100
Chicago *(G-3714)*
Automated Systems & Control Co .... G 847 735-8310
Lake Bluff *(G-12172)*
▲ **Bar Codes Inc** .... D 800 351-9962
Chicago *(G-3828)*
Barcodesource Inc .... G 630 545-9590
Glen Ellyn *(G-10397)*
Bigtime Fantasy Sports Inc .... G 630 605-7544
Lombard *(G-13043)*
Bishop Image Group Inc .... G 312 735-8153
Chicago *(G-3900)*
Black Box Corporation .... G 847 439-5000
Elk Grove Village *(G-8868)*
Black Box Corporation .... F 312 656-8807
Tinley Park *(G-19812)*
Bowe Bell + Hwell Scanners LLC .... E 847 675-7600
Wheeling *(G-20864)*
Bycap Inc .... E 773 561-4976
Chicago *(G-3988)*
CDI Computers US Corporation .... G 888 226-5727
Chicago *(G-4048)*
CDs Office Systems Inc .... D 800 367-1508
Springfield *(G-19343)*
Cisco Systems Inc .... B 847 678-6600
Des Plaines *(G-7747)*
Cobius Halthcare Solutions LLC .... G 847 656-8700
Northbrook *(G-15363)*
Commscope Technologies LLC .... B 779 435-6000
Joliet *(G-11845)*
Computerprox .... F 847 516-8560
Elgin *(G-8548)*
◆ **Contemporary Ctrl Systems Inc** .... D 630 963-7070
Downers Grove *(G-7980)*
Corporate Graphics Inc .... G 630 762-9000
Saint Charles *(G-18176)*
Dennis Wright .... G 847 816-6110
Vernon Hills *(G-20049)*
▲ **Digital Check Corp** .... E 847 446-2285
Northbrook *(G-15376)*
Domino Amjet Inc .... E 847 662-3148
Gurnee *(G-10869)*
Domino Lasers Inc .... E 847 855-1364
Gurnee *(G-10872)*
◆ **Dover Corporation** .... C 630 541-1540
Downers Grove *(G-7989)*
Election Systems & Sftwr LLC .... F 815 397-8144
Rockford *(G-17394)*
Epix Inc .... G 847 465-1818
Buffalo Grove *(G-2535)*
Gb Marketing Inc .... F 847 367-0101
Vernon Hills *(G-20055)*
Hafner Duplicating Company .... G 312 362-0120
Chicago *(G-4766)*
▲ **Hoffman J&M Farm Holdings Inc** .... D 847 671-6280
Schiller Park *(G-18813)*
Ibs Conversions Inc .... D 630 571-9100
Oak Brook *(G-15626)*
Ig US Holdings Inc .... G 312 884-0179
Chicago *(G-4879)*
Illinois Tool Works Inc .... D 618 997-1716
Marion *(G-13518)*
Illinois Tool Works Inc .... C 847 724-7500
Des Plaines *(G-7784)*
Imageworks Manufacturing Inc .... E 708 503-1122
Park Forest *(G-16255)*
John Harland Company .... G 815 293-4350
Romeoville *(G-17836)*
Lexmark International Inc .... E 847 318-5700
Rosemont *(G-18030)*
Mediarecall Holdings LLC .... G 847 513-6710
Northbrook *(G-15430)*
Micros Systems Inc .... F 443 285-6000
Itasca *(G-11702)*
Oceancomm Incorporated .... G 800 757-3266
Chicago *(G-5653)*
Omex Technologies Inc .... G 847 850-5858
Wheeling *(G-20949)*
▲ **Omni Vision Inc** .... E 630 893-1720
Glendale Heights *(G-10481)*
Paradise Group LLC .... G 779 207-9077
Chicago *(G-5757)*
Pos Plus LLC .... F 618 993-7587
Marion *(G-13529)*
Poynting Products Inc .... G 708 386-2139
Oak Park *(G-15769)*
Precision Computer Methods .... G 630 208-8000
Elburn *(G-8469)*
◆ **Printjet Corporation** .... F 815 877-7511
Machesney Park *(G-13368)*
Richardson Electronics Ltd .... C 630 208-2278
Lafox *(G-12137)*
Riverbed Technology Inc .... G 217 344-8091
Champaign *(G-3343)*
Scadaware Inc .... F 309 665-0135
Normal *(G-15224)*
Sg2 .... G 847 779-5500
Skokie *(G-19029)*
Singer Data Products Inc .... G 630 860-6500
Bensenville *(G-1893)*
Source Software Inc .... G 815 922-7717
Lockport *(G-13024)*
▲ **Spartanics Ltd** .... E 847 394-5700
Rolling Meadows *(G-17777)*
Sparton Aydin LLC .... G 800 772-7866
Schaumburg *(G-18716)*
Tangent Systems Inc .... F 847 882-3833
Hoffman Estates *(G-11466)*
▲ **Tech Global Inc** .... F 847 532-4882
Elgin *(G-8746)*
Teledyne Lecroy Inc .... E 847 888-0450
Elgin *(G-8749)*
Timeout Devices Inc .... F 847 729-6543
Glenview *(G-10632)*
Tomantron Inc .... F 708 532-2456
Tinley Park *(G-19860)*
◆ **Tripp Manufacturing Company** .... B 773 869-1111
Chicago *(G-6429)*
United Universal Inds Inc .... E 815 727-4445
Joliet *(G-11939)*
Verdasee Solutions Inc .... G 847 265-9441
Gurnee *(G-10944)*
Xerox Corporation .... E 630 573-1000
Hinsdale *(G-11383)*
Yfy Jupiter Inc .... E 312 419-8565
Chicago *(G-6699)*
Zebra Retail Solutions LLC .... G 847 634-6700
Lincolnshire *(G-12803)*
▲ **Zebra Technologies Corporation** .... B 847 634-6700
Lincolnshire *(G-12804)*
Zebra Technologies Corporation .... D 847 793-5911
Buffalo Grove *(G-2625)*
Zebra Technologies Corporation .... G 630 548-1370
Naperville *(G-14993)*
Zebra Technologies Corporation .... B 847 634-6700
Chicago *(G-6711)*
◆ **Zebra Technologies Intl LLC** .... G 847 634-6700
Lincolnshire *(G-12805)*
▲ **Zih Corp** .... G 847 634-6700
Lincolnshire *(G-12807)*
Zih Corp .... E 847 634-6700
Lincolnshire *(G-12808)*

3578 Calculating & Accounting Eqpt

Asai Chicago .... F 708 239-0133
Alsip *(G-419)*
Barcodesource Inc .... G 630 545-9590
Glen Ellyn *(G-10397)*
Business Valuation Group Inc .... G 312 595-1900
Chicago *(G-3982)*
Chase Home Finance .... G 630 617-4747
Elmhurst *(G-9343)*
Creative Merchandising Systems .... G 847 955-9990
Lincolnshire *(G-12756)*
◆ **Cummins-Allison Corp** .... B 800 786-5528
Mount Prospect *(G-14523)*
Diebold Nixdorf Incorporated .... D 847 598-3300
Schaumburg *(G-18506)*
Kahuna LLC .... F 888 357-8472
Bloomington *(G-2066)*
Micros Systems Inc .... F 443 285-6000
Itasca *(G-11702)*
OHare Shell Partners Inc .... G 847 678-1900
Schiller Park *(G-18829)*
PNC Financial Svcs Group Inc .... G 630 420-8400
Naperville *(G-14900)*
Pos Plus LLC .... F 618 993-7587
Marion *(G-13529)*
Singer Data Products Inc .... G 630 860-6500
Bensenville *(G-1893)*
▲ **Talaris Inc** .... C 630 577-1000
Lisle *(G-12948)*

3579 Office Machines, NEC

Acco Brands USA LLC .... E 708 280-4702
Addison *(G-14)*
American Perforator Company .... G 815 469-4300
Frankfort *(G-9766)*
Connies Home Health Care .... G 708 790-4000
Park Forest *(G-16253)*
Copar Corporation .... E 708 496-1859
Burbank *(G-2635)*
Cummins - Allison Corp .... D 847 299-9550
Mount Prospect *(G-14521)*
Cummins - Allison Corp .... C 847 299-9550
Mount Prospect *(G-14522)*
Cummins - Allison Corp .... F 630 833-2285
Elmhurst *(G-9357)*

Employee Codes: A=Over 500 employees, B=251-500
C=101-250, D=51-100, E=20-50, F=10-19, G=3-9
2020 Harris Illinois
Industrial Directory
969

35 INDUSTRIAL AND COMMERCIAL MACHINERY AND COMPUTER EQUIPMENT SIC SECTION

◆ Deluxe Stitcher Company Inc............D....... 847 455-4400
 Franklin Park *(G-9931)*
Direct Mail Equipment Services............G....... 815 485-7010
 New Lenox *(G-15030)*
Election Works............G....... 630 232-4030
 Geneva *(G-10268)*
Fluence Automation LLC............C....... 847 423-7400
 Arlington Heights *(G-737)*
H N C Products Inc............E....... 217 935-9100
 Clinton *(G-6921)*
▲ Holdings Liquidation Inc............A....... 312 541-9300
 Wheeling *(G-20910)*
▲ Identification Products Mfg Co............G....... 847 367-6452
 Lake Forest *(G-12264)*
Inscerco Mfg Inc............E....... 708 597-8777
 Midlothian *(G-13992)*
Ives Way Products Inc............G....... 847 223-1020
 Grayslake *(G-10784)*
◆ Klai-Co Idntification Pdts Inc............E....... 847 573-0375
 Lake Forest *(G-12270)*
Laminting Bnding Solutions Inc............G....... 847 573-0375
 Lake Forest *(G-12271)*
Lane Industries Inc............E....... 847 498-6650
 Northbrook *(G-15417)*
Multimail Solutions............G....... 847 516-9977
 Cary *(G-3181)*
Neopost R Meadows............G....... 630 467-0604
 Itasca *(G-11710)*
Pitney Bowes Inc............E....... 312 209-2216
 Schaumburg *(G-18674)*
Pitney Bowes Inc............E....... 773 755-5808
 Chicago *(G-5813)*
Pitney Bowes Inc............D....... 630 435-7500
 Lisle *(G-12927)*
Pitney Bowes Inc............E....... 800 784-4224
 Itasca *(G-11719)*
▲ Plastic Binding Laminating Inc............G....... 847 573-0375
 Lake Forest *(G-12291)*
▲ SBA Wireless Inc............E....... 847 215-8720
 Buffalo Grove *(G-2595)*
Singer Data Products Inc............G....... 630 860-6500
 Bensenville *(G-1893)*
Stenograph LLC............D....... 630 532-5100
 Elmhurst *(G-9429)*
▲ Sws Industries Inc............E....... 904 482-0091
 Woodstock *(G-21438)*
Taloc Usa Inc............G....... 847 665-8222
 Libertyville *(G-12714)*
▲ Your Supply Depot Limited............G....... 815 568-4115
 Marengo *(G-13497)*

3581 Automatic Vending Machines

Advanced Technologies Inc............G....... 847 329-9875
 Park Ridge *(G-16264)*
Classic Vending Inc............E....... 773 252-7000
 Chicago *(G-4171)*
Laurel Metal Products Inc............E....... 847 674-0064
 Lincolnwood *(G-12827)*
◆ Lucky Yuppy Puppy Co............G....... 847 437-7879
 Arlington Heights *(G-772)*
▲ Manufctrng-Resourcing Intl Inc............F....... 217 821-3733
 Shumway *(G-18904)*
▲ Partec Inc............C....... 847 678-9520
 Franklin Park *(G-10014)*
◆ Seaga Manufacturing Inc............D....... 815 297-9500
 Freeport *(G-10141)*
Singer Data Products Inc............G....... 630 860-6500
 Bensenville *(G-1893)*
Success Vending Mfg Co LLC............E....... 773 262-1685
 Chicago *(G-6263)*

3582 Commercial Laundry, Dry Clean & Pressing Mchs

B-Clean Laundromat Inc............G....... 678 983-5492
 Chicago *(G-3809)*
◆ Chicago Dryer Company............C....... 773 235-4430
 Chicago *(G-4101)*
▼ Cmv Sharper Finish Inc............E....... 773 276-4800
 Chicago *(G-4185)*
◆ Ellis Corporation............D....... 630 250-9222
 Itasca *(G-11648)*
Eminent Technologies LLC............G....... 630 416-2311
 Naperville *(G-14824)*
Extractor Corporation............F....... 847 742-3532
 South Elgin *(G-19144)*
Jetin Systems Inc............F....... 815 726-4686
 Joliet *(G-11885)*
L T P LLC............C....... 815 723-9400
 Joliet *(G-11893)*

New Spin Cycle............G....... 773 952-7490
 Chicago *(G-5580)*
Ross and White Company............F....... 847 516-3900
 Cary *(G-3187)*

3585 Air Conditioning & Heating Eqpt

Advanced Cooler Inc............G....... 630 443-8933
 Saint Charles *(G-18142)*
Air Duct Manufacturing Inc............G....... 630 620-9866
 Lisle *(G-12859)*
American Event Services LLC............G....... 217 709-1811
 Danville *(G-7319)*
American Fuel Economy Inc............G....... 815 433-3226
 Ottawa *(G-16037)*
American Soda Ftn Exch Inc............F....... 312 733-5000
 Chicago *(G-3668)*
◆ Amsted Industries Incorporated............B....... 312 645-1700
 Chicago *(G-3685)*
◆ Banner Equipment Co............G....... 815 941-9600
 Morris *(G-14294)*
▲ Bergstrom Climate Systems LLC............B....... 815 874-7821
 Rockford *(G-17319)*
Bergstrom Inc............D....... 815 874-7821
 Rockford *(G-17322)*
Bernard Cffey Vtrans Fundation............G....... 630 687-0033
 Naperville *(G-14779)*
◆ Bevstream Corp............G....... 630 761-0060
 Batavia *(G-1357)*
Big M Manufacturing LLC............G....... 217 824-9372
 Taylorville *(G-19750)*
Brunet Snow Service Company............G....... 847 846-0037
 Wood Dale *(G-21172)*
Buell Manufacturing Company............G....... 708 447-6320
 Lyons *(G-13304)*
Cardinal Construction Co............G....... 618 842-5553
 Fairfield *(G-9621)*
◆ Cerro Flow Products LLC............C....... 618 337-6000
 Sauget *(G-18392)*
◆ Chill Passion............G....... 847 778-6121
 Schaumburg *(G-18476)*
Cisco Heating & Cooling............G....... 309 637-6809
 Peoria *(G-16422)*
Clarios............F....... 630 871-7700
 Carol Stream *(G-2961)*
Commercial Rfrgn Centl III Inc............E....... 217 235-5016
 Mattoon *(G-13634)*
Continental Materials Corp............F....... 312 541-7200
 Chicago *(G-4228)*
◆ Cornelius Inc............B....... 630 539-6850
 Glendale Heights *(G-10445)*
Danfoss LLC............G....... 717 261-5000
 Loves Park *(G-13205)*
◆ Dover Corporation............C....... 630 541-1540
 Downers Grove *(G-7989)*
Durable Manufacturing Company............F....... 630 766-0398
 Bensenville *(G-1791)*
Elkay Manufacturing Company............C....... 815 493-8850
 Lanark *(G-12480)*
Elkay Manufacturing Company............B....... 708 681-1880
 Broadview *(G-2434)*
Elkay Manufacturing Company............G....... 800 223-5529
 Downers Grove *(G-7999)*
Elkay Manufacturing Company............B....... 815 273-7001
 Savanna *(G-18404)*
Enertech Global LLC............G....... 605 996-7180
 Greenville *(G-10833)*
Evapco Inc............C....... 217 923-3431
 Greenup *(G-10820)*
EZ Comfort Heating & AC............G....... 630 289-2020
 Elgin *(G-8582)*
Flinn & Dreffein Engrg Co............E....... 847 272-6374
 Northbrook *(G-15391)*
▲ Frigel North America Inc............E....... 847 540-0160
 East Dundee *(G-8196)*
Galmar Enterprises Inc............G....... 815 463-9826
 New Lenox *(G-15035)*
Gateway Industrial Power Inc............G....... 309 821-1035
 Bloomington *(G-2049)*
Goodman Manufacturing Co LP............G....... 618 234-2781
 Swansea *(G-19692)*
Goose Island Mfg & Supply Corp............G....... 708 343-4225
 Lansing *(G-12495)*
▲ Green Box America Inc............G....... 630 616-5400
 Schaumburg *(G-18541)*
▼ H A Phillips & Co............G....... 630 377-0050
 Dekalb *(G-7683)*
Habegger Corporation............G....... 217 789-4328
 Springfield *(G-19377)*
Habegger Corporation............G....... 309 793-7172
 Rock Island *(G-17221)*

Haskris Co............D....... 847 956-6420
 Elk Grove Village *(G-9028)*
Heatcraft Rfrgn Pdts LLC............B....... 217 446-3710
 Danville *(G-7344)*
▲ Heaven Fresh USA Inc............G....... 800 642-0367
 Plainfield *(G-16671)*
Henry Technologies Inc............D....... 217 483-2406
 Chatham *(G-3422)*
▲ Henry Technologies Inc............G....... 217 483-2406
 Chatham *(G-3421)*
Highland Park Mechanical Inc............G....... 847 269-3863
 Zion *(G-21517)*
Hohlflder A H Shtmtl Htg Coolg............G....... 815 965-9134
 Rockford *(G-17451)*
Honeywell International Inc............D....... 847 797-4000
 Des Plaines *(G-7778)*
▲ Howe Corporation............E....... 773 235-0200
 Chicago *(G-4851)*
ICC Intrntonal Celsius Concept............G....... 773 993-4405
 Cicero *(G-6853)*
Illinois Tool Works Inc............G....... 847 724-7500
 Glenview *(G-10560)*
Illinois Tool Works Inc............C....... 630 372-2150
 Bartlett *(G-1288)*
Illinois Tool Works Inc............C....... 847 783-5500
 Elgin *(G-8621)*
Industrial Thermo Products............G....... 847 398-8600
 Rolling Meadows *(G-17740)*
J D Refrigeration............G....... 618 345-0041
 Collinsville *(G-6963)*
John Bean Technologies Corp............D....... 312 861-5900
 Chicago *(G-5036)*
John F Mate Co............G....... 847 381-8131
 Lake Barrington *(G-12154)*
Kackert Enterprises Inc............G....... 630 898-9339
 Aurora *(G-1120)*
Kap Holdings LLC............F....... 708 948-0226
 Oak Park *(G-15759)*
▲ Kelco Industries Inc............G....... 815 334-3600
 Woodstock *(G-21398)*
▲ Kkt Chillers Inc............E....... 847 734-1600
 Wood Dale *(G-21204)*
Kool Technologies Inc............G....... 630 483-2256
 Streamwood *(G-19581)*
Leaders Bev Consulting Inc............F....... 312 497-5602
 Chicago *(G-5190)*
Lennox Industries Inc............D....... 630 378-7054
 Romeoville *(G-17842)*
M & I Heating and Cooling Inc............G....... 773 743-7073
 Chicago *(G-5296)*
◆ Maid O Mist LLC............E....... 773 685-7300
 Chicago *(G-5319)*
◆ Marshall Middleby Inc............C....... 847 741-3300
 Elgin *(G-8649)*
Marvin Schumaker Plbg Inc............G....... 815 626-8130
 Sterling *(G-19516)*
Micro Matic Usa Inc............F....... 815 968-7557
 Machesney Park *(G-13359)*
▲ Natural Choice Corporation............F....... 815 874-4444
 Loves Park *(G-13240)*
Parks Industries LLC............F....... 618 997-9608
 Marion *(G-13524)*
◆ Peerless America Incorporated............C....... 217 342-0400
 Effingham *(G-8418)*
Perfection Equipment Inc............E....... 847 244-7200
 Gurnee *(G-10911)*
◆ Polyscience Inc............D....... 847 647-0611
 Niles *(G-15161)*
Pure N Natural Systems Inc............F....... 630 372-9681
 Streamwood *(G-19591)*
Quality Filter Services............G....... 618 654-3716
 Highland *(G-11236)*
Raytheon Technologies Corp............B....... 815 226-6000
 Rockford *(G-17567)*
Reedy Industries Inc............G....... 847 729-9450
 Glenview *(G-10610)*
Ring Sheet Metal Heating & AC............G....... 309 289-4213
 Knoxville *(G-12069)*
Rukel Management LLC............A....... 630 377-8886
 Saint Charles *(G-18262)*
Ruyle Incorporated............E....... 309 674-6644
 Springfield *(G-19437)*
Scotsman Group Inc............D....... 847 215-4500
 Vernon Hills *(G-20092)*
◆ Scotsman Industries Inc............G....... 847 215-4500
 Vernon Hills *(G-20093)*
Sendra Service Corp............G....... 815 462-0061
 New Lenox *(G-15058)*
▲ Spirotherm Inc............D....... 630 307-2662
 Glendale Heights *(G-10497)*

35 INDUSTRIAL AND COMMERCIAL MACHINERY AND COMPUTER EQUIPMENT

▲ Standard Refrigeration LLC ....D...... 608 855-5800
  Wood Dale *(G-21242)*
Synergy Mech Solutions Inc ....G...... 847 437-4500
  Elk Grove Village *(G-9262)*
◆ Taylor Coml Foodservice Inc ....F...... 815 624-8333
  Rockton *(G-17703)*
Tds Inc ....E...... 847 678-2084
  Schiller Park *(G-18847)*
Temp-Air Inc ....F...... 847 931-7700
  Elgin *(G-8751)*
Temperature Equipment Corp ....G...... 815 229-2935
  Rockford *(G-17655)*
◆ Thermal Care Inc ....C...... 847 966-2260
  Niles *(G-15180)*
Thermoelectric Coolg Amer Corp ....F...... 773 342-4900
  Chicago *(G-6362)*
Trane US Inc ....C...... 630 734-3200
  Willowbrook *(G-21063)*
Trane US Inc ....G...... 708 532-8004
  Tinley Park *(G-19861)*
Ventfabrics Inc ....F...... 773 775-4477
  Chicago *(G-6534)*
▲ Voges Inc ....D...... 618 233-2760
  Belleville *(G-1608)*
York International Corporation ....D...... 815 946-2351
  Polo *(G-16761)*

3586 Measuring & Dispensing Pumps

◆ Cornelius Inc ....B...... 630 539-6850
  Glendale Heights *(G-10445)*
◆ Dover Corporation ....C...... 630 541-1540
  Downers Grove *(G-7989)*
Dromont Corporation ....G...... 404 615-2336
  Palatine *(G-16114)*
Franklin Fueling Systems Inc ....F...... 207 283-0156
  Chicago *(G-4631)*
Gfi Innovations LLC ....G...... 847 263-9000
  Antioch *(G-612)*
▲ March Manufacturing Inc ....D...... 847 729-5300
  Glenview *(G-10587)*
▲ Standard Lifts & Equipment Inc ....G...... 414 444-1000
  Hanover Park *(G-11015)*
◆ Tuthill Corporation ....E...... 630 382-4900
  Burr Ridge *(G-2727)*

3589 Service Ind Machines, NEC

◆ A J Antunes & Co ....C...... 630 784-1000
  Carol Stream *(G-2922)*
Advanage Diversified Pdts Inc ....F...... 708 331-8390
  Harvey *(G-11069)*
Advanced Ozone Tech Inc ....F...... 630 964-1300
  Downers Grove *(G-7949)*
Ali Group North America Corp ....C...... 847 215-6565
  Vernon Hills *(G-20040)*
Alternative Wastewater Systems ....G...... 630 761-8720
  Batavia *(G-1345)*
Amber Soft Inc ....F...... 630 377-6945
  Lake Barrington *(G-12141)*
Ambi-Design Incorporated ....G...... 815 964-7568
  Rockford *(G-17300)*
▲ American Vacuum Company ....G...... 847 674-8383
  Niles *(G-15102)*
American Watersource LLC ....E...... 630 778-9900
  Naperville *(G-14957)*
Amsoil Inc ....G...... 630 595-8385
  Bensenville *(G-1745)*
Applied Mechanical Tech LLC ....G...... 815 472-2700
  Momence *(G-14182)*
▼ Aquion Inc ....C...... 847 725-3000
  Roselle *(G-17938)*
Arbortech Corporation ....G...... 847 462-1111
  Johnsburg *(G-11801)*
Area Disposal Service Inc ....F...... 217 935-1300
  Clinton *(G-6919)*
Asbestos Control & Envmtl Svc ....F...... 630 690-0189
  Eola *(G-9469)*
▲ Avw Equipment Company Inc ....E...... 708 343-7738
  Maywood *(G-13661)*
Azcon Inc ....F...... 815 548-7000
  Sterling *(G-19499)*
Best Way Carpet & Uphl Clg ....G...... 618 544-8585
  Robinson *(G-17108)*
Big R Car Wash Inc ....G...... 217 367-4958
  Urbana *(G-19974)*
Bissell Inc ....G...... 815 423-1300
  Elwood *(G-9461)*
▼ Blastline USA Inc ....G...... 630 871-0147
  Carol Stream *(G-2951)*
▲ Bravilor Bonamat LLC ....F...... 630 423-9400
  Aurora *(G-926)*

Brite-O-Matic Mfg Inc ....D...... 847 956-1100
  Arlington Heights *(G-709)*
Bunn-O-Matic Corporation ....G...... 217 529-6601
  Springfield *(G-19331)*
Bunn-O-Matic Corporation ....G...... 217 528-8739
  Springfield *(G-19333)*
Bunn-O-Matic Corporation ....G...... 217 529-6601
  Springfield *(G-19334)*
Butterfield Cleaners ....G...... 847 816-7060
  Mundelein *(G-14669)*
◆ C Cretors & Co ....G...... 847 616-6900
  Wood Dale *(G-21173)*
C2 Water Inc ....G...... 312 550-1159
  Kenilworth *(G-12014)*
Carlinville Waste Water Plants ....G...... 217 854-6506
  Carlinville *(G-2868)*
Carney Flow Technics LLC ....G...... 815 277-2600
  Frankfort *(G-9777)*
▲ Carter Hoffmann LLC ....C...... 847 362-5500
  Mundelein *(G-14674)*
◆ Charger Water Conditioning Inc ....F...... 847 967-9558
  Morton Grove *(G-14395)*
Chemical Pump ....G...... 815 464-1908
  Frankfort *(G-9779)*
City of Edwardsville ....G...... 618 692-7053
  Edwardsville *(G-8352)*
City of Toulon ....G...... 309 286-7073
  Toulon *(G-19890)*
Coe Equipment Inc ....G...... 217 498-7200
  Rochester *(G-17164)*
Covington Service Installation ....G...... 309 376-4921
  Carlock *(G-2885)*
◆ Culligan International Company ....E...... 847 430-2800
  Rosemont *(G-18013)*
Cutting Edge Document Dstrctn ....F...... 630 620-0193
  Lombard *(G-13062)*
▲ D R Sperry & Co ....D...... 630 892-4361
  Aurora *(G-1083)*
Detrex Corporation ....G...... 708 345-3806
  Melrose Park *(G-13849)*
Diskin Systems Inc ....G...... 815 276-7288
  Algonquin *(G-370)*
Dml LLC ....G...... 630 231-8873
  West Chicago *(G-20572)*
▲ Dontech Industries Inc ....F...... 847 428-8222
  Gilberts *(G-10353)*
Dubois Chemicals Inc ....G...... 847 457-1813
  Rosemont *(G-18021)*
Dun-Rite Tool & Machine Co ....G...... 815 758-5464
  Cortland *(G-7020)*
Durable Manufacturing Company ....G...... 630 766-0398
  Bensenville *(G-1791)*
Earthwise Environmental Inc ....G...... 630 475-3070
  Wood Dale *(G-21183)*
◆ Ecodyne Water Treatment LLC ....E...... 630 961-5043
  Naperville *(G-14820)*
◆ Ellis Corporation ....D...... 630 250-9222
  Itasca *(G-11648)*
Enterprises One Stop ....G...... 773 924-5506
  Chicago *(G-4515)*
Equipsolutions LLC ....G...... 630 351-9070
  Roselle *(G-17953)*
◆ Evac North America Inc ....E...... 815 654-8300
  Cherry Valley *(G-3439)*
Evoqua Water Technologies LLC ....F...... 815 921-8325
  Rockford *(G-17404)*
Evoqua Water Technologies LLC ....F...... 618 451-1205
  Granite City *(G-10705)*
Extol Hydro Technologies Inc ....F...... 708 717-4371
  Palos Park *(G-16210)*
Fna Ip Holdings Inc ....D...... 847 348-1500
  Elk Grove Village *(G-9001)*
Galesburg Manufacturing Co ....E...... 309 342-3173
  Galesburg *(G-10192)*
▲ Gehrke Technology Group Inc ....F...... 847 498-7320
  Wauconda *(G-20353)*
Gillespie City Water ....G...... 217 839-3279
  Gillespie *(G-10375)*
Glo Heat Treat Services LLC ....G...... 815 601-5728
  Durand *(G-8152)*
H-O-H Water Technology Inc ....E...... 847 358-7400
  Palatine *(G-16121)*
H2o Solutions LLC ....G...... 618 219-2905
  Granite City *(G-10713)*
Heat Transfer Laboratories ....G...... 708 715-4300
  Oakbrook Terrace *(G-15801)*
◆ Heico Companies LLC ....F...... 312 419-8220
  Chicago *(G-4798)*
◆ Holden Industries Inc ....F...... 847 940-1500
  Deerfield *(G-7616)*

Hpd LLC ....C...... 815 609-2032
  Plainfield *(G-16673)*
Hydrotec Systems Company Inc ....G...... 815 624-6644
  Tiskilwa *(G-19873)*
◆ Illinois Water Tech Inc ....E...... 815 636-8884
  Roscoe *(G-17911)*
Industrial Specialty Chem Inc ....E...... 708 339-1313
  South Holland *(G-19224)*
▲ Inlet & Pipe Protection Inc ....D...... 630 355-3288
  Naperville *(G-14974)*
International Water Werks Inc ....G...... 847 669-1902
  Huntley *(G-11544)*
J II Inc ....D...... 847 432-8979
  Highland Park *(G-11275)*
James A Freund LLC ....G...... 630 664-7692
  Oswego *(G-16009)*
Jetin Systems Inc ....F...... 815 726-4686
  Joliet *(G-11885)*
Keating of Chicago Inc ....E...... 815 569-2324
  Capron *(G-2834)*
Lane Industries Inc ....E...... 847 498-6650
  Northbrook *(G-15417)*
▲ Liquitech Inc ....C...... 630 693-0500
  Lombard *(G-13097)*
M & M Pump Co ....G...... 217 935-2517
  Clinton *(G-6926)*
Markham Division 9 Inc ....E...... 708 503-0657
  Park Forest *(G-16257)*
Marmon Group LLC ....D...... 847 647-8200
  Skokie *(G-18984)*
◆ Marmon Holdings Inc ....D...... 312 372-9500
  Chicago *(G-5343)*
◆ Marmon Industrial LLC ....G...... 312 372-9500
  Chicago *(G-5344)*
Masters Hand Enterprises LLC ....G...... 312 933-7674
  Chicago *(G-5362)*
McDowell Inc ....G...... 309 467-2335
  Eureka *(G-9483)*
▼ McNish Corporation ....D...... 630 892-7921
  Aurora *(G-1128)*
▲ Meyer Machine & Equipment Inc ....E...... 847 395-2977
  Antioch *(G-625)*
Microplasma Ozone Tech Inc ....F...... 217 693-7950
  Champaign *(G-3321)*
▲ Midco International Inc ....E...... 773 604-8700
  Chicago *(G-5433)*
Middleby Corporation ....E...... 847 741-3300
  Elgin *(G-8660)*
Middleby Corporation ....E...... 847 741-3300
  Elgin *(G-8661)*
Midwest Water Group Inc ....E...... 866 526-6558
  Crystal Lake *(G-7230)*
◆ Minuteman International Inc ....C...... 630 627-6900
  Pingree Grove *(G-16622)*
Minuteman International Inc ....D...... 847 683-5210
  Hampshire *(G-10980)*
▲ Mullarkey Associates Inc ....F...... 708 597-5555
  Tinley Park *(G-19846)*
Nano Gas Technologies Inc ....G...... 847 317-0656
  Deerfield *(G-7640)*
Nano2 LLC ....G...... 217 563-2942
  Nokomis *(G-15195)*
▲ Natural Choice Corporation ....F...... 815 874-4444
  Loves Park *(G-13240)*
Nijhuis Water Technology Inc ....G...... 312 466-9900
  Chicago *(G-5601)*
◆ Nikro Industries Inc ....F...... 630 530-0558
  Villa Park *(G-20162)*
North Shore Wtr Rclamation Dst ....E...... 847 623-6060
  Waukegan *(G-20470)*
◆ Omni Containment Systems LLC ....G...... 847 468-1772
  Elgin *(G-8679)*
▼ Optimal Automatics Co ....G...... 847 439-9110
  Elk Grove Village *(G-9165)*
Palmyra Modesto Water Comm ....G...... 217 436-2519
  Palmyra *(G-16180)*
◆ Pentair Fltrtion Solutions LLC ....E...... 630 307-3000
  Hanover Park *(G-11012)*
▼ Powerboss Inc ....C...... 630 627-6900
  Pingree Grove *(G-16623)*
◆ Prince Castle LLC ....G...... 630 462-8800
  Carol Stream *(G-3050)*
Princeton Fast Stop ....F...... 815 872-0706
  Princeton *(G-16818)*
Prinzings of Rockford ....G...... 815 874-9654
  Rockford *(G-17560)*
Pristine Water Solutions Inc ....F...... 847 689-1100
  Waukegan *(G-20482)*
Producers Envmtl Pdts LLC ....G...... 630 482-5995
  Batavia *(G-1406)*

35 INDUSTRIAL AND COMMERCIAL MACHINERY AND COMPUTER EQUIPMENT — SIC SECTION

Pure N Natural Systems Inc .... F 630 372-9681
 Streamwood (G-19591)
▲ Pureline Treatment Systems LLC .... C 847 963-8465
 Bensenville (G-1877)
Quantum Technical Services Inc .... E 815 464-1540
 Frankfort (G-9829)
Rays Power Wshg Svc Peggy Ray ...... G 618 939-6306
 Waterloo (G-20295)
Regency Hand Laundry .... G 773 871-3950
 Chicago (G-6001)
Regunathan & Assoc Inc .... G 630 653-0387
 Wheaton (G-20818)
Ross and White Company .... F 847 516-3900
 Cary (G-3187)
▲ RPS Products Inc .... E 847 683-3400
 Hampshire (G-10986)
▲ Safe Water Technologies Inc .... G 847 888-6900
 Elgin (G-8723)
Selrok Inc .... G 630 876-8322
 West Chicago (G-20640)
Servetech Water Solutions Inc .... G 630 784-9050
 Wheaton (G-20823)
Sewer Equipment Co America .... C 815 835-5566
 Dixon (G-7917)
Siemens Industry Inc .... G 815 672-2653
 Streator (G-19622)
Star Industries Inc .... E 708 240-4862
 Highland Park (G-11300)
Superior Water Services Inc .... G 309 691-9287
 Peoria (G-16531)
◆ Taylor Coml Foodservice Inc .... F 815 624-8333
 Rockton (G-17703)
Tkg Sweeping & Services LLC .... G 847 505-1400
 Waukegan (G-20506)
Toppert Jetting Service Inc .... G 309 755-2240
 East Moline (G-8244)
▲ Tornado Industries LLC .... D 817 551-6507
 West Chicago (G-20653)
Towne Towing Inc .... G 847 705-1710
 Palatine (G-16165)
Triwater Holdings LLC .... G 847 457-1812
 Lake Forest (G-12318)
U Wash Equipment Co .... G 618 466-9442
 Alton (G-575)
Umf Corporation .... G 224 251-7822
 Niles (G-15184)
◆ Umf Corporation .... F 847 920-0370
 Skokie (G-19049)
Veolia Water Technologies Inc .... E 815 609-2000
 Plainfield (G-16726)
Walter Louis Chem & Assoc Inc .... F 217 223-2017
 Quincy (G-16954)
Water Dynamics Inc .... G 630 584-8475
 Saint Charles (G-18297)
Waterco of Central States Inc .... C 630 576-4782
 Lombard (G-13153)
We Clean .... G 708 574-2551
 Oak Forest (G-15692)
White Diamond Bubbles Hand .... G 773 417-3237
 Chicago (G-6617)
Will County Well & Pump Co Inc .... G 815 485-2413
 New Lenox (G-15069)
William N Pasulka .... G 815 339-6300
 Peru (G-16598)
▲ William W Meyer and Sons .... D 847 918-0111
 Libertyville (G-12726)

3592 Carburetors, Pistons, Rings & Valves

Borgwarner Inc .... C 815 288-1462
 Dixon (G-7892)
▲ Burgess-Norton Mfg Co Inc .... B 630 232-4100
 Geneva (G-10256)
Extreme Force Valve Inc .... G 618 494-5795
 Jerseyville (G-11790)
Hantemp Corporation .... G 630 537-1049
 Westmont (G-20746)
Helio Precision Products Inc .... E 585 697-5434
 Lake Bluff (G-12186)
▲ Helio Precision Products Inc .... C 847 473-1300
 Lake Bluff (G-12187)
Kuhn Special Steel N Amer Inc .... G 262 788-9358
 Chicago (G-5135)
Milliken Valve Co Inc .... C 217 425-7410
 Decatur (G-7526)
Mueller Co LLC .... E 217 423-4471
 Decatur (G-7528)
Research and Testing Worx Inc .... G 815 734-7346
 Mount Morris (G-14501)
▲ Riken Corporation of America ...... C 847 673-1400
 Skokie (G-19023)

United Carburetor Inc .... E 773 777-1223
 Schiller Park (G-18849)
▲ United Remanufacturing Co Inc .... E 773 777-1223
 Schiller Park (G-18850)
United Remanufacturing Co Inc .... E 847 678-2233
 Schiller Park (G-18851)

3593 Fluid Power Cylinders & Actuators

Advance Automation Company .... F 773 539-7633
 Chicago (G-3553)
▲ Bimba Manufacturing Company .... B 708 534-8544
 University Park (G-19949)
Bimba Manufacturing Company .... E 708 534-7997
 Manteno (G-13444)
Bimba Manufacturing Company .... G 815 654-7775
 Machesney Park (G-13329)
Bimba Manufacturing Company .... E 708 534-8544
 Frankfort (G-9772)
◆ Blac Inc .... D 630 279-6400
 Elmhurst (G-9335)
Brake Parts Inc LLC .... G 217 324-2161
 Litchfield (G-12961)
Catching Hydraulics Co Ltd .... E 708 344-2334
 Melrose Park (G-13839)
◆ Dover Prtg Identification Inc .... D 630 541-1540
 Downers Grove (G-7992)
Dresser LLC .... D 847 437-5940
 Elk Grove Village (G-8955)
Ergo-Help Inc .... G 847 593-0722
 Fox River Grove (G-9757)
▼ Gpe Controls Inc .... F 708 236-6000
 Hillside (G-11340)
Hadady Machining Company Inc ...... F 708 474-8620
 Lansing (G-12496)
Illinois Pneumatic Inc .... G 815 654-9301
 Roscoe (G-17910)
Ken Elliott Co .... G 618 466-8200
 Godfrey (G-10654)
▲ Kitagawa Usa Inc .... E 847 310-8198
 Schaumburg (G-18587)
Kocsis Technologies Inc .... G 708 597-4177
 Alsip (G-466)
Kocsis Technologies Inc .... G 708 597-4177
 Alsip (G-467)
Manitowoc Lifts and Mfg LLC .... G 815 748-9500
 Dekalb (G-7690)
Master Hydraulics & Machining .... F 847 895-5578
 Schaumburg (G-18623)
MEA Inc .... E 847 766-9040
 Elk Grove Village (G-9114)
▲ Mead Fluid Dynamics Inc .... E 773 685-6800
 University Park (G-19959)
Ortman Fluid Power Inc .... E 217 277-0321
 Quincy (G-16919)
▲ Rdc Linear Enterprises LLC .... E 815 547-1106
 Belvidere (G-1697)
RE-Do-It Corp .... E 708 343-7125
 Broadview (G-2463)
Regent Automotive Engineering ...... G 773 889-5744
 Chicago (G-6002)
▲ Rehobot Inc .... G 815 385-7777
 McHenry (G-13786)
◆ Sarco Hydraulics Inc .... E 217 324-6577
 Litchfield (G-12977)
SMC Corporation of America .... E 630 449-0600
 Aurora (G-1017)
T J Brooks Co .... G 847 680-0350
 Libertyville (G-12713)
◆ Tuxco Corporation .... F 847 244-2220
 Gurnee (G-10940)
Walach Manufacturing Co Inc .... F 773 836-2060
 Chicago (G-6585)
Xtreme Cylinders LLC .... G 877 219-9001
 Tinley Park (G-19870)

3594 Fluid Power Pumps & Motors

▲ American Electronic Pdts Inc .... F 630 889-9977
 Oak Brook (G-15592)
Brock Equipment Company .... E 815 459-4210
 Woodstock (G-21367)
Bucher Hydraulics Inc .... G 847 429-0700
 Elgin (G-8526)
Caterpillar Inc .... B 815 729-5511
 Joliet (G-11838)
Central Hydraulics Inc .... G 309 527-5238
 El Paso (G-8434)
Danfoss Power Solutions US Co .... C 815 233-4200
 Freeport (G-10105)
Deltrol Corp .... C 708 547-0500
 Bellwood (G-1621)

Grand Specialties Co .... F 630 629-8000
 Oak Brook (G-15625)
Highland Mch & Screw Pdts Co .... D 618 654-2103
 Highland (G-11218)
▲ Hydro-Gear Inc .... C 217 728-2581
 Sullivan (G-19668)
Idex Corporation .... C 847 498-7070
 Lake Forest (G-12265)
▼ Ifh Group Inc .... D 800 435-7003
 Rock Falls (G-17187)
Ifh Group Inc .... G 815 380-2367
 Galt (G-10225)
Kocsis Technologies Inc .... G 708 597-4177
 Alsip (G-467)
▲ Leading Edge Group Inc .... C 815 316-3500
 Rockford (G-17492)
Mandus Group LLC .... G 309 786-1507
 Rock Island (G-17228)
Mechanical Engineering Pdts .... G 312 421-3375
 Chicago (G-5380)
▲ Mechanical Tool & Engrg Co .... C 815 397-4701
 Rockford (G-17513)
Mechanical Tool & Engrg Co .... C 815 397-4701
 Rockford (G-17514)
Parker-Hannifin Corporation .... E 216 896-3000
 Chicago (G-5767)
Parker-Hannifin Corporation .... C 847 258-6200
 Elk Grove Village (G-9169)
Parker-Hannifin Corporation .... D 815 636-4100
 Machesney Park (G-13362)
Parker-Hannifin Corporation .... C 847 955-5000
 Lincolnshire (G-12792)
Parker-Hannifin Corporation .... C 309 266-2200
 Morton (G-14377)
Rdh Inc of Rockford .... F 815 874-9421
 Rockford (G-17568)
▲ Rehobot Inc .... G 815 385-7777
 McHenry (G-13786)
▲ Rhino Tool Company .... F 309 853-5555
 Kewanee (G-12040)
Roberts Electric Company .... G 773 725-7323
 Chicago (G-6044)
Settima Usa Inc .... G 630 812-1433
 Wood Dale (G-21240)
Sunsource Holdings Inc .... G 630 317-2700
 Addison (G-298)
Tomenson Machine Works Inc .... D 630 377-7670
 West Chicago (G-20652)
Tramco Pump Co .... E 312 243-5800
 Romeoville (G-17881)
◆ Tuxco Corporation .... F 847 244-2220
 Gurnee (G-10940)
Wes-Tech Inc .... G 847 541-5070
 Buffalo Grove (G-2620)

3596 Scales & Balances, Exc Laboratory

Advanced Weighing Systems Inc ...... G 630 916-6179
 Addison (G-22)
Belt-Way Scales Inc .... E 815 625-5573
 Rock Falls (G-17176)
Brian Burcar .... G 815 856-2271
 Leonore (G-12611)
◆ Doran Scales Inc .... E 630 879-1200
 Saint Charles (G-18186)
E Rowe Foundry & Machine Co .... D 217 382-4135
 Martinsville (G-13583)
EJ Cady & Company .... G 847 537-2239
 Wheeling (G-20888)
G & H Balancer Service .... G 773 509-1988
 Chicago (G-4647)
▲ Glenview Systems Inc .... F 847 724-2691
 Glenview (G-10552)
▲ Heng Tuo Usa Inc .... G 630 317-7672
 Oakbrook Terrace (G-15802)
Howard Schwartz .... G 847 540-8260
 Round Lake Beach (G-18089)
International Rd Dynamics Corp ...... E 815 675-1430
 Spring Grove (G-19277)
▲ Lllb LLC .... F 630 315-3300
 Elk Grove Village (G-9097)
◆ Medela LLC .... C 800 435-8316
 McHenry (G-13768)
Meto-Grafics Inc .... F 847 639-0044
 Crystal Lake (G-7226)
Mettler-Toledo LLC .... G 630 446-7700
 Aurora (G-1002)
Morrison Weighing Systems Inc .... G 309 799-7311
 Milan (G-14019)
◆ Newell Operating Company .... C 815 235-4171
 Freeport (G-10129)

SIC SECTION
35 INDUSTRIAL AND COMMERCIAL MACHINERY AND COMPUTER EQUIPMENT

◆ **Pelstar LLC** .... E 708 377-0600
Countryside *(G-7067)*
Southern Ill Scale & Cnstr Inc .... G 618 723-2303
Noble *(G-15192)*

3599 Machinery & Eqpt, Indl & Commercial, NEC

2 M Tool Company Inc .... F 773 282-0722
Chicago *(G-3462)*
3-V Industries Inc .... G 217 835-4453
Benld *(G-1717)*
3d Industries Inc .... E 630 616-8702
Bensenville *(G-1719)*
3d Manufacturing Corporation .... G 815 806-9200
Frankfort *(G-9763)*
A & A Machine Co Inc .... G 847 985-4619
Elk Grove Village *(G-8790)*
A & B Machine Shop .... G 815 397-0495
Rockford *(G-17279)*
A & M Tool Co Inc .... E 847 215-8140
Wheeling *(G-20835)*
A & R Machine Inc .... G 708 388-4764
Alsip *(G-406)*
A J Horne Inc .... G 630 231-8686
West Chicago *(G-20530)*
A K Tool & Manufacturing Inc .... G 630 889-9220
Lombard *(G-13033)*
A R Tech & Tool Inc .... G 708 599-5745
Bridgeview *(G-2317)*
A W Radtke Tool Corporation .... G 847 662-7373
Waukegan *(G-20404)*
A&S Machining & Welding Inc .... E 708 442-4544
Mc Cook *(G-13689)*
A-1 Lapping & Machine Inc .... F 815 398-1465
Rockford *(G-17282)*
Aarstar Precision Grinding .... G 847 678-4880
Franklin Park *(G-9858)*
AB Machine Shop LLC .... G 618 467-6474
Godfrey *(G-10646)*
Abacus Manufacturing Group Inc .... G 815 654-7050
Rockford *(G-17284)*
▲ **Abbott Machine Co** .... F 618 465-1898
Alton *(G-540)*
▲ **Abbott Scott Manufacturing Co** .... E 773 342-7200
Chicago *(G-3505)*
Abet Industries Corporation .... G 708 482-8282
La Grange Park *(G-12094)*
Able Barmilling & Mfg Co Inc .... F 708 343-5666
Wauconda *(G-20325)*
Absolute Grinding and Mfg .... F 815 964-1999
Rockford *(G-17289)*
Absolute Turn Inc .... E 847 459-4629
Wheeling *(G-20839)*
Accro Precision Grinding Inc .... G 708 681-0520
Chicago *(G-3516)*
Accu Cut Inc .... G 815 229-3525
Rockford *(G-17291)*
Accurate CNc Machining Inc .... G 815 623-6516
Roscoe *(G-17897)*
Accurate Metal Components Inc .... F 847 520-5900
Niles *(G-15099)*
Accurate Metal Fabricating LLC .... D 773 235-0400
Chicago *(G-3518)*
Accurate Metallizing Inc .... G 708 424-7747
Oak Lawn *(G-15695)*
Accurate Tool Inc .... G 847 437-8544
Arlington Heights *(G-682)*
Accutech Machining Inc .... E 630 350-2066
Bensenville *(G-1725)*
Ace Coating Enterprises Inc .... E 708 547-6680
Hillside *(G-11325)*
Ace Precision Tool & Mfg Co .... G 847 690-0111
Elk Grove Village *(G-8802)*
Acme Grinding & Manufacturing .... C 815 323-1380
Belvidere *(G-1644)*
▲ **Acme Industries Inc** .... C 847 296-3346
Elk Grove Village *(G-8804)*
Action Carbide Grinding Co .... G 847 891-9026
Schaumburg *(G-18427)*
Active Grinding & Mfg Co .... F 708 344-0510
Broadview *(G-2414)*
Adams Machine Shop .... G 630 851-6060
Naperville *(G-14765)*
Addison Precision Products .... F 815 857-4466
Amboy *(G-577)*
Adermanns Welding & Mch & Co .... G 217 342-3234
Effingham *(G-8383)*
Advance Machining .... G 630 521-9392
Bensenville *(G-1728)*
Advance Printers Machine Shop .... G 773 588-3169
Chicago *(G-3557)*
◆ **Advanced Fltration Systems Inc** .... C 217 351-3073
Champaign *(G-3260)*
▼ **Advanced Machine & Engrg Co** .... C 815 962-6076
Rockford *(G-17296)*
Advanced Prcsion Machining Ltd .... G 630 860-2549
Bensenville *(G-1731)*
Advantage Machining Inc .... E 630 897-1220
Aurora *(G-1042)*
Aero Apmc Inc .... F 630 766-0910
Franklin Park *(G-9861)*
Aero Plastics and Supply .... G 815 975-9305
Belvidere *(G-1645)*
Aero Plastics and Supply Co .... G 847 553-5578
Belvidere *(G-1646)*
▲ **Afc Cable Systems Inc** .... B 508 998-1131
Harvey *(G-11070)*
Affri Inc .... G 224 374-0931
Wood Dale *(G-21156)*
AGS Machine Co Inc .... G 630 766-7777
Bensenville *(G-1733)*
Air Caster LLC .... E 217 877-1237
Decatur *(G-7436)*
▲ **Air Stamping Inc** .... F 217 342-1283
Effingham *(G-8384)*
▲ **Airo Tool & Manufacturing Inc** .... F 815 547-7588
Belvidere *(G-1647)*
Ajax Tool Works Inc .... G 847 737-2600
Franklin Park *(G-9863)*
Alanson Manufacturing LLC .... F 773 762-2530
Chicago *(G-3596)*
Alicona Manufacturing Inc .... G 630 736-2718
Bartlett *(G-1263)*
All Cnc Solutions Inc .... G 847 972-1139
Skokie *(G-18913)*
All Cut Inc .... G 630 910-6505
Darien *(G-7400)*
All Precision Mfg LLC .... E 217 563-7070
Nokomis *(G-15193)*
Allans Welding & Machine Inc .... G 618 392-3708
Olney *(G-15851)*
Allied Machine Tool & Dye .... G 708 388-7676
Crestwood *(G-7106)*
Alpine Amusement Co Inc .... G 708 233-9131
Oak Lawn *(G-15699)*
Alsip Mfg Inc .... E 708 333-4446
Harvey *(G-11072)*
Alster Machining Corp .... F 773 384-2370
Chicago *(G-3633)*
▲ **AM Precision Machine Inc** .... E 847 439-9955
Schaumburg *(G-18436)*
American Cnc Machine Co Inc .... E 630 628-6490
Addison *(G-31)*
American Drilling Inc .... E 847 850-5090
Wheeling *(G-20847)*
▼ **American Engraving Inc** .... G 630 543-2525
Bensenville *(G-1742)*
◆ **American Extrusion Intl Corp** .... E 815 624-6616
South Beloit *(G-19081)*
American Grinding & Machine Co .... D 773 889-4343
Chicago *(G-3653)*
American Machining Inc .... G 815 498-1593
Ottawa *(G-16038)*
▲ **American Machining & Wldg Inc** .... E 773 586-2585
Chicago *(G-3659)*
American Precision Machining .... F 847 455-1720
Franklin Park *(G-9867)*
American Quality Mfg Inc .... E 815 226-9301
Rockford *(G-17301)*
American Tool Design Inc .... G 847 690-1010
Elk Grove Village *(G-8825)*
American Total Engine Co .... G 847 623-2737
Ingleside *(G-11578)*
Americut Wire Edm Inc .... F 847 675-1754
Skokie *(G-18919)*
Anah Machine Mfg Co .... F 847 228-6450
Elk Grove Village *(G-8830)*
Anamet Inc .... G 217 234-8844
Glen Ellyn *(G-10394)*
Anderson Tage Co .... G 815 397-3040
Rockford *(G-17304)*
Andersson Tool & Die LLP .... F 847 746-8866
Zion *(G-21508)*
Andrew Toschak .... G 630 553-3434
Yorkville *(G-21472)*
Anpec Industries Inc .... E 815 239-2303
Pecatonica *(G-16320)*
AP Machine Inc .... F 708 450-1010
Melrose Park *(G-13826)*
Apex Manufacturing Inc .... G 815 728-0108
Ringwood *(G-17039)*
Apex Mfg & Design Inc .... G 618 997-0512
Marion *(G-13504)*
Apex Mfg & Design Inc .... G 618 252-5529
Galatia *(G-10162)*
Aphelion Precision Tech Corp .... E 847 215-7285
Elk Grove Village *(G-8835)*
Apollo Machine & Manufacturing .... G 847 677-6444
Skokie *(G-18921)*
Archer Manufacturing Corp .... E 773 585-7181
Chicago *(G-3725)*
Arcline Fabrication LLC .... G 207 468-1997
Rockdale *(G-17256)*
Ardekin Precision LLC .... C 815 986-4359
Rockford *(G-17306)*
▲ **Argo Manufacturing Co** .... F 630 377-1750
Wasco *(G-20260)*
Armitage Machine Co Inc .... F 309 697-9050
Peoria *(G-16386)*
Arnette Pattern Co Inc .... E 618 451-7700
Granite City *(G-10698)*
Aro Metal Stamping Company Inc .... E 630 351-7676
Wood Dale *(G-21166)*
Arrow Edm Inc .... F 217 893-4277
Rantoul *(G-16967)*
Arrow Gear Company .... E 630 969-7640
Downers Grove *(G-7956)*
Art Technologies Inc .... G 773 557-3896
Bensenville *(G-1747)*
Asteroid Precision Inc .... D 847 298-8109
Wheeling *(G-20852)*
◆ **Astro Machine Corporation** .... E 847 364-6363
Elk Grove Village *(G-8844)*
Astro-Craft Inc .... E 815 675-1500
Spring Grove *(G-19265)*
Atlas Manufacturing Ltd .... F 815 943-1400
Harvard *(G-11047)*
Atlas Material Tstg Tech LLC .... G 773 327-4520
Chicago *(G-3766)*
Atlas Material Tstg Tech LLC .... E 773 327-4520
Chicago *(G-3767)*
▲ **Atlas Material Tstg Tech LLC** .... C 773 327-4520
Mount Prospect *(G-14512)*
Atomic Engineering Co .... F 847 228-1387
Elk Grove Village *(G-8846)*
Atomic Industrial Machine Inc .... F 847 228-1387
Elk Grove Village *(G-8847)*
◆ **Ats Sortimat USA LLC** .... D 847 925-1234
Rolling Meadows *(G-17713)*
Aura Systems Inc .... E 217 423-4100
Decatur *(G-7461)*
◆ **Aurora Metals Division LLC** .... C 630 844-4900
Montgomery *(G-14231)*
Austin Tool & Die Co .... D 847 509-5800
Northbrook *(G-15344)*
Auto Head and Engine Exchange .... G 708 448-8762
Worth *(G-21454)*
Autocut Machine Company Inc .... G 815 436-1900
Elwood *(G-9460)*
Automated Design Corp .... G 630 783-1150
Romeoville *(G-17797)*
Automated Mfg Solutions Inc .... F 815 477-2428
Crystal Lake *(G-7165)*
Automation Design & Mfg Inc .... G 630 896-4206
Aurora *(G-1060)*
Automotive Engine Specialties .... G 847 956-1244
Elk Grove Village *(G-8849)*
Avan Tool & Die Co Inc .... F 773 287-1670
Chicago *(G-3782)*
Avers Machine & Mfg Inc .... E 847 447-3430
Schiller Park *(G-18788)*
Awerkamp Machine Co .... E 217 222-3480
Quincy *(G-16859)*
Awerkamp Machine Co .... F 217 222-3490
Quincy *(G-16860)*
Axis Manufacturing Inc .... F 847 350-0200
Elk Grove Village *(G-8852)*
Azimuth Cnc Inc .... F 815 399-4433
Rockford *(G-17310)*
B & B Specialty Company Inc .... G 708 652-9234
Lemont *(G-12555)*
B & B Tool Co .... E 815 229-5792
Rockford *(G-17311)*
B & G Machine Inc .... G 618 262-2269
Mount Carmel *(G-14466)*
◆ **B & L Machine Sales Inc** .... E 217 342-3918
Effingham *(G-8388)*
B & M Machine Inc .... G 630 350-8950
Bensenville *(G-1749)*

S I C

Employee Codes: A=Over 500 employees, B=251-500
C=101-250, D=51-100, E=20-50, F=10-19, G=3-9
2020 Harris Illinois
Industrial Directory
973

B & R Grinding Co ....G.... 630 595-7789
Franklin Park *(G-9881)*
B & W Machine Company Inc ....G.... 847 364-4500
Elk Grove Village *(G-8853)*
B A P Enterprises Inc ....G.... 708 849-0900
Dolton *(G-7931)*
B M W Inc ....E.... 847 439-0095
Wheeling *(G-20855)*
B Radtke and Sons Inc ....G.... 847 546-3999
Round Lake Park *(G-18095)*
B S Grinding Inc ....G.... 847 787-0770
Elk Grove Village *(G-8854)*
▲ **B T M Industries Inc** ....G.... 815 338-6464
Woodstock *(G-21362)*
B&B Machining Incorporated ....F.... 630 898-3009
Aurora *(G-920)*
Bahr Tool & Die Co ....G.... 847 392-4447
Wheeling *(G-20856)*
Balas Incorporated ....F.... 630 406-7971
Batavia *(G-1353)*
Baley Enterprises Inc ....G.... 708 681-0900
Melrose Park *(G-13830)*
▲ **Ballco Manufacturing Co Inc** ....D.... 630 898-1600
Aurora *(G-922)*
▲ **Banner Service Corporation** ....C.... 630 653-7500
Carol Stream *(G-2944)*
Barnes Machine Shop LLC ....G.... 217 774-5308
Shelbyville *(G-18876)*
Bartech Precision Machining Co ....F.... 630 243-9068
Lemont *(G-12556)*
▲ **Barton Manufacturing LLC** ....E.... 217 428-0711
Decatur *(G-7462)*
▲ **Bbs Automation Chicago Inc** ....C.... 630 351-3000
Bartlett *(G-1268)*
Bc Machine ....G.... 815 962-7884
Rockford *(G-17316)*
Bear Machine Tool & Die Inc ....G.... 815 932-4204
Bradley *(G-2277)*
Bedford Rakim ....G.... 773 749-3086
Lansing *(G-12485)*
Bem Mold Inc ....E.... 847 805-9750
Schaumburg *(G-18459)*
Bendplex Compand ....G.... 630 797-5808
Saint Charles *(G-18154)*
▲ **Big 3 Precision Products Inc** ....C.... 618 533-3251
Centralia *(G-3222)*
▲ **Bills Machine & Power Transm** ....E.... 618 392-2500
Olney *(G-15856)*
Bluechip Fabrication ....G.... 618 496-3569
Tamaroa *(G-19741)*
Bold Machine Works Inc ....F.... 217 428-6644
Decatur *(G-7466)*
Boley Tool & Machine Works Inc ....C.... 309 694-2722
East Peoria *(G-8254)*
Boring Industries ....F.... 815 986-1172
Rockford *(G-17326)*
BR Machine Inc ....F.... 815 434-0427
Ottawa *(G-16042)*
Bradley Machining Inc ....F.... 630 543-2875
Addison *(G-53)*
Brenco Machine and Tool Inc ....F.... 815 356-5100
Crystal Lake *(G-7171)*
Brian Burcar ....G.... 815 856-2271
Leonore *(G-12611)*
Bridgeview Cnc Inc ....G.... 708 599-4641
Bridgeview *(G-2329)*
Bridgeview Machining Inc ....G.... 708 599-4060
Bridgeview *(G-2331)*
Brock Industrial Services LLC ....E.... 815 730-3350
Joliet *(G-11834)*
Brucher Machining Inc ....F.... 630 876-1661
West Chicago *(G-20555)*
▲ **Bryco Machine Inc** ....E.... 708 614-1900
Tinley Park *(G-19814)*
BSB International Corp ....G.... 847 791-9272
Bensenville *(G-1759)*
Budapest Tool ....G.... 630 250-0711
Itasca *(G-11630)*
Burgess Manufacturing Inc ....F.... 847 680-1724
Libertyville *(G-12641)*
Burke Tool & Manufacturing Inc ....G.... 618 542-6441
Du Quoin *(G-8116)*
Burmac Manufacturing Inc ....G.... 815 434-1660
Ottawa *(G-16043)*
Burns Machine Company ....E.... 815 434-3131
Ottawa *(G-16044)*
▲ **Burns Machine Company** ....E.... 815 434-1660
Ottawa *(G-16045)*
Byrne & Schaefer Inc ....G.... 815 727-5000
Lockport *(G-12985)*

C & D Machining Inc ....F.... 815 778-4946
Lyndon *(G-13286)*
C & F Machine Corp ....F.... 630 924-0300
Bloomingdale *(G-1983)*
C D Tools Machining Inc ....G.... 773 859-2028
Addison *(G-59)*
C E R Machining & Tooling Ltd ....G.... 708 442-9614
Lyons *(G-13305)*
C N C Central Inc ....G.... 630 595-1453
Bensenville *(G-1760)*
C N C Hi-Tech Inc ....G.... 847 431-4335
Wauconda *(G-20338)*
C Tri Co ....E.... 309 467-4715
Eureka *(G-9477)*
Caffero Tool & Mfg ....D.... 224 293-2600
Streamwood *(G-19564)*
Calco Controls Inc ....F.... 847 639-3858
Crystal Lake *(G-7176)*
▲ **CAM Co Inc** ....F.... 630 556-3110
Big Rock *(G-1969)*
Camco Manufacturing Inc ....F.... 708 597-4288
Crestwood *(G-7108)*
Camshop Industrial LLC ....G.... 708 597-4288
Crestwood *(G-7109)*
Capitol City Machine ....G.... 217 529-0293
Springfield *(G-19338)*
Car Shop Inc ....G.... 309 797-4188
Moline *(G-14135)*
Carmona Gear Cutting ....G.... 815 963-8236
Rockford *(G-17337)*
Carr Machine & Tool Inc ....G.... 847 593-8003
Elk Grove Village *(G-8879)*
Casward Tool Works Inc ....G.... 773 486-4900
Orland Park *(G-15946)*
Catapult Integrated Svcs LLC ....G.... 312 216-4460
Chicago *(G-4042)*
CB Machine & Tool Corp ....G.... 847 288-1807
Franklin Park *(G-9901)*
Celinco Inc ....G.... 815 964-2256
Rockford *(G-17341)*
Centerless Grinding Co ....F.... 847 455-7660
Franklin Park *(G-9902)*
Central Machining Inc ....G.... 217 854-6646
Carlinville *(G-2870)*
CF Gear Holdings LLC ....E.... 847 376-8322
Des Plaines *(G-7742)*
CH Machining Company ....G.... 630 595-1050
Bensenville *(G-1766)*
Chadwick Manufacturing Ltd ....G.... 815 684-5152
Chadwick *(G-3257)*
Chamfermatic Inc ....G.... 815 636-5082
Machesney Park *(G-13333)*
Chicago Cnc Machining Co ....G.... 708 352-1255
Hodgkins *(G-11386)*
Chicago Grinding & Machine Co ....E.... 708 343-4399
Melrose Park *(G-13843)*
▼ **Chicago Powdered Metal Pdts Co** ....D.... 847 678-2836
Schiller Park *(G-18793)*
▼ **Chicago Turnrite Co Inc** ....E.... 773 626-8404
Chicago *(G-4135)*
Chicago Waterjet Inc ....G.... 847 350-1898
Elk Grove Village *(G-8896)*
Chips Manufacturing Inc ....D.... 630 682-4477
West Chicago *(G-20561)*
▲ **Chrome Crankshaft Company LLC** ..F.... 815 725-9030
Joliet *(G-11840)*
Circle Boring & Machine Co ....G.... 815 398-4150
Rockford *(G-17348)*
Circle Boring & Machine Co ....G.... 815 397-3040
Rockford *(G-17349)*
▲ **Circle Gear & Machine Co Inc** ....E.... 708 652-1000
Cicero *(G-6835)*
Cirrus Products LLC ....G.... 630 501-1881
Burr Ridge *(G-2662)*
CK Grinding and Machining Inc ....G.... 847 541-0960
Wheeling *(G-20870)*
Class A Grinding ....G.... 815 874-2118
Rockford *(G-17352)*
Classic Automation & Tool ....G.... 708 388-6311
Crestwood *(G-7112)*
▲ **Clean and Science USA Co Ltd** ....G.... 847 461-9292
Rolling Meadows *(G-17722)*
Clinkenbeard & Associates Inc ....E.... 815 226-0291
South Beloit *(G-19087)*
Cmg Precision Machining Co Inc ....G.... 630 759-8080
Romeoville *(G-17810)*
Cnc Chicago Corp ....G.... 847 671-3319
Addison *(G-75)*
Cnc Swiss Inc ....G.... 630 543-9595
Addison *(G-76)*

Cnh Industrial America LLC ....E.... 309 965-2233
Goodfield *(G-10672)*
Cobalt Tool & Manufacturing ....G.... 630 530-8898
Villa Park *(G-20139)*
▲ **Cold Headers Inc** ....F.... 773 775-7900
Chicago *(G-4197)*
Comet Roll & Machine Company ....E.... 630 268-1407
Saint Charles *(G-18172)*
Commercial Dynamics Inc ....G.... 847 439-5300
Arlington Heights *(G-717)*
Commercial Machine Services ....F.... 847 806-1901
Elk Grove Village *(G-8905)*
Compak Inc ....E.... 815 399-2699
Machesney Park *(G-13335)*
▲ **Component Products Inc** ....E.... 847 301-1000
Elmhurst *(G-9352)*
▲ **Component Specialty Inc** ....F.... 847 742-4400
Elgin *(G-8547)*
Component Tool & Mfg Co ....F.... 708 672-5505
Crete *(G-7136)*
Concentric Components Inc ....G.... 224 422-0638
Island Lake *(G-11606)*
Concepts and Controls Inc ....F.... 847 478-9296
Buffalo Grove *(G-2527)*
Concorde Mfg & Fabrication Inc ....F.... 815 344-3788
McHenry *(G-13729)*
Conform Industries Inc ....F.... 630 285-0272
Schaumburg *(G-18484)*
Connell Mc Machine & Welding ....G.... 815 868-2275
Mc Connell *(G-13688)*
Contour Machining Inc ....G.... 847 364-0111
Elk Grove Village *(G-8911)*
Contour Screw Products Inc ....E.... 847 357-1190
Arlington Heights *(G-719)*
Cope Plastics Inc ....D.... 618 466-0221
Alton *(G-549)*
Corrigan Manufacturing Co ....F.... 815 399-9326
Rockford *(G-17358)*
Cosmopolitan Machine Rebuilder ....G.... 630 595-8141
Bensenville *(G-1778)*
County Tool & Die ....G.... 217 324-6527
Litchfield *(G-12962)*
▲ **Creative Machining Tech LLC** ....D.... 309 755-7700
Highland Park *(G-11260)*
Crown Machine Inc ....E.... 815 877-7700
Rockford *(G-17361)*
Crv Industries Inc ....F.... 630 595-3777
Bensenville *(G-1781)*
Custom Cut EDM Inc ....G.... 847 647-9500
Skokie *(G-18947)*
Custom Machine Inc ....G.... 815 284-3820
Dixon *(G-7895)*
Custom Machining Company ....G.... 630 766-2600
Bensenville *(G-1783)*
Custom Millers Supply Inc ....G.... 309 734-6312
Monmouth *(G-14216)*
Custom Precision Inc ....G.... 847 278-7877
Schaumburg *(G-18502)*
Custom Superfinishing Grinding ....G.... 847 699-9710
Rosemont *(G-18016)*
Cutting Edge Machining Inc ....G.... 847 427-1392
Elk Grove Village *(G-8928)*
Cutting Edge Water Jet Service ....G.... 815 389-0100
South Beloit *(G-19088)*
D & H Precision Tooling Co ....G.... 815 653-9611
Wonder Lake *(G-21144)*
D & J Machine Shop Inc ....G.... 815 472-6057
Momence *(G-14184)*
D & K Machine and Tool Inc ....G.... 847 439-8691
Elk Grove Village *(G-8933)*
D & M Tool Llc ....G.... 847 731-3600
Zion *(G-21511)*
D & R Autochuck Inc ....E.... 815 394-1744
Rockford *(G-17364)*
D & R Machine Company Inc ....G.... 618 465-5611
Alton *(G-550)*
D & S Manufacturing Inc ....G.... 815 637-8889
Loves Park *(G-13202)*
D and K Plastics ....G.... 712 723-5372
Yorkville *(G-21476)*
▲ **D E Specialty Tool & Mfg Inc** ....E.... 847 678-0004
Franklin Park *(G-9925)*
D Machine Inc ....G.... 815 877-5991
Loves Park *(G-13203)*
Dagger Tool Co Inc ....G.... 630 279-5050
Addison *(G-86)*
Daley Automation LLC ....G.... 630 384-9900
Naperville *(G-14812)*
Datum Machine Works Inc ....F.... 815 877-8502
Rockford *(G-17369)*

Datum Tool and Mfg Inc ....F 847 742-4092
South Elgin *(G-19142)*
Daves Auto Repair ....G 630 682-4411
Carol Stream *(G-2973)*
David L Knoche ....G 618 466-7120
Godfrey *(G-10651)*
Davis Machine Company Inc ....G 815 723-9121
Joliet *(G-11854)*
Deedrick Machine Inc ....E 217 598-2366
Sadorus *(G-18131)*
Delta Centerless Grinding Inc ....F 847 288-0300
Franklin Park *(G-9930)*
▲ **Delta Design Inc** ....F 708 424-9400
Evergreen Park *(G-9592)*
▲ **Design Corrugating Company** ....E 314 821-4300
Taylorville *(G-19754)*
Design Enhanced Mfg Co ....G 815 946-3562
Polo *(G-16755)*
Design Metals Fabrication Inc ....G 630 752-9060
Carol Stream *(G-2976)*
Device Technologies Inc ....G 630 553-7178
Yorkville *(G-21479)*
Dial Industries Inc ....F 815 397-7994
Rockford *(G-17375)*
Dial Machine Inc ....E 815 397-6660
Rockford *(G-17376)*
Diamond Industrial Sales Ltd ....G 630 858-3687
Glen Ellyn *(G-10400)*
Die Cast Quality Services Inc ....G 708 582-3584
Park Ridge *(G-16273)*
Die Cutters Inc ....F 618 532-3448
Centralia *(G-3228)*
Disco Machine & Mfg Inc ....E 708 456-0835
Norridge *(G-15233)*
Diversified Machining Inc ....G 815 316-8561
Rockford *(G-17381)*
Djw Assembly Inc ....F 847 956-5330
Arlington Heights *(G-729)*
DK Precision Inc ....G 847 985-8008
Schaumburg *(G-18508)*
Dkb Partners Inc ....G 618 632-6718
O Fallon *(G-15572)*
DMS Industries Inc ....F 708 895-8000
Lansing *(G-12491)*
DNp Enterprises Inc ....G 630 628-7210
Addison *(G-95)*
Dodge Machine Tool ....G 815 544-0967
Belvidere *(G-1666)*
Donaldson Company Inc ....C 309 667-2885
New Windsor *(G-15072)*
Donaldson Company Inc ....E 815 288-3374
Dixon *(G-7898)*
Donnelly Automotive Machine ....F 217 428-7414
Decatur *(G-7491)*
Donson Machine ....G 708 468-8392
Orland Park *(G-15952)*
▲ **Donson Machine Company** ....D 708 388-0880
Alsip *(G-440)*
Dooling Machine Products Inc ....G 618 254-0724
Hartford *(G-11034)*
Double-Disc Grinding Corp ....G 708 410-1770
Melrose Park *(G-13853)*
Dovin Machine Shop Inc ....G 815 672-5247
Streator *(G-19607)*
Du All Precision LLC ....E 630 543-4243
Addison *(G-102)*
Du Page Precision Products Co ....F 630 849-2940
Aurora *(G-953)*
Du Page Precision Products Co ....D 630 849-2940
Aurora *(G-954)*
Du Page Precision Products Co ....E 630 849-2940
Naperville *(G-14818)*
Dugan Tool and Die Inc ....F 618 259-1351
East Alton *(G-8164)*
Dundick Corporation ....E 708 656-6363
Cicero *(G-6843)*
Dunteman and Co ....G 309 772-2166
Bushnell *(G-2742)*
▲ **Duraflex Inc** ....E 847 462-1007
Cary *(G-3156)*
Duragrind Inc ....E 815 625-6500
Sterling *(G-19506)*
Durite Screw Corporation ....E 773 622-3410
Chicago *(G-4413)*
Durr - All Corporation ....G 815 943-1032
Harvard *(G-11053)*
Dyers Machine Service Inc ....G 708 496-8100
Summit Argo *(G-19678)*
Dynamac Inc ....E 630 543-0033
Addison *(G-104)*
Dynamic Machining Inc ....G 815 675-3330
Spring Grove *(G-19273)*
Dynamic Precision Products ....F 847 526-2054
Wauconda *(G-20346)*
▲ **Dynomax Inc** ....B 847 680-8833
Wheeling *(G-20883)*
E & E Machine & Engineering Co ....G 708 841-5208
Riverdale *(G-17071)*
▲ **E & F Tool Company Inc** ....F 815 729-1305
Joliet *(G-11856)*
E & J Precision Machining Inc ....G 815 363-2522
McHenry *(G-13740)*
E B Bronson & Co Inc ....E 708 385-3600
Blue Island *(G-2119)*
E C Machining Inc ....E 708 496-0116
Justice *(G-11952)*
E M Glabus Co Inc ....F 630 766-3027
Bensenville *(G-1792)*
Eagle Gear & Manufacturing Co ....F 630 628-6100
Addison *(G-110)*
Eagle Machine Company ....G 312 243-7407
Chicago *(G-4429)*
Eaglestone Inc ....F 630 587-1115
Saint Charles *(G-18192)*
Eastwood Enterprises Inc ....D 847 940-4008
Deerfield *(G-7607)*
Eaw Machining ....G 847 865-5162
Wauconda *(G-20347)*
Ed Hartwig Trucking & Excvtg ....G 309 364-3672
Henry *(G-11163)*
Ed Weitekamp Inc ....G 217 229-4239
Raymond *(G-16989)*
EDM Dept Inc ....E 630 736-0531
Bartlett *(G-1276)*
EDM Scorpio Inc ....G 847 931-5164
Elgin *(G-8573)*
Edwardsville Mch & Wldg Co Inc ....G 618 656-5145
Edwardsville *(G-8360)*
Eeco Services Inc ....F 312 226-6030
Chicago *(G-4462)*
Eenigenburg Mfg Inc ....G 708 474-0850
Lansing *(G-12492)*
◆ **Elastec Inc** ....C 618 382-2525
Carmi *(G-2904)*
▲ **Elburn Metal Stamping Inc** ....E 630 365-2500
Elburn *(G-8452)*
◆ **Electri-Flex Company** ....D 630 529-2920
Roselle *(G-17952)*
▲ **Electroform Company** ....E 815 633-1113
Machesney Park *(G-13341)*
Elliott Machine & Tool Corp ....G 630 543-6755
Addison *(G-114)*
EM Smith & Co ....E 309 691-6812
Peoria *(G-16435)*
EMC Machining Inc ....F 630 860-7076
Bensenville *(G-1795)*
Emerald Machine Inc ....G 773 924-3659
Chicago *(G-4495)*
Empire Hard Chrome Inc ....B 773 762-3156
Chicago *(G-4500)*
Emtech Machining & Grinding ....G 815 338-1580
Woodstock *(G-21385)*
Engelhardt Enterprises Inc ....G 847 277-7070
Inverness *(G-11600)*
Engineering Design & Dev ....E 309 266-6298
Morton *(G-14359)*
Engle Manufacturing Co ....F 815 738-2282
Leaf River *(G-12541)*
ENR General Machining Co ....E 773 523-2944
Chicago *(G-4512)*
▲ **ERA Industries Inc** ....C 847 357-1320
Elk Grove Village *(G-8981)*
Erickson Tool & Machine Co ....G 815 397-2653
Rockford *(G-17400)*
Eton Machine Co Ltd ....F 847 426-3380
Elgin *(G-8581)*
Eww Enterprise Inc ....G 815 463-9607
New Lenox *(G-15034)*
Exact Machine Company Inc ....G 815 963-7905
Rockford *(G-17406)*
Excel Machine & Tool ....G 815 467-1177
Channahon *(G-3383)*
Excel Machining Inc ....G 773 585-6666
Chicago *(G-4543)*
Execl Machine Technology ....G 847 439-8434
Elk Grove Village *(G-8990)*
Express Grinding Inc ....G 847 434-5827
Elk Grove Village *(G-8992)*
Express Machining & Molds ....G 630 350-8480
Franklin Park *(G-9942)*
F N Smith Corporation ....E 815 732-2171
Oregon *(G-15919)*
Fabricators Unlimited Inc ....G 847 223-7986
Grayslake *(G-10772)*
Fabtec Manufacturing Inc ....F 847 671-4888
Franklin Park *(G-9943)*
Fanmar Inc ....E 847 621-2010
Elk Grove Village *(G-8995)*
Fern Manufacturing Company ....G 630 260-9350
Carol Stream *(G-2983)*
FH Ayer Manufacturing Co ....E 708 755-0550
Chicago Heights *(G-6746)*
▲ **Flex-Weld Inc** ....D 815 334-3662
Woodstock *(G-21387)*
Flextron Inc ....F 630 543-5995
Addison *(G-125)*
Flores Precision Products ....G 630 264-2222
Aurora *(G-1096)*
Folk Race Cars ....G 815 629-2418
Durand *(G-8151)*
Folkerts Manufacturing Inc ....G 815 968-7426
Rockford *(G-17417)*
Forest City Grinding Inc ....G 815 874-2424
Rockford *(G-17419)*
▼ **Fosbinder Fabrication Inc** ....E 309 764-0913
Moline *(G-14146)*
Four-Tech Industries Co ....G 708 444-8230
Tinley Park *(G-19828)*
Fox Machine & Tool Inc ....G 847 357-1845
Elk Grove Village *(G-9006)*
Fox Tool & Manufacturing Inc ....F 815 338-3046
Woodstock *(G-21390)*
▲ **Franklin Automation Inc** ....F 630 466-1900
Sugar Grove *(G-19645)*
Frey Wiss Prcsion McHining Inc ....E 630 595-9073
Wood Dale *(G-21191)*
Furry Inc ....F 217 446-0084
Danville *(G-7337)*
Future Tool Inc ....F 815 395-0012
Rockford *(G-17426)*
G & Z Industries Inc ....E 847 215-2300
Wheeling *(G-20903)*
G L Doemelt ....F 217 268-4243
Arcola *(G-649)*
G P Cole Inc ....F 217 431-3029
Danville *(G-7338)*
G&D Integrated Mfg LLC ....E 309 284-6700
Morton *(G-14361)*
G&G Machine Shop Inc ....G 217 892-9696
Rantoul *(G-16976)*
G&R Machining Inc ....G 847 526-7364
Island Lake *(G-11608)*
G3 Machining LLC ....G 309 323-8310
Bloomington *(G-2048)*
Galactic Tool Co ....G 815 962-3420
Rockford *(G-17427)*
Galaxy Precision Mfg Inc ....F 847 238-9066
Elk Grove Village *(G-9011)*
▲ **Galaxy Sourcing Inc** ....G 630 532-5003
Addison *(G-133)*
Gardner Products Inc ....F 815 562-6011
Rochelle *(G-17142)*
Gartech Manufacturing Co ....E 217 324-6527
Litchfield *(G-12963)*
Gates Inc ....G 217 335-2378
Barry *(G-1250)*
Gavin Woodworking Inc ....G 815 786-2242
Sandwich *(G-18371)*
Gebco Machine Inc ....F 618 452-6120
Granite City *(G-10710)*
General Grind & Machine Inc ....C 309 582-5959
Aledo *(G-356)*
General Grinding Co ....G 630 543-9088
Addison *(G-137)*
General Machine Inc ....E 618 234-1919
Freeburg *(G-10090)*
General Machine & Tl Works Inc ....F 312 337-2177
Chicago *(G-4673)*
General Machine and Tool Inc ....G 815 727-5270
Joliet *(G-11869)*
General Machine and Tool Inc ....G 815 727-4342
Lockport *(G-12996)*
General Machining Service Inc ....G 708 636-4848
Oak Lawn *(G-15718)*
General Precision Mfg LLC ....F 847 624-4969
Elk Grove Village *(G-9012)*
▲ **Geo T Schmidt Inc** ....D 847 647-7117
Niles *(G-15124)*
Gett Industries Ltd ....D 309 799-5131
Milan *(G-14012)*

Employee Codes: A=Over 500 employees, B=251-500
C=101-250, D=51-100, E=20-50, F=10-19, G=3-9

2020 Harris Illinois
Industrial Directory

975

35 INDUSTRIAL AND COMMERCIAL MACHINERY AND COMPUTER EQUIPMENT SIC SECTION

◆ **GF Machining Solutions LLC** ....D 847 913-5300
Lincolnshire *(G-12766)*

Gibbs Machine Corp ....E 815 336-9000
Coleta *(G-6949)*

Gibson Insurance Inc ....G 217 864-4877
Mount Zion *(G-14646)*

▲ **Global Gear & Machining LLC** ....C 630 969-9400
Downers Grove *(G-8013)*

Goellner Inc ....C 815 962-6076
Rockford *(G-17430)*

Gordys Machine and Tool Inc ....F 618 842-9331
Fairfield *(G-9626)*

Goreville Auto Parts & Mch Sp ....G 618 995-2375
Goreville *(G-10680)*

GPI Industries Incorporated ....D 708 877-8200
Thornton *(G-19787)*

GPM Mfg Inc ....F 847 550-8200
Lake Zurich *(G-12418)*

Graffs Tooling Center Inc ....G 618 357-5005
Pinckneyville *(G-16616)*

Gray Machine & Welding Inc ....F 309 788-2501
Rock Island *(G-17220)*

Grebner Machine & Tool Inc ....G 309 248-7768
Washburn *(G-20263)*

Green Technologies Inc ....G 815 624-8011
Rockton *(G-17698)*

Greens Machine Shop ....G 618 532-4631
Centralia *(G-3234)*

Griffin Machining Inc ....G 847 360-0098
Gurnee *(G-10884)*

Grind Lap Services Inc ....E 630 458-1111
Addison *(G-143)*

▲ **Grindal Company** ....E 630 250-8950
Itasca *(G-11662)*

Griswold Machine Co ....G 708 333-4258
South Holland *(G-19217)*

Groth Manufacturing ....E 847 428-5950
Carpentersville *(G-3103)*

Gti Spindle Technology Inc ....F 309 820-7887
Bloomington *(G-2054)*

Gymtek Incorporated ....F 815 547-0771
Belvidere *(G-1675)*

H & B Machine Corporation ....G 312 829-4850
Chicago *(G-4756)*

H & D Motor Service ....G 217 342-3262
Altamont *(G-533)*

H & H Machining ....G 309 365-7010
Lexington *(G-12619)*

H & K Precision Machining Co ....G 847 382-0288
Lake Barrington *(G-12149)*

H & M Machining Inc ....F 815 877-5623
Machesney Park *(G-13346)*

H & M Thread Rolling Co Inc ....G 847 451-1570
Franklin Park *(G-9955)*

H & R Tool & Machine Co ....G 618 344-7683
Caseyville *(G-3213)*

H B Products Incorporated ....G 773 735-0936
Palos Park *(G-16211)*

H Felde Tool & Machine Co ....F 309 692-5870
Peoria *(G-16449)*

H M C Products Inc ....E 815 885-1900
Machesney Park *(G-13319)*

H&S Machine & Tools Inc ....G 618 451-0164
Granite City *(G-10712)*

Hadady Machining Company Inc ....F 708 474-8620
Lansing *(G-12496)*

Hadco Tool Co LLC ....G 847 677-6263
Skokie *(G-18963)*

Halter Machine Shop Inc ....G 618 943-2224
Lawrenceville *(G-12534)*

Harbor Manufacturing Inc ....D 708 543-1740
Frankfort *(G-9800)*

Harbor Tool Manufacturing Co ....E 708 614-6400
Tinley Park *(G-19835)*

Harmony Metal Fabrication Inc ....E 847 426-8900
Gilberts *(G-10356)*

Hattan Tool Company ....G 708 597-9308
Alsip *(G-455)*

Haveco Tool & Mfg Inc ....G 847 603-1893
Lake Villa *(G-12354)*

Headco Industries Inc ....F 847 640-6490
Elk Grove Village *(G-9031)*

Headco Industries Inc ....G 815 729-4016
Joliet *(G-11875)*

Heartland Machine and Sup LLC ....F 217 543-2678
Arthur *(G-861)*

Henning Machine & Die Works ....G 217 286-3393
Henning *(G-11161)*

Hess Machine Inc ....G 618 887-4444
Marine *(G-13498)*

Hfo Chicago LLC ....F 847 258-2850
Elk Grove Village *(G-9034)*

▲ **Hfr Precision Machining Inc** ....E 630 556-4325
Sugar Grove *(G-19646)*

HI Tech Machining & Welding ....G 708 331-3608
South Holland *(G-19221)*

▼ **Hi-Grade Welding and Mfg LLC** ....E 847 640-8172
Schaumburg *(G-18548)*

Hi-Tech Manufacturing LLC ....C 847 678-1616
Schiller Park *(G-18812)*

Hidden Hollow Stables Inc ....G 309 243-7979
Dunlap *(G-8133)*

Highland Mch & Screw Pdts Co ....D 618 654-2103
Highland *(G-11218)*

Highland Metal Inc ....E 708 544-6641
Hillside *(G-11342)*

Hillers Sheet Metal Works ....G 217 532-2595
Hillsboro *(G-11314)*

HI Precision Manufacturing LLC ....D 217 398-6881
Champaign *(G-3302)*

Holmes Bros Inc ....E 217 442-1430
Danville *(G-7345)*

Holshouser Machine & Tool Inc ....G 618 451-0164
Granite City *(G-10715)*

Hopkins Machine Corporation ....G 773 772-2800
Chicago *(G-4840)*

Hottenrott Company Inc ....G 618 473-2531
Hecker *(G-11155)*

HPp Precision Machine Co Inc ....G 815 469-2608
Frankfort *(G-9802)*

▲ **Hy-Tek Manufacturing Co Inc** ....E 630 466-7664
Sugar Grove *(G-19647)*

I D Rockford Shop Inc ....G 815 335-1150
Winnebago *(G-21120)*

I-N-I Machining Inc ....G 309 496-1002
East Moline *(G-8229)*

Ideal Machine Inc ....G 217 925-5109
Dieterich *(G-7877)*

▲ **Illiana Machine & Mfg Corp** ....D 708 479-1333
Mokena *(G-14090)*

Illini Precision Machining Inc ....G 217 425-5780
Decatur *(G-7504)*

Illinois Pro-Turn Inc ....G 847 462-1870
Cary *(G-3170)*

Illinois Valley Machine Sp Inc ....F 815 586-4511
Ransom *(G-16965)*

Illinois Weld & Machine Inc ....F 309 565-0533
Hanna City *(G-10993)*

Imh Fabrication Inc ....F 815 537-2381
Prophetstown *(G-16833)*

IMI Manufacturing Inc ....G 630 771-0003
Bolingbrook *(G-2190)*

In-Place Machining Co Inc ....G 847 669-3006
Huntley *(G-11542)*

Indiana Precision Inc ....F 765 361-0247
Danville *(G-7351)*

Industrial Graphite Products ....G 630 350-0155
Franklin Park *(G-9964)*

Industrial Tool and Repair ....G 309 633-0939
Peoria *(G-16458)*

Innovative Gringing Inc ....G 630 766-4567
Bensenville *(G-1822)*

Innovative Machine Inc ....G 309 945-9445
Geneseo *(G-10244)*

▲ **Insync Manufacturing LLC** ....F 815 304-6300
Kankakee *(G-11978)*

International Revere Co ....G 773 248-1841
Chicago *(G-4955)*

Inventive Mfg Inc ....F 847 647-9500
Skokie *(G-18969)*

IPM Precision Inc ....G 847 304-7900
Lake Barrington *(G-12152)*

Irmko Tool Works Inc ....E 630 350-7550
Bensenville *(G-1825)*

Itc Inc ....G 309 634-1825
Dunlap *(G-8134)*

J & A Sheet Metal Shop Inc ....E 773 276-3739
Chicago *(G-4981)*

▲ **J & I Son Tool Company Inc** ....G 847 455-4200
Franklin Park *(G-9967)*

J & L Cnc Machining Inc ....G 708 388-2090
Alsip *(G-461)*

J & S Machine Works Inc ....G 708 344-2101
Melrose Park *(G-13885)*

J D Machining ....G 847 428-8690
Gilberts *(G-10360)*

J K Manufacturing Co ....D 708 563-2500
Bedford Park *(G-1475)*

J T Fennell Co Inc ....D 309 274-2145
Chillicothe *(G-6819)*

Jacksonville Machine Inc ....D 217 243-1119
Jacksonville *(G-11771)*

Jaday Industries ....F 847 928-1033
Franklin Park *(G-9971)*

Jakes McHning Rbilding Svc Inc ....E 630 892-3291
Aurora *(G-1116)*

▲ **James Walker Mfg Co** ....E 708 754-4020
Glenwood *(G-10641)*

Janssen Machine Inc ....F 815 877-9901
Loves Park *(G-13221)*

Jav Machine Craft Inc ....G 708 867-8608
Chicago *(G-5011)*

Jay RS Steel & Welding Inc ....G 847 949-9353
Mundelein *(G-14703)*

Jbw Machining Inc ....E 847 451-0276
Franklin Park *(G-9974)*

JC Precision Milling LLC ....E 815 654-1070
Machesney Park *(G-13352)*

▲ **Jdb Machining Inc** ....G 708 749-9596
Forest View *(G-9730)*

▲ **Jdb Manufacturing Company** ....G 708 749-9596
Forest View *(G-9731)*

Jefco Screw Machine Products ....F 815 282-2000
Loves Park *(G-13224)*

Jem Tool & Manufacturing Co ....F 630 595-1686
Bensenville *(G-1829)*

Jen-Sko-Vec Machining & Engrg ....G 773 776-7400
Chicago *(G-5017)*

Jet Grinding & Manufacturing ....F 847 956-8646
Arlington Heights *(G-761)*

Jet Industries Inc ....E 773 586-8900
Chicago *(G-5024)*

Jewel Machine Inc ....G 815 765-3636
Poplar Grove *(G-16781)*

Jim Sterner Machines ....G 815 962-8983
Rockford *(G-17474)*

Jingdiao North America Inc ....F 847 906-8888
Mount Prospect *(G-14540)*

JM Die Tooling Co ....E 630 616-7776
Bensenville *(G-1831)*

JMr Precision Machining Inc ....G 847 279-3982
Mundelein *(G-14704)*

John & Helen Inc ....F 815 654-1070
Loves Park *(G-13225)*

John H Best & Sons Inc ....E 309 932-2124
Galva *(G-10234)*

Johnson Pattern & Mch Works ....E 815 433-2775
Ottawa *(G-16057)*

Jones Garrison Sons Mch Works ....G 618 847-2161
Fairfield *(G-9629)*

Jr Tech Inc ....G 847 214-8860
Elgin *(G-8635)*

K & A Precision Machine Inc ....D 847 998-1933
Glenview *(G-10577)*

K & B Machining ....G 847 663-9534
Morton Grove *(G-14416)*

K & C Design and Manufacturing ....G 630 543-3386
Addison *(G-163)*

K & H Tool Co ....G 630 766-4588
Bensenville *(G-1834)*

K & K Tool & Die Inc ....F 309 829-4479
Bloomington *(G-2065)*

K D L Machining Inc ....G 309 477-3036
Pekin *(G-16341)*

K P Enterprises Inc ....G 630 509-2174
Bensenville *(G-1836)*

K R J Inc ....G 309 925-5123
Tremont *(G-19897)*

K R N Machine and Laser Center ....G 618 942-6064
Herrin *(G-11173)*

▲ **Kaas Industries Inc** ....G 847 298-9106
Rosemont *(G-18029)*

Kadon Precision Machining Inc ....D 815 874-5850
Rockford *(G-17479)*

Kaman Tool Corporation ....G 708 652-9023
Cicero *(G-6858)*

Kaskaskia Tool and Machine Inc ....E 618 475-3301
New Athens *(G-15020)*

Keeper Corp ....G 630 773-9393
Itasca *(G-11682)*

Kegley Machine Co ....G 309 346-8914
Pekin *(G-16342)*

▲ **Kelco Industries Inc** ....G 815 334-3600
Woodstock *(G-21398)*

Kemp Manufacturing Company ....E 309 682-7292
Peoria *(G-16465)*

Kemper Industries ....G 217 826-5712
Marshall *(G-13573)*

▲ **Kksp Precision Machining LLC** ....D 630 260-1735
Glendale Heights *(G-10464)*

SIC SECTION
35 INDUSTRIAL AND COMMERCIAL MACHINERY AND COMPUTER EQUIPMENT

Klapperich Tool Inc .... F 847 608-8471
South Elgin *(G-19160)*
KLM Tool Company .... E 630 458-1700
Addison *(G-172)*
▲ **Kocsis Brothers Machine Co** .... D 708 597-8110
Alsip *(G-465)*
Koenig Machine & Welding Inc .... G 217 228-6538
Quincy *(G-16904)*
Koerner Aviation Inc .... G 815 932-4222
Kankakee *(G-11988)*
Kohlert Manufacturing Corp .... G 630 584-0013
Saint Charles *(G-18221)*
▲ **Komax Corporation** .... D 888 465-6629
Buffalo Grove *(G-2556)*
Kopis Machine Co Inc .... E 630 543-4138
Addison *(G-175)*
Kormex Metal Craft Inc .... E 630 953-8856
Lombard *(G-13093)*
Kreis Tool & Mfg Co Inc .... E 847 289-3700
Elgin *(G-8639)*
Kremer Precision Machine Inc .... F 217 868-2627
Shumway *(G-18903)*
Kresser Precision Inds Inc .... G 815 899-2202
Davis Junction *(G-7425)*
▲ **Kris Dee and Associates Inc** .... D 630 503-4093
South Elgin *(G-19161)*
Krygier Machine Company Inc .... G 708 331-5255
South Holland *(G-19228)*
Kuchar Products Inc .... G 815 405-3692
New Lenox *(G-15038)*
Kw Fabrication .... G 773 523-2420
Chicago *(G-5137)*
L A T Enterprise Inc .... G 630 543-5533
Addison *(G-176)*
L K Beutel Machining Co Inc .... G 847 895-5310
Schaumburg *(G-18595)*
L M C Automotive Inc .... G 618 235-5242
Belleville *(G-1567)*
▲ **L W Schneider Inc** .... E 815 875-3835
Princeton *(G-16812)*
L-V Industries Inc .... F 630 595-9251
Bensenville *(G-1839)*
Lake County Technologies Inc .... F 847 977-1330
East Dundee *(G-8204)*
Lake County Tool Works North .... G 847 662-4542
Wadsworth *(G-20210)*
Lancer Manufacturing Inc .... F 630 595-1150
Barrington *(G-1223)*
Lane Tool & Mfg Co Inc .... E 847 622-1506
South Elgin *(G-19166)*
Lavezzi Precision Inc .... C 630 582-1230
Bloomingdale *(G-1997)*
Lays Mining Service Inc .... E 618 244-6570
Mount Vernon *(G-14621)*
▲ **Lb Steel LLC** .... B 708 331-2600
Harvey *(G-11092)*
▲ **Leading Edge Group Inc** .... C 815 316-3500
Rockford *(G-17492)*
Lehman Fast Tech .... G 847 742-5202
Elgin *(G-8641)*
Lenrok Industries Inc .... G 630 628-1946
Addison *(G-182)*
Leppala Machining Inc .... G 847 625-0270
Beach Park *(G-1443)*
Lesmark Tool Company .... G 815 725-7430
Rockdale *(G-17266)*
Lester Manufacturing Inc .... E 815 986-1172
Rockford *(G-17495)*
Lho Enterprises Inc .... G 708 499-0017
Chicago Ridge *(G-6801)*
Licon Inc .... G 618 485-2222
Ashley *(G-885)*
Line Craft Tool Company Inc .... C 630 932-1182
Lombard *(G-13096)*
Linne Machine Company Inc .... G 217 446-5746
Danville *(G-7359)*
Linx Global Mfg LLC .... G 847 910-5303
Chicago *(G-5233)*
Lion Tool & Die Co .... F 847 658-8898
Algonquin *(G-377)*
▲ **Littell LLC** .... E 630 916-6662
Schaumburg *(G-18609)*
Livingston Products Inc .... F 847 808-0900
Waukegan *(G-20460)*
▼ **Ln Engineering LLC** .... F 815 472-2939
Momence *(G-14187)*
Lorbern Mfg Inc .... E 847 301-8600
Schaumburg *(G-18612)*
Luebbers Welding & Mfg Inc .... F 618 594-2489
Carlyle *(G-2893)*
Lunquist Manufacturing Corp .... E 815 874-2437
Rockford *(G-17499)*
M & J Manufacturing Co Inc .... F 847 364-6066
Elk Grove Village *(G-9100)*
▲ **M & R Precision Machining Inc** .... E 847 364-1050
Elk Grove Village *(G-9101)*
M & S Industrial Co Inc .... E 773 252-1616
Chicago *(G-5297)*
M & W Grinding of Rockford .... G 815 874-9481
Rockford *(G-17500)*
M S —action Machining Corp .... E 815 344-3770
McHenry *(G-13760)*
Mac-Weld Inc .... G 618 529-1828
Carbondale *(G-2850)*
Machine & Design .... G 630 858-6416
Glen Ellyn *(G-10411)*
◆ **Machine Technology Inc** .... G 815 444-4837
Crystal Lake *(G-7221)*
Machine Technology Inc .... F 815 795-6818
Marseilles *(G-13560)*
Machine Tool Acc & Mfg Co .... G 773 489-0903
Chicago *(G-5309)*
Machine Tool Bearing & ACC Inc .... G 847 357-1793
Elk Grove Village *(G-9104)*
Machine Works of Decatur Inc .... G 217 428-3896
Decatur *(G-7519)*
Machined Concepts LLC .... G 847 708-4923
Elgin *(G-8646)*
Machined Metals Manufacturing .... E 847 364-6116
Elk Grove Village *(G-9105)*
Machining Systems Corporation .... G 708 385-7903
Crestwood *(G-7122)*
▼ **Machining Technology Inc** .... G 815 469-0400
Lemont *(G-12570)*
Madden Ventures Inc .... G 847 487-0644
Mundelein *(G-14712)*
Magnet-Schultz Amer Holdg LLC .... F 630 789-0600
Westmont *(G-20755)*
▲ **Magnet-Schultz America Inc** .... D 630 789-0600
Westmont *(G-20756)*
Magnum Machining LLC .... G 815 862-2040
Richmond *(G-17018)*
▲ **Mah Machine Company** .... C 708 656-1826
Cicero *(G-6864)*
Main Source Machining .... G 815 962-8770
Rockford *(G-17503)*
Manhattan Mechanical Svcs LLC .... E 815 478-9940
Manhattan *(G-13434)*
Manteno Metal Works .... G 815 468-6128
Manteno *(G-13452)*
Manufctring Mint Solutions Inc .... E 309 263-6077
Pekin *(G-16343)*
Marathon Technologies Inc .... E 847 378-8572
Elk Grove Village *(G-9111)*
Marble Machine Inc .... E 217 431-3014
Danville *(G-7361)*
Marion Tool & Die Inc .... D 309 266-6551
Morton *(G-14364)*
Maritool Incorporated .... G 888 352-7773
Wood Dale *(G-21213)*
Mark Lahey .... G 217 243-4433
Jacksonville *(G-11775)*
Martin Precision Inc .... G 815 873-1000
Rockford *(G-17506)*
Marvel Machining Co Inc .... G 630 350-0075
Bensenville *(G-1847)*
Master Cut E D M Inc .... G 847 534-0343
Schaumburg *(G-18622)*
Master Hydraulics & Machining .... F 847 895-5578
Schaumburg *(G-18623)*
Matis Inc .... F 708 425-7100
Chicago Ridge *(G-6802)*
Matrix Machine & Tool Mfg .... G 708 452-8707
River Grove *(G-17063)*
▲ **Mattsn/Witt Precision Pdts Inc** .... E 847 382-7810
Lake Barrington *(G-12159)*
MB Machine Inc .... F 815 864-3555
Shannon *(G-18871)*
MBA Manufacturing Inc .... G 847 566-2555
Bensenville *(G-1849)*
MBR Tool Inc .... G 847 671-4491
Schiller Park *(G-18822)*
Mc Henry Machine Co Inc .... G 815 875-1953
Princeton *(G-16813)*
McArthur Machining Inc .... G 847 838-6998
Antioch *(G-624)*
McBride & Shoff Inc .... E 309 367-4193
Metamora *(G-13963)*
McGill Machine Works Inc .... G 847 301-8000
Schaumburg *(G-18624)*
▲ **Mechanical Devices Company** .... G 309 663-2843
Bloomington *(G-2073)*
▲ **Mechanical Products Corp** .... F 630 543-4842
Addison *(G-194)*
Mechanical Tool & Engrg Co .... C 815 397-4701
Rockford *(G-17514)*
Mennies Machine Company .... F 815 339-2227
Granville *(G-10757)*
Mercury Eqp Fabg & Machining .... G 847 288-0079
Franklin Park *(G-9992)*
Messer Machine .... G 815 398-6248
Rockford *(G-17518)*
▲ **Meta TEC Development Inc** .... G 309 246-2960
Lacon *(G-12131)*
Meta TEC of Illinois Inc .... D 309 246-2960
Lacon *(G-12132)*
Metal Works Machine Inc .... G 217 868-5111
Shumway *(G-18905)*
Meteer Manufacturing Co .... G 217 636-8109
Athens *(G-899)*
Metric Machine Shop Inc .... G 847 439-9891
Elk Grove Village *(G-9120)*
Metro East Manufacturing .... F 618 233-0182
Swansea *(G-19693)*
Meyer Tool & Manufacturing Inc .... E 708 425-9080
Oak Lawn *(G-15727)*
Microlution Inc .... E 773 282-6495
Chicago *(G-5424)*
Microtech Machine Inc .... E 847 870-0707
Wheeling *(G-20940)*
Mid-West Screw Products Inc .... E 773 283-6032
Chicago *(G-5432)*
Midaco Corporation .... E 847 593-8420
Elk Grove Village *(G-9123)*
Midstate Manufacturing Company .... C 309 342-9555
Galesburg *(G-10210)*
Midway Grinding Inc .... E 847 439-7424
Elk Grove Village *(G-9124)*
Midway Machine & Tool Co Inc .... G 708 385-3450
Alsip *(G-477)*
Midwest EDM Specialties Inc .... G 815 521-2130
Channahon *(G-3390)*
Midwest Hardfacing LLC .... F 815 622-9420
Rock Falls *(G-17190)*
▲ **Midwest Machine Company Ltd** .... G 630 628-0485
Addison *(G-212)*
Midwest Machine Service Inc .... F 708 229-1122
Alsip *(G-479)*
Midwest Machine Tool Inc .... G 815 427-8665
Saint Anne *(G-18136)*
Midwest Metal Castings Inc .... G 773 762-3009
Chicago *(G-5444)*
Midwestern Mch Hydraulics Inc .... F 618 246-9440
Mount Vernon *(G-14625)*
Milans Machining & Mfg Co Inc .... D 708 780-6600
Cicero *(G-6867)*
Milco Precision Machining Inc .... F 630 628-5730
Addison *(G-216)*
Miller Machine .... G 815 845-2508
Scales Mound *(G-18421)*
Miller Roger Weston .... G 217 352-0476
Champaign *(G-3322)*
Mills Machine Inc .... G 815 273-4707
Savanna *(G-18409)*
Mills Machining .... G 815 933-9193
Bradley *(G-2287)*
Mister Inc of Chicago .... G 773 342-7200
Chicago *(G-5468)*
Mitsubishi Chemical Advncd Mtr .... C 847 367-0110
Libertyville *(G-12682)*
Mitsubishi Heavy Inds Amer Inc .... F 630 693-4700
Addison *(G-220)*
Mk Systems Incorporated .... F 847 709-6180
Elk Grove Village *(G-9129)*
Moore Machine Works .... G 815 625-0536
Sterling *(G-19521)*
▲ **Morgan Bronze Products Inc** .... D 847 526-6000
Lake Zurich *(G-12435)*
Morris Midwest LLC .... G 630 351-1901
Roselle *(G-17971)*
Moultri Cnty Hstrcl/Gnlgcl Sct .... F 217 728-4085
Sullivan *(G-19672)*
Mt Carmel Machine Shop Inc .... F 618 262-4591
Mount Carmel *(G-14480)*
Mtech Cnc Machining Inc .... G 224 848-0818
Lake Zurich *(G-12437)*
▲ **Multax Corporation** .... D 309 266-9765
Morton *(G-14372)*
Multimetal Products Corp .... E 847 662-9110
Gurnee *(G-10901)*

S
I
C

Employee Codes: A=Over 500 employees, B=251-500
C=101-250, D=51-100, E=20-50, F=10-19, G=3-9
2020 Harris Illinois
Industrial Directory
977

35 INDUSTRIAL AND COMMERCIAL MACHINERY AND COMPUTER EQUIPMENT SIC SECTION

Mushro Machine & Tool Co ... F ... 815 672-5848
Streator (G-19617)

N J Tech Inc ... G ... 847 428-1001
Gilberts (G-10363)

N K C Inc ... G ... 630 628-9159
Addison (G-225)

Napier Machine & Welding Inc ... G ... 217 525-8740
Springfield (G-19410)

National Component Sales Inc ... F ... 847 439-0333
Arlington Heights (G-780)

National Machine Repair Inc ... F ... 708 672-7711
Crete (G-7142)

National Tool & Machine Co ... F ... 618 271-6445
East Saint Louis (G-8316)

National Tool & Mfg Co ... D ... 847 806-9800
East Dundee (G-8206)

▲ Nationwide Precision Pdts Corp ... B ... 585 272-7100
Lake Bluff (G-12197)

Natura Products Inc ... F ... 847 509-5835
Northbrook (G-15439)

Nett Industries ... G ... 847 838-3300
Antioch (G-628)

New Cie Inc ... E ... 815 224-1511
Peru (G-16584)

New Dimensions Precision Mac ... D ... 815 923-8300
Union (G-19941)

New Lenox Machine Co Inc ... F ... 815 584-4866
Dwight (G-8156)

Newssor Manufacturing Inc ... G ... 618 259-1174
East Alton (G-8167)

Nex Gen Manufacturing Inc ... G ... 847 487-7077
Wauconda (G-20381)

▲ Nicholas Machine & Tool Inc ... G ... 847 298-2035
Rosemont (G-18038)

Niese Walter Machine Mfg Co ... G ... 773 774-7337
Des Plaines (G-7811)

Nor Service Inc ... E ... 815 232-8379
Freeport (G-10130)

Northwest Mold & Machine Corp ... G ... 847 690-1501
Elk Grove Village (G-9155)

Northwest Tool Co Inc ... G ... 630 350-4770
Bensenville (G-1860)

▲ Norton Machine Co ... G ... 217 748-6115
Rossville (G-18066)

NS Precision Lathe Inc ... G ... 708 867-5023
Maywood (G-13675)

▲ Nu-Way Industries Inc ... C ... 847 298-7710
Des Plaines (G-7812)

O & L Machine Inc ... G ... 815 963-6600
Rockford (G-17541)

O Brien Bill ... G ... 630 980-5571
Geneva (G-10294)

O K Jobbers Inc ... G ... 217 728-7378
Sullivan (G-19674)

▼ Obsidian Mfg Inds Inc ... F ... 815 962-8700
Rockford (G-17542)

Octane Motorsports LLC ... G ... 224 419-5460
Waukegan (G-20473)

OHare Precision Metals LLC ... E ... 847 640-6050
Arlington Heights (G-783)

Oldendorf Machining & Fabg ... G ... 708 946-2498
Beecher (G-1519)

Olney Machine & Design Inc ... F ... 618 392-6634
Olney (G-15881)

Olson Machining Inc ... E ... 815 675-2900
Spring Grove (G-19291)

Omega Manufacturing LLC ... G ... 708 345-8505
Melrose Park (G-13899)

On Target Grinding and Mfg ... G ... 708 418-3905
Lynwood (G-13296)

Oostman Fabricating & Wldg Inc ... F ... 630 241-1315
Westmont (G-20763)

Orat Inc ... G ... 630 567-6728
Saint Charles (G-18238)

Orbit Machining Company ... E ... 847 678-1050
Schiller Park (G-18830)

Orient Machining & Welding Inc ... E ... 708 371-3500
Dixmoor (G-7886)

Orion Tool Die & Machine Co ... E ... 309 526-3303
Orion (G-15930)

Orland Precision Machine LLC ... E ... 815 464-9210
Frankfort (G-9818)

P & A Driveline & Machine Inc ... F ... 630 860-7474
Bensenville (G-1865)

P & G Machine & Tool Inc ... G ... 618 283-0273
Vandalia (G-20018)

◆ P & H Manufacturing Co ... D ... 217 774-2123
Shelbyville (G-18882)

P M Armor Inc ... E ... 847 797-9940
Mount Prospect (G-14557)

P M Mfg Services Inc ... G ... 630 553-6924
Yorkville (G-21496)

P R Manufacturing Co ... G ... 309 596-2986
Viola (G-20181)

▲ Pacific Bearing Corp ... C ... 815 389-5600
Roscoe (G-17921)

Parallel Machine Products Inc ... F ... 847 359-1012
Palatine (G-16148)

Paramount Sintered Pdts LLP ... G ... 847 746-8866
Zion (G-21524)

Paris Machine & Welding ... G ... 217 463-2894
Paris (G-16238)

Park Engineering Inc ... E ... 847 455-1424
Franklin Park (G-10013)

Parker Tool & Die Co ... G ... 847 566-2229
Mundelein (G-14723)

Parsons Company Inc ... B ... 309 467-9100
Roanoke (G-17104)

Part Stop Inc ... G ... 618 377-5238
Bethalto (G-1965)

Patkus Machine Co ... G ... 815 398-7818
Rockford (G-17548)

Patlin Enterprises Inc ... F ... 815 675-6606
Spring Grove (G-19292)

Paul & Ron Manufacturing Inc ... F ... 309 596-2986
Viola (G-20182)

PDQ Machine Inc ... G ... 815 282-7575
Machesney Park (G-13363)

Performance Automotive ... G ... 618 377-0020
Bethalto (G-1966)

Performance Pattern & Mch Inc ... E ... 309 676-0907
Peoria (G-16496)

Peters Machine Works Inc ... F ... 708 496-3005
Oak Lawn (G-15732)

Pgi Mfg LLC ... C ... 815 224-7540
Peru (G-16589)

Pgi Mfg LLC ... D ... 800 821-3475
Rockford (G-17552)

PH Tool Manufacturing ... G ... 847 952-9441
Des Plaines (G-7821)

Phillip Rodgers ... G ... 815 877-5461
Loves Park (G-13244)

▲ Phoenix Tool Corp ... F ... 847 956-1886
Elk Grove Village (G-9178)

Pioneer Grinding & Mfg Co ... G ... 847 678-6565
Franklin Park (G-10018)

Pittsfield Mch Tl & Wldg Co ... G ... 217 656-4000
Payson (G-16317)

▲ Planter Inc ... D ... 773 637-7777
Chicago (G-5817)

Plastak Inc ... G ... 630 466-4100
Sugar Grove (G-19649)

Platinum Tooling Technologies ... G ... 847 749-0633
Prospect Heights (G-16845)

Playing With Fusion Inc ... G ... 309 258-7259
Mackinaw (G-13385)

PM Machine Shop ... G ... 217 854-3504
Carlinville (G-2883)

Pmb Industries Inc ... G ... 708 442-4515
La Grange (G-12086)

PMI Aerospace Inc ... G ... 815 397-3894
Rockford (G-17555)

Popular Ridge Machine Met Cft ... G ... 618 687-1656
Murphysboro (G-14757)

Prairie Manufacturing Inc ... G ... 815 498-1593
Somonauk (G-19072)

Precision Cnncting Rod Svc Inc ... F ... 708 345-3700
Broadview (G-2458)

Precision Dynamics Inc ... F ... 815 877-1592
Machesney Park (G-13366)

Precision Engineering & Dev Co ... E ... 630 834-5956
Villa Park (G-20165)

Precision Grinding Inc ... G ... 847 238-1000
Elk Grove Village (G-9189)

Precision Ground ... F ... 815 578-2613
Lakemoor (G-12475)

Precision Inc ... G ... 847 593-2947
Elk Grove Village (G-9190)

Precision Laser Marking Inc ... G ... 630 628-8575
Addison (G-250)

Precision Machine and ... F ... 618 997-8795
Marion (G-13530)

Precision Machine Products ... G ... 630 860-0861
Wood Dale (G-21230)

Precision Machining & Tool Co ... G ... 847 674-7111
Skokie (G-19009)

Precision Masters Inc ... E ... 815 397-3894
Rockford (G-17558)

Precision Metal Crafters Inc ... F ... 847 816-3244
Libertyville (G-12698)

Precision Prismatic Inc ... G ... 708 424-0905
Chicago Ridge (G-6808)

Precision Waterjet Inc ... G ... 847 462-9381
Crystal Lake (G-7245)

Premier Tool & Machine Inc ... G ... 618 445-9066
Albion (G-352)

Premium Manufacturing Inc ... E ... 309 787-3882
Rock Island (G-17233)

Press Brake Tool and Supply ... G ... 847 776-9201
Palatine (G-16149)

Price Machine Inc ... G ... 217 892-8958
Dewey (G-7874)

Pride Machine & Tool Co Inc ... F ... 708 343-7190
Melrose Park (G-13905)

▲ Prince Industries Inc ... B ... 630 588-0088
Carol Stream (G-3052)

Pro-Beam USA Inc ... G ... 630 327-6909
Plainfield (G-16708)

Pro-Qua Inc ... G ... 630 543-5644
Addison (G-256)

Pro-Tech Machining Inc ... G ... 773 406-9297
Bensenville (G-1872)

Production Manufacturing ... G ... 217 256-4211
Warsaw (G-20259)

▲ Production Tool Corporation ... E ... 773 288-4400
Chicago (G-5894)

Prospan Manufacturing Co ... G ... 630 860-1930
Bensenville (G-1874)

Prospect Grinding Incorporated ... G ... 847 229-9240
Wheeling (G-20966)

Puskar Precision Machining Co ... F ... 847 888-2929
Elgin (G-8704)

Quadrant Tool and Mfg Co ... E ... 847 352-6977
Schaumburg (G-18691)

Quality Cnc Incorporated ... F ... 630 406-0101
Batavia (G-1407)

Quality Fabricators Inc ... D ... 630 543-0540
Addison (G-261)

Quality Machine ... G ... 708 499-0021
Oak Lawn (G-15733)

Quality Machine Tool Services ... G ... 847 776-0073
Schaumburg (G-18692)

Quality Metal Products Inc ... C ... 309 692-8014
Peoria (G-16505)

Quality Metal Works Inc ... G ... 309 379-5311
Stanford (G-19473)

▲ Quality Tool Inc ... G ... 847 288-9330
Franklin Park (G-10030)

Quantum Precision Inc ... E ... 630 692-1545
West Chicago (G-20634)

R & B Metal Products Inc ... E ... 815 338-1890
Woodstock (G-21427)

R & D Machine LLC ... G ... 618 282-6262
Red Bud (G-16999)

R & N Machine Co ... F ... 708 841-5555
Riverdale (G-17075)

R & S Steel Corporation ... G ... 309 448-2645
Congerville (G-7001)

R A E Tool and Manufacturing ... G ... 815 485-2506
New Lenox (G-15053)

R A Zweig Inc ... C ... 847 832-9001
Glenview (G-10607)

R B M Tool Inc ... G ... 630 422-7065
Elk Grove Village (G-9209)

R C Sales & Manufacturing Inc ... G ... 815 645-8898
Stillman Valley (G-19545)

R D S Co ... G ... 630 893-2990
Bloomingdale (G-2010)

R G Hanson Company Inc ... F ... 309 661-9200
Bloomington (G-2087)

R K Precision Machine Inc ... G ... 574 293-0231
Alsip (G-500)

R L Lewis Industries Inc ... E ... 309 353-7670
Pekin (G-16358)

R M Armstrong & Son Inc ... G ... 847 669-3988
Huntley (G-11562)

R M Tool & Manufacturing Co ... G ... 847 888-0433
Elgin (G-8713)

R Machining Inc ... G ... 217 532-2174
Butler (G-2749)

R T M Precision Machining Inc ... G ... 630 595-0946
Carol Stream (G-3058)

R-M Industries Inc ... F ... 630 543-3071
Addison (G-264)

R/K Industries Inc ... F ... 847 526-2222
Wauconda (G-20387)

Radius Machine & Tool Inc ... F ... 847 662-7690
Gurnee (G-10922)

Rah Enterprises Inc ... G ... 217 223-1970
Quincy (G-16938)

Rajner Quality Machine Works ....G....... 847 394-8999
Wheeling (G-20968)
Ramco Tool & Manufacturing Inc ....F....... 847 639-9899
Cary (G-3184)
Rapco Ltd ....G....... 618 249-6614
Richview (G-17033)
Rapid Motion Cnc LLC ....G....... 224 372-9000
Lake Villa (G-12366)
Raycar Gear & Machine Company ....E....... 815 874-3948
Rockford (G-17566)
Rays Machine & Mfg Co Inc ....F....... 309 699-2121
East Peoria (G-8286)
Reba Machine Corp ....G....... 630 595-1272
Wood Dale (G-21234)
Rebco Machine Specialties Inc............F....... 630 852-3419
Westmont (G-20769)
Regent Automotive Engineering ....G....... 773 889-5744
Chicago (G-6002)
Reliance Tool Inc............G....... 815 636-2770
Loves Park (G-13252)
Remmers Welding and Machine............G....... 815 689-2765
Cullom (G-7301)
Research and Testing Worx Inc............G....... 815 734-7346
Mount Morris (G-14501)
Reyco Precision Welding Inc............F....... 847 593-2947
Lake Zurich (G-12450)
Reynolds Manufacturing Company.......E....... 309 787-8600
Milan (G-14025)
RF Mau Co............F....... 847 329-9731
Lincolnwood (G-12838)
▲ Ri-Del Mfg Inc............D....... 312 829-8720
Chicago (G-6024)
Rice Precision Machining ....F....... 630 543-7220
Addison (G-274)
Richard A Anderson............G....... 815 895-5627
Sycamore (G-19729)
Richardson Manufacturing Co............D....... 217 546-2249
Springfield (G-19434)
Richland County Machine Inc............G....... 618 392-2892
Olney (G-15886)
Riser Machine Corporation ....F....... 708 532-2313
New Lenox (G-15055)
Riverside Tool & Die Co ....F....... 309 689-0104
Peoria (G-16511)
Rj Cnc Works Inc ....G....... 847 671-9120
Franklin Park (G-10037)
▼ Rj Link International Inc ....F....... 815 874-8110
Rockford (G-17576)
Rjd Machining LLC ....G....... 217 684-5100
Longview (G-13175)
RMH Enterprises............G....... 630 525-5552
Wheaton (G-20819)
Robert C Weisheit Co Inc ....E....... 847 648-4991
Glendale Heights (G-10489)
Rockford Burrall Mch Co Inc ....E....... 815 877-7428
Rockford (G-17589)
Rockford Jobbing Service Inc ....G....... 815 398-8661
Rockford (G-17596)
Rockford Linear Actuation............G....... 815 986-4400
Rockford (G-17597)
Rockford Precision Machine............F....... 815 873-1018
Rockford (G-17601)
Rockford Quality Grinding Inc............F....... 815 227-9001
Rockford (G-17603)
Rockford Secondary Co............G....... 815 398-0401
Rockford (G-17605)
Rockford Tool and Mfg Co ....F....... 815 398-5876
Rockford (G-17607)
Roe Machine Inc............E....... 618 983-5524
West Frankfort (G-20681)
▲ Rogers Precision Machining............F....... 815 233-0065
Freeport (G-10138)
Rogus Tool Inc............G....... 847 824-5939
Des Plaines (G-7838)
Rohbi Enterprises Inc............G....... 708 343-2004
Broadview (G-2467)
Roll Rite Inc............G....... 815 645-8600
Davis Junction (G-7426)
Roll-Kraft Northern Inc ....G....... 815 469-0205
Frankfort (G-9832)
Romed Industries Corporation............G....... 847 362-3900
Lake Zurich (G-12452)
Romtech Machining Inc............G....... 630 543-7039
Addison (G-276)
Roscoe Tool & Manufacturing ....E....... 815 633-8808
Roscoe (G-17929)
Royal Machine Works Inc............G....... 815 465-6879
Grant Park (G-10752)
Royal Machining Corporation............G....... 708 338-3387
Melrose Park (G-13911)

RT Blackhawk Mch Pdts Inc ....G....... 815 389-3632
South Beloit (G-19111)
Runge Enterprises Inc............G....... 630 365-2000
Elburn (G-8472)
Rusco Manufacturing Inc............F....... 815 654-3930
Machesney Park (G-13372)
S & B Jig Grinding Inc............G....... 815 654-7907
Loves Park (G-13262)
S & J Machine Inc ....G....... 815 297-1594
Freeport (G-10139)
S & K Boring Inc............G....... 815 227-4394
Rockford (G-17619)
S & W Machine Works Inc............G....... 708 597-6043
Alsip (G-508)
S D Custom Machining............G....... 618 544-7007
Robinson (G-17125)
S&R Precision Machine LLC............F....... 815 469-6544
Frankfort (G-9835)
Sam Solutions Inc............G....... 708 594-0480
Summit Argo (G-19681)
▼ Sandbagger LLC ....D....... 630 876-2400
Elmhurst (G-9422)
Sandbagger Corp............F....... 630 876-2400
Elmhurst (G-9423)
Sanks Machining Inc ....G....... 618 635-8279
Staunton (G-19477)
Sas Industrial Machinery Inc ....G....... 847 455-5526
Franklin Park (G-10044)
Savex Manufacturing Company ....G....... 630 668-7219
Carol Stream (G-3064)
Schaffer Tool & Design Inc ....G....... 630 876-3800
Saint Charles (G-18266)
Schmid Tool & Engineering Corp..........E....... 630 333-1733
Villa Park (G-20171)
Schold Holdings Inc ....E....... 708 458-3788
Chicago (G-6114)
Schram Enterprises Inc............E....... 708 345-2252
Melrose Park (G-13914)
Schultes Precision Mfg Inc ....D....... 847 465-0300
Buffalo Grove (G-2596)
Scot Industries Inc............D....... 630 466-7591
Sugar Grove (G-19653)
SEC Design Technologies Inc ....F....... 847 680-0439
Libertyville (G-12704)
◆ Senior Holdings Inc............D....... 630 837-1811
Bartlett (G-1309)
Senior Operations LLC............A....... 630 837-1811
Bartlett (G-1310)
◆ Senior Operations LLC ....B....... 630 372-3500
Bartlett (G-1311)
Senior PLC............G....... 630 372-3511
Bartlett (G-1312)
Service Auto Supply ....F....... 309 444-9704
Washington (G-20280)
Service Machine Company Inc ....F....... 815 654-2310
Loves Park (G-13264)
Service Machine Jobs ....G....... 815 986-3033
Rockford (G-17626)
SF Holdings Group LLC ....F....... 630 543-6682
Addison (G-287)
Shaner Quality Machining Inc............G....... 815 985-7209
Rockford (G-17628)
Share Machine Inc ....F....... 630 906-1810
Aurora (G-1156)
Sigma Tool & Machining ....G....... 815 874-0500
Rockford (G-17631)
Sikora Automation Incorporated ....G....... 630 833-0298
Addison (G-291)
Sikora Precision Inc............G....... 847 468-0900
Elgin (G-8732)
Silver Machine Shop Inc............G....... 217 359-5717
Champaign (G-3348)
Silverlight Cnc Inc............G....... 847 450-1099
Barrington (G-1244)
Skild Manufacturing Inc ....E....... 847 437-1717
Elk Grove Village (G-9243)
▲ Smith & Richardson Mfg Co ....E....... 630 232-2581
Geneva (G-10306)
Smith and Son Machine Shop ....G....... 217 260-3257
Broadlands (G-2410)
Sobot Tool & Manufacturing Co ....E....... 847 480-0560
Northbrook (G-15482)
▲ Sollami Company............E....... 618 988-1521
Herrin (G-11179)
Solutions Manufacturing Inc............E....... 847 310-4506
Hoffman Estates (G-11461)
Sonic Manufacturing Corp............F....... 847 228-0015
Elk Grove Village (G-9246)
Source United LLC............G....... 847 956-1459
Elk Grove Village (G-9248)

Southern IL Crankshaft Inc ....F....... 618 282-4100
Red Bud (G-17002)
Southern Illinois Crankshafts ....F....... 618 282-4100
Ruma (G-18107)
Southwest Tool & Machine ....G....... 708 349-4441
Orland Park (G-15982)
Southwick Machine & Design Co ....G....... 309 949-2868
Colona (G-6980)
Specialty Enterprises Inc ....G....... 630 595-7808
Franklin Park (G-10050)
Spectrum Machining Co............E....... 630 562-9400
West Chicago (G-20645)
Spyco Industries Inc............E....... 630 655-5900
Burr Ridge (G-2721)
Spytek Aerospace Corporation ....G....... 847 318-7515
Bensenville (G-1898)
▲ Sst Forming Roll Inc ....G....... 847 215-6812
Buffalo Grove (G-2608)
St Charles Screw Products Inc............G....... 815 943-8060
Harvard (G-11067)
Standard Machine & Tool Corp............F....... 309 762-6431
Moline (G-14179)
▲ Standard Precision Grinding Co ......F....... 708 474-1211
Lansing (G-12517)
▲ Stanley Machining & Tool Corp ....D....... 847 426-4560
Carpentersville (G-3120)
Star Cnc Machine Tool Corp ....G....... 847 437-8300
Elk Grove Village (G-9254)
Starmont Manufacturing Co............G....... 815 939-1041
Kankakee (G-12007)
Starro Precision Products Inc ....E....... 847 741-9400
Elgin (G-8739)
Stateline Swiss Mfg LLC ....F....... 815 282-5181
Roscoe (G-17935)
Sterling Tool & Manufacturing............G....... 847 304-1800
Barrington (G-1245)
Strategic Mfg Partner LLC............G....... 262 878-5213
Northbrook (G-15488)
▲ Strausak Inc............G....... 847 281-8550
Mundelein (G-14739)
Streator Machine Company ....G....... 815 672-2436
Streator (G-19627)
Stuart Moore Racing Ltd ....G....... 847 949-9100
Mundelein (G-14740)
Stuhlman Family LLC ....G....... 815 436-2432
Plainfield (G-16719)
Suburban Indus Tl & Mfg Co............F....... 708 597-7788
Alsip (G-513)
Suburban Machine & Tool............G....... 815 469-2221
Mokena (G-14118)
Suburban Machine Corporation ....E....... 847 808-9095
Wheeling (G-20992)
Sugar River Machine Shop ....E....... 815 624-0214
South Beloit (G-19115)
▼ Sun Centre Usa Inc ....F....... 224 699-9058
Crystal Lake (G-7271)
Supreme Manufacturing Company ....E....... 847 297-8212
Des Plaines (G-7854)
Swebco Mfg Inc............E....... 815 636-7160
Machesney Park (G-13377)
Swiss E D M Wirecut Inc ....F....... 847 459-4310
Prospect Heights (G-16847)
▲ Swiss Precision Machining Inc..........D....... 847 647-7111
Wheeling (G-20995)
▲ Sycamore Precision............D....... 815 784-5151
Genoa (G-10324)
Symbol Tool Inc ....G....... 847 674-1080
Skokie (G-19041)
T & K Precision Grinding ....G....... 708 450-0565
Melrose Park (G-13920)
T & K Tool & Manufacturing Co ....G....... 815 338-0954
Woodstock (G-21439)
T & T Machine Shop............G....... 847 244-2020
Gurnee (G-10932)
T R Machine Inc............E....... 815 865-5711
Davis (G-7419)
T/J Fabricators Inc ....D....... 630 543-2293
Addison (G-303)
Tag-Barton LLC ....G....... 217 428-0711
Decatur (G-7556)
Tait Machine Tool Inc............G....... 815 932-2011
Kankakee (G-12010)
Tal-Mar Cstm Met Fbrctors Corp ....D....... 708 371-0333
Crestwood (G-7131)
Tane Corporation ....G....... 847 705-7125
Palatine (G-16161)
Tar-B Precision Machining Corp ....G....... 630 521-9771
Bensenville (G-1900)
Target Laser & Machining Inc ....E....... 815 963-6706
Rockford (G-17652)

SIC

Employee Codes: A=Over 500 employees, B=251-500
C=101-250, D=51-100, E=20-50, F=10-19, G=3-9
2020 Harris Illinois
Industrial Directory
979

35 INDUSTRIAL AND COMMERCIAL MACHINERY AND COMPUTER EQUIPMENT

Tarney Inc .... E 773 235-0331
  Chicago (G-6327)
Taylor Design Inc .... G 815 389-3991
  Roscoe (G-17936)
Taylor Made Machining Inc .... G 815 339-6267
  Mark (G-13547)
Tazewell Machine Works Inc .... C 309 347-3181
  Pekin (G-16365)
Tbw Machining Inc .... F 847 524-1501
  Schaumburg (G-18740)
TDS Machining Inc .... F 630 964-0004
  Darien (G-7413)
Tech-Max Machine Inc .... E 630 875-0054
  Itasca (G-11744)
Tech-Tool Enterprise .... G 630 639-9425
  Roselle (G-17992)
Technical Metals Inc .... D 815 692-4643
  Fairbury (G-9614)
Technox Machine & Mfg Inc .... E 773 745-6800
  Chicago (G-6335)
Techny Precision Mfg Inc .... F 630 543-7065
  Addison (G-305)
Tekmill Inc .... E 217 353-5111
  Champaign (G-3358)
Telco Machine & Manufacturing .... E 773 725-4441
  Chicago (G-6338)
Telco Machine & Manufacturing .... G 773 725-4441
  Chicago (G-6339)
Temco Grinding Inc .... E 815 282-9405
  Loves Park (G-13272)
Tent Maker Industrial Sup Inc .... G 847 469-6070
  Wauconda (G-20398)
Ter-Son Corporation .... D 309 274-6227
  Chillicothe (G-6822)
Terracycle Regulated Waste LLC .... E 800 909-9709
  Lisle (G-12950)
Thomason Machine Works Inc .... F 815 874-8217
  Rockford (G-17660)
Thompson Industries Inc .... E 815 899-6670
  Sycamore (G-19735)
Threads Up Inc .... G 630 595-2297
  Palatine (G-16163)
Thryselius Machining Inc .... F 630 365-9191
  Elburn (G-8476)
Thunderbird LLC .... E 847 718-9300
  Elk Grove Village (G-9272)
Tibor Machine Products Inc .... D 708 499-0017
  Bridgeview (G-2393)
Tibor Machine Products Inc .... E 309 786-3052
  Rock Island (G-17250)
Tinney Tool & Machine Co .... G 618 236-7273
  Belleville (G-1598)
Titan Tool Works LLC .... F 630 221-1080
  Carol Stream (G-3081)
▲ Titus Tool Company Inc .... E 847 243-8801
  Franklin Park (G-10062)
Tnp Machinery Co Inc .... G 708 344-7750
  Westchester (G-20714)
Tolerance Manufacturing Inc .... F 847 244-8836
  Waukegan (G-20508)
Tolerances Grinding Co Inc .... E 630 543-6066
  Addison (G-311)
Tomenson Machine Works Inc .... D 630 377-7670
  West Chicago (G-20652)
Tomko Machine Works Inc .... G 630 244-0902
  Lemont (G-12593)
Tomsons Products Inc .... G 708 479-7030
  Orland Park (G-15987)
Tomsons Products Inc .... G 708 479-7030
  Mokena (G-14123)
Tool Form Inc .... G 815 654-0035
  Loves Park (G-13275)
Tool Rite Industries Inc .... G 630 406-6161
  Batavia (G-1431)
Tool-Masters Tool & Stamp Inc .... G 815 465-6830
  Grant Park (G-10753)
Toolex Corporation .... G 630 458-0001
  Addison (G-312)
Top Notch Tool & Supply Inc .... G 815 633-6295
  Cherry Valley (G-3447)
▲ Torrence Machine & Tool Co .... G 815 469-1850
  Mokena (G-14124)
Total Engineered Products Inc .... G 630 543-9006
  Addison (G-315)
Total Titanium Inc .... E 866 208-6446
  Red Bud (G-17003)
Toth Automotive .... F 708 474-5137
  Lansing (G-12522)
Tower Tool & Engineering Inc 815 654-1115
  Machesney Park (G-13378)

Towne Machine Tool Company .... F 217 442-4910
  Danville (G-7389)
Trailers Inc .... G 217 472-6000
  Chapin (G-3396)
▲ Transcedar Limited .... E 618 262-4153
  Mount Carmel (G-14488)
▲ Traxco Inc .... E 847 669-1545
  Huntley (G-11569)
Tri-J Machine Works .... E 618 542-2663
  Du Quoin (G-8125)
Tribus Aerospace LLC .... E 312 876-7267
  Chicago (G-6427)
Trident Machine Co .... G 815 968-1585
  Rockford (G-17668)
Trinity Machined Products Inc .... E 630 876-6992
  Aurora (G-1028)
Triple Edge Manufacturing Inc .... G 847 468-9156
  South Elgin (G-19178)
Triwire Inc .... G 815 633-7707
  Loves Park (G-13278)
Tru Grind Inc .... G 847 749-3163
  Arlington Heights (G-823)
Tru-Cut Machine Incorporated .... G 815 422-5047
  Saint Anne (G-18138)
Tru-Cut Production Inc .... G 815 335-2215
  Winnebago (G-21121)
Tru-Machine Co Inc .... G 815 675-6735
  Spring Grove (G-19305)
▲ Trufab Group USA LLC .... E 630 994-3286
  Schaumburg (G-18758)
Tsd Manufacturing Co Inc .... F 630 238-8750
  Elk Grove Village (G-9288)
Turbo Tool & Mold Co .... G 708 615-1730
  Broadview (G-2473)
Uhlir Manufacturing Corp .... G 773 376-5289
  Chicago (G-6455)
▲ Ulrich Kaeppler .... G 847 290-0220
  Elk Grove Village (G-9290)
Ultimate Machining & Engrg Inc .... E 815 439-8361
  Plainfield (G-16724)
Ultra Specialties Incorporated .... E 847 437-8110
  Elk Grove Village (G-9292)
Ultra Specialty Holdings Inc .... E 847 437-8110
  Elk Grove Village (G-9293)
Ultra-Metric Tool Co .... F 773 281-4200
  Chicago (G-6459)
Umw Inc .... F 847 352-5252
  Schaumburg (G-18763)
Unique Mold & Machine Inc .... E 630 406-8305
  Batavia (G-1436)
United Craftsmen Ltd .... F 815 626-7802
  Sterling (G-19539)
United Machine Works Inc .... F 847 352-5252
  Schaumburg (G-18766)
United Maint Wldg & McHy C .... F 708 458-1705
  Bedford Park (G-1508)
United Standard Industries Inc .... D 847 724-0350
  Glenview (G-10635)
Universal-Spc Inc .... E 847 742-4400
  Elgin (G-8770)
◆ US Hose Corp .... G 815 886-1140
  Romeoville (G-17883)
USA Industrial Export Corp .... G 312 391-5552
  Northbrook (G-15497)
V & A Manufacturing .... G 630 595-1072
  Bensenville (G-1906)
V & L Enterprises Inc .... F 847 541-1760
  Wheeling (G-21006)
V Brothers Machine Co .... E 708 652-0062
  Cicero (G-6886)
V W Broaching Service Inc .... F 773 533-9000
  Chicago (G-6516)
Vandeventer Mfg Co Inc .... E 630 879-2511
  Batavia (G-1439)
Variable Operations Tech Inc .... E 815 479-8528
  Crystal Lake (G-7288)
▲ Vector Engineering & Mfg Corp .... E 708 474-3900
  Lansing (G-12524)
Vek Screw Machine Products .... G 630 543-5557
  Addison (G-327)
Vicari Tool & Plastics Inc .... E 847 671-9430
  Franklin Park (G-10078)
Visos Machine Shop & Mfg .... E 630 372-3925
  Streamwood (G-19601)
W & K Machining Inc .... E 708 430-9000
  Alsip (G-523)
W E S Inc .... F 815 436-1732
  Joliet (G-11943)
W-D Tool Engineering Company .... F 773 638-2688
  Chicago (G-6580)

Wabel Tool Company .... E 217 429-3656
  Decatur (G-7568)
Walach Manufacturing Co Inc .... F 773 836-2060
  Chicago (G-6585)
▲ Walco Tool & Engineering Corp .... D 815 834-0225
  Romeoville (G-17886)
Walern Form Grinding Inc .... G 815 874-7000
  Rockford (G-17676)
Wallys Precision Machining .... G 708 205-2950
  Melrose Park (G-13927)
Walter Tool & Mfg Inc .... F 847 697-7230
  Elgin (G-8774)
Ward Cnc Machining .... G 815 637-1490
  Loves Park (G-13280)
▲ Warner Industries Inc .... D 708 458-0627
  Bedford Park (G-1510)
Weber Metal Products Inc .... G 815 844-3169
  Chenoa (G-3435)
West Machine Products Inc .... E 847 740-2404
  Round Lake (G-18086)
▲ West Side Machine Inc .... F 630 243-1069
  Lemont (G-12594)
Whale Manufacturing Inc .... G 847 357-9192
  Lombard (G-13155)
Wherry Machine & Welding Inc .... G 309 828-5423
  Bloomington (G-2107)
White Jig Grinding .... G 847 888-2260
  South Elgin (G-19180)
▲ White Racker Co Inc .... G 847 758-1640
  Elk Grove Village (G-9308)
Wilczak Industrial Parts Inc .... G 847 260-5559
  Franklin Park (G-10085)
William Davis & Co .... G 847 395-6860
  Antioch (G-644)
Willoughbys Auto & Mch Sp .... G 815 448-2281
  Mazon (G-13685)
Wilmouth Machine Works Inc .... G 618 372-3189
  Brighton (G-2405)
Wilson Tool Corporation .... E 815 226-0147
  Rockford (G-17687)
Wirco Inc .... D 217 398-3200
  Champaign (G-3371)
Wk Machine .... G 618 426-3423
  Campbell Hill (G-2819)
World Class Tool & Machine .... G 815 962-2081
  South Beloit (G-19125)
Wright Technologies Inc .... G 847 439-4150
  Elk Grove Village (G-9313)
▲ X-Cel Technologies Inc .... E 708 802-7400
  Tinley Park (G-19869)
X-Tech Innovations Inc .... G 815 962-4127
  Rockford (G-17691)
Xact Wire EDM Corp .... F 847 516-0903
  Cary (G-3197)
▼ Z & L Machining Inc .... E 847 623-9500
  Waukegan (G-20521)
Z-Tech Inc .... G 815 335-7395
  Winnebago (G-21122)
Zaxis Factory Inc 888 299-5516
  Chicago (G-6708)
Ziglers & Mch & Metalworks LLC .... F 815 255-8200
  Dixon (G-7927)
Zj Industries Inc .... E 630 543-6400
  Addison (G-342)

36 ELECTRONIC AND OTHER ELECTRICAL EQUIPMENT AND COMPONENTS, EXCEPT COMPUTER

3612 Power, Distribution & Specialty Transformers

Aldonex Inc .... F 708 547-5663
  Bellwood (G-1613)
American Cips .... G 618 393-5641
  Olney (G-15852)
Coiltechnic Inc .... F 815 675-9260
  Spring Grove (G-19271)
Communication Coil Inc .... D 847 671-1333
  Schiller Park (G-18795)
Cymatics Inc .... G 630 420-7117
  Naperville (G-14811)
Dex Blue Corp .... F 847 916-7744
  Morton Grove (G-14399)
Dresser LLC .... D 847 437-5940
  Elk Grove Village (G-8955)
Dukane Corporation .... G 630 797-4900
  Saint Charles (G-18190)

Equus Power I LP ... G ... 847 908-2878
Schaumburg *(G-18519)*

▲ Ferrite International Company ... E ... 847 249-4900
Wadsworth *(G-20209)*

Forest Electric Company ... E ... 708 681-0180
Melrose Park *(G-13868)*

Gsg Industries ... F ... 618 544-7976
Robinson *(G-17115)*

Hubbell Power Systems Inc ... F ... 618 797-5000
Edwardsville *(G-8365)*

▲ Inglot Electronics Corp ... D ... 773 286-5881
Chicago *(G-4921)*

◆ Intermatic Incorporated ... A ... 815 675-7000
Spring Grove *(G-19276)*

Invenergy Wind Fin Co III LLC ... G ... 312 224-1400
Chicago *(G-4963)*

Ipr Systems Inc ... G ... 708 385-7500
Alsip *(G-458)*

▲ Lenco Electronics Inc ... E ... 815 344-2900
McHenry *(G-13756)*

Magnetic Coil Manufacturing Co ... E ... 630 787-1948
Wood Dale *(G-21212)*

Magnetic Devices Inc ... G ... 815 459-0077
Crystal Lake *(G-7222)*

Methode Development Co ... D ... 708 867-6777
Chicago *(G-5408)*

Micron Engineering Co ... G ... 815 455-2888
Crystal Lake *(G-7228)*

▲ Micron Industries Corporation ... C ... 630 516-1222
Oak Brook *(G-15645)*

Micron Industries Corporation ... D ... 815 380-2222
Sterling *(G-19519)*

▲ Mitsubishi Elc Automtn Inc ... C ... 847 478-2100
Vernon Hills *(G-20075)*

▲ Newhaven Display Intl Inc ... E ... 847 844-8795
Elgin *(G-8668)*

◆ Olsun Electrics Corporation ... G ... 815 678-2421
Richmond *(G-17019)*

▲ Orei LLC ... G ... 847 983-4761
Skokie *(G-19001)*

Pactra Corp ... G ... 847 281-0308
Vernon Hills *(G-20081)*

Peterson Elc Panl Mfg Co Inc ... F ... 708 449-2270
Berkeley *(G-1943)*

Powell Industries Inc ... G ... 708 409-1200
Northlake *(G-15557)*

▲ Power House Tool Inc ... E ... 815 727-6301
Joliet *(G-11915)*

◆ Power-Volt Inc ... D ... 630 628-9999
Addison *(G-249)*

Precision Components Inc ... D ... 630 462-9110
Saint Charles *(G-18249)*

▲ Radionic Industries Inc ... C ... 773 804-0100
Chicago *(G-5961)*

Relay Services Mfg Corp ... F ... 773 252-2700
Chicago *(G-6008)*

▲ Saachi Inc ... G ... 630 775-1700
Roselle *(G-17982)*

Saturn Electrical Services Inc ... G ... 630 980-0300
Roselle *(G-17983)*

▼ Simplex Inc ... C ... 217 483-1600
Springfield *(G-19446)*

Storage Battery Systems LLC ... G ... 630 221-1700
Carol Stream *(G-3078)*

▲ Thomas Research Products LLC ... F ... 224 654-8626
Elgin *(G-8754)*

TLC Dental Care LLC ... G ... 425 442-9000
Elgin *(G-8755)*

▲ Transformer Manufacturers Inc ... E ... 708 457-1200
Norridge *(G-15245)*

U S Co-Tronics Corp ... E ... 815 692-3204
Fairbury *(G-9615)*

▲ V and F Transformer Corp ... D ... 630 497-8070
Elgin *(G-8771)*

Wicc Ltd ... D ... 309 444-4125
Washington *(G-20284)*

3613 Switchgear & Switchboard Apparatus

A C Gentrol Inc ... E ... 309 274-5486
Chillicothe *(G-6812)*

Agnes & Chris Gulik ... G ... 847 931-9641
Elgin *(G-8499)*

AKD Controls Inc ... G ... 815 633-4586
Machesney Park *(G-13324)*

Allocator Logistics Co ... G ... 708 339-5678
South Holland *(G-19190)*

◆ Appleton Grp LLC ... C ... 847 268-6000
Rosemont *(G-17999)*

Automated Systems & Control Co ... G ... 847 735-8310
Lake Bluff *(G-12172)*

◆ Boltswitch Inc ... E ... 815 459-6900
Crystal Lake *(G-7170)*

Cable Electric Company Inc ... G ... 708 458-8900
Oak Lawn *(G-15706)*

Calo Corporation ... E ... 630 879-2202
North Aurora *(G-15256)*

Chicago Switchboard Co Inc ... E ... 630 833-2266
Elmhurst *(G-9345)*

Clark Tashaunda ... G ... 708 247-8274
Calumet Park *(G-2796)*

Control Panels Inc ... F ... 815 654-6000
Rockford *(G-17357)*

▲ Control Solutions LLC ... D ... 630 806-7062
Aurora *(G-941)*

Control Works Inc ... G ... 630 444-1942
Saint Charles *(G-18174)*

Custom Power Products Inc ... G ... 309 249-2704
Edelstein *(G-8332)*

Cymatics Inc ... G ... 630 420-7117
Naperville *(G-14811)*

David Jeskey ... G ... 630 659-6337
Saint Charles *(G-18180)*

Don Johns Inc ... E ... 630 454-4700
Batavia *(G-1374)*

▲ E N M Company ... D ... 773 775-8400
Chicago *(G-4425)*

Eaton Corporation ... A ... 217 732-3131
Lincoln *(G-12729)*

Elcon Inc ... E ... 815 467-9500
Minooka *(G-14059)*

◆ Elenco Electronics Inc ... E ... 847 541-3800
Wheeling *(G-20889)*

◆ Emac Inc ... E ... 618 529-4525
Carbondale *(G-2841)*

▲ Emerge Technology Group LLC ... G ... 224 603-2161
Lake Villa *(G-12350)*

◆ Enercon Engineering Inc ... C ... 800 218-8831
East Peoria *(G-8266)*

Enercon Engineering Inc ... D ... 309 694-1418
East Peoria *(G-8267)*

Engineered Fluid Inc ... C ... 618 533-1351
Centralia *(G-3230)*

Excel Ltd Inc ... G ... 847 543-9138
Grayslake *(G-10771)*

Fixture Company ... G ... 847 214-3100
Chicago *(G-4600)*

▼ G & F Manufacturing Co Inc ... E ... 708 424-4170
Oak Lawn *(G-15716)*

GE Zenith Controls Inc ... G ... 773 299-6600
Oakbrook Terrace *(G-15800)*

General Electric Company ... E ... 630 334-0054
Oak Brook *(G-15624)*

General Electric Company ... C ... 309 664-1513
Bloomington *(G-2050)*

◆ Grayhill Inc ... B ... 708 354-1040
La Grange *(G-12077)*

Grayhill Inc ... G ... 708 482-1411
Mc Cook *(G-13691)*

▲ Gus Berthold Electric Company ... D ... 312 243-5767
Chicago *(G-4752)*

Honeywell International Inc ... D ... 815 235-5500
Freeport *(G-10118)*

Hubbell Power Systems Inc ... E ... 618 797-5000
Edwardsville *(G-8366)*

Illinois Switchboard Corp ... F ... 630 543-0910
Addison *(G-154)*

Illinois Tool Works Inc ... C ... 847 724-7500
Des Plaines *(G-7784)*

Industrial Electric Svc Inc ... G ... 708 997-2090
Bartlett *(G-1289)*

Inland Tech Holdings LLC ... E ... 618 476-7678
Millstadt *(G-14048)*

Inman Electric Motors Inc ... E ... 815 223-2288
La Salle *(G-12115)*

Its Solar LLC ... E ... 618 476-7678
Waterloo *(G-20291)*

J & A Sheet Metal Shop Inc ... E ... 773 276-3739
Chicago *(G-4981)*

Kenyeri Consulting LLC ... G ... 630 920-3497
Downers Grove *(G-8039)*

Kinney Electrical Mfg Co ... D ... 847 742-9600
Elgin *(G-8636)*

◆ Kms Industries LLC ... G ... 331 225-2671
Addison *(G-173)*

Langham Engineering ... G ... 815 223-5250
Peru *(G-16580)*

▲ Littelfuse Inc ... A ... 773 628-1000
Chicago *(G-5238)*

Lumenite Control Technology ... F ... 847 455-1450
Franklin Park *(G-9982)*

Machine Control Systems Inc ... G ... 708 597-1200
Alsip *(G-471)*

Machine Control Systems Inc ... G ... 708 389-2160
Palos Heights *(G-16190)*

Marshall Electric Inc ... F ... 618 382-3932
Carmi *(G-2910)*

◆ Marshall Wolf Automation Inc ... E ... 847 658-8130
Algonquin *(G-378)*

Methode Electronics Inc ... A ... 217 357-3941
Carthage *(G-3139)*

Meto-Grafics Inc ... F ... 847 639-0044
Crystal Lake *(G-7226)*

Midwest Control Corp ... F ... 708 599-1331
Bridgeview *(G-2365)*

▲ Mitsubishi Elc Automtn Inc ... C ... 847 478-2100
Vernon Hills *(G-20075)*

Morton Automatic Electric Co ... G ... 309 263-7577
Morton *(G-14369)*

▲ Motec Inc ... G ... 630 241-9595
Downers Grove *(G-8060)*

Mpc Products Corporation ... G ... 847 673-8300
Niles *(G-15150)*

New Cie Inc ... F ... 815 224-1485
La Salle *(G-12118)*

Numerical Control Incorporated ... G ... 708 389-8140
Alsip *(G-486)*

▼ Nutherm International Inc ... E ... 618 244-6000
Mount Vernon *(G-14631)*

Oakland Industries Ltd ... E ... 847 827-7600
Mount Prospect *(G-14555)*

Panel Authority Inc ... F ... 815 838-0488
Plainfield *(G-16699)*

Panelshopnet Inc ... G ... 630 692-0214
Naperville *(G-14982)*

Peterson Elc Panl Mfg Co Inc ... F ... 708 449-2270
Berkeley *(G-1943)*

Platt Industrial Control Inc ... G ... 630 833-4388
Addison *(G-243)*

Power Distribution Eqp Co Inc ... E ... 847 455-2500
Franklin Park *(G-10021)*

▲ Prater Industries Inc ... D ... 630 679-3200
Bolingbrook *(G-2228)*

Product Service Craft Inc ... F ... 630 964-5160
Downers Grove *(G-8085)*

Protection Controls Inc ... E ... 773 763-3110
Skokie *(G-19017)*

Quantum Design Inc ... D ... 815 885-1300
Machesney Park *(G-13321)*

R G Controls Inc ... G ... 847 438-3981
Barrington *(G-1239)*

Rauckman High Voltage Sales ... G ... 618 239-0399
Swansea *(G-19696)*

Recora LLC ... G ... 630 879-2202
North Aurora *(G-15273)*

RLC Industries Inc ... G ... 708 837-7300
La Grange *(G-12088)*

Ronk Electrical Industries Inc ... E ... 217 563-8333
Nokomis *(G-15198)*

RWS Design and Controls Inc ... E ... 815 654-6000
Roscoe *(G-17930)*

◆ S & C Electric Company ... A ... 773 338-1000
Chicago *(G-6083)*

▲ SAI Advanced Pwr Solutions Inc ... D ... 708 450-0990
Franklin Park *(G-10041)*

Schneider Electric Usa Inc ... G ... 312 697-4770
Chicago *(G-6112)*

Schneider Electric Usa Inc ... E ... 847 441-2526
Schaumburg *(G-18708)*

Schubert Controls Corporation ... G ... 847 526-8200
Wauconda *(G-20390)*

▼ Simplex Inc ... C ... 217 483-1600
Springfield *(G-19446)*

▲ Switchcraft Inc ... B ... 773 792-2700
Chicago *(G-6299)*

▲ Switchcraft Holdco Inc ... G ... 773 792-2700
Chicago *(G-6300)*

Texas Instruments Incorporated ... D ... 630 836-2827
Warrenville *(G-20253)*

Venture Design Incorporated ... F ... 630 369-1148
Naperville *(G-14941)*

Venturedyne Ltd ... E ... 708 597-7550
Chicago *(G-6535)*

◆ Woodward Controls Inc ... C ... 847 673-8300
Skokie *(G-19058)*

Xylem Lnc ... G ... 847 966-3700
Morton Grove *(G-14451)*

3621 Motors & Generators

▲ A E Iskra Inc ... G ... 815 874-4022
Rockford *(G-17280)*

SIC

Employee Codes: A=Over 500 employees, B=251-500
C=101-250, D=51-100, E=20-50, F=10-19, G=3-9

2020 Harris Illinois
Industrial Directory

981

36 ELECTRONIC AND OTHER ELECTRICAL EQUIPMENT AND COMPONENTS, EXCEPT COMPUTER SIC SECTION

ABB Motors and Mechanical Inc............C....... 630 296-1400
Bolingbrook *(G-2146)*
Active Tool and Machine Inc..................F....... 708 599-0022
Oak Lawn *(G-15697)*
Advanced Enrgy Solutions Group........F....... 618 988-0888
Carterville *(G-3128)*
◆ **Alfa Controls Inc**................................G....... 847 978-9245
Wheeling *(G-20844)*
▲ **Alin Machining Company Inc**...........C....... 708 681-1043
Melrose Park *(G-13821)*
▲ **Altorfer Power Systems**....................G....... 309 697-1234
Bartonville *(G-1328)*
▲ **American Electronic Pdts Inc**...........F....... 630 889-9977
Oak Brook *(G-15592)*
American Rotors Inc..............................E....... 847 263-1300
Gurnee *(G-10860)*
American Total Engine Co.....................G....... 847 623-2737
Ingleside *(G-11578)*
Arcosa Wind Towers Inc.......................F....... 217 935-7900
Clinton *(G-6918)*
Atlas Copco Compressors LLC............F....... 281 590-7500
Chicago *(G-3762)*
Awem Corporation.................................G....... 217 670-1451
Springfield *(G-19322)*
Becsis LLC...G....... 630 400-6454
South Elgin *(G-19136)*
Bill West Enterprises Inc.......................G....... 217 886-2591
Jacksonville *(G-11757)*
◆ **Bison Gear & Engineering Corp**........C....... 630 377-4327
Saint Charles *(G-18156)*
◆ **Bodine Electric Company**..................B....... 773 478-3515
Northfield *(G-15509)*
▲ **Bolingbrook Communications Inc**...A....... 630 759-9500
Lisle *(G-12874)*
Broad-Ocean Motor LLC........................E....... 630 908-4720
Westmont *(G-20730)*
▲ **Brown Line Metal Works LLC**...........G....... 312 884-7644
Chicago *(G-3968)*
▲ **Calumet Armature and Elc LLC**........E....... 708 841-6880
Riverdale *(G-17070)*
Cemec Inc..G....... 630 495-9696
Downers Grove *(G-7966)*
CGprofessional Services Inc.................G....... 708 389-4110
Orland Park *(G-15947)*
Charles Industries LLC..........................D....... 217 826-2318
Marshall *(G-13566)*
Charles R Frontczak...............................G....... 224 392-4151
Rockford *(G-17345)*
Coilform Company..................................E....... 630 232-8000
Geneva *(G-10262)*
Communication Coil Inc.........................D....... 847 671-1333
Schiller Park *(G-18795)*
Con-Trol-Cure Inc....................................F....... 773 248-0099
Chicago *(G-4211)*
Crescent Ridge LLC................................G....... 815 646-4119
Tiskilwa *(G-19872)*
Datasource..G....... 312 405-9152
Calumet City *(G-2774)*
Ddu Magnetics Inc..................................G....... 708 325-6587
Lynwood *(G-13293)*
Digitaldrive Tech.....................................G....... 630 510-1580
Wheaton *(G-20796)*
Djh Industries Inc...................................E....... 309 246-8456
Lacon *(G-12126)*
▲ **Dlt Electric LLC**....................................F....... 630 552-4115
Plano *(G-16730)*
Eco Green Analytics LLC.......................G....... 847 691-1148
Deerfield *(G-7608)*
Ees Inc..G....... 708 343-1800
Stone Park *(G-19553)*
Encap Technologies Inc..........................C....... 847 202-3443
Grayslake *(G-10768)*
Encap Technologies Inc..........................F....... 510 337-2700
Palatine *(G-16116)*
Encap Technologies Inc..........................B....... 510 337-2700
Palatine *(G-16117)*
Engine Rebuilders & Supply..................G....... 708 338-1113
Stone Park *(G-19554)*
Federal Prison Industries.......................C....... 309 346-8588
Pekin *(G-16333)*
Flolo Corporation....................................G....... 847 249-0880
Gurnee *(G-10878)*
▲ **Forest City Auto Electric Co**...............F....... 815 963-4350
Rockford *(G-17418)*
▲ **Fulling Motor USA Inc**.........................G....... 847 894-6238
Park Ridge *(G-16277)*
▲ **General Manufacturing LLC**...............D....... 708 345-8600
Melrose Park *(G-13873)*
Ghetzler Aero-Power Corp.....................G....... 224 513-5636
Vernon Hills *(G-20056)*
Ground Cover Industries Inc..................G....... 800 550-4424
Kildeer *(G-12048)*
▲ **Hallmark Industries Inc**.......................F....... 847 301-8050
Streamwood *(G-19577)*
Hamilton Sundstrand Corp....................F....... 815 226-6000
Rockford *(G-17440)*
Haran Ventures LLC................................G....... 217 239-1628
Champaign *(G-3299)*
Hardin Industries LLC............................E....... 309 246-8456
Lacon *(G-12127)*
Harvey Bros Inc.......................................F....... 309 342-3137
Galesburg *(G-10199)*
▲ **Heng Tuo Usa Inc**.................................G....... 630 317-7672
Oakbrook Terrace *(G-15802)*
Hinetics LLC..G....... 217 239-1628
Champaign *(G-3301)*
Hopcroft Electric Inc...............................G....... 618 288-7302
Glen Carbon *(G-10388)*
◆ **Howland Technology Inc**.....................F....... 847 965-9808
Morton Grove *(G-14411)*
Illinois Tool Works Inc.............................C....... 847 724-7500
Des Plaines *(G-7784)*
Industrial Welder Rebuilders..................G....... 708 371-5688
Alsip *(G-457)*
▲ **Inglot Electronics Corp**.........................D....... 773 286-5881
Chicago *(G-4921)*
Inman Electric Motors Inc......................E....... 815 223-2288
La Salle *(G-12115)*
Integrated Power Services LLC..............E....... 708 877-5310
Thornton *(G-19789)*
International Supply Co..........................D....... 309 249-6211
Edelstein *(G-8333)*
▲ **Inventus Power (illinois) LLC**...............C....... 630 410-7900
Woodridge *(G-21317)*
Jardis Industries Inc...............................F....... 630 773-5600
Itasca *(G-11681)*
Jasiek Motor Rebuilding Inc...................G....... 815 883-3678
Oglesby *(G-15842)*
Jomar Electric Coil Mfg Inc....................G....... 630 279-1494
Villa Park *(G-20153)*
◆ **Jordan Industries Inc**..........................F....... 847 945-5591
Deerfield *(G-7621)*
Kackert Enterprises Inc..........................G....... 630 898-9339
Aurora *(G-1120)*
Kap Holdings LLC....................................F....... 708 948-0226
Oak Park *(G-15759)*
Kaybee Engineering Company Inc..........E....... 630 968-7100
Westmont *(G-20751)*
L & H Company Inc..................................F....... 630 571-7200
Oak Brook *(G-15630)*
Lakeview Energy LLC...............................E....... 312 386-5897
Chicago *(G-5167)*
Lenhardt Tool and Die Company..............D....... 618 462-1075
Alton *(G-563)*
Lionheart Critical Pow.............................E....... 847 291-1413
Huntley *(G-11552)*
◆ **Luon Energy LLC**..................................G....... 217 419-2678
Savoy *(G-18415)*
M R Glenn Electric Inc.............................E....... 708 479-9200
Lockport *(G-13009)*
Magnetic Coil Manufacturing Co..............E....... 630 787-1948
Wood Dale *(G-21212)*
Magnetic Devices Inc................................G....... 815 459-0077
Crystal Lake *(G-7222)*
◆ **Marmon Industries LLC**.......................G....... 312 372-9500
Chicago *(G-5345)*
Maurey Instrument Corp..........................F....... 708 388-9898
Alsip *(G-474)*
◆ **Mecc Alte Inc**...F....... 815 344-0530
McHenry *(G-13767)*
▲ **Moons Industries America Inc**..............A....... 630 833-5940
Itasca *(G-11705)*
Morrell Incorporated.................................F....... 630 858-4600
Glendale Heights *(G-10477)*
◆ **Mpc Products Corporation**....................A....... 847 673-8300
Niles *(G-15149)*
Nelco Coil Supply Company......................E....... 847 259-7517
Mount Prospect *(G-14550)*
Netgain Motors Inc....................................G....... 630 243-9100
Lockport *(G-13016)*
Nidec Motor Corporation..........................G....... 815 444-1229
Crystal Lake *(G-7238)*
Nidec Motor Corporation..........................D....... 847 439-3760
Elk Grove Village *(G-9148)*
Nidec Motor Corporation..........................B....... 847 585-8430
Elgin *(G-8673)*
North Point Investments Inc.....................G....... 312 977-4386
Chicago *(G-5620)*
Northrop Grumman Systems Corp.............A....... 847 259-9600
Rolling Meadows *(G-17755)*
Performance Battery Group Inc................G....... 630 293-5505
West Chicago *(G-20628)*
Power Enclosures Inc................................F....... 309 274-9000
Chillicothe *(G-6821)*
Powersource Generator Rentals................G....... 847 587-3991
Fox Lake *(G-9752)*
▲ **Pre Fnish Mtals Mrrisville Inc**...............D....... 847 439-2211
Elk Grove Village *(G-9188)*
◆ **Progress Rail Locomotive Inc**................A....... 800 255-5355
Mc Cook *(G-13699)*
Progress Rail Locomotive Inc...................F....... 708 387-5510
Mc Cook *(G-13700)*
Provisur Technologies...............................G....... 312 284-4698
Chicago *(G-5908)*
Qcircuits Inc..E....... 618 662-8365
Flora *(G-9690)*
Rathje Enterprises Inc...............................F....... 217 443-0022
Danville *(G-7377)*
Roberts Electric Company..........................G....... 773 725-7323
Chicago *(G-6044)*
Ronk Electrical Industries Inc....................E....... 217 563-8333
Nokomis *(G-15198)*
Rotary Dryer Parts Inc................................G....... 217 877-2787
Decatur *(G-7544)*
Ruby Automation LLC................................F....... 815 624-5959
South Beloit *(G-19112)*
Ruby Automation LLC................................F....... 847 273-9050
Schaumburg *(G-18699)*
Santucci Enterprises..................................G....... 773 286-5629
Chicago *(G-6102)*
▲ **Schneider Elc Buildings LLC**...................B....... 815 381-5000
Rockford *(G-17622)*
▲ **Schneider Elc Holdings Inc**......................A....... 717 944-5460
Schaumburg *(G-18707)*
Scot Inc..G....... 630 969-0620
Downers Grove *(G-8091)*
Sexton Wind Power LLC..............................G....... 224 212-1250
Lake Bluff *(G-12209)*
Sfc of Illinois Inc...E....... 815 745-2100
Warren *(G-20224)*
▲ **Spg Usa Inc**..G....... 847 439-4949
Schaumburg *(G-18723)*
Stable Beginning Corporation....................E....... 815 745-2100
Warren *(G-20225)*
Stanton Wind Energy LLC...........................F....... 312 224-1400
Chicago *(G-6232)*
Synergy Power Group LLC..........................E....... 618 247-3200
Sandoval *(G-18365)*
Teledyne Lecroy Inc.....................................E....... 847 888-0450
Elgin *(G-8749)*
▲ **Torqeedo Inc**...G....... 815 444-8806
Crystal Lake *(G-7284)*
Tracy Electric Inc..E....... 618 943-6205
Lawrenceville *(G-12538)*
▲ **Transformer Manufacturers Inc**..................E....... 708 457-1200
Norridge *(G-15245)*
Transfrmtional Enrgy Solutions....................G....... 828 226-7821
Decatur *(G-7562)*
U S Co-Tronics Corp......................................E....... 815 692-3204
Fairbury *(G-9615)*
▼ **Ultrasonic Power Corporation**....................E....... 815 235-6020
Freeport *(G-10148)*
UPS Power Management Inc........................F....... 844 877-2288
Chicago *(G-6490)*
Voss Electric Inc..G....... 708 596-6000
Harvey *(G-11100)*
Wagenate Entps Holdings LLC.....................G....... 773 503-1306
Riverdale *(G-17078)*
▲ **Warfield Electric Company Inc**...................E....... 815 469-4094
Frankfort *(G-9851)*
Weldon Corporation......................................E....... 708 343-4700
Maywood *(G-13680)*
◆ **Wellington Drive Tech US**..........................G....... 847 922-5098
Buffalo Grove *(G-2619)*
▲ **Western Motor Mfg Co**...............................G....... 815 986-2214
Rockford *(G-17681)*
White Oak Energy LLC..................................G....... 815 824-2182
Carlock *(G-2888)*
Willow Creek Energy LLC.............................G....... 312 224-1400
Chicago *(G-6633)*
Wodack Electric Tool Corp............................F....... 773 287-9866
Chicago *(G-6661)*
Xform Power and Eqp Sups LLC..................G....... 773 260-0209
Chicago *(G-6694)*
Xylem Lnc...G....... 847 966-3700
Morton Grove *(G-14451)*
◆ **Yaskawa America Inc**.................................C....... 847 887-7000
Waukegan *(G-20520)*
Yaskawa America Inc....................................C....... 847 887-7909
Des Plaines *(G-7869)*

3624 Carbon & Graphite Prdts

▲ **Aero Industries Inc**............F 800 747-3553
Harvard *(G-11041)*
AMS Seals Inc............G....... 815 609-4977
Plainfield *(G-16642)*
Becker Brothers Graphite Corp............G....... 708 410-0700
Maywood *(G-13662)*
Cabot Corporation............D....... 217 253-5752
Tuscola *(G-19925)*
Carbon Solutions Group LLC............F 312 638-9077
Chicago *(G-4025)*
Frantz Manufacturing Company............D....... 815 625-7063
Sterling *(G-19509)*
▲ **Graphtek LLC**............F 847 279-1925
Northbrook *(G-15396)*
Industrial Graphite Sales LLC............G....... 815 943-5502
Harvard *(G-11057)*
J Ream Manufacturing............G....... 630 983-6945
Naperville *(G-14852)*
Kirkman Composites............G....... 309 734-5606
Monmouth *(G-14222)*
Process Engineering Corp............F 815 459-1734
Crystal Lake *(G-7250)*
Rnfl Acquisition LLC............E 651 442-6011
Chicago *(G-6041)*
▲ **Starex Inc**............G....... 847 918-5555
Libertyville *(G-12709)*
Superior Graphite Co............E 708 458-0006
Chicago *(G-6281)*

3625 Relays & Indl Controls

▲ **7 Mile Solutions Inc**............E 847 588-2280
Niles *(G-15096)*
Advanced Technologies Inc............G....... 847 329-9875
Park Ridge *(G-16264)*
American Control Elec LLC............G....... 815 624-6950
South Beloit *(G-19080)*
American Controls & Automation............G....... 630 293-8841
West Chicago *(G-20537)*
◆ **Arens Controls Company LLc**............D....... 847 844-4700
Arlington Heights *(G-694)*
Automated Systems & Control Co............G....... 847 735-8310
Lake Bluff *(G-12172)*
Autotech Tech Ltd Partnr............E 563 359-7501
Chicago *(G-3780)*
Baldwin Technology Company Inc............C....... 618 842-2664
Fairfield *(G-9618)*
◆ **Blachford Investments Inc**............C....... 630 231-8300
West Chicago *(G-20552)*
◆ **Bodine Electric Company**............B 773 478-3515
Northfield *(G-15509)*
Box of Rain Ltd............G....... 847 640-6996
Arlington Heights *(G-707)*
BTR Controls Inc............G....... 847 608-9500
Elgin *(G-8525)*
Burke Tool & Manufacturing Inc............G....... 618 542-6441
Du Quoin *(G-8116)*
Capable Controls Inc............D....... 630 860-6514
Bensenville *(G-1761)*
Capsonic Automotive Inc............F 847 888-7300
Elgin *(G-8529)*
▲ **Capsonic Automotive Inc**............F 847 888-7300
Elgin *(G-8530)*
Capsonic Automotive Inc............B 915 872-3585
Chicago *(G-4020)*
Caterpillar Inc............B 815 729-5511
Joliet *(G-11838)*
◆ **Chamberlain Manufacturing Corp**............A 630 279-3600
Oak Brook *(G-15608)*
Competition Electronics Inc............G....... 815 874-8001
Rockford *(G-17356)*
Con-Trol-Cure Inc............F 773 248-0099
Chicago *(G-4211)*
Connor-Winfield Corp............C....... 630 851-4722
Aurora *(G-1079)*
Continental Auto Systems Inc............G....... 847 862-5000
Deer Park *(G-7579)*
Control Designs Inc............G....... 847 672-9514
Gurnee *(G-10865)*
Control Research Inc............G....... 847 352-4920
Schaumburg *(G-18488)*
▲ **Control Solutions LLC**............D....... 630 806-7062
Aurora *(G-941)*
Control System Innovators Inc............G....... 847 741-0007
Elgin *(G-8553)*
Control Systems Inc............G....... 847 438-6228
Long Grove *(G-13159)*
Controllink Incorporated............E 847 622-1100
Elgin *(G-8554)*
Copar Corporation............E 708 496-1859
Burbank *(G-2635)*
Crane Dorray Corporation............G....... 630 893-7553
Addison *(G-83)*
Creative Controls Systems Inc............G....... 815 629-2358
Rockton *(G-17696)*
◆ **CTS Automotive LLC**............C....... 630 577-8800
Lisle *(G-12880)*
CTS Automotive LLC............E 815 385-9480
McHenry *(G-13734)*
▲ **Danfoss Inc**............G....... 815 639-8600
Loves Park *(G-13204)*
Danfoss LLC............C....... 888 326-3677
Loves Park *(G-13206)*
Danfoss LLC............G....... 717 261-5000
Loves Park *(G-13205)*
Deltrol Corp............C....... 708 547-0500
Bellwood *(G-1621)*
Dgm Electronics Inc............G....... 815 389-2040
Roscoe *(G-17904)*
Domino Engineering Corp............F 217 824-9441
Taylorville *(G-19756)*
Don Johns Inc............E 630 454-4700
Batavia *(G-1374)*
Dresser LLC............D....... 847 437-5940
Elk Grove Village *(G-8955)*
▲ **E N M Company**............D....... 773 775-8400
Chicago *(G-4425)*
Eaton Corporation............C....... 815 562-2107
Rochelle *(G-17138)*
Elcon Inc............E 815 467-9500
Minooka *(G-14059)*
Electro-Matic Products Co............F 773 235-4010
Chicago *(G-4477)*
Elemech Inc............E 630 417-2845
Aurora *(G-956)*
◆ **Elenco Electronics Inc**............E 847 541-3800
Wheeling *(G-20889)*
Enercon Engineering Inc............D....... 309 694-1418
East Peoria *(G-8267)*
◆ **Enercon Engineering Inc**............C....... 800 218-8831
East Peoria *(G-8266)*
Envirnmntal Ctrl Solutions Inc............G....... 217 793-8966
Springfield *(G-19363)*
▲ **Environmental Specialties Inc**............G....... 630 860-7070
Itasca *(G-11651)*
▲ **Essex Electro Engineers Inc**............E 847 891-4444
Schaumburg *(G-18522)*
Fivecubits Inc............F 925 273-1862
Oak Brook *(G-15621)*
Flolo Corporation............G....... 847 249-0880
Gurnee *(G-10878)*
Four-Most Inc............G....... 815 282-9788
Rockford *(G-17422)*
FSI Technologies Inc............E 630 932-9380
Lombard *(G-13080)*
General Electric Company............C....... 309 664-1513
Bloomington *(G-2050)*
▼ **Gpe Controls Inc**............F 708 236-6000
Hillside *(G-11340)*
◆ **Grayhill Inc**............B 708 354-1040
La Grange *(G-12077)*
Grayhill Inc............G....... 708 482-1411
Mc Cook *(G-13691)*
Guardian Consolidated Tech Inc............G....... 815 334-3600
Woodstock *(G-21392)*
▲ **Guardian Electric Mfg Co**............D....... 815 334-3600
Woodstock *(G-21393)*
Hamilton Sundstrand Corp............F 815 226-6000
Rockford *(G-17440)*
▲ **Harrington Signal Inc**............E 309 762-0731
Moline *(G-14148)*
Harris Precision Tools Inc............G....... 708 422-5808
Chicago Ridge *(G-6797)*
Harvey Bros Inc............F 309 342-3137
Galesburg *(G-10199)*
Hauhinco LP............E 618 993-5399
Marion *(G-13514)*
Hausermann Controls Co............F 630 543-6688
Addison *(G-147)*
Heico Companies LLC............G....... 847 258-0300
Elmhurst *(G-9370)*
Hella Corporate Center USA Inc............B 734 414-0900
Flora *(G-9682)*
Hella Corporate Center USA Inc............B 618 662-4402
Flora *(G-9683)*
Hella Electronics Corporation............A 618 662-5186
Flora *(G-9684)*
▲ **I P C Automation Inc**............G....... 815 759-3934
McHenry *(G-13749)*
ICT Power USA Inc............F 630 313-4941
Saint Charles *(G-18209)*
Ideal Industries Inc............C....... 815 895-1108
Sycamore *(G-19715)*
Industrial Controls Inc............G....... 630 752-8100
Geneva *(G-10278)*
▲ **Industrial Motion Control LLC**............C....... 847 459-5200
Wheeling *(G-20915)*
Industrial Sensing and Safety............G....... 630 264-8249
Aurora *(G-1112)*
Industrial Service Solutions............C....... 917 609-6979
Chicago *(G-4910)*
Instrmntation Ctrl Systems Inc............F 630 543-6200
Roselle *(G-17959)*
Intersol Industries Inc............F 630 238-0385
Bensenville *(G-1824)*
Invektek Llc............G....... 312 343-0600
Chicago *(G-4961)*
▲ **Italvibras Usa Inc**............G....... 815 872-1350
Princeton *(G-16811)*
Joliet Technologies LLC............G....... 815 725-9696
Crest Hill *(G-7089)*
◆ **Jordan Industries Inc**............F 847 945-5591
Deerfield *(G-7621)*
▲ **Jtekt Toyoda Americas Corp**............C....... 847 253-0340
Arlington Heights *(G-764)*
Justice Manufacturing Inc............G....... 217 877-2250
Decatur *(G-7512)*
K & W Auto Electric............F 217 857-1717
Teutopolis *(G-19770)*
Kackert Enterprises Inc............G....... 630 898-9339
Aurora *(G-1120)*
▲ **Kelco Industries Inc**............G....... 815 334-3600
Woodstock *(G-21398)*
Keonix Corporation............G....... 847 259-9430
Arlington Heights *(G-765)*
Knowles Elec Holdings Inc............A 630 250-5100
Itasca *(G-11687)*
Kz Manufacturing Co............G....... 708 937-8097
Mc Cook *(G-13694)*
▲ **Las Systems Inc**............E 847 462-8100
Woodstock *(G-21404)*
Light of Mine LLC............G....... 312 840-8570
Chicago *(G-5220)*
Littelfuse Inc............E 773 628-1000
Chicago *(G-5239)*
Loda Electronics Co............G....... 217 386-2554
Loda *(G-13029)*
Lumenite Control Technology............F 847 455-1450
Franklin Park *(G-9982)*
M-1 Tool Works Inc............E 815 344-1275
McHenry *(G-13761)*
Machine Control Systems Inc............G....... 708 389-2160
Palos Heights *(G-16190)*
Machine Control Systems Inc............G....... 708 597-1200
Alsip *(G-471)*
Magnet-Schultz Amer Holdg LLC............F 630 789-0600
Westmont *(G-20755)*
▲ **Magnet-Schultz America Inc**............D....... 630 789-0600
Westmont *(G-20756)*
▼ **Magnetrol International Inc**............C....... 630 723-6600
Aurora *(G-1001)*
◆ **Martin Automatic Inc**............C....... 815 654-4800
Rockford *(G-17505)*
▼ **Master Control Systems Inc**............E 847 295-1010
Lake Bluff *(G-12195)*
Maurey Instrument Corp............F 708 388-9898
Alsip *(G-474)*
Meister Industries Inc............G....... 815 623-8919
Roscoe *(G-17917)*
Mektronix Technology Inc............G....... 847 680-3300
Libertyville *(G-12677)*
Methode Electronics Inc............A 217 357-3941
Carthage *(G-3139)*
Meto-Grafics Inc............F 847 639-0044
Crystal Lake *(G-7226)*
Meyer Systems............G....... 815 436-7077
Joliet *(G-11900)*
Microware Inc............G....... 847 943-9113
Glenview *(G-10588)*
Mission Control Systems Inc............F 847 956-7650
Elk Grove Village *(G-9127)*
Morton Automatic Electric Co............G....... 309 263-7577
Morton *(G-14369)*
Mpc Products Corporation............G....... 847 673-8300
Niles *(G-15150)*
◆ **Mpc Products Corporation**............A 847 673-8300
Niles *(G-15149)*
New Cie Inc............F 815 224-1485
La Salle *(G-12118)*

S I C

Employee Codes: A=Over 500 employees, B=251-500
C=101-250, D=51-100, E=20-50, F=10-19, G=3-9
2020 Harris Illinois
Industrial Directory
983

▲ **Nidec Mobility America Corp**............A....... 630 443-6800
Saint Charles *(G-18234)*
Niles Auto Parts..................................G....... 847 215-2549
Lincolnshire *(G-12788)*
▲ **O C Keckley Company**.....................E....... 847 674-8422
Skokie *(G-18997)*
▲ **Ohmite Holding LLC**........................E....... 847 258-0300
Warrenville *(G-20243)*
▲ **Olympic Controls Corp**.....................E....... 847 742-3566
Elgin *(G-8678)*
Panatrol Corporation............................E....... 630 655-4700
Burr Ridge *(G-2713)*
Parking Systems Inc..............................G....... 847 891-3819
Schaumburg *(G-18666)*
Pilz Automtn Safety Ltd Partnr.............G....... 734 354-0272
Chicago *(G-5808)*
Power-Io Inc...E....... 630 717-7335
Naperville *(G-14901)*
Pro-Quip Incorporated...........................F....... 708 352-5732
La Grange *(G-12087)*
Process and Control Systems...............F....... 708 293-0557
Alsip *(G-498)*
Process Technologies Group................G....... 630 393-4777
Warrenville *(G-20250)*
Protection Controls Inc.........................E....... 773 763-3110
Skokie *(G-19017)*
▲ **Questek Manufacturing Corp**...........D....... 847 428-0300
Elgin *(G-8710)*
R & D Electronics Inc............................G....... 847 583-9080
Niles *(G-15163)*
Relay Services Mfg Corp.......................F....... 773 252-2700
Chicago *(G-6008)*
Rensel-Chicago Inc.................................E....... 773 235-2100
Chicago *(G-6015)*
Rimtec Corporation................................F....... 630 628-0036
Addison *(G-275)*
Robert Higgins...D....... 217 337-0734
Urbana *(G-19999)*
Rockdale Controls Co Inc.......................F....... 815 436-6181
Plainfield *(G-16711)*
Rockwell Automation Inc.......................F....... 901 367-4220
Champaign *(G-3344)*
Rockwell Automation Inc.......................D....... 630 789-5900
Lisle *(G-12934)*
Ruby Automation LLC............................F....... 815 624-5959
South Beloit *(G-19112)*
◆ **S & C Electric Company**....................A....... 773 338-1000
Chicago *(G-6083)*
▲ **Schneider Elc Buildings LLC**...........B....... 815 381-5000
Rockford *(G-17622)*
▲ **Schneider Elc Holdings Inc**..............A....... 717 944-5460
Schaumburg *(G-18707)*
Scientific Instruments Inc.....................G....... 847 679-1242
Schaumburg *(G-18709)*
▲ **SE Relays LLC**.....................................G....... 847 441-2540
Schaumburg *(G-18710)*
◆ **Siemens Industry Inc**..........................A....... 847 215-1000
Buffalo Grove *(G-2600)*
Siemens Industry Inc.............................G....... 217 824-6833
Taylorville *(G-19762)*
▼ **Simplex Inc**...C....... 217 483-1600
Springfield *(G-19446)*
▲ **Smart Systems Inc**.............................E....... 630 343-3333
Bolingbrook *(G-2242)*
Sound Seal Inc...E....... 630 844-1999
North Aurora *(G-15276)*
Sparton Aydin LLC..................................G....... 800 772-7866
Schaumburg *(G-18716)*
Sparton Onyx Holdings LLC.................G....... 847 762-5800
Schaumburg *(G-18720)*
▲ **Spectrum Cos International**..............G....... 630 879-8008
Batavia *(G-1418)*
▼ **Steel-Guard Safety Corp**....................G....... 708 589-4588
South Holland *(G-19246)*
Sterling Systems & Controls.................F....... 815 625-0852
Sterling *(G-19536)*
Sumitomo Machinery Corp Amer..........E....... 630 752-0200
Glendale Heights *(G-10504)*
Tc Electric Controls LLC.......................G....... 815 213-7680
Sterling *(G-19538)*
Tc Electric Controls LLC.......................G....... 815 213-7680
Schaumburg *(G-18741)*
Tomantron Inc..F....... 708 532-2456
Tinley Park *(G-19860)*
Tough Electric Inc...................................G....... 630 236-8332
Aurora *(G-1163)*
Unitrol Electronics Inc...........................E....... 847 480-0115
Northbrook *(G-15496)*
USA Drives Inc..E....... 630 323-1282
Burr Ridge *(G-2730)*
Value Added Services & Tech...............G....... 847 888-8232
Elgin *(G-8772)*
Warming Systems...................................G....... 800 663-7831
Lake Villa *(G-12371)*
Warner Electric LLC...............................E....... 815 547-1106
South Beloit *(G-19121)*
Wgi Innovations Ltd................................G....... 800 847-8269
Plano *(G-16747)*
Win Technologies Incorporated.............E....... 630 236-1020
Aurora *(G-1037)*
Woodward Inc...F....... 847 673-8300
Skokie *(G-19057)*
◆ **Woodward Controls Inc**.....................C....... 847 673-8300
Skokie *(G-19058)*
◆ **Yaskawa America Inc**.........................C....... 847 887-7000
Waukegan *(G-20520)*

3629 Electrical Indl Apparatus, NEC

10g LLC...F....... 630 754-2400
Woodridge *(G-21269)*
A J R International Inc...........................D....... 800 232-3965
Glendale Heights *(G-10435)*
Advanced Enrgy Solutions Group.........F....... 618 988-0888
Carterville *(G-3128)*
▲ **American Electronic Pdts Inc**...........F....... 630 889-9977
Oak Brook *(G-15592)*
Ametek Inc..C....... 847 596-7000
Waukegan *(G-20416)*
B&Bimc LLC..D....... 815 433-5100
Ottawa *(G-16040)*
Battery Systems LLC................................G....... 833 487-6937
Naperville *(G-14777)*
Beyond Components West Inc.................G....... 847 465-0480
Wheeling *(G-20858)*
◆ **Charles Industries LLC**.......................D....... 847 806-6300
Schaumburg *(G-18474)*
Charles Industries LLC.............................D....... 217 932-2068
Casey *(G-3199)*
▲ **Delta-Unibus Corp**...............................C....... 708 409-1200
Northlake *(G-15545)*
Divergent Alliance LLC.............................G....... 847 531-0559
West Dundee *(G-20662)*
Ees Inc..G....... 708 343-1800
Stone Park *(G-19553)*
Electro-Matic Products Co.......................F....... 773 235-4010
Chicago *(G-4477)*
◆ **Engineered Abrasives Inc**.................E....... 662 582-4143
Alsip *(G-445)*
Exide Technologies LLC..........................D....... 678 566-9000
Lombard *(G-13075)*
Hauhinco LP...E....... 618 993-5399
Marion *(G-13514)*
Innovation Plus Power Systems.............F....... 630 457-1105
Saint Charles *(G-18213)*
◆ **Inventus Power Inc**.............................C....... 630 410-7900
Woodridge *(G-21316)*
Jf Industries Inc..G....... 773 775-8840
Chicago *(G-5028)*
Ksm Electronics Inc..................................C....... 630 393-9310
Warrenville *(G-20241)*
◆ **La Marche Mfg Co**...............................C....... 847 299-1188
Des Plaines *(G-7795)*
▼ **Master Control Systems Inc**...............E....... 847 295-1010
Lake Bluff *(G-12195)*
▲ **Motor Capacitors Inc**..........................F....... 773 774-6666
Wood Dale *(G-21217)*
Panatrol Corporation...............................E....... 630 655-4700
Burr Ridge *(G-2713)*
Powell Electrical Systems Inc..................C....... 708 409-1200
Northlake *(G-15555)*
Powell Electrical Systems Inc..................C....... 708 409-1200
Northlake *(G-15556)*
Powerone Corp...G....... 630 443-6500
Saint Charles *(G-18248)*
▲ **Powervar Inc**..C....... 847 596-7000
Waukegan *(G-20480)*
Radionic Hi-Tech Inc.................................D....... 773 804-0100
Chicago *(G-5960)*
▲ **Rauckman Utility Products LLC**........F....... 618 234-0001
Belleville *(G-1587)*
◆ **Schumacher Electric Corp**................D....... 847 385-1600
Mount Prospect *(G-14569)*
Seidel Diesel Group..................................D....... 877 373-6659
Bolingbrook *(G-2236)*
▲ **Slaughter Company Inc**......................E....... 847 932-3662
Lake Forest *(G-12303)*
▲ **We International**..................................G....... 618 549-1784
Carbondale *(G-2863)*

3631 Household Cooking Eqpt

▲ **Apache Supply**.......................................G....... 708 409-1040
Bartlett *(G-1264)*
▲ **Axis International Marketing**.............C....... 847 297-0744
Des Plaines *(G-7735)*
◆ **Belson Outdoors LLC**.........................E....... 630 897-8489
Naperville *(G-14778)*
BR Machine Inc..F....... 815 434-0427
Ottawa *(G-16042)*
Chadwick Manufacturing Ltd...................G....... 815 684-5152
Chadwick *(G-3257)*
▲ **Empire Comfort Systems Inc**............C....... 618 233-7420
Belleville *(G-1551)*
▲ **Global Contract Mfg Inc**.....................G....... 312 432-6200
Chicago *(G-4695)*
Home & Leisure Lifestyles LLC..............G....... 618 651-0358
Highland *(G-11227)*
▼ **Kalamazoo Outdoor Gourmet LLC**..G....... 312 423-8770
Chicago *(G-5077)*
◆ **Marshall Middleby Inc**........................C....... 847 741-3300
Elgin *(G-8649)*
Microwave RES & Applications..............G....... 630 480-7456
Carol Stream *(G-3029)*
◆ **Peerless-Premier Appliance Co**........C....... 618 233-0475
Belleville *(G-1585)*
◆ **Taylor Coml Foodservice Inc**............F....... 815 624-8333
Rockton *(G-17703)*
◆ **Weber-Stephen Products LLC**...........B....... 847 934-5700
Palatine *(G-16173)*
Weber-Stephen Products LLC.................F....... 224 836-8536
Palatine *(G-16174)*
Weber-Stephen Products LLC.................F....... 847 669-4900
Huntley *(G-11573)*

3632 Household Refrigerators & Freezers

▼ **Craig Industries Inc**.............................D....... 217 228-2421
Quincy *(G-16873)*
Dover Corporation....................................G....... 212 922-1640
Downers Grove *(G-7990)*
Flurida Group Inc......................................G....... 310 513-0888
Naperville *(G-14966)*
▼ **H A Phillips & Co**..................................E....... 630 377-0050
Dekalb *(G-7683)*
Lambright Distributors.............................G....... 217 543-2083
Arthur *(G-865)*
◆ **Scotsman Industries Inc**....................D....... 847 215-4500
Vernon Hills *(G-20093)*
Sphinx Panel and Door Inc.......................G....... 618 351-9266
Cobden *(G-6944)*
Tri-State Food Equipment........................G....... 217 228-1550
Quincy *(G-16952)*

3633 Household Laundry Eqpt

5 Alarm Coin Laundry Inc.........................G....... 815 298-0585
Rockford *(G-17278)*
C Streeter Enterprise................................G....... 773 858-4388
Chicago *(G-3995)*
Coin Macke Laundry.................................G....... 847 459-1109
Wheeling *(G-20874)*
Eastgate Cleaners.....................................G....... 630 627-9494
Lombard *(G-13071)*
Iron-A-Way LLC..E....... 309 266-7232
Morton *(G-14363)*
Monqui Suds LLC.......................................G....... 217 479-0090
Jacksonville *(G-11777)*

3634 Electric Household Appliances

Alpha Bedding LLC....................................F....... 847 550-5110
Lake Zurich *(G-12383)*
American Fuel Economy Inc.....................G....... 815 433-3226
Ottawa *(G-16037)*
Baier Home Center....................................G....... 815 457-2300
Cissna Park *(G-6894)*
▲ **Bestair Pro**..G....... 847 683-3400
Hampshire *(G-10964)*
▲ **Blueair Inc**..F....... 888 258-3247
Chicago *(G-3915)*
Bunn-O-Matic Corporation.......................E....... 562 926-0764
Springfield *(G-19332)*
Cabot Microelectronics Corp....................D....... 630 375-6631
Aurora *(G-932)*
◆ **Conair Corporation**.............................G....... 203 351-9000
Rantoul *(G-16972)*
Expo Engineered Inc.................................G....... 708 780-7155
Cicero *(G-6847)*
Extractor Corporation...............................F....... 847 742-3532
South Elgin *(G-19144)*
General Electric Company.........................F....... 708 780-2600
Cicero *(G-6848)*

36 ELECTRONIC AND OTHER ELECTRICAL EQUIPMENT AND COMPONENTS, EXCEPT COMPUTER

Hamilton Beach Brands Inc ....E....... 847 252-7036
 Inverness (G-11596)
▲ Heaven Fresh USA Inc ....G....... 800 642-0367
 Plainfield (G-16671)
High Rise Specialty Products ....G....... 708 343-9265
 Maywood (G-13669)
Hotvapes Ltd ....F....... 775 468-8273
 Niles (G-15130)
Imh Fabrication Inc ....F....... 815 537-2381
 Prophetstown (G-16833)
▼ Kalb Corporation ....F....... 309 483-3600
 Oneida (G-15903)
Keating of Chicago Inc ....E....... 815 569-2324
 Capron (G-2834)
Lighthouse Marketing Inc ....G....... 949 542-4558
 Chicago (G-5221)
Matthews-Gerbar Ltd ....G....... 847 680-9043
 Libertyville (G-12674)
▲ Matthews-Gerbar Ltd ....G....... 847 680-9043
 Libertyville (G-12675)
▲ Menk Usa LLC ....E....... 815 626-9730
 Sterling (G-19518)
Mh Equipment Company ....D....... 217 443-7210
 Danville (G-7366)
▲ Newhaven Display Intl Inc ....E....... 847 844-8795
 Elgin (G-8668)
▲ O2cool LLC ....E....... 312 951-6700
 Chicago (G-5647)
Quick Nic Juice LLC ....F....... 815 315-8523
 Sandwich (G-18383)
Radovent Illinois LLC ....E....... 847 637-0297
 Naperville (G-14984)
▲ Sensible Designs Online Inc ....G....... 708 267-8924
 Orland Park (G-15978)
◆ Taylor Coml Foodservice Inc ....F....... 815 624-8333
 Rockton (G-17703)
▲ Tempro International Corp ....G....... 847 677-5370
 Skokie (G-19044)
▲ Thermosoft International Corp ....E....... 847 279-3800
 Vernon Hills (G-20105)
Tifb Media Group Inc ....G....... 844 862-4391
 Burbank (G-2638)
Tonjon Company ....F....... 630 208-1173
 Geneva (G-10312)
▲ Tri-Lite Inc ....E....... 773 384-7765
 Chicago (G-6422)
Upper Limits Midwest Inc ....G....... 217 679-4315
 Springfield (G-19467)
▲ Winchester Interconnect Rugged ....G....... 708 594-5890
 Broadview (G-2475)
▲ World Dryer Corporation ....E....... 800 323-0701
 Bensenville (G-1914)

3635 Household Vacuum Cleaners

Campanella Clg Solutions Inc ....G....... 847 949-4222
 Mundelein (G-14671)
Dyson Inc ....G....... 847 995-8010
 Schaumburg (G-18510)
▲ Dyson Inc ....D....... 312 469-5950
 Chicago (G-4416)
▲ Dyson B2b Inc ....E....... 312 469-5950
 Chicago (G-4417)
Dyson Direct Inc ....G....... 312 469-5950
 Chicago (G-4418)
Lee Sauzek ....G....... 618 539-5815
 Freeburg (G-10091)
Wodack Electric Tool Corp ....F....... 773 287-9866
 Chicago (G-6661)

3639 Household Appliances, NEC

Appliance Repair ....G....... 708 456-1020
 Norridge (G-15230)
◆ Belson Outdoors LLC ....E....... 630 897-8489
 Naperville (G-14778)
◆ Mic Quality Service Inc ....E....... 847 778-5676
 Chicago (G-5422)
Rampro Facilities Svcs Corp ....G....... 224 639-6378
 Waukegan (G-20487)
▲ Tablecraft Products Co Inc ....D....... 847 855-9000
 Gurnee (G-10933)
Unique Indoor Comfort ....F....... 847 362-1910
 Libertyville (G-12719)

3641 Electric Lamps

▲ AAA Press Specialists Inc ....F....... 847 818-1100
 Arlington Heights (G-681)
Acculight LLC ....G....... 630 847-1000
 Elk Grove Village (G-8799)
Aco Inc ....E....... 773 774-5200
 Chicago (G-3529)

▲ Advanced Micro Lites Inc ....G....... 630 365-5450
 Elburn (G-8442)
▲ Advanced Strobe Products Inc ...D....... 708 867-3100
 Chicago (G-3567)
Aero-Tech Light Bulb Co ....D....... 847 352-4900
 Schaumburg (G-18430)
▲ Amglo Kemlite Laboratories Inc .....D....... 630 238-3031
 Bensenville (G-1744)
Anixter Inc ....C....... 800 323-8167
 Glenview (G-10526)
Benko Lamps Ltd ....F....... 708 458-7965
 Bridgeview (G-2328)
▲ Cec Industries Ltd ....E....... 847 821-1199
 Lincolnshire (G-12748)
Ddk Scientific Corporation ....G....... 618 235-2849
 Belleville (G-1543)
▲ Dontech Industries Inc ....F....... 847 428-8222
 Gilberts (G-10353)
Eden Park Illumination Inc ....E....... 217 403-1866
 Champaign (G-3287)
Keating of Chicago Inc ....E....... 815 569-2324
 Capron (G-2834)
Lamp Works Inc ....F....... 630 871-7663
 Carol Stream (G-3015)
▲ Lampholders Assemblies Inc .....G....... 773 205-0005
 Chicago (G-5173)
▲ Light Matrix Inc ....G....... 847 590-0856
 Palatine (G-16136)
Malcolite Corporation ....E....... 847 562-1350
 Deerfield (G-7634)
▲ Mattson Lamp Plant ....E....... 217 258-9390
 Mattoon (G-13647)
Modern Lighting Tech LLC ....G....... 312 624-9267
 Chicago (G-5478)
North American Lighting Inc ....A....... 618 548-6249
 Salem (G-18348)
Radionic Hi-Tech Inc ....D....... 773 804-0100
 Chicago (G-5960)
▼ Royal Haeger Lamp Co ....E....... 309 837-9966
 Macomb (G-13400)
S A W Co ....G....... 630 678-5400
 Lombard (G-13126)
Santas Best ....F....... 847 459-3301
 Vernon Hills (G-20091)
Universal Lighting Corporation ....G....... 773 927-2000
 Chicago (G-6481)
Vision Engineering Labs ....F....... 630 350-9470
 Bensenville (G-1910)
◆ Waters Industries Inc ....E....... 847 783-5900
 West Dundee (G-20667)

3643 Current-Carrying Wiring Devices

ABB Power Protection LLC ....F....... 804 236-3300
 Chicago (G-3501)
Aco Inc ....E....... 773 774-5200
 Chicago (G-3529)
Alan Manufacturing Corp ....G....... 815 568-6836
 Marengo (G-13478)
Alcon Tool & Mfg Co Inc ....F....... 773 545-8742
 Chicago (G-3598)
American Bare Conductor Inc ....E....... 815 224-3422
 La Salle (G-12102)
▲ Amerline Enterprises Co Inc ....E....... 847 671-6554
 Schiller Park (G-18786)
◆ Amphenol Eec Inc ....C....... 773 463-8343
 Des Plaines (G-7731)
◆ Appleton Grp LLC ....C....... 847 268-6000
 Rosemont (G-17999)
Belden Energy Solutions Inc ....G....... 800 235-3361
 Elmhurst (G-9330)
▲ Bright Image Corporation ....D....... 708 449-5656
 Broadview (G-2423)
▲ Central Rubber Company ....E....... 815 544-2191
 Belvidere (G-1661)
Chicago Freight Car Leasing Co ....D....... 847 318-8000
 Schaumburg (G-18475)
Cinch Connectors Inc ....D....... 630 705-6001
 Lombard (G-13055)
◆ Coleman Cable LLC ....E....... 847 672-2300
 Lincolnshire (G-12752)
Connector Concepts Inc ....F....... 847 541-4020
 Mundelein (G-14680)
◆ CTS Automotive LLC ....C....... 630 577-8800
 Lisle (G-12880)
Cutshaw Instls Inc ....E....... 847 426-9208
 East Dundee (G-8190)
David Jeskey ....G....... 630 659-6337
 Saint Charles (G-18180)
Dcx-Chol Enterprises Inc ....E....... 309 353-4455
 Pekin (G-16327)

Dollar Express ....G....... 815 399-9719
 Rockford (G-17384)
Dqm Inc ....F....... 630 692-0633
 Montgomery (G-14243)
▲ Eastco Inc ....E....... 708 499-1701
 Oak Lawn (G-15714)
▲ Emerge Technology Group LLC .....G....... 224 603-2161
 Lake Villa (G-12350)
▲ Excel Specialty Corp ....E....... 773 262-7575
 Lake Forest (G-12248)
▲ Flex-Weld Inc ....D....... 815 334-3662
 Woodstock (G-21387)
Gateway Cable Inc ....F....... 630 766-7969
 Lisle (G-12893)
General Electric Company ....C....... 309 664-1513
 Bloomington (G-2050)
Grayhill Inc ....C....... 847 428-6990
 Carpentersville (G-3102)
▲ Grayhill Inc ....B....... 708 354-1040
 La Grange (G-12077)
Grayhill Inc ....G....... 708 482-1411
 Mc Cook (G-13691)
▲ Gus Berthold Electric Company .....D....... 312 243-5767
 Chicago (G-4752)
▲ Harger Inc ....E....... 847 548-8700
 Grayslake (G-10780)
Hauhinco LP ....E....... 618 993-5399
 Marion (G-13514)
▲ Heil Sound Ltd ....F....... 618 257-3000
 Fairview Heights (G-9646)
Honeywell International Inc ....C....... 815 745-2131
 Warren (G-20223)
Hubbell Incorporated ....F....... 972 756-1184
 Aurora (G-1110)
Ideal Industries Inc ....C....... 815 895-1108
 Sycamore (G-19715)
Ideal Industries Inc ....C....... 815 895-5181
 Sycamore (G-19716)
◆ Ideal Industries Inc ....C....... 815 895-5181
 Sycamore (G-19714)
IL Tool Work ....G....... 630 972-6400
 Bolingbrook (G-2189)
Illinois Tool Works Inc ....C....... 847 724-7500
 Des Plaines (G-7784)
▲ Inglot Electronics Corp ....D....... 773 286-5881
 Chicago (G-4921)
Itron Corporation Del ....F....... 708 222-5320
 Cicero (G-6857)
J P Goldenne Incorporated ....F....... 847 776-5063
 Palatine (G-16132)
▲ Ki Industries Inc ....E....... 708 449-1990
 Berkeley (G-1941)
Leviton Manufacturing Co Inc ....C....... 630 443-0500
 Saint Charles (G-18226)
Leviton Manufacturing Co Inc ....B....... 630 350-2656
 Bensenville (G-1844)
▲ Lutamar Electrical Assemblies ....E....... 847 679-5400
 Skokie (G-18981)
M E Barber Co Inc ....G....... 217 428-4591
 Decatur (G-7518)
◆ Maclean Senior Industries LLC .....G....... 630 350-1600
 Wood Dale (G-21210)
▼ Magnetrol International Inc ....G....... 630 723-6600
 Aurora (G-1001)
Methode Development Co ....D....... 708 867-6777
 Chicago (G-5408)
Methode Electronics Inc ....C....... 847 577-9545
 Rolling Meadows (G-17750)
Methode Electronics Inc ....A....... 217 357-3941
 Carthage (G-3139)
◆ Methode Electronics Inc ....B....... 708 867-6777
 Chicago (G-5409)
Micro West Ltd ....G....... 630 766-7160
 Bensenville (G-1850)
Midwest Fiber Solutions ....G....... 217 971-7400
 Springfield (G-19407)
◆ Molex LLC ....A....... 630 969-4550
 Lisle (G-12911)
Molex LLC ....G....... 630 527-4363
 Bolingbrook (G-2216)
Molex LLC ....F....... 630 512-8787
 Downers Grove (G-8059)
▲ Molex International Inc ....F....... 630 969-4550
 Lisle (G-12914)
▲ Molex Premise Networks Inc ......A....... 866 733-6659
 Lisle (G-12915)
Morrell Incorporated ....F....... 630 858-4600
 Glendale Heights (G-10477)
Mpc Products Corporation ....E....... 847 673-8300
 Niles (G-15150)

36 ELECTRONIC AND OTHER ELECTRICAL EQUIPMENT AND COMPONENTS, EXCEPT COMPUTER SIC SECTION

Pancon Illinois LLC....G....630 972-6400
Bolingbrook (G-2224)
Panduit Corp....E....815 836-1800
Lockport (G-13018)
Plug Electric LLC....G....630 788-1018
Chicago Ridge (G-6807)
Porch Electric LLC....G....815 368-3230
Lostant (G-13177)
Possehl Connector Svcs SC Inc....E....803 366-8316
Elk Grove Village (G-9184)
Process Screw Products Inc....E....815 864-2220
Shannon (G-18872)
Radionic Hi-Tech Inc....D....773 804-0100
Chicago (G-5960)
▲ Remke Industries Inc....D....847 541-3780
Vernon Hills (G-20085)
▲ Rockford Rigging Inc....F....309 263-0566
Roscoe (G-17926)
◆ S & C Electric Company....A....773 338-1000
Chicago (G-6083)
S-P Products Inc....F....847 593-8595
Elk Grove Village (G-9227)
▲ Safco LLC....E....847 677-3204
Skokie (G-19026)
Schneider Electric Usa Inc....E....847 441-2526
Schaumburg (G-18708)
Shattuc Cord Specialties Inc....F....847 360-9500
Waukegan (G-20494)
▼ Simplex Inc....C....217 483-1600
Springfield (G-19446)
Skach Manufacturing Co Inc....E....847 395-3560
Antioch (G-635)
Special Mine Services Inc....D....618 932-2151
West Frankfort (G-20684)
▲ Switchcraft Inc....B....773 792-2700
Chicago (G-6299)
▲ Switchcraft Holdco Inc....G....773 792-2700
Chicago (G-6300)
Telegartner Inc....E....630 616-7600
Franklin Park (G-10059)
Triton Manufacturing Co Inc....C....708 587-4000
Monee (G-14210)
Twin City Electric Inc....E....309 827-0636
Bloomington (G-2105)
U S Tool & Manufacturing Co....E....630 953-1000
Addison (G-321)
United Universal Inds Inc....E....815 727-4445
Joliet (G-11939)
Unlimited Svcs Wisconsin Inc....E....815 399-0282
Machesney Park (G-13383)
Western-Cullen-Hayes Inc....D....773 254-9600
Chicago (G-6609)
▲ Winchester Interconnect Rugged....G....708 594-5890
Broadview (G-2475)
▲ Woodhead Industries LLC....B....847 353-2500
Lincolnshire (G-12802)
◆ Woodward Controls Inc....C....847 673-8300
Skokie (G-19058)

3644 Noncurrent-Carrying Wiring Devices

Aco Inc....E....773 774-5200
Chicago (G-3529)
▲ Anamet Electrical Inc....C....217 234-8844
Mattoon (G-13630)
Anamet Inc....G....217 234-8844
Glen Ellyn (G-10394)
◆ Appleton Grp LLC....C....847 268-6000
Rosemont (G-17999)
▲ Beacon Fas & Components Inc....E....847 541-0404
Wheeling (G-20857)
▲ Cable Management Products Inc....G....630 723-0470
Aurora (G-929)
Chase Corporation....F....630 752-3622
Wheaton (G-20793)
Chicago Switchboard Co Inc....E....630 833-2266
Elmhurst (G-9345)
Dells Raceway Park Inc....G....815 494-0074
Roscoe (G-17903)
Eaton Corporation....A....217 732-3131
Lincoln (G-12729)
◆ Electri-Flex Company....D....630 529-2920
Roselle (G-17952)
Electric Conduit Cnstr Co....C....630 293-4474
Elburn (G-8453)
Electric Conduit Construction....F....630 859-9310
Elburn (G-8454)
▲ Excel Specialty Corp....E....773 262-7575
Lake Forest (G-12248)
Guardian Energy Tech Inc....F....800 516-0949
Riverwoods (G-17091)
Illinois Tool Works Inc....D....815 943-4785
Lincolnshire (G-12774)
J & A Sheet Metal Shop Inc....E....773 276-3739
Chicago (G-4981)
John Maneely Company....C....773 254-0617
Chicago (G-5043)
▲ Lew Electric Fittings Co....F....630 665-2075
Carol Stream (G-3017)
Linear Solutions Inc....G....724 426-6384
Chicago (G-5228)
▲ Lutamar Electrical Assemblies....E....847 679-5400
Skokie (G-18981)
◆ Maclean Senior Industries LLC....G....630 350-1600
Wood Dale (G-21210)
Methode Development Co....D....708 867-6777
Chicago (G-5408)
Midwest-Design Inc....G....708 615-1572
Broadview (G-2452)
▲ Minerallac Company....E....630 543-7080
Hampshire (G-10979)
Panduit Corp....E....815 836-1800
Lockport (G-13018)
◆ Panduit Corp....A....708 532-1800
Tinley Park (G-19848)
▲ Questek Manufacturing Corp....D....847 428-0300
Elgin (G-8710)
Resinite Corporation....C....847 537-4250
Wheeling (G-20973)
Southern IL Raceway....G....618 201-0500
Marion (G-13536)
Taurus Safety Products Inc....G....630 620-7940
Lombard (G-13140)
▲ Thermamax Inc....F....630 340-5682
Aurora (G-1022)
Vertiv Group Corporation....E....630 579-5000
Lombard (G-13150)
Windy City RC....G....847 818-8354
Arlington Heights (G-834)

3645 Residential Lighting Fixtures

▲ Advanced Micro Lites Inc....G....630 365-5450
Elburn (G-8442)
◆ Afx Inc....C....847 249-5970
Waukegan (G-20410)
Astral Power Systems Inc....G....630 518-1741
Aurora (G-1055)
Benko Lamps Ltd....F....708 458-7965
Bridgeview (G-2328)
◆ Blg McC Enterprises Inc....E....847 455-0188
Franklin Park (G-9888)
Cooper Lighting LLC....G....312 595-2770
Elk Grove Village (G-8913)
Cooper Lighting LLC....D....847 956-8400
Elk Grove Village (G-8914)
Cosas Inc....G....312 492-6100
Chicago (G-4243)
▲ Eclipse Lighting Inc....E....847 260-0333
Schiller Park (G-18802)
▲ Elcast Manufacturing Inc....E....630 628-1992
Addison (G-111)
Fanmar Inc....E....847 621-2010
Elk Grove Village (G-8995)
Fli Products LLC....G....630 520-0017
West Chicago (G-20584)
▲ Gerber Manufacturing (gm) LLC....F....708 478-0100
Tinley Park (G-19830)
Grow Masters....G....224 399-9877
Gurnee (G-10885)
▲ H A Framburg & Company....E....708 547-5757
Bellwood (G-1627)
H E Associates Inc....F....630 553-6382
Yorkville (G-21487)
◆ Intermatic Incorporated....A....815 675-7000
Spring Grove (G-19276)
▲ Io Lighting LLC....E....847 735-7000
Vernon Hills (G-20067)
▲ K&I Light Kandi Led Inc....G....773 745-1533
Chicago (G-5068)
Lamp Co of America Inc....G....630 584-4001
Saint Charles (G-18224)
Lamp Works Inc....F....630 871-7663
Carol Stream (G-3015)
▲ Lampshade Inc....F....773 522-2300
Chicago (G-5174)
Lli Architectural Lighting LLC....F....847 412-4880
Buffalo Grove (G-2564)
▲ Lllb LLC....F....630 315-3300
Elk Grove Village (G-9097)
▲ Lumenart Ltd....G....773 254-0744
Chicago (G-5281)
McAteers Wholesale....G....618 233-3400
Belleville (G-1573)
McKenzie & Keim LLC....G....317 443-6663
Chicago (G-5377)
▲ Metomic Corporation....E....773 247-4716
Chicago (G-5410)
Midwest Sun-Ray Lighting & Sig....F....618 656-2884
Granite City (G-10726)
▲ New Metal Crafts Inc....E....312 787-6991
Lincolnwood (G-12832)
◆ Pace Industries Inc....C....312 226-5500
Chicago (G-5737)
◆ Productworks LLC....F....224 406-8810
Northbrook (G-15468)
▲ Rgb Lights Inc....F....312 421-6080
Chicago (G-6021)
▼ Royal Haeger Lamp Co....E....309 837-9966
Macomb (G-13400)
▲ Smart Solar Inc....F....813 343-5770
Libertyville (G-12708)
▲ Sternberg Lanterns Inc....C....847 588-3400
Roselle (G-17991)
Stone Lighting LLC....F....312 240-0400
Flossmoor (G-9703)
▲ Uncommon Radiant....G....773 640-1674
Chicago (G-6461)
▲ Vaxcel International Co Ltd....E....630 260-0067
Carol Stream (G-3084)
Western Lighting Inc....F....847 451-7200
Franklin Park (G-10084)

3646 Commercial, Indl & Institutional Lighting Fixtures

555 International Inc....E....773 869-0555
Chicago (G-3475)
555 International Inc....E....773 847-1400
Chicago (G-3474)
▲ Advanced Specialty Lighting....C....708 867-3140
Harwood Heights (G-11101)
◆ Afx Inc....C....847 249-5970
Waukegan (G-20410)
Amerilights Inc....G....847 219-1476
Bloomingdale (G-1976)
◆ Appleton Grp LLC....C....847 268-6000
Rosemont (G-17999)
Astral Power Systems Inc....G....630 518-1741
Aurora (G-1055)
Avtec Inc....F....618 337-7800
East Saint Louis (G-8298)
Blackjack Lighting....G....847 941-0588
Buffalo Grove (G-2518)
◆ Blg McC Enterprises Inc....E....847 455-0188
Franklin Park (G-9888)
▲ Challenger Lighting Co Inc....E....847 717-4700
Batavia (G-1365)
Conservation Tech III LLC....F....847 559-5500
Northbrook (G-15365)
◆ Conservation Technology Ltd....D....847 559-5500
Northbrook (G-15366)
Contemprary Enrgy Slutions LLC....F....630 768-3743
Naperville (G-14963)
Cooper Lighting LLC....D....847 956-8400
Elk Grove Village (G-8914)
Dado Lighting LLC....G....708 243-9059
Brookfield (G-2481)
Dado Lighting LLC....G....877 323-6584
Western Springs (G-20720)
Dado Lighting LLC....G....877 323-6584
Countryside (G-7050)
Dva Mayday Corporation....G....847 848-7555
Village of Lakewood (G-20178)
▲ Eclipse Lighting Inc....E....847 260-0333
Schiller Park (G-18802)
◆ Esco Lighting Inc....E....773 427-7000
Chicago (G-4530)
◆ Eti Solid State Lighting Inc....E....855 384-7754
Wheeling (G-20895)
First Light Inc....G....630 520-0017
West Chicago (G-20583)
Fli Products LLC....G....630 520-0017
West Chicago (G-20584)
Focal Point Lighting Inc....C....773 247-9494
Chicago (G-4613)
▲ Focal Point LLC....E....773 247-9494
Chicago (G-4614)
◆ Glamox Aqua Signal Corporation....F....847 639-6412
Cary (G-3165)
▲ H A Framburg & Company....E....708 547-5757
Bellwood (G-1627)

36 ELECTRONIC AND OTHER ELECTRICAL EQUIPMENT AND COMPONENTS, EXCEPT COMPUTER

▲ Holiday Bright Lights Inc ....G....... 312 226-8281
Chicago (G-4830)
▲ Jarvis Corp ....E....... 800 363-1075
Schaumburg (G-18575)
Lamp Co of America Inc ....G....... 630 584-4001
Saint Charles (G-18224)
Lava World International Inc ....G....... 630 315-3300
Carol Stream (G-3016)
Led Business Solutions LLC ....F....... 844 464-5337
Downers Grove (G-8043)
Ledil Inc ....F....... 815 766-3204
Sycamore (G-19721)
▲ Louvers International Inc ....E....... 630 782-9977
Elmhurst (G-9394)
▲ Luxo Corporation ....F....... 914 345-0067
Cary (G-3176)
Morris Kurtzon Incorporated ....E....... 773 277-2121
Chicago (G-5500)
▲ New Metal Crafts Inc ....E....... 312 787-6991
Lincolnwood (G-12832)
▲ North Star Lighting LLC ....D....... 708 681-4330
Elmhurst (G-9405)
Omnilight Inc ....G....... 773 696-1602
Chicago (G-5676)
Paul D Metal Products Inc ....D....... 773 847-1400
Chicago (G-5771)
Pineapple Led Inc ....G....... 847 255-3710
Barrington (G-1235)
Premier Lighting and Sup LLC ....G....... 708 612-9693
Oak Forest (G-15687)
◆ Productworks LLC ....F....... 224 406-8810
Northbrook (G-15468)
▲ Pure Lighting LLC ....F....... 773 770-1130
Chicago (G-5917)
◆ Rainbow Lighting ....E....... 847 480-1136
Northbrook (G-15470)
▲ Rgb Lights Inc ....F....... 312 421-6080
Chicago (G-6021)
S-P Products Inc ....F....... 847 593-8595
Elk Grove Village (G-9227)
Sensio America LLC ....G....... 877 501-5337
Carol Stream (G-3067)
▲ Sternberg Lanterns Inc ....C....... 847 588-3400
Roselle (G-17991)
Sustanble Sltions Amer Led LLC .....F....... 866 323-3494
Chicago (G-6291)
▲ Tri-Lite Inc ....E....... 773 384-7765
Chicago (G-6422)
Twin Supplies Ltd ....F....... 630 590-5138
Oak Brook (G-15667)
▲ Wallace/Haskin Corp ....G....... 630 789-2882
Downers Grove (G-8105)
Western Lighting Inc ....F....... 847 451-7200
Franklin Park (G-10084)

3647 Vehicular Lighting Eqpt

Astronics Cnnctvity Systems Cr ....F....... 847 821-3059
Waukegan (G-20419)
▲ Elc Industries Corp ....E....... 630 851-1616
Aurora (G-1088)
Esafety Lights LLC ....F....... 800 236-8621
Chicago (G-4529)
◆ Federal Signal Corporation ....D....... 630 954-2000
Oak Brook (G-15618)
◆ Glamox Aqua Signal Corporation ....F....... 847 639-6412
Cary (G-3165)
L & T Services Inc ....G....... 815 397-6260
Rockford (G-17487)
▲ Lecip Inc ....F....... 312 626-2525
Bensenville (G-1842)
Master Fog LLC ....G....... 773 918-9080
Romeoville (G-17845)
North American Lighting Inc ....B....... 217 465-7800
Paris (G-16236)
▲ North American Lighting Inc ....A....... 217 465-6600
Paris (G-16237)
North American Lighting Inc ....A....... 618 548-6249
Salem (G-18348)
North American Lighting Inc ....B....... 618 662-4483
Flora (G-9686)
Outbound Lighting LLC ....E....... 314 330-0696
Lincolnwood (G-12835)
◆ Progress Rail Locomotive Inc ....A....... 800 255-5355
Mc Cook (G-13699)
Progress Rail Locomotive Inc ....F....... 708 387-5510
Mc Cook (G-13700)
River View Motor Sports Inc ....G....... 309 467-4569
Congerville (G-7003)
▲ Tiger Accessory Group LLC ....F....... 847 821-9630
Long Grove (G-13171)

Tool Automation Enterprises ....G....... 708 799-6847
East Hazel Crest (G-8218)
▲ Tri-Lite Inc ....E....... 773 384-7765
Chicago (G-6422)

3648 Lighting Eqpt, NEC

A Burst of Sun Inc ....G....... 815 335-2331
Winnebago (G-21118)
Acuity Brands Lighting Inc ....F....... 847 827-9880
Des Plaines (G-7722)
▲ Advanced Cstm Enrgy Sltons Inc .....D....... 312 428-9540
Chicago (G-3563)
Akt Corporation ....E....... 414 475-5020
Elgin (G-8501)
▲ Big Beam Emergency Systems Inc ....E....... 815 459-6100
Crystal Lake (G-7169)
Bilt-Rite Metal Products Inc ....E....... 815 495-2211
Leland (G-12547)
Boston Warehouse Trading Corp .....G....... 630 992-5604
Aurora (G-925)
▲ Carmen Matthew LLC ....D....... 630 784-7500
Rolling Meadows (G-17720)
City of Pekin ....F....... 309 477-2325
Pekin (G-16325)
CU Layer Inc ....G....... 630 802-7873
Batavia (G-1369)
Cyclops Industrial Inc. ....G....... 815 962-1984
Rockford (G-17363)
D2 Lighting LLC ....G....... 708 243-9059
La Grange Highlands (G-12092)
David Michael Productions ....G....... 630 972-9640
Woodridge (G-21293)
Designed For Just For You ....G....... 309 221-2667
Macomb (G-13391)
Duroweld Company Inc ....E....... 847 680-3064
Lake Bluff (G-12179)
Eagle High Mast Ltg Co Inc ....G....... 847 473-3800
Waukegan (G-20440)
Eclipse Lighting Inc ....G....... 847 916-2623
Franklin Park (G-9936)
Ecurrent LLC ....G....... 888 815-5786
Wood Dale (G-21184)
Efficient Energy Lighting Inc ....G....... 630 272-9388
Saint Charles (G-18193)
▲ Elcast Manufacturing Inc ....E....... 630 628-1992
Addison (G-111)
Esafety Lights LLC ....F....... 800 236-8621
Chicago (G-4529)
Est Lighting Inc ....G....... 847 612-1705
Richmond (G-17013)
◆ First Alert Inc ....C....... 630 499-3295
Aurora (G-962)
First-Light Usa LLC ....F....... 217 687-4048
Seymour (G-18868)
Flex Lighting II LLC ....G....... 312 929-3488
Chicago (G-4603)
Genesis Ltg Managemet Svcs ....F....... 630 986-3900
Willowbrook (G-21044)
◆ Good Earth Lighting Inc ....E....... 847 808-1133
Mount Prospect (G-14531)
Group O Inc ....D....... 309 736-8660
Milan (G-14013)
Hangout Lighting LLC ....G....... 224 817-4101
Chicago (G-4777)
Hubbell Lighting Inc ....G....... 847 515-3057
Rolling Meadows (G-17736)
Illuminight Lighting LLC ....F....... 312 685-4448
Highland Park (G-11272)
Inliten LLC ....G....... 847 486-4200
Glenview (G-10568)
Intex Lighting LLC ....G....... 847 380-2027
Schaumburg (G-18566)
Jr Lighting Design Inc ....G....... 708 460-6319
Tinley Park (G-19842)
▲ Lampholders Assemblies Inc ....G....... 773 205-0005
Chicago (G-5173)
▲ Lbl Lighting LLC ....F....... 708 755-2100
Skokie (G-18978)
▲ Lighting Innovations Inc ....E....... 630 889-8100
Saint Charles (G-18228)
Lightitech LLC ....G....... 847 910-4177
Chicago (G-5222)
Lightolier Genlyte Inc ....D....... 847 364-8250
Elk Grove Village (G-9095)
Lightscape Inc ....E....... 847 247-8800
Libertyville (G-12670)
Litetronics Technologies Inc ....G....... 708 333-6707
Chicago (G-5235)
Microlite Corporation ....G....... 630 876-0500
West Chicago (G-20617)

Midwest Sign & Lighting Inc ....G....... 708 365-5555
Country Club Hills (G-7042)
▲ Modern Home Products Corp ....E....... 847 395-6556
Antioch (G-627)
Musco Sports Lighting LLC ....E....... 630 876-0500
Batavia (G-1396)
Nicks Emergency Ltg & More ....G....... 815 780-8327
Peru (G-16585)
◆ North American Signal Co ....E....... 847 537-8888
Wheeling (G-20945)
Northern Lighting & Power Inc ....G....... 708 383-9926
Oak Park (G-15766)
Patty Style Shop ....G....... 618 654-2015
Highland (G-11234)
▲ Plastic Technologies Inc ....E....... 847 841-8610
Elgin (G-8688)
▲ Press A Light Corporation ....F....... 630 231-6566
West Chicago (G-20632)
◆ Productworks LLC ....F....... 224 406-8810
Northbrook (G-15468)
Promier Products Inc ....F....... 815 223-3393
Peru (G-16591)
Radionic Hi-Tech Inc ....D....... 773 804-0100
Chicago (G-5960)
SC Lighting ....G....... 630 849-3384
Schaumburg (G-18705)
▲ Schreder Lighting LLC ....E....... 847 621-5130
Oak Brook (G-15662)
Sensio America LLC ....G....... 877 501-5337
Carol Stream (G-3067)
Spurt Inc ....G....... 847 571-6497
Northbrook (G-15486)
▲ Sternberg Lanterns Inc ....C....... 847 588-3400
Roselle (G-17991)
Tactical Lighting Systems Inc ....F....... 800 705-0518
Lombard (G-13138)
Telser Lighting Associates LLC ....G....... 630 800-5312
East Dundee (G-8211)
▲ Tri-Lite Inc ....E....... 773 384-7765
Chicago (G-6422)
Twin Supplies Ltd ....F....... 630 590-5138
Oak Brook (G-15667)
◆ Waters Industries Inc ....E....... 847 783-5900
West Dundee (G-20667)
Western Lighting Inc ....F....... 847 451-7200
Franklin Park (G-10084)
▲ Winchester Interconnect Rugged ....G....... 708 594-5890
Broadview (G-2475)

3651 Household Audio & Video Eqpt

A and T Labs Incorporated ....G....... 630 668-8562
Wheaton (G-20783)
Aco Inc ....E....... 773 774-5200
Chicago (G-3529)
◆ Acoustic Avenue Inc ....F....... 217 544-9810
Springfield (G-19315)
Advance Tools LLC ....G....... 630 337-5904
Glenview (G-10520)
Alexander Brewster LLC ....E....... 618 346-8580
Collinsville (G-6954)
▲ Alumapro Inc ....G....... 224 569-3650
Huntley (G-11527)
◆ Amplivox Sound Systems LLC ....E....... 800 267-5486
Northbrook (G-15336)
▲ Audio Installers Inc ....F....... 815 969-7500
Loves Park (G-13193)
AVI-Spl Employee ....G....... 847 437-7712
Schaumburg (G-18453)
▲ Bem Wireless LLC ....F....... 815 337-0541
Schaumburg (G-18460)
Billinium Records LLC ....G....... 800 651-8059
Chicago (G-3887)
Bose Corporation ....G....... 630 575-8044
Hinsdale (G-11366)
Bose Corporation ....G....... 630 585-6654
Aurora (G-924)
◆ Bretford Manufacturing Inc ....B....... 847 678-2545
Franklin Park (G-9892)
Cco Holdings LLC ....G....... 618 505-3505
Troy (G-19912)
Cco Holdings LLC ....G....... 618 651-6486
Highland (G-11208)
◆ Chamberlain Manufacturing Corp ....A....... 630 279-3600
Oak Brook (G-15608)
▲ Clearsounds Communications Inc ....F....... 630 321-2300
Naperville (G-14800)
Connecteriors LLC ....G....... 773 549-3333
Chicago (G-4218)
Crystal Partners Inc ....G....... 847 882-0467
Schaumburg (G-18498)

Employee Codes: A=Over 500 employees, B=251-500
C=101-250, D=51-100, E=20-50, F=10-19, G=3-9

2020 Harris Illinois
Industrial Directory

987

36 ELECTRONIC AND OTHER ELECTRICAL EQUIPMENT AND COMPONENTS, EXCEPT COMPUTER SIC SECTION

▲ **Elexa Consumer Products Inc**.........B....... 773 794-1300
Bannockburn *(G-1200)*
Epic Eye.........G....... 309 210-6212
Grand Ridge *(G-10688)*
Fire CAM.........G....... 618 416-8390
Belleville *(G-1552)*
Fire CAM LLC.........G....... 618 416-8390
Belleville *(G-1553)*
G T C Industries Inc.........G....... 708 369-9815
Naperville *(G-14832)*
Guys Hi-Def Inc.........G....... 708 261-7487
Joliet *(G-11872)*
▲ **Hammond Suzuki Usa Inc**.........E....... 630 543-0277
Addison *(G-145)*
Harman International Inds Inc.........D....... 847 996-8118
Vernon Hills *(G-20059)*
▲ **Heil Sound Ltd**.........F....... 618 257-3000
Fairview Heights *(G-9646)*
Identatronics Inc.........E....... 847 437-2654
Crystal Lake *(G-7208)*
Ionit Technologies Inc.........E....... 847 205-9651
Northfield *(G-15518)*
J P Goldenne Incorporated.........F....... 847 776-5063
Palatine *(G-16132)*
James R Chittick.........G....... 217 446-0925
Danville *(G-7353)*
▲ **Japan Electronic Manufacturers**.........F....... 972 735-0463
Wilmette *(G-21080)*
John Hardy Co.........G....... 847 864-8060
Evanston *(G-9542)*
K C Audio.........G....... 708 636-4928
Alsip *(G-462)*
Knowles Corporation.........E....... 630 250-5100
Itasca *(G-11685)*
Knowles Elec Holdings Inc.........A....... 630 250-5100
Itasca *(G-11687)*
Linx Enterprises LLC.........G....... 224 409-2206
Chicago *(G-5232)*
◆ **Maxxsonics Usa Inc**.........E....... 847 540-7700
Libertyville *(G-12676)*
Mechanical Music Corp.........F....... 847 398-5444
Arlington Heights *(G-775)*
Metronet Integration Inc.........G....... 312 781-0045
Chicago *(G-5412)*
Mitek Corporation.........C....... 608 328-5560
Winslow *(G-21139)*
Mitek Corporation.........C....... 815 367-3000
Winslow *(G-21140)*
▲ **Nantsound Inc**.........F....... 847 939-6101
Park Ridge *(G-16289)*
▲ **Newhaven Display Intl Inc**.........E....... 847 844-8795
Elgin *(G-8668)*
Northrop Grumman Systems Corp.........A....... 847 259-9600
Rolling Meadows *(G-17755)*
▲ **Orei LLC**.........G....... 847 983-4761
Skokie *(G-19001)*
Organized Noise Inc.........G....... 630 820-9855
Aurora *(G-1004)*
Othernet Inc.........G....... 773 688-4320
Long Grove *(G-13168)*
Peterson Intl Entp Ltd.........F....... 847 541-3700
Wheeling *(G-20958)*
Prager Associates.........G....... 309 691-1565
Peoria *(G-16501)*
Prescotts Inc.........G....... 815 626-2996
Sterling *(G-19525)*
Pyar & Co LLC.........G....... 312 451-5073
Chicago *(G-5920)*
▲ **Quam-Nichols Company**.........C....... 773 488-5800
Chicago *(G-5932)*
Rexroat Sound.........G....... 309 764-1663
Colona *(G-6978)*
▲ **Robotics Technologies Inc**.........E....... 815 722-7650
Joliet *(G-11927)*
▲ **SBA Wireless Inc**.........E....... 847 215-8720
Buffalo Grove *(G-2595)*
▲ **Senario LLC**.........F....... 847 882-0677
Schaumburg *(G-18711)*
Sho Technologies Inc.........G....... 217 954-0020
Champaign *(G-3346)*
Shure Incorporated.........F....... 847 520-4404
Wheeling *(G-20984)*
Signify North America Corp.........E....... 708 307-3000
Roselle *(G-17989)*
Sonistic.........G....... 217 377-9698
Champaign *(G-3350)*
Sony Electronics Inc.........C....... 630 773-7500
Carol Stream *(G-3071)*
▲ **Sound Enhancement Products Inc**..E....... 847 639-4646
Glendale Heights *(G-10496)*
Studio Technologies Inc.........F....... 847 676-9177
Skokie *(G-19038)*
Tech Upgraders.........G....... 877 324-8940
Maywood *(G-13678)*
Techpol Automation Inc.........G....... 847 347-4765
Des Plaines *(G-7855)*
United States Audio Corp.........F....... 312 316-2929
Glenview *(G-10636)*
United States Audio Corp.........G....... 312 316-2929
Chicago *(G-6476)*
Victoria Amplifier Company.........F....... 630 369-3527
Naperville *(G-14991)*
William N Pasulka.........G....... 815 339-6300
Peru *(G-16598)*
▲ **Wireless Chamberlain Products**.........E....... 800 282-6225
Elmhurst *(G-9446)*
Wirelessusa Inc.........G....... 217 222-4300
Quincy *(G-16957)*
▲ **Zenith Electronics Corporation**.........E....... 847 941-8000
Lincolnshire *(G-12806)*
Zmf Inc.........G....... 603 667-1672
Lyons *(G-13316)*

3652 Phonograph Records & Magnetic Tape

Abbey Products LLP.........G....... 636 922-5577
Troy *(G-19909)*
Acta Publications.........G....... 773 989-3036
Chicago *(G-3533)*
Advanced Audio Technology Inc.........G....... 630 665-3344
Carol Stream *(G-2925)*
▼ **Alligator Rec & Artist MGT Inc**.........F....... 773 973-7736
Chicago *(G-3620)*
◆ **B D C Inc**.........E....... 847 741-2233
Elgin *(G-8519)*
BRANCh.........G....... 312 213-0138
Chicago *(G-3945)*
Cedille Chicago Nfp.........G....... 773 989-2515
Chicago *(G-4052)*
Chicago Producers Inc.........F....... 312 226-6900
Forest Park *(G-9709)*
Corporate Disk Company.........D....... 800 634-3475
McHenry *(G-13730)*
Crusade Enterprises Inc.........G....... 618 662-4461
Flora *(G-9679)*
Csiteq Studio LLC.........F....... 312 265-1509
Rosemont *(G-18012)*
Datasis Corporation.........F....... 847 427-0909
Elk Grove Village *(G-8938)*
Delmark Records LLC.........G....... 773 539-5001
Chicago *(G-4334)*
▲ **Drag City**.........G....... 312 455-1015
Chicago *(G-4396)*
Ev Interactive LLC.........G....... 847 907-4689
Palatine *(G-16118)*
Fultonworks LLC.........G....... 312 544-9639
Chicago *(G-4642)*
Lmno Technologies LLC.........G....... 773 418-2875
Chicago *(G-5246)*
Modular Wood Systems Inc.........G....... 847 251-6401
Wilmette *(G-21088)*
Private Studios.........G....... 217 367-3530
Urbana *(G-19995)*
Qsrsoft.........G....... 630 995-9642
Lombard *(G-13124)*
Replay S Disc Cook-Kankaee LLC.........F....... 312 371-5018
Monee *(G-14207)*
Sparrow Sound Design.........G....... 773 281-8510
Chicago *(G-6209)*
Tony Patterson.........G....... 773 487-4000
Chicago *(G-6390)*
▲ **Towers Media Holdings Inc**.........D....... 312 993-1550
Northfield *(G-15534)*
United Cmra Binocular Repr LLC.........E....... 630 595-2525
Elk Grove Village *(G-9296)*

3661 Telephone & Telegraph Apparatus

A T Products Inc.........G....... 815 943-3590
Harvard *(G-11038)*
Advantage Optics Inc.........F....... 630 548-9870
Naperville *(G-14767)*
Alltemated Inc.........D....... 847 394-5800
Wheeling *(G-20845)*
▲ **American Comm & Networks**.........E....... 630 241-2800
Downers Grove *(G-7950)*
AT&T Corp.........F....... 312 602-4108
Chicago *(G-3755)*
Axon Telecom LLC.........G....... 618 278-4606
Dorsey *(G-7943)*
▲ **Best-Tronics Mfg Inc**.........C....... 708 802-9677
Tinley Park *(G-19810)*
◆ **Charles Industries LLC**.........D....... 847 806-6300
Schaumburg *(G-18474)*
Charles Industries LLC.........D....... 217 826-2318
Marshall *(G-13566)*
Charles Industries LLC.........D....... 217 893-8335
Rantoul *(G-16970)*
Charles Industries LLC.........D....... 217 932-2068
Casey *(G-3199)*
Charles Industries LLC.........D....... 217 932-5292
Casey *(G-3200)*
Cml Technologies Inc.........G....... 708 450-1911
Westchester *(G-20694)*
◆ **Coleman Cable LLC**.........D....... 847 672-2300
Lincolnshire *(G-12752)*
Coleman Cable LLC.........D....... 847 672-2300
Lincolnshire *(G-12753)*
Connor-Winfield Corp.........D....... 630 499-2121
Aurora *(G-1078)*
Coriant North America LLC.........A....... 630 798-8800
Naperville *(G-14806)*
▲ **Coriant Operations Inc**.........E....... 630 798-8800
Naperville *(G-14807)*
Cronus Technologies Inc.........D....... 847 839-0088
Schaumburg *(G-18496)*
Cutting Edge Communications.........G....... 815 788-9419
Crystal Lake *(G-7191)*
▲ **D & S Communications Inc**.........D....... 847 628-4195
Elgin *(G-8562)*
Datasource.........G....... 312 405-9152
Calumet City *(G-2774)*
Elanza Technologies Inc.........E....... 312 396-4187
Chicago *(G-4475)*
▲ **Elexa Consumer Products Inc**.........B....... 773 794-1300
Bannockburn *(G-1200)*
Elite Fiber Optics LLC.........E....... 630 225-9454
Franklin Park *(G-9938)*
▲ **Etcon Corp**.........F....... 630 325-6100
Burr Ridge *(G-2672)*
Excel Photonics Inc.........G....... 732 829-2667
Elk Grove Village *(G-8987)*
▲ **Firefly Mobile Inc**.........E....... 305 538-2777
Schaumburg *(G-18529)*
HI Tech.........G....... 708 957-4210
Homewood *(G-11496)*
IL Green Pastures Fiber Co-Op.........G....... 815 751-0887
Kirkland *(G-12061)*
Kuna Corp.........G....... 815 675-0140
Spring Grove *(G-19282)*
Ledcor Construction Inc.........F....... 630 916-1200
Oakbrook Terrace *(G-15805)*
Mako Networks Sales & Mktg Inc.........D....... 847 752-5566
Elgin *(G-8647)*
Medical Cmmnctions Systems Inc.........G....... 708 895-4500
Lansing *(G-12508)*
Mitel Networks Inc.........F....... 312 479-9000
Chicago *(G-5471)*
Motorola Solutions Inc.........C....... 847 576-5000
Chicago *(G-5511)*
Motorola Solutions Inc.........C....... 847 576-8600
Schaumburg *(G-18637)*
Netgear Inc.........G....... 630 955-0080
Naperville *(G-14881)*
O & M Electronic Inc.........F....... 708 203-1947
Oak Lawn *(G-15730)*
Olfb Corporation.........G....... 309 283-0825
Moline *(G-14164)*
◆ **Parts Specialists Inc**.........G....... 708 371-2444
Posen *(G-16800)*
Pentegra Systems LLC.........E....... 630 941-6000
Addison *(G-235)*
Photon Partners LLC.........G....... 773 991-9788
Chicago *(G-5805)*
Pitney Bowes Inc.........E....... 800 784-4224
Itasca *(G-11719)*
Precision Components Inc.........D....... 630 462-9110
Saint Charles *(G-18249)*
Primo Microphone Inc.........G....... 630 837-6119
Streamwood *(G-19589)*
Quen-Tel Communication Svc Inc.........G....... 815 463-1800
New Lenox *(G-15052)*
Quintum Technologies Inc.........F....... 847 348-7730
Schaumburg *(G-18694)*
Ruckus Wireless Inc.........E....... 630 281-3000
Lisle *(G-12935)*
Sandmancom Inc.........G....... 630 980-7710
Glendale Heights *(G-10490)*
Smart Choice Mobile Inc.........F....... 708 581-4904
Hickory Hills *(G-11203)*
Stellar Manufacturing Company.........D....... 618 823-3761
Cahokia *(G-2764)*

SIC SECTION 36 ELECTRONIC AND OTHER ELECTRICAL EQUIPMENT AND COMPONENTS, EXCEPT COMPUTER

▲ **Switchcraft Inc** .... B 773 792-2700
Chicago *(G-6299)*
▲ **Switchcraft Holdco Inc** .... G 773 792-2700
Chicago *(G-6300)*
Tancher Corp .... F 847 668-8765
Park Ridge *(G-16299)*
Tekno Industries Inc .... F 630 766-6960
Glen Ellyn *(G-10421)*
Tellabs Mexico Inc .... F 630 445-5333
Naperville *(G-14928)*
Tellabs Tg Inc .... G 630 798-8800
Naperville *(G-14929)*
Unified Solutions Corp .... E 847 478-9100
Arlington Heights *(G-824)*
Vertiv Group Corporation .... E 630 579-5000
Lombard *(G-13150)*
Wescom Products .... G 217 932-5292
Casey *(G-3209)*
▲ **Westell Inc** .... D 630 898-2500
Aurora *(G-1035)*
Westell Technologies Inc .... E 630 898-2500
Aurora *(G-1036)*
▲ **Wireless Chamberlain Products** .... E 800 282-6225
Elmhurst *(G-9446)*

3663 Radio & T V Communications, Systs & Eqpt, Broadcast/Studio

Acp Tower Holdings LLC .... C 800 835-8527
Chicago *(G-3531)*
Advance Technologies Inc .... G 815 297-1771
Freeport *(G-10097)*
AF Antronics Inc .... G 217 328-0800
Villa Grove *(G-20121)*
Ale USA Inc .... G 630 713-5194
Naperville *(G-14770)*
Allcom Products Illinois LLC .... E 847 468-8830
South Elgin *(G-19131)*
▲ **Amphenol T&M Antennas Inc** .... F 847 478-5600
Lincolnshire *(G-12746)*
◆ **Amplivox Sound Systems LLC** .... E 800 267-5486
Northbrook *(G-15336)*
Andrew International Svcs Corp .... A 779 435-6000
Joliet *(G-11823)*
Andrew New Zealand Inc .... E 708 873-3507
Orland Park *(G-15940)*
▲ **Andrew Systems Inc** .... E 708 873-3855
Orland Park *(G-15941)*
▲ **Antenex Inc** .... D 847 839-6910
Schaumburg *(G-18441)*
Anywave Communication Tech Inc .... F 847 415-2258
Vernon Hills *(G-20042)*
AVI-Spl Employee .... B 847 437-7712
Schaumburg *(G-18453)*
BEI Electronics LLC .... F 217 224-9600
Quincy *(G-16863)*
BEI Holding Corporation .... G 217 224-9600
Quincy *(G-16864)*
Big Ten Network Services LLC .... D 312 329-3666
Chicago *(G-3883)*
Boeing Company .... C 312 544-2000
Chicago *(G-3925)*
Boeing Irving Company .... A 312 544-2000
Chicago *(G-3928)*
▲ **Bolingbrook Communications Inc** .... A 630 759-9500
Lisle *(G-12874)*
◆ **Broadcast Electronics Inc** .... C 217 224-9600
Quincy *(G-16869)*
▲ **Cable Company** .... E 847 437-5267
Elk Grove Village *(G-8877)*
▲ **Callpod Inc** .... F 312 829-2680
Chicago *(G-4007)*
Cco Holdings LLC .... G 618 505-3505
Troy *(G-19912)*
Cco Holdings LLC .... G 618 651-6486
Highland *(G-11208)*
Charles Electronics LLC .... G 815 244-7981
Mount Carroll *(G-14494)*
Checkpoint Systems Inc .... D 630 771-4240
Romeoville *(G-17806)*
Coleman Cable LLC .... D 847 672-2300
Lincolnshire *(G-12753)*
Colt Technology Services LLC .... F 312 465-2484
Chicago *(G-4205)*
Commscope Inc North Carolina .... C 779 435-6000
Joliet *(G-11843)*
Commscope Connectivity LLC .... F 779 435-6000
Joliet *(G-11844)*
Commscope Solutions Intl Inc .... G 828 324-2200
Westchester *(G-20695)*
Commscope Technologies LLC .... B 779 435-6000
Joliet *(G-11845)*
Commscope Technologies LLC .... G 847 397-6307
Schaumburg *(G-18481)*
Community Advantage Network .... G 847 376-8943
Des Plaines *(G-7748)*
▲ **Conquest Sound Inc** .... F 708 534-0309
Manteno *(G-13445)*
▲ **Crescend Technologies LLC** .... E 847 908-5400
Schaumburg *(G-18494)*
D W Ram Manufacturing Co .... E 708 633-7900
Tinley Park *(G-19821)*
Driver Services .... G 505 267-8686
Bensenville *(G-1789)*
Dtv Innovations LLC .... F 847 919-3550
Elgin *(G-8571)*
Easy Trac Gps Inc .... G 630 359-5804
Chicago *(G-4436)*
Ed Co .... E 708 614-0695
Tinley Park *(G-19822)*
▼ **Elite Rf LLC** .... E 847 592-6350
Hoffman Estates *(G-11420)*
▲ **Evanston Graphic Imaging Inc** .... G 847 869-7446
Evanston *(G-9516)*
Forest City Satellite .... G 815 639-0500
Davis Junction *(G-7422)*
Fred Kennerly .... G 815 398-6861
Rockford *(G-17424)*
FSI Technologies Inc .... E 630 932-9380
Lombard *(G-13080)*
Gatesair Inc .... C 800 622-0022
Quincy *(G-16886)*
Gogo Intermediate Holdings LLC .... G 630 647-1400
Chicago *(G-4710)*
Gogo LLC .... D 630 647-1400
Bensenville *(G-1813)*
Gogo LLC .... B 630 647-1400
Chicago *(G-4711)*
◆ **Heico Companies LLC** .... F 312 419-8220
Chicago *(G-4798)*
▲ **Heil Sound Ltd** .... F 618 257-3000
Fairview Heights *(G-9646)*
Hi-Def Communications .... G 217 258-6679
Mattoon *(G-13637)*
Huawei Technologies USA Inc .... G 425 463-8275
Rolling Meadows *(G-17735)*
Iheartcommunications Inc .... E 312 255-5100
Chicago *(G-4882)*
▲ **Inclusion Solutions LLC** .... G 847 869-2500
Evanston *(G-9537)*
Innovative AV Systems Inc .... G 312 265-6282
Elmhurst *(G-9379)*
Invisio Communications Inc .... G 412 327-6578
Chicago *(G-4965)*
Isco International Inc .... G 630 283-3100
Schaumburg *(G-18572)*
Jai-S Record Label .... G 708 351-4279
Park Forest *(G-16256)*
Jklein Enterprises Inc .... G 618 664-4554
Greenville *(G-10836)*
Kokes Kid Zone .... G 217 483-4615
Chatham *(G-3423)*
Kvh Industries Inc .... E 708 444-2800
Tinley Park *(G-19843)*
L3 Technologies Inc .... F 212 697-1111
Rolling Meadows *(G-17747)*
Langham Engineering .... G 815 223-5250
Peru *(G-16580)*
▲ **Las Systems Inc** .... E 847 462-8100
Woodstock *(G-21404)*
Latino Arts & Communications .... G 773 501-0029
Chicago *(G-5180)*
◆ **Lemko Corporation** .... E 630 948-3025
Schaumburg *(G-18603)*
LL Electronics .... G 217 586-6477
Mahomet *(G-13425)*
Locusview Solutions Inc .... E 312 548-3848
Chicago *(G-5248)*
Meshplusplus Inc .... G 847 494-6325
Chicago *(G-5402)*
Metro Service Center .... G 618 524-8583
Metropolis *(G-13973)*
Motorola Intl Dev Corp .... E 847 576-5000
Schaumburg *(G-18635)*
▲ **Motorola Mobility Holdings LLC** .... F 800 668-6765
Chicago *(G-5508)*
Motorola Mobility LLC .... F 847 576-5000
Chicago *(G-5509)*
▲ **Motorola Mobility LLC** .... B 847 523-5000
Chicago *(G-5510)*
Motorola Solutions Inc .... C 847 576-5000
Chicago *(G-5511)*
Motorola Solutions Inc .... G 847 341-3485
Oak Brook *(G-15647)*
Motorola Solutions Inc .... G 217 894-6451
Clayton *(G-6910)*
Motorola Solutions Inc .... E 847 523-5000
Libertyville *(G-12683)*
Motorola Solutions Inc .... C 630 308-9394
Schaumburg *(G-18636)*
Motorola Solutions Inc .... G 630 353-8000
Downers Grove *(G-8061)*
Motorola Solutions Inc .... G 847 523-5000
Libertyville *(G-12684)*
Motorola Solutions Inc .... C 847 540-8815
Arlington Heights *(G-779)*
Motorola Solutions Inc .... G 847 523-5000
Libertyville *(G-12685)*
Motorola Solutions Inc .... C 708 476-8226
Schaumburg *(G-18638)*
Motorola Solutions Inc .... C 800 331-6456
Schaumburg *(G-18639)*
Motorola Solutions Inc .... C 847 576-5000
Elgin *(G-8665)*
Motorola Solutions Inc .... C 847 576-8600
Schaumburg *(G-18637)*
Northern Information Tech .... F 800 528-4343
Rolling Meadows *(G-17754)*
Northrop Grumman Systems Corp .... A 847 259-9600
Rolling Meadows *(G-17755)*
Nucurrent Inc .... F 312 575-0388
Chicago *(G-5640)*
▲ **Omni Vision Inc** .... E 630 893-1720
Glendale Heights *(G-10481)*
Othernet Inc .... G 773 688-4320
Long Grove *(G-13168)*
Pc-Tel Inc .... C 630 372-6800
Bloomingdale *(G-2008)*
Portable Cmmnctons Spclsts .... G 630 458-1800
Addison *(G-246)*
Prime Time Sports LLC .... F 847 637-3500
Arlington Heights *(G-790)*
Progressive Concepts .... G 630 736-9822
Streamwood *(G-19590)*
Qaboss Partners .... B 312 203-4290
Chicago *(G-5922)*
Radio Frequency Systems Inc .... E 800 321-4700
Naperville *(G-14906)*
Ram Systems & Communication .... G 847 487-7575
McHenry *(G-13785)*
Research In Motion Rf Inc .... G 815 444-1095
Crystal Lake *(G-7255)*
Ruckus Wireless Inc .... E 630 281-3000
Lisle *(G-12935)*
Safemobile Inc .... F 847 818-1649
Rolling Meadows *(G-17772)*
Saga Communications Inc .... G 248 631-8099
Springfield *(G-19438)*
Skybitz Tank Monitoring Corp .... E 312 379-8397
Chicago *(G-6183)*
▲ **Spectrum Cos International** .... G 630 879-8008
Batavia *(G-1418)*
State of Illinois .... C 312 836-9500
Chicago *(G-6235)*
▼ **STC Inc** .... E 618 643-2555
Mc Leansboro *(G-13708)*
Studio Technologies Inc .... F 847 676-9177
Skokie *(G-19038)*
Sure-Response Inc .... G 888 530-5668
Carbondale *(G-2861)*
▲ **Switchcraft Inc** .... B 773 792-2700
Chicago *(G-6299)*
▲ **Switchcraft Holdco Inc** .... G 773 792-2700
Chicago *(G-6300)*
T-Mobile Usa Inc .... F 847 289-9988
South Elgin *(G-19176)*
Talk-A-Phone LLC .... D 773 539-1100
Niles *(G-15178)*
▲ **Telular Corporation** .... D 800 835-8527
Chicago *(G-6341)*
Temco Japan Co Ltd .... G 847 359-3277
South Barrington *(G-19078)*
▲ **Tribeam Inc** .... G 847 409-9497
Arlington Heights *(G-821)*
Twr3 Inc .... G 847 784-5251
Northfield *(G-15536)*
Vincor Ltd .... F 708 534-0008
Monee *(G-14211)*
▼ **Visiplex Inc** .... F 847 229-0250
Buffalo Grove *(G-2618)*

S I C

Employee Codes: A=Over 500 employees, B=251-500
C=101-250, D=51-100, E=20-50, F=10-19, G=3-9

36 ELECTRONIC AND OTHER ELECTRICAL EQUIPMENT AND COMPONENTS, EXCEPT COMPUTER SIC SECTION

Winston Privacy Inc..............G....... 312 282-0162
Chicago *(G-6647)*
▲ **Wireless Chamberlain Products**.......E....... 800 282-6225
Elmhurst *(G-9446)*
▲ **Xentris Wireless LLC**..............D....... 844 936-8747
Addison *(G-339)*
▲ **Zenith Electronics Corporation**........E....... 847 941-8000
Lincolnshire *(G-12806)*

3669 Communications Eqpt, NEC

Ademco Inc..............G....... 708 599-1390
Bridgeview *(G-2319)*
Ademco Inc..............E....... 847 472-2900
Elk Grove Village *(G-8807)*
Aimtron Systems LLC..............E....... 262 947-8400
Palatine *(G-16092)*
All Tech Systems & Install..............G....... 815 609-0685
Plainfield *(G-16641)*
AR Concepts USA Inc..............G....... 847 392-4608
Palatine *(G-16093)*
AVI-Spl Employee..............B....... 847 437-7712
Schaumburg *(G-18453)*
◆ **Brk Brands Inc**..............C....... 630 851-7330
Aurora *(G-927)*
Buell Manufacturing Company..............G....... 708 447-6320
Lyons *(G-13304)*
Data Comm For Business Inc..............F....... 217 897-1741
Dewey *(G-7873)*
Extentel Wrless Communications.........G....... 847 809-3131
Inverness *(G-11595)*
◆ **Federal Signal Corporation**..............D....... 630 954-2000
Oak Brook *(G-15618)*
◆ **First Alert Inc**..............C....... 630 499-3295
Aurora *(G-962)*
Global Fire Control Inc..............G....... 309 755-6352
East Moline *(G-8227)*
Gretta Transportation Inc..............E....... 252 202-7714
Westmont *(G-20743)*
▲ **Harrington Signal Inc**..............E....... 309 762-0731
Moline *(G-14148)*
▲ **Jeron Electronic Systems Inc**..........D....... 773 275-1900
Niles *(G-15136)*
John Thomas Inc..............E....... 815 288-2343
Dixon *(G-7902)*
Km Enterprises Inc..............F....... 618 204-0888
Mount Vernon *(G-14620)*
Lares Technologies LLC..............G....... 630 408-4368
Oswego *(G-16010)*
▲ **Lecip Inc**..............F....... 312 626-2525
Bensenville *(G-1842)*
Legrand AV Inc..............G....... 719 661-8134
Chicago *(G-5203)*
Lumentum Operations LLC..............G....... 408 546-5483
Chicago *(G-5282)*
▼ **Lund Industries Inc**..............E....... 847 459-1460
Northbrook *(G-15424)*
▲ **Marine Technologies Inc**..............E....... 847 546-9001
Volo *(G-20203)*
McC Technology Inc..............F....... 630 377-7200
Saint Charles *(G-18231)*
▲ **Minelab Americas Inc**..............F....... 630 401-8150
Naperville *(G-14871)*
Mobotrex Inc..............G....... 847 546-1616
Volo *(G-20204)*
N E S Traffic Safety..............F....... 312 603-7444
Chicago *(G-5533)*
Nafisco Inc..............F....... 815 372-3300
Romeoville *(G-17858)*
Neovision Usa Inc..............F....... 847 533-0541
Deer Park *(G-7582)*
◆ **North American Signal Co**..............E....... 847 537-8888
Wheeling *(G-20945)*
▲ **Pacific Custom Components Corp**...F....... 815 206-5450
Woodstock *(G-21419)*
▲ **Procomm Inc Hoopeston Illinois**......E....... 815 268-4303
Onarga *(G-15902)*
Quality Service & Installation..............G....... 847 352-4000
Schaumburg *(G-18693)*
Regional Emergency Dispatch..............F....... 847 498-5748
Northbrook *(G-15471)*
▲ **RF Technologies Inc**..............E....... 618 377-2654
Buffalo Grove *(G-2592)*
Securecom Inc..............G....... 219 314-4537
Lansing *(G-12515)*
Siemens Industry Inc..............D....... 630 444-4316
Saint Charles *(G-18269)*
◆ **Siemens Industry Inc**..............A....... 847 215-1000
Buffalo Grove *(G-2600)*
Signalmasters Inc..............F....... 708 534-3330
Monee *(G-14208)*
Stenograph LLC..............D....... 630 532-5100
Elmhurst *(G-9429)*
▲ **Telular Corporation**..............D....... 800 835-8527
Chicago *(G-6341)*
Tool Automation Enterprises..............G....... 708 799-6847
East Hazel Crest *(G-8218)*
▲ **Track Group Inc**..............E....... 877 260-2010
Naperville *(G-14936)*
Traffco Products LLC..............G....... 773 374-6645
Chicago *(G-6404)*
▲ **Tri-Lite Inc**..............E....... 773 384-7765
Chicago *(G-6422)*
Western Remac Inc..............E....... 630 972-7770
Woodridge *(G-21347)*
Western-Cullen-Hayes Inc..............D....... 773 254-9600
Chicago *(G-6609)*
▲ **Wireless Chamberlain Products**.......E....... 800 282-6225
Elmhurst *(G-9446)*
Xomi Instruments Co Ltd..............G....... 847 660-4614
Vernon Hills *(G-20113)*

3671 Radio & T V Receiving Electron Tubes

Dcx-Chol Enterprises Inc..............E....... 309 353-4455
Pekin *(G-16327)*
F & L Electronics LLC..............F....... 217 586-2132
Mahomet *(G-13423)*
▲ **Futaba Corporation of America**........F....... 847 884-1444
Schaumburg *(G-18532)*
King S Court Exterior..............G....... 630 904-4305
Naperville *(G-14976)*
Light of Mine LLC..............G....... 312 840-8570
Chicago *(G-5220)*
Northrop Grumman Systems Corp.......A....... 847 259-9600
Rolling Meadows *(G-17755)*
Rcl Electronics..............G....... 630 834-0156
Addison *(G-268)*
◆ **Richardson Electronics Ltd**..............C....... 630 208-2200
Lafox *(G-12138)*
Starfire Industries LLC..............E....... 217 721-4165
Champaign *(G-3356)*
Thomas Electronics Inc..............E....... 315 923-2051
Addison *(G-307)*
▲ **Zenith Electronics Corporation**........E....... 847 941-8000
Lincolnshire *(G-12806)*

3672 Printed Circuit Boards

Accelerated Assemblies Inc..............E....... 630 616-6680
Elk Grove Village *(G-8798)*
Accutrace Inc..............F....... 847 290-9900
Elk Grove Village *(G-8801)*
▲ **Advanced Electronics Inc**..............D....... 630 293-3300
West Chicago *(G-20531)*
▲ **Aerotronic Controls Co**..............F....... 847 228-6504
Chicago *(G-3575)*
Allfavor Technologies Inc..............G....... 630 913-4263
Schaumburg *(G-18432)*
◆ **Alpha Circuit Corporation**..............E....... 630 617-5555
Elmhurst *(G-9325)*
▲ **Alpha Pcb Designs Inc**..............G....... 773 631-5543
Chicago *(G-3631)*
American Circuit Services Inc..............G....... 847 895-0500
Elk Grove Village *(G-8822)*
American Circuit Systems Inc..............E....... 630 543-4450
Addison *(G-30)*
American Controls & Automation.........G....... 630 293-8841
West Chicago *(G-20537)*
◆ **American Precision Elec Inc**..............D....... 630 510-8080
Carol Stream *(G-2936)*
American Progressive Circuits..............E....... 630 495-6900
Addison *(G-34)*
▲ **American Standard Circuits Inc**........C....... 630 639-5444
West Chicago *(G-20539)*
▲ **Amitron Inc**..............C....... 847 290-9800
Elk Grove Village *(G-8828)*
Ampel Incorporated..............E....... 847 952-1900
Elk Grove Village *(G-8829)*
Answer Call..............G....... 773 573-6369
Chicago *(G-3703)*
▲ **ARC-Tronics Inc**..............C....... 847 437-0211
Elk Grove Village *(G-8837)*
Asg-Uniaero..............G....... 773 941-5053
Dolton *(G-7930)*
Astral Power Systems Inc..............G....... 630 518-1741
Aurora *(G-1055)*
▲ **Aurora Circuits Inc**..............D....... 630 978-3830
Aurora *(G-915)*
▼ **Aurora Circuits LLC**..............D....... 630 978-3830
Aurora *(G-916)*
Bandjwet Enterprises Inc..............G....... 847 797-9250
Rolling Meadows *(G-17716)*
Bandjwet Enterprises Inc..............E....... 847 797-9250
Rolling Meadows *(G-17717)*
Bartec Orb Inc..............E....... 773 927-8600
Chicago *(G-3843)*
Benchmark Electronics Inc..............B....... 309 822-8587
Metamora *(G-13959)*
Bestproto Inc..............F....... 224 387-3280
South Elgin *(G-19138)*
Bishop Engineering Company..............F....... 630 305-9538
Lisle *(G-12872)*
Brigitflex Inc..............F....... 847 741-1452
Elgin *(G-8524)*
Camtek Inc..............D....... 309 661-0348
Bloomington *(G-2029)*
▲ **Cck Automations Inc**..............E....... 217 243-6040
Jacksonville *(G-11761)*
Chicago Circuits Corporation..............F....... 847 238-1623
Elk Grove Village *(G-8891)*
Circom Inc..............E....... 630 595-4460
Bensenville *(G-1770)*
▲ **Circuit Engineering LLC**..............E....... 847 806-7777
Elk Grove Village *(G-8899)*
▲ **Circuit Works Corporation**..............D....... 847 283-8600
Waukegan *(G-20428)*
▲ **Circuit World Inc**..............E....... 630 250-1100
Itasca *(G-11637)*
Circuitronics..............E....... 630 668-5407
Elgin *(G-8540)*
Creative Hi-Tech Ltd..............E....... 224 653-4000
Schaumburg *(G-18492)*
Daves Electronic Service..............F....... 217 283-5010
Hoopeston *(G-11507)*
Delta Circuits Inc..............E....... 630 876-0691
West Chicago *(G-20569)*
▲ **Delta Precision Circuits Inc**..............E....... 847 758-8000
Elk Grove Village *(G-8943)*
Eagle Capital Group Inc..............D....... 847 891-5800
Schaumburg *(G-18512)*
Ecmc Inc..............E....... 847 352-5015
Schaumburg *(G-18514)*
Edgo Technical Sales Inc..............G....... 630 961-8398
Naperville *(G-14965)*
Elcon Inc..............E....... 815 467-9500
Minooka *(G-14059)*
Electro-Circuits Inc..............E....... 630 339-3389
Schaumburg *(G-18516)*
Electronic Design & Mfg Inc..............D....... 847 550-1912
Lake Zurich *(G-12406)*
Electronic Interconnect Corp..............D....... 847 364-4848
Elk Grove Village *(G-8971)*
Electronic Resources Corp..............G....... 331 225-3450
Addison *(G-112)*
▲ **Emerge Technology Group LLC**......G....... 224 603-2161
Lake Villa *(G-12350)*
Excel Electro Assembly Inc..............F....... 847 621-2500
Elk Grove Village *(G-8986)*
▲ **Excell Electronics Corporation**.........E....... 847 766-7455
Elk Grove Village *(G-8988)*
◆ **Fine Circuits Inc**..............F....... 630 213-8700
Bartlett *(G-1280)*
▲ **Galaxy Circuits Inc**..............E....... 630 462-1010
Carol Stream *(G-2989)*
General Electro Corporation..............F....... 630 595-8989
Bensenville *(G-1810)*
Get A Quote For Your Pcb..............G....... 847 952-1900
Elk Grove Village *(G-9014)*
Hytel Group Inc..............E....... 847 683-9800
Hampshire *(G-10974)*
Illinois Tool Works Inc..............E....... 630 825-7900
Glendale Heights *(G-10460)*
Image Circuit Inc..............G....... 847 622-3300
Elk Grove Village *(G-9045)*
Imagineering Inc..............E....... 847 806-0003
Elk Grove Village *(G-9047)*
▲ **International Control Svcs Inc**..........C....... 217 422-6700
Decatur *(G-7508)*
Intratek Inc..............G....... 847 640-0007
Elk Grove Village *(G-9059)*
Journey Circuits Inc..............G....... 630 283-0604
Schaumburg *(G-18579)*
▲ **K Trox Sales Inc**..............G....... 815 568-1521
Marengo *(G-13487)*
Kay & Cee..............G....... 773 425-9169
Calumet Park *(G-2798)*
King Circuit..............E....... 630 629-7300
Schaumburg *(G-18586)*
Landmeier Corp..............G....... 847 709-2823
Elk Grove Village *(G-9083)*
Light of Mine LLC..............G....... 312 840-8570
Chicago *(G-5220)*

36 ELECTRONIC AND OTHER ELECTRICAL EQUIPMENT AND COMPONENTS, EXCEPT COMPUTER

M-Wave Controls LLC ..... E 630 562-5550
  Glendale Heights (G-10470)
▲ M-Wave International LLC ..... E 630 562-5550
  Glendale Heights (G-10471)
Manu Industries Inc ..... F 847 891-6412
  Schaumburg (G-18618)
Manu-TEC of Illinois LLC ..... F 630 543-3022
  Addison (G-191)
▲ Mega Circuit Inc ..... D 630 543-8460
  Addison (G-196)
Mektronix Technology Inc ..... G 847 680-3300
  Libertyville (G-12677)
Methode Development Co ..... D 708 867-6777
  Chicago (G-5408)
◆ Methode Electronics Inc ..... B 708 867-6777
  Chicago (G-5409)
Meyer Electronic Mfg Svcs Inc ..... G 309 808-4100
  Normal (G-15209)
Michele Terrell ..... G 312 305-0876
  Evanston (G-9551)
Micro Circuit Inc ..... F 630 628-5760
  Addison (G-205)
Microsun Electronics Corp ..... F 630 410-7900
  Woodridge (G-21323)
Milplex Circuits Inc ..... E 630 250-1580
  Addison (G-217)
Milplex Electronics Inc ..... E 630 250-1580
  Addison (G-218)
Mr Rakesh Avichal ..... G 224 735-0505
  Elk Grove Village (G-9136)
◆ National Technology Inc ..... E 847 506-1300
  Rolling Meadows (G-17752)
Ncab Group Usa Inc ..... F 630 562-5550
  Itasca (G-11709)
▲ Novatronix Inc ..... G 847 860-4300
  Wood Dale (G-21223)
Online Electronics Inc ..... E 847 871-1700
  Elk Grove Village (G-9164)
▲ Paramount Laminates Inc ..... G 630 594-1840
  Wood Dale (G-21227)
Parth Consultants Inc ..... E 847 758-1400
  Schaumburg (G-18667)
▲ Patriot Materials LLC ..... G 630 501-0260
  Elmhurst (G-9409)
Pcb Express Inc ..... G 847 952-8896
  Elk Grove Village (G-9171)
Plexus Corp ..... B 847 793-4400
  Buffalo Grove (G-2587)
Price Circuits LLC ..... E 847 742-4700
  Elgin (G-8694)
Printing Circuit Boards ..... F 630 543-3453
  Addison (G-255)
▲ Qcircuits Inc ..... D 847 797-6678
  Elk Grove Village (G-9203)
Qcircuits Inc ..... E 618 662-8365
  Flora (G-9690)
Quality Surface Mount Inc ..... E 630 350-8556
  Wood Dale (G-21233)
Rw Technologies US LLC ..... F 815 444-6887
  Crystal Lake (G-7259)
Siemens Manufacturing Co Inc ..... C 618 539-3000
  Freeburg (G-10094)
Siemens Manufacturing Co Inc ..... C 618 475-3325
  New Athens (G-15021)
Sigmatron International Inc ..... G 847 586-5200
  Elgin (G-8730)
▲ Sigmatron International Inc ..... G 847 956-8000
  Elk Grove Village (G-9238)
▲ Sparton Corporation ..... B 847 762-5800
  Schaumburg (G-18717)
Sparton Design Services LLC ..... G 847 762-5800
  Schaumburg (G-18718)
Sparton Parent Inc ..... G 847 762-5800
  Schaumburg (G-18721)
Srr Manufacturing Services ..... G 847 404-3527
  Gilberts (G-10372)
▲ Sunrise Electronics Inc ..... E 847 357-0500
  Elk Grove Village (G-9260)
▲ Surya Electronics Inc ..... C 630 858-0000
  Glendale Heights (G-10507)
Taranda Specialties Inc ..... G 815 469-3041
  Frankfort (G-9844)
▲ Tecnova Electronics Inc ..... D 847 336-6160
  Waukegan (G-20502)
▲ The Syntek Group Inc ..... G 773 279-0131
  Chicago (G-6360)
Triad Circuits Inc ..... E 847 283-8600
  Waukegan (G-20510)
Twisted Traces Inc ..... G 630 345-5400
  Elk Grove Village (G-9289)

▲ United Electronics Corp Inc ..... D 847 671-6034
  Franklin Park (G-10069)
Universal Scientific Ill Inc ..... E 847 228-6464
  Chicago (G-6483)
Wand Enterprises Inc ..... F 847 433-0231
  Highland Park (G-11304)
▲ Y 2 K Electronics Inc ..... F 847 238-9024
  Elk Grove Village (G-9315)

3674 Semiconductors

Accelerated Assemblies Inc ..... E 630 616-6680
  Elk Grove Village (G-8798)
Akhan Semiconductor Inc ..... G 847 855-8400
  Gurnee (G-10856)
Altera Corporation ..... G 847 240-0313
  Schaumburg (G-18435)
Amoco Technology Company ..... C 312 861-6000
  Chicago (G-3682)
Analog Devices Inc ..... G 847 519-3669
  Schaumburg (G-18439)
Angela Yang Chingjui ..... G 630 724-0596
  Darien (G-7401)
▲ B+b Smartworx Inc ..... D 815 433-5100
  Ottawa (G-16041)
Bare Development Inc ..... F 708 352-2273
  Countryside (G-7044)
Bold Renewables Holdings LLC ..... G 541 312-3832
  Chicago (G-3931)
▲ BP Solar International Inc ..... A 301 698-4200
  Naperville (G-14785)
Broadcom Corporation ..... G 773 965-1600
  Lake Barrington (G-12142)
Brocade Cmmnctions Systems LLC ..... F 630 273-5530
  Schaumburg (G-18465)
▲ Capsonic Automotive Inc ..... F 847 888-7300
  Elgin (G-8530)
Chicago Pixels SRC ..... G 312 513-7949
  Chicago (G-4123)
Coinstar Procurement LLC ..... G 630 424-4788
  Oakbrook Terrace (G-15794)
Convergent Bill Ete Ort T ..... G 847 387-4059
  Hoffman Estates (G-11416)
Csi2d Inc ..... G 312 282-7407
  Hoffman Estates (G-11472)
◆ CTS Automotive LLC ..... G 630 577-8800
  Lisle (G-12880)
▲ CTS Corporation ..... G 630 577-8800
  Lisle (G-12881)
▲ Dauber Company Inc ..... E 815 442-3569
  Tonica (G-19888)
Digital Optics Tech Inc ..... G 847 358-2592
  Rolling Meadows (G-17727)
◆ Dover Corporation ..... G 630 541-1540
  Downers Grove (G-7989)
Drs Ntwork Imaging Systems LLC ..... E 214 215-5960
  Bolingbrook (G-2169)
Dynawave Corporation ..... F 630 232-4945
  Geneva (G-10267)
Effimax Solar ..... G 217 550-2422
  Champaign (G-3288)
Epir Inc ..... G 630 842-4486
  Bolingbrook (G-2174)
Epir Technologies Inc ..... E 630 771-0203
  Bolingbrook (G-2175)
▲ Epiworks Inc ..... D 217 373-1590
  Champaign (G-3291)
FSI Technologies Inc ..... E 630 932-9380
  Lombard (G-13080)
GBA Systems Integrators LLC ..... G 913 492-0400
  Moline (G-14147)
General Lattice Inc ..... G 312 374-3158
  Chicago (G-4671)
▲ General Products International ..... E 847 458-6357
  Lake In The Hills (G-12335)
Hologram Inc ..... G 716 771-8308
  Chicago (G-4831)
Hytel Group Inc ..... E 847 683-9800
  Hampshire (G-10974)
Inland Tech Holdings LLC ..... E 618 476-7678
  Millstadt (G-14048)
Integrated Lighting Tech Inc ..... G 630 750-3786
  Bolingbrook (G-2193)
Intel Corporation ..... F 408 765-8080
  Chicago (G-4941)
Intel East ..... G 312 725-2014
  Mount Prospect (G-14536)
Intelligent SCM LLC ..... G 630 625-7229
  Wood Dale (G-21202)
▼ Interplex Daystar Inc ..... D 847 455-2424
  Franklin Park (G-9966)

Ipr Systems Inc ..... G 708 385-7500
  Alsip (G-458)
JAD Group Inc ..... G 847 223-1804
  Grayslake (G-10785)
Jql Technologies Corporation ..... F 800 236-9828
  Mundelein (G-14705)
Laird Connectivity Inc ..... G 847 839-6000
  Schaumburg (G-18596)
LED Rite LLC ..... G 847 683-8000
  Hampshire (G-10977)
Linear Technology LLC ..... G 847 925-0860
  Schaumburg (G-18607)
▲ Luminaid Lab LLC ..... G 312 600-8997
  Chicago (G-5284)
Lynk Labs Inc ..... G 847 783-0123
  Elgin (G-8643)
◆ Methode Electronics Inc ..... B 708 867-6777
  Chicago (G-5409)
Microchip Technology Inc ..... E 630 285-0071
  Itasca (G-11701)
Microlink Devices Inc ..... D 847 588-3001
  Niles (G-15146)
Micron Technology Inc ..... G 208 368-4000
  Chicago (G-5425)
Motorola International Capital ..... G 847 576-5000
  Schaumburg (G-18634)
Motorola Solutions Inc ..... C 847 576-8600
  Schaumburg (G-18637)
Motorola Solutions Inc ..... G 847 341-3485
  Oak Brook (G-15647)
New Vision Display ..... G 224 268-3345
  Elgin (G-8667)
Nhanced Semiconductors Inc ..... F 408 759-4060
  Naperville (G-14884)
Nxp Usa Inc ..... B 847 843-6824
  Hoffman Estates (G-11441)
Plug Power Inc Ctc ..... G 518 782-7700
  Romeoville (G-17863)
Seasonal Magnets ..... G 708 499-3235
  Evergreen Park (G-9600)
Shakthi Solar Inc ..... G 630 842-0893
  Bolingbrook (G-2238)
Sigenics Inc ..... F 312 448-8000
  Chicago (G-6164)
Smart Controls LLC ..... G 618 394-0300
  Fairview Heights (G-9648)
▲ Solid State Luminaires LLC ..... G 877 775-4733
  Saint Charles (G-18272)
Sparton Design Services LLC ..... G 847 762-5800
  Schaumburg (G-18718)
Sparton Emt LLC ..... G 800 772-7866
  Schaumburg (G-18719)
Sparton Parent Inc ..... G 847 762-5800
  Schaumburg (G-18721)
Tagore Technology Inc ..... F 847 790-3799
  Arlington Heights (G-816)
Tech Oasis International Inc ..... F 847 302-1590
  Gurnee (G-10934)
Telehealth Sensors LLC ..... E 630 879-3101
  North Aurora (G-15279)
▲ Tempro International Corp ..... G 847 677-5370
  Skokie (G-19044)
Tezzaron Semiconductor Corp ..... C 630 505-0404
  Naperville (G-14931)
Toshiba America Electronic ..... G 847 484-2400
  Buffalo Grove (G-2613)
▲ Touchsensor Technologies LLC ..... B 630 221-9000
  Wheaton (G-20829)
Value Engineered Products ..... E 708 867-6777
  Rolling Meadows (G-17784)
Vega Wave Systems Inc ..... G 630 562-9433
  West Chicago (G-20657)
Wilmar Group LLC ..... G 847 421-6595
  Lake Forest (G-12322)
Xelerated Inc ..... G 408 222-2500
  Chicago (G-6692)
Xtremedata Inc ..... E 847 871-0379
  Schaumburg (G-18778)
Xylem Lnc ..... G 847 966-3700
  Morton Grove (G-14451)
Yash Technologies Inc ..... E 309 755-0433
  East Moline (G-8248)
▲ Zenith Electronics Corporation ..... E 847 941-8000
  Lincolnshire (G-12806)

3675 Electronic Capacitors

10g LLC ..... F 630 754-2400
  Woodridge (G-21269)
Aisin Light Metals LLC ..... G 618 997-9800
  Marion (G-13500)

Employee Codes: A=Over 500 employees, B=251-500
C=101-250, D=51-100, E=20-50, F=10-19, G=3-9

36 ELECTRONIC AND OTHER ELECTRICAL EQUIPMENT AND COMPONENTS, EXCEPT COMPUTER

Bycap Inc .... E 773 561-4976
　Chicago (G-3988)
Illinois Capacitor Inc .... B 847 675-1760
　Des Plaines (G-7783)
▲ Jbsmwg Corp .... F 847 675-1865
　Lincolnwood (G-12824)
Knowles Corporation .... C 630 250-5100
　Itasca (G-11686)
Knowles Corporation .... E 630 250-5100
　Itasca (G-11685)
▲ Motor Capacitors Inc .... F 773 774-6666
　Wood Dale (G-21217)
Murata Electronics N Amer Inc .... G 847 330-9200
　Schaumburg (G-18641)
Standard Condenser Corporation ..... F 847 965-2722
　Morton Grove (G-14441)
▲ United Chemi-Con Inc .... E 847 696-2000
　Rolling Meadows (G-17783)

3676 Electronic Resistors

▲ CTS Corporation .... C 630 577-8800
　Lisle (G-12881)
Elematec USA Corporation .... G 858 527-1700
　Itasca (G-11647)
Maurey Instrument Corp .... F 708 388-9898
　Alsip (G-474)
◆ Methode Electronics Inc .... B 708 867-6777
　Chicago (G-5409)
◆ Mpc Products Corporation .... A 847 673-8300
　Niles (G-15149)
Voltronics Inc .... F 773 625-1779
　Chicago (G-6568)

3677 Electronic Coils & Transformers

▲ Altran Corp .... E 815 455-5650
　Crystal Lake (G-7158)
▲ Arnold Engineering Co .... D 815 568-2000
　Marengo (G-13479)
AT&T Corp .... F 312 602-4108
　Chicago (G-3755)
Barnes International Inc .... C 815 964-8661
　Rockford (G-17312)
▲ Becker Specialty Corporation .... E 847 766-3555
　Elk Grove Village (G-8860)
Blocksmoy Inc .... F 847 260-9070
　Franklin Park (G-9889)
Cemec Inc .... G 630 495-9696
　Downers Grove (G-7966)
◆ Charles Industries LLC .... D 847 806-6300
　Schaumburg (G-18474)
Charles Industries LLC .... D 217 826-2318
　Marshall (G-13566)
Coilcraft Incorporated .... D 815 288-7051
　Oregon (G-15915)
Coilform Company .... E 630 232-8000
　Geneva (G-10262)
Communication Coil Inc .... D 847 671-1333
　Schiller Park (G-18795)
Daly Engineered Filtration Inc .... G 708 355-1550
　Naperville (G-14813)
Datasource .... G 312 405-9152
　Calumet City (G-2774)
Eis .... G 630 530-7500
　Elmhurst (G-9359)
Erbeck One Chem & Lab Sup Inc ... G 312 203-0078
　Manhattan (G-13432)
Forest Electric Company .... E 708 681-0180
　Melrose Park (G-13868)
Gsg Industries .... F 618 544-7976
　Robinson (G-17115)
▲ Induction Innovations Inc .... G 847 836-6933
　Elgin (G-8625)
▲ Inglot Electronics Corp .... D 773 286-5881
　Chicago (G-4921)
Ipr Systems Inc .... G 708 385-7500
　Alsip (G-458)
▲ Lenco Electronics Inc .... E 815 344-2900
　McHenry (G-13756)
Magnetic Coil Manufacturing Co ..... E 630 787-1948
　Wood Dale (G-21212)
Magnetic Devices Inc .... G 815 459-0077
　Crystal Lake (G-7222)
MEI Realty Ltd .... E 847 358-5000
　Inverness (G-11597)
Michele Terrell .... G 312 305-0876
　Evanston (G-9551)
◆ Muntz Industries Inc .... E 847 949-8280
　Mundelein (G-14718)
Nelco Coil Supply Company .... E 847 259-7517
　Mount Prospect (G-14550)

◆ Netcom Inc .... C 847 537-6300
　Wheeling (G-20943)
North Point Investments Inc .... G 312 977-4386
　Chicago (G-5620)
◆ Olympic Controls Corp .... E 847 742-3566
　Elgin (G-8678)
◆ Perma-Pipe Intl Holdings Inc .... E 847 966-1000
　Niles (G-15158)
Pnc Inc .... D 815 946-2328
　Polo (G-16758)
◆ Power House Tool Inc .... E 815 727-6301
　Joliet (G-11915)
◆ Power-Volt Inc .... D 630 628-9999
　Addison (G-249)
◆ Qcircuits Inc .... E 847 797-6678
　Elk Grove Village (G-9203)
Qcircuits Inc .... E 618 662-8365
　Flora (G-9690)
◆ Qse Inc .... E 815 432-5281
　Watseka (G-20315)
Sam Electronics Worldwide Inc .... F 847 290-1720
　Rolling Meadows (G-17773)
Santucci Enterprises .... G 773 286-5629
　Chicago (G-6102)
◆ Schumacher Electric Corp .... D 847 385-1600
　Mount Prospect (G-14569)
Sigmatron International Inc .... G 847 586-5200
　Elgin (G-8730)
▲ Sigmatron International Inc .... G 847 956-8000
　Elk Grove Village (G-9238)
Starfire Industries LLC .... E 217 721-4165
　Champaign (G-3356)
▼ STC Inc .... E 618 643-2555
　Mc Leansboro (G-13708)
Stryde Technologies Inc .... E 510 786-8890
　Chicago (G-6255)
Taycorp Inc .... E 630 530-7500
　Elmhurst (G-9433)
▲ Taycorp Inc .... E 708 629-0921
　Alsip (G-514)
Te Connectivity Corporation .... D 847 680-7400
　Mundelein (G-14742)
▲ Transformer Manufacturers Inc .... E 708 457-1200
　Norridge (G-15245)
U S Co-Tronics Corp .... E 815 692-3204
　Fairbury (G-9615)
▲ V and F Transformer Corp .... D 630 497-8070
　Elgin (G-8771)
◆ Wattcore Inc .... G 571 482-6777
　Morton Grove (G-14448)

3678 Electronic Connectors

▲ Advantage Components Inc .... E 815 725-8644
　Joliet (G-11817)
▲ Aiwa Corporation .... G 305 394-4119
　Chicago (G-3591)
Amphenol Corporation .... D 800 944-6446
　Lisle (G-12863)
Amphenol Corporation .... G 847 478-5600
　Lincolnshire (G-12745)
▲ Amphenol Fiber Optic Products .... E 630 960-1010
　Lisle (G-12864)
Belden Energy Solutions Inc .... G 800 235-3361
　Elmhurst (G-9330)
C D T Manufacturing Inc .... G 847 679-2361
　Skokie (G-18935)
▲ Central Rubber Company .... E 815 544-2191
　Belvidere (G-1661)
◆ Cinch Cnnctivity Solutions Inc ...... C 630 705-6000
　Lombard (G-13054)
Cinch Connectors Inc .... C 630 705-6001
　Lombard (G-13055)
Conxall Corporation .... C 630 834-7504
　Villa Park (G-20141)
Cord Sets Inc .... E 847 427-1185
　Elk Grove Village (G-8915)
◆ CTS Corporation .... C 630 577-8800
　Lisle (G-12881)
Data Accessories Inc .... G 847 669-3640
　Huntley (G-11533)
David Jeskey .... E 630 659-6337
　Saint Charles (G-18180)
◆ Dynomax Inc .... B 847 680-8833
　Wheeling (G-20883)
◆ Eastco Inc .... G 708 499-1701
　Oak Lawn (G-15714)
Evoys Corp .... G 773 736-4200
　Chicago (G-4540)
Gage Applied Technologies LLC ..... E 815 838-0005
　Lockport (G-12995)

Glenair Inc .... E 847 679-8833
　Lincolnwood (G-12823)
Harting Inc of North America .... E 847 741-2700
　Elgin (G-8608)
▲ Harting Inc of North America ...... E 847 741-1500
　Elgin (G-8609)
Harting Manufacturing Inc .... G 847 741-1500
　Elgin (G-8610)
Hirose Electric (usa) Inc .... D 630 282-6700
　Downers Grove (G-8024)
Industrial Electronic Contrls .... F 815 873-1980
　Rockford (G-17458)
▲ Ip Media Holdings .... E 847 714-1177
　Wheeling (G-20917)
▲ Konnectronix Inc .... E 847 672-8685
　Waukegan (G-20456)
Kylon Midwest .... G 773 699-3640
　Chicago (G-5139)
◆ Mac Lean-Fogg Company .... D 847 566-0010
　Mundelein (G-14710)
Methode Development Co .... E 708 867-6777
　Chicago (G-5408)
◆ Methode Electronics Inc .... B 708 867-6777
　Chicago (G-5409)
Methode Electronics Inc .... C 847 577-9545
　Rolling Meadows (G-17750)
Methode Electronics Inc .... A 217 357-3941
　Carthage (G-3139)
Microway Systems Inc .... E 847 679-8833
　Lincolnwood (G-12830)
Molex LLC .... G 630 969-4550
　Naperville (G-14873)
Molex LLC .... G 630 527-4357
　Lisle (G-12912)
Molex LLC .... F 630 512-8787
　Downers Grove (G-8059)
Molex Electronic Tech LLC .... G 630 969-4550
　Lisle (G-12913)
▲ Molex International Inc .... F 630 969-4550
　Lisle (G-12914)
Newko Tool & Engineering Co .... G 847 359-1670
　Palatine (G-16142)
▲ Nobility Corporation .... E 847 677-3204
　Skokie (G-18996)
North Ridge Properties LLC .... G 815 434-7800
　Ottawa (G-16064)
P K Neuses Incorporated .... G 847 253-6555
　Rolling Meadows (G-17758)
▲ Switchcraft Inc .... B 773 792-2700
　Chicago (G-6299)
▲ Switchcraft Holdco Inc .... G 773 792-2700
　Chicago (G-6300)
Te Connectivity Corporation .... D 847 680-7400
　Mundelein (G-14742)
United Universal Inds Inc .... E 815 727-4445
　Joliet (G-11939)
▲ Woodhead Industries LLC .... B 847 353-2500
　Lincolnshire (G-12802)
Woodhead Industries Inc .... G 847 236-9300
　Deerfield (G-7660)

3679 Electronic Components, NEC

Accelerated Assemblies Inc .... E 630 616-6680
　Elk Grove Village (G-8798)
▲ Access Assembly LLC .... E 847 894-1047
　Mundelein (G-14659)
▲ Advanced Strobe Products Inc .... D 708 867-3100
　Chicago (G-3567)
Advanced Technologies Inc .... G 847 329-9875
　Park Ridge (G-16264)
▲ Aerotronic Controls Co .... F 847 228-6504
　Chicago (G-3575)
▲ Aimtron Corporation .... D 630 372-7500
　Palatine (G-16091)
▲ Air802 Corporation .... G 630 966-2501
　Oswego (G-15991)
Andrew New Zealand Inc .... E 708 873-3507
　Orland Park (G-15940)
Andrew Technologies Inc .... G 847 520-5770
　Wheeling (G-20849)
▲ ARC-Tronics Inc .... C 847 437-0211
　Elk Grove Village (G-8837)
Aria Corporation .... G 847 327-9000
　Libertyville (G-12630)
◆ B D C Inc .... E 847 741-2233
　Elgin (G-8519)
▲ Bem Wireless LLC .... F 815 337-0541
　Schaumburg (G-18460)
▲ Bestar Technologies Inc .... G 847 261-2850
　Saint Charles (G-18155)

▲ Bias Power Inc ....G.... 847 419-9180
Buffalo Grove (G-2517)
Big Joes Sealcoati ....G.... 630 935-7032
Lisle (G-12871)
▲ Bircher America Inc ....G.... 847 952-3730
Schaumburg (G-18462)
▲ Blockmaster Electronics Inc ....G.... 847 956-1680
Elk Grove Village (G-8869)
Bozki Inc ....G.... 312 767-2122
Wheeling (G-20865)
C & B Services ....G.... 847 462-8484
Cary (G-3151)
C & S Electric Specialties ....G.... 630 406-6170
Bolingbrook (G-2154)
C Hofbauer Inc ....G.... 630 920-1222
Burr Ridge (G-2659)
C L Greenslade Sales Inc ....G.... 847 593-3450
Arlington Heights (G-713)
C R V Electronics Corp ....D.... 815 675-6500
Spring Grove (G-19269)
Cal-Tronics Systems Inc ....E.... 630 350-0044
Wood Dale (G-21174)
Capital Advanced Technologies ....G.... 630 690-1696
Carol Stream (G-2955)
▲ Capsonic Automotive Inc ....F.... 847 888-7300
Elgin (G-8530)
Casco Manufacturing Inc ....E.... 630 771-9555
Bolingbrook (G-2155)
Central Industries of Indiana ....G.... 618 943-2311
Lawrenceville (G-12528)
▲ Central Rubber Company ....E.... 815 544-2191
Belvidere (G-1661)
Chicago Cardinal Communication ....F.... 708 424-1446
Oak Lawn (G-15708)
Chicago Technical Sales Inc ....G.... 630 889-7121
Oakbrook Terrace (G-15792)
▲ Cinch Cnnctivity Solutions Inc ....C.... 630 705-6000
Lombard (G-13054)
Circom Inc ....E.... 630 595-4460
Bensenville (G-1770)
▲ Cita Technologies LLC ....G.... 847 419-9118
Buffalo Grove (G-2525)
Cmetrix Inc ....G.... 630 595-9800
Wood Dale (G-21177)
Commscope Technologies LLC ....B.... 779 435-6000
Joliet (G-11845)
Compu Doc Inc ....G.... 630 554-5800
Oswego (G-15997)
Connor-Winfield Corp ....C.... 630 851-4722
Aurora (G-1079)
◆ Consolidated Elec Wire & Cable ....D.... 847 455-8830
Franklin Park (G-9913)
▲ Continental Assembly Inc ....F.... 773 472-8004
Chicago (G-4226)
▲ CTS Corporation ....C.... 630 577-8800
Lisle (G-12881)
▲ Daesam Corporation ....G.... 917 653-2000
Grayslake (G-10765)
Dalco Marketing Services ....G.... 630 961-3366
Carol Stream (G-2971)
◆ De Amertek Corporation Inc ....D.... 630 572-0800
Lombard (G-13063)
Delta Circuits Inc ....E.... 630 876-0691
West Chicago (G-20569)
▲ Delta Design Inc ....F.... 708 424-9400
Evergreen Park (G-9592)
Dynamac Microwave Inc ....G.... 630 543-0033
Addison (G-105)
▲ Elan Industries Inc ....F.... 630 679-2000
Bolingbrook (G-2172)
Electronic Design & Mfg Inc ....D.... 847 550-1912
Lake Zurich (G-12406)
▲ Essex Electro Engineers Inc ....E.... 847 891-4444
Schaumburg (G-18522)
▲ Excel Specialty Corp ....E.... 773 262-7575
Lake Forest (G-12248)
Flp Industries LLC ....F.... 847 215-8650
Wheeling (G-20897)
Formcraft Tool Company ....F.... 773 476-8727
Chicago (G-4620)
▲ Four Star Tool Inc ....D.... 224 735-2419
Rolling Meadows (G-17733)
G T C Industries Inc ....G.... 708 369-9815
Naperville (G-14832)
Gateway Cable Inc ....G.... 630 766-7969
Bensenville (G-1808)
▲ Global Display Solutions Inc ....E.... 815 282-2328
Rockford (G-17429)
◆ Grand Products Inc ....B.... 800 621-6101
Elk Grove Village (G-9020)
Grayhill Inc ....C.... 847 428-6990
Carpentersville (G-3102)
◆ Grayhill Inc ....B.... 708 354-1040
La Grange (G-12077)
Grayhill Inc ....G.... 708 482-1411
Mc Cook (G-13691)
▲ Guardian Electric Mfg Co ....D.... 815 334-3600
Woodstock (G-21393)
Hart Electric LLC ....E.... 815 368-3341
Lostant (G-13176)
Hubbell Power Systems Inc ....F.... 618 797-5000
Edwardsville (G-8365)
▲ Ikonix Group Inc ....G.... 847 367-4671
Lake Forest (G-12266)
Illinois Tool Works Inc ....C.... 847 724-7500
Des Plaines (G-7784)
▼ IMS Companies LLC ....D.... 847 391-8100
Des Plaines (G-7786)
Innolux Technology USA Inc ....G.... 847 490-5315
Hoffman Estates (G-11430)
Integrated Circuits Research ....G.... 630 830-9024
Hanover Park (G-11007)
▲ Inventus Power (illinois) LLC ....C.... 630 410-7900
Woodridge (G-21317)
Ipr Systems Inc ....G.... 708 385-7500
Alsip (G-458)
Jds Labs Inc ....G.... 618 550-9359
Collinsville (G-6964)
Joseph C Rakers ....G.... 618 670-6995
Pocahontas (G-16752)
Journey Circuits Inc ....G.... 630 283-0604
Schaumburg (G-18579)
Knowles Elec Holdings Inc ....A.... 630 250-5100
Itasca (G-11687)
▲ Knowles Electronics LLC ....C.... 630 250-5100
Itasca (G-11688)
Kraus & Naimer Inc ....G.... 847 298-2450
Des Plaines (G-7794)
Ksm Electronics Inc ....C.... 630 393-9310
Warrenville (G-20241)
◆ L I K Inc ....F.... 630 213-1282
Streamwood (G-19583)
Lace Technologies Inc ....F.... 630 528-8083
Addison (G-180)
▲ Limitless Innovations Inc ....E.... 855 843-4828
McHenry (G-13758)
▲ Littelfuse Inc ....A.... 773 628-1000
Chicago (G-5238)
Loda Electronics Co ....G.... 217 386-2554
Loda (G-13029)
Lodan Electronics Inc ....C.... 847 398-5311
Arlington Heights (G-771)
Lynn Electronics Corp ....G.... 972 412-7240
Bolingbrook (G-2208)
Manu-TEC of Illinois LLC ....F.... 630 543-3022
Addison (G-191)
Matrix Circuits LLC ....G.... 319 367-5000
Lake Villa (G-12360)
Midwest Aero Support Inc ....E.... 815 398-9202
Machesney Park (G-13360)
▲ Millennium Electronics Inc ....D.... 815 479-9755
Crystal Lake (G-7231)
Mk Test Systems Americas Inc ....G.... 773 569-3778
Lake Barrington (G-12161)
◆ Molex LLC ....A.... 630 969-4550
Lisle (G-12911)
Molex LLC ....G.... 630 527-4363
Bolingbrook (G-2216)
Molex LLC ....F.... 630 512-8787
Downers Grove (G-8059)
▲ Molex International Inc ....F.... 630 969-4550
Lisle (G-12914)
▲ Molex Premise Networks Inc ....A.... 866 733-6659
Lisle (G-12915)
▲ Monnex International Inc ....E.... 847 850-5263
Buffalo Grove (G-2576)
▲ Motec Inc ....G.... 630 241-9595
Downers Grove (G-8060)
Murata Electronics N Amer Inc ....G.... 847 330-9200
Schaumburg (G-18641)
Navatek Resources Inc ....G.... 847 301-0174
Schaumburg (G-18645)
Navitas Electronics Corp ....E.... 702 293-4670
Woodridge (G-21325)
▲ Nep Electronics Inc ....C.... 630 595-8500
Wood Dale (G-21221)
◆ Netcom Inc ....C.... 847 537-6300
Wheeling (G-20943)
Northrop Grumman Systems Corp ....A.... 847 259-9600
Rolling Meadows (G-17755)
Novel Electronic Designs Inc ....G.... 309 224-9945
Chillicothe (G-6820)
Nu-Way Electronics Inc ....E.... 847 437-7120
Elk Grove Village (G-9156)
Omnitronix Corporation ....F.... 630 837-1400
Streamwood (G-19587)
Ot Systems Limited ....G.... 630 554-9178
Plano (G-16737)
Othernet Inc ....G.... 773 688-4320
Long Grove (G-13168)
▲ Partec Inc ....C.... 847 678-9520
Franklin Park (G-10014)
Perfectvision Mfg Inc ....F.... 630 226-9890
Bolingbrook (G-2225)
▲ Peterson Elctr-Msical Pdts Inc ....E.... 708 388-3311
Alsip (G-490)
Pintsch Tiefenbach Us Inc ....G.... 618 993-8513
Marion (G-13527)
Polyera Corporation ....E.... 847 677-7517
Skokie (G-19006)
Power Equipment Company ....E.... 815 754-4090
Cortland (G-7026)
◆ Power-Volt Inc ....D.... 630 628-9999
Addison (G-249)
Precision Circuits Inc ....F.... 630 515-9100
Downers Grove (G-8083)
▲ Qcircuits Inc ....D.... 847 797-6678
Elk Grove Village (G-9203)
Quality Cable & Components Inc ....E.... 309 695-3435
Wyoming (G-21461)
Relay Services Mfg Corp ....F.... 773 252-2700
Chicago (G-6008)
Richardson Electronics Ltd ....C.... 630 208-2278
Lafox (G-12137)
◆ Richardson Electronics Ltd ....C.... 630 208-2200
Lafox (G-12138)
▲ Rubicon Technology Inc ....E.... 847 295-7000
Bensenville (G-1887)
Safemobile Inc ....F.... 847 818-1649
Rolling Meadows (G-17772)
Sandes Quynetta ....G.... 815 275-4876
Freeport (G-10140)
Satellink Inc ....G.... 618 983-5555
Johnston City (G-11812)
Seaco Data Systems Inc ....D.... 630 876-2169
Carol Stream (G-3066)
Sigmatron International Inc ....G.... 847 586-5200
Elgin (G-8730)
▲ Sigmatron International Inc ....G.... 847 956-8000
Elk Grove Village (G-9238)
Simple Circuits Inc ....G.... 708 671-9600
Palos Park (G-16214)
Skyfly Networks Inc ....G.... 312 429-4580
Des Plaines (G-7846)
▲ Skyline International Inc ....F.... 847 357-9077
Palatine (G-16159)
Sota Service Ctr By Bodinets ....G.... 608 538-3500
Dekalb (G-7704)
▲ Sub-Sem Inc ....E.... 815 459-4139
Crystal Lake (G-7270)
Sumida America Inc ....E.... 847 545-6700
Schaumburg (G-18729)
▲ Switchcraft Inc ....B.... 773 792-2700
Chicago (G-6299)
▲ Switchcraft Holdco Inc ....G.... 773 792-2700
Chicago (G-6300)
Switchee Bandz Usa LLC ....G.... 312 415-1100
Highland Park (G-11301)
▲ T&L International Mfg/Dist Inc ....G.... 309 830-7238
Farmer City (G-9658)
Tanvas Inc ....G.... 773 295-6220
Chicago (G-6325)
Tech Star Design and Mfg ....F.... 847 290-8676
Elk Grove Village (G-9268)
Tedds Cstm Installations Inc ....G.... 815 485-6800
New Lenox (G-15063)
◆ Teejet Technologies LLC ....D.... 630 665-5002
Springfield (G-19462)
Teledyne Defense Elec LLC ....C.... 630 754-3300
Woodridge (G-21344)
Triton Manufacturing Co Inc ....C.... 708 587-4000
Monee (G-14210)
Tvh Parts Co ....E.... 847 223-1000
Grayslake (G-10803)
▲ Uico LLC ....E.... 630 592-4400
Elmhurst (G-9439)
Unlimited Svcs Wisconsin Inc ....E.... 815 399-0282
Machesney Park (G-13383)
Vl Inc ....G.... 618 277-8703
Belleville (G-1606)

Employee Codes: A=Over 500 employees, B=251-500
C=101-250, D=51-100, E=20-50, F=10-19, G=3-9
2020 Harris Illinois
Industrial Directory
993

36 ELECTRONIC AND OTHER ELECTRICAL EQUIPMENT AND COMPONENTS, EXCEPT COMPUTER SIC SECTION

Weldon Corporation ....E 708 343-4700
Maywood *(G-13680)*
▲ **Wintek Electro-Optics Corp** ....F 734 477-5480
Glenview *(G-10638)*
▲ **Woodhead Industries LLC** ....B 847 353-2500
Lincolnshire *(G-12802)*
Zero Ground LLC ....F 847 360-9500
Waukegan *(G-20522)*
ZF Active Safety & Elec US LLC ....B 217 826-3011
Marshall *(G-13580)*
Zic Incorporated ....G 847 680-8833
Wheeling *(G-21016)*

3691 Storage Batteries

▲ **All Cell Technologies LLC** ....E 872 281-7606
Chicago *(G-3607)*
Batteries Plus 287 ....G 630 279-3478
Villa Park *(G-20132)*
Battery Builders LLC ....D 630 851-5800
Naperville *(G-14961)*
Battery Sales Inc ....G 708 489-6645
Matteson *(G-13619)*
C & C 1 LLC ....G 630 903-6345
Elmhurst *(G-9340)*
Clarios ....F 630 871-7700
Carol Stream *(G-2961)*
Clarios LLC ....B 630 232-4270
Geneva *(G-10260)*
Crown Battery Manufacturing Co ....G 630 530-8060
Villa Park *(G-20143)*
Duracell Company ....G 203 796-4000
Chicago *(G-4410)*
Duracell Distributing LLC ....G 203 796-4000
Chicago *(G-4411)*
Duracell US Operations Inc ....G 312 469-5266
Chicago *(G-4412)*
East Penn Manufacturing Co ....A 610 682-6361
Naperville *(G-14819)*
Ecolocap Solutions Inc ....G 312 585-6670
Morton Grove *(G-14403)*
Enersys ....D 630 455-4872
Lisle *(G-12889)*
Exide Technologies ....G 630 862-2200
Lombard *(G-13074)*
Exide Technologies LLC ....D 678 566-9000
Lombard *(G-13075)*
Firefly International Enrgy Co ....G 309 402-0701
Peoria *(G-16438)*
Glidepath Power LLC ....G 312 375-6034
Elmhurst *(G-9367)*
Hubbell Power Systems Inc ....F 618 797-5000
Edwardsville *(G-8365)*
Interstate All Battery Center ....F 217 214-1069
Quincy *(G-16894)*
Interstate Btry Sys Intl Inc ....G 708 424-2288
Oak Lawn *(G-15720)*
◆ **Inventus Power Inc** ....C 630 410-7900
Woodridge *(G-21316)*
Inventus Power Holdings Inc ....G 630 410-7900
Woodridge *(G-21318)*
▲ **Iterna LLC** ....E 630 585-7400
Aurora *(G-989)*
Itta Corporation ....G 872 221-4882
Chicago *(G-4978)*
▲ **National Power LLC** ....E 773 685-2662
Chicago *(G-5551)*
▲ **Navitas Systems LLC** ....F 630 755-7920
Woodridge *(G-21326)*
P L R Sales Inc ....G 217 733-2245
Fairmount *(G-9644)*
▲ **Palladium Energy Group Inc** ....E 630 410-7900
Woodridge *(G-21330)*
Performance Battery Group Inc ....G 630 293-5505
West Chicago *(G-20628)*
Rayovac Corp ....G 815 285-6500
Dixon *(G-7909)*
Spectrum Brands Inc ....G 815 285-6500
Dixon *(G-7919)*
Storage Battery Systems LLC ....G 630 221-1700
Carol Stream *(G-3078)*
◆ **Technical Power Systems Inc** ....E 630 719-1471
Lisle *(G-12949)*
Veteran Wire and Cable LLC ....G 630 327-5849
Addison *(G-329)*

3692 Primary Batteries: Dry & Wet

Exide Technologies LLC ....D 678 566-9000
Lombard *(G-13075)*

3694 Electrical Eqpt For Internal Combustion Engines

▲ **A E Iskra Inc** ....G 815 874-4022
Rockford *(G-17280)*
Aerodyne Incorporated ....G 773 588-2905
Chicago *(G-3572)*
Aeromotive Services Inc ....F 224 535-9220
Elgin *(G-8498)*
▲ **Amerline Enterprises Co Inc** ....E 847 671-6554
Schiller Park *(G-18786)*
Appliance Information and Repr ....G 217 698-8858
Rochester *(G-17163)*
Ark De Mexico LLC ....B 630 240-9483
Saint Charles *(G-18148)*
◆ **Ark Technologies Inc** ....D 630 377-8855
Saint Charles *(G-18149)*
Bill West Enterprises Inc ....G 217 886-2591
Jacksonville *(G-11757)*
▲ **Carnation Enterprises** ....G 847 804-5928
Niles *(G-15108)*
Charlotte Louise Tate ....G 773 849-3236
Chicago *(G-4076)*
▲ **County Packaging Inc** ....D 708 597-1100
Crestwood *(G-7114)*
Egan Wagner Corporation ....G 630 985-8007
Woodridge *(G-21298)*
▲ **Elc Industries Corp** ....E 630 851-1616
Aurora *(G-1088)*
▲ **Excel Specialty Corp** ....E 773 262-7575
Lake Forest *(G-12248)*
Harvey Bros Inc ....F 309 342-3137
Galesburg *(G-10199)*
Innovation Specialists Inc ....G 815 372-9001
New Lenox *(G-15037)*
Joes Automotive Inc ....G 815 937-9281
Kankakee *(G-11982)*
K & W Auto Electric ....F 217 857-1717
Teutopolis *(G-19770)*
▼ **Kold-Ban International Ltd** ....E 847 658-8561
Lake In The Hills *(G-12338)*
Major Wire Incorporated ....F 708 457-0121
Norridge *(G-15239)*
▲ **Mat Engine Technologies LLC** ....G 847 821-9630
Long Grove *(G-13164)*
▲ **Midtronics Inc** ....D 630 323-2800
Willowbrook *(G-21050)*
Midwest Aero Support Inc ....E 815 398-9202
Machesney Park *(G-13360)*
Monona Holdings LLC ....G 630 946-0630
Naperville *(G-14875)*
Motorola Solutions Inc ....C 847 576-8600
Schaumburg *(G-18637)*
▲ **MTA USA Corp** ....G 847 847-5503
Elk Grove Village *(G-9138)*
Nidec Motor Corporation ....D 847 439-3760
Des Plaines *(G-7810)*
Niles Auto Parts ....G 847 215-2549
Lincolnshire *(G-12788)*
Plasmatreat USA Inc ....F 847 783-0622
Elgin *(G-8687)*
Powermaster ....G 630 957-4019
West Chicago *(G-20631)*
Quick Start Pdts & Solutions ....F 815 562-5414
Rochelle *(G-17153)*
◆ **Robert Bosch LLC** ....B 917 421-7209
Broadview *(G-2466)*
Sk Express Inc ....C 815 748-4388
Dekalb *(G-7702)*
Southern Ill Auto Elec Inc ....F 618 587-3308
Tilden *(G-19792)*
UNI Electric Enterprise Inc ....G 630 372-6312
Bartlett *(G-1258)*
W W Williams Company LLC ....F 309 756-1068
Rock Island *(G-17253)*
Xenia Mfg Inc ....C 618 678-2218
Xenia *(G-21469)*
Xenia Mfg Inc ....E 618 392-7212
Olney *(G-15894)*

3695 Recording Media

Acro Magnetics Inc ....G 815 943-5018
Harvard *(G-11040)*
Acta Publications ....G 773 989-3036
Chicago *(G-3533)*
Adsensa Corporation ....G 312 559-2881
Chicago *(G-3552)*
▲ **Ats Commercial Group LLC** ....F 815 686-2705
Piper City *(G-16625)*
Bpn Chicago ....E 312 799-4100
Chicago *(G-3940)*
Brandmuscle Inc ....G 866 236-8481
Chicago *(G-3946)*
Estad Stamping & Mfg Co ....E 217 442-4600
Danville *(G-7331)*
Imperial Technical Services ....F 708 403-1564
Orland Park *(G-15961)*
◆ **Jvc Advanced Media USA Inc** ....G 630 237-2439
Schaumburg *(G-18581)*
Lssp Corporation ....G 630 428-0099
Lisle *(G-12909)*
M K Advantage Inc ....F 773 902-5272
Chicago *(G-5302)*
Magna-Flux International ....G 815 623-7634
Roscoe *(G-17914)*
Magnetic Occasions & More Inc ....G 815 462-4141
New Lenox *(G-15040)*
Mak-System Corp ....F 847 803-4863
Des Plaines *(G-7799)*
Sammy USA Corp ....E 847 364-9787
Elk Grove Village *(G-9228)*
Tdm Systems Inc ....G 847 605-1269
Schaumburg *(G-18742)*

3699 Electrical Machinery, Eqpt & Splys, NEC

AAC Microtec North America Inc ....E 602 284-7997
Columbia *(G-6982)*
Accurate Security & Lock Corp ....G 815 455-0133
Lake In The Hills *(G-12326)*
Aemm A Electric ....G 708 403-6700
Orland Park *(G-15935)*
Agrowtek Inc ....G 847 380-3009
Gurnee *(G-10854)*
Aim Inc ....G 630 941-0027
Elmhurst *(G-9322)*
▲ **Alliance Laser Sales Inc** ....E 847 487-1945
Wauconda *(G-20328)*
◆ **Allmetal Inc** ....D 630 250-8090
Itasca *(G-11619)*
Ambient Lightning and Electric ....G 708 529-3434
Oak Lawn *(G-15700)*
American Holiday Lights Inc ....G 630 769-9999
Woodridge *(G-21274)*
◆ **Appleton Grp LLC** ....C 847 268-6000
Rosemont *(G-17999)*
Assa Abloy ACC Door Cntrls Gro ....D 704 283-2101
Franklin Park *(G-9876)*
Assa Abloy Entrance Systems US ....F 847 228-5600
Elk Grove Village *(G-8843)*
Associate General Labs Inc ....G 847 678-2717
Franklin Park *(G-9877)*
Azilsa Inc ....E 312 919-1741
Schaumburg *(G-18455)*
Azz Incorporated ....D 815 723-5000
Joliet *(G-11826)*
▲ **Bechara Sim** ....F 847 913-9950
Buffalo Grove *(G-2514)*
Best Rep Company Corporation ....G 847 451-6644
Franklin Park *(G-9886)*
◆ **Blg McC Enterprises Inc** ....E 847 455-0188
Franklin Park *(G-9888)*
Blustor Pmc Inc ....G 312 265-3058
Chicago *(G-3919)*
Boaleeco Inc ....G 847 428-3085
Gilberts *(G-10351)*
Buss Boyz Customs Inc ....G 815 369-2803
Lena *(G-12598)*
◆ **Bystronic Inc** ....C 847 214-0300
Hoffman Estates *(G-11410)*
Calx Trading Corporation ....E 630 456-6721
Naperville *(G-14962)*
Carey Electric Co Inc ....G 847 949-9294
Grayslake *(G-10761)*
Cdc Enterprises Inc ....G 815 790-4205
Johnsburg *(G-11802)*
Cecomp Electronics Inc ....E 847 918-3510
Libertyville *(G-12642)*
◆ **Chamberlain Group Inc** ....B 630 279-3600
Oak Brook *(G-15606)*
Chamberlain Group Inc ....F 630 705-0300
Addison *(G-67)*
Chamberlain Group Inc ....E 630 279-3600
Oak Brook *(G-15607)*
◆ **Chamberlain Manufacturing Corp** ....A 630 279-3600
Oak Brook *(G-15608)*
Chase Security Systems Inc ....G 773 594-1919
Chicago *(G-4078)*
Checkpoint Systems Inc ....D 630 771-4240
Romeoville *(G-17806)*
Coles Craft Corporation ....G 630 858-8171
Glen Ellyn *(G-10398)*

Connor Electric Services Inc ....E 630 823-8230
Schaumburg *(G-18485)*

CTS of Illinois Inc ....G 630 892-2355
Montgomery *(G-14242)*

Custom Tool Inc ....F 217 465-8538
Paris *(G-16228)*

Delta-Therm Corporation ....F 847 526-2407
Crystal Lake *(G-7193)*

Domino Amjet Inc ....E 847 662-3148
Gurnee *(G-10869)*

Domino Lasers Inc ....E 847 855-1364
Gurnee *(G-10872)*

▲ Dukane Corporation ....C 630 797-4900
Saint Charles *(G-18189)*

Duvas USA Limited ....G 312 266-1420
Chicago *(G-4415)*

▲ E N M Company ....D 773 775-8400
Chicago *(G-4425)*

East West Martial Arts Sups ....G 773 878-7711
Chicago *(G-4434)*

Eazypower Corporation ....E 773 278-5000
Chicago *(G-4439)*

◆ Eazypower Corporation ....G 773 278-5000
Chicago *(G-4440)*

Elec Easel ....G 815 444-9700
Crystal Lake *(G-7196)*

◆ Electri-Flex Company ....D 630 529-2920
Roselle *(G-17952)*

Electro-Technic Products Inc ....F 773 561-2349
Chicago *(G-4478)*

◆ Elenco Electronics Inc ....E 847 541-3800
Wheeling *(G-20889)*

Engineered SEC & Sound Inc ....G 630 876-8853
West Chicago *(G-20573)*

Enginuity Communications Corp ....E 630 444-0778
Saint Charles *(G-18198)*

Extreme Flight Simulation ....G 224 656-5546
Gurnee *(G-10877)*

Eztech Manufacturing Inc ....F 630 293-0010
West Chicago *(G-20582)*

▲ Fisa North America Inc ....G 847 593-2080
Elk Grove Village *(G-8998)*

Gate Systems Corporation ....G 847 731-6700
Gurnee *(G-10882)*

Gerardo and Quintana Auto Elc ....G 773 424-0634
Chicago *(G-4686)*

Giba Electric ....G 773 685-4420
Chicago *(G-4690)*

Global Manufacturing ....G 630 908-7633
Willowbrook *(G-21045)*

Herrmann Ultrasonics Inc ....E 630 626-1626
Bartlett *(G-1285)*

▲ Heuft Usa Inc ....F 630 395-9521
Downers Grove *(G-8021)*

▲ HK America Inc ....G 630 916-0200
Bartlett *(G-1286)*

HK Laser and Systems ....G 630 916-0200
Bartlett *(G-1287)*

Hopcroft Electric Inc ....G 618 288-7302
Glen Carbon *(G-10388)*

Hubbell Power Systems Inc ....F 618 797-5000
Edwardsville *(G-8365)*

▲ IMS Engineered Products LLC ....C 847 391-8100
Des Plaines *(G-7787)*

▼ Industrial Enclosure Corp ....E 630 898-7499
Aurora *(G-1111)*

Interior Tectonics LLC ....G 312 515-7779
Chicago *(G-4947)*

Intermountain Electronics Inc ....G 618 339-6743
Centralia *(G-3235)*

▲ Inventus Power (illinois) LLC ....C 630 410-7900
Woodridge *(G-21317)*

Invisible Fencing of Quad City ....G 309 797-1688
Moline *(G-14151)*

James J Sandoval ....G 734 717-7555
Lombard *(G-13089)*

Jardis Industries Inc ....F 630 773-5600
Itasca *(G-11681)*

Jescorp Inc ....D 847 378-1200
Elk Grove Village *(G-9068)*

Jk Audio Inc ....F 815 786-2929
Sandwich *(G-18375)*

Kamstra Door Service Inc ....G 708 895-9990
Lansing *(G-12500)*

Kavanaugh Electric Inc ....G 708 503-1310
Frankfort *(G-9812)*

Kaybee Engineering Company Inc ....E 630 968-7100
Westmont *(G-20751)*

Kohns Electric ....G 309 463-2331
Varna *(G-20032)*

Laser Energy Systems ....G 815 282-8200
Loves Park *(G-13232)*

▲ Lecip Inc ....F 312 626-2525
Bensenville *(G-1842)*

Lt Security Inc ....E 630 348-8088
Elk Grove Village *(G-9099)*

▲ Lutamar Electrical Assemblies ....E 847 679-5400
Skokie *(G-18981)*

Maco-Sys LLC ....F 779 888-3260
Rockford *(G-17502)*

▼ Magnetrol International Inc ....C 630 723-6600
Aurora *(G-1001)*

◆ Marbil Enterprises Inc ....G 618 257-1810
Belleville *(G-1570)*

Marmon Engineered Components ....G 312 372-9500
Chicago *(G-5341)*

Mason Electric ....G 618 457-8900
Carterville *(G-3133)*

Maxi-Vac Inc ....G 630 620-6669
East Dundee *(G-8205)*

Mi-Jack Systems & Tech LLC ....F 708 596-3780
Hazel Crest *(G-11134)*

Midwest Tool Inc ....G 773 588-1313
Chicago *(G-5449)*

Midwest Treasure Detectors ....G 217 223-4769
Quincy *(G-16915)*

Migatron Corporation ....E 815 338-5800
Woodstock *(G-21411)*

◆ Min Sheng Technology Inc ....G 815 569-4496
Schaumburg *(G-18631)*

Mobiloc LLC ....G 773 742-1329
Alsip *(G-481)*

Moog Inc ....E 770 987-7550
Northbrook *(G-15435)*

Motor Sport Marketing Group ....E 618 654-6750
Highland *(G-11232)*

▲ Newhaven Display Intl Inc ....E 847 844-8795
Elgin *(G-8668)*

▲ Nitek International LLC ....G 847 259-8900
Rolling Meadows *(G-17753)*

Novanta Inc ....G 781 266-5700
Newton *(G-15089)*

Occly LLC ....G 773 969-5080
Chicago *(G-5652)*

Omron Electronics LLC ....D 847 843-7900
Hoffman Estates *(G-11442)*

P & J Technologies ....G 847 995-1108
Schaumburg *(G-18661)*

◆ Panduit Corp ....A 708 532-1800
Tinley Park *(G-19848)*

Panduit Corp ....E 815 836-1800
Lockport *(G-13018)*

Pipeline Trading Systems LLC ....G 312 212-4288
Chicago *(G-5811)*

▲ Power Port Products Inc ....E 630 628-9102
Addison *(G-248)*

Powertech Systems ....G 847 553-1867
Wauconda *(G-20383)*

Prime Devices Corporation ....F 847 729-2550
Willow Springs *(G-21027)*

▲ Pro Access Systems Inc ....F 630 426-0022
Elburn *(G-8470)*

Protection Controls Inc ....E 773 763-3110
Skokie *(G-19017)*

Quality Intgrted Solutions Inc ....G 815 464-4772
Tinley Park *(G-19852)*

◆ Raynor Mfg Co ....A 815 288-1431
Dixon *(G-7908)*

Raytheon Technologies Corp ....B 815 226-6000
Rockford *(G-17567)*

▲ Rf Ideas Inc ....D 847 870-1723
Rolling Meadows *(G-17771)*

Rockford Linear Motion LLC ....G 815 961-7900
Rockford *(G-17598)*

◆ Roundtble Hlthcare Partners LP ....E 847 739-3200
Lake Forest *(G-12299)*

RTS Sentry Inc ....F 618 257-7100
Belleville *(G-1594)*

Santas Best ....F 847 459-3301
Vernon Hills *(G-20091)*

Sciaky Inc ....E 708 594-3841
Chicago *(G-6116)*

Scis Air Security Corporation ....G 847 671-9502
Schiller Park *(G-18843)*

▲ Sennco Solutions Inc ....E 815 577-3400
Plainfield *(G-16713)*

▼ Simformotion LLC ....F 309 263-7595
Peoria *(G-16524)*

Simulation Technology LLC ....G 630 365-3400
Elburn *(G-8473)*

Sound Design Inc ....G 630 548-7000
Plainfield *(G-16715)*

▲ Spartanics Ltd ....E 847 394-5700
Rolling Meadows *(G-17777)*

Sparton Onyx Holdings LLC ....G 847 762-5800
Schaumburg *(G-18720)*

Sphere Laser LLC ....F 317 752-1604
Saint Charles *(G-18274)*

◆ Sphere Laser LLC ....G 317 752-1604
McHenry *(G-13793)*

Spurt Inc ....G 847 571-6497
Northbrook *(G-15486)*

Stabiloc LLC ....G 586 412-1147
Carol Stream *(G-3074)*

Standard Electric Supply Inc ....G 217 239-0800
Champaign *(G-3354)*

Starfire Industries LLC ....E 217 721-4165
Champaign *(G-3356)*

Sustanable Infrastructures Inc ....G 815 341-1447
Frankfort *(G-9842)*

▲ Temple Display Ltd ....G 630 851-3331
Oswego *(G-16026)*

◆ Tenneco Automotive Oper Co Inc ....C 847 482-5000
Lake Forest *(G-12308)*

Three Hands Technologies ....G 847 680-5358
Vernon Hills *(G-20106)*

Tii Technical Educatn Systems ....G 847 428-3085
Gilberts *(G-10373)*

Toho Technology Inc ....G 773 583-7183
Chicago *(G-6385)*

Tri Cable Inc ....G 847 815-6082
Libertyville *(G-12717)*

Tricor Systems Inc ....E 847 742-5542
Elgin *(G-8760)*

Tylu Wireless Technology LLC ....G 312 260-7934
Chicago *(G-6450)*

Unified Tool Die & Mfg Co Inc ....F 847 678-3773
Schiller Park *(G-18848)*

Unique Product Productions Inc ....G 708 259-1500
Richton Park *(G-17032)*

▲ United Amercn Healthcare Corp ....E 313 393-4571
Chicago *(G-6469)*

United Universal Inds Inc ....E 815 727-4445
Joliet *(G-11939)*

Usl Lock Corporation ....G 815 739-4707
Bartlett *(G-1320)*

Victoria Amplifier Company ....F 630 369-3527
Naperville *(G-14991)*

◆ Videojet Technologies Inc ....A 630 860-7300
Wood Dale *(G-21255)*

Vlahos Electric Service Dr ....G 224 764-2335
Arlington Heights *(G-828)*

Wesco International Inc ....G 630 513-4864
Elmhurst *(G-9445)*

▲ Wildlife Materials Inc ....E 618 687-3505
Murphysboro *(G-14762)*

Windy City Laser Service Inc ....G 773 995-0188
Chicago *(G-6642)*

Wittenstein Arspc Smlation Inc ....G 630 540-5300
Bartlett *(G-1326)*

37 TRANSPORTATION EQUIPMENT

3711 Motor Vehicles & Car Bodies

4x4 Headquarters LLC ....G 217 540-5337
Effingham *(G-8381)*

AEP Nvh Opco LLC ....F 708 758-0211
Chicago Heights *(G-6729)*

Alexis Fire Equipment Company ....D 309 482-6121
Alexis *(G-364)*

Amerex Corporation ....E 309 382-4389
North Pekin *(G-15326)*

Bergstrom Inc ....D 847 394-4013
Joliet *(G-11831)*

Bill West Enterprises Inc ....G 217 886-2591
Jacksonville *(G-11757)*

Blackjack Customs ....G 847 361-5225
North Chicago *(G-15307)*

Brunos Automotive Products ....G 630 458-0043
Addison *(G-56)*

▼ Chassis Service Unlimited ....G 847 336-2305
Waukegan *(G-20427)*

Crete Twp ....G 708 672-3111
Crete *(G-7138)*

Dakkota Integrated Systems LLC ....D 517 694-6500
Chicago *(G-4308)*

Dierzen-Kewanee Heavy Inds ....D 309 853-2316
Kewanee *(G-12030)*

Direct Dimension Inc ....G 815 479-1936
Algonquin *(G-369)*

S
I
C

37 TRANSPORTATION EQUIPMENT

ED Etnyre & Co ....B....... 815 732-2116
  Oregon *(G-15917)*
Enterprise Service Corporation ....G....... 773 589-2727
  Des Plaines *(G-7758)*
FCA US LLC ....G....... 630 724-2321
  Lisle *(G-12890)*
Federal Signal Corporation ....E....... 708 534-4756
  University Park *(G-19952)*
Federal Signal Corporation ....E....... 708 534-3400
  University Park *(G-19954)*
◆ Federal Signal Corporation ....D....... 630 954-2000
  Oak Brook *(G-15618)*
Folk Race Cars ....G....... 815 629-2418
  Durand *(G-8151)*
◆ Fs Depot Inc ....G....... 847 468-2350
  University Park *(G-19955)*
Fuji Oozx America Inc ....G....... 281 888-2247
  Schaumburg *(G-18531)*
Heartland Classics Inc. ....G....... 618 783-4444
  Newton *(G-15084)*
Hertz Corporation ....G....... 630 897-0956
  Montgomery *(G-14247)*
High Speed Welding Inc ....G....... 630 971-8929
  Westmont *(G-20747)*
Hopperstad Customs ....G....... 815 547-7534
  Belvidere *(G-1677)*
Illinois Sterling Ltd ....G....... 847 526-5151
  Wauconda *(G-20360)*
Innova Uev LLC ....F....... 630 568-5609
  Burr Ridge *(G-2687)*
Jenner Precision Inc ....F....... 815 692-6655
  Fairbury *(G-9609)*
John Beyer Race Cars ....G....... 773 779-5313
  Chicago *(G-5037)*
Jorge A Cruz ....G....... 773 722-2828
  Chicago *(G-5049)*
Kens Street Rod Repair ....G....... 815 874-1811
  Rockford *(G-17482)*
Koenig Body & Equipment Inc ....G....... 309 673-7435
  West Peoria *(G-20687)*
Kurts Carstar Collision Ctr ....F....... 618 345-4519
  Maryville *(G-13591)*
Legend Racing Enterprises Inc ......G....... 847 923-8979
  Schaumburg *(G-18602)*
Liberty Coach Inc ....D....... 847 578-4600
  North Chicago *(G-15316)*
Light of Mine LLC ....G....... 312 840-8570
  Chicago *(G-5220)*
Long Wolf Express Inc ....G....... 708 673-1583
  South Holland *(G-19230)*
Mares Service Inc. ....G....... 708 656-1660
  Cicero *(G-6865)*
Maxim Inc. ....F....... 217 544-7015
  Springfield *(G-19403)*
Mickey Truck Bodies Inc ....F....... 309 827-8227
  Bloomington *(G-2076)*
Midwest Coach Builders Inc ....G....... 630 690-1420
  Carol Stream *(G-3030)*
Midwest Hot Rods Inc. ....F....... 815 254-7637
  Plainfield *(G-16689)*
Midwest Remanufacturing LLC ......G....... 708 496-9100
  Bedford Park *(G-1484)*
Motor Coach Inds Intl Inc ....C....... 847 285-2000
  Des Plaines *(G-7804)*
Motor Coach Industries ....G....... 847 285-2000
  Des Plaines *(G-7805)*
◆ Navistar Inc ....C....... 331 332-5000
  Lisle *(G-12917)*
Navistar Inc. ....D....... 331 332-5000
  Lisle *(G-12918)*
Navistar Inc ....C....... 331 332-5000
  Joliet *(G-11907)*
Navistar Inc ....D....... 708 865-3333
  Melrose Park *(G-13895)*
Navistar Defense LLC ....G....... 662 494-3421
  Lisle *(G-12920)*
◆ Navistar International Corp ....A....... 331 332-5000
  Lisle *(G-12921)*
Neckbone Skunks Logistics & Te ...F....... 312 218-0281
  Chicago *(G-5561)*
▲ Nippon Sharyo Mfg LLC ....G....... 815 562-8600
  Rochelle *(G-17151)*
Nissan ....G....... 630 957-4360
  West Chicago *(G-20622)*
Odin Fire Protection District ....E....... 618 775-8292
  Odin *(G-15835)*
◆ Oshkosh Specialty Vehicles Inc ...C....... 708 868-5071
  Calumet City *(G-2784)*
Oshkosh/Mcnlus Fncl Svcs Prtnr ...G....... 630 466-5100
  Sugar Grove *(G-19648)*

Park License Service Inc ....G....... 815 633-5511
  Loves Park *(G-13243)*
Phils Auto Body ....G....... 773 847-7156
  Chicago *(G-5801)*
R & S Automotive Inc ....G....... 847 622-8838
  Elgin *(G-8711)*
◆ R/A Hoerr Inc ....E....... 309 691-8789
  Edwards *(G-8340)*
Rahn Equipment Company ....G....... 217 431-1232
  Danville *(G-7376)*
Restorations Unlimited II Inc ....G....... 847 639-5818
  Cary *(G-3186)*
Rj Race Cars Inc. ....F....... 309 343-7575
  Galesburg *(G-10218)*
SAE Customs Inc ....G....... 855 723-2878
  Round Lake *(G-18082)*
Sentinel Emrgncy Solutions LLC ...E....... 618 539-3863
  Freeburg *(G-10093)*
Subaru of America Inc ....E....... 630 250-4740
  Itasca *(G-11741)*
T J Van Der Bosch & Associates ...G....... 815 344-3210
  McHenry *(G-13805)*
T R Z Motorsports Inc ....G....... 815 806-0838
  Frankfort *(G-9843)*
Taylor Off Road Racing ....G....... 815 544-4500
  Belvidere *(G-1703)*
Tenneco Intl Holdg Corp ....F....... 847 482-5000
  Lake Forest *(G-12313)*
Tesla Inc ....F....... 312 733-9780
  Chicago *(G-6354)*
Tesla Motors ....G....... 630 541-1214
  Westmont *(G-20776)*
Vanderbosch Tj & Assoc Inc ....G....... 815 344-3210
  McHenry *(G-13806)*

3713 Truck & Bus Bodies

▲ ATI Oldco Inc ....C....... 630 860-5600
  Bartlett *(G-1266)*
◆ Auto Truck Group LLC ....G....... 630 860-5600
  Bartlett *(G-1267)*
Bruder Tank Inc ....E....... 217 292-9058
  Sullivan *(G-19662)*
C I F Industries Inc. ....E....... 618 635-2010
  Staunton *(G-19476)*
▲ C S O Corp ....D....... 630 365-6600
  Virgil *(G-20190)*
Campbell International Inc ....E....... 408 661-0794
  Wauconda *(G-20339)*
Caterpillar Inc ....A....... 217 475-4000
  Decatur *(G-7471)*
City Utility Equipment ....F....... 815 254-6673
  Plainfield *(G-16651)*
Dierzen Trailer Co ....D....... 815 695-5291
  Newark *(G-15076)*
Donermen LLC ....G....... 773 430-2828
  Chicago *(G-4382)*
Entrans International LLC ....E....... 618 548-3660
  Salem *(G-18337)*
Erie Vehicle Company ....F....... 773 536-6300
  Chicago *(G-4526)*
▲ Gvw Group LLC ....G....... 847 681-8417
  Highland Park *(G-11269)*
Herr Display Vans Inc ....G....... 708 755-7926
  Sauk Village *(G-18400)*
Imperial Oil Inc ....G....... 773 866-1235
  Chicago *(G-4898)*
Independent Antique RAD Mfg ....G....... 847 458-7400
  Algonquin *(G-374)*
Jarco Inc ....E....... 888 681-3660
  Salem *(G-18343)*
Knapheide Manufacturing Co ....F....... 217 222-7134
  Quincy *(G-16901)*
Kurts Carstar Collision Ctr ....F....... 618 345-4519
  Maryville *(G-13591)*
◆ Lmt Inc ....F....... 217 568-8265
  Galva *(G-10235)*
▲ McLaughlin Body Co ....D....... 309 762-7755
  Moline *(G-14159)*
Mickey Truck Bodies Inc ....F....... 309 827-8227
  Bloomington *(G-2076)*
Mid-America Truck Corporation .....D....... 815 672-3211
  Streator *(G-19614)*
Motor Coach Inds Intl Inc ....C....... 847 285-2000
  Des Plaines *(G-7804)*
Navistar Inc ....B....... 662 494-3421
  Lisle *(G-12919)*
◆ Navistar International Corp ....A....... 331 332-5000
  Lisle *(G-12921)*
Newf LLC ....G....... 630 330-5462
  Naperville *(G-14883)*

Pafco Truck Bodies Inc ....F....... 309 699-4613
  East Peoria *(G-8281)*
Paramount Truck Body Co Inc. ......E....... 312 666-6441
  Chicago *(G-5762)*
Phils Auto Body ....G....... 773 847-7156
  Chicago *(G-5801)*
Pools Welding Inc ....G....... 309 787-2083
  Milan *(G-14020)*
Quad County Fire Equipment ....G....... 815 832-4475
  Saunemin *(G-18402)*
R & L Truck Service Inc ....F....... 847 489-7135
  Wadsworth *(G-20212)*
Robinsport LLC ....G....... 630 724-9280
  Woodridge *(G-21337)*
Sauber Manufacturing Company ....D....... 630 365-6600
  Virgil *(G-20191)*
Summit Tank & Equipment Co ....F....... 708 594-3040
  Mc Cook *(G-13703)*
Thule Inc ....C....... 847 455-2420
  Forest Park *(G-9725)*
Tondinis Wrecker Service ....G....... 618 997-9884
  Marion *(G-13541)*
Tri-County Truck Tops Inc ....G....... 847 740-4004
  Round Lake *(G-18085)*
▲ Triseal Corporation ....E....... 815 648-2473
  Hebron *(G-11151)*
Wag Industries Inc ....F....... 847 329-8932
  Skokie *(G-19053)*

3714 Motor Vehicle Parts & Access

▲ A&G Manufacturing Inc ....F....... 815 562-2107
  Rochelle *(G-17129)*
Accurate Auto Manufacturing Co ...G....... 618 244-0727
  Mount Vernon *(G-14595)*
Accurate Engine & Machine Inc ....G....... 773 237-4942
  Chicago *(G-3517)*
Accuride Corporation ....C....... 630 568-3914
  Hinsdale *(G-11360)*
Acd USA Inc ....G....... 929 428-1744
  Wood Dale *(G-21154)*
Acme Auto Electric Co ....G....... 708 754-5420
  S Chicago Hts *(G-18115)*
Adient US LLC ....C....... 815 895-2095
  Sycamore *(G-19699)*
▲ Advance Wheel Corporation ......D....... 773 471-5734
  Chicago *(G-3560)*
Air Land and Sea Interiors ....G....... 630 834-1717
  Villa Park *(G-20129)*
Air-X Remanufacturing Corp ....G....... 708 598-0044
  Bridgeview *(G-2320)*
Airbrake Products Inc ....F....... 708 594-1110
  Orland Park *(G-15936)*
▲ Aircraft Gear Corporation ....D....... 815 877-7473
  Loves Park *(G-13185)*
◆ Airtex Products LP ....E....... 618 842-2111
  Fairfield *(G-9617)*
◆ Aisin Electronics Illinois LLC ......C....... 618 997-9800
  Marion *(G-13499)*
Aisin Mfg Illinois LLC ....G....... 618 998-8333
  Marion *(G-13501)*
▲ Aisin Mfg Illinois LLC ....A....... 618 998-8333
  Marion *(G-13502)*
Alloy Tech ....G....... 217 253-3939
  Tuscola *(G-19922)*
Aluminum Drive Line Products ......G....... 708 946-9777
  Beecher *(G-1516)*
Amerex Corporation ....E....... 309 382-4389
  North Pekin *(G-15326)*
▲ American Diesel Tube Corp ....F....... 630 628-1830
  Addison *(G-32)*
American Speed Enterprises ....G....... 309 764-3601
  Moline *(G-14131)*
▲ American Vulko Tread Corp ....F....... 847 956-1300
  Elk Grove Village *(G-8826)*
American Wheel Corp. ....E....... 708 458-9141
  Chicago *(G-3673)*
Amsoil Inc ....G....... 630 595-8385
  Bensenville *(G-1745)*
Andersen Machine & Welding Inc ..G....... 815 232-4664
  Freeport *(G-10101)*
Android Indstres- Blvidere LLC .....C....... 815 547-3742
  Belvidere *(G-1649)*
◆ Anthony Liftgates Inc ....G....... 815 842-3383
  Pontiac *(G-16765)*
Antolin Interiors Usa Inc ....B....... 618 327-4416
  Nashville *(G-14994)*
Arco Automotive Elec Svc Co ....G....... 708 422-2976
  Oak Lawn *(G-15701)*
▲ Area Diesel Service Inc ....E....... 217 854-2641
  Carlinville *(G-2867)*

SIC SECTION
37 TRANSPORTATION EQUIPMENT

Ark De Mexico LLC ....B 630 240-9483
Saint Charles *(G-18148)*
▲ **Arrow Gear Company** ....B 630 969-7640
Downers Grove *(G-7955)*
◆ **Ascent Tranz Group LLC** ....G....... 844 424-7347
Chicago *(G-3747)*
▲ **Auto Meter Products Inc**....C....... 815 895-8141
Sycamore *(G-19702)*
◆ **Autonomous Stuff LLC** ....G....... 309 291-0966
Morton *(G-14353)*
▲ **Autospec Inc**....G....... 773 254-2288
Chicago *(G-3779)*
▲ **Barcar Manufacturing Inc**....G....... 630 365-5200
Elburn *(G-8445)*
Bedford Rakim ....G....... 773 759-3947
South Holland *(G-19199)*
Belvidere Brose Inc ....F 779 552-7600
Belvidere *(G-1654)*
Bergstrom Inc....D....... 815 874-7821
Rockford *(G-17322)*
Bergstrom Inc....D 847 394-4013
Joliet *(G-11831)*
▲ **Bi-Phase Technologies LLC**....F 952 886-6450
Wood Dale *(G-21168)*
Bill Weeks Inc....G....... 217 523-8735
Springfield *(G-19326)*
◆ **Bison Gear & Engineering Corp**....C....... 630 377-4327
Saint Charles *(G-18156)*
Boler Company ....C....... 630 910-2800
Woodridge *(G-21279)*
◆ **Boler Company**....F....... 630 773-9111
Itasca *(G-11628)*
Boler Ventures LLC....D 630 773-9111
Itasca *(G-11629)*
Borg Warner Automotive - B....E....... 248 754-9200
Dixon *(G-7891)*
Borg-Warner Automotive Inc ....G....... 815 469-2721
Frankfort *(G-9774)*
Borgwarner Inc....E 248 754-9200
Bellwood *(G-1617)*
Borgwarner Inc....E 248 754-9200
Frankfort *(G-9775)*
Borgwarner Inc....C....... 815 288-1462
Dixon *(G-7892)*
Borgwarner Transm Systems Inc....A 708 547-2600
Bellwood *(G-1618)*
Borgwarner Transm Systems Inc....B 815 469-2721
Frankfort *(G-9776)*
Borgwarner Transm Systems Inc....B 815 469-7819
Chicago *(G-3936)*
Borgwarner Transm Systems Inc....F 708 731-4540
Melrose Park *(G-13834)*
Boyce Industries Inc....F 708 345-0455
Melrose Park *(G-13836)*
Bpi Holdings International Inc....C....... 815 363-9000
McHenry *(G-13722)*
◆ **Brake Parts Inc India LLC**....G....... 815 363-9000
McHenry *(G-13723)*
Brake Parts Inc LLC....B 815 363-8181
McHenry *(G-13724)*
◆ **Brake Parts Inc LLC** ....C....... 815 363-9000
McHenry *(G-13725)*
Brake Parts Inc LLC....G....... 217 324-2161
Litchfield *(G-12961)*
Brunos Automotive Products ....G....... 630 458-0043
Addison *(G-56)*
Buell Manufacturing Company....G....... 708 447-6320
Lyons *(G-13304)*
Byd Motors Inc....G....... 847 590-9002
Arlington Heights *(G-712)*
C & M Engineering....G....... 815 932-3388
Bourbonnais *(G-2257)*
Caldwell & Moten LLC ....G....... 773 619-2584
Chicago *(G-4003)*
California Muffler and Brakes....G....... 773 776-8990
Chicago *(G-4004)*
Caterpillar Inc....B 815 842-6000
Pontiac *(G-16767)*
Cavanaugh Government Group LLC....F 630 210-8668
Bridgeview *(G-2332)*
CC Distributing Services Inc....G....... 800 931-2668
Crestwood *(G-7110)*
Central Hydraulics Inc....G....... 309 527-5238
El Paso *(G-8434)*
Cft Performance Inc....G....... 618 781-3981
Maryville *(G-13590)*
◆ **Champion Laboratories Inc**....A 618 445-6011
Albion *(G-347)*
Champion Laboratories Inc ....F 618 445-5407
Albion *(G-348)*
Champion Laboratories Inc ....F....... 618 445-6011
Bannockburn *(G-1198)*
Chicago Drive Line Inc ....G....... 708 385-1900
Alsip *(G-427)*
Chucking Machine Products Inc ....D 847 678-1192
Franklin Park *(G-9907)*
City Subn Auto Svc Goodyear....G....... 773 355-5550
Chicago *(G-4162)*
Clarios....D 630 279-0050
Elmhurst *(G-9347)*
Clarios....F 630 871-7700
Carol Stream *(G-2961)*
Clark Filter Inc....E 216 896-3000
Chicago *(G-4167)*
Clement Industries Inc Del....E 708 458-9141
Bedford Park *(G-1463)*
Clutch Systems Inc....G....... 815 282-7960
Machesney Park *(G-13334)*
Cnh Industrial America LLC....E 309 965-2233
Goodfield *(G-10672)*
Continental Auto Systems Inc ....B 847 862-6300
Deer Park *(G-7580)*
▲ **Crawford Heating & Cooling Co** ....E 309 794-1000
Rock Island *(G-17212)*
◆ **CTS Automotive LLC**....C....... 630 577-8800
Lisle *(G-12880)*
Dana ....G....... 419 887-3000
Sterling *(G-19503)*
Dana Driveshaft Mfg LLC ....E 815 626-6700
Sterling *(G-19504)*
Dana Incorporated ....E 630 271-0001
Lisle *(G-12883)*
Dana Sealing Manufacturing LLC....G....... 618 544-8651
Robinson *(G-17112)*
Dana Sealing Manufacturing LLC....B 618 544-8651
Robinson *(G-17113)*
Dana Sealing Products LLC....D 630 960-4200
Lisle *(G-12884)*
Danfoss Power Solutions US Co....C....... 815 233-4200
Freeport *(G-10105)*
David Horton ....G....... 312 917-8610
Chicago *(G-4325)*
◆ **Doga USA Corporation** ....F 847 669-8529
Huntley *(G-11535)*
Driv Automotive Inc....G....... 847 482-5000
Lake Forest *(G-12244)*
Driv Incorporated....G....... 857 842-5000
Lake Forest *(G-12245)*
Drive Shaft Unlimited Inc ....G....... 708 447-2211
Lyons *(G-13307)*
DTE Enterprises LLC ....G....... 630 307-9355
Addison *(G-100)*
▲ **Dynamic Manufacturing Inc** ....D 708 343-8753
Hillside *(G-11336)*
Dynamic Manufacturing Inc....D 708 681-0682
Melrose Park *(G-13855)*
Dynamic Manufacturing Inc....D 708 547-7081
Hillside *(G-11337)*
Dynamic Manufacturing Inc....E 708 343-8753
Melrose Park *(G-13856)*
Dynamic Manufacturing Inc....B 708 547-9011
Hillside *(G-11338)*
◆ **Eagle Wings Industries Inc**....B 217 892-4322
Rantoul *(G-16974)*
▲ **Eakas Corporation** ....B 815 223-8811
Peru *(G-16575)*
Eaton Corporation....C....... 815 562-2107
Rochelle *(G-17138)*
▲ **Elgin Industries Inc**....C....... 847 742-1720
Elgin *(G-8574)*
Engine Rebuilders & Supply....G 708 338-1113
Stone Park *(G-19554)*
▲ **Engine Solutions Inc** ....G....... 815 979-2312
Rockford *(G-17397)*
Exress Motor and Lift Parts ....G....... 630 327-2000
Frankfort *(G-9792)*
▲ **Ezee Roll Manufacturing Co** ....G....... 217 339-2279
Hoopeston *(G-11508)*
▲ **Fabricated Metals Co**....C....... 847 718-1300
Elk Grove Village *(G-8994)*
FCA US LLC....G....... 630 724-2321
Lisle *(G-12890)*
FCA US LLC....A 630 637-3000
Naperville *(G-14828)*
Federal-Mogul Motorparts LLC....A 847 674-7700
Skokie *(G-18954)*
Federal-Mogul Motorparts LLC....C....... 773 478-0404
Chicago *(G-4571)*
Federal-Mogul Motorparts LLC....E 248 354-7700
Berwyn *(G-1954)*
Fire Chariot LLC....G....... 815 561-3688
Rochelle *(G-17141)*
▲ **Flender Corporation** ....C....... 847 931-1990
Elgin *(G-8588)*
Flex-N-Gate Corporation ....D 217 442-4018
Danville *(G-7334)*
Flex-N-Gate Corporation ....A 217 255-5025
Urbana *(G-19983)*
▲ **Flex-N-Gate LLC**....B 217 384-6600
Urbana *(G-19984)*
Flex-N-Gate LLC....G....... 773 437-5686
Chicago *(G-4604)*
Flex-N-Gate LLC....A 217 278-2400
Urbana *(G-19985)*
Fram Group Holdings Inc....A 847 482-2045
Lake Forest *(G-12249)*
Frantz Manufacturing Company ....D....... 815 564-0991
Sterling *(G-19510)*
Gates Corporation ....C....... 309 343-7171
Galesburg *(G-10196)*
Gem Manufacturing Corporation....G....... 630 458-0014
Naperville *(G-14834)*
Genuine Parts Company ....F 630 293-1300
Chicago *(G-4681)*
Glk Enterprises Inc ....G....... 847 395-7368
Antioch *(G-614)*
Gray Machine & Welding Inc....F 309 788-2501
Rock Island *(G-17220)*
Great Lakes Forge Company....G....... 773 277-2800
Chicago *(G-4735)*
Grupo Antolin Illinois Inc ....C....... 815 544-8020
Belvidere *(G-1674)*
Gs Custom Works Inc....G....... 815 233-4724
Freeport *(G-10113)*
▲ **Gunite Corporation**....B 815 490-6260
Rockford *(G-17436)*
Gunite Corporation....B 815 964-3301
Rockford *(G-17437)*
H R Larke Corp....G....... 847 204-2776
Crystal Lake *(G-7204)*
Harbison-Fischer Inc ....G....... 618 375-3841
Grayville *(G-10808)*
Hardy Radiator Repair....F 217 223-8320
Quincy *(G-16889)*
Hd Turbo Llc....G....... 847 636-7586
Elk Grove Village *(G-9030)*
Hendrickson Holdings LLC....G....... 630 910-2800
Itasca *(G-11664)*
Hendrickson International Corp ....C....... 815 727-4031
Joliet *(G-11876)*
◆ **Hendrickson International Corp**....E 630 874-9700
Woodridge *(G-21311)*
Hendrickson Usa LLC....E 630 910-2800
Woodridge *(G-21312)*
◆ **Hendrickson Usa LLC** ....E 630 874-9700
Itasca *(G-11665)*
◆ **Hendrickson Usa LLC** ....C....... 630 910-2844
Woodridge *(G-21313)*
Hendrickson Usa LLC....D 815 727-4031
Joliet *(G-11877)*
Hendrix Industrial Gastrux Inc....G....... 847 526-1700
Mundelein *(G-14696)*
High Impact Fabricating LLC ....G....... 708 235-8912
University Park *(G-19956)*
HM Manufacturing Inc ....F 847 487-8700
Wauconda *(G-20356)*
Honeywell International Inc ....B 269 428-6305
Saint Joseph *(G-18317)*
Hoosier Stamping & Mfg Corp....E 618 375-2057
Grayville *(G-10810)*
Hyperaktive Prfmce Solutions....G....... 847 321-1982
Antioch *(G-615)*
Iggys Auto Parts ....F 708 452-9790
Norridge *(G-15237)*
Illinois Tool Works Inc ....E 630 993-9990
Elmhurst *(G-9376)*
Illinois Tool Works Inc ....D 630 993-9990
Elmhurst *(G-9377)*
Illinois Tool Works Inc ....C....... 708 479-7200
Mokena *(G-14091)*
Illinois Tool Works Inc ....C....... 815 448-7300
Mazon *(G-13681)*
Illinois Tool Works Inc ....G....... 708 479-3346
Tinley Park *(G-19838)*
▼ **IMS Companies LLC** ....D 847 391-8100
Des Plaines *(G-7786)*
Independent Antique RAD Mfg ....G....... 847 458-7400
Algonquin *(G-374)*
Industrial Opprtnity Prtners L....E 847 556-3460
Evanston *(G-9538)*

S I C

Employee Codes: A=Over 500 employees, B=251-500
C=101-250, D=51-100, E=20-50, F=10-19, G=3-9
2020 Harris Illinois
Industrial Directory
997

Infinitybox LLC G 847 232-1991
Elk Grove Village *(G-9051)*

Interstate Power Systems Inc F 630 871-1111
Carol Stream *(G-3006)*

Interstate Power Systems Inc D 952 854-2044
Rockford *(G-17470)*

ITW Global Investments LLC G 847 724-7500
Glenview *(G-10574)*

Jasiek Motor Rebuilding Inc G 815 883-3678
Oglesby *(G-15842)*

▲ Johnson Power Ltd E 708 345-4300
Broadview *(G-2445)*

◆ Jordan Industries Inc F 847 945-5591
Deerfield *(G-7621)*

▲ Jsn Inc E 708 410-1800
Maywood *(G-13670)*

▲ Just Parts Inc G 815 756-2184
Cortland *(G-7022)*

K & W Auto Electric F 217 857-1717
Teutopolis *(G-19770)*

Kackert Enterprises Inc G 630 898-9339
Aurora *(G-1120)*

Kccdd Inc D 309 344-2030
Galesburg *(G-10205)*

▲ Kiene Diesel Accessories Inc E 630 543-7170
Addison *(G-169)*

Kleinhoffer Manufacturing Inc G 815 725-3638
Joliet *(G-11890)*

▲ Koehler Enterprises Inc G 847 451-4966
Franklin Park *(G-9978)*

L & M Screw Machine Products F 630 801-0455
Montgomery *(G-14253)*

Larry Pontnack G 815 732-7751
Oregon *(G-15923)*

Lemfco Inc E 815 777-0242
Galena *(G-10176)*

Lgb Industries G 847 639-1691
Cary *(G-3175)*

Line Craft Tool Company Inc C 630 932-1182
Lombard *(G-13096)*

Little Egypt Gas A & Wldg Sups G 618 937-2271
West Frankfort *(G-20677)*

Lkq Corporation C 312 621-1950
Chicago *(G-5243)*

▲ Mag Daddy LLC G 847 719-5600
Wauconda *(G-20371)*

Magna Exteriors America Inc A 618 327-4381
Nashville *(G-14999)*

Magna Exteriors America Inc B 618 327-2136
Nashville *(G-15000)*

Maintenance Inc G 708 598-1390
La Grange *(G-12082)*

Makerite Mfg Co Inc E 815 389-3902
Roscoe *(G-17916)*

Mann+hummel Filtration Tech F 800 407-9263
McHenry *(G-13762)*

Mann+hummel Filtration Technol G 815 759-7744
McHenry *(G-13763)*

◆ Marmon Industries LLC G 312 372-9500
Chicago *(G-5345)*

◆ Mat Holdings Inc D 847 821-9630
Long Grove *(G-13165)*

Matrix International Ltd G 815 389-3771
South Beloit *(G-19099)*

▲ Mattoon Precision Mfg C 217 235-6000
Mattoon *(G-13645)*

Maxim Inc F 217 544-7015
Springfield *(G-19403)*

Mendota Welding & Mfg G 815 539-6944
Mendota *(G-13949)*

▲ Mercury Products Corp C 847 524-4400
Schaumburg *(G-18627)*

Methode Electronics Inc A 217 357-3941
Carthage *(G-3139)*

Michelangelo & Donata Burdi F 773 427-1437
Chicago *(G-5423)*

Midwest Converters Inc F 815 229-9808
Rockford *(G-17525)*

Mike Mulcahy Motorsports LLC G 630 567-0298
Morris *(G-14315)*

Mobis Parts America LLC B 630 907-4700
Aurora *(G-1136)*

▲ Molor Products Company F 630 375-5999
Oswego *(G-16015)*

◆ Morse Automotive Corporation A 773 843-9000
Buffalo Grove *(G-2577)*

▲ Motec Inc G 630 241-9595
Downers Grove *(G-8060)*

Motor Coach Inds Intl Inc C 847 285-2000
Des Plaines *(G-7804)*

Motor Parts & Equipment Corp E 217 877-7456
Decatur *(G-7527)*

Motor Row Development Corp G 773 525-3311
Chicago *(G-5507)*

Mouldtec Inc G 815 893-0908
Crystal Lake *(G-7234)*

Mr Auto Electric G 217 523-3659
Springfield *(G-19409)*

▲ Nascote Industries Inc A 618 327-4381
Nashville *(G-15002)*

Nascote Industries Inc C 618 478-2092
Nashville *(G-15003)*

◆ National Cycle Inc C 708 343-0400
Maywood *(G-13674)*

National Porges Radiator Corp F 773 224-3000
Chicago *(G-5550)*

◆ Navistar Inc C 331 332-5000
Lisle *(G-12917)*

Navistar Inc D 708 865-3333
Melrose Park *(G-13895)*

◆ Navistar International Corp A 331 332-5000
Lisle *(G-12921)*

Naylor Automotive Engrg Co Inc F 773 582-6900
Chicago *(G-5558)*

NGK Spark Plugs (usa) Inc E 630 595-7894
Wood Dale *(G-21222)*

▲ Nidec Mobility America Corp A 630 443-6800
Saint Charles *(G-18234)*

Nivelco USA LLC G 630 848-2100
Naperville *(G-14885)*

▲ Nta Precision Axle Corporation B 630 690-6300
Carol Stream *(G-3041)*

Oakley Industries Sub Assembly F 815 544-6666
Belvidere *(G-1692)*

Ogden Top & Trim Shop Inc G 708 484-5422
Berwyn *(G-1958)*

▲ Old World Global LLC G 800 323-5440
Northbrook *(G-15445)*

Old World Inds Holdings LLC G 800 323-5440
Northbrook *(G-15446)*

▲ Olympic Controls Corp E 847 742-3566
Elgin *(G-8678)*

◆ Oshkosh Specialty Vehicles Inc C 708 868-5071
Calumet City *(G-2784)*

▲ Otr Wheel Engineering Inc E 217 223-7705
Quincy *(G-16920)*

Parker Fabrication Inc E 309 266-8413
Morton *(G-14376)*

Performance Gear Systems Inc E 630 739-6666
Plainfield *(G-16700)*

Performance Manufacturing G 630 231-8099
West Chicago *(G-20629)*

Php Racengines Inc G 847 526-9393
Wauconda *(G-20382)*

Piston Automotive LLC C 313 541-8789
Belvidere *(G-1694)*

◆ Plews Inc C 815 288-3344
Dixon *(G-7906)*

Pma Friction Products Inc D 630 406-9119
Batavia *(G-1404)*

Pmw Holdings Inc G 815 672-0551
Streator *(G-19621)*

Polar Container Corporation G 847 299-5030
Bensenville *(G-1869)*

▲ Power Plus Products Inc F 773 788-9794
Bedford Park *(G-1492)*

Powerstop G 708 442-6761
Mc Cook *(G-13698)*

▲ Powertrain Rockford Inc C 815 633-7460
Loves Park *(G-13248)*

▲ Precision Governors LLC E 815 229-5300
Rockford *(G-17556)*

Precision Remanufacturing Inc F 773 489-7225
Chicago *(G-5858)*

Precision Truck Products Inc E 618 548-9011
Salem *(G-18352)*

Premiere Motorsports LLC G 708 634-0007
Plainfield *(G-16706)*

Prestige Motor Works Inc G 630 780-6439
Naperville *(G-14983)*

▼ Pryco Inc E 217 364-4467
Mechanicsburg *(G-13811)*

Quarter Master Industries Inc E 847 540-8999
Lake Zurich *(G-12447)*

Qwik-Tip Inc G 847 640-7387
Elk Grove Village *(G-9207)*

R & R Engines and Parts Inc G 630 628-1545
Addison *(G-263)*

▲ R2c Performance Products LLC F 708 488-8211
Mundelein *(G-14730)*

◆ Randall Manufacturing LLC D 630 782-0001
Elmhurst *(G-9414)*

RE-Do-It Corp G 708 343-7125
Broadview *(G-2463)*

▲ Realwheels Corporation E 847 662-7722
Gurnee *(G-10923)*

Rebuilders Enterprises Inc G 708 430-0030
Bridgeview *(G-2380)*

Redhorse Performance Inc G 708 430-1603
Hickory Hills *(G-11202)*

Rj Race Cars Inc F 309 343-7575
Galesburg *(G-10218)*

Robert Bosch LLC F 708 865-5415
Broadview *(G-2465)*

◆ Robert Bosch LLC B 917 421-7209
Broadview *(G-2466)*

Rogers Motorcycle Shop Inc G 309 828-3242
Bloomington *(G-2090)*

▲ S A Gear Company Inc E 708 496-0395
Bedford Park *(G-1502)*

SKF USA Inc D 847 742-0700
Elgin *(G-8736)*

SLF Motion LLC G 217 891-8384
Pawnee *(G-16306)*

Splice Energy Solutions LLC G 815 861-8402
Mchenry *(G-13794)*

▲ Strange Engineering Inc D 847 663-1701
Morton Grove *(G-14443)*

Suburban Driveline Inc G 630 941-7101
Villa Park *(G-20174)*

Suburban Plastics Co E 708 681-1475
Broadview *(G-2471)*

Sumitomo Machinery Corp Amer E 630 752-0200
Glendale Heights *(G-10504)*

Sure Plus Manufacturing Co D 708 756-3100
Chicago Heights *(G-6777)*

Surge Clutch & Drive Line Co G 708 331-1352
South Holland *(G-19247)*

Symbol Tool Inc G 847 674-1080
Skokie *(G-19041)*

T & T Machine Shop G 847 244-2020
Gurnee *(G-10932)*

T G Automotive E 630 916-7818
Lombard *(G-13137)*

T J Van Der Bosch & Associates E 815 344-3210
McHenry *(G-13805)*

▲ T/CCI Manufacturing LLC D 217 423-0066
Decatur *(G-7555)*

▲ Taap Corp F 224 676-0653
Wheeling *(G-20996)*

Taw Enterprises LLC G 618 466-0134
Godfrey *(G-10664)*

Tbc Retail Group Inc G 630 692-0232
Montgomery *(G-14271)*

◆ Tenneco Automotive Oper Co Inc C 847 482-5000
Lake Forest *(G-12308)*

Tenneco Automotive Oper Co Inc C 847 821-0757
Lincolnshire *(G-12798)*

Tenneco Automotive Rsa Company G 847 482-5000
Lake Forest *(G-12309)*

◆ Tenneco Europe Limited G 847 482-5000
Lake Forest *(G-12310)*

Tenneco Global Holdings Inc G 847 482-5000
Lake Forest *(G-12311)*

Tenneco Inc G 847 774-1636
Lincolnwood *(G-12844)*

◆ Tenneco Inc D 847 482-5000
Lake Forest *(G-12312)*

Tenneco Intl Holdg Corp F 847 482-5000
Lake Forest *(G-12313)*

Tesla Inc F 312 733-9780
Chicago *(G-6354)*

Thyssenkrupp Crankshaft Co LLC C 217 444-5500
Danville *(G-7385)*

◆ Thyssenkrupp Crankshaft Co LLC C 217 431-0060
Danville *(G-7383)*

◆ Thyssenkrupp North America Inc E 312 525-2800
Chicago *(G-6375)*

Thyssenkrupp Presta Cold Forgi E 217 431-4212
Danville *(G-7386)*

◆ Thyssnkrupp Prsta Danville LLC B 217 444-5500
Danville *(G-7387)*

Titan International Inc C 217 228-6011
Quincy *(G-16948)*

◆ Titan Wheel Corp Illinois A 217 228-6023
Quincy *(G-16950)*

Topy America Inc G 847 350-6399
Elk Grove Village *(G-9276)*

▲ Toyo USA Manufacturing Inc F 309 827-8836
Bloomington *(G-2103)*

▲ Toyota Boshoku Illinois LLC...B ... 618 943-5300
Lawrenceville (G-12537)
▲ Transcedar Limited...E ... 618 262-4153
Mount Carmel (G-14488)
Transomatic Des Plaines LLC...G ... 847 625-1500
Des Plaines (G-7859)
◆ Tuxco Corporation...F ... 847 244-2220
Gurnee (G-10940)
▲ U G N Inc...D ... 773 437-2400
Tinley Park (G-19863)
U S Tool & Manufacturing Co...E ... 630 953-1000
Addison (G-321)
▲ Ucal Holdings Inc...D ... 847 695-8030
Elgin (G-8765)
▲ Ucal Systems Inc...C ... 847 695-8030
Elgin (G-8767)
United Carburetor Inc...E ... 773 777-1223
Schiller Park (G-18849)
▲ United Gasket Corporation...D ... 708 656-3700
Cicero (G-6885)
▲ United Remanufacturing Co Inc...E ... 773 777-1223
Schiller Park (G-18850)
United Remanufacturing Co Inc...E ... 847 678-2233
Schiller Park (G-18851)
United States Gear Corporation...G ... 773 821-5450
Chicago (G-6477)
US Tsubaki Power Transm LLC...C ... 847 459-9500
Wheeling (G-21004)
◆ Vehicle Improvement Pdts Inc...G ... 847 395-7250
Antioch (G-642)
Velasquez & Sons Muffler Shop...G ... 847 740-6990
Round Lake Beach (G-18093)
Vfn Fiberglass Inc...F ... 630 543-0232
Addison (G-330)
Vibracoustic Usa Inc...C ... 618 382-2318
Carmi (G-2917)
Vipar Heavy Duty Inc...F ... 815 788-1700
Crystal Lake (G-7291)
Vitesco Technologies Usa LLC...G ... 847 862-5000
Deer Park (G-7583)
Vogel Manufacturing Co Inc...G ... 217 536-6946
Effingham (G-8429)
Walters Distributing Company...G ... 847 468-0941
Elgin (G-8775)
▲ Waltz Brothers Inc...E ... 847 520-1122
Wheeling (G-21011)
▲ Wanxiang USA Holdings Corp...F ... 847 622-8838
Elgin (G-8776)
▲ Warner Electric LLC...C ... 815 389-4300
South Beloit (G-19122)
Windy City Engineering Inc...F ... 773 254-8113
Chicago (G-6640)
Winhere Brake Parts Inc...G ... 630 307-0158
Bartlett (G-1324)
▲ Woodbridge Inc...F ... 847 229-1741
Wheeling (G-21015)
Wpg US Holdco LLC...B ... 312 517-3750
Chicago (G-6681)
Ycl International Inc...E ... 630 873-0768
Woodridge (G-21350)
Zeigler Chrysler Dodge...G ... 708 956-7700
Berwyn (G-1963)
ZF Chassis Components LLC...B ... 773 371-4550
Chicago (G-6718)
ZF North America Inc...C ... 847 478-6868
Vernon Hills (G-20114)
◆ ZF Services LLC...B ... 847 478-6868
Vernon Hills (G-20115)

3715 Truck Trailers

A & S Steel Specialties Inc...E ... 815 838-8188
Lockport (G-12979)
Advanced Mobility &...E ... 708 235-2800
Monee (G-14195)
Azcon Inc...F ... 815 548-7000
Sterling (G-19499)
Barrington Financial Services...G ... 847 404-1767
Lake In The Hills (G-12330)
Barron 2m Inc...G ... 847 219-3650
Schaumburg (G-18456)
Classic Roadliner Corporation...G ... 708 769-0666
Justice (G-11950)
D D Sales Inc...E ... 217 857-3196
Teutopolis (G-19768)
Dolche Truckload Corp...G ... 800 719-4921
Palatine (G-16113)
Dundee Truck & Trlr Works LLC...G ... 224 484-8182
East Dundee (G-8195)
Entrans International LLC...E ... 618 548-3660
Salem (G-18337)
Fleetpride Inc...C ... 708 430-2081
Bridgeview (G-2347)
Great Dane LLC...C ... 309 854-0407
Kewanee (G-12036)
Great Dane LLC...B ... 309 854-0407
Kewanee (G-12037)
Great Dane LLC...D ... 773 254-5533
Kewanee (G-12038)
◆ Great Dane LLC...D ... 773 254-5533
Chicago (G-4733)
Groovy Logistics Inc...G ... 847 946-1491
Joliet (G-11871)
Hunter Logistics...G ... 309 299-7015
Wataga (G-20286)
Imperial Group Mfg Inc...B ... 615 325-9224
Chicago (G-4897)
Jhb Group Inc...G ... 657 888-3473
Cary (G-3173)
Load Redi Inc...G ... 217 784-4200
Gibson City (G-10340)
Maple Park Trucking Inc...G ... 815 899-1958
Maple Park (G-13465)
Matt Snell and Sons...G ... 618 695-3555
Vienna (G-20118)
Mickey Truck Bodies Inc...F ... 309 827-8227
Bloomington (G-2076)
▲ Midland Manufacturing Corp...C ... 847 677-0333
Skokie (G-18990)
Mmm Uno Corp...G ... 773 577-7329
Streamwood (G-19586)
Paramount Truck Body Co Inc...E ... 312 666-6441
Chicago (G-5762)
Peter Built...E ... 618 337-4000
East Saint Louis (G-8318)
Pk Corporation...G ... 847 879-1070
Elk Grove Village (G-9180)
Quality Trailer Sales Inc...G ... 630 739-2495
Morton (G-14380)
Roadex Carriers Inc...G ... 773 454-8772
Wheeling (G-20975)
Robert Davis & Son Inc...G ... 815 889-4168
Milford (G-14036)
Seat Trans Inc...G ... 224 522-1007
Lake In The Hills (G-12343)
STI Holdings Inc...F ... 630 789-2713
Burr Ridge (G-2722)
Summit Tank & Equipment Co...F ... 708 594-3040
Mc Cook (G-13703)
Timpte Industries Inc...D ... 309 820-1095
Bloomington (G-2102)
U S Intermodal Inc...E ... 708 448-9862
Frankfort (G-9848)
Vaughan Equipment Inc...G ... 618 842-3500
Fairfield (G-9638)

3716 Motor Homes

Liberty Coach Inc...D ... 847 578-4600
North Chicago (G-15316)

3721 Aircraft

A & S Helicopters Inc...G ... 618 337-2600
Cahokia (G-2760)
A R B C Inc...F ... 815 777-6006
Galena (G-10163)
Aerostars Inc...G ... 847 736-8171
Cary (G-3145)
Aerovision Engine Services LLC...E ... 231 799-9000
Chicago (G-3576)
Aviation Services Group Inc...G ... 708 425-4700
Chicago Ridge (G-6788)
Boeing Company...C ... 312 544-2000
Chicago (G-3925)
Boeing Company...G ... 618 746-4062
Scott Afb (G-18856)
Boeing Global Holdings Corp...G ... 312 544-2000
Chicago (G-3926)
Boeing International Corp...E ... 312 544-2000
Chicago (G-3927)
Boeing LTS Inc...B ... 312 544-2000
Chicago (G-3929)
Calumet Motorsports Inc...G ... 708 895-0398
Lansing (G-12487)
Elan Express Inc...E ... 815 713-1190
Rockford (G-17393)
Gulfstream Aerospace Corp...A ... 630 470-9146
Naperville (G-14839)
Gulfstream Aerospace Corp...G ... 815 469-1509
Frankfort (G-9798)
Helivalues...G ... 847 487-8258
Wauconda (G-20355)
Ibanum Manufacturing LLC...G ... 815 262-5373
Rockford (G-17455)
Inav LLC...F ... 847 847-3600
Crystal Lake (G-7209)
Jet Aviation St Louis Inc...D ... 618 646-8000
Cahokia (G-2761)
Learjet Inc...B ... 847 553-0172
Des Plaines (G-7797)
Mitchell Arcft Expendables LLC...E ... 847 516-3773
Cary (G-3180)
Quad City Ultralight Aircraft...F ... 309 764-3515
Moline (G-14171)
Raytheon Technologies Corp...B ... 815 226-6000
Rockford (G-17567)
Ruby Industrial Tech LLC...E ... 317 248-8355
Wood Dale (G-21235)
SC Aviation Inc...G ... 800 416-4176
Saint Charles (G-18264)
Southern Ill Helicopters LLC...G ... 618 997-0101
Marion (G-13537)
▲ Strauss Facter Assoc Inc...G ... 847 759-1100
Park Ridge (G-16297)
Textron Aviation Inc...G ... 630 443-5080
West Chicago (G-20650)
Tribus Aerospace Corp...G ... 312 876-2683
Chicago (G-6426)

3724 Aircraft Engines & Engine Parts

▲ AAR Corp...D ... 630 227-2000
Wood Dale (G-21149)
Acra Products...G ... 847 346-9889
Addison (G-17)
▼ Aero-Cables Corp...G ... 815 609-6600
Oswego (G-15990)
Aerovision Engine Services LLC...E ... 231 799-9000
Chicago (G-3576)
▲ Aertrade LLC...G ... 630 428-4440
Aurora (G-910)
▲ Area Diesel Service Inc...E ... 217 854-2641
Carlinville (G-2867)
▲ Arrow Gear Company...B ... 630 969-7640
Downers Grove (G-7955)
Chemring Energetic Devices Inc...C ... 630 969-0620
Downers Grove (G-7968)
▲ CTS Electronic Components Inc...D ... 630 577-8800
Lisle (G-12882)
Danville Metal Stamping Co Inc...F ... 217 446-0647
Danville (G-7328)
Danville Metal Stamping Co Inc...F ... 217 446-0647
Danville (G-7329)
Dynomax Inc...E ... 847 680-8833
Wheeling (G-20882)
▲ Dynomax Inc...B ... 847 680-8833
Wheeling (G-20883)
▲ Essex Electro Engineers Inc...E ... 847 891-4444
Schaumburg (G-18522)
GE Ges Inc...G ... 815 307-0595
Ingleside (G-11583)
General Machinery & Mfg Co...F ... 773 235-3700
Chicago (G-4674)
Green Apu LLC...G ... 310 736-2211
Lemont (G-12565)
Heligear Acquisition Co...C ... 708 728-2000
Bedford Park (G-1471)
Honeywell...E ... 815 235-5500
Freeport (G-10115)
Honeywell Inc...F ... 618 546-1671
Robinson (G-17117)
Honeywell International Inc...F ... 847 251-3510
Freeport (G-10116)
Honeywell International Inc...A ... 630 960-5282
Darien (G-7407)
Honeywell International Inc...A ... 630 922-0138
Naperville (G-14973)
Honeywell International Inc...G ... 630 554-5342
Oswego (G-16007)
Honeywell International Inc...D ... 815 266-3209
Freeport (G-10117)
Honeywell International Inc...E ... 847 797-4612
Des Plaines (G-7779)
Honeywell International Inc...A ... 401 573-6821
Moline (G-14149)
Honeywell International Inc...A ... 480 353-3020
Chicago (G-4837)
Honeywell International Inc...A ... 847 701-3038
Palatine (G-16125)
Honeywell International Inc...C ... 815 663-2011
Spring Valley (G-19308)
Honeywell International Inc...C ... 815 777-2780
Galena (G-10174)

SIC

Employee Codes: A=Over 500 employees, B=251-500
C=101-250, D=51-100, E=20-50, F=10-19, G=3-9
2020 Harris Illinois
Industrial Directory
999

37 TRANSPORTATION EQUIPMENT

Honeywell International Inc ....B....... 630 377-6580
  Saint Charles (G-18207)
Honeywell International Inc ....G....... 847 634-2802
  Lincolnshire (G-12771)
Honeywell International Inc ....A....... 973 455-2000
  Chicago (G-4838)
Honeywell International Inc ....A....... 309 383-4045
  Metamora (G-13961)
Honeywell International Inc 217 431-3710
  Danville (G-7346)
I D Rockford Shop Inc ....G....... 815 335-1150
  Winnebago (G-21120)
▲ Ihi Turbo America Co ....D....... 217 774-9571
  Shelbyville (G-18880)
Innovative Design and RES Inc ....G....... 217 322-3907
  Rushville (G-18111)
Jetpower LLC ....F....... 847 856-8359
  Gurnee (G-10889)
Midwest Fuel Injction Svc Corp ....F....... 847 991-7867
  Palatine (G-16140)
Pietro Carnaghi USA Inc ....G....... 779 368-0564
  Rockford (G-17554)
Precoat Metals Corp ....D....... 618 451-0909
  Granite City (G-10731)
Raytheon Technologies Corp ....B....... 630 516-3460
  Elmhurst (G-9415)
Raytheon Technologies Corp 815 226-6000
  Rockford (G-17567)
Superior Joining Tech Inc ....E....... 815 282-7581
  Machesney Park (G-13376)
Universal Trnspt Systems LLC ....F....... 312 994-2349
  Chicago (G-6484)
Woodward Inc ....A....... 815 877-7441
  Loves Park (G-13282)

3728 Aircraft Parts & Eqpt, NEC

A J R Industries Inc ....E....... 847 439-0380
  Elk Grove Village (G-8791)
▲ AAR Aircraft & Eng Sls & Lsg ....G....... 630 227-2000
  Wood Dale (G-21147)
▼ AAR Allen Services Inc ....D....... 630 227-2410
  Wood Dale (G-21148)
AAR Government Services Inc ....E....... 630 227-2000
  Wood Dale (G-21150)
▲ AAR Supply Chain Inc ....D....... 630 227-2000
  Wood Dale (G-21151)
ACS Parts Group LLC 815 211-4707
  Park Forest (G-16249)
Aero Aviation Company Inc 618 797-6630
  Granite City (G-10690)
Air Land and Sea Interiors ....G....... 630 834-1717
  Villa Park (G-20129)
▲ Aircraft Gear Corporation ....D....... 815 877-7473
  Loves Park (G-13185)
Airport Aviation Professionals ....G....... 773 948-6631
  Chicago (G-3589)
American Concorde Systems ....F....... 773 342-9951
  Streamwood (G-19561)
American Science and Tech Corp ......G....... 312 433-3800
  Chicago (G-3666)
Armstrong Aerospace Inc ....D....... 847 244-4500
  Waukegan (G-20418)
Art Technologies Inc 773 557-3896
  Bensenville (G-1747)
Astronics Cnnctvty Systems Cr ....F....... 847 821-3059
  Waukegan (G-20419)
Auxitrol SA ....G....... 815 874-2471
  Rockford (G-17309)
Azimuth Cnc Inc ....F....... 815 399-4433
  Rockford (G-17310)
▲ Bison Aerospace and Def LLC 618 795-2678
  Savanna (G-18403)
Boaleeco Inc ....G....... 847 428-3085
  Gilberts (G-10351)
Boeing Company ....C....... 312 544-2000
  Chicago (G-3925)
Brunswick International Ltd 847 735-4700
  Mettawa (G-13980)
Calport Aviation Company ....G....... 630 588-8091
  Bartlett (G-1254)
CEF Industries LLC 630 628-2299
  Addison (G-65)
Certifynation Inc ....G....... 775 237-8439
  Elmhurst (G-9342)
Chicago Midway Airport ....G....... 773 838-0600
  Chicago (G-4117)
Chucking Machine Products Inc ....D....... 847 678-1192
  Franklin Park (G-9907)
CMC Electronics Aurora LLC ....D....... 630 556-9619
  Sugar Grove (G-19640)

Cyn Industries Inc ....F....... 773 895-4324
  Chicago (G-4295)
Direct Aerosystems Inc ....F....... 630 509-2141
  Aurora (G-952)
Electronica Aviation LLC ....G....... 407 498-1092
  Chicago (G-4479)
▲ Frasca International Inc ....C....... 217 344-9200
  Urbana (G-19986)
GE Aviation Systems LLC 779 203-8100
  Loves Park (G-13214)
Goodrich Corporation ....F....... 815 226-5915
  Rockford (G-17433)
▼ Gpe Controls Inc ....G....... 708 236-6000
  Hillside (G-11340)
Hamilton Sndstrand Space Syste .....G....... 815 226-6000
  Rockford (G-17439)
Hamilton Sundstrand Corp ....A....... 815 226-6000
  Rockford (G-17441)
Helitune Inc 847 228-0985
  Elk Grove Village (G-9032)
Ibanum Manufacturing LLC 815 262-5373
  Rockford (G-17455)
Ingenium Aerospace LLC 815 525-2000
  Rockford (G-17460)
Jet X Aerospace LLC 630 238-1920
  Bensenville (G-1830)
Jetpower LLC ....F....... 847 856-8359
  Gurnee (G-10889)
▲ Jsn Inc ....E....... 708 410-1800
  Maywood (G-13670)
Kellstrom Coml Arospc Inc 847 233-5800
  Roselle (G-17961)
Kemell Enterprises LLC 618 671-1513
  Belleville (G-1561)
Logan Actuator Co 815 943-9500
  Harvard (G-11059)
Makerite Mfg Co Inc 815 389-3902
  Roscoe (G-17916)
Mitchell Aircraft Products 815 331-8609
  McHenry (G-13771)
▲ Mitchell Aircraft Spares Inc ....E....... 847 516-3773
  Cary (G-3179)
◆ Mpc Products Corporation ....A....... 847 673-8300
  Niles (G-15149)
▲ Multax Corporation ....D....... 309 266-9765
  Morton (G-14372)
New Gen Aerospace Corp ....G....... 847 740-2216
  Lake Villa (G-12361)
Northstar Aerospace (usa) Inc ....F....... 708 728-2000
  Bedford Park (G-1486)
▲ Nsa (chi) Liquidating Corp ....F....... 708 728-2000
  Elmhurst (G-9406)
Prograf LLC 815 234-4848
  Villa Park (G-20166)
Quad City Ultralight Aircraft ....F....... 309 764-3515
  Moline (G-14171)
Qualiseal Technology LLC ....E....... 708 887-6080
  Harwood Heights (G-11108)
S I A Inc 708 361-3100
  Palos Heights (G-16191)
▼ Seginus Inc 630 800-2795
  Oswego (G-16025)
Shadowtech Labs Inc ....G....... 630 413-4478
  Willowbrook (G-21060)
Skandia Inc ....D....... 800 945-7135
  Davis Junction (G-7427)
South Subn Logistics Sups Corp ....G....... 312 804-3401
  Harvey (G-11096)
Systems & Electronics Inc 847 228-0985
  Elk Grove Village (G-9263)
Textron Aviation Inc 630 443-5080
  West Chicago (G-20650)
Thales Visionix Inc ....D....... 630 375-2008
  Aurora (G-1161)
TI International Ltd 847 689-0233
  North Chicago (G-15322)
Trident Machine Co 815 968-1585
  Rockford (G-17668)
Triumph Group Inc 312 498-2516
  Willowbrook (G-21064)
▲ Vestergaard Company Inc ....G....... 815 759-9102
  McHenry (G-13807)
◆ Video Refurbishing Svcs Inc ....E....... 847 844-7366
  Carpentersville (G-3122)
Vonberg Valve Inc ....E....... 847 259-3800
  Rolling Meadows (G-17785)
Wittenstein Arspc Smlation Inc 630 540-5300
  Bartlett (G-1326)
Woodward Inc ....B....... 815 877-7441
  Loves Park (G-13281)

Woodward Governor Hlth Svcs Tr ....G....... 815 877-7441
  Loves Park (G-13283)

3731 Shipbuilding & Repairing

▲ Chicago Flyhouse Incorporated .....F....... 773 533-1590
  Chicago (G-4104)
Full Circle Shipyard LLC ....G....... 630 343-2264
  Lemont (G-12564)
▲ Midland Manufacturing Corp ....C....... 847 677-0333
  Skokie (G-18990)
▲ Mikes Inc ....D....... 618 254-4491
  South Roxana (G-19253)
▲ National Maint & Repr Inc 618 254-7451
  Hartford (G-11036)
Rinker Boat Company ....E....... 574 457-5731
  Chicago (G-6034)
Williamson J Hunter & Company 847 441-7888
  Winnetka (G-21137)

3732 Boat Building & Repairing

Advocations Inc ....G....... 815 568-7505
  Woodstock (G-21356)
Air Land and Sea Interiors 630 834-1717
  Villa Park (G-20129)
Akema Inc ....G....... 708 482-3148
  La Grange (G-12070)
◆ Brunswick Corporation ....B....... 847 735-4700
  Mettawa (G-13979)
Brunswick Family Boat Co Inc 847 735-4700
  Lake Forest (G-12234)
Brunswick International Ltd ....E....... 847 735-4700
  Mettawa (G-13980)
▼ Chicago Sea Ray Inc ....E....... 815 385-2720
  Volo (G-20197)
Crowleys Yacht Yard Lakeside ....F....... 773 221-9990
  Chicago (G-4276)
Custom Fiberglass of Illinois 309 344-7727
  Galesburg (G-10189)
Elite Power Boats Inc 618 654-6292
  Highland (G-11215)
Karma Yacht Sales LLC ....G....... 773 254-0200
  Chicago (G-5083)
▼ Leisure Properties LLC ....A....... 618 937-6426
  West Frankfort (G-20675)
Mastercraft Auto Rebuilding ....F....... 847 487-8787
  Wauconda (G-20373)
Metro East Fiberglass Repair 618 235-9217
  Belleville (G-1577)
▼ Nautic Global Group LLC 574 457-5731
  Chicago (G-5555)
Oquawka Boats and Fabrications 309 867-2213
  Oquawka (G-15906)
Outback USA Inc 863 699-2220
  Saint Charles (G-18240)
Rinalli Boat Co Inc ....G....... 618 467-8850
  Godfrey (G-10660)
Scf Services LLC ....E....... 314 436-7559
  Sauget (G-18398)
Sereen LLC 386 527-4876
  Rockford (G-17625)
Tls Windsled Inc 815 262-5791
  Belvidere (G-1704)
Union Ave Auto Inc 708 754-3899
  Steger (G-19495)
◆ Wave Pads LLC 224 444-9283
  Plainfield (G-16728)
Waypoint Enterprises 847 551-9213
  Algonquin (G-395)

3743 Railroad Eqpt

A & S Steel Specialties Inc ....E....... 815 838-8188
  Lockport (G-12979)
▲ Aldon Co ....F....... 847 623-8800
  Waukegan (G-20412)
Alliance Wheel Services LLC ....G....... 309 444-4334
  Washington (G-20265)
▼ Amfab LLC 630 783-2570
  Lemont (G-12553)
◆ Amsted Industries Incorporated ....B....... 312 645-1700
  Chicago (G-3685)
Amsted Rail Company Inc ....D....... 312 258-8000
  Chicago (G-3688)
Amsted Rail Company Inc 618 452-2111
  Granite City (G-10695)
Amsted Rail Company Inc ....B....... 618 225-6463
  Granite City (G-10695)
Anchor Brake Shoe Company LLC ....F....... 630 293-1110
  West Chicago (G-20541)
▲ Cardwell Westinghouse Company ..D....... 773 483-7575
  Chicago (G-4027)

37 TRANSPORTATION EQUIPMENT

▲ Clark Industrial Prpts Inc ....G....... 815 265-7210
  Gilman *(G-10377)*
Creative Rlcar Mktg Svcs II LL...........G....... 773 396-1114
  Chicago *(G-4266)*
Creative Rlcar Mktg Svcs II LL...........G....... 773 396-1114
  Chicago *(G-4267)*
Eagle Freight Inc ....G....... 708 202-0651
  Franklin Park *(G-9935)*
▲ Freight Car Services Inc ....B....... 217 443-4106
  Danville *(G-7336)*
◆ Freightcar America Inc ....D....... 800 458-2235
  Chicago *(G-4635)*
Fugiel Railroad Supply Corp................G....... 847 516-6862
  Cary *(G-3160)*
Gateway Rail Services Inc..................F....... 618 451-0100
  Madison *(G-13412)*
▲ GE Transportation Parts LLC.........E....... 814 875-2755
  Chicago *(G-4666)*
▲ Hadady Corporation ....E....... 219 322-7417
  South Holland *(G-19218)*
▲ Holden America II LLC ....G....... 708 552-4070
  Chicago *(G-4829)*
◆ Holland LP ....C....... 708 672-2300
  Crete *(G-7140)*
▲ Illini Castings LLC ....F....... 217 446-6365
  Danville *(G-7349)*
▲ Illinois Transit Assembly Corp........F....... 618 451-0100
  Madison *(G-13415)*
Jaix Leasing Company ....G....... 312 928-0850
  Chicago *(G-5000)*
Kevin Robinson......................................G....... 618 410-3083
  Caseyville *(G-3217)*
Locodocs Inc ....G....... 815 448-2100
  Mazon *(G-13682)*
▲ Maclean Fastener Services LLC ....G....... 847 353-8402
  Buffalo Grove *(G-2566)*
◆ Marmon Holdings Inc ....D....... 312 372-9500
  Chicago *(G-5343)*
◆ Marmon Industrial LLC ....G....... 312 372-9500
  Chicago *(G-5344)*
Meadoweld Machine Inc ....G....... 815 623-3939
  South Beloit *(G-19102)*
Midland Railway Supply Inc................E....... 618 467-6305
  Godfrey *(G-10657)*
Midwest Railcar Corporation ....E....... 618 692-5575
  Edwardsville *(G-8371)*
◆ MWK Rail LLC ....G....... 815 671-5217
  Urbana *(G-19989)*
Narita Manufacturing Inc ....F....... 248 345-1777
  Belvidere *(G-1688)*
National Railway Equipment Co.........D....... 708 388-4781
  Dixmoor *(G-7884)*
National Railway Equipment Co.........C....... 309 755-6800
  Silvis *(G-18908)*
National Railway Equipment Co.........E....... 708 388-6002
  Dixmoor *(G-7885)*
National Railway Equipment Co.........G....... 618 241-9270
  Mount Vernon *(G-14630)*
▲ National Trackwork Inc...................E....... 630 250-0600
  Itasca *(G-11708)*
Nis Express Inc ....G....... 708 880-4090
  Hickory Hills *(G-11201)*
Nordco Inc ....E....... 414 766-2180
  Arcola *(G-660)*
Pintsch Tiefenbach Us Inc ....G....... 618 993-8513
  Marion *(G-13527)*
Prairie Island Inc ....G....... 630 395-9846
  Westmont *(G-20767)*
Precision Screw Machining Co...........F....... 773 205-4280
  Chicago *(G-5859)*
Professional RR Solutions LLC...........G....... 815 209-7473
  Roscoe *(G-17922)*
Progress Rail Services Corp.................E....... 618 451-0072
  Granite City *(G-10734)*
Progress Rail Services Corp.................F....... 309 343-6170
  Galesburg *(G-10216)*
Rail Exchange Inc ....E....... 708 757-3317
  Chicago Heights *(G-6767)*
Railway & Industrial Svcs Inc ....C....... 815 726-4224
  Crest Hill *(G-7094)*
Railway Program Services Inc............G....... 708 552-4000
  Chicago *(G-5964)*
Ramptech Inc ....G....... 303 936-3641
  Chicago *(G-5966)*
▲ Ramptech Inc ....E....... 708 594-2179
  Chicago *(G-5967)*
Relco Locomotives Inc ....D....... 630 968-0670
  Burr Ridge *(G-2716)*
Rescar Companies Inc ....G....... 618 875-3234
  East Saint Louis *(G-8320)*

Right Rail LLC ....G....... 630 882-9335
  Yorkville *(G-21500)*
Russell Enterprises Inc ....B....... 847 692-6050
  Park Ridge *(G-16295)*
Salco Products Inc................................D....... 630 783-2570
  Lemont *(G-12588)*
Seec Trasportation Corp......................G....... 800 215-4003
  Chicago *(G-6132)*
◆ Standard Car Truck Company ......E....... 847 692-6050
  Rosemont *(G-18051)*
Standard Car Truck Company ....D....... 630 860-5511
  Bensenville *(G-1899)*
Teleweld Inc ....F....... 815 672-4561
  Streator *(G-19629)*
Tenneco Intl Holdg Corp ....F....... 847 482-5000
  Lake Forest *(G-12313)*
▲ Transco Railway Products Inc ......C....... 312 427-2818
  Chicago *(G-6409)*
◆ Union Tank Car Company ....E....... 312 431-3111
  Chicago *(G-6466)*
Union Tank Car Company ....G....... 815 942-7391
  Morris *(G-14336)*
Union Tank Car Company ....C....... 312 431-3111
  Chicago *(G-6467)*
UTC Railcar Repair Svcs LLC ....A....... 312 431-5053
  Chicago *(G-6508)*
Voestalpine Nortrak Inc ....D....... 217 876-9160
  Decatur *(G-7567)*
Voestalpine Nortrak Inc ....G....... 708 753-2125
  Chicago Heights *(G-6786)*
Wallace Industries Inc ....G....... 815 389-8999
  South Beloit *(G-19119)*
▲ Western Railway Devices Corp .....G....... 847 625-8500
  Lake Bluff *(G-12216)*
Western-Cullen-Hayes Inc..................D....... 773 254-9600
  Chicago *(G-6609)*
◆ Whiting Corporation ....C....... 800 861-5744
  Monee *(G-14212)*
Willims-Hyward Intl Ctings Inc............F....... 708 458-0015
  Argo *(G-678)*

3751 Motorcycles, Bicycles & Parts

Black Magic Customs Inc.....................G....... 815 786-1977
  Sandwich *(G-18366)*
▲ Brg Sports Inc ....D....... 224 585-5200
  Des Plaines *(G-7741)*
Chopper Mm LLC ....G....... 309 875-3544
  Maquon *(G-13477)*
▲ Colnago America Inc ....G....... 312 239-6666
  Chicago *(G-4202)*
David Taylor..E....... 217 222-6480
  Quincy *(G-16875)*
Franks Maintenance & Engrg ....G....... 847 475-1003
  Evanston *(G-9523)*
Gs Custom Works Inc...........................G....... 815 233-4724
  Freeport *(G-10113)*
Industrial Opprtnity Prtners L...............E....... 847 556-3460
  Evanston *(G-9538)*
▲ Joe Hunt...G....... 618 392-2000
  Olney *(G-15866)*
▲ Kyosei International Corp ....G....... 847 821-0341
  Buffalo Grove *(G-2558)*
Midwest Recumbent Bicycles..............G....... 618 343-1885
  Mascoutah *(G-13604)*
Monahan Partners Inc ....F....... 217 268-5758
  Arcola *(G-658)*
◆ National Cycle Inc ....C....... 708 343-0400
  Maywood *(G-13674)*
Pacific Cycle Inc....................................E....... 618 393-2508
  Olney *(G-15882)*
Pruett Enterprises Inc...........................E....... 618 235-6184
  Belleville *(G-1586)*
Quality Plating......................................G....... 815 626-5223
  Sterling *(G-19526)*
◆ Sram LLC ....D....... 312 664-8800
  Chicago *(G-6223)*
Taurus Cycle...G....... 309 454-1565
  Bloomington *(G-2099)*
Valley Racing Inc..................................G....... 708 946-1440
  Beecher *(G-1523)*
W L & J Enterprises Inc ....G....... 708 946-0999
  Beecher *(G-1524)*
World of Soul Inc ....G....... 773 840-4839
  Chicago *(G-6676)*
Wrench ....G....... 773 609-1698
  Chicago *(G-6684)*

3761 Guided Missiles & Space Vehicles

Boeing Company ....C....... 312 544-2000
  Chicago *(G-3925)*

Branmark Strategy Group LLC ....G....... 847 849-9080
  Glenview *(G-10534)*
National Def Intelligence Inc................C....... 312 233-2318
  Naperville *(G-14980)*

3764 Guided Missile/Space Vehicle Propulsion Units & parts

Atks Inc ....G....... 715 914-0395
  Chicago *(G-3760)*
Boeing Company ....C....... 312 544-2000
  Chicago *(G-3925)*

3769 Guided Missile/Space Vehicle Parts & Eqpt, NEC

AAC Microtec North America Inc ....E....... 602 284-7997
  Columbia *(G-6982)*
Azimuth Cnc Inc....................................F....... 815 399-4433
  Rockford *(G-17310)*
Chemring Energetic Devices ....C....... 310 784-2100
  Downers Grove *(G-7967)*
▲ Duraflex Inc ....E....... 847 462-1007
  Cary *(G-3156)*
Spytek Aerospace Corporation ....G....... 847 318-7515
  Bensenville *(G-1898)*
Wilson Tool Corporation ....E....... 815 226-0147
  Rockford *(G-17687)*

3792 Travel Trailers & Campers

A & S Steel Specialties Inc..................E....... 815 838-8188
  Lockport *(G-12979)*
Arthur Leo Kuhl ....G....... 618 752-5473
  Ingraham *(G-11591)*
Boyd Spotting Inc ....G....... 217 669-2418
  Cisco *(G-6891)*
Brumleve Industries Inc ....F....... 217 857-3777
  Teutopolis *(G-19764)*
▲ Davison Co Ltd ....G....... 815 966-2905
  Rockford *(G-17370)*
Dedicated Tcs LLC ....F....... 815 467-9560
  Channahon *(G-3378)*
I94 Rv LLC ....G....... 847 395-9500
  Russell *(G-18114)*
Lakeshore Lacrosse LLC......................G....... 773 350-4356
  Wheaton *(G-20810)*
▲ Rieco-Titan Products Inc................E....... 815 464-7400
  Frankfort *(G-9831)*
◆ Travel Caddy Inc ....E....... 847 621-7000
  Franklin Park *(G-10065)*

3795 Tanks & Tank Components

Bruder Tank Inc....................................E....... 217 292-9058
  Sullivan *(G-19662)*
Chelsea Framing Products Inc ....G....... 847 550-5556
  Lake Zurich *(G-12393)*
◆ Navistar Defense LLC ....E....... 708 617-4500
  Melrose Park *(G-13896)*
◆ Protectoseal Company ....G....... 630 595-0800
  Bensenville *(G-1876)*

3799 Transportation Eqpt, NEC

▲ Advance Metalworking Company...E....... 309 853-3387
  Kewanee *(G-12019)*
◆ Brennan Equipment and Mfg Inc ..D....... 708 534-5500
  University Park *(G-19950)*
Brewer Utility Systems Inc...................G....... 217 224-5975
  Quincy *(G-16868)*
Custom Millers Supply Inc...................G....... 309 734-6312
  Monmouth *(G-14216)*
Great Lakes Forge Company ....G....... 773 277-2800
  Chicago *(G-4735)*
Grs Holding LLC ....F....... 630 355-1660
  Naperville *(G-14838)*
◆ Howland Technology Inc ....F....... 847 965-9808
  Morton Grove *(G-14411)*
IPC Group Purchasing ....G....... 630 276-5485
  Naperville *(G-14850)*
▲ Kerins Industries Inc ....G....... 630 515-9111
  Darien *(G-7408)*
Knight Bros Inc ....G....... 618 439-9626
  Benton *(G-1930)*
Loraines Logistics LLC.........................G....... 800 839-6943
  Chicago *(G-5259)*
M & C Powersports ....G....... 207 713-3128
  Kankakee *(G-11990)*
New World Trnsp Systems ....C....... 773 509-5931
  Chicago *(G-5583)*
▲ Scaletta Moloney Armoring ....C....... 708 924-0099
  Bedford Park *(G-1503)*

Employee Codes: A=Over 500 employees, B=251-500
C=101-250, D=51-100, E=20-50, F=10-19, G=3-9

2020 Harris Illinois
Industrial Directory

1001

▲ **Smart Solar Inc**.....F.....813 343-5770
Libertyville *(G-12708)*
Synergy Power Group LLC.....E.....618 247-3200
Sandoval *(G-18365)*
T & D Metal Products LLC.....G.....815 432-4938
Watseka *(G-20318)*
T & E Enterprises Herscher Inc.....F.....815 426-2761
Herscher *(G-11188)*
Triple B Manufacturing Co Inc.....G.....618 566-2888
Mascoutah *(G-13607)*
◆ **Wise Equipment & Rentals Inc**.....F.....847 895-5555
Schaumburg *(G-18774)*

38 MEASURING, ANALYZING AND CONTROLLING INSTRUMENTS; PHOTOGRAPHIC, MEDICAL AN

3812 Search, Detection, Navigation & Guidance Systs & Instrs

2nd Amendment Defense Inc.....G.....815 218-2847
Rockford *(G-17276)*
▲ **Acl Inc**.....F.....773 285-0295
Chicago *(G-3525)*
Andrew New Zealand Inc.....E.....708 873-3507
Orland Park *(G-15940)*
ARINC Incorporated.....E.....800 633-6882
O Fallon *(G-15567)*
Auxitrol SA.....G.....815 874-2471
Rockford *(G-17309)*
Bizstarterscom LLC.....G.....847 305-4626
Arlington Heights *(G-705)*
Black Bear Defense LLC.....G.....708 357-7233
Chicago *(G-3906)*
Blaxtair Inc.....G.....312 299-5590
Chicago *(G-3910)*
Boeing Company.....C.....312 544-2000
Chicago *(G-3925)*
▲ **Bolingbrook Communications Inc**.....A.....630 759-9500
Lisle *(G-12874)*
Bring Your Own Auto Parts Inc.....F.....815 730-6900
Crest Hill *(G-7084)*
Brunswick International Ltd.....E.....847 735-4700
Mettawa *(G-13980)*
▲ **CAM Co Inc**.....F.....630 556-3110
Big Rock *(G-1969)*
Cedar Elec Holdings Corp.....G.....630 862-7282
Chicago *(G-4051)*
CEF Industries LLC.....C.....630 628-2299
Addison *(G-65)*
Checkpoint Systems Inc.....D.....630 771-4240
Romeoville *(G-17806)*
Chemring Energetic Devices Inc.....C.....630 969-0620
Downers Grove *(G-7968)*
Contego Defense Group.....G.....630 532-1063
Woodridge *(G-21287)*
▼ **Csiteq LLC**.....F.....312 265-1509
Rosemont *(G-18011)*
Ctg Advanced Materials LLC.....E.....630 226-9080
Bolingbrook *(G-2161)*
D W Terry Welding Company.....G.....618 433-9722
Alton *(G-551)*
Dapper Defense LLC.....G.....309 922-9203
East Peoria *(G-8265)*
Ecolotech Asl Inc.....G.....630 859-0485
Aurora *(G-1086)*
Electro-Technic Products Inc.....F.....773 561-2349
Chicago *(G-4478)*
Engility Corporation.....G.....847 583-1216
Skokie *(G-18951)*
Engility Corporation.....G.....708 596-8245
Harvey *(G-11083)*
Epir Technologies Inc.....E.....630 771-0203
Bolingbrook *(G-2175)*
Frostdefense Envirotech Inc.....G.....217 979-3052
Champaign *(G-3293)*
FSI Technologies Inc.....E.....630 932-9380
Lombard *(G-13080)*
Graceland Custom Products Inc.....F.....630 616-4143
Bensenville *(G-1815)*
Graceland Ferray Products.....G.....847 258-3828
Arlington Heights *(G-743)*
Guardian Personal Defense Tng.....G.....630 272-9811
Oswego *(G-16006)*
Honeywell International Inc.....A.....401 573-6821
Moline *(G-14149)*
Ihi Terrasun Solutions Inc.....G.....312 878-8532
Chicago *(G-4883)*
Illinois Ticket Defense Firm.....G.....954 467-1965
Saint Charles *(G-18210)*
Intex Systems Corp.....G.....630 636-6594
Oswego *(G-16008)*
Kaney Capital LLC.....G.....815 986-4359
Rockford *(G-17480)*
Kaney Group LLC.....F.....815 986-4359
Rockford *(G-17481)*
Kogan Self Defense.....G.....847 877-4711
Buffalo Grove *(G-2555)*
Kvh Industries Inc.....E.....708 444-2800
Tinley Park *(G-19843)*
L A M Inc De.....G.....630 860-9700
Wood Dale *(G-21206)*
Learjet Inc.....B.....847 553-0172
Des Plaines *(G-7797)*
Lg Innotek USA Inc.....G.....847 941-8713
Lincolnshire *(G-12780)*
Lockheed Martin Corporation.....G.....618 628-0700
O Fallon *(G-15579)*
Magnetec Inspection Inc.....F.....815 802-1363
Bradley *(G-2286)*
▲ **Marine Technologies Inc**.....E.....847 546-9001
Volo *(G-20203)*
Measurement Devices US LLC.....F.....281 646-0050
Dundee *(G-8129)*
MidAmerican Technology Inc.....G.....815 496-2400
Serena *(G-18864)*
Midwest Aero Support Inc.....E.....815 398-9202
Machesney Park *(G-13360)*
Motorola Solutions Inc.....C.....847 576-8600
Schaumburg *(G-18637)*
Motorola Solutions Inc.....G.....847 341-3485
Oak Brook *(G-15647)*
◆ **Mpc Products Corporation**.....A.....847 673-8300
Niles *(G-15149)*
National Aerospace Corp.....G.....847 566-5834
Hawthorn Woods *(G-11125)*
◆ **Navistar Defense LLC**.....E.....708 617-4500
Melrose Park *(G-13896)*
▲ **Navman Wireless Holdings LP**.....D.....866 527-9896
Glenview *(G-10592)*
Northrop Grumman Systems Corp.....D.....847 259-9600
Rolling Meadows *(G-17756)*
Oceancomm Incorporated.....G.....800 757-3266
Chicago *(G-5653)*
Open Hand Self Defense.....G.....815 718-3994
Morrison *(G-14346)*
Quartix Inc.....F.....855 913-6663
Chicago *(G-5934)*
Raytheon Company.....B.....630 295-6394
Rolling Meadows *(G-17770)*
Research In Motion Rf Inc.....G.....815 444-1095
Crystal Lake *(G-7255)*
Ridge Road Defense.....G.....630 820-8906
Aurora *(G-1148)*
S Flying Inc.....F.....618 586-9999
Palestine *(G-16179)*
Sextant Company.....G.....847 680-6550
Gurnee *(G-10926)*
Sharp Defense LLC.....G.....630 205-3502
Elgin *(G-8728)*
Smart Pixel Inc.....G.....630 771-0206
Bolingbrook *(G-2241)*
▲ **Teletrac Navman US Ltd**.....E.....866 527-9896
Glenview *(G-10631)*
Tomahawk Defense.....G.....773 871-7268
Chicago *(G-6388)*
Trident Machine Co.....G.....815 968-1585
Rockford *(G-17668)*
UTC Aerospace Systems.....G.....877 808-7575
Rockford *(G-17674)*
Vanguard Defense Group.....G.....850 218-4233
Island Lake *(G-11612)*
▲ **Waltz Brothers Inc**.....E.....847 520-1122
Wheeling *(G-21011)*
Winn Star Inc.....G.....618 964-1811
Carbondale *(G-2865)*

3821 Laboratory Apparatus & Furniture

1 Federal Supply Source Inc.....G.....708 964-2222
Steger *(G-19486)*
Aalborg Company.....G.....708 246-8858
Western Springs *(G-20718)*
Amity Hospital Services Inc.....G.....708 206-3970
Country Club Hills *(G-7035)*
Amoco Technology Company.....C.....312 861-6000
Chicago *(G-3682)*
▲ **Atlas Material Tstg Tech LLC**.....C.....773 327-4520
Mount Prospect *(G-14512)*
B T Technology Inc.....G.....217 322-3768
Rushville *(G-18108)*
Bea Electro Sales Inc.....G.....847 238-1420
Elk Grove Village *(G-8859)*
Biosynergy Inc.....G.....847 956-0471
Elk Grove Village *(G-8867)*
Celinco Inc.....G.....815 964-2256
Rockford *(G-17341)*
Chicago Lab Products.....G.....312 942-0730
Chicago *(G-4109)*
Cole-Parmer Instrument Co LLC.....C.....847 381-7050
Lake Barrington *(G-12144)*
Cubic Group Inc.....G.....859 494-5834
Arlington Heights *(G-722)*
Cymatics Inc.....G.....630 420-7117
Naperville *(G-14811)*
David Martin.....G.....217 564-2440
Ivesdale *(G-11756)*
Dual Mfg Co Inc.....F.....773 267-4457
Franklin Park *(G-9933)*
◆ **Flinn Scientific Inc**.....C.....800 452-1261
Batavia *(G-1378)*
Florida Metrology LLC.....F.....630 833-3800
Villa Park *(G-20147)*
Gardner Denver Inc.....E.....847 676-8800
Niles *(G-15123)*
▼ **Grieve Corporation**.....D.....847 546-8225
Round Lake *(G-18078)*
Hcs Hahn Calibration Service.....G.....847 567-2500
Lincolnshire *(G-12769)*
Heidolph NA LLC.....F.....224 265-9600
Wood Dale *(G-21197)*
◆ **Humboldt Mfg Co**.....E.....708 456-6300
Elgin *(G-8617)*
Illinois Tool Works Inc.....C.....847 295-6500
Lake Bluff *(G-12189)*
Innovative Projects Lab Inc.....G.....847 605-2125
Schaumburg *(G-18562)*
◆ **Innovtive Prcess Applctons LLC**.....G.....708 844-6100
Crestwood *(G-7119)*
Intermerican Clinical Svcs Inc.....F.....773 252-1147
Chicago *(G-4949)*
Kewaunee Scientific Corp.....G.....847 675-7744
Highland Park *(G-11278)*
L A M Inc De.....G.....630 860-9700
Wood Dale *(G-21206)*
Labjackscom Inc.....G.....847 537-2099
Deerfield *(G-7628)*
▲ **Laboratory Builders Inc**.....G.....630 598-0216
Burr Ridge *(G-2695)*
▲ **Leica Microsystems Inc**.....C.....847 405-0123
Buffalo Grove *(G-2563)*
Leybold USA Inc.....E.....724 327-5700
Chicago *(G-5214)*
Ludwig Medical Inc.....G.....217 342-6570
Effingham *(G-8408)*
Mettler-Toledo LLC.....E.....630 446-7700
Aurora *(G-1002)*
Norman P Moeller.....G.....847 991-3933
Lake Barrington *(G-12162)*
Novel Products Inc.....G.....815 624-4888
Rockton *(G-17700)*
OBrien Scntfic GL Blowing LLC.....G.....217 762-3636
Monticello *(G-14283)*
▼ **Parr Instrument Company**.....C.....309 762-7716
Moline *(G-14165)*
Perten Instruments Inc.....E.....217 585-9440
Springfield *(G-19424)*
▲ **Preferred Freezer Services of**.....F.....773 254-9500
Chicago *(G-5860)*
◆ **Preston Industries Inc**.....C.....847 647-0611
Niles *(G-15162)*
◆ **Prime Industries Inc**.....E.....630 725-9200
Lisle *(G-12929)*
Quincy Lab Inc.....E.....773 622-2428
Chicago *(G-5938)*
R L Kolbi Company.....F.....847 506-1440
Arlington Heights *(G-795)*
Scanlab America Inc.....G.....630 797-2044
Saint Charles *(G-18265)*
Scientific Instruments Inc.....G.....847 679-1242
Schaumburg *(G-18709)*
Sirius Automation Group Inc.....F.....847 607-9378
Buffalo Grove *(G-2606)*
Sterigenics US LLC.....E.....847 855-0727
Gurnee *(G-10930)*
▼ **Suburban Surgical Co**.....C.....847 537-9320
Wheeling *(G-20993)*
Supertek Scientific LLC.....G.....630 345-3450
Addison *(G-300)*

Vac Serve Inc..........G....... 224 766-6445
Skokie *(G-19052)*
▲ **Wrightwood Technologies Inc**..........G....... 312 238-9512
Chicago *(G-6685)*

3822 Automatic Temperature Controls

A&B Reliable..........G....... 708 228-6148
Lemont *(G-12551)*
Ademco Inc..........G....... 708 599-1390
Bridgeview *(G-2319)*
Ademco Inc..........E....... 847 472-2900
Elk Grove Village *(G-8807)*
Automatic Building Contrls LLC..........D....... 847 296-4000
Rolling Meadows *(G-17714)*
Automax Corporation..........G....... 630 972-1919
Woodridge *(G-21277)*
Baldwin Technology Company Inc..........C....... 618 842-2664
Fairfield *(G-9618)*
Beneficial Reuse MGT LLC..........F....... 312 784-0300
Chicago *(G-3867)*
Biosynergy Inc..........G....... 847 956-0471
Elk Grove Village *(G-8867)*
Boyleston 21st Century LLC..........G....... 708 387-2012
Brookfield *(G-2479)*
Building Technologies Inc..........G....... 800 743-6367
Buffalo Grove *(G-2521)*
▲ **Candy Manufacturing Company**..........F....... 847 588-2639
Niles *(G-15107)*
◆ **Catalytic Products Intl Inc**..........E....... 847 438-0334
Lake Zurich *(G-12390)*
Caterpillar Inc..........B....... 815 729-5511
Joliet *(G-11838)*
Cdc Enterprises Inc..........G....... 815 790-4205
Johnsburg *(G-11802)*
Clarios..........E....... 815 397-5147
Rockford *(G-17351)*
Clarios..........D....... 708 474-1717
Calumet City *(G-2773)*
Clarios..........F....... 630 871-7700
Carol Stream *(G-2961)*
Control Equipment Company Inc..........F....... 847 891-7500
Schaumburg *(G-18487)*
Crandall Stats and Sensors Inc..........E....... 815 316-8600
Machesney Park *(G-13336)*
Creative Controls Systems Inc..........G....... 815 629-2358
Rockton *(G-17696)*
Danfoss LLC..........G....... 717 261-5000
Loves Park *(G-13205)*
▲ **Dickson/Unigage Inc**..........E....... 630 543-3747
Addison *(G-92)*
◆ **Dometic Corporation**..........A....... 847 447-7190
Rosemont *(G-18019)*
Dundee Design LLC..........G....... 847 494-2360
East Dundee *(G-8194)*
E George Special Services LLC..........G....... 773 934-7878
Glenwood *(G-10640)*
◆ **Eclipse Inc**..........D....... 815 877-3031
Rockford *(G-17388)*
Elcon Inc..........E....... 815 467-9500
Minooka *(G-14059)*
▲ **Global Green Products LLC**..........G....... 708 341-3670
Orland Park *(G-15955)*
Goodrich Sensor Systems..........G....... 847 546-5749
Round Lake *(G-18077)*
Green Ladder Technologies LLC..........E....... 630 457-1872
Batavia *(G-1382)*
▲ **Gus Berthold Electric Company**..........D....... 312 243-5767
Chicago *(G-4752)*
▼ **H A Phillips & Co**..........E....... 630 377-0050
Dekalb *(G-7683)*
◆ **Hansen Technologies Corp**..........D....... 706 335-5551
Burr Ridge *(G-2682)*
▲ **Holland Safety Equipment Inc**..........G....... 847 680-9930
Libertyville *(G-12659)*
Homecontrolplus Incorporated..........G....... 847 823-8414
Park Ridge *(G-16283)*
Indesco Oven Products Inc..........G....... 217 622-6345
Petersburg *(G-16602)*
Industrial Thermo Products..........G....... 847 398-8600
Rolling Meadows *(G-17740)*
▲ **Intech Industries Inc**..........F....... 847 487-5599
Wauconda *(G-20361)*
Interactive Bldg Solutions LLC..........F....... 815 724-0525
Joliet *(G-11882)*
ITW Motion..........E....... 708 720-0300
Frankfort *(G-9809)*
Jql Technologies Corporation..........F....... 800 236-9828
Mundelein *(G-14705)*
Kingfisher Controls LLC..........G....... 425 359-5601
Illiopolis *(G-11574)*
Lopez Plumbing Systems Inc..........G....... 773 424-8225
Chicago *(G-5258)*
▲ **Mitsubishi Elc Automtn Inc**..........C....... 847 478-2100
Vernon Hills *(G-20075)*
New Century Mfg..........G....... 847 998-0960
Glenview *(G-10594)*
Precision Control Systems..........D....... 630 521-0234
Lisle *(G-12928)*
Professional Freezing Svcs LLC..........G....... 773 847-7500
Chicago *(G-5896)*
R & D Electronics Inc..........G....... 847 583-9080
Niles *(G-15163)*
Reliable Appliance and Ref..........G....... 847 581-9520
Morton Grove *(G-14438)*
◆ **Robertshaw Controls Company**..........C....... 630 260-3400
Itasca *(G-11727)*
▲ **Schneider Elc Buildings LLC**..........B....... 815 381-5000
Rockford *(G-17622)*
Schneider Elc Buildings LLC..........E....... 815 227-4000
Rockford *(G-17623)*
▲ **Schneider Elc Holdings Inc**..........A....... 717 944-5460
Schaumburg *(G-18707)*
Scientific Instruments Inc..........G....... 847 679-1242
Schaumburg *(G-18709)*
Siemens Industry Inc..........D....... 847 520-9084
Buffalo Grove *(G-2599)*
Siemens Industry Inc..........G....... 309 664-2460
Bloomington *(G-2094)*
Siemens Industry Inc..........G....... 847 941-5050
Buffalo Grove *(G-2601)*
Siemens Industry Inc..........D....... 630 444-4316
Saint Charles *(G-18269)*
Siemens Industry Inc..........D....... 847 215-1000
Buffalo Grove *(G-2602)*
◆ **Siemens Industry Inc**..........A....... 847 215-1000
Buffalo Grove *(G-2600)*
SMC Corporation of America..........E....... 630 449-0600
Aurora *(G-1017)*
▲ **Solidyne Corporation**..........F....... 847 394-3333
Rolling Meadows *(G-17775)*
Solidyne Corporation..........G....... 847 394-3333
Hoffman Estates *(G-11460)*
Sonne Industries LLC..........G....... 630 235-6734
Naperville *(G-14917)*
Spring Brook Nature Center..........G....... 630 773-5572
Itasca *(G-11739)*
Temperature Equipment Corp..........G....... 847 429-0818
Elgin *(G-8752)*
▲ **Temprite Company**..........E....... 630 293-5910
West Chicago *(G-20649)*
▲ **Tempro International Corp**..........G....... 847 677-5370
Skokie *(G-19044)*
Unitrol Electronics Inc..........E....... 847 480-0115
Northbrook *(G-15496)*
Vent Ure Air..........G....... 708 652-7200
Chicago *(G-6533)*

3823 Indl Instruments For Meas, Display & Control

Active Grinding & Mfg Co..........F....... 708 344-0510
Broadview *(G-2414)*
Advanced Technologies Inc..........G....... 847 329-9875
Park Ridge *(G-16264)*
▲ **Air Gage Company**..........C....... 847 695-0911
Elgin *(G-8500)*
Alti LLC..........G....... 951 505-3148
Highland Park *(G-11252)*
Ametek Inc..........E....... 630 621-3121
Warrenville *(G-20230)*
▲ **ARI Industries Inc**..........D....... 630 953-9100
Addison *(G-38)*
▲ **Atlas Material Tstg Tech LLC**..........C....... 773 327-4520
Mount Prospect *(G-14512)*
▲ **Auto Meter Products Inc**..........C....... 815 895-8141
Sycamore *(G-19702)*
Automated Logic Corporation..........F....... 630 852-1700
Lisle *(G-12870)*
Autrol Corporation of AME..........G....... 847 874-7545
Crystal Lake *(G-7166)*
▲ **Autrol Corporation of America**..........F....... 847 779-5000
Schaumburg *(G-18450)*
Axode Corp..........G....... 312 578-9897
Chicago *(G-3796)*
Azcon Inc..........F....... 815 548-7000
Sterling *(G-19499)*
Barcor Inc..........F....... 847 940-0750
Bannockburn *(G-1192)*
Benetech Inc..........G....... 630 806-7888
Montgomery *(G-14232)*
Benetech Inc..........E....... 630 844-1300
Aurora *(G-1063)*
Benetech (taiwan) LLC..........G....... 630 844-1300
Aurora *(G-1064)*
Caterpillar Inc..........B....... 815 729-5511
Joliet *(G-11838)*
Champion Comm Svcs Inc..........G....... 815 654-8607
Rockford *(G-17344)*
▲ **Charnor Inc**..........D....... 309 787-2427
Milan *(G-14002)*
Clean Energy Renewables LLC..........E....... 309 797-4844
Moline *(G-14136)*
Cognex Corporation..........G....... 630 505-9990
Naperville *(G-14801)*
Competition Electronics Inc..........G....... 815 874-8001
Rockford *(G-17356)*
Controlled Thermal Processing..........G....... 847 651-5511
Streamwood *(G-19567)*
County of Piatt..........G....... 217 762-7009
Monticello *(G-14280)*
Creative Controls Systems Inc..........G....... 815 629-2358
Rockton *(G-17696)*
Dadant & Sons Inc..........F....... 217 852-3324
Dallas City *(G-7313)*
Danaher Corporation..........C....... 815 568-8001
Marengo *(G-13483)*
Danfoss LLC..........C....... 888 326-3677
Loves Park *(G-13206)*
Decatur Aeration and Temp..........F....... 217 733-2800
Fairmount *(G-9642)*
▲ **Dickson/Unigage Inc**..........E....... 630 543-3747
Addison *(G-92)*
◆ **Dometic Corporation**..........A....... 847 447-7190
Rosemont *(G-18019)*
▲ **Durex International Corp**..........B....... 847 639-5600
Cary *(G-3157)*
E+e Elektronik Corporation..........G....... 847 490-0520
Schaumburg *(G-18511)*
◆ **Eclipse Inc**..........D....... 815 877-3031
Rockford *(G-17388)*
Electro-Matic Products Co..........F....... 773 235-4010
Chicago *(G-4477)*
Electronic System Design Inc..........G....... 847 358-8212
Bensenville *(G-1794)*
◆ **Emac Inc**..........E....... 618 529-4525
Carbondale *(G-2841)*
Embedor Technologies Inc..........G....... 202 681-0359
Champaign *(G-3289)*
Emerson Electric Co..........D....... 847 585-8300
Elgin *(G-8578)*
Emerson Electric Co..........E....... 847 268-6000
Rosemont *(G-18023)*
Emerson Electric Co..........E....... 312 803-4321
Chicago *(G-4497)*
Emerson Electric Co..........G....... 708 263-6100
Tinley Park *(G-19824)*
Enerstar Inc..........G....... 847 350-3400
Bensenville *(G-1797)*
Erdco Engineering Corporation..........E....... 847 328-0550
Evanston *(G-9514)*
Fisher Controls Intl LLC..........D....... 847 956-8020
Chicago *(G-4596)*
Fms USA Inc..........G....... 847 519-4400
Hoffman Estates *(G-11424)*
Fox Meter Inc..........G....... 630 968-3635
Lisle *(G-12892)*
▼ **Frequency Devices Inc**..........F....... 815 434-7800
Ottawa *(G-16053)*
FSI Technologies Inc..........E....... 630 932-9380
Lombard *(G-13080)*
◆ **Fuel Tech Inc**..........C....... 630 845-4500
Warrenville *(G-20237)*
▲ **Fusion Systems Incorporated**..........E....... 630 323-4115
Burr Ridge *(G-2675)*
G-M Services..........G....... 618 532-2324
Centralia *(G-3232)*
Goodrich Corporation..........D....... 815 226-6000
Rockford *(G-17432)*
Hadady Machining Company Inc..........F....... 708 474-8620
Lansing *(G-12496)*
Harry J Trainor..........G....... 630 493-1163
Downers Grove *(G-8017)*
Hauhinco LP..........E....... 618 993-5399
Marion *(G-13514)*
▲ **Heng Tuo Usa Inc**..........G....... 630 317-7672
Oakbrook Terrace *(G-15802)*
Hexagon Metrology Inc..........G....... 312 624-8786
Chicago *(G-4811)*
Hexagon Metrology Inc..........G....... 847 469-3344
Elgin *(G-8615)*

S I C

Employee Codes: A=Over 500 employees, B=251-500
C=101-250, D=51-100, E=20-50, F=10-19, G=3-9
2020 Harris Illinois
Industrial Directory
1003

38 MEASURING, ANALYZING AND CONTROLLING INSTRUMENTS; PHOTOGRAPHIC, MEDICAL AN

Humidity 2 Optimization LLC ....F....... 847 991-7488
 East Dundee *(G-8200)*
Imacc LLC ....G....... 512 341-8189
 Palatine *(G-16126)*
Imada Inc ....E....... 847 562-0834
 Northbrook *(G-15403)*
Indev Gauging Systems Inc ....G....... 815 282-4463
 Loves Park *(G-13219)*
Industrial Thermo Products ....G....... 847 398-8600
 Rolling Meadows *(G-17740)*
Innovative Marine Safety Inc ....G....... 618 254-9470
 Wood River *(G-21264)*
Innovative Werks Inc ....G....... 312 767-8618
 Naperville *(G-14848)*
Instrument & Valve Services Co ....D....... 708 535-5120
 Oak Forest *(G-15684)*
Instrument & Valve Services Co ....F....... 281 998-6673
 Chicago *(G-4939)*
Janco Process Controls Inc ....E....... 847 526-0800
 Wauconda *(G-20363)*
Jjs Technical Services ....G....... 847 999-4313
 Schaumburg *(G-18577)*
Lake Electronics Inc ....F....... 847 201-1270
 Volo *(G-20202)*
▲ Landairsea Systems Inc ....F....... 847 462-8100
 Woodstock *(G-21403)*
Level Developments Ltd ....G....... 312 465-1082
 Chicago *(G-5210)*
◆ Liquid Controls LLC ....C....... 847 295-1050
 Lake Bluff *(G-12194)*
▲ Liquitech Inc ....E....... 630 693-0500
 Lombard *(G-13097)*
Liveone Inc ....G....... 312 282-2320
 Chicago *(G-5242)*
Lumenite Control Technology ....F....... 847 455-1450
 Franklin Park *(G-9982)*
Luse Thermal Technologies LLC ....G....... 630 862-2600
 Aurora *(G-1000)*
▼ Magnetrol International Inc ....C....... 630 723-6600
 Aurora *(G-1001)*
◆ Martin Automatic Inc ....C....... 815 654-4800
 Rockford *(G-17505)*
▼ Master Control Systems Inc ....E....... 847 295-1010
 Lake Bluff *(G-12195)*
▼ Mech-Tronics Corporation ....D....... 708 344-9823
 Melrose Park *(G-13891)*
Metrology Resource Group Inc ....G....... 815 703-3141
 Rockford *(G-17520)*
Mettler-Toledo LLC ....E....... 630 446-1700
 Aurora *(G-1002)*
▲ Mid-American Elevator Co Inc ......C....... 773 486-6900
 Chicago *(G-5428)*
Mid-American Elevator Co Inc ....E....... 815 740-1204
 Joliet *(G-11902)*
Mid-American Elevator Eqp Co ....E....... 773 486-6900
 Chicago *(G-5429)*
Midwest Energy Management Inc .....G....... 630 759-6007
 Lombard *(G-13101)*
Millpro LLC ....G....... 630 608-9241
 Aurora *(G-1135)*
Modern Fluid Technology Inc ....G....... 815 356-0001
 Crystal Lake *(G-7232)*
▲ Monitor Technologies LLC ....G....... 630 365-9403
 Elburn *(G-8463)*
National Micro Systems Inc ....G....... 312 566-0414
 Chicago *(G-5549)*
Nordson Asymtek Inc ....C....... 760 431-1919
 Chicago *(G-5615)*
Nuance Incorporated ....G....... 207 449-6398
 Chicago *(G-5638)*
Oakland Industries Ltd ....E....... 847 827-7600
 Mount Prospect *(G-14555)*
◆ Omron Healthcare Inc ....D....... 847 680-6200
 Lake Forest *(G-12276)*
Oxytech Systems Inc ....F....... 847 888-8611
 Carpentersville *(G-3110)*
▲ Pan America Environmental Inc ....G....... 815 344-2960
 McHenry *(G-13775)*
Perkinelmer Hlth Sciences Inc ....C....... 630 969-6000
 Downers Grove *(G-8073)*
Principal Instruments Inc ....G....... 815 469-8159
 Frankfort *(G-9827)*
Process Mechanical Inc ....G....... 630 416-7021
 Naperville *(G-14902)*
Process Technologies Group ....G....... 630 393-4777
 Warrenville *(G-20250)*
Prostat Corporation ....F....... 630 238-8883
 Bensenville *(G-1875)*
Protection Controls Inc ....E....... 773 763-3110
 Skokie *(G-19017)*

Pullman Company ....G....... 847 482-5000
 Lake Forest *(G-12293)*
Robertshaw Controls Company ....E....... 815 591-2417
 Hanover *(G-10997)*
◆ Robertshaw Controls Company ....C....... 630 260-3400
 Itasca *(G-11727)*
Rosemount Inc ....G....... 217 877-5278
 Decatur *(G-7543)*
Ruby Automation LLC ....F....... 815 624-5959
 South Beloit *(G-19112)*
▲ Schneider Elc Buildings LLC ....B....... 815 381-5000
 Rockford *(G-17622)*
▲ Schneider Elc Holdings Inc ....A....... 717 944-5460
 Schaumburg *(G-18707)*
Schrader-Bridgeport Intl Inc ....G....... 815 288-3344
 Dixon *(G-7916)*
▲ Semler Industries Inc ....E....... 847 671-5650
 Franklin Park *(G-10046)*
Sendele Wireless Solutions ....G....... 815 227-4212
 Rockford *(G-17624)*
Sensor Synergy ....G....... 847 353-8200
 Vernon Hills *(G-20097)*
Silicon Control Inc ....G....... 847 215-7947
 Deerfield *(G-7649)*
Sun Infrared Technologies Inc ....G....... 618 632-3013
 O Fallon *(G-15585)*
Superior Graphite Co ....E....... 708 458-0006
 Chicago *(G-6281)*
▲ Surya Electronics Inc ....G....... 630 858-8000
 Glendale Heights *(G-10507)*
T T T Inc ....G....... 630 860-7499
 Wood Dale *(G-21245)*
Technical Sales Midwest Inc ....G....... 847 855-2457
 Gurnee *(G-10935)*
▲ Tempro International Corp ....E....... 847 677-5370
 Skokie *(G-19044)*
Tenco Hydro Inc of Illinois ....G....... 708 387-0700
 Brookfield *(G-2496)*
Thread & Gage Co Inc ....G....... 815 675-2305
 Spring Grove *(G-19302)*
Tii Technical Educatn Systems ....G....... 847 428-3085
 Gilberts *(G-10373)*
Tomantron Inc ....F....... 708 532-2456
 Tinley Park *(G-19860)*
Tricor Systems Inc ....E....... 847 742-5542
 Elgin *(G-8760)*
Uic Inc ....G....... 815 744-4477
 Joliet *(G-11937)*
Village Hampshire Trtmnt Plant ....G....... 847 683-2064
 Hampshire *(G-10989)*
Village Hebron Water Sewage ....G....... 815 648-2353
 Hebron *(G-11154)*
Vorne Industries Inc ....E....... 630 875-3600
 Itasca *(G-11751)*
Xco International Incorporated ....F....... 847 428-2400
 East Dundee *(G-8215)*
◆ Yaskawa America Inc ....C....... 847 887-7000
 Waukegan *(G-20520)*

3824 Fluid Meters & Counters

◆ Advance Engineering Corp ....E....... 847 760-9421
 Elgin *(G-8496)*
▲ ARC-Tronics Inc ....C....... 847 437-0211
 Elk Grove Village *(G-8837)*
▲ Auto Meter Products Inc ....C....... 815 895-8141
 Sycamore *(G-19702)*
Bc Enterprises ....G....... 618 655-0784
 Edwardsville *(G-8348)*
▲ Dynapar Corporation ....C....... 847 662-2666
 Gurnee *(G-10873)*
▲ E N M Company ....D....... 773 775-8400
 Chicago *(G-4425)*
Erdco Engineering Corporation ....E....... 847 328-0550
 Evanston *(G-9514)*
Flodyne Inc ....G....... 630 563-3600
 Hanover Park *(G-11004)*
▲ G H Meiser & Co ....E....... 708 388-7867
 Mokena *(G-14085)*
Langham Engineering ....G....... 815 223-5250
 Peru *(G-16580)*
Line Group Inc ....E....... 847 593-6810
 Arlington Heights *(G-769)*
▲ Metraflex Company ....D....... 312 738-3800
 Chicago *(G-5411)*
Midwest Meter Inc ....E....... 217 623-4064
 Edinburg *(G-8335)*
▲ Nep Electronics Inc ....C....... 630 595-8500
 Wood Dale *(G-21221)*
Nichiden USA Corp ....G....... 224 266-2928
 Elk Grove Village *(G-9147)*

▲ O E M Marketing Inc ....F....... 847 985-9490
 Schaumburg *(G-18655)*
▲ Opw Fuel MGT Systems Inc ....G....... 708 352-9617
 Hodgkins *(G-11392)*
Otak International Inc ....G....... 630 373-9229
 Melrose Park *(G-13900)*
Perkinelmer Hlth Sciences Inc ....C....... 630 969-6000
 Downers Grove *(G-8073)*
Professional Meters Inc ....C....... 815 942-7000
 Morris *(G-14323)*
Shoppertrak Rct Corporation ....F....... 312 529-5300
 Chicago *(G-6156)*
▲ Spartanics Ltd ....E....... 847 394-5700
 Rolling Meadows *(G-17777)*
▲ Tml Inc ....G....... 847 382-1550
 Barrington *(G-1247)*
Walk 4 Life Inc ....G....... 815 439-2340
 Oswego *(G-16031)*
Woodward Inc ....G....... 847 673-8300
 Skokie *(G-19057)*

3825 Instrs For Measuring & Testing Electricity

10g LLC ....F....... 630 754-2400
 Woodridge *(G-21269)*
ABM Marking Services Ltd ....G....... 618 277-3773
 Belleville *(G-1527)*
Accushim Inc ....G....... 708 442-6448
 Lyons *(G-13300)*
▲ Acl Inc ....F....... 773 285-0295
 Chicago *(G-3525)*
Adams Elevator Equipment Co ....E....... 847 581-2900
 Chicago *(G-3538)*
Agilent Technologies Inc ....E....... 800 227-9770
 Chicago *(G-3582)*
Agilent Technologies Inc ....A....... 847 690-0431
 Arlington Heights *(G-685)*
Aiknow Inc ....F....... 312 391-9452
 Naperville *(G-14953)*
▲ Air Gage Company ....C....... 847 695-0911
 Elgin *(G-8500)*
Amerinet of Michigan Inc ....G....... 708 466-0110
 Naperville *(G-14958)*
▲ Associated Research Inc ....E....... 847 367-4077
 Lake Forest *(G-12229)*
▲ Atlas Material Tstg Tech LLC ....C....... 773 327-4520
 Mount Prospect *(G-14512)*
▲ Auto Meter Products Inc ....C....... 815 895-8141
 Sycamore *(G-19702)*
B T Technology Inc ....G....... 217 322-3768
 Rushville *(G-18108)*
▲ B+b Smartworx Inc ....D....... 815 433-5100
 Ottawa *(G-16041)*
Bluenrgy LLC ....D....... 802 865-3866
 Chicago *(G-3917)*
▲ Bolingbrook Communications Inc ...A....... 630 759-9500
 Lisle *(G-12874)*
Brandt Assoc ....G....... 847 362-0556
 Lake Bluff *(G-12174)*
C E R Machining & Tooling Ltd ....G....... 708 442-9614
 Lyons *(G-13305)*
Centurion Non Destructive Tstg ....F....... 630 736-5500
 Streamwood *(G-19565)*
Cobalt Tool & Manufacturing ....G....... 630 530-8898
 Villa Park *(G-20139)*
Creative Science Activities ....G....... 847 870-1746
 Prospect Heights *(G-16837)*
Cyber Tech Corp ....G....... 630 472-3200
 Oak Brook *(G-15615)*
Cymatics Inc ....G....... 630 420-7117
 Naperville *(G-14811)*
▲ Davies Molding LLC ....C....... 630 510-8188
 Carol Stream *(G-2974)*
▲ Design Technology Inc ....E....... 630 920-1300
 Westmont *(G-20736)*
Dgm Electronics Inc ....G....... 815 389-2040
 Roscoe *(G-17904)*
Dytec Midwest Inc ....E....... 847 255-3200
 Rolling Meadows *(G-17728)*
Electronic System Design Inc ....G....... 847 358-8212
 Bensenville *(G-1794)*
◆ Elenco Electronics Inc ....F....... 847 541-3800
 Wheeling *(G-20889)*
Erdco Engineering Corporation ....E....... 847 328-0550
 Evanston *(G-9514)*
▲ Etcon Corp ....F....... 630 325-6100
 Burr Ridge *(G-2672)*
F T I Inc ....E....... 312 943-4015
 Chicago *(G-4552)*

SIC SECTION 38 MEASURING, ANALYZING AND CONTROLLING INSTRUMENTS; PHOTOGRAPHIC, MEDICAL AN

Falex Corporation ... E ... 630 556-3679
Sugar Grove *(G-19643)*
▼ **Frequency Devices Inc** ... F ... 815 434-7800
Ottawa *(G-16053)*
FSI Technologies Inc ... E ... 630 932-9380
Lombard *(G-13080)*
Gld Industries Inc ... G ... 217 390-9594
Champaign *(G-3296)*
Greenlee Textron Inc ... C ... 815 784-5127
Genoa *(G-10318)*
Haynes-Bent Inc ... F ... 630 845-3316
Wilmington *(G-21100)*
◆ **Hd Electric Company** ... E ... 847 473-4980
Rockford *(G-17444)*
▲ **Heidenhain Corporation** ... D ... 847 490-1191
Schaumburg *(G-18545)*
Hipskind Tech Sltons Group Inc ... D ... 630 920-0960
Oakbrook Terrace *(G-15803)*
Huygen Corporation ... F ... 815 455-2200
Crystal Lake *(G-7207)*
▲ **I P C Automation Inc** ... G ... 815 759-3934
McHenry *(G-13749)*
◆ **Ideal Industries Inc** ... C ... 815 895-5181
Sycamore *(G-19714)*
Ideal Industries Inc ... C ... 815 895-1108
Sycamore *(G-19715)*
Illinois Tool Works Inc ... E ... 847 657-5300
Glenview *(G-10562)*
Illinois Tool Works Inc ... C ... 847 295-6500
Lake Bluff *(G-12189)*
Innovative Sports Training Inc ... G ... 773 244-6470
Chicago *(G-4932)*
▼ **Integral Automation Inc** ... F ... 630 654-4300
Burr Ridge *(G-2688)*
International Electro Magnetic ... G ... 847 358-4622
Wheeling *(G-20916)*
Langham Engineering ... G ... 815 223-5250
Peru *(G-16580)*
Lindgren Family LLC ... G ... 630 307-7200
Glendale Heights *(G-10469)*
Maurey Instrument Corp ... F ... 708 388-9898
Alsip *(G-474)*
◆ **Methode Electronics Inc** ... B ... 708 867-6777
Chicago *(G-5409)*
▲ **Midtronics Inc** ... D ... 630 323-2800
Willowbrook *(G-21050)*
Monolithic Industries Inc ... G ... 630 985-6009
Woodridge *(G-21324)*
▲ **Nidec-Shimpo America Corp** ... E ... 630 924-7138
Glendale Heights *(G-10479)*
Nu Vision Media Inc ... G ... 773 495-5254
Chicago *(G-5636)*
Oso Technologies Inc ... G ... 844 777-2575
Urbana *(G-19991)*
P K Neuses Incorporated ... G ... 847 253-6555
Rolling Meadows *(G-17758)*
Premium Test Equipment Corp ... G ... 630 400-2681
Warrenville *(G-20248)*
Professional Meters Inc ... C ... 815 942-7000
Morris *(G-14323)*
Prostat Corporation ... F ... 630 238-8883
Bensenville *(G-1875)*
Protec Equipment Resources Inc ... G ... 847 434-5808
Schaumburg *(G-18686)*
Radio Controlled Models Inc ... G ... 847 740-8726
Round Lake Beach *(G-18092)*
▲ **Richardson Rfpd Inc** ... D ... 630 262-6800
Geneva *(G-10302)*
▲ **Righthand Technologies Inc** ... E ... 773 774-7600
Chicago *(G-6033)*
S Himmelstein and Company ... E ... 847 843-3300
Hoffman Estates *(G-11452)*
Schweitzer Engrg Labs Inc ... D ... 847 362-8304
Lake Zurich *(G-12455)*
▲ **Serene One LLC** ... F ... 630 285-1500
Itasca *(G-11731)*
Sfc of Illinois Inc ... E ... 815 745-2100
Warren *(G-20224)*
Sigmatron International Inc ... G ... 847 586-5200
Elgin *(G-8730)*
▲ **Sigmatron International Inc** ... G ... 847 956-8000
Elk Grove Village *(G-9238)*
Silicon Control Inc ... G ... 847 215-7947
Deerfield *(G-7649)*
Singer Data Products Inc ... G ... 630 860-6500
Bensenville *(G-1893)*
Singer Medical Products Inc ... G ... 630 860-6500
Bensenville *(G-1894)*
Sk Hynix America Inc ... G ... 847 925-0196
Schaumburg *(G-18713)*

Spectral Dynamics Inc ... E ... 630 595-4288
Itasca *(G-11738)*
Stevens Instrument Company ... G ... 847 336-9375
Waukegan *(G-20498)*
Suffolk Business Group Inc ... G ... 847 404-2486
Bartlett *(G-1315)*
TEC Rep Corporation ... F ... 630 627-9110
Lombard *(G-13141)*
Telcom Innovations Group LLC ... E ... 630 350-0700
Itasca *(G-11745)*
Teledyne Lecroy Inc ... E ... 847 888-0450
Elgin *(G-8749)*
Teradyne Inc ... F ... 847 981-0400
Arlington Heights *(G-819)*
▲ **Transformer Manufacturers Inc** ... E ... 708 457-1200
Norridge *(G-15245)*

3826 Analytical Instruments

▲ **Abbott Laboratories** ... A ... 224 667-6100
Abbott Park *(G-1)*
Abbott Laboratories ... G ... 800 551-5838
Lake Forest *(G-12218)*
Abbott Laboratories ... A ... 847 932-7900
North Chicago *(G-15293)*
Abbott Molecular Inc ... G ... 224 361-7800
Des Plaines *(G-7719)*
▲ **Abbott Molecular Inc** ... D ... 224 361-7800
Des Plaines *(G-7720)*
Ag-Defense Systems Inc ... G ... 309 495-7258
Peoria *(G-16376)*
Alexeter Technologies LLC ... F ... 847 419-1507
Wheeling *(G-20843)*
Alti LLC ... G ... 951 505-3148
Highland Park *(G-11252)*
Amoco Technology Company ... C ... 312 861-6000
Chicago *(G-3682)*
Beckman Coulter Inc ... G ... 800 526-3821
Wood Dale *(G-21167)*
Bio-RAD Laboratories Inc ... B ... 847 699-2217
Des Plaines *(G-7739)*
Blanke Industries Incorporated ... G ... 847 487-2780
Wauconda *(G-20335)*
Cambridge Sensors USA LLC ... G ... 877 374-4062
Plainfield *(G-16647)*
Carlson Scientific Inc ... G ... 708 258-6377
Peotone *(G-16551)*
Cbana Labs Inc ... G ... 217 819-5201
Champaign *(G-3277)*
Chinchilla Scientific LLC ... G ... 630 645-0600
Oak Brook *(G-15610)*
Dionex Corporation ... G ... 847 295-7500
Bannockburn *(G-1199)*
EJ Cady & Company ... G ... 847 537-2239
Wheeling *(G-20888)*
EMD Millipore Corporation ... C ... 815 937-8270
Kankakee *(G-11968)*
EMD Millipore Corporation ... B ... 815 932-9017
Kankakee *(G-11969)*
Enhanced Plasmonics LLC ... G ... 904 238-9270
Evanston *(G-9513)*
Fisher Scientific Company LLC ... C ... 412 490-8300
Hanover Park *(G-11003)*
Gaertner Scientific Corp ... E ... 847 673-5006
Skokie *(G-18958)*
Grays Laser & Instrument RPR ... G ... 618 222-1791
Smithton *(G-19064)*
Hach Company ... C ... 800 227-4224
Chicago *(G-4763)*
Huygen Corporation ... F ... 815 455-2200
Crystal Lake *(G-7207)*
Igt Testing Systems Inc ... G ... 847 952-2448
Arlington Heights *(G-755)*
Illinois Bone & Joint Inst LLC ... D ... 847 724-4470
Glenview *(G-10559)*
Illinois Instruments Inc ... E ... 815 344-6212
Johnsburg *(G-11805)*
Illinois Tool Works Inc ... C ... 847 295-6500
Lake Bluff *(G-12189)*
Imed Glenview ... G ... 847 298-2200
Glenview *(G-10566)*
Instruments & Technology ... G ... 815 838-5909
Lockport *(G-13002)*
ISs (usa) Inc ... E ... 217 359-8681
Champaign *(G-3310)*
◆ **Jrd Labs LLC** ... G ... 847 818-1076
Elk Grove Village *(G-9070)*
Kw Fabrication Inc ... G ... 773 294-8584
Riverside *(G-17086)*
L A M Inc De ... G ... 630 860-9700
Wood Dale *(G-21206)*

Lachata Design Ltd ... G ... 708 946-2757
Beecher *(G-1518)*
Laser Products Industries Inc ... G ... 877 679-1300
Romeoville *(G-17839)*
McCrone Associates Inc ... G ... 630 887-7100
Westmont *(G-20758)*
Mettler-Toledo LLC ... E ... 630 446-7700
Aurora *(G-1002)*
Mk Environmental Inc ... G ... 630 848-0585
Lombard *(G-13102)*
Moisture Detection Inc ... G ... 847 426-0464
Hoffman Estates *(G-11437)*
O2m Technologies LLC ... G ... 773 910-8533
Chicago *(G-5648)*
Omex Technologies Inc ... G ... 847 850-5858
Wheeling *(G-20949)*
▲ **Orochem Technologies Inc** ... E ... 630 210-8300
Naperville *(G-14889)*
▼ **Parr Instrument Company** ... C ... 309 762-7716
Moline *(G-14165)*
Peoria Open M R I ... G ... 309 692-7674
Peoria *(G-16494)*
Perkinelmer Inc ... G ... 331 229-3012
Naperville *(G-14895)*
Pine Environmental Svcs LLC ... G ... 847 718-1246
Lombard *(G-13120)*
Prairie Glen Imaging Ctr LLC ... G ... 847 296-5366
Des Plaines *(G-7829)*
Presence Legacy Association ... F ... 815 741-7555
Joliet *(G-11916)*
▲ **Prime Systems Inc** ... E ... 630 681-2100
Carol Stream *(G-3049)*
Quest Integrity ... G ... 779 205-3068
Shorewood *(G-18901)*
Scientific Instruments Inc ... G ... 847 679-1242
Schaumburg *(G-18709)*
Sensor 21 Inc ... G ... 847 561-6233
Mundelein *(G-14736)*
▲ **Sherwood Industries Inc** ... F ... 847 626-0300
Niles *(G-15170)*
Smart Scan Mri LLC ... G ... 847 623-4000
Gurnee *(G-10928)*
Spectroclick Inc ... G ... 217 356-4829
Champaign *(G-3351)*
St Imaging Inc ... F ... 847 501-3344
Northbrook *(G-15487)*
Standard Safety Equipment Co ... E ... 815 363-8565
McHenry *(G-13795)*
Supertek Scientific LLC ... G ... 630 345-3450
Addison *(G-300)*
▲ **Swan Analytical Usa Inc** ... F ... 847 229-1290
Wheeling *(G-20994)*
Talis Biomedical Corporation ... G ... 312 589-5000
Chicago *(G-6314)*
Thermo Fisher Scientific Inc ... G ... 847 295-7500
Bannockburn *(G-1211)*
Thermo Fisher Scientific Inc ... G ... 815 968-7970
Rockford *(G-17657)*
Thermo Fisher Scientific Inc ... D ... 847 381-7050
Bartlett *(G-1316)*
Verson Enterprises Inc ... F ... 847 364-2600
Elk Grove Village *(G-9302)*
Warbler of Illinois Company ... G ... 301 520-0438
Champaign *(G-3369)*
Waters Technologies Corp ... F ... 630 766-6249
Wood Dale *(G-21256)*
Waters Technologies Corp ... F ... 508 482-8365
Chicago *(G-6589)*
Western Analytical Products ... G ... 800 541-8421
Vernon Hills *(G-20110)*

3827 Optical Instruments

4 U Optical ... G ... 847 459-8598
Buffalo Grove *(G-2502)*
Abet Technologies LLC ... F ... 847 682-5541
Evanston *(G-9485)*
Alicona Corporation ... G ... 630 372-9900
Itasca *(G-11618)*
Astro-Physics Inc ... F ... 815 282-1513
Machesney Park *(G-13328)*
Beastgrip Co ... G ... 312 283-5283
Des Plaines *(G-7738)*
Cabot McRlectronics Polsg Corp ... E ... 630 543-6682
Addison *(G-61)*
Cipp Robotics LLC ... G ... 815 202-6628
La Salle *(G-12108)*
Elmed Incorporated ... E ... 224 353-6446
Glendale Heights *(G-10448)*
Fjw Optical Systems Inc ... F ... 847 358-2500
Palatine *(G-16119)*

SIC

Employee Codes: A=Over 500 employees, B=251-500
C=101-250, D=51-100, E=20-50, F=10-19, G=3-9
2020 Harris Illinois
Industrial Directory
1005

Gaertner Scientific Corp E 847 673-5006
Skokie *(G-18958)*
H L Clausing Inc G 847 676-0330
Skokie *(G-18962)*
Illinois Tool Works Inc C 847 295-6500
Lake Bluff *(G-12189)*
Inprentus Inc F 217 239-9862
Champaign *(G-3308)*
Intra Action Corp E 708 547-6644
Bellwood *(G-1628)*
J A K Enterprises Inc G 217 422-3881
Decatur *(G-7509)*
Jme Technologies Inc E 815 477-8800
Crystal Lake *(G-7213)*
Karl Lambrecht Corp E 773 472-5442
Chicago *(G-5082)*
▲ Kollmorgen Corp G 815 568-8001
Marengo *(G-13488)*
Kreischer Optics Ltd F 815 344-4220
McHenry *(G-13754)*
Laurel Industries Inc E 847 432-8204
Highland Park *(G-11281)*
Leica McRosystems Holdings Inc F 800 248-0123
Buffalo Grove *(G-2561)*
Leica Microsystems Inc G 847 405-0123
Buffalo Grove *(G-2562)*
▲ Leica Microsystems Inc C 847 405-0123
Buffalo Grove *(G-2563)*
Lens Lenticlear Lenticular F 630 467-0900
Elk Grove Village *(G-9093)*
Lockwood Custom Optics Inc G 217 684-2170
Philo *(G-16607)*
McCrone Associates Inc G 630 887-7100
Westmont *(G-20758)*
Night Vision Specialists LLC G 618 614-8626
Makanda *(G-13429)*
Omex Technologies Inc G 847 850-5858
Wheeling *(G-20949)*
Opti-Vue Inc G 630 274-6121
Bensenville *(G-1862)*
PHI Optics Inc G 217 819-1570
Champaign *(G-3332)*
Precision Vision Inc G 815 223-2022
Woodstock *(G-21423)*
Quality Optical Inc G 773 561-0870
Chicago *(G-5930)*
Scopedawg Optics LLC G 618 401-3342
Highland *(G-11239)*
Strausbrger Assoc Sls Mktg Inc G 630 768-6179
Yorkville *(G-21501)*
Tonjon Company F 630 208-1173
Geneva *(G-10312)*
Two Tower Frames Inc G 773 517-0394
Chicago *(G-6448)*
Vega Technology & Systems G 630 855-5068
Bartlett *(G-1259)*
Vibgyor Optical Systems Corp E 847 818-0788
Arlington Heights *(G-826)*
Vibgyor Optics Inc E 847 818-0788
Arlington Heights *(G-827)*
Wayne Engineering G 416 943-6271
Skokie *(G-19054)*

3829 Measuring & Controlling Devices, NEC

▲ 7 Mile Solutions Inc E 847 588-2280
Niles *(G-15096)*
7000 Inc F 312 800-3612
Bolingbrook *(G-2143)*
Aixacct Systems Inc G 952 303-4077
Wheaton *(G-20787)*
Alphagage G 815 391-6400
Rockford *(G-17299)*
Amerex Corporation E 309 382-4389
North Pekin *(G-15326)*
Anamet Inc G 217 234-8844
Glen Ellyn *(G-10394)*
Apollo Sensors Inc F 630 293-5820
West Chicago *(G-20542)*
Asm Sensors Inc F 630 832-3202
Elmhurst *(G-9326)*
Assurance Technologies Inc F 630 550-5000
Bartlett *(G-1265)*
▲ Auto Meter Products Inc C 815 895-8141
Sycamore *(G-19702)*
Avalign Technologies Inc D 855 282-5446
Bannockburn *(G-1189)*
◆ Aw Dynamometer Inc F 815 844-6968
Pontiac *(G-16766)*
Barcor Inc F 847 831-2650
Highland Park *(G-11254)*
Barcor Inc F 847 940-0750
Bannockburn *(G-1192)*
◆ Binks Industries Inc G 630 801-1100
Montgomery *(G-14233)*
Biosynergy Inc G 847 956-0471
Elk Grove Village *(G-8867)*
C & L Manufacturing Entps G 618 465-7623
Alton *(G-546)*
Cabot McRlectronics Polsg Corp E 630 543-6682
Addison *(G-61)*
▲ CAM Co Inc F 630 556-3110
Big Rock *(G-1969)*
Cd LLC F 312 275-5747
Chicago *(G-4047)*
Celinco Inc G 815 964-2256
Rockford *(G-17341)*
Centurion Non Destructive Tstg F 630 736-5500
Streamwood *(G-19565)*
▲ Chicago Dial Indicator Company E 847 827-7186
Des Plaines *(G-7744)*
Circle Systems Inc F 815 286-3271
Hinckley *(G-11357)*
Clean Energy Renewables LLC E 309 797-4844
Moline *(G-14136)*
Coinstar Procurement LLC G 630 424-4788
Oakbrook Terrace *(G-15794)*
Controls Group USA Inc G 847 551-5775
Elgin *(G-8555)*
Convergence Fuel Systems LLC G 970 498-3430
Loves Park *(G-13195)*
Converging Systems Inc G 847 519-0232
Schaumburg *(G-18489)*
▲ CTS Corporation C 630 577-8800
Lisle *(G-12881)*
Cubic Trnsp Systems Inc G 312 257-3242
Chicago *(G-4282)*
▲ D O D Technologies Inc E 815 788-5200
Cary *(G-3153)*
▲ Deatak Inc F 815 322-2013
McHenry *(G-13735)*
Deere & Company E 309 765-2960
Moline *(G-14140)*
Diehl Metering LLC G 331 204-6540
Naperville *(G-14816)*
Double K Towers Inc G 773 964-3104
Chicago *(G-4388)*
Dual Mfg Co Inc F 773 267-4457
Franklin Park *(G-9933)*
▲ Durex International Corp B 847 639-5600
Cary *(G-3157)*
▼ Dynamicsignals LLC E 815 838-0005
Lockport *(G-12992)*
E-Motion LLC G 815 825-4411
Fairbury *(G-9606)*
EJ Cady & Company G 847 537-2239
Wheeling *(G-20888)*
Elcon Inc E 815 467-9500
Minooka *(G-14059)*
Elektro-Physik USA Inc G 847 437-6616
Arlington Heights *(G-732)*
Emissions Systems Incorporated G 847 669-8044
Lake In The Hills *(G-12333)*
Erdco Engineering Corporation E 847 328-0550
Evanston *(G-9514)*
▲ Ewikon Molding Tech Inc G 815 874-7270
Rockford *(G-17405)*
Falex Corporation E 630 556-3679
Sugar Grove *(G-19643)*
◆ First Alert Inc C 630 499-3295
Aurora *(G-962)*
Fluid Manufacturing Services G 800 458-5262
Lake Bluff *(G-12181)*
Gamma Products Inc F 708 974-4100
Palos Hills *(G-16201)*
Germann Instruments Inc G 847 329-9999
Evanston *(G-9524)*
▼ Gpe Controls Inc F 708 236-6000
Hillside *(G-11340)*
▲ H S I Fire and Safety Group G 847 427-8340
Elk Grove Village *(G-9026)*
Hamilton Maurer Intl Inc G 713 468-6805
Hudson *(G-11518)*
Holmes Bros Inc E 217 442-1430
Danville *(G-7345)*
▲ Honeywell Analytics Inc C 847 955-8200
Lincolnshire *(G-12770)*
◆ Humboldt Mfg Co E 708 456-6300
Elgin *(G-8617)*
▲ I C Innovations Inc G 847 279-7888
Highland Park *(G-11271)*
Illinois Tool Works Inc E 847 657-5300
Glenview *(G-10562)*
Illinois Tool Works Inc C 847 295-6500
Lake Bluff *(G-12189)*
Industrial Msrment Systems Inc G 630 236-5901
Aurora *(G-981)*
Industrial Thermo Products G 847 398-8600
Rolling Meadows *(G-17740)*
▲ Innoquest Inc G 815 337-8555
Woodstock *(G-21396)*
James Instruments Inc F 773 463-6565
Chicago *(G-5002)*
Jones Medical Instrument Co E 630 571-1980
Oak Brook *(G-15627)*
Jordan Industrial Controls Inc E 217 864-4444
Mount Zion *(G-14648)*
Joseph Ringelstein G 708 955-7467
Norridge *(G-15238)*
▲ Keson Industries Inc E 630 820-4200
Aurora *(G-993)*
▲ Kiene Diesel Accessories Inc E 630 543-7170
Addison *(G-169)*
Kocour Co E 773 847-1111
Chicago *(G-5114)*
L & J Engineering Inc E 708 236-6000
Hillside *(G-11344)*
L & J Holding Company Ltd D 708 236-6000
Hillside *(G-11345)*
L A M Inc De G 630 860-9700
Wood Dale *(G-21206)*
Laboratory Technologies Inc G 630 365-1000
Elburn *(G-8456)*
Landauer Inc C 708 755-7000
Glenwood *(G-10642)*
◆ Lcr Hallcrest Llc E 847 998-8580
Glenview *(G-10584)*
Libco Industries Inc F 815 623-7677
Roscoe *(G-17912)*
◆ Livorsi Marine Inc E 847 548-5900
Grayslake *(G-10788)*
▲ Luster Leaf Products Inc F 815 337-5560
Woodstock *(G-21407)*
▲ M I E America Inc F 847 981-6100
Elk Grove Village *(G-9102)*
◆ Martin Engineering Company C 309 852-2384
Neponset *(G-15018)*
Mech-Tronics Corporation G 708 344-0202
Melrose Park *(G-13892)*
Melt Design Inc F 630 443-4000
Saint Charles *(G-18232)*
Midwest Ultrasonics Inc G 630 434-9458
Darien *(G-7409)*
Migatron Corporation E 815 338-5800
Woodstock *(G-21411)*
▲ Mitsubishi Elc Automtn Inc C 847 478-2100
Vernon Hills *(G-20075)*
MWM Express Inc G 630 401-0528
Chicago Ridge *(G-6805)*
Norman P Moeller G 847 991-3933
Lake Barrington *(G-12162)*
◆ Omron Healthcare Inc D 847 680-6200
Lake Forest *(G-12276)*
Oneplus Systems Inc E 847 498-0955
Northbrook *(G-15447)*
Outdoor Environments LLC G 847 325-5000
Buffalo Grove *(G-2583)*
Parking Systems Inc G 847 891-3819
Schaumburg *(G-18666)*
Parsonics Corp G 815 338-6509
Woodstock *(G-21420)*
Perfection Probes Inc G 847 726-8868
Lake Zurich *(G-12442)*
Perkinelmer Hlth Sciences Inc C 630 969-6000
Downers Grove *(G-8073)*
Polmax LLC C 708 843-8300
Alsip *(G-494)*
▲ Power House Tool Inc E 815 727-6301
Joliet *(G-11915)*
Praxsym Inc F 217 897-1744
Fisher *(G-9667)*
Product Feeding Solutions Inc G 630 709-9546
Chicago Ridge *(G-6809)*
Prostat Corporation F 630 238-8883
Bensenville *(G-1875)*
Psylotech Inc G 847 328-7100
Evanston *(G-9572)*
Reliefband Technologies LLC G 877 735-2263
Rosemont *(G-18047)*
Rockford Rams Products Inc G 815 226-0016
Rockford *(G-17604)*

SIC SECTION 38 MEASURING, ANALYZING AND CONTROLLING INSTRUMENTS; PHOTOGRAPHIC, MEDICAL AN

Romus Incorporated..........G....... 414 350-6233
Roselle *(G-17979)*
▲ **Ryeson Corporation**..........D....... 847 455-8677
Carol Stream *(G-3061)*
▲ **S & W Manufacturing Co Inc**..........E....... 630 595-5044
Bensenville *(G-1888)*
Santec Systems Inc..........F....... 847 215-8884
Arlington Heights *(G-804)*
Schultes Precision Mfg Inc..........D....... 847 465-0300
Buffalo Grove *(G-2596)*
Scientific Instruments Inc..........G....... 847 679-1242
Schaumburg *(G-18709)*
Siemens Med Solutions USA Inc..........D....... 847 304-7700
Hoffman Estates *(G-11458)*
Sikora Automation Incorporated..........G....... 630 833-0298
Addison *(G-291)*
SKF USA Inc..........D....... 847 742-0700
Elgin *(G-8736)*
Somat Corporation..........E....... 800 578-4260
Champaign *(G-3349)*
▼ **Sonoscan Inc**..........D....... 847 437-6400
Elk Grove Village *(G-9247)*
Star Test Dynamometer Inc..........G....... 309 452-0371
Normal *(G-15225)*
Stevens Instrument Company..........G....... 847 336-9375
Waukegan *(G-20498)*
◆ **Technics Inc**..........F....... 630 938-4709
Bolingbrook *(G-2248)*
Tektrol LLC..........F....... 847 857-6076
Crystal Lake *(G-7279)*
Teledyne Lecroy Inc..........E....... 847 888-0450
Elgin *(G-8749)*
Teledyne Monitor Labs Inc..........F....... 303 792-3300
Chicago *(G-6340)*
◆ **Tempco Electric Heater Corp**..........B....... 630 350-2252
Wood Dale *(G-21248)*
▲ **Tempro International Corp**..........G....... 847 677-5370
Skokie *(G-19044)*
Touhy Diagnostic At Home LLC..........F....... 847 803-1111
Des Plaines *(G-7858)*
TRC Environmental Corp..........G....... 630 953-9046
Burr Ridge *(G-2724)*
Tricor Systems Inc..........E....... 847 742-5542
Elgin *(G-8760)*
Trinity Brand Industries Inc..........F....... 708 482-4980
Burr Ridge *(G-2725)*
▼ **Ultrasonic Power Corporation**..........E....... 815 235-6020
Freeport *(G-10148)*
Venturedyne Ltd..........E....... 708 597-7090
Alsip *(G-521)*
Vibra-Tech Engineers Inc..........G....... 630 858-0681
Glen Ellyn *(G-10423)*
Water Services Company of Ill..........G....... 847 697-6623
Elgin *(G-8777)*
Watlow Electric Mfg Co..........G....... 314 878-4600
Richmond *(G-17025)*
Wellness Center Usa Inc..........F....... 847 925-1885
Hoffman Estates *(G-11471)*
Wilkens-Anderson Company..........E....... 773 384-4433
Chicago *(G-6626)*
▲ **Worth-Pfaff Innovations Inc**..........G....... 847 940-9305
Deerfield *(G-7661)*
▲ **Ziv USA Inc**..........G....... 224 735-3961
Rolling Meadows *(G-17786)*

3841 Surgical & Medical Instrs & Apparatus

1 Federal Supply Source Inc..........G....... 708 964-2222
Steger *(G-19486)*
3M Company..........B....... 309 654-2291
Cordova *(G-7005)*
7000 Inc..........F....... 312 800-3612
Bolingbrook *(G-2143)*
▲ **Abbott Laboratories**..........A....... 224 667-6100
Abbott Park *(G-1)*
Abbott Laboratories..........G....... 800 551-5838
Lake Forest *(G-12218)*
Abbott Laboratories..........G....... 847 937-6100
North Chicago *(G-15294)*
Abbott Laboratories..........A....... 847 932-7900
North Chicago *(G-15293)*
◆ **Abbott Laboratories Inc**..........C....... 224 668-2076
Abbott Park *(G-2)*
Abrasive West LLC..........G....... 630 736-0818
Bartlett *(G-1262)*
Access Medical Supply Inc..........G....... 847 891-6210
Schaumburg *(G-18425)*
Addition Technology Inc..........F....... 847 297-8419
Lombard *(G-13035)*
Adhereon Corporation..........G....... 312 997-5002
Chicago *(G-3545)*
ADM Imaging Inc..........G....... 630 834-7100
Wheaton *(G-20786)*
Advanced Cooling Therapy Inc..........E....... 888 534-4873
Chicago *(G-3562)*
Advanced Microderm Inc..........E....... 630 980-3300
Schaumburg *(G-18428)*
Advanced Retinal Institute Inc..........G....... 617 821-5597
Oak Park *(G-15742)*
Aerogenaerogen..........G....... 312 624-9598
Chicago *(G-3573)*
AG Industries LLC..........E....... 636 349-4466
Chicago *(G-3580)*
Aksys Ltd..........D....... 847 229-2020
Lincolnshire *(G-12743)*
Alicona Manufacturing Inc..........G....... 630 736-2718
Bartlett *(G-1263)*
Amar Plastics Inc..........F....... 630 627-4105
Addison *(G-28)*
Amer Surgical Instruments Inc..........F....... 630 986-8032
Westmont *(G-20727)*
▲ **American Biooptics LLC**..........G....... 847 467-0628
Evanston *(G-9493)*
American Medical Industries..........G....... 847 918-9800
Lake Bluff *(G-12169)*
Anchor Products Company..........E....... 630 543-9124
Addison *(G-35)*
Aplicare Products LLC..........G....... 847 949-5500
Northfield *(G-15506)*
Argentum Medical LLC..........E....... 888 551-0188
Geneva *(G-10253)*
Arpwave Usa LLC..........G....... 773 835-0122
Chicago *(G-3732)*
Avalign Grman Specialty Instrs..........E....... 847 908-0292
Schaumburg *(G-18451)*
Avalign Technologies Inc..........D....... 855 282-5446
Bannockburn *(G-1189)*
Avant Diagnostics Inc..........G....... 732 410-9810
Chicago *(G-3783)*
Bandgrip Inc..........G....... 844 968-6322
Chicago *(G-3825)*
Bard Brachytherapy Inc..........E....... 630 933-7610
Carol Stream *(G-2945)*
▼ **Baxalta Export Corporation**..........C....... 224 948-2000
Bannockburn *(G-1193)*
Baxalta World Trade LLC..........G....... 224 940-2000
Bannockburn *(G-1195)*
Baxalta Worldwide LLC..........C....... 224 948-2000
Deerfield *(G-7590)*
▼ **Baxter Global Holdings II Inc**..........E....... 224 948-1812
Deerfield *(G-7591)*
Baxter Healthcare Corporation..........G....... 847 270-4757
Wonder Lake *(G-21143)*
Baxter Healthcare Corporation..........C....... 847 948-3206
Spring Grove *(G-19267)*
Baxter Healthcare Corporation..........D....... 847 270-5720
Round Lake *(G-18069)*
Baxter Healthcare Corporation..........F....... 847 948-4770
Round Lake *(G-18070)*
Baxter Healthcare Corporation..........C....... 847 367-2544
Vernon Hills *(G-20045)*
Baxter Healthcare Corporation..........B....... 847 948-2000
Deerfield *(G-7593)*
Baxter Healthcare Corporation..........B....... 847 940-6599
Round Lake *(G-18072)*
Baxter Healthcare Corporation..........B....... 847 948-2000
Deerfield *(G-7594)*
Baxter Healthcare Corporation..........E....... 847 578-4671
Waukegan *(G-20422)*
Baxter International Inc..........A....... 224 948-2000
Deerfield *(G-7595)*
Baxter World Trade Corporation..........F....... 224 948-2000
Deerfield *(G-7596)*
Becton Dickinson and Company..........G....... 630 743-2006
Downers Grove *(G-7959)*
Beecken Petty Okeefe & Co LLC..........A....... 312 435-0300
Chicago *(G-3858)*
Biosynergy Inc..........G....... 847 956-0471
Elk Grove Village *(G-8867)*
Bird Products Corporation..........G....... 872 757-0114
Mettawa *(G-13978)*
Bold Diagnostics LLC..........G....... 806 543-5743
Chicago *(G-3930)*
▲ **Brainlab Inc**..........C....... 800 784-7700
Westchester *(G-20692)*
Briteseed LLC..........G....... 206 384-0311
Chicago *(G-3960)*
C & S Chemicals Inc..........G....... 815 722-6671
Joliet *(G-11837)*
Cardinal Health Inc..........B....... 847 578-4443
Waukegan *(G-20424)*
Cardinal Health 200 LLC..........E....... 847 689-8410
Waukegan *(G-20425)*
Carematix Inc..........E....... 312 627-9300
Chicago *(G-4028)*
▲ **Carstens Incorporated**..........D....... 708 669-1500
Chicago *(G-4032)*
Chronos Imaging LLC..........D....... 630 296-9220
Aurora *(G-938)*
Chucking Machine Products Inc..........D....... 847 678-1192
Franklin Park *(G-9907)*
Clariance Inc..........F....... 773 868-7041
Chicago *(G-4166)*
Coeur Inc..........F....... 815 648-1093
Hebron *(G-11141)*
Cook Polymer Technology..........G....... 309 740-2342
Canton *(G-2825)*
Covidien Holding Inc..........G....... 618 664-2111
Greenville *(G-10831)*
Cr Bard Inc..........D....... 630 933-7653
Carol Stream *(G-2968)*
Cryonize..........G....... 773 935-8803
Chicago *(G-4278)*
Csl Behring LLC..........B....... 815 932-6773
Bradley *(G-2279)*
◆ **D-M-S Holdings Inc**..........E....... 515 327-6416
Waukegan *(G-20433)*
Diagnostic Photonics Inc..........G....... 312 320-5478
Chicago *(G-4351)*
Doctors Choice Inc..........G....... 312 666-1111
Chicago *(G-4378)*
Elas Tek Molding Inc..........E....... 815 675-9012
Spring Grove *(G-19274)*
Eldest Daughter LLC..........G....... 949 677-7385
Chicago *(G-4476)*
Elmed Incorporated..........E....... 224 353-6446
Glendale Heights *(G-10448)*
▲ **Emergency Medical Instruments**..........G....... 630 365-2001
Maple Park *(G-13462)*
Endofix Ltd..........G....... 708 715-3472
Brookfield *(G-2482)*
Endotronix Inc..........G....... 630 504-2861
Lisle *(G-12888)*
Eriem Surgical Inc..........G....... 847 549-1410
Lake Forest *(G-12247)*
▲ **Esma Inc**..........G....... 708 331-0456
South Holland *(G-19211)*
Feelsure Health Corparation..........G....... 847 823-0137
Park Ridge *(G-16275)*
Fetzer Surgical LLC..........G....... 630 635-2520
Schaumburg *(G-18527)*
Fisher Scientific Company LLC..........G....... 800 528-0494
Chicago *(G-4597)*
Gema Inc..........F....... 773 508-6690
Chicago *(G-4668)*
Global Endoscopy Inc..........G....... 847 910-5836
Elk Grove Village *(G-9015)*
Glooko..........G....... 513 307-0903
Chicago *(G-4701)*
▲ **Good Lite Co**..........G....... 847 841-1145
Elgin *(G-8598)*
Graymont Prof Pdts Ip LLC..........F....... 312 374-4376
Chicago *(G-4731)*
Hearing Screening Assoc LLC..........G....... 855 550-9427
Arlington Heights *(G-747)*
Hill-Rom Holdings Inc..........B....... 312 819-7200
Chicago *(G-4819)*
◆ **Hollister Incorporated**..........B....... 847 680-1000
Libertyville *(G-12660)*
◆ **Hospira Inc**..........A....... 224 212-2000
Lake Forest *(G-12259)*
Hospira Inc..........C....... 224 212-6244
Lake Forest *(G-12260)*
◆ **Hospira Worldwide LLC**..........G....... 224 212-2000
Lake Forest *(G-12261)*
▲ **Hospital Therapy Products Inc**..........F....... 630 766-7101
Wood Dale *(G-21198)*
Imh Fabrication Inc..........F....... 815 537-2381
Prophetstown *(G-16833)*
Inland Midwest Corporation..........E....... 773 775-2111
Elmhurst *(G-9378)*
Integrated Medical Tech Inc..........G....... 309 662-3614
Bloomington *(G-2062)*
ISS Medical Inc..........G....... 217 359-8681
Champaign *(G-3311)*
Jointechlabs Inc..........G....... 773 954-1076
Wheeling *(G-20921)*
Jones Medical Instrument Co..........E....... 630 571-1980
Oak Brook *(G-15627)*
▲ **Jstone Inc**..........E....... 847 325-5660
Mundelein *(G-14706)*

S I C

Employee Codes: A=Over 500 employees, B=251-500
C=101-250, D=51-100, E=20-50, F=10-19, G=3-9
2020 Harris Illinois
Industrial Directory
1007

38 MEASURING, ANALYZING AND CONTROLLING INSTRUMENTS; PHOTOGRAPHIC, MEDICAL AN

Kdk Upset Forging Co ....E 708 388-8770
  Blue Island (G-2128)
Konica Minolta Healthcare ....G....... 815 893-0691
  Crystal Lake (G-7218)
Leica Microsystems Inc ....G....... 847 405-0123
  Buffalo Grove (G-2562)
▲ Leica Microsystems Inc ....C....... 847 405-0123
  Buffalo Grove (G-2563)
Life Spine Inc ....D....... 847 884-6117
  Huntley (G-11551)
◆ Lsl Industries Inc ....D....... 773 878-1100
  Niles (G-15141)
Ltc Holdings Inc ....C....... 847 249-5900
  Waukegan (G-20464)
Ludwig Medical Inc ....G....... 217 342-6570
  Effingham (G-8408)
Luminex Corporation ....G....... 847 400-9000
  Northbrook (G-15423)
▲ Manan Medical Products Inc ....D....... 847 637-3333
  Wheeling (G-20936)
Manan Tool & Manufacturing ....A....... 847 637-3333
  Wheeling (G-20937)
Mc Squared Group Inc ....G....... 815 322-2485
  Spring Grove (G-19283)
MD Technologies Inc ....F....... 815 598-3143
  Elizabeth (G-8788)
Medical Adherence Tech Inc ....G....... 847 525-6300
  Winnetka (G-21133)
Medicate Dme Inc ....F....... 618 874-3000
  East Saint Louis (G-8314)
Medifix Inc ....G....... 847 965-1898
  Morton Grove (G-14427)
Medigroup Inc ....G....... 630 554-5533
  Oswego (G-16013)
◆ Medline Industries Inc ....A....... 847 949-5500
  Northfield (G-15523)
Medline Industries Inc ....B....... 847 949-2056
  Mundelein (G-14715)
Medline Industries Inc ....B....... 847 949-5500
  Waukegan (G-20466)
Medtex Health Services Inc ....G....... 630 789-0330
  Clarendon Hills (G-6900)
Medtronic Inc ....F....... 815 444-2500
  Crystal Lake (G-7225)
Medtronic Inc ....E....... 630 627-6677
  Lombard (G-13099)
Mindful Mdispa Mediclinic Pllc ....G....... 847 922-4768
  Barrington (G-1229)
Minute Mlcular Diagnostics Inc ....G....... 847 849-0263
  Evanston (G-9554)
Mobile Health & Wellness Inc ....G....... 773 697-9892
  Chicago (G-5475)
Monogen Inc ....E....... 847 573-6700
  Chicago (G-5492)
Murray Inc ....E....... 847 620-7990
  North Barrington (G-15287)
Nanosphere LLC ....C....... 847 400-9000
  Northbrook (G-15438)
◆ Nemera Buffalo Grove LLC ....E....... 847 541-7900
  Buffalo Grove (G-2580)
Nemera Buffalo Grove LLC ....G....... 847 325-3629
  Buffalo Grove (G-2581)
Nemera Buffalo Grove LLC ....G....... 847 325-3628
  Buffalo Grove (G-2582)
▲ Newmedical Technology Inc ....E....... 847 412-1000
  Northbrook (G-15441)
Nordent Manufacturing Inc ....E....... 847 437-4780
  Elk Grove Village (G-9150)
Northgate Technologies Inc ....E....... 847 608-8900
  Elgin (G-8674)
Novo Surgical Inc ....E....... 877 860-6686
  Oak Brook (G-15650)
Nrtx LLC ....G....... 224 717-0465
  Chicago (G-5635)
▲ Oakridge Products LLC ....G....... 815 363-4700
  McHenry (G-13772)
Oberg Medical Products Co LLC ....E....... 847 364-4750
  Elk Grove Village (G-9158)
Odin Technologies LLC ....G....... 408 309-1925
  Chicago (G-5655)
◆ Ohio Medical LLC ....D....... 847 855-0500
  Gurnee (G-10907)
Omc Investors LLC ....G....... 847 855-6220
  Gurnee (G-10908)
Omnicare Group Inc ....G....... 708 949-8502
  Homer Glen (G-11485)
◆ Omron Healthcare Inc ....D....... 847 680-6200
  Lake Forest (G-12276)
Opticent Inc ....G....... 410 829-7384
  Evanston (G-9563)

▲ Organ Recovery Systems Inc ....F....... 847 824-2600
  Itasca (G-11714)
Phenome Technologies Inc ....G....... 847 962-1273
  Skokie (G-19004)
Photonicare Inc ....G....... 866 411-3277
  Champaign (G-3333)
Precision Medical Mfg LLC ....G....... 847 229-1551
  Wheeling (G-20964)
Precision Products Mfg Intl ....G....... 847 299-8500
  Des Plaines (G-7831)
Precision Vision Inc ....G....... 815 223-2022
  Woodstock (G-21423)
Provena Randalwood Open Mri ....E....... 630 587-9917
  Geneva (G-10300)
Quadrant Medical Corporation ....G....... 312 800-1294
  Aurora (G-1011)
RAD Source Technologies Inc ....G....... 815 477-1291
  Algonquin (G-385)
Resonance Medical LLC ....G....... 229 292-2094
  Chicago (G-6017)
Revolutionary Medical Dvcs Inc ....F....... 520 464-4299
  Mettawa (G-13981)
Reznik Instrument Co ....G....... 847 673-3444
  Skokie (G-19022)
▼ Richard Wolf Med Instrs Corp ....C....... 847 913-1113
  Vernon Hills (G-20086)
Riverbank Laboratories Inc ....G....... 630 232-2207
  Geneva (G-10303)
Rti Surgical Holdings Inc ....G....... 386 418-8888
  Deerfield (G-7647)
◆ Salter Labs ....F....... 847 739-3224
  Lake Forest (G-12300)
Salter Medical Holdings Corp ....E....... 800 421-0024
  Lake Forest (G-12301)
Sensormedics Corporation ....G....... 872 757-0114
  Mettawa (G-13982)
Shanks Veterinary Equipment ....G....... 815 225-7700
  Milledgeville (G-14040)
▲ Siemens Hlthcare Dgnostics Inc ....C....... 847 267-5300
  Deerfield (G-7648)
Siemens Med Solutions USA Inc ....D....... 847 304-7700
  Schaumburg (G-18712)
Simpex Medical Inc ....G....... 847 757-9928
  Mount Prospect (G-14571)
▲ Smiths Medical ....G....... 847 383-1400
  Vernon Hills (G-20098)
Southwestern Hearing Centers ....G....... 618 651-4199
  Highland (G-11241)
Sparton Onyx Holdings LLC ....G....... 847 762-5800
  Schaumburg (G-18720)
▲ Star Cushion Products Inc ....F....... 618 539-7070
  Freeburg (G-10096)
Star Ophthalmic Instrs Inc ....F....... 630 655-4500
  Orland Park (G-15984)
Stereo Optical Company Inc ....F....... 773 867-0380
  Chicago (G-6244)
Stradis Medical LLC ....F....... 847 887-8400
  Waukegan (G-20499)
Stretch CHI ....G....... 773 420-9355
  Chicago (G-6253)
Stryker Corporation ....G....... 630 616-0606
  Wood Dale (G-21244)
Stryker Corporation ....G....... 847 829-5238
  Cary (G-3192)
Stryker Corporation ....B....... 312 386-9780
  Chicago (G-6256)
Stryker Enterprises LLC ....G....... 815 975-5167
  Loves Park (G-13267)
◆ Summit Industries LLC ....D....... 773 353-4000
  Niles (G-15176)
▲ Sunset Halthcare Solutions Inc ....E....... 877 578-6738
  Chicago (G-6278)
Superior Surgical Instrumen TS ....G....... 630 628-8437
  Addison (G-299)
Supertek Scientific LLC ....G....... 630 345-3450
  Addison (G-300)
Surgical Innovation Assoc Inc ....G....... 626 372-4884
  Chicago (G-6289)
Surgical Innovation Assoc Inc ....G....... 847 548-8499
  Libertyville (G-12711)
Surgical Instrument Svcs & Sav ....G....... 847 646-2000
  Northfield (G-15533)
Surgical Solutions LLC ....C....... 847 607-6098
  Deerfield (G-7650)
◆ Sysmex America Inc ....C....... 847 996-4500
  Lincolnshire (G-12797)
Teleflex Incorporated ....D....... 847 259-7400
  Arlington Heights (G-818)
Teleflex Medical OEM LLC ....C....... 847 596-3100
  Gurnee (G-10936)

Thermatome Corporation ....G....... 312 772-2201
  Chicago (G-6361)
Thrift Medical Products ....G....... 630 857-3548
  Naperville (G-14933)
Tianhe Stem Cell Biotechnolgie ....F....... 630 723-1968
  Lisle (G-12952)
Total Titanium Inc ....E....... 866 208-6446
  Red Bud (G-17003)
▲ United Amercn Healthcare Corp ....E....... 313 393-4571
  Chicago (G-6469)
Uresil LLC ....E....... 847 982-0200
  Skokie (G-19050)
Varian Medical Systems Inc ....F....... 847 279-5100
  Lincolnshire (G-12800)
Viant Wheeling Inc ....G....... 847 520-1553
  Wheeling (G-21009)
Vital Care Reps ....G....... 708 342-2680
  Tinley Park (G-19867)
Vital Signs Inc ....G....... 872 757-0114
  Mettawa (G-13983)
Vyaire Company ....G....... 833 327-3284
  Mettawa (G-13984)
Vyaire Medical Inc ....C....... 833 327-3284
  Mettawa (G-13985)
Vyaire Medical LLC ....G....... 833 327-3284
  Mettawa (G-13986)
Vyaire Medical Mx LLC ....B....... 872 757-0114
  Mettawa (G-13987)
Vyaire Medical Payroll LLC ....G....... 224 544-5436
  Mettawa (G-13988)
Welkins LLC ....G....... 877 319-3504
  Downers Grove (G-8108)
Whitney Products Inc ....F....... 847 966-6161
  Niles (G-15187)
Wholesale Point Inc ....F....... 630 986-1700
  Burr Ridge (G-2735)
Wisdom Medical Technology LLC ....G....... 630 803-6383
  Oswego (G-16033)
Ziemer Usa Inc ....F....... 618 462-9301
  Alton (G-576)
Zimmer Smith & Associates Inc ....F....... 217 788-5800
  Springfield (G-19471)

3842 Orthopedic, Prosthetic & Surgical Appliances/Splys

1 Federal Supply Source Inc ....G....... 708 964-2222
  Steger (G-19486)
▲ 20 20 Medical Systems Inc ....G....... 815 455-7161
  Crystal Lake (G-7152)
Accurate Radiation Shielding ....G....... 847 639-5533
  Cary (G-3143)
Accutone Hearing Aid Inc ....G....... 773 545-3279
  Evanston (G-9487)
Advanced Bionics LLC ....G....... 708 946-3406
  Warrenville (G-20229)
Advanced O&P Solutions ....E....... 708 878-2241
  Hickory Hills (G-11193)
▲ Anatomical Worldwide LLC ....G....... 312 224-4772
  Evanston (G-9494)
Argentum Medical LLC ....E....... 888 551-0188
  Geneva (G-10253)
Artistic Dental Studio Inc ....E....... 630 679-8686
  Bolingbrook (G-2149)
B & D Independence Inc ....E....... 618 262-7117
  Mount Carmel (G-14465)
▼ Baxalta Export Corporation ....C....... 224 948-2000
  Bannockburn (G-1193)
Baxalta World Trade LLC ....G....... 224 940-2000
  Bannockburn (G-1195)
Baxalta Worldwide LLC ....C....... 224 948-2000
  Deerfield (G-7590)
Baxter Healthcare Corporation ....E....... 847 578-4671
  Waukegan (G-20422)
Baxter International Inc ....A....... 224 948-2000
  Deerfield (G-7595)
Becks Medical & Indus Gases ....F....... 618 273-9019
  Eldorado (G-8479)
Beltone Corporation ....C....... 847 832-3300
  Glenview (G-10530)
Bergmann Orthotic Lab Inc ....G....... 847 446-3616
  Northfield (G-15508)
Bergmann Orthotic Laboratory ....G....... 847 729-7923
  Glenview (G-10531)
Bioconcepts Inc ....G....... 630 986-0007
  Burr Ridge (G-2656)
Bionic Chicago ....G....... 773 698-6269
  Chicago (G-3897)
Blue Sky Bio LLC ....F....... 718 376-0422
  Libertyville (G-12638)

SIC SECTION 38 MEASURING, ANALYZING AND CONTROLLING INSTRUMENTS; PHOTOGRAPHIC, MEDICAL AN

▲ Boss Manufacturing Holdings ....F 309 852-2781
Kewanee (G-12025)
Brandt Interiors ....G 847 251-3543
Wilmette (G-21071)
Brasel Products Inc ....G 630 879-3759
Batavia (G-1360)
C & S Chemicals Inc ....G 815 722-6671
Joliet (G-11837)
C R Kesner Company ....G 630 232-8118
Geneva (G-10258)
Cape Prosthetics-Orthotics Inc ....G 618 457-4692
Marion (G-13507)
Cast21 Inc ....G 847 772-8547
Chicago (G-4036)
▲ Comfort Companies LLC ....E 406 522-8560
Belleville (G-1540)
Cornucopia Supply Corp ....G 847 532-9365
Morton Grove (G-14397)
Cosmedent Inc ....E 312 644-9388
Chicago (G-4245)
D J Peters Orthopedics Ltd ....G 309 664-6930
Bloomington (G-2037)
Dabir Surfaces Inc ....F 708 867-6777
Harwood Heights (G-11103)
Daniel Zimmer Associates ....F 847 697-9393
North Barrington (G-15283)
David Rotter Prosthetics Ltd ....G 815 255-3220
Joliet (G-11853)
Dean Prsthtic Orthtic Svcs Ltd ....G 847 475-7080
Evanston (G-9508)
Deborah Morris Gulbrandson Pt ....F 847 639-4140
Cary (G-3154)
Dental Craft Corp ....F 815 385-7132
Ringwood (G-17041)
Dreher Orthopedic Industries ....G 708 848-4646
Western Springs (G-20721)
Dura-Crafts Corp ....F 815 464-3561
Frankfort (G-9789)
Duroweld Company Inc ....E 847 680-3064
Lake Bluff (G-12179)
E&B Exercise LLC ....G 844 425-5025
Chicago (G-4426)
E-Z Cuff Inc ....G 847 549-1550
Libertyville (G-12648)
East West Martial Arts Sups ....G 773 878-7711
Chicago (G-4434)
Ecomed Solutions LLC ....E 866 817-7114
Mundelein (G-14685)
Elginex Corporation ....G 815 786-8406
Sandwich (G-18368)
Elmed Incorporated ....E 224 353-6446
Glendale Heights (G-10448)
Eln Group LLC ....G 847 477-1496
Winnetka (G-21128)
Enespro LLC ....G 630 332-2801
Oak Brook (G-15617)
Etymotic Research Inc ....E 847 228-0006
Elk Grove Village (G-8984)
Fall Protection Systems Inc ....E 618 452-7000
Madison (G-13411)
◆ Firm of John Dickinson ....D 847 680-1000
Libertyville (G-12652)
G & M Industries Inc ....G 618 344-6655
Collinsville (G-6962)
Gema Inc ....F 773 508-6690
Chicago (G-4668)
General Bandages Inc ....F 847 966-8383
Park Ridge (G-16280)
Go Steady LLC ....G 630 293-3243
West Chicago (G-20588)
Gohear LLC ....G 847 574-7829
Lake Forest (G-12252)
Great Ideas Inc ....F 800 611-5515
Highland Park (G-11267)
Gregory Lamar & Assoc Inc ....G 312 595-1545
Chicago (G-4741)
▲ Guardian Equipment Inc ....E 312 447-8100
Chicago (G-4747)
Hanger Inc ....E 847 695-6955
McHenry (G-13747)
Hanger Inc ....F 708 679-1006
Matteson (G-13624)
Hanger Prosthetics & ....G 217 429-6656
Decatur (G-7499)
Hanger Prosthetics & ....G 630 986-0007
Burr Ridge (G-2680)
Hanger Prosthetics & ....G 630 986-0007
Burr Ridge (G-2681)
Hanger Prosthetics & ....G 847 623-6080
Gurnee (G-10886)

Hanger Prosthetics & ....G 630 820-5656
Aurora (G-977)
Hanger Prsthetcs & Ortho Inc ....G 309 585-2349
Normal (G-15204)
Hanger Prsthetcs & Ortho Inc ....G 217 429-6656
Decatur (G-7500)
Hanger Prsthtics Orthotics Inc ....G 309 637-6581
Peoria (G-16451)
Hanger Prsthtics Orthotics Inc ....G 815 744-9944
Joliet (G-11873)
Hanger Prsthtics Orthtics E In ....G 618 997-1451
Herrin (G-11172)
Hearing Aid Warehouse Inc ....G 217 431-4700
Danville (G-7343)
Heart 4 Heart Inc ....G 217 544-2699
Springfield (G-19379)
Hogg Welding Inc ....G 708 339-0033
Harvey (G-11089)
◆ Hollister Incorporated ....B 847 680-1000
Libertyville (G-12660)
Honeywell Safety Pdts USA Inc ....C 630 343-3731
Bolingbrook (G-2185)
Howmedica Osteonics Corp ....G 309 663-6414
Bloomington (G-2059)
Illiana Orthopedics Inc ....G 708 532-0061
Tinley Park (G-19836)
Imhear Corporation ....G 630 395-9628
Downers Grove (G-8029)
Integrated Medical Tech Inc ....G 309 662-3614
Bloomington (G-2062)
JP Orthotics ....G 217 885-3047
Quincy (G-16898)
▲ Kinsman Enterprises Inc ....G 618 932-3838
West Frankfort (G-20674)
▲ Knowles Electronics LLC ....C 630 250-5100
Itasca (G-11688)
Koebers Prosthetic Orthpd Lab ....G 309 676-2276
Chicago (G-5117)
Lemaitre Vascular Inc ....F 847 462-2191
Fox River Grove (G-9760)
▲ Lester L Brossard Co ....F 815 338-7825
Woodstock (G-21405)
Logan Actuator Co ....G 815 943-9500
Harvard (G-11059)
◆ Lsl Industries Inc ....D 773 878-1100
Niles (G-15141)
M2m Enterprises LLC ....G 847 899-7565
Elgin (G-8644)
◆ MAC Medical Inc ....C 618 476-3550
Millstadt (G-14051)
◆ Magid Glove Safety Mfg Co LLC ....B 773 384-2070
Romeoville (G-17844)
▲ Manan Medical Products Inc ....D 847 637-3333
Wheeling (G-20936)
Mandis Dental Laboratory ....G 618 345-3777
Collinsville (G-6968)
MD Orthotic Prosthetic Lab Inc ....E 708 387-9700
Brookfield (G-2488)
Medbot Inc ....G 213 200-6658
Chicago (G-5381)
▲ Medgyn Products Inc ....D 630 627-4105
Addison (G-195)
Medline Industries Inc ....B 847 949-5500
Waukegan (G-20466)
Merry Walker Corporation ....G 847 837-9580
Mundelein (G-14716)
Mhub ....G 773 580-1485
Chicago (G-5420)
Microguide Inc ....G 630 964-3335
Downers Grove (G-8054)
Midwest Orthotic & Technology ....G 773 930-3770
Burr Ridge (G-2703)
Midwest Water Group Inc ....E 866 526-6558
Crystal Lake (G-7230)
Milvia ....G 312 527-3403
Chicago (G-5463)
Mimosa Acoustics Inc ....G 217 359-9740
Champaign (G-3323)
Mio Med Orthopedics Inc ....G 773 477-8991
Chicago (G-5466)
Mobility Connection Inc ....G 815 965-8090
Rockford (G-17531)
Modern Aids Inc ....E 847 437-8600
Elk Grove Village (G-9130)
Neo Orthotics Inc ....G 309 699-0354
East Peoria (G-8279)
New Step Orthotic Lab Inc ....F 618 208-4444
Maryville (G-13592)
▲ Newmedical Technology Inc ....E 847 412-1000
Northbrook (G-15441)

Northern Prosthetics ....G 815 226-0444
Rockford (G-17539)
O & P Kinetic ....G 815 401-7260
Bourbonnais (G-2267)
One Way Safety LLC ....E 708 579-0229
La Grange (G-12085)
Opportunity Inc ....D 847 831-9400
Highland Park (G-11290)
Optech Ortho & Prosth Svcs ....G 708 364-9700
Orland Park (G-15972)
Optech Ortho & Prosth Svcs ....F 815 932-8564
Kankakee (G-11995)
▲ Pal Health Technologies Inc ....D 309 347-8785
Pekin (G-16351)
Payne Chauna ....G 618 580-2584
Belleville (G-1583)
▲ Phonak LLC ....A 630 821-5000
Warrenville (G-20245)
Plastic Specialists America ....G 847 406-7547
Gurnee (G-10912)
PR Manufacturing Entps LLC ....E 309 347-8785
Pekin (G-16354)
PR Orthotics & Ot ....G 224 470-8550
Skokie (G-19008)
▲ Pres-On Corporation ....E 630 628-2255
Bolingbrook (G-2229)
Prointegration Tech LLC ....G 618 409-3233
Highland (G-11235)
Prosthetic Orthotic Specialist ....F 309 454-8733
Normal (G-15219)
Prosthetics Orthotics Han ....G 847 695-6955
McHenry (G-13784)
Psyonic Inc ....G 888 779-6642
Champaign (G-3340)
Punch Products Manufacturing ....E 773 533-2800
Chicago (G-5915)
Quad City Prosthetics Inc ....F 309 676-2276
Rock Island (G-17236)
Quincy Lab Inc ....E 773 622-2428
Chicago (G-5938)
R G H & Associates Inc ....G 630 357-5915
Naperville (G-14904)
R W G Manufacturing Inc ....G 708 755-8035
S Chicago Hts (G-18127)
Research Design Inc ....G 708 246-8166
Western Springs (G-20724)
Respironics Inc ....C 708 923-6200
Palos Park (G-16213)
Robert B Scott Ocularists Ltd ....E 312 782-3558
Chicago (G-6042)
Roho Inc ....D 618 277-9173
Belleville (G-1592)
Ronald S Lefors Bs Cpo ....G 618 259-1969
East Alton (G-8170)
▲ Rondex Products Incorporated ....F 815 226-0452
Rockford (G-17615)
Rti Surgical Holdings Inc ....F 386 418-8888
Deerfield (G-7647)
◆ Sage Products LLC ....C 815 455-4700
Cary (G-3188)
Sage Products Holdings II LLC ....G 800 323-2220
Cary (G-3189)
◆ Salisbury Elec Safety LLC ....B 877 406-4501
Bolingbrook (G-2234)
SC Industries LLC ....F 407 484-2081
Chicago (G-6109)
Scheck Siress Prosthetics Inc ....G 312 757-5270
Chicago (G-6111)
Scheck Siress Prosthetics Inc ....C 630 424-0392
Oak Park (G-15771)
Serola Biomechanics Inc ....F 815 636-2780
Loves Park (G-13263)
Sonova USA Inc ....C 763 744-3300
Aurora (G-1018)
▲ Sourcennex International Co ....G 847 251-5500
Wilmette (G-21093)
Standard Safety Equipment Co ....E 815 363-8565
McHenry (G-13795)
▲ Star Cushion Products Inc ....F 618 539-7070
Freeburg (G-10096)
▼ Steel-Guard Safety Corp ....G 708 589-4588
South Holland (G-19246)
▲ Steiner Industries Inc ....D 773 588-3444
Chicago (G-6240)
Stellar Orthtics Prsthtics LLC ....F 847 410-2751
Glenview (G-10626)
Steris Corporation ....F 847 455-2881
Franklin Park (G-10052)
Surgical Instrument Service Co ....F 630 221-1988
Glendale Heights (G-10506)

S I C

38 MEASURING, ANALYZING AND CONTROLLING INSTRUMENTS; PHOTOGRAPHIC, MEDICAL AN

Teleflex Incorporated .... D 847 259-7400
 Arlington Heights (G-818)
▲ Tetra Medical Supply Corp .... F 847 647-0590
 Niles (G-15179)
Therapeutic Envisions Inc .... G 720 323-7032
 Libertyville (G-12716)
◆ Tradex International Inc .... D 216 651-4788
 Elwood (G-9465)
Tri R .... G 224 399-7786
 Libertyville (G-12718)
Triad Controls Inc .... D 630 443-9320
 Saint Charles (G-18291)
Trigon International LLC .... D 630 978-9990
 Aurora (G-1027)
Tuu Duc Le Inc .... G 630 897-6363
 North Aurora (G-15280)
United Seating & Mobility LLC .... G 309 699-0509
 East Peoria (G-8293)
Weeb Enterprises LLC .... G 815 861-2625
 Wauconda (G-20402)
Welkins LLC .... G 877 319-3504
 Downers Grove (G-8108)
Wheaton Resource Corp .... G 630 690-5795
 Carol Stream (G-3088)
Whitney Products Inc .... F 847 966-6161
 Niles (G-15187)
▲ Williams Halthcare Systems LLC .. D 847 741-3650
 Elgin (G-8782)
World Class Technologies Inc ...... G 312 758-3114
 Chicago (G-6672)

3843 Dental Eqpt & Splys

Acquamed Technologies Inc .... G 630 728-4014
 Oswego (G-15989)
Apex Dental Materials Inc .... G 847 719-1133
 Lake Zurich (G-12385)
Artistic Dental Studio Inc .... E 630 679-8686
 Bolingbrook (G-2149)
▲ Astron Dental Corporation .... F 847 726-8787
 Lake Zurich (G-12386)
Bennett Technologies Inc .... F 708 389-9501
 Tinley Park (G-19809)
▲ Bisco Inc .... D 847 534-6000
 Schaumburg (G-18464)
Ched Markay Inc .... G 847 566-3307
 Mundelein (G-14675)
Cislak Manufacturing Inc .... E 847 647-1819
 Niles (G-15110)
Denbur Inc .... G 630 986-9667
 Westmont (G-20735)
Dental Arts Laboratories Inc .... G 309 342-3117
 Galesburg (G-10190)
Dental Craft Corp .... F 815 385-7132
 Ringwood (G-17041)
Dental Crafts Lab Inc .... G 815 872-3221
 Princeton (G-16806)
Dental Laboratory Inc .... E 630 262-3700
 Geneva (G-10265)
▲ Dental Technologies Inc .... D 847 677-5500
 Lincolnwood (G-12816)
Dentalez Alabama Inc .... C 773 624-4330
 Chicago (G-4341)
Dentsply Sirona Inc .... G 847 640-4800
 Elgin (G-8565)
Dove Dental Studio .... G 847 679-2434
 Niles (G-15116)
Duquoin Dental Associates .... G 618 542-8832
 Du Quoin (G-8118)
Fred Pigg Dental Lab .... G 618 439-6829
 Mount Vernon (G-14611)
Fricke Dental Manufacturing Co .... G 630 540-1900
 Streamwood (G-19575)
◆ Gc America Inc .... C 708 597-0900
 Alsip (G-446)
Gc Manufacturing America LLC .... D 708 597-0900
 Alsip (G-447)
Goldman Products Inc .... E 847 526-1166
 Wauconda (G-20354)
Healthdentl LLC .... G 800 845-5172
 Plainfield (G-16670)
Holland Specialty Co .... E 309 697-9262
 Peoria (G-16453)
▲ Hu-Friedy Mfg Co LLC .... C 773 975-3975
 Chicago (G-4858)
Integrated Medical Tech Inc .... G 309 662-3614
 Bloomington (G-2062)
J L Lawrence & Co .... G 217 235-3622
 Mattoon (G-13638)
James Street Dental P C .... G 630 232-9535
 Geneva (G-10286)

◆ Lang Dental Mfg Co Inc .... F 847 215-6622
 Wheeling (G-20929)
Lmpl Management Corporation .... G 708 636-2443
 Oak Lawn (G-15725)
M & N Dental .... G 815 678-0036
 Richmond (G-17017)
Mandis Dental Laboratory .... G 618 345-3777
 Collinsville (G-6968)
Martin Dental Laboratory Inc .... F 708 597-8880
 Lockport (G-13011)
Myerson LLC .... G 312 432-8200
 Chicago (G-5531)
Nordent Manufacturing Inc .... E 847 437-4780
 Elk Grove Village (G-9150)
◆ Odl Inc .... D 815 434-0655
 Ottawa (G-16067)
Oratech Inc .... E 217 793-2735
 Springfield (G-19418)
Ortho Arch Company Inc .... E 847 885-7805
 Schaumburg (G-18660)
▲ Prime Dental Manufacturing .... E 773 283-2914
 Chicago (G-5873)
Proalliance Corp .... G 815 207-8556
 Harvard (G-11064)
Reliance Dental Mfg Co .... G 708 597-6694
 Alsip (G-502)
Smile Lee Faces .... C 773 376-9999
 Chicago (G-6192)
Strictly Dentures .... G 815 969-0531
 Rockford (G-17647)
▲ Sunstar Americas Inc .... B 847 794-4157
 Schaumburg (G-18730)
Tanaka Dental Enterprises Inc ..... F 847 679-1610
 Skokie (G-19042)
Underwood Dental Laboratories .... G 217 398-0090
 Champaign (G-3360)
▲ Young Innovations Inc .... D 847 458-5400
 Algonquin (G-397)
Young Innovations Inc .... E 847 458-5400
 Algonquin (G-398)
Young Mydent LLC .... F 631 434-3190
 Algonquin (G-399)
Young Os LLC .... E 847 458-5400
 Algonquin (G-400)

3844 X-ray Apparatus & Tubes

▲ 7 Mile Solutions Inc .... E 847 588-2280
 Niles (G-15096)
Abbott Laboratories .... A 847 932-7900
 North Chicago (G-15293)
Arquilla Inc .... F 815 455-2470
 Crystal Lake (G-7163)
Assurance Technologies Inc .... F 630 550-5000
 Bartlett (G-1265)
Brand X-Ray Company .... F 630 543-5331
 Addison (G-54)
Faxitron X-Ray LLC .... E 847 465-9729
 Lincolnshire (G-12763)
▲ Gama Electronics Inc .... F 815 356-9600
 Woodstock (G-21391)
General Electric Company .... C 630 588-8853
 Carol Stream (G-2990)
Lixi Inc .... G 630 620-4646
 Downers Grove (G-8045)
Mark Industries .... G 847 487-8670
 Wauconda (G-20372)
Material Control Inc .... F 630 892-4274
 Batavia (G-1393)
Medical Radiation Concepts .... G 630 289-1515
 Bartlett (G-1297)
Midmark Corporation .... D 800 643-6275
 Buffalo Grove (G-2574)
Philips North America LLC .... C 630 585-2000
 Aurora (G-1008)
Poersch Metal Manufacturing Co .. F 773 722-0890
 Chicago (G-5828)
▲ Sedecal Usa Inc .... E 847 394-6960
 Arlington Heights (G-806)
Starfire Industries LLC .... E 217 721-4165
 Champaign (G-3356)
Superior X Ray Tube Company ..... G 815 338-4424
 Woodstock (G-21437)
Varex Imaging Corporation .... D 847 279-5121
 Franklin Park (G-10076)
Wallace Enterprises Inc .... G 309 496-1230
 East Moline (G-8247)
▲ X-Ray Cassette Repair Co Inc .... E 815 356-8181
 Crystal Lake (G-7296)

3845 Electromedical & Electrotherapeutic Apparatus

7000 Inc .... F 312 800-3612
 Bolingbrook (G-2143)
Aed Essentials .... G 815 977-5920
 Rockford (G-17297)
Aespheptics Medical Ltd .... G 630 416-1400
 Lombard (G-13037)
Amcor Flexibles LLC .... F 847 362-9000
 Mundelein (G-14662)
Amigo Mobility Center .... G 630 268-8670
 Oakbrook Terrace (G-15784)
Apana Inc .... G 309 303-4007
 Peoria (G-16384)
Arxium Inc .... C 847 808-2600
 Buffalo Grove (G-2513)
Axiosonic LLC .... F 217 342-3412
 Effingham (G-8387)
Barrington Clinical Partners .... G 847 508-9737
 Barrington (G-1214)
Cardiac Imaging Inc .... G 630 834-7100
 Oakbrook Terrace (G-15791)
Cortek Endoscopy Inc .... G 847 526-2266
 Wauconda (G-20340)
Ctg Advanced Materials LLC .... E 630 226-9080
 Bolingbrook (G-2161)
◆ CTS Automotive LLC .... C 630 577-8800
 Lisle (G-12880)
Dermatique Laser & Skin .... F 630 262-2515
 Geneva (G-10266)
Domino Lasers Inc .... E 847 855-1364
 Gurnee (G-10872)
Dupage Chropractic Centre Ltd .... G 630 858-9780
 Glen Ellyn (G-10402)
Elmed Incorporated .... E 224 353-6446
 Glendale Heights (G-10448)
General Electric Company .... B 847 304-7400
 Hoffman Estates (G-11428)
Healthlight LLC .... F 224 231-0342
 Schaumburg (G-18544)
Henderson Engineering Co Inc .... G 815 786-9471
 Sandwich (G-18374)
Interexpo Ltd .... F 847 489-7056
 Kildeer (G-12049)
Isovac Products LLC .... G 630 679-1740
 Romeoville (G-17834)
IV & Respiratory Care Services .... E 618 398-2720
 Belleville (G-1559)
Jones Medical Instrument Co .... E 630 571-1980
 Oak Brook (G-15627)
Keebomed Inc .... G 630 888-2888
 Mount Prospect (G-14542)
Lifeline Scientific Inc .... E 847 294-0300
 Itasca (G-11691)
Lifewatch Corp .... G 847 720-2100
 Rosemont (G-18031)
Lifewatch Services Inc .... G 847 720-2100
 Rosemont (G-18032)
▲ Lifewatch Technologies Inc .... D 847 720-2100
 Rosemont (G-18033)
Medical Specialties Distrs LLC .... G 630 307-6200
 Hanover Park (G-11009)
Medtex Health Services Inc .... G 630 789-0330
 Clarendon Hills (G-6900)
Metritrack Inc .... G 630 607-9311
 Hillside (G-11347)
Mobile Endoscopix LLC .... G 847 380-8992
 Northbrook (G-15434)
Nanocytomics LLC .... G 847 467-2868
 Evanston (G-9556)
Neopenda Pbc .... G 919 622-2487
 Chicago (G-5570)
Northgate Technologies Inc .... E 847 608-8900
 Elgin (G-8674)
Odin Technologies LLC .... G 408 309-1925
 Chicago (G-5655)
Omex Technologies Inc .... G 847 850-5858
 Wheeling (G-20949)
◆ Omron Healthcare Inc .... D 847 680-6200
 Lake Forest (G-12276)
Output Medical Inc .... G 630 430-8024
 Chicago (G-5716)
Positron Corporation .... E 317 576-0183
 Westmont (G-20765)
Retmap Inc .... G 312 224-8938
 Grayslake (G-10797)
Samel Botros .... G 847 466-5905
 Bloomingdale (G-2014)
Siemens Med Solutions USA Inc .. D 847 304-7700
 Hoffman Estates (G-11458)

Smart Scan Mri LLC ....G.... 847 623-4000
Gurnee (G-10928)
Snap Diagnostics LLC ....F.... 847 777-0000
Wheeling (G-20988)
Sullivan Home Health Products ....G.... 217 532-6366
Hillsboro (G-11320)
System Science Corporation ....G.... 708 214-2264
Chicago (G-6304)
Thermatome Corporation ....G.... 312 772-2201
Chicago (G-6361)
Universal Holdings Inc ....F.... 224 353-6198
Hoffman Estates (G-11470)
Verena Solutions LLC ....G.... 314 651-1908
Chicago (G-6536)
Victory Pharmacy Decatur Inc ....G.... 708 801-9626
Calumet City (G-2792)
Virtusense Technologies Inc ....E.... 855 443-5744
Peoria (G-16544)
Vivotronix Inc ....G.... 312 536-3130
Chicago (G-6563)
Vpr Unlimited Inc ....G.... 708 830-6285
Bridgeview (G-2397)

3851 Ophthalmic Goods

Alcon Vision LLC ....E.... 312 751-6200
Chicago (G-3599)
Asico LLC ....F.... 630 986-8032
Westmont (G-20729)
C & S Chemicals Inc ....G.... 815 722-6671
Joliet (G-11837)
Clear Sight Inc ....G.... 630 323-3590
Westmont (G-20732)
Dean B Scott ....G.... 630 960-4455
Downers Grove (G-7984)
Edgebrook Eyecare ....F.... 815 397-5959
Rockford (G-17390)
Ellison Eyewear Inc ....G.... 312 880-7609
Chicago (G-4487)
Essilor Laboratories Amer Inc ....E.... 309 787-2727
Rock Island (G-17219)
Eye Surgeons of Libertyville ....G.... 847 362-3811
Libertyville (G-12650)
Eyewearplanet Com Inc ....G.... 847 513-6203
Northbrook (G-15387)
First Look Wholesale Lab Inc ....G.... 618 462-9042
Wood River (G-21261)
Illmo R/X Service ....F.... 217 877-1192
Decatur (G-7505)
Independent Eyewear Mfg LLC ....D.... 847 537-0008
Vernon Hills (G-20066)
Innova Systems Inc ....G.... 630 920-8880
Burr Ridge (G-2686)
Jim Maui Inc ....G.... 888 666-5905
Peoria (G-16462)
▲ M & S Technologies Inc ....F.... 847 763-0500
Niles (G-15142)
Midwest Uncuts Inc ....F.... 312 664-3131
Chicago (G-5450)
Night Vision Corporation ....G.... 847 677-7611
Lincolnwood (G-12833)
One Way Safety LLC ....E.... 708 579-0229
La Grange (G-12085)
◆ Opticote Inc ....E.... 847 678-8900
Franklin Park (G-10012)
Quality Optical Inc ....G.... 773 561-0870
Chicago (G-5930)
Robert B Scott Ocularists Ltd ....E.... 312 782-3558
Chicago (G-6042)
▲ Scuba Optics Inc ....G.... 815 625-7272
Rock Falls (G-17195)
Spectacle Zoom LLC ....G.... 504 352-7237
Des Plaines (G-7849)
Tammy Smith ....G.... 618 372-8410
Brighton (G-2404)
Vicron Optical Inc ....F.... 847 412-5530
Deerfield (G-7657)
Village Optical Shop ....G.... 847 295-3290
Lake Bluff (G-12212)
Vision Assessment Corporation ....G.... 847 239-5889
Elk Grove Village (G-9305)
Walman Optical Company ....E.... 309 787-0000
Milan (G-14030)
◆ Waters Industries Inc ....E.... 847 783-5900
West Dundee (G-20667)
Wesley-Jessen Corporation Del ....A.... 847 294-3000
Des Plaines (G-7868)
Western Ilinois Optical Inc ....G.... 309 837-2000
Macomb (G-13401)

3861 Photographic Eqpt & Splys

2nd Cine Inc ....G.... 773 455-5808
Elgin (G-8488)
9 Dots Solutions LLC ....G.... 877 919-9349
Mundelein (G-14656)
A Division of A&A Studios Inc ....F.... 312 278-1144
Chicago (G-3487)
Alpha Laser of Chicago ....G.... 708 478-0464
Mokena (G-14070)
ARX Nimbus LLC ....G.... 888 422-6584
Chicago (G-3744)
▲ AV Stumpfl Usa Corp ....F.... 630 359-0999
Elmhurst (G-9327)
AVI-Spl Employee ....B.... 847 437-7712
Schaumburg (G-18453)
Base-Line II Inc ....G.... 847 336-8403
Gurnee (G-10862)
Bka Inc ....G.... 847 831-3535
Highland Park (G-11255)
Brahman Spirit Tribe ....F.... 773 957-2828
Chicago (G-3942)
◆ Bretford Manufacturing Inc ....B.... 847 678-2545
Franklin Park (G-9892)
Canon Solutions America Inc ....D.... 630 351-1227
Itasca (G-11633)
CDs Office Systems Inc ....D.... 800 367-1508
Springfield (G-19343)
Chicago Film Archive Nfp ....G.... 773 478-3799
Chicago (G-4103)
Clover Imaging Group LLC ....B.... 815 431-8100
Ottawa (G-16048)
◆ Clover Technologies Group LLC ....A.... 866 734-6548
Hoffman Estates (G-11414)
Cushing and Company ....E.... 312 266-8228
Chicago (G-4287)
▲ Dukane Corporation ....C.... 630 797-4900
Saint Charles (G-18189)
▲ Essannay Show It Inc ....G.... 312 733-5511
Chicago (G-4532)
Fire CAM ....G.... 618 416-8390
Belleville (G-1552)
Fujifilm Elctrnic Mtls USA Inc ....G.... 312 924-5800
Hanover Park (G-11006)
▲ Funk Family Holdings Corp ....G.... 847 276-2700
Buffalo Grove (G-2541)
George Wilson ....G.... 847 342-1111
Prospect Heights (G-16841)
Good Vibes Sound Inc ....F.... 217 351-0909
Champaign (G-3298)
Imac Asset Sales Corp ....G.... 847 741-4622
Elgin (G-8622)
Innovatech It Svc Solutions ....G.... 815 484-9940
Rockford (G-17464)
▲ Ishot Products Inc ....G.... 312 497-4190
Bolingbrook (G-2195)
Kinetic BEI LLC ....F.... 847 888-8060
South Elgin (G-19159)
▲ Koll Ltd ....G.... 224 544-5418
Mundelein (G-14708)
Laser Pro ....G.... 847 742-1055
Elgin (G-8640)
Letter-Rite Express LLC ....F.... 847 678-1100
Aurora (G-998)
Lochman Ref Silk Screen Co ....F.... 847 475-6266
Evanston (G-9547)
Midwest Laser Incorporated ....G.... 708 974-0084
Palos Hills (G-16202)
Moog Inc ....C.... 847 498-0704
Northbrook (G-15436)
Motus Digital Llc ....E.... 972 943-0008
Des Plaines (G-7806)
Nexus Office Systems Inc ....F.... 847 836-1095
Elgin (G-8671)
Norvida USA Inc ....G.... 618 282-2992
Sparta (G-19258)
Ops 3 LLC ....G.... 312 243-8265
Chicago (G-5683)
Paulmar Industries Inc ....F.... 847 395-2520
Antioch (G-629)
Plate and Pre-Press Management ....G.... 847 352-0462
Schaumburg (G-18676)
Poersch Metal Manufacturing Co ....F.... 773 722-0890
Chicago (G-5828)
▲ Promark International Inc ....D.... 630 830-2500
Bartlett (G-1301)
Proofing Technologies Ltd ....G.... 847 222-7100
Rolling Meadows (G-17768)
Purple Onyx LLC ....G.... 708 756-1500
Park Forest (G-16258)
Rensel-Chicago Inc ....E.... 773 235-2100
Chicago (G-6015)
Research Technology Intl Co ....E.... 847 677-3000
Lincolnwood (G-12837)
Rmf Products Inc ....G.... 630 879-0020
Batavia (G-1411)
▲ Robotics Technologies Inc ....E.... 815 722-7650
Joliet (G-11927)
Rotation Dynamics Corporation ....E.... 630 769-9700
Chicago (G-6065)
Screen North Amer Holdings Inc ....F.... 847 870-7400
Rolling Meadows (G-17774)
Seaport Digital LLC ....G.... 847 235-2319
Mundelein (G-14734)
▲ Speedotron Corporation ....G.... 630 246-5001
Bartlett (G-1314)
▲ Team Play Inc ....F.... 847 952-7533
Elk Grove Village (G-9267)
Trend Setters Ltd ....F.... 309 929-7012
Tremont (G-19901)
▲ Tri Industries Nfp ....E.... 773 754-3100
Vernon Hills (G-20107)
Wesling Products Inc ....G.... 773 533-2850
Chicago (G-6603)
Xerox Corporation ....D.... 630 983-0172
Naperville (G-14951)
Xerox Corporation ....E.... 630 573-1000
Hinsdale (G-11383)

3873 Watch & Clock Devices & Parts

Chicago Lighthouse Industries ....D.... 312 666-1331
Chicago (G-4110)
Claessens Kids Inc ....G.... 973 551-8528
Morton Grove (G-14396)
▲ Hampden Corporation ....E.... 312 583-3000
Chicago (G-4775)
Indigo Time ....G.... 847 255-4818
Mount Prospect (G-14534)
Instrument Services Inc ....G.... 815 623-2993
Machesney Park (G-13350)
Kl Watch Service Inc ....G.... 847 368-8780
Bartlett (G-1293)
Lumenite Control Technology ....F.... 847 455-1450
Franklin Park (G-9982)
Tammy Banks ....G.... 312 280-1388
Chicago (G-6317)
Zantech Inc ....G.... 309 692-8307
Peoria (G-16548)

SIC

39 MISCELLANEOUS MANUFACTURING INDUSTRIES

3911 Jewelry: Precious Metal

A G Mitchells Jewelers Ltd ....F.... 847 394-0820
Arlington Heights (G-680)
A M Lee Inc ....G.... 847 291-1777
Northbrook (G-15329)
Accents By Fred ....G.... 708 366-9850
Forest Park (G-9707)
Alan Rocca Ltd ....E.... 630 323-5800
Oak Brook (G-15590)
▲ Alomar Inc ....G.... 312 855-0714
Chicago (G-3627)
▲ Award Concepts Inc ....E.... 630 513-7801
Saint Charles (G-18153)
Award Emblem Mfg Co Inc ....F.... 630 739-0800
Bolingbrook (G-2153)
Azteca Jewelry ....G.... 773 929-0796
Chicago (G-3803)
Barrett NJide Yvonne ....F.... 312 701-3962
Chicago (G-3838)
Bee-Jay Industries Inc ....F.... 708 867-4431
Bloomingdale (G-1979)
Bliss Ring Company Inc ....F.... 847 446-3440
Winnetka (G-21127)
Burdeens Jewelry Ltd ....G.... 847 459-8980
Buffalo Grove (G-2522)
Cabanas Manufacturing Jewelers ....G.... 312 726-0333
Chicago (G-3999)
Casting House Inc ....F.... 312 782-7160
Chicago (G-4037)
Charles Horberg Jewelers Inc ....G.... 312 263-4924
Chicago (G-4074)
Club Jewelry Manufacturing Inc ....G.... 847 541-0700
Wheeling (G-20873)
D & M Perlman Fine Jewelry ....G.... 847 426-8881
West Dundee (G-20661)
David Nelson Exquisite Jewelry ....G.... 815 741-4702
Joliet (G-11852)

Employee Codes: A=Over 500 employees, B=251-500
C=101-250, D=51-100, E=20-50, F=10-19, G=3-9
2020 Harris Illinois
Industrial Directory
1011

Edgar H Fey Jewelers Inc E 708 352-4115
Naperville *(G-14821)*

Emerald City Jewelry Inc G 217 222-8896
Quincy *(G-16880)*

Empire Corp G 630 887-8228
Willowbrook *(G-21042)*

Eve J Alfille Ltd E 847 869-7920
Evanston *(G-9518)*

Fashion Craft Corporation E 847 998-0092
Highland Park *(G-11262)*

Faye Jewellery Chez G 815 477-1818
Crystal Lake *(G-7198)*

Fine Gold Mfg Jewelers G 630 323-9600
Hinsdale *(G-11368)*

Frank S Bender Inc G 847 441-7370
Northfield *(G-15514)*

G Blando Jewelers Inc G 630 627-7963
Countryside *(G-7053)*

General Design Jewelers Inc G 312 201-9047
Chicago *(G-4669)*

H Watson Jewelry Co G 312 236-1104
Chicago *(G-4761)*

Hakimian Gem Co G 312 236-6969
Chicago *(G-4770)*

Herff Jones LLC F 815 756-4743
Dekalb *(G-7684)*

Herff Jones LLC D 773 463-1144
Chicago *(G-4807)*

Herff Jones LLC F 217 351-9500
Champaign *(G-3300)*

Herff Jones LLC G 708 425-0130
Oak Lawn *(G-15719)*

Herff Jones LLC C 317 612-3705
Hillside *(G-11341)*

Ho Brothers LLC G 312 854-3008
Chicago *(G-4826)*

Hustedt Manufacturing Jewelers G 217 784-8462
Gibson City *(G-10339)*

▼ Hy Spreckman & Sons Inc F 312 236-2173
Skokie *(G-18966)*

ISA Chicago G 630 317-7169
Carol Stream *(G-3007)*

Jason Lau Jewelry G 312 750-1028
Chicago *(G-5010)*

John Buechner Inc G 312 263-2226
Chicago *(G-5038)*

Joseph C Wolf G 312 332-3135
Chicago *(G-5053)*

Kaye Lee & Company Inc G 312 236-9686
Chicago *(G-5086)*

Kesher Stam G 773 973-7826
Chicago *(G-5097)*

Lana Unlimited Co G 312 226-7050
Lake Forest *(G-12272)*

Leo A Bachrach Jewelers Inc G 312 263-3111
Chicago *(G-5204)*

Lester Lampert Inc E 312 944-6888
Chicago *(G-5208)*

M B Jewelers Inc G 312 853-3490
Chicago *(G-5299)*

Made As Intended Inc F 630 789-3494
Oak Brook *(G-15639)*

Masud Jewelers Inc G 312 236-0547
Chicago *(G-5363)*

Medaowview Ventures II Inc E 847 965-1700
Morton Grove *(G-14426)*

Michael P Jones G 217 787-7457
Springfield *(G-19406)*

Mint Masters Inc E 847 451-1133
Franklin Park *(G-10000)*

Mtm Jostens Inc G 815 875-1111
Princeton *(G-16816)*

Mtm Recognition Corporation C 815 875-1111
Princeton *(G-16817)*

Norkin Jewelry Co Inc E 312 782-7311
Chicago *(G-5616)*

Norridge Jewelry G 312 984-1036
Chicago *(G-5617)*

Park-Ohio Industries Inc D 708 652-6691
Chicago *(G-5766)*

Perle & Sons Jewelers Inc G 630 357-3357
Naperville *(G-14896)*

▲ R S Owens & Co Inc B 773 282-6000
Chicago *(G-5953)*

Rahmanims Imports Inc G 312 236-2200
Chicago *(G-5963)*

◆ Razny Jewelers Ltd E 630 932-4900
Addison *(G-267)*

Richards Fine Jewelry & Design G 847 697-4053
South Elgin *(G-19172)*

Rodger Murphy G 309 582-2202
Aledo *(G-359)*

Roger Burke Jewelers Inc F 309 692-0210
Peoria *(G-16514)*

Ross Designs Ltd G 847 831-7669
Highland Park *(G-11295)*

S G Nelson & Co G 630 668-7900
Wheaton *(G-20822)*

Simon Zelikman G 847 338-8031
Oakwood Hills *(G-15822)*

Trebor Enterprises Ltd G 815 235-1700
Freeport *(G-10147)*

Tri-City Gold Exchange Inc F 708 331-5995
Harvey *(G-11098)*

Ulla of Finland G 773 763-0700
Chicago *(G-6457)*

Unicorn Designs G 847 295-5230
Lake Forest *(G-12319)*

V & O Style Jewelry Mfg Co G 312 372-2454
Chicago *(G-6510)*

Victor Levy Jewelry Co Inc G 312 782-5297
Chicago *(G-6545)*

Vintaj Natural Brass Co G 815 776-9300
Galena *(G-10180)*

White Diamonds Inc G 708 868-4006
Calumet City *(G-2793)*

3914 Silverware, Plated & Stainless Steel Ware

All American Trophy King Inc F 708 597-2121
Crestwood *(G-7105)*

AMG International Inc G 847 439-1001
Elk Grove Village *(G-8827)*

Baroque Silversmith Inc G 312 357-2813
Chicago *(G-3835)*

Budget Signs F 618 259-4460
Wood River *(G-21260)*

Captains Emporium Inc G 773 972-7609
Chicago *(G-4021)*

Crown Brands LLC E 224 513-2917
Lincolnshire *(G-12757)*

▲ Empire Bronze Corp F 630 916-9722
Lombard *(G-13073)*

Fusion Tech Integrated Inc D 309 774-4275
Roseville *(G-18062)*

Mint Masters Inc E 847 451-1133
Franklin Park *(G-10000)*

Mtm Recognition Corporation C 815 875-1111
Princeton *(G-16817)*

▲ Nelson-Whittaker Ltd E 815 459-6000
Crystal Lake *(G-7237)*

Omni-Rinse LLC G 708 860-3250
Palatine *(G-16146)*

▲ RS Owens Div St Regis LLC D 773 282-6000
Itasca *(G-11730)*

Rudon Enterprises Inc G 618 457-0441
Carbondale *(G-2857)*

▲ Stellar Recognition Inc D 773 282-8060
Chicago *(G-6243)*

▼ Suburban Surgical Co C 847 537-9320
Wheeling *(G-20993)*

Trophies By George G 630 497-1212
Bartlett *(G-1318)*

3915 Jewelers Findings & Lapidary Work

144 International Inc F 847 426-8881
West Dundee *(G-20660)*

Alex and Ani LLC G 708 403-4450
Orland Park *(G-15937)*

▲ C D Nelson Consulting Inc G 847 487-4870
Wauconda *(G-20336)*

Edmund D Schmelzie & Sons G 312 782-7230
Chicago *(G-4453)*

Israel Levy Diamnd Cutters Inc E 312 368-8540
Chicago *(G-4974)*

M B Jewelers Inc G 312 853-3490
Chicago *(G-5299)*

Micro Lapping & Grinding Co E 847 455-5446
Franklin Park *(G-9997)*

▲ Precise Lapping Grinding Corp F 708 615-0240
Melrose Park *(G-13904)*

S G Nelson & Co G 630 668-7900
Wheaton *(G-20822)*

Steinmetz R (us) Ltd G 312 332-0990
Chicago *(G-6241)*

3931 Musical Instruments

▲ American Plating & Mfg Co F 773 890-4907
Chicago *(G-3664)*

Analog Outfitters Inc G 217 202-6134
Rantoul *(G-16966)*

Berghaus Pipe Organ Builders E 708 544-4052
Bellwood *(G-1616)*

▲ Buzard Pipe Organ Builders LLC F 217 352-1955
Champaign *(G-3273)*

C P O Inc G 630 898-7733
Aurora *(G-1068)*

Century Mallet Instr Svc LLC G 773 248-7733
Chicago *(G-4061)*

Daves Electronic Service F 217 283-5010
Hoopeston *(G-11507)*

◆ Demont Guitars LLC G 347 433-6668
Oswego *(G-16001)*

Fabry Inc G 847 395-1919
Fox Lake *(G-9746)*

Fugate Inc G 309 472-6830
Morton *(G-14360)*

Gibson Brands Inc E 800 544-2766
Elgin *(G-8594)*

▲ Hammond Suzuki Usa Inc E 630 543-0277
Addison *(G-145)*

Harrison Harmonicas LLC G 312 379-9427
Chicago *(G-4783)*

▲ Intelligent Instrument Sy G 630 323-3911
Burr Ridge *(G-2689)*

Lothson Guitars G 815 756-2031
Dekalb *(G-7688)*

▲ Lyon & Healy Harps Inc G 312 786-1881
Chicago *(G-5293)*

▲ Lyon & Healy Holding Corp E 312 786-1881
Chicago *(G-5294)*

Mathew Lucante Violins LLC G 773 320-2997
Skokie *(G-18985)*

Mechanical Music Corp F 847 398-5444
Arlington Heights *(G-775)*

Music Solutions F 630 759-3033
Bolingbrook *(G-2218)*

North Okaw Woodworking G 217 856-2178
Humboldt *(G-11524)*

▲ Peterson Elctr-Msical Pdts Inc E 708 388-3311
Alsip *(G-490)*

▲ Pjla Music G 847 382-3212
Barrington *(G-1236)*

▲ Schaff International LLC E 847 438-4560
Lake Zurich *(G-12453)*

Schilke Music Products Inc E 708 343-8858
Melrose Park *(G-13913)*

Schneider Pipe Organs Inc G 217 871-4807
Kenney *(G-12016)*

Suntimez Entertainment G 630 747-0712
Cicero *(G-6877)*

Tom Crown Mute Co G 773 930-4979
Chicago *(G-6386)*

Trick Percussion Products Inc G 847 342-2019
Arlington Heights *(G-822)*

Umphreys McGee Inc G 773 880-0024
Chicago *(G-6460)*

Village of Burnham G 708 868-0661
Chicago *(G-6552)*

Westheimer Corp G 847 498-9850
Lake Zurich *(G-12470)*

▲ Wicks Organ Company E 618 654-2191
Highland *(G-11249)*

3942 Dolls & Stuffed Toys

◆ Enesco LLC B 630 875-5300
Itasca *(G-11650)*

◆ First & Main Inc E 630 587-1000
Saint Charles *(G-18199)*

▲ Hunter Mfg LLP D 859 254-7573
Lake Forest *(G-12262)*

▲ North American Bear Co Inc E 773 376-3457
Chicago *(G-5618)*

Shawnimals LLC G 312 235-2625
Chicago *(G-6150)*

Unique Novelty & Manufacturing G 217 538-2014
Fillmore *(G-9666)*

3944 Games, Toys & Children's Vehicles

▲ Accurail Inc F 630 365-6400
Elburn *(G-8441)*

▲ Aeromax Industries Inc G 847 756-4085
Lake Barrington *(G-12140)*

AGS Partners LLC D 630 446-7777
Itasca *(G-11616)*

Airgun Designs USA Inc G 847 520-7507
Cary *(G-3146)*

▲ Amav Enterprises Ltd G 630 761-3077
Batavia *(G-1346)*

American Science & Surplus Inc ... F ... 773 763-0313
Chicago (G-3665)
American Specialty Toy ... G ... 312 222-0984
Chicago (G-3669)
Aqua Golf Inc ... G ... 217 824-2097
Taylorville (G-19749)
Arkadian Gaming LLC ... G ... 708 377-5656
Orland Park (G-15942)
Branch Lines Ltd ... G ... 847 256-4294
Wilmette (G-21070)
Central RC Hobbies ... G ... 309 686-8004
Peoria (G-16418)
Chicago Contract Bridge Assn ... G ... 630 355-5560
Naperville (G-14797)
Cino Incorporated ... G ... 630 377-7242
Saint Charles (G-18166)
Circuitron Inc ... G ... 815 886-9010
Romeoville (G-17809)
▲ Click-Block Corporation ... E ... 847 749-1651
Rolling Meadows (G-17723)
Craft World Inc ... G ... 800 654-6114
Loves Park (G-13198)
▲ Du Bro Products Inc ... E ... 847 526-2136
Wauconda (G-20344)
E J Kupjack & Associates Inc ... G ... 847 823-6661
Chicago (G-4424)
Edwin Waldmire & Virginia ... G ... 217 498-9375
Rochester (G-17165)
▲ Fun Incorporated ... E ... 773 745-3837
Wheeling (G-20902)
Gamestop Inc ... G ... 773 568-0457
Chicago (G-4658)
Gamestop Corp ... G ... 618 258-8611
Wood River (G-21262)
Gift of Games Ltd ... G ... 847 370-1541
Grayslake (G-10775)
Goat Wolf & Cabbage LLC ... G ... 563 580-0617
Chicago (G-4708)
Harris Skokie ... G ... 847 675-6300
Skokie (G-18965)
Hart Puzzles Inc ... G ... 847 910-2290
Bensenville (G-1817)
▲ Henes Usa Inc ... D ... 312 448-6130
Glenview (G-10556)
Huff & Puff Industries Ltd ... G ... 847 381-8255
North Barrington (G-15286)
Ing Bank Fsb ... G ... 312 981-1236
Chicago (G-4920)
◆ Jcw Investments Inc ... G ... 708 478-7323
Orland Park (G-15962)
▲ Kaskey Kids Inc ... G ... 847 441-3092
Winnetka (G-21131)
▲ Kato USA Inc ... G ... 847 781-9500
Schaumburg (G-18585)
Kd-Kidz Dlight Interactive LLC ... G ... 630 724-0223
Downers Grove (G-8038)
Kei Keis Kreation Kafe ... F ... 708 982-6560
Hazel Crest (G-11130)
Lake County C V Joints Inc ... G ... 847 537-7588
Wheeling (G-20928)
Lego Systems Inc ... G ... 312 202-0946
Chicago (G-5202)
▲ Liberty Classics Inc ... G ... 847 367-1288
Libertyville (G-12667)
Made By Hands Inc ... G ... 773 761-4200
Chicago (G-5310)
Manseemanwant LLC ... G ... 217 610-8888
Springfield (G-19402)
Midwest Rail Junction ... G ... 815 963-0200
Rockford (G-17527)
Narita Manufacturing Inc ... F ... 248 345-1777
Belvidere (G-1688)
▲ Nelson-Whittaker Ltd ... E ... 815 459-6000
Crystal Lake (G-7237)
Novomatic Americas Sales LLC ... F ... 224 802-2974
Mount Prospect (G-14553)
Oakridge Corporation ... G ... 630 435-5900
Lemont (G-12574)
Octura Models Inc ... G ... 847 674-7351
Skokie (G-18998)
Pacific Cycle Inc ... C ... 618 393-2508
Olney (G-15882)
▲ Paragon Packaging Inc ... G ... 707 786-4004
Chicago (G-5758)
Petronics Inc ... G ... 608 630-6527
Champaign (G-3331)
Powers Sports LLC ... G ... 815 436-6769
Plainfield (G-16703)
Pro-Line Winning Ways & Penlan ... G ... 309 745-8530
Washington (G-20277)
Puzzles Bus Off Solutions Inc ... G ... 773 891-7688
Chicago (G-5918)
Quicker Engineering ... G ... 815 675-6516
Spring Grove (G-19297)
Racine Paper Box Manufacturing ... E ... 773 227-3900
Chicago (G-5958)
◆ Radio Flyer Inc ... E ... 773 637-7100
Chicago (G-5959)
▲ Rapid Displays Inc ... C ... 773 927-5000
Chicago (G-5971)
◆ Raw Thrills Inc ... D ... 847 679-8373
Skokie (G-19019)
Rust-Oleum Corporation ... D ... 815 967-4258
Rockford (G-17617)
▲ Safe Traffic System Inc ... G ... 847 233-0365
Lincolnwood (G-12842)
Scale Railroad Equipment ... G ... 630 682-9170
Carol Stream (G-3065)
◆ Shure Products Inc ... F ... 773 227-1001
Chicago (G-6162)
▲ Standard Container Co of Edgar ... E ... 847 438-1510
Lake Zurich (G-12460)
Star Sleigh ... F ... 630 858-2576
Glen Ellyn (G-10420)
▲ Sunnywood Incorporated ... G ... 815 675-9777
McHenry (G-13799)
▲ Testor Corporation ... D ... 815 962-6654
Rockford (G-17656)
▲ Trivial Development Corp ... E ... 630 860-2500
Itasca (G-11748)
Video Gaming Technologies Inc ... G ... 847 776-3516
Palatine (G-16170)
Virtu ... G ... 773 235-3790
Chicago (G-6555)
Vmm USA Unique Master Mod ... G ... 847 537-0867
Deerfield (G-7658)
Wells-Gardner Technologies Inc ... G ... 630 819-8219
Burr Ridge (G-2732)
Wiliams Interactive LLC ... C ... 773 961-1920
Chicago (G-6625)

3949 Sporting & Athletic Goods, NEC

All American Athletics Ltd ... G ... 815 432-8326
Watseka (G-20304)
Allied Scoring Tables Inc ... G ... 815 654-8807
Loves Park (G-13187)
▲ Altamont Co ... D ... 800 626-5774
Thomasboro (G-19775)
◆ Amer Sports Company ... B ... 773 714-6400
Chicago (G-3646)
Andrew C Arnold ... G ... 815 220-0282
Peru (G-16564)
◆ Arachnid 360 LLC ... E ... 815 654-0212
Loves Park (G-13190)
▲ Athletic Specialties Inc ... G ... 847 487-7880
Wauconda (G-20333)
▲ Bell Racing Usa LLC ... G ... 217 239-5355
Champaign (G-3271)
Bell Sports Inc ... D ... 217 893-9300
Rantoul (G-16968)
Best Technology Systems Inc ... E ... 815 254-9554
Plainfield (G-16644)
◆ Big Dog Treestand Inc ... G ... 309 263-6800
Morton (G-14354)
▲ Big Game Gut Glove ... G ... 847 544-8806
Frankfort (G-9771)
Biospawn Lure Co ... G ... 773 458-0752
Evanston (G-9500)
Bluetown Skateboard Co LLC ... G ... 312 718-4786
Chicago (G-3918)
Bob Folder Lures Co ... F ... 217 787-1116
Springfield (G-19328)
Bobs Business Inc ... G ... 630 238-5790
Bensenville (G-1755)
Bodysmart USA Inc ... G ... 630 682-9701
Wheaton (G-20790)
▲ Boss Manufacturing Holdings ... F ... 309 852-2781
Kewanee (G-12025)
Bowl-Tronics Enterprises Inc ... G ... 847 741-4500
Elgin (G-8523)
Bowlero Corp ... D ... 847 473-2600
Waukegan (G-20423)
Bowtree Inc ... G ... 217 430-8884
Quincy (G-16867)
Brg Sports Inc ... F ... 217 892-4704
Rantoul (G-16969)
▲ Brg Sports Inc ... D ... 224 585-5200
Des Plaines (G-7741)
Brunswick Corporation ... B ... 847 288-3300
Franklin Park (G-9894)
◆ Brunswick Corporation ... B ... 847 735-4700
Mettawa (G-13979)
Brunswick International Ltd ... E ... 847 735-4700
Mettawa (G-13980)
BSN Sports LLC ... G ... 217 788-0914
Springfield (G-19330)
Burt Coyote Co ... F ... 309 358-1602
Yates City (G-21470)
C6 Agility LLC ... G ... 734 548-0008
Chicago (G-3997)
Cast Industries Inc ... E ... 217 522-8292
Springfield (G-19342)
Castillo Leather Goods ... G ... 773 491-0018
Oak Lawn (G-15707)
▲ Ccsi International Inc ... E ... 815 544-8385
Garden Prairie (G-10236)
City Sports & Stage Door Dance ... E ... 708 687-9950
Oak Forest (G-15673)
◆ Coleman Company Inc ... C ... 316 832-2653
Chicago (G-4198)
College Bound Athlete LLC ... G ... 708 259-7713
Downers Grove (G-7976)
Compound Bow Rifle Sight Inc ... G ... 618 526-4427
Breese (G-2301)
Crooked Creek Outdoors ... G ... 309 837-3000
Macomb (G-13390)
Crown Gym Mats Inc ... F ... 847 381-8282
Lake Barrington (G-12145)
Custom Golf By Tanis ... G ... 708 481-4433
Matteson (G-13622)
Custom Rods By Grandt Ltd ... G ... 847 577-0848
Arlington Heights (G-723)
Dark Speed Works ... G ... 312 772-3275
Wheaton (G-20795)
David Hall ... E ... 309 797-9721
Moline (G-14137)
Davis Athletic Equipment Co ... F ... 708 563-9006
Bedford Park (G-1466)
Dinger Bats LLC ... G ... 618 272-7250
Ridgway (G-17036)
Dj Illinois River Valley Calls ... G ... 309 348-2112
Pekin (G-16330)
Donaldson & Associates Inc ... G ... 708 633-1090
Lockport (G-12988)
EJL Custom Golf Clubs Inc ... G ... 630 654-8887
Willowbrook (G-21041)
▲ Empire Comfort Systems Inc ... C ... 618 233-7420
Belleville (G-1551)
▲ Enjoylife Inc ... G ... 847 966-3377
Morton Grove (G-14405)
Evergreen Pool & Spa LLC ... G ... 618 247-3555
Sandoval (G-18363)
▼ Flex Court International Inc ... F ... 309 852-0899
Kewanee (G-12033)
◆ Flora Bowl ... G ... 618 662-4561
Flora (G-9680)
◆ Frabill Inc ... E ... 630 552-9426
Plano (G-16732)
Geneva Running Outfitters LLC ... G ... 331 248-0221
Geneva (G-10272)
▼ Gill Athletics ... G ... 217 367-8438
Champaign (G-3294)
▲ Golfco Inc ... E ... 773 777-7877
Chicago (G-4714)
H2o Pod Inc ... G ... 630 240-1769
Glen Ellyn (G-10404)
Hampster Industries Inc ... G ... 866 280-2287
Mundelein (G-14695)
Headball Inc ... G ... 618 628-2656
Belleville (G-1555)
Heartland Inspection Company ... G ... 630 788-3607
Sycamore (G-19713)
▲ Hunter Mfg LLP ... D ... 859 254-7573
Lake Forest (G-12262)
▲ Hunter-Nusport Inc ... G ... 815 254-7520
Plainfield (G-16674)
Iler Brands Inc ... G ... 314 799-3833
O Fallon (G-15574)
Illinois State Usbc Wba ... G ... 309 827-6355
Bloomington (G-2061)
▲ Infiniti Golf ... G ... 630 520-0626
West Chicago (G-20594)
International Wood Products ... G ... 630 530-6164
Aurora (G-988)
Jack & Lidias Resort Inc ... G ... 847 356-1389
Lake Villa (G-12356)
James G Carter ... G ... 309 543-2634
Havana (G-11115)
Jerrys Tackle and Guns ... G ... 618 654-3235
Highland (G-11228)

S I C

Employee Codes: A=Over 500 employees, B=251-500
C=101-250, D=51-100, E=20-50, F=10-19, G=3-9
2020 Harris Illinois
Industrial Directory
1013

39 MISCELLANEOUS MANUFACTURING INDUSTRIES SIC SECTION

Kayser Lure Corp ..... G 217 964-2110
Ursa *(G-20004)*
Kps Capital Partners LP ..... A 847 288-3300
Franklin Park *(G-9979)*
▲ Kranos Corporation ..... C 217 324-3978
Litchfield *(G-12969)*
Kuldisak LLC ..... G 847 772-7412
Northbrook *(G-15416)*
L L Bean Inc ..... G 847 568-3600
Skokie *(G-18974)*
Lax Shop ..... G 847 945-8529
Highwood *(G-11308)*
◆ Litania Sports Group Inc ..... C 217 367-8438
Champaign *(G-3317)*
▲ Luck E Strike Corporation ..... F 630 313-2408
Geneva *(G-10289)*
Lumos Holdings US Acquisition ..... G 847 288-3300
Rosemont *(G-18034)*
Mallardtone Game Calls ..... G 309 798-2481
Taylor Ridge *(G-19746)*
Mettle Sports LLC ..... G 312 757-6373
Evanston *(G-9550)*
◆ Midwest Canvas Corp ..... C 773 287-4400
Chicago *(G-5440)*
Miha Bodytec Inc ..... G 833 367-6442
Addison *(G-214)*
Moreno and Sons Inc ..... G 815 725-8600
Crest Hill *(G-7092)*
▲ Mullarkey Associates Inc ..... F 708 597-5555
Tinley Park *(G-19846)*
Nameplate Robinson & Precision ..... G 847 678-2255
Franklin Park *(G-10005)*
▲ New Archery Products LLC ..... D 708 488-2500
Forest Park *(G-9722)*
New Wave Lax LLC ..... G 630 219-3919
Plainfield *(G-16694)*
Nichols Net & Twine Inc ..... G 618 797-0211
Granite City *(G-10728)*
Normal Cornbelters ..... G 309 451-3432
Normal *(G-15212)*
Oak Leaf Outdoors Inc ..... F 309 691-9653
Brimfield *(G-2407)*
Oban Composites LLC ..... G 866 607-0284
Chicago *(G-5649)*
Obies Tackle Co Inc ..... G 618 234-5638
Belleville *(G-1581)*
▲ Orthotech Sports - Med Eqp Inc ..... F 618 942-6611
Herrin *(G-11176)*
Orvis Company Inc ..... F 312 440-0662
Chicago *(G-5707)*
Oso900 Nfp ..... G 312 206-4219
Chicago *(G-5711)*
▼ Par Golf Supply Inc ..... E 847 891-1222
Schaumburg *(G-18663)*
▲ Park View Manufacturing Corp ..... D 618 548-9054
Salem *(G-18350)*
Peak Healthcare Advisors LLC ..... G 646 479-0005
Chicago *(G-5775)*
Perry Adult Living Inc ..... G 618 542-5421
Du Quoin *(G-8123)*
Plastech Inc ..... F 630 595-7222
Bensenville *(G-1868)*
Polyair Inter Pack Inc ..... D 773 995-1818
Chicago *(G-5838)*
◆ Porter Athletic Equipment Co ..... C 888 277-7778
Champaign *(G-3337)*
Pritchard Enterprises Inc ..... G 217 832-8588
Camargo *(G-2801)*
Pro Circle Golf Centers Inc ..... G 815 675-2747
Spring Grove *(G-19295)*
Pro-AM Team Sports LLC ..... F 708 995-1511
Mokena *(G-14110)*
ProAm Sports Products ..... G 708 841-4200
Dolton *(G-7939)*
▲ Protactic Golf Enterprises ..... F 708 209-1120
River Forest *(G-17054)*
Prototech Industries Inc ..... G 847 223-9808
Gurnee *(G-10918)*
Qcfec LLC ..... G 309 517-1158
Moline *(G-14169)*
▲ Quality Sport Nets Inc ..... G 618 533-0700
Centralia *(G-3247)*
Quality Targets ..... G 618 245-6515
Farina *(G-9653)*
Quincy Bow Pro ..... G 217 222-2222
Quincy *(G-16929)*
Rainbo Sports LLC ..... G 847 784-9857
Northfield *(G-15528)*
Rainbow Midwest Inc ..... G 847 955-9300
Vernon Hills *(G-20084)*
Rasoi Resturaunt ..... G 847 455-8888
Roselle *(G-17977)*
Reagent Chemical & RES Inc ..... G 618 271-8140
East Saint Louis *(G-8319)*
Reeves Lure Co ..... G 217 864-3493
Lovington *(G-13285)*
Reflex Fitness Products Inc ..... F 309 756-1050
Milan *(G-14024)*
▲ Riddell Inc ..... C 847 292-1472
Des Plaines *(G-7837)*
Road Runner Sports Inc ..... F 847 719-8941
Palatine *(G-16154)*
Roger Jolly Skateboards ..... G 618 277-7113
Belleville *(G-1591)*
◆ Roller Derby Skate Corp ..... E 217 324-3961
Litchfield *(G-12976)*
Royal Fiberglass Pools Inc ..... D 618 266-7089
Dix *(G-7882)*
Scuba Sports Inc ..... G 217 787-3483
Springfield *(G-19440)*
Sentry Pool & Chemical Supply ..... E 309 797-9721
Moline *(G-14177)*
◆ Septic Solutions Inc ..... G 217 925-5992
Dieterich *(G-7878)*
Shuffle Tech International LLC ..... G 312 787-7780
Chicago *(G-6161)*
Siggs Rigs ..... G 847 456-4012
Crystal Lake *(G-7266)*
Southern Illinois Miners ..... F 618 969-8506
Marion *(G-13538)*
Spinball Sports LLC ..... G 314 503-3194
Skokie *(G-19035)*
▲ Strikeforce Bowling LLC ..... E 800 297-8555
Melrose Park *(G-13917)*
Superior Table Pad Co ..... G 773 248-7232
Chicago *(G-6284)*
Topgolf International Inc ..... G 630 595-4653
Wood Dale *(G-21250)*
Total Control Sports Inc ..... G 708 486-5800
Broadview *(G-2472)*
True Lacrosse LLC ..... G 630 359-3857
Lombard *(G-13148)*
▲ Tweeten Fibre Co ..... E 312 733-7878
Chicago *(G-6445)*
▲ U S Weight Inc ..... E 618 392-0408
Olney *(G-15891)*
▲ Ultra Play Systems Inc ..... E 618 282-8200
Red Bud *(G-17004)*
◆ Vista Outdoor Inc ..... G 309 693-2746
Rantoul *(G-16985)*
Wagner International LLC ..... G 224 619-9247
Vernon Hills *(G-20109)*
Warphole LLC ..... G 866 471-6464
Glen Ellyn *(G-10424)*
Warthog Inc ..... G 815 540-7197
Rockford *(G-17677)*
Welkins LLC ..... G 877 319-3504
Downers Grove *(G-8108)*
White Rhino LLC ..... G 309 691-9653
Brimfield *(G-2408)*
White Whale LLC ..... G 309 303-0028
Mossville *(G-14462)*
Wilson Sporting Goods Co ..... C 773 714-6500
Chicago *(G-6636)*
◆ Wilson Sporting Goods Co ..... B 773 714-6400
Chicago *(G-6635)*
Woodland Fence Forest Pdts Inc ..... G 630 393-2220
Warrenville *(G-20257)*
World Class Technologies Inc ..... G 312 758-3114
Chicago *(G-6672)*
Xmt Solutions LLC ..... G 703 338-9422
Chicago *(G-6696)*
Zarc International Inc ..... F 309 807-2565
Minonk *(G-14056)*

3951 Pens & Mechanical Pencils

Alexander Manufacturing Co ..... D 309 728-2224
Towanda *(G-19892)*
◆ Essentra Holdings Corp ..... G 804 518-0322
Westchester *(G-20698)*
▲ Eversharp Pen Company ..... E 847 366-5030
Franklin Park *(G-9940)*
Fayco Enterprises Inc ..... C 618 283-0638
Vandalia *(G-20011)*
Gillette Company ..... D 847 689-3111
North Chicago *(G-15312)*
Icandee LLC ..... G 773 754-0493
Chicago *(G-4871)*
Perkins Pencil Co ..... G 708 363-9249
Lansing *(G-12511)*
Pilot Corporation of America ..... G 773 792-1111
Park Ridge *(G-16292)*
▲ Premier Packaging Corp ..... G 815 469-7951
Frankfort *(G-9825)*
▲ U Mark Inc ..... E 618 235-7500
Belleville *(G-1604)*
UNI-Ball Corporation ..... G 310 505-5926
Wheaton *(G-20830)*

3952 Lead Pencils, Crayons & Artist's Mtrls

Alexander Manufacturing Co ..... D 309 728-2224
Towanda *(G-19892)*
▲ Badger Air Brush Co ..... D 847 678-3104
Franklin Park *(G-9883)*
Cushing and Company ..... E 312 266-8228
Chicago *(G-4287)*
Erasermitt Incorporated ..... G 312 842-2855
Chicago *(G-4525)*
Fernandez Windows Corp ..... G 773 762-2365
Chicago *(G-4581)*
▲ Graphic Chemical & Ink Co ..... F 630 832-6004
Villa Park *(G-20149)*
Hydro Ink Corp ..... G 847 674-0057
Skokie *(G-18967)*
James Howard Co ..... G 815 497-2831
Compton *(G-6996)*
▲ Lectro Stik Corp ..... E 630 894-1355
Glendale Heights *(G-10466)*
Miller Pallet ..... F 217 589-4411
Roodhouse *(G-17893)*
Moldworks Inc ..... G 815 520-8819
Roscoe *(G-17918)*
On Paint It Company ..... G 219 765-5639
Dekalb *(G-7697)*
Perkins Pencil Co ..... G 708 363-9249
Lansing *(G-12511)*
Plastruct Inc ..... D 626 912-7017
Des Plaines *(G-7824)*
◆ Polyform Products Company ..... E 847 427-0020
Elk Grove Village *(G-9182)*
Rust-Oleum Corporation ..... D 815 967-4258
Rockford *(G-17617)*
Stentech Inc ..... G 630 833-4747
Elmhurst *(G-9430)*
▲ Testor Corporation ..... D 815 962-6654
Rockford *(G-17656)*

3953 Marking Devices

A & E Rubber Stamp Corp ..... G 312 575-1416
Chicago *(G-3481)*
A 1 Marking Products ..... G 309 762-6096
Moline *(G-14130)*
A To Z Engraving Co Inc ..... G 847 526-7396
Wauconda *(G-20324)*
ABM Marking Services Ltd ..... G 618 277-3773
Belleville *(G-1527)*
Anderson Safford Mkg Graphics ..... F 847 827-8968
Des Plaines *(G-7732)*
B&H Machine Inc ..... F 618 281-3737
Columbia *(G-6984)*
Bendsen Signs & Graphics Inc ..... F 217 877-2345
Decatur *(G-7464)*
Bertco Enterprises Inc ..... G 618 234-9283
Belleville *(G-1535)*
Blue Monkey Graphics Inc ..... G 708 488-9501
Forest Park *(G-9708)*
◆ C H Hanson Company ..... D 630 848-2000
Naperville *(G-14786)*
Chicago Silk Screen Sup Co Inc ..... E 312 666-1213
Chicago *(G-4129)*
Custom Cut Stencil Company Inc ..... G 618 277-5077
Belleville *(G-1542)*
Education Partners Project Ltd ..... G 773 675-6643
Chicago *(G-4458)*
Hookset Enterprises LLC ..... F 224 374-1935
Wheeling *(G-20911)*
Iemco Corporation ..... G 773 728-4400
Chicago *(G-4878)*
Illinois Tool Works Inc ..... D 618 997-1716
Marion *(G-13518)*
◆ Jackson Marking Products Co ..... F 618 242-7901
Mount Vernon *(G-14617)*
Joes Printing ..... G 773 545-6063
Chicago *(G-5034)*
K and A Graphics Inc ..... G 847 244-2345
Gurnee *(G-10890)*
Kellogg Printing Co ..... F 309 734-8388
Monmouth *(G-14220)*
Keneal Industries Inc ..... F 815 886-1300
Romeoville *(G-17837)*

▲ Keson Industries Inc E 630 820-4200
Aurora (G-993)
Kiwi Coders Corp E 847 541-4511
Wheeling (G-20925)
Letters Unlimited Inc G 847 891-7811
Schaumburg (G-18604)
Mich Enterprises Inc F 630 616-9000
Wood Dale (G-21216)
Nameplate Robinson & Precision G 847 678-2255
Franklin Park (G-10005)
Nathan Winston Service Inc G 815 758-4545
Dekalb (G-7692)
National Rubber Stamp Co Inc G 773 281-6522
Chicago (G-5552)
Navitor Inc B 800 323-0253
Harwood Heights (G-11106)
Nelson - Harkins Inds Inc E 773 478-6243
Lake Bluff (G-12199)
▲ Pro-Pak Industries Inc F 630 876-1050
West Chicago (G-20633)
Professional Sales Associates G 847 487-1900
Wauconda (G-20384)
▼ Promoframes LLC G 866 566-7224
Schaumburg (G-18685)
Pylon Plastics Inc G 630 968-6374
Lisle (G-12930)
Richards & Stehman LLC G 217 522-6801
Springfield (G-19433)
S and S Associates Inc G 847 584-0033
Elk Grove Village (G-9224)
Shawver Press Inc G 815 772-4700
Morrison (G-14348)
Take Your Mark Sports LLC G 708 655-0525
Western Springs (G-20726)
Trodat Usa Inc E 847 806-1750
Elk Grove Village (G-9287)
▲ U Mark Inc E 618 235-7500
Belleville (G-1604)
Village Press Inc G 847 362-1856
Libertyville (G-12724)
▲ Wagner Zip-Change Inc E 708 681-4100
Melrose Park (G-13926)
Weakley Printing & Sign Shop G 847 473-4466
North Chicago (G-15323)

3955 Carbon Paper & Inked Ribbons

Active Office Solutions F 773 539-3333
Chicago (G-3536)
Aim Graphic Machinery Ltd F 847 215-8000
Buffalo Grove (G-2506)
Allen Paper Company G 312 454-4500
Chicago (G-3615)
Alternative TS G 618 257-0230
Belleville (G-1529)
Cartridge World Decatur G 217 875-0465
Decatur (G-7470)
Dauphin Enterprise Inc G 630 893-6300
Bloomingdale (G-1987)
Illinois Tool Works Inc E 708 720-0300
Frankfort (G-9807)
Ink Stop Inc G 847 478-0631
Buffalo Grove (G-2550)
Next Day Toner Supplies Inc E 708 478-1000
Orland Park (G-15971)
▲ Rpt Toner LLC E 630 694-0400
Bensenville (G-1886)
Shoppers Planet F 877 232-5435
Olympia Fields (G-15898)
▼ Tonerhead Inc E 815 331-3200
Spring Grove (G-19304)
Troy McDaniel G 309 369-6225
Pekin (G-16366)

3961 Costume Jewelry & Novelties

Acme Button & Buttonhole Co G 773 907-8400
Chicago (G-3526)
◆ Alessco Inc F 773 327-7919
Chicago (G-3602)
Anthos and Co LLC G 773 744-6813
Inverness (G-11594)
Bee-Jay Industries Inc F 708 867-4431
Bloomingdale (G-1979)
Bird Dog Bay Inc G 312 631-3108
Chicago (G-3899)
D & D Sukach Inc G 815 895-3377
Sycamore (G-19704)
Daniels Jewelry & Mfg Co G 847 998-5222
Glenview (G-10542)
▲ Diamondaire Corp G 630 355-7464
Saint Charles (G-18184)
Hustedt Manufacturing Jewelers G 217 784-8462
Gibson City (G-10339)
Jewerly and Beyond G 312 833-6785
Schaumburg (G-18576)
Jordan Gold Inc G 708 430-7008
Oak Lawn (G-15722)
JP Leatherworks Inc G 847 317-9804
Deerfield (G-7623)
K Fleye Designs G 773 531-0716
Chicago (G-5066)
Medical ID Fashions Company G 847 404-6789
Deerfield (G-7636)
Noor Jewels LLC G 847 505-9849
Chicago (G-5613)
Pearl Perfect Inc E 847 679-6251
Morton Grove (G-14432)
▲ R S Owens & Co Inc B 773 282-6000
Chicago (G-5953)
Richards Fabulous Finds G 773 943-0710
Chicago (G-6025)
Smart Creations Inc G 847 433-3451
Highland Park (G-11298)
Solari R Mfg Jewelers G 847 823-4354
Park Ridge (G-16296)
▲ Sunnywood Incorporated G 815 675-9777
McHenry (G-13799)
Swarovski North America Ltd G 708 364-0090
Orland Park (G-15985)
Swarovski North America Ltd G 847 680-5150
Vernon Hills (G-20102)
Swarovski North America Ltd G 847 413-9960
Schaumburg (G-18733)
Swarovski US Holding Limited G 847 679-8670
Skokie (G-19040)

3965 Fasteners, Buttons, Needles & Pins

Acme Button & Buttonhole Co G 773 907-8400
Chicago (G-3526)
Aerofast Inc E 630 668-6575
Carol Stream (G-2926)
▲ Afi Industries Inc E 630 462-0400
Carol Stream (G-2927)
Agrati Inc G 704 747-1200
Park Forest (G-16250)
Ambrit Inc G 847 593-3301
Elk Grove Village (G-8820)
◆ Ample Supply Company E 815 895-3500
Sycamore (G-19700)
Anixter Inc E 512 989-4254
Glenview (G-10525)
▲ Buildex Divison of ITW G 630 595-3500
Itasca (G-11631)
▲ Classic Fasteners LLC G 630 605-0195
Saint Charles (G-18170)
▲ Ecf Holdings LLC G 224 723-5524
Northbrook (G-15379)
▲ Engineered Components Co E 847 985-8000
Elgin (G-8579)
Forest City Technologies Inc E 815 965-5880
Rockford (G-17420)
▲ Hawk Fastener Services F 708 489-2000
Alsip (G-456)
▲ Ideal Supply Inc G 847 961-5900
Huntley (G-11541)
Illinois Tool Works Inc B 847 724-7500
Glenview (G-10560)
Illinois Tool Works Inc C 630 372-2150
Bartlett (G-1288)
Illinois Tool Works Inc C 847 783-5500
Elgin (G-8621)
Illinois Tool Works Inc C 847 299-2222
Des Plaines (G-7785)
▲ Inland Fastener Inc F 630 293-3800
West Chicago (G-20596)
Jahm Inc F 847 647-7650
Niles (G-15135)
Jason Incorporated C 630 627-7000
Addison (G-158)
Jinhap US Corporation G 630 833-2880
Elmhurst (G-9382)
Just Another Button F 618 667-8531
Troy (G-19916)
L & M Screw Machine Products F 630 801-0455
Montgomery (G-14253)
Leggett & Platt Incorporated D 847 768-6139
Des Plaines (G-7798)
◆ Lehigh Consumer Products LLC C 630 851-7330
Aurora (G-997)
Lhs Inc G 630 832-3875
Elmhurst (G-9391)
Linda Levinson Designs Inc G 312 951-6943
Chicago (G-5226)
▲ Lre Products Inc E 630 238-8321
Bensenville (G-1845)
Magic Solutions Inc G 312 647-8688
Chicago (G-5315)
◆ Marmon Industrial LLC G 312 372-9500
Chicago (G-5344)
Matchless Parisian Novelty Inc G 773 924-1515
Chicago (G-5364)
Matthew Warren Inc G 630 860-7766
Bensenville (G-1848)
▲ Minigrip Inc D 845 680-2710
Ottawa (G-16061)
▲ Multitech Cold Forming LLC E 630 949-8200
Carol Stream (G-3034)
Nbs Corporation G 847 860-8856
Elk Grove Village (G-9145)
◆ Newell Operating Company C 815 235-4171
Freeport (G-10129)
▲ Pecson Distributors LLC G 815 342-7977
Beecher (G-1520)
Peter Fox G 847 428-2249
East Dundee (G-8208)
◆ R-B Industries Inc E 847 647-4020
Morton Grove (G-14436)
Safety Socket LLC E 224 484-6222
Gilberts (G-10368)
Sanco Industries Inc F 847 243-8675
Kildeer (G-12052)
▲ STA-Rite Ginnie Lou Inc F 217 774-3921
Shelbyville (G-18887)
Sullivans Inc F 815 331-8347
McHenry (G-13796)
▲ Supreme Screw Inc G 630 226-9000
Romeoville (G-17879)
▲ Swd Inc D 630 543-3003
Addison (G-301)

3991 Brooms & Brushes

Concorde Laboratories Inc G 630 717-5300
Lisle (G-12878)
▲ Don Leventhal Group LLC E 618 783-4424
Newton (G-15082)
▲ E Gornell & Sons Inc E 773 489-2330
Chicago (G-4423)
Federal Prison Industries C 309 346-8588
Pekin (G-16333)
▲ Freudenberg Household Pdts LP C 630 270-1400
Aurora (G-964)
Gosia Cartage Ltd G 312 613-8735
Hodgkins (G-11389)
Humboldt Broom Company G 217 268-3718
Arcola (G-652)
Jim Jolly Sales Inc G 847 669-7570
Huntley (G-11546)
Jones Software Corp G 312 952-0011
Chicago (G-5047)
Klm Commercial Sweeping Inc G 618 978-9276
Belleville (G-1563)
◆ Libman Company C 217 268-4200
Arcola (G-655)
Luco Mop Company G 217 235-1992
Mattoon (G-13643)
◆ Newell Operating Company C 815 235-4171
Freeport (G-10129)
◆ Nexstep Commercial Pdts LLC G 217 379-2377
Paxton (G-16309)
▲ Quinn Broom Works Inc E 217 923-3181
Greenup (G-10822)
Re-Maid Incorporated G 815 315-0500
Freeport (G-10136)
Rejuv-A-Roller LLC G 815 975-9635
Belvidere (G-1698)
Sherwin-Williams Company G 847 251-6115
Kenilworth (G-12015)
Team Technologies Inc D 630 937-0380
Batavia (G-1426)
True Value Company LLC E 847 639-5383
Cary (G-3196)
◆ True Value Company LLC B 773 695-5000
Chicago (G-6437)
Zimmerman Brush Co D 773 761-6331
Chicago (G-6719)

3993 Signs & Advertising Displays

A & E Rubber Stamp Corp G 312 575-1416
Chicago (G-3481)
A & J Signs F 815 476-0128
Wilmington (G-21095)

Employee Codes: A=Over 500 employees, B=251-500
C=101-250, D=51-100, E=20-50, F=10-19, G=3-9

2020 Harris Illinois
Industrial Directory

1015

39 MISCELLANEOUS MANUFACTURING INDUSTRIES

A 1 Trophies Awards & Engrv ....G...... 630 837-6000
 Streamwood (G-19558)
A Plus Signs Inc ....G...... 708 534-2030
 Monee (G-14194)
A To Z Engraving Co Inc ....G...... 847 526-7396
 Wauconda (G-20324)
A Trustworthy Sup Source Inc ....G...... 773 480-0255
 Chicago (G-3492)
Ability Plastics Inc ....E...... 708 458-4480
 Justice (G-11949)
Academy Screenprinting Awards ....G...... 309 686-0026
 Peoria (G-16374)
Accurate Metal Fabricating LLC ....D...... 773 235-0400
 Chicago (G-3518)
Accurate Repro Inc ....F...... 630 428-4433
 Naperville (G-14763)
Ace Sign Co ....E...... 217 522-8417
 Springfield (G-19314)
Acrylic Service Inc ....G...... 630 543-0336
 Addison (G-18)
Action Graphics and Signs Inc ....G...... 618 939-5755
 Columbia (G-6983)
Ad Deluxe Sign Company Inc ....G...... 815 556-8469
 Blue Island (G-2109)
Ad Special TZ Inc ....G...... 847 845-6767
 Buffalo Grove (G-2504)
Adams Outdoor Advg Ltd Partnr ....E...... 309 692-2482
 Peoria (G-16375)
Addison Engraving Inc ....G...... 630 833-9123
 Villa Park (G-20127)
Addison Pro Plastics Inc ....G...... 630 543-6770
 Addison (G-21)
Adnama Inc ....G...... 312 922-0509
 Chicago (G-3549)
Advance Press Sign Inc ....G...... 630 833-1600
 Villa Park (G-20128)
Advertising Premiums Inc ....G...... 888 364-9710
 Mount Prospect (G-14509)
Advertising Products Inc ....G...... 847 758-0415
 Elk Grove Village (G-8812)
Albright Enterprises Inc ....G...... 630 357-2300
 Naperville (G-14769)
Alex Displays & Co ....F...... 312 829-2948
 Chicago (G-3603)
Alexander Manufacturing Co ....D...... 309 728-2224
 Towanda (G-19892)
Alexander Signs & Designs Inc ....G...... 815 933-3100
 Bourbonnais (G-2255)
All Signs & Wonders Co ....G...... 630 232-9019
 Geneva (G-10250)
All Signs Inc ....G...... 847 324-5500
 Skokie (G-18914)
▲ All-American Sign Co Inc ....E...... 708 422-2203
 Oak Lawn (G-15698)
All-Right Sign Inc ....F...... 708 754-6366
 Steger (G-19487)
▲ All-Steel Structures Inc ....E...... 708 210-1313
 South Holland (G-19189)
▲ Allied Die Casting Corporation ....E...... 815 385-9330
 McHenry (G-13717)
Alphabet Shop Inc ....E...... 847 888-3150
 Elgin (G-8505)
◆ Altco Inc ....D...... 847 549-0321
 Vernon Hills (G-20041)
▲ AM Ko Oriental Foods ....G...... 217 398-2922
 Champaign (G-3262)
◆ AMD Industries Inc ....D...... 708 863-8900
 Oak Brook (G-15591)
American Name Plate & Metal De ....E...... 773 376-1400
 Chicago (G-3663)
▲ American Sign & Lighting Co ....E...... 847 258-8151
 Chicago (G-3667)
Anbek Inc ....G...... 815 672-6087
 La Salle (G-12103)
Anbek Inc ....F...... 815 223-0734
 La Salle (G-12104)
Anbek Inc ....F...... 815 434-7340
 Ottawa (G-16039)
Antlia Displays LLC ....G...... 773 353-2223
 Chicago (G-3706)
Antolak Management Co Inc ....G...... 312 464-1800
 Chicago (G-3707)
Arrow Sign Company Inc ....G...... 630 620-9803
 Addison (G-40)
Arrow Signs ....F...... 618 466-0818
 Godfrey (G-10649)
Arrow Signs ....G...... 618 466-0818
 Godfrey (G-10650)
Art & Son Sign Inc ....F...... 847 526-7205
 Wauconda (G-20332)

Art Wire Works Inc ....F...... 708 458-3993
 Bedford Park (G-1457)
Artisan Graphics Co ....G...... 847 841-9200
 Streamwood (G-19562)
Arts & Letters Marshall Signs ....G...... 773 927-4442
 Chicago (G-3743)
Associated Attractions Entps ....F...... 773 376-1900
 Chicago (G-3750)
▲ Athena Design Group Inc ....E...... 312 733-2828
 Chicago (G-3758)
Atlantis Entp Investments Inc ....G...... 432 237-0404
 Chicago (G-3761)
Aubrey Sign Co Inc ....G...... 630 482-9901
 Batavia (G-1351)
◆ Authentic Street Signs Inc ....G...... 618 349-8878
 Saint Peter (G-18322)
Award Emblem Mfg Co Inc ....G...... 630 739-0800
 Bolingbrook (G-2153)
Awnings Express ....G...... 773 579-1437
 Chicago (G-3793)
Azusa Inc ....G...... 618 244-6591
 Mount Vernon (G-14597)
▲ B W M Global ....G...... 847 785-1355
 Waukegan (G-20421)
Bannerville USA Inc ....F...... 630 455-0304
 Burr Ridge (G-2654)
▲ Bards Products Inc ....G...... 800 323-5499
 Mundelein (G-14665)
Barry Signs Inc ....G...... 773 327-1183
 Chicago (G-3841)
Baum Holdings Inc ....G...... 847 488-0650
 South Elgin (G-19135)
Bee-Jay Industries Inc ....F...... 708 867-4431
 Bloomingdale (G-1979)
Bella Sign Co ....G...... 630 539-0343
 Roselle (G-17940)
◆ Benchmarc Display Incorporated .....E...... 847 541-2828
 Vernon Hills (G-20046)
Bendsen Signs & Graphics Inc ....F...... 217 877-2345
 Decatur (G-7464)
Best Advertising Spc & Prtg ....G...... 708 448-1110
 Worth (G-21455)
Best Neon Sign Co ....G...... 773 586-2700
 Chicago (G-3872)
Bick Broadcasting Inc ....G...... 217 223-9693
 Quincy (G-16885)
Biron Studio General Svcs Inc ....G...... 708 229-2600
 Oak Lawn (G-15703)
◆ Bish Creative Display Inc ....E...... 847 438-1500
 Lake Zurich (G-12388)
▲ Blu Prime Inc ....G...... 800 709-5413
 Chicago (G-3912)
Blue Diamond Athletic Disp Inc ....G...... 847 414-9971
 Downers Grove (G-7960)
Boatman Signs ....G...... 618 548-6567
 Salem (G-18332)
Braeside Holdings LLC ....F...... 847 395-8500
 Antioch (G-606)
Bright Light Sign Company Inc ....G...... 847 550-8902
 Lake Zurich (G-12389)
Briscoe Signs LLC ....G...... 630 529-1616
 Roselle (G-17942)
Budget Signs ....F...... 618 259-4460
 Wood River (G-21260)
C M F Enterprises Inc ....F...... 847 526-9499
 Wauconda (G-20337)
Cachera and Klemm Inc ....G...... 217 876-7446
 Decatur (G-7468)
Cacini Inc ....G...... 847 884-1162
 Schaumburg (G-18466)
Campbell Management Services ....G...... 847 566-9020
 Mundelein (G-14672)
Canham Graphics ....G...... 217 585-5085
 Springfield (G-19337)
Captivating Signs LLC ....G...... 630 470-6161
 Naperville (G-14788)
Castino & Associates Inc ....G...... 847 291-7446
 Northbrook (G-15354)
Central Illinois Sign Company ....G...... 217 523-4740
 Springfield (G-19346)
Central State Finds ....G...... 630 359-4706
 Elk Grove Village (G-8885)
Century Signs Inc ....F...... 217 224-7419
 Quincy (G-16871)
Chicago I and D Services Inc ....G...... 312 623-8071
 Chicago (G-4107)
Chicago Scenic Studios Inc ....D...... 312 274-9900
 Chicago (G-4127)
▲ Chicago Show Inc ....E...... 847 955-0200
 Buffalo Grove (G-2524)

Chicago Sign & Light Company ....G...... 630 407-0802
 Carol Stream (G-2958)
▲ Chicago Sign Group ....G...... 847 899-9021
 Vernon Hills (G-20048)
Churchill Wilmslow Corporation ....G...... 312 759-8911
 Chicago (G-4147)
CJ Signs ....G...... 309 676-9999
 Peoria (G-16424)
Cks Signs Inc ....G...... 847 423-3456
 Skokie (G-18943)
Classic Midwest Die Mold Inc ....F...... 773 227-8000
 Chicago (G-4169)
Classique Signs & Engrv Inc ....G...... 217 228-7446
 Quincy (G-16872)
Clover Signs ....G...... 773 588-2828
 Chicago (G-4181)
Cnc Graphics ....G...... 630 766-6308
 Bensenville (G-1771)
CNE Inc ....G...... 847 534-7135
 Schaumburg (G-18480)
Color Communications LLC ....G...... 312 223-0204
 Chicago (G-4204)
Color Signs ....G...... 847 368-0101
 Arlington Heights (G-716)
Comet Neon ....G...... 630 668-6366
 Lombard (G-13056)
Concepts Magnet ....G...... 847 253-3351
 Mount Prospect (G-14520)
Consolidated Displays Co Inc ....G...... 630 851-8666
 Oswego (G-15998)
Contempo Autographic & Signs ....G...... 708 371-5499
 Crestwood (G-7113)
Cook Fabrication Signs Graphic ....G...... 309 360-3805
 Deer Creek (G-7573)
Corporate Identification Solut ....E...... 773 763-9600
 Chicago (G-4240)
Corporate Sign Systems Inc ....F...... 847 882-6100
 Roselle (G-17948)
Corpro Screen Tech Inc ....G...... 815 633-1201
 Loves Park (G-13196)
Crown Publications Inc ....G...... 217 893-4856
 Rantoul (G-16973)
Crown Trophy ....G...... 309 699-1766
 East Peoria (G-8264)
CST Sign & Manufacturing LLC ....G...... 312 222-0020
 Chicago (G-4281)
Cubby Hole of Carlinville Inc ....F...... 217 854-8511
 Carlinville (G-2872)
Custom Enterprises ....G...... 618 439-6626
 Benton (G-1923)
Custom Sign Consultants Inc ....G...... 312 533-2302
 Chicago (G-4292)
Custom Signs On Metal LLC ....F...... 217 443-5347
 Tilton (G-19795)
Custom Telephone Printing Co ....F...... 815 338-0000
 Woodstock (G-21379)
Custom Trophies ....G...... 217 422-3353
 Decatur (G-7480)
Cutting Edge Graphics ....G...... 630 717-9233
 Plainfield (G-16654)
Cutting Edge Graphics Ltd ....G...... 630 717-9233
 Naperville (G-14964)
Cypress Multigraphics LLC ....E...... 708 633-1166
 Tinley Park (G-19820)
D E Signs & Storage LLC ....G...... 618 939-8050
 Waterloo (G-20289)
D&J Arlington Heights Inc ....G...... 847 577-8200
 Arlington Heights (G-724)
DAmico Associates Inc ....G...... 847 291-7446
 Northbrook (G-15373)
▲ Dard Products Inc ....C...... 847 328-5000
 Wauconda (G-20341)
Darnall Printing ....G...... 309 827-7212
 Bloomington (G-2039)
Dazzling Displays Inc ....F...... 708 262-6340
 Morris (G-14302)
DE Asbury Inc ....E...... 217 222-0617
 Quincy (G-16876)
Decal Solutions Unlimited Inc ....G...... 847 590-5405
 Arlington Heights (G-727)
Demond Signs Inc ....F...... 618 624-7260
 O Fallon (G-15571)
Derse Inc ....D...... 847 473-2149
 Waukegan (G-20435)
Design Group Signage Corp ....F...... 847 390-0350
 Des Plaines (G-7756)
▲ Design Phase Inc ....E...... 847 473-0077
 Waukegan (G-20436)
Designovations Inc ....G...... 815 645-8598
 Loves Park (G-13207)

Designs Unlimited ..... G 618 357-6728
Pinckneyville *(G-16613)*

Desk & Door Nameplate Company ..... F 815 806-8670
Frankfort *(G-9785)*

Dewrich Inc ..... G 847 249-7445
Gurnee *(G-10868)*

◆ **Dgs Import LLC** ..... E 800 211-9646
Chicago *(G-4350)*

Diamond Sign Design ..... G 630 543-4900
Addison *(G-89)*

▲ **Dicke Tool Company** ..... D 630 969-0050
Downers Grove *(G-7988)*

Dickey Sign Co ..... G 618 797-1262
Granite City *(G-10703)*

Digital Artz LLC ..... G 618 651-1500
Highland *(G-11213)*

Digital Edge Signs Inc ..... G 847 838-4760
Antioch *(G-609)*

Digital Factory Tech Inc ..... E 513 560-4074
Chicago *(G-4358)*

Digital Greensigns Inc ..... G 312 624-8550
Chicago *(G-4359)*

Digital Minds Inc ..... G 847 430-3390
Rosemont *(G-18017)*

Display Link Inc ..... G 815 968-0778
Rockford *(G-17380)*

Display Signs & Design ..... G 800 782-1558
Chicago *(G-4367)*

Distinctive SIGns& The Neon Ex ..... G 847 245-7159
Grayslake *(G-10767)*

Diva Dream Signs ..... G 618 201-4348
Christopher *(G-6824)*

Divine Signs Inc ..... G 847 534-9220
Schaumburg *(G-18507)*

Doyle Signs Inc ..... D 630 543-9490
Addison *(G-97)*

E A A Enterprises Inc ..... G 630 279-0150
Villa Park *(G-20145)*

E B G B Inc ..... G 847 228-9333
Elk Grove Village *(G-8962)*

E K Kuhn Inc ..... G 815 899-9211
Sycamore *(G-19709)*

E Z Sign Co Inc ..... G 815 469-4080
Oak Forest *(G-15675)*

East Bank Neon Inc ..... G 618 345-9517
Collinsville *(G-6958)*

Eberhart Sign & Lighting Co ..... G 618 656-7256
Edwardsville *(G-8359)*

Edventure Promotions Inc ..... G 312 440-1800
Chicago *(G-4460)*

Effingham Signs & Graphics ..... G 217 347-8711
Effingham *(G-8398)*

Eisendrath Inc ..... G 847 432-3899
Highland Park *(G-11261)*

▲ **Elk Grove Signs Inc** ..... G 847 427-0005
Elk Grove Village *(G-8973)*

Enchanted Signs of Rockford ..... G 815 874-5100
Rockford *(G-17396)*

Engravings Plus ..... G 217 784-8426
Gibson City *(G-10337)*

Enterprise Signs Inc ..... G 708 691-1273
Blue Island *(G-2121)*

Exclusively Expo ..... F 630 378-4600
Romeoville *(G-17819)*

Exex Holding Corporation ..... G 815 703-7295
Romeoville *(G-17820)*

Express Signs & Lighting Maint ..... F 815 725-9080
Shorewood *(G-18896)*

▲ **Exsel Exhibits Inc** ..... F 847 647-1012
Des Plaines *(G-7762)*

Fast Signs ..... G 773 698-8115
Chicago *(G-4564)*

Fast Signs ..... G 815 730-7828
Mokena *(G-14080)*

Fast Signs 590 ..... G 815 937-1855
Kankakee *(G-11970)*

Fastsigns ..... G 312 344-1765
Chicago *(G-4565)*

Fastsigns ..... G 847 981-1965
Elk Grove Village *(G-8997)*

Fastsigns ..... G 630 932-0001
Oakbrook Terrace *(G-15798)*

Fastsigns ..... G 847 675-1600
Lincolnwood *(G-12818)*

Fastsigns ..... G 847 680-7446
Libertyville *(G-12651)*

Fastsigns LLC ..... G 630 541-8901
Downers Grove *(G-8001)*

Fastsigns International ..... G 847 967-7222
Morton Grove *(G-14407)*

Federal Signal Corporation ..... D 708 534-3400
University Park *(G-19953)*

Fedex Office & Print Svcs Inc ..... E 309 685-4093
Peoria *(G-16437)*

Fedex Office & Print Svcs Inc ..... E 847 670-4100
Arlington Heights *(G-736)*

▲ **Flow-Eze Company** ..... F 815 965-1062
Rockford *(G-17416)*

FM Graphic Impressions Inc ..... E 630 897-8788
Aurora *(G-1097)*

Forest Awards & Engraving ..... G 630 595-2242
Wood Dale *(G-21189)*

Fourth Quarter Holdings Inc ..... G 847 249-7445
Gurnee *(G-10879)*

▲ **Frank O Carlson & Co Inc** ..... F 773 847-6900
Chicago *(G-4630)*

Freedom Design & Decals Inc ..... G 815 806-8172
Mokena *(G-14084)*

Friendly Signs Inc ..... G 815 933-7070
Kankakee *(G-11973)*

▲ **Fun Incorporated** ..... E 773 745-3837
Wheeling *(G-20902)*

G & J Associates Inc ..... G 847 255-0123
Arlington Heights *(G-738)*

G and D Enterprises Inc ..... E 847 981-8661
Arlington Heights *(G-739)*

G D S Professional Bus Display ..... E 309 829-3298
Bloomington *(G-2047)*

G M Sign Inc ..... D 847 546-0424
Round Lake *(G-18075)*

Gabel & Schubert Bronze ..... F 773 878-6800
Chicago *(G-4653)*

Galesburg Sign & Lighting ..... G 309 342-9798
Galesburg *(G-10194)*

Gaytan Signs & Co Inc ..... G 815 726-2975
Joliet *(G-11868)*

Geebees Inc ..... G 309 682-5300
Peoria *(G-16443)*

▲ **Gemini Industries Inc** ..... D 618 251-3352
Roxana *(G-18100)*

General Motor Sign ..... G 847 546-0424
Round Lake *(G-18076)*

Geneva Sign Corporation ..... G 630 262-1700
Geneva *(G-10273)*

George Lauterer Corporation ..... E 312 913-1881
Chicago *(G-4682)*

Grate Signs Inc ..... E 815 729-9700
Joliet *(G-11870)*

Graymon Graphics Inc ..... G 773 737-0176
Chicago *(G-4730)*

Grimco Inc ..... F 630 530-7756
Bolingbrook *(G-2181)*

Gz Sign Designs Inc ..... G 630 307-7446
Roselle *(G-17956)*

▲ **Hanover Displays Inc** ..... F 773 334-9934
Elk Grove Village *(G-9027)*

Harder Signs Inc ..... F 815 874-7777
Rockford *(G-17443)*

Haus Sign Incorporated ..... G 708 598-8740
Bridgeview *(G-2354)*

Hazen Display Corporation ..... E 815 248-2925
Davis *(G-7418)*

Heavy Hitters LLC ..... G 630 258-2991
Calumet City *(G-2780)*

Heffner Designs ..... F 630 854-2852
Naperville *(G-14840)*

Heiman Sign Studio ..... G 815 397-6909
Rockford *(G-17447)*

Hercl Signs & Service Inc ..... G 847 471-4015
South Elgin *(G-19151)*

Heritage Signs Ltd ..... G 847 549-1942
Libertyville *(G-12658)*

Hermann Gene Signs & Service ..... G 618 244-3681
Mount Vernon *(G-14613)*

Heron Bay Inc ..... G 309 661-1300
Bloomington *(G-2057)*

Herrmann Signs & Service ..... G 618 246-6537
Mount Vernon *(G-14614)*

▼ **HM Witt & Co** ..... E 773 250-5000
Chicago *(G-4824)*

Holland Design Group Inc ..... F 847 526-8848
Wauconda *(G-20357)*

Holmes Associates Inc ..... G 847 336-4515
Gurnee *(G-10887)*

Horizon Downing LLC ..... E 815 758-6867
Dekalb *(G-7685)*

▲ **House of Doolittle Ltd** ..... E 847 228-9591
Arlington Heights *(G-751)*

Hughes & Son Inc ..... G 815 459-1887
Crystal Lake *(G-7206)*

Icon Identity Solutions Inc ..... C 847 364-2250
Rolling Meadows *(G-17738)*

ID Sign and Lighting Inc ..... G 630 844-3565
Montgomery *(G-14249)*

▲ **Ideal Box Co** ..... C 708 594-3100
Chicago *(G-4875)*

Idek Graphics LLC ..... G 630 530-1232
Elmhurst *(G-9373)*

Identiti Resources Ltd ..... E 866 477-4467
Schaumburg *(G-18554)*

Idot North Side Sign Shop ..... G 847 705-4033
Schaumburg *(G-18555)*

▲ **Ilight Technologies Inc** ..... F 312 876-8630
Chicago *(G-4887)*

Image Fx Corp ..... G 630 655-2850
Burr Ridge *(G-2685)*

Image Signs Inc ..... F 815 282-4141
Loves Park *(G-13218)*

Imagecare Maintenance Svcs LLC ..... F 847 631-3306
Rolling Meadows *(G-17739)*

Images Alive Ltd ..... G 847 498-5550
Highland Park *(G-11273)*

Imageworks Manufacturing Inc ..... E 708 503-1122
Park Forest *(G-16255)*

Impact Signs & Graphics Inc ..... G 708 469-7178
La Grange *(G-12080)*

In Sight Sign Company Inc ..... G 773 267-4002
Chicago *(G-4903)*

Infinity Communications Group ..... F 708 352-1086
Countryside *(G-7060)*

Insignia Design Ltd ..... G 301 254-9221
Rolling Meadows *(G-17741)*

Integrity Sign Company ..... F 708 532-5038
Mokena *(G-14092)*

Interstate Graphics Inc ..... E 815 877-6777
Machesney Park *(G-13351)*

Isates Inc ..... G 309 691-8822
Peoria *(G-16460)*

Its A Sign ..... G 708 848-7446
Oak Park *(G-15758)*

Ivan Carlson Associates Inc ..... E 312 829-4616
Chicago *(G-4979)*

J & B Signs Inc ..... G 312 640-8181
Chicago *(G-4982)*

J & D Instant Signs ..... G 847 965-2800
Morton Grove *(G-14414)*

J R Fridrich Inc ..... F 847 439-1554
Elk Grove Village *(G-9064)*

▲ **Jacobson Acqstion Holdings LLC** ..... C 847 623-1414
Waukegan *(G-20452)*

Jamali Kopy Kat Printing Inc ..... G 708 544-6164
Bellwood *(G-1629)*

James D Ahern Company ..... F 773 254-0717
Chicago *(G-5001)*

▼ **Janis Plastics Inc** ..... D 847 838-5500
Antioch *(G-617)*

JAS Dahern Signs ..... G 773 254-0717
Chicago *(G-5009)*

Jem Solutions Inc ..... G 815 436-0880
Plainfield *(G-16677)*

Jenkins Displays Co ..... G 618 335-3874
Vandalia *(G-20013)*

▲ **Joans Trophy & Plaque Co** ..... E 309 674-6500
Peoria *(G-16463)*

Jodaat Inc ..... G 630 916-7776
Lombard *(G-13091)*

John Cornbleet Inc ..... G 630 357-3278
Naperville *(G-14855)*

John Omalley ..... G 847 924-8670
Elgin *(G-8634)*

John Parker Advertising Co ..... G 217 892-4118
Rantoul *(G-16979)*

Johnson Sign Co ..... G 847 678-2092
Franklin Park *(G-9975)*

Joliet Pattern Works Inc ..... D 815 726-5373
Crest Hill *(G-7088)*

Jonem Grp Inc DBA Sign A Rama ..... G 224 848-4620
Lake Barrington *(G-12155)*

Joseph D Smithies ..... G 618 632-6141
Caseyville *(G-3216)*

K and A Graphics Inc ..... G 847 244-2345
Gurnee *(G-10890)*

K-Display Corp ..... F 773 586-2042
Chicago *(G-5071)*

Kane Graphical Corporation ..... E 773 384-1200
Chicago *(G-5080)*

Kdn Signs Inc ..... F 847 721-3848
Bensenville *(G-1837)*

Kellys Sign Shop ..... G 217 477-0167
Danville *(G-7356)*

Ken Young Construction Co ....G....... 847 358-3026
Hoffman Estates *(G-11433)*
Keyesport Manufacturing Inc ....G....... 618 749-5510
Keyesport *(G-12043)*
Keystone Display Inc ....D....... 815 648-2456
Hebron *(G-11144)*
Keystone Printing & Publishing ....G....... 815 678-2591
Richmond *(G-17016)*
Kieffer Holding Co ....G....... 877 543-3337
Lincolnshire *(G-12776)*
Kornick Enterprises LLC ....G....... 847 884-1162
Schaumburg *(G-18591)*
Krick Enterprises Inc ....G....... 630 515-1085
Downers Grove *(G-8041)*
Ksem Inc ....G....... 618 656-5388
Edwardsville *(G-8367)*
L & C Imaging Inc ....G....... 309 829-1802
Bloomington *(G-2069)*
Lakeview Sign Co ....G....... 773 698-8104
Chicago *(G-5168)*
Lambert Print Source Llc ....G....... 630 708-0505
Yorkville *(G-21491)*
Lange Sign Group ....G....... 815 747-2448
East Dubuque *(G-8178)*
Laux Grafix Inc ....G....... 618 337-4558
East Saint Louis *(G-8313)*
Legacy 3d LLC ....F....... 815 727-5454
Crest Hill *(G-7090)*
Legible Signs Group Corp ....F....... 815 654-0100
Loves Park *(G-13233)*
Lena Sign Shop ....G....... 815 369-9090
Lena *(G-12604)*
Leo Burnett Company Inc ....C....... 312 220-5959
Chicago *(G-5205)*
Leos Sign ....G....... 773 227-2460
Chicago *(G-5206)*
Lettering Specialists Inc ....F....... 847 674-3414
Skokie *(G-18979)*
Lettermen Signage Inc ....G....... 708 479-5161
Mokena *(G-14095)*
Letters Unlimited Inc ....G....... 847 891-7811
Schaumburg *(G-18604)*
Light Waves LLC ....F....... 847 251-1622
Wilmette *(G-21084)*
Lightning Graphic ....G....... 815 623-1937
Roscoe *(G-17913)*
Lincolnland Archtctral Grphics ....G....... 217 629-9009
Glenarm *(G-10426)*
Link Media Florida LLC ....G....... 815 224-4742
La Salle *(G-12117)*
Lonelino Sign Company Inc ....G....... 217 243-2444
Jacksonville *(G-11773)*
M & R Media Inc ....G....... 847 884-6300
Schaumburg *(G-18616)*
M G M Displays Inc ....G....... 708 594-3699
Chicago *(G-5300)*
Magnetic Signs ....G....... 773 476-6551
Chicago *(G-5317)*
Main Street Visuals Inc ....G....... 847 869-7446
Morton Grove *(G-14425)*
Mark Collins ....G....... 847 324-5500
Skokie *(G-18983)*
Mark Your Space Inc ....G....... 630 289-7082
Bartlett *(G-1295)*
Marking Specialists/Poly ....F....... 847 793-8100
Buffalo Grove *(G-2568)*
Massey Grafix ....G....... 815 644-4620
Watseka *(G-20310)*
Matrex Exhibits Inc ....D....... 630 628-2233
Addison *(G-193)*
Maxs Screen Machine Inc ....G....... 773 878-4949
Chicago *(G-5370)*
Mbm Business Assistance Inc ....G....... 217 398-6600
Champaign *(G-3318)*
McKernin Exhibits Inc ....F....... 708 333-4500
South Holland *(G-19231)*
Meagher Sign & Graphics Inc ....G....... 618 662-7446
Flora *(G-9685)*
Mekanism Inc ....F....... 415 908-4000
Chicago *(G-5390)*
Meltdown Creative Works Inc ....G....... 309 310-1978
Bloomington *(G-2074)*
Mer-Pla Inc ....F....... 847 530-9798
Chicago *(G-5393)*
▲ Mercury Plastics Inc ....E....... 888 884-1864
Chicago *(G-5394)*
Mersigns ....G....... 618 234-4450
Belleville *(G-1575)*
▲ Metal Box International LLC ....C....... 847 455-8500
Franklin Park *(G-9994)*
Mich Enterprises Inc ....F....... 630 616-9000
Wood Dale *(G-21216)*
Michael Reggis Clark ....G....... 618 533-3841
Centralia *(G-3238)*
▲ Midway Displays Inc ....E....... 708 563-2323
Bedford Park *(G-1482)*
Midwest Nameplate Corp ....G....... 708 614-0606
Orland Park *(G-15968)*
Midwest Promotional Group Co ....E....... 708 563-0600
Burr Ridge *(G-2705)*
Midwest Sign & Lighting Inc ....G....... 708 365-5555
Country Club Hills *(G-7042)*
Midwest Signs & Structures Inc ....G....... 847 249-8398
Gurnee *(G-10898)*
Midwest Signworks ....G....... 815 942-3517
Morris *(G-14314)*
Midwest Sun-Ray Lighting & Sig ....F....... 618 656-2884
Granite City *(G-10726)*
Minerva Sportswear Inc ....F....... 309 661-2387
Bloomington *(G-2080)*
Mission Signs Inc ....G....... 630 243-6731
Lemont *(G-12572)*
▲ Mk Signs Inc ....E....... 773 545-4444
Chicago *(G-5473)*
▼ Mmxix Capital Inc ....D....... 815 441-2647
Sterling *(G-19520)*
Monitor Sign Co ....F....... 217 234-2412
Mattoon *(G-13651)*
Mostert & Ferguson Signs ....G....... 815 485-1212
Orland Park *(G-15969)*
Mount Vernon Neon Sign Co ....C....... 618 242-0645
Mount Vernon *(G-14626)*
Murphys Sign Studio ....G....... 630 963-0677
Westmont *(G-20762)*
N Bujarski Inc ....G....... 847 884-1600
Schaumburg *(G-18643)*
Nafisco Inc ....F....... 815 372-3300
Romeoville *(G-17858)*
Nameplate Robinson & Precision ....G....... 847 678-2255
Franklin Park *(G-10005)*
Nathan Winston Service Inc ....G....... 815 758-4545
Dekalb *(G-7692)*
Navitor Inc ....B....... 800 323-0253
Harwood Heights *(G-11106)*
▲ Neil International Inc ....C....... 847 549-7627
Vernon Hills *(G-20078)*
Nelson - Harkins Inds Inc ....E....... 773 478-6243
Lake Bluff *(G-12199)*
Neon Art ....G....... 773 588-5883
Chicago *(G-5566)*
Neon Design Inc ....G....... 773 880-5020
Evanston *(G-9558)*
Neon Express Signs ....G....... 773 463-7335
Chicago *(G-5567)*
Neon Prism Electric Sign Co ....G....... 630 879-1010
Batavia *(G-1400)*
Neon Shop Inc ....G....... 773 227-0303
Chicago *(G-5569)*
◆ Nevco Sports LLC ....D....... 618 664-0360
Greenville *(G-10840)*
Newport Printing Services Inc ....G....... 847 632-1000
Schaumburg *(G-18648)*
Nimlok Co ....G....... 855 764-6565
Woodridge *(G-21327)*
Nite Lite Signs & Balloons Inc ....G....... 630 953-2866
Addison *(G-229)*
Nordmeyer Graphics ....G....... 815 697-2634
Chebanse *(G-3430)*
North Shore Sign Company ....E....... 847 816-7020
Libertyville *(G-12690)*
Noteworthy Group Inc ....G....... 618 549-2505
Carbondale *(G-2851)*
Nu Glo Sign Company ....F....... 847 223-6160
Grayslake *(G-10793)*
Nu-Art Printing ....G....... 618 533-9971
Centralia *(G-3242)*
◆ Nu-Dell Manufacturing Co Inc ....F....... 847 803-4500
Chicago *(G-5637)*
Nutheme Sign Company ....G....... 847 230-0067
Downers Grove *(G-8067)*
Nycor Products Inc ....G....... 815 727-9883
Joliet *(G-11910)*
O Signs Inc ....G....... 312 888-3386
Chicago *(G-5646)*
Oakley Signs & Graphics Inc ....F....... 224 612-5045
Des Plaines *(G-7813)*
Ogden Offset Printers Inc ....G....... 773 284-7797
Chicago *(G-5663)*
Olympic Signs Inc ....E....... 630 424-6100
Lombard *(G-13112)*
Olympic Trophy and Awards Co ....F....... 773 631-9500
Chicago *(G-5672)*
Omega Sign & Lighting Inc ....E....... 630 237-4397
Addison *(G-231)*
Orbit Enterprises Inc ....G....... 630 469-3405
Oak Brook *(G-15654)*
◆ Orbus LLC ....C....... 630 226-1155
Woodridge *(G-21328)*
Outdoor Solutions Team Inc ....E....... 312 446-4220
Northbrook *(G-15450)*
P & D Sign Co ....G....... 815 224-9220
Peru *(G-16588)*
▲ P & L Mark-It Inc ....E....... 630 879-7590
Batavia *(G-1402)*
P N K Ventures Inc ....G....... 630 527-0500
Naperville *(G-14891)*
Paddock Industries Inc ....F....... 618 277-1580
Smithton *(G-19068)*
Paldo Sign and Display Company ....G....... 708 456-1711
River Grove *(G-17065)*
Parvin-Clauss Sign Co Inc ....E....... 866 490-2877
Carol Stream *(G-3045)*
Patt Supply Corporation ....F....... 708 442-3901
Lyons *(G-13312)*
Pellegrini Enterprises Inc ....G....... 815 717-6408
Orland Park *(G-15974)*
Peterson Brothers Plastics ....F....... 773 286-5666
Chicago *(G-5795)*
Photo Techniques Corp ....E....... 630 690-9360
Carol Stream *(G-3046)*
Plainfield Signs Inc ....G....... 815 439-1063
Plainfield *(G-16702)*
Platts Printing Company ....G....... 309 228-1069
Farmington *(G-9663)*
Prairie Display Chicago Inc ....F....... 630 834-8773
Elmhurst *(G-9411)*
Prairie Signs Inc ....F....... 309 452-0463
Normal *(G-15218)*
Preformance Signs ....G....... 815 544-5044
Belvidere *(G-1695)*
Premier Signs Creations Inc ....G....... 309 637-6890
Peoria *(G-16502)*
Prime Market Targeting Inc ....E....... 815 469-4555
Frankfort *(G-9826)*
Printing Plus of Roselle Inc ....G....... 630 893-0410
Roselle *(G-17974)*
▲ Procon General Services Inc ....G....... 773 227-8258
Chicago *(G-5891)*
Promotional Co of Illinois ....G....... 847 382-0239
Inverness *(G-11603)*
Pronto Signs and Engraving ....G....... 847 249-7874
Waukegan *(G-20483)*
Pry-Bar Company ....F....... 815 436-3383
Joliet *(G-11918)*
Q SC Design ....G....... 815 933-6777
Bradley *(G-2289)*
Qt Sign Inc ....G....... 847 524-7950
Schaumburg *(G-18690)*
▲ Quantum Sign Corporation ....F....... 630 466-0372
Sugar Grove *(G-19652)*
Quick Quality Printing Inc ....G....... 708 895-5885
Lansing *(G-12513)*
Quick Signs Inc ....G....... 630 554-7370
Oswego *(G-16023)*
Quincy Electric & Sign Company ....F....... 217 223-8404
Quincy *(G-16930)*
R & L Signs Inc ....G....... 708 233-0112
Bridgeview *(G-2377)*
▲ R D Niven & Associates Ltd ....E....... 630 580-6000
Carol Stream *(G-3057)*
R-Signs Service and Design Inc ....G....... 815 722-0283
Joliet *(G-11921)*
Rainbow Signs ....F....... 815 675-6750
Spring Grove *(G-19298)*
Real Neon Inc ....F....... 630 543-0995
Villa Park *(G-20168)*
Realt Images Inc ....G....... 217 567-3487
Tower Hill *(G-19894)*
Rebechini Studio Inc ....F....... 847 437-9030
Elk Grove Village *(G-9215)*
◆ Rico Industries Inc ....D....... 312 427-0313
Niles *(G-15166)*
Right Way Signs LLC ....G....... 773 930-4361
Chicago *(G-6032)*
Rjw Graphics Inc ....G....... 847 336-4515
Waukegan *(G-20488)*
Rkm Enterprises ....G....... 217 348-5437
Charleston *(G-3411)*
Rmkc Inc ....G....... 630 932-0001
Oakbrook Terrace *(G-15814)*

Road Ready Signs ....F 309 828-1007
Bloomington *(G-2089)*
▲ **Roeda Signs Inc** ....E 708 333-3021
Chicago Heights *(G-6772)*
Roman Signs ....G 847 381-3425
Barrington *(G-1241)*
Ron Meyer ....G 847 844-9880
Gilberts *(G-10367)*
Roth Neon Sign Company Inc ....G 618 942-6378
Herrin *(G-11177)*
Rout A Bout Shop Inc ....G 309 829-0674
Bloomington *(G-2091)*
Rowdy Star Custom Creations ....G 217 497-1789
Danville *(G-7379)*
RTC Industries Inc ....D 847 640-2400
Chicago *(G-6075)*
Rutke Signs Inc ....G 708 841-6464
Westchester *(G-20709)*
S and S Associates Inc ....G 847 584-0033
Elk Grove Village *(G-9224)*
S D Custom Machining ....G 618 544-7007
Robinson *(G-17125)*
Sadannah Group LLC ....G 630 357-2300
Naperville *(G-14912)*
Same Day Signs ....G 773 697-4896
Chicago *(G-6097)*
Samsung Sign Corp ....G 847 816-1374
Libertyville *(G-12703)*
Sandee Manufacturing Co ....E 847 671-1335
Franklin Park *(G-10042)*
Sandra E Greene ....G 815 469-0092
Frankfort *(G-9836)*
Saturn Sign ....G 847 520-9009
Wheeling *(G-20978)*
Savino Displays Inc ....G 630 574-0777
Hinsdale *(G-11378)*
Schellerer Corporation Inc ....D 630 980-4567
Hanover Park *(G-11013)*
Service Sheet Metal Works Inc ....F 773 229-0031
Chicago *(G-6143)*
▲ **Sharn Enterprises Inc** ....E 815 464-9715
Frankfort *(G-9838)*
Shawcraft Sign Co ....G 815 282-4105
Machesney Park *(G-13374)*
Shinn Enterprises ....G 217 698-3344
Springfield *(G-19443)*
Sign ....G 630 351-8400
Glendale Heights *(G-10495)*
Sign & Banner Express ....G 630 783-9700
Bolingbrook *(G-2239)*
Sign A Rama ....G 630 293-7300
West Chicago *(G-20642)*
Sign A Rama Inc ....G 630 359-5125
Villa Park *(G-20172)*
Sign America Inc ....G 773 262-7800
Chicago *(G-6165)*
Sign Appeal Inc ....G 847 587-4300
Fox Lake *(G-9754)*
Sign Authority ....G 630 462-9850
Wheaton *(G-20824)*
Sign Central ....G 847 543-7600
Round Lake *(G-18083)*
Sign Centre ....G 847 595-7300
Elk Grove Village *(G-9239)*
Sign City Corp ....G 847 382-3838
Lake Barrington *(G-12165)*
Sign Contractors ....G 708 795-1761
Burr Ridge *(G-2720)*
Sign Express Inc ....G 708 524-8811
Oak Park *(G-15773)*
Sign Fx ....G 630 466-7446
Sugar Grove *(G-19656)*
Sign Girls Inc ....G 847 336-4002
Gurnee *(G-10927)*
Sign Identity Inc ....G 630 942-1400
Glen Ellyn *(G-10419)*
Sign O Rama ....G 815 744-8702
Joliet *(G-11930)*
Sign Outlet Inc ....G 708 824-2222
Alsip *(G-510)*
Sign Palace Inc ....G 847 228-7446
Elk Grove Village *(G-9240)*
Sign Pro of Quincy Inc ....G 217 223-9693
Quincy *(G-16945)*
Sign Shop Express ....G 630 964-3500
Downers Grove *(G-8094)*
Sign Solutions ....G 618 443-6565
Sparta *(G-19259)*
Sign Team Inc ....G 309 302-0017
East Moline *(G-8240)*
Sign-A-Rama ....G 312 922-0509
Chicago *(G-6166)*
Sign-A-Rama of Buffalo Grove ....G 847 215-1535
Buffalo Grove *(G-2604)*
Signarama ....G 847 543-4870
Grayslake *(G-10800)*
Signature Screen Printing Corp ....G 773 866-0070
Chicago *(G-6169)*
Signcraft Screenprint Inc ....C 815 777-3030
Galena *(G-10178)*
Signcrafters Enterprises Inc ....G 815 648-4484
Hebron *(G-11150)*
Signet Sign Company ....G 630 830-8242
Bartlett *(G-1313)*
Signkraft Co ....G 217 787-7105
Springfield *(G-19444)*
Signs By Custom Cutting Inc ....G 630 759-2734
Bolingbrook *(G-2240)*
Signs By Design ....G 708 599-9970
Palos Hills *(G-16207)*
◆ **Signs Direct Inc** ....F 309 820-1070
Bloomington *(G-2095)*
Signs For Success Inc ....F 847 800-4870
Buffalo Grove *(G-2605)*
Signs In Dundee Inc ....G 847 742-9530
Elgin *(G-8731)*
Signs Now ....G 847 427-0005
Elk Grove Village *(G-9242)*
Signs Now ....G 800 356-3373
Chicago *(G-6170)*
Signs of Distinction Inc ....G 847 520-0787
Wheeling *(G-20986)*
Signs Plus ....G 847 489-9009
Des Plaines *(G-7844)*
Signs Today Inc ....G 847 934-9777
Palatine *(G-16158)*
Signscapes Inc ....G 847 719-2610
Lake Zurich *(G-12457)*
Signwise Inc ....G 630 932-3204
Addison *(G-290)*
Signworx Sign & Lighting Co ....G 217 413-2532
Springfield *(G-19445)*
Signx Co Inc ....G 847 639-7917
Cary *(G-3190)*
Simply Signs ....G 309 849-9016
Metamora *(G-13968)*
Skyward Promotions Inc ....G 815 969-0909
Rockford *(G-17633)*
Solar Traffic Systems Inc ....G 331 318-8500
Lemont *(G-12590)*
South Water Signs LLC ....E 630 333-4900
Elmhurst *(G-9428)*
Southwest Signs Inc ....G 773 585-3530
Chicago *(G-6207)*
Specialty Graphics Supply Inc ....G 630 584-8202
Saint Charles *(G-18273)*
Speedpro North Shore ....G 847 983-0095
Skokie *(G-19034)*
Speedpro of Dupage ....G 630 812-5080
Lombard *(G-13134)*
Staar Bales Lestarge Inc ....G 618 259-6366
East Alton *(G-8171)*
Stans Sportsworld Inc ....G 217 359-8474
Champaign *(G-3355)*
Stecker Graphics Inc ....G 309 786-4973
Rock Island *(G-17246)*
▲ **Stellar Recognition Inc** ....D 773 282-8060
Chicago *(G-6243)*
Stelmont Inc ....G 847 870-0200
Arlington Heights *(G-812)*
Stevens Exhibits & Displays ....E 773 523-3900
Chicago *(G-6246)*
▲ **Stevens Sign Co Inc** ....G 708 562-4888
Northlake *(G-15560)*
Sticker Dude Inc ....G 815 322-2480
Johnsburg *(G-11810)*
Store 409 Inc ....F 708 478-5751
Mokena *(G-14117)*
Strictly Neon Inc ....G 708 597-1616
Crestwood *(G-7130)*
▲ **Sub-Surface Sign Co Ltd** ....E 847 675-6530
Skokie *(G-19039)*
Suburban Accents Inc ....G 847 776-7474
Rolling Meadows *(G-17778)*
Summit Signworks Inc ....G 847 870-0937
Arlington Heights *(G-815)*
Super Sign Service ....F 309 829-9241
Bloomington *(G-2098)*
Syndigo LLC ....C 309 690-5231
Peoria *(G-16532)*
T & J Electric Company Inc ....F 309 347-2196
Pekin *(G-16364)*
T Graphics ....G 618 592-4145
Oblong *(G-15830)*
T Ham Sign Inc ....E 618 242-2010
Opdyke *(G-15905)*
T J Marche Ltd ....G 618 445-2314
Albion *(G-353)*
Targin Sign Systems Inc ....G 630 766-7667
Wood Dale *(G-21246)*
Technicraft Supply Co ....G 309 495-5245
Peoria *(G-16537)*
Teds Shirt Shack Inc ....G 217 224-9705
Quincy *(G-16946)*
Tfa Signs ....G 773 267-6007
Chicago *(G-6357)*
Thermo-Graphic LLC ....E 630 350-2226
Bensenville *(G-1901)*
Tierneys Signs Inc ....G 847 395-8224
Lake Villa *(G-12369)*
Timothy Anderson Corporation ....F 815 398-8371
Rockford *(G-17663)*
Timothy Darrey ....G 847 231-2277
Des Plaines *(G-7856)*
Toms Signs ....G 630 377-8525
Saint Charles *(G-18290)*
Trophytime Inc ....G 217 351-7958
Champaign *(G-3359)*
Turnroth Sign Company Inc ....F 815 625-1155
Rock Falls *(G-17198)*
Twin City Awards ....G 309 452-9291
Normal *(G-15226)*
Ultimate Sign Co ....G 773 282-4595
Chicago *(G-6458)*
Unistrut International Corp ....D 630 773-3460
Addison *(G-323)*
Varsity Striping & Cnstr Co ....E 217 352-2203
Champaign *(G-3362)*
▲ **Vindee Industries Inc** ....E 815 469-3300
Frankfort *(G-9850)*
Vinyl Graphics Inc ....G 708 579-1234
Countryside *(G-7077)*
Vision Signs Inc ....G 815 530-0870
Joliet *(G-11941)*
▲ **Visual Marketing Inc** ....E 312 664-9177
Chicago *(G-6559)*
Visual Marketing Solutions ....G 815 589-3848
Fulton *(G-10159)*
Visucom ....G 708 460-3001
Mokena *(G-14126)*
Vital Signs USA ....G 630 832-9600
Elmhurst *(G-9442)*
W G N Flag & Decorating Co ....F 773 768-8076
Chicago *(G-6573)*
▲ **Wagner Zip-Change Inc** ....E 708 681-4100
Melrose Park *(G-13926)*
Walnut Creek Hardwood ....G 815 389-3317
South Beloit *(G-19120)*
▲ **Watchfire Enterprises Inc** ....E 217 442-0611
Danville *(G-7393)*
◆ **Watchfire Signs LLC** ....B 217 442-0611
Danville *(G-7394)*
Watchfire Tech Holdings I Inc ....G 217 442-6971
Danville *(G-7395)*
Watchfire Tech Holdings II Inc ....G 217 442-0611
Danville *(G-7396)*
Wave Mechanics Neon ....G 312 829-9283
Chicago *(G-6591)*
Weakley Printing & Sign Shop ....G 847 473-4466
North Chicago *(G-15323)*
Weatherford Signs ....G 618 529-2000
Carbondale *(G-2864)*
Weiskamp Screen Printing ....G 217 398-8428
Champaign *(G-3370)*
West Zwick Corp ....G 217 222-0228
Quincy *(G-16955)*
Western Lighting Inc ....F 847 451-7200
Franklin Park *(G-10084)*
Western Remac Inc ....E 630 972-7770
Woodridge *(G-21347)*
White Way Sign & Maint Co ....C 847 391-0200
Chicago *(G-6619)*
Willdon Corp ....E 773 276-7080
Chicago *(G-6628)*
◆ **William Frick & Company** ....E 847 918-3700
Libertyville *(G-12725)*
Windy City Plastics Inc ....G 773 533-1099
Chicago *(G-6643)*
▲ **Wiremasters Incorporated** ....E 773 254-3700
Chicago *(G-6649)*

SIC

Employee Codes: A=Over 500 employees, B=251-500
C=101-250, D=51-100, E=20-50, F=10-19, G=3-9
2020 Harris Illinois
Industrial Directory
1019

39 MISCELLANEOUS MANUFACTURING INDUSTRIES

Wow Signs Inc .... G 847 910-4405
  Deerfield *(G-7662)*
Wright Quick Signs Inc .... G 708 652-6020
  Cicero *(G-6889)*
Xpressigns Inc .... G 888 303-0640
  Arlington Heights *(G-837)*
Xtrem Graphix Solutions Inc .... G 217 698-6424
  Springfield *(G-19469)*
Ye Olde Sign Shoppe .... G 847 228-7446
  Elk Grove Village *(G-9316)*
Zainab Enterprises Inc .... G 630 739-0110
  Romeoville *(G-17891)*
Zendavor Signs & Graphics Inc ..... G 309 691-8822
  Peoria *(G-16549)*
Zimmerman Enterprises Inc .... F 847 297-3177
  Des Plaines *(G-7871)*

3995 Burial Caskets

Dixline Corporation .... D 309 932-2011
  Galva *(G-10231)*
▲ Greenwood Inc .... F 800 798-4900
  Danville *(G-7341)*
Hoffman Burial Supplies Inc .... G 708 233-1567
  Bridgeview *(G-2355)*
J Garvin Industries Inc .... G 708 297-7400
  Posen *(G-16796)*
J Garvin Industries Inc .... G 708 297-7400
  Evergreen Park *(G-9595)*
Tolar Group LLC .... E 847 662-8000
  Waukegan *(G-20507)*

3996 Linoleum & Hard Surface Floor Coverings, NEC

Armstrong Flooring Inc .... B 815 939-2501
  Kankakee *(G-11958)*
Kitchen & Bath Gallery .... G 217 214-0310
  Quincy *(G-16900)*
Owens Corning Sales LLC .... E 708 594-6935
  Argo *(G-675)*
◆ Surface Shields Inc .... E 708 226-9810
  Tinley Park *(G-19859)*

3999 Manufacturing Industries, NEC

1803 Candles .... G 815 264-3009
  Waterman *(G-20297)*
3 Goldenstar Inc .... F 847 963-0451
  Palatine *(G-16088)*
3dp Unlimited LLC .... G 815 389-5667
  Roscoe *(G-17896)*
◆ 3M Dekalb Distribution .... E 815 756-5087
  Dekalb *(G-7664)*
425 Manufacturing .... G 815 873-7066
  Rockford *(G-17277)*
◆ A and T Cigarettes Imports .... G 847 836-9134
  East Dundee *(G-8186)*
A Stucki Company .... E 618 498-4442
  Jerseyville *(G-11785)*
A Wiley & Associates .... G 815 343-7401
  Ottawa *(G-16036)*
AAM Manufacturing .... G 708 606-9360
  Bolingbrook *(G-2144)*
ABC Beverage Mfg Inc .... G 708 449-2600
  Northlake *(G-15538)*
Acme Design Inc .... G 847 841-7400
  Elgin *(G-8492)*
Acme Finishing Company LLC .... F 847 640-7890
  Elk Grove Village *(G-8803)*
Acquired Sales Corp .... G 847 915-2446
  Lake Forest *(G-12219)*
Advance Manufacturing .... G 618 245-6515
  Farina *(G-9649)*
◆ Afam Concept Inc .... C 773 838-1336
  Chicago *(G-3578)*
Albert F Amling LLC .... C 630 333-1720
  Elmhurst *(G-9324)*
Alliance For Illinois Mfg .... G 773 594-9292
  Chicago *(G-3616)*
Alpha Industries Inc .... G 847 945-1740
  Deerfield *(G-7584)*
Amerex Corporation .... E 309 382-4389
  North Pekin *(G-15326)*
America Display Inc .... F 708 430-7000
  Bridgeview *(G-2322)*
American Fur Enterprises .... G 618 542-2018
  Du Quoin *(G-8115)*
American Tape Measures .... G 312 208-0282
  Chicago *(G-3670)*
Ameriguard Corporation .... G 630 986-1900
  Burr Ridge *(G-2652)*

Amk Enterprises Chicago Inc .... G 312 523-7212
  Chicago *(G-3681)*
Andrew C Arnold .... G 815 220-0282
  Peru *(G-16564)*
▲ Anfinsen Plastic Moulding Inc ... E 630 554-4100
  Oswego *(G-15992)*
Apollo Aerosol Industries LLC .... G 770 433-0210
  Downers Grove *(G-7953)*
Aquadine Inc .... G 800 497-3463
  Harvard *(G-11046)*
AR Industries .... G 630 543-0282
  Addison *(G-37)*
◆ Assemblers Inc .... G 773 378-3000
  Chicago *(G-3749)*
Associated Design Inc .... F 708 974-9100
  Palos Hills *(G-16195)*
▲ Atlas Manufacturing .... G 773 327-3005
  Chicago *(G-3765)*
Avondale Adventures .... G 773 588-5761
  Chicago *(G-3789)*
▲ AWego Enterprises Inc .... G 815 765-1957
  Belvidere *(G-1651)*
Axxent Energy Inc .... E 312 288-8640
  Chicago *(G-3797)*
B and B Amusement Illinois LLC ... G 309 585-2077
  Bloomington *(G-2025)*
◆ Badge-A-Minit Ltd .... G 815 883-8822
  Oglesby *(G-15839)*
Baessler Carl Dgn Mfg Rep .... G 779 994-4103
  Crystal Lake *(G-7167)*
▲ Baker Manufacturing LLC .... G 847 362-3663
  Lake Bluff *(G-12173)*
◆ Beachwaver Co .... E 201 751-5625
  Libertyville *(G-12637)*
Bella Casa .... G 630 455-5900
  Hinsdale *(G-11365)*
▲ Belvedere Usa LLC .... C 815 544-3131
  Belvidere *(G-1653)*
Bentleys Pet Stuff LLC .... G 847 793-0500
  Long Grove *(G-13157)*
Bentleys Pet Stuff LLC .... G 773 857-7600
  Chicago *(G-3869)*
▲ Bestpysanky Inc .... G 877 797-2659
  Morton Grove *(G-14391)*
Bezarr .... G 651 200-5641
  Willowbrook *(G-21031)*
Big City Sets Inc .... G 312 421-3210
  Chicago *(G-3881)*
Blac Cultivation LLC .... G 309 532-6325
  Normal *(G-15199)*
▼ Bocks Cattle-Identi Co Inc .... G 217 234-6634
  Mattoon *(G-13632)*
Bogart Industries LLC .... G 224 242-4578
  Elburn *(G-8446)*
Bone A Fide Pet Grooming .... G 217 872-0907
  Decatur *(G-7467)*
Boombox Beverage LLC .... G 312 607-1038
  Skokie *(G-18930)*
Bork Industries .... G 630 365-5517
  Maple Park *(G-13460)*
Borse Industries Inc .... G 630 325-1210
  Willowbrook *(G-21032)*
Boss Manufacturing Holdings ..... G 309 852-2131
  Kewanee *(G-12026)*
Boss Pet Products Inc .... G 216 332-0832
  Kewanee *(G-12027)*
Brees Studio Inc .... F 618 687-3331
  Murphysboro *(G-14752)*
Broc LLC .... F 773 709-9931
  Chicago *(G-3961)*
Buff & Go Inc .... F 773 719-4436
  Chicago *(G-3972)*
Buhrke Industries LLC .... E 630 412-2028
  Elk Grove Village *(G-8873)*
Burke Whistles Inc .... G 618 534-7953
  Murphysboro *(G-14753)*
Busy Beaver Button Company ... G 773 645-3359
  Chicago *(G-3985)*
Bw Industries .... G 630 784-1020
  Winfield *(G-21108)*
C Becky & Company Inc .... G 847 818-1021
  Mount Prospect *(G-14516)*
◆ C H Hanson Company .... D 630 848-2000
  Naperville *(G-14786)*
Candle Crest LLC .... G 815 704-3809
  Rockford *(G-17334)*
Candle Enterprises Inc .... G 618 526-8070
  Breese *(G-2300)*
Candle-Licious .... G 847 488-9982
  Morrison *(G-14341)*

Candleart Candle Company Inc ... G 217 925-5905
  Dieterich *(G-7875)*
Cane Plus .... G 217 522-4035
  Springfield *(G-19336)*
Capital Pttern Model Works Inc ... G 630 469-8200
  Glendale Heights *(G-10440)*
Cargo Support Industries Inc .... G 847 744-0786
  Inverness *(G-11599)*
Ccar Industries .... E 217 345-3300
  Charleston *(G-3397)*
Chicago Art Center Co .... G 773 817-2725
  Chicago *(G-4091)*
Chicago Candle Company .... G 773 637-5279
  Chicago *(G-4094)*
Chicago Scenic Studios Inc .... D 312 274-9900
  Chicago *(G-4127)*
Chronx Global Industries Ltd .... G 773 770-5753
  Round Lake *(G-18073)*
Cindys Nail & Hair Care .... G 847 234-0780
  Lake Forest *(G-12237)*
Circle T Manufacturing LLC .... G 217 728-4834
  Sullivan *(G-19665)*
Cleats Mfg Inc .... F 773 542-0453
  Chicago *(G-4176)*
Clown Global Brands LLC .... G 847 564-5950
  Northbrook *(G-15362)*
▲ Cobraco Manufacturing Inc ..... E 847 726-5800
  Lake Zurich *(G-12395)*
◆ Conair Corporation .... G 203 351-9000
  Rantoul *(G-16972)*
Consolidated Displays Co Inc ...... G 630 851-8666
  Oswego *(G-15998)*
CPM Industries .... G 630 469-8200
  Glendale Heights *(G-10446)*
Creative Werks LLC .... E 630 860-2222
  Bartlett *(G-1274)*
▲ Creative Werks LLC .... E 630 860-2222
  Elk Grove Village *(G-8920)*
Crystal Clear Cndle Design LLC ... F 847 749-4782
  Arlington Heights *(G-721)*
Crystal Nails McHenry .... G 815 363-5498
  McHenry *(G-13733)*
Cultivated Energy Group Inc .... G 312 203-8833
  Hebron *(G-11142)*
Curlee Mfg .... G 847 268-6517
  Rosemont *(G-18014)*
Custom Karts and More LLC .... G 815 703-6438
  Davis *(G-7416)*
◆ Dadant & Sons Inc .... D 217 847-3324
  Hamilton *(G-10954)*
Dal Acres West Kennel .... G 217 793-3647
  Springfield *(G-19359)*
◆ Denoyer - Geppert Science Co ... E 800 621-1014
  Skokie *(G-18948)*
▲ Design Plus Industries Inc ...... F 309 697-9778
  Peoria *(G-16430)*
Diamond Industries LLC .... G 612 859-1210
  Chicago *(G-4352)*
Diamond Quality Manufacturing .. G 815 521-4184
  Channahon *(G-3379)*
Discuss Music Education Co .... G 773 561-2796
  Chicago *(G-4365)*
DMJ Group Inc .... G 847 322-7533
  Algonquin *(G-371)*
◆ Dometic Corporation .... A 847 447-7190
  Rosemont *(G-18019)*
DPM Solutions LLC .... G 630 285-1170
  Addison *(G-98)*
Dura-Crafts Corp .... F 815 464-3561
  Frankfort *(G-9789)*
Dyno Manufacturing Inc .... G 618 451-6609
  Madison *(G-13409)*
E J Kupjack & Associates Inc ...... G 847 823-6661
  Chicago *(G-4424)*
E2 Manufacturing Group LLC ...... G 224 399-9608
  Waukegan *(G-20439)*
▲ Ecologic Industries LLC .... E 847 234-5855
  Waukegan *(G-20441)*
Edmark Visual Identification .... G 800 923-8333
  Chicago *(G-4452)*
Elan Furs .... F 317 255-6100
  Morton Grove *(G-14404)*
Elia Day Spa .... F 708 535-1450
  Oak Forest *(G-15676)*
Elite Industries .... G 224 433-6988
  Gurnee *(G-10876)*
Enz (usa) Inc .... G 630 692-7880
  Aurora *(G-958)*
Erell Manufacturing Company ... F 847 427-3000
  Elk Grove Village *(G-8982)*

Essentra Corp G 814 899-7671
Westchester (G-20697)
◆ Essentra Holdings Corp G 804 518-0322
Westchester (G-20698)
Evergreen Scale Models Inc F 224 567-8099
Des Plaines (G-7761)
Evo Exhibits LLC G 630 520-0710
West Chicago (G-20577)
Eyes Forward Innovations Corp G 281 755-5826
West Chicago (G-20581)
◆ First Alert Inc C 630 499-3295
Aurora (G-962)
Flame Guard Usa LLC G 815 219-4074
Vernon Hills (G-20054)
Flight Manufacturing Corp G 815 876-1616
Princeton (G-16809)
Floralstar Enterprises G 847 726-0124
Hawthorn Woods (G-11123)
Flurry Industries Inc G 630 882-8361
Yorkville (G-21482)
▲ Franklin Display Group Inc D 815 544-6676
Belvidere (G-1668)
Freitas P Sabah G 708 386-8934
Oak Park (G-15754)
Fun Industries Inc F 309 755-5021
East Moline (G-8226)
Fuyao Glass Illinois Inc C 217 864-2392
Decatur (G-7495)
G & M Industries Inc G 618 344-6655
Collinsville (G-6962)
Gabel & Schubert Bronze F 773 878-6800
Chicago (G-4653)
Galvanize Labs Inc G 630 258-1476
Palos Heights (G-16184)
Gateway Seed Company Inc G 618 327-8000
Nashville (G-14997)
Genetics Development Corp G 847 283-9780
Lake Bluff (G-12182)
Gillons Inc E 773 531-8900
Homewood (G-11495)
Gilster-Mary Lee Corporation G 618 826-3102
Chester (G-3455)
GM Partners G 847 895-7627
Schaumburg (G-18536)
Goble Manufacturing Inc G 217 932-5615
Casey (G-3202)
Gpi Prototype & Mfg Svcs LLC E 847 615-8900
Lake Bluff (G-12185)
◆ Grand Products Inc B 800 621-6101
Elk Grove Village (G-9020)
Grevan Enterprises Inc G 708 799-3422
Flossmoor (G-9699)
H and D Distribution Inc G 847 247-2011
Libertyville (G-12656)
▲ H Hal Kramer Co G 847 441-0213
Northfield (G-15516)
H V Manufacturing Vanguar G 847 229-5502
Wheeling (G-20905)
Hagen Manufacturing Inc G 224 735-2099
Wheeling (G-20906)
Hair Plus Studios LLC G 530 487-4247
Chicago (G-4768)
Hairline Creations Inc F 773 282-5454
Chicago (G-4769)
Heartland Candle Co G 815 698-2200
Ashkum (G-883)
Hendrick Manufacturing G 847 608-2047
Elgin (G-8611)
Houghton Mifflin Harcourt Co G 630 467-6049
Itasca (G-11666)
Houghton Mifflin Harcourt Co G 303 504-9312
Geneva (G-10276)
Houghton Mifflin Harcourt Co G 800 225-5425
Evanston (G-9533)
Hu-Friedy Mfg Co LLC F 847 257-4500
Des Plaines (G-7781)
▲ Hue Circle Inc G 224 567-8116
Glenview (G-10558)
▲ Hunter Mfg LLP D 859 254-7573
Lake Forest (G-12262)
I T C W Inc B 630 305-8849
Naperville (G-14842)
Igd Group LLC F 630 240-6736
Elmhurst (G-9374)
▲ Ihi Turbo America Co D 217 774-9571
Shelbyville (G-18880)
▲ Illinois Bottle Mfg Co D 847 595-9000
Elk Grove Village (G-9040)
Illumivation Studios LLC G 312 261-5561
Chicago (G-4892)
▼ Imagination Products Corp E 309 274-6223
Chillicothe (G-6818)
Imagine That Candle Co G 708 481-6370
Matteson (G-13625)
In Aaw Hair Emporium LLC G 779 227-1450
Joliet (G-11880)
Industrial Tech Centl LLC G 312 785-2520
Chicago (G-4911)
Infamous Industries Inc G 708 789-2326
Hickory Hills (G-11198)
Integrated Industries Inc G 773 299-1970
Chicago (G-4940)
▲ Integrated Mfg Tech LLC E 618 282-8306
Red Bud (G-16996)
Interesting Products Inc G 773 265-1100
Chicago (G-4944)
▼ Ironwood Manufacturing Inc G 630 969-1100
Naperville (G-14975)
▲ ITW Bldg Components Group G 847 634-1900
Glenview (G-10571)
J and J International G 847 842-8628
Barrington (G-1222)
J B Burling Group Ltd G 773 327-5362
Chicago (G-4986)
◆ James Coleman Company F 847 963-8100
Rolling Meadows (G-17742)
Jamtec USA LLC G 224 392-1258
Arlington Heights (G-760)
Jf Industries Inc G 773 775-8840
Chicago (G-5028)
▲ Jing MEI Industrial USA Inc E 847 671-0800
Rosemont (G-18028)
JM Industries LLC G 708 758-2600
Chicago Heights (G-6752)
Jr Industries LLC F 773 908-5317
Chicago (G-5056)
▲ K M I International Corp G 630 627-6300
Addison (G-166)
Kemis Kollections G 773 431-2307
Chicago (G-5094)
Kemp Manufacturing Company E 309 682-7292
Peoria (G-16465)
▲ Keys Manufacturing Company Inc E 217 465-4001
Paris (G-16231)
Km4 Manufacturing G 708 924-5150
Bedford Park (G-1476)
▲ Kmp Products LLC G 630 956-0438
Westmont (G-20754)
Knapheide Mfg Co E 217 223-1848
Quincy (G-16903)
Kop Industries Corporated Inc G 630 930-9516
Glen Ellyn (G-10407)
Kriese Mfg G 815 748-2683
Cortland (G-7023)
▲ Lcg Sales Inc D 773 378-7455
Chicago (G-5188)
◆ Learning Resources Inc D 847 573-8400
Vernon Hills (G-20072)
Learning Seed LLC G 847 540-8855
Chicago (G-5193)
Ledretrofitting Inc G 815 347-5047
Glen Ellyn (G-10408)
▲ Lenze Americas G 224 653-8119
Glendale Heights (G-10467)
Liv Labs Inc G 630 373-1471
Chicago (G-5240)
LMD Industries Inc G 630 383-9546
Oswego (G-16011)
Love Journey Inc G 773 447-5591
Chicago (G-5268)
Lumen Technologies Inc G 708 363-7758
Elmhurst (G-9395)
Lumentum Operations LLC G 408 546-5483
Chicago (G-5282)
Luminescence Media Group Nfp G 312 602-3302
Chicago (G-5285)
▲ Luxury Living Inc G 847 845-3863
Cary (G-3177)
M & A Grocery G 708 749-9786
Stickney (G-19543)
Mac Medical Inc F 618 719-6757
Belleville (G-1569)
Manhattan Eyelash EXT Sew On G 847 818-8774
Arlington Heights (G-774)
Marca Industries Inc G 773 884-4500
Burbank (G-2636)
Marking Specialists/Poly F 847 793-8100
Buffalo Grove (G-2568)
Marley Candles E 815 485-6604
Mokena (G-14097)
Masterbolt LLC F 847 834-5191
Lake In The Hills (G-12340)
Mat Capital LLC G 847 821-9630
Long Grove (G-13163)
Matrix Industries Inc G 847 975-7701
Wauconda (G-20374)
Mbs Manufacturing G 630 227-0300
Franklin Park (G-9986)
Mgn Tool & Mfg Co Inc G 630 849-3575
Carol Stream (G-3027)
Ml Vape Co F 815 582-3838
Joliet (G-11901)
▲ Midwest Foods Mfg Inc E 847 455-4636
Franklin Park (G-9999)
Midwest Nameplate Corp G 708 614-0606
Orland Park (G-15968)
▲ Ming Trading LLC G 773 442-2221
Chicago (G-5464)
Mint Masters Inc E 847 451-1133
Franklin Park (G-10000)
Models Plus Inc E 847 231-4300
Grayslake (G-10789)
▲ Modern Specialties Company G 312 648-5800
Chicago (G-5481)
Modern Sprout LLC G 312 342-2114
Chicago (G-5482)
Mold Repair and Manufacturing G 815 477-1332
Crystal Lake (G-7233)
▲ Molor Products Company F 630 375-5999
Oswego (G-16015)
▲ Mondelez Global LLC C 847 943-4000
Deerfield (G-7637)
Monty Burcenski G 815 838-0934
Lockport (G-13014)
Mp Manufacturing Inc G 815 334-1112
Woodstock (G-21414)
Murff Enterprises LLC G 203 685-5556
Chicago (G-5526)
Nature House Inc D 217 833-2393
Griggsville (G-10850)
Northfield Industries G 847 981-7530
Elk Grove Village (G-9154)
Northlake Industries G 847 358-6875
Palatine (G-16143)
Northwoods Wreaths Company E 847 615-9491
Lake Forest (G-12275)
Northwstern Globl Hlth Fndtion G 214 207-9485
Chicago (G-5626)
Nutraid Manufacturing G 847 214-4860
Elgin (G-8675)
Orbus Holdings Inc D 630 226-1155
Woodridge (G-21329)
▲ Orlandi Statuary Company D 773 489-0303
Chicago (G-5704)
Oval Fire Products Corporation G 630 635-5000
Glendale Heights (G-10482)
Ozcut Inc G 630 605-7398
Peru (G-16587)
Paradigm Development Group Inc F 847 545-9600
Winfield (G-21114)
Pawz & Klawz G 630 257-0245
Lemont (G-12580)
Pegasus Mfg Inc F 309 342-9337
Galesburg (G-10215)
Performance Manufacturing G 630 231-8099
West Chicago (G-20629)
▲ Pet Factory Inc C 847 837-8900
Mundelein (G-14724)
▲ Petote LLC G 312 455-0873
Chicago (G-5796)
▲ Phoenix Industries Inc G 708 478-5474
Mokena (G-14107)
▲ Plastic Container Corporation D 217 352-2722
Urbana (G-19993)
Platinum Touch Industries LLC G 773 775-9988
Des Plaines (G-7826)
Polish Your Lf Nail Salon LLC G 312 838-1018
Cicero (G-6870)
Posh Lash Inc G 630 388-6828
Chicago (G-5846)
Potash Holding Company Inc G 847 849-4200
Northbrook (G-15462)
▲ Prevue Pet Products Inc E 773 722-1052
Chicago (G-5870)
▲ Prime Vector International LLC G 847 348-1060
Palatine (G-16150)
Prospan Manufacturing G 847 815-0191
Rosemont (G-18044)
Prote USA LLC G 773 576-9079
Chicago (G-5905)

Employee Codes: A=Over 500 employees, B=251-500
C=101-250, D=51-100, E=20-50, F=10-19, G=3-9
2020 Harris Illinois
Industrial Directory
1021

Pru Dent Mfg Inc ....G 847 301-1170
Schaumburg ***(G-18687)***
Psimet LLC ....G 847 871-7005
Elgin ***(G-8703)***
Quad-Illinois Inc ....F 847 836-1115
Elgin ***(G-8706)***
◆ Quality Technology Intl Inc ....E 847 649-9300
Elgin ***(G-8709)***
R L Allen Industries ....G 618 667-2544
Troy ***(G-19919)***
▲ R S Owens & Co Inc ....B 773 282-6000
Chicago ***(G-5953)***
Ramona Sedivy ....G 630 983-1902
Naperville ***(G-14907)***
Replogle Globes Partners LLC ....G 708 593-3995
Hillside ***(G-11354)***
Research Mannikins Inc ....F 618 426-3456
Ava ***(G-1177)***
Ringmaster Mfg ....G 815 675-4230
Spring Grove ***(G-19299)***
▲ River City Sign Company Inc ....G 309 796-3606
Silvis ***(G-18909)***
Riverside Assessments LLC ....G 800 767-8420
Itasca ***(G-11725)***
Riverside Memorial Co ....G 217 323-1280
Beardstown ***(G-1450)***
Riverview Mfg House SA ....G 815 625-1459
Rock Falls ***(G-17193)***
Riviera Tan Spa ....G 618 466-1012
Godfrey ***(G-10661)***
▲ Roberts Colonial House Inc ....F 708 331-6233
South Holland ***(G-19241)***
Robs Aquatics ....G 708 444-7627
Tinley Park ***(G-19854)***
Rock Island Cannon Company ....G 309 786-1507
Rock Island ***(G-17245)***
Roll-A-Way Conveyors Inc ....F 847 336-5033
Gurnee ***(G-10924)***
▲ Rome Industries Inc ....G 309 691-7120
Peoria ***(G-16517)***
Roses Moulding By Design Inc ....E 847 549-9200
Mundelein ***(G-14733)***
Rudon Enterprises Inc ....G 618 457-0441
Carbondale ***(G-2857)***
S & S Mfg Solutions LLC ....G 815 838-1960
Lockport ***(G-13022)***
Sashe Lux LLC ....G 312 593-1379
Chicago ***(G-6106)***
Sassy Primitives Ltd ....G 815 385-9302
McCullom Lake ***(G-13712)***
Schmit Laboratories Inc ....E 773 476-0072
Glendale Heights ***(G-10491)***
Scientific Manufacturing Inc ....G 847 414-5658
Sleepy Hollow ***(G-19062)***
Scimatco Office ....E 630 879-1306
Batavia ***(G-1414)***
Scs Absorbent Mfg Inc ....G 502 417-1365
Monticello ***(G-14285)***
Sean Matthew Innovations Inc ....G 815 455-4525
Crystal Lake ***(G-7261)***
Shaw Industries ....G 847 844-9190
Elgin ***(G-8729)***
Shedrain Corporation ....G 708 848-5212
Oak Park ***(G-15772)***
Shermar Industries LLC ....G 847 378-8073
Des Plaines ***(G-7843)***
Singer Equities Inc ....F 815 874-5364
Rockford ***(G-17632)***
▲ Slagel Manufacturing Inc ....E 815 688-3318
Forrest ***(G-9738)***
Smith Industrial Rubber & Plas ....F 815 874-5364
Rockford ***(G-17636)***
Snowball Industries ....G 773 316-0051
Chicago ***(G-6195)***
Sport Electronics Inc ....G 847 564-5575
Northbrook ***(G-15485)***
Star Freeport Company LLC ....E 815 758-6400
Freeport ***(G-10145)***
Star Lite Mfg ....G 630 595-8338
Wood Dale ***(G-21243)***
State Street Jewelers Inc ....F 630 232-2085
Geneva ***(G-10307)***
▲ Stellar Recognition Inc ....D 773 282-8060
Chicago ***(G-6243)***
Steve C Gough ....G 618 529-7423
Carbondale ***(G-2860)***
Sturtevant Inc ....G 630 613-8968
Lombard ***(G-13135)***
Sun Pattern & Model Inc ....E 630 293-3366
West Chicago ***(G-20648)***
▲ Sunscape Time Inc ....G 708 345-8791
Melrose Park ***(G-13919)***
Synergetic Industries ....G 309 321-8145
Morton ***(G-14385)***
T P R Resources Inc ....G 630 443-9060
Saint Charles ***(G-18284)***
Tank In A Box LLC ....G 847 624-1234
Chicago ***(G-6322)***
Tatine ....G 312 733-0173
Chicago ***(G-6329)***
◆ Technical Power Systems Inc ....E 630 719-1471
Lisle ***(G-12949)***
Thrilled LLC ....G 312 404-1929
Chicago ***(G-6373)***
Tii Technical Educatn Systems ....G 847 428-3085
Gilberts ***(G-10373)***
Timber Industries LLC ....E 815 857-3674
Dixon ***(G-7922)***
Tiny Human Food Inc ....G 630 397-9936
Naperville ***(G-14934)***
Tishma Engineering LLC ....G 847 755-1200
Elk Grove Village ***(G-9275)***
Top Dollar Slots ....G 779 210-4884
Loves Park ***(G-13276)***
◆ Tradex International Inc ....D 216 651-4788
Elwood ***(G-9465)***
Trident Industries ....F 847 285-1316
Schaumburg ***(G-18757)***
Tropar Trophy Manufacturing Co ....E 630 787-1900
Wood Dale ***(G-21252)***
Trustar Holdings LLC ....G 847 598-8800
Schaumburg ***(G-18759)***
Truvanity Beauty LLC ....G 312 778-6499
Chicago ***(G-6441)***
Two Cards Innovation LLC ....G 815 793-2517
Rockton ***(G-17705)***
Twoinspireyou LLC ....G 630 849-8214
Geneva ***(G-10314)***
UIC ....F 312 413-7697
Chicago ***(G-6456)***
▼ US International Inc ....G 312 671-9207
Chicago ***(G-6501)***
Utlx Manufacturing Inc ....G 312 431-3111
Chicago ***(G-6509)***
◆ Veeco Manufacturing Inc ....F 312 666-0900
Melrose Park ***(G-13925)***
Vim Recyclers LP ....C 630 892-2559
Aurora ***(G-1166)***
Visionary Solutions Inc ....G 847 296-9615
Des Plaines ***(G-7865)***
◆ Wahl Clipper Corporation ....A 815 625-6525
Sterling ***(G-19540)***
Wahl Clipper Corporation ....F 815 625-6525
Sterling ***(G-19541)***
Waterway Rv LLC Mfg Home ....G 312 207-1835
Chicago ***(G-6590)***
Waxman Candles Inc ....G 773 929-3000
Chicago ***(G-6593)***
Western Sand & Gravel Co ....F 815 433-1600
Ottawa ***(G-16085)***
Wexford Home Corp ....G 331 225-0979
Countryside ***(G-7078)***
Whyte Gate Incorporated ....F 847 201-7000
Grayslake ***(G-10804)***
Wielgus Product Models Inc ....E 312 432-1950
Chicago ***(G-6624)***
Williams Electronic Games De ....B 773 961-1000
Chicago ***(G-6630)***
Williams Electronic Games De ....G 773 961-1000
Chicago ***(G-6631)***
◆ Wilton Brands Inc ....F 815 823-8547
Joliet ***(G-11945)***
Wingfield Manufacturing LLC ....G 800 637-6712
Urbana ***(G-20003)***
Wish Bone Rescue ....G 309 212-9210
Bloomington ***(G-2108)***
WMS Games Inc ....F 773 728-2300
Chicago ***(G-6657)***
WMS Gaming Inc ....C 773 961-1747
Chicago ***(G-6658)***
◆ WMS Gaming Inc ....A 773 961-1000
Chicago ***(G-6659)***
WMS Industries Inc ....E 847 785-3000
Chicago ***(G-6660)***
Write Stuff ....G 630 365-4425
Saint Charles ***(G-18303)***
Xd Industries Inc ....G 847 293-0796
Prospect Heights ***(G-16849)***
Xl Manufacture ....G 773 271-8900
Chicago ***(G-6695)***
Yetter M Co Inc Emp B Tr ....G 309 776-4111
Colchester ***(G-6947)***
Yetter Manufacturing Company ....E 309 833-1445
Macomb ***(G-13403)***
Zeta Manufacturing Company ....G 708 301-3766
Crete ***(G-7147)***
Zing Enterprises LLC ....G 608 201-9490
Oswego ***(G-16034)***

73 BUSINESS SERVICES

7372 Prepackaged Software

3vue LLC ....G 630 796-7441
Woodridge ***(G-21270)***
4c Insights Inc ....F 602 881-9127
Chicago ***(G-3471)***
4degrees AV Inc ....G 903 253-7398
Chicago ***(G-3472)***
4ever Printing Inc ....G 847 222-1525
Arlington Heights ***(G-679)***
A M P Software Inc ....G 630 240-5922
Elk Grove Village ***(G-8792)***
A Trustworthy Sup Source Inc ....G 773 480-0255
Chicago ***(G-3492)***
Abki Tech Service Inc ....F 847 818-8403
Des Plaines ***(G-7721)***
Above Waves Inc ....G 708 341-9123
Mokena ***(G-14068)***
Access International Inc ....E 312 920-9366
Chicago ***(G-3514)***
Accuity Inc ....B 847 676-9600
Evanston ***(G-9486)***
Accuware Incorporated ....F 630 858-8409
Glen Ellyn ***(G-10393)***
Acp Tower Holdings LLC ....C 800 835-8527
Chicago ***(G-3531)***
Acresso Software Inc ....G 408 642-3865
Schaumburg ***(G-18426)***
Active Simulations Inc ....G 630 747-8393
Oak Park ***(G-15740)***
Adams Telephone Co-Operative ....E 217 224-9566
Quincy ***(G-16850)***
Adaptive Testing Tech Inc ....F 312 878-6490
Chicago ***(G-3539)***
Adept Coalescence LLC ....G 440 503-1808
Rockford ***(G-17295)***
Adeptia Inc ....E 312 229-1727
Chicago ***(G-3543)***
Adesso Solutions LLC ....F 847 342-1095
Rolling Meadows ***(G-17709)***
Adflow Networks ....G 866 423-3569
Chicago ***(G-3544)***
Aerial Intelligence Inc ....F 312 914-1259
Chicago ***(G-3571)***
Aeverie Inc ....G 844 238-3743
Buffalo Grove ***(G-2505)***
Agile Health Technologies Inc ....E 331 457-5167
Naperville ***(G-14952)***
Aginity Inc ....D 224 307-2656
Evanston ***(G-9489)***
Ahead Inc ....A 312 753-7967
Oak Brook ***(G-15589)***
Ahead Inc ....D 312 924-4492
Chicago ***(G-3584)***
Ahead Data Blue LLC ....G 866 577-2902
Chicago ***(G-3585)***
Airport Park and Fly LLC ....G 708 310-2442
Chicago ***(G-3590)***
Akamai Technologies Inc ....E 312 893-7900
Chicago ***(G-3593)***
Alliance Technology MGT Corp ....G 847 574-9752
Northfield ***(G-15504)***
Allscripts Healthcare LLC ....G 312 506-1200
Chicago ***(G-3621)***
Allscripts Holdings LLC ....G 800 334-8534
Chicago ***(G-3622)***
Allscrpts Hlthcare Sltions Inc ....C 800 334-8534
Chicago ***(G-3623)***
Amada America Inc ....G 877 262-3287
Itasca ***(G-11620)***
Amariko Inc ....G 630 734-1000
Clarendon Hills ***(G-6899)***
◆ American Labelmark Company ....C 773 478-0900
Chicago ***(G-3656)***
Amoco Technology Company ....C 312 861-6000
Chicago ***(G-3682)***
Angsten Group Inc ....G 888 222-7126
Elgin ***(G-8511)***
Anju Software Inc ....E 630 243-9810
Lisle ***(G-12866)***

Anylogic N Amer Ltd Lblty Co ...F ... 312 635-3344 Oakbrook Terrace *(G-15785)*
Applied Systems Inc ...A ... 708 534-5575 University Park *(G-19946)*
Approved Contact LLC ...G ... 800 449-7137 Springfield *(G-19319)*
Appsanity Advisory LLC ...G ... 847 638-1172 Winnetka *(G-21125)*
Aprimo US LLC ...D ... 877 794-8556 Chicago *(G-3715)*
Aptean Inc ...F ... 773 975-3100 Chicago *(G-3716)*
Aqueous Solutions LLC ...F ... 217 531-1206 Champaign *(G-3266)*
AR Inet Corp ...G ... 603 380-3903 Aurora *(G-913)*
Ariba Inc ...G ... 630 649-7600 Lisle *(G-12868)*
Armarius Software Inc ...G ... 630 639-6332 Aurora *(G-914)*
Arvamont ...G ... 630 926-2468 Hinsdale *(G-11361)*
Ascent Innovations LLC ...E ... 847 572-8000 Schaumburg *(G-18445)*
Askric LLC ...G ... 309 360-3125 Germantown Hills *(G-10333)*
Associate Computer Systems ...G ... 618 997-3653 Marion *(G-13505)*
Associated Agri-Business Inc ...G ... 618 498-2977 Jerseyville *(G-11786)*
Associated Agri-Business Inc ...G ... 618 498-2977 Eldred *(G-8487)*
Ats Communications Netwrk Corp ...G ... 309 673-6733 Peoria *(G-16388)*
Auto Injury Solutions Inc ...E ... 312 229-2704 Chicago *(G-3775)*
Automated Insights Inc ...C ... 919 442-8865 Chicago *(G-3776)*
◆ Autonomous Stuff LLC ...G ... 309 291-0966 Morton *(G-14353)*
Avaya Inc ...F ... 847 885-3598 Schaumburg *(G-18452)*
Axiomatics Inc ...F ... 312 374-3443 Chicago *(G-3794)*
Bantix Technologies LLC ...G ... 630 446-0886 Glen Ellyn *(G-10396)*
Banyan Technologies Inc ...G ... 312 967-9885 Chicago *(G-3826)*
Barcodesource Inc ...G ... 630 545-9590 Glen Ellyn *(G-10397)*
Bc Asi Capital II Inc ...A ... 708 534-5575 University Park *(G-19948)*
Bdna Corporation ...D ... 650 625-9530 Itasca *(G-11627)*
Beacon Annuity Solutions LLC ...G ... 847 864-5447 Northfield *(G-15507)*
Bi Software Inc ...G ... 224 622-4706 Hoffman Estates *(G-11408)*
Big Game Software LLC ...F ... 630 592-8082 Elmhurst *(G-9333)*
Bighand Inc ...F ... 312 893-5906 Chicago *(G-3884)*
Bigtime Software Inc ...E ... 312 346-4646 Chicago *(G-3885)*
Bitsio Inc ...G ... 217 793-2827 Springfield *(G-19327)*
Blue Software LLC ...D ... 773 957-1600 Chicago *(G-3914)*
BMC Software Inc ...E ... 331 777-8700 Oakbrook Terrace *(G-15790)*
Braindok LLC ...G ... 847 877-1586 Buffalo Grove *(G-2520)*
Brainware Company ...G ... 773 250-6465 Chicago *(G-3943)*
Brechts Database Solutions ...G ... 618 654-6960 Highland *(G-11205)*
Brevity LLC ...F ... 949 250-0701 Chicago *(G-3951)*
Bridgeline Digital Inc ...G ... 312 784-5720 Chicago *(G-3955)*
Brokerassist LLC ...G ... 847 858-2357 River Forest *(G-17050)*
Bundlar LLC ...G ... 773 839-3976 Chicago *(G-3974)*
Business Systems Consultants ...F ... 312 553-1253 Chicago *(G-3981)*
Busways LLC ...G ... 617 697-2009 Chicago *(G-3984)*
Buyersvine Inc ...G ... 630 235-6804 Hinsdale *(G-11367)*
Bytebin LLC ...G ... 312 286-0740 Chicago *(G-3989)*
C W Publications Inc ...G ... 800 554-5537 Sterling *(G-19502)*
Ca Inc ...G ... 312 201-8557 Chicago *(G-3998)*
Call Potential LLC ...F ... 877 552-2557 Naperville *(G-14787)*
Capers North America LLC ...F ... 708 995-7500 Willowbrook *(G-21034)*
Capital Merchant Solutions Inc ...F ... 309 452-5990 Bloomington *(G-2030)*
Capsim MGT Simulations Inc ...E ... 312 477-7200 Chicago *(G-4019)*
Carlease Inc ...F ... 847 714-1414 Northbrook *(G-15352)*
Cassetica Software Inc ...G ... 312 546-3668 Chicago *(G-4035)*
Catalytic Inc ...E ... 844 787-4268 Chicago *(G-4041)*
Catapult Communications Corp ...G ... 847 884-0048 Schaumburg *(G-18468)*
CDK Global Inc ...A ... 847 397-1700 Hoffman Estates *(G-11412)*
Centrex Technologies LLC ...G ... 800 768-0700 Oak Brook *(G-15605)*
Ch Group Holdings Inc ...G ... 888 428-6614 Schaumburg *(G-18473)*
Champion Medical Tech Inc ...E ... 866 803-3720 Lake Zurich *(G-12392)*
Chartnet Technologies Inc ...F ... 630 385-4100 Yorkville *(G-21475)*
Cheetah Digital Inc ...D ... 312 858-8200 Chicago *(G-4081)*
Chewy Software LLC ...G ... 773 935-2627 Chicago *(G-4084)*
Chicago Data Solutions Inc ...G ... 847 370-4609 Willowbrook *(G-21035)*
Chwey Software LLC ...E ... 773 525-6445 Chicago *(G-4149)*
Cision Ltd ...E ... 866 639-5087 Chicago *(G-4153)*
Cityzenith LLC ...F ... 312 883-5554 Chicago *(G-4164)*
Classroom Technologies LLC ...F ... 708 548-1642 Frankfort *(G-9780)*
Clean Coders LLC ...G ... 847 370-4098 Libertyville *(G-12643)*
Cleartrial LLC ...F ... 877 206-4846 Chicago *(G-4174)*
Cleo Communications Inc ...E ... 815 654-8110 Rockford *(G-17353)*
Cliqster LLC ...G ... 847 732-1457 Highland Park *(G-11259)*
Cloud 9 Infosystems Inc ...C ... 855 225-6839 Downers Grove *(G-7974)*
Cognizant Tech Solutions Corp ...E ... 630 955-0617 Lisle *(G-12877)*
Comdata Inc ...G ... 630 847-6988 Somonauk *(G-19069)*
Common Goal Systems Inc ...E ... 630 592-4200 Elmhurst *(G-9351)*
Comptia Learning LLC ...F ... 630 678-8490 Downers Grove *(G-7977)*
Compusystems Inc ...C ... 708 344-9070 Downers Grove *(G-7978)*
Computer Maintenance Inc ...G ... 630 953-1555 Addison *(G-79)*
▼ Computer Pwr Solutions III Ltd ...E ... 618 281-8898 Columbia *(G-6988)*
Computer Svcs & Consulting Inc ...E ... 855 482-2267 Burr Ridge *(G-2666)*
Computerized Fleet Analysis ...G ... 630 543-1410 Addison *(G-80)*
Computhink Inc ...E ... 630 705-9050 Lombard *(G-13057)*
Computing Integrity Inc ...G ... 217 355-4469 Champaign *(G-3282)*
Comvigo Inc ...G ... 312 933-3385 Willowbrook *(G-21037)*
Condata Global Inc ...E ... 708 390-2500 Mokena *(G-14076)*
Configure One Inc ...E ... 630 368-9950 Oak Brook *(G-15612)*
Connelly & Associates ...E ... 847 372-5001 Palatine *(G-16103)*
Conor Sports LLC ...G ... 847 903-6639 Chicago *(G-4221)*
Conscisys Corp ...E ... 630 810-4444 Downers Grove *(G-7979)*
Convr Enterprises Inc ...E ... 888 507-9733 Schaumburg *(G-18490)*
Coorens Communications Inc ...G ... 773 235-8688 Chicago *(G-4233)*
Cozent LLC ...G ... 630 781-2822 Naperville *(G-14810)*
Createasoft Inc ...F ... 630 851-9474 Aurora *(G-943)*
Credit & Management Systems ...F ... 618 654-3500 Highland *(G-11211)*
Crestwood Associates LLC ...F ... 847 394-8820 Schaumburg *(G-18495)*
Crowdmatrix Fx LLC ...G ... 312 329-1170 Chicago *(G-4275)*
Crowdsource Solutions Inc ...G ... 855 276-9376 Swansea *(G-19691)*
Cunningham Electronics Corp ...G ... 618 833-7775 Anna *(G-582)*
Cyborg Systems Inc ...C ... 312 279-7000 Chicago *(G-4293)*
Datafordummies ...G ... 618 421-2323 Flat Rock *(G-9671)*
Datair Employee Benefit Systems ...E ... 630 325-2600 Westmont *(G-20734)*
Datix (usa) Inc ...G ... 312 724-7776 Chicago *(G-4322)*
David Corporation ...E ... 781 587-3008 Chicago *(G-4324)*
Decision Systems Company ...G ... 815 885-3000 Roscoe *(G-17902)*
Delante Group Inc ...G ... 312 493-4371 Chicago *(G-4332)*
Dell Software Inc ...D ... 630 836-0503 Buffalo Grove *(G-2531)*
Designa Access Corporation ...E ... 630 891-3105 Westmont *(G-20737)*
Dev Base LLC ...E ... 319 321-3014 Chicago *(G-4346)*
Devnet Incorporated ...E ... 815 899-6850 Sycamore *(G-19707)*
Digi Trax Corporation ...E ... 847 613-2100 Lincolnshire *(G-12759)*
Digital Ignite LLC ...F ... 630 317-7904 Lombard *(G-13066)*
Digital Minds Inc ...G ... 847 430-3390 Rosemont *(G-18017)*
Digital Realty Inc ...E ... 630 428-7979 Naperville *(G-14817)*
Docket Technologies Inc ...G ... 415 489-0127 Chicago *(G-4377)*
Drawn LLC ...E ... 312 982-0040 Chicago *(G-4397)*
Dynami Solutions LLC ...G ... 618 363-2771 Edwardsville *(G-8357)*
Earshot Inc ...F ... 773 383-1798 Chicago *(G-4433)*
Easy Ware Corp ...G ... 773 755-7732 Chicago *(G-4437)*
Eatsee Inc ...G ... 312 846-1492 Chicago *(G-4438)*
Ecd-Network LLC ...G ... 917 670-0821 Chicago *(G-4444)*
Education Equity Inc ...B ... 800 339-7985 Chicago *(G-4457)*
Effici Inc ...G ... 401 584-2266 Schaumburg *(G-18515)*
Eighty Nine Robotics LLC ...G ... 512 573-9091 Chicago *(G-4463)*
Electronics Boutique Amer Inc ...G ... 618 465-3125 Alton *(G-555)*
Elitegen Corp ...F ... 630 637-6917 Naperville *(G-14823)*
Embassy Security Group Inc ...E ... 800 627-1325 Mokena *(G-14079)*
Embedur Systems Inc ...G ... 847 749-3665 Rolling Meadows *(G-17731)*
EMC Corporation ...D ... 630 505-3273 Lisle *(G-12887)*
Emx Digital LLC ...G ... 212 792-6810 Chicago *(G-4503)*
Endure Holdings Inc ...G ... 224 558-1828 Bloomingdale *(G-1992)*
Energy Services Group LLC ...G ... 630 581-4840 Oak Brook *(G-15616)*
Enrollment Rx LLC ...F ... 847 233-0088 Schiller Park *(G-18804)*
Entappia LLC ...G ... 630 546-4531 Aurora *(G-957)*
Entience ...G ... 217 649-2590 Urbana *(G-19982)*

SIC

Employee Codes: A=Over 500 employees, B=251-500
C=101-250, D=51-100, E=20-50, F=10-19, G=3-9
2020 Harris Illinois
Industrial Directory
1023

73 BUSINESS SERVICES SIC SECTION

Envestnet Inc....G.... 866 924-8912
Chicago (G-4517)
Envestnet Inc....C.... 312 827-2800
Chicago (G-4518)
Envestnet Rtrment Slutions LLC....G.... 312 827-7957
Chicago (G-4519)
Environmental Systems Res Inst....G.... 312 609-0966
Chicago (G-4520)
▲ Ep Technology Corporation USA....D.... 217 351-7888
Champaign (G-3290)
Epazz Inc....G.... 312 955-8161
Wheeling (G-20892)
Epublishing Inc....G.... 312 768-6800
Chicago (G-4522)
Equilibrium Contact Center Inc....G.... 888 708-1405
Rockford (G-17398)
Equisoft Inc....G.... 815 629-2789
Winnebago (G-21119)
Equity Concepts Co Inc....G.... 815 226-1300
Rockford (G-17399)
Evention LLC....E.... 773 733-4256
Chicago (G-4539)
Eyelation Inc....F.... 888 308-4703
Tinley Park (G-19826)
Family Time Computing Inc....F.... 309 664-1742
Bloomington (G-2041)
Ferenbach Marucco Stoddard....E.... 217 698-3535
Springfield (G-19366)
Fibroblast Inc....F.... 800 396-6463
Chicago (G-4586)
▲ Fivecubits Inc....G.... 630 749-4182
Oak Brook (G-15620)
Fleetwood Press Inc....G.... 708 485-6811
Brookfield (G-2483)
Flexera Holdings LP....G.... 847 466-4000
Itasca (G-11659)
Flexera Software LLC....A.... 847 466-4000
Itasca (G-11660)
Floydware LLC....G.... 630 469-1078
Lombard (G-13077)
Focus Health and Fitness LLC....G.... 847 975-8687
Woodstock (G-21389)
Follett School Solutions Inc....C.... 815 759-1700
McHenry (G-13745)
Forecast 5 Analytics Inc....E.... 630 955-7500
Naperville (G-14830)
Forte Incorporated....G.... 815 224-8300
La Salle (G-12112)
Foster Learning LLC....G.... 618 656-6836
Edwardsville (G-8362)
Fresh Software Solutions LLC....G.... 630 995-4350
Naperville (G-14831)
Friedman Corporation....E.... 847 948-7180
Rosemont (G-18024)
Friedrich Klatt and Associates....G.... 773 753-1806
Chicago (G-4636)
G2 Crowd Inc....D.... 847 748-7559
Chicago (G-4652)
Gather Voices Inc....G.... 312 476-9465
Chicago (G-4661)
GE Intelligent Platforms Inc....D.... 630 829-4000
Lisle (G-12894)
Genisys Decision Corporation....G.... 708 524-5100
Oak Park (G-15755)
Glidera Inc....G.... 773 350-4000
Elmhurst (G-9368)
Global Tech & Resources Inc....G.... 630 364-4260
Rolling Meadows (G-17734)
Go Mango Interactive Corp....G.... 224 214-9528
Mundelein (G-14690)
Goeducation LLC....G.... 312 800-1838
Chicago (G-4709)
Govqa Inc....F.... 630 985-1300
Woodridge (G-21305)
Great Software Laboratory Inc....G.... 630 655-8905
Chicago (G-4738)
Gtx Surgery Inc....G.... 847 920-8489
Evanston (G-9528)
Guidance Software Inc....G.... 847 994-7324
Chicago (G-4751)
H&R Block Inc....F.... 847 566-5557
Mundelein (G-14694)
▲ Havi Global Solutions LLC....B.... 630 493-7400
Downers Grove (G-8018)
Healthcare Research LLC....F.... 773 592-3508
Chicago (G-4792)
Healthy-Txt LLC....G.... 630 945-1787
Chicago (G-4794)
Help/Systems LLC....G.... 847 605-1311
Schaumburg (G-18547)

Hera Cnsltng Interntnl Opratn....F.... 630 515-8819
Lisle (G-12897)
High Tech Research Inc....F.... 847 215-9797
Deerfield (G-7615)
Hostforweb Incorporated....G.... 312 343-4678
Chicago (G-4845)
Hucuai LLC....G.... 312 608-6101
Chicago (G-4860)
Humaginarium LLC....G.... 312 788-7719
Oak Park (G-15757)
Hybris (us) Corporation....E.... 312 265-5010
Chicago (G-4861)
Hyperera Inc....F.... 312 842-2288
Chicago (G-4865)
I2c LLC....G.... 630 281-2330
Naperville (G-14843)
Idevconcepts Inc....G.... 312 351-1615
Chicago (G-4877)
Iep Quality Inc....G.... 217 840-0570
Champaign (G-3305)
Ifs North America Inc....E.... 888 437-4968
Itasca (G-11670)
Illinois Assn Cnty Officials....F.... 217 585-9065
Springfield (G-19385)
Illumen Studios LLC....G.... 847 440-2222
Grayslake (G-10782)
Imaging Systems Inc....F.... 630 875-1100
Itasca (G-11674)
Imanage LLC....C.... 312 667-7000
Chicago (G-4895)
Imcp Inc....G.... 630 477-8600
Itasca (G-11675)
Independent Network Tv LLC....G.... 312 953-8508
Forest Park (G-9720)
Industrial Finance Systems....G.... 847 592-0200
Itasca (G-11676)
Industrial Phrm Resources Inc....F.... 630 823-4700
Bartlett (G-1290)
Infiniscene Inc....G.... 630 567-0452
Chicago (G-4912)
Infinite Cnvrgnce Slutions Inc....G.... 224 764-3400
Arlington Heights (G-758)
Infogix Inc....C.... 630 505-1800
Naperville (G-14846)
Infor (us) Inc....D.... 312 279-1245
Chicago (G-4914)
Informatica LLC....G.... 360 393-7576
Naperville (G-14847)
Information Builders Inc....E.... 630 971-6700
Schaumburg (G-18558)
Information Resources Inc....G.... 312 474-3380
Chicago (G-4917)
Information Resources Inc....B.... 312 474-3154
Bartlett (G-1255)
Information Resources Inc....A.... 312 474-8900
Chicago (G-4918)
Infosys Limited....E.... 630 482-5000
Lisle (G-12901)
Injury Sciences LLC....F.... 210 691-0674
Chicago (G-4925)
Innerworkings Inc....D.... 312 642-3700
Chicago (G-4927)
Innolitica Labs LLC....G.... 224 434-1238
Chicago (G-4928)
▲ Innovations For Learning Inc....G.... 800 975-3452
Evanston (G-9539)
Innovative Custom Software Inc....G.... 630 892-5022
Aurora (G-983)
Innovative SEC Systems Inc....F.... 217 355-6308
Savoy (G-18414)
Inrule Technology Inc....E.... 312 648-1800
Chicago (G-4933)
Instana Inc....G.... 415 340-2777
Chicago (G-4936)
Intel Corporation....D.... 408 765-8080
Chicago (G-4941)
Intermedix Holdings Inc....G.... 312 324-7820
Chicago (G-4948)
Intravation Inc....G.... 847 299-6423
Des Plaines (G-7789)
Invisible Institute....G.... 415 669-4691
Chicago (G-4964)
Ironsafe LLC....G.... 877 297-1833
Naperville (G-14851)
Isewa LLC....G.... 847 877-1586
Buffalo Grove (G-2551)
Isoprime Corporation....G.... 630 737-0963
Lisle (G-12902)
Janitor Ltd....G.... 773 936-3389
Chicago (G-5004)

Jellyvision Inc....D.... 312 266-0606
Chicago (G-5015)
Jlg Innovations Inc....G.... 618 363-2323
Breese (G-2305)
John Galt Development Inc....G.... 312 701-9026
Chicago (G-5040)
Jones Software Corp....G.... 312 952-0011
Chicago (G-5047)
Juniper Networks Inc....E.... 773 632-1200
Chicago (G-5060)
K-Tron Inc....G.... 708 460-2128
Orland Park (G-15964)
Kana Software Inc....G.... 312 447-5600
Chicago (G-5079)
Key Resources Inc....G.... 800 574-1339
Lake Villa (G-12357)
Kinaxis Corp....F.... 613 592-5780
Chicago (G-5105)
King of Software Inc....G.... 847 354-8745
Des Plaines (G-7793)
Knowledgeshift Inc....G.... 630 221-8759
Wheaton (G-20809)
Konveau Inc....G.... 312 476-9385
Chicago (G-5122)
Koombea Inc....G.... 408 786-5290
Chicago (G-5123)
Kronos Incorporated....F.... 847 969-6501
Schaumburg (G-18592)
Ksr Software LLC....G.... 847 705-0100
Palatine (G-16135)
L Street Collaborative LLC....F.... 630 243-5783
Chicago (G-5143)
L-Data Corporation....E.... 312 552-7855
Chicago (G-5144)
Larsen & Toubro Infotech Ltd....G.... 847 303-3900
Schaumburg (G-18600)
Lattice Incorporated....E.... 630 949-3250
Wheaton (G-20811)
Lbe Ltd....G.... 847 907-4959
Kildeer (G-12050)
Legal Files Software Inc....E.... 217 726-6000
Springfield (G-19398)
Legistek Corporation....G.... 312 399-4891
Chicago (G-5201)
Lexray LLC....F.... 630 664-6740
Downers Grove (G-8044)
Liaison Home Automation LLC....G.... 888 279-1235
Decatur (G-7517)
Liders LLC....G.... 312 873-1112
Chicago (G-5219)
Linkedhealth Solutions....F.... 312 600-6684
Chicago (G-5230)
Liquidfire....G.... 312 376-7448
Chicago (G-5234)
Loadsys Consulting Inc....G.... 708 873-1750
Bourbonnais (G-2265)
Localfix Solutions LLC....G.... 312 569-0619
Winfield (G-21112)
Logical Design Solutions Inc....G.... 630 786-5999
Naperville (G-14865)
Logicgate Inc....C.... 312 279-2775
Chicago (G-5250)
Lonelybrand LLC....G.... 312 880-7506
Chicago (G-5254)
Lottobot LLC....G.... 773 909-6656
Chicago (G-5265)
LP Software Inc....G.... 708 361-4310
Orland Park (G-15966)
Lutheran Church-Missouri Synod....E.... 630 607-0300
Oak Brook (G-15638)
M&M Restaurant Group LLC....F.... 773 253-5326
Chicago (G-5307)
Manscore LLC....G.... 630 297-7502
Downers Grove (G-8050)
Manufacturing Tech Group Inc....G.... 815 966-2300
Rockford (G-17504)
Marin Software Incorporated....G.... 312 267-2083
Chicago (G-5338)
McConnell Chase Software Works....G.... 312 540-1508
Chicago (G-5374)
Mealplot Inc....G.... 217 419-2681
Champaign (G-3319)
Mediafly Inc....E.... 312 281-5175
Chicago (G-5384)
Mediaocean....F.... 312 676-4646
Chicago (G-5385)
Memorable Inc....G.... 847 272-8207
Northbrook (G-15431)
Message Mediums LLC....F.... 312 566-4300
Chicago (G-5403)

SIC SECTION
73 BUSINESS SERVICES

Company	Code	Phone
Metamation Inc, Hoffman Estates (G-11434)	F	775 826-1717
Michaels Ross and Cole Inc, Oak Brook (G-15644)	F	630 916-0662
Micrograms Inc, Rockford (G-17523)	G	815 877-4455
Microsoft Corporation, Evanston (G-9552)	E	847 864-4777
Microsoft Corporation, Downers Grove (G-8055)	D	630 725-4000
Microsoft Corporation, Bloomington (G-2077)	D	309 665-0113
Microsoft Corporation, Northlake (G-15551)	D	708 409-4759
Mike Howerton, Quincy (G-16916)	G	217 242-9676
Mirus Research, Normal (G-15210)	E	309 828-3100
Mobile 7 Group Inc, Chicago Heights (G-6760)	E	312 600-8952
Mobilehop Technology LLC, Chicago (G-5476)	G	312 504-3773
Moduslink Corporation, Bedford Park (G-1485)	E	708 496-7800
Monotype Imaging Inc, Elk Grove Village (G-9131)	F	847 631-1111
Mosaic Construction, Northbrook (G-15437)	G	847 504-0177
Motivequest LLC, Chicago (G-5506)	F	847 905-6100
Music Plug LLC, Colfax (G-6950)	G	309 826-5238
My Local Beacon Llc, Chicago (G-5529)	G	888 482-6691
Myeccho LLC, Des Plaines (G-7809)	G	224 639-3068
Myhomeeq LLC, Chicago (G-5532)	G	773 328-7034
Nanex LLC, Winnetka (G-21134)	G	847 501-4787
Napersoft Inc, Naperville (G-14879)	F	630 420-1515
Narrative Health Network Inc, Chicago (G-5541)	G	312 600-9154
Nautilus Medical, Barrington (G-1232)	G	847 323-1334
Navipoint Genomics LLC, Naperville (G-14981)	G	630 464-8013
Navistarsinfosoft Inc, Chicago (G-5557)	E	877 270-3543
NE Desktop Software Inc, Schaumburg (G-18646)	F	800 211-8332
Neon One LLC, Chicago (G-5568)	E	888 860-6366
Nerd Island Studios LLC, Highland Park (G-11288)	G	224 619-5361
Netsuite Inc, Chicago (G-5572)	F	312 273-4100
Network Harbor Inc, Peoria (G-16485)	G	309 633-9118
Newera Software Inc, Kingston (G-12056)	G	815 784-3345
Newport Media Inc, Oswego (G-16016)	G	630 551-1651
Nexlp Inc, Chicago (G-5592)	F	773 383-4114
Next Generation Inc, Plainfield (G-16695)	G	312 739-0520
Nextpoint Inc, Chicago (G-5593)	E	773 929-4000
Niche Interactive Media Inc, Chicago (G-5596)	F	312 498-7933
Nimbl Worldwide Inc, Chicago (G-5603)	E	303 800-0245
Novaspect Inc, Schaumburg (G-18653)	C	847 956-8020
Ntt America Solutions Inc, Schaumburg (G-18654)	F	847 278-6413
Office of Experience LLC, Chicago (G-5658)	G	872 228-5126
Onefire Media Group Inc, Peoria (G-16487)	E	309 740-0345
Onoffblock Inc, New Lenox (G-15046)	F	312 899-6360
Onoffblock Inc, New Lenox (G-15047)	F	312 899-6360
Onx USA LLC, Lisle (G-12925)	F	630 343-8940
Opex Analytics LLC, Chicago (G-5682)	E	847 733-7439
Optimus Advantage LLC, Chicago (G-5685)	G	847 905-1000
Optionscity Software Inc, Chicago (G-5686)	G	312 605-4500
Oracle Bigmachines LLC, Deerfield (G-7641)	D	847 572-0300
Oracle Corporation, Chicago (G-5688)	B	773 404-9300
Oracle Corporation, Chicago (G-5689)	C	312 692-5270
Oracle Corporation, Itasca (G-11713)	B	630 931-6400
Oracle Corporation, Chicago (G-5690)	B	262 957-3000
Oracle Hcm User Group Inc, Chicago (G-5691)	G	312 222-9350
Oracle Systems Corporation, Chicago (G-5692)	G	312 673-5863
Oracle Systems Corporation, Westchester (G-20706)	D	708 409-7800
Orbit Enterprises Inc, Oak Brook (G-15654)	G	630 469-3405
Orecx, Chicago (G-5696)	F	312 895-5292
Origami Risk LLC, Chicago (G-5699)	E	312 546-6515
Original Software Inc, Westmont (G-20764)	E	630 413-5762
Orinoco Systems LLC, Wheaton (G-20814)	F	630 510-0775
Otus LLC, Chicago (G-5714)	E	312 229-7648
Overgrad Inc, Chicago (G-5717)	G	312 324-4952
Own The Night App, Chicago (G-5721)		773 216-0245
P B R W Enterprises Inc, Woodstock (G-21418)	G	815 337-5519
Pagepath Technologies Inc, Plano (G-16738)	F	630 689-4111
Panatech Computer Management, Lincolnshire (G-12789)	G	847 678-8848
Paragon International Inc, Schaumburg (G-18664)	F	847 240-2981
Parallel Solutions LLC, Schaumburg (G-18665)	G	847 708-9227
Parathon Recovery Service LLC, Naperville (G-14893)	G	630 689-0450
Patientbond LLC, Elmhurst (G-9408)	E	312 445-8751
Paylocity Holding Corporation, Schaumburg (G-18670)	C	847 463-3200
Paylocity Holding Corporation, Naperville (G-14894)	C	331 701-7975
Peak Computer Systems Inc, Belleville (G-1584)	F	618 398-5612
Peapod Digital Labs LLC, Chicago (G-5776)		800 573-2763
Pearl Bath Bombs Inc, Chicago (G-5777)	F	312 661-2881
Peopleadmin Inc, Chicago (G-5786)	E	877 637-5800
Perficient Inc, Chicago (G-5790)	F	312 291-9035
Performitiv LLC, Chicago (G-5791)	G	312 307-5716
Perry Johnson Inc, Rosemont (G-18041)	F	847 635-0010
Personify Inc, Chicago (G-5792)	F	855 747-9940
Personify Inc, Urbana (G-19992)	G	217 840-2638
Pervasive Health Inc, Chicago (G-5793)	G	312 257-2967
Phillip Grigalanz, Jerseyville (G-11795)	G	219 628-6706
Physician Software Systems LLC, Lisle (G-12926)	F	630 717-8192
Picis Clinical Solutions Inc, Rosemont (G-18042)	F	847 993-2200
Pinnakle Technologies Inc, Aurora (G-1009)	F	630 352-0070
Pitney Bowes Inc, Itasca (G-11719)	E	800 784-4224
Playground Pointers, Hinsdale (G-11375)	G	952 200-4168
Politech Inc, Trout Valley (G-19908)	F	847 516-2717
Polysystems Inc, Chicago (G-5839)	D	312 332-2114
Popular Pays Inc, Chicago (G-5844)	G	435 767-7297
Power102jamz, Urbana (G-19994)	G	312 912-2766
Powerschool Group LLC, Chicago (G-5850)	F	610 867-9200
Prairie Area Library System, Coal Valley (G-6938)	E	309 799-3155
Prairie Wi-FI Systems, Chicago (G-5852)	G	515 988-3260
Premier Intl Entps Inc, Chicago (G-5862)	E	312 857-2200
Presspage Inc, Chicago (G-5869)	F	312 256-9985
Price Fx Inc, Chicago (G-5871)	G	312 763-3121
Prism Esolutions Dv Andy Frain, Aurora (G-1010)	F	630 820-3820
Priva Mobility Inc, Evanston (G-9571)	G	248 410-3702
Privacy One LLC, Chicago (G-5886)	G	312 872-3757
Producepro Inc, Woodridge (G-21335)	F	630 395-9700
Productive Edge LLC, Chicago (G-5895)	D	312 561-9000
Proquis Inc, Elgin (G-8700)	F	847 278-3230
Proship Inc, Chicago (G-5904)	G	312 332-7447
Protepo Ltd, Elk Grove Village (G-9200)	G	847 466-1023
Ptc/User Inc, Chicago (G-5910)	G	619 417-2050
Pubpal LLC, Washington (G-20278)	G	309 222-5062
Pumpkin Patch Ventures Inc, Chicago (G-5914)	G	708 699-4396
Pycas Design Innovations LLC, Glenview (G-10604)	E	847 656-5000
Quadramed Corporation, Chicago (G-5926)	E	312 396-0700
Questily LLC, Chicago (G-5935)	G	312 636-6657
Questily LLC, Chicago (G-5936)	G	312 636-6657
Quiddity Solutions LLC, Chicago (G-5937)	G	773 844-2058
R & J Systems Inc, Bartlett (G-1257)	F	630 289-3010
Radius Solutions Incorporated, Chicago (G-5962)	F	312 648-0800
React Computer Services Inc, Willowbrook (G-21058)	D	630 323-6200
Recsolu Inc, Chicago (G-5990)	E	312 517-3200
Reflection Software Inc, Aurora (G-1013)	E	630 270-1200
Relativity Oda LLC, Chicago (G-6007)	C	312 263-1177
Reliefwatch Inc, Chicago (G-6011)	G	646 678-2336
Rivalfly National Network LLC, Chicago (G-6036)	G	847 867-8660
Robis Elections Inc, Wheaton (G-20820)	F	630 752-0220
Roger Cantu & Assocs, Oak Brook (G-15661)	G	630 573-9215
Rosewood Software Inc, Palatine (G-16155)	G	847 438-2185
Sales & Marketing Resources, Fox River Grove (G-9761)	G	847 910-9169
Salesforcecom Inc, Chicago (G-6093)	G	312 361-3555
Salesforcecom Inc, Chicago (G-6094)	F	312 288-3600
Sap America Inc, Downers Grove (G-8089)	E	630 395-2700
Scholarship Solutions LLC, Chicago (G-6113)	F	847 859-5629
School Town LLC, Northbrook (G-15477)	G	847 943-9115
Schwider Systems, Frankfort (G-9837)	G	815 469-2834
Scientific Cmpt Assoc Corp, River Forest (G-17056)	G	708 771-4567
Sct Alternative Inc, Buffalo Grove (G-2598)	F	847 215-7488
Secure Data Inc, O Fallon (G-15583)	F	618 726-5225

Employee Codes: A=Over 500 employees, B=251-500, C=101-250, D=51-100, E=20-50, F=10-19, G=3-9

73 BUSINESS SERVICES

Company	Code	Phone
Secureslice Inc — Chicago (G-6128)	E	800 984-0494
Sedona Inc — Moline (G-14176)	C	309 736-4104
See What You Send Inc — Chicago (G-6131)	G	781 780-1483
Sellers Commerce LLC — Northbrook (G-15479)	F	858 345-1212
Seoclarity — Des Plaines (G-7842)	F	773 831-4500
Serrala Solutions US Corp — Chicago (G-6139)	G	650 655-3939
Servicenow Inc — Downers Grove (G-8092)	G	630 963-4608
Sharpedge Solutions Inc — Naperville (G-14987)	F	630 792-9639
Shipbob Inc — Chicago (G-6154)	B	217 819-8539
Shipbob Inc — Chicago (G-6155)	F	844 474-4726
Showcase Corporation — Chicago (G-6158)	C	312 651-3000
Siemens Industry Software Inc — Downers Grove (G-8093)	E	630 437-6700
Signal Digital Inc — Chicago (G-6167)	E	312 685-1911
Signs & Wonders Unlimited LLC — Libertyville (G-12707)	G	847 816-9734
Simplement Inc — Northfield (G-15530)	G	702 560-5332
Single Path LLC — Lombard (G-13130)	E	708 653-4100
Smartbyte Solutions Inc — Palatine (G-16160)	F	847 925-1870
Social Qnect LLC — Northbrook (G-15483)	G	847 997-0077
Socialcloak Inc — East Dubuque (G-8184)	G	650 549-4412
Soft O Soft Inc — Schaumburg (G-18714)	E	630 741-4414
Softhaus Ltd — Alton (G-572)	G	618 463-1140
Softlabz Corporation — Highland Park (G-11299)	G	847 780-7076
Softtech LLC — Fox River Grove (G-9762)	G	847 809-8801
Softwareidm Inc — Wheaton (G-20825)	G	331 218-0001
Soloinsight Inc — Chicago (G-6198)	F	312 846-6729
Spl Software Alliance LLC — Morton (G-14383)	G	309 266-0304
Spooky Cool Labs LLC — Chicago (G-6218)	F	773 577-5555
Springcoin Inc — Chicago (G-6220)	G	323 577-9322
Sprout Social Inc — Chicago (G-6221)	D	866 878-3231
Srv Professional Publications — Schaumburg (G-18727)	G	847 330-1260
Starlight Software System Inc — Hudson (G-11519)	G	309 454-7349
Storiant Inc — Chicago (G-6250)	E	617 431-8000
Streamlinx LLC — Naperville (G-14920)	F	630 864-3043
Structurepoint LLC — Skokie (G-19037)	F	847 966-4357
Su Enterprise Inc — Arlington Heights (G-814)	G	847 394-1656
Sunrise Futures LLC — Chicago (G-6275)	G	312 612-1041
Supply Vision Inc — Chicago (G-6285)	G	847 388-0064
Swapp Technologies Inc — Chicago (G-6293)	G	312 912-1515
Swift Education Systems Inc — Chicago (G-6295)	G	312 257-3751
Swift Technologies Inc — Marengo (G-13494)	G	815 568-8402
Symfact Inc — Chicago (G-6301)	E	847 380-4174
Synergy Technology Group Inc — Chicago (G-6303)	F	773 305-3500
Synopsys Inc — Schaumburg (G-18734)	F	847 706-2000
Systems Live Ltd — Crystal Lake (G-7273)	G	815 455-3383
Systemslogix LLC — Glendale Heights (G-10509)	G	630 784-3113
Teenfitnation LLC — South Barrington (G-19077)	G	847 322-2953
Tegratecs Development Corp — Schaumburg (G-18743)	G	847 397-0088
Telemedicine Solutions LLC — Schaumburg (G-18744)	F	847 519-3500
Tempus Labs Inc — Chicago (G-6347)	E	312 784-4400
Textura Corporation — Deerfield (G-7654)	C	866 839-8872
Thinkcercacom Inc — Chicago (G-6365)	F	224 412-3722
Thomas A Doan — Evanston (G-9584)	G	847 864-8772
Thomson Quantitative Analytics — Chicago (G-6368)	E	847 610-0574
Thoughtly Corp — Chicago (G-6371)	G	772 559-2008
Thyng LLC — Chicago (G-6374)	G	312 262-5703
◆ Timepilot Corporation — Batavia (G-1430)	G	630 879-6400
◆ Tom Zosel Associates Ltd — Long Grove (G-13172)	D	847 540-6543
Torgo Inc — Riverwoods (G-17096)	G	800 360-5910
Track My Foreclosures LLC — Monticello (G-14288)	G	877 782-8187
Traena Inc — Chicago (G-6403)	G	630 605-3087
Tri-Tech Sltons Consulting Inc — Mount Prospect (G-14576)	G	847 941-0199
Trident Software Corp — Niles (G-15182)	G	847 219-8777
Trinket Studios — Chicago (G-6428)	G	773 888-3454
Trivaeo LLC — Paris (G-16245)	G	760 505-4751
Truepad LLC — Chicago (G-6438)	G	847 274-6898
Trustwave Holdings Inc — Chicago (G-6440)	F	312 750-0950
Turfmapp Inc — Chicago (G-6443)	G	703 473-5678
Turner Agward — Chicago (G-6444)	G	773 669-8559
Twocanoes Software Inc — Naperville (G-14937)	G	630 305-9601
Tzee Inc — Lisle (G-12953)	G	630 857-3425
Uber Technologies Inc — Chicago (G-6454)	E	612 600-4737
Ubipass Inc — Willowbrook (G-21066)	G	312 626-4624
Ultimate Software Group Inc — Rosemont (G-18056)	E	847 273-1701
Usmedexport Company — Wheeling (G-21005)	G	847 749-5520
Uxm Studio Inc — Villa Park (G-20175)	F	773 359-1333
V2 Solutions Inc — Schaumburg (G-18769)	G	312 528-9050
Vaimo Inc — Chicago (G-6517)	G	502 767-9550
Val P Enterprises — Chicago (G-6518)	G	708 982-6561
Varsity Logistics Inc — Rosemont (G-18059)	E	650 392-7979
Vauto Inc — Oakbrook Terrace (G-15818)	E	630 590-2000
Velocity Software LLC — Lombard (G-13149)	F	800 351-6893
Veloflip Inc — Northfield (G-15537)	G	847 757-4972
Vertex Consulting Services Inc — Schaumburg (G-18771)	F	313 492-5154
Vertical Software Inc — Bartonville (G-1336)	F	309 633-0700
Viclarity Inc — Chicago (G-6543)	G	201 214-5405
Victor Consulting — Lincolnshire (G-12801)	G	847 267-8012
Vigilanz Corporation — Oak Park (G-15778)	E	708 383-3008
Vision I Systems — Chicago (G-6556)	G	312 326-9188
Visual Information Tech Inc — Champaign (G-3367)	G	217 841-2155
Vizr Tech LLC — Chicago (G-6564)	G	312 420-4466
Vlc Solutions LLC — Schaumburg (G-18772)	D	630 447-9852
Vodori Inc — Chicago (G-6566)	D	312 324-3992
W A M Computers International — Litchfield (G-12978)	G	217 324-6926
Wargaming (usa) Inc — Chicago (G-6587)	E	312 258-0500
Wavsys LLC — Chicago (G-6592)	F	773 442-0888
Webqa Incorporated — Woodridge (G-21346)	D	630 985-1300
Websolutions Technology Inc — Aurora (G-1033)	E	630 375-6833
Wellsky Corporation — Oak Brook (G-15670)	G	630 218-2700
Whospoppin Enterprises Inc — Chicago (G-6621)	G	312 912-8480
Wincademy Inc — Grayslake (G-10805)	G	847 445-7886
Winscribe Usa Inc — Chicago (G-6645)	F	773 399-1608
Wolfram Research Inc — Champaign (G-3372)	C	217 398-0700
World Class Tae Kwon — Aurora (G-1039)	G	630 870-9293
Wow Bao LLC — Chicago (G-6680)	D	888 496-9226
Written Word Inc — Roselle (G-17996)	G	630 671-9803
Xaptum Inc — Chicago (G-6691)	G	312 852-1595
Yesimpact — Darien (G-7415)	G	765 413-9667
Yhlsoft Inc — Chicago (G-6700)	F	844 829-0039
Yield Management Systems LLC — Chicago (G-6701)	G	312 665-1595
Zirmed Inc — Chicago (G-6721)	E	312 207-0889

76 MISCELLANEOUS REPAIR SERVICES

7692 Welding Repair

Company	Code	Phone
A&S Machining & Welding Inc — Mc Cook (G-13689)	E	708 442-4544
Ability Welding Service Inc — Bensenville (G-1723)	G	630 595-3737
Ablaze Welding & Fabricating — Rockford (G-17287)	G	815 965-0046
Abzenco Welding Inc — Batavia (G-1339)	G	630 234-8021
Accurate Auto Manufacturing Co — Mount Vernon (G-14595)	G	618 244-0727
Adams Steel Service Inc — McHenry (G-13715)	E	815 385-9100
Adermanns Welding & Mch & Co — Effingham (G-8383)		217 342-3234
Advanced Welding Ltd — Addison (G-23)	F	708 205-4559
Affordable Welding Us Inc — Chicago (G-3579)	G	773 374-2000
Aileys 3 Welding — Crescent City (G-7081)	G	815 683-2181
Alberto Daza — Chicago (G-3597)	F	773 638-9880
Aledo Welding Enterprises Inc — Aledo (G-354)	G	309 582-2019
All Metal Machine — South Beloit (G-19079)	G	815 389-0168
All Pro Welding Services Inc — Mahomet (G-13420)	G	217 586-5383
Allans Welding & Machine Inc — Olney (G-15851)	G	618 392-3708
Allied Welding Inc — Chillicothe (G-6813)	E	309 274-6227
Alloy Welding Corp — Melrose Park (G-13822)	E	708 345-6756
Alloyweld Inspection Co Inc — Bensenville (G-1738)	E	630 595-2145
American Grinding & Machine Co — Chicago (G-3653)		773 889-4343
▲ American Machining & Wldg Inc — Chicago (G-3659)	E	773 586-2585
American Metal Installers & FA — Villa Park (G-20131)	G	630 993-0812
American Welding & Gas Inc — Stone Park (G-19551)	E	630 527-2550

SIC SECTION
76 MISCELLANEOUS REPAIR SERVICES

Anchor Welding & Fabrication ....G....... 815 937-1640
  Aroma Park (G-839)
Andel Services Inc ....G....... 630 566-0210
  Aurora (G-1052)
Andersen Machine & Welding Inc .....G....... 815 232-4664
  Freeport (G-10101)
Apollo Machine & Manufacturing ....G....... 847 677-6444
  Skokie (G-18921)
Armitage Welding ....G....... 773 772-1442
  Chicago (G-3731)
◆ Arndt Enterprise Ltd ....G....... 847 234-5736
  Lake Forest (G-12226)
AS Fabricating Inc ....G....... 618 242-7438
  Mount Vernon (G-14596)
Ascent Mfg Co ....E....... 847 806-6600
  Elk Grove Village (G-8841)
Assured Welding Service Inc ....G....... 847 671-1414
  West Chicago (G-20545)
Atlas Boiler & Welding Company ....G....... 815 963-3360
  Elgin (G-8517)
◆ Ats Sortimat USA LLC ....D....... 847 925-1234
  Rolling Meadows (G-17713)
Awerkamp Machine Co ....E....... 217 222-3480
  Quincy (G-16859)
B & W Machine Company Inc ....G....... 847 364-4500
  Elk Grove Village (G-8853)
B J Fehr Machine Co ....G....... 309 923-8691
  Roanoke (G-17099)
B T Brown Manufacturing ....G....... 815 947-3633
  Kent (G-12017)
Bales Mold Service Inc ....E....... 630 852-4665
  Downers Grove (G-7957)
Baley Enterprises Inc ....G....... 708 681-0900
  Melrose Park (G-13830)
Barton Manufacturing LLC ....F....... 217 428-0726
  Decatur (G-7463)
Bc Welding Inc ....G....... 708 258-0076
  Peotone (G-16550)
Bear Machine Tool & Die Inc ....G....... 815 932-4204
  Bradley (G-2277)
Bear Mtal Wldg Fabrication Inc ....G....... 630 261-9353
  Villa Park (G-20133)
Beaver Creek Enterprises Inc ....F....... 815 723-9455
  Joliet (G-11829)
Beesing Welding & Eqp Repr ....G....... 815 732-7552
  Oregon (G-15913)
Bellinis Custom Welding and A ....G....... 815 284-4175
  Dixon (G-7889)
Bessler Welding Inc ....F....... 309 699-6224
  East Peoria (G-8253)
Bi State Steel Co ....G....... 309 755-0668
  East Moline (G-8223)
Bierman Welding Inc ....F....... 217 342-2050
  Effingham (G-8389)
Bill Welding & Fabrication LLC ....G....... 312 871-2623
  Chicago (G-3886)
Botts Welding and Trck Svc Inc ....E....... 815 338-0594
  Woodstock (G-21366)
Brian D Obermiller ....G....... 815 830-3100
  Tonica (G-19887)
Bulaw Welding & Engineering Co .....D....... 630 228-8300
  Itasca (G-11632)
Burgess Manufacturing Inc ....F....... 847 680-1724
  Libertyville (G-12641)
Burke Tool & Manufacturing Inc ......G....... 618 542-6441
  Du Quoin (G-8116)
Burns Machine Company ....E....... 815 434-3131
  Ottawa (G-16044)
Bushnell Welding & Radiator ....G....... 309 772-9289
  Bushnell (G-2740)
C & B Welders Inc ....G....... 773 722-0097
  Chicago (G-3990)
C E R Machining & Tooling Ltd ....G....... 708 442-9614
  Lyons (G-13305)
C I F Industries Inc ....E....... 618 635-2010
  Staunton (G-19476)
C J Holdings Inc ....G....... 309 274-3141
  Chillicothe (G-6815)
C Keller Manufacturing Inc ....E....... 630 833-5593
  Villa Park (G-20136)
Carrolls Welding & Fabrication ....G....... 217 728-8720
  Sullivan (G-19663)
Casward Tool Works Inc ....G....... 773 486-4900
  Orland Park (G-15946)
CB Machine & Tool Corp ....G....... 847 288-1807
  Franklin Park (G-9901)
Certiweld Inc ....G....... 708 389-0148
  Crestwood (G-7111)
Cervones Welding Service Inc ....G....... 847 985-6865
  Schaumburg (G-18471)

Chicago Tube and Iron Company ......E....... 815 834-2500
  Romeoville (G-17807)
Cokel Dj Welding Bay & Muffler ....G....... 309 385-4567
  Princeville (G-16825)
Cokel Welding Shop ....G....... 217 357-3312
  Carthage (G-3134)
Colfax Welding & Fabricating ....G....... 847 359-4433
  Palatine (G-16101)
Comers Welding Service Inc ....G....... 630 892-0168
  Montgomery (G-14241)
Comet Fabricating & Welding Co .....E....... 815 229-0468
  Rockford (G-17354)
Commercial Machine Services ....F....... 847 806-1901
  Elk Grove Village (G-8905)
Component Tool & Mfg Co ....F....... 708 672-5505
  Crete (G-7136)
Concept Industries Inc ....G....... 847 258-3545
  Elk Grove Village (G-8907)
Connell Mc Machine & Welding ....G....... 815 868-2275
  Mc Connell (G-13688)
▲ Coras Welding Shop Inc ....G....... 815 672-7950
  Streator (G-19606)
Corrugated Converting Eqp ....F....... 618 532-2138
  Centralia (G-3227)
County Tool & Die ....G....... 217 324-6527
  Litchfield (G-12962)
Cr Welding Met Fabrication Inc ......G....... 224 789-7825
  Gurnee (G-10867)
Custom Fabricators LLC ....G....... 630 372-4399
  Streamwood (G-19569)
Cyclops Welding Co ....G....... 815 223-0685
  La Salle (G-12109)
Cylinder Services Inc ....G....... 630 466-9820
  Sugar Grove (G-19641)
D & H Precision Tooling Co ....G....... 815 653-9611
  Wonder Lake (G-21144)
D & M Welding Inc ....G....... 708 233-6080
  Bridgeview (G-2339)
D M Manufacturing 2 Inc ....G....... 618 455-3550
  Sainte Marie (G-18325)
D N Welding & Fabricating Inc ....G....... 847 244-6410
  Waukegan (G-20432)
D W Terry Welding Company ....G....... 618 433-9722
  Alton (G-551)
Daniel Mfg Inc ....F....... 309 963-4227
  Carlock (G-2886)
Darnell Welding ....G....... 618 945-9538
  Bridgeport (G-2312)
Daves Welding Service Inc ....G....... 630 655-3224
  Darien (G-7405)
David Schutte ....G....... 217 223-5464
  Quincy (G-16874)
Device Technologies Inc ....G....... 630 553-7178
  Yorkville (G-21479)
Dons Welding ....G....... 847 526-1177
  Wauconda (G-20343)
Dooling Machine Products Inc ....G....... 618 254-0724
  Hartford (G-11034)
▼ Du Page Welding Inc ....G....... 630 543-8511
  Addison (G-103)
Duroweld Company Inc ....E....... 847 680-3064
  Lake Bluff (G-12179)
Dyers Machine Service Inc ....G....... 708 496-8100
  Summit Argo (G-19678)
E & E Machine & Engineering Co ....G....... 708 841-5208
  Riverdale (G-17071)
Eagle Machine Company ....G....... 312 243-7407
  Chicago (G-4429)
Edward F Data ....G....... 708 597-0158
  Alsip (G-444)
Edwardsville Mch & Wldg Co Inc .....G....... 618 656-5145
  Edwardsville (G-8360)
Eenigenburg Mfg Inc ....G....... 708 474-0850
  Lansing (G-12492)
▼ Ehrhardt Tool & Machine LLC .....C....... 314 436-6900
  Granite City (G-10704)
▲ Ekstrom Carlson Fabg Co Inc ......G....... 815 226-1511
  Rockford (G-17392)
Emerald Machine Inc ....G....... 773 924-3659
  Chicago (G-4495)
Emv Welding Inc ....G....... 630 264-0893
  Aurora (G-1089)
▲ Erva Tool & Die Company ....G....... 773 533-7806
  Chicago (G-4528)
Estructuras Inc ....F....... 773 522-2200
  Chicago (G-4534)
Eton Machine Co Ltd ....F....... 847 426-3380
  Elgin (G-8581)
Eveready Welding Service Inc ....G....... 708 532-2432
  Tinley Park (G-19825)

Extreme Welding & Machine Serv ....G....... 618 272-7237
  Eldorado (G-8481)
F Vogelmann and Company ....F....... 815 469-2285
  Frankfort (G-9793)
Fabco Enterprises Inc ....G....... 708 333-4644
  Harvey (G-11084)
Fabricating & Welding Corp ....E....... 773 928-2050
  Chicago (G-4555)
Fast Forward Welding Inc ....G....... 815 254-1901
  Plainfield (G-16664)
Fehring Ornamental Iron Works ......G....... 217 483-6727
  Rochester (G-17166)
Floyds Welding Service ....G....... 618 395-2414
  Olney (G-15861)
Folk Race Cars ....G....... 815 629-2418
  Durand (G-8151)
Force Manufacturing Inc ....G....... 847 265-6500
  Lake Villa (G-12351)
Franklin Maintenance ....G....... 815 284-6806
  Dixon (G-7900)
Franks Ideal Welding Inc ....G....... 708 344-4409
  Broadview (G-2438)
Fred Stollenwerk ....G....... 309 852-3794
  Kewanee (G-12034)
Gengler-Lowney Laser Works ....F....... 630 801-4840
  Aurora (G-1103)
Gma Inc ....G....... 630 595-1255
  Bensenville (G-1812)
Golden Hydraulic & Machine ....G....... 708 597-4265
  Blue Island (G-2124)
Graham Welding Inc ....G....... 217 422-1423
  Decatur (G-7497)
Great Lakes Mech Svcs Inc ....F....... 708 672-5900
  Lincolnshire (G-12768)
Greens Machine Shop ....G....... 618 532-4631
  Centralia (G-3234)
Gridley Welding Inc ....G....... 309 747-2325
  Gridley (G-10845)
Grimm Metal Fabricators Inc ....E....... 630 792-1710
  Lombard (G-13083)
Grover Welding Company ....G....... 847 966-3119
  Skokie (G-18961)
GV Welding Inc ....G....... 312 863-0071
  Chicago (G-4753)
H & H Services Inc ....F....... 618 633-2837
  Hamel (G-10949)
Halter Machine Shop Inc ....G....... 618 943-2224
  Lawrenceville (G-12534)
Harbor Manufacturing Inc ....D....... 708 543-1740
  Frankfort (G-9800)
Hattan Tool Company ....G....... 708 597-9308
  Alsip (G-455)
Hedricks Welding & Fabrication ....G....... 217 846-3230
  Foosland (G-9705)
Heiss Welding Inc ....F....... 815 434-1838
  Ottawa (G-16055)
▲ Hfr Precision Machining Inc ....E....... 630 556-4325
  Sugar Grove (G-19646)
Higgs Welding LLC ....G....... 217 925-5999
  Dieterich (G-7876)
High Speed Welding Inc ....G....... 630 971-8929
  Westmont (G-20747)
Hofmeister Welding Inc ....G....... 217 407-4091
  Griggsville (G-10849)
Hogg Welding Inc ....G....... 708 339-0033
  Harvey (G-11079)
Holshouser Machine & Tool Inc ....G....... 618 451-0164
  Granite City (G-10715)
Holstein Garage Inc ....G....... 630 668-0328
  Wheaton (G-20802)
Hts Coatings LLC ....E....... 618 215-8161
  Madison (G-13414)
Hutton Welding Service Inc ....G....... 217 932-5585
  Casey (G-3203)
ILmachine Company Inc ....F....... 847 243-9900
  Wheeling (G-20913)
Incline Construction Inc ....G....... 815 577-8881
  Joliet (G-11881)
Industrial Mint Wldg Machining ......D....... 773 376-6526
  Chicago (G-4908)
Industrial Welding Inc ....F....... 815 535-9300
  Rock Falls (G-17188)
J & B Welding LLC ....G....... 309 887-4151
  Fulton (G-10153)
▲ J & I Son Tool Company Inc ....G....... 847 455-4200
  Franklin Park (G-9967)
J & M Fab Metals Inc ....G....... 815 758-0354
  Marengo (G-13486)
J B Metal Works Inc ....G....... 847 824-4253
  Des Plaines (G-7790)

Employee Codes: A=Over 500 employees, B=251-500
C=101-250, D=51-100, E=20-50, F=10-19, G=3-9

2020 Harris Illinois
Industrial Directory

76 MISCELLANEOUS REPAIR SERVICES

Company	Code	Phone
Jacksonville Machine Inc	D	217 243-1119
Jacksonville (G-11771)		
Jacob Chambliss	G	618 731-6632
Dahlgren (G-7308)		
Jacobs Boiler & Mech Inds Inc	E	773 385-9900
Chicago (G-4998)		
Jakes McHning Rbilding Svc Inc	E	630 892-3291
Aurora (G-1116)		
Jarvis Welding Co	G	309 647-0033
Canton (G-2827)		
Jasiek Motor Rebuilding Inc	G	815 883-3678
Oglesby (G-15842)		
Jav Machine Craft Inc	G	708 867-8608
Chicago (G-5011)		
Jayne Excavating & Welding LLC	G	618 553-1149
Newton (G-15085)		
Jet Industries Inc	E	773 586-8900
Chicago (G-5024)		
Jim Cokel Welding	G	309 734-5063
Monmouth (G-14219)		
Joint Field Services Inc	E	815 795-3714
Marseilles (G-13559)		
JW Welding	G	618 228-7213
Aviston (G-1180)		
K & K Tool & Die Inc	F	309 829-4479
Bloomington (G-2065)		
K & P Welding	G	217 536-5245
Watson (G-20322)		
K D Welding Inc	G	815 591-3545
Hanover (G-10996)		
K Three Welding Service Inc	G	708 563-2911
Chicago (G-5067)		
Karly Iron Works Inc	G	815 477-3430
Crystal Lake (G-7215)		
Kemper Industries	G	217 826-5712
Marshall (G-13573)		
Kenneth W Templeman	G	847 912-2740
Volo (G-20200)		
Kim Gough	G	309 734-3511
Monmouth (G-14221)		
Koerner Aviation Inc	G	815 932-4222
Kankakee (G-11988)		
Kopp Welding Inc	G	847 593-2070
Elk Grove Village (G-9079)		
Ksem Inc	G	618 656-5388
Edwardsville (G-8367)		
Lake Fabrication Inc	G	217 832-2761
Villa Grove (G-20124)		
Larrys Garage & Machine Shop	G	815 968-8416
Rockford (G-17491)		
Laystrom Manufacturing Co	D	773 342-4800
Chicago (G-5186)		
Lee Brothers Welding Inc	G	309 342-6017
Galesburg (G-10207)		
Legna Iron Works Inc	E	630 894-8056
Roselle (G-17964)		
Leroys Welding & Fabg Inc	F	847 215-6151
Wheeling (G-20931)		
Lewis Process Systems Inc	F	630 510-8200
Carol Stream (G-3018)		
Linne Machine Company Inc	G	217 446-5746
Danville (G-7359)		
Luebbers Welding & Mfg Inc	F	618 594-2489
Carlyle (G-2893)		
M & F Fabrication & Welding	G	217 457-2221
Concord (G-6998)		
M & J Manufacturing Co Inc	F	847 364-6066
Elk Grove Village (G-9100)		
M & M Welding Inc	G	815 895-3955
Sycamore (G-19723)		
Magnetic Inspection Lab Inc	D	847 437-4488
Elk Grove Village (G-9106)		
Mark Lahey	G	217 243-4433
Jacksonville (G-11775)		
Mark S Machine Shop Inc	G	815 895-3955
Sycamore (G-19724)		
Marlboro Wire Ltd	E	217 224-7989
Quincy (G-16910)		
Mason Welding Inc	G	708 755-0621
S Chicago Hts (G-18123)		
Matrix Machine & Tool Mfg	G	708 452-8707
River Grove (G-17063)		
MB Machine Inc	G	815 864-3555
Shannon (G-18871)		
McCloskey Eyman Mlone Mfg Svcs	G	309 647-4000
Canton (G-2830)		
McFarland Welding and Machine	G	618 627-2838
Thompsonville (G-19779)		
Meadoweld Machine Inc	G	815 623-3939
South Beloit (G-19102)		
Melrose Mold & Machine Co Inc	G	847 233-9970
Franklin Park (G-9991)		
Mendota Welding & Mfg	G	815 539-6944
Mendota (G-13949)		
Merritt Farm Equipment Inc	G	217 746-5331
Carthage (G-3138)		
Meteer Manufacturing Co	G	217 636-8109
Athens (G-899)		
Method Molds Inc	G	815 877-0191
Loves Park (G-13236)		
Metzger Welding Service	G	217 234-2851
Mattoon (G-13649)		
Mevert Automotive Inc	G	618 965-9609
Steeleville (G-19484)		
Mfw Services Inc	G	708 522-5879
South Holland (G-19232)		
▲ Micro Products Company	E	630 406-9550
Peoria (G-16472)		
Midway Machine & Tool Co Inc	G	708 385-3450
Alsip (G-477)		
Mihalis Marine	G	773 445-6220
Chicago (G-5455)		
Milans Machining & Mfg Co Inc	D	708 780-6600
Cicero (G-6867)		
Millers Eureka Inc	F	312 666-9383
Chicago (G-5459)		
Misselhorn Welding & Machines	G	618 426-3714
Campbell Hill (G-2818)		
Moline Welding Inc	F	309 756-0643
Milan (G-14018)		
Mt Vernon Mold Works Inc	E	618 242-6040
Mount Vernon (G-14629)		
Mushro Machine & Tool Co	F	815 672-5848
Streator (G-19617)		
Napier Machine & Welding Inc	G	217 525-8740
Springfield (G-19410)		
National Tool & Machine Co	F	618 271-6445
East Saint Louis (G-8316)		
Natural Fiber Welding Inc	E	309 339-7794
Peoria (G-16483)		
Neals Trailer Sales	G	217 792-5136
Lincoln (G-12736)		
Needham Shop Inc	G	630 557-9019
Kaneville (G-11955)		
▲ Nehring Electrical Works Co	C	815 756-2741
Dekalb (G-7693)		
Nelson Stud Welding Inc	F	708 430-3770
Tinley Park (G-19847)		
Newman Welding & Machine Shop	G	618 435-5591
Benton (G-1934)		
North Shore Truck & Equipment	F	847 887-0200
Lake Bluff (G-12201)		
▲ Norton Machine Co	F	217 748-6115
Rossville (G-18066)		
Odom Tool and Technology Inc	G	815 895-8545
Sycamore (G-19726)		
On Site Mechanical Svcs Inc	F	708 367-0470
Crete (G-7143)		
Oostman Fabricating & Wldg Inc	F	630 241-1315
Westmont (G-20763)		
Orient Machining & Welding Inc	E	708 371-3500
Dixmoor (G-7886)		
▲ Orsolinis Welding & Fabg	G	773 722-9855
Chicago (G-5705)		
P & G Machine & Tool Inc	G	618 283-0273
Vandalia (G-20018)		
Palatine Welding Company	E	847 358-1075
Rolling Meadows (G-17759)		
Parker Fabrication Inc	G	309 266-8413
Morton (G-14376)		
Patkus Machine Co	G	815 398-7818
Rockford (G-17548)		
▲ Pauls Machine & Welding Corp	D	217 832-2541
Villa Grove (G-20125)		
Pedraza Inc	F	773 874-9020
Chicago (G-5780)		
Pekin Weldors Inc	F	309 382-3627
North Pekin (G-15327)		
Performance Welding LLC	G	217 412-5722
Maroa (G-13554)		
Phoenix Welding Co Inc	F	630 616-1700
Franklin Park (G-10016)		
PM Woodwind Repair Inc	G	847 869-7049
Evanston (G-9567)		
Precision Tool Welding	G	630 285-9844
Elk Grove Village (G-9193)		
Pro Arc Inc	E	815 877-1804
Loves Park (G-13249)		
Pro-Fab Metals Inc	G	618 283-2986
Vandalia (G-20020)		
Production Fabg & Stamping Inc	F	708 755-5468
S Chicago Hts (G-18126)		
Production Manufacturing	G	217 256-4211
Warsaw (G-20259)		
Professional Metal Works LLC	F	618 539-2214
Freeburg (G-10092)		
Quality Metal Works Inc	G	309 379-5311
Stanford (G-19473)		
Quality Tool & Machine Inc	G	773 721-8655
Chicago (G-5931)		
R & R Machining Inc	G	217 835-4579
Benld (G-1718)		
R Machining Inc	G	217 532-2174
Butler (G-2749)		
R-M Industries Inc	G	630 543-3071
Addison (G-264)		
Ramsey Welding Inc	E	618 483-6248
Altamont (G-537)		
Ramseys Machine Co	G	217 824-2320
Taylorville (G-19761)		
Rapco Ltd	G	618 249-6614
Richview (G-17033)		
Reber Welding Service	G	217 774-3441
Shelbyville (G-18885)		
Recendiz Welding Inc	G	708 205-8759
Elmwood Park (G-9456)		
Reco of IL Inc	G	630 898-2010
Aurora (G-1147)		
Regal Steel Erectors LLC	E	847 888-3500
Elgin (G-8716)		
Rex Radiator and Welding Co	G	847 428-1112
East Dundee (G-8209)		
Rex Radiator and Welding Co	G	312 421-1531
Chicago (G-6020)		
Rex Radiator and Welding Co	G	630 595-4664
Bensenville (G-1883)		
Rex Radiator and Welding Co	G	815 725-6655
Rockdale (G-17271)		
▲ Ri-Del Mfg Inc	D	312 829-8720
Chicago (G-6024)		
Rk Maintenance Inc	G	708 429-2215
Tinley Park (G-19853)		
Robert Davis & Son Inc	G	815 889-4168
Milford (G-14036)		
Robertson Repair	G	618 895-2593
Sims (G-18910)		
Rockford Precision Machine	F	815 873-1018
Rockford (G-17601)		
Rodney Tite Welding	G	618 845-9072
Ullin (G-19936)		
Rw Welding Inc	G	847 541-5508
Arlington Heights (G-802)		
S & S Welding & Fabrication	G	847 742-7344
Elgin (G-8722)		
▲ S & W Manufacturing Co Inc	E	630 595-5044
Bensenville (G-1888)		
S D Custom Machining	G	618 544-7007
Robinson (G-17125)		
Service Cutting & Welding	G	773 622-8366
Chicago (G-6142)		
Service Sheet Metal Works Inc	F	773 229-0031
Chicago (G-6143)		
Shanks Veterinary Equipment	G	815 225-7700
Milledgeville (G-14040)		
Shannon & Sons Welding	G	630 898-7778
Aurora (G-1155)		
Sheas Iron Works Inc	E	847 356-2922
Lake Villa (G-12367)		
Shup Tool & Machine Co	G	618 931-2596
Granite City (G-10737)		
Sigel Welding	G	217 844-2412
Sigel (G-18907)		
Silver Machine Shop Inc	G	217 359-5717
Champaign (G-3348)		
Sivco Welding Company	G	309 944-5171
Geneseo (G-10247)		
Smith Welding LLC	G	618 829-5414
Saint Elmo (G-18312)		
South Side Bler Wldg Works Inc	G	708 478-1714
Orland Park (G-15981)		
South Subn Wldg & Fabg Co Inc	G	708 385-7160
Posen (G-16801)		
Southwick Machine & Design Co	G	309 949-2868
Colona (G-6980)		
Spaeth Welding Inc	F	618 588-3596
New Baden (G-15024)		
Spannuth Boiler Co	G	708 386-1882
Oak Park (G-15774)		
Special Tool Engineering Co	F	773 767-6690
Chicago (G-6212)		

SIC SECTION

76 MISCELLANEOUS REPAIR SERVICES

Company	Code	Phone
Spencer Welding Service Inc	G	847 272-0580
Northbrook (G-15484)		
Springfield Welding & Auto Bdy	E	217 523-5365
Springfield (G-19457)		
Steel Services Enterprises	G	708 259-1181
Lansing (G-12519)		
Stevenson Fabrication Svcs Inc	E	815 468-7941
Manteno (G-13458)		
Stockton Stainless Inc	E	815 947-2168
Stockton (G-19550)		
Stuhlman Family LLC	G	815 436-2432
Plainfield (G-16719)		
Suburban Welding & Steel LLC	F	847 678-1264
Franklin Park (G-10057)		
Superior Joining Tech Inc	E	815 282-7581
Machesney Park (G-13376)		
Superior Welding Inc	F	618 544-8822
Robinson (G-17126)		
Tait Machine Tool Inc	G	815 932-2011
Kankakee (G-12010)		
Taylor Design Inc	G	815 389-3991
Roscoe (G-17936)		
Taylor Off Road Racing	G	815 544-4500
Belvidere (G-1703)		
Tdw Welding LLC	G	217 690-3521
Wheeler (G-20833)		
▲ Technology One Welding Inc	G	630 871-1296
Carol Stream (G-3080)		
Telza Welding Inc	G	773 777-4467
Chicago (G-6342)		
Tewell Bros Machine Inc	F	217 253-6303
Tuscola (G-19931)		
Titan Tool Works LLC	G	630 221-1080
Carol Stream (G-3081)		
Toledo Machine & Welding Inc	G	217 849-2251
Toledo (G-19880)		
Tomko Machine Works Inc	G	630 244-0902
Lemont (G-12593)		
Tony Weishaar	G	217 774-2774
Shelbyville (G-18888)		
Tonys Welding Service Inc	G	618 532-9353
Centralia (G-3253)		
Toolweld Inc	G	847 854-8013
Algonquin (G-389)		
▲ Torrence Machine & Tool Co	G	815 469-1850
Mokena (G-14124)		
Trailers Inc	G	217 472-6000
Chapin (G-3396)		
Tri-Cunty Wldg Fabrication LLC	E	217 543-3304
Arthur (G-881)		
Trotters Manufacturing Co	G	217 364-4540
Buffalo (G-2501)		
United Machine Works Inc	G	847 352-5252
Schaumburg (G-18766)		
United Maint Wldg & McHy C	F	708 458-1705
Bedford Park (G-1508)		
United Tool and Engineering Co	D	815 389-3021
South Beloit (G-19118)		
Universal Broaching Inc	F	847 228-1440
Elk Grove Village (G-9298)		
US Dept Agriculture Forest Svc	G	618 285-5211
Golconda (G-10669)		
V Brothers Machine Co	E	708 652-0062
Cicero (G-6886)		
Vaughn & Sons Machine Shop	G	618 842-9048
Fairfield (G-9639)		
VG Ates and Welding	G	847 263-4416
Waukegan (G-20515)		
▲ Vindee Industries Inc	G	815 469-3300
Frankfort (G-9850)		
Vrn Welding & Fabrication Inc	G	847 735-7270
Lake Bluff (G-12213)		
▲ Walco Tool & Engineering Corp	D	815 834-0225
Romeoville (G-17886)		
Wardzala Industries Inc	F	847 288-9909
Franklin Park (G-10083)		
Warner Brothers Inc	G	217 643-7950
Rantoul (G-16987)		
WEb Production & Fabg Inc	F	312 733-6800
Chicago (G-6595)		
▲ Wegener Welding LLC	F	630 789-0990
Burr Ridge (G-2731)		
Weiland Welding Inc	G	815 580-8079
Cherry Valley (G-3448)		
Weld-Rite Service Inc	E	708 458-6000
Bedford Park (G-1512)		
▲ Welding By K &K LLC	G	847 360-1190
Waukegan (G-20517)		
▼ Welding Company of America	E	630 806-2000
Aurora (G-1168)		
Welding Shop	G	773 785-1305
Chicago (G-6599)		
Welding Specialties	G	708 798-5388
East Hazel Crest (G-8219)		
Wemco Inc	F	708 388-1980
Alsip (G-524)		
West End Tool & Die Inc	G	815 462-3040
New Lenox (G-15068)		
Wherry Machine & Welding Inc	G	309 828-5423
Bloomington (G-2107)		
Williams Welding Service	G	217 235-1758
Humboldt (G-11525)		
Wirfs Industries Inc	F	815 344-0635
McHenry (G-13809)		
Wissmiller & Evans Road Eqp	G	309 725-3598
Cooksville (G-7004)		
Xd Industries Inc	F	630 766-2843
Bensenville (G-1916)		

7694 Armature Rewinding Shops

Company	Code	Phone
Accurate Elc Mtr & Pump Co	G	708 448-2792
Worth (G-21453)		
Acme Control Service Inc	E	773 774-9191
Chicago (G-3527)		
Addison Electric Inc	E	800 517-4871
Addison (G-19)		
All Electric Mtr Repr Svc Inc	G	773 925-2404
Chicago (G-3609)		
▲ Amj Industries Inc	G	815 654-9000
Rockford (G-17302)		
Apex Industrial Automation LLC	G	866 924-2808
Romeoville (G-17795)		
Armature Motor & Pump Company	G	309 829-3600
East Peoria (G-8251)		
Avana Electric Motors Inc	F	847 588-0400
Elk Grove Village (G-8850)		
Bak Electric	G	708 458-3578
Bridgeview (G-2327)		
Bellwood Electric Motors Inc	G	708 544-7223
Bellwood (G-1615)		
BP Elc Mtrs Pump & Svc Inc	G	773 539-4343
Skokie (G-18931)		
C and C Machine Tool Service	G	630 810-0484
Downers Grove (G-7962)		
▲ Calumet Armature and Elc LLC	E	708 841-6880
Riverdale (G-17070)		
Cameron Electric Motor Corp	F	312 939-5770
Chicago (G-4012)		
Cox Electric Motor Service	G	217 344-2458
Urbana (G-19980)		
Decatur Industrial Elc Inc	E	618 244-1066
Mount Vernon (G-14607)		
Decatur Industrial Elc Inc	G	217 428-6621
Decatur (G-7487)		
Dependable Electric	G	618 592-3314
Oblong (G-15826)		
Dreisilker Electric Motors Inc	C	630 469-7510
Glen Ellyn (G-10401)		
Eastland Industries Inc	G	708 547-6500
Hillside (G-11339)		
Ebling Electric Company	F	312 455-1885
Chicago (G-4441)		
Elmot Inc	G	773 791-7039
Chicago (G-4489)		
Endeavor Technologies Inc	G	630 562-0300
Saint Charles (G-18197)		
Erbes Electric	G	815 849-5508
Sublette (G-19636)		
▲ Fdf Armature Inc	G	630 458-0452
Addison (G-120)		
First Electric Motor Shop Inc	G	217 698-0672
Springfield (G-19368)		
Fleetpride Inc	F	630 455-6881
Willowbrook (G-21043)		
Flolo Corporation	G	630 595-1010
West Chicago (G-20585)		
Flolo Corporation	G	847 249-0880
Gurnee (G-10878)		
Fluid Pump Service Inc	G	847 228-0750
Elk Grove Village (G-9000)		
Fontela Electric Incorporated	F	630 932-1600
Addison (G-127)		
Four-Most Inc	G	563 323-3233
Peoria (G-16440)		
Gem Electric Motor Repair	G	815 756-5317
Dekalb (G-7682)		
Goding Electric Company	F	630 858-7700
Glendale Heights (G-10455)		
H & H Motor Service Inc	G	708 652-6100
Cicero (G-6850)		
Harvey Bros Inc	F	309 342-3137
Galesburg (G-10199)		
Heise Industries Inc	G	847 223-2410
Grayslake (G-10781)		
Hills Electric Motor Service	G	815 625-0305
Rock Falls (G-17184)		
Hopcroft Electric Inc	G	618 288-7302
Glen Carbon (G-10388)		
Iesco Inc	E	708 594-1250
Romeoville (G-17831)		
▲ Illinois Electric Works Inc	E	618 451-6900
Granite City (G-10717)		
Industrial Service Solutions	C	917 609-6979
Chicago (G-4910)		
Inman Electric Motors Inc	E	815 223-2288
La Salle (G-12115)		
Integrated Power Services LLC	E	708 877-5310
Thornton (G-19789)		
J & J Electric Motor Repair Sp	G	217 529-0015
Springfield (G-19391)		
Jasiek Motor Rebuilding Inc	G	815 883-3678
Oglesby (G-15842)		
Joes Automotive Inc	G	815 937-9281
Kankakee (G-11982)		
Kankakee Industrial Tech	F	815 933-6683
Bradley (G-2285)		
L A Motors Incorporated	G	773 736-7305
Chicago (G-5142)		
Lakenburges Motor Co	G	618 523-4231
Germantown (G-10331)		
Lange Electric Inc	G	217 347-7626
Effingham (G-8407)		
Lawrence Maddock	F	847 394-1698
Arlington Heights (G-768)		
Lee Foss Electric Motor Svc	G	708 681-5335
Stone Park (G-19556)		
M H Electric Motor & Ctrl Corp	G	630 393-3736
Warrenville (G-20242)		
M R Glenn Electric Inc	G	708 479-9200
Lockport (G-13009)		
Metroeast Motorsports Inc	G	618 628-2466
O Fallon (G-15580)		
Metzka Inc	G	815 932-6363
Kankakee (G-11991)		
▲ Mid-America Taping Reeling Inc	D	630 629-6646
Glendale Heights (G-10475)		
Midwest Elc Mtr Inc Danville	G	217 442-5656
Danville (G-7367)		
New Cie Inc	F	815 224-1485
La Salle (G-12118)		
New Cie Inc	E	815 224-1511
Peru (G-16584)		
OReilly Automotive Stores Inc	G	847 882-4384
Schaumburg (G-18659)		
OReilly Automotive Stores Inc	G	847 360-0012
Waukegan (G-20474)		
OReilly Automotive Stores Inc	G	708 430-8155
Bridgeview (G-2370)		
Park Electric Motor Service	G	217 442-1977
Danville (G-7372)		
Pillarhouse USA Inc	F	847 593-9080
Elk Grove Village (G-9179)		
Precision Drive & Control Inc	G	815 235-7595
Freeport (G-10133)		
Prompt Motor Rewinding Service	G	847 675-7155
Skokie (G-19016)		
Quality Armature Inc	G	773 622-3951
Chicago (G-5929)		
Rathje Enterprises Inc	B	217 423-2593
Decatur (G-7540)		
Richards Electric Motor Co	E	217 222-7154
Quincy (G-16940)		
Rockford Electric Equipment Co	G	815 398-4096
Rockford (G-17593)		
Sandner Electric Co Inc	G	618 932-2179
West Frankfort (G-20682)		
Schaeffer Electric Co	G	618 592-3231
Oblong (G-15829)		
Service Pro Electric Mtr Repr	G	630 766-1215
Bensenville (G-1892)		
Steiner Electric Company	E	312 421-7220
Chicago (G-6239)		
Tracy Electric Inc	E	618 943-6205
Lawrenceville (G-12538)		
Vandalia Electric Mtr Svc Inc	G	618 283-0068
Vandalia (G-20027)		
Voss Electric Inc	G	708 596-6000
Harvey (G-11100)		
▲ Warfield Electric Company Inc	E	815 469-4094
Frankfort (G-9851)		

Employee Codes: A=Over 500 employees, B=251-500
C=101-250, D=51-100, E=20-50, F=10-19, G=3-9

76 MISCELLANEOUS REPAIR SERVICES

Xylem Water Solutions USA Inc ....F 856 467-3636
  Mokena *(G-14129)*

◆ Yaskawa America Inc ....C 847 887-7000
  Waukegan *(G-20520)*

ALPHABETIC SECTION

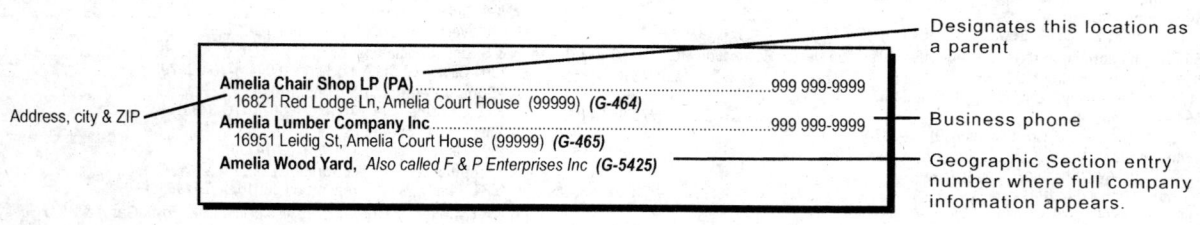

See footnotes for symbols and codes identification.
* Companies listed alphabetically.
* Complete physical or mailing address.

1 Engineering, Batavia *Also called Bevstream Corp (G-1357)*
1 Federal Supply Source Inc 708 964-2222
   30 E 34th St Steger (60475) *(G-19486)*
1 Heavy Equipment Loading Inc 773 581-7374
   6535 S Austin Ave Bedford Park (60638) *(G-1451)*
10 4 Irp Inc 708 485-1040
   8846 47th St Brookfield (60513) *(G-2476)*
1035 Kiss, Chicago *Also called Iheartcommunications Inc (G-4882)*
10g LLC 630 754-2400
   100 Morey Dr Woodridge (60517) *(G-21269)*
10th Magnitude LLC (PA) 224 628-9047
   20 N Wacker Dr Ste 3250 Chicago (60606) *(G-3461)*
10x Microstructures LLC 847 215-7448
   420 Harvester Ct Wheeling (60090) *(G-20834)*
11th Street Express Prtg Inc 815 968-0208
   2135 11th St Rockford (61104) *(G-17275)*
13rf Rental & Fabrication, Murphysboro *Also called Thirteen Rf Inc (G-14761)*
13th Ward Office, Chicago *Also called City of Chicago (G-4158)*
144 International Inc 847 426-8881
   740 S 8th St West Dundee (60118) *(G-20660)*
15679 Wadsworth Inc 847 662-4561
   15679 W Wadsworth Rd Wadsworth (60083) *(G-20207)*
1776 Fabrication LLC 773 895-7590
   735 N Edgewood Ave Ste J Wood Dale (60191) *(G-21146)*
1803 Candles 815 264-3009
   360 E Lincoln Hwy Waterman (60556) *(G-20297)*
1883 Properties Inc (HQ) 847 537-8800
   600 Knightsbridge Pkwy Lincolnshire (60069) *(G-12740)*
2 Koi, Gurnee *Also called Speedpro Imaging (G-10929)*
2 M Tool Company Inc 773 282-0722
   6530 W Dakin St Chicago (60634) *(G-3462)*
20 20 Medical Systems Inc 815 455-7161
   111 Erick St Ste 125 Crystal Lake (60014) *(G-7152)*
20/20 Imaging, Crystal Lake *Also called Konica Minolta Healthcare (G-7218)*
2000plus Groups Inc 630 528-3220
   2607 W 22nd St Ste 39 Oak Brook (60523) *(G-15587)*
2000plus Groups Inc (PA) 800 939-6268
   4343 W 44th Pl Chicago (60632) *(G-3463)*
21 Holdings LLC 630 876-4886
   501 Conde St West Chicago (60185) *(G-20528)*
21st Century Us-Sino Services 312 808-9328
   500 W 18th St Fl 1 Chicago (60616) *(G-3464)*
22nd Century Media 847 272-4565
   60 Revere Dr Northbrook (60062) *(G-15328)*
22nd Century Media (PA) 708 326-9170
   11516 W 183rd St U Sw 3 Orland Park (60467) *(G-15931)*
24land Express Inc 630 766-2424
   1460 Mark St Elk Grove Village (60007) *(G-8789)*
2bald Inc 815 403-8870
   3420 N Richmond Rd Johnsburg (60051) *(G-11800)*
2l Technologies LLC 312 526-3900
   445 N Franklin St Chicago (60654) *(G-3465)*
2m Control Systems Inc 630 709-6225
   245 W Roosevelt Rd Ste 86 West Chicago (60185) *(G-20529)*
2nd Amendment Defense Inc 815 218-2847
   4304 Maray Dr Rockford (61107) *(G-17276)*
2nd Cine Inc 773 455-5808
   637 Frazier St Ste 2 Elgin (60123) *(G-8488)*
3 Angels, Addison *Also called Three Angels Printing Svcs Inc (G-308)*
3 Goldenstar Inc 847 963-0451
   545 E Dundee Rd Palatine (60074) *(G-16088)*
3 Point Ink LLC 618 664-1550
   1550 E City Route 40 Greenville (62246) *(G-10825)*
3-Switch LLC 217 721-4546
   2940 N Albany Ave Chicago (60618) *(G-3466)*
3-V Industries Inc 217 835-4453
   110 W Oak St Benld (62009) *(G-1717)*

300 Below Inc 217 423-3070
   2999 E Parkway Dr Decatur (62526) *(G-7431)*
300 P S I, Olney *Also called Harris Drilling Fluids Inc (G-15864)*
355 Pallet Service 773 431-6688
   704 W Diversey Ave Apt C Addison (60101) *(G-12)*
360 Cabinetry Inc 630 879-0701
   1417 Paramount Pkwy Batavia (60510) *(G-1338)*
360 Digital Print Inc 630 682-3601
   262 Tubeway Dr Carol Stream (60188) *(G-2921)*
360 Yield Center LLC 309 263-4360
   180 Detroit Ave Morton (61550) *(G-14352)*
3abn 618 627-4651
   6020 Green Meadow Rd Thompsonville (62890) *(G-19777)*
3b Media Inc 312 563-9363
   401 N Michigan Ave # 1200 Chicago (60611) *(G-3467)*
3d Industries Inc 630 616-8702
   500 Frontier Way Bensenville (60106) *(G-1719)*
3d Manufacturing Corporation 815 806-9200
   9218 Corsair Rd Unit 5 Frankfort (60423) *(G-9763)*
3d Platform, Roscoe *Also called 3dp Unlimited LLC (G-17896)*
3d Printer Experience LLC 312 896-3399
   350 N Clark St Ste 400 Chicago (60654) *(G-3468)*
3dp Unlimited LLC 815 389-5667
   6402 E Rockton Rd Roscoe (61073) *(G-17896)*
3dpx, Chicago *Also called 3d Printer Experience LLC (G-3468)*
3M Company 309 654-2291
   22614 Route 84 N Cordova (61242) *(G-7005)*
3M Dekalb Distribution 815 756-5087
   12101 Barber Greene Rd Dekalb (60115) *(G-7664)*
3p Works, Chicago *Also called L Street Collaborative LLC (G-5143)*
3primedx Inc 312 621-0643
   191 N Wacker Dr Ste 1500 Chicago (60606) *(G-3469)*
3rd Coast Imaging Inc 312 322-3111
   228 S Wabash Ave Ste 350 Chicago (60604) *(G-3470)*
3v Pallet 708 620-7790
   133 W 154th St South Holland (60473) *(G-19185)*
3v Pallet 708 333-1113
   2205 Thornton Lansing Rd Lansing (60438) *(G-12483)*
3vue LLC 630 796-7441
   6440 Main St Ste 330 Woodridge (60517) *(G-21270)*
4 Elements Company 773 236-2284
   520 Cardinal Pl Mundelein (60060) *(G-14655)*
4 Seasons Sales and Marketing, Park Ridge *Also called Strauss Facter Assoc Inc (G-16297)*
4 U Optical 847 459-8598
   125 E Lake Cook Rd # 110 Buffalo Grove (60089) *(G-2502)*
4200 Kirchoff Corp 773 551-1541
   4200 Kirchoff Rd Rolling Meadows (60008) *(G-17707)*
425 Manufacturing 815 873-7066
   5004 27th Ave Rockford (61109) *(G-17277)*
4c Insights Inc 602 881-9127
   1 E Wacker Dr Ste 700 Chicago (60601) *(G-3471)*
4degrees AV Inc 903 253-7398
   5254 S Dorchester Ave # 205 Chicago (60615) *(G-3472)*
4ever Design Studio, Arlington Heights *Also called 4ever Printing Inc (G-679)*
4ever Printing Inc 847 222-1525
   3401b N Kennicott Ave Arlington Heights (60004) *(G-679)*
4knines, Vernon Hills *Also called Seat Cover Pro LLC (G-20094)*
4l Technologies Inc (HQ) 815 431-8100
   122 W Madison St Ottawa (61350) *(G-16035)*
4l Waterjet, Winchester *Also called Lashcon Inc (G-21106)*
4urhair, Chicago *Also called Hair Plus Studios LLC (G-4768)*
4x4 Headquarters LLC 217 540-5337
   18086 N Highway 45 Effingham (62401) *(G-8381)*
5 Alarm Coin Laundry Inc 815 298-0585
   3939 W Riverside Blvd E Rockford (61101) *(G-17278)*
5 B'S Catering Service, Waterman *Also called William Badal (G-20303)*
503b FDA Outsourcing Facility, Glenview *Also called Bella Pharmaceuticals Inc (G-10529)*

(PA)=Parent Co (HQ)=Headquarters (DH)=Div Headquarters

ALPHABETIC SECTION

51 Elements..847 712-5550
550 Cherbourg Ct S Buffalo Grove (60089) *(G-2503)*
510 Holdings Company LLC..................................618 659-8600
1019 Century Dr Ste 10 Edwardsville (62025) *(G-8343)*
555 Design Fabrication MGT, Chicago Also called 555 Design Fabrication MGT Inc *(G-3473)*
555 Design Fabrication MGT Inc..........................773 869-0555
4501 S Western Blvd Chicago (60609) *(G-3473)*
555 International Inc..773 847-1400
2225 W Pershing Rd Chicago (60609) *(G-3474)*
555 International Inc..773 869-0555
4000 S Bell Ave Chicago (60609) *(G-3475)*
555 International Inc (PA)................................773 869-0555
4501 S Western Blvd Chicago (60609) *(G-3476)*
5h Consulting & Design LLC................................618 317-5822
8211 Oakdale Rd Ellis Grove (62241) *(G-9319)*
5inch, Chicago Also called T 26 Inc *(G-6306)*
680 Design, Elk Grove Village Also called Rebechini Studio Inc *(G-9215)*
6965 North Hamlin LLC..847 673-8900
6965 N Hamlin Ave Lincolnwood (60712) *(G-12809)*
7 Mile Solutions Inc..847 588-2280
7540 N Caldwell Ave Niles (60714) *(G-15096)*
7 Up, East Alton Also called Flowers Distributing Inc *(G-8165)*
7-Up-The American Bottling Co, Loves Park Also called American Bottling Company *(G-13188)*
7000 Inc..312 800-3612
856 Fieldcrest Dr Bolingbrook (60490) *(G-2143)*
773 LLC (PA)..312 707-8780
1629 S Clinton St Chicago (60616) *(G-3477)*
773 LLC..312 707-8780
564 W Randolph St Chicago (60661) *(G-3478)*
78 Brand Co..312 344-1602
1655 S Blue Island Ave Chicago (60608) *(G-3479)*
78 Red Ketchup, Chicago Also called 78 Brand Co *(G-3479)*
8 Electronic Cigarette Inc....................................630 708-6803
1830 Wallace Ave Ste 201 Saint Charles (60174) *(G-18140)*
8 Electronic Cigarettes, Saint Charles Also called 8 Electronic Cigarette Inc *(G-18140)*
815 Pallets Inc..815 678-0012
11600 Sterling Pkwy Richmond (60071) *(G-17006)*
847 696-9278, Rolling Meadows Also called United Chemi-Con Inc *(G-17783)*
87p, LLC, Carol Stream Also called Fresh Factory *(G-2988)*
89robotics, Chicago Also called Eighty Nine Robotics LLC *(G-4463)*
9 Dots Solutions LLC..877 919-9349
112 Terrace Dr Mundelein (60060) *(G-14656)*
9.solutions, Mundelein Also called 9 Dots Solutions LLC *(G-14656)*
9161 Corporation..847 470-8828
9161 N Milwaukee Ave Niles (60714) *(G-15097)*
A & A Cabinet Creations Inc................................630 350-1560
468 Country Club Dr Bensenville (60106) *(G-1720)*
A & A Graphx, Champaign Also called Dabel Incorporated *(G-3284)*
A & A Machine Co Inc..847 985-4619
1530 Jarvis Ave Elk Grove Village (60007) *(G-8790)*
A & A Magnetics Inc..815 338-6054
520 Magnet Way Woodstock (60098) *(G-21352)*
A & A Steel Fabricating Co....................................708 389-4499
14100 S Harrison Ave Posen (60469) *(G-16789)*
A & B Machine Shop..815 397-0495
1920 20th Ave Rockford (61104) *(G-17279)*
A & B Metal Polishing Inc....................................773 847-1077
1900 S Washtenaw Ave Chicago (60608) *(G-3480)*
A & B Printing Service Inc....................................217 789-9034
2122 N Republic St Springfield (62702) *(G-19313)*
A & C Mold Company Inc....................................630 587-0177
3870 Swenson Ave Saint Charles (60174) *(G-18141)*
A & E Forge, Forest Park Also called Clark Caster Co *(G-9710)*
A & E Rubber Stamp Corp....................................312 575-1416
215 N Desplaines St 2n Chicago (60661) *(G-3481)*
A & F Pallet Service Inc..773 767-9500
4333 S Knox Ave Chicago (60632) *(G-3482)*
A & H Bindery, The, Buffalo Grove Also called Ricter Corporation *(G-2593)*
A & H Manufacturing Inc....................................630 543-5900
200 W Laura Dr Addison (60101) *(G-13)*
A & J Finishers..847 352-5408
623 Lunt Ave Schaumburg (60193) *(G-18423)*
A & J Signs..815 476-0128
2104 Woodview Dr Wilmington (60481) *(G-21095)*
A & L Construction Inc..708 343-1660
1951 Cornell Ave Melrose Park (60160) *(G-13816)*
A & M Cabinets, Batavia Also called Anderson & Marter Cabinets *(G-1349)*
A & M Products Company....................................815 875-2667
575 Elm Pl Princeton (61356) *(G-16803)*
A & M Tool Co Inc..847 215-8140
5 W Waltz Dr Wheeling (60090) *(G-20835)*
A & M Wood Products Inc..................................630 323-2555
9900 S Madison St Unit A Burr Ridge (60527) *(G-2647)*
A & R Machine Inc..708 388-4764
12340 S Keeler Ave Alsip (60803) *(G-406)*
A & R Screening LLC..708 598-2480
4611 136th St Crestwood (60418) *(G-7103)*

A & S Arms Inc..224 267-5670
847 Forest View Way Antioch (60002) *(G-593)*
A & S Helicopters Inc..618 337-2600
4000 Vector Dr Cahokia (62206) *(G-2760)*
A & S Steel Specialties Inc....................................815 838-8188
1001 Clinton St Ste A Lockport (60441) *(G-12979)*
A - Square Manufacturing Inc (PA)....................800 628-6720
1100 S Kostner Ave Chicago (60624) *(G-3483)*
A 1 Marking Products..309 762-6096
1801 5th Ave Moline (61265) *(G-14130)*
A 1 Trophies Awards & Engrv..............................630 837-6000
1534 Brandy Pkwy Streamwood (60107) *(G-19558)*
A A A Cylinder, West Frankfort Also called Little Egypt Gas A & Wldg Sups *(G-20677)*
A A Coil Products, University Park Also called M Lizen Manufacturing Co *(G-19958)*
A A N S, Rolling Meadows Also called American Assn Nurosurgeons Inc *(G-17710)*
A A Swift Print Inc..847 301-1122
30 Standish Ln Schaumburg (60193) *(G-18424)*
A and J Development Plus LLC..............................630 470-9539
10101 S Mandel St Ste A Plainfield (60585) *(G-16639)*
A and P Directional Drlg LLC................................708 715-1192
11629 S Mayfield Ave Alsip (60803) *(G-407)*
A and P Directional Drlg LLC (PA)......................708 715-1192
10842 Eleanor Ln Orland Park (60467) *(G-15932)*
A and R Custom Chrome......................................708 728-1005
6528 S Lavergne Ave Chicago (60638) *(G-3484)*
A and T Cigarettes Imports..................................847 836-9134
105 Prairie Lake Rd East Dundee (60118) *(G-8186)*
A and T Labs Incorporated..................................630 668-8562
1926 Berkshire Pl Wheaton (60189) *(G-20783)*
A Arbec Company, Lockport Also called Printing Plus *(G-13019)*
A Ashland Lock Company (PA)............................773 348-5106
2510 N Ashland Ave Chicago (60614) *(G-3485)*
A B, Waukegan Also called AB Specialty Silicones LLC *(G-20405)*
A B C Blind Inc..708 877-7100
108 S Julian St Thornton (60476) *(G-19784)*
A B C Truss, Jerseyville Also called Atlas Building Components Inc *(G-11787)*
A B Kelly Inc..847 639-1022
212 W Main St Ste 5 Cary (60013) *(G-3142)*
A B S Embroidery Inc..708 597-7785
4814 W 129th St Alsip (60803) *(G-408)*
A Barr Ftn Beverage Sls & Svc..............................708 442-2000
16300 103rd St Lemont (60439) *(G-12550)*
A Burst of Sun Inc..815 335-2331
817 N Elida St Winnebago (61088) *(G-21118)*
A C A, Streamwood Also called Aluminum Coil Anodizing Corp *(G-19560)*
A C Gentrol Inc..309 274-5486
100 S 4th St Chillicothe (61523) *(G-6812)*
A C H Retail Products, Oakbrook Terrace Also called Ach Food Companies Inc *(G-15781)*
A Closet Wholesaler..312 654-1400
1155 N Howe St Chicago (60610) *(G-3486)*
A Cnc Manufacturing Facility, Bensenville Also called Art Technologies Inc *(G-1747)*
A Corporate Printing Service................................630 515-0432
7705 Dalewood Pkwy Woodridge (60517) *(G-21271)*
A D Skylights Inc..847 854-2900
206 Berg St Algonquin (60102) *(G-365)*
A D Specialty Sewing..847 639-0390
410 Northwest Hwy Fox River Grove (60021) *(G-9756)*
A Division of A&A Studios Inc..............................312 278-1144
350 N Ogden Ave Ste 10 Chicago (60607) *(G-3487)*
A Division of TEC, Elgin Also called Temperature Equipment Corp *(G-8752)*
A Divison of Da, Montgomery Also called Viking Metal Cabinet Company *(G-14274)*
A E Frasz Inc..630 232-6223
1n545 Brundige Rd Elburn (60119) *(G-8440)*
A E Iskra Inc..815 874-4022
4814 American Rd Rockford (61109) *(G-17280)*
A E Micek Engineering Corp................................847 455-8181
9239 Cherry Ave Franklin Park (60131) *(G-9857)*
A F C, Lake In The Hills Also called Advanced Flxble Composites Inc *(G-12327)*
A F I, Carol Stream Also called Afi Industries Inc *(G-2927)*
A Finkl & Sons Co (HQ)......................................773 975-2510
412 S Wells St Ste 500 Chicago (60607) *(G-3488)*
A Flores, Aurora Also called Flores Precision Products *(G-1096)*
A G Mitchells Jewelers Ltd..................................847 394-0820
10 N Dunton Ave Arlington Heights (60005) *(G-680)*
A Hartlett & Sons Inc..815 338-0109
406 N Eastwood Dr Woodstock (60098) *(G-21353)*
A I 2, Chicago Also called Access International Inc *(G-3514)*
A I I, Danville Also called Automation International Inc *(G-7321)*
A I R, Rochester Also called Appliance Information and Repr *(G-17163)*
A I Satellite Distributing, Loves Park Also called Audio Installers Inc *(G-13193)*
A J Adhesives Inc..708 210-1111
15461 La Salle St South Holland (60473) *(G-19186)*
A J Antunes & Co (PA)......................................630 784-1000
180 Kehoe Blvd Carol Stream (60188) *(G-2922)*
A J Carbide Grinding..847 675-5112
8509 E Prairie Rd Skokie (60076) *(G-18911)*

ALPHABETIC SECTION
Aak Mechanical Inc

A J Funk & Co 847 741-6760
1471 Timber Dr Elgin (60123) *(G-8489)*

A J Horne Inc 630 231-8686
893 Industrial Dr West Chicago (60185) *(G-20530)*

A J Kay Co 224 475-0370
304 Washington Blvd Mundelein (60060) *(G-14657)*

A J Manufacturing Co Inc 630 832-2828
437 W Wrightwood Ave Elmhurst (60126) *(G-9321)*

A J R Industries Inc 847 439-0380
117 Gordon St Elk Grove Village (60007) *(G-8791)*

A J R International Inc (PA) 800 232-3965
300 Regency Dr Glendale Heights (60139) *(G-10435)*

A J Wagner & Son 773 935-1414
1120 N Rand Rd Frnt 1 Wauconda (60084) *(G-20323)*

A K Tool & Manufacturing Inc 630 889-9220
260 Cortland Ave Ste 4 Lombard (60148) *(G-13033)*

A Lakin & Sons Inc (PA) 773 871-6360
2001 Greenfield Rd Montgomery (60538) *(G-14229)*

A Len Complete Auto Svc Ctr, Downers Grove *Also called A Len Radiator Shoppe Inc (G-7948)*

A Len Radiator Shoppe Inc 630 852-5445
333 Ogden Ave Downers Grove (60515) *(G-7948)*

A Lucas & Sons 309 673-8547
1328 Sw Washington St Peoria (61602) *(G-16372)*

A M A, Chicago *Also called American Medical Association (G-3660)*

A M Lee Inc 847 291-1777
2778 Dundee Rd Northbrook (60062) *(G-15329)*

A M P Software Inc 630 240-5922
455 Vermont Dr Elk Grove Village (60007) *(G-8792)*

A M T, Elk Grove Village *Also called American Molding Tech Inc (G-8824)*

A M Tool, Rolling Meadows *Also called Precision Metal Spinning Corp (G-17764)*

A M Tool & Die 847 398-7530
1000 Carnegie St Rolling Meadows (60008) *(G-17708)*

A New Dairy Company 312 421-1234
1234 W Randolph St Chicago (60607) *(G-3489)*

A P L Plastics 773 265-1370
3501 W Fillmore St Chicago (60624) *(G-3490)*

A P Livestock Division G S I 217 226-4449
1004 E Illinois St Assumption (62510) *(G-887)*

A P M, Nokomis *Also called All Precision Mfg LLC (G-15193)*

A P M, Woodstock *Also called American Packaging McHy Inc (G-21358)*

A P S Gas Turbine Inc 708 262-2939
5324 W 124th St Alsip (60803) *(G-409)*

A Plus Apparel 815 675-2117
9902 Fox Bluff Ln Spring Grove (60081) *(G-19262)*

A Plus Signs Inc 708 534-2030
25807 S Governors Hwy Monee (60449) *(G-14194)*

A R B C Inc 815 777-6006
11440 Dandar St Galena (61036) *(G-10163)*

A R C O, Niles *Also called American Vacuum Company (G-15102)*

A R K, Saint Charles *Also called Ark Technologies Inc (G-18149)*

A R Tech & Tool Inc 708 599-5745
8620 S Thomas Ave Bridgeview (60455) *(G-2317)*

A Seamless Gutters, Lombard *Also called Seamless Gutter Corp (G-13128)*

A Stucki Company 618 498-4442
27128 Crystal Lake Rd Jerseyville (62052) *(G-11785)*

A T Products Inc 815 943-3590
1600 S Division St Harvard (60033) *(G-11038)*

A T S, Lawrenceville *Also called Toyota Boshoku Illinois LLC (G-12537)*

A To Z Engraving Co Inc 847 526-7396
1150 Brown St Ste G Wauconda (60084) *(G-20324)*

A To Z Engrvg, Wauconda *Also called A To Z Engraving Co Inc (G-20324)*

A To Z Tool Inc 630 787-0478
400 W Saint Charles Rd # 1 Villa Park (60181) *(G-20126)*

A To Z Type & Graphic Inc 312 587-1887
1703 N Vine St Chicago (60614) *(G-3491)*

A Touch of Beauty Inc 708 387-0360
9034 Brookfield Ave Brookfield (60513) *(G-2477)*

A Touch of Beauty Brass, Brookfield *Also called A Touch of Beauty Inc (G-2477)*

A Trustworthy Sup Source Inc 773 480-0255
6047 N Central Park Ave Chicago (60659) *(G-3492)*

A W Enterprises Inc 708 458-8989
6543 S Laramie Ave Bedford Park (60638) *(G-1452)*

A W Radtke Tool Corporation 847 662-7373
111 E Greenwood Ave Waukegan (60087) *(G-20404)*

A Wheels Inc 847 699-7000
666 Garland Pl Des Plaines (60016) *(G-7717)*

A Wiley & Associates 815 343-7401
707 E Dayton Rd Ottawa (61350) *(G-16036)*

A Z Z, Joliet *Also called AAA Galvanizing - Joliet Inc (G-11816)*

A&B Apparel 815 962-5070
1029 Broadway Frnt Rockford (61104) *(G-17281)*

A&B Reliable 708 228-6148
190 Munster Rd Lemont (60439) *(G-12551)*

A&E Plastics, Lake Bluff *Also called E A M & J Inc (G-12180)*

A&G Manufacturing Inc 815 562-2107
200 E Avenue G Rochelle (61068) *(G-17129)*

A&J Paving Inc 773 889-9133
1911 N Sayre Ave Chicago (60707) *(G-3493)*

A&S Machining & Welding Inc 708 442-4544
4828 S Lawndale Ave Ste 3 Mc Cook (60525) *(G-13689)*

A&W Stone Masonry LLC 618 499-7239
2005 Walnut Grove Rd Harrisburg (62946) *(G-11019)*

A&W Tool Inc 815 653-1700
5309 Bus Pkwy Unit 101 Ringwood (60072) *(G-17037)*

A-1 Food & Liquor, Decatur *Also called Jamiel Inc (G-7510)*

A-1 Lapping & Machine Inc 815 398-1465
539 Grable St Rockford (61109) *(G-17282)*

A-1 Tool Corporation 708 345-5000
1425 Armitage Ave Melrose Park (60160) *(G-13817)*

A-B Die Mold Inc 847 658-1199
5n701 Meadowlark Dr Bartlett (60103) *(G-1261)*

A-Creations Inc 630 541-5801
8102 Lemont Rd Ste 1500 Woodridge (60517) *(G-21272)*

A-Flex Label LLC 630 325-7265
655 Executive Dr Willowbrook (60527) *(G-21028)*

A-Korn Roller Inc (PA) 773 254-5700
3545 S Morgan St Chicago (60609) *(G-3494)*

A-L-L Equipment Company 815 877-7000
5619 Pike Rd Loves Park (61111) *(G-13181)*

A-Line, Chicago *Also called Ascent Tranz Group LLC (G-3747)*

A-Ok Inc 815 943-7431
711 W Brown St Harvard (60033) *(G-11039)*

A-Punch Products Mfg Co, Chicago *Also called Punch Products Manufacturing (G-5915)*

A-Reliable Printing 630 790-2525
604 Roosevelt Rd Glen Ellyn (60137) *(G-10392)*

A-S Medication Solutions LLC (PA) 847 680-3515
2401 Commerce Dr Libertyville (60048) *(G-12624)*

A-Squared Woodworking Inc 773 742-7234
7900 W 75th St Bridgeview (60455) *(G-2318)*

A-Z Sales Inc 630 334-2869
3717 N Cicero Ave Chicago (60641) *(G-3495)*

A-Z Stepping Stones, Bolingbrook *Also called Mandys Soul Food Kitchen LLC (G-2209)*

A.M.H. Products, Chicago *Also called AM Harper Products Inc (G-3640)*

A.P.e, Carol Stream *Also called American Precision Elec Inc (G-2936)*

A.W.T. World Trade, Chicago *Also called Advance World Trade Inc (G-3561)*

A1 Skilled Staffing 309 281-1400
915 15th Ave East Moline (61244) *(G-8221)*

A2 Creative Inc 855 344-5667
1115 N 2nd St Edwardsville (62025) *(G-8344)*

A2 Sales LLC (PA) 708 924-1200
6499 W 65th St Bedford Park (60638) *(G-1453)*

A2z Green Lighting, Bloomingdale *Also called Amerilights Inc (G-1976)*

AA Pallet Inc 773 536-3699
900 W 49th Pl Chicago (60609) *(G-3496)*

AA Rigoni Brothers Inc 815 838-9770
112 Connor Ave Lockport (60441) *(G-12980)*

AA Superb Food Corporation 773 927-3233
2455 S Damen Ave Chicago (60608) *(G-3497)*

AAA Cnc Manufacturing Corp 708 288-2678
14005 Kostner Ave Crestwood (60418) *(G-7104)*

AAA Galvanizing - Joliet Inc 815 284-5001
310 E Progress Dr Dixon (61021) *(G-7887)*

AAA Galvanizing - Joliet Inc (HQ) 815 723-5000
625 Mills Rd Joliet (60433) *(G-11816)*

AAA Galvanizing - Peoria Inc 309 697-4100
6718 W Plank Rd Ste 2 Peoria (61604) *(G-16373)*

AAA Galvanizing of Dixon, Dixon *Also called AAA Galvanizing - Joliet Inc (G-7887)*

AAA Mold Finishers Inc 773 775-3977
7208 W Pratt Ave Chicago (60631) *(G-3498)*

AAA Press International, Arlington Heights *Also called AAA Press Specialists Inc (G-681)*

AAA Press Specialists Inc 847 818-1100
3166 N Kennicott Ave Arlington Heights (60004) *(G-681)*

AAA Tool and Machine, O Fallon *Also called Dkb Partners Inc (G-15572)*

AAA Trash 618 775-1365
408 S Merritt St Odin (62870) *(G-15833)*

Aabbitt Adhesives Inc (PA) 773 227-2700
2403 N Oakley Ave Chicago (60647) *(G-3499)*

Aabbitt Adhesives Inc 773 723-6780
601 W 81st Chicago (60620) *(G-3500)*

Aable License Consultants 708 836-1235
2600 S 25th Ave Ste B Broadview (60155) *(G-2411)*

AAC Microtec North America Inc 602 284-7997
5 Berry Patch Ln Columbia (62236) *(G-6982)*

Aaction Printing 951 788-5111
652 Lowry St Pittsfield (62363) *(G-16627)*

AAF International, Chicago *Also called American Air Filter Co Inc (G-3647)*

Aaii, Chicago *Also called American Association of Indivi (G-3649)*

Aais Services Corporation (PA) 630 681-8347
701 Warrenville Rd # 100 Lisle (60532) *(G-12856)*

Aais Services Corporation 630 457-3263
701 Wrrnvlle Rd Ste 100 Lisle (60532) *(G-12857)*

Aak Mechanical Inc 217 935-8501
10962 Riddle Rd Clinton (61727) *(G-6917)*

ALPHABETIC

Aalborg Company.....708 246-8858
4521 Harvey Ave Western Springs (60558) ***(G-20718)***
AAM Manufacturing.....708 606-9360
455 Gibraltar Dr Bolingbrook (60440) ***(G-2144)***
AAM-Ro Corporation.....708 343-5543
3110 S 26th Ave Broadview (60155) ***(G-2412)***
Aana Publishing Inc.....847 692-7050
222 S Prospect Ave Park Ridge (60068) ***(G-16262)***
AAR Aircraft & Eng Sls & Lsg.....630 227-2000
1100 N Wood Dale Rd Wood Dale (60191) ***(G-21147)***
AAR Allen Services Inc (HQ).....630 227-2410
1100 N Wood Dale Rd Wood Dale (60191) ***(G-21148)***
AAR Corp (PA).....630 227-2000
1100 N Wood Dale Rd Wood Dale (60191) ***(G-21149)***
AAR Defense Systems Logistics, Wood Dale *Also called AAR Supply Chain Inc* ***(G-21151)***
AAR Doing It Right, Wood Dale *Also called AAR Corp* ***(G-21149)***
AAR Government Services Inc (HQ).....630 227-2000
1100 N Wood Dale Rd Wood Dale (60191) ***(G-21150)***
AAR Supply Chain Inc (HQ).....630 227-2000
1100 N Wood Dale Rd Wood Dale (60191) ***(G-21151)***
Aardvark Pharma LLC.....630 248-2380
2 Mid America Plz Ste 800 Oakbrook Terrace (60181) ***(G-15779)***
Aardvark Pharmaceuticals, Oakbrook Terrace *Also called Aardvark Pharma LLC* ***(G-15779)***
Aargus Industries, Wheeling *Also called Aargus Plastics Inc* ***(G-20837)***
Aargus Industries Inc.....847 325-4444
540 Allendale Dr Ste 100a Wheeling (60090) ***(G-20836)***
Aargus Plastics Inc.....847 325-4444
540 Allendale Dr Ste 100a Wheeling (60090) ***(G-20837)***
Aaro Roller Corp.....815 398-7655
4338 11th St Rockford (61109) ***(G-17283)***
Aaron Co, Lincolnwood *Also called Gerald Graff* ***(G-12822)***
Aarstar Precision Grinding.....847 678-4880
9007 Exchange Ave Franklin Park (60131) ***(G-9858)***
Aat, Carol Stream *Also called Advanced Audio Technology Inc* ***(G-2925)***
Aaxis Engravers Inc.....224 629-4045
230 William St Ste A Bensenville (60106) ***(G-1721)***
AB & D Custom Cabinets, Homewood *Also called AB&d Custom Furniture Inc* ***(G-11487)***
AB Machine Shop LLC.....618 467-6474
6344 Lake Dr Godfrey (62035) ***(G-10646)***
AB Specialty Silicones LLC (PA).....908 273-8015
3725 Hawthorne Ct Waukegan (60087) ***(G-20405)***
AB&d Custom Furniture Inc.....708 922-9061
17200 Palmer Blvd Homewood (60430) ***(G-11487)***
Aba Custom Woodworking.....815 356-9663
765 Duffy Dr Ste B Crystal Lake (60014) ***(G-7153)***
Abacus Manufacturing Group Inc.....815 654-7050
516 18th Ave Rockford (61104) ***(G-17284)***
Abb Inc.....630 759-7428
1 Territorial Ct Ste A Bolingbrook (60440) ***(G-2145)***
ABB Motors and Mechanical Inc.....630 296-1400
1055 Remington Blvd Ste B Bolingbrook (60440) ***(G-2146)***
ABB Power Protection LLC.....804 236-3300
29029 Network Pl Chicago (60673) ***(G-3501)***
Abbacus Injection Molding Inc.....815 637-9222
1248 Shappert Dr Machesney Park (61115) ***(G-13322)***
Abbco Inc.....630 595-7115
304 Meyer Rd Bensenville (60106) ***(G-1722)***
Abbey Copying Support Svcs Inc.....618 466-3300
3312 Godfrey Rd Godfrey (62035) ***(G-10647)***
Abbey Metal Services Inc.....773 568-0330
820 W 120th St Chicago (60643) ***(G-3502)***
Abbey Products LLP.....636 922-5577
112 Willing Way Troy (62294) ***(G-19909)***
Abbey Ridge Brewery & Tap Room, Pomona *Also called Abbey Ridge LLC* ***(G-16762)***
Abbey Ridge LLC.....618 713-2537
24 Brewster Vly Pomona (62975) ***(G-16762)***
Abbott Health Products Inc (HQ).....847 937-6100
100 Abbott Park Rd North Chicago (60064) ***(G-15290)***
Abbott Interfast LLC.....847 459-6200
190 Abbott Dr Ste A Wheeling (60090) ***(G-20838)***
Abbott Label Inc.....630 773-3614
1414 Norwood Ave Itasca (60143) ***(G-11614)***
Abbott Laboratories (PA).....224 667-6100
100 Abbott Park Rd Abbott Park (60064) ***(G-1)***
Abbott Laboratories.....224 330-0271
279 Adler Dr Libertyville (60048) ***(G-12625)***
Abbott Laboratories.....847 937-2210
6235 N Newark Ave Chicago (60631) ***(G-3503)***
Abbott Laboratories.....847 938-3220
3561 Burwood Dr Waukegan (60085) ***(G-20406)***
Abbott Laboratories.....800 551-5838
75 Remittance Dr Chicago (60675) ***(G-3504)***
Abbott Laboratories.....847 735-0573
26525 N Riverwoods Blvd Mettawa (60045) ***(G-13977)***
Abbott Laboratories.....847 937-6100
Mrtn Lthr Kng Dr Rr 41 North Chicago (60064) ***(G-15291)***
Abbott Laboratories.....847 937-6100
3629 Burwood Dr Waukegan (60085) ***(G-20407)***
Abbott Laboratories.....224 361-7129
1800 Brummel Ave Elk Grove Village (60007) ***(G-8793)***
Abbott Laboratories.....800 551-5838
100 Saunders Rd Lake Forest (60045) ***(G-12218)***
Abbott Laboratories.....847 938-4196
Bldg Ap 52 200 Ab Dept 36 North Chicago (60064) ***(G-15292)***
Abbott Laboratories.....847 932-7900
1401 Sheridan Rd North Chicago (60064) ***(G-15293)***
Abbott Laboratories.....847 935-8130
1136 Laurel Ln Gurnee (60031) ***(G-10852)***
Abbott Laboratories.....312 944-0660
2355 Waukegan Rd Ste 300 Bannockburn (60015) ***(G-1188)***
Abbott Laboratories.....847 937-6100
215 E Washington St Des Plaines (60016) ***(G-7718)***
Abbott Laboratories.....847 855-9217
1175 Tri State Pkwy Gurnee (60031) ***(G-10853)***
Abbott Laboratories.....847 937-6100
200 Abbott Park Rd North Chicago (60064) ***(G-15294)***
Abbott Laboratories.....847 937-6100
1150 S Northpoint Blvd Waukegan (60085) ***(G-20408)***
Abbott Laboratories Inc.....224 668-2076
200 Abbott Park Rd Abbott Park (60064) ***(G-2)***
Abbott Laboratories Intl Co (HQ).....847 937-6100
100 Abbott Park Rd North Chicago (60064) ***(G-15295)***
Abbott Laboratories PCF Ltd (HQ).....847 937-6100
100 Abbott Park Rd North Chicago (60064) ***(G-15296)***
Abbott Laboratories Svcs Corp (HQ).....708 937-6100
1 Abbott Park Rd North Chicago (60064) ***(G-15297)***
Abbott Labs Hlth Care Tr.....224 667-6100
100 Abbott Park Rd Abbott Park (60064) ***(G-3)***
Abbott Machine Co (PA).....618 465-1898
700 W Broadway Alton (62002) ***(G-540)***
Abbott Molecular Inc.....224 361-7800
1300 E Touhy Ave Des Plaines (60018) ***(G-7719)***
Abbott Molecular Inc (HQ).....224 361-7800
1300 E Touhy Ave Des Plaines (60018) ***(G-7720)***
ABBOTT NUTRITION, Abbott Park *Also called Abbott Laboratories* ***(G-1)***
Abbott Nutrition, Chicago *Also called Abbott Laboratories* ***(G-3504)***
Abbott Nutrition, Lake Forest *Also called Abbott Laboratories* ***(G-12218)***
Abbott Nutrition Mfg Inc.....614 624-6083
200 Abbott Park Rd Abbott Park (60064) ***(G-4)***
Abbott Pharmaceutical Corp, Abbott Park *Also called Abbvie Holdings Inc* ***(G-8)***
Abbott Plastics & Supply Co.....815 874-8500
3302 Lonergan Dr Rockford (61109) ***(G-17285)***
Abbott Point of Care Inc.....847 937-6100
100 Abbott Park Rd Abbott Park (60064) ***(G-5)***
Abbott Products Inc (HQ).....847 937-6100
100 Abbott Park Rd Abbott Park (60064) ***(G-6)***
Abbott Scott Manufacturing Co.....773 342-7200
4215 W Grand Ave Chicago (60651) ***(G-3505)***
Abbott Universal LLC (HQ).....224 667-6100
100 Abbott Park Rd Abbott Park (60064) ***(G-7)***
Abbott-Abbvie Multiple Employe.....847 473-2053
100 Abbott Park Rd North Chicago (60064) ***(G-15298)***
Abbotts Minute Printing Inc.....708 339-6010
611 E 170th St South Holland (60473) ***(G-19187)***
Abbvie.....847 946-8753
1027 Aberdeen Ln Mundelein (60060) ***(G-14658)***
Abbvie.....847 548-1016
480 S Us Highway 45 Grayslake (60030) ***(G-10758)***
Abbvie Endocrinology Inc.....888 857-0668
1 N Waukegan Rd Apt 5ne North Chicago (60064) ***(G-15299)***
Abbvie Holdings Inc.....847 937-7632
100 Abbott Park Rd Abbott Park (60064) ***(G-8)***
Abbvie Inc.....847 367-7621
75 N Fairway Dr Vernon Hills (60061) ***(G-20038)***
Abbvie Inc.....847 937-4566
200 Abbott Park Rd Abbott Park (60064) ***(G-9)***
Abbvie Inc (PA).....847 932-7900
1 N Waukegan Rd North Chicago (60064) ***(G-15300)***
Abbvie Inc.....847 932-7900
1401 Sheridan Rd North Chicago (60064) ***(G-15301)***
Abbvie Inc.....847 473-4787
1150 S Northpoint Blvd Waukegan (60085) ***(G-20409)***
Abbvie Inc.....847 938-2042
1675 Lakeside Ave J23 North Chicago (60064) ***(G-15302)***
Abbvie Respiratory LLC.....847 937-6100
100 Abbott Park Rd North Chicago (60064) ***(G-15303)***
Abbvie US LLC.....800 255-5162
1 N Waukegan Rd North Chicago (60064) ***(G-15304)***
Abc Inc.....312 980-1000
190 N State St Fl 7 Chicago (60601) ***(G-3506)***
ABC Beverage Mfg Inc.....708 449-2600
400 N Wolf Rd Ste A Northlake (60164) ***(G-15538)***
ABC Business Forms Inc.....773 774-8282
5654 N Elston Ave Chicago (60646) ***(G-3507)***
ABC Coating Company III Inc.....708 258-9633
1160 N Boudreau Rd Manteno (60950) ***(G-13443)***
ABC Imaging of Washington.....312 253-0040
161 W Harrison St C-101 Chicago (60605) ***(G-3508)***

ABC Printing, Chicago *Also called ABC Business Forms Inc* ***(G-3507)***
Abco Metals Corporations.....773 881-1504
1020 W 94th St Chicago (60620) ***(G-3509)***
Abct Corporation.....773 427-1010
3924 W Devon Ave Ste 300 Lincolnwood (60712) ***(G-12810)***
Abel Howe Crane, Woodridge *Also called Columbus McKinnon Corporation* ***(G-21286)***
Abel Vault & Monument Co Inc.....309 647-0105
1001 E Linn St Canton (61520) ***(G-2820)***
Abelei Inc.....630 859-1410
194 Alder Dr North Aurora (60542) ***(G-15253)***
Aberdeen Group, Rosemont *Also called Hw Holdco LLC* ***(G-18026)***
Aberdeen Technologies Inc.....630 665-8590
272 Commonwealth Dr Carol Stream (60188) ***(G-2923)***
Aberdeen Window Shade Service, Chicago *Also called Shade Brookline Co* ***(G-6145)***
Aberdon Enterprises.....847 228-1300
225 Bond St Elk Grove Village (60007) ***(G-8794)***
Abet Industries Corporation.....708 482-8282
111 Kemman Ave La Grange Park (60526) ***(G-12094)***
Abet Technologies LLC.....847 682-5541
9446 Hamlin Ave Evanston (60203) ***(G-9485)***
ABG Bag Inc.....815 963-9525
1925 Elmwood Rd Rockford (61103) ***(G-17286)***
Ability Cabinet Co Inc.....847 678-6678
3503 Martens St Franklin Park (60131) ***(G-9859)***
Ability Engineering, South Holland *Also called Ae2009 Technologies Inc* ***(G-19188)***
Ability Engineering Technology, South Holland *Also called Bennu Group Inc* ***(G-19200)***
Ability Fasteners Inc.....847 593-4230
685 Fargo Ave Elk Grove Village (60007) ***(G-8795)***
Ability Metal Company.....847 437-7040
1355 Greenleaf Ave Elk Grove Village (60007) ***(G-8796)***
Ability Plastics Inc.....708 458-4480
8721 Industrial Dr Justice (60458) ***(G-11949)***
Ability Welding Service Inc.....630 595-3737
500 Meyer Rd Bensenville (60106) ***(G-1723)***
Abitec Corporation.....217 465-8577
1800 S Main St Paris (61944) ***(G-16223)***
Abitzy Inc.....847 659-9228
945 Sivert Dr Wood Dale (60191) ***(G-21152)***
Abki Tech Service Inc.....847 818-8403
764 Meadow Dr Des Plaines (60016) ***(G-7721)***
Abkitech, Des Plaines *Also called Abki Tech Service Inc* ***(G-7721)***
Ablaze Welding & Fabricating.....815 965-0046
2003 Kishwaukee St Rockford (61104) ***(G-17287)***
Able American Plastics Inc.....815 678-4646
9703 Us Highway 12 Frnt Unit Richmond (60071) ***(G-17007)***
Able Barmilling & Mfg Co Inc.....708 343-5666
1111 N Old Rand Rd Wauconda (60084) ***(G-20325)***
Able Barmilling & Mfg Inc, Wauconda *Also called Able Barmilling & Mfg Co Inc* ***(G-20325)***
Able Die Casting Corporation.....847 678-1991
3907 Wesley Ter Schiller Park (60176) ***(G-18781)***
Able Electropolishing, Chicago *Also called Metco Treating and Dev Co* ***(G-5407)***
Able Electropolishing Co Inc.....773 277-1600
2001 S Kilbourn Ave Chicago (60623) ***(G-3510)***
Able Printing Service Inc.....708 788-7115
6837 Stanley Ave Berwyn (60402) ***(G-1947)***
ABM Marking Ltd.....618 277-3773
2799 S Belt W Belleville (62226) ***(G-1526)***
ABM Marking Services Ltd.....618 277-3773
2799 S Belt W Belleville (62226) ***(G-1527)***
Abner Trucking Co Inc.....618 676-1301
207 S 1st St Se Clay City (62824) ***(G-6902)***
About Face Designs Inc.....847 914-9040
1510 Old Deerfield Rd # 211 Highland Park (60035) ***(G-11250)***
About Learning Inc.....847 487-1800
441 W Bonner Rd Wauconda (60084) ***(G-20326)***
Above & Beyond Black Oxiding.....708 345-7100
1029 N 27th Ave Melrose Park (60160) ***(G-13818)***
Above Waves Inc.....708 341-9123
11600 N Brightway Dr Mokena (60448) ***(G-14068)***
Abrading Machinery Division, Broadview *Also called AAM-Ro Corporation* ***(G-2412)***
Abrasic 90 Inc.....847 647-5994
7525 N Oak Park Ave Niles (60714) ***(G-15098)***
Abrasive.....630 893-7800
454 Scott Dr Bloomingdale (60108) ***(G-1973)***
Abrasive Rubber Wheel Co.....847 587-0900
135 S Us Highway 12 Fox Lake (60020) ***(G-9743)***
Abrasive Technology Inc.....847 888-7100
1175 Bowes Rd Elgin (60123) ***(G-8490)***
Abrasive West LLC.....630 736-0818
1292 Humbracht Cir Ste F Bartlett (60103) ***(G-1262)***
Abrasive-Form LLC (PA).....630 220-3437
454 Scott Dr Bloomingdale (60108) ***(G-1974)***
Abraxis Bioscience LLC.....310 437-7715
1300 Chase Ave Elk Grove Village (60007) ***(G-8797)***
Abraxis Bioscience LLC.....310 883-1300
2020 N Ruby St Melrose Park (60160) ***(G-13819)***
ABS Equipment Division, Itasca *Also called ABS Graphics Inc* ***(G-11615)***
ABS Graphics Inc (PA).....630 495-2400
900 N Rohlwing Rd Itasca (60143) ***(G-11615)***
ABS Tool & Machine Inc.....815 968-4630
1202 20th Ave Rockford (61104) ***(G-17288)***
Absolute Grinding and Mfg.....815 964-1999
2400 11th St Rockford (61104) ***(G-17289)***
Absolute Indus Fabricators, Addison *Also called Aif Inc* ***(G-24)***
Absolute Turn Inc.....847 459-4629
1704 S Wolf Rd Wheeling (60090) ***(G-20839)***
Absolute Windows Inc.....708 599-9191
9630 S 76th Ave Oak Lawn (60457) ***(G-15693)***
Absolutely Custom, Spring Grove *Also called Sportdecals Inc* ***(G-19301)***
Abundance House Treasure Nfp.....312 788-4316
1309 S Kedzie Ave Chicago (60623) ***(G-3511)***
Abundant Living Christian Ctr.....708 896-6181
14540 Lincoln Ave Dolton (60419) ***(G-7928)***
Abyss Salon Inc.....312 880-0263
67 E 16th St Ste 5 Chicago (60616) ***(G-3512)***
Abzenco Welding Inc.....630 234-8021
1183 Pierson Dr Batavia (60510) ***(G-1339)***
AC Americos.....312 366-2943
633 S Plymouth Ct Apt 201 Chicago (60605) ***(G-3513)***
AC Mold, Saint Charles *Also called A & C Mold Company Inc* ***(G-18141)***
Academy of Awards II, Peoria *Also called Academy Screenprinting Awards* ***(G-16374)***
Academy Screenprinting Awards.....309 686-0026
1316 E War Memorial Dr Peoria (61614) ***(G-16374)***
Accel Corporation.....630 579-6961
900 Douglas Rd Batavia (60510) ***(G-1340)***
Accelerated Assemblies Inc.....630 616-6680
725 Nicholas Blvd Elk Grove Village (60007) ***(G-8798)***
Accelerated Pharma Inc (PA).....773 517-0789
15w155 81st St Burr Ridge (60527) ***(G-2648)***
Accelrted Mch Design Engrg LLC.....815 316-6381
3044 Eastrock Ct Rockford (61109) ***(G-17290)***
Accent Metal Finishing Inc.....847 678-7420
9331 Byron St Schiller Park (60176) ***(G-18782)***
Accents By Fred.....708 366-9850
7519 Madison St Forest Park (60130) ***(G-9707)***
Access Assembly LLC.....847 894-1047
1047 E High St Mundelein (60060) ***(G-14659)***
Access International Inc.....312 920-9366
180 N Stetson Ave # 3660 Chicago (60601) ***(G-3514)***
Access Medical Supply Inc.....847 891-6210
658 Albion Ave Schaumburg (60193) ***(G-18425)***
Acciona Windpower N Amer LLC.....319 643-9463
333 W Wacker Dr Ste 1500 Chicago (60606) ***(G-3515)***
Acclaim Sign Company, Saint Charles *Also called Toms Signs* ***(G-18290)***
Acco Brands Inc.....847 541-9500
4 Corporate Dr Lake Zurich (60047) ***(G-12373)***
Acco Brands Corporation (PA).....847 541-9500
4 Corporate Dr Lake Zurich (60047) ***(G-12374)***
Acco Brands International Inc.....847 541-9500
4 Corporate Dr Lake Zurich (60047) ***(G-12375)***
Acco Brands USA LLC (HQ).....800 222-6462
4 Corporate Dr Lake Zurich (60047) ***(G-12376)***
Acco Brands USA LLC.....708 280-4702
2171 W Executive Dr # 500 Addison (60101) ***(G-14)***
Acco Brands USA LLC.....847 272-3700
500 Bond St Lincolnshire (60069) ***(G-12741)***
Acco Europe Fin Holdings LLC.....800 222-6462
4 Corporate Dr Lake Zurich (60047) ***(G-12377)***
Acco Intl Holdings Inc.....800 222-6462
4 Corporate Dr Lake Zurich (60047) ***(G-12378)***
Accord Carton Co.....708 272-3050
6155 W 115th St Alsip (60803) ***(G-410)***
Accord Packaging, Alsip *Also called Accord Carton Co* ***(G-410)***
Accord Packaging LLC.....708 272-3050
6155 W 115th St Alsip (60803) ***(G-411)***
Accounting Department, Chicago *Also called Newly Weds Foods Inc* ***(G-5586)***
Accro Precision Grinding Inc.....708 681-0520
6648 S Narragansett Ave Chicago (60638) ***(G-3516)***
Accu Cast 2 Inc.....423 622-4344
412 N State St Elgin (60123) ***(G-8491)***
Accu Cut Inc.....815 229-3525
1617 Magnolia St Rockford (61104) ***(G-17291)***
Accu-Chem Industries Inc.....708 344-0900
1930 George St Ste 3 Melrose Park (60160) ***(G-13820)***
Accu-Cut Diamond Tool Company (PA).....708 457-8800
423840 N Sayre Ave Norridge (60706) ***(G-15228)***
Accu-Cut Dmnd Bore Szing Syste (HQ).....708 457-8800
4238 N Sayre Ave Norridge (60706) ***(G-15229)***
Accu-Fab Incorporated.....847 541-4230
1550 Abbott Dr Wheeling (60090) ***(G-20840)***
Accu-Grind Manufacturing Inc.....847 526-2700
386 Hollow Hill Rd Wauconda (60084) ***(G-20327)***
Accu-Wright Fiberglass Inc.....618 337-3318
2393 Carol St East Saint Louis (62206) ***(G-8295)***
Accubow LLC.....815 250-0607
350 5th St Ste 266 Peru (61354) ***(G-16563)***
Accucast Inc.....815 394-1875
5113 27th Ave Rockford (61109) ***(G-17292)***

ALPHABETIC

Accudata, Moline *Also called L C Inn Partners* ***(G-14156)***
Accuity Inc (HQ)....847 676-9600
1007 Church St Ste 600 Evanston (60201) ***(G-9486)***
Acculight LLC....630 847-1000
2570 United Ln Elk Grove Village (60007) ***(G-8799)***
Accumation Inc....815 455-6250
6211 Factory Rd Crystal Lake (60014) ***(G-7154)***
Accurail Inc....630 365-6400
400 W Nebraska St Elburn (60119) ***(G-8441)***
Accurate Anodizing Div, Cicero *Also called Saporito Finishing Co* ***(G-6874)***
Accurate Anodizing Division, Chicago *Also called Saporito Finishing Co* ***(G-6103)***
Accurate Auto Manufacturing Co....618 244-0727
1804 S 8th St Mount Vernon (62864) ***(G-14595)***
Accurate Business Controls Inc....815 633-5500
7846 Burden Rd Machesney Park (61115) ***(G-13323)***
Accurate Cnc Machine, Roscoe *Also called Accurate CNc Machining Inc* ***(G-17897)***
Accurate CNc Machining Inc....815 623-6516
5365 Edith Ln Roscoe (61073) ***(G-17897)***
Accurate Color Compounding Inc....630 978-1227
1666 Dearborn Ave Aurora (60505) ***(G-1041)***
Accurate Cstm Sash Mllwk Corp....708 423-0423
5516 W 110th St Ste 1 Oak Lawn (60453) ***(G-15694)***
Accurate Custom Cabinets Inc....630 458-0460
115 W Fay Ave Addison (60101) ***(G-15)***
Accurate Die Cutting Inc....847 437-7215
120 Joey Dr Elk Grove Village (60007) ***(G-8800)***
Accurate Elc Mtr & Pump Co....708 448-2792
6955 W 111th St Worth (60482) ***(G-21453)***
Accurate Engine & Machine Inc....773 237-4942
5053 W Diversey Ave Chicago (60639) ***(G-3517)***
Accurate Fabricators Inc....618 451-1886
1603 Cleveland Blvd Granite City (62040) ***(G-10689)***
Accurate Finishers....630 543-8575
1213 W Capitol Dr 1 Addison (60101) ***(G-16)***
Accurate Grinding Co Inc....708 371-1887
14003 S Harrison Ave Posen (60469) ***(G-16790)***
Accurate Metal Components Inc....847 520-5900
7540 N Caldwell Ave Niles (60714) ***(G-15099)***
Accurate Metal Fabricating LLC....773 235-0400
1657 N Kostner Ave Chicago (60639) ***(G-3518)***
Accurate Metal Finishing Co....847 428-7705
359 Sola Dr Gilberts (60136) ***(G-10349)***
Accurate Metallizing Inc....708 424-7747
5340 W 111th St Ste 2 Oak Lawn (60453) ***(G-15695)***
Accurate Metals Illinois LLC....815 966-6320
2524 11th St Rockford (61104) ***(G-17293)***
Accurate Partitions Corp....708 442-6801
160 Tower Dr Burr Ridge (60527) ***(G-2649)***
Accurate Parts Mfg Co....630 616-4125
220 Gateway Rd Bensenville (60106) ***(G-1724)***
Accurate Perforating Co Inc....773 254-3232
3636 S Kedzie Ave Chicago (60632) ***(G-3519)***
Accurate Printing Inc....708 824-0058
4749 W 136th St Midlothian (60445) ***(G-13989)***
Accurate Products Incorporated....773 878-2200
4645 N Ravenswood Ave Chicago (60640) ***(G-3520)***
Accurate Radiation Shielding....847 639-5533
206 Cleveland St Cary (60013) ***(G-3143)***
Accurate Reliable Technology, Bridgeview *Also called Art Cnc Machining LLC* ***(G-2325)***
Accurate Repro Inc....630 428-4433
2368 Corporate Ln Ste 100 Naperville (60563) ***(G-14763)***
Accurate Rivet Manufacturing....630 766-3401
343 Beinoris Dr Wood Dale (60191) ***(G-21153)***
Accurate Security & Lock Corp....815 455-0133
5533 Danbury Cir Lake In The Hills (60156) ***(G-12326)***
Accurate Spring Tech Inc....815 344-3333
5801 W Hill St McHenry (60050) ***(G-13713)***
Accurate Tool Inc....847 437-8544
2460 E Oakton St Arlington Heights (60005) ***(G-682)***
Accurate Wire Strip Frming Inc....630 260-1000
175 Tubeway Dr Carol Stream (60188) ***(G-2924)***
Accuride Corporation....630 568-3914
201 E Ogden Ave Ste 220 Hinsdale (60521) ***(G-11360)***
Accushim Inc (PA)....708 442-6448
4601 Lawndale Ave Lyons (60534) ***(G-13300)***
Accusol Incorporated....773 283-4686
9632 S Kildare Ave Oak Lawn (60453) ***(G-15696)***
Accutech Machining Inc....630 350-2066
381 Evergreen Ave Bensenville (60106) ***(G-1725)***
Accutone Hearing Aid Inc....773 545-3279
1580 Sherman Ave Evanston (60201) ***(G-9487)***
Accutrace Inc....847 290-9900
2425 Touhy Ave Elk Grove Village (60007) ***(G-8801)***
Accuware Incorporated....630 858-8409
799 Roosevelt Rd 3-218 Glen Ellyn (60137) ***(G-10393)***
Acd USA Inc....929 428-1744
1001 Mittel Dr Wood Dale (60191) ***(G-21154)***
Ace Anodizing Impregnating Inc....708 547-6680
4161 Butterfield Rd Hillside (60162) ***(G-11324)***
Ace Bakeries....312 225-4973
3241 S Halsted St Chicago (60608) ***(G-3521)***
Ace Coating Enterprises Inc (PA)....708 547-6680
4161 Butterfield Rd Hillside (60162) ***(G-11325)***
Ace Custom Upholstery & Rod Sp....618 842-2913
200 W Delaware St Fairfield (62837) ***(G-9616)***
Ace Engraving & Specialties Co....815 759-2093
4204 Ponca St McHenry (60050) ***(G-13714)***
Ace Graphics Inc....630 357-2244
2052 Corporate Ln Naperville (60563) ***(G-14764)***
Ace Grease Service Inc (PA)....618 781-1207
9035 State Route 163 Millstadt (62260) ***(G-14041)***
Ace Grease Service Inc....618 337-0974
9011 State Route 163 Millstadt (62260) ***(G-14042)***
Ace Industries, Chicago *Also called Acme Spinning Company Inc* ***(G-3528)***
Ace Industries, Chicago *Also called Ace Plating Company* ***(G-3522)***
Ace Machine & Tool Inc....815 793-5077
300 W Lincoln Hwy Ste 6 Cortland (60112) ***(G-7015)***
Ace Metal Crafts Company....847 455-1010
484 Thomas Dr Bensenville (60106) ***(G-1726)***
Ace Metal Refinishers Inc....800 323-7147
2001 Spring Rd Oak Brook (60523) ***(G-15588)***
Ace Metal Refinishers Inc (PA)....630 778-9200
978 N Dupage Ave Lombard (60148) ***(G-13034)***
Ace Metal Spinning Inc....708 389-5635
11630 S Mayfield Ave Alsip (60803) ***(G-412)***
Ace of Diamonds, Chicago *Also called Hakimian Gem Co* ***(G-4770)***
Ace Pcb Design Inc....847 674-8745
5138 Conrad St Skokie (60077) ***(G-18912)***
Ace Plastic Inc....815 635-3737
7942 N 3350 East Rd Chatsworth (60921) ***(G-3425)***
Ace Plating Company....773 927-2711
3433 W 48th Pl Chicago (60632) ***(G-3522)***
Ace Precision Tool & Mfg Co....847 690-0111
1612 Landmeier Rd Elk Grove Village (60007) ***(G-8802)***
Ace Printing Co....618 259-2711
615 E Airline Dr East Alton (62024) ***(G-8162)***
Ace Sand Blast, Chicago *Also called Ace Sandblast Company* ***(G-3523)***
Ace Sandblast Company....773 777-6654
4601 W Roscoe St Chicago (60641) ***(G-3523)***
Ace Sign Co....217 522-8417
2540 S 1st St Springfield (62704) ***(G-19314)***
Aces, Chicago *Also called Advanced Cstm Enrgy Sltons Inc* ***(G-3563)***
Ach Food Companies Inc....866 386-8282
1 Parkview Plz Ste 500 Oakbrook Terrace (60181) ***(G-15780)***
Ach Food Companies Inc (HQ)....866 386-8282
1 Parkview Plz Ste 500 Oakbrook Terrace (60181) ***(G-15781)***
Ach Food Companies Inc....708 458-8690
6400 S Archer Rd Summit Argo (60501) ***(G-19676)***
Aci, Spring Valley *Also called Aqua Control Inc* ***(G-19307)***
Aci Illinois, LLC, Williamsville *Also called Icg Illinois LLC* ***(G-21023)***
Acj Partners LLC....630 745-1335
11552 S Bell Ave Chicago (60643) ***(G-3524)***
Acl Inc....773 285-0295
840 W 49th Pl Chicago (60609) ***(G-3525)***
Acm Inc....847 473-1991
2254 Commonwealth Ave North Chicago (60064) ***(G-15305)***
Acme Alliance, Northbrook *Also called Acme Die Casting LLC* ***(G-15331)***
Acme Alliance LLC (HQ)....847 272-9520
3610 Commercial Ave Northbrook (60062) ***(G-15330)***
Acme Auto Electric Co....708 754-5420
2626 Chicago Rd S Chicago Hts (60411) ***(G-18115)***
Acme Awning Co....847 446-0153
1500 Old Deerfield Rd # 21 Highland Park (60035) ***(G-11251)***
Acme Awning Co Inc....847 446-0153
325 Pebblecreek Dr Lake Zurich (60047) ***(G-12379)***
Acme Button & Buttonhole Co....773 907-8400
4638 N Ravenswood Ave # 2 Chicago (60640) ***(G-3526)***
Acme Control Service Inc....773 774-9191
6140 W Higgins Ave Chicago (60630) ***(G-3527)***
Acme Design Inc....847 841-7400
37 N Union St Elgin (60123) ***(G-8492)***
Acme Die Casting LLC....847 272-9520
3610 Commercial Ave Northbrook (60062) ***(G-15331)***
Acme Finishing Company LLC....847 640-7890
1595 Oakton St Elk Grove Village (60007) ***(G-8803)***
Acme Grinding & Manufacturing....815 323-1380
6871 Belford Indus Dr Belvidere (61008) ***(G-1644)***
Acme Industrial Company (HQ)....847 428-3911
441 Maple Ave Carpentersville (60110) ***(G-3090)***
Acme Industries Inc....847 296-3346
1325 Pratt Blvd Elk Grove Village (60007) ***(G-8804)***
Acme Marble Co Inc....630 964-7162
1103 Belair Dr Darien (60561) ***(G-7399)***
Acme Sales, Chicago *Also called Acme Button & Buttonhole Co* ***(G-3526)***
Acme Scale Systems, Villa Park *Also called Florida Metrology LLC* ***(G-20147)***
Acme Screw Co (PA)....630 665-2200
1201 W Union Ave Wheaton (60187) ***(G-20784)***

ALPHABETIC SECTION

Acme Screw Co 815 332-7548
  125 E State St Cherry Valley (61016) *(G-3436)*
Acme Spinning Company Inc 773 927-2711
  3433 W 48th Pl Fl 1 Chicago (60632) *(G-3528)*
Acme Wire Products LLC 708 345-4430
  2915 S 18th Ave Fl 1 Broadview (60155) *(G-2413)*
Acmealliance, Northbrook *Also called Acme Alliance LLC (G-15330)*
Acnc, Downers Grove *Also called American Comm & Networks (G-7950)*
Aco Inc 773 774-5200
  5656 N Northwest Hwy Chicago (60646) *(G-3529)*
Acomtech Mold Inc 847 741-3537
  39w433 Highland Ave Ste 1 Elgin (60124) *(G-8493)*
ACORN BOOK, Springfield *Also called Elliot Inst For Scial Scnces R (G-19361)*
Acorn Diversified Inc 708 478-1051
  17809 New Jersey Ct # 14 Orland Park (60467) *(G-15933)*
Acorn Wire and Iron Works LLC 312 243-6414
  2415 W 21st St Chicago (60608) *(G-3530)*
Acoustic Avenue Inc 217 544-9810
  3023 E Sangamon Ave Springfield (62702) *(G-19315)*
ACP PUBLICATIONS, South Holland *Also called American Catholic Press Inc (G-19191)*
Acp Tower Holdings LLC 800 835-8527
  311 S Wacker Dr Ste 4300 Chicago (60606) *(G-3531)*
Acquamed Technologies Inc 630 728-4014
  195 Kendall Point Dr # 16 Oswego (60543) *(G-15989)*
Acquaviva Winery LLC 630 365-0333
  47 W 614 Rr 38 Maple Park (60151) *(G-13459)*
Acquired Sales Corp (PA) 847 915-2446
  31 N Suffolk Ln Lake Forest (60045) *(G-12219)*
Acra Products 847 346-9889
  1820 Kings Point Dr S Addison (60101) *(G-17)*
Acresso Software Inc 408 642-3865
  1000 E Wdfield Rd Ste 400 Schaumburg (60173) *(G-18426)*
Acro Magnetics Inc 815 943-5018
  24005 Il Route 173 Harvard (60033) *(G-11040)*
Acro Tech Corporation 630 408-2248
  1540 Spero Ct Wheaton (60187) *(G-20785)*
Acrofab 630 350-7941
  1100 Entry Dr Unit 1 Bensenville (60106) *(G-1727)*
Acrylic Design Works Inc 773 843-1300
  5023 W 66th St Chicago (60638) *(G-3532)*
Acrylic Service Inc 630 543-0336
  1060 W Republic Dr Addison (60101) *(G-18)*
Acrylic Ventures Inc 847 901-4440
  1921 Pickwick Ln Glenview (60026) *(G-10517)*
ACS, Chicago *Also called Antares Computer Systems Inc (G-3704)*
ACS Parts Group LLC 815 211-4707
  129 Hemlock St Park Forest (60466) *(G-16249)*
ACS Susico, Skokie *Also called Sub-Surface Sign Co Ltd (G-19039)*
Acta Publications 773 989-3036
  4848 N Clark St Chicago (60640) *(G-3533)*
Actega North America Inc 847 690-9310
  1550 Carmen Dr Bldg 7 Elk Grove Village (60007) *(G-8805)*
Action Advertising Inc 312 791-0660
  2420 S Michigan Ave Chicago (60616) *(G-3534)*
Action Cabinet Sales Inc 847 717-0011
  1150 Davis Rd Ste K Elgin (60123) *(G-8494)*
Action Carbide Grinding Co 847 891-9026
  1118 Lunt Ave Ste B Schaumburg (60193) *(G-18427)*
Action Electric Sales Co Inc (PA) 773 539-1800
  3900 N Rockwell St Chicago (60618) *(G-3535)*
Action Graphics and Signs Inc 618 939-5755
  8802 Summer Rd Columbia (62236) *(G-6983)*
Action Packaging, Machesney Park *Also called Compak Inc (G-13335)*
Action Painting & Cleaning, Franklin Park *Also called Production Chemical Co Inc (G-10027)*
Action Prcsion Crbide Grinding, Schaumburg *Also called Action Carbide Grinding Co (G-18427)*
Action Pump Co 847 516-3636
  170 Chicago St Cary (60013) *(G-3144)*
Action Screen Print Inc 630 393-1990
  30 W 260 Bttrfeld Rd Ste Warrenville (60555) *(G-20228)*
Action Tool & Mfg Inc 815 874-5775
  5573 Sandy Hollow Rd Rockford (61109) *(G-17294)*
Action Turbine Repair Svc Inc 708 924-9601
  5120 W Lawndale Ave Summit Argo (60501) *(G-19677)*
Active Automation Inc 847 427-8100
  530 Bennett Rd Elk Grove Village (60007) *(G-8806)*
Active Copier, Chicago *Also called Active Office Solutions (G-3536)*
Active Graphics Inc 708 656-8900
  5500 W 31st St Cicero (60804) *(G-6827)*
Active Grinding & Mfg Co 708 344-0510
  1796 Parkes Dr Broadview (60155) *(G-2414)*
Active Office Solutions 773 539-3333
  3839 W Devon Ave Chicago (60659) *(G-3536)*
Active Simulations Inc 630 747-8393
  312 S Lombard Ave Oak Park (60302) *(G-15740)*
Active Tool and Machine Inc 708 599-0022
  8445 Beloit Ave Oak Lawn (60455) *(G-15697)*

Active Wireworks, Bartlett *Also called Elite Wireworks Corporation (G-1277)*
Acuity Brands Lighting Inc 847 827-9880
  1300 S Wolf Rd Des Plaines (60018) *(G-7722)*
Acument Tm Global Technologies, Belvidere *Also called Camcar LLC (G-1659)*
Acura Pharmaceuticals Inc (PA) 847 705-7709
  616 N North Ct Ste 120 Palatine (60067) *(G-16089)*
Ad Cabinetry, Albers *Also called Architctlly Designed Cabinetry (G-343)*
Ad Deluxe Sign Company Inc 815 556-8469
  2747 York St Blue Island (60406) *(G-2109)*
AD Huesing Corporation (PA) 309 788-5652
  527 37th Ave Rock Island (61201) *(G-17199)*
Ad Images 847 956-1887
  1729 Pebble Beach Ct Hoffman Estates (60169) *(G-11403)*
Ad Special TZ Inc 847 845-6767
  2456 Palazzo Ct Buffalo Grove (60089) *(G-2504)*
Ad Works Inc 217 342-9688
  17866 N Us Highway 45 Effingham (62401) *(G-8382)*
Ad-Deluxe Sign Co, Blue Island *Also called Ad Deluxe Sign Company Inc (G-2109)*
Ada Holding Company Inc (HQ) 312 440-2897
  211 E Chicago Ave B29 Chicago (60611) *(G-3537)*
Ada Metal Products Inc 847 673-1190
  7120 N Capitol Dr Lincolnwood (60712) *(G-12811)*
Adams & Masterson Memorials, Pana *Also called Pana Monument Co (G-16220)*
Adams Apple Distributing LP 847 832-9900
  2301 Ravine Way Glenview (60025) *(G-10518)*
Adams Elevator Equipment Co (HQ) 847 581-2900
  100 S Wacker Dr Ste 1250 Chicago (60606) *(G-3538)*
Adams Machine Shop 630 851-6060
  1223 Arthur Rd Naperville (60540) *(G-14765)*
Adams Memorials, Charleston *Also called Wendell Adams (G-3416)*
Adams Network, Quincy *Also called Adams Telephone Co-Operative (G-16850)*
Adams Outdoor Advg Ltd Partnr 309 692-2482
  911 Sw Adams St Peoria (61602) *(G-16375)*
Adams Outdoor Advg Peoria, Peoria *Also called Adams Outdoor Advg Ltd Partnr (G-16375)*
Adams Printing Co 618 529-2396
  315 E College St Carbondale (62901) *(G-2838)*
Adams Steel Service Inc 815 385-9100
  2022 S Il Route 31 Ste A McHenry (60050) *(G-13715)*
Adams Telephone Co-Operative 217 224-9566
  301 Oak St Quincy (62301) *(G-16850)*
Adaptive Testing Tech Inc 312 878-6490
  217 N Jefferson St # 601 Chicago (60661) *(G-3539)*
Adazon Inc 847 235-2700
  1485 N Western Ave Lake Forest (60045) *(G-12220)*
ADC, Carlinville *Also called Area Diesel Service Inc (G-2867)*
ADC 360, Romeoville *Also called Automated Design Corp (G-17797)*
Adco Amrcn Day Camp Outfitters, Skokie *Also called Cloz Companies Inc (G-18944)*
Adco Global Inc (HQ) 847 282-3485
  100 Tri State Intl # 135 Lincolnshire (60069) *(G-12742)*
Adcraft Printers Inc 815 932-6432
  1355 W Jeffery St Kankakee (60901) *(G-11956)*
Addison Electric Inc 800 517-4871
  502 W Factory Rd Addison (60101) *(G-19)*
Addison Electro Polishing Div, Addison *Also called K & P Industries Inc (G-165)*
Addison Engraving Inc 630 833-9123
  204 W Ridge Rd Villa Park (60181) *(G-20127)*
Addison Interiors Company 630 628-1345
  711 W Fullerton Ave Ste A Addison (60101) *(G-20)*
Addison Precision Products 815 857-4466
  200 E Kellen Dr Amboy (61310) *(G-577)*
Addison Precision Tech LLC 773 626-4747
  4343 S Oakley Ave Chicago (60609) *(G-3540)*
Addison Pro Plastics Inc 630 543-6770
  503 S Westgate St Ste D Addison (60101) *(G-21)*
Addison Steel Inc 847 998-9445
  1340 Bonnie Glen Ln Glenview (60025) *(G-10519)*
Addition Technology Inc 847 297-8419
  820 Oak Creek Dr Lombard (60148) *(G-13035)*
Addvalue2print LLC 847 551-1570
  737 N Central Ave Wood Dale (60191) *(G-21155)*
Ade Inc (PA) 773 646-3400
  1430 E 130th St Chicago (60633) *(G-3541)*
Adel Tool Co LLP 708 867-8530
  1516 Marguerite St Park Ridge (60068) *(G-16263)*
Adel Woodworks (PA) 815 886-9006
  15523 Weber Rd Ste 104 Romeoville (60446) *(G-17787)*
Adello Biologics LLC 312 620-1500
  3440 S Dearborn St # 300 Chicago (60616) *(G-3542)*
Ademco Inc 708 599-1390
  9745 Industrial Dr Ste 2 Bridgeview (60455) *(G-2319)*
Ademco Inc 847 472-2900
  509 Busse Rd Elk Grove Village (60007) *(G-8807)*
Adept Coalescence LLC 440 503-1808
  3538 Golden Prairie Ave Rockford (61109) *(G-17295)*
Adeptia Inc 312 229-1727
  343 W Erie St Ste 430 Chicago (60654) *(G-3543)*
Adermanns Welding & Mch & Co 217 342-3234
  1310 Pike Ave Effingham (62401) *(G-8383)*

Alphabetic Section

Adesso Solutions LLC 847 342-1095
3701 Algonquin Rd Ste 270 Rolling Meadows (60008) *(G-17709)*

Adflow Networks 866 423-3569
203 N Lasalle St Ste 2100 Chicago (60601) *(G-3544)*

Adhereon Corporation 312 997-5002
222 Mdse Mart Plz # 1230 Chicago (60654) *(G-3545)*

Adhes Tape Technology Inc 847 496-7949
3339 N Ridge Ave Arlington Heights (60004) *(G-683)*

Adhesive Coating Tech Inc 847 215-8355
420 Northgate Pkwy Wheeling (60090) *(G-20841)*

ADI Global Distribution, Bridgeview *Also called Ademco Inc* *(G-2319)*

ADI Global Distribution, Elk Grove Village *Also called Ademco Inc* *(G-8807)*

Adient US LLC 815 895-2095
1701 Bethany Rd Sycamore (60178) *(G-19699)*

Adjustable Clamp Company (PA) 312 666-0640
404 N Armour St Chicago (60642) *(G-3546)*

Adk Products Inc 847 710-0021
2821 Old Higgins Rd Elk Grove Village (60007) *(G-8808)*

Adkins Energy LLC 815 369-9173
4350 W Galena Rd Lena (61048) *(G-12597)*

ADM, Chicago *Also called Archer-Daniels-Midland Company* *(G-3728)*
ADM, Macon *Also called Archer-Daniels-Midland Company* *(G-13404)*
ADM, Decatur *Also called Archer-Daniels-Midland Company* *(G-7441)*
ADM, Decatur *Also called Archer-Daniels-Midland Company* *(G-7442)*
ADM, Edgewood *Also called Archer-Daniels-Midland Company* *(G-8334)*
ADM, Decatur *Also called Archer-Daniels-Midland Company* *(G-7443)*
ADM, Peoria *Also called Archer-Daniels-Midland Company* *(G-16385)*
ADM, Martinton *Also called Archer-Daniels-Midland Company* *(G-13589)*
ADM, Altamont *Also called Archer-Daniels-Midland Company* *(G-530)*
ADM, Bushnell *Also called Archer-Daniels-Midland Company* *(G-2737)*
ADM, Mount Auburn *Also called Archer-Daniels-Midland Company* *(G-14464)*
ADM, Decatur *Also called Archer-Daniels-Midland Company* *(G-7445)*
ADM, Decatur *Also called Archer-Daniels-Midland Company* *(G-7446)*
ADM, Decatur *Also called Archer-Daniels-Midland Company* *(G-7447)*
ADM, Decatur *Also called Archer-Daniels-Midland Company* *(G-7448)*
ADM, Meredosia *Also called Archer-Daniels-Midland Company* *(G-13955)*
ADM, Mendota *Also called Archer-Daniels-Midland Company* *(G-13936)*
ADM, Decatur *Also called Archer-Daniels-Midland Company* *(G-7449)*
ADM, Decatur *Also called Archer-Daniels-Midland Company* *(G-7450)*
ADM, Decatur *Also called Archer-Daniels-Midland Company* *(G-7451)*
ADM, Saint Charles *Also called Ark De Mexico LLC* *(G-18148)*
ADM, Effingham *Also called Archer-Daniels-Midland Company* *(G-8385)*
ADM, Fairbury *Also called Archer-Daniels-Midland Company* *(G-9603)*
ADM, Peru *Also called Archer-Daniels-Midland Company* *(G-16566)*
ADM, Decatur *Also called Archer-Daniels-Midland Company* *(G-7452)*
ADM, Hume *Also called Archer-Daniels-Midland Company* *(G-11526)*
ADM, Quincy *Also called Archer-Daniels-Midland Company* *(G-16856)*
ADM, Crystal Lake *Also called Archer-Daniels-Midland Company* *(G-7162)*
ADM, Quincy *Also called Archer-Daniels-Midland Company* *(G-16857)*
ADM, Patoka *Also called Archer-Daniels-Midland Company* *(G-16302)*
ADM, Decatur *Also called Archer-Daniels-Midland Company* *(G-7456)*
ADM, Decatur *Also called Archer-Daniels-Midland Company* *(G-7458)*
ADM, Quincy *Also called Archer-Daniels-Midland Company* *(G-16858)*
ADM, Decatur *Also called Archer-Daniels-Midland Company* *(G-7459)*
ADM, Decatur *Also called Archer-Daniels-Midland Company* *(G-7460)*

ADM Custome Cabinet Chicago 773 688-5379
1900 N Austin Ave Chicago (60639) *(G-3547)*

ADM Grain Company 217 424-5200
4666 E Faries Pkwy Decatur (62526) *(G-7432)*

ADM Holdings LLC 217 422-7281
350 N Water St Decatur (62523) *(G-7433)*

ADM Holdings LLC 312 634-8100
191 N Wacker Dr Ste 1500 Chicago (60606) *(G-3548)*

ADM Holdings LLC (HQ) 217 424-5200
4666 E Faries Pkwy Decatur (62526) *(G-7434)*

ADM Imaging Inc 630 834-7100
100 W Roosevelt Rd A1-20 Wheaton (60187) *(G-20786)*

ADM Milling, Decatur *Also called Archer-Daniels-Midland Company* *(G-7444)*
ADM Research, Decatur *Also called Archer-Daniels-Midland Company* *(G-7457)*

Admo Inc 847 741-5777
2550 Decade Ct Ste A Elgin (60124) *(G-8495)*

Adnama Inc 312 922-0509
1513 S State St Chicago (60605) *(G-3549)*

Adolph Kiefer & Associates LLC (PA) 309 451-5858
903 Morrissey Dr Bloomington (61701) *(G-2021)*

Adora Bella Medspa LLC 779 206-8331
3035 W Wilson Ave Chicago (60625) *(G-3550)*

ADP Pallet Inc 773 638-3800
7300 S Kostner Ave Chicago (60629) *(G-3551)*

Adrenaline Prints 618 277-9600
126 E Main St Belleville (62220) *(G-1528)*

ADS, Lake Forest *Also called Amity Die and Stamping Co* *(G-12224)*
ADS, Peoria *Also called Ag-Defense Systems Inc* *(G-16376)*

ADS LLC 256 430-3366
144 Tower Dr Burr Ridge (60527) *(G-2650)*

Adsensa Corporation 312 559-2881
404 S Wells St Fl 5 Chicago (60607) *(G-3552)*

Advanage Diversified Pdts Inc 708 331-8390
16615 Halsted St Harvey (60426) *(G-11069)*

Advance Adhesives, Chicago *Also called Aabbitt Adhesives Inc* *(G-3499)*
Advance Adhesives, Chicago *Also called Aabbitt Adhesives Inc* *(G-3500)*

Advance Automation Company 773 539-7633
3526 N Elston Ave Chicago (60618) *(G-3553)*

Advance Awnair Corp 708 422-2730
15418 S 70th Ct Orland Park (60462) *(G-15934)*

Advance Enameling Co 773 737-7356
5849 S Bishop St Chicago (60636) *(G-3554)*

Advance Engineering Corp 847 760-9421
440 S Mclean Blvd Elgin (60123) *(G-8496)*

Advance Equipment Mfg Co 773 287-8220
4615 W Chicago Ave Chicago (60651) *(G-3555)*

Advance Iron Works Inc 708 798-3540
1325 171st St East Hazel Crest (60429) *(G-8216)*

Advance Machining 630 521-9392
405 Evergreen Ave Bensenville (60106) *(G-1728)*

Advance Manufacturing 618 245-6515
204 Through St Farina (62838) *(G-9649)*

Advance Metalworking Company 309 853-3387
3726 Us Highway 34 Kewanee (61443) *(G-12019)*

Advance Pallet Incorporated 847 697-5700
600 Woodbury St South Elgin (60177) *(G-19128)*

Advance Plastic Corp 773 637-5922
4866 W Cortland St Chicago (60639) *(G-3556)*

Advance Press Sign Inc 630 833-1600
719 N Addison Rd Villa Park (60181) *(G-20128)*

Advance Printers Machine Shop 773 588-3169
4271 N Elston Ave Chicago (60618) *(G-3557)*

Advance Quick Print 708 848-2200
900 Madison St Oak Park (60302) *(G-15741)*

Advance Security Products, Belleville *Also called Marbil Enterprises Inc* *(G-1570)*

Advance Steel Services Inc 773 619-2977
4722 W Harrison St Chicago (60644) *(G-3558)*

Advance Technologies Inc 815 297-1771
430 Challenge St Freeport (61032) *(G-10097)*

Advance Tools LLC (PA) 630 337-5904
2456 Saranac Ln Glenview (60026) *(G-10520)*

Advance Uniform Company 312 922-1797
33 E 13th St Ste 1 Chicago (60605) *(G-3559)*

Advance Ureathane, West Chicago *Also called Innocor Inc* *(G-20597)*

Advance Wheel Corporation 773 471-5734
5335 S Western Blvd Ste H Chicago (60609) *(G-3560)*

Advance World Trade Inc (PA) 773 777-7100
4321 N Knox Ave Chicago (60641) *(G-3561)*

Advanced Asphalt Co (PA) 815 872-9911
308 W Railroad Ave Princeton (61356) *(G-16804)*

Advanced Assembly 630 379-6158
703 Blue Ridge Dr Streamwood (60107) *(G-19559)*

Advanced Audio Technology Inc 630 665-3344
200 Easy St Ste E Carol Stream (60188) *(G-2925)*

Advanced Biological Concepts, Osco *Also called Helfter Enterprises Inc* *(G-15988)*

Advanced Bionics LLC 708 946-3406
4520 Weaver Pkwy Warrenville (60555) *(G-20229)*

Advanced Cabinets Corp 847 928-0001
9200 Belmont Ave Franklin Park (60131) *(G-9860)*

Advanced Cooler Inc 630 443-8933
515 Illinois St Saint Charles (60174) *(G-18142)*

Advanced Cooling Therapy Inc 888 534-4873
3440 S Dearborn St 215-S Chicago (60616) *(G-3562)*

Advanced Cstm Enrgy Sltons Inc 312 428-9540
2545 W Diversey Ave Chicago (60647) *(G-3563)*

Advanced Custom Metals Inc 847 803-2090
1024 North Ave Des Plaines (60016) *(G-7723)*

Advanced Custom Shapes 618 684-2222
550 N 19th St Murphysboro (62966) *(G-14749)*

Advanced Diamond Tech Inc 815 293-0900
2100 Sanders Rd Ste 170 Northbrook (60062) *(G-15332)*

Advanced Digital & Mold Inc 630 595-8242
833 Eagle Dr Bensenville (60106) *(G-1729)*

Advanced Drainage Systems Inc 815 539-2160
1600 Industrial Dr Mendota (61342) *(G-13933)*

Advanced Electronics Inc 630 293-3300
721 Winston St West Chicago (60185) *(G-20531)*

Advanced Enrgy Solutions Group 618 988-0888
1804 Supply Rd Carterville (62918) *(G-3128)*

Advanced Fiber Products LLC 847 768-9001
200 Howard Ave Ste 244 Des Plaines (60018) *(G-7724)*

Advanced Flexible Mtls LLC 312 961-9231
150 N Wacker Dr Ste 2160 Chicago (60606) *(G-3564)*

Advanced Fltration Systems Inc (HQ) 217 351-3073
3206 Farber Dr Champaign (61822) *(G-3260)*

Advanced Flxble Composites Inc (PA) 847 658-3938
14 Walter Ct Lake In The Hills (60156) *(G-12327)*

ALPHABETIC SECTION

Advanced Galvanics 630 422-5157
772 Foster Ave Bensenville (60106) *(G-1730)*
Advanced Graphics Tech Inc 817 481-8561
1101 Windham Pkwy Romeoville (60446) *(G-17788)*
Advanced Heat Treating Inc 815 877-8593
980 Industrial Ct Loves Park (61111) *(G-13182)*
Advanced Lubrication Inc (PA) 815 932-3288
4517 E 2000n Rd Kankakee (60901) *(G-11957)*
Advanced Machine & Engrg Co 815 962-6076
2500 Latham St Rockford (61103) *(G-17296)*
Advanced Machine and Engrg, Rockford Also called Goellner Inc *(G-17430)*
Advanced Machine Co Inc 773 545-9790
4450 W Belmont Ave Chicago (60641) *(G-3565)*
Advanced Micro Lites Inc 630 365-5450
205 Dempsey St Ste A Elburn (60119) *(G-8442)*
Advanced Microderm Inc 630 980-3300
904 S Roselle Rd 302 Schaumburg (60193) *(G-18428)*
Advanced Mobility & 708 235-2800
6370 W Emerald Pkwy # 107 Monee (60449) *(G-14195)*
Advanced Molding Tech Inc 815 334-3600
1425 Lake Ave Woodstock (60098) *(G-21354)*
Advanced O&P Solutions 708 878-2241
8647 W 95th St Hickory Hills (60457) *(G-11193)*
Advanced On-Site Concrete Inc 773 622-7836
5308 W Grand Ave Chicago (60639) *(G-3566)*
Advanced Ozone Tech Inc 630 964-1300
2743 Curtiss St Downers Grove (60515) *(G-7949)*
Advanced Pattern Works LLC 618 346-9039
305 Railroad Ave Collinsville (62234) *(G-6952)*
Advanced Plastic Corp 847 674-2070
3725 W Lunt Ave Lincolnwood (60712) *(G-12812)*
Advanced Plbg & Pipe Fitting 618 554-2677
15498 N 1590th St Newton (62448) *(G-15079)*
Advanced Polymer Alloys LLC 847 836-8119
400 Maple Ave Ste A Carpentersville (60110) *(G-3091)*
Advanced Prcsion Machining Ltd 630 860-2549
766 Birginal Dr Bensenville (60106) *(G-1731)*
Advanced Prototype Molding 847 202-4200
263 N Woodwork Ln Palatine (60067) *(G-16090)*
Advanced Refr Instllation Tech 847 741-3105
1150 Davis Rd Ste G Elgin (60123) *(G-8497)*
Advanced Retinal Institute Inc 617 821-5597
1123 N Oak Park Ave Oak Park (60302) *(G-15742)*
Advanced Robotics Research 630 544-0040
791 Sigmund Rd Naperville (60563) *(G-14766)*
Advanced Seal Technology Inc 815 861-4010
5306 Bus Pkwy Unit 107 Ringwood (60072) *(G-17038)*
Advanced Specialty Lighting 708 867-3140
7227 W Wilson Ave Harwood Heights (60706) *(G-11101)*
Advanced Steel Fabrication 847 956-6565
181 Randall St Elk Grove Village (60007) *(G-8809)*
Advanced Strobe Products, Harwood Heights Also called Advanced Specialty Lighting *(G-11101)*
Advanced Strobe Products Inc 708 867-3100
7227 W Wilson Ave Chicago (60706) *(G-3567)*
Advanced Technologies Inc 847 329-9875
310 Busse Hwy Ste 241 Park Ridge (60068) *(G-16264)*
Advanced Thermal Processing 630 595-9000
501 Eastern Ave Bensenville (60106) *(G-1732)*
Advanced Valve Tech LLC (HQ) 847 364-3700
800 Busse Rd Elk Grove Village (60007) *(G-8810)*
Advanced Valve Tech LLC 877 489-4909
12601 Homan Ave Blue Island (60406) *(G-2110)*
Advanced Web Technologies LLC 847 985-3833
393 Joseph Dr South Elgin (60177) *(G-19129)*
Advanced Weighing Systems Inc 630 916-6179
1433 W Fullerton Ave H Addison (60101) *(G-22)*
Advanced Welding Ltd 708 205-4559
760 W Factory Rd Addison (60101) *(G-23)*
Advanced Window Corp 773 379-3500
4935 W Le Moyne St Chicago (60651) *(G-3568)*
Advangene Consumables Inc 847 295-2539
21 N Skokie Hwy Ste 104 Lake Bluff (60044) *(G-12168)*
Advantage Components Inc 815 725-8644
2240 Oak Leaf St Joliet (60436) *(G-11817)*
Advantage Machining Inc 630 897-1220
601 W New York St Frnt Aurora (60506) *(G-1042)*
Advantage Manufacturing Inc 773 626-2200
1458 N Lamon Ave Chicago (60651) *(G-3569)*
Advantage News 618 463-0612
192a Alton Square Mall Dr Alton (62002) *(G-541)*
Advantage Optics Inc 630 548-9870
1555 Bond St Ste 117 Naperville (60563) *(G-14767)*
Advantage Press Inc 630 960-5305
3033 Ogden Ave Ste 110 Lisle (60532) *(G-12858)*
Advantage Printing Inc 630 627-7468
1920 S Highland Ave # 300 Lombard (60148) *(G-13036)*
Advantage Seal Inc 630 226-0200
694 Veterans Pkwy Ste A Bolingbrook (60440) *(G-2147)*

Advantage Structures LLC 773 734-9305
10554 S Muskegon Ave Chicago (60617) *(G-3570)*
Advantage Tool and Mold Inc 847 301-9020
1501 Kathleen Way Elk Grove Village (60007) *(G-8811)*
Advantage Unlimited, Bensenville Also called R N I Industries Inc *(G-1881)*
Advantage Worldwide Wholesale, Arlington Heights Also called Mechanical Music Corp *(G-775)*
Advantech Bb Smartworx, Ottawa Also called B+b Smartworx Inc *(G-16041)*
Advantech Limited 815 289-7678
601 N Russell Ave Aurora (60506) *(G-1043)*
Advantech Plastics LLC 815 338-8383
2500 S Eastwood Dr Woodstock (60098) *(G-21355)*
Advantex Inc of Illinois 618 505-0701
326 Bargraves Blvd Troy (62294) *(G-19910)*
Advantex Inc 618 505-0701
326 Bargraves Blvd Troy (62294) *(G-19911)*
Advent Tool & Mfg Inc 847 395-9707
710 Anita Ave Antioch (60002) *(G-594)*
Advent Tool and Mfg 847 395-9707
712 Anita Ave Antioch (60002) *(G-595)*
Adventure Advertising, Ottawa Also called Ottawa Publishing Co Inc *(G-16069)*
Adventures Unlimited (PA) 815 253-6390
303 Main St Kempton (60946) *(G-12013)*
Advert Display Products Inc 815 513-5432
3727 N Division St Morris (60450) *(G-14290)*
Advertising Age, Chicago Also called Crain Communications Inc *(G-4259)*
Advertising Designs, Crestwood Also called Fanning Communications Inc *(G-7118)*
Advertising Premiums Inc 888 364-9710
800 W Central Rd Ste 162 Mount Prospect (60056) *(G-14509)*
Advertising Products Inc 847 758-0415
680 Fargo Ave Elk Grove Village (60007) *(G-8812)*
Advocate 815 694-2122
330 N 4th St Clifton (60927) *(G-6913)*
Advocate Print Shop 847 390-3594
799 Biermann Ct Ste 110 Mount Prospect (60056) *(G-14510)*
Advocate Printing, Clifton Also called Advocate *(G-6913)*
Advocations Inc 815 568-7505
17709 Collins Rd Woodstock (60098) *(G-21356)*
Advyzon, Chicago Also called Yhlsoft Inc *(G-6700)*
Ae2009 Technologies Inc 708 331-0025
16140 Vincennes Ave South Holland (60473) *(G-19188)*
AEC, Elgin Also called Advance Engineering Corp *(G-8496)*
Aechem Scientific Corporation (PA) 630 364-5106
2055 University Dr Naperville (60565) *(G-14768)*
Aed Essentials (PA) 815 977-5920
6775 Fincham Dr Ste 3 Rockford (61108) *(G-17297)*
Aemm A Electric 708 403-6700
8448 Camelia Ln Orland Park (60462) *(G-15935)*
Aen Industries Inc 708 758-3000
1522 Union Ave Chicago Heights (60411) *(G-6728)*
AEP Inc 618 466-7668
1225 Cabin Club Dr Alton (62002) *(G-542)*
AEP Nvh Opco LLC 708 758-0211
1001 State St Chicago Heights (60411) *(G-6729)*
Aerial Intelligence Inc 312 914-1259
100 S State St Chicago (60603) *(G-3571)*
Aeries Riverview Winery Inc 618 786-7477
600 Timber Ridge Dr Grafton (62037) *(G-10683)*
Aero Alehouse LLC 815 977-5602
6164 E Riverside Blvd Loves Park (61111) *(G-13183)*
Aero Apmc Inc 630 766-0910
411 S County Line Rd Franklin Park (60131) *(G-9861)*
Aero Aviation Company Inc (PA) 618 797-6630
3701 State Route 162 Granite City (62040) *(G-10690)*
Aero Industries Inc 800 747-3553
450 Commanche Cir Harvard (60033) *(G-11041)*
Aero Metals Alliance Inc (HQ) 225 236-1441
555 Skokie Blvd Ste 555 # 555 Northbrook (60062) *(G-15333)*
Aero Plastics and Supply 815 975-9305
754 Landmark Dr Belvidere (61008) *(G-1645)*
Aero Plastics and Supply Co 847 553-5578
756 Landmark Dr Belvidere (61008) *(G-1646)*
Aero Precision Machining, Franklin Park Also called Aero Apmc Inc *(G-9861)*
Aero Products Holdings Inc 847 485-3200
1834 Walden Office Sq # 300 Schaumburg (60173) *(G-18429)*
Aero Products International, Schaumburg Also called Aero Products Holdings Inc *(G-18429)*
Aero Rubber Company Inc 800 662-1009
8100 185th St Tinley Park (60487) *(G-19798)*
Aero Tool & Stamping, Franklin Park Also called S&L Tool Company Inc *(G-10039)*
Aero Vac Brazing Heat Treating, Itasca Also called Bulaw Welding & Engineering Co *(G-11632)*
Aero-Cables Corp 815 609-6600
114 Kirkland Cir Ste A Oswego (60543) *(G-15990)*
Aero-Tech Light Bulb Co (PA) 847 352-4900
534 Pratt Ave N Schaumburg (60193) *(G-18430)*
Aerodine Magazine 847 358-4355
1514 Banbury Rd Inverness (60067) *(G-11592)*

Aerodyne Incorporated 773 588-2905
2612 W Barry Ave Chicago (60618) *(G-3572)*
Aerofast Inc 630 668-6575
360 Gundersen Dr Carol Stream (60188) *(G-2926)*
Aerogen-Tek, Paris *Also called Meco Company LLC (G-16234)*
Aerogenaerogen 312 624-9598
410 N Michigan Ave Chicago (60611) *(G-3573)*
Aeromax Industries Inc 847 756-4085
28 W079 Industrial Ave Lake Barrington (60010) *(G-12140)*
Aeromotive, Chicago *Also called Aerodyne Incorporated (G-3572)*
Aeromotive Services Inc 224 535-9220
345 Willard Ave Elgin (60120) *(G-8498)*
Aeronautical Electric Company, Chicago *Also called Aco Inc (G-3529)*
Aeropharm Technology LLC 847 937-6100
100 Abbott Park Rd North Chicago (60064) *(G-15306)*
Aerosols Danville Inc 773 816-5132
340 E 138th St Chicago (60827) *(G-3574)*
Aerosols Danville Inc (HQ) 217 442-1400
1 W Hegeler Ln Danville (61832) *(G-7318)*
Aerosourcex LLC 314 565-4026
9 Cascade Ct South Elgin (60177) *(G-19130)*
Aerospace Metals LLC 888 600-7811
2401 Mississippi Ave Sauget (62201) *(G-18387)*
Aerostars Inc 847 736-8171
6413 Kingsbridge Dr Cary (60013) *(G-3145)*
Aerotronic Controls Co (PA) 847 228-6504
1512 N Fremont St Ste 103 Chicago (60642) *(G-3575)*
Aerovision Engine Services LLC 231 799-9000
500 W Madison St Ste 2800 Chicago (60661) *(G-3576)*
Aertrade LLC (PA) 630 428-4440
1585 Beverly Ct Ste 128 Aurora (60502) *(G-910)*
Aerus Electrolux, Mundelein *Also called Campanella Clg Solutions Inc (G-14671)*
AES Solar, Carterville *Also called Advanced Enrgy Solutions Group (G-3128)*
Aespheptics Medical Ltd 630 416-1400
477 E Bttrfeld Rd Ste 408 Lombard (60148) *(G-13037)*
Aetna Engineering Works Inc 773 785-0489
12001 S Calumet Ave Chicago (60628) *(G-3577)*
Aetna Plywood Inc (PA) 708 343-1515
1401 Saint Charles Rd Maywood (60153) *(G-13658)*
Aeverie Inc 844 238-3743
129 Manchester Ct Buffalo Grove (60089) *(G-2505)*
AF, Chicago *Also called Art-Flo Shirt & Lettering Co (G-3738)*
AF Antronics Inc 217 328-0800
2 N Main St Villa Grove (61956) *(G-20121)*
Afam Concept Inc 773 838-1336
7401 S Pulaski Rd Ste A Chicago (60629) *(G-3578)*
Afar Imports & Interiors Inc (PA) 217 744-3262
3125 S Douglas Ave Springfield (62704) *(G-19316)*
Afc Cable Systems Inc (HQ) 508 998-1131
16100 Lathrop Ave Harvey (60426) *(G-11070)*
Afc Machining Division, Mundelein *Also called Muntz Industries Inc (G-14718)*
Afco Industries Inc 618 742-6469
8161 State Highway 37 Olmsted (62970) *(G-15850)*
Afco Lite American Fluorescent, Waukegan *Also called Afx Inc (G-20410)*
Afco Products Incorporated 847 299-1055
1030 Commerce Dr Lake Zurich (60047) *(G-12380)*
Affectionately Yours Ent 708 275-6333
609 Old Meadow Rd Matteson (60443) *(G-13616)*
Affirmed LLC 847 550-0170
280a N Rand Rd Ste A Lake Zurich (60047) *(G-12381)*
Affordable Welding Us Inc 773 374-2000
3100 E 87th St Chicago (60617) *(G-3579)*
Affordable Welding Ironworks, Chicago *Also called Affordable Welding Us Inc (G-3579)*
Affri Inc 224 374-0931
850 Dillon Dr Wood Dale (60191) *(G-21156)*
Affton Fabg & Wldg Co Inc 314 781-4100
1635 Sauget Business Blvd Sauget (62206) *(G-18388)*
Affy Tapple LLC 773 338-1100
6300 W Gross Point Rd Niles (60714) *(G-15100)*
Afi Industries Inc 630 462-0400
475 Kehoe Blvd Carol Stream (60188) *(G-2927)*
Afm Heatsheets, Chicago *Also called Advanced Flexible Mtls LLC (G-3564)*
African-American Images Inc 708 672-4909
24906 S Wllow Broke Trl Crete (60417) *(G-7134)*
Afs Classico LLC 309 786-8833
507 34th Ave Rock Island (61201) *(G-17200)*
Afs Inc 847 437-2345
3232 Nordic Rd Arlington Heights (60005) *(G-684)*
Afton Chemical Corporation 618 583-1000
501 Monsanto Ave East Saint Louis (62206) *(G-8296)*
Afton Chemical Corporation 708 728-1546
7201 W 65th St Bedford Park (60638) *(G-1454)*
Afx Inc (PA) 847 249-5970
2345 Ernie Krueger Cir Waukegan (60087) *(G-20410)*
AG Hohlfelder Sheet Metal, Rockford *Also called Hohlflder A H Shtmtl Htg Coolg (G-17451)*
AG Industries LLC 636 349-4466
28782 Network Pl Chicago (60673) *(G-3580)*
AG Manufacturing - Illinois, Rochelle *Also called A&G Manufacturing Inc (G-17129)*

AG Medical Systems Inc 847 458-3100
13 Prosper Ct Ste B Lake In The Hills (60156) *(G-12328)*
AG Solutions, Paxton *Also called Plastic Designs Inc (G-16314)*
Ag-Defense Systems Inc 309 495-7258
801 W Main St Ste A118 Peoria (61606) *(G-16376)*
Agate Publishing Inc 847 475-4457
1328 Greenleaf St Evanston (60202) *(G-9488)*
AGCO Corporation 630 293-9905
1160 Powis Rd West Chicago (60185) *(G-20532)*
AGCO Corporation 630 406-3248
1500 N Raddant Rd Batavia (60510) *(G-1341)*
AGCO Recycling LLC 217 224-9048
4425 Gardner Expy Quincy (62305) *(G-16851)*
Agena Manufacturing Co 630 668-5086
360 Gundersen Dr Carol Stream (60188) *(G-2928)*
Aggregate Industries MGT Inc (HQ) 773 372-1000
8700 W Bryn Mawr Ave # 300 Chicago (60631) *(G-3581)*
Aggregate Materials Company 815 747-2430
18525 Us Highway 20 W East Dubuque (61025) *(G-8174)*
Aggresive Motor Sports 630 761-1550
201 Oswald Ave Batavia (60510) *(G-1342)*
Aggressive Graphics, Highland *Also called BT Steelle Investments Inc (G-11206)*
Aggressive Motorsports Inc 847 846-7488
227 Oswald Ave Batavia (60510) *(G-1343)*
Agi Corp 815 708-0502
6075 Material Ave Ste 100 Loves Park (61111) *(G-13184)*
Agi-Yargus, Marshall *Also called Yargus Manufacturing Inc (G-13579)*
Agie Charmilles, Lincolnshire *Also called GF Machining Solutions LLC (G-12766)*
Agile Health Technologies Inc 331 457-5167
2728 Forgue Dr Ste 106 Naperville (60564) *(G-14952)*
Agilent Technologies Inc 800 227-9770
4187 Collection Center Dr Chicago (60693) *(G-3582)*
Agilent Technologies Inc 847 690-0431
720 W Algonquin Rd Arlington Heights (60005) *(G-685)*
Aginity Inc 224 307-2656
1007 Church St Ste 700 Evanston (60201) *(G-9489)*
Agmaco, Broadview *Also called Active Grinding & Mfg Co (G-2414)*
Agnes & Chris Gulik 847 931-9641
408 W Amberside Dr Elgin (60124) *(G-8499)*
Agrati Inc (HQ) 704 747-1200
24000 S Western Ave Park Forest (60466) *(G-16250)*
Agrati - Park Forest LLC (HQ) 708 228-5193
24000 S Western Ave Park Forest (60466) *(G-16251)*
Agrati USA Corp 708 228-5193
24000 S Western Ave Park Forest (60466) *(G-16252)*
Agresearch Inc 815 726-0410
1 Genstar Ln Joliet (60435) *(G-11818)*
Agri-Fab Inc 217 728-8388
701 W Eden St Sullivan (61951) *(G-19659)*
Agri-Fab Inc 217 875-7051
3490 L & A Industrial Dr Decatur (62521) *(G-7435)*
Agri-News Publications Inc (HQ) 815 223-2558
426 2nd St La Salle (61301) *(G-12100)*
Agriscience Inc 212 365-4214
5115 N Martha St Peoria (61614) *(G-16377)*
Agritech Worldwide Inc (PA) 847 549-6002
1011 Campus Dr Mundelein (60060) *(G-14660)*
Agro Chem West, Saybrook *Also called Agro-Chem Inc (G-18418)*
Agro-Chem Inc 309 475-8311
127 S Center St Saybrook (61770) *(G-18418)*
Agrochem Inc 847 564-1304
3703 Pebble Beach Rd Northbrook (60062) *(G-15334)*
Agrofresh Inc (HQ) 267 317-9135
222 N Lasalle St Chicago (60601) *(G-3583)*
Agrowtek Inc 847 380-3009
173 Ambrogio Dr Ste A Gurnee (60031) *(G-10854)*
AGS Machine Co Inc 630 766-7777
872 Eagle Dr Bensenville (60106) *(G-1733)*
AGS Partners LLC 630 446-7777
905 W Irving Park Rd Itasca (60143) *(G-11616)*
AGS Technology Inc 847 534-6600
951 Douglas Rd Batavia (60510) *(G-1344)*
Agsco Corporation (PA) 847 520-4455
160 W Hintz Rd Wheeling (60090) *(G-20842)*
Agt Products, Addison *Also called American Gasket Tech Inc (G-33)*
Agusta Mill Works 309 787-4616
117 17th St E Milan (61264) *(G-13999)*
Agvision, Springfield *Also called Brandt Consolidated Inc (G-19329)*
Ah, Freeport *Also called Anchor-Harvey Components LLC (G-10100)*
Ah Tensor International LLC 630 739-9600
10330 Argonne Woods Dr # 300 Woodridge (60517) *(G-21273)*
Ahead Inc 312 753-7967
1515 W 22nd St Ste 200 Oak Brook (60523) *(G-15589)*
Ahead Inc (HQ) 312 924-4492
401 N Michigan Ave # 3400 Chicago (60611) *(G-3584)*
Ahead Data Blue LLC (PA) 866 577-2902
401 N Michigan Ave # 3400 Chicago (60611) *(G-3585)*
Ahlstrm-Munksjo Filtration LLC 217 824-9611
1200 E Elm St Taylorville (62568) *(G-19748)*

Ai Ind ... 773 265-6640
4015 W Carroll Ave Chicago (60624) *(G-3586)*
Ai Industries, Chicago *Also called Ai Ind (G-3586)*
Aic, Gurnee *Also called American Industrial Company (G-10859)*
Aid For Women Northern Lk Cnty ... 847 249-2700
4606 Old Grand Ave Apt 2 Gurnee (60031) *(G-10855)*
Aidar Express Inc ... 773 757-3447
2814 W Arthur Ave Apt 1 Chicago (60645) *(G-3587)*
Aidarex Pharmaceuticals LLC ... 800 657-4724
2401 Commerce Dr Libertyville (60048) *(G-12626)*
Aif Inc ... 630 495-0077
1393 W Jeffrey Dr Addison (60101) *(G-24)*
Aiknow Inc ... 312 391-9452
2243 Glouceston Ln Naperville (60564) *(G-14953)*
Aileys 3 Welding ... 815 683-2181
Rr 24 Box West Crescent City (60928) *(G-7081)*
Aim LLC ... 727 544-3000
11939 S Central Ave Ste B Alsip (60803) *(G-413)*
Aim Business Printers, Buffalo Grove *Also called Aim Graphic Machinery Ltd (G-2506)*
AIM Distribution Inc ... 815 986-2770
510 18th Ave Rockford (61104) *(G-17298)*
Aim Graphic Machinery Ltd ... 847 215-8000
1374 Abbott Ct Buffalo Grove (60089) *(G-2506)*
Aim Inc ... 630 941-0027
586 S Rex Blvd Elmhurst (60126) *(G-9322)*
Aim Mail Centers, Alsip *Also called Aim LLC (G-413)*
Aim Screen Printing Supply LLC ... 630 357-4293
2731 Willow Ridge Dr Naperville (60564) *(G-14954)*
Aimee M Ford ... 630 308-9785
1005 Summerhill Dr Aurora (60506) *(G-1044)*
Aimtron Corporation (PA) ... 630 372-7500
555 S Vermont St Palatine (60067) *(G-16091)*
Aimtron Systems LLC ... 262 947-8400
500 S Hicks Rd Palatine (60067) *(G-16092)*
Air Land and Sea Interiors ... 630 834-1717
220 E Saint Charles Rd Villa Park (60181) *(G-20129)*
Air Caddy ... 708 383-5541
310 Lake St Ste 8 Oak Park (60302) *(G-15743)*
Air Caster LLC ... 217 877-1237
2887 N Woodford St Decatur (62526) *(G-7436)*
Air Duct Manufacturing Inc ... 630 620-9866
4810 Venture St Lisle (60532) *(G-12859)*
Air Flow Company Inc ... 630 628-1138
850 W Fullerton Ave Addison (60101) *(G-25)*
Air Gage Company ... 847 695-0911
516 Slade Ave Elgin (60120) *(G-8500)*
Air Liquide America LP ... 815 747-6803
16675 Us Highway 20 W # 1 East Dubuque (61025) *(G-8175)*
Air Liquide Industrial U S, East Dubuque *Also called Air Liquide America LP (G-8175)*
Air Mite Devices Inc ... 224 338-0071
606 Long Lake Dr Round Lake (60073) *(G-18067)*
Air Products and Chemicals Inc ... 618 452-5335
2200 Monroe St Granite City (62040) *(G-10691)*
Air Products and Chemicals Inc ... 815 223-2924
318 Civic Rd La Salle (61301) *(G-12101)*
Air Products and Chemicals Inc ... 618 451-0577
35 N Gate Indus Dr Granite City (62040) *(G-10692)*
Air Products and Chemicals Inc ... 815 423-5032
25915 S Frontage Rd Channahon (60410) *(G-3373)*
Air Pure LLC ... 815 275-8990
1103 Hillcrest Dr Freeport (61032) *(G-10098)*
Air Source Corp ... 630 355-7655
825 W State St Ste 109 Geneva (60134) *(G-10249)*
Air Stamping Inc ... 217 342-1283
3 Legend Park Effingham (62401) *(G-8384)*
Air Vent Inc ... 309 692-6969
7700 N Harker Dr Ste B Peoria (61615) *(G-16378)*
Air-Drive Inc ... 847 625-0226
576 Stockbridge Ct Lake Forest (60045) *(G-12221)*
Air-Duct Manufacturing Inc ... 630 620-9866
319 E Benton St Aurora (60505) *(G-1045)*
Air-X Remanufacturing Corp ... 708 598-0044
8909 Odell Ave Bridgeview (60455) *(G-2320)*
Air802 Corporation ... 630 966-2501
1981d Wiesbrook Rd Oswego (60543) *(G-15991)*
Airbrake Products Inc ... 708 594-1110
10334 Alveston St Orland Park (60462) *(G-15936)*
Aircraft Gear Corporation (PA) ... 815 877-7473
611 Beacon St Loves Park (61111) *(G-13185)*
Aircraft Plywood Mfg Inc ... 618 654-6740
806 Cedar St Highland (62249) *(G-11204)*
Aircraft Wheel & Brake Div, Chicago *Also called Parker-Hannifin Corporation (G-5767)*
Aires Press Inc ... 847 698-6813
227 Murphy Lake Ln Park Ridge (60068) *(G-16265)*
Airgas Inc ... 773 785-3000
12722 S Wentworth Ave Chicago (60628) *(G-3588)*
Airgas Usa LLC ... 708 354-0813
5235 9th Ave Countryside (60525) *(G-7043)*
Airgas Usa LLC ... 618 439-7207
12238 Petroff Rd Benton (62812) *(G-1917)*
Airgas Usa LLC ... 630 231-9260
1250 W Washington St West Chicago (60185) *(G-20533)*
Airgun Designs USA Inc ... 847 520-7507
401 Florine Ct Cary (60013) *(G-3146)*
Airmite Devices Inc Cylndrs, Round Lake *Also called Air Mite Devices Inc (G-18067)*
Airo Tool & Manufacturing Inc ... 815 547-7588
6823 Irene Rd Belvidere (61008) *(G-1647)*
Airport Aviation Professionals ... 773 948-6631
5757 S Cicero Ave Chicago (60638) *(G-3589)*
Airport Park and Fly LLC ... 708 310-2442
4901 4925 W 47th Chicago (60638) *(G-3590)*
Airtex Products LP (HQ) ... 618 842-2111
407 W Main St Fairfield (62837) *(G-9617)*
Aisin Electronics Illinois LLC (HQ) ... 618 997-9800
11000 Redco Dr Marion (62959) *(G-13499)*
Aisin Light Metals LLC ... 618 997-9800
11000 Redco Dr Marion (62959) *(G-13500)*
Aisin Mfg Illinois LLC ... 618 998-8333
1100 Glenn Clarida Dr Marion (62959) *(G-13501)*
Aisin Mfg Illinois LLC (HQ) ... 618 998-8333
11000 Redco Dr Marion (62959) *(G-13502)*
Aiwa Corporation (PA) ... 305 394-4119
965 W Chicago Ave Chicago (60642) *(G-3591)*
Aixacct Systems Inc ... 952 303-4077
715 N Wheaton Ave Wheaton (60187) *(G-20787)*
Aj Auto ... 847 678-8200
4918 River Rd Schiller Park (60176) *(G-18783)*
AJ Oster LLC ... 630 260-1040
180 Alexandra Way Carol Stream (60188) *(G-2929)*
Aj Welding Services ... 708 843-2701
3640 S Kedzie Ave Chicago (60632) *(G-3592)*
Ajax Tool Works Inc ... 847 455-5420
10801 Franklin Ave Franklin Park (60131) *(G-9862)*
Ajax Tool Works Inc ... 847 737-2600
10530 Anderson Pl Franklin Park (60131) *(G-9863)*
Ajax Tools, Franklin Park *Also called Ajax Tool Works Inc (G-9862)*
Aji Custom Cabinets ... 847 312-7847
5720 Wilmot Rd McHenry (60051) *(G-13716)*
Ajinomoto Food Ingredients LLC ... 773 714-1436
1300 N Arlington Hts Rd Itasca (60143) *(G-11617)*
Ajinomoto Foods North Amer Inc ... 815 452-2559
110 N Main St Toluca (61369) *(G-19885)*
Ajinomoto Foods North Amer Inc ... 815 452-2361
301 W 3rd St Toluca (61369) *(G-19886)*
Ajr Enterprises Inc ... 630 377-8886
1200 Rukel Way Saint Charles (60174) *(G-18143)*
AJS Ministry ... 773 403-4166
632 Primrose Cir Matteson (60443) *(G-13617)*
Ajs Premier Printing Inc ... 847 838-6350
893 Main St Antioch (60002) *(G-596)*
AJS Publications ... 847 526-5027
229 Brier Ct Island Lake (60042) *(G-11604)*
AK Steel Corporation ... 815 267-3838
24036 Nightingale Ct Plainfield (60585) *(G-16640)*
Akamai Technologies Inc ... 312 893-7900
444 N Michigan Ave Chicago (60611) *(G-3593)*
AKD Controls Inc ... 815 633-4586
10340 Product Dr Machesney Park (61115) *(G-13324)*
Akema Inc ... 708 482-3148
637 S Waiola Ave La Grange (60525) *(G-12070)*
Akers Packaging Service Inc ... 773 731-2900
1037 E 87th St Chicago (60619) *(G-3594)*
Akers Packaging Solutions Inc ... 217 468-2396
7573 N State Route 48 Oreana (62554) *(G-15910)*
Akers Packg Solutions Decatur, Oreana *Also called Akers Packaging Solutions Inc (G-15910)*
Akerue Industries LLC ... 847 395-3300
90 Mcmillen Rd Antioch (60002) *(G-597)*
Akhan Semiconductor Inc ... 847 855-8400
940 Lakeside Dr Gurnee (60031) *(G-10856)*
Akorn Inc ... 847 625-1100
5605 Centerpoint Ct Ste B Gurnee (60031) *(G-10857)*
Akorn Inc (PA) ... 847 279-6100
1925 W Field Ct Ste 300 Lake Forest (60045) *(G-12222)*
Akorn Inc ... 217 428-1100
150 S Wyckles Rd Decatur (62522) *(G-7437)*
Akorn Inc ... 217 423-9715
1222 W Grand Ave Decatur (62522) *(G-7438)*
Akorn Inc ... 847 279-6166
50 Lakeview Pkwy Ste 112 Vernon Hills (60061) *(G-20039)*
Akorn Pharmaceuticals, Lake Forest *Also called Akorn Inc (G-12222)*
Akorn Pharmaceuticals, Decatur *Also called Akorn Inc (G-7438)*
Akorn Pharmaceuticals ... 800 932-5676
1925 W Field Ct Lake Forest (60045) *(G-12223)*
Akr Industries Inc ... 732 998-5662
9710 N Megan Ct Peoria (61615) *(G-16379)*
Akrylix Inc (PA) ... 773 869-9005
171 Ontario St Frankfort (60423) *(G-9764)*
Akshar Plastic Inc ... 815 635-3536
1101 Bell St Bloomington (61701) *(G-2022)*

ALPHABETIC

ALPHABETIC SECTION

Aksys Ltd 847 229-2020
  2 Marriott Dr Lincolnshire (60069) *(G-12743)*
Akt Corporation 414 475-5020
  909 Grace St Elgin (60120) *(G-8501)*
Akt Corporation of Wisconsin, Elgin *Also called Akt Corporation (G-8501)*
Akzo Nobel Aerospace Coatings, Waukegan *Also called Akzo Nobel Coatings Inc (G-20411)*
Akzo Nobel Coatings Inc 630 792-1619
  931 N Du Page Ave Lombard (60148) *(G-13038)*
Akzo Nobel Coatings Inc 847 623-4200
  E Water St Waukegan (60085) *(G-20411)*
Akzo Nobel Coatings Inc 312 544-7057
  131 S Dearborn St # 1000 Chicago (60603) *(G-3595)*
Akzonobel, Chicago *Also called Nouryon Functional Chem LLC (G-5631)*
Al Bar Laboratories Inc 847 251-1218
  127 Green Bay Rd Wilmette (60091) *(G-21068)*
Al Bar-Wilmette Platers, Wilmette *Also called Al Bar Laboratories Inc (G-21068)*
Al Gelato Chicago LLC 847 455-5355
  3220 Mannheim Rd Franklin Park (60131) *(G-9864)*
Al3 Inc 847 441-7888
  170 Linden St Winnetka (60093) *(G-21123)*
Alagor Industries Incorporated (PA) 630 766-2910
  489 Thomas Dr Bensenville (60106) *(G-1734)*
Alali Enterprises Inc 630 827-9231
  1228 Narragansett Dr Carol Stream (60188) *(G-2930)*
Alan Manufacturing Corp 815 568-6836
  5017 Ritz Rd Marengo (60152) *(G-13478)*
Alan Rocca Ltd 630 323-5800
  3824 York Rd Ste B Oak Brook (60523) *(G-15590)*
Alan Rocca Fine Jewelery, Oak Brook *Also called Alan Rocca Ltd (G-15590)*
Alan Stamping, Marengo *Also called Alan Manufacturing Corp (G-13478)*
Alang Pattern Inc 773 722-9481
  3635 S 61st Ave Cicero (60804) *(G-6828)*
Alanson Manufacturing LLC 773 762-2530
  4408 W Cermak Rd Chicago (60623) *(G-3596)*
Alao Temitope 331 454-3333
  29 Brookhill Ct Collinsville (62234) *(G-6953)*
Albax Inc 630 758-1072
  521 W Wrightwood Ave Elmhurst (60126) *(G-9323)*
Albert F Amling LLC (PA) 630 333-1720
  331 N York St Elmhurst (60126) *(G-9324)*
Albert Vivo Upholstery Co Inc 312 226-7779
  836 Lakeview Ln Burr Ridge (60527) *(G-2651)*
Albert Whitman & Company 847 232-2800
  250 S Northwest Hwy # 320 Park Ridge (60068) *(G-16266)*
Alberto Daza 773 638-9880
  4243 W Arthington St Chicago (60624) *(G-3597)*
Albright Enterprises Inc 630 357-2300
  426 W 5th Ave Naperville (60563) *(G-14769)*
Alca Industrial Instrs Svc, Franklin Park *Also called Best Rep Company Corporation (G-9886)*
Alcast Company (PA) 309 691-5513
  8821 N University St Peoria (61615) *(G-16380)*
Alcast Company 309 691-5513
  8820 N Pioneer Rd Peoria (61615) *(G-16381)*
Alcast Company 309 691-5513
  8600 N Industrial Rd Peoria (61615) *(G-16382)*
Alco Locomotive Company, Dixmoor *Also called National Railway Equipment Co (G-7884)*
Alco Manufacturing Corp LLC 815 708-5540
  4950 Marlin Dr Machesney Park (61115) *(G-13325)*
Alco Spring Industries Inc 708 755-0438
  2300 Euclid Ave Chicago Heights (60411) *(G-6730)*
Alcon Tool & Mfg Co Inc 773 545-8742
  5266 N Elston Ave Chicago (60630) *(G-3598)*
Alcon Vision LLC 312 751-6200
  400 W Superior St Chicago (60654) *(G-3599)*
Alconix Usa Inc 847 717-7407
  25 Northwest Point Blvd # 800 Elk Grove Village (60007) *(G-8813)*
Alden & Ott Printing Inks Co (HQ) 847 956-6830
  616 E Brook Dr Arlington Heights (60005) *(G-686)*
Alden & Ott Printing Inks Co 847 364-6817
  2050 S Carboy Rd Mount Prospect (60056) *(G-14511)*
Aldi Inc 815 877-0861
  1545 W Lane Rd Machesney Park (61115) *(G-13326)*
Aldon Co 847 623-8800
  3410 Sunset Ave Waukegan (60087) *(G-20412)*
Aldonex Inc 708 547-5663
  2917 Saint Charles Rd Bellwood (60104) *(G-1613)*
Aldrich Company, Wyoming *Also called Aldrico Inc (G-21457)*
Aldrico Inc 309 695-2311
  341 E Williams St Wyoming (61491) *(G-21457)*
Ale Syndicate Brewers LLC 773 340-2337
  2601 W Diversey Ave Chicago (60647) *(G-3600)*
Ale USA Inc 630 713-5194
  1960 Nperville Wheaton Rd Naperville (60563) *(G-14770)*
Alecto Industries Inc 708 344-1488
  148 S 8th Ave Maywood (60153) *(G-13659)*
Aledo Welding Enterprises Inc 309 582-2019
  1802 Se 3rd St Aledo (61231) *(G-354)*
Alef Sausage & Deli, Mundelein *Also called Ifa International Inc (G-14698)*

Alegra Printing, Elgin *Also called Allegra Print & Imaging Inc (G-8502)*
Alegria Company 608 726-2336
  2952 N Kilbourn Ave Chicago (60641) *(G-3601)*
Alert Manufacturing, Elk Grove Village *Also called All-State Industries Inc (G-8815)*
Alert Screw Products Corp 847 587-1360
  100 Honing Rd Fox Lake (60020) *(G-9744)*
Alert Tubing Fabricators Inc 815 633-5065
  8019 Commercial Ave Loves Park (61111) *(G-13186)*
Alessco Inc (PA) 773 327-7919
  2237 N Janssen Ave Chicago (60614) *(G-3602)*
Alex and Ani LLC 708 403-4450
  544 Orland Square Dr E12 Orland Park (60462) *(G-15937)*
Alex Displays & Co 312 829-2948
  401 N Leavitt St Chicago (60612) *(G-3603)*
Alex Smart Inc 773 244-9275
  1800 W Grace St Apt 322 Chicago (60613) *(G-3604)*
Alexander Brewster LLC 618 346-8580
  1401 N Bluff Rd Collinsville (62234) *(G-6954)*
Alexander Lumber Co 815 754-1000
  160 S Loves Rd Cortland (60112) *(G-7016)*
Alexander Manufacturing Co 309 728-2224
  114 N Lincoln St Towanda (61776) *(G-19892)*
Alexander Signs & Designs Inc 815 933-3100
  1511 Commerce Dr Bourbonnais (60914) *(G-2255)*
Alexander Technique 847 337-7926
  1830 Sherman Ave Ste 302 Evanston (60201) *(G-9490)*
Alexeter Technologies LLC (PA) 847 419-1507
  830 Seton Ct Ste 6 Wheeling (60090) *(G-20843)*
Alexi's One Stop Shop, Bridgeview *Also called Amis Inc (G-2323)*
Alexia Foods 312 374-3449
  222 Merchandise Mart Plz Chicago (60654) *(G-3605)*
Alexis Fire Equipment Company 309 482-6121
  109 E Broadway Ave Alexis (61412) *(G-364)*
Alfa Controls Inc 847 978-9245
  311 Egidi Dr Wheeling (60090) *(G-20844)*
Alfa Laval Standard, Wood Dale *Also called Standard Refrigeration LLC (G-21242)*
Alfa Mfg Industries Inc 847 470-9595
  7845 Merrimac Ave Morton Grove (60053) *(G-14388)*
Alfa Tools, Morton Grove *Also called Sandtech Inc (G-14439)*
Alfa Tools, Morton Grove *Also called Alfa Mfg Industries Inc (G-14388)*
Alfa-Pet Inc (PA) 314 865-0400
  7319 Ingham Ln Godfrey (62035) *(G-10648)*
Alfredos Iron Works Inc 815 748-1177
  280 W Lincoln Hwy Cortland (60112) *(G-7017)*
Algus Packaging Inc 815 756-1881
  200 N Peace Rd Dekalb (60115) *(G-7665)*
Ali Group North America Corp (HQ) 847 215-6565
  101 Corporate Woods Pkwy Vernon Hills (60061) *(G-20040)*
Ali VS Kitchen LLC 312 852-5090
  110 W Kinzie St Fl 3 Chicago (60654) *(G-3606)*
Alicona Corporation 630 372-9900
  150 E Pierce Rd Ste 130 Itasca (60143) *(G-11618)*
Alicona Manufacturing Inc 630 736-2718
  1261 Humbracht Cir Ste A Bartlett (60103) *(G-1263)*
Align Production Systems LLC 217 423-6001
  2230 N Brush College Rd Decatur (62526) *(G-7439)*
Alignlife, Wood River *Also called Ican Clinic LLC (G-21263)*
Alin Machining Company Inc (PA) 708 681-1043
  3131 N Soffel Ave Melrose Park (60160) *(G-13821)*
Aline International LLC 708 478-2471
  9100 W 191st St Ste 103 Mokena (60448) *(G-14069)*
Alisun Business Printing, Westchester *Also called Alisun Inc (G-20691)*
Alisun Inc 708 571-3451
  937 S Mannheim Rd Ste 2 Westchester (60154) *(G-20691)*
All American Athletics Ltd 815 432-8326
  100 Laird Ln Watseka (60970) *(G-20304)*
All American Nut & Candy Corp 630 595-6473
  255 Beinoris Dr Wood Dale (60191) *(G-21157)*
All American Ready Mix 217 931-2344
  2510 Richards Ln Springfield (62702) *(G-19317)*
All American Spring Stamping 847 928-9468
  10220 Franklin Ave Franklin Park (60131) *(G-9865)*
All American Trophy King Inc 708 597-2121
  13811 Cicero Ave Crestwood (60418) *(G-7105)*
All American Washer Werks Inc 847 566-9091
  912 E High St Mundelein (60060) *(G-14661)*
All American Wood Register Co 815 356-1000
  7103 Sands Rd Crystal Lake (60014) *(G-7155)*
All Cell Technologies LLC 872 281-7606
  2321 W 41st St Chicago (60609) *(G-3607)*
All City Brick Staining LLC 312 459-8937
  3635 W Dickens Ave Apt 1b Chicago (60647) *(G-3608)*
All Cnc Solutions Inc 847 972-1139
  7617 Parkside Ave Skokie (60077) *(G-18913)*
All Container Inc 847 677-2100
  7060 N Lawndale Ave Lincolnwood (60712) *(G-12813)*
All Cut Inc 630 910-6505
  8195 S Lemont Rd Darien (60561) *(G-7400)*

All Dental 708 749-0277
6721 Cermak Rd Berwyn (60402) ***(G-1948)***
All Electric Mtr Repr Svc Inc (PA) 773 925-2404
6726 S Ashland Ave Chicago (60636) ***(G-3609)***
All Foam Industries, Elmhurst *Also called K & S Service & Rental Corp* ***(G-9384)***
All Foam Products 847 913-9341
2546 Live Oak Ln Buffalo Grove (60089) ***(G-2507)***
All Fresh Food Products (PA) 847 864-5030
2156 Green Bay Rd Evanston (60201) ***(G-9491)***
All Gear Inc 847 564-9016
3014 Commercial Ave Northbrook (60062) ***(G-15335)***
All In Stitches 309 944-4084
100 E Main St Geneseo (61254) ***(G-10238)***
All Line Inc 630 820-1800
31w310 91st St Naperville (60564) ***(G-14955)***
All Metal Machine 815 389-0168
14305 Dorr Rd South Beloit (61080) ***(G-19079)***
All Metal Recycling Company 847 530-4825
409 N Addison Rd Villa Park (60181) ***(G-20130)***
All Metal Solutions Inc (PA) 312 483-4178
2044 N Whipple St Chicago (60647) ***(G-3610)***
All Nation Line Division, Carol Stream *Also called Scale Railroad Equipment* ***(G-3065)***
All Pallet Service 618 451-7545
1459 State St Granite City (62040) ***(G-10693)***
All Precision Mfg LLC 217 563-7070
153 N 5th St Nokomis (62075) ***(G-15193)***
All Printing & Graphics Inc 773 553-3049
125 S Clark St Fl 3 Chicago (60603) ***(G-3611)***
All Printing & Graphics Inc (PA) 708 450-1512
2250 S 14th Ave Broadview (60155) ***(G-2415)***
All Pro Welding Services Inc 217 586-5383
157 County Road 2300 N Mahomet (61853) ***(G-13420)***
All Products Gasket 877 255-8700
618 Anderson Dr Ste B Romeoville (60446) ***(G-17789)***
All Right Sales Inc 773 558-4800
28w240 Trieste Ln West Chicago (60185) ***(G-20534)***
All Rite Industries Inc 847 540-0300
470 Oakwood Rd Lake Zurich (60047) ***(G-12382)***
All Rite Spring Co 815 675-1350
2200 Spring Ridge Dr Spring Grove (60081) ***(G-19263)***
All Rite Spring Company 815 675-1350
2302 Spring Ridge Dr Spring Grove (60081) ***(G-19264)***
All Saints Monument Co Inc 847 824-1248
20 S River Rd Des Plaines (60016) ***(G-7725)***
All Seasons Co, Decatur *Also called All Seasons Heating & AC* ***(G-7440)***
All Seasons Heating & AC 217 429-2022
167 S Excelsior St Decatur (62521) ***(G-7440)***
All Seasons Screen Prtg & EMB, Chicago *Also called Wellspring Investments LLC* ***(G-6602)***
All She Wrote 773 529-0100
825 W Armitage Ave Chicago (60614) ***(G-3612)***
All Signs & Wonders Co 630 232-9019
1020 W Fabyan Pkwy Geneva (60134) ***(G-10250)***
All Signs Inc 847 324-5500
8088 Mccormick Blvd Skokie (60076) ***(G-18914)***
All Spun Metal Products, Lombard *Also called Spectracrafts Ltd* ***(G-13133)***
All Star Custom Awards 630 428-1515
1203 Hidden Spring Dr Naperville (60540) ***(G-14771)***
All Star Injection Molders Inc 630 978-4046
24w959 Ramm Dr Unit 5 Naperville (60564) ***(G-14956)***
All Star Publishing 630 428-1515
1203 Hidden Spring Dr Naperville (60540) ***(G-14772)***
All Stars -N- Stitches Inc 618 435-5555
418 E Main St Benton (62812) ***(G-1918)***
All Stone Inc 815 529-1754
1525 Azalea Cir Romeoville (60446) ***(G-17790)***
All Suburban Generator, Willowbrook *Also called Michael Wilton Cstm Homes Inc* ***(G-21049)***
All Tech Systems & Install 815 609-0685
11952 S Spaulding Schl Dr Plainfield (60585) ***(G-16641)***
All Type Hydraulics Corp 618 585-4844
149 S Washington St Bunker Hill (62014) ***(G-2632)***
All Weather Courts Inc 217 364-4546
Rr Box 276 Dawson (62520) ***(G-7428)***
All Weather Products Co LLC 847 981-0386
1500 Greenleaf Ave Elk Grove Village (60007) ***(G-8814)***
All West Plastics Inc 847 395-8830
606 Drom Ct Antioch (60002) ***(G-598)***
All-American Sign Co Inc 708 422-2203
5501 W 109th St Ste 1 Oak Lawn (60453) ***(G-15698)***
All-Brite Anodizing Co Inc (PA) 708 562-0502
100 W Lake St Northlake (60164) ***(G-15539)***
All-Feed Proc & Packg Inc (PA) 309 629-0001
210 S 1st St Alpha (61413) ***(G-405)***
All-Feed Proc & Packg Inc 309 932-3119
717 W Division St Galva (61434) ***(G-10226)***
All-Pak Manufacturing Corp 630 851-5859
1221 Jackson St Ste A-B Aurora (60505) ***(G-1046)***
All-Right Sign Inc 708 754-6366
3628 Union Ave Ste 1 Steger (60475) ***(G-19487)***
All-State Industries Inc 847 350-0460
2651 Carl Blvd Elk Grove Village (60007) ***(G-8815)***
All-Steel Structures Inc 708 210-1313
16301 Vincennes Ave South Holland (60473) ***(G-19189)***
All-Style Custom Tops 708 532-6606
5555 175th St Tinley Park (60477) ***(G-19799)***
All-Vac Industries Inc 847 675-2290
7350 Central Park Ave Skokie (60076) ***(G-18915)***
All-Ways Quick Print 708 403-8422
14609 Birch St Orland Park (60462) ***(G-15938)***
Allan Brooks & Associates Inc 847 537-7500
95 W Grand Ave Ste 120 Lake Villa (60046) ***(G-12345)***
Allans Welding & Machine Inc 618 392-3708
3815 E Ilinois Hwy 250 Olney (62450) ***(G-15851)***
Allcell Technologies, Chicago *Also called All Cell Technologies LLC* ***(G-3607)***
Allcom Products Illinois LLC 847 468-8830
695 Sundown Rd South Elgin (60177) ***(G-19131)***
Allegion Lcn & Falcon Closers, Princeton *Also called Allegion S&S Holding Co Inc* ***(G-16805)***
Allegion S&S Holding Co Inc 815 875-3311
121 W Railroad Ave Princeton (61356) ***(G-16805)***
Allegra Marketing Print & Mail, Elk Grove Village *Also called Woogl Corporation* ***(G-9312)***
Allegra Marketing Print Mail, Romeoville *Also called Allegra Network LLC* ***(G-17791)***
Allegra Marketing Print Mail 630 790-0444
1945 Wright Blvd Schaumburg (60193) ***(G-18431)***
Allegra Marketing Print Web, Aurora *Also called Bat Business Services Inc* ***(G-1062)***
Allegra Mktg Print Mail, Naperville *Also called Spell It With Color Inc* ***(G-14919)***
Allegra Network LLC (PA) 331 253-2775
1340 Enterprise Dr Romeoville (60446) ***(G-17791)***
Allegra Network LLC 630 801-9335
987 Oak Ave Aurora (60506) ***(G-1047)***
Allegra Print & Imaging, Evanston *Also called Evanston Graphic Imaging Inc* ***(G-9516)***
Allegra Print & Imaging, Alsip *Also called Anikam Inc* ***(G-415)***
Allegra Print & Imaging, Rolling Meadows *Also called M & R Printing Inc* ***(G-17749)***
Allegra Print & Imaging, Glendale Heights *Also called Rightway Printing Inc* ***(G-10488)***
Allegra Print & Imaging, Northbrook *Also called Officers Printing Inc* ***(G-15444)***
Allegra Print & Imaging, Aurora *Also called Allegra Network LLC* ***(G-1047)***
Allegra Print & Imaging 630 963-9100
2200 Ogden Ave Ste 500a Lisle (60532) ***(G-12860)***
Allegra Print & Imaging Inc 847 697-1434
909 Davis Rd Elgin (60123) ***(G-8502)***
Allegro Publishing Inc 847 565-9083
2421 N Artesian Ave Chicago (60647) ***(G-3613)***
Allen Awards, Streamwood *Also called A 1 Trophies Awards & Engrv* ***(G-19558)***
Allen Entertainment Management 630 752-0903
471 Essex Pl Carol Stream (60188) ***(G-2931)***
Allen Larson 773 454-2210
1914 N Washtenaw Ave Chicago (60647) ***(G-3614)***
Allen Paper Company 312 454-4500
641 W Lake St Ste L101 Chicago (60661) ***(G-3615)***
Allendale Gravel Co Inc 618 263-3521
18306 Wabash 18 Ave Allendale (62410) ***(G-402)***
Allens Farm Quality Meats 217 896-2532
Rr 49 Homer (61849) ***(G-11474)***
Allenton Lumber Company, Hampshire *Also called Ht Lumber & Crates Inc* ***(G-10973)***
Allergan Inc 714 246-4500
605 Tri State Pkwy Gurnee (60031) ***(G-10858)***
Allerton Charter Coach 217 344-2600
714 S 6th St Champaign (61820) ***(G-3261)***
Allerton Supply Company 217 896-2522
1050 N &Amp 2600 E Homer (61849) ***(G-11475)***
Allfavor Technologies Inc 630 913-4263
905 Albion Ave Schaumburg (60193) ***(G-18432)***
Allform Manufacturing Co 847 680-0144
342 4th St Libertyville (60048) ***(G-12627)***
Allfresh Food Products Inc (HQ) 847 869-3100
2156 Green Bay Rd Evanston (60201) ***(G-9492)***
Alliance Creative Group Inc (PA) 847 885-1800
160 Windsor Dr East Dundee (60118) ***(G-8187)***
Alliance Display, Dekalb *Also called Westrock Rkt LLC* ***(G-7713)***
Alliance Door and Hardware LLC 630 451-7070
225 Fencl Ln Hillside (60162) ***(G-11326)***
Alliance Envelope & Print LLC 847 446-4079
854 Prospect Ave Winnetka (60093) ***(G-21124)***
Alliance For Illinois Mfg 773 594-9292
8420 W Bryn Mawr Ave Chicago (60631) ***(G-3616)***
Alliance Graphics 312 280-8000
1652 W Ogden Ave Apt 4 Chicago (60612) ***(G-3617)***
Alliance Industries Inc 847 288-9090
2120 Roberts Dr Ste A Broadview (60155) ***(G-2416)***
Alliance Investment Corp 847 933-0400
9150 Kenneth Ave Skokie (60076) ***(G-18916)***
Alliance Laser Sales Inc (PA) 847 487-1945
275 Industrial Dr Wauconda (60084) ***(G-20328)***
Alliance Plastics 888 643-1432
830 Fairway Dr Ste 104 Bensenville (60106) ***(G-1735)***
Alliance Printing Inc 630 613-9529
1785 W Cortland Ct Addison (60101) ***(G-26)***
Alliance Specialties Corp 847 487-1945
275 Industrial Dr Wauconda (60084) ***(G-20329)***
Alliance Steel, Bedford Park *Also called A2 Sales LLC* ***(G-1453)***

ALPHABETIC

Alliance Technology MGT Corp (PA)....847 574-9752
790 W Frontage Rd Ste 716 Northfield (60093) **(G-15504)**
Alliance Tool & Manufacturing....708 345-5444
91 Wilcox St Maywood (60153) **(G-13660)**
Alliance Wheel Services LLC....309 444-4334
302 W Holland St Washington (61571) **(G-20265)**
Allie Woodworking....847 244-1919
3035 Sunset Ave Waukegan (60087) **(G-20413)**
Allied Asphalt Paving Co Inc (PA)....630 289-6080
1100 Brandt Dr Elgin (60120) **(G-8503)**
Allied Asphalt Paving Company, Hoffman Estates *Also called Plote Construction Inc* **(G-11445)**
Allied Die Casting Company III, Franklin Park *Also called RCM Industries Inc* **(G-10033)**
Allied Die Casting Corporation....815 385-9330
3923 W West Ave McHenry (60050) **(G-13717)**
Allied Garage Door Inc....630 279-0795
310 W Gerri Ln Addison (60101) **(G-27)**
Allied Gear Co....773 287-8742
1034 Keystone Ave River Forest (60305) **(G-17049)**
Allied Graphics Inc....847 419-8830
1398 Busch Pkwy Buffalo Grove (60089) **(G-2508)**
Allied Machine Tool & Dye....708 388-7676
13430 Kolmar Ave Crestwood (60418) **(G-7106)**
Allied Metal Co (PA)....312 225-2800
1300 N Kostner Ave Chicago (60651) **(G-3618)**
Allied Print & Copy, Chicago *Also called Allied Printing Inc* **(G-3619)**
Allied Printing Inc....773 334-5200
5640 N Broadway St Chicago (60660) **(G-3619)**
Allied Production Drilling....815 969-0940
5746 N Hales Corner Rd Stillman Valley (61084) **(G-19544)**
Allied Rivet Inc....630 208-0120
1172 Commerce Dr Geneva (60134) **(G-10251)**
Allied Scoring Tables Inc....815 654-8807
5417 Forest Hills Ct Loves Park (61111) **(G-13187)**
Allied Stone, Milan *Also called Riverstone Group Inc* **(G-14026)**
Allied Tube & Conduit Corp (HQ)....708 339-1610
16100 Lathrop Ave Harvey (60426) **(G-11071)**
Allied Welding, Chillicothe *Also called Ter-Son Corporation* **(G-6822)**
Allied Welding Inc....309 274-6227
1820 N Santa Fe Ave Chillicothe (61523) **(G-6813)**
Allied-Locke Industries Inc....800 435-7752
1020 Subic Rd Dixon (61021) **(G-7888)**
Alligator Rec & Artist MGT Inc....773 973-7736
1441 W Devon Ave Chicago (60660) **(G-3620)**
Allison's Comfort Shoes, Maryville *Also called New Step Orthotic Lab Inc* **(G-13592)**
Allkut Tool Incorporated....815 476-9656
601 Davy Ln Wilmington (60481) **(G-21096)**
Allmetal Inc (PA)....630 250-8090
1 Pierce Pl Ste 295w Itasca (60143) **(G-11619)**
Allmetal Inc....630 766-8500
636 Thomas Dr Bensenville (60106) **(G-1736)**
Allmetal Inc....630 766-1407
224-230 Foster Ave Bensenville (60106) **(G-1737)**
Allmetal Inc....630 350-2524
377 Balm Ct Wood Dale (60191) **(G-21158)**
Allocator Logistics Co....708 339-5678
22 W 154th St South Holland (60473) **(G-19190)**
Alloy Chrome Inc....847 678-2880
9328 Bernice Ave Schiller Park (60176) **(G-18784)**
Alloy Engineering & Casting Co, Champaign *Also called Illinois Ni Cast LLC* **(G-3307)**
Alloy Rod Products Inc....815 562-8200
601 W New York St Ste 4 Aurora (60506) **(G-1048)**
Alloy Rod Products Inc....815 562-8200
100 Quarry Rd Rochelle (61068) **(G-17130)**
Alloy Sling Chains Inc (PA)....708 647-4900
1406 175th St East Hazel Crest (60429) **(G-8217)**
Alloy Specialties Inc....815 586-4728
32028 N 1500 East Rd Blackstone (61313) **(G-1970)**
Alloy Tech....217 253-3939
608 E Pinzon St Tuscola (61953) **(G-19922)**
Alloy Welding Corp....708 345-6756
2033 Janice Ave Melrose Park (60160) **(G-13822)**
Alloys Tech Inc....708 248-5041
3305 Butler St S Chicago Hts (60411) **(G-18116)**
Alloyweld Inspection Co Inc....630 595-2145
796 Maple Ln Bensenville (60106) **(G-1738)**
Allprint Graphics Inc....847 519-9898
1034 National Pkwy Schaumburg (60173) **(G-18433)**
Allprint Inc....847 726-0658
66 Tournament Dr S Hawthorn Woods (60047) **(G-11121)**
Allquip Co Inc....309 944-6153
524 E Exchange St Geneseo (61254) **(G-10239)**
Allscripts Healthcare LLC....312 506-1200
222 Merchandise Mart Plz Chicago (60654) **(G-3621)**
Allscripts Holdings LLC....800 334-8534
222 Merchandise Mart Plz # 2024 Chicago (60654) **(G-3622)**
Allscrpts Hlthcare Sltions Inc (PA)....800 334-8534
222 Merchandise Mart Plz Chicago (60654) **(G-3623)**
Allsep Techonlogies, Wheeling *Also called Sielc Technologies Corporation* **(G-20985)**

Allstar Embroidery....847 913-1133
240 Blackthorn Dr Buffalo Grove (60089) **(G-2509)**
Allstar Fasteners Inc....847 640-7827
1550 Arthur Ave Elk Grove Village (60007) **(G-8816)**
Allstar Tool & Molds Inc....630 766-0162
799 Eagle Dr Ste A Bensenville (60106) **(G-1739)**
Allstate Metal Fabricators Inc....630 860-1500
365 Beinoris Dr Wood Dale (60191) **(G-21159)**
Allstates Rubber & Tool Corp....708 342-1030
8201 183rd St Ste M Tinley Park (60487) **(G-19800)**
Alltec Gates Inc (PA)....708 301-9361
15941 Harlem Ave Ste 325 Tinley Park (60477) **(G-19801)**
Alltech Associates Inc (HQ)....773 261-2252
415 S Kilpatrick Ave Chicago (60644) **(G-3624)**
Alltech Plastics Inc....847 352-2309
821 Thornton Ct Apt 2b Schaumburg (60193) **(G-18434)**
Alltemated Inc (PA)....847 394-5800
541 Northgate Pkwy Wheeling (60090) **(G-20845)**
Allured Publishing Corporation....630 653-2155
336 Gundersen Dr Ste A Carol Stream (60188) **(G-2932)**
Ally Global Corporation....773 822-3373
6033 N Sheridan Rd 23d Chicago (60660) **(G-3625)**
Ally International Trading, Chicago *Also called Ally Global Corporation* **(G-3625)**
Alm Distributors LLC....708 865-8000
2060 Janice Ave Melrose Park (60160) **(G-13823)**
Alm Fine Cabinetry Inc....815 562-6667
314 N 6th St Rochelle (61068) **(G-17131)**
Alm Positioners Inc....309 787-6200
8080 Centennial Expy Rock Island (61201) **(G-17201)**
Almacen Inc....847 934-7955
927 Kirkwood Dr Inverness (60067) **(G-11593)**
Aloha Document Services Inc....312 542-1300
141 W Jackson Blvd A10a Chicago (60604) **(G-3626)**
Aloha Print Group, Chicago *Also called Aloha Document Services Inc* **(G-3626)**
Alois Box Co Inc....708 681-4090
2000 N Mannheim Rd Melrose Park (60160) **(G-13824)**
Alomar Inc....312 855-0714
5 S Wabash Ave Ste 316 Chicago (60603) **(G-3627)**
Alpha Acrylic Design....847 818-8178
3359 N Ridge Ave Ste A Arlington Heights (60004) **(G-687)**
Alpha AG Inc (PA)....217 546-2724
8295 Bomke Rd Pleasant Plains (62677) **(G-16749)**
Alpha Assembly Solutions Inc....847 426-4241
2541 Technology Dr Elgin (60124) **(G-8504)**
Alpha Bag Group, Rockford *Also called ABG Bag Inc* **(G-17286)**
Alpha Bedding LLC....847 550-5110
1290 Ensell Rd Lake Zurich (60047) **(G-12383)**
Alpha Circuit Corporation....630 617-5555
730 N Oaklawn Ave Elmhurst (60126) **(G-9325)**
Alpha Coating Technologies LLC....630 268-8787
1725 Western Dr West Chicago (60185) **(G-20535)**
Alpha Consultings....773 251-0053
2240 N Leavitt St Chicago (60647) **(G-3628)**
Alpha Form Technologies, Elgin *Also called Master Machine Group Inc* **(G-8650)**
Alpha Industries Inc....847 945-1740
1720 Christopher Dr Deerfield (60015) **(G-7584)**
Alpha Industries MGT Inc....773 359-8000
1650 E 95th St Chicago (60617) **(G-3629)**
Alpha Laser of Chicago....708 478-0464
9632 194th Pl Mokena (60448) **(G-14070)**
Alpha Natural Resources Inc....618 298-2394
1000 Beall Woods Dr Keensburg (62852) **(G-12012)**
Alpha Omega Plastics Company....847 956-8777
1099 Touhy Ave Elk Grove Village (60007) **(G-8817)**
Alpha Omega Profile Extrusion....847 956-8777
1099 Touhy Ave Elk Grove Village (60007) **(G-8818)**
Alpha Packaging Minnesota Inc....507 454-3830
6824 Paysphere Cir Chicago (60674) **(G-3630)**
Alpha Pcb Designs Inc....773 631-5543
6815 W Higgins Ave Chicago (60656) **(G-3631)**
Alpha Precision Inc....630 553-7331
9750 Rte 126 Yorkville (60560) **(G-21471)**
Alpha Products Inc (PA)....708 594-3883
5570 W 70th Pl Bedford Park (60638) **(G-1455)**
Alpha Products Inc....708 387-1580
9128 47th St Brookfield (60513) **(G-2478)**
Alpha Star Tool and Mold Inc....815 455-2802
11 Burdent Dr Crystal Lake (60014) **(G-7156)**
Alpha Swiss Industries Inc....815 455-3031
700 Tek Dr Crystal Lake (60014) **(G-7157)**
Alpha Tekniko, Lake Zurich *Also called Alpha Bedding LLC* **(G-12383)**
Alphabet Shop Inc....847 888-3150
300 Elgin Ave Elgin (60120) **(G-8505)**
Alphadigital Inc....708 482-4488
712 E Elm Ave La Grange (60525) **(G-12071)**
Alphagage....815 391-6400
5245 27th Ave Rockford (61109) **(G-17299)**
AlphaGraphics, Chicago *Also called Moran Graphics Inc* **(G-5497)**
AlphaGraphics, Aurora *Also called Cynlar Inc* **(G-949)**

AlphaGraphics, Chicago *Also called Graphics 255 LLC* ***(G-4728)***
AlphaGraphics, Vernon Hills *Also called P H C Enterprises Inc* ***(G-20080)***
AlphaGraphics, Schaumburg *Also called Cifuentes Luis & Nicole Inc* ***(G-18477)***
AlphaGraphics, Bannockburn *Also called Print & Design Services LLC* ***(G-1206)***
AlphaGraphics, Saint Charles *Also called Avid of Illinois Inc* ***(G-18152)***
AlphaGraphics, La Grange *Also called Alphadigital Inc* ***(G-12071)***
AlphaGraphics, Park Ridge *Also called Gamma Alpha Visual Communicatn* ***(G-16279)***
AlphaGraphics, Chicago *Also called Basswood Associates Inc* ***(G-3845)***
AlphaGraphics 468, Wood Dale *Also called Bitforms Inc* ***(G-21169)***
AlphaGraphics Printshops ... 630 964-9600
1997 Ohio St Ste B Lisle (60532) ***(G-12861)***
AlphaGraphics US 590, Crystal Lake *Also called Jamether Incorporated* ***(G-7211)***
Alpine Amusement Co Inc ... 708 233-9131
8037 Neva Ave Oak Lawn (60459) ***(G-15699)***
Alpine Imports, Loves Park *Also called Craft World Inc* ***(G-13198)***
Alpine Refrigeration, Streamwood *Also called Kool Technologies Inc* ***(G-19581)***
Alply Insulated Panels LLC ... 217 324-6700
1401 Eilerman Ave Litchfield (62056) ***(G-12959)***
Alps ... 847 437-0665
2445 E Oakton St Arlington Heights (60005) ***(G-688)***
Alps Group Inc (PA) ... 815 469-3800
8779 W Laraway Rd Frankfort (60423) ***(G-9765)***
Alps Group Inc ... 815 469-3800
55 E Monroe St Ste 3800 Chicago (60603) ***(G-3632)***
Alps Group, The, Frankfort *Also called Alps Group Inc* ***(G-9765)***
Alsip Express Newspaper, Midlothian *Also called Southwest Messenger Press Inc* ***(G-13996)***
Alsip Mfg Inc ... 708 333-4446
16700 Carse Ave Harvey (60426) ***(G-11072)***
Alsip Minimill LLC ... 708 625-0098
13101 S Pulaski Rd Ste 1 Alsip (60803) ***(G-414)***
Alstat Wood Products ... 618 684-5167
456 Highway 4 Murphysboro (62966) ***(G-14750)***
Alster Machining Corp ... 773 384-2370
4243 W Diversey Ave Chicago (60639) ***(G-3633)***
Alston Race Cars, Antioch *Also called Glk Enterprises Inc* ***(G-614)***
Alta Vista Solutions Inc ... 312 473-3050
2035 W Grand Ave Chicago (60612) ***(G-3634)***
Altair Corporation (HQ) ... 847 634-9540
350 Barclay Blvd Lincolnshire (60069) ***(G-12744)***
Altair Corporation Del, Lincolnshire *Also called Altair Corporation* ***(G-12744)***
Altak Inc ... 630 622-0300
250 Covington Dr Bloomingdale (60108) ***(G-1975)***
Altamira Art Glass ... 708 848-3799
202 And A Half S Mrion St Oak Park (60302) ***(G-15744)***
Altamont Co ... 800 626-5774
901 N Church St Thomasboro (61878) ***(G-19775)***
Altamont News ... 618 483-6176
7 Do It Dr Altamont (62411) ***(G-529)***
Altathera Pharmaceuticals LLC ... 312 445-8900
311 S Wacker Dr Ste 2275a Chicago (60606) ***(G-3635)***
Altco Inc ... 847 549-0321
1000 Woodlands Pkwy Vernon Hills (60061) ***(G-20041)***
Alter Recycling, Bartonville *Also called Alter Trading Corporation* ***(G-1327)***
Alter Scrap, Quincy *Also called Alter Trading Corporation* ***(G-16852)***
Alter Trading Corporation ... 217 223-0156
2834 Gardner Expy Quincy (62305) ***(G-16852)***
Alter Trading Corporation ... 309 828-6084
501 E Stewart St Bloomington (61701) ***(G-2023)***
Alter Trading Corporation ... 309 697-6161
7000 S Adams St Ste 2 Bartonville (61607) ***(G-1327)***
Altera Corporation ... 847 240-0313
425 N Martingale Rd # 1320 Schaumburg (60173) ***(G-18435)***
Alternative TS ... 618 257-0230
5300 N Belt W Belleville (62226) ***(G-1529)***
Alternative Wastewater Systems ... 630 761-8720
1815 Phelps Dr Batavia (60510) ***(G-1345)***
Alti LLC ... 951 505-3148
826 Pleasant Ave Highland Park (60035) ***(G-11252)***
Altium Packaging ... 815 943-7828
875 W Diggins St Harvard (60033) ***(G-11042)***
Altium Packaging ... 630 231-7150
1300 Northwest Ave West Chicago (60185) ***(G-20536)***
Altivity Packaging, Carol Stream *Also called Graphic Packaging Intl LLC* ***(G-2993)***
Altivity Packaging, Romeoville *Also called Mondi Bags Usa LLC* ***(G-17856)***
Altivity Packaging, Carol Stream *Also called Graphic Packaging Intl LLC* ***(G-2994)***
Altman & Koehler Foundry ... 773 373-7737
505 W Root St Chicago (60609) ***(G-3636)***
Altman Manufacturing Co Inc ... 630 963-0031
1990 Ohio St Lisle (60532) ***(G-12862)***
Altman Pattern and Foundry Co ... 773 586-9100
6820 W 63rd St Chicago (60638) ***(G-3637)***
Alto Vineyards Limited (PA) ... 618 893-4898
8515 Highway 127 Alto Pass (62905) ***(G-538)***
Alton Sheet Metal Corp ... 618 462-0609
801 E Broadway Alton (62002) ***(G-543)***
Altona Co ... 815 232-7819
70 E Monterey St Freeport (61032) ***(G-10099)***
Altonat, Altamont *Also called Better News Papers Inc* ***(G-531)***
Altorfer Power Systems ... 309 697-1234
6315 W Fauber Rd Bartonville (61607) ***(G-1328)***
Altra Division 5 Llc ... 708 534-1100
650 Central Ave University Park (60484) ***(G-19945)***
Altran Corp ... 815 455-5650
365 E Terra Cotta Ave Crystal Lake (60014) ***(G-7158)***
Altran Magnetics LLC ... 815 632-3150
1741 Industrial Dr # 14 Sterling (61081) ***(G-19497)***
Alturdyne Power Systems LLC ... 619 440-5531
5023 N Clark St Chicago (60640) ***(G-3638)***
Alu-Bra Foundry Inc ... 630 766-3112
630 E Green St Bensenville (60106) ***(G-1740)***
Alum-I-Tank Inc ... 800 652-6630
201 Ratzlaff St Harvard (60033) ***(G-11043)***
Alum-I-Tank Inc (PA) ... 815 943-6649
11317 N Us Highway 14 Harvard (60033) ***(G-11044)***
Alumapro Inc ... 224 569-3650
1 Union Special Plz Huntley (60142) ***(G-11527)***
Aluminite of Paris ... 217 463-2233
2009 S Main St Paris (61944) ***(G-16224)***
Aluminum and Zinc Die, Schiller Park *Also called Soldy Manufacturing Inc* ***(G-18844)***
Aluminum Castings Corporation ... 309 343-8910
340 S Kellogg St Galesburg (61401) ***(G-10184)***
Aluminum Coil Anodizing Corp (PA) ... 630 837-4000
501 E Lake St Streamwood (60107) ***(G-19560)***
Aluminum Drive Line Products ... 708 946-9777
746 Penfield St Beecher (60401) ***(G-1516)***
Alumitank, Harvard *Also called Alum-I-Tank Inc* ***(G-11044)***
Alva/MCO Phrmcal Companies Inc ... 847 663-0700
7711 N Merrimac Ave Niles (60714) ***(G-15101)***
Alvar Inc ... 309 248-7523
112 State Route 89 Washburn (61570) ***(G-20262)***
Alvarez & Marsal Inc ... 312 601-4220
540 W Madison St Fl 18 Chicago (60661) ***(G-3639)***
Alvin F Lambright ... 618 835-2050
209 County Road 1715 N Xenia (62899) ***(G-21465)***
Alwan Printing Inc ... 708 598-9600
7825 S Roberts Rd Bridgeview (60455) ***(G-2321)***
Always Faithful Dog Traning ... 630 696-2572
73 Highgate Crse Saint Charles (60174) ***(G-18144)***
Always There Express Corp ... 773 931-3744
29 Forestwood Ct Ste 6 Romeoville (60446) ***(G-17792)***
Alyce Designs Inc (PA) ... 847 966-6933
7901 Caldwell Ave Morton Grove (60053) ***(G-14389)***
Alyce Paris, Morton Grove *Also called Alyce Designs Inc* ***(G-14389)***
AM Harper Products Inc ... 312 767-8283
2300 W Jarvis Ave Apt 3 Chicago (60645) ***(G-3640)***
AM Ko Oriental Foods ... 217 398-2922
101 E Springfield Ave Champaign (61820) ***(G-3262)***
AM PM Printers, Cortland *Also called Michael Burza* ***(G-7024)***
AM Precision Machine Inc ... 847 439-9955
1310 Lorraine Pl Schaumburg (60173) ***(G-18436)***
AM Swiss Screw Mch Pdts Inc ... 847 468-9300
345 Industrial Dr South Elgin (60177) ***(G-19132)***
Am-Don Partnership ... 217 355-7750
1819 S Neil St Ste A Champaign (61820) ***(G-3263)***
Am-Ko Oriental Grocery, Champaign *Also called AM Ko Oriental Foods* ***(G-3262)***
Am2pat Inc (PA) ... 847 726-9443
3034 W Devon Ave Chicago (60659) ***(G-3641)***
Amada America Inc ... 877 262-3287
1091 W Hawthorn Dr Itasca (60143) ***(G-11620)***
Amag Manufacturing Inc ... 773 667-5184
4940 S East End Ave 11c Chicago (60615) ***(G-3642)***
Amaitis and Associates Inc (PA) ... 847 428-1269
810 Lively Blvd Wood Dale (60191) ***(G-21160)***
Amani Froyo LLC ... 941 744-1111
2005 S Meyers Rd Apt 427 Oakbrook Terrace (60181) ***(G-15782)***
Amar Plastics Inc ... 630 627-4105
100 W Industrial Rd Addison (60101) ***(G-28)***
Amariko Inc ... 630 734-1000
123 Ogden Ave Clarendon Hills (60514) ***(G-6899)***
Amav Enterprises Ltd ... 630 761-3077
1921 W Wilson St Ste A Batavia (60510) ***(G-1346)***
Amazing Mascots ... 727 475-0255
4913 W Montrose Ave 3 Chicago (60641) ***(G-3643)***
Ambassador Printing, Oak Forest *Also called Babak Inc* ***(G-15672)***
Amber Engineering and Mfg Co ... 847 595-6966
2400 Brickvale Dr Elk Grove Village (60007) ***(G-8819)***
Amber Soft Inc ... 630 377-6945
28214 W Northwest Hwy Lake Barrington (60010) ***(G-12141)***
Amberaw Asphalt Materials, Lawrenceville *Also called Asphalt Products Inc* ***(G-12527)***
Amberleaf Cabinetry Inc ... 773 247-8282
1400 W 37th St Chicago (60609) ***(G-3644)***
Ambi-Design Incorporated ... 815 964-7568
4654 Crested Butte Trl Rockford (61114) ***(G-17300)***
Ambient Lightning and Electric ... 708 529-3434
10033 Menard Ave Oak Lawn (60453) ***(G-15700)***

Ambir Technology Inc......630 530-5400
820 Sivert Dr Wood Dale (60191) *(G-21161)*
Amboy News......815 857-2311
245 E Main St Amboy (61310) *(G-578)*
Ambraw Asphalt Materials Inc......618 943-4716
S 15th St Lawrenceville (62439) *(G-12526)*
Ambrit Inc......847 593-3301
1191 E Higgins Rd Ste 100 Elk Grove Village (60007) *(G-8820)*
Ambrotos Inc......815 355-8217
4219 Belson Ln Crystal Lake (60014) *(G-7159)*
Amcast Inc......630 766-7450
350 Meyer Rd Bensenville (60106) *(G-1741)*
Amco Machines Division, Somonauk *Also called Precision Entps Fndry Mch Inc (G-19074)*
Amcol, Belvidere *Also called American Colloid Company (G-1648)*
Amcol, Hoffman Estates *Also called American Colloid Company (G-11406)*
Amcol Hlth Buty Solutions Inc (HQ)......847 851-1300
2870 Forbs Ave Hoffman Estates (60192) *(G-11404)*
Amcol International......847 392-4673
1500 W Shure Dr Ste 500 Arlington Heights (60004) *(G-689)*
Amcol International Corp (HQ)......847 851-1500
2870 Forbs Ave Hoffman Estates (60192) *(G-11405)*
Amcor, Chicago *Also called American Metal Chemical Corp (G-3661)*
Amcor Flexibles Healthcare, Mundelein *Also called Amcor Flexibles LLC (G-14662)*
Amcor Flexibles LLC (HQ)......224 313-7000
2150 E Lake Cook Rd Buffalo Grove (60089) *(G-2510)*
Amcor Flexibles LLC......847 362-9000
1919 S Butterfield Rd Mundelein (60060) *(G-14662)*
Amcor Phrm Packg USA LLC......847 298-5626
1731 S Mount Prospect Rd Des Plaines (60018) *(G-7726)*
Amcor Rigid Packaging Usa LLC......630 628-5859
1035 W Republic Dr Addison (60101) *(G-29)*
Amcor Rigid Packaging Usa LLC......630 773-3235
750 Expressway Dr Itasca (60143) *(G-11621)*
Amcor Rigid Plastics Usa LLC......630 406-3500
1300 S River St Batavia (60510) *(G-1347)*
Amcraft Manufacturing Inc......847 439-4565
580 Lively Blvd Elk Grove Village (60007) *(G-8821)*
AMD Industries Inc (PA)......708 863-8900
815 Saint Stephens Grn Oak Brook (60523) *(G-15591)*
Amedico Laboratories LLC......347 857-7546
17w173 16th St Oakbrook Terrace (60181) *(G-15783)*
Amelio Bros Meats......708 300-2920
4322 Whitehall Ln Richton Park (60471) *(G-17027)*
Amenities Home Design......312 421-2450
1529 W Glenlake Ave Chicago (60660) *(G-3645)*
Amer Needle & Novelty, Buffalo Grove *Also called American Needle Inc (G-2511)*
Amer Nitrogen Co......847 681-1068
184 Leonard Wood S # 107 Highland Park (60035) *(G-11253)*
Amer Sports Company (HQ)......773 714-6400
8750 W Bryn Mawr Ave Chicago (60631) *(G-3646)*
Amer Surgical Instruments Inc......630 986-8032
26 Plaza Dr Westmont (60559) *(G-20727)*
Ameralloy Steel Corporation......847 967-0600
7848 Merrimac Ave Morton Grove (60053) *(G-14390)*
Amerex Corporation......309 382-4389
540 S Main St North Pekin (61554) *(G-15326)*
Ameri Label Company......847 895-8000
2015 Pennsbury Ln Bartlett (60133) *(G-1253)*
Ameri Rolls and Guides......815 588-0486
337 Clover Ridge Dr Lockport (60441) *(G-12981)*
Ameri-Tex......847 247-0777
1520 Mccormick Blvd Mundelein (60060) *(G-14663)*
Ameribest Fasteners, Schiller Park *Also called Gayton Group Inc (G-18809)*
America Display Inc......708 430-7000
10061 S 76th Ave Bridgeview (60455) *(G-2322)*
America International Dist, Chicago *Also called Sign America Inc (G-6165)*
America Printing Inc......847 229-8358
716 Gregor Ln Wheeling (60090) *(G-20846)*
American Acrylics Inc......847 674-7800
8124 Central Park Ave Skokie (60076) *(G-18917)*
American Ad Bag Company Inc......815 338-0300
1510 Lamb Rd Woodstock (60098) *(G-21357)*
American Air Filter Co Inc......502 637-0011
24828 Network Pl Chicago (60673) *(G-3647)*
American Alum Extrusion Co LLC......815 525-3100
5253 Mccurry Rd Roscoe (61073) *(G-17898)*
American Apparels & Promotions, Lake In The Hills *Also called Graphic Source Group Inc (G-12336)*
American Asp Surfc Recycl Inc......708 448-9540
13301 Southwest Hwy Ste H Orland Park (60462) *(G-15939)*
American Assn Endodontists......312 266-7255
180 N Stetson Ave # 1500 Chicago (60601) *(G-3648)*
American Assn Nurosurgeons Inc (PA)......847 378-0500
5550 Meadowbrook Dr Rolling Meadows (60008) *(G-17710)*
American Association of Indivi (PA)......312 280-0170
625 N Michigan Ave # 1900 Chicago (60611) *(G-3649)*
American Bakeware, Northbrook *Also called Harris Potteries LP (G-15397)*
American Bar Association (PA)......312 988-5000
321 N Clark St Ste Ll2 Chicago (60654) *(G-3650)*
American Bare Conductor Inc......815 224-3422
2969 Chartres St La Salle (61301) *(G-12102)*
American Bee Journal, The, Hamilton *Also called Dadant & Sons Inc (G-10954)*
American Bell Screen Prtg Co......815 623-5522
11447 2nd St Ste 1 Roscoe (61073) *(G-17899)*
American Binding, Itasca *Also called Phoenix Binding Corp (G-11717)*
American Biooptics LLC......847 467-0628
1801 Maple Ave Ste 4316 Evanston (60201) *(G-9493)*
American Bottling Company......217 356-0577
815 Pioneer St Champaign (61820) *(G-3264)*
American Bottling Company......708 947-5000
400 N Wolf Rd Ste A Northlake (60164) *(G-15540)*
American Bottling Company......815 877-7777
5300 Forest Hills Rd Loves Park (61111) *(G-13188)*
American Bottling Company......309 693-2777
7215 N Kckapoo Edwards Rd Edwards (61528) *(G-8336)*
American Boxboard LLC......708 924-9810
1400 Paramount Pkwy Batavia (60510) *(G-1348)*
American Broom Company, Mattoon *Also called Luco Mop Company (G-13643)*
American Buildings Company......309 527-5420
2101 E Main St El Paso (61738) *(G-8433)*
American Bullnose Co Midw......630 238-1300
640 Pond Dr Ste C Wood Dale (60191) *(G-21162)*
American Cast Products Inc......708 895-5152
17730 Chicago Ave Frnt Lansing (60438) *(G-12484)*
American Cast Stone......630 291-0250
14563 136th St Lemont (60439) *(G-12552)*
American Catholic Press Inc......708 331-5485
16565 State St South Holland (60473) *(G-19191)*
American Chemet Corporation (PA)......847 948-0800
740 Waukegan Rd Ste 202 Deerfield (60015) *(G-7585)*
American Chemet Export, Deerfield *Also called American Chemet Corporation (G-7585)*
American Chemical & Eqp Inc......815 675-9199
128 W Lake St 130 Northlake (60164) *(G-15541)*
American Church Supply......847 464-4140
41w699 Foxtail Cir Saint Charles (60175) *(G-18145)*
American Chute Systems Inc......815 723-7632
603 E Washington St Joliet (60433) *(G-11819)*
American Cips......618 393-5641
4978 N Il 130 Olney (62450) *(G-15852)*
American Circuit Services Inc......847 895-0500
80 Martin Ln Elk Grove Village (60007) *(G-8822)*
American Circuit Systems Inc......630 543-4450
712 S Westgate St Addison (60101) *(G-30)*
American City Bus Journals Inc......312 873-2200
141 W Jackson Blvd # 1795 Chicago (60604) *(G-3651)*
American Classic Rebar Corp......708 225-1010
15810 Suntone Dr South Holland (60473) *(G-19192)*
American Cllege Chest Physcans (PA)......224 521-9800
2595 Patriot Blvd Glenview (60026) *(G-10521)*
American Cnc Machine Co Inc......630 628-6490
749 W Fullerton Ave Addison (60101) *(G-31)*
American Coal Company (HQ)......618 268-6311
9085 Highway 34 N Galatia (62935) *(G-10161)*
American Colloid Company......618 452-8143
1601 Walnut St Granite City (62040) *(G-10694)*
American Colloid Company......304 882-2123
3422 Cameron Dr Elgin (60124) *(G-8506)*
American Colloid Company......800 527-9948
1500 W Shure Dr Fl 7 Arlington Heights (60004) *(G-690)*
American Colloid Company......815 547-5369
2786 Newburg Rd Belvidere (61008) *(G-1648)*
American Colloid Company (HQ)......847 851-1700
2870 Forbs Ave Hoffman Estates (60192) *(G-11406)*
American Comm & Networks......630 241-2800
2516 Wisconsin Ave Downers Grove (60515) *(G-7950)*
American Concorde Systems......773 342-9951
1548 Burgundy Pkwy Streamwood (60107) *(G-19561)*
American Control Elec LLC......815 624-6950
14300 De La Tour Dr South Beloit (61080) *(G-19080)*
American Controls & Automation......630 293-8841
897 Industrial Dr West Chicago (60185) *(G-20537)*
American Convenience Inc......815 344-6040
2102 W Il Route 120 McHenry (60051) *(G-13718)*
American Cooner, Sesser *Also called C and H Publishing Co (G-18865)*
American Cotton Products Div, Chicago *Also called Sea-Rich Corp (G-6124)*
American Couplings Co......630 323-4442
40 Chestnut Ave Westmont (60559) *(G-20728)*
American Custom Publishing......847 816-8660
328 W Lincoln Ave Libertyville (60048) *(G-12628)*
American Custom Woodworking......847 526-5900
1247 Karl Ct Wauconda (60084) *(G-20330)*
American Dawn Inc......312 961-2909
1269 N Wood Dale Rd Wood Dale (60191) *(G-21163)*
American Deck & Sunroom C......217 586-4840
2603 Appaloosa Ln Mahomet (61853) *(G-13421)*
American Die Supplies Acquisit......630 766-6226
618 N Edgewood Ave Wood Dale (60191) *(G-21164)*
American Diesel Tube Corp......630 628-1830
1240 W Capitol Dr Addison (60101) *(G-32)*

American Digital Corporation....847 637-4300
25 Northwest Point Blvd # 200 Elk Grove Village (60007) ***(G-8823)***
American Dragway Trophy Co, Chicago *Also called American Trophy & Award Co Inc* ***(G-3672)***
American Drilling Inc....847 850-5090
625 Glenn Ave Wheeling (60090) ***(G-20847)***
American Electronic Pdts Inc....630 889-9977
2001 Midwest Rd Ste 105 Oak Brook (60523) ***(G-15592)***
American Engraving Inc....630 543-2525
151 Wilson Ct Bensenville (60106) ***(G-1742)***
American Enlightenment LLC....773 687-8996
2023 W Carroll Ave # 303 Chicago (60612) ***(G-3652)***
American Equipment & Mch Inc....618 533-3857
2400 S Wabash Ave Centralia (62801) ***(G-3221)***
American Event Services LLC....217 709-1811
1706 Warrington Ave Danville (61832) ***(G-7319)***
American Extrusion Intl Corp (PA)....815 624-6616
498 Prairie Hill Rd South Beloit (61080) ***(G-19081)***
American Fastening Systems, Glendale Heights *Also called Si Enterprises Inc* ***(G-10494)***
American Flange & Mfg Co Inc (HQ)....630 665-7900
290 Fullerton Ave Carol Stream (60188) ***(G-2933)***
American Fuel Economy Inc....815 433-3226
1772 N 2753rd Rd Ottawa (61350) ***(G-16037)***
American Fur Enterprises....618 542-2018
413 S Greenwood Ave Du Quoin (62832) ***(G-8115)***
American Gasket & Rubber, Schaumburg *Also called Plastic Specialties & Tech Inc* ***(G-18675)***
American Gasket Tech Inc....630 543-1510
10 W Laura Dr Addison (60101) ***(G-33)***
American Gear Inc....815 537-5111
910 Swanson Dr Prophetstown (61277) ***(G-16830)***
American Graphic Systems Inc....708 614-7007
7650 185th St Ste A Tinley Park (60477) ***(G-19802)***
American Graphics Network Inc....847 729-7220
1625 Glenview Rd Unit 309 Glenview (60025) ***(G-10522)***
American Grinders Inc....815 943-4902
3 Lincoln St Ste 3 # 3 Harvard (60033) ***(G-11045)***
American Grinding & Machine Co (PA)....773 889-4343
2000 N Mango Ave Chicago (60639) ***(G-3653)***
American Hao Feng Co, Riverwoods *Also called JAm International Co Ltd* ***(G-17094)***
American Header Tool Tech, Rockford *Also called Amtech Inc* ***(G-17303)***
American Holiday Lights Inc....630 769-9999
6813 Hobson Valley Dr # 102 Woodridge (60517) ***(G-21274)***
American Home Aluminium Co....773 925-9442
12127 S Paulina St Calumet Park (60827) ***(G-2794)***
American Home Aluminum Co, Calumet Park *Also called American Home Aluminium Co* ***(G-2794)***
American Hosp Assn Svcs Del (HQ)....312 422-2000
155 N Wacker Dr Ste 400 Chicago (60606) ***(G-3654)***
American Inds A Div A Stucki, Jerseyville *Also called A Stucki Company* ***(G-11785)***
American Industrial Company....847 855-9200
1080 Tri State Pkwy Gurnee (60031) ***(G-10859)***
American Industrial Direct LLC (PA)....800 382-1200
2545 Millennium Dr Elgin (60124) ***(G-8507)***
American Inks and Coatings Co....630 226-0994
1225 Lakeside Dr 1 Romeoville (60446) ***(G-17793)***
American Inquiry LLC....312 922-1910
3238 N Wolcott Ave Fl 2 Chicago (60657) ***(G-3655)***
American Kitchen Delights Inc....708 210-3200
15320 Cooper Ave Harvey (60426) ***(G-11073)***
American Label Company....630 830-4444
1678 Wright Blvd Ste D Schaumburg (60193) ***(G-18437)***
American Labelmark Company (PA)....773 478-0900
5724 N Pulaski Rd Chicago (60646) ***(G-3656)***
American Library Association....312 280-5718
50 E Huron St Chicago (60611) ***(G-3657)***
American Litho Incorporated....630 682-0600
175 Mercedes Dr Carol Stream (60188) ***(G-2934)***
American Litho Incorporated....630 462-1700
175 Mercedes Dr Carol Stream (60188) ***(G-2935)***
American Louver Company (PA)....847 470-0400
7700 Austin Ave Skokie (60077) ***(G-18918)***
American Louver Company....800 772-0355
100 Howard Ave Des Plaines (60018) ***(G-7727)***
American Machine....815 539-6558
215 E 12th St Mendota (61342) ***(G-13934)***
American Machine Pdts & Svcs....708 743-9088
11863 W Josephine Dr Mokena (60448) ***(G-14071)***
American Machine Tools Inc....773 775-6285
5864 N Northwest Hwy Chicago (60631) ***(G-3658)***
American Machining Inc....815 498-1593
350 W Marquette St Ottawa (61350) ***(G-16038)***
American Machining & Wldg Inc....773 586-2585
6009 S New England Ave Chicago (60638) ***(G-3659)***
American Marble & Granite Inc....815 741-1710
1930 Donmaur Dr Crest Hill (60403) ***(G-7083)***
American Medical Association (PA)....312 464-5000
330 N Wabash Ave # 39300 Chicago (60611) ***(G-3660)***
American Medical Industries....847 918-9800
28915 N Herky Dr Ste 107 Lake Bluff (60044) ***(G-12169)***
American Metal Chemical Corp (PA)....773 254-1818
3546 S Morgan St Chicago (60609) ***(G-3661)***
American Metal Coil Works Inc....708 562-2645
130 W Lake St Northlake (60164) ***(G-15542)***
American Metal Fibers Inc (PA)....847 295-8166
13420 Rockland Rd Lake Bluff (60044) ***(G-12170)***
American Metal Installers & FA....630 993-0812
55 W Home Ave Villa Park (60181) ***(G-20131)***
American Metal Mfg Inc....847 651-6097
6323 N Avondale Ave # 125 Chicago (60631) ***(G-3662)***
American Metalcraft Inc....800 333-9133
3708 River Rd Ste 800 Franklin Park (60131) ***(G-9866)***
American Milling Company....309 347-6888
1811 American St Pekin (61554) ***(G-16323)***
American Molding Tech Inc....847 437-6900
2350 Lunt Ave Elk Grove Village (60007) ***(G-8824)***
American Monument Co....618 993-8968
306 S Court St Marion (62959) ***(G-13503)***
American Name Plate & Metal De....773 376-1400
4501 S Kildare Ave Chicago (60632) ***(G-3663)***
American Needle Inc (PA)....847 215-0011
1275 Busch Pkwy Buffalo Grove (60089) ***(G-2511)***
American NTN Bearing Mfg Corp (HQ)....847 741-4545
1525 Holmes Rd Elgin (60123) ***(G-8508)***
American NTN Bearing Mfg Corp....847 671-5450
9515 Winona Ave Schiller Park (60176) ***(G-18785)***
American Outfitters Ltd....847 623-3959
3700 Sunset Ave Waukegan (60087) ***(G-20414)***
American Packaging McHy Inc....815 337-8580
2550 S Eastwood Dr Woodstock (60098) ***(G-21358)***
American Pallet Co Inc....847 662-5525
1105 Greenfield Ave Waukegan (60085) ***(G-20415)***
American Pallet Industries Inc....815 678-0680
9821 Route 12 Richmond (60071) ***(G-17008)***
American Partsmith Inc....630 520-0432
901 Atlantic Dr West Chicago (60185) ***(G-20538)***
American Perforator Company....815 469-4300
22803 S Mustang Rd Ste A Frankfort (60423) ***(G-9766)***
American Phrm Partners Inc....847 969-2700
1501 E Woodfield Rd Schaumburg (60173) ***(G-18438)***
American Piping Group Inc....815 772-7470
800 French Creek Rd Morrison (61270) ***(G-14340)***
American Piping Products Inc....708 339-1753
15801 Van Drunen Rd South Holland (60473) ***(G-19193)***
American Plastics Technoligies, Morton Grove *Also called RAO Design International Inc* ***(G-14437)***
American Plating & Mfg Co....773 890-4907
3941 S Keeler Ave Chicago (60632) ***(G-3664)***
American Powder Coatings Inc....630 762-0100
420 38th Ave Saint Charles (60174) ***(G-18146)***
American Precision Elec Inc (PA)....630 510-8080
25w624 Saint Charles Rd Carol Stream (60188) ***(G-2936)***
American Precision Machining....847 455-1720
11135 Franklin Ave Franklin Park (60131) ***(G-9867)***
American Process Systems Div, Gurnee *Also called Eirich Machines Inc* ***(G-10875)***
American Progressive Circuits....630 495-6900
1772 W Armitage Ct Addison (60101) ***(G-34)***
American Quality Mfg Inc....815 226-9301
3519 Kishwaukee St Ste 1 Rockford (61109) ***(G-17301)***
American Rotors Inc....847 263-1300
3873 Clearview Ct Gurnee (60031) ***(G-10860)***
American Rubber Mfg Inc....331 551-9600
766 Foster Ave Bensenville (60106) ***(G-1743)***
American Science & Surplus Inc....773 763-0313
5316w N Milwaukee Ave Chicago (60630) ***(G-3665)***
American Science and Tech Corp (PA)....312 433-3800
1367 W Chicago Ave Chicago (60642) ***(G-3666)***
American Screw Machine Co....847 455-4308
2833 N Comm St Franklin Park (60131) ***(G-9868)***
American Shtmtl Fabricators....708 877-7200
665 W Armory Dr South Holland (60473) ***(G-19194)***
American Sign & Lighting Co....847 258-8151
350 N La Salle Dr # 1100 Chicago (60654) ***(G-3667)***
American Slide-Chart Co (PA)....630 665-3333
25w 550 Geneva Rd Carol Stream (60188) ***(G-2937)***
American Soc HM Inspectors Inc (PA)....847 759-2820
932 Lee St Ste 101 Des Plaines (60016) ***(G-7728)***
American Soc Plastic Surgeons (PA)....847 228-9900
444 E Algonquin Rd # 100 Arlington Heights (60005) ***(G-691)***
American Soda Ftn Exch Inc....312 733-5000
455 N Oakley Blvd Chicago (60612) ***(G-3668)***
American Specialty Toy....312 222-0984
432 N Clark St Ste 305 Chicago (60654) ***(G-3669)***
American Speed Enterprises....309 764-3601
3006 Avenue Of The Cities Moline (61265) ***(G-14131)***
American Speedy Printing, East Peoria *Also called Selnar Inc* ***(G-8290)***
American Speedy Printing, Pekin *Also called We-B-Print Inc* ***(G-16368)***
American Speedy Printing, Chicago *Also called Josco Inc* ***(G-5051)***

ALPHABETIC

American Speedy Printing, Galesburg *Also called Marnic Inc* ***(G-10208)***
American Sportswear Inc 630 859-8998
250 Heritage Dr Aurora (60506) ***(G-1049)***
American Standard Circuits Inc 630 639-5444
475 Industrial Dr West Chicago (60185) ***(G-20539)***
American Steel Carports Inc 800 487-4010
832 N East St Kewanee (61443) ***(G-12020)***
American Steel Fabricators Inc 847 807-4200
1985 Anson Dr Melrose Park (60160) ***(G-13825)***
American Steel Services Inc 815 774-0677
840 Brian Dr Joliet (60403) ***(G-11820)***
American Store Fixtures, Skokie *Also called American Louver Company* ***(G-18918)***
American Supply Association (PA) 630 467-0000
1200 N Arlngton Hts 150 Itasca (60143) ***(G-11622)***
American Tape Measures 312 208-0282
6717 W Foster Ave Chicago (60656) ***(G-3670)***
American Technologies Inc 630 548-8150
1150 Shore Rd Naperville (60563) ***(G-14773)***
American Tire Distributors 708 680-5150
9450 W Sergo Dr Ste A La Grange Highlands (60525) ***(G-12091)***
American Tool Design Inc 847 690-1010
680 Lunt Ave Elk Grove Village (60007) ***(G-8825)***
American Total Engine Co 847 623-2737
27840 W Concrete Dr Ste B Ingleside (60041) ***(G-11578)***
American Trade Magazines LLC 312 497-7707
650 W Lake St Ste 320 Chicago (60661) ***(G-3671)***
American Tristar Inc 630 262-5500
2089 Pillsbury Dr Geneva (60134) ***(G-10252)***
American Trophy & Award Co Inc 312 939-3252
1006 S Michigan Ave # 503 Chicago (60605) ***(G-3672)***
American Vacuum Company 847 674-8383
6700 W Touhy Ave Niles (60714) ***(G-15102)***
American Vulko Tread Corp 847 956-1300
690 Chase Ave Elk Grove Village (60007) ***(G-8826)***
American Watersource LLC 630 778-9900
1228 Bards Ave Naperville (60564) ***(G-14957)***
American Welding & Gas Inc 630 527-2550
3900 W North Ave Stone Park (60165) ***(G-19551)***
American Wheel Corp 708 458-9141
5939 W 66th St Chicago (60638) ***(G-3673)***
American Wilbert Vault Corp 773 238-2746
11118 S Rockwell St Chicago (60655) ***(G-3674)***
American Wilbert Vault Corp (PA) 708 366-3210
4415 Harrison St Ste 246 Hillside (60162) ***(G-11327)***
American Wilbert Vault Corp 847 824-4415
165 S River Rd Des Plaines (60016) ***(G-7729)***
American Wilbert Vault Corp 847 741-3089
954 Bluff City Blvd Elgin (60120) ***(G-8509)***
American Woodworks 630 279-1629
718 Hillcrest Dr Sleepy Hollow (60118) ***(G-19061)***
American/Jebco Corporation 847 455-3150
3250 S Central Ave Cicero (60804) ***(G-6829)***
Americana Building Pdts Inc (PA) 618 548-2800
2 Industrial Dr Salem (62881) ***(G-18328)***
Americana Building Products, Salem *Also called Americana Powder Finishing LLC* ***(G-18329)***
Americana Powder Finishing LLC 618 548-2800
2 Industrial Dr Salem (62881) ***(G-18329)***
Americas Community Bankers 312 644-3100
363 W Erie St Fl 4 Chicago (60654) ***(G-3675)***
Americas Styrenics LLC 815 418-6403
26332 S Frontage Rd Channahon (60410) ***(G-3374)***
Americhem Systems Inc 630 495-9300
1740 Molitor Rd Aurora (60505) ***(G-1050)***
Americlean Inc 314 741-8901
23 E Ferguson Ave Wood River (62095) ***(G-21259)***
Americn Foreign Lang Newspaper 312 368-4815
55 E Jackson Blvd Ste 920 Chicago (60604) ***(G-3676)***
Americo Chemical Products Inc 630 588-0830
551 Kimberly Dr Carol Stream (60188) ***(G-2938)***
Americoats, Franklin Park *Also called Coatings International Inc* ***(G-9912)***
Americraft Carton 630 225-7311
2809 Butterfield Rd Oak Brook (60523) ***(G-15593)***
Americut Wire Edm Inc 847 675-1754
8045 Ridgeway Ave Skokie (60076) ***(G-18919)***
Ameriflon Ltd (PA) 847 541-6000
930 Seton Ct Wheeling (60090) ***(G-20848)***
AmeriGas 708 544-1131
4158 Division St Hillside (60162) ***(G-11328)***
Amerigreen Pallets 309 698-3463
280 Fondulac Dr East Peoria (61611) ***(G-8250)***
Ameriguard Corporation 630 986-1900
7701 S Grant St Burr Ridge (60527) ***(G-2652)***
Ameriken Die Supply Inc 630 766-6226
618 N Edgewood Ave Wood Dale (60191) ***(G-21165)***
Amerilights Inc 847 219-1476
146 Roundtree Ct Bloomingdale (60108) ***(G-1976)***
Amerinet of Michigan Inc 708 466-0110
3909 White Eagle Dr W Naperville (60564) ***(G-14958)***

Ameriplate Inc 815 744-8585
600 Joyce Rd Joliet (60436) ***(G-11821)***
Ameriscan Designs Inc 773 542-1291
4147 W Ogden Ave Chicago (60623) ***(G-3677)***
Amerisun Inc 800 791-9458
1131 W Bryn Mawr Ave Itasca (60143) ***(G-11623)***
Ameritex Industries Inc 217 324-4044
14 Litchfield Plz Ste 1a Litchfield (62056) ***(G-12960)***
Amerline Enterprises Co Inc 847 671-6554
9509 Winona Ave Schiller Park (60176) ***(G-18786)***
Ameroc Export Inc 818 961-6169
4126 Miller Dr Glenview (60026) ***(G-10523)***
Ameroc Lubricants Export, Glenview *Also called Ameroc Export Inc* ***(G-10523)***
Ameropan Oil Corp 773 847-4400
3301 S California Ave Chicago (60608) ***(G-3678)***
Ametek Inc 847 596-7000
1450 S Lakeside Dr Waukegan (60085) ***(G-20416)***
Ametek Inc 630 621-3121
27755 Diehl Rd Ste 300 Warrenville (60555) ***(G-20230)***
Ametek Power Instruments, Warrenville *Also called Ametek Inc* ***(G-20230)***
Ametek Powervar, Waukegan *Also called Ametek Inc* ***(G-20416)***
Amex Nooter LLC 708 429-8300
18501 Maple Creek Dr # 900 Tinley Park (60477) ***(G-19803)***
Amfab LLC 630 783-2570
1385 101st St Ste A Lemont (60439) ***(G-12553)***
Amfi, Lake Bluff *Also called American Metal Fibers Inc* ***(G-12170)***
Amfotek, Tinley Park *Also called Big Tent Inc* ***(G-19811)***
AMG International Inc 847 439-1001
1480 E Devon Ave Elk Grove Village (60007) ***(G-8827)***
Amglo Kemlite Laboratories Inc (PA) 630 238-3031
215 Gateway Rd Bensenville (60106) ***(G-1744)***
Amiberica Inc 773 247-3600
3701 S Ashland Ave Chicago (60609) ***(G-3679)***
Amic Global Inc 847 600-3590
353 Hastings Dr Buffalo Grove (60089) ***(G-2512)***
Amigo Mobility Center 630 268-8670
17w620 14th St Ste 101 Oakbrook Terrace (60181) ***(G-15784)***
Amigoni Construction 309 923-3701
800 N State St Roanoke (61561) ***(G-17098)***
Amis Inc 708 598-9700
7506 W 90th St Bridgeview (60455) ***(G-2323)***
Amitron Inc 847 290-9800
2001 Landmeier Rd Elk Grove Village (60007) ***(G-8828)***
Amity Die and Stamping Co 847 680-6600
13870 W Polo Trail Dr Lake Forest (60045) ***(G-12224)***
Amity Hospital Services Inc 708 206-3970
4921 173rd St Ste 2 Country Club Hills (60478) ***(G-7035)***
Amity Packing Company Inc (PA) 312 942-0270
4220 S Kildare Ave Chicago (60632) ***(G-3680)***
Amj Industries Inc 815 654-9000
4000 Auburn St Unit 104 Rockford (61101) ***(G-17302)***
Amk Automation Corp 804 348-2125
256 S Washington St 1 Carpentersville (60110) ***(G-3092)***
Amk Enterprises Chicago Inc 312 523-7212
3605 S Calumet Ave Chicago (60653) ***(G-3681)***
Amkine Inc 847 526-7088
230 Industrial Dr Wauconda (60084) ***(G-20331)***
Amkus Inc 630 515-1800
2700 Wisconsin Ave Downers Grove (60515) ***(G-7951)***
Amkus Rescue Systems, Downers Grove *Also called Amkus Inc* ***(G-7951)***
Amling Donuts Inc 847 426-5327
98 N Kennedy Dr Carpentersville (60110) ***(G-3093)***
Amling's Flowerland, Elmhurst *Also called Albert F Amling LLC* ***(G-9324)***
Ammentorp Tool Company Inc 847 671-9290
9828 Franklin Ave Franklin Park (60131) ***(G-9869)***
Ammeraal Beltech Inc (HQ) 847 673-6720
7501 Saint Louis Ave Skokie (60076) ***(G-18920)***
Amnetic LLC 877 877-3678
1645 S River Rd Ste 8 Des Plaines (60018) ***(G-7730)***
Amoco, Naperville *Also called BP Products North America Inc* ***(G-14783)***
Amoco Technology Company (HQ) 312 861-6000
200 E Randolph St # 3500 Chicago (60601) ***(G-3682)***
Amoco Technology Company Del, Chicago *Also called Amoco Technology Company* ***(G-3682)***
Amos Industries Inc 630 393-0606
1080 Corporate Blvd Aurora (60502) ***(G-911)***
AMP Americas LLC (PA) 312 300-6700
811 W Evergreen Ave # 201 Chicago (60642) ***(G-3683)***
AMP CNG, Chicago *Also called AMP Americas LLC* ***(G-3683)***
Ampac Flexibles, Hanover Park *Also called Ampac Flexicon LLC* ***(G-10999)***
Ampac Flexibles, Cary *Also called Ampac Flexicon LLC* ***(G-3147)***
Ampac Flexicon LLC 630 439-3160
825 Turnberry Ct Hanover Park (60133) ***(G-10998)***
Ampac Flexicon LLC 952 541-0730
825 Turnberry Ct Hanover Park (60133) ***(G-10999)***
Ampac Flexicon LLC (HQ) 847 639-3530
165 Chicago St Cary (60013) ***(G-3147)***

Ampel Incorporated (PA) 847 952-1900
925 Estes Ave Elk Grove Village (60007) *(G-8829)*
Amperite Co., Elgin *Also called Olympic Controls Corp (G-8678)*
Ampex Screw Mfg Inc 847 228-1202
2936 Malmo Dr Arlington Heights (60005) *(G-692)*
Amphenol Corporation 800 944-6446
2100 Western Ct Ste 300 Lisle (60532) *(G-12863)*
Amphenol Corporation 847 478-5600
100 Tristate Intl Lincolnshire (60069) *(G-12745)*
Amphenol Eec Inc 773 463-8343
1701 Birchwood Ave Des Plaines (60018) *(G-7731)*
Amphenol Fiber Optic Products 630 960-1010
2100 Western Ct Ste 300 Lisle (60532) *(G-12864)*
Amphenol T&M Antennas Inc (HQ) 847 478-5600
100 Tri State Intl # 255 Lincolnshire (60069) *(G-12746)*
Amphix Bio Inc 720 840-7327
57 E Del Pl Apt 2802 Chicago (60611) *(G-3684)*
Amplate, Chicago *Also called American Plating & Mfg Co (G-3664)*
Ample Supply Company 815 895-3500
1401 S Prairie Dr Sycamore (60178) *(G-19700)*
Amplivox Prtable Sound Systems, Northbrook *Also called Amplivox Sound Systems LLC (G-15336)*
Amplivox Sound Systems LLC (PA) 800 267-5486
650 Anthony Trl Ste D Northbrook (60062) *(G-15336)*
Amric Resources 309 664-0391
2422 E Washington St # 102 Bloomington (61704) *(G-2024)*
Amron Stair Works Inc (PA) 847 426-4800
152 Industrial Dr Gilberts (60136) *(G-10350)*
AMS, Lake In The Hills *Also called AG Medical Systems Inc (G-12328)*
AMS Seals Inc 815 609-4977
12149 Rhea Dr Plainfield (60585) *(G-16642)*
Amsoil Inc 630 595-8385
485 Thomas Dr Bensenville (60106) *(G-1745)*
Amst, Monee *Also called Advanced Mobility & (G-14195)*
Amstadt Industries, Lombard *Also called Line Craft Tool Company Inc (G-13096)*
Amsted Industries Incorporated (PA) 312 645-1700
180 N Stetson Ave # 1800 Chicago (60601) *(G-3685)*
Amsted Industries Incorporated 312 645-1700
2 Prudential Plaza 180 Chicago (60601) *(G-3686)*
Amsted Industries Incorporated 312 819-1181
205 N Michigan Ave Chicago (60601) *(G-3687)*
Amsted Rail Company Inc 312 258-8000
10 S Riverside Plz Fl 10 # 10 Chicago (60606) *(G-3688)*
Amsted Rail Company Inc 618 452-2111
1700 Walnut St Granite City (62040) *(G-10695)*
Amsted Rail Company Inc 618 225-6463
1078 19th St Granite City (62040) *(G-10696)*
Amsty 815 418-6430
26332 S Frontage Rd Channahon (60410) *(G-3375)*
Amsysco Inc 630 296-8383
1200 Windham Pkwy Romeoville (60446) *(G-17794)*
Amt Group LLC 847 324-4411
7350 N Croname Rd Niles (60714) *(G-15103)*
Amt Kikai, Barrington *Also called Miyanohitec Machinery Inc (G-1230)*
Amtab Manufacturing Corp 630 301-7600
600 Eagle Dr Bensenville (60106) *(G-1746)*
Amtec Molded Products Inc 815 226-0187
1355 Holmes Rd Ste A Elgin (60123) *(G-8510)*
Amtec Precision Products, Elgin *Also called Ucal Systems Inc (G-8766)*
Amtec Precision Products, Elgin *Also called Ucal Systems Inc (G-8767)*
Amtec Precision Products, Inc., Elgin *Also called Ucal Holdings Inc (G-8765)*
Amtech Inc 815 962-0500
1819 9th St Rockford (61104) *(G-17303)*
Amtex, Glendale Heights *Also called Surya Electronics Inc (G-10507)*
Amtex Chemicals LLC 630 268-0085
450 E 22nd St Ste 164 Lombard (60148) *(G-13039)*
Amv International, Machesney Park *Also called Saws International Inc (G-13373)*
Amv International Inc 815 282-9990
7814 Forest Hills Rd Loves Park (61111) *(G-13189)*
Amwell 630 898-6900
1740 Molitor Rd Aurora (60505) *(G-1051)*
Amy Schutt 618 994-7405
420 N Thompson St Carrier Mills (62917) *(G-3123)*
Amy Wertheim (PA) 309 830-4361
1865 2200th St Bldg 2 Atlanta (61723) *(G-904)*
Amylu Foods LLC (PA) 312 829-2250
1400 W 44th St Chicago (60609) *(G-3689)*
An Affliate of Heico Companies, Warrenville *Also called Pettibone LLC (G-20244)*
Anah Machine Mfg Co 847 228-6450
801 Pratt Blvd Elk Grove Village (60007) *(G-8830)*
Analog Devices Inc 847 519-3669
1901 N Roselle Rd Ste 100 Schaumburg (60195) *(G-18439)*
Analog Outfitters Inc 217 202-6134
701 Pacesetter Dr Rantoul (61866) *(G-16966)*
Anamet Electrical Inc 217 234-8844
1000 Broadway Ave E Mattoon (61938) *(G-13630)*
Anamet Inc (PA) 217 234-8844
799 Roosevelt Rd 4-313 Glen Ellyn (60137) *(G-10394)*
Anart Inc 708 447-0225
440 Repton Rd Riverside (60546) *(G-17080)*
Anash Educational Institute 773 338-7704
2929 W Greenleaf Ave Chicago (60645) *(G-3690)*
Anatomical Worldwide LLC 312 224-4772
1630 Darrow Ave Evanston (60201) *(G-9494)*
Anbek Inc 815 672-6087
222 3rd St La Salle (61301) *(G-12103)*
Anbek Inc 815 223-0734
222 3rd St La Salle (61301) *(G-12104)*
Anbek Inc (PA) 815 434-7340
104 W Madison St Ottawa (61350) *(G-16039)*
Anbm, Elgin *Also called American NTN Bearing Mfg Corp (G-8508)*
Anchor Abrasives Company 708 444-4300
7651 185th St Tinley Park (60477) *(G-19804)*
Anchor Brake Shoe Company LLC 630 293-1110
1111 Harvester Rd West Chicago (60185) *(G-20540)*
Anchor Brake Shoe Company LLC (HQ) 630 293-1110
1920 Downs Dr West Chicago (60185) *(G-20541)*
Anchor Mechanical Inc (PA) 312 492-6994
255 N California Ave Chicago (60612) *(G-3691)*
Anchor Products Company 630 543-9124
52 W Official Rd Addison (60101) *(G-35)*
Anchor Welding & Fabrication 815 937-1640
2950 N Lowe Rd Aroma Park (60910) *(G-839)*
Anchor-Harvey Components LLC 815 233-3833
600 W Lamm Rd Freeport (61032) *(G-10100)*
Ancillary Genomic Systems LLC 765 714-3799
1524 E 59th St Apt B1 Chicago (60637) *(G-3692)*
Andee Boiler & Welding Co, Chicago *Also called Pedraza Inc (G-5780)*
Andel Services Inc 630 566-0210
1145 S Union St Aurora (60505) *(G-1052)*
Andersen Machine & Welding Inc 815 232-4664
1441 W Demeter Dr Freeport (61032) *(G-10101)*
Andersen Welding, Chicago *Also called Welding Shop (G-6599)*
Anderson & Marter Cabinets 630 406-9840
845 E Wilson St Batavia (60510) *(G-1349)*
Anderson & Vreeland-Illinois 847 255-2110
525 W University Dr Arlington Heights (60004) *(G-693)*
Anderson Copper & Brass Co LLC (HQ) 708 535-9030
255 Industry Ave Frankfort (60423) *(G-9767)*
Anderson Fittings, Frankfort *Also called Anderson Copper & Brass Co LLC (G-9767)*
Anderson House Foundation 630 461-7254
258 Harwarden St Glen Ellyn (60137) *(G-10395)*
Anderson Lanette 217 284-6603
1045 N Osburn Ave Springfield (62702) *(G-19318)*
Anderson Msnry Refr Spcalist I, Lake Zurich *Also called Anderson Msnry Refr Spcialists (G-12384)*
Anderson Msnry Refr Spcialists 847 540-8885
25675 N Stoney Kirk Ct Lake Zurich (60047) *(G-12384)*
Anderson Safford Mkg Graphics 847 827-8968
570 E Northwest Hwy Ste 7 Des Plaines (60016) *(G-7732)*
Anderson Shumaker Company, Chicago *Also called As 1902 LLC (G-3746)*
Anderson Tage Co 815 397-3040
2316 7th Ave Rockford (61104) *(G-17304)*
Anderson Truss Company 618 982-9228
12418 Poordo Rd Pittsburg (62974) *(G-16626)*
Anderson, Richard Shop, Sycamore *Also called Richard A Anderson (G-19729)*
Andersons Candy Shop Inc (PA) 815 678-6000
10301 N Main St Richmond (60071) *(G-17009)*
Andersson Tool & Die LLP 847 746-8866
1717 Kenosha Rd Zion (60099) *(G-21508)*
Andover Junction Publications 815 538-3060
467 N 46th Rd Mendota (61342) *(G-13935)*
Andrea and ME and ME Too 708 955-3850
4206 Lindenwood Dr 1ne Matteson (60443) *(G-13618)*
Andrew C Arnold 815 220-0282
2228 4th St Peru (61354) *(G-16564)*
Andrew Corporation 779 435-6000
2700 Ellis Rd Joliet (60433) *(G-11822)*
Andrew International Svcs Corp 779 435-6000
2700 Ellis Rd Joliet (60433) *(G-11823)*
Andrew McDonald 618 867-2323
100 N Ash St De Soto (62924) *(G-7430)*
Andrew New Zealand Inc 708 873-3507
10500 W 153rd St Orland Park (60462) *(G-15940)*
Andrew Solutions, Joliet *Also called Commscope Technologies LLC (G-11845)*
Andrew Systems Inc 708 873-3855
10500 W 153rd St Orland Park (60462) *(G-15941)*
Andrew Technologies Inc 847 520-5770
305 Alderman Ave Wheeling (60090) *(G-20849)*
Andrew Toschak 630 553-3434
1025 Mchugh Rd Yorkville (60560) *(G-21472)*
Andrews Automotive Company 773 768-1122
10055 S Torrence Ave Chicago (60617) *(G-3693)*
Andrews Converting LLC 708 352-2555
707 E 47th St La Grange (60525) *(G-12072)*
Andrews Decal & Label Company, Chicago *Also called Gallas Label & Decal (G-4656)*
Andria Lieu, Chicago *Also called Laqueus Inc (G-5176)*

Andria's Steak Sauce, O Fallon *Also called Andrias Food Group Inc* ***(G-15565)***
Andria's Steak Sauce, O Fallon *Also called Andrias Food Group Inc* ***(G-15566)***
Andrias Food Group Inc (PA)....618 632-4866
6805 Old Collinsville Rd O Fallon (62269) ***(G-15565)***
Andrias Food Group Inc....618 632-3118
6813 Old Collinsville Rd O Fallon (62269) ***(G-15566)***
Androck Hardware Corporation....815 229-1144
711 19th St Rockford (61104) ***(G-17305)***
Android Indstres- Blvidere LLC....815 547-3742
1222 Crosslink Pkwy Belvidere (61008) ***(G-1649)***
Andscot Co Inc....847 455-5800
9117 Medill Ave Franklin Park (60131) ***(G-9870)***
Andy Dallas & Co....217 351-5974
101 E University Ave Champaign (61820) ***(G-3265)***
Andys Deli and Mikolajczyk (PA)....773 722-1000
4021 W Kinzie St Chicago (60624) ***(G-3694)***
Andys Pet Shop, Peru *Also called Andrew C Arnold* ***(G-16564)***
Anees Upholstery....312 243-2919
1500 S Western Ave Ste 3 Chicago (60608) ***(G-3695)***
Anfinsen Plastic Moulding Inc....630 554-4100
445b Treasure Dr Unit B Oswego (60543) ***(G-15992)***
Angel Equipment LLC....847 730-3938
1941 Johns Dr Glenview (60025) ***(G-10524)***
Angel Rose Energy LLC....618 392-3700
4368 N Holly Rd Olney (62450) ***(G-15853)***
Angel Wind Energy Inc....815 471-2020
113 N Pine St Onarga (60955) ***(G-15901)***
Angel's Envy, Chicago *Also called Angels Share Brands LLC* ***(G-3697)***
Angela Yang Chingjui....630 724-0596
1026 Sean Cir Darien (60561) ***(G-7401)***
Angels Heavenly Funeral Home....773 239-8700
10634 S Wallace St Chicago (60628) ***(G-3696)***
Angels Share Brands LLC....312 494-1100
119 W Hubbard St Fl 5 Chicago (60654) ***(G-3697)***
Angle Metal Manufacturing Co....847 437-8666
1497 Tonne Rd Elk Grove Village (60007) ***(G-8831)***
Angle Press Inc....847 439-6388
3701 Algonquin Rd Ste 340 Rolling Meadows (60008) ***(G-17711)***
Angle Sheet Metal, Elk Grove Village *Also called Angle Metal Manufacturing Co* ***(G-8831)***
Angle Tool Company....847 593-7572
425 Crossen Ave Elk Grove Village (60007) ***(G-8832)***
Angleboard, Kankakee *Also called Signode Industrial Group LLC* ***(G-12003)***
Angsten Group Inc....888 222-7126
2175 Point Blvd Ste 100 Elgin (60123) ***(G-8511)***
Anheuser-Busch LLC....630 512-9002
1011 Warrenville Rd # 350 Lisle (60532) ***(G-12865)***
Anikam Inc....708 385-0200
12549 S Holiday Dr Alsip (60803) ***(G-415)***
Animal Center International....217 214-0536
4124 Kochs Ln Quincy (62305) ***(G-16853)***
Animal Health Div, Chicago Heights *Also called Zoetis LLC* ***(G-6787)***
Animated Advg Techniques Inc....312 372-4694
210 S Desplaines St Chicago (60661) ***(G-3698)***
Animated Manufacturing Company....708 333-6688
106 W 154th St South Holland (60473) ***(G-19195)***
Animated Printing & Packaging, Itasca *Also called The Web Cmmnications Group Inc* ***(G-11746)***
Anixter Inc....512 989-4254
2301 Patriot Blvd Glenview (60026) ***(G-10525)***
Anixter Inc....800 323-8167
2301 Patriot Blvd Glenview (60026) ***(G-10526)***
Anju Software Inc....630 243-9810
4343 Commerce Ct Ste 501 Lisle (60532) ***(G-12866)***
Ann Taylor, Peoria *Also called Anntaylor Retail Inc* ***(G-16383)***
Anna Plant, Anna *Also called Illini Ready Mix Inc* ***(G-585)***
Anna Quarries Inc....618 833-5121
1000 Quarry Rd Anna (62906) ***(G-581)***
Annas Draperies & Associates....773 282-1365
5908 W Montrose Ave Chicago (60634) ***(G-3699)***
Anns Bakery Inc....773 384-5562
2158 W Chicago Ave Chicago (60622) ***(G-3700)***
Anntaylor Retail Inc....309 693-2762
5201 W War Memorial Dr # 54 Peoria (61615) ***(G-16383)***
Anodizing Specialists Ltd....847 437-9495
210 Crossen Ave Elk Grove Village (60007) ***(G-8833)***
Anonymous Press Inc....509 779-4094
1658 N Milwaukee Ave Chicago (60647) ***(G-3701)***
Another Chance Community Dev....773 998-1641
1641 W 79th St Chicago (60620) ***(G-3702)***
Anp Inc....309 757-0372
1515 5th Ave Ste 428 Moline (61265) ***(G-14132)***
Anpec Industries Inc....815 239-2303
216 Main St Pecatonica (61063) ***(G-16320)***
ANR Pipeline Company....309 667-2158
296 N 600th Ave New Windsor (61465) ***(G-15071)***
Anritsu Indus Slutions USA Inc, Elk Grove Village *Also called Anritsu Infivis Inc* ***(G-8834)***
Anritsu Infivis Inc....847 419-9729
1001 Cambridge Dr Elk Grove Village (60007) ***(G-8834)***
Anscor, Schiller Park *Also called Tds Inc* ***(G-18847)***
Anselmo Die and Index Co Inc....847 397-1200
2235 Hammond Dr Ste F Schaumburg (60173) ***(G-18440)***
Anselmo Index, Schaumburg *Also called Anselmo Die and Index Co Inc* ***(G-18440)***
Answer Call....773 573-6369
10633 S Green St Chicago (60643) ***(G-3703)***
Antares Computer Systems Inc....773 783-8855
8114 S Maryland Ave # 12 Chicago (60619) ***(G-3704)***
Antek Madison Plastics USA Ltd....773 933-0900
8822 S Dobson Ave Chicago (60619) ***(G-3705)***
Antenex Inc....847 839-6910
1751 Wilkening Ct Schaumburg (60173) ***(G-18441)***
Anthony Liftgates Inc....815 842-3383
1037 W Howard St Pontiac (61764) ***(G-16765)***
Anthony's, East Peoria *Also called Chips Aleeces Pita* ***(G-8260)***
Anthos and Co LLC....773 744-6813
2010 Dundee Rd Inverness (60067) ***(G-11594)***
Anti-Seize Technology, Franklin Park *Also called AST Industries Inc* ***(G-9878)***
Antigua Casa Sherry-Brener (PA)....773 737-1711
2801 W Jefferson St Ofc C Joliet (60435) ***(G-11824)***
Antioch Fine Arts Foundation....847 838-2274
41380 N Il Route 83 Antioch (60002) ***(G-599)***
Antique Mirror Glass Company, Bureau *Also called Timeless Reflections* ***(G-2639)***
Antlia Displays LLC....773 353-2223
1720 W Division St 2 Chicago (60622) ***(G-3706)***
Antolak Management Co Inc....312 464-1800
447 E Ohio St Chicago (60611) ***(G-3707)***
Antolin Interiors Usa Inc....618 327-4416
18355 Enterprise Ave Nashville (62263) ***(G-14994)***
Anton-Argires Inc....708 388-6250
12345 S Latrobe Ave Alsip (60803) ***(G-416)***
Anvil Acquisition Corp....309 365-8270
500 S Spencer St Lexington (61753) ***(G-12617)***
Anvil International LLC....708 534-1414
7979 183rd St Ste D Tinley Park (60477) ***(G-19805)***
Anvil International Inc....603 418-2800
24023 Network Pl Chicago (60673) ***(G-3708)***
Anylogic N Amer Ltd Lblty Co....312 635-3344
1 Tower Ln Ste 2655 Oakbrook Terrace (60181) ***(G-15785)***
Anytime Heating & AC....630 851-6696
10s264 Schoger Dr Ste 2 Naperville (60564) ***(G-14959)***
Anytime Window Cleaning Inc....773 235-5677
2517 N Monticello Ave Chicago (60647) ***(G-3709)***
Anywave Communication Tech Inc....847 415-2258
100 N Fairway Dr Vernon Hills (60061) ***(G-20042)***
Ao Corporate, Naperville *Also called Advantage Optics Inc* ***(G-14767)***
AP, Broadview *Also called Arrow Pneumatics Inc* ***(G-2418)***
AP Machine Inc....708 450-1010
1975 N 17th Ave Melrose Park (60160) ***(G-13826)***
APAC II LLC....618 426-1338
39 Schatte Rd Campbell Hill (62916) ***(G-2813)***
APAC Unlimited Inc....847 441-4282
790 W Frontage Rd Ste 214 Northfield (60093) ***(G-15505)***
Apache Supply....708 409-1040
647 Philip Dr Bartlett (60103) ***(G-1264)***
Apana Inc....309 303-4007
7201 N Drake Ct Peoria (61615) ***(G-16384)***
Apco Enterprises Inc....708 430-7333
9901 S 76th Ave Bridgeview (60455) ***(G-2324)***
Apergy Energy Automation LLC (HQ)....630 541-1540
3005 Highland Pkwy Downers Grove (60515) ***(G-7952)***
Apex Colors....219 764-3301
1031 W Bryn Mawr Ave 1a Chicago (60660) ***(G-3710)***
Apex Dental Materials Inc....847 719-1133
330 Telser Rd Lake Zurich (60047) ***(G-12385)***
Apex Engineering Products Corp....630 820-8888
1241 Shoreline Dr Aurora (60504) ***(G-912)***
Apex Industrial Automation LLC (PA)....866 924-2808
737 Oakridge Dr Romeoville (60446) ***(G-17795)***
Apex Manufacturing Inc....815 728-0108
5409 Craftwell Dr Ste A Ringwood (60072) ***(G-17039)***
Apex Mfg & Design Inc (PA)....618 997-0512
1800 E Boyton St Marion (62959) ***(G-13504)***
Apex Mfg & Design Inc....618 252-5529
125 Highland Rd Galatia (62935) ***(G-10162)***
Apex Tool Works Inc....847 394-5810
3200 Tollview Dr Rolling Meadows (60008) ***(G-17712)***
Apex Wire Products Company Inc....847 671-1830
9030 Gage Ave Franklin Park (60131) ***(G-9871)***
Apf US Inc....217 304-0027
2204 Kickapoo Dr Danville (61832) ***(G-7320)***
Aph Custom Wood & Metal Pdts....708 410-1274
2801 S 25th Ave Broadview (60155) ***(G-2417)***
Aphelion Precision Tech Corp....847 215-7285
1800 Greenleaf Ave Elk Grove Village (60007) ***(G-8835)***
API, Elk Grove Village *Also called Advertising Products Inc* ***(G-8812)***
API Publishing Services LLC....312 644-6610
330 N Wabash Ave Ste 2000 Chicago (60611) ***(G-3711)***

ALPHABETIC SECTION

APL Engineered Materials Inc 217 367-1340
2401 Willow Rd Urbana (61802) *(G-19972)*
APL Logistics Americas Ltd 630 783-0200
2649 Internationale Pkwy Woodridge (60517) *(G-21275)*
Aplicare Products LLC 847 949-5500
3 Lakes Dr Northfield (60093) *(G-15506)*
APM Process Center, Dekalb *Also called L M C Inc* *(G-7687)*
Apoc, Abbott Park *Also called Abbott Point of Care Inc* *(G-5)*
Apollo Aerosol Industries LLC 770 433-0210
2651 Warrenville Rd # 300 Downers Grove (60515) *(G-7953)*
Apollo Colors, Rockdale *Also called Scientific Colors Inc* *(G-17273)*
Apollo Colors Mfg Plant, Rockdale *Also called Scientific Colors Inc* *(G-17274)*
Apollo Machine & Manufacturing 847 677-6444
7617 Parkside Ave Skokie (60077) *(G-18921)*
Apollo Plastics Corporation 773 282-9222
5333 N Elston Ave Chicago (60630) *(G-3712)*
Apollo Sensors Inc 630 293-5820
778 W Hawthorne Ln West Chicago (60185) *(G-20542)*
Apostrophe Brands 312 832-0300
225 W Hubbard St Ste 600 Chicago (60654) *(G-3713)*
App Pharmaceuticals Inc 847 969-2700
1501 E Woodfield Rd 300e Schaumburg (60173) *(G-18442)*
Apparel Works Intl LLC 847 778-9559
51 Sherwood Ter Ste G Lake Bluff (60044) *(G-12171)*
Apple Graphics Inc 630 389-2222
934 Paramount Pkwy Batavia (60510) *(G-1350)*
Apple Press Inc 815 224-1451
2428 4th St Peru (61354) *(G-16565)*
Apple Print, Itasca *Also called George Vaggelatos* *(G-11661)*
Apple Rush Company 847 730-5324
4300 Dipaolo Ctr Glenview (60025) *(G-10527)*
Appleton Group, Rosemont *Also called Appleton Grp LLC* *(G-17999)*
Appleton Grp LLC (HQ) 847 268-6000
9377 W Higgins Rd Rosemont (60018) *(G-17999)*
Appliance Information and Repr 217 698-8858
10190 Buckhart Rd Rochester (62563) *(G-17163)*
Appliance Repair 708 456-1020
4911 N Delphia Ave Norridge (60706) *(G-15230)*
Applied Acoustic International, Chicago Heights *Also called AEP Nvh Opco LLC* *(G-6729)*
Applied Arts & Sciences Inc 407 288-8228
21432 Prestancia Dr Mokena (60448) *(G-14072)*
Applied Mechanical Tech LLC 815 472-2700
135 Industrial Dr Momence (60954) *(G-14182)*
Applied Polymer System Inc 847 301-1712
507 Estes Ave Schaumburg (60193) *(G-18443)*
Applied Products Inc 815 633-3825
12000 Product Dr Machesney Park (61115) *(G-13327)*
Applied Systems Inc (PA) 708 534-5575
200 Applied Pkwy University Park (60484) *(G-19946)*
Applied Tech Publications Inc 847 382-8100
535 Plainfield Rd Ste A Willowbrook (60527) *(G-21029)*
Applus Technologies Inc (HQ) 312 661-1700
120 S La Salle St # 1450 Chicago (60603) *(G-3714)*
Apprize Promotional Pdts Inc 630 468-2043
18w100 22nd St Ste 125 Oakbrook Terrace (60181) *(G-15786)*
Approved Contact LLC (PA) 800 449-7137
1 The Elms Springfield (62712) *(G-19319)*
Appsanity Advisory LLC 847 638-1172
335 Auburn Ave Winnetka (60093) *(G-21125)*
Apr Graphics Inc 847 329-7800
4825 Main St Skokie (60077) *(G-18922)*
Aprimo Marketing Operations Uk, Chicago *Also called Aprimo US LLC* *(G-3715)*
Aprimo US LLC 877 794-8556
230 W Monroe St Ste 1200 Chicago (60606) *(G-3715)*
Apser Laboratory Inc 630 543-3333
625 W Factory Rd Ste B Addison (60101) *(G-36)*
Apser Labs, Addison *Also called Apser Laboratory Inc* *(G-36)*
APT Tool Inc 815 337-0051
1301 Cobblestone Way Woodstock (60098) *(G-21359)*
Aptargroup Inc 847 816-9400
901 Technology Way Libertyville (60048) *(G-12629)*
Aptargroup Inc (PA) 815 477-0424
265 Exchange Dr Ste 100 Crystal Lake (60014) *(G-7160)*
Aptargroup Inc 847 462-3900
4900 Prime Pkwy McHenry (60050) *(G-13719)*
Aptargroup Inc 847 639-2124
1160 Silver Lake Rd Cary (60013) *(G-3148)*
Aptargroup International LLC 815 477-0424
475 W Terra Cotta Ave E. Crystal Lake (60014) *(G-7161)*
Aptean Inc 773 975-3100
2000 N Racine Ave Chicago (60614) *(G-3716)*
Aqua Belle Manufacturing Co, Highland Park *Also called J II Inc* *(G-11275)*
Aqua Coat Inc 815 209-0808
1061 Davis Rd Elgin (60123) *(G-8512)*
Aqua Control Inc 815 664-4900
6a Wolfer Industrial Park Spring Valley (61362) *(G-19307)*
Aqua Golf Inc (PA) 217 824-2097
6 Manor Ct Taylorville (62568) *(G-19749)*
Aqua Marine Pools, Loves Park *Also called Rockford Sewer Co Inc* *(G-13259)*

Aqua-Tech Co 847 383-7075
1875 Big Timber Rd Ste C Elgin (60123) *(G-8513)*
Aquadine Inc (PA) 800 497-3463
495 Commanche Cir Harvard (60033) *(G-11046)*
Aquadine Nutritional System, Harvard *Also called Aquadine Inc* *(G-11046)*
Aquagreen Dispositions LLC 708 606-0211
25731 S Bristol Ln Monee (60449) *(G-14196)*
Aquagreen Dispositions LLC 708 606-0211
1514 E 168th St South Holland (60473) *(G-19196)*
Aquarius Metal Products Inc (PA) 847 659-9266
12795 Muir Dr Huntley (60142) *(G-11528)*
Aquatrol Inc 630 365-2363
600 E North St Elburn (60119) *(G-8443)*
Aquaviva Winery (PA) 815 899-4444
219 W State St Sycamore (60178) *(G-19701)*
Aqueous Solutions LLC 217 531-1206
301 N Neil St Ste 400 Champaign (61820) *(G-3266)*
Aquion Inc (HQ) 847 725-3000
101 S Gary Ave Unit A Roselle (60172) *(G-17938)*
Aquion Partners Ltd Partnr 847 437-9400
2080 Lunt Ave Elk Grove Village (60007) *(G-8836)*
AR Concepts USA Inc 847 392-4608
520 N Hicks Rd Ste 120 Palatine (60067) *(G-16093)*
AR Impex Inc 404 649-4581
106 Somerset Ln Bolingbrook (60440) *(G-2148)*
AR Industries 630 543-0282
1405 W Bernard Dr Ste C Addison (60101) *(G-37)*
AR Inet Corp 603 380-3903
2336 Pagosa Springs Dr Aurora (60503) *(G-913)*
Ar-En Party Printers Inc 847 673-7390
3416 Oakton St Skokie (60076) *(G-18923)*
Arachnid 360 LLC (PA) 815 654-0212
6212 Material Ave Loves Park (61111) *(G-13190)*
Aracon Drpery Vntian Blind Ltd 773 252-1281
3015 N Kedzie Ave Chicago (60618) *(G-3717)*
Aracon Venetian Blind-Drapery, Chicago *Also called Aracon Drpery Vntian Blind Ltd* *(G-3717)*
Arbee Sales, Chicago *Also called Roberts Electric Company* *(G-6044)*
Arbetman & Associates 708 386-8586
635 S Humphrey Ave Oak Park (60304) *(G-15745)*
Arbor Investments, Chicago *Also called Arbor Private Inv Co LLC* *(G-3718)*
Arbor Printing & Graphics Inc 630 969-2277
438 Angelo Ln Lisle (60532) *(G-12867)*
Arbor Private Inv Co LLC (PA) 312 981-3770
676 N Michigan Ave # 3400 Chicago (60611) *(G-3718)*
Arbor Products 847 653-6210
614 Wisner St Park Ridge (60068) *(G-16267)*
Arbortech Corporation 847 462-1111
3607 Chapel Hill Rd Ste M Johnsburg (60051) *(G-11801)*
Arby Graphic Service Inc 847 763-0900
676 Willow Tree Ln Glencoe (60022) *(G-10428)*
ARC Industries Inc 847 303-5005
2020 Hammond Dr Schaumburg (60173) *(G-18444)*
ARC-Tronics Inc 847 437-0211
1150 Pagni Dr Elk Grove Village (60007) *(G-8837)*
Arcade Beauty, Dixon *Also called Dixon Direct LLC* *(G-7896)*
Arcadia Press Inc 847 451-6390
10915 Franklin Ave Ste L Franklin Park (60131) *(G-9872)*
Arcam Cad To Metal Inc 630 357-5700
55 Shuman Blvd Ste 850 Naperville (60563) *(G-14774)*
Arcelormittal Hennepin LLC (HQ) 815 925-2311
10726 Steel Dr Hennepin (61327) *(G-11156)*
Arcelormittal Intl Amer LLC (HQ) 312 899-3400
1 S Dearborn St Ste 1800 Chicago (60603) *(G-3719)*
Arcelormittal North America, Chicago *Also called Arcelormittal USA LLC* *(G-3723)*
Arcelormittal Riverdale LLC 708 849-8803
13500 S Perry Ave Riverdale (60827) *(G-17067)*
Arcelormittal South Chicago 312 899-3300
1 S Dearborn St Ste 2100 Chicago (60603) *(G-3720)*
Arcelormittal USA Inc 312 899-3500
1 S Dearborn St Ste 1800 Chicago (60603) *(G-3721)*
Arcelormittal USA LLC 312 899-3400
1 S Dearborn St Ste 2100 Chicago (60603) *(G-3722)*
Arcelormittal USA LLC (HQ) 312 346-0300
1 S Dearborn St Ste 1800 Chicago (60603) *(G-3723)*
Arcelormittal USA of Chicago, Chicago *Also called Arcelormittal USA LLC* *(G-3722)*
Arcelrmttal N Amer Hldngs LLC (HQ) 312 899-3400
1 S Dearborn St Ste 1900 Chicago (60603) *(G-3724)*
Arch Chemicals Inc 630 365-1720
809 Hicks Dr Ste A Elburn (60119) *(G-8444)*
Arch Coal Inc 217 566-3000
5945 Lester Rd Williamsville (62693) *(G-21022)*
Arch Printing 630 896-6610
710 Morton Ave North Aurora (60542) *(G-15254)*
Arch Printing Inc 630 966-0235
710 Morton Ave Ste N Aurora (60506) *(G-1053)*
Archer Engineering Company 773 247-3501
2015 S Frontage Rd Darien (60561) *(G-7402)*

Archer General Contg & Fabg 708 757-7902
22498 Miller Rd Steger (60475) ***(G-19488)***

Archer Manufacturing Corp 773 585-7181
4439 S Knox Ave Chicago (60632) ***(G-3725)***

Archer Metal & Paper Co 773 585-3030
4619 S Knox Ave Chicago (60632) ***(G-3726)***

Archer Screw Products Inc (PA) 847 451-1150
11341 Melrose Ave Franklin Park (60131) ***(G-9873)***

Archer Tinning & Re-Tinning Co (PA) 773 927-7240
1019 W 47th St Chicago (60609) ***(G-3727)***

Archer Wire International Corp (PA) 708 563-1700
7300 S Narragansett Ave Bedford Park (60638) ***(G-1456)***

Archer-Daniels-Midland Company (PA) 312 634-8100
77 W Wacker Dr Ste 4600 Chicago (60601) ***(G-3728)***

Archer-Daniels-Midland Company 217 764-3345
200 Front St Macon (62544) ***(G-13404)***

Archer-Daniels-Midland Company 217 424-5882
3665 E Division Decatur (62525) ***(G-7441)***

Archer-Daniels-Midland Company 217 451-8909
3095 E Parkway Dr Decatur (62526) ***(G-7442)***

Archer-Daniels-Midland Company 217 222-7100
1000 N 30th St Quincy (62301) ***(G-16854)***

Archer-Daniels-Midland Company 618 238-4800
406 Route 37 Edgewood (62426) ***(G-8334)***

Archer-Daniels-Midland Company 217 424-5236
466 Ferrys Pkwy Decatur (62525) ***(G-7443)***

Archer-Daniels-Midland Company 309 673-7828
1 Edmund St Peoria (61602) ***(G-16385)***

Archer-Daniels-Midland Company 815 428-7513
104 S 1st Martinton (60951) ***(G-13589)***

Archer-Daniels-Midland Company 217 419-5100
2021 S 1st St Champaign (61820) ***(G-3267)***

Archer-Daniels-Midland Company 800 257-5743
4666 E Faries Pkwy Ste 1 Decatur (62526) ***(G-7444)***

Archer-Daniels-Midland Company 618 483-6171
601 W Division St Altamont (62411) ***(G-530)***

Archer-Daniels-Midland Company 309 772-2141
160 E Main St Bushnell (61422) ***(G-2737)***

Archer-Daniels-Midland Company 309 699-9581
910 Wesley Rd Creve Coeur (61610) ***(G-7148)***

Archer-Daniels-Midland Company 815 384-4011
Rr 38 Box E Rochelle (61068) ***(G-17132)***

Archer-Daniels-Midland Company 815 857-2058
1193 Rock Rd Amboy (61310) ***(G-579)***

Archer-Daniels-Midland Company 217 676-3811
503 S Auger St Mount Auburn (62547) ***(G-14464)***

Archer-Daniels-Midland Company 217 424-5806
3605 E Division St Decatur (62526) ***(G-7445)***

Archer-Daniels-Midland Company 217 451-4460
3350 N 27th St Decatur (62526) ***(G-7446)***

Archer-Daniels-Midland Company 217 424-5413
350 N Water St Decatur (62523) ***(G-7447)***

Archer-Daniels-Midland Company 217 228-0805
436 S Front St Quincy (62301) ***(G-16855)***

Archer-Daniels-Midland Company 217 424-5200
2235 N Brush College Rd Decatur (62526) ***(G-7448)***

Archer-Daniels-Midland Company 217 754-3300
1673 Growmark Ln Meredosia (62665) ***(G-13955)***

Archer-Daniels-Midland Company 815 538-3771
3648 Meridian Rd Mendota (61342) ***(G-13936)***

Archer-Daniels-Midland Company 217 424-5200
4666 E Faries Pkwy Ste 1 Decatur (62526) ***(G-7449)***

Archer-Daniels-Midland Company 217 424-5830
4083 E Faries Pkwy Decatur (62526) ***(G-7450)***

Archer-Daniels-Midland Company 217 451-8169
2311 N 22nd St Decatur (62525) ***(G-7451)***

Archer-Daniels-Midland Company 815 539-6219
581 N 43rd Rd Mendota (61342) ***(G-13937)***

Archer-Daniels-Midland Company 217 342-3986
1200 Mcgrath Ave Effingham (62401) ***(G-8385)***

Archer-Daniels-Midland Company 815 692-2324
Rr 24 Box E Fairbury (61739) ***(G-9603)***

Archer-Daniels-Midland Company 815 223-7907
100 Foot Of Brunner St Peru (61354) ***(G-16566)***

Archer-Daniels-Midland Company 217 424-5660
3601 E Division St Decatur (62526) ***(G-7452)***

Archer-Daniels-Midland Company 217 424-5858
3883 E Faries Pkwy Decatur (62526) ***(G-7453)***

Archer-Daniels-Midland Company 217 887-2514
10 Center St Hume (61932) ***(G-11526)***

Archer-Daniels-Midland Company 217 224-1800
2100 Gardner Expy Quincy (62305) ***(G-16856)***

Archer-Daniels-Midland Company 815 459-1600
8550 Ridgefield Rd Crystal Lake (60012) ***(G-7162)***

Archer-Daniels-Midland Company 217 429-3054
2254 N 40th St Decatur (62526) ***(G-7454)***

Archer-Daniels-Midland Company 217 424-5785
3615 E Faries Pkwy Decatur (62526) ***(G-7455)***

Archer-Daniels-Midland Company 217 224-1800
1900 Gardner Expy Quincy (62301) ***(G-16857)***

Archer-Daniels-Midland Company 618 432-7194
408 S Railroad St Patoka (62875) ***(G-16302)***

Archer-Daniels-Midland Company 217 451-4481
3210 E Parkway Dr Decatur (62526) ***(G-7456)***

Archer-Daniels-Midland Company 217 451-6528
1001 N Brush College Rd Decatur (62521) ***(G-7457)***

Archer-Daniels-Midland Company 217 423-2788
2120 N 40th St Decatur (62526) ***(G-7458)***

Archer-Daniels-Midland Company 217 224-1875
2701 Refinery Rd Quincy (62305) ***(G-16858)***

Archer-Daniels-Midland Company 217 424-5200
3700 E Division St Decatur (62526) ***(G-7459)***

Archer-Daniels-Midland Company 217 424-5669
2505 N Jasper St Decatur (62526) ***(G-7460)***

Architctlly Designed Cabinetry 618 248-5931
207 E Dwight St Albers (62215) ***(G-343)***

Architectual Woodworking 847 259-3331
305 Brian Ln Prospect Heights (60070) ***(G-16835)***

Architectural Cast Ston 630 377-4800
2775 Norton Creek Dr West Chicago (60185) ***(G-20543)***

Architectural Cast Stone LLC 630 377-4800
2775 Norton Creek Dr West Chicago (60185) ***(G-20544)***

Architectural Fan Coil Inc 312 399-1203
3900 W Palmer St Chicago (60647) ***(G-3729)***

Architectural Limestone Inc 847 623-0100
2180 Swanson Ct Gurnee (60031) ***(G-10861)***

Architectural Mall Inc 630 543-5253
323 Saint Paul Blvd Carol Stream (60188) ***(G-2939)***

Architectural Metal Solutions, Alsip *Also called Doralco Inc* ***(G-441)***

Architectural Metals LLC 815 654-2370
6200 Forest Hills Rd Loves Park (61111) ***(G-13191)***

Architectural Wdwkg Design Inc 630 810-1604
4401 Roslyn Rd Downers Grove (60515) ***(G-7954)***

Architectural Wood Expressions 708 731-2355
3200 W Le Moyne Ave Stone Park (60165) ***(G-19552)***

Arcline Fabrication LLC 207 468-1997
12 Graham Dr Unit A Rockdale (60436) ***(G-17256)***

Arco Automobile, Oak Lawn *Also called Arco Automotive Elec Svc Co* ***(G-15701)***

Arco Automotive Elec Svc Co 708 422-2976
10707 S Cicero Ave Oak Lawn (60453) ***(G-15701)***

Arco Brand, Lake Villa *Also called C & F Packing Co Inc* ***(G-12348)***

Arcoa Group Inc (PA) 847 693-7519
3300 Washington St Waukegan (60085) ***(G-20417)***

Arcoa USA, Waukegan *Also called Arcoa Group Inc* ***(G-20417)***

Arcola Rcord Hrld-Rankin Publr, Arcola *Also called Arcola Record Herald* ***(G-645)***

Arcola Record Herald 217 268-4950
118 E Main St Arcola (61910) ***(G-645)***

Arconic Corporation 217 431-3800
1 Customer Pl Danville (61834) ***(G-7321)***

Arcorp Structures LLC 773 791-1648
7301 W 25th St Unit 199 Riverside (60546) ***(G-17081)***

Arcosa Wind Towers Inc 217 935-7900
10000 Tabor Rd Clinton (61727) ***(G-6918)***

Arcsec Digital LLC 312 324-4794
717 Forest Ave Fl 2 Lake Forest (60045) ***(G-12225)***

Arctic Blast Co, Lake Bluff *Also called Duroweld Company Inc* ***(G-12179)***

Arcturus Performance Pdts LLC 630 204-0211
3955 Commerce Dr Saint Charles (60174) ***(G-18147)***

Ardagh Glass Inc 847 869-7248
1 Rotary Ctr Evanston (60201) ***(G-9495)***

Ardagh Glass Inc 708 849-4010
13850 Cottage Grove Ave Dolton (60419) ***(G-7929)***

Ardekin Precision LLC 815 986-4359
1300 Capital Dr Rockford (61109) ***(G-17306)***

Ardent Mills LLC 618 826-2371
101 Water St Chester (62233) ***(G-3449)***

Area Diesel Service Inc (PA) 217 854-2641
1300 University St Carlinville (62626) ***(G-2867)***

Area Disposal Service Inc 217 935-1300
9550 Heritage Rd Clinton (61727) ***(G-6919)***

Area Fabricators 217 455-3426
1735 Highway 24 Coatsburg (62325) ***(G-6940)***

Area Marketing Inc 815 806-8844
10221 W Lincoln Hwy Frankfort (60423) ***(G-9768)***

Area Rigging & Millwright Svcs, Rockford *Also called Patrick Holdings Inc* ***(G-17549)***

Arena Sports Usa Inc 847 809-7268
820 Black Partridge Rd McHenry (60051) ***(G-13720)***

Arens Controls Company LLc 847 844-4700
3602 N Kennicott Ave Arlington Heights (60004) ***(G-694)***

Argentum Medical LLC 888 551-0188
2571 Kaneville Ct Geneva (60134) ***(G-10253)***

Argo Manufacturing Co 630 377-1750
4n944 Old Lafox Rd Wasco (60183) ***(G-20260)***

Argon Medical, Wheeling *Also called Manan Medical Products Inc* ***(G-20936)***

Argus Systems Group, Savoy *Also called Innovative SEC Systems Inc* ***(G-18414)***

Argyle Cut Stone Co 847 456-6210
1046 Woodlawn Ave Des Plaines (60016) ***(G-7733)***

ARI Industries Inc 630 953-9100
381 S Ari Ct Addison (60101) ***(G-38)***

ALPHABETIC SECTION

Aria Corporation 847 327-9000
  29471 N Northwoods Dr Libertyville (60048) *(G-12630)*
Ariba Inc 630 649-7600
  3333 Warrenville Rd # 130 Lisle (60532) *(G-12868)*
Arid Technologies Inc 630 681-8500
  323 S Hale St Wheaton (60187) *(G-20788)*
ARINC Incorporated 800 633-6882
  8 Eagle Ctr Ste 4 O Fallon (62269) *(G-15567)*
Arizon Strctures Worldwide LLC 618 451-7250
  1200 W 7th St Granite City (62040) *(G-10697)*
Arjay Instant Printing 847 438-9059
  26481 N Il Route 83 Mundelein (60060) *(G-14664)*
Ark De Mexico LLC (PA) 630 240-9483
  902 S Randall Rd Saint Charles (60174) *(G-18148)*
Ark Technologies Inc (PA) 630 377-8855
  3655 Ohio Ave Saint Charles (60174) *(G-18149)*
Arkadian Gaming LLC 708 377-5656
  11227 Distinctive Dr Orland Park (60467) *(G-15942)*
Arkema Coating Resins, Alsip Also called Arkema Inc *(G-417)*
Arkema Inc 708 396-3001
  12840 S Pulaski Rd Alsip (60803) *(G-417)*
Arkema Inc 708 385-2188
  12840 S Pulaski Rd Alsip (60803) *(G-418)*
Arla Graphics Inc 847 470-0005
  875 Mountain Dr Deerfield (60015) *(G-7586)*
Arlington Plating Company 847 359-1490
  600 S Vermont St Palatine (60067) *(G-16094)*
Arlington Signs & Banners, Arlington Heights Also called Stelmont Inc *(G-812)*
Arlington Strl Stl Co Inc 847 577-2200
  1727 E Davis St Arlington Heights (60005) *(G-695)*
Armacell LLC 708 596-9501
  16800 S Canal St South Holland (60473) *(G-19197)*
Armada Nutrition LLC 931 451-7808
  285 Fullerton Ave Carol Stream (60188) *(G-2940)*
Armarius Software Inc 630 639-6332
  2415 Wilson Creek Cir Aurora (60503) *(G-914)*
Armature Motor & Pump Company 309 829-3600
  3011 N Main St Ste B East Peoria (61611) *(G-8251)*
Armbrust Paper Tubes Inc 773 586-3232
  6255 S Harlem Ave Chicago (60638) *(G-3730)*
Armil/Cfs Inc 708 339-6810
  15660 La Salle St South Holland (60473) *(G-19198)*
Armin Industries, South Elgin Also called Armin Molding Corp *(G-19133)*
Armin Molding Corp 847 742-1864
  1500 N La Fox St South Elgin (60177) *(G-19133)*
Armin Tool and Mfg Co (PA) 847 742-1864
  1500 N Lafox St South Elgin (60177) *(G-19134)*
Armitage Machine Co Inc 309 697-9050
  6035 Washington St Peoria (61607) *(G-16386)*
Armitage Welding 773 772-1442
  3212 W Armitage Ave Chicago (60647) *(G-3731)*
Armoloy of Illinois Inc 815 758-6657
  114 Simonds Ave Dekalb (60115) *(G-7666)*
Armor Contract Mfg Inc 847 981-9800
  2301 Estes Ave Elk Grove Village (60007) *(G-8838)*
Armstrong Aerospace Inc (HQ) 847 244-4500
  804 S Northpoint Blvd Waukegan (60085) *(G-20418)*
Armstrong Flooring Inc 815 939-2501
  1401 N Hobbie Ave Kankakee (60901) *(G-11958)*
Armstrong Hydraulic, Carmi Also called Armstrong Tool LLC *(G-2899)*
Armstrong Tool LLC 618 382-4184
  1403 E Main St Carmi (62821) *(G-2899)*
Armstrong USA, Kankakee Also called Armstrong Flooring Inc *(G-11958)*
Armstrong World Industries Inc 847 362-8720
  1821 Industrial Dr Libertyville (60048) *(G-12631)*
Armstrong-Alar Chain, Prospect Heights Also called Armstrong/Alar Inc *(G-16836)*
Armstrong/Alar Inc 847 808-8885
  15 E Palatine Rd Ste 108 Prospect Heights (60070) *(G-16836)*
Army Navy Supply Depot, Marengo Also called Your Supply Depot Limited *(G-13497)*
Arndt Enterprise Ltd 847 234-5736
  674 Timber Ln Ste 200 Lake Forest (60045) *(G-12226)*
Arndt's Hallmark Shop, Newton Also called Arndts Stores Inc *(G-15080)*
Arndts Stores Inc (PA) 618 783-2511
  106 W Washington St Newton (62448) *(G-15080)*
Arnel Industries Inc 630 543-6500
  57 W Interstate Rd Addison (60101) *(G-39)*
Arnette Pattern Co Inc 618 451-7700
  3203 Missouri Ave Granite City (62040) *(G-10698)*
Arnold Engineering Co (HQ) 815 568-2000
  300 N West St Marengo (60152) *(G-13479)*
Arnold Magnetic Tech Corp 815 568-2000
  300 N West St Marengo (60152) *(G-13480)*
Arnold Monument Co Inc (PA) 217 546-2102
  1621 Wabash Ave Springfield (62704) *(G-19320)*
Arntzen Corporation 815 334-0788
  14600 Washington St Woodstock (60098) *(G-21360)*
Aro Metal Stamping Company Inc 630 351-7676
  935 N Central Ave Wood Dale (60191) *(G-21166)*
Arpac LLC (PA) 847 678-9034
  9555 Irving Park Rd Schiller Park (60176) *(G-18787)*
Arpwave Usa LLC 773 835-0122
  1354 W Taylor St Chicago (60607) *(G-3732)*
Arquilla Inc 815 455-2470
  4220 Waller St Ste 1 Crystal Lake (60012) *(G-7163)*
Arro Corporation 708 352-8200
  7250 Santa Fe Dr Ste 1 Hodgkins (60525) *(G-11384)*
Arro Corporation 773 978-1251
  10459 S Muskegon Ave Chicago (60617) *(G-3733)*
Arro Corporation 708 352-7412
  7550 Santa Fe Dr Hodgkins (60525) *(G-11385)*
Arro Liquid Division, Hodgkins Also called Arro Corporation *(G-11385)*
Arro Packing, Chicago Also called Arro Corporation *(G-3733)*
Arrow Aluminum Castings Inc 815 338-4480
  2617 S Il Route 47 Woodstock (60098) *(G-21361)*
Arrow Edm Inc 217 893-4277
  1120 Veterans Pkwy Rantoul (61866) *(G-16967)*
Arrow Engineering Inc 815 397-0862
  5191 27th Ave Rockford (61109) *(G-17307)*
Arrow Gear Company (PA) 630 969-7640
  2301 Curtiss St Downers Grove (60515) *(G-7955)*
Arrow Gear Company 630 969-7640
  5240 Belmont Rd Downers Grove (60515) *(G-7956)*
Arrow Group Industries, Breese Also called Arrow Shed LLC *(G-2296)*
Arrow Pin and Products Inc 708 755-7575
  51 E 34th St S Chicago Hts (60411) *(G-18117)*
Arrow Pneumatics Inc 708 343-6177
  2111 W 21st St Broadview (60155) *(G-2418)*
Arrow Road Construction Co (PA) 847 437-0700
  1445 Oakton St Elk Grove Village (60007) *(G-8839)*
Arrow Shed LLC (HQ) 618 526-4546
  1101 N 4th St Breese (62230) *(G-2296)*
Arrow Sheet Metal Company 815 455-2019
  1032 Ascot Dr Crystal Lake (60014) *(G-7164)*
Arrow Sign Company Inc 630 620-9803
  415 W Belden Ave Ste F Addison (60101) *(G-40)*
Arrow Signs (PA) 618 466-0818
  4545 N Alby Rd Godfrey (62035) *(G-10649)*
Arrow Signs 618 466-0818
  6203 Godfrey Rd Godfrey (62035) *(G-10650)*
Arrowhead Brick Pavers Inc 630 393-1584
  30w218 Bttrfeld Rd Unit A Warrenville (60555) *(G-20231)*
Arrows Up Inc 847 305-2550
  3 W College Dr Rear 1 Arlington Heights (60004) *(G-696)*
Arrowtech Pallet & Crating 815 547-9300
  860 E Jackson St Belvidere (61008) *(G-1650)*
Art & Son Design, Wauconda Also called Art & Son Sign Inc *(G-20332)*
Art & Son Sign Inc 847 526-7205
  1090 Brown St Wauconda (60084) *(G-20332)*
Art Bookbinders of America 312 226-4100
  451 N Claremont Ave Chicago (60612) *(G-3734)*
Art Cnc Machining LLC 708 907-3090
  9824 Industrial Dr Bridgeview (60455) *(G-2325)*
Art Crystal II Enterprises Inc 630 739-0222
  7852 47th St Lyons (60534) *(G-13301)*
Art House Coffee LLC 618 659-0571
  206 E Linden St Edwardsville (62025) *(G-8345)*
Art In Print Review 773 697-9478
  3500 N Lake Shore Dr Chicago (60657) *(G-3735)*
Art Jewel Enterprises Ltd 630 260-0400
  460 Randy Rd Carol Stream (60188) *(G-2941)*
Art Media Resources Inc 312 663-5351
  1965 W Pershing Rd Ste 4 Chicago (60609) *(G-3736)*
Art Newvo Incorporated 847 838-0304
  25819 W Grail Lk Rd Ste 1 Antioch (60002) *(G-600)*
Art of Running, The, Glencoe Also called Panache Editions Ltd *(G-10433)*
Art of Shaving - Fl LLC 630 495-7316
  441 E Roosevelt Rd Lombard (60148) *(G-13040)*
Art of Shaving - Fl LLC 312 527-1604
  520 N Michigan Ave # 122 Chicago (60611) *(G-3737)*
Art of Shaving - Fl LLC 630 684-0277
  100 Oakbrook Ctr Oak Brook (60523) *(G-15594)*
Art Technologies Inc 773 557-3896
  450 Frontier Way Ste B Bensenville (60106) *(G-1747)*
Art Wire Works Inc 708 458-3993
  6711 S Leclaire Ave Bedford Park (60638) *(G-1457)*
Art-Craft Printers 847 455-2201
  9108 Belden Ave Franklin Park (60131) *(G-9874)*
Art-Flo Shirt & Lettering Co 708 656-5422
  6939 W 59th St Chicago (60638) *(G-3738)*
Artganiks, Naperville Also called I T C W Inc *(G-14842)*
Arthur Coyle Press 773 465-8418
  2730 W Coyle Ave Chicago (60645) *(G-3739)*
Arthur Custom Tank LLC 217 543-4022
  510 E Progress St Arthur (61911) *(G-841)*
Arthur Graphic Clarion 217 543-2151
  113 E Illinois St Arthur (61911) *(G-842)*
Arthur Leo Kuhl 618 752-5473
  1023 N 500th St Ingraham (62434) *(G-11591)*

Arthur R Baker Inc — ALPHABETIC SECTION

Arthur R Baker Inc 708 301-4828
13507 W Oakwood Ct Homer Glen (60491) *(G-11477)*

Arthur Schuman Inc 847 851-8500
2589 Technology Dr Elgin (60124) *(G-8514)*

Arthur Schuman Midwest LLC 847 851-8500
2589 Technology Dr Elgin (60124) *(G-8515)*

Arthur/Busse Properties Inc 847 289-1800
2299 Busse Rd Elk Grove Village (60007) *(G-8840)*

Artisan Element 630 229-5654
6128 Allan Dr Woodridge (60517) *(G-21276)*

Artisan Graphics Co 847 841-9200
1527 Burgundy Pkwy Streamwood (60107) *(G-19562)*

Artisan Handprints Inc 773 725-1799
4234 N Pulaski Rd Chicago (60641) *(G-3740)*

Artisan Millwork LLC 847 417-5236
902 S Randall Rd Ste C335 Saint Charles (60174) *(G-18150)*

Artisan Signs, Orland Park Also called Mostert & Ferguson Signs *(G-15969)*

Artisan Signs & Lighting, Orland Park Also called Pellegrini Enterprises Inc *(G-15974)*

Artistic Carton Company, Elgin Also called Gpi Midwest LLC *(G-8599)*

Artistic Dental Studio Inc 630 679-8686
470 Woodcreek Dr Bolingbrook (60440) *(G-2149)*

Artistic Embroidery Creations 815 385-8854
5203 Home Ave McHenry (60050) *(G-13721)*

Artistic Framing Inc (PA) 847 808-0200
860 Chaddick Dr Ste F Wheeling (60090) *(G-20850)*

Artistries By Tommy Musto Inc 630 674-8667
159 W Lake St Ste 1 Bloomingdale (60108) *(G-1977)*

Artistry Engraving & Embossing 773 775-4888
6000 N Northwest Hwy Chicago (60631) *(G-3741)*

Artline Screen Printing Inc 815 963-8125
1309 7th St Rockford (61104) *(G-17308)*

Artpol Printing Inc 773 622-0498
7011 W Higgins Ave Chicago (60656) *(G-3742)*

Arts & Letters Marshall Signs 773 927-4442
3610 S Albany Ave Chicago (60632) *(G-3743)*

Arts Tamales 309 367-2850
1453 Hickory Point Rd Metamora (61548) *(G-13958)*

Arttig Art 847 804-8001
100 Chaddick Dr Wheeling (60090) *(G-20851)*

Artwear 618 234-5522
1916 Lebanon Ave Belleville (62221) *(G-1530)*

Arvamont 630 926-2468
549 W 58th St Hinsdale (60521) *(G-11361)*

Arvens Technology Inc 650 776-5443
801 W Main St Peoria (61606) *(G-16387)*

Arway Confections, Chicago Also called Baldi Candy Co *(G-3818)*

Arway Confections, Chicago Also called Baldi Candy Co *(G-3819)*

ARX Nimbus LLC 888 422-6584
323 E Wacker Dr Ste 300 Chicago (60601) *(G-3744)*

Arxium Inc 847 808-2600
1400 Busch Pkwy Buffalo Grove (60089) *(G-2513)*

Aryzta Great Kitchens, Romeoville Also called Aryzta LLC *(G-17796)*

Aryzta LLC 815 306-7171
300 Innovation Dr Romeoville (60446) *(G-17796)*

Aryzta LLC 708 757-4671
401 E Joe Orr Rd Chicago Heights (60411) *(G-6731)*

Aryzta LLC 312 836-2300
350 N Orleans St 7500s Chicago (60654) *(G-3745)*

As 1902 LLC 773 287-0874
824 S Central Ave Chicago (60644) *(G-3746)*

AS Fabricating Inc 618 242-7438
15518 N Il Highway 37 Mount Vernon (62864) *(G-14596)*

As Lawn & Land LLC 309 246-5012
301 4th St Lacon (61540) *(G-12125)*

Asa, Itasca Also called American Supply Association *(G-11622)*

Asahi Kasei Bioprocess Inc 847 834-0800
1855 Elmdale Ave Glenview (60026) *(G-10528)*

Asai Chicago 708 239-0133
12559 S Holiday Dr Ste C Alsip (60803) *(G-419)*

ASAP Pallets Inc (PA) 630 350-7689
480 Podlin Dr Franklin Park (60131) *(G-9875)*

ASAP Pallets Inc 630 917-0180
2711 Washington Blvd Bellwood (60104) *(G-1614)*

ASAP Printing, Morton Grove Also called Printing Source Inc *(G-14433)*

ASap Specialties Inc Del 847 223-7699
888 E Belvidere Rd # 111 Grayslake (60030) *(G-10759)*

Asbestos Control & Envmtl Svc 630 690-0189
31 W 780 Poss Rd Eola (60519) *(G-9469)*

ASC, West Chicago Also called American Standard Circuits Inc *(G-20539)*

ASC Fasteners, Sycamore Also called Ample Supply Company *(G-19700)*

Ascent Innovations LLC 847 572-8000
475 N Martingale Rd # 820 Schaumburg (60173) *(G-18445)*

Ascent Mfg Co 847 806-6600
123 Scott St Elk Grove Village (60007) *(G-8841)*

Ascent Tranz Group LLC (PA) 844 424-7347
5620 W 51st St Chicago (60638) *(G-3747)*

Asco LP 630 789-2082
443 S Banbury Rd Arlington Heights (60005) *(G-697)*

Asg-Uniaero 773 941-5053
13829 Park Ave Dolton (60419) *(G-7930)*

Ash Pallet Management Inc 847 473-5700
61 Mcmillen Rd Antioch (60002) *(G-601)*

ASHI, Des Plaines Also called American Soc HM Inspectors Inc *(G-7728)*

Ashland ABC Choice Inc 773 488-7800
7903 S Ashland Ave Chicago (60620) *(G-3748)*

Ashland Door Solutions LLC 773 348-5106
185 Martin Ln Elk Grove Village (60007) *(G-8842)*

Ashland Lock & SEC Solutions, Chicago Also called A Ashland Lock Company *(G-3485)*

Ashland Screening Corporation 708 758-8800
475 E Joe Orr Rd Chicago Heights (60411) *(G-6732)*

Ashley Lauren 847 733-9470
636 Church St Ste 701 Evanston (60201) *(G-9496)*

Ashley Lauren Natural Products, Evanston Also called Ashley Lauren *(G-9496)*

Ashley Oil Co 217 932-2112
508 Deere Run Ln Casey (62420) *(G-3198)*

Ashley's Cutom Stationary, Hinsdale Also called Ashleys Inc *(G-11362)*

Ashleys Inc 630 794-0804
30 E 1st St Hinsdale (60521) *(G-11362)*

Ashton Diversified Enterprises 630 739-0981
19w442 Deerpath Ln Lemont (60439) *(G-12554)*

Asi, Crystal Lake Also called Alpha Swiss Industries Inc *(G-7157)*

Asico, Westmont Also called Amer Surgical Instruments Inc *(G-20727)*

Asico LLC 630 986-8032
26 Plaza Dr Westmont (60559) *(G-20729)*

Ask Power, Aurora Also called Ask Products Inc *(G-1054)*

Ask Products Inc 630 896-4056
544 N Highland Ave Aurora (60506) *(G-1054)*

Askric LLC 309 360-3125
406 Johnson Ct Germantown Hills (61548) *(G-10333)*

Asm Sensors Inc 630 832-3202
650 W Grand Ave Ste 205 Elmhurst (60126) *(G-9326)*

Asmw, Mc Cook Also called A&S Machining & Welding Inc *(G-13689)*

Aspen API Inc (HQ) 847 635-0985
2136 S Wolf Rd Des Plaines (60018) *(G-7734)*

Aspen Carpet Designs 815 483-8501
11335 Stratford Rd Mokena (60448) *(G-14073)*

Aspen Foods, Chicago Also called Koch Meat Co Inc *(G-5113)*

Aspen Foods, Park Ridge Also called Jcg Industries Inc *(G-16286)*

Aspen Foods Inc 312 829-7282
1300 Higgins Rd Ste 100 Park Ridge (60068) *(G-16268)*

Aspen Guard LLC 708 325-0400
5858 W 73rd St Bedford Park (60638) *(G-1458)*

Aspen Industries Inc 630 238-0611
480 Country Club Dr Bensenville (60106) *(G-1748)*

Aspen Manufacturing Company 630 495-0922
1001 W Republic Dr Ste 6 Addison (60101) *(G-41)*

Aspen Printing Services LLC 630 357-3203
405 S River Rd Naperville (60540) *(G-14775)*

Aspen Shutters Inc 847 979-0166
2235 Hammond Dr Ste F Schaumburg (60173) *(G-18446)*

Asphalt Mtls DBA Hrtg Asp LLC 773 735-2233
4950 W 41st St Cicero (60804) *(G-6830)*

Asphalt Products Inc 618 943-4716
6574 Akin Rd Lawrenceville (62439) *(G-12527)*

Assa Abloy ACC Door Cntrls Gro 704 283-2101
9100 Belmont Ave Franklin Park (60131) *(G-9876)*

Assa Abloy Entrance Systems US 847 228-5600
1630 Jarvis Ave Elk Grove Village (60007) *(G-8843)*

Assa Abloy Pry 630 682-8800
235 E Lies Rd Carol Stream (60188) *(G-2942)*

Assemble and Mail Group Inc 309 473-2006
508 S Buchanan St Heyworth (61745) *(G-11189)*

Assemblers Inc (PA) 773 378-3000
2850 W Columbus Ave Chicago (60652) *(G-3749)*

Assertio Holdings Inc (PA) 224 419-7106
100 Saunders Rd Ste 300 Lake Forest (60045) *(G-12227)*

Assertio Therapeutics Inc (HQ) 224 419-7106
100 Saunders Rd Ste 300 Lake Forest (60045) *(G-12228)*

Associate Computer Systems 618 997-3653
211 N Market St Ste A Marion (62959) *(G-13505)*

Associate General Labs Inc 847 678-2717
9035 Exchange Ave Franklin Park (60131) *(G-9877)*

Associated Agri-Business Inc 618 498-2977
100 S State St Jerseyville (62052) *(G-11786)*

Associated Agri-Business Inc (PA) 618 498-2977
229 Elm St Eldred (62027) *(G-8487)*

Associated Attractions Entps 773 376-1900
4834 S Halsted St 14 Chicago (60609) *(G-3750)*

Associated Design Inc 708 974-9100
11160 Southwest Hwy Ste B Palos Hills (60465) *(G-16195)*

Associated Design Service, Palos Hills Also called Associated Design Inc *(G-16195)*

Associated Equipment Distrs (PA) 630 574-0650
650 E Algonquin Rd # 305 Schaumburg (60173) *(G-18447)*

Associated Group Holdings LLC (PA) 312 662-5488
156 N Jefferson St # 300 Chicago (60661) *(G-3751)*

Associated Metal Mfg, Chicago Also called Kcp Metal Fabrications Inc *(G-5088)*

Associated Printers Inc....847 548-8929
43215 N Grandview Ter Antioch (60002) *(G-602)*
Associated Professionals....847 931-0095
665 Tollgate Rd Ste F Elgin (60123) *(G-8516)*
Associated Publications Inc....312 266-8680
875 N Michigan Ave # 3100 Chicago (60611) *(G-3752)*
Associated Research Inc....847 367-4077
13860 W Laurel Dr Lake Forest (60045) *(G-12229)*
Associates Engraving Company....217 523-4565
2601 Colt Rd Springfield (62707) *(G-19321)*
Association Management Center....847 375-4700
8735 W Higgins Rd Ste 300 Chicago (60631) *(G-3753)*
Assurance Clg Restoration LLC....630 444-3600
3740 Stern Ave Saint Charles (60174) *(G-18151)*
Assurance Technologies Inc....630 550-5000
1251 Humbracht Cir Ste A Bartlett (60103) *(G-1265)*
Assured Welding Service Inc....847 671-1414
975 Aster Ln West Chicago (60185) *(G-20545)*
AST Industries Inc....847 455-2300
2345 17th St Franklin Park (60131) *(G-9878)*
Asta Service Inc....630 271-0960
5821 Iris Ln Lisle (60532) *(G-12869)*
Astec Mobile Screens Inc....815 626-6374
2704 W Le Fevre Rd Sterling (61081) *(G-19498)*
Astellas Pharma Global Dev Inc....224 205-8800
1 Astellas Way Northbrook (60062) *(G-15337)*
Astellas Pharma Inc....800 695-4321
1 Astellas Way Northbrook (60062) *(G-15338)*
Astellas Pharma Us Inc (HQ)....800 888-7704
1 Astellas Way Northbrook (60062) *(G-15339)*
Astellas RES Inst Amer LLC....847 933-7400
8045 Lamon Ave Skokie (60077) *(G-18924)*
Astellas Scntfic Med Affirs In....224 205-5452
1 Astellas Way Northbrook (60062) *(G-15340)*
Astellas US Holding Inc (HQ)....224 205-8800
1 Astellas Way Northbrook (60062) *(G-15341)*
Astellas US LLC....800 888-7704
3 Parkway North Blvd Deerfield (60015) *(G-7587)*
Astellas US Technologies Inc....847 317-8800
3 Parkway North Blvd # 300 Deerfield (60015) *(G-7588)*
Asteroid Precision Inc....847 298-8109
1075 Chaddick Dr Wheeling (60090) *(G-20852)*
Astoria Wire & Metal Products, Bedford Park *Also called Astoria Wire Products Inc (G-1459)*
Astoria Wire Products Inc....708 496-9950
5303 W 74th Pl Bedford Park (60638) *(G-1459)*
Astral Power Systems Inc....630 518-1741
31 W Downer Pl Ste 408 Aurora (60506) *(G-1055)*
Astro Machine Corporation....847 364-6363
630 Lively Blvd Elk Grove Village (60007) *(G-8844)*
Astro Plastic Containers Inc....708 458-7100
903 Carlow Dr Bolingbrook (60490) *(G-2150)*
Astro Printing Inc....773 436-0500
6550 S Kedzie Ave Fl 1 Chicago (60629) *(G-3754)*
Astro Tool Co Inc....630 876-3402
1200 Atlantic Dr West Chicago (60185) *(G-20546)*
Astro-Craft Inc....815 675-1500
7509 Spring Grove Rd Spring Grove (60081) *(G-19265)*
Astro-Physics Inc....815 282-1513
11250 Forest Hills Rd Machesney Park (61115) *(G-13328)*
Astron Dental Corporation....847 726-8787
815 Oakwood Rd Ste G Lake Zurich (60047) *(G-12386)*
Astronics Armstrong Aerospace, Waukegan *Also called Armstrong Aerospace Inc (G-20418)*
Astronics Cnnctvity Systems Cr (HQ)....847 821-3059
804 S Northpoint Blvd Waukegan (60085) *(G-20419)*
Astronics CSC, Waukegan *Also called Astronics Cnnctvity Systems Cr (G-20419)*
Asutra, Chicago *Also called Proximity Capital Partners LLC (G-5909)*
At Home Magazine....217 351-5282
15 E Main St Champaign (61820) *(G-3268)*
AT&I Resources LLC (HQ)....918 925-0154
444 W Interstate Rd Addison (60101) *(G-42)*
AT&T Corp....630 693-5000
851 Oak Creek Dr Lombard (60148) *(G-13041)*
AT&T Corp....312 602-4108
1 S Wacker Dr Ste 3900 Chicago (60606) *(G-3755)*
AT&T Midwest, Chicago *Also called AT&T Teleholdings Inc (G-3756)*
AT&T Teleholdings Inc (HQ)....800 288-2020
30 S Wacker Dr Fl 34 Chicago (60606) *(G-3756)*
Ata Finishing Corp....847 677-8560
8225 Kimball Ave Skokie (60076) *(G-18925)*
Ataraxia LLC....618 446-3219
884 Industrial St Albion (62806) *(G-346)*
Atbc LLC....847 648-2822
1580 N Northwest Hwy Park Ridge (60068) *(G-16269)*
Ateco Automotive, Ingleside *Also called American Total Engine Co (G-11578)*
Atelier Juvence Cstm Stonework, Chicago *Also called Atelier Jvnce Stncarving Tiles (G-3757)*
Atelier Jvnce Stncarving Tiles....312 492-7922
1601 S Ind Ave Ste 209 Chicago (60616) *(G-3757)*
Athena Design Group Inc....312 733-2828
3500 S Morgan St 1 Chicago (60609) *(G-3758)*
Athena Precision Machining, Bensenville *Also called JM Tool & Die LLC (G-1832)*
Athenex Pharmaceutical Div LLC....847 922-8041
10 N Martingale Rd # 230 Schaumburg (60173) *(G-18448)*
Athenian Foods Co....708 343-6700
1814 N 15th Ave Melrose Park (60160) *(G-13827)*
Athenian Pastries & Food, Melrose Park *Also called Athenian Foods Co (G-13827)*
Atherton Foundry Products Inc....708 849-4615
13000 S Halsted St Riverdale (60827) *(G-17068)*
Athletic & Sports Seating....630 837-5566
676 Bonded Pkwy Ste L Streamwood (60107) *(G-19563)*
Athletic Fundraising.com, Pekin *Also called Varsity Publications Inc (G-16367)*
Athletic Image....217 347-7377
510 W Jaycee Ave Ste 3 Effingham (62401) *(G-8386)*
Athletic Outfitters Inc....815 942-6696
409 Liberty St Morris (60450) *(G-14291)*
Athletic Sewing Mfg Co (PA)....773 589-0361
7449 W Irving Park Rd # 1 Chicago (60634) *(G-3759)*
Athletic Specialties Inc....847 487-7880
1230 Karl Ct Unit A Wauconda (60084) *(G-20333)*
Athllete LLC....773 829-3752
948 W Briarcliff Rd Bolingbrook (60440) *(G-2151)*
ATI Flat Rlled Pdts Hldngs LLC....708 974-8801
8687 S 77th Ave Bridgeview (60455) *(G-2326)*
ATI Oldco Inc (HQ)....630 860-5600
1420 Brewster Creek Blvd Bartlett (60103) *(G-1266)*
ATI Wah Chang, Northbrook *Also called Tdy Industries LLC (G-15492)*
Atk Foods, Chicago *Also called Amylu Foods LLC (G-3689)*
Atk Home Services, O Fallon *Also called Atk Services Inc (G-15568)*
Atk Services Inc....618 726-5114
1392 Frontage Rd Ste 9 O Fallon (62269) *(G-15568)*
Atkore International Inc (HQ)....708 339-1610
16100 Lathrop Ave Harvey (60426) *(G-11074)*
Atkore International Group Inc (PA)....708 339-1610
16100 Lathrop Ave Harvey (60426) *(G-11075)*
Atkore Intl Holdings Inc (HQ)....708 225-2051
16100 Lathrop Ave Harvey (60426) *(G-11076)*
Atkore Rmcp Inc (HQ)....708 339-1610
16100 Lathrop Ave Harvey (60426) *(G-11077)*
Atks Inc....715 914-0395
2946 N Clybourn Ave # 101 Chicago (60618) *(G-3760)*
Atlanta Warehouse 1023, Chicago *Also called Leggett & Platt Incorporated (G-5200)*
Atlantic Beverage Company Inc (PA)....847 412-6200
1033 Skokie Blvd Ste 600 Northbrook (60062) *(G-15342)*
Atlantic Engineering....847 782-1762
42008 N Delany Rd Zion (60099) *(G-21509)*
Atlantis Entp Investments Inc....432 237-0404
3432 W Diversey Ave Fl 2 Chicago (60647) *(G-3761)*
Atlantis Products Inc....630 971-9680
586 Territorial Dr Ste H Bolingbrook (60440) *(G-2152)*
Atlas Boiler & Welding Company....815 963-3360
424 N Grove Ave Elgin (60120) *(G-8517)*
Atlas Building Components Inc....618 639-0222
5 Industrial Dr Jerseyville (62052) *(G-11787)*
Atlas Components Inc....815 332-4904
4055 S Perryville Rd Cherry Valley (61016) *(G-3437)*
Atlas Copco Compressors LLC....847 640-6067
2501 Landmeier Rd Ste 110 Elk Grove Village (60007) *(G-8845)*
Atlas Copco Compressors LLC....281 590-7500
75 Remittance Dr # 3009 Chicago (60675) *(G-3762)*
Atlas Die LLC....630 351-5140
2000 Bloomingdale Rd # 235 Glendale Heights (60139) *(G-10436)*
Atlas Energy Products, East Moline *Also called Atlas Roofing Corporation (G-8222)*
Atlas Fibre Company (PA)....847 674-1234
3411 Woodhead Dr Northbrook (60062) *(G-15343)*
Atlas Holding Inc (HQ)....773 646-4500
1855 E 122nd St Chicago (60633) *(G-3763)*
Atlas Maintenance Service Inc....773 486-3386
2055 N Kedzie Ave Chicago (60647) *(G-3764)*
Atlas Manufacturing....773 327-3005
4114 N Ravenswood Ave Chicago (60613) *(G-3765)*
Atlas Manufacturing Ltd....815 943-1400
1001 W Roosevelt St Harvard (60033) *(G-11047)*
Atlas Material Tstg Tech LLC (HQ)....773 327-4520
1500 Bishop Ct Mount Prospect (60056) *(G-14512)*
Atlas Material Tstg Tech LLC....773 327-4520
1800 W Belle Plaine Ave Chicago (60613) *(G-3766)*
Atlas Material Tstg Tech LLC....773 327-4520
1800 W Belle Plaine Ave F Chicago (60613) *(G-3767)*
Atlas Putty Products Co....708 429-5858
8351 185th St Tinley Park (60487) *(G-19806)*
Atlas Ready Mix Inc....618 271-0774
2901 Missouri Ave East Saint Louis (62205) *(G-8297)*
Atlas Roofing Corporation....309 752-7121
3110 Morton Dr East Moline (61244) *(G-8222)*
Atlas Screen Supply Co., Schiller Park *Also called Damy Corp (G-18798)*
Atlas Tool & Die Works Inc....708 442-1661
4633 Lawndale Ave Lyons (60534) *(G-13302)*

A L P H A B E T I C

Atlas Trade Solutions LLC 618 954-6119
18 Powder Valley Dr Belleville (62223) ***(G-1531)***

Atlas Tube (chicago) LLC 312 275-1672
1855 E 122nd St Chicago (60633) ***(G-3768)***

Atlas Uniform Company 312 492-8527
1412 W Wa Blvd Fl 2 Chicago (60607) ***(G-3769)***

Atm America Corp 800 298-0030
1900 N Austin Ave Ste 69 Chicago (60639) ***(G-3770)***

Atmark Trading Inc 312 933-7907
1965 W Pershing Rd Chicago (60609) ***(G-3771)***

Atmi Dynacore LLC 815 838-9492
960 Ridgeway Ave Ste 1 Aurora (60506) ***(G-1056)***

Atmi Plant, Aurora *Also called Atmi Precast Inc* ***(G-1058)***

Atmi Precast Inc (PA) 630 897-0577
960 Ridgeway Ave Fl 2 Aurora (60506) ***(G-1057)***

Atmi Precast Inc 630 897-0577
930 Ridgeway Ave Aurora (60506) ***(G-1058)***

Atmosphere Global LLC 630 660-2833
55 W Goethe St Unit 1241 Chicago (60610) ***(G-3772)***

Ato Systems, Lake Forest *Also called Perfect Circle Projectiles LLC* ***(G-12286)***

Atometric Inc 815 505-2582
7320 Forest Hills Rd Loves Park (61111) ***(G-13192)***

Atomic Engineering Co 847 228-1387
365 Kent Ave Elk Grove Village (60007) ***(G-8846)***

Atomic Industrial Machine Inc 847 228-1387
365 Kent Ave Elk Grove Village (60007) ***(G-8847)***

Ats Acoustics, Piper City *Also called Ats Commercial Group LLC* ***(G-16625)***

Ats Commercial Group LLC 815 686-2705
15 W Main St Piper City (60959) ***(G-16625)***

Ats Communications Netwrk Corp 309 673-6733
1500 Ne Jefferson Ave Peoria (61603) ***(G-16388)***

Ats Sortimat USA LLC 847 925-1234
5655 Meadowbrook Indus Ct Rolling Meadows (60008) ***(G-17713)***

Atsp Innovations Inc 217 778-4400
60 Hazelwood Dr Ste 145 Champaign (61820) ***(G-3269)***

Attic Gifts, Mundelein *Also called In The Attic Inc* ***(G-14699)***

Attune Medical, Chicago *Also called Advanced Cooling Therapy Inc* ***(G-3562)***

Atturo Tire Corp 855 632-8031
3250 N Oak Grove Ave Waukegan (60087) ***(G-20420)***

Atwood-Hamlin Mfg Co Inc 815 678-7291
5614 Kenosha St Richmond (60071) ***(G-17010)***

Atwoot Herald, Mount Zion *Also called Village of Mt Zion* ***(G-14650)***

Aubrey Sign Co Inc 630 482-9901
1847 Suncast Ln Batavia (60510) ***(G-1351)***

Audio Installers Inc 815 969-7500
5061 Contractors Dr Loves Park (61111) ***(G-13193)***

Audio Tech Bus Bk Summaries 630 734-0500
1314 Kensington Rd # 4953 Oak Brook (60523) ***(G-15595)***

August Hill Winery 815 224-8199
21 N 2551st Rd Peru (61354) ***(G-16567)***

Augusta Eagle 217 392-2715
600 Main St Augusta (62311) ***(G-909)***

Augusta Label Corp 630 537-1961
7938 S Madison St Burr Ridge (60527) ***(G-2653)***

Augustan, Oak Brook *Also called NRR Corp* ***(G-15651)***

Augusthill Winery Co 815 667-5211
106 Mill St Utica (61373) ***(G-20005)***

Aunt Ems Gourmet Popcorn Inc 309 447-6612
405 E 1st Ave Deer Creek (61733) ***(G-7571)***

Auntie Mmmms 217 509-6012
105 N Ohio St Camp Point (62320) ***(G-2809)***

Aura Systems Inc 217 423-4100
2345 E Garfield Ave Decatur (62526) ***(G-7461)***

Aurel Construction LLC 312 998-5000
9209 S Peoria St Chicago (60620) ***(G-3773)***

Aurora Bearing Company 630 897-8941
901 Aucutt Rd Montgomery (60538) ***(G-14230)***

Aurora Circuits Inc 630 978-3830
2250 White Oak Cir Aurora (60502) ***(G-915)***

Aurora Circuits LLC 630 978-3830
2250 White Oak Cir Aurora (60502) ***(G-916)***

Aurora Cord & Cable Company, Aurora *Also called Elc Industries Corp* ***(G-1088)***

Aurora Fastprint Inc 630 896-5980
54 E Galena Blvd Aurora (60505) ***(G-1059)***

Aurora Line 847 670-1600
3407 N Ridge Ave Ste A Arlington Heights (60004) ***(G-698)***

Aurora Metals Division LLC 630 844-4900
1995 Greenfield Rd Montgomery (60538) ***(G-14231)***

Aurora Narinder 773 275-2100
4549 N Clark St Chicago (60640) ***(G-3774)***

Aurora Orthopedic Laboratories, North Aurora *Also called Tuu Duc Le Inc* ***(G-15280)***

Aurora Packing Company Inc 630 897-0551
125 S Grant St North Aurora (60542) ***(G-15255)***

Aurora Pump, North Aurora *Also called Pentair Flow Technologies LLC* ***(G-15269)***

Aurora Service Center, Aurora *Also called Grundfos CBS Inc* ***(G-975)***

Aurora Spclty Txtles Group Inc 800 864-0303
2705 N Bridge St Yorkville (60560) ***(G-21473)***

Aurora Tent & Awning Co, Plainfield *Also called Stritzel Awnng Svc/Aurra Tent* ***(G-16718)***

Aurora Textile Finishing Co, Aurora *Also called Meridian Industries Inc* ***(G-1131)***

Aurubis Buffalo Inc 630 980-8400
129 Fairfield Way Ste 308 Bloomingdale (60108) ***(G-1978)***

Austin Tool & Die Co (PA) 847 509-5800
3555 Woodhead Dr Northbrook (60062) ***(G-15344)***

Austins Saloon & Eatery 847 549-1972
481 Peterson Rd Libertyville (60048) ***(G-12632)***

Authentic Street Signs Inc 618 349-8878
183 Main St Saint Peter (62880) ***(G-18322)***

Authority Screenprint & EMB 630 236-0289
10148 Clow Creek Rd Ste D Plainfield (60585) ***(G-16643)***

Auto Body Tool Mart, Elgin *Also called American Industrial Direct LLC* ***(G-8507)***

Auto Head and Engine Exchange 708 448-8762
6603 W 111th St Worth (60482) ***(G-21454)***

Auto Injury Solutions Inc (HQ) 312 229-2704
222 Merchandise Mart Plz # 900 Chicago (60654) ***(G-3775)***

Auto Meter Products Inc 815 895-8141
413 W Elm St Sycamore (60178) ***(G-19702)***

Auto Truck, Bartlett *Also called ATI Oldco Inc* ***(G-1266)***

Auto Truck Group LLC (HQ) 630 860-5600
1420 Brewster Creek Blvd Bartlett (60103) ***(G-1267)***

Auto Truck Grp Wyn Flt Equipme, Bartlett *Also called Auto Truck Group LLC* ***(G-1267)***

Auto-Owners Insurance, Mount Zion *Also called Gibson Insurance Inc* ***(G-14646)***

Autocut Machine Company Inc 815 436-1900
23702 S Vetter Rd Elwood (60421) ***(G-9460)***

Autograph, Chicago *Also called Signature Screen Printing Corp* ***(G-6169)***

Autojet Technologies, Glendale Heights *Also called Spraying Systems Co* ***(G-10498)***

Automated Design Corp 630 783-1150
1404 N Joliet Rd Ste D Romeoville (60446) ***(G-17797)***

Automated Forms & Graphics Inc 630 887-9811
200 W 11th St Ste 2sw Lockport (60441) ***(G-12982)***

Automated Insights Inc 919 442-8865
203 N La Salle St # 2200 Chicago (60601) ***(G-3776)***

Automated Logic Chicago, Lisle *Also called Automated Logic Corporation* ***(G-12870)***

Automated Logic Corporation 630 852-1700
2400 Ogden Ave Ste 100 Lisle (60532) ***(G-12870)***

Automated Material Hdlg Svcs (PA) 630 947-7605
725 Hunter Dr Batavia (60510) ***(G-1352)***

Automated Mfg Solutions Inc 815 477-2428
6096 Commercial Rd Crystal Lake (60014) ***(G-7165)***

Automated Systems & Control Co 847 735-8310
11 N Skokie Hwy Ste 115 Lake Bluff (60044) ***(G-12172)***

Automatic Anodizing Corp 773 478-3304
3340 W Newport Ave Chicago (60618) ***(G-3777)***

Automatic Building Contrls LLC (PA) 847 296-4000
3315 Algonquin Rd Ste 550 Rolling Meadows (60008) ***(G-17714)***

Automatic Feeder Company Inc 847 534-2300
921 Albion Ave Schaumburg (60193) ***(G-18449)***

Automatic Fire Controls, Mokena *Also called Fire Systems Holdings Inc* ***(G-14081)***

Automatic Precision Inc 708 867-1116
4609 N Ronald St Chicago (60706) ***(G-3778)***

Automatic Production Eqp Inc 847 439-1448
815 Touhy Ave Elk Grove Village (60007) ***(G-8848)***

Automatic Spring Coiling, Bensenville *Also called Mw Industries Inc* ***(G-1855)***

Automatic Swiss Corporation 630 543-3888
1130 W National Ave Ste A Addison (60101) ***(G-43)***

Automation Design & Mfg Inc 630 896-4206
841 S River St Aurora (60506) ***(G-1060)***

Automation International Inc 217 446-9500
1020 Bahls St Danville (61832) ***(G-7322)***

Automation Specialist Svcs LLC 847 792-1692
44w110 Us Highway 20 A Hampshire (60140) ***(G-10962)***

Automation Systems Inc 847 671-9515
2001 N 17th Ave Melrose Park (60160) ***(G-13828)***

Automax Corporation 630 972-1919
1940 Intrntonale Pkwy # 550 Woodridge (60517) ***(G-21277)***

Automotive Engine Specialties 847 956-1244
173 Randall St Elk Grove Village (60007) ***(G-8849)***

Automtic Lquid Packg Solutions, Arlington Heights *Also called Diamond Machine Werks Inc* ***(G-728)***

Automtic Lquid Pckg Sltons LLC 847 372-3336
2445 E Oakton St Arlington Heights (60005) ***(G-699)***

Autonamic Corporation 815 675-6300
7806 Industrial Dr Spring Grove (60081) ***(G-19266)***

Autonetics Inc 847 426-8525
425 Maple Ave Carpentersville (60110) ***(G-3094)***

Autonomic Materials Inc 217 863-2023
495 County Road 1300 N Champaign (61822) ***(G-3270)***

Autonomous Stuff LLC (HQ) 309 291-0966
306 Erie Ave Morton (61550) ***(G-14353)***

Autonomoustuff, Morton *Also called Autonomous Stuff LLC* ***(G-14353)***

Autospec Inc 773 254-2288
1464 W 37th St Chicago (60609) ***(G-3779)***

Autotech Tech Ltd Partnr 563 359-7501
28617 Network Pl Chicago (60673) ***(G-3780)***

Autotype Americas Incorporated 847 818-8262
1675 Winnetka Cir Rolling Meadows (60008) ***(G-17715)***

Autrol America, Schaumburg *Also called Autrol Corporation of America* ***(G-18450)***

Autrol Corporation of AME....847 874-7545
796 Tek Dr Crystal Lake (60014) ***(G-7166)***
Autrol Corporation of America....847 779-5000
10 N Martingale Rd # 470 Schaumburg (60173) ***(G-18450)***
Autumn Mill....217 795-3399
13014 Cemetery Rd Argenta (62501) ***(G-671)***
Autumn Woods Ltd....630 868-3535
112 N Main St Wheaton (60187) ***(G-20789)***
Autumn Woods Ltd (PA)....630 668-2080
375 Gundersen Dr Carol Stream (60188) ***(G-2943)***
Aux Sable Liquid Products, Morris *Also called Aux Sable Midstream LLC* ***(G-14293)***
Aux Sable Liquid Products LP (PA)....815 941-5800
6155 E Us Route 6 Morris (60450) ***(G-14292)***
Aux Sable Midstream LLC....815 941-5800
6155 E Us Route 6 Morris (60450) ***(G-14293)***
Aux Sable Sand & Gravel, Morris *Also called Lafarge Aux Sable LLC* ***(G-14309)***
Auxitrol SA....815 874-2471
3358 N Publishers Dr Rockford (61109) ***(G-17309)***
AV Franklin, Elmhurst *Also called AV Stumpfl Usa Corp* ***(G-9327)***
AV Stumpfl Usa Corp....630 359-0999
960 N Industrial Dr Ste 3 Elmhurst (60126) ***(G-9327)***
Available Business Group Inc....773 247-4141
3944 S Morgan St Chicago (60609) ***(G-3781)***
Available Spring and Mfg Co....847 520-4854
350 Holbrook Dr Wheeling (60090) ***(G-20853)***
Avalign Grman Specialty Instrs....847 908-0292
626 Cooper Ct Schaumburg (60173) ***(G-18451)***
Avalign Technologies Inc (PA)....855 282-5446
2275 Half Day Rd Ste 126 Bannockburn (60015) ***(G-1189)***
Avan Precast Concrete Pdts Inc....708 757-6200
3201 211th St Lynwood (60411) ***(G-13291)***
Avan Tool & Die Co Inc....773 287-1670
4612 W Maypole Ave Chicago (60644) ***(G-3782)***
Avana Electric Motors Inc....847 588-0400
1445 Brummel Ave Elk Grove Village (60007) ***(G-8850)***
Avana Electrotek, Elk Grove Village *Also called Avana Electric Motors Inc* ***(G-8850)***
Avani Spices LLC....847 532-1075
1690 Stone Ridge Ln Algonquin (60102) ***(G-366)***
Avant Diagnostics Inc (PA)....732 410-9810
40 E 9th St Apt 804 Chicago (60605) ***(G-3783)***
Avant Tecno USA Inc....847 380-1308
3020 Malmo Dr Arlington Heights (60005) ***(G-700)***
Avanti Engineering Inc (PA)....630 260-1333
200 W Lake Dr Glendale Heights (60139) ***(G-10437)***
Avanti Foods Company....815 379-2155
109 Depot St Walnut (61376) ***(G-20216)***
Avanti Motor Carriers Inc....630 313-9160
4440 White Ash Ln Naperville (60564) ***(G-14960)***
Avasarala Inc....847 969-0630
1 E Northwest Hwy Ste 214 Palatine (60067) ***(G-16095)***
Avatar Corporation....708 534-5511
500 Central Ave University Park (60484) ***(G-19947)***
Avaya Inc....847 885-3598
2500 W Higgins Rd Schaumburg (60195) ***(G-18452)***
Ave Inc....815 727-0153
126 S Des Plaines St Joliet (60436) ***(G-11825)***
Avec Inc....815 577-3122
762 Shoreline Dr Ste 100 Aurora (60504) ***(G-917)***
Avenir Publishing Inc....872 228-2830
1 N State St Ste 1500 Chicago (60602) ***(G-3784)***
Aventine Rnwble Enrgy Hldngs L (HQ)....309 347-9200
1300 S 2nd St Pekin (61554) ***(G-16324)***
Aventine Rnwble Enrgy Holdings, Pekin *Also called Pacific Ethanol Pekin LLC* ***(G-16350)***
Avenue Metal Manufacturing Co....312 243-3483
1640 W Ogden Ave Chicago (60612) ***(G-3785)***
Avers Machine & Mfg Inc....847 447-3430
3999 25th Ave Schiller Park (60176) ***(G-18788)***
Averus Usa Inc (PA)....800 913-7034
2410 Vantage Dr Elgin (60124) ***(G-8518)***
Avery Dennison Corporation....877 214-0909
7542 N Natchez Ave Niles (60714) ***(G-15104)***
Avery Dennison Corporation....847 824-7450
902 Feehanville Dr Mount Prospect (60056) ***(G-14513)***
Avery Dennison Rfid Company....626 304-2000
13424 Collection Ctr Dr Chicago (60693) ***(G-3786)***
Avery Dnnson Ret Info Svcs LLC....626 304-2000
15178 Collection Ctr Dr Chicago (60693) ***(G-3787)***
Avexis....847 964-9948
3 Parkway North Blvd Deerfield (60015) ***(G-7589)***
Avexis Inc (HQ)....847 572-8280
2275 Half Day Rd Ste 200 Bannockburn (60015) ***(G-1190)***
Avexis Inc....847 572-8280
1940 Usg Dr Libertyville (60048) ***(G-12633)***
Avexis Inc....847 572-8280
600 N Us Highway 45 Libertyville (60048) ***(G-12634)***
AVI-Spl Employee....847 437-7712
2266 Palmer Dr Schaumburg (60173) ***(G-18453)***
Aviation Services Group Inc....708 425-4700
10524 Major Ave Chicago Ridge (60415) ***(G-6788)***
Aviation Services Group of IL, Chicago Ridge *Also called Aviation Services Group Inc* ***(G-6788)***
Avid of Illinois Inc....847 698-2775
2740 E Main St Saint Charles (60174) ***(G-18152)***
Avis Commercial Anodizing, Chicago *Also called P B A Corp* ***(G-5728)***
Avlon Industries Inc....708 344-0709
1999 N 15th Ave Melrose Park (60160) ***(G-13829)***
Avoca Ridge Ltd....815 692-4772
310 S 7th St Ste 2 Fairbury (61739) ***(G-9604)***
Avocet Polymer Tech Inc....773 523-2872
4047 W 40th St Chicago (60632) ***(G-3788)***
Avondale Adventures....773 588-5761
3817 N Pulaski Rd Chicago (60641) ***(G-3789)***
Avondale Cstm Bldg Fabrication, Chicago *Also called Avondale Customs Inc* ***(G-3790)***
Avondale Customs Inc....773 680-4631
3241 N Lawndale Ave Chicago (60618) ***(G-3790)***
Avt Service Technologies, Blue Island *Also called Advanced Valve Tech LLC* ***(G-2110)***
Avtec Inc....618 337-7800
6 Industrial Dr East Saint Louis (62206) ***(G-8298)***
Avw Equipment Company Inc....708 343-7738
105 S 9th Ave Maywood (60153) ***(G-13661)***
Aw Dynamometer Inc....815 844-6968
1001 W North St Pontiac (61764) ***(G-16766)***
Awa, Wood Dale *Also called Intelligent SCM LLC* ***(G-21202)***
Awa, Ottawa *Also called A Wiley & Associates* ***(G-16036)***
Award Concepts Inc....630 513-7801
110 S 11th Ave Saint Charles (60174) ***(G-18153)***
Award Concepts Mfg Co, Saint Charles *Also called Award Concepts Inc* ***(G-18153)***
Award Emblem Mfg Co Inc....630 739-0800
179 E South Frontage Rd Bolingbrook (60440) ***(G-2153)***
Award/Visionps Inc....331 318-7800
208 S Jefferson St # 203 Chicago (60661) ***(G-3791)***
Awards and More Inc....773 581-7771
8544 S Pulaski Rd Chicago (60652) ***(G-3792)***
Awardspring, Chicago *Also called Scholarship Solutions LLC* ***(G-6113)***
AWego Enterprises Inc....815 765-1957
2967 Country Meadow Ln Belvidere (61008) ***(G-1651)***
Awem Corporation....217 670-1451
1 W Old State Capitol Plz # 703 Springfield (62701) ***(G-19322)***
Awerkamp Machine Co (PA)....217 222-3480
237 N 7th St Quincy (62301) ***(G-16859)***
Awerkamp Machine Co....217 222-3490
321 Broadway St Quincy (62301) ***(G-16860)***
Awerkamp Steel, Quincy *Also called Awerkamp Machine Co* ***(G-16860)***
Awesome Amusements Co., Addison *Also called Nite Lite Signs & Balloons Inc* ***(G-229)***
AWI / Titanium....708 263-9970
15146 Geoffrey Rd Oak Forest (60452) ***(G-15671)***
Awnings By Zip Dee Inc....847 640-0460
96 Crossen Ave Elk Grove Village (60007) ***(G-8851)***
Awnings Express....773 579-1437
2415 W 24th Pl Chicago (60608) ***(G-3793)***
Awnings Over Chicagoland Inc....847 233-0310
10204 Franklin Ave Franklin Park (60131) ***(G-9879)***
Axiomatics Inc....312 374-3443
525 W Monroe St Ste 2310 Chicago (60661) ***(G-3794)***
Axiomm, Essex *Also called Tatty Stick LLC* ***(G-9476)***
Axiosonic LLC....217 342-3412
2600 S Raney St Effingham (62401) ***(G-8387)***
Axis Design Architectual Mllwk....630 466-4549
239 State Route 47 Sugar Grove (60554) ***(G-19637)***
Axis Display Group Inc....513 342-1884
8272 Douglas Ave South Beloit (61080) ***(G-19082)***
Axis International Marketing....847 297-0744
1800 S Wolf Rd Ste 2 Des Plaines (60018) ***(G-7735)***
Axis Manufacturing Inc....847 350-0200
2436 Delta Ln Elk Grove Village (60007) ***(G-8852)***
Axletech International....773 264-1234
1120 W 119th St Chicago (60643) ***(G-3795)***
Axode Corp....312 578-9897
35 E Wacker Dr Ste 670 Chicago (60601) ***(G-3796)***
Axon Cable Inc (HQ)....847 230-7813
1316 N Plum Grove Rd Schaumburg (60173) ***(G-18454)***
Axon Telecom LLC....618 278-4606
177 Snake Rd Dorsey (62021) ***(G-7943)***
Axxent Energy Inc....312 288-8640
W 1016 Ste 502 Chicago (60601) ***(G-3797)***
Aydin Displays, Schaumburg *Also called Sparton Aydin LLC* ***(G-18716)***
AZ Foods, Chicago *Also called A-Z Sales Inc* ***(G-3495)***
AZ Plastics Inc (PA)....773 679-0988
5300 W Roscoe St Chicago (60641) ***(G-3798)***
AZ Plastics Inc....773 679-0988
1232 Mckinley Ave Chicago (60641) ***(G-3799)***
Azcon Inc....815 548-7000
101 Avenue K Sterling (61081) ***(G-19499)***
Azek Company, The, Chicago *Also called Cpg International LLC* ***(G-4252)***
Azilsa Inc....312 919-1741
1425 W Schaumburg Rd Schaumburg (60194) ***(G-18455)***

ALPHABETIC

Azimuth Cnc Inc 815 399-4433
4801 White Oak Ave Rockford (61114) *(G-17310)*
Aztec Material Service Corp (PA) 773 521-0909
3624 W 26th St Fl 2 Chicago (60623) *(G-3800)*
Aztec Plastic Company 312 733-0900
1747 W Carroll Ave Chicago (60612) *(G-3801)*
Aztec Products 217 726-8631
3321 Blueberry Ln Springfield (62711) *(G-19323)*
Azteca Foods Inc (PA) 708 563-6600
5005 S Nagle Ave Chicago (60638) *(G-3802)*
Azteca Jewelry (PA) 773 929-0796
3334 N Lincoln Ave Chicago (60657) *(G-3803)*
Aztech Engineering Inc 630 236-3200
2675 White Oak Cir Ste 1 Aurora (60502) *(G-918)*
Aztech Locknut Company, Aurora *Also called Aztech Engineering Inc (G-918)*
Azul 3d Inc 321 277-7807
8111 Saint Louis Ave # 2 Skokie (60076) *(G-18926)*
Azusa Inc 618 244-6591
15179 N Il Highway 37 Mount Vernon (62864) *(G-14597)*
Azusa Printing, Mount Vernon *Also called Azusa Inc (G-14597)*
Azz Incorporated 815 723-5000
625 Mills Rd Joliet (60433) *(G-11826)*
B & B Custom TS & Gifts 618 463-0443
2714 Corner Ct Alton (62002) *(G-544)*
B & B Equipment 217 562-2511
401 S Business 5 Assumption (62510) *(G-888)*
B & B Fabrications LLC 217 620-3210
901 W Jefferson St Sullivan (61951) *(G-19660)*
B & B Formica Appliers Inc 773 804-1015
5617 W Grand Ave Chicago (60639) *(G-3804)*
B & B Machine Inc 309 786-3279
1221 2nd Ave Rock Island (61201) *(G-17202)*
B & B Printing, Kewanee *Also called Bailleu & Bailleu Printing Inc (G-12021)*
B & B Printing Company 217 285-6072
115 E Washington St A Pittsfield (62363) *(G-16628)*
B & B Specialty Company Inc 708 652-9234
139 Timberline Dr Lemont (60439) *(G-12555)*
B & B Tank Truck Construction (PA) 618 378-3337
760 Us Highway 45 Norris City (62869) *(G-15246)*
B & B Tool Co 815 229-5792
5005 27th Ave Rockford (61109) *(G-17311)*
B & D Independence Inc 618 262-7117
1024 Empire St Mount Carmel (62863) *(G-14465)*
B & D Murray Manufacturing Co 815 568-6176
3911 N Il Route 23 Marengo (60152) *(G-13481)*
B & G Machine Inc 618 262-2269
421 W 9th St Mount Carmel (62863) *(G-14466)*
B & H Biotechnologies LLC 630 915-3227
6520 Chaucer Rd Willowbrook (60527) *(G-21030)*
B & H Industries, Warrenville *Also called Robal Company Inc (G-20252)*
B & J Wet Enterprises, Rolling Meadows *Also called Bandjwet Enterprises Inc (G-17717)*
B & J Wire Inc 877 787-9473
1919 S Fairfield Ave # 1 Chicago (60608) *(G-3805)*
B & L Machine & Design, Effingham *Also called B & L Machine Sales Inc (G-8388)*
B & L Machine Sales Inc 217 342-3918
1 Legend Park Effingham (62401) *(G-8388)*
B & M Automotive 309 637-4977
1811 S Oakwood Ave Peoria (61605) *(G-16389)*
B & M Machine Inc 630 350-8950
768 Industrial Dr Bensenville (60106) *(G-1749)*
B & M Plastic Inc 847 258-4437
3737 Acorn Ln Franklin Park (60131) *(G-9880)*
B & R Alarm Co, Decatur *Also called Justice Manufacturing Inc (G-7512)*
B & R Grinding Co 630 595-7789
459 Podlin Dr Franklin Park (60131) *(G-9881)*
B & T Polishing Co 847 658-6415
2433 W Fulton St Chicago (60612) *(G-3806)*
B & W Machine Company Inc 847 364-4500
71 Gordon St Elk Grove Village (60007) *(G-8853)*
B A Die Mold Inc 630 978-4747
3685 Prairie Lake Ct Aurora (60504) *(G-919)*
B A I Publishers 847 537-1300
190 Abbott Dr Ste A Wheeling (60090) *(G-20854)*
B A P Enterprises Inc 708 849-0900
14235 Cottage Grove Ave Dolton (60419) *(G-7931)*
B A Precast Inc 309 645-0639
29794 N County Highway 2 Ellisville (61431) *(G-9320)*
B Allan Graphics Inc 708 396-1704
11629 S Mayfield Ave Alsip (60803) *(G-420)*
B and A Screen Printing 217 762-2632
350 W Burnside Rd Monticello (61856) *(G-14277)*
B and B Amusement Illinois LLC 309 585-2077
1404 Mrtin Luther King Dr Bloomington (61701) *(G-2025)*
B B M Packing Co Inc 312 243-1061
874 N Milwaukee Ave Chicago (60642) *(G-3807)*
B B Milling Co Inc 217 376-3131
300 North St Emden (62635) *(G-9466)*
B C Die & Mold Inc 630 543-5090
1046 W Republic Dr Addison (60101) *(G-44)*
B C I, Libertyville *Also called BCI Acrylic Inc (G-12636)*
B C T, Machesney Park *Also called Business Cards Tomorrow (G-13332)*
B C T, Machesney Park *Also called Business Card Systems Inc (G-13331)*
B Creative Screen Print Co 815 806-3037
8844 W Steger Rd Frankfort (60423) *(G-9769)*
B D, Downers Grove *Also called Becton Dickinson and Company (G-7959)*
B D C Inc 847 741-2233
1185 Jansen Farm Ct Elgin (60123) *(G-8519)*
B D Enterprises 618 462-5861
655 E Broadway Alton (62002) *(G-545)*
B D Sport Photos and Trophies, Alton *Also called B D Enterprises (G-545)*
B E, Quincy *Also called Broadcast Electronics Inc (G-16869)*
B E A Electro-Optics, Elk Grove Village *Also called Bea Electro Sales Inc (G-8859)*
B F I, Chicago *Also called Beverage Flavors Intl LLC (G-3876)*
B F Shaw Printing Company 815 625-3600
3200 E Lincolnway Sterling (61081) *(G-19500)*
B I L, Mettawa *Also called Brunswick International Ltd (G-13980)*
B J Fehr Machine Co 309 923-8691
209 N Main St Roanoke (61561) *(G-17099)*
B J Plastic Molding Co (PA) 630 766-3200
435 S County Line Rd Franklin Park (60131) *(G-9882)*
B J Plastic Molding Co 630 766-8750
778 County Line Rd Bensenville (60106) *(G-1750)*
B JS Printables 618 656-8625
1501 Troy Rd B Edwardsville (62025) *(G-8346)*
B L I Tool & Die Inc 217 434-9106
1468 Highway 24 Fowler (62338) *(G-9742)*
B M S Tool & Equipment Co, Bridgeport *Also called Bridgeport Air Comprsr & Tl Co (G-2310)*
B M W Inc 847 439-0095
110 Carpenter Ave Wheeling (60090) *(G-20855)*
B N Blance Enrgy Solutions LLC 847 287-7466
2019 N Wainwright Ct Palatine (60074) *(G-16096)*
B N K Inc 630 231-5640
330 S Neltnor Blvd West Chicago (60185) *(G-20547)*
B P I Printing & Duplicating (PA) 773 327-7300
3223 N Lakewood Ave Chicago (60657) *(G-3808)*
B P I Printing & Duplicating 773 822-0111
2801 Lakeside Dr Ste 110 Bannockburn (60015) *(G-1191)*
B Quad Oil Inc 618 656-4419
1405 Troy Rd Ste B Edwardsville (62025) *(G-8347)*
B R I Operations, Flora *Also called Booth Resources Inc (G-9676)*
B Radtke and Sons Inc 847 546-3999
101 W Main St Ste 2 Round Lake Park (60073) *(G-18095)*
B S Grinding Inc 847 787-0770
2535 United Ln Elk Grove Village (60007) *(G-8854)*
B T Brown Manufacturing 815 947-3633
14871 E Airport Rd Kent (61044) *(G-12017)*
B T M Industries Inc 815 338-6464
604 Washington St Woodstock (60098) *(G-21362)*
B T Technology Inc 217 322-3768
320 N Railroad St Rushville (62681) *(G-18108)*
B W M Global 847 785-1355
3740 Hawthorne Ct Waukegan (60087) *(G-20421)*
B&A Livestock Feed Company LLC 618 245-6422
201 E Jefferson Ave Farina (62838) *(G-9650)*
B&B Machining Incorporated 630 898-3009
24 Gastville St Aurora (60503) *(G-920)*
B&Bimc LLC 815 433-5100
707 E Dayton Rd Ottawa (61350) *(G-16040)*
B&H Machine Inc 618 281-3737
251 Southwoods Ctr Ste 1 Columbia (62236) *(G-6984)*
B+b Smartworx Inc (HQ) 815 433-5100
707 E Dayton Rd Ottawa (61350) *(G-16041)*
B-Clean Laundromat Inc 678 983-5492
5419 S Halsted St Chicago (60609) *(G-3809)*
B-O-F Corporation 630 585-0020
2453 Prospect Dr Ste A Aurora (60502) *(G-921)*
B.E.S.t, Rolling Meadows *Also called Bandjwet Enterprises Inc (G-17716)*
B/E Aerospace Inc 561 791-5000
1220 Central Ave Hanover Park (60133) *(G-11000)*
Ba Le Meat Processing & Whl Co 773 506-2499
2405 W Ardmore Ave Chicago (60659) *(G-3810)*
Babak Inc 312 419-8686
15411 Cicero Ave Oak Forest (60452) *(G-15672)*
Babbletees 815 780-1953
3322 W Washington Blvd Chicago (60624) *(G-3811)*
Babylon Travel & Tour Service, Skokie *Also called Ganji Klames (G-18959)*
Bach & Associates 618 277-1652
120 N 36th St Belleville (62226) *(G-1532)*
Bach Plastic Works Inc 847 680-4342
1711 Young Dr B Libertyville (60048) *(G-12635)*
Bach Timber & Pallet Inc 815 885-3774
8858 Grove St Caledonia (61011) *(G-2768)*
Bachi Company Div, Itasca *Also called Jardis Industries Inc (G-11680)*
Back Forty WD Works & Nurs LLC 618 898-1241
1431 County Road 740 E Johnsonville (62850) *(G-11811)*
Back of Yards Coffee LLC 773 475-6381
2059 W 47th St Fl 1 Chicago (60609) *(G-3812)*

Background Investigator, The, Morton Grove *Also called Steven Brownstein* **(G-14442)**
Backyard Bucket Co.....773 771-0743
1726 S Halsted St Chicago (60608) **(G-3813)**
Backyard Creations.....217 836-5678
14389 State Highway 97 Petersburg (62675) **(G-16600)**
Bact Process Systems Inc.....847 577-0950
3345 N Arlington Hts B Arlington Heights (60004) **(G-701)**
Bad Boys Neons, Springfield *Also called Shinn Enterprises* **(G-19443)**
Bade Herman & Son Trucking, Villa Grove *Also called Herman Bade & Sons* **(G-20123)**
Badge-A-Minit Ltd (HQ).....815 883-8822
345 N Lewis Ave Oglesby (61348) **(G-15839)**
Badger Air Brush Co.....847 678-3104
9128 Belmont Ave Franklin Park (60131) **(G-9883)**
Badger Basket Co, Lake Zurich *Also called Standard Container Co of Edgar* **(G-12460)**
Baessler Carl Dgn Mfg Rep.....779 994-4103
360 Memorial Dr Crystal Lake (60014) **(G-7167)**
Bag and Barrier Corporation.....217 849-3271
505 E Rte 121 Toledo (62468) **(G-19874)**
Bag Tags Inc.....847 983-4732
3415 Howard St Ste 101 Skokie (60076) **(G-18927)**
Bagcraftpapercon I LLC (HQ).....620 856-2800
3900 W 43rd St Chicago (60632) **(G-3814)**
Bagcraftpapercon II LLC (HQ).....773 843-8000
3900 W 43rd St Chicago (60632) **(G-3815)**
Bagmakers Inc.....815 923-2247
6606 S Union Rd Union (60180) **(G-19937)**
Bahr Tool & Die Co.....847 392-4447
2201 Foster Ave Wheeling (60090) **(G-20856)**
Baier Home Center.....815 457-2300
120 S 2nd St Cissna Park (60924) **(G-6894)**
Baier Publishing Company.....815 457-2245
119 W Garfield Ave Cissna Park (60924) **(G-6895)**
Bailey Business Group.....618 548-3566
3089 State Route 37 Salem (62881) **(G-18330)**
Bailey Hardwoods Inc.....217 529-6800
628 Kimble Ct Springfield (62703) **(G-19324)**
Bailleu & Bailleu Printing Inc.....309 852-2517
214 S Main St Ste A Kewanee (61443) **(G-12021)**
Baily International Inc (PA).....618 451-8878
2501 W 20th St Granite City (62040) **(G-10699)**
Baily International Inc.....773 927-3233
3823 S Halsted St 27 Chicago (60609) **(G-3816)**
Baird Inc.....217 526-3407
577 Illinois Route 48 Morrisonville (62546) **(G-14350)**
Bak Electric.....708 458-3578
7951 S Oketo Ave Bridgeview (60455) **(G-2327)**
Baka Vitaliy.....773 370-5522
2224 W Chicago Ave Chicago (60622) **(G-3817)**
Baker & Taylor LLC.....815 802-2444
501 Gladiolus St Momence (60954) **(G-14183)**
Baker Atlas, Olney *Also called Baker Hghes Olfld Oprtions LLC* **(G-15854)**
Baker Avenue Investments Inc.....309 427-2500
205 Eastgate Dr Washington (61571) **(G-20266)**
Baker Drapery Corporation.....309 691-3295
4211 W Simpson Dr Dunlap (61525) **(G-8132)**
Baker Elements Inc.....630 660-8100
159 N Marion St Oak Park (60301) **(G-15746)**
Baker Hghes Olfld Oprtions LLC.....618 393-2919
930 S West St Olney (62450) **(G-15854)**
Baker La Russo.....630 788-5108
911 Joan Ct Naperville (60540) **(G-14776)**
Baker Manufacturing LLC.....847 362-3663
1349 Rockland Rd Lake Bluff (60044) **(G-12173)**
Baker Petrolite LLC.....618 966-3688
315 S State St Crossville (62827) **(G-7149)**
Baker's Custom Lettering, Naperville *Also called Baker La Russo* **(G-14776)**
Bakery Feeds, Seneca *Also called Griffin Industries LLC* **(G-18858)**
Bakery McHy & Fabrication LLC.....815 224-1306
307 Bakery Ave Peru (61354) **(G-16568)**
Bal-Craft Screw Machine Co.....847 398-7688
985 Lively Blvd Elk Grove Village (60007) **(G-8855)**
Bala & Anula Fuels Inc.....630 766-1807
154 S York Rd Bensenville (60106) **(G-1751)**
Balanceuticals Group, Chicago *Also called Health King Enterprise Inc* **(G-4791)**
Balancing Services, Elk Grove Village *Also called Balanstar Corporation* **(G-8856)**
Balanstar Corporation (PA).....773 261-5034
170 Lively Blvd Elk Grove Village (60007) **(G-8856)**
Balas Incorporated.....630 406-7971
1080 Kingsland Dr Batavia (60510) **(G-1353)**
Baldi Candy Co (PA).....773 267-5770
3425 N Kimball Ave Chicago (60618) **(G-3818)**
Baldi Candy Co.....773 267-5770
3323 W Newport Ave Chicago (60618) **(G-3819)**
Baldwin Americas, Fairfield *Also called Baldwin Technology Company Inc* **(G-9618)**
Baldwin OXY-Dry Corporation (HQ).....630 595-3651
1210 N Swift Rd Addison (60101) **(G-45)**
Baldwin Richardson Foods Co (PA).....815 464-9994
1 Tower Ln Ste 2390 Oakbrook Terrace (60181) **(G-15787)**
Baldwin Technology Company Inc.....618 842-2664
600 Us Highway 45 Ste A Fairfield (62837) **(G-9618)**
Baldwin Technology Company Inc.....618 842-2664
3350 W Salt Creek Ln # 110 Arlington Heights (60005) **(G-702)**
Bales Mold Service Inc.....630 852-4665
2824 Hitchcock Ave Ste A Downers Grove (60515) **(G-7957)**
Baley Enterprises Inc.....708 681-0900
1206 N 31st Ave Melrose Park (60160) **(G-13830)**
Ball Foster Glass Container.....708 849-1500
13850 Cottage Grove Ave Dolton (60419) **(G-7932)**
Ball Plastic Container Div, Batavia *Also called Amcor Rigid Plastics Usa LLC* **(G-1347)**
Ball Publishing.....630 208-9080
622 Town Rd West Chicago (60185) **(G-20548)**
Ballard Bros Inc.....217 374-2137
420 E Lincoln St White Hall (62092) **(G-21017)**
Ballard Bros Con Pdts & Excav, White Hall *Also called Ballard Bros Inc* **(G-21017)**
Ballco Manufacturing Co Inc (PA).....630 898-1600
2375 Liberty St Aurora (60502) **(G-922)**
Ballert Orthopedic of Chicago, Chicago *Also called Gema Inc* **(G-4668)**
Ballotready Inc.....301 706-0708
1626 N Honore St Chicago (60622) **(G-3820)**
Bally Foil Graphics Inc.....847 427-1509
1701 Elmhurst Rd Elk Grove Village (60007) **(G-8857)**
Balon International Corp.....773 379-7779
5410 W Roosevelt Rd 133a Chicago (60644) **(G-3821)**
Balsley Fast Printing, Rockton *Also called Balsley Printing Inc* **(G-17692)**
Balsley Printing Inc (PA).....815 624-7515
119 E Main St Rockton (61072) **(G-17692)**
Balsley Printing Inc.....815 624-7515
119 E Main St Rockton (61072) **(G-17693)**
Balton Corporation.....773 933-7927
1001 E 99th St Chicago (60628) **(G-3822)**
Bam Operating Inc.....254 629-8561
2145 Pioneer Rd Evanston (60201) **(G-9497)**
Bamberger Polymers Inc.....630 773-8626
1 Pierce Pl Ste 255c Itasca (60143) **(G-11624)**
Bamenda Coffee Company Inc.....214 566-8175
924 E High Park Blvd Chicago (60615) **(G-3823)**
Band of Shoppers Inc.....312 857-4250
2669 N Greenview Ave F Chicago (60614) **(G-3824)**
Bandage, The Div, Lanark *Also called Hygienic Fabrics & Filters Inc* **(G-12482)**
Bandgrip Inc.....844 968-6322
311 S Wacker Dr Ste 650 Chicago (60606) **(G-3825)**
Bandjwet Enterprises Inc.....847 797-9250
3603 Edison Pl Rolling Meadows (60008) **(G-17716)**
Bandjwet Enterprises Inc.....847 797-9250
3603 Edison Pl Rolling Meadows (60008) **(G-17717)**
Bando Usa Inc (HQ).....630 773-6600
1149 W Bryn Mawr Ave Itasca (60143) **(G-11625)**
Bangert Casing Pulling Corp.....618 676-1411
1 Industrial Park Rd Clay City (62824) **(G-6903)**
Bankier Companies Inc (PA).....847 647-6565
6151 W Gross Point Rd Niles (60714) **(G-15105)**
Bankmark Inc.....847 683-9834
46w299 Middleton Rd Hampshire (60140) **(G-10963)**
Banner Equipment Co.....815 941-9600
922 Armstrong St Morris (60450) **(G-14294)**
Banner Medical, Carol Stream *Also called Banner Service Corporation* **(G-2944)**
Banner Moulded Products.....708 452-0033
3050 River Rd River Grove (60171) **(G-17057)**
Banner Publications.....309 338-3294
350 N 1st St Cuba (61427) **(G-7297)**
Banner Sale Management Service, Cuba *Also called Banner Publications* **(G-7297)**
Banner Service Corporation (HQ).....630 653-7500
494 E Lies Rd Carol Stream (60188) **(G-2944)**
Banner Up Signs, Sycamore *Also called E K Kuhn Inc* **(G-19709)**
Bannerville USA Inc.....630 455-0304
8168 S Madison St Burr Ridge (60527) **(G-2654)**
Bannon Enterprises Inc.....847 529-9265
2627 Lorraine Cir Geneva (60134) **(G-10254)**
Bantix Technologies LLC.....630 446-0886
490 Pennsylvania Ave Glen Ellyn (60137) **(G-10396)**
Banyan Technologies Inc.....312 967-9885
1452 E 53rd St Fl 2 Chicago (60615) **(G-3826)**
Baps Investors Group LLC.....847 818-8444
3940 Industrial Ave Rolling Meadows (60008) **(G-17718)**
Baptist General Conference (PA).....800 323-4215
2002 S Arlington Hts Rd Arlington Heights (60005) **(G-703)**
Bar Code Dr Inc.....815 547-1001
4337 S Perryville Rd Cherry Valley (61016) **(G-3438)**
Bar Code Graphics Inc.....312 664-0700
65 E Wacker Pl Ste 1800 Chicago (60601) **(G-3827)**
Bar Codes Inc.....800 351-9962
200 W Monroe St Ste 2300 Chicago (60606) **(G-3828)**
Bar Processing Corporation.....708 757-4570
1601 Wentworth Ave Ste 33 Chicago Heights (60411) **(G-6733)**
Bar Stool Depotcom.....815 727-7294
816 Caton Ave Joliet (60435) **(G-11827)**

ALPHABETIC

Bar-B-Que Industries Inc 773 227-5400
4460 W Armitage Ave Chicago (60639) *(G-3829)*
Bar/Bri Group, Chicago *Also called West Publishing Corporation (G-6605)*
Barbecue Select Inc 773 847-0230
1421 W 47th St Chicago (60609) *(G-3830)*
Barbeque Select, Chicago *Also called New Specialty Products Inc (G-5579)*
Barber Steel Foundry Corp 231 894-1830
6400 Shafer Ct Ste 450 Rosemont (60018) *(G-18000)*
Barcar Manufacturing Inc 630 365-5200
1 N 081 Thryselius Dr Elburn (60119) *(G-8445)*
Barco Stamping Co (PA) 630 293-5155
1095 Carolina Dr West Chicago (60185) *(G-20549)*
Barcodesource Inc (PA) 630 545-9590
435 Pennsylvania Ave # 147 Glen Ellyn (60137) *(G-10397)*
Barcodesupplies.com, Glen Ellyn *Also called Barcodesource Inc (G-10397)*
Barcor Inc 847 940-0750
1413 Aitken Dr Bannockburn (60015) *(G-1192)*
Barcor Inc 847 831-2650
1510 Old Deerfield Rd # 206 Highland Park (60035) *(G-11254)*
Bard Brachytherapy Inc 630 933-7610
295 E Lies Rd Carol Stream (60188) *(G-2945)*
Bard Optical, Decatur *Also called J A K Enterprises Inc (G-7509)*
Bardash & Bukowski Inc 312 829-2080
329 W 18th St Ste 908 Chicago (60616) *(G-3831)*
Bards Products Inc (PA) 800 323-5499
1427 Armour Blvd Mundelein (60060) *(G-14665)*
Bare Development Inc 708 352-2273
5425 9th Ave Countryside (60525) *(G-7044)*
Bare Metals Inc 773 583-1100
3065 N Rockwell St Chicago (60618) *(G-3832)*
Barilla America Inc (HQ) 515 956-4400
885 Sunset Ridge Rd Northbrook (60062) *(G-15345)*
Bark Project Management Inc 630 964-5876
7017 Roberts Dr Woodridge (60517) *(G-21278)*
Barker Metalcraft Inc 773 588-9300
2955 N California Ave Chicago (60618) *(G-3833)*
Barks Publications Inc 312 321-9440
17 N State St Ste 1650 Chicago (60602) *(G-3834)*
Barnaby Complete Printing Svcs, Aurora *Also called Barnaby Inc (G-1061)*
Barnaby Inc 815 895-6555
1600 Mountain St Aurora (60505) *(G-1061)*
Barnant, Bartlett *Also called Thermo Fisher Scientific Inc (G-1316)*
Barnes & Noble College 309 677-2320
830 N Elmwood Ave Peoria (61606) *(G-16390)*
Barnes International Inc (PA) 815 964-8661
814 Chestnut St Rockford (61102) *(G-17312)*
Barnes Machine Shop LLC 217 774-5308
8 Boarman Dr Shelbyville (62565) *(G-18876)*
Barnett Bob Redi-Mix, Harrisburg *Also called Bob Barnett Redi-Mix Inc (G-11020)*
Barnett Redi-Mix Inc 618 276-4298
11300 Highway 1 Junction (62954) *(G-11948)*
Barneys Aluminum Specialties 815 723-5341
340 Ruby St Joliet (60435) *(G-11828)*
Barnstormer Distilleries 314 397-1100
6969 S Main St Rockford (61102) *(G-17313)*
Baron Manufacturing Co LLC 630 628-9110
730 Baker Dr Itasca (60143) *(G-11626)*
Baroque Silversmith Inc (PA) 312 357-2813
55 E Washington St # 302 Chicago (60602) *(G-3835)*
Barrel 312 754-0156
2015 S Damen Ave Ste A Chicago (60608) *(G-3836)*
Barrel Maker Printing 773 490-3065
3065 N Rockwell St Ste 8 Chicago (60618) *(G-3837)*
Barrett NJide Yvonne 312 701-3962
1011 W 18th St Chicago (60608) *(G-3838)*
Barrett Graphic Services, Sycamore *Also called Tel-Comm Incorporated (G-19734)*
Barriersafe Solutions Intl Inc 866 931-3613
150 N Field Dr Ste 210 Lake Forest (60045) *(G-12230)*
Barrington Automation Ltd 847 458-0900
9116 Virginia Rd Lake In The Hills (60156) *(G-12329)*
Barrington Cardinal Whse LLC 847 387-3676
340 W Northwest Hwy Barrington (60010) *(G-1213)*
Barrington Clinical Partners 847 508-9737
25377 N Wagon Wheel Ct Barrington (60010) *(G-1214)*
Barrington Company 815 933-3233
195 N Euclid Ave Bradley (60915) *(G-2276)*
Barrington Financial Services 847 404-1767
3 Sunvalley Ct Lake In The Hills (60156) *(G-12330)*
Barrington Packaging Systems 847 382-8063
835 Barrington Point Rd Barrington (60010) *(G-1215)*
Barrington Packg Systems Group, Barrington *Also called Barrington Packaging Systems (G-1215)*
Barron 2m Inc 847 219-3650
1031 S Braintree Dr Schaumburg (60193) *(G-18456)*
Barron Metal Finishing LLC 815 962-8053
2219 Kishwaukee St Rockford (61104) *(G-17314)*
Barry Callebaut USA LLC 312 496-7300
2144 Paysphere Cir Chicago (60610) *(G-3839)*
Barry Callebaut USA LLC (HQ) 312 496-7300
600 W Chicago Ave Ste 860 Chicago (60654) *(G-3840)*
Barry Callebaut USA LLC 312 496-7372
1401 W Main St Robinson (62454) *(G-17106)*
Barry Electric Div, Maywood *Also called National Cycle Inc (G-13674)*
Barry Signs Inc 773 327-1183
6950 W Imlay St Chicago (60631) *(G-3841)*
Barry-Whmller Cont Systems Inc (HQ) 630 759-6800
1305 Lakeview Dr Romeoville (60446) *(G-17798)*
Barsanti Woodwork Corporation 773 284-6888
3838 W 51st St Chicago (60632) *(G-3842)*
Bartec Orb Inc 773 927-8600
4724 S Christiana Ave Chicago (60632) *(G-3843)*
Bartech Precision Machining Co 630 243-9068
16135 New Ave Ste 3 Lemont (60439) *(G-12556)*
Bartell Corporation 847 854-3232
3671 Persimmon Dr Algonquin (60102) *(G-367)*
Bartesian Corp 847 302-4467
303 W Erie St Ste 320 Chicago (60654) *(G-3844)*
Barth Wind Elan Furs, Morton Grove *Also called Elan Furs (G-14404)*
Bartlett Farms, Dallas City *Also called Jack Bartlett (G-7314)*
Barton Manufacturing LLC (HQ) 217 428-0711
1395 S Taylorville Rd Decatur (62521) *(G-7462)*
Barton Manufacturing LLC 217 428-0726
600 E Wabash Ave Decatur (62523) *(G-7463)*
Barudan America Inc 815 227-1359
6191 Abington Dr Rockford (61109) *(G-17315)*
Base 2 Marketing and Supply 847 516-0012
720 Industrial Dr Ste 103 Cary (60013) *(G-3149)*
Base-Line II Inc 847 336-8403
2001 N Delany Rd Gurnee (60031) *(G-10862)*
Baseball Digest, Gurnee *Also called Grandstand Publishing LLC (G-10883)*
Baseline Graphics Inc 630 964-9566
5424 Webster St Downers Grove (60515) *(G-7958)*
Baseline Services Inc 618 678-2753
1360 Ironwood Rd Xenia (62899) *(G-21466)*
Basement Dewatering Systems 309 647-0331
3100 N Main St Canton (61520) *(G-2821)*
Basement Flood Protector Inc 847 438-6770
100 Oakwood Rd Ste F Lake Zurich (60047) *(G-12387)*
BASF Corporation 815 932-6751
2525 S Kensington Ave Kankakee (60901) *(G-11959)*
Basic Industries, Hecker *Also called Hottenrott Company Inc (G-11155)*
Basic Wire & Cable Co, Chicago *Also called Action Electric Sales Co Inc (G-3535)*
Basin Transports 618 829-3323
112 E 4th St Saint Elmo (62458) *(G-18305)*
Basnett Investments 618 842-4040
215 Se 3rd St Ste 208 Fairfield (62837) *(G-9619)*
Basnett, John, Fairfield *Also called Basnett Investments (G-9619)*
Basor Electric Inc (HQ) 618 476-6300
604 S Mulberry St Millstadt (62260) *(G-14043)*
Basor Electric Inc 618 476-6300
900 W Adams St Millstadt (62260) *(G-14044)*
Bass Brother Incorporated (PA) 800 252-1114
2720 S River Rd Ste 146 Des Plaines (60018) *(G-7736)*
Bass Company LLC 618 526-7211
8060 Old Us Highway 50 Breese (62230) *(G-2297)*
Bass-Mollett Publishers Inc 618 664-3141
507 Monroe St Greenville (62246) *(G-10826)*
Basswood Associates Inc (PA) 312 240-9400
1017 W Washington Blvd Chicago (60607) *(G-3845)*
Bat Business Services Inc 630 801-9335
987 Oak Ave Aurora (60506) *(G-1062)*
Batavia Bio Processing Limited 630 761-1180
970 Douglas Rd Batavia (60510) *(G-1354)*
Batavia Container Inc 630 879-2100
1400 Paramount Pkwy Batavia (60510) *(G-1355)*
Batavia Foundry and Machine Co 630 879-1319
717 First St Batavia (60510) *(G-1356)*
Batavia Instant Print 630 262-0370
33w480 Fabyan Pkwy # 104 West Chicago (60185) *(G-20550)*
Bathwraps 630 227-1737
401 S Gary Ave Unit A Roselle (60172) *(G-17939)*
Batteries Plus 287 ....630 279-3478
240 E Roosevelt Rd Villa Park (60181) *(G-20132)*
Battery Builders LLC 630 851-5800
31w238 91st St Naperville (60564) *(G-14961)*
Battery Sales Inc 708 489-6645
5545 Miller Circle Dr Matteson (60443) *(G-13619)*
Battery Systems LLC 833 487-6937
2135 City Gate Ln Ste 300 Naperville (60563) *(G-14777)*
Battle Balls Bubble Soccer, Chicago *Also called Peak Healthcare Advisors LLC (G-5775)*
Bauermeister Inc 901 363-0921
601 Corporate Woods Pkwy Vernon Hills (60061) *(G-20043)*
Bauhaus Zwick Co, Quincy *Also called West Zwick Corp (G-16955)*
Baum Holdings Inc 847 488-0650
506 Sundown Rd South Elgin (60177) *(G-19135)*
Baumer Financial Publishing, Chicago *Also called Imagination Publishing LLC (G-4894)*

Bavius Technologie Inc....847 844-3300
205 Prairie Lake Rd Ste B East Dundee (60118) *(G-8188)*
Baxalta Export Corporation....224 948-2000
1200 Lakeside Dr Bannockburn (60015) *(G-1193)*
Baxalta Incorporated (HQ)....224 940-2000
1200 Lakeside Dr Bannockburn (60015) *(G-1194)*
Baxalta US Inc....312 648-2244
135 S Lasalle St Ste 3425 Chicago (60603) *(G-3846)*
Baxalta US Inc....847 948-2000
25212 W Il Route 120 Round Lake (60073) *(G-18068)*
Baxalta World Trade LLC (HQ)....224 940-2000
1200 Lakeside Dr Bannockburn (60015) *(G-1195)*
Baxalta Worldwide LLC....224 948-2000
1 Baxter Pkwy Deerfield (60015) *(G-7590)*
Baxter Gene Therapy Unit, Round Lake *Also called Baxter Healthcare Corporation (G-18069)*
Baxter Global Holdings II Inc (HQ)....224 948-1812
1 Baxter Pkwy Deerfield (60015) *(G-7591)*
Baxter Healthcare Corporation....847 522-8600
400 Lakeview Pkwy Vernon Hills (60061) *(G-20044)*
Baxter Healthcare Corporation....800 422-9837
1 Baxter Pkwy Deerfield (60015) *(G-7592)*
Baxter Healthcare Corporation....847 270-4757
7621 Center Dr Wonder Lake (60097) *(G-21143)*
Baxter Healthcare Corporation....847 948-3206
1606 Beech St Spring Grove (60081) *(G-19267)*
Baxter Healthcare Corporation....847 270-5720
Wilson Rd Rr 120 Round Lake (60073) *(G-18069)*
Baxter Healthcare Corporation....847 948-4770
25212 W Il Route 120 Round Lake (60073) *(G-18070)*
Baxter Healthcare Corporation....224 270-6300
32360 N Wilson Rd Round Lake (60073) *(G-18071)*
Baxter Healthcare Corporation....847 367-2544
440 N Fairway Dr Vernon Hills (60061) *(G-20045)*
Baxter Healthcare Corporation....847 578-4671
2105 S Waukegan Rd Waukegan (60085) *(G-20422)*
Baxter Healthcare Corporation....847 948-2000
1435 Lake Cook Rd Deerfield (60015) *(G-7593)*
Baxter Healthcare Corporation....847 940-6599
25212 W Illinois Rte 120 Round Lake (60073) *(G-18072)*
Baxter Healthcare Corporation....847 948-2000
1 Baxter Pkwy Deerfield (60015) *(G-7594)*
Baxter International Inc (PA)....224 948-2000
1 Baxter Pkwy Df2-1w Deerfield (60015) *(G-7595)*
Baxter Vineyards....217 453-2528
2010 Parley St Nauvoo (62354) *(G-15013)*
Baxter World Trade Corporation (HQ)....224 948-2000
1 Baxter Pkwy Deerfield (60015) *(G-7596)*
Bay Plastics....847 299-2045
1245 E Forest Ave Ste 8 Des Plaines (60018) *(G-7737)*
Bay Valley Foods LLC....815 239-2631
215 W 3rd St Pecatonica (61063) *(G-16321)*
Bay Valley Foods LLC....773 927-7700
4401 W 44th Pl Chicago (60632) *(G-3847)*
Bayer Corporation....847 725-6320
25 Northwest Point Blvd # 560 Elk Grove Village (60007) *(G-8858)*
Bb Services LLC....630 941-8122
205 E Butterfield Rd Elmhurst (60126) *(G-9328)*
BBC, Wood Dale *Also called Boswell Building Contrs Inc (G-21171)*
BBC Fasteners Inc....708 597-9100
4210 W Shirley Ln Alsip (60803) *(G-421)*
BBC Innovation Corporation....847 458-2334
7900 S Illinois Rte 31 Crystal Lake (60014) *(G-7168)*
Bbq Smokewagon Inc....309 271-7002
245 Farmdale Rd East Peoria (61611) *(G-8252)*
Bbs Automation Chicago Inc....630 351-3000
1580 Hecht Ct Bartlett (60103) *(G-1268)*
Bc Asi Capital II Inc....708 534-5575
200 Applied Pkwy University Park (60484) *(G-19948)*
Bc Enterprises....618 655-0784
99 Shore Dr Sw Edwardsville (62025) *(G-8348)*
Bc International....847 674-7384
4909 Old Orchard Ctr Skokie (60077) *(G-18928)*
Bc Machine....815 962-7884
1704 16th Ave Rockford (61104) *(G-17316)*
Bc Welding Inc....708 258-0076
308 E Crawford St Peotone (60468) *(G-16550)*
Bc Welding Service and Repair, Peotone *Also called Bc Welding Inc (G-16550)*
Bcbg, Northbrook *Also called Runway Liquidation LLC (G-15476)*
Bce-USA LLC....815 556-8037
3500 Martens St Franklin Park (60131) *(G-9884)*
BCI Acrylic Inc....847 963-8827
1800 Industrial Dr Libertyville (60048) *(G-12636)*
Bcr Elevators Incorporated....219 689-5951
20608 S Driftwood Dr Frankfort (60423) *(G-9770)*
Bcs Industries, Chicago *Also called Charles N Benner Inc (G-4075)*
Bdna Corporation....650 625-9530
300 Park Blvd Ste 500 Itasca (60143) *(G-11627)*
Be Group Inc....312 436-0301
4850 S Lake Park Ave # 1906 Chicago (60615) *(G-3848)*
Be McGonagle Inc....847 394-0413
858 S Arthur Ave Arlington Heights (60005) *(G-704)*
Be Products Inc....312 201-9669
180 W Washington St Fl 10 Chicago (60602) *(G-3849)*
Be Something Studio, Melrose Park *Also called Zagone Studios LLC (G-13932)*
Bea Electro Sales Inc....847 238-1420
1400 Howard St Elk Grove Village (60007) *(G-8859)*
Bea's Best, Chicago *Also called City Foods Inc (G-4155)*
Beachwaver Co....201 751-5625
850 Technology Way Libertyville (60048) *(G-12637)*
Beacon Annuity Solutions LLC....847 864-5447
790 W Frontage Rd Ste 335 Northfield (60093) *(G-15507)*
Beacon Fas & Components Inc....847 541-0404
198 Carpenter Ave Wheeling (60090) *(G-20857)*
Beacon Inc....708 544-9900
12223 S Laramie Ave Alsip (60803) *(G-422)*
Beacon Solutions Inc....303 513-0469
111 E Wacker Dr Ste 3000 Chicago (60601) *(G-3850)*
Beacon Terminal Pin, Wheeling *Also called Beacon Fas & Components Inc (G-20857)*
Beall Manufacturing Inc (PA)....618 307-9589
420 N Main St Edwardsville (62025) *(G-8349)*
Beam Global Spirits & Wine LLC (HQ)....847 948-8888
222 Merchandise Mart Plz # 1600 Chicago (60654) *(G-3851)*
Beam Suntory, Chicago *Also called Beam Global Spirits & Wine LLC (G-3851)*
Beam Suntory Inc (HQ)....312 964-6999
222 Merchandise Mart Plz # 1600 Chicago (60654) *(G-3852)*
Bean and Body, Chicago *Also called Fast Forward Energy Inc (G-4562)*
Bean Products Inc....312 666-3600
1500 S Western Ave Ste 40 Chicago (60608) *(G-3853)*
Beans Printing Inc....217 223-5555
3710 Broadway St Quincy (62305) *(G-16861)*
Bear Creek Truss Inc....217 543-3329
615 N County Road 250 E Tuscola (61953) *(G-19923)*
Bear Machine Tool & Die Inc....815 932-4204
928 E Broadway St Bradley (60915) *(G-2277)*
Bear Mtal Wldg Fabrication Inc....630 261-9353
111 W Home Ave Villa Park (60181) *(G-20133)*
Bear-Stewart Corporation (PA)....773 276-0400
1025 N Damen Ave Chicago (60622) *(G-3854)*
Beardsley Printery Inc....309 788-4041
1103 51st Ave Rock Island (61201) *(G-17203)*
Beardstown Newspapers Inc....217 323-1010
1210 Wall St Beardstown (62618) *(G-1445)*
Beardstown Tube Plant, Beardstown *Also called Caraustar Industrial and Con (G-1446)*
Bearing Division, Sterling *Also called Frantz Manufacturing Company (G-19510)*
Bearing Headquarters Co, Elk Grove Village *Also called Headco Industries Inc (G-9031)*
Bearing Headquarters Co, Joliet *Also called Headco Industries Inc (G-11875)*
Bearing Sales Corporation....773 282-8686
4153 N Kostner Ave Chicago (60641) *(G-3855)*
Bearings Manufacturing Company....773 583-6703
1033 N Kolmar Ave Chicago (60651) *(G-3856)*
Bearmoon LLC....815 312-2327
508 S 7th St Oregon (61061) *(G-15912)*
Bearning Sales, Chicago *Also called Isostatic Industries Inc (G-4973)*
Bearse Manufacturing Co....773 235-8710
3815 W Cortland St Chicago (60647) *(G-3857)*
Bearse USA, Chicago *Also called Bearse Manufacturing Co (G-3857)*
Beastgrip Co....312 283-5283
1269 Rand Rd Des Plaines (60016) *(G-7738)*
Beastman Tea LLC....636 362-4594
3815 Sequoia Dr Edwardsville (62025) *(G-8350)*
Beau-Brehm L Ranches, Mount Vernon *Also called Brehm Oil Inc (G-14600)*
Beauticontrol....217 223-0382
1702 Locust St Quincy (62301) *(G-16862)*
Beautiful Displays, Carbondale *Also called Noteworthy Group Inc (G-2851)*
Beaver Creek Enterprises Inc (PA)....815 723-9455
801 Rowell Ave Joliet (60433) *(G-11829)*
Beaver Creek Golf Carts, Joliet *Also called Beaver Creek Enterprises Inc (G-11829)*
Bechara Sim....847 913-9950
121 Willow Pkwy Buffalo Grove (60089) *(G-2514)*
Becker Brothers Graphite Corp....708 410-0700
39 Legion St Maywood (60153) *(G-13662)*
Becker Jules D Wood Products....847 526-8002
25250 W Old Rand Rd Wauconda (60084) *(G-20334)*
Becker Specialty Corporation (HQ)....847 766-3555
2526 Delta Ln Elk Grove Village (60007) *(G-8860)*
Beckman Coulter Inc....800 526-3821
1500 N Mittel Blvd Wood Dale (60191) *(G-21167)*
Becks Light Gauge Aluminum Co....847 290-9990
1425 Tonne Rd Elk Grove Village (60007) *(G-8861)*
Becks Medical & Indus Gases....618 273-9019
1411 Locust St Eldorado (62930) *(G-8479)*
Becsis LLC....630 400-6454
2197 Brookwood Dr South Elgin (60177) *(G-19136)*
Becton Dickinson and Company....630 743-2006
1400 Opus Pl Ste 805 Downers Grove (60515) *(G-7959)*
Bedding Group Inc (PA)....309 788-0401
2350 5th St Rock Island (61201) *(G-17204)*

ALPHABETIC

Bedding Group, The, Rock Island *Also called Bedding Group Inc* ***(G-17204)***
Bedford Rakim....773 749-3086
3022 Bernice Ave Apt 3s Lansing (60438) ***(G-12485)***
Bedford Rakim....773 759-3947
17125 Evans Dr South Holland (60473) ***(G-19199)***
Bee Boat Co Inc....217 379-2605
209 E Green St Paxton (60957) ***(G-16307)***
Bee Clean Specialties LLC....847 451-0844
550 Albion Ave Ste 50 Schaumburg (60193) ***(G-18457)***
Bee Designs Embroidery & Scree....815 393-4593
20733 E Welty Rd Esmond (60129) ***(G-9475)***
Bee Line Service Inc....815 233-1812
2291 Us Highway 20 E Freeport (61032) ***(G-10102)***
Bee Sales Company (PA)....847 600-4400
6330 W Touhy Ave Niles (60714) ***(G-15106)***
Bee-Jay Industries Inc....708 867-4431
148 Paxton Rd Bloomingdale (60108) ***(G-1979)***
Beechner Heat Treating Co Inc....815 397-4314
905 Brooke Rd Rockford (61109) ***(G-17317)***
Beecken Petty Okeefe & Co LLC (PA)....312 435-0300
131 S Dearborn St Ste 122 Chicago (60603) ***(G-3858)***
Beelman Ready-Mix Inc....618 357-6120
5780 State Route 154 Pinckneyville (62274) ***(G-16611)***
Beelman Ready-Mix Inc....618 478-2044
17558 Mockingbird Rd Nashville (62263) ***(G-14995)***
Beelman Ready-Mix Inc....618 526-0260
8200 Old Us Highway 50 Breese (62230) ***(G-2298)***
Beelman Ready-Mix Inc (PA)....618 646-5300
1 Racehorse Dr East Saint Louis (62205) ***(G-8299)***
Beelman Ready-Mix Inc....618 244-9600
13425 N Shiloh Dr Mount Vernon (62864) ***(G-14598)***
Beelman Ready-Mix Inc....618 247-3866
100 Cemetery Rd Sandoval (62882) ***(G-18362)***
Beelman Slag Sales....618 452-8120
2000 Edwardsville Rd Madison (62060) ***(G-13405)***
Beeman & Sons Inc....217 232-4268
5815 E Snake Trail Rd Martinsville (62442) ***(G-13581)***
Beesing Welding & Eqp Repr....815 732-7552
2506 S Il Route 2 Oregon (61061) ***(G-15913)***
Befco Manufactoring Co., Oak Lawn *Also called G & F Manufacturing Co Inc* ***(G-15716)***
Befco Manufacturing Co Inc....708 424-4170
5555 W 109th St Oak Lawn (60453) ***(G-15702)***
Begel Industries, Chicago *Also called Tmb Industries Inc* ***(G-6382)***
Begoun Inc....630 617-0200
655 W Grand Ave Ste 200 Elmhurst (60126) ***(G-9329)***
Beh IL Corp (PA)....630 616-1850
15 Salt Creek Ln Ste 412 Hinsdale (60521) ***(G-11363)***
Beh IL Sub LLC (HQ)....630 616-1850
15 Salt Creek Ln Ste 412 Hinsdale (60521) ***(G-11364)***
Behabelt USA....630 521-9835
2300 W Windsor Ct Ste D Addison (60101) ***(G-46)***
Behr Process Corporation....630 289-6247
950 S Il Route 59 Bartlett (60103) ***(G-1269)***
Behr Process Corporation....708 753-0136
21701 Mark Collins Dr # 200 Chicago Heights (60411) ***(G-6734)***
Behr Process Corporation....708 753-1820
21399 Torrence Ave Ste 1 Lynwood (60411) ***(G-13292)***
Behr Process Corporation....708 757-6350
270 State St Ste 1 Chicago Heights (60411) ***(G-6735)***
BEI Electronics LLC (HQ)....217 224-9600
4100 N 24th St Quincy (62305) ***(G-16863)***
BEI Holding Corporation....217 224-9600
4100 N 24th St Quincy (62305) ***(G-16864)***
Beijing Jingdiao Group, Mount Prospect *Also called Jingdiao North America Inc* ***(G-14540)***
Bel Americas Inc....646 454-8220
30 S Wacker Dr Ste 3000 Chicago (60606) ***(G-3859)***
Bel Brands Usa Inc (PA)....312 462-1500
30 S Wacker Dr Ste 3000 Chicago (60606) ***(G-3860)***
Bel Mar Wire Products Inc....773 342-3800
2343 N Damen Ave Chicago (60647) ***(G-3861)***
Bel-Air Manufacturing Inc....773 276-7550
3525 W Potomac Ave Chicago (60651) ***(G-3862)***
Belair Hd Studios LLC....312 254-5188
2233 S Throop St Chicago (60608) ***(G-3863)***
Belboz Corp....708 856-6099
742 Evans Ct Dolton (60419) ***(G-7933)***
Belcar Products Inc....630 462-1950
500 Randy Rd Ste B Carol Stream (60188) ***(G-2946)***
Belden Energy Solutions Inc....800 235-3361
719 S Berkley Ave Elmhurst (60126) ***(G-9330)***
Belden Enterprises LP....618 829-3274
801 N Elm St Saint Elmo (62458) ***(G-18306)***
Belden Machine Corporation....708 344-4600
2500 Braga Dr Broadview (60155) ***(G-2419)***
Belden Tools Inc....708 344-4600
4100 Madison St Hillside (60162) ***(G-11329)***
Belden Universal, Hillside *Also called Belden Tools Inc* ***(G-11329)***
Belford Electronics Inc....630 705-3020
1460 W Jeffrey Dr Addison (60101) ***(G-47)***
Belgian Chocolatier Piron Inc....847 864-5504
509 Main St Fl A Evanston (60202) ***(G-9498)***
Bell & Gossett, Morton Grove *Also called Fluid Handling LLC* ***(G-14408)***
Bell Aromatics, Northbrook *Also called Bell Flavors & Fragrances Inc* ***(G-15346)***
Bell Brothers....618 544-2157
201 N Jefferson St Robinson (62454) ***(G-17107)***
Bell Cabinet & Millwork Co....708 425-1200
10542 S Michael Dr Palos Hills (60465) ***(G-16196)***
Bell Flavors & Fragrances Inc (PA)....847 291-8300
500 Academy Dr Northbrook (60062) ***(G-15346)***
Bell Flavors & Fragrances Inc....847 291-8300
501 Lindberg Ln Northbrook (60062) ***(G-15347)***
Bell Litho Inc (PA)....847 952-3300
370 Crossen Ave Elk Grove Village (60007) ***(G-8862)***
Bell Litho Inc....847 290-9300
1820 Lunt Ave Elk Grove Village (60007) ***(G-8863)***
Bell Racing Co, Champaign *Also called Bell Racing Usa LLC* ***(G-3271)***
Bell Racing Usa LLC....217 239-5355
301 Mercury Dr Ste 8 Champaign (61822) ***(G-3271)***
Bell Sports Inc....217 893-9300
1001 Innovation Rd Rantoul (61866) ***(G-16968)***
Bella Architectural Products....708 339-4782
16910 Lathrop Ave Harvey (60426) ***(G-11078)***
Bella Cabinet, Bridgeview *Also called Eddie Gapastione* ***(G-2344)***
Bella Casa....630 455-5900
322 N Adams St Hinsdale (60521) ***(G-11365)***
Bella Pharmaceuticals Inc....847 722-1692
4301 Regency Dr Glenview (60025) ***(G-10529)***
Bella Salon, Lake Forest *Also called Cindys Nail & Hair Care* ***(G-12237)***
Bella Sign Co....630 539-0343
9 Presidential Dr Roselle (60172) ***(G-17940)***
Bella T Winery, Creal Springs *Also called Bella Terra Winery LLC* ***(G-7080)***
Bella Terra Winery LLC....618 658-8882
755 Parker City Rd Creal Springs (62922) ***(G-7080)***
Belle Aire Creations, Mundelein *Also called Belle-Aire Fragrances Inc* ***(G-14666)***
Belle-Aire Fragrances Inc (PA)....847 816-3500
1600 Baskin Rd Mundelein (60060) ***(G-14666)***
Bellen Container Corporation....847 741-5600
1460 Bowes Rd Elgin (60123) ***(G-8520)***
Belleville Automotive, Belleville *Also called L M C Automotive Inc* ***(G-1567)***
Belleville News Democrat, Belleville *Also called McClatchy Newspapers Inc* ***(G-1574)***
Belleville News Democrat....618 239-2552
120 S Illinois St Belleville (62220) ***(G-1533)***
Belleville News Democrat, The, Belleville *Also called Belleville News Democrat* ***(G-1533)***
Bellinis Custom Welding and A....815 284-4175
1577 Eldena Rd Dixon (61021) ***(G-7889)***
Bellisario Holdings LLC....847 867-2960
117 Elmore St Park Ridge (60068) ***(G-16270)***
Bellman-Melcor Holdings Inc....708 532-5000
7575 183rd St Tinley Park (60477) ***(G-19807)***
Bellota Agrsltions Tls USA LLC....309 787-2491
4415 85th Ave W Rock Island (61201) ***(G-17205)***
Bellows Shoppe....847 446-5533
1048 Gage St Ste 301 Winnetka (60093) ***(G-21126)***
Bellwood Electric Motors Inc....708 544-7223
200 25th Ave Bellwood (60104) ***(G-1615)***
Bellwood Industries Inc (PA)....773 522-1002
4351 W Roosevelt Rd Chicago (60624) ***(G-3864)***
Belmont Plating Works Inc (PA)....847 678-0200
9145 King St Franklin Park (60131) ***(G-9885)***
Belmont Sausage Company....847 357-1515
2201 Estes Ave Elk Grove Village (60007) ***(G-8864)***
Belmonte Printing Co....847 352-8841
525 W Wise Rd Ste D Schaumburg (60193) ***(G-18458)***
Beloit Pattern Works....815 389-2578
819 Ingersoll Pl South Beloit (61080) ***(G-19083)***
Beloit Tool Inc (PA)....815 389-2300
215 Elmwood Ave South Beloit (61080) ***(G-19084)***
Belrock Printing Inc....815 547-1096
915 W Perry St Belvidere (61008) ***(G-1652)***
Belson Outdoors LLC....630 897-8489
627 Amersale Dr Naperville (60563) ***(G-14778)***
Belson Steel Center Scrap Inc....815 932-7416
1685 N State Route 50 Bourbonnais (60914) ***(G-2256)***
Belt-Way Scales Inc....815 625-5573
1 Beltway Rd Rock Falls (61071) ***(G-17176)***
Beltone Corporation (HQ)....847 832-3300
2601 Patriot Blvd Glenview (60026) ***(G-10530)***
Beltoutlet.com, Bolingbrook *Also called Phoenix Leather Goods LLC* ***(G-2227)***
Belvedere Usa LLC (PA)....815 544-3131
1 Belvedere Blvd Belvidere (61008) ***(G-1653)***
Belvidere Brose Inc....779 552-7600
725 Logistics Dr Belvidere (61008) ***(G-1654)***
Belvidere Daily Republican Co....815 547-0084
130 S State St Ste 101 Belvidere (61008) ***(G-1655)***
Belvin J & F Sheet Metal Co....312 666-5222
675 N Milwaukee Ave Chicago (60642) ***(G-3865)***
Belzona Gateway Inc....888 774-2984
8124 Bunkum Rd Caseyville (62232) ***(G-3210)***

Bem Cnc, Schaumburg Also called Bem Mold Inc (G-18459)
Bem Mold Inc 847 805-9750
410 Remington Rd Schaumburg (60173) (G-18459)
Bem Wireless LLC 815 337-0541
1325 Remington Rd Ste H Schaumburg (60173) (G-18460)
Bema Inc 630 279-7800
744 N Oaklawn Ave Elmhurst (60126) (G-9331)
Bemis Hydraulics, Galesburg Also called Midwest Hydra-Line Inc (G-10211)
Benchmarc Display Incorporated (PA) 847 541-2828
1001 Woodlands Pkwy Vernon Hills (60061) (G-20046)
Benchmark Cabinets & Mllwk Inc 309 697-5855
5913 W Plank Rd Peoria (61604) (G-16391)
Benchmark Electronics Inc 309 822-8587
388 Riverview Blf Metamora (61548) (G-13959)
Benchmark Properties Ltd 618 395-7023
5076 N Il 130 Olney (62450) (G-15855)
Benda Manufacturing Inc 708 633-4600
18504 West Creek Dr Ste B Tinley Park (60477) (G-19808)
Bende Inc 847 913-0304
925 Corporate Woods Pkwy Vernon Hills (60061) (G-20047)
Bender Mat Fctry Fton Slepshop (PA) 217 328-1700
1206 N Cunningham Ave A Urbana (61802) (G-19973)
Benders Mat Fctry Sleep Shoppe, Urbana Also called Bender Mat Fctry Fton Slepshop (G-19973)
Bending Specialists LLC 815 726-6281
3051 S State St Lockport (60441) (G-12983)
Bendinger Bruce Crtve Comm In 773 871-1179
2144 N Hudson Ave Ste 1 Chicago (60614) (G-3866)
Bendplex Compand 630 797-5808
36w610 Marguerite St A Saint Charles (60174) (G-18154)
Bendsen Signs & Graphics Inc 217 877-2345
1506 E Mcbride Ave Decatur (62526) (G-7464)
Beneficial Reuse MGT LLC (PA) 312 784-0300
372 W Ontario St Ste 501 Chicago (60654) (G-3867)
Benessere Vineyard Inc (PA) 708 560-9840
2100 Clearwater Dr # 250 Oak Brook (60523) (G-15596)
Benestar Brands LLC (PA) 773 254-7400
4118 S Halsted St Chicago (60609) (G-3868)
Benetech Inc 630 806-7888
1851 Albright Rd Montgomery (60538) (G-14232)
Benetech Inc (HQ) 630 844-1300
2245 Sequoia Dr Ste 300 Aurora (60506) (G-1063)
Benetech (taiwan) LLC (HQ) 630 844-1300
2245 Sequoia Dr Ste 300 Aurora (60506) (G-1064)
Benko Lamps Ltd 708 458-7965
7400 S Harlem Ave Bridgeview (60455) (G-2328)
Benko Manufacturing Co, Bridgeview Also called Benko Lamps Ltd (G-2328)
Bennett Industries, Peotone Also called North America Packaging Corp (G-16555)
Bennett Metal Products Inc 618 244-1911
700 Rackaway St Mount Vernon (62864) (G-14599)
Bennett Technologies Inc 708 389-9501
17049 Harlem Ave Tinley Park (60477) (G-19809)
Bennu Group Inc 708 331-0025
16140 Vincennes Ave South Holland (60473) (G-19200)
Beno J Gundlach Company 618 233-1781
211 N 21st St Belleville (62226) (G-1534)
Bensenville Screw Products 630 860-5222
796 County Line Rd Bensenville (60106) (G-1752)
Bent River Brewing Co (PA) 309 797-2722
1413 5th Ave Moline (61265) (G-14133)
Bentleys Pet Stuff LLC 847 793-0500
4196 Illinois Rte 83 Long Grove (60047) (G-13157)
Bentleys Pet Stuff LLC 773 857-7600
3657 N Suthport Ave Ste 1 Chicago (60613) (G-3869)
Benton Evening News Co 618 438-5611
111 E Church St Benton (62812) (G-1919)
Benton Gazette 618 438-6397
104 W Main St Benton (62812) (G-1920)
Bentronics, Bensenville Also called General Electro Corporation (G-1810)
Benzinger Printing 815 784-6560
673 Park Ave Ste 1 Genoa (60135) (G-10315)
Berens Inc 815 932-0913
1650 E Sheridan St Kankakee (60901) (G-11960)
Berens Inc 815 935-3237
1269 E 5000s Rd Saint Anne (60964) (G-18132)
Berg Industries Inc 815 874-1588
3455 S Mulford Rd Rockford (61109) (G-17318)
Berge Plating Works Inc (PA) 309 788-2831
617 25th Ave Rock Island (61201) (G-17206)
Bergeron Group Inc 815 741-1635
99 Republic Ave Joliet (60435) (G-11830)
Berghaus Pipe Organ Builders 708 544-4052
2151 Madison St Ste 1 Bellwood (60104) (G-1616)
Bergmann Orthotic Lab Inc 847 446-3616
1730 Holder Ln Northfield (60093) (G-15508)
Bergmann Orthotic Laboratory 847 729-7923
1864 Johns Dr Glenview (60025) (G-10531)
Bergst Engineering, Addison Also called Bergst Special Tools Inc (G-48)

Bergst Special Tools Inc 630 543-1020
723 W Annoreno Dr Addison (60101) (G-48)
Bergstrom Climate Systems LLC (HQ) 815 874-7821
2390 Blackhawk Rd Rockford (61109) (G-17319)
Bergstrom Elctrfied Systems LL 815 874-7821
2390 Blackhawk Rd Rockford (61109) (G-17320)
Bergstrom Inc (PA) 815 874-7821
2390 Blackhawk Rd Rockford (61109) (G-17321)
Bergstrom Inc 815 874-7821
5910 Falcon Rd Rockford (61109) (G-17322)
Bergstrom Inc 847 394-4013
4060 Mound Rd Joliet (60436) (G-11831)
Bergstrom Parts LLC 815 874-7821
5910 Falcon Rd Rockford (61109) (G-17323)
Berland Communications, Bannockburn Also called Berland Printing Inc (G-1196)
Berland Printing Inc 773 702-1999
2801 Lakeside Dr Ste 110 Bannockburn (60015) (G-1196)
Bernard C Turner, Chicago Also called Highlight of Chicago Bress (G-4818)
Bernard Cffey Vtrans Fundation 630 687-0033
1634 Mulligan Dr Naperville (60563) (G-14779)
Bernard Food Industries Inc (PA) 847 869-5222
1125 Hartrey Ave Evanston (60202) (G-9499)
Berner Food & Beverage LLC (PA) 815 563-4222
2034 E Factory Rd Dakota (61018) (G-7311)
Berner Food & Beverage LLC 815 865-5136
10010 N Rock City Rd Rock City (61070) (G-17174)
Berner Foods, Dakota Also called Berner Food & Beverage LLC (G-7311)
Bernhard Woodwork Ltd 847 291-1040
3670 Woodhead Dr Northbrook (60062) (G-15348)
Berny Metal Products Inc 847 742-8500
655 Sundown Rd South Elgin (60177) (G-19137)
Berridge Manufacturing Company 630 231-7495
1175 Carolina Dr West Chicago (60185) (G-20551)
Berry Global Inc 815 334-5225
1008 Courtaulds Dr Woodstock (60098) (G-21363)
Berry Global Inc 847 884-1200
1228 Tower Rd Schaumburg (60173) (G-18461)
Berry Global Inc 847 541-7900
800 Corporate Grove Dr Buffalo Grove (60089) (G-2515)
Berry Global Inc 630 375-0358
999 Bilter Rd Aurora (60502) (G-923)
Berry Global Inc 630 896-6200
921 Industrial Dr Aurora (60506) (G-1065)
Berry Global Films LLC 708 239-4619
12900 S Pulaski Rd Alsip (60803) (G-423)
Bertco Enterprises Inc 618 234-9283
108 N Jackson St Belleville (62220) (G-1535)
Bertsche Engineering Corp 847 537-8757
711 Dartmouth Ln Buffalo Grove (60089) (G-2516)
Bes Designs & Associates Inc (PA) 217 443-4619
2412 Georgetown Rd Danville (61832) (G-7323)
Besam Entrance Solutions, Elk Grove Village Also called Assa Abloy Entrance Systems US (G-8843)
Besco Awards & Embroidery 847 395-4862
43085 N Crawford Rd Antioch (60002) (G-603)
Besco Marketing, Antioch Also called Besco Awards & Embroidery (G-603)
Beslow Associates Inc 847 559-2703
633 Skokie Blvd Ste 200 Northbrook (60062) (G-15349)
Besly Cutting Tools Inc 815 389-2231
16200 Woodmint Ln South Beloit (61080) (G-19085)
Bessco Tube Bending Pipe Fabg 708 339-3977
16000 Van Drunen Rd South Holland (60473) (G-19201)
Bessler Welding Inc 309 699-6224
5313 N Main St East Peoria (61611) (G-8253)
Best Advertising Spc & Prtg 708 448-1110
11437 S Natoma Ave Worth (60482) (G-21455)
Best Air, Hampshire Also called RPS Products Inc (G-10986)
Best Brake Die Inc 708 388-1896
13434 Kolmar Ave Crestwood (60418) (G-7107)
Best Bus Sales, Des Plaines Also called Zimmerman Enterprises Inc (G-7871)
Best Chicago Meat Company LLC 773 523-8161
4649 W Armitage Ave Chicago (60639) (G-3870)
Best Cutting Die Co (PA) 847 675-5522
8080 Mccormick Blvd Skokie (60076) (G-18929)
Best Designs Inc 618 985-4445
11521 Kevin Ln Carterville (62918) (G-3129)
Best Diamond Plastics LLC 773 336-3485
1401 E 98th St Chicago (60628) (G-3871)
Best Display Systems, Galva Also called John H Best & Sons Inc (G-10234)
Best Foods Baking Group, Summit Argo Also called Ach Food Companies Inc (G-19676)
Best In Printing Inc 630 833-7366
114 N Walnut St Elmhurst (60126) (G-9332)
Best Metal Corporation 815 337-0420
925 Dieckman St Woodstock (60098) (G-21364)
Best Metal Extrusions Inc 847 981-0797
1900 E Devon Ave Elk Grove Village (60007) (G-8865)
Best Neon Sign Co 773 586-2700
6025 S New England Ave Chicago (60638) (G-3872)

Best Newspapers In Ill Inc ...217 728-7381
100 W Monroe St Sullivan (61951) ***(G-19661)***
Best Pallet Company LLC ...815 637-1500
1110 Widsor Rd Loves Park (61111) ***(G-13194)***
Best Pallet Company LLC (PA) ...312 242-4009
166 W Washington St # 300 Chicago (60602) ***(G-3873)***
Best Rep Company Corporation ...847 451-6644
9224 Grand Ave Ste 2 Franklin Park (60131) ***(G-9886)***
Best Technology Systems Inc ...815 254-9554
12024 S Aero Dr Plainfield (60585) ***(G-16644)***
Best Veneer Company LLC ...630 541-8312
16w273 83rd St Ste A Burr Ridge (60527) ***(G-2655)***
Best Way Carpet & Uphl Clg ...618 544-8585
1401 N Johnson St Robinson (62454) ***(G-17108)***
Best-Tronics Mfg Inc ...708 802-9677
18500 Graphic Ct Tinley Park (60477) ***(G-19810)***
Bestair Pro ...847 683-3400
281 Keyes Ave Hampshire (60140) ***(G-10964)***
Bestairpro, Hampshire *Also called Bestair Pro* ***(G-10964)***
Bestar Technologies Inc ...847 261-2850
761 N 17th St Ste 4 Saint Charles (60174) ***(G-18155)***
Bestmetal, A Division of PSM, Woodstock *Also called PSM Industries Inc* ***(G-21425)***
Bestproto Inc ...224 387-3280
1627 Louise Dr South Elgin (60177) ***(G-19138)***
Bestpysanky Inc ...877 797-2659
6212 Madison Ct Morton Grove (60053) ***(G-14391)***
Bestwords Org Corp ...618 939-4324
8934 Trolley Rd Columbia (62236) ***(G-6985)***
Beta Pak Inc ...708 466-7844
1600 Beta Dr Sugar Grove (60554) ***(G-19638)***
Bethany Pharmacol Co Inc ...217 665-3395
131 Hwy 121 E Bethany (61914) ***(G-1967)***
Bets, Chicago *Also called Bishops Engrv & Trophy Svc Inc* ***(G-3901)***
Bettendorf Stanford Inc ...618 548-3555
1370 W Main St Salem (62881) ***(G-18331)***
Better Built Buildings ...217 267-7824
604 E Kelly Ave Westville (61883) ***(G-20778)***
Better Earth LLC (PA) ...844 243-6333
2444 W 16th St Ste 4r Chicago (60608) ***(G-3874)***
Better Earth Premium Compost ...309 697-0963
1400 S Cameron Ln Peoria (61607) ***(G-16392)***
Better Gaskets Inc ...847 276-7635
26218 W Ingleside Ave Ingleside (60041) ***(G-11579)***
Better Gaskets Sealing Systems, Ingleside *Also called Better Gaskets Inc* ***(G-11579)***
Better Mens Wear, Chicago *Also called BMW Sportswear Inc* ***(G-3921)***
Better News Papers Inc (PA) ...618 566-8282
314 E Church St Ste 1 Mascoutah (62258) ***(G-13593)***
Better News Papers Inc ...618 483-6176
118 N Main St Altamont (62411) ***(G-531)***
Betty Watters ...618 232-1150
Rr 1 Box 27 Hamburg (62045) ***(G-10948)***
Beutel Corporation (PA) ...309 786-8134
1800 11th St Rock Island (61201) ***(G-17207)***
Bev Art HM Brewing Winemaking, Chicago *Also called Beverage Art Inc* ***(G-3875)***
Bevel Granite, Indian Head Park *Also called Rogan Granitindustrie Inc* ***(G-11577)***
Bevel Granite Company Inc ...708 371-4191
6544 Pontiac Dr Indian Head Park (60525) ***(G-11576)***
Beverage Art Inc ...773 881-9463
9030 S Hermitage Ave Chicago (60620) ***(G-3875)***
Beverage Flavors Intl LLC ...773 248-3860
3150 N Campbell Ave Chicago (60618) ***(G-3876)***
Beverage-Air, A Div of, Rockton *Also called Taylor Coml Foodservice Inc* ***(G-17703)***
Beverly Fndry Prcsion McHining, Lansing *Also called American Cast Products Inc* ***(G-12484)***
Beverly Materials, Hoffman Estates *Also called Plote Construction Inc* ***(G-11444)***
Beverly Materials LLC ...847 695-9300
1100 Brandt Dr Hoffman Estates (60192) ***(G-11407)***
Beverly Review, Chicago *Also called T R Communications Inc* ***(G-6307)***
Beverly Shear Mfg Corporation ...773 233-2063
3004 W 111th St Ste 1a Chicago (60655) ***(G-3877)***
Bevolution Group, Chicago *Also called Lx/Jt Intermediate Holdings* ***(G-5291)***
Bevolution Group, Chicago *Also called Juice Tyme Inc* ***(G-5058)***
Bevstream Corp ...630 761-0060
600 Kingsland Dr Batavia (60510) ***(G-1357)***
Bevwrap LLC ...773 580-5434
420 Bonnie Ln Elk Grove Village (60007) ***(G-8866)***
Beyond Components West Inc ...847 465-0480
505 Chaddick Dr Wheeling (60090) ***(G-20858)***
Beyond Limits Media Group LLC ...773 948-9296
9930 S Bensley Ave Chicago (60617) ***(G-3878)***
Bezarr ...651 200-5641
10s515 Ivy Ln Willowbrook (60527) ***(G-21031)***
Bfafv, Benton *Also called Bio Fuels By American Farmers* ***(G-1921)***
Bfc Forms Service Inc ...630 879-9240
1051 N Kirk Rd Batavia (60510) ***(G-1358)***
Bfc Print ...630 879-9240
1051 N Kirk Rd Batavia (60510) ***(G-1359)***
BFI Waste Systems N Amer Inc ...847 429-7370
1330 Gasket Dr Elgin (60120) ***(G-8521)***
Bfw Coating ...847 639-2155
740 Industrial Dr Ste G Cary (60013) ***(G-3150)***
Bg Die Mold Inc ...847 961-5861
11520 Smith Dr Huntley (60142) ***(G-11529)***
Bh Sports, Chicago *Also called Bhs Media LLC* ***(G-3879)***
Bhs Media LLC ...312 701-0000
29 E Madison St Ste 809 Chicago (60602) ***(G-3879)***
Bi Protec, Dekalb *Also called Armoloy of Illinois Inc* ***(G-7666)***
Bi Software Inc ...224 622-4706
808 Linden Cir Hoffman Estates (60169) ***(G-11408)***
Bi State Steel Co ...309 755-0668
503 7th St East Moline (61244) ***(G-8223)***
Bi-Link Metal Specialties Inc (PA) ...630 858-5900
125 Fairfield Way Ste 310 Bloomingdale (60108) ***(G-1980)***
Bi-Petro Inc (PA) ...217 535-0181
3150 Executive Park Dr Springfield (62703) ***(G-19325)***
Bi-Phase Technologies LLC ...952 886-6450
201 Mittel Dr Wood Dale (60191) ***(G-21168)***
Bi-Torq Valve Automation, Lafox *Also called Strahman Valves Inc* ***(G-12139)***
Bi-Torq Valve Automation Inc ...630 208-9343
1n046 Linlar Dr Lafox (60147) ***(G-12135)***
Biagios Gourmet Foods Inc ...708 867-4641
7319 W Lawrence Ave Chicago (60706) ***(G-3880)***
Bias Power Inc (PA) ...847 419-9180
975 Deerfield Pkwy Buffalo Grove (60089) ***(G-2517)***
Bible Students Publications ...630 595-0984
900 Brentwood Dr Bensenville (60106) ***(G-1753)***
Bible Truth Publishers Inc ...630 543-1441
59 W Industrial Rd Addison (60101) ***(G-49)***
Bick Broadcasting Inc ...217 223-9693
408 N 24th St Quincy (62301) ***(G-16865)***
Bidwells Candies, Humboldt *Also called Bobbie Haycraft* ***(G-11522)***
Bierdeman Box LLC ...847 256-0302
3445 Riverside Dr Wilmette (60091) ***(G-21069)***
Bierman Welding Inc ...217 342-2050
1103 S Willow St Effingham (62401) ***(G-8389)***
Biewer Fabricating Inc ...630 530-8922
208 W Stone Rd Villa Park (60181) ***(G-20134)***
Biewer John A Co of Seneca, Seneca *Also called John A Biewer Lumber Company* ***(G-18859)***
Big 3 Precision Products Inc (HQ) ...618 533-3251
2923 S Wabash Ave Centralia (62801) ***(G-3222)***
Big Als Machines Inc ...618 963-2619
204 Il Highway 14 Enfield (62835) ***(G-9468)***
Big Beam Emergency Systems Inc ...815 459-6100
290 E Prairie St Crystal Lake (60014) ***(G-7169)***
Big Bolt LLC ...630 539-9400
140 Covington Dr Bloomingdale (60108) ***(G-1981)***
Big City Sets Inc ...312 421-3210
4318 W Carroll Ave Chicago (60624) ***(G-3881)***
Big Creek Forestry & Logging L ...217 822-8282
75 Archer Ave Marshall (62441) ***(G-13565)***
Big Dog Treestand Inc ...309 263-6800
120 Detroit Pkwy Morton (61550) ***(G-14354)***
Big Frontire, Paxton *Also called Paxton Packing LLC* ***(G-16312)***
Big Game Gut Glove ...847 544-8806
19500 E Hillside Dr Frankfort (60423) ***(G-9771)***
Big Game Software LLC ...630 592-8082
110 E Schiller St Ste 302 Elmhurst (60126) ***(G-9333)***
Big Joe Forklift, Lombard *Also called Big Lift LLC* ***(G-13042)***
Big Joes Sealcoati ...630 935-7032
6563 Fernwood Dr Lisle (60532) ***(G-12871)***
Big Kser Precision Tooling Inc ...847 228-7660
2600 Huntington Blvd Hoffman Estates (60192) ***(G-11409)***
Big Lift LLC (PA) ...630 916-2600
1060 N Garfield St Lombard (60148) ***(G-13042)***
Big M Manufacturing LLC ...217 824-9372
928 E 1090 North Rd Taylorville (62568) ***(G-19750)***
Big R Car Wash Inc (PA) ...217 367-4958
501 E University Ave Urbana (61802) ***(G-19974)***
Big River Prairie Gold LLC ...319 753-1100
1100 Se 2nd St Galva (61434) ***(G-10227)***
Big River Resources Galva LLC ...309 932-2033
1100 Se 2nd St Galva (61434) ***(G-10228)***
Big River Zinc Corporation ...618 274-5000
2401 Mississippi Ave Sauget (62201) ***(G-18389)***
Big Rver Rsrces W Brlngton LLC ...309 734-8423
903 S Sunny Ln Monmouth (61462) ***(G-14214)***
Big Shoulders Coffee Works (PA) ...312 888-3042
2415 W 19th St Ste 1c Chicago (60608) ***(G-3882)***
Big T Graphics, Sparta *Also called Norvida USA Inc* ***(G-19258)***
Big Ten Network Services LLC ...312 329-3666
600 W Chicago Ave Ste 875 Chicago (60654) ***(G-3883)***
Big Tent Inc ...708 532-1222
7700 185th St Tinley Park (60477) ***(G-19811)***
Big Time Bats, Mundelein *Also called Hampster Industries Inc* ***(G-14695)***
Bigfoot Construction Eqp Inc ...888 743-7320
1111 Broadway Ct Woodstock (60098) ***(G-21365)***

Bighand Inc (HQ) 312 893-5906
  125 S Wacker Dr Ste 300 Chicago (60606) *(G-3884)*
Bigmachines A G, Deerfield Also called Oracle Bigmachines LLC *(G-7641)*
Bigtime Fantasy Sports Inc 630 605-7544
  149 W Washington Blvd Lombard (60148) *(G-13043)*
Bigtime Software Inc 312 346-4646
  311 S Wacker Dr Ste 2300 Chicago (60606) *(G-3885)*
Bill Chandler Farms 618 752-7551
  5182 Bucktown Ln Noble (62868) *(G-15188)*
Bill Peterson 815 378-8633
  25007 Flat Iron Rd Harvard (60033) *(G-11048)*
Bill Rodgers Drlg & Producing, West Salem Also called Rodgers Bill Oil Min Bits Svc *(G-20688)*
Bill Weeks Inc 217 523-8735
  229 N Grand Ave W Springfield (62702) *(G-19326)*
Bill Welding & Fabrication LLC 312 871-2623
  939 W North Ave Ste 750 Chicago (60642) *(G-3886)*
Bill West Enterprises Inc 217 886-2591
  2170 Arcadia Rd Jacksonville (62650) *(G-11757)*
Bill's Auto & Truck Repair, Des Plaines Also called Signs Plus *(G-7844)*
Biller Press & Manufacturing 847 395-4111
  966 Victoria St Antioch (60002) *(G-604)*
Billiards Digest, Chicago Also called Luby Publishing Inc *(G-5276)*
Billing Office, Urbana Also called Mid-America Sand & Gravel *(G-19988)*
Billinium Films, Chicago Also called Billinium Records LLC *(G-3887)*
Billinium Records LLC 800 651-8059
  200 W Madison St Ste 2100 Chicago (60606) *(G-3887)*
Bills Best Feeds, Emden Also called B B Milling Co Inc *(G-9466)*
Bills Machine & Power Transm (PA) 618 392-2500
  4678 Weinmann Dr Ste B Olney (62450) *(G-15856)*
Bills Shade & Blind Service (PA) 773 493-5000
  6029 1/2 S Harper Ave Chicago (60637) *(G-3888)*
Billy Cash For Gold Inc 773 905-2447
  101 N 19th Ave Melrose Park (60160) *(G-13831)*
Bilt-Rite Metal Products, Leland Also called Bilt-Rite Metal Products Inc *(G-12547)*
Bilt-Rite Metal Products Inc 815 495-2211
  100 E North St Leland (60531) *(G-12547)*
Bilz Tool Company 630 495-3996
  1140 N Main St Lombard (60148) *(G-13044)*
Bimba Manufacturing Company (HQ) 708 534-8544
  25150 S Governors Hwy University Park (60484) *(G-19949)*
Bimba Manufacturing Company 708 534-7997
  500 S Spruce St Manteno (60950) *(G-13444)*
Bimba Manufacturing Company 815 654-7775
  10914 N 2nd St Machesney Park (61115) *(G-13329)*
Bimba Manufacturing Company 708 534-8544
  9450 W Laraway Rd Frankfort (60423) *(G-9772)*
Bimbo Bakehouse LLC (HQ) 800 550-6810
  8550 W Bryn Mawr Ave Chicago (60631) *(G-3889)*
Bimbo Bakeries Usa Inc 630 469-4579
  1695 Glen Ellyn Rd Glendale Heights (60139) *(G-10438)*
Bimbo Bakeries Usa Inc 773 254-3578
  2503 S Blue Island Ave Chicago (60608) *(G-3890)*
Bimbo Bakeries Usa Inc 815 626-6797
  1204 12th Ave Rock Falls (61071) *(G-17177)*
Bimbo Bakeries Usa Inc 217 235-3181
  3801 Dewitt Ave Mattoon (61938) *(G-13631)*
Bimbo Bakeries Usa Inc 309 797-4968
  5205 22nd Ave Moline (61265) *(G-14134)*
Bimbo Qsr Chicago LLC 773 376-4444
  1801 W 31st Pl Chicago (60608) *(G-3891)*
Bimbo Qsr Us LLC (HQ) 740 450-3869
  1801 W 31st Pl Chicago (60608) *(G-3892)*
Bimeda Animal Health Inc 630 928-0361
  1 Tower Ln Ste 2250 Oakbrook Terrace (60181) *(G-15788)*
Binder Tool Inc 847 678-4222
  9833 Franklin Ave Franklin Park (60131) *(G-9887)*
Bindery & Distribution Service 847 550-7000
  9 Overbrook Rd South Barrington (60010) *(G-19075)*
Bindery Maintenance Services 618 945-7480
  777 E State St Bridgeport (62417) *(G-2309)*
Bingaman Metal Spinning, Rolling Meadows Also called Bingamn-Prcsion Mtal Spnning C *(G-17719)*
Bingamn-Prcsion Mtal Spnning C 847 392-5620
  1000 Carnegie St Rolling Meadows (60008) *(G-17719)*
Binks Industries Inc 630 801-1100
  1997a Aucutt Rd Montgomery (60538) *(G-14233)*
Binnys Beverage Depot, Springfield Also called Gold Standard Enterprises Inc *(G-19375)*
Binzel Industries LLC 847 506-0003
  3051 S State St Lockport (60441) *(G-12984)*
Bio Ascend LLC 888 476-9129
  980 N Michigan Ave # 1400 Chicago (60611) *(G-3893)*
BIO BIDET, Crystal Lake Also called BBC Innovation Corporation *(G-7168)*
Bio Fuels By American Farmers 561 859-6251
  10163 Sugar Creek Rd Benton (62812) *(G-1921)*
Bio Industries Inc 847 215-8999
  540 Allendale Dr Ste B Wheeling (60090) *(G-20859)*
Bio Services Inc 630 808-2125
  4917 Butterfield Rd Hillside (60162) *(G-11330)*
Bio Star Films LLC 773 254-5959
  4848 S Hoyne Ave Chicago (60609) *(G-3894)*
Bio-Bridge Science Inc 630 328-0213
  1801 S Meyers Rd Ste 220 Oakbrook Terrace (60181) *(G-15789)*
Bio-RAD Laboratories Inc 847 699-2217
  1400 E Touhy Ave Des Plaines (60018) *(G-7739)*
Bioaffinity Inc 815 988-5077
  641 S Main St Rockford (61101) *(G-17324)*
Bioanalytics Inc 217 649-6820
  2067 Coyote Run Rd Monticello (61856) *(G-14278)*
Bioblend Lubricants Intl 630 227-1800
  2439 Reeves Rd Joliet (60436) *(G-11832)*
Biocare Labs Inc 708 496-8657
  14800 S Mckinley Ave B Posen (60469) *(G-16791)*
Biochemical Lab 708 447-3923
  247 Addison Rd Riverside (60546) *(G-17082)*
Bioconcepts Inc (HQ) 630 986-0007
  100 Tower Dr Ste 101 Burr Ridge (60527) *(G-2656)*
Bioelements Inc 773 525-3509
  4619 N Ravenswood Ave 202a Chicago (60640) *(G-3895)*
Biogreen Organics Inc 847 740-9637
  30937 N Gilmer Rd Volo (60073) *(G-20196)*
Biolife Plasma LLC 224 940-7611
  1200 Lakeside Dr Bannockburn (60015) *(G-1197)*
Biologos Inc 630 801-4740
  2235 Cornell Ave Montgomery (60538) *(G-14234)*
Biomerieux Inc 630 600-5516
  1113 N Main St Lombard (60148) *(G-13045)*
Biomerieux Inc 630 628-6055
  1105 N Main St Lombard (60148) *(G-13046)*
Bion Dillos Baking Co 773 921-8282
  4900 W Division St Chicago (60651) *(G-3896)*
Bion Enterprises Ltd 847 544-5044
  455 State St Ste 100 Des Plaines (60016) *(G-7740)*
Bionic Chicago 773 698-6269
  4315 N Lincoln Ave Chicago (60618) *(G-3897)*
Biospawn Lure Co 773 458-0752
  9332 Hamlin Ave Evanston (60203) *(G-9500)*
Biosynergy Inc (PA) 847 956-0471
  1940 E Devon Ave Elk Grove Village (60007) *(G-8867)*
Biovie Inc (PA) 978 998-4756
  25 W 15th St Apt B Chicago (60605) *(G-3898)*
Bircher America Inc 847 952-3730
  870 Pratt Ave N Schaumburg (60193) *(G-18462)*
Bird Dog Bay Inc 312 631-3108
  2010 W Fulton St F280b Chicago (60612) *(G-3899)*
Bird Products Corporation 872 757-0114
  26125 N Riverwoods Blvd Mettawa (60045) *(G-13978)*
Bird-X Inc 312 226-2473
  845 N Larch Ave Elmhurst (60126) *(G-9334)*
Birdco Fabricators Inc (PA) 217 408-8744
  500 Allen Ave Jacksonville (62650) *(G-11758)*
Birdsell Machine & Orna Inc 217 243-5849
  531 W Independence Ave Jacksonville (62650) *(G-11759)*
Birkeys Construction Equipment, Urbana Also called Birkeys Farm Store Inc *(G-19975)*
Birkeys Farm Store Inc 217 337-1772
  2202 S High Cross Rd Urbana (61802) *(G-19975)*
Birnberg Machinery Inc 847 673-5242
  1450 Northwoods Rd Deerfield (60015) *(G-7597)*
Birom Cabinetry LLC 312 286-7132
  7440 Forest Hill Rd Burr Ridge (60527) *(G-2657)*
Biron Studio General Svcs Inc 708 229-2600
  6253 W 95th St Ste 1 Oak Lawn (60453) *(G-15703)*
Bisco Enterprise Inc 630 628-1831
  550 Albion Ave Ste 40 Schaumburg (60193) *(G-18463)*
Bisco Inc 847 534-6000
  1100 W Irving Park Rd Schaumburg (60193) *(G-18464)*
Bisco Intl Inc 708 544-6308
  543 Granville Ave Hillside (60162) *(G-11331)*
Bish Creative Display Inc 847 438-1500
  945 Telser Rd Lake Zurich (60047) *(G-12388)*
Bishop Engineering Company (PA) 630 305-9538
  6495 Bannister Ct Lisle (60532) *(G-12872)*
Bishop Image Group Inc 312 735-8153
  5244 N Elston Ave Chicago (60630) *(G-3900)*
Bishops Engrv & Trophy Svc Inc 773 777-5014
  6708 W Belmont Ave Chicago (60634) *(G-3901)*
Bison Aerospace and Def LLC 618 795-2678
  3297 Crim Dr Savanna (61074) *(G-18403)*
Bison Gear & Engineering Corp (PA) 630 377-4327
  3850 Ohio Ave Saint Charles (60174) *(G-18156)*
Bissell Inc 815 423-1300
  20200 W Ira Morgan Rd Elwood (60421) *(G-9461)*
Bit Brokers International Ltd 618 435-5811
  5568 Logan Rd West Frankfort (62896) *(G-20668)*
Bitforms Inc 630 595-6800
  165 Hansen Ct Ste 111e Wood Dale (60191) *(G-21169)*
Bits of Gold Jewelry, Nashville Also called Marion Oelze *(G-15001)*

Bitsio Inc 217 793-2827
920 S Spring St Ste 1200 Springfield (62704) *(G-19327)*
Bitter End Yacht Club Intl 312 506-6205
875 N Michigan Ave # 3707 Chicago (60611) *(G-3902)*
Biz 3 Publicity 773 342-3331
1321 N Milwaukee Ave Chicago (60622) *(G-3903)*
Bizbash Media Inc 312 436-2525
5437 N Ashland Ave Chicago (60640) *(G-3904)*
Bizstarterscom Inc 847 305-4626
126 E Wing St Ste 321 Arlington Heights (60004) *(G-705)*
BJ Mold & Die Inc 630 595-1797
780 Creel Dr Ste 1 Wood Dale (60191) *(G-21170)*
BJs Welding Services Etc Co 773 964-5836
1521 E 83rd St Chicago (60619) *(G-3905)*
Bka Inc 847 831-3535
1999 Castlewood Rd Highland Park (60035) *(G-11255)*
Bkbg Enterprises Inc 847 228-7070
440 Mission St Carol Stream (60188) *(G-2947)*
BL Downey Company LLC 708 345-8000
2125 Gardner Rd Broadview (60155) *(G-2420)*
Blac Cultivation LLC 309 532-6325
1715 Rockingham Dr Apt B Normal (61761) *(G-15199)*
Blac Inc 630 279-6400
195 W Spangler Ave Ste A Elmhurst (60126) *(G-9335)*
Blachford Corporation 815 464-2100
401 Center Rd Frankfort (60423) *(G-9773)*
Blachford Investments Inc 630 231-8300
1400 Nuclear Dr West Chicago (60185) *(G-20552)*
Black & Decker Corporation 630 521-1097
901 S Rohlwing Rd Ste A Addison (60101) *(G-50)*
Black Band LLC 309 208-0323
1000 Sw Adams St Peoria (61602) *(G-16393)*
Black Bear Defense LLC 708 357-7233
1350 E 75th St Chicago (60619) *(G-3906)*
Black Bison Water Services LLC (PA) 630 272-5935
953 W Fulton St U 2 2 U Chicago (60607) *(G-3907)*
Black Box Corporation 847 439-5000
1850 Jarvis Ave Elk Grove Village (60007) *(G-8868)*
Black Box Corporation 312 656-8807
9365 Windsor Pkwy Tinley Park (60487) *(G-19812)*
Black Bros Co (PA) 815 539-7451
501 9th Ave Mendota (61342) *(G-13938)*
Black Fodder Coffee, Chicago *Also called Wolfart Maciej* *(G-6663)*
Black Lab LLC 440 285-3189
3624 E 2351st Rd Serena (60549) *(G-18863)*
Black Magic Customs Inc 815 786-1977
4686 E 29th St Sandwich (60548) *(G-18366)*
Black Market Parts Inc 630 562-9400
776 W Hawthorne Ln West Chicago (60185) *(G-20553)*
Black Mountain Products Inc 224 655-5955
7705 Industrial Dr Ste B Spring Grove (60081) *(G-19268)*
Black Rock Milling and Pav Co 847 952-0700
2400 Terminal Dr Arlington Heights (60005) *(G-706)*
Black Start Labs Inc 630 444-1800
1500 Foundry St Ste 8 Saint Charles (60174) *(G-18157)*
Black Swan Manufacturing Co 773 227-3700
4540 W Thomas St Chicago (60651) *(G-3908)*
Blackberry Historical Farm, Aurora *Also called Fox Valley Park District* *(G-1100)*
Blackburn Sampling Inc 309 342-8429
77 S Henderson St Galesburg (61401) *(G-10185)*
Blackfriars Corp (PA) 818 597-3754
555 Skokie Blvd Ste 555 # 555 Northbrook (60062) *(G-15350)*
Blackhawk Biofuels LLC 217 431-6600
210 W Spring St Ste 1 Freeport (61032) *(G-10103)*
Blackhawk Corrugated LLC 844 270-2296
700 Kimberly Dr Carol Stream (60188) *(G-2948)*
Blackhawk Courtyards LLC 416 298-8101
700 Kimberly Dr Carol Stream (60188) *(G-2949)*
Blackhawk Industrial Dist Inc 773 736-9600
245 E Lies Rd Carol Stream (60188) *(G-2950)*
Blackhawk Molding Co Inc (PA) 630 628-6218
120 W Interstate Rd Addison (60101) *(G-51)*
Blackhawk Molding Co Inc 630 543-3900
138 W Interstate Rd Addison (60101) *(G-52)*
Blackjack Customs 847 361-5225
2920 Frontenac St North Chicago (60064) *(G-15307)*
Blackjack Lighting 847 941-0588
1547 Barclay Blvd Buffalo Grove (60089) *(G-2518)*
Blaige 312 337-5200
980 N Michigan Ave # 1080 Chicago (60611) *(G-3909)*
Blake Awning, Rockford *Also called Blake Co Inc* *(G-17325)*
Blake Co Inc 815 962-3852
1135 Charles St Rockford (61104) *(G-17325)*
Blando's Marry ME Jewelry, Countryside *Also called G Blando Jewelers Inc* *(G-7053)*
Blanke Industries Incorporated 847 487-2780
1099 Brown St Ste 103 Wauconda (60084) *(G-20335)*
Blast Products, Madison *Also called Damco Products Inc* *(G-13407)*
Blast Products Inc 618 452-4700
224 State St Madison (62060) *(G-13406)*
Blastline USA, Carol Stream *Also called Blastline USA Inc* *(G-2951)*

Blastline USA Inc 630 871-0147
226 S Westgate Dr Ste B Carol Stream (60188) *(G-2951)*
Blaum Brothers Distilling Co 815 777-1000
9380 W Us Highway 20 Galena (61036) *(G-10164)*
Blaxtair Inc 312 299-5590
330 N Wabash Ave Fl 23 Chicago (60611) *(G-3910)*
Blaz Cartage, Chicago *Also called Scott Janczak* *(G-6120)*
Blazing Color Inc 618 826-3001
1007 State St Chester (62233) *(G-3450)*
Bleigh Construction Company 217 222-5005
3522 S 6th St Quincy (62305) *(G-16866)*
Blending and Transfer Systems, Chicago *Also called Emerson Electric Co* *(G-4497)*
Blending and Transfer Systems, Chicago *Also called FMC Technologies Inc* *(G-4612)*
Blew Chemical Company 708 448-5780
12501 S Richard Ave Palos Heights (60463) *(G-16181)*
Blg McC Enterprises Inc 847 455-0188
3700 Sandra St Franklin Park (60131) *(G-9888)*
Bli Legacy Inc (PA) 847 428-6059
1013 Tamarac Dr Carpentersville (60110) *(G-3095)*
Bliss Ring Company Inc 847 446-3440
1095 Willow Rd Winnetka (60093) *(G-21127)*
Blissful Brownies Inc 541 308-0226
619 Highview Ter Lake Forest (60045) *(G-12231)*
Blistex Global Inc 630 571-2870
1800 Swift Dr Oak Brook (60523) *(G-15597)*
Blistex Inc (PA) 630 571-2870
1800 Swift Dr Oak Brook (60523) *(G-15598)*
Blistex Inc 630 571-2870
100 Windsor Dr Oak Brook (60523) *(G-15599)*
Block and Company Inc (HQ) 847 537-7200
1111 Wheeling Rd Wheeling (60090) *(G-20860)*
Block Midland Group, Wheeling *Also called Block and Company Inc* *(G-20860)*
Blockmaster Electronics Inc 847 956-1680
1400 Howard St Elk Grove Village (60007) *(G-8869)*
Blocksmoy Inc 847 260-9070
10632 Grand Ave Franklin Park (60131) *(G-9889)*
Blomberg Bros Inc 618 245-6321
Hwy 37 S Farina (62838) *(G-9651)*
Blommer Chocolate Company 800 621-1606
600 W Kinzie St Chicago (60654) *(G-3911)*
Bloomberg Bna, Chicago *Also called Bureau of National Affairs Inc* *(G-3975)*
Blooming Color Inc 630 705-9200
230 Eisenhower Ln N Lombard (60148) *(G-13047)*
Bloomington Offset Process Inc 309 662-3395
1705 S Veterans Pkwy Bloomington (61701) *(G-2026)*
Bloomington Tent & Awning Inc 309 828-3411
226 E Market St Bloomington (61701) *(G-2027)*
Blount International Inc 800 319-6637
2606 S Il Route 2 Oregon (61061) *(G-15914)*
Blowers LLC 708 594-1800
835 N Industrial Dr Elmhurst (60126) *(G-9336)*
Bls Enterprises Inc 630 766-1300
1120 Thorndale Ave Bensenville (60106) *(G-1754)*
Blu Prime Inc 800 709-5413
1030 W North Ave Ste 104 Chicago (60642) *(G-3912)*
Bluco Corporation 630 637-1820
1510 Frontenac Rd Naperville (60563) *(G-14780)*
Blue Book of Building & Cnstr, Lombard *Also called Contractors Register Inc* *(G-13058)*
Blue Brothers Coatings 847 265-5400
2415 N Quaker Hollow Ln Round Lake Beach (60073) *(G-18087)*
Blue Chip Construction Inc 630 208-5254
435 Stevens Dr Geneva (60134) *(G-10255)*
Blue Chip Mfg LLC 630 553-6321
37 Stonehill Rd Oswego (60543) *(G-15993)*
Blue Comet Transport Inc 773 617-9512
4919 W Parker Ave Chicago (60639) *(G-3913)*
Blue Diamond Athletic Disp Inc 847 414-9971
1933 Loomes Ave Downers Grove (60516) *(G-7960)*
Blue Gem Computers Inc. 708 562-5524
822 East St Morris (60450) *(G-14295)*
Blue Island Beer Co 708 954-8085
13357 Olde Western Ave Blue Island (60406) *(G-2111)*
Blue Island Newspaper Prtg Inc 708 333-1006
262 W 147th St Harvey (60426) *(G-11079)*
Blue Island Sun 708 388-9033
12607 Artesian Ave Blue Island (60406) *(G-2112)*
Blue Light Inc 630 400-4539
1440 Maple Ave Ste 5b Lisle (60532) *(G-12873)*
Blue Monkey Graphics Inc. 708 488-9501
7540 Roosevelt Rd Ste 4 Forest Park (60130) *(G-9708)*
Blue Nile Trucking LLC 618 215-1077
404 N 27th St East Saint Louis (62205) *(G-8300)*
Blue Pearl Stone Tech LLC 708 698-5700
333 Washington Ave La Grange (60525) *(G-12073)*
Blue Ridge Fiberboard 800 233-8721
300 Industrial Dr Hampshire (60140) *(G-10965)*
Blue Ridge Forge Inc 309 274-5377
316 W Cedar St Chillicothe (61523) *(G-6814)*
Blue Ridge Land and Cattle 217 762-9652
1068 E 1765 North Rd Monticello (61856) *(G-14279)*

ALPHABETIC SECTION — Bond Broadcasting Inc

Blue Sky Bio LLC 718 376-0422
800 Liberty Dr Libertyville (60048) *(G-12638)*

Blue Sky Vineyard 618 995-9463
3150 S Rocky Comfort Rd Makanda (62958) *(G-13427)*

Blue Software LLC 773 957-1600
8430 W Bryn Mawr Ave # 1100 Chicago (60631) *(G-3914)*

Blue Yonder Inc 630 701-1492
280 Shuman Blvd Ste 105 Naperville (60563) *(G-14781)*

Blueair Inc 888 258-3247
100 N La Salle St # 1900 Chicago (60602) *(G-3915)*

Blueberry Woodworking Inc 773 230-7179
2824 Birch St Franklin Park (60131) *(G-9890)*

Bluechip Fabrication 618 496-3569
25 N Chestnut St Tamaroa (62888) *(G-19741)*

Bluegrass Enterprises LLC 630 544-3781
1501 Indiana Ave Saint Charles (60174) *(G-18158)*

Bluemastiff Group LLC 708 704-3529
903 W 35th St Ste 562 Chicago (60609) *(G-3916)*

Bluenrgy LLC 802 865-3866
410 S Michigan Ave # 933 Chicago (60605) *(G-3917)*

Bluestone Specialty Chem LLC 815 727-3010
10 Industry Ave Joliet (60435) *(G-11833)*

Bluesun Hitech, Naperville Also called Lightfoot Technologies Inc *(G-14864)*

Bluetown Skateboard Co LLC 312 718-4786
1344 N Oakley Blvd Ste 2 Chicago (60622) *(G-3918)*

Bluewater Thermal Solutions, Northlake Also called Bwt LLC *(G-15544)*

Bluewater Thermal Solutions, Rockford Also called Bwt LLC *(G-17331)*

Bluffs Vineyard & Winery L L C 618 763-4447
1505 Business Highway 13 Murphysboro (62966) *(G-14751)*

Blumthal Gas Geologist, Olney Also called Benchmark Properties Ltd *(G-15855)*

Bluprime Playing Cards, Chicago Also called Blu Prime Inc *(G-3912)*

Blustor Pmc Inc 312 265-3058
401 N Michigan Ave # 1200 Chicago (60611) *(G-3919)*

Bm Machine & Fabrication, Olney Also called Bills Machine & Power Transm *(G-15856)*

Bm Welding, Addison Also called Gallon Industries Inc *(G-134)*

Bmac Usa Inc 630 279-5500
1415 W 22nd St Towe Fl Oak Brook (60523) *(G-15600)*

BMC, Chicago Also called Bearings Manufacturing Company *(G-3856)*

BMC 1092 Inc 708 544-2200
2200 Parkes Dr Broadview (60155) *(G-2421)*

BMC Software Inc 331 777-8700
18w140 Bttrfeld Rd Ste 10 Oakbrook Terrace (60181) *(G-15790)*

Bmg Seltec, Oak Brook Also called Fivecubits Inc *(G-15620)*

Bmi Products Northern Ill Inc 847 395-7110
28919 W Il Route 173 Antioch (60002) *(G-605)*

Bms Manufacturing Company Inc 309 787-3158
651 8th Ave W Milan (61264) *(G-14000)*

Bmt Prntng Crtgraph Espclists 773 646-4700
12941 S Exchange Ave Chicago (60633) *(G-3920)*

BMW Sportswear Inc 773 265-0110
3967 W Madison St Chicago (60624) *(G-3921)*

Bn National Trail 618 783-8709
8810 Commercial Ave Newton (62448) *(G-15081)*

BNP Media Inc 847 205-5660
155 N Pfingsten Rd Deerfield (60015) *(G-7598)*

Bo Inc 312 459-0013
10725 Forestview Rd Countryside (60525) *(G-7045)*

Boaleeco Inc 847 428-3085
56 E End Dr Gilberts (60136) *(G-10351)*

Boaters World, Chicago Also called Cyn Industries Inc *(G-4295)*

Boatman Signs 618 548-6567
1700 E Main St Salem (62881) *(G-18332)*

Bob Barnett Redi-Mix Inc (PA) 618 252-3581
285 Garden Heights Rd Harrisburg (62946) *(G-11020)*

Bob C Beverages LLC 847 520-7582
419 Harvester Ct Wheeling (60090) *(G-20861)*

Bob Chinn's Premium Beverages, Wheeling Also called Bob C Beverages LLC *(G-20861)*

Bob Evans Farms Inc 309 932-2194
1001 Sw 2nd St Galva (61434) *(G-10229)*

Bob Folder Lures Co 217 787-1116
2071 Hazlett Rd Springfield (62707) *(G-19328)*

Bobak Sausage Company 773 735-5334
4551 W Adams St Chicago (60624) *(G-3922)*

Bobbi Screen Printing 773 847-8200
4573 S Archer Ave Chicago (60632) *(G-3923)*

Bobbie Haycraft 217 856-2194
110 Homann Ct Humboldt (61931) *(G-11522)*

Bobble, Chicago Also called O2cool LLC *(G-5647)*

Bobs Business Inc 630 238-5790
730 Thomas Dr Bensenville (60106) *(G-1755)*

Bobs Market & Greenhouse 217 442-8155
1118 E Voorhees St Danville (61832) *(G-7324)*

Bobs Tshirt Store 618 567-1730
419 Jackson St Mascoutah (62258) *(G-13594)*

Boc Global Helium Inc 630 897-1900
1998 Albright Rd Montgomery (60538) *(G-14235)*

Bock's Identi Co., Mattoon Also called Bocks Cattle-Identi Co Inc *(G-13632)*

Bocks Cattle-Identi Co Inc 217 234-6634
3101 Cedar Ave Mattoon (61938) *(G-13632)*

Bodine Electric Company (PA) 773 478-3515
201 Northfield Rd Northfield (60093) *(G-15509)*

Bodine Electric of Decatur, Decatur Also called Rathje Enterprises Inc *(G-7540)*

Bodine Electric of Decatur, Danville Also called Rathje Enterprises Inc *(G-7377)*

Bodines Baking Company 217 853-7707
2136 N Dennis Ave Decatur (62526) *(G-7465)*

Body Wipe Corporation 847 687-9321
1027 E High St Mundelein (60060) *(G-14667)*

Bodycote Thermal Proc Inc 708 236-5360
1975 N Ruby St Melrose Park (60160) *(G-13832)*

Bodycote Thermal Proc Inc 630 221-0385
194 Internationale Blvd Glendale Heights (60139) *(G-10439)*

Bodysmart USA Inc 630 682-9701
2077 W Roosevelt Rd Wheaton (60187) *(G-20790)*

Boe Intermediate Holding Corp 773 890-3300
3200 S Kilbourn Ave Chicago (60623) *(G-3924)*

Boeing Company (PA) 312 544-2000
100 N Riverside Plz Chicago (60606) *(G-3925)*

Boeing Company 618 746-4062
205 Hangar Rd Bldg 470 Scott Afb (62225) *(G-18856)*

Boeing Global Holdings Corp (HQ) 312 544-2000
100 N Riverside Plz Chicago (60606) *(G-3926)*

Boeing International Corp (HQ) 312 544-2000
100 N Riverside Plz Chicago (60606) *(G-3927)*

Boeing Irving Company 312 544-2000
100 N Riverside Plz Fl 35 Chicago (60606) *(G-3928)*

Boeing LTS Inc 312 544-2000
100 N Riverside Plz Chicago (60606) *(G-3929)*

Boekeloo Heating & Sheet Metal 708 877-6560
601 N Williams St Thornton (60476) *(G-19785)*

Boetje Foods Inc 309 788-4352
2736 12th St Rock Island (61201) *(G-17208)*

Bofa Americas Inc 618 205-5007
303 S Madison St Staunton (62088) *(G-19474)*

Bogart Industries LLC 224 242-4578
315 E Reader St Elburn (60119) *(G-8446)*

Bohl Machine & Tool Company 309 799-5122
4405 78th Ave Milan (61264) *(G-14001)*

Bohler 630 883-3000
2505 Millennium Dr Elgin (60124) *(G-8522)*

Boiler Tube & Fabrication Div, Romeoville Also called Chicago Tube and Iron Company *(G-17807)*

Boise Cascade Company 618 491-7030
1201 W 1st St Ste 310 Granite City (62040) *(G-10700)*

Boise Paper, Elk Grove Village Also called Packaging Corporation America *(G-9168)*

Boise White Paper LLC (HQ) 847 482-3000
1 N Field Ct Lake Forest (60045) *(G-12232)*

Boise White Paper LLC 208 805-1424
1955 W Field Ct Lake Forest (60045) *(G-12233)*

Bolchazy-Carducci Publishers 847 526-4344
1570 Baskin Rd Mundelein (60060) *(G-14668)*

Bold Diagnostics LLC 806 543-5743
222 Merchandise Mart Plz Chicago (60654) *(G-3930)*

Bold Machine Works Inc 217 428-6644
1677 S Taylorville Rd Decatur (62521) *(G-7466)*

Bold Renewables Holdings LLC (PA) 541 312-3832
222 N Lasalle Ste 705 Chicago (60601) *(G-3931)*

Boler Company (PA) 630 773-9111
500 Park Blvd Ste 1010 Itasca (60143) *(G-11628)*

Boler Company 630 910-2800
800 S Frontage Rd Woodridge (60517) *(G-21279)*

Boler Ventures LLC (PA) 630 773-9111
500 Park Blvd Ste 1010 Itasca (60143) *(G-11629)*

Boley Tool & Machine Works Inc 309 694-2722
1044 Spring Bay Rd East Peoria (61611) *(G-8254)*

Bolhuis Woodworking Co 708 333-5100
14250 W Joliet Rd Manhattan (60442) *(G-13431)*

Bolingbrook Communications Inc 630 759-9500
1938 University Ln Ste C Lisle (60532) *(G-12874)*

Bolingbrook Quarry, Plainfield Also called Legacy Vulcan LLC *(G-16683)*

Bolt & Hide Co 773 231-2002
321 N Clark St Ste 2300 Chicago (60654) *(G-3932)*

Boltswitch Inc 815 459-6900
6208 Commercial Rd Crystal Lake (60014) *(G-7170)*

Bolzoni Auramo Inc (HQ) 708 957-8809
17635 Hoffman Way Homewood (60430) *(G-11488)*

Bombardier Learjet, Des Plaines Also called Learjet Inc *(G-7797)*

Bomel Tool Manufacturing Co 708 343-3663
2111 Roberts Dr Broadview (60155) *(G-2422)*

Bona Fide Corp 847 970-8693
100 Shepard Ave Wheeling (60090) *(G-20862)*

Bonanno Vintners LLC 773 477-8351
2614 N Paulina St Chicago (60614) *(G-3933)*

Bond & Fayette County Shopper 618 664-4566
201 N 3rd St Ste Frnt Greenville (62246) *(G-10827)*

Bond Broadcasting Inc 618 664-3300
309 W Main St Greenville (62246) *(G-10828)*

Bond Brothers & Co............708 442-5510
7826 47th St Lyons (60534) ***(G-13303)***
Bond Brothers Hardwoods............618 272-4811
412 W Main St Ridgway (62979) ***(G-17035)***
Bondfire LLC............630 742-8022
133 Chapin Way Oswego (60543) ***(G-15994)***
Bone A Fide Pet Grooming............217 872-0907
1220 E Pershing Rd Ste 1 Decatur (62526) ***(G-7467)***
Bonell Manufacturing Company............708 849-1770
13521 S Halsted St Fl 1 Riverdale (60827) ***(G-17069)***
Bonnell Industries Inc............815 284-3819
1385 Franklin Grove Rd Dixon (61021) ***(G-7890)***
Bonnie's Slick Printing, Gurnee *Also called Proforma Quality Business Svcs* ***(G-10916)***
Bonsal American Inc............847 678-6220
10352 Franklin Ave Franklin Park (60131) ***(G-9891)***
Bookends Publishing............312 988-1500
2001 N Halsted St Ste 201 Chicago (60614) ***(G-3934)***
Booklist, Chicago *Also called American Library Association* ***(G-3657)***
Boom Company Inc............847 459-6199
161 Wheeling Rd Wheeling (60090) ***(G-20863)***
Boombox Beverage LLC............312 607-1038
7415 Saint Louis Ave Skokie (60076) ***(G-18930)***
Boone County Shopper Inc............815 544-2166
112 Leonard Ct Belvidere (61008) ***(G-1656)***
Booth Resources Inc............618 662-4955
7965 Old Highway 50 Flora (62839) ***(G-9676)***
Bopi............312 320-1109
1705 S Veterans Pkwy Bloomington (61701) ***(G-2028)***
Borders Metals Recovery............217 586-2501
1203 S Sunny Acres Rd Mahomet (61853) ***(G-13422)***
Boree Unlimited LLC............773 498-6591
3014 W 63rd St Chicago (60629) ***(G-3935)***
Borg Warner Automotive, Bellwood *Also called Borgwarner Transm Systems Inc* ***(G-1618)***
Borg Warner Automotive - B............248 754-9200
1350 Franklin Grove Rd Dixon (61021) ***(G-7891)***
Borg-Warner Automotive Inc............815 469-2721
300 S Maple St Frankfort (60423) ***(G-9774)***
Borg-Warner Emissions Systems, Dixon *Also called Borgwarner Inc* ***(G-7892)***
Borgwarner Inc............815 288-1462
1350 Franklin Grove Rd Dixon (61021) ***(G-7892)***
Borgwarner Inc............248 754-9200
700 25th Ave Bellwood (60104) ***(G-1617)***
Borgwarner Inc............248 754-9200
300 S Maple St Frankfort (60423) ***(G-9775)***
Borgwarner Inc............708 731-4540
2437 W North Ave Melrose Park (60160) ***(G-13833)***
Borgwarner Transm Systems Inc............708 547-2600
700 25th Ave Bellwood (60104) ***(G-1618)***
Borgwarner Transm Systems Inc............815 469-2721
300 S Maple St Frankfort (60423) ***(G-9776)***
Borgwarner Transm Systems Inc............815 469-7819
10807 S Fairfield Ave Chicago (60655) ***(G-3936)***
Borgwarner Transm Systems Inc............708 731-4540
2437 W North Ave Melrose Park (60160) ***(G-13834)***
Boring Industries............815 986-1172
2219 N Central Ave Rockford (61101) ***(G-17326)***
Bork Industries............630 365-5517
44w508 Ic Trl Maple Park (60151) ***(G-13460)***
Borns Picture Frames............630 876-1709
540 Belleview Ave West Chicago (60185) ***(G-20554)***
Borse Industries Inc............630 325-1210
7409 S Quincy St Willowbrook (60527) ***(G-21032)***
Bos Machine Tool Services Inc............309 658-2223
621 Main St Hillsdale (61257) ***(G-11321)***
Bosch Auto Svc Solutions Inc............815 407-3900
1385 N Weber Rd Romeoville (60446) ***(G-17799)***
Bosch Engineering North Amer, Broadview *Also called Robert Bosch LLC* ***(G-2466)***
Bose Corporation............630 575-8044
65 Oakbrook Ctr Hinsdale (60523) ***(G-11366)***
Bose Corporation............630 585-6654
1650 Premium Outlet Blvd # 1257 Aurora (60502) ***(G-924)***
Bose Factory Store, Aurora *Also called Bose Corporation* ***(G-924)***
Bose Showcase Store, Hinsdale *Also called Bose Corporation* ***(G-11366)***
Boss Balloon Company Inc............309 852-2131
1221 Page St Kewanee (61443) ***(G-12022)***
Boss Holdings Inc (PA)............309 852-2131
1221 Page St Kewanee (61443) ***(G-12023)***
Boss Manufacturing Company (HQ)............309 852-2131
1221 Page St Kewanee (61443) ***(G-12024)***
Boss Manufacturing Holdings (HQ)............309 852-2781
1221 Page St Kewanee (61443) ***(G-12025)***
Boss Manufacturing Holdings............309 852-2131
1221 Page St Kewanee (61443) ***(G-12026)***
Boss Pet Products Inc............216 332-0832
1501 Burlington Ave Kewanee (61443) ***(G-12027)***
Bost Corporation (PA)............708 344-7023
601 Saint Charles Rd Maywood (60153) ***(G-13663)***
Bost Corporation............708 450-9234
2780 Thomas St Melrose Park (60160) ***(G-13835)***
Bostic Publishing Company............773 551-7065
3236 N Sacramento Ave Chicago (60618) ***(G-3937)***
Boston Leather Inc............815 622-1635
1801 Eastwood Dr Sterling (61081) ***(G-19501)***
Boston Warehouse Trading Corp............630 992-5604
2600 Beverly Dr Aurora (60502) ***(G-925)***
Boswell Building Contrs Inc............630 595-5027
933 Dillon Dr Wood Dale (60191) ***(G-21171)***
Botkin Lumber Company Inc............217 287-2127
201 S Baughman Rd Taylorville (62568) ***(G-19751)***
Botti Studio of Architectural (PA)............847 869-5933
1225 Harms Rd Glenview (60025) ***(G-10532)***
Botts Welding and Trck Svc Inc (PA)............815 338-0594
335 N Eastwood Dr Woodstock (60098) ***(G-21366)***
Boudin Bakery, Addison *Also called Chicago Bread Company* ***(G-69)***
Bound + D Termined Inc............847 696-1501
60 S Dee Rd Apt E Park Ridge (60068) ***(G-16271)***
Bourn & Bourn Inc............815 965-4013
2500 Kishwaukee St Rockford (61104) ***(G-17327)***
Bourn & Koch Inc (PA)............815 965-4013
2500 Kishwaukee St Rockford (61104) ***(G-17328)***
Bourrette Logging............815 591-3761
1012 Blackhawk B Hanover (61041) ***(G-10995)***
Bow Brothers Co Inc............217 359-0555
3108 W Springfield Ave Champaign (61822) ***(G-3272)***
Bowe Bell + Hwell Scanners LLC............847 675-7600
760 S Wolf Rd Wheeling (60090) ***(G-20864)***
Bowebellhowell, Wheeling *Also called Holdings Liquidation Inc* ***(G-20910)***
Bowhunting.com, Huntley *Also called Hunting Network LLC* ***(G-11540)***
Bowl Doctors Inc............815 282-6009
7664 Hawks Rdg Machesney Park (61115) ***(G-13330)***
Bowl-Tronics Enterprises Inc............847 741-4500
1115 Sherwood Ave Elgin (60120) ***(G-8523)***
Bowlero Corp............847 473-2600
385 Frederick Plz Waukegan (60085) ***(G-20423)***
Bowne Enterprise Solutions, Chicago *Also called Donnelley Financial LLC* ***(G-4384)***
Bows Arts Inc............847 501-3161
1944 Lehigh Ave Ste C Glenview (60026) ***(G-10533)***
Bowtie Inc............630 515-9493
477 E Bttrfeld Rd Ste 200 Lombard (60148) ***(G-13048)***
Bowtree Inc............217 430-8884
720 E Tolton Dr Quincy (62305) ***(G-16867)***
Box Enclsres Assembly Svcs Inc............847 932-4700
14092 W Lambs Ln Libertyville (60048) ***(G-12639)***
Box Form Inc............773 927-8808
1334 W 43rd St Chicago (60609) ***(G-3938)***
Box Manufacturing Inc............309 637-6228
201 Spring St Peoria (61603) ***(G-16394)***
Box of Rain Ltd............847 640-6996
1504 E Algonquin Rd Arlington Heights (60005) ***(G-707)***
Box Office Magazine, Chicago *Also called R L D Communications Inc* ***(G-5946)***
Box USA............708 562-6000
401 Northwest Ave Northlake (60164) ***(G-15543)***
Boyce Industries Inc............708 345-0455
4915 Division St Melrose Park (60160) ***(G-13836)***
Boyd Sawmill............618 735-2056
19775 N Boyd Ln Dix (62830) ***(G-7881)***
Boyd Spotting Inc............217 669-2418
1310 N 300 East Rd Cisco (61830) ***(G-6891)***
Boyer Corporation............708 352-2553
9600 W Ogden Ave La Grange (60525) ***(G-12074)***
Boyleston 21st Century LLC............708 387-2012
9118 47th St Ste 3 Brookfield (60513) ***(G-2479)***
Bozki Inc............312 767-2122
325 N Milwaukee Ave Wheeling (60090) ***(G-20865)***
BP America Inc (HQ)............630 420-5111
4101 Winfield Rd Ste 200 Warrenville (60555) ***(G-20232)***
BP Amoco Chemical Company............630 420-5111
150 W Warrenville Rd Naperville (60563) ***(G-14782)***
BP Elc Mtrs Pump & Svc Inc............773 539-4343
8135 Ridgeway Ave Skokie (60076) ***(G-18931)***
BP Products North America Inc............630 420-4300
150 W Warrenville Rd Naperville (60563) ***(G-14783)***
BP Products North America Inc............312 594-7689
30 S Wacker Dr Ste 900 Chicago (60606) ***(G-3939)***
BP Shipping............630 393-1032
150 W Warrenville Rd Naperville (60563) ***(G-14784)***
BP Solar International Inc............301 698-4200
150 W Warrenville Rd Naperville (60563) ***(G-14785)***
Bpi Holdings International Inc (HQ)............815 363-9000
4400 Prime Pkwy McHenry (60050) ***(G-13722)***
Bpn Chicago............312 799-4100
875 N Michigan Ave # 1850 Chicago (60611) ***(G-3940)***
Bpo Assistant, Monticello *Also called Track My Foreclosures LLC* ***(G-14288)***
Bprex Healthcare Packaging Inc (HQ)............800 537-0178
600 Deerfield Pkwy Buffalo Grove (60089) ***(G-2519)***
Bps Fuels Inc............217 452-7608
352 N Morgan St Virginia (62691) ***(G-20192)***
BR Concepts International Inc............847 674-9481
7436 Kildare Ave Skokie (60076) ***(G-18932)***

BR Machine Inc....815 434-0427
3312 E 2153rd Rd Ottawa (61350) ***(G-16042)***
Braceunder, Libertyville *Also called Therapeutic Envisions Inc* ***(G-12716)***
Brad Martz....217 825-5855
1250 State Highway 128 Shelbyville (62565) ***(G-18877)***
Braden Rock Bit....618 435-4519
14447 State Highway 34 Benton (62812) ***(G-1922)***
Bradley Adhsive Applctions Inc (PA)....630 443-8424
3635 Swenson Ave Saint Charles (60174) ***(G-18159)***
Bradley Group, The, Saint Charles *Also called Bradley Adhsive Applctions Inc* ***(G-18159)***
Bradley Machining Inc....630 543-2875
136 W Official Rd Addison (60101) ***(G-53)***
Bradley Smoker USA Inc....309 343-1124
644 Enterprise Ave Galesburg (61401) ***(G-10186)***
Bradley Systems, Des Plaines *Also called Bass Brother Incorporated* ***(G-7736)***
Bradley Terrace Inc....773 775-6579
8770 W Bryn Mawr Ave # 1300 Chicago (60631) ***(G-3941)***
Bradley Terrace Outdoor Furn, Chicago *Also called Bradley Terrace Inc* ***(G-3941)***
Bradley University Bookstore, Peoria *Also called Barnes & Noble College* ***(G-16390)***
Braeside Displays, Antioch *Also called Braeside Holdings LLC* ***(G-606)***
Braeside Holdings LLC....847 395-8500
945 Anita Ave Antioch (60002) ***(G-606)***
Brahman Spirit Tribe....773 957-2828
5841 S Peoria St Chicago (60621) ***(G-3942)***
Brahman Spirit Tribe, The, Chicago *Also called Brahman Spirit Tribe* ***(G-3942)***
Braindok LLC....847 877-1586
2104 Birchwood Ln Buffalo Grove (60089) ***(G-2520)***
Brainerd Chemical Midwest LLC....918 622-1214
209 Brewer Rd Danville (61834) ***(G-7325)***
Brainlab Inc....800 784-7700
5 Westbrook Corp Ctr Westchester (60154) ***(G-20692)***
Brainware Company....773 250-6465
4802 N Broadway St 201a Chicago (60640) ***(G-3943)***
Brainworx Studio....773 743-8200
6531 N Albany Ave Chicago (60645) ***(G-3944)***
Brake Drum Tool Co America Div, Waukegan *Also called Illinois Carbide Tool Co Inc* ***(G-20447)***
Brake Parts Inc India LLC (HQ)....815 363-9000
4400 Prime Pkwy McHenry (60050) ***(G-13723)***
Brake Parts Inc LLC....815 363-8181
1380 Corporate Dr McHenry (60050) ***(G-13724)***
Brake Parts Inc LLC (HQ)....815 363-9000
4400 Prime Pkwy McHenry (60050) ***(G-13725)***
Brake Parts Inc LLC....217 324-2161
725 Mckinley Ave Litchfield (62056) ***(G-12961)***
Brakur Custom Cabinetry Inc....630 355-2244
18656 S State Route 59 Shorewood (60404) ***(G-18893)***
Bramic Industries, Addison *Also called Lenrok Industries Inc* ***(G-182)***
Bran-Zan Holdings LLC (PA)....847 342-0000
1655 N Arlington Heights Arlington Heights (60004) ***(G-708)***
Branatt Enterprises LLC....630 632-3532
400 N Walnut St Byron (61010) ***(G-2750)***
BRANCh....312 213-0138
500 E 33rd St Apt 801 Chicago (60616) ***(G-3945)***
Branch Lines Ltd....847 256-4294
1200 N Branch Rd Wilmette (60091) ***(G-21070)***
Branchfield Casting Inc (PA)....309 932-2278
2580 130th Ave Matherville (61263) ***(G-13614)***
Brand X-Ray Company....630 543-5331
910 S Westwood Ave Addison (60101) ***(G-54)***
Branding Iron Holdings Inc (PA)....618 337-8400
1682 Sauget Business Blvd Sauget (62206) ***(G-18390)***
Brandmuscle Inc....866 236-8481
4141 S Peoria St Chicago (60609) ***(G-3946)***
Brandt Assoc....847 362-0556
1002 Muir Ave Lake Bluff (60044) ***(G-12174)***
Brandt Consolidated Inc (PA)....217 547-5800
2935 S Koke Mill Rd Springfield (62711) ***(G-19329)***
Brandt Consolidated Inc....217 626-1123
788 E 3070 North Rd Farmer City (61842) ***(G-9654)***
Brandt Consolidated Inc....217 438-6158
300 W Jefferson St Auburn (62615) ***(G-906)***
Brandt Consolidated Inc....309 365-7201
610 W Main St Lexington (61753) ***(G-12618)***
Brandt Interiors....847 251-3543
803 Ridge Rd Wilmette (60091) ***(G-21071)***
Brandt Printing, Morris *Also called D G Brandt Inc* ***(G-14301)***
Braner Usa Inc (PA)....847 671-6210
9301 W Bernice St Schiller Park (60176) ***(G-18789)***
Branmark Strategy Group LLC....847 849-9080
2013 Burr Oak Dr W Glenview (60025) ***(G-10534)***
Branstiter Printing Co....217 245-6533
217 E Morgan St Jacksonville (62650) ***(G-11760)***
Brasel Products Inc....630 879-3759
715 Hunter Dr Batavia (60510) ***(G-1360)***
Braun Manufacturing Co Inc....847 635-2050
1350 Feehanville Dr Mount Prospect (60056) ***(G-14514)***
Brave Products Inc....815 672-0551
1705 N Shabbona St Streator (61364) ***(G-19605)***
Bravilor Bonamat LLC....630 423-9400
1204 Bilter Rd Aurora (60502) ***(G-926)***
Bravura Moulding Company....262 633-1882
28915 N Herky Dr Ste 103 Lake Bluff (60044) ***(G-12175)***
BRC Manufacturing Co, Skokie *Also called BR Concepts International Inc* ***(G-18932)***
Brd Development Group LLC....312 912-7110
253 E Delaware Pl Apt 21c Chicago (60611) ***(G-3947)***
Breachers Tape, Wauconda *Also called Fontana Associates Inc* ***(G-20352)***
Breaker Press Co Inc....773 927-1666
2421 S Western Ave Chicago (60608) ***(G-3948)***
Breakfast Fuel LLC....847 251-3835
1222 Washington Ct Wilmette (60091) ***(G-21072)***
Breakroom Brewery....773 564-9534
2925 W Montrose Ave Chicago (60618) ***(G-3949)***
Breal Time, Chicago *Also called Emx Digital LLC* ***(G-4503)***
Brechts Database Solutions....618 654-6960
1000 Broadway Ste 300 Highland (62249) ***(G-11205)***
Breckenridge Material Company....618 398-4141
10 Tucker Dr Caseyville (62232) ***(G-3211)***
Breedlove Sporting Goods Inc (PA)....309 852-2434
123 W 2nd St Kewanee (61443) ***(G-12028)***
Breedlove Sporting Goods Inc....309 852-2434
215 W 2nd St Kewanee (61443) ***(G-12029)***
Breedlove's, Kewanee *Also called Breedlove Sporting Goods Inc* ***(G-12028)***
Brees Studio Inc....618 687-3331
430 S 19th St Murphysboro (62966) ***(G-14752)***
Breese Journal, Breese *Also called Breese Publishing Co Inc* ***(G-2299)***
Breese Publishing Co Inc (PA)....618 526-7211
8060 Old Us Highway 50 Breese (62230) ***(G-2299)***
Breeze Printing Company (PA)....217 824-2233
212 S Main St Taylorville (62568) ***(G-19752)***
Breeze-Courier, Taylorville *Also called Breeze Printing Company* ***(G-19752)***
Brehm Oil Inc (PA)....618 242-4620
1915 Broadway St Mount Vernon (62864) ***(G-14600)***
Bremner-Davis Eductl Systems, Chicago *Also called Fox International Corp* ***(G-4627)***
Brenco Machine and Tool Inc....815 356-5100
6117 Factory Rd Crystal Lake (60014) ***(G-7171)***
Brenda Miller....618 678-2639
130 Old Highway 50 Xenia (62899) ***(G-21467)***
Brennan Engineering, Danville *Also called Estad Stamping & Mfg Co* ***(G-7331)***
Brennan Equipment and Mfg Inc....708 534-5500
730 Central Ave University Park (60484) ***(G-19950)***
Brenneman Welding & Equipment, Percy *Also called Rudy Brenneman* ***(G-16560)***
Brenner Tank Services LLC....773 468-6390
803 E 120th St Chicago (60628) ***(G-3950)***
Brent Pumps Supply, Norris City *Also called William R Becker* ***(G-15252)***
Bretford Manufacturing Inc (PA)....847 678-2545
11000 Seymour Ave Franklin Park (60131) ***(G-9892)***
Brevity LLC....949 250-0701
3838 N Kenneth Ave Chicago (60641) ***(G-3951)***
Brewer Company....708 339-9000
3852 W 159th Pl Harvey (60428) ***(G-11080)***
Brewer Utility Systems Inc....217 224-5975
1628 Madison St Quincy (62301) ***(G-16868)***
Brewers Bottlers & Bev Corp....773 262-9711
7233 N Sheridan Rd Ste 5 Chicago (60626) ***(G-3952)***
Brewster Cheese Company....815 947-3361
300 W Railroad Ave Stockton (61085) ***(G-19548)***
Brex-Arlington Incorporated....847 255-6284
800 W Central Rd Ste 101n Mount Prospect (60056) ***(G-14515)***
Brg Sports Inc....217 892-4704
105 W Flessner Ave Rantoul (61866) ***(G-16969)***
Brg Sports Inc (HQ)....224 585-5200
1700 E Higgins Rd Ste 500 Des Plaines (60018) ***(G-7741)***
Brian Bequette Cabinetry....618 670-5427
18630 White City Rd Staunton (62088) ***(G-19475)***
Brian Burcar....815 856-2271
310 Walnut St Leonore (61332) ***(G-12611)***
Brian D Obermiller....815 830-3100
124 S Peru St Louis Tonica (61370) ***(G-19887)***
Brian Hobbs....618 758-1303
207 E Mill St Coulterville (62237) ***(G-7029)***
Brian K Wattleworth....847 356-2103
36345 N Yew Tree Dr Lake Villa (60046) ***(G-12346)***
Brian Kinney....309 206-4219
1529 28th St Rock Island (61201) ***(G-17209)***
Brian Lindstrom....309 463-2388
2412 Wenona Rd Varna (61375) ***(G-20031)***
Brian Robert Awning Co....847 679-1140
8152 Lawndale Ave Skokie (60076) ***(G-18933)***
Briannas Pancake Cafe....630 365-4770
151 Il Route 38 Elburn (60119) ***(G-8447)***
Bricks Inc (PA)....630 897-6926
723 S Lasalle St Aurora (60505) ***(G-1066)***
Bricks Inc....773 523-5718
3425 S Kedzie Ave Ste 1 Chicago (60623) ***(G-3953)***
Bridge City Mechanical Inc....309 944-4873
777 E Culver Ct Geneseo (61254) ***(G-10240)***

ALPHABETIC

(PA)=Parent Co (HQ)=Headquarters (DH)=Div Headquarters
2020 Harris Illinois
Industrial Directory
1069

Bridge Printing & Promotional (PA) 847 776-0200
52 Congress Cir W Roselle (60172) *(G-17941)*
Bridge Printing & Promotional 312 929-1456
70 W Madison St Chicago (60602) *(G-3954)*
Bridge Street Foods, Yorkville *Also called Gerard Mitchell Company LLC (G-21485)*
Bridge Wave Electronics, Darien *Also called Angela Yang Chingjui (G-7401)*
Bridgeline Digital Inc 312 784-5720
30 N La Salle St Ste 2000 Chicago (60602) *(G-3955)*
Bridgeport Air Comprsr & TI Co 618 945-7163
745 Monroe St Bridgeport (62417) *(G-2310)*
Bridgeport Pharmacy Inc 312 791-9000
3201 S Wallace St Chicago (60616) *(G-3956)*
Bridgeport Steel Sales Inc 312 326-4800
2730 S Hillock Ave Chicago (60608) *(G-3957)*
Bridgestone Americas 309 452-4411
1600 Fort Jesse Rd Normal (61761) *(G-15200)*
Bridgestone Company Inc 847 325-5172
41 Century Dr Wheeling (60090) *(G-20866)*
Bridgeview Cnc Inc 708 599-4641
9019 Odell Ave Bridgeview (60455) *(G-2329)*
Bridgeview Custom Kit Cabinets 708 598-1221
8655 Beloit Ave Bridgeview (60455) *(G-2330)*
Bridgeview Machining Inc 708 599-4060
9009 S Thomas Ave Bridgeview (60455) *(G-2331)*
Bridgford Foods Corporation 312 733-0300
170 N Green St Chicago (60607) *(G-3958)*
Bridgford Marketing, Chicago *Also called Bridgford Foods Corporation (G-3958)*
Briergate Tool & Engrg Co 630 766-7050
1007 Industrial Dr Bensenville (60106) *(G-1756)*
Bright Brain 844 272-4645
108 W Schick Rd Unit 6130 Bloomingdale (60108) *(G-1982)*
Bright Image Corporation 708 449-5656
2830 S 18th Ave Broadview (60155) *(G-2423)*
Bright Light Sign Company Inc 847 550-8902
310 Telser Rd Lake Zurich (60047) *(G-12389)*
Brighton Cabinetry Inc 217 235-1978
2908 Lake Land Blvd Mattoon (61938) *(G-13633)*
Brighton Cabinetry Inc (PA) 217 895-3000
1095 Industrial Park Ave Neoga (62447) *(G-15016)*
Brighton Collectibles LLC 847 674-6719
4999 Old Orchard Ctr M17 Skokie (60077) *(G-18934)*
Brigitflex Inc 847 741-1452
1725 Fleetwood Dr Elgin (60123) *(G-8524)*
Brijen Electronics, Schaumburg *Also called Parth Consultants Inc (G-18667)*
Brilliant Color Corp 847 367-3300
14044 W Petronella Dr # 3 Libertyville (60048) *(G-12640)*
Bring Your Own Auto Parts Inc 815 730-6900
2123 Plainfield Rd Crest Hill (60403) *(G-7084)*
Brinkman Company Inc 630 595-3640
460 Evergreen Ave Bensenville (60106) *(G-1757)*
Briscoe Signs LLC 630 529-1616
119 N Bokelman St Roselle (60172) *(G-17942)*
Bristar 847 678-5000
3541 Martens St Ste 304 Franklin Park (60131) *(G-9893)*
Bristol Blacktop, Aurora *Also called Andel Services Inc (G-1052)*
Bristol Hose & Fitting Inc 708 492-3456
1950 N Mannheim Rd Ste 1 Melrose Park (60160) *(G-13837)*
Bristol Towing & Transport, Melrose Park *Also called Bristol Transport Inc (G-13838)*
Bristol Transport Inc 708 343-6411
1950 N Mannheim Rd Ste 1 Melrose Park (60160) *(G-13838)*
Brite One Inc 708 481-8005
21649 Richmond Rd Matteson (60443) *(G-13620)*
Brite Site Supply Inc 773 772-7300
4616 W Fullerton Ave Chicago (60639) *(G-3959)*
Brite-O-Matic Mfg Inc 847 956-1100
527 W Algonquin Rd Arlington Heights (60005) *(G-709)*
Briteseed LLC 206 384-0311
4660 N Ravenswood Ave Chicago (60640) *(G-3960)*
British Converting Solutions 630 219-1906
650 W Grand Ave Ste 201 Elmhurst (60126) *(G-9337)*
Britt Industries Inc 847 640-1177
3010 Malmo Dr Arlington Heights (60005) *(G-710)*
Brk Brands Inc (HQ) 630 851-7330
3901 Liberty St Aurora (60504) *(G-927)*
Broad-Ocean Motor LLC 630 908-4720
910 Pasquinelli Dr Westmont (60559) *(G-20730)*
Broadcast Electronics, Quincy *Also called BEI Holding Corporation (G-16864)*
Broadcast Electronics, Quincy *Also called BEI Electronics LLC (G-16863)*
Broadcast Electronics Inc (HQ) 217 224-9600
4100 N 24th St Quincy (62305) *(G-16869)*
Broadcom Corporation 773 965-1600
25949 Oak Hills Rd Lake Barrington (60010) *(G-12142)*
Broadwind Energy Inc (PA) 708 780-4800
3240 S Central Ave Cicero (60804) *(G-6831)*
Broc LLC 773 709-9931
5100 W Grand Ave # 390645 Chicago (60639) *(G-3961)*
Brocade Cmmnctions Systems LLC 630 273-5530
20 N Martingale Rd # 290 Schaumburg (60173) *(G-18465)*

Brock Equipment Company (PA) 815 459-4210
1001 Rail Dr Unit 4 Woodstock (60098) *(G-21367)*
Brock Industrial Services LLC 815 730-3350
2210 Oak Leaf St Joliet (60436) *(G-11834)*
Brockway Standard Inc 773 893-2100
1440 S Kilbourn Ave Chicago (60623) *(G-3962)*
Brodie's, Galesburg *Also called J Brodie Meat Products Inc (G-10202)*
Broken Earth Winery 847 383-5052
219 Rbert Prker Coffin Rd Long Grove (60047) *(G-13158)*
Broken Oar Inc 847 639-9468
614 Rawson Bridge Rd Port Barrington (60010) *(G-16785)*
Brokerassist LLC 847 858-2357
31 Forest Ave River Forest (60305) *(G-17050)*
Brokers Print Mail Rsource Inc 708 532-9900
17732 Oak Park Ave Tinley Park (60477) *(G-19813)*
Brolite Products Incorporated 630 830-0340
1335 Schiferl Rd Bartlett (60103) *(G-1270)*
Brombereks Flagstone Co Inc (PA) 630 257-0686
910 Singer Ave Lemont (60439) *(G-12557)*
Bromine Systems Inc 331 209-9881
1001 W Republic Dr Ste 9 Addison (60101) *(G-55)*
Bronson & Bratton Inc 630 986-1815
220 Shore Dr Burr Ridge (60527) *(G-2658)*
Bronson Machine Shop, Blue Island *Also called E B Bronson & Co Inc (G-2119)*
Bronze Memorial Inc 773 276-7972
1842 N Elston Ave Chicago (60642) *(G-3963)*
Brooke Burial Vault Co, Ottawa *Also called Oakwood Memorial Park Inc (G-16066)*
Brooke Graphics LLC 847 593-1300
1331 Greenleaf Ave Elk Grove Village (60007) *(G-8870)*
Brooks Allan, Lake Villa *Also called Allan Brooks & Associates Inc (G-12345)*
Brookside Flavors Ingredients, Addison *Also called Flavorfocus LLC (G-124)*
Brookstone Resources Inc 618 382-2893
1615 Oak St Carmi (62821) *(G-2900)*
Broome & Greene Online LLC 312 584-1580
222 Merchandise Mart Plz Chicago (60654) *(G-3964)*
Bros Lithographing Company 312 666-0919
1326 W Washington Blvd Chicago (60607) *(G-3965)*
Brothers Decorating 815 648-2214
10305 Vanderkarr Rd Hebron (60034) *(G-11139)*
Brothers Leal LLC 708 385-4400
12007 S Cicero Ave Alsip (60803) *(G-424)*
Brothers Pallets Co 773 306-2695
7711 S Claremont Ave Chicago (60620) *(G-3966)*
Brown & Miller Literary Assoc 312 922-3063
410 S Michigan Ave # 460 Chicago (60605) *(G-3967)*
Brown Adhesives & Equipment, Elk Grove Village *Also called Brown Packaging LLC (G-8871)*
Brown Line Metal Works LLC 312 884-7644
4001 N Ravenswood Ave 303a Chicago (60613) *(G-3968)*
Brown Metal Products Ltd 309 936-7384
513 N Spring Atkinson (61235) *(G-901)*
Brown Packaging LLC 224 415-3182
901 Cambridge Dr Elk Grove Village (60007) *(G-8871)*
Brown Packing Company Inc 708 849-7990
15801 Greenwood Rd South Holland (60473) *(G-19202)*
Brown Printing, Woodstock *Also called Quad/Graphics Inc (G-21426)*
Brown Wood Products Company (PA) 847 673-4780
7040 N Lawndale Ave Lincolnwood (60712) *(G-12814)*
Brown Woodworking 815 477-8333
1804 Blue Island Dr Crystal Lake (60012) *(G-7172)*
Browns Global Exchange 708 345-0955
1928 S 21st Ave Maywood (60153) *(G-13664)*
Bruce McCullough 217 773-3130
1161 980n Ave Mount Sterling (62353) *(G-14589)*
Bruce Offset, Elk Grove Village *Also called R R Donnelley & Sons Company (G-9210)*
Brucher Machining Inc 630 876-1661
1030 Atlantic Dr West Chicago (60185) *(G-20555)*
Bruder Tank Inc 217 292-9058
901 W Jefferson St Sullivan (61951) *(G-19662)*
Brumleve Canvas Products, Teutopolis *Also called Brumleve Industries Inc (G-19764)*
Brumleve Industries Inc 217 857-3777
1317 W Main St Teutopolis (62467) *(G-19764)*
Brunet Snow Service Company 847 846-0037
174 Hawthorne Ave Wood Dale (60191) *(G-21172)*
Brunner & Lay Inc 847 678-3232
300 Evergreen Ave Bensenville (60106) *(G-1758)*
Brunos Automotive Products 630 458-0043
14 W Industrial Rd Ste A Addison (60101) *(G-56)*
Brunswick Corporation (PA) 847 735-4700
26125 N Riverwoods Blvd # 500 Mettawa (60045) *(G-13979)*
Brunswick Corporation 847 288-3300
10600 Belmont Ave Franklin Park (60131) *(G-9894)*
Brunswick Family Boat Co Inc 847 735-4700
1 N Field Ct Lake Forest (60045) *(G-12234)*
Brunswick International Ltd (HQ) 847 735-4700
26125 N Riverwoods Blvd # 500 Mettawa (60045) *(G-13980)*
Brush Creek Quarry, Mode *Also called Iola Quarry Inc (G-14067)*
Brush Foil, Palatine *Also called Transcenda Inc (G-16166)*

Brusic-Rose Inc 708 458-9900
7300 S Central Ave Bedford Park (60638) *(G-1460)*
Bruss Company (HQ) 773 282-2900
3548 N Kostner Ave Chicago (60641) *(G-3969)*
Bryan Metals LLC (HQ) 419 636-4571
305 Lewis And Clark Blvd East Alton (62024) *(G-8163)*
Bryco Machine Inc 708 614-1900
8059 185th St Tinley Park (60487) *(G-19814)*
Brynolf Manufacturing Inc 815 873-8878
412 18th Ave Rockford (61104) *(G-17329)*
BSB International Corp 847 791-9272
225 James St Ste 4 Bensenville (60106) *(G-1759)*
BSC Imports Incorporated 773 844-4788
213 N Morgan St Unit 2c Chicago (60607) *(G-3970)*
BSN Sports LLC 217 788-0914
510 E Apple Orchard Rd # 107 Springfield (62703) *(G-19330)*
Bssi, Lake Forest Also called Barriersafe Solutions Intl Inc *(G-12230)*
Bst North America Inc (HQ) 630 833-9900
655 W Grand Ave Ste 220 Elmhurst (60126) *(G-9338)*
BT & E Co 815 544-6431
6877 Belford Indus Dr Belvidere (61008) *(G-1657)*
BT Steelle Investments Inc 618 410-0534
3649 George St Highland (62249) *(G-11206)*
BT Tech, Rushville Also called B T Technology Inc *(G-18108)*
Btd Manufacturing Inc 309 444-1268
118 Muller Rd Washington (61571) *(G-20267)*
Bti Dental, Tinley Park Also called Bennett Technologies Inc *(G-19809)*
Btn, Chicago Also called Big Ten Network Services LLC *(G-3883)*
BTR Controls Inc 847 608-9500
1570 Todd Farm Dr Elgin (60123) *(G-8525)*
Bu National, Bartlett Also called Fine Circuits Inc *(G-1280)*
Bubble Bubble Inc 815 455-2366
35 Berkshire Dr Ste 3 Crystal Lake (60014) *(G-7173)*
Bucher Hydraulics Inc 847 429-0700
2545 Northwest Pkwy Elgin (60124) *(G-8526)*
Bucket Mart Inc 813 390-8626
300 W Longstreet Rd Marion (62959) *(G-13506)*
Buckeye Diamond Logistics Inc 630 236-1174
2453 Prospect Dr Ste A Aurora (60502) *(G-928)*
Buckeye Partners LP 217 342-2336
18264 N Highway 45 Effingham (62401) *(G-8390)*
Buckley Powder Co 217 285-5531
1353 W Washington St Pittsfield (62363) *(G-16629)*
Buckner Sand Co 630 653-3700
1500 N Main St 200 Wheaton (60187) *(G-20791)*
Bucktown Polymers 312 436-1460
1658 N Milwaukee Ave # 421 Chicago (60647) *(G-3971)*
Bucthel Metal Finishing Corp 847 427-8704
1945 Touhy Ave Elk Grove Village (60007) *(G-8872)*
Budapest Tool 630 250-0711
1300 Industrial Dr Ste A Itasca (60143) *(G-11630)*
Budding Polishing & Met Finshg 708 396-1166
130 E 168th St South Holland (60473) *(G-19203)*
Budget Printing Center 618 655-1636
3709 Edwardsville Rd # 1 Edwardsville (62025) *(G-8351)*
Budget Signs 618 259-4460
333 E Edwardsville Rd Wood River (62095) *(G-21260)*
Budget Signs Trophies Plaques, Wood River Also called Budget Signs *(G-21260)*
Budmark Oil Company Inc 618 937-2495
106 E Oak St West Frankfort (62896) *(G-20669)*
Budnick Converting Inc 618 281-8090
340 Parkway Dr Columbia (62236) *(G-6986)*
Budnick Supply, Columbia Also called Budnick Converting Inc *(G-6986)*
Buell Airhorns, Lyons Also called Buell Manufacturing Company *(G-13304)*
Buell Manufacturing Company 708 447-6320
8125 47th St Lyons (60534) *(G-13304)*
Buff & Go Inc 773 719-4436
4345 S Langley Ave Apt 1n Chicago (60653) *(G-3972)*
Buhl Press 708 449-8989
5656 Mcdermott Dr Berkeley (60163) *(G-1939)*
Buhlwork Design Guild 630 325-5340
320 Luthin Rd Oak Brook (60523) *(G-15601)*
Buhrke Industries LLC (HQ) 847 981-7550
511 W Algonquin Rd Arlington Heights (60005) *(G-711)*
Buhrke Industries LLC 630 412-2028
2771 Busse Rd Elk Grove Village (60007) *(G-8873)*
Builders Cabinet Supply, Chicago Also called Orchard Hill Cabinetry Inc *(G-5695)*
Builders Chicago Corporation 224 654-2122
9820 W Foster Ave Rosemont (60018) *(G-18001)*
Builders Ironworks Inc 708 754-4092
3242 Louis Sherman Dr Steger (60475) *(G-19489)*
Builders Ironworks Inc (PA) 708 672-1047
399 Greenbriar Dr Crete (60417) *(G-7135)*
Builders Ready-Mix Co 847 866-6300
2525 Oakton St Evanston (60202) *(G-9501)*
Builders Warehouse Inc 309 672-1760
2115 Sw Washington St Peoria (61602) *(G-16395)*
Buildex Division of ITW 630 595-3500
1349 W Bryn Mawr Ave Itasca (60143) *(G-11631)*

Building Maintenance Dept, Mattoon Also called Lsc Communications Us LLC *(G-13642)*
Building Products Corp (PA) 618 233-4427
950 Freeburg Ave Belleville (62220) *(G-1536)*
Building Technologies Inc 800 743-6367
1000 Deerfield Pkwy Buffalo Grove (60089) *(G-2521)*
Buildingpoint Midwest LLC 855 332-7527
12360 S Industrial Dr E # 1 Plainfield (60585) *(G-16645)*
Bulaw Welding & Engineering Co 630 228-8300
750 N Rohlwing Rd Itasca (60143) *(G-11632)*
Bulk Lift International, Carpentersville Also called Bli Legacy Inc *(G-3095)*
Bulk Molding Compounds Inc (HQ) 630 377-1065
1600 Powis Ct West Chicago (60185) *(G-20556)*
Bulk-Strap, Elburn Also called Turf Inc *(G-8478)*
Bull Moose Tube Company 708 757-7700
555 E 16th St Chicago Heights (60411) *(G-6736)*
Bull Valley Hardwood (PA) 815 701-9400
18014 Collins Rd Woodstock (60098) *(G-21368)*
Bull Valley Hardwood 815 701-9400
820 E Terra Cotta Ave # 244 Crystal Lake (60014) *(G-7174)*
Bullards Bakery 618 842-6666
906 E Main St Fairfield (62837) *(G-9620)*
Bullen Midwest Inc (PA) 773 785-2300
900 E 103rd St Ste D Chicago (60628) *(G-3973)*
Bulletin 618 553-9764
103 W Main St Ste 4 Oblong (62449) *(G-15824)*
Bullseye Imprinting & EMB 630 834-8175
846 N York St Ste C Elmhurst (60126) *(G-9339)*
Bumper Scuffs 847 489-7926
37254 N Piper Ln Lake Villa (60046) *(G-12347)*
Bumper Works, Danville Also called Flex-N-Gate Corporation *(G-7334)*
Bundlar LLC 773 839-3976
222 Merchandise Mart Plz Chicago (60654) *(G-3974)*
Bunge Loders Croklaan, Channahon Also called Loders Croklaan Usa LLC *(G-3387)*
Bunge North America Foundation 217 784-8261
Rts 9 & 47 # 9 Gibson City (60936) *(G-10335)*
Bunker Hill Publication 618 585-4411
150 N Washington St Bunker Hill (62014) *(G-2633)*
Bunn-O-Matic Corporation 217 529-6601
1400 Stevenson Dr Springfield (62703) *(G-19331)*
Bunn-O-Matic Corporation 562 926-0764
5020 Ash Grove Dr Springfield (62711) *(G-19332)*
Bunn-O-Matic Corporation 217 528-8739
825 S Airport Dr Springfield (62707) *(G-19333)*
Bunn-O-Matic Corporation 217 529-6601
1500 Stevenson Dr Springfield (62703) *(G-19334)*
Bunzl, Morton Grove Also called Keenpac LLC *(G-14418)*
Bunzl Retail LLC 847 733-1469
8338 Austin Ave Morton Grove (60053) *(G-14392)*
Bunzl Retail Services LLC 847 966-2550
8338 Austin Ave Morton Grove (60053) *(G-14393)*
Burdeens Jewelry Ltd 847 459-8980
1151 W Lake Cook Rd Buffalo Grove (60089) *(G-2522)*
Burdett Burner Mfg Inc 630 617-5060
335 S Ardmore Ave Villa Park (60181) *(G-20135)*
Burdzy Tool & Die Co 847 671-6666
9355 Byron St Schiller Park (60176) *(G-18790)*
Bureau County Republican, Princeton Also called The b F Shaw Printing Co *(G-16823)*
Bureau of National Affairs Inc 773 775-8801
6692 N Sioux Ave Chicago (60646) *(G-3975)*
Bureau Valley Chief 815 646-4731
108 W Main St Tiskilwa (61368) *(G-19871)*
Burgess & Burgess Inc 847 855-1048
157 S Hunt Club Rd Gurnee (60031) *(G-10863)*
Burgess Manufacturing Inc 847 680-1724
1911 Industrial Dr Libertyville (60048) *(G-12641)*
Burgess-Norton Mfg Co Inc (HQ) 630 232-4100
737 Peyton St Geneva (60134) *(G-10256)*
Burgess-Norton Mfg Co Inc 630 232-4100
500 Western Ave Geneva (60134) *(G-10257)*
Burghof Engineering & Mfg Co 847 634-0737
16051 W Deerfield Pkwy # 1 Lincolnshire (60069) *(G-12747)*
Burgopak Limited 312 255-0827
213 W Institute Pl # 301 Chicago (60610) *(G-3976)*
Burke Tool & Manufacturing Inc 618 542-6441
339 E Olive St Du Quoin (62832) *(G-8116)*
Burke Whistles Inc 618 534-7953
389 Wells St Murphysboro (62966) *(G-14753)*
Burke, Roger G Jewelers, Peoria Also called Roger Burke Jewelers Inc *(G-16514)*
Burmac Manufacturing Inc 815 434-1660
4000 Burmac Rd Ottawa (61350) *(G-16043)*
Burnex Corporation 815 728-1317
5418 Business Pkwy Ringwood (60072) *(G-17040)*
Burnham Village Pump Station, Chicago Also called Village of Burnham *(G-6552)*
Burns Machine Company 815 434-3131
4000 Burmac Rd Ottawa (61350) *(G-16044)*
Burns Machine Company (PA) 815 434-1660
4000 Burmac Rd Ottawa (61350) *(G-16045)*
Burrell Beverage Co 708 581-6953
22 W Washington St # 1500 Chicago (60602) *(G-3977)*

Burrito Beach LLC....312 861-1986
233 N Michigan Ave C023 Chicago (60601) *(G-3978)*
Burry Foodservice, Saint Charles *Also called Quality Bakeries LLC (G-18255)*
Burstan Inc....847 787-0380
2530 United Ln Elk Grove Village (60007) *(G-8874)*
Burt Coyote Co....309 358-1602
104 N Union St Yates City (61572) *(G-21470)*
Bury Industrial Service LLC....847 235-2053
222 E Wscnsin Ave Ste 206 Lake Forest (60045) *(G-12235)*
Busatis Inc....630 844-9803
1755 Aucutt Rd Montgomery (60538) *(G-14236)*
Bushnell Illinois Tank Co....309 772-3106
650 W Davis St Bushnell (61422) *(G-2738)*
Bushnell Locker Service....309 772-2783
330 Green St Bushnell (61422) *(G-2739)*
Bushnell Welding & Radiator....309 772-9289
120 Charles St Bushnell (61422) *(G-2740)*
Business Card Systems Inc....815 877-0990
11025 Raleigh Ct Machesney Park (61115) *(G-13331)*
Business Cards Etc....847 470-8848
6437 Dempster St Morton Grove (60053) *(G-14394)*
Business Cards Tomorrow....815 877-0990
11025 Raleigh Ct Machesney Park (61115) *(G-13332)*
Business Express R & A Prtg, Chicago *Also called Negs & Litho Inc (G-5563)*
Business Forms Finishing Svc....773 229-0230
5410 S Sayre Ave Chicago (60638) *(G-3979)*
Business Graphics, Elmhurst *Also called Stevens Group LLC (G-9431)*
Business Insurance (PA)....877 812-1587
150 N Michigan Ave # 1800 Chicago (60601) *(G-3980)*
Business Magazine, Arcola *Also called Rankin Publishing Inc (G-664)*
Business Systems Consultants....312 553-1253
333 N Michigan Ave # 912 Chicago (60601) *(G-3981)*
Business Valuation Group Inc....312 595-1900
400 N La Salle Dr # 3905 Chicago (60654) *(G-3982)*
Businessmine LLC....630 541-8480
784 Oak Creek Dr Lombard (60148) *(G-13049)*
Buss Boyz Customs Inc....815 369-2803
216 S Center St Lena (61048) *(G-12598)*
Buster Services Inc....773 247-2070
3301 W 47th Pl Chicago (60632) *(G-3983)*
Busways LLC....617 697-2009
445 W Barry Ave Apt 329 Chicago (60657) *(G-3984)*
Busy Beaver Button Company....773 645-3359
3407 W Armitage Ave Chicago (60647) *(G-3985)*
Butcher Block Furn By Oneill....312 666-9144
555 W 16th St Chicago (60616) *(G-3986)*
Butera Finer Foods Inc....708 456-5939
4411 N Cumberland Ave Norridge (60706) *(G-15231)*
Butera Markets, Norridge *Also called Butera Finer Foods Inc (G-15231)*
Butler Bros Steel Rule Die Co....815 630-4629
303 Amendodge Dr Shorewood (60404) *(G-18894)*
Butterball LLC....800 575-3365
2125 Rochester Rd Montgomery (60538) *(G-14237)*
Buttercrumb Bakery, Hickory Hills *Also called G & K Baking LLC (G-11196)*
Butterfield Cleaners....847 816-7060
1420 S Butterfield Rd Mundelein (60060) *(G-14669)*
Butterfield Color Inc (HQ)....630 906-1980
625 W Illinois Ave Aurora (60506) *(G-1067)*
Butternut Bread, Darien *Also called Chicago Baking Company (G-7404)*
Button Man Printing Inc....630 549-0438
7 E Main St Saint Charles (60174) *(G-18160)*
Buww Coverings Incorporated (PA)....815 394-1985
4462 Boeing Dr Rockford (61109) *(G-17330)*
Buyersvine Inc....630 235-6804
641 S Bodin St Hinsdale (60521) *(G-11367)*
Buzard Pipe Organ Builders LLC....217 352-1955
112 W Hill St Champaign (61820) *(G-3273)*
Buzard Pipe Organ Craftsmen, Champaign *Also called Buzard Pipe Organ Builders LLC (G-3273)*
Buzz Sales Company Inc....815 459-1170
6110 Official Rd Crystal Lake (60014) *(G-7175)*
Buzzi Unicem USA Inc....815 768-3660
450 Railroad St Joliet (60436) *(G-11835)*
Buzzi Unicem USA Inc....610 882-5000
625 1st Ave Rock Island (61201) *(G-17210)*
Bvc, Burr Ridge *Also called Best Veneer Company LLC (G-2655)*
Bvc Veneer, Lisle *Also called R S Bacon Veneer Company (G-12932)*
Bw Exhibits....847 697-9224
41 Prairie Pkwy Gilberts (60136) *(G-10352)*
Bw Industries....630 784-1020
27w230 Beecher Ave Ste 1 Winfield (60190) *(G-21108)*
Bw Integrated Systems, Romeoville *Also called Barry-Whmller Cont Systems Inc (G-17798)*
Bway Corporation....847 956-0750
1350 Arthur Ave Elk Grove Village (60007) *(G-8875)*
Bway Corporation....773 254-8700
3200 S Kilbourn Ave Chicago (60623) *(G-3987)*
Bwt LLC....708 410-8000
75 E Lake St Northlake (60164) *(G-15544)*
Bwt LLC....630 210-4577
5136 27th Ave Rockford (61109) *(G-17331)*
Bycap Inc....773 561-4976
5505 N Wolcott Ave Chicago (60640) *(G-3988)*
Byd Motors Inc....847 590-9002
1500 W Shure Dr Ste 250 Arlington Heights (60004) *(G-712)*
Byelkaycom Sales Inc....630 574-8484
2222 Camden Ct Oak Brook (60523) *(G-15602)*
Byers Printing Company, Springfield *Also called Springfield Printing Inc (G-19454)*
Byrne & Schaefer Inc....815 727-5000
1061 Caton Farm Rd Lockport (60441) *(G-12985)*
Byron Blacktop Inc....815 234-2225
3499 E Tower Rd Byron (61010) *(G-2751)*
Byron Ready Mix, Oregon *Also called Rogers Ready Mix & Mtls Inc (G-15926)*
Bystronic Inc (HQ)....847 214-0300
2200 W Central Rd Hoffman Estates (60192) *(G-11410)*
Bystronic Mfg Americas LLC....847 214-0300
2200 W Central Rd Hoffman Estates (60192) *(G-11411)*
Bytebin LLC....312 286-0740
516 N Ogden Ave 55 Chicago (60642) *(G-3989)*
Byttow Enterprises Inc....708 372-4450
18683 Forest View Ln Lansing (60438) *(G-12486)*
Byus Steel Inc....630 879-2200
1750 Hubbard Ave Batavia (60510) *(G-1361)*
C & B Services....847 462-8484
6305 Lake Shore Dr Cary (60013) *(G-3151)*
C & B Welders Inc....773 722-0097
2645 W Monroe St Chicago (60612) *(G-3990)*
C & C 1 LLC....630 903-6345
159 S Kenmore Ave Elmhurst (60126) *(G-9340)*
C & C Bakery Inc....773 276-4233
2655 W Huron St Chicago (60612) *(G-3991)*
C & C Can Co Inc....312 421-2372
1838 W Grand Ave Chicago (60622) *(G-3992)*
C & C Embroidery Inc....815 777-6167
800 Spring St Ste 201 Galena (61036) *(G-10165)*
C & C Printing Controls Inc....630 810-0484
5015 Chase Ave Downers Grove (60515) *(G-7961)*
C & C Publications....815 723-0325
254 E Cass St Joliet (60432) *(G-11836)*
C & C Sport Stop....618 632-7812
115 N Lincoln Ave O Fallon (62269) *(G-15569)*
C & C Tooling Inc (PA)....630 543-5523
344 W Interstate Rd Addison (60101) *(G-57)*
C & D Machining Inc....815 778-4946
207 E Commercial St Lyndon (61261) *(G-13286)*
C & E Specialties Inc....815 229-9230
2530 Laude Dr Rockford (61109) *(G-17332)*
C & F Forge Company (PA)....847 455-6609
9100 Parklane Ave Franklin Park (60131) *(G-9895)*
C & F Machine Corp....630 924-0300
176 Covington Dr Bloomingdale (60108) *(G-1983)*
C & F Packing Co Inc....847 245-2000
515 Park Ave Lake Villa (60046) *(G-12348)*
C & H Gravel C Inc....217 857-3425
14046 N 1600th St Teutopolis (62467) *(G-19765)*
C & J Metal Products Inc....847 455-0766
11119 Franklin Ave Franklin Park (60131) *(G-9896)*
C & K Custom Signs, Decatur *Also called Cachera and Klemm Inc (G-7468)*
C & L Manufacturing Entps....618 465-7623
2109 Holland St Alton (62002) *(G-546)*
C & L Printing Company....312 235-0380
228 S Wabash Ave Ste 260 Chicago (60604) *(G-3993)*
C & L Supreme Mfg Co, Des Plaines *Also called Supreme Manufacturing Company (G-7854)*
C & L Tiling Inc (PA)....217 773-3357
196 Us 24 1075n Ave Timewell (62375) *(G-19797)*
C & M Engineering....815 932-3388
110 Mooney Dr Ste 8 Bourbonnais (60914) *(G-2257)*
C & M Recycling Inc....847 578-1066
1600 Morrow Ave North Chicago (60064) *(G-15308)*
C & R Industries, Joliet *Also called C & S Chemicals Inc (G-11837)*
C & R Scrap Metal, Chicago *Also called Archer Metal & Paper Co (G-3726)*
C & S Chemicals Inc....815 722-6671
1306 Mckinley St Joliet (60436) *(G-11837)*
C & S Electric Specialties....630 406-6170
250 Gibraltar Dr Bolingbrook (60440) *(G-2154)*
C & S Steel Rule Die Co Inc....773 254-4027
4305 S Homan Ave Chicago (60632) *(G-3994)*
C A C, Carol Stream *Also called Cac Corporation (G-2953)*
C A Larson & Son Inc....847 717-6010
5n200 Wooley Rd Maple Park (60151) *(G-13461)*
C and C Machine Tool Service....630 810-0484
5015 Chase Ave Downers Grove (60515) *(G-7962)*
C and H Gravel, Teutopolis *Also called C & H Gravel C Inc (G-19765)*
C and H Publishing Co (PA)....618 625-2711
114 E Franklin St Sesser (62884) *(G-18865)*
C and S Carpentry LLC....224 523-8064
164 E Chicago St Elgin (60120) *(G-8527)*

C B E Inc 630 571-2610
110 Oak Brook Rd Oak Brook (60523) ***(G-15603)***
C B Ferrari Incorporated 847 756-4100
22179 N Pepper Rd Lake Barrington (60010) ***(G-12143)***
C B M Plastics Inc 217 543-3870
398 E St Rt 133 Arthur (61911) ***(G-843)***
C Becky & Company Inc 847 818-1021
708 S Na Wa Ta Ave Mount Prospect (60056) ***(G-14516)***
C C I, Sugar Grove *Also called Finishes Unlimited Inc* ***(G-19644)***
C C P Express Inc 773 315-0317
2630 Highland Ave Berwyn (60402) ***(G-1949)***
C C T, Volo *Also called Composite Cutter Tech Inc* ***(G-20198)***
C CN Chicago Corp 847 671-3319
421 S Irmen Dr Ste B Addison (60101) ***(G-58)***
C Cretors & Co (PA) 847 616-6900
176 Mittel Dr Wood Dale (60191) ***(G-21173)***
C D Nelson Consulting Inc 847 487-4870
27421 N Darrell Rd Wauconda (60084) ***(G-20336)***
C D S Office Technologies, Springfield *Also called CDs Office Systems Inc* ***(G-19344)***
C D T Manufacturing Inc 847 679-2361
8020 Monticello Ave Skokie (60076) ***(G-18935)***
C D Tools Machining Inc 773 859-2028
33 W Fullerton Ave Addison (60101) ***(G-59)***
C E Dienberg Printing Company 708 848-4406
114 Madison St Lowr 1 Oak Park (60302) ***(G-15747)***
C E R Machining & Tooling Ltd 708 442-9614
8214 47th St Lyons (60534) ***(G-13305)***
C F C Interantional 708 753-0679
385 E Joe Orr Rd Chicago Heights (60411) ***(G-6737)***
C H Hanson Company (PA) 630 848-2000
2000 N Aurora Rd Naperville (60563) ***(G-14786)***
C Hofbauer Inc 630 920-1222
11433 Ridgewood Ln Burr Ridge (60527) ***(G-2659)***
C I F Industries Inc 618 635-2010
20988 Old Route 66 Staunton (62088) ***(G-19476)***
C J Holdings Inc 309 274-3141
110 W Walnut St Chillicothe (61523) ***(G-6815)***
C J T, Carol Stream *Also called Cjt Koolcarb Inc* ***(G-2960)***
C Johnson Sign Co, Franklin Park *Also called Johnson Sign Co* ***(G-9975)***
C K North America Inc 815 524-4246
1243 Naperville Dr Romeoville (60446) ***(G-17800)***
C Keller Manufacturing Inc 630 833-5593
925 N Ellsworth Ave Villa Park (60181) ***(G-20136)***
C L Graphics Marketing Inc 815 455-0900
365 Industrial Dr South Elgin (60177) ***(G-19139)***
C L Greenslade Sales Inc (PA) 847 593-3450
505 E Golf Rd Ste H Arlington Heights (60005) ***(G-713)***
C L Vault & Safe Srv 708 237-0039
6754 W 89th Pl Oak Lawn (60453) ***(G-15704)***
C Line Products Inc (PA) 847 827-6661
1100 E Business Center Dr Mount Prospect (60056) ***(G-14517)***
C M C, Joliet *Also called CMC America Corporation* ***(G-11842)***
C M C Industries Inc 630 377-0530
2525 Production Dr Saint Charles (60174) ***(G-18161)***
C M F Enterprises Inc 847 526-9499
950 N Rand Rd Ste 113 Wauconda (60084) ***(G-20337)***
C M J Associates Inc 708 636-2995
10745 S Kolmar Ave Oak Lawn (60453) ***(G-15705)***
C M Products, Lake Zurich *Also called R and R Brokerage Co* ***(G-12448)***
C N C Central Inc 630 595-1453
177 Il Route 83 Bensenville (60106) ***(G-1760)***
C N C Hi-Tech Inc 847 431-4335
1150 Brown St Ste H Wauconda (60084) ***(G-20338)***
C N F, Saint Charles *Also called Strathmore Press* ***(G-18280)***
C N Tool, Elk Grove Village *Also called Source United LLC* ***(G-9248)***
C P, Lake Forest *Also called Colbert Packaging Corporation* ***(G-12238)***
C P Environmental Inc 630 759-8866
1336 Enterprise Dr Ste 2 Romeoville (60446) ***(G-17801)***
C P O Inc 630 898-7733
1500 Dearborn Ave Ofc Aurora (60505) ***(G-1068)***
C R Kesner Company 630 232-8118
1624 Kummer Ct Geneva (60134) ***(G-10258)***
C R L, Highland Park *Also called Laurel Industries Inc* ***(G-11281)***
C R Plastics Inc 847 541-3601
851 Seton Ct Ste 1c Wheeling (60090) ***(G-20867)***
C R V Electronics Corp 815 675-6500
2249 Pierce Dr Spring Grove (60081) ***(G-19269)***
C Rockelmann Co, Saint Charles *Also called American Church Supply* ***(G-18145)***
C S I, Downers Grove *Also called Compusystems Inc* ***(G-7978)***
C S I, Raleigh *Also called Centrifugal Services Inc* ***(G-16959)***
C S O Corp (PA) 630 365-6600
10 N Sauber Rd Virgil (60151) ***(G-20190)***
C Streeter Enterprise 773 858-4388
28 E Jackson Blvd Fl 10 Chicago (60604) ***(G-3995)***
C Tri Co 309 467-4715
1035 W Center St Eureka (61530) ***(G-9477)***
C U Plastic LLC 888 957-9993
100 4th Ave Rochelle (61068) ***(G-17133)***
C W Publications Inc 800 554-5537
1705 37th Ave Sterling (61081) ***(G-19502)***
C&C Sealants 708 717-0686
576 Covered Bridge Dr Elgin (60124) ***(G-8528)***
C&R Directional Boring 630 458-0055
880 S Fiene Dr Addison (60101) ***(G-60)***
C&R Scrap Iron & Metal 847 459-9815
251 E Dundee Rd Wheeling (60090) ***(G-20868)***
C-V Cstom Cntrtops Cbinets Inc 708 388-5066
12525 Irving Ave Blue Island (60406) ***(G-2113)***
C. R. G., Chicago *Also called Channeled Resources Inc* ***(G-4069)***
C.A. Zoes Mfg Co, Chicago *Also called Zoes Mfgco LLC* ***(G-6722)***
C.E. Printed Products, Carol Stream *Also called Chicago Envelope Inc* ***(G-2957)***
C2 Imaging LLC 847 439-7834
1200 Chase Ave Elk Grove Village (60007) ***(G-8876)***
C2 Imaging LLC 312 238-3800
600 W Van Buren St # 604 Chicago (60607) ***(G-3996)***
C2 Publishing Inc 630 834-4994
4415 Harrison St Ste 412 Hillside (60162) ***(G-11332)***
C2 Water Inc 312 550-1159
732 Cummings Ave Kenilworth (60043) ***(G-12014)***
C4 Petrolum Transport Inc 815 690-0356
1624 Arborwood Cir Romeoville (60446) ***(G-17802)***
C6 Agility LLC 734 548-0008
1415 W Winona St Chicago (60640) ***(G-3997)***
Ca Inc 312 201-8557
123 N Wacker Dr Ste 2125 Chicago (60606) ***(G-3998)***
CA Custom Woodworking 630 201-6154
14690 County Line Rd Newark (60541) ***(G-15074)***
Cab Communications Inc 847 963-8740
50 N Brockway St Ste 4-11 Palatine (60067) ***(G-16097)***
Cabanas Manufacturing Jewelers 312 726-0333
9 N Wabash Ave Ste 555 Chicago (60602) ***(G-3999)***
Cabcraft, Carpentersville *Also called Donald Kranz* ***(G-3101)***
Cabinet Creations Plus 847 245-3800
515 N Lake St Mundelein (60060) ***(G-14670)***
Cabinet Factories Outlet, Arthur *Also called Masterbrand Cabinets Inc* ***(G-868)***
Cabinet Gallery LLC 618 882-4801
205 Madison St Highland (62249) ***(G-11207)***
Cabinet Stiles Inc 630 553-8639
1165 N Bridge St Yorkville (60560) ***(G-21474)***
Cabinet Wholesale Supply Inc 708 536-7090
17532 Duvan Dr Tinley Park (60477) ***(G-19815)***
Cabinetland of Springfield 217 523-7253
4340 N Peoria Rd Springfield (62702) ***(G-19335)***
Cabinetry Solutions Imprvs LLC (PA) 630 333-9195
6944 Kingery Hwy Willowbrook (60527) ***(G-21033)***
Cabinets & Granite Direct LLC 630 588-8886
1175 N Gary Ave Carol Stream (60188) ***(G-2952)***
Cabinets By Custom Craft Inc 815 637-4001
5261 Swanson Rd Roscoe (61073) ***(G-17900)***
Cabinets City 847 440-3371
1650 W Algonquin Rd Mount Prospect (60056) ***(G-14518)***
Cabinets Doors and More LLC 847 395-6334
25819 W Grass Lake Rd Antioch (60002) ***(G-607)***
Cabinetwerks, Wilmette *Also called Orren Pickell Builders Inc* ***(G-21090)***
Cable Company (PA) 847 437-5267
498 Bonnie Ln Elk Grove Village (60007) ***(G-8877)***
Cable Electric Company Inc 708 458-8900
7640 Archer Rd Oak Lawn (60458) ***(G-15706)***
Cable Management Products Inc 630 723-0470
1005 N Commons Dr Aurora (60504) ***(G-929)***
Cable X-Perts Inc 800 828-3340
721 Amsterdam St Woodstock (60098) ***(G-21369)***
Cablofil Inc 618 566-3230
8319 State Route 4 Mascoutah (62258) ***(G-13595)***
Cablofil/Legrand, Mascoutah *Also called Cablofil Inc* ***(G-13595)***
Cabot Corporation 217 253-3370
700 E Us Highway 36 Tuscola (61953) ***(G-19924)***
Cabot Corporation 217 253-5752
700 E Us Highway 36 Tuscola (61953) ***(G-19925)***
Cabot McRlectronics Globl Corp (HQ) 630 375-6631
870 N Commons Dr Aurora (60504) ***(G-930)***
Cabot McRlectronics Polsg Corp 630 543-6682
39 W Official Rd Addison (60101) ***(G-61)***
Cabot Microelectronics Corp (PA) 630 375-6631
870 N Commons Dr Aurora (60504) ***(G-931)***
Cabot Microelectronics Corp 630 375-6631
845 Enterprise St Aurora (60504) ***(G-932)***
Cabot Microelectronics Corp 630 375-6631
500 N Commons Dr Aurora (60504) ***(G-933)***
Cac Corporation (PA) 630 221-5200
307 E Lies Rd Carol Stream (60188) ***(G-2953)***
Cachera and Klemm Inc 217 876-7446
2271 W Packard St Decatur (62522) ***(G-7468)***
Cacini Inc 847 884-1162
711 E Golf Rd Schaumburg (60173) ***(G-18466)***
Cadaco Division, Chicago *Also called Rapid Displays Inc* ***(G-5971)***
Cadbury, Loves Park *Also called Mondelez Global LLC* ***(G-13238)***

ALPHABETIC

Caddy, Wheeling Also called EJ Cady & Company *(G-20888)*

Cade Communications Inc 773 477-7184
3018 N Sheridan Rd Apt 2s Chicago (60657) *(G-4000)*

Cadillac Products Packaging Co 217 463-1444
2005 S Main St Paris (61944) *(G-16225)*

Cadillac Tank Met Fbrctors Inc 630 543-2600
225 W Gerri Ln Addison (60101) *(G-62)*

Cadore-Miller Printing Inc 708 430-7091
9901 S 78th Ave Hickory Hills (60457) *(G-11194)*

Caduceus Communications Inc 773 549-4800
4043 N Ravenswood Ave # 309 Chicago (60613) *(G-4001)*

Caffero Tool & Mfg 224 293-2600
1537 Brandy Pkwy Streamwood (60107) *(G-19564)*

Cahokia Rice 618 661-1060
31778 Lynns Ln Mc Clure (62957) *(G-13686)*

Caibros Americas LLC 312 593-3128
116 Deere Park Ct Highland Park (60035) *(G-11256)*

Caid Tronics, Naperville Also called Hemmerle Jr Irvin *(G-14841)*

Cain Millwork Inc 815 561-9700
1 Cain Pkwy Rochelle (61068) *(G-17134)*

Cain Tubular Products Inc 630 584-5330
310 Kirk Rd Saint Charles (60174) *(G-18162)*

Cains Foods Inc (HQ) 978 772-0300
2021 Spring Rd Ste 600 Oak Brook (60523) *(G-15604)*

Cairo Diagnostic Center 618 734-1500
13289 Kessler Rd Cairo (62914) *(G-2765)*

Cairo Dry Kilns Inc 618 734-1039
14372 State Highway 37 Cairo (62914) *(G-2766)*

Cais, Oak Brook Also called Lutheran Church-Missouri Synod *(G-15638)*

Caisson Inc (PA) 815 547-5925
720 Logistics Dr Belvidere (61008) *(G-1658)*

Cake Factory 708 897-0872
4018 W 127th St Alsip (60803) *(G-425)*

Cal-Ill Gasket Co 773 287-9605
4716 W Rice St Chicago (60651) *(G-4002)*

Cal-Tronics Systems Inc 630 350-0044
729 Creel Dr Wood Dale (60191) *(G-21174)*

Calco, Richmond Also called 815 Pallets Inc *(G-17006)*

Calco Controls Inc 847 639-3858
439 S Dartmoor Dr Crystal Lake (60014) *(G-7176)*

Calco Cutaways, Crystal Lake Also called Calco Controls Inc *(G-7176)*

Calcon Machine Inc 815 495-9227
210 E Lincoln Ave Leland (60531) *(G-12548)*

Caldwell & Moten LLC 773 619-2584
910 S Michigan Ave # 1010 Chicago (60605) *(G-4003)*

Caldwell Letter Service Inc 773 847-0708
10500 163rd Pl Orland Park (60467) *(G-15943)*

Caldwell Plumbing Co 630 588-8900
821 Childs St Wheaton (60187) *(G-20792)*

Calhoun Quarry Incorporated (PA) 618 396-2229
25 Main St Batchtown (62006) *(G-1442)*

Calhoun Quarry Incorporated 618 576-9223
Eldred Rd Hardin (62047) *(G-11016)*

California Muffler and Brakes 773 776-8990
5059 S California Ave Chicago (60632) *(G-4004)*

California Pure Delite Juice &, Chicago Also called Florida Fruit Juices Inc *(G-4611)*

California Technical Pltg Corp 818 365-8205
3758 W Belmont Ave Chicago (60618) *(G-4005)*

Calihan Pork Processors Inc 309 674-9175
1 South St Peoria (61602) *(G-16396)*

Call Potential LLC 877 552-2557
24047 W Lockport St Naperville (60540) *(G-14787)*

Callahan Industries, Lombard Also called Frank R Walker Company *(G-13079)*

Callahan Mining Corporation 312 489-5800
104 S Michigan Ave # 900 Chicago (60603) *(G-4006)*

Callen Die Casting, Bannockburn Also called Mumford Metal Casting LLC *(G-1204)*

Callender Construction Co Inc (PA) 217 285-2161
928 W Washington St Pittsfield (62363) *(G-16630)*

Callies Cuties Inc 815 566-6885
24860 Madison St Plainfield (60544) *(G-16646)*

Callison Distributing LLC 618 277-4300
4 Premier Dr Belleville (62220) *(G-1537)*

Callpod Inc (PA) 312 829-2680
850 W Jackson Blvd # 500 Chicago (60607) *(G-4007)*

Calma Optima Foods 847 962-8329
10915 Franklin Ave Ste A Franklin Park (60131) *(G-9897)*

Calmark Group LLC (PA) 708 728-0101
6755 S Sayre Ave Bedford Park (60638) *(G-1461)*

Calmark Group, The, Bedford Park Also called Calmark Group LLC *(G-1461)*

Calmer Corn Heads Inc 309 629-9000
3056 N 700th Ave Lynn Center (61262) *(G-13288)*

Calo Corporation 630 879-2202
197 Alder Dr North Aurora (60542) *(G-15256)*

Calport Aviation Company 630 588-8091
4n220 84 Ct Bartlett (60133) *(G-1254)*

Calumet Armature and Elc LLC 708 841-6880
1050 W 134th St Riverdale (60827) *(G-17070)*

Calumet Brass Foundry Inc 708 849-3040
14610 Lakeside Ave Dolton (60419) *(G-7934)*

Calumet Motorsports Inc 708 895-0398
3441 Washington St Lansing (60438) *(G-12487)*

Calumet Refining LLC 708 832-2463
14000 S Mackinaw Ave Burnham (60633) *(G-2644)*

Calumet Rubber Corp 773 536-6350
3545 S Normal Ave Ste A Chicago (60609) *(G-4008)*

Calumet Screw Machine Products 708 479-1660
19600 97th Ave Mokena (60448) *(G-14074)*

Calutech Inc 708 614-0228
15646 S 70th Ct 1 Orland Park (60462) *(G-15944)*

Calvert Systems 309 523-3262
21114 94th Ave N Port Byron (61275) *(G-16786)*

Calx Trading Corporation 630 456-6721
1245 Amaranth Dr Naperville (60564) *(G-14962)*

CAM Co Inc 630 556-3110
400 Rhodes Ave Big Rock (60511) *(G-1969)*

CAM Systems 800 208-3244
30 S Wacker Dr Ste 2200 Chicago (60606) *(G-4009)*

CAM Tek Lubricants Inc 708 477-3000
9540 W 144th Pl Ste 2a Orland Park (60462) *(G-15945)*

Cama Group, Buffalo Grove Also called Cama USA Inc *(G-2523)*

Cama USA Inc 847 607-8797
901 Corporate Grove Dr Buffalo Grove (60089) *(G-2523)*

Cambrdg Printing Corp 630 510-2100
780 W Army Trail Rd Carol Stream (60188) *(G-2954)*

Cambridge Brands Mfg Inc (HQ) 773 838-3400
7401 S Cicero Ave Chicago (60629) *(G-4010)*

Cambridge Business Publishers 630 321-0173
102 Chestnut Ave Westmont (60559) *(G-20731)*

Cambridge Chronicle 309 937-3303
119 W Exchange St Cambridge (61238) *(G-2802)*

Cambridge Monument Co, Rock Island Also called Beutel Corporation *(G-17207)*

Cambridge Pattern Works 309 937-5370
105 E Railroad St Cambridge (61238) *(G-2803)*

Cambridge Resources, Chicago Also called Coda Resources Ltd *(G-4189)*

Cambridge Resources, Chicago Also called Coda Resources Ltd *(G-4190)*

Cambridge Sensor Limited, Plainfield Also called Cambridge Sensors USA LLC *(G-16647)*

Cambridge Sensors USA LLC 877 374-4062
23866 W Industrial Dr N Plainfield (60585) *(G-16647)*

Camcar, Belvidere Also called Ring Screw LLC *(G-1699)*

Camcar LLC 815 544-7574
826 E Madison St Belvidere (61008) *(G-1659)*

Camco Manufacturing, Crestwood Also called Camshop Industrial LLC *(G-7109)*

Camco Manufacturing 708 597-4288
13933 Kildare Ave Crestwood (60418) *(G-7108)*

Camco Screw Machine Products, Crestwood Also called Camco Manufacturing Inc *(G-7108)*

Camcraft Inc (PA) 630 582-6001
1080 Muirfield Dr Hanover Park (60133) *(G-11001)*

Cameo Container Corporation 773 254-1030
1415 W 44th St Chicago (60609) *(G-4011)*

Cameo Mold & Duplicating, West Chicago Also called Cameo Mold Corp *(G-20557)*

Cameo Mold Corp 630 876-1340
1125 Carolina Dr West Chicago (60185) *(G-20557)*

Cameron Electric Motor Corp 312 939-5770
551 W Lexington St Chicago (60607) *(G-4012)*

Cameron Printing Inc 630 231-3301
1275 W Roosevelt Rd # 119 West Chicago (60185) *(G-20558)*

Camet, Schiller Park Also called Chicago Powdered Metal Pdts Co *(G-18793)*

Camfil USA Inc 815 459-6600
500 S Main St Crystal Lake (60014) *(G-7177)*

Camilles of Canton Inc 309 647-7403
1400 S Avenue B Canton (61520) *(G-2822)*

Camis Mold & Tool Co 847 593-6620
1350 Brummel Ave Elk Grove Village (60007) *(G-8878)*

Cammun LLC 312 628-1201
345 N Canal St Apt 1408 Chicago (60606) *(G-4013)*

Campanella Clg Solutions Inc 847 949-4222
900 N Lake St Ste 100 Mundelein (60060) *(G-14671)*

Campbell Cab, Wauconda Also called Campbell International Inc *(G-20339)*

Campbell Camie Inc 314 968-3222
2651 Warrenville Rd # 300 Downers Grove (60515) *(G-7963)*

Campbell Energy LLC 618 382-3939
1238 County Road 1500 N Carmi (62821) *(G-2901)*

Campbell International Inc 408 661-0794
120 Kent Ave Wauconda (60084) *(G-20339)*

Campbell Management Services 847 566-9020
25727 N Hillview Ct Mundelein (60060) *(G-14672)*

Campbell Publishing Co Inc 618 498-1234
832 S State St Jerseyville (62052) *(G-11788)*

Campbell Publishing Co Inc 217 285-2345
115 W Jefferson St Pittsfield (62363) *(G-16631)*

Campbell Publishing Inc 217 742-3313
4 S Hill St Winchester (62694) *(G-21104)*

Campbell Science Corp 815 962-7415
641 S Main St Rockford (61101) *(G-17333)*

Campbell Soup Company 618 548-3001
1824 W Main St Salem (62881) *(G-18333)*

Campbell Soup Company 630 241-6200
230 2nd St Downers Grove (60515) *(G-7964)*

Campeche Restaurant & Bar, Galena *Also called Campeche Restaurant Inc* ***(G-10166)***
Campeche Restaurant Inc 815 776-9950
230 N Commerce St Galena (61036) ***(G-10166)***
Campus Cardboard 847 373-7673
600 Waukegan Rd Northbrook (60062) ***(G-15351)***
Campus Cardboard 847 251-2594
5115 Church St Ste 104 Skokie (60077) ***(G-18936)***
Campus Sportswear Incorporated 217 344-0944
710 S 6th St Ste B Champaign (61820) ***(G-3274)***
Camryn Industries LLC 815 544-1900
3458 Morreim Dr Belvidere (61008) ***(G-1660)***
Camshop Industrial LLC 708 597-4288
13933 Kildare Ave Crestwood (60418) ***(G-7109)***
Camtek Inc 309 661-0348
2402 E Empire St Bloomington (61704) ***(G-2029)***
Canada Organization & Dev LLC (HQ) 630 743-2563
3005 Highland Pkwy Downers Grove (60515) ***(G-7965)***
Canadian Harvest LP 309 343-7808
701 W 6th St Galesburg (61401) ***(G-10187)***
Canam Steel Corporation 815 224-9588
9 Unytite Dr Peru (61354) ***(G-16569)***
Canconex Inc 847 458-9955
901 Armstrong St Algonquin (60102) ***(G-368)***
Candle Crest LLC 815 704-3809
604 N London Ave Rockford (61107) ***(G-17334)***
Candle Enterprises Inc 618 526-8070
580 N 2nd St Breese (62230) ***(G-2300)***
Candle-Licious 847 488-9982
634 E Lincolnway Morrison (61270) ***(G-14341)***
Candleart Candle Company Inc 217 925-5905
10084 N 1950th St Dieterich (62424) ***(G-7875)***
Candoc, Chicago *Also called Cudner & OConnor Co* ***(G-4283)***
Candriene Logistics LLC 312 260-0740
1016 W Jackson Blvd Chicago (60607) ***(G-4014)***
Candy Controls, Niles *Also called Candy Manufacturing Company* ***(G-15107)***
Candy Manufacturing Company 847 588-2639
5633 W Howard St Niles (60714) ***(G-15107)***
Cane Plus 217 522-4035
2225 S Whittier Ave Springfield (62704) ***(G-19336)***
Canham Graphics 217 585-5085
4524 Industrial Ave Springfield (62703) ***(G-19337)***
Cannon Ball Marketing Inc 630 971-2127
701 59th St Lisle (60532) ***(G-12875)***
Canny Tool & Mold Corporation 847 548-1573
888 E Belvidere Rd # 207 Grayslake (60030) ***(G-10760)***
Cano Container Corporation (PA) 630 585-7500
3920 Enterprise Ct Ste A Aurora (60504) ***(G-934)***
Canon Solutions America Inc 630 351-1227
1800 Bruning Dr W Itasca (60143) ***(G-11633)***
Canright & Paule Inc 888 202-3894
333 S Wabash Ave Ste 2700 Chicago (60604) ***(G-4015)***
Canright Communications, Chicago *Also called Canright & Paule Inc* ***(G-4015)***
Canton Noodle Company, Chicago *Also called YMC Corp* ***(G-6702)***
Canton Redi-Mix Inc 309 668-2261
22381 N State Highway 78 Canton (61520) ***(G-2823)***
Canton Redi-Mix Inc 309 647-0019
1130 W Locust St Canton (61520) ***(G-2824)***
Canyon Foods Inc 773 890-9888
1150 W 40th St Chicago (60609) ***(G-4016)***
Cap & Seal Co., Elgin *Also called Cs Legacy Corp* ***(G-8558)***
Cap & Seal Company, Elgin *Also called Sealco Industries Inc* ***(G-8725)***
Cap Factory 618 273-9662
816 State St Eldorado (62930) ***(G-8480)***
Cap Today 847 832-7377
325 Waukegan Rd Northfield (60093) ***(G-15510)***
Capable Controls Inc (PA) 630 860-6514
1062 Tower Ln Bensenville (60106) ***(G-1761)***
Cape Prosthetics-Orthotics Inc 618 457-4692
118 Airway Dr Marion (62959) ***(G-13507)***
Capers North America LLC 708 995-7500
632 Executive Dr Willowbrook (60527) ***(G-21034)***
Capital Advanced Technologies 630 690-1696
309 Village Dr Carol Stream (60188) ***(G-2955)***
Capital Engineering & Mfg Co, Barrington *Also called Cem LLC* ***(G-1217)***
Capital Merchant Solutions Inc 309 452-5990
3005 Gill St Ste 2 Bloomington (61704) ***(G-2030)***
Capital Printing & Die-Cutting, Aurora *Also called Capital Prtg & Die Cutng Inc* ***(G-1069)***
Capital Prtg & Die Cutng Inc 630 896-5520
303 S Highland Ave Aurora (60506) ***(G-1069)***
Capital Pttern Model Works Inc 630 469-8200
410 Windy Point Dr Glendale Heights (60139) ***(G-10440)***
Capital Rubber Corporation 630 595-6644
1140 Tower Ln Bensenville (60106) ***(G-1762)***
Capitol Carton Company (PA) 312 563-9690
346 N Justine St Ste 406 Chicago (60607) ***(G-4017)***
Capitol Carton Company 312 491-2220
1917 W Walnut St Chicago (60612) ***(G-4018)***
Capitol City Machine 217 529-0293
2840 Adlai Stevenson Dr B Springfield (62703) ***(G-19338)***
Capitol City Tool & Design 217 544-9250
1330 Taylor Ave Springfield (62703) ***(G-19339)***
Capitol Coil Inc 847 891-1390
821 Albion Ave Ste B Schaumburg (60193) ***(G-18467)***
Capitol Containers, Chicago *Also called Capitol Carton Company* ***(G-4017)***
Capitol Impressions Inc 309 633-1400
1622 W Moss Ave Peoria (61606) ***(G-16397)***
Capitol Ready-Mix Inc (PA) 217 528-1100
1900 E Mason St Springfield (62702) ***(G-19340)***
Capitol Wood Works LLC 217 522-5553
1010 E Edwards St Springfield (62703) ***(G-19341)***
Caples-El Transport Inc 708 300-2727
560 Buffalo Ave Calumet City (60409) ***(G-2772)***
Capol LLC 224 545-5095
707 Lake Cook Rd Ste 320 Deerfield (60015) ***(G-7599)***
Capron Mfg Co (PA) 815 569-2301
200 Burr Oak Rd Capron (61012) ***(G-2832)***
Capsim MGT Simulations Inc 312 477-7200
55 E Monroe St Ste 3210 Chicago (60603) ***(G-4019)***
Capsonic Automotive Inc 847 888-7300
495 Renner Dr Elgin (60123) ***(G-8529)***
Capsonic Automotive Inc (PA) 847 888-7300
460 2nd St Elgin (60123) ***(G-8530)***
Capsonic Automotive Inc 915 872-3585
4219 Solutions Ctr Chicago (60677) ***(G-4020)***
Capsonic Group, Elgin *Also called Capsonic Automotive Inc* ***(G-8529)***
Capsonic Group LLC (PA) 847 888-7264
460 2nd St Elgin (60123) ***(G-8531)***
Capstone Dev Svcs Co LLC 847 999-0131
9450 Bryn Mawr Ave # 200 Rosemont (60018) ***(G-18002)***
Capstone Therapeutics Corp (PA) 602 286-5520
5141 W 122nd St Alsip (60803) ***(G-426)***
Captain Hook Inc 309 565-7676
5125 S Hnna Cy Glsford Rd Hanna City (61536) ***(G-10991)***
Captains Emporium Inc 773 972-7609
1200 W 35th St Chicago (60609) ***(G-4021)***
Captivating Signs LLC (PA) 630 470-6161
612 W 5th Ave Ste A Naperville (60563) ***(G-14788)***
Car - Mon Products Inc 847 695-9000
1225 Davis Rd Elgin (60123) ***(G-8532)***
Car Shop Inc 309 797-4188
1214 17th Ave Moline (61265) ***(G-14135)***
Cara ANAM Enterprises Inc 630 587-8700
216 Kirk Rd Saint Charles (60174) ***(G-18163)***
Caraustar Industrial and Con 217 323-5225
100 Forest Ln Beardstown (62618) ***(G-1446)***
Caraustar Industries Inc 773 308-7622
555 N Tripp Ave Chicago (60624) ***(G-4022)***
Caravan Ingredients Inc 708 849-8590
14622 Lakeside Ave Dolton (60419) ***(G-7935)***
Carbco Manufacturing Inc 630 377-1410
2525 Production Dr Saint Charles (60174) ***(G-18164)***
Carbit Corporation (PA) 312 280-2300
927 W Blackhawk St Chicago (60642) ***(G-4023)***
Carbit Paint Co, Chicago *Also called Carbit Corporation* ***(G-4023)***
Carbon Clean Solutions USA Inc 872 206-0197
1712 N Wood St Apt 3w Chicago (60622) ***(G-4024)***
Carbon Solutions Group LLC 312 638-9077
1130 W Monroe St Ste 1 Chicago (60607) ***(G-4025)***
Carbondale Night Life 618 549-2799
2015 W Main St Ste 105 Carbondale (62901) ***(G-2839)***
Carbondale Times, Carbondale *Also called Carbondale Night Life* ***(G-2839)***
Carbondale Trophy Co, Carbondale *Also called Rudon Enterprises Inc* ***(G-2857)***
Card Dynamix LLC 630 685-4060
1120 Windham Pkwy Romeoville (60446) ***(G-17803)***
Card Prsnlzation Solutions LLC 630 543-2630
80 Internationale Blvd C Glendale Heights (60139) ***(G-10441)***
Cardiac Imaging Inc 630 834-7100
2 Transam Plaza Dr # 420 Oakbrook Terrace (60181) ***(G-15791)***
Cardinal Cattle 309 479-1302
Rr 2 Box 181 Wyoming (61491) ***(G-21458)***
Cardinal Colorprint Prtg Corp 630 467-1000
1270 Ardmore Ave Itasca (60143) ***(G-11634)***
Cardinal Construction Co 618 842-5553
705 S 1st St Fairfield (62837) ***(G-9621)***
Cardinal Engineering Inc 309 342-7474
1640 N Kellogg St Galesburg (61401) ***(G-10188)***
Cardinal Enterprises 618 994-4454
562 Ferrel Rd Stonefort (62987) ***(G-19557)***
Cardinal Health Inc 847 578-4443
1500 S Waukegan Rd Waukegan (60085) ***(G-20424)***
Cardinal Health 200 LLC 847 689-8410
1430 S Waukegan Rd Waukegan (60085) ***(G-20425)***
Cardinal Hill Candles & Crafts, Rochester *Also called Edwin Waldmire & Virginia* ***(G-17165)***
Cardinal Medical Services, Waukegan *Also called Cardinal Health Inc* ***(G-20424)***
Cardinal Pallet Co 773 725-5387
505 W 43rd St Chicago (60609) ***(G-4026)***
Cardinal Plating Solutions Inc 309 582-6215
802 Se 19th Ave Aledo (61231) ***(G-355)***

ALPHABETIC

Cardon Mold Finishing Inc 630 543-5431
703 W Annoreno Dr Ste 4 Addison (60101) ***(G-63)***
Cardthartic LLC 217 239-5895
30102 Research Rd Champaign (61822) ***(G-3275)***
Cardwell Westinghouse Company....773 483-7575
8400 S Stewart Ave Chicago (60620) ***(G-4027)***
Care Creations, Skokie *Also called Laser Reproductions Inc* ***(G-18977)***
Care Education Group Inc 708 361-4110
126 Commons Dr Palos Park (60464) ***(G-16208)***
Carematix Inc....312 627-9300
209 W Jackson Blvd # 401 Chicago (60606) ***(G-4028)***
Carey Color Inc....630 761-2605
2500 Enterprise Cir # 100 West Chicago (60185) ***(G-20559)***
Carey Electric Co Inc....847 949-9294
24809 W Chardon Rd Grayslake (60030) ***(G-10761)***
Cargill Incorporated 773 374-3808
12201 S Torrence Ave Chicago (60617) ***(G-4029)***
Cargill Incorporated 618 662-8070
6 Industrial Park Flora (62839) ***(G-9677)***
Cargill Incorporated 815 942-0932
301 Griggs St Morris (60450) ***(G-14296)***
Cargill Incorporated 217 872-7653
765 E Pythian Ave Decatur (62526) ***(G-7469)***
Cargill Incorporated 630 739-1746
10420 Woodward Ave Woodridge (60517) ***(G-21280)***
Cargill Incorporated 773 375-7255
12200 S Torrence Ave Chicago (60617) ***(G-4030)***
Cargill Incorporated....309 587-8111
408 1st St New Boston (61272) ***(G-15026)***
Cargill Incorporated 309 827-7100
115 S Euclid Ave Bloomington (61701) ***(G-2031)***
Cargill Incorporated 630 505-7788
954 W Wa Blvd Ste 225 Chicago (60607) ***(G-4031)***
Cargill Dry Corn Ingrdents Inc (HQ)....217 465-5331
616 S Jefferson St Paris (61944) ***(G-16226)***
Cargill Food Distribution, Woodridge *Also called Cargill Meat Solutions Corp* ***(G-21281)***
Cargill Meat Solutions Corp 630 739-1746
10420 Woodward Ave Woodridge (60517) ***(G-21281)***
Cargo Support Industries Inc....847 744-0786
242 Willow St Inverness (60010) ***(G-11599)***
Carl Buddig and Company (PA) 708 798-0900
950 175th St Homewood (60430) ***(G-11489)***
Carl Gorr Printing Co 815 338-3191
1002 Mchenry Ave Woodstock (60098) ***(G-21370)***
Carl Manufacturing USA Inc 847 884-2842
100 E Pierce Rd Ste 100 # 100 Itasca (60143) ***(G-11635)***
Carl Stahl Decorcable LLC, Burr Ridge *Also called Carl Stahl Decrcabl Innovtns I* ***(G-2660)***
Carl Stahl Decrcabl Innovtns I....312 474-1100
8080 S Madison St Burr Ridge (60527) ***(G-2660)***
Carlease Inc 847 714-1414
1945 Techny Rd Ste 8 Northbrook (60062) ***(G-15352)***
Carlin Mfg A Div Grs Holdg LLC....559 276-0123
131 W Jefferson Ave # 223 Naperville (60540) ***(G-14789)***
Carlinville Waste Water Plants 217 854-6506
1345 Mayo St Carlinville (62626) ***(G-2868)***
Carlisle Construction Mtls LLC 847 671-2516
9201 Belmont Ave Franklin Park (60131) ***(G-9898)***
Carlisle Syn TEC Inc....618 664-4540
1825 E City Route 40 Greenville (62246) ***(G-10829)***
Carlson Capitol Mfg Co, Rockford *Also called Carlson Capitol Mfg Co* ***(G-17335)***
Carlson Capitol Mfg Co 815 398-3110
2319 23rd Ave Rockford (61104) ***(G-17335)***
Carlson Scientific Inc....708 258-6377
514 S Third St Peotone (60468) ***(G-16551)***
Carlson STI, Elgin *Also called Carlson Tool & Machine Company* ***(G-8534)***
Carlson Sti Inc 630 232-2460
1875 Big Timber Rd Ste A Elgin (60123) ***(G-8533)***
Carlson Tool & Machine Company 630 232-2460
1875 Big Timber Rd Ste A Elgin (60123) ***(G-8534)***
Carlyle Brewing Co....815 963-2739
215 E State St Rockford (61104) ***(G-17336)***
Carlyle Sand & Gravel Ltd 618 594-8263
11842 State Route 127 Carlyle (62231) ***(G-2889)***
Carmen Matthew LLC....630 784-7500
2100 Golf Rd Ste 460 Rolling Meadows (60008) ***(G-17720)***
Carmi Times....618 382-4176
323 E Main St Carmi (62821) ***(G-2902)***
Carmona Gear Cutting 815 963-8236
1707 Magnolia St Rockford (61104) ***(G-17337)***
Carnaghi Towing & Repair Inc....217 446-0333
2000 Georgetown Rd Tilton (61833) ***(G-19793)***
Carnation Enterprises....847 804-5928
8630 N National Ave Niles (60714) ***(G-15108)***
Carney Flow Technics LLC....815 277-2600
181 Ontario St Frankfort (60423) ***(G-9777)***
Carol Andrzejewski....630 369-9711
2339 Kalamazoo Dr Naperville (60565) ***(G-14790)***
Carol Douglas Company, Silvis *Also called River City Sign Company Inc* ***(G-18909)***
Caroline Cole Inc 618 233-0600
711 S Illinois St Belleville (62220) ***(G-1538)***
Caroline Rose Inc 708 386-1011
741 Madison St Oak Park (60302) ***(G-15748)***
Carols Cookies Inc 847 831-4500
3184 Macarthur Blvd Northbrook (60062) ***(G-15353)***
Carousel Checks Inc....708 613-2452
11152 Southwest Hwy Ste A Palos Hills (60465) ***(G-16197)***
Carpenters Millwork Co 708 339-7707
16046 Vandustrial Ln South Holland (60473) ***(G-19204)***
Carpenters Millwork Co (PA) 708 339-7707
224 W Stone Rd Villa Park (60181) ***(G-20137)***
Carpentersville Quarry Inc....847 836-1550
800 Bolz Rd Carpentersville (60110) ***(G-3096)***
Carpet One, Chicago *Also called L & L Flooring Inc* ***(G-5140)***
Carquest Auto Parts, Decatur *Also called Donnelly Automotive Machine* ***(G-7491)***
Carr Machine & Tool Inc....847 593-8003
1301 Jarvis Ave Elk Grove Village (60007) ***(G-8879)***
Carrera Stone Systems of Chica....847 566-2277
675 Tower Rd Mundelein (60060) ***(G-14673)***
Carroll County Locker....815 493-2370
122 E Carroll St Lanark (61046) ***(G-12478)***
Carroll County Review 815 259-2131
809 W Main St Thomson (61285) ***(G-19780)***
Carroll Distrg & Cnstr Sup Inc....630 892-4855
1031 W Lake St Aurora (60506) ***(G-1070)***
Carroll Distrg & Cnstr Sup Inc....630 243-0272
13087 Main St Lemont (60439) ***(G-12558)***
Carroll Distrg & Cnstr Sup Inc....815 941-1548
460 Briscoe Dr Morris (60450) ***(G-14297)***
Carroll Distrg & Cnstr Sup Inc....309 449-6044
201 Ford Ave Hopedale (61747) ***(G-11516)***
Carroll Distrg & Cnstr Sup Inc....630 369-6520
1700 Quincy Ave Naperville (60540) ***(G-14791)***
Carroll Distrg & Cnstr Sup Inc....815 464-0100
121 Industry Ave Frankfort (60423) ***(G-9778)***
Carroll Industrial Molds Inc 815 225-7250
202 N Washington St Milledgeville (61051) ***(G-14038)***
Carroll International Corp 630 983-5979
55 N Mayflower Rd Lake Forest (60045) ***(G-12236)***
Carrolls Welding & Fabrication 217 728-8720
819 N Market St Sullivan (61951) ***(G-19663)***
Carson Printing Inc 847 836-0900
1110 Heinz Dr Ste C East Dundee (60118) ***(G-8189)***
Carson Properties Inc (PA) 630 832-3322
953 N Larch Ave Elmhurst (60126) ***(G-9341)***
Carstens Incorporated 708 669-1500
7310 W Wilson Ave Chicago (60706) ***(G-4032)***
Carstin Brands Inc....217 543-3331
520 E 2nd St Arthur (61911) ***(G-844)***
Cartec, Mount Vernon *Also called Dennis Carnes* ***(G-14608)***
Cartel Holdings Inc (PA)....815 334-0250
3 Lincoln St Ste 2a Harvard (60033) ***(G-11049)***
Carter Anna Brooks LLC....618 382-3939
1238 County Road 1500 N Carmi (62821) ***(G-2903)***
Carter Hoffmann LLC 847 362-5500
1551 Mccormick Blvd Mundelein (60060) ***(G-14674)***
Carter Motor Company, Warren *Also called Stable Beginning Corporation* ***(G-20225)***
Carter Printing Co Inc 217 227-4464
607 Elevator St Farmersville (62533) ***(G-9659)***
Carterville Courier 618 985-6187
122 S Division St Carterville (62918) ***(G-3130)***
Cartpac Inc....630 283-8979
245 E North Ave Carol Stream (60188) ***(G-2956)***
Cartridge World Bloomingdale, Bloomingdale *Also called Dauphin Enterprise Inc* ***(G-1987)***
Cartridge World Decatur....217 875-0465
215 E Ash Ave Ste D Decatur (62526) ***(G-7470)***
Carus Chemical Company, La Salle *Also called Carus LLC* ***(G-12106)***
Carus Corporation....815 223-1565
1500 8th St La Salle (61301) ***(G-12105)***
Carus Group Inc (PA) 815 223-1500
315 5th St Peru (61354) ***(G-16570)***
Carus LLC (HQ)....815 223-1500
315 5th St Peru (61354) ***(G-16571)***
Carus LLC 815 223-1500
1500 8th St La Salle (61301) ***(G-12106)***
Carus Publishing Company (HQ) 603 924-7209
70 E Lake St Ste 800 Chicago (60601) ***(G-4033)***
Carus Publishing Company....312 701-1720
70 E Lake St Ste 800 Chicago (60601) ***(G-4034)***
Carver Custom Woodworks, Milan *Also called Agusta Mill Works* ***(G-13999)***
Carver Plastic Products Inc....708 588-0081
512 W Burlington Ave # 208 La Grange (60525) ***(G-12075)***
Cary Physcl Therapy Spt Rehab, Cary *Also called Deborah Morris Gulbrandson Pt* ***(G-3154)***
Casa Di Castronovo Inc 815 962-4731
722 N Main St Rockford (61103) ***(G-17338)***
Casa Nostra Bakery Co Inc....847 455-5175
3140 Mannheim Rd Franklin Park (60131) ***(G-9899)***
Cascades Enviropac Aurora, Aurora *Also called Cascades Plastics Inc* ***(G-935)***
Cascades Plastics Inc....450 469-3389
2300 Raddant Rd Ste B Aurora (60502) ***(G-935)***

ALPHABETIC SECTION Caterpillar Inc

Casco Manufacturing Inc....630 771-9555
600 Territorial Dr Ste C Bolingbrook (60440) ***(G-2155)***
Case Guys, Bedford Park *Also called A W Enterprises Inc* ***(G-1452)***
Case New Holl Burr Ridge Opera, Burr Ridge *Also called Cnh Industrial America LLC* ***(G-2664)***
Case/D M I, Goodfield *Also called Cnh Industrial America LLC* ***(G-10672)***
Casey Spring Co Inc....708 867-8949
1516 Marguerite St Park Ridge (60068) ***(G-16272)***
Casey Stone Co....217 857-3425
14046 N 1600th St Teutopolis (62467) ***(G-19766)***
CASS COUNTY STAR GAZZETTE, Beardstown *Also called Beardstown Newspapers Inc* ***(G-1445)***
Cass Meats....217 452-3072
5815 Il Route 78 Virginia (62691) ***(G-20193)***
Cassetica Software Inc....312 546-3668
22 W Washington St # 1500 Chicago (60602) ***(G-4035)***
Cassini Cabinetry....847 244-9755
701 Belvidere Rd Waukegan (60085) ***(G-20426)***
Cast Aluminum Solutions LLC....630 482-5325
1310 Kingsland Dr Batavia (60510) ***(G-1362)***
Cast Films Inc....847 808-0363
401 Chaddick Dr Wheeling (60090) ***(G-20869)***
Cast Glassworks....847 831-0222
1975 Northland Ave Highland Park (60035) ***(G-11257)***
Cast Industries Inc....217 522-8292
580 North St Springfield (62704) ***(G-19342)***
Cast Products Inc....708 457-1500
4200 N Nordica Ave Norridge (60706) ***(G-15232)***
Cast Technologies Inc (PA)....309 676-1715
1100 Sw Washington St Peoria (61602) ***(G-16398)***
Cast Technologies Inc....309 674-1402
2718 Sw Adams St Peoria (61602) ***(G-16399)***
Cast21 Inc....847 772-8547
965 W Chicago Ave Chicago (60642) ***(G-4036)***
Caster Warehouse Inc....847 836-5712
1011 Tamarac Dr Carpentersville (60110) ***(G-3097)***
Castillo Leather Goods....773 491-0018
9233 S 51st Ave Oak Lawn (60453) ***(G-15707)***
Casting House Inc....312 782-7160
5 S Wabash Ave Ste 614 Chicago (60603) ***(G-4037)***
Casting Impregnators Inc (PA)....847 455-1000
11150 Addison Ave Franklin Park (60131) ***(G-9900)***
Castino & Associates Inc....847 291-7446
3065 Dundee Rd Northbrook (60062) ***(G-15354)***
Castle Craft Products Inc....630 279-7494
1133 N Ellsworth Ave Villa Park (60181) ***(G-20138)***
Castle Metal Finishing Corp....847 678-6041
4631 25th Ave Schiller Park (60176) ***(G-18791)***
Castle Metal Products Corp....847 806-4540
1947 Quincy Ct Glendale Heights (60139) ***(G-10442)***
Castle-Printech Inc....815 758-5484
121 Industrial Dr Dekalb (60115) ***(G-7667)***
Castlegate Publishers Inc....847 382-6420
25597 W Drake Rd Barrington (60010) ***(G-1216)***
Castro Foods Wholesale Inc....773 869-0641
1365 W 37th St Chicago (60609) ***(G-4038)***
Castrol Industrial N Amer Inc (HQ)....877 641-1600
150 W Warrenville Rd Naperville (60563) ***(G-14792)***
Castronovo's Bridal Shop, Rockford *Also called Casa Di Castronovo Inc* ***(G-17338)***
Castwell Products LLC....847 966-5050
7800 Austin Ave Skokie (60077) ***(G-18937)***
Casward Tool Works Inc....773 486-4900
8062 Pickens Dr Orland Park (60462) ***(G-15946)***
Cat I Manufacturing Inc....847 931-8986
865 Commerce Dr South Elgin (60177) ***(G-19140)***
Cat-I Glass, South Elgin *Also called Cat I Manufacturing Inc* ***(G-19140)***
Catalent Pharma Solutions LLC....815 338-9500
2210 Lake Shore Dr Woodstock (60098) ***(G-21371)***
Catalent Pharma Solutions Inc....815 338-9500
2210 Lake Shore Dr Woodstock (60098) ***(G-21372)***
Catalina Coating & Plas Inc....847 806-1340
870 Greenleaf Ave Elk Grove Village (60007) ***(G-8880)***
Catalina Graphic Films, Elk Grove Village *Also called Catalina Coating & Plas Inc* ***(G-8880)***
Catalina Graphics Inc....773 973-7780
2325 W Farwell Ave Apt 3s Chicago (60645) ***(G-4039)***
Catalog Designers Inc....847 228-0025
106 Buckingham Ct Elk Grove Village (60007) ***(G-8881)***
Catalyst Chicago....312 427-4830
332 S Michigan Ave Ste 37 Chicago (60604) ***(G-4040)***
Catalytic Inc....844 787-4268
954 W Wa Blvd Ste 700 Chicago (60607) ***(G-4041)***
Catalytic Products Intl Inc....847 438-0334
980 Ensell Rd Lake Zurich (60047) ***(G-12390)***
Catalyze, Chicago *Also called Mhub* ***(G-5420)***
Catapult Communications Corp....847 884-0048
1821 Walden Office Sq # 120 Schaumburg (60173) ***(G-18468)***
Catapult Global LLC....847 364-8149
1000 Lee St Elk Grove Village (60007) ***(G-8882)***
Catapult Integrated Svcs LLC....312 216-4460
104 S Michigan Ave # 1500 Chicago (60603) ***(G-4042)***
Catching Hydraulics Co Ltd....708 344-2334
1733 N 25th Ave Melrose Park (60160) ***(G-13839)***
Cater Chemical Co....630 980-2300
30 Monaco Dr Roselle (60172) ***(G-17943)***
Caterpilar, Carrier Mills *Also called Caterpillar Globl Min Amer LLC* ***(G-3124)***
Caterpillar Authorized Dealer, Morton *Also called Spl Software Alliance LLC* ***(G-14383)***
Caterpillar Authorized Dealer, Bartonville *Also called Altorfer Power Systems* ***(G-1328)***
Caterpillar Brazil LLC....309 675-1000
100 Ne Adams St Peoria (61629) ***(G-16400)***
Caterpillar Forest Pdts Inc....309 675-1000
330 Sw Adams St Peoria (61602) ***(G-16401)***
Caterpillar Foundation....309 675-4232
100 Ne Adams St Peoria (61629) ***(G-16402)***
Caterpillar Gb LLC....309 675-1000
100 Ne Adams St Peoria (61629) ***(G-16403)***
Caterpillar Global Mining LLC....618 378-3441
635 Il Highway 1 Norris City (62869) ***(G-15247)***
Caterpillar Globl Min Amer LLC....618 982-9000
9580 Highway 13 W Carrier Mills (62917) ***(G-3124)***
Caterpillar Inc....309 578-2185
48 Cranbarry Mossville (61552) ***(G-14452)***
Caterpillar Inc....309 675-1000
2000 Carver Ln East Peoria (61611) ***(G-8255)***
Caterpillar Inc (PA)....224 551-4000
510 Lake Cook Rd Ste 100 Deerfield (60015) ***(G-7600)***
Caterpillar Inc....815 729-5511
540 Joyce Rd Joliet (60436) ***(G-11838)***
Caterpillar Inc....630 859-5000
325 S Rte 31 Montgomery (60538) ***(G-14238)***
Caterpillar Inc....217 475-4000
3000 N 27th St Decatur (62525) ***(G-7471)***
Caterpillar Inc....309 675-1000
100 Ne Adams St Peoria (61629) ***(G-16404)***
Caterpillar Inc....309 675-2545
100 Tractor Dr East Peoria (61630) ***(G-8249)***
Caterpillar Inc....309 675-1000
600 W Washington St East Peoria (61611) ***(G-8256)***
Caterpillar Inc....309 578-6118
14009 Old Galena Rd Mossville (61552) ***(G-14453)***
Caterpillar Inc....309 675-5681
7022 W Middle Rd Peoria (61607) ***(G-16405)***
Caterpillar Inc....217 475-4355
3125 N 22nd St Decatur (62526) ***(G-7472)***
Caterpillar Inc....309 633-8788
8826 W Us Highway 24 Mapleton (61547) ***(G-13468)***
Caterpillar Inc....309 578-2086
28194 Caterpillar Ln Washington (61571) ***(G-20268)***
Caterpillar Inc....309 675-8327
5801 N Smith Rd Edwards (61528) ***(G-8337)***
Caterpillar Inc....304 327-7793
500 N Morton Ave Morton (61550) ***(G-14355)***
Caterpillar Inc....217 424-1809
2701 Pershing Rd Decatur (62526) ***(G-7473)***
Caterpillar Inc....309 266-4294
1900 E Old Galena Rd Mossville (61552) ***(G-14454)***
Caterpillar Inc....903 712-4505
14009 Old Galena Rd Mossville (61552) ***(G-14455)***
Caterpillar Inc....309 495-9216
600 W Washington St East Peoria (61611) ***(G-8257)***
Caterpillar Inc....309 578-4643
8201 N University St # 2 Peoria (61615) ***(G-16406)***
Caterpillar Inc....888 614-4328
501 Sw Jefferson Ave Peoria (61605) ***(G-16407)***
Caterpillar Inc....309 675-1000
100 Ne Adams St Peoria (61629) ***(G-16408)***
Caterpillar Inc....217 475-4322
2500 N 22nd St Decatur (62526) ***(G-7474)***
Caterpillar Inc....815 842-6000
1300 4h Park Rd Pontiac (61764) ***(G-16767)***
Caterpillar Inc....309 578-2473
Old Galena Rd Ste H Mossville (61552) ***(G-14456)***
Caterpillar Inc....309 675-1000
14009 Old Galena Rd Mossville (61552) ***(G-14457)***
Caterpillar Inc....309 675-3183
901 W Washington St East Peoria (61611) ***(G-8258)***
Caterpillar Inc....309 675-1000
1335 Sw Washington St Peoria (61602) ***(G-16409)***
Caterpillar Inc....309 675-6223
Illinois Rte 29 Mossville (61552) ***(G-14458)***
Caterpillar Inc....309 494-0858
Rr 31 Box S Aurora (60507) ***(G-1071)***
Caterpillar Inc....309 578-1615
Ac 6123 Mossville (61552) ***(G-14459)***
Caterpillar Inc....309 675-1000
100 Ne Adams St Peoria (61629) ***(G-16410)***
Caterpillar Inc....217 255-8500
1901 S 1st St Ste C1 Champaign (61820) ***(G-3276)***

ALPHABETIC

Caterpillar Inc   ALPHABETIC SECTION

Caterpillar Inc 309 675-6590
2400 Sw Washington St Peoria (61602) *(G-16411)*
Caterpillar Intl Lsg LLC 309 675-1000
100 Ne Adams St Peoria (61629) *(G-16412)*
Caterpillar Luxembourg LLC (HQ) 309 675-1000
100 Ne Adams St Peoria (61629) *(G-16413)*
Caterpillar Power Systems Inc 309 675-1000
100 Ne Adams St Peoria (61629) *(G-16414)*
Caterpillar World Trading Corp 309 675-1000
100 Ne Adams St Peoria (61629) *(G-16415)*
Cathay Industries (usa) Inc (HQ) 219 531-5359
2340 Kenyon Rd Bartlett (60103) *(G-1271)*
Cathay Pigments, Bartlett Also called Cathay Industries (usa) Inc *(G-1271)*
Catholic Book Covers, Franklin Park Also called J S Printing Inc *(G-9970)*
Catholic Press Assn of The US 312 380-6789
205 W Monroe St Chicago (60606) *(G-4043)*
Cathys Sweet Creations 815 886-6769
519 W Lockport Rd Plainfield (60544) *(G-16648)*
Cavallo Tool Service Inc 630 620-4445
1714 W Armitage Ct Addison (60101) *(G-64)*
Cavanaugh Government Group LLC 630 210-8668
8432 Beloit Ave Bridgeview (60455) *(G-2332)*
Cavco Printers 618 988-8011
406 N Pershing St Energy (62933) *(G-9467)*
Cavco Printers Prtg & Copy Ctr, Energy Also called Cavco Printers *(G-9467)*
Cavero Coatings Company LLC 630 616-2868
422 County Line Rd Bensenville (60106) *(G-1763)*
Caxton Club 312 266-8825
60 W Walton St Chicago (60610) *(G-4044)*
Caxton Club Chicago, The, Chicago Also called Caxton Club *(G-4044)*
Cayenne Couture Atelier 773 408-4664
1665 E 79th St Chicago (60649) *(G-4045)*
CB & I Water, Bourbonnais Also called CB&i LLC *(G-2258)*
CB Machine & Tool Corp 847 288-1807
9321 Schiller Blvd Franklin Park (60131) *(G-9901)*
CB&i LLC 815 936-5440
1035 E 5000n Rd Bourbonnais (60914) *(G-2258)*
CB&i Tyler LLC 281 774-2200
14105 S Route 59 Plainfield (60544) *(G-16649)*
Cb2, Northbrook Also called Euromarket Designs Inc *(G-15386)*
Cbana Labs Inc (PA) 217 819-5201
2021 S 1st St Ste 206 Champaign (61820) *(G-3277)*
Cbc Restaurant Corp 773 463-0665
2711 W George St Chicago (60618) *(G-4046)*
CC Distributing Services Inc 800 931-2668
13655 Kenton Ave Crestwood (60418) *(G-7110)*
Ccar Industries 217 345-3300
200 W Locust Ave Charleston (61920) *(G-3397)*
CCC Brands, Chicago Also called Chicago Coml Consmr Brands LLC *(G-4098)*
CCC Cabinets, Elk Grove Village Also called CCC Chicago Cabinet Center LLC *(G-8883)*
CCC Chicago Cabinet Center LLC 855 508-5525
300 King St Elk Grove Village (60007) *(G-8883)*
CCH Incorporated (HQ) 847 267-7000
2700 Lake Cook Rd Riverwoods (60015) *(G-17090)*
CCI Manufacturing IL Corp 630 739-0606
15550 Canal Bank Rd Lemont (60439) *(G-12559)*
CCI Redi Mix, Effingham Also called Contractors Concrete Inc *(G-8394)*
Cck Automations Inc 217 243-6040
500 Capitol Way Jacksonville (62650) *(G-11761)*
CCL Construction Inc (PA) 219 237-2911
18161 Morris Ave Ste 204 Homewood (60430) *(G-11490)*
CCL Label (chicago) Inc 630 406-9991
1862 Suncast Ln Batavia (60510) *(G-1363)*
Ccmha, Taylorville Also called Christian Cnty Mntal Hlth Assn *(G-19753)*
Cco Holdings LLC 618 505-3505
523 Troy Plz Troy (62294) *(G-19912)*
Cco Holdings LLC 618 651-6486
2762 Troxler Way Highland (62249) *(G-11208)*
CCS Contractor Eqp & Sup Inc (PA) 630 393-9020
1567 Frontenac Rd Naperville (60563) *(G-14793)*
Ccsi, Lansing Also called Construction Contg Svcs Inc *(G-12489)*
Ccsi International Inc 815 544-8385
8642 Us Highway 20 Garden Prairie (61038) *(G-10236)*
Ccty USA Bearing Co 847 540-8196
1111 Rose Rd Lake Zurich (60047) *(G-12391)*
Cd LLC 312 275-5747
363 W Erie St Ste 400w Chicago (60654) *(G-4047)*
CD Magic Inc 708 582-3496
116 S Prospect St Roselle (60172) *(G-17944)*
Cda Industries Inc 630 357-7654
1228 Jane Ave Naperville (60540) *(G-14794)*
Cdc Enterprises Inc 815 790-4205
1512 River Terrace Dr Johnsburg (60051) *(G-11802)*
Cdg Operations LLC 618 943-8700
8528 N Frontage Ln Bridgeport (62417) *(G-2311)*
CDI Computer Dealers, Chicago Also called CDI Computers US Corporation *(G-4048)*
CDI Computers US Corporation 888 226-5727
500 N Michigan Ave # 600 Chicago (60611) *(G-4048)*

CDI Corp 773 205-2960
3440 N Knox Ave Chicago (60641) *(G-4049)*
CDK Global Inc (PA) 847 397-1700
1950 Hassell Rd Hoffman Estates (60169) *(G-11412)*
Cds Engineering, Elgin Also called Agnes & Chris Gulik *(G-8499)*
CDs Office Systems Inc (PA) 800 367-1508
612 S Dirksen Pkwy Springfield (62703) *(G-19343)*
CDs Office Systems Inc 217 351-5046
3108 Farber Dr Ofc Champaign (61822) *(G-3278)*
CDs Office Systems Inc 630 305-9034
612 S Dirksen Pkwy Springfield (62703) *(G-19344)*
Cds Office Technologies, Springfield Also called CDs Office Systems Inc *(G-19343)*
Cdv, Rockford Also called Stuhr Manufacturing Co *(G-17648)*
Cdv Corp 815 397-3903
5085 27th Ave Rockford (61109) *(G-17339)*
Cdw Merchants, Morton Grove Also called Bunzl Retail LLC *(G-14392)*
Cec Industries Ltd 847 821-1199
599 Bond St Lincolnshire (60069) *(G-12748)*
Cec, The Ozone Co, Downers Grove Also called Advanced Ozone Tech Inc *(G-7949)*
Cecomp Electronics Inc 847 918-3510
1220 American Way Libertyville (60048) *(G-12642)*
Cedar Concepts Corporation 773 890-5790
4100 S Packers Ave Chicago (60609) *(G-4050)*
Cedar Elec Holdings Corp (PA) 630 862-7282
6500 W Cortland St Chicago (60707) *(G-4051)*
Cedar Rustic Fence Co., Joliet Also called Bergeron Group Inc *(G-11830)*
Cedille Chicago Nfp 773 989-2515
1205 W Balmoral Ave Chicago (60640) *(G-4052)*
CEDILLE RECORDS, Chicago Also called Cedille Chicago Nfp *(G-4052)*
CEF Industries LLC (HQ) 630 628-2299
320 S Church St Addison (60101) *(G-65)*
Ceg Subsidiary LLC (PA) 618 262-8666
714 N Walnut St Mount Carmel (62863) *(G-14467)*
Ceg Subsidiary LLC 618 262-8666
714 N Walnut St Mount Carmel (62863) *(G-14468)*
Celco Tool & Engineering Inc 847 671-2520
9300 Bernice Ave Schiller Park (60176) *(G-18792)*
Celectiv, Chicago Also called Liders LLC *(G-5219)*
Celerity Pharmaceuticals LLC 847 999-0131
9450 Bryn Mawr Ave # 200 Rosemont (60018) *(G-18003)*
Celgene Corporation 908 673-9000
2045 Cornell Ave Melrose Park (60160) *(G-13840)*
Celinco Inc 815 964-2256
2320 Kishwaukee St Rockford (61104) *(G-17340)*
Celinco Inc (PA) 815 964-2256
2320 Kishwaukee St Rockford (61104) *(G-17341)*
Cell Parts Manufacturing Co 847 669-9690
10675 Wolf Dr Huntley (60142) *(G-11530)*
Cellar LLC (PA) 618 956-9900
326 Vermont Rd Carterville (62918) *(G-3131)*
Cellas Confections Inc (HQ) 773 838-3400
7401 S Cicero Ave Chicago (60629) *(G-4053)*
Cellmark Inc 630 775-9500
1 Tiffany Pt Ste 300 Bloomingdale (60108) *(G-1984)*
Cellusuede Products Inc 815 964-8619
1515 Elmwood Rd Rockford (61103) *(G-17342)*
Celtic Environmental 708 442-5823
6640 99th Pl Chicago Ridge (60415) *(G-6789)*
Cem LLC 708 333-3761
6000 Garlands Ln Ste 120 Barrington (60010) *(G-1217)*
Cemec Inc (PA) 630 495-9696
1516 Centre Cir Downers Grove (60515) *(G-7966)*
Cemex Cement Inc 773 995-5100
12101 S Doty Ave Chicago (60633) *(G-4054)*
Centec Automation Inc 847 791-9430
420 S Vermont St Palatine (60067) *(G-16098)*
Centech Plastics Inc 847 364-4433
855 Touhy Ave Elk Grove Village (60007) *(G-8884)*
Center Ethanol Company LLC 618 875-3008
231 Monsanto Ave Sauget (62201) *(G-18391)*
Center Tool Company 847 683-7559
250 Industrial Dr Hampshire (60140) *(G-10966)*
Center-111 W Burnham Wash LLC 312 368-5320
111 W Washington St # 1017 Chicago (60602) *(G-4055)*
Centerless Grinding Co 847 455-7660
2330 17th St Unit B Franklin Park (60131) *(G-9902)*
Centor North America Inc 630 957-1000
966 Corporate Blvd # 130 Aurora (60502) *(G-936)*
Central Autmtc Screw Pdts Inc 630 766-7966
372 Meyer Rd Bensenville (60106) *(G-1764)*
Central Can Company Inc 773 254-8700
3200 S Kilbourn Ave Chicago (60623) *(G-4056)*
Central Decal Company Inc 630 325-9892
6901 High Grove Blvd Burr Ridge (60527) *(G-2661)*
Central Die Cutting, Chicago Also called Animated Advg Techniques Inc *(G-3698)*
Central Graphics Corp 630 759-1696
1302 Enterprise Dr Romeoville (60446) *(G-17804)*
Central Hydraulics Inc 309 527-5238
513 State Route 251 El Paso (61738) *(G-8434)*

Central IL Business Magazine.....217 351-5281
15 E Main St Champaign (61820) *(G-3279)*
Central Ill Communications LLC.....217 753-2226
1240 S 6th St Springfield (62703) *(G-19345)*
Central Ill Fbrcation Whse Inc.....217 367-2323
510 E Main St Urbana (61802) *(G-19976)*
Central Illinois Bus Publs Inc.....309 683-3060
5005 N Glen Park Place Rd Peoria (61614) *(G-16416)*
Central Illinois Glass &.....309 367-4242
506 W Mount Vernon St Metamora (61548) *(G-13960)*
Central Illinois Hardwood.....309 352-2363
15634 Toboggan Ave Green Valley (61534) *(G-10816)*
Central Illinois Homes Guide.....309 688-6419
7307 N Willow Lake Ct Peoria (61614) *(G-16417)*
Central Illinois Newspapers.....217 935-3171
111 S Monroe St Clinton (61727) *(G-6920)*
Central Illinois Poultry Proc.....217 543-2937
119 N Cr 000 E Arthur (61911) *(G-845)*
Central Illinois Sign Company.....217 523-4740
3040 E Linden Ave Springfield (62702) *(G-19346)*
Central Illinois Steel Company (PA).....217 854-3251
21050 Route 4 Carlinville (62626) *(G-2869)*
Central Illinois Truss (PA).....309 447-6644
105 Prospect Dr Deer Creek (61733) *(G-7572)*
Central Illinois Truss.....309 266-8787
919 Detroit Ct Ste 2 Morton (61550) *(G-14356)*
Central Industries of Indiana.....618 943-2311
13301 Tinker St Lawrenceville (62439) *(G-12528)*
Central Ink Corporation (PA).....630 231-6500
1100 Harvester Rd West Chicago (60185) *(G-20560)*
Central Ink of Wisconsin Div, West Chicago *Also called Central Ink Corporation* *(G-20560)*
Central Limestone Company Inc.....815 736-6341
16805 Quarry Rd Morris (60450) *(G-14298)*
Central Machining Inc.....217 854-6646
502 W 1st North St Carlinville (62626) *(G-2870)*
Central Manufacturing Company.....309 387-6591
4258 Springfield Rd East Peoria (61611) *(G-8259)*
Central Molded Products LLC.....773 622-4000
1978 N Lockwood Ave Chicago (60639) *(G-4057)*
Central Newspaper Incorporated.....630 416-4191
40 Shuman Blvd Ste 305 Naperville (60563) *(G-14795)*
Central Printers & Graphics.....773 586-3711
6109 W 63rd St Bedford Park (60638) *(G-1462)*
Central Radiator Cabinet Co (PA).....773 539-1700
8857 N 5 Corners Rd Lena (61048) *(G-12599)*
Central RC Hobbies.....309 686-8004
Peoria Hts Peoria (61616) *(G-16418)*
Central Rubber Company.....815 544-2191
844 E Jackson St Belvidere (61008) *(G-1661)*
Central Sheet Metal Pdts Inc.....773 583-2424
7251 Linder Ave Skokie (60077) *(G-18938)*
Central Specialties, Crystal Lake *Also called Nelson-Whittaker Ltd* *(G-7237)*
Central State Coca-Cola Peru.....815 220-3100
3808 Progress Blvd Peru (61354) *(G-16572)*
Central State Finds.....630 359-4706
221 King St Elk Grove Village (60007) *(G-8885)*
Central States Pallets.....217 494-2710
26 Highland Ln Chatham (62629) *(G-3418)*
Central Steel Fabricators.....708 652-2037
2100 Parkes Dr Broadview (60155) *(G-2424)*
Central Stone Company.....217 335-2615
Hwy 36 Barry (62312) *(G-1248)*
Central Stone Company.....309 776-3900
5533 E 400th St Colchester (62326) *(G-6946)*
Central Stone Company.....217 327-4300
38084 County Highway 21 Chambersburg (62323) *(G-3259)*
Central Stone Company.....217 723-4410
26176 487th St Pittsfield (62363) *(G-16632)*
Central Stone Company.....217 224-7330
8514 Rock Quarry Rd Quincy (62305) *(G-16870)*
Central Tool Specialities Co.....630 543-6351
325 W Factory Rd Ste A Addison (60101) *(G-66)*
Central Township Road & Bridge.....618 704-5517
920 E Bowman Dr Greenville (62246) *(G-10830)*
Central Welding Shop, Kewanee *Also called Fred Stollenwerk* *(G-12034)*
Central Wire Inc (HQ).....800 435-8317
6509 Olson Rd Union (60180) *(G-19938)*
Central Wood LLC.....217 543-2662
210 E County Road 200n Arcola (61910) *(G-646)*
Central Wood Products Inc.....217 728-4412
1809 Cr 1300e Sullivan (61951) *(G-19664)*
Centralia Machine & Fab Inc.....618 533-9010
306 S Chestnut St Centralia (62801) *(G-3223)*
Centralia Morning Sentinel.....618 532-5601
232 E Broadway Centralia (62801) *(G-3224)*
Centralia Press Ltd (PA).....618 532-5604
232 E Broadway Centralia (62801) *(G-3225)*
Centralia Press Ltd.....618 246-2000
1808 Broadway St Mount Vernon (62864) *(G-14601)*
Centralia Sentinel, Centralia *Also called Centralia Press Ltd* *(G-3225)*
Centrex Technologies LLC.....800 768-0700
2021 Midwest Rd Ste 200 Oak Brook (60523) *(G-15605)*
Centric Mfg Solutions Inc.....815 315-9258
875 N Michigan Ave # 3614 Chicago (60611) *(G-4058)*
Centrifugal & Mechanical Inds, Raleigh *Also called Elgin National Industries Inc* *(G-16960)*
Centrifugal Services Inc.....618 268-4850
5595 Highway 34 N Raleigh (62977) *(G-16959)*
Centro Inc.....309 751-9700
1001 13th St East Moline (61244) *(G-8224)*
Centroid and Cardinal Engrg, Galesburg *Also called Cardinal Engineering Inc* *(G-10188)*
Centurion NDT, Streamwood *Also called Centurion Non Destructive Tstg* *(G-19565)*
Centurion Non Destructive Tstg.....630 736-5500
1400 Yorkshire Dr Streamwood (60107) *(G-19565)*
Century Aluminum Company (PA).....312 696-3101
1 S Wacker Dr Ste 1000 Chicago (60606) *(G-4059)*
Century Automatics LLC.....847 515-1188
11962 Oak Creek Pkwy Huntley (60142) *(G-11531)*
Century Fasteners & Mch Co Inc.....773 463-3900
4901 Fairview Ln Ste 1 Skokie (60077) *(G-18939)*
Century Filter Products Inc.....773 477-1790
2939 N Oakley Ave Chicago (60618) *(G-4060)*
Century Kitchen & Bath Inc.....847 395-3418
39133 N Us Highway 41 Wadsworth (60083) *(G-20208)*
Century Mallet Instr Svc LLC.....773 248-7733
1770 W Berteau Ave # 204 Chicago (60613) *(G-4061)*
Century Metal Spinning Co Inc.....630 595-3900
430 Meyer Rd Bensenville (60106) *(G-1765)*
Century Mold & Tool Co.....847 364-5858
855 Touhy Ave Elk Grove Village (60007) *(G-8886)*
Century Pipe Organ Company, Aurora *Also called C P O Inc* *(G-1068)*
Century Printing.....618 632-2486
510 Pepperwood Ct O Fallon (62269) *(G-15570)*
Century Signs Inc.....217 224-7419
2704 N 30th St Quincy (62305) *(G-16871)*
Century Spring Corporation.....800 237-5225
4045 W Thorndale Ave Chicago (60646) *(G-4062)*
Cenveo Worldwide Limited.....636 240-5817
3001 N Rockwell St Chicago (60618) *(G-4063)*
Ceragem 26th St.....773 277-0672
3948 W 26th St Ste 207 Chicago (60623) *(G-4064)*
Ceramic Designs Unlimited.....708 758-0690
475 E Joe Orr Rd Chicago Heights (60411) *(G-6738)*
Ceratizit Chicago Holding Inc (HQ).....847 923-8400
2050 Mitchell Blvd Schaumburg (60193) *(G-18469)*
Ceratizit Chicago Inc.....847 923-8400
2050 Mitchell Blvd Schaumburg (60193) *(G-18470)*
Cerro Flow Products LLC (HQ).....618 337-6000
3000 Mississippi Ave Sauget (62206) *(G-18392)*
Certified Asphalt Paving.....847 441-5000
540 W Frontage Rd # 3175 Northfield (60093) *(G-15511)*
Certified Business Forms Inc.....773 286-8194
5732 W Patterson Ave Chicago (60634) *(G-4065)*
Certified Heat Treating Co.....309 693-7711
8917 N University St Peoria (61615) *(G-16419)*
Certified Polymers Inc.....630 515-0007
4479 Lawn Ave Western Springs (60558) *(G-20719)*
Certified Tank & Mfg LLC.....217 525-1433
2500 Richards Ln Springfield (62702) *(G-19347)*
Certifynation Inc.....775 237-8439
650 W Grand Ave Ste 105 Elmhurst (60126) *(G-9342)*
Certiweld Inc.....708 389-0148
13953 Kostner Ave Crestwood (60418) *(G-7111)*
Certus Industries N Amer LLC.....847 217-2537
301 E Congress Pkwy Crystal Lake (60039) *(G-7178)*
Cervantes/Salgado LLC.....630 806-4864
1001 Aucutt Rd Ste C Montgomery (60538) *(G-14239)*
Cervones Welding Service Inc.....847 985-6865
1104 Lunt Ave Schaumburg (60193) *(G-18471)*
Ces, Hoffman Estates *Also called Clover Technologies Group LLC* *(G-11414)*
Ces Material Handling, Eureka *Also called Crane Equipment & Services Inc* *(G-9479)*
Cetco, Hoffman Estates *Also called Colloid Envmtl Tech Co LLC* *(G-11415)*
CF Gear Holdings LLC (PA).....847 376-8322
2064 Mannheim Rd Des Plaines (60018) *(G-7742)*
CF Industries Inc (HQ).....847 405-2400
4 Parkway North Blvd # 400 Deerfield (60015) *(G-7601)*
CF Industries Holdings Inc (PA).....847 405-2400
4 Parkway North Blvd # 400 Deerfield (60015) *(G-7602)*
CF Industries Nitrogen LLC (HQ).....847 405-2400
4 Parkway North Blvd # 400 Deerfield (60015) *(G-7603)*
CF Solutions Co.....630 413-9058
725 E Weathersfield Way Schaumburg (60193) *(G-18472)*
Cfa Software, Addison *Also called Computerized Fleet Analysis* *(G-80)*
Cfc Inc (PA).....847 257-8920
30 E Oakton St Des Plaines (60018) *(G-7743)*
CFC Applied Holographics, Chicago Heights *Also called CFC International Corporation* *(G-6740)*
CFC International Inc.....708 891-3456
500 State St Chicago Heights (60411) *(G-6739)*

ALPHABETIC

CFC International Corporation (HQ) 708 323-4131
500 State St Chicago Heights (60411) *(G-6740)*
CFC Wire Forms Inc 630 879-7575
1000 Douglas Rd Batavia (60510) *(G-1364)*
Cfcl, Schaumburg *Also called Chicago Freight Car Leasing Co* *(G-18475)*
Cfpg Ltd (HQ) 630 679-1420
2500 Intrntonale Pkwy Woodridge (60517) *(G-21282)*
CFS Crtive Fbrction Sltons LLC 309 264-3946
5807 Washington St Peoria (61607) *(G-16420)*
Cft Performance Inc 618 781-3981
18 Schiber Ct Maryville (62062) *(G-13590)*
Cg Nutritionals Inc 224 667-6100
100 Abbott Park Rd North Chicago (60064) *(G-15309)*
CGC Corporation 773 838-3400
7401 S Cicero Ave Chicago (60629) *(G-4066)*
Cgi Automated Mfg Inc 815 221-5300
275 Innovation Dr Romeoville (60446) *(G-17805)*
Cgk Enterprises Inc 847 888-1362
695 Church Rd Elgin (60123) *(G-8535)*
CGprofessional Services Inc 708 389-4110
10711 165th St Ste F Orland Park (60467) *(G-15947)*
CGR Technologies Inc 847 934-7622
350 W Colfax St Palatine (60067) *(G-16099)*
Cgw Camel Grinding Wheels, USA, Niles *Also called Abrasic 90 Inc* *(G-15098)*
Ch Distillery, Chicago *Also called 773 LLC* *(G-3477)*
Ch Group Holdings Inc 888 428-6614
900 National Pkwy Ste 100 Schaumburg (60173) *(G-18473)*
CH Machining Company 630 595-1050
1044 Fairway Dr Bensenville (60106) *(G-1766)*
Chad Mazeika 815 298-8118
3705 Burrmont Rd Rockford (61107) *(G-17343)*
Chad's Ford Snow Removal & Con, Aurora *Also called Aimee M Ford* *(G-1044)*
Chadwick Manufacturing Ltd 815 684-5152
224 N Main St Chadwick (61014) *(G-3257)*
Challenge Printers 773 252-0212
4354 W Armitage Ave Chicago (60639) *(G-4067)*
Challenge Publications L T D 309 421-0392
1948 Riverview Dr Macomb (61455) *(G-13388)*
Challenge Tool Co 847 640-8085
60 Joey Dr Elk Grove Village (60007) *(G-8887)*
Challenger Fabricators Inc 815 704-0077
4095 Prairie Hill Rd South Beloit (61080) *(G-19086)*
Challenger Lighting Co Inc 847 717-4700
1400 Kingsland Dr Batavia (60510) *(G-1365)*
Challinor Wood Products Inc 847 256-8828
1213 Wilmette Ave Ste 208 Wilmette (60091) *(G-21073)*
Chalon Wood Products Inc 630 243-9793
12670 111th St Lemont (60439) *(G-12560)*
Chamberlain Group Inc (HQ) 630 279-3600
300 Windsor Dr Oak Brook (60523) *(G-15606)*
Chamberlain Group Inc 630 705-0300
1350 N Greenbriar Dr Addison (60101) *(G-67)*
Chamberlain Group Inc 630 279-3600
300 Windsor Dr Oak Brook (60523) *(G-15607)*
Chamberlain Manufacturing Corp (HQ) 630 279-3600
300 Windsor Dr Oak Brook (60523) *(G-15608)*
Chambers Gasket & Mfg Co 773 626-8800
4701 W Rice St Chicago (60651) *(G-4068)*
Chambers Marketing Options 847 584-2626
1008 Bonaventure Dr Elk Grove Village (60007) *(G-8888)*
Chambliss Welding, Dahlgren *Also called Jacob Chambliss* *(G-7308)*
Chamfermatic Inc 815 636-5082
7842 Burden Rd Machesney Park (61115) *(G-13333)*
Champaign Cnty Tent & Awng Co 217 328-5749
308 E Anthony Dr Urbana (61802) *(G-19977)*
Champion A Gardner Denver Co, Princeton *Also called Gardner Denver Inc* *(G-16810)*
Champion Chisel Works Inc (PA) 815 535-0647
804 E 18th St Rock Falls (61071) *(G-17178)*
Champion Comm Svcs Inc 815 654-8607
1090 Broadway Rockford (61104) *(G-17344)*
Champion Container Corp 630 530-1990
1455 N Michael Dr Wood Dale (60191) *(G-21175)*
Champion Foods LLC 815 648-2725
9910 Main St Hebron (60034) *(G-11140)*
Champion Healthcare Tech, Lake Zurich *Also called Champion Medical Tech Inc* *(G-12392)*
Champion Laboratories Inc (HQ) 618 445-6011
200 S 4th St Albion (62806) *(G-347)*
Champion Laboratories Inc 618 445-5407
329 Industrial Dr Albion (62806) *(G-348)*
Champion Laboratories Inc 618 445-6011
2201 Waukegan Rd Ste 140 Bannockburn (60015) *(G-1198)*
Champion Medical Tech Inc 866 803-3720
765 Ela Rd Ste 200 Lake Zurich (60047) *(G-12392)*
Champion Packaging & Dist Inc 630 972-0100
2501 Internationale Pkwy Woodridge (60517) *(G-21283)*
Champion Pizza, Hebron *Also called Champion Foods LLC* *(G-11140)*
Champion Silkscreen & EMB, Park Forest *Also called Ronald J Nixon* *(G-16259)*
Champion Wood Pallets Inc 630 801-8036
105 Hankes Ave Ste 100 Aurora (60505) *(G-1072)*

Championx LLC 618 740-1279
3340 Selmaville Rd Salem (62881) *(G-18334)*
Champs Sports, Lombard *Also called Foot Locker Retail Inc* *(G-13078)*
Channeled Resources Inc (PA) 312 733-4200
240 N Ashland Ave Ste 130 Chicago (60607) *(G-4069)*
Chaos Ai Art LLC 847 274-9158
410 N Paulina St Chicago (60622) *(G-4070)*
Char Crust Co Inc 773 528-0600
3017 N Lincoln Ave Chicago (60657) *(G-4071)*
Charger Water Conditioning Inc (HQ) 847 967-9558
8150 Lehigh Ave Ste A Morton Grove (60053) *(G-14395)*
Charles Atwater Assoc Inc 815 678-4813
5705 George St Richmond (60071) *(G-17011)*
Charles Autin Limited 312 432-0888
1801 S Canal St Chicago (60616) *(G-4072)*
Charles C Thomas Publisher 217 789-8980
2600 S 1st St Springfield (62704) *(G-19348)*
Charles Chauncey Wells Inc 708 524-0695
735 N Grove Ave Oak Park (60302) *(G-15749)*
Charles Cicero Fingerhut (PA) 708 652-3643
5537 W Cermak Rd Chicago (60804) *(G-4073)*
Charles E Mahoney Company 618 235-3355
209 Service St Swansea (62226) *(G-19690)*
Charles Electronics LLC 815 244-7981
302 S East St Mount Carroll (61053) *(G-14494)*
Charles Fingerhut Bakeries, Chicago *Also called Charles Cicero Fingerhut* *(G-4073)*
Charles H Luck Envelope Inc 847 451-1500
10551 Anderson Pl Franklin Park (60131) *(G-9903)*
Charles Horberg Jewelers Inc 312 263-4924
5 S Wabash Ave Ste 706 Chicago (60603) *(G-4074)*
Charles Horn Lumber Company 773 847-7397
4700 W 19th St Cicero (60804) *(G-6832)*
Charles Industries LLC (HQ) 847 806-6300
1450 American Ln Fl 20 Schaumburg (60173) *(G-18474)*
Charles Industries LLC 217 826-2318
16265 E National Rd Marshall (62441) *(G-13566)*
Charles Industries LLC 217 893-8335
201 Shellhouse Dr Rantoul (61866) *(G-16970)*
Charles Industries LLC 217 932-2068
400 Se 8th St Casey (62420) *(G-3199)*
Charles Industries LLC 217 932-5292
503 Ne 15th St Casey (62420) *(G-3200)*
Charles K Eichen 217 854-9751
20002 Claremont Rd Carlinville (62626) *(G-2871)*
Charles N Benner Inc 312 829-4300
401 N Western Ave Ste 4 Chicago (60612) *(G-4075)*
Charles R Frontczak 224 392-4151
4816 Mohawk Rd Rockford (61107) *(G-17345)*
Charles Selon Associates, Northbrook *Also called A M Lee Inc* *(G-15329)*
Charles Sheridan and Sons 847 903-7209
2331 Church St Evanston (60201) *(G-9502)*
Charleston Concrete Supply Co 217 345-6404
2417 18th St Charleston (61920) *(G-3398)*
Charleston County Market 217 345-7031
551 W Lincoln Ave Charleston (61920) *(G-3399)*
Charleston Farrier Contruction, Charleston *Also called Charleston Concrete Supply Co* *(G-3398)*
Charleston Ready Mix, Charleston *Also called Mid-Illinois Concrete Inc* *(G-3407)*
Charleston Stone Company 217 345-6292
9709 N County Rd 2000 E Ashmore (61912) *(G-886)*
Charlie, Northbrook *Also called Mosaic Construction* *(G-15437)*
Charlotte Louise Tate 773 849-3236
1304 E 87th St Chicago (60619) *(G-4076)*
Charnor Inc 309 787-2427
1711 1st Ave E Milan (61264) *(G-14002)*
Charter Dura-Bar Inc (HQ) 815 338-3900
2100 W Lake Shore Dr Woodstock (60098) *(G-21373)*
Charter Dura-Bar Inc 815 338-7800
1800 W Lake Shore Dr Woodstock (60098) *(G-21374)*
Charter Precision LLC 847 214-8400
1145 Jansen Farm Dr Elgin (60123) *(G-8536)*
Chartnet Technologies Inc 630 385-4100
220 Garden St Yorkville (60560) *(G-21475)*
Chartwell Studio Inc 847 868-8674
320 W Ohio St Ste 3w Chicago (60654) *(G-4077)*
Chas Levy Circulating Co 630 353-2500
815 Ogden Ave Lisle (60532) *(G-12876)*
Chas O Larson Co 815 625-0503
2602 E Rock Falls Rd Rock Falls (61071) *(G-17179)*
Chase Corporation 630 752-3622
1800 S Naperville Rd Wheaton (60189) *(G-20793)*
Chase Corporation 847 866-8500
1527 Lyons St Evanston (60201) *(G-9503)*
Chase Fasteners Inc 708 345-0335
1539 N 25th Ave Melrose Park (60160) *(G-13841)*
Chase Group LLC 847 564-2000
305 Era Dr Northbrook (60062) *(G-15355)*
Chase Home Finance 630 617-4747
163 N York St Elmhurst (60126) *(G-9343)*

ALPHABETIC SECTION
Chicago Can Conveyor Corp

Chase Manhattan, Elmhurst *Also called Chase Home Finance* ***(G-9343)***
Chase Products Co 708 865-1000
2727 Gardner Rd Broadview (60155) ***(G-2425)***
Chase Security Systems Inc 773 594-1919
5947 N Milwaukee Ave Chicago (60646) ***(G-4078)***
Chassis Service Unlimited 847 336-2305
2984 W Wadsworth Rd Waukegan (60087) ***(G-20427)***
Chateau Food Products Inc 708 863-4207
6137 W Cermak Rd Chicago (60804) ***(G-4079)***
Chatham Clarion, Auburn *Also called South County Publications* ***(G-907)***
Chatham Corporation (PA) 847 634-5506
350 Barclay Blvd Lincolnshire (60069) ***(G-12749)***
Chatham Plastics Inc 217 483-1481
7 Kemp Dr Chatham (62629) ***(G-3419)***
Cheap Dumpster For Rent 773 770-4334
1210 W Granville Ave # 200 Chicago (60660) ***(G-4080)***
Checkpoint Systems Inc 630 771-4240
1140 Windham Pkwy Romeoville (60446) ***(G-17806)***
Ched Markay Inc 847 566-3307
1065 E High St Mundelein (60060) ***(G-14675)***
Cheers Food and Fuel 240 .... 618 995-9153
845 S Broadway Goreville (62939) ***(G-10679)***
Cheers Food Fuel 618 827-4836
510 Ne Front St Dongola (62926) ***(G-7942)***
Cheese Cake, Chicago *Also called Jr Bakery* ***(G-5055)***
Cheese Merchants America LLC 630 221-0580
1301 Schiferl Rd Bartlett (60103) ***(G-1272)***
Cheetah Digital Inc (HQ) 312 858-8200
72 W Adams St Fl 8 Chicago (60603) ***(G-4081)***
Chef Lmt Foods LLC 847 279-6490
1655 N Arlington Heights Arlington Heights (60004) ***(G-714)***
Chef M J Brando, Arlington Heights *Also called Bran-Zan Holdings LLC* ***(G-708)***
Chelar Tool & Die Inc 618 234-6550
11 N Florida Ave Belleville (62221) ***(G-1539)***
Chelsea Framing Products Inc 847 550-5556
333 Enterprise Pkwy Lake Zurich (60047) ***(G-12393)***
Chelsea's Beads, Highland Park *Also called Smart Creations Inc* ***(G-11298)***
Chem Free Solutions (PA) 630 541-7931
8420 Evergreen Ln Darien (60561) ***(G-7403)***
Chem Processing Inc (PA) 815 874-8118
3910 Linden Oaks Dr Rockford (61109) ***(G-17346)***
Chem Processing Inc 815 965-1037
715 N Madison St Rockford (61107) ***(G-17347)***
Chem Rx - Chicago LLC 708 449-7600
150 Fencl Ln Hillside (60162) ***(G-11333)***
Chem Trade Global 847 675-2682
3832 Dobson St Skokie (60076) ***(G-18940)***
Chem-Cast Ltd 217 443-5532
1009 Lynch Rd Danville (61834) ***(G-7326)***
Chem-Plate Industries Inc 708 345-3588
30 N 8th Ave Maywood (60153) ***(G-13665)***
Chem-Plate Industries Inc (PA) 847 640-1600
1800 Touhy Ave Elk Grove Village (60007) ***(G-8889)***
Chem-Tainer Industries Inc 630 932-7778
2 N 225 Grace Lombard (60148) ***(G-13050)***
Chemalloy Company LLC 847 696-2400
9550 W Higgins Rd Ste 380 Rosemont (60018) ***(G-18004)***
Chemblend of America LLC 630 521-1600
240 Foster Ave Bensenville (60106) ***(G-1767)***
Chemi-Flex LLC 630 627-9650
1040 N Ridge Ave Lombard (60148) ***(G-13051)***
Chemical Mgmt Systems, Roselle *Also called Equipsolutions LLC* ***(G-17953)***
Chemical Processing & Acc 847 793-2387
175 Old Hlf Day Rd 140-10 Lincolnshire (60069) ***(G-12750)***
Chemical Pump 815 464-1908
23233 S Center Rd Frankfort (60423) ***(G-9779)***
Chemical Specialties Mfg Corp 309 697-5400
8316 W Route 24 Mapleton (61547) ***(G-13469)***
Chemix Corp 708 754-2150
330 W 194th St Glenwood (60425) ***(G-10639)***
Chemquest International Inc 630 628-1900
200 W Laura Dr Addison (60101) ***(G-68)***
Chemring Energetic Devices 310 784-2100
2525 Curtiss St Downers Grove (60515) ***(G-7967)***
Chemring Energetic Devices Inc 630 969-0620
2525 Curtiss St Downers Grove (60515) ***(G-7968)***
Chemsci Technologies Inc 815 608-9135
6574 Revlon Dr Belvidere (61008) ***(G-1662)***
Chemstation Chicago LLC 630 279-2857
934 N Oaklawn Ave Ste 1 Elmhurst (60126) ***(G-9344)***
Chemtech Plastics Inc 630 503-6000
765 Church Rd Elgin (60123) ***(G-8537)***
Chemtech Services Inc 815 838-4800
20648 Gaskin Dr Lockport (60446) ***(G-12986)***
Chemtool Inc 815 459-1250
8200 Ridgefield Rd Crystal Lake (60012) ***(G-7179)***
Chemtool Incorporated (HQ) 815 957-4140
801 W Rockton Rd Rockton (61072) ***(G-17694)***
Chemtool Incorporated 815 459-1250
8200 Ridgefield Rd Crystal Lake (60012) ***(G-7180)***
Chemtool Incorporated 815 389-0250
1165 Prairie Hill Rd Rockton (61072) ***(G-17695)***
Chemtrade Chemicals US LLC 618 274-4363
2500 Kingshighway East Saint Louis (62201) ***(G-8301)***
Chemtrade Logistics (us) Inc 704 369-2496
2250 E 130th St Chicago (60633) ***(G-4082)***
Chemtura Corporation 309 633-9480
8220 W Us Highway 24 Mapleton (61547) ***(G-13470)***
Chenoa Locker Inc 815 945-7323
113 N Veto St Chenoa (61726) ***(G-3432)***
Chep/Millwood, Melrose Park *Also called Millwood Inc* ***(G-13893)***
Cherith Agro Inc 847 258-3865
921 Oakton St Elk Grove Village (60007) ***(G-8890)***
Cherokee Printing & Svcs Inc 847 566-6116
442 N Seymour Ave Mundelein (60060) ***(G-14676)***
Cherry Instruments, Chicago *Also called Wrightwood Technologies Inc* ***(G-6685)***
Cherry Meat Packers Inc 773 927-1200
4750 S California Ave Chicago (60632) ***(G-4083)***
Cherry Street Printing & Award 618 252-6814
211 E Poplar St Ste 2 Harrisburg (62946) ***(G-11021)***
Chesley Limited 847 562-9292
3170 Macarthur Blvd Northbrook (60062) ***(G-15356)***
Chester Brass and Aluminum 618 826-2391
600 Barron St Chester (62233) ***(G-3451)***
Chester Dairy Company Inc (PA) 618 826-2394
1915 State St Chester (62233) ***(G-3452)***
Chester Dairy Company Inc 618 826-2395
1912 Swanwick St Chester (62233) ***(G-3453)***
Chester Foundry, Chester *Also called Chester Brass and Aluminum* ***(G-3451)***
Chester White Swine Rcord Assn 309 691-0151
6320 N Sheridan Rd Ste A Peoria (61614) ***(G-16421)***
Chesterfield Awning Co Inc (PA) 708 596-4434
16999 Van Dam Rd South Holland (60473) ***(G-19205)***
Chevron Commercial Inc 618 654-5555
3545 George St Highland (62249) ***(G-11209)***
Chewy Software LLC 773 935-2627
507 W Aldine Ave Apt 1b Chicago (60657) ***(G-4084)***
Chgo Daily Law Bulletin 217 525-6735
401 S 2nd St Springfield (62701) ***(G-19349)***
CHi Doors Holdings Inc (HQ) 217 543-2135
1485 Sunrise Dr Arthur (61911) ***(G-846)***
CHI Home Improvement Mag Inc 630 801-7788
2031 Bryn Mawr Dr Aurora (60506) ***(G-1073)***
CHI Montes, Cicero *Also called Tele Guia Spanish TV Guide* ***(G-6879)***
CHI Overhead Doors, Arthur *Also called CHi Doors Holdings Inc* ***(G-846)***
CHI-Town Printing Inc 773 577-2500
6025 N Cicero Ave Chicago (60646) ***(G-4085)***
Chicago 847 437-7700
2045 S Arlington Heights Arlington Heights (60005) ***(G-715)***
Chicago Adhesive Products 630 978-7766
1105 S Frontenac St Aurora (60504) ***(G-937)***
Chicago Aerosol LLC 708 598-7100
8407 S 77th Ave Bridgeview (60455) ***(G-2333)***
Chicago Agent Magazine 773 296-6001
2000 N Racine Ave Chicago (60614) ***(G-4086)***
Chicago Alum Castings Co Inc 773 762-3009
205 W Wacker Dr Ste 1818 Chicago (60606) ***(G-4087)***
Chicago Aluminum Castings, Chicago *Also called Midwest Metal Castings Inc* ***(G-5444)***
Chicago American Mfg LLC 773 376-0100
4500 W 47th St Chicago (60632) ***(G-4088)***
Chicago and Suburbs 773 306-3787
3325 N Nottingham Ave Chicago (60634) ***(G-4089)***
Chicago Anodizing Company 773 533-3737
4112 W Lake St Chicago (60624) ***(G-4090)***
Chicago Art Center Co 773 817-2725
6540 N Washtenaw Ave Chicago (60645) ***(G-4091)***
Chicago Baking Company (HQ) 630 684-2335
6818 Rte 83 Darien (60561) ***(G-7404)***
Chicago Blind Company 815 553-5525
20607 Burl Ct Joliet (60433) ***(G-11839)***
Chicago Block, Berwyn *Also called Northfield Block Company* ***(G-1957)***
Chicago Boating Publications 312 266-8400
851 N La Salle Dr Chicago (60610) ***(G-4092)***
Chicago Booth Mfg Inc 773 378-8400
5000 W Roosevelt Rd # 202 Chicago (60644) ***(G-4093)***
Chicago Bottling Industries 847 885-8093
2075 Stonington Ave Hoffman Estates (60169) ***(G-11413)***
Chicago Bread Company 630 620-1849
1405 W Fullerton Ave Addison (60101) ***(G-69)***
Chicago Brick Oven LLC (PA) 630 359-4793
1020 Davey Rd Ste 300 Woodridge (60517) ***(G-21284)***
Chicago Bullet Proof, University Park *Also called Metaltek Fabricating Inc* ***(G-19960)***
Chicago Cabinet & Fixture Co 630 616-8071
316 Meyer Rd Bensenville (60106) ***(G-1768)***
Chicago Cabinet Co 708 429-5100
22000 S Schoolhouse Rd New Lenox (60451) ***(G-15027)***
Chicago Can Conveyor Corp 708 430-0988
8912 Moore Dr Bridgeview (60455) ***(G-2334)***

ALPHABETIC

Chicago Candle Company....773 637-5279
2701 N Sayre Ave Chicago (60707) ***(G-4094)***
Chicago Car Seal Company....773 278-9400
594 Brookside Rd Chicago (60612) ***(G-4095)***
Chicago Cardinal Communication....708 424-1446
10232 S Kenton Ave # 204 Oak Lawn (60453) ***(G-15708)***
Chicago Carton Plant, Chicago *Also called Caraustar Industries Inc* ***(G-4022)***
Chicago Catalog, Chicago *Also called Ryan Partnership LLC* ***(G-6080)***
Chicago Chain and Transm Co (PA)....630 482-9000
650 E Plainfield Rd Countryside (60525) ***(G-7046)***
Chicago Chinese Times....630 717-4567
424 Fort Hill Dr Ste 100 Naperville (60540) ***(G-14796)***
Chicago Circuits Corporation....847 238-1623
2685 United Ln Elk Grove Village (60007) ***(G-8891)***
Chicago Citizen Newsppr Group (PA)....773 783-1251
806 E 78th St Chicago (60619) ***(G-4096)***
Chicago Clamp Company....708 343-8311
2350 S 27th Ave Broadview (60155) ***(G-2426)***
Chicago Cnc Machining Co....708 352-1255
6880 River Rd Unit 2 Hodgkins (60525) ***(G-11386)***
Chicago Collection Magazine, Chicago *Also called Northwest Publishing LLC* ***(G-5624)***
Chicago Coml & Consmr Brands....773 484-5771
501 W 82nd St Chicago (60620) ***(G-4097)***
Chicago Coml Consmr Brands LLC....773 488-2639
7437 S Vincennes Ave Chicago (60621) ***(G-4098)***
Chicago Contract Bridge Assn (PA)....630 355-5560
1624 Masters Ct Naperville (60563) ***(G-14797)***
Chicago Crate Inc....708 380-4716
440 Roe Ct Downers Grove (60516) ***(G-7969)***
Chicago Creative Directory, Chicago *Also called Creative Directory Inc* ***(G-4262)***
Chicago Cremation Supplies, Posen *Also called J Garvin Industries Inc* ***(G-16796)***
Chicago Cremation Supplies, Evergreen Park *Also called J Garvin Industries Inc* ***(G-9595)***
Chicago Crusader News Group (PA)....773 752-2500
6429 S King Dr Chicago (60637) ***(G-4099)***
Chicago Cutting Die Co....847 509-5800
3555 Woodhead Dr Northbrook (60062) ***(G-15357)***
Chicago Data Solutions Inc....847 370-4609
146 Somerset Rd Willowbrook (60527) ***(G-21035)***
Chicago Defender Newspaper, Chicago *Also called Real Times II LLC* ***(G-5985)***
Chicago Dial Indicator Company....847 827-7186
1372 Redeker Rd Des Plaines (60016) ***(G-7744)***
Chicago Die Casting Mfg Co....847 671-5010
9148 King St Franklin Park (60131) ***(G-9904)***
Chicago Direct Mail, Oak Brook *Also called Flyerinc Corporation* ***(G-15622)***
Chicago Drive Line Inc....708 385-1900
11500 S Central Ave Alsip (60803) ***(G-427)***
Chicago Dropcloth Tarpaulin Co....773 588-3123
3719 W Lawrence Ave Chicago (60625) ***(G-4100)***
Chicago Dryer Company....773 235-4430
2200 N Pulaski Rd Chicago (60639) ***(G-4101)***
Chicago Dscovery Solutions LLC....815 609-2071
23561 W Main St Plainfield (60544) ***(G-16650)***
Chicago Dye Works....847 931-7968
18 N State St Elgin (60123) ***(G-8538)***
Chicago Enclosures....708 344-6600
1975 N 17th Ave Melrose Park (60160) ***(G-13842)***
Chicago Envelope Inc (PA)....630 668-0400
685 Kimberly Dr Carol Stream (60188) ***(G-2957)***
Chicago Export Packing Co....773 247-8911
1501 W 38th St Chicago (60609) ***(G-4102)***
Chicago Film Archive Nfp....773 478-3799
5746 N Drake Ave Chicago (60659) ***(G-4103)***
Chicago Flameproof WD Spc Corp (PA)....630 859-0009
1200 S Lake St Montgomery (60538) ***(G-14240)***
Chicago Floral Planters Inc....708 423-2754
10139 S Harlem Ave Chicago Ridge (60415) ***(G-6790)***
Chicago Flyhouse Incorporated....773 533-1590
2925 W Carroll Ave Chicago (60612) ***(G-4104)***
Chicago Freight Car Leasing Co (HQ)....847 318-8000
425 N Martingale Rd Fl 6 Schaumburg (60173) ***(G-18475)***
Chicago Going Out Guide, Chicago *Also called Real Estate News Corp* ***(G-5983)***
Chicago Gourmet Wholesale Bky, Elk Grove Village *Also called New Chicago Wholesale Bky Inc* ***(G-9146)***
Chicago Grinding & Machine Co....708 343-4399
1950 N 15th Ave Melrose Park (60160) ***(G-13843)***
Chicago Group Acquisition LLC....312 755-0720
350 N Orleans St Fl 10-S Chicago (60654) ***(G-4105)***
Chicago Hardware and Fix Co (PA)....847 455-6609
9100 Parklane Ave Franklin Park (60131) ***(G-9905)***
Chicago Heights Pallets Co....708 757-7641
1200 State St Chicago Heights (60411) ***(G-6741)***
Chicago Heights Star Tool and....708 758-2525
640 217th St Chicago Heights (60411) ***(G-6742)***
Chicago Heights Steel, Chicago Heights *Also called CHS Acquisition Corp* ***(G-6743)***
Chicago Home Improvement Mag, Aurora *Also called CHI Home Improvement Mag Inc* ***(G-1073)***
Chicago Honeymooners LLC....312 399-5699
3341 W Sunnyside Ave # 2 Chicago (60625) ***(G-4106)***
Chicago I and D Services Inc....312 623-8071
5600 S Melvina Ave Chicago (60638) ***(G-4107)***
Chicago Ink & Research Co Inc....847 395-1078
97 Ida Ave Antioch (60002) ***(G-608)***
Chicago Iron Works Corporation (PA)....312 829-1062
439 N Western Ave Chicago (60612) ***(G-4108)***
Chicago Jet Group LLC (PA)....630 466-3600
43 W 522 Rr 30 Sugar Grove (60554) ***(G-19639)***
Chicago Jewish News....847 966-0606
4638 Church St Skokie (60076) ***(G-18941)***
Chicago Jewish Star, Skokie *Also called Star Media Group* ***(G-19036)***
Chicago Knitting Mills....773 463-1464
2424 Hampton Ln Northbrook (60062) ***(G-15358)***
Chicago Lab Products....312 942-0730
660 N Union Ave Chicago (60654) ***(G-4109)***
Chicago Laboratory Pdts Inc, Chicago *Also called Guardian Equipment Inc* ***(G-4747)***
Chicago Lifesttyle, The, Carol Stream *Also called Allen Entertainment Management* ***(G-2931)***
Chicago Lighthouse Industries....312 666-1331
1850 W Roosevelt Rd Ste 1 Chicago (60608) ***(G-4110)***
Chicago Local Foods LLC....312 432-6575
1427 W Willow St Chicago (60642) ***(G-4111)***
Chicago Magazine, Chicago *Also called Tribune Publishing Company LLC* ***(G-6425)***
Chicago Magnesium....708 926-9531
14050 Wood St Dixmoor (60426) ***(G-7883)***
Chicago Mailing Tube Company....312 243-6050
400 N Leavitt St Chicago (60612) ***(G-4112)***
Chicago Materials Corporation....630 257-5600
13769 Main St Lemont (60439) ***(G-12561)***
Chicago Meat Authority Inc....773 254-3811
1120 W 47th Pl Chicago (60609) ***(G-4113)***
Chicago Meat, The, Chicago *Also called Cherry Meat Packers Inc* ***(G-4083)***
Chicago Menu Co, Glenview *Also called Greek Art Printing & Pubg Co* ***(G-10553)***
Chicago Metal Fabricators Inc....773 523-5755
3724 S Rockwell St Ste 1 Chicago (60632) ***(G-4114)***
Chicago Metal Rolled Pdts Co (PA)....773 523-5757
3715 S Rockwell St Chicago (60632) ***(G-4115)***
Chicago Metal Supply Inc....773 417-7439
4930 W Grand Ave Chicago (60639) ***(G-4116)***
Chicago Midway Airport....773 838-0600
5700 S Cicero Ave Ste 57 Chicago (60638) ***(G-4117)***
Chicago Mltlingua Graphics Inc (PA)....847 386-7187
550 W Frontage Rd # 2700 Northfield (60093) ***(G-15512)***
Chicago Mold Engrg Co Inc....630 584-1311
615 Stetson Ave Saint Charles (60174) ***(G-18165)***
Chicago Molding Outlet....773 471-6870
5858 S Kedzie Ave Ste 1 Chicago (60629) ***(G-4118)***
Chicago Mtal Sup Fbrcation Inc....773 227-6200
4940 W Grand Ave Chicago (60639) ***(G-4119)***
Chicago Neon and Sign LLC....708 255-5284
4140 Sunnyside Ave Brookfield (60513) ***(G-2480)***
Chicago Off Set, Elk Grove Village *Also called Sung Ji USA Inc* ***(G-9258)***
Chicago Offset, Elk Grove Village *Also called FL 1* ***(G-8999)***
Chicago Oriental Cnstr Inc....312 733-9633
1835 S Canal St 2f Chicago (60616) ***(G-4120)***
Chicago Oriental Wholesale Mkt, Chicago *Also called Chicago Oriental Cnstr Inc* ***(G-4120)***
Chicago Ornamental Iron Inc....773 321-9635
1237 51 W 47th St Chicago (60609) ***(G-4121)***
Chicago Pallet Service Inc....847 439-8330
1305 S 1st Ave Maywood (60153) ***(G-13666)***
Chicago Pallet Service Inc (HQ)....847 439-8754
1875 Greenleaf Ave Elk Grove Village (60007) ***(G-8892)***
Chicago Pallet Service II Inc (PA)....847 439-8330
1875 Greenleaf Ave Elk Grove Village (60007) ***(G-8893)***
Chicago Panel & Truss Inc....630 870-1300
875 Aurora Ave Ste 1 Aurora (60505) ***(G-1074)***
Chicago Paper Tub & Can, Chicago *Also called Multi Packaging Solutions Inc* ***(G-5523)***
Chicago Paper Tube & Can Co., Chicago *Also called Rolled Edge Inc* ***(G-6054)***
Chicago Parent News Magazine, Chicago *Also called Wednesday Journal Inc* ***(G-6597)***
Chicago Pastry Inc....630 529-6161
142 N Bloomingdale Rd Bloomingdale (60108) ***(G-1985)***
Chicago Pastry Inc....630 972-0404
556 Saint James Gate Bolingbrook (60440) ***(G-2156)***
Chicago Pipe Bending & Coil Co....773 379-1918
4535 W Lake St Chicago (60624) ***(G-4122)***
Chicago Pixels SRC....312 513-7949
3600 W Sunnyside Ave 1 Chicago (60625) ***(G-4123)***
Chicago Plastic Systems Inc....815 455-4599
161 Virginia Rd Crystal Lake (60014) ***(G-7181)***
Chicago Poetry Center, Chicago *Also called Poetry Center* ***(G-5829)***
Chicago Powdered Metal Pdts Co....847 678-2836
9700 Waveland Ave Schiller Park (60131) ***(G-18793)***
Chicago Premier Meats Inc....773 847-5400
822 W Exchange Ave Chicago (60609) ***(G-4124)***
Chicago Prepress Color Inc....708 385-3465
14650 Kostner Ave Midlothian (60445) ***(G-13990)***
Chicago Press Corporation....773 276-1500
1880 Busse Rd Elk Grove Village (60007) ***(G-8894)***

ALPHABETIC SECTION Christopher Wagner

Chicago Print Group Inc 312 251-1962
12901 S Throop St Calumet Park (60827) *(G-2795)*
Chicago Print Partners LLC 312 525-2015
120 W Laura Dr Addison (60101) *(G-70)*
Chicago Printers Guild 303 819-6197
1009 N Mozart St 2 Chicago (60622) *(G-4125)*
Chicago Printing and EMB Inc 630 628-1777
60 W Fay Ave Addison (60101) *(G-71)*
Chicago Printing Center, Schaumburg *Also called Wide Image Incorporated (G-18773)*
Chicago Producers Inc 312 226-6900
7507 Madison St Ste D4 Forest Park (60130) *(G-9709)*
Chicago Quadrill Co 847 824-4196
1840 Busse Hwy Des Plaines (60016) *(G-7745)*
Chicago Reader, Chicago *Also called Stm Reader LLC (G-6249)*
Chicago Reader, Chicago *Also called Sun-Times Media LLC (G-6270)*
Chicago Retractable Awnings, Antioch *Also called Midwest Screens LLC (G-626)*
Chicago Review Press Inc (PA) 312 337-0747
814 N Franklin St Ste 100 Chicago (60610) *(G-4126)*
Chicago Rivet & Machine Co (PA) 630 357-8500
901 Frontenac Rd Naperville (60563) *(G-14798)*
Chicago Roll Co Inc 630 627-8888
970 N Lombard Rd Lombard (60148) *(G-13052)*
Chicago Sales & Dist Ctr, Downers Grove *Also called Green Bay Packaging Inc (G-8014)*
Chicago Salt Company Inc 708 906-4718
2924 River Rd River Grove (60171) *(G-17058)*
Chicago Salt Service, Chicago *Also called Morton Salt Inc (G-5501)*
Chicago Scenic Studios Inc 312 274-9900
955 W Cermak Rd Chicago (60608) *(G-4127)*
Chicago School Woodworking LLC 773 275-1170
5680 N Northwest Hwy Chicago (60646) *(G-4128)*
Chicago Sea Ray Inc 815 385-2720
31535 N Us Highway 12 Volo (60073) *(G-20197)*
Chicago Shade Makers Inc 708 597-5590
12617 S Kroll Dr Alsip (60803) *(G-428)*
Chicago Sheet Plant, Bedford Park *Also called Packaging Corporation America (G-1489)*
Chicago Show Inc 847 955-0200
1358 Busch Pkwy Buffalo Grove (60089) *(G-2524)*
Chicago Sign & Light Company 630 407-0802
26w 535 St Charles Rd 8 26 W Carol Stream (60188) *(G-2958)*
Chicago Sign Designs, Elk Grove Village *Also called E B G B Inc (G-8962)*
Chicago Sign Group 847 899-9021
305 Albert Dr Vernon Hills (60061) *(G-20048)*
Chicago Silk Screen Sup Co Inc 312 666-1213
882 N Milwaukee Ave Chicago (60642) *(G-4129)*
Chicago Slitter, Itasca *Also called Rdi Group Inc (G-11724)*
Chicago Soy Dairy, Addison *Also called We Love Soy Inc (G-332)*
Chicago Speedpro Imaging, Chicago *Also called Corps Levl Ventures Inc (G-4242)*
Chicago Sports Media Inc 847 676-1900
5940 W Touhy Ave Ste 230 Niles (60714) *(G-15109)*
Chicago Steaks, Chicago *Also called Tomcyndi Inc (G-6389)*
Chicago Steel Inc 800 344-3032
875 N Michigan Ave Fl 31 Chicago (60611) *(G-4130)*
Chicago Sun-Times Features Inc (HQ) 312 321-3000
350 N Orleans St Fl 10 Chicago (60654) *(G-4131)*
Chicago Switchboard Co Inc 630 833-2266
470 W Wrightwood Ave Elmhurst (60126) *(G-9345)*
Chicago T-Shirt Authority, Glendale Heights *Also called Sunburst Sportswear Inc (G-10505)*
Chicago Tank Lining Sales 847 328-0500
3603 Hillside Rd Evanston (60201) *(G-9504)*
Chicago Technical Sales Inc 630 889-7121
17w755 Butterfield Rd Oakbrook Terrace (60181) *(G-15792)*
Chicago Tempered Glass Inc 773 583-2300
2945 N Mozart St Chicago (60618) *(G-4132)*
Chicago Toffee Co, Glenview *Also called Chocolate Potpourri Ltd (G-10535)*
Chicago Tribune Company 312 222-3232
777 W Chicago Ave Chicago (60654) *(G-4133)*
Chicago Tribune Company LLC (HQ) 312 222-3232
160 N Stetson Ave Chicago (60601) *(G-4134)*
Chicago Tube and Iron Company 815 834-2500
1 Chicago Tube Dr Romeoville (60446) *(G-17807)*
Chicago Tube and Iron Company 309 787-4947
1040 11th St W Milan (61264) *(G-14003)*
Chicago Turnrite Co Inc 773 626-8404
4459 W Lake St Chicago (60624) *(G-4135)*
Chicago Valves & Controls LLC 312 637-3551
885 Cambridge Dr Elk Grove Village (60007) *(G-8895)*
Chicago Waterjet Inc 847 350-1898
42 Martin Ln Elk Grove Village (60007) *(G-8896)*
Chicago Wedding Resouce, Northbrook *Also called Gail McGrath & Associates Inc (G-15392)*
Chicago Weekend, Chicago *Also called Chicago Citizen Newsppr Group (G-4096)*
Chicago Weekly 773 702-7718
1131 E 57th St Chicago (60637) *(G-4136)*
Chicago White Metal Cast Inc 630 595-4424
649 Il Route 83 Bensenville (60106) *(G-1769)*
Chicago Wicker & Trading Co 708 563-2890
5625 W 115th St Alsip (60803) *(G-429)*
Chicago Wire, Chicago *Also called Reino Tool & Manufacturing Co (G-6005)*
Chicago/West Michigan, Willowbrook *Also called Trane US Inc (G-21063)*
Chicagoland Closets LLC 630 906-0000
850 Ridgeway Ave Ste A Aurora (60506) *(G-1075)*
Chicagoland Metal Fabricators 847 260-5320
10355 Franklin Ave Franklin Park (60131) *(G-9906)*
Chicagoland Tails, Chicago *Also called Tails Inc (G-6311)*
Chicagone Developers Inc 773 783-2105
1350 E 75th St Chicago (60619) *(G-4137)*
Chicagos Finest Iron Works 773 646-4484
3319 W Washington Blvd Chicago (60624) *(G-4138)*
Chicagos Finest Ironworks 708 895-4484
17564 Chicago Ave Lansing (60438) *(G-12488)*
Chickens & Things, Naperville *Also called Ramona Sedivy (G-14907)*
Chicks and Salsa LLC 815 735-6660
427 Smith St Verona (60479) *(G-20116)*
Chicor Inc 630 953-6154
2021 Midwest Rd Ste 200 Oak Brook (60523) *(G-15609)*
Chii Clothing Company 312 243-8304
1151 W 40th St Chicago (60609) *(G-4139)*
Chikki Bars, Des Plaines *Also called Soni Mohnish (G-7848)*
Child Evngelism Fellowship Inc 630 983-7708
365 Du Pahze St Naperville (60565) *(G-14799)*
Chill Passion (PA) 847 778-6121
760 N Brookdale Dr Schaumburg (60194) *(G-18476)*
China Journal Inc 312 326-3228
2146a S Archer Ave Chicago (60616) *(G-4140)*
Chinchilla Scientific LLC 630 645-0600
900 Jorie Blvd Ste 35 Oak Brook (60523) *(G-15610)*
Chinese American News 312 225-5600
610 W 31st St Chicago (60616) *(G-4141)*
Chip's Tool & Machine Works, Peoria *Also called Synergetic Holdings LLC (G-16533)*
Chipita America Inc (HQ) 708 731-2434
1 Westbrook Corporate Ctr Westchester (60154) *(G-20693)*
Chips Aleeces Pita 309 699-8859
308 Illini Dr East Peoria (61611) *(G-8260)*
Chips Manufacturing Inc 630 682-4477
741 Winston St West Chicago (60185) *(G-20561)*
Chiquita, Princeville *Also called Seneca Foods Corporation (G-16829)*
Chisholm, Boyd & White Company, Chicago *Also called Venturedyne Ltd (G-6535)*
Chisholm-Boyd & White 708 597-7550
4101 W 126th St Ste 1 Alsip (60803) *(G-430)*
Chocolate Potpourri Ltd 847 729-8878
3908 Kiess Dr Glenview (60026) *(G-10535)*
Choi Brands Inc 773 489-2800
3401 W Division St Chicago (60651) *(G-4142)*
Choice Cabinet Chicago 630 599-1099
2000 Bloomingdale Rd # 135 Glendale Heights (60139) *(G-10443)*
Choice Furnishings Inc 847 329-0004
7518 Saint Louis Ave # 1053 Skokie (60076) *(G-18942)*
Chopper Mm LLC 309 875-3544
500 Knox Road 900 E Maquon (61458) *(G-13477)*
Chris Dj Mix LLC 312 725-3838
1408 W Fillmore St Chicago (60607) *(G-4143)*
Chris Industries Inc (PA) 847 729-9292
2810 Old Willow Rd Northbrook (60062) *(G-15359)*
Chris Plating Inc 847 729-9271
2810 Old Willow Rd Northbrook (60062) *(G-15360)*
Chrisman Fuel 217 463-3400
102 Mcmillan St Paris (61944) *(G-16227)*
Christ Bros Products LLC 618 537-6174
820 S Fritz St Lebanon (62254) *(G-12543)*
Christensen Precision Products 630 543-6525
1056 W Republic Dr Addison (60101) *(G-72)*
Christian Century 312 263-7510
104 S Michigan Ave # 1100 Chicago (60603) *(G-4144)*
Christian Cnty Mntal Hlth Assn (PA) 217 824-9675
707 Mcadam Dr Taylorville (62568) *(G-19753)*
Christian National Womans (PA) 847 864-1396
1730 Chicago Ave Ste 4585 Evanston (60201) *(G-9505)*
Christian Specialized Services 217 546-7338
2312 S Wiggins Ave Springfield (62704) *(G-19350)*
Christian Wolf Inc 618 667-9522
12618 Pioneer Rd Bartelso (62218) *(G-1252)*
Christianica Center 847 657-3818
1807 Prairie St Glenview (60025) *(G-10536)*
Christianity Today Intl 630 260-6200
465 Gundersen Dr Carol Stream (60188) *(G-2959)*
Christiansen Sawmill and Log 815 315-7520
20080 Grade School Rd Caledonia (61011) *(G-2769)*
Christopher Concrete Products 618 724-2951
110 N Mine Rd Buckner (62819) *(G-2499)*
Christopher Glass & Aluminum 312 256-8500
832 N Industrial Dr Elmhurst (60126) *(G-9346)*
Christopher R Cline Prtg Ltd 847 981-0500
931 Oakton St Elk Grove Village (60007) *(G-8897)*
Christopher Wagner 630 205-9200
563 Cardinal Ave Oswego (60543) *(G-15995)*

ALPHABETIC

Christos Woodworking 708 975-5045
5865 W 124th St Alsip (60803) ***(G-431)***
Christys Kitchen 815 735-6791
2203 Aplington St La Salle (61301) ***(G-12107)***
Chroma Color Corporation (PA) 877 385-8777
3900 W Dayton St McHenry (60050) ***(G-13726)***
Chromatech Printing Inc 847 699-0333
16 Mary St Des Plaines (60016) ***(G-7746)***
Chrome Crankshaft Company LLC 815 725-9030
4166 Mound Rd Joliet (60436) ***(G-11840)***
Chrome Shop The, Rock Island *Also called Berge Plating Works Inc* ***(G-17206)***
Chrometec LLC 630 792-8777
192 S Lombard Ave Lombard (60148) ***(G-13053)***
Chromium Industries Inc 773 287-3716
4645 W Chicago Ave Chicago (60651) ***(G-4145)***
Chromium Industries LLC 773 287-3716
4645 W Chicago Ave Chicago (60651) ***(G-4146)***
Chromold Plating Inc 815 344-8644
1631 Oak Dr McHenry (60050) ***(G-13727)***
Chronicle Newspapers Inc 630 845-5247
1000 Randall Rd Geneva (60134) ***(G-10259)***
Chronos Imaging LLC 630 296-9220
555 N Commerce St Aurora (60504) ***(G-938)***
Chronx Global Industries Ltd 773 770-5753
1787 S Hamlin Ln Round Lake (60073) ***(G-18073)***
CHS Acquisition Corp 708 756-5648
211 E Main St Chicago Heights (60411) ***(G-6743)***
CHS Annawan, Annawan *Also called Patriot Renewable Fuels LLC* ***(G-592)***
CHS Rochelle, Rochelle *Also called Illinois River Energy LLC* ***(G-17146)***
Chucking Machine Products Inc 847 678-1192
3550 Birch St Franklin Park (60131) ***(G-9907)***
Church of Brethren Inc (PA) 847 742-5100
1451 Dundee Ave Elgin (60120) ***(G-8539)***
Church Street Brewing Co LLC 630 438-5725
1480 Industrial Dr Ste C Itasca (60143) ***(G-11636)***
Churchill Cabinet Company 708 780-0070
4616 W 19th St Cicero (60804) ***(G-6833)***
Churchill Wilmslow Corporation 312 759-8911
162 N Franklin St Ste 200 Chicago (60606) ***(G-4147)***
Churny Company Inc 847 646-5500
200 E Randolph St Chicago (60601) ***(G-4148)***
Chwey Software LLC 773 525-6445
4809 N Ravenswood Ave # 422 Chicago (60640) ***(G-4149)***
CIC North America Inc 847 873-0860
5410 Newport Dr Ste 40 Rolling Meadows (60008) ***(G-17721)***
Cicero Iron Metal & Paper Inc 708 863-8601
5901 W Ogden Ave Ste 7 Cicero (60804) ***(G-6834)***
Cicero Plastic Products Inc 815 886-9522
121 Anton Dr Romeoville (60446) ***(G-17808)***
Cicerone Certification Program 773 549-4800
4043 N Ravenswood Ave # 306 Chicago (60613) ***(G-4150)***
Cie Source, Chicago *Also called IB Source Inc* ***(G-4869)***
Cifuentes Luis & Nicole Inc 847 490-3660
636 Remington Rd Ste D Schaumburg (60173) ***(G-18477)***
Cigtechs (PA) 630 855-6513
173 W Irving Park Rd Roselle (60172) ***(G-17945)***
Cim-Tech Plastics Inc 847 350-0900
2670 United Ln Elk Grove Village (60007) ***(G-8898)***
Cimc Capital Inc., Oakbrook Terrace *Also called Cimc Leasing Usa Inc* ***(G-15793)***
Cimc Leasing Usa Inc 630 785-6875
2 Transam Plaza Dr # 320 Oakbrook Terrace (60181) ***(G-15793)***
Cimentos N Votorantim Amer Inc (PA) 708 458-0400
7601 W 79th St Bridgeview (60455) ***(G-2335)***
Cinch Cnnctivity Solutions Inc (HQ) 630 705-6000
1700 S Finley Rd Lombard (60148) ***(G-13054)***
Cinch Connectors Inc (HQ) 630 705-6001
1700 S Finley Rd Lombard (60148) ***(G-13055)***
Cindys Nail & Hair Care 847 234-0780
950 N Western Ave Ste G Lake Forest (60045) ***(G-12237)***
Cindys Pocket Kitchen 815 388-8385
23802 Chemung St Harvard (60033) ***(G-11050)***
Cino Incorporated 630 377-7242
3n264 Loretta Dr Saint Charles (60175) ***(G-18166)***
Cintas Corporation 708 563-2626
5600 W 73rd St Chicago (60638) ***(G-4151)***
Cintas Corporation No 2 ....708 424-4747
9525 S Cicero Ave Oak Lawn (60453) ***(G-15709)***
Cipher Tech Solutions, Montgomery *Also called CTS of Illinois Inc* ***(G-14242)***
Cipp Robotics LLC 815 202-6628
320 Raccuglia Dr La Salle (61301) ***(G-12108)***
Circle Bolt & Nut Company, Glenview *Also called Optimas Oe Solutions LLC* ***(G-10595)***
Circle Boring & Machine Co (PA) 815 398-4150
3161 Forest View Rd Rockford (61109) ***(G-17348)***
Circle Boring & Machine Co 815 397-3040
2316 7th Ave Rockford (61104) ***(G-17349)***
Circle Caster Engineering Co 847 455-2206
10706 Grand Ave Ste 1 Franklin Park (60131) ***(G-9908)***
Circle Cutting Tools Inc 815 398-4153
3161 Forest View Rd Rockford (61109) ***(G-17350)***
Circle Gear & Machine Co Inc 708 652-1000
1501 S 55th Ct Cicero (60804) ***(G-6835)***
Circle K Industries Inc 847 949-0363
25563 N Gilmer Rd Mundelein (60060) ***(G-14677)***
Circle Metal Specialties Inc 708 597-1700
4029 W 123rd St Alsip (60803) ***(G-432)***
Circle Studio Stained Glass 847 432-7249
946 Central Ave Highland Park (60035) ***(G-11258)***
Circle Studio Stained Glass 773 588-4848
3928 N Elston Ave Chicago (60618) ***(G-4152)***
Circle Systems Inc (PA) 815 286-3271
479 W Lincoln Ave Hinckley (60520) ***(G-11357)***
Circle T Manufacturing LLC 217 728-4834
1801a Cr 1300e Sullivan (61951) ***(G-19665)***
Circom Inc 630 595-4460
505 W Main St Bensenville (60106) ***(G-1770)***
Circuit Assembly & Mfg, Bloomington *Also called Camtek Inc* ***(G-2029)***
Circuit Engineering LLC 847 806-7777
1390 Lunt Ave Elk Grove Village (60007) ***(G-8899)***
Circuit Works Corporation (PA) 847 283-8600
3135 N Oak Grove Ave Waukegan (60087) ***(G-20428)***
Circuit World Inc 630 250-1100
751 Hilltop Dr Itasca (60143) ***(G-11637)***
Circuitron Inc 815 886-9010
211 Rocbaar Dr Romeoville (60446) ***(G-17809)***
Circuitronics 630 668-5407
1300 Holmes Rd Elgin (60123) ***(G-8540)***
Cirrus Products LLC 630 501-1881
220 Shore Dr Burr Ridge (60527) ***(G-2662)***
CIS Systems Inc 847 827-0747
4338 Regency Dr Glenview (60025) ***(G-10537)***
Cisco, Carlinville *Also called Central Illinois Steel Company* ***(G-2869)***
Cisco Heating & Cooling 309 637-6809
3304 W Linda Ln Peoria (61605) ***(G-16422)***
Cisco Systems Inc 847 678-6600
9501 Tech Blvd Ste 100 Des Plaines (60018) ***(G-7747)***
Cision Ltd (HQ) 866 639-5087
130 E Randolph St Fl 7 Chicago (60601) ***(G-4153)***
Cision US Inc (HQ) 312 922-2400
130 E Randolph St Fl 7 Chicago (60601) ***(G-4154)***
Ciske & Dresch 630 251-9200
1125 Paramount Pkwy Ste F Batavia (60510) ***(G-1366)***
Cislak Manufacturing Inc 847 647-1819
7450 N Natchez Ave Niles (60714) ***(G-15110)***
Cissna Park News, Cissna Park *Also called Baier Publishing Company* ***(G-6895)***
Cita Technologies LLC 847 419-9118
975 Deerfield Pkwy Buffalo Grove (60089) ***(G-2525)***
Citadel Specialty Products Inc 630 820-4134
657 Wolverine Dr Ste 3 Aurora (60502) ***(G-939)***
Citation Oil & Gas Corp 618 676-1044
3943 Big Four Rd Clay City (62824) ***(G-6904)***
Citation Oil & Gas Corp 618 966-2101
Hwy 14 E Crossville (62827) ***(G-7150)***
Citation Oil & Gas Corp 618 548-2331
2302 Hoots Chapel Rd Odin (62870) ***(G-15834)***
Citgo Petroleum Corporation 847 818-1800
1201 Ogden Ave Downers Grove (60515) ***(G-7970)***
Citgo Refinery, Lemont *Also called Pdv Midwest Refining LLC* ***(G-12581)***
Citizenprime LLC 708 995-1241
8940 W 192nd St Ste I Mokena (60448) ***(G-14075)***
Citrus Systems 608 271-3000
2001 Butterfield Rd # 600 Downers Grove (60515) ***(G-7971)***
City Business Journals Network, Chicago *Also called American City Bus Journals Inc* ***(G-3651)***
City Foods Inc 773 523-1566
4230 S Racine Ave Chicago (60609) ***(G-4155)***
City Iron Works, Elgin *Also called City Ornamental Iron Works* ***(G-8541)***
City Living Design Inc 312 335-0711
401 E Ontario St Apt 1302 Chicago (60611) ***(G-4156)***
City of Chicago 312 744-0940
6441 N Ravenswood Ave # 49 Chicago (60626) ***(G-4157)***
City of Chicago 773 581-8000
6500 S Pulaski Rd Ste 2 Chicago (60629) ***(G-4158)***
City of Chicago 312 746-6583
4211 W Ferdinand St Chicago (60624) ***(G-4159)***
City of Danville 217 442-1564
5 Southgate Ct Tilton (61833) ***(G-19794)***
City of Edwardsville 618 692-7053
3735 Wanda Rd Edwardsville (62025) ***(G-8352)***
City of Pekin 309 477-2325
1208 Koch St Pekin (61554) ***(G-16325)***
City of Toulon 309 286-7073
120 N Franklin St Toulon (61483) ***(G-19890)***
City Ornamental Iron Works 847 888-8898
1140 Morningside Dr Elgin (60123) ***(G-8541)***
City Press Juice & Bottle 773 360-7226
2931 N Broadway St Chicago (60657) ***(G-4160)***
City Screen Inc (PA) 773 588-5642
5540 N Kedzie Ave Chicago (60625) ***(G-4161)***

City Sports & Stage Door Dance 708 687-9950
15801 Oak Park Ave Oak Forest (60452) *(G-15673)*
City Subn Auto Svc Goodyear 773 355-5550
5674 N Northwest Hwy Chicago (60646) *(G-4162)*
City Utility Equipment 815 254-6673
22414 W 143rd St Plainfield (60544) *(G-16651)*
City Wide Pallet 773 891-2561
4045 S Wallace St Chicago (60609) *(G-4163)*
City Zenith, Chicago *Also called Cityzenith LLC (G-4164)*
Cityblue Technologies LLC (PA) 309 550-5000
404 Sw Adams St Peoria (61602) *(G-16423)*
Citywide Printing, Des Plaines *Also called Jph Enterprises Inc (G-7792)*
Cityzenith LLC 312 883-5554
2506 N Clark St Ste 235 Chicago (60614) *(G-4164)*
Civil Constrs Inc Illinois, Elizabeth *Also called Civil Constructors Inc (G-8786)*
Civil Constructors Inc 815 858-2691
1307 W Longhollow Rd Elizabeth (61028) *(G-8786)*
Civiq Smartscapes LLC 312 300-4776
200 S Michigan Ave # 1305 Chicago (60604) *(G-4165)*
CJ Anderson & Company 708 867-4002
4751 N Olcott Ave Harwood Heights (60706) *(G-11102)*
CJ Drilling Inc 847 669-8000
19n041 Galligan Rd Dundee (60118) *(G-8126)*
CJ Signs 309 676-9999
4024 Sw Adams St Peoria (61605) *(G-16424)*
Cjt Automotive Inc 847 671-0800
10275 W Higgins Rd # 470 Rosemont (60018) *(G-18005)*
Cjt Koolcarb Inc (PA) 630 690-5933
494 Mission St Carol Stream (60188) *(G-2960)*
CK Grinding and Machining Inc 847 541-0960
169 Wheeling Rd Wheeling (60090) *(G-20870)*
Ckd, Lake Zurich *Also called Coordinated Kitchen Dev Inc (G-12396)*
Ckd USA Corporation (HQ) 847 368-0539
1605 N Penny Ln Schaumburg (60173) *(G-18478)*
Cks Signs Inc 847 423-3456
3437 Dempster St Skokie (60076) *(G-18943)*
Clad-Rex Steel LLC 847 455-7373
11500 King St Franklin Park (60131) *(G-9909)*
Claessens Kids Inc 973 551-8528
6350 Kirk St Morton Grove (60053) *(G-14396)*
Claire Manufacturing, Downers Grove *Also called Claire-Sprayway Inc (G-7972)*
Claire-Sprayway Inc (HQ) 630 628-3000
2651 Warrenville Rd # 300 Downers Grove (60515) *(G-7972)*
Claire-Sprayway Inc 630 628-3000
2651 Warrenville Rd # 300 Downers Grove (60515) *(G-7973)*
Clarence Hancock Sawmill Inc 618 854-2232
1191 E White Ln Noble (62868) *(G-15189)*
Clariance Inc 773 868-7041
4809 N Ravenswood Ave # 119 Chicago (60640) *(G-4166)*
Clariant Plas Coatings USA LLC 630 562-9700
625 Wegner Dr West Chicago (60185) *(G-20562)*
Claridge Products 847 991-8822
923 N State St Elgin (60123) *(G-8542)*
Claridge Products and Eqp Inc 847 991-8822
923 N State St Elgin (60123) *(G-8543)*
Clarios 815 288-3859
629 N Galena Ave Ste 210 Dixon (61021) *(G-7893)*
Clarios 309 427-2800
3850 N Main St East Peoria (61611) *(G-8261)*
Clarios 630 573-0897
78 Oakbrook Ctr Oak Brook (60523) *(G-15611)*
Clarios 815 397-5147
7316 Argus Dr 1 Rockford (61107) *(G-17351)*
Clarios 708 474-1717
1500 Huntington Dr Calumet City (60409) *(G-2773)*
Clarios 630 871-7700
883 Carol Ct Carol Stream (60188) *(G-2961)*
Clarios 331 212-3800
3600 Thayer Ct Ste 300 Aurora (60504) *(G-940)*
Clarios 630 562-4602
1800 W Hawthorne Ln E2 West Chicago (60185) *(G-20563)*
Clarios 630 279-0050
450 W Wrightwood Ave Elmhurst (60126) *(G-9347)*
Clarios 630 351-9407
153 Stratford Square Mall Bloomingdale (60108) *(G-1986)*
Clarios LLC 630 232-4270
300 S Glengarry Dr Geneva (60134) *(G-10260)*
Clark Tashaunda 708 247-8274
12406 S Morgan St Calumet Park (60827) *(G-2796)*
Clark Caster Co 708 366-1913
7310 Roosevelt Rd Forest Park (60130) *(G-9710)*
Clark County Ready Mix, Martinsville *Also called Mid-Illinois Concrete Inc (G-13586)*
Clark Filter Inc 216 896-3000
13000 Collections Ctr Dr Chicago (60693) *(G-4167)*
Clark Gear Works Inc 630 561-2320
1218 Saratoga Dr Carol Stream (60188) *(G-2962)*
Clark Industrial Prpts Inc 815 265-7210
104 E Butterfield Trl Gilman (60938) *(G-10377)*
Clark Printing & Marketing 217 363-5300
501 Mercury Dr Champaign (61822) *(G-3280)*
Clark Wire & Cable Co Inc 847 949-9944
408 Washington Blvd Ste A Mundelein (60060) *(G-14678)*
Clarke Aquatic Services Inc 630 894-2000
675 Sidwell Ct Saint Charles (60174) *(G-18167)*
Clarke Div, Batavia *Also called Tegrant Corporation (G-1428)*
Clarke Equipment Company 701 241-8700
2649 Internationale Pkwy Woodridge (60517) *(G-21285)*
Clarke Group Inc 630 894-2000
675 Sidwell Ct Saint Charles (60174) *(G-18168)*
Clarke Mosquito Ctrl Pdts Inc (PA) 630 894-2000
675 Sidwell Ct Saint Charles (60174) *(G-18169)*
Clarkson Soy Products LLC 217 763-9511
320 E South St Cerro Gordo (61818) *(G-3256)*
Clarkwestern Dietrich Building 815 561-2360
501 S Steward Rd Rochelle (61068) *(G-17135)*
Clarus Therapeutics Inc 847 562-4300
555 Skokie Blvd Ste 340 Northbrook (60062) *(G-15361)*
Class, Palatine *Also called Complete Lawn and Snow Service (G-16102)*
Class A Grinding 815 874-2118
3704 Samuelson Rd Rockford (61109) *(G-17352)*
Class Printing, Schaumburg *Also called Allprint Graphics Inc (G-18433)*
Classic Automation & Tool 708 388-6311
4329 136th Ct Crestwood (60418) *(G-7112)*
Classic Color Inc 708 484-0000
2424 S 25th Ave Broadview (60155) *(G-2427)*
Classic Embroidery Inc 708 485-7034
6939 W 59th St Chicago (60638) *(G-4168)*
Classic Fasteners LLC 630 605-0195
3540 Stern Ave Saint Charles (60174) *(G-18170)*
Classic Foods, Chicago *Also called Danziger Kosher Catering Inc (G-4316)*
Classic Group, The, Chicago *Also called Classic Vending Inc (G-4171)*
Classic Management, Hainesville *Also called Classic Printery Inc (G-10946)*
Classic Metal Company Inc 815 252-0104
115 16th St Mendota (61342) *(G-13939)*
Classic Metal Vaults 217 826-6302
806 N 2nd St Marshall (62441) *(G-13567)*
Classic Midwest Die Mold Inc 773 227-8000
1140 N Kostner Ave Chicago (60651) *(G-4169)*
Classic Molding Co Inc 847 671-7888
3800 Wesley Ter Schiller Park (60176) *(G-18794)*
Classic Printery Inc 847 546-6555
336 W Main St Hainesville (60073) *(G-10946)*
Classic Printing Co Inc 217 428-1733
529 N Martin Luther King Decatur (62523) *(G-7475)*
Classic Products Inc 815 344-0051
4010 W Albany St McHenry (60050) *(G-13728)*
Classic Prtg Thermography Inc 630 595-7765
735 N Edgewood Ave Ste F Wood Dale (60191) *(G-21176)*
Classic Remix 312 915-0521
116 W Illinois St Fl 6w-B Chicago (60654) *(G-4170)*
Classic Roadliner Corporation 708 769-0666
8027 Marion Dr Apt 1e Justice (60458) *(G-11950)*
Classic Screen Printing Inc 708 771-9355
1401 Circle Ave Ste 1n Forest Park (60130) *(G-9711)*
Classic Sheet Metal Inc 630 694-0300
1515 W Wrightwood Ct A Addison (60101) *(G-73)*
Classic Vending Inc 773 252-7000
2155 S Carpenter St Chicago (60608) *(G-4171)*
Classic Woodwork Inc 815 356-9000
6704 Pingree Rd Ste 2 Crystal Lake (60014) *(G-7182)*
Classical Statuary & Decor 815 462-3408
21621 S Schoolhouse Rd New Lenox (60451) *(G-15028)*
Classique Signs & Engrv Inc 217 228-7446
1702 Harrison St Quincy (62301) *(G-16872)*
Classroom Technologies LLC 708 548-1642
9227 Gulfstream Rd Frankfort (60423) *(G-9780)*
Claviers Piano Explorer, Northbrook *Also called Instrumentalists Inc (G-15406)*
Clawmounts Mfg Inc 708 525-7552
2595 Bond St University Park (60484) *(G-19951)*
Clay Cnty Rhbilitation Ctr Inc 618 662-6607
1 Commercial Dr Flora (62839) *(G-9678)*
Clay County Industries, Flora *Also called Clay Cnty Rhbilitation Ctr Inc (G-9678)*
Clay County Republican, Louisville *Also called Danny Fender (G-13178)*
Clay Vollmar Products Co 847 540-5850
124 N Buesching Rd Lake Zurich (60047) *(G-12394)*
Clay Vollmar Products Co (PA) 773 774-1234
5835 W Touhy Ave Chicago (60646) *(G-4172)*
Claymount, Franklin Park *Also called Varex Imaging Corporation (G-10076)*
CLC Lubricants Company (PA) 630 232-7900
0n902 Old Kirk Rd Geneva (60134) *(G-10261)*
Clean and Science USA Co Ltd 847 461-9292
2775 Algonquin Rd Ste 110 Rolling Meadows (60008) *(G-17722)*
Clean Coders LLC 847 370-4098
1520 Artaius Pkwy # 7038 Libertyville (60048) *(G-12643)*
Clean Energy Renewables LLC 309 797-4844
4709 15th Street A Moline (61265) *(G-14136)*
Clean Harbors Wichita LLC 815 675-1272
2500 Westward Dr Spring Grove (60081) *(G-19270)*

ALPHABETIC

Clean Hrbors Es Indus Svcs Inc 708 652-0575
6001 W Pershing Rd Cicero (60804) *(G-6836)*
Clean Motion Inc 607 323-1778
4444 W Chicago Ave Chicago (60651) *(G-4173)*
Clean Rite Products, Long Grove *Also called Tiger Accessory Group LLC (G-13171)*
Clean Shop Division, Chicago Heights *Also called Aen Industries Inc (G-6728)*
Clean Sweep Environmental Inc 630 879-8750
1805 Phelps Dr Batavia (60510) *(G-1367)*
Clear Focus Imaging Inc (PA) 707 544-7990
9201 Belmont Ave Ste 100c Franklin Park (60131) *(G-9910)*
Clear Lake Sand & Gravel Co 217 725-6999
2500 Shadow Chaser Dr Springfield (62711) *(G-19351)*
Clear Pack Company 847 957-6282
11610 Copenhagen Ct Franklin Park (60131) *(G-9911)*
Clear Print Inc 815 795-6225
768 Adams St Ottawa (61350) *(G-16046)*
Clear Sight Inc 630 323-3590
220 Rosewood Ct Westmont (60559) *(G-20732)*
Clear Stand, Brighton *Also called Piasa Plastics Inc (G-2403)*
Clear View Industries Inc 815 267-3593
2429 Von Esch Rd Unit G Plainfield (60586) *(G-16652)*
Clearly Kosher Foods 630 546-2052
8s696 Barnes Rd Aurora (60506) *(G-1076)*
Clearsounds Communications Inc (PA) 630 321-2300
1743 Quincy Ave Ste 155 Naperville (60540) *(G-14800)*
Cleartrial LLC 877 206-4846
233 S Wacker Dr Ste 4500 Chicago (60606) *(G-4174)*
Cleats Manufacturing Company, Chicago *Also called Cleats Mfg Inc (G-4175)*
Cleats Mfg Inc (PA) 773 521-0300
1855 S Kilbourn Ave Chicago (60623) *(G-4175)*
Cleats Mfg Inc 773 542-0453
1701 S Kostner Ave Chicago (60623) *(G-4176)*
Cleavenger Associates Inc 630 221-0007
27w474 Jewell Rd Ste 2w Winfield (60190) *(G-21109)*
Clement Industries Inc Del 708 458-9141
5939 W 66th St Bedford Park (60638) *(G-1463)*
Clement Wheel, Bedford Park *Also called Clement Industries Inc Del (G-1463)*
Clementi Printing Inc 773 622-0795
2832 N Narragansett Ave Chicago (60634) *(G-4177)*
Cleo Communications Inc (PA) 815 654-8110
4949 Harrison Ave Ste 200 Rockford (61108) *(G-17353)*
Cleveland Folder Service 847 782-5850
4330 Lee Ave Gurnee (60031) *(G-10864)*
Cleveland Hdwr & Forging Co 630 896-9850
138 Pierce St Aurora (60505) *(G-1077)*
Cleveland Quarry, Cleveland *Also called Riverstone Group Inc (G-6912)*
Cleveland Steel Container Corp 708 258-0700
117 E Lincoln St Peotone (60468) *(G-16552)*
Click Block, Rolling Meadows *Also called Click-Block Corporation (G-17723)*
Click-Block Corporation 847 749-1651
1100 Hicks Rd Rolling Meadows (60008) *(G-17723)*
Cliffe Printing Company 708 345-1665
112 S 5th Ave Maywood (60153) *(G-13667)*
Clifford W Estes Co Inc 815 433-0944
1289 W Marquette St Ottawa (61350) *(G-16047)*
Cliffords Pub Inc 847 259-3000
1503 N Rand Rd Palatine (60074) *(G-16100)*
Clifton Chemical Company (PA) 815 697-2343
160 S Locust St Chebanse (60922) *(G-3429)*
Climate Guard Design 773 873-0000
155 W 84th St Chicago (60620) *(G-4178)*
Climateguard, Chicago *Also called Climate Guard Design (G-4178)*
Climco Coils Company 815 772-3717
701 Klimstra Ct Morrison (61270) *(G-14342)*
Clinard Ready Mix Inc 217 773-3965
Rr 24 Box West Mount Sterling (62353) *(G-14590)*
Cline Concrete Products 217 283-5012
438 W Thompson Ave Hoopeston (60942) *(G-11505)*
Clinkenbeard & Associates Inc 815 226-0291
810 Progressive Ln South Beloit (61080) *(G-19087)*
Clintex Laboratories Inc 773 493-9777
140 W 62nd St Chicago (60621) *(G-4179)*
Clinton County Materials Corp 618 533-4252
100 Rhodes St Centralia (62801) *(G-3226)*
Clinton Daily Journal, Clinton *Also called Central Illinois Newspapers (G-6920)*
Clinton Journal 309 242-3900
14 Kenfield Cir Bloomington (61704) *(G-2032)*
Clinton Oil Corp 815 356-1124
250 N Il Route 31 176 Crystal Lake (60014) *(G-7183)*
Cliqster LLC 847 732-1457
212 Pine Point Dr Highland Park (60035) *(G-11259)*
Cll Engineering LLC 630 628-8393
5 W Laura Dr Addison (60101) *(G-74)*
Clodfelter Engraving Inc 314 968-8418
2109 Holland St Alton (62002) *(G-547)*
Cloos Robotic Welding Inc (HQ) 847 923-9988
911 Albion Ave Schaumburg (60193) *(G-18479)*
Cloos Robotics De Mexico, Schaumburg *Also called Cloos Robotic Welding Inc (G-18479)*
Clopay Building Pdts Co Inc 708 346-0901
10047 Virginia Ave Ste A Chicago Ridge (60415) *(G-6791)*
Clorox Company 510 271-7000
7201 S Adams St Willowbrook (60527) *(G-21036)*
Clorox Hidden Valley Mfg 847 229-5500
1197 Willis Ave Wheeling (60090) *(G-20871)*
Clorox Manufacturing Company 847 229-5500
1197 Willis Ave Wheeling (60090) *(G-20872)*
Closet Concept 217 375-4214
1881 E 300 North Rd Milford (60953) *(G-14033)*
Closet Concpts By Shlvng Unlim, Cherry Valley *Also called Shelving and Bath Unlimited (G-3446)*
Closet Works Division, Elmhurst *Also called Carson Properties Inc (G-9341)*
Closets By Design, Aurora *Also called Chicagoland Closets LLC (G-1075)*
Cloud 9 Division, Inverness *Also called Mason Engineering & Designing (G-11602)*
Cloud 9 Infosystems Inc 855 225-6839
1333 Butterfield Rd # 401 Downers Grove (60515) *(G-7974)*
Clover Club Bottling Co Inc 773 261-7100
356 N Kilbourn Ave Chicago (60624) *(G-4180)*
Clover Custom Counters Inc 708 598-8912
9220 S Octavia Ave Bridgeview (60455) *(G-2336)*
Clover Global, Ottawa *Also called 4l Technologies Inc (G-16035)*
Clover Imaging Group LLC 815 431-8100
700 E Dayton Rd Ottawa (61350) *(G-16048)*
Clover Plastics LLC 630 473-6488
1145 Howard Dr West Chicago (60185) *(G-20564)*
Clover Signs 773 588-2828
2944 W Montrose Ave Apt 1 Chicago (60618) *(G-4181)*
Clover Technologies Group LLC (HQ) 866 734-6548
2700 W Higgins Rd Ste 100 Hoffman Estates (60169) *(G-11414)*
Clover US Holdings LLC (HQ) 630 967-3600
3333 Finley Rd Ste 800 Downers Grove (60515) *(G-7975)*
Clover Usa, LLC, Downers Grove *Also called Hearthside Usa LLC (G-8020)*
Cloverleaf Feed Co Inc 217 589-5010
Rr 267 Box S Roodhouse (62082) *(G-17892)*
Clown Global Brands LLC 847 564-5950
3184 Doolittle Dr Northbrook (60062) *(G-15362)*
Cloz Companies Inc (PA) 773 247-8879
5550 Touhy Ave Ste 202 Skokie (60077) *(G-18944)*
Clp Foodservice, Lincolnshire *Also called Crown Brands LLC (G-12757)*
Club House Designs, Chicago *Also called Orland Sports Ltd (G-5703)*
Club Jewelry Manufacturing Inc 847 541-0700
137 N Milwaukee Ave Wheeling (60090) *(G-20873)*
Clugston Tibbitts Funeral Home (PA) 309 833-2188
303 E Washington St Macomb (61455) *(G-13389)*
Clugston-Tibbots Monument Co, Macomb *Also called Clugston Tibbitts Funeral Home (G-13389)*
Clutch Systems Inc 815 282-7960
10901 N 2nd St Machesney Park (61115) *(G-13334)*
Clybourn 1200 ....312 477-7442
1249 N Clybourn Ave # 300 Chicago (60610) *(G-4182)*
Clybourn Metal Finishing Co 773 525-8162
2240 N Clybourn Ave Chicago (60614) *(G-4183)*
Clyde Printing Company 773 847-5900
3520 S Morgan St Fl 2a Chicago (60609) *(G-4184)*
Clyde's Delicious Donuts, Addison *Also called Herman Seekamp Inc (G-149)*
CM Associates, Tinley Park *Also called Cypress Multigraphics LLC (G-19820)*
CM Woodwords Inc 847 945-7689
20968 Deerrun Dr Deerfield (60015) *(G-7604)*
Cma Inc 847 848-0674
929 Kelly Ave Joliet (60435) *(G-11841)*
Cma Inc (PA) 630 551-3100
19 Stonehill Rd Oswego (60543) *(G-15996)*
Cma, Flodyne, Hydradyne, Hanover Park *Also called Flodyne Inc (G-11004)*
Cmb Printing Inc 630 323-1110
15w700 79th St Unit 4 Burr Ridge (60527) *(G-2663)*
CMC America Corporation 815 726-4337
208 S Center St Joliet (60436) *(G-11842)*
CMC Electronics Aurora LLC 630 556-9619
84 N Dugan Rd Sugar Grove (60554) *(G-19640)*
Cmd Conveyor Inc 708 237-0996
10008 Anderson Ave Chicago Ridge (60415) *(G-6792)*
Cmetrix Inc 630 595-9800
165 Mittel Dr Wood Dale (60191) *(G-21177)*
Cmg Precision Machining Co Inc 630 759-8080
1342 Enterprise Dr Romeoville (60446) *(G-17810)*
CMI, Streamwood *Also called Copy-Mor Inc (G-19568)*
CMI, Chicago *Also called Craftmaster Manufacturing Inc (G-4256)*
CMI Display, Chicago *Also called Continental Marketing Inc (G-4227)*
Cml Technologies Inc 708 450-1911
10330 W Roosevelt Rd # 205 Westchester (60154) *(G-20694)*
Cmp Anodizing, Elk Grove Village *Also called Cmp Associates Inc (G-8900)*
Cmp Associates Inc 847 956-1313
1340 Howard St Elk Grove Village (60007) *(G-8900)*
Cmp Millwork Co 630 832-6462
601 S Il Route 83 Ste 100 Elmhurst (60126) *(G-9348)*
Cmt, Elk Grove Village *Also called Centech Plastics Inc (G-8884)*

Cmt International Inc 618 549-1829
1400 N Wood Rd Murphysboro (62966) *(G-14754)*
Cmv Sharper Finish Inc 773 276-4800
4500 W Augusta Blvd Chicago (60651) *(G-4185)*
Cmworks Acquisition LLC, Elgin *Also called Charter Precision LLC (G-8536)*
Cnc / Machine Shop, Cortland *Also called Ace Machine & Tool Inc (G-7015)*
Cnc Chicago Corp 847 671-3319
421 S Irmen Dr Ste B Addison (60101) *(G-75)*
Cnc Graphics 630 766-6308
501 Frontier Way Bensenville (60106) *(G-1771)*
Cnc Machining, Arcola *Also called G L Doemelt (G-649)*
Cnc Milling & Turning, Crestwood *Also called AAA Cnc Manufacturing Corp (G-7104)*
Cnc Swiss Inc 630 543-9595
761 W Racquet Club Dr A Addison (60101) *(G-76)*
CNE Inc 847 534-7135
1018 Lunt Ave Schaumburg (60193) *(G-18480)*
Cnh America LLC 309 965-2217
600 E Peoria St Goodfield (61742) *(G-10671)*
Cnh Industrial America LLC 847 263-5793
2450 W Air Ln Waukegan (60087) *(G-20429)*
Cnh Industrial America LLC 309 965-2233
1498 Us Highway 150 Goodfield (61742) *(G-10672)*
Cnh Industrial America LLC 309 965-2217
600 E Peoria St Goodfield (61742) *(G-10673)*
Cnh Industrial America LLC 630 887-2233
6900 Veterans Blvd Burr Ridge (60527) *(G-2664)*
Cnh Industrial Capitl Amer LLC (PA) 630 887-2233
6900 Veterans Blvd Burr Ridge (60527) *(G-2665)*
Cnhi LLC 217 774-2161
201 N Banker St Effingham (62401) *(G-8391)*
Cnlc-Stc Inc (HQ) 312 321-3000
350 N Orleans St Chicago (60654) *(G-4186)*
Cnv Enterprises Inc 815 405-6762
8282 Old Ridge Rd Plainfield (60544) *(G-16653)*
Co-Fair Corporation 847 626-1500
7301 Saint Louis Ave Skokie (60076) *(G-18945)*
Co-Ordinated Packaging Inc 847 559-8877
1001 Entry Dr Bensenville (60106) *(G-1772)*
Co-Rect Bar Products, Lincolnshire *Also called Co-Rect Products Inc (G-12751)*
Co-Rect Products Inc (PA) 763 542-9200
300 Knightsbridge Pkwy # 400 Lincolnshire (60069) *(G-12751)*
Coach House Inc 217 543-3761
700 E Mill St Arthur (61911) *(G-847)*
Coach House Garages, Arthur *Also called Coach House Inc (G-847)*
Coaching For Excelence, Country Club Hills *Also called Coaching For Excellence LLC (G-7036)*
Coaching For Excellence LLC 708 957-6047
4131 191st Pl Country Club Hills (60478) *(G-7036)*
Coal City Courant 815 634-0315
271 S Broadway St Coal City (60416) *(G-6930)*
Coal City Redi-Mix Co Inc 815 634-4455
640 S Mazon St Coal City (60416) *(G-6931)*
Coalesse 312 622-6269
222 Merchds Mrt Plz 1032 Chicago (60654) *(G-4187)*
Coates Screen, Saint Charles *Also called Sun Chemical Corporation (G-18281)*
Coating Methods Incorporated 847 428-8800
853 Commerce Pkwy Carpentersville (60110) *(G-3098)*
Coating Specialty Inc 708 754-3311
3311 Holeman Ave Ste 7 S Chicago Hts (60411) *(G-18118)*
Coatings International Inc 847 455-1400
3429 Runge St Franklin Park (60131) *(G-9912)*
Cobalt Chains Inc 309 698-9250
200 Catherine St East Peoria (61611) *(G-8262)*
Cobalt Tool & Manufacturing 630 530-8898
131 W Home Ave Villa Park (60181) *(G-20139)*
Cobatco Inc 309 676-2663
1215 Ne Adams St Peoria (61603) *(G-16425)*
Cobius Halthcare Solutions LLC 847 656-8700
853 Sanders Rd Ste 313 Northbrook (60062) *(G-15363)*
Cobra Coal Inc 630 560-1050
3n060 Powis Rd West Chicago (60185) *(G-20565)*
Cobra Metal Works Inc 847 214-8400
1140 Jansen Farm Dr Elgin (60123) *(G-8544)*
Cobraa Inc 618 228-7380
350 W 4th St Aviston (62216) *(G-1178)*
Cobraco Manufacturing Inc (PA) 847 726-5800
300 E Il Route 22 Lake Zurich (60047) *(G-12395)*
Coca Cola 630 588-8786
775 East Dr Carol Stream (60188) *(G-2963)*
Coca Cola Bottling Compan 847 227-6766
9700 W Higgins Rd Rosemont (60018) *(G-18006)*
Coca Cola Fleet Service 847 600-2279
7500 N Oak Park Ave Niles (60714) *(G-15111)*
Coca-Cola, Chicago *Also called Emmert John (G-4499)*
Coca-Cola, Niles *Also called Coca Cola Fleet Service (G-15111)*
Coca-Cola, Carol Stream *Also called Coca Cola (G-2963)*
Coca-Cola Btlg Wisconsin Del 847 647-0200
7400 N Oak Park Ave Niles (60714) *(G-15112)*
Coca-Cola Company 847 647-0200
7400 N Oak Park Ave Niles (60714) *(G-15113)*
Coca-Cola Refreshments USA Inc 630 513-5247
105 Industrial Dr Saint Charles (60174) *(G-18171)*
Coca-Cola Refreshments USA Inc 217 348-1001
1321 Loxa Rd Charleston (61920) *(G-3400)*
Coca-Cola Refreshments USA Inc 708 597-6700
5321 W 122nd St Alsip (60803) *(G-433)*
Coca-Cola Refreshments USA Inc 847 647-0200
7425 N Oak Park Ave Niles (60714) *(G-15114)*
Coca-Cola Refreshments USA Inc 708 597-4700
12200 S Laramie Ave Chicago (60803) *(G-4188)*
Coca-Cola Refreshments USA Inc 309 697-8600
5001 S Becker Dr Bartonville (61607) *(G-1329)*
Coca-Cola Refreshments USA Inc 217 544-4892
3495 E Sangamon Ave Springfield (62707) *(G-19352)*
Coca-Cola Refreshments USA Inc 217 367-1761
2809 N Lincoln Ave Urbana (61802) *(G-19978)*
Coca-Cola Refreshments USA Inc 813 298-1000
6250 N River Rd Ste 9000 Rosemont (60018) *(G-18007)*
Coca-Cola Refreshments USA Inc 618 542-2101
Hwy 51 S Du Quoin (62832) *(G-8117)*
Cocajo Blades & Leather 217 370-6634
481 Oxley Rd Franklin (62638) *(G-9854)*
Coda Resources Ltd 718 649-1666
600 N Kilbourn Ave Chicago (60624) *(G-4189)*
Coda Resources Ltd 718 649-1666
4444 W Ferdinand St Chicago (60624) *(G-4190)*
Code B Magazine, Chicago *Also called Code Black LLC (G-4191)*
Code Black LLC 773 493-4500
9 W Washington St Chicago (60602) *(G-4191)*
Cody Metal Finishing Inc 773 252-2026
1620 N Throop St Chicago (60642) *(G-4192)*
Coe Equipment Inc 217 498-7200
5953 Cherry St Rochester (62563) *(G-17164)*
Coeur Inc 815 648-1093
11411 Price Rd Hebron (60034) *(G-11141)*
Coeur Capital Inc 312 489-5800
104 S Michigan Ave Chicago (60603) *(G-4193)*
Coeur Mining Inc (PA) 312 489-5800
104 S Michigan Ave # 800 Chicago (60603) *(G-4194)*
Coeur Rochester Inc 312 661-2436
104 S Michigan Ave Chicago (60603) *(G-4195)*
Cofair Products Inc 847 626-1500
7301 Saint Louis Ave Skokie (60076) *(G-18946)*
Coffee Brewmasters Usa LLC 773 294-9665
351 Hastings Dr Buffalo Grove (60089) *(G-2526)*
Coffee News of Dupage County, Carol Stream *Also called Alali Enterprises Inc (G-2930)*
Cognex Corporation 630 505-9990
800 E Diehl Rd Ste 125 Naperville (60563) *(G-14801)*
Cognizant Tech Solutions Corp 630 955-0617
3333 Warrenville Rd # 350 Lisle (60532) *(G-12877)*
Cohera Medical Inc 602 418-8788
10 S La Salle St Ste 3300 Chicago (60603) *(G-4196)*
Coi Company, Chicago *Also called Chicago Ornamental Iron Inc (G-4121)*
Coil It, Elk Grove Village *Also called Majestic Spring Inc (G-9108)*
Coil Sales and Manufacturing, Marshall *Also called Charles Industries LLC (G-13566)*
Coilcraft Incorporated 815 288-7051
9 Clay St Oregon (61061) *(G-15915)*
Coilform Company (PA) 630 232-8000
2571 Kaneville Ct Geneva (60134) *(G-10262)*
Coiltechnic Inc 815 675-9260
2402 Spring Ridge Dr C Spring Grove (60081) *(G-19271)*
Coin Macke Laundry 847 459-1109
124b Messner Dr Wheeling (60090) *(G-20874)*
Coinstar Procurement LLC 630 424-4788
1 Tower Ln Ste 900 Oakbrook Terrace (60181) *(G-15794)*
Cokel D J Wldg Stl Fabricators, Princeville *Also called Cokel Dj Welding Bay & Muffler (G-16825)*
Cokel Dj Welding Bay & Muffler 309 385-4567
224 E Evans St Princeville (61559) *(G-16825)*
Cokel Jim Prtble Wldg Sp Servi, Monmouth *Also called Jim Cokel Welding (G-14219)*
Cokel Welding Shop 217 357-3312
117 S Madison St Carthage (62321) *(G-3134)*
Cokel's Welding, Aledo *Also called Aledo Welding Enterprises Inc (G-354)*
Colbert Custom Framing Inc 630 717-1448
1283 S Naper Blvd Naperville (60540) *(G-14802)*
Colbert Packaging Corporation (PA) 847 367-5990
28355 N Bradley Rd Lake Forest (60045) *(G-12238)*
Colborne Acquisition Co LLC 847 371-0101
28495 N Ballard Dr Lake Forest (60045) *(G-12239)*
Cold Headers Inc (PA) 773 775-7900
5514 N Elston Ave 14 Chicago (60630) *(G-4197)*
Cole Pallet Services Corp 815 758-3226
1600 S 7th St Dekalb (60115) *(G-7668)*
Cole-Parmer Instrument Co LLC 847 381-7050
28092 W Commercial Ave Lake Barrington (60010) *(G-12144)*
Coleman Cable LLC (HQ) 847 672-2300
1 Overlook Pt Ste 265 Lincolnshire (60069) *(G-12752)*

ALPHABETIC

Coleman Cable LLC   **ALPHABETIC SECTION**

Coleman Cable LLC 847 672-2300
  1 Overlook Pt Lincolnshire (60069) *(G-12753)*
Coleman Company Inc (HQ) 316 832-2653
  180 N Lasalle St Ste 700 Chicago (60601) *(G-4198)*
Coles Appliance & Furn Co 773 525-1797
  4026 N Lincoln Ave Chicago (60618) *(G-4199)*
Coles Craft Corporation 630 858-8171
  868 Baker Ct Glen Ellyn (60137) *(G-10398)*
Colfax Welding & Fabricating 847 359-4433
  605 W Colfax St Palatine (60067) *(G-16101)*
Collagen Usa Inc 708 716-0251
  3048 N Milwaukee Ave Chicago (60618) *(G-4200)*
Colleagues of Beer Inc 847 727-3318
  520 Laurie Ct Grayslake (60030) *(G-10762)*
Colleens Confection 630 653-2231
  190 Easy St Ste I Carol Stream (60188) *(G-2964)*
College Bound Athlete LLC 708 259-7713
  2659 Wisconsin Ave Downers Grove (60515) *(G-7976)*
College Bound Publications 773 262-5810
  7658 N Rogers Ave Chicago (60626) *(G-4201)*
Colley Elevator Company 630 766-7230
  226 William St Bensenville (60106) *(G-1773)*
Collins Bros, Mount Vernon *Also called Collins Brothers Oil Corp (G-14602)*
Collins Brothers Oil Corp (PA) 618 244-1093
  218 N 9th St Mount Vernon (62864) *(G-14602)*
Collinson Stone Co (PA) 309 787-7983
  225 1st St E Milan (61264) *(G-14004)*
Collinsville Ice & Fuel Co 618 344-3272
  800 N Bluff Rd Collinsville (62234) *(G-6955)*
Colloid Envmtl Tech Co LLC (HQ) 847 851-1500
  2870 Forbs Ave Hoffman Estates (60192) *(G-11415)*
Colnago America Inc 312 239-6666
  1528 W Adams St Ste 4b Chicago (60607) *(G-4202)*
Colonade Interiors II, Burr Ridge *Also called Ameriguard Corporation (G-2652)*
Colonial Bag Corporation 630 690-3999
  205 Fullerton Ave Carol Stream (60188) *(G-2965)*
Colony Display LLC (HQ) 847 426-5300
  2531 Tech Dr Ste 314 Elgin (60124) *(G-8545)*
Color Communications LLC 773 638-1400
  4000 W Fillmore St Chicago (60624) *(G-4203)*
Color Communications LLC (PA) 312 223-0204
  230 W Monroe St Ste 2000 Chicago (60606) *(G-4204)*
Color Signs 847 368-0101
  3110 N Arlington Hts Rd Arlington Heights (60004) *(G-716)*
Color Smiths Inc 708 562-0061
  747 N Church Rd Ste E6 Elmhurst (60126) *(G-9349)*
Color Tone Printing 708 385-1442
  2619 Orchard St Blue Island (60406) *(G-2114)*
Color4 .... 847 996-6880
  28100 N Ashley Cir Ste 10 Libertyville (60048) *(G-12644)*
Colorex Chemical Co Inc 630 238-3124
  834 Foster Ave Bensenville (60106) *(G-1774)*
Colorforms, Clinton *Also called R R Donnelley & Sons Company (G-6928)*
Colorful Fire, Zion *Also called Philmar LLC (G-21525)*
Colorkraft Roll Products Inc (PA) 217 382-4967
  1 Harry Glynn Dr Martinsville (62442) *(G-13582)*
Colors For Plastics Inc (PA) 847 437-0033
  2245 Pratt Blvd Elk Grove Village (60007) *(G-8901)*
Colorsmith Stained GL Studio 708 447-8763
  8 E Quincy St Riverside (60546) *(G-17083)*
Colson Group Holdings LLC (PA) 630 613-2941
  1815 S Meyers Rd Ste 750 Oakbrook Terrace (60181) *(G-15795)*
Colson Publications, Mount Sterling *Also called Democrat Message (G-14591)*
Colt Technology Services LLC 312 465-2484
  141 W Jackson Blvd # 2808 Chicago (60604) *(G-4205)*
Columbia Chutes LLC 847 520-5989
  610 Moen Ave Rockdale (60436) *(G-17257)*
Columbia Metal Spinning Co, Chicago *Also called Craft Metal Spinning Co (G-4255)*
Columbia Metal Spinning Co 773 685-2800
  4351 N Normandy Ave Chicago (60634) *(G-4206)*
Columbia Quarry Company (PA) 618 281-7631
  210 State Route 158 Columbia (62236) *(G-6987)*
Columbia Quarry Company 618 939-8833
  5440 Quarry Dr Waterloo (62298) *(G-20288)*
Columbia Tool & Gage Co., Niles *Also called Accurate Metal Components Inc (G-15099)*
Columbia Woodworks Corporation 202 526-2387
  230 W Laura Dr Addison (60101) *(G-77)*
Columbian Home Products LLC (PA) 847 307-8600
  404 N Rand Rd North Barrington (60010) *(G-15282)*
Columbia Foods Company, Des Plaines *Also called Cfc Inc (G-7743)*
Columbus McKinnon Corporation 800 548-2930
  801 W Center St Eureka (61530) *(G-9478)*
Columbus McKinnon Corporation 630 783-1195
  10321 Werch Dr Ste 100 Woodridge (60517) *(G-21286)*
Columbus Meats Inc 312 829-2480
  906 W Randolph St Fl 1 Chicago (60607) *(G-4207)*
Colvin Printing 708 331-4580
  12958 Ashland Ave Blue Island (60406) *(G-2115)*

Com-Graphics Inc 312 226-0900
  329 W 18th St Fl 10 Chicago (60616) *(G-4208)*
Combe Laboratories Inc 217 893-4490
  200 Shellhouse Dr Rantoul (61866) *(G-16971)*
Combined Metals Chicago LLC 847 683-0500
  1 Hauk Rd Hampshire (60140) *(G-10967)*
Combined Metals Holding Inc 708 547-8800
  2401 Grant Ave Bellwood (60104) *(G-1619)*
Combined Technologies Inc (PA) 847 968-4855
  732 Florsheim Dr Ste 14 Libertyville (60048) *(G-12645)*
Comdata Inc 630 847-6988
  239 W Lasalle St Somonauk (60552) *(G-19069)*
Comers Welding Service Inc 630 892-0168
  1105 S Lake St Montgomery (60538) *(G-14241)*
Comet Conection Inc 312 243-5400
  5040 W 127th St Alsip (60803) *(G-434)*
Comet Die & Engraving Company 630 833-5600
  909 N Larch Ave Elmhurst (60126) *(G-9350)*
Comet Fabricating & Welding Co. 815 229-0468
  5620 Falcon Rd Rockford (61109) *(G-17354)*
Comet Neon 630 668-6366
  1120 N Ridge Ave Lombard (60148) *(G-13056)*
Comet Press, Alsip *Also called Comet Conection Inc (G-434)*
Comet Roll & Machine Company 630 268-1407
  405 Stone Dr Saint Charles (60174) *(G-18172)*
Comet Supply Inc 309 444-2712
  312 Muller Rd Washington (61571) *(G-20269)*
Comet Tool Inc 847 956-0126
  880 Nicholas Blvd Elk Grove Village (60007) *(G-8902)*
Comfort Companies LLC (HQ) 406 522-8560
  100 N Florida Ave Belleville (62221) *(G-1540)*
Commercial Copy Printing Ctr 847 981-8590
  520 Bennett Rd Elk Grove Village (60007) *(G-8903)*
Commercial Dynamics Inc. 847 439-5300
  2025 S Arlington Hts Rd Arlington Heights (60005) *(G-717)*
Commercial Fabricators Inc (PA) 708 594-1199
  7247 S 78th Ave Ste 1 Bridgeview (60455) *(G-2337)*
Commercial Finishes Co Ltd 847 981-9222
  540 Lively Blvd Elk Grove Village (60007) *(G-8904)*
Commercial Machine Services 847 806-1901
  1099 Touhy Ave Elk Grove Village (60007) *(G-8905)*
Commercial Metals Company 815 928-9600
  780 Eastgate Indus Pkwy Kankakee (60901) *(G-11961)*
Commercial Pallet Inc 312 226-6699
  2029 W Hubbard St Chicago (60612) *(G-4209)*
Commercial Plastics Company (PA) 847 566-1700
  800 Allanson Rd Mundelein (60060) *(G-14679)*
Commercial Printers, Chicago *Also called Breaker Press Co Inc (G-3948)*
Commercial Product Group, Moline *Also called Harrington Signal Inc (G-14148)*
Commercial Prtg Graphics Arts, Oakbrook Terrace *Also called Printed Impressions Inc (G-15813)*
Commercial Prtg of Rockford 815 965-4759
  1120 2nd Ave Rockford (61104) *(G-17355)*
Commercial Rfrgn Centl III Inc 217 235-5016
  2020 Prairie Ave Mattoon (61938) *(G-13634)*
Commercial Stainless Svcs Inc 847 349-1560
  1201 Busse Rd Elk Grove Village (60007) *(G-8906)*
Common Culture Brewing Co 847 584-2337
  821 Chicago Ave Evanston (60202) *(G-9506)*
Common Goal Systems Inc 630 592-4200
  188 W Industrial Dr # 240 Elmhurst (60126) *(G-9351)*
Common Ground Publishing LLC 217 721-6839
  2001 S 1st St Ste 202 Champaign (61820) *(G-3281)*
Common Scents Mom 309 389-3216
  10812 W Timber Rd Mapleton (61547) *(G-13471)*
Commscope Inc North Carolina 779 435-6000
  2700 Ellis Rd Joliet (60433) *(G-11843)*
Commscope Connectivity LLC 779 435-6000
  2700 Ellis Rd Joliet (60433) *(G-11844)*
Commscope Solutions Intl Inc (HQ) 828 324-2200
  4 Westbrook Corp Ctr Westchester (60154) *(G-20695)*
Commscope Technologies LLC 779 435-6000
  2700 Ellis Rd Joliet (60433) *(G-11845)*
Commscope Technologies LLC 847 397-6307
  1821 Walden Office Sq # 400 Schaumburg (60173) *(G-18481)*
Communication Coil Inc 847 671-1333
  9601 Soreng Ave Schiller Park (60176) *(G-18795)*
Communication Technologies Inc 630 384-0900
  188 Internationale Blvd Glendale Heights (60139) *(G-10444)*
Communications Integrators, Harvey *Also called Afc Cable Systems Inc (G-11070)*
Communications Resource Inc 630 860-1661
  1175 Tower Rd Schaumburg (60173) *(G-18482)*
Community Advantage Network (PA) 847 376-8943
  1163 Lee St Des Plaines (60016) *(G-7748)*
Community Magazine Group 312 880-0370
  1550 S Indiana Ave Chicago (60605) *(G-4210)*
Community Rady Mix of Pttsfeld 217 285-5548
  1503 Kamar Dr Pittsfield (62363) *(G-16633)*

Community Ready Mix Pittsfield, Pittsfield *Also called Community Rady Mix of Pittsfeld* ***(G-16633)***
Community Readymix Inc 217 245-6668
710 Brooklyn Ave Jacksonville (62650) ***(G-11762)***
Community Support Systems (PA) 217 705-4300
618 W Main St Teutopolis (62467) ***(G-19767)***
Compact Industries Inc 630 513-9600
3945 Ohio Ave Saint Charles (60174) ***(G-18173)***
Compak Inc 815 399-2699
539 Chicory St Machesney Park (61115) ***(G-13335)***
Competition Electronics Inc 815 874-8001
3469 Precision Dr Rockford (61109) ***(G-17356)***
Competitive Edge Opportunities 815 981-4060
910 E Burnett Rd Island Lake (60042) ***(G-11605)***
Complete Conveying Svcs LLC 815 695-5176
15583 State Route 71 Newark (60541) ***(G-15075)***
Complete Custom Woodworks 309 644-1911
3 Crestview Dr Coal Valley (61240) ***(G-6934)***
Complete Lawn and Snow Service 847 776-7287
544 W Colfax St Ste 5 Palatine (60067) ***(G-16102)***
Complete Mold Polishing Inc 630 406-7668
1219 Paramount Pkwy Batavia (60510) ***(G-1368)***
Complete Woman, Chicago *Also called Associated Publications Inc* ***(G-3752)***
Complex Woodwork Inc 630 651-3637
601 N Chicago St Joliet (60432) ***(G-11846)***
Component Parts Company 815 477-2323
7301 Foxfire Dr Crystal Lake (60012) ***(G-7184)***
Component Plastics Inc 847 695-9200
700 Tollgate Rd Elgin (60123) ***(G-8546)***
Component Precast Supply Inc 630 483-2900
4n325 Powis Rd West Chicago (60185) ***(G-20566)***
Component Products Inc 847 301-1000
764 N Oaklawn Ave Elmhurst (60126) ***(G-9352)***
Component Sales Incorporated 630 543-9666
130 S Fairbank St Addison (60101) ***(G-78)***
Component Specialty Inc (HQ) 847 742-4400
412 N State St Elgin (60123) ***(G-8547)***
Component Tool & Mfg Co 708 672-5505
25416 S Dixie Hwy Ste 1 Crete (60417) ***(G-7136)***
Componenta USA LLC 309 691-7000
8515 N University St Peoria (61615) ***(G-16426)***
Composite Bearings Mfg 630 595-8334
720 N Edgewood Ave Wood Dale (60191) ***(G-21178)***
Composite Cutter Tech Inc 847 740-6875
31632 N Ellis Dr Unit 210 Volo (60073) ***(G-20198)***
Composition One Inc 630 588-1900
400 Lake St Ste 110b Roselle (60172) ***(G-17946)***
Compound Bow Rifle Sight Inc 618 526-4427
1004 S Walnut St Breese (62230) ***(G-2301)***
Compressed Air Advisors Inc 877 247-2381
2215 S Wolf Rd Ste 127 Hillside (60162) ***(G-11334)***
Comptia Learning LLC 630 678-8490
3500 Lacey Rd Ste 100 Downers Grove (60515) ***(G-7977)***
Comptons Encyclopedia, Chicago *Also called Success Publishing Group Inc* ***(G-6262)***
Compu Doc Inc 630 554-5800
105 Theodore Dr Ste A Oswego (60543) ***(G-15997)***
Compusystems Inc (PA) 708 344-9070
2651 Warrenville Rd # 400 Downers Grove (60515) ***(G-7978)***
Computaforms, Waukegan *Also called Medical Records Co* ***(G-20465)***
Computer Industry Almanac Inc 847 758-1926
1013 S Belmont Ave Arlington Heights (60005) ***(G-718)***
Computer Maintenance Inc 630 953-1555
1433 W Fullerton Ave M Addison (60101) ***(G-79)***
Computer Pwr Solutions Ill Ltd 618 281-8898
235 Southwoods Ctr Columbia (62236) ***(G-6988)***
Computer Svcs & Consulting Inc 855 482-2267
16w241 S Frontage Rd # 4 Burr Ridge (60527) ***(G-2666)***
Computerized Fleet Analysis 630 543-1410
1020 W Fullerton Ave A Addison (60101) ***(G-80)***
Computerprox 847 516-8560
163 E Chicago St Fl 2 Elgin (60120) ***(G-8548)***
Computhink Inc 630 705-9050
151 E 22nd St Lombard (60148) ***(G-13057)***
Computing Integrity Inc 217 355-4469
3102 Valleybrook Dr Champaign (61822) ***(G-3282)***
Compx Fort, Grayslake *Also called Fort Lock Corporation* ***(G-10773)***
Compx International Inc 847 234-1864
915 Sherwood Dr Lake Bluff (60044) ***(G-12176)***
Compx Security Products Inc 847 234-1864
715 Center St Grayslake (60030) ***(G-10763)***
Compx Timberline, Grayslake *Also called Compx Security Products Inc* ***(G-10763)***
Comtec Industries Ltd 630 759-9000
586 Territorial Dr Ste F Bolingbrook (60440) ***(G-2157)***
Comvigo Inc 312 933-3385
410 Woodgate Ct Willowbrook (60527) ***(G-21037)***
Comwell (PA) 618 282-6233
10257 State Route 3 Red Bud (62278) ***(G-16991)***
Con Form Industry Inc 847 278-1143
561 Estes Ave Schaumburg (60193) ***(G-18483)***
Con-Tech, Northbrook *Also called Conservation Technology Ltd* ***(G-15366)***
Con-Temp Cabinets Inc 630 892-7300
201 Poplar Pl North Aurora (60542) ***(G-15257)***
Con-Trol-Cure Inc 773 248-0099
1229 W Cortland St Chicago (60614) ***(G-4211)***
Conagra, Chester *Also called Ardent Mills LLC* ***(G-3449)***
Conagra Brands Inc (PA) 312 549-5000
222 Mdse Mart Plz Chicago (60654) ***(G-4212)***
Conagra Brands Inc 630 857-1000
750 E Diehl Rd Ste 111 Naperville (60563) ***(G-14803)***
Conagra Dairy Foods Company (HQ) 630 848-0975
222 Merchandise Mart Plz # 1300 Chicago (60654) ***(G-4213)***
Conair Corporation 203 351-9000
205 Shellhouse Dr Rantoul (61866) ***(G-16972)***
Concentric Components Inc 224 422-0638
811 Longacre Ct Island Lake (60042) ***(G-11606)***
Concentric Itasca Inc 630 773-3355
800 Hollywood Ave Itasca (60143) ***(G-11638)***
Concep Machine Co Inc 847 498-9740
1800 Holste Rd Northbrook (60062) ***(G-15364)***
Concept and Design Services 847 259-1675
807 S Golfview Pl Mount Prospect (60056) ***(G-14519)***
Concept Industries Inc 847 258-3545
199 Gaylord St Elk Grove Village (60007) ***(G-8907)***
Concept Laboratories Inc 773 395-7300
1400 W Wabansia Ave Chicago (60642) ***(G-4214)***
Concept One Design Inc 708 807-3111
1034 Forest View Ct Naperville (60563) ***(G-14804)***
Concept Printers (PA) 708 481-2430
209 Glenwood Rd Chicago Heights (60411) ***(G-6744)***
Concepts and Controls Inc 847 478-9296
2530 Apple Hill Ct N Buffalo Grove (60089) ***(G-2527)***
Concepts Magnet 847 253-3351
515 S Edward St Mount Prospect (60056) ***(G-14520)***
Conchemco, Chicago *Also called Consolidated Chem Works Ltd* ***(G-4222)***
Concierge Preferred 312 360-1770
101 W Grand Ave Ste 404 Chicago (60654) ***(G-4215)***
Concord Cabinets Inc (PA) 217 894-6507
1276 E 2575th St Clayton (62324) ***(G-6909)***
Concord Oil & Gas Corporation 618 393-2124
1712 S Whittle Ave Olney (62450) ***(G-15857)***
Concord Printing Inc 847 734-1616
1550 E Higgins Rd Ste 113 Elk Grove Village (60007) ***(G-8908)***
Concord Steel, Harvey *Also called Lb Metals LLC* ***(G-11091)***
Concord Well Service Inc 618 395-4405
1102 N East St Olney (62450) ***(G-15858)***
Concorde Laboratories Inc 630 717-5300
4504 Concorde Pl Lisle (60532) ***(G-12878)***
Concorde Mfg & Fabrication Inc 815 344-3788
1620 S Schroeder Ln McHenry (60050) ***(G-13729)***
Concorde Prtg Dgtal Imging Inc 312 552-3006
180 N Michigan Ave # 1700 Chicago (60601) ***(G-4216)***
Concrete 1 Inc 630 357-1329
429 E 8th Ave Naperville (60563) ***(G-14805)***
Concrete Products 815 339-6395
304 E Harper Ave Granville (61326) ***(G-10754)***
Concrete Products Ziano, Granville *Also called Concrete Products* ***(G-10754)***
Concrete Specialities Co Inc 847 608-1200
1375 Gifford Rd Elgin (60120) ***(G-8549)***
Concrete Specialties Co (PA) 847 608-1200
1375 Gifford Rd Elgin (60120) ***(G-8550)***
Concrete Supply LLC 618 646-5300
1 Racehorse Dr East Saint Louis (62205) ***(G-8302)***
Concrete Supply of Illinois, East Saint Louis *Also called Concrete Supply LLC* ***(G-8302)***
Concrete Supply Tolono Inc 217 485-3100
1466 County Road 1100 N Urbana (61802) ***(G-19979)***
Condata Global Inc (PA) 708 390-2500
9830 W 190th St Ste M Mokena (60448) ***(G-14076)***
Condominiums Northbrook Cort 1 ....847 498-1640
830 Audubon Way Apt 217 Lincolnshire (60069) ***(G-12754)***
Condominiums Northbrook Court, Lincolnshire *Also called Condominiums Northbrook Cort 1* ***(G-12754)***
Condor Granites Intl Inc 847 635-7214
1605 Dundee Ave Ste H Elgin (60120) ***(G-8551)***
Condor Labels Inc 708 429-0707
8506 W 119th Pl Palos Park (60464) ***(G-16209)***
Condor Machine Tool 773 767-5985
5315 W 63rd St Chicago (60638) ***(G-4217)***
Condor Tool & Manufacturing 630 628-8200
321 W Gerri Ln Addison (60101) ***(G-81)***
Condy Holdings LLC (PA) 815 223-1500
315 5th St Peru (61354) ***(G-16573)***
Conex Cable LLC 800 877-8089
1007 E Locust St Dekalb (60115) ***(G-7669)***
Confab Systems Inc 708 388-4103
14831 S Mckinley Ave Posen (60469) ***(G-16792)***
Conferences I/O, Chicago *Also called Goeducation LLC* ***(G-4709)***
Configure One Inc (PA) 630 368-9950
900 Jorie Blvd Ste 190 Oak Brook (60523) ***(G-15612)***

ALPHABETIC

(PA)=Parent Co (HQ)=Headquarters (DH)=Div Headquarters

Conform Industries Inc........630 285-0272
561 Estes Ave Schaumburg (60193) ***(G-18484)***
Congress Drive Inc........972 875-6060
1189 Wilmette Ave Wilmette (60091) ***(G-21074)***
Conley Steel Inc........630 393-1193
3s710 Mignin Dr Warrenville (60555) ***(G-20233)***
Conmat Inc........815 238-3885
1246 S River Rd Galena (61036) ***(G-10167)***
Conmat Inc (HQ)........815 235-2200
2283 Us Highway 20 E Freeport (61032) ***(G-10104)***
Connecteriors LLC........773 549-3333
3100 N Clybourn Ave Chicago (60618) ***(G-4218)***
Connections........217 553-7920
511 E Ash St Springfield (62703) ***(G-19353)***
Connections Company, Carol Stream *Also called Dalco Marketing Services* ***(G-2971)***
Connector Concepts Inc........847 541-4020
1530 Mccormick Blvd Mundelein (60060) ***(G-14680)***
Connell Mc Machine & Welding........815 868-2275
8934 N Korth Rd Mc Connell (61050) ***(G-13688)***
Connelly & Associates........847 372-5001
892 E Glencoe St Palatine (60074) ***(G-16103)***
Connelly-Gpm Inc........773 247-7231
3154 S California Ave Chicago (60608) ***(G-4219)***
Connies Home Health Care........708 790-4000
453 Saugatuck St Park Forest (60466) ***(G-16253)***
Connor Electric Services Inc........630 823-8230
649 Estes Ave Schaumburg (60193) ***(G-18485)***
Connor Sports Flooring LLC (HQ)........847 290-9020
595 Supreme Dr Bensenville (60106) ***(G-1775)***
Connor Voice and Data Tech, Schaumburg *Also called Connor Electric Services Inc* ***(G-18485)***
Connor-Winfield Corp........630 499-2121
2111 Comprehensive Dr Aurora (60505) ***(G-1078)***
Connor-Winfield Corp (PA)........630 851-4722
2111 Comprehensive Dr Aurora (60505) ***(G-1079)***
Conopco Inc........773 916-4400
2816 S Kilbourn Ave Chicago (60623) ***(G-4220)***
Conor Sports LLC........847 903-6639
444 N Michigan Ave # 3600 Chicago (60611) ***(G-4221)***
Conquest Sound Inc........708 534-0309
209 Cypress Dr Manteno (60950) ***(G-13445)***
Conquest Sound Company, Manteno *Also called Conquest Sound Inc* ***(G-13445)***
Conscisys Corp........630 810-4444
1125 Mistwood Pl Downers Grove (60515) ***(G-7979)***
Conservation Tech III LLC........847 559-5500
725 Landwehr Rd Northbrook (60062) ***(G-15365)***
Conservation Technology Ltd........847 559-5500
725 Landwehr Rd Northbrook (60062) ***(G-15366)***
Consolidated Carqueville Prtg........630 246-6451
1536 Bourbon Pkwy Streamwood (60107) ***(G-19566)***
Consolidated Chem Works Ltd........312 226-6150
400 N Ashland Ave Ste 2 Chicago (60622) ***(G-4222)***
Consolidated Displays Co Inc........630 851-8666
1210 Us Highway 34 Oswego (60543) ***(G-15998)***
Consolidated Elec Wire & Cable........847 455-8830
11044 King St Franklin Park (60131) ***(G-9913)***
Consolidated Foam Inc........847 850-5011
1670 Barclay Blvd Buffalo Grove (60089) ***(G-2528)***
Consolidated Materials Inc (PA)........815 568-1538
8920 S Rt 23 Marengo (60152) ***(G-13482)***
Consolidated Materials Inc........847 658-4342
1320 S Virginia Rd Crystal Lake (60014) ***(G-7185)***
Consolidated Mill Supply Inc (PA)........847 706-6715
1530 E Dundee Rd Ste 200 Palatine (60074) ***(G-16104)***
Consolidated Paving Inc........309 693-3505
6918 N Galena Rd Peoria (61614) ***(G-16427)***
Consolidated Printing Co Inc........773 631-2800
1715 Elmhurst Rd Elk Grove Village (60007) ***(G-8909)***
Constrction Sltons Chicago Inc........630 834-1929
222 W Stone Rd Villa Park (60181) ***(G-20140)***
Construction Bus Media LLC........847 359-6493
579 N 1st Bank Dr Ste 220 Palatine (60067) ***(G-16105)***
Construction Contg Svcs Inc........219 779-0900
1965 Bernice Rd Ste 1nw Lansing (60438) ***(G-12489)***
Consulate General Lithuania........312 397-0382
455 N Ctyfrnt Plz Dr # 800 Chicago (60611) ***(G-4223)***
Consumer Guide, Morton Grove *Also called Publications International Ltd* ***(G-14434)***
Consumer Vinegar and Spice........708 354-1144
745 S Ashland Ave La Grange (60525) ***(G-12076)***
Consumerbase LLC........312 600-8000
33 N Dearborn St Ste 200 Chicago (60602) ***(G-4224)***
Consumers Packing Co Inc........708 344-0047
1301 Carson Dr Melrose Park (60160) ***(G-13844)***
Container Graphics Corp........847 584-0299
492 Lunt Ave Schaumburg (60193) ***(G-18486)***
Container Hdlg Systems Corp........708 482-9900
621 E Plainfield Rd Countryside (60525) ***(G-7047)***
Container Service Group Inc........815 744-8693
2132 Gould Ct Unit A Rockdale (60436) ***(G-17258)***
Container Specialties Inc........708 615-1400
10800 Belmont Ave Ste 200 Franklin Park (60131) ***(G-9914)***
Containers Inc........708 442-2000
4424 Prescott Ave Lyons (60534) ***(G-13306)***
Contech Engnered Solutions LLC........217 529-5461
1110 Stevenson Dr Springfield (62703) ***(G-19354)***
Contech Engnered Solutions LLC........630 573-1110
1200 Harger Rd Ste 707 Oak Brook (60523) ***(G-15613)***
Contech Lighting, Northbrook *Also called Conservation Tech III LLC* ***(G-15365)***
Contego Defense Group........630 532-1063
7546 Janes Ave Woodridge (60517) ***(G-21287)***
Contempo Autographic & Signs........708 371-5499
13866 Cicero Ave Crestwood (60418) ***(G-7113)***
Contempo Industries Inc........815 337-6267
455 Borden St Woodstock (60098) ***(G-21375)***
Contempo Marble & Granite Inc........312 455-0022
411 N Paulina St Chicago (60622) ***(G-4225)***
Contemporary Ctrl Systems Inc (PA)........630 963-7070
2431 Curtiss St Downers Grove (60515) ***(G-7980)***
Contemporary Marble Inc........618 281-6200
8533 Hanover Indus Dr Columbia (62236) ***(G-6989)***
Contemprary Enrgy Slutions LLC........630 768-3743
2951 Beth Ln Naperville (60564) ***(G-14963)***
Content That Works, Chicago *Also called F M Aquisition Corp* ***(G-4551)***
Context Software Systems........630 654-0291
601 Oakmont Ln Fl 2 Westmont (60559) ***(G-20733)***
Contigo, Chicago *Also called Ignite Usa LLC* ***(G-4880)***
Continent Corp........773 733-1584
227 Tiger St Bolingbrook (60490) ***(G-2158)***
Continental Assembly Inc........773 472-8004
4317 N Ravenswood Ave Chicago (60613) ***(G-4226)***
Continental Auto Systems Inc........847 862-5000
21440 W Lake Cook Rd Deer Park (60010) ***(G-7579)***
Continental Auto Systems Inc........847 862-6300
21440 W Lake Cook Rd Deer Park (60010) ***(G-7580)***
Continental Bindery Corp........847 439-6811
1250 Pratt Blvd Elk Grove Village (60007) ***(G-8910)***
Continental Carbonic Pdts Inc........309 346-7515
140 Distillery Rd Pekin (61554) ***(G-16326)***
Continental Carbonic Pdts Inc (HQ)........217 428-2068
3985 E Harrison Ave Decatur (62526) ***(G-7476)***
Continental Concepts, Cicero *Also called Royal Box Group LLC* ***(G-6872)***
Continental Cutoff Machine, Addison *Also called Kiene Diesel Accessories Inc* ***(G-169)***
Continental Datalabel Inc (PA)........847 742-1600
1855 Fox Ln Elgin (60123) ***(G-8552)***
Continental Marketing Inc........773 467-8300
5696 N Milwaukee Ave Chicago (60646) ***(G-4227)***
Continental Materials Corp (HQ)........312 541-7200
440 S La Salle St # 3100 Chicago (60605) ***(G-4228)***
Continental Midland........708 441-1000
1340 W 127th St Calumet Park (60827) ***(G-2797)***
Continental Mills Inc........800 426-0955
600 W Chicago Ave Ste 670 Chicago (60654) ***(G-4229)***
Continental Mills Inc........217 540-4000
1200 Stevens Ave Effingham (62401) ***(G-8392)***
Continental Resources Ill Inc (PA)........618 242-1717
830 Il Highway 15 E Mount Vernon (62864) ***(G-14603)***
Continental Sales Inc........847 381-6530
213 W Main St Barrington (60010) ***(G-1218)***
Continental Screws Mch Pdts........847 459-7766
160 Abbott Dr Wheeling (60090) ***(G-20875)***
Continental Studios Inc........773 542-0309
1300 S Kostner Ave Chicago (60623) ***(G-4230)***
Continental Supply Co........708 448-2728
21 Carriage Trl Palos Heights (60463) ***(G-16182)***
Continental Tire Americas LLC........618 242-7100
11525 N Il Highway 142 Mount Vernon (62864) ***(G-14604)***
Continental Tire Americas LLC........618 246-2585
10075 Progress Pkwy Mascoutah (62258) ***(G-13596)***
Continental Tire Mt. Vernon, Mount Vernon *Also called Continental Tire Americas LLC* ***(G-14604)***
Continental Web Press Inc (PA)........630 773-1903
1430 Industrial Dr Itasca (60143) ***(G-11639)***
Continental Web Press KY Inc (PA)........630 773-1903
1430 Industrial Dr Itasca (60143) ***(G-11640)***
Continental Window and GL Corp........773 794-1600
4311 W Belmont Ave Chicago (60641) ***(G-4231)***
Continental Window South Inc........773 767-1300
4600 S Kolmar Ave Chicago (60632) ***(G-4232)***
Continental/Midland, LLC, Park Forest *Also called Agrati - Park Forest LLC* ***(G-16251)***
Continuous Cast Alloys LLC........815 562-8200
100 Quarry Rd Rochelle (61068) ***(G-17136)***
Contmid Inc........708 747-1200
24000 S Western Ave Park Forest (60466) ***(G-16254)***
Contour Machining Inc........847 364-0111
640 Fargo Ave Elk Grove Village (60007) ***(G-8911)***
Contour Saws Inc (PA)........800 259-6834
900 Graceland Ave Des Plaines (60016) ***(G-7749)***

Contour Saws Inc 800 259-6834
1217 E Thacker St Des Plaines (60016) *(G-7750)*
Contour Screw Products Inc 847 357-1190
3014 Malmo Dr Arlington Heights (60005) *(G-719)*
Contour Tool Works Inc 847 947-4700
1712 N Lee Ct Palatine (60074) *(G-16106)*
Contract Industries Inc 708 458-8150
6641 S Narragansett Ave Bedford Park (60638) *(G-1464)*
Contract Transportation Sys Co 217 342-5757
711 W Wabash Ave Effingham (62401) *(G-8393)*
Contractor Advisors, Chicago *Also called Be Group Inc (G-3848)*
Contractor Concrete, Marshall *Also called Contractors Concrete (G-13568)*
Contractors Concrete 217 826-2290
16996 N Quality Lime Rd Marshall (62441) *(G-13568)*
Contractors Concrete Inc 217 342-2299
2604 N Haarmann St Effingham (62401) *(G-8394)*
Contractors Ready-Mix Inc 217 482-5530
210 E Elm St Mason City (62664) *(G-13610)*
Contractors Ready-Mix Inc (PA) 217 735-2565
601 S Kickapoo St Lincoln (62656) *(G-12728)*
Contractors Register Inc 630 519-3480
555 Waters Edge Ste 150 Lombard (60148) *(G-13058)*
Control Designs Inc 847 672-9514
4006 Grove Ave Gurnee (60031) *(G-10865)*
Control Equipment Company Inc 847 891-7500
1115 Morse Ave Schaumburg (60193) *(G-18487)*
Control Panels Inc 815 654-6000
1350 Harder Ct Rockford (61103) *(G-17357)*
Control Research Inc 847 352-4920
908 Albion Ave Schaumburg (60193) *(G-18488)*
Control Solutions LLC 630 806-7062
2520 Diehl Rd Aurora (60502) *(G-941)*
Control System Innovators Inc 847 741-0007
1760 Britannia Dr Ste 1 Elgin (60124) *(G-8553)*
Control Systems Inc 847 438-6228
8603 Crestview Dr Long Grove (60047) *(G-13159)*
Control Works Inc 630 444-1942
2701 Dukane Dr Ste B Saint Charles (60174) *(G-18174)*
Controlled Thermal Processing (PA) 847 651-5511
1521 Bourbon Pkwy Streamwood (60107) *(G-19567)*
Controllink Incorporated 847 622-1100
1650 Cambridge Dr Elgin (60123) *(G-8554)*
Controls Group USA Inc 847 551-5775
2521 Tech Dr Ste 203 Elgin (60124) *(G-8555)*
Controlweigh, Round Lake Beach *Also called Howard Schwartz (G-18089)*
Convergence Fuel Systems LLC 970 498-3430
1 Woodward Loves Park (61111) *(G-13195)*
Convergent Bill Ete Ort T 847 387-4059
2000 W Att Center Dr Rm 4 Hoffman Estates (60192) *(G-11416)*
Converting Systems Inc 847 519-0232
1045 Remington Rd Schaumburg (60173) *(G-18489)*
Converting Technology Inc 847 290-0590
1557 Carmen Dr Elk Grove Village (60007) *(G-8912)*
Conveyor Specialties Inc 815 727-7638
841 Brian Dr Ste A Joliet (60403) *(G-11847)*
Conveyor Systems & Engineering 847 593-2900
855 E Golf Rd Arlington Heights (60005) *(G-720)*
Conveyors Plus Inc 708 361-1512
13301 Southwest Hwy Ste J Orland Park (60462) *(G-15948)*
Convr Enterprises Inc 888 507-9733
425 N Martingale Rd # 700 Schaumburg (60173) *(G-18490)*
Conwed Plas Acquisition V LLC 630 293-3737
390 Wegner Dr Ste B West Chicago (60185) *(G-20567)*
Conxall Corporation 630 834-7504
601 E Wildwood Ave Villa Park (60181) *(G-20141)*
Cook Chocolate Company, Chicago *Also called Worlds Finest Chocolate Inc (G-6677)*
Cook Communications Minis 847 741-5168
850 N Grove Ave Elgin (60120) *(G-8556)*
Cook Communications Ministries 847 741-0800
850 N Grove Ave Elgin (60120) *(G-8557)*
Cook Fabrication Signs Graphic 309 360-3805
325 N Deer Crk Deer Creek (61733) *(G-7573)*
Cook JV Printing 708 799-0007
4061 183rd St Country Club Hills (60478) *(G-7037)*
Cook Polymer Technology 309 740-2342
225 S 3rd Ave Canton (61520) *(G-2825)*
Cook Portable Warehouses, Cobden *Also called Cook Sales Inc (G-6941)*
Cook Sales Inc (PA) 618 893-2114
3455 Old Highway 51 N Cobden (62920) *(G-6941)*
Cook, David C, Elgin *Also called Cook Communications Ministries (G-8557)*
Cookie Kingdom Inc 815 883-3331
1201 E Walnut St Oglesby (61348) *(G-15840)*
Cool Fluidics Inc 815 861-4063
123 S Eastwood Dr Ste 145 Woodstock (60098) *(G-21376)*
Cooler Concepts Inc 815 462-3866
21753 S Center Ave New Lenox (60451) *(G-15029)*
Cooley Wire Products Mfg Co 847 678-8585
5025 River Rd Schiller Park (60176) *(G-18796)*
Coon Run Drainage & Levee Dst 217 248-5511
826 Arenzville Rd Arenzville (62611) *(G-670)*
Cooper B-Line Inc (HQ) 618 654-2184
509 W Monroe St Highland (62249) *(G-11210)*
Cooper B-Line Inc 618 357-5353
3764 Longspur Rd Pinckneyville (62274) *(G-16612)*
Cooper Equipment Company Inc 708 367-1291
763 W Old Monee Rd Crete (60417) *(G-7137)*
Cooper Lake Millworks Inc 217 847-2681
1202 N State Highway 96 Hamilton (62341) *(G-10951)*
Cooper Lighting LLC 312 595-2770
2550 United Ln Elk Grove Village (60007) *(G-8913)*
Cooper Lighting LLC 847 956-8400
400 Busse Rd Elk Grove Village (60007) *(G-8914)*
Cooper Oil Co 708 349-2893
9500 W 159th St Orland Park (60467) *(G-15949)*
Coopers Hawk Intrmdate Hldg LL (PA) 708 839-2920
3500 Lacey Rd Ste 1000 Downers Grove (60515) *(G-7981)*
Coopers Hawk Intrmdate Hldg LL 708 215-5674
430 E Plainfield Rd Countryside (60525) *(G-7048)*
Coopers Hawk Production LLC 708 839-2920
430 E Plainfield Rd Countryside (60525) *(G-7049)*
Coopers Hawk Winery 630 940-1000
3710 E M St Saint Charles (60174) *(G-18175)*
Coopers Hawk Winery & Rest, Downers Grove *Also called Coopers Hawk Intrmdate Hldg LL (G-7981)*
Coopers Hwk Intermedte Holdng 708 215-5674
9016 Murphy Rd Ste 200 Woodridge (60517) *(G-21288)*
Coordinate Machine Company 630 894-9880
59 Congress Cir W Roselle (60172) *(G-17947)*
Coordinated Kitchen Dev Inc 847 847-7692
1525 Coral Reef Way Lake Zurich (60047) *(G-12396)*
Coordinated Packaging, Bensenville *Also called Co-Ordinated Packaging Inc (G-1772)*
Coorens Communications Inc 773 235-8688
2134 W Pierce Ave Chicago (60622) *(G-4233)*
Copar Corporation 708 496-1859
5744 W 77th St Burbank (60459) *(G-2635)*
Copar International, Burbank *Also called Copar Corporation (G-2635)*
Cope & Sons Asphalt 618 462-2207
3510 Thomas Ave Alton (62002) *(G-548)*
Cope Plastics Inc (PA) 618 466-0221
4441 Indl Dr Alton (62002) *(G-549)*
Cope Plastics Inc 309 787-4465
630 High Point Ln East Peoria (61611) *(G-8263)*
Copies Overnight Inc (PA) 630 690-2000
262 Commonwealth Dr Carol Stream (60188) *(G-2966)*
Copper Dock 618 669-2675
498 White Oak Ln Pocahontas (62275) *(G-16751)*
Copper Fiddle Distilery 847 847-7613
532 W Il Route 22 Lake Zurich (60047) *(G-12397)*
Coppolinos Itln BF Grill & Bar, Chicago *Also called Joseph Coppolino (G-5054)*
Copresco, Carol Stream *Also called Copies Overnight Inc (G-2966)*
Copy Express Inc 815 338-7161
301 E Calhoun St Ste 2 Woodstock (60098) *(G-21377)*
Copy Mat Printing 309 452-1392
1103 Martin Luther King D Bloomington (61701) *(G-2033)*
Copy Service Inc 815 758-1151
1005 W Lincoln Hwy Dekalb (60115) *(G-7670)*
COPY WORKS, Oak Forest *Also called In-Print Graphics Inc (G-15683)*
Copy Workshop, The, Chicago *Also called Bendinger Bruce Crtve Comm In (G-3866)*
Copy-Mor Inc 312 666-4000
1536 Bourbon Pkwy Streamwood (60107) *(G-19568)*
Copyco Printing Inc 847 824-4400
9500 Bryn Mawr Ave # 130 Rosemont (60018) *(G-18008)*
Copyset Shop Inc 847 768-2679
1801 E Oakton St Des Plaines (60018) *(G-7751)*
Cora Lee Candies Inc 847 724-2754
1844 Waukegan Rd Glenview (60025) *(G-10538)*
Coral Chemical Company 847 246-6666
1915 Industrial Ave Zion (60099) *(G-21510)*
Coral Lake, Marengo *Also called Consolidated Materials Inc (G-13482)*
Coras Trailer Manufacturing, Streator *Also called Coras Welding Shop Inc (G-19606)*
Coras Welding Shop Inc 815 672-7950
1901 N Shabbona St Streator (61364) *(G-19606)*
Corbett Accel Healthcare Grp C 312 475-2505
225 N Michigan Ave Chicago (60601) *(G-4234)*
Corcom, Mundelein *Also called Te Connectivity Corporation (G-14742)*
Cord Sets Inc 847 427-1185
1822 Elmhurst Rd Elk Grove Village (60007) *(G-8915)*
Core Finishing Inc 630 521-9635
717 Thomas Dr Bensenville (60106) *(G-1776)*
Core Integrated Marketing, Chicago Heights *Also called Poll Enterprises Inc (G-6764)*
Core Pipe, Carol Stream *Also called Gerlin Inc (G-2991)*
Core Pipe Products Inc 630 690-7000
170 Tubeway Dr Carol Stream (60188) *(G-2967)*
Corefx Ingredients LLC 773 271-2663
12495 N Pleasant Hill Rd Orangeville (61060) *(G-15908)*
Coregistics, Wheeling *Also called Iam Acquisition LLC (G-20912)*
Corelle Brands Holdings Inc (PA) 847 233-8600
9525 Bryn Mawr Ave Ste 30 Rosemont (60018) *(G-18009)*

ALPHABETIC

Corelle Brands LLC (HQ) 847 233-8600
9525 Bryn Mawr Ave Rosemont (60018) ***(G-18010)***

Cores For You Inc 217 847-3233
160 Industrial Park Hamilton (62341) ***(G-10952)***

Coretechs Corp 847 295-3720
245 Butler Dr Lake Forest (60045) ***(G-12240)***

Corey Steel Company 708 735-8000
2800 S 61st Ct Cicero (60804) ***(G-6837)***

Coriant North America LLC 630 798-8800
1415 W Diehl Rd Naperville (60563) ***(G-14806)***

Coriant Operations Inc (PA) 630 798-8800
1415 W Diehl Rd Naperville (60563) ***(G-14807)***

Corken Inc (HQ) 405 946-5576
105 Albrecht Dr Lake Bluff (60044) ***(G-12177)***

Corn Products International, Chicago *Also called Ingredion Incorporated* ***(G-4923)***

Cornelius Inc (HQ) 630 539-6850
101 Regency Dr Glendale Heights (60139) ***(G-10445)***

Cornelius Renew Inc 309 734-9505
1301 N Main St Ste 3 Monmouth (61462) ***(G-14215)***

Cornell Forge Company 708 458-1582
6666 W 66th St Chicago (60638) ***(G-4235)***

Corner Bakery Cafe, Chicago *Also called Cbc Restaurant Corp* ***(G-4046)***

Corner Stone, Chicago *Also called Cornerstone Communications* ***(G-4236)***

Cornerstone Building Products 217 543-2829
226 E Cr 600 N Arthur (61911) ***(G-848)***

Cornerstone Communications 773 989-2087
920 W Wilson Ave Chicago (60640) ***(G-4236)***

Cornerstone Community Outreach 773 506-4904
4615 N Clifton Ave Chicago (60640) ***(G-4237)***

Cornerstone Fdsrvice Group Inc (PA) 630 527-8600
127 Ambassador Dr Ste 147 Naperville (60540) ***(G-14808)***

Cornerstone Polishing Company 618 777-2754
85 Zach Ln Ozark (62972) ***(G-16087)***

Cornfields LLC 847 263-7000
3830 Sunset Ave Waukegan (60087) ***(G-20430)***

Cornucopia Supply Corp 847 532-9365
8305 Gross Point Rd Morton Grove (60053) ***(G-14397)***

Coronado Conservation Inc 301 512-4671
5807 S Woodlawn Ave Chicago (60637) ***(G-4238)***

Corplex Usa LLC 630 755-3132
208 Suth Pnnacle Dr Ste D Romeoville (60446) ***(G-17811)***

Corporate Business Card Ltd 847 455-5760
9611 Franklin Ave Franklin Park (60131) ***(G-9915)***

Corporate Disk Company (PA) 800 634-3475
4610 Prime Pkwy McHenry (60050) ***(G-13730)***

Corporate Graphics Inc 630 762-9000
3710 Illinois Ave Saint Charles (60174) ***(G-18176)***

Corporate Graphics America Inc 773 481-2100
5312 N Elston Ave Chicago (60630) ***(G-4239)***

Corporate Identification Solut 773 763-9600
5563 N Elston Ave Chicago (60630) ***(G-4240)***

Corporate Print Source Inc 847 724-1150
1969 Johns Dr Glenview (60025) ***(G-10539)***

Corporate Sign Systems Inc 847 882-6100
900 Central Ave Roselle (60172) ***(G-17948)***

Corporate Textiles Inc 847 433-4111
6529 N Lincoln Ave 5 Lincolnwood (60712) ***(G-12815)***

Corporation Supply Co Inc (PA) 312 726-3375
205 W Randolph St Ste 610 Chicago (60606) ***(G-4241)***

Corpro Screen Tech Inc 815 633-1201
5129 Forest Hills Ct Loves Park (61111) ***(G-13196)***

Corps Levl Ventures Inc 312 846-1441
2028 S Michigan Ave # 101 Chicago (60616) ***(G-4242)***

Corr-Pak Corporation 708 442-7806
8000 Joliet Rd Ste 100 Mc Cook (60525) ***(G-13690)***

Correct Tool Inc 630 595-6055
869 Fairway Dr Bensenville (60106) ***(G-1777)***

Correctional Technologies Inc 630 455-0811
7530 Plaza Ct Willowbrook (60527) ***(G-21038)***

Corrective Asphalt Mtls LLC 618 254-3855
300 Daniel Boone Trl South Roxana (62087) ***(G-19252)***

Corrigan Corporation America 800 462-6478
104 Ambrogio Dr Gurnee (60031) ***(G-10866)***

Corrigan Manufacturing Co (PA) 815 399-9326
1818 Christina St Rockford (61104) ***(G-17358)***

Corro-Shield International Inc 847 298-7770
2575 United Ln Elk Grove Village (60007) ***(G-8916)***

Corrpak Inc 618 758-2755
1231 State Route 13 Coulterville (62237) ***(G-7030)***

Corrugated Converting Eqp 618 532-2138
306 S Chestnut St Centralia (62801) ***(G-3227)***

Corrugated Metals Inc 815 323-1310
6550 Revlon Dr Belvidere (61008) ***(G-1663)***

Corrugated Solutions LLC 847 220-8348
276 E Deerpath 421 Lake Forest (60045) ***(G-12241)***

Corrugated Supplies Co LLC (PA) 708 458-5525
5043 W 67th St Bedford Park (60638) ***(G-1465)***

Corsaw Hardwood Lumber Inc 309 293-2055
26015 N County Highway 2 Smithfield (61477) ***(G-19063)***

Corsetti Structural Steel Inc 815 726-0186
2515 New Lenox Rd Joliet (60433) ***(G-11848)***

Corsicana Bedding LLC 708 331-9000
970 S Lake St Aurora (60506) ***(G-1080)***

Cortech USA, Willowbrook *Also called Correctional Technologies Inc* ***(G-21038)***

Cortek Endoscopy Inc 847 526-2266
206 Jamie Ln Wauconda (60084) ***(G-20340)***

Cortelyou Excavating 309 772-2922
494 W Davis St Bushnell (61422) ***(G-2741)***

Cortina Companies Inc 847 455-2800
10706 Grand Ave Ste 1 Franklin Park (60131) ***(G-9916)***

Cortina Companies, The, Franklin Park *Also called Cortina Companies Inc* ***(G-9916)***

Cortina Safety Products, Franklin Park *Also called Cortina Tool & Molding Co* ***(G-9917)***

Cortina Tool & Molding Co 847 455-2800
10706 Grand Ave Ste 1 Franklin Park (60131) ***(G-9917)***

Cortube Products Co 708 429-6700
18500 Spring Creek Dr Tinley Park (60477) ***(G-19816)***

Corus America Inc 847 585-2599
475 N Martingale Rd # 400 Schaumburg (60173) ***(G-18491)***

Corwin Printing 618 263-3936
1004 Landes St Mount Carmel (62863) ***(G-14469)***

Corydon Converting Company Inc 630 898-9896
1350 Shore Rd Ste 120 Naperville (60563) ***(G-14809)***

Corydon Converting Company Inc (PA) 630 983-1900
932 E Benton St Aurora (60505) ***(G-1081)***

Cosas Inc 312 492-6100
2170 S Canalport Ave Chicago (60608) ***(G-4243)***

Cositas Cupcakes & More 773 992-7088
4138 W 57th St Chicago (60629) ***(G-4244)***

Cosmedent Inc 312 644-9388
401 N Michigan Ave # 2500 Chicago (60611) ***(G-4245)***

Cosmo Films Inc (HQ) 317 790-9547
775 W Belden Ave Ste D Addison (60101) ***(G-82)***

Cosmopolitan Foot Care 312 984-5111
1 S Wacker Dr Fl 11 Chicago (60606) ***(G-4246)***

Cosmopolitan Machine Rebuilder 630 595-8141
346 Evergreen Ave Bensenville (60106) ***(G-1778)***

Cosmos Manufacturing Inc 708 756-1400
111 E 34th St S Chicago Hts (60411) ***(G-18119)***

Cosmos Plastics Company 847 451-1307
3630 Wolf Rd Franklin Park (60131) ***(G-9918)***

Cottage Door Press LLC 224 228-6000
5005 Newport Dr Ste 300 Rolling Meadows (60008) ***(G-17724)***

Cotton Goods Manufacturing Co 773 265-0088
259 N California Ave Chicago (60612) ***(G-4247)***

Coudal Partners Inc 312 243-1107
401 N Racine Ave Chicago (60642) ***(G-4248)***

Coulson Publications, Pittsfield *Also called Pike County Express* ***(G-16638)***

Counter 312 666-5335
666 W Diversey Pkwy Chicago (60614) ***(G-4249)***

Counter Cft Svc Systems & Pdts 630 629-7336
720 Concord Ln Lombard (60148) ***(G-13059)***

Counter Craft Inc 847 336-8205
2113 Northwestern Ave Waukegan (60087) ***(G-20431)***

Counter-Intelligence 708 974-3326
8150 W 107th St Palos Hills (60465) ***(G-16198)***

Countertop Creations 618 736-2700
6th St And Hwy 142 Dahlgren (62828) ***(G-7306)***

Counting House, Martinsville *Also called Pap-R Products Company* ***(G-13587)***

Country Donut, Schaumburg *Also called Joshi Brothers Inc* ***(G-18578)***

Country Donuts, Carpentersville *Also called Amling Donuts Inc* ***(G-3093)***

Country Home Magazine, Chicago *Also called Meredith Corp* ***(G-5395)***

Country Journal Publishing Co 217 877-9660
3065 Pershing Ct Decatur (62526) ***(G-7477)***

Country Side Woodworking, Arthur *Also called David L Kaufman* ***(G-851)***

Country Stone Inc (PA) 309 787-1744
6300 75th Ave Ste A Milan (61264) ***(G-14005)***

Country Village Meats 815 849-5532
401 N Pennsylvania St Sublette (61367) ***(G-19635)***

Country Workshop 217 543-4094
651 N Cr 125 E Arthur (61911) ***(G-849)***

County Asphalt Inc 618 224-9033
427 S Madison St Trenton (62293) ***(G-19902)***

County Journal, Percy *Also called Willis Publishing* ***(G-16561)***

County Line Tool, East Peoria *Also called Tag Tool Services Incorporated* ***(G-8292)***

County Market, Quincy *Also called Niemann Foods Inc* ***(G-16918)***

County Materials Corp 217 352-4181
702 N Edwin St Champaign (61821) ***(G-3283)***

County of Piatt 217 762-7009
101 W Washington St # 214 Monticello (61856) ***(G-14280)***

County Packaging Inc 708 597-1100
13600 Kildare Ave Crestwood (60418) ***(G-7114)***

County Tool & Die 217 324-6527
1400 W Hudson Dr Litchfield (62056) ***(G-12962)***

Couplings Company Inc 847 634-8990
570 Bond St Lincolnshire (60069) ***(G-12755)***

Coupon Magazine, Elgin *Also called Progressive Publications Inc* ***(G-8699)***

Cour Pharmaceuticals Dev 773 621-3241
2215 Sanders Rd Ste 428 Northbrook (60062) ***(G-15367)***
Courier Publishing Co, Washington *Also called Washington Courier* ***(G-20282)***
Coursons Coring & Drilling 618 349-8765
Nr Hwy 185 Saint Peter (62880) ***(G-18323)***
Courtesy Metal Polishing 630 832-1862
735 N Addison Rd Ste B Villa Park (60181) ***(G-20142)***
Coutland Components, Cortland *Also called Alexander Lumber Co* ***(G-7016)***
Covachem LLC 779 500-0918
5055 28th Ave Ste 3 Rockford (61109) ***(G-17359)***
Covachem LLC 815 714-8421
6260 E Riverside Blvd Loves Park (61111) ***(G-13197)***
Cover Connection, Wauconda *Also called C M F Enterprises Inc* ***(G-20337)***
Covey Machine Inc 773 650-1530
3604 S Morgan St Chicago (60609) ***(G-4250)***
Covia Holdings Corporation 618 747-2355
110 Railroad St Tamms (62988) ***(G-19742)***
Covia Holdings Corporation 815 732-2121
1446 W Devils Backbone Rd Oregon (61061) ***(G-15916)***
Covia Holdings Corporation 815 539-6734
S Peru St Troy Grove (61372) ***(G-19920)***
Covia Holdings Corporation 618 747-2338
32079 State Highway 127 Tamms (62988) ***(G-19743)***
Covia Holdings Corporation 203 966-8880
776 Centennial Dr Ottawa (61350) ***(G-16049)***
Covidien Holding Inc 618 664-2111
100 Louis Latzer Dr Greenville (62246) ***(G-10831)***
Covington Service Installation 309 376-4921
1907 County Road 275 N Carlock (61725) ***(G-2885)***
Cowtan and Tout Inc 312 644-0717
222 Merchds Mart Plz 638 Chicago (60654) ***(G-4251)***
Cox Electric Motor Service 217 344-2458
1409 Triumph Dr Urbana (61802) ***(G-19980)***
Cox Metal Processing, Chicago *Also called National Material LP* ***(G-5547)***
Coyote Transportation Inc 630 204-5729
600 Thomas Dr Bensenville (60106) ***(G-1779)***
Cozent LLC 630 781-2822
2135 City Gate Ln Ste 300 Naperville (60563) ***(G-14810)***
Cozzini LLC 773 478-9700
2567 Greenleaf Ave Elk Grove Village (60007) ***(G-8917)***
CP Diesel Inc 815 979-9600
289 N 1700 East Rd Cissna Park (60924) ***(G-6896)***
CP Screw Machine Products 630 766-2313
211 Beeline Dr Ste 3 Bensenville (60106) ***(G-1780)***
Cpg International LLC (HQ) 570 558-8000
1330 W Fulton St Ste 350 Chicago (60607) ***(G-4252)***
Cpg Newco LLC 877 275-2935
1330 W Fulton St Ste 350 Chicago (60607) ***(G-4253)***
Cpg Printing & Graphics 309 820-1392
1103 Martin Luther King D Bloomington (61701) ***(G-2034)***
CPI, Norridge *Also called Cast Products Inc* ***(G-15232)***
CPI, Rockford *Also called Chem Processing Inc* ***(G-17346)***
CPI Satcom Division- Lisle, Lisle *Also called Bolingbrook Communications Inc* ***(G-12874)***
Cpiprint, East Dundee *Also called Carson Printing Inc* ***(G-8189)***
CPM Co Inc 815 385-7700
1805 Dot St McHenry (60050) ***(G-13731)***
CPM Industries 630 469-8200
410 Windy Point Dr Glendale Heights (60139) ***(G-10446)***
Cpp, Edelstein *Also called Custom Power Products Inc* ***(G-8332)***
Cppc, Paris Plant, Paris *Also called Cadillac Products Packaging Co* ***(G-16225)***
Cpr Printing Inc (PA) 630 377-8420
321 Stevens St Ste E Geneva (60134) ***(G-10263)***
CPS, Vernon Hills *Also called Rust-Leum Con Prtction Systems* ***(G-20087)***
CPSI, Columbia *Also called Computer Pwr Solutions Ill Ltd* ***(G-6988)***
Cq Industries Inc 630 530-0177
477 W Fullerton Ave Elmhurst (60126) ***(G-9353)***
Cr Bard Inc 630 933-7653
295 E Lies Rd Carol Stream (60188) ***(G-2968)***
Cr Laurence, Chicago *Also called US Aluminium IL* ***(G-6498)***
Cr Welding Met Fabrication Inc (PA) 224 789-7825
4190 Grove Ave Gurnee (60031) ***(G-10867)***
Craft Beer Institute, Chicago *Also called Caduceus Communications Inc* ***(G-4001)***
Craft Die Casting Corporation 773 237-9710
1831 N Lorel Ave Chicago (60639) ***(G-4254)***
Craft Metal Spinning Co 773 685-4700
4351 N Normandy Ave Chicago (60634) ***(G-4255)***
Craft Pallet Inc 618 437-5382
1620 N Benton Ln INA (62846) ***(G-11575)***
Craft World Inc 800 654-6114
6836 Forest Hills Rd Loves Park (61111) ***(G-13198)***
Craftmaster Manufacturing Inc 800 405-2233
500 W Monroe St Ste 2010 Chicago (60661) ***(G-4256)***
Crafts Technology, Elk Grove Village *Also called Craftstech Inc* ***(G-8918)***
Craftsman Custom Metals LLC 847 655-0040
3838 River Rd Schiller Park (60176) ***(G-18797)***
Craftsman Pltg & Tinning Corp (PA) 773 477-1040
1250 W Melrose St Chicago (60657) ***(G-4257)***
Craftsman Tool & Mold Co 630 851-8700
2750 Church Rd Aurora (60502) ***(G-942)***
Craftsmen Printing 217 283-9574
217 Bank St Hoopeston (60942) ***(G-11506)***
Craftstech Inc 847 758-3100
91 Joey Dr Elk Grove Village (60007) ***(G-8918)***
Craftwood Inc 630 758-1740
889 N Larch Ave Ste 100 Elmhurst (60126) ***(G-9354)***
Craig Alan Salon, Naperville *Also called Second Chance Inc* ***(G-14986)***
Craig Industries Inc 217 228-2421
401 Delaware St Quincy (62301) ***(G-16873)***
Craiger Custom Design, Crystal Lake *Also called Craiger Inc* ***(G-7186)***
Craiger Inc 815 479-9660
2510 Rte 176 Unit D Crystal Lake (60014) ***(G-7186)***
Crain Communications Inc (PA) 312 649-5200
150 N Michigan Ave # 1800 Chicago (60601) ***(G-4258)***
Crain Communications Inc 312 649-5200
150 E Michigan Ave Chicago (60601) ***(G-4259)***
Crandall Stats and Sensors Inc 815 316-8600
9918 N Alpine Rd Machesney Park (61115) ***(G-13336)***
Crane Composites Inc (HQ) 815 467-8600
23525 W Eames St Channahon (60410) ***(G-3376)***
Crane Composites Inc 630 378-9580
594 Territorial Dr Ste D Bolingbrook (60440) ***(G-2159)***
Crane Composites Inc 815 467-1437
23525 W Eames St Channahon (60410) ***(G-3377)***
Crane Dorray Corporation 630 893-7553
320 S Lombard Rd Addison (60101) ***(G-83)***
Crane Equipment & Services Inc (HQ) 309 467-6262
801 W Center St Eureka (61530) ***(G-9479)***
Crane Nuclear Inc 630 226-4900
860 Remington Blvd Bolingbrook (60440) ***(G-2160)***
Crane Quality Equipment LLC 815 258-5375
188 E 3100 North Rd Clifton (60927) ***(G-6914)***
Crane Valve Services, Bolingbrook *Also called Crane Nuclear Inc* ***(G-2160)***
Crash Candles, Mount Prospect *Also called C Becky & Company Inc* ***(G-14516)***
Crate and Pallet Packg Co LLC 217 679-2681
401 Colbrook Dr Springfield (62702) ***(G-19355)***
Crawford Company, Rock Island *Also called Crawford Heating & Cooling Co* ***(G-17211)***
Crawford County Oil LLC 618 544-3493
7005 E 1050th Ave Robinson (62454) ***(G-17109)***
Crawford Heating & Cooling Co (PA) 309 788-4573
1306 Mill St Rock Island (61201) ***(G-17211)***
Crawford Heating & Cooling Co 309 794-1000
1306 Mill St Rock Island (61201) ***(G-17212)***
Crawford Sausage Co Inc 773 277-3095
2310 S Pulaski Rd Chicago (60623) ***(G-4260)***
Crazy Llama Brewing Co LLC 779 200-1878
5312 Williams Dr Roscoe (61073) ***(G-17901)***
Crazy Quilt Patch Factory, Elmhurst *Also called Cq Industries Inc* ***(G-9353)***
Crd Enterprises Inc 847 438-4299
549 Capital Dr Lake Zurich (60047) ***(G-12398)***
Crea and Crea 630 292-5625
1115 Struckman Blvd Bartlett (60103) ***(G-1273)***
Creamery Inc 708 479-5706
191000 Wolf Rd Mokena (60448) ***(G-14077)***
Creasey Printing Services Inc 217 787-1055
1905 Morning Sun Ln Springfield (62711) ***(G-19356)***
Createasoft Inc 630 851-9474
3909 75th St Ste 105 Aurora (60504) ***(G-943)***
Creative Cabinets Countertops 217 446-6406
3817 N Vermilion St Danville (61832) ***(G-7327)***
Creative Cakes LLC 708 614-9755
16649 Oak Park Ave Ste F Tinley Park (60477) ***(G-19817)***
Creative Clothing Created 4 U 847 543-0051
488 Wood Duck Ct Grayslake (60030) ***(G-10764)***
Creative Concepts Fabrication 630 940-0500
3725 Stern Ave Saint Charles (60174) ***(G-18177)***
Creative Contract Packg LLC 630 851-6226
3777 Exchange Ave Aurora (60504) ***(G-944)***
Creative Controls Systems Inc 815 629-2358
15929 Hauley Rd Rockton (61072) ***(G-17696)***
Creative Conveniences By K&E 847 975-8526
55 N Buesching Rd Apt 312 Lake Zurich (60047) ***(G-12399)***
Creative Covers Inc 708 233-6880
7508 W 90th St Bridgeview (60455) ***(G-2338)***
Creative Curricula Inc 815 363-9419
1621 Park St McHenry (60050) ***(G-13732)***
Creative Design, Somonauk *Also called Peddlers Den Inc* ***(G-19071)***
Creative Design Builders, Chicago *Also called Creative Designs Kitc* ***(G-4261)***
Creative Designs Kitc 773 327-8400
4355 N Ravenswood Ave Chicago (60613) ***(G-4261)***
Creative Directory Inc 773 427-7777
5219 W Belle Plaine Ave Chicago (60641) ***(G-4262)***
Creative Graphic Arts Inc 847 498-2678
3690 Oak Ave Northbrook (60062) ***(G-15368)***
Creative Hi-Tech Ltd 224 653-4000
710 Cooper Ct Schaumburg (60173) ***(G-18492)***

ALPHABETIC

Creative Ideas Inc 217 245-1378
  4 Sunnydale Ave Jacksonville (62650) *(G-11763)*
Creative Image Inc 708 647-2860
  3615 Briar Ln Hazel Crest (60429) *(G-11128)*
Creative Inds Terrazzo Pdts 773 235-9088
  1753 N Spaulding Ave Chicago (60647) *(G-4263)*
Creative Iron 217 267-7797
  108 Westville Ln Westville (61883) *(G-20779)*
Creative Kitchens & Baths, Bloomington Also called Thoennes & Thoennes Inc *(G-2101)*
Creative Label Inc (PA) 847 956-6960
  2450 Estes Ave Elk Grove Village (60007) *(G-8919)*
Creative Lithocraft Inc (PA) 847 352-7002
  1730 Wright Blvd Schaumburg (60193) *(G-18493)*
Creative Machining Tech LLC 309 755-7700
  1949 Saint Johns Ave # 200 Highland Park (60035) *(G-11260)*
Creative Menu's Plus, Burr Ridge Also called Rick Styfer *(G-2717)*
Creative Merchandising Systems 847 955-9990
  425 Village Grn Unit 307 Lincolnshire (60069) *(G-12756)*
Creative Metal Products 773 638-3200
  1101 S Kilbourn Ave Chicago (60624) *(G-4264)*
Creative Millwork LLC 630 762-0002
  3700 Illinois Ave Saint Charles (60174) *(G-18178)*
Creative Panel Systems Inc 630 625-5002
  1401 Glenlake Ave Itasca (60143) *(G-11641)*
Creative Perky Cuisine LLC 312 870-0282
  6601 Martin France Cir Tinley Park (60477) *(G-19818)*
Creative Pig Minds Designwear 815 968-7447
  105 Hall St Rockford (61107) *(G-17360)*
Creative Powder Coating Inc 815 260-3124
  920 Brian Dr Crest Hill (60403) *(G-7085)*
Creative Printing, Dixon Also called Tlm Enterprises Inc *(G-7923)*
Creative Prtg & Smart Ideas 773 481-6522
  3406 N Cicero Ave Chicago (60641) *(G-4265)*
Creative Rlcar Mktg Svcs II LL 773 396-1114
  1700 W Irving Park Rd # 3 Chicago (60613) *(G-4266)*
Creative Rlcar Mktg Svcs II LL 773 396-1114
  1700 W Irving Park Rd # 310 Chicago (60613) *(G-4267)*
Creative Science Activities 847 870-1746
  2 E Clarendon St Prospect Heights (60070) *(G-16837)*
Creative Werks LLC 630 860-2222
  1350 Munger Rd Bartlett (60103) *(G-1274)*
Creative Werks LLC (PA) 630 860-2222
  1460 Brummel Ave Elk Grove Village (60007) *(G-8920)*
Creative Wood Concepts Inc 773 384-9960
  1680 N Ada St Chicago (60642) *(G-4268)*
Credit & Management Systems 618 654-3500
  13648 Alpine Way Highland (62249) *(G-11211)*
Credit Card Systems Inc 847 459-8320
  180 Shepard Ave Wheeling (60090) *(G-20876)*
Creed Group LLC 708 261-8387
  66 Kenneth St Matteson (60443) *(G-13621)*
Creekside Exterior Solutions 618 326-7654
  99 E 1300 Ave Mulberry Grove (62262) *(G-14653)*
Creekside Printing, Elgin Also called Taykit Inc *(G-8745)*
Creekstone Kettle Works Ltd 217 246-5355
  509 S Obannon St Raymond (62560) *(G-16988)*
Crescend Technologies LLC (PA) 847 908-5400
  140 E State Pkwy Schaumburg (60173) *(G-18494)*
Crescent Cardboard Company, Wheeling Also called Potomac Corporation *(G-20962)*
Crescent Cardboard Company LLC 888 293-3956
  100 W Willow Rd Wheeling (60090) *(G-20877)*
Crescent Foods, Chicago Also called 2000plus Groups Inc *(G-3463)*
Crescent Ridge LLC 815 646-4119
  6250 1475 East St Tiskilwa (61368) *(G-19872)*
Crest Greetings Inc 708 210-0800
  444 W 31st St Chicago (60616) *(G-4269)*
Crest Metal Craft Inc 773 978-0950
  2900 E 95th St Chicago (60617) *(G-4270)*
Crestwood Associates LLC 847 394-8820
  1501 E Wdfeld Rd Ste 113e Schaumburg (60173) *(G-18495)*
Crestwood Custom Cabinets 708 385-3167
  13960 Kildare Ave Crestwood (60418) *(G-7115)*
Crestwood Industries Inc 847 680-9088
  1345 Wilhelm Rd Mundelein (60060) *(G-14681)*
Creswell Woodworking CA 847 381-9222
  911 Rail Dr Unit C Woodstock (60098) *(G-21378)*
Crete Twp 708 672-3111
  26730 S Stoney Island Ave Crete (60417) *(G-7138)*
Cricket Magazine Group, Chicago Also called Carus Publishing Company *(G-4033)*
Cricket Publishing, Chicago Also called Carus Publishing Company *(G-4034)*
Crippa Usa LLC 630 659-7720
  65 N River Ln Ste 209 Geneva (60134) *(G-10264)*
Crisp Container Corporation 618 998-0400
  700 Skyline Dr Marion (62959) *(G-13508)*
Criss Cross Express Illinois, Rantoul Also called Jancorp LLC *(G-16977)*
Cristaux Inc 312 778-8800
  1343 Brummel Ave Elk Grove Village (60007) *(G-8921)*
Cristaux International, Elk Grove Village Also called Cristaux Inc *(G-8921)*
Critical18, Naperville Also called National Def Intelligence Inc *(G-14980)*

Crj Cabinets 331 303-0326
  1925 W 51st St Chicago (60609) *(G-4271)*
Crl Industries Inc 847 940-3550
  500 Lake Cook Rd Ste 430 Deerfield (60015) *(G-7605)*
Crli Acceptance Corp 847 940-1500
  500 Lake Cook Rd Ste 400 Deerfield (60015) *(G-7606)*
Crm North America LLC 708 603-3475
  2308 17th St Franklin Park (60131) *(G-9919)*
Crms, Chicago Also called Creative Rlcar Mktg Svcs II LL *(G-4267)*
Crocs Inc 630 820-3572
  1650 Premium Outlet Blvd # 931 Aurora (60502) *(G-945)*
Cronus Chemicals LLC 312 863-8638
  150 N Michigan Ave # 2800 Chicago (60601) *(G-4272)*
Cronus Technologies Inc 847 839-0088
  424 E State Pkwy Schaumburg (60173) *(G-18496)*
Crooked Creek Outdoors 309 837-3000
  1025 W Grant St Macomb (61455) *(G-13390)*
Crooked Oak LLC 708 344-6955
  1920 Beach St Broadview (60155) *(G-2428)*
Crooked Trails Sawmill 618 244-1547
  18058 E Il Highway 142 Opdyke (62872) *(G-15904)*
Crosby Group LLC 708 333-3005
  16868 Lathrop Ave Harvey (60426) *(G-11081)*
Cross Container Corporation 847 844-3200
  400 Maple Ave Ste B Carpentersville (60110) *(G-3099)*
Cross Express Company 847 439-7457
  153 Crest Ave Elk Grove Village (60007) *(G-8922)*
Cross Oil & Well Service Inc 618 592-4609
  104 E Missouri St Oblong (62449) *(G-15825)*
Crosscom Inc 630 871-5500
  528 W Roosevelt Rd Lla Wheaton (60187) *(G-20794)*
Crossmark Printing Inc (PA) 708 532-8263
  18400 76th Ave Ste A Tinley Park (60477) *(G-19819)*
Crossmark Printing Inc 708 754-4000
  410 Ashland Ave Ste 300 Chicago Heights (60411) *(G-6745)*
Crossroad Crating & Pallet 815 657-8409
  27700 E 700 North Rd Forrest (61741) *(G-9732)*
Crosstech Communications Inc 312 382-0111
  111 N Jefferson St Chicago (60661) *(G-4273)*
Crosstree Inc 773 227-1234
  1906 N Milwaukee Ave Chicago (60647) *(G-4274)*
Crossway Bibles, Nfp, Wheaton Also called Good News Publishers *(G-20801)*
Crosswind Printing 847 356-1009
  588 Crosswind Ln Lindenhurst (60046) *(G-12853)*
Crosswords Club, The, Lisle Also called MTS Publishing Co *(G-12916)*
Crowdmatrix Fx LLC 312 329-1170
  333 W Hubbard St Apt 901 Chicago (60654) *(G-4275)*
Crowdsource Solutions Inc (PA) 855 276-9376
  33 Bronze Pointe Blvd Swansea (62226) *(G-19691)*
Crowley-Sheppard Asphalt Inc 708 499-2900
  6525 99th Pl Chicago Ridge (60415) *(G-6793)*
Crowleys Yacht Yard Lakeside 773 221-9990
  3434 E 95th St Chicago (60617) *(G-4276)*
Crown Battery Manufacturing Co 630 530-8060
  1199 N Ellsworth Ave Villa Park (60181) *(G-20143)*
Crown Brands LLC (PA) 224 513-2917
  300 Knightsbridge Pkwy Lincolnshire (60069) *(G-12757)*
Crown Coatings Company 630 365-9925
  215 W Nebraska St Elburn (60119) *(G-8448)*
Crown Concepts Corporation 815 941-1081
  7080 Lisbon Rd Morris (60450) *(G-14299)*
Crown Cork & Seal Usa Inc 708 239-5555
  5555 W 115th St Alsip (60803) *(G-435)*
Crown Cork & Seal Usa Inc 815 933-9351
  1035 E North St Bradley (60915) *(G-2278)*
Crown Cork & Seal Usa Inc 708 239-5000
  11535 S Central Ave Alsip (60803) *(G-436)*
Crown Cork & Seal Usa Inc 708 385-8670
  11535 S Central Ave Alsip (60803) *(G-437)*
Crown Cork & Seal Usa Inc 217 672-3533
  970 W North St Warrensburg (62573) *(G-20226)*
Crown Cork & Seal Usa Inc 217 872-6100
  255 W Pershing Rd Decatur (62526) *(G-7478)*
Crown Cork & Seal Usa Inc 630 851-7774
  3737 Exchange Ave Aurora (60504) *(G-946)*
Crown Corned Beef and Foods 312 738-0099
  351 N Justine St Chicago (60607) *(G-4277)*
Crown Coverings Inc 630 546-2959
  814 Central Ave Roselle (60172) *(G-17949)*
Crown Custom Cabinetry Inc 815 942-0432
  1110 E Washington St Morris (60450) *(G-14300)*
Crown Equipment Corporation 847 397-1900
  2055 Hammond Dr Schaumburg (60173) *(G-18497)*
Crown Equipment Corporation 815 773-0022
  4100 Olympic Blvd Joliet (60431) *(G-11849)*
Crown Equipment Corporation 309 663-9200
  1714 E Hamilton Rd Bloomington (61704) *(G-2035)*
Crown Gym Mats Inc 847 381-8282
  27929 W Industrial Ave Lake Barrington (60010) *(G-12145)*

Crown Industrial 607 745-8709
1020 Subic Rd Dixon (61021) *(G-7894)*
Crown Kandy Enterprise Ltd 708 580-6494
1127 S Mannheim Rd # 313 Westchester (60154) *(G-20696)*
Crown Kandy Publishing, Westchester *Also called Crown Kandy Enterprise Ltd (G-20696)*
Crown Lift Trucks, Schaumburg *Also called Crown Equipment Corporation (G-18497)*
Crown Lift Trucks, Joliet *Also called Crown Equipment Corporation (G-11849)*
Crown Lift Trucks, Bloomington *Also called Crown Equipment Corporation (G-2035)*
Crown Machine Inc 815 877-7700
2707 N Main St Rockford (61103) *(G-17361)*
Crown Metal Manufacturing Co 630 279-9800
765 S Il Route 83 Elmhurst (60126) *(G-9355)*
Crown Polymers LLC 847 683-0800
44w104 Us Highway 20 Hampshire (60140) *(G-10968)*
Crown Polymers Corporation 847 659-0300
11111 Kiley Dr Huntley (60142) *(G-11532)*
Crown Premiums Inc (PA) 815 469-8789
22774 Citation Rd Unit A Frankfort (60423) *(G-9781)*
Crown Publications Inc 217 893-4856
515 S Tanner St Rantoul (61866) *(G-16973)*
Crown Trophy 309 699-1766
235 E Washington St Ste C East Peoria (61611) *(G-8264)*
Crownline Boats, West Frankfort *Also called Leisure Properties LLC (G-20675)*
Cruise Boiler and Repr Co Inc 630 279-7111
824 N Addison Ave Elmhurst (60126) *(G-9356)*
Crusade Enterprises Inc 618 662-4461
200 E North Ave Flora (62839) *(G-9679)*
Crush Stone, Quincy *Also called Central Stone Company (G-16870)*
Crv Industries Inc 630 595-3777
777 Maple Ln Bensenville (60106) *(G-1781)*
Crv Lancaster Cams & Indexers, Bensenville *Also called Crv Industries Inc (G-1781)*
Crw Finishing Inc 630 495-4994
1470 W Jeffrey Dr Addison (60101) *(G-84)*
Cryogenic Systems Equipment 708 385-4216
2363 136th St Blue Island (60406) *(G-2116)*
Cryonize 773 935-8803
2716 N Ashland Ave Ste 1 Chicago (60614) *(G-4278)*
Crystal Cave 847 251-1160
1946 Lehigh Ave Ste E Glenview (60026) *(G-10540)*
Crystal Clear Cndle Design LLC 847 749-4782
1313 N Rand Rd Arlington Heights (60004) *(G-721)*
Crystal Die and Mold Inc 847 658-6535
5521 Meadowbrook Indus Ct Rolling Meadows (60008) *(G-17725)*
Crystal Edge, Itasca *Also called Slee Corporation (G-11733)*
Crystal L Smith 773 817-2797
636 Church St Ste 510 Evanston (60201) *(G-9507)*
Crystal Lake Beer Company 779 220-9288
150 N Main St Crystal Lake (60014) *(G-7187)*
Crystal Lake Brewing, Crystal Lake *Also called Crystal Lake Beer Company (G-7187)*
Crystal Lake Pallets 815 526-3637
650 W Terra Cotta Ave Crystal Lake (60014) *(G-7188)*
Crystal Nails McHenry 815 363-5498
2030 N Richmond Rd McHenry (60051) *(G-13733)*
Crystal Partners Inc 847 882-0467
838 Prince Charles Ct Schaumburg (60195) *(G-18498)*
Crystal Precision Drilling 815 633-5460
5122 Torque Rd Loves Park (61111) *(G-13199)*
Crystal Productions Co 847 657-8144
3701 Coml Ave Ste 10 Northbrook (60062) *(G-15369)*
Crystal Rain Distillery I 224 508-9361
28468 N Ballard Dr Lake Forest (60045) *(G-12242)*
Crystatech Inc 847 768-0500
1700 S Mount Prospect Rd Des Plaines (60018) *(G-7752)*
Cs Elements LLC 219 508-9270
2619 W Agatite Ave Apt 1b Chicago (60625) *(G-4279)*
Cs Legacy Corp 847 741-3101
1591 Fleetwood Dr Elgin (60123) *(G-8558)*
Cs Magazine Front Desk Chicago, Chicago *Also called Modern Luxury Media LLC (G-5479)*
CSC Learning, Burr Ridge *Also called Computer Svcs & Consulting Inc (G-2666)*
Csd, Dorsey *Also called Axon Telecom LLC (G-7943)*
Csi Chicago Inc 773 665-2226
2216 W Winnemac Ave Chicago (60625) *(G-4280)*
CSI Cutting Specialist Inc 731 352-5351
420 N Main St Edwardsville (62025) *(G-8353)*
Csi Manufacturing Inc 309 937-2653
Hwy 81 E Cambridge (61238) *(G-2804)*
Csi of Tolono, Urbana *Also called Concrete Supply Tolono Inc (G-19979)*
Csi2d Inc 312 282-7407
4907 Turnberry Dr Hoffman Estates (60010) *(G-11472)*
Csiteq LLC (PA) 312 265-1509
5600 N River Rd Rosemont (60018) *(G-18011)*
Csiteq Group, Rosemont *Also called Csiteq LLC (G-18011)*
Csiteq Studio LLC 312 265-1509
5600 N River Rd Rosemont (60018) *(G-18012)*
Csl Behring LLC 815 932-6773
1201 N Kinzie Ave Bradley (60915) *(G-2279)*
Csl Plasma Inc 708 343-8845
1977 N Mannheim Rd Melrose Park (60160) *(G-13845)*

CSM Tube Usa Inc 847 640-6447
1599 Lunt Ave Elk Grove Village (60007) *(G-8923)*
CSP Information Group Inc 630 574-5075
1100 Jorie Blvd Ste 260 Oak Brook (60523) *(G-15614)*
CSP Magazine, Oak Brook *Also called CSP Information Group Inc (G-15614)*
CST Sign & Manufacturing LLC 312 222-0020
4108 W Division St Chicago (60651) *(G-4281)*
CT Group Inc 708 466-8277
408 Lawrence Ave Glen Ellyn (60137) *(G-10399)*
Ctc Machine Service Inc 630 876-5120
756 W Hawthorne Ln West Chicago (60185) *(G-20568)*
Ctg Advanced Materials LLC 630 226-9080
479 Quadrangle Dr Ste E Bolingbrook (60440) *(G-2161)*
CTI, Libertyville *Also called Combined Technologies Inc (G-12645)*
CTI, Elk Grove Village *Also called Converting Technology Inc (G-8912)*
CTI Industries Corporation (PA) 847 382-1000
22160 N Pepper Rd Lake Barrington (60010) *(G-12146)*
CTI Industries Corporation 800 284-5605
800 Church St Lake Zurich (60047) *(G-12400)*
CTI/Usa Inc 847 258-1000
350 Randy Rd Ste 1 Carol Stream (60188) *(G-2969)*
CTS Advanced Materials LLC 630 577-8800
4925 Indiana Ave Lisle (60532) *(G-12879)*
CTS Automotive LLC (HQ) 630 577-8800
4925 Indiana Ave Lisle (60532) *(G-12880)*
CTS Automotive LLC 815 385-9480
5213 Prime Pkwy McHenry (60050) *(G-13734)*
CTS Corporation (PA) 630 577-8800
4925 Indiana Ave Lisle (60532) *(G-12881)*
CTS Electronic Components Inc (HQ) 630 577-8800
4925 Indiana Ave Lisle (60532) *(G-12882)*
CTS of Illinois Inc 630 892-2355
1556 Crescent Lake Dr Montgomery (60538) *(G-14242)*
CU Layer Inc 630 802-7873
214 Mill St Batavia (60510) *(G-1369)*
Cub Foods Inc 309 689-0140
5001 N Big Hollow Rd Peoria (61615) *(G-16428)*
Cub Foods 83, Springfield *Also called Niemann Foods Inc (G-19411)*
Cubby Hole of Carlinville Inc (PA) 217 854-8511
12472 Route 108 Carlinville (62626) *(G-2872)*
Cubby Hole, The, Carlinville *Also called Cubby Hole of Carlinville Inc (G-2872)*
Cube Tomato Inc 224 653-2655
636 Remington Rd Ste B Schaumburg (60173) *(G-18499)*
Cubic Group Inc 859 494-5834
445 E Algonquin Rd Ste 2 Arlington Heights (60005) *(G-722)*
Cubic Trnsp Systems Inc 312 257-3242
221 N La Salle St Ste 500 Chicago (60601) *(G-4282)*
Cucchi-BLT America Inc 224 829-1400
1520 Industrial Dr Unit C Lake In The Hills (60156) *(G-12331)*
Cudner & OConnor Co 773 826-0200
4035 W Kinzie St Chicago (60624) *(G-4283)*
Culinary Co-Pack Inc 847 451-1551
9140 Belden Ave Franklin Park (60131) *(G-9920)*
Culinary Co-Pack Incorporated 847 451-1551
2300 N 17th Ave Franklin Park (60131) *(G-9921)*
Culligan, Lombard *Also called Waterco of Central States Inc (G-13153)*
Culligan International Company (PA) 847 430-2800
9399 W Higgins Rd # 1100 Rosemont (60018) *(G-18013)*
Cullinan & Sons Inc (PA) 309 925-2711
121 W Park St Tremont (61568) *(G-19895)*
Cultivated Energy Group Inc 312 203-8833
10702 Seaman Rd Hebron (60034) *(G-11142)*
Cultor Food Science Danis 815 259-3311
10994 Three Mile Rd Thomson (61285) *(G-19781)*
Culture Media Supplies Inc 630 499-5000
118 Kirkland Cir Ste D Oswego (60543) *(G-15999)*
Culture Studio, Chicago *Also called Chii Clothing Company (G-4139)*
Cumberland Engrg Entps Inc 314 727-5550
1100 E Wdfield Rd Ste 550 Schaumburg (60173) *(G-18500)*
Cummins - Allison Corp 847 299-9550
891 Feehanville Dr Mount Prospect (60056) *(G-14521)*
Cummins - Allison Corp 847 299-9550
851 Feehanville Dr Mount Prospect (60056) *(G-14522)*
Cummins - Allison Corp 630 833-2285
851 N Addison Ave Elmhurst (60126) *(G-9357)*
Cummins Allison, Mount Prospect *Also called Cummins-Allison Corp (G-14523)*
Cummins Crosspoint LLC 309 452-4454
450 W Northtown Rd Normal (61761) *(G-15201)*
Cummins Diesel Sales, Hodgkins *Also called Cummins Npower LLC (G-11387)*
Cummins Dist Holdco Inc 309 787-4300
7820 42nd St W Rock Island (61201) *(G-17213)*
Cummins Great Plains Diesel, Rock Island *Also called Cummins Dist Holdco Inc (G-17213)*
Cummins Inc 309 787-4300
7820 42nd St W Rock Island (61201) *(G-17214)*
Cummins Npower LLC 708 579-9222
7145 Santa Fe Dr Hodgkins (60525) *(G-11387)*
Cummins-Allison Corp (HQ) 800 786-5528
852 Feehanville Dr Mount Prospect (60056) *(G-14523)*

ALPHABETIC

Cummins-American Corp....847 299-9550
852 Feehanville Dr Mount Prospect (60056) ***(G-14524)***
Cunningham Electronics Corp....618 833-7775
120 N Main St Anna (62906) ***(G-582)***
Cup O Joe Coffee LLC....877 828-7656
2032 W Iowa St Chicago (60622) ***(G-4284)***
Cupcake Holdings LLC....800 794-5866
2240 75th St Woodridge (60517) ***(G-21289)***
Cupcakeologist LLC....630 656-2272
2124 Country Club Dr Woodridge (60517) ***(G-21290)***
Curatek Pharmaceuticals LLC....702 215-5700
1965 Pratt Blvd Elk Grove Village (60007) ***(G-8924)***
Curbside Splendor....224 515-6512
2816 N Kedzie Ave Chicago (60618) ***(G-4285)***
Curl Mix Popup Party, Chicago *Also called Curlmix Inc* ***(G-4286)***
Curlee Mfg....847 268-6517
9377 W Higgins Rd Rosemont (60018) ***(G-18014)***
Curlmix Inc....773 234-6891
325 N Hoyne Ave Ste C318 Chicago (60612) ***(G-4286)***
Curran Contracting Company....815 758-8113
2220 County Farm Rd Dekalb (60115) ***(G-7671)***
Curran Contracting Company (HQ)....815 455-5100
286 Memorial Ct Crystal Lake (60014) ***(G-7189)***
Curran Group Inc (PA)....815 455-5100
286 Memorial Ct Crystal Lake (60014) ***(G-7190)***
Curry Ready Mix of Mason City, Mason City *Also called Contractors Ready-Mix Inc* ***(G-13610)***
Curry Ready Mix of Petersburg....217 632-2516
1106 N 7th St Petersburg (62675) ***(G-16601)***
Curry Ready-Mix of Decatur....217 428-7177
2200 N Woodford St Decatur (62526) ***(G-7479)***
Curt Herrmann Construction Inc....815 748-0531
512 Maplewood Ave Dekalb (60115) ***(G-7672)***
Curt Smith Sporting Goods Inc (PA)....618 233-5177
213 E Main St Belleville (62220) ***(G-1541)***
Curtis 1000 Inc....309 663-0325
2 Hardman Dr Bloomington (61701) ***(G-2036)***
Curtis Metal Finishing Company....815 282-1433
10911 N 2nd St Machesney Park (61115) ***(G-13337)***
Curtis Metal Finishing Company....815 633-6693
9917 N Alpine Rd Machesney Park (61115) ***(G-13338)***
Curtis Thermal Processing, Machesney Park *Also called Curtis Metal Finishing Company* ***(G-13337)***
Curtis Woodworking Inc....815 544-3543
4820 Newburg Rd Belvidere (61008) ***(G-1664)***
Curto-Ligonier Foundries Co....708 345-2250
1215 N 31st Ave Melrose Park (60160) ***(G-13846)***
Curv Group LLC....847 636-0101
860 Bonnie Ln Elk Grove Village (60007) ***(G-8925)***
Cushing and Company (PA)....312 266-8228
213 W Institute Pl # 200 Chicago (60610) ***(G-4287)***
Cushioneer Inc....815 748-5505
1651 Pleasant St Dekalb (60115) ***(G-7673)***
Custom & Hard To Find Wigs....773 777-0222
4065 N Milwaukee Ave Chicago (60641) ***(G-4288)***
Custom Accents, Elk Grove Village *Also called Custom Plastics Inc* ***(G-8926)***
Custom Aluminum Products Inc....847 717-5000
312 Eureka St Genoa (60135) ***(G-10316)***
Custom Aluminum Products Inc (PA)....847 717-5000
414 Division St South Elgin (60177) ***(G-19141)***
Custom Assembly Solutions Inc....847 224-5800
101 E State Pkwy Schaumburg (60173) ***(G-18501)***
Custom Bindery Services, Addison *Also called Hopkins Printing & Envelope Co* ***(G-152)***
Custom Blades & Tools Inc....630 860-7650
1084 Fairway Dr Bensenville (60106) ***(G-1782)***
Custom Blending & Pckaging of....618 286-1140
108 Coulter Rd Dupo (62239) ***(G-8135)***
Custom Blow Molding....630 820-9700
2560 White Oak Cir # 140 Aurora (60502) ***(G-947)***
Custom Boxes Inc (PA)....630 364-3944
681 W Briarcliff Rd Bolingbrook (60440) ***(G-2162)***
Custom Cabinet Refacers Inc....847 695-8800
2482 Technology Dr Elgin (60124) ***(G-8559)***
Custom Calendar Corp....708 547-6191
875 E 22nd St Apt 202 Lombard (60148) ***(G-13060)***
Custom Calender, Lombard *Also called Custom Calendar Corp* ***(G-13060)***
Custom Canvas LLC....847 587-0225
26463 W Grand Ave Ingleside (60041) ***(G-11580)***
Custom Case Co Inc....773 585-1164
6045 S Knox Ave Chicago (60629) ***(G-4289)***
Custom Chemical Engineering, Springfield *Also called Custom Chemical Inc* ***(G-19357)***
Custom Chemical Inc....217 529-0878
4524 Industrial Ave Springfield (62703) ***(G-19357)***
Custom Chrome & Polishing....618 885-9499
18416 Stagecoach Rd Jerseyville (62052) ***(G-11789)***
Custom Coating Innovations Inc....618 808-0500
30 Commerce Dr Lebanon (62254) ***(G-12544)***
Custom Copper Hoods Inc....224 577-9000
103 Harding Ave Libertyville (60048) ***(G-12646)***
Custom Crafted Door Inc....309 527-5075
2810 County Road 520 N El Paso (61738) ***(G-8435)***
Custom Culinary Inc (HQ)....630 928-4898
2505 S Finley Rd Ste 100 Lombard (60148) ***(G-13061)***
Custom Culinary Inc....630 299-0500
2100 Wiesbrook Rd Oswego (60543) ***(G-16000)***
Custom Cut EDM Inc....847 647-9500
5423 Fargo Ave Skokie (60077) ***(G-18947)***
Custom Cut Stencil Company Inc....618 277-5077
132 Iowa Ave Belleville (62220) ***(G-1542)***
Custom Cutting Tools Inc....815 986-0320
5405 Forest Hills Ct Loves Park (61111) ***(G-13200)***
Custom Cuttingedge Tool Inc....847 622-0457
1217 Paramount Pkwy Batavia (60510) ***(G-1370)***
Custom Design Services & Assoc....815 226-9747
220 E State St Rockford (61104) ***(G-17362)***
Custom Designs By Georgio....847 233-0410
9955 Pacific Ave Franklin Park (60131) ***(G-9922)***
Custom Direct Inc....630 529-1936
715 E Irving Park Rd Roselle (60172) ***(G-17950)***
Custom Enterprises....618 439-6626
131 Industrial Park Rd Benton (62812) ***(G-1923)***
Custom Fabrications Inc....847 531-5912
1625 Weld Rd Ste B Elgin (60123) ***(G-8560)***
Custom Fabricators LLC (PA)....630 372-4399
302 Roma Jean Pkwy Streamwood (60107) ***(G-19569)***
Custom Fabricators LLC....773 814-2757
106 Heine Dr Streamwood (60107) ***(G-19570)***
Custom Fbrication Coatings Inc....618 452-9540
1107 22nd St Granite City (62040) ***(G-10701)***
Custom Feeder Co of Rockford....815 654-2444
6207 Material Ave Ste 1 Loves Park (61111) ***(G-13201)***
Custom Fiberglass of Illinois....309 344-7727
875 Enterprise Ave Galesburg (61401) ***(G-10189)***
Custom Films Inc....217 826-2326
1400 Archer Ave Marshall (62441) ***(G-13569)***
Custom Filter LLC....630 906-2100
2300 Raddant Rd Ste A Aurora (60502) ***(G-948)***
Custom Flooring Insets, East Dundee *Also called Grads Inc* ***(G-8198)***
Custom Foam Works Inc....618 920-2810
31 Sequoia Dr Troy (62294) ***(G-19913)***
Custom Food Products, Oswego *Also called Custom Culinary Inc* ***(G-16000)***
Custom Framework Inc....618 401-8494
3865 Ridge View Rd Edwardsville (62025) ***(G-8354)***
Custom Golf By Tanis....708 481-4433
21750 Main St Unit 17 Matteson (60443) ***(G-13622)***
Custom Graphics Inc....309 633-0850
4100 Ricketts Ave Bartonville (61607) ***(G-1330)***
Custom Hard Chrome Service Co....847 759-1420
7083 Barry St Rosemont (60018) ***(G-18015)***
Custom Hardwoods LLC....815 784-9974
446 Alden Dr Sycamore (60178) ***(G-19703)***
Custom Karts and More LLC....815 703-6438
1570 Chadbourne Dr Davis (61019) ***(G-7416)***
Custom Machine Inc....815 284-3820
895 Shop Rd Dixon (61021) ***(G-7895)***
Custom Machining Company....630 766-2600
401 Evergreen Ave Bensenville (60106) ***(G-1783)***
Custom Menu Insights LLC....312 237-3860
73 W Monroe St 215 Chicago (60603) ***(G-4290)***
Custom Metal Products, Rockford *Also called Klinck Inc* ***(G-17484)***
Custom Millers Supply Inc....309 734-6312
511 S 3rd St Monmouth (61462) ***(G-14216)***
Custom Mold Services Inc....847 364-6589
1605 W Algonquin Rd Mount Prospect (60056) ***(G-14525)***
Custom Monogramming....815 625-9044
1204 Lincoln St Rock Falls (61071) ***(G-17180)***
Custom Plastics Inc....847 439-6770
1940 Lunt Ave Elk Grove Village (60007) ***(G-8926)***
Custom Plastics Inc....847 439-6770
1940 Lunt Ave Elk Grove Village (60007) ***(G-8927)***
Custom Plastics of Peoria....309 697-2888
4623 Enterprise Dr Bartonville (61607) ***(G-1331)***
Custom Power Products Inc....309 249-2704
19727 N State Route 40 Edelstein (61526) ***(G-8332)***
Custom Precision Inc....847 278-7877
555 Estes Ave Schaumburg (60193) ***(G-18502)***
Custom Product Innovations....618 628-0111
40 Commerce Dr Lebanon (62254) ***(G-12545)***
Custom Railz & Stairs Inc....773 592-7210
7808 La Crosse Ave Oak Lawn (60459) ***(G-15710)***
Custom Railz & Stairz Inc....773 592-7210
6740 S Belt Circle Dr Chicago (60638) ***(G-4291)***
Custom Rods By Grandt Ltd....847 577-0848
203 S Highland Ave Arlington Heights (60005) ***(G-723)***
Custom Screen Printing....217 543-3691
111 N Vine St Arthur (61911) ***(G-850)***
Custom Seal & Rubber Products....888 356-2966
112 E Hitt St Mount Morris (61054) ***(G-14499)***

ALPHABETIC SECTION
D & W Mfg Co Inc

Custom Sign Consultants Inc 312 533-2302
1928 W Fulton St Ste 5 Chicago (60612) *(G-4292)*
Custom Signs On Metal LLC 217 443-5347
301 Mayfield St Tilton (61833) *(G-19795)*
Custom Stainless Steel Inc (PA) 618 435-2605
350 Industrial Park Dr Benton (62812) *(G-1924)*
Custom Stone Works Inc 815 748-2109
165 W Stephenie Dr Cortland (60112) *(G-7018)*
Custom Stone Wrks Acqstion Inc 630 669-1119
165 W Stephenie Dr Cortland (60112) *(G-7019)*
Custom Superfinishing Grinding 847 699-9710
7083 Barry St Rosemont (60018) *(G-18016)*
Custom Systems Inc 314 355-4575
3660 State Route 111 Granite City (62040) *(G-10702)*
Custom Telephone Printing Co 815 338-0000
1002 Mchenry Ave Woodstock (60098) *(G-21379)*
Custom Tool Inc 217 465-8538
926 N Central Ave Paris (61944) *(G-16228)*
Custom Towels Inc 618 539-5005
6410 Hilgard Memorial Dr Freeburg (62243) *(G-10088)*
Custom Trophies 217 422-3353
947 N Water St Decatur (62523) *(G-7480)*
Custom Window Accents 815 943-7651
900 W Diggins St Harvard (60033) *(G-11051)*
Custom Wood & Laminate Ltd 815 727-4168
1102 Davison St Joliet (60433) *(G-11850)*
Custom Wood Creations 618 346-2208
776 Timberlane Dr Collinsville (62234) *(G-6956)*
Custom Wood Designs Inc 708 799-3439
14237 Kilbourne Ave Crestwood (60418) *(G-7116)*
Custom Woodwork & Interiors (PA) 217 546-0006
3208 S Douglas Ave Springfield (62704) *(G-19358)*
Customeyes, Rock Island *Also called Essilor Laboratories Amer Inc (G-17219)*
Cut - To - Size Technology Inc 630 543-8328
345 S Fairbank St Addison (60101) *(G-85)*
Cut Rate Printers, Chicago *Also called Swift Impressions Inc (G-6296)*
Cutco Abrasive Co, Saint Charles *Also called C M C Industries Inc (G-18161)*
Cutn Edge Cstm Fabrication LLC 779 774-4991
10469 Product Dr Machesney Park (61115) *(G-13339)*
Cutshaw Instls Inc 847 426-9208
216 Dundee Ave East Dundee (60118) *(G-8190)*
Cutting Edge Communications 815 788-9419
764 Grandview Dr Crystal Lake (60014) *(G-7191)*
Cutting Edge Document Dstrctn 630 620-0193
10 E 22nd St Lombard (60148) *(G-13062)*
Cutting Edge Graphics 630 717-9233
10160 Clow Creek Rd Plainfield (60585) *(G-16654)*
Cutting Edge Graphics Ltd 630 717-9233
1329 Marengo Ct Naperville (60564) *(G-14964)*
Cutting Edge Industries Inc 847 678-1777
9015 Exchange Ave Franklin Park (60131) *(G-9923)*
Cutting Edge Machining Inc 847 427-1392
105 Randall St Ste B Elk Grove Village (60007) *(G-8928)*
Cutting Edge Water Jet Service 815 389-0100
441 Clark St South Beloit (61080) *(G-19088)*
Cutting Specialists Inc 731 352-5351
420 N Main St Edwardsville (62025) *(G-8355)*
Cutting Tool Innovations Inc 630 766-4839
759 Industrial Dr Bensenville (60106) *(G-1784)*
Cvp Systems LLC 630 852-1190
1675 Todd Farm Dr Elgin (60123) *(G-8561)*
Cwh LLC 847 489-7907
100 Lexington Dr Ste 201 Buffalo Grove (60089) *(G-2529)*
Cws Cabinets 847 258-4468
225 Stanley St Elk Grove Village (60007) *(G-8929)*
Cy-Tec Inc 815 756-8416
221 Industrial Dr Dekalb (60115) *(G-7674)*
Cyber Tech Corp 630 472-3200
1301 W 22nd St Ste 308 Oak Brook (60523) *(G-15615)*
Cyborg Systems Inc (HQ) 312 279-7000
233 S Wacker Dr Lob -001 Chicago (60606) *(G-4293)*
Cyclops Industrial Inc 815 962-1984
126 Monroe St Rockford (61101) *(G-17363)*
Cyclops Welding Co 815 223-0685
11 Joliet St La Salle (61301) *(G-12109)*
Cygnet Midwest, Naperville *Also called Media Unlimited Inc (G-14867)*
Cygnus Corp Packaging Div, Chicago *Also called Cygnus Corporation (G-4294)*
Cygnus Corporation 773 785-2845
340 E 138th St Chicago (60827) *(G-4294)*
Cygnus D/B/A Marietta Chicago, Chicago *Also called Marietta Corporation (G-5337)*
Cylinder Services Inc 630 466-9820
629 N Heartland Dr Sugar Grove (60554) *(G-19641)*
Cymatics Inc 630 420-7117
31w280 Diehl Rd Ste 104 Naperville (60563) *(G-14811)*
Cyn Industries Inc 773 895-4324
1661 N Elston Ave Chicago (60642) *(G-4295)*
Cynlar Inc 630 820-2200
1585 Beverly Ct Ste 125 Aurora (60502) *(G-949)*
Cynthia Espy, Chicago *Also called Amenities Home Design (G-3645)*
Cypress Multigraphics LLC (PA) 708 633-1166
8500 185th St Ste A Tinley Park (60487) *(G-19820)*
Cyrus Shank Company 331 212-5488
575 Exchange Ct Aurora (60504) *(G-950)*
Cyrus Shank Company (HQ) 708 652-2700
4645 W Roosevelt Rd Cicero (60804) *(G-6838)*
Czarnik Memorials Inc 708 458-4443
7300 Archer Rd Justice (60458) *(G-11951)*
Czarnik Precision Grinding Mch 708 229-9639
5530 W 110th St Ste 8 Oak Lawn (60453) *(G-15711)*
Czech American TV Herald 708 813-0028
124 Sunset Ridge Rd Willowbrook (60527) *(G-21039)*
D & B Fabricators & Distrs 630 325-3811
16w065 Jeans Rd Ste A Lemont (60439) *(G-12562)*
D & D Business Inc 630 935-3522
10s428 Carrington Cir Willowbrook (60527) *(G-21040)*
D & D Construction Co LLC 217 852-6631
220 Cherry St Dallas City (62330) *(G-7312)*
D & D Embroidery 309 266-7092
140 S Main St Morton (61550) *(G-14357)*
D & D Jewelers, Sycamore *Also called D & D Sukach Inc (G-19704)*
D & D Manufacturing 815 339-9100
6th St Rr 26 Hennepin (61327) *(G-11157)*
D & D Manufacturing Inc 888 300-6869
500 Territorial Dr Bolingbrook (60440) *(G-2163)*
D & D Manufacturing Entps, Bolingbrook *Also called D & D Tooling and Mfg Inc (G-2164)*
D & D Printing Inc 708 425-2080
9737 Southwest Hwy Oak Lawn (60453) *(G-15712)*
D & D Sukach Inc 815 895-3377
1733 Dekalb Ave Sycamore (60178) *(G-19704)*
D & D Tooling and Mfg Inc (PA) 888 300-6869
500 Territorial Dr Bolingbrook (60440) *(G-2164)*
D & D Tooling Inc 630 759-0015
500 Territorial Dr Bolingbrook (60440) *(G-2165)*
D & G Pallet Service Inc 773 265-8470
4445 W 5th Ave Chicago (60624) *(G-4296)*
D & G Welding Supply Company 815 675-9890
7705 Industrial Dr Ste E Spring Grove (60081) *(G-19272)*
D & H Granite and Marble Sup 773 869-9988
1520 W Pershing Rd Chicago (60609) *(G-4297)*
D & H Precision Tooling Co 815 653-9611
7522 Barnard Mill Rd Wonder Lake (60097) *(G-21144)*
D & J International Inc 847 966-9260
7793 N Caldwell Ave Niles (60714) *(G-15115)*
D & J Machine Shop Inc 815 472-6057
2120 N 11250e Rd Momence (60954) *(G-14184)*
D & J Metalcraft Company Inc 773 878-6446
4451 N Ravenswood Ave Chicago (60640) *(G-4298)*
D & J Plastics Inc 847 534-0601
1775 Illinois St Roselle (60172) *(G-17951)*
D & K Custom Machine Design 847 956-4757
1795 Commerce Dr Elk Grove Village (60007) *(G-8930)*
D & K Group Inc (PA) 847 956-0160
1795 Commerce Dr Elk Grove Village (60007) *(G-8931)*
D & K International Inc (HQ) 847 956-0160
1795 Commerce Dr Elk Grove Village (60007) *(G-8932)*
D & K Machine and Tool Inc 847 439-8691
1080 Howard St Elk Grove Village (60007) *(G-8933)*
D & K Tanks 618 553-3186
7875 N 600th St Robinson (62454) *(G-17110)*
D & M Custom Injection M 847 683-2054
150 French Rd Burlington (60109) *(G-2640)*
D & M Perlman Fine Jewelry 847 426-8881
740 S 8th St West Dundee (60118) *(G-20661)*
D & M Plastics, Burlington *Also called D & M Custom Injection M (G-2640)*
D & M Tool Llc 847 731-3600
2013 Horizon Ct Zion (60099) *(G-21511)*
D & M Welding Inc 708 233-6080
8314 S 77th Ave Bridgeview (60455) *(G-2339)*
D & N Deburring Co Inc 847 451-7702
2919 Birch St Franklin Park (60131) *(G-9924)*
D & P Construction Co Inc (PA) 773 714-9330
5521 N Cmderland Ste 1106 Chicago (60656) *(G-4299)*
D & R Autochuck Inc 815 394-1744
5248 27th Ave Rockford (61109) *(G-17364)*
D & R Ekstrom Carlson Co 815 394-1744
5248 27th Ave Rockford (61109) *(G-17365)*
D & R Machine Company Inc (PA) 618 465-5611
4131 Alby St Alton (62002) *(G-550)*
D & R Press 708 452-0500
7959 W Grand Ave Elmwood Park (60707) *(G-9450)*
D & S Communications Inc (PA) 847 628-4195
1355 N Mclean Blvd Elgin (60123) *(G-8562)*
D & S Manufacturing Inc 815 637-8889
5604 Pike Rd Loves Park (61111) *(G-13202)*
D & S Wire Inc 847 766-5520
2531 E Devon Ave Elk Grove Village (60007) *(G-8934)*
D & W Mfg Co Inc 773 533-1542
3237 W Lake St Chicago (60624) *(G-4300)*

ALPHABETIC

D & Z Exploration Inc 618 829-3274
901 N Elm St Saint Elmo (62458) ***(G-18307)***
D A Matot Inc 708 547-1888
2501 Van Buren St Bellwood (60104) ***(G-1620)***
D and D Pallets 630 800-1102
725 S Broadway Aurora (60505) ***(G-1082)***
D and K Plastics 712 723-5372
2127 State Route 47 Yorkville (60560) ***(G-21476)***
D and R Tech 224 353-6693
1118 Lunt Ave Ste F Schaumburg (60193) ***(G-18503)***
D and S Molding & Dctg Inc 815 399-2734
2816 Kishwaukee St Rockford (61109) ***(G-17366)***
D C Cooper Corporation 309 924-1941
Junction 116 & 94 Stronghurst (61480) ***(G-19633)***
D C Estate Winery 815 218-0573
8925 Stateline Rd South Beloit (61080) ***(G-19089)***
D C T/Precision LLC 217 475-0141
1260 E North St Decatur (62521) ***(G-7481)***
D Castris, Rockford *Also called Midwest Stitch* ***(G-17528)***
D D G Inc (PA) 847 412-0277
1955 Shermer Rd Ste 300 Northbrook (60062) ***(G-15370)***
D D Sales Inc 217 857-3196
1608 W Main St Teutopolis (62467) ***(G-19768)***
D E Asbury Inc (PA) 217 222-0617
1479 Keokuk St Hamilton (62341) ***(G-10953)***
D E Signs & Storage LLC 618 939-8050
6167 State Route 3 Waterloo (62298) ***(G-20289)***
D E Specialty Tool & Mfg Inc 847 678-0004
9865 Franklin Ave Franklin Park (60131) ***(G-9925)***
D G Brandt Inc 815 942-4064
901 Liberty St Morris (60450) ***(G-14301)***
D G Printing Inc 847 397-7779
69 Falcon Dr Hawthorn Woods (60047) ***(G-11122)***
D J Peters Orthopedics Ltd 309 664-6930
908 N Hershey Rd Ste 1 Bloomington (61704) ***(G-2037)***
D Kersey Construction Co 847 919-4980
4130 Timberlane Dr Northbrook (60062) ***(G-15371)***
D L Austin Steel Supply Corp (PA) 618 345-7200
500 Camelot Dr Collinsville (62234) ***(G-6957)***
D L S, Roselle *Also called RR Donnelley Logistics SE* ***(G-17981)***
D L S, Itasca *Also called Diversfied Lbling Slutions Inc* ***(G-11643)***
D L Sheet Metal 708 599-5538
8717 W 98th Pl Palos Hills (60465) ***(G-16199)***
D L V Printing Service Inc 773 626-1661
5825 W Corcoran Pl Chicago (60644) ***(G-4301)***
D Little Drilling 618 943-3721
4734 Country Club Rd Saint Francisville (62460) ***(G-18313)***
D M C Mold & Tool Corp 847 639-3098
740 Industrial Dr Ste H Cary (60013) ***(G-3152)***
D M L, Schaumburg *Also called Dml Distribution Inc* ***(G-18509)***
D M Manufacturing 2 Inc 618 455-3550
490 S Main St Sainte Marie (62459) ***(G-18325)***
D Machine Inc 815 877-5991
921 River Ln Loves Park (61111) ***(G-13203)***
D N D Coating 309 379-3021
313 W Main St Stanford (61774) ***(G-19472)***
D N Welding & Fabricating Inc 847 244-6410
3627 Washington St Bldg 5 Waukegan (60085) ***(G-20432)***
D O D Technologies Inc 815 788-5200
675 Industrial Dr Cary (60013) ***(G-3153)***
D R Sperry & Co 630 892-4361
623 Rathbone Ave Aurora (60506) ***(G-1083)***
D R Walters 618 926-6337
65 County Road 300 N Norris City (62869) ***(G-15248)***
D S A, Lake Barrington *Also called D S Arms Incorporated* ***(G-12147)***
D S Arms Incorporated 847 277-7258
27996 W Industrial Ave # 1 Lake Barrington (60010) ***(G-12147)***
D S Precision Tool Company 630 627-0696
1420 Brook Dr Downers Grove (60515) ***(G-7982)***
D W Machine Products Inc 618 654-2161
1111 6th St Highland (62249) ***(G-11212)***
D W Ram Manufacturing Co 708 633-7900
18530 Spring Creek Dr # 1 Tinley Park (60477) ***(G-19821)***
D W Terry Welding Company 618 433-9722
1860 E Broadway Alton (62002) ***(G-551)***
D&J Arlington Heights Inc 847 577-8200
1814 N Arlington Hts Rd Arlington Heights (60004) ***(G-724)***
D&M Plastics, Burlington *Also called Owen Plastics LLC* ***(G-2642)***
D&W Fine Pack Holdings LLC (HQ) 847 378-1200
777 Mark St Wood Dale (60191) ***(G-21179)***
D&W Fine Pack LLC 800 323-0422
800 Ela Rd Lake Zurich (60047) ***(G-12401)***
D&W Fine Pack LLC 215 362-1501
777 Mark St Wood Dale (60191) ***(G-21180)***
D-M-S Holdings Inc (HQ) 515 327-6416
1931 Norman Dr Waukegan (60085) ***(G-20433)***
D-Orum Corporation 773 567-2064
325 W 103rd St Chicago (60628) ***(G-4302)***
D.P. Filters, Peoria *Also called Dust Patrol Inc* ***(G-16432)***
D/C Export & Domestic Pkg Inc (PA) 847 593-4200
1300 E Devon Ave Elk Grove Village (60007) ***(G-8935)***
D/C Group The, Elk Grove Village *Also called D/C Export & Domestic Pkg Inc* ***(G-8935)***
D2 Lighting LLC 708 243-9059
5718 Harvey Ave La Grange Highlands (60525) ***(G-12092)***
D5 Design Met Fabrication LLC 773 770-4705
2439 N Pulaski Rd Chicago (60639) ***(G-4303)***
Da Closet 708 206-1414
4139 167th St Country Club Hills (60478) ***(G-7038)***
Dabecca Natural Foods Inc 773 291-1428
700 E 107th St Chicago (60628) ***(G-4304)***
Dabel Incorporated 217 398-3389
602 E Green St Champaign (61820) ***(G-3284)***
Dabir Surfaces Inc (HQ) 708 867-6777
7447 W Wilson Ave Harwood Heights (60706) ***(G-11103)***
Dabrico Inc 815 939-0580
1555 Commerce Dr Bourbonnais (60914) ***(G-2259)***
Dach Fence Co, Rockford *Also called William Dach* ***(G-17685)***
Dadant & Sons Inc (PA) 217 847-3324
51 S 2nd St Ste 2 Hamilton (62341) ***(G-10954)***
Dadant & Sons Inc 217 852-3324
Hwy 9 S Dallas City (62330) ***(G-7313)***
Dado Lighting LLC 708 243-9059
9100 Plainfield Rd Ste 9 Brookfield (60513) ***(G-2481)***
Dado Lighting LLC 877 323-6584
4700 Gilbert Ave 47-217 Western Springs (60558) ***(G-20720)***
Dado Lighting LLC 877 323-6584
5446 Dansher Rd Countryside (60525) ***(G-7050)***
Dadum Die & Design, Buffalo Grove *Also called Dadum Inc* ***(G-2530)***
Dadum Inc 847 541-7851
950 Beechwood Rd Buffalo Grove (60089) ***(G-2530)***
Daesam Corporation 917 653-2000
888 E Belvidere Rd # 306 Grayslake (60030) ***(G-10765)***
Dagger Tool Co Inc 630 279-5050
501 W Interstate Rd Addison (60101) ***(G-86)***
Daily American, The, West Frankfort *Also called Gatehouse Media LLC* ***(G-20673)***
Daily Dollar Savings LLC 860 883-0351
9448 Skokie Blvd Morton Grove (60053) ***(G-14398)***
Daily Egyptian Siu Newspaper 618 536-3311
1100 Lincoln Dr Rm 1259 Carbondale (62901) ***(G-2840)***
Daily Fastner 847 907-9830
1304 W Northwest Hwy Palatine (60067) ***(G-16107)***
Daily General LLC 217 273-0719
2757 W Le Moyne St Apt 2 Chicago (60622) ***(G-4305)***
Daily Herald, Arlington Heights *Also called Paddock Publications Inc* ***(G-786)***
Daily Herald, Schaumburg *Also called Paddock Publications Inc* ***(G-18662)***
Daily Herald, Libertyville *Also called Paddock Publications Inc* ***(G-12693)***
Daily Highway Express, Winthrop Harbor *Also called Rd Daily Enterprises* ***(G-21142)***
Daily Journal, The, Kankakee *Also called Kankakee Daily Journal Co LLC* ***(G-11985)***
Daily Kratom 815 768-7104
4010 Brenton Dr Joliet (60431) ***(G-11851)***
Daily Lawrenceville Record 618 943-2331
1209 State St Lawrenceville (62439) ***(G-12529)***
Daily Lawrenceville Record (PA) 618 544-2101
1209 State St Lawrenceville (62439) ***(G-12530)***
Daily Leader Newspaper, Pontiac *Also called Gatehouse Media LLC* ***(G-16771)***
Daily Money Matters LLC 847 729-8393
2200 Goldenrod Ln Glenview (60026) ***(G-10541)***
Daily News Condominium Assn 312 492-8526
222 S Racine Ave Chicago (60607) ***(G-4306)***
Daily News Tribune Inc (PA) 815 223-2558
426 2nd St La Salle (61301) ***(G-12110)***
Daily News/Daily Record, Lawrenceville *Also called Daily Lawrenceville Record* ***(G-12530)***
DAILY NORTHWESTERN NEWSPAPER, Evanston *Also called Students Publishing Company In* ***(G-9579)***
Daily Register, Harrisburg *Also called Gatehouse Media LLC* ***(G-11024)***
Daily Republican Register, Mount Carmel *Also called Mt Carmel Register Co Inc* ***(G-14481)***
Daily Robinson News Inc 618 544-2101
302 S Cross St Robinson (62454) ***(G-17111)***
Daily Times, The, Ottawa *Also called Ottawa Publishing Co Inc* ***(G-16068)***
Daily Whale 312 787-5204
222 W Ontario St Chicago (60654) ***(G-4307)***
Dainichi Machinery Inc 630 681-1572
745 Kimberly Dr Carol Stream (60188) ***(G-2970)***
Dairy Dynamics LLC 847 758-7300
17820 Washington St Elk Grove Village (60007) ***(G-8936)***
Daito Pharmaceuticals Amer Inc 847 205-0800
707 Skokie Blvd Ste 210 Northbrook (60062) ***(G-15372)***
Daito USA Inc 847 437-6788
1470 Elmhurst Rd Elk Grove Village (60007) ***(G-8937)***
Dakkota Integrated Systems LLC 517 694-6500
12525 S Carondolet Ave Chicago (60633) ***(G-4308)***
Dal Acres West Kennel 217 793-3647
2508 W Jefferson St Springfield (62702) ***(G-19359)***
Dalco Marketing Services 630 961-3366
362 Sherwood Dr Carol Stream (60188) ***(G-2971)***
Dale K Brown 815 338-0222
130 Wshngton St Unit Rear Woodstock (60098) ***(G-21380)***

Dale's Diesel Service, Teutopolis *Also called D D Sales Inc (G-19768)*
Daley Automation LLC (PA) 630 384-9900
1111 S Washington St Naperville (60540) **(G-14812)**
Dallas & Co Costumes & Magic, Champaign *Also called Andy Dallas & Co (G-3265)*
Dallas Corporation 630 322-8000
4340 Cross St Downers Grove (60515) **(G-7983)**
Daly Engineered Filtration Inc 708 355-1550
942 E Hillside Rd Naperville (60540) **(G-14813)**
DAmatos Bakery Inc 312 733-6219
1332 W Grand Ave Chicago (60642) **(G-4309)**
Damco Products Inc 618 452-4700
224 State St Madison (62060) **(G-13407)**
Damen Carbide Tool Company Inc 630 766-7875
344 Beinoris Dr Wood Dale (60191) **(G-21181)**
DAmico Associates Inc 847 291-7446
3065 Dundee Rd Northbrook (60062) **(G-15373)**
Damien Corporation 630 369-3549
6s204 Cohasset Rd Naperville (60540) **(G-14814)**
Damron Corporation 773 265-2724
4433 W Ohio St Chicago (60624) **(G-4310)**
Damron Tea, Chicago *Also called Damron Corporation (G-4310)*
Damy Corp 847 233-0515
9353 Seymour Ave Schiller Park (60176) **(G-18798)**
Dan Moy 217 243-2572
806 Woodland Pl Jacksonville (62650) **(G-11764)**
Dana 419 887-3000
2001 Eastwood Dr Sterling (61081) **(G-19503)**
Dana Corp Power Tech Group, Robinson *Also called Dana Sealing Manufacturing LLC (G-17113)*
Dana Driveshaft Mfg LLC 815 626-6700
2001 Eastwood Dr Sterling (61081) **(G-19504)**
Dana Driveshaft Products, Sterling *Also called Dana Driveshaft Mfg LLC (G-19504)*
Dana Incorporated 630 271-0001
1945 Ohio St Lisle (60532) **(G-12883)**
Dana Plastic Container Corp (HQ) 847 670-0650
6 N Hickory Ave Arlington Heights (60004) **(G-725)**
Dana Plastic Container Corp 630 529-7878
200 W Central Rd Schaumburg (60195) **(G-18504)**
Dana Sealing Manufacturing LLC 618 544-8651
1201 S Eaton St Robinson (62454) **(G-17112)**
Dana Sealing Manufacturing LLC 618 544-8651
1201 E Victor Dana Rd Robinson (62454) **(G-17113)**
Dana Sealing Products LLC 630 960-4200
1945 Ohio St Lisle (60532) **(G-12884)**
Danaher Corporation 815 568-8001
1300 N State St Marengo (60152) **(G-13483)**
Danaher Indus Sensors Contrls, Gurnee *Also called Dynapar Corporation (G-10873)*
Danco Converting 630 949-8112
455 E North Ave Carol Stream (60188) **(G-2972)**
Dancyn Recovery Systems 309 829-5450
707 N East St Bloomington (61701) **(G-2038)**
Dandelion Distributors Inc 815 675-9800
888 E Belvidere Rd # 114 Grayslake (60030) **(G-10766)**
Dandurand Custom Woodworking 708 489-6440
2606 W Walter Zimny Dr Posen (60469) **(G-16793)**
Dane Industries LLC 815 234-2811
602 E Blackhawk Dr Byron (61010) **(G-2752)**
Danfoss Inc 815 639-8600
7500 Beverage Blvd Loves Park (61111) **(G-13204)**
Danfoss LLC 717 261-5000
4401 N Bell School Rd Loves Park (61111) **(G-13205)**
Danfoss LLC 888 326-3677
4401 N Bell School Rd Loves Park (61111) **(G-13206)**
Danfoss Power Electronics, Loves Park *Also called Danfoss LLC (G-13206)*
Danfoss Power Solutions US Co 815 233-4200
580 N Henderson Rd Freeport (61032) **(G-10105)**
Dangios Fine Art Inc 773 533-3000
3050 W Taylor St Chicago (60612) **(G-4311)**
Daniel & Sons Mech Contrs Inc 618 997-2822
105 Hilltop Ln Marion (62959) **(G-13509)**
Daniel Bruce LLC 917 583-1538
2365 N Irene Dr Palatine (60074) **(G-16108)**
Daniel J Nickel & Assocs PC 312 345-1850
3052 N Haussen Ct Chicago (60618) **(G-4312)**
Daniel M Powers & Assoc Ltd 630 685-8400
575 W Crossroads Pkwy B Bolingbrook (60440) **(G-2166)**
Daniel Mfg Inc 309 963-4227
273 County Road 1850 E Carlock (61725) **(G-2886)**
Daniel Zimmer Associates 847 697-9393
77 Hillburn Ln North Barrington (60010) **(G-15283)**
Daniels Health, Chicago *Also called Daniels Sharpsmart Inc (G-4313)*
Daniels Jewelry & Mfg Co 847 998-5222
1436 Waukegan Rd Glenview (60025) **(G-10542)**
Daniels Printing & Office Sup, Oak Forest *Also called Dans Printing & Off Sups Inc (G-15674)*
Daniels Sharpsmart Inc (HQ) 312 546-8900
111 W Jackson Blvd # 1900 Chicago (60604) **(G-4313)**
Danielson Food Products Inc 773 285-2111
215 W Root St Chicago (60609) **(G-4314)**

Danisco Sweeteners, Thomson *Also called E I Du Pont De Nemours & Co (G-19783)*
Danisco USA Inc 815 259-3311
10994 Three Mile Rd Thomson (61285) **(G-19782)**
Danish Maid Butter Company 773 731-8787
8512 S Commercial Ave Chicago (60617) **(G-4315)**
Danko Industries 630 882-6070
181 Wolf St Unit C Yorkville (60560) **(G-21477)**
Danlee Wood Products Inc 815 938-9016
207 S Chestnut St Forreston (61030) **(G-9739)**
Danny Fender 618 665-3135
124 S Church St Louisville (62858) **(G-13178)**
Dans Printing & Off Sups Inc 708 687-3055
14800 Cicero Ave Ste 101 Oak Forest (60452) **(G-15674)**
Danville Brass and Aluminum, Danville *Also called Marble Machine Inc (G-7362)*
Danville Metal Stamping Co Inc (PA) 217 446-0647
20 Oakwood Ave Danville (61832) **(G-7328)**
Danville Metal Stamping Co Inc 217 446-0647
17 Oakwood Ave Danville (61832) **(G-7329)**
Danze Inc 630 754-0277
2500 Internationale Pkwy Woodridge (60517) **(G-21291)**
Danziger Kosher Catering Inc 847 982-1818
3931 S Leavitt St Chicago (60609) **(G-4316)**
Dapper Defense LLC 309 922-9203
232 Pershing Pl East Peoria (61611) **(G-8265)**
Daprato Rigali Studios Inc 773 763-5511
6030 N Northwest Hwy Chicago (60631) **(G-4317)**
Dar Enterprises Inc 815 961-8748
217 7th St Rockford (61104) **(G-17367)**
Darbe Products Company Inc 630 985-0769
2936 Two Paths Dr Woodridge (60517) **(G-21292)**
Dard Products Inc 847 328-5000
1230 Karl Ct Unit A Wauconda (60084) **(G-20341)**
Darda Enterprises Inc 847 270-0410
301 N Dean Dr Palatine (60074) **(G-16109)**
Darios Pallets Corp 312 421-3413
339 N California Ave Chicago (60612) **(G-4318)**
Dark Matter Printing 217 791-4059
7 Ridge Dr Decatur (62521) **(G-7482)**
Dark Speed Works 312 772-3275
122 N Wheaton Ave # 551 Wheaton (60187) **(G-20795)**
Darling Ingredients Inc 773 376-5550
3443 S Lawndale Ave Chicago (60623) **(G-4319)**
Darling Ingredients Inc 618 271-8190
2 Exchange Ave National Stock Yards (62071) **(G-15012)**
Darling Ingredients Inc 217 482-3261
1000 S Main St Mason City (62664) **(G-13611)**
Darling Ingredients Inc 708 388-3223
3000 Wireton Rd Blue Island (60406) **(G-2117)**
Darling Ingredients Inc 309 476-8111
202 Bengston St Lynn Center (61262) **(G-13289)**
Darling Intl Grse Trp Pump Div, Blue Island *Also called Darling Ingredients Inc (G-2117)*
Darlington Climate Control, Collinsville *Also called J D Refrigeration (G-6963)*
Darnall Printing 309 827-7212
801 W Chestnut St Ste B Bloomington (61701) **(G-2039)**
Darnell Welding 618 945-9538
9210 Lanterman Rd Bridgeport (62417) **(G-2312)**
Darrell Fickas 618 599-3632
16749 N Campground Ln Mount Vernon (62864) **(G-14605)**
Darrell Fickas Sawmill, Mount Vernon *Also called Darrell Fickas (G-14605)*
Dart Castings Inc 708 388-4914
12400 S Lombard Ln Alsip (60803) **(G-438)**
Dart Container Corp Illinois 630 896-4631
310 Evergreen Dr North Aurora (60542) **(G-15258)**
Dart Container Corp Illinois 800 367-2877
300 Tri State Intl Ste 20 Lincolnshire (60069) **(G-12758)**
Darwill Inc 708 449-7770
11900 Roosevelt Rd Hillside (60162) **(G-11335)**
Das Brothers LLC 925 980-6180
997 S Butternut Cir Frankfort (60423) **(G-9782)**
Das Foods LLC 224 715-9289
2041 W Carroll Ave C222 Chicago (60612) **(G-4320)**
Dasco Pro Inc 815 962-3727
340 Blackhawk Park Ave Rockford (61104) **(G-17368)**
Dasher Dependable Reindeer LLC 630 513-7737
3010 Royal Queens Ct Saint Charles (60174) **(G-18179)**
Dat Metal Fabricating, Fairmount *Also called Decatur Aeration and Temp (G-9642)*
Data Accessories Inc 847 669-3640
40w735 Powers Rd Huntley (60142) **(G-11533)**
Data Cable Technologies Inc 630 226-5600
1306 Enterprise Dr Ste E Romeoville (60446) **(G-17812)**
Data Com PLD Inc 708 267-5657
153 Santa Fe Ln Willow Springs (60480) **(G-21025)**
Data Comm For Business Inc (PA) 217 897-1741
2949 County Road 1000 E Dewey (61840) **(G-7873)**
Data Management Center, Glendale Heights *Also called Communication Technologies Inc (G-10444)*
Data Service Solutions, Bolingbrook *Also called Segerdahl Corp (G-2235)*
Datafordummies 618 421-2323
32 N 1550th St Flat Rock (62427) **(G-9671)**

ALPHABETIC

Datair Employee Beneft Systems 630 325-2600
735 N Cass Ave Westmont (60559) ***(G-20734)***

Datamax Oneil Printer Supplies, Robinson *Also called Pioneer Labels Inc* ***(G-17121)***

Datasis Corporation 847 427-0909
1687 Elmhurst Rd Elk Grove Village (60007) ***(G-8938)***

Datasite Global Corporation 312 263-3524
311 S Wacker Dr Ste 2450 Chicago (60606) ***(G-4321)***

Datasource 312 405-9152
1931 Wilson Ave Apt 7 Calumet City (60409) ***(G-2774)***

Datix (usa) Inc 312 724-7776
311 S Wacker Dr Ste 4900 Chicago (60606) ***(G-4322)***

Datum Machine Works Inc 815 877-8502
2219 N Central Ave Rockford (61101) ***(G-17369)***

Datum Tool and Mfg Inc 847 742-4092
200 Kane St South Elgin (60177) ***(G-19142)***

Dauber Company Inc 815 442-3569
577 N 18th Rd Tth Tonica (61370) ***(G-19888)***

Daubert Cromwell LLC (PA) 708 293-7750
12701 S Ridgeway Ave Alsip (60803) ***(G-439)***

Daubert Industries Inc (PA) 630 203-6800
700 S Central Ave Burr Ridge (60527) ***(G-2667)***

Daubert Vci Inc (HQ) 630 203-6800
1333 Burr Ridge Pkwy # 200 Burr Ridge (60527) ***(G-2668)***

Dauphin Enterprise Inc 630 893-6300
358 W Army Trail Rd # 150 Bloomingdale (60108) ***(G-1987)***

Dave White 618 898-1130
1269 Conty Rod 970 E Cisne (62823) ***(G-6892)***

Daves Auto Repiar 630 682-4411
211 E Saint Charles Rd Carol Stream (60188) ***(G-2973)***

Daves Electronic Service 217 283-5010
105 E Penn St Hoopeston (60942) ***(G-11507)***

Daves Welding Service Inc 630 655-3224
7201 Leonard Dr Darien (60561) ***(G-7405)***

David Architectural Metals Inc 773 376-3200
3100 S Kilbourn Ave Chicago (60623) ***(G-4323)***

David Corporation (PA) 781 587-3008
227 W Monroe St Ste 650 Chicago (60606) ***(G-4324)***

David H Pool 847 695-5007
1405 Timber Dr Ste B Elgin (60123) ***(G-8563)***

David H Vander Ploeg 708 331-7700
534 W 162nd St South Holland (60473) ***(G-19206)***

David Hall 309 797-9721
1529 46th Ave Moline (61265) ***(G-14137)***

David Horton 312 917-8610
1530 S State St Apt 17g Chicago (60605) ***(G-4325)***

David Jeskey 630 659-6337
1523 Banbury Ave Saint Charles (60174) ***(G-18180)***

David L Kaufman 217 543-4190
550 N Cr 240 E Arthur (61911) ***(G-851)***

David L Knoche 618 466-7120
611 Armsway Blvd Godfrey (62035) ***(G-10651)***

David Linderholm 847 336-3755
2210 Grand Ave Unit 2 Waukegan (60085) ***(G-20434)***

David Martin 217 564-2440
504 E 4th St Ivesdale (61851) ***(G-11756)***

David Michael Productions 630 972-9640
1340 Internationale Pkwy # 100 Woodridge (60517) ***(G-21293)***

David Nelson Exquisite Jewelry 815 741-4702
1312 W Jefferson St Ste 2 Joliet (60435) ***(G-11852)***

David Rotter Prosthetics Ltd 815 255-3220
121 Springfield Ave Ste 3 Joliet (60435) ***(G-11853)***

David S Smith Hldings Amer Inc (PA) 630 296-2000
1201 Windham Pkwy Romeoville (60446) ***(G-17813)***

David Schutte 217 223-5464
1226 N 14th St Quincy (62301) ***(G-16874)***

David Taylor 217 222-6480
2201 N 24th St Quincy (62301) ***(G-16875)***

David V Michals 847 671-6767
9505 Winona Ave Schiller Park (60176) ***(G-18799)***

David Yates 618 656-7879
6407 Sworm Ln Edwardsville (62025) ***(G-8356)***

Davidson Farms of Creston, Creston *Also called Davidson Grain Incorporated* ***(G-7101)***

Davidson Grain Incorporated 815 384-3208
5960 S Woodlawn Rd Creston (60113) ***(G-7101)***

Davidson Redi-Mix Concrete, Oak Forest *Also called T H Davidson & Co Inc* ***(G-15690)***

Davies Mfg, Fulton *Also called Fulton Corporation* ***(G-10152)***

Davies Molding LLC 630 510-8188
350 Kehoe Blvd Carol Stream (60188) ***(G-2974)***

Davis Athletic Equipment Co 708 563-9006
5021 W 66th St Bedford Park (60638) ***(G-1466)***

Davis Machine Company Inc 815 723-9121
312 Henderson Ave Joliet (60432) ***(G-11854)***

Davis Welding, Milford *Also called Robert Davis & Son Inc* ***(G-14036)***

Davis Welding & Manfctg Inc 217 784-5480
511 W 8th St Gibson City (60936) ***(G-10336)***

Davison Co Ltd 815 966-2905
1812 Harlem Blvd Rockford (61103) ***(G-17370)***

Davitz Mold Co Inc 847 426-4848
570 Rock Road Dr Ste D East Dundee (60118) ***(G-8191)***

Dawe's Laboratories, Arlington Heights *Also called Dawes LLC* ***(G-726)***

Dawes LLC (PA) 847 577-2020
3355 N Arlington Hts Rd Arlington Heights (60004) ***(G-726)***

Dawn Equipment Company Inc 815 899-8000
370 N Cross St Sycamore (60178) ***(G-19705)***

Dawn Food Products Inc 815 933-0600
785 N Kinzie Ave Bradley (60915) ***(G-2280)***

Dawn Food Products Inc 815 468-6286
1340 W Sycamore Rd Manteno (60950) ***(G-13446)***

Dax Steel Rule Dies Inc 708 448-4436
13250 Jean Creek Dr Orland Park (60462) ***(G-15950)***

Daxam Inc 847 214-1733
1550 Executive Dr Elgin (60123) ***(G-8564)***

Day International, Batavia *Also called Varn International Inc* ***(G-1440)***

Day International Group Inc 630 406-6501
1333 N Kirk Rd Batavia (60510) ***(G-1371)***

Day Star Systems LLC 618 426-1868
14226 Highway 4 Campbell Hill (62916) ***(G-2814)***

Dayton Superior Corporation (HQ) 847 391-4700
2400 Arthur Ave Elk Grove Village (60007) ***(G-8939)***

Dayton Superior Corporation 219 476-4106
2150b S Us Highway 45 52 Kankakee (60901) ***(G-11962)***

Dayton Superior Corporation 815 936-3300
2150b S Us Highway 45 52 Kankakee (60901) ***(G-11963)***

Dayton Superior Corporation 815 936-3300
2150 W Jeffery St Kankakee (60901) ***(G-11964)***

Dazzling Displays Inc 708 262-6340
3727 N Division St Morris (60450) ***(G-14302)***

Db Professionals, Rolling Meadows *Also called Global Tech & Resources Inc* ***(G-17734)***

Dcc Propane LLC (PA) 217 395-2648
204 N Highway 54 Roberts (60962) ***(G-17105)***

DCS Mechanical, Aurora *Also called Tin Man Heating & Cooling Inc* ***(G-1162)***

Dct, Decatur *Also called D C T/Precision LLC* ***(G-7481)***

Dct Mount Vernon, Mount Vernon *Also called Decatur Custom Tool Inc* ***(G-14606)***

Dcx-Chol Enterprises Inc 309 353-4455
225 Enterprise Dr Pekin (61554) ***(G-16327)***

Ddazzledistributors, Calumet Park *Also called Clark Tashaunda* ***(G-2796)***

Ddc Journal, Chicago *Also called Avenir Publishing Inc* ***(G-3784)***

Ddi Printing, Willowbrook *Also called D & D Business Inc* ***(G-21040)***

Ddk Scientific Corporation 618 235-2849
1 11th Fairway Ct Belleville (62220) ***(G-1543)***

DDN Industries Inc 847 885-8595
2155 Stnngton Ave Ste 221 Hoffman Estates (60169) ***(G-11417)***

Ddu Magnetics Inc 708 325-6587
20152 Cypress Ave Lynwood (60411) ***(G-13293)***

De Amertek Corporation Inc (PA) 630 572-0800
2000 S Finley Rd Lombard (60148) ***(G-13063)***

DE Asbury Inc 217 222-0617
2615 Ellington Rd Quincy (62305) ***(G-16876)***

De Boer & Associates 630 972-1600
736 Dorchester Dr Bolingbrook (60440) ***(G-2167)***

De Enterprises Inc 708 345-8088
1945 Gardner Rd Broadview (60155) ***(G-2429)***

De Kalb Plating Co Inc 815 756-6112
221 Grove St Dekalb (60115) ***(G-7675)***

De Vine Distributors LLC 773 248-7005
3034 W Devon Ave Ste 104 Chicago (60659) ***(G-4326)***

De Vries International Inc 773 248-6695
3139 N Lincoln Ave Chicago (60657) ***(G-4327)***

De-Sta-Co Camco Products, Wheeling *Also called Industrial Motion Control LLC* ***(G-20915)***

Deadline Prtg Clor Copying LLC 847 437-9000
963 Kentucky Ln Elk Grove Village (60007) ***(G-8940)***

Deal Mold Polishing Inc 815 363-8200
1242 Manchester Dr Crystal Lake (60014) ***(G-7192)***

Dealer Tire LLC 847 671-0683
3708 River Rd Ste 600 Franklin Park (60131) ***(G-9926)***

Dealers Edge, Waterloo *Also called D E Signs & Storage LLC* ***(G-20289)***

Dealers Transmission Exchange, Addison *Also called DTE Enterprises LLC* ***(G-100)***

Dean B Scott 630 960-4455
1319 Butterfield Rd # 524 Downers Grove (60515) ***(G-7984)***

Dean Dairy Fluid LLC 815 490-5578
1126 Kilburn Ave Rockford (61101) ***(G-17371)***

Dean Dairy Fluid LLC 815 943-7375
6303 Maxon Rd Harvard (60033) ***(G-11052)***

Dean Dairy Fluid LLC 847 669-5508
11710 Mill St Huntley (60142) ***(G-11534)***

Dean Dairy Fluid LLC 217 428-6726
965 S Wyckles Rd Decatur (62522) ***(G-7483)***

Dean Dairy Ice Cream LLC 815 544-2105
630 Meadow St Belvidere (61008) ***(G-1665)***

Dean Dairy Ice Cream LLC 937 323-5777
3600 River Rd Franklin Park (60131) ***(G-9927)***

Dean Dairy Ice Cream LLC 630 879-0800
1253 Kingsland Dr Batavia (60510) ***(G-1372)***

Dean Food Products Company 847 678-1680
3600 River Rd Franklin Park (60131) ***(G-9928)***

Dean P & O Services, Evanston *Also called Dean Prsthtic Orthtic Svcs Ltd* ***(G-9508)***

Dean Printing Systems 847 526-9545
166 Waltonian Ter Fox Lake (60020) ***(G-9745)***

ALPHABETIC SECTION

Dean Prsthtic Orthtic Svcs Ltd..................847 475-7080
2530 Crawford Ave Ste 218 Evanston (60201) *(G-9508)*
Dearborn Denim & Apparel, Chicago Also called Four Star Denim and AP LLC *(G-4626)*
Dearborn Tool & Mfg Inc..................630 655-1260
7749 S Grant St Burr Ridge (60527) *(G-2669)*
Deatak Inc..................815 322-2013
4004 W Dayton St McHenry (60050) *(G-13735)*
Debbie Harshman..................217 335-2112
725 Bainbridge St Barry (62312) *(G-1249)*
Debcor Inc..................708 333-2191
513 W Taft Dr South Holland (60473) *(G-19207)*
Deborah Morris Gulbrandson Pt..................847 639-4140
2615 3 Oaks Rd Ste 1a Cary (60013) *(G-3154)*
Deborah Zeitler Associates Inc..................312 527-3733
222 Merchandise Mart Plz Chicago (60654) *(G-4328)*
Debourg Corp..................815 338-7852
10004 Bull Valley Rd Bull Valley (60098) *(G-2627)*
Dec Art Designs Inc..................312 329-0553
2970 Maria Ave Ste 226 Northbrook (60062) *(G-15374)*
Dec Tool Corp..................630 513-9883
2651 Dukane Dr Saint Charles (60174) *(G-18181)*
Decal Solutions Unlimited Inc..................847 590-5405
3110 N Arlington Hts Rd Arlington Heights (60004) *(G-727)*
Decal Works LLC..................815 784-4000
2021 Johnson Ct Kingston (60145) *(G-12055)*
Decardy Diecasting, Chicago Also called Vogel/Hill Corporation *(G-6567)*
Decatur Aeration and Temp..................217 733-2800
101 N Main St Fairmount (61841) *(G-9642)*
Decatur Blue Print Company..................217 423-7589
230 W Wood St Decatur (62523) *(G-7484)*
Decatur Bottling Co..................217 429-5415
2112 N Brush College Rd Decatur (62526) *(G-7485)*
Decatur Custom Tool Inc..................618 244-4078
5101 Lake Ter Ne Mount Vernon (62864) *(G-14606)*
Decatur Foundry Inc..................217 429-5261
1745 N Illinois St Decatur (62526) *(G-7486)*
Decatur Industrial Elc Inc (PA)..................217 428-6621
1650 E Garfield Ave Decatur (62526) *(G-7487)*
Decatur Industrial Elc Inc..................618 244-1066
1313 Harlan Rd Mount Vernon (62864) *(G-14607)*
Decatur Plating & Mfg Co..................217 422-8514
1147 E Garfield Ave Decatur (62526) *(G-7488)*
Decatur Ras LLC..................217 433-2794
2121 S Imboden Ct Decatur (62521) *(G-7489)*
Decatur Tribune, Decatur Also called Osborne Publications Inc *(G-7534)*
Decision Systems Company..................815 885-3000
8937 Sheringham Dr Roscoe (61073) *(G-17902)*
Deco Adhesive Pdts 1985 Ltd..................847 472-2100
500 Thorndale Ave Ste H Elk Grove Village (60007) *(G-8941)*
Deco Labels & Tags, Elk Grove Village Also called Deco Adhesive Pdts 1985 Ltd *(G-8941)*
Decoplate, Wheeling Also called Hookset Enterprises LLC *(G-20911)*
Decor Rv Locks, Franklin Park Also called Suburban Metalcraft Inc *(G-10056)*
Decorative Industries Inc..................773 229-0015
6935 W 62nd St Chicago (60638) *(G-4329)*
Decorators Supply Corporation..................773 847-6300
3610 S Morgan St Ste 2 Chicago (60609) *(G-4330)*
Decorators Vault, Mokena Also called Tanya Shipley *(G-14121)*
Decore Tool & Mfg Inc..................630 681-9760
159 Easy St Carol Stream (60188) *(G-2975)*
Decore-Ative Specialties..................630 947-6294
387 Oakmont Dr Cary (60013) *(G-3155)*
Dedicated Tcs LLC..................815 467-9560
23330 S Frontage Rd W Channahon (60410) *(G-3378)*
Dee Drilling Co (PA)..................618 262-4136
431 N Market St Mount Carmel (62863) *(G-14470)*
Dee Erectors Inc..................630 327-1185
8314 Old Fence Ct Downers Grove (60517) *(G-7985)*
Deedrick Machine Inc..................217 598-2366
105 E Market St Sadorus (61872) *(G-18131)*
Deelone Distributing Inc..................309 788-1444
1419 9th St Rock Island (61201) *(G-17215)*
Deem Woodworks..................217 832-9614
22 N Deer Lk Villa Grove (61956) *(G-20122)*
Deep Coat LLC..................630 466-1505
550 N Heartland Dr Sugar Grove (60554) *(G-19642)*
Deep Rock Energy Corporation..................618 548-2779
631 S Broadway Ave Salem (62881) *(G-18335)*
Deep Rock Energy Corporation..................618 548-2779
7601 Oleary Rd Kinmundy (62854) *(G-12058)*
Deephole Drilling Service, Rockford Also called Pgi Mfg LLC *(G-17551)*
Deer Creek Flange Pipe Co Inc..................309 447-6981
300 N Logan St Deer Creek (61733) *(G-7574)*
Deer Processing..................309 799-5994
11928 Niabi Zoo Rd Coal Valley (61240) *(G-6935)*
Deere & Company (PA)..................309 765-8000
1 John Deere Pl Moline (61265) *(G-14138)*
Deere & Company..................309 765-8275
John Deere Moline (61266) *(G-14139)*
Deere & Company..................309 765-2960
1 John Deere Pl Moline (61265) *(G-14140)*
Deerland Dairy, Freeport Also called Douglas Graybill *(G-10106)*
Defender Steel Door & Window (PA)..................708 780-7320
6119 W 35th St Cicero (60804) *(G-6839)*
Deines-Nitz Solutions LLC..................309 658-9985
721 Chase Rd Erie (61250) *(G-9472)*
Deja Investments Inc (PA)..................630 408-9222
279 Marquette Dr Bolingbrook (60440) *(G-2168)*
Dekalb Blower Inc..................630 553-8831
319 E Van Emmon St Yorkville (60560) *(G-21478)*
Dekalb Confectionary Inc (PA)..................815 758-5990
149 N 2nd St Dekalb (60115) *(G-7676)*
Deks North America Inc..................312 219-2110
2700 W Roosevelt Rd Chicago (60608) *(G-4331)*
Del Great Frame Up Systems Inc (PA)..................847 808-1955
9335 Belmont Ave Ste 100 Franklin Park (60131) *(G-9929)*
Del Monte Foods Inc..................309 968-7033
812 S Adams St Manito (61546) *(G-13437)*
Del Storm Products Inc..................217 446-3377
2003 E Voorhees St Danville (61834) *(G-7330)*
Delair Publishing Company Inc..................708 345-7000
2085 Cornell Ave Melrose Park (60160) *(G-13847)*
Delaney Sheet Metal Co..................847 991-9579
116 N Benton St Palatine (60067) *(G-16110)*
Delaney Sheetmetal, Palatine Also called Delaney Sheet Metal Co *(G-16110)*
Delante Group Inc..................312 493-4371
401 N Michigan Ave Chicago (60611) *(G-4332)*
Delavan Times..................309 244-7111
314 S Locust St Delavan (61734) *(G-7715)*
Delco West LLC..................309 799-7543
7507 50th St Milan (61264) *(G-14006)*
Deli Star Ventures Inc..................618 233-0400
3 Amann Ct Belleville (62220) *(G-1544)*
Delicious Treats LLC..................618 410-6722
1905 Marseilles Dr East Saint Louis (62206) *(G-8303)*
Deliteful Taste Foods Inc..................708 251-5121
18241 West St Ste 205 Lansing (60438) *(G-12490)*
Dell Cove Spice Co..................312 339-8389
4900 N Hermitage Ave 3 Chicago (60640) *(G-4333)*
Dell Software Inc..................630 836-0503
975 Weiland Rd Unit 200 Buffalo Grove (60089) *(G-2531)*
Delleman Associates & Corp..................708 345-9520
8 N 6th Ave Maywood (60153) *(G-13668)*
Dells Raceway Park Inc..................815 494-0074
13750 Metric Rd Roscoe (61073) *(G-17903)*
Delmark Records LLC..................773 539-5001
4121 N Rockwell St Chicago (60618) *(G-4334)*
Delobian Foods..................773 564-0913
7424 N Western Ave Chicago (60645) *(G-4335)*
Dels Metal Co..................309 788-1993
1605 1st St Rock Island (61201) *(G-17216)*
Delta Centerless Grinding Inc..................847 288-0300
921820 W Chestnut Ave Franklin Park (60131) *(G-9930)*
Delta Circuits Inc..................630 876-0691
730 W Hawthorne Ln West Chicago (60185) *(G-20569)*
Delta Design Inc..................708 424-9400
3140 W 92nd St Evergreen Park (60805) *(G-9592)*
Delta Erectors Inc..................708 267-9721
18w178 Buckingham Ln Villa Park (60181) *(G-20144)*
Delta Golf, Chicago Also called Golfco Inc *(G-4714)*
Delta Label Inc..................618 233-8984
920 Scheel St Belleville (62221) *(G-1545)*
Delta Laboratories Inc..................630 351-1798
2690 Delta Ln Elk Grove Village (60007) *(G-8942)*
Delta Metal Products Co..................773 745-9220
1953 N Latrobe Ave Chicago (60639) *(G-4336)*
Delta Power Company (PA)..................815 397-6628
4484 Boeing Dr Rockford (61109) *(G-17372)*
Delta Precision Circuits Inc..................847 758-8000
1370 Lively Blvd Elk Grove Village (60007) *(G-8943)*
Delta Press Inc..................847 671-3200
756 W Kimball Ave Palatine (60067) *(G-16111)*
Delta Products Group Inc..................630 357-5544
1655 Eastwood Dr Aurora (60506) *(G-1084)*
Delta Secondary Inc..................630 766-1180
1000 Industrial Dr Ste 3d Bensenville (60106) *(G-1785)*
Delta Steel Boilers Div, Elmhurst Also called Cruise Boiler and Repr Co Inc *(G-9356)*
Delta Structures Inc..................630 694-8700
18w675 18th St Lombard (60148) *(G-13064)*
Delta Waseca, Naperville Also called Newf LLC *(G-14883)*
Delta-Ha, Inc., Westmont Also called Ha-Usa Inc *(G-20745)*
Delta-Therm Corporation..................847 526-2407
6711 Sands Rd Ste A Crystal Lake (60014) *(G-7193)*
Delta-Unibus Corp..................708 409-1200
515 N Railroad Ave Northlake (60164) *(G-15545)*
Deltar Body Interior, Frankfort Also called Illinois Tool Works Inc *(G-9808)*
Deltrol Corp..................708 547-0500
3001 Grant Ave Bellwood (60104) *(G-1621)*

Deltrol Fluid Products, Bellwood *Also called Deltrol Corp* ***(G-1621)***
Deluxe Check Printers, Des Plaines *Also called Deluxe Corporation* ***(G-7753)***
Deluxe Corporation 847 635-7200
1600 E Touhy Ave Des Plaines (60018) ***(G-7753)***
Deluxe Fixture, Franklin Park *Also called Deluxe Stitcher Company Inc* ***(G-9931)***
Deluxe Johnson 847 635-7200
1600 E Touhy Ave Des Plaines (60018) ***(G-7754)***
Deluxe Printing 312 225-0061
2816 S Wentworth Ave # 1 Chicago (60616) ***(G-4337)***
Deluxe Stitcher Company Inc 847 455-4400
3747 Acorn Ln Franklin Park (60131) ***(G-9931)***
Demand One, Aurora *Also called Kelvyn Press Inc* ***(G-991)***
Demarco Industrial Vacuum Corp 815 344-2222
1030 Lutter Dr Crystal Lake (60014) ***(G-7194)***
Dematic Corp 630 852-9200
750 Warrenville Rd # 101 Lisle (60532) ***(G-12885)***
Demco Inc 708 345-4822
2975 W Soffel Ave Melrose Park (60160) ***(G-13848)***
Demco Products Inc 708 636-6240
4644 W 92nd St Oak Lawn (60453) ***(G-15713)***
Demeter Millwork LLC 312 224-4440
135 W Carroll Ave Chicago (60612) ***(G-4338)***
Democrat Company Corp 217 357-2149
31 N Washington St Carthage (62321) ***(G-3135)***
Democrat Message 217 773-3371
123 W Main St Mount Sterling (62353) ***(G-14591)***
Demond Signs Inc 618 624-7260
93 Betty Ln O Fallon (62269) ***(G-15571)***
Demont Guitars LLC (PA) 347 433-6668
61a Stonehill Rd Oswego (60543) ***(G-16001)***
Demoulin Brothers & Company (PA) 618 664-2000
1025 S 4th St Greenville (62246) ***(G-10832)***
Demuth Steel Products Inc 815 997-1116
3939 S Central Ave Rockford (61102) ***(G-17373)***
Den Graphix Inc 309 962-2000
111 S Chestnut St Le Roy (61752) ***(G-12539)***
Denbur Inc (PA) 630 986-9667
650 Blackhawk Dr Westmont (60559) ***(G-20735)***
Dendro Co 312 772-6836
481 Scotland Rd Unit 102 Lakemoor (60051) ***(G-12471)***
Dennco Inc (PA) 708 862-0070
14350 S Saginaw Ave Burnham (60633) ***(G-2645)***
Dennis Carnes 618 244-1770
2118 Brownsville Rd Mount Vernon (62864) ***(G-14608)***
Dennis Kellogg Ofc 773 588-3421
4104 N Elston Ave Chicago (60618) ***(G-4339)***
Dennis Wright 847 816-6110
229 Augusta Dr Vernon Hills (60061) ***(G-20049)***
Denoninational Headquarters, Elgin *Also called Church of Brethren Inc* ***(G-8539)***
Denor Graphics Inc 847 364-1130
665 Lunt Ave Elk Grove Village (60007) ***(G-8944)***
Denovx LLC (PA) 910 333-6689
3440 S Dearborn St Ste 20 Chicago (60616) ***(G-4340)***
Denoyer - Geppert Science Co 800 621-1014
7514 Saint Louis Ave Skokie (60076) ***(G-18948)***
Denta Treet LLC 618 384-1028
17707 E Angling Rd Mount Vernon (62864) ***(G-14609)***
Dental Arts Laboratories Inc 309 342-3117
1172 Monroe St Ste 5 Galesburg (61401) ***(G-10190)***
Dental Craft Corp 815 385-7132
5414 Craftwell Dr Ringwood (60072) ***(G-17041)***
Dental Crafts Lab Inc 815 872-3221
211 S 5th St Princeton (61356) ***(G-16806)***
Dental Laboratory Inc 630 262-3700
37w391 Keslinger Rd Geneva (60134) ***(G-10265)***
Dental Sealants & More 309 692-6435
214 W Wolf Rd Peoria (61614) ***(G-16429)***
Dental Technologies Inc 847 677-5500
6901 N Hamlin Ave Lincolnwood (60712) ***(G-12816)***
Dentalez Alabama Inc 773 624-4330
5000 S Halsted St Chicago (60609) ***(G-4341)***
Dentsply Sirona Inc 847 640-4800
385 Airport Rd Ste 104 Elgin (60123) ***(G-8565)***
Deny Machine Shop, Lansing *Also called DMS Industries Inc* ***(G-12491)***
Department Streets Sanitation, Chicago *Also called City of Chicago* ***(G-4157)***
Dependable Electric 618 592-3314
728 E State Hwy 33 Oblong (62449) ***(G-15826)***
Dept 28 Inc 847 285-1343
1169 Tower Rd Schaumburg (60173) ***(G-18505)***
Depth Action Marketing Group 847 475-7122
2512 Lawndale Ave Evanston (60201) ***(G-9509)***
Depue Mechanical Inc (PA) 815 447-2267
216 W 4th S Depue (61322) ***(G-7716)***
Deputante Inc 773 545-9531
4113 W Newport Ave Chicago (60641) ***(G-4342)***
Der Holtzmacher Ltd 815 895-4887
1649 Afton Rd Sycamore (60178) ***(G-19706)***
Der-Holtzmacher, Sycamore *Also called Der Holtzmacher Ltd* ***(G-19706)***
Derbytech Inc 309 755-2662
700 16th Ave East Moline (61244) ***(G-8225)***
Derbyteescom 309 264-1033
622 Gateway Dr Henry (61537) ***(G-11162)***
Dermatique Laser & Skin 630 262-2515
407 S 3rd St Ste 240 Geneva (60134) ***(G-10266)***
Derse Inc 847 473-2149
3696 Burwood Dr Waukegan (60085) ***(G-20435)***
Des Moines Stamp Mfg Co, Moline *Also called A 1 Marking Products* ***(G-14130)***
Des Plaines Journal Inc 847 299-5511
622 Graceland Ave Des Plaines (60016) ***(G-7755)***
Des Plaines Printing LLC 847 465-3300
999 Commerce Ct Buffalo Grove (60089) ***(G-2532)***
Des Plaines Valley News, Summit Argo *Also called Heritage Media Svcs Co of Ill* ***(G-19679)***
Des4ta, Chicago *Also called Desforte LLC* ***(G-4343)***
Desco Dryers, Elk Grove Village *Also called Desco Inc* ***(G-8945)***
Desco Inc 847 439-2130
1240 Howard St Elk Grove Village (60007) ***(G-8945)***
Desforte LLC 224 301-5364
5634 N Kenmore Ave # 106 Chicago (60660) ***(G-4343)***
Deshamusic Inc 818 257-2716
1645 W Ogden Ave Unit 713 Chicago (60612) ***(G-4344)***
Desi Talk LLC 212 675-7515
2652 W Devon Ave Ste B Chicago (60659) ***(G-4345)***
Desi Talk Chicago, Chicago *Also called Desi Talk LLC* ***(G-4345)***
Design and Woodworks, Fairbury *Also called Avoca Ridge Ltd* ***(G-9604)***
Design Corrugating Company 314 821-4300
400 S Baughman Rd Taylorville (62568) ***(G-19754)***
Design Enhanced Mfg Co 815 946-3562
9796 W Il Route 64 Polo (61064) ***(G-16755)***
Design Graphics Inc 815 462-3323
23007 Long Beach Dr Frankfort (60423) ***(G-9783)***
Design Group Signage Corp 847 390-0350
2135 Frontage Rd Des Plaines (60018) ***(G-7756)***
Design Lab, Chicago *Also called Interesting Products Inc* ***(G-4944)***
Design Loft Imaging Inc 847 439-2486
393 Bianco Dr Elk Grove Village (60007) ***(G-8946)***
Design Manufacturing & Eqp Co 217 824-9219
400 S Baughman Rd Taylorville (62568) ***(G-19755)***
Design Metals Fabrication Inc 630 752-9060
361 Randy Rd Ste 106 Carol Stream (60188) ***(G-2976)***
Design On Time 815 464-5750
9645 Lincolnway Ln # 103 Frankfort (60423) ***(G-9784)***
Design Phase Inc 847 473-0077
1771 S Lakeside Dr Waukegan (60085) ***(G-20436)***
Design Plus Industries Inc (PA) 309 697-9778
6311 W Development Dr Peoria (61604) ***(G-16430)***
Design Systems Inc 309 263-7706
361 Erie Ave Morton (61550) ***(G-14358)***
Design Technology Inc 630 920-1300
768 Burr Oak Dr Westmont (60559) ***(G-20736)***
Design Woodworks 847 566-6603
27266 N Owens Rd Mundelein (60060) ***(G-14682)***
Designa Access Corporation (HQ) 630 891-3105
777 Oakmont Ln Ste 2000 Westmont (60559) ***(G-20737)***
Designation Inc 847 367-9100
1352 Armour Blvd Ste A Mundelein (60060) ***(G-14683)***
Designed Eqp Acquisition Corp 847 647-5000
1510 Lunt Ave Elk Grove Village (60007) ***(G-8947)***
Designed For Just For You 309 221-2667
106 Pam Ln Macomb (61455) ***(G-13391)***
Designed Plastics Inc 630 694-7300
1133 Bryn Mawr Ave Bensenville (60106) ***(G-1786)***
Designed Stairs Inc (PA) 815 786-2021
1480 E 6th St Sandwich (60548) ***(G-18367)***
Designer Blinds, Naperville *Also called Carol Andrzejewski* ***(G-14790)***
Designers Point Inc 224 578-7043
2150 Plum Grove Rd Rolling Meadows (60008) ***(G-17726)***
Designovations Inc 815 645-8598
8020 Commercial Ave Loves Park (61111) ***(G-13207)***
Designs & Signs By Anderson, Ottawa *Also called Anbek Inc* ***(G-16039)***
Designs and Signs By Anderson, La Salle *Also called Anbek Inc* ***(G-12104)***
Designs Unlimited 618 357-6728
1242 S Main St Pinckneyville (62274) ***(G-16613)***
Desk & Door Nameplate Company 815 806-8670
9310 Gulfstream Rd Frankfort (60423) ***(G-9785)***
Deslauriers Inc (PA) 708 544-4455
1245 Barnsdale Rd La Grange Park (60526) ***(G-12095)***
Dessertwerks Inc (PA) 847 487-8239
1421 Allyson Ct Libertyville (60048) ***(G-12647)***
Details Etc 708 932-5543
19256 85th Ct Mokena (60448) ***(G-14078)***
Detonics Defense Technologies, Millstadt *Also called Double Nickel LLC* ***(G-14045)***
Detrex Corporation 708 345-3806
2537 W Le Moyne St Melrose Park (60160) ***(G-13849)***
Deublin Company (PA) 847 689-8600
2050 Norman Dr Waukegan (60085) ***(G-20437)***
Deuce Development Corp 309 353-6324
100 Broadway St Pekin (61554) ***(G-16328)***

ALPHABETIC SECTION

Dev Base LLC 319 321-3014
111 W Wacker Dr Apt 4607 Chicago (60601) *(G-4346)*
Devanco Foods, Carol Stream Also called Bkbg Enterprises Inc *(G-2947)*
Devansoy Inc 712 792-9665
10010 N Rock City Rd Rock City (61070) *(G-17175)*
Devco Casting 312 456-0076
5 S Wabash Ave Ste 407 Chicago (60603) *(G-4347)*
Device Technologies Inc 630 553-7178
1211 Badger St Ste H Yorkville (60560) *(G-21479)*
Devil Dog Arms Inc 847 790-4004
650 Telser Rd Lake Zurich (60047) *(G-12402)*
Devils Due Publishing 773 412-6427
3021 W Diversey Ave Apt 2 Chicago (60647) *(G-4348)*
Devnet Incorporated 815 899-6850
1709 Afton Rd Sycamore (60178) *(G-19707)*
Devon Discount Pharmacy, Chicago Also called Power Partners LLC *(G-5847)*
Devon Precision Machine Pdts 847 233-9700
10140 Pacific Ave Franklin Park (60131) *(G-9932)*
Dewrich Inc 847 249-7445
1379 Saint Paul Ave Gurnee (60031) *(G-10868)*
Dex Blue Corp 847 916-7744
6321 Dempster St 174 Morton Grove (60053) *(G-14399)*
Dexton Enterprises 309 788-1881
1324 2nd St Rock Island (61201) *(G-17217)*
Deyco Inc 630 553-5666
102 Beaver St Yorkville (60560) *(G-21480)*
Dezign Sewing Inc 773 549-4336
4001 N Rvnswd Ave 505 Chicago (60613) *(G-4349)*
Df Fan Services Inc 630 876-1495
495 Wegner Dr West Chicago (60185) *(G-20570)*
Df Goldsmith, Evanston Also called Dfg Mercury Corp *(G-9510)*
Dfg Mercury Corp 847 869-7800
909 Pitner Ave Evanston (60202) *(G-9510)*
Dfk America Inc 630 324-6793
2464 Wisconsin Ave Downers Grove (60515) *(G-7986)*
Dg Digital Printing 815 961-0000
728 N Prospect St Ste 1 Rockford (61107) *(G-17374)*
Dg Wood Processing 217 543-2128
120 E Cr 200 N Arthur (61911) *(G-852)*
Dgm Electronics Inc 815 389-2040
13654 Metric Rd Roscoe (61073) *(G-17904)*
Dgs Import LLC 800 211-9646
5513 N Cumberland Ave # 707 Chicago (60656) *(G-4350)*
Dharti Food, Chicago Also called Vhrk Food Inc *(G-6541)*
Di Stefani T Shirt Printing 618 282-2380
4716 Stefani Rd Red Bud (62278) *(G-16992)*
Di-Carr Printing Company 708 863-0069
1630 S Cicero Ave Cicero (60804) *(G-6840)*
Diablo Furnaces LLC 815 636-7502
7723 Burden Rd Machesney Park (61115) *(G-13340)*
Diageo 815 267-4499
24460 W 143rd St Plainfield (60544) *(G-16655)*
Diageo North America Inc 815 267-4400
24440 W 143rd St Plainfield (60544) *(G-16656)*
Diager USA Inc 630 762-8443
1820 Wallace Ave Ste 122 Saint Charles (60174) *(G-18182)*
Diagnostic Photonics Inc 312 320-5478
222 Merchandise Mart Plz # 1230 Chicago (60654) *(G-4351)*
Diagraph MSP & ITW Company, Marion Also called Illinois Tool Works Inc *(G-13518)*
Diagrind Inc 708 460-4333
10491 164th Pl Orland Park (60467) *(G-15951)*
Dial Industries Inc 815 397-7994
2902 Eastrock Dr Rockford (61109) *(G-17375)*
Dial Machine Inc 815 397-6660
2902 Eastrock Dr Rockford (61109) *(G-17376)*
Dial Tool Industries Inc 630 543-3600
201 S Church St Addison (60101) *(G-87)*
Diamant Toys Unlimited, Batavia Also called Amav Enterprises Ltd *(G-1346)*
Diamond Bag & Print Co, Northbrook Also called Diamond Cellophane Pdts Inc *(G-15375)*
Diamond Blast Corporation 708 681-2640
1741 N 30th Ave Melrose Park (60160) *(G-13850)*
Diamond Cellophane Pdts Inc 847 418-3000
2855 Shermer Rd Northbrook (60062) *(G-15375)*
Diamond Coat, Batavia Also called Aggressive Motorsports Inc *(G-1343)*
Diamond Die & Bevel Cutng LLC 224 387-3200
2087 Foster Ave Wheeling (60090) *(G-20878)*
Diamond Edge Manufacturing 630 458-1630
644 W Winthrop Ave Addison (60101) *(G-88)*
Diamond Envelope Corporation (PA) 630 499-2800
2270 White Oak Cir Aurora (60502) *(G-951)*
Diamond Graphics of Berwyn 708 749-2500
6625 26th St Ste 1 Berwyn (60402) *(G-1950)*
Diamond Heat Treat Inc 815 873-1348
3691 Publishers Dr Rockford (61109) *(G-17377)*
Diamond Icic Corporation 309 269-8652
916 21st St Rock Island (61201) *(G-17218)*
Diamond Industrial Sales Ltd 630 858-3687
175 Cortland Ct Glen Ellyn (60137) *(G-10400)*

Diamond Industries LLC 612 859-1210
3041 S Shields Ave Chicago (60616) *(G-4352)*
Diamond Machine Werks Inc 847 437-0665
2445 E Oakton St Arlington Heights (60005) *(G-728)*
Diamond Marketing Solutions, Carol Stream Also called National Data Svcs Chicago Inc *(G-3038)*
Diamond Plating Company Inc 618 451-7740
5 Caine Dr Madison (62060) *(G-13408)*
Diamond Quality Manufacturing 815 521-4184
24109 S Northern Ill Dr Channahon (60410) *(G-3379)*
Diamond Ready Mix Inc 630 355-5414
27w742 North Ln Naperville (60540) *(G-14815)*
Diamond Screen Process Inc 847 439-6200
321 Bond St Elk Grove Village (60007) *(G-8948)*
Diamond Sign Design 630 543-4900
603 W Factory Rd Addison (60101) *(G-89)*
Diamond Spray Painting Inc 630 513-5600
1840 Production Dr Saint Charles (60174) *(G-18183)*
Diamond Teez & More LLC 618 579-9876
4134 Alby St Alton (62002) *(G-552)*
Diamond Tool & Mold Inc 630 543-7011
1212 W National Ave Addison (60101) *(G-90)*
Diamond Web Printing LLC 630 663-0351
2820 Hitchcock Ave Downers Grove (60515) *(G-7987)*
Diamond Wholesale Group LLC 708 529-7495
7325 W 87th St Bridgeview (60455) *(G-2340)*
Diamondaire Corp 630 355-7464
117 W Main St Ste 110 Saint Charles (60174) *(G-18184)*
Dianas Bananas Inc 773 638-6800
2733 W Harrison St Chicago (60612) *(G-4353)*
Diaz Pallets II Corporation 630 340-3736
760 Prairie St Aurora (60506) *(G-1085)*
Diaz Printing 773 887-3366
4725 W Grand Ave Chicago (60639) *(G-4354)*
Dibi Accessories, Palatine Also called Daniel Bruce LLC *(G-16108)*
Dice Mold & Engineering Inc 630 773-3595
75 N Prospect Ave Itasca (60143) *(G-11642)*
Dicianni Graphics Incorporated 630 833-5100
421 S Addison Rd Addison (60101) *(G-91)*
Dicke Safety Products, Downers Grove Also called Dicke Tool Company *(G-7988)*
Dicke Tool Company (PA) 630 969-0050
1201 Warren Ave Downers Grove (60515) *(G-7988)*
Dickey Sign Co 618 797-1262
116 Springfield Dr Granite City (62040) *(G-10703)*
Dicks Asphalt Service 815 932-7157
2695 E 3500s Rd Kankakee (60901) *(G-11965)*
Dicks Custom Cabinet Shop 815 358-2663
202 W Main St Cornell (61319) *(G-7012)*
Dickson Company, The, Addison Also called Dickson/Unigage Inc *(G-92)*
Dickson/Unigage Inc 630 543-3747
930 S Westwood Ave Addison (60101) *(G-92)*
Dicom Transportation Group LP (PA) 312 255-4800
676 N Michigan Ave # 3700 Chicago (60611) *(G-4355)*
Die Cast Machinery LLC 847 360-9170
3246 W Monroe St Waukegan (60085) *(G-20438)*
Die Cast Quality Services Inc 708 582-3584
438 S Dee Rd Park Ridge (60068) *(G-16273)*
Die Cut Group Inc 630 629-9211
850 N Du Page Ave Ste 5 Lombard (60148) *(G-13065)*
Die Cut Plates, Dolton Also called T A U Inc *(G-7940)*
Die Cutters Inc 618 532-3448
306 S Chestnut St Centralia (62801) *(G-3228)*
Die Darrell 309 282-9112
106 W Burton Ave Eureka (61530) *(G-9480)*
Die Mold Jig Grinding & Mfg 847 228-1444
1485 Landmeier Rd Ste M Elk Grove Village (60007) *(G-8949)*
Die Pros Inc 630 543-2025
1233 W Capitol Dr Ste B Addison (60101) *(G-93)*
Die Specialty Co 312 303-5738
1510 Cleveland Ave La Grange Park (60526) *(G-12096)*
Die World Steel Rule Dies 815 399-8675
2519 15th Ave Rockford (61108) *(G-17378)*
Diebold Nixdorf Incorporated 847 598-3300
900 National Pkwy Ste 420 Schaumburg (60173) *(G-18506)*
Diebolds Cabinet Shop 773 772-3076
1938 N Springfield Ave Chicago (60647) *(G-4356)*
Diecrafters Inc 708 656-3336
1349 S 55th Ct Cicero (60804) *(G-6841)*
Diehl Metering LLC 331 204-6540
1813 N Mill St Ste C Naperville (60563) *(G-14816)*
Diemasters Manufacturing Inc 847 640-9900
2100 Touhy Ave Elk Grove Village (60007) *(G-8950)*
Diemold Service Company 847 885-6007
1591 Elmhurst Rd Elk Grove Village (60007) *(G-8951)*
Diequa Corporation (PA) 630 980-1133
180 Covington Dr Bloomingdale (60108) *(G-1988)*
Dierzen Trailer Co 815 695-5291
101 N Fayette St Newark (60541) *(G-15076)*
Dierzen-Kewanee Heavy Inds 309 853-2316
101 Franklin St Kewanee (61443) *(G-12030)*

Dies Plus Inc 630 285-1065
  2 E Main St Carpentersville (60110) *(G-3100)*
Diesel Radiator Co (PA) 800 345-9244
  1990 Janice Ave Melrose Park (60160) *(G-13851)*
Diesel Radiator Co 708 865-7299
  3030 W Hirsch St Melrose Park (60160) *(G-13852)*
Dietrich Industries Inc 815 207-0110
  3901 Olympic Blvd Joliet (60431) *(G-11855)*
Dietzgen Corporation 217 348-8111
  1555 N 5th St Charleston (61920) *(G-3401)*
Digi Trax Corporation 847 613-2100
  650 Heathrow Dr Lincolnshire (60069) *(G-12759)*
Digistitch Embroidery & Design 773 229-8630
  6535 W Archer Ave Chicago (60638) *(G-4357)*
Digital Artz LLC 618 651-1500
  188 Woodcrest Dr Highland (62249) *(G-11213)*
Digital Check Corp (PA) 847 446-2285
  630 Dundee Rd Ste 210 Northbrook (60062) *(G-15376)*
Digital Check Technologies, Northbrook Also called Digital Check Corp *(G-15376)*
Digital Edge Signs Inc 847 838-4760
  248 W Depot St A Antioch (60002) *(G-609)*
Digital Factory Tech Inc 513 560-4074
  801 S Financial Pl # 2310 Chicago (60605) *(G-4358)*
Digital Greensigns Inc 312 624-8550
  1606 W Grace St Chicago (60613) *(G-4359)*
Digital H2o Inc 847 456-8424
  18 S Michigan Ave Fl 12 Chicago (60603) *(G-4360)*
Digital Homes Technologies, Palatine Also called J P Goldenne Incorporated *(G-16132)*
Digital Hub LLC 312 943-6161
  5656 Mcdermott Dr Berkeley (60163) *(G-1940)*
Digital Ignite LLC (HQ) 630 317-7904
  101 W 22nd St Ste 104 Lombard (60148) *(G-13066)*
Digital Minds Inc 847 430-3390
  9501 W Devon Ave Ste 603 Rosemont (60018) *(G-18017)*
Digital Optics Tech Inc 847 358-2592
  1645 Hicks Rd Ste H Rolling Meadows (60008) *(G-17727)*
Digital Printing & Total Graph 630 627-7400
  70 Eisenhower Ln N Lombard (60148) *(G-13067)*
Digital Prtg & Total Graphics 630 627-7400
  123 Eisenhower Ln N Lombard (60148) *(G-13068)*
Digital Publishing Group, Chicago Also called A To Z Type & Graphic Inc *(G-3491)*
Digital Realty Inc 630 428-7979
  303 N Mill St Naperville (60540) *(G-14817)*
Digitaldrive Tech 630 510-1580
  1601 E Prairie Ave Wheaton (60187) *(G-20796)*
Dike-O-Seal Incorporated 773 254-3224
  3965 S Keeler Ave Chicago (60632) *(G-4361)*
Dilars Embroidery & Monograms 815 338-6066
  1320 Zimmerman Rd Woodstock (60098) *(G-21381)*
Dimension Molding Corporation 630 628-0777
  777 W Annoreno Dr Addison (60101) *(G-94)*
Dimples Donuts 630 406-0303
  328 E Wilson St Batavia (60510) *(G-1373)*
Dines Machine & Manufacturing, Danville Also called G P Cole Inc *(G-7338)*
Dinger Bat Company, Ridgway Also called Dinger Bats LLC *(G-17036)*
Dinger Bats LLC 618 272-7250
  109 S Kimbro St Ridgway (62979) *(G-17036)*
Dingo Inc 217 868-5615
  14480 N 1025th St Effingham (62401) *(G-8395)*
Dinkels Bakery Inc 773 281-7300
  3329 N Lincoln Ave Chicago (60657) *(G-4362)*
Dino Design Incorporated 773 763-4223
  9023 Oriole Ave Morton Grove (60053) *(G-14400)*
Dino Publishing LLC 312 822-9266
  350 W Hubbard St Ste 400 Chicago (60654) *(G-4363)*
Dionex Corporation 847 295-7500
  3000 Lakeside Dr Ste 116n Bannockburn (60015) *(G-1199)*
Dip Seal Plastics Inc 815 398-3533
  2311 23rd Ave Rockford (61104) *(G-17379)*
Dippit Inc 630 762-6500
  1879 N Neltnor Blvd 326 West Chicago (60185) *(G-20571)*
Direct Aerosystems Inc 630 509-2141
  2680 Diehl Rd Aurora (60502) *(G-952)*
Direct Dimension Inc (PA) 815 479-1936
  8195 Pyott Rd Algonquin (60156) *(G-369)*
Direct Envelope, Wheeling Also called Managed Marketing Inc *(G-20935)*
Direct Impressions, Champaign Also called News-Gazette Inc *(G-3325)*
Direct Mail Equipment Services 815 485-7010
  14460 W Edison Dr Ste D New Lenox (60451) *(G-15030)*
Direct Pallet Inc 847 697-1019
  1144 Saint Charles St Elgin (60120) *(G-8566)*
Direct Selling Strategies 847 993-3188
  5600 N River Rd Ste 800 Rosemont (60018) *(G-18018)*
Directions Magazine, Glencoe Also called Elliott Jsj & Associates Inc *(G-10429)*
Dirk Vander Noot 224 558-1878
  811 Andover Ct Prospect Heights (60070) *(G-16838)*
Dirtt Envmtl Solutions Inc 312 245-2870
  325 N Wells St Ste 1000 Chicago (60654) *(G-4364)*
Disa Holding Corp (HQ) 630 820-3000
  80 Kendall Point Dr Oswego (60543) *(G-16002)*
Disco Machine & Mfg Inc 708 456-0835
  7327 W Agatite Ave Norridge (60706) *(G-15233)*
Discount Computer Supply Inc 847 883-8743
  871 Shambliss Ln Buffalo Grove (60089) *(G-2533)*
Discount Eyewear, Rock Falls Also called Scuba Optics Inc *(G-17195)*
Discuss Music Education Co 773 561-2796
  2720 W Winnemac Ave Apt 1 Chicago (60625) *(G-4365)*
Disk.com, McHenry Also called Corporate Disk Company *(G-13730)*
Diskin Systems Inc 815 276-7288
  9550 S Il Route 31 Algonquin (60102) *(G-370)*
Dispense-Rite, Northbrook Also called Diversified Metal Products Inc *(G-15377)*
Display Link Inc 815 968-0778
  311 S Main St Rockford (61101) *(G-17380)*
Display Plan Lpdg 773 525-3787
  1901 N Clybourn Ave # 400 Chicago (60614) *(G-4366)*
Display Signs & Design 800 782-1558
  5578 N Northwest Hwy Chicago (60630) *(G-4367)*
Displayplan US, Chicago Also called Display Plan Lpdg *(G-4366)*
Distillery Geeks Inc 630 240-7259
  2020 N California Ave Chicago (60647) *(G-4368)*
Distillery Wine & Allied 309 347-1444
  300 Mclean St Pekin (61554) *(G-16329)*
Distinctive Foods LLC (PA) 847 459-3600
  654 Wheeling Rd Wheeling (60090) *(G-20879)*
Distinctive Foods LLC 847 459-3600
  450 Evergreen Ave Bensenville (60106) *(G-1787)*
Distinctive SIGns& The Neon Ex 847 245-7159
  1868 E Belvidere Rd A Grayslake (60030) *(G-10767)*
Distribution Center, Bensenville Also called Fresenius Kabi LLC *(G-1805)*
Distribution Center, Ottawa Also called Clover Imaging Group LLC *(G-16048)*
Distribution Enterprises Inc 847 582-9276
  28457 N Ballard Dr Ste A1 Lake Forest (60045) *(G-12243)*
District 32820, Elk Grove Village Also called R R Donnelley & Sons Company *(G-9211)*
District 97 .... 708 289-7064
  254 Pleasant St Apt 2 Oak Park (60302) *(G-15750)*
Div. 5, Chicago Also called Summit Architectural Mtls LLC *(G-6265)*
Diva Dream Signs 618 201-4348
  807 E Main St Christopher (62822) *(G-6824)*
Divergent Alliance LLC 847 531-0559
  511 Eichler Dr West Dundee (60118) *(G-20662)*
Diversatech Metalfab LLC 309 747-4159
  108 S Center St Gridley (61744) *(G-10843)*
Diversfied III Green Works LLC 773 544-7777
  2419 W Byron St Chicago (60618) *(G-4369)*
Diversfied Lbling Slutions Inc (HQ) 630 625-1225
  1285 Hamilton Pkwy Itasca (60143) *(G-11643)*
Diversified CPC Intl Inc (HQ) 815 424-2000
  24338 W Durkee Rd Channahon (60410) *(G-3380)*
Diversified Fleet MGT Inc 815 578-1051
  776 Ridgeview Dr McHenry (60050) *(G-13736)*
Diversified Machining Inc 815 316-8561
  6151 Montague Rd Rockford (61102) *(G-17381)*
Diversified Metal Products Inc 847 753-9595
  2205 Carlson Dr Northbrook (60062) *(G-15377)*
Diversified Print Group 630 893-8920
  358 W Army Trail Rd # 140 Bloomingdale (60108) *(G-1989)*
Diversifoam Products, Mendota Also called Minnesota Diversified Pdts Inc *(G-13950)*
Divine Signs & Graphics, Schaumburg Also called Divine Signs Inc *(G-18507)*
Divine Signs Inc 847 534-9220
  601 Estes Ave Schaumburg (60193) *(G-18507)*
Division 5 Metals Inc 815 901-5001
  2314 Old State Rd Kirkland (60146) *(G-12059)*
Division of Monoxivent, Rock Island Also called Crawford Heating & Cooling Co *(G-17212)*
Division Sonoco Products Co, Franklin Park Also called Clear Pack Company *(G-9911)*
Dix-Mcguire Commodities - LLC 847 496-5320
  201 E Dundee Rd Ste 2 Palatine (60074) *(G-16112)*
Dixie Carbonic Inc 217 428-2068
  3985 E Harrison Ave Decatur (62526) *(G-7490)*
Dixie Cream Donut Shop 618 937-4866
  510 W Main St West Frankfort (62896) *(G-20670)*
Dixline Corporation (PA) 309 932-2011
  136 Exchange St Galva (61434) *(G-10230)*
Dixline Corporation 309 932-2011
  26 Sw 4th Ave Galva (61434) *(G-10231)*
Dixmor Division, Chicago Heights Also called Ptc Group Holdings Corp *(G-6766)*
Dixon Brass 630 323-3716
  40 Chestnut Ave Westmont (60559) *(G-20738)*
Dixon Direct LLC (HQ) 815 284-2211
  1226 W 7th St Dixon (61021) *(G-7896)*
Dixon Graphics Incorporated 217 351-6100
  105 W John St Champaign (61820) *(G-3285)*
Dixon Pallet Service 773 238-9569
  10340 S Lowe Ave Chicago (60628) *(G-4370)*
Dixon Telegraph 815 284-2224
  113 S Peoria Ave Ste 1 Dixon (61021) *(G-7897)*
Dixon-Marquette Cement, Dixon Also called Southfield Corporation *(G-7918)*

Diy Cabinet Warehouse, Arthur *Also called Masterbrand Cabinets Inc* ***(G-869)***
Dj Illinois River Valley Calls....309 348-2112
7949 State Rte 78 Pekin (61554) ***(G-16330)***
Dj Liquors Inc....815 645-1145
5657 N Junction Way Davis Junction (61020) ***(G-7421)***
Dj Titanium....312 823-2963
4016 S California Ave Chicago (60632) ***(G-4371)***
DJB Corporation....815 469-7533
9527 Corsair Rd Ste 2w Frankfort (60423) ***(G-9786)***
Djh Industries Inc....309 246-8456
400 N Commercial St Lacon (61540) ***(G-12126)***
Djr Inc....773 581-5204
5900 W 65th St Chicago (60638) ***(G-4372)***
Djw Assembly Inc....847 956-5330
2912 Malmo Dr Arlington Heights (60005) ***(G-729)***
Djw Machining & Assembly, Arlington Heights *Also called Djw Assembly Inc* ***(G-729)***
DK Knutsen....815 626-4388
609 W 3rd St Sterling (61081) ***(G-19505)***
DK Precision Inc....847 985-8008
614 Lunt Ave Schaumburg (60193) ***(G-18508)***
Dkb Partners Inc....618 632-6718
230 Obernuefemann Rd O Fallon (62269) ***(G-15572)***
Dla Document Services....618 256-4686
901 South Dr Bldg 700e Scott Air Force Base (62225) ***(G-18857)***
DLM Manufacturing Inc....815 964-3800
919 Taylor St Rockford (61101) ***(G-17382)***
Dlp Coating, Elk Grove Village *Also called Durable Longlasting* ***(G-8957)***
DLS Custom Embroidery Inc....847 593-5957
1665 Tonne Rd Elk Grove Village (60007) ***(G-8952)***
DLS Printing & Promotions, Elk Grove Village *Also called DLS Custom Embroidery Inc* ***(G-8952)***
Dlt Electric LLC....630 552-4115
202 W Main St Plano (60545) ***(G-16730)***
Dlux Brand LLC....630 215-5557
1s072 Luther Ave Lombard (60148) ***(G-13069)***
DMarv Design Specialty Prtrs....708 389-4420
13010 Western Ave Blue Island (60406) ***(G-2118)***
Dmg Charlotte LLC (HQ)....704 583-1193
2400 Huntington Blvd Hoffman Estates (60192) ***(G-11418)***
Dmg Mori Seiki U.S.a, Hoffman Estates *Also called Dmg Mori Usa Inc* ***(G-11419)***
Dmg Mori Usa Inc (HQ)....847 593-5400
2400 Huntington Blvd Hoffman Estates (60192) ***(G-11419)***
Dmi Information Process Center....773 378-2644
5090 W Harrison St Chicago (60644) ***(G-4373)***
DMJ Group Inc....847 322-7533
2413 W Algonquin Rd # 227 Algonquin (60102) ***(G-371)***
Dmk Specialties....815 919-7282
17435 Tanglewood Lockport (60441) ***(G-12987)***
Dml Distribution Inc....630 839-9041
1814 W Weathersfield Way Schaumburg (60193) ***(G-18509)***
Dml LLC....630 231-8873
419 Colford Ave West Chicago (60185) ***(G-20572)***
Dms Inc....847 726-2828
1120 Ensell Rd Lake Zurich (60047) ***(G-12403)***
DMS Industries Inc (PA)....708 895-8000
1925 177th St Lansing (60438) ***(G-12491)***
Dmtg North America LLC....815 637-8500
1301 Eddy Ave Rockford (61103) ***(G-17383)***
Dnepr Techologies Inc....773 603-3360
3304 N Broadway St # 163 Chicago (60657) ***(G-4374)***
DNp Enterprises Inc (PA)....630 628-7210
1213 W Capitol Dr Addison (60101) ***(G-95)***
Do It Best, Monee *Also called Wille Bros Co* ***(G-14213)***
Do It Best, Chicago *Also called Dumore Supplies Inc* ***(G-4403)***
Do You See Entertainment, Chicago *Also called Do You See What I See Entertai* ***(G-4375)***
Do You See What I See Entertai....773 612-1269
2544 W North Ave Apt 3d Chicago (60647) ***(G-4375)***
Do-Rite Die & Engineering Co....708 754-4355
3344 Butler St S Chicago Hts (60411) ***(G-18120)***
Dober Chemical Corp (PA)....630 410-7300
11230 Katherines Crossin Woodridge (60517) ***(G-21294)***
Dober Group, Woodridge *Also called Dober Chemical Corp* ***(G-21294)***
Dobinski Marketing....773 248-5880
3843 N Fremont St Chicago (60613) ***(G-4376)***
Dobratz Sales Company Inc....224 569-3081
5945 Lucerne Ln Lake In The Hills (60156) ***(G-12332)***
Docket Technologies Inc....415 489-0127
211 W Wacker Dr Ste 1703 Chicago (60606) ***(G-4377)***
Doctors Choice Inc....312 666-1111
600 W Cermak Rd Ste 1a Chicago (60616) ***(G-4378)***
Doctors Interior Plantscaping....708 333-3323
255 W Taft Dr South Holland (60473) ***(G-19208)***
Document Capture Technologies, Wood Dale *Also called Ambir Technology Inc* ***(G-21161)***
Document Centre, Roselle *Also called Composition One Inc* ***(G-17946)***
Document Publishing Group....847 783-0670
2511 Tech Dr Ste 102 Elgin (60124) ***(G-8567)***
Document Services, Champaign *Also called University of Illinois* ***(G-3361)***
Dodge Machine Tool....815 544-0967
204 S Main St Belvidere (61008) ***(G-1666)***
Doerock Inc....217 543-2101
901 E Columbia St Arthur (61911) ***(G-853)***
Doga USA Corporation....847 669-8529
12060 Raymond Ct Huntley (60142) ***(G-11535)***
Doh Services Inc....708 331-3811
16525 Van Dam Rd Ste 2 South Holland (60473) ***(G-19209)***
Doings Newspaper, Hinsdale *Also called Pioneer Newspapers Inc* ***(G-11374)***
Dolche Truckload Corp....800 719-4921
473 W Northwest Hwy 2e Palatine (60067) ***(G-16113)***
Doll Furniture Co Inc....309 452-2606
400 N Beech St Normal (61761) ***(G-15202)***
Dollar Express....815 399-9719
4225 Charles St Rockford (61108) ***(G-17384)***
Dolls Lettering Inc....815 467-8000
110 Industrial Dr Unit A Minooka (60447) ***(G-14057)***
Dolphin, Chicago *Also called Serrala Solutions US Corp* ***(G-6139)***
Dom Plastic Div, Saint Anne *Also called Eastern Illinois Clay Company* ***(G-18133)***
Domeny Tool & Stamping Company....847 526-5700
354 Hollow Hill Rd Wauconda (60084) ***(G-20342)***
Dometic Corporation....847 447-7190
5600 N River Rd Ste 250 Rosemont (60018) ***(G-18019)***
Dometic Group, Rosemont *Also called Dometic Corporation* ***(G-18019)***
Dominicks Finer Foods Inc....630 584-1750
2063 Lincoln Hwy Saint Charles (60174) ***(G-18185)***
Dominique Graves....773 368-5289
1929 S 14th Ave Broadview (60155) ***(G-2430)***
Domino Amjet Inc....847 662-3148
4321 Lee Ave Gurnee (60031) ***(G-10869)***
Domino Amjet Inc (HQ)....847 244-2501
1290 Lakeside Dr Gurnee (60031) ***(G-10870)***
Domino Engineering Corp....217 824-9441
208 S Spresser St Taylorville (62568) ***(G-19756)***
Domino Foods Inc....773 254-8282
2905 S Western Ave Chicago (60608) ***(G-4379)***
Domino Foods Inc....773 646-2203
2400 E 130th St Chicago (60633) ***(G-4380)***
Domino Holdings Inc (HQ)....847 244-2501
1290 Lakeside Dr Gurnee (60031) ***(G-10871)***
Domino Lasers Inc....847 855-1364
1290 Lakeside Dr Gurnee (60031) ***(G-10872)***
Domino Sugar, Chicago *Also called Domino Foods Inc* ***(G-4379)***
Domino Sugar, Chicago *Also called Domino Foods Inc* ***(G-4380)***
Domino's Pastry Shop, Hickory Hills *Also called Dominos Pastries Inc* ***(G-11195)***
Dominos Pastries Inc....773 889-3549
7731 W 98th St Ste E Hickory Hills (60457) ***(G-11195)***
Dominos Pizza LLC....630 783-0738
10410 Woodward Ave # 100 Woodridge (60517) ***(G-21295)***
Domor Equipment LLC....309 467-3483
925 W Center St Eureka (61530) ***(G-9481)***
Doms Incorporated....847 838-6723
940 Anita Ave Antioch (60002) ***(G-610)***
Don Anderson Co....618 495-2511
101 S Hickory St Hoffman (62250) ***(G-11402)***
Don Churro, Chicago *Also called El Moro De Letran Churros & Ba* ***(G-4465)***
Don Johns Inc (PA)....630 454-4700
701 N Raddant Rd Batavia (60510) ***(G-1374)***
Don Leventhal Group LLC....618 783-4424
1508 W Jourdan St Newton (62448) ***(G-15082)***
Don's Custom Draperies, McHenry *Also called Dons Drapery Service* ***(G-13737)***
Donald J Leventhal....309 662-8080
606 Iaa Dr Bloomington (61701) ***(G-2040)***
Donald Kranz....847 428-1616
10 W Main St Fl 1 Carpentersville (60110) ***(G-3101)***
Donaldson & Associates Inc....708 633-1090
12141 W 159th St Ste A Lockport (60491) ***(G-12988)***
Donaldson Company Inc....309 667-2885
3230 65th Ave New Windsor (61465) ***(G-15072)***
Donaldson Company Inc....815 288-3374
815 W Progress Dr Dixon (61021) ***(G-7898)***
Donato Remodeling, Wadsworth *Also called Century Kitchen & Bath Inc* ***(G-20208)***
Donchef Inc....224 619-2223
1408 W Diversey Pkwy Chicago (60614) ***(G-4381)***
Donermen LLC....773 430-2828
2849 W Belmont Ave A Chicago (60618) ***(G-4382)***
Donghia Showrooms Inc....312 822-0766
631 Merchandise Mart 63 Chicago (60654) ***(G-4383)***
Donkey Brands LLC....630 251-2007
281 Carlton Dr Carol Stream (60188) ***(G-2977)***
Donkey Chips, Carol Stream *Also called Donkey Brands LLC* ***(G-2977)***
Donnas House of Type Inc....217 522-5050
23267 Railsplitter Ln Athens (62613) ***(G-896)***
Donnelley Financial LLC (HQ)....844 866-4337
35 W Wacker Dr Chicago (60601) ***(G-4384)***
Donnelley Financial LLC....630 963-9494
4101 Winfield Rd Warrenville (60555) ***(G-20234)***
Donnelley Financial Solutions, Warrenville *Also called Donnelley Financial LLC* ***(G-20234)***

ALPHABETIC

Donnells Printing & Off Pdts — 815 842-6541
708 W Howard St Pontiac (61764) *(G-16768)*

Donnelly Automotive Machine — 217 428-7414
1298 E Eldorado St Decatur (62521) *(G-7491)*

Dons Drapery Service — 815 385-4759
2210 Orchard Beach Rd McHenry (60050) *(G-13737)*

Dons Meat Market — 309 968-6026
203 W Market St Manito (61546) *(G-13438)*

Dons Welding — 847 526-1177
552 S Rand Rd Wauconda (60084) *(G-20343)*

Donson Machine — 708 468-8392
15440 S 70th Ct Orland Park (60462) *(G-15952)*

Donson Machine Company — 708 388-0880
12416 S Kedvale Ave Alsip (60803) *(G-440)*

Dontech Industries Inc — 847 428-8222
76 Center Dr Gilberts (60136) *(G-10353)*

Doody Enterprises Inc — 312 239-6226
1100 Lake St Ste Ll25 Oak Park (60301) *(G-15751)*

Dooley Brothers Plumbing & Htg — 309 852-2720
306 N Tremont St Kewanee (61443) *(G-12031)*

Dooling Machine Products Inc (PA) — 618 254-0724
107 N Delmar Ave Hartford (62048) *(G-11034)*

Doosan, Crestwood Also called County Packaging Inc *(G-7114)*

Doral Inc — 630 543-5523
344 W Interstate Rd Addison (60101) *(G-96)*

Doralco Inc — 708 388-9324
5919 W 118th St Alsip (60803) *(G-441)*

Doran Oil Properties — 618 283-2460
415 1/2 W Gallatin St Vandalia (62471) *(G-20010)*

Doran Scales Inc — 630 879-1200
883 Enterprise Ct Saint Charles (60174) *(G-18186)*

Doras Spinning Wheel Inc — 618 466-1900
96 Northport Dr Alton (62002) *(G-553)*

Dorbin Metal Strip Mfg Co — 708 656-2333
2404 S Cicero Ave Cicero (60804) *(G-6842)*

Dordan Manufacturing Company — 815 334-0087
2025 Castle Rd Woodstock (60098) *(G-21382)*

Doreen's Gourmet Frozen Pizza, Calumet City Also called Doreens Pizza Inc *(G-2775)*

Doreens Pizza Inc — 708 862-7499
130 State St Calumet City (60409) *(G-2775)*

Dorenfest Group Ltd — 312 464-3000
444 N Michigan Ave # 1200 Chicago (60611) *(G-4385)*

Doric Products Inc (PA) — 217 826-6302
201 W Us Highway 40 Marshall (62441) *(G-13570)*

Doris Bridal Boutique — 847 433-2575
448 Sheridan Rd Ste 1 Highwood (60040) *(G-11306)*

Doris Company — 224 302-5605
30 Porter Dr Round Lake Park (60073) *(G-18096)*

Dormakaba USA Inc — 847 295-2700
924 Sherwood Dr Lake Bluff (60044) *(G-12178)*

Dormakaba USA Inc — 618 965-3491
1003 W Broadway Steeleville (62288) *(G-19480)*

Dormer Pramet LLC — 800 877-3745
2511 Tech Dr Ste 113 Elgin (60124) *(G-8568)*

Dos Bro Corp — 773 334-1919
1208 W Glenlake Ave Chicago (60660) *(G-4386)*

Dosimetry Medicine Group, Schaumburg Also called Siemens Med Solutions USA Inc *(G-18712)*

DOT Sharper Printing Inc — 847 581-9033
8120 River Dr Ste 1 Morton Grove (60053) *(G-14401)*

Dots UT Inc — 217 390-3286
2716 W Clark Rd Ste E Champaign (61822) *(G-3286)*

Dottikon Es America Inc — 215 295-2295
3559 N Cumberland Ave # 106 Chicago (60634) *(G-4387)*

Doty & Sons Concrete Products — 815 895-2884
1275 E State St Sycamore (60178) *(G-19708)*

Doubet Window & Door, Peoria Also called Sheraton Road Lumber *(G-16523)*

Double Image Press Inc — 630 893-6777
151 N Brandon Dr Glendale Heights (60139) *(G-10447)*

Double K Towers Inc — 773 964-3104
5114 N Western Ave Chicago (60625) *(G-4388)*

Double M Machine Inc — 815 692-4676
614 W Pine St Fairbury (61739) *(G-9605)*

Double Nickel LLC — 618 476-3200
609 S Breese St Ste 101 Millstadt (62260) *(G-14045)*

Double Nickel Holdings LLC — 618 476-3200
609 S Breese St Ste 101 Millstadt (62260) *(G-14046)*

Double R Manufacturing Co, Leonore Also called Brian Burcar *(G-12611)*

Double-Disc Grinding Corp — 708 410-1770
2041 Janice Ave Melrose Park (60160) *(G-13853)*

Doubletake Marketing Inc — 845 598-3175
54 Williamsburg Rd Evanston (60203) *(G-9511)*

Dougherty E J Oil & Stone Sup — 618 271-4414
1501 Lincoln Ave East Saint Louis (62204) *(G-8304)*

Doughman Don & Assoc — 312 321-1011
222 Merchandise Mart Plz # 947 Chicago (60654) *(G-4389)*

Doughnut Boy — 773 463-6328
250 Parkway Dr Ste 270 Lincolnshire (60069) *(G-12760)*

Douglas County Mil Moldings — 217 268-4689
326 E County Road 100n Arcola (61910) *(G-647)*

Douglas County Molding, Arcola Also called Douglas County Mil Moldings *(G-647)*

Douglas County Wood Products — 217 543-2888
491 N Cr 100 E Arthur (61911) *(G-854)*

Douglas Graybill — 815 218-1749
3693 N Dakota Rd Freeport (61032) *(G-10106)*

Douglas Press Inc — 800 323-0705
2810 Madison St Bellwood (60104) *(G-1622)*

Doumak Inc (PA) — 800 323-0318
1004 Fairway Dr Bensenville (60106) *(G-1788)*

Doumak Inc — 847 981-2180
2491 Estes Ave Elk Grove Village (60007) *(G-8953)*

Dove Dental Studio — 847 679-2434
6201 W Howard St Ste 202 Niles (60714) *(G-15116)*

Dove Foundation — 312 217-3683
5056 N Marine Dr Apt C4 Chicago (60640) *(G-4390)*

Dove Industries Inc — 618 234-4509
229 Taft St Belleville (62220) *(G-1546)*

Dove Products Inc — 815 727-4683
3357 S State St Lockport (60441) *(G-12989)*

Dove Steel Inc — 815 588-3772
16035 W Red Cloud Dr Lockport (60441) *(G-12990)*

Dovee Manufacturing Inc — 847 437-8122
640 Church Rd Elgin (60123) *(G-8569)*

Dover Corporation (PA) — 630 541-1540
3005 Highland Pkwy # 200 Downers Grove (60515) *(G-7989)*

Dover Corporation — 212 922-1640
3005 Highland Pkwy # 200 Downers Grove (60515) *(G-7990)*

Dover Energy, Inc., Oakbrook Terrace Also called Dover Pmps Prcess Sltons Sgmen *(G-15796)*

Dover Europe Inc (HQ) — 630 541-1540
3005 Highland Pkwy # 200 Downers Grove (60515) *(G-7991)*

Dover Industrial Chrome Inc — 773 478-2022
2929 N Campbell Ave Chicago (60618) *(G-4391)*

Dover Pmps Prcess Sltons Sgmen (HQ) — 630 487-2240
1815 S Meyers Rd Oakbrook Terrace (60181) *(G-15796)*

Dover Prtg Identification Inc (HQ) — 630 541-1540
3005 Highland Pkwy # 200 Downers Grove (60515) *(G-7992)*

Dovetail Brewery Inc — 773 683-1414
1800 W Belle Plaine Ave Chicago (60613) *(G-4392)*

Dovin Machine Shop Inc — 815 672-5247
521 Lundy St Streator (61364) *(G-19607)*

Dow Agrosciences LLC — 815 844-3128
18078 N 1500 East Rd Pontiac (61764) *(G-16769)*

Dow Chemical Company — 847 439-2240
2401 Pratt Blvd Elk Grove Village (60007) *(G-8954)*

Dow Chemical Company — 815 423-5921
26332 S Frontage Rd Channahon (60410) *(G-3381)*

Dow Chemical Company — 815 653-2411
5005 Barnard Mill Rd Ringwood (60072) *(G-17042)*

Dow Chemical Company — 815 933-8900
1400 Harvard Dr Kankakee (60901) *(G-11966)*

Dow Chemical Company — 708 396-3009
12840 S Pulaski Rd Alsip (60803) *(G-442)*

Dow Jones & Company Inc — 618 651-2300
915 Hemlock St Highland (62249) *(G-11214)*

Dow Jones & Company Inc — 312 580-1023
1 S Wacker Dr Ste 1700 Chicago (60606) *(G-4393)*

Down River, Blue Island Also called Signode Industrial Group LLC *(G-2140)*

Downen Enterprises, Shawneetown Also called Jader Fuel Co Inc *(G-18875)*

Downey Investments Inc — 708 345-8000
2125 Gardner Rd Broadview (60155) *(G-2431)*

Doxa Enterprises LLC — 618 515-4470
1798 Summit Ave East Saint Louis (62205) *(G-8305)*

Doyle Signs Inc (PA) — 630 543-9490
232 W Interstate Rd Addison (60101) *(G-97)*

Dpcac LLC — 630 741-7900
1345 Norwood Ave Itasca (60143) *(G-11644)*

Dpe Incorporated — 773 306-0105
7647 S Kedzie Ave Chicago (60652) *(G-4394)*

DPM Solutions LLC — 630 285-1170
724 W Racquet Club Dr Addison (60101) *(G-98)*

Dps Digital Print Svc — 847 836-7734
555 Plate Dr Ste 4 East Dundee (60118) *(G-8192)*

Dqm, Montgomery Also called Sealtec *(G-14268)*

Dqm Inc — 630 692-0633
1551 Aucutt Rd Montgomery (60538) *(G-14243)*

Dr & Dr Property Leasing — 309 965-3200
211 N Eureka St Goodfield (61742) *(G-10674)*

Dr Earles LLC — 312 225-7200
2930 S Michigan Ave # 100 Chicago (60616) *(G-4395)*

Dr Pepper Snapple Group, Loves Park Also called Keurig Dr Pepper Inc *(G-13228)*

Dr Pepper/7 Up Bottling Group — 217 585-1496
4600 Industrial Ave Springfield (62703) *(G-19360)*

Drag City — 312 455-1015
2921 N Cicero Ave Chicago (60641) *(G-4396)*

Dragon Die Mold Inc — 630 836-0699
30w250 Butterfield Rd # 311 Warrenville (60555) *(G-20235)*

Drake Envelope Printing Co — 217 374-2772
207 White St White Hall (62092) *(G-21018)*

Draker, Chicago *Also called Bluenrgy LLC* ***(G-3917)***
Dramatic Publishing Company 815 338-7170
311 Washington St Woodstock (60098) ***(G-21383)***
Drapery Room Inc 708 301-3374
15757 Annico Dr Ste 5 Homer Glen (60491) ***(G-11478)***
Draperyland Inc 630 521-1000
368 Georgetown Sq Wood Dale (60191) ***(G-21182)***
DRAUGAS PUBLISHING, Chicago *Also called Lithuanian Catholic Press* ***(G-5236)***
Drawing Technology Inc 815 877-5133
1550 Elmwood Rd Rockford (61103) ***(G-17385)***
Drawn LLC 312 982-0040
35 E Wacker Dr Fl 14 Chicago (60601) ***(G-4397)***
Drawn Metal Products, Niles *Also called Jahm Inc* ***(G-15135)***
Dreamwrks Grphic Cmmnctons LLC 847 679-6710
2323 Ravine Way Glenview (60025) ***(G-10543)***
Dreher Orthopedic Industries (PA) 708 848-4646
5129 Woodland Ave Western Springs (60558) ***(G-20721)***
Dreisilker Electric Motors Inc (PA) 630 469-7510
352 Roosevelt Rd Glen Ellyn (60137) ***(G-10401)***
Dresbach Distributing Co 815 223-0116
102 Pike St Peru (61354) ***(G-16574)***
Dresser LLC 847 437-5940
1550 Greenleaf Ave Elk Grove Village (60007) ***(G-8955)***
Drewrys Brewing Company 815 385-9115
5402 Brittany Dr McHenry (60050) ***(G-13738)***
Drexel House of Drapes Inc 618 624-5415
3721 Lebanon Ave Belleville (62221) ***(G-1547)***
Drexel Vinisitian and Blind, Belleville *Also called Drexel House of Drapes Inc* ***(G-1547)***
Dreymiller & Kray Inc 847 683-2271
140 S State St Hampshire (60140) ***(G-10969)***
DRG Molding & Pad Printing Inc 847 223-3398
1631 Wood St Round Lake Beach (60073) ***(G-18088)***
Drig Corporation 312 265-1509
5600 N River Rd Rosemont (60018) ***(G-18020)***
Driv Automotive Inc 847 482-5000
500 N Field Dr Lake Forest (60045) ***(G-12244)***
Driv Incorporated 857 842-5000
500 N Field Dr Lake Forest (60045) ***(G-12245)***
Drive Shaft Unlimited Inc 708 447-2211
4323 Joliet Rd Lyons (60534) ***(G-13307)***
Driver Services 505 267-8686
120 George St Apt 517 Bensenville (60106) ***(G-1789)***
Drives & Motion Division, Waukegan *Also called Yaskawa America Inc* ***(G-20520)***
Drivetrain Svc & Components, Bensenville *Also called P & A Driveline & Machine Inc* ***(G-1865)***
Dromont Corporation 404 615-2336
220 N Smith St Ste 414 Palatine (60067) ***(G-16114)***
Drp Solutions Inc 815 782-2014
24322 W 143rd St Plainfield (60544) ***(G-16657)***
Drr Construction, McHenry *Also called Reliable Sand and Gravel Co* ***(G-13787)***
Drs Electrostatic Painting 708 681-5535
4113 Butterfield Rd Bellwood (60104) ***(G-1623)***
Drs Ntwork Imaging Systems LLC 214 215-5960
590 Territorial Dr Ste B Bolingbrook (60440) ***(G-2169)***
Drum Manufacturing 217 923-5625
804 E York Rd Greenup (62428) ***(G-10819)***
Drumbeaters of America Inc 630 365-5527
215 W Nebraska St Elburn (60119) ***(G-8449)***
Drumheller Bag Corporation 309 676-1006
1114 Sw Adams St Peoria (61602) ***(G-16431)***
Drummond Industries Inc 773 637-1264
639 Thomas Dr Bensenville (60106) ***(G-1790)***
Dry Systems Technologies LLC (HQ) 630 427-2051
10420 Rising Ct Woodridge (60517) ***(G-21296)***
Dry Systems Technologies LLC 618 658-3000
1430 Us Highway 45 N Vienna (62995) ***(G-20117)***
Drywear Apparel LLC 847 687-8540
21231 W Brandon Rd Kildeer (60047) ***(G-12046)***
DS Air & Heating Inc (PA) 773 826-7411
549 N Monticello Ave Chicago (60624) ***(G-4398)***
Ds Containers Inc (PA) 630 406-9600
1789 Hubbard Ave Batavia (60510) ***(G-1375)***
Ds Production LLC 708 873-3142
16101 108th Ave Orland Park (60467) ***(G-15953)***
Ds Services of America Inc 773 586-8600
6055 S Harlem Ave Chicago (60638) ***(G-4399)***
Ds Services of America Inc 800 322-6272
2425 Laude Dr Rockford (61109) ***(G-17386)***
Ds Services of America Inc 815 469-7100
9409 Gulfstream Rd Frankfort (60423) ***(G-9787)***
Ds Smith, Romeoville *Also called Corplex Usa LLC* ***(G-17811)***
Dset Laboratories, Chicago *Also called Atlas Material Tstg Tech LLC* ***(G-3766)***
Dsi Inc 309 965-5110
401 State Route 117 Goodfield (61742) ***(G-10675)***
DSI Spaceframes Inc 630 607-0045
509 S Westgate St Addison (60101) ***(G-99)***
DSM Desotech Inc (HQ) 847 697-0400
1122 Saint Charles St Elgin (60120) ***(G-8570)***
DSM Functional Materials, Elgin *Also called DSM Desotech Inc* ***(G-8570)***
Dspc Company (PA) 815 997-1116
3939 S Central Ave Rockford (61102) ***(G-17387)***
Dsr Screenprinting 630 855-2790
676 Bonded Pkwy Ste L Streamwood (60107) ***(G-19571)***
Dss Inc 630 587-1169
3550 Stern Ave Saint Charles (60174) ***(G-18187)***
Dss Competition Engines, Saint Charles *Also called Dss Inc* ***(G-18187)***
Dss Rapak Inc 630 296-2000
1201 Windham Pkwy Ste D Romeoville (60446) ***(G-17814)***
Dt Metronic Inc 224 567-8414
1253 Rand Rd Des Plaines (60016) ***(G-7757)***
Dtc Products Inc 630 513-3323
2651 Dukane Dr Saint Charles (60174) ***(G-18188)***
DTE Enterprises LLC 630 307-9355
2350 W Pinehurst Blvd Addison (60101) ***(G-100)***
Dti, Rockford *Also called Drawing Technology Inc* ***(G-17385)***
Dti Molding Technologies Inc 630 543-3600
201 S Church St Addison (60101) ***(G-101)***
Dtk Construction Inc 312 296-2762
296 W Palatine Rd Wheeling (60090) ***(G-20880)***
Dtk Stone Works, Wheeling *Also called Dtk Construction Inc* ***(G-20880)***
Dtmf, Gridley *Also called Diversatech Metalfab LLC* ***(G-10843)***
Dtrs Enterprises Inc 630 296-6890
1317 Rosemary Dr Bolingbrook (60490) ***(G-2170)***
DTS America Inc 847 783-0401
427 E 4th St East Dundee (60118) ***(G-8193)***
Dtv Innovations LLC (PA) 847 919-3550
2402 Millennium Dr Elgin (60124) ***(G-8571)***
Du All Precision LLC 630 543-4243
1025 W National Ave Addison (60101) ***(G-102)***
Du Bro Products Inc 847 526-2136
480 W Bonner Rd Wauconda (60084) ***(G-20344)***
Du Page Precision Products Co (PA) 630 849-2940
3695 Darlene Ct Ste 101 Aurora (60504) ***(G-953)***
Du Page Precision Products Co 630 849-2940
811 Shoreline Dr Aurora (60504) ***(G-954)***
Du Page Precision Products Co 630 849-2940
433 Spring Ave Naperville (60540) ***(G-14818)***
Du Page Welding Inc 630 543-8511
847 S Westgate St Addison (60101) ***(G-103)***
Du Pont Delaware Inc 630 285-2700
500 Park Blvd Ste 545 Itasca (60143) ***(G-11645)***
Du Quoin, IL Plant, Du Quoin *Also called General Cable Industries Inc* ***(G-8122)***
Du-Call Miller Plastics Inc 630 964-6020
704 E North St Elburn (60119) ***(G-8450)***
Dual Mfg Co Inc 773 267-4457
3522 Martens St Franklin Park (60131) ***(G-9933)***
Dubois Chemicals, Chicago *Also called Metal Finishing Research Corp* ***(G-5404)***
Dubois Chemicals Inc 847 457-1813
5600 N River Rd Ste 800 Rosemont (60018) ***(G-18021)***
Dubois Chemicals Group Inc 708 458-2000
7025 W 66th Pl Chicago (60638) ***(G-4400)***
Duckys Formal Wear Inc 309 342-5914
309 E Main St Galesburg (61401) ***(G-10191)***
Dude Products Inc 800 898-7304
3501 N Southport Ave 476c Chicago (60657) ***(G-4401)***
Dudek & Bock Spring Mfg Co (PA) 773 379-4100
5100 W Roosevelt Rd Chicago (60644) ***(G-4402)***
Dugan Tool and Die Inc 618 259-1351
1145 E Airline Dr East Alton (62024) ***(G-8164)***
Duhack Lehn & Associates Inc 815 777-3460
1228 N Blackjack Rd Galena (61036) ***(G-10168)***
Dukane Corporation (PA) 630 797-4900
2900 Dukane Dr Saint Charles (60174) ***(G-18189)***
Dukane Corporation 630 797-4900
2900 Dukane Dr Saint Charles (60174) ***(G-18190)***
Dukane Ias LLC (PA) 630 797-4900
2900 Dukane Dr Saint Charles (60174) ***(G-18191)***
Dulce Vida Juice Bar LLC 224 236-5045
2003 Irving Park Rd Hanover Park (60133) ***(G-11002)***
Dumore Supplies Inc 312 949-6260
2525 S Wabash Ave Chicago (60616) ***(G-4403)***
Dumpster Dave LLC 618 475-3835
10121 Marissa Twp Line Rd Lenzburg (62255) ***(G-12610)***
Dun-Rite Tool & Machine Co 815 758-5464
55 W Lincoln Hwy Cortland (60112) ***(G-7020)***
Dun-Rite Tooling, Cortland *Also called Dun-Rite Tool & Machine Co* ***(G-7020)***
Dun-Wel Lithograph Co Inc 773 327-8811
3338 N Ravenswood Ave Chicago (60657) ***(G-4404)***
Dunajec Bakery & Deli 773 585-9611
8339 S Harlem Ave Bridgeview (60455) ***(G-2341)***
Dunamis International 773 504-5733
1239 W Madison St Chicago (60607) ***(G-4405)***
Dunbar Systems Inc (PA) 630 257-2900
1186 Walter St Lemont (60439) ***(G-12563)***
Duncan Oil Company Inc 618 548-2923
300 S Washington St Salem (62881) ***(G-18336)***
Dundee Design LLC 847 494-2360
570 Rock Road Dr Ste P East Dundee (60118) ***(G-8194)***

ALPHABETIC

Dundee Truck & Trlr Works LLC 224 484-8182
407 Christina Dr East Dundee (60118) ***(G-8195)***
Dundee Truck Repair & Wash, East Dundee *Also called Dundee Truck & Trlr Works LLC* ***(G-8195)***
Dundick Corporation 708 656-6363
4616 W 20th St Cicero (60804) ***(G-6843)***
Dune Manufacturing Company 708 681-2905
1800 N 15th Ave Melrose Park (60160) ***(G-13854)***
Dunham Designs Inc 815 462-0100
1043 Industry Rd New Lenox (60451) ***(G-15031)***
Dunhill Corp 815 806-8600
9218 Corsair Rd Unit 1 Frankfort (60423) ***(G-9788)***
Dunigan Custom Woodworking 708 351-5213
1426 Ridge Rd Homewood (60430) ***(G-11491)***
Dunkin Donuts 708 460-3088
14461 S La Grange Rd Orland Park (60462) ***(G-15954)***
Dunkin' Donuts, Chicago *Also called Union Foods Inc* ***(G-6465)***
Dunkin' Donuts, West Chicago *Also called B N K Inc* ***(G-20547)***
Dunkin' Donuts, Palos Heights *Also called Walter & Kathy Anczerewicz* ***(G-16194)***
Dunkin' Donuts, Wheaton *Also called Express Donuts Enterprise Inc* ***(G-20798)***
Dunkin' Donuts, Lake Zurich *Also called Jay Elka* ***(G-12426)***
Dunteman and Co 309 772-2166
115 E Twyman St Bushnell (61422) ***(G-2742)***
Duo Display, Chicago *Also called Duo Usa Incorporated* ***(G-4407)***
Duo Graphics 847 228-7080
1612 Landmeier Rd Ste C Elk Grove Village (60007) ***(G-8956)***
Duo North America 312 421-7755
329 W 18th St Ste 607 Chicago (60616) ***(G-4406)***
Duo Plex Glass Ltd (PA) 708 532-4422
10655 S Michael Dr Palos Hills (60465) ***(G-16200)***
Duo Usa Incorporated 312 421-7755
332 S Michigan Ave # 900 Chicago (60604) ***(G-4407)***
Dupage Chropractic Centre Ltd 630 858-9780
45 S Park Blvd Ste 155 Glen Ellyn (60137) ***(G-10402)***
Dupage Products Group 630 969-7200
2250 Curtiss St Downers Grove (60515) ***(G-7993)***
Dupli Group Inc 773 549-5285
3628 N Lincoln Ave Chicago (60613) ***(G-4408)***
Dupont, Itasca *Also called Du Pont Delaware Inc* ***(G-11645)***
Dupont, El Paso *Also called E I Du Pont De Nemours & Co* ***(G-8436)***
Dupont, Morton Grove *Also called E I Du Pont De Nemours & Co* ***(G-14402)***
Dupont, Rochelle *Also called E I Du Pont De Nemours & Co* ***(G-17137)***
Dupont Nutrition & Health, Gibson City *Also called Solae LLC* ***(G-10347)***
Duquoin Dental Associates 618 542-8832
1266 S Washington St Du Quoin (62832) ***(G-8118)***
Dura Bar Division, Woodstock *Also called Charter Dura-Bar Inc* ***(G-21374)***
Dura Feed Inc 815 395-1115
7542 Forest Hills Rd Loves Park (61111) ***(G-13208)***
Dura Operating LLC 815 947-3333
301 S Simmons St Stockton (61085) ***(G-19549)***
Dura Wax Company 815 385-5000
4101 W Albany St McHenry (60050) ***(G-13739)***
Dura-Bar Div, Woodstock *Also called Charter Dura-Bar Inc* ***(G-21373)***
Dura-Crafts Corp 815 464-3561
9408 Gulfstream Rd Frankfort (60423) ***(G-9789)***
Durabilt Dyvex Inc 708 397-4673
2545 S 25th Ave Broadview (60155) ***(G-2432)***
Durable Longlasting 847 350-0113
2301 Eastern Ave Elk Grove Village (60007) ***(G-8957)***
Durable Design Products Inc 708 707-1147
1520 Franklin Ave River Forest (60305) ***(G-17051)***
Durable Engravers Inc 630 766-6420
521 S County Line Rd Franklin Park (60131) ***(G-9934)***
Durable Inc (PA) 847 541-4400
750 Northgate Pkwy Wheeling (60090) ***(G-20881)***
Durable Manufacturing Company 630 766-0398
232 Evergreen Ave Unit B Bensenville (60106) ***(G-1791)***
Durable Packaging Intl, Wheeling *Also called Durable Inc* ***(G-20881)***
Durable Technologies, Franklin Park *Also called Visimark Inc* ***(G-10079)***
Durabuilt Die Corp 847 437-2086
619 Woodview Ave Elk Grove Village (60007) ***(G-8958)***
Duracare Seating Company Inc 888 592-1102
4800 W Roosevelt Rd # 201 Chicago (60644) ***(G-4409)***
Duracell Company 203 796-4000
181 W Madison St Fl 44 Chicago (60602) ***(G-4410)***
Duracell Distributing LLC 203 796-4000
181 W Madison St Ste 4400 Chicago (60602) ***(G-4411)***
Duracell US Operations Inc 312 469-5266
135 S La Salle St Chicago (60603) ***(G-4412)***
Duraclean International Inc 847 704-7100
220 W Campus Dr Ste A Arlington Heights (60004) ***(G-730)***
Duraco Specialty Tapes LLC (PA) 866 800-0775
7400 Industrial Dr Forest Park (60130) ***(G-9712)***
Duracrest Fabrics 847 350-0030
2474 Delta Ln Elk Grove Village (60007) ***(G-8959)***
Duraflex Inc 847 462-1007
765 Industrial Dr Cary (60013) ***(G-3156)***
Duragrind Inc 815 625-6500
2910 W Le Fevre Rd Sterling (61081) ***(G-19506)***
Duratech Corporation 618 533-8891
2520 S Wabash Ave Centralia (62801) ***(G-3229)***
Duratrack Inc 847 806-0202
950 Morse Ave Elk Grove Village (60007) ***(G-8960)***
Duravant (PA) 630 635-3910
3500 Lacey Rd Ste 290 Downers Grove (60515) ***(G-7994)***
Duravant LLC (HQ) 630 635-3910
3500 Lacey Rd Ste 290 Downers Grove (60515) ***(G-7995)***
Durex Industries, Cary *Also called Durex International Corp* ***(G-3157)***
Durex International Corp 847 639-5600
190 Detroit St Cary (60013) ***(G-3157)***
Durite Screw Corporation 773 622-3410
1815 N Long Ave 35 Chicago (60639) ***(G-4413)***
Duro Bag Manufacturing Company 708 385-8674
12245 S Central Ave Alsip (60803) ***(G-443)***
Duro Cast Inc 815 498-2317
145 E Market St Somonauk (60552) ***(G-19070)***
Duro-Chrome Industries Inc 847 487-2900
275 Indl Dr Wauconda (60084) ***(G-20345)***
Duroweld Company Inc 847 680-3064
1565 Rockland Rd Lake Bluff (60044) ***(G-12179)***
Durr - All Corporation 815 943-1032
1001 W Diggins St Ste 2 Harvard (60033) ***(G-11053)***
Dust Logging LLC 217 844-2305
16666 E 2050th Ave Effingham (62401) ***(G-8396)***
Dust Patrol Inc 309 676-1161
1620 W Chanute Rd Ste D Peoria (61615) ***(G-16432)***
Dustcatchers Inc 773 768-1440
8801 S South Chicago Ave Chicago (60617) ***(G-4414)***
Dusty Lane Wood Products 618 426-9045
295 Dusty Ln Campbell Hill (62916) ***(G-2815)***
Dutch American Foods 708 304-2648
25393 S Dixie Hwy Crete (60417) ***(G-7139)***
Dutch Prairie Conveyors 618 349-6177
844 N 1625 St Shobonier (62885) ***(G-18892)***
Dutch Valley Veal, South Holland *Also called Brown Packing Company Inc* ***(G-19202)***
Duvas USA Limited 312 266-1420
676 N Michigan Ave # 2800 Chicago (60611) ***(G-4415)***
Dva Mayday Corporation 847 848-7555
8108 Redtail Dr Village of Lakewood (60014) ***(G-20178)***
Dva Metal Fabrication Inc 224 577-8217
1427 Tonne Rd Elk Grove Village (60007) ***(G-8961)***
Dva Metal Fabrication Inc 224 577-8217
1656 Brighton Dr Mundelein (60060) ***(G-14684)***
Dvcc Inc 630 323-3105
40 Chestnut Ave Westmont (60559) ***(G-20739)***
DVine Wine Crafters LLC 847 658-4900
2380 Esplanade Dr Algonquin (60102) ***(G-372)***
Dvoraks Creations Inc 815 838-2214
1521 Daviess Ave Lockport (60441) ***(G-12991)***
Dwyer Products & Services, Itasca *Also called Dpcac LLC* ***(G-11644)***
Dyco-TEC Products Ltd (PA) 630 837-6410
29w600 Schick Rd Bartlett (60103) ***(G-1275)***
Dyer's Superchargers, Summit Argo *Also called Dyers Machine Service Inc* ***(G-19678)***
Dyers Machine Service Inc 708 496-8100
7665 W 63rd St Summit Argo (60501) ***(G-19678)***
Dyna Cut Industries, Carol Stream *Also called Dynacut Industries Inc* ***(G-2978)***
Dyna-Burr Chicago Inc 708 250-6744
65 E Lake St Northlake (60164) ***(G-15546)***
Dynacast, Rockford *Also called Taurus 80 LLC* ***(G-17653)***
Dynacast LLC 847 608-2200
195 Corporate Dr Elgin (60123) ***(G-8572)***
Dynachem Inc 217 662-2136
15662 E 980 North Rd Westville (61883) ***(G-20780)***
Dynaco Door, Mundelein *Also called Entrematic HPD North Amer Inc* ***(G-14687)***
Dynacoil Inc 847 731-3300
2000 Lewis Ave Zion (60099) ***(G-21512)***
Dynacut Industries Inc 630 462-1900
500 Randy Rd Ste A Carol Stream (60188) ***(G-2978)***
Dynagraphics Incorporated 217 876-9950
3220 N Woodford St Decatur (62526) ***(G-7492)***
Dynamac Inc 630 543-0033
1229 W Capitol Dr Addison (60101) ***(G-104)***
Dynamac Microwave Inc 630 543-0033
1229 W Capitol Dr Addison (60101) ***(G-105)***
Dynamesh Inc., Batavia *Also called NBC Meshtec Americas Inc* ***(G-1398)***
Dynami Solutions LLC 618 363-2771
2 Loggers Trl Edwardsville (62025) ***(G-8357)***
Dynamic Automation Inc 312 782-8555
3445 W Arthur Ave Lincolnwood (60712) ***(G-12817)***
Dynamic Colors Inc 847 721-8834
1019 Florence Ave Evanston (60202) ***(G-9512)***
Dynamic Machining Inc 815 675-3330
2304 Spring Ridge Dr C Spring Grove (60081) ***(G-19273)***
Dynamic Manufacturing Inc (PA) 708 343-8753
4201 Raymond Dr Hillside (60162) ***(G-11336)***

Dynamic Manufacturing Inc......708 681-0682
1800 N 30th Ave Ste 1 Melrose Park (60160) *(G-13855)*
Dynamic Manufacturing Inc......708 547-7081
4300 Madison St Hillside (60162) *(G-11337)*
Dynamic Manufacturing Inc......708 343-8753
1930 N Mannheim Rd Melrose Park (60160) *(G-13856)*
Dynamic Manufacturing Inc......708 547-9011
4211 Madison St Hillside (60162) *(G-11338)*
Dynamic Manufacturing Inc......708 343-8753
1801 N 32nd Ave Melrose Park (60160) *(G-13857)*
Dynamic Mfg Torque Converters, Melrose Park *Also called Dynamic Manufacturing Inc (G-13856)*
Dynamic Powertrain Reman LLC......708 343-5444
3003 W Hirsch St Melrose Park (60160) *(G-13858)*
Dynamic Precision Products......847 526-2054
1280 Kyle Ct Wauconda (60084) *(G-20346)*
Dynamicsignals LLC (PA)......815 838-0005
900 N State St Lockport (60441) *(G-12992)*
Dynapar Corporation (HQ)......847 662-2666
1675 N Delany Rd Gurnee (60031) *(G-10873)*
Dynasty Mold Builders, Wauconda *Also called Illinois Mold Builders Inc (G-20359)*
Dynawave Corporation......630 232-4945
1624 Kummer Ct Geneva (60134) *(G-10267)*
Dyne Inc......815 521-1111
7280 E Us Highway 6 Minooka (60447) *(G-14058)*
Dyneer Corporation......217 228-6011
2701 Spruce St Quincy (62301) *(G-16877)*
Dyno Manufacturing Inc......618 451-6609
2 Fox Industrial Dr Madison (62060) *(G-13409)*
Dyno Nobel Inc......217 285-5531
1353 W Washington St Detroit (62363) *(G-7872)*
Dynomax Inc......847 680-8833
230 W Palatine Rd Wheeling (60090) *(G-20882)*
Dynomax Inc (PA)......847 680-8833
1535 Abbott Dr Wheeling (60090) *(G-20883)*
Dyson Inc......847 995-8010
1025 E Golf Rd Schaumburg (60173) *(G-18510)*
Dyson Inc (HQ)......312 469-5950
1330 W Fulton St Fl 5 Chicago (60607) *(G-4416)*
Dyson B2b Inc......312 469-5950
1330 W Fulton St Ste 500 Chicago (60607) *(G-4417)*
Dyson Direct Inc (HQ)......312 469-5950
1330 W Fulton St Ste 500 Chicago (60607) *(G-4418)*
Dytec Midwest Inc (PA)......847 255-3200
1855 Rohlwing Rd Ste C Rolling Meadows (60008) *(G-17728)*
Dzro-Bans International Inc......779 324-2740
3011 183rd St Homewood (60430) *(G-11492)*
E A M & J Inc......847 622-9200
65 Waukegan Rd Lake Bluff (60044) *(G-12180)*
E & C Custom Plastic Inc......630 543-3325
466 S Vista Ave Addison (60101) *(G-106)*
E & E Machine & Engineering Co......708 841-5208
14016 S Indiana Ave Riverdale (60827) *(G-17071)*
E & F Tool Company Inc......815 729-1305
213 Amendodge Dr Joliet (60404) *(G-11856)*
E & H Graphic Service Inc......708 748-5656
21750 Main St Unit 21 Matteson (60443) *(G-13623)*
E & H Tubing Inc (PA)......773 522-3100
4401 W Roosevelt Rd Chicago (60624) *(G-4419)*
E & J Gallo Winery......630 505-4000
4225 Naperville Rd # 330 Lisle (60532) *(G-12886)*
E & J Precision Machining Inc......815 363-2522
4215 W Orleans St McHenry (60050) *(G-13740)*
E & L Communication......773 890-1656
2644 W 47th St Chicago (60632) *(G-4420)*
E & R Media LLC......618 790-9376
104 E Main St Du Quoin (62832) *(G-8119)*
E & R Powder Coatings Inc......773 523-9510
3729 W 49th St Chicago (60632) *(G-4421)*
E & T Plastic Mfg Co Inc......630 628-9048
140 S Fairbank St Addison (60101) *(G-107)*
E & T Plastics of Illinois, Addison *Also called E & T Plastic Mfg Co Inc (G-107)*
E A, Alsip *Also called Engineered Abrasives Inc (G-445)*
E A A Enterprises Inc......630 279-0150
250 E Saint Charles Rd Villa Park (60181) *(G-20145)*
E and J Polishing and Buffing......773 569-0661
4729 S Kostner Ave Chicago (60632) *(G-4422)*
E B Bronson & Co Inc......708 385-3600
12826 Irving Ave Blue Island (60406) *(G-2119)*
E B G B Inc......847 228-9333
220 Lively Blvd Elk Grove Village (60007) *(G-8962)*
E B Inc......815 758-6646
116 S State St De Kalb (60115) *(G-7429)*
E C Machining Inc......708 496-0116
8267 S 86th Ct Justice (60458) *(G-11952)*
E C S, Broadview *Also called Elevator Cable & Supply Co (G-2433)*
E C Schultz & Co Inc......847 640-1190
333 Crossen Ave Elk Grove Village (60007) *(G-8963)*
E D M, Lake Zurich *Also called Electronic Design & Mfg Inc (G-12406)*

E F I, Centralia *Also called Engineered Fluid Inc (G-3230)*
E George Special Services LLC......773 934-7878
642 E 192nd St Glenwood (60425) *(G-10640)*
E Gornell & Sons Inc......773 489-2330
2241 N Knox Ave Chicago (60639) *(G-4423)*
E H Baare Corporation......618 546-1575
500 S Heath Toffee Ave Robinson (62454) *(G-17114)*
E H Wachs, Lincolnshire *Also called Illinois Tool Works Inc (G-12774)*
E H Wachs......815 943-4785
600 Knightsbridge Pkwy Lincolnshire (60069) *(G-12761)*
E H Wachs......815 943-4785
600 Knightsbridge Pkwy Lincolnshire (60069) *(G-12762)*
E H Wachs Company, Lincolnshire *Also called 1883 Properties Inc (G-12740)*
E I Du Pont De Nemours & Co......309 527-5115
2830 Us Highway 24 El Paso (61738) *(G-8436)*
E I Du Pont De Nemours & Co......847 965-6580
7828 Merrimac Ave Morton Grove (60053) *(G-14402)*
E I Du Pont De Nemours & Co......815 562-7570
13239 E Il Route 38 Rochelle (61068) *(G-17137)*
E I Du Pont De Nemours & Co......815 259-3311
10994 Three Mile Rd Thomson (61285) *(G-19783)*
E J Basler Co......847 678-8880
9511 Ainslie St Schiller Park (60176) *(G-18800)*
E J Kupjack & Associates Inc......847 823-6661
2233 S Throop St Apt 319 Chicago (60608) *(G-4424)*
E J Self Furniture (PA)......847 394-0899
332 S Rammer Ave Arlington Heights (60004) *(G-731)*
E J Somerville, Melrose Park *Also called Ej Somerville Plating Co (G-13862)*
E J Welch Co Inc......847 238-0100
2601 Lively Blvd Elk Grove Village (60007) *(G-8964)*
E K Kuhn Inc......815 899-9211
1170 E State St Sycamore (60178) *(G-19709)*
E M C Industry......217 543-2894
441 E Cr 400 N Arthur (61911) *(G-855)*
E M F Y & Associates, Rockford *Also called Charles R Frontczak (G-17345)*
E M Glabus Co Inc......630 766-3027
420 County Line Rd Bensenville (60106) *(G-1792)*
E M S, Lake In The Hills *Also called Emissions Systems Incorporated (G-12333)*
E Mc......217 228-1280
906 Vermont St Quincy (62301) *(G-16878)*
E N M Company......773 775-8400
5617 N Northwest Hwy Chicago (60646) *(G-4425)*
E N M Digital Counters, Chicago *Also called E N M Company (G-4425)*
E N P Inc (PA)......800 255-4906
603 14th St Mendota (61342) *(G-13940)*
E N P Inc......815 539-7471
2001 E Main St Mendota (61342) *(G-13941)*
E P Computer, Champaign *Also called Ep Technology Corporation USA (G-3290)*
E Rowe Foundry & Machine Co......217 382-4135
147 W Cumberland St Martinsville (62442) *(G-13583)*
E S I, Itasca *Also called Environmental Specialties Inc (G-11651)*
E S I Steel Fabrication, Salem *Also called Esi Steel & Fabrication (G-18338)*
E T News Report, Effingham *Also called Effingham Ttplis News Rport In (G-8399)*
E W I, Rantoul *Also called Eagle Wings Industries Inc (G-16974)*
E Z Sign Co Inc......815 469-4080
15347 Cicero Ave Rear Oak Forest (60452) *(G-15675)*
E Z Trail Inc (PA)......217 543-3471
1050 E Columbia St Arthur (61911) *(G-856)*
E&B Exercise LLC......844 425-5025
55 W Monroe St Ste 2350 Chicago (60603) *(G-4426)*
E&D Printing Services Inc......815 609-8222
15857 Spanglers Farm Dr Plainfield (60544) *(G-16658)*
E+e Elektronik Corporation......847 490-0520
333 E State Pkwy Schaumburg (60173) *(G-18511)*
E-Intrctive Mktg Solutions Inc......312 241-1692
7551 W 99th St Bridgeview (60455) *(G-2342)*
E-J Industries Inc......312 226-5023
1275 S Campbell Ave Chicago (60608) *(G-4427)*
E-Jay Plastics Co......630 543-4000
115 W Laura Dr Addison (60101) *(G-108)*
E-Lite Tool & Mfg Co......618 236-1580
122 Industrial Dr Belleville (62220) *(G-1548)*
E-M Metal Fabricator......847 593-9970
145 Joey Dr Elk Grove Village (60007) *(G-8965)*
E-Motion LLC......815 825-4411
124 W Locust St Fairbury (61739) *(G-9606)*
E-Quip Manufacturing Co......815 464-0053
230 Industry Ave Frankfort (60423) *(G-9790)*
E-T-A Circuit Breakers, Mount Prospect *Also called Oakland Industries Ltd (G-14555)*
E-Z Cuff Inc......847 549-1550
1840 Industrial Dr # 260 Libertyville (60048) *(G-12648)*
E-Z Mix, Chicago *Also called Hymans Auto Supply Co (G-4864)*
E-Z Products Inc......847 551-9199
92 E End Dr Gilberts (60136) *(G-10354)*
E-Z Rotational Molder Inc......847 806-1327
1001 Nicholas Blvd Ste F Elk Grove Village (60007) *(G-8966)*
E-Z Tree Recycling Inc......773 493-8600
7050 S Dorchester Ave Chicago (60637) *(G-4428)*

ALPHABETIC

E2 Manufacturing Group LLC.....224 399-9608
3776 Hawthorne Ct Waukegan (60087) *(G-20439)*
E3 Artisan Inc.....815 575-9315
140 Cass St Woodstock (60098) *(G-21384)*
Ea Mackay Enterprises Inc.....630 627-7010
104 N West Rd Lombard (60148) *(G-13070)*
Eager Polymers, Chicago *Also called Savannah Industries Inc (G-6107)*
Eagle Burial Vault.....815 722-8660
9535 W Steger Rd Frankfort (60423) *(G-9791)*
Eagle Capital Group Inc.....847 891-5800
1735 Mitchell Blvd Schaumburg (60193) *(G-18512)*
Eagle Carpet Services Ltd.....956 971-8560
135 S Fairbank St Addison (60101) *(G-109)*
Eagle Companies Inc.....309 686-9054
4214 E Rome Rd Chillicothe (61523) *(G-6816)*
Eagle Electronics, Schaumburg *Also called Eagle Capital Group Inc (G-18512)*
Eagle Express Mail LLC.....618 377-6245
333 W Bethalto Dr Ste C Bethalto (62010) *(G-1964)*
Eagle Forum (PA).....618 462-5415
322 State St Ste 301 Alton (62002) *(G-554)*
Eagle Freight Inc.....708 202-0651
3710 River Rd Ste 200 Franklin Park (60131) *(G-9935)*
Eagle Gear & Manufacturing Co.....630 628-6100
740 W Racquet Club Dr Addison (60101) *(G-110)*
Eagle Grips, Carol Stream *Also called Art Jewel Enterprises Ltd (G-2941)*
Eagle High Mast Ltg Co Inc.....847 473-3800
1070a S Northpoint Blvd Waukegan (60085) *(G-20440)*
Eagle Machine Company.....312 243-7407
1725 W Walnut St Chicago (60612) *(G-4429)*
Eagle Panel System Inc.....618 326-7132
127 N Maple St Mulberry Grove (62262) *(G-14654)*
Eagle Plastics & Supply Inc.....708 331-6232
814 W 120th St Chicago (60643) *(G-4430)*
Eagle Press, Crystal Lake *Also called LAC Enterprises Inc (G-7219)*
Eagle Printing Company.....309 762-0771
2957 12th Ave Moline (61265) *(G-14141)*
Eagle Publications Inc.....618 345-5400
11 Executive Dr Ste 10 Fairview Heights (62208) *(G-9645)*
Eagle Screen Print Inds Inc.....708 579-0454
5326 East Ave Countryside (60525) *(G-7051)*
Eagle Stone and Brick Inc.....618 282-6722
450 N Main St Red Bud (62278) *(G-16993)*
Eagle Wings Industries Inc.....217 892-4322
400 Shellhouse Dr Rantoul (61866) *(G-16974)*
Eaglestone Inc.....630 587-1115
3705 Swenson Ave Saint Charles (60174) *(G-18192)*
Eakas Corporation.....815 223-8811
6251 State Route 251 Peru (61354) *(G-16575)*
Eam Pallets.....708 333-0596
15224 Dixie Hwy Ste A Harvey (60426) *(G-11082)*
Earl Ad Inc.....312 666-7106
2201 S Union Ave Ste 2 Chicago (60616) *(G-4431)*
Earl G Graves Pubg Co Inc.....312 274-0682
625 N Michigan Ave # 401 Chicago (60611) *(G-4432)*
Earl Mich, Wood Dale *Also called Mich Enterprises Inc (G-21216)*
Earlville Cold Stor Lckr LLC.....815 246-9469
101 N East St Earlville (60518) *(G-8160)*
Early Bird Advertising Inc.....847 253-1423
502 Grego Ct Prospect Heights (60070) *(G-16839)*
Earnest Earth Agriculture Inc.....217 766-4401
4655 Il Hwy 81 Lynn Center (61262) *(G-13290)*
Earshot Inc.....773 383-1798
560 W Washington Blvd # 240 Chicago (60661) *(G-4433)*
Earth Friendly Products, Addison *Also called Venus Laboratories Inc (G-328)*
Earth Stone Products Ill Inc.....847 671-3000
4535 25th Ave Schiller Park (60176) *(G-18801)*
Earthchoice, Lake Forest *Also called Pactiv LLC (G-12279)*
Earthcomber LLC.....708 366-1600
110 N Marion St Oak Park (60301) *(G-15752)*
Earthgrains.....630 859-8782
321 Airport Rd North Aurora (60542) *(G-15259)*
Earthgrains Refrigertd Dough P.....630 455-5200
3250 Lacey Rd Ste 600 Downers Grove (60515) *(G-7996)*
Earthwise Environmental Inc.....630 475-3070
777 N Edgewood Ave Wood Dale (60191) *(G-21183)*
Earthwise Recycled Pallet.....618 286-6015
336 Mcbride Ave Dupo (62239) *(G-8136)*
East Balt Bakeries, Chicago *Also called Bimbo Qsr Chicago LLC (G-3891)*
East Balt Bakery, Chicago *Also called Bimbo Qsr Us LLC (G-3892)*
East Bank Neon Inc.....618 345-9517
8146 Gass Ln Collinsville (62234) *(G-6958)*
East Central Communications Co.....217 892-9613
1332 Harmon Dr Rantoul (61866) *(G-16975)*
East Dbque Ntrgn Frtlizers LLC.....815 747-3101
16675 Us Highway 20 W East Dubuque (61025) *(G-8176)*
East Moline Sheet Metal Co.....309 755-1422
3001 48th Ave Moline (61265) *(G-14142)*
East Penn Manufacturing Co.....610 682-6361
1651 Frontenac Rd Naperville (60563) *(G-14819)*
East Side Cafe, Warrenville *Also called Preziosio Ltd (G-20249)*
East Side Jersey Dairy Inc (HQ).....217 854-2547
1100 Broadway Carlinville (62626) *(G-2873)*
East Side Jersey Dairy Inc.....662 289-3344
3744 Staunton Rd Edwardsville (62025) *(G-8358)*
East Side Tool & Die Co Inc.....618 397-1633
2762 N 89th St Caseyville (62232) *(G-3212)*
East St Louis Monitor Pubg Co, East Saint Louis *Also called Monitor Newspaper Inc (G-8315)*
East St Louis Trml & Stor Co.....618 271-2185
1501 Lincoln Ave East Saint Louis (62204) *(G-8306)*
East West Intergrated Therapys.....815 788-0574
2719 Red Barn Rd Crystal Lake (60012) *(G-7195)*
East West Martial Arts Sups.....773 878-7711
5544 N Western Ave Chicago (60625) *(G-4434)*
Eastco Inc.....708 499-1701
5500 W 111th St Oak Lawn (60453) *(G-15714)*
Eastern Accents Inc.....773 604-7300
4201 W Belmont Ave Chicago (60641) *(G-4435)*
Eastern Company.....847 537-1800
301 W Hintz Rd Wheeling (60090) *(G-20884)*
Eastern Illinois Clay Company (PA).....815 427-8144
460 S Elm Ave Saint Anne (60964) *(G-18133)*
Eastern Services, Norris City *Also called B & B Tank Truck Construction (G-15246)*
Eastgate Cleaners.....630 627-9494
837 Westmore-Myers Rd A10 Lombard (60148) *(G-13071)*
Eastland Fabrication LLC.....815 493-8399
14273 Il Route 73 Lanark (61046) *(G-12479)*
Eastland Industries Inc.....708 547-6500
4115 Washington Blvd Hillside (60162) *(G-11339)*
Eastman Chemical Company.....618 482-6409
500 Monsanto Ave Sauget (62206) *(G-18393)*
Easton Bell Sports, Rantoul *Also called Brg Sports Inc (G-16969)*
Eastwood Enterprises Inc.....847 940-4008
1020 Chapel Ct Deerfield (60015) *(G-7607)*
Easy Heat Inc.....847 268-6000
9377 W Higgins Rd Rosemont (60018) *(G-18022)*
Easy Trac Gps Inc.....630 359-5804
233 S Wacker Dr Fl 8 Chicago (60606) *(G-4436)*
Easy Ware Corp.....773 755-7732
2052 N Lincoln Park W Chicago (60614) *(G-4437)*
Easyshow LLC.....847 480-7177
450 Skokie Blvd Ste 1200 Northbrook (60062) *(G-15378)*
Eaton, Highland *Also called Cooper B-Line Inc (G-11210)*
Eaton Cor Actuator & Sensor Di, Rochelle *Also called Eaton Corporation (G-17138)*
Eaton Corporation.....217 732-3131
1725 1200th Ave Lincoln (62656) *(G-12729)*
Eaton Corporation.....815 562-2107
200 E Avenue G Rochelle (61068) *(G-17138)*
Eatsee Inc.....312 846-1492
1132 S Wabash Ave Ste 606 Chicago (60605) *(G-4438)*
Eaw Machining.....847 865-5162
1205 Karl Ct Wauconda (60084) *(G-20347)*
Eazypower Corporation.....773 278-5000
2321 N Keystone Ave Chicago (60639) *(G-4439)*
Eazypower Corporation (PA).....773 278-5000
60639 W Belden St Ste 10 Chicago (60639) *(G-4440)*
Eb Brands, Chicago *Also called E&B Exercise LLC (G-4426)*
Ebe Industrial LLC.....815 379-2400
507 W North St Walnut (61376) *(G-20217)*
Eberhart Sign & Lighting Co (PA).....618 656-7256
104 1st Ave Edwardsville (62025) *(G-8359)*
Eberle Manufacturing Company.....847 215-0100
230 Larkin Dr Wheeling (60090) *(G-20885)*
Ebers Drilling Co.....618 826-5398
4318 State Route 150 Chester (62233) *(G-3454)*
Ebk Containers, Lake In The Hills *Also called Jodi Maurer (G-12337)*
Ebling Electric Company.....312 455-1885
2222 W Hubbard St Chicago (60612) *(G-4441)*
Ebonyenergy Publishing Inc Nfp.....773 851-5159
10960 S Prospect Ave Chicago (60643) *(G-4442)*
Ebooks2go.....847 598-1145
1111 N Plaza Dr Ste 652 Schaumburg (60173) *(G-18513)*
Ebro Foods Inc.....773 696-0150
1330 W 43rd St Chicago (60609) *(G-4443)*
Ebro Packing Company, Chicago *Also called Ebro Foods Inc (G-4443)*
Ebway Industries Inc.....630 860-5959
1201 Ardmore Ave Itasca (60143) *(G-11646)*
EC Harms Met Fabricators Inc.....309 385-2132
1017 N Santa Fe Ave Princeville (61559) *(G-16826)*
Eccofab, Rockford *Also called Ekstrom Carlson Fabg Co Inc (G-17392)*
Ecd-Network LLC.....917 670-0821
320 W Ohio St Ste 3w Chicago (60654) *(G-4444)*
Ecf Holdings LLC.....224 723-5524
3550 Woodhead Dr Northbrook (60062) *(G-15379)*
Echelon Capital LLC (PA).....312 263-0263
121 W Wacker Dr Chicago (60601) *(G-4445)*
Echo Incorporated (HQ).....847 540-8400
400 Oakwood Rd Lake Zurich (60047) *(G-12404)*

ALPHABETIC SECTION

Echo Incorporated 847 540-3500
   1000 Rose Rd Lake Zurich (60047) *(G-12405)*
Ecker-Erhardt, Chicago Also called Eeco Services Inc *(G-4462)*
Eckert Orchards Inc (PA) 618 233-0513
   951 S Green Mount Rd Belleville (62220) *(G-1549)*
Ecli Products LLC (HQ) 630 449-5000
   3851 Exchange Ave Aurora (60504) *(G-955)*
Eclipse Inc (HQ) 815 877-3031
   1665 Elmwood Rd Rockford (61103) *(G-17388)*
Eclipse Awnings Inc 708 636-3160
   3609 W 95th St Evergreen Park (60805) *(G-9593)*
Eclipse Combustion Inc (HQ) 815 877-3031
   1665 Elmwood Rd Rockford (61103) *(G-17389)*
Eclipse Lighting Inc 847 916-2623
   3506 River Rd Franklin Park (60131) *(G-9936)*
Eclipse Lighting Inc (PA) 847 260-0333
   9245 Ivanhoe St Schiller Park (60176) *(G-18802)*
Ecmc Inc 847 352-5015
   1517 Wright Blvd Schaumburg (60193) *(G-18514)*
Eco Green Analytics LLC 847 691-1148
   735 Castlewood Ln Deerfield (60015) *(G-7608)*
Eco Print Mail Consultants, Chicago Also called Grace Enterprises Inc *(G-4721)*
Eco Safety Lights, Chicago Also called Esafety Lights LLC *(G-4529)*
Eco-Light, Mount Prospect Also called Good Earth Lighting Inc *(G-14531)*
Eco-Pur Solutions LLC 630 917-8789
   694 Veterans Pkwy Ste F Chicago (60606) *(G-4446)*
Eco-Pur Solutions LLC 630 226-2300
   1245 Naperville Dr Romeoville (60446) *(G-17815)*
Eco-Smart Flooring Company 847 404-5032
   550 W Wshnton Blvd Ste 20 Chicago (60661) *(G-4447)*
Eco-Tech Plastics LLC 262 539-3811
   1519 Woodlark Dr Northbrook (60062) *(G-15380)*
Ecoco Inc 773 745-7700
   1830 N Lamon Ave Chicago (60639) *(G-4448)*
Ecodyne Water Treatment LLC 630 961-5043
   1270 Frontenac Rd Naperville (60563) *(G-14820)*
Ecolab Inc 815 389-3441
   5151 E Rockton Rd Roscoe (61073) *(G-17905)*
Ecolab Inc 815 729-7334
   3001 Channahon Rd Joliet (60436) *(G-11857)*
Ecolab Inc 708 496-5378
   6236 W 124th Pl Palos Heights (60463) *(G-16183)*
Ecolab Inc 847 350-2229
   1060 Thorndale Ave Elk Grove Village (60007) *(G-8967)*
Ecolab Inc 847 350-2229
   1060 Thorndale Ave Elk Grove Village (60007) *(G-8968)*
Ecolocap Solutions Inc 312 585-6670
   6240 Oakton St Morton Grove (60053) *(G-14403)*
Ecologic LLC (PA) 630 869-0495
   18w140 Butterfield Rd # 1180 Oakbrook Terrace (60181) *(G-15797)*
Ecologic Industries LLC 847 234-5755
   3742 Hawthorne Ct Waukegan (60087) *(G-20441)*
Ecology Tech, Aurora Also called S & S Metal Recyclers Inc *(G-1152)*
Ecolotech Asl Inc 630 859-0485
   611 Phoenix Ct Aurora (60505) *(G-1086)*
Ecomed Solutions LLC 866 817-7114
   214 Terrace Dr Mundelein (60060) *(G-14685)*
Econodome Kits, Sullivan Also called Faze Change Produx *(G-19667)*
Economy Iron Inc 708 343-1777
   3132 W Hirsch St Melrose Park (60160) *(G-13859)*
Econopin 708 599-5002
   8540 S Thomas Ave Bridgeview (60455) *(G-2343)*
Ecosystem Protective Coatings 815 725-6343
   1214 Colorado Ave Joliet (60435) *(G-11858)*
Ecoturf Midwest Inc 630 350-9500
   789 Golf Ln Bensenville (60106) *(G-1793)*
Ecp Incorporated 630 754-4200
   11210 Katherines Xing # 100 Woodridge (60517) *(G-21297)*
Ecsi, Springfield Also called Envirnmntal Ctrl Solutions Inc *(G-19363)*
Ecurrent LLC 888 815-5786
   740 N Edgewood Ave Wood Dale (60191) *(G-21184)*
Ecurrent Led, Wood Dale Also called Ecurrent LLC *(G-21184)*
Ed Bell Investments Inc 618 345-0799
   34 Empire Dr Ste 1 Belleville (62220) *(G-1550)*
Ed Co 708 614-0695
   8304 Lilac Ln Tinley Park (60477) *(G-19822)*
ED Etnyre & Co 815 732-2116
   1333 S Daysville Rd Oregon (61061) *(G-15917)*
Ed Garvey and Company (PA) 847 647-1900
   7400 N Lehigh Ave Niles (60714) *(G-15117)*
Ed Hartwig Trucking & Excvtg 309 364-3672
   312 Jefferson St Henry (61537) *(G-11163)*
Ed Hill S Custom Canvas 815 476-5042
   8655 E Mallard Ln Wilmington (60481) *(G-21097)*
Ed Kabrick Beef Inc 217 656-3263
   218 E Main St Plainville (62365) *(G-16729)*
Ed Stan Fabricating Co 708 863-7668
   4859 W Ogden Ave Chicago (60804) *(G-4449)*

Ed Weitekamp Inc 217 229-4239
   5046 N 23rd Ave Raymond (62560) *(G-16989)*
Eddie Gapastione 708 430-3881
   8927 S Octavia Ave Bridgeview (60455) *(G-2344)*
Eddie Z'S, Westmont Also called EZ Blinds and Drapery Inc *(G-20742)*
Eden Fuels LLC 847 676-9470
   5025 Old Orchard Rd Skokie (60077) *(G-18949)*
Eden Park Illumination Inc 217 403-1866
   903 N Country Fair Dr Champaign (61821) *(G-3287)*
Eden's and Old Orchard's Shell, Skokie Also called Eden Fuels LLC *(G-18949)*
Edgar A Weber & Company 847 215-1980
   549 Palwaukee Dr Wheeling (60090) *(G-20886)*
Edgar A Weber & Company 847 215-1980
   549 Palwaukee Dr Wheeling (60090) *(G-20887)*
Edgar County Locker Service 217 466-5000
   116 E Steidl Rd Paris (61944) *(G-16229)*
Edgar H Fey Jewelers Inc (PA) 708 352-4115
   833 N Washington St Naperville (60563) *(G-14821)*
Edgar Pallets 773 454-8919
   4122 W Ogden Ave Chicago (60623) *(G-4450)*
Edgars Custom Cabinets 847 928-0922
   3315 Dora St Franklin Park (60131) *(G-9937)*
Edge Capital Group Inc 773 295-4774
   55 E Monroe St Ste 3800 Chicago (60603) *(G-4451)*
Edge Carrier, Chicago Also called Edge Capital Group Inc *(G-4451)*
Edge Communication 708 749-7818
   3825 Kenilworth Ave Berwyn (60402) *(G-1951)*
Edgebrook Eyecare 815 397-5959
   1603 N Alpine Rd Ste 121 Rockford (61107) *(G-17390)*
Edgetool Industrial Supplies, Waukegan Also called David Linderholm *(G-20434)*
Edgewater Products Company Inc 708 345-9200
   3315 W North Ave Melrose Park (60160) *(G-13860)*
Edgewell Per Care Brands LLC 708 544-5550
   5000 Proviso Dr Melrose Park (60163) *(G-13861)*
Edgo Technical Sales Inc 630 961-8398
   9s131 Skylane Dr Naperville (60564) *(G-14965)*
Edison Pallet & Wood Products 630 653-3416
   371 County Farm Rd Winfield (60190) *(G-21110)*
Edk Construction Inc 630 853-3484
   1325 Chapman Dr Darien (60561) *(G-7406)*
Edlong Corporation (PA) 847 439-9230
   225 Scott St Elk Grove Village (60007) *(G-8969)*
Edlong Flavors, Elk Grove Village Also called Edlong Corporation *(G-8969)*
EDM Department, Bartlett Also called EDM Dept Inc *(G-1276)*
EDM Dept Inc 630 736-0531
   1261 Humbracht Cir Ste A Bartlett (60103) *(G-1276)*
EDM Products LLC 630 785-2554
   484 W Wrightwood Ave Elmhurst (60126) *(G-9358)*
EDM Scorpio Inc 847 931-5164
   84 Joslyn Dr Elgin (60120) *(G-8573)*
Edmark Visual Identification 800 923-8333
   4552 N Kilbourn Ave Chicago (60630) *(G-4452)*
Edmik Inc 847 263-0460
   3850 Grove Ave Gurnee (60031) *(G-10874)*
Edmik Plastics, Gurnee Also called Edmik Inc *(G-10874)*
Edmpartscom Inc 630 427-1603
   958 N Du Page Ave Lombard (60148) *(G-13072)*
Edmund D Schmelzie & Sons 312 782-7230
   29 E Madison St Ste 1214 Chicago (60602) *(G-4453)*
Edoc Communications, Mount Prospect Also called PHI Group Inc *(G-14561)*
Edr Electronics, Arlington Heights Also called Box of Rain Ltd *(G-707)*
Eds Pallet Service 618 248-5386
   409 N Commercial St Albers (62215) *(G-344)*
Edsal Manufacturing Co LLC (PA) 773 475-3000
   4400 S Packers Ave Chicago (60609) *(G-4454)*
Edsal Manufacturing Co LLC 773 475-3165
   4000 S Racine Ave Chicago (60609) *(G-4455)*
Edsal Manufacturing Co LLC 773 475-3013
   1555 W 44th St Chicago (60609) *(G-4456)*
Eduardo Enterprises Inc 708 599-9700
   7461 W 93rd St Ste Unitf Bridgeview (60455) *(G-2345)*
Education Equity Inc 800 339-7985
   30 W Webster Ave Unit A Chicago (60614) *(G-4457)*
Education Partners Project Ltd 773 675-6643
   4800 S Chicago Beach Dr 1901s Chicago (60615) *(G-4458)*
Educational Insights, Vernon Hills Also called Learning Resources Inc *(G-20072)*
Edv District 7 Clringhouse Vine (PA) 312 380-1349
   8034 S Ellis Ave Apt 1w Chicago (60619) *(G-4459)*
Edventure Promotions Inc 312 440-1800
   1953 N Clybourn Ave Ste R Chicago (60614) *(G-4460)*
Edward F Data 708 597-0158
   12625 S Kroll Dr Alsip (60803) *(G-444)*
Edward Fields Incorporated 312 644-0400
   222 Merchandise Mart Plz # 635 Chicago (60654) *(G-4461)*
Edward Hull Cabinet Shop 217 864-3011
   1310 N State Route 121 Mount Zion (62549) *(G-14645)*
Edward J Warren Jr 630 882-8817
   2921 Alden Ave Yorkville (60560) *(G-21481)*

Edwards Acquisition Corp 309 944-2117
210 S Chicago St Geneseo (61254) ***(G-10241)***
Edwards County Concrete LL 618 445-2711
210 N Commercial St Harrisburg (62946) ***(G-11022)***
Edwards County Concrete LLC 618 445-2711
327 Industrial Dr Albion (62806) ***(G-349)***
Edwards Creative Services LLC 309 756-0199
435 1st St E Milan (61264) ***(G-14007)***
Edwards Readymix Co., Geneseo *Also called Edwards Acquisition Corp* ***(G-10241)***
Edwardsville Intelligencer, Edwardsville *Also called Edwardsville Publishing Co* ***(G-8361)***
Edwardsville Mch & Wldg Co Inc 618 656-5145
1509 Troy Rd Edwardsville (62025) ***(G-8360)***
Edwardsville Publishing Co 618 656-4700
116 N Main St Edwardsville (62025) ***(G-8361)***
Edwin M Knowles China Company 847 581-8354
9333 N Milwaukee Ave Niles (60714) ***(G-15118)***
Edwin Waldmire & Virginia 217 498-9375
Hc 2 Rochester (62563) ***(G-17165)***
Eeco Services Inc 312 226-6030
2347 W 18th St Chicago (60608) ***(G-4462)***
Eenigenburg Mfg Inc 708 474-0850
19530 Burnham Ave Lansing (60438) ***(G-12492)***
Ees Inc 708 343-1800
4300 W North Ave Stone Park (60165) ***(G-19553)***
Efco Corporation 630 378-4720
595 Territorial Dr Ste A Bolingbrook (60440) ***(G-2171)***
Effective Energy Assoc LLC 815 248-9280
1979 Sunline Dr Davis (61019) ***(G-7417)***
Effici Inc 401 584-2266
939 N Plum Grove Rd Schaumburg (60173) ***(G-18515)***
Efficient Energy Lighting Inc 630 272-9388
35w912 Rock Glen Rd Saint Charles (60175) ***(G-18193)***
Effimax Solar 217 550-2422
60 Hazelwood Dr Champaign (61820) ***(G-3288)***
Effingham Daily News, Effingham *Also called Newspaper Holding Inc* ***(G-8415)***
Effingham Equity 217 268-5128
912 E County Road 600n Arcola (61910) ***(G-648)***
Effingham Monument Co Inc 217 857-6085
Rr 33 Box E Effingham (62401) ***(G-8397)***
Effingham Printing Company, Effingham *Also called Rusty & Angela Buzzard* ***(G-8423)***
Effingham Signs & Graphics 217 347-8711
1009 S Oak St Effingham (62401) ***(G-8398)***
Effingham Ttplis News Rport In 217 342-5583
1901 S 4th St Effingham (62401) ***(G-8399)***
Egan Wagner Corporation 630 985-8007
2929 Two Paths Dr Woodridge (60517) ***(G-21298)***
Egd Manufacturing Inc 815 964-2900
2320 Kishwaukee St Rockford (61104) ***(G-17391)***
Egg Cream America Inc (PA) 847 559-2700
633 Skokie Blvd Ste 200 Northbrook (60062) ***(G-15381)***
Eggology Inc 818 610-2222
968 S Kent Rd Pearl City (61062) ***(G-16319)***
Egp, Chicago *Also called Engineered Glass Products LLC* ***(G-4508)***
Ehrhardt Engineered Solutions, Granite City *Also called Ehrhardt Tool & Machine LLC* ***(G-10704)***
Ehrhardt Tool & Machine LLC 314 436-6900
25 Central Industrial Dr Granite City (62040) ***(G-10704)***
Ehs Solutions LLC (PA) 309 282-9121
8800 N Allen Rd Ste 1 Peoria (61615) ***(G-16433)***
Eichen Lumber Co Inc 217 854-9751
20002 Claremont Rd Carlinville (62626) ***(G-2874)***
Eichen's Saw Mill, Carlinville *Also called Charles K Eichen* ***(G-2871)***
Eickmans Processing Co Inc 815 247-8451
3226 S Pecatonica Rd Seward (61077) ***(G-18867)***
Eiesland Builders Inc 847 998-1731
2041 Johns Dr Glenview (60025) ***(G-10544)***
Eiesland Woodwork, Glenview *Also called Eiesland Builders Inc* ***(G-10544)***
Eifeler Coatings Tech Inc 630 587-1220
3800 Commerce Dr Saint Charles (60174) ***(G-18194)***
Eighty Nine Robotics LLC 512 573-9091
965 W Chicago Ave Chicago (60642) ***(G-4463)***
Eikenberry Sheet Metal Works 815 625-0955
412 E 3rd St Sterling (61081) ***(G-19507)***
Einstein Crest 847 965-7791
9347 N Milwaukee Ave Niles (60714) ***(G-15119)***
Eirich Machines Inc 847 336-2444
4033 Ryan Rd Gurnee (60031) ***(G-10875)***
Eis 630 530-7500
752 N Larch Ave Elmhurst (60126) ***(G-9359)***
Eisendrath Inc 847 432-3899
716 Central Ave Apt B Highland Park (60035) ***(G-11261)***
Eisenhower High School - Blue 708 385-6815
12700 Sacramento Ave Blue Island (60406) ***(G-2120)***
EJ Cady & Company 847 537-2239
135 Wheeling Rd Wheeling (60090) ***(G-20888)***
Ej Pierogi 773 318-3383
1700 Oakton St Elk Grove Village (60007) ***(G-8970)***
Ej Somerville Plating Co 708 345-5100
1305 N 31st Ave Melrose Park (60160) ***(G-13862)***
Ej Usa Inc 815 740-1640
310 Garnet Dr New Lenox (60451) ***(G-15032)***
EJL Custom Golf Clubs Inc (PA) 630 654-8887
825 75th St Ste F Willowbrook (60527) ***(G-21041)***
Eklund Metal Treating Inc 815 877-7436
721 Beacon St Loves Park (61111) ***(G-13209)***
Ekstrom Carlson Fabg Co Inc 815 226-1511
1204 Milford Ave Rockford (61109) ***(G-17392)***
El Campeon Food Products, Chicago *Also called Sparrer Sausage Company Inc* ***(G-6208)***
El Dia Newspaper 708 956-7282
6331 26th St Apt 1 Berwyn (60402) ***(G-1952)***
El Encanto Products Inc 773 940-1807
4041 W Ogden Ave Ste 12 Chicago (60623) ***(G-4464)***
El Giloy Specialty Metals, Hampshire *Also called Combined Metals Chicago LLC* ***(G-10967)***
El Moro De Letran Churros & Ba 312 733-3173
1626 S Blue Island Ave Chicago (60608) ***(G-4465)***
El Paso Journal 309 527-8595
51 W Front St El Paso (61738) ***(G-8437)***
El Popocatapetl Industries Inc 773 843-0888
4246 W 47th St Chicago (60632) ***(G-4466)***
El Popocatapetl Industries Inc (PA) 312 421-6143
1854 W 21st St Chicago (60608) ***(G-4467)***
El Sol Dechicago Newspaper 773 235-7655
4217 W Fullerton Ave Chicago (60639) ***(G-4468)***
El Superior Mexican Foods, Chicago *Also called Roca Inc* ***(G-6047)***
El Tradicional 773 925-0335
7647 S Kedzie Ave Chicago (60652) ***(G-4469)***
El Valle Florido 630 898-0689
1028 Cypress Dr Aurora (60506) ***(G-1087)***
El-Milagro Inc (PA) 773 579-6120
3050 W 26th St Chicago (60623) ***(G-4470)***
El-Milagro Inc 773 650-1614
2919 S Western Ave Fl 1 Chicago (60608) ***(G-4471)***
El-Milagro Inc 773 299-1216
2759 S Kedzie Ave Chicago (60623) ***(G-4472)***
El-Ranchero Food Products 773 843-0430
4457 S Kildare Ave Chicago (60632) ***(G-4473)***
El-Ranchero Food Products (PA) 773 847-9167
4545 S Tripp Ave Chicago (60632) ***(G-4474)***
Elan Express Inc 815 713-1190
3815 N Mulford Rd Ste 4 Rockford (61114) ***(G-17393)***
Elan Furs 317 255-6100
3841 E 82nd St Morton Grove (60053) ***(G-14404)***
Elan Industries Inc 630 679-2000
650 S Schmidt Rd Ste A Bolingbrook (60440) ***(G-2172)***
Elanza Technologies Inc 312 396-4187
500 N Michigan Ave # 600 Chicago (60611) ***(G-4475)***
Elas Tek Molding Inc 815 675-9012
7517 Meyer Rd Ste 1 Spring Grove (60081) ***(G-19274)***
Elastec Inc (PA) 618 382-2525
1309 W Main St Carmi (62821) ***(G-2904)***
Elastec / American Marine, Carmi *Also called Elastec Inc* ***(G-2904)***
Elastek Molding, Spring Grove *Also called Elas Tek Molding Inc* ***(G-19274)***
Elba Tool Co Inc 847 895-4100
220 Covington Dr Bloomingdale (60108) ***(G-1990)***
Elburn Herald, Saint Charles *Also called Kaneland Publications Inc* ***(G-18220)***
Elburn Market Inc 630 365-6461
250 S Main St Elburn (60119) ***(G-8451)***
Elburn Metal Stamping Inc 630 365-2500
44w210 Keslinger Rd Elburn (60119) ***(G-8452)***
Elc Industries Corp 630 851-1616
401 Hankes Ave Aurora (60505) ***(G-1088)***
Elcast Lighting, Addison *Also called Elcast Manufacturing Inc* ***(G-111)***
Elcast Manufacturing Inc 630 628-1992
815 S Kay Ave Ste B Addison (60101) ***(G-111)***
Elco Laboratories Inc (PA) 708 534-3000
1300 E North St Coal City (60416) ***(G-6932)***
Elcon Inc (PA) 815 467-9500
600 Twin Rail Dr Minooka (60447) ***(G-14059)***
Eldest Daughter LLC 949 677-7385
1305 N Damen Ave Chicago (60622) ***(G-4476)***
Elec Easel 815 444-9700
2600 Behan Rd Crystal Lake (60014) ***(G-7196)***
Election Services Division, Rockford *Also called Election Systems & Sftwr LLC* ***(G-17394)***
Election Systems & Sftwr LLC 815 397-8144
929 S Alpine Rd Ste 301 Rockford (61108) ***(G-17394)***
Election Works 630 232-4030
0s096 Catlin Sq Geneva (60134) ***(G-10268)***
Electri-Flex Company 630 529-2920
222 Central Ave Roselle (60172) ***(G-17952)***
Electric Conduit Cnstr Co 630 293-4474
816 Hicks Dr Elburn (60119) ***(G-8453)***
Electric Conduit Construction 630 859-9310
601 E North St Elburn (60119) ***(G-8454)***
Electric Supply Direct, Burr Ridge *Also called Etcon Corp* ***(G-2672)***
Electrical Safety Testing Eqp, Lake Forest *Also called Ikonix Group Inc* ***(G-12266)***
Electrmchnical Bench Reference, Chicago *Also called Barks Publications Inc* ***(G-3834)***
Electro Freeze, East Moline *Also called HC Duke & Son LLC* ***(G-8228)***

Electro Motive Diesel, Mc Cook *Also called Progress Rail Locomotive Inc* **(G-13699)**
Electro-Circuits Inc 630 339-3389
1651 Mitchell Blvd Schaumburg (60193) **(G-18516)**
Electro-Matic Products Co 773 235-4010
2235 N Knox Ave Chicago (60639) **(G-4477)**
Electro-Max Inc 847 683-4100
105 Rowell Rd Ste D Hampshire (60140) **(G-10970)**
Electro-Technic Products Inc 773 561-2349
4642 N Ravenswood Ave Chicago (60640) **(G-4478)**
Electroform Company 815 633-1113
11070 Raleigh Ct Machesney Park (61115) **(G-13341)**
Electron Beam Technologies Inc 815 935-2211
1275 Harvard Dr Kankakee (60901) **(G-11967)**
Electronic Design & Mfg Inc 847 550-1912
1225 Flex Ct Lake Zurich (60047) **(G-12406)**
Electronic Equipment Exchange, Danville *Also called Vermilion Steel Fabrication* **(G-7391)**
Electronic Interconnect Corp 847 364-4848
2375 Estes Ave Elk Grove Village (60007) **(G-8971)**
Electronic Plating Co 708 652-8100
1821 S 54th Ave Cicero (60804) **(G-6844)**
Electronic Resources Corp 331 225-3450
817 S Kay Ave Ste 6 Addison (60101) **(G-112)**
Electronic System Design Inc 847 358-8212
225 Foster Ave Bensenville (60106) **(G-1794)**
Electronic Technology Group, South Holland *Also called Techno - Grphics Trnsltons Inc* **(G-19248)**
Electronica Aviation LLC 407 498-1092
150 S Wacker Dr Ste 2403 Chicago (60606) **(G-4479)**
Electronics Boutique Amer Inc 618 465-3125
128 Alton Sq Alton (62002) **(G-555)**
Electrowire, Schaumburg *Also called Hamalot Inc* **(G-18542)**
Elegance In Awards & Gifts, Chicago *Also called R S Owens & Co Inc* **(G-5953)**
Elegant Acquisition LLC 708 652-3400
5253 W Roosevelt Rd Cicero (60804) **(G-6845)**
Elegant Concepts Ltd 708 456-9590
7444 W Grand Ave Elmwood Park (60707) **(G-9451)**
Elegant Embroidery Inc 847 540-8003
100 Oakwood Rd Ste C Lake Zurich (60047) **(G-12407)**
Elegant Packaging, Cicero *Also called Elegant Acquisition LLC* **(G-6845)**
Elektro-Physik USA Inc 847 437-6616
778 W Algonquin Rd Arlington Heights (60005) **(G-732)**
Elektron N Magnesium Amer Inc (HQ) 618 452-5190
1001 College St Madison (62060) **(G-13410)**
Elematec USA Corporation 858 527-1700
500 Park Blvd Ste 760 Itasca (60143) **(G-11647)**
Elemech Inc 630 417-2845
2275 White Oak Cir Aurora Aurora (60502) **(G-956)**
Element Bars Inc 888 411-3536
1140 S Washtenaw Ave Chicago (60612) **(G-4480)**
Element Collection 217 898-5175
2731 County Road 100 N Allerton (61810) **(G-403)**
Element Events LLC 630 717-2800
123 Water St Naperville (60540) **(G-14822)**
Elemental Art Jewelry 773 844-4812
5917 N Broadway St Chicago (60660) **(G-4481)**
Elementbars.com, Chicago *Also called Element Bars Inc* **(G-4480)**
Elements Group 312 664-2252
2033 N Larrabee St Chicago (60614) **(G-4482)**
Elenco Electronics Inc 847 541-3800
150 Carpenter Ave Wheeling (60090) **(G-20889)**
Elevance Rnewable Sciences Inc (PA) 630 296-8880
2501 Davey Rd Woodridge (60517) **(G-21299)**
Elevate Digital, Chicago *Also called Civiq Smartscapes LLC* **(G-4165)**
Elevator Cable & Supply Co 708 338-9700
2807 S 25th Ave Broadview (60155) **(G-2433)**
Elexa Commercial Products, Bannockburn *Also called Elexa Consumer Products Inc* **(G-1200)**
Elexa Consumer Products Inc 773 794-1300
2275 Half Day Rd Ste 160 Bannockburn (60015) **(G-1200)**
Elfi LLC 815 439-1833
6001 S Knox Ave Chicago (60629) **(G-4483)**
Elfi Wall Systems, Chicago *Also called Elfi LLC* **(G-4483)**
Elg Metals Inc 773 374-1500
103rd St The Calumet Riv Chicago (60617) **(G-4484)**
Elgalabwater LLC 630 343-5251
5 Earl Ct Ste 100 Woodridge (60517) **(G-21300)**
Elgiloy Specialty Metals 847 683-0500
1 Hauk Rd Hampshire (60140) **(G-10971)**
Elgin Die Mold Co 847 464-0140
14n002 Prairie St Pingree Grove (60140) **(G-16621)**
Elgin Engineering Center, Elgin *Also called Nidec Motor Corporation* **(G-8673)**
Elgin Equipment Group LLC (HQ) 630 434-7200
2001 Bttrfeld Rd Ste 1020 Downers Grove (60515) **(G-7997)**
Elgin Fastener Group LLC 847 465-0048
288 Holbrook Dr Wheeling (60090) **(G-20890)**
Elgin Granite Works, Saint Charles *Also called St Charles Memorial Works Inc* **(G-18275)**
Elgin Industries Inc 847 742-1720
1100 Jansen Farm Dr Elgin (60123) **(G-8574)**
Elgin Instant Print 847 931-9006
293 S Aldine St Elgin (60123) **(G-8575)**
Elgin Molded Plastics Inc (PA) 847 931-2455
909 Grace St Elgin (60120) **(G-8576)**
Elgin National Industries Inc (PA) 630 434-7200
2001 Bttrfeld Rd Ste 1020 Downers Grove (60515) **(G-7998)**
Elgin National Industries Inc 314 776-2848
5595 Highway 34 N Raleigh (62977) **(G-16960)**
Elgin Sweeper Company 847 741-5370
1300 W Bartlett Rd Elgin (60120) **(G-8577)**
Elgin World Trade, Elgin *Also called Elgin Industries Inc* **(G-8574)**
Elginex Corporation 815 786-8406
1002 E 3rd St Sandwich (60548) **(G-18368)**
Elia Day Spa 708 535-1450
5251 147th St Ste 3 Oak Forest (60452) **(G-15676)**
Elim Pdtric Phrmaceuticals Inc (PA) 412 266-5968
Corp Ctr 1600 Rolling Meadows (60008) **(G-17729)**
Elim Pdtric Phrmaceuticals Inc 412 266-5968
1141 Tower Rd Schaumburg (60173) **(G-18517)**
Elim Pdtric Phrmaceuticals Inc 412 266-5968
Corp Ctr 1600 Glf Rd 12 Rolling Meadows (60008) **(G-17730)**
Elimparcial Newspaper, Cicero *Also called Teleguia Inc* **(G-6880)**
Elis Cheesecake Company 773 205-3800
6701 W Forest Preserve Dr Chicago (60634) **(G-4485)**
Elise S Allen 309 673-2613
1600 Mrtn Lthr Kng Jr Dr Peoria (61605) **(G-16434)**
Elite Custom Woodworking 630 888-4322
219 S Water St Batavia (60510) **(G-1376)**
Elite Die & Finishing Inc 708 389-4848
18650 Graphic Ct Tinley Park (60477) **(G-19823)**
Elite Extrusion Technology Inc 630 485-2020
3620 Ohio Ave Saint Charles (60174) **(G-18195)**
Elite Fabrication Inc 773 274-4474
1524 W Jarvis Ave Chicago (60626) **(G-4486)**
Elite Fasteners Inc 815 397-8848
2005 15th St Rockford (61104) **(G-17395)**
Elite Fiber Optics LLC 630 225-9454
10029 Pacific Ave Franklin Park (60131) **(G-9938)**
Elite Impressions & Graphics 847 695-3730
645 Stevenson Rd South Elgin (60177) **(G-19143)**
Elite Industries 224 433-6988
5710 Des Plaines Ct Gurnee (60031) **(G-10876)**
Elite Manufacturing Tech Inc 630 351-5757
333 Munroe Dr Bloomingdale (60108) **(G-1991)**
Elite Monument Co 217 532-6080
1119 School St Hillsboro (62049) **(G-11310)**
Elite Power Boats Inc 618 654-6292
3645 George St Highland (62249) **(G-11215)**
Elite Rf LLC 847 592-6350
2155 Stnngton Ave Ste 217 Hoffman Estates (60169) **(G-11420)**
Elite Wireworks Corporation 630 837-9100
1239 Humbracht Cir Bartlett (60103) **(G-1277)**
Elitegen Corp 630 637-6917
1112 Sheldon Ct Naperville (60540) **(G-14823)**
Elk Grove Corrugated Plant, Elk Grove Village *Also called Weyerhaeuser Company* **(G-9307)**
Elk Grove Custom Sheet Metal 847 352-2845
106 N Lively Blvd Elk Grove Village (60007) **(G-8972)**
Elk Grove Recycle, Elk Grove Village *Also called Legacy Vulcan LLC* **(G-9092)**
Elk Grove Rubber & Plastic Co 630 543-5656
99 W Commercial Ave Addison (60101) **(G-113)**
Elk Grove Signs Inc 847 427-0005
1670 Greenleaf Ave Elk Grove Village (60007) **(G-8973)**
Elkay Manufacturing Company 815 493-8850
105 N Rochester St Lanark (61046) **(G-12480)**
Elkay Manufacturing Company 630 377-0150
2530 Production Dr Saint Charles (60174) **(G-18196)**
Elkay Manufacturing Company 708 681-1880
2700 S 17th Ave Broadview (60155) **(G-2434)**
Elkay Manufacturing Company 800 223-5529
1333 Butterfield Rd # 200 Downers Grove (60515) **(G-7999)**
Elkay Manufacturing Company 815 273-7001
6400 Penn Ave Savanna (61074) **(G-18404)**
Ella Engineering Incorporated 847 354-4767
800 Morse Ave Elk Grove Village (60007) **(G-8974)**
Elle Magazine, Chicago *Also called Hearst Corporation* **(G-4795)**
Elliot Inst For Scial Scnces R 217 525-8202
524 E Lawrence Ave Springfield (62703) **(G-19361)**
Elliott Aviation Arcft Sls Inc 309 799-3183
6601 74th Ave Milan (61264) **(G-14008)**
Elliott Jsj & Associates Inc 847 242-0412
194 Green Bay Rd Glencoe (60022) **(G-10429)**
Elliott Machine & Tool Corp 630 543-6755
511 W Interstate Rd Addison (60101) **(G-114)**
Elliott Publishing Inc 217 645-3033
103 E Hannibal St Liberty (62347) **(G-12622)**
Elliott Publishing Inc 217 593-6515
202 E State St Camp Point (62320) **(G-2810)**
Ellis Corporation (PA) 630 250-9222
1400 W Bryn Mawr Ave Itasca (60143) **(G-11648)**

ALPHABETIC

ALPHABETIC SECTION

Ellison Eyewear Inc 312 880-7609
314 W Institute Pl Ste 2e Chicago (60610) *(G-4487)*
Ellwood Group Inc 815 725-9030
4166 Mound Rd Joliet (60436) *(G-11859)*
Elm Street Industries Inc 309 854-7000
206 W 4th St Kewanee (61443) *(G-12032)*
Elm Tool and Manufacturing Co 847 455-6805
10257 Dickens Ave Melrose Park (60164) *(G-13863)*
Elmed Incorporated 224 353-6446
35 N Brandon Dr Glendale Heights (60139) *(G-10448)*
Elmer L Larson L C (PA) 815 895-4837
21218 Airport Rd Sycamore (60178) *(G-19710)*
Elmhurst-Chicago Stone Company (PA) 630 832-4000
400 W 1st St Elmhurst (60126) *(G-9360)*
Elmhurst-Chicago Stone Company 630 557-2446
45 W 371 Main Kaneville (60144) *(G-11954)*
Elmhurst-Chicago Stone Company 630 983-6410
351 Royce Rd Bolingbrook (60440) *(G-2173)*
Elmos Tombstone Service 773 643-0200
6023 S State St Chicago (60621) *(G-4488)*
Elmot Inc 773 791-7039
4923 W Fullerton Ave Chicago (60639) *(G-4489)*
Elmwood Locker Service, Elmwood *Also called Powers John* *(G-9449)*
Eln Group LLC 847 477-1496
39 Longmeadow Rd Winnetka (60093) *(G-21128)*
Elongated Plastics Inc 224 456-0559
677 Alice Dr Northbrook (60062) *(G-15382)*
Elorac Inc (PA) 847 362-8200
100 N Fairway Dr Ste 134 Vernon Hills (60061) *(G-20050)*
Elpress Inc 331 814-2910
900 Oakmont Ln Ste 207 Westmont (60559) *(G-20740)*
Elston Materials LLC 773 235-3100
1420 N Elston Ave Chicago (60642) *(G-4490)*
EM Smith & Co 309 691-6812
826 W Detweiller Dr Peoria (61615) *(G-16435)*
Emac Inc 618 529-4525
2390 Emac Ln Carbondale (62902) *(G-2841)*
Emalex Biosciences LLC (PA) 847 715-0577
1033 Skokie Blvd Northbrook (60062) *(G-15383)*
Embassy Security Group Inc 800 627-1325
9960 191st St Ste N Mokena (60448) *(G-14079)*
Embeddedkits 847 401-7488
1025 Oakland Dr Streamwood (60107) *(G-19572)*
Embedor Technologies Inc 202 681-0359
60 Hazelwood Dr Champaign (61820) *(G-3289)*
Embedur Systems Inc 847 749-3665
3601 Algonquin Rd Ste 608 Rolling Meadows (60008) *(G-17731)*
Emberglo Div of Midco Intl, Chicago *Also called Midco International Inc* *(G-5433)*
Embroid ME, Peoria *Also called Sew Wright Embroidery Inc* *(G-16521)*
Embroid ME 847 272-9000
2845 Dundee Rd Northbrook (60062) *(G-15384)*
Embroid ME 815 485-4155
2399 E Joliet Hwy New Lenox (60451) *(G-15033)*
Embroidea Custom Embroidery 217 698-6422
60 Providence Ln Springfield (62711) *(G-19362)*
Embroidery Experts Inc 847 403-0200
595 Lakeview Pkwy Vernon Hills (60061) *(G-20051)*
Embroidery House, Peoria *Also called Senn Enterprises Inc* *(G-16520)*
Embroidery Services Inc 847 588-2660
6287 W Howard St Niles (60714) *(G-15120)*
Embroidme 847 301-1010
36595 N Yew Tree Dr Lake Villa (60046) *(G-12349)*
Embroidme-Fox River Valley, Saint Charles *Also called Cara ANAM Enterprises Inc* *(G-18163)*
EMC Corporation 630 505-3273
4225 Naperville Rd # 500 Lisle (60532) *(G-12887)*
EMC Corporation 312 577-0026
4246 Collection Center Dr Chicago (60693) *(G-4491)*
EMC Corporation 312 577-0026
353 N Clark St 19th Chicago (60654) *(G-4492)*
EMC Fire Inc 480 225-5498
22824 W Winchester Dr Channahon (60410) *(G-3382)*
EMC Innovations Inc 815 741-2546
1252 Woodland Ct Joliet (60436) *(G-11860)*
EMC Machining Inc 630 860-7076
905 Fairway Dr Bensenville (60106) *(G-1795)*
Emco Chemical Distributors Inc 262 427-0400
2100 Commonwealth Ave North Chicago (60064) *(G-15310)*
Emco Gears Inc (PA) 847 220-4327
160 King St Elk Grove Village (60007) *(G-8975)*
Emco Metals LLC 312 925-1553
1505 S Laramie Ave Cicero (60804) *(G-6846)*
Emco Wheaton Usa Inc (HQ) 217 222-5400
1800 Gardner Expy Quincy (62305) *(G-16879)*
EMD, Mc Cook *Also called Progress Rail Locomotive Inc* *(G-13700)*
EMD Millipore Corporation 815 937-8270
195 W Birch St Kankakee (60901) *(G-11968)*
EMD Millipore Corporation 815 932-9017
2407 Eastgate Pkwy Kankakee (60901) *(G-11969)*

Emecole Inc 815 372-2493
50 Montrose Romeoville (60446) *(G-17816)*
Emeelys Socks and More 847 529-3026
2415 1/2 W 63rd St Chicago (60629) *(G-4493)*
Emerald Biofuels LLC (PA) 847 420-0898
300 N La Salle Dr # 4925 Chicago (60654) *(G-4494)*
Emerald City Jewelers, Quincy *Also called Emerald City Jewelry Inc* *(G-16880)*
Emerald City Jewelry Inc 217 222-8896
3236 Broadway St Quincy (62301) *(G-16880)*
Emerald Machine Inc 773 924-3659
4641 S Halsted St Chicago (60609) *(G-4495)*
Emerald One LLC 601 529-6793
300 N La Salle Dr # 4925 Chicago (60654) *(G-4496)*
Emerald Performance Mtls LLC 309 364-2311
1550 County Road 1450 N Henry (61537) *(G-11164)*
Emerald Polymer Additives LLC 309 364-2311
1550 County Road 1450 N Henry (61537) *(G-11165)*
Emerge Technology Group LLC 224 603-2161
1600 N Milwaukee Ave # 708 Lake Villa (60046) *(G-12350)*
Emergency Medical Instruments 630 365-2001
44 W 528 Rt 64 Maple Park (60151) *(G-13462)*
Emerson, Oak Forest *Also called Instrument & Valve Services Co* *(G-15684)*
Emerson, Chicago *Also called Instrument & Valve Services Co* *(G-4939)*
Emerson Automation Solutions 309 946-5205
121 W 1st St Geneseo (61254) *(G-10242)*
Emerson Electric Co 847 585-8300
1901 South St Elgin (60123) *(G-8578)*
Emerson Electric Co 847 268-6000
9377 W Higgins Rd Rosemont (60018) *(G-18023)*
Emerson Electric Co 312 803-4321
222 W Adams St Ste 400 Chicago (60606) *(G-4497)*
Emerson Electric Co 708 263-6100
7650 185th St Ste D Tinley Park (60477) *(G-19824)*
Emerson Industries LLC (PA) 630 279-0920
680 Baker Dr Itasca (60143) *(G-11649)*
Emerson Press, Divernon *Also called Leonard Emerson* *(G-7880)*
Emerson Process Management 708 535-5120
4320 166th St Oak Forest (60452) *(G-15677)*
Emhart Teknologies LLC 877 364-2781
12337 Collections Ctr Dr Chicago (60693) *(G-4498)*
EMI, Grayslake *Also called Engineered Mills Inc* *(G-10770)*
EMI, Maple Park *Also called Emergency Medical Instruments* *(G-13462)*
Eminent Technologies LLC 630 416-2311
215 Shuman Blvd Ste 403 Naperville (60563) *(G-14824)*
Emissions Systems Incorporated 847 669-8044
480 Wright Dr Lake In The Hills (60156) *(G-12333)*
Emlin Cosmetics Inc (PA) 630 860-5773
290 Beeline Dr Bensenville (60106) *(G-1796)*
Emmel Inc 847 254-5178
13 Baldwin Ct Lake In The Hills (60156) *(G-12334)*
Emmert John 773 292-6580
1401 N Cicero Ave Chicago (60651) *(G-4499)*
Emmett's Ale House, Wheaton *Also called Emmetts Tavern & Brewing Co* *(G-20797)*
Emmett's Ale House, Palatine *Also called Emmetts Tavern & Brewing Co* *(G-16115)*
Emmetts Tavern & Brewing Co 630 434-8500
5200 Main St Downers Grove (60515) *(G-8000)*
Emmetts Tavern & Brewing Co 630 480-7181
121 W Front St Wheaton (60187) *(G-20797)*
Emmetts Tavern & Brewing Co 847 359-1533
110 N Brockway St Palatine (60067) *(G-16115)*
Emmetts Tavern & Brewing Co (PA) 847 428-4500
128 W Main St West Dundee (60118) *(G-20663)*
Empco-Lite Div, Elgin *Also called Elgin Molded Plastics Inc* *(G-8576)*
Empcor, Chicago *Also called Expanded Metal Products Corp* *(G-4544)*
Empire Acoustical Systems Inc 815 261-0072
1111 Ace Rd Princeton (61356) *(G-16807)*
Empire Bronze Corp 630 916-9722
1130 N Ridge Ave Lombard (60148) *(G-13073)*
Empire Comfort Systems Inc 618 233-7420
918 Freeburg Ave Belleville (62220) *(G-1551)*
Empire Corp 630 887-8228
6262 Kingery Hwy Ste 307 Willowbrook (60527) *(G-21042)*
Empire Hard Chrome Inc (PA) 773 762-3156
1615 S Kostner Ave Chicago (60623) *(G-4500)*
Empire Hard Chrome Inc 312 226-7548
1537 S Wood St Chicago (60608) *(G-4501)*
Empire Screw Manufacturing Co 630 833-7060
747 N Yale Ave Villa Park (60181) *(G-20146)*
Empowered Press LLC 630 400-3127
139 Pineridge Dr S Oswego (60543) *(G-16003)*
EMR Manufacturing Inc 630 766-3366
617 N Central Ave Wood Dale (60191) *(G-21185)*
Ems Acrylics & Silk Screener (PA) 773 777-5656
4840 W Diversey Ave Chicago (60639) *(G-4502)*
Ems Industrial and Service Co 815 678-2700
10800 N Main St Richmond (60071) *(G-17012)*
Emsur USA LLC (HQ) 847 367-8787
2800 Carl Blvd Elk Grove Village (60007) *(G-8976)*
Emt, Rockford *Also called Ewikon Molding Tech Inc* *(G-17405)*

Emt, Bloomingdale *Also called Elite Manufacturing Tech Inc (G-1991)*
Emt International Inc 630 655-4145
760 Pasquinelli Dr # 300 Westmont (60559) ***(G-20741)***
Emtech Machining & Grinding 815 338-1580
911 Rail Dr Woodstock (60098) ***(G-21385)***
Emulsicoat Inc (HQ) 217 344-7775
705 E University Ave Urbana (61802) ***(G-19981)***
Emulsions Inc 618 943-2615
1105 Adams St Lawrenceville (62439) ***(G-12531)***
Emv Welding Inc 630 264-0893
544 S River St Aurora (60506) ***(G-1089)***
Emx Digital LLC 212 792-6810
222 N Lasalle St Chicago (60601) ***(G-4503)***
En Es Cee Technology, Elk Grove Village *Also called North Shore Consultants Inc (G-9153)*
En Pointe Cabinetry LLC (PA) 847 787-0777
950 Thorndale Ave Elk Grove Village (60007) ***(G-8977)***
En-Chro Plating Inc 708 450-1250
2755 W Lake St Melrose Park (60160) ***(G-13864)***
Enameled Steel and Sign Co 773 481-2270
4568 W Addison St Chicago (60641) ***(G-4504)***
Enbarr LLC 630 217-2101
431 Ford Ln Bartlett (60103) ***(G-1278)***
Encap Technologies Inc 847 202-3443
61 S Seymour Ave Grayslake (60030) ***(G-10768)***
Encap Technologies Inc (PA) 510 337-2700
707 S Vermont St Palatine (60067) ***(G-16116)***
Encap Technologies Inc 510 337-2700
640 S Vermont St Palatine (60067) ***(G-16117)***
Enchanted Signs of Rockford 815 874-5100
4626 Shropshire Dr Rockford (61109) ***(G-17396)***
Enclosures Inc (HQ) 847 678-2020
9200 Ivanhoe St Schiller Park (60176) ***(G-18803)***
Encompass Group LLC 847 680-3388
955 Campus Dr Mundelein (60060) ***(G-14686)***
Encon Environmental Concepts 630 543-1583
643 W Winthrop Ave Addison (60101) ***(G-115)***
Encore Fastners, Northbrook *Also called Ecf Holdings LLC (G-15379)*
Encyclopaedia Britannica Inc (HQ) 312 347-7000
325 N Lasalle St Ste 200 Chicago (60654) ***(G-4505)***
Endeavor Technologies Inc 630 562-0300
417 Stone Dr Saint Charles (60174) ***(G-18197)***
Enders Engineering, Glendale Heights *Also called Enders Process Equipment Corp (G-10449)*
Enders Process Equipment Corp 630 469-3787
746 Armitage Ave Glendale Heights (60139) ***(G-10449)***
Endofix Ltd 708 715-3472
9118 Ogden Ave Ste 1 Brookfield (60513) ***(G-2482)***
Endoplus, Mundelein *Also called Jstone Inc (G-14706)*
Endotronix Inc (PA) 630 504-2861
815 Ogden Ave Lisle (60532) ***(G-12888)***
Endura Paint Chicago 815 630-5083
2239 Muriel Ct Joliet (60433) ***(G-11861)***
Endure Holdings Inc 224 558-1828
125 Fairfield Way Ste 108 Bloomingdale (60108) ***(G-1992)***
Eneos, Schaumburg *Also called Jx Nippon Oil & Energy USA Inc (G-18583)*
Enercon Engineering Inc (PA) 800 218-8831
201 Altorfer Ln East Peoria (61611) ***(G-8266)***
Enercon Engineering Inc 309 694-1418
301 Altorfer Ln East Peoria (61611) ***(G-8267)***
Energy Absorption Systems Inc (HQ) 312 467-6750
70 W Madison St Ste 2350 Chicago (60602) ***(G-4506)***
Energy Group Inc (PA) 847 836-2000
14 N 679 Il Rt 25 Ste C Dundee (60118) ***(G-8127)***
Energy Parts Solutions Inc 224 653-9412
820 Estes Ave Schaumburg (60193) ***(G-18518)***
Energy Services Group LLC 630 581-4840
700 Commerce Dr Ste 500 Oak Brook (60523) ***(G-15616)***
Energy Solutions Inc 618 465-5404
1520 Worden Ave Alton (62002) ***(G-556)***
Energy Tees 708 771-0000
1401 Circle Ave Ste 1n Forest Park (60130) ***(G-9713)***
Energy-Glazed Systems Inc 847 223-4500
350 Center St Grayslake (60030) ***(G-10769)***
Enerstar Inc 847 350-3400
838 Foster Ave Bensenville (60106) ***(G-1797)***
Enersys 630 455-4872
801 Warrenville Rd # 250 Lisle (60532) ***(G-12889)***
Enertech Global LLC 605 996-7180
2506 S Elm St Greenville (62246) ***(G-10833)***
Enesco LLC (PA) 630 875-5300
225 Windsor Dr Itasca (60143) ***(G-11650)***
Enespro LLC 630 332-2801
122 W 22nd St Ste 1 Oak Brook (60523) ***(G-15617)***
Engelhardt Enterprises Inc 847 277-7070
710 Bradwell Rd Inverness (60010) ***(G-11600)***
Engelhardt Gear Co 847 766-7070
2526 American Ln Elk Grove Village (60007) ***(G-8978)***
Engert Co Inc 847 673-1633
8103 Monticello Ave Skokie (60076) ***(G-18950)***
Engility Corporation 847 583-1216
5600 Old Orchard Rd Bsmt Skokie (60077) ***(G-18951)***
Engility Corporation 708 596-8245
16501 Kedzie Ave Ph Rm245 Harvey (60428) ***(G-11083)***
Engine Efficiency Systems LLC 630 590-5241
6125 S Madison St Burr Ridge (60527) ***(G-2670)***
Engine Rebuilders & Supply 708 338-1113
4010 W North Ave Stone Park (60165) ***(G-19554)***
Engine Solutions Inc 815 979-2312
1928 12th St Rockford (61104) ***(G-17397)***
Engineered Abrasives Inc 662 582-4143
11631 S Austin Ave Alsip (60803) ***(G-445)***
Engineered Components Co (PA) 847 985-8000
1100 Davis Rd Ste A Elgin (60123) ***(G-8579)***
Engineered Custom Lubricants, Aurora *Also called Ecli Products LLC (G-955)*
Engineered Finishing Systems, Elmhurst *Also called Engineering Finshg Systems LLC (G-9361)*
Engineered Fluid Inc (PA) 618 533-1351
1308 N Maple St Centralia (62801) ***(G-3230)***
Engineered Fluid Inc 618 533-1351
1308 N Maple St Centralia (62801) ***(G-3231)***
Engineered Foam Solutions Inc 708 769-4130
16000 Van Drunen Rd # 600 South Holland (60473) ***(G-19210)***
Engineered Glass Products LLC 773 843-1964
929 W Exchange Ave Chicago (60609) ***(G-4507)***
Engineered Glass Products LLC (PA) 312 326-4710
2857 S Halsted St Chicago (60608) ***(G-4508)***
ENGINEERED GLASS PRODUCTS, L.L.C., Chicago *Also called Engineered Glass Products LLC (G-4507)*
Engineered Iron Works Inc 773 887-5701
1071 Waveland Ave Chicago (60639) ***(G-4509)***
Engineered Materials Inc (PA) 847 821-8280
89 Chestnut Ter Buffalo Grove (60089) ***(G-2534)***
Engineered Mills Inc 847 548-0044
888 E Belvidere Rd Grayslake (60030) ***(G-10770)***
Engineered Plastic Pdts Corp 847 952-8400
1848 S Elmhurst Rd Mount Prospect (60056) ***(G-14526)***
Engineered Plastic Systems LLC 800 480-2327
885 Church Rd Elgin (60123) ***(G-8580)***
Engineered Plumbing Spc LLC 630 682-1555
2312 Oak Leaf St Joliet (60436) ***(G-11862)***
Engineered Polymer Systems Div, Elgin *Also called Parker-Hannifin Corporation (G-8685)*
Engineered SEC & Sound Inc 630 876-8853
1275 W Roosevelt Rd # 110 West Chicago (60185) ***(G-20573)***
Engineered Storage Products Co, Dekalb *Also called Tank Wind-Down Corp (G-7707)*
Engineering Design & Dev 309 266-6298
1001 W Jefferson St Morton (61550) ***(G-14359)***
Engineering Finshg Systems LLC (PA) 815 893-6090
202 E Bttrfield Rd Ste 20 Elmhurst (60126) ***(G-9361)***
Engineering Products Company 815 436-9055
15125 S Meadow Ln Plainfield (60544) ***(G-16659)***
Engineering Resources, Vernon Hills *Also called Steamgard LLC (G-20100)*
Enginred Molding Solutions Inc 815 363-9600
4913 Prime Pkwy McHenry (60050) ***(G-13741)***
Enginuity Communications Corp 630 444-0778
3545 Stern Ave Saint Charles (60174) ***(G-18198)***
Engis Corporation (PA) 847 808-9400
105 W Hintz Rd Wheeling (60090) ***(G-20891)***
Engle Manufacturing Co 815 738-2282
214 Main St Leaf River (61047) ***(G-12541)***
Englewood Co Op 773 873-1201
900 W 63rd Pkwy Chicago (60621) ***(G-4510)***
Engravings Plus 217 784-8426
421 S Lott Blvd Gibson City (60936) ***(G-10337)***
Enhanced Plasmonics LLC 904 238-9270
820 Davis St Ste 216 Evanston (60201) ***(G-9513)***
Enjoy Life Foods, Chicago *Also called Enjoy Life Natural Brands LLC (G-4511)*
Enjoy Life Natural Brands LLC (HQ) 773 632-2163
8770 W Bryn Mawr Ave Chicago (60631) ***(G-4511)***
Enjoylife Inc 847 966-3377
8244 Lehigh Ave Morton Grove (60053) ***(G-14405)***
Ennis Inc 815 875-2000
200 W Railroad Ave Princeton (61356) ***(G-16808)***
Enp Investments LLC 815 539-7471
2001 W Main St Mendota (61342) ***(G-13942)***
ENR General Machining Co 773 523-2944
3725 W 49th St Chicago (60632) ***(G-4512)***
Enrollment Rx LLC 847 233-0088
9511 River St Ste 100 Schiller Park (60176) ***(G-18804)***
Ensembleiq Inc 847 438-7357
20909 N Middleton Dr Kildeer (60047) ***(G-12047)***
Ensign Emblem Ltd 217 877-8224
2435 E Federal Dr Decatur (62526) ***(G-7493)***
Ensource Inc 312 912-1048
2826 S Union Ave Chicago (60616) ***(G-4513)***
Entappia LLC 630 546-4531
1052 Sundew Ct Aurora (60504) ***(G-957)***
Entec Polymers LLC 866 598-8941
24210 W 143rd St Plainfield (60544) ***(G-16660)***

ALPHABETIC

Entech Fabrications Inc 708 597-5568
14002 S Harrison Ave Posen (60469) ***(G-16794)***
Enterprise AC & Htg Co 708 430-2212
6112 111th St Chicago Ridge (60415) ***(G-6794)***
Enterprise Oil Co 312 487-2025
3200 S Western Ave Chicago (60608) ***(G-4514)***
Enterprise Pallet Inc 815 928-8546
1166 E 6000n Rd Bourbonnais (60914) ***(G-2260)***
Enterprise Printing, Downers Grove *Also called Perryco Inc* ***(G-8074)***
Enterprise Products Company 708 534-6266
23313 S Ridgeland Ave Monee (60449) ***(G-14197)***
Enterprise Service Corporation 773 589-2727
5400 Milton Pkwy Des Plaines (60018) ***(G-7758)***
Enterprise Signs Inc 708 691-1273
2538 New St Blue Island (60406) ***(G-2121)***
Enterprises One Stop 773 924-5506
48 E Garfield Blvd Chicago (60615) ***(G-4515)***
Entience 217 649-2590
305 W Michigan Ave Urbana (61801) ***(G-19982)***
Entrac Systems, Mount Vernon *Also called Km Enterprises Inc* ***(G-14620)***
Entrans International LLC 618 548-3660
1414 S Broadway Ave Salem (62881) ***(G-18337)***
Entrematic HPD North Amer Inc (HQ) 847 562-4910
935 Campus Dr Mundelein (60060) ***(G-14687)***
Entrepreneur Media Inc 312 923-0818
205 W Wacker Dr Ste 1820 Chicago (60606) ***(G-4516)***
Entrigue Designs 708 647-6159
825 Maple Ave Homewood (60430) ***(G-11493)***
Entropy Cab Solutions Inc USA 630 834-3872
918 N Oaklawn Ave Elmhurst (60126) ***(G-9362)***
Entrust Services LLC (PA) 630 699-9132
608 S Washington St Naperville (60540) ***(G-14825)***
Envelope Division, Danville *Also called Westrock Mwv LLC* ***(G-7397)***
Envelopes Only Inc 630 213-2500
2000 S Park Ave Streamwood (60107) ***(G-19573)***
Envestnet Inc 866 924-8912
35 E Wacker Dr Ste 2400 Chicago (60601) ***(G-4517)***
Envestnet Inc (PA) 312 827-2800
35 E Wacker Dr Ste 2400 Chicago (60601) ***(G-4518)***
Envestnet PMC Prtflio MGT Cons, Chicago *Also called Envestnet Inc* ***(G-4517)***
Envestnet Rtrment Slutions LLC (HQ) 312 827-7957
35 E Wacker Dr Chicago (60601) ***(G-4519)***
Envirnmntal Ctrl Solutions Inc (PA) 217 793-8966
2020 Timberbrook Dr Springfield (62702) ***(G-19363)***
Enviro Tech International Inc 708 343-6641
1800 N 25th Ave Melrose Park (60160) ***(G-13865)***
Enviro-Buildings, Quincy *Also called Craig Industries Inc* ***(G-16873)***
Enviro-Chem Inc 847 549-7797
228 Alexandria Dr Vernon Hills (60061) ***(G-20052)***
Enviro-Safe Refrigerants Inc 309 346-1110
400 Hanna Dr Pekin (61554) ***(G-16331)***
Envirocoat Inc 847 673-3649
7440 Saint Louis Ave Skokie (60076) ***(G-18952)***
Environetics Inc 815 838-8331
1201 Commerce St Lockport (60441) ***(G-12993)***
Environmental Inks & Coatings, West Chicago *Also called Siegwerk Eic LLC* ***(G-20641)***
Environmental Inks & Coding (PA) 630 231-7313
450 Wegner Dr West Chicago (60185) ***(G-20574)***
Environmental Products Co Div, Batavia *Also called Material Control Inc* ***(G-1393)***
Environmental Solutions Intl, Batavia *Also called Producers Envmtl Pdts LLC* ***(G-1406)***
Environmental Specialties Inc 630 860-7070
1600 Glenlake Ave Itasca (60143) ***(G-11651)***
Environmental Systems Res Inst 312 609-0966
221 N La Salle St Ste 863 Chicago (60601) ***(G-4520)***
Envision 3, Bloomingdale *Also called Envision Graphics LLC* ***(G-1993)***
Envision Graphics LLC 630 825-1200
225 Madsen Dr Bloomingdale (60108) ***(G-1993)***
Envision Inc 847 735-0789
40 N Ahwahnee Rd Lake Forest (60045) ***(G-12246)***
Envision Unlimited 773 651-1100
8562 S Vincennes Ave Chicago (60620) ***(G-4521)***
Enz (usa) Inc 630 692-7880
1585 Beverly Ct Ste 115 Aurora (60502) ***(G-958)***
Enzyme Mechanisms Conference 847 491-5653
755 Sheridan Rd Winnetka (60093) ***(G-21129)***
Enzymes Incorporated 847 487-5401
1099 Brown St Ste 102 Wauconda (60084) ***(G-20348)***
Eoe Inc 847 550-1665
590 Telser Rd Ste A Lake Zurich (60047) ***(G-12408)***
Ep Technology Corporation USA 217 351-7888
1401 Interstate Dr Champaign (61822) ***(G-3290)***
Epazz Inc (PA) 312 955-8161
325 N Milwaukee Ave Ste G Wheeling (60090) ***(G-20892)***
Epco, Plainfield *Also called Engineering Products Company* ***(G-16659)***
Epcor Industrial Inc 847 545-9212
1325 Louis Ave Elk Grove Village (60007) ***(G-8979)***
Epe Industries Usa Inc 800 315-0336
1109 Kirk St Elk Grove Village (60007) ***(G-8980)***
Epe Industries USA Chicago, Elk Grove Village *Also called Epe Industries Usa Inc* ***(G-8980)***
Epic Eye 309 210-6212
1869 E 19th Rd Grand Ridge (61325) ***(G-10688)***
Epic Metals Corporation 847 803-6411
2400 E Devon Ave Ste 205 Des Plaines (60018) ***(G-7759)***
Epir Inc 630 842-4486
586 Territorial Dr Ste A Bolingbrook (60440) ***(G-2174)***
Epir Technologies Inc 630 771-0203
590 Territorial Dr Ste H Bolingbrook (60440) ***(G-2175)***
Epiworks Inc 217 373-1590
1606 Rion Dr Champaign (61822) ***(G-3291)***
Epix Inc 847 465-1818
381 Lexington Dr Buffalo Grove (60089) ***(G-2535)***
Epix Tube Co Inc 630 844-0960
500 N Broadway Aurora (60505) ***(G-1090)***
Epoxy Chemicals, Kirkland *Also called Euclid Chemical Company* ***(G-12060)***
Epp Composites Inc 847 612-3495
129 Fairfield Way Bloomingdale (60108) ***(G-1994)***
EPS Solutions Incorporated 815 206-0868
1525 W Lake Shore Dr Woodstock (60098) ***(G-21386)***
Epscca 815 568-3020
1400 N State St Marengo (60152) ***(G-13484)***
Epublishing Inc 312 768-6800
720 N Franklin St Chicago (60654) ***(G-4522)***
Equa Star Chemical Corp 815 942-7011
8805 Tabler Rd Morris (60450) ***(G-14303)***
Equi-Chem International Inc 630 784-0432
510 Tower Blvd Carol Stream (60188) ***(G-2979)***
Equilibrium Contact Center Inc 888 708-1405
1410 Auburn St Rockford (61103) ***(G-17398)***
Equilon Enterprises LLC 312 733-1849
1001 W Jackson Blvd Chicago (60607) ***(G-4523)***
Equinox Group Inc 312 226-7002
329 W 18th St Ste 1000 Chicago (60616) ***(G-4524)***
EQUIPMENT MONITOR & CONTROL, Carbondale *Also called Emac Inc* ***(G-2841)***
Equipment Rent and Royalty, Northbrook *Also called ER&r Inc* ***(G-15385)***
Equipmentbag.com, Wheaton *Also called Wyckoff Advertising Inc* ***(G-20832)***
Equipsolutions LLC (PA) 630 351-9070
31 Presidential Dr Roselle (60172) ***(G-17953)***
Equipto Electronics Corp (PA) 630 897-4691
351 Woodlawn Ave Aurora (60506) ***(G-1091)***
Equisoft Inc 815 629-2789
8176 W Oliver Rd Winnebago (61088) ***(G-21119)***
Equistar, Morris *Also called Lyondell Chemical Company* ***(G-14311)***
Equistar Chemicals LP 217 253-3311
625 E Us Highway 36 Tuscola (61953) ***(G-19926)***
Equity Concepts Co Inc (PA) 815 226-1300
5758 Elaine Dr Rockford (61108) ***(G-17399)***
Equus Power I LP (PA) 847 908-2878
1900 E Golf Rd Ste 1030 Schaumburg (60173) ***(G-18519)***
Equustock LLC 866 962-4686
8179 Starwood Dr Ste 1 Loves Park (61111) ***(G-13210)***
ER&r Inc 847 791-5671
800 Midway Rd Apt 2n Northbrook (60062) ***(G-15385)***
Er2 Image Group, Hanover Park *Also called Schellerer Corporation Inc* ***(G-11013)***
ERA Industries Inc 847 357-1320
1800 Greenleaf Ave Elk Grove Village (60007) ***(G-8981)***
ERA Tool and Manufacturing Co 847 298-6333
3200 16th St Zion (60099) ***(G-21513)***
Erasermitt Incorporated 312 842-2855
2001 S Michigan Ave 18q Chicago (60616) ***(G-4525)***
Erbeck One Chem & Lab Sup Inc 312 203-0078
16279 Celtic Cir Manhattan (60442) ***(G-13432)***
Erbes Electric 815 849-5508
409 W Main St Sublette (61367) ***(G-19636)***
Erdco Engineering Corporation 847 328-0550
721 Custer Ave Evanston (60202) ***(G-9514)***
Erect - O -Veyor Corporation 630 766-1200
421 S County Line Rd Franklin Park (60131) ***(G-9939)***
Erect-A-Tube Inc 815 943-4091
701 W Park St Harvard (60033) ***(G-11054)***
Erell Manufacturing Company 847 427-3000
2678 Coyle Ave Elk Grove Village (60007) ***(G-8982)***
Ergo-Help Inc 847 593-0722
728 Northwest Hwy # 152 Fox River Grove (60021) ***(G-9757)***
Ergo-Help Pneumatics, Fox River Grove *Also called Ergo-Help Inc* ***(G-9757)***
Ergo-Tech Incorporated 630 773-2222
217 Catalpa Ave Itasca (60143) ***(G-11652)***
Ergonomic Office Chairs, Lake Forest *Also called The United Group Inc* ***(G-12314)***
Ergoseal Inc 630 462-9370
344 Commerce Dr Carol Stream (60188) ***(G-2980)***
Ergoseal Inc (PA) 630 462-9600
346 Commerce Dr Carol Stream (60188) ***(G-2981)***
Eric Harr 618 538-7889
7508 Triple Lakes Rd East Carondelet (62240) ***(G-8172)***
Erickson Tool & Machine Co 815 397-2653
1903 20th Ave Rockford (61104) ***(G-17400)***
Ericson S Log & Lumber Co (PA) 309 667-2147
11 State Highway 17 New Windsor (61465) ***(G-15073)***

Erie Group International Inc 309 659-2233
1201 S Main St Rochelle (61068) ***(G-17139)***
Erie Vehicle Company 773 536-6300
60 E 51st St Chicago (60615) ***(G-4526)***
Eriem Surgical Inc 847 549-1410
28438 N Ballard Dr Lake Forest (60045) ***(G-12247)***
Erin Rope Corporation 708 377-1084
2661 139th St Blue Island (60406) ***(G-2122)***
Ermak Usa Inc 847 640-7765
2860 S River Rd Ste 145 Des Plaines (60018) ***(G-7760)***
Erowa Technology Inc 847 290-0295
2535 S Clearbrook Dr Arlington Heights (60005) ***(G-733)***
Erq Systems Inc 815 469-1072
10439 S Maplewood Ave Chicago (60655) ***(G-4527)***
Erva Tool & Die Company 773 533-7806
3100 W Grand Ave Chicago (60622) ***(G-4528)***
Erwin Wiczer Industries Inc 847 541-9556
500 Harvester Ct Ste 8 Wheeling (60090) ***(G-20893)***
Esafety Lights LLC 800 236-8621
7144 N Harlem Ave Ste 113 Chicago (60631) ***(G-4529)***
Esc Integris, South Beloit *Also called Cutting Edge Water Jet Service* ***(G-19088)***
Escalade Sports, Olney *Also called U S Weight Inc* ***(G-15891)***
Esco Lighting Inc 773 427-7000
3254 N Kilbourn Ave Chicago (60641) ***(G-4530)***
Esd, Prospect Heights *Also called Creative Science Activities* ***(G-16837)***
Esi Fuel & Energy Group LLC 716 465-4289
1997 Lemontree Ln Collinsville (62234) ***(G-6959)***
Esi Steel & Fabrication 618 548-3017
1645 N Broadway Ave Salem (62881) ***(G-18338)***
Esma Inc 708 331-0456
450 Taft Dr Ste 101 South Holland (60473) ***(G-19211)***
Esmark, Hinsdale *Also called Severstal US Holdings II Inc* ***(G-11379)***
ESP Properties LLC 312 725-5100
123 N Wacker Dr Ste 880 Chicago (60606) ***(G-4531)***
Espe Manufacturing Co 847 678-8950
9220 Ivanhoe St Schiller Park (60176) ***(G-18805)***
Espee Biopharma & Finechem LLC 224 355-5950
1701 E Wdfield Rd Ste 636 Schaumburg (60173) ***(G-18520)***
Espee Biopharma & Finechem LLC 888 851-6667
1701 E Woodfield Rd # 636 Schaumburg (60173) ***(G-18521)***
Esri, Chicago *Also called Environmental Systems Res Inst* ***(G-4520)***
Essannay Show It Inc 312 733-5511
451 W Grand Ave Chicago (60642) ***(G-4532)***
Essen Nutrition Corporation 630 739-6700
1414 Sherman Rd Romeoville (60446) ***(G-17817)***
Essential Creat Chicago Inc 773 238-1700
2112 W 95th St Chicago (60643) ***(G-4533)***
Essential Laser and Skin Inst 815 381-7005
534 Roxbury Rd Rockford (61107) ***(G-17401)***
Essentra Corp (HQ) 814 899-7671
2 Westbrook Corp Ctr # 200 Westchester (60154) ***(G-20697)***
Essentra Holdings Corp (HQ) 804 518-0322
2 Westbrook Corporate Ctr # 200 Westchester (60154) ***(G-20698)***
Essentra Packaging US Inc (HQ) 704 418-8692
2 Westbrook Corp Ctr Westchester (60154) ***(G-20699)***
Essex Electro Engineers Inc 847 891-4444
2015 Mitchell Blvd Schaumburg (60193) ***(G-18522)***
Essex Group Inc 630 628-7841
758 W Racquet Club Dr Addison (60101) ***(G-116)***
Essilor Laboratories Amer Inc 309 787-2727
4470 48th Avenue Ct Rock Island (61201) ***(G-17219)***
Est Lighting Inc 847 612-1705
10305 Covell St Richmond (60071) ***(G-17013)***
Estad Stamping & Mfg Co 217 442-4600
1005 Griggs St Danville (61832) ***(G-7331)***
Estes Laser & Mfg Inc 847 301-8231
930 Lunt Ave Schaumburg (60193) ***(G-18523)***
Estima, Evanston *Also called Thomas A Doan* ***(G-9584)***
Estructuras Inc 773 522-2200
2232 S Pulaski Rd Chicago (60623) ***(G-4534)***
Estwing Manufacturing Co Inc 815 397-9521
2647 8th St Rockford (61109) ***(G-17402)***
ET Products LLC 800 325-5746
8128 S Madison St Burr Ridge (60527) ***(G-2671)***
ET Simonds Materials Company 618 457-8191
1500 N Oakland Ave Carbondale (62901) ***(G-2842)***
Etch-Tech Inc 630 833-4234
494 W Wrightwood Ave Elmhurst (60126) ***(G-9363)***
Etcon Corp 630 325-6100
7750 S Grant St Burr Ridge (60527) ***(G-2672)***
Etel Inc 847 519-3380
333 E State Pkwy Schaumburg (60173) ***(G-18524)***
Eternal Quality Group 309 799-3800
910 10th Ave W Milan (61264) ***(G-14009)***
Ethan Company Incorporated 815 715-2283
306 Harvard Ct Shorewood (60404) ***(G-18895)***
Ethereal Confections, Woodstock *Also called E3 Artisan Inc* ***(G-21384)***
Ethnic Media LLC 224 676-0778
704 S Milwaukee Ave Wheeling (60090) ***(G-20894)***
Ethos Seafood Group LLC 312 858-3474
6800 Santa Fe Dr Ste L Hodgkins (60525) ***(G-11388)***
Ethyl Corp 618 583-1292
501 Monsanto Ave East Saint Louis (62206) ***(G-8307)***
Eti Solid State Lighting Inc 855 384-7754
720 Northgate Pkwy Wheeling (60090) ***(G-20895)***
Etlon Enterprises 847 258-5265
1441 Elmhurst Rd Elk Grove Village (60007) ***(G-8983)***
Etnyre International Ltd (PA) 815 732-2116
1333 S Daysville Rd Oregon (61061) ***(G-15918)***
Eton Machine Co Ltd 847 426-3380
1485 Davis Rd Ste B Elgin (60123) ***(G-8581)***
Eton Pharmaceuticals Inc (PA) 847 787-7361
21925 W Feld Pkwy Ste 235 Deer Park (60010) ***(G-7581)***
Etti, Wauconda *Also called Extrusion Tooling Technology* ***(G-20350)***
Etymotic Research Inc 847 228-0006
61 Martin Ln Elk Grove Village (60007) ***(G-8984)***
Euclid Chemical Company 815 522-2308
3835 State Route 72 Kirkland (60146) ***(G-12060)***
Eugene Ewbank 630 705-0400
118 Kirkland Cir Ste B Oswego (60543) ***(G-16004)***
Euphoria Catering and Events 630 301-4369
611 Pennsylvania Ave Aurora (60506) ***(G-1092)***
Eureka Locker Inc 309 467-2731
110 4h Park Rd Eureka (61530) ***(G-9482)***
Eureka Printing & Stationery, Eureka *Also called Paul D Burton* ***(G-9484)***
Euro Marble Supply Ltd 847 233-0700
4552 Ruby St Schiller Park (60176) ***(G-18806)***
Euro-Tech Cabinetry Rmdlg Corp 815 254-3876
12515 Rhea Dr Plainfield (60585) ***(G-16661)***
Euromarket Designs Inc (HQ) 847 272-2888
1250 Techny Rd Northbrook (60062) ***(G-15386)***
European American Industries, Lake Bluff *Also called American Medical Industries* ***(G-12169)***
European Ornamental Iron Works 630 705-9300
1786 W Armitage Ct Addison (60101) ***(G-117)***
European Wood Works Inc 773 662-6607
1151 Woodlake Dr Carol Stream (60188) ***(G-2982)***
Euroview Enterprises LLC 630 227-3300
342 W Carol Ln Elmhurst (60126) ***(G-9364)***
Ev Interactive LLC 847 907-4689
675 N North Ct Ste 140 Palatine (60067) ***(G-16118)***
Eva's Bridal, Orland Park *Also called Halanick Enterprises Inc* ***(G-15958)***
Evac Environmental Solutions, Cherry Valley *Also called Evac North America Inc* ***(G-3439)***
Evac North America Inc 815 654-8300
1445 Huntwood Dr Cherry Valley (61016) ***(G-3439)***
Evac Systems Fire & Rescue 309 764-7812
400 24th St Moline (61265) ***(G-14143)***
Evang Lthn Ch Dr Mrtn Luth KG 773 380-2540
8765 W Higgins Rd Ste 600 Chicago (60631) ***(G-4535)***
Evangers Dog and Cat Fd Co Inc 847 537-0102
2210 W 162nd St Markham (60428) ***(G-13548)***
Evans Food Group Ltd (HQ) 773 254-7400
4118 S Halsted St Chicago (60609) ***(G-4536)***
Evans Foods Inc (HQ) 773 254-7400
4118 S Halsted St Chicago (60609) ***(G-4537)***
Evans Heating and Air Inc 217 483-8440
6172 Lick Rd Chatham (62629) ***(G-3420)***
Evans Manufacturing, Rock Island *Also called Premium Manufacturing Inc* ***(G-17233)***
Evans Talaiha 618 327-8200
550 W Saint Louis St Nashville (62263) ***(G-14996)***
Evans Tool & Manufacturing 630 897-8656
6s252 Hankes Rd Aurora (60506) ***(G-1093)***
Evanston Awning Company 847 864-4520
2801 Central St Evanston (60201) ***(G-9515)***
Evanston Graphic Imaging Inc 847 869-7446
1255 Hartrey Ave Evanston (60202) ***(G-9516)***
Evanston Woman Magazine 847 722-5654
1881 Oak Ave Apt 513w Evanston (60201) ***(G-9517)***
Evapco Inc 410 756-2600
62140 Collection Ctr Chicago (60693) ***(G-4538)***
Evapco Inc 217 923-3431
1723 E York Rd Greenup (62428) ***(G-10820)***
Evapco Midwest, Greenup *Also called Evapco Inc* ***(G-10820)***
Eve J Alfille Gallery & Studio, Evanston *Also called Eve J Alfille Ltd* ***(G-9518)***
Eve J Alfille Ltd 847 869-7920
623 Grove St Evanston (60201) ***(G-9518)***
Evenson Explosives LLC 815 942-5800
2019 Dunn Rd Morris (60450) ***(G-14304)***
Evention LLC 773 733-4256
121 W Wacker Dr Ste 3200 Chicago (60601) ***(G-4539)***
Ever Ready Pin & Manufacturing 815 874-4949
5560 International Dr Rockford (61109) ***(G-17403)***
Everbrite LLC 618 242-0645
1 Neon Dr Mount Vernon (62864) ***(G-14610)***
Eveready Welding Service Inc 708 532-2432
18111 Harlem Ave Tinley Park (60477) ***(G-19825)***
Everede Tool Company LLC (HQ) 623 414-4800
850 W Hawthorne Ln West Chicago (60185) ***(G-20575)***

ALPHABETIC

Everede Tool Company LLC 773 467-4200
850 W Hawthorne Ln West Chicago (60185) *(G-20576)*
Evergreen Drive Systems, Morton Grove Also called Howland Technology Inc *(G-14411)*
Evergreen Energy LLC 618 384-9295
645 W Illinois Hwy 14 Carmi (62821) *(G-2905)*
Evergreen Fs Inc 815 934-5422
19484 N 3000 East Rd Cullom (60929) *(G-7298)*
Evergreen Manufacturing Inc 217 382-5108
1 Harry Glynn Dr Martinsville (62442) *(G-13584)*
Evergreen Marathon 708 636-5700
2755 W 87th St Evergreen Park (60805) *(G-9594)*
Evergreen Pool & Spa Center, Sandoval Also called Evergreen Pool & Spa LLC *(G-18363)*
Evergreen Pool & Spa LLC 618 247-3555
Us Hwys 50 & 51 Sandoval (62882) *(G-18363)*
Evergreen Scale Models Inc 224 567-8099
65 Bradrock Dr Des Plaines (60018) *(G-7761)*
Evergreen Tank Solutions Inc 708 235-0487
25896 S Sunset Dr Monee (60449) *(G-14198)*
Everlast Portable Buildings 217 543-4080
1565 Cr 1800n Sullivan (61951) *(G-19666)*
Everon Polymers LLC 815 681-8800
420 Woodruff Rd Joliet (60432) *(G-11863)*
Everpure, Hanover Park Also called Pentair Fltrtion Solutions LLC *(G-11012)*
Eversharp Pen Company 847 366-5030
9240 Belmont Ave Unit A Franklin Park (60131) *(G-9940)*
Everything Xclusive 309 370-7450
4010 N Brandywine Dr Peoria (61614) *(G-16436)*
Evo Exhibits LLC 630 520-0710
399 Wegner Dr West Chicago (60185) *(G-20577)*
Evolution Sorbent Products LLC 630 293-8055
1270 Nuclear Dr West Chicago (60185) *(G-20578)*
Evolution Sorbent Products LLC (PA) 630 293-8055
1149 Howard Dr West Chicago (60185) *(G-20579)*
Evonik Corporation 309 697-6220
8300 W Route 24 Mapleton (61547) *(G-13472)*
Evonik Corporation 630 230-0176
7420 S County Line Rd Burr Ridge (60527) *(G-2673)*
Evoqua Water Technologies LLC 815 921-8325
4669 Shepherd Trl Rockford (61103) *(G-17404)*
Evoqua Water Technologies LLC 618 451-1205
3202 W 20th St Granite City (62040) *(G-10705)*
Evoys Corp 773 736-4200
4142 W Lawrence Ave Chicago (60630) *(G-4540)*
Evraz Inc NA (HQ) 312 533-3555
71 S Wacker Dr Ste 1700 Chicago (60606) *(G-4541)*
Evraz Oregon Steel, Chicago Also called Evraz Inc NA *(G-4541)*
Evsco Inc 847 362-7068
2309 N Ringwood Rd Ste M McHenry (60050) *(G-13742)*
EW Bredemeier and Co 773 237-1600
6625 W Diversey Ave Chicago (60707) *(G-4542)*
Ewab Engineering Inc 847 247-0015
1971 Kelley Ct Libertyville (60048) *(G-12649)*
Ewellix USA LLC 618 392-3647
3519 N Union Dr Olney (62450) *(G-15859)*
Ewert, Inc., Alsip Also called MJT Incorporated *(G-480)*
Ewikon Molding Tech Inc 815 874-7270
5652 International Dr Rockford (61109) *(G-17405)*
Eww Enterprise Inc 815 463-9607
1311 S Schoolhouse Rd # 2 New Lenox (60451) *(G-15034)*
Ex-Cell Kaiser LLC 847 451-0451
11240 Melrose Ave Franklin Park (60131) *(G-9941)*
Exact Data, Chicago Also called Consumerbase LLC *(G-4224)*
Exact Machine Company Inc 815 963-7905
2502 Preston St Rockford (61102) *(G-17406)*
Exact Tool Company Inc 847 632-1140
2123 Foster Ave Wheeling (60090) *(G-20896)*
Examiner Publications Inc 630 830-4145
4n781 Gerber Rd Bartlett (60103) *(G-1279)*
Examiner, The, Bartlett Also called Examiner Publications Inc *(G-1279)*
Excalibur Pr-Keyed Shafting Inc 800 487-0514
1111 N Old Rand Rd Wauconda (60084) *(G-20349)*
Excel Ltd Inc 847 543-9138
888 E Belvidere Rd # 105 Grayslake (60030) *(G-10771)*
Excel Bottling Co 618 526-7159
488 S Broadway Breese (62230) *(G-2302)*
Excel Color Corporation 847 734-1270
220 Bond St Elk Grove Village (60007) *(G-8985)*
Excel Displays & Packaging, Aurora Also called Georg-Pcific Corrugated IV LLC *(G-967)*
Excel Electro Assembly Inc 847 621-2500
1595 Brummel Ave Elk Grove Village (60007) *(G-8986)*
Excel Forms Inc 630 801-1936
760 Donna Ave Aurora (60505) *(G-1094)*
Excel Foundry & Machine Inc 309 347-6155
1 Excel Way Pekin (61554) *(G-16332)*
Excel Gear Inc 815 623-3414
11865 Main St Roscoe (61073) *(G-17906)*
Excel Glass Inc 847 801-5200
10507 Delta Pkwy Schiller Park (60176) *(G-18807)*
Excel Group Holdings Inc (PA) 630 773-1815
800 Baker Dr Itasca (60143) *(G-11653)*
Excel Machine & Tool 815 467-1177
24050 S Northern Ill Dr Channahon (60410) *(G-3383)*
Excel Machining Inc 773 585-6666
5654 W 65th St Chicago (60638) *(G-4543)*
Excel Photonics Inc 732 829-2667
1595 Brummel Ave Elk Grove Village (60007) *(G-8987)*
Excel Screen Prtg & EMB Inc 847 801-5200
10507 Delta Pkwy Schiller Park (60176) *(G-18808)*
Excel Specialty Corp 773 262-7575
28101 N Ballard Dr Ste A Lake Forest (60045) *(G-12248)*
Excell Electronics Corporation 847 766-7455
2425 American Ln Elk Grove Village (60007) *(G-8988)*
Excellent Bindery Inc 630 766-9050
500 Eastern Ave Bensenville (60106) *(G-1798)*
Excelsior Inc 815 987-2900
4982 27th Ave Rockford (61109) *(G-17407)*
Excelsior Inc 815 987-2900
4982 27th Ave Rockford (61109) *(G-17408)*
Exclusive Boarding, Elburn Also called Harry Otto Printing Company *(G-8455)*
Exclusive Pro Sports Ltd 815 877-8585
5035 28th Ave Rockford (61109) *(G-17409)*
Exclusive Publications Inc 847 963-0400
3830 Bordeaux Dr Hoffman Estates (60192) *(G-11421)*
Exclusive Stone 847 593-6963
1361 Jarvis Ave Elk Grove Village (60007) *(G-8989)*
Exclusively Expo (PA) 630 378-4600
1225 Naperville Dr Romeoville (60446) *(G-17818)*
Exclusively Expo 630 378-4600
1201 Naperville Dr Romeoville (60446) *(G-17819)*
Execl Machine Technology 847 439-8434
1625 Tonne Rd Elk Grove Village (60007) *(G-8990)*
Executive Performance Fuel LLC 847 364-1933
1060 Talbots Ln Elk Grove Village (60007) *(G-8991)*
Exex Holding Corporation 815 703-7295
1201 Naperville Dr Romeoville (60446) *(G-17820)*
Exide Technologies 630 862-2200
1051 N Main St Ste B Lombard (60148) *(G-13074)*
Exide Technologies LLC 678 566-9000
829 Parkview Blvd Lombard (60148) *(G-13075)*
Exo Fabrication Inc 630 501-1136
1140 W Fullerton Ave Addison (60101) *(G-118)*
Exopack, Chicago Also called Transcontinental Tech LLC *(G-6411)*
Expandable Habitats 815 624-6784
11022 N Main St Rockton (61072) *(G-17697)*
Expanded Metal Products Corp 773 735-4500
4633 S Knox Ave Chicago (60632) *(G-4544)*
Expercolor Inc 773 465-3400
3737 Chase Ave Skokie (60076) *(G-18953)*
Experimental Aircraft Examiner 847 226-0777
69 Mohawk St Cary (60013) *(G-3158)*
Experior Transport, Alsip Also called Polmax LLC *(G-494)*
Expert Manufacturing Systems, Deerfield Also called High Tech Research Inc *(G-7615)*
Expert Metal Finishing Inc 708 583-2550
2120 West St River Grove (60171) *(G-17059)*
Expo Engineered Inc 708 780-7155
1824 S Cicero Ave Cicero (60804) *(G-6847)*
Export Packaging Co Inc (PA) 309 756-4288
525 10th Ave E Milan (61264) *(G-14010)*
Express Cutting Tools Inc 815 964-0410
5026 27th Ave Rockford (61109) *(G-17410)*
Express Donuts Enterprise Inc 630 510-9310
15 Danada Sq E Wheaton (60189) *(G-20798)*
Express Flighting, Princeton Also called Princeton Flighting Corp *(G-16819)*
Express Grinding Inc 847 434-5827
119 Joey Dr Elk Grove Village (60007) *(G-8992)*
Express LLC 708 453-0566
4122 N Harlem Ave Norridge (60706) *(G-15234)*
Express Machining & Molds 630 350-8480
456 Dominic Ct Franklin Park (60131) *(G-9942)*
Express Publishing Inc 773 725-6218
6121 W Belmont Ave Chicago (60634) *(G-4545)*
Express Signs & Lighting Maint 815 725-9080
212 Amendodge Dr Shorewood (60404) *(G-18896)*
Expressions By Christine Inc 217 223-2750
711 Maine St Quincy (62301) *(G-16881)*
Expri Publishing & Printing 773 274-5955
6220 N Hermitage Ave Chicago (60660) *(G-4546)*
Exress Motor and Lift Parts 630 327-2000
1018 Lambrecht Dr Frankfort (60423) *(G-9792)*
Exsel Exhibits Inc 847 647-1012
111 Rawls Rd Des Plaines (60018) *(G-7762)*
Extentel Wrless Communications 847 809-3131
90 Dirleton Ln Inverness (60067) *(G-11595)*
Extol Hydro Technologies Inc 708 717-4371
13020 Ridgewood Dr Palos Park (60464) *(G-16210)*
Exton Corp 847 391-8100
1 Innovation Dr Des Plaines (60016) *(G-7763)*
Exton Corporation, Des Plaines Also called Exton Corp *(G-7763)*

ALPHABETIC SECTION
Falcon Technologies Inc

Extractor Corporation 847 742-3532
685 Martin Dr South Elgin (60177) ***(G-19144)***
Extreme Flight Simulation 224 656-5546
1350 Tri State Pkwy # 128 Gurnee (60031) ***(G-10877)***
Extreme Force Valve Inc 618 494-5795
515 Mound St Jerseyville (62052) ***(G-11790)***
Extreme Glass, Melrose Park *Also called Glass Dimensions Inc* ***(G-13874)***
Extreme Tools Inc 630 202-8324
740 Frontenac Rd Naperville (60563) ***(G-14826)***
Extreme Welding & Machine Serv 618 272-7237
1506 Us Highway 45 N Eldorado (62930) ***(G-8481)***
Extreme Woodworking Inc 224 338-8179
24650 W Luther Ave Apt B Round Lake (60073) ***(G-18074)***
Extrude Hone LLC 847 669-5355
10663 Wolf Dr Huntley (60142) ***(G-11536)***
Extruded Solutions Inc 630 871-6450
1185 W Hawthorne Ln West Chicago (60185) ***(G-20580)***
Extrusion Science, Savanna *Also called Metform LLC* ***(G-18407)***
Extrusion Tooling Technology 847 526-1606
1000 N Rand Rd Ste 210 Wauconda (60084) ***(G-20350)***
Exxon Mobil Corporation 217 854-3291
14491 Brushy Mound Rd Carlinville (62626) ***(G-2875)***
Exxonmobil Pipeline Company 815 423-5571
Interstate 55 & Smth Brg Elwood (60421) ***(G-9462)***
Eye Surgeons of Libertyville 847 362-3811
1880 W Winchester Rd # 105 Libertyville (60048) ***(G-12650)***
Eyeball Music, Chicago *Also called Alligator Rec & Artist MGT Inc* ***(G-3620)***
Eyelation Inc 888 308-4703
18501 Maple Creek Dr # 400 Tinley Park (60477) ***(G-19826)***
Eyes Forward Innovations Corp 281 755-5826
1s735 Pamela Ct West Chicago (60185) ***(G-20581)***
Eyewearplanet Com Inc 847 513-6203
3150 Commercial Ave Northbrook (60062) ***(G-15387)***
EZ Blinds and Drapery Inc (PA) 708 246-6600
550 Quail Ridge Dr Westmont (60559) ***(G-20742)***
EZ Comfort Heating & AC 630 289-2020
1290 Evergreen Ln Elgin (60123) ***(G-8582)***
Ezee Roll Manufacturing Co 217 339-2279
20 N 3000 East Rd Hoopeston (60942) ***(G-11508)***
Eztech Manufacturing Inc 630 293-0010
1200 Howard Dr West Chicago (60185) ***(G-20582)***
F & B Distributors, Arthur *Also called F & B Woodworking Inc* ***(G-857)***
F & B Woodworking Inc 217 543-2531
1702 Cr 2300n Arthur (61911) ***(G-857)***
F & L Drapery Inc 815 932-8997
6279 Warren St Saint Anne (60964) ***(G-18134)***
F & L Electronics LLC 217 586-2132
103 N Prairieview Rd Mahomet (61853) ***(G-13423)***
F & R Plastics Inc 847 336-1330
642 Westmoreland Ave Waukegan (60085) ***(G-20442)***
F & S Engraving Inc 847 870-8400
1620 W Central Rd Mount Prospect (60056) ***(G-14527)***
F and F Screw Products 815 968-7330
2136 12th St Rockford (61104) ***(G-17411)***
F and L Pallets Inc 773 364-0798
3018 S Spaulding Ave Fl 1 Chicago (60623) ***(G-4547)***
F and S Enterprises Plainfield 815 439-9655
2035 Havenhill Dr Plainfield (60586) ***(G-16662)***
F C L Kelloggs 815 467-8198
6225 E Minooka Rd Minooka (60447) ***(G-14060)***
F H Leinweber Co Inc (PA) 708 424-7000
9812 S Cicero Ave Oak Lawn (60453) ***(G-15715)***
F H Leinweber Co Inc 773 568-7722
346 W 107th Pl Chicago (60628) ***(G-4548)***
F Hyman & Co 312 664-3810
1329 N Clybourn Ave Fl 1 Chicago (60610) ***(G-4549)***
F J Murphy & Son Inc 217 787-3477
1800 Factory St Springfield (62702) ***(G-19364)***
F K Pattern & Foundry Company 847 578-5260
1400 Morrow Ave North Chicago (60064) ***(G-15311)***
F Kreutzer & Co 773 826-5767
2646 W Madison St Chicago (60612) ***(G-4550)***
F L C, Sugar Grove *Also called Falex Corporation* ***(G-19643)***
F M Aquisition Corp 773 728-8351
3750 N Lake Shore Dr 8d Chicago (60613) ***(G-4551)***
F M I, Lincolnshire *Also called Flexan LLC* ***(G-12764)***
F N Smith Corporation 815 732-2171
1200 S 2nd St Oregon (61061) ***(G-15919)***
F P M Heat Treating, Elk Grove Village *Also called F P M LLC* ***(G-8993)***
F P M LLC (PA) 847 228-2525
1501 Lively Blvd Elk Grove Village (60007) ***(G-8993)***
F P M LLC 815 332-4961
648 Bypass Us Hwy 20 Cherry Valley (61016) ***(G-3440)***
F P S, Northfield *Also called Financial Publishing Svcs Co* ***(G-15513)***
F S Gateway Inc 618 458-6588
3145 Maeystown Rd Fults (62244) ***(G-10160)***
F T I Inc 312 943-4015
416 W Erie St Chicago (60654) ***(G-4552)***
F V M, Plano *Also called Fox Valley Molding Inc* ***(G-16731)***
F Vogelmann and Company 815 469-2285
440 Center Rd Frankfort (60423) ***(G-9793)***
F Weber Printing Co Inc 815 468-6152
450 N Locust St Manteno (60950) ***(G-13447)***
F&A Specialty Foods Inc 312 887-1344
2nd Fl E 53rd St St Flr Chicago (60615) ***(G-4553)***
F-C Enterprises Inc 815 254-7295
12249 Rhea Dr Ste 3 Plainfield (60585) ***(G-16663)***
F1r Wheels, Chicago *Also called Autospec Inc* ***(G-3779)***
F5d Inc 815 953-9183
70 Tobey Dr Herscher (60941) ***(G-11183)***
Fab Werks Inc 815 724-0317
911 Brian Dr Crest Hill (60403) ***(G-7086)***
Fabbri Sausage Manufacturing 312 829-6363
166 N Aberdeen St Chicago (60607) ***(G-4554)***
Fabco Enterprises Inc 708 333-4644
16812 Lathrop Ave Harvey (60426) ***(G-11084)***
Fabcorr, Coulterville *Also called Corrpak Inc* ***(G-7030)***
Faber Builders Discount, Sterling *Also called Ronnie P Faber* ***(G-19529)***
Fabick Mining LLC 618 982-9000
635 Illinois Highway 1 Norris City (62869) ***(G-15249)***
Fabracraft Manufacturing, Elk Grove Village *Also called Amcraft Manufacturing Inc* ***(G-8821)***
Fabri-Tek, Naperville *Also called Fabritek LLC* ***(G-14827)***
Fabric Images Inc 847 488-9877
325 Corporate Dr Elgin (60123) ***(G-8583)***
Fabricated Metal Systems Inc 815 886-6200
646 Forestwood Dr Ste C Romeoville (60446) ***(G-17821)***
Fabricated Metals Co 847 718-1300
2121 Landmeier Rd Elk Grove Village (60007) ***(G-8994)***
Fabricated Products Co Inc 630 898-6460
1875 Plain Ave Aurora (60502) ***(G-959)***
Fabricating & Welding Corp 773 928-2050
12246 S Halsted St Chicago (60628) ***(G-4555)***
Fabricating Machinery & Eqp, Wood Dale *Also called Fabricating Machinery Sales* ***(G-21186)***
Fabricating Machinery Sales 630 350-2266
640 Pond Dr Ste A Wood Dale (60191) ***(G-21186)***
Fabricators & Mfrs Assn Intl (PA) 815 399-8700
2135 Point Blvd Elgin (60123) ***(G-8584)***
Fabricators and Mfrs Assn, Elgin *Also called Tube & Pipe Association Intl* ***(G-8763)***
Fabricators Unlimited Inc 847 223-7986
55 S Barron Blvd Grayslake (60030) ***(G-10772)***
Fabrick Molded Plastic Div, McHenry *Also called CTS Automotive LLC* ***(G-13734)***
Fabrik Industries Inc 815 385-9480
5213 Prime Pkwy McHenry (60050) ***(G-13743)***
Fabrik Molded Plastics, McHenry *Also called Fabrik Industries Inc* ***(G-13743)***
Fabritek LLC 630 983-0211
216 Briarheath Ln Naperville (60565) ***(G-14827)***
Fabry Inc (PA) 847 395-1919
8315 Evergreen Ct Fox Lake (60020) ***(G-9746)***
Fabtec Manufacturing Inc 847 671-4888
9896 Franklin Ave Franklin Park (60131) ***(G-9943)***
Fabtek Aero Ltd 630 552-3622
775 Duvick Ave Sandwich (60548) ***(G-18369)***
Facemakers Inc (PA) 815 273-3944
140 N 5th St Savanna (61074) ***(G-18405)***
Facemakers Inc 815 273-3944
800 Chicago Ave Savanna (61074) ***(G-18406)***
Fact NA LLC 847 421-1125
2125 Bonita Ln Hoffman Estates (60192) ***(G-11422)***
Fairbanks Wire Corporation 847 683-2600
260 Industrial Dr Ste B Hampshire (60140) ***(G-10972)***
Fairbury Division, Fairbury *Also called Ptc Tubular Products LLC* ***(G-9612)***
Fairbury Fair Association, Fairbury *Also called John Joda Post 54* ***(G-9610)***
Fairchild Industries Inc 847 550-9580
475 Capital Dr Lake Zurich (60047) ***(G-12409)***
Fairdeal Jumbo Packaging USA, Naperville *Also called Kobawala Poly-Pack Inc* ***(G-14859)***
Fairfield Acid and Frac Co 618 842-9186
Hwy 15 W Fairfield (62837) ***(G-9622)***
Fairfield Processing Corp 618 452-8404
1201 W 1st St Granite City (62040) ***(G-10706)***
Fairfield Ready Mix Inc 618 842-9462
County Rte 45 N Fairfield (62837) ***(G-9623)***
Fairmont Central LLC (PA) 815 433-2449
776 Centennial Dr Ottawa (61350) ***(G-16050)***
Fairmount Redi-Mix, Fairmount *Also called Ferber George & Sons* ***(G-9643)***
Fairmount Santrol Inc 815 433-2449
776 Centennial Dr Ottawa (61350) ***(G-16051)***
Fairmount Santrol Inc 815 587-4410
776 Centennial Dr Ottawa (61350) ***(G-16052)***
Fairmount Santrol Inc 815 538-2645
300 S Vermillion St Troy Grove (61372) ***(G-19921)***
Fairview Heights Tribune, Mascoutah *Also called Herald Publications* ***(G-13599)***
Faith Printing 217 675-2191
824 Bills Rd Franklin (62638) ***(G-9855)***
Falcon Press Inc 815 455-9099
341 E Crystal Lake Ave Crystal Lake (60014) ***(G-7197)***
Falcon Technologies Inc 847 550-1866
1050 Ensell Rd Lake Zurich (60047) ***(G-12410)***

ALPHABETIC

(PA)=Parent Co (HQ)=Headquarters (DH)=Div Headquarters
2020 Harris Illinois
Industrial Directory
1119

Falex Corporation...630 556-3679
1020 Airpark Dr Sugar Grove (60554) **(G-19643)**
Fall Protection Systems Inc (PA)...618 452-7000
2901 Old Nickel Plate Rd Madison (62060) **(G-13411)**
Falling Springs Quarry, Dupo *Also called Stolle Casper Quar & Contg Co* **(G-8146)**
False Hope Brand Co...312 265-1364
1211 S Wstn Ave Ste 205 Chicago (60608) **(G-4556)**
Famar Flavor LLC...708 926-2951
4711 137th St Crestwood (60418) **(G-7117)**
Family Health Foods, Arthur *Also called Helmuth Custom Kitchens LLC* **(G-862)**
Family Record, Palos Heights *Also called Graphic Communicators Inc* **(G-16186)**
Family Time Computing Inc...309 664-1742
4 Yount Dr Bloomington (61704) **(G-2041)**
Family Time Magazine, Frankfort *Also called Area Marketing Inc* **(G-9768)**
Famous Fossil Vinyard & Winery...815 563-4665
395 W Cedarville Rd Freeport (61032) **(G-10107)**
Famous Lubricants Inc...773 268-2555
124 W 47th St Chicago (60609) **(G-4557)**
Fanmar Inc...847 621-2010
901 Greenleaf Ave Elk Grove Village (60007) **(G-8995)**
Fannie May Cnfctons Brands Inc (HQ)...330 494-0833
9 W Washington St Chicago (60602) **(G-4558)**
Fannie May Fine Chocolate, Chicago *Also called Fannie May Cnfctons Brands Inc* **(G-4558)**
Fanning Communications Inc...708 293-1430
4701 Midlothian Tpke # 4 Crestwood (60418) **(G-7118)**
Fantastic Lettering Inc...773 685-7650
5644 W Lawrence Ave Chicago (60630) **(G-4559)**
Fantus Paper Products, Chicago *Also called P S Greetings Inc* **(G-5729)**
Fanuc America Corporation...847 898-5000
1800 Lakewood Blvd Hoffman Estates (60192) **(G-11423)**
Fapme...815 624-8538
810 Progressive Ln South Beloit (61080) **(G-19090)**
Far East Food Inc...312 733-1688
1836 S Canal St Chicago (60616) **(G-4560)**
Far East Trading Co, Chicago *Also called Far East Food Inc* **(G-4560)**
Far West Print Solutions LLC...630 879-9500
714 Fairfield Way North Aurora (60542) **(G-15260)**
Fareva Morton Grove Inc...847 966-0200
6901 Golf Rd Morton Grove (60053) **(G-14406)**
Farina News...618 245-6216
109 N Walnut St Farina (62838) **(G-9652)**
Fariss John...815 433-3803
3700 N Shore Dr Moline (61265) **(G-14144)**
Fariss Step & Railing Co, Moline *Also called Fariss John* **(G-14144)**
Farm Fresh Str D&M Dar Stores, Chester *Also called Chester Dairy Company Inc* **(G-3452)**
Farm Plastic Supply Inc (PA)...312 625-1024
1555 Industrial Dr Itasca (60143) **(G-11654)**
Farm Week...309 557-3140
1701 Towanda Ave Bloomington (61701) **(G-2042)**
Farmer Bros Co...217 787-7565
3430c Constitution Dr Springfield (62711) **(G-19365)**
Farmer's Fridge, Chicago *Also called Romaine Empire Inc* **(G-6056)**
Farmercityjournal.com, Bloomington *Also called Pantagraph Publishing Co* **(G-2085)**
Farmers Brothers Coffee, Springfield *Also called Farmer Bros Co* **(G-19365)**
Farmers Manufacturing Company...618 377-6237
5635 Loop Rd Dorsey (62021) **(G-7944)**
Farmers Packing Inc...618 445-3822
747 Illinois Route 130 Albion (62806) **(G-350)**
Farmhouse Lb, Chicago *Also called Leo Burnett Company Inc* **(G-5205)**
Farmington Crematory, Farmington *Also called Farmington Wilbert Vault Corp* **(G-9662)**
Farmington Foods Inc (PA)...708 771-3600
7419 Franklin St Forest Park (60130) **(G-9714)**
Farmington Locker/Ice Plant Co...309 245-4621
101 W Fort St Farmington (61531) **(G-9661)**
Farmington Wilbert Vault Corp (PA)...309 245-2133
22413 E State Route 116 Farmington (61531) **(G-9662)**
Farmstead Business Solutions, Chicago *Also called Ogwuru Uzoaku* **(G-5664)**
Farmweld Inc...217 857-6423
605 E Main St Teutopolis (62467) **(G-19769)**
Farrow Lumber Co...618 734-0255
Hwy 37 N Cairo (62914) **(G-2767)**
Fas-Trak Industries Inc...708 570-0650
4654 W Crocus Ave Monee (60449) **(G-14199)**
Fashahnn Corporation...773 994-3132
8016 S Cottage Grove Ave Chicago (60619) **(G-4561)**
Fashion Craft Corporation...847 998-0092
1421 Old Deerfield Rd Highland Park (60035) **(G-11262)**
Fashionaire, Oak Park *Also called Unitex Industries Inc* **(G-15777)**
Faspro Technologies Inc...847 364-9999
165 King St Elk Grove Village (60007) **(G-8996)**
Faspro Technologies Inc (PA)...847 392-9500
500 W Campus Dr Arlington Heights (60004) **(G-734)**
Fast Color, North Aurora *Also called Janssen Avenue Boys Inc* **(G-15265)**
Fast Forward Energy Inc...312 860-0978
2023 W Carroll Ave Chicago (60612) **(G-4562)**
Fast Forward Welding Inc...815 254-1901
23840 W Andrew Rd Ste 4 Plainfield (60585) **(G-16664)**
Fast Impressions, Decatur *Also called Dynagraphics Incorporated* **(G-7492)**
Fast Lane Threads Custom EMB...815 544-9898
1467 Mckinley Ave Ste A Belvidere (61008) **(G-1667)**
Fast Pipe Lining Inc...815 712-8646
320 Raccuglia Dr La Salle (61301) **(G-12111)**
Fast Print Shop...618 997-1976
501 W Deyoung St Ste 7 Marion (62959) **(G-13510)**
Fast Printing of Joliet Inc...815 723-0080
842 Plainfield Rd Joliet (60435) **(G-11864)**
Fast Radius Inc (PA)...866 222-5458
113 N May St Chicago (60607) **(G-4563)**
Fast Signs...773 698-8115
1101 W Belmont Ave Chicago (60657) **(G-4564)**
Fast Signs...815 730-7828
19404 S La Grange Rd Mokena (60448) **(G-14080)**
Fast Signs 590...815 937-1855
601a N 5th Ave Kankakee (60901) **(G-11970)**
Fast Technologies Corp...815 234-4744
4600 N River Rd Oregon (61061) **(G-15920)**
Fasteners For Retail Inc...847 296-5511
1600 Birchwood Ave Des Plaines (60018) **(G-7764)**
Fastrack Stairs & Rails Ltd...847 531-6252
303 N 11th St Dekalb (60115) **(G-7677)**
Fastron Co...630 766-5000
2040 Janice Ave Melrose Park (60160) **(G-13866)**
Fastsigns, Chicago *Also called Fast Signs* **(G-4564)**
Fastsigns, Gurnee *Also called Holmes Associates Inc* **(G-10887)**
Fastsigns, Kankakee *Also called Fast Signs 590* **(G-11970)**
Fastsigns, Northbrook *Also called Castino & Associates Inc* **(G-15354)**
Fastsigns, Skokie *Also called Cks Signs Inc* **(G-18943)**
Fastsigns, Oakbrook Terrace *Also called Rmkc Inc* **(G-15814)**
Fastsigns, Waukegan *Also called Rjw Graphics Inc* **(G-20488)**
Fastsigns, Arlington Heights *Also called D&J Arlington Heights Inc* **(G-724)**
Fastsigns, Champaign *Also called Mbm Business Assistance Inc* **(G-3318)**
Fastsigns, Chicago *Also called Antolak Management Co Inc* **(G-3707)**
Fastsigns, Bloomington *Also called Heron Bay Inc* **(G-2057)**
Fastsigns, Naperville *Also called John Cornbleet Inc* **(G-14855)**
Fastsigns, Northbrook *Also called DAmico Associates Inc* **(G-15373)**
Fastsigns, Mokena *Also called Fast Signs* **(G-14080)**
Fastsigns, Schaumburg *Also called M & R Media Inc* **(G-18616)**
Fastsigns, Peoria *Also called Geebees Inc* **(G-16443)**
Fastsigns...312 344-1765
118 N Halsted St Chicago (60661) **(G-4565)**
Fastsigns...847 981-1965
1701 Howard St Ste C Elk Grove Village (60007) **(G-8997)**
Fastsigns...630 932-0001
17w608 14th St Oakbrook Terrace (60181) **(G-15798)**
Fastsigns...847 675-1600
3450 W Devon Ave Lincolnwood (60712) **(G-12818)**
Fastsigns...847 680-7446
1350 S Milwaukee Ave Libertyville (60048) **(G-12651)**
Fastsigns LLC...630 541-8901
408 75th St Downers Grove (60516) **(G-8001)**
Fastsigns International...847 967-7222
7911 Golf Rd Morton Grove (60053) **(G-14407)**
Fastway Printing Inc...847 882-0950
14 E Schaumburg Rd Ste 3 Schaumburg (60194) **(G-18525)**
Fastway Printing Service, Schaumburg *Also called Fastway Printing Inc* **(G-18525)**
Father & Daughters Printing...708 749-8286
6237 Roosevelt Rd Berwyn (60402) **(G-1953)**
Father and Son Commercial...773 424-3301
4940 S Kilbourn Ave Chicago (60632) **(G-4566)**
Father Marcellos & Son...312 654-2565
645 W North Ave Chicago (60610) **(G-4567)**
Fattah Trading Company Inc (PA)...773 227-2525
4545 W Armitage Ave Chicago (60639) **(G-4568)**
Faulstich Printing Company Inc...217 442-4994
2001 E Voorhees St Danville (61834) **(G-7332)**
Fausto's Bread Bakery, Arlington Heights *Also called Faustos Bakery* **(G-735)**
Faustos Bakery...847 255-9049
16 S Evergreen Ave Arlington Heights (60005) **(G-735)**
Faxitron X-Ray LLC...847 465-9729
575 Bond St Lincolnshire (60069) **(G-12763)**
Fay Electric Wire, Elmhurst *Also called Taycorp Inc* **(G-9433)**
Fayco Enterprises Inc (PA)...618 283-0638
1313 Sunset Dr Vandalia (62471) **(G-20011)**
Faye Jewellery Chez...815 477-1818
6314 Tilgee Rd Crystal Lake (60012) **(G-7198)**
Faze Change Produx...217 728-2184
1331 Cr 1470e Sullivan (61951) **(G-19667)**
FBC Industries Inc (PA)...847 241-6143
1933 N Meacham Rd Ste 550 Schaumburg (60173) **(G-18526)**
FBC Industries Inc...847 839-0880
110 E Avenue H Rochelle (61068) **(G-17140)**
Fbs Group Inc...773 229-8675
6513 W 64th St Chicago (60638) **(G-4569)**

ALPHABETIC SECTION
Fiberglass Innovations LLC

Fbsa LLC 773 524-2440
4545 W Augusta Blvd Chicago (60651) **(G-4570)**
Fc Lighting, Saint Charles *Also called Lighting Innovations Inc* **(G-18228)**
Fca LLC 309 949-3999
2212 Us Highway 6 Coal Valley (61240) **(G-6936)**
Fca LLC 309 385-2588
610 S Walnut St Princeville (61559) **(G-16827)**
Fca LLC (PA) 309 792-3444
7601 John Deere Pkwy Moline (61265) **(G-14145)**
FCA Packaging, Moline *Also called Fca LLC* **(G-14145)**
FCA US LLC 630 724-2321
901 Warrenville Rd # 550 Lisle (60532) **(G-12890)**
FCA US LLC 630 637-3000
1980 High Grove Ln Naperville (60540) **(G-14828)**
Fci Flavors 630 373-1707
1208 N Swift Rd Addison (60101) **(G-119)**
FCL Graphics Inc 708 867-5500
4600 N Olcott Ave Harwood Heights (60706) **(G-11104)**
Fcm Mills, Lombard *Also called Sturtevant Inc* **(G-13135)**
Fdf Armature Inc 630 458-0452
220 W Gerri Ln Addison (60101) **(G-120)**
Feathersound, Chicago *Also called Eastern Accents Inc* **(G-4435)**
Fedder Oil Co Inc 618 344-0050
417 Short St Collinsville (62234) **(G-6960)**
Federal Envelope Company 630 595-2000
608 Country Club Dr Bensenville (60106) **(G-1799)**
Federal Equipment & Svcs Inc 847 731-9002
3200 16th St Zion (60099) **(G-21514)**
Federal Mogul Driveline Pdts, Berwyn *Also called Federal-Mogul Motorparts LLC* **(G-1954)**
Federal Prison Industries 618 664-6361
Us Rt 40 4th St Greenville (62246) **(G-10834)**
Federal Prison Industries 309 346-8588
2600 S 2nd St Pekin (61554) **(G-16333)**
Federal Screw Products, Gurnee *Also called Fsp LLC* **(G-10880)**
Federal Signal Corporation 708 534-4756
2645 Federal Signal Dr University Park (60484) **(G-19952)**
Federal Signal Corporation (PA) 630 954-2000
1415 W 22nd St Ste 1100 Oak Brook (60523) **(G-15618)**
Federal Signal Corporation 708 534-3400
2645 Federal Signal Dr University Park (60484) **(G-19953)**
Federal Signal Corporation 708 534-3400
2645 Federal Signal Dr University Park (60484) **(G-19954)**
Federal Signal-Codespear, University Park *Also called Federal Signal Corporation* **(G-19952)**
Federal-Mogul Motorparts LLC 847 674-7700
7450 Mccormick Blvd Skokie (60076) **(G-18954)**
Federal-Mogul Motorparts LLC 773 478-0404
3440 N Kedzie Ave Chicago (60618) **(G-4571)**
Federal-Mogul Motorparts LLC 248 354-7700
4929 S Mason Berwyn (60402) **(G-1954)**
Federated Paint Mfg Co (PA) 708 345-4848
5812 S Homan Ave Chicago (60629) **(G-4572)**
Fedex Corporation 847 918-7730
281 W Townline Rd Ste 100 Vernon Hills (60061) **(G-20053)**
Fedex Ground Package Sys Inc 800 463-3339
115 W Lake Dr Ste 100 Glendale Heights (60139) **(G-10450)**
Fedex Office & Print Svcs Inc 312 341-9644
71 E Jackson Blvd Chicago (60604) **(G-4573)**
Fedex Office & Print Svcs Inc 847 475-8650
2518 Green Bay Rd Evanston (60201) **(G-9519)**
Fedex Office & Print Svcs Inc 312 755-0325
540 N Michigan Ave Chicago (60611) **(G-4574)**
Fedex Office & Print Svcs Inc 815 229-0033
6234 Mulford Village Dr Rockford (61107) **(G-17412)**
Fedex Office & Print Svcs Inc 312 595-0768
505 N Michigan Ave Chicago (60611) **(G-4575)**
Fedex Office & Print Svcs Inc 847 329-9464
6829 N Lincoln Ave Lincolnwood (60712) **(G-12819)**
Fedex Office & Print Svcs Inc 217 355-3400
505 S Mattis Ave Champaign (61821) **(G-3292)**
Fedex Office & Print Svcs Inc 847 729-3030
1623 Waukegan Rd Glenview (60025) **(G-10545)**
Fedex Office & Print Svcs Inc 309 685-4093
3465 N University St Peoria (61604) **(G-16437)**
Fedex Office & Print Svcs Inc 630 759-5784
251 S Weber Rd Bolingbrook (60490) **(G-2176)**
Fedex Office & Print Svcs Inc 847 459-8008
76 W Dundee Rd Buffalo Grove (60089) **(G-2536)**
Fedex Office & Print Svcs Inc 708 452-0149
1720 N Harlem Ave Elmwood Park (60707) **(G-9452)**
Fedex Office & Print Svcs Inc 847 823-9360
678 N Northwest Hwy Park Ridge (60068) **(G-16274)**
Fedex Office & Print Svcs Inc 312 663-1149
720 S Michigan Ave Chicago (60605) **(G-4576)**
Fedex Office & Print Svcs Inc 847 670-7283
1 W Rand Rd Ste F Mount Prospect (60056) **(G-14528)**
Fedex Office & Print Svcs Inc 630 894-1800
369 W Army Trail Rd Bloomingdale (60108) **(G-1995)**
Fedex Office & Print Svcs Inc 847 670-4100
205 W Rand Rd Arlington Heights (60004) **(G-736)**
Fedex Office & Print Svcs Inc 312 670-4460
444 N Wells St Fl 1 Chicago (60654) **(G-4577)**
Feelsure Health Corparation 847 823-0137
120 Columbia Ave Park Ridge (60068) **(G-16275)**
Fehr Cab Interiors 815 692-3355
10116 N 1900 East Rd Fairbury (61739) **(G-9607)**
Fehrenbacher Ready-Mix Inc 618 395-2306
1401 S Whittle Ave Olney (62450) **(G-15860)**
Fehring Ornamental Iron Works 217 483-6727
10685 E State Route 29 Rochester (62563) **(G-17166)**
Felco, Melrose Park *Also called Forest Electric Company* **(G-13868)**
Felice Hosiery Co Inc (PA) 312 922-3710
632 W Roosevelt Rd Chicago (60607) **(G-4578)**
Felice Hosiery Company Inc 312 922-3710
632 W Roosevelt Rd Chicago (60607) **(G-4579)**
Felix Partners LLC 847 648-8449
1845 Hicks Rd Ste C Rolling Meadows (60008) **(G-17732)**
Feller Oilfield Service Inc 618 267-5650
Hwy 40 W Saint Elmo (62458) **(G-18308)**
Felpak, Chicago *Also called Mercury Plastics Inc* **(G-5394)**
Felste Co Inc 217 283-4884
217 N 9th Ave Hoopeston (60942) **(G-11509)**
Femina Sport Inc 630 271-1876
5100 Walnut Ave Downers Grove (60515) **(G-8002)**
Femsa, Frankfort *Also called Paratech Incorporated* **(G-9821)**
Fenix Manufacturing LLC 815 208-0755
2001 9th St Fulton (61252) **(G-10151)**
Fenwal Inc (HQ) 800 333-6925
3 Corporate Dr Ste 300 Lake Zurich (60047) **(G-12411)**
Feralloy Corporation (HQ) 503 286-8869
8755 W Higgins Rd Ste 970 Chicago (60631) **(G-4580)**
Ferber George & Sons 217 733-2184
102 S Pine St Fairmount (61841) **(G-9643)**
Ferenbach Marucco Stoddard 217 698-3535
3445 Liberty Dr Springfield (62704) **(G-19366)**
Fern Manufacturing Company 630 260-9350
333 Kimberly Dr Carol Stream (60188) **(G-2983)**
Fernandez Windows Corp 773 762-2365
2535 S Ridgeway Ave Chicago (60623) **(G-4581)**
Fernwood Printers Ltd 630 964-9449
14955 Mission Ave Oak Forest (60452) **(G-15678)**
Ferrara Candy Company (HQ) 708 366-0500
404 W Harrison St 650s Chicago (60607) **(G-4582)**
Ferrara Candy Company 800 323-1768
1445 Norwood Ave Itasca (60143) **(G-11655)**
Ferrara Candy Company 630 366-0500
7301 Harrison St Forest Park (60130) **(G-9715)**
Ferrara Candy Company 630 378-4197
910 Dalton Ln Bolingbrook (60490) **(G-2177)**
Ferrara Candy Company 507 452-3433
404 W Harrison St 650s Chicago (60607) **(G-4583)**
Ferrara Candy Company 708 432-4407
3000 Washington Blvd Bellwood (60104) **(G-1624)**
Ferrara Candy Company 708 488-1892
7525 Industrial Dr Forest Park (60130) **(G-9716)**
Ferrara Pan Candy Co, Forest Park *Also called Ferrara Candy Company* **(G-9715)**
Ferrellgas LP 815 877-7333
10522 N 2nd St Machesney Park (61115) **(G-13342)**
Ferrite International Company 847 249-4900
39105 Magnetics Blvd Wadsworth (60083) **(G-20209)**
Ferro Corporation 847 623-0370
1219 Glen Rock Ave Waukegan (60085) **(G-20443)**
Fetco, Lake Zurich *Also called Food Equipment Technologies Co* **(G-12412)**
Fetzer Surgical LLC 630 635-2520
1019 W Wise Rd Ste 201 Schaumburg (60193) **(G-18527)**
Fey & Company, Naperville *Also called Edgar H Fey Jewelers Inc* **(G-14821)**
Ffr Merchandising, Des Plaines *Also called Fasteners For Retail Inc* **(G-7764)**
Fg Manufacturing, Vernon Hills *Also called Flame Guard Usa LLC* **(G-20054)**
Fgfi LLC 708 598-0909
411 E Plainfield Rd Countryside (60525) **(G-7052)**
Fgs Inc 312 421-3060
815 W Van Buren St # 302 Chicago (60607) **(G-4584)**
Fgs - Fulfillment Services, Broadview *Also called Financial Graphic Services Inc* **(G-2437)**
Fgs-IL LLC (HQ) 630 375-8500
780 Mcclure Rd Aurora (60502) **(G-960)**
Fgwa 630 759-6800
1305 Lakeview Dr Romeoville (60446) **(G-17822)**
FH Ayer Manufacturing Co 708 755-0550
2015 S Halsted St Chicago Heights (60411) **(G-6746)**
FHP-Berner USA LP 630 270-1400
2188a Diehl Rd Aurora (60502) **(G-961)**
Fiber Options Div, Chicago *Also called Buster Services Inc* **(G-3983)**
Fiberbasin Inc 630 978-0705
1500 Dearborn Ave Ste 13 Aurora (60505) **(G-1095)**
Fibergel Technologies Inc 847 549-6002
1011 Campus Dr Mundelein (60060) **(G-14688)**
Fiberglass Innovations LLC 815 962-9338
2219 Kishwaukee St Rockford (61104) **(G-17413)**

ALPHABETIC

Fiberglass Innovations LLC 815 962-3727
340 Blackhawk Park Ave Rockford (61104) *(G-17414)*
Fiberglass International, Aroma Park *Also called New Dimension Models (G-840)*
Fiberglass Solutions Corp 630 458-0756
436 W Belden Ave Addison (60101) *(G-121)*
Fiberlink LLC 312 951-8500
230 E Ohio St Ste 212 Chicago (60611) *(G-4585)*
Fiberteq LLC 217 431-2111
3650 Southgate Dr Danville (61834) *(G-7333)*
Fibertex Nonwovens LLC 815 349-3200
27981 W Concrete Dr Ingleside (60041) *(G-11581)*
Fibre Drum Company 815 933-3222
1650 E Sheridan St Kankakee (60901) *(G-11971)*
Fibro Inc (HQ) 815 229-1300
139 Harrison Ave Rockford (61104) *(G-17415)*
Fibroblast Inc 800 396-6463
222 Merchandise Mart Plz # 1230 Chicago (60654) *(G-4586)*
Fibromanta, Rockford *Also called Fibro Inc (G-17415)*
FIC America Corp (HQ) 630 871-7609
485 E Lies Rd Carol Stream (60188) *(G-2984)*
Fidelity Bindery Company 708 343-6833
2829 S 18th Ave Broadview (60155) *(G-2435)*
Fidelity Print Cmmncations LLC 708 343-6833
2829 S 18th Ave 33 Broadview (60155) *(G-2436)*
Fidelity Tool & Mold Ltd (PA) 630 879-2300
1885 Suncast Ln Batavia (60510) *(G-1377)*
Field Holdings LLC (PA) 847 509-2250
400 Skokie Blvd Ste 860 Northbrook (60062) *(G-15388)*
Field Notes, Chicago *Also called Coudal Partners Inc (G-4248)*
Field Outfitting Co., The, Chicago *Also called Tfo Group LLC (G-6358)*
Field Roast Grain Meat Co, Elmhurst *Also called Greenleaf Foods Spc (G-9369)*
Field Ventures LLC 847 509-2250
400 Skokie Blvd Ste 860 Northbrook (60062) *(G-15389)*
Fielders Choice 618 937-2294
25 Frankfort Dr West Frankfort (62896) *(G-20671)*
Fifth Quarter 618 346-6659
1770 Triad Rd Saint Jacob (62281) *(G-18316)*
File System Labs LLC 617 431-4313
3387 Commercial Ave Northbrook (60062) *(G-15390)*
Fill-Weigh Inc 815 254-4704
23900 W Industrial Dr S # 6 Plainfield (60585) *(G-16665)*
Fillo's Frijoles, North Aurora *Also called Sofrito Foods LLC (G-15275)*
Filmfax Magazine Inc 847 866-7155
1320 Oakton St Evanston (60202) *(G-9520)*
Filter Friend Z Inc 847 824-4049
2280 Magnolia St Des Plaines (60018) *(G-7765)*
Filter Kleen Inc 708 447-4666
8432 44th Pl Lyons (60534) *(G-13308)*
Filter Monkey LLC 630 773-4402
424 S Lombard Rd Itasca (60143) *(G-11656)*
Filter Renew Tecnologies 815 344-2200
3205 Lakeside Ct McCullom Lake (60050) *(G-13711)*
Filter Services, Elk Grove Village *Also called GAG Industries Inc (G-9008)*
Filter Technology Inc 773 523-7200
7200 S Leamington Ave Bedford Park (60638) *(G-1467)*
Filters To You 815 939-0700
183 E North St Bradley (60915) *(G-2281)*
Filtertek Inc (HQ) 815 648-2410
11411 Price Rd Hebron (60034) *(G-11143)*
Filtran Holdings LLC (PA) 847 635-6670
875 Seegers Rd Des Plaines (60016) *(G-7766)*
Filtran LLC (HQ) 847 635-6670
875 Seegers Rd Des Plaines (60016) *(G-7767)*
Filtration Group Corporation (PA) 512 593-7999
600 W 22nd St Ste 300 Oak Brook (60523) *(G-15619)*
Filtration Group LLC 815 726-4600
912 E Washington St Ste 1 Joliet (60433) *(G-11865)*
Fim Engineering LLC 773 880-8841
2199 E 1120 North Rd Milford (60953) *(G-14034)*
Fin North America Holding Inc (HQ) 815 349-3219
27981 W Concrete Dr Ingleside (60041) *(G-11582)*
Final Call Inc 773 602-1230
734 W 79th St Chicago (60620) *(G-4587)*
Final Call Newspaper, The, Chicago *Also called Final Call Inc (G-4587)*
Financial and Professional Reg 217 782-2127
325 W Adams St Lbby Springfield (62704) *(G-19367)*
Financial Graphic Service, Broadview *Also called Kelvyn Press Inc (G-2448)*
Financial Graphic Services Inc (PA) 708 343-0448
2910 S 18th Ave Broadview (60155) *(G-2437)*
Financial Publishing Svcs Co 847 501-4120
1883 Old Willow Rd Northfield (60093) *(G-15513)*
Finchs Beer Company LLC 312 929-4773
1800 W Walnut St Chicago (60612) *(G-4588)*
Fine Arts Engraving Co 800 688-4400
311 S Wacker Dr Ste 300 Chicago (60606) *(G-4589)*
Fine Circuits Inc 630 213-8700
848 W Bartlett Rd Ste 9 Bartlett (60103) *(G-1280)*
Fine Gold Mfg Jewelers 630 323-9600
777 N York Rd Ste 27 Hinsdale (60521) *(G-11368)*
Fine Line Printing 773 582-9709
5181 S Archer Ave Chicago (60632) *(G-4590)*
Finer Line Inc 847 884-1611
1701 Glenlake Ave Itasca (60143) *(G-11657)*
Finer Line Engraving, Itasca *Also called Finer Line Inc (G-11657)*
Fingers, Chicago *Also called Gregory Lamar & Assoc Inc (G-4741)*
Finish Line USA Inc 847 608-7800
1750 Todd Farm Dr Ste A Elgin (60123) *(G-8585)*
Finished Metals Incorporated 773 229-1600
6146 S New England Ave Chicago (60638) *(G-4591)*
Finishers Exchange 847 462-0533
744 Northwest Hwy Fox River Grove (60021) *(G-9758)*
Finishes Unlimited Inc 630 466-4881
482 Wheeler Rd Sugar Grove (60554) *(G-19644)*
Finishing Company 630 559-0808
136 W Commercial Ave Addison (60101) *(G-122)*
Finishing Group 847 884-4890
1300 Basswood Rd Ste 200r Schaumburg (60173) *(G-18528)*
Finishing Touch Inc 773 774-7349
5580 N Northwest Hwy Chicago (60630) *(G-4592)*
Finite Resources Ltd 618 252-3733
520 S Mckinley St Harrisburg (62946) *(G-11023)*
Finkl Steel - Chicago, Chicago *Also called A Finkl & Sons Co (G-3488)*
Finkl Steel - Houston LLC (HQ) 773 975-2540
412 S Wells St Ste 500 Chicago (60607) *(G-4593)*
Finks Oil Co Inc 618 548-5757
519 W Boone St Salem (62881) *(G-18339)*
Finzer Holding LLC (PA) 847 390-6200
129 Rawls Rd Des Plaines (60018) *(G-7768)*
Finzer Roller Inc 410 939-1850
129 Rawls Rd Des Plaines (60018) *(G-7769)*
Finzer Roller Inc (PA) 847 390-6200
129 Rawls Rd Des Plaines (60018) *(G-7770)*
Finzer Roller Inc 812 829-1455
129 Rawls Rd Des Plaines (60018) *(G-7771)*
Finzer Roller Indiana, Des Plaines *Also called Finzer Roller Inc (G-7771)*
Finzer Roller Maryland, Des Plaines *Also called Finzer Roller Inc (G-7769)*
Finzer Roller Pennsylvania, Des Plaines *Also called Finzer Holding LLC (G-7768)*
Fire & Ice Imports LLC 310 871-1695
1222 Andrea Ct Morris (60450) *(G-14305)*
Fire CAM 618 416-8390
525 W Main St Ste 100 Belleville (62220) *(G-1552)*
Fire CAM LLC 618 416-8390
321 Clearwater Dr Belleville (62220) *(G-1553)*
Fire Chariot LLC 815 561-3688
770 Wiscold Dr Rochelle (61068) *(G-17141)*
Fire House Press 217 864-2864
5070 E Firehouse Rd Decatur (62521) *(G-7494)*
Fire Orb LLC 847 454-9198
300 Elm St Prospect Heights (60070) *(G-16840)*
Fire Place By Ignite, Darien *Also called Tagitsold Inc (G-7412)*
Fire Systems Holdings Inc 708 333-4130
8940 W 192nd St Ste M Mokena (60448) *(G-14081)*
Firefly International Enrgy Co (PA) 309 402-0701
8306 N University St Peoria (61615) *(G-16438)*
Firefly Mobile Inc 305 538-2777
1325 Remington Rd Ste H Schaumburg (60173) *(G-18529)*
Fireground Supply, Plainfield *Also called Response Graphics & EMB LLC (G-16710)*
Firepenny, Mokena *Also called Citizenprime LLC (G-14075)*
Firm of John Dickinson 847 680-1000
2000 Hollister Dr Libertyville (60048) *(G-12652)*
First & Main Inc 630 587-1000
2400 E Main St Ste 103-35 Saint Charles (60174) *(G-18199)*
First Alert, Aurora *Also called Brk Brands Inc (G-927)*
First Alert Inc (HQ) 630 499-3295
3901 Liberty St Aurora (60504) *(G-962)*
First American Restoration Inc 800 209-3609
6935 W Gunnison St Harwood Heights (60706) *(G-11105)*
First Amrcn Plstic Mlding Entp 815 624-8538
810 Progressive Ln South Beloit (61080) *(G-19091)*
First Ayd Corporation 847 622-0001
1325 Gateway Dr Elgin (60124) *(G-8586)*
First Electric Motor Shop Inc 217 698-0672
1130 W Reynolds St Springfield (62702) *(G-19368)*
First Element Solutions 847 691-8381
505 W Henry St Mount Prospect (60056) *(G-14529)*
First Header Die Inc 815 282-5161
1313 Anvil Rd Machesney Park (61115) *(G-13343)*
First Impression 815 883-3357
211 S Columbia Ave Oglesby (61348) *(G-15841)*
First Impression of Chicago 773 224-3434
218 E 79th St Chicago (60619) *(G-4594)*
First Light Inc 630 520-0017
245 W Roosevelt Rd Ste 3 West Chicago (60185) *(G-20583)*
First Look Wholesale Lab Inc 618 462-9042
90 Enviro Way Wood River (62095) *(G-21261)*
First Priority Inc (PA) 847 531-1215
1590 Todd Farm Dr Elgin (60123) *(G-8587)*

First Stage Fabrication Inc 618 282-8320
340 Kennedy Dr Red Bud (62278) ***(G-16994)***
First Step Womens Center 217 523-0100
104 E North Grand Ave A Springfield (62702) ***(G-19369)***
First String Enterprises Inc (PA) 708 614-1200
18650 Graphic Ct Tinley Park (60477) ***(G-19827)***
First-Light Usa LLC 217 687-4048
205 S Main St Seymour (61875) ***(G-18868)***
Fisa North America Inc 847 593-2080
260 Stanley St Elk Grove Village (60007) ***(G-8998)***
Fischer Paper Products Inc (PA) 847 395-6060
179 Ida Ave Antioch (60002) ***(G-611)***
Fischer Stone & Materials LLC 815 233-3232
1567 N Heine Rd Freeport (61032) ***(G-10108)***
Fish King Inc 773 736-4974
5228 W Giddings St Chicago (60630) ***(G-4595)***
Fish Oven and Equipment Corp 847 526-8686
120 Kent Ave Wauconda (60084) ***(G-20351)***
Fish Window Cleaning, Oswego *Also called James A Freund LLC* ***(G-16009)***
Fisher & Ludlow, Bourbonnais *Also called Harris Steel Ulc* ***(G-2262)***
Fisher Container Holdings LLC (PA) 847 541-0000
1111 Busch Pkwy Buffalo Grove (60089) ***(G-2537)***
Fisher Controls Intl LLC 847 956-8020
1124 Tower Rd Chicago (60673) ***(G-4596)***
Fisher Diagnostics, Chicago *Also called Fisher Scientific Company LLC* ***(G-4597)***
Fisher Midwest, Camargo *Also called Pritchard Enterprises Inc* ***(G-2801)***
Fisher Printing Inc 708 598-1500
8640 S Oketo Ave Bridgeview (60455) ***(G-2346)***
Fisher Safety, Hanover Park *Also called Fisher Scientific Company LLC* ***(G-11003)***
Fisher Scientific Company LLC 412 490-8300
4500 Turnberry Dr Hanover Park (60133) ***(G-11003)***
Fisher Scientific Company LLC 800 528-0494
13795 Collections Ctr Dr Chicago (60693) ***(G-4597)***
Fisheye Grahphics, Chicago *Also called Fisheye Services Incorporated* ***(G-4598)***
Fisheye Services Incorporated 773 942-6314
5443 N Broadway St Chicago (60640) ***(G-4598)***
Fishing Facts, Burr Ridge *Also called Midwest Outdoors Ltd* ***(G-2704)***
Fishstone Studio Inc 815 276-0299
110 East St Crystal Lake (60014) ***(G-7199)***
Fitness Wear Inc 847 486-1704
1940 Lehigh Ave Ste B Glenview (60026) ***(G-10546)***
Fitz Chem LLC (HQ) 630 467-8383
450 E Devon Ave Ste 300 Itasca (60143) ***(G-11658)***
Fitzpatrick Bros Inc 217 592-3500
309 Radio Rd Quincy (62305) ***(G-16882)***
Five Brother Inc 309 663-6323
2905 Gill St Ste B Bloomington (61704) ***(G-2043)***
Five P Drilling Inc 618 943-9771
10585 Cabin Hill Dr Bridgeport (62417) ***(G-2313)***
Five Star Desserts and Foods 773 375-5100
8559 S Constance Ave Chicago (60617) ***(G-4599)***
Five Star Industries Inc (PA) 618 542-4880
1308 Wells Street Rd Du Quoin (62832) ***(G-8120)***
Five Star Pallets Inc 847 613-8488
3939 W Albany St McHenry (60050) ***(G-13744)***
Five Star Printing Inc 217 965-3355
169 W Jackson St Virden (62690) ***(G-20184)***
Fivecubits Inc (HQ) 630 749-4182
1315 W 22nd St Ste 300 Oak Brook (60523) ***(G-15620)***
Fivecubits Inc 925 273-1862
1315 W 22nd St Ste 300 Oak Brook (60523) ***(G-15621)***
Fives Landis Corp 815 389-2251
481 Gardner St South Beloit (61080) ***(G-19092)***
Fix It Fast Ltd 708 401-8320
14922 Lawndale Ave Midlothian (60445) ***(G-13991)***
Fixture Company 847 214-3100
8770 W Bryn Mawr Ave Chicago (60631) ***(G-4600)***
Fixture Displays 630 296-4190
2333 Wisconsin Ave Downers Grove (60515) ***(G-8003)***
Fixture Hardware Co (PA) 773 777-6100
2800 W Lake St Melrose Park (60160) ***(G-13867)***
Fjcj LLC 618 785-2217
11000 Baldwin Rd Baldwin (62217) ***(G-1184)***
Fjw Optical Systems Inc 847 358-2500
322 N Woodwork Ln Palatine (60067) ***(G-16119)***
Fkm Usa LLC 815 469-2473
21950 S La Grange Rd A Frankfort (60423) ***(G-9794)***
FL 1 ....847 956-9400
128 N Lively Blvd Fl 1 Elk Grove Village (60007) ***(G-8999)***
Flagsource, Batavia *Also called J C Schultz Enterprises Inc* ***(G-1388)***
Flaherty Incorporated 773 472-8456
9047 Terminal Ave Skokie (60077) ***(G-18955)***
Flame Guard Usa LLC 815 219-4074
1000 Bttrfeld Rd Ste 1029 Vernon Hills (60061) ***(G-20054)***
Flash Printing Inc 847 288-9101
9224 Grand Ave Ste 1 Franklin Park (60131) ***(G-9944)***
Flashcut Cnc, Deerfield *Also called Worth-Pfaff Innovations Inc* ***(G-7661)***
Flat-Tech Inc 847 364-4333
3330 Old Glenview Rd # 14 Wilmette (60091) ***(G-21075)***
Flatland Forge & Design, De Soto *Also called Andrew McDonald* ***(G-7430)***
Flatout Gaskets, Mundelein *Also called Flatout Group Llc* ***(G-14689)***
Flatout Group Llc 847 837-9200
668 Tower Rd Mundelein (60060) ***(G-14689)***
Flavor Concepts Inc 630 520-9060
1208 N Swift Rd Addison (60101) ***(G-123)***
Flavor Savor Inc 630 868-0350
285 Fullerton Ave Carol Stream (60188) ***(G-2985)***
Flavorchem Corporation (PA) 630 932-8100
1525 Brook Dr Downers Grove (60515) ***(G-8004)***
Flavorfocus LLC 630 520-9060
1210 N Swift Rd Addison (60101) ***(G-124)***
Fleetchem LLC (PA) 708 957-5311
1222 Brassie Ave Ste 19 Flossmoor (60422) ***(G-9698)***
Fleetpride Inc 630 455-6881
7630 S Madison St Willowbrook (60527) ***(G-21043)***
Fleetpride Inc 708 430-2081
7400 W 87th St Bridgeview (60455) ***(G-2347)***
Fleetwood Fixtures 773 271-3390
848 W Eastman St Chicago (60642) ***(G-4601)***
Fleetwood Press Inc 708 485-6811
9321 Ogden Ave Brookfield (60513) ***(G-2483)***
Fleischmanns Vinegar Co Inc 773 523-2817
4801 S Oakley Ave Chicago (60609) ***(G-4602)***
Fleming Music Technology Ctr 708 316-8662
408 W Elm St Wheaton (60189) ***(G-20799)***
Flender Corporation 847 931-1990
1401 Madeline Ln Elgin (60124) ***(G-8588)***
Flex Court Electronic, Kewanee *Also called Flex Court International Inc* ***(G-12033)***
Flex Court International Inc 309 852-0899
4328 Us Highway 34 Kewanee (61443) ***(G-12033)***
Flex Lighting II LLC 312 929-3488
11 W Illinois St Fl 3 Chicago (60654) ***(G-4603)***
Flex Lighting,, Chicago *Also called Flex Lighting II LLC* ***(G-4603)***
Flex N Gate, Chicago *Also called Flex-N-Gate LLC* ***(G-4604)***
Flex N Gate Plastics, Danville *Also called Flex-N-Gate Corporation* ***(G-7335)***
Flex-N-Gate Corporation 217 442-4018
3403 Lynch Creek Dr Danville (61834) ***(G-7334)***
Flex-N-Gate Corporation 217 255-5025
502 E Anthony Dr Urbana (61802) ***(G-19983)***
Flex-N-Gate Corporation 217 442-4018
3403 Lynch Creek Dr Danville (61834) ***(G-7335)***
Flex-N-Gate LLC (PA) 217 384-6600
1306 E University Ave Urbana (61802) ***(G-19984)***
Flex-N-Gate LLC 773 437-5686
2924 E 126th St Chicago (60633) ***(G-4604)***
Flex-N-Gate LLC 217 278-2400
601 Guardian Way Urbana (61802) ***(G-19985)***
Flex-O-Glass Inc (PA) 773 261-5200
4647 W Augusta Blvd Ste 1 Chicago (60651) ***(G-4605)***
Flex-O-Glass Inc 773 379-7878
1100 N Cicero Ave Ste 1 Chicago (60651) ***(G-4606)***
Flex-O-Glass Inc 815 288-1424
1200 Warp Rd Dixon (61021) ***(G-7899)***
Flex-Weld Inc 815 334-3662
1425 Lake Ave Woodstock (60098) ***(G-21387)***
Flexan LLC (HQ) 224 543-0003
500 Bond St Lincolnshire (60069) ***(G-12764)***
Flexan LLC 773 685-6446
6626 W Dakin St Chicago (60634) ***(G-4607)***
Flexan Chicago, Chicago *Also called Flexan LLC* ***(G-4607)***
Flexera Holdings LP 847 466-4000
300 Park Blvd Ste 500 Itasca (60143) ***(G-11659)***
Flexera Software LLC (HQ) 847 466-4000
300 Park Blvd Ste 500 Itasca (60143) ***(G-11660)***
Flexible Metal Tubing Conduit, Addison *Also called Flextron Inc* ***(G-125)***
Flexible Safety Zoning Co, Romeoville *Also called Nafisco Inc* ***(G-17858)***
Flexicore Slab, East Saint Louis *Also called St Louis Flexicore Inc* ***(G-8324)***
Flexicraft Industries Inc 312 428-4750
2323 W Hubbard St Chicago (60612) ***(G-4608)***
Flexicraft Industries Inc 312 229-7550
2315 W Hubbard St Chicago (60612) ***(G-4609)***
Flexicraft Industries Inc (PA) 312 738-3588
2315 W Hubbard St Chicago (60612) ***(G-4610)***
Flexisnake, Chillicothe *Also called Imagination Products Corp* ***(G-6818)***
Flexitech Inc (HQ) 309 665-0658
1719 E Hamilton Rd Bloomington (61704) ***(G-2044)***
Flexo Prepress Solutions, Oswego *Also called Eugene Ewbank* ***(G-16004)***
Flexografix Inc 630 350-0100
27 W 136 St Charles Carol Stream (60188) ***(G-2986)***
Flextron Inc 630 543-5995
130 W Fay Ave Addison (60101) ***(G-125)***
Flextronics Intl USA Inc 847 383-1529
700 Corporate Grove Dr Buffalo Grove (60089) ***(G-2538)***
Fli Products, West Chicago *Also called First Light Inc* ***(G-20583)***
Fli Products LLC 630 520-0017
245 W Roosevelt Rd Ste 3 West Chicago (60185) ***(G-20584)***

ALPHABETIC

Flight Manufacturing Corp....815 876-1616
2750 Tradition Princeton (61356) **(G-16809)**
Flink Company (PA)....815 673-4321
502 N Vermillion St Streator (61364) **(G-19608)**
Flinn & Dreffein Engrg Co....847 272-6374
4025 Michelline Ln Northbrook (60062) **(G-15391)**
Flinn Scientific Inc....800 452-1261
770 N Raddant Rd Batavia (60510) **(G-1378)**
Flint Group US LLC....630 526-9903
1333 N Kirk Rd Batavia (60510) **(G-1379)**
Flint Group US LLC....920 725-0101
1225 Lakeside Dr 1 Romeoville (60446) **(G-17823)**
Flint Group US LLC....618 349-8384
619 N 2200 St Saint Peter (62880) **(G-18324)**
Flint Hills Resources LP....815 224-5232
501 Brunner St Peru (61354) **(G-16576)**
Flint Ink North America Div, Romeoville *Also called Flint Group US LLC* **(G-17823)**
Flip Flop Puzzle Mats, Chicago *Also called Alessco Inc* **(G-3602)**
Flix Candy, Niles *Also called Imaginings 3 Inc* **(G-15131)**
Flocon Inc....815 527-7990
11595 Mcconnell Rd Woodstock (60098) **(G-21388)**
Flocon Inc (PA)....815 444-1500
339 Cary Point Dr Cary (60013) **(G-3159)**
Flodyne Inc....630 563-3600
1000 Muirfield Dr Hanover Park (60133) **(G-11004)**
Floline Archtctral Systems LLC (PA)....630 922-0550
16108 S Route 59 Ste 108 Plainfield (60586) **(G-16666)**
Flolo Corporation (PA)....630 595-1010
1400 Harvester Rd West Chicago (60185) **(G-20585)**
Flolo Corporation....847 249-0880
1401 N Delany Rd Gurnee (60031) **(G-10878)**
Floor-Chem Inc....630 789-2152
1313 Enterprise Dr Ste D Romeoville (60446) **(G-17824)**
Flooring Warehouse Direct Inc....815 730-6767
14126 Camdan Rd Homer Glen (60491) **(G-11479)**
Flora Bowl....618 662-4561
927 W North Ave Flora (62839) **(G-9680)**
Flora Ready Mix Inc....618 662-4818
11170 Old Highway 50 Flora (62839) **(G-9681)**
Floralstar Enterprises....847 726-0124
68 Tournament Dr N Hawthorn Woods (60047) **(G-11123)**
Flores Precision Products....630 264-2222
413 Cleveland Ave Aurora (60506) **(G-1096)**
Florida Fruit Juices Inc....773 586-6200
7001 W 62nd St Chicago (60638) **(G-4611)**
Florida Metrology LLC....630 833-3800
1100 N Villa Ave Villa Park (60181) **(G-20147)**
Florock, Chicago *Also called Tennant Company* **(G-6350)**
Flotek Inc....815 943-6816
1000 Northfield Ave Harvard (60033) **(G-11055)**
Flow Control US Holding Corp....630 307-3000
1040 Muirfield Dr Hanover Park (60133) **(G-11005)**
Flow Pro Products Inc....815 836-1900
618 Anderson Dr Ste A Romeoville (60446) **(G-17825)**
Flow Valves International LLC....847 866-1188
500 Davis St Ste 600 Evanston (60201) **(G-9521)**
Flow-Eze Company....815 965-1062
3209 Auburn St Rockford (61101) **(G-17416)**
Flowers Baking, Dupo *Also called Flowers Foods Inc* **(G-8137)**
Flowers Distributing Inc....618 255-1021
4605 Hedge Rd East Alton (62024) **(G-8165)**
Flowers Foods Inc....618 286-3300
731 Prairie Dupont Dr Dupo (62239) **(G-8137)**
Flowers Foods Inc....217 347-2308
2305 Hoffman Dr Effingham (62401) **(G-8400)**
Flowserve Corporation....630 762-4100
1400 Powis Ct West Chicago (60185) **(G-20586)**
Flowserve Corporation....630 543-4240
409 S Vista Ave Addison (60101) **(G-126)**
Flowserve Corporation....630 435-9596
10 Eisenhower Ln N Lombard (60148) **(G-13076)**
Flowserve US Inc....630 783-1468
1020 Davey Rd Ste 100 Woodridge (60517) **(G-21301)**
Flowserve US Inc....630 655-5700
161 Tower Dr Ste D Burr Ridge (60527) **(G-2674)**
Floyd Steel Erectors Inc....630 238-8383
310 Richert Rd Wood Dale (60191) **(G-21187)**
Floyds Welding Service....618 395-2414
3519 N Union Dr Olney (62450) **(G-15861)**
Floydware LLC....630 469-1078
1020 Parkview Blvd Lombard (60148) **(G-13077)**
Flp Industries LLC....847 215-8650
404 Mercantile Ct Wheeling (60090) **(G-20897)**
FLS Pekin, Pekin *Also called Flsmidth Pekin LLC* **(G-16335)**
Flsmidth Inc....309 347-3031
1 Excel Way Pekin (61554) **(G-16334)**
Flsmidth Pekin LLC (HQ)....309 347-3031
14425 Wagonseller Rd Pekin (61554) **(G-16335)**
Fluence Automation LLC....847 423-7400
3323 N Kennicott Ave Arlington Heights (60004) **(G-737)**
Fluid Air, Aurora *Also called Spraying Systems Co* **(G-1020)**
Fluid Handling LLC....773 267-1600
8200 Austin Ave Morton Grove (60053) **(G-14408)**
Fluid Logic Inc....847 459-2202
1001 Commerce Ct Buffalo Grove (60089) **(G-2539)**
Fluid Management Inc (HQ)....847 537-0880
1023 Wheeling Rd Wheeling (60090) **(G-20898)**
Fluid Manufacturing Services....800 458-5262
105 Albrecht Dr Lake Bluff (60044) **(G-12181)**
Fluid Mnagement Operations LLC (HQ)....847 537-0880
1023 Wheeling Rd Wheeling (60090) **(G-20899)**
Fluid Pump Service Inc....847 228-0750
435 Bennett Rd Elk Grove Village (60007) **(G-9000)**
Fluid Pump Systems, Elk Grove Village *Also called Fluid Pump Service Inc* **(G-9000)**
Fluid-Aire Dynamics Inc....847 678-8388
530 Albion Ave Schaumburg (60193) **(G-18530)**
Flurida Group Inc....310 513-0888
2439 Haider Ave Naperville (60564) **(G-14966)**
Flurry Industries Inc....630 882-8361
2002 Prairie Rose Ln Yorkville (60560) **(G-21482)**
Fly Ball, Chicago *Also called Miglio Di Mario Uomo Inc* **(G-5454)**
Flyerinc Corporation....630 655-3400
700 Commerce Dr Ste 500 Oak Brook (60523) **(G-15622)**
Flying S, Palestine *Also called S Flying Inc* **(G-16179)**
FM, Wheeling *Also called Fluid Management Inc* **(G-20898)**
FM Graphic Impressions Inc....630 897-8788
84 S Lasalle St Aurora (60505) **(G-1097)**
FMA, Elgin *Also called Fabricators & Mfrs Assn Intl* **(G-8584)**
Fma Communicatons Inc....815 227-8284
2135 Point Blvd Elgin (60123) **(G-8589)**
FMC Corporation....309 695-2571
Hwy 17 E Wyoming (61491) **(G-21459)**
FMC Corporation....309 695-2571
Hwy 17 Wyoming (61491) **(G-21460)**
FMC Technologies Inc....312 803-4321
222 W Adams St Ste 400 Chicago (60606) **(G-4612)**
Fmi LLC....847 350-1535
500 Bond St Lincolnshire (60069) **(G-12765)**
FML Terminal Logistics LLC....815 433-2449
2069 N 3462 Rd Wedron (60557) **(G-20524)**
Fms, Trivoli *Also called Frame Material Supply Inc* **(G-19906)**
Fms of Wisconsin Div, Mokena *Also called Frank Miller & Sons Inc* **(G-14083)**
Fms USA Inc....847 519-4400
2155 Stnngton Ave Ste 119 Hoffman Estates (60169) **(G-11424)**
Fna Ip Holdings Inc....847 348-1500
1825 Greenleaf Ave Elk Grove Village (60007) **(G-9001)**
Fnh Ready Mix Inc....815 235-1400
751 Il Route 26 N Freeport (61032) **(G-10109)**
Foba Pdts Aplicat Ctr Svc Ctr, Wood Dale *Also called Videojet Technologies Inc* **(G-21255)**
Focal Point Lighting, Chicago *Also called Focal Point LLC* **(G-4614)**
Focal Point Lighting Inc....773 247-9494
4201 S Pulaski Rd Chicago (60632) **(G-4613)**
Focal Point LLC (HQ)....773 247-9494
4141 S Pulaski Rd Chicago (60632) **(G-4614)**
Focus Health and Fitness LLC....847 975-8687
123 S Eastwood Dr Woodstock (60098) **(G-21389)**
Focus Marketing Group Inc....815 363-2525
3320 Rocky Beach Rd Johnsburg (60051) **(G-11803)**
Fog Software Group, Rosemont *Also called Friedman Corporation* **(G-18024)**
Fola Community Action Services....773 487-4310
8014 S Ashland Ave Chicago (60620) **(G-4615)**
Folding Guard, Bedford Park *Also called L & P Guarding LLC* **(G-1477)**
Folding Guard, Bedford Park *Also called Aspen Guard LLC* **(G-1458)**
Foliar-Pak, Mendota *Also called Enp Investments LLC* **(G-13942)**
Folk Race Cars....815 629-2418
9027 Freeport Rd Durand (61024) **(G-8151)**
Folkerts Manufacturing Inc....815 968-7426
2229 23rd Ave Rockford (61104) **(G-17417)**
Follett School Solutions Inc....815 759-1700
1340 Ridgeview Dr McHenry (60050) **(G-13745)**
Folsoms Bakery Inc....815 622-7870
319 1st Ave Rock Falls (61071) **(G-17181)**
Foltz Welding Ltd....618 432-7777
501 E Clinton Ave Patoka (62875) **(G-16303)**
Fona Distribution Center, Saint Charles *Also called Fona International Inc* **(G-18200)**
Fona International, Geneva *Also called Interntnal Ingredient Mall LLC* **(G-10285)**
Fona International Inc....630 578-8600
1100 N Raddant Rd Batavia (60510) **(G-1380)**
Fona International Inc....630 578-8600
3940 Swenson Ave Saint Charles (60174) **(G-18200)**
Fona International Inc (PA)....630 578-8600
1900 Averill Rd Geneva (60134) **(G-10269)**
Fona Uk Ltd....331 442-5779
1900 Averill Rd Geneva (60134) **(G-10270)**
Fontana Associates Inc....888 707-8273
282 Jamie Ln Wauconda (60084) **(G-20352)**
Fontela Electric Incorporated (PA)....630 932-1600
1406 W Jeffrey Dr Addison (60101) **(G-127)**

Fonterra (usa) Inc (HQ) 847 928-1600
8700 W Bryn Mawr Ave 500s Chicago (60631) ***(G-4616)***
Food Bikes, Chicago *Also called Wrench* ***(G-6684)***
Food Equipment Technologies Co 847 719-3000
600 Rose Rd Lake Zurich (60047) ***(G-12412)***
Food Evolution, Schiller Park *Also called Rt Wholesale* ***(G-18841)***
Food Industry News, Des Plaines *Also called Food Service Publishing Co* ***(G-7772)***
Food Processing Magazine, Schaumburg *Also called Putman Media Inc* ***(G-18689)***
Food Purveyors Logistics 630 229-6168
760 Inland Cir Apt 101 Naperville (60563) ***(G-14829)***
Food Service 815 933-0725
1501 E Maple St Kankakee (60901) ***(G-11972)***
Food Service Products Division, Oakbrook Terrace *Also called McCain Foods Usa Inc* ***(G-15808)***
Food Service Publishing Co 847 699-3300
3166 S River Rd Ste 40 Des Plaines (60018) ***(G-7772)***
Food Service Publishing Co 847 699-3300
1440 Renaissance Dr # 210 Park Ridge (60068) ***(G-16276)***
Foodhandler Inc (HQ) 866 931-3613
2301 Lunt Ave Elk Grove Village (60007) ***(G-9002)***
Foods & Things Inc 618 526-4478
604 N 1st St Breese (62230) ***(G-2303)***
Foodservice Database Co Inc 773 745-9400
5724 W Diversey Ave Chicago (60639) ***(G-4617)***
Foot Locker Retail Inc 630 678-0155
112 Yorktown Ctr Lombard (60148) ***(G-13078)***
For Our Generation Inc 312 282-1257
944 Woodward Ave Deerfield (60015) ***(G-7609)***
Forbo Siegling LLC 630 595-4031
918 N Central Ave Wood Dale (60191) ***(G-21188)***
Force America Inc 815 730-3600
500 Brookforest Ave Joliet (60404) ***(G-11866)***
Force Enterprises, Tinley Park *Also called First String Enterprises Inc* ***(G-19827)***
Force Manufacturing Inc 847 265-6500
266 Park Ave Lake Villa (60046) ***(G-12351)***
Forcerl 847 432-7588
1350 Forest Ave Highland Park (60035) ***(G-11263)***
Ford Gum & Machine Company Inc 847 955-0003
1615 Barclay Blvd Buffalo Grove (60089) ***(G-2540)***
Ford Marble and Tile Inc 618 475-2987
203 S Van Buren St New Athens (62264) ***(G-15019)***
Ford Motor Company 708 757-5700
1000 E Lincoln Hwy Ford Heights (60411) ***(G-9706)***
Ford Tool & Machining Inc (PA) 815 633-5727
2205 Range Rd Loves Park (61111) ***(G-13211)***
Ford-Tool, Loves Park *Also called Triwire Inc* ***(G-13278)***
Forecast 5 Analytics Inc (PA) 630 955-7500
2135 City Gate Ln Ste 420 Naperville (60563) ***(G-14830)***
Foreclosure Report, Lake Barrington *Also called John C Grafft* ***(G-12153)***
Foreman Tool & Mold Corp 630 377-6389
3850 Swenson Ave Saint Charles (60174) ***(G-18201)***
Foreman Tool and Mold, Saint Charles *Also called Ps3 Tool Mold & Assembly LLC* ***(G-18253)***
Foreman Tool and Mold 630 377-6389
3627 Stern Ave Saint Charles (60174) ***(G-18202)***
Foremost Industrial Tech, Peoria *Also called Four-Most Inc* ***(G-16440)***
Foremost Industrial Tech, Rockford *Also called Four-Most Inc* ***(G-17422)***
Foremost Plastic Pdts Co Inc 708 452-5300
7834 W Grand Ave Elmwood Park (60707) ***(G-9453)***
Foremost Plastics, Elmwood Park *Also called Foremost Plastic Pdts Co Inc* ***(G-9453)***
Forest Awards & Engraving 630 595-2242
336 E Irving Park Rd Wood Dale (60191) ***(G-21189)***
Forest City Auto Electric Co 815 963-4350
1255 23rd Ave Rockford (61104) ***(G-17418)***
Forest City Counter Tops Inc 815 633-8602
6050 Broadcast Pkwy Loves Park (61111) ***(G-13212)***
Forest City Grinding Inc 815 874-2424
4844 Stenstrom Rd Rockford (61109) ***(G-17419)***
Forest City Industry Inc 815 877-4084
6100 Material Ave Loves Park (61111) ***(G-13213)***
Forest City Satellite 815 639-0500
432 Heartland Dr Davis Junction (61020) ***(G-7422)***
Forest City Technologies Inc 815 965-5880
892 Southrock Dr Rockford (61102) ***(G-17420)***
Forest Electric Company 708 681-0180
1301 Armitage Ave Ste B Melrose Park (60160) ***(G-13868)***
Forest Envelope Company 630 515-1200
309 E Crossroads Pkwy Bolingbrook (60440) ***(G-2178)***
Forest Lee LLC 312 379-0032
440 N Wells St Ste 530 Chicago (60654) ***(G-4618)***
Forest Packaging Corporation 847 981-7000
1955 Estes Ave Elk Grove Village (60007) ***(G-9003)***
Forest Plating Co 708 366-2071
930 Des Plaines Ave Forest Park (60130) ***(G-9717)***
Forest Printing Co 708 366-5100
7214 Madison St Ste 1 Forest Park (60130) ***(G-9718)***
Forestech Wood Products 217 279-3659
204 W Washington St West Union (62477) ***(G-20690)***

Forever Fly LLC 312 981-9161
934 N Waller Ave Chicago (60651) ***(G-4619)***
Forge Group Dekalb LLC (PA) 815 756-3538
1801 Pleasant St Dekalb (60115) ***(G-7678)***
Forge Group Star LLC 815 758-6400
1801 S Ihm Blvd Freeport (61032) ***(G-10110)***
Forge Resources Group, Dekalb *Also called Forge Group Dekalb LLC* ***(G-7678)***
Forge Resources Group LLC (PA) 815 758-6400
1832 Pleasant St Dekalb (60115) ***(G-7679)***
Forge Resources Group LLC 815 758-6400
1801 Pleasant St Dekalb (60115) ***(G-7680)***
Forge Resources Group LLC (PA) 815 758-6400
1832 Pleasant St Dekalb (60115) ***(G-7681)***
Forgings & Stampings Inc (PA) 815 962-5597
1025 23rd Ave Rockford (61104) ***(G-17421)***
Fork Standards, Lombard *Also called FSI Technologies Inc* ***(G-13080)***
Forking By Frank, Evanston *Also called Franks Maintenance & Engrg* ***(G-9523)***
Forklift Firm LLC 708 770-7207
12139 White Pine Trl Homer Glen (60491) ***(G-11480)***
Form Plastics Company 630 443-1400
3825 Stern Ave Saint Charles (60174) ***(G-18203)***
Form Relief Tool Co Inc 815 393-4263
14499 E Il Route 72 Davis Junction (61020) ***(G-7423)***
Form-All Spring Stamping Inc 630 595-8833
380 Meyer Rd Bensenville (60106) ***(G-1800)***
Forman Co Inc 309 734-3413
609 W Broadway Monmouth (61462) ***(G-14217)***
Formar Inc 630 543-1151
1049 W Republic Dr Addison (60101) ***(G-128)***
Formax Inc 708 479-3000
9150 W 191st St Mokena (60448) ***(G-14082)***
Formco Metal Products Inc 630 766-4441
556 Clayton Ct Wood Dale (60191) ***(G-21190)***
Formco Plastics Inc 630 860-7998
904 Fairway Dr Bensenville (60106) ***(G-1801)***
Formcraft Tool Company 773 476-8727
6453 S Bell Ave Chicago (60636) ***(G-4620)***
Formed Fastener Mfg Inc 708 496-1219
7247 S 78th Ave Ste 1 Bridgeview (60455) ***(G-2348)***
Forming America Ltd (PA) 888 993-1304
1200 N Prince Crossing Rd West Chicago (60185) ***(G-20587)***
Forms Design Plus Coleman Prtg 309 685-6000
1105 E War Memorial Dr # 1 Peoria (61616) ***(G-16439)***
Forms Press Inc 815 455-4466
1006 Bennington Dr Crystal Lake (60014) ***(G-7200)***
Formtek Inc (HQ) 630 285-1500
711 Ogden Ave Lisle (60532) ***(G-12891)***
Formula Systems North America 847 350-0655
2300 Eastern Ave Elk Grove Village (60007) ***(G-9004)***
Formulations Inc 847 674-9141
8050 Ridgeway Ave Skokie (60076) ***(G-18956)***
Forno Palese Baking Company 630 595-5502
1235 Humbracht Cir Ste 1 Bartlett (60103) ***(G-1281)***
Forrest Consulting 630 730-9619
479 N Main St Ste 220 Glen Ellyn (60137) ***(G-10403)***
Forrest Pallet Service, Poplar Grove *Also called Steve Forrest* ***(G-16784)***
Forrest Redi-Mix Inc 815 657-8241
321 W Krack St Forrest (61741) ***(G-9733)***
Forreston Tool Inc 815 938-3626
400 E Avon St Forreston (61030) ***(G-9740)***
Forster Products Inc 815 493-6360
310 Se Lanark Ave Lanark (61046) ***(G-12481)***
Forster Tool & Mfg Co Inc 630 616-8177
1135 Industrial Dr Bensenville (60106) ***(G-1802)***
Forsyth Brothers Concrete Pdts 217 548-2770
104 E North Sherman St Fithian (61844) ***(G-9669)***
Fort Dearborn Company 773 774-4321
6035 W Gross Point Rd Niles (60714) ***(G-15121)***
Fort Lock Corporation (HQ) 708 456-1100
715 Center St Grayslake (60030) ***(G-10773)***
Forte Automation Systems Inc 815 316-6247
8155 Burden Rd Machesney Park (61115) ***(G-13344)***
Forte Incorporated 815 224-8300
601 2nd St Ste 3 La Salle (61301) ***(G-12112)***
Forte Print Corporation 773 391-0105
3139 W Chicago Ave Chicago (60622) ***(G-4621)***
Fortella Company Inc 312 567-9000
214 W 26th St Chicago (60616) ***(G-4622)***
Fortella Forture Cookies, Chicago *Also called Fortella Company Inc* ***(G-4622)***
Forterra Pressure Pipe Inc (PA) 815 389-4800
4416 Prairie Hill Rd South Beloit (61080) ***(G-19093)***
Fortman & Associates Ltd 847 524-0741
472 Potomac Ln Elk Grove Village (60007) ***(G-9005)***
Fortuna Baking Company 630 681-3000
149 Easy St Carol Stream (60188) ***(G-2987)***
Fortune Brands Home & SEC Inc (PA) 847 484-4400
520 Lake Cook Rd Deerfield (60015) ***(G-7610)***
Fortune International Tech LLC 847 429-9791
5883 Chatham Dr Hoffman Estates (60192) ***(G-11425)***

A
L
P
H
A
B
E
T
I
C

Fortune Metal Midwest LLC 630 778-7776
1212 E 6th St Sandwich (60548) *(G-18370)*
Fortune Rope & Metal Co Inc 630 787-9715
700 County Line Rd Bensenville (60106) *(G-1803)*
Forza Customs 708 474-6625
17809 Torrence Ave Lansing (60438) *(G-12493)*
Fosbinder Fabrication Inc 309 764-0913
130 35th St Moline (61265) *(G-14146)*
Foseco, Champaign Also called Vesuvius U S A Corporation *(G-3366)*
Foster Learning LLC 618 656-6836
900 Timberlake Dr Edwardsville (62025) *(G-8362)*
Fotofab LLC 773 463-6211
3758 W Belmont Ave Chicago (60618) *(G-4623)*
Fotofabrication, Chicago Also called Fotofab LLC *(G-4623)*
Fotowatch, Chicago Also called Tammy Banks *(G-6317)*
Found Inc 773 279-3000
3401 N Kedzie Ave Chicago (60618) *(G-4624)*
Foundation Lithuanian Minor 630 969-1316
908 Rob Roy Pl Downers Grove (60516) *(G-8005)*
Foundry Printers Row Crossfit 312 566-7201
730 S Clark St Chicago (60605) *(G-4625)*
Fountain Products Inc 630 991-7237
2769 Cascade Falls Cir Elgin (60124) *(G-8590)*
Fountain Technologies Ltd 847 537-3677
423 Dennistion Ct Wheeling (60090) *(G-20900)*
Four Acre Wood Products 217 543-2971
553 N Cr 240 E Arthur (61911) *(G-858)*
Four Season Pallets Inc 708 940-5545
16140 Clinton St Harvey (60426) *(G-11085)*
Four Seasons Ace Hardware 618 439-2101
11230 State Highway 37 Benton (62812) *(G-1925)*
Four Seasons Gutter Prote 309 694-4565
1815 Meadow Ave East Peoria (61611) *(G-8268)*
Four Star Denim and AP LLC 847 707-6365
3333 W Harrison St Chicago (60624) *(G-4626)*
Four Star Tool Inc 224 735-2419
5521 Meadowbrook Ct Rolling Meadows (60008) *(G-17733)*
Four-Most Inc (PA) 563 323-3233
6518 W Plank Rd Peoria (61604) *(G-16440)*
Four-Most Inc 815 282-9788
1550 Elmwood Rd Rockford (61103) *(G-17422)*
Four-Tech Industries Co 708 444-8230
18545 West Creek Dr Tinley Park (60477) *(G-19828)*
Fourell Corp 217 742-3186
410 E Jefferson St Winchester (62694) *(G-21105)*
Fourier Systems Inc 708 478-5333
12610 W Hank Ct E Homer Glen (60491) *(G-11481)*
Fournie Farms Inc 618 344-8527
925 Mcdonough Lake Rd Collinsville (62234) *(G-6961)*
Fourth Quarter Holdings Inc 847 249-7445
1379 Saint Paul Ave Gurnee (60031) *(G-10879)*
Fox International Corp 773 465-3634
7366 N Greenview Ave Chicago (60626) *(G-4627)*
Fox Machine & Tool Inc 847 357-1845
985 Lively Blvd Elk Grove Village (60007) *(G-9006)*
Fox Meter Inc 630 968-3635
5403 Patton Dr Ste 218 Lisle (60532) *(G-12892)*
Fox Redi-Mix Inc 217 774-2110
870 County Highway 6 Shelbyville (62565) *(G-18878)*
Fox Tool & Manufacturing Inc 815 338-3046
900 Dieckman St Woodstock (60098) *(G-21390)*
Fox Valley Chemical Company 815 653-2660
5201 Mann Dr Ringwood (60072) *(G-17043)*
Fox Valley Iron & Metal Corp 630 897-5907
1440 W Downer Pl Aurora (60506) *(G-1098)*
Fox Valley Labor News Inc 630 897-4022
726 N Edgelawn Dr Aurora (60506) *(G-1099)*
Fox Valley Molding Inc (PA) 630 552-3176
113 S Center St Plano (60545) *(G-16731)*
Fox Valley Park District 630 892-1550
100 S Barnes Rd Aurora (60506) *(G-1100)*
Fox Valley Pregnancy Center (PA) 847 697-0200
101 E State St South Elgin (60177) *(G-19145)*
Fox Valley Sandblasting Inc 630 553-6050
1211 Badger St Yorkville (60560) *(G-21483)*
Fox Valley Stamping Company 847 741-2277
385 Production Dr South Elgin (60177) *(G-19146)*
Fox Valley Tree Professionals, McHenry Also called Platinum Inc *(G-13780)*
Fox Valley Windows LLC 630 210-6400
2711 E New York St Aurora (60502) *(G-963)*
Fox Valley Winery Inc 630 554-0404
5600 Us Highway 34 Oswego (60543) *(G-16005)*
FP International, Deerfield Also called Free-Flow Packaging Intl Inc *(G-7611)*
FP International, Homewood Also called Free-Flow Packaging Intl Inc *(G-11494)*
Fpm Heat Treating 815 332-4961
648 Us Highway 20 Cherry Valley (61016) *(G-3441)*
Fra No 3800 W Division 708 338-0690
3800 Division St Stone Park (60165) *(G-19555)*
Fra-Milco Cabinets Co Inc ....
386 Nevada A Ct Frankfort (60423) *(G-9795)*

Frabill Inc 630 552-9426
431 E South St Plano (60545) *(G-16732)*
Fragrance Island Inc 773 488-2700
641 E 79th St Chicago (60619) *(G-4628)*
Fragrance Master, Saint Charles Also called Odorite International Inc *(G-18236)*
Frain Group, Carol Stream Also called Cartpac Inc *(G-2956)*
Fram Group Holdings Inc 847 482-2045
1900 W Field Ct Lake Forest (60045) *(G-12249)*
Frame Game 573 754-2385
119 E Quincy St Pleasant Hill (62366) *(G-16748)*
Frame House Inc 708 383-1616
163 S Oak Park Ave Oak Park (60302) *(G-15753)*
Frame House Passport Photos, Oak Park Also called Frame House Inc *(G-15753)*
Frame Mart Inc 309 452-0658
1211 Silver Oak Cir Normal (61761) *(G-15203)*
Frame Material Supply Inc 309 362-2323
520 N Trivoli Rd Trivoli (61569) *(G-19906)*
Frame World, Lake In The Hills Also called Barrington Automation Ltd *(G-12329)*
Framery 618 656-5749
216 E Park St Edwardsville (62025) *(G-8363)*
Franch & Sons Trnsp Inc 630 392-3307
329 N Mill Rd Unit 108 Addison (60101) *(G-129)*
Francis L Morris 618 676-1724
1377 Angling Rd Clay City (62824) *(G-6905)*
Francis Screw Products Co Inc 847 647-9462
7400 N Milwaukee Ave Niles (60714) *(G-15122)*
Frank A Edmunds & Co Inc (PA) 773 586-2772
6111 S Sayre Ave Chicago (60638) *(G-4629)*
Frank Bender Jewels, Northfield Also called Frank S Bender Inc *(G-15514)*
Frank E Galloway 618 948-2578
4808 Moffett Ln Sumner (62466) *(G-19686)*
Frank Miller & Sons Inc (PA) 708 201-7200
10002 W 190th Pl Mokena (60448) *(G-14083)*
Frank O Carlson & Co Inc 773 847-6900
3622 S Morgan St Ste 2r Chicago (60609) *(G-4630)*
Frank R Walker Company 630 613-9312
700 Springer Dr Lombard (60148) *(G-13079)*
Frank S Bender Inc 847 441-7370
316 Happ Rd Northfield (60093) *(G-15514)*
Frank S Johnson & Company Inc 847 492-1660
818 Lake St Evanston (60201) *(G-9522)*
Frankenstitch Promotions LLC 847 459-4840
311 Egidi Dr Wheeling (60090) *(G-20901)*
Frankfort Machine & Tools Inc 815 469-9902
285 Industry Ave Frankfort (60423) *(G-9796)*
Franklin Automation Inc 630 466-1900
1981 Bucktail Ln Sugar Grove (60554) *(G-19645)*
Franklin Display Group Inc (PA) 815 544-6676
910 E Lincoln Ave Belvidere (61008) *(G-1668)*
Franklin Display Group Inc 815 544-5300
725 Landmark Dr Belvidere (61008) *(G-1669)*
Franklin Fueling Systems Inc 207 283-0156
21054 Network Pl Chicago (60673) *(G-4631)*
Franklin Maintenance 815 284-6806
1597 Nachusa Rd Dixon (61021) *(G-7900)*
Franklin Park Building Mtls 847 455-3985
9400 Chestnut Ave Franklin Park (60131) *(G-9945)*
Franklin Screw Products Inc 815 784-8500
600 S Sycamore St Unit 1 Genoa (60135) *(G-10317)*
Franklin Well Services Inc 812 494-2800
10483 May Chapel Rd Lawrenceville (62439) *(G-12532)*
Franklin Wire Works Inc 815 544-6676
2519 Business Route 20 Belvidere (61008) *(G-1670)*
Franks Auto Insurance A Div BR, Evanston Also called Frank S Johnson & Company Inc *(G-9522)*
Franks Dgtal Prtg Off Sups Inc 630 892-2511
723 Aurora Ave Aurora (60505) *(G-1101)*
Franks Ideal Welding Inc 708 344-4409
2600 S 25th Ave Ste P Broadview (60155) *(G-2438)*
Franks Maintenance & Engrg 847 475-1003
945 Pitner Ave Evanston (60202) *(G-9523)*
Franmar Chemical 309 829-5952
11 Mary Ellen Way Bloomington (61701) *(G-2045)*
Frantz Bearing Division, Sterling Also called Frantz Manufacturing Company *(G-19508)*
Frantz Manufacturing Company (PA) 815 625-3333
3201 W Lefevre Rd Sterling (61081) *(G-19508)*
Frantz Manufacturing Company 815 625-7063
3809 W Lincoln Hwy Sterling (61081) *(G-19509)*
Frantz Manufacturing Company 815 564-0991
3201 W Le Fevre Rd Sterling (61081) *(G-19510)*
Frasca Air Services, Urbana Also called Frasca International Inc *(G-19986)*
Frasca International Inc (PA) 217 344-9200
906 Airport Rd Urbana (61802) *(G-19986)*
Fraser Millwork Inc 708 447-3262
8109 Ogden Ave Lyons (60534) *(G-13309)*
Frazier Management LLC 815 484-8900
1635 New Milford Schl Rd Rockford (61109) *(G-17423)*
Fred Kennerly 815 398-6861
1619 Arden Ave Rockford (61107) *(G-17424)*

ALPHABETIC SECTION

Fred Pigg Dental Lab..618 439-6829
14544 N Wing Ln Mount Vernon (62864) *(G-14611)*
Fred Stollenwerk...309 852-3794
801 Elmwood Ave Kewanee (61443) *(G-12034)*
Freddie Bear Sports..708 532-4133
17250 Oak Park Ave Tinley Park (60477) *(G-19829)*
Freddie Bear Sports.com, Tinley Park Also called Freddie Bear Sports *(G-19829)*
Frederick P Schall, McHenry Also called Deatak Inc *(G-13735)*
Frederics Frame Studio Inc....................................312 243-2950
680 N Lk Shr Dr Apt 903 Chicago (60611) *(G-4632)*
Frederking Construction Co..................................618 483-5031
8595 N 300th St Altamont (62411) *(G-532)*
Fredette Racing Products, Beecher Also called W L & J Enterprises Inc *(G-1524)*
Fredman Bros Furniture Co Inc.............................309 674-2011
908 Sw Washington St Peoria (61602) *(G-16441)*
Free Press Advocate, Wilmington Also called Free Press Newspapers *(G-21098)*
Free Press Newspapers, Coal City Also called Coal City Courant *(G-6930)*
Free Press Newspapers..815 476-7966
111 S Water St Wilmington (60481) *(G-21098)*
Free-Flow Packaging Intl Inc (HQ).........................650 261-5300
1650 Lake Cook Rd Ste 400 Deerfield (60015) *(G-7611)*
Free-Flow Packaging Intl Inc.................................708 589-6500
905 175th St Fl 3 Homewood (60430) *(G-11494)*
Freeburg Printing & Publishing..............................618 539-3320
820 S State St Freeburg (62243) *(G-10089)*
Freedman Seating Company (PA).........................773 524-3255
4545 W Augusta Blvd Chicago (60651) *(G-4633)*
Freedom Design & Decals Inc...............................815 806-8172
18811 90th Ave Ste G Mokena (60448) *(G-14084)*
Freedom Fastener Inc..847 891-3686
1084 Industrial Dr Ste 6 Bensenville (60106) *(G-1804)*
Freedom Fuel & Food Inc......................................773 233-5350
8950 S Ashland Ave Chicago (60620) *(G-4634)*
Freedom Graphic Systems, Aurora Also called Fgs-IL LLC *(G-960)*
Freedom Material Resources Inc..........................618 937-6415
1186 State Highway 37 West Frankfort (62896) *(G-20672)*
Freedom Pines, Skokie Also called Lanzatech Inc *(G-18976)*
Freedom Sausage Inc..815 792-8276
4155 E 1650th Rd Earlville (60518) *(G-8161)*
Freeman Energy Corporation (HQ)......................217 698-3949
3008 Happy Landing Dr Springfield (62711) *(G-19370)*
Freeman Products Worldwide, Elk Grove Village Also called AMG International Inc *(G-8727)*
Freeman United Coal Mining Co...........................217 627-2161
22393 Crown Two Mine Rd 2 Mine Girard (62640) *(G-10381)*
Freeman United Coal Mining Co (HQ)..................217 698-3300
4440 Ash Grove Dr Ste A Springfield (62711) *(G-19371)*
Freeport Journal Standard, Freeport Also called Journal Standard *(G-10122)*
Freeport Press Inc..815 232-1181
1031 W Empire St Freeport (61032) *(G-10111)*
Freesen Inc...309 827-4554
1523 Cottage Ave Bloomington (61701) *(G-2046)*
Freeway-Rockford Inc...815 397-6425
4701 Boeing Dr Rockford (61109) *(G-17425)*
Freight Car Services Inc.......................................217 443-4106
2313 Cannon St Ste 2 Danville (61832) *(G-7336)*
Freight House Kit & Bath Str, Dixon Also called Scheffler Custom Woodworking *(G-7915)*
Freightcar America Inc (PA)..................................800 458-2235
125 S Wacker Dr Ste 1500 Chicago (60606) *(G-4635)*
Freitas P Sabah..708 386-8934
6105 1/2 North Ave Oak Park (60302) *(G-15754)*
French Studio Ltd..618 942-5328
821 S Park Ave Stop 1 Herrin (62948) *(G-11171)*
Frequency Devices, Ottawa Also called North Ridge Properties LLC *(G-16064)*
Frequency Devices Inc..815 434-7800
1784 Chessie Ln Unit 1 Ottawa (61350) *(G-16053)*
Fresco Plaster Finishes Inc..................................847 277-1484
228 James St Ste 2 Barrington (60010) *(G-1219)*
Fresenius Kabi LLC (HQ)......................................847 550-2300
3 Corporate Dr Lake Zurich (60047) *(G-12413)*
Fresenius Kabi LLC...630 350-7150
600 Supreme Dr Bensenville (60106) *(G-1805)*
Fresenius Kabi Pharm (HQ)..................................847 550-2300
3 Corporate Dr Lake Zurich (60047) *(G-12414)*
Fresenius Kabi Usa Inc...708 450-7500
2020 N Ruby St Melrose Park (60160) *(G-13869)*
Fresenius Kabi Usa Inc...708 410-4761
2020 N Ruby St Melrose Park (60160) *(G-13870)*
Fresenius Kabi Usa Inc...708 345-6170
2020 N Ruby St Melrose Park (60160) *(G-13871)*
Fresenius Kabi Usa LLC (HQ)...............................847 550-2300
3 Corporate Dr Fl 3 # 3 Lake Zurich (60047) *(G-12415)*
Fresenius Kabi Usa LLC.......................................847 983-7100
The Illinois Scienc Skokie (60077) *(G-18957)*
Fresenius Kabi Usa LLC.......................................847 550-2300
3 Corporate Dr Ste 300 Lake Zurich (60047) *(G-12416)*
Fresh Concept Enterprises Inc.............................815 254-7295
12249 Rhea Dr Plainfield (60585) *(G-16667)*
Fresh Express Incorporated.................................630 736-3900
1109 E Lake St Streamwood (60107) *(G-19574)*

Fresh Facs...618 357-9697
612 County Rd Pinckneyville (62274) *(G-16614)*
Fresh Factory...630 580-9038
238 Tubeway Dr Carol Stream (60188) *(G-2988)*
Fresh Look & Sons..815 325-9692
406 E Main St Morris (60450) *(G-14306)*
Fresh Software Solutions LLC..............................630 995-4350
1717 N Naper Blvd Ste 207 Naperville (60563) *(G-14831)*
Fresh Solutions For Your Home, Coal City Also called Elco Laboratories Inc *(G-6932)*
Freudenberg & Co, Aurora Also called Freudenberg Household Pdts LP *(G-964)*
Freudenberg Household Pdts LP.........................630 270-1400
2188 Diehl Rd Aurora (60502) *(G-964)*
Frey Wiss Prcsion McHining Inc..........................630 595-9073
384 Beinoris Dr Wood Dale (60191) *(G-21191)*
Fri Jado Inc..630 633-7944
1401 Davey Rd Ste 100 Woodridge (60517) *(G-21302)*
Fricke Dental Manufacturing Co..........................630 540-1900
165 Roma Jean Pkwy Streamwood (60107) *(G-19575)*
Friedman Corporation (HQ)..................................847 948-7180
10275 W Higgins Rd # 250 Rosemont (60018) *(G-18024)*
Friedrich Klatt and Associates.............................773 753-1806
5240 S Hyde Park Blvd Chicago (60615) *(G-4636)*
Friend Oil Co..618 842-9161
Enterprise Rd Rr 3 Fairfield (62837) *(G-9624)*
Friendly Remedies, Woodridge Also called Symbria Rx Services LLC *(G-21342)*
Friendly Signs Inc...815 933-7070
1281 N Schuyler Ave Kankakee (60901) *(G-11973)*
Friends Fuel...773 434-9387
8200 S Kedzie Ave Chicago (60652) *(G-4637)*
Friends Pyramid State Park Inc............................618 318-3992
804 Belle Ave Pinckneyville (62274) *(G-16615)*
Frigel North America Inc......................................847 540-0160
150 Prairie Lake Rd Ste A East Dundee (60118) *(G-8196)*
Frigid Fluid Company..708 836-1215
11631 W Grand Ave Melrose Park (60164) *(G-13872)*
Frito-Lay North America Inc.................................217 532-5040
1400 E Tremont St Hillsboro (62049) *(G-11311)*
Frito-Lay North America Inc.................................815 468-3940
450 N Grove St Manteno (60950) *(G-13448)*
Frito-Lay North America Inc.................................708 331-7200
4170 166th St Oak Forest (60452) *(G-15679)*
Fromm Airpad Inc..630 393-9790
3s320 Rockwell St Warrenville (60555) *(G-20236)*
Frontida Biopharm Inc..215 620-3527
2500 Molitor Rd Aurora (60502) *(G-965)*
Frontier Soups, Gurnee Also called K M J Enterprises Inc *(G-10892)*
Frostdefense Envirotech Inc.................................217 979-3052
509 S Garfield Ave Champaign (61821) *(G-3293)*
Fruit Fancy...708 724-2613
1116 W 110th St Chicago (60643) *(G-4638)*
Frye-Williamson Press Inc...................................217 522-7744
901 N Macarthur Blvd Springfield (62702) *(G-19372)*
Fryer To Fuel Inc...309 654-2875
26700 171st Ave N Cordova (61242) *(G-7006)*
Fs Depot Inc..847 468-2350
2645 Federal Signal Dr University Park (60484) *(G-19955)*
FSI Technologies Inc..630 932-9380
668 E Western Ave Lombard (60148) *(G-13080)*
Fsp LLC..773 992-2600
245 Ambrogio Dr Gurnee (60031) *(G-10880)*
FTC Family of Companies, Bloomington Also called Family Time Computing Inc *(G-2041)*
Fuchs Corporation (HQ).......................................800 323-7755
17050 Lathrop Ave Harvey (60426) *(G-11086)*
Fuchs Lubricants Co, Harvey Also called Fuchs Corporation *(G-11086)*
Fuel Tech Inc (PA)...630 845-4500
27601 Bella Vista Pkwy Warrenville (60555) *(G-20237)*
Fugate Inc..309 472-6830
1349 W Birchwood St Morton (61550) *(G-14360)*
Fugate Instruments, Morton Also called Fugate Inc *(G-14360)*
Fugiel Railroad Supply Corp.................................847 516-6862
700 Industrial Dr Ste E Cary (60013) *(G-3160)*
Fuji Impulse American Corp.................................847 236-9190
1735 Lisa Marie Ct Deerfield (60015) *(G-7612)*
Fuji Oozx America Inc..281 888-2247
1051 Perimeter Dr # 1175 Schaumburg (60173) *(G-18531)*
Fuji Robotics, Elk Grove Village Also called Fuji Yusoki Kogyo Co Ltd *(G-9007)*
Fuji Yusoki Kogyo Co Ltd....................................425 522-0722
1220 Landmeier Rd Elk Grove Village (60007) *(G-9007)*
Fujifilm Elctronic Mtls USA Inc.............................312 924-5800
850 Central Ave Hanover Park (60133) *(G-11006)*
Fujifilm NDT Systems, Hanover Park Also called Fujifilm Elctrnic Mtls USA Inc *(G-11006)*
Fulfillment Center, The, Downers Grove Also called MPS Chicago Inc *(G-8062)*
Full Circle Shipyard LLC.......................................630 343-2264
13108 Grant Rd Lemont (60439) *(G-12564)*
Full Court Press Inc..773 779-1135
9146 S Pleasant Ave Chicago (60643) *(G-4639)*
Full Line Printing Inc..312 642-8080
361 W Chicago Ave Chicago (60654) *(G-4640)*

Fuller Asphalt & Landscape....618 797-1169
4353 Lake Dr Granite City (62040) ***(G-10707)***
Fuller Brothers Ready Mix....217 532-2422
935 Ash St Hillsboro (62049) ***(G-11312)***
Fulling Motor USA Inc....847 894-6238
1601 Park Ridge Pt Park Ridge (60068) ***(G-16277)***
Fully Equipped Inc....312 978-9936
1751d W Howard St 103 Chicago (60626) ***(G-4641)***
Fulton Corporation (PA)....815 589-3211
303 8th Ave Fulton (61252) ***(G-10152)***
Fulton County Democrat, Canton *Also called Martin Publishing Co* ***(G-2828)***
Fulton County Rehabilitation (PA)....309 647-6510
500 N Main St Canton (61520) ***(G-2826)***
Fulton Metal Works Inc....217 476-8223
1763 Ashland Rd Ashland (62612) ***(G-884)***
Fultonworks LLC....312 544-9639
1165 N Clark St Chicago (60610) ***(G-4642)***
Fun Incorporated....773 745-3837
333 Alice St Wheeling (60090) ***(G-20902)***
Fun Industries Inc....309 755-5021
627 15th Ave East Moline (61244) ***(G-8226)***
Funeral Register Books Inc....217 627-3235
499 Rachel Rd Girard (62640) ***(G-10382)***
Funk Family Holdings Corp (PA)....847 276-2700
1081 Johnson Dr Buffalo Grove (60089) ***(G-2541)***
Funk Linko Group Inc....708 757-7421
26815 S Winfield Rd Monee (60449) ***(G-14200)***
Funks Grove Pure Maple Syrup....309 874-3360
5257 Old Route 66 Shirley (61772) ***(G-18891)***
Funny Valentine Press Inc....773 769-6552
4923 N Oakley Ave Chicago (60625) ***(G-4643)***
Fura Inc....847 451-0000
9224 Chestnut Ave Franklin Park (60131) ***(G-9946)***
Fura International, Franklin Park *Also called Fura Inc* ***(G-9946)***
Furdge Trucking Inc....773 800-5431
7704 S Loomis Blvd Chicago (60620) ***(G-4644)***
Furnace Fixers Inc....630 736-0670
308a Roma Jean Pkwy Streamwood (60107) ***(G-19576)***
Furnel Inc (PA)....630 543-0885
350 S Stewart Ave Addison (60101) ***(G-130)***
Furniture Doctor, The, Girard *Also called Robert Harlan Ernst* ***(G-10385)***
Furniture Manufacture, Algonquin *Also called What We Make Inc* ***(G-396)***
Furry Inc....217 446-0084
2005 E Voorhees St Danville (61834) ***(G-7337)***
Furst-Mcness Company (PA)....800 435-5100
120 E Clark St Freeport (61032) ***(G-10112)***
Fusibond Piping Systems Inc....630 969-4488
2615 Curtiss St Downers Grove (60515) ***(G-8006)***
Fusion Chemical Corporation....847 656-5285
350 S Northwest Hwy # 300 Park Ridge (60068) ***(G-16278)***
Fusion Fabrication....815 214-9148
627 E 10th St Lockport (60441) ***(G-12994)***
Fusion Gates LLC....618 650-9170
2412 Little Round Top Dr Edwardsville (62025) ***(G-8364)***
Fusion OEM, Burr Ridge *Also called Fusion Systems Incorporated* ***(G-2675)***
Fusion Systems Incorporated....630 323-4115
6951 High Grove Blvd Burr Ridge (60527) ***(G-2675)***
Fusion Tech Integrated Inc (PA)....309 774-4275
218 20th Ave Roseville (61473) ***(G-18062)***
Futaba Corporation of America (HQ)....847 884-1444
711 E State Pkwy Schaumburg (60173) ***(G-18532)***
Futters Nut Butters....847 540-0565
2400 Hassell Rd Ste 300 Hoffman Estates (60169) ***(G-11426)***
Future Brands LLC (HQ)....847 444-1880
222 Merchandise Mart Plz # 1600 Chicago (60654) ***(G-4645)***
Future Tool Inc....815 395-0012
2029 23rd Ave Rockford (61104) ***(G-17426)***
Futures Magazine Inc....312 846-4600
107 W Van Buren St # 203 Chicago (60605) ***(G-4646)***
Fuyao Glass Illinois Inc....217 864-2392
2768 E Elwin Rd Decatur (62521) ***(G-7495)***
G & C Enterprises Inc....618 747-2272
18837 County Line Rd Jonesboro (62952) ***(G-11946)***
G & E Automatic....815 654-7766
10462 Product Dr Ste B Machesney Park (61115) ***(G-13345)***
G & F Manufacturing Co Inc....708 424-4170
5555 W 109th St Oak Lawn (60453) ***(G-15716)***
G & G Printing, Bradley *Also called G & G Studios /Broadway Prtg* ***(G-2282)***
G & G Studios /Broadway Prtg....815 933-8181
345 W Broadway St Bradley (60915) ***(G-2282)***
G & H Balancer Service....773 509-1988
2919 W Irving Park Rd Chicago (60618) ***(G-4647)***
G & J Associates Inc....847 255-0123
1315 E Davis St Arlington Heights (60005) ***(G-738)***
G & J Hall Tools Inc....314 968-5040
77 Eisenhower Ln S Lombard (60148) ***(G-13081)***
G & K Baking LLC....708 741-7260
7731 W 98th St Ste E Hickory Hills (60457) ***(G-11196)***
G & M Die Casting Company Inc....630 595-2340
284 Richert Rd Wood Dale (60191) ***(G-21192)***
G & M Embroidery....708 636-7005
260 Chicago Ridge Mall Chicago Ridge (60415) ***(G-6795)***
G & M Fabricating Inc....815 282-1744
9014 Swanson Dr Roscoe (61073) ***(G-17907)***
G & M Industries Inc....618 344-6655
208 Yorktown Dr Collinsville (62234) ***(G-6962)***
G & M Manufacturing Corp....815 455-1900
111 S Main St Crystal Lake (60014) ***(G-7201)***
G & M Metal Fabricators Inc....847 678-6501
9120 Gage Ave Franklin Park (60131) ***(G-9947)***
G & M Steel Fabricating, Granite City *Also called Accurate Fabricators Inc* ***(G-10689)***
G & M Woodworking Inc....708 425-4013
5656 W 88th Pl Oak Lawn (60453) ***(G-15717)***
G & R Stained Glass....847 455-7026
2919 Emerson St Franklin Park (60131) ***(G-9948)***
G & S Asphalt Inc....217 826-2421
16870 N Quality Lime Rd Marshall (62441) ***(G-13571)***
G & S Manufacturing Inc....847 674-7666
2345 Waukegan Rd Ste 155 Bannockburn (60015) ***(G-1201)***
G & S Pallets....630 574-2741
66 Windsor Dr Oak Brook (60523) ***(G-15623)***
G & W Electric Company....708 388-6363
3450 127th St Blue Island (60406) ***(G-2123)***
G & W Technical Corporation....847 487-0990
578 E Burnett Rd Island Lake (60042) ***(G-11607)***
G & Z Industries Inc....847 215-2300
541 Chaddick Dr Wheeling (60090) ***(G-20903)***
G A I M Engineering, Bensenville *Also called GAim Plastics Incorporated* ***(G-1806)***
G and D Enterprises Inc....847 981-8661
1425 E Algonquin Rd Arlington Heights (60005) ***(G-739)***
G B C Velobind, Addison *Also called Acco Brands USA LLC* ***(G-14)***
G B Holdings Inc....773 265-3000
600 N Kilbourn Ave Chicago (60624) ***(G-4648)***
G Blando Jewelers Inc....630 627-7963
3 Countryside Plz Countryside (60525) ***(G-7053)***
G Branch Corp....630 458-1909
409 S Vista Ave Unit B Addison (60101) ***(G-131)***
G D S Professional Bus Display....309 829-3298
1103 Martin Luther King D Bloomington (61701) ***(G-2047)***
G E Mathis Company....773 586-3800
6100 S Oak Park Ave Chicago (60638) ***(G-4649)***
G F Ltd....708 333-8300
16255 Vincennes Ave South Holland (60473) ***(G-19212)***
G F Printing....618 797-0576
2439 Hemlock Ave Granite City (62040) ***(G-10708)***
G Force Labels & Printing Inc....630 552-8911
405 E South St Plano (60545) ***(G-16733)***
G H Meiser & Co....708 388-7867
18770 88th Ave Unit B Mokena (60448) ***(G-14085)***
G I A Publications Inc (PA)....708 496-3800
7404 S Mason Ave Chicago (60638) ***(G-4650)***
G I C, Orland Park *Also called Graphic Image Corporation* ***(G-15956)***
G I W, Aurora *Also called Garbe Iron Works Inc* ***(G-1102)***
G J Nikolas & Co Inc....708 544-0320
2800 Washington Blvd Bellwood (60104) ***(G-1625)***
G K Enterprises Inc (PA)....708 587-2150
26000 S Whiting Way Ste 2 Monee (60449) ***(G-14201)***
G K L Corporation....815 886-5900
5 Greenwood Ave Romeoville (60446) ***(G-17826)***
G L Beaumont Lumber Company (PA)....618 423-2323
Rr 51 Box S Ramsey (62080) ***(G-16964)***
G L Doemelt....217 268-4243
299 Egyptian Trl Arcola (61910) ***(G-649)***
G L Tool and Manufacturing Co....630 628-1992
815 S Kay Ave Ste A Addison (60101) ***(G-132)***
G M Sign Inc....847 546-0424
704 Sunset Dr Round Lake (60073) ***(G-18075)***
G M T, Buffalo Grove *Also called Global Material Tech Inc* ***(G-2542)***
G N F, Oak Lawn *Also called Befco Manufacturing Co Inc* ***(G-15702)***
G P Albums, Chicago *Also called General Products* ***(G-4678)***
G P Cole Inc....217 431-3029
1120 Industrial St Danville (61832) ***(G-7338)***
G P Concrete & Iron Works....815 842-2270
1217 E Indiana Ave Pontiac (61764) ***(G-16770)***
G P I, Lake In The Hills *Also called General Products International* ***(G-12335)***
G P International, Crystal Lake *Also called Vulcan Ladder Usa LLC* ***(G-7292)***
G R Leonard & Co Inc (PA)....847 797-8101
115 E University Dr Arlington Heights (60004) ***(G-740)***
G S F, South Elgin *Also called Graphic Screen Fashion Ltd* ***(G-19149)***
G S Foundry Mfg....618 282-4114
210 Kaskaskia Dr Red Bud (62278) ***(G-16995)***
G S I Group, Assumption *Also called A P Livestock Division G S I* ***(G-887)***
G T C Industries Inc....708 369-9815
609 Sara Ln Naperville (60565) ***(G-14832)***
G T Express Ltd....708 338-0303
2233 West St River Grove (60171) ***(G-17060)***
G T I Spindle, Bloomington *Also called Gti Spindle Technology Inc* ***(G-2054)***

G T L Technologies Inc 630 469-9818
413 2nd Pl Ste 100 Glendale Heights (60139) ***(G-10451)***
G T Services of Illionois Inc 309 925-5111
22387 State Route 9 Tremont (61568) ***(G-19896)***
G Y Industries LLC 708 210-0800
70 W Madison St Ste 2300 Chicago (60602) ***(G-4651)***
G&D Integrated Mfg LLC 309 284-6700
50 Commerce Dr Morton (61550) ***(G-14361)***
G&D Integrated Services Inc 309 284-6700
50 Commerce Dr Morton (61550) ***(G-14362)***
G&G Machine Shop Inc 217 892-9696
1580 E Grove Ave Ste 2 Rantoul (61866) ***(G-16976)***
G&K-Vijuk Intern Corp 630 530-2203
715 N Church Rd Elmhurst (60126) ***(G-9365)***
G&R Machining Inc 847 526-7364
3205 Poplar Dr Island Lake (60042) ***(G-11608)***
G-Fast Distribution Inc 847 926-0722
1954 1st St 228 Highland Park (60035) ***(G-11264)***
G-III Apparel Group Ltd 630 236-8900
1650 Premium Outlet Blvd Aurora (60502) ***(G-966)***
G-M Services 618 532-2324
309 Country Club Rd Centralia (62801) ***(G-3232)***
G-P Manufacturing Co Inc 847 473-9001
1535 S Lakeside Dr Waukegan (60085) ***(G-20444)***
G-W Communications Inc 815 476-7966
111 S Water St Wilmington (60481) ***(G-21099)***
G.T.L. International, Glendale Heights *Also called G T L Technologies Inc* ***(G-10451)***
G1 Industries Co, Joy *Also called Robin L Barnhouse* ***(G-11947)***
G2 Crowd Inc (PA) 847 748-7559
20 N Wacker Dr Ste 1800 Chicago (60606) ***(G-4652)***
G2 Labs, Chicago *Also called G2 Crowd Inc* ***(G-4652)***
G3 Machining LLC 309 323-8310
915 E Oakland Ave Bloomington (61701) ***(G-2048)***
Gabel & Schubert Bronze 773 878-6800
4500 N Ravenswood Ave Chicago (60640) ***(G-4653)***
Gabriel Enterprises 773 342-8705
1734 W North Ave Chicago (60622) ***(G-4654)***
Gadgetworld Enterprises Inc 773 703-0796
10956 S Western Ave Chicago (60643) ***(G-4655)***
Gaertner Scientific Corp 847 673-5006
3650 Jarvis Ave Skokie (60076) ***(G-18958)***
Gafco, Melrose Park *Also called Graphic Arts Finishing Company* ***(G-13875)***
GAG Industries Inc 847 616-8710
1065 Chase Ave Elk Grove Village (60007) ***(G-9008)***
Gage Applied Technologies LLC 815 838-0005
900 N State St Lockport (60441) ***(G-12995)***
Gage Assembly Co 847 679-5180
3771 W Morse Ave Lincolnwood (60712) ***(G-12820)***
Gage Grinding Company Inc (PA) 847 639-3888
40 Detroit St Unit D Cary (60013) ***(G-3161)***
Gage Manufacturing Inc 847 228-7300
820 Touhy Ave Elk Grove Village (60007) ***(G-9009)***
Gage Tool & Manufacturing Inc 847 640-1069
1025 Pauly Dr Elk Grove Village (60007) ***(G-9010)***
Gail Glasser Brickman, Skokie *Also called Century Fasteners & Mch Co Inc* ***(G-18939)***
Gail McGrath & Associates Inc 847 770-4620
3453 Commercial Ave Northbrook (60062) ***(G-15392)***
GAim Plastics Incorporated (PA) 630 350-9500
789 Golf Ln Bensenville (60106) ***(G-1806)***
Gain Wireline Services Inc 618 842-2914
306a Petroleum Blvd Fairfield (62837) ***(G-9625)***
Gaither Tool Co 217 245-0545
2255 W Morton Ave Jacksonville (62650) ***(G-11765)***
Galactic Clothing, Chicago *Also called Allen Larson* ***(G-3614)***
Galactic Tool Co 815 962-3420
1402 18th Ave Rockford (61104) ***(G-17427)***
Galaxy Circuits Inc 630 462-1010
383 Randy Rd Carol Stream (60188) ***(G-2989)***
Galaxy Industries Inc 847 639-8580
231 Jandus Rd Cary (60013) ***(G-3162)***
Galaxy Precision Mfg Inc 847 238-9066
2636 United Ln Elk Grove Village (60007) ***(G-9011)***
Galaxy Sourcing Inc 630 532-5003
15 W Commercial Ave Addison (60101) ***(G-133)***
Galena Cellars Winery (PA) 815 777-3330
515 S Main St Galena (61036) ***(G-10169)***
Galena Cellars Winery 815 777-3429
4746 N Ford Rd Galena (61036) ***(G-10170)***
Galena Road Gravel Inc 309 274-6388
5129 E Truitt Rd Chillicothe (61523) ***(G-6817)***
Galenas Kandy Kitchen 815 777-0241
100 N Main St Galena (61036) ***(G-10171)***
Galesburg Manufacturing Co (PA) 309 342-3173
1835 Lacon Dr Galesburg (61401) ***(G-10192)***
Galesburg Register-Mail (HQ) 309 343-7181
140 S Prairie St Galesburg (61401) ***(G-10193)***
Galesburg Sign & Lighting 309 342-9798
1518 S Henderson St Galesburg (61401) ***(G-10194)***
Gall Machine Co 708 352-2800
9640 Joliet Rd Countryside (60525) ***(G-7054)***
Gallagher Asphalt Corporation (PA) 708 877-7160
18100 Indiana Ave Thornton (60476) ***(G-19786)***
Gallagher Corporation 847 249-3440
3908 Morrison Dr Gurnee (60031) ***(G-10881)***
Gallas Label & Decal 773 775-1000
6559 N Avondale Ave Chicago (60631) ***(G-4656)***
Gallasi Cut Stone & Marble LLC 708 479-9494
10001 191st St Mokena (60448) ***(G-14086)***
Galleon Industries Inc 708 478-5444
16714 Cherry Creek Ct Joliet (60433) ***(G-11867)***
Galleon Printing Co, Joliet *Also called Galleon Industries Inc* ***(G-11867)***
Gallimore Industries Inc 847 356-3331
200 Park Ave Ste B Lake Villa (60046) ***(G-12352)***
Gallon Industries Inc 630 628-1020
341 W Factory Rd Addison (60101) ***(G-134)***
Galloway Como Processing 815 626-0305
24578 Stone St Sterling (61081) ***(G-19511)***
Galloway Logging, Sumner *Also called Frank E Galloway* ***(G-19686)***
Galloway Meats & Poultry, Sterling *Also called Galloway Como Processing* ***(G-19511)***
Galloy and Van Etten Inc (PA) 773 928-4800
11756 S Halsted St Chicago (60628) ***(G-4657)***
Galmar Enterprises Inc 815 463-9826
14408 W Edison Dr Ste F New Lenox (60451) ***(G-15035)***
Galva Iron and Metal Co Inc 309 932-3450
625 Se Industrial Ave Galva (61434) ***(G-10232)***
Galvanize Labs Inc 630 258-1476
6728 W Highland Dr Palos Heights (60463) ***(G-16184)***
Galvanized Stairs, East Lynn *Also called Greene Welding & Hardware Inc* ***(G-8220)***
Gam Enterprises Inc 847 649-2500
901 E Business Center Dr Mount Prospect (60056) ***(G-14530)***
Gama Electronics Inc 815 356-9600
1240 Cobblestone Way Woodstock (60098) ***(G-21391)***
Game Day Incentives Inc 630 854-0581
1731 Princess Cir Naperville (60564) ***(G-14967)***
Gamestop Inc 773 568-0457
800 N Kedzie Ave Chicago (60651) ***(G-4658)***
Gamestop Corp 618 258-8611
662 Wesley Dr Wood River (62095) ***(G-21262)***
Gametime Snacks LLC 309 517-6342
2224 1st St W Milan (61264) ***(G-14011)***
Gamma Alpha Visual Communicatn 847 956-0633
642 Busse Hwy Park Ridge (60068) ***(G-16279)***
Gamma Products Inc 708 974-4100
7730 W 114th Pl Ste 1 Palos Hills (60465) ***(G-16201)***
Gamma Quality, Norridge *Also called Joseph Ringelstein* ***(G-15238)***
Ganji Klames 773 478-9000
4455 Oakton St Skokie (60076) ***(G-18959)***
Gannett Health Care Group, Hoffman Estates *Also called Gannett Stllite Info Ntwrk LLC* ***(G-11427)***
Gannett Stllite Info Ntwrk LLC 630 629-1280
136 Bertram Dr Unit C Yorkville (60560) ***(G-21484)***
Gannett Stllite Info Ntwrk LLC 847 839-1700
1721 Moon Lake Blvd # 540 Hoffman Estates (60169) ***(G-11427)***
Gannon Graphics, Schaumburg *Also called Marty Gannon* ***(G-18620)***
Gannon Graphics 847 895-1043
1025 Morse Ave Schaumburg (60193) ***(G-18533)***
Gano Welding Supplies Inc 217 345-3777
320 Railroad Ave Charleston (61920) ***(G-3402)***
Gantec Pubg Solutions LLC 847 598-1144
1827 Walden Office Sq # 260 Schaumburg (60173) ***(G-18534)***
Garbe Iron Works Inc 630 897-5100
456 N Broadway Aurora (60505) ***(G-1102)***
Garcoa Inc 708 905-5118
8838 Brookfield Ave Brookfield (60513) ***(G-2484)***
Gard, Ron, Chicago *Also called Guess Whackit & Hope Inc* ***(G-4750)***
Garden Prrie Pool Spa Enclsres, Garden Prairie *Also called Ccsi International Inc* ***(G-10236)***
Garden Watering, Mount Prospect *Also called Robert Bosch Tool Corporation* ***(G-14566)***
Gardien, Buffalo Grove *Also called Consolidated Foam Inc* ***(G-2528)***
Gardner Abrasive Products, South Beloit *Also called Fives Landis Corp* ***(G-19092)***
Gardner Asphalt Corporation 800 237-1155
4718 W Roosevelt Rd Chicago (60644) ***(G-4659)***
Gardner Denver Inc 770 632-5000
1800 Gardner Expy Quincy (62305) ***(G-16883)***
Gardner Denver Inc 217 222-5400
1800 Gardner Expy Quincy (62305) ***(G-16884)***
Gardner Denver Inc 800 231-3628
1860 Gardner Expy Quincy (62305) ***(G-16885)***
Gardner Denver Inc 815 875-3321
1301 N Euclid Ave Princeton (61356) ***(G-16810)***
Gardner Denver Inc 847 676-8800
5621 W Howard St Niles (60714) ***(G-15123)***
Gardner Denver Nash LLC 331 457-5377
2808 Hillcrest Cir Naperville (60564) ***(G-14968)***
Gardner Products Inc 815 562-6011
224 4th Ave Rochelle (61068) ***(G-17142)***
Gardner-Gibson, Chicago *Also called Gardner Asphalt Corporation* ***(G-4659)***
Garfilds Bev Whse - Barrington, Barrington *Also called Barrington Cardinal Whse LLC* ***(G-1213)***

ALPHABETIC

Garman Trucking, Fairfield *Also called Fairfield Ready Mix Inc* ***(G-9623)***
Garratt-Callahan Company 630 543-4411
340 S La Londe Ave Addison (60101) ***(G-135)***
Garren Sawmill & Farm, Dix *Also called Boyd Sawmill* ***(G-7881)***
Gartech Manufacturing Co 217 324-6527
1400 W Hudson Dr Litchfield (62056) ***(G-12963)***
Garver Feeds (PA) 217 422-2201
222 E Wabash Ave Decatur (62523) ***(G-7496)***
Garver Inc 217 932-2441
10234 N 230th St Casey (62420) ***(G-3201)***
Garvey Group, The, Niles *Also called Ed Garvey and Company* ***(G-15117)***
Garvey Group, The, Niles *Also called Tru Line Lithographing Inc* ***(G-15183)***
Garvin Electrical Manufacturer, Franklin Park *Also called Blg McC Enterprises Inc* ***(G-9888)***
Gary & Larry Brown Trucking (PA) 618 268-6377
5525 Highway 34 N Raleigh (62977) ***(G-16961)***
Gary Bryan Kitchens & Bath, Springfield *Also called Custom Woodwork & Interiors* ***(G-19358)***
Gary Galassi and Sons Inc 815 886-3906
44 Devonwood Ave Romeoville (60446) ***(G-17827)***
Gary Galassi Stone & Steel, Romeoville *Also called Gary Galassi and Sons Inc* ***(G-17827)***
Gary Grimm & Associates Inc 217 357-3401
1204 Buchanan St Carthage (62321) ***(G-3136)***
Gary Quarries, Hamilton *Also called Gray Quarries Inc* ***(G-10955)***
Gas Compression Systems Inc 630 766-6049
1035 Entry Dr Bensenville (60106) ***(G-1807)***
Gas Depot Inc 847 581-0303
8930 Waukegan Rd Ste 230 Morton Grove (60053) ***(G-14409)***
Gasket & Seal Fabricators Inc 314 241-3673
1640 Sauget Indl Pkwy East Saint Louis (62206) ***(G-8308)***
Gaskoa Inc 708 339-5000
16928 State St South Holland (60473) ***(G-19213)***
Gast Monuments Inc (PA) 773 262-2400
1900 W Peterson Ave Chicago (60660) ***(G-4660)***
Gate Systems Corporation 847 731-6700
690 Chandler Rd Apt 401 Gurnee (60031) ***(G-10882)***
Gatehouse Media LLC 309 852-2181
105 E Central Blvd Kewanee (61443) ***(G-12035)***
Gatehouse Media LLC 618 783-2324
700 W Washington St Newton (62448) ***(G-15083)***
Gatehouse Media LLC 217 788-1300
1 Copley Plz Springfield (62701) ***(G-19373)***
Gatehouse Media LLC 618 393-2931
206 S Whittle Ave Olney (62450) ***(G-15862)***
Gatehouse Media LLC 618 937-2850
111 S Emma St West Frankfort (62896) ***(G-20673)***
Gatehouse Media LLC 585 598-0030
18w140 Butterfield Rd # 450 Oakbrook Terrace (60181) ***(G-15799)***
Gatehouse Media LLC 815 842-1153
318 N Main St Pontiac (61764) ***(G-16771)***
Gatehouse Media LLC 618 253-7146
35 S Vine St Harrisburg (62946) ***(G-11024)***
Gatehouse Media - Wstn Ill Div 309 299-6135
140 S Prairie St Galesburg (61401) ***(G-10195)***
Gatehouse Media Ill Holdings 585 598-0030
1 News Plz Peoria (61643) ***(G-16442)***
Gatehuse Mdia Ill Hldngs II In 217 788-1300
1 Copley Plz Springfield (62701) ***(G-19374)***
Gates Corporation 309 343-7171
630 Us Highway 150 E Galesburg (61401) ***(G-10196)***
Gates Inc 217 335-2378
134 Smith St Barry (62312) ***(G-1250)***
Gates Repair & Machine, Barry *Also called Gates Inc* ***(G-1250)***
Gates Rubber Co, The, Galesburg *Also called Gates Corporation* ***(G-10196)***
Gatesair Inc 800 622-0022
3200 Wisman Ln Quincy (62301) ***(G-16886)***
Gateway Cable Inc (PA) 630 766-7969
1998 Ohio St Ste 100 Lisle (60532) ***(G-12893)***
Gateway Cable Inc 630 766-7969
11 Gateway Rd Bensenville (60106) ***(G-1808)***
Gateway Crushing & Screening 618 337-1954
3936 Mississippi Ave East Saint Louis (62206) ***(G-8309)***
GATEWAY F. S. INC, Fults *Also called F S Gateway Inc* ***(G-10160)***
Gateway Fabricators Inc 618 271-5700
633 Collinsville Ave East Saint Louis (62201) ***(G-8310)***
Gateway Fbrction Solutions LLC 618 612-3170
5819 Lrc Rd Waterloo (62298) ***(G-20290)***
Gateway Fs Inc 618 824-6631
18 N Mill Rd Venedy (62214) ***(G-20034)***
Gateway Fuels Inc 618 248-5000
5260 State Route 161 Albers (62215) ***(G-345)***
Gateway Impressions 618 505-7544
218 Edwardsville Rd Troy (62294) ***(G-19914)***
Gateway Industrial Power Inc 309 821-1035
13958 Roberto Rd Ste 2 Bloomington (61705) ***(G-2049)***
Gateway Mine, Coulterville *Also called Peabody Coal Company* ***(G-7033)***
Gateway North Mine 618 758-1515
12968 State Route 13 Coulterville (62237) ***(G-7031)***
Gateway Packaging Company LLC 618 451-0010
20 Central Industrial Dr Granite City (62040) ***(G-10709)***
Gateway Printing, Huntley *Also called Rohrer Corporation* ***(G-11564)***
Gateway Rail Services Inc 618 451-0100
1980 3rd St Madison (62060) ***(G-13412)***
Gateway Screw & Rivet Inc 630 539-2232
301 High Grove Blvd Glendale Heights (60139) ***(G-10452)***
Gateway Seed Company Inc (PA) 618 327-8000
5517 Van Buren Rd Nashville (62263) ***(G-14997)***
Gather Voices Inc 312 476-9465
4021 N Broadway St Chicago (60613) ***(G-4661)***
Gator Die Supplies, Rockford *Also called Rockform Tooling & Machinery* ***(G-17611)***
Gator Products Inc 847 836-0581
80 Industrial Dr Unit 105 Gilberts (60136) ***(G-10355)***
Gatorade Company (HQ) 312 821-1000
555 W Monroe St Fl 1 Chicago (60661) ***(G-4662)***
Gatto Industrial Platers Inc 773 287-0100
4620 W Roosevelt Rd Chicago (60644) ***(G-4663)***
Gaunt Industries Inc 847 671-0776
9828 Franklin Ave Franklin Park (60131) ***(G-9949)***
Gavel Company Div, The, Lincolnwood *Also called Brown Wood Products Company* ***(G-12814)***
Gavin Machine & Manufacturing, Sandwich *Also called Gavin Woodworking Inc* ***(G-18371)***
Gavin Woodworking Inc 815 786-2242
16119 Chicago Rd Sandwich (60548) ***(G-18371)***
Gaw-Ohara Envelope Co (PA) 773 638-1200
500 N Sacramento Blvd Chicago (60612) ***(G-4664)***
Gayety Candy Co Inc (PA) 708 418-0062
3306 Ridge Rd Lansing (60438) ***(G-12494)***
Gayetys Chocolates & Ice Cream, Lansing *Also called Gayety Candy Co Inc* ***(G-12494)***
Gaylee Corporation Saws 586 803-1100
215 Elmwood Ave South Beloit (61080) ***(G-19094)***
Gaytan Signs & Co Inc 815 726-2975
317 Mcdonough St Joliet (60436) ***(G-11868)***
Gayton Group Inc 847 233-0509
9353 Seymour Ave Schiller Park (60176) ***(G-18809)***
Gazette (PA) 815 777-0105
716 S Bench St Galena (61036) ***(G-10172)***
Gazette Democrat 618 833-2150
108 Lafayette St 112 Anna (62906) ***(G-583)***
Gazette News Office, Bunker Hill *Also called Bunker Hill Publication* ***(G-2633)***
Gazette Newspapers, Loves Park *Also called Rock Valley Publishing LLC* ***(G-13255)***
Gazette Printing Co 309 389-2811
508 W Main St Glasford (61533) ***(G-10387)***
Gazette-Democrat 618 833-2158
112 Lafayette St Anna (62906) ***(G-584)***
Gb Marketing Inc 847 367-0101
200 N Fairway Dr Ste 202 Vernon Hills (60061) ***(G-20055)***
GBA Systems Integrators LLC 913 492-0400
1701 River Dr Ste 100 Moline (61265) ***(G-14147)***
Gbh Walnut Inc (PA) 815 379-2151
300 Wyanet Rd Walnut (61376) ***(G-20218)***
GBS Document Solutions, Princeton *Also called Ennis Inc* ***(G-16808)***
Gc America Inc (HQ) 708 597-0900
3737 W 127th St Alsip (60803) ***(G-446)***
Gc Custom Woodworking LLC 847 724-7292
3418 Winchester Ln Glenview (60026) ***(G-10547)***
GC Laser Systems Inc 844 532-1064
900 Des Plaines Ave Forest Park (60130) ***(G-9719)***
Gc Manufacturing America LLC 708 597-0900
3737 W 127th St Alsip (60803) ***(G-447)***
Gcb Metal Building Systems LLC 224 268-3792
800 Dundee Ave Elgin (60120) ***(G-8591)***
Gcg Corp 847 298-2285
4344 Regency Dr Glenview (60025) ***(G-10548)***
GCI, Bolingbrook *Also called General Converting Inc* ***(G-2179)***
Gcm, Chicago *Also called Global Contract Mfg Inc* ***(G-4695)***
Gcm Chicago, Schiller Park *Also called Hi-Tech Manufacturing LLC* ***(G-18812)***
Gcp Applied Technologies 708 728-2420
6051 W 65th St Chicago (60638) ***(G-4665)***
Gcp Applied Technologies Inc 617 876-1400
2051 Waukegan Rd Bannockburn (60015) ***(G-1202)***
Gcpro LLC 773 764-2776
220 Eisenhower Ln N Lombard (60148) ***(G-13082)***
Gcpro Restoration, Lombard *Also called Gcpro LLC* ***(G-13082)***
Gdi, Granite City *Also called Grain Densification Intl LLC* ***(G-10711)***
Gdm Seeds Inc (PA) 317 752-6783
454 E 300n Rd Gibson City (60936) ***(G-10338)***
Gds, Bloomington *Also called G D S Professional Bus Display* ***(G-2047)***
Gds Enterprises 217 543-3681
399 E Progress St Arthur (61911) ***(G-859)***
GE Aviation Systems LLC 779 203-8100
1354 Clifford Ave Ste 100 Loves Park (61111) ***(G-13214)***
GE Fairchild Mining Equipment 618 559-3216
707 N Hickory St Du Quoin (62832) ***(G-8121)***
GE Ges Inc 815 307-0595
411 Garfield Rd Ingleside (60041) ***(G-11583)***

GE Healthcare Holdings Inc 847 398-8400
3350 N Ridge Ave Arlington Heights (60004) ***(G-741)***

GE Healthcare Inc 774 249-6290
3350 N Ridge Ave Arlington Heights (60004) ***(G-742)***

GE Healthcare Inc 630 595-6642
945 N Edgewood Ave Ste A1 Wood Dale (60191) ***(G-21193)***

GE Intelligent Platforms Inc 630 829-4000
901 Warrenville Rd # 300 Lisle (60532) ***(G-12894)***

GE Transportation Parts LLC (HQ) 814 875-2755
500 W Monroe St Chicago (60661) ***(G-4666)***

GE Zenith Controls Inc 773 299-6600
18w140 Butterfield Rd # 350 Oakbrook Terrace (60181) ***(G-15800)***

Gea Farm Technologies Inc (HQ) 630 548-8200
1880 Country Farm Dr Naperville (60563) ***(G-14833)***

Gea Farm Technologies Inc 630 369-8100
1354 Enterprise Dr Romeoville (60446) ***(G-17828)***

Gear & Repair 708 387-0144
9100 Plainfield Rd Ste 13 Brookfield (60513) ***(G-2485)***

Gear Technology, Elk Grove Village *Also called Randall Publishing Inc* ***(G-9214)***

Gearon Company, The, Chicago *Also called Metomic Corporation* ***(G-5410)***

Gebco Machine Inc 618 452-6120
2900 Emzee Ave Granite City (62040) ***(G-10710)***

Geebees Inc 309 682-5300
3024 N University St Peoria (61604) ***(G-16443)***

Gehl Company, Belvidere *Also called Manitou Americas Inc* ***(G-1684)***

Gehrke Technology Group Inc (PA) 847 498-7320
1050 N Rand Rd Wauconda (60084) ***(G-20353)***

Geib Industries Inc 847 455-4550
901 E Jefferson St Bensenville (60106) ***(G-1809)***

Geka Manufacturing Corporation 224 238-5080
1690 Cambridge Dr Elgin (60123) ***(G-8592)***

Gelita USA Chicago 708 891-8400
10 Wentworth Ave Calumet City (60409) ***(G-2776)***

Gelita USA Inc 708 891-8400
10 Wentworth Ave Calumet City (60409) ***(G-2777)***

Gelnex, Chicago *Also called In3gredients Inc* ***(G-4904)***

Gem Acquisition Company Inc 773 735-3300
5942 S Central Ave Chicago (60638) ***(G-4667)***

Gem Business Forms, Chicago *Also called Gem Acquisition Company Inc* ***(G-4667)***

Gem Electric Motor Repair 815 756-5317
1400 E Lincoln Hwy Dekalb (60115) ***(G-7682)***

Gem Equipment & Mfg LLC 309 923-7312
1503 W Front St Roanoke (61561) ***(G-17100)***

Gem Equipment & Mfg LLC 309 923-7312
1503 W Front St Roanoke (61561) ***(G-17101)***

Gem Manufacturing Corporation 630 458-0014
1922 Springside Dr Naperville (60565) ***(G-14834)***

Gema Inc (PA) 773 508-6690
2434 W Peterson Ave Chicago (60659) ***(G-4668)***

Gemco (PA) 217 446-7900
1019 Griggs St Danville (61832) ***(G-7339)***

Gemini Digital Inc 630 894-9430
860 Lake St Ste 606 Roselle (60172) ***(G-17954)***

Gemini Industries Inc 618 251-3352
1 Gemini Industrial Dr Roxana (62084) ***(G-18100)***

Gemini Steel Inc (PA) 815 472-4462
1450 N 11250e Rd Momence (60954) ***(G-14185)***

Gemini Tool & Manufacturing 847 678-5000
3541 Martens St Franklin Park (60131) ***(G-9950)***

Gemtar Inc 618 548-1353
138 Woodland Dr Salem (62881) ***(G-18340)***

Gemworld International Inc 847 657-0555
2640 Patriot Blvd Ste 240 Glenview (60026) ***(G-10549)***

Genacc LLC 309 253-9034
60 State St Ste 101 Peoria (61602) ***(G-16444)***

Genentech Inc 650 225-1045
329 Laurel Ave Libertyville (60048) ***(G-12653)***

General Acrylics, Mount Vernon *Also called Gunner Energy Corporation* ***(G-14612)***

General Assembly & Mfg Corp 847 516-6462
750 Industrial Dr Ste B Cary (60013) ***(G-3163)***

General Bandages Inc 847 966-8383
717 N Washington Ave Park Ridge (60068) ***(G-16280)***

General Cable Industries Inc 618 542-4761
1453 S Washington St Du Quoin (62832) ***(G-8122)***

General Contractor Inc 618 533-5213
190 Industrial Park Dr Sandoval (62882) ***(G-18364)***

General Converting Inc 630 378-9800
250 W Crossroads Pkwy Bolingbrook (60440) ***(G-2179)***

General Cutng Tl Svc & Mfg Inc 847 677-8770
6440 N Ridgeway Ave Lincolnwood (60712) ***(G-12821)***

General Design Jewelers Inc 312 201-9047
5 S Wabash Ave Ste 217 Chicago (60603) ***(G-4669)***

General Dynamics Corporation 618 993-9207
6658 Route 148 Marion (62959) ***(G-13511)***

General Dynamics Ordnance 618 985-8211
6658 Route 148 Marion (62959) ***(G-13512)***

General Dynmics Mssion Systems 703 876-3000
50 S La Salle St Chicago (60603) ***(G-4670)***

General Electric Company 309 664-1513
1601 General Electric Rd Bloomington (61704) ***(G-2050)***

General Electric Company 630 588-8853
775 East Dr Carol Stream (60188) ***(G-2990)***

General Electric Company 708 780-2600
1543 S 54th Ave Cicero (60804) ***(G-6848)***

General Electric Company 630 334-0054
2015 Spring Rd Ste 400 Oak Brook (60523) ***(G-15624)***

General Electric Company 847 304-7400
2501 Barrington Rd Hoffman Estates (60192) ***(G-11428)***

General Electro Corporation 630 595-8989
1069 Bryn Mawr Ave Bensenville (60106) ***(G-1810)***

General Engineering Works 630 543-8000
1025 W National Ave Addison (60101) ***(G-136)***

General Forging Die Co Inc 815 874-4224
4635 Hydraulic Rd Rockford (61109) ***(G-17428)***

General Grind & Machine Inc 309 582-5959
2103 Se 5th St Aledo (61231) ***(G-356)***

General Grinding Co 630 543-9088
1514 W Wrightwood Ct Addison (60101) ***(G-137)***

General Laminating Company 847 639-8770
179 Northwest Hwy Ste 3 Cary (60013) ***(G-3164)***

General Lattice Inc 312 374-3158
2415 W 19th St Chicago (60608) ***(G-4671)***

General Loose Leaf Bindery Inc 847 244-9700
350 N La Salle Dr # 1100 Chicago (60654) ***(G-4672)***

General Lrng Communications, Northbrook *Also called M I T Financial Group Inc* ***(G-15425)***

General Machine Inc 618 234-1919
6038 Schiermeier Rd Freeburg (62243) ***(G-10090)***

General Machine & Tl Works Inc 312 337-2177
990 N Lk Shr Dr Apt 20e Chicago (60611) ***(G-4673)***

General Machine and Tool Inc 815 727-5270
615 Mills Rd Joliet (60433) ***(G-11869)***

General Machine and Tool Inc (PA) 815 727-4342
348 Caton Farm Rd Lockport (60441) ***(G-12996)***

General Machinery & Mfg Co 773 235-3700
2634 N Keeler Ave Chicago (60639) ***(G-4674)***

General Machining Service Inc 708 636-4848
5521 W 110th St Ste 6 Oak Lawn (60453) ***(G-15718)***

General Manufacturing LLC 708 345-8600
1725 N 33rd Ave Melrose Park (60160) ***(G-13873)***

General Methods Co, Morton *Also called Morton Automatic Electric Co* ***(G-14369)***

General Mills Inc 630 844-1125
1370 Orchard Rd Montgomery (60538) ***(G-14244)***

General Mills Inc 630 231-1140
1600 Huntington Dr Calumet City (60409) ***(G-2778)***

General Mills Inc 309 342-9165
1557 S Henderson St Galesburg (61401) ***(G-10197)***

General Mills Inc 815 544-7399
915 E Pleasant St Belvidere (61008) ***(G-1671)***

General Mills Green Giant 815 547-5311
725 Landmark Dr Belvidere (61008) ***(G-1672)***

General Mills Operations LLC 630 844-1125
1370 Orchard Rd Montgomery (60538) ***(G-14245)***

General Motor Sign 847 546-0424
704 Sunset Dr Round Lake (60073) ***(G-18076)***

General Packaging Products Inc (HQ) 312 226-5611
1700 S Canal St Chicago (60616) ***(G-4675)***

General Pallet 773 660-8550
13513 S Calumet Ave Chicago (60827) ***(G-4676)***

General Plating Co Inc 630 543-0088
303 W Fay Ave Addison (60101) ***(G-138)***

General Precision Mfg LLC 847 624-4969
2670 Greenleaf Ave Elk Grove Village (60007) ***(G-9012)***

General Press Colors Ltd 630 543-7878
53 W Jackson Blvd # 1115 Chicago (60604) ***(G-4677)***

General Products 773 463-2424
4045 N Rockwell St Chicago (60618) ***(G-4678)***

General Products International 847 458-6357
9245 S Il Route 31 Lake In The Hills (60156) ***(G-12335)***

General Sand & Gravel, Rock Island *Also called Riverstone Group Inc* ***(G-17243)***

General Steel & Materials, Mattoon *Also called Mervis Industries Inc* ***(G-13648)***

General Surface Hardening Inc (PA) 312 226-5472
2108 W Fulton St Chicago (60612) ***(G-4679)***

Genes Ice Cream Inc 309 846-5925
2 Lake Pointe Ct Bloomington (61704) ***(G-2051)***

Geneseo Publication, Cambridge *Also called Liberty Group Publishing* ***(G-2805)***

Geneseo Republic, The, Geneseo *Also called Liberty Group Publishing* ***(G-10245)***

Genesis Comics Group 312 544-7473
2631 S Ind Ave Apt 1410 Chicago (60616) ***(G-4680)***

Genesis Duragrind Inc 815 625-6500
2910 W Le Fevre Rd Sterling (61081) ***(G-19512)***

Genesis III Inc 815 537-7900
5575 Lyndon Rd Prophetstown (61277) ***(G-16831)***

Genesis Inc (PA) 630 351-4400
980 Central Ave Roselle (60172) ***(G-17955)***

Genesis Ltg Managemet Svcs 630 986-3900
7320 S Mddson Ave Unit 10 Willowbrook (60527) ***(G-21044)***

Genesis Mold Corp 847 573-9431
854 Liberty Dr Ste C Libertyville (60048) ***(G-12654)***

Genetics Development Corp 847 283-9780
21 N Skokie Hwy Ste 104 Lake Bluff (60044) ***(G-12182)***

(PA)=Parent Co (HQ)=Headquarters (DH)=Div Headquarters

2020 Harris Illinois
Industrial Directory

1131

Geneva Cabinet Gallery   **ALPHABETIC SECTION**

Geneva Cabinet Gallery 630 232-9500
   321 Stevens St Geneva (60134) *(G-10271)*
Geneva Construction Company 630 892-6536
   216 Butterfield Rd North Aurora (60542) *(G-15261)*
Geneva Running Outfitters LLC 331 248-0221
   221 W State St Geneva (60134) *(G-10272)*
Geneva Sign Corporation 630 262-1700
   726 E State St Geneva (60134) *(G-10273)*
Gengler-Lowney Laser Works 630 801-4840
   899 Sullivan Rd Aurora (60506) *(G-1103)*
Genie Pro Sales Center, Itasca *Also called Overhead Door Corporation* *(G-11715)*
Genisys Decision Corporation 708 524-5100
   1150 S Taylor Ave Ste 200 Oak Park (60304) *(G-15755)*
Gennco International Inc 847 541-3333
   3162 Doriann Dr Northbrook (60062) *(G-15393)*
Genoa Business Forms Inc 815 895-2800
   445 Park Ave Sycamore (60178) *(G-19711)*
Genoa Manufacturing Center, Genoa *Also called Greenlee Textron Inc* *(G-10318)*
Gensler Gardens Inc (PA) 815 874-9634
   8631 11th St Davis Junction (61020) *(G-7424)*
Gentry Small Engine Repair 217 849-3378
   124 Court House Sq Toledo (62468) *(G-19875)*
Genuine Parts Company 630 293-1300
   1225 W Roosevelt Rd Chicago (60608) *(G-4681)*
Genwoods Holdco LLC 815 732-2141
   2606 S Illinois Rte 2 Oregon (61061) *(G-15921)*
Geo B Carpenter Co Division, Elmhurst *Also called Tri Vantage LLC* *(G-9438)*
Geo J Rothan Co 309 674-5189
   1200 W Johnson St Peoria (61605) *(G-16445)*
Geo Lauterer, Chicago *Also called George Lauterer Corporation* *(G-4682)*
Geo T Schmidt Inc (PA) 847 647-7117
   6151 W Howard St Niles (60714) *(G-15124)*
Geocap Financial Solutions, Burr Ridge *Also called Cnh Industrial Capitl Amer LLC* *(G-2665)*
Geocyn Company Inc 331 213-2851
   5s250 Frontenac Rd Naperville (60563) *(G-14835)*
Geomentum Inc (HQ) 630 729-7500
   3025 Highland Pkwy # 700 Downers Grove (60515) *(G-8007)*
Geomentum Inc 630 729-7500
   3025 Highland Pkwy Downers Grove (60515) *(G-8008)*
Geomentum Solutions, Downers Grove *Also called Geomentum Inc* *(G-8007)*
Georg-Pcific Corrugated IV LLC 630 896-3610
   4390 Liberty St Aurora (60504) *(G-967)*
George Drowne Cabinet Sand 847 234-1487
   517 Lincoln Ave Lake Bluff (60044) *(G-12183)*
George Hansen & Co Inc 630 628-8700
   50 W Laura Dr Addison (60101) *(G-139)*
George Industries LLC 847 394-3610
   2200 Foster Ave Wheeling (60090) *(G-20904)*
George Lauterer Corporation 312 913-1881
   310 S Racine Ave Chicago (60607) *(G-4682)*
George Nottoli & Sons Inc 773 589-1010
   7652 W Belmont Ave Chicago (60634) *(G-4683)*
George Pagels Company 708 478-7036
   9910 W 190th St Ste H Mokena (60448) *(G-14087)*
George Press Inc 217 324-2242
   905 N Old Route 66 Litchfield (62056) *(G-12964)*
George S Music Room 773 767-4676
   600 E Grand Ave Chicago (60611) *(G-4684)*
George Vaggelatos 847 361-3880
   400 W Center St Itasca (60143) *(G-11661)*
George Wilson 847 342-1111
   477 Greystone Ln Prospect Heights (60070) *(G-16841)*
George's Farm Supply, West Salem *Also called West Salem Knox County Htchy* *(G-20689)*
Georges Printwear, Lake Zurich *Also called JLJ Corp* *(G-12427)*
Georgetown Waste Water 217 662-2525
   208 S Walnut St Georgetown (61846) *(G-10326)*
Georgetown Wood and Pallet Co 217 662-2563
   5781 State Route 1 Georgetown (61846) *(G-10327)*
Georgia-Pacific LLC 815 423-9990
   21837 W Mississippi Ave Elwood (60421) *(G-9463)*
Georgia-Pacific LLC 217 999-2511
   900 S Old Route 66 Mount Olive (62069) *(G-14503)*
Georgies Greek Tasty Food Inc 773 987-1298
   2527 W Carmen Ave Chicago (60625) *(G-4685)*
Gepco International Inc (HQ) 847 795-9555
   1770 Birchwood Ave Des Plaines (60018) *(G-7773)*
Gerald Graff 312 343-2612
   6818 N Kildare Ave Lincolnwood (60712) *(G-12822)*
Gerald R Page Corporation (PA) 847 398-5575
   309 E Kenilworth Ave Prospect Heights (60070) *(G-16842)*
Gerali Custom Design Inc 847 760-0500
   1482 Sheldon Dr Elgin (60120) *(G-8593)*
Gerard Mitchell Company LLC 708 205-0828
   291 Walsh Cir Yorkville (60560) *(G-21485)*
Gerard Printing Company 847 437-6442
   710 Bonnie Ln Elk Grove Village (60007) *(G-9013)*
Gerardo and Quintana Auto Elc 773 424-0634
   4034 W 63rd St Chicago (60629) *(G-4686)*

Gerb Vibration Control Systems 630 724-1660
   1950 Ohio St Lisle (60532) *(G-12895)*
Gerber Manufacturing (gm) LLC 708 478-0100
   18700 Ridgeland Ave Tinley Park (60477) *(G-19830)*
Gerber Plumbing Fixtures, Woodridge *Also called Cfpg Ltd* *(G-21282)*
Gerber Plumbing Fixtures LLC 630 679-1420
   2500 Intrntonale Pkwy Woodridge (60517) *(G-21303)*
Gerdau Ameristeel US Inc 800 237-0230
   13535 S Torrence Ave # 5 Chicago (60633) *(G-4687)*
Gerdau Ameristeel US Inc 815 547-0400
   2595 Tripp Rd Belvidere (61008) *(G-1673)*
Gerdau Long Steel, Chicago *Also called Gerdau Ameristeel US Inc* *(G-4687)*
Gerhard Designing & Mfg Inc 708 599-4664
   8540 S Thomas Ave Ste A Bridgeview (60455) *(G-2349)*
Gerlin Inc 630 653-5232
   170 Tubeway Dr Carol Stream (60188) *(G-2991)*
German American Nat Congress (PA) 773 561-9181
   4740 N Western Ave Fl 2 Chicago (60625) *(G-4688)*
Germann Instruments Inc 847 329-9999
   8845 Forestview Rd Evanston (60203) *(G-9524)*
Gerresheimer Glass Inc 708 843-4246
   1131 Arnold St Chicago Heights (60411) *(G-6747)*
Geske & Sons, Crystal Lake *Also called Geske and Sons Inc* *(G-7203)*
Geske and Sons Inc (PA) 815 459-2407
   400 E Terra Cotta Ave Crystal Lake (60014) *(G-7202)*
Geske and Sons Inc 815 459-2407
   400 E Terra Cotta Ave Crystal Lake (60014) *(G-7203)*
Get A Quote For Your Pcb 847 952-1900
   925 Estes Ave Elk Grove Village (60007) *(G-9014)*
Getex Corporation 630 993-1300
   2158 Ogden Ave Aurora (60504) *(G-968)*
Gett Industries Ltd 309 799-5131
   7307 50th St Milan (61264) *(G-14012)*
GF Machining Solutions LLC (HQ) 847 913-5300
   560 Bond St Lincolnshire (60069) *(G-12766)*
Gfc, Pittsfield *Also called God Family Country LLC* *(G-16634)*
Gfi Innovations LLC 847 263-9000
   861 Anita Ave Antioch (60002) *(G-612)*
Gfi Metal Treating, Rockford *Also called Golfers Family Corporation* *(G-17431)*
Gfl Environmental Svcs USA Inc (HQ) 866 579-6900
   19701 97th Ave Mokena (60448) *(G-14088)*
Gfx International LLC (HQ) 847 543-7179
   333 Barron Blvd Grayslake (60030) *(G-10774)*
Ggc Corp 847 671-6500
   4300 United Pkwy Schiller Park (60176) *(G-18810)*
Ggi, Medinah *Also called Great Guy Inc* *(G-13813)*
Gh Cranes Corporation 815 277-5328
   9134 Gulfstream Rd Frankfort (60423) *(G-9797)*
Gh Printing Co Inc 630 663-0351
   2820 Hitchcock Ave Downers Grove (60515) *(G-8009)*
Gh Printing Co Inc (PA) 630 960-4115
   5207 Walnut Ave Downers Grove (60515) *(G-8010)*
Ghetzler Aero-Power Corp 224 513-5636
   26 Manchester Ln Vernon Hills (60061) *(G-20056)*
Gholson Pump & Repairs Co 618 382-4730
   725 County Road 1450 N Carmi (62821) *(G-2906)*
Ghp Group Inc (PA) 847 324-5900
   6440 W Howard St Niles (60714) *(G-15125)*
Gianni Incorporated 708 863-6696
   4615 W Roosevelt Rd Cicero (60804) *(G-6849)*
Giant Finishing Inc 708 343-6900
   600 W Factory Rd Addison (60101) *(G-140)*
Giant Globes Inc 773 772-2917
   4433 W Montana St Chicago (60639) *(G-4689)*
Giba Electric 773 685-4420
   4054 W Warwick Ave Chicago (60641) *(G-4690)*
Gibbs Machine Corp 815 336-9000
   411 S Main Coleta (61081) *(G-6949)*
Gibraltar Chemical Works Inc 708 333-0600
   114 E 168th St South Holland (60473) *(G-19214)*
Gibson Brands Inc 800 544-2766
   1150 Bowes Rd Elgin (60123) *(G-8594)*
Gibson Insurance Inc 217 864-4877
   300 N State Route 121 Mount Zion (62549) *(G-14646)*
Gift Check Program 2013 Inc 630 986-5081
   1400 Opus Pl Ste 810 Downers Grove (60515) *(G-8011)*
Gift of Games Ltd 847 370-1541
   82 Center St Unit W Grayslake (60030) *(G-10775)*
Gift of Games, The, Grayslake *Also called Gift of Games Ltd* *(G-10775)*
Gift Wraping Center, Skokie *Also called Wrap & Send Services* *(G-19059)*
Giftware News, Chicago *Also called Talcott Communications Corp* *(G-6313)*
Gig Karasek LLC 630 549-0394
   3955 Commerce Dr Saint Charles (60174) *(G-18204)*
Gilbert Spring Corporation 773 486-6030
   2301 N Knox Ave Chicago (60639) *(G-4691)*
Gilberts Craft Sausages LLC 630 923-8969
   123 W Front St Ste 210 Wheaton (60187) *(G-20800)*
Gilco Real Estate Company 847 298-1717
   515 Jarvis Ave Des Plaines (60018) *(G-7774)*

Gilday Service Company, Antioch *Also called Gilday Services* ***(G-613)***
Gilday Services...847 395-0853
25870 W Hermann Ave Antioch (60002) ***(G-613)***
Gill Athletics, Champaign *Also called Litania Sports Group Inc* ***(G-3317)***
Gill Athletics...217 367-8438
2808 Gemini Ct Champaign (61822) ***(G-3294)***
Gillespie City Water...217 839-3279
400 Pear St Gillespie (62033) ***(G-10375)***
Gillette Company...847 689-3111
3500 16th St North Chicago (60064) ***(G-15312)***
Gillons Inc...773 531-8900
17341 Palmer Blvd Homewood (60430) ***(G-11495)***
Gilman Star Inc...815 265-7332
203 N Central St 7 Gilman (60938) ***(G-10378)***
Gilster-Mary Lee, Chester *Also called Mary Lee Packaging Corporation* ***(G-3458)***
Gilster-Mary Lee Corporation...618 826-3102
111 Industrial Dr Chester (62233) ***(G-3455)***
Gilster-Mary Lee Corporation (HQ)...618 826-2361
1037 State St Chester (62233) ***(G-3456)***
Ginas Jams...773 622-1051
1941 N Newcastle Ave Chicago (60707) ***(G-4692)***
Ginger Windmill Brew LLC...630 677-2850
2600 Keslinger Rd Ste 15 Geneva (60134) ***(G-10274)***
Gingerich Custom Woodworking...217 578-3491
750 N Cr 250 E Arthur (61911) ***(G-860)***
Gino's Pizza, Walnut *Also called Avanti Foods Company* ***(G-20216)***
Giovanni Rana, Oak Brook *Also called Rana Meal Solutions LLC* ***(G-15659)***
Girard Chemical Company...630 293-5886
605 Country Club Dr Ste F Bensenville (60106) ***(G-1811)***
Girls In The Garage, Carrier Mills *Also called Amy Schutt* ***(G-3123)***
Girlygirl...708 633-7290
17037 Odell Ave Tinley Park (60477) ***(G-19831)***
Givaudan Flavors Corporation...630 682-5600
195 Alexandra Way Carol Stream (60188) ***(G-2992)***
Givaudan Flavors Corporation...847 608-6200
580 Tollgate Rd Ste A Elgin (60123) ***(G-8595)***
Givaudan Fragrances Corp...847 735-0221
1720 N Waukegan Rd Lake Forest (60045) ***(G-12250)***
Givaudan Fragrances Corp...847 645-7000
580 Tollgate Rd Ste A Elgin (60123) ***(G-8596)***
GL Downs Inc...618 993-9777
1805 Wolff Dr Marion (62959) ***(G-13513)***
GL Precision Tube, Aurora *Also called Great Lakes Precision Tube Inc* ***(G-1105)***
Glamox Aqua Signal Corporation (HQ)...847 639-6412
1125 Alexander Ct Cary (60013) ***(G-3165)***
Glanbia Performance Ntrtn Inc...630 256-7445
948 Meridian Lake Dr Aurora (60504) ***(G-969)***
Glanbia Performance Ntrtn Inc...630 236-0097
975 Medidian Lake Dr Aurora (60504) ***(G-970)***
Glanbia Performance Ntrtn Inc...800 336-2183
600 N Commerce St Aurora (60504) ***(G-971)***
Glanbia Prfmce Ntrtn NA Inc (HQ)...630 236-0097
3500 Lacey Rd Downers Grove (60515) ***(G-8012)***
Glaser USA Inc...847 362-7878
14181 W Hawthorne Ave Lake Forest (60045) ***(G-12251)***
Glasford Gazette, Glasford *Also called Gazette Printing Co* ***(G-10387)***
Glass & Wood Work Inc...708 945-9558
10004 S 76th Ave Ste H Bridgeview (60455) ***(G-2350)***
Glass America Midwest Inc., Elmhurst *Also called Glass America Midwest LLC* ***(G-9366)***
Glass America Midwest LLC (HQ)...877 743-7237
977 N Oaklawn Ave Ste 200 Elmhurst (60126) ***(G-9366)***
Glass Artistry...847 998-5800
1908 Janke Dr Northbrook (60062) ***(G-15394)***
Glass Cleaner, Elgin *Also called A J Funk & Co* ***(G-8489)***
Glass Dimensions Inc...708 410-2305
1942 N 15th Ave Melrose Park (60160) ***(G-13874)***
Glass Fx...217 359-0048
202 S 1st St Champaign (61820) ***(G-3295)***
Glass Haus...815 459-5849
2412 S Justen Rd McHenry (60050) ***(G-13746)***
Glass Management Services Inc...312 462-3257
1002 E 87th St Chicago (60619) ***(G-4693)***
Glasstek Inc...630 978-9897
10s059 Schoger Dr Unit 40 Naperville (60564) ***(G-14969)***
Glazed Structures Inc...847 223-4560
350 Center St Grayslake (60030) ***(G-10776)***
GLC Engineering, Addison *Also called GLC Industries Inc* ***(G-141)***
GLC Industries Inc...630 628-5870
326 W Gerri Ln Addison (60101) ***(G-141)***
Gld Industries Inc...217 390-9594
4411 Southford Trace Dr Champaign (61822) ***(G-3296)***
Glen Oak Foods, Aurora *Also called OSI International Foods Ltd* ***(G-1005)***
Glen Products...847 998-1361
927 Harms Rd Glenview (60025) ***(G-10550)***
Glen-Gery Corporation...815 795-6911
1401 Broadway St Marseilles (61341) ***(G-13555)***
Glenair Inc...847 679-8833
7000 N Lawndale Ave Lincolnwood (60712) ***(G-12823)***
Glendale Woodworking...630 545-1520
641 E North Ave Glendale Heights (60139) ***(G-10453)***
Glenmark Burgers, Chicago *Also called Best Chicago Meat Company LLC* ***(G-3870)***
Glenmark Industries Ltd...773 927-4800
4545 S Racine Ave Ste 1 Chicago (60609) ***(G-4694)***
Glenraven Inc...847 515-1321
40w260 Apache Ln Huntley (60142) ***(G-11537)***
Glenview Custom Cabinets Inc...847 345-5754
1921 Pickwick Ln Glenview (60026) ***(G-10551)***
Glenview Health Systems, Glenview *Also called Glenview Systems Inc* ***(G-10552)***
Glenview Systems Inc...847 724-2691
3048 N Lake Ter Glenview (60026) ***(G-10552)***
Glenwood Tool & Mold Inc...630 289-3400
1251 Humbracht Cir Ste D Bartlett (60103) ***(G-1282)***
Glidden Professional Paint Ctr, Meredosia *Also called PPG Architectural Finishes Inc* ***(G-13956)***
Glidden Professional Paint Ctr, Peoria *Also called PPG Architectural Finishes Inc* ***(G-16500)***
Glideaway Bed Carriage Mf, Peoria *Also called Fredman Bros Furniture Co Inc* ***(G-16441)***
Glidepath Power LLC...312 375-6034
132 N York St Apt 3l Elmhurst (60126) ***(G-9367)***
Glidera Inc...773 350-4000
188 W Industrial Dr # 240 Elmhurst (60126) ***(G-9368)***
Glitter Your Pallet...708 516-8494
14350 S Saddle Brook Ln Homer Glen (60491) ***(G-11482)***
Glk Enterprises Inc...847 395-7368
248 E Depot St Unit 2 Antioch (60002) ***(G-614)***
Glo Document Solutions, Elk Grove Village *Also called Bell Litho Inc* ***(G-8862)***
Glo Heat Treat Services LLC...815 601-5728
1207 Cameron Dr Durand (61024) ***(G-8152)***
Glo-Mold Inc...847 671-1762
3800 Wesley Ter Schiller Park (60176) ***(G-18811)***
Global Abrasive Products Inc...630 543-9466
39 W Factory Rd Addison (60101) ***(G-142)***
Global Brass and Copper Inc (HQ)...502 873-3000
305 Lewis And Clark Blvd East Alton (62024) ***(G-8166)***
Global Brass Cop Holdings Inc (HQ)...847 240-4700
475 N Martingale Rd # 1050 Schaumburg (60173) ***(G-18535)***
Global Contract Mfg Inc...312 432-6200
156 N Jefferson St # 300 Chicago (60661) ***(G-4695)***
Global Cosmetics Industry, Carol Stream *Also called Allured Publishing Corporation* ***(G-2932)***
Global Display Solutions Inc...815 282-2328
5217 28th Ave Rockford (61109) ***(G-17429)***
Global Endoscopy Inc...847 910-5836
878 Cass Ln Elk Grove Village (60007) ***(G-9015)***
Global Fastener Engrg Inc...847 929-9563
505 Oakwood Rd Ste 200 Lake Zurich (60047) ***(G-12417)***
Global Fire Control Inc...309 755-6352
1033 7th St Ste 1 East Moline (61244) ***(G-8227)***
Global Gear & Machining LLC...630 969-9400
2500 Curtiss St Downers Grove (60515) ***(G-8013)***
Global General Contractors LLC...708 663-0476
9018 Walnut Ln Tinley Park (60487) ***(G-19832)***
Global Green Products LLC (PA)...708 341-3670
8617 Golfview Dr Orland Park (60462) ***(G-15955)***
Global Industries Inc...630 681-2818
1879 Internationale Blvd Glendale Heights (60139) ***(G-10454)***
Global Maintenance LLC...270 933-1281
5357 Industrial Park Dr Metropolis (62960) ***(G-13971)***
Global Manufacturing...630 908-7633
324 Central Ave Willowbrook (60527) ***(G-21045)***
Global Material Tech Inc (PA)...847 495-4700
750 W Lake Cook Rd # 480 Buffalo Grove (60089) ***(G-2542)***
Global Material Tech Inc...773 247-6000
2825 W 31st St Chicago (60623) ***(G-4696)***
Global Medical Services LLC (PA)...847 460-8086
12904 Rockfish Ln Plainfield (60585) ***(G-16668)***
Global Packaging Dev LLC...847 209-3270
540 N State St Apt 2504 Chicago (60654) ***(G-4697)***
Global Pharma Device Solutions...708 212-5801
6454 W 74th St Chicago (60638) ***(G-4698)***
Global Signs & Printing, Chicago *Also called Atlantis Entp Investments Inc* ***(G-3761)***
Global Tech & Resources Inc...630 364-4260
3601 Algonquin Rd Ste 650 Rolling Meadows (60008) ***(G-17734)***
Global Technologies I LLC (PA)...312 255-8350
980 N Michigan Ave # 1400 Chicago (60611) ***(G-4699)***
Global Telephony Magazine...312 840-8405
330 N Wabash Ave Ste 2300 Chicago (60611) ***(G-4700)***
Global Tool & Die Inc...847 956-1200
1355 Tonne Rd Elk Grove Village (60007) ***(G-9016)***
Global Track Property USA Inc...630 213-6863
31w300 W Bartlett Rd Bartlett (60103) ***(G-1283)***
Global Track Warehouse USA, Bartlett *Also called Global Track Property USA Inc* ***(G-1283)***
Global Water Technology Inc...708 349-9991
354 W Armory Dr South Holland (60473) ***(G-19215)***
Global Web Systems Inc...630 782-9690
742 Cutter Ln Elk Grove Village (60007) ***(G-9017)***
Globaltech International LLC (PA)...630 327-6909
3909 75th St Ste 105 Aurora (60504) ***(G-972)***

ALPHABETIC

Globe Telecom, Bensenville *Also called Driver Services* ***(G-1789)***
Globe Ticket, Carol Stream *Also called CTI/Usa Inc* ***(G-2969)***
Globe Union Group Inc (HQ) 630 679-1420
2500 Internationale Pkwy Woodridge (60517) ***(G-21304)***
Globepharm Inc 224 904-3352
306 Basswood Dr Northbrook (60062) ***(G-15395)***
Globetec Midwest Partners LLC 847 608-9300
403 Joseph Dr South Elgin (60177) ***(G-19147)***
Globus Food Products LLC 847 378-8221
2258 Landmeier Rd Ste A Elk Grove Village (60007) ***(G-9018)***
Glooko 513 307-0903
303 E Wacker Dr Ste 339 Chicago (60601) ***(G-4701)***
Glorius Renditions 815 315-0177
508 E Third St Leaf River (61047) ***(G-12542)***
Glover Oil Field Service Inc 618 395-3624
4993 N Il 130 Olney (62450) ***(G-15863)***
Glucosentient Inc 217 487-4087
2100 S Oak St Ste 101 Champaign (61820) ***(G-3297)***
Glue Inc 312 451-4018
5701 N Sheridan Rd Apt 4m Chicago (60660) ***(G-4702)***
Gluetech Inc 847 455-2707
701 Creel Dr Wood Dale (60191) ***(G-21194)***
Glunz Cellars, Grayslake *Also called Glunz Fmly Winery Cellars Inc* ***(G-10777)***
Glunz Fmly Winery Cellars Inc (PA) 847 548-9463
888 E Belvidere Rd # 205 Grayslake (60030) ***(G-10777)***
GM Lighting, Tinley Park *Also called Gerber Manufacturing (gm) LLC* ***(G-19830)***
GM Partners 847 895-7627
219 Lundy Ln Schaumburg (60193) ***(G-18536)***
GM Scrap Metals 618 259-8570
220 Franklin Ave Cottage Hills (62018) ***(G-7028)***
Gma Inc 630 595-1255
756 Birginal Dr Bensenville (60106) ***(G-1812)***
Gmb Partners LLC (PA) 773 248-4038
4257 N Lincoln Ave Chicago (60618) ***(G-4703)***
GMC Technologies Inc 847 426-8618
215 Prairie Lake Rd Ste A East Dundee (60118) ***(G-8197)***
Gmd Mobile Pressure Wshg Svcs 773 826-1903
539 N Saint Louis Ave Chicago (60624) ***(G-4704)***
Gmh Metal Fabrication Inc 309 253-6429
136 Fleur De Lis Dr East Peoria (61611) ***(G-8269)***
GMI Packaging Co 734 972-7389
1600 E 122nd St Chicago (60633) ***(G-4705)***
Gmk Finishing 630 837-0568
1967 Southfield Dr Bartlett (60103) ***(G-1284)***
Gmm Holdings LLC 312 255-9830
175 E Delaware Pl Unit 6 Chicago (60611) ***(G-4706)***
Gmmco, Chicago *Also called General Machinery & Mfg Co* ***(G-4674)***
Gmp Metal Products, Schaumburg *Also called Wozniak Industries Inc* ***(G-18776)***
Gmt Inc 847 697-8161
180 S Melrose Ave Elgin (60123) ***(G-8597)***
GNB Industrial Global Business, Lombard *Also called Exide Technologies LLC* ***(G-13075)***
Gnk Technologies Inc 847 382-1185
200 James St Barrington (60010) ***(G-1220)***
Gnome Brew LLC 773 961-7750
2026 W Montrose Ave Chicago (60618) ***(G-4707)***
Go Mango Interactive Corp 224 214-9528
1664 Templeton Ct Mundelein (60060) ***(G-14690)***
Go Steady LLC 630 293-3243
505 Wegner Dr West Chicago (60185) ***(G-20588)***
Go To Steel Inc (PA) 773 814-3017
7625 W Norridge St Norridge (60706) ***(G-15235)***
Go Van Goghs Tee Shirt 309 342-1112
237 E Tompkins St Galesburg (61401) ***(G-10198)***
Go2 Partners, Des Plaines *Also called Print Management Partners Inc* ***(G-7833)***
Goat Wolf & Cabbage LLC 563 580-0617
1917 N Elston Ave Chicago (60642) ***(G-4708)***
Goble Manufacturing Inc 217 932-5615
704 W Main St Casey (62420) ***(G-3202)***
God Family Country LLC 217 285-6487
34273 210th Ave Pittsfield (62363) ***(G-16634)***
Goding Electric Company 630 858-7700
686 E Fullerton Ave Glendale Heights (60139) ***(G-10455)***
Godiva Chocolatier Inc 630 820-5842
1650 Premium Outlet Blvd # 1213 Aurora (60502) ***(G-973)***
Goeducation LLC 312 800-1838
222 Merchandise Mart Plz # 1225 Chicago (60654) ***(G-4709)***
Goelitz Confectionery Company 847 689-2225
1501 Morrow Ave North Chicago (60064) ***(G-15313)***
Goellner Inc (PA) 815 962-6076
2500 Latham St Rockford (61103) ***(G-17430)***
Gogo Intermediate Holdings LLC (HQ) 630 647-1400
111 N Canal St Fl 15 Chicago (60606) ***(G-4710)***
Gogo LLC (HQ) 630 647-1400
111 N Canal St Fl 15 Chicago (60606) ***(G-4711)***
Gogo LLC 630 647-1400
814 Thorndale Ave Bensenville (60106) ***(G-1813)***
Gohear LLC 847 574-7829
100 Saunders Rd Lake Forest (60045) ***(G-12252)***
Gold Leaf, Albion *Also called Ataraxia LLC* ***(G-346)***
Gold Market Publications, Virden *Also called Five Star Printing Inc* ***(G-20184)***
Gold Medal Products Co 630 860-2525
450 N York Rd Bensenville (60106) ***(G-1814)***
Gold Nugget Publications Inc (PA) 217 965-3355
169 W Jackson St Virden (62690) ***(G-20185)***
Gold Seal Cabinets Countertops 630 906-0366
1750 Eastwood Dr Aurora (60506) ***(G-1104)***
Gold Standard Baking Inc (PA) 773 523-2333
3700 S Kedzie Ave Chicago (60632) ***(G-4712)***
Gold Standard Enterprises Inc 217 546-1633
2490 Wabash Ave Springfield (62704) ***(G-19375)***
Gold Star Fs Inc 309 659-2801
9087 Moline Rd Erie (61250) ***(G-9473)***
Golda House 773 927-0140
3128 W 41st St Chicago (60632) ***(G-4713)***
Golda Inc 217 895-3602
100 Trowbridge Rd Neoga (62447) ***(G-15017)***
Golden Grain Company 708 458-7020
7700 W 71st St Bridgeview (60455) ***(G-2351)***
Golden Grape Estate, Naperville *Also called Prp Wine International Inc* ***(G-14903)***
Golden Hydraulic & Machine 708 597-4265
2966 Wireton Rd Blue Island (60406) ***(G-2124)***
Golden Locker Inc (PA) 217 696-4456
1880 E 2400th St Camp Point (62320) ***(G-2811)***
Golden Prairie News 217 226-3721
301 S Chestnut St Assumption (62510) ***(G-889)***
Golden Trophy Steaks, Chicago *Also called Bruss Company* ***(G-3969)***
Golden Valley Hardscapes LLC 309 654-2261
18715 Route 84 N Cordova (61242) ***(G-7007)***
Goldman Dental, Wauconda *Also called Goldman Products Inc* ***(G-20354)***
Goldman Products Inc 847 526-1166
379 Hollow Hill Rd Wauconda (60084) ***(G-20354)***
Goldmax Carrier Inc 773 366-1718
2625 Greenleaf Ave Elk Grove Village (60007) ***(G-9019)***
Goldsmith, The, Aledo *Also called Rodger Murphy* ***(G-359)***
Goldy Metals Trading, Aurora *Also called Avec Inc* ***(G-917)***
Golf Gazette 815 838-0184
428 S Washington St Lockport (60441) ***(G-12997)***
Golf Tee Printers Inc 973 328-4008
550 Pratt Ave N Schaumburg (60193) ***(G-18537)***
Golf Trucks, Countryside *Also called Bare Development Inc* ***(G-7044)***
Golfcar Utility Systems, Quincy *Also called Brewer Utility Systems Inc* ***(G-16868)***
Golfco Inc 773 777-7877
4727 W Montrose Ave Chicago (60641) ***(G-4714)***
Golfers Family Corporation 815 968-0094
1531 Preston St Rockford (61102) ***(G-17431)***
Golosinas El Canto 847 625-5103
1115 Washington St Waukegan (60085) ***(G-20445)***
Gone For Good 217 753-0414
101 N 16th St Springfield (62703) ***(G-19376)***
Gonnella Baking Co (PA) 312 733-2020
1117 Wiley Rd Schaumburg (60173) ***(G-18538)***
Gonnella Baking Co 312 733-2020
1117 Wiley Rd Schaumburg (60173) ***(G-18539)***
Gonnella Baking Co 630 820-3433
2435 Church Rd Aurora (60502) ***(G-974)***
Gonnella Frozen Products LLC (HQ) 847 884-8829
1117 Wiley Rd Schaumburg (60173) ***(G-18540)***
Gooch & Associates Printing, Springfield *Also called J Gooch & Associates Inc* ***(G-19392)***
Good Earth Lighting Inc 847 808-1133
1400 E Business Center Dr # 108 Mount Prospect (60056) ***(G-14531)***
Good Foods Inc 773 260-9110
700 E 107th St Chicago (60628) ***(G-4715)***
Good Impressions Inc 847 831-4317
3150 Skokie Valley Rd # 24 Highland Park (60035) ***(G-11265)***
Good Lite Co (PA) 847 841-1145
1155 Jansen Farm Dr Elgin (60123) ***(G-8598)***
Good News Printing 708 389-1127
5535 W 131st St Palos Heights (60463) ***(G-16185)***
Good News Publishers (PA) 630 682-4300
1300 Crescent St Wheaton (60187) ***(G-20801)***
Good Sam Enterprises LLC (HQ) 847 229-6720
250 Parkway Dr Ste 270 Lincolnshire (60069) ***(G-12767)***
Good Vibes Sound Inc (PA) 217 351-0909
2010 Round Barn Rd Champaign (61821) ***(G-3298)***
Good World Noodle Inc 312 326-0441
2522 S Halsted St Chicago (60608) ***(G-4716)***
Goodale Corporation 312 421-9663
1619-1635 S Canal St 1 Chicago (60616) ***(G-4717)***
Goodco Products LLC 630 258-6384
6688 Joliet Rd Ste 185 Countryside (60525) ***(G-7055)***
Gooder-Henrichsen Company Inc 708 757-5030
2900 State St Chicago Heights (60411) ***(G-6748)***
Goodfield Milling Co, Goodfield *Also called Dr & Dr Property Leasing LLC* ***(G-10674)***
Goodheart Wilcox Publisher, Tinley Park *Also called Goodheart-Willcox Company Inc* ***(G-19833)***
Goodheart-Willcox Company Inc (PA) 708 687-0315
18604 West Creek Dr Tinley Park (60477) ***(G-19833)***

Goodman Manufacturing Co LP...618 234-2781
120 Corporate Dr Swansea (62226) ***(G-19692)***
Goodman Packaging Equipment, Waukegan *Also called Prototype Equipment Corp* ***(G-20484)***
Goodman Sawmill...309 547-3597
114 N Broadway St Lewistown (61542) ***(G-12615)***
Goodrich Corporation...815 226-6000
4747 Harrison Ave Rockford (61108) ***(G-17432)***
Goodrich Corporation...815 226-5915
2421 11th St Rockford (61104) ***(G-17433)***
Goodrich Sensor Systems...847 546-5749
34232 N Bluestem Rd Round Lake (60073) ***(G-18077)***
Goodwood Country Firewood, Chicago *Also called Goodale Corporation* ***(G-4717)***
Goodyear Tire & Rubber Company...815 389-8222
16049 Willowbrook Rd South Beloit (61080) ***(G-19095)***
Goose Holdings Inc...312 226-1119
1800 W Fulton St Chicago (60612) ***(G-4718)***
Goose Island Brewer, Chicago *Also called Goose Holdings Inc* ***(G-4718)***
Goose Island Mfg & Supply Corp...708 343-4225
17725 Volbrecht Rd Ste 1 Lansing (60438) ***(G-12495)***
Goose Printing Co...847 673-1414
8833 Ewing Ave Evanston (60203) ***(G-9525)***
Gophercentral...708 478-4500
7851 185th St Ste 106 Tinley Park (60477) ***(G-19834)***
Gord Industrial Plastics Inc...815 786-9494
1310 E 6th St Sandwich (60548) ***(G-18372)***
Gordon Burke John Publisher...847 866-8625
1032 Cleveland St Evanston (60202) ***(G-9526)***
Gordon Hann...630 761-1835
154 W Wilson St Batavia (60510) ***(G-1381)***
Gordys Machine and Tool Inc...618 842-9331
1101 Sw 3rd St Fairfield (62837) ***(G-9626)***
Goreville Auto Parts & Mch Sp...618 995-2375
Rr 37 Goreville (62939) ***(G-10680)***
Goreville Concrete Inc...618 995-2670
301 N Hubbard Ave Goreville (62939) ***(G-10681)***
Gorman & Associates...309 691-9087
7501 N University St # 122 Peoria (61614) ***(G-16446)***
Gorman Brothers Ready Mix Inc...618 498-2173
721 S State St Jerseyville (62052) ***(G-11791)***
Gorman Ready Mix, Jerseyville *Also called Gorman Brothers Ready Mix Inc* ***(G-11791)***
Gorr Communication Products, Woodstock *Also called Carl Gorr Printing Co* ***(G-21370)***
Goshen Coffee, Edwardsville *Also called Art House Coffee LLC* ***(G-8345)***
Gosia Cartage Ltd...312 613-8735
6400 River Rd Hodgkins (60525) ***(G-11389)***
Gossett Printing Inc...618 548-2583
2100 Old Texas Ln Salem (62881) ***(G-18341)***
Got 2b Scrappin...217 347-3600
1901 S 4th St Ste 11 Effingham (62401) ***(G-8401)***
Gotham Greens Pullman LLC...779 379-0307
720 E 11th St Chicago (60628) ***(G-4719)***
Goulds Pumps LLC...708 563-1220
6733 W 73rd St Bedford Park (60638) ***(G-1468)***
Gourmet Frog Pastry Shop...847 433-7038
316 Green Bay Rd Highland Park (60035) ***(G-11266)***
Gourmet Gorilla Inc (PA)...877 219-3663
1200 W Cermak Rd Chicago (60608) ***(G-4720)***
Govqa Inc...630 985-1300
900 S Frontage Rd Ste 110 Woodridge (60517) ***(G-21305)***
GP, Zion *Also called Graphic Partners Inc* ***(G-21515)***
Gpe Controls Inc (HQ)...708 236-6000
5911 Butterfield Rd Hillside (60162) ***(G-11340)***
Gpi Manufacturing Inc...847 615-8900
940 W North Shore Dr Lake Bluff (60044) ***(G-12184)***
Gpi Midwest LLC (HQ)...847 741-0247
1975 Big Timber Rd Elgin (60123) ***(G-8599)***
Gpi Prototype & Mfg Svcs, Lake Bluff *Also called Gpi Manufacturing Inc* ***(G-12184)***
Gpi Prototype & Mfg Svcs LLC...847 615-8900
940 N Shore Dr Lake Bluff (60044) ***(G-12185)***
GPI Industries Incorporated...708 877-8200
395 Armory Dr Thornton (60476) ***(G-19787)***
GPM Mfg Inc...847 550-8200
1199 Flex Ct Lake Zurich (60047) ***(G-12418)***
Gr8 Seas Holdings Inc...630 862-5099
803 N Bridge St Ste A Yorkville (60560) ***(G-21486)***
Grab Brothers Ir Works Co Corp...847 288-1055
2302 17th St Franklin Park (60131) ***(G-9951)***
Graber Building Sup & Hdwr Inc...217 268-3014
111 W Springfield Rd Arcola (61910) ***(G-650)***
Graber Concrete Pipe Company...630 894-5950
24w121 Army Trail Rd Bloomingdale (60108) ***(G-1996)***
Grace and Truth...217 442-1120
210 Chestnut St Danville (61832) ***(G-7340)***
Grace Dvson Discovery Sciences, Chicago *Also called Alltech Associates Inc* ***(G-3624)***
Grace Enterprises Inc (PA)...847 423-2100
2050 W Devon Ave Ste 2 Chicago (60659) ***(G-4721)***
Grace Printing and Mailing...847 423-2100
8130 Saint Louis Ave Skokie (60076) ***(G-18960)***

Graceland Custom Products Inc...630 616-4143
1017 Graceland Ave Bensenville (60106) ***(G-1815)***
Graceland Ferray Products...847 258-3828
736 W Algonquin Rd Arlington Heights (60005) ***(G-743)***
Grads Inc...847 426-3904
205 Prairie Lake Rd Ste C East Dundee (60118) ***(G-8198)***
Graf Ink Printing Inc...618 273-4231
24 W Church St Harrisburg (62946) ***(G-11025)***
Grafcor Packaging Inc...815 639-2380
1030 River Ln Loves Park (61111) ***(G-13215)***
Grafcor Packaging Inc (PA)...815 963-1300
121 Loomis St Rockford (61101) ***(G-17434)***
Graff-Pinkert & Co...708 535-2200
4235 166th St Oak Forest (60452) ***(G-15680)***
Graffs Tooling Center Inc...618 357-5005
801 S Main St Pinckneyville (62274) ***(G-16616)***
Grafton Winery Inc...618 786-3001
300 W Main St Grafton (62037) ***(G-10684)***
Graham Packaging Co Europe LLC...630 293-8616
1760 W Hawthorne Ln West Chicago (60185) ***(G-20589)***
Graham Packaging Co Europe LLC...630 562-5912
1445 Northwest Ave West Chicago (60185) ***(G-20590)***
Graham Packaging Company LP...630 739-9150
2400 Internationale Pkwy # 1 Woodridge (60517) ***(G-21306)***
Graham Welding Inc...217 422-1423
813 E North St Decatur (62521) ***(G-7497)***
Grain Densification Intl LLC...618 823-5122
1350 4th St Granite City (62040) ***(G-10711)***
Grain Journal, Decatur *Also called Country Journal Publishing Co* ***(G-7477)***
Grain Systems, Vandalia *Also called Gsi Group LLC* ***(G-20012)***
Grain Systems, Paris *Also called Gsi Group LLC* ***(G-16230)***
Grain Systems Inc (HQ)...888 474-2467
1004 E Illinois St Assumption (62510) ***(G-890)***
Graized LLC...815 615-1012
2912 N 645 East Rd Moweaqua (62550) ***(G-14651)***
Gram Colossal Inc...847 223-5757
888 E Belvidere Rd # 113 Grayslake (60030) ***(G-10778)***
Granadino Food Services Corp...708 717-2930
7506 W 85th Pl Bridgeview (60455) ***(G-2352)***
Grand Forms & Systems Inc...847 259-4600
910 W Miner St Arlington Heights (60005) ***(G-744)***
Grand Printing & Graphics Inc...312 218-6780
105 W Madison St Ste 1100 Chicago (60602) ***(G-4722)***
Grand Products Inc (PA)...800 621-6101
1718 Hampshire Dr Elk Grove Village (60007) ***(G-9020)***
Grand Specialties Co...630 629-8000
110 Oakbrook Ctr Oak Brook (60523) ***(G-15625)***
Grand Trunk, Skokie *Also called Travel Hammock Inc* ***(G-19047)***
Grandma Mauds Inc...773 493-5353
1525 E 55th St Ste 304 Chicago (60615) ***(G-4723)***
Grandstand Publishing LLC...847 491-6440
1800 Nations Dr Ste 117 Gurnee (60031) ***(G-10883)***
Grandt's Custom Fishing Rods, Arlington Heights *Also called Custom Rods By Grandt Ltd* ***(G-723)***
Grangrit, Baldwin *Also called Fjcj LLC* ***(G-1184)***
Granite City Works, Granite City *Also called United States Steel Corp* ***(G-10748)***
Granite Mountain Inc...708 774-1442
538 E Illinois Hwy Ste A New Lenox (60451) ***(G-15036)***
Graniteworks...815 288-3350
1220 S Galena Ave Dixon (61021) ***(G-7901)***
Granja & Sons Printing...773 762-3840
2707 S Pulaski Rd Chicago (60623) ***(G-4724)***
Grant J Grapperhaus...618 410-4428
470 Pike Dr E Highland (62249) ***(G-11216)***
Grant Park Packing Company Inc...312 421-4096
3434 Runge St Franklin Park (60131) ***(G-9952)***
Grant Technologies LLC...847 370-9306
111 E Wacker Dr Chicago (60601) ***(G-4725)***
Grant View Distillery, Rockford *Also called Barnstormer Distilleries* ***(G-17313)***
Grantco Inc...941 567-9259
102 Terrace Dr Mundelein (60060) ***(G-14691)***
Granville Ready Mix, Granville *Also called J W Ossola Company Inc* ***(G-10755)***
Granville Ready Mix, Granville *Also called JW Ossola Co Inc* ***(G-10756)***
Graph-Pak, Franklin Park *Also called Graphic Packaging Corporation* ***(G-9953)***
Graphic Arts Bindery LLC...708 416-4290
1020 S Main St Rochelle (61068) ***(G-17143)***
Graphic Arts Finishing Company...708 345-8484
1990 N Mannheim Rd Melrose Park (60160) ***(G-13875)***
Graphic Arts Services Inc (PA)...630 629-7770
333 W Saint Charles Rd Villa Park (60181) ***(G-20148)***
Graphic Arts Studio Inc (PA)...847 381-1105
28 W 111 Coml Ave Commercial Barrington (60010) ***(G-1221)***
Graphic Chemical & Ink Co...630 832-6004
728 N Yale Ave Villa Park (60181) ***(G-20149)***
Graphic Communicators Inc...708 385-7550
12500 S Meade Ave Palos Heights (60463) ***(G-16186)***
Graphic Engravers Inc...630 595-0400
691 Country Club Dr Bensenville (60106) ***(G-1816)***

ALPHABETIC

(PA)=Parent Co (HQ)=Headquarters (DH)=Div Headquarters
2020 Harris Illinois
Industrial Directory
1135

Graphic Image Corporation.....312 829-7800
10500 163rd Pl Orland Park (60467) ***(G-15956)***
Graphic Industries Inc.....847 357-9870
645 Stevenson Rd South Elgin (60177) ***(G-19148)***
Graphic Innovators Inc.....847 718-1516
855 Morse Ave Elk Grove Village (60007) ***(G-9021)***
Graphic Marking Systems, Lake Forest *Also called Distribution Enterprises Inc* ***(G-12243)***
Graphic Packaging Corporation.....847 451-7400
11250 Addison Ave Franklin Park (60131) ***(G-9953)***
Graphic Packaging Intl LLC.....630 260-6500
400 E North Ave Carol Stream (60188) ***(G-2993)***
Graphic Packaging Intl LLC.....618 533-2721
2333 S Wabash Ave Centralia (62801) ***(G-3233)***
Graphic Packaging Intl LLC.....630 260-6500
400 E North Ave Carol Stream (60188) ***(G-2994)***
Graphic Pallet & Transport.....630 904-4951
10225 Bode St Plainfield (60585) ***(G-16669)***
Graphic Partners Inc.....847 872-9445
4300 Il Route 173 Zion (60099) ***(G-21515)***
Graphic Parts Intl Inc.....773 725-4900
4321 N Knox Ave Chicago (60641) ***(G-4726)***
Graphic Photo Engravers, Bensenville *Also called Graphic Engravers Inc* ***(G-1816)***
Graphic Press.....312 909-6100
545 N Dearborn St # 3002 Chicago (60654) ***(G-4727)***
Graphic Press Inc.....847 272-6000
6511 Oakton St Morton Grove (60053) ***(G-14410)***
Graphic Promotions Inc.....815 726-3288
405 Earl Rd Shorewood (60404) ***(G-18897)***
Graphic Sciences Inc.....630 226-0994
582 Territorial Dr Ste A Bolingbrook (60440) ***(G-2180)***
Graphic Score Book Co Inc.....847 823-7382
306 Busse Hwy Park Ridge (60068) ***(G-16281)***
Graphic Screen Fashion Ltd.....847 695-5566
365 Woodbury St South Elgin (60177) ***(G-19149)***
Graphic Screen Printing Inc.....708 429-3330
15640 S 70th Ct Orland Park (60462) ***(G-15957)***
Graphic Source Group Inc.....847 854-2670
1119 W Algonquin Rd Ste B Lake In The Hills (60156) ***(G-12336)***
Graphicmark Inc.....708 293-1200
5659 W 120th St Alsip (60803) ***(G-448)***
Graphics 2000 Inc.....630 920-0022
161 Tower Dr Ste A Burr Ridge (60527) ***(G-2676)***
Graphics 255 LLC (PA).....312 266-9266
811 W Evergreen Ave 101a Chicago (60642) ***(G-4728)***
Graphics Group LLC.....708 867-5500
4600 N Olcott Ave Chicago (60706) ***(G-4729)***
Graphtek LLC (PA).....847 279-1925
600 Academy Dr Ste 100 Northbrook (60062) ***(G-15396)***
Grasso Graphics Inc.....708 489-2060
5156 W 125th Pl Alsip (60803) ***(G-449)***
Grate Signs Inc.....815 729-9700
4044 Mcdonough St Joliet (60431) ***(G-11870)***
Gravure Ink, Franklin Park *Also called Patrick Industries Inc* ***(G-10015)***
Gray Machine & Welding Inc.....309 788-2501
710 30th Ave Rock Island (61201) ***(G-17220)***
Gray Quarries Inc.....217 847-2712
750 E County Road 1220 Hamilton (62341) ***(G-10955)***
Grayhill Inc (PA).....708 354-1040
561 W Hillgrove Ave La Grange (60525) ***(G-12077)***
Grayhill Inc.....708 482-1411
4800 S Vernon Ave Mc Cook (60525) ***(G-13691)***
Grayhill Inc.....847 428-6990
459 Maple Ave Carpentersville (60110) ***(G-3102)***
Graymills Corporation.....773 477-4100
2601 S 25th Ave Broadview (60155) ***(G-2439)***
Graymon Graphics Inc.....773 737-0176
4934 S Rockwell St Chicago (60632) ***(G-4730)***
Graymont Prof Pdts Ip LLC.....312 374-4376
1621 W Carroll Ave Chicago (60612) ***(G-4731)***
Grays Cabinet Co.....618 948-2211
Rr 1 Saint Francisville (62460) ***(G-18314)***
Grays Laser & Instrument RPR.....618 222-1791
214 Suburban Dr Smithton (62285) ***(G-19064)***
Grayslake Feed Sales Inc.....847 223-4855
81 E Belvidere Rd Grayslake (60030) ***(G-10779)***
Graziano Tl Inc (PA).....847 741-1900
1450 Bowes Rd Elgin (60123) ***(G-8600)***
Great American Popcorn Company.....815 777-4116
110 S Main St Galena (61036) ***(G-10173)***
Great Books Foundation.....312 332-5870
233 N Michigan Ave # 420 Chicago (60601) ***(G-4732)***
Great Dane LLC.....309 854-0407
324 N Main St Kewanee (61443) ***(G-12036)***
Great Dane LLC.....309 854-0407
2006 Kentville Rd Kewanee (61443) ***(G-12037)***
Great Dane LLC.....773 254-5533
2006 Kentville Rd Kewanee (61443) ***(G-12038)***
Great Dane LLC (HQ).....773 254-5533
222 N Lasalle St Ste 920 Chicago (60601) ***(G-4733)***
Great Dane Trailers, Chicago *Also called Great Dane LLC* ***(G-4733)***
Great Dane Trlrs-Kewanee Plant, Kewanee *Also called Great Dane LLC* ***(G-12037)***
Great Display Company Llc.....309 821-1037
704 S Mclean St Bloomington (61701) ***(G-2052)***
Great Guy Inc.....312 203-9872
22 W 220 Woodview Dr Medinah (60157) ***(G-13813)***
Great Holloween Stores, Elgin *Also called Orr Marketing Corp* ***(G-8680)***
Great Ideas Inc.....800 611-5515
1633 Ravine Ln Highland Park (60035) ***(G-11267)***
Great Impressions Inc.....847 367-6725
19071 W Casey Rd Libertyville (60048) ***(G-12655)***
Great Lakes Bag & Vinyl, Highland Park *Also called Morton Group Ltd* ***(G-11286)***
Great Lakes Boating Magazine, Chicago *Also called Chicago Boating Publications* ***(G-4092)***
Great Lakes Clay & Supply Inc.....224 535-8127
927 N State St Elgin (60123) ***(G-8601)***
Great Lakes Coca-Cola Dist LLC (HQ).....847 227-6500
6250 N River Rd Ste 9000 Rosemont (60018) ***(G-18025)***
Great Lakes Envmtl Mar Del.....312 332-3377
39 S La Salle St Ste 308 Chicago (60603) ***(G-4734)***
Great Lakes Finishing Eqp Inc.....708 345-5300
842 Schneider Dr South Elgin (60177) ***(G-19150)***
Great Lakes Forge Company.....773 277-2800
2141 S Spaulding Ave Chicago (60623) ***(G-4735)***
Great Lakes GL & Mirror Corp.....847 647-1036
6261 W Howard St Niles (60714) ***(G-15126)***
Great Lakes Lbr & Pallet Inc.....773 243-6839
3333 W 47th Pl Chicago (60632) ***(G-4736)***
Great Lakes Lifting.....815 931-4825
4910 Wilshire Blvd Country Club Hills (60478) ***(G-7039)***
Great Lakes Lumber and Pallet.....773 243-6839
2137 N Home Ave Park Ridge (60068) ***(G-16282)***
Great Lakes Mech Svcs Inc.....708 672-5900
100 Tri State Intl Lincolnshire (60069) ***(G-12768)***
Great Lakes Packing Co Intl.....773 927-6660
1535 W 43rd St Chicago (60609) ***(G-4737)***
Great Lakes Pallet, Chicago *Also called Best Pallet Company LLC* ***(G-3873)***
Great Lakes Pallet Company, Loves Park *Also called Best Pallet Company LLC* ***(G-13194)***
Great Lakes Precision Tube Inc.....630 859-8940
237 S Highland Ave Aurora (60506) ***(G-1105)***
Great Lakes Region, Itasca *Also called Subaru of America Inc* ***(G-11741)***
Great Lakes Service Center, Romeoville *Also called Tdw Services Inc* ***(G-17880)***
Great Lakes Stair & Steel Inc.....708 430-2323
10130 Virginia Ave Chicago Ridge (60415) ***(G-6796)***
Great Lakes Tool & Mold Inc.....630 964-7121
6817 Hobson Valley Dr # 116 Woodridge (60517) ***(G-21307)***
Great Lakes Washer Company.....630 887-7447
127 Tower Dr Burr Ridge (60527) ***(G-2677)***
Great Revivalist Brew Lab, Geneseo *Also called Great Revivalist Brewing LLC* ***(G-10243)***
Great Revivalist Brewing LLC.....309 944-5466
1225 S Oakwood Ave Geneseo (61254) ***(G-10243)***
Great River Printing, Hamilton *Also called D E Asbury Inc* ***(G-10953)***
Great River Ready Mix Inc.....217 847-3515
750 E County Road 1220 Hamilton (62341) ***(G-10956)***
Great Software Laboratory Inc.....630 655-8905
60 E Monroe St Unit 4301 Chicago (60603) ***(G-4738)***
Great Spirit Hardwoods LLC.....224 801-1969
7 Jackson St East Dundee (60118) ***(G-8199)***
Greater Than, Highland Park *Also called Team Sider Inc* ***(G-11303)***
Greatlkes Archtctral Mllwrks L.....312 829-7110
2135 W Fulton St Chicago (60612) ***(G-4739)***
Grebner Machine & Tool Inc.....309 248-7768
1866 County Road 00 N Washburn (61570) ***(G-20263)***
Grecian Delight Foods Inc (PA).....847 364-1010
1201 Tonne Rd Elk Grove Village (60007) ***(G-9022)***
Grecian Delight Foods, Inc Del, Elk Grove Village *Also called Grecian Delight Foods Inc* ***(G-9022)***
Greco Graphics Inc.....217 483-2877
22 Sugar Creek Ln Glenarm (62536) ***(G-10425)***
Greek Art Printing & Pubg Co.....847 724-8860
2921 Covert Rd Glenview (60025) ***(G-10553)***
Green Apu LLC.....310 736-2211
13067 Main St Lemont (60439) ***(G-12565)***
Green Around Sills LLC.....847 868-8957
1233 Judson Ave Evanston (60202) ***(G-9527)***
Green Bay Packaging Inc.....847 455-2553
2200 Warrenville Rd Downers Grove (60515) ***(G-8014)***
Green Book Lenders Guide, The, Elgin *Also called Reid Communications Inc* ***(G-8717)***
Green Box America Inc.....630 616-5400
1900 E Golf Rd Ste 950 Schaumburg (60173) ***(G-18541)***
Green Earth Technologies Inc.....847 991-0436
617 S Middleton Ave Palatine (60067) ***(G-16120)***
Green Gables Country Store.....309 897-7160
201 Bonita Ave Bradford (61421) ***(G-2273)***
Green Ladder Technologies LLC.....630 457-1872
1540 Louis Bork Dr Batavia (60510) ***(G-1382)***
Green Organics Inc.....630 871-0108
290 S Main Pl Ste 103 Carol Stream (60188) ***(G-2995)***
Green Plains Partners LP.....618 451-4420
395 Bissell St Madison (62060) ***(G-13413)***

Green Products LLC 815 407-0900
221 Rocbaar Dr Romeoville (60446) *(G-17829)*
Green Roof Solutions Inc 847 297-7936
3126 W Lake Ave Glenview (60026) *(G-10554)*
Green Technologies Inc 815 624-8011
112 Hawick St Rockton (61072) *(G-17698)*
Green Thumb Industries, Chicago *Also called Gti Rock Island LLC (G-4746)*
Green Thumb Industries Inc (PA) 312 471-6720
325 W Huron St Ste 412 Chicago (60654) *(G-4740)*
Green Valley Mfg Ill Inc 217 864-4125
100 Green Valley Dr Mount Zion (62549) *(G-14647)*
Greenberg Casework Company Inc 815 624-0288
14328 Commercial Pkwy South Beloit (61080) *(G-19096)*
Greencycle of Indiana Inc (HQ) 847 441-6606
400 Central Ave Ste 115 Northfield (60093) *(G-15515)*
Greene Jersey Shoppers (PA) 217 942-3626
428 N Main St Carrollton (62016) *(G-3126)*
Greene Welding & Hardware Inc 217 375-4244
41774 N Main St East Lynn (60932) *(G-8220)*
Greenfield Contractors LLC 309 385-1859
1012 N Santa Fe Ave Ste B Princeville (61559) *(G-16828)*
Greenfield Products LLC (PA) 708 596-5200
3111 167th St Hazel Crest (60429) *(G-11129)*
Greenleaf Foods Spc (HQ) 800 268-3708
180 E Park Ave Ste 300 Elmhurst (60126) *(G-9369)*
Greenlee Diamond Tool Co 866 451-3316
2375 Touhy Ave Elk Grove Village (60007) *(G-9023)*
Greenlee Textron Inc 815 784-5127
702 W Main St Genoa (60135) *(G-10318)*
Greenlee Tools Inc (HQ) 800 435-0786
4455 Boeing Dr Rockford (61109) *(G-17435)*
Greenridge Farm Inc 847 434-1803
2355 Greenleaf Ave Elk Grove Village (60007) *(G-9024)*
Greens Machine Shop 618 532-4631
315 E Kell St Centralia (62801) *(G-3234)*
Greenville Advocate Inc 618 664-3144
305 S 2nd St Greenville (62246) *(G-10835)*
Greenville Ready Mix, Greenville *Also called Mid-Illinois Concrete Inc (G-10838)*
Greenwood Inc (PA) 800 798-4900
1126 N Kimball St Danville (61832) *(G-7341)*
Greenwood Inc 217 431-6034
1126 N Kimball St Danville (61832) *(G-7342)*
Greenwood Associates Inc 847 579-5500
6280 W Howard St Niles (60714) *(G-15127)*
Greenwood Plastics, Danville *Also called Greenwood Inc (G-7341)*
Greenwood Plastics Industries, Danville *Also called Greenwood Inc (G-7342)*
Greg Lambert Construction 815 468-7361
5485 N 5000e Rd Bourbonnais (60914) *(G-2261)*
Greg Screw Machine Products 630 694-8875
647 N Central Ave Ste 103 Wood Dale (60191) *(G-21195)*
Gregor Jonsson Associates Inc 847 247-4200
13822 W Laurel Dr Lake Forest (60045) *(G-12253)*
Gregory Gravel Co 618 943-2796
11403 Club Kilroy Rd Lawrenceville (62439) *(G-12533)*
Gregory Lamar & Assoc Inc 312 595-1545
345 N La Salle Dr # 2103 Chicago (60654) *(G-4741)*
Gregory Martin 815 265-4527
325 E Park Ct Gilman (60938) *(G-10379)*
Gregory's Gravel Pit, Lawrenceville *Also called Gregory Gravel Co (G-12533)*
Gregs Frozen Custard Company 847 837-4175
1490 S Lake St Mundelein (60060) *(G-14692)*
Greif Inc 815 838-7210
1225 Daviess Ave Lockport (60441) *(G-12998)*
Greif Inc 708 371-4777
4300 W 130th St Alsip (60803) *(G-450)*
Greif Inc 815 935-7575
150 E North St Bradley (60915) *(G-2283)*
Greif Inc 217 468-2396
7573 N Rte 48 Oreana (62554) *(G-15911)*
Greif Inc 630 753-1859
5s220 Frontenac Rd Naperville (60563) *(G-14836)*
Greif Inc 630 961-1842
5 S 220 Frontenace Rd Naperville (60540) *(G-14837)*
Grem Machining Division, Lemont *Also called Machining Technology Inc (G-12570)*
Gremp Steel Co 708 389-7393
14100 S Western Ave Ste 2 Posen (60469) *(G-16795)*
Gretta Transportation Inc 252 202-7714
133 Hampton Ave Westmont (60559) *(G-20743)*
Grevan Enterprises Inc 708 799-3422
3007 Lawrence Cres Flossmoor (60422) *(G-9699)*
Grey Shirt Guys LLC 800 787-4478
419 Jackson St Mascoutah (62258) *(G-13597)*
Gridley Division, Gridley *Also called United Animal Health Inc (G-10848)*
Gridley Meat Products LLC 309 747-2120
205 E 3rd St Gridley (61744) *(G-10844)*
Gridley Welding Inc 309 747-2325
116 E 3rd St Gridley (61744) *(G-10845)*
Gridley Welding Shop, Gridley *Also called Gridley Welding Inc (G-10845)*

Grier Abrasive Co Inc 708 333-6445
123 W Taft Dr South Holland (60473) *(G-19216)*
Grieve Corporation 847 546-8225
500 Hart Rd Round Lake (60073) *(G-18078)*
Griffard & Associates LLC 217 316-1732
1022 Kochs Ln Quincy (62305) *(G-16887)*
Griffin John 708 301-2316
15751 Annico Dr Ste 2 Lockport (60491) *(G-12999)*
Griffin Industries LLC 815 357-8200
410 Shipyard Rd Seneca (61360) *(G-18858)*
Griffin Machining Inc 847 360-0098
4170 Grove Ave Gurnee (60031) *(G-10884)*
Griffin Plating Co Inc 773 342-5181
1636 W Armitage Ave Chicago (60622) *(G-4742)*
Griffith Foods Group Inc (PA) 708 371-0900
1 Griffith Ctr Alsip (60803) *(G-451)*
Griffith Foods Inc (HQ) 708 371-0900
1 Griffith Ctr Alsip (60803) *(G-452)*
Griffith Foods Inc 773 523-7509
1437 W 37th St Chicago (60609) *(G-4743)*
Griffith Foods Worldwide Inc (HQ) 708 371-0900
12200 S Central Ave Alsip (60803) *(G-453)*
Griffith Laboratories, Alsip *Also called Griffith Foods Worldwide Inc (G-453)*
Grifols Shared Svcs N Amer Inc 309 827-3031
511 W Washington St Bloomington (61701) *(G-2053)*
Grigalanz Software Enterprises, Jerseyville *Also called Phillip Grigalanz (G-11795)*
Grimco Inc 630 530-7756
575 W Crssrads Pkwy Ste B Bolingbrook (60440) *(G-2181)*
Grimm Metal Fabricators Inc 630 792-1710
1121 N Garfield St Lombard (60148) *(G-13083)*
Grind Lap Services Inc 630 458-1111
1045 W National Ave Addison (60101) *(G-143)*
Grindal Company 630 250-8950
1551 Industrial Dr Itasca (60143) *(G-11662)*
Grinding Specialty Co Inc 847 724-6493
1879 N Neltnor Blvd West Chicago (60185) *(G-20591)*
Griswold Feed Inc 815 432-2811
450 S Cips St Watseka (60970) *(G-20305)*
Griswold Machine Co (PA) 708 333-4258
241 W Taft Dr South Holland (60473) *(G-19217)*
Gro Alliance LLC 217 792-3355
247 1500th Ave Mount Pulaski (62548) *(G-14587)*
Gro-Mar Industries Inc 708 343-5901
2725 Thomas St Melrose Park (60160) *(G-13876)*
Groff Testing Corporation 815 939-1153
1410 Stanford Dr Kankakee (60901) *(G-11974)*
Grohne Concrete Products Co 217 877-4197
2594 N Water St Decatur (62526) *(G-7498)*
Groovjoint LLC (PA) 312 803-2627
155 N Wacker Dr Ste 4250 Chicago (60606) *(G-4744)*
Groovy Logistics Inc 847 946-1491
1120 Manhattan Rd Joliet (60433) *(G-11871)*
GROsse&sons Htg &SHeet Met Inc 708 447-8397
4236 Elm Ave Lyons (60534) *(G-13310)*
Groth Manufacturing 847 428-5950
845 Commerce Pkwy Carpentersville (60110) *(G-3103)*
Ground Cover Industries Inc (PA) 800 550-4424
21333 N Middleton Dr Kildeer (60047) *(G-12048)*
Ground Cover Marketing, Kewanee *Also called Rhino Tool Company (G-12040)*
Group Industries Inc 708 877-6200
459 N Williams St Thornton (60476) *(G-19788)*
Group O Inc 309 736-8660
7300 50th St Milan (61264) *(G-14013)*
Group O Inc 309 736-8311
120 4th Ave E Milan (61264) *(G-14014)*
Group O Inc 309 736-8100
4905 77th Ave E Milan (61264) *(G-14015)*
Group O Supply Chain Solution, Milan *Also called Group O Inc (G-14013)*
Groupe Lacasse LLC 312 670-9100
222 Merchandise Mart Plz # 1042 Chicago (60654) *(G-4745)*
Grovak Instant Printing Co 847 675-2414
701 S Meier Rd Mount Prospect (60056) *(G-14532)*
Grove Industrial 815 385-4800
3915 Spring Grove Rd Johnsburg (60051) *(G-11804)*
Grove Plastic Inc 847 678-8244
10352 Front Ave Franklin Park (60131) *(G-9954)*
Grove Plating Company Inc 847 639-7651
400 Algonquin Rd Fox River Grove (60021) *(G-9759)*
Grover Welding Company 847 966-3119
9120 Terminal Ave Skokie (60077) *(G-18961)*
Grow Masters 224 399-9877
4641 Old Grand Ave Gurnee (60031) *(G-10885)*
Grower Equipment & Supply Co 847 223-3100
294 E Belvidere Rd Hainesville (60030) *(G-10947)*
Grphic Richards Communications 708 547-6000
2700 Van Buren St Bellwood (60104) *(G-1626)*
Grs Holding LLC (PA) 630 355-1660
131 W Jefferson Ave # 223 Naperville (60540) *(G-14838)*
Grundfos CBS Inc 331 401-0057
3905 Enterprise Ct Aurora (60504) *(G-975)*

ALPHABETIC

Grundfos Water Utility Inc 630 236-5500
3905 Enterprise Ct Aurora (60504) ***(G-976)***
Grupo Antolin Illinois Inc 815 544-8020
642 Crystal Pkwy Belvidere (61008) ***(G-1674)***
Gs Custom Works Inc 815 233-4724
2110 Park Crest Dr Freeport (61032) ***(G-10113)***
Gs Metals Corp 618 357-5353
3764 Longspur Rd Pinckneyville (62274) ***(G-16617)***
GSE, Lincolnshire *Also called Good Sam Enterprises LLC* ***(G-12767)***
Gsg Industries 618 544-7976
1708 W Main St Robinson (62454) ***(G-17115)***
Gsi, Assumption *Also called Grain Systems Inc* ***(G-890)***
Gsi Group LLC 618 283-9792
110 S Coles St Vandalia (62471) ***(G-20012)***
Gsi Group LLC 217 463-1612
13217 Illinois Hwy 133 W Paris (61944) ***(G-16230)***
Gsi Group LLC 217 226-4421
1004 E Illinois St Assumption (62510) ***(G-891)***
Gsi Group LLC 217 287-6244
2400 S Spresser St Taylorville (62568) ***(G-19757)***
Gsi Holdings Corp (HQ) 217 226-4421
1004 E Illinois St Assumption (62510) ***(G-892)***
Gsil Holding Corp, Quincy *Also called Hollister-Whitney Elev Co LLC* ***(G-16892)***
Gsipc LLC 630 325-8181
311 Shore Dr Burr Ridge (60527) ***(G-2678)***
Gt Business Services, Tremont *Also called G T Services of Illionois Inc* ***(G-19896)***
Gt Flow Technology Inc 815 636-9982
5364 Mainsail Dr Roscoe (61073) ***(G-17908)***
Gti, Chicago *Also called Green Thumb Industries Inc* ***(G-4740)***
Gti Rock Island LLC (PA) 312 664-5050
325 W Huron St Ste 412 Chicago (60654) ***(G-4746)***
Gti Spindle Technology Inc 309 820-7887
14015 Carole Dr Ste 2 Bloomington (61705) ***(G-2054)***
Gtx Inc 847 699-7421
300 E Touhy Ave Des Plaines (60018) ***(G-7775)***
Gtx Surgery Inc 847 920-8489
848 Dodge Ave Unit 384 Evanston (60202) ***(G-9528)***
Guaranteed Ink, Pekin *Also called Troy McDaniel* ***(G-16366)***
Guardian Angel Outreach 815 672-4567
111 Spring St Streator (61364) ***(G-19609)***
Guardian Consolidated Tech Inc (HQ) 815 334-3600
1425 Lake Ave Woodstock (60098) ***(G-21392)***
Guardian Construction Pdts Inc 630 820-8899
10s359 Normantown Rd Naperville (60564) ***(G-14970)***
Guardian Electric Mfg Co (HQ) 815 334-3600
1425 Lake Ave Woodstock (60098) ***(G-21393)***
Guardian Energy Tech Inc 800 516-0949
2033 Milwaukee Ave # 136 Riverwoods (60015) ***(G-17091)***
Guardian Equipment Inc 312 447-8100
1140 N North Branch St Chicago (60642) ***(G-4747)***
Guardian Horse Bedding, Loves Park *Also called Equustock LLC* ***(G-13210)***
Guardian Personal Defense Tng 630 272-9811
403 Lennox Ct Oswego (60543) ***(G-16006)***
Guardian Rollform LLC 847 382-8074
27951 W Industrial Ave Lake Barrington (60010) ***(G-12148)***
Guardian West, Urbana *Also called Flex-N-Gate LLC* ***(G-19985)***
Gue Liquidation Delivery Inc (HQ) 630 719-7800
3113 Woodcreek Dr Downers Grove (60515) ***(G-8015)***
Gueros Pallets Inc 312 523-5561
355 N Lavergne Ave Chicago (60644) ***(G-4748)***
Guerrero Industries LLC 773 968-8648
12605 S Melvina Ave Palos Heights (60463) ***(G-16187)***
Guess Inc 312 440-9592
605 N Michigan Ave # 200 Chicago (60611) ***(G-4749)***
Guess Whackit & Hope Inc 773 342-4273
1883 N Milwaukee Ave Chicago (60647) ***(G-4750)***
Guidance Software Inc 847 994-7324
300 S Wacker Dr Ste 1100 Chicago (60606) ***(G-4751)***
Guide Line Industries Inc 815 777-3722
1453 W Schapville Rd Scales Mound (61075) ***(G-18420)***
Gulf Coast Exploration Inc 847 226-4654
983 Harvard Ct Highland Park (60035) ***(G-11268)***
Gulfstream Aerospace Corp 630 470-9146
472 Quail Dr Naperville (60565) ***(G-14839)***
Gulfstream Aerospace Corp 815 469-1509
9416 Gulfstream Rd Ste 1a Frankfort (60423) ***(G-9798)***
Gumball Machine Factory.com, Arlington Heights *Also called Lucky Yuppy Puppy Co* ***(G-772)***
Gundlach Equipment Corporation 618 233-7208
1 Freedom Dr Belleville (62226) ***(G-1554)***
Gunite Corporation (HQ) 815 490-6260
302 Peoples Ave Rockford (61104) ***(G-17436)***
Gunite Corporation 815 964-3301
302 Peoples Ave Rockford (61104) ***(G-17437)***
Gunner Energy Corporation 618 237-2829
1200 Hill St Mount Vernon (62864) ***(G-14612)***
Gurman Food Co 847 837-1100
906 Tower Rd Mundelein (60060) ***(G-14693)***
Gus Berthold Electric Company (PA) 312 243-5767
1900 W Carroll Ave Chicago (60612) ***(G-4752)***
Gusco Silicone Rbr & Svcs LLC 773 770-5008
1500 Dearborn Ave Aurora (60505) ***(G-1106)***
Gutter Masters 309 686-1234
2117 E Cornell St Peoria (61614) ***(G-16447)***
Guys Hi-Def Inc 708 261-7487
1948 Essington Rd Ste C Joliet (60435) ***(G-11872)***
Guzzler Manufacturing Inc 815 672-3171
1621 S Illinois St Streator (61364) ***(G-19610)***
GV Welding Inc 312 863-0071
4849 W Grand Ave Chicago (60639) ***(G-4753)***
Gvw Group LLC (PA) 847 681-8417
625 Roger Williams Ave Highland Park (60035) ***(G-11269)***
Gvw Holdings, Highland Park *Also called Gvw Group LLC* ***(G-11269)***
Gycor International Ltd 630 754-8070
10216 Werch Dr Ste 108 Woodridge (60517) ***(G-21308)***
Gymtek Incorporated 815 547-0771
6853 Indy Dr Belvidere (61008) ***(G-1675)***
Gyood 773 360-8810
2048 W Belmont Ave Chicago (60618) ***(G-4754)***
Gyro Processing Inc 800 491-0733
3338 N Ashland Ave Chicago (60657) ***(G-4755)***
Gz Sign Designs Inc 630 307-7446
912 Central Ave Roselle (60172) ***(G-17956)***
H & B Hams 618 372-8690
202 W Plum St Brighton (62012) ***(G-2400)***
H & B Machine Corporation 312 829-4850
1943 W Walnut St Chicago (60612) ***(G-4756)***
H & B Quality Tooling Inc 217 223-2387
2723 S Commercial Dr Quincy (62305) ***(G-16888)***
H & D Motor Service 217 342-3262
901 W Cumberland Rd Altamont (62411) ***(G-533)***
H & H Drilling Co 618 529-3697
59 Pineview Rd Carbondale (62901) ***(G-2843)***
H & H Fabric Cutters 773 772-1904
4431 W Rice St Chicago (60651) ***(G-4757)***
H & H Graphics LLC 847 383-6285
450 Corporate Woods Pkwy Vernon Hills (60061) ***(G-20057)***
H & H Graphics Illinois Inc 847 383-6285
450 Corporate Woods Pkwy Vernon Hills (60061) ***(G-20058)***
H & H Machining 309 365-7010
500 S Spencer St Lexington (61753) ***(G-12619)***
H & H Motor Service Inc 708 652-6100
5130 W 16th St Cicero (60804) ***(G-6850)***
H & H Printing 847 866-9520
1800 Dempster St Evanston (60202) ***(G-9529)***
H & H Services Inc 618 633-2837
391 N Old Us Route 66 Hamel (62046) ***(G-10949)***
H & H Stone LLC 815 782-5700
1421 W 135th St Bolingbrook (60490) ***(G-2182)***
H & K Precision Machining Co 847 382-0288
7 Hillside Dr Ste B Lake Barrington (60010) ***(G-12149)***
H & M Machining Inc 815 877-5623
1209 Shappert Dr Machesney Park (61115) ***(G-13346)***
H & M Thread Rolling Co Inc 847 451-1570
9212 Grand Ave Franklin Park (60131) ***(G-9955)***
H & M Woodworks 608 289-3141
1610 N County Road 1200 Hamilton (62341) ***(G-10957)***
H & R Block, Mundelein *Also called H&R Block Inc* ***(G-14694)***
H & R Tool & Machine Co 618 344-7683
19 W Scates St Caseyville (62232) ***(G-3213)***
H & S Mechanical Inc 309 696-7066
5607 Washington St Peoria (61607) ***(G-16448)***
H A Framburg & Company (PA) 708 547-5757
941 Cernan Dr Bellwood (60104) ***(G-1627)***
H A Friend & Company Inc (PA) 847 746-1248
1535 Lewis Ave Zion (60099) ***(G-21516)***
H A Phillips & Co (PA) 630 377-0050
770 Enterprise Ave Dekalb (60115) ***(G-7683)***
H and D Distribution Inc 847 247-2011
28045 N Ashley Cir Unit 1 Libertyville (60048) ***(G-12656)***
H B Products Incorporated 773 735-0936
42 Parklane Dr Palos Park (60464) ***(G-16211)***
H B Taylor Co 773 254-4805
4830 S Christiana Ave Chicago (60632) ***(G-4758)***
H C Schau & Son Inc 630 783-1000
10350 Argonne Dr Ste 400 Woodridge (60517) ***(G-21309)***
H D A Fans Inc 630 627-2087
1455 Brummel Ave 300 Elk Grove Village (60007) ***(G-9025)***
H D C, Burr Ridge *Also called Medtext Inc* ***(G-2702)***
H E Associates Inc 630 553-6382
201 Beaver St Yorkville (60560) ***(G-21487)***
H F I, West Chicago *Also called Howler Fabrication & Wldg Inc* ***(G-20593)***
H Felde Tool & Machine Co 309 692-5870
2324 W Altorfer Dr Peoria (61615) ***(G-16449)***
H Field & Sons Inc 847 434-0970
2605 S Clearbrook Dr Arlington Heights (60005) ***(G-745)***
H G & N Fertilizer, Clinton *Also called Harbach Gillan & Nixon Inc* ***(G-6922)***

ALPHABETIC SECTION Hamilton Sundstrand Corp

H G Acquisition Corp (PA)....630 382-1000
7020 High Grove Blvd Burr Ridge (60527) ***(G-2679)***
H H Interantional Inc....847 697-7805
1010 Douglas Rd Elgin (60120) ***(G-8602)***
H Hal Kramer Co (PA)....847 441-0213
1865 Old Willow Rd # 231 Northfield (60093) ***(G-15516)***
H J M P Corp (HQ)....708 345-5370
1930 George St Ste 2 Melrose Park (60160) ***(G-13877)***
H J Mohr & Sons Company....708 366-0338
915 S Maple Ave Oak Park (60304) ***(G-15756)***
H Kramer & Co....312 226-6600
1345 W 21st St Chicago (60608) ***(G-4759)***
H L Clausing Inc....847 676-0330
8038 Monticello Ave Skokie (60076) ***(G-18962)***
H M C Products Inc....815 885-1900
7165 Greenlee Dr Machesney Park (61011) ***(G-13319)***
H M I, Hudson *Also called Hamilton Maurer Intl Inc* ***(G-11518)***
H N C Products Inc (PA)....309 319-2151
1619 Commerce Pkwy Bloomington (61704) ***(G-2055)***
H N C Products Inc....217 935-9100
8631 Sunset Rd Clinton (61727) ***(G-6921)***
H P Tops, Highland Park *Also called Larry & Myra Stone* ***(G-11280)***
H R Larke Corp....847 204-2776
999 Saddle Creek Ln Crystal Lake (60014) ***(G-7204)***
H R Slater Co Inc....312 666-1855
2050 W 18th St Chicago (60608) ***(G-4760)***
H S Crocker Company Inc (PA)....847 669-3600
12100 Smith Dr Huntley (60142) ***(G-11538)***
H S I Fire and Safety Group (PA)....847 427-8340
107 Garlisch Dr Elk Grove Village (60007) ***(G-9026)***
H V Manufacturing Vanguar....847 229-5502
1197 Willis Ave Wheeling (60090) ***(G-20905)***
H W Hostetler & Sons....815 438-7816
27445 Hurd Rd Deer Grove (61243) ***(G-7577)***
H Watson Jewelry Co....312 236-1104
29 E Madison St Ste 1007 Chicago (60602) ***(G-4761)***
H&H Crushing Inc....309 275-0643
2401 W Rhodora Ave West Peoria (61604) ***(G-20686)***
H&H Die Manufacturing Inc....708 479-6267
22772 Challenger Rd A Frankfort (60423) ***(G-9799)***
H&K Perforating LLC (PA)....773 626-1800
5470 W Roosevelt Rd Chicago (60644) ***(G-4762)***
H&R Block Inc....847 566-5557
1527 S Lake St Mundelein (60060) ***(G-14694)***
H&S Machine & Tools Inc....618 451-0164
35 Central Industrial Dr Granite City (62040) ***(G-10712)***
H&Z Fuel & Food Inc....815 399-9108
3420 E State St Rockford (61108) ***(G-17438)***
H-O-H Water Technology Inc (PA)....847 358-7400
500 S Vermont St Palatine (60067) ***(G-16121)***
H. E. Wisdom & Sons, Inc., Elgin *Also called Wisdom Adhesives LLC* ***(G-8783)***
H.B. Fuller Construction Pdts, Aurora *Also called HB Fuller Cnstr Pdts Inc* ***(G-978)***
H2o, East Dundee *Also called Humidity 2 Optimization LLC* ***(G-8200)***
H2o Filter Inc....630 963-3303
4407 Chelsea Ave Lisle (60532) ***(G-12896)***
H2o Mobil, Tiskilwa *Also called Hydrotec Systems Company Inc* ***(G-19873)***
H2o Pod Inc....630 240-1769
490 Pennsylvania Ave Glen Ellyn (60137) ***(G-10404)***
H2o Solutions LLC....618 219-2905
40 Georgetown Dr Granite City (62040) ***(G-10713)***
H3 Group LLC....309 222-6027
900 Sw Adams St Peoria (61602) ***(G-16450)***
Ha International, Westmont *Also called Ha-International LLC* ***(G-20744)***
Ha-International LLC (HQ)....630 575-5700
630 Oakmont Ln Westmont (60559) ***(G-20744)***
Ha-International LLC....815 732-3898
1449 W Devils Backbone Rd Oregon (61061) ***(G-15922)***
Ha-Usa Inc (HQ)....630 575-5700
630 Oakmont Ln Westmont (60559) ***(G-20745)***
Haaker Mold Co Inc....847 253-8103
628 N Salem Ave Arlington Heights (60004) ***(G-746)***
Haakes Awning....618 529-4808
2525 Edgewood Ln Carbondale (62901) ***(G-2844)***
Habegger Corporation....309 793-7172
437 2nd St Rock Island (61201) ***(G-17221)***
Habegger Corporation....217 789-4328
2900 Old Rochester Rd Springfield (62703) ***(G-19377)***
Hach Company....800 227-4224
2207 Collection Center Dr Chicago (60693) ***(G-4763)***
Hackett Precision Company Inc....615 227-3136
70 W Madison St Ste 2300 Chicago (60602) ***(G-4764)***
Hadady Corporation (PA)....219 322-7417
510 W 172nd St South Holland (60473) ***(G-19218)***
Hadady Machining Company Inc (PA)....708 474-8620
16730 Chicago Ave Lansing (60438) ***(G-12496)***
Hadco Tool Co LLC....847 677-6263
8105 Monticello Ave Skokie (60076) ***(G-18963)***
Haddock Tool & Manufacturing....815 786-2739
917 E Railroad St Sandwich (60548) ***(G-18373)***
Hadley Capital Fund II LP (PA)....847 906-5300
1200 Central Ave Ste 300 Wilmette (60091) ***(G-21076)***
Hadley Gear Manufacturing Co....773 722-1030
4444 W Roosevelt Rd Chicago (60624) ***(G-4765)***
Hafner Duplicating Company....312 362-0120
601 S La Salle St Chicago (60605) ***(G-4766)***
Hafner Printing Co Inc....312 362-0120
111 N Jefferson St Chicago (60661) ***(G-4767)***
Hagen Manufacturing Inc....224 735-2099
318 Holbrook Dr Wheeling (60090) ***(G-20906)***
Haggard Well Services Inc....618 262-5060
710 Poplar St Mount Carmel (62863) ***(G-14471)***
Hahn Industries....815 689-2133
300 S Walnut St Cullom (60929) ***(G-7299)***
Haight Company....224 407-0763
166 Symphony Way Elgin (60120) ***(G-8603)***
Haight, The, Elgin *Also called Haight Company* ***(G-8603)***
Haimer Usa LLC....630 833-1500
134 E Hill St Villa Park (60181) ***(G-20150)***
Hair Plus Studios LLC....530 487-4247
2860 N Broadway St Ste 12 Chicago (60657) ***(G-4768)***
Hairline Creations Inc (PA)....773 282-5454
5850 W Montrose Ave 54 Chicago (60634) ***(G-4769)***
Hairy Ant Inc....630 338-7194
601 Sidwell Ct Ste F Saint Charles (60174) ***(G-18205)***
Hakimian Gem Co....312 236-6969
5 S Wabash Ave Ste 1212 Chicago (60603) ***(G-4770)***
Hako Minuteman Inc....630 627-6900
111 S Rohlwing Rd Addison (60101) ***(G-144)***
Hakwood Inc....630 219-3388
2244 95th St Ste 200 Naperville (60564) ***(G-14971)***
Hal Mather & Sons Incorporated....815 338-4000
11803 Highway 120 Woodstock (60098) ***(G-21394)***
Halanick Enterprises Inc....708 403-3334
14428 John Humphrey Dr Orland Park (60462) ***(G-15958)***
Halas Vocational Center, Chicago *Also called Envision Unlimited* ***(G-4521)***
Haleys Corker Inc....708 228-1427
1323 Park Ave River Forest (60305) ***(G-17052)***
Half Acre Beer Company, Chicago *Also called Gmb Partners LLC* ***(G-4703)***
Half Price Bks Rec Mgzines Inc....847 588-2286
5605 W Touhy Ave Niles (60714) ***(G-15128)***
Hall Fabrication Inc....217 322-2212
121 N Liberty St Rushville (62681) ***(G-18109)***
Hall Shrpning Stnes A Rh Pryda, Chicago *Also called Rh Preyda Company* ***(G-6022)***
Hallen Burial Vault Inc....815 544-6138
3690 Newburg Rd Belvidere (61008) ***(G-1676)***
Hallmark Cabinet Company....708 757-7807
251 Switchgrass Dr Minooka (60447) ***(G-14061)***
Hallmark Industries Inc....847 301-8050
411 E North Ave Streamwood (60107) ***(G-19577)***
Hallmark Surfaces, Minooka *Also called Hallmark Cabinet Company* ***(G-14061)***
Hallstar....330 945-5292
5350 W 70th Pl Bedford Park (60638) ***(G-1469)***
Hallstar Company....901 948-8663
120 S Riverside Plz # 1620 Chicago (60606) ***(G-4771)***
Hallstar Company (PA)....312 554-7400
120 S Riverside Plz # 1620 Chicago (60606) ***(G-4772)***
Hallstar Company....708 594-5947
5851 W 73rd St Bedford Park (60638) ***(G-1470)***
Hallstar Services Corp....312 554-7400
120 S Riverside Plz # 1620 Chicago (60606) ***(G-4773)***
Halper Publishing Company....847 542-9793
913 Forest Ave Apt 2s Evanston (60202) ***(G-9530)***
Halsted Packing House Co....312 421-5147
445 N Halsted St Chicago (60642) ***(G-4774)***
Halter Machine Shop Inc....618 943-2224
9452 Peachtree Rd Lawrenceville (62439) ***(G-12534)***
Hamalot Inc (PA)....847 944-1500
933 Remington Rd Schaumburg (60173) ***(G-18542)***
Hamel Tire and Concrete Pdts....618 633-2405
200 Hamel Ave Hamel (62046) ***(G-10950)***
Hamel Tire Service, Hamel *Also called Hamel Tire and Concrete Pdts* ***(G-10950)***
Hamilton Beach Brands Inc....847 252-7036
142 Crichton Ln Inverness (60067) ***(G-11596)***
Hamilton Concrete Products Co....217 847-3118
400 Windy Woods Dr Hamilton (62341) ***(G-10958)***
Hamilton Construction Co, Hamilton *Also called Hamilton Concrete Products Co* ***(G-10958)***
Hamilton County Coal LLC....618 648-2603
18033 County Road 500 E Dahlgren (62828) ***(G-7307)***
Hamilton Fbrcation Stl Sup Inc....618 466-0012
311 Tolle Ln Godfrey (62035) ***(G-10652)***
Hamilton Maurer Intl Inc....713 468-6805
14431 E 2400 North Rd Hudson (61748) ***(G-11518)***
Hamilton Sndstrand Space Syste (HQ)....815 226-6000
4747 Harrison Ave Rockford (61108) ***(G-17439)***
Hamilton Sundstrand Corp....815 226-6000
2421 11th St Rockford (61104) ***(G-17440)***
Hamilton Sundstrand Corp....815 226-6000
4747 Harrison Ave Rockford (61108) ***(G-17441)***

ALPHABETIC

Hammer Down Construction, Springfield *Also called Jeff E Allen* ***(G-19394)***
Hammer Enterprises Inc 217 662-8225
5781 State Route 1 Georgetown (61846) ***(G-10328)***
Hammer Source, The, Naperville *Also called Ironwood Manufacturing Inc* ***(G-14975)***
Hammond Printing 847 724-1539
1622 Pickwick Ln Glenview (60026) ***(G-10555)***
Hammond Suzuki Usa Inc 630 543-0277
733 W Annoreno Dr Addison (60101) ***(G-145)***
Hampden Corporation 312 583-3000
1550 W Carroll Ave # 207 Chicago (60607) ***(G-4775)***
Hampster Industries Inc 866 280-2287
26400 N Pheasant Run Mundelein (60060) ***(G-14695)***
Hamsher Lakeside Funerals 847 587-2100
12 N Pistakee Lake Rd Fox Lake (60020) ***(G-9747)***
Han-Win Products Inc 630 897-1591
726 S Broadway Aurora (60505) ***(G-1107)***
Hancock County Journal-Pilot, Carthage *Also called Democrat Company Corp* ***(G-3135)***
Hancock County Shopper 217 847-6628
1830 Keokuk St Hamilton (62341) ***(G-10959)***
Hand Tool America 847 947-2866
45 Buckingham Ln Buffalo Grove (60089) ***(G-2543)***
Handcrafted By Jackie Turbot 815 708-7200
671 Purple Sage Dr Roscoe (61073) ***(G-17909)***
Handcut Foods LLC 312 239-0381
1441 W Willow St Chicago (60642) ***(G-4776)***
Handi-Foil Corp (PA) 847 520-1000
135 E Hintz Rd Wheeling (60090) ***(G-20907)***
Handi-Foil of America, Wheeling *Also called Hfa Inc* ***(G-20908)***
Handling Systems Intl Inc 708 352-1213
8000 Joliet Rd Bldg 1 Mc Cook (60525) ***(G-13692)***
Hands To Work Railroading 708 489-9776
12217 S Cicero Ave Alsip (60803) ***(G-454)***
Handy Filler Systems, Carterville *Also called Jon Cagle* ***(G-3132)***
Handy Helper Fencing, Coulterville *Also called Brian Hobbs* ***(G-7029)***
Hanger Inc 847 695-6955
649 Ridgeview Dr McHenry (60050) ***(G-13747)***
Hanger Inc 708 679-1006
4525 Lincoln Hwy Matteson (60443) ***(G-13624)***
Hanger Clinic, Decatur *Also called Hanger Prosthetics &* ***(G-7499)***
Hanger Clinic, Herrin *Also called Hanger Prsthtics Orthtics E In* ***(G-11172)***
Hanger Clinic, Gurnee *Also called Hanger Prosthetics &* ***(G-10886)***
Hanger Clinic, Aurora *Also called Hanger Prosthetics &* ***(G-977)***
Hanger Clinic, Matteson *Also called Hanger Inc* ***(G-13624)***
Hanger Prosthetics & 217 429-6656
1910 S Mount Zion Rd D Decatur (62521) ***(G-7499)***
Hanger Prosthetics & 630 986-0007
100 Tower Dr Ste 101 Burr Ridge (60527) ***(G-2680)***
Hanger Prosthetics & 630 986-0007
100 Tower Dr Ste 101 Burr Ridge (60527) ***(G-2681)***
Hanger Prosthetics & 847 623-6080
35 Tower Ct Ste C Gurnee (60031) ***(G-10886)***
Hanger Prosthetics & 630 820-5656
4400 Mccoy Dr Ste 100 Aurora (60504) ***(G-977)***
Hanger Prsthetcs & Ortho Inc 309 585-2349
211 Landmark Dr Ste A5 Normal (61761) ***(G-15204)***
Hanger Prsthetcs & Ortho Inc 217 429-6656
1910 S Mount Zion Rd D Decatur (62521) ***(G-7500)***
Hanger Prsthtics Orthotics Inc 309 637-6581
311 W Romeo B Garrett Ave Peoria (61605) ***(G-16451)***
Hanger Prsthtics Orthotics Inc 815 744-9944
694 Essington Rd Unit B Joliet (60435) ***(G-11873)***
Hanger Prsthtics Orthtics E In 618 997-1451
404 Rushing Dr Herrin (62948) ***(G-11172)***
Hangerjack, Mokena *Also called Applied Arts & Sciences Inc* ***(G-14072)***
Hangout Lighting LLC 224 817-4101
2100 W Grand Ave Ste 2 Chicago (60612) ***(G-4777)***
Hanigs Footwear Inc 773 248-1977
1515 Sheridan Rd Ste 2 Wilmette (60091) ***(G-21077)***
Hanley Design Inc 309 682-9665
2519 N Rockwood Dr Peoria (61604) ***(G-16452)***
Hanley Industries Inc 618 465-8892
3640 Seminary St Alton (62002) ***(G-557)***
Hanlon Group Ltd 773 525-3666
1872 N Clybourn Ave # 604 Chicago (60614) ***(G-4778)***
Hanna Steel Corporation 309 478-3800
220 Hanna Dr Pekin (61554) ***(G-16336)***
Hanover Displays Inc 773 334-9934
1601 Tonne Rd Elk Grove Village (60007) ***(G-9027)***
Hanover Park Press, McHenry *Also called McHenry Printing Services* ***(G-13765)***
Hansel Walter J & Assoc Inc (PA) 815 678-6065
4311 Hill Rd Richmond (60071) ***(G-17014)***
Hansels Custom Tech Inc 815 496-2345
405 E Si Johnson Ave Sheridan (60551) ***(G-18889)***
Hansen Custom Cabinet Inc 847 356-1100
23418 W Apollo Ct Lake Villa (60046) ***(G-12353)***
Hansen Packing Co 618 498-3714
807 State Highway 16 Jerseyville (62052) ***(G-11792)***
Hansen Plastics Corp 847 741-4510
2758 Alft Ln Elgin (60124) ***(G-8604)***
Hansen Plastics Corp 847 741-4510
1300 Abbott Dr Elgin (60123) ***(G-8605)***
Hansen Printing Co Inc 708 599-1500
9745 Industrial Dr Ste 10 Bridgeview (60455) ***(G-2353)***
Hansen Technologies Corp (HQ) 706 335-5551
681 Commerce St Burr Ridge (60527) ***(G-2682)***
Hansens Mfrs Win Coverings (PA) 815 935-0010
235 N Kinzie Ave Bradley (60915) ***(G-2284)***
Hanson Aggregates East LLC 815 398-2300
5011 E State St Rockford (61108) ***(G-17442)***
Hanson Material Service, Romeoville *Also called Material Service Corporation* ***(G-17846)***
Hanson Material Service, Westchester *Also called Material Service Corporation* ***(G-20705)***
Hansvedt, Rantoul *Also called Arrow Edm Inc* ***(G-16967)***
Hantemp Controls, Westmont *Also called Hantemp Corporation* ***(G-20746)***
Hantemp Corporation 630 537-1049
33 Chestnut Ave Westmont (60559) ***(G-20746)***
Haran Technologies, Champaign *Also called Haran Ventures LLC* ***(G-3299)***
Haran Ventures LLC 217 239-1628
1804 Vale St Champaign (61822) ***(G-3299)***
Harbach Gillan & Nixon Inc (PA) 217 935-8378
618 W Van Buren St Clinton (61727) ***(G-6922)***
Harbach Gillan & Nixon Inc 217 794-5117
40 Ag Rd Maroa (61756) ***(G-13552)***
Harbach Nixon & Willson Inc (HQ) 217 935-8378
618 W Van Buren St Clinton (61727) ***(G-6923)***
Harbison Fischer Sales Co, Grayville *Also called Harbison-Fischer Inc* ***(G-10808)***
Harbison-Fischer Inc 618 375-3841
1421 N Court St Grayville (62844) ***(G-10808)***
Harbisonwalker Intl Inc 708 474-5350
1400 Huntington Dr Calumet City (60409) ***(G-2779)***
Harbor Manufacturing Inc 708 543-1740
458 Ohio Rd Frankfort (60423) ***(G-9800)***
Harbor Tool Manufacturing Co 708 614-6400
8300 185th St Tinley Park (60487) ***(G-19835)***
Harbor Village LLC 773 338-2222
2241 W Howard St Chicago (60645) ***(G-4779)***
Hard Reset Printing Inc 773 850-9277
109 3rd Ave Joliet (60433) ***(G-11874)***
Hardball Chemical Co, Lincoln *Also called Vernon Micheal* ***(G-12739)***
Harder Signs Inc 815 874-7777
4695 Stenstrom Rd Rockford (61109) ***(G-17443)***
Hardin Industries LLC 309 246-8456
400 N Commercial St Lacon (61540) ***(G-12127)***
Hardin Ready Mix Inc 618 576-9313
19321 Illinois River Rd Hardin (62047) ***(G-11017)***
Hardinge Grinding Group Inc (HQ) 847 888-0148
1524 Davis Rd Elgin (60123) ***(G-8606)***
Hardscape Outpost LLC 630 551-6105
326 Butterfield Rd North Aurora (60542) ***(G-15262)***
Hardschellreport 773 972-2500
1246 Hinman Ave Evanston (60202) ***(G-9531)***
Hardware Representatives, Bridgeview *Also called Formed Fastener Mfg Inc* ***(G-2348)***
Hardwood Connection 815 895-8733
1810 W State St Sycamore (60178) ***(G-19712)***
Hardwood Furniture & Design, Addison *Also called Columbia Woodworks Corporation* ***(G-77)***
Hardwood Line Manufacturing Co 773 463-2600
4045 N Elston Ave Chicago (60618) ***(G-4780)***
Hardwood Lumber Products Co 309 538-4411
21046 E Cr 800n Kilbourne (62655) ***(G-12044)***
Hardy Company, The, Evanston *Also called John Hardy Co* ***(G-9542)***
Hardy Radiator Repair 217 223-8320
1710 N 12th St Quincy (62301) ***(G-16889)***
Hardy's Auto Sales, Quincy *Also called Hardy Radiator Repair* ***(G-16889)***
Harger Inc (PA) 847 548-8700
301 Ziegler Dr Grayslake (60030) ***(G-10780)***
Harger Lightning & Grounding, Grayslake *Also called Harger Inc* ***(G-10780)***
Harig Manufacturing Corp 847 647-9500
5423 Fargo Ave Skokie (60077) ***(G-18964)***
Harig Products Inc 847 695-1000
1875 Big Timber Rd Elgin (60123) ***(G-8607)***
Harlan Vance Company 309 888-4804
1741 Hovey Ave Normal (61761) ***(G-15205)***
Harman International Inds Inc 847 996-8118
702 N Deerpath Dr Vernon Hills (60061) ***(G-20059)***
Harmon Inc 630 759-8060
100 E Crssrads Pkwy Ste B Bolingbrook (60440) ***(G-2183)***
Harmony House, Morton Grove *Also called Success Journal Corp* ***(G-14444)***
Harmony Metal Fabrication Inc 847 426-8900
148 Industrial Dr Gilberts (60136) ***(G-10356)***
Harners Bakery Restaurant 630 892-5545
10 W State St North Aurora (60542) ***(G-15263)***
Harold L Ray Truck & Trctr Svc 618 673-2701
Hwy 45 N Cisne (62823) ***(G-6893)***
Harold Prefinished Wood Inc 618 548-1414
5318 State Route 37 Salem (62881) ***(G-18342)***

Harold Printing & Graphics, Murphysboro *Also called Schwebel Printing* ***(G-14759)***
Harrier Interior Products 847 934-1310
319 W Colfax St Palatine (60067) ***(G-16122)***
Harrington King Prforating Inc 773 626-1800
5655 W Fillmore St Chicago (60644) ***(G-4781)***
Harrington Signal Inc 309 762-0731
2519 4th Ave Moline (61265) ***(G-14148)***
Harris Bmo Bank National Assn 815 886-1900
630 N Independence Blvd Romeoville (60446) ***(G-17830)***
Harris Bookbinding LLC 773 287-9414
5375 Walnut Ave Downers Grove (60515) ***(G-8016)***
Harris Companies Inc 217 578-2231
521 N Illinois St Atwood (61913) ***(G-905)***
Harris Container Corp 630 553-0027
113 Riverside Dr Yorkville (60560) ***(G-21488)***
Harris Drilling Fluids Inc 618 395-7395
1015 S Whittle Ave Olney (62450) ***(G-15864)***
Harris Equipment Corporation 708 343-0866
2040 N Hawthorne Ave Melrose Park (60160) ***(G-13878)***
Harris Lubricants 708 849-1935
14335 Dorchester Ave Dolton (60419) ***(G-7936)***
Harris Metals & Recycling 217 235-1808
1213 N 11th St Mattoon (61938) ***(G-13635)***
Harris Potteries LP (PA) 847 564-5544
707 Skokie Blvd Ste 220 Northbrook (60062) ***(G-15397)***
Harris Precision Tools Inc 708 422-5808
10081 Anderson Ave Chicago Ridge (60415) ***(G-6797)***
Harris Skokie 847 675-6300
9731 Skokie Blvd Skokie (60077) ***(G-18965)***
Harris Steel Company (PA) 708 656-5500
1223 S 55th Ct Cicero (60804) ***(G-6851)***
Harris Steel Ulc 815 932-1200
1115 E 5000n Rd Bourbonnais (60914) ***(G-2262)***
Harris William & Company Inc (PA) 312 621-0590
191 N Wacker Dr Ste 1500 Chicago (60606) ***(G-4782)***
Harrison Harmonicas LLC 312 379-9427
4541 N Ravenswood Ave # 203 Chicago (60640) ***(G-4783)***
Harrison Martha Print Studio 949 290-8630
3222 Carrington Dr Crystal Lake (60014) ***(G-7205)***
Harry J Trainor 630 493-1163
2113 Oxnard Dr Downers Grove (60516) ***(G-8017)***
Harry Otto Printing Company 630 365-6111
707 E North St Ste A Elburn (60119) ***(G-8455)***
Harsco Corporation 309 347-1962
13090 E Manito Rd Pekin (61554) ***(G-16337)***
Harsco Corporation 217 237-4335
226 E 1640 Rd Pawnee (62558) ***(G-16304)***
Hart & Cooley Inc 630 665-5549
815 Kimberly Dr Carol Stream (60188) ***(G-2996)***
Hart - Clayton Inc 217 525-1610
2000 E Cornell Ave Ste 2 Springfield (62703) ***(G-19378)***
Hart Electric LLC 815 368-3341
102 S Main St Lostant (61334) ***(G-13176)***
Hart Puzzles Inc 847 910-2290
661 Frontier Way Bensenville (60106) ***(G-1817)***
Hart Schaffner & Marx, Des Plaines *Also called W Diamond Group Corporation* ***(G-7866)***
Harting Elektronik, Elgin *Also called Harting Inc of North America* ***(G-8608)***
Harting Inc of North America 847 741-2700
1375 Crispin Dr Elgin (60123) ***(G-8608)***
Harting Inc of North America (HQ) 847 741-1500
1370 Bowes Rd Elgin (60123) ***(G-8609)***
Harting Manufacturing Inc 847 741-1500
1370 Bowes Rd Elgin (60123) ***(G-8610)***
Hartland Cutting Tools Inc 847 639-9400
240 Jandus Rd Cary (60013) ***(G-3166)***
Hartmann 618 684-6814
29 Steven Dr Murphysboro (62966) ***(G-14755)***
Hartrich Meats Inc 618 455-3172
326 W Embarras St Sainte Marie (62459) ***(G-18326)***
Harts Top and Cabinet Shop 708 957-4666
4941 173rd St Ste 1 Country Club Hills (60478) ***(G-7040)***
Harts Top Shop, Country Club Hills *Also called Harts Top and Cabinet Shop* ***(G-7040)***
Hartwig Roll Off Containers, Henry *Also called Ed Hartwig Trucking & Excvtg* ***(G-11163)***
Harvard Building Products, Harvard *Also called A-Ok Inc* ***(G-11039)***
Harvest Publications Div, Arlington Heights *Also called Baptist General Conference* ***(G-703)***
Harvey Bros Inc 309 342-3137
2181 Grand Ave Galesburg (61401) ***(G-10199)***
Harvey Cement Products Inc 708 333-1900
16030 Park Ave Harvey (60426) ***(G-11087)***
Harvey Fuels 708 339-0777
2 E 159th St Harvey (60426) ***(G-11088)***
Harvey Pallets Inc 708 293-1831
2200 138th St Blue Island (60406) ***(G-2125)***
Haskris Co 847 956-6420
100 Kelly St Elk Grove Village (60007) ***(G-9028)***
Hass and Associates, Northbrook *Also called Sport Electronics Inc* ***(G-15485)***
Hassebrock Asphalt Sealing 618 566-7214
111 W Poplar St Mascoutah (62258) ***(G-13598)***

Hastie Min & Trckg Ltd Partnr (PA) 618 289-4536
Hwy 146 Cave In Rock (62919) ***(G-3219)***
Hastie Mining & Trucking 618 285-3600
68 Bohn St Rosiclare (62982) ***(G-18063)***
Hastings Printing 217 253-5086
111 Sale St Tuscola (61953) ***(G-19927)***
Hatcher Associates Inc 773 252-2171
1612 N Throop St Chicago (60642) ***(G-4784)***
Hats For You 773 481-1611
7509 W Belmont Ave Chicago (60634) ***(G-4785)***
Hattan Tool Company 708 597-9308
4909 W 128th Pl Alsip (60803) ***(G-455)***
Hatzer Ready Mix, Streator *Also called Joe Hatzer & Son Inc* ***(G-19612)***
Hatzer Ready Mix, Streator *Also called Joe Hatzer & Son Inc* ***(G-19613)***
Hauhinco LP 618 993-5399
810 Skyline Dr Marion (62959) ***(G-13514)***
Haus Sign Incorporated 708 598-8740
7325 W 90th St Bridgeview (60455) ***(G-2354)***
Hausermann Abrading Process Co 630 543-6688
300 W Laura Dr Addison (60101) ***(G-146)***
Hausermann Controls Co 630 543-6688
1047 W Compton Pt Addison (60101) ***(G-147)***
Hausermann Die & Machine, Addison *Also called Hausermann Controls Co* ***(G-147)***
Hausner Hard - Chrome Inc (PA) 847 439-6010
670 Greenleaf Ave Elk Grove Village (60007) ***(G-9029)***
Haussermann Usa LLC 847 272-9850
425 Huehl Rd Bldg 10 Northbrook (60062) ***(G-15398)***
Haute Diggity Dawgs 773 801-0195
3043 W 5th Ave Chicago (60612) ***(G-4786)***
Haute Noir Magzine, Chicago *Also called Haute Noir Media Group Inc* ***(G-4787)***
Haute Noir Media Group Inc 312 869-4526
220 N Green St Chicago (60607) ***(G-4787)***
Havana Independent Shopper, Lewistown *Also called Independent Shoppers* ***(G-12616)***
Havana Metal Culverts Division, Havana *Also called Metal Culverts Inc* ***(G-11117)***
Havanah Fuel 309 543-2211
520 E Laurel Ave Havana (62644) ***(G-11114)***
Havas Barn 312 640-6800
36 E Grand Ave Chicago (60611) ***(G-4788)***
Haveco Tool & Mfg Inc 847 603-1893
1600 N Milwaukee Ave Lake Villa (60046) ***(G-12354)***
Havi Global Solutions LLC (HQ) 630 493-7400
3500 Lacey Rd Ste 600 Downers Grove (60515) ***(G-8018)***
Having A Good Time 847 330-8460
1710 E Woodfield Rd Schaumburg (60173) ***(G-18543)***
Havoline Xpress Lube LLC 847 221-5724
1402 N Rand Rd Palatine (60074) ***(G-16123)***
Hawk Fastener Services 708 489-2000
12324 S Laramie Ave Alsip (60803) ***(G-456)***
Hawk Molding Inc 224 523-2888
435 Andrea Ct Harvard (60033) ***(G-11056)***
Hawk Technology, Rock Island *Also called JC Automation Inc* ***(G-17226)***
Hawkins Inc 708 258-3797
32040 S Route 45 Peotone (60468) ***(G-16553)***
Hawthorne Press 708 652-9000
5615 W Roosevelt Rd Cicero (60804) ***(G-6852)***
Hawthorne Press Inc 847 587-0582
208 Chateau Dr Spring Grove (60081) ***(G-19275)***
Hayden Mills Inc 618 962-3136
119 Washington Ave Omaha (62871) ***(G-15900)***
Hayes Abrasives Inc 217 532-6850
120 Smith Ln # 120 Hillsboro (62049) ***(G-11313)***
Haymarket Brewing Company LLC 312 638-0700
737 W Randolph St Chicago (60661) ***(G-4789)***
Haymarket Pub & Brewery, Chicago *Also called Haymarket Brewing Company LLC* ***(G-4789)***
Haynes-Bent Inc 630 845-3316
35179 S Old Chicago Rd Wilmington (60481) ***(G-21100)***
Hazen Display Corporation (PA) 815 248-2925
537 Baintree Rd Davis (61019) ***(G-7418)***
HB Fuller Adhesives LLC 815 357-6726
7440 W Dupont Rd Morris (60450) ***(G-14307)***
HB Fuller Cnstr Pdts Inc (HQ) 630 978-7766
1105 S Frontenac St Aurora (60504) ***(G-978)***
HB Plastics, Freeport *Also called Hbp Inc* ***(G-10114)***
HBm Electro Chemical Company 708 895-7710
2800 Bernice Rd Ste 18 Lansing (60438) ***(G-12497)***
Hbm Somat, Champaign *Also called Hottinger Bldwin Msrements Inc* ***(G-3303)***
Hbp Inc 815 235-3000
107 N Henderson Rd Freeport (61032) ***(G-10114)***
HC Duke & Son LLC (HQ) 309 755-4553
2116 8th Ave East Moline (61244) ***(G-8228)***
Hc Materials, Bolingbrook *Also called Ctg Advanced Materials LLC* ***(G-2161)***
Hcc Inc 815 539-9371
1501 1st Ave Mendota (61342) ***(G-13943)***
Hcf Building Corporation 630 595-2040
840 Lively Blvd Wood Dale (60191) ***(G-21196)***
Hci Cabinetry and Design Inc 630 584-0266
305 S Fairbank St Addison (60101) ***(G-148)***
Hcs Hahn Calibration Service 847 567-2500
20575 N William Ave Lincolnshire (60069) ***(G-12769)***

ALPHABETIC

(PA)=Parent Co (HQ)=Headquarters (DH)=Div Headquarters
2020 Harris Illinois
Industrial Directory
1141

Hd Electric Company ... 847 473-4980
4455 Boeing Dr Rockford (61109) *(G-17444)*
Hd Turbo Llc ... 847 636-7586
352 Lively Blvd Elk Grove Village (60007) *(G-9030)*
Headball Inc ... 618 628-2656
41 Acorn Lake Dr Belleville (62221) *(G-1555)*
Headco Industries Inc ... 847 640-6490
109 N Lively Blvd Elk Grove Village (60007) *(G-9031)*
Headco Industries Inc ... 815 729-4016
2104 Oak Leaf St Unit D Joliet (60436) *(G-11875)*
Header Die and Tool Inc ... 815 397-0123
3022 Eastrock Ct Rockford (61109) *(G-17445)*
Headly Manufacturing Co (PA) ... 708 338-0800
2700 23rd St Broadview (60155) *(G-2440)*
Headly Manufacturing Co ... 708 338-0800
2111 Roberts Dr Broadview (60155) *(G-2441)*
Headly Mfg, Broadview *Also called Headly Manufacturing Co (G-2441)*
Headquarters, Chicago *Also called Flexicraft Industries Inc (G-4610)*
Healing Scents ... 815 874-0924
1986 Will James Rd Rockford (61109) *(G-17446)*
Health Administration Press ... 312 424-2800
1 N Franklin St Ste 1600 Chicago (60606) *(G-4790)*
Health King Enterprise Inc ... 312 567-9978
238 W 31st St Ste 1 Chicago (60616) *(G-4791)*
Health O Meter Professional, Countryside *Also called Pelstar LLC (G-7067)*
Healthcare Labels Inc ... 847 382-3993
245 Honey Lake Ct North Barrington (60010) *(G-15284)*
Healthcare Research LLC ... 773 592-3508
744 N Wells St Fl 3 Chicago (60654) *(G-4792)*
Healthdentl LLC ... 800 845-5172
10052 Bode St Ste E Plainfield (60585) *(G-16670)*
Healthful Habits LLC ... 224 489-4256
245 W Roosevelt Rd # 143 West Chicago (60185) *(G-20592)*
Healthleaders Inc ... 312 932-0848
1404 N Cleveland Ave Chicago (60610) *(G-4793)*
Healthlight LLC ... 224 231-0342
920 E State Pkwy Unit B Schaumburg (60173) *(G-18544)*
Healthsmart International, Waukegan *Also called D-M-S Holdings Inc (G-20433)*
Healthware Systems, Elgin *Also called Document Publishing Group (G-8567)*
Healthy Body LLC ... 208 409-6602
2740 Columbus St Ste 300 Ottawa (61350) *(G-16054)*
Healthy Life Nutraceutics Inc ... 201 253-9053
500 Lake Cook Rd Ste 350 Deerfield (60015) *(G-7613)*
Healthy-Txt LLC ... 630 945-1787
950 W Monroe St Unit 813 Chicago (60607) *(G-4794)*
Hearing Aid Warehouse Inc ... 217 431-4700
1005 N Gilbert St Danville (61832) *(G-7343)*
Hearing Screening Assoc LLC ... 855 550-9427
3333 N Kennicott Ave Arlington Heights (60004) *(G-747)*
Hearst Communications Inc ... 309 829-9000
301 W Washington St Bloomington (61701) *(G-2056)*
Hearst Corporation ... 618 463-2500
219 Piasa St Alton (62002) *(G-558)*
Hearst Corporation ... 217 245-6121
235 W State St Jacksonville (62650) *(G-11766)*
Hearst Corporation ... 312 984-5100
333 W Wacker Dr Ste 950 Chicago (60606) *(G-4795)*
Heart & Soul Memories Inc ... 847 478-1931
1938 Sheridan Rd Buffalo Grove (60089) *(G-2544)*
Heart 4 Heart Inc (PA) ... 217 544-2699
2924 N Dirksen Pkwy Springfield (62702) *(G-19379)*
Heart Printing & Form Service, Arlington Heights *Also called Heart Printing Inc (G-748)*
Heart Printing Inc ... 847 259-2100
1624 W Northwest Hwy Arlington Heights (60004) *(G-748)*
Heartfelt Framing Gallery, Kewanee *Also called Heartfelt Gifts Inc (G-12039)*
Heartfelt Gifts Inc ... 309 852-2296
224 N Main St Kewanee (61443) *(G-12039)*
Hearthside, Downers Grove *Also called Clover US Holdings LLC (G-7975)*
Hearthside Food Solutions LLC ... 815 853-4348
775 State Route 251 Wenona (61377) *(G-20526)*
Hearthside Food Solutions LLC (PA) ... 630 967-3600
3500 Lacey Rd Ste 300 Downers Grove (60515) *(G-8019)*
Hearthside USA ... 630 845-9400
1100 Remington Blvd Bolingbrook (60490) *(G-2184)*
Hearthside Usa LLC ... 630 783-1000
10350 Argonne Dr Ste 400 Woodridge (60517) *(G-21310)*
Hearthside Usa LLC (HQ) ... 978 716-2530
3333 Finley Rd Ste 800 Downers Grove (60515) *(G-8020)*
Heartland Bench and Pew, Sandwich *Also called Designed Stairs Inc (G-18367)*
Heartland Candle Co ... 815 698-2200
2739 N 700 East Rd Ashkum (60911) *(G-883)*
Heartland Classics Inc ... 618 783-4444
1705 W Jourdan St Newton (62448) *(G-15084)*
Heartland Coca-Cola Btlg LLC ... 217 544-4891
3495 E Sangamon Ave Springfield (62707) *(G-19380)*
Heartland Coca-Cola Btlg LLC ... 217 223-3336
2620 Ellington Rd Quincy (62305) *(G-16890)*
Heartland Coca-Cola Btlg LLC ... 217 367-1761
2809 N Lincoln Ave Urbana (61802) *(G-19987)*
Heartland Coca-Cola Btlg LLC ... 309 697-8600
5001 S Becker Dr Bartonville (61607) *(G-1332)*
Heartland Coca-Cola Btlg LLC ... 217 348-1001
1321 Loxa Rd Charleston (61920) *(G-3403)*
Heartland Fabrication LLC ... 309 448-2644
210 W Lantz St Congerville (61729) *(G-6999)*
Heartland Hardwoods Inc ... 217 844-3312
20871 N 1600th St Effingham (62401) *(G-8402)*
Heartland Harvest Inc ... 815 932-2100
2401 Eastgate Indus Pkwy Kankakee (60901) *(G-11975)*
Heartland Inspection Company ... 630 788-3607
510 Nathan Lattin Ln Sycamore (60178) *(G-19713)*
Heartland Labels Inc ... 217 826-8324
17135 N Quality Lime Rd Marshall (62441) *(G-13572)*
Heartland Machine and Sup LLC ... 217 543-2678
337 E Sr 133 Arthur (61911) *(G-861)*
Heartland News ... 217 856-2332
3240 E County Road 1550n Humboldt (61931) *(G-11523)*
Heartland Printing, Bloomington *Also called Donald J Leventhal (G-2040)*
Heartland Publications Inc ... 217 529-9506
7900 Olde Carriage Way Springfield (62712) *(G-19381)*
Heat and Control Inc ... 847 381-0290
1027 Ridgeview Dr Inverness (60010) *(G-11601)*
Heat and Control Inc ... 309 342-5518
1721 Us Highway 164 Galesburg (61401) *(G-10200)*
Heat Seal Tooling Corporation ... 815 626-6009
300 Avenue A Rock Falls (61071) *(G-17182)*
Heat Systems Instrs Svc Co LLC ... 630 404-6884
10s115 Clarendon Hills Rd Willowbrook (60527) *(G-21046)*
Heat Transfer Laboratories ... 708 715-4300
2 Mid America Plz Ste 800 Oakbrook Terrace (60181) *(G-15801)*
Heat Treat, Chicago *Also called Axletech International (G-3795)*
Heatcraft Refrigeration Pdts, Danville *Also called Heatcraft Rfrgn Pdts LLC (G-7344)*
Heatcraft Rfrgn Pdts LLC ... 217 446-3710
1001 E Voorhees St Ste B Danville (61832) *(G-7344)*
Heathrow Scientific LLC ... 847 816-5070
620 Lakeview Pkwy Vernon Hills (60061) *(G-20060)*
Heaven Fresh USA Inc ... 800 642-0367
10057 Bode St Plainfield (60585) *(G-16671)*
Heaven Hill Distillery Inc ... 773 564-9791
4418 N Wolcott Ave Chicago (60640) *(G-4796)*
Heavenly Enterprises ... 773 783-2981
8401 S 85th Ct Hickory Hills (60457) *(G-11197)*
Heavy Hitters LLC ... 630 258-2991
304 153rd Pl Calumet City (60409) *(G-2780)*
Heavy Quip Incorporated ... 312 368-7997
55 W Wacker Dr Ste 1120 Chicago (60601) *(G-4797)*
Heckmann Building Products Inc ... 708 865-2403
1501 N 31st Ave Melrose Park (60160) *(G-13879)*
Hedman Orchard and Vineyard ... 618 893-4923
560 Chestnut St Alto Pass (62905) *(G-539)*
Hedricks Welding & Fabrication ... 217 846-3230
201 Main St Foosland (61845) *(G-9705)*
Heffner Designs ... 630 854-2852
2827 Aurora Ave Naperville (60540) *(G-14840)*
Heggerty Phonemic Awareness, Oak Park *Also called Literacy Resources LLC (G-15763)*
Heico Companies LLC ... 847 258-0300
360 W Butterfield Rd Elmhurst (60126) *(G-9370)*
Heico Companies LLC (PA) ... 312 419-8220
70 W Madison St Ste 5600 Chicago (60602) *(G-4798)*
Heico Holding Inc (PA) ... 630 353-5100
27501 Bella Vista Pkwy Warrenville (60555) *(G-20238)*
Heidenhain Corporation (HQ) ... 847 490-1191
333 E State Pkwy Schaumburg (60173) *(G-18545)*
Heidenhain Holding Inc (HQ) ... 716 661-1700
333 E State Pkwy Schaumburg (60173) *(G-18546)*
Heidolph NA LLC ... 224 265-9600
1235 N Mittel Blvd B Wood Dale (60191) *(G-21197)*
Heidolph North America, Wood Dale *Also called Heidolph NA LLC (G-21197)*
Heidtman Steel Products Inc ... 618 451-0052
10 Northgate Indus Dr Granite City (62040) *(G-10714)*
Heil Sound Ltd ... 618 257-3000
5800 N Illinois St Fairview Heights (62208) *(G-9646)*
Heiman Sign Studio ... 815 397-6909
6909 Canter Ct Rockford (61108) *(G-17447)*
Heinkels Packing Company Inc ... 217 428-4401
2005 N 22nd St Decatur (62526) *(G-7501)*
Heise Industries Inc ... 847 223-2410
123 Hawley St Grayslake (60030) *(G-10781)*
Heiss Welding Inc ... 815 434-1838
260 W Marquette St Ottawa (61350) *(G-16055)*
Helander Metal Spinning Co ... 630 268-9292
931 N Ridge Ave Lombard (60148) *(G-13084)*
Helena Agri-Enterprises LLC ... 217 234-2726
3559 E County Road 1000n Mattoon (61938) *(G-13636)*
Helena Agri-Enterprises LLC ... 217 382-4241
9666 E Angling Rd Martinsville (62442) *(G-13585)*
Helfter Enterprises Inc ... 309 522-5505
301 Main St Osco (61274) *(G-15988)*

Heligear Acquisition Co (PA)....708 728-2000
6006 W 73rd St Bedford Park (60638) ***(G-1471)***
Helio Precision Products Inc....585 697-5434
601 N Skokie Hwy Ste A Lake Bluff (60044) ***(G-12186)***
Helio Precision Products Inc (PA)....847 473-1300
601 N Skokie Hwy Ste B Lake Bluff (60044) ***(G-12187)***
Helitune Inc....847 228-0985
190 Gordon St Elk Grove Village (60007) ***(G-9032)***
Helivalues....847 487-8258
1001 N Old Rand Rd # 101 Wauconda (60084) ***(G-20355)***
Helix International Inc (PA)....847 709-0666
900 Hollywood Ave Itasca (60143) ***(G-11663)***
Helix International Mch Div, Itasca *Also called Helix International Inc* ***(G-11663)***
Helix Re Inc....415 254-2724
515 N State St Fl 15 Chicago (60654) ***(G-4799)***
Hella Corporate Center USA Inc....734 414-0900
50 Industrial Park Flora (62839) ***(G-9682)***
Hella Corporate Center USA Inc....618 662-4402
1101 Vincennes Ave Flora (62839) ***(G-9683)***
Hella Electronics, Flora *Also called Hella Corporate Center USA Inc* ***(G-9682)***
Hella Electronics Corporation....618 662-5186
1101 Vincennes Ave Flora (62839) ***(G-9684)***
Hello Delicious Brands LLC....844 845-4544
707 Skokie Blvd Ste 580 Northbrook (60062) ***(G-15399)***
Helm Tool Company Incorporated....847 952-9528
1290 Brummel Ave Elk Grove Village (60007) ***(G-9033)***
Helmuth Custom Kitchens LLC....217 543-3588
2004 Cr 1800e Arthur (61911) ***(G-862)***
Help/Systems LLC....847 605-1311
1920 Thoreau Dr N Ste 165 Schaumburg (60173) ***(G-18547)***
Hemingway Chimney Inc....708 333-0355
16940 Vincennes Ave South Holland (60473) ***(G-19219)***
Hemmerle Jr Irvin....630 334-4392
1526 Treeline Ct Naperville (60565) ***(G-14841)***
Hempel Group Inc....630 389-2222
934 Paramount Pkwy Batavia (60510) ***(G-1383)***
Henderson Co Inc....773 628-7216
6020 N Keating Ave Chicago (60646) ***(G-4800)***
Henderson County Quill, Stronghurst *Also called Henderson Hancock Quill Inc* ***(G-19634)***
Henderson Engineering Co Inc (PA)....815 786-9471
95 N Main St Sandwich (60548) ***(G-18374)***
Henderson Family....309 236-6783
208 N College Ave Aledo (61231) ***(G-357)***
Henderson Hancock Quill Inc....309 924-1871
102 N Broadway St Stronghurst (61480) ***(G-19634)***
Henderson Products Inc....847 836-4996
124 Industrial Dr Gilberts (60136) ***(G-10357)***
Henderson Products Inc....847 515-3482
11921 Smith Dr Huntley (60142) ***(G-11539)***
Henderson Truck Equipment, Gilberts *Also called Henderson Products Inc* ***(G-10357)***
Henderson Water District....618 498-6418
1004 State Highway 16 Jerseyville (62052) ***(G-11793)***
Hendrick Manufacturing....847 608-2047
1320 Gateway Dr Elgin (60124) ***(G-8611)***
Hendrick Metal Products LLC....847 742-7002
1320 Gateway Dr Elgin (60124) ***(G-8612)***
Hendrickson, Woodridge *Also called Boler Company* ***(G-21279)***
Hendrickson Bumper and Trim, Joliet *Also called Hendrickson Usa LLC* ***(G-11877)***
Hendrickson Holdings LLC....630 910-2800
500 Park Blvd Ste 1010 Itasca (60143) ***(G-11664)***
Hendrickson International Corp....815 727-4031
501 Caton Farm Rd Joliet (60434) ***(G-11876)***
Hendrickson International Corp (HQ)....630 874-9700
840 S Frontage Rd Woodridge (60517) ***(G-21311)***
Hendrickson Truck Suspension, Woodridge *Also called Hendrickson Usa LLC* ***(G-21313)***
Hendrickson Usa LLC....630 910-2800
800 S Frontage Rd Woodridge (60517) ***(G-21312)***
Hendrickson Usa LLC (HQ)....630 874-9700
500 Park Blvd Ste 450 Itasca (60143) ***(G-11665)***
Hendrickson Usa LLC (HQ)....630 910-2844
800 S Frontage Rd Woodridge (60517) ***(G-21313)***
Hendrickson Usa LLC....815 727-4031
501 Caton Farm Rd Joliet (60435) ***(G-11877)***
Hendrix Industrial Gastrux Inc....847 526-1700
327 Rye Rd Mundelein (60060) ***(G-14696)***
Henes Usa Inc....312 448-6130
125 Milwaukee Ave Ste 301 Glenview (60025) ***(G-10556)***
Heng Tuo Usa Inc (PA)....630 317-7672
1 Transam Plaza Dr # 545 Oakbrook Terrace (60181) ***(G-15802)***
Henkel Consumer Goods Inc....630 892-4381
2000 Aucutt Rd Montgomery (60538) ***(G-14246)***
Henkel Consumer Goods Inc....847 426-4552
1122 N Clark St Apt 2007 Chicago (60610) ***(G-4801)***
Henkel Technology Corporation (PA)....708 924-9582
6050 W 51st St Chicago (60638) ***(G-4802)***
Henkel US Operations Corp....847 468-9200
1345 Gasket Dr Elgin (60120) ***(G-8613)***
Henkelman Inc....331 979-2013
493 W Fullerton Ave Elmhurst (60126) ***(G-9371)***
Hennessy Sheet Metal....708 754-6342
3256 Butler St S Chicago Hts (60411) ***(G-18121)***
Hennig Gasket & Seals Inc....312 243-8270
2350 W Cullerton St Chicago (60608) ***(G-4803)***
Hennig Inc (HQ)....815 636-9900
9900 N Alpine Rd Machesney Park (61115) ***(G-13347)***
Henning Machine & Die Works....217 286-3393
4 N Main St Henning (61848) ***(G-11161)***
Henry J'S Famous Foods, Chicago *Also called Bar-B-Que Industries Inc* ***(G-3829)***
Henry News Republican....309 364-3250
709 3rd St Henry (61537) ***(G-11166)***
Henry Pratt Company LLC (HQ)....630 844-4000
401 S Highland Ave Aurora (60506) ***(G-1108)***
Henry Pratt Company LLC....620 208-8100
500 W Eldorado St Decatur (62522) ***(G-7502)***
Henry Printing Inc....618 529-3040
975 Charles Rd Carbondale (62901) ***(G-2845)***
Henry Tech Inc Intl Sls Co, Chatham *Also called Henry Technologies Inc* ***(G-3421)***
Henry Technologies Inc (HQ)....217 483-2406
701 S Main St Chatham (62629) ***(G-3421)***
Henry Technologies Inc....217 483-2406
701 S Main St Chatham (62629) ***(G-3422)***
Henry-Lee & Company LLC....312 242-2501
909 Rollingwood Rd Highland Park (60035) ***(G-11270)***
Hensaal Management Group Inc....312 624-8133
4632 W Monroe St Chicago (60644) ***(G-4804)***
Hentzen Coatings Inc....414 353-4200
1500 Lathem St Batavia (60510) ***(G-1384)***
Hepalink USA Inc (PA)....630 206-1788
233 S Wacker Dr Ste 9300 Chicago (60606) ***(G-4805)***
Hera Cnsltng Interntnl Opratn....630 515-8819
4307 Westerhoff Dr Lisle (60532) ***(G-12897)***
Herald & Review, Decatur *Also called Lee Enterprises Incorporated* ***(G-7515)***
Herald Mount Olive....217 999-3941
102 E Main St Mount Olive (62069) ***(G-14504)***
Herald Newspapers Inc....773 643-8533
1525 E 53rd St Ste 920 Chicago (60615) ***(G-4806)***
Herald Publications (PA)....618 566-8282
314 E Church St Ste 1 Mascoutah (62258) ***(G-13599)***
Herald Whig Quincy....217 222-7600
130 N 5th St Quincy (62301) ***(G-16891)***
Herbs Bakery Inc....847 741-0249
1020 Larkin Ave Elgin (60123) ***(G-8614)***
Herbs License Service, Collinsville *Also called Precision Service* ***(G-6972)***
Hercl Signs & Service Inc....847 471-4015
23 Barcroft Ct South Elgin (60177) ***(G-19151)***
Hercules Industrial Division, Addison *Also called Suez Wts Usa Inc* ***(G-297)***
Here Holdings LLC (PA)....563 723-1008
238 Tubeway Dr Carol Stream (60188) ***(G-2997)***
Herff Jones LLC....217 268-4543
901 Bob King Dr Arcola (61910) ***(G-651)***
Herff Jones LLC....815 756-4743
901 N 1st St Ste 7 Dekalb (60115) ***(G-7684)***
Herff Jones LLC....773 463-1144
3333 N Elston Ave Chicago (60618) ***(G-4807)***
Herff Jones LLC....217 351-9500
1000 N Market St Champaign (61820) ***(G-3300)***
Herff Jones LLC....708 425-0130
6305 W 95th St Ste 1w Oak Lawn (60453) ***(G-15719)***
Herff Jones LLC....317 612-3705
125 Fencl Ln Hillside (60162) ***(G-11341)***
Heritage Custom Trailers, Benton *Also called Knight Bros Inc* ***(G-1930)***
Heritage Media Svcs Co of Ill....708 594-9340
7676 W 63rd St Summit Argo (60501) ***(G-19679)***
Heritage Mold Incorporated....815 397-1117
3170 Forest View Rd Rockford (61109) ***(G-17448)***
Heritage Moulding Inc....630 961-0001
10233 Clow Creek Rd Plainfield (60585) ***(G-16672)***
Heritage Packaging LLC....217 735-4406
2350 5th St Lincoln (62656) ***(G-12730)***
Heritage Press Inc....847 362-9699
312 Peterson Rd Libertyville (60048) ***(G-12657)***
Heritage Printing (PA)....815 537-2372
219 Washington St Prophetstown (61277) ***(G-16832)***
Heritage Products Corporation....847 419-8835
1398 Busch Pkwy Buffalo Grove (60089) ***(G-2545)***
Heritage Sheet Metal Inc....847 724-8449
2049 Johns Dr Glenview (60025) ***(G-10557)***
Heritage Signs Ltd....847 549-1942
1840 Industrial Dr # 240 Libertyville (60048) ***(G-12658)***
Heritage Structures Inc....618 895-8028
6267 County Road 400 N Mc Leansboro (62859) ***(G-13706)***
Herman Bade & Sons....217 832-9444
608 N Henson Rd Villa Grove (61956) ***(G-20123)***
Herman L Loeb LLC....618 943-2227
600 Country Club Rd Lawrenceville (62439) ***(G-12535)***
Herman Seekamp Inc....630 628-6555
1120 W Fullerton Ave Addison (60101) ***(G-149)***
Herman's World of Embroidery, Rock Island *Also called Hermans Inc* ***(G-17222)***

ALPHABETIC

Hermanitas Cupcakes ... 708 620-9396
1067 Stewart Ave Calumet City (60409) ***(G-2781)***

Hermann Gene Signs & Service ... 618 244-3681
12436 E Lakewood Dr Mount Vernon (62864) ***(G-14613)***

Hermans Inc ... 309 206-4892
2820 46th Ave Rock Island (61201) ***(G-17222)***

Hermitage Group Inc ... 773 561-3773
5151 N Ravenswood Ave Chicago (60640) ***(G-4808)***

Herner-Geissler Wdwkg Corp ... 312 226-3400
400 N Hermitage Ave Chicago (60622) ***(G-4809)***

Heron Bay Inc ... 309 661-1300
1605 General Elc Rd Ste 1 Bloomington (61704) ***(G-2057)***

Herr Display Vans Inc ... 708 755-7926
22401 Joshua Dr Sauk Village (60411) ***(G-18400)***

Herrin News Litho, Herrin *Also called French Studio Ltd* ***(G-11171)***

Herris Group LLC ... 630 908-7393
10410 163rd Pl Orland Park (60467) ***(G-15959)***

Herrmann Signs & Service ... 618 246-6537
12436 E Lakewood Dr Mount Vernon (62864) ***(G-14614)***

Herrmann Ultrasonics Inc ... 630 626-1626
1261 Hardt Cir Bartlett (60103) ***(G-1285)***

Herschberger Window Inc ... 217 543-2106
623 N County Road 250 E Tuscola (61953) ***(G-19928)***

Herschberger Wood Working ... 217 543-4075
145 E Cr 300 N Arthur (61911) ***(G-863)***

Hershey Company ... 800 468-1714
1751 Lake Cook Rd Deerfield (60015) ***(G-7614)***

Hershey Company ... 618 544-3111
1401 W Main St Robinson (62454) ***(G-17116)***

Hershey Creamery Company ... 708 339-4656
601 W 167th St South Holland (60473) ***(G-19220)***

Hersheys Metal Meister, Claremont *Also called Hersheys Metal Meister LLC* ***(G-6898)***

Hersheys Metal Meister LLC ... 217 234-4700
7405 E Mount Pleasant Ln Claremont (62421) ***(G-6898)***

Hertz Corporation ... 630 897-0956
1375 Bohr Ave Montgomery (60538) ***(G-14247)***

Hertzberg Ernst & Sons ... 773 525-3518
1751 W Belmont Ave Chicago (60657) ***(G-4810)***

Hess Machine Inc ... 618 887-4444
10724 Pocahontas Rd Marine (62061) ***(G-13498)***

Hester Cabinets & Millwork ... 815 634-4555
655 S Marguerite St Coal City (60416) ***(G-6933)***

Heuft Usa Inc ... 630 395-9521
2820 Thatcher Rd Downers Grove (60515) ***(G-8021)***

Hevco Industries ... 708 344-1342
1500 Dearborn Ave Ste 10 Aurora (60505) ***(G-1109)***

Hexacomb Corporation (HQ) ... 847 955-7984
1296 Barclay Blvd Buffalo Grove (60089) ***(G-2546)***

Hexagon Marketing, Chicago *Also called Hexagon Metrology Inc* ***(G-4811)***

Hexagon Metrology Inc ... 312 624-8786
455 N Ctyfrnt Plz Dr # 3030 Chicago (60611) ***(G-4811)***

Hexagon Metrology Inc ... 847 469-3344
755 Tollgate Rd Elgin (60123) ***(G-8615)***

Hexion Inc ... 708 728-8834
8600 W 71st St Bedford Park (60501) ***(G-1472)***

Hfa Inc ... 847 520-1000
135 E Hintz Rd Wheeling (60090) ***(G-20908)***

Hfd Graphics Equipment, Waukegan *Also called Hfd Manufacturing Inc* ***(G-20446)***

Hfd Manufacturing Inc ... 847 263-5050
1813 W Glen Flora Ave Waukegan (60085) ***(G-20446)***

Hfo Chicago LLC ... 847 258-2850
555 Busse Rd Elk Grove Village (60007) ***(G-9034)***

Hfr Precision Machining Inc ... 630 556-4325
1015 Airpark Dr Sugar Grove (60554) ***(G-19646)***

Hg-Farley Holdings LLC (PA) ... 815 874-1400
6833 Stalter Dr Rockford (61108) ***(G-17449)***

Hg-Farley Laserlab USA Inc ... 815 874-1400
4635 Colt Rd Rockford (61109) ***(G-17450)***

Hgh Products, Godfrey *Also called David L Knoche* ***(G-10651)***

HH Backer Associates Inc ... 312 578-1818
18 S Michigan Ave # 1100 Chicago (60603) ***(G-4812)***

HI India ... 773 552-6083
2544 W Devon Ave Chicago (60659) ***(G-4813)***

HI Prcision TI Makers McHy Inc ... 630 694-0200
774 Foster Ave Bensenville (60106) ***(G-1818)***

HI Tech ... 708 957-4210
1551 187th St Homewood (60430) ***(G-11496)***

HI Tech Colorants ... 630 762-0368
5n634 Lostview Ln Saint Charles (60175) ***(G-18206)***

HI Tech Machining & Welding ... 708 331-3608
16120 Vincennes Ave South Holland (60473) ***(G-19221)***

HI Tek Tool & Machining Inc ... 847 836-6422
2413 W Algonquin Rd Algonquin (60102) ***(G-373)***

Hi-Cone Div, Itasca *Also called Illinois Tool Works Inc* ***(G-11673)***

Hi-Def Communications ... 217 258-6679
3116 Pine Ave Mattoon (61938) ***(G-13637)***

Hi-Grade Egg Producers, Loda *Also called Midwest Poultry Services LP* ***(G-13030)***

Hi-Grade Welding & Mfg, Schaumburg *Also called Hi-Grade Welding and Mfg LLC* ***(G-18548)***

Hi-Grade Welding and Mfg LLC ... 847 640-8172
140 Commerce Dr Schaumburg (60173) ***(G-18548)***

Hi-Perfrmnce Fastening Systems, Bensenville *Also called Matthew Warren Inc* ***(G-1848)***

Hi-Tech Manufacturing LLC ... 847 678-1616
9815 Leland Ave Schiller Park (60176) ***(G-18812)***

Hi-Tech Polymers Inc ... 815 282-2272
7967 Crest Hills Dr Loves Park (61111) ***(G-13216)***

Hi-Tech Welding Services Inc ... 630 595-8160
233 William St Bensenville (60106) ***(G-1819)***

Hiatt Brothers, De Kalb *Also called E B Inc* ***(G-7429)***

Hickman Williams & Company ... 630 574-2150
7800 W College Dr Ste 1e Palos Heights (60463) ***(G-16188)***

Hickory Street Cabinets ... 618 667-9676
208 S Hickory St Troy (62294) ***(G-19915)***

Hidalgo Fine Cabinetry ... 630 753-9323
8952 Hanslik Ct Ste 22 Naperville (60564) ***(G-14972)***

Hidden Hollow Stables Inc ... 309 243-7979
9222 Brimfield Jubilee Rd Dunlap (61525) ***(G-8133)***

Hidden Lake Winery Ltd ... 618 228-9111
10580 Wellen Rd Aviston (62216) ***(G-1179)***

Hidrostal LLC ... 630 240-6271
2225 White Oak Cir Aurora (60502) ***(G-979)***

Hidrostal Pumps, Aurora *Also called Hidrostal LLC* ***(G-979)***

HIG Chemicals Holdings ... 773 376-9000
4650 S Racine Ave Chicago (60609) ***(G-4814)***

Higgins Bros Inc ... 773 523-0124
1428 W 37th St Chicago (60609) ***(G-4815)***

Higgins Forms & Systems, Des Plaines *Also called Higgins Quick Print* ***(G-7776)***

Higgins Glass Studio LLC ... 708 447-2787
33 E Quincy St Ste A Riverside (60546) ***(G-17084)***

Higgins Handcrafted Glass, Riverside *Also called Higgins Glass Studio LLC* ***(G-17084)***

Higgins Quick Print ... 847 635-7700
2410 S River Rd Des Plaines (60018) ***(G-7776)***

Higgs Welding LLC ... 217 925-5999
101 Zumbahlen Ave Dieterich (62424) ***(G-7876)***

High Impact Fabricating LLC ... 708 235-8912
1149 Central Ave University Park (60484) ***(G-19956)***

High Performance Entp Inc ... 773 283-1778
3500 N Kostner Ave Chicago (60641) ***(G-4816)***

High Performance Lubr LLC ... 815 468-3535
500 S Spruce St Manteno (60950) ***(G-13449)***

High Performance Packaging, Island Lake *Also called Competitive Edge Opportunities* ***(G-11605)***

High Performance Uniforms, Chicago *Also called High Performance Entp Inc* ***(G-4816)***

High Point Recovery Company ... 217 821-7777
603 County Road 500 E Toledo (62468) ***(G-19876)***

High Pointe Publishing, O Fallon *Also called Highpoint Publishing Inc* ***(G-15573)***

High Power Inc ... 773 581-7650
8457 S Pulaski Rd Chicago (60652) ***(G-4817)***

High Rise Specialty Products ... 708 343-9265
912 N Maywood Dr Maywood (60153) ***(G-13669)***

High Speed Welding Inc ... 630 971-8929
728 Vandustrial Dr Ste 5 Westmont (60559) ***(G-20747)***

High Tech Research Inc (PA) ... 847 215-9797
1020 Milwaukee Ave # 330 Deerfield (60015) ***(G-7615)***

High-5 Printwear Inc ... 847 818-0081
3311 N Ridge Ave Arlington Heights (60004) ***(G-749)***

High-Life Products Inc ... 847 991-9449
615 W Colfax St Palatine (60067) ***(G-16124)***

Highland Baking Company Inc ... 847 677-2789
2301 Shermer Rd Northbrook (60062) ***(G-15400)***

Highland Journal Printing Inc (PA) ... 618 654-4131
1014 Laurel St Highland (62249) ***(G-11217)***

Highland Mch & Screw Pdts Co ... 618 654-2103
700 5th St Highland (62249) ***(G-11218)***

Highland Metal Inc ... 708 544-6641
541 Hyde Park Ave Hillside (60162) ***(G-11342)***

Highland Mfg & Sls Co (PA) ... 618 654-2161
1111 6th St Highland (62249) ***(G-11219)***

Highland News Leader ... 618 654-2366
1 Woodcrest Prof Park Highland (62249) ***(G-11220)***

Highland Park Mechanical Inc ... 847 269-3863
3204 16th St Zion (60099) ***(G-21517)***

Highland Printers ... 618 654-5880
1005 Broadway Ste A Highland (62249) ***(G-11221)***

Highland Southern Wire Inc (PA) ... 618 654-2161
1111 6th St Highland (62249) ***(G-11222)***

Highland Spring & Specialty ... 618 654-3831
150 Matter Dr Highland (62249) ***(G-11223)***

Highland Supply, Highland *Also called Highland Mfg & Sls Co* ***(G-11219)***

Highland Supply, Highland *Also called Highland Southern Wire Inc* ***(G-11222)***

Highland Supply Corporation (PA) ... 618 654-2161
1111 6th St Highland (62249) ***(G-11224)***

Highland Wire Inc (PA) ... 618 654-2161
1111 6th St Highland (62249) ***(G-11225)***

Highlandnews Leader, Highland *Also called McClatchy Newspapers Inc* ***(G-11231)***

Highlight of Chicago Bress ... 773 944-0085
912 W Sunnyside Ave 1e Chicago (60640) ***(G-4818)***

Highpoint Publishing Inc 928 717-0100
305 Orange Jewel Ct O Fallon (62269) **(G-15573)**
Higman LLC 618 785-2545
609 W Myrtle St Baldwin (62217) **(G-1185)**
Hilander 00805, Rockford *Also called Kroger Co* **(G-17485)**
Hill Design, McHenry *Also called Accurate Spring Tech Inc* **(G-13713)**
Hill Design Products Inc 815 344-3333
5801 W Hill St McHenry (60050) **(G-13748)**
Hill Engineering Inc 630 315-5070
373 Randy Rd Carol Stream (60188) **(G-2998)**
Hill Holdings Inc 815 625-6600
2700 E Hill Dr Rock Falls (61071) **(G-17183)**
Hill Printing and Office Sup, Marion *Also called Sigley Printing & Off Sup Co* **(G-13535)**
Hill Reporter LLC 309 532-4794
404 W 4th St El Paso (61738) **(G-8438)**
Hill Top Pallet 618 426-9810
612 Bollman Rd Ava (62907) **(G-1172)**
Hill-Rom Holdings Inc (PA) 312 819-7200
130 E Randolph St # 1000 Chicago (60601) **(G-4819)**
Hillers Sheet Metal Works 217 532-2595
150 N Oak St Hillsboro (62049) **(G-11314)**
Hills Electric Motor Service 815 625-0305
305 1st Ave Rock Falls (61071) **(G-17184)**
Hillsboro Energy LLC 217 532-7310
925 S Main St Ste 2 Hillsboro (62049) **(G-11315)**
Hillsboro Journal Inc 217 532-3933
431 S Main St Hillsboro (62049) **(G-11316)**
Hillshire Brands Company (HQ) 312 614-6000
400 S Jefferson St Fl 1 Chicago (60607) **(G-4820)**
Hillshire Brands Company 312 614-6000
400 S Jefferson St Fl 1 Chicago (60607) **(G-4821)**
Hillshire Brands Company 800 727-2533
600 Wiscold Dr Rochelle (61068) **(G-17144)**
Hillshire Brands Company 888 317-5867
400 S Jefferson St Fl 1 Chicago (60607) **(G-4822)**
Hillshire Brands Company 847 956-7575
1325 Chase Ave Elk Grove Village (60007) **(G-9035)**
Hillshire Brands Company 312 614-6000
3500 Lacey Rd Downers Grove (60515) **(G-8022)**
Hillshire Brands Company 847 310-9400
1355 Remington Rd Ste U Schaumburg (60173) **(G-18549)**
Hillshire Brands Company 630 991-5100
3131 Woodcreek Dr Downers Grove (60515) **(G-8023)**
Hilltop Group Home, Dixon *Also called Kreider Services Incorporated* **(G-7903)**
Hillyer Inc 309 837-6434
1420 E Carroll St Macomb (61455) **(G-13392)**
Hillyer's U-Store-It, Macomb *Also called Hillyer Inc* **(G-13392)**
Hilscher North America Inc 630 505-5301
2525 Cabot Dr Ste 200 Lisle (60532) **(G-12898)**
Hilti Inc 847 364-9818
135 W Diversey Ave Elmhurst (60126) **(G-9372)**
Hinckley & Schmitt Inc 773 586-8600
6055 S Harlem Ave Chicago (60638) **(G-4823)**
Hinckley Concrete Products Co 815 286-3235
540 W Lincoln Ave Hinckley (60520) **(G-11358)**
Hinckley Spring, Rockford *Also called Ds Services of America Inc* **(G-17386)**
Hinckley Springs, Chicago *Also called Hinckley & Schmitt Inc* **(G-4823)**
Hinckley Springs, Chicago *Also called Ds Services of America Inc* **(G-4399)**
Hinckley Springs, Frankfort *Also called Ds Services of America Inc* **(G-9787)**
Hinetics LLC 217 239-1628
1804 Vale St Champaign (61822) **(G-3301)**
Hipro Manufacturing Inc 815 432-5271
1909 E 1800 N Rd Watseka (60970) **(G-20306)**
Hipskind Tech Sltons Group Inc 630 920-0960
17w220 22nd St Ste 450 Oakbrook Terrace (60181) **(G-15803)**
Hire-Nelson Company Inc 630 543-9400
325 W Factory Rd Ste B Addison (60101) **(G-150)**
Hirise Promotions & Marketing, Chicago *Also called Information Usa Inc* **(G-4919)**
Hirose Electric (usa) Inc (HQ) 630 282-6700
2300 Warrenville Rd # 150 Downers Grove (60515) **(G-8024)**
Historcal Genealogical Soc Mou, Sullivan *Also called Moultri Cnty Hstrcl/Gnlgcl Sct* **(G-19672)**
Historic Timber & Plank Inc 618 372-4546
16092 Lageman Ln Brighton (62012) **(G-2401)**
Hiwood USA, Lake Zurich *Also called Seshin USA Inc* **(G-12456)**
HK America Inc 630 916-0200
1296 Humbracht Cir Bartlett (60103) **(G-1286)**
HK Laser and Systems 630 916-0200
1296 Humbracht Cir Bartlett (60103) **(G-1287)**
HK Paper (usa) Inc (PA) 847 969-9600
943 N Plum Grove Rd Ste A Schaumburg (60173) **(G-18550)**
HK Woodwork 773 964-2468
925 Seton Ct Ste 7 Wheeling (60090) **(G-20909)**
Hl Metals LLC 312 590-3360
910 Spruce St Winnetka (60093) **(G-21130)**
Hl Precision Manufacturing LLC 217 398-6881
2110 Round Barn Rd Champaign (61821) **(G-3302)**

HM Manufacturing Inc 847 487-8700
1200 Henri Dr Wauconda (60084) **(G-20356)**
HM Witt & Co 773 250-5000
3313 W Newport Ave Chicago (60618) **(G-4824)**
HMC, Sugar Grove *Also called Hy-Tek Manufacturing Co Inc* **(G-19647)**
HMC Holdings LLC (PA) 800 874-6625
720 Dartmouth Ln Buffalo Grove (60089) **(G-2547)**
Hmg, Bolingbrook *Also called 7000 Inc* **(G-2143)**
Hmh, Itasca *Also called Houghton Mifflin Harcourt Co* **(G-11666)**
Hmh, Geneva *Also called Houghton Mifflin Harcourt Co* **(G-10276)**
Hmh, Evanston *Also called Houghton Mifflin Harcourt Co* **(G-9533)**
Hmh Sports LLC 773 330-3789
2727 Eastwood Ave Evanston (60201) **(G-9532)**
Hml Elevators Inc 757 822-8285
70 W Madison St Ste 5750 Chicago (60602) **(G-4825)**
HMM Pallets Inc 773 927-3448
20500 Stoney Island Ave Chicago Heights (60411) **(G-6749)**
Hmt Manufacturing Inc 847 473-2310
2323 Commonwealth Ave North Chicago (60064) **(G-15314)**
Hn Precision, Lake Bluff *Also called Helio Precision Products Inc* **(G-12186)**
Hn Precision, Lake Bluff *Also called Helio Precision Products Inc* **(G-12187)**
Hn Precision-Ny, Lake Bluff *Also called Nationwide Precision Pdts Corp* **(G-12197)**
Hnrc Dissolution Co 618 758-4501
12626 Sarah Rd Coulterville (62237) **(G-7032)**
Ho Brothers LLC 312 854-3008
5 S Wabash Ave Ste 1503 Chicago (60603) **(G-4826)**
Ho-Ka Turkey Farm, Waterman *Also called Kauffman Poultry Farms Inc* **(G-20298)**
Hobsource 847 229-9120
834 E Rand Rd Ste 2 Mount Prospect (60056) **(G-14533)**
Hocking Oil Company Inc 618 263-3258
123 W 4th St Ste 103 Mount Carmel (62863) **(G-14472)**
Hoeing Die & Mold Engraving 630 543-0006
441 W Interstate Rd Addison (60101) **(G-151)**
Hoerbiger-Origa Corporation 800 283-1377
100 W Lake Dr Glendale Heights (60139) **(G-10456)**
Hoerr Racing Products, Edwards *Also called R/A Hoerr Inc* **(G-8340)**
Hoffer Plastics Corporation 847 741-5740
500 N Collins St South Elgin (60177) **(G-19152)**
Hoffman Air & Filtration, Quincy *Also called Gardner Denver Inc* **(G-16883)**
Hoffman Burial Supplies Inc 708 233-1567
7501 W 99th Pl Bridgeview (60455) **(G-2355)**
Hoffman J&M Farm Holdings Inc 847 671-6280
3999 25th Ave Schiller Park (60176) **(G-18813)**
Hoffman Nuclear Medicine Group, Hoffman Estates *Also called Siemens Med Solutions USA Inc* **(G-11458)**
Hoffman Tool Inc 815 692-4643
1301 W Oak St Fairbury (61739) **(G-9608)**
Hofhaus, Chicago *Also called John Hofmeister & Son Inc* **(G-5041)**
Hofmeister Welding Inc 217 407-4091
402 N Wall St Griggsville (62340) **(G-10849)**
Hogan Woodwork Inc 708 354-4525
5328 East Ave Countryside (60525) **(G-7056)**
Hogback Hardwoods, Orangeville *Also called Hogback Haven Maple Farm* **(G-15909)**
Hogback Haven Maple Farm 815 291-9440
13800 N Hogback Rd Orangeville (61060) **(G-15909)**
Hogg Hollow Winery LLC 618 695-9463
48 E Glendale Rd Golconda (62938) **(G-10665)**
Hogg Welding Inc 708 339-0033
16201 Clinton St Harvey (60426) **(G-11089)**
Hohlfider A H Shtmtl Htg Coolg 815 965-9134
2911 Prairie Rd Rockford (61102) **(G-17451)**
Hohmann & Barnard Illinois LLC 773 586-6700
9999 Virginia Ave Chicago Ridge (60415) **(G-6798)**
Hohmann & Barnard Inc 773 586-6700
9999 Virginia Ave Chicago Ridge (60415) **(G-6799)**
Holcim (us) Inc (HQ) 773 372-1000
8700 W Bryn Mawr Ave Chicago (60631) **(G-4827)**
Holcim Participations US Inc (HQ) 773 372-1000
8700 W Bryn Mawr Ave Chicago (60631) **(G-4828)**
Holcim USA, Chicago *Also called Holcim (us) Inc* **(G-4827)**
Holcomb Hollow 847 837-9123
580 Woodcrest Dr Mundelein (60060) **(G-14697)**
Holden America II LLC 708 552-4070
6235 S Oak Park Ave Chicago (60638) **(G-4829)**
Holden Industries Inc (PA) 847 940-1500
500 Lake Cook Rd Ste 400 Deerfield (60015) **(G-7616)**
Holder Publishing Corporation 309 828-7533
25 Monarch Dr Bloomington (61704) **(G-2058)**
Holdings Liquidation Inc 312 541-9300
760 S Wolf Rd Wheeling (60090) **(G-20910)**
Hole In The Wall Screen Arts 217 243-9100
112 Park St Jacksonville (62650) **(G-11767)**
Holey Cards, Chicago *Also called Avondale Adventures* **(G-3789)**
Holiday Bright Lights Inc (PA) 312 226-8281
954 W Wa Blvd Ste 705 Chicago (60607) **(G-4830)**
Holiday Gift Check Program, Downers Grove *Also called Gift Check Program 2013 Inc* **(G-8011)**

ALPHABETIC

Holidynamics, Chicago *Also called Holiday Bright Lights Inc* ***(G-4830)***
Holland LP (HQ) 708 672-2300
1000 Holland Dr Crete (60417) ***(G-7140)***
Holland Applied Technologies (HQ) 630 325-5130
7050 High Grove Blvd Burr Ridge (60527) ***(G-2683)***
Holland Company, Crete *Also called Holland LP* ***(G-7140)***
Holland Design Group Inc 847 526-8848
1090 Brown St Wauconda (60084) ***(G-20357)***
Holland Laboratories, Peoria *Also called Holland Specialty Co* ***(G-16453)***
Holland Manufacturing Corp 708 849-1000
13901 Indiana Ave Dolton (60419) ***(G-7937)***
Holland Printing Inc 708 596-9000
922 E 162nd St South Holland (60473) ***(G-19222)***
Holland Safety Equipment Inc 847 680-9930
726 Mckinley Ave Libertyville (60048) ***(G-12659)***
Holland Specialty Co 309 697-9262
4611 W Middle Rd Peoria (61605) ***(G-16453)***
Hollingsworth & Vose Company 847 222-9228
4256 N Arlington Hts Rd Arlington Heights (60004) ***(G-750)***
Hollingworth Candies Inc 815 838-2275
926 N State St Lockport (60441) ***(G-13000)***
Hollister Incorporated (PA) 847 680-1000
2000 Hollister Dr Libertyville (60048) ***(G-12660)***
Hollister-Whitney Elev Co LLC 217 222-0466
2603 N 24th St Quincy (62305) ***(G-16892)***
Holly Press, The, Grayslake *Also called Dandelion Distributors Inc* ***(G-10766)***
Hollymatic Corporation 708 579-3700
600 E Plainfield Rd Countryside (60525) ***(G-7057)***
Hollywood Traders LLC 630 943-6461
1154 E Addison Ave Lombard (60148) ***(G-13085)***
Holmes Associates Inc 847 336-4515
4949 Grand Ave Ste 2 Gurnee (60031) ***(G-10887)***
Holmes Bros Inc 217 442-1430
510 Junction St Danville (61832) ***(G-7345)***
Hologram Inc (PA) 716 771-8308
1 N Lasalle St Ste 850 Chicago (60602) ***(G-4831)***
Holshouser Machine & Tool Inc 618 451-0164
35 Central Industrial Dr Granite City (62040) ***(G-10715)***
Holsolutions Inc 888 847-5467
21200 S La Grange Rd # 119 Frankfort (60423) ***(G-9801)***
Holstein Garage Inc 630 668-0328
309 W Front St Wheaton (60187) ***(G-20802)***
Holt Building, Newton *Also called Jesse B Holt Inc* ***(G-15086)***
Holt Publications Inc 618 654-6206
12047 Travis Ln Highland (62249) ***(G-11226)***
Holten Meat Inc 618 337-8400
1682 Sauget Business Blvd Sauget (62206) ***(G-18394)***
Holton Food Products Company 708 352-5599
500 W Burlington Ave La Grange (60525) ***(G-12078)***
Holy Cow Sports Incorporated 630 852-9001
5004 Chase Ave Downers Grove (60515) ***(G-8025)***
Holy Hill Gourmet, Chicago *Also called Chicago Candle Company* ***(G-4094)***
Homan Bindery 773 276-1500
1112 N Homan Ave Chicago (60651) ***(G-4832)***
Home & Leisure Lifestyles LLC 618 651-0358
907 Washington St Highland (62249) ***(G-11227)***
Home Chef, Chicago *Also called Relish Labs LLC* ***(G-6012)***
Home City Ice (PA) 773 622-9400
2248 N Natchez Ave Chicago (60707) ***(G-4833)***
Home Fires Inc 815 967-4100
1102 10th St Rockford (61104) ***(G-17452)***
Home Juice Co of Memphis, Melrose Park *Also called H J M P Corp* ***(G-13877)***
Home Juice Corp 708 345-5370
1930 George St Ste 2 Melrose Park (60160) ***(G-13880)***
Home Pdts Intl - N Amer Inc (HQ) 773 890-1010
4501 W 47th St Chicago (60632) ***(G-4834)***
Home Run Inn Frozen Foods Corp 630 783-9696
1300 Internationale Pkwy Woodridge (60517) ***(G-21314)***
Home School Enrichment Inc 309 347-1392
124 Thrush Ave Pekin (61554) ***(G-16338)***
Home Style 847 455-5000
11125 Franklin Ave Franklin Park (60131) ***(G-9956)***
Home Water Products, Peru *Also called William N Pasulka* ***(G-16598)***
Home World Business, Lincolnshire *Also called Icd Publications Inc* ***(G-12773)***
Homecontrolplus Incorporated 847 823-8414
1884 Fenton Ln Park Ridge (60068) ***(G-16283)***
Homer Vintage Bakery 217 896-2538
111 S Main St Homer (61849) ***(G-11476)***
Homers Ice Cream Inc 847 251-0477
1237 Green Bay Rd Wilmette (60091) ***(G-21078)***
Homers Rest & Ice Cream Parlor, Wilmette *Also called Homers Ice Cream Inc* ***(G-21078)***
Hometown Food Company (PA) 312 500-7710
500 W Madison St Chicago (60661) ***(G-4835)***
Hometown Foods, Chicago *Also called Hometown Food Company* ***(G-4835)***
Hometown Phone Book, Fairview Heights *Also called Eagle Publications Inc* ***(G-9645)***
Homeway Homes Inc 309 965-2312
100 Homeway Ct Deer Creek (61733) ***(G-7575)***
Homewerks Worldwide LLC 224 543-1529
55 Albrecht Dr Lake Bluff (60044) ***(G-12188)***
Homewood-Flossmoor Chronicle 630 728-2661
1361 Olive Rd Homewood (60430) ***(G-11497)***
Homnay Magazine 773 334-6655
1114 W Argyle St Chicago (60640) ***(G-4836)***
Homwarehouse 224 500-3367
1683 S Mount Prospect Rd Des Plaines (60018) ***(G-7777)***
Homz, Chicago *Also called Home Pdts Intl - N Amer Inc* ***(G-4834)***
Honey Fluff Doughnuts 708 579-1826
6566 Joliet Rd Countryside (60525) ***(G-7058)***
Honey Foods Inc 847 989-8186
4028 Tugwell St Franklin Park (60131) ***(G-9957)***
Honeywell 815 235-5500
315 E Stephenson St Freeport (61032) ***(G-10115)***
Honeywell Analytics Inc (HQ) 847 955-8200
405 Barclay Blvd Lincolnshire (60069) ***(G-12770)***
Honeywell Authorized Dealer, Joliet *Also called Interactive Bldg Solutions LLC* ***(G-11882)***
Honeywell Authorized Dealer, Loves Park *Also called National Metal Works Inc* ***(G-13239)***
Honeywell Authorized Dealer, Arlington Heights *Also called Ibbotson Heating Co* ***(G-752)***
Honeywell Inc 618 546-1671
7656 E 700th Ave Robinson (62454) ***(G-17117)***
Honeywell International Inc 847 251-3510
11 W Spring St Freeport (61032) ***(G-10116)***
Honeywell International Inc 815 745-2131
814 Anson St Warren (61087) ***(G-20223)***
Honeywell International Inc 618 524-2111
2768 N Us Hwy 45 N Metropolis (62960) ***(G-13972)***
Honeywell International Inc 630 960-5282
7714 Baker Ct Darien (60561) ***(G-7407)***
Honeywell International Inc 630 922-0138
4412 Buttermilk Ct Naperville (60564) ***(G-14973)***
Honeywell International Inc 630 554-5342
637 Salem Cir Oswego (60543) ***(G-16007)***
Honeywell International Inc 815 266-3209
670 N Greenfield Dr Freeport (61032) ***(G-10117)***
Honeywell International Inc 847 797-4000
95 E Algonquin Rd Bldg D Des Plaines (60016) ***(G-7778)***
Honeywell International Inc 815 235-5500
315 E Stephenson St Freeport (61032) ***(G-10118)***
Honeywell International Inc 847 797-4612
200 E Algonquin Rd Des Plaines (60016) ***(G-7779)***
Honeywell International Inc 401 573-6821
2052 Ave Moline (61265) ***(G-14149)***
Honeywell International Inc 480 353-3020
1 Bank One Plz Chicago (60670) ***(G-4837)***
Honeywell International Inc 847 701-3038
407 N Quentin Rd Palatine (60067) ***(G-16125)***
Honeywell International Inc 815 663-2011
410 Richard A Mautino Dr Spring Valley (61362) ***(G-19308)***
Honeywell International Inc 847 391-2000
25 E Algonquin Rd Des Plaines (60016) ***(G-7780)***
Honeywell International Inc 815 777-2780
11309 W Chetlain Ln Galena (61036) ***(G-10174)***
Honeywell International Inc 630 377-6580
3825 Ohio Ave Saint Charles (60174) ***(G-18207)***
Honeywell International Inc 847 634-2802
405 Barclay Blvd Lincolnshire (60069) ***(G-12771)***
Honeywell International Inc 269 428-6305
3737 Red Arrow Hwy Saint Joseph (61873) ***(G-18317)***
Honeywell International Inc 973 455-2000
24004 Network Pl Chicago (60673) ***(G-4838)***
Honeywell International Inc 309 383-4045
539 Justa Rd Metamora (61548) ***(G-13961)***
Honeywell International Inc 217 431-3710
3401 Lynch Creek Dr Danville (61834) ***(G-7346)***
Honeywell Safety Pdts USA Inc 630 343-3731
101 E Crssrads Pkwy Ste A Bolingbrook (60440) ***(G-2185)***
Honeywell Safety Pdts USA Inc 309 786-7741
101 13th Ave Rock Island (61201) ***(G-17223)***
Hong Kong Market, Chicago *Also called Hop Kee Incorporated* ***(G-4839)***
Hontech International Corp 847 364-9800
1000 Lee St Elk Grove Village (60007) ***(G-9036)***
Hoogwegt US Inc 847 918-8787
100 Saunders Rd Ste 200 Lake Forest (60045) ***(G-12254)***
Hooker Custom Harness Inc 815 233-5478
324 E Stephenson St Freeport (61032) ***(G-10119)***
Hooker Harness, Freeport *Also called Hooker Custom Harness Inc* ***(G-10119)***
Hookset Enterprises LLC 224 374-1935
1120 Larkin Dr Ste A Wheeling (60090) ***(G-20911)***
Hoopeston Foods, Hoopeston *Also called Teasdale Foods Inc* ***(G-11514)***
Hooray Puree Inc 312 515-0266
310 Busse Hwy Ste 322 Park Ridge (60068) ***(G-16284)***
Hoosier Stamping & Mfg Corp 812 426-2778
399 Industrial Park Dr Grayville (62844) ***(G-10809)***
Hoosier Stamping & Mfg Corp 618 375-2057
832 W Spring St Grayville (62844) ***(G-10810)***
Hop Brewery LLC 866 724-4677
203 W Market St Christopher (62822) ***(G-6825)***

ALPHABETIC SECTION

Hop Kee Incorporated (PA) 312 791-9111
   2425 S Wallace St Chicago (60616) *(G-4839)*
Hopcroft Electric Inc 618 288-7302
   606 Glen Crossing Rd Glen Carbon (62034) *(G-10388)*
Hope Pallet Inc 815 412-4606
   936 Moen Ave Ste 16 Rockdale (60436) *(G-17259)*
Hope Publishing Company 630 665-3200
   380 S Main Pl Carol Stream (60188) *(G-2999)*
Hopkins Grease Company, Lake In The Hills Also called MW Hopkins & Sons Inc *(G-12341)*
Hopkins Machine Corporation 773 772-2800
   4243 W Diversey Ave Chicago (60639) *(G-4840)*
Hopkins Printing & Envelope Co 630 543-8227
   120 W Laura Dr Addison (60101) *(G-152)*
Hopkins Saws & Cart, Belle Rive Also called Hopkins Saws & Karts Inc *(G-1525)*
Hopkins Saws & Karts Inc 618 756-2778
   9398 N Markham Ln Belle Rive (62810) *(G-1525)*
Hopper Graphics Inc 708 489-0459
   6106 W 127th St Palos Heights (60463) *(G-16189)*
Hopperstad Customs 815 547-7534
   6860 Imron Dr Belvidere (61008) *(G-1677)*
Horizon Downing LLC 815 758-6867
   1115 E Locust St Dekalb (60115) *(G-7685)*
Horizon Fuel Cell Americas 312 316-8050
   18 S Michigan Ave # 1200 Chicago (60603) *(G-4841)*
Horizon Medicines LLC 224 383-3110
   150 Saunders Rd Lake Forest (60045) *(G-12255)*
Horizon Metals, Niles Also called Monett Metals Inc *(G-15148)*
Horizon Metals Inc 773 478-8888
   5739 W Howard St Niles (60714) *(G-15129)*
Horizon Mfg Entps Inc 847 438-0888
   1230 Karl Ct Unit C Wauconda (60084) *(G-20358)*
Horizon Pharma Inc (HQ) 224 383-3000
   150 Saunders Rd Ste 400 Lake Forest (60045) *(G-12256)*
Horizon Pharmaceuticals, Lake Forest Also called Horizon Therapeutics Usa Inc *(G-12258)*
Horizon Phrma Rheumatology LLC 224 383-3000
   150 Saunders Rd Ste 150 # 150 Lake Forest (60045) *(G-12257)*
Horizon Publications Inc (PA) 618 993-1711
   1120 N Carbon St Ste 100 Marion (62959) *(G-13515)*
Horizon Publications (2003) (PA) 618 993-1711
   1120 N Carbon St Ste 100 Marion (62959) *(G-13516)*
Horizon Sperfinishing Grinding, Rosemont Also called Custom Superfinishing Grinding *(G-18016)*
Horizon Steel Treating Inc 847 639-4030
   231 Jandus Rd Cary (60013) *(G-3167)*
Horizon Therapeutics Usa Inc 224 383-3000
   1 Takeda Pkwy Deerfield (60015) *(G-7617)*
Horizon Therapeutics Usa Inc 312 332-1401
   150 S Wacker Dr Chicago (60606) *(G-4842)*
Horizon Therapeutics Usa Inc (HQ) 224 383-3000
   150 Saunders Rd Ste 150 # 150 Lake Forest (60045) *(G-12258)*
Horizon, The, Marion Also called Review *(G-13533)*
Hormann LLC (HQ) 630 859-3000
   5050 Baseline Rd Montgomery (60538) *(G-14248)*
Horse Creek Outfitters 217 544-2740
   600 S Dirksen Pkwy 600a Springfield (62703) *(G-19382)*
Horween Leather Company 773 772-2026
   2015 N Elston Ave Ste 1 Chicago (60614) *(G-4843)*
Hospira Inc (HQ) 224 212-2000
   275 N Field Dr Lake Forest (60045) *(G-12259)*
Hospira Inc 224 212-6244
   375 N Field Dr Bldg H3 Lake Forest (60045) *(G-12260)*
Hospira Worldwide LLC (HQ) 224 212-2000
   275 N Field Dr Lake Forest (60045) *(G-12261)*
Hospital Hlth Care Systems Inc (PA) 708 863-3400
   7830 47th St Ste 1 Lyons (60534) *(G-13311)*
Hospital Labels Co Div, Chicago Also called Labels Unlimited Incorporated *(G-5152)*
Hospital Therapy Products Inc 630 766-7101
   757 N Central Ave Wood Dale (60191) *(G-21198)*
Hospitology Products LLC 630 359-5075
   300 S Lombard Rd Addison (60101) *(G-153)*
Hostess Brands LLC 773 745-9800
   2035 N Narragansett Ave Chicago (60639) *(G-4844)*
Hostforweb Incorporated 312 343-4678
   7061 N Kedzie Ave Ste 302 Chicago (60645) *(G-4845)*
Hostmann Steinberg Inc (HQ) 502 968-5961
   2850 Festival Dr Kankakee (60901) *(G-11976)*
Hot Food Boxes Inc 773 533-5912
   4109 W Lake St Chicago (60624) *(G-4846)*
Hot Mexican Peppers Inc 773 843-9774
   2215 W 47th St Chicago (60609) *(G-4847)*
Hot Shots Nm LLC 815 484-0500
   4330 Charles St Rockford (61108) *(G-17453)*
Hot Topic Inc 708 453-1216
   4104 N Harlem Ave Ste 132 Norridge (60706) *(G-15236)*
Hotel Amerika 219 508-9418
   434 W Briar Pl Apt 4 Chicago (60657) *(G-4848)*
Hottenrott Company Inc 618 473-2531
   351 S Main St Hecker (62248) *(G-11155)*
Hottinger Bldwin Msrements Inc 217 328-5359
   1806 Fox Dr Ste A Champaign (61820) *(G-3303)*
Hotvapes Ltd 775 468-8273
   7240 N Milwaukee Ave Niles (60714) *(G-15130)*
Hough General Homes, Hillsboro Also called Elite Monument Co *(G-11310)*
Houghton International Inc 610 666-4000
   6600 S Nashville Ave Chicago (60638) *(G-4849)*
Houghton Mifflin Harcourt 928 467-9599
   1900 S Batavia Ave Geneva (60134) *(G-10275)*
Houghton Mifflin Harcourt Co 630 467-6049
   761 District Dr Itasca (60143) *(G-11666)*
Houghton Mifflin Harcourt Co 303 504-9312
   1900 S Batavia Ave Geneva (60134) *(G-10276)*
Houghton Mifflin Harcourt Co 800 225-5425
   909 Davis St Ste 300 Evanston (60201) *(G-9533)*
Houghton Mifflin Harcourt Pubg 630 208-5704
   1900 S Batavia Ave Geneva (60134) *(G-10277)*
Houghton Mifflin Harcourt Pubg 630 467-6095
   425 Spring Lake Dr Itasca (60143) *(G-11667)*
Houghton Mifflin Harcourt Pubg 847 869-2300
   909 Davis St Ste 300 Evanston (60201) *(G-9534)*
Houghton Mifflin Harcourt Pubg 708 869-2300
   909 Davis St Ste 300 Evanston (60201) *(G-9535)*
Houpt Revolving Cutters Inc 618 395-1913
   516 W Butler St Olney (62450) *(G-15865)*
House Granite & Marble Corp 847 928-1111
   5136 Pearl St Schiller Park (60176) *(G-18814)*
House of Atlas LLC 847 491-1800
   1578 Sherman Ave Fl 2 Evanston (60201) *(G-9536)*
House of Color 708 352-3222
   9912 W 55th St Countryside (60525) *(G-7059)*
House of Doolittle Ltd (PA) 847 228-9591
   3001 Malmo Dr Arlington Heights (60005) *(G-751)*
House of Graphics 630 682-0810
   370 Randy Rd Carol Stream (60188) *(G-3000)*
House of Rattan Inc (PA) 630 627-8160
   18w375 Roosevelt Rd Lombard (60148) *(G-13086)*
House On The Hill Inc 630 279-4455
   2206 N Main St Wheaton (60187) *(G-20803)*
Houser Meats 217 322-4994
   180 Rr 2 Rushville (62681) *(G-18110)*
Hovi Industries Incorporated (PA) 815 512-7500
   380 Veterans Pkwy Ste 110 Bolingbrook (60440) *(G-2186)*
How To Be Good For Santa Inc 281 961-4002
   261 Kimberly Rd North Barrington (60010) *(G-15285)*
Howard Custom Transfers Inc 847 695-8195
   1925 Holmes Rd Ste 400 Elgin (60123) *(G-8616)*
Howard Energy Corporation 618 263-3000
   519 W 3rd St Mount Carmel (62863) *(G-14473)*
Howard Medical Company 773 278-1440
   3450 N Kostner Ave Chicago (60641) *(G-4850)*
Howard Press Printing Inc 708 345-7437
   303 E North Ave Lowr 100 Northlake (60164) *(G-15547)*
Howard Schwartz 847 540-8260
   2189 N Rte 83 Ste 335 Round Lake Beach (60073) *(G-18089)*
Howe Corporation 773 235-0200
   1650 N Elston Ave Chicago (60642) *(G-4851)*
Howlan Inc 847 478-1760
   880 Corporate Woods Pkwy Vernon Hills (60061) *(G-20061)*
Howland Technology Inc 847 965-9808
   8129 Austin Ave Morton Grove (60053) *(G-14411)*
Howler Fabrication & Wldg Inc 630 293-9300
   1100 Carolina Dr West Chicago (60185) *(G-20593)*
Howmedica Osteonics Corp 309 663-6414
   7 Westport Ct Bloomington (61704) *(G-2059)*
Howmet Aerospace Inc 773 581-7200
   5414 S Archer Ave Chicago (60638) *(G-4852)*
Howmet Aerospace Inc 217 324-4469
   108 Historic Old Rte 66 Litchfield (62056) *(G-12965)*
Howmet Aerospace Inc 309 674-0065
   2616 Sw Jefferson Ave Peoria (61605) *(G-16454)*
Howw Manufacturing Company Inc 847 382-4380
   28020 W Commercial Ave Lake Barrington (60010) *(G-12150)*
Hoyer Outdoor Equipment Inc 618 564-2080
   7402 Unionville Rd Brookport (62910) *(G-2498)*
Hp Inc 650 857-1501
   303 E Wacker Dr Ste 2700 Chicago (60601) *(G-4853)*
Hp Inc 309 664-4000
   303 N Hershey Rd Bloomington (61704) *(G-2060)*
Hp Inc 650 857-1501
   1124 Tower Rd Schaumburg (60173) *(G-18551)*
Hp Inc 650 857-1501
   100 N Riverside Plz # 152 Chicago (60606) *(G-4854)*
HP Interactive Inc 773 681-4440
   2461 W Balmoral Ave Chicago (60625) *(G-4855)*
Hp2000 Apu, Marion Also called Parks Industries LLC *(G-13524)*
Hpc Automation, Chicago Also called Hackett Precision Company Inc *(G-4764)*
Hpc of Pennsylvania Inc 618 993-1711
   1120 N Carbon St Ste 100 Marion (62959) *(G-13517)*

(PA)=Parent Co (HQ)=Headquarters (DH)=Div Headquarters

Hpd LLC 815 609-2032
23563 W Main St Plainfield (60544) *(G-16673)*
HPD Evporation Crystallization, Plainfield Also called Veolia Water Technologies Inc *(G-16726)*
HPD Evporation Crystallization, Plainfield Also called Hpd LLC *(G-16673)*
Hpfs, Bensenville Also called Lre Products Inc *(G-1845)*
Hpi North America Inc 773 890-8927
4501 W 47th St Chicago (60632) *(G-4856)*
Hpl Stampings Inc (PA) 847 540-1400
425 Enterprise Pkwy Lake Zurich (60047) *(G-12419)*
Hpmillwork LLC 630 220-4387
3007 Commercial Ave Northbrook (60062) *(G-15401)*
HPp Precision Machine Co Inc 815 469-2608
22829 S Mustang Rd Frankfort (60423) *(G-9802)*
Hq Printers Inc 312 782-2020
200 N La Salle St Lbby 2 Chicago (60601) *(G-4857)*
Hqf Manufacturing, East Dundee Also called Peter Fox *(G-8208)*
HRB America Corporation 630 513-1800
3485 Swenson Ave Saint Charles (60174) *(G-18208)*
Hsa, Arlington Heights Also called Hearing Screening Assoc LLC *(G-747)*
Hsa Chicago Office, Schaumburg Also called Sk Hynix America Inc *(G-18713)*
Hst Materials Inc 847 640-1803
1631 Brummel Ave Elk Grove Village (60007) *(G-9037)*
Ht Lumber & Crates Inc 847 683-0200
200 Industrial Dr Unit C Hampshire (60140) *(G-10973)*
Hts Chicago Inc 630 352-3690
107 W Willow Ave Wheaton (60187) *(G-20804)*
Hts Coatings LLC 618 215-8161
932 Fairway Park Dr Madison (62060) *(G-13414)*
Hts Hancock Transcriptions Svc (PA) 217 379-9241
136 S Market St Paxton (60957) *(G-16308)*
Hu-Friedy Mfg Co LLC (HQ) 773 975-3975
3232 N Rockwell St Chicago (60618) *(G-4858)*
Hu-Friedy Mfg Co LLC 847 257-4500
1666 E Touhy Ave Des Plaines (60018) *(G-7781)*
Huawei Technologies USA Inc 425 463-8275
3601 Algonquin Rd Rolling Meadows (60008) *(G-17735)*
Hub Manufacturing Company Inc 773 252-1373
1212 N Central Park Ave Chicago (60651) *(G-4859)*
Hub Printing & Office Supplies, Rochelle Also called Hub Printing Company Inc *(G-17145)*
Hub Printing Company Inc 815 562-7057
101 Maple Ave Rochelle (61068) *(G-17145)*
Hub Stamping & Mfg Co, Chicago Also called Hub Manufacturing Company Inc *(G-4859)*
Hubba, Oswego Also called Newport Media Inc *(G-16016)*
Hubbell Incorporated 972 756-1184
1455 Sequoia Dr Ste 113 Aurora (60506) *(G-1110)*
Hubbell Lighting Inc 847 515-3057
2100 Golf Rd Ste 460 Rolling Meadows (60008) *(G-17736)*
Hubbell Lighting Components, Rolling Meadows Also called Hubbell Lighting Inc *(G-17736)*
Hubbell Power Systems Inc 618 797-5000
131 Enterprise Dr Edwardsville (62025) *(G-8365)*
Hubbell Power Systems Inc 618 797-5000
131 Enterprise Dr Edwardsville (62025) *(G-8366)*
Huber Carbonates LLC 217 224-8737
3150 Gardner Expy Quincy (62305) *(G-16893)*
Hubergroup North America, Rolling Meadows Also called Hubergroup Usa Inc *(G-17737)*
Hubergroup Usa Inc (HQ) 815 929-9293
1701 Golf Rd Ste 3-201 Rolling Meadows (60008) *(G-17737)*
Hucks Food Fuel 618 286-5111
110 S Main St Dupo (62239) *(G-8138)*
Hucuai LLC 312 608-6101
222 Merchandise Mart Plz Chicago (60654) *(G-4860)*
Hudapack Mtal Treating Ill Inc 630 793-1916
550 Mitchell Rd Glendale Heights (60139) *(G-10457)*
Hudson Boiler & Tank Company 312 666-4780
3101 S State St Lockport (60441) *(G-13001)*
Hudson Technologies Inc 217 373-1414
3402 N Mattis Ave Champaign (61822) *(G-3304)*
Hudson Tool & Die Co 847 678-8710
3845 Carnation St Franklin Park (60131) *(G-9958)*
Hue Circle Inc 224 567-8116
4259 Commercial Way Glenview (60025) *(G-10558)*
Hueber LLC (PA) 815 393-4879
110 S Main St Creston (60113) *(G-7102)*
Hueber LLC 815 625-4546
105 Dixon Ave Rock Falls (61071) *(G-17185)*
Huels Oil Company 877 338-6277
16320 Old Us Highway 50 Carlyle (62231) *(G-2890)*
Huetone Imprints Inc 630 694-9610
90 N Lively Blvd Elk Grove Village (60007) *(G-9038)*
Huff & Puff Industries Ltd 847 381-8255
125 Arrowhead Ln North Barrington (60010) *(G-15286)*
Hugh Courtright & Co Ltd 708 534-8400
26749 S Governors Hwy Monee (60449) *(G-14202)*
Hughes & Son Inc 815 459-1887
305 Dearborn Ct Crystal Lake (60014) *(G-7206)*
Hughes Sign Co, Crystal Lake Also called Hughes & Son Inc *(G-7206)*

Hugo Boss Usa Inc 847 517-1461
5 Woodfield Mall Schaumburg (60173) *(G-18552)*
Hulse Excavating 815 796-4106
20289 N 400 East Rd Flanagan (61740) *(G-9670)*
Humaginarium LLC 312 788-7719
325 S Grove Ave Oak Park (60302) *(G-15757)*
Human Factor RES Group Inc 618 476-3200
609 Suth Brese St Ste 101 Millstadt (62260) *(G-14047)*
Human Service Center, Red Bud Also called Comwell *(G-16991)*
Humboldt Broom Company 217 268-3718
901 E County Road 300n Arcola (61910) *(G-652)*
Humboldt Mfg Co (PA) 708 456-6300
875 Tollgate Rd Elgin (60123) *(G-8617)*
Humid-A-Mist, New Lenox Also called Galmar Enterprises Inc *(G-15035)*
Humidity 2 Optimization LLC 847 991-7488
105 Prairie Lake Rd Ste D East Dundee (60118) *(G-8200)*
Huml Industries Inc 847 426-8061
78 E End Dr Gilberts (60136) *(G-10358)*
Humpsman, Peru Also called Nova Chemicals Inc *(G-16586)*
Hunt Charles 217 793-5151
3161 W White Oaks Dr Springfield (62704) *(G-19383)*
Hunt Enterprises Inc 708 354-8464
4201 166th St Oak Forest (60452) *(G-15681)*
Hunt Foods Company, Naperville Also called Conagra Brands Inc *(G-14803)*
Hunt Printing & Graphics, Oak Forest Also called Hunt Enterprises Inc *(G-15681)*
Hunter Foundry Machinery Corp 847 397-5110
2222 Hammond Dr Schaumburg (60196) *(G-18553)*
Hunter Logistics 309 299-7015
280 Knox Road 2200 N Wataga (61488) *(G-20286)*
Hunter Mfg LLP 859 254-7573
227 Northgate St Ste 3 Lake Forest (60045) *(G-12262)*
Hunter-Nusport Inc 815 254-7520
24317 W 143rd St Ste 103 Plainfield (60544) *(G-16674)*
Hunter-Stevens Company Inc 847 671-5014
4003 Fleetwood Dr Franklin Park (60131) *(G-9959)*
Hunting Network LLC 847 659-8200
11964 Oak Creek Pkwy Huntley (60142) *(G-11540)*
Huntley & Associates Inc 224 381-8500
47 Carolyn Ct Lake Zurich (60047) *(G-12420)*
Huntsman Expndable Polymers Lc 815 224-5463
501 Brunner St Peru (61354) *(G-16577)*
Huntsman International LLC 815 653-1500
5015 Barnard Mill Rd Ringwood (60072) *(G-17044)*
Hunzinger Williams Inc 847 381-1878
27w982 Commercial Ave Lake Barrington (60010) *(G-12151)*
Hurst Chemical Company 815 964-0451
2020 Cunningham Rd Rockford (61102) *(G-17454)*
Hurst Manufacturing Co Inc 309 756-9960
823 9th St W Milan (61264) *(G-14016)*
Husar Abatement Ltd 847 349-9105
10215 Franklin Ave Franklin Park (60131) *(G-9960)*
Husar Picture Frame, Chicago Also called J R Husar Inc *(G-4994)*
Husky Injection Molding 708 479-9049
8845 W 192nd St Ste B Mokena (60448) *(G-14089)*
Hussain Shaheen 630 405-8009
1900 Danube Way Bolingbrook (60490) *(G-2187)*
Hustedt Manufacturing Jewelers 217 784-8462
113 N Sangamon Ave Gibson City (60936) *(G-10339)*
Huston Patterson Printers, Decatur Also called Huston-Patterson Corporation *(G-7503)*
Huston-Patterson Corporation (PA) 217 429-5161
123 W North St Fl 4 Decatur (62522) *(G-7503)*
Hutchens-Bit Service Inc 618 439-9485
11898 Commerce Ln Benton (62812) *(G-1926)*
Hutton Welding Service Inc 217 932-5585
11995 N 180th St Casey (62420) *(G-3203)*
Huyear Trucking Inc 217 854-3551
708 Sumner St Carlinville (62626) *(G-2876)*
Huygen Corporation (PA) 815 455-2200
1025 Lutter Dr Crystal Lake (60014) *(G-7207)*
Hw Holdco LLC 773 824-2400
5600 N River Rd Ste 250 Rosemont (60018) *(G-18026)*
HWI, Ottawa Also called Heiss Welding Inc *(G-16055)*
Hy Spreckman & Sons Inc 312 236-2173
9725 Woods Dr Unit 1302 Skokie (60077) *(G-18966)*
Hy-Dac Rubber Mfg Co, Smithton Also called Hydac Rubber Manufacturing *(G-19065)*
Hy-Tek Manufacturing Co Inc 630 466-7664
1998 Bucktail Ln Sugar Grove (60554) *(G-19647)*
Hybris (us) Corporation (HQ) 312 265-5010
20 N Wacker Dr Ste 2900 Chicago (60606) *(G-4861)*
Hydac Rubber Manufacturing 618 233-2129
301 S Main St Smithton (62285) *(G-19065)*
Hydac Technology Corp 630 545-0800
445 Windy Point Dr Glendale Heights (60139) *(G-10458)*
Hyde Park Herald, Chicago Also called Herald Newspapers Inc *(G-4806)*
Hydra Fold Auger Inc 217 379-2614
931 N 1600e Rd Loda (60948) *(G-13028)*
Hydra-Stop, Burr Ridge Also called ADS LLC *(G-2650)*
Hydra-Stop LLC 708 389-5111
144 Tower Dr Ste A Burr Ridge (60527) *(G-2684)*

ALPHABETIC SECTION

Hydraforce Inc (PA) 847 793-2300
  500 Barclay Blvd Lincolnshire (60069) *(G-12772)*
Hydralic Cartridge Systems Div, Lincolnshire Also called Parker-Hannifin Corporation *(G-12792)*
Hydraulic Accumulator, Machesney Park Also called Parker-Hannifin Corporation *(G-13362)*
Hydraulic Division, Glendale Heights Also called Hydac Technology Corp *(G-10458)*
Hydraulic Hoses & Fittings, Melrose Park Also called Bristol Hose & Fitting Inc *(G-13837)*
Hydro Extrusion Usa LLC (HQ) 877 710-7272
  6250 N River Rd Ste 5000 Rosemont (60018) *(G-18027)*
Hydro Ink Corp 847 674-0057
  7331 Monticello Ave Skokie (60076) *(G-18967)*
Hydro-Gear Inc (HQ) 217 728-2581
  1411 S Hamilton St Sullivan (61951) *(G-19668)*
Hydrogen Education Council 630 681-1732
  1115 Aurora Way Wheaton (60189) *(G-20805)*
Hydrology Inc 312 832-9000
  435 N La Salle Dr Ste 100 Chicago (60654) *(G-4862)*
Hydrosil International Ltd 847 741-1600
  125 Prairie Lake Rd East Dundee (60118) *(G-8201)*
Hydrotec Systems Company Inc (PA) 815 624-6644
  145 E Main St Tiskilwa (61368) *(G-19873)*
Hydrox Chemical Company Inc 847 468-9400
  825 Tollgate Rd Ste B Elgin (60123) *(G-8618)*
Hydrox Laboratories, Elgin Also called Hydrox Chemical Company Inc *(G-8618)*
Hygienic Fabrics & Filters Inc (PA) 815 493-2502
  118 S Broad St Lanark (61046) *(G-12482)*
Hylan Design Ltd 312 243-7341
  329 W 18th St Ste 700 Chicago (60616) *(G-4863)*
Hymans Auto Supply Co (PA) 773 978-8221
  8600-8614 S Coml Ave Chicago (60617) *(G-4864)*
Hyperaktive Prfmce Solutions 847 321-1982
  423 Joren Trl Antioch (60002) *(G-615)*
Hyperera Inc 312 842-2288
  2316 S Wentworth Ave Fl 1 Chicago (60616) *(G-4865)*
Hypermax Engineering Inc 847 428-5655
  255 Higgins Rd Gilberts (60136) *(G-10359)*
Hyperstitch 815 568-0590
  219 E Grant Hwy Marengo (60152) *(G-13485)*
Hyponex Corporation 815 772-2167
  9349 Garden Plain Rd Morrison (61270) *(G-14343)*
Hyspan Precision Products Inc 773 277-0700
  17111 Wallace St South Holland (60473) *(G-19223)*
Hyster Co 217 443-7000
  1010 E Fairchild St Danville (61832) *(G-7347)*
Hyster-Yale Group Inc 217 443-7416
  1010 E Fairchild St Danville (61832) *(G-7348)*
Hytel Group Inc (PA) 847 683-9800
  290 Industrial Dr Hampshire (60140) *(G-10974)*
Hznp Usa Inc 224 383-3000
  150 Saunders Rd Ste 200 Lake Forest (60045) *(G-12263)*
I AM A Print Shoppe, Chicago Also called Klein Printing Inc *(G-5108)*
I B P, Goodfield Also called Tyson Fresh Meats Inc *(G-10678)*
I C Innovations Inc 847 279-7888
  1101 Golf Ave Highland Park (60035) *(G-11271)*
I C S, Roselle Also called Instrmntation Ctrl Systems Inc *(G-17959)*
I C S, Decatur Also called International Control Svcs Inc *(G-7508)*
I C T W Ink (PA) 630 893-4658
  968 Lake St Ste A Roselle (60172) *(G-17957)*
I C Universal Inc 630 766-1169
  1040 Fairway Dr Bensenville (60106) *(G-1820)*
I D Rockford Shop Inc 815 335-1150
  105 N Pecatonica St Winnebago (61088) *(G-21120)*
I D T, Elgin Also called Tri-Dim Filter Corporation *(G-8759)*
I D Togs 618 235-1538
  67 Cheshire Dr Belleville (62223) *(G-1556)*
I D Tool Specialty Company 815 432-2007
  819 N Jefferson St Watseka (60970) *(G-20307)*
I E C, Rockford Also called Industrial Electronic Contrls *(G-17458)*
I E C, Aurora Also called Industrial Enclosure Corp *(G-1111)*
I E Press & Graphics, Belvidere Also called Ink Enterprises Inc *(G-1679)*
I F & G Metal Craft Co 847 488-0630
  405 Industrial Dr South Elgin (60177) *(G-19153)*
I F I, Melrose Park Also called Industrial Fiberglass Inc *(G-13882)*
I F S, Potomac Also called Illini Fs Inc *(G-16802)*
I F S C O Industries, Chicago Also called Illinois Fibre Specialty Co *(G-4890)*
I Forge Company LLC 815 535-0600
  2900 E Rock Falls Rd Rock Falls (61071) *(G-17186)*
I Hardware Direct Inc 708 325-0000
  642 Blackhawk Dr Westmont (60559) *(G-20748)*
I Kustom Cabinets Inc 773 343-6858
  220 Oakridge Ave Highwood (60040) *(G-11307)*
I M M Inc 773 767-3700
  5262 S Kolmar Ave Chicago (60632) *(G-4866)*
I P C Automation Inc 815 759-3934
  4615 Prime Pkwy McHenry (60050) *(G-13749)*
I P G, South Elgin Also called Integrated Print Graphics Inc *(G-19155)*

I P G Warehouse Ltd 773 722-5527
  600 N Pulaski Rd Chicago (60624) *(G-4867)*
I P R, Bartlett Also called Industrial Phrm Resources Inc *(G-1290)*
I P S, Rockford Also called Ingersoll Prod Systems LLC *(G-17463)*
I Pulloma Paints 847 426-4140
  1 Day Ln Carpentersville (60110) *(G-3104)*
I Q Infinity LLC 773 651-2556
  7624 S Wood St Chicago (60620) *(G-4868)*
I S C America Inc (PA) 630 616-1331
  750 Creel Dr Wood Dale (60191) *(G-21199)*
I S C O, Morton Grove Also called International Spring Company *(G-14413)*
I T Audit Search, Wheaton Also called Nano Technologies Inc *(G-20813)*
I T C W Inc 630 305-8849
  584 Beaconsfield Ave Naperville (60565) *(G-14842)*
I T R Inc 217 245-4478
  21 Harold Cox Dr Jacksonville (62650) *(G-11768)*
I T W Affrdbl Hsing Invstments, Glenview Also called ITW International Holdings LLC *(G-10575)*
I T W Chronotherm, Elmhurst Also called Illinois Tool Works Inc *(G-9377)*
I T W Ramset 630 825-7900
  700 High Grove Blvd Glendale Heights (60139) *(G-10459)*
I Tech, Rolling Meadows Also called Northern Information Tech *(G-17754)*
I TW Deltar Insert Molded Pdts 847 593-8811
  830 Lee St Elk Grove Village (60007) *(G-9039)*
I W M Corporation 847 695-0700
  399 Hammond Ave Elgin (60120) *(G-8619)*
I-N-I Machining Inc 309 496-1002
  17128 Route 2 & 92 East Moline (61244) *(G-8229)*
I2c LLC 630 281-2330
  1708 Chepstow Ct Naperville (60540) *(G-14843)*
I94 Rv LLC 847 395-9500
  16125 Russel Rd Russell (60075) *(G-18114)*
IAC Belvidere, Belvidere Also called International Automotive Compo *(G-1680)*
IACO, Springfield Also called Illinois Assn Cnty Officials *(G-19385)*
Iam Acquisition LLC 847 259-7800
  230 W Palatine Rd Wheeling (60090) *(G-20912)*
IB Source Inc 312 698-7062
  516 N Ogden Ave Ste 111 Chicago (60642) *(G-4869)*
Ibanum Manufacturing LLC 815 262-5373
  5963 Cambridge Chase Rockford (61107) *(G-17455)*
Ibarra Group LLC 773 650-0503
  3100 S Homan Ave Chicago (60623) *(G-4870)*
Ibbotson Heating Co 847 253-0866
  514 S Arthur Ave Arlington Heights (60005) *(G-752)*
Iberia Foods Corp 847 678-2200
  121 Foster Ave Bensenville (60106) *(G-1821)*
Ibi, Cary Also called Illinois Blower Inc *(G-3168)*
IBM, Chicago Also called International Bus Mchs Corp *(G-4951)*
Ibs Conversions Inc 630 571-9100
  2625 Bttrfield Rd Ste 114w Oak Brook (60523) *(G-15626)*
Ican Clinic LLC 618 254-2273
  203 E Ferguson Ave Wood River (62095) *(G-21263)*
Icandee LLC 773 754-0493
  954 W Carmen Ave Chicago (60640) *(G-4871)*
Icandee Marketing, Chicago Also called Icandee LLC *(G-4871)*
ICC Intrntonal Celsius Concept 773 993-4405
  2385 S 59th Ct Cicero (60804) *(G-6853)*
Iccn Holdings, Woodridge Also called Inventus Power Holdings Inc *(G-21318)*
Icd Publications Inc 847 913-8295
  175 Old Hlf Day Rd # 240 Lincolnshire (60069) *(G-12773)*
Ice Maid, Evansville Also called Voges Inc *(G-9590)*
Iceberg Enterprises LLC (PA) 847 685-9500
  2700 S River Rd Ste 303 Des Plaines (60018) *(G-7782)*
Iced 217 774-2247
  118 E Main St Shelbyville (62565) *(G-18879)*
Icg Illinois 217 947-2332
  781 600th St Elkhart (62634) *(G-9318)*
Icg Illinois LLC (HQ) 217 566-3000
  5945 Lester Rd Williamsville (62693) *(G-21023)*
ICI Fiberite 708 403-3788
  14342 Beacon Ave Orland Park (60462) *(G-15960)*
Icon Acquisition Holdings LP (PA) 312 751-8000
  680 N Lake Shore Dr Chicago (60611) *(G-4872)*
Icon Co 630 545-2345
  1s640 Sunnybrook Rd Glen Ellyn (60137) *(G-10405)*
Icon Identity Solutions Inc (HQ) 847 364-2250
  1701 Golf Rd Ste 1-900 Rolling Meadows (60008) *(G-17738)*
Icon Mech Cnstr & Engrg LLC 618 452-0035
  1616 Cleveland Blvd Granite City (62040) *(G-10716)*
Icon Metalcraft Inc 630 766-5600
  940 Dillon Dr Wood Dale (60191) *(G-21200)*
Icon Power Roller Inc 630 545-2345
  2882 E 24th Rd Marseilles (61341) *(G-13556)*
Iconic USA, Lake Forest Also called Slaughter Company Inc *(G-12303)*
ICP Industrial Inc (HQ) 630 227-1692
  1600 Glenlake Ave Itasca (60143) *(G-11668)*
ICP Industries LLC 888 672-2123
  1600 Glenlake Ave Itasca (60143) *(G-11669)*

Icream Group LLC ... 773 342-2834
1537 N Milwaukee Ave # 1 Chicago (60622) ***(G-4873)***
Ics Saint Louis, Venice *Also called Sho Pak LLC* ***(G-20036)***
ICT Power USA Inc ... 630 313-4941
3960 Commerce Dr Saint Charles (60174) ***(G-18209)***
ID Additives Inc ... 708 588-0081
512 W Burlington Ave # 208 La Grange (60525) ***(G-12079)***
ID Direct, Crystal Lake *Also called Identatronics Inc* ***(G-7208)***
ID Label Inc (PA) ... 847 265-1200
425 Park Ave Lake Villa (60046) ***(G-12355)***
ID Sign and Lighting Inc ... 630 844-3565
2287 Cornell Ave Montgomery (60538) ***(G-14249)***
Id3 Inc ... 847 734-9781
768 W Algonquin Rd Arlington Heights (60005) ***(G-753)***
Idaho Timber, Rochelle *Also called Southeast Wood Treating Inc* ***(G-17160)***
Iddc, Long Grove *Also called International Drug Dev Cons* ***(G-13160)***
Idea Tool & Manufacturing Co ... 312 476-1080
5615 S Claremont Ave Chicago (60636) ***(G-4874)***
Ideal Advertising & Printing (PA) ... 815 965-1713
116 N Winnebago St Rockford (61101) ***(G-17456)***
Ideal Box Co (PA) ... 708 594-3100
4800 S Austin Ave Chicago (60638) ***(G-4875)***
Ideal Cabinet Solutions Inc ... 618 514-7087
1105 W Main St Alhambra (62001) ***(G-401)***
Ideal Fabricators Inc ... 217 999-7017
621 S Main St Mount Olive (62069) ***(G-14505)***
Ideal Gerit Drum Ring Mfg, Chicago *Also called Meyer Steel Drum Inc* ***(G-5417)***
Ideal Industries Inc (PA) ... 815 895-5181
1375 Park Ave Sycamore (60178) ***(G-19714)***
Ideal Industries Inc ... 815 895-1108
434 Borden Ave Dock14 Sycamore (60178) ***(G-19715)***
Ideal Industries Inc ... 815 895-5181
1000 Park Ave Sycamore (60178) ***(G-19716)***
Ideal Machine Inc ... 217 925-5109
400 Amy St Dieterich (62424) ***(G-7877)***
Ideal Media LLC (PA) ... 312 456-2822
200 E Randolph St # 7000 Chicago (60601) ***(G-4876)***
Ideal Roller, Chicago *Also called Rotation Dynamics Corporation* ***(G-6066)***
Ideal Stitcher & Manufacturing, Chicago *Also called W R Pabich Mfg Co Inc* ***(G-6578)***
Ideal Supply Inc (PA) ... 847 961-5900
11400 Kreutzer Rd Huntley (60142) ***(G-11541)***
Ideal Turf Inc ... 309 691-3362
614 W Ravinwoods Rd Peoria (61615) ***(G-16455)***
Ideas Inc (PA) ... 630 620-2010
625 S Main St Lombard (60148) ***(G-13087)***
Ideas Inc ... 708 596-1055
16131 Clinton St Harvey (60426) ***(G-11090)***
Idek Graphics LLC ... 630 530-1232
926 S Prospect Ave Elmhurst (60126) ***(G-9373)***
Idemia America Corp ... 630 551-0792
2764 Golfview Rd Naperville (60563) ***(G-14844)***
Identatronics Inc ... 847 437-2654
2510 Il Route 176 Ste E Crystal Lake (60014) ***(G-7208)***
Identco International Corp (PA) ... 815 385-0011
28164 W Concrete Dr Ingleside (60041) ***(G-11584)***
Identco West LLC ... 815 385-0011
28164 W Concrete Dr Ingleside (60041) ***(G-11585)***
Identi-Graphics Inc ... 630 801-4845
101 Knell St Montgomery (60538) ***(G-14250)***
Identification Products Mfg Co (PA) ... 847 367-6452
13777 W Laurel Dr Lake Forest (60045) ***(G-12264)***
Identiti Resources Ltd ... 866 477-4467
425 N Martingale Rd # 1800 Schaumburg (60173) ***(G-18554)***
Idevconcepts Inc ... 312 351-1615
100 E 14th St Apt 904 Chicago (60605) ***(G-4877)***
Idex Corporation (PA) ... 847 498-7070
1925 W Field Ct Ste 200 Lake Forest (60045) ***(G-12265)***
IDI Fabrication Inc ... 630 783-2246
1385 101st St Lemont (60439) ***(G-12566)***
Idlr USA Inc ... 630 375-0101
2121 Ridge Ave Ste 103 Aurora (60504) ***(G-980)***
Idot North Side Sign Shop ... 847 705-4033
201 Center Ct Schaumburg (60196) ***(G-18555)***
Idrc, Rushville *Also called Innovative Design and RES Inc* ***(G-18111)***
IDS Lift-Net, Cicero *Also called Integrated Display Systems Inc* ***(G-6856)***
Ieg Sponsorship Conference, Chicago *Also called ESP Properties LLC* ***(G-4531)***
Iei, Bolingbrook *Also called Institutional Equipment Inc* ***(G-2192)***
IEM, Vernon Hills *Also called Independent Eyewear Mfg LLC* ***(G-20066)***
Iemco Corporation ... 773 728-4400
4530 N Ravenswood Ave Chicago (60640) ***(G-4878)***
Iep Quality Inc ... 217 840-0570
2705 N Salisbury Ct Champaign (61821) ***(G-3305)***
Iepa Printing, Springfield *Also called State Attorney Appellate* ***(G-19458)***
Iesco Inc ... 708 594-1250
737 Oakridge Dr Romeoville (60446) ***(G-17831)***
If Walls Could Talk ... 847 219-5527
323 W Harvard Cir South Elgin (60177) ***(G-19154)***
Ifa International Inc ... 847 566-0008
354356 Townline Rd Mundelein (60060) ***(G-14698)***
Ifastgroupe Usa LLC ... 450 658-7148
2626 Warrenville Rd # 400 Downers Grove (60515) ***(G-8026)***
Ifco ... 630 226-0650
400 W Crssrads Pkwy Ste A Bolingbrook (60440) ***(G-2188)***
Ifh Group Inc (PA) ... 800 435-7003
3300 E Rock Falls Rd Rock Falls (61071) ***(G-17187)***
Ifh Group Inc ... 815 380-2367
5505 Anne St Galt (61037) ***(G-10225)***
Ifm, Litchfield *Also called International Filter Mfg Corp* ***(G-12966)***
Ifs North America Inc (HQ) ... 888 437-4968
300 Park Blvd Ste 555 Itasca (60143) ***(G-11670)***
Ig US Holdings Inc ... 312 884-0179
200 W Jackson Blvd # 1450 Chicago (60606) ***(G-4879)***
Igar Bridal Inc ... 224 318-2337
723 E Dundee Rd Arlington Heights (60004) ***(G-754)***
Igd Display LLC ... 630 916-0700
2804 Centre Cir Downers Grove (60515) ***(G-8027)***
Igd Group LLC ... 630 240-6736
140 E Saint Charles Rd Elmhurst (60126) ***(G-9374)***
Iggys Auto Parts ... 708 452-9790
7230 W Montrose Ave Norridge (60706) ***(G-15237)***
Igm Solutions Inc ... 847 918-1790
1900 Enterprise Ct Libertyville (60048) ***(G-12661)***
Ignite Usa LLC ... 312 432-6223
180 N La Salle St Ste 700 Chicago (60601) ***(G-4880)***
Igt Testing Systems Inc ... 847 952-2448
543 W Golf Rd Arlington Heights (60005) ***(G-755)***
Iguanamed LLC ... 312 546-4182
363 W Erie St Ste 200e Chicago (60654) ***(G-4881)***
Iheartcommunications Inc ... 312 255-5100
875 N Michigan Ave # 4000 Chicago (60611) ***(G-4882)***
Ihi Terrasun Solutions Inc ... 312 878-8532
100 N Riverside Plz # 220 Chicago (60606) ***(G-4883)***
Ihi Turbo America Co (HQ) ... 217 774-9571
1598 State Highway 16 Shelbyville (62565) ***(G-18880)***
Iht, Crystal Lake *Also called Induction Heat Treating Corp* ***(G-7210)***
IICLE, Springfield *Also called Illinois Inst Cntng Legl Ed* ***(G-19386)***
Ikan Creations LLC ... 312 204-7333
2010 S Wabash Ave Ste H Chicago (60616) ***(G-4884)***
Iko Midwest Inc ... 815 936-9600
6600 S Central Ave Chicago (60638) ***(G-4885)***
Ikonix Group Inc (PA) ... 847 367-4671
28105 N Keith Dr Lake Forest (60045) ***(G-12266)***
IL Green Pastures Fiber Co-Op ... 815 751-0887
28668 Bell Rd Kirkland (60146) ***(G-12061)***
IL International LLC (PA) ... 773 276-0070
1720 N Elston Ave Chicago (60642) ***(G-4886)***
IL Tool Work ... 630 972-6400
309 E Crossroads Pkwy Bolingbrook (60440) ***(G-2189)***
Ileesh Products LLC ... 224 424-4682
100 N Fairway Dr Ste 114 Vernon Hills (60061) ***(G-20062)***
Iler Brands Inc ... 314 799-3833
1350 Bossler Ln O Fallon (62269) ***(G-15574)***
Ilf Technologies LLC ... 630 789-9770
7001 S Adams St Willowbrook (60527) ***(G-21047)***
Ilf Technologies LLC ... 630 759-1776
1215 S Laramie Ave Cicero (60804) ***(G-6854)***
Ilight Technologies Inc (PA) ... 312 876-8630
118 S Clinton St Ste 370 Chicago (60661) ***(G-4887)***
Ilikecrochet.com, Northbrook *Also called Prime Publishing LLC* ***(G-15466)***
Ill Dept Natural Resources ... 217 498-9208
9898 Cascade Rd Rochester (62563) ***(G-17167)***
Ill Dept Natural Resources ... 217 782-4970
1 Natural Resources Way # 100 Springfield (62702) ***(G-19384)***
Illco Inc ... 815 725-9100
2106 Mcdonough St Joliet (60436) ***(G-11878)***
Illiana Cores Inc ... 618 586-9800
10156 N 1725th St Palestine (62451) ***(G-16178)***
Illiana Financial Inc ... 630 941-3838
833 N Church Rd Elmhurst (60126) ***(G-9375)***
Illiana Machine & Mfg Corp ... 708 479-1333
19700 97th Ave Mokena (60448) ***(G-14090)***
Illiana Orthopedics Inc ... 708 532-0061
17378 Overhill Ave Tinley Park (60477) ***(G-19836)***
Illiana Real Log Homes Inc ... 815 471-4004
107 N Fritz Dr Milford (60953) ***(G-14035)***
Illini Castings LLC ... 217 446-6365
1940 E Fairchild St Danville (61832) ***(G-7349)***
Illini Concrete Inc (PA) ... 618 235-4141
1300 E A St Belleville (62221) ***(G-1557)***
Illini Concrete Inc ... 618 398-4141
10 Tucker Dr Caseyville (62232) ***(G-3214)***
Illini Coolant Management Corp (PA) ... 847 966-1079
8011 Parkside Ave Morton Grove (60053) ***(G-14412)***
Illini Digital Printing Co ... 618 271-6622
680 N 20th St East Saint Louis (62205) ***(G-8311)***
Illini Foundry Co Inc ... 309 697-3142
6523 N Galena Rd Peoria (61614) ***(G-16456)***

ALPHABETIC SECTION

Illinois Tool Works Inc

Illini Fs Inc 217 442-4737
6637 E 3050 North Rd Potomac (61865) **(G-16802)**

Illini Line, Ltd., Vernon Hills *Also called Altco Inc* **(G-20041)**

Illini Media Co (PA) 217 337-8300
1001 S Wright St Champaign (61820) **(G-3306)**

Illini Precast 815 795-6161
2649 E Us Highway 6 Marseilles (61341) **(G-13557)**

Illini Precast LLC 708 562-7700
2255 Entp Dr Ste 5501 Westchester (60154) **(G-20700)**

Illini Precision Machining Inc 217 425-5780
750 E Prairie Ave Decatur (62523) **(G-7504)**

Illini Ready Mix Inc 618 833-7321
300 Mckinley St Anna (62906) **(G-585)**

Illini Ready Mix Inc (PA) 618 734-0287
801 W Industrial Park Rd Carbondale (62901) **(G-2846)**

Illini Tech Services, Carlinville *Also called Integrated Media Inc* **(G-2877)**

Illinoi Eye Surgns/Quantm Visn 618 315-6560
3000 Broadway St Mount Vernon (62864) **(G-14615)**

Illinois Agricultural Assn, Bloomington *Also called Farm Week* **(G-2042)**

Illinois Assn Cnty Officials 217 585-9065
1417 James St Springfield (62703) **(G-19385)**

Illinois Baking 773 995-7200
10839 S Langley Ave Chicago (60628) **(G-4888)**

Illinois Blower Inc 847 639-5500
750 Industrial Dr Ste E Cary (60013) **(G-3168)**

Illinois Bone & Joint Inst LLC 847 724-4470
2350 Ravine Way Ste 600 Glenview (60025) **(G-10559)**

Illinois Bottle Mfg Co 847 595-9000
701 E Devon Ave Elk Grove Village (60007) **(G-9040)**

Illinois Box & Pallet, Taylorville *Also called Botkin Lumber Company Inc* **(G-19751)**

Illinois Broaching Company (PA) 847 678-3080
4200 Grace St Schiller Park (60176) **(G-18815)**

Illinois Capacitor Inc 847 675-1760
2400 E Devon Ave Ste 292 Des Plaines (60018) **(G-7783)**

Illinois Carbide Tool Co Inc (PA) 847 244-1110
1322 Belvidere Rd Waukegan (60085) **(G-20447)**

Illinois Cement Company LLC (HQ) 815 224-2112
1601 Rockwell Rd La Salle (61301) **(G-12113)**

Illinois Conveyor Service Inc 630 469-1300
21w161 Hill Ave Glen Ellyn (60137) **(G-10406)**

Illinois Corn Processing LLC 309 353-3990
1301 S Front St Pekin (61554) **(G-16339)**

Illinois Dermatological Center, Elk Grove Village *Also called Michael A Greenberg MD Ltd* **(G-9122)**

Illinois Electric Works Inc 618 451-6900
2161 Adams St Granite City (62040) **(G-10717)**

Illinois Electro Deburring Co (PA) 847 678-5010
2915 Birch St Franklin Park (60131) **(G-9961)**

Illinois Embroidery Service 618 526-8006
580 N 2nd St Breese (62230) **(G-2304)**

Illinois Engineered Pdts Inc 312 850-3710
2415 W 21st St Chicago (60608) **(G-4889)**

Illinois Engraving & Mfg Co, Chicago *Also called Iemco Corporation* **(G-4878)**

Illinois Expedited Express Inc 217 926-2171
18227 Olde Farm Rd Lansing (60438) **(G-12498)**

Illinois Fibre Specialty Co (PA) 773 376-1122
4301 S Western Blvd Chicago (60609) **(G-4890)**

Illinois Forge Company, Rock Falls *Also called I Forge Company LLC* **(G-17186)**

Illinois Foundation Seeds Inc 217 485-6420
1178 County Road 900 N Tolono (61880) **(G-19883)**

Illinois Fuel Company LLC 618 275-4486
920 Gape Hollow Rd Herod (62947) **(G-11170)**

Illinois Glove Company 847 291-1700
650 Anthony Trl Ste A Northbrook (60062) **(G-15402)**

Illinois Green Cnstr Inc 847 975-2312
3651 N Nora Ave Chicago (60634) **(G-4891)**

Illinois Inst Cntng Legl Ed 217 787-2080
2395 W Jefferson St Springfield (62702) **(G-19386)**

Illinois Instruments Inc 815 344-6212
2401 Hiller Rdg Ste A Johnsburg (60051) **(G-11805)**

Illinois Lift Equipment Inc 888 745-0577
640 Industrial Dr Cary (60013) **(G-3169)**

Illinois Meter Inc 618 438-6039
1500 W Webster St Benton (62812) **(G-1927)**

Illinois Mold Builders Inc 847 526-0400
250 Jamie Ln Wauconda (60084) **(G-20359)**

Illinois Newspaper In Educatn 847 427-4388
1 Copley Plz Springfield (62701) **(G-19387)**

Illinois Ni Cast LLC 217 398-3200
1700 W Washington St Champaign (61821) **(G-3307)**

Illinois Office Sup Elect Prtg 815 434-0186
1119 La Salle St Ottawa (61350) **(G-16056)**

Illinois Oil Marketing Eqp Inc (PA) 309 347-1819
850 Brenkman Dr Pekin (61554) **(G-16340)**

Illinois Oil Marketing Eqp Inc 217 935-5107
601 E Leander St Clinton (61727) **(G-6924)**

Illinois Oil Products Inc 309 788-1896
2715 36th St Rock Island (61201) **(G-17224)**

Illinois Pallets Inc 773 640-9228
8075 Tec Air Ave Willow Springs (60480) **(G-21026)**

Illinois Pneumatic Inc 815 654-9301
9325 Starboard Dr Ste B Roscoe (61073) **(G-17910)**

Illinois Pneumatic Tool Co, Addison *Also called Ivan Schwenker* **(G-156)**

Illinois Printing Services Inc 217 728-2786
800 S Patterson Rd Sullivan (61951) **(G-19669)**

Illinois Pro-Turn Inc 847 462-1870
309 Cary Point Dr Ste F Cary (60013) **(G-3170)**

Illinois Pulley & Gear Inc 847 407-9595
611 Lunt Ave Ste C Schaumburg (60193) **(G-18556)**

Illinois Rack Enterprises Inc 815 385-5750
480 Scotland Rd Ste A Lakemoor (60051) **(G-12472)**

Illinois Radio Network, Springfield *Also called Saga Communications Inc* **(G-19438)**

Illinois River Energy LLC 815 561-0650
4000 N Division Rochelle (61068) **(G-17146)**

Illinois Road Contractors Inc (PA) 217 245-6181
520 N Webster Ave Jacksonville (62650) **(G-11769)**

Illinois Sports News, Chicago *Also called Wabash Publishing Co Inc* **(G-6581)**

Illinois State Usbc Wba 309 827-6355
402 W Hamilton Rd Bloomington (61704) **(G-2061)**

Illinois Sterling Ltd 847 526-5151
540 S Rand Rd Wauconda (60084) **(G-20360)**

Illinois Switchboard Corp 630 543-0910
125 W Laura Dr Addison (60101) **(G-154)**

Illinois Tag Co 773 626-0542
287 Commonwealth Dr Carol Stream (60188) **(G-3001)**

Illinois Ticket Defense Firm 954 467-1965
39w745 Goldenrod Dr Saint Charles (60175) **(G-18210)**

Illinois Times, Springfield *Also called Central Ill Communications LLC* **(G-19345)**

Illinois Tool Works Inc 630 825-7900
700 High Grove Blvd Glendale Heights (60139) **(G-10460)**

Illinois Tool Works Inc (PA) 847 724-7500
155 Harlem Ave Glenview (60025) **(G-10560)**

Illinois Tool Works Inc 708 325-2300
7201 S 78th Ave Bridgeview (60455) **(G-2356)**

Illinois Tool Works Inc 630 372-2150
1452 Brewster Creek Blvd Bartlett (60103) **(G-1288)**

Illinois Tool Works Inc 847 724-7500
195 E Algonquin Rd Des Plaines (60016) **(G-7784)**

Illinois Tool Works Inc 708 681-3891
2550 S 27th Ave Broadview (60155) **(G-2442)**

Illinois Tool Works Inc 630 773-9300
1140 W Bryn Mawr Ave Itasca (60143) **(G-11671)**

Illinois Tool Works Inc 708 720-0300
250 Industry Ave Frankfort (60423) **(G-9803)**

Illinois Tool Works Inc 847 657-4639
3640 W Lake Ave Glenview (60026) **(G-10561)**

Illinois Tool Works Inc 630 595-3500
1349 W Bryn Mawr Ave Itasca (60143) **(G-11672)**

Illinois Tool Works Inc 708 720-0300
21601 S Harlem Ave Frankfort (60423) **(G-9804)**

Illinois Tool Works Inc 630 752-4000
475 N Gary Ave Carol Stream (60188) **(G-3002)**

Illinois Tool Works Inc 847 634-1900
888 Forest Edge Dr Vernon Hills (60061) **(G-20063)**

Illinois Tool Works Inc 630 595-3500
86 Chancellor Dr Roselle (60172) **(G-17958)**

Illinois Tool Works Inc 708 720-2600
21555 S Harlem Ave Frankfort (60423) **(G-9805)**

Illinois Tool Works Inc 630 993-9990
935 N Oaklawn Ave Elmhurst (60126) **(G-9376)**

Illinois Tool Works Inc 217 345-2166
1140 W Bryn Mawr Ave Itasca (60143) **(G-11673)**

Illinois Tool Works Inc 630 787-3298
950 Pratt Blvd Elk Grove Village (60007) **(G-9041)**

Illinois Tool Works Inc 630 315-2150
425 N Gary Ave Carol Stream (60188) **(G-3003)**

Illinois Tool Works Inc 708 720-7070
21701 S Harlem Ave Frankfort (60423) **(G-9806)**

Illinois Tool Works Inc 708 479-3346
8402 183rd St Ste D Tinley Park (60487) **(G-19837)**

Illinois Tool Works Inc 847 593-8811
830 Lee St Elk Grove Village (60007) **(G-9042)**

Illinois Tool Works Inc 847 350-0193
2471 Brickvale Dr Elk Grove Village (60007) **(G-9043)**

Illinois Tool Works Inc 847 741-7900
1201 Saint Charles St Elgin (60120) **(G-8620)**

Illinois Tool Works Inc 217 345-2166
155 5th St Charleston (61920) **(G-3404)**

Illinois Tool Works Inc 847 918-6473
14050 W Lambs Ln Unit 1 Libertyville (60048) **(G-12662)**

Illinois Tool Works Inc 708 720-7800
22501 Bohlmann Pkwy Richton Park (60471) **(G-17028)**

Illinois Tool Works Inc 847 634-1900
888 Forest Edge Dr Vernon Hills (60061) **(G-20064)**

Illinois Tool Works Inc 847 821-2170
888 Forest Edge Dr Vernon Hills (60061) **(G-20065)**

Illinois Tool Works Inc 847 299-2222
195 E Algonquin Rd Des Plaines (60016) **(G-7785)**

ALPHABETIC

(PA)=Parent Co (HQ)=Headquarters (DH)=Div Headquarters

2020 Harris Illinois
Industrial Directory

1151

Illinois Tool Works Inc..........708 681-3891
2550 S 27th Ave Broadview (60155) ***(G-2443)***
Illinois Tool Works Inc..........618 997-1716
5307 Meadowland Pkwy Marion (62959) ***(G-13518)***
Illinois Tool Works Inc..........708 720-0300
250 Industry Ave Frankfort (60423) ***(G-9807)***
Illinois Tool Works Inc..........847 657-5300
155 Harlem Ave Glenview (60025) ***(G-10562)***
Illinois Tool Works Inc..........708 479-7200
9629 197th St Mokena (60448) ***(G-14091)***
Illinois Tool Works Inc..........815 654-1510
10818 N 2nd St Machesney Park (61115) ***(G-13348)***
Illinois Tool Works Inc..........847 215-8925
180 Hastings Dr Buffalo Grove (60089) ***(G-2548)***
Illinois Tool Works Inc..........847 724-6100
3650 W Lake Ave Glenview (60026) ***(G-10563)***
Illinois Tool Works Inc..........847 783-5500
2501 Galvin Dr Elgin (60124) ***(G-8621)***
Illinois Tool Works Inc..........563 422-5686
3700 W Lake Ave Glenview (60026) ***(G-10564)***
Illinois Tool Works Inc..........815 654-1510
10818 N 2nd St Machesney Park (61115) ***(G-13349)***
Illinois Tool Works Inc..........815 448-7300
804 Commercial Dr Mazon (60444) ***(G-13681)***
Illinois Tool Works Inc..........708 458-7320
7701 W 71st St Bridgeview (60455) ***(G-2357)***
Illinois Tool Works Inc..........847 766-9000
2700 York Rd Elk Grove Village (60007) ***(G-9044)***
Illinois Tool Works Inc..........815 943-4785
600 Knightsbridge Pkwy Lincolnshire (60069) ***(G-12774)***
Illinois Tool Works Inc..........630 993-9990
935 N Oaklawn Ave Elmhurst (60126) ***(G-9377)***
Illinois Tool Works Inc..........847 295-6500
41 Waukegan Rd Lake Bluff (60044) ***(G-12189)***
Illinois Tool Works Inc..........708 720-3541
21701 S Harlem Ave Frankfort (60423) ***(G-9808)***
Illinois Tool Works Inc..........847 724-7500
2550 Millbrook Dr Buffalo Grove (60089) ***(G-2549)***
Illinois Tool Works Inc..........708 479-3346
8402 183rd St Ste D Tinley Park (60487) ***(G-19838)***
Illinois Tool Works Inc..........847 657-4022
3660 W Lake Ave Glenview (60026) ***(G-10565)***
Illinois Transit Assembly Corp..........618 451-0100
1980 3rd St Madison (62060) ***(G-13415)***
Illinois Valley Container Inc..........815 223-7200
2 Terminal Rd Peru (61354) ***(G-16578)***
Illinois Valley Glass & Mirror..........309 682-6603
3300 Ne Adams St Ste A Peoria (61603) ***(G-16457)***
Illinois Valley Machine Sp Inc..........815 586-4511
108 N Lincoln St Ransom (60470) ***(G-16965)***
Illinois Valley Minerals LLC..........815 442-8402
575 N 18th Rd Tonica (61370) ***(G-19889)***
Illinois Valley Paving Co Inc..........217 422-1010
Rr 51 Box S Elwin (62532) ***(G-9459)***
Illinois Valley Plastics, Washington *Also called Iplastics LLC* ***(G-20270)***
Illinois Valley Press East..........217 586-2512
303 E Main St Ste D Mahomet (61853) ***(G-13424)***
Illinois Water Tech Inc..........815 636-8884
5443 Swanson Ct Roscoe (61073) ***(G-17911)***
Illinois Weld & Machine Inc..........309 565-0533
123 S 2nd St Hanna City (61536) ***(G-10992)***
Illinois Weld & Machine Inc (PA)..........309 565-0533
101 S 2nd St Hanna City (61536) ***(G-10993)***
Illinois Wood Fiber Products..........847 836-6176
99 Day Ln Carpentersville (60110) ***(G-3105)***
Illmo R/X Service..........217 877-1192
3373 N Woodford St Decatur (62526) ***(G-7505)***
Illmo R/X Services, Decatur *Also called Illmo R/X Service* ***(G-7505)***
Illumen Studios LLC..........847 440-2222
314 Lexington Ln Grayslake (60030) ***(G-10782)***
Illuminight Lighting LLC..........312 685-4448
1954 1st St 394 Highland Park (60035) ***(G-11272)***
Illumivation Studios LLC..........312 261-5561
4425 S Western Blvd Ste 1 Chicago (60609) ***(G-4892)***
ILmachine Company Inc..........847 243-9900
421 Harvester Ct Wheeling (60090) ***(G-20913)***
Ilmo Products Company (PA)..........217 245-2183
7 Eastgate Dr Jacksonville (62650) ***(G-11770)***
Iloilo Custom Framing..........773 334-2844
850 W Argyle St Apt 506 Chicago (60640) ***(G-4893)***
Ilpea Industries Inc..........309 343-3332
611 S Linwood Rd Galesburg (61401) ***(G-10201)***
Ima Automation North America, Loves Park *Also called Ima Automation Usa Inc* ***(G-13217)***
Ima Automation Usa Inc..........815 885-8800
4608 Interstate Blvd Loves Park (61111) ***(G-13217)***
Imac Asset Sales Corp..........847 741-4622
2521 Tech Dr Ste 212 Elgin (60124) ***(G-8622)***
Imacc LLC..........512 341-8189
500 W Wood St Palatine (60067) ***(G-16126)***
Imada Inc..........847 562-0834
3100 Dundee Rd Ste 707 Northbrook (60062) ***(G-15403)***
Image 360 - Mokena, Mokena *Also called Store 409 Inc* ***(G-14117)***
Image Circuit Inc..........847 622-3300
925 Estes Ave Elk Grove Village (60007) ***(G-9045)***
Image Fx Corp..........630 655-2850
16w109 83rd St Burr Ridge (60527) ***(G-2685)***
Image Pact Printing..........708 460-6070
18650 Graphic Ct Tinley Park (60477) ***(G-19839)***
Image Plus Inc..........630 852-4920
4248 Belle Aire Ln Ste 1 Downers Grove (60515) ***(G-8028)***
Image Print Inc (PA)..........815 672-1068
31070 N 600 East Rd Streator (61364) ***(G-19611)***
Image Signs Inc..........815 282-4141
7323 N Alpine Rd Loves Park (61111) ***(G-13218)***
Image Systems Bus Slutions LLC..........847 378-8249
1776 Commerce Dr Elk Grove Village (60007) ***(G-9046)***
Image360 Gurnee, Gurnee *Also called Fourth Quarter Holdings Inc* ***(G-10879)***
Imagecare Maintenance Svcs LLC..........847 631-3306
1701 Golf Rd Ste 1-900 Rolling Meadows (60008) ***(G-17739)***
Images Alive Ltd..........847 498-5550
875 Pleasant Ave Highland Park (60035) ***(G-11273)***
Imageworks Creative Group, Highland *Also called Digital Artz LLC* ***(G-11213)***
Imageworks Manufacturing Inc..........708 503-1122
49 South St Park Forest (60466) ***(G-16255)***
Imagination Products Corp..........309 274-6223
227 W Cedar St Chillicothe (61523) ***(G-6818)***
Imagination Publishing LLC..........312 887-1000
600 W Fulton St Ste 600 # 600 Chicago (60661) ***(G-4894)***
Imagine That Candle Co..........708 481-6370
4107 Applewood Ln Matteson (60443) ***(G-13625)***
Imagineering Inc..........847 806-0003
2425 Touhy Ave Elk Grove Village (60007) ***(G-9047)***
Imaging Equipment Sales, Highland Park *Also called Bka Inc* ***(G-11255)***
Imaging Systems Inc (PA)..........630 875-1100
1009 W Hawthorn Dr Itasca (60143) ***(G-11674)***
Imaginings 3 Inc..........847 647-1370
6401 W Gross Point Rd Niles (60714) ***(G-15131)***
Imago Manufacturing..........815 333-5272
321 Schryver Ave Woodstock (60098) ***(G-21395)***
Imanage LLC (PA)..........312 667-7000
540 W Madison St Ste 300 Chicago (60661) ***(G-4895)***
Imap, Grayslake *Also called International Mold & Prod LLC* ***(G-10783)***
Imbert Construction Inds Inc..........847 588-3170
7030 N Austin Ave Niles (60714) ***(G-15132)***
Imbibe, Niles *Also called Amt Group LLC* ***(G-15103)***
IMC Outdoor Living..........314 373-1171
315 Tolle Ln Godfrey (62035) ***(G-10653)***
Imco, Benton *Also called Illinois Meter Inc* ***(G-1927)***
Imco Precast LLC..........217 742-5300
4390 Jeffory St Springfield (62703) ***(G-19388)***
Imcp Inc..........630 477-8600
900 N Arlington Itasca (60143) ***(G-11675)***
Imds, Geneva *Also called Innovative Molecular Diagnosti* ***(G-10283)***
Imed Glenview..........847 298-2200
1247 Milwaukee Ave # 100 Glenview (60025) ***(G-10566)***
Imedia Network Inc..........847 331-1774
2532 W Irving Park Rd 1e Chicago (60618) ***(G-4896)***
Imerys Refractory Mnrl USA Inc..........618 285-6558
Ferrell Rd Rosiclare (62982) ***(G-18064)***
Imh Fabrication Inc..........815 537-2381
326 W 5th St Prophetstown (61277) ***(G-16833)***
Imhear Corporation..........630 395-9628
2711 Curtiss St Ste B Downers Grove (60515) ***(G-8029)***
IMI Manufacturing Inc..........630 771-0003
694 Veterans Pkwy Ste B Bolingbrook (60440) ***(G-2190)***
IMI McR Inc..........309 734-6282
1301 N Main St Ste 3 Monmouth (61462) ***(G-14218)***
IMI Precision Engineering, Machesney Park *Also called Bimba Manufacturing Company* ***(G-13329)***
Imp, Niles *Also called Industrial Market Place* ***(G-15133)***
Impac Group Inc..........708 344-9100
1950 N Ruby St Melrose Park (60160) ***(G-13881)***
Impac Products, Chicago *Also called J B Watts Company Inc* ***(G-4987)***
Impact Bronze Plaques, La Grange *Also called Impact Signs & Graphics Inc* ***(G-12080)***
Impact Polymer LLC..........847 441-2394
790 W Frontage Rd Northfield (60093) ***(G-15517)***
Impact Prtrs & Lithographers..........847 981-9676
1370 E Higgins Rd Elk Grove Village (60007) ***(G-9048)***
Impact Signs & Graphics Inc..........708 469-7178
26 E Burlington Ave La Grange (60525) ***(G-12080)***
Imperial Glass Structures Co..........847 253-6150
2120 Foster Ave Wheeling (60090) ***(G-20914)***
Imperial Group Mfg Inc..........615 325-9224
640 N La Salle Dr Ste 670 Chicago (60654) ***(G-4897)***
Imperial Kitchens & Bath Inc..........708 485-0020
8918 Ogden Ave Brookfield (60513) ***(G-2486)***

ALPHABETIC SECTION

Imperial Mfg Group Inc 618 465-3133
   1450 Discovery Pkwy Alton (62002) *(G-559)*
Imperial Oil Inc 773 866-1235
   4346 N Western Ave Chicago (60618) *(G-4898)*
Imperial Pizza, Streamwood Also called Randolph Packing Co *(G-19592)*
Imperial Plating Company III 773 586-3500
   7030 W 60th St Chicago (60638) *(G-4899)*
Imperial Punch & Manufacturing 815 226-8200
   2016 23rd Ave Rockford (61104) *(G-17457)*
Imperial Steel Tank 773 779-4284
   10439 S Maplewood Ave Chicago (60655) *(G-4900)*
Imperial Store Fixtures Inc 773 348-1137
   3768 N Clark St Chicago (60613) *(G-4901)*
Imperial Technical Services 708 403-1564
   14001 Thomas Dr Orland Park (60462) *(G-15961)*
Imperial Woodworking Company (PA) 847 221-2107
   310 N Woodwork Ln Palatine (60067) *(G-16127)*
Imperial Woodworking Entps Inc 847 358-6920
   310 N Woodwork Ln Palatine (60067) *(G-16128)*
Impossible Objects Inc 847 400-9582
   3455 Commercial Ave Northbrook (60062) *(G-15404)*
Impress Printing & Design Inc 815 730-9440
   1325 W Jefferson St Joliet (60435) *(G-11879)*
Impression Printing 708 614-8660
   4901 Lorin Ln Oak Forest (60452) *(G-15682)*
Impressions Count Printing 847 395-2445
   907 Main St Antioch (60002) *(G-616)*
Impressive Impressions 312 432-0501
   329 W 18th St Ste 306 Chicago (60616) *(G-4902)*
Imprex International Inc 847 364-4930
   2916 Malmo Dr Arlington Heights (60005) *(G-756)*
Impro Graphics, Arlington Heights Also called Impro International Inc *(G-757)*
Impro Industries Usa Inc 630 759-0280
   375 Sw Frontage Rd Ste D Bolingbrook (60440) *(G-2191)*
Impro International Inc 847 398-3870
   3110 N Arlington Hts Rd Arlington Heights (60004) *(G-757)*
IMS, Bourbonnais Also called Tms International LLC *(G-2271)*
IMS Buhrke-Olson, Arlington Heights Also called Olson Metal Products LLC *(G-784)*
IMS Buhrke-Olson, Arlington Heights Also called Buhrke Industries LLC *(G-711)*
IMS Buhrke-Olson, Elk Grove Village Also called Buhrke Industries LLC *(G-8873)*
IMS Companies   LLC (PA) 847 391-8100
   1 Innovation Dr Des Plaines (60016) *(G-7786)*
IMS Engineered Products   LLC 847 391-8100
   1 Innovation Dr Des Plaines (60016) *(G-7787)*
IMS Olson   LLC 630 969-9400
   2500 Curtiss St Downers Grove (60515) *(G-8030)*
Imtran Industries Inc 630 752-4000
   475 N Gary Ave Carol Stream (60188) *(G-3004)*
In Aaw Hair Emporium LLC 779 227-1450
   423 Buell Ave 1 Joliet (60435) *(G-11880)*
In Color Graphics Coml Prtg 847 697-0003
   1855 Fox Ln Elgin (60123) *(G-8623)*
In Focus Restaurant & Bar Sup, Joliet Also called Bar Stool Depotcom *(G-11827)*
In Sight Sign Company Inc 773 267-4002
   3910 W Grand Ave Chicago (60651) *(G-4903)*
In Style Magazine, Chicago Also called TI Gotham Inc *(G-6376)*
In The Attic Inc 847 949-5077
   1955 Buckingham Rd Mundelein (60060) *(G-14699)*
In These Times, Chicago Also called Institute For Public Affairs *(G-4938)*
In-Place Machining Co Inc 847 669-3006
   11414 Smith Dr Unit D Huntley (60142) *(G-11542)*
In-Print Graphics Inc (PA) 708 396-1010
   4201 166th St Oak Forest (60452) *(G-15683)*
In3gredients Inc 312 577-4275
   30 N Michigan Ave Ste 505 Chicago (60602) *(G-4904)*
Inav LLC 847 847-3600
   300 Exchange Dr Ste C Crystal Lake (60014) *(G-7209)*
Inc Midwest Die Mold 224 353-6417
   624 Lunt Ave Schaumburg (60193) *(G-18557)*
Inc., Dix McGuire Intl, Palatine Also called Dix-Mcguire Commodities - LLC *(G-16112)*
Incline Construction Inc 815 577-8881
   131 Airport Dr Unit H Joliet (60431) *(G-11881)*
Incline Welding & Construction, Joliet Also called Incline Construction Inc *(G-11881)*
Inclusion Solutions   LLC 847 869-2500
   2000 Greenleaf St Ste 3 Evanston (60202) *(G-9537)*
Incobrasa Industries   Ltd 815 265-4803
   540 E Us Highway 24 Gilman (60938) *(G-10380)*
Incon Industries Inc 630 728-4014
   3955 Commerce Dr Saint Charles (60174) *(G-18211)*
Incon Processing   LLC (HQ) 630 305-8556
   970 Douglas Rd Batavia (60510) *(G-1385)*
Incredible Threads   LLC 847 970-0183
   300 Moseley St Elgin (60123) *(G-8624)*
Independence Tube Corporation, Chicago Also called Nucor Tubular Products Inc *(G-5639)*
Independent Antique RAD Mfg 847 458-7400
   200 Berg St Algonquin (60102) *(G-374)*
Independent Awning Co, South Holland Also called Chesterfield Awning Co Inc *(G-19205)*

Independent Eyewear Mfg LLC 847 537-0008
   255 Corp Woods Pkwy Vernon Hills (60061) *(G-20066)*
Independent Network Tv LLC 312 953-8508
   1525 Circle Ave Ste 3 Forest Park (60130) *(G-9720)*
Independent News 217 662-6001
   2202 Kickapoo Dr Danville (61832) *(G-7350)*
Independent News, The, Danville Also called Independent News *(G-7350)*
Independent Publishers Group, Chicago Also called I P G Warehouse Ltd *(G-4867)*
Independent Publishers Group, Chicago Also called Chicago Review Press Inc *(G-4126)*
Independent Shoppers 309 647-5200
   154 W Washington Ave Lewistown (61542) *(G-12616)*
Indesco Oven Products Inc 217 622-6345
   15935 Whisper Ln Petersburg (62675) *(G-16602)*
Indev Gauging Systems Inc 815 282-4463
   6830 Forest Hills Rd Loves Park (61111) *(G-13219)*
India Bulletin Inc 847 674-7941
   4332 Emerson St Skokie (60076) *(G-18968)*
India Tribune Ltd Corporation (PA) 773 588-5077
   3304 W Peterson Ave Chicago (60659) *(G-4905)*
Indian Creek Development, Aurora Also called Louis J Hansen Enterprises Inc *(G-1124)*
Indian Point Oil & Gas, Salem Also called Jerry D Graham Oil *(G-18344)*
Indiana Agri-News Inc 317 726-5391
   420 2nd St La Salle (61301) *(G-12114)*
Indiana Precision Inc 765 361-0247
   130 N Jackson St Danville (61832) *(G-7351)*
Indiana Steel & Tube, Chicago Also called E & H Tubing Inc *(G-4419)*
Indigo Time 847 255-4818
   800 W Central Rd Ste 162 Mount Prospect (60056) *(G-14534)*
Indilab Inc 847 928-1050
   10367 Franklin Ave Franklin Park (60131) *(G-9962)*
Indium Corporation of America 847 439-9134
   80 Scott St Elk Grove Village (60007) *(G-9049)*
Indorama Ventures Oxide & Glyl (HQ) 800 365-0794
   2610 Lake Cook Rd Ste 133 Riverwoods (60015) *(G-17092)*
Indorama Vntres USA Hldings LP (HQ) 847 943-3100
   2610 Lake Cook Rd Riverwoods (60015) *(G-17093)*
Induction Heat Treating Corp 815 477-7788
   775 Tek Dr Crystal Lake (60014) *(G-7210)*
Induction Innovations Inc 847 836-6933
   1175 Jansen Farm Ct Elgin (60123) *(G-8625)*
Induspac Rtp Inc. 919 484-9484
   8100 77th Ave Bridgeview (60455) *(G-2358)*
Industrial Controls Inc 630 752-8100
   512 Nelson Dr Geneva (60134) *(G-10278)*
Industrial Cstm Powdr Coating, Decatur Also called Industrial Cstm Pwdr Cting Inc *(G-7506)*
Industrial Cstm Pwdr Cting Inc 217 423-4272
   661 E Wood St Decatur (62523) *(G-7506)*
Industrial Diamond Products 847 272-7840
   3045 Macarthur Blvd Northbrook (60062) *(G-15405)*
Industrial Electric Svc Inc (PA) 708 997-2090
   1055 Martingale Dr Bartlett (60103) *(G-1289)*
Industrial Electronic Contrls 815 873-1980
   4689 Stenstrom Rd Rockford (61109) *(G-17458)*
Industrial Enclosure Corp. 630 898-7499
   619 N Loucks St Ste A Aurora (60505) *(G-1111)*
Industrial Fence Inc 773 521-9900
   1300 S Kilbourn Ave Chicago (60623) *(G-4906)*
Industrial Fiberglass Inc 708 681-2707
   1100 Main St Melrose Park (60160) *(G-13882)*
Industrial Filter Pump Mfg Co 708 656-7800
   5900 W Ogden Ave Cicero (60804) *(G-6855)*
Industrial Finance Systems 847 592-0200
   300 Park Blvd Itasca (60143) *(G-11676)*
Industrial Finishing   Inc 847 451-4230
   2337 17th St Franklin Park (60131) *(G-9963)*
Industrial Gas Products Inc 618 337-1030
   2350 Falling Springs Rd East Saint Louis (62206) *(G-8312)*
Industrial Graphite Products 630 350-0155
   429 S County Line Rd Franklin Park (60131) *(G-9964)*
Industrial Graphite Sales LLC 815 943-5502
   450 Commanche Cir Harvard (60033) *(G-11057)*
Industrial Hard Chrome   Ltd 630 208-7000
   501 Fluid Power Dr Geneva (60134) *(G-10279)*
Industrial Instrument Svc Corp 773 581-3355
   5643 W 63rd Pl Chicago (60638) *(G-4907)*
Industrial Kinetics Inc (PA) 630 655-0300
   2535 Curtiss St Downers Grove (60515) *(G-8031)*
Industrial Market Place 847 676-1900
   5940 W Touhy Ave Ste 230 Niles (60714) *(G-15133)*
Industrial Mint Wldg Machining 773 376-6526
   1431 W Pershing Rd Chicago (60609) *(G-4908)*
Industrial Modern Pattern 847 296-4930
   970 Nicholas Blvd Elk Grove Village (60007) *(G-9050)*
Industrial Molded Products 847 358-2160
   800 Allanson Rd Mundelein (60060) *(G-14700)*
Industrial Molds Inc (PA) 815 397-2971
   5175 27th Ave Rockford (61109) *(G-17459)*
Industrial Motion Control LLC (HQ) 847 459-5200
   1444 S Wolf Rd Wheeling (60090) *(G-20915)*

Industrial Msrment Systems Inc..........630 236-5901
2760 Beverly Dr Ste 4 Aurora (60502) ***(G-981)***
Industrial Opprtnity Prtners L (PA)..........847 556-3460
1603 Orrington Ave # 700 Evanston (60201) ***(G-9538)***
Industrial Packaging Division, Chicago *Also called Flex-O-Glass Inc* ***(G-4606)***
Industrial Pallets LLC..........708 351-8783
1462 Glen Ellyn Rd Glendale Heights (60139) ***(G-10461)***
Industrial Park Machine & Tool..........708 754-7080
3326 Butler St S Chicago Hts (60411) ***(G-18122)***
Industrial Phrm Resources Inc (PA)..........630 823-4700
1241 Hardt Cir Bartlett (60103) ***(G-1290)***
Industrial Pipe and Supply Co..........708 652-7511
5100 W 16th St Chicago (60804) ***(G-4909)***
Industrial Proccess and Sensor, Alton *Also called C & L Manufacturing Entps* ***(G-546)***
Industrial Roller Co (PA)..........618 234-0740
301 S Main St Smithton (62285) ***(G-19066)***
Industrial Roller Co..........618 234-0740
211 N Smith St Smithton (62285) ***(G-19067)***
Industrial Rubber & Sup Entp..........217 429-3747
2670 E Garfield Ave Decatur (62526) ***(G-7507)***
Industrial Sensing and Safety..........630 264-8249
1936 School House Ln Aurora (60506) ***(G-1112)***
Industrial Service Solutions (PA)..........917 609-6979
875 N Michigan Ave Chicago (60611) ***(G-4910)***
Industrial Specialty Chem Inc (HQ)..........708 339-1313
410 W 169th St South Holland (60473) ***(G-19224)***
Industrial Steel Cnstr Inc (PA)..........630 232-7473
413 Old Kirk Rd Geneva (60134) ***(G-10280)***
Industrial Tech Centl LLC..........312 785-2520
333 S Wabash Ave Ste 2700 Chicago (60604) ***(G-4911)***
Industrial Technology, Chicago *Also called Tower Oil & Technology Co* ***(G-6401)***
Industrial Thermo Products..........847 398-8600
1051 Rohlwing Rd Ste C Rolling Meadows (60008) ***(G-17740)***
Industrial Tool and Repair..........309 633-0939
218 S Starr Ln Ste A Peoria (61604) ***(G-16458)***
Industrial Waste Elimination..........312 498-0880
5115 N Martha St Peoria (61614) ***(G-16459)***
Industrial Water Management, Elgin *Also called I W M Corporation* ***(G-8619)***
Industrial Welder Rebuilders..........708 371-5688
11700 S Mayfield Ave Alsip (60803) ***(G-457)***
Industrial Welding Inc..........815 535-9300
805 Antec Rd Rock Falls (61071) ***(G-17188)***
Industrial Wire & Cable Corp..........847 726-8910
66 N Buesching Rd Lake Zurich (60047) ***(G-12421)***
Industrial Wire Cable II Corp..........847 726-8910
66 N Buesching Rd Lake Zurich (60047) ***(G-12422)***
Industrialexport.net, Northbrook *Also called USA Industrial Export Corp* ***(G-15497)***
Industries Publication Inc..........630 357-5269
4412 Black Partridge Ln Lisle (60532) ***(G-12899)***
Inelco, Chicago *Also called Inglot Electronics Corp* ***(G-4921)***
Ineos Americas LLC..........630 857-7463
150 W Warrenville Rd Naperville (60563) ***(G-14845)***
Ineos Americas LLC..........630 857-7000
3030 Warrenville Rd # 650 Lisle (60532) ***(G-12900)***
Ineos Joliet LLC (HQ)..........815 467-3200
23425 Amoco Rd Channahon (60410) ***(G-3384)***
Ineos Styrolution America LLC..........815 423-5541
25846 S Frontage Rd Channahon (60410) ***(G-3385)***
Ineos Styrolution America LLC (HQ)..........630 820-9500
4245 Meridian Pkwy # 151 Aurora (60504) ***(G-982)***
Ineos Technologies, Lisle *Also called Ineos Americas LLC* ***(G-12900)***
Infamous Industries Inc..........708 789-2326
9253 S 89th Ct Hickory Hills (60457) ***(G-11198)***
Infiniscene Inc..........630 567-0452
25 W Hubbard St Fl 5 Chicago (60654) ***(G-4912)***
Infinite Cnvrgnce Slutions Inc (HQ)..........224 764-3400
3231 N Wilke Rd Arlington Heights (60004) ***(G-758)***
Infiniti Golf..........630 520-0626
245 W Roosevelt Rd Ste 9 West Chicago (60185) ***(G-20594)***
Infinity Communications Group..........708 352-1086
5350 East Ave Countryside (60525) ***(G-7060)***
Infinity Metal Spinning Inc..........773 731-4467
10247 S Avenue O Chicago (60617) ***(G-4913)***
Infinity Signs, Countryside *Also called Infinity Communications Group* ***(G-7060)***
Infinity Tool Mfg LLC..........618 439-4042
11648 Skylane Dr Benton (62812) ***(G-1928)***
Infinitybox LLC..........847 232-1991
1410 Brummel Ave Elk Grove Village (60007) ***(G-9051)***
Inflight Entertainment Pdts, Carpentersville *Also called Video Refurbishing Svcs Inc* ***(G-3122)***
Infogix Inc (PA)..........630 505-1800
1240 E Diehl Rd Ste 400 Naperville (60563) ***(G-14846)***
Infor (us) Inc..........312 279-1245
8725 W Higgins Rd Chicago (60631) ***(G-4914)***
Informa Business Media Inc..........312 595-1080
200 W Madison St Ste 2610 Chicago (60606) ***(G-4915)***
Informa Media Inc..........212 204-4200
24652 Network Pl Chicago (60673) ***(G-4916)***

Informatica LLC..........360 393-7576
2135 City Gate Ln Ste 340 Naperville (60563) ***(G-14847)***
Information Builders Inc..........630 971-6700
20 N Martingale Rd # 430 Schaumburg (60173) ***(G-18558)***
Information Resources Inc..........312 474-3380
150 N Clinton St Chicago (60661) ***(G-4917)***
Information Resources Inc..........312 474-3154
1201 Nashua Ln Bartlett (60133) ***(G-1255)***
Information Resources Inc..........312 474-8900
550 W Washington Blvd # 6 Chicago (60661) ***(G-4918)***
Information Usa Inc..........312 943-6288
1555 N Dearborn Pkwy Ofc Chicago (60610) ***(G-4919)***
Informative Systems Inc..........217 523-8422
5119 Old Route 36 Springfield (62707) ***(G-19389)***
Infosys Limited..........630 482-5000
2300 Cabot Dr Ste 250 Lisle (60532) ***(G-12901)***
Infra Red Heating, La Grange *Also called Maintenance Inc* ***(G-12082)***
Infrastructure Def Tech LLC..........800 379-1822
6550 Revlon Dr Belvidere (61008) ***(G-1678)***
Infratrol LLC..........779 475-3098
602 E Blackhawk Dr Byron (61010) ***(G-2753)***
Ing Bank Fsb..........312 981-1236
21 E Chestnut St Chicago (60611) ***(G-4920)***
Ingenious Concepts Inc..........630 539-8059
22w313 Temple Dr Medinah (60157) ***(G-13814)***
Ingenium Aerospace LLC..........815 525-2000
5389 International Dr Rockford (61109) ***(G-17460)***
Ingersoll Cutting Tool Company (HQ)..........815 387-6600
845 S Lyford Rd Rockford (61108) ***(G-17461)***
Ingersoll Machine Tools Inc (HQ)..........815 987-6000
707 Fulton Ave Rockford (61103) ***(G-17462)***
Ingersoll Prod Systems LLC (HQ)..........815 637-8500
1301 Eddy Ave Rockford (61103) ***(G-17463)***
Ingersoll-Rand, Elmhurst *Also called Trane Technologies Company LLC* ***(G-9436)***
Ingersoll-Rand, Chicago *Also called Trane Technologies Company LLC* ***(G-6406)***
Inglese Box Co Ltd..........847 669-1700
13851 Prime Point Rd Huntley (60142) ***(G-11543)***
Inglot Electronics Corp..........773 286-5881
4878 N Elston Ave Chicago (60630) ***(G-4921)***
Ingram, Rockford *Also called Celinco Inc* ***(G-17341)***
Ingram Gauge Co, Rockford *Also called Celinco Inc* ***(G-17340)***
Ingram Vault Co, Jerseyville *Also called Unique Concrete Concepts Inc* ***(G-11797)***
Ingredients Golden Hill..........773 852-5112
2020 N California Ave Chicago (60647) ***(G-4922)***
Ingredion Incorporated (PA)..........708 551-2600
5 Westbrook Corporate Ctr # 500 Westchester (60154) ***(G-20701)***
Ingredion Incorporated..........309 550-9136
8310 W Rte 24 Mapleton (61547) ***(G-13473)***
Ingredion Incorporated..........708 551-2600
141 W Jackson Blvd # 340 Chicago (60604) ***(G-4923)***
Ingredion Incorporated..........708 728-3535
6400 S Archer Rd Summit Argo (60501) ***(G-19680)***
Ingredion Incorporated..........708 563-2400
6400 S Archer Rd Bldg 90 Argo (60501) ***(G-673)***
Inhance Technologies LLC..........630 231-7515
829 W Hawthorne Ln West Chicago (60185) ***(G-20595)***
Inheris Biopharma Inc..........415 482-5652
150 N Riverside Plz # 1840 Chicago (60606) ***(G-4924)***
Inheris Pharmaceuticals, Inc., Chicago *Also called Inheris Biopharma Inc* ***(G-4924)***
Initial Choice..........847 234-5884
226 E Westminster Lake Forest (60045) ***(G-12267)***
Initial Impressions Inc..........630 208-9399
405 Stevens St Geneva (60134) ***(G-10281)***
Initially Ewe..........708 246-7777
1058 Hillgrove Ave Western Springs (60558) ***(G-20722)***
Injury Sciences LLC..........210 691-0674
222 Merchandise Mart Plz # 900 Chicago (60654) ***(G-4925)***
Ink Enterprises Inc..........815 547-5515
9594 Ruth Ct Belvidere (61008) ***(G-1679)***
Ink Solution, Flossmoor *Also called Springbox Inc* ***(G-9702)***
Ink Solutions LLC (PA)..........847 593-5200
800 Estes Ave Elk Grove Village (60007) ***(G-9052)***
Ink Spot Printing..........773 528-0288
2 N Riverside Plz Ste 365 Chicago (60606) ***(G-4926)***
Ink Spot Silk Screen..........847 724-6234
84 Park Dr Glenview (60025) ***(G-10567)***
Ink Spots Prtg & Meida Design..........708 754-1300
1131 175th St Ste B Homewood (60430) ***(G-11498)***
Ink Stop Inc..........847 478-0631
330 Foxford Dr Buffalo Grove (60089) ***(G-2550)***
Ink Systems Inc..........847 427-2200
800 Estes Ave Elk Grove Village (60007) ***(G-9053)***
Ink Well, Lombard *Also called Mormor Incorporated* ***(G-13104)***
Ink Well, Chicago *Also called Jans Graphics Inc* ***(G-5006)***
Ink Well..........618 398-1427
10603 Lincoln Trl Fairview Heights (62208) ***(G-9647)***
Ink Well Printing & Design Ltd..........847 923-8060
604 Albion Ave Schaumburg (60193) ***(G-18559)***

ALPHABETIC SECTION — Instruments & Technology

Ink Your Wear Inc 708 329-4444
  3222 Harlem Ave Riverside (60546) *(G-17085)*
Ink2image, Glenview Also called CIS Systems Inc *(G-10537)*
Inkjet Inc 800 280-3245
  4225 Winston Dr Hoffman Estates (60192) *(G-11429)*
Inkn Tees 847 244-2266
  2901 N Delany Rd Ste 105 Waukegan (60087) *(G-20448)*
Inkorporated Designs 217 965-4653
  423 N Springfield St Virden (62690) *(G-20186)*
Inky Printers (PA) 815 235-3700
  122 N Van Buren Ave Freeport (61032) *(G-10120)*
Inland Broaching and TI Co LLC 847 233-0033
  1441 Timber Dr Elgin (60123) *(G-8626)*
Inland Fastener Inc 630 293-3800
  750 W Hawthorne Ln West Chicago (60185) *(G-20596)*
Inland Midwest Corporation (HQ) 773 775-2111
  612 W Lamont Rd Elmhurst (60126) *(G-9378)*
Inland Plastics Inc 815 933-3500
  1310 E Birch St Kankakee (60901) *(G-11977)*
Inland Tech Holdings LLC 618 476-7678
  609 S Breese St Millstadt (62260) *(G-14048)*
Inland Tool Company 217 792-3206
  727 N Topper Dr Mount Pulaski (62548) *(G-14588)*
Inlet & Pipe Protection Inc 630 355-3288
  24137 111th St Ste A Naperville (60564) *(G-14974)*
Inliten LLC 847 486-4200
  2350 Ravine Way Ste 300 Glenview (60025) *(G-10568)*
Inman Electric Motors Inc 815 223-2288
  314 Civic Rd La Salle (61301) *(G-12115)*
Inn Intl Newspaper Network 309 764-5314
  1521 47th Ave Moline (61265) *(G-14150)*
Innerweld Cover Co 847 497-3009
  21227 W Coml Dr Ste E Mundelein (60060) *(G-14701)*
Innerworkings Inc (PA) 312 642-3700
  203 N Lasalle St Ste 1800 Chicago (60601) *(G-4927)*
Innocor Inc 630 231-0622
  1700 Downs Dr Ste 200 West Chicago (60185) *(G-20597)*
Innocor Foam Tech W Chcago LLC 732 945-6222
  1750 Downs Dr West Chicago (60185) *(G-20598)*
Innocor Foam Technologies LLC 630 293-0780
  1750 Downs Dr West Chicago (60185) *(G-20599)*
Innolitica Labs LLC 224 434-1238
  1620 S Michigan Ave # 910 Chicago (60616) *(G-4928)*
Innolux Technology USA Inc (HQ) 847 490-5315
  2300 Barrington Rd # 400 Hoffman Estates (60169) *(G-11430)*
Innophos Inc 708 757-6111
  1101 Arnold St Chicago Heights (60411) *(G-6750)*
Innophos Inc 773 468-2300
  512 E 138th St Chicago (60803) *(G-4929)*
Innoquest Inc 815 337-8555
  910 Hobe Rd Woodstock (60098) *(G-21396)*
Innotech Manufacturing LLC 618 244-6261
  915 S 13th St Mount Vernon (62864) *(G-14616)*
Innova Print Fulfillment Inc 630 845-3215
  2000 S Batavia Ave # 310 Geneva (60134) *(G-10282)*
Innova Systems Inc 630 920-8880
  8330 S Madison St Ste 60 Burr Ridge (60527) *(G-2686)*
Innova Uev LLC 630 568-5609
  16w235 83rd St Ste A Burr Ridge (60527) *(G-2687)*
Innovant Inc 646 368-6254
  222 Merchandise Mart Plz Chicago (60654) *(G-4930)*
Innovate Technologies Inc 630 587-4220
  761 N 17th St Saint Charles (60174) *(G-18212)*
Innovatech It Svc Solutions (PA) 815 484-9940
  730 N Church St Ste 201 Rockford (61103) *(G-17464)*
Innovation Center, Ottawa Also called Fairmount Santrol Inc *(G-16051)*
Innovation Plus Power Systems 630 457-1105
  3960 Commerce Dr Saint Charles (60174) *(G-18213)*
Innovation Specialists Inc 815 372-9001
  2328 E Lincoln Hwy # 356 New Lenox (60451) *(G-15037)*
Innovations For Learning Inc (PA) 800 975-3452
  518 Davis St Evanston (60201) *(G-9539)*
Innovative Automation 708 418-8720
  3116 192nd St Lansing (60438) *(G-12499)*
Innovative AV Systems Inc 312 265-6282
  909 S Il Route 83 Elmhurst (60126) *(G-9379)*
Innovative Components Inc 847 885-9050
  1050 National Pkwy Schaumburg (60173) *(G-18560)*
Innovative Custom Software Inc 630 892-5022
  2731 Beverly Dr Aurora (60502) *(G-983)*
Innovative Design & Graphics, Evanston Also called Innovtive Design Graphics Corp *(G-9540)*
Innovative Design and RES Inc 217 322-3907
  338 W Lafayette St Rushville (62681) *(G-18111)*
Innovative Fix Solutions LLC 815 395-8500
  1122 Milford Ave Rockford (61109) *(G-17465)*
Innovative Fix Solutions LLC 815 395-8500
  1122 Milford Ave Rockford (61109) *(G-17466)*
Innovative Gringing Inc 630 766-4567
  690 County Line Rd Bensenville (60106) *(G-1822)*

Innovative Growers Eqp Inc 815 991-5010
  421 N California St Sycamore (60178) *(G-19717)*
Innovative Hess Products LLC 847 676-3260
  1407 S Cypress Dr Mount Prospect (60056) *(G-14535)*
Innovative Industrial Svcs LLC 309 527-2035
  600 S Fayette St Ste 4 El Paso (61738) *(G-8439)*
Innovative Machine Inc 309 945-9445
  925 Dilenbeck Dr Geneseo (61254) *(G-10244)*
Innovative Mag Drive LLC 630 543-4240
  6911 W 59th St Chicago (60638) *(G-4931)*
Innovative Mag-Drive LLC 630 543-4240
  409 S Vista Ave Addison (60101) *(G-155)*
Innovative Marine Safety Inc 618 254-9470
  35 W Ferguson Ave Wood River (62095) *(G-21264)*
Innovative Mktg Solutions Inc 630 227-4300
  1320 N Plum Grove Rd Schaumburg (60173) *(G-18561)*
Innovative Molecular Diagnosti 630 845-8246
  1436 Fargo Blvd Geneva (60134) *(G-10283)*
Innovative Plastech Inc 630 232-1808
  1260 Kingsland Dr Batavia (60510) *(G-1386)*
Innovative Projects Lab Inc 847 605-2125
  150 N Martingale Rd # 838 Schaumburg (60173) *(G-18562)*
Innovative Rack & Gear Company 630 766-2652
  365 Balm Ct Wood Dale (60191) *(G-21201)*
Innovative SEC Systems Inc 217 355-6308
  1809 Woodfield Dr Savoy (61874) *(G-18414)*
Innovative Sports Training Inc 773 244-6470
  3711 N Ravenswood Ave # 150 Chicago (60613) *(G-4932)*
Innovative Werks Inc 312 767-8618
  800 W 5th Ave Ste 203c Naperville (60563) *(G-14848)*
Innovo Corp 847 616-0063
  2385 United Ln Elk Grove Village (60007) *(G-9054)*
Innovtive Design Graphics Corp 847 475-7772
  1327 Greenleaf St 1 Evanston (60202) *(G-9540)*
Innovtive Prcess Applctons LLC 708 844-6100
  14011 Kostner Ave Crestwood (60418) *(G-7119)*
Inplex Custom Extruders LLC 847 827-7046
  1657 Frontenac Rd Naperville (60563) *(G-14849)*
Inprentus Inc 217 239-9862
  51 E Kenyon Rd Champaign (61820) *(G-3308)*
Inprentus Precision Optics, Champaign Also called Inprentus Inc *(G-3308)*
Inpro/Seal LLC 309 787-8940
  4221 81st Ave W Rock Island (61201) *(G-17225)*
Inrule Technology Inc 312 648-1800
  651 W Washington Blvd # 500 Chicago (60661) *(G-4933)*
Inscerco Mfg Inc 708 597-8777
  4621 W 138th St Midlothian (60445) *(G-13992)*
Insertech LLC (PA) 847 516-6184
  711 Indl Dr Cary (60013) *(G-3171)*
Insertech International Inc 847 416-6184
  711 Industrial Dr Cary (60013) *(G-3172)*
Inservio3 LLC 310 343-3486
  17 N State St Ste 1520 Chicago (60602) *(G-4934)*
Inside Beverages 847 438-1338
  635 Oakwood Rd Lake Zurich (60047) *(G-12423)*
Inside Council 312 654-3500
  222 S Riverside Plz # 620 Chicago (60606) *(G-4935)*
Inside Track Trading 630 585-9218
  2905 Lahinch Ct Aurora (60503) *(G-984)*
Insight Beverages Inc 847 438-1598
  750 Oakwood Rd Lake Zurich (60047) *(G-12424)*
Insight Beverages Inc (HQ) 847 438-1598
  635 Oakwood Rd Lake Zurich (60047) *(G-12425)*
Insignia Design Ltd 301 254-9221
  2118 Plum Grove Rd 191 Rolling Meadows (60008) *(G-17741)*
Instana Inc (PA) 415 340-2777
  222 S Riverside Plz # 1500 Chicago (60606) *(G-4936)*
Instant Collating Service Inc 312 243-4703
  2443 W 16th St Chicago (60608) *(G-4937)*
Institute For Public Affairs 773 772-0100
  2040 N Milwaukee Ave Fl 2 Chicago (60647) *(G-4938)*
Institutional Equipment Inc (PA) 630 771-0990
  704 Veterans Pkwy Ste B Bolingbrook (60440) *(G-2192)*
Institutional Foods Packing Co 847 904-5250
  2350 Ravine Way Ste 200 Glenview (60025) *(G-10569)*
Instrmntation Ctrl Systems Inc 630 543-6200
  360 Heritage Dr Roselle (60172) *(G-17959)*
Instrument & Valve Services Co 708 535-5120
  4320 166th St Oak Forest (60452) *(G-15684)*
Instrument & Valve Services Co 281 998-6673
  4320 W 166 St Chicago (60673) *(G-4939)*
Instrument Laboratories Div, Wheeling Also called International Electro Magnetic *(G-20916)*
Instrument Services Inc 815 623-2993
  4075 Steele Dr Machesney Park (61115) *(G-13350)*
Instrumentalists Inc 847 446-5000
  1838 Techny Ct Northbrook (60062) *(G-15406)*
Instrumentics, Rosemont Also called Lifewatch Technologies Inc *(G-18033)*
Instruments & Technology 815 838-5909
  700 N Glenmore St Lockport (60441) *(G-13002)*

Insty Prints Palatine Inc ... 847 963-0000
453 S Vermont St Ste A Palatine (60067) ***(G-16129)***
Insty-Prints, Waukegan *Also called Instyprints of Waukegan Inc* ***(G-20449)***
Insty-Prints, Elk Grove Village *Also called Valee Inc* ***(G-9300)***
Insty-Prints, Palatine *Also called Insty Prints Palatine Inc* ***(G-16129)***
Instyprints of Waukegan Inc ... 847 336-5599
1711 Grand Ave Ste 1 Waukegan (60085) ***(G-20449)***
Insulated Transport Products, Glenview *Also called Signode Industrial Group LLC* ***(G-10618)***
Insulators Supply Inc ... 847 394-2836
741 Pinecrest Dr Prospect Heights (60070) ***(G-16843)***
Insync Manufacturing LLC ... 815 304-6300
601a N 5th Ave Kankakee (60901) ***(G-11978)***
Intec-Mexico LLC ... 847 358-0088
666 S Vermont St Palatine (60067) ***(G-16130)***
Intecells Inc ... 586 612-9811
2541 Tech Dr Ste 407 Elgin (60124) ***(G-8627)***
Intech Industries Inc ... 847 487-5599
1101 Brown St Wauconda (60084) ***(G-20361)***
Integra Graphics and Forms Inc ... 708 385-0950
4749 136th St Crestwood (60418) ***(G-7120)***
Integra Print & Data Services ... 708 337-6265
940 N Milwaukee Ave Ste C Libertyville (60048) ***(G-12663)***
Integral Automation Inc ... 630 654-4300
16 W 171 Shore Ct Burr Ridge (60527) ***(G-2688)***
Integratech, Elgin *Also called Integrity Technologies LLC* ***(G-8628)***
Integrated Circuits Research ... 630 830-9024
6600 Appletree St Hanover Park (60133) ***(G-11007)***
Integrated Display Systems Inc (PA) ... 708 298-9661
5130 W 16th St Cicero (60804) ***(G-6856)***
Integrated Document Tech, Itasca *Also called Imaging Systems Inc* ***(G-11674)***
Integrated Graphics Inc ... 630 482-6100
1198 Nagel Blvd Batavia (60510) ***(G-1387)***
Integrated Industries Inc ... 773 299-1970
4201 W 36th St Ste 1 Chicago (60632) ***(G-4940)***
Integrated Label Corporation ... 815 874-2500
3407 Pyramid Dr Rockford (61109) ***(G-17467)***
Integrated Lighting Tech Inc (PA) ... 630 750-3786
1317 Rosemary Dr Bolingbrook (60490) ***(G-2193)***
Integrated Media Inc ... 217 854-6260
21709 Route 4 Carlinville (62626) ***(G-2877)***
Integrated Medical Tech Inc (PA) ... 309 662-3614
2422 E Washington St # 103 Bloomington (61704) ***(G-2062)***
Integrated Mfg Tech LLC ... 618 282-8306
401 Randolph St Red Bud (62278) ***(G-16996)***
Integrated Packg & Fastener ... 847 439-5730
1678 Carmen Dr Elk Grove Village (60007) ***(G-9055)***
Integrated Power Services LLC ... 708 877-5310
17001 Vincennes Rd Thornton (60476) ***(G-19789)***
Integrated Print Graphics Inc (PA) ... 847 695-6777
645 Stevenson Rd South Elgin (60177) ***(G-19155)***
Integrated Print Graphics Inc ... 847 888-2880
635 Stevenson Rd South Elgin (60177) ***(G-19156)***
Integrating Green Technologies, Bolingbrook *Also called Integrated Lighting Tech Inc* ***(G-2193)***
Integrity Manufacturing Inc ... 815 514-8230
1351 Enterprise Dr Romeoville (60446) ***(G-17832)***
Integrity Metals LLC ... 630 963-4126
1351 Enterprise Dr Romeoville (60446) ***(G-17833)***
Integrity Prtg McHy Svcs LLC ... 847 834-9484
1650 Glen Lake Rd Hoffman Estates (60169) ***(G-11431)***
Integrity Sign Company ... 708 532-5038
18770 88th Ave Unit A Mokena (60448) ***(G-14092)***
Integrity Technologies LLC ... 850 240-6089
1140 Peachtree Ln Unit B Elgin (60120) ***(G-8628)***
Intek Strength, Herrin *Also called Orthotech Sports - Med Eqp Inc* ***(G-11176)***
Intel Corporation ... 408 765-8080
21003 Network Pl Chicago (60673) ***(G-4941)***
Intel East ... 312 725-2014
660 W Pickwick Ct Apt 1w Mount Prospect (60056) ***(G-14536)***
Intel Printing Inc ... 708 343-1144
1805 Beach St Broadview (60155) ***(G-2444)***
Intelex Usa LLC ... 844 927-6437
105 Prairie Lake Rd East Dundee (60118) ***(G-8202)***
Intelligent Flrg Systems LLC ... 630 587-1800
3830 Commerce Dr Saint Charles (60174) ***(G-18214)***
Intelligent Instrument Sy ... 630 323-3911
16w251 S Frontage Rd # 23 Burr Ridge (60527) ***(G-2689)***
Intelligent SCM LLC ... 630 625-7229
1263 N Wood Dale Rd Wood Dale (60191) ***(G-21202)***
Intelliginix Consulting Svcs, Chicago *Also called Turner Agward* ***(G-6444)***
Intelligrated Systems Inc ... 630 985-4350
9014 Heritage Pkwy # 308 Woodridge (60517) ***(G-21315)***
Intellisource Inc ... 847 426-7400
2531 Tech Dr Ste 301 Elgin (60124) ***(G-8629)***
Inter Solutions Co ... 773 657-4437
6134 N Milwaukee Ave C Chicago (60646) ***(G-4942)***
Inter Swiss Ltd ... 773 379-0400
5410 W Roosevelt Rd # 242 Chicago (60644) ***(G-4943)***
Inter-Continental Trdg USA Inc ... 847 640-1777
1601 W Algonquin Rd Mount Prospect (60056) ***(G-14537)***
Inter-Market Inc ... 847 729-5330
1946 Lehigh Ave Ste A Glenview (60026) ***(G-10570)***
Inter-State Studio & Pubg Co ... 815 874-0342
3446 Colony Bay Dr Rockford (61109) ***(G-17468)***
Interactive Bldg Solutions LLC ... 815 724-0525
1919 Cherry Hill Rd Joliet (60433) ***(G-11882)***
Interactive Data Technologies, Athens *Also called Donnas House of Type Inc* ***(G-896)***
Interactive Inks Coatings Corp ... 847 289-8710
1610 Shanahan Dr South Elgin (60177) ***(G-19157)***
Interesting Products Inc ... 773 265-1100
328 N Albany Ave Chicago (60612) ***(G-4944)***
Interexpo Ltd ... 847 489-7056
22438 N Clayton Ct Kildeer (60047) ***(G-12049)***
Interfaceflor LLC ... 312 836-3389
440 N Wells St Ste 200 Chicago (60654) ***(G-4945)***
Interfaceflor LLC ... 312 822-9640
222 Merchandise Mart Plz # 130 Chicago (60654) ***(G-4946)***
Interflo Industries Inc ... 847 228-0606
695 Lunt Ave Elk Grove Village (60007) ***(G-9056)***
Intergrted Thrmforming Systems ... 630 906-6895
305 Hankes Ave Aurora (60505) ***(G-1113)***
Interior Fashions Contract ... 847 358-6050
120 S Northwest Hwy Palatine (60074) ***(G-16131)***
Interior Tectonics LLC ... 312 515-7779
1716 N Cleveland Ave Chicago (60614) ***(G-4947)***
Interlake Mecalux Inc (HQ) ... 708 344-9999
1600 N 25th Ave Melrose Park (60160) ***(G-13883)***
Interlake Mecalux Inc ... 815 844-7191
701 N Interlake Dr Pontiac (61764) ***(G-16772)***
Intermatic Incorporated (PA) ... 815 675-7000
7777 Winn Rd Spring Grove (60081) ***(G-19276)***
Intermedix Holdings Inc (HQ) ... 312 324-7820
401 N Michigan Ave # 2700 Chicago (60611) ***(G-4948)***
Intermerican Clinical Svcs Inc ... 773 252-1147
2651 W Division St Chicago (60622) ***(G-4949)***
Intermet Metals Services Inc ... 847 605-1300
1375 E Wdfield Rd Ste 520 Schaumburg (60173) ***(G-18563)***
Interminal Services ... 773 978-8129
2040 E 106th St Chicago (60617) ***(G-4950)***
Intermolding Technology LLC ... 847 376-8517
1420 Wright Blvd Schaumburg (60193) ***(G-18564)***
Intermountain Electronics Inc ... 618 339-6743
400 Swan Ave Centralia (62801) ***(G-3235)***
International Automotive Compo ... 815 544-2102
1236 Crosslink Pkwy Belvidere (61008) ***(G-1680)***
International Bus Mchs Corp ... 312 423-6640
222 S Riverside Plz # 1 Chicago (60606) ***(G-4951)***
International College Surgeons (PA) ... 312 642-6502
1516 N Lake Shore Dr Fl 3 Chicago (60610) ***(G-4952)***
International Control Svcs Inc ... 217 422-6700
606 W Imboden Dr Decatur (62521) ***(G-7508)***
International Conveyors Amer ... 630 549-4007
10 W State St Ste 108 Geneva (60134) ***(G-10284)***
International Cutting Die Inc ... 708 343-3333
2030 Janice Ave Melrose Park (60160) ***(G-13884)***
International Drug Dev Cons ... 847 634-9586
1549 Rfd Long Grove (60047) ***(G-13160)***
International Electro Magnetic ... 847 358-4622
1033 Noel Ave Wheeling (60090) ***(G-20916)***
International Filter Mfg Corp ... 217 324-2303
713 W Columbian Blvd S Litchfield (62056) ***(G-12966)***
International Golden Foods Inc ... 630 860-5552
819 Industrial Dr Bensenville (60106) ***(G-1823)***
International Graphics & Assoc ... 630 584-2248
38w598 Clubhouse Dr Saint Charles (60175) ***(G-18215)***
International Locksmith, Glencoe *Also called International Silver Plating* ***(G-10430)***
International Marketing & Mfg, Chicago *Also called I M M Inc* ***(G-4866)***
International Mold & Prod LLC ... 313 617-5251
1397 Mayfair Ln Grayslake (60030) ***(G-10783)***
International Molding Mch Co ... 708 354-1380
1201 Barnsdale Rd Ste 1 La Grange Park (60526) ***(G-12097)***
INTERNATIONAL MUSEUM OF SURGIC, Chicago *Also called International College Surgeons* ***(G-4952)***
International News ... 773 283-8323
4917 N Milwaukee Ave 14 Chicago (60630) ***(G-4953)***
International Paint LLC ... 847 623-4200
1 E Water St Waukegan (60085) ***(G-20450)***
International Paper Company ... 708 728-8200
5300 W 73rd St Chicago (60638) ***(G-4954)***
International Paper Company ... 618 233-5460
3001 Otto St Belleville (62226) ***(G-1558)***
International Paper Company ... 630 896-2061
1001 Knell St Montgomery (60538) ***(G-14251)***
International Paper Company ... 815 398-2100
2100 23rd Ave Rockford (61104) ***(G-17469)***
International Paper Company ... 708 562-6000
401 Northwest Ave Northlake (60164) ***(G-15548)***

ALPHABETIC SECTION

International Paper Company 217 735-1221
   1601 5th St Lincoln (62656) *(G-12731)*
International Paper Company 630 449-7200
   2540 Prospect Ct Aurora (60502) *(G-985)*
International Paper Company 630 585-3300
   4140 Campus Dr Aurora (60504) *(G-986)*
International Paper Company 630 653-3500
   139 Fullerton Ave Carol Stream (60188) *(G-3005)*
International Paper Company 847 390-1300
   100 E Oakton St Des Plaines (60018) *(G-7788)*
International Paper Company 847 228-7227
   25 Northwest Point Blvd # 300 Elk Grove Village (60007) *(G-9057)*
International Paper Company 708 728-1000
   7333 S Lockwood Ave Bedford Park (60638) *(G-1473)*
International Paper Company 630 585-3400
   4160 Campus Dr Aurora (60504) *(G-987)*
International Paper Company 630 250-1300
   1225 W Bryn Mawr Ave Itasca (60143) *(G-11677)*
International Plating Svc LLC (PA) 619 734-2335
   11142 Addison Ave Franklin Park (60131) *(G-9965)*
International Proc Co Amer 847 437-8400
   1485 Lively Blvd Elk Grove Village (60007) *(G-9058)*
International Rd Dynamics Corp 815 675-1430
   2402 Spring Ridge Dr E Spring Grove (60081) *(G-19277)*
International Revere Co 773 248-1841
   2333 W Nelson St Chicago (60618) *(G-4955)*
International Services, Chicago Also called Success Vending Mfg Co LLC *(G-6263)*
International Silver Plating 847 835-0705
   364 Park Ave Glencoe (60022) *(G-10430)*
International Source Solutions 847 251-8265
   3229 Wilmette Ave Wilmette (60091) *(G-21079)*
International Spring Company 847 470-8170
   7901 Nagle Ave Morton Grove (60053) *(G-14413)*
International Supply Co 309 249-6211
   2717 W North St Edelstein (61526) *(G-8333)*
International Technologies Inc 847 301-9005
   627 Estes Ave Schaumburg (60193) *(G-18565)*
International Water Werks Inc 847 669-1902
   11470 Kreutzer Rd Huntley (60142) *(G-11544)*
International Wood Design Inc 773 227-9270
   941 N California Ave Chicago (60622) *(G-4956)*
International Wood Products 630 530-6164
   2812 Stuart Kaplan Ct Aurora (60503) *(G-988)*
Internet Industry Almanac, Arlington Heights Also called Computer Industry Almanac Inc *(G-718)*
Internet Retailer, Chicago Also called Vertical Web Media LLC *(G-6539)*
Interntional Casings Group Inc, Chicago Also called Van Hessen USA Inc *(G-6519)*
Interntional Chem Formulations, Broadview Also called De Enterprises Inc *(G-2429)*
Interntional Cmpt Concepts Inc 847 808-7789
   300 Wainwright Dr Northbrook (60062) *(G-15407)*
Interntional Grnhse Contrs Inc (PA) 217 443-0600
   70 Eastgate Dr Danville (61834) *(G-7352)*
Interntional Metal Finshg Svcs 815 234-5254
   8692 Glacier Dr Byron (61010) *(G-2754)*
Interntnal Awekening Ministries 630 653-8616
   123 N Washington St Wheaton (60187) *(G-20806)*
Interntnal Cmmnctons For MGT G, Chicago Also called Thg International Publishing *(G-6363)*
Interntnal Ice Bgging Systems 312 633-4000
   234 Dennis Ln Glencoe (60022) *(G-10431)*
Interntnal Ingredient Mall LLC 630 462-1414
   1900 Averill Rd Geneva (60134) *(G-10285)*
Interntonal Creative RES Group, Chicago Also called Baka Vitaliy *(G-3817)*
Interplex Daystar Inc 847 455-2424
   11130 King St 1 Franklin Park (60131) *(G-9966)*
Interra Global Corporation 847 292-8600
   800 Busse Hwy Ste 101 Park Ridge (60068) *(G-16285)*
Interserve, Belvidere Also called Caisson Inc *(G-1658)*
Intersol Industries Inc 630 238-0385
   241 James St Bensenville (60106) *(G-1824)*
Intersports Screen Printing 773 489-7383
   2407 N Central Park Ave Chicago (60647) *(G-4957)*
Interstate All Battery Center 217 214-1069
   101 N 48th St Quincy (62305) *(G-16894)*
Interstate Btry Sys Intl Inc 708 424-2288
   10336 S Cicero Ave Oak Lawn (60453) *(G-15720)*
Interstate Cargo Inc 630 701-7744
   380 Internationale Dr A Bolingbrook (60440) *(G-2194)*
Interstate Graphics Inc 815 877-6777
   7817 Burden Rd Machesney Park (61115) *(G-13351)*
Interstate Mechanical Inc 312 961-9291
   1882 S Normal Ave Ste 1 Chicago (60616) *(G-4958)*
Interstate Power Systemd, Carol Stream Also called Interstate Power Systems Inc *(G-3006)*
Interstate Power Systems Inc 630 871-1111
   210 Alexandra Way Carol Stream (60188) *(G-3006)*
Interstate Power Systems Inc 952 854-2044
   3736 11th St Rockford (61109) *(G-17470)*
Interstuhl USA Inc 312 385-0240
   625 W Adams St Chicago (60661) *(G-4959)*

Intertape Polymer Corp 618 549-2131
   2200 N Mcroy Dr Carbondale (62901) *(G-2847)*
Intertape Polymer Group, Carbondale Also called Intertape Polymer Corp *(G-2847)*
Intervarsity Press, Westmont Also called Intervrsity Chrstn Fllwshp/Usa *(G-20749)*
Intervrsity Chrstn Fllwshp/Usa 630 734-4000
   430 Plaza Dr Frnt Westmont (60559) *(G-20749)*
Intex Lighting LLC 847 380-2027
   1300 E Wdfield Rd Ste 400 Schaumburg (60173) *(G-18566)*
Intex Systems Corp 630 636-6594
   22 Crestview Dr Oswego (60543) *(G-16008)*
Intra Action Corp 708 547-6644
   3719 Warren Ave Bellwood (60104) *(G-1628)*
Intra-Cut Die Cutting Inc 773 775-6228
   5559 N Northwest Hwy Chicago (60630) *(G-4960)*
Intratek Inc 847 640-0007
   54 N Lively Blvd Elk Grove Village (60007) *(G-9059)*
Intravation Inc (PA) 847 299-6423
   1113 Hewitt Dr Des Plaines (60016) *(G-7789)*
Intrepid Molding Inc 847 526-9477
   285 Industrial Dr Wauconda (60084) *(G-20362)*
Invektek Llc 312 343-0600
   2039 N Lincoln Ave Unit P Chicago (60614) *(G-4961)*
Invenergy 815 795-4964
   2192 E 25th Rd Marseilles (61341) *(G-13558)*
Invenergy Investment Company L 312 224-1400
   1 S Wacker Dr Ste 1800 Chicago (60606) *(G-4962)*
Invenergy Wind Fin Co III LLC 312 224-1400
   1 S Wacker Dr Ste 1900 Chicago (60606) *(G-4963)*
Invensys Controls, Hanover Also called Robertshaw Controls Company *(G-10997)*
Invensys Environmental Contrls, Rockford Also called Schneider Elc Buildings LLC *(G-17622)*
Inventex Medical, Niles Also called Inventive Display Group LLC *(G-15134)*
Inventive Display Group LLC 847 588-1100
   7415 N Melvina Ave Niles (60714) *(G-15134)*
Inventive Mfg Inc 847 647-9500
   5423 Fargo Ave Skokie (60077) *(G-18969)*
Inventus Power Inc (HQ) 630 410-7900
   1200 Internationale Pkwy Woodridge (60517) *(G-21316)*
Inventus Power (illinois) LLC 630 410-7900
   1200 Internationale Pkwy Woodridge (60517) *(G-21317)*
Inventus Power Holdings Inc (PA) 630 410-7900
   1200 Internationale Pkwy Woodridge (60517) *(G-21318)*
Inverom Corporation 630 568-5609
   16w235 83rd St Ste A Burr Ridge (60527) *(G-2690)*
Invisible Fencing of Quad City 309 797-1688
   5202 38th Ave Ste 2 Moline (61265) *(G-14151)*
Invisible Institute 415 669-4691
   6100 S Blackstone Ave Chicago (60637) *(G-4964)*
Invisio Communications Inc 412 327-6578
   150 N Michigan Ave # 1950 Chicago (60601) *(G-4965)*
Invitation Creations Inc 847 432-4441
   580 Roger Williams Ave # 24 Highland Park (60035) *(G-11274)*
INX Digital International Co 630 382-1800
   150 N Martingale Rd # 700 Schaumburg (60173) *(G-18567)*
INX Group 847 441-0600
   651 Bonnie Ln Elk Grove Village (60007) *(G-9060)*
INX Group Ltd 708 799-1993
   1000 Maple Rd Homewood (60430) *(G-11499)*
INX Group Ltd (HQ) 630 382-1800
   150 N Martingale Rd # 700 Schaumburg (60173) *(G-18568)*
INX International Ink Co (HQ) 630 382-1800
   150 N Martingale Rd # 700 Schaumburg (60173) *(G-18569)*
INX International Ink Co 708 799-1993
   1000 Maple Rd Homewood (60430) *(G-11500)*
INX International Ink Co 630 681-7200
   1860 Western Dr West Chicago (60185) *(G-20600)*
INX International Ink Co 708 496-3600
   5001 S Mason Ave Chicago (60638) *(G-4966)*
INX International Ink Co 800 233-4657
   150 N Martingale Rd # 700 Schaumburg (60173) *(G-18570)*
INX International Ink Co 630 382-1800
   1419 W Carroll Ave Chicago (60607) *(G-4967)*
INX International Ink Co 630 382-1800
   150 N Martingale Rd # 700 Schaumburg (60173) *(G-18571)*
INX International Ink Co 630 681-7100
   1760 Western Dr West Chicago (60185) *(G-20601)*
Io Lighting LLC 847 735-7000
   370 Corporate Woods Pkwy Vernon Hills (60061) *(G-20067)*
Iodon Inc 708 799-4062
   18610 John Ave Country Club Hills (60478) *(G-7041)*
Iola Quarry Inc 217 682-3865
   2671 County Hwy 6 Mode (62444) *(G-14067)*
Ion Inc 224 875-1313
   14702 W Mayland Villa Rd Lincolnshire (60069) *(G-12775)*
Ionit Technologies Inc 847 205-9651
   2311 Dorina Dr Northfield (60093) *(G-15518)*
Iop, Evanston Also called Industrial Opprtnity Prtners L *(G-9538)*
Iosso Products, Elk Grove Village Also called International Proc Co Amer *(G-9058)*

Ip Media Holdings.....847 714-1177
55 E Hintz Rd Wheeling (60090) ***(G-20917)***
IPC Group Purchasing.....630 276-5485
1151 E Warrenville Rd M Naperville (60563) ***(G-14850)***
Iplastics LLC (PA).....309 444-8884
300 N Cummings Ln Washington (61571) ***(G-20270)***
IPM Precision Inc.....847 304-7900
22179 N Pepper Rd Lake Barrington (60010) ***(G-12152)***
Ipr Group, Carol Stream *Also called Stand Fast Group LLC* ***(G-3075)***
Ipr Systems Inc.....708 385-7500
11651 S Mayfield Ave Alsip (60803) ***(G-458)***
Ips & Luggage Co Inc.....630 894-2414
685 Washington Ct Roselle (60172) ***(G-17960)***
Ipsen Inc.....815 239-2385
325 John St Pecatonica (61063) ***(G-16322)***
Ipsen Inc (HQ).....815 332-4941
984 Ipsen Rd Cherry Valley (61016) ***(G-3442)***
Ireco LLC.....630 741-0155
577 W Lamont Rd Elmhurst (60126) ***(G-9380)***
Irene Quary, Belvidere *Also called William Charles Cnstr Co LLC* ***(G-1711)***
Iretired LLC.....630 285-9500
700 District Dr Itasca (60143) ***(G-11678)***
Iria Pharma Inc.....217 979-1417
60 Hazelwood Dr Ste 245 Champaign (61820) ***(G-3309)***
Irish Dancing Magazine.....630 279-7521
110 E Schiller St Ste 206 Elmhurst (60126) ***(G-9381)***
Irmko Tool Works Inc.....630 350-7550
205 Park St Bensenville (60106) ***(G-1825)***
Iron & Wire LLC.....773 255-2672
3600 W Potomac Ave Chicago (60651) ***(G-4968)***
Iron Castle Inc.....773 890-0575
3847 S Kedzie Ave Chicago (60632) ***(G-4969)***
Iron-A-Way LLC.....309 266-7232
220 W Jackson St Morton (61550) ***(G-14363)***
Ironform Holdings Co (PA).....312 374-4810
640 N La Salle Dr Ste 670 Chicago (60654) ***(G-4970)***
Ironsafe LLC.....877 297-1833
1807 W Diehl Rd Naperville (60563) ***(G-14851)***
Ironwood Industries Inc.....847 362-8681
115 S Bradley Rd Libertyville (60048) ***(G-12664)***
Ironwood Manufacturing Inc.....630 969-1100
2863 95th St Ste 14 Naperville (60564) ***(G-14975)***
Irving Press Inc.....847 595-6650
2530 United Ln Elk Grove Village (60007) ***(G-9061)***
Irwin Industrial Tool Company.....815 235-4171
29 E Stephenson St Freeport (61032) ***(G-10121)***
Irwin Seating Company.....618 483-6157
610 E Cumberland Rd Altamont (62411) ***(G-534)***
Irwin Telescopic Seating Co.....618 483-6157
610 E Cumberland Rd Altamont (62411) ***(G-535)***
ISA Chicago.....630 317-7169
470 Mission St Unit 7 Carol Stream (60188) ***(G-3007)***
ISachs Sons Inc.....312 733-2815
4500 S Kolin Ave Ste 1a Chicago (60632) ***(G-4971)***
Isates Inc.....309 691-8822
2251 W Altorfer Dr Peoria (61615) ***(G-16460)***
Isbir Bulk Bag Usa LLC.....972 722-9200
27475 Ferry Rd Warrenville (60555) ***(G-20239)***
Isbs, Elk Grove Village *Also called Image Systems Bus Slutions LLC* ***(G-9046)***
ISC Water Solutions, South Holland *Also called Industrial Specialty Chem Inc* ***(G-19224)***
Isco International Inc (PA).....630 283-3100
444 E State Pkwy Ste A Schaumburg (60173) ***(G-18572)***
Isenberg Bath Corporation.....972 510-5916
1325 W Irving Park Rd Bensenville (60106) ***(G-1826)***
Isewa LLC.....847 877-1586
2104 Birchwood Ln Buffalo Grove (60089) ***(G-2551)***
Ishot Products Inc.....312 497-4190
558 Payton Ln Bolingbrook (60440) ***(G-2195)***
ISI Building Products, East Peoria *Also called Meyer Enterprises LLC* ***(G-8278)***
ISI Printing, Springfield *Also called Informative Systems Inc* ***(G-19389)***
Isky North America Inc (PA).....937 641-1368
47 W Polk St Ste 208 Chicago (60605) ***(G-4972)***
Isoflex Packaging, Chicago *Also called Alpha Industries MGT Inc* ***(G-3629)***
Isoprime Corporation.....630 737-0963
505 Warrenville Rd # 104 Lisle (60532) ***(G-12902)***
Isostatic Industries Inc.....773 286-3444
4153 N Kostner Ave Fl 1 Chicago (60641) ***(G-4973)***
Isovac Products LLC.....630 679-1740
1306 Enterprise Dr Ste A Romeoville (60446) ***(G-17834)***
Isp, Homewood *Also called Ink Spots Prtg & Meida Design* ***(G-11498)***
Israel Levy Diamnd Cutters Inc.....312 368-8540
29 E Madison St Ste 700 Chicago (60602) ***(G-4974)***
ISS, Champaign *Also called ISs (usa) Inc* ***(G-3310)***
ISs (usa) Inc.....217 359-8681
1602 Newton Dr Champaign (61822) ***(G-3310)***
ISS Medical Inc.....217 359-8681
1602 Newton Dr Champaign (61822) ***(G-3311)***
It For Whats Inc.....847 949-6522
3 Cayuga Ct Hawthorn Woods (60047) ***(G-11124)***
It Transportation Company.....773 383-5073
5156 W Winnemac Ave Chicago (60630) ***(G-4975)***
Italia Foods Inc.....847 397-4479
2127 Hammond Dr Schaumburg (60173) ***(G-18573)***
Italmatch Chemicals Group, Bedford Park *Also called Italmatch Sc LLC* ***(G-1474)***
Italmatch Sc LLC.....708 929-9657
7201 W 65th St Bedford Park (60638) ***(G-1474)***
Italvibras Usa Inc.....815 872-1350
1940 Vans Way Princeton (61356) ***(G-16811)***
Itasca Plastics Inc.....630 443-4446
3750 Ohio Ave Saint Charles (60174) ***(G-18216)***
Itc Inc.....309 634-1825
11808 N Hickory Grove Rd Dunlap (61525) ***(G-8134)***
Iterative Therapeutics Inc.....773 455-7203
2201 W Campbell Park Dr Chicago (60612) ***(G-4976)***
Iterna LLC.....630 585-7400
2600 Beverly Dr Ste 107 Aurora (60502) ***(G-989)***
Iterum Therapeutics US Limited.....312 763-3975
200 S Wacker Dr Ste 650 Chicago (60606) ***(G-4977)***
Itg Brands LLC.....217 529-5746
900 Christopher Ln Ste 7 Springfield (62712) ***(G-19390)***
Itron Corporation Del (PA).....708 222-5320
3131 S Austin Blvd Cicero (60804) ***(G-6857)***
Its A Sign.....708 848-7446
6140 Roosevelt Rd Oak Park (60304) ***(G-15758)***
Its Easy With Jesus Printing, Franklin *Also called Faith Printing* ***(G-9855)***
Its Solar LLC.....618 476-7678
946 Park St Ste A Waterloo (62298) ***(G-20291)***
ITT, Bedford Park *Also called Goulds Pumps LLC* ***(G-1468)***
ITT Water & Wastewater USA Inc.....708 342-0484
8402 W 183 Th Ste A Tinley Park (60477) ***(G-19840)***
Itta Corporation.....872 221-4882
2449 W Coyle Ave Chicago (60645) ***(G-4978)***
ITW, Glenview *Also called Illinois Tool Works Inc* ***(G-10560)***
ITW, Lincolnshire *Also called E H Wachs* ***(G-12762)***
ITW Bldg Components Group (PA).....847 634-1900
155 Harlem Ave Glenview (60025) ***(G-10571)***
ITW Blding Cmponents Group Inc.....217 324-0303
7 Skyview Dr Litchfield (62056) ***(G-12967)***
ITW Brands, Bartlett *Also called Illinois Tool Works Inc* ***(G-1288)***
ITW Buildex, Roselle *Also called Illinois Tool Works Inc* ***(G-17958)***
ITW Covid Security Group Inc (HQ).....847 724-7500
155 Harlem Ave Glenview (60025) ***(G-10572)***
ITW Delpro, Frankfort *Also called Illinois Tool Works Inc* ***(G-9804)***
ITW Deltar Bdy Intr Richton Pk, Richton Park *Also called Illinois Tool Works Inc* ***(G-17028)***
ITW Deltar Fuel Systems, Tinley Park *Also called Illinois Tool Works Inc* ***(G-19837)***
ITW Deltar Fuel Systems, Tinley Park *Also called Illinois Tool Works Inc* ***(G-19838)***
ITW Deltar Ipac, Frankfort *Also called Illinois Tool Works Inc* ***(G-9806)***
ITW Deltar Seat Component, Elmhurst *Also called Illinois Tool Works Inc* ***(G-9376)***
ITW Dynatec.....847 657-4830
3600 W Lake Ave Glenview (60026) ***(G-10573)***
ITW Filtration, Elk Grove Village *Also called Illinois Tool Works Inc* ***(G-9042)***
ITW Flter Pdts Trnsm Fltration, Hebron *Also called Filtertek Inc* ***(G-11143)***
ITW Fluids North America.....630 384-0146
475 N Gary Ave Carol Stream (60188) ***(G-3008)***
ITW Global Investments Inc., Glenview *Also called ITW Global Investments LLC* ***(G-10574)***
ITW Global Investments LLC (HQ).....847 724-7500
155 Harlem Ave Glenview (60025) ***(G-10574)***
ITW Hi-Cone, Charleston *Also called Illinois Tool Works Inc* ***(G-3404)***
ITW International Holdings LLC (HQ).....847 724-7500
3600 W Lake Ave Glenview (60026) ***(G-10575)***
ITW Minigrip/Zip-Pak, Ottawa *Also called Minigrip Inc* ***(G-16061)***
ITW Motion.....708 720-0300
21601 S Harlem Ave Frankfort (60423) ***(G-9809)***
ITW Paslode, Vernon Hills *Also called Illinois Tool Works Inc* ***(G-20063)***
ITW Paslode, Vernon Hills *Also called Illinois Tool Works Inc* ***(G-20064)***
ITW Paslode, Glenview *Also called ITW Bldg Components Group* ***(G-10571)***
ITW Paslode, Elgin *Also called Illinois Tool Works Inc* ***(G-8621)***
ITW Ramset Red Head, Elk Grove Village *Also called Illinois Tool Works Inc* ***(G-9043)***
ITW Shake Proof Auto Division, Machesney Park *Also called Illinois Tool Works Inc* ***(G-13349)***
ITW Shakeproof Automotive, Machesney Park *Also called Illinois Tool Works Inc* ***(G-13348)***
ITW Shakeproof Group, Broadview *Also called Illinois Tool Works Inc* ***(G-2442)***
ITW Shakeproof-Elk Grove, Elk Grove Village *Also called Illinois Tool Works Inc* ***(G-9044)***
ITW Switches, Des Plaines *Also called Illinois Tool Works Inc* ***(G-7784)***
IV & Respiratory Care Services.....618 398-2720
65 S 65th St Ste 1 Belleville (62223) ***(G-1559)***
Ivan Carlson Associates Inc.....312 829-4616
2224 W Fulton St Chicago (60612) ***(G-4979)***
Ivan Schwenker.....630 543-7798
1480 W Bernard Dr Ste A Addison (60101) ***(G-156)***
Ivanhoe Industries Inc.....847 872-3311
3333 20th St Mundelein (60060) ***(G-14702)***
Ivans Insurance Solutions, University Park *Also called Applied Systems Inc* ***(G-19946)***

ALPHABETIC SECTION

Ives Way Products Inc 847 223-1020
  683 Center St Ste E Grayslake (60030) *(G-10784)*
Ives-Way Products Inc 847 740-0658
  2030 N Nicole Ln Round Lake Beach (60073) *(G-18090)*
IVEX Specialty Paper LLC 309 686-3830
  1 Sloan St Peoria (61603) *(G-16461)*
Ivp Plastics of Missouri LLC 309 444-8884
  300 N Cummings Ln Washington (61571) *(G-20271)*
Ixmation North America, Bartlett Also called Bbs Automation Chicago Inc *(G-1268)*
Ixtapa Foods 773 788-9701
  6135 S Nottingham Ave Chicago (60638) *(G-4980)*
Iya Foods LLC 630 854-7107
  348 Smoketree Bsn Dr North Aurora (60542) *(G-15264)*
J & A Sheet Metal Shop Inc 773 276-3739
  1800 N Campbell Ave Chicago (60647) *(G-4981)*
J & B Signs Inc 312 640-8181
  105 W Chicago Ave Chicago (60654) *(G-4982)*
J & B Welding LLC 309 887-4151
  11280 Elston Rd Fulton (61252) *(G-10153)*
J & D Instant Signs 847 965-2800
  5614 Dempster St Morton Grove (60053) *(G-14414)*
J & E Seating LLC 847 956-1700
  125 Connell Ave Rockdale (60436) *(G-17260)*
J & F Engineering, Addison Also called Doral Inc *(G-96)*
J & G Fabricating Inc 708 385-9147
  12653 Irving Ave Blue Island (60406) *(G-2126)*
J & I Resources LLC 773 436-4028
  5301 S Western Blvd Ste 1 Chicago (60609) *(G-4983)*
J & I Son Tool Company Inc 847 455-4200
  9219 Parklane Ave Franklin Park (60131) *(G-9967)*
J & J Carbide & Tool Inc 708 489-0300
  5656 W 120th St Alsip (60803) *(G-459)*
J & J Electric Motor Repair Sp 217 529-0015
  2800 S 11th St Springfield (62703) *(G-19391)*
J & J Equipment Inc 309 449-5442
  260 4th Ave Hopedale (61747) *(G-11517)*
J & J Express Envelopes Inc 847 253-7146
  645 Stevenson Rd South Elgin (60177) *(G-19158)*
J & J Fish, Rockford Also called Dar Enterprises Inc *(G-17367)*
J & J Inc of Illinois 217 306-0787
  20224 Big Oak Ave Greenview (62642) *(G-10823)*
J & J Industries Inc 630 595-8878
  708 S Edgewood Ln Mount Prospect (60056) *(G-14538)*
J & J Manufacturing, Chillicothe Also called C J Holdings Inc *(G-6815)*
J & J Mr Quick Print Inc 773 767-7776
  5740 S Archer Ave Ste 1 Chicago (60638) *(G-4984)*
J & J Powder Coating, Zion Also called Joseph Kristan *(G-21518)*
J & J Printing, Chicago Also called J & J Mr Quick Print Inc *(G-4984)*
J & J Quality Pallets Inc 618 262-6426
  226 W 11th St Mount Carmel (62863) *(G-14474)*
J & J Silk Screening 773 838-9000
  5316 S Monitor Ave Chicago (60638) *(G-4985)*
J & J Snack Foods Corp 708 377-0400
  3701 W 128th Pl Alsip (60803) *(G-460)*
J & K Cabinetry Inc 847 758-7808
  1655 Busse Rd Elk Grove Village (60007) *(G-9062)*
J & L Cnc Machining Inc 708 388-2090
  12633 S Springfield Ave Alsip (60803) *(G-461)*
J & L Gear Incorporated 630 832-1880
  726 N Princeton Ave Ste C Villa Park (60181) *(G-20151)*
J & M Custom Cabinets 217 677-2229
  202 W North 2nd St La Place (61936) *(G-12099)*
J & M Fab Metals Inc 815 758-0354
  6710 S Grant Hwy Marengo (60152) *(G-13486)*
J & M Plating Inc 815 964-4975
  4500 Kishwaukee St Rockford (61109) *(G-17471)*
J & S Machine Works Inc 708 344-2101
  1733 N 25th Ave Melrose Park (60160) *(G-13885)*
J A K Enterprises Inc 217 422-3881
  288 N Park St Decatur (62523) *(G-7509)*
J and D Installers Inc 847 288-0783
  9330 Franklin Ave Franklin Park (60131) *(G-9968)*
J and J International 847 842-8628
  1016 S Summit St Barrington (60010) *(G-1222)*
J and J Prfmce Powdr Coating 309 376-4340
  410 E Washington St Carlock (61725) *(G-2887)*
J and K Molding 224 276-3355
  31632 N Ellis Dr Unit 201 Volo (60073) *(G-20199)*
J and K Printing 708 229-9558
  5629 W 84th Pl Oak Lawn (60459) *(G-15721)*
J B Burling Group Ltd 773 327-5362
  540 W Aldine Ave Ste 6 Chicago (60657) *(G-4986)*
J B Metal Works Inc 847 824-4253
  1325 Lee St Des Plaines (60018) *(G-7790)*
J B Oil Field Cnstr & Sup 618 936-2350
  218 E Sycamore St Sumner (62466) *(G-19687)*
J B Watts Company Inc 773 643-1855
  6224 S Vernon Ave Chicago (60637) *(G-4987)*
J Brodie Meat Products Inc 309 342-1500
  605 W 6th St Galesburg (61401) *(G-10202)*

J C Communications Company 312 236-5122
  318 W Adams St Ste 1406 Chicago (60606) *(G-4988)*
J C Decaux New York Inc 312 456-2999
  3959 S Morgan St Chicago (60609) *(G-4989)*
J C Embroidery & Screen Print 630 595-4670
  406 Industrial Dr Bensenville (60106) *(G-1827)*
J C Hose & Tube Inc 630 543-4747
  236 S La Londe Ave Ste C Addison (60101) *(G-157)*
J C Products Inc 847 208-9616
  1961 Tunbridge Ct Algonquin (60102) *(G-375)*
J C Schultz Enterprises Inc 800 323-9127
  951 Swanson Dr Batavia (60510) *(G-1388)*
J D Graphic Co Inc 847 364-4000
  1101 Arthur Ave Elk Grove Village (60007) *(G-9063)*
J D M Coatings Inc 708 755-6300
  3300 Louis Sherman Dr Steger (60475) *(G-19490)*
J D Machining 847 428-8690
  57 Center Dr Ste B Gilberts (60136) *(G-10360)*
J D Plating Works Inc 847 662-6484
  1424 12th St Waukegan (60085) *(G-20451)*
J D Refrigeration 618 345-0041
  6849 Fedder Ln Collinsville (62234) *(G-6963)*
J Design Works Inc 847 812-0891
  210 Ironbark Way Bolingbrook (60440) *(G-2196)*
J E Tomes & Associates Inc 708 653-5100
  2513 140th Pl Blue Island (60406) *(G-2127)*
J F Schroeder Company Inc 847 357-8600
  2616 S Clearbrook Dr Arlington Heights (60005) *(G-759)*
J F Wagner Printing Co, Northbrook Also called Wagner John *(G-15498)*
J Francis & Assoc 309 697-5931
  4603 Carol Ct Bartonville (61607) *(G-1333)*
J G B Uniforms & Career AP, Chicago Also called J G Uniforms Inc *(G-4990)*
J G Uniforms Inc 773 545-4644
  5949 W Irving Park Rd Chicago (60634) *(G-4990)*
J Garvin Industries Inc (PA) 708 297-7400
  14750 S Campbell Ave Posen (60469) *(G-16796)*
J Garvin Industries Inc 708 297-7400
  3513 W 97th St Evergreen Park (60805) *(G-9595)*
J Gayleen Hammond, Rushville Also called Stitchables Embroidery *(G-18113)*
J Gooch & Associates Inc 217 522-7575
  140 W Lenox Ave Springfield (62704) *(G-19392)*
J H Benedict Co Inc 309 694-3111
  3211 N Main St East Peoria (61611) *(G-8270)*
J H Botts LLC 815 726-5885
  253 Bruce St Joliet (60432) *(G-11883)*
J H H of Illinois Inc 630 293-0739
  1331 Howard Dr West Chicago (60185) *(G-20602)*
J H Robison & Associates Ltd (PA) 847 559-9662
  905 Voltz Rd Northbrook (60062) *(G-15408)*
J Hoffman Lumber Co Inc 815 899-2260
  1330 E State St Sycamore (60178) *(G-19718)*
J II Inc 847 432-8979
  1292 Old Skokie Rd Highland Park (60035) *(G-11275)*
J J Collins Sons Inc (PA) 630 960-2525
  2300 Warrenville Rd # 190 Downers Grove (60515) *(G-8032)*
J J Collins Sons Inc 217 345-7606
  2351 Madison Ave Charleston (61920) *(G-3405)*
J J Mata Inc 773 750-0643
  2524 W Devon Ave Chicago (60659) *(G-4991)*
J K Creative Printers, Quincy Also called Jost & Kiefer Printing Company *(G-16897)*
J K Custom Countertops 630 495-2324
  820 N Ridge Ave Ste A Lombard (60148) *(G-13088)*
J K Manufacturing Co 708 563-2500
  7301 W 66th St Bedford Park (60638) *(G-1475)*
J K Printing & Mailing Inc 847 432-7717
  2090 Green Bay Rd Highland Park (60035) *(G-11276)*
J L Lawrence & Co 217 235-3622
  1921 Richmond Ave Mattoon (61938) *(G-13638)*
J L M Plastics Corporation 815 722-0066
  1012 Collins St Joliet (60432) *(G-11884)*
J M Fabricating Inc 815 359-2024
  214 S 1st St Harmon (61042) *(G-11018)*
J M Lustig Custom Cabinets Co 217 342-6661
  921 E Fayette Ave Effingham (62401) *(G-8403)*
J M Office Products, Crest Hill Also called J M Printers Inc *(G-7087)*
J M Printers Inc (PA) 815 727-1579
  510 Pasadena Ave Crest Hill (60403) *(G-7087)*
J Mac Metals Inc 309 932-3001
  330 Se Industrial Ave Galva (61434) *(G-10233)*
J N Machinery Corp 224 699-9161
  1081 Rock Road Ln East Dundee (60118) *(G-8203)*
J N P, Blue Island Also called Color Tone Printing *(G-2114)*
J N R Custo-Matic Screw Inc 630 260-1333
  200 W Lake Dr Glendale Heights (60139) *(G-10462)*
J Oshana & Son Printing 773 283-8311
  4021 W Irving Park Rd Chicago (60641) *(G-4992)*
J P Goldenne Incorporated 847 776-5063
  346 N Northwest Hwy Palatine (60067) *(G-16132)*
J P Printing Inc 773 626-5222
  5639 W Division St Chicago (60651) *(G-4993)*

J P Vincent & Sons Inc..........815 777-2365
11340 W Us Highway 20 Galena (61036) ***(G-10175)***
J R Finishers Inc..........847 301-2556
616 Albion Ave Schaumburg (60193) ***(G-18574)***
J R Fridrich Inc..........847 439-1554
1830 Lunt Ave Elk Grove Village (60007) ***(G-9064)***
J R Husar Inc..........312 243-7888
1631 W Carroll Ave Chicago (60612) ***(G-4994)***
J R Mold Inc..........630 289-2192
65 Sangra Ct Streamwood (60107) ***(G-19578)***
J R Short Milling Company (PA)..........800 544-8734
1580 Grinnell Rd Kankakee (60901) ***(G-11979)***
J R Short Milling Company..........815 937-2633
1580 Grinnell Rd Kankakee (60901) ***(G-11980)***
J Ream Manufacturing..........630 983-6945
31w280 Diehl Rd Ste 101 Naperville (60563) ***(G-14852)***
J S, West Chicago *Also called Jel Sert Co* ***(G-20603)***
J S Paluch Co Inc (PA)..........847 678-9300
3708 River Rd Ste 400 Franklin Park (60131) ***(G-9969)***
J S Printing Inc..........847 678-6300
9832 Franklin Ave Franklin Park (60131) ***(G-9970)***
J Schneerberger Corp..........847 888-3498
1160 Abbott Dr Elgin (60123) ***(G-8630)***
J Stilling Enterprises Inc..........630 584-5050
330 S 2nd St Ste A Saint Charles (60174) ***(G-18217)***
J T C Inc..........773 292-9262
4710 W North Ave Chicago (60639) ***(G-4995)***
J T Fennell Co Inc (PA)..........309 274-2145
1104 N Front St Chillicothe (61523) ***(G-6819)***
J W Ossola Company Inc..........815 339-6112
502 E Harper Ave Granville (61326) ***(G-10755)***
J W Reynolds Monument Co Inc..........618 833-6014
517 E Vienna St Ste A Anna (62906) ***(G-586)***
J W Rudy Co Inc..........618 676-1616
506 S 1st St Se Clay City (62824) ***(G-6906)***
J W Todd Co..........630 406-5715
709 Morton Ave Aurora (60506) ***(G-1114)***
J Wallace & Associates Inc..........630 960-4221
1409 Centre Cir Downers Grove (60515) ***(G-8033)***
J&A Mtchell Stl Fbricators Inc..........815 939-2144
2524 S 8000w Rd Kankakee (60901) ***(G-11981)***
J&A Pallets Service Inc..........708 333-6601
1225 Arnold St Chicago Heights (60411) ***(G-6751)***
J&E Storm Services Inc..........630 401-3793
17807 65th Ct Tinley Park (60477) ***(G-19841)***
J&I Tool Company, Franklin Park *Also called J & I Son Tool Company Inc* ***(G-9967)***
J&J Ready Mix Inc..........309 676-0579
100 Cass St East Peoria (61611) ***(G-8271)***
J&M Acrylics, Lake Zurich *Also called Motherboard Gifts & More LLC* ***(G-12436)***
J&M Food Products Company, Chicago *Also called My Own Meals Inc* ***(G-5530)***
J-Industries Inc..........815 654-0055
5129 Forest Hills Ct Loves Park (61111) ***(G-13220)***
J-Soft Tech, Chicago *Also called Jones Software Corp* ***(G-5047)***
J-TEC Metal Products Inc..........630 875-1300
1320 Ardmore Ave Itasca (60143) ***(G-11679)***
J. J. Collins Printers, Downers Grove *Also called J J Collins Sons Inc* ***(G-8032)***
J. P. Bell Fabricating, Inc., Wood Dale *Also called EMR Manufacturing Inc* ***(G-21185)***
J.H. Botts, Joliet *Also called J H Botts LLC* ***(G-11883)***
J/B Industries Inc..........630 851-9444
601 N Farnsworth Ave Aurora (60505) ***(G-1115)***
J6 Polymers LLC..........815 517-1179
601 Derby Line Rd Genoa (60135) ***(G-10319)***
Ja-T & Associates Inc..........773 744-2094
37 N Long Ave Chicago (60644) ***(G-4996)***
Jack & Lidias Resort Inc..........847 356-1389
3610 N Edgewood St Lake Villa (60046) ***(G-12356)***
Jack Bartlett..........217 659-3575
2745 N County Road 2150 Dallas City (62330) ***(G-7314)***
Jack Beall Vertical Service In..........847 426-7958
109 W Snyder St Abingdon (61410) ***(G-10)***
Jack Ruch Archtctral Mouldings, Bloomington *Also called Jack Ruch Quality Homes Inc* ***(G-2063)***
Jack Ruch Quality Homes Inc..........309 663-6595
2908 Gill St Ste 2 Bloomington (61704) ***(G-2063)***
Jack Shepard Logging..........618 845-3496
14225 Shepard Ln Ullin (62992) ***(G-19935)***
Jack Walters & Sons Corp..........618 842-2642
204 E Main St Fairfield (62837) ***(G-9627)***
Jackhammer..........773 743-5772
6406 N Clark St Chicago (60626) ***(G-4997)***
Jackson & Partners LLC..........630 219-1598
1717 N Naper Blvd Ste 108 Naperville (60563) ***(G-14853)***
Jackson County Sand & Grav Co..........618 763-4711
1 Sickler Rd Gorham (62940) ***(G-10682)***
Jackson Marking Products Co..........618 242-7901
9105 N Rainbow Ln Mount Vernon (62864) ***(G-14617)***
Jackson Oil Corporation..........618 263-6521
809 W 9th St Mount Carmel (62863) ***(G-14475)***
Jackson Spring & Mfg Co..........847 952-8850
299 Bond St Elk Grove Village (60007) ***(G-9065)***
Jacksonville Machine Inc..........217 243-1119
2265 W Morton Ave Jacksonville (62650) ***(G-11771)***
Jacksonville Monument Co..........217 245-2514
330 E State St Jacksonville (62650) ***(G-11772)***
Jacob Chambliss..........618 731-6632
127 County Road 600 E Dahlgren (62828) ***(G-7308)***
Jacob Hay Company..........847 215-8880
509 N Wolf Rd Wheeling (60090) ***(G-20918)***
Jacobs Boiler & Mech Inds Inc..........773 385-9900
6632 W Diversey Ave Chicago (60707) ***(G-4998)***
Jacobs Reproduction..........618 374-2198
25116 Beltrees Rd Elsah (62028) ***(G-9458)***
Jacobsen Lntclar Tl Cylnder En, Elk Grove Village *Also called Lens Lenticlear Lenticular* ***(G-9093)***
Jacobson Acqstion Holdings LLC..........847 623-1414
1414 Jacobson Dr Waukegan (60085) ***(G-20452)***
JAD Group Inc..........847 223-1804
888 E Belvidere Rd # 213 Grayslake (60030) ***(G-10785)***
Jada Specialties Inc..........847 272-7799
3834 Normandy Ln Northbrook (60062) ***(G-15409)***
Jaday Industries..........847 928-1033
10002 Pacific Ave Franklin Park (60131) ***(G-9971)***
Jade Screen Printing..........618 463-2325
220 Main St Alton (62002) ***(G-560)***
Jader Fuel Co Inc..........618 269-3101
117 S Edison St Shawneetown (62984) ***(G-18875)***
Jaeger Saw & Cutter Works, Rockford *Also called Jaeger Saw and Cutter Inc* ***(G-17472)***
Jaeger Saw and Cutter Inc..........815 963-0313
81005 5th Ave Rockford (61104) ***(G-17472)***
Jaffee Investment Partnr LP..........312 321-1515
410 N Michigan Ave # 400 Chicago (60611) ***(G-4999)***
Jagjita Corp..........217 374-6016
654 N Main St White Hall (62092) ***(G-21019)***
Jahm Inc..........847 647-7650
6143 W Howard St Niles (60714) ***(G-15135)***
Jai-S Record Label..........708 351-4279
22011 Central Park Ave Park Forest (60466) ***(G-16256)***
Jaix Leasing Company..........312 928-0850
2 N Riverside Plz Chicago (60606) ***(G-5000)***
Jakes McHning Rbilding Svc Inc..........630 892-3291
580 S Lake St Aurora (60506) ***(G-1116)***
Jakes World Design..........217 348-3043
2736 N County Road 1100e Lerna (62440) ***(G-12613)***
Jalaa Fiberglass Inc..........217 923-3433
1654 County Road 350n Greenup (62428) ***(G-10821)***
Jalor Company..........847 202-1172
545 Tollgate Rd Ste E Elgin (60123) ***(G-8631)***
JAm International Co Ltd..........847 827-6391
302 Saunders Rd Ste 200 Riverwoods (60015) ***(G-17094)***
Jamaica Pyrotechnics (PA)..........217 649-2902
212 Franks Dr Philo (61864) ***(G-16606)***
Jamali Kopy Kat Printing Inc..........708 544-6164
2501 Saint Charles Rd Bellwood (60104) ***(G-1629)***
Jamar Packaging, West Chicago *Also called J H H of Illinois Inc* ***(G-20602)***
Jamco Products Inc (HQ)..........815 624-0400
1 Jamco Ct South Beloit (61080) ***(G-19097)***
Jamco Tool & Cams Inc..........847 678-0280
10151 Franklin Ave Franklin Park (60131) ***(G-9972)***
James A Freund LLC..........630 664-7692
26 Longford Ct Oswego (60543) ***(G-16009)***
James B Beam Import, Deerfield *Also called Jim Beam Brands Co* ***(G-7620)***
James Coleman Company..........847 963-8100
1500 Hicks Rd Rolling Meadows (60008) ***(G-17742)***
James D Ahern Company (PA)..........773 254-0717
3257 S Harding Ave Chicago (60623) ***(G-5001)***
James G Carter..........309 543-2634
15907 Sr 97 Havana (62644) ***(G-11115)***
James Howard Co..........815 497-2831
623 W Chestnut St Compton (61318) ***(G-6996)***
James Injection Molding Co..........847 564-3820
300 Pfingsten Rd Northbrook (60062) ***(G-15410)***
James Instruments Inc (PA)..........773 463-6565
3727 N Kedzie Ave Chicago (60618) ***(G-5002)***
James J Sandoval..........734 717-7555
333 N Grace St Lombard (60148) ***(G-13089)***
James L Tracey Co..........630 907-8999
1480 Sequoia Dr Ste A2 Aurora (60506) ***(G-1117)***
James Precious Metals Plating..........773 774-8700
5700 N Northwest Hwy Chicago (60646) ***(G-5003)***
James R Chittick..........217 446-0925
32 N Jackson St Danville (61832) ***(G-7353)***
James R Wilbat Glass Studio..........847 940-0015
924 Woodward Ave Deerfield (60015) ***(G-7618)***
James Randall..........309 444-8765
201 Monroe St Washington (61571) ***(G-20272)***
James Ray Monroe Corporation (PA)..........618 532-4575
308 W Noleman St Centralia (62801) ***(G-3236)***

James Rosenbaum Co 847 859-7660
425 Davis St Unit 903 Evanston (60201) ***(G-9541)***
James Street Dental P C 630 232-9535
22 James St Ste 3 Geneva (60134) ***(G-10286)***
James W Smith Printing Company 847 244-6486
1573 Saint Paul Ave Gurnee (60031) ***(G-10888)***
James Walker Mfg Co 708 754-4020
511 W 195th St Glenwood (60425) ***(G-10641)***
Jameson Steel Fabrication Inc 217 354-2205
19965 Newtown Rd Oakwood (61858) ***(G-15820)***
Jamether Incorporated 815 444-9971
6294 Northwest Hwy Crystal Lake (60014) ***(G-7211)***
Jamiel Inc 217 423-1000
151 N Jasper St Decatur (62521) ***(G-7510)***
Jamtec USA LLC 224 392-1258
2622 N Stratford Rd Arlington Heights (60004) ***(G-760)***
Jan-Air Inc 815 678-4516
10815 Commercial St Richmond (60071) ***(G-17015)***
Janco Process Controls Inc 847 526-0800
368 W Liberty St Wauconda (60084) ***(G-20363)***
Jancorp LLC (PA) 217 892-4830
608 Kopman St Rantoul (61866) ***(G-16977)***
Jane Stodden Bridals 815 223-2091
955 Marquette St La Salle (61301) ***(G-12116)***
Janelle Publications Inc 815 756-2300
116 Twombly Rd Dekalb (60115) ***(G-7686)***
Janik Custom Millwork Inc 708 482-4844
6017 Lenzi Ave Ste 1 Hodgkins (60525) ***(G-11390)***
Janis Plastics Inc 847 838-5500
330 North Ave Antioch (60002) ***(G-617)***
Janitor Ltd 773 936-3389
218 N Jefferson St # 202 Chicago (60661) ***(G-5004)***
Janler Corporation 773 774-0166
6545 N Avondale Ave Chicago (60631) ***(G-5005)***
Jans Graphics Inc 312 644-4700
2 N Riverside Plz Ste 365 Chicago (60606) ***(G-5006)***
Janssen Avenue Boys Inc 630 627-0202
200 Alder Dr A North Aurora (60542) ***(G-15265)***
Janssen Machine Inc 815 877-9901
985 Industrial Ct Loves Park (61111) ***(G-13221)***
Janssen Pharmaceuticals Inc 312 750-0507
20 N Wacker Dr Ste 1442 Chicago (60606) ***(G-5007)***
Janssen, Ron, Loves Park *Also called Janssen Machine Inc* ***(G-13221)***
Japan Electronic Manufacturers 972 735-0463
1000 Skokie Blvd Ste 120 Wilmette (60091) ***(G-21080)***
Jarco, Salem *Also called Entrans International LLC* ***(G-18337)***
Jarco Inc 888 681-3660
8 Carpenter Dr Salem (62881) ***(G-18343)***
Jardis Industries Inc (PA) 630 860-5959
1201 Ardmore Ave Itasca (60143) ***(G-11680)***
Jardis Industries Inc 630 773-5600
1201 Ardmore Ave Itasca (60143) ***(G-11681)***
Jarr Printing Co 815 363-5435
5435 Bull Valley Rd # 300 McHenry (60050) ***(G-13750)***
Jarries Shoe Bags 773 379-4044
107 S Parkside Ave Chicago (60644) ***(G-5008)***
Jarvis Corp 800 363-1075
1078 National Pkwy Schaumburg (60173) ***(G-18575)***
Jarvis Drilling Co 217 422-3120
132 S Water St Ste 331 Decatur (62523) ***(G-7511)***
Jarvis Lighting, Schaumburg *Also called Jarvis Corp* ***(G-18575)***
Jarvis Welding Co 309 647-0033
124 E Pine St Canton (61520) ***(G-2827)***
JAS Dahern Signs 773 254-0717
3257 S Harding Ave Chicago (60623) ***(G-5009)***
JAS Express Inc 847 836-7984
8307 Seeman Rd Union (60180) ***(G-19939)***
Jasch North America Company 815 282-4463
6830 Forest Hills Rd Loves Park (61111) ***(G-13222)***
Jasco Tool & Manufacturing 815 271-5158
6000 Tomlinson Dr McHenry (60050) ***(G-13751)***
Jasiek Motor Rebuilding Inc 815 883-3678
451 E State Route 71 Oglesby (61348) ***(G-15842)***
Jason Incorporated 630 627-7000
201 S Swift Rd Addison (60101) ***(G-158)***
Jason Industrial, Carol Stream *Also called Megadyne America LLC* ***(G-3023)***
Jason Lau Jewelry 312 750-1028
29 E Madison St Ste 1107 Chicago (60602) ***(G-5010)***
Jav Machine Craft Inc 708 867-8608
4624 N Oketo Ave Chicago (60706) ***(G-5011)***
Java Express 217 525-2430
1827 N Peoria Rd Springfield (62702) ***(G-19393)***
Javamania Coffee Roastery Inc 815 885-4661
8179 Starwood Dr Ste 4 Loves Park (61111) ***(G-13223)***
Jax Asphalt Company Inc 618 244-0500
1800 Waterworks Rd Mount Vernon (62864) ***(G-14618)***
Jay A Morris (PA) 815 432-6440
2238 E Township Road 165 Watseka (60970) ***(G-20308)***
Jay Cee Plastic Fabricators 773 276-1920
2133 W Mclean Ave Chicago (60647) ***(G-5012)***
Jay Elka 847 540-7776
1180 Heather Dr Lake Zurich (60047) ***(G-12426)***
Jay Morris Trucking, Watseka *Also called Jay A Morris* ***(G-20308)***
Jay Printing 847 934-6103
553 N Hicks Rd Palatine (60067) ***(G-16133)***
Jay RS Steel & Welding Inc 847 949-9353
840 Tower Rd Mundelein (60060) ***(G-14703)***
Jayne Excavating & Welding LLC 618 553-1149
11477 E 1500th Ave Newton (62448) ***(G-15085)***
JB & S Machining 815 258-4007
1675 Enterprise Way Bourbonnais (60914) ***(G-2263)***
JB Enterprises II Inc (PA) 630 372-8300
375 Roma Jean Pkwy Streamwood (60107) ***(G-19579)***
JB Metalfab Mfg Inc 630 422-7420
708 County Line Rd Bensenville (60106) ***(G-1828)***
JB Metals, Bensenville *Also called JB Metalfab Mfg Inc* ***(G-1828)***
JB Mfg & Screw Machine 630 850-6978
16w154 Hillside Ln Burr Ridge (60527) ***(G-2691)***
JB Mfg & Screw Machine PR 847 451-0892
9243 Parklane Ave Franklin Park (60131) ***(G-9973)***
Jbc Holding Co (PA) 217 347-7701
3601 S Banker St Effingham (62401) ***(G-8404)***
Jbl - Alton 618 466-0411
2345 State St Alton (62002) ***(G-561)***
Jbs USA Food Company 217 323-6200
8295 Arenzville Rd Beardstown (62618) ***(G-1447)***
Jbsmwg Corp 847 675-1865
7170 N Ridgeway Ave Lincolnwood (60712) ***(G-12824)***
JBT, Chicago *Also called John Bean Technologies Corp* ***(G-5036)***
Jbw Machining Inc 847 451-0276
2826 Birch St Franklin Park (60131) ***(G-9974)***
JC Automation Inc 309 270-7000
8072 Centennial Expy Rock Island (61201) ***(G-17226)***
JC Metalcrafters Inc 815 942-9891
1360 East St Morris (60450) ***(G-14308)***
JC Precision Milling LLC 815 654-1070
1275 Turret Dr Machesney Park (61115) ***(G-13352)***
JC Tool and Mold Inc 630 483-2203
1529 Burgundy Pkwy Streamwood (60107) ***(G-19580)***
JC Tooling Company Inc 618 327-9379
560 National Mine Rd Nashville (62263) ***(G-14998)***
Jcb Inc 912 704-2995
800 Bilter Rd Ste A Aurora (60502) ***(G-990)***
Jcdecaux Chicago LLC 312 456-2999
3959 S Morgan St Chicago (60609) ***(G-5013)***
Jcg Industries Inc 312 829-7282
1300 Higgins Rd Ste 100 Park Ridge (60068) ***(G-16286)***
Jcw Investments Inc 708 478-7323
11415 183rd Pl Ste E Orland Park (60467) ***(G-15962)***
JD Norman Industries Inc (PA) 630 458-3700
787 W Belden Ave Addison (60101) ***(G-159)***
JD Pro Productions Inc 708 485-2126
4123 Maple Ave Brookfield (60513) ***(G-2487)***
Jdb Machining Inc 708 749-9596
4635 S Harlem Ave Forest View (60402) ***(G-9730)***
Jdb Manufacturing Company 708 749-9596
4635 S Harlem Ave Forest View (60402) ***(G-9731)***
Jdi Mold and Tool LLC 815 759-5646
2510 Hiller Rdg Johnsburg (60051) ***(G-11806)***
Jdis Dealers 309 765-8000
1400 13th St East Moline (61244) ***(G-8230)***
Jdl Graphics 815 401-1120
4489a S 4500e Rd Saint Anne (60964) ***(G-18135)***
Jdl Graphics Inc 815 694-2979
3043 N 1600 East Rd Clifton (60927) ***(G-6915)***
JDM Engines Chicago LLC 214 235-5071
1583 Elmhurst Rd Elk Grove Village (60007) ***(G-9066)***
Jdp Therapeutics LLC 847 739-0490
520 Lake Cook Rd Ste 500 Deerfield (60015) ***(G-7619)***
Jds Labs Inc 618 550-9359
909 N Bluff Rd Collinsville (62234) ***(G-6964)***
Jds Printing Inc 630 208-1195
1709 President St Glendale Heights (60139) ***(G-10463)***
Jeannie Wagner 815 477-2700
835 Virginia Rd Ste G Crystal Lake (60014) ***(G-7212)***
Jebco" Screw" and Speciality, Cicero *Also called American/Jebco Corporation* ***(G-6829)***
Jedi Corporation 815 344-5334
4450 Bull Valley Rd Ste 2 McHenry (60050) ***(G-13752)***
Jefco Screw Machine Products 815 282-2000
6203 Material Ave Loves Park (61111) ***(G-13224)***
Jeff E Allen 217 801-6878
1928 E Watch Ave Springfield (62702) ***(G-19394)***
Jeff's Soda, Northbrook *Also called Egg Cream America Inc* ***(G-15381)***
Jefferies Orchard Sawmill 217 487-7582
1016 Jefferies Rd Springfield (62707) ***(G-19395)***
Jefferson County Ready Mix, Mount Vernon *Also called Quad-County Ready Mix Corp* ***(G-14635)***
Jefferson Ice, Chicago *Also called Home City Ice* ***(G-4833)***

ALPHABETIC

Jeffrey Jae Inc...847 808-2002
1125 Wheeling Rd Wheeling (60090) ***(G-20919)***
Jeffs Small Engine Inc...630 904-6840
12438 S Route 59 Plainfield (60585) ***(G-16675)***
Jel Sert Co (PA)...630 231-7590
Conde St Rr 59 West Chicago (60185) ***(G-20603)***
Jelco Inc...847 459-5207
450 Wheeling Rd Wheeling (60090) ***(G-20920)***
Jeld-Wen Inc...312 544-5041
500 W Monroe St Ste 2010 Chicago (60661) ***(G-5014)***
Jeld-Wen Inc...217 893-4444
201 Evans Rd Rantoul (61866) ***(G-16978)***
Jeld-Wen Windows, Rantoul *Also called Jeld-Wen Inc* ***(G-16978)***
Jeleniz...217 235-6789
1414 Broadway Ave Mattoon (61938) ***(G-13639)***
Jelinek & Sons Inc...630 355-3474
25400 W Hafenrichter Rd Plainfield (60585) ***(G-16676)***
Jelly Belly Candy Company...847 689-2225
1501 Morrow Ave North Chicago (60064) ***(G-15315)***
Jellyvision Inc...312 266-0606
848 W Eastman St Ste 104 Chicago (60642) ***(G-5015)***
Jem Associates Ltd (PA)...847 808-8377
5206 N Meade Ave Chicago (60630) ***(G-5016)***
Jem Solutions Inc...815 436-0880
16200 S Lincoln Hwy # 100 Plainfield (60586) ***(G-16677)***
Jem Tool & Manufacturing Co...630 595-1686
797 Industrial Dr Bensenville (60106) ***(G-1829)***
Jema, Wilmette *Also called Japan Electronic Manufacturers* ***(G-21080)***
Jen-Sko-Vec Machining & Engrg...773 776-7400
5335 S Western Blvd Chicago (60609) ***(G-5017)***
Jenco Metal Products Inc...847 956-0550
1690 W Imperial Ct Mount Prospect (60056) ***(G-14539)***
Jenkins Displays Co...618 335-3874
1910 Hollow Dr Vandalia (62471) ***(G-20013)***
Jenkins Truck & Farm, Vandalia *Also called Jenkins Displays Co* ***(G-20013)***
Jenner Precision Inc...815 692-6655
8735 N 2000 East Rd Fairbury (61739) ***(G-9609)***
Jenny Capp Co...773 217-0057
6605 S Harvard Ave Chicago (60621) ***(G-5018)***
Jensen and Son Inc...815 895-3855
353 N Maple St Sycamore (60178) ***(G-19719)***
Jensen Plating Works Inc (PA)...773 252-7733
183844 N Western Ave Chicago (60647) ***(G-5019)***
Jeremiah Fleming Music Sites, Wheaton *Also called Fleming Music Technology Ctr* ***(G-20799)***
Jerhen Industries Inc...815 397-0400
5196 27th Ave Rockford (61109) ***(G-17473)***
Jerjerb LLC...917 415-3319
6715 N Ionia Ave Chicago (60646) ***(G-5020)***
Jernberg Industries LLC (HQ)...773 268-3004
328 W 40th Pl Chicago (60609) ***(G-5021)***
Jernberg Industries LLC...630 972-7000
455 Gibraltar Dr Bolingbrook (60440) ***(G-2197)***
Jernberg of Bolingbrook, Bolingbrook *Also called Jernberg Industries LLC* ***(G-2197)***
Jero Medical Eqp & Sups Inc...773 305-4193
4444 W Chicago Ave Chicago (60651) ***(G-5022)***
Jerome Remien Corporation...847 806-0888
409 Busse Rd Elk Grove Village (60007) ***(G-9067)***
Jeron Electronic Systems Inc...773 275-1900
7501 N Natchez Ave Niles (60714) ***(G-15136)***
Jerry Berry Contracting Co...618 594-3339
1691 Kane St Carlyle (62231) ***(G-2891)***
Jerry D Graham Oil...618 548-5540
1213 S Broadway Ave Salem (62881) ***(G-18344)***
Jerrys Tackle and Guns...618 654-3235
604 12th St Highland (62249) ***(G-11228)***
Jersey County Journal, Jerseyville *Also called Campbell Publishing Co Inc* ***(G-11788)***
Jescorp Inc...847 378-1200
1900 Pratt Blvd Elk Grove Village (60007) ***(G-9068)***
Jesse B Holt Inc...618 783-3075
13 Hillcrest Dr Newton (62448) ***(G-15086)***
Jessis Hideout...618 343-4346
421 S Main St Caseyville (62232) ***(G-3215)***
Jessup Manufacturing Company (PA)...815 385-6650
2815 W Rte 120 Mchenry (60051) ***(G-13753)***
Jessup Manufacturing Company...847 362-0961
1701 Rockland Rd Lake Bluff (60044) ***(G-12190)***
Jesus People USA Full Gos...773 989-2083
5242 N Elston Ave Chicago (60630) ***(G-5023)***
Jesus People USA Full Gospel M, Chicago *Also called Lakefront Roofing Supply* ***(G-5163)***
Jet Aviation St Louis Inc (HQ)...618 646-8000
6400 Curtiss Steinberg Dr Cahokia (62206) ***(G-2761)***
Jet Finishers Inc...847 718-0501
136 W Commercial Ave Addison (60101) ***(G-160)***
Jet Grinding & Manufacturing...847 956-8646
2309 E Oakton St Ste A Arlington Heights (60005) ***(G-761)***
Jet Industries Inc...773 586-8900
6025 S Oak Park Ave Chicago (60638) ***(G-5024)***
Jet Precast & Redimix Inc...618 632-3594
570 W 3rd St O Fallon (62269) ***(G-15575)***
Jet Rack Corp...773 586-2150
6200 S New England Ave Chicago (60638) ***(G-5025)***
Jet X Aerospace LLC...630 238-1920
400 N York Rd Bensenville (60106) ***(G-1830)***
Jetin Systems Inc...815 726-4686
800 Railroad St Joliet (60436) ***(G-11885)***
Jetpower LLC...847 856-8359
880 Lakeside Dr Ste 3 Gurnee (60031) ***(G-10889)***
Jets Computing Inc...618 585-6676
200 S Brighton St Bunker Hill (62014) ***(G-2634)***
Jewel - Osco 3316, Hoffman Estates *Also called Jewel Osco Inc* ***(G-11432)***
Jewel Machine Inc...815 765-3636
302 Kingsbury Dr Se Poplar Grove (61065) ***(G-16781)***
Jewel Osco Inc...630 355-2172
1759 W Ogden Ave Ste A Naperville (60540) ***(G-14854)***
Jewel Osco Inc...847 882-6477
1071 N Roselle Rd Hoffman Estates (60169) ***(G-11432)***
Jewel Osco Inc...630 226-1892
1200 W Boughton Rd Bolingbrook (60440) ***(G-2198)***
Jewel Osco Inc...773 728-7730
5516 N Clark St Chicago (60640) ***(G-5026)***
Jewel Osco Inc...773 784-1922
5343 N Broadway St Chicago (60640) ***(G-5027)***
Jewel Osco Inc...847 296-7786
1500 Lee St Des Plaines (60018) ***(G-7791)***
Jewel Osco Inc...847 677-3331
9449 Skokie Blvd Skokie (60077) ***(G-18970)***
Jewel Osco Inc...708 352-0120
5545 S Brainard Ave Countryside (60525) ***(G-7061)***
Jewel Osco Inc...630 584-4594
2073 Prairie St Saint Charles (60174) ***(G-18218)***
Jewel Osco Inc...630 859-1212
1952 W Galena Blvd Aurora (60506) ***(G-1118)***
Jewel Osco Inc...815 464-5352
21164 N Lagrange Rd Frankfort (60423) ***(G-9810)***
Jewel Osco Inc...847 428-3547
1250 W Main St West Dundee (60118) ***(G-20664)***
Jewel-Osco 3013, Bolingbrook *Also called Jewel Osco Inc* ***(G-2198)***
Jewel-Osco 3052, Frankfort *Also called Jewel Osco Inc* ***(G-9810)***
Jewel-Osco 3059, Naperville *Also called Jewel Osco Inc* ***(G-14854)***
Jewel-Osco 3154, Countryside *Also called Jewel Osco Inc* ***(G-7061)***
Jewel-Osco 3252, Aurora *Also called Jewel Osco Inc* ***(G-1118)***
Jewel-Osco 3331, Saint Charles *Also called Jewel Osco Inc* ***(G-18218)***
Jewel-Osco 3407, Chicago *Also called Jewel Osco Inc* ***(G-5026)***
Jewel-Osco 3425, Des Plaines *Also called Jewel Osco Inc* ***(G-7791)***
Jewel-Osco 3443, Chicago *Also called Jewel Osco Inc* ***(G-5027)***
Jewel-Osco 3465, Skokie *Also called Jewel Osco Inc* ***(G-18970)***
Jewell Resources Corporation (HQ)...276 935-8810
1011 Warrenville Rd # 600 Lisle (60532) ***(G-12903)***
Jewerly and Beyond...312 833-6785
608 Newbury Ln B Schaumburg (60173) ***(G-18576)***
Jf Industries Inc...773 775-8840
7751 W Rosedale Ave Chicago (60631) ***(G-5028)***
Jf Labs, Chicago *Also called Afam Concept Inc* ***(G-3578)***
Jfb Hart Coatings Inc (PA)...630 783-1917
5337 Maplewood Pl Downers Grove (60515) ***(G-8034)***
Jgr Commercial Solutions Inc...847 669-7010
11414 Smith Dr Unit G Huntley (60142) ***(G-11545)***
Jhb Group Inc...657 888-3473
766 Industrial Dr Ste G Cary (60013) ***(G-3173)***
Jhelsa Metal Polsg Fabrication...773 385-6628
1900 N Austin Ave Ste 71 Chicago (60639) ***(G-5029)***
Jht Robertson Lumber Inc...618 842-2004
408 Airport Rd Fairfield (62837) ***(G-9628)***
Jiffy Metal Products Inc...773 626-8090
5025 W Lake St Chicago (60644) ***(G-5030)***
Jigsaw Solutions Inc...630 926-1948
1296 Lakeview Dr Romeoville (60446) ***(G-17835)***
Jim Beam Brands Co (HQ)...847 948-8903
510 Lake Cook Rd Ste 200 Deerfield (60015) ***(G-7620)***
Jim Cokel Welding...309 734-5063
204 E 6th Ave Monmouth (61462) ***(G-14219)***
Jim Haley Oil Production Co...618 382-7338
1415 W Main St Carmi (62821) ***(G-2907)***
Jim Jolly Sales Inc...847 669-7570
11225 Giordano Ct Huntley (60142) ***(G-11546)***
Jim Maui Inc...888 666-5905
1 Aloha Ln Peoria (61615) ***(G-16462)***
Jim Sterner Machines...815 962-8983
2500 N Main St Ste 25 Rockford (61103) ***(G-17474)***
Jim's Plumbing, Streamwood *Also called Caffero Tool & Mfg* ***(G-19564)***
Jindilli Beverages LLC...630 581-5697
8100 S Madison St Burr Ridge (60527) ***(G-2692)***
Jing MEI Industrial USA Inc (PA)...847 671-0800
10275 W Higgins Rd # 470 Rosemont (60018) ***(G-18028)***

ALPHABETIC SECTION
Johnos Inc (PA)

Jingdiao North America Inc....847 906-8888
1400 E Bus Ctr Dr Ste 103 Mount Prospect (60056) *(G-14540)*
Jinhap US Corporation (HQ)....630 833-2880
900 N Church Rd Elmhurst (60126) *(G-9382)*
Jinny Corp....773 588-7200
3505 N Kimball Ave Chicago (60618) *(G-5031)*
Jireh Inc....217 335-3276
1103 Highway 106 Barry (62312) *(G-1251)*
Jj Collins Printers, Charleston *Also called J J Collins Sons Inc* *(G-3405)*
Jj Wood Working....708 426-6854
9016 Odell Ave Bridgeview (60455) *(G-2359)*
Jjc Epoxy Inc....630 231-5600
1105 Carolina Dr West Chicago (60185) *(G-20604)*
Jjm Printing Inc....815 499-3067
311 1st Ave Sterling (61081) *(G-19513)*
Jjm Products LLC....630 319-9325
1052 Zygmunt Cir Westmont (60559) *(G-20750)*
Jjs Technical Services....847 999-4313
1900 E Golf Rd Ste 950 Schaumburg (60173) *(G-18577)*
Jk Audio Inc....815 786-2929
1311 E 6th St Sandwich (60548) *(G-18375)*
Jk Cabinets Plus LLC....952 237-1825
6614 S Union Rd Union (60180) *(G-19940)*
Jk Installs, Greenville *Also called Jklein Enterprises Inc* *(G-10836)*
JK Williams Distilling LLC (PA)....309 839-0591
526 High Point Ln East Peoria (61611) *(G-8272)*
Jklein Enterprises Inc....618 664-4554
505a W South Ave Greenville (62246) *(G-10836)*
JKS Ventures Inc (PA)....708 345-9344
2035 Indian Boundry Dr Melrose Park (60160) *(G-13886)*
JL Clark LLC....815 961-5677
2300 S 6th St Rockford (61104) *(G-17475)*
JL Clark LLC (HQ)....815 961-5609
923 23rd Ave Rockford (61104) *(G-17476)*
Jlg Innovations Inc....618 363-2323
920 N 7th St Breese (62230) *(G-2305)*
JLJ Corp....847 726-9795
250 Telser Rd Ste D Lake Zurich (60047) *(G-12427)*
Jlm Woodworking....309 275-8259
500 Orlando Ave Normal (61761) *(G-15206)*
Jlo Metal Products Co A Corp....773 889-6242
5841 W Dickens Ave Chicago (60639) *(G-5032)*
Jls Industries Inc....630 261-9445
1015 E Wilson Ave Lombard (60148) *(G-13090)*
JM Circle Enterprise Inc....708 946-3333
28255 S Cottage Grove Ave Beecher (60401) *(G-1517)*
JM Die Tooling Co....630 616-7776
466 Meyer Rd Bensenville (60106) *(G-1831)*
JM Huber Corporation....217 224-1100
3150 Gardner Expy Quincy (62305) *(G-16895)*
JM Huber Corporation....217 224-1123
1700 Turtle Lake Rd Quincy (62305) *(G-16896)*
JM Industries LLC....708 849-4700
1000 W 142nd St Riverdale (60827) *(G-17072)*
JM Industries LLC....708 758-2600
330 E Joe Orr Rd Chicago Heights (60411) *(G-6752)*
JM Tool & Die LLC....630 616-7776
299 Beeline Dr Bensenville (60106) *(G-1832)*
Jmc Steel Group, Chicago *Also called Zekelman Industries Inc* *(G-6712)*
Jme Technologies Inc....815 477-8800
2520 Rt 176 Bldg 3 Unit 3 Crystal Lake (60014) *(G-7213)*
Jmjocs LLC....708 769-7981
6119 103rd St Chicago Ridge (60415) *(G-6800)*
JMr Precision Machining Inc....847 279-3982
630 S Wheeling Rd Mundelein (60060) *(G-14704)*
JMS Auto Electric, Lombard *Also called James J Sandoval* *(G-13089)*
JMS Manufacturing, Lakemoor *Also called Podrez Enterprise LLC* *(G-12474)*
JMS Metals Inc....618 443-1000
1255 W Broadway St Sparta (62286) *(G-19255)*
Jn Pump Holdings Inc (PA)....708 754-2940
1249 Center Ave Chicago Heights (60411) *(G-6753)*
Jns Glass & Coatings, Yorkville *Also called Strausbrger Assoc Sls Mktg Inc* *(G-21501)*
Jo Davies County Transit, Galena *Also called Workshop* *(G-10183)*
Jo Snow Inc....773 732-3045
4536 W Altgeld St Chicago (60639) *(G-5033)*
Joans Trophy & Plaque Co....309 674-6500
508 Ne Jefferson Ave Peoria (61603) *(G-16463)*
Jodaat Inc....630 916-7776
18w333 Roosevelt Rd Ste 1 Lombard (60148) *(G-13091)*
Jodi Maurer....847 961-5347
5001 Princeton Ln Lake In The Hills (60156) *(G-12337)*
Joe Anthony & Associates....708 935-0804
5151 Sauk Trl Richton Park (60471) *(G-17029)*
Joe Chicken & Fish, Richton Park *Also called Joe Anthony & Associates* *(G-17029)*
Joe Hatzer & Son Inc (PA)....815 673-5571
602 Lundy St Streator (61364) *(G-19612)*
Joe Hatzer & Son Inc....815 672-2161
2515 1/2 N Bloomington St Streator (61364) *(G-19613)*
Joe Hunt....618 392-2000
1911 E Main St Olney (62450) *(G-15866)*
Joe Zsido Sales & Design Inc....618 435-2605
350 Industrial Park Rd Benton (62812) *(G-1929)*
Joes Automotive Inc....815 937-9281
560 S Washington Ave Kankakee (60901) *(G-11982)*
Joes Printing....773 545-6063
6025 N Cicero Ave Chicago (60646) *(G-5034)*
John & Helen Inc....815 654-1070
988 Industrial Ct Loves Park (61111) *(G-13225)*
John A Biewer Lumber Company....815 357-6792
524 E Union St Seneca (61360) *(G-18859)*
John B Sanfilippo & Son Inc (PA)....847 289-1800
1703 N Randall Rd Elgin (60123) *(G-8632)*
John B Sanfilippo & Son Inc....847 690-8432
2350 Fox Ln Elgin (60123) *(G-8633)*
John Bean Technologies Corp....845 340-9727
2707 Solutions Ctr Chicago (60677) *(G-5035)*
John Bean Technologies Corp (PA)....312 861-5900
70 W Madison St Ste 4400 Chicago (60602) *(G-5036)*
John Beyer Race Cars....773 779-5313
10718 S Homan Ave Chicago (60655) *(G-5037)*
John Buechner Inc....312 263-2226
8 S Michigan Ave Ste 607 Chicago (60603) *(G-5038)*
John C Grafft (PA)....847 842-9200
28045 Roberts Rd Lake Barrington (60010) *(G-12153)*
John Cornbleet Inc....630 357-3278
931 E Ogden Ave Ste 127 Naperville (60563) *(G-14855)*
John Crane Inc (HQ)....312 605-7800
227 W Monroe St Ste 1800 Chicago (60606) *(G-5039)*
John Crane Inc....815 459-0420
29-31 Burdent Dr Crystal Lake (60014) *(G-7214)*
John Crane Inc....630 410-4444
175 E Crossroads Pkwy Bolingbrook (60440) *(G-2199)*
John Crane Inc....847 967-2400
6400 Oakton St Morton Grove (60053) *(G-14415)*
John Dagys Media LLC....708 373-0180
8011 W 125th St Palos Park (60464) *(G-16212)*
John Deere, Moline *Also called Deere & Company* *(G-14138)*
John Deere Accounts Payble, Moline *Also called Deere & Company* *(G-14139)*
John Deere AG Holdings Inc (HQ)....309 765-8000
1 John Deere Pl Moline (61265) *(G-14152)*
John Deere Authorized Dealer, Rockford *Also called West Side Tractor Sales Co* *(G-17680)*
John F Mate Co....847 381-8131
27930 W Industrial Ave # 5 Lake Barrington (60010) *(G-12154)*
John Galt Development Inc....312 701-9026
17 N State St Ste 1890 Chicago (60602) *(G-5040)*
John Gillen Company, Cicero *Also called Tvo Acquisition Corporation* *(G-6882)*
John H Best & Sons Inc....309 932-2124
1 Burlington Rd Galva (61434) *(G-10234)*
John Hardy Co....847 864-8060
1728 Brummel St Evanston (60202) *(G-9542)*
John Harland Company....815 293-4350
1003 Birch Ln Romeoville (60446) *(G-17836)*
John Hofmeister & Son Inc....773 847-0700
2386 S Blue Island Ave Chicago (60608) *(G-5041)*
John J Moesle Whl Meats Inc....773 847-4900
4725 S Talman Ave Chicago (60632) *(G-5042)*
John J Monaco Products Co Inc....708 344-3333
3120 W Lake St Melrose Park (60160) *(G-13887)*
John J Rickhoff Shtmtl Co Inc....708 331-2970
320 E 152nd St Phoenix (60426) *(G-16608)*
John Joda Post 54....815 692-3222
600 S 3rd St Fairbury (61739) *(G-9610)*
John Maneely Company....773 254-0617
4435 S Western Blvd Chicago (60609) *(G-5043)*
John Omalley....847 924-8670
170 River Bluff Rd Elgin (60120) *(G-8634)*
John Parker Advertising Co....217 892-4118
520 E Grove Ave Rantoul (61866) *(G-16979)*
John R Nalbach Engrg Co Inc....708 579-9100
621 E Plainfield Rd Countryside (60525) *(G-7062)*
John Rietveld Farms LLC....815 936-9800
4067 E 4000n Rd Bourbonnais (60914) *(G-2264)*
John S Swift Company Inc (PA)....847 465-3300
999 Commerce Ct Buffalo Grove (60089) *(G-2552)*
John S Swift of Des Plaines, Buffalo Grove *Also called Des Plaines Printing LLC* *(G-2532)*
John Sakash Company Inc (PA)....630 833-3940
700 N Walnut St Elmhurst (60126) *(G-9383)*
John Thomas Inc....815 288-2343
1560 Lovett Dr Dixon (61021) *(G-7902)*
John Thomas Company, Dixon *Also called John Thomas Inc* *(G-7902)*
John Tobin Millwork Co (PA)....630 832-3780
231 W North Ave Villa Park (60181) *(G-20152)*
Johnny Rckets Firewrks Display....847 501-1270
4410 N Hamilton Ave Chicago (60625) *(G-5044)*
Johnny Vans Smokehouse....773 750-1589
924 W Gordon Ter Apt 3 Chicago (60613) *(G-5045)*
Johnos Inc (PA)....630 897-6929
1804 E New York St Aurora (60505) *(G-1119)*

A
L
P
H
A
B
E
T
I
C

Johns Manville Corporation 815 744-1545
2151 Channahon Rd Rockdale (60436) ***(G-17261)***

Johns-Byrne Company (PA) 847 583-3100
6701 W Oakton St Niles (60714) ***(G-15137)***

Johnsbyrne, Niles *Also called Johns-Byrne Company* ***(G-15137)***

Johnsbyrne Graphic Tech Corp 847 583-3100
6701 W Oakton St Niles (60714) ***(G-15138)***

Johnson & Johnson 847 640-5400
1350 Estes Ave Elk Grove Village (60007) ***(G-9069)***

Johnson & Johnson 815 282-5671
5500 Forest Hills Rd Loves Park (61111) ***(G-13226)***

Johnson Bag Co Inc 847 438-2424
1001 N Old Rand Rd 103a Wauconda (60084) ***(G-20364)***

Johnson Contrls Authorized Dlr, Joliet *Also called Ecolab Inc* ***(G-11857)***

Johnson Contrls Authorized Dlr, Joliet *Also called Illco Inc* ***(G-11878)***

Johnson Contrls Authorized Dlr, Elk Grove Village *Also called Ecolab Inc* ***(G-8968)***

Johnson Controls, Dixon *Also called Clarios* ***(G-7893)***

Johnson Controls, East Peoria *Also called Clarios* ***(G-8261)***

Johnson Controls, Oak Brook *Also called Clarios* ***(G-15611)***

Johnson Controls, Rockford *Also called Clarios* ***(G-17351)***

Johnson Controls, Calumet City *Also called Clarios* ***(G-2773)***

Johnson Controls, Carol Stream *Also called Clarios* ***(G-2961)***

Johnson Controls, Aurora *Also called Clarios* ***(G-940)***

Johnson Controls, West Chicago *Also called Clarios* ***(G-20563)***

Johnson Controls, Elmhurst *Also called Clarios* ***(G-9347)***

Johnson Controls, Bloomingdale *Also called Clarios* ***(G-1986)***

Johnson Controls Inc 847 549-2350
859 W End Ct Vernon Hills (60061) ***(G-20068)***

Johnson Controls Inc 847 364-1500
3007 Malmo Dr Arlington Heights (60005) ***(G-762)***

Johnson Custom Cabinets 815 675-9690
7609 Blivin St Spring Grove (60081) ***(G-19278)***

Johnson Group, Des Plaines *Also called Deluxe Johnson* ***(G-7754)***

Johnson Matthey Inc 630 268-6300
2 Transam Plaza Dr # 230 Oakbrook Terrace (60181) ***(G-15804)***

Johnson Oil Company, Wheaton *Also called R H Johnson Oil Co Inc* ***(G-20817)***

Johnson Pattern & Mch Works 815 433-2775
350 W Marquette St Ottawa (61350) ***(G-16057)***

Johnson Power Ltd (PA) 708 345-4300
2530 Braga Dr Broadview (60155) ***(G-2445)***

Johnson Press America Inc 815 844-5161
800 N Court St Pontiac (61764) ***(G-16773)***

Johnson Printing 630 595-8815
729 Il Route 83 Ste 323 Bensenville (60106) ***(G-1833)***

Johnson Pumps America Inc 847 671-7867
5885 11th St Rockford (61109) ***(G-17477)***

Johnson Rolan Co Inc 309 674-9671
718 Sw Adams St Peoria (61602) ***(G-16464)***

Johnson Seat & Canvas Shop 815 756-2037
25 S Somonauk Rd Cortland (60112) ***(G-7021)***

Johnson Sign Co 847 678-2092
9615 Waveland Ave Franklin Park (60131) ***(G-9975)***

Johnson Steel Rule & Die 708 547-1726
2600 Washington Blvd A Bellwood (60104) ***(G-1630)***

Johnson Steel Rule Die Co 773 921-4334
5410 W Roosevelt Rd # 228 Chicago (60644) ***(G-5046)***

Johnson Tool Company 708 453-8600
11528 Smith Dr 3 Huntley (60142) ***(G-11547)***

Johnsons Processing Plant 815 684-5183
201 Il Route 40 E Chadwick (61014) ***(G-3258)***

Johnsons Screen Printing 630 262-8210
419 Stevens St Ste C Geneva (60134) ***(G-10287)***

Johnston & Jennings Inc 708 757-5375
1200 State St Ste 1 Chicago Heights (60411) ***(G-6754)***

Joiner Sheet Metal & Roofg Inc 618 664-9488
205 Madison St Highland (62249) ***(G-11229)***

Joint Field Services Inc 815 795-3714
1020 Broadway St Marseilles (61341) ***(G-13559)***

Jointechlabs Inc 773 954-1076
505 N Wolf Rd Wheeling (60090) ***(G-20921)***

Joliet Cabinet Company Inc 815 727-4096
405 Caton Farm Rd Lockport (60441) ***(G-13003)***

Joliet Herald Newspaper 815 280-4100
2175 Oneida St Joliet (60435) ***(G-11886)***

Joliet Pattern Works Inc 815 726-5373
508 Pasadena Ave Crest Hill (60403) ***(G-7088)***

Joliet Refinery, Elwood *Also called Exxonmobil Pipeline Company* ***(G-9462)***

Joliet Sand and Gravel Company 815 741-2090
2509 Mound Rd Rockdale (60436) ***(G-17262)***

Joliet Technologies LLC 815 725-9696
1724 Tomich Ct Crest Hill (60403) ***(G-7089)***

Joliet Times Weekly, Joliet *Also called C & C Publications* ***(G-11836)***

Jomar Electric Coil Mfg Inc 630 279-1494
218 W Stone Rd Villa Park (60181) ***(G-20153)***

Jon Cagle 618 559-3578
1611 Lindbergh Rd Carterville (62918) ***(G-3132)***

Jonem Grp Inc DBA Sign A Rama 224 848-4620
28039 W Coml Ave Ste 9 Lake Barrington (60010) ***(G-12155)***

Jones Design Group Ltd 630 462-9340
27w230 Beecher Ave Ste 1 Winfield (60190) ***(G-21111)***

Jones Garrison Sons Mch Works 618 847-2161
Hwy 15 W Fairfield (62837) ***(G-9629)***

Jones Medical Instrument Co 630 571-1980
200 Windsor Dr Ste A Oak Brook (60523) ***(G-15627)***

Jones Packing Co 815 943-4488
22701 Oak Grove Rd Harvard (60033) ***(G-11058)***

Jones Products Co, Woodstock *Also called Shannon Industries Inc* ***(G-21433)***

Jones Software Corp 312 952-0011
531 S Plymouth Ct Ste 104 Chicago (60605) ***(G-5047)***

Jones Watch and Jewelry Repair, Springfield *Also called Michael P Jones* ***(G-19406)***

Jones Wood Products 618 826-2682
11801 Ebenezer Rd Rockwood (62280) ***(G-17706)***

Joong-Ang Daily News 847 228-7200
3501 Algonquin Rd Ste 250 Rolling Meadows (60008) ***(G-17743)***

Jordan Gold Inc 708 430-7008
8741 Ridgeland Ave Oak Lawn (60453) ***(G-15722)***

Jordan Industrial Controls Inc 217 864-4444
215 Casa Park Dr Mount Zion (62549) ***(G-14648)***

Jordan Industries Inc (PA) 847 945-5591
1751 Lake Cook Rd Ste 550 Deerfield (60015) ***(G-7621)***

Jordan Paper Box Company 773 287-5362
5045 W Lake St Chicago (60644) ***(G-5048)***

Jordan Services 630 416-6701
2100 Scarlet Oak Ln Lisle (60532) ***(G-12904)***

Jordan Specialty Plastics Inc (HQ) 847 945-5591
1751 Lake Cook Rd Ste 550 Deerfield (60015) ***(G-7622)***

Jorge A Cruz 773 722-2828
240 N Harding Ave Chicago (60624) ***(G-5049)***

Joriki LLC 312 848-1136
1220 W Wrightwood Ave Chicago (60614) ***(G-5050)***

Josco Inc 708 867-7189
4830 N Harlem Ave Chicago (60706) ***(G-5051)***

Jose Pallets 773 376-8320
4506 S Mcdowell Ave Chicago (60609) ***(G-5052)***

Joseph B Krisher 618 677-2016
9950 Drum Hill Rd Mascoutah (62258) ***(G-13600)***

Joseph B Pigato MD Ltd 815 937-2122
375 N Wall St Ste P630 Kankakee (60901) ***(G-11983)***

Joseph C Rakers 618 670-6995
209 Pocahontas St Pocahontas (62275) ***(G-16752)***

Joseph C Wolf 312 332-3135
5 S Wabash Ave Ste 1018 Chicago (60603) ***(G-5053)***

Joseph Coppolino 773 735-8647
4455 W 55th St Chicago (60632) ***(G-5054)***

Joseph D Smithies 618 632-6141
7409 N Illinois St Caseyville (62232) ***(G-3216)***

Joseph Kristan 847 731-3131
2805 Ebenezer Ave Zion (60099) ***(G-21518)***

Joseph Ringelstein 708 955-7467
4110 1/2 N Octavia Ave Norridge (60706) ***(G-15238)***

Joseph Taylor Inc 309 762-5323
708 18th Avenue A Moline (61265) ***(G-14153)***

Joseph Woodworking Corporation 847 233-9766
4226 Grace St Schiller Park (60176) ***(G-18816)***

Josephs Food Products Co Inc 708 338-4090
2759 S 25th Ave Broadview (60155) ***(G-2446)***

Josephs Printing Service 847 724-4429
1739 Chestnut Ave Ste 107 Glenview (60025) ***(G-10576)***

Joshi Brothers Inc 847 895-0200
1218 S Roselle Rd Schaumburg (60193) ***(G-18578)***

Jost & Kiefer Printing Company 217 222-5145
2029 Hllster Whitney Pkwy Quincy (62305) ***(G-16897)***

Journal, Kankakee *Also called Small Newspaper Group* ***(G-12004)***

Journal & Topics Newspapers, Des Plaines *Also called Des Plaines Journal Inc* ***(G-7755)***

Journal Fabrication, Mount Olive *Also called Herald Mount Olive* ***(G-14504)***

Journal News 217 532-3933
431 S Main St Hillsboro (62049) ***(G-11317)***

Journal News 217 324-6604
510 N State St Litchfield (62056) ***(G-12968)***

Journal of Banking and Fin 618 203-9074
4 Oxford Ln Glen Carbon (62034) ***(G-10389)***

Journal Standard 815 232-1171
50 W Douglas St Ste 900 Freeport (61032) ***(G-10122)***

Journal-Courier, Jacksonville *Also called Hearst Corporation* ***(G-11766)***

Journey Circuits Inc 630 283-0604
830 E Higgins Rd Ste 111h Schaumburg (60173) ***(G-18579)***

Joy Global Underground Min LLC 618 242-3650
4111 N Water Tower Pl B Mount Vernon (62864) ***(G-14619)***

JP Leatherworks Inc 847 317-9804
1038 Somerset Ave Deerfield (60015) ***(G-7623)***

JP O'Callaghan, Chicago *Also called Regent Window Fashions LLC* ***(G-6003)***

JP Orthotics 217 885-3047
9234 Broadway St Quincy (62305) ***(G-16898)***

Jph Enterprises Inc 847 390-0900
420 Lee St Des Plaines (60016) ***(G-7792)***

Jpi, Philo *Also called Jamaica Pyrotechnics* ***(G-16606)***
Jql Technologies Corporation (PA)........800 236-9828
1255 Armour Blvd Mundelein (60060) ***(G-14705)***
Jr Bakery........773 465-6733
2841 W Howard St Chicago (60645) ***(G-5055)***
JR Edwrds Brshes Rollers Inc........815 933-3742
1325 Harvard Dr Kankakee (60901) ***(G-11984)***
Jr Industries LLC........773 908-5317
4218 N California Ave Chicago (60618) ***(G-5056)***
Jr Lighting Design Inc........708 460-6319
18464 West Creek Dr Tinley Park (60477) ***(G-19842)***
Jr Sons Welding, Alsip *Also called Edward F Data* ***(G-444)***
Jr Tech Inc........847 214-8860
1600 Todd Farm Dr Ste A Elgin (60123) ***(G-8635)***
Jrb Attachments LLC........319 378-3696
2211 York Rd Ste 320 Oak Brook (60523) ***(G-15628)***
Jrd Labs LLC........847 818-1076
2613 Greenleaf Ave Elk Grove Village (60007) ***(G-9070)***
Jrm International Inc........815 282-9330
5701 Industrial Ave Loves Park (61111) ***(G-13227)***
JRS J Rettenmaier and Soh........309 343-7808
701 W 6th St Galesburg (61401) ***(G-10203)***
Js Poole Inc........847 241-8441
3553 W Peterson Ave # 101 Chicago (60659) ***(G-5057)***
Jsa Tool & Engineering, Northbrook *Also called Strategic Mfg Partner LLC* ***(G-15488)***
Jsc Freight Solutions LLC........708 731-0448
1427 Regency Ridge Dr Joliet (60436) ***(G-11887)***
Jsc Products Inc........847 290-9520
2270 Elmhurst Rd Elk Grove Village (60007) ***(G-9071)***
Jsn Inc........708 410-1800
611 Saint Charles Rd Maywood (60153) ***(G-13670)***
Jsn Printing Inc........815 582-4014
1400 Essington Rd Joliet (60435) ***(G-11888)***
Jsolo Corp........847 964-9188
607 Carriage Way Deerfield (60015) ***(G-7624)***
Jsp Mold LLC........815 225-7110
404 E 4th St Milledgeville (61051) ***(G-14039)***
Jsq Inc........847 731-8800
2817 Ezra Ave Zion (60099) ***(G-21519)***
Jstone Inc........847 325-5660
750 Tower Rd Spc A Mundelein (60060) ***(G-14706)***
JT Cullen Co Inc........815 589-2412
901 31st Ave Fulton (61252) ***(G-10154)***
Jtec Industries Inc........309 698-9301
201 Carver Ln East Peoria (61611) ***(G-8273)***
Jtekt Toyoda Americas Corp........847 253-0340
316 W University Dr Arlington Heights (60004) ***(G-763)***
Jtekt Toyoda Americas Corp (HQ)........847 253-0340
316 W University Dr Arlington Heights (60004) ***(G-764)***
Juice Tyme Inc (HQ)........773 579-1291
4401 S Oakley Ave Chicago (60609) ***(G-5058)***
July 25th Corporation........309 664-6444
1708 E Hamilton Rd Ste B Bloomington (61704) ***(G-2064)***
Juniors Custom Cabinets........773 495-6962
2539 W Moffat St Chicago (60647) ***(G-5059)***
Juniper Networks Inc........773 632-1200
8755 W Higgins Rd Ste 960 Chicago (60631) ***(G-5060)***
Junker Inc........630 231-3770
391 Wegner Dr Ste A West Chicago (60185) ***(G-20605)***
Juno Lighting, Des Plaines *Also called Acuity Brands Lighting Inc* ***(G-7722)***
Jupiter Industries Inc (PA)........847 925-5120
1821 Walden Office Sq # 400 Schaumburg (60173) ***(G-18580)***
Jupiter Machine Tool Inc........309 297-1920
1124 Enterprise Ave Galesburg (61401) ***(G-10204)***
Jura Films North America LLC........630 261-1226
230 S Fairbank St Addison (60101) ***(G-161)***
Jury Verdict Reporter........312 644-7800
415 N State St Ste 1 Chicago (60654) ***(G-5061)***
Juskie Printing Corp........630 663-8833
2820 Hitchcock Ave Ste E Downers Grove (60515) ***(G-8035)***
Just Another Button........618 667-8531
116 W Market St Troy (62294) ***(G-19916)***
Just Ice Inc........773 301-7323
1400 W 46th St Chicago (60609) ***(G-5062)***
Just Parts Inc (PA)........815 756-2184
121 W Elm Ave Cortland (60112) ***(G-7022)***
Just Rite Rental, Naperville *Also called CCS Contractor Eqp & Sup Inc* ***(G-14793)***
Just Your Type Inc........847 864-8890
1800 Dempster St Evanston (60202) ***(G-9543)***
Justice Manufacturing Inc........217 877-2250
291 Michael Ave Decatur (62526) ***(G-7512)***
Justrite Manufacturing Co LLC........800 798-9250
1751 Lake Cook Rd Ste 370 Deerfield (60015) ***(G-7625)***
Justrite Mfg, Deerfield *Also called Justrite Manufacturing Co LLC* ***(G-7625)***
Jvc Advanced Media USA Inc........630 237-2439
10 N Martingale Rd # 575 Schaumburg (60173) ***(G-18581)***
Jvi Inc........847 675-1560
7131 N Ridgeway Ave Lincolnwood (60712) ***(G-12825)***
Jvk Precision Hard Chrome Inc........630 628-0810
29 W Commercial Ave Addison (60101) ***(G-162)***
JW Ossola Co Inc........815 339-6113
And Elm St Rr 71 Granville (61326) ***(G-10756)***
JW Sealants Inc........630 398-1010
1478 Beaumont Cir Bartlett (60103) ***(G-1291)***
JW Welding........618 228-7213
11 S Clement Dr Aviston (62216) ***(G-1180)***
JWT Farms Inc........618 664-3429
1072 Il Route 143 Pocahontas (62275) ***(G-16753)***
Jx Nippon Oil & Energy Lubrica........847 413-2188
20 N Martingale Rd # 300 Schaumburg (60173) ***(G-18582)***
Jx Nippon Oil & Energy USA Inc (HQ)........847 413-2188
20 N Martingale Rd # 325 Schaumburg (60173) ***(G-18583)***
K & A Precision Machine Inc........847 998-1933
2500 Ravine Way Glenview (60025) ***(G-10577)***
K & B Machining........847 663-9534
6206 Madison Ct Morton Grove (60053) ***(G-14416)***
K & C Design and Manufacturing........630 543-3386
422 S Irmen Dr Addison (60101) ***(G-163)***
K & G Men's Superstore, Orland Park *Also called K&G Mens Company Inc* ***(G-15963)***
K & H Tool Co........630 766-4588
164 Devon Ave Bensenville (60106) ***(G-1834)***
K & J Phillips Corporation........630 355-0660
526 W 5th Ave Naperville (60563) ***(G-14856)***
K & J Synthetic Lubricants........630 628-1011
405 W Myrick Ave Addison (60101) ***(G-164)***
K & K Abrasives & Supplies........773 582-9500
5161 S Millard Ave Chicago (60632) ***(G-5063)***
K & K Buildings, Ewing *Also called K & K Storage Barns LLC* ***(G-9602)***
K & K Iron Works LLC........773 619-6899
2340 S Springfield Ave Chicago (60623) ***(G-5064)***
K & K Iron Works LLC (PA)........708 924-0000
5100 S Lawndale Ave Ste 7 Mc Cook (60525) ***(G-13693)***
K & K Storage Barns LLC (PA)........618 927-0533
19867 Ketterman Ln Ewing (62836) ***(G-9602)***
K & K Tool & Die Inc........309 829-4479
915 E Oakland Ave Bloomington (61701) ***(G-2065)***
K & L Looseleaf Products Inc........847 357-9733
425 Bonnie Ln Elk Grove Village (60007) ***(G-9072)***
K & M Printing Company Inc........847 884-1100
1410 N Meacham Rd Frnt Schaumburg (60173) ***(G-18584)***
K & N Laboratories Inc........708 482-3240
633 S La Grange Rd La Grange (60525) ***(G-12081)***
K & P Industries Inc........630 628-6676
1120 W Republic Dr Ste H Addison (60101) ***(G-165)***
K & P Welding........217 536-5245
12374 E 550th Ave Watson (62473) ***(G-20322)***
K & S Engineering, Chicago *Also called Midwest Model Aircraft Co* ***(G-5446)***
K & S Manufacturing Co Inc........815 232-7519
24 S Hooker Ave Freeport (61032) ***(G-10123)***
K & S Precision Metals Co........773 586-8503
6911 W 59th St Chicago (60638) ***(G-5065)***
K & S Printing Services........815 899-2923
510 N Main St Ste 1 Sycamore (60178) ***(G-19720)***
K & S Service & Rental Corp (PA)........630 279-4292
471 W Monroe St Elmhurst (60126) ***(G-9384)***
K & W Auto Electric........217 857-1717
103 N Automotive Dr Teutopolis (62467) ***(G-19770)***
K and A Graphics Inc........847 244-2345
4090 Ryan Rd Ste A Gurnee (60031) ***(G-10890)***
K B Metal Company........309 248-7355
1172 County Road 2100 N Washburn (61570) ***(G-20264)***
K B Sales & Service, Geneva *Also called O Brien Bill* ***(G-10294)***
K B Tool Inc........630 595-4340
211 Beeline Dr Ste 7 Bensenville (60106) ***(G-1835)***
K C Audio........708 636-4928
4824 W 129th St Alsip (60803) ***(G-462)***
K C Printing Services Inc........847 382-8822
22292 N Pepper Rd Ste A Lake Barrington (60010) ***(G-12156)***
K Chae Corp........847 763-0077
3630 W Pratt Ave Lincolnwood (60712) ***(G-12826)***
K D Custom Sawing Logging........309 231-4805
6570 Illinois Route 29 Green Valley (61534) ***(G-10817)***
K D Iron Works........847 991-3039
542 W Colfax St Ste 5 Palatine (60067) ***(G-16134)***
K D L Machining Inc........309 477-3036
1917 S 2nd St Pekin (61554) ***(G-16341)***
K D R Productions, Hoffman Estates *Also called Ken Young Construction Co* ***(G-11433)***
K D Welding Inc........815 591-3545
2 River Bend Dr Hanover (61041) ***(G-10996)***
K Fleye Designs........773 531-0716
532 N Long Ave Chicago (60644) ***(G-5066)***
K H Huppert Co........708 339-2020
16850 State St South Holland (60473) ***(G-19225)***
K H M Plastics Inc........847 249-4910
4090 Ryan Rd Ste B Gurnee (60031) ***(G-10891)***
K K O Inc........815 569-2324
100 E Grove St Capron (61012) ***(G-2833)***
K M I International Corp........630 627-6300
1411 W Jeffrey Dr Addison (60101) ***(G-166)***

ALPHABETIC

K M J Enterprises Inc 847 688-1200
2001 Swanson Ct Gurnee (60031) ***(G-10892)***
K M K, Trenton *Also called Kmk Metal Fabricators Inc* ***(G-19903)***
K O G Mfg & Bindery Corp 847 263-5050
1813 W Glen Flora Ave Waukegan (60085) ***(G-20453)***
K P Enterprises Inc 630 509-2174
792 County Line Rd Ste A Bensenville (60106) ***(G-1836)***
K R J Inc 309 925-5123
101 S West St Tremont (61568) ***(G-19897)***
K R Komarek Inc (HQ) 847 956-0060
548 Clayton Ct Wood Dale (60191) ***(G-21203)***
K R N Machine & Laser Center, Herrin *Also called K R N Machine and Laser Center* ***(G-11173)***
K R N Machine and Laser Center 618 942-6064
516 N Park Ave Herrin (62948) ***(G-11173)***
K Systems Corporation 708 449-0400
4931 Butterfield Rd Hillside (60162) ***(G-11343)***
K Three Welding Service Inc 708 563-2911
814 W 120th St Chicago (60643) ***(G-5067)***
K Transco Inc 630 881-5411
13207 W Hunt Master Ln Lemont (60439) ***(G-12567)***
K Trox Sales Inc 815 568-1521
6807 Paulson Dr Marengo (60152) ***(G-13487)***
K V F Company (PA) 847 437-5100
950 Lively Blvd Elk Grove Village (60007) ***(G-9073)***
K V F Company 847 437-5019
1325 Landmeier Rd Elk Grove Village (60007) ***(G-9074)***
K&Company, Naperville *Also called Wilton Brands LLC* ***(G-14948)***
K&G Mens Company Inc 708 349-2579
180 Orland Park Pl Orland Park (60462) ***(G-15963)***
K&H Fuel 815 405-4364
22193 Clove Dr Frankfort (60423) ***(G-9811)***
K&I Light Kandi Led Inc 773 745-1533
2600 N Cicero Ave Chicago (60639) ***(G-5068)***
K&J Finishing Inc 815 965-9655
716 Cedar St Rockford (61102) ***(G-17478)***
K&S International Inc 847 229-0202
760 Glenn Ave Wheeling (60090) ***(G-20922)***
K+s Montana Holdings LLC (HQ) 312 807-2000
123 N Wacker Dr Chicago (60606) ***(G-5069)***
K+s Salt LLC (HQ) 844 789-3991
444 W Lake St Ste 3000 Chicago (60606) ***(G-5070)***
K-C Tool Co 630 983-5960
552 S Washington St Naperville (60540) ***(G-14857)***
K-Display Corp 773 586-2042
6150 S Oak Park Ave Chicago (60638) ***(G-5071)***
K-G Spray-Pak Inc 630 543-7600
2651 Warrenville Rd # 300 Downers Grove (60515) ***(G-8036)***
K-Met Industries Inc 708 534-3300
25911 S Ridgeland Ave Monee (60449) ***(G-14203)***
K-Pro US LLC 872 529-5776
475 Regency Park Ste 175 O Fallon (62269) ***(G-15576)***
K-Technology Inc 708 458-4890
6200 W 51st St Ste 6 Chicago (60638) ***(G-5072)***
K-Tron Inc 708 460-2128
9704 Hummingbird Hill Dr Orland Park (60467) ***(G-15964)***
K2 Tables, Crystal Lake *Also called 20 20 Medical Systems Inc* ***(G-7152)***
KA Steel Chemicals Inc 630 257-3900
1001 31st St Ste 200 Downers Grove (60515) ***(G-8037)***
Kaages News Service 847 529-7199
6700 N Northwest Hwy Chicago (60631) ***(G-5073)***
Kaas Industries Inc 847 298-9106
7035 Barry St Rosemont (60018) ***(G-18029)***
Kabat American Inc 870 739-1430
410 38th Ave Saint Charles (60174) ***(G-18219)***
Kabert Industries Inc (PA) 630 833-2115
321 W Saint Charles Rd Villa Park (60181) ***(G-20154)***
Kabinet Kraft 618 395-1047
536 E Cherry St Olney (62450) ***(G-15867)***
Kackert Enterprises Inc 630 898-9339
824 2nd Ave Aurora (60505) ***(G-1120)***
Kaco Signs, Centralia *Also called Michael Reggis Clark* ***(G-3238)***
Kadon Precision Machining Inc 815 874-5850
5876 Sandy Hollow Rd Rockford (61109) ***(G-17479)***
Kae Dj Publishing 773 233-2609
12003 S Pulaski Rd # 202 Chicago (60803) ***(G-5074)***
Kaelco Entrmt Holdings Inc 217 600-7815
3 Henson Pl Ste 1 Champaign (61820) ***(G-3312)***
Kaeppler Machining, Elk Grove Village *Also called Ulrich Kaeppler* ***(G-9290)***
Kafka Manufacturing Co 708 771-0970
7600 Industrial Dr Forest Park (60130) ***(G-9721)***
Kafko International Ltd 847 763-0333
3555 Howard St Skokie (60076) ***(G-18971)***
Kagan Industries, Chicago *Also called Creative Metal Products* ***(G-4264)***
Kahuna Atm, Bloomington *Also called Kahuna LLC* ***(G-2066)***
Kahuna LLC 888 357-8472
807 Arcadia Dr Ste B Bloomington (61704) ***(G-2066)***
Kai Lee Couture Inc 773 426-1668
5612 S King Dr Chicago (60637) ***(G-5075)***
Kaiser Mfg Co 773 235-4705
4700 W Le Moyne St Chicago (60651) ***(G-5076)***
Kalamazoo Outdoor Gourmet LLC (HQ) 312 423-8770
810 W Washington Blvd Chicago (60607) ***(G-5077)***
Kalb Corporation 309 483-3600
110 W Depot St Oneida (61467) ***(G-15903)***
Kalena LLC 773 598-0033
1937 N Mohawk St Chicago (60614) ***(G-5078)***
Kalle USA Inc 847 775-0781
5750 Centerpoint Ct Ste B Gurnee (60031) ***(G-10893)***
Kam Group Inc 630 679-9668
486 W North Frontage Rd Bolingbrook (60440) ***(G-2200)***
Kam Tool and Mold 815 338-8360
1300 Cobblestone Way Woodstock (60098) ***(G-21397)***
Kaman Tool Corporation 708 652-9023
3147 S Austin Blvd Cicero (60804) ***(G-6858)***
Kamflex Conveyor Corporation 630 682-1555
2312 Oak Leaf St Joliet (60436) ***(G-11889)***
Kamflex, LLC, Joliet *Also called Engineered Plumbing Spc LLC* ***(G-11862)***
Kamstra Door Service Inc 708 895-9990
2007 Thornton Lansing Rd Lansing (60438) ***(G-12500)***
Kana Software Inc 312 447-5600
30 S Wacker Dr Ste 1300 Chicago (60606) ***(G-5079)***
Kanaflex Corporation Illinois (HQ) 847 634-6100
800 Woodlands Pkwy Vernon Hills (60061) ***(G-20069)***
Kanan Fashions Inc (PA) 630 240-1234
1010 Jorie Blvd Ste 324 Oak Brook (60523) ***(G-15629)***
Kanbo International (us) Inc 630 873-6320
650 Warrenville Rd # 100 Lisle (60532) ***(G-12905)***
Kane County Chronicle, Crystal Lake *Also called Shaw Suburban Media Group Inc* ***(G-7264)***
Kane Graphical Corporation 773 384-1200
2255 W Logan Blvd Chicago (60647) ***(G-5080)***
Kaneland Publications Inc 630 365-6446
333 N Randall Rd Ste 111 Saint Charles (60174) ***(G-18220)***
Kaney Capital LLC 815 986-4359
801 Airport Dr Rockford (61109) ***(G-17480)***
Kaney Group LLC (PA) 815 986-4359
1300 Capital Dr Rockford (61109) ***(G-17481)***
Kankakee Daily Journal Co LLC (HQ) 815 937-3300
8 Dearborn Sq Kankakee (60901) ***(G-11985)***
Kankakee Industrial Tech 815 933-6683
359 S Kinzie Ave Bradley (60915) ***(G-2285)***
Kankakee Industrial Technology, Decatur *Also called Decatur Industrial Elc Inc* ***(G-7487)***
Kankakee Tent & Awning Co 815 932-8000
679b W 2000s Rd Kankakee (60901) ***(G-11986)***
Kanneberg Custom Kitchens Inc 815 654-1110
1242 Shappert Dr Machesney Park (61115) ***(G-13353)***
Kap Holdings LLC (PA) 708 948-0226
137 N Oak Park Ave # 214 Oak Park (60301) ***(G-15759)***
Kapak Company LLC 952 541-0730
825 Turnberry Ct Hanover Park (60133) ***(G-11008)***
Kapp Company LLC 618 676-1000
3600 E White Ln Olney (62450) ***(G-15868)***
Kapstone Kraft Paper Corp (HQ) 252 533-6000
1101 Skokie Blvd Ste 300 Northbrook (60062) ***(G-15411)***
Kara Graphics Inc 630 964-8122
6823 Hobson Valley Dr # 201 Woodridge (60517) ***(G-21319)***
Karen Young 312 202-0142
10 W Elm St Apt 900 Chicago (60610) ***(G-5081)***
Karimi Saifuddin 630 943-8808
14017 S Lakeridge Dr Plainfield (60544) ***(G-16678)***
Karimi Enterprise, Plainfield *Also called Karimi Saifuddin* ***(G-16678)***
Karl Lambrecht Corp 773 472-5442
4204 N Lincoln Ave Chicago (60618) ***(G-5082)***
Karlin Foods Corp 847 441-8330
1845 Oak St Ste 19 Northfield (60093) ***(G-15519)***
Karly Iron Works Inc 815 477-3430
4014 Northwest Hwy Ste 4c Crystal Lake (60014) ***(G-7215)***
Karma Yacht Sales LLC (PA) 773 254-0200
3434 E 95th St Chicago (60617) ***(G-5083)***
Karnak Midwest LLC 708 338-3388
2601 Gardner Rd Broadview (60155) ***(G-2447)***
Kaser Power Equipment Inc 309 289-2176
480 Henderson Rd Knoxville (61448) ***(G-12068)***
Kasha Industries Inc 618 375-2511
1 Plastic Ln Grayville (62844) ***(G-10811)***
Kasha Industries Inc 618 375-2511
1 Plastics Ln Grayville (62844) ***(G-10812)***
Kashiv Biosciences LLC 908 895-1576
3440 S Dearborn St # 300 Chicago (60616) ***(G-5084)***
Kaskaskia Mechanical Insul Co 618 768-4526
6606 State Route 15 Mascoutah (62258) ***(G-13601)***
Kaskaskia Tool and Machine Inc 618 475-3301
107 S Benton St New Athens (62264) ***(G-15020)***
Kaskey Kids Inc 847 441-3092
1485 Scott Ave Winnetka (60093) ***(G-21131)***
Kastalon Inc 708 389-2210
4100 W 124th Pl Alsip (60803) ***(G-463)***
Kastalon Polyurethane Products, Alsip *Also called Kastalon Inc* ***(G-463)***

Kastelic Canvas Inc 815 436-8160
15940 S Lincoln Hwy Plainfield (60586) ***(G-16679)***
Kastle Therapeutics LLC 312 883-5695
181 W Madison St Ste 3745 Chicago (60602) ***(G-5085)***
Kathleen A Badasch 618 462-5881
31 E Broadway Alton (62002) ***(G-562)***
Kathys Kitchen LLC 217 452-3035
201 N Pitt St Virginia (62691) ***(G-20194)***
Kato USA Inc 847 781-9500
100 Remington Rd Schaumburg (60173) ***(G-18585)***
Kats Meow 815 747-2113
288 Sinsinawa Ave East Dubuque (61025) ***(G-8177)***
Katy Lynn Winery LLC 618 964-1818
1801 Sneed Rd Carbondale (62902) ***(G-2848)***
Katy's Goodness, Oak Park *Also called Katys LLC* ***(G-15760)***
Katys LLC (PA) 708 522-9814
1040 S Maple Ave Oak Park (60304) ***(G-15760)***
Kauffman Poultry Farms Inc 815 264-3470
8519 Leland Rd Waterman (60556) ***(G-20298)***
Kaufman Woodworking 217 543-3607
29 E Cr 100 N Arthur (61911) ***(G-864)***
Kaufman-Worthen Machinery Inc 847 360-9170
2326 W Wadsworth Rd Waukegan (60087) ***(G-20454)***
Kaufmans Custom Cabinets 217 268-4330
363 E County Road 200n Arcola (61910) ***(G-653)***
Kavalierglass North Amer Inc 847 364-7303
1301 Brummel Ave Elk Grove Village (60007) ***(G-9075)***
Kavanaugh Electric Inc 708 503-1310
9511 Corsair Rd Ste B Frankfort (60423) ***(G-9812)***
Kawneer Company Inc 815 224-2708
2528 7th St Peru (61354) ***(G-16579)***
Kay & Cee 773 425-9169
1204 W 127th St Calumet Park (60827) ***(G-2798)***
Kay Home Products, Antioch *Also called Akerue Industries LLC* ***(G-597)***
Kay Manufacturing Company LLC 708 862-6800
602 State St Calumet City (60409) ***(G-2782)***
Kaybee Engineering Company Inc 630 968-7100
100 E Quincy St Westmont (60559) ***(G-20751)***
Kaybee Engnrng, Westmont *Also called Kaybee Engineering Company Inc* ***(G-20751)***
Kaydon Acquisition Xii Inc 217 443-3592
130 N Jackson St Danville (61832) ***(G-7354)***
Kaye Lee & Company Inc 312 236-9686
5 S Wabash Ave Ste 200 Chicago (60603) ***(G-5086)***
Kaylen Industries Inc (PA) 847 671-6767
9505 Winona Ave Schiller Park (60176) ***(G-18817)***
Kayser Lure Corp 217 964-2110
107 Junction St Ursa (62376) ***(G-20004)***
Kazmier Tooling Inc 773 586-0300
6001 S Oak Park Ave Chicago (60638) ***(G-5087)***
KB Publishing Inc (PA) 708 331-6352
924 E 162nd St South Holland (60473) ***(G-19226)***
KB Publishing Inc 708 331-6352
930 E 162nd St South Holland (60473) ***(G-19227)***
Kccdd Inc 309 344-2030
1200 Monmouth Blvd Galesburg (61401) ***(G-10205)***
Kci Chemical, Matteson *Also called Konzen Chemicals Inc* ***(G-13626)***
Kci Satellite 800 664-2602
101 N Industrial Park Dr Pittsfield (62363) ***(G-16635)***
Kcp Metal Fabrications Inc 773 775-0318
5475 N Northwest Hwy Chicago (60630) ***(G-5088)***
Kd Steel Incorporated 630 201-1619
420 N Park St Westmont (60559) ***(G-20752)***
Kd-Kidz Dlight Interactive LLC 630 724-0223
1431 Opus Pl Ste 110 Downers Grove (60515) ***(G-8038)***
Kdk Upset Forging Co 708 388-8770
2645 139th St Blue Island (60406) ***(G-2128)***
Kdm Enterprises LLC 877 591-9768
820 Commerce Pkwy Carpentersville (60110) ***(G-3106)***
Kdn Signs Inc 847 721-3848
890 Eagle Dr Bensenville (60106) ***(G-1837)***
Keane Inc 847 952-9700
1697 W Imperial Ct Mount Prospect (60056) ***(G-14541)***
Keane Gillette Publishing LLC 630 279-7521
110 E Schiller St Ste 206 Elmhurst (60126) ***(G-9385)***
Keating of Chicago Inc 815 569-2324
100 E Grove St Capron (61012) ***(G-2834)***
Keats Manufacturing Co (PA) 847 520-1133
350 Holbrook Dr Wheeling (60090) ***(G-20923)***
Keckley Manufacturing Company 847 674-8422
3400 Cleveland St Skokie (60076) ***(G-18972)***
Keebler Foods Company (HQ) 630 833-2900
677 N Larch Ave Elmhurst (60126) ***(G-9386)***
Keebomed Inc 630 888-2888
832 E Rand Rd Ste 22 Mount Prospect (60056) ***(G-14542)***
Keene Technology Inc 815 624-8989
7550 Quantum Ct Machesney Park (61011) ***(G-13320)***
Keenpac LLC 845 291-8680
8338 Austin Ave Morton Grove (60053) ***(G-14417)***
Keenpac LLC (HQ) 845 291-8680
8338 Austin Ave Morton Grove (60053) ***(G-14418)***
Keeper Corp 630 773-9393
1345 Industrial Dr Itasca (60143) ***(G-11682)***
Keeper Thermal Bag Co Inc 630 213-0125
1006 Poplar Ln Bartlett (60103) ***(G-1292)***
Keepes Funeral Home Inc 618 262-5200
1500 N Cherry St Mount Carmel (62863) ***(G-14476)***
Keflex, Woodstock *Also called Flex-Weld Inc* ***(G-21387)***
Kegley Machine Co 309 346-8914
615 Main St Pekin (61554) ***(G-16342)***
Kei Keis Kreation Kafe 708 982-6560
2801 Lexington Dr Hazel Crest (60429) ***(G-11130)***
Keil-Forness Comfort Systems 618 233-3039
301 N Illinois St Belleville (62220) ***(G-1560)***
Kelch, Bob Floors, Peoria *Also called T J P Investments Inc* ***(G-16534)***
Kelco Construction Inc 773 853-2974
5572 N Lynch Ave Chicago (60630) ***(G-5089)***
Kelco Industries Inc (PA) 815 334-3600
1425 Lake Ave Woodstock (60098) ***(G-21398)***
Keleen Leathers Inc 630 590-5300
1010 Executive Dr Ste 400 Westmont (60559) ***(G-20753)***
Keller Grain & Livestock Inc 618 455-3634
7031 N 1900th St Willow Hill (62480) ***(G-21024)***
Keller Group Inc (PA) 847 446-7550
1 Northfield Plz Ste 510 Northfield (60093) ***(G-15520)***
Kellermann Manufacturing Co, Wauconda *Also called Kellermann Manufacturing Inc* ***(G-20365)***
Kellermann Manufacturing Inc 847 526-7266
1000 N Rand Rd Ste 224 Wauconda (60084) ***(G-20365)***
Kelley Construction Inc 217 422-1800
2454 N 27th St Decatur (62526) ***(G-7513)***
Kelley Crematory, Champaign *Also called Kelley Vault Co Inc* ***(G-3313)***
Kelley Iron Works, East Peoria *Also called Kelley Ornamental Iron LLC* ***(G-8274)***
Kelley Ornamental Iron LLC (PA) 309 697-9870
4303 N Main St East Peoria (61611) ***(G-8274)***
Kelley Ornamental Iron LLC 309 820-7540
1206 Towanda Ave Ste 1 Bloomington (61701) ***(G-2067)***
Kelley Vault Co Inc 217 355-5551
1901 W Springer Dr Champaign (61821) ***(G-3313)***
Kellogg Company 773 254-0900
2945 W 31st St Chicago (60623) ***(G-5090)***
Kellogg Company 630 941-0300
545 W Lamont Rd Elmhurst (60126) ***(G-9387)***
Kellogg Company 217 258-3251
3801 Dewitt Ave Mattoon (61938) ***(G-13640)***
Kellogg Company 773 995-7200
750 E 110th St Chicago (60628) ***(G-5091)***
Kellogg Printing Co 309 734-8388
95 Public Sq Monmouth (61462) ***(G-14220)***
Kellogg's, Elmhurst *Also called Kellogg Company* ***(G-9387)***
Kellstrom Aerospace, Roselle *Also called Kellstrom Coml Arospc Inc* ***(G-17961)***
Kellstrom Coml Arospc Inc (HQ) 847 233-5800
450 Medinah Rd Roselle (60172) ***(G-17961)***
Kelly & Son Forestry & Log LLC 815 275-6877
1783 Ashford Ln Crystal Lake (60014) ***(G-7216)***
Kelly Corned Beef Co Chicago 773 588-2882
3531 N Elston Ave Chicago (60618) ***(G-5092)***
Kelly Eisenberg, Chicago *Also called Kelly Corned Beef Co Chicago* ***(G-5092)***
Kelly Printing Co Inc 217 443-1792
205 Oregon Ave Danville (61832) ***(G-7355)***
Kelly Systems Inc (PA) 312 733-3224
422 N Western Ave Chicago (60612) ***(G-5093)***
Kellyjo Makes Scents 618 281-4241
3050 Steppig Rd Columbia (62236) ***(G-6990)***
Kellys Sign Shop 217 477-0167
1004 N Vermilion St Danville (61832) ***(G-7356)***
Kelmscott Communications, Berkeley *Also called Voris Communication Co Inc* ***(G-1946)***
Kelvyn Press Inc (HQ) 708 343-0448
2910 S 18th Ave Broadview (60155) ***(G-2448)***
Kelvyn Press Inc 630 585-8160
880 Enterprise St Ste F Aurora (60504) ***(G-991)***
Kemco Portable Machining, Hillsdale *Also called Bos Machine Tool Services Inc* ***(G-11321)***
Kemell Enterprises LLC 618 671-1513
612 Ganim Dr Belleville (62221) ***(G-1561)***
Kemis Kollections 773 431-2307
240 E 115th St Chicago Chicago (60628) ***(G-5094)***
Kemlite Sequentia Products, Channahon *Also called Crane Composites Inc* ***(G-3377)***
Kemp Manufacturing Company (PA) 309 682-7292
4310 N Voss St Peoria (61616) ***(G-16465)***
Kempco Window Treatments Inc 708 754-4484
74 E 23rd St Chicago Heights (60411) ***(G-6755)***
Kemper Industries 217 826-5712
1017 Clarksville Rd Marshall (62441) ***(G-13573)***
Kempner Company Inc 312 733-1606
629 W Cermak Rd Ste 201 Chicago (60616) ***(G-5095)***
Ken Elliott Co 618 466-8200
3704 Riehl Ln Godfrey (62035) ***(G-10654)***
Ken Matthews & Associates Inc 630 628-6470
415 W Belden Ave Ste H Addison (60101) ***(G-167)***

ALPHABETIC

Ken Young Construction Co 847 358-3026
1185 Ash Rd Hoffman Estates (60169) *(G-11433)*
Kencor Stairs & Woodworking 630 279-8980
311 W Stone Rd Villa Park (60181) *(G-20155)*
Kendall County Concrete Inc 630 851-9197
695 Route 34 Aurora (60503) *(G-992)*
Kendall County Record (PA) 630 553-7034
109 W Veterans Pkwy Yorkville (60560) *(G-21489)*
Kendall Printing Co 630 553-9200
948 N Bridge St Yorkville (60560) *(G-21490)*
Kendel Witte Die & Mold, Freeport *Also called Witte Kendel Die & Mold (G-10150)*
Keneal Graphic Solutions, Romeoville *Also called Keneal Industries Inc (G-17837)*
Keneal Industries Inc 815 886-1300
679 Parkwood Ave Romeoville (60446) *(G-17837)*
Kenent Screw Machine Products 815 624-7216
4843 Yale Bridge Rd Rockton (61072) *(G-17699)*
Kenilworth Press Incorporated 847 256-5210
1223 Green Bay Rd Wilmette (60091) *(G-21081)*
Kenmode Tool and Engrg Inc 847 658-5041
820 W Algonquin Rd Algonquin (60102) *(G-376)*
Kennametal Inc 309 578-1888
Olglena Rd Mossville (61552) *(G-14460)*
Kenneth W Templeman 847 912-2740
382 Minuet Cir Volo (60073) *(G-20200)*
Kens Quick Print Inc 847 831-4410
1500 Old Deerfield Rd # 5 Highland Park (60035) *(G-11277)*
Kens Street Rod Repair 815 874-1811
5521 International Dr Rockford (61109) *(G-17482)*
Kensen Tool & Die Inc 847 455-0150
9200 Parklane Ave Franklin Park (60131) *(G-9976)*
Kent Nutrition Group Inc 815 874-2411
1612 S Bend Rd Rockford (61109) *(G-17483)*
Kent Nutrition Group Inc 217 323-1216
8679 Kent Feed Rd Beardstown (62618) *(G-1448)*
Kent Precision Foods Group Inc 630 226-0071
1000 Dalton Ln Ste A Bolingbrook (60490) *(G-2201)*
Kent Precision Foods Group Inc 630 226-0071
850 Remington Blvd Bolingbrook (60440) *(G-2202)*
Kenwood Electrical Systems, Machesney Park *Also called Unlimited Svcs Wisconsin Inc (G-13383)*
Kenyeri Consulting LLC 630 920-3497
2300 Wscnsin Ave Ste 218 Downers Grove (60515) *(G-8039)*
Kenyeri Engineering & Mfg, Downers Grove *Also called Kenyeri Consulting LLC (G-8039)*
Keonix Corporation 847 259-9430
922 N Chicago Ave Arlington Heights (60004) *(G-765)*
Kep Woodworking 847 480-9545
12260 Lisbon Rd Newark (60541) *(G-15077)*
Kepner Products Company 630 279-1550
995 N Ellsworth Ave Villa Park (60181) *(G-20156)*
Kerala Express Newspaper 773 465-5359
2050 W Devon Ave Apt 1w Chicago (60659) *(G-5096)*
Kerins Industries Inc 630 515-9111
8408 Wilmette Ave Ste A Darien (60561) *(G-7408)*
Kernel Kutter Inc 815 877-1515
10509 Tartan Ct Machesney Park (61115) *(G-13354)*
Kerogen Resources Inc 618 382-3114
645 Il Highway 14 Carmi (62821) *(G-2908)*
Kerrigan Corporation 847 251-8994
811 Ridge Rd Wilmette (60091) *(G-21082)*
Kerry Inc 847 595-1003
1301 Mark St Elk Grove Village (60007) *(G-9076)*
Kerry Inc 708 450-3260
3141 W North Ave Melrose Park (60160) *(G-13888)*
Kerry Ingredients, Melrose Park *Also called Kerry Inc (G-13888)*
Kerry Ingredients & Flavours 847 595-1003
1301 Mark St Elk Grove Village (60007) *(G-9077)*
Kerry Ingredients and Flavours, Elk Grove Village *Also called Kerry Inc (G-9076)*
Kerry Zurich, Lake Zurich *Also called Insight Beverages Inc (G-12425)*
Kesher Stam 773 973-7826
2817 W Touhy Ave Chicago (60645) *(G-5097)*
Keson Industries Inc 630 820-4200
810 N Commerce St Aurora (60504) *(G-993)*
Kester LLC 630 616-6882
940 W Thorndale Ave Itasca (60143) *(G-11683)*
Kester LLC (HQ) 630 616-4000
800 W Thorndale Ave Itasca (60143) *(G-11684)*
Kestler Digital Printing Inc 773 581-5918
2845 W 48th Pl Chicago (60632) *(G-5098)*
Kettler Casting Co Inc 618 234-5303
2640 Old Freeburg Rd Belleville (62220) *(G-1562)*
Keurig Dr Pepper Inc 708 947-5000
401 N Railroad Ave Northlake (60164) *(G-15549)*
Keurig Dr Pepper Inc 815 877-7777
5300 Forest Hills Rd Loves Park (61111) *(G-13228)*
Kevin Kewney 217 228-7444
410 S 10th St Quincy (62301) *(G-16899)*
Kevin Robinson 618 410-3083
8898 Bunkum Rd Caseyville (62232) *(G-3217)*
Kevins Small Engine Repair 309 897-2026
15080 Township Rd 1250 N Bradford (61421) *(G-2274)*
Kevron Printing & Design Inc 708 229-7725
9831 S 78th Ave Ste F Hickory Hills (60457) *(G-11199)*
Kevs Kans Inc 309 303-3999
1501 W Front St Roanoke (61561) *(G-17102)*
Kewanee Star Courier, Kewanee *Also called Gatehouse Media LLC (G-12035)*
Kewanee Triangle Concrete, Kewanee *Also called Triangle Concrete Co Inc (G-12042)*
Kewaunee Scientific Corp 847 675-7744
3150 Skokie Valley Rd # 8 Highland Park (60035) *(G-11278)*
Key Colony Inc 630 783-8572
16300 103rd St Lemont (60439) *(G-12568)*
Key Magazine, Chicago *Also called This Week In Chicago Inc (G-6367)*
Key Printing 815 933-1800
111 E Court St Kankakee (60901) *(G-11987)*
Key Resources Inc 800 574-1339
36467 S Nathan Hale Dr Lake Villa (60046) *(G-12357)*
Key Smart, Elk Grove Village *Also called Curv Group LLC (G-8925)*
Key Source, Peoria *Also called Need To Know Inc (G-16484)*
Key West Metal Industries Inc 708 371-1470
13831 Kostner Ave Crestwood (60418) *(G-7121)*
Keyesport Manufacturing Inc 618 749-5510
1610 Mulberry St Keyesport (62253) *(G-12043)*
Keyleaf, Batavia *Also called Batavia Bio Processing Limited (G-1354)*
Keyrock Energy LLC 618 982-9710
20227 Thorn Rd Thompsonville (62890) *(G-19778)*
Keys Manufacturing Company Inc 217 465-4001
13338 N 1900th St Paris (61944) *(G-16231)*
Keystone Aniline, Chicago *Also called Milliken & Company (G-5461)*
Keystone Bar Products Inc 708 753-1200
317 E 11th St Chicago Heights (60411) *(G-6756)*
Keystone Consolidated Inds Inc 309 697-7020
7000 S Adams St Peoria (61641) *(G-16466)*
Keystone Consolidated Inds Inc 708 753-1200
317 E 11th St Chicago Heights (60411) *(G-6757)*
Keystone Display Inc 815 648-2456
11916 Maple Ave Hebron (60034) *(G-11144)*
Keystone Printing & Publishing 815 678-2591
5512 May Ave Richmond (60071) *(G-17016)*
Keystone Printing Service, Richmond *Also called Keystone Printing & Publishing (G-17016)*
Keystone Printing Services 773 622-7210
2451 N Harlem Ave Chicago (60707) *(G-5099)*
Keystone Wire & Cable, Bolingbrook *Also called Lynn Electronics Corp (G-2208)*
Keystroke Graphics, Montgomery *Also called Silent W Communications Inc (G-14270)*
Kf Control, Illiopolis *Also called Kingfisher Controls LLC (G-11574)*
Kfi, Rolling Meadows *Also called Komatsu Forklift USA LLC (G-17744)*
KG Lift Inc 815 908-1855
1214 W Capitol Dr Ste 8 Addison (60101) *(G-168)*
Kgbal Manufacturing LLC 312 841-3545
493 Mission St Carol Stream (60188) *(G-3009)*
Khc Corporation 815 337-7630
333 E Judd St Woodstock (60098) *(G-21399)*
Khm, Gurnee *Also called K H M Plastics Inc (G-10891)*
Ki, Chicago *Also called Krueger International Inc (G-5134)*
Ki Industries Inc 708 449-1990
5540 Mcdermott Dr Berkeley (60163) *(G-1941)*
Ki Machine Tools & Productions 815 484-9216
2107 Charmar Dr Loves Park (61111) *(G-13229)*
Kibar Americas Inc 312 285-2553
1 N Wacker Dr Ste 1900 Chicago (60606) *(G-5100)*
Kickapoo Creek Winery 309 495-9463
6605 N Smith Rd Edwards (61528) *(G-8338)*
Kidsbooks LLC (PA) 773 509-0707
3535 W Peterson Ave Chicago (60659) *(G-5101)*
Kiefer Sports Group, Bloomington *Also called Adolph Kiefer & Associates LLC (G-2021)*
Kieffer Holding Co (PA) 877 543-3337
585 Bond St Lincolnshire (60069) *(G-12776)*
Kieft Bros Inc 630 832-8090
837 S Riverside Dr Elmhurst (60126) *(G-9388)*
Kiene Diesel Accessories Inc 630 543-7170
325 S Fairbank St Addison (60101) *(G-169)*
Kienstra Pipe & Precast LLC 618 482-3283
1072 Eagle Park Rd Madison (62060) *(G-13416)*
Kienstra-Illinois LLC 618 251-6345
201 W Ferguson Ave Wood River (62095) *(G-21265)*
Kier Mfg Co 630 953-9500
1450 W Jeffrey Dr Addison (60101) *(G-170)*
Kik Custom Products, Inc., Danville *Also called Aerosols Danville Inc (G-7318)*
Kik International Inc 905 660-0444
780 W Army Trail Rd 209 Carol Stream (60188) *(G-3010)*
Kile Machine & Tool Inc 217 446-8616
3231 Illini Rd Danville (61834) *(G-7357)*
Killeen Confectionery LLC (PA) 312 804-0009
600 20th St Wilmette (60091) *(G-21083)*
Kim Gough 309 734-3511
1201 N Main St Ste 2 Monmouth (61462) *(G-14221)*
Kimball Office Inc 800 349-9827
325 N Wells St Ste 100 Chicago (60654) *(G-5102)*

Kimberly-Clark Corporation 312 371-5166
2275 Half Day Rd Ste 350 Deerfield (60015) ***(G-7626)***
Kimberly-Clark Corporation 815 886-7872
740 Pro Logis Pkwy Romeoville (60446) ***(G-17838)***
Kimberly-Clark Corporation 847 885-1050
20 N Wacker Dr Ste 4200 Chicago (60606) ***(G-5103)***
Kimberly-Clark Corporation 708 409-8500
505 Northwest Ave Ste C Northlake (60164) ***(G-15550)***
Kimco U S A, Marshall *Also called Kimco USA Inc* ***(G-13574)***
Kimco USA Inc 800 788-1133
118 E Trefz Dr Marshall (62441) ***(G-13574)***
Kimmaterials Inc 618 466-0352
9434 Godfrey Rd Godfrey (62035) ***(G-10655)***
Kimmykakes Co 312 927-3933
2616 W 85th Pl Chicago (60652) ***(G-5104)***
Kinaxis Corp 613 592-5780
40 E Chicago Ave Chicago (60611) ***(G-5105)***
Kincaid Oil Producers Inc 618 686-3084
6166 Bible Grove Ln Louisville (62858) ***(G-13179)***
Kindlon Enterprises Inc (PA) 708 367-4000
2300 Raddant Rd Ste B Aurora (60502) ***(G-994)***
Kindred Spirits Distillery 815 910-7116
1701 Milwaukee Ave Mendota (61342) ***(G-13944)***
Kinesis Vaccines LLC 847 543-7725
1495 Colbee Benton Rd Grayslake (60030) ***(G-10786)***
Kinetic BEI LLC 847 888-8060
2197 Brookwood Dr South Elgin (60177) ***(G-19159)***
King & Sons Monuments 815 786-6321
131 E Center St Ste 1 Sandwich (60548) ***(G-18376)***
King Circuit 630 629-7300
1651 Mitchell Blvd Schaumburg (60193) ***(G-18586)***
King Metal Co 708 388-3845
4200 W 122nd St Alsip (60803) ***(G-464)***
King Midas Seafood Entps Inc 847 566-2192
309 N Lake St Ste 200 Mundelein (60060) ***(G-14707)***
King of Software Inc 847 354-8745
1232 Willow Ave Des Plaines (60016) ***(G-7793)***
King S Court Exterior 630 904-4305
2328 Skylane Dr Naperville (60564) ***(G-14976)***
King Systems Inc (PA) 309 879-2668
1130 Lakeview Rd S Dahinda (61428) ***(G-7305)***
King's Food Products, Belleville *Also called Deli Star Ventures Inc* ***(G-1544)***
Kingery Printing Company (PA) 217 347-5151
3012 S Banker St Effingham (62401) ***(G-8405)***
Kingery Steel Fabricators Inc 708 474-6665
16895 Chicago Ave Lansing (60438) ***(G-12501)***
Kingfisher Controls LLC 425 359-5601
208 Prairie Run Illiopolis (62539) ***(G-11574)***
Kingport Industries LLC 847 480-5745
1912 Shermer Rd Northbrook (60062) ***(G-15412)***
Kingsbury Enterprises Inc 708 535-7590
15007 Moorings Ln Oak Forest (60452) ***(G-15685)***
Kingspan Light & Air LLC 847 816-1060
28662 N Ballard Dr Lake Forest (60045) ***(G-12268)***
Kinney Electrical Mfg Co 847 742-9600
678 Buckeye St Elgin (60123) ***(G-8636)***
Kinoco Inc 618 378-3802
1000 County Road 300 E Norris City (62869) ***(G-15250)***
Kinser Woodworks 618 549-4540
120 Old Lower Cobden Rd Makanda (62958) ***(G-13428)***
Kinsman Enterprises Inc 618 932-3838
10804 Mark Twain Rd West Frankfort (62896) ***(G-20674)***
Kipp Manufacturing Company Inc 630 768-9051
375 Hollow Hill Rd Wauconda (60084) ***(G-20366)***
Kirby Lester LLC (HQ) 847 984-3377
13700 W Irma Lee Ct Lake Forest (60045) ***(G-12269)***
Kirby Sheet Metal Works Inc 773 247-6477
4209 S Western Blvd Chicago (60609) ***(G-5106)***
Kirk Wood Products Inc 309 829-6661
10424 E 1400 North Rd Bloomington (61705) ***(G-2068)***
Kirkland Sawmill Inc 815 522-6150
606 W Main St Kirkland (60146) ***(G-12062)***
Kirkman Composites 309 734-5606
1201 N Main St Ste 2 Monmouth (61462) ***(G-14222)***
Kirkwood Crates LLC 651 373-5945
335 W Depot St Kirkwood (61447) ***(G-12067)***
Kishknows Inc 708 252-3648
3831 Janis Dr Richton Park (60471) ***(G-17030)***
Kiss ME Comix 773 982-8334
9654 S Forest Ave Chicago (60628) ***(G-5107)***
Kit Artisan Cab Refinishers 630 922-9714
10200 S Mandel St Ste D Plainfield (60585) ***(G-16680)***
Kitagawa Usa Inc 847 310-8198
301 Commerce Dr Schaumburg (60173) ***(G-18587)***
Kitagawa-Northtech Inc 847 310-8787
301 Commerce Dr Schaumburg (60173) ***(G-18588)***
Kitamura Machinery USA Inc (HQ) 847 520-7755
78 Century Dr Wheeling (60090) ***(G-20924)***
Kitchen & Bath Cabinet Company 217 352-1900
1806 Camp Dr Champaign (61821) ***(G-3314)***
Kitchen & Bath Gallery 217 214-0310
615 Jersey St Quincy (62301) ***(G-16900)***
Kitchen Cooked, Farmington *Also called Utz Quality Foods LLC* ***(G-9664)***
Kitchen Cooked, Bushnell *Also called Utz Quality Foods LLC* ***(G-2747)***
Kitchen Design Studio, Addison *Also called Mica Furniture Mfg Inc* ***(G-203)***
Kitchen Krafters Inc 815 675-6061
7801 Industrial Dr Ste D Spring Grove (60081) ***(G-19279)***
Kitchen Supply Wholesale 224 603-1208
438 Birchwood Dr Antioch (60002) ***(G-618)***
Kitchens To Go LLC 630 364-3083
131 W Jefferson Ave # 223 Naperville (60540) ***(G-14858)***
Kitchens To Go Built By Carlin, Naperville *Also called Grs Holding LLC* ***(G-14838)***
Kitchy Koo Gourmet Co 708 499-5236
7845 Lamon Ave Oak Lawn (60459) ***(G-15723)***
Kitty Pallets, Bellwood *Also called R K J Pallets Inc* ***(G-1636)***
Kiwi Coders Corp 847 541-4511
265 Messner Dr Wheeling (60090) ***(G-20925)***
Kjellberg Printing 630 653-2244
805 W Liberty Dr Wheaton (60187) ***(G-20807)***
KK Stevens Publishing Co 309 329-2151
100 N Pearl St Astoria (61501) ***(G-893)***
Kksp Precision Machining LLC (PA) 630 260-1735
1688 Glen Ellyn Rd Glendale Heights (60139) ***(G-10464)***
Kkt Chillers Inc 847 734-1600
765 Dillon Dr Wood Dale (60191) ***(G-21204)***
Kl Watch Service Inc 847 368-8780
191 Amherst Dr Bartlett (60103) ***(G-1293)***
Klai-Co Idntification Pdts Inc 847 573-0375
13777 W Laurel Dr Lake Forest (60045) ***(G-12270)***
Klaman Hardwood 217 972-7888
4351 N Macarthur Rd Decatur (62526) ***(G-7514)***
Klapperich Tool Inc 847 608-8471
857 Schneider Dr South Elgin (60177) ***(G-19160)***
Klean-Ko Inc 630 620-1860
952 N Du Page Ave Lombard (60148) ***(G-13092)***
Kleen Cut Tool Inc 630 447-7020
30w250 Bttrfeld Rd Unit 3 Warrenville (60555) ***(G-20240)***
Kleer Pak Mfg Co Inc 630 543-0208
320 S La Londe Ave Addison (60101) ***(G-171)***
Klehm Family Winery LLC 847 609-9997
44w637 Il Route 72 Hampshire (60140) ***(G-10975)***
Klein Plastics Company LLC 616 863-9900
450 Bond St Lincolnshire (60069) ***(G-12777)***
Klein Printing Inc 773 235-2121
3035 W Fullerton Ave Chicago (60647) ***(G-5108)***
Klein Tools Inc (PA) 847 821-5500
450 Bond St Lincolnshire (60069) ***(G-12778)***
Klein Tools Inc 847 249-4930
2920 W Aviation Dr Waukegan (60087) ***(G-20455)***
Klein Tools Inc 847 228-6999
2300 E Devon Ave Elk Grove Village (60007) ***(G-9078)***
Klein Tools Inc 847 821-5500
450 Bond St Lincolnshire (60069) ***(G-12779)***
Kleinhoffer Manufacturing Inc 815 725-3638
1852 Terry Dr Joliet (60436) ***(G-11890)***
Klh Printing Corp 847 459-0115
664 Wheeling Rd Wheeling (60090) ***(G-20926)***
Klimp Industries Inc 630 682-0752
175 Tubeway Dr Carol Stream (60188) ***(G-3011)***
Klimp Industries Inc 630 790-0600
175 Tubeway Dr Carol Stream (60188) ***(G-3012)***
Klinck Inc 815 397-3306
1827 Broadway Rockford (61104) ***(G-17484)***
Kliux Energies Intl Inc 312 985-7717
300 N La Salle Dr # 4925 Chicago (60654) ***(G-5109)***
Klm Commercial Sweeping Inc 618 978-9276
320 Saint Sabre Dr Belleville (62226) ***(G-1563)***
KLM Tool Company 630 458-1700
930 S Stiles Dr Addison (60101) ***(G-172)***
Km Cabinet Supply 312 927-8860
3841 W 95th St Evergreen Park (60805) ***(G-9596)***
Km Enterprises Inc 618 204-0888
320 S 11th St Ste 2 Mount Vernon (62864) ***(G-14620)***
Km Press Incorporated 618 277-1222
120 Iowa Ave Belleville (62220) ***(G-1564)***
Km4 Manufacturing 708 924-5150
7420 S Meade Ave Bedford Park (60638) ***(G-1476)***
Kmf Enterprises Inc 630 858-2210
20 Danada Sq W Wheaton (60189) ***(G-20808)***
Kmk Metal Fabricators Inc 618 224-2000
408 E Broadway Trenton (62293) ***(G-19903)***
Kmp Products LLC 630 956-0438
1060 Zygmunt Cir Westmont (60559) ***(G-20754)***
Kmp Tool Grinding Inc 847 205-9640
1808 Janke Dr Ste J Northbrook (60062) ***(G-15413)***
Kms Industries LLC 331 225-2671
923 W National Ave Addison (60101) ***(G-173)***
Knaack LLC 815 459-6020
420 E Terra Cotta Ave Crystal Lake (60014) ***(G-7217)***
Knaack Manufacturing, Crystal Lake *Also called Knaack LLC* ***(G-7217)***

ALPHABETIC

(PA)=Parent Co (HQ)=Headquarters (DH)=Div Headquarters
2020 Harris Illinois Industrial Directory
1169

Knack, Crystal Lake *Also called Werner Co* ***(G-7294)***
Knapheide Manufacturing Co....217 222-7134
436 S 6th St Quincy (62301) ***(G-16901)***
Knapheide Manufacturing Co....217 223-1848
1848 Westphalia Strasse Quincy (62305) ***(G-16902)***
Knapheide Mfg Co....217 223-1848
3109 N 30th St Quincy (62305) ***(G-16903)***
Knapp Industrial Wood....815 657-8854
820 N Center St Forrest (61741) ***(G-9734)***
Knauer Industries Ltd....815 725-0246
19505 Ne Frontage Rd Joliet (60404) ***(G-11891)***
Kniffen Brothers Sawmill....618 629-2437
16794 Buxton Rd Whittington (62897) ***(G-21020)***
Knight Bros Inc....618 439-9626
10764 Industrial Park Rd Benton (62812) ***(G-1930)***
Knight Hawk Coal LLC (PA)....618 426-3662
500 Cutler Trico Rd Percy (62272) ***(G-16559)***
Knight Hawk Coal LLC....618 497-2768
7290 County Line Rd Cutler (62238) ***(G-7304)***
Knight Packaging Group, Bridgeview *Also called Knight Paper Box Company* ***(G-2360)***
Knight Paper Box Company (PA)....773 585-2035
8811 S 77th Ave Bridgeview (60455) ***(G-2360)***
Knight Plastics LLC....815 334-1240
1008 Courtaulds Dr Woodstock (60098) ***(G-21400)***
Knight Printing and Litho Svcs, Island Lake *Also called Knight Prtg & Litho Svc Ltd* ***(G-11609)***
Knight Prtg & Litho Svc Ltd....847 487-7700
706 E Burnett Rd Island Lake (60042) ***(G-11609)***
Knight Tool Works Inc....847 678-1237
1200 Abbott Dr Ste C Elgin (60123) ***(G-8637)***
Knighthouse Media Inc....312 676-1100
150 N Michigan Ave # 900 Chicago (60601) ***(G-5110)***
Knighthouse Publishing, Chicago *Also called Knighthouse Media Inc* ***(G-5110)***
Knights of Immaculata, Libertyville *Also called Marytown* ***(G-12673)***
Knock On Metal Inc (PA)....312 372-4569
221 N La Salle St # 3315 Chicago (60601) ***(G-5111)***
Knockout LLC Evanston....224 714-3007
1029 Davis St Evanston (60201) ***(G-9544)***
Knoll Inc....312 454-6920
811 W Fulton Market Chicago (60607) ***(G-5112)***
Knoll Steel Inc....815 675-9400
2851 N Us Highway 12 Spring Grove (60081) ***(G-19280)***
Knoll Textiles, Chicago *Also called Knoll Inc* ***(G-5112)***
Knotty By Nature....618 610-2481
15 E Main St Grafton (62037) ***(G-10685)***
Knowledgeshift Inc....630 221-8759
26w245 Grand Ave Ste 200 Wheaton (60187) ***(G-20809)***
Knowles Corporation (PA)....630 250-5100
1151 Maplewood Dr Itasca (60143) ***(G-11685)***
Knowles Corporation....630 250-5100
1151 Maplewood Dr Itasca (60143) ***(G-11686)***
Knowles Elec Holdings Inc....630 250-5100
1151 Maplewood Dr Itasca (60143) ***(G-11687)***
Knowles Electronics LLC (HQ)....630 250-5100
1151 Maplewood Dr Itasca (60143) ***(G-11688)***
Kns Companies Inc....630 665-9010
475 Randy Rd Carol Stream (60188) ***(G-3013)***
Ko-Polymer Inc....847 742-7700
1380 Gateway Dr Ste 7 Elgin (60124) ***(G-8638)***
Koala Cabinets....630 818-1289
333 Charles Ct West Chicago (60185) ***(G-20606)***
Kobac....847 520-6000
1007 Commerce Ct Buffalo Grove (60089) ***(G-2553)***
Kobawala Poly-Pack Inc (PA)....312 664-3810
800 W 5th Ave Ste 212 Naperville (60563) ***(G-14859)***
Kobelco Advnced Cting Amer Inc....847 520-6000
1007 Commerce Ct Buffalo Grove (60089) ***(G-2554)***
Koch Meat Co Inc....847 384-5940
4404 W Berteau Ave Chicago (60641) ***(G-5113)***
Koch Poultry....847 455-0902
2155 25th Ave Franklin Park (60131) ***(G-9977)***
Kocisis Brothers Machine, Alsip *Also called Kocsis Technologies Inc* ***(G-467)***
Kocour Co....773 847-1111
4800 S Saint Louis Ave Chicago (60632) ***(G-5114)***
Kocsis Brothers Machine Co (PA)....708 597-8110
11755 S Austin Ave Alsip (60803) ***(G-465)***
Kocsis Technologies Inc (PA)....708 597-4177
11755 S Austin Ave Alsip (60803) ***(G-466)***
Kocsis Technologies Inc....708 597-4177
11755 S Austin Ave Alsip (60803) ***(G-467)***
Koderhandt Inc....618 233-4808
1651 N Charles St Belleville (62221) ***(G-1565)***
Kodiak LLC....248 545-7520
4320 S Knox Ave Chicago (60632) ***(G-5115)***
Kodiak LLC....773 284-9975
4320 S Knox Ave Chicago (60632) ***(G-5116)***
Koebers Prosthetic Orthpd Lab (PA)....309 676-2276
3834 W Irving Park Rd # 1 Chicago (60618) ***(G-5117)***
Koehler Bindery Inc....773 539-7979
4315 Main St Skokie (60076) ***(G-18973)***
Koehler Enterprises Inc....847 451-4966
2960 Hart Ct Franklin Park (60131) ***(G-9978)***
Koenemann Sausage Co....815 385-6260
27090 Volo Village Rd Volo (60073) ***(G-20201)***
Koenig Body & Equipment Inc....309 673-7435
2428 W Farmington Rd West Peoria (61604) ***(G-20687)***
Koenig Machine & Welding Inc....217 228-6538
2707 N 24th St Quincy (62305) ***(G-16904)***
Koerner Aviation Inc....815 932-4222
1520 S State Route 115 Kankakee (60901) ***(G-11988)***
Koflo Corporation....847 516-3700
309 Cary Point Dr Ste A Cary (60013) ***(G-3174)***
Kogan Self Defense....847 877-4711
1549 Barclay Blvd Buffalo Grove (60089) ***(G-2555)***
Kohler Co....920 457-4441
91283 Collections Ctr Dr Chicago (60693) ***(G-5118)***
Kohler Co....847 734-1777
11449 Morning Glory Ln Huntley (60142) ***(G-11548)***
Kohler Co....630 323-7674
775 Village Center Dr Burr Ridge (60527) ***(G-2693)***
Kohler Co....847 635-8071
1180 Milwaukee Ave Glenview (60025) ***(G-10578)***
Kohler K&B Store, Glenview *Also called Kohler Co* ***(G-10578)***
Kohlert Manufacturing Corp....630 584-0013
2851 Dukane Dr Saint Charles (60174) ***(G-18221)***
Kohnens Concrete Products Inc....618 277-2120
503 Green St Germantown (62245) ***(G-10330)***
Kohns Electric....309 463-2331
1555 Key Ct S Varna (61375) ***(G-20032)***
Kohout Woodwork Inc....630 628-6257
759 W Factory Rd Addison (60101) ***(G-174)***
Koi Computers Inc....630 627-8811
1341 Warren Ave Ste B Downers Grove (60515) ***(G-8040)***
Kokes Kid Zone....217 483-4615
1033 Jason Pl Chatham (62629) ***(G-3423)***
Kokoku Rubber Inc (HQ)....847 517-6770
1375 E Wdfield Rd Ste 560 Schaumburg (60173) ***(G-18589)***
Kolb-Lena Inc....815 369-4577
3990 N Sunnyside Rd Lena (61048) ***(G-12600)***
Kolb-Lena Bresse Bleu, Inc., Lena *Also called Kolb-Lena Inc* ***(G-12600)***
Kolbi Pipe Marker Co, Arlington Heights *Also called R L Kolbi Company* ***(G-795)***
Kolcraft Enterprises Inc (PA)....312 361-6315
1100 W Monroe St Ste 1 Chicago (60607) ***(G-5119)***
Kold-Ban International Ltd....847 658-8561
8390 Pingree Rd Lake In The Hills (60156) ***(G-12338)***
Koll Ltd (PA)....224 544-5418
112 Terrace Dr Mundelein (60060) ***(G-14708)***
Kollmorgen Corp....815 568-8001
1300 N State St Marengo (60152) ***(G-13488)***
Kolorcure Corporation....630 879-9050
1180 Lyon Rd Batavia (60510) ***(G-1389)***
Komar Screw Corp (PA)....847 965-9090
7790 N Merrimac Ave Niles (60714) ***(G-15139)***
Komatsu America Corp (HQ)....847 437-5800
8770 W Bryn Mawr Ave Chicago (60631) ***(G-5120)***
Komatsu Forklift USA LLC (HQ)....847 437-5800
1701 Golf Rd Ste 1 Rolling Meadows (60008) ***(G-17744)***
Komax Corporation (HQ)....888 465-6629
1100 E Corp Grove Dr Buffalo Grove (60089) ***(G-2556)***
Komet, Schaumburg *Also called Martin Tool Works Inc* ***(G-18619)***
Komet of America Holding, Inc., Schaumburg *Also called Ceratizit Chicago Holding Inc* ***(G-18469)***
Komet of America, Inc., Schaumburg *Also called Ceratizit Chicago Inc* ***(G-18470)***
Komodo Brands LLC....312 788-2730
150 S Wacker Dr Ste 2400 Chicago (60606) ***(G-5121)***
Komori America Corporation (HQ)....847 806-9000
5520 Meadowbrook Indus Ct Rolling Meadows (60008) ***(G-17745)***
Kon Printing Inc....630 879-2211
316 E Wilson St Batavia (60510) ***(G-1390)***
Kone Elevator (HQ)....309 764-6771
1 Kone Ct Moline (61265) ***(G-14154)***
Kone Escalator Div, Coal Valley *Also called Kone Inc* ***(G-6937)***
Kone Inc (HQ)....630 577-1650
4225 Naperville Rd # 400 Lisle (60532) ***(G-12906)***
Kone Inc....309 945-4961
2266 Us Highway 6 Coal Valley (61240) ***(G-6937)***
Kongskilde Industries Inc....309 452-3300
1802 Industrial Park Dr A Normal (61761) ***(G-15207)***
Konica Minolta....630 893-8238
1000 Stevenson Ct Ste 109 Roselle (60172) ***(G-17962)***
Konica Minolta Healthcare....815 893-0691
829 Virginia Rd Ste A Crystal Lake (60014) ***(G-7218)***
Konica Mnlta Bus Sltons USA In....309 671-1360
401 Sw Water St Peoria (61602) ***(G-16467)***
Konnectronix Inc....847 672-8685
2340 Ernie Krueger Cir Waukegan (60087) ***(G-20456)***

Konveau Inc 312 476-9385
805 E Drexel Sq Chicago (60615) *(G-5122)*
Konzen Chemicals Inc 708 878-7636
4248 Oakwood Ln Matteson (60443) *(G-13626)*
Kool Technologies Inc 630 483-2256
714 Bonded Pkwy Ste A Streamwood (60107) *(G-19581)*
Koombea Inc 408 786-5290
3409 N Paulina St Chicago (60657) *(G-5123)*
Kop Industries Corporated Inc 630 930-9516
22w440 Armitage Ave Glen Ellyn (60137) *(G-10407)*
Kop-Coat Inc 847 272-2278
1608 Barclay Blvd Buffalo Grove (60089) *(G-2557)*
Kopis Machine Co Inc 630 543-4138
329 W Interstate Rd Addison (60101) *(G-175)*
Kopp Welding Inc 847 593-2070
991 Oakton St Elk Grove Village (60007) *(G-9079)*
Koppers Industries Inc 309 343-5157
Rr 41 Box S Galesburg (61402) *(G-10206)*
Koppers Industries Inc 708 656-5900
3900 S Laramie Ave Cicero (60804) *(G-6859)*
Korea Times 847 626-0388
615 Milwaukee Ave Ste 12 Glenview (60025) *(G-10579)*
Korea Times Chicago Inc 847 626-0388
615 Milwaukee Ave Ste 12 Glenview (60025) *(G-10580)*
Korea Tribune Inc 847 956-9101
1699 Wall St Ste 200k Mount Prospect (60056) *(G-14543)*
Korean Media Group LLC 847 391-4112
3520 Milwaukee Ave Fl 2 Northbrook (60062) *(G-15414)*
Korex Chicago LLC 708 458-4890
6200 W 51st St Ste 7 Chicago (60638) *(G-5124)*
Korhumel Inc 847 330-0335
230 Parktrail Ct Schaumburg (60173) *(G-18590)*
Korinek & Co Inc 708 652-2870
4828 W 25th St Cicero (60804) *(G-6860)*
Kormex Metal Craft Inc 630 953-8856
961 Dupage Ave Lombard (60148) *(G-13093)*
Kornick Enterprises LLC 847 884-1162
711 E Golf Rd Schaumburg (60173) *(G-18591)*
Korte Meat Processing, Highland *Also called Korte Meat Processors Inc (G-11230)*
Korte Meat Processors Inc 618 654-3813
810 Deal St Highland (62249) *(G-11230)*
Kory Farm Equipment Division, Schaumburg *Also called Korhumel Inc (G-18590)*
Kosmos Tool Inc 815 675-2200
2727 N Us Highway 12 Spring Grove (60081) *(G-19281)*
Koson Tool Inc 815 277-2107
9235 Corsair Rd Ste B Frankfort (60423) *(G-9813)*
Kostelac Grease Service Inc 314 436-7166
8105 Pecan Tree Ln Belleville (62223) *(G-1566)*
Kosto Food Products Company 847 487-2600
1325 N Old Rand Rd Wauconda (60084) *(G-20367)*
Koswell Pattern Works Inc 708 757-5225
3149 Glenwood Dyer Rd H Lynwood (60411) *(G-13294)*
Kothe Distilling Tech Inc 312 878-7766
5121 N Ravenswood Ave Chicago (60640) *(G-5125)*
Kotter Ready Mix, Metropolis *Also called Metropolis Ready Mix Inc (G-13974)*
Koval Distillery, Chicago *Also called Koval Inc (G-5127)*
Koval Inc 312 878-7988
5121 N Ravenswood Ave Grw Chicago (60640) *(G-5126)*
Koval Inc (PA) 773 944-0089
4241 N Ravenswood Ave # 2 Chicago (60613) *(G-5127)*
Kowal Custom Cabinet & Furn 708 597-3367
2900 Wireton Rd Blue Island (60406) *(G-2129)*
Kowalik Brothers, Chicago *Also called United States Audio Corp (G-6476)*
Kowalski Memorials Inc 630 462-7226
195 Kehoe Blvd Ste 1 Carol Stream (60188) *(G-3014)*
Koza 773 646-0958
13548 S Burley Ave Chicago (60633) *(G-5128)*
Kozaczka Inc 224 435-6180
3350 N Carriageway Dr Arlington Heights (60004) *(G-766)*
Kpi Machining Inc 815 496-2246
225 W Plum St Sheridan (60551) *(G-18890)*
Kps Capital Partners LP 630 972-7000
455 Gibraltar Dr Bolingbrook (60440) *(G-2203)*
Kps Capital Partners LP 847 288-3300
10601 Belmont Ave Franklin Park (60131) *(G-9979)*
Kr Machine 815 248-2250
15322 Eicks Rd Durand (61024) *(G-8153)*
Kr Strikeforce Bowling, Melrose Park *Also called Strikeforce Bowling LLC (G-13917)*
Kraft Foods, Glenview *Also called Kraft Heinz Foods Company (G-10582)*
Kraft Foods, Granite City *Also called Kraft Heinz Foods Company (G-10718)*
Kraft Foods, Northfield *Also called Kraft Heinz Foods Company (G-15521)*
Kraft Foods, Champaign *Also called Kraft Heinz Foods Company (G-3315)*
Kraft Foods, Naperville *Also called Mondelez Global LLC (G-14874)*
Kraft Foods Asia PCF Svcs LLC (HQ) 847 943-4000
3 Parkway North Blvd # 300 Deerfield (60015) *(G-7627)*
Kraft Heinz Company 847 646-2000
200 E Randolph St # 7300 Chicago (60601) *(G-5129)*
Kraft Heinz Foods Company 847 291-3900
2301 Shermer Rd Northbrook (60062) *(G-15415)*
Kraft Heinz Foods Company 815 338-7000
1300 Claussen Dr Woodstock (60098) *(G-21401)*
Kraft Heinz Foods Company 847 646-3690
801 Waukegan Rd Glenview (60025) *(G-10581)*
Kraft Heinz Foods Company 630 907-2590
1700 N Edgelawn Dr Aurora (60506) *(G-1121)*
Kraft Heinz Foods Company 412 456-5700
Aon Center 200 E St Aon Cent Chicago (60601) *(G-5130)*
Kraft Heinz Foods Company 630 505-0170
3030 Warrenville Rd # 200 Lisle (60532) *(G-12907)*
Kraft Heinz Foods Company 847 646-2000
801 Waukegan Rd Glenview (60025) *(G-10582)*
Kraft Heinz Foods Company 618 451-4820
2901 Missouri Ave Granite City (62040) *(G-10718)*
Kraft Heinz Foods Company 847 646-2000
3 Lakes Dr 2b Northfield (60093) *(G-15521)*
Kraft Heinz Foods Company 217 378-1900
1701 W Bradley Ave Champaign (61821) *(G-3315)*
Kraft Heinz Receivables LLC 847 646-2000
200 E Randolph St # 7600 Chicago (60601) *(G-5131)*
Kraft Pizza Company, Inc, Glenview *Also called Nestle Pizza Company Inc (G-10593)*
Krafty Kabinets 815 369-5250
106 W Provost St Lena (61048) *(G-12601)*
Kraly Tire Repair Materials 708 863-5981
5936 W 35th St Cicero (60804) *(G-6861)*
Kram Digital Solutions Inc (PA) 312 222-0431
1717 Chestnut Ave Glenview (60025) *(G-10583)*
Kramer Window Co 708 343-4780
1219 Orchard Ave Maywood (60153) *(G-13671)*
Kranos Corporation (PA) 217 324-3978
710 Industrial Dr Litchfield (62056) *(G-12969)*
Kraus & Naimer Inc 847 298-2450
200 Howard Ave Ste 270 Des Plaines (60018) *(G-7794)*
Krebs Custom Guns, Wauconda *Also called Krebs Custom Inc (G-20368)*
Krebs Custom Inc 847 487-7776
1000 N Rand Rd Ste 106 Wauconda (60084) *(G-20368)*
Kreg Medical Inc 312 829-8904
1940 Janice Ave Melrose Park (60160) *(G-13889)*
Kreider Services Incorporated (PA) 815 288-6691
500 Anchor Rd Dixon (61021) *(G-7903)*
Kreis Tool & Mfg Co Inc 847 289-3700
1615 Cambridge Dr Elgin (60123) *(G-8639)*
Kreischer Optics Ltd 815 344-4220
1729 Oak Dr McHenry (60050) *(G-13754)*
Krel Laboratories Inc 773 826-4487
388 N Avers Ave Chicago (60624) *(G-5132)*
Kremer Precision Machine Inc 217 868-2627
10748 E 1850th Ave Shumway (62461) *(G-18903)*
Kress Corporation (PA) 309 446-3395
227 W Illinois St Brimfield (61517) *(G-2406)*
Kresser Precision Inds Inc 815 899-2202
700 Golden Prairie Dr Davis Junction (61020) *(G-7425)*
Krick Enterprises Inc 630 515-1085
1548 Ogden Ave Downers Grove (60515) *(G-8041)*
Kriese Mfg 815 748-2683
231 N Juniper St Cortland (60112) *(G-7023)*
Kris Dee and Associates Inc 630 503-4093
755 Schneider Dr South Elgin (60177) *(G-19161)*
Krisdee, South Elgin *Also called Kris Dee and Associates Inc (G-19161)*
Kristel Displays, Saint Charles *Also called Kristel Limited Partnership (G-18222)*
Kristel Limited Partnership 630 443-1290
555 Kirk Rd Unit C Saint Charles (60174) *(G-18222)*
Kristine Van Stockum's Hand PA, Deerfield *Also called Van Stockum Kristine (G-7656)*
Kroger Co 815 332-7267
2206 Barnes Blvd Rockford (61112) *(G-17485)*
Kroger Co 309 694-6298
201 S Main St East Peoria (61611) *(G-8275)*
Kroh-Wagner Inc 773 252-2031
2331 N Pulaski Rd Chicago (60639) *(G-5133)*
Kronos Foods Corp (PA) 224 353-5400
1 Kronos Glendale Heights (60139) *(G-10465)*
Kronos Incorporated 847 969-6501
475 N Martingale Rd # 900 Schaumburg (60173) *(G-18592)*
Kropp Forge, Chicago *Also called Park-Hio Frged McHned Pdts LLC (G-5765)*
Krueger and Company 630 833-5650
900 N Industrial Dr Elmhurst (60126) *(G-9389)*
Krueger International Inc 312 467-6850
1181 Merchandise Mart Chicago (60654) *(G-5134)*
Krueger Steel & Wire, Elmhurst *Also called Krueger and Company (G-9389)*
Krug-Northwest Electric Motors, Grayslake *Also called Heise Industries Inc (G-10781)*
Kruger North America Inc 708 851-3670
1010 Lake St Ste 106 Oak Park (60301) *(G-15761)*
Krum Kreations 815 772-8296
22585 Carroll Rd Morrison (61270) *(G-14344)*
Kryder Wood Products LLC 815 494-1208
5150 8th St Rockford (61109) *(G-17486)*
Krygier Design Inc 620 766-1001
635 Wheat Ln Wood Dale (60191) *(G-21205)*

ALPHABETIC

Krygier Machine Company Inc 708 331-5255
15938 Suntone Dr South Holland (60473) *(G-19228)*
Ksem Inc 618 656-5388
6471 Miller Dr Edwardsville (62025) *(G-8367)*
Ksi Conveyor Inc 815 457-2403
454 N State Route 49 Cissna Park (60924) *(G-6897)*
Ksm Electronics Inc 630 393-9310
27745 Diehl Rd Warrenville (60555) *(G-20241)*
Ksm Electronics Midwest, Warrenville *Also called Ksm Electronics Inc (G-20241)*
Kso Metalfab Inc 630 372-1200
250 Roma Jean Pkwy Streamwood (60107) *(G-19582)*
Ksr Software LLC 847 705-0100
388 N Chalary Ct Palatine (60067) *(G-16135)*
Kta Trucking Services Inc 224 788-8312
346 North Ave Antioch (60002) *(G-619)*
Ktm Industries Inc 217 224-5861
2701 Weiss Ln Quincy (62305) *(G-16905)*
Ktm Lab Service Co Inc 708 351-6780
716 Morse Ave Schaumburg (60193) *(G-18593)*
Kubota Authorized Dealer, Metropolis *Also called Michaels Equipment Co (G-13975)*
Kuchar Combine Performance 217 854-9838
18995 Route 4 Carlinville (62626) *(G-2878)*
Kuchar High Perfomance Parts, Carlinville *Also called Kuchar Combine Performance (G-2878)*
Kuchar Products Inc 815 405-3692
12559 Old Plank Dr New Lenox (60451) *(G-15038)*
Kuche Fine Cabinetry 217 342-2244
814 E Fayette Ave Effingham (62401) *(G-8406)*
Kuhl's Trailer Sales, Ingraham *Also called Arthur Leo Kuhl (G-11591)*
Kuhn Special Steel N Amer Inc 262 788-9358
55 W Monroe St Ste 2900 Chicago (60603) *(G-5135)*
Kuldisak LLC 847 772-7412
3342 Commercial Ave Northbrook (60062) *(G-15416)*
Kult of Athena, Elgin *Also called Proton Multimedia Inc (G-8701)*
Kuna Corp 815 675-0140
1512 Spring Ct Spring Grove (60081) *(G-19282)*
Kuna Food Service, Dupo *Also called Kuna Meat Company Inc (G-8139)*
Kuna Meat Company Inc 618 286-4000
704 Kuna Industrial Ct Dupo (62239) *(G-8139)*
Kunde Woodwork Inc 847 669-2030
11901 Smith Dr Huntley (60142) *(G-11549)*
Kuntry Kettle 618 426-1600
178 Gordon Rd Ava (62907) *(G-1173)*
Kunverji Enterprise Corp 847 683-2954
395 S Main St Burlington (60109) *(G-2641)*
Kunz Carpentry (PA) 618 224-7892
16 E Broadway Trenton (62293) *(G-19904)*
Kunz Engineering Inc 815 539-6954
2100 Welland Rd Mendota (61342) *(G-13945)*
Kunz Glove Co Inc 312 733-8780
1532 W Fulton St Chicago (60607) *(G-5136)*
Kunz Industries Inc 708 596-7717
15800 Suntone Dr South Holland (60473) *(G-19229)*
Kure Steel Inc 815 836-8027
422 N State St Lockport (60441) *(G-13004)*
Kuriyama of America Inc (HQ) 847 755-0360
360 E State Pkwy Schaumburg (60173) *(G-18594)*
Kurland Steel Company, Urbana *Also called Central Ill Fbrcation Whse Inc (G-19976)*
Kurts Carstar Collision Ctr 618 345-4519
1 Mueller Dr Maryville (62062) *(G-13591)*
Kurtzon Lighting, Chicago *Also called Morris Kurtzon Incorporated (G-5500)*
Kurz Transfer Products LP 847 228-0001
220 Martin Ln Elk Grove Village (60007) *(G-9080)*
Kusmierek Industries Inc 708 258-3100
6434 W North Peotone Rd Peotone (60468) *(G-16554)*
Kut-Rite Tool Co., Streamwood *Also called Retondo Enterprises Inc (G-19593)*
Kuusakoski Philadelphia LLC 215 533-8323
13543 S Route 30 Plainfield (60544) *(G-16681)*
Kvd Enterprises LLC 618 726-5114
1392 Frontage Rd Ste 10 O Fallon (62269) *(G-15577)*
Kvd Sewer, O Fallon *Also called Kvd Enterprises LLC (G-15577)*
Kvf-Quad Corporation 563 529-1916
808 13th St East Moline (61244) *(G-8231)*
Kvh Industries Inc 708 444-2800
8412 185th St Tinley Park (60487) *(G-19843)*
Kw Container, Chicago *Also called Kw Plastics (G-5138)*
Kw Fabrication 773 523-2420
4724 S Christiana Ave Chicago (60632) *(G-5137)*
Kw Fabrication Inc 773 294-8584
270 Maplewood Rd Riverside (60546) *(G-17086)*
Kw Plastics 708 757-5140
270 S State St Chicago (60604) *(G-5138)*
Kw Precast LLC (PA) 708 562-7700
2255 Entp Dr Ste 1510 Westchester (60154) *(G-20702)*
Kwalyti Tling McHy Rblding Inc 630 761-8040
1690 E Fabyan Pkwy Batavia (60510) *(G-1391)*
Kwik Kopy Printing, Alsip *Also called Grasso Graphics Inc (G-449)*
Kwik Kopy Printing, Rantoul *Also called Crown Publications Inc (G-16973)*
Kwik Kopy Printing, Saint Charles *Also called West Vly Graphics & Print Inc (G-18298)*
Kwik Kopy Printing, Peoria *Also called Ro-Web Inc (G-16512)*
Kwik Kopy Printing, Chicago *Also called Wolfam Holdings Corporation (G-6662)*
Kwik Mark Inc 815 363-8268
4071 W Albany St McHenry (60050) *(G-13755)*
Kwik Print Inc 630 773-3225
206 W Irving Park Rd Itasca (60143) *(G-11689)*
Kwik-Wall Company, Springfield *Also called Capitol Wood Works LLC (G-19341)*
Kwikee, Peoria *Also called Syndigo LLC (G-16532)*
Kwikset Corporation 630 577-0500
4225 Naperville Rd # 340 Lisle (60532) *(G-12908)*
Kwm Gutterman Inc 815 725-9205
795 S Larkin Ave Rockdale (60436) *(G-17263)*
Kwok's Food Service, Chicago *Also called Charles Autin Limited (G-4072)*
Kws Cereals Usa LLC 815 200-2666
4101 Colleen Dr Champaign (61822) *(G-3316)*
Kylon Midwest 773 699-3640
238 E 108th St Apt 2w Chicago (60628) *(G-5139)*
Kyosei International Corp 847 821-0341
1000 Asbury Dr Ste 5 Buffalo Grove (60089) *(G-2558)*
Kyowa Industrial Co Ltd USA 847 459-3500
711 Glenn Ave Wheeling (60090) *(G-20927)*
Kz Manufacturing Co 708 937-8097
8312 Joliet Rd Unit 6 Mc Cook (60525) *(G-13694)*
L & C Imaging Inc 309 829-1802
908 White Oak Rd Bloomington (61701) *(G-2069)*
L & D Group Inc 630 892-8941
420 N Main St Montgomery (60538) *(G-14252)*
L & H Company Inc (PA) 630 571-7200
1220 Kensington Rd 210 Oak Brook (60523) *(G-15630)*
L & J Engineering Inc (HQ) 708 236-6000
5911 Butterfield Rd Hillside (60162) *(G-11344)*
L & J Holding Company Ltd (PA) 708 236-6000
5911 Butterfield Rd Hillside (60162) *(G-11345)*
L & J Industrial Staples Inc 815 864-3337
15 W Market St Shannon (61078) *(G-18870)*
L & J Producers Inc 217 932-5639
3795 E 700th Rd Casey (62420) *(G-3204)*
L & J Technologies, Hillside *Also called L & J Engineering Inc (G-11344)*
L & J Technologies, Hillside *Also called L & J Holding Company Ltd (G-11345)*
L & L Flooring Inc 773 935-9314
3071 N Lincoln Ave Chicago (60657) *(G-5140)*
L & M Hardware Ltd 630 493-1026
145 Tower Dr Ste 5 Burr Ridge (60527) *(G-2694)*
L & M Screw Machine Products 630 801-0455
321 Webster St Montgomery (60538) *(G-14253)*
L & M Tool & Die Co Inc 847 364-9760
1570 Louis Ave Elk Grove Village (60007) *(G-9081)*
L & N Structures Inc (PA) 815 426-2164
104 S Park Rd Herscher (60941) *(G-11184)*
L & P Guarding LLC 708 325-0400
5858 W 73rd St Bedford Park (60638) *(G-1477)*
L & S Label Printing Inc 815 964-6753
4337 S Perryville Rd # 102 Cherry Valley (61016) *(G-3443)*
L & T Services Inc 815 397-6260
1004 Samuelson Rd Rockford (61109) *(G-17487)*
L & W Bedding Inc 309 762-6019
1211 16th Ave Moline (61265) *(G-14155)*
L & W Fuels 815 848-8360
5484 N 2100 East Rd Fairbury (61739) *(G-9611)*
L & W Tool & Screw Mch Pdts 847 238-1212
1447 Ardmore Ave Itasca (60143) *(G-11690)*
L A Bedding Corp 773 715-9641
3421 W 48th Pl Chicago (60632) *(G-5141)*
L A D Specialties 708 430-1588
9010 Beloit Ave Ste F Oak Lawn (60455) *(G-15724)*
L A M Inc De 630 860-9700
620 Wheat Ln Ste B Wood Dale (60191) *(G-21206)*
L A Motors Incorporated 773 736-7305
4034 N Tripp Ave Chicago (60641) *(G-5142)*
L A T Enterprise Inc 630 543-5533
423 W Interstate Rd Addison (60101) *(G-176)*
L C Inn Partners (PA) 309 743-0800
1510 47th Ave Moline (61265) *(G-14156)*
L C Mold Inc 847 593-5004
3640 Edison Pl Rolling Meadows (60008) *(G-17746)*
L C Neelydrilling Inc 618 544-2726
702 N Jackson St Robinson (62454) *(G-17118)*
L D Redmer Screw Pdts Inc (PA) 630 787-0504
515 Thomas Dr Bensenville (60106) *(G-1838)*
L I K Inc 630 213-1282
304 Roma Jean Pkwy Streamwood (60107) *(G-19583)*
L J Iron Works, Morton Grove *Also called Lichtnwald - Johnston Ir Works (G-14419)*
L K Beutel Machining Co Inc 847 895-5310
536 Morse Ave Schaumburg (60193) *(G-18595)*
L L Bean Inc 847 568-3600
4999 Old Orchard Ctr F18 Skokie (60077) *(G-18974)*
L Land Hardwoods 708 496-9000
6247 W 74th St Bedford Park (60638) *(G-1478)*

L M C Inc...815 758-3514
1142 Glidden Ave Dekalb (60115) ***(G-7687)***
L M C Automotive Inc...618 235-5242
1200 W Main St Belleville (62220) ***(G-1567)***
L M J Tooling & Manufacturing, Woodstock *Also called Serien Manufacturing Inc* ***(G-21431)***
L M Sheet Metal Inc...815 654-1837
6727 Elm Ave Loves Park (61111) ***(G-13230)***
L P M Inc...847 866-9777
1553 Sherman Ave Evanston (60201) ***(G-9545)***
L P S Express Inc...217 636-7683
1620 S 5th St Ste A Springfield (62703) ***(G-19396)***
L P T, Lake Zurich *Also called Loch Precision Technologies* ***(G-12429)***
L R Gregory and Son Inc...847 247-0216
1233 Rockland Rd Lake Bluff (60044) ***(G-12191)***
L S Diesel Repair Inc...217 283-5537
220 N 10th Ave Hoopeston (60942) ***(G-11510)***
L S Starrett Co...847 816-9999
50 Lakeview Pkwy Ste 107 Vernon Hills (60061) ***(G-20070)***
L Street Collaborative LLC (PA)...630 243-5783
20 N Upper Wacker Chicago (60606) ***(G-5143)***
L Surges Custom Woodwork...815 774-9663
225 Maple St Joliet (60432) ***(G-11892)***
L T L Co...815 874-0913
4801 American Rd Rockford (61109) ***(G-17488)***
L T P LLC...815 723-9400
490 Mills Rd Joliet (60433) ***(G-11893)***
L W Schneider Inc...815 875-3835
1180 N 6th St Princeton (61356) ***(G-16812)***
L&P Plastics...618 594-3692
2510 Franklin St Carlyle (62231) ***(G-2892)***
L-Data Corporation...312 552-7855
203 N La Salle St # 2169 Chicago (60601) ***(G-5144)***
L-R Systems, Schaumburg *Also called Tsm North America Inc* ***(G-18760)***
L-V Industries Inc...630 595-9251
508 Meyer Rd Bensenville (60106) ***(G-1839)***
L.A.B. Equipment, Itasca *Also called Spectral Dynamics Inc* ***(G-11738)***
L/J Fabricators Inc...815 397-9099
944 Research Pkwy Rockford (61109) ***(G-17489)***
L2 Supply DBA Ica Cab Supp Ly...773 382-8037
4250 N Milwaukee Ave Chicago (60641) ***(G-5145)***
L3 Technologies Inc...212 697-1111
1200 Hicks Rd Rolling Meadows (60008) ***(G-17747)***
La Autentica Michoacana Never...630 516-1888
507 S Addison Rd Addison (60101) ***(G-177)***
La Criolla Inc...312 243-8882
12828 S Ridgeway Ave Alsip (60803) ***(G-468)***
La Dolce Bella Cupcakes...847 987-3738
1228 Newbridge Ave Lockport (60441) ***(G-13005)***
La Espanola Food Dist Corp...312 733-0775
401 N Oakley Blvd Chicago (60612) ***(G-5146)***
La Force Inc...630 325-1950
7501 S Quincy St Ste 180 Willowbrook (60527) ***(G-21048)***
La Force Inc...847 415-5107
280 Corporate Woods Pkwy Vernon Hills (60061) ***(G-20071)***
La Hispamex Food Products Inc...708 780-1808
6955 S Harlem Ave Chicago (60638) ***(G-5147)***
La Luc Bakery Inc...847 740-0303
246 N Cedar Lake Rd Frnt Round Lake (60073) ***(G-18079)***
La Marche Mfg Co (PA)...847 299-1188
106 Bradrock Dr Des Plaines (60018) ***(G-7795)***
La Mexicana Food Prducts, Chicago *Also called La Espanola Food Dist Corp* ***(G-5146)***
La Mexicana Tortilleria Inc...773 247-5443
2703 S Kedzie Ave Chicago (60623) ***(G-5148)***
La Quinta Gas Pipeline Company...217 430-6781
1416 Donlee St Quincy (62305) ***(G-16906)***
La Raza Chicago Inc...312 870-7000
605 N Michigan Ave # 400 Chicago (60611) ***(G-5149)***
La Raza Newspaper, Chicago *Also called La Raza Chicago Inc* ***(G-5149)***
La Salle Co Esda...815 433-5622
711 E Etna Rd Ottawa (61350) ***(G-16058)***
La Salle Mfg & Mch Co, Rockford *Also called Pgi Mfg LLC* ***(G-17552)***
La Tropicana Inc...773 476-1107
5646 S Kedzie Ave Chicago (60629) ***(G-5150)***
La-Co Industries Inc (PA)...847 956-7600
1201 Pratt Blvd Elk Grove Village (60007) ***(G-9082)***
Lab TEC Cosmt By Marzena Inc...630 396-3970
1470 W Bernard Dr Addison (60101) ***(G-178)***
Lab Ten LLC...815 877-1410
5029 Willow Creek Rd Machesney Park (61115) ***(G-13355)***
Labaquette Kedzie Inc...773 925-0455
5859 S Kedzie Ave Chicago (60629) ***(G-5151)***
Label Design...815 462-4949
19633 Snowmass Rd Mokena (60448) ***(G-14093)***
Label Graphics Co Inc...815 648-2478
12024 3rd Ave Hebron (60034) ***(G-11145)***
Label Printers LP...630 897-6970
1710 Landmark Rd Aurora (60506) ***(G-1122)***
Label Tek Inc...630 820-8499
3505 Thayer Ct Ste 200 Aurora (60504) ***(G-995)***
Labelmaster Division, Chicago *Also called American Labelmark Company* ***(G-3656)***
Labelquest Inc...630 833-9400
493 W Fullerton Ave Elmhurst (60126) ***(G-9390)***
Labels & Specialty Pdts LLC...630 513-8060
3915 Stern Ave Saint Charles (60174) ***(G-18223)***
Labels Unlimited Incorporated...773 523-7500
3400 W 48th Pl Chicago (60632) ***(G-5152)***
Labeltape Group, Willowbrook *Also called A-Flex Label LLC* ***(G-21028)***
Labjackscom Inc...847 537-2099
151 S Pfingsten Rd Ste N Deerfield (60015) ***(G-7628)***
Laboratory Builders Inc...630 598-0216
166 Shore Dr Burr Ridge (60527) ***(G-2695)***
Laboratory Media Corporation...630 897-8000
1731 Commerce Dr Montgomery (60538) ***(G-14254)***
Laboratory Technologies Inc...630 365-1000
4n645 Mohican Ln Elburn (60119) ***(G-8456)***
Labriola Baking, Alsip *Also called J & J Snack Foods Corp* ***(G-460)***
Labtec Cosmetics...630 359-4569
715 W Racquet Club Dr Addison (60101) ***(G-179)***
LAC Enterprises Inc...815 455-5044
2530 Il Route 176 Ste 9 Crystal Lake (60014) ***(G-7219)***
Lacava...773 637-9600
1100 W Cermak Rd B-403 Chicago (60608) ***(G-5153)***
Lacava LLC...773 637-9600
6630 W Wrightwood Ave Chicago (60707) ***(G-5154)***
Lacava Design, Chicago *Also called Lacava LLC* ***(G-5154)***
Lace Technologies Inc...630 528-8083
315 S Fairbank St Addison (60101) ***(G-180)***
Lacey-Bauer, Pearl *Also called Martha Lacey* ***(G-16318)***
Lachata Design Ltd...708 946-2757
3006 E Indiana Ave Beecher (60401) ***(G-1518)***
Lacon Home Journal...309 246-2865
204 S Washington St Lacon (61540) ***(G-12128)***
Lafarge Aggregates Ill Inc (HQ)...847 742-6060
7n394 S Mclean Blvd South Elgin (60177) ***(G-19162)***
Lafarge Aggregates Ill Inc...630 365-3600
1s194 Il Route 47 Elburn (60119) ***(G-8457)***
Lafarge Aux Sable LLC...815 941-1423
4225 Dellos Rd Morris (60450) ***(G-14309)***
Lafarge Building Materials Inc (HQ)...678 746-2000
8700 W Bryn Mawr Ave 300n Chicago (60631) ***(G-5155)***
Lafarge North America Inc...630 892-1616
105 Conco St North Aurora (60542) ***(G-15266)***
Lafarge North America Inc (HQ)...773 372-1000
8700 W Bryn Mawr Ave Chicago (60631) ***(G-5156)***
Lafarge North America Inc...847 742-6060
1310 Rt 31 South Elgin (60177) ***(G-19163)***
Lafarge North America Inc...815 741-2090
2509 Mound Rd Rockdale (60436) ***(G-17264)***
Lafarge North America Inc...773 372-1000
501 Il Route 146 34 Golconda (62938) ***(G-10666)***
Lafarge North America Inc...618 543-7541
2500 Portland Rd Grand Chain (62941) ***(G-10687)***
Lafarge North America Inc...847 244-3800
315 E Sea Horse Dr Waukegan (60085) ***(G-20457)***
Lafarge North America Inc...773 372-1000
8700 W Bryn Mawr Ave Chicago (60631) ***(G-5157)***
Lafarge North America Inc...773 646-5228
2150 E 130th St Chicago (60633) ***(G-5158)***
Lafargeholcim, Waukegan *Also called Lafarge North America Inc* ***(G-20457)***
Lafeber Distribution LLC...630 524-4845
24981 N 1400 East Rd Cornell (61319) ***(G-7013)***
Lafox Manufacturing Corp...630 232-0266
1 N 278 Lafox Rd Lafox (60147) ***(G-12136)***
Lafox Screw Products Inc...847 695-1732
440 N Gilbert St South Elgin (60177) ***(G-19164)***
Lagunitas Brewing Company...773 522-1308
2607 W 17th St Chicago (60608) ***(G-5159)***
Lah Inc...815 282-4939
6309 Material Ave Ste 2 Loves Park (61111) ***(G-13231)***
Lahood Construction Inc...309 699-5080
3305 N Main St East Peoria (61611) ***(G-8276)***
Laird Connectivity Inc...847 839-6000
1751 Wilkening Ct Schaumburg (60173) ***(G-18596)***
Laird Technologies Inc...847 839-6000
1751 Wilkening Ct Schaumburg (60173) ***(G-18597)***
Lake Area Disposal Service Inc...217 522-9271
2742 S 6th St Springfield (62703) ***(G-19397)***
Lake Area Recycling Services, Springfield *Also called Lake Area Disposal Service Inc* ***(G-19397)***
Lake Cable LLC (PA)...888 518-8086
529 Thomas Dr Bensenville (60106) ***(G-1840)***
Lake Cook C V, Wheeling *Also called Lake County C V Joints Inc* ***(G-20928)***
Lake Copper Conductors LLC...847 378-7006
529 Thomas Dr Bensenville (60106) ***(G-1841)***
Lake County C V Joints Inc...847 537-7588
133 Wheeling Rd Wheeling (60090) ***(G-20928)***
Lake County Grading Co LLC (PA)...847 362-2590
32901 N Hwy 21 Libertyville (60048) ***(G-12665)***

ALPHABETIC

Lake County Press Inc (PA).....847 336-4333
98 Noll St Waukegan (60085) ***(G-20458)***
Lake County Technologies Inc.....847 977-1330
120 Prairie Lake Rd Ste E East Dundee (60118) ***(G-8204)***
Lake County Tool Works North.....847 662-4542
15986 Hwy 173 Wadsworth (60083) ***(G-20210)***
Lake Effect Medical Ip, Chicago *Also called Graymont Prof Pdts Ip LLC* ***(G-4731)***
Lake Electronics Inc.....847 201-1270
31632 N Ellis Dr Unit 203 Volo (60073) ***(G-20202)***
Lake Fabrication Inc.....217 832-2761
4 S Sycamore St Villa Grove (61956) ***(G-20124)***
Lake Hill Winery Inc.....217 357-2675
1822 E County Road 1540 N Carthage (62321) ***(G-3137)***
Lake Iron Inc.....708 870-0546
5520 W Lake St Chicago (60644) ***(G-5160)***
Lake Pacific Partners LLC.....312 578-1110
120 S La Salle St # 1510 Chicago (60603) ***(G-5161)***
Lake Process Systems Inc.....847 381-7663
27930 W Commercial Ave Lake Barrington (60010) ***(G-12157)***
Lake Shore Stair Co Inc (PA).....815 363-7777
28090 W Concrete Dr Ingleside (60041) ***(G-11586)***
Lake Shore Stair Co Inc.....847 362-3262
615 E Park Ave Libertyville (60048) ***(G-12666)***
Lake Street Pallets.....773 889-2266
4600 W Armitage Ave Chicago (60639) ***(G-5162)***
Lakefront Roofing Supply (HQ).....773 509-0400
2950 N Western Ave Chicago (60618) ***(G-5163)***
Lakefront Sculpture Exhibit.....312 719-0207
1807 N Orleans St Ste 1s Chicago (60614) ***(G-5164)***
Lakefront Supply, Chicago *Also called Jesus People USA Full Gos* ***(G-5023)***
Lakeland Boating Magazine.....312 276-0610
630 Davis St Ste 301 Evanston (60201) ***(G-9546)***
Lakeland Pallets Inc.....616 949-9515
2080 Gary Ln Ste 3 Geneva (60134) ***(G-10288)***
Lakenburges Motor Co.....618 523-4231
806 Walnut St Germantown (62245) ***(G-10331)***
Lakes Reg Prtg & Graphics LLC.....847 838-5838
25325 W Hickory St Antioch (60002) ***(G-620)***
Lakeshore Lacrosse LLC.....773 350-4356
20 Danada Sq W Ste 289 Wheaton (60189) ***(G-20810)***
Lakeshore Operating LLC.....844 557-4763
2637 N Sawyer Ave Chicago (60647) ***(G-5165)***
Lakeside Lithography LLC.....312 243-3001
1600 S Laflin St Chicago (60608) ***(G-5166)***
Lakeside Publishing Co LLC.....847 491-6440
1800 Nations Dr Ste 117 Gurnee (60031) ***(G-10894)***
Lakeside Screw Products Inc.....630 495-1606
1395 W Jeffrey Dr Addison (60101) ***(G-181)***
Lakeview Energy LLC (PA).....312 386-5897
300 W Adams St Ste 830 Chicago (60606) ***(G-5167)***
Lakeview Metals Inc (PA).....847 838-9800
905 Anita Ave Antioch (60002) ***(G-621)***
Lakeview Prcsion Machining Inc.....847 742-7170
751 Schneider Dr South Elgin (60177) ***(G-19165)***
Lakeview Sign Co.....773 698-8104
1101 W Belmont Ave Chicago (60657) ***(G-5168)***
Lakewood Countertop, Bloomingdale *Also called Pearl Design Group LLC* ***(G-2009)***
Lakin General, Montgomery *Also called A Lakin & Sons Inc* ***(G-14229)***
Lakin General Corporation.....773 871-6360
2001 Greenfield Rd Montgomery (60538) ***(G-14255)***
Lakone Company.....630 892-4251
1003 Aucutt Rd Montgomery (60538) ***(G-14256)***
Lambda Publications Inc.....773 871-7610
5443 N Broadway St # 101 Chicago (60640) ***(G-5169)***
Lambert Bridge & Iron, Bourbonnais *Also called Greg Lambert Construction* ***(G-2261)***
Lambert Print Source Llc.....630 708-0505
301 Walsh Cir Yorkville (60560) ***(G-21491)***
Lamboo Inc.....866 966-2999
311 W Edwards St Litchfield (62056) ***(G-12970)***
Lamboo Technologies LLC.....866 966-2999
311 W Edwards St Litchfield (62056) ***(G-12971)***
Lambright Distributors.....217 543-2083
35 E Cr 200 N Arthur (61911) ***(G-865)***
Lamco Advertising Specialties, Chicago *Also called Laminet Cover Company* ***(G-5171)***
Lamco Slings & Rigging Inc.....309 764-7400
4960 41st Street Ct Moline (61265) ***(G-14157)***
Lamico Designers Deerfield Inc.....847 465-8850
3300 Skokie Valley Rd Highland Park (60035) ***(G-11279)***
Lamin-Art LLC.....800 323-7624
1670 Basswood Rd Schaumburg (60173) ***(G-18598)***
Laminarp.....847 884-9298
1670 Basswood Rd Schaumburg (60173) ***(G-18599)***
Laminate Craft, Lincolnwood *Also called Yazdan Essie* ***(G-12852)***
Laminated Components Inc.....815 648-4811
12204 Hansen Rd Hebron (60034) ***(G-11146)***
Laminated Designs Countertops.....815 877-7222
9731 N 2nd St Machesney Park (61115) ***(G-13356)***
Lamination Specialties LLC.....773 254-7500
4444 S Kildare Ave Chicago (60632) ***(G-5170)***
Lamination Specialties LLC (HQ).....312 243-2181
1400 16th St Oak Brook (60523) ***(G-15631)***
Laminet Cover Company.....773 622-6700
4900 W Bloomingdale Ave Chicago (60639) ***(G-5171)***
Laminting Bnding Solutions Inc.....847 573-0375
27885 Irma Lee Cir Lake Forest (60045) ***(G-12271)***
Lamka Enterprises Inc.....630 659-5965
8700 Crystal Springs Rd Woodstock (60098) ***(G-21402)***
Lamonica Ornamental Iron Works.....773 638-6633
3311 W Chicago Ave Chicago (60651) ***(G-5172)***
Lamont Wells Industrial.....804 299-2557
5215 Old Orchard Rd # 725 Skokie (60077) ***(G-18975)***
Lamp Co of America Inc.....630 584-4001
214 S 13th Ave Saint Charles (60174) ***(G-18224)***
Lamp Works Inc.....630 871-7663
332 Commerce Dr Carol Stream (60188) ***(G-3015)***
Lampe Publications.....309 741-9790
401 W Main St Elmwood (61529) ***(G-9448)***
Lampholders Assemblies Inc.....773 205-0005
4106 N Nashville Ave Chicago (60634) ***(G-5173)***
Lampley Oil Inc.....618 439-6288
720 W Main St Ste B Benton (62812) ***(G-1931)***
Lampshade Inc.....773 522-2300
4041 W Ogden Ave Ste 1 Chicago (60623) ***(G-5174)***
Lamson Oil Company (HQ).....815 226-8090
2217 20th Ave Rockford (61104) ***(G-17490)***
Lana Jewelry, Lake Forest *Also called Lana Unlimited Co* ***(G-12272)***
Lana Unlimited Co (PA).....312 226-7050
736 N Western Ave Ste 308 Lake Forest (60045) ***(G-12272)***
Lancaster Traditions LLC.....847 428-5446
100 W Higgins Rd Unit E5 South Barrington (60010) ***(G-19076)***
Lancer Manufacturing Inc (PA).....630 595-1150
1021 Oakland Dr Barrington (60010) ***(G-1223)***
Lanco International Inc (PA).....708 596-5200
3111 167th St Hazel Crest (60429) ***(G-11131)***
Land O'Lake Purina Seed, Vandalia *Also called Purina Animal Nutrition LLC* ***(G-20021)***
Land OFrost Inc (PA).....708 474-7100
16850 Chicago Ave Lansing (60438) ***(G-12502)***
Land-O-Tackle, Bensenville *Also called Plastech Inc* ***(G-1868)***
Landairsea Systems Inc.....847 462-8100
2040 Dillard Ct Woodstock (60098) ***(G-21403)***
Landauer Inc (HQ).....708 755-7000
2 Science Rd Glenwood (60425) ***(G-10642)***
Landmarx Screen Printing.....217 223-4601
3902 Payson Rd Quincy (62305) ***(G-16907)***
Landmeier Corp.....847 709-2823
180 Martin Ln Elk Grove Village (60007) ***(G-9083)***
Landquist & Son Inc.....847 674-6600
9850 W 190th St Ste L Mokena (60448) ***(G-14094)***
Landsberg Chicago, Lombard *Also called Orora North America* ***(G-13114)***
Lane Industries Inc (PA).....847 498-6650
1200 Shermer Rd Ste 400 Northbrook (60062) ***(G-15417)***
Lane Tool & Mfg Co Inc.....847 622-1506
655 Sundown Rd South Elgin (60177) ***(G-19166)***
Lang Dental Mfg Co Inc.....847 215-6622
175 Messner Dr Wheeling (60090) ***(G-20929)***
Lang Exterior Inc (PA).....773 737-4500
2323 W 59th St Chicago (60636) ***(G-5175)***
Lang Exterior Mfg Co, Chicago *Also called Lang Exterior Inc* ***(G-5175)***
Lange Electric Inc.....217 347-7626
912 E Fayette Ave Effingham (62401) ***(G-8407)***
Lange Sign Group.....815 747-2448
1780 Il Route 35 N East Dubuque (61025) ***(G-8178)***
Langham Engineering.....815 223-5250
1414 Shooting Park Rd Peru (61354) ***(G-16580)***
Langheim Ready Mix Inc.....217 625-2351
110 E Jefferson St Girard (62640) ***(G-10383)***
Langston Bag of Peoria LLC.....309 676-1006
1114 Sw Adams St Peoria (61602) ***(G-16468)***
Lanigan Holdings LLC (PA).....708 596-5200
3111 167th St Hazel Crest (60429) ***(G-11132)***
Laninver USA Inc (PA).....847 367-8787
2800 Carl Bulevard Elk Grove Village (60007) ***(G-9084)***
Lanmar Inc.....800 233-5520
3160 Doolittle Dr Northbrook (60062) ***(G-15418)***
Lans Printing Inc.....708 895-6226
2581 Glenwd Lansing Rd A Lynwood (60411) ***(G-13295)***
Lansing Cut Stone Co.....708 474-7515
3125 Glenwood Lansing Rd Lansing (60438) ***(G-12503)***
Lansing Wings Inc.....708 895-3300
3720 Ridge Rd Lansing (60438) ***(G-12504)***
Lantech Logistics, Hazel Crest *Also called Lanco International Inc* ***(G-11131)***
Lanxess Solutions US Inc.....309 633-9480
8220 W Route 24 Mapleton (61547) ***(G-13474)***
Lanzatech Inc (HQ).....630 439-3050
8045 Lamon Ave Ste 400 Skokie (60077) ***(G-18976)***
Lapham-Hickey Steel Corp (PA).....708 496-6111
5500 W 73rd St Bedford Park (60638) ***(G-1479)***
Laqueus Inc.....773 508-1993
7435 N Western Ave Chicago (60645) ***(G-5176)***

Laredo Foods Inc 773 762-1500
3401 W Cermak Rd Chicago (60623) *(G-5177)*
Laredo Spices & Herbs, Chicago *Also called Laredo Foods Inc (G-5177)*
Lares Technologies LLC 630 408-4368
748 Charismatic Dr Oswego (60543) *(G-16010)*
Larry & Myra Stone 847 433-0540
667 Central Ave Ste 5 Highland Park (60035) *(G-11280)*
Larry Musgrave Logging 618 842-6386
414 Nw 6th St Fairfield (62837) *(G-9630)*
Larry Pontnack 815 732-7751
6309 E Brick Rd Oregon (61061) *(G-15923)*
Larrys Garage & Machine Shop 815 968-8416
101 Vista Ter Rockford (61102) *(G-17491)*
Larsen & Toubro Infotech Ltd 847 303-3900
1821 Walden Office Sq # 400 Schaumburg (60173) *(G-18600)*
Larsen Envelope Co Inc 847 952-9020
165 Gaylord St Elk Grove Village (60007) *(G-9085)*
Larsen Manufacturing LLC (PA) 847 970-9600
1201 Allanson Rd Mundelein (60060) *(G-14709)*
Larson Hardware Manufacturing, Rock Falls *Also called Chas O Larson Co (G-17179)*
Larson-Juhl US LLC 630 307-9700
550 Congress Cir N Roselle (60172) *(G-17963)*
Las Systems Inc 847 462-8100
2040 Dillard Ct Woodstock (60098) *(G-21404)*
Laser Center Corporation 630 523-1600
1001 Morse Ave Schaumburg (60193) *(G-18601)*
Laser Creations, South Beloit *Also called Walnut Creek Hardwood (G-19120)*
Laser Energy Systems 815 282-8200
4924 Torque Rd Loves Park (61111) *(G-13232)*
Laser Expressions Ltd 847 419-9600
165 N Arlngton Hgts Rd Buffalo Grove (60089) *(G-2559)*
Laser Images, Quincy *Also called Kevin Kewney (G-16899)*
Laser Plus Technologies LLC 847 787-9017
2450 American Ln Elk Grove Village (60007) *(G-9086)*
Laser Pro 847 742-1055
978 N Mclean Blvd Elgin (60123) *(G-8640)*
Laser Products Industries Inc 877 679-1300
1344 Enterprise Dr Romeoville (60446) *(G-17839)*
Laser Reproductions Inc 847 410-0397
8228 Mccormick Blvd Skokie (60076) *(G-18977)*
Laser Technologies Inc 630 761-1200
1120 Frontenac Rd Naperville (60563) *(G-14860)*
Laser Technology Group Inc 847 524-4088
1029 Charlela Ln Apt 407 Elk Grove Village (60007) *(G-9087)*
Laser Tek Industries, Spring Grove *Also called Tonerhead Inc (G-19304)*
Laserage, Waukegan *Also called Ltc Holdings Inc (G-20464)*
Lasersketch Ltd 630 243-6360
1319 Enterprise Dr Romeoville (60446) *(G-17840)*
Lashcon Inc 217 742-3186
540 Coultas Rd Winchester (62694) *(G-21106)*
Lasner Beauty Supply, Chicago *Also called Lasner Bros Inc (G-5178)*
Lasner Bros Inc 773 935-7383
3649 N Ashland Ave Chicago (60613) *(G-5178)*
Lasons Label Co 773 775-2606
5666 N Northwest Hwy Chicago (60646) *(G-5179)*
Last Minute Gourmet, Chicago *Also called Taylor Farms Illinois Inc (G-6331)*
Lathom Pin - Div, Loves Park *Also called Ford Tool & Machining Inc (G-13211)*
Latino Arts & Communications 773 501-0029
3514 W Diversey Ave 212 Chicago (60647) *(G-5180)*
Lattice Incorporated 630 949-3250
1751 S Nprvlle Rd Ste 100 Wheaton (60189) *(G-20811)*
Lau Nae Winery Inc 618 282-9463
806 White Oak Dr Red Bud (62278) *(G-16997)*
Laughing Dog Graphics 309 392-3330
207 N Main Ave Minier (61759) *(G-14054)*
Launch Press 773 669-8372
325 N Martha St Lombard (60148) *(G-13094)*
Laundry Services Company 630 327-9329
4805 Pershing Ave Downers Grove (60515) *(G-8042)*
Laundryworld, Chicago *Also called Lloyd M Hughes Enterprises Inc (G-5245)*
Laurel Industries Inc 847 432-8204
544 Michigan Ave Highland Park (60035) *(G-11281)*
Laurel Metal Products Inc 847 674-0064
3500 W Touhy Ave Lincolnwood (60712) *(G-12827)*
Laurenceleste Inc 708 383-3432
230 Clinton Ave Oak Park (60302) *(G-15762)*
Laux Grafix Inc 618 337-4558
3709 Mississippi Ave East Saint Louis (62206) *(G-8313)*
Lava World International Inc 630 315-3300
430 Kimberly Dr Carol Stream (60188) *(G-3016)*
Lavell General Handyman Svcs 773 691-3101
8150 S Anthony Ave Chicago (60617) *(G-5181)*
Lavender Crest Winery 309 949-2565
5401 Us Highway 6 Colona (61241) *(G-6975)*
Laverns Wood Items 217 268-4544
421 E County Road 200n Arcola (61910) *(G-654)*
Lavezzi Precision Inc 630 582-1230
250 Madsen Dr Bloomingdale (60108) *(G-1997)*
Law Bulletin Publishing Co (PA) 312 644-2763
415 N State St Ste 1 Chicago (60654) *(G-5182)*
Law Bulletin Publishing Co 847 883-9100
1360 Abbott Ct Buffalo Grove (60089) *(G-2560)*
Lawlor Family Winery, Galena *Also called Galena Cellars Winery (G-10169)*
Lawlor Family Winery, Galena *Also called Galena Cellars Winery (G-10170)*
Lawlor Marketing 847 357-1080
2035 S Arlington Hts Rd Arlington Heights (60005) *(G-767)*
Lawndale Forging & Tool Works 773 277-2800
2141 S Spaulding Ave Chicago (60623) *(G-5183)*
Lawndale News, Cicero *Also called Lawndale Press Inc (G-6862)*
Lawndale Press Inc (PA) 708 656-6900
5533 W 25th St Cicero (60804) *(G-6862)*
Lawrence Allen 618 786-3794
21031 State Highway 3 Grafton (62037) *(G-10686)*
Lawrence Brand Shot 618 798-6112
1200 16th St Granite City (62040) *(G-10719)*
Lawrence Foods Inc 847 437-2400
2200 Lunt Ave Elk Grove Village (60007) *(G-9088)*
Lawrence J L & Co Dental Labs, Mattoon *Also called J L Lawrence & Co (G-13638)*
Lawrence Maddock 847 394-1698
500 S Arthur Ave Arlington Heights (60005) *(G-768)*
Lawrence Oil Company Inc 618 262-4138
801 W 9th St Rm 208 Mount Carmel (62863) *(G-14477)*
Lawrence Rgan Cmmnications Inc 312 960-4100
10 S La Salle St Ste 310 Chicago (60603) *(G-5184)*
Lawrence Screw Products Inc 217 735-1230
437 8th St Lincoln (62656) *(G-12732)*
Lawter Inc (HQ) 312 662-5700
200 N La Salle St # 2600 Chicago (60601) *(G-5185)*
Lax Shop 847 945-8529
108 Washington Ave Highwood (60040) *(G-11308)*
Layer Saver LLC 630 325-7287
9075 Turnberry Dr Burr Ridge (60527) *(G-2696)*
Lays Mining Service Inc 618 244-6570
1121 S 10th St Mount Vernon (62864) *(G-14621)*
Laystrom Manufacturing Co 773 342-4800
3900 W Palmer St Chicago (60647) *(G-5186)*
Lazare Printing Co Inc 773 871-2500
709 W Wrightwood Ave # 1 Chicago (60614) *(G-5187)*
Lb Metals LLC 708 331-2600
15700 Lathrop Ave Harvey (60426) *(G-11091)*
Lb Staley Elmwood, Canton *Also called Canton Redi-Mix Inc (G-2823)*
Lb Steel LLC 708 331-2600
15700 Lathrop Ave Harvey (60426) *(G-11092)*
Lbe Ltd 847 907-4959
21038 N Andover Rd Kildeer (60047) *(G-12050)*
Lbl Lighting LLC (PA) 708 755-2100
7400 Linder Ave Skokie (60077) *(G-18978)*
Lbp Manufacturing LLC (PA) 800 545-6200
1325 S Cicero Ave Cicero (60804) *(G-6863)*
Lc Holdings of Delaware Inc (PA) 847 940-3550
500 Lake Cook Rd Ste 430 Deerfield (60015) *(G-7629)*
LC Industries Inc 312 455-0500
2781 Katherine Way Elk Grove Village (60007) *(G-9089)*
Lcg Sales Inc 773 378-7455
5410 W Roosevelt Rd # 231 Chicago (60644) *(G-5188)*
Lcr Hallcrest Llc 847 998-8580
1911 Pickwick Ln Glenview (60026) *(G-10584)*
Lcv Company 309 738-6452
919 15th Ave East Moline (61244) *(G-8232)*
LDI Industries Inc 847 669-7510
12901 Jim Dhamer Dr Huntley (60142) *(G-11550)*
Le Chocolat Bky & Chocolates, Naperville *Also called Le Chocolat Du Bouchard LLC (G-14861)*
Le Chocolat Du Bouchard LLC (PA) 630 355-5720
127-129 S Washington St Naperville (60563) *(G-14861)*
Le Petit Pain Holdings LLC (PA) 312 981-3770
676 N Michigan Ave Chicago (60611) *(G-5189)*
Le Print Express, Dekalb *Also called Nancy J Perkins (G-7691)*
Lea & Sachs Inc (PA) 847 296-8000
1267 Rand Rd Des Plaines (60016) *(G-7796)*
Lead n Glass Tm 847 255-2074
2039 Foster Ave Ste A Wheeling (60090) *(G-20930)*
Leader Newspaper, East Moline *Also called Small Nwsppr Group Shred Svcs (G-8242)*
Leaders Bev Consulting Inc 312 497-5602
4038 N Nshvlle Ave Chcago Chicago Chicago (60634) *(G-5190)*
Leading Americas Inc 815 568-2199
130 Arrowhead Dr Unit 13 Hampshire (60140) *(G-10976)*
Leading Edge Group Inc (PA) 815 316-3500
1800 16th Ave Rockford (61104) *(G-17492)*
Leading Edge Hydraulics, Rockford *Also called Leading Edge Group Inc (G-17492)*
Leading Lady Company, Neoga *Also called Golda Inc (G-15017)*
Leaffilter North LLC 630 595-9605
587 N Edgewood Ave Wood Dale (60191) *(G-21207)*
Leahy-Ifp Company, Glenview *Also called Institutional Foods Packing Co (G-10569)*
Lean Protein Team LLC 440 525-1532
235 W Van Buren St Chicago (60607) *(G-5191)*

ALPHABETIC

(PA)=Parent Co (HQ)=Headquarters (DH)=Div Headquarters
2020 Harris Illinois Industrial Directory
1175

ALPHABETIC SECTION

Leapfrog Product Dev LLC..312 229-0089
159 N Racine Ave Ste 3e Chicago (60607) *(G-5192)*
Learjet Inc...847 553-0172
251 Wille Rd Ste A Des Plaines (60018) *(G-7797)*
Learning Curve International (HQ)..........................630 573-7200
1111 W 22nd St Ste 320 Oak Brook (60523) *(G-15632)*
Learning Resources Inc (PA)...................................847 573-8400
380 N Fairway Dr Vernon Hills (60061) *(G-20072)*
Learning Seed LLC..847 540-8855
208 S Jefferson St # 205 Chicago (60661) *(G-5193)*
Leas Baking Company LLC.....................................708 710-3404
14660 Pebble Creek Ct Homer Glen (60491) *(G-11483)*
Leasing Dynamics, Saint Charles *Also called Water Dynamics Inc (G-18297)*
Lebanon Chemical, Danville *Also called Lebanon Seaboard Corporation (G-7358)*
Lebanon Seaboard Corporation..............................217 446-0983
508 W Ross Ln Danville (61834) *(G-7358)*
Lechler Inc..630 377-6611
445 Kautz Rd Saint Charles (60174) *(G-18225)*
Lecip Inc..312 626-2525
881 Il Route 83 Bensenville (60106) *(G-1842)*
Lectro Stik Corp...630 894-1355
1957 Quincy Ct Glendale Heights (60139) *(G-10466)*
Led Business Solutions LLC..................................844 464-5337
433 Maple Ave Downers Grove (60515) *(G-8043)*
LED Rite LLC..847 683-8000
120 Rowell Rd Hampshire (60140) *(G-10977)*
Ledcor Construction Inc..630 916-1200
18w140 Bttrfeld Rd Ste 15 Oakbrook Terrace (60181) *(G-15805)*
Ledil Inc..815 766-3204
228 W Page St Ste D Sycamore (60178) *(G-19721)*
Ledretrofitting Inc...815 347-5047
2n138 Bernice Ave Glen Ellyn (60137) *(G-10408)*
Lee Armand & Co Ltd...312 455-1200
840 N Milwaukee Ave Chicago (60642) *(G-5194)*
Lee Brothers Welding Inc.......................................309 342-6017
575 Lincoln St Galesburg (61401) *(G-10207)*
Lee Enterprises Incorporated.................................309 829-9000
301 W Washington St Bloomington (61701) *(G-2070)*
Lee Enterprises Incorporated.................................309 743-0800
1521 47th Ave Moline (61265) *(G-14158)*
Lee Enterprises Incorporated.................................618 998-8499
3000 W Deyoung St Ste 336 Marion (62959) *(G-13519)*
Lee Enterprises Incorporated.................................217 421-6920
601 E William St Decatur (62523) *(G-7515)*
Lee Enterprises Incorporated.................................618 529-5454
710 N Illinois Ave Carbondale (62901) *(G-2849)*
Lee Foss Electric Motor Svc....................................708 681-5335
3418 W North Ave Stone Park (60165) *(G-19556)*
Lee Gilster-Mary Corporation..................................618 826-2361
981 State St Chester (62233) *(G-3457)*
Lee Gilster-Mary Corporation..................................618 965-3426
705 N Sparta St Steeleville (62288) *(G-19481)*
Lee Gilster-Mary Corporation..................................618 443-5676
403 E 4th St Sparta (62286) *(G-19256)*
Lee Gilster-Mary Corporation..................................618 533-4808
100 W Calumet St Centralia (62801) *(G-3237)*
Lee Gilster-Mary Corporation..................................815 472-6456
305 E Washington St Momence (60954) *(G-14186)*
Lee Gilster-Mary Corporation..................................618 965-3449
10 Industrial Park Steeleville (62288) *(G-19482)*
Lee Jensen Sales Co Inc (PA)................................815 459-0929
101 W Terra Cotta Ave Crystal Lake (60014) *(G-7220)*
Lee Quarry Inc...815 547-7141
1473 Flora Church Rd Kirkland (60146) *(G-12063)*
Lee Quigley Company..708 563-1600
5301 W 65th St Ste D Chicago (60638) *(G-5195)*
Lee Sauzek..618 539-5815
316 Silverthorne Dr Freeburg (62243) *(G-10091)*
Lee-Wel Printing Corporation.................................630 682-0935
1554 S County Farm Rd Wheaton (60189) *(G-20812)*
Leesons Cakes Inc..708 429-1330
6713 163rd Pl Tinley Park (60477) *(G-19844)*
Leg Up LLC..312 282-2725
639 W Diversey Pkwy # 205 Chicago (60614) *(G-5196)*
Legacy 3d LLC...815 727-5454
2020 N Raynor Ave Crest Hill (60403) *(G-7090)*
Legacy Audio, Springfield *Also called Acoustic Avenue Inc (G-19315)*
Legacy Foods Mfg LLC..224 639-5297
498 Franklin Ln Elk Grove Village (60007) *(G-9090)*
Legacy Foods Mfg LLC..847 595-9106
1550 Greenleaf Ave Elk Grove Village (60007) *(G-9091)*
Legacy International Assoc LLC.............................847 823-1602
1420 Park Ridge Blvd Park Ridge (60068) *(G-16287)*
Legacy Plastics Inc...815 226-3013
5040 27th Ave Rockford (61109) *(G-17493)*
Legacy Prints..815 946-9112
607 S Division Ave Polo (61064) *(G-16756)*
Legacy Vulcan LLC...815 468-8141
6141 N Rte 50 Manteno (60950) *(G-13450)*
Legacy Vulcan LLC...847 437-4181
1520 Midway Ct Elk Grove Village (60007) *(G-9092)*
Legacy Vulcan LLC...217 932-2611
9129 N 230th St Casey (62420) *(G-3205)*
Legacy Vulcan LLC...815 726-6900
595 W Laraway Rd Joliet (60436) *(G-11894)*
Legacy Vulcan LLC...815 937-7928
1277 S 7000w Rd Kankakee (60901) *(G-11989)*
Legacy Vulcan LLC...773 890-2360
3910 S Racine Ave Chicago (60609) *(G-5197)*
Legacy Vulcan LLC...217 963-2196
2855 S Lincoln Memorial P Decatur (62522) *(G-7516)*
Legacy Vulcan LLC...630 739-0182
1361 N Joliet Rd Romeoville (60446) *(G-17841)*
Legacy Vulcan LLC...217 498-7263
1200 Jostes Rd Rochester (62563) *(G-17168)*
Legacy Vulcan LLC...708 485-6602
5500 Joliet Rd Mc Cook (60525) *(G-13695)*
Legacy Vulcan LLC...815 895-6501
12502 Lloyd Rd Sycamore (60178) *(G-19722)*
Legacy Vulcan LLC...217 963-2196
2855 Lincoln Pkwy Harristown (62537) *(G-11032)*
Legacy Vulcan LLC...815 436-3535
Rr 126 Plainfield (60544) *(G-16682)*
Legacy Vulcan LLC...847 578-9622
29821 N Skokie Hwy Lake Bluff (60044) *(G-12192)*
Legacy Vulcan LLC...630 904-1110
22933 W Hassert Blvd Plainfield (60585) *(G-16683)*
Legacy Woodwork Inc..847 451-7602
9137 Cherry Ave Franklin Park (60131) *(G-9980)*
Legal Files Software Inc.......................................217 726-6000
801 S Durkin Dr Ste A Springfield (62704) *(G-19398)*
Legend Creative Group, Lake Zurich *Also called Legend Promotions (G-12428)*
Legend Dynamix Inc..847 789-7007
77 Mcmillen Rd Ste 106 Antioch (60002) *(G-622)*
Legend Engraving Company, Antioch *Also called Legend Dynamix Inc (G-622)*
Legend Promotions...847 438-3528
815 Oakwood Rd Ste B Lake Zurich (60047) *(G-12428)*
Legend Racing Enterprises Inc...............................847 923-8979
616 Morse Ave Schaumburg (60193) *(G-18602)*
Leggett & Platt Incorporated.................................773 907-0261
13535 S Torrence Ave Chicago (60633) *(G-5198)*
Leggett & Platt Incorporated.................................630 851-0101
969 Corporate Blvd Aurora (60502) *(G-996)*
Leggett & Platt Incorporated.................................847 768-6139
1798 Sherwin Ave Des Plaines (60018) *(G-7798)*
Leggett & Platt Incorporated.................................815 233-0022
1555 Il Route 75 E Ste 2 Freeport (61032) *(G-10124)*
Leggett & Platt 0338, Chicago *Also called Leggett & Platt Incorporated (G-5199)*
Leggett & Platt 0351, Freeport *Also called Leggett & Platt Incorporated (G-10124)*
Leggett & Platt 0n09, North Aurora *Also called Leggett & Platt Incorporated (G-15267)*
Leggett & Platt 6003, Aurora *Also called Leggett & Platt Incorporated (G-996)*
Leggett & Platt Incorporated..................................312 529-2053
205 W Wacker Dr Ste 1020 Chicago (60606) *(G-5199)*
Leggett & Platt Incorporated..................................630 801-0609
241 Airport Rd North Aurora (60542) *(G-15267)*
Leggett & Platt Incorporated..................................800 699-0607
6755 W 65th St Chicago (60638) *(G-5200)*
Leggs Manufacturing...618 842-9847
900 W Delaware St Fairfield (62837) *(G-9631)*
Legible Signs Group Corp......................................815 654-0100
2221 Nimtz Rd Loves Park (61111) *(G-13233)*
Legistek Corporation...312 399-4891
211 W Wacker Dr Ste 201 Chicago (60606) *(G-5201)*
Legna Iron Works Inc...630 894-8056
80 Central Ave Roselle (60172) *(G-17964)*
Lego Systems Inc..312 202-0946
835 N Michigan Ave # 3000 Chicago (60611) *(G-5202)*
Legrand AV Inc...719 661-8134
15457 Collection Ctr Dr Chicago (60693) *(G-5203)*
Lehigh Consumer Products LLC (HQ)....................630 851-7330
3901 Liberty St Aurora (60504) *(G-997)*
Lehman Fast Tech...847 742-5202
37w468 Elmer Ct Elgin (60124) *(G-8641)*
Lei Graphics, Alsip *Also called Luttrell Engraving Inc (G-470)*
Leica McRosystems Holdings Inc..........................800 248-0123
1700 Leider Ln Buffalo Grove (60089) *(G-2561)*
Leica Microsystems Inc..847 405-0123
1700 Leider Ln Buffalo Grove (60089) *(G-2562)*
Leica Microsystems Inc (HQ)................................847 405-0123
1700 Leider Ln Buffalo Grove (60089) *(G-2563)*
Leisure Properties LLC..618 937-6426
11884 Country Club Rd West Frankfort (62896) *(G-20675)*
LELAND HOUSE, Chicago *Also called Cornerstone Community Outreach (G-4237)*
Lemaitre Vascular Inc..847 462-2191
912 Northwest Hwy Ste 106 Fox River Grove (60021) *(G-9760)*
Lemanski Heating & AC..815 232-4519
1398 S Armstrong Ave Freeport (61032) *(G-10125)*

ALPHABETIC SECTION — Liberty Diversified Intl Inc

Lemfco Inc 815 777-0242
100 S Comm St Galena (61036) *(G-10176)*

Lemko Corporation 630 948-3025
846 E Algonquin Rd # 101 Schaumburg (60173) *(G-18603)*

Lemont Scrap Processing 630 257-6532
16229 New Ave Lemont (60439) *(G-12569)*

Lena AJS Maid Meats 815 369-4522
500 W Main St Lena (61048) *(G-12602)*

Lena Mercantile 815 369-9955
101 W Railroad St Lena (61048) *(G-12603)*

Lena Sign Shop 815 369-9090
109 W Railroad St Lena (61048) *(G-12604)*

Lenco Electronics Inc 815 344-2900
1330 S Belden St McHenry (60050) *(G-13756)*

Lenhardt Tool and Die Company 618 462-1075
3400 Bloomer Dr Alton (62002) *(G-563)*

Lennox Industries Inc 630 378-7054
187 S South Creek Pkwy Romeoville (60446) *(G-17842)*

Lenova Inc (PA) 312 733-1098
4580 Roosevelt Rd Hillside (60162) *(G-11346)*

Lenrok Industries Inc 630 628-1946
542 W Winthrop Ave Addison (60101) *(G-182)*

Lens Lenticlear Lenticular 630 467-0900
2515 Pan Am Blvd Elk Grove Village (60007) *(G-9093)*

Lenze Americas 224 653-8119
125 Wall St Glendale Heights (60139) *(G-10467)*

Leo A Bachrach Jewelers Inc 312 263-3111
55 E Washington St # 801 Chicago (60602) *(G-5204)*

Leo Bachrach and Son, Chicago Also called Leo A Bachrach Jewelers Inc *(G-5204)*

Leo Burnett Company Inc (HQ) 312 220-5959
35 W Wacker Dr Fl 21 Chicago (60601) *(G-5205)*

Leonard A Unes Printing Co 309 674-4942
619 Spring St Peoria (61603) *(G-16469)*

Leonard Associates Inc 815 226-9609
6733 Hedgewood Rd Rockford (61108) *(G-17494)*

Leonard Emerson 217 628-3441
103 W Dodds St Divernon (62530) *(G-7880)*

Leonard's Guide, Arlington Heights Also called G R Leonard & Co Inc *(G-740)*

Leonards Unit Step Co 815 744-1263
1515 Channahon Rd Rockdale (60436) *(G-17265)*

Leonards Unit Step of Moline 309 792-9641
24415 Ridge Rd Colona (61241) *(G-6976)*

Leos Dancewear Inc 773 889-7700
7601 North Ave River Forest (60305) *(G-17053)*

Leos Gluten Free LLC 847 233-9211
10130 Pacific Ave Franklin Park (60131) *(G-9981)*

Leos Sign 773 227-2460
1334 N Kostner Ave Chicago (60651) *(G-5206)*

Leos Sweet Sensations Inc 773 237-1200
1900 N Austin Ave Chicago (60639) *(G-5207)*

Leppala Machining Inc 847 625-0270
12726d W Wadsworth Rd Beach Park (60087) *(G-1443)*

Lerner New York, Geneva Also called New York & Company Inc *(G-10293)*

Leroy E Ritzert 815 737-8210
9092 Randall Rd Capron (61012) *(G-2835)*

Leroys Plastic Co Inc 630 898-7006
1650 Mountain St Aurora (60505) *(G-1123)*

Leroys Welding & Fabg Inc 847 215-6151
363 Alice St Wheeling (60090) *(G-20931)*

Les Wilson Inc 618 382-4667
205 Industrial Ave Carmi (62821) *(G-2909)*

Lesker Company Inc 708 343-2277
528 N York Rd Bensenville (60106) *(G-1843)*

Lesmark Tool Company 815 725-7430
1808 Moen Ave Rockdale (60436) *(G-17266)*

Less Cost Copy Center Inc 618 345-3121
2103 Vandalia St Collinsville (62234) *(G-6965)*

Lessabah Arts Center, Oak Park Also called Freitas P Sabah *(G-15754)*

Lessy Messy LLC 708 790-7589
3143 Aviara Ct Naperville (60564) *(G-14977)*

Lester Building Systems LLC 217 364-8664
750 W State St Charleston (61920) *(G-3406)*

Lester L Brossard Co 815 338-7825
930 Dieckman St Woodstock (60098) *(G-21405)*

Lester Lampert Inc 312 944-6888
7 E Huron St Chicago (60611) *(G-5208)*

Lester Lampert Jewelers, Chicago Also called Lester Lampert Inc *(G-5208)*

Lester Manufacturing Inc 815 986-1172
2219 N Central Ave Rockford (61101) *(G-17495)*

Let There Be Distillers LLC 217 741-0392
1815 W Berteau Ave Chicago (60613) *(G-5209)*

Letellier Material Hdlg Eqp, South Holland Also called Peerless Chain Company *(G-19239)*

Letraw Manufacturing LLC 815 987-9670
200 Quaker Rd Ste 2 Rockford (61104) *(G-17496)*

Letter-Rite Express LLC 847 678-1100
1660 Wind Song Ln Aurora (60504) *(G-998)*

Lettering Specialists Inc 847 674-3414
8020 Lawndale Ave Skokie (60076) *(G-18979)*

Lettermen Signage Inc 708 479-5161
19912 Wolf Rd Mokena (60448) *(G-14095)*

Letters Unlimited Inc 847 891-7811
1010 Morse Ave Ste E Schaumburg (60193) *(G-18604)*

Level Developments Ltd 312 465-1082
1016 W Jackson Blvd 251 Chicago (60607) *(G-5210)*

Levelor Corporation 815 233-8684
29 E Stephenson St Freeport (61032) *(G-10126)*

Levi Strauss & Co 773 486-3900
1552 N Milwaukee Ave Chicago (60622) *(G-5211)*

Levi Strauss & Co 847 619-0655
5 Woodfeld Shopg Ctr 11 # 114 Schaumburg (60173) *(G-18605)*

Leviton Manufacturing Co Inc 630 443-0500
3837 E Main St Ste 331 Saint Charles (60174) *(G-18226)*

Leviton Manufacturing Co Inc 630 350-2656
700 Golf Ln Bensenville (60106) *(G-1844)*

Levolor Inc 800 346-3278
2707 Butterfield Rd Oak Brook (60523) *(G-15633)*

Lew Electric Fittings Co 630 665-2075
371 Randy Rd Carol Stream (60188) *(G-3017)*

Lew-El Tool & Manufacturing Co 773 804-1133
1935 N Leclaire Ave Chicago (60639) *(G-5212)*

Lewibelle Company, The, Chicago Also called Ade Inc *(G-3541)*

Lewis Acquisition Corp 773 486-5660
712 W Winthrop Ave Addison (60101) *(G-183)*

Lewis Brothers Bakeries Inc 708 531-6435
1955 W North Ave Melrose Park (60160) *(G-13890)*

Lewis N Clark Travel ACC, Elk Grove Village Also called LC Industries Inc *(G-9089)*

Lewis Paper Place Inc 847 808-1343
220 E Marquardt Rd Wheeling (60090) *(G-20932)*

Lewis Plastics, Addison Also called Lewis Acquisition Corp *(G-183)*

Lewis Process Systems Inc 630 510-8200
294 Commonwealth Dr Carol Stream (60188) *(G-3018)*

Lewis Spring and Mfg Company (PA) 847 588-7030
7500 N Natchez Ave Niles (60714) *(G-15140)*

Lex Holding Co 708 594-9200
1400 16th St Ste 250 Oak Brook (60523) *(G-15634)*

Lexcentral Steel, Bedford Park Also called Lexington Steel Corporation *(G-1480)*

Lexington Leather Goods Co 773 287-5500
5414 W Roosevelt Rd Chicago (60644) *(G-5213)*

Lexington Steel Corporation 708 594-9200
5443 W 70th Pl Bedford Park (60638) *(G-1480)*

Lexisnexis, Chicago Also called Relx Inc *(G-6013)*

Lexmark International Inc 847 318-5700
9700 W Higgins Rd Ste 930 Rosemont (60018) *(G-18030)*

Lexpress Inc 773 517-7095
1176 Cove Dr Prospect Heights (60070) *(G-16844)*

Lexray LLC 630 664-6740
3041 Woodcreek Dr Ste 200 Downers Grove (60515) *(G-8044)*

Leybold USA Inc 724 327-5700
25968 Network Pl Chicago (60673) *(G-5214)*

Leyden Lawn Sprinklers 630 665-5520
23w274 North Ave Glen Ellyn (60137) *(G-10409)*

Lezza Spumoni and Desserts Inc 708 547-5969
4009 Saint Charles Rd Bellwood (60104) *(G-1631)*

LFA Industries Inc 630 762-7391
1820 Wallace Ave Ste 122 Saint Charles (60174) *(G-18227)*

Lg Innotek USA Inc 847 941-8713
2000 Millbrook Dr Lincolnshire (60069) *(G-12780)*

Lgb Industries 847 639-1691
91 Fairfield Ln Cary (60013) *(G-3175)*

Lho Enterprises Inc (PA) 708 499-0017
6350 Birmingham St Chicago Ridge (60415) *(G-6801)*

Lhs Inc 630 832-3875
188 W Industrial Dr # 26 Elmhurst (60126) *(G-9391)*

LI Chou Metals Inc 312 451-4834
2150b S Archer Ave Chicago (60616) *(G-5215)*

LI Gear Inc 630 226-1688
1292 Lakeview Dr Romeoville (60446) *(G-17843)*

Liaison Home Automation LLC 888 279-1235
288 N Park St Decatur (62523) *(G-7517)*

Liam Brex 630 848-0222
222 S Main St Naperville (60540) *(G-14862)*

Libaerty LLC 312 330-2767
1343 W Irving Park Rd Chicago (60613) *(G-5216)*

Libation Container Inc 312 636-7206
4519 N Mozart St Chicago (60625) *(G-5217)*

Libbey Inc 630 818-3400
1850 Blackhawk Dr West Chicago (60185) *(G-20607)*

Libco Industries Inc 815 623-7677
10567 Main St Roscoe (61073) *(G-17912)*

Liberty Bee, Liberty Also called Elliott Publishing Inc *(G-12622)*

Liberty Chemical Corp 773 657-1282
1503 Carmen Dr Elk Grove Village (60007) *(G-9094)*

Liberty Classics Inc 847 367-1288
1860 W Winchester Rd # 103 Libertyville (60048) *(G-12667)*

Liberty Coach Inc 847 578-4600
1400 Morrow Ave North Chicago (60064) *(G-15316)*

Liberty Diversified Intl Inc 217 935-8361
10670 State Highway 10 Clinton (61727) *(G-6925)*

Liberty Diversified Intl Inc 309 787-6161
3402 78th Ave W Rock Island (61201) *(G-17227)*

Liberty Engineering Company, Roscoe *Also called Libco Industries Inc* ***(G-17912)***
Liberty Feed Mill 217 645-3441
408 Liberty St Liberty (62347) ***(G-12623)***
Liberty Flags, Waukegan *Also called Seasonal Designs Inc* ***(G-20493)***
Liberty Group Publishing (PA) 309 944-1779
108 W 1st St Geneseo (61254) ***(G-10245)***
Liberty Group Publishing 309 937-3303
119 W Exchange St Cambridge (61238) ***(G-2805)***
Liberty Group Publishing 618 937-2850
111 S Emma St West Frankfort (62896) ***(G-20676)***
Liberty Limestone Inc 815 385-5011
430 W Wegner Rd McHenry (60051) ***(G-13757)***
Liberty Machinery Company 847 276-2761
111 Schelter Rd Lincolnshire (60069) ***(G-12781)***
Liberty Publishing, Macomb *Also called McDonough County Shopper Inc* ***(G-13393)***
Liberty Spclity Stels Amer Inc 847 521-6464
20 N Martingale Rd # 200 Schaumburg (60173) ***(G-18606)***
Liberty Suburban Chicago 630 368-1100
709 Enterprise Dr Oak Brook (60523) ***(G-15635)***
Liberty Systems, Plainfield *Also called Fill-Weigh Inc* ***(G-16665)***
Liberty Tire Recycling LLC 773 871-6360
2044 N Dominick St Chicago (60614) ***(G-5218)***
Libertyville Brewing Company 847 362-6688
345 N Milwaukee Ave Libertyville (60048) ***(G-12668)***
Libertyville Monuments 641 295-3506
120 W Park Ave Libertyville (60048) ***(G-12669)***
Libman Company (PA) 217 268-4200
1 Libman Way Arcola (61910) ***(G-655)***
Liborio Baking Co Inc 708 452-7222
8212 Grand Ave River Grove (60171) ***(G-17061)***
Lice B Gone, Belleville *Also called Safe Effective Alternatives* ***(G-1595)***
Lichtnwald - Johnston Ir Works 847 966-1100
7840 Lehigh Ave Morton Grove (60053) ***(G-14419)***
Lickenbrock & Sons Inc 618 632-4977
328 W State St O Fallon (62269) ***(G-15578)***
Licon Inc 618 485-2222
23297 County Highway 7 Ashley (62808) ***(G-885)***
Liders LLC 312 873-1112
155 N Wacker Dr Ste 4250 Chicago (60606) ***(G-5219)***
Lids Corporation 708 873-9606
416 Orland Square Dr Orland Park (60462) ***(G-15965)***
Liese Lumber Co Inc 618 234-0105
2215 S Belt W Belleville (62226) ***(G-1568)***
Life Fitness Mfg Fcilty, Franklin Park *Also called Kps Capital Partners LP* ***(G-9979)***
Life Fitness US, Franklin Park *Also called Brunswick Corporation* ***(G-9894)***
Life Spine Inc 847 884-6117
13951 Quality Dr Huntley (60142) ***(G-11551)***
Life Tronics International, Chicago *Also called Litetronics Technologies Inc* ***(G-5235)***
Lifeline Scientific Inc (PA) 847 294-0300
1 Pierce Pl Ste 475w Itasca (60143) ***(G-11691)***
Lifetime Creations 708 895-2770
17838 Chappel Ave Lansing (60438) ***(G-12505)***
Lifetime Roof Tile, Naperville *Also called Lifetime Rooftile Company* ***(G-14863)***
Lifetime Rooftile Company (PA) 630 355-7922
1805 High Grove Ln Naperville (60540) ***(G-14863)***
Lifetrients, Lake Bluff *Also called Nourishlife LLC* ***(G-12202)***
Lifewatch Corp (HQ) 847 720-2100
10255 W Higgins Rd # 100 Rosemont (60018) ***(G-18031)***
Lifewatch Services Inc (HQ) 847 720-2100
10255 W Higgins Rd # 100 Rosemont (60018) ***(G-18032)***
Lifewatch Technologies Inc 847 720-2100
10255 W Higgins Rd # 100 Rosemont (60018) ***(G-18033)***
Lifeway Foods Inc (PA) 847 967-1010
6431 Oakton St Morton Grove (60053) ***(G-14420)***
Lifeway Kefir Shop LLC 847 967-1010
6431 Oakton St Morton Grove (60053) ***(G-14421)***
Lift-All Company Inc 800 909-1964
1414 Norwood Ave Itasca (60143) ***(G-11692)***
Lift-All Company Inc 630 534-6860
1620 Fullerton Ct Ste 400 Glendale Heights (60139) ***(G-10468)***
Liftmaster, Oak Brook *Also called Chamberlain Group Inc* ***(G-15606)***
Lifts of Illinois Inc 309 923-7450
415 W Front St Roanoke (61561) ***(G-17103)***
Liftseat Corporation 630 424-2840
2001 Midwest Rd Ste 204 Oak Brook (60523) ***(G-15636)***
Light Efficient Design, Cary *Also called Tadd LLC* ***(G-3194)***
Light Matrix Inc 847 590-0856
339 S Valor Ct Palatine (60074) ***(G-16136)***
Light of Mine LLC 312 840-8570
401 N Michigan Ave # 1200 Chicago (60611) ***(G-5220)***
Light The Lamp Brewery, Grayslake *Also called Colleagues of Beer Inc* ***(G-10762)***
Light Waves LLC 847 251-1622
1000 Skokie Blvd Wilmette (60091) ***(G-21084)***
Lightfoot Technologies Inc 331 302-1297
2135 City Gate Ln Ste 300 Naperville (60563) ***(G-14864)***
Lighthouse Marketing Inc (PA) 949 542-4558
343 W Erie St Ste 320 Chicago (60654) ***(G-5221)***
Lighthouse Marketing Services 630 482-9900
1484 Anderson Rd Elburn (60119) ***(G-8458)***
Lighthouse Printing Inc 708 479-7776
21754 S Center Ave New Lenox (60451) ***(G-15039)***
Lighting Control Systems, West Chicago *Also called Microlite Corporation* ***(G-20617)***
Lighting Innovations Inc 630 889-8100
3609 Swenson Ave Saint Charles (60174) ***(G-18228)***
Lightitech LLC 847 910-4177
200 W Superior St Ste 400 Chicago (60654) ***(G-5222)***
Lightlife Foods Inc (HQ) 413 774-9000
180 E Park Ave Ofc 1 Elmhurst (60126) ***(G-9392)***
Lightning Graphic 815 623-1937
10444 Rock Ln Roscoe (61073) ***(G-17913)***
Lightolier Genlyte Inc 847 364-8250
951 Busse Rd Elk Grove Village (60007) ***(G-9095)***
Lights On Service, Byron *Also called Interntional Metal Finshg Svcs* ***(G-2754)***
Lightscape Inc 847 247-8800
342 4th St Libertyville (60048) ***(G-12670)***
Lightworks Communcation Inc 847 966-1110
5632 Carol Ave Morton Grove (60053) ***(G-14422)***
Ligo Products Inc 708 478-1800
9100 W 191st St Ste 101 Mokena (60448) ***(G-14096)***
Lil Beaver Brewery LLC 309 808-2590
16 Currency Dr Unit B Bloomington (61704) ***(G-2071)***
Lilipi Brands, Vernon Hills *Also called Ileesh Products LLC* ***(G-20062)***
Lilly Air Systems Co Inc 630 773-2225
217 Catalpa Ave Itasca (60143) ***(G-11693)***
Lilly Industries Inc 630 773-2222
427 W Irving Park Rd Itasca (60143) ***(G-11694)***
Lilly Steam Trap, Itasca *Also called Lilly Industries Inc* ***(G-11694)***
Limitless Coffee LLC 630 779-3778
676 N Kingsbury St # 402 Chicago (60654) ***(G-5223)***
Limitless Innovations Inc 855 843-4828
4800 Metalmaster Dr McHenry (60050) ***(G-13758)***
Limitless Sparkling, Chicago *Also called Limitless Coffee LLC* ***(G-5223)***
Lincoln Bark LLC 800 428-4027
858 W Armitage Ave 240 Chicago (60614) ***(G-5224)***
Lincoln Electric Company 630 783-3600
115 E Crlroads Pkwy Ste A Bolingbrook (60440) ***(G-2204)***
Lincoln Generating Fcilty LLC 815 478-3799
27150 S Kankakee St Manhattan (60442) ***(G-13433)***
Lincoln Heritage Winery LLC 618 833-3783
772 Kaolin Rd Cobden (62920) ***(G-6942)***
Lincoln Land Enterprises, Posen *Also called Parts Specialists Inc* ***(G-16800)***
Lincoln Office, Washington *Also called Baker Avenue Investments Inc* ***(G-20266)***
Lincoln Office LLC (PA) 309 427-2500
205 Eastgate Dr Washington (61571) ***(G-20273)***
Lincoln Printers Inc 217 732-3121
711 Broadway St Lincoln (62656) ***(G-12733)***
Lincoln Square Printing 773 334-9030
4607 N Western Ave Fl 1 Chicago (60625) ***(G-5225)***
Lincoln State Steel Div, Rockford *Also called Mc Chemical Company* ***(G-17511)***
Lincolndailynewscom 217 732-7443
601 Keokuk St Lincoln (62656) ***(G-12734)***
Lincolnland Archtctral Grphics 217 629-9009
12 Covered Bridge Acres Glenarm (62536) ***(G-10426)***
Lincolnland Graphics, Glenarm *Also called Lincolnland Archtctral Grphics* ***(G-10426)***
Lincolnshire Printing Inc 815 578-0740
4004 W Dayton St McHenry (60050) ***(G-13759)***
Linda Levinson Designs Inc 312 951-6943
111 E Oak St 3 Chicago (60611) ***(G-5226)***
Linde Gas North America LLC 630 857-6460
2000 S 25th Ave Ste S Broadview (60155) ***(G-2449)***
Linde Gas North America LLC 630 257-3108
810 E 135th St Lockport (60441) ***(G-13006)***
Lindemann Chimney Co, Lake Bluff *Also called Lindemann Chimney Service Inc* ***(G-12193)***
Lindemann Chimney Service Inc (PA) 847 918-7994
86 Albrecht Dr Lake Bluff (60044) ***(G-12193)***
Lindgren Family LLC 630 307-7200
400 High Grove Blvd Glendale Heights (60139) ***(G-10469)***
Lindsay Metal Madness Inc 815 568-4560
13706 Washington St Woodstock (60098) ***(G-21406)***
Lindstrand Balloons USA, Galena *Also called A R B C Inc* ***(G-10163)***
Lindstrom Farm, Varna *Also called Brian Lindstrom* ***(G-20031)***
Line Craft Inc 630 932-1182
10 W North Ave Lombard (60148) ***(G-13095)***
Line Craft Tool Company Inc 630 932-1182
10 W North Ave Lombard (60148) ***(G-13096)***
Line Group Inc (PA) 847 593-6810
539 W Algonquin Rd Arlington Heights (60005) ***(G-769)***
Line of Advance Nfp 312 768-0043
2126 W Armitage Ave Apt 3 Chicago (60647) ***(G-5227)***
Line Tool & Stamping Co, Arlington Heights *Also called Line Group Inc* ***(G-769)***
Linear Kinetics Inc 630 365-0075
48 W 989 Rr 64 Maple Park (60151) ***(G-13463)***
Linear Solutions Inc 724 426-6384
1727 S Ind Ave Apt 211 Chicago (60616) ***(G-5228)***

Linear Technology LLC 847 925-0860
2040 E Algonquin Rd Schaumburg (60173) ***(G-18607)***
Liners Direct, Roselle *Also called Bathwraps* ***(G-17939)***
Lingle Design Group Inc 815 369-9155
158 W Main St Lena (61048) ***(G-12605)***
Link Media Florida LLC 815 224-4742
2968 Saint Vincent Ave La Salle (61301) ***(G-12117)***
Link Tools Intl (usa) Inc 773 549-3000
2440 N Lakeview Ave Chicago (60614) ***(G-5229)***
Linkedhealth Solutions 312 600-6684
700 N Green St Chicago (60642) ***(G-5230)***
Linmore Publishing Co 847 382-7606
409 South St Barrington (60010) ***(G-1224)***
Linn West Paper Company 773 561-3839
4649 N Magnolia Ave Chicago (60640) ***(G-5231)***
Linne Machine Company Inc 217 446-5746
209 Avenue C Danville (61832) ***(G-7359)***
Linpac Ropak Packaging Central, Elk Grove Village *Also called Ropak Central Inc* ***(G-9221)***
Lintec of America Inc 847 229-0547
935 National Pkwy # 93553 Schaumburg (60173) ***(G-18608)***
Linx Enterprises LLC 224 409-2206
5051 S Forrestville Ave Chicago (60615) ***(G-5232)***
Linx Global Mfg LLC 847 910-5303
4809 N Ravenswood Ave Chicago (60640) ***(G-5233)***
Linz Electric Inc 847 595-1473
3005 Commercial Ave Northbrook (60062) ***(G-15419)***
Lion Concrete Products Inc 630 892-7304
111 N Railroad St Montgomery (60538) ***(G-14257)***
Lion Ornamental Concrete Pdts, Montgomery *Also called Lion Concrete Products Inc* ***(G-14257)***
Lion Tool & Die Co 847 658-8898
910 W Algonquin Rd Algonquin (60102) ***(G-377)***
Lion Trans Group Inc 970 402-8073
5300 Carriageway Dr Rolling Meadows (60008) ***(G-17748)***
Lionheart Critical Pow 847 291-1413
13151 Executive Ct Huntley (60142) ***(G-11552)***
Lipscomb Engineering Inc 630 231-3833
1215 W Washington St West Chicago (60185) ***(G-20608)***
Liqua Fit Inc (PA) 630 965-8067
100 N Atkinson Rd Ste 102 Grayslake (60030) ***(G-10787)***
Liquid Controls LLC (HQ) 847 295-1050
105 Albrecht Dr Lake Bluff (60044) ***(G-12194)***
Liquid Lf Sprators Systems Div, Aurora *Also called Thomas Pump Company* ***(G-1023)***
Liquid Resin International 618 392-3590
4295 N Holly Rd Olney (62450) ***(G-15869)***
Liquidfire 312 376-7448
8554 W Rascher Ave Apt 2n Chicago (60656) ***(G-5234)***
Liquitech Inc 630 693-0500
421 Eisenhower Ln S Lombard (60148) ***(G-13097)***
Liquitube Industries LLC 618 985-4445
721 E Herrin St Herrin (62948) ***(G-11174)***
Litania Sports Group Inc 217 367-8438
601 Mercury Dr Champaign (61822) ***(G-3317)***
Litchfield News Herald Inc 217 324-2121
112 E Ryder St Litchfield (62056) ***(G-12972)***
Literacy Resources LLC 708 366-5947
711 South Blvd Ste 12 Oak Park (60302) ***(G-15763)***
Litestage Lighting Systems, Bensenville *Also called Formco Plastics Inc* ***(G-1801)***
Litetronics Technologies Inc 708 333-6707
6969 W 73rd St Chicago (60638) ***(G-5235)***
Lith Liqure 847 458-5180
461 N Randall Rd Lake In The Hills (60156) ***(G-12339)***
Litho Research Incorporated 630 860-7070
1600 Glenlake Ave Itasca (60143) ***(G-11695)***
Litho Type LLC 708 895-3720
16710 Chicago Ave Lansing (60438) ***(G-12506)***
Lithographic Industries Inc 773 921-7955
2445 Gardner Rd Broadview (60155) ***(G-2450)***
Lithotype Company Inc 630 771-1920
594 Territorial Dr Ste G Bolingbrook (60440) ***(G-2205)***
Lithuanian Catholic Press 773 585-9500
4545 W 63rd St Chicago (60629) ***(G-5236)***
Lithuanian Press Inc 773 776-3399
2711 W 71st St Chicago (60629) ***(G-5237)***
Litt Aluminium & Shtmtl Co 708 366-4720
9825 W Roosevelt Rd Westchester (60154) ***(G-20703)***
Littelfuse Inc (PA) 773 628-1000
8755 W Higgins Rd Ste 500 Chicago (60631) ***(G-5238)***
Littelfuse Inc 773 628-1000
8755 W Higgins Rd Ste 300 Chicago (60631) ***(G-5239)***
Littell LLC 630 916-6662
1211 Tower Rd Schaumburg (60173) ***(G-18609)***
Littell International Inc 630 622-4950
1211 Tower Rd Schaumburg (60173) ***(G-18610)***
Little Creek Woodworking 217 543-2815
1473 Cr 1675e Arthur (61911) ***(G-866)***
Little Egypt Gas A & Wldg Sups 618 937-2271
10603 Bencie Ln West Frankfort (62896) ***(G-20677)***
Little Giant, University Park *Also called Brennan Equipment and Mfg Inc* ***(G-19950)***
Little Journeys Limited 847 677-0350
7914 Kildare Ave Skokie (60076) ***(G-18980)***
Little Lady Foods Inc (PA) 847 806-1440
2323 Pratt Blvd Elk Grove Village (60007) ***(G-9096)***
Little Miss Muffin, Lincolnshire *Also called Doughnut Boy* ***(G-12760)***
Little River Research & Design, Carbondale *Also called Steve C Gough* ***(G-2860)***
Little Shop of Papers Ltd 847 382-7733
740 W Northwest Hwy Barrington (60010) ***(G-1225)***
Little Village Printing Inc 708 749-4414
3210 Grove Ave Apt 2w Berwyn (60402) ***(G-1955)***
Liturgical Conference 847 866-3875
1125 Wilmette Ave Wilmette (60091) ***(G-21085)***
Litwiller Machine and Supply, Tremont *Also called K R J Inc* ***(G-19897)***
Liv Labs Inc 630 373-1471
5516 S Everett Ave 2nd Chicago (60637) ***(G-5240)***
Live Daily LLC 312 286-6706
2627 W Lunt Ave Chicago (60645) ***(G-5241)***
Live Wire & Cable Co 847 577-5483
409 W University Dr Arlington Heights (60004) ***(G-770)***
Liveone Inc 312 282-2320
333 N Michigan Ave # 2800 Chicago (60601) ***(G-5242)***
Living Laminates Inc 847 741-2004
50w485 Il Route 64 Maple Park (60151) ***(G-13464)***
Living Royal 312 906-7600
500 Quail Hollow Dr Wheeling (60090) ***(G-20933)***
Living Royal Inc 312 906-7600
333 W Hintz Rd Wheeling (60090) ***(G-20934)***
Livingston Innovations LLC 847 808-0900
3242 W Monroe St Waukegan (60085) ***(G-20459)***
Livingston Products Inc 847 808-0900
3242 W Monroe St Waukegan (60085) ***(G-20460)***
Livorsi Marine Inc 847 548-5900
715 Center St Grayslake (60030) ***(G-10788)***
Lixi Inc 630 620-4646
1438 Brook Dr Downers Grove (60515) ***(G-8045)***
Lizotte Sheet Metal Inc 618 656-3066
632 W Schwarz St Edwardsville (62025) ***(G-8368)***
Lj Fabricators, Rockford *Also called L/J Fabricators Inc* ***(G-17489)***
Ljm Equipment Co 847 291-0162
205 Huehl Rd Northbrook (60062) ***(G-15420)***
Lkq Corporation (PA) 312 621-1950
500 W Madison St Ste 2800 Chicago (60661) ***(G-5243)***
LL Display Group Ltd 847 982-0231
5414 W Roosevelt Rd B Chicago (60644) ***(G-5244)***
LL Electronics 217 586-6477
103 S Prairieview Rd Mahomet (61853) ***(G-13425)***
Lla Exploration Inc 217 623-4096
1747 N 800 East Rd Taylorville (62568) ***(G-19758)***
LLC Urban Farmer 815 468-7200
1551 N Boudreau Rd Manteno (60950) ***(G-13451)***
Lli Architectural Lighting LLC 847 412-4880
1555 Barclay Blvd Buffalo Grove (60089) ***(G-2564)***
Lllb LLC 630 315-3300
1200 Thorndale Ave Elk Grove Village (60007) ***(G-9097)***
Lloyd M Hughes Enterprises Inc 773 363-6331
6331 S Martin L King Dr Chicago (60637) ***(G-5245)***
Lloyd Midwest Graphics 815 282-8828
7103 N 2nd St Machesney Park (61115) ***(G-13357)***
LMD Industries Inc 630 383-9546
316 Hemlock Ct Oswego (60543) ***(G-16011)***
Lmk Technologies LLC 815 433-1275
1779 Chessie Ln Ottawa (61350) ***(G-16059)***
Lmno Technologies LLC 773 418-2875
1720 S Michigan Ave # 25 Chicago (60616) ***(G-5246)***
Lmpl Management Corporation 708 636-2443
5757 W 95th St Ste 3 Oak Lawn (60453) ***(G-15725)***
LMS Innovations Inc 312 613-2345
2734 W Leland Ave Apt 3 Chicago (60625) ***(G-5247)***
Lmsys, Chicago *Also called World Class Technologies Inc* ***(G-6672)***
Lmt Inc 217 568-8265
1105 Se 2nd St Galva (61434) ***(G-10235)***
Lmt Onsrud LP 847 362-1560
1081 S Northpoint Blvd Waukegan (60085) ***(G-20461)***
Lmt Usa Inc 630 969-5412
1081 S Northpoint Blvd Waukegan (60085) ***(G-20462)***
Ln Engineering LLC 815 472-2939
125 Gladiolus St Ste A Momence (60954) ***(G-14187)***
Lo Riser Trailers, Kewanee *Also called Advance Metalworking Company* ***(G-12019)***
Lo-Ko Performance Coatings 708 424-7863
5340 W 111th St Ste 1 Oak Lawn (60453) ***(G-15726)***
Load Redi Inc 217 784-4200
1124 S Sangamon Ave Gibson City (60936) ***(G-10340)***
Loadsys Consulting Inc 708 873-1750
5645 Gatehouse Way Bourbonnais (60914) ***(G-2265)***
Local 46 Training Program Tr 217 528-4041
2888 E Cook St Springfield (62703) ***(G-19399)***
Local Wine Tours, Lake Bluff *Also called Terlato Wine Group Ltd* ***(G-12210)***
Localfix Solutions LLC 312 569-0619
26w194 Prestwick Ln Winfield (60190) ***(G-21112)***

ALPHABETIC

Loch Precision Technologies....847 438-1400
1215 Berkley Rd Lake Zurich (60047) ***(G-12429)***
Lochman Ref Silk Screen Co....847 475-6266
2405 Oakton St Evanston (60202) ***(G-9547)***
Lock & Roll Trailer Hitch, Chicago *Also called Great Lakes Forge Company* ***(G-4735)***
Locker Room Screen Printing....630 759-2533
253 S Schmidt Rd Bolingbrook (60440) ***(G-2206)***
Lockheed Martin Corporation....618 628-0700
4 Eagle Ctr Ste 1 O Fallon (62269) ***(G-15579)***
Locknut Technology Inc....630 628-5330
351 S Lombard Rd Addison (60101) ***(G-184)***
Lockport Fish Pantry....815 588-3543
604 E 9th St Lockport (60441) ***(G-13007)***
Lockport Steel Fabricators LLC....815 726-6281
3051 S State St Lockport (60441) ***(G-13008)***
Lockwood Custom Optics Inc....217 684-2170
648 County Road 1700 E Philo (61864) ***(G-16607)***
Locodocs Inc (PA)....815 448-2100
1000 Front St Mazon (60444) ***(G-13682)***
Locusview Solutions Inc....312 548-3848
626 W Randolph St Chicago (60661) ***(G-5248)***
Loda Electronics Co....217 386-2554
307 S Elm St Loda (60948) ***(G-13029)***
Lodaat LLC (PA)....630 248-2380
1415 W 22nd St Ste Tower Oak Brook (60523) ***(G-15637)***
Lodaat LLC....630 852-7544
410 40th St Downers Grove (60515) ***(G-8046)***
Lodan Electronics Inc....847 398-5311
3311 N Kennicott Ave Arlington Heights (60004) ***(G-771)***
Loders Croklaan BV....815 730-5200
24708 W Durkee Rd Channahon (60410) ***(G-3386)***
Loders Croklaan Usa LLC....815 730-5200
24708 W Durkee Rd Channahon (60410) ***(G-3387)***
Loeb Oil, Lawrenceville *Also called Herman L Loeb LLC* ***(G-12535)***
Loeffel Steel Products Inc (PA)....847 382-6770
27951 W Industrial Ave Lake Barrington (60010) ***(G-12158)***
Lofthouse Bakery Products Inc....630 455-5229
3250 Lacey Rd Ste 600 Downers Grove (60515) ***(G-8047)***
Logan Actuator Co....815 943-9500
550 Chippewa Rd Harvard (60033) ***(G-11059)***
Logan Graphic Products Inc....847 526-5515
1100 Brown St Wauconda (60084) ***(G-20369)***
Logan Mason Rehabilitation, Lincoln *Also called Mental Health Ctrs Centl Ill* ***(G-12735)***
Logan Square Aluminum Sup Inc....847 985-1700
1450 Mitchell Blvd Schaumburg (60193) ***(G-18611)***
Logan Square Aluminum Sup Inc....847 676-4767
4767 W Touhy Ave Lincolnwood (60712) ***(G-12828)***
Logan Square Aluminum Sup Inc....773 278-3600
2622 N Pulaski Rd Chicago (60639) ***(G-5249)***
Logic Printing, Downers Grove *Also called S G S Inc* ***(G-8088)***
Logical Design Solutions Inc....630 786-5999
280 Shuman Blvd Ste 106 Naperville (60563) ***(G-14865)***
Logicds, Naperville *Also called Logical Design Solutions Inc* ***(G-14865)***
Logicgate Inc....312 279-2775
320 W Ohio St Ste 5e Chicago (60654) ***(G-5250)***
Logicon Group LLC....618 558-7757
100 Traver Tine Cir Millstadt (62260) ***(G-14049)***
Logistic Department, Lisle *Also called Molex LLC* ***(G-12912)***
Logo Wear Unlimited Inc....309 367-2333
104 S Menard St Metamora (61548) ***(G-13962)***
Logo Works....815 942-4700
824 Liberty St Ste A Morris (60450) ***(G-14310)***
Logo's & More, Breese *Also called Illinois Embroidery Service* ***(G-2304)***
Logoplaste Chicago LLC....815 230-6961
14420 N Van Dyke Rd Plainfield (60544) ***(G-16684)***
Logoplaste Fort Worth LLC....815 230-6961
14420 N Van Dyke Rd Plainfield (60544) ***(G-16685)***
Logoplaste Racine LLC....815 230-6961
14420 N Van Dyke Rd Plainfield (60544) ***(G-16686)***
Logoplaste Usa Inc (HQ)....815 230-6961
14420 N Van Dyke Rd Plainfield (60544) ***(G-16687)***
Logoskirt Corporation....773 584-7300
4500 W 46th St Chicago (60632) ***(G-5251)***
Lohr Quarry, Godfrey *Also called Kimmaterials Inc* ***(G-10655)***
Lokman Enterprises Inc....773 654-0525
7240 N Ridge Blvd Apt 102 Chicago (60645) ***(G-5252)***
Lom, Chicago *Also called Light of Mine LLC* ***(G-5220)***
Lombard Archtctral Prcast Pdts....708 389-1060
4245 W 123rd St Chicago (60803) ***(G-5253)***
Lombard Investment Company (PA)....708 389-1060
4245 W 123rd St Alsip (60803) ***(G-469)***
Lombard Swiss Screw Company....630 576-5096
420 S Rohlwing Rd Addison (60101) ***(G-185)***
London Shoe Shop & Western Wr....618 345-9570
125 W Main St Collinsville (62234) ***(G-6966)***
Lone Star Industries Inc....815 883-3173
490 Portland Ave Oglesby (61348) ***(G-15843)***
Lone Wolf Portable Treestand, Brimfield *Also called Oak Leaf Outdoors Inc* ***(G-2407)***
Lonelino Sign Company Inc....217 243-2444
2122 E Morton Ave Jacksonville (62650) ***(G-11773)***
Lonelybrand LLC (PA)....312 880-7506
118 W Kinzie St Chicago (60654) ***(G-5254)***
Loneoak Timber & Veneere Co....618 426-3065
45 Longhorn Trl Ava (62907) ***(G-1174)***
Long Construction Services....217 443-2876
617 1/2 E Voorhees St Danville (61832) ***(G-7360)***
Long Elevator and Mch Co Inc (HQ)....217 629-9648
2908 Old Rochester Rd Springfield (62703) ***(G-19400)***
Long Grove Apple Haus, Long Grove *Also called Mangel and Co* ***(G-13162)***
Long Grove Confectionery Co (PA)....847 459-3100
333 Lexington Dr Buffalo Grove (60089) ***(G-2565)***
Long Screw, Loves Park *Also called Lsl Precision Machining Inc* ***(G-13234)***
Long View Publishing Co Inc....773 446-9920
3339 S Halsted St Ste 4 Chicago (60608) ***(G-5255)***
Long Wolf Express Inc....708 673-1583
16260 Louis Ave South Holland (60473) ***(G-19230)***
Lonnie Hickam....618 893-4223
2726 Sadler Rd Pomona (62975) ***(G-16763)***
Lonza LLC....309 697-7200
8316 W Route 24 Mapleton (61547) ***(G-13475)***
Loomcraft Textile & Supply Co....847 680-0000
647 Lakeview Pkwy Vernon Hills (60061) ***(G-20073)***
Loop Attachment Co....847 922-0642
1509 N Hudson Ave Apt 3 Chicago (60610) ***(G-5256)***
Loop Automotive LLC....847 912-9090
303 W Ohio St Apt 2609 Chicago (60654) ***(G-5257)***
Loop Belt Industries Inc....630 469-1300
21w171 Hill Ave Glen Ellyn (60137) ***(G-10410)***
Loose Petals, Chicago *Also called Karen Young* ***(G-5081)***
Lopez Plumbing Systems Inc....773 424-8225
5816 S Claremont Ave Chicago (60636) ***(G-5258)***
Loraines Logistics LLC....800 839-6943
1014 N Mason Ave 2 Chicago (60651) ***(G-5259)***
Lorbern Mfg Inc....847 301-8600
708 Morse Ave Schaumburg (60193) ***(G-18612)***
Lordahl Engineering, Long Grove *Also called Lordahl Manufacturing Co* ***(G-13161)***
Lordahl Engineering Co, Waukegan *Also called Lordahl Manufacturing Co* ***(G-20463)***
Lordahl Manufacturing Co (PA)....847 244-0448
1001 S Lewis Ave Waukegan (60085) ***(G-20463)***
Lordahl Manufacturing Co....847 244-0448
1571 Rfd Long Grove (60047) ***(G-13161)***
Lorette Dies Inc....630 279-9682
246 E 2nd St Elmhurst (60126) ***(G-9393)***
Lorton Group LLC....844 352-5089
940 Seneca Rd Wilmette (60091) ***(G-21086)***
Los Angelos Times, Chicago *Also called Los Angles Tmes Cmmnctions LLC* ***(G-5260)***
Los Angles Tmes Cmmnctions LLC....312 467-4670
435 N Michigan Ave Fl 2 Chicago (60611) ***(G-5260)***
Los Gamas Inc....872 829-3514
3333 W Armitage Ave Chicago (60647) ***(G-5261)***
Los Mangos....815 630-2611
1701 N Larkin Ave Crest Hill (60403) ***(G-7091)***
Los Mangos....773 542-1522
3058 S Avers Ave Chicago (60623) ***(G-5262)***
Los Mangos I, Chicago *Also called Los Mangos* ***(G-5262)***
Los Primos Pallets Inc....773 418-3584
2013 W Ferdinand St Chicago (60612) ***(G-5263)***
Loso Trucking Inc....312 601-2231
55 E Monroe St Ste 3800 Chicago (60603) ***(G-5264)***
Lothson Guitars....815 756-2031
10580 Keslinger Rd Dekalb (60115) ***(G-7688)***
Lottobot LLC....773 909-6656
1116 W Hubbard St Apt 4e Chicago (60642) ***(G-5265)***
Lotton Art Glass Co....708 672-1400
24760 S Country Ln Crete (60417) ***(G-7141)***
Lottus Inc....847 691-9464
3216 Ronald Rd Glenview (60025) ***(G-10585)***
Lotus Creative Innovations LLC....815 440-8999
970 Melugins Grove Rd Compton (61318) ***(G-6997)***
Louis J Hansen Enterprises Inc....630 956-3765
1500 Dearborn Ave Ste 12a Aurora (60505) ***(G-1124)***
Louis Marsch Inc....217 526-3723
601 Carlin St Morrisonville (62546) ***(G-14351)***
Louis Meskan Aluminum & Brass....773 637-8236
2000 N Parkside Ave Chicago (60639) ***(G-5266)***
Louis Meskan Brass Foundry Inc....773 237-7662
2007 N Major Ave Chicago (60639) ***(G-5267)***
Louisville Ladder Inc....309 692-1895
7921 N Hale Ave Peoria (61615) ***(G-16470)***
Louvers International Inc....630 782-9977
851 N Church Ct Elmhurst (60126) ***(G-9394)***
Love Journey Inc....773 447-5591
8121 S Colfax Ave Chicago (60617) ***(G-5268)***
Love Joy Technology, Downers Grove *Also called Powdered Metal Tech LLC* ***(G-8080)***
Love ME Tenders LLC....773 502-8000
833 Laurel Ave Unit 202 Highland Park (60035) ***(G-11282)***

ALPHABETIC SECTION

Lovejoy Inc (HQ) 630 852-0500
  2655 Wisconsin Ave Downers Grove (60515) *(G-8048)*
Lovejoy Industries Inc (PA) 859 873-6828
  3610 Commercial Ave Northbrook (60062) *(G-15421)*
Loves Travel Stops 618 931-1575
  1201 Denham Dr Granite City (62040) *(G-10720)*
Loyalty Publishing Inc 309 693-0840
  4414 Entec Dr Bartonville (61607) *(G-1334)*
Loyola Paper Company 847 956-7770
  951 Lunt Ave Elk Grove Village (60007) *(G-9098)*
Loyola Press 800 621-1008
  3441 N Ashland Ave Chicago (60657) *(G-5269)*
LP Software Inc 708 361-4310
  15255 S 94th Ave Ste 500 Orland Park (60462) *(G-15966)*
LPI Worldwide Inc 773 826-8600
  4821 S Aberdeen St Chicago (60609) *(G-5270)*
Lpz Inc 773 579-6120
  2919 S Western Ave Chicago (60608) *(G-5271)*
Lre, Schaumburg Also called Legend Racing Enterprises Inc *(G-18602)*
Lre Products Inc 630 238-8321
  733 Maple Ln Bensenville (60106) *(G-1845)*
Lrwmotivequest, Chicago Also called Motivequest LLC *(G-5506)*
Lsa United Inc 773 476-7439
  1020 E Emerson Ave Lombard (60148) *(G-13098)*
Lsc Communications Inc (PA) 773 272-9200
  191 N Wacker Dr Ste 1400 Chicago (60606) *(G-5272)*
Lsc Communications Inc 217 258-2832
  6821 E County Road 1100n Mattoon (61938) *(G-13641)*
Lsc Communications Mm LLC 815 844-1819
  191 N Wacker Dr Ste 1400 Chicago (60606) *(G-5273)*
Lsc Communications Us LLC (HQ) 844 572-5720
  191 N Wacker Dr Ste 1400 Chicago (60606) *(G-5274)*
Lsc Communications Us LLC 815 844-5181
  1600 N Main St Pontiac (61764) *(G-16774)*
Lsc Communications Us LLC 217 235-0561
  6821 1100n Mattoon (61938) *(G-13642)*
Lsk Import 847 342-8447
  100 S Wacker Dr Ste 700 Chicago (60606) *(G-5275)*
Lsl Healthcare, Niles Also called Lsl Industries Inc *(G-15141)*
Lsl Industries Inc 773 878-1100
  6200 W Howard St Niles (60714) *(G-15141)*
Lsl Precision Machining Inc 815 633-4701
  2210 Nimtz Rd Loves Park (61111) *(G-13234)*
Lsp Industries Inc (PA) 815 226-8090
  5060 27th Ave Rockford (61109) *(G-17497)*
Lssp Corporation 630 428-0099
  4300 Commerce Ct Lisle (60532) *(G-12909)*
Lt Construction 815 243-6807
  1288 Anee Dr Rockford (61108) *(G-17498)*
Lt Security Inc 630 348-8088
  1459 Elmhurst Rd Elk Grove Village (60007) *(G-9099)*
Ltb Graphics Inc 630 238-1754
  749 N Edgewood Ave Wood Dale (60191) *(G-21208)*
Ltc Holdings Inc 847 249-5900
  3021 N Delany Rd Waukegan (60087) *(G-20464)*
Lte-Little Timber Enterprises 224 321-0361
  1331 Carriage Ln Lake Villa (60046) *(G-12358)*
Lub-Tek Petroleum Products (PA) 815 741-0414
  2439 Reeves Rd Joliet (60436) *(G-11895)*
Lube Rite 217 267-7766
  802 S State St Westville (61883) *(G-20781)*
Lubeq Corporation 847 931-1020
  1380 Gateway Dr Ste 6 Elgin (60124) *(G-8642)*
Luby Publishing Inc 312 341-1110
  55 E Jackson Blvd Ste 401 Chicago (60604) *(G-5276)*
Lucas Coatings, Alsip Also called RM Lucas Co *(G-504)*
Luck E Strike Corporation 630 313-2408
  2100 Enterprise Ave Geneva (60134) *(G-10289)*
Luck E Strike USA, Geneva Also called Luck E Strike Corporation *(G-10289)*
Lucksfood 773 878-7778
  1109 W Argyle St Chicago (60640) *(G-5277)*
Lucky Games Inc 773 549-9051
  574 Alice Dr Northbrook (60062) *(G-15422)*
Lucky Yuppy Puppy Co 847 437-7879
  533 W Golf Rd Arlington Heights (60005) *(G-772)*
Luckyprints, Chicago Also called American Enlightenment LLC *(G-3652)*
Lucmia Enterprises Inc 800 785-3157
  8308 Fullerton Ave River Grove (60171) *(G-17062)*
Luco Mop Company 217 235-1992
  1200 Moultrie Ave Mattoon (61938) *(G-13643)*
Lucrezia F. O'Brien, Naperville Also called Lucrezia LLC *(G-14866)*
Lucrezia LLC 630 263-0088
  7 Baker Ln Naperville (60565) *(G-14866)*
Ludis Foods Adams Inc 312 939-2877
  23 E Adams St Chicago (60603) *(G-5278)*
Ludwig Medical Inc 217 342-6570
  1010 N Parkview St Effingham (62401) *(G-8408)*
Luebbers Welding & Mfg Inc 618 594-2489
  2420 Old State Rd Carlyle (62231) *(G-2893)*

Luke Graphics Inc 773 775-6733
  6000 N Northwest Hwy Chicago (60631) *(G-5279)*
Lulus 773 865-8978
  2401 S Ridgeway Ave Chicago (60623) *(G-5280)*
Lulus Real Froyo 630 299-3854
  1147 N Eola Rd Aurora (60502) *(G-999)*
Lumberyard Suppliers Inc 217 965-4911
  700 S Springfield St Virden (62690) *(G-20187)*
Lumen Technologies Inc 708 363-7758
  423 N Emery Ln Elmhurst (60126) *(G-9395)*
Lumenart Lighting Solutions, Chicago Also called Lumenart Ltd *(G-5281)*
Lumenart Ltd 773 254-0744
  3333 W 47th St Chicago (60632) *(G-5281)*
Lumenite Control Technology 847 455-1450
  2331 17th St Franklin Park (60131) *(G-9982)*
Lumenite Electronic, Franklin Park Also called Lumenite Control Technology *(G-9982)*
Lumentum Operations LLC 408 546-5483
  33186 Collection Ctr Dr Chicago (60693) *(G-5282)*
Lumina Inc 312 829-8970
  512 N Racine Ave Chicago (60642) *(G-5283)*
Luminaid Lab LLC 312 600-8997
  211 W Wacker Dr Chicago (60606) *(G-5284)*
Luminescence Media Group Nfp 312 602-3302
  3740 N Lake Shore Dr Chicago (60613) *(G-5285)*
Luminex Corporation 847 400-9000
  4088 Commercial Ave Northbrook (60062) *(G-15423)*
Lumos Holdings US Acquisition (HQ) 847 288-3300
  9525 Bryn Mawr Ave Rosemont (60018) *(G-18034)*
Luna Azul Communications Inc 773 616-0007
  1340 Hackberry Rd Deerfield (60015) *(G-7630)*
Luna Medical Inc 800 380-4339
  1057 W Grand Ave Ste 1 Chicago (60642) *(G-5286)*
Lund Industries Inc 847 459-1460
  3175 Macarthur Blvd Northbrook (60062) *(G-15424)*
Lundbeck LLC (HQ) 847 282-1000
  6 Parkway North Blvd # 400 Deerfield (60015) *(G-7631)*
Lundbeck Pharmaceuticals LLC 847 282-1000
  6 Parkway North Blvd # 400 Deerfield (60015) *(G-7632)*
Lundmark Inc 630 628-1199
  350 S La Londe Ave Addison (60101) *(G-186)*
Lundmark Wax Co, Addison Also called Lundmark Inc *(G-186)*
Lunquist Manufacturing Corp 815 874-2437
  5681 11th St Rockford (61109) *(G-17499)*
Luon Energy LLC 217 419-2678
  605 Buttercup Dr Savoy (61874) *(G-18415)*
Lure Group LLC 630 222-6515
  5 Privett Ct Bolingbrook (60490) *(G-2207)*
Luse Thermal Technologies LLC 630 862-2600
  3990 Enterprise Ct Aurora (60504) *(G-1000)*
Luster Leaf Products Inc (PA) 815 337-5560
  1961 Dillard Ct Woodstock (60098) *(G-21407)*
Luster Products Inc (PA) 773 579-1800
  1104 W 43rd St Chicago (60609) *(G-5287)*
Lutamar Electrical Assemblies 847 679-5400
  8030 Ridgeway Ave Skokie (60076) *(G-18981)*
Lutheran Church-Missouri Synod 630 607-0300
  1200 Jorie Blvd Ste 308 Oak Brook (60523) *(G-15638)*
Lutheran General Printing Svcs 847 298-8040
  799 Biermann Ct Ste 130 Mount Prospect (60056) *(G-14544)*
Lutheran Magazine, Chicago Also called Evang Lthn Ch Dr Mrtn Luth KG *(G-4535)*
Luthers Form Grinding Company, Loves Park Also called Lah Inc *(G-13231)*
Luttrell Engraving Inc 708 489-3800
  5000 W 128th Pl Alsip (60803) *(G-470)*
Lutz Corp 800 203-7740
  208 N Parkside Rd Normal (61761) *(G-15208)*
Lutz Sales Company, Schaumburg Also called Trellborg Sling Sltions US Inc *(G-18753)*
Luvo Usa LLC (PA) 847 485-8595
  2095 Hammond Dr Schaumburg (60173) *(G-18613)*
Luvo Usa LLC 847 485-8595
  2095 Hammond Dr Schaumburg (60173) *(G-18614)*
Luxe Classic Kitchens & Interi 630 774-9337
  135 E Van Emmon St Ste 1 Yorkville (60560) *(G-21492)*
Luxfer Graphic Arts, Madison Also called Elektron N Magnesium Amer Inc *(G-13410)*
Luxis International Inc 800 240-1473
  1292 S 7th St Dekalb (60115) *(G-7689)*
Luxo Corporation 914 345-0067
  1125 Alexander Ct Cary (60013) *(G-3176)*
Luxon Printing Inc 630 293-7710
  375 Wegner Dr West Chicago (60185) *(G-20609)*
Luxurious Lathers Ltd 844 877-7627
  15 Spinning Wheel Rd Hinsdale (60521) *(G-11369)*
Luxury Bath Systems, Streator Also called Murray Cabinetry & Tops Inc *(G-19616)*
Luxury Living Inc 847 845-3863
  5 Tamarack Ct Cary (60013) *(G-3177)*
Luxury MBL & Gran Design Inc 773 656-2125
  3206 N Kilpatrick Ave Chicago (60641) *(G-5288)*
Luxury Upgrade Inc 773 875-8018
  987 W Happfield Dr Arlington Heights (60004) *(G-773)*

Lv Ventures Inc (PA).....312 993-1800
440 S La Salle St Chicago (60605) ***(G-5289)***
Lv Ventures Inc.....312 993-1758
440 S La Salle St Chicago (60605) ***(G-5290)***
Lx/Jt Intermediate Holdings (PA).....773 369-2652
4401 S Oakley Ave Chicago (60609) ***(G-5291)***
Lyko Woodworking & Cnstr.....773 583-4561
4157 N Elston Ave Chicago (60618) ***(G-5292)***
Lyle James.....217 675-2191
880 S Main St Jacksonville (62650) ***(G-11774)***
Lynda Hervas.....847 985-1690
800 Morse Ave Schaumburg (60193) ***(G-18615)***
Lynfred Winery Inc (PA).....630 529-9463
15 S Roselle Rd Roselle (60172) ***(G-17965)***
Lynk Labs Inc.....847 783-0123
2511 Tech Dr Ste 108 Elgin (60124) ***(G-8643)***
Lynn Electronics Corp.....972 412-7240
386 Internationale Dr H Bolingbrook (60440) ***(G-2208)***
Lynns Printing Co.....618 465-7701
3050 Homer M Adams Pkwy Alton (62002) ***(G-564)***
Lyon LLC (HQ).....630 892-8941
420 N Main St Montgomery (60538) ***(G-14258)***
Lyon LLC.....815 432-4595
475 N Veterans Pkwy Watseka (60970) ***(G-20309)***
Lyon & Dittrich Holding Co, Montgomery *Also called L & D Group Inc* ***(G-14252)***
Lyon & Healy Harps Inc.....312 786-1881
168 N Ogden Ave Chicago (60607) ***(G-5293)***
Lyon & Healy Holding Corp (HQ).....312 786-1881
168 N Ogden Ave Chicago (60607) ***(G-5294)***
Lyon LLC.....217 465-6321
13571 Il Highway 133 Paris (61944) ***(G-16232)***
Lyon Workspace Products Inc.....630 892-8941
420 N Main St Montgomery (60538) ***(G-14259)***
Lyondell Chemical Company.....815 942-7011
8805 Tabler Rd Morris (60450) ***(G-14311)***
Lyondllbsell Advnced Plymers I.....847 426-3350
400 Maple Ave Ste A Carpentersville (60110) ***(G-3107)***
Lyre Glass Press LLC.....847 834-9643
3616 Glenlake Dr Glenview (60026) ***(G-10586)***
M & A Grocery.....708 749-9786
6719 Pershing Rd Stickney (60402) ***(G-19543)***
M & B Services Ltd Inc.....217 463-2162
213 E Union St Paris (61944) ***(G-16233)***
M & B Supply Inc.....309 944-3206
208 W 1st St Geneseo (61254) ***(G-10246)***
M & C Powersports.....207 713-3128
1548 S 6th Ave Kankakee (60901) ***(G-11990)***
M & D Industries Inc.....847 362-8720
1821 Industrial Dr Libertyville (60048) ***(G-12671)***
M & D Printing Div, Effingham *Also called Kingery Printing Company* ***(G-8405)***
M & D Supplies, Gilman *Also called Gregory Martin* ***(G-10379)***
M & F Fabrication & Welding.....217 457-2221
2243 Mud Creek Rd Concord (62631) ***(G-6998)***
M & G Graphics Inc.....773 247-1596
3500 W 38th St Chicago (60632) ***(G-5295)***
M & G Simplicitees.....224 372-7426
39420 N Il Route 59 # 4 Lake Villa (60046) ***(G-12359)***
M & I Acid Company Inc.....618 676-1638
1107 S Main St Clay City (62824) ***(G-6907)***
M & I Heating and Cooling Inc.....773 743-7073
6405 N Campbell Ave Chicago (60645) ***(G-5296)***
M & J Manufacturing Co Inc.....847 364-6066
1450 Jarvis Ave Elk Grove Village (60007) ***(G-9100)***
M & L Well Service Inc.....618 393-7144
3648 N Illinois 130 Olney (62450) ***(G-15870)***
M & L Well Service Inc.....618 395-4538
800 E Main St Olney (62450) ***(G-15871)***
M & M Exposed Aggregate Co.....847 551-1818
155 S Washington St Carpentersville (60110) ***(G-3108)***
M & M Paltech Inc.....630 350-7890
860 E Jackson St Belvidere (61008) ***(G-1681)***
M & M Patio Stone Company, Carpentersville *Also called M & M Exposed Aggregate Co* ***(G-3108)***
M & M Pump Co.....217 935-2517
404 S Portland Pl Apt 2 Clinton (61727) ***(G-6926)***
M & M Tooling Inc.....630 595-8834
395 E Potter St Wood Dale (60191) ***(G-21209)***
M & M Welding Inc.....815 895-3955
410 N Main St Sycamore (60178) ***(G-19723)***
M & N Dental.....815 678-0036
9716 Ill Route 12 Richmond (60071) ***(G-17017)***
M & R Custom Millwork Inc.....815 547-8549
1979 Belford North Dr Belvidere (61008) ***(G-1682)***
M & R Graphics Inc.....708 534-6621
2401 Bond St University Park (60484) ***(G-19957)***
M & R Media Inc.....847 884-6300
1084 National Pkwy Schaumburg (60173) ***(G-18616)***
M & R Precision Machining Inc.....847 364-1050
680 Lively Blvd Elk Grove Village (60007) ***(G-9101)***
M & R Printing Inc.....847 398-2500
5100 Newport Dr Ste 4 Rolling Meadows (60008) ***(G-17749)***
M & R Printing Equipment Inc (HQ).....630 858-6101
440 Medinah Rd Roselle (60172) ***(G-17966)***
M & R Sales and Service, Roselle *Also called M & R Printing Equipment Inc* ***(G-17966)***
M & S Industrial Co Inc.....773 252-1616
4334 W Division St Chicago (60651) ***(G-5297)***
M & S Oil Well Cementing Co (PA).....618 262-7962
Hwy 1 N Mount Carmel (62863) ***(G-14478)***
M & S Technologies Inc.....847 763-0500
5715 W Howard St Niles (60714) ***(G-15142)***
M & W Curios, Xenia *Also called Brenda Miller* ***(G-21467)***
M & W Feed Service.....815 858-2412
201 S Ash St Elizabeth (61028) ***(G-8787)***
M & W Gear Company, Gibson City *Also called Rhinoag Inc* ***(G-10343)***
M & W Grinding of Rockford.....815 874-9481
4697 Hydraulic Rd Rockford (61109) ***(G-17500)***
M A I, Carol Stream *Also called Media Associates Intl Inc* ***(G-3022)***
M and M Box Partition Co.....773 276-8400
4141 W Grand Ave Chicago (60651) ***(G-5298)***
M and M Pallet Inc.....708 272-4447
2810 Vermont St Blue Island (60406) ***(G-2130)***
M B E, Gilberts *Also called R & I Ornamental Iron Inc* ***(G-10366)***
M B Jewelers Inc.....312 853-3490
29 E Madison St Ste 1835 Chicago (60602) ***(G-5299)***
M Buckman & Son Co.....815 663-9411
200 S Greenwood St Spring Valley (61362) ***(G-19309)***
M C F Printing Company.....630 279-0301
118 S York St Ste 212 Elmhurst (60126) ***(G-9396)***
M C S Inc.....708 323-9233
7230 171st St Unit 344 Tinley Park (60477) ***(G-19845)***
M C Steel Inc.....847 350-9618
43160 N Crawford Rd Antioch (60002) ***(G-623)***
M CA Chicago.....312 384-1220
7065 Veterans Blvd Burr Ridge (60527) ***(G-2697)***
M Cor Inc.....630 860-1150
227 James St Ste 6 Bensenville (60106) ***(G-1846)***
M D Harmon Inc (PA).....618 662-8925
752 Jupiter Dr Xenia (62899) ***(G-21468)***
M E Barber Co Inc.....217 428-4591
1660 S Taylorville Rd Decatur (62521) ***(G-7518)***
M E F Corp.....815 965-8604
1614 Christina St Rockford (61104) ***(G-17501)***
M G A, Gurnee *Also called Metropolitan Graphic Arts Inc* ***(G-10896)***
M G M Displays Inc.....708 594-3699
4956 S Monitor Ave Chicago (60638) ***(G-5300)***
M H Detrick Company.....708 479-5085
7231 W Laraway Rd Frankfort (60423) ***(G-9814)***
M H Electric Motor & Ctrl Corp.....630 393-3736
30w250 Calumet Ave W Warrenville (60555) ***(G-20242)***
M I E America Inc.....847 981-6100
420 Bennett Rd Elk Grove Village (60007) ***(G-9102)***
M I L, Elk Grove Village *Also called Magnetic Inspection Lab Inc* ***(G-9106)***
M I T Financial Group Inc.....847 205-3000
900 Skokie Blvd Ste 200 Northbrook (60062) ***(G-15425)***
M Inc.....312 853-0512
205 W Wacker Dr Ste 307 Chicago (60606) ***(G-5301)***
M J Burton Engraving Co.....217 223-7273
824 Maine St Quincy (62301) ***(G-16908)***
M J Celco Inc (PA).....847 671-1900
3900 Wesley Ter Schiller Park (60176) ***(G-18818)***
M J Kull LLC.....217 246-5952
1911 3rd St Lerna (62440) ***(G-12614)***
M J Molding, Hebron *Also called Sherwood Tool Inc* ***(G-11149)***
M K Advantage Inc.....773 902-5272
1055 W Bryn Mawr Ave F216 Chicago (60660) ***(G-5302)***
M L Rongo Inc.....630 540-1120
1281 Humbracht Cir Ste A Bartlett (60103) ***(G-1294)***
M L S Printing Co Inc.....847 948-8902
537 Hermitage Dr Deerfield (60015) ***(G-7633)***
M Lizen Manufacturing Co.....708 755-7213
2625 Federal Signal Dr University Park (60484) ***(G-19958)***
M M Marketing.....815 459-7968
522 S Rand Rd Wauconda (60084) ***(G-20370)***
M Martinez Inc.....847 740-6364
828 Warrior St Round Lake Heights (60073) ***(G-18094)***
M Mauritzon & Company Inc.....773 235-6000
3939 W Belden Ave Chicago (60647) ***(G-5303)***
M O W Printing Inc.....618 345-5525
526 Vandalia St Collinsville (62234) ***(G-6967)***
M P I Labels Systems, University Park *Also called Miller Products Inc* ***(G-19962)***
M Putterman & Co LLC (HQ).....773 927-4120
815 W Van Buren St # 550 Chicago (60607) ***(G-5304)***
M R C, Oak Brook *Also called Michaels Ross and Cole Inc* ***(G-15644)***
M R Glenn Electric Inc.....708 479-9200
200 W 6th St Lockport (60441) ***(G-13009)***
M R O Solutions LLC.....847 588-2480
5645 W Howard St Niles (60714) ***(G-15143)***

M S —action Machining Corp.......815 344-3770
4061 W Dayton St McHenry (60050) ***(G-13760)***
M S A Printing Co.......847 593-5699
850 Touhy Ave Elk Grove Village (60007) ***(G-9103)***
M S Tool & Engineering.......630 876-3437
1200 Atlantic Dr West Chicago (60185) ***(G-20610)***
M SM, Sterling *Also called Westwood Machine & Tool Co* ***(G-19542)***
M T E Hydraulics, Rockford *Also called Mechanical Tool & Engrg Co* ***(G-17514)***
M T I Industries, Volo *Also called Marine Technologies Inc* ***(G-20203)***
M Ward Manufacturing Co Inc.......847 864-4786
2222 2230 Main St Evanston (60202) ***(G-9548)***
M Wells Printing Co.......312 455-0400
329 W 18th St Ste 502 Chicago (60616) ***(G-5305)***
M&J Hauling Inc.......312 342-6596
2048 W Hubbard St Chicago (60612) ***(G-5306)***
M&M Mars, Chicago *Also called Mars Chocolate North Amer LLC* ***(G-5347)***
M&M Restaurant Group LLC.......773 253-5326
1463 W Leland Ave Chicago (60640) ***(G-5307)***
M&R Holdings Inc (PA).......630 858-6101
440 Medinah Rd Roselle (60172) ***(G-17967)***
M&R Printing, Roselle *Also called M&R Holdings Inc* ***(G-17967)***
M-1 Tool Works Inc.......815 344-1275
1419 S Belden St McHenry (60050) ***(G-13761)***
M-Prime Company.......630 834-9400
649 N Ardmore Ave Villa Park (60181) ***(G-20157)***
M-Tek, Elgin *Also called Middleby Packg Solutions LLC* ***(G-8662)***
M-Wave Controls LLC (PA).......630 562-5550
100 High Grove Blvd Glendale Heights (60139) ***(G-10470)***
M-Wave International LLC.......630 562-5550
100 High Grove Blvd Glendale Heights (60139) ***(G-10471)***
M.S.i, Broadview *Also called Multi Swatch Corporation* ***(G-2456)***
M.S.I., Addison *Also called Mexacali Silkscreen Inc* ***(G-201)***
M13 Graphics, Schaumburg *Also called M13 Inc* ***(G-18617)***
M13 Inc.......847 310-1913
1300 Basswood Rd Ste 100 Schaumburg (60173) ***(G-18617)***
M2m Enterprises LLC.......847 899-7565
361 N Alfred Ave Elgin (60123) ***(G-8644)***
M4 Steel LLC.......309 222-6027
1208 Dorchester Ct Washington (61571) ***(G-20274)***
Maac Machinery Co Inc.......630 665-1700
590 Tower Blvd Carol Stream (60188) ***(G-3019)***
Maasdam Pow'r-Pull, Schaumburg *Also called Pullr Holding Company LLC* ***(G-18688)***
Maass - Midwest Mfg Inc (PA).......847 669-5135
11283 Dundee Rd Huntley (60142) ***(G-11553)***
Maass Midwest, Huntley *Also called Maass - Midwest Mfg Inc* ***(G-11553)***
Mab Equipment Company.......630 551-4017
51 Stonehill Rd Oswego (60543) ***(G-16012)***
Mab Pharmacy Inc.......773 342-5878
2724 W Division St Ste A Chicago (60622) ***(G-5308)***
Mac American Corporation.......847 277-9450
530 Fox Glen Ct Barrington (60010) ***(G-1226)***
Mac Construction.......618 541-4092
10 Pine St Millstadt (62260) ***(G-14050)***
Mac Graphics Group Inc.......630 620-7200
17w703 Butterfield Rd D Oakbrook Terrace (60181) ***(G-15806)***
Mac Lean-Fogg Company (PA).......847 566-0010
1000 Allanson Rd Mundelein (60060) ***(G-14710)***
Mac Medical Inc.......618 719-6757
325 W Main St Belleville (62220) ***(G-1569)***
MAC Medical Inc.......618 476-3550
820 S Mulberry St Millstadt (62260) ***(G-14051)***
Mac Plastics Manufacturing Inc.......618 392-3010
715 N West St Olney (62450) ***(G-15872)***
Mac Ster Inc.......847 359-3640
724 W Peregrine Dr Palatine (60067) ***(G-16137)***
Mac's Snacks, Chicago *Also called Evans Foods Inc* ***(G-4537)***
Mac-Ster Inc.......847 830-7013
1420 W Bernard Dr Addison (60101) ***(G-187)***
Mac-Weld Inc.......618 529-1828
612 San Diego Rd Carbondale (62901) ***(G-2850)***
Mac-Weld Partnership, Carbondale *Also called Mac-Weld Inc* ***(G-2850)***
Macari Appliance Center, Shelbyville *Also called Macari Service Center Inc* ***(G-18881)***
Macari Service Center Inc (PA).......217 774-4214
502 N Peter St Ste A Shelbyville (62565) ***(G-18881)***
Maccarb Inc.......877 427-2499
2430 Millennium Dr Elgin (60124) ***(G-8645)***
Mace Iron Works Inc (PA).......708 479-2456
221 Industry Ave Frankfort (60423) ***(G-9815)***
Mach Mechanical Group LLC.......630 674-6224
28w016 Country View Dr Naperville (60564) ***(G-14978)***
Mach Mining LLC.......618 983-3020
16468 Liberty School Rd Marion (62959) ***(G-13520)***
Machine & Design.......630 858-6416
767 Willis St Glen Ellyn (60137) ***(G-10411)***
Machine Control Systems Inc (PA).......708 389-2160
12424 S Austin Ave Palos Heights (60463) ***(G-16190)***
Machine Control Systems Inc.......708 597-1200
12549 S Laramie Ave Alsip (60803) ***(G-471)***
Machine Job Shop, Milan *Also called Gett Industries Ltd* ***(G-14012)***
Machine Medics LLC.......309 633-5454
5726 W Plank Rd Peoria (61604) ***(G-16471)***
Machine Solution Providers Inc.......630 717-7040
2659 Wisconsin Ave Downers Grove (60515) ***(G-8049)***
Machine Tech Services, Marseilles *Also called Machine Technology Inc* ***(G-13560)***
Machine Technology Inc.......815 444-4837
221 Erick St Crystal Lake (60014) ***(G-7221)***
Machine Technology Inc (PA).......815 795-6818
1020 Broadway St Marseilles (61341) ***(G-13560)***
Machine Tool Acc & Mfg Co.......773 489-0903
1915 W Fullerton Ave Chicago (60614) ***(G-5309)***
Machine Tool Bearing & ACC Inc.......847 357-1793
590 Bonnie Ln Elk Grove Village (60007) ***(G-9104)***
Machine Tools Div., Addison *Also called Mitsubishi Heavy Inds Amer Inc* ***(G-220)***
Machine Works of Decatur Inc.......217 428-3896
2035 E Garfield Ave Decatur (62526) ***(G-7519)***
Machined Concepts LLC.......847 708-4923
1760 Britannia Dr Ste 8 Elgin (60124) ***(G-8646)***
Machined Metals Manufacturing.......847 364-6116
1450 Jarvis Ave Elk Grove Village (60007) ***(G-9105)***
Machined Products, Elk Grove Village *Also called Fabricated Metals Co* ***(G-8994)***
Machining Systems Corporation.......708 385-7903
14003 Kostner Ave Crestwood (60418) ***(G-7122)***
Machining Technology Inc.......815 469-0400
418 Keepataw Dr Lemont (60439) ***(G-12570)***
Macholl Metal Fabrication.......815 597-1908
6934 Garden Prairie Rd Garden Prairie (61038) ***(G-10237)***
Mackenzie Johnson.......630 244-2367
1826 S 10th Ave Maywood (60153) ***(G-13672)***
Macklin Inc (PA).......815 562-4803
6089 Dement Rd Rochelle (61068) ***(G-17147)***
Maclean Fastener Services LLC.......847 353-8402
355 W Dundee Rd Ste 105 Buffalo Grove (60089) ***(G-2566)***
Maclean Fasteners, Mundelein *Also called Mac Lean-Fogg Company* ***(G-14710)***
Maclean Senior Industries LLC.......630 350-1600
610 Pond Dr Wood Dale (60191) ***(G-21210)***
Maclee Chemical Company Inc.......847 480-0953
1316 Edgewood Ln Northbrook (60062) ***(G-15426)***
Maclen-Fogg Cmpnent Sltons LLC (HQ).......248 853-2525
1000 Allanson Rd Mundelein (60060) ***(G-14711)***
Maco Antennas, Mount Carroll *Also called Charles Electronics LLC* ***(G-14494)***
Maco Business Forms, Peoria *Also called Proform* ***(G-16503)***
Maco-Sys LLC.......779 888-3260
3415 Precision Dr B Rockford (61109) ***(G-17502)***
Macomb Concrete Products Inc.......309 772-3826
11 Hillcrest Dr Bushnell (61422) ***(G-2743)***
Macon Construction, Bradford *Also called Macon Gc LLC* ***(G-2275)***
Macon Gc LLC.......309 897-8216
201 Bonita Ave Bradford (61421) ***(G-2275)***
Macon Resources Inc.......217 875-1910
2121 Hubbard Ave Decatur (62526) ***(G-7520)***
Macon Sand & Gravel, Decatur *Also called Legacy Vulcan LLC* ***(G-7516)***
Macoupin County Enquirer Inc.......217 854-2534
125 E Main St Carlinville (62626) ***(G-2879)***
Macoupin Energy LLC.......217 854-3291
14300 Brushy Mound Rd Carlinville (62626) ***(G-2880)***
Macoupin Energy LLC.......217 854-3291
14300 Brushy Mound Rd Carlinville (62626) ***(G-2881)***
Madden Communications Inc (PA).......630 787-2200
901 Mittel Dr Wood Dale (60191) ***(G-21211)***
Madden Communications Inc.......630 784-4325
355 Longview Dr Bloomingdale (60108) ***(G-1998)***
Madden Ventures Inc.......847 487-0644
1045 Campus Dr Ste A Mundelein (60060) ***(G-14712)***
Made As Intended Inc.......630 789-3494
3423 Spring Rd Oak Brook (60523) ***(G-15639)***
Made By Hands Inc.......773 761-4200
3501 N Southport Ave # 352 Chicago (60657) ***(G-5310)***
Made Rite Bedding Company.......847 349-5886
11221 Melrose Ave Franklin Park (60131) ***(G-9983)***
Mademoiselle Inc.......773 394-4555
4200 W Schubert Ave Chicago (60639) ***(G-5311)***
Madison Capital Partners Corp (PA).......312 277-0323
500 W Madison St Ste 3890 Chicago (60661) ***(G-5312)***
Madison Farms Butter Company (PA).......217 854-2547
1100 Broadway Carlinville (62626) ***(G-2882)***
Madison Inds Holdings LLC (PA).......312 277-0156
500 W Madison St Ste 3890 Chicago (60661) ***(G-5313)***
Mafomsic Incorporated.......630 279-2005
756 N Industrial Dr Elmhurst (60126) ***(G-9397)***
Mag Daddy LLC.......847 719-5600
278 Jamie Ln Wauconda (60084) ***(G-20371)***
Mag MO Systems.......815 625-0125
302 Wallace St Sterling (61081) ***(G-19514)***
Magazine Plus.......773 281-4106
2445 N Clark St Chicago (60614) ***(G-5314)***
Magenta LLC (PA).......773 777-5050
15160 New Ave Lockport (60441) ***(G-13010)***

ALPHABETIC

(PA)=Parent Co (HQ)=Headquarters (DH)=Div Headquarters
2020 Harris Illinois Industrial Directory
1183

Magic Mist, The, Lincolnshire *Also called Paralleldirect LLC* ***(G-12791)***
Magic Mold Removal 630 486-0912
689 Wood St Aurora (60505) ***(G-1125)***
Magic Solutions Inc 312 647-8688
5455 N Sheridan Rd # 3809 Chicago (60640) ***(G-5315)***
Magick Woods Inc 630 229-0121
1600 Sequoia Dr Aurora (60506) ***(G-1126)***
Magid Glove Safety Mfg Co LLC (PA) 773 384-2070
1300 Naperville Dr Romeoville (60446) ***(G-17844)***
Magid Glove Safety Mfg Co LLC 773 384-2070
1805 N Hamlin Ave Chicago (60647) ***(G-5316)***
Magiglide, Mokena *Also called Landquist & Son Inc* ***(G-14094)***
Magna Exteriors America Inc 779 552-7400
675 Corporate Pkwy Belvidere (61008) ***(G-1683)***
Magna Exteriors America Inc 618 327-4381
18310 Enterprise Ave Nashville (62263) ***(G-14999)***
Magna Exteriors America Inc 618 327-2136
18355 Enterprise Ave Nashville (62263) ***(G-15000)***
Magna-Flux International 815 623-7634
11898 Burnside Ln Roscoe (61073) ***(G-17914)***
Magneco Inc (HQ) 630 543-6660
223 W Interstate Rd Addison (60101) ***(G-188)***
Magneco Inc 630 543-6660
206 W Factory Rd Addison (60101) ***(G-189)***
Magneco/Metrel Inc (PA) 630 543-6660
223 W Interstate Rd Addison (60101) ***(G-190)***
Magnet-Schultz Amer Holdg LLC (HQ) 630 789-0600
401 Plaza Dr Westmont (60559) ***(G-20755)***
Magnet-Schultz America Inc 630 789-0600
401 Plaza Dr Westmont (60559) ***(G-20756)***
Magnetec Inspection Inc (PA) 815 802-1363
1159 E North St Bradley (60915) ***(G-2286)***
Magnetic Coil Manufacturing Co 630 787-1948
325 Beinoris Dr Ste A Wood Dale (60191) ***(G-21212)***
Magnetic Devices Inc 815 459-0077
150 Virginia Rd Ste 5 Crystal Lake (60014) ***(G-7222)***
Magnetic Inspection Lab Inc 847 437-4488
1401 Greenleaf Ave Elk Grove Village (60007) ***(G-9106)***
Magnetic Occasions & More Inc 815 462-4141
21605 S Schoolhouse Rd New Lenox (60451) ***(G-15040)***
Magnetic Signs 773 476-6551
4922 S Western Ave Chicago (60609) ***(G-5317)***
Magnetrol International Inc (PA) 630 723-6600
705 Enterprise St Aurora (60504) ***(G-1001)***
Magnetstreet, Carol Stream *Also called Master Marketing Intl Inc* ***(G-3021)***
Magnify Peace, Chicago *Also called Dove Foundation* ***(G-4390)***
Magnum International Inc 708 889-9999
1965 Bernice Rd Ste 2se Lansing (60438) ***(G-12507)***
Magnum Machining LLC 815 862-2040
11427 Coml Ave Unit 19 Richmond (60071) ***(G-17018)***
Magnum Steel Works Inc 618 244-5190
200 Shiloh Dr Mount Vernon (62864) ***(G-14622)***
Magnus Screw Products Co 773 889-2344
1818 N Latrobe Ave Chicago (60639) ***(G-5318)***
Magnuson Group Inc 630 783-8100
1400 Internationale Pkwy Woodridge (60517) ***(G-21320)***
Magrabar LLC 847 965-7550
6100 Madison Ct Morton Grove (60053) ***(G-14423)***
Magros Processing 217 438-2880
3150 Stanton St Springfield (62703) ***(G-19401)***
Mah Machine Company 708 656-1826
3301 S Central Ave Cicero (60804) ***(G-6864)***
Mahans Fiberglass 309 562-7349
106 E Main St Easton (62633) ***(G-8330)***
Maher Publications Inc 630 941-2030
102 N Haven Rd Elmhurst (60126) ***(G-9398)***
Mahoney Asphalt, Swansea *Also called Charles E Mahoney Company* ***(G-19690)***
Mahoney Environmental Inc (PA) 815 730-2087
712 Essington Rd Joliet (60435) ***(G-11896)***
Mahoney Foundries Inc 309 784-2311
29 N Main St Vermont (61484) ***(G-20037)***
Mahoney Publishing Inc 815 369-5384
707 Maple St Lena (61048) ***(G-12606)***
MAI Apparel, Oak Brook *Also called Made As Intended Inc* ***(G-15639)***
Maid O Mist LLC 773 685-7300
3217 N Pulaski Rd Chicago (60641) ***(G-5319)***
Maiers Bakery 847 967-8042
9328 Waukegan Rd Morton Grove (60053) ***(G-14424)***
Mail Box Store, The, Bethalto *Also called Eagle Express Mail LLC* ***(G-1964)***
Mailbox Plus 847 577-1737
1516 N Elmhurst Rd Mount Prospect (60056) ***(G-14545)***
Mailcrafters, Midlothian *Also called Inscerco Mfg Inc* ***(G-13992)***
Mailers Company, Elk Grove Village *Also called Pulver Inc* ***(G-9202)***
Main Office, Ramsey *Also called G L Beaumont Lumber Company* ***(G-16964)***
Main Source Machining 815 962-8770
2411 Latham St Rockford (61103) ***(G-17503)***
Main Steel - Corporate 6001, Elk Grove Village *Also called Main Steel Polishing Co Inc* ***(G-9107)***
Main Steel Polishing Co Inc (PA) 847 916-1220
2200 Pratt Blvd Elk Grove Village (60007) ***(G-9107)***
Main Street Market Roscoe Inc 815 623-6328
9515 N 2nd St Roscoe (61073) ***(G-17915)***
Main Street Meat Co, Roscoe *Also called Main Street Market Roscoe Inc* ***(G-17915)***
Main Street Records 618 244-2737
313 S 10th St Mount Vernon (62864) ***(G-14623)***
Main Street Visuals Inc 847 869-7446
8340 Callie Ave Unit 110 Morton Grove (60053) ***(G-14425)***
Main Surplus Store, Aurora *Also called Johnos Inc* ***(G-1119)***
Mainstream Renewable Power 815 379-2784
108 Jackson St Walnut (61376) ***(G-20219)***
Maintenance Inc 708 598-1390
11055 80th Pl La Grange (60525) ***(G-12082)***
Maintenance Tech Training, Willowbrook *Also called Applied Tech Publications Inc* ***(G-21029)***
Majestic Archtctural Wdwrk Inc 708 240-8484
2150 Madison St Bellwood (60104) ***(G-1632)***
Majestic Spring Inc 847 593-8887
1390 Jarvis Ave Elk Grove Village (60007) ***(G-9108)***
Majesty Cases Inc 847 546-2558
34550 N Wilson Rd Ingleside (60041) ***(G-11587)***
Major Die & Engineering Co 630 773-3444
1352 Industrial Dr Itasca (60143) ***(G-11696)***
Major Wire Incorporated 708 457-0121
7014 W Cullom Ave Norridge (60706) ***(G-15239)***
Mak Design Group Incorporated 847 682-4504
1023 W 55th St Ste A Countryside (60525) ***(G-7063)***
Mak-System Corp 847 803-4863
2720 S River Rd Ste 225 Des Plaines (60018) ***(G-7799)***
Makerite Mfg Co Inc 815 389-3902
13571 Metric Rd Roscoe (61073) ***(G-17916)***
Makers Mark Distillery Inc 312 964-6999
222 Merchandise Mart Plz # 1600 Chicago (60654) ***(G-5320)***
Makkah Printing 630 980-2315
1979 Bloomingdale Rd Glendale Heights (60139) ***(G-10472)***
Mako Mold Corporation 630 377-9010
3820 Ohio Ave Ste 7 Saint Charles (60174) ***(G-18229)***
Mako Networks Sales & Mktg Inc 847 752-5566
1355 N Mclean Blvd Elgin (60123) ***(G-8647)***
Makowskis Real Sausage Co 312 842-5330
2710 S Poplar Ave Chicago (60608) ***(G-5321)***
Makray Manufacturing Company (PA) 708 456-7100
4400 N Harlem Ave Norridge (60706) ***(G-15240)***
Makray Manufacturing Company 847 260-5408
9515 Seymour Ave Schiller Park (60176) ***(G-18819)***
Malca-Amit North America Inc 312 346-1507
5 S Wabash Ave Ste 1414 Chicago (60603) ***(G-5322)***
Malcolite Corporation (PA) 847 562-1350
1161 Lake Cook Rd Ste I Deerfield (60015) ***(G-7634)***
Mall Graphic Inc 847 668-7600
12693 Cold Springs Dr Huntley (60142) ***(G-11554)***
Mall Publishing, Huntley *Also called Mall Graphic Inc* ***(G-11554)***
Mallard Handling Solutions LLC (PA) 815 625-9491
101 Mallard Rd Sterling (61081) ***(G-19515)***
Mallard Manufacturing, Sterling *Also called Mallard Handling Solutions LLC* ***(G-19515)***
Mallardtone Game Calls 309 798-2481
10406 96th Street Ct W Taylor Ridge (61284) ***(G-19746)***
Mallof Abruzino Nash Mktg Inc 630 929-5200
765 Kimberly Dr Carol Stream (60188) ***(G-3020)***
Malthandlingcom LLC 773 888-7718
800 N Winthrop Ave S 2 Chicago (60660) ***(G-5323)***
Malvaes Solutions Incorporated 773 823-1034
4243 W Ogden Ave Chicago (60623) ***(G-5324)***
Mama Bosso Pizza, Rock Island *Also called Afs Classico LLC* ***(G-17200)***
Mamagreen LLC (PA) 312 953-3557
222 Merchandise Mart Plz 1519a Chicago (60654) ***(G-5325)***
Mamagreen Sstnble Otdoor Lxury, Chicago *Also called Mamagreen LLC* ***(G-5325)***
Mamata Enterprises Inc (HQ) 941 205-0227
2275 Cornell Ave Montgomery (60538) ***(G-14260)***
Man Marketing, Carol Stream *Also called Mallof Abruzino Nash Mktg Inc* ***(G-3020)***
Managed Marketing Inc 847 279-8260
2232 Foster Ave Wheeling (60090) ***(G-20935)***
Manan Medical Products Inc (HQ) 847 637-3333
241 W Palatine Rd Wheeling (60090) ***(G-20936)***
Manan Tool & Manufacturing 847 637-3333
241 W Palatine Rd Wheeling (60090) ***(G-20937)***
Manchester Tank & Equipment Co 217 224-7600
3400 Wisman Ln Quincy (62301) ***(G-16909)***
Mancillas International Ltd (PA) 847 441-7748
47 Longmeadow Rd Winnetka (60093) ***(G-21132)***
Mancillas Intl, Winnetka *Also called Mancillas International Ltd* ***(G-21132)***
Mancuso Cheese Company 815 722-2475
612 Mills Rd Ste 1 Joliet (60433) ***(G-11897)***
Mandel Metals Inc (PA) 847 455-6606
11400 Addison Ave Franklin Park (60131) ***(G-9984)***
Mandis Dental Laboratory 618 345-3777
607 Vandalia St Ste 300 Collinsville (62234) ***(G-6968)***
Mandus Group LLC 309 786-1507
2408 4th Ave Rock Island (61201) ***(G-17228)***

ALPHABETIC SECTION

Mandys Soul Food Kitchen LLC 630 485-7291
   431u N Bolingbrook Dr Bolingbrook (60440) *(G-2209)*
Mangel & Co, Buffalo Grove *Also called Long Grove Confectionery Co (G-2565)*
Mangel and Co (PA) 847 459-3100
   333 Lexington Dr Buffalo Grove (60089) *(G-2567)*
Mangel and Co 847 634-0730
   230 Rbert Prker Coffin Rd Long Grove (60047) *(G-13162)*
Mangelsdorf Seed Co, Teutopolis *Also called Siemer Enterprises Inc (G-19772)*
Mangold Networks 224 402-0068
   1068 Bayside Rd Elgin (60123) *(G-8648)*
Manhattan Eyelash EXT Sew On 847 818-8774
   8 S Dunton Ave Arlington Heights (60005) *(G-774)*
Manhattan Island 312 762-5152
   209 S Lasalle Ste 1200 Chicago (60604) *(G-5326)*
Manhattan Mechanical Svcs LLC 815 478-9940
   25630 S Gougar Rd 3 Manhattan (60442) *(G-13434)*
Manitex International Inc (PA) 708 430-7500
   9725 Industrial Dr Bridgeview (60455) *(G-2361)*
Manitou Americas Inc 262 334-9461
   888 Landmark Dr Belvidere (61008) *(G-1684)*
Manitowoc Lifts and Mfg LLC 815 748-9500
   155 Harvestore Dr Dekalb (60115) *(G-7690)*
Mann+hummel Filtration Tech 800 407-9263
   4500 Prime Pkwy McHenry (60050) *(G-13762)*
Mann+hummel Filtration Technol 815 759-7744
   1380 Corporate Dr McHenry (60050) *(G-13763)*
Manner Plating Inc 815 877-7791
   926 River Ln Loves Park (61111) *(G-13235)*
Manor Tool and Mfg Co (PA) 847 678-2020
   9200 Ivanhoe St Schiller Park (60176) *(G-18820)*
Manroland Goss Web Systems Int (HQ) 630 796-7560
   9018 Heritage Pkwy # 1200 Woodridge (60517) *(G-21321)*
Manroland Inc (HQ) 630 920-2000
   800 E Oakhill Dr Westmont (60559) *(G-20757)*
Manroland Websystems, Westmont *Also called Manroland Inc (G-20757)*
Manscore LLC 630 297-7502
   1239 Gilbert Ave Downers Grove (60515) *(G-8050)*
Manseemanwant LLC 217 610-8888
   4055 W Jefferson St Springfield (62707) *(G-19402)*
Manteno Metal Works 815 468-6128
   4192 E 7000n Rd Manteno (60950) *(G-13452)*
Manteno Quarry, Manteno *Also called Legacy Vulcan LLC (G-13450)*
Manticore Arms Inc 630 715-0334
   747 Herra St Unit A Elburn (60119) *(G-8459)*
Manu Industries Inc 847 891-6412
   977 Lunt Ave Schaumburg (60193) *(G-18618)*
Manu-TEC of Illinois LLC 630 543-3022
   415 W Belden Ave Ste E Addison (60101) *(G-191)*
Manufactured Specialties Inc 630 444-1992
   3575 Stern Ave Saint Charles (60174) *(G-18230)*
Manufacturers Alliance Corp 847 696-1600
   320 W Saint Charles Rd Villa Park (60181) *(G-20158)*
Manufacturers Custom Products 630 988-5055
   3510 Hobson Rd Ste 101c Woodridge (60517) *(G-21322)*
Manufacturers News Inc 847 864-7000
   1633 Central St Evanston (60201) *(G-9549)*
Manufacturing Tech Group Inc 815 966-2300
   3520 N Main St Rockford (61103) *(G-17504)*
Manufasteners House Iq Inc 847 705-6538
   427 S Middleton Ave Palatine (60067) *(G-16138)*
Manufctrers Clring Hse III Inc (PA) 773 545-6300
   4875 N Elston Ave Chicago (60630) *(G-5327)*
Manufctring Mint Solutions Inc 309 263-6077
   14646 Watson Rd Pekin (61554) *(G-16343)*
Manufctrng-Resourcing Intl Inc 217 821-3733
   5265 E 1800th Ave Shumway (62461) *(G-18904)*
Manufcture Dsign Innvation Inc 773 526-7773
   1760 Metoyer Ct Unit F West Chicago (60185) *(G-20611)*
Map Oil Co Inc 618 375-7616
   139 County Road 990 E Grayville (62844) *(G-10813)*
Mapei Corporation 630 293-5800
   430 Industrial Dr West Chicago (60185) *(G-20612)*
Mapei Corporation 630 293-5800
   530 Industrial Dr West Chicago (60185) *(G-20613)*
Mapes & Sprowl LLC 847 364-0055
   1100 E Devon Ave Elk Grove Village (60007) *(G-9109)*
Mapes & Sprowl Steel LLC 800 777-1025
   1100 E Devon Ave Elk Grove Village (60007) *(G-9110)*
Maple Hill Creamery LLC (PA) 518 758-7777
   540 Lake Cook Rd Ste 120 Deerfield (60015) *(G-7635)*
Maple Park Landscape Supplies, Maple Park *Also called Maple Park Trucking Inc (G-13465)*
Maple Park Trucking Inc 815 899-1958
   50w 363 Isle Rr 64 St 50 Maple Park (60151) *(G-13465)*
Maplehurst Farms Inc (PA) 815 562-8723
   936 S Moore Rd Rochelle (61068) *(G-17148)*
Mar Cor Purification Inc 630 435-1017
   2850 Hitchcock Ave Downers Grove (60515) *(G-8051)*
Mar Graphics 618 935-2111
   523 S Meyer Ave Valmeyer (62295) *(G-20009)*

Maranatha Christian Revival Ch, Chicago *Also called Marantha Wrld Rvval Ministries (G-5328)*
Marantha Wrld Rvval Ministries (PA) 773 384-7717
   4301 W Diversey Ave Chicago (60639) *(G-5328)*
Marathon Cutting Die Inc 847 398-5165
   2340 Foster Ave Wheeling (60090) *(G-20938)*
Marathon Gas, Rolling Meadows *Also called 4200 Kirchoff Corp (G-17707)*
Marathon Manufacturing Inc 630 543-6262
   110 W Laura Dr Addison (60101) *(G-192)*
Marathon Petroleum Company LP 618 544-2121
   400 S Marathon Ave Robinson (62454) *(G-17119)*
Marathon Petroleum Company LP 618 829-3288
   200 E 4th St Saint Elmo (62458) *(G-18309)*
Marathon Technologies Inc 847 378-8572
   800 Nicholas Blvd Elk Grove Village (60007) *(G-9111)*
Marbil Enterprises Inc 618 257-1810
   129 Wild Rose Dr Belleville (62221) *(G-1570)*
Marble Emporium Inc (PA) 847 205-4000
   2200 Carlson Dr Northbrook (60062) *(G-15427)*
Marble Machine Inc (PA) 217 431-3014
   21204 Rileysburg Rd Danville (61834) *(G-7361)*
Marble Machine Inc 217 442-0746
   205 Oakwood Ave Danville (61832) *(G-7362)*
Marble Works, South Elgin *Also called Wienmar Inc (G-19181)*
Marc Business Forms Inc 847 568-9200
   6416 N Ridgeway Ave Lincolnwood (60712) *(G-12829)*
Marca Industries Inc (PA) 773 884-4500
   5901 W 79th St 400 Burbank (60459) *(G-2636)*
Marcal Rope & Rigging Inc (PA) 618 462-0172
   1862 E Broadway Alton (62002) *(G-565)*
Marcells Pallet Inc (PA) 773 265-1200
   4221 W Ferdinand St Chicago (60624) *(G-5329)*
March Industries Inc 224 654-6500
   150 Arrowhead Dr Hampshire (60140) *(G-10978)*
March Manufacturing Inc (PA) 847 729-5300
   1819 Pickwick Ln Glenview (60026) *(G-10587)*
March Pumps, Glenview *Also called March Manufacturing Inc (G-10587)*
Marco Lighting Components Inc (PA) 312 829-6900
   457 N Leavitt St Chicago (60612) *(G-5330)*
Marconi, Des Plaines *Also called V Formusa Co (G-7863)*
Marcoot Jersey Creamery LLC 618 664-1110
   526 Dudleyville Rd Greenville (62246) *(G-10837)*
Marcor, Downers Grove *Also called Mar Cor Purification Inc (G-8051)*
Marcres Manufacturing Inc 847 439-1808
   600 W Carboy Rd Mount Prospect (60056) *(G-14546)*
Marcres Metal Works, Mount Prospect *Also called Marcres Manufacturing Inc (G-14546)*
Marcus Press 630 351-1857
   168 Constitution Dr Bloomingdale (60108) *(G-1999)*
Marcy Enterprises Inc 708 352-7220
   250 Kings Ct La Grange Park (60526) *(G-12098)*
Marcy Laboratories Inc 630 377-6655
   4n215 Powis Rd West Chicago (60185) *(G-20614)*
Marena Marena Two Inc 773 327-0619
   665 W Sheridan Rd Chicago (60613) *(G-5331)*
Marengo Tool & Die Works Inc 815 568-7411
   201 E Railroad St Marengo (60152) *(G-13489)*
Marengo Union Times 815 568-5400
   709 Lura Ln Marengo (60152) *(G-13490)*
Mares Service Inc 708 656-1660
   4611 W 34th St Cicero (60804) *(G-6865)*
Mareta Ravioli & Noodle, Leonore *Also called Mareta Ravioli Inc (G-12612)*
Mareta Ravioli Inc 815 856-2621
   303 Gary St Leonore (61332) *(G-12612)*
Marfa Cabinets Inc 847 701-5558
   3426 W Touhy Ave Skokie (60076) *(G-18982)*
Margies Brands Inc 773 643-1417
   6122 S Dorchester Ave Chicago (60637) *(G-5332)*
Maria Salazar Rivas, Oak Forest *Also called We Clean (G-15692)*
Mariachi Monumental De Mexico 520 878-8688
   4550 W 57th St Chicago (60629) *(G-5333)*
Mariah Media Inc 312 222-1100
   444 N Michigan Ave # 3350 Chicago (60611) *(G-5334)*
Marias Bakery Inc 847 266-0811
   410 Sheridan Rd Highwood (60040) *(G-11309)*
Marias Chicken ATI Atihan 847 699-3113
   9054 W Golf Rd Niles (60714) *(G-15144)*
Marie Gere Corporation 847 540-1154
   1275 Ensell Rd Lake Zurich (60047) *(G-12430)*
Marie's Salad Dressings, Thornton *Also called Ventura Foods LLC (G-19791)*
Mariegold Bake Shoppe 773 561-1978
   5752 N California Ave Chicago (60659) *(G-5335)*
Maries Custom Made Choir Robes 773 826-1214
   3838 W Madison St Chicago (60624) *(G-5336)*
Marietta Corporation 773 816-5137
   340 E 138th St Chicago (60827) *(G-5337)*
Marin Software Incorporated 312 267-2083
   140 S Dearborn St 300a Chicago (60603) *(G-5338)*
Marine Acquisition Corp 217 324-9400
   1 Sierra Pl Litchfield (62056) *(G-12973)*

Marine Technologies Inc — 847 546-9001
31632 N Ellis Dr Unit 301 Volo (60073) *(G-20203)*

Marion Oelze (PA) — 618 327-9224
11872 County Highway 27 # 3 Nashville (62263) *(G-15001)*

Marion Star — 618 997-7827
1205 Tower Square Plz Marion (62959) *(G-13521)*

Marion Tool & Die Inc — 309 266-6551
701 Flint Ave Morton (61550) *(G-14364)*

Maritool Incorporated — 888 352-7773
242 Beinoris Dr Wood Dale (60191) *(G-21213)*

Marjan Hot Tinning, Montgomery Also called Marjan Inc *(G-14261)*

Marjan Inc — 630 906-0053
1801 Albright Rd Montgomery (60538) *(G-14261)*

Marjo Graphics Inc — 847 367-1305
1510 Bull Creek Dr Libertyville (60048) *(G-12672)*

Mark Anthony Brewing Inc (HQ) — 312 202-3700
300 W Hubbard St Ste 301 Chicago (60654) *(G-5339)*

Mark Collins — 847 324-5500
4443 Oakton St Skokie (60076) *(G-18983)*

Mark Development Corporation — 815 339-2226
Mennie Dr Rr 71 Mark (61340) *(G-13545)*

Mark Industries — 847 487-8670
535 N Legion Ct Wauconda (60084) *(G-20372)*

Mark Lahey — 217 243-4433
107 S Johnson St Jacksonville (62650) *(G-11775)*

Mark Power International — 815 877-5984
7897 Burden Rd Machesney Park (61115) *(G-13358)*

Mark Radtke Co Division, Chicago Also called Kirby Sheet Metal Works Inc *(G-5106)*

Mark S Machine Shop Inc — 815 895-3955
416 N Main St Sycamore (60178) *(G-19724)*

Mark Twain Press Inc — 847 255-2700
3312 Sheridan Ln Mundelein (60060) *(G-14713)*

Mark Your Space Inc — 630 289-7082
1235 Humbracht Cir Ste 9 Bartlett (60103) *(G-1295)*

Mark-It Company, Batavia Also called P & L Mark-It Inc *(G-1402)*

Markal Company, Elk Grove Village Also called La-Co Industries Inc *(G-9082)*

Market Ready Inc — 847 689-1000
30 Porter Dr Round Lake Park (60073) *(G-18097)*

Marketing & Technology Group — 312 266-3311
1415 N Dayton St Ste 115 Chicago (60642) *(G-5340)*

Marketing Card Technology LLC — 630 985-7900
1213 Butterfield Rd Downers Grove (60515) *(G-8052)*

Markham Cabinet Works Inc — 708 687-3074
4235 151st St Midlothian (60445) *(G-13993)*

Markham Division 9 Inc — 708 503-0657
2213 W Wolpers Rd Park Forest (60466) *(G-16257)*

Markham Industry Inc — 815 338-0116
2220 Tech Ct Woodstock (60098) *(G-21408)*

Marking Specialists Group, Buffalo Grove Also called Marking Specialists/Poly *(G-2568)*

Marking Specialists/Poly — 847 793-8100
1000 Asbury Dr Ste 2 Buffalo Grove (60089) *(G-2568)*

Markman Peat Corp — 815 772-4014
13161 Fenton Rd Morrison (61270) *(G-14345)*

Marko International, Inc, Chicago Also called Trotta Enterprises Inc *(G-6433)*

Marks Custom Seating — 630 980-8270
816 Central Ave Roselle (60172) *(G-17968)*

Markus Cabinet Manufacturing Inc — 618 228-7376
601 S Clinton St Aviston (62216) *(G-1181)*

Marland Clutch — 800 216-3515
449 Gardner St South Beloit (61080) *(G-19098)*

Marlboro Wire Ltd — 217 224-7989
2403 N 24th St Quincy (62305) *(G-16910)*

Marley Candles — 815 485-6604
12525 187th St Mokena (60448) *(G-14097)*

Marmon Engineered Components (HQ) — 312 372-9500
181 W Madison St Fl 26 Chicago (60602) *(G-5341)*

Marmon Group LLC (HQ) — 312 372-9500
181 W Madison St Ste 2600 Chicago (60602) *(G-5342)*

Marmon Group LLC — 847 647-8200
5215 Old Orchard Rd # 725 Skokie (60077) *(G-18984)*

Marmon Holdings Inc (HQ) — 312 372-9500
181 W Madison St Ste 2600 Chicago (60602) *(G-5343)*

Marmon Industrial LLC (HQ) — 312 372-9500
181 W Madison St Fl 26 Chicago (60602) *(G-5344)*

Marmon Industries LLC (HQ) — 312 372-9500
181 W Madison St Ste 2600 Chicago (60602) *(G-5345)*

Marmon Retail Technologies Co (HQ) — 312 332-0317
181 W Madison St Chicago (60602) *(G-5346)*

Marnic Inc (PA) — 309 343-1418
439 N Henderson St Galesburg (61401) *(G-10208)*

Maro Carton Inc — 708 649-9982
333 31st Ave Bellwood (60104) *(G-1633)*

Maroa AG, Maroa Also called Harbach Gillan & Nixon Inc *(G-13552)*

Marquardt Printing Company — 630 887-8500
161 Tower Dr Ste A Burr Ridge (60527) *(G-2698)*

Marquis Energy LLC — 815 925-7300
11953 Prairie Indus Pkwy Hennepin (61327) *(G-11158)*

Marquis Marine Inc — 815 925-9125
7548 W Power Plant Rd Hennepin (61327) *(G-11159)*

Marqutte Stl Sup Fbrcation Inc — 815 433-0178
800 W Marquette St Ottawa (61350) *(G-16060)*

Mars Incorporated — 630 293-9066
120 N Aurora St West Chicago (60185) *(G-20615)*

Mars Chocolate North Amer LLC — 662 335-8000
2019 N Oak Park Ave Chicago (60707) *(G-5347)*

Mars Chocolate North Amer LLC — 630 850-9898
15w660 79th St Burr Ridge (60527) *(G-2699)*

Mars Snackfood US — 773 637-0659
2019 N Oak Park Ave Chicago (60707) *(G-5348)*

Marsco Glass Products LLC (HQ) — 312 326-4710
2857 S Halsted St Chicago (60608) *(G-5349)*

Marsh Products, Batavia Also called Spectrum Cos International *(G-1418)*

Marsh Shipping Supply Co LLC (PA) — 618 343-1006
926 Mcdonough Lake Rd E Collinsville (62234) *(G-6969)*

Marshall Advocate, Marshall Also called Strohm Newspapers Inc *(G-13578)*

Marshall County Publishing Co — 309 246-2865
204 S Washington St Lacon (61540) *(G-12129)*

Marshall Electric Inc — 618 382-3932
1707 Oak St Ste B Carmi (62821) *(G-2910)*

Marshall Middleby Inc (HQ) — 847 741-3300
1400 Toastmaster Dr Elgin (60120) *(G-8649)*

Marshall Mold & Engineering, Glendale Heights Also called Marshall Mold Inc *(G-10473)*

Marshall Mold Inc — 630 582-1800
1934 Bentley Ct Ste A Glendale Heights (60139) *(G-10473)*

Marshall Pubg & Promotions — 224 238-3530
123 S Hough St Barrington (60010) *(G-1227)*

Marshall Sign Co, Chicago Also called Arts & Letters Marshall Signs *(G-3743)*

Marshall Wolf Automation Inc (PA) — 847 658-8130
923 S Main St Algonquin (60102) *(G-378)*

Martha Lacey — 217 723-4380
47424 212th Ave Pearl (62361) *(G-16318)*

Martin Automatic Inc — 815 654-4800
1661 Northrock Ct Rockford (61103) *(G-17505)*

Martin Dental Laboratory Inc — 708 597-8880
411 New Ave Unit 2 Lockport (60441) *(G-13011)*

Martin Engineering Company (PA) — 309 852-2384
1 Martin Pl Neponset (61345) *(G-15018)*

Martin Engineering USA, Neponset Also called Martin Engineering Company *(G-15018)*

Martin Exploration Mgt Co (PA) — 708 385-6500
4501 W 127th St Alsip (60803) *(G-472)*

Martin Glass Company (PA) — 618 277-1946
25 Center Plz Belleville (62220) *(G-1571)*

Martin Machine Co, Ivesdale Also called David Martin *(G-11756)*

Martin Marietta Materials Inc — 618 285-6267
Missouri Portland Rd Golconda (62938) *(G-10667)*

Martin Oil, Alsip Also called Martin Exploration Mgt Co *(G-472)*

Martin Precision Inc — 815 873-1000
3230 Pyramid Dr Rockford (61109) *(G-17506)*

Martin Publishing Co — 309 647-9501
31 S Main St Canton (61520) *(G-2828)*

Martin Publishing Co (PA) — 309 543-2000
217 W Market St Havana (62644) *(G-11116)*

Martin Publishing Co — 309 647-9501
31 S Main St Canton (61520) *(G-2829)*

Martin Publishing Company, Canton Also called Martin Publishing Co *(G-2829)*

Martin Sprocket & Gear Inc — 847 298-8844
1505 Birchwood Ave Des Plaines (60018) *(G-7800)*

Martin Steel Fabrication Inc — 618 410-7066
508 S Railway St Mascoutah (62258) *(G-13602)*

Martin Stees LLC — 630 664-6273
2289 Copley St Aurora (60506) *(G-1127)*

Martin Tool Works Inc — 847 923-8400
2050 Mitchell Blvd Schaumburg (60193) *(G-18619)*

Martinez Management Inc — 847 822-7202
2413 W Algonquin Rd Algonquin (60102) *(G-379)*

Martinez Printing LLC — 773 732-8108
2714 N Mulligan Ave Chicago (60639) *(G-5350)*

Marty Gannon — 847 895-1059
1025 Morse Ave Schaumburg (60193) *(G-18620)*

Marty Lundeen — 630 250-8917
311 Willow St Itasca (60143) *(G-11697)*

Maruichi Leavitt Pipe Tube LLC — 800 532-8488
3655 Solutions Ctr Chicago (60677) *(G-5351)*

Maruichi Leavitt Pipe Tube LLC (HQ) — 773 239-7700
1717 W 115th St Chicago (60643) *(G-5352)*

Marv's Scooters, Belleville Also called Pruett Enterprises Inc *(G-1586)*

Marv-O-Lus Manufacturing Co (PA) — 773 826-1717
220 N Washtenaw Ave Chicago (60612) *(G-5353)*

Marvel Group Inc — 773 523-4804
3800 W 44th St Chicago (60632) *(G-5354)*

Marvel Group Inc (PA) — 773 523-4804
3843 W 43rd St Chicago (60632) *(G-5355)*

Marvel Group Inc — 773 523-4804
4417 S Springfield Ave Chicago (60632) *(G-5356)*

Marvel Industries Incorporated (PA) — 847 325-2930
700 Dartmouth Ln Buffalo Grove (60089) *(G-2569)*

Marvel Machining Co Inc — 630 350-0075
231 Evergreen Ave Bensenville (60106) *(G-1847)*

Marvin Schumaker Plbg Inc......815 626-8130
25457 Front St Sterling (61081) *(G-19516)*
Marvin Suckow......618 483-5570
5267 N 700th St Mason (62443) *(G-13608)*
Mary Hill Memorials, Chicago *Also called Venetian Monument Company (G-6531)*
Mary Lee Packaging Corporation (PA)......618 826-2361
1037 State St Chester (62233) *(G-3458)*
Mary McHelle Winery Vinyrd LLC......217 942-6250
54 Ponderosa Ln Carrollton (62016) *(G-3127)*
Marytown......847 367-7800
1600 W Park Ave Libertyville (60048) *(G-12673)*
Marzeya Bakery Inc......773 374-7855
8908 S Commercial Ave Chicago (60617) *(G-5357)*
Masa Uno Inc......708 749-4866
6311 Cermak Rd Ste 2 Berwyn (60402) *(G-1956)*
Masco Corporation......847 303-3088
1821 Walden Office Sq # 400 Schaumburg (60173) *(G-18621)*
Mascoutah Herald, Mascoutah *Also called Better News Papers Inc (G-13593)*
Mashburn Well Drilling......217 794-3728
214 N Pine St Maroa (61756) *(G-13553)*
Mason City Banner Times......217 482-3276
126 N Tonica St Mason City (62664) *(G-13612)*
Mason County Democrat, Havana *Also called Martin Publishing Co (G-11116)*
Mason Electric......618 457-8900
1300 Pin Oak Dr Carterville (62918) *(G-3133)*
Mason Engineering & Designing......630 595-5000
505 W Lancaster Ct Inverness (60010) *(G-11602)*
Mason Welding Inc......708 755-0621
3321 Holeman Ave S Chicago Hts (60411) *(G-18123)*
Masonite Corporation......630 584-6330
1955 Powis Rd West Chicago (60185) *(G-20616)*
Massage Chair Deals, Burbank *Also called Tifb Media Group Inc (G-2638)*
Massey Grafix......815 644-4620
1637 E 1900 North Rd Watseka (60970) *(G-20310)*
Mast Harness Shop......217 543-3463
488 Post Oak Rd Campbell Hill (62916) *(G-2816)*
Master Builders LLC......847 249-4080
1810 Northwestern Ave Gurnee (60031) *(G-10895)*
Master Cabinets......847 639-1323
209 Cleveland St Ste D Cary (60013) *(G-3178)*
Master Control Systems Inc (PA)......847 295-1010
910 N Shore Dr Lake Bluff (60044) *(G-12195)*
Master Cut E D M Inc......847 534-0343
1025 Lunt Ave Ste C Schaumburg (60193) *(G-18622)*
Master Engraving......217 965-5885
246 E Dean St Virden (62690) *(G-20188)*
Master Fog LLC......773 918-9080
148 S Pinnacle Dr Romeoville (60446) *(G-17845)*
Master Foundry Inc......217 223-7396
4808 Ellington Rd Quincy (62305) *(G-16911)*
Master Graphics LLC......815 562-5800
1100 S Main St Rochelle (61068) *(G-17149)*
Master Hydraulics & Machining......847 895-5578
540 Morse Ave Schaumburg (60193) *(G-18623)*
Master Machine Craft Inc......815 874-3078
6483 Falcon Rd Rockford (61109) *(G-17507)*
Master Machine Group Inc......847 472-9940
1515 Commerce Dr Elgin (60123) *(G-8650)*
Master Manufacturing Co......630 833-7060
747 N Yale Ave Villa Park (60181) *(G-20159)*
Master Marketing Intl Inc (PA)......630 653-5525
280 Gerzevske Ln Carol Stream (60188) *(G-3021)*
Master Mechanic Mfg Inc......847 573-3812
970 Campus Dr Mundelein (60060) *(G-14714)*
Master Molded Products LLC......847 695-9700
1000 Davis Rd Elgin (60123) *(G-8651)*
Master Paper Box Company Inc......773 927-0252
3641 S Iron St Chicago (60609) *(G-5358)*
Master Polishing & Buffing......773 731-3883
10247 S Avenue O Chicago (60617) *(G-5359)*
Master Spring & Wire Form Co......708 453-2570
1340 Ardmore Ave Itasca (60143) *(G-11698)*
Master Tape Printers Inc......773 283-8273
4517 N Elston Ave Chicago (60630) *(G-5360)*
Master Tech Tool Inc......815 363-4001
4539 Prime Pkwy McHenry (60050) *(G-13764)*
Master-Halco Inc......618 395-4365
4633 E Radio Tower Ln Olney (62450) *(G-15873)*
Masterbolt LLC......847 834-5191
8015 Pyott Rd Lake In The Hills (60156) *(G-12340)*
Masterbrand Cabinets Inc......217 543-3311
501 W Progress St Arthur (61911) *(G-867)*
Masterbrand Cabinets Inc......217 543-3466
N Arthur Atwood Rd Arthur (61911) *(G-868)*
Masterbrand Cabinets Inc......503 241-4964
100 N Vine St Arthur (61911) *(G-869)*
Mastercoil Spring, McHenry *Also called Classic Products Inc (G-13728)*
Mastercraft Auto Rebuilding......847 487-8787
265 Industrial Dr Wauconda (60084) *(G-20373)*
Mastercraft Furn Rfnishing Inc......773 722-5730
3140 W Chicago Ave Chicago (60622) *(G-5361)*
Masterfeed Corporation......630 879-1133
1326 Hollister Dr Batavia (60510) *(G-1392)*
Mastermolding Inc......815 741-1230
1715 Terry Dr Joliet (60436) *(G-11898)*
Masterpiece Cabinetry Design......217 258-6880
69 Kingswood Mattoon (61938) *(G-13644)*
Masters & Alloy LLC......312 582-1880
12841 S Pulaski Rd Alsip (60803) *(G-473)*
Masters & Yates Machine, Rockford *Also called Masters Yates Inc (G-17509)*
Masters Billiard Chalk, Chicago *Also called Tweeten Fibre Co (G-6445)*
Masters Hand Enterprises LLC......312 933-7674
4021 W Harrison St Chicago (60624) *(G-5362)*
Masters Plating Co Inc......815 226-8846
2228 20th Ave Rockford (61104) *(G-17508)*
Masters Shop......217 643-7826
1621 County Road 2500 N Thomasboro (61878) *(G-19776)*
Masters Yates Inc......815 227-9585
1188 N Crest Dr Rockford (61107) *(G-17509)*
Masud Jewelers Inc......312 236-0547
17 N Wabash Ave Ste 430 Chicago (60602) *(G-5363)*
Mat Capital LLC (PA)......847 821-9630
6700 Wildlife Way Long Grove (60047) *(G-13163)*
Mat Engine Technologies LLC (HQ)......847 821-9630
6700 Wildlife Way Long Grove (60047) *(G-13164)*
Mat Holdings Inc (PA)......847 821-9630
6700 Wildlife Way Long Grove (60047) *(G-13165)*
Mat Industries LLC (HQ)......847 821-9630
6700 Wildlife Way Long Grove (60047) *(G-13166)*
Matchless Parisian Novelty Inc (PA)......773 924-1515
840 W 49th Pl Chicago (60609) *(G-5364)*
Matcon, East Moline *Also called Material Control Systems Inc (G-8233)*
Matcon 2, Cordova *Also called Material Control Systems Inc (G-7009)*
Matcon Manufacturing Inc......309 755-1020
15509 Route 84 N Cordova (61242) *(G-7008)*
Matcon Usa Inc......856 256-1330
832 N Industrial Dr Elmhurst (60126) *(G-9399)*
Matcor Metal Fabrication Group, Morton *Also called Matcor Mtal Fbrication III Inc (G-14365)*
Matcor Mtal Fbrication III Inc (HQ)......309 263-1707
1021 W Birchwood St Morton (61550) *(G-14365)*
Mate Technologies Inc......847 289-1010
1695 Todd Farm Dr Elgin (60123) *(G-8652)*
Material Control Inc......630 892-4274
525 N River St Ste 100 Batavia (60510) *(G-1393)*
Material Control Systems Inc (PA)......309 523-3774
375 36th St East Moline (61244) *(G-8233)*
Material Control Systems Inc......309 654-9031
15509 Route 84 N Cordova (61242) *(G-7009)*
Material Sciences Corporation......847 439-2210
2250 Pratt Blvd Elk Grove Village (60007) *(G-9112)*
Material Service Corporation......815 838-2400
681 S Material Rd Romeoville (60446) *(G-17846)*
Material Service Corporation......847 658-4559
Rr 31 Algonquin (60102) *(G-380)*
Material Service Corporation......708 877-6540
620 W 183rd St Thornton (60476) *(G-19790)*
Material Service Corporation......708 447-1100
2235 Entp Dr Ste 3504 Westchester (60154) *(G-20704)*
Material Service Corporation (HQ)......708 731-2600
2235 Entp Dr Ste 3504 Westchester (60154) *(G-20705)*
Material Service Corporation......217 563-2531
22283 Taylorville Rd Nokomis (62075) *(G-15194)*
Material Service Corporation......815 942-1830
125 N Independence Blvd Romeoville (60446) *(G-17847)*
Material Service Corporation......217 732-2117
25142 Quarry Ave Athens (62613) *(G-897)*
Material Service Corporation......708 485-8211
9101 W 47th St Mc Cook (60525) *(G-13696)*
Material Service Corporation......815 838-3420
125 N Independence Blvd Romeoville (60446) *(G-17848)*
Material Service Yard 12, Nokomis *Also called Material Service Corporation (G-15194)*
Material Svc Yard 67, Romeoville *Also called Material Service Corporation (G-17848)*
Materion Brush Inc......630 832-9650
606 W Lamont Rd Elmhurst (60126) *(G-9400)*
Mather Dataforms, Woodstock *Also called Hal Mather & Sons Incorporated (G-21394)*
Matheson Tri-Gas Inc......815 727-2202
200 Alessio Dr Joliet (60433) *(G-11899)*
Matheson Tri-Gas Inc......309 697-1933
7700 W Wheeler Rd Mapleton (61547) *(G-13476)*
Matheu Tool Works Inc......773 327-9274
2426 N Clybourn Ave Fl 1 Chicago (60614) *(G-5365)*
Mathew Equipment Company, Crystal Lake *Also called Mathews Company (G-7223)*
Mathew Lucante Violins LLC......773 320-2997
4200 Enfield Ave Skokie (60076) *(G-18985)*
Mathews Company......815 459-2210
500 Industrial Rd Crystal Lake (60012) *(G-7223)*
Mathews Fan Company, Libertyville *Also called Matthews-Gerbar Ltd (G-12674)*

ALPHABETIC

Mathis Energy LLC....309 925-3177
701 E Pearl St Tremont (61568) **(G-19898)**
Matis Inc....708 425-7100
10235 Southwest Hwy Chicago Ridge (60415) **(G-6802)**
Matrex Exhibits Inc....630 628-2233
301 S Church St Addison (60101) **(G-193)**
Matrix Circuits LLC (PA)....319 367-5000
37575 N Il Route 59 Lake Villa (60046) **(G-12360)**
Matrix Design LLC....847 841-8260
1361 Schiferl Rd Bartlett (60103) **(G-1296)**
Matrix Industries Inc (PA)....847 975-7701
375 Hollow Hill Rd Wauconda (60084) **(G-20374)**
Matrix International Ltd....815 389-3771
449 Gardner St South Beloit (61080) **(G-19099)**
Matrix IV Inc....815 338-4500
610 E Judd St Woodstock (60098) **(G-21409)**
Matrix Legacy Holdings, Bartlett *Also called Matrix Design LLC* **(G-1296)**
Matrix Machine & Tool Mfg....708 452-8707
8044 Grand Ave River Grove (60171) **(G-17063)**
Matrix Nac, Chicago *Also called Matrix North Amercn Cnstr Inc* **(G-5366)**
Matrix North Amercn Cnstr Inc (HQ)....312 754-6605
1 E Wacker Dr Ste 1110 Chicago (60601) **(G-5366)**
Matrix Plastic Products Inc....630 595-6144
949 Aec Dr Wood Dale (60191) **(G-21214)**
Matrix Service Inc....618 466-4862
3403 E Broadway Alton (62002) **(G-566)**
Matrix Tooling, Wood Dale *Also called Matrix Plastic Products Inc* **(G-21214)**
Matt Pak Inc....847 451-4018
2910 Commerce St Franklin Park (60131) **(G-9985)**
Matt Snell and Sons....618 695-3555
4530 Mount Shelter Rd Vienna (62995) **(G-20118)**
Mattaliano Furniture, Chicago *Also called M Inc* **(G-5301)**
Mattarusky Inc....630 469-4125
1n272 Pleasant Ave Glen Ellyn (60137) **(G-10412)**
Matthew Warren Inc....847 364-5000
989 Pauly Dr Elk Grove Village (60007) **(G-9113)**
Matthew Warren Inc....630 860-7766
733 Maple Ln Bensenville (60106) **(G-1848)**
Matthew Warren Inc....847 671-6767
9505 Winona Ave Schiller Park (60176) **(G-18821)**
Matthew Warren Inc (HQ)....847 349-5760
9501 Tech Blvd Ste 401 Rosemont (60018) **(G-18035)**
Matthews Fan Company, Libertyville *Also called Matthews-Gerbar Ltd* **(G-12675)**
Matthews-Gerbar Ltd....847 680-9043
1881 Industrial Dr Libertyville (60048) **(G-12674)**
Matthews-Gerbar Ltd (PA)....847 680-9043
1881 Industrial Dr Libertyville (60048) **(G-12675)**
Mattoon Precision Mfg....217 235-6000
2408 S 14th St Mattoon (61938) **(G-13645)**
Mattoon Printing Center....217 234-3100
212 N 20th St Mattoon (61938) **(G-13646)**
Mattoon-Charleston Ready Mix, Mattoon *Also called Mid-Illinois Concrete Inc* **(G-13650)**
Matts Cookie Company....847 537-3888
482 N Milwaukee Ave Wheeling (60090) **(G-20939)**
Mattsn/Witt Precision Pdts Inc....847 382-7810
28005 W Industrial Ave Lake Barrington (60010) **(G-12159)**
Mattson Lamp Plant....217 258-9390
1501 S 19th St Mattoon (61938) **(G-13647)**
Maurey Instrument Corp....708 388-9898
5959 W 115th St Alsip (60803) **(G-474)**
Mauser Pckg Sltons Intrmdate I (PA)....770 645-4800
1515 W 22nd St Ste 1100 Oak Brook (60523) **(G-15640)**
Mauser Usa LLC....773 261-2332
903 N Kilpatrick Ave Chicago (60651) **(G-5367)**
Mautino Distributing Co Inc....815 664-4311
501 W 1st St Spring Valley (61362) **(G-19310)**
Maverick Ales & Lagers LLC....408 605-1508
2137 W Walnut St Chicago (60612) **(G-5368)**
MAX FIRE BOX, Godfrey *Also called Max Fire Training Inc* **(G-10656)**
Max Fire Training Inc....618 210-2079
901 Hampton Ct Godfrey (62035) **(G-10656)**
Max Miller....708 758-7760
3000 State St S Chicago Hts (60411) **(G-18124)**
Max-Block Development LLC....773 220-6214
10500 S Hamilton Ave Chicago (60643) **(G-5369)**
Maxant Technologies, Niles *Also called 7 Mile Solutions Inc* **(G-15096)**
Maxco Ready Mix, Washington *Also called Maxheimer Construction Inc* **(G-20275)**
Maxheimer Construction Inc....309 444-4200
25130 Schuck Rd Washington (61571) **(G-20275)**
Maxi-Vac Inc....630 620-6669
1437 Holmes Rd Elgin (60123) **(G-8653)**
Maxi-Vac Inc....630 620-6669
120 Prairie Lake Rd Ste C East Dundee (60118) **(G-8205)**
Maxim Inc....217 544-7015
2709 E Ash St Springfield (62703) **(G-19403)**
Maximum Prtg & Graphics Inc....630 737-0270
911 Burlington Ave Downers Grove (60515) **(G-8053)**
Maximum Sealants LLC....815 985-7183
3086 Alliance Ave Rockford (61101) **(G-17510)**
Maxit, Antioch *Also called Bmi Products Northern Ill Inc* **(G-605)**
Maxon Plastics Inc....630 761-3667
1069 Kingsland Dr Batavia (60510) **(G-1394)**
Maxs One Stop....618 235-4005
1319 N 17th St Belleville (62226) **(G-1572)**
Maxs Screen Machine Inc (PA)....773 878-4949
6125 N Nrthwst Hwy Frnt 1 Chicago (60631) **(G-5370)**
Maxwell Counters Inc....309 928-2848
324 S Plum St Farmer City (61842) **(G-9655)**
Maxxsonics Usa Inc....847 540-7700
851 E Park Ave Libertyville (60048) **(G-12676)**
May Sand and Gravel Inc....815 338-4761
3013 Thompson Rd Wonder Lake (60097) **(G-21145)**
May Wood Industries Inc....708 489-1515
12636 S Springfield Ave Alsip (60803) **(G-475)**
Maya Romanoff Corporation (PA)....773 465-6909
3435 Madison St Skokie (60076) **(G-18986)**
Mayco Manufacturing LLC....618 451-4400
1200 16th St Granite City (62040) **(G-10721)**
Mayco-Granite City Inc....618 451-4400
1200 16th St Granite City (62040) **(G-10722)**
Mayfair Metal Spinning Co Inc....847 358-7450
538 S Vermont St Palatine (60067) **(G-16139)**
Maylan Skincare, Oakbrook Terrace *Also called Amedico Laboratories LLC* **(G-15783)**
Mayline Investments Inc (PA)....847 948-9340
555 Skokie Blvd Northbrook (60062) **(G-15428)**
Maynard Inc....773 235-5225
1421 S Plymouth Ct Chicago (60605) **(G-5371)**
Maytec Inc....847 429-0321
901 Wesemann Dr Dundee (60118) **(G-8128)**
Maze Nails Div, Peru *Also called W H Maze Company* **(G-16596)**
Mazel & Co Inc (PA)....773 533-1600
4300 W Ferdinand St Chicago (60624) **(G-5372)**
MB Box Inc....815 589-3043
1201 4th St Fulton (61252) **(G-10155)**
MB Corp & Associates....847 214-8843
445 Renner Dr Elgin (60123) **(G-8654)**
MB Machine Inc....815 864-3555
10214 N Mount Vernon Rd Shannon (61078) **(G-18871)**
MB Quart Entertainment, Libertyville *Also called Maxxsonics Usa Inc* **(G-12676)**
MBA Manufacturing Inc....847 566-2555
1086 Industrial Dr Ste 3 Bensenville (60106) **(G-1849)**
Mbacase, Plainfield *Also called Ohrvall Media LLC* **(G-16698)**
MBC Cmpsite Bring Mnfactioring, Wood Dale *Also called Composite Bearings Mfg* **(G-21178)**
Mbc-Aerosol, Elgin *Also called MB Corp & Associates* **(G-8654)**
Mbexpress, Bloomingdale *Also called Madden Communications Inc* **(G-1998)**
Mbh Promotions Inc....847 634-2411
1108 Gail Dr Buffalo Grove (60089) **(G-2570)**
MBI Tools LLC....815 844-0937
15116 E 2100 North Rd Pontiac (61764) **(G-16775)**
MBL Bion, Des Plaines *Also called Bion Enterprises Ltd* **(G-7740)**
Mbm Business Assistance Inc....217 398-6600
313 N Mattis Ave Ste 114 Champaign (61821) **(G-3318)**
Mbo Painting, Shelbyville *Also called Brad Martz* **(G-18877)**
MBR Tool Inc....847 671-4491
5118 Pearl St Schiller Park (60176) **(G-18822)**
Mbs Manufacturing....630 227-0300
1100 E Green St Franklin Park (60131) **(G-9986)**
Mc Adams Multigraphics Inc....630 990-1707
900 Jorie Blvd Ste 26 Oak Brook (60523) **(G-15641)**
Mc Brady Engineering Inc....815 744-8900
1251 S Larkin Ave Rockdale (60436) **(G-17267)**
Mc Brady Exports, Rockdale *Also called Mc Brady Engineering Inc* **(G-17267)**
Mc Chemical Company....618 965-3668
1208 N Cherry St Steeleville (62288) **(G-19483)**
Mc Chemical Company (PA)....815 964-7687
720 South St Rockford (61102) **(G-17511)**
Mc Cleary Equipment Inc....815 389-3053
239 Oak Grove Ave South Beloit (61080) **(G-19100)**
Mc Cook Manufacturing Plant, Mc Cook *Also called UOP LLC* **(G-13704)**
Mc Henry Machine Co Inc....815 875-1953
1309 Il Highway 26 Princeton (61356) **(G-16813)**
Mc Kinney Steel & Sales Inc....847 746-3344
813 29th St Zion (60099) **(G-21520)**
Mc Laminated Cabinets....773 301-0393
3115 Dora St Franklin Park (60131) **(G-9987)**
Mc Lean County Concrete Co, Bloomington *Also called McLean County Asphalt Co* **(G-2072)**
Mc Mechanical Contractors Inc....708 460-0075
15774 S La Grange Rd # 245 Orland Park (60462) **(G-15967)**
Mc Metals & Fabricating Inc....847 961-5242
10683 Wolf Dr Huntley (60142) **(G-11555)**
Mc Squared Group Inc....815 322-2485
7801 Industrial Dr Ste F Spring Grove (60081) **(G-19283)**
McAllister Equipment Co....217 789-0351
100 Tri State Intl # 215 Lincolnshire (60069) **(G-12782)**
McArthur Machining Inc....847 838-6998
303 Main St Ste 100a Antioch (60002) **(G-624)**

McAteer's Landscape Lighting, Belleville *Also called McAteers Wholesale* ***(G-1573)***
McAteers Wholesale....618 233-3400
3101 S Belt W Belleville (62226) ***(G-1573)***
McBride & Shoff Inc....309 367-4193
723 N Wiedman St Metamora (61548) ***(G-13963)***
McC Technology Inc....630 377-7200
2422 W Main St Unit 4d Saint Charles (60175) ***(G-18231)***
McCain Foods Usa Inc (HQ)....630 955-0400
1 Tower Ln Fl 11 Oakbrook Terrace (60181) ***(G-15807)***
McCain Foods Usa Inc....920 563-6625
1 Tower Ln Ste Uppr Oakbrook Terrace (60181) ***(G-15808)***
McCain Foodservice, Oakbrook Terrace *Also called McCain Foods Usa Inc* ***(G-15807)***
McCain Usa Inc (HQ)....800 938-7799
1 Tower Ln Ste Uppr Oakbrook Terrace (60181) ***(G-15809)***
McCann Concrete Products Inc....618 377-3888
8709 N State Route 159 Dorsey (62021) ***(G-7945)***
McCarren Group, The, Rockford *Also called Flow-Eze Company* ***(G-17416)***
McCarty's Contemporary Marble, Columbia *Also called Contemporary Marble Inc* ***(G-6989)***
McClatchy Newspapers Inc....618 239-2624
120 S Illinois St Belleville (62220) ***(G-1574)***
McClatchy Newspapers Inc....618 654-2366
1 Woodcrest Prof Park Highland (62249) ***(G-11231)***
McClatchy Newspapers Inc....618 443-2145
116 W Main St Sparta (62286) ***(G-19257)***
McCleary Inc (PA)....815 389-3053
239 Oak Grove Ave South Beloit (61080) ***(G-19101)***
McClendon Holdings Affiliates, Chicago *Also called McClendon Holdings LLC* ***(G-5373)***
McClendon Holdings LLC....773 251-2314
7200 S Exchange Ave Ste A Chicago (60649) ***(G-5373)***
McCloskey Eyman Mlone Mfg Svcs....309 647-4000
37 S 1st Ave Canton (61520) ***(G-2830)***
McCloud Mtlwrks Indus Svcs Inc....618 713-2318
114 John Dr Chester (62233) ***(G-3459)***
McConnell Chase Software Works....312 540-1508
360 E Randolph St # 3202 Chicago (60601) ***(G-5374)***
McCracken Label Co....773 581-8860
5303 S Keeler Ave Chicago (60632) ***(G-5375)***
McCrone Associates Inc....630 887-7100
850 Pasquinelli Dr Westmont (60559) ***(G-20758)***
McCurdy Tool & Machining Co....815 765-2117
1912 Krupke Rd Caledonia (61011) ***(G-2770)***
McDonnell Components Inc....815 547-9555
828 Landmark Dr Belvidere (61008) ***(G-1685)***
McDonough County Shopper Inc....309 833-2114
26 W Side Sq Macomb (61455) ***(G-13393)***
McDonough Democrat Inc....309 772-2129
358 E Main St Bushnell (61422) ***(G-2744)***
McDowell Inc....309 467-2335
809 W Center St Eureka (61530) ***(G-9483)***
McElroy Metal Mill Inc....217 935-9421
10940 State Hwy 10 Clinton (61727) ***(G-6927)***
McEnglevan Indus Frnc Mfg Inc....217 446-0941
708 Griggs St Danville (61832) ***(G-7363)***
McFarland Welding and Machine....618 627-2838
4066 N Thompsonville Rd Thompsonville (62890) ***(G-19779)***
McGill, Woodstock *Also called Sws Industries Inc* ***(G-21438)***
McGill Asphalt Construction Co....708 924-1755
4956 S Monitor Ave Chicago (60638) ***(G-5376)***
McGill Machine Works Inc....847 301-8000
638 Lunt Ave Schaumburg (60193) ***(G-18624)***
McGinley Kawasaki, Highland *Also called Motor Sport Marketing Group* ***(G-11232)***
McGrath Press Inc....815 356-5246
740 Duffy Dr Crystal Lake (60014) ***(G-7224)***
McGrath Printing Custom Ap, Crystal Lake *Also called McGrath Press Inc* ***(G-7224)***
McHenry Printing Services....815 385-7600
4901 Pyndale Dr McHenry (60050) ***(G-13765)***
McHenry Screw Products Inc....815 344-4638
4515 Prime Pkwy McHenry (60050) ***(G-13766)***
Mcli, Des Plaines *Also called Motor Coach Inds Intl Inc* ***(G-7804)***
Mcllvaine Co....847 784-0012
191 Waukegan Rd Ste 208 Northfield (60093) ***(G-15522)***
McIntyre & Associates....847 639-8050
41 Nippersink Rd Apt 3 Fox Lake (60020) ***(G-9748)***
McKean Pallet Co....309 246-7543
1046 State Route 26 Lacon (61540) ***(G-12130)***
McKenzie & Keim LLC....317 443-6663
2850 N Pulaski Rd Ste 1r Chicago (60641) ***(G-5377)***
McKernin Exhibits Inc....708 333-4500
570 W Armory Dr South Holland (60473) ***(G-19231)***
McKillip Industries Inc (PA)....815 439-1050
207 Beaver St Yorkville (60560) ***(G-21493)***
McKlein Company LLC....773 235-0600
4447 W Cortland St Ste A Chicago (60639) ***(G-5378)***
McKlein USA, Chicago *Also called McKlein Company LLC* ***(G-5378)***
McKnight's Assisted Living, Northbrook *Also called McKnights Long Term Care News* ***(G-15429)***
McKnights Long Term Care News....847 559-2884
900 Skokie Blvd Ste 114 Northbrook (60062) ***(G-15429)***
McLaughlin Body Co (PA)....309 762-7755
2430 River Dr Moline (61265) ***(G-14159)***
McLaughlin Body Co....309 736-6105
1400 5th St East Moline (61244) ***(G-8234)***
McLean County Asphalt Co (PA)....309 827-6115
1100 W Market St Bloomington (61701) ***(G-2072)***
McLean Machine Tools, Lake Barrington *Also called McLean Manufacturing Company* ***(G-12160)***
McLean Manufacturing Company....847 277-9912
28040 W Industrial Ave Lake Barrington (60010) ***(G-12160)***
McLean Subsurface Utility....336 988-2520
2150 N Main St Decatur (62526) ***(G-7521)***
McNdt Pipeline Ltd (PA)....815 467-5200
24154 S Northern Ill Dr Channahon (60410) ***(G-3388)***
McNish Corporation (PA)....630 892-7921
840 N Russell Ave Aurora (60506) ***(G-1128)***
MCR Technologies Group Inc....815 622-3181
1704 Westwood Dr Sterling (61081) ***(G-19517)***
MCS Booths, Roselle *Also called Marks Custom Seating* ***(G-17968)***
MCS Midwest LLC....314 398-8107
5506 Dial Dr Granite City (62040) ***(G-10723)***
MCS Midwest LLC....630 393-7402
85 Hankes Ave Aurora (60505) ***(G-1129)***
McShares Inc....217 762-2561
226 W Livingston St Monticello (61856) ***(G-14281)***
McX Press....630 784-4325
355 Longview Dr Bloomingdale (60108) ***(G-2000)***
MD Labs, Brookfield *Also called MD Orthotic Prosthetic Lab Inc* ***(G-2488)***
MD Orthotic Prosthetic Lab Inc (PA)....708 387-9700
8400 Brookfield Ave Brookfield (60513) ***(G-2488)***
MD Technologies Inc....815 598-3143
6965 S Pleasant Hill Rd Elizabeth (61028) ***(G-8788)***
Mdhearingaid, Chicago *Also called SC Industries LLC* ***(G-6109)***
Mdi-Co, West Chicago *Also called Manufcture Dsign Innvation Inc* ***(G-20611)***
Mdm Communications Inc....708 582-9667
8737 Central Park Ave Skokie (60076) ***(G-18987)***
Mdm Construction Supply LLC....815 847-7340
815 N Church St Ste 3 Rockford (61103) ***(G-17512)***
Mdt Customs LLC....573 316-5995
34734 Grapevine Trl Mc Clure (62957) ***(G-13687)***
ME and Gia Inc....708 583-1111
7434 W North Ave Elmwood Park (60707) ***(G-9454)***
MEA Inc....847 766-9040
2600 American Ln Elk Grove Village (60007) ***(G-9114)***
Mead Fluid Dynamics Inc....773 685-6800
25150 S Governors Hwy University Park (60484) ***(G-19959)***
Mead Johnson Nutrition Company (HQ)....312 466-5800
225 N Canal St Fl 25 Chicago (60606) ***(G-5379)***
Meade Electric Co, Oak Brook *Also called L & H Company Inc* ***(G-15630)***
Meaden Precision....630 655-0888
16w210 83rd St Burr Ridge (60527) ***(G-2700)***
Meaden Precision Machined Pdts....630 655-0888
16w210 83rd St Burr Ridge (60527) ***(G-2701)***
Meaden Screw Products Company, Burr Ridge *Also called Meaden Precision Machined Pdts* ***(G-2701)***
Meador Industries Inc....847 671-5042
10031 Franklin Ave Franklin Park (60131) ***(G-9988)***
Meadoweld Machine Inc....815 623-3939
530 Eastern Ave South Beloit (61080) ***(G-19102)***
Meadoworks LLC....847 640-8580
935 National Pkwy # 93510 Schaumburg (60173) ***(G-18625)***
Meadowvale Inc....630 553-0202
1305 E 6th St Sandwich (60548) ***(G-18377)***
Meagher Sign & Graphics Inc....618 662-7446
225 Hagen Dr Flora (62839) ***(G-9685)***
Mealplot Inc....217 419-2681
60 Hazelwood Dr Champaign (61820) ***(G-3319)***
Measurement Devices US LLC....281 646-0050
1001 Wesemann Dr Dundee (60118) ***(G-8129)***
Meats By Linz Inc (PA)....708 862-0830
414 State St Calumet City (60409) ***(G-2783)***
Meau, Vernon Hills *Also called Mitsubishi Elc Automtn Inc* ***(G-20075)***
Mecc Alte Inc....815 344-0530
1229 Adams Dr McHenry (60051) ***(G-13767)***
Mech-Tronics Corporation (PA)....708 344-9823
1635 N 25th Ave Melrose Park (60160) ***(G-13891)***
Mech-Tronics Corporation....708 344-0202
1701 N 25th Ave Melrose Park (60160) ***(G-13892)***
Mech-Tronics Nucleaur Div, Melrose Park *Also called Mech-Tronics Corporation* ***(G-13892)***
Mechanical Devices Company....309 663-2843
2005 General Electric Rd Bloomington (61704) ***(G-2073)***
Mechanical Engineering Pdts....312 421-3375
1319 W Lake St Chicago (60607) ***(G-5380)***
Mechanical Indus Stl Svcs Inc (PA)....815 521-1725
24226 S Northern Ill Dr Channahon (60410) ***(G-3389)***
Mechanical Music Corp....847 398-5444
3319 N Ridge Ave Arlington Heights (60004) ***(G-775)***
Mechanical Power Inc....847 487-0070
135 Kerry Ln Wauconda (60084) ***(G-20375)***

ALPHABETIC

(PA)=Parent Co (HQ)=Headquarters (DH)=Div Headquarters
2020 Harris Illinois Industrial Directory
1189

Mechanical Products Corp 630 543-4842
330 W Gerri Ln Addison (60101) *(G-194)*
Mechanical Tool & Engrg Co (PA) 815 397-4701
4701 Kishwaukee St Rockford (61109) *(G-17513)*
Mechanical Tool & Engrg Co 815 397-4701
4700 Boeing Dr Rockford (61109) *(G-17514)*
Mechanics Planing Mill Inc 618 288-3000
1 Cottonwood Indus Park Glen Carbon (62034) *(G-10390)*
Mechanovent, Effingham Also called New York Blower Company *(G-8414)*
Meck Print 708 358-0600
830 S Kenilworth Ave Oak Park (60304) *(G-15764)*
Meco Company LLC 217 465-5620
2121 S Main St Paris (61944) *(G-16234)*
Meda Pharmaceuticals, Decatur Also called Mylan Inc *(G-7532)*
Medaowview Ventures II Inc (PA) 847 965-1700
8350 Lehigh Ave Morton Grove (60053) *(G-14426)*
Medbot Inc 213 200-6658
856 W Nelson St Apt 1006 Chicago (60657) *(G-5381)*
Medefil Inc (PA) 630 682-4600
250 Windy Point Dr Glendale Heights (60139) *(G-10474)*
Medela LLC (HQ) 800 435-8316
1101 Corporate Dr McHenry (60050) *(G-13768)*
Mederer Group 630 860-4587
733 Lee St Ste 206 Des Plaines (60016) *(G-7801)*
Medexus Pharma Inc 312 854-0500
29 N Wacker Dr Ste 704 Chicago (60606) *(G-5382)*
Medford Aero Arms LLC 773 961-7686
4541 N Ravenswood Ave Chicago (60640) *(G-5383)*
Medgyn Products Inc 630 627-4105
100 W Industrial Rd Addison (60101) *(G-195)*
Media Associates Intl Inc 630 260-9063
351 S Main Pl Ste 230 Carol Stream (60188) *(G-3022)*
Media Services, Vernon Hills Also called Moor Printing Services Inc *(G-20076)*
Media Unlimited Inc 630 527-0900
1701 Quincy Ave Ste 25 Naperville (60540) *(G-14867)*
Mediafly Inc (PA) 312 281-5175
150 N Michigan Ave # 2000 Chicago (60601) *(G-5384)*
Mediaocean 312 676-4646
120 S Riverside Plz # 1900 Chicago (60606) *(G-5385)*
Mediarecall Holdings LLC 847 513-6710
3363 Commercial Ave Northbrook (60062) *(G-15430)*
Mediatec Publishing (PA) 312 676-9900
111 E Wacker Dr Ste 1200 Chicago (60601) *(G-5386)*
Mediatec Publishing Inc 510 834-0100
150 N Michigan Ave # 550 Chicago (60601) *(G-5387)*
Medical Adherence Tech Inc 847 525-6300
825 Heather Ln Winnetka (60093) *(G-21133)*
Medical Cmmnctions Systems Inc (PA) 708 895-4500
17595 Paxton Ave Lansing (60438) *(G-12508)*
Medical ID Fashions Company 847 404-6789
408 Swan Blvd Deerfield (60015) *(G-7636)*
Medical Liability Monitor Inc 312 944-7900
7234 W North Ave Ste 101 Elmwood Park (60707) *(G-9455)*
Medical Memories LLC 847 478-0078
2274 Avalon Dr Buffalo Grove (60089) *(G-2571)*
Medical Murray, North Barrington Also called Murray Inc *(G-15287)*
Medical Radiation Concepts 630 289-1515
857 Marina Ter W Bartlett (60103) *(G-1297)*
Medical Records Co 847 662-6373
317 Stewart Ave Waukegan (60085) *(G-20465)*
Medical Specialties Distrs LLC 630 307-6200
1549 Hunter Rd Hanover Park (60133) *(G-11009)*
Medicate Dme Inc 618 874-3000
1833 Kingshighway East Saint Louis (62204) *(G-8314)*
Medicate Pharmacy Inc 618 482-2002
911 Water St Cahokia (62206) *(G-2762)*
Medicate Pharmacy Dme, Cahokia Also called Medicate Pharmacy Inc *(G-2762)*
Medifix Inc 847 965-1898
8727 Narragansett Ave Morton Grove (60053) *(G-14427)*
Medigroup Inc 630 554-5533
14a Stonehill Rd Oswego (60543) *(G-16013)*
Medline Industries (PA) 847 949-5500
3 Lakes Dr Northfield (60093) *(G-15523)*
Medline Industries Inc 618 283-4036
1015 W Jefferson St Vandalia (62471) *(G-20014)*
Medline Industries Inc 847 949-2056
1200 Townline Rd Mundelein (60060) *(G-14715)*
Medline Industries Inc 847 949-5500
1170 S Northpoint Blvd Waukegan (60085) *(G-20466)*
Medplast Group Inc 630 706-5500
1520 Kensington Rd # 313 Oak Brook (60523) *(G-15642)*
Medtex Health Services Inc 630 789-0330
554 Willowcreek Ct Clarendon Hills (60514) *(G-6900)*
Medtext Inc 630 325-3277
15w560 89th St Burr Ridge (60527) *(G-2702)*
Medtorque, Elmhurst Also called Inland Midwest Corporation *(G-9378)*
Medtronic Inc 815 444-2500
815 Tek Dr Crystal Lake (60014) *(G-7225)*
Medtronic Inc 630 627-6677
1 E 22nd St Ste 407 Lombard (60148) *(G-13099)*

Mef Construction Inc 847 741-8601
707 Mariner Ct Elgin (60120) *(G-8655)*
Mega Corporation 847 985-1900
516 Morse Ave Schaumburg (60193) *(G-18626)*
Mega Circuit Inc 630 543-8460
1040 S Westgate St Addison (60101) *(G-196)*
Mega Equipment Inc 309 764-5310
1834 46th St Moline (61265) *(G-14160)*
Mega Manufacturing Inc 620 663-1127
650 Race St Rockford (61101) *(G-17515)*
Mega Polymers Inc 815 230-0092
1343 Enterprise Dr Romeoville (60446) *(G-17849)*
Megadyne America LLC 630 752-0600
221 S Westgate Dr Ste N2 Carol Stream (60188) *(G-3023)*
Megli Lawn Care, Sterling Also called Mag MO Systems *(G-19514)*
MEI, Buffalo Grove Also called Bechara Sim *(G-2514)*
MEI, La Grange Park Also called Marcy Enterprises Inc *(G-12098)*
MEI LLC 630 285-1505
315 N Linden St Itasca (60143) *(G-11699)*
MEI Realty Ltd 847 358-5000
1601 W Colonial Pkwy Inverness (60067) *(G-11597)*
Meier Granite Company 847 678-7300
9966 Pacific Ave Franklin Park (60131) *(G-9989)*
Meilahn Manufacturing Company, Chicago Also called Djr Inc *(G-4372)*
Meinhardt Diamond Tool Co 773 267-3260
3800 W Belmont Ave Chicago (60618) *(G-5388)*
Meinhart Grain Farm Inc 217 683-2692
3546 E 1900th Ave Montrose (62445) *(G-14289)*
Meister Industries Inc 815 623-8919
6608 Saladino Dr Roscoe (61073) *(G-17917)*
Meitheal Pharmaceuticals Inc 773 951-6542
8700 W Bryn Mawr Ave 600s Chicago (60631) *(G-5389)*
Mej 1933 Inc (PA) 847 678-5151
9233 King St Franklin Park (60131) *(G-9990)*
Mekanism Inc 415 908-4000
950 W Washington Blvd Chicago (60607) *(G-5390)*
Mektronix Technology Inc 847 680-3300
530 N Milwaukee Ave Ste B Libertyville (60048) *(G-12677)*
Mel Price Company Inc (PA) 217 442-9092
16395 Lewis Rd Danville (61834) *(G-7364)*
Mel Price Containers, Danville Also called Mel Price Company Inc *(G-7364)*
Mel-O-Cream Donuts, Springfield Also called O-Donuts Inc *(G-19415)*
Mel-O-Cream Donuts Intl Inc 217 483-1825
5456 International Pkwy Springfield (62711) *(G-19404)*
Melinda I Rhodes (PA) 815 569-2789
15423 Capron Rd Capron (61012) *(G-2836)*
Melinta Subsidiary Corp (HQ) 203 624-5606
300 Tristate Intl Ste 272 Lincolnshire (60069) *(G-12783)*
Melinta Subsidiary Corp 203 624-5606
300 Tristate Intl Ste 272 Lincolnshire (60069) *(G-12784)*
Melon Ink Screen Print 847 726-0003
100 Oakwood Rd Ste B Lake Zurich (60047) *(G-12431)*
Melrose Mold & Machine Co Inc 847 233-9970
10085 Pacific Ave Franklin Park (60131) *(G-9991)*
Melt Design Inc 630 443-4000
3803 Illinois Ave Saint Charles (60174) *(G-18232)*
Meltdown Creative Works Inc 309 310-1978
409 E Washington St Bloomington (61701) *(G-2074)*
Melters and More 815 419-2043
512 N Division St Chenoa (61726) *(G-3433)*
Melyx Inc (PA) 309 654-2551
18715 Route 84 N Cordova (61242) *(G-7010)*
Meminger Metal Finishing Inc (PA) 309 582-3363
2107 Se 8th St Aledo (61231) *(G-358)*
Memorable Inc 847 272-8207
3336 Commercial Ave Northbrook (60062) *(G-15431)*
Menard Inc 815 474-6767
2611 Eldamain Rd Plano (60545) *(G-16734)*
Menard Inc 708 346-9144
9100 S Western Ave Evergreen Park (60805) *(G-9597)*
Menard Inc 715 876-5911
2619 Eldamain Rd Bldg 220 Plano (60545) *(G-16735)*
Menasha Corp 630 679-8000
465 W Crossroads Pkwy Bolingbrook (60440) *(G-2210)*
Menasha Packaging Company LLC 630 263-4547
710 N Mattis Ave Champaign (61821) *(G-3320)*
Menasha Packaging Company LLC 773 227-6000
4545 W Palmer St Chicago (60639) *(G-5391)*
Menasha Packaging Company LLC 312 880-4620
350 N Clark St Ste 300 Chicago (60654) *(G-5392)*
Menasha Packaging Company LLC 618 931-7805
21 W Gtwy Commerce Ctr Dr Edwardsville (62025) *(G-8369)*
Menasha Packaging Company LLC 630 236-4011
1700 N Edgelawn Dr Aurora (60506) *(G-1130)*
Menasha Packaging Company LLC 708 552-8946
7770 W 71st St Bridgeview (60455) *(G-2362)*
Menasha Packaging Company LLC 618 501-6040
9 Gatway Cmmerce Ctr Dr E Edwardsville (62025) *(G-8370)*
Menasha Packaging Company LLC 708 482-7619
800 S Weber Rd Ste A Bolingbrook (60490) *(G-2211)*

ALPHABETIC SECTION — **Metal Impregnating Corp**

Menasha Packaging Company LLC 773 489-8332
 1935 Techny Rd Ste 14 Northbrook (60062) *(G-15432)*
Menasha Packaging Company LLC 708 552-8946
 7800 W 71st St Bridgeview (60455) *(G-2363)*
Menasha Packaging Company LLC 312 880-4631
 1251 115th St Ste B Bolingbrook (60490) *(G-2212)*
Menasha Packaging Company LLC 630 391-1741
 456 International Pkwy Minooka (60447) *(G-14062)*
Menasha Packaging Company LLC 708 853-5450
 11671 S Central Ave Alsip (60803) *(G-476)*
Menasha Packaging Company LLC 309 787-1747
 7800 14th St W Rock Island (61201) *(G-17229)*
Mencarini Enterprises Inc 815 398-9565
 4911 26th Ave Rockford (61109) *(G-17516)*
Mendota Agri-Products Inc (PA) 815 539-5633
 448 N 3973rd Rd Mendota (61342) *(G-13946)*
Mendota Monument Co 815 539-7276
 606 Main St Mendota (61342) *(G-13947)*
Mendota Reporter 815 539-9396
 703 Illinois Ave Mendota (61342) *(G-13948)*
Mendota Welding & Mfg 815 539-6944
 1605 One Half 13th Ave Mendota (61342) *(G-13949)*
Mengarelli Enterprises Inc 847 272-6980
 2926 Macarthur Blvd Northbrook (60062) *(G-15433)*
Menges Roller Co Inc 847 487-8877
 260 Industrial Dr Wauconda (60084) *(G-20376)*
Menk Usa LLC 815 626-9730
 2207 Enterprise Dr Sterling (61081) *(G-19518)*
Mennel Milling Co 217 999-2161
 415 E Main St Mount Olive (62069) *(G-14506)*
Mennies Machine Company (PA) 815 339-2226
 Mennie Dr Mark Rr 71 Mark (61340) *(G-13546)*
Mennies Machine Company 815 339-2227
 508 N Saint Paul St Granville (61326) *(G-10757)*
Mennon Rbr & Safety Pdts Inc 847 678-8250
 4932 River Rd Schiller Park (60176) *(G-18823)*
Meno Stone Co Inc 630 257-9220
 10800 Route 83 Lemont (60439) *(G-12571)*
Menoni & Mocogni Inc 847 432-0850
 2160 Skokie Valley Rd Highland Park (60035) *(G-11283)*
Mental Health Ctrs Centl Ill 217 735-1413
 760 S Postville Dr Lincoln (62656) *(G-12735)*
Menus To Go 630 483-0848
 676 Bonded Pkwy Ste A Streamwood (60107) *(G-19584)*
Mer-Pla Inc 847 530-9798
 4535 W Fullerton Ave Chicago (60639) *(G-5393)*
Merchants Metals LLC 847 249-4086
 2800 Northwestern Ave Waukegan (60087) *(G-20467)*
Mercury Eqp Fabg & Machining 847 288-0079
 11415 Melrose Ave Bldg 1 Franklin Park (60131) *(G-9992)*
Mercury Plastics Inc 888 884-1864
 4535 W Fullerton Ave Chicago (60639) *(G-5394)*
Mercury Products Corp (PA) 847 524-4400
 1201 Mercury Dr Schaumburg (60193) *(G-18627)*
Mercurys Green LLC 708 865-9134
 9201 King St Franklin Park (60131) *(G-9993)*
Meredith Corp 312 580-1623
 130 E Randolph St # 1700 Chicago (60601) *(G-5395)*
Merichem Catalyst & Tech Sls, Schaumburg Also called *Merichem Chem Rfinery Svcs LLC* *(G-18628)*
Merichem Chem Rfinery Svcs LLC 847 285-3850
 650 E Algonquin Rd Schaumburg (60173) *(G-18628)*
Meridian Healthcare 815 633-5326
 1718 Northrock Ct Rockford (61103) *(G-17517)*
Meridian Industries Inc 630 892-7651
 911 N Lake St Aurora (60506) *(G-1131)*
Meridian Laboratories Inc 847 808-0081
 1130 W Lake Cook Rd # 202 Buffalo Grove (60089) *(G-2572)*
Meridian Parts Inc 630 718-1995
 445 Jackson Ave Ste 202 Naperville (60540) *(G-14868)*
Merisant Company (HQ) 312 840-6000
 125 S Wacker Dr Ste 3150 Chicago (60606) *(G-5396)*
Merisant Foreign Holdings I (HQ) 312 840-6000
 33 N Dearborn St Ste 200 Chicago (60602) *(G-5397)*
Merisant Us Inc (HQ) 312 840-6000
 125 S Wacker Dr Ste 3150 Chicago (60606) *(G-5398)*
Merisant Us Inc 815 929-2700
 125 S Wacker Dr Ste 3150 Chicago (60606) *(G-5399)*
Merit Emplyment Assssment Svcs 815 320-3680
 342 Alana Dr New Lenox (60451) *(G-15041)*
Merkel Woodworking Inc 630 458-0700
 300 S Stewart Ave Addison (60101) *(G-197)*
Merrill Corporation 312 386-2200
 200 W Jackson Blvd Fl 11 Chicago (60606) *(G-5400)*
Merrill Fine Arts Engrv Inc (HQ) 312 786-6300
 311 S Wacker Dr Ste 300 Chicago (60606) *(G-5401)*
Merrimac Lab, Geneva Also called *Dental Laboratory Inc* *(G-10265)*
Merritt & Edwards Corporation 309 828-4741
 302 E Washington St Bloomington (61701) *(G-2075)*

Merritt Farm Equipment Inc 217 746-5331
 1875 E County Road 2000 N Carthage (62321) *(G-3138)*
Merritt Rv, Carthage Also called *Merritt Farm Equipment Inc* *(G-3138)*
Merry Walker Corporation 847 837-9580
 21350 W Sylvan Dr S Mundelein (60060) *(G-14716)*
Mersigns 618 234-4450
 1700 N Belt E Belleville (62221) *(G-1575)*
Mertel Gravel Company Inc 815 223-0468
 2400 Water St Peru (61354) *(G-16581)*
Mervis Industries Inc (PA) 217 442-5300
 3295 E Main St Ste C Danville (61834) *(G-7365)*
Mervis Industries Inc 217 235-5575
 612 N Logan St Mattoon (61938) *(G-13648)*
Mervis Industries Inc 217 753-1492
 1100 S 9th St Springfield (62703) *(G-19405)*
Mervis Iron & Metal Div, Danville Also called *Mervis Industries Inc* *(G-7365)*
Mervis Recycling, Springfield Also called *Mervis Industries Inc* *(G-19405)*
Meryll 200000 Mile Check, Yorkville Also called *Deyco Inc* *(G-21480)*
Merz Air Conditioning and Htg 217 342-2323
 509 S Willow St Effingham (62401) *(G-8409)*
Merz Vault Company Inc 618 548-2859
 2918 State Route 37 Salem (62881) *(G-18345)*
Meshplusplus Inc 847 494-6325
 935 W Chestnut St Ste 505 Chicago (60642) *(G-5402)*
Mesic Vale LLC 309 335-8521
 161 S Cherry St Ste 207 Galesburg (61401) *(G-10209)*
Meskan Foundry, Chicago Also called *Louis Meskan Brass Foundry Inc* *(G-5267)*
Message Mediums LLC 312 566-4300
 222 Merchandise Mart Plz # 1818 Chicago (60654) *(G-5403)*
Messenger 618 235-9601
 2620 Lebanon Ave Unit 2 Belleville (62221) *(G-1576)*
Messer LLC 309 353-9717
 125 Distillery Rd Pekin (61554) *(G-16344)*
Messer LLC 630 690-3010
 640 Kimberly Dr Carol Stream (60188) *(G-3024)*
Messer LLC 630 515-2576
 1751 W Diehl Rd Ste 300 Naperville (60563) *(G-14869)*
Messer LLC 618 251-5217
 1200 S Delmar Ave Hartford (62048) *(G-11035)*
Messer Machine 815 398-6248
 2327 20th Ave Rockford (61104) *(G-17518)*
Messer North America Inc 630 897-1900
 1998 Albright Rd Montgomery (60538) *(G-14262)*
Messer North America Inc 630 257-3612
 810 E Romeo Rd Lockport (60441) *(G-13012)*
Met Plastics, Elk Grove Village Also called *Met2plastic LLC* *(G-9116)*
Met Plastics 847 228-5070
 333 King St Elk Grove Village (60007) *(G-9115)*
Met-Pro Technologies LLC 630 775-0707
 905 Sivert Dr Wood Dale (60191) *(G-21215)*
Met2plastic LLC 847 228-5070
 701 Lee St Elk Grove Village (60007) *(G-9116)*
Meta TEC Development Inc (PA) 309 246-2960
 125 N Commercial St Lacon (61540) *(G-12131)*
Meta TEC of Illinois Inc 309 246-2960
 125 N Commercial St Lacon (61540) *(G-12132)*
Meta-Meg Tool Corporation 847 742-3600
 1434 Davis Rd Elgin (60123) *(G-8656)*
Metal Acesories, Elk Grove Village Also called *Dayton Superior Corporation* *(G-8939)*
Metal Arts Finishing Inc 630 892-6744
 1001 S Lake St Aurora (60506) *(G-1132)*
Metal Box International LLC 847 455-8500
 11600 King St Franklin Park (60131) *(G-9994)*
Metal Briquetters, Rosemont Also called *Chemalloy Company LLC* *(G-18004)*
Metal Center News 630 571-1067
 1010 Jorie Blvd Ste 44 Oak Brook (60523) *(G-15643)*
Metal Ceramics Inc 847 678-2293
 9306 Belmont Ave Franklin Park (60131) *(G-9995)*
Metal Construction News, Skokie Also called *Modern Trade Communications* *(G-18992)*
Metal Crafters, Monmouth Also called *Kim Gough* *(G-14221)*
Metal Culverts Inc 309 543-2271
 15732 Rte 97 S Havana (62644) *(G-11117)*
Metal Decor, Springfield Also called *Associates Engraving Company* *(G-19321)*
Metal Edge Inc 708 756-4696
 624 Anderson Dr Ste A Romeoville (60446) *(G-17850)*
Metal Finishers, Arlington Heights Also called *Britt Industries Inc* *(G-710)*
Metal Finishing Pros Corp 630 883-8339
 41 N Union St Elgin (60123) *(G-8657)*
Metal Finishing Research Corp 773 373-0800
 4025 S Princeton Ave Chicago (60609) *(G-5404)*
Metal Images Inc 847 488-9877
 325 Corporate Dr Elgin (60123) *(G-8658)*
Metal Impact LLC 847 718-0192
 1501 Oakton St Elk Grove Village (60007) *(G-9117)*
Metal Impact South LLC 847 718-9300
 1501 Oakton St Elk Grove Village (60007) *(G-9118)*
Metal Impregnating Corp 630 543-3443
 121 W Official Rd Addison (60101) *(G-198)*

(PA)=Parent Co (HQ)=Headquarters (DH)=Div Headquarters

2020 Harris Illinois Industrial Directory

Metal Improvement Company LLC 630 543-4950
678 W Winthrop Ave Addison (60101) ***(G-199)***
Metal Improvement Company LLC 630 620-6808
129 Eisenhower Ln S Lombard (60148) ***(G-13100)***
Metal Management Inc 773 721-1100
9331 S Ewing Ave Chicago (60617) ***(G-5405)***
Metal Management Inc 773 489-1800
1509 W Cortland St Chicago (60642) ***(G-5406)***
Metal Mfg LLC 815 432-4595
475 N Veterans Pkwy Watseka (60970) ***(G-20311)***
Metal Prep Services Inc 815 874-7631
5434 International Dr Rockford (61109) ***(G-17519)***
Metal Products Sales Corp 708 301-6844
15700 S Parker Rd Lockport (60491) ***(G-13013)***
Metal Resources Intl LLC 847 806-7200
1965 Pratt Blvd Elk Grove Village (60007) ***(G-9119)***
Metal Sales Manufacturing Corp 309 787-1200
8111 29th St W Rock Island (61201) ***(G-17230)***
Metal Spinners Inc 815 625-0390
802 E 11th St Rock Falls (61071) ***(G-17189)***
Metal Strip Buiding Products 847 742-8500
1345 Norwood Ave Itasca (60143) ***(G-11700)***
Metal Substrates, Carpentersville *Also called Performance Industries Inc* ***(G-3111)***
Metal Tech Inc 630 529-7400
80 Monaco Dr Roselle (60172) ***(G-17969)***
Metal Works, Northbrook *Also called We Innovex Inc* ***(G-15500)***
Metal Works Machine Inc 217 868-5111
11100 E 1850th Ave Shumway (62461) ***(G-18905)***
Metal-Matic Inc 708 594-7553
7200 S Narragansett Ave Bedford Park (60638) ***(G-1481)***
Metal-Rite Inc 708 656-3832
3140 S 61st Ave Cicero (60804) ***(G-6866)***
Metalex Corporation, Libertyville *Also called Metalex LLC* ***(G-12678)***
Metalex LLC 847 362-5400
700 Liberty Dr Libertyville (60048) ***(G-12678)***
Metals & Metals LLC 630 866-4200
999 Remington Blvd Ste C Bolingbrook (60440) ***(G-2213)***
Metals and Services Inc 630 627-2900
145 N Swift Rd Addison (60101) ***(G-200)***
Metals Technology Corporation 630 221-2500
120 N Schmale Rd Carol Stream (60188) ***(G-3025)***
Metalstamp Inc 815 467-7800
6800 E Minooka Rd Minooka (60447) ***(G-14063)***
Metalsupermarkets LLC, Bolingbrook *Also called Metals & Metals LLC* ***(G-2213)***
Metaltek Fabricating Inc 708 534-9102
2595 Bond St University Park (60484) ***(G-19960)***
Metamation Inc (PA) 775 826-1717
1900 W Central Rd Hoffman Estates (60192) ***(G-11434)***
Metamora Industries LLC 309 367-2368
723 N Wiedman St Metamora (61548) ***(G-13964)***
Metco Treating and Dev Co 773 277-1600
2001 S Kilbourn Ave Chicago (60623) ***(G-5407)***
Meteer Inc 217 636-7280
16592 Kincaid St Athens (62613) ***(G-898)***
Meteer Manufacturing Co 217 636-8109
25904 Meteer Ln Athens (62613) ***(G-899)***
Metform LLC 815 273-2201
2551 Wacker Rd Savanna (61074) ***(G-18407)***
Metform LLC 815 273-0230
7034 Rte 84 S Savanna (61074) ***(G-18408)***
Metform LLC (HQ) 847 566-0010
1000 Allanson Rd Mundelein (60060) ***(G-14717)***
Metform LLC 815 273-2201
905 S Jackson St Mount Carroll (61053) ***(G-14495)***
Method Molds Inc 815 877-0191
5085 Contractors Dr Loves Park (61111) ***(G-13236)***
Methode Development Co 708 867-6777
7401 W Wilson Ave Chicago (60706) ***(G-5408)***
Methode Electronics Inc (PA) 708 867-6777
8750 W Bryn Mawr Ave # 1000 Chicago (60631) ***(G-5409)***
Methode Electronics Inc 847 577-9545
1700 Hicks Rd Rolling Meadows (60008) ***(G-17750)***
Methode Electronics Inc 217 357-3941
111 W Buchanan St Carthage (62321) ***(G-3139)***
Meto-Grafics Inc 847 639-0044
111 Erick St Ste 116 Crystal Lake (60014) ***(G-7226)***
Metokote Corporation 815 223-1190
5750 State Route 251 Peru (61354) ***(G-16582)***
Metomic Corporation 773 247-4716
2944 W 26th St Chicago (60623) ***(G-5410)***
Metraflex Company 312 738-3800
2323 W Hubbard St Chicago (60612) ***(G-5411)***
Metric Machine Shop Inc 847 439-9891
101 Kelly St Ste D Elk Grove Village (60007) ***(G-9120)***
Metrie 815 717-2660
2200 W Haven Ave New Lenox (60451) ***(G-15042)***
Metritrack Inc 630 607-9311
4415 Harrison St Ste 243 Hillside (60162) ***(G-11347)***
Metro Cabinet Refinishers 217 498-7174
7032 Ramblewood Dr Rochester (62563) ***(G-17169)***
Metro East Fiberglass Repair 618 235-9217
1166 Heneral Ave Belleville (62220) ***(G-1577)***
Metro East Manufacturing 618 233-0182
1120 N Illinois St Swansea (62226) ***(G-19693)***
Metro Paint Supplies 708 385-7701
14032 Kostner Ave Unit G Midlothian (60445) ***(G-13994)***
Metro Printing & Pubg Inc 618 476-9587
109 W Washington St Millstadt (62260) ***(G-14052)***
Metro Service Center 618 524-8583
103 W 10th St Ste B Metropolis (62960) ***(G-13973)***
Metro Tool Company 847 673-6790
8315 Ridgeway Ave Skokie (60076) ***(G-18988)***
Metroeast Motorsports Inc 618 628-2466
1714 Frontage Rd O Fallon (62269) ***(G-15580)***
Metrology Resource Group Inc 815 703-3141
316 Warren Ave Rockford (61107) ***(G-17520)***
Metrom LLC (not Llc) 847 847-7233
904 Donata Ct Lake Zurich (60047) ***(G-12432)***
Metrom Rail LLC 855 943-8726
1125 Mitchell Ct Crystal Lake (60014) ***(G-7227)***
Metronet Integration Inc 312 781-0045
811 W Oakdale Ave Apt G Chicago (60657) ***(G-5412)***
Metropolis Ready Mix Inc (PA) 618 524-8221
1200 E 2nd St Metropolis (62960) ***(G-13974)***
Metropolitan Brewing LLC 773 474-6893
3057 N Rockwell St Chicago (60618) ***(G-5413)***
Metropolitan Graphic Arts Inc 847 566-9502
3818 Grandville Ave Gurnee (60031) ***(G-10896)***
Metropolitan Industries Inc 815 886-9200
37 Forestwood Dr Romeoville (60446) ***(G-17851)***
Metropolitan Newspapers, The, Oakbrook Terrace *Also called Gatehouse Media LLC* ***(G-15799)***
Metropolitan Printers 309 694-1114
109 E Washington St East Peoria (61611) ***(G-8277)***
Metropolitan Pump Company, Romeoville *Also called Metropolitan Industries Inc* ***(G-17851)***
Mettes Cabinet Corner Inc 217 342-9552
3240 S Banker St Effingham (62401) ***(G-8410)***
Mettle Sports LLC 312 757-6373
1555 Sherman Ave Ste 22 Evanston (60201) ***(G-9550)***
Mettler-Toledo LLC 630 446-7700
2640 White Oak Cir Ste A Aurora (60502) ***(G-1002)***
Metzger Welding & Machine, Mattoon *Also called Metzger Welding Service* ***(G-13649)***
Metzger Welding Service 217 234-2851
2900 Marshall Ave Mattoon (61938) ***(G-13649)***
Metzka Inc 815 932-6363
431 S Washington Ave Kankakee (60901) ***(G-11991)***
Mevert Automotive Inc 618 965-9609
1014 W Broadway Steeleville (62288) ***(G-19484)***
Mevert Automotive & Welding, Steeleville *Also called Mevert Automotive Inc* ***(G-19484)***
Mexacali Silkscreen Inc 630 628-9313
931 W National Ave Addison (60101) ***(G-201)***
Mexicali Hard Chrome Corp 630 543-0646
502 W Winthrop Ave Addison (60101) ***(G-202)***
Mexicandy Distributor Inc 773 847-0024
2332 S Blue Island Ave Chicago (60608) ***(G-5414)***
Mexichem Specialty Resins Inc 309 364-2154
1546 County Road 1450 N Henry (61537) ***(G-11167)***
Mexico Enterprise Corporation 920 568-8900
6859 W 64th Pl Chicago (60638) ***(G-5415)***
Mexinox USA Inc 224 533-6700
2275 Half Day Rd Ste 300 Bannockburn (60015) ***(G-1203)***
Meyer E M S, Normal *Also called Meyer Electronic Mfg Svcs Inc* ***(G-15209)***
Meyer Electronic Mfg Svcs Inc 309 808-4100
440 Wylie Dr Normal (61761) ***(G-15209)***
Meyer Engineering Co 847 746-1500
1139 Lewis Ave Winthrop Harbor (60096) ***(G-21141)***
Meyer Enterprises LLC (PA) 309 698-0062
401 Truck Haven Rd East Peoria (61611) ***(G-8278)***
Meyer Machine & Equipment Inc (PA) 847 395-2977
351 Main St Antioch (60002) ***(G-625)***
Meyer Material Co Merger Corp 847 658-7811
10500 S Il Route 31 Algonquin (60102) ***(G-381)***
Meyer Material Co Merger Corp 847 824-4111
1s194 Il Route 47 Elburn (60119) ***(G-8460)***
Meyer Material Co Merger Corp 815 943-2605
20806 Mcguire Rd Harvard (60033) ***(G-11060)***
Meyer Material Co Merger Corp 815 331-7200
1021 Frances Dr Streamwood (60107) ***(G-19585)***
Meyer Material Co Merger Corp 847 689-9200
30288 N Skokie Hwy Lake Bluff (60044) ***(G-12196)***
Meyer Metal Systems Inc 847 468-0500
1111 Davis Rd Elgin (60123) ***(G-8659)***
Meyer Mtl Streamwood Yard 3, Streamwood *Also called Meyer Material Co Merger Corp* ***(G-19585)***
Meyer Signs & Graphics, Gilberts *Also called Ron Meyer* ***(G-10367)***
Meyer Steel Drum Inc 773 522-3030
2000 S Kilbourn Ave Chicago (60623) ***(G-5416)***
Meyer Steel Drum Inc (PA) 773 376-8376
3201 S Millard Ave Chicago (60623) ***(G-5417)***

ALPHABETIC SECTION Microsoft Corporation

Meyer Systems 815 436-7077
25035 W Black Rd Joliet (60404) ***(G-11900)***

Meyer Tool & Manufacturing Inc 708 425-9080
4601 Southwest Hwy Oak Lawn (60453) ***(G-15727)***

Meyercord Revenue Inc 630 682-6200
475 Village Dr Carol Stream (60188) ***(G-3026)***

MFC, Peoria *Also called Midwest Hydra-Line Inc* ***(G-16475)***

Mfi Industries Inc 708 841-0727
14000 S Stewart Ave Riverdale (60827) ***(G-17073)***

Mfp Holding Co (HQ) 312 666-3366
1414 S Western Ave Chicago (60608) ***(G-5418)***

Mfr Manufacturing Corp Inc 815 552-3333
1065 Sill Ave Aurora (60506) ***(G-1133)***

Mfs Holdings LLC 815 385-7700
1805 Dot St McHenry (60050) ***(G-13769)***

Mfw Services Inc 708 522-5879
215 W 155th St South Holland (60473) ***(G-19232)***

MGA Innovation Inc 847 672-9947
3818 Grandville Ave Gurnee (60031) ***(G-10897)***

Mgb Engineering Company (PA) 847 956-7444
1099 Touhy Ave Elk Grove Village (60007) ***(G-9121)***

Mgi Services, Aurora *Also called Mid-America Underground LLC* ***(G-1134)***

Mgn Tool & Mfg Co Inc 630 849-3575
373 Randy Rd Carol Stream (60188) ***(G-3027)***

Mgp Holding Corp 847 967-5600
6451 Main St Morton Grove (60053) ***(G-14428)***

Mgp Ingredients Illinois Inc 309 353-3990
1301 S Front St Pekin (61554) ***(G-16345)***

Mgpi Processing Inc 309 353-3990
1301 S Front St Pekin (61554) ***(G-16346)***

Mgr Imports, Lincolnwood *Also called Quay Corporation Inc* ***(G-12836)***

Mgs Group North America Inc 847 371-1158
14050 W Lambs Ln Ste 4 Libertyville (60048) ***(G-12679)***

Mgs Manufacturing Group, Antioch *Also called All West Plastics Inc* ***(G-598)***

Mgs Mfg Group Inc 847 968-4335
14050 Lands Ln Ste 2 Libertyville (60048) ***(G-12680)***

Mgsolutions Inc 630 530-2005
451 N York St Elmhurst (60126) ***(G-9401)***

Mh Equipment Company 217 443-7210
1010 E Fairchild St Danville (61832) ***(G-7366)***

MHS Ltd 773 736-3333
6616 W Irving Park Rd Chicago (60634) ***(G-5419)***

Mhub 773 580-1485
965 W Chicago Ave Chicago (60642) ***(G-5420)***

Mhwp 618 228-7600
307 W Harrison St Aviston (62216) ***(G-1182)***

MI Vape Co 815 582-3838
1112 W Jefferson St Joliet (60435) ***(G-11901)***

Mi-Jack Products Inc (HQ) 708 596-5200
3111 167th St Hazel Crest (60429) ***(G-11133)***

Mi-Jack Systems & Tech LLC 708 596-3780
3111 167th St Hazel Crest (60429) ***(G-11134)***

Mi-Te Fast Printers Inc 312 236-3278
311 Park Ave Glencoe (60022) ***(G-10432)***

Mi-Te Fast Printers Inc (PA) 312 236-8352
180 W Washington St Fl 2 Chicago (60602) ***(G-5421)***

Mi-Te Printing & Graphics, Glencoe *Also called Mi-Te Fast Printers Inc* ***(G-10432)***

Mi-Te Printing & Graphics, Chicago *Also called Mi-Te Fast Printers Inc* ***(G-5421)***

Mic Quality Service Inc 847 778-5676
3500 S Morgan St Chicago (60609) ***(G-5422)***

Mica Furniture Mfg Inc 708 430-1150
1130 W Fullerton Ave Addison (60101) ***(G-203)***

Micanan Systems Inc 630 501-1909
721 W Racquet Club Dr Addison (60101) ***(G-204)***

Mich Enterprises Inc 630 616-9000
720 Creel Dr Wood Dale (60191) ***(G-21216)***

Michael A Greenberg MD Ltd 847 364-4717
800 Biesterfield Rd # 3002 Elk Grove Village (60007) ***(G-9122)***

Michael Burza 815 909-0233
122 E Meadow Dr Cortland (60112) ***(G-7024)***

Michael Christopher Ltd 815 308-5018
1007 Trakk Ln Woodstock (60098) ***(G-21410)***

Michael P Jones 217 787-7457
3124 Montvale Dr Ste C Springfield (62704) ***(G-19406)***

Michael Reggis Clark 618 533-3841
1308 N Elm St Centralia (62801) ***(G-3238)***

Michael Wilton Cstm Homes Inc 630 508-1200
6458 Cambridge Rd Willowbrook (60527) ***(G-21049)***

Michaels Ross and Cole Inc (PA) 630 916-0662
2001 Midwest Rd Ste 310 Oak Brook (60523) ***(G-15644)***

Michaels Equipment Co 618 524-8560
5481 Illinois 145 Rd Metropolis (62960) ***(G-13975)***

Michel Fertilizer & Equipment 618 242-6000
1313 Shawnee St Mount Vernon (62864) ***(G-14624)***

Michel's Frame Shop & Gallery, Niles *Also called Michels Frame Shop* ***(G-15145)***

Michelangelo & Donata Burdi 773 427-1437
6411 W Addison St Chicago (60634) ***(G-5423)***

Michele Baking Company 847 451-9481
3140 Mannheim Rd Franklin Park (60131) ***(G-9996)***

Michele Terrell 312 305-0876
230 Dodge Ave Unit C Evanston (60202) ***(G-9551)***

Michelmann Steel Cnstr Co 217 222-0555
137 N 2nd St Quincy (62301) ***(G-16912)***

Michels Frame Shop 847 647-7366
7120 W Touhy Ave Niles (60714) ***(G-15145)***

Michigan Renewable Carbon, Chicago *Also called Rnfl Acquisition LLC* ***(G-6041)***

Mickey Finns Brewery, Libertyville *Also called Libertyville Brewing Company* ***(G-12668)***

Mickey Truck Bodies Inc 309 827-8227
14661 Old Colonial Rd Bloomington (61705) ***(G-2076)***

Mickhali Local Distributors, Chicago *Also called Charlotte Louise Tate* ***(G-4076)***

Micro Circuit Inc 630 628-5760
1225 W National Ave Addison (60101) ***(G-205)***

Micro Craft Manufacturing Co 847 679-2022
7248 Saint Louis Ave Skokie (60076) ***(G-18989)***

Micro Lapping & Grinding Co 847 455-5446
2330 17th St Unit B Franklin Park (60131) ***(G-9997)***

Micro Matic Usa Inc 815 968-7557
10726 N 2nd St Machesney Park (61115) ***(G-13359)***

Micro Mold Corporation 630 628-0777
777 W Annoreno Dr Addison (60101) ***(G-206)***

Micro Products Company 630 406-9550
6523 N Galena Rd Peoria (61614) ***(G-16472)***

Micro Products Company 309 697-1216
6523 N Galena Rd Peoria (61614) ***(G-16473)***

Micro Punch & Die Co 815 874-5544
5536 International Dr Rockford (61109) ***(G-17521)***

Micro Screw Machine Co Inc 815 397-2115
2115 15th St Rockford (61104) ***(G-17522)***

Micro Surface Corporation 815 942-4221
465 Briscoe Dr Morris (60450) ***(G-14312)***

Micro West Ltd 630 766-7160
326 Evergreen Ave Bensenville (60106) ***(G-1850)***

Microchip Technology Inc 630 285-0071
333 W Pierce Rd Ste 180 Itasca (60143) ***(G-11701)***

Microcut Engineering, Gilberts *Also called Gator Products Inc* ***(G-10355)***

Microdynamics Corporation (PA) 630 276-0527
1400 Shore Rd Naperville (60563) ***(G-14870)***

Microdynamics Group, Naperville *Also called Microdynamics Corporation* ***(G-14870)***

Micrograms Inc 815 877-4455
805 Hemlock Ln Rockford (61107) ***(G-17523)***

Micrograms Software, Rockford *Also called Micrograms Inc* ***(G-17523)***

Microguide Inc 630 964-3335
1635 Plum Ct Downers Grove (60515) ***(G-8054)***

Microlink Devices Inc 847 588-3001
6457 W Howard St Niles (60714) ***(G-15146)***

Microlink Graphics, Schaumburg *Also called Communications Resource Inc* ***(G-18482)***

Microlite, Batavia *Also called Musco Sports Lighting LLC* ***(G-1396)***

Microlite Corporation (HQ) 630 876-0500
1150 Powis Rd Ste 8 West Chicago (60185) ***(G-20617)***

Microlution Inc 773 282-6495
6635 W Irving Park Rd Chicago (60634) ***(G-5424)***

Micromatic Spring Stamping Inc (PA) 630 607-0141
45 N Church St Addison (60101) ***(G-207)***

Micron Engineering Co 815 455-2888
2125 E Dean Woodstock Crystal Lake (60039) ***(G-7228)***

Micron Filter Cartridge Corp., Elmhurst *Also called Micron Filter Cartridges Corp* ***(G-9402)***

Micron Filter Cartridges Corp 630 337-3877
506 S Spring Rd Ste 3 Elmhurst (60126) ***(G-9402)***

Micron Industries Corporation (PA) 630 516-1222
1211 W 22nd St Ste 200 Oak Brook (60523) ***(G-15645)***

Micron Industries Corporation 815 380-2222
1801 Westwood Dr Ste 2 Sterling (61081) ***(G-19519)***

Micron Metal Finishing LLC 708 599-0055
8585 S 77th Ave Bridgeview (60455) ***(G-2364)***

Micron Mold & Mfg Inc 630 871-9531
1085 Idaho St Carol Stream (60188) ***(G-3028)***

Micron Power, Oak Brook *Also called Micron Industries Corporation* ***(G-15645)***

Micron Power, Sterling *Also called Micron Industries Corporation* ***(G-19519)***

Micron Semiconductor, Chicago *Also called Micron Technology Inc* ***(G-5425)***

Micron Technology Inc 208 368-4000
12829 Collections Ctr Dr Chicago (60693) ***(G-5425)***

Micronics Engineered Filtrtion, Romeoville *Also called C P Environmental Inc* ***(G-17801)***

Microplasma Ozone Tech Inc 217 693-7950
2105 W Park Ct Champaign (61821) ***(G-3321)***

Microprint Inc 630 969-1710
1294 Lakeview Dr Romeoville (60446) ***(G-17852)***

Micros Systems Inc 443 285-6000
2 Pierce Pl Ste 1700 Itasca (60143) ***(G-11702)***

Microsoft Corporation 847 864-4777
1822 Ridge Ave Ste 210 Evanston (60201) ***(G-9552)***

Microsoft Corporation 630 725-4000
3025 Highland Pkwy # 300 Downers Grove (60515) ***(G-8055)***

Microsoft Corporation 309 665-0113
2203 E Empire St Ste J Bloomington (61704) ***(G-2077)***

Microsoft Corporation 708 409-4759
601 Northwest Ave Northlake (60164) ***(G-15551)***

ALPHABETIC

Microsun Electronics Corp 630 410-7900
1200 Internationale Pkwy # 101 Woodridge (60517) *(G-21323)*
Microtech Machine Inc 847 870-0707
222 Camp Mcdonald Rd Wheeling (60090) *(G-20940)*
Microtek Pattern Inc 217 428-0433
2035 N Jasper St Decatur (62526) *(G-7522)*
Microthincom Inc 630 543-0501
661 Frontier Way Bensenville (60106) *(G-1851)*
Microware Inc 847 943-9113
2418 Swainwood Dr Glenview (60025) *(G-10588)*
Microwave RES & Applications 630 480-7456
190 Easy St Ste A Carol Stream (60188) *(G-3029)*
Microway Systems Div Glenair, Lincolnwood *Also called Glenair Inc (G-12823)*
Microway Systems Inc 847 679-8833
7000 N Lawndale Ave Lincolnwood (60712) *(G-12830)*
Mid America Chemical, Glenview *Also called Mid America Intl Inc (G-10589)*
Mid America Intl Inc 847 635-8303
1245 Milwaukee Ave # 202 Glenview (60025) *(G-10589)*
Mid America Recycling, Mahomet *Also called Mid-America Sand & Gravel (G-13426)*
Mid America Web Solutions, Belleville *Also called Headball Inc (G-1555)*
Mid Central Printing & Mailing 847 251-4040
1211 Wilmette Ave Wilmette (60091) *(G-21087)*
Mid City Printing Service 773 777-5400
5566 N Northwest Hwy Chicago (60630) *(G-5426)*
Mid Illinois Quarry Company 217 932-2611
9129 N 230th St Casey (62420) *(G-3206)*
Mid Oaks Investments LLC (PA) 847 215-3475
750 W Lake Cook Rd # 460 Buffalo Grove (60089) *(G-2573)*
Mid Pack 773 626-3500
4610 W West End Ave Chicago (60644) *(G-5427)*
Mid River Minerals Inc 815 941-7524
4675 Weitz Rd Morris (60450) *(G-14313)*
Mid State Graphics (PA) 309 772-3843
496 W Harris Ave Bushnell (61422) *(G-2745)*
Mid States Corporation 708 754-1760
3245 Holeman Ave S Chicago Hts (60411) *(G-18125)*
Mid States Distributing, Fairfield *Also called Mid States Salvage (G-9632)*
Mid States Salvage 618 842-6741
6 Petroleum Blvd Fairfield (62837) *(G-9632)*
Mid States Tool & Cutter, Bensenville *Also called Midstates Cutting Tools Inc (G-1852)*
Mid West Investors Solutions, Geneva *Also called R & R Creative Graphics Inc (G-10301)*
Mid-America Carbonates LLC 618 944-6171
Il 146 Cave In Rock (62919) *(G-3220)*
Mid-America Carbonates LLC 217 222-3500
520 N 30th St Quincy (62301) *(G-16913)*
Mid-America Government Supply, Glendale Heights *Also called Mid-America Taping Reeling Inc (G-10475)*
Mid-America Plastic Company 815 938-3110
500 E Avon St Forreston (61030) *(G-9741)*
Mid-America Sand & Gravel (PA) 217 586-4536
250 County Rd 2050 N Mahomet (61853) *(G-13426)*
Mid-America Sand & Gravel 217 355-1307
2906 N Oak St Urbana (61802) *(G-19988)*
Mid-America Taping Reeling Inc (PA) 630 629-6646
121 Exchange Blvd Glendale Heights (60139) *(G-10475)*
Mid-America Truck Corporation 815 672-3211
1807 N Bloomington St Streator (61364) *(G-19614)*
Mid-America Underground LLC 630 443-9999
901 Ridgeway Ave Aurora (60506) *(G-1134)*
Mid-American Elevator Co Inc (PA) 773 486-6900
820 N Wolcott Ave Chicago (60622) *(G-5428)*
Mid-American Elevator Co Inc 815 740-1204
1000 Sak Dr Unit A Joliet (60403) *(G-11902)*
Mid-American Elevator Eqp Co 773 486-6900
820 N Wolcott Ave Chicago (60622) *(G-5429)*
Mid-Amrica Prtctive Ctings Inc 630 628-4501
85 W Industrial Rd Addison (60101) *(G-208)*
Mid-Central Business Forms 309 692-9090
1413 W Sunnyview Dr Peoria (61614) *(G-16474)*
Mid-City Die & Mold Corp 773 278-4844
1743 N Keating Ave Chicago (60639) *(G-5430)*
Mid-Illinois Concrete Inc 217 235-5858
1413 Dewitt Ave E Mattoon (61938) *(G-13650)*
Mid-Illinois Concrete Inc 217 382-6650
1001 N Ridgelawn Rd Martinsville (62442) *(G-13586)*
Mid-Illinois Concrete Inc 618 664-1340
1311 S 4th St Greenville (62246) *(G-10838)*
Mid-Illinois Concrete Inc 618 283-1600
1021 Janette Dr Vandalia (62471) *(G-20015)*
Mid-Illinois Concrete Inc 217 345-6404
2417 18th St Charleston (61920) *(G-3407)*
Mid-Oak Distillery Inc 708 926-9131
14800 S Mckinley Ave Posen (60469) *(G-16797)*
Mid-State Industries Oper Inc (PA) 217 268-3900
908 Bob King Dr Arcola (61910) *(G-656)*
Mid-State Tank Co Inc 217 728-8383
1357 Johnson Creek Rd Sullivan (61951) *(G-19670)*
Mid-States Concrete Inds LLC 815 389-2277
500 S Park Ave 550 South Beloit (61080) *(G-19103)*
Mid-States Door and Hardware, Quincy *Also called Michelmann Steel Cnstr Co (G-16912)*
Mid-States Forging Die-Tool 815 226-2313
2844 Eastrock Dr Rockford (61109) *(G-17524)*
Mid-States Services LLC 618 842-4726
6 Petroleum Blvd Fairfield (62837) *(G-9633)*
Mid-States Wire Proc Corp 773 379-3775
4642 W Maypole Ave Chicago (60644) *(G-5431)*
Mid-West Feeder Inc 815 544-2994
601 E Pleasant St Belvidere (61008) *(G-1686)*
Mid-West Millwork Wholesale 618 407-5940
9 W Green St Mascoutah (62258) *(G-13603)*
Mid-West Screw Products Inc (PA) 773 283-6032
3523 N Kenton Ave Chicago (60641) *(G-5432)*
Mid-West Spring & Stamping Inc (HQ) 630 739-3800
1404 N Joliet Rd Ste C Romeoville (60446) *(G-17853)*
Mid-West Spring & Stamping Inc 630 739-3800
1404 Joliet Rd Ste C Romeoville (60446) *(G-17854)*
Mid-West Spring and Stamping, Romeoville *Also called Mid-West Spring Mfg Co (G-17855)*
Mid-West Spring Mfg Co, Romeoville *Also called Mid-West Spring & Stamping Inc (G-17854)*
Mid-West Spring Mfg Co (PA) 630 739-3800
1404 N Joliet Rd Ste C Romeoville (60446) *(G-17855)*
Midaco Corporation 847 593-8420
2000 Touhy Ave Elk Grove Village (60007) *(G-9123)*
MidAmerican Prtg Systems Inc 312 663-4720
3838 River Rd Schiller Park (60176) *(G-18824)*
MidAmerican Technology Inc 815 496-2400
3708 E 25th Rd Serena (60549) *(G-18864)*
Midas 8793, Montgomery *Also called Tbc Retail Group Inc (G-14271)*
Midco Exploration Inc 630 655-2198
414 Plaza Dr Ste 204 Westmont (60559) *(G-20759)*
Midco International Inc 773 604-8700
4140 W Victoria St Chicago (60646) *(G-5433)*
Midco Petroleum Inc 630 655-2198
336 S Cass Ave Westmont (60559) *(G-20760)*
Midco Production Co Inc (PA) 630 655-2198
414 Plaza Dr Ste 204 Westmont (60559) *(G-20761)*
Middleby Cooking Systems Group, Elgin *Also called Marshall Middleby Inc (G-8649)*
Middleby Corporation (PA) 847 741-3300
1400 Toastmaster Dr Elgin (60120) *(G-8660)*
Middleby Corporation 847 741-3300
1400 Toastmaster Dr Elgin (60120) *(G-8661)*
Middleby Packg Solutions LLC 847 741-3500
1675 Todd Farm Dr Elgin (60123) *(G-8662)*
Middleby Worldwide Inc (HQ) 847 741-3300
1400 Toastmaster Dr Elgin (60120) *(G-8663)*
Middletons Mouldings Inc 517 278-6610
1325 Remington Rd Ste H Schaumburg (60173) *(G-18629)*
Middletown Coke Company LLC 630 284-1755
1011 Warrenville Rd # 600 Lisle (60532) *(G-12910)*
Midland Coal Company 309 362-2795
2203 N Trivoli Rd Trivoli (61569) *(G-19907)*
Midland Davis Corporation (PA) 309 277-1617
3301 4th Ave Moline (61265) *(G-14161)*
Midland Industries Inc 312 664-7300
1424 N Halsted St Chicago (60642) *(G-5434)*
Midland Manufacturing Corp 847 677-0333
7733 Gross Point Rd Skokie (60077) *(G-18990)*
Midland Paper Company (PA) 847 777-2700
101 E Palatine Rd Wheeling (60090) *(G-20941)*
Midland Paper Packaging & Sups, Wheeling *Also called Midland Paper Company (G-20941)*
Midland Plastics Inc 262 938-7000
295 W Walnut St Roselle (60172) *(G-17970)*
Midland Printing, Skokie *Also called Alliance Investment Corp (G-18916)*
Midland Railway Supply Inc (PA) 618 467-6305
1815 W Delmar Ave Godfrey (62035) *(G-10657)*
Midland Stamping and Fabg Corp (PA) 847 678-7573
9521 Ainslie St Schiller Park (60176) *(G-18825)*
Midland Wood Products 618 344-5640
105 Greer Ct Collinsville (62234) *(G-6970)*
Midmark Corporation 800 643-6275
1001 Asbury Dr Buffalo Grove (60089) *(G-2574)*
Midnight Marble, Palatine *Also called Wasowski Jacek (G-16172)*
Midpoint Packaging LLC 630 613-9922
2512 Wisconsin Ave Downers Grove (60515) *(G-8056)*
Midpoint Trade Books Inc (PA) 212 727-0190
814 N Franklin St Ste 100 Chicago (60610) *(G-5435)*
Midstate Core Co 217 429-2673
777 E William St Decatur (62521) *(G-7523)*
Midstate Iron & Metals, Taylorville *Also called Midstate Salvage Corp (G-19759)*
Midstate Manufacturing Company 309 342-9555
750 W 3rd St Galesburg (61401) *(G-10210)*
Midstate Salvage Corp 217 824-6047
1402 W South St Taylorville (62568) *(G-19759)*
Midstates Cutting Tools Inc 630 595-0700
304 Meyer Rd Bensenville (60106) *(G-1852)*
Midstates Rail LLC 708 758-7245
901 State St Chicago Heights (60411) *(G-6758)*
Midtown Fuels 217 347-7191
503 W Jefferson Ave Effingham (62401) *(G-8411)*

ALPHABETIC SECTION

Midtronics Inc (PA) 630 323-2800
7000 Monroe St Willowbrook (60527) *(G-21050)*
Midway Cap Company 773 384-0911
1239 W Madison St Fl 3 Chicago (60607) *(G-5436)*
Midway Cap Company 773 384-0911
4513 W Armitage Ave Chicago (60639) *(G-5437)*
Midway Displays Inc 708 563-2323
6554 S Austin Ave Bedford Park (60638) *(G-1482)*
Midway Grinding Inc 847 439-7424
1451 Lunt Ave Elk Grove Village (60007) *(G-9124)*
Midway Industries Inc 708 594-2600
6750 S Belt Circle Dr Chicago (60638) *(G-5438)*
Midway Machine & Tool Co Inc 708 385-3450
5828 W 117th Pl Alsip (60803) *(G-477)*
Midway Machine Products & Svcs 847 860-8180
2690 American Ln Elk Grove Village (60007) *(G-9125)*
Midway Windows and Doors, Chicago Also called Midway Industries Inc *(G-5438)*
Midwest Aero Support Inc 815 398-9202
1303 Turret Dr Machesney Park (61115) *(G-13360)*
Midwest Agracultural RES Ctr, Seymour Also called Valent USA LLC *(G-18869)*
Midwest Air Pro Inc 773 622-4566
2054 N New England Ave Chicago (60707) *(G-5439)*
Midwest Architectural Millwork 847 621-2013
125 Joey Dr Elk Grove Village (60007) *(G-9126)*
Midwest Awnings Inc 309 762-3339
2201 155th St Cameron (61423) *(G-2808)*
Midwest Bio Manufacturing Div 815 542-6417
310 2650 N Ave Tampico (61283) *(G-19744)*
Midwest Bio-Systems Inc 815 438-7200
28933 35 E St Tampico (61283) *(G-19745)*
Midwest Biofluids Inc 630 790-9708
22w080 Glen Valley Dr Glen Ellyn (60137) *(G-10413)*
Midwest Block and Brick Inc 618 939-7600
8605 State Route 3 Waterloo (62298) *(G-20292)*
Midwest Blow Molding LLC 618 283-9223
1111 Imco Dr Vandalia (62471) *(G-20016)*
Midwest Brass Forging Co 847 678-7023
10015 Franklin Ave 21 Franklin Park (60131) *(G-9998)*
Midwest Business Center, Lisle Also called FCA US LLC *(G-12890)*
Midwest Cage Company 815 806-0005
9217 Gulfstream Rd # 101 Frankfort (60423) *(G-9816)*
Midwest Canvas Corp (PA) 773 287-4400
4635 W Lake St Chicago (60644) *(G-5440)*
Midwest Cement Products Inc 815 284-2342
809 Central St Woosung (61091) *(G-21452)*
Midwest Cnstr Svcs Inc Peoria (PA) 309 697-1000
4200 Ricketts Ave Bartonville (61607) *(G-1335)*
Midwest Coach Builders Inc 630 690-1420
200 Easy St Ste I Carol Stream (60188) *(G-3030)*
Midwest Coast Brewing Company, Chicago Also called Maverick Ales & Lagers LLC *(G-5368)*
Midwest Coatings Inc 815 717-8914
157 Oakwood Dr Bolingbrook (60440) *(G-2214)*
Midwest Control, Wauconda Also called Intech Industries Inc *(G-20361)*
Midwest Control Corp 708 599-1331
9063 S Octavia Ave Bridgeview (60455) *(G-2365)*
Midwest Converters Inc 815 229-9808
5112 28th Ave Rockford (61109) *(G-17525)*
Midwest Converting Inc 708 924-1510
6634 W 68th St Bedford Park (60638) *(G-1483)*
Midwest Cortland Inc 847 671-0376
235 W Laura Dr Addison (60101) *(G-209)*
Midwest Custom Case Inc (PA) 708 672-2900
425 Crossing Dr Unit A University Park (60484) *(G-19961)*
Midwest Display & Mfg Inc 815 962-2199
127 N Wyman St Apt 4 Rockford (61101) *(G-17526)*
Midwest EDM Specialties Inc 815 521-2130
24108 S Northern Ill Dr Channahon (60410) *(G-3390)*
Midwest Elc Mtr Inc Danville 217 442-5656
819 N Bowman Ave Danville (61832) *(G-7367)*
Midwest Energy Management Inc 630 759-6007
10 E 22nd St Ste 111 Lombard (60148) *(G-13101)*
Midwest Feeder, Belvidere Also called Mid-West Feeder Inc *(G-1686)*
Midwest Fiber Inc Decatur 217 424-9460
1781 Hubbard Ave Decatur (62526) *(G-7524)*
Midwest Fiber Solutions 217 971-7400
1600 Hunter Ridge Dr Springfield (62704) *(G-19407)*
Midwest Fibre Products Inc 309 596-2955
2819 95th Ave Viola (61486) *(G-20180)*
Midwest Fillers 309 567-2957
16861 Ncr 1800 E Havana (62644) *(G-11118)*
Midwest Finishers Pwdrctng 217 536-9098
10235 N 800th St Effingham (62401) *(G-8412)*
Midwest Foods Mfg Inc 847 455-4636
11359 Franklin Ave Franklin Park (60131) *(G-9999)*
Midwest Foundry Products, Palatine Also called Darda Enterprises Inc *(G-16109)*
Midwest Fuel Injction Svc Corp 847 991-7867
543 S Vermont St Ste A Palatine (60067) *(G-16140)*

Midwest Galvanizing Inc 773 434-2682
7400 S Damen Ave Chicago (60636) *(G-5441)*
Midwest Glass Co, Hillside Also called Shoreline Glass Co Inc *(G-11356)*
Midwest Gold Stampers Inc 773 775-5253
5707 N Northwest Hwy Chicago (60646) *(G-5442)*
Midwest Grain Products, Pekin Also called Mgpi Processing Inc *(G-16346)*
Midwest Graphic Industries 630 509-2972
605 Country Club Dr Ste A Bensenville (60106) *(G-1853)*
Midwest Graphics, Bensenville Also called Midwest Graphic Industries *(G-1853)*
Midwest Ground Effects 708 516-5874
1713 Fox Ridge Dr Plainfield (60586) *(G-16688)*
Midwest Hardfacing LLC 815 622-9420
205 E 4th St Rock Falls (61071) *(G-17190)*
Midwest Hose & Fittings Inc 815 578-9040
3218 N Richmond Rd Unit 5 Johnsburg (60051) *(G-11807)*
Midwest Hot Rods Inc 815 254-7637
23533 W Main St Plainfield (60544) *(G-16689)*
Midwest Hydra-Line Inc 309 674-6570
817 Ne Adams St Peoria (61603) *(G-16475)*
Midwest Hydra-Line Inc (HQ) 309 342-6171
698 Us Highway 150 E Galesburg (61401) *(G-10211)*
Midwest Ice Cream Company LLC 815 544-2105
630 Meadow St Belvidere (61008) *(G-1687)*
Midwest Imperial Steel 815 469-1072
5555 W 109th St Oak Lawn (60453) *(G-15728)*
Midwest Index Inc 847 995-8425
2121 W Army Trail Rd # 105 Addison (60101) *(G-210)*
Midwest Industrial Packaging, Glenview Also called Illinois Tool Works Inc *(G-10564)*
Midwest Ink Co 708 345-7177
2701 S 12th Ave Broadview (60155) *(G-2451)*
Midwest Innovations Inc 815 578-1401
4137 W Orleans St McHenry (60050) *(G-13770)*
Midwest Innovative Pdts LLC 888 945-4545
3225 Corporate Dr Unit C Joliet (60431) *(G-11903)*
Midwest Innovative Tech Inc 618 740-0074
400 S Broadway Ave Salem (62881) *(G-18346)*
Midwest Insert Composite Mold, Rolling Meadows Also called Baps Investors Group LLC *(G-17718)*
Midwest Intgrted Companies LLC 847 426-6354
275 Sola Dr Gilberts (60136) *(G-10361)*
Midwest Label Resorces, Addison Also called AT&I Resources LLC *(G-42)*
Midwest Labels and Decals Inc (PA) 630 543-7556
1235 W Capitol Dr Ste D Addison (60101) *(G-211)*
Midwest Labs, Chicago Also called Midwest Uncuts Inc *(G-5450)*
Midwest Laser Incorporated 708 974-0084
10639 S 82nd Ct Palos Hills (60465) *(G-16202)*
Midwest Lifting Products Inc 214 356-7102
1635 W 1st St Ste 312 Granite City (62040) *(G-10724)*
Midwest Linen Recovery LLC 217 675-2766
115 Blaine St Franklin (62638) *(G-9856)*
Midwest Lminating Coatings Inc 708 653-9500
12650 S Laramie Ave Alsip (60803) *(G-478)*
Midwest Machine Company Ltd 630 628-0485
1001 W Republic Dr Ste 13 Addison (60101) *(G-212)*
Midwest Machine Service Inc 708 229-1122
5632 Pleasant Blvd Alsip (60803) *(G-479)*
Midwest Machine Tool Inc 815 427-8665
485 S Oak St Saint Anne (60964) *(G-18136)*
Midwest Machining & Fabg, Granite City Also called Arnette Pattern Co Inc *(G-10698)*
Midwest Manufacturing & Distrg 773 866-1010
6025 N Keystone Ave Chicago (60646) *(G-5443)*
Midwest Marine Div, Chicago Also called ONeill Products Inc *(G-5678)*
Midwest Marketing Distrs Inc 309 663-6972
904 S Eldorado Rd Bloomington (61704) *(G-2078)*
Midwest Marketing Distrs Inc (PA) 309 688-8858
2000 E War Memorial Dr # 2 Peoria (61614) *(G-16476)*
Midwest Material Management, Gilberts Also called Midwest Intgrted Companies LLC *(G-10361)*
Midwest Metal Castings Inc 773 762-3009
1838 N Elston Ave 42 Chicago (60642) *(G-5444)*
Midwest Metal Coatings LLC 618 451-2971
9 Konzen Ct Granite City (62040) *(G-10725)*
Midwest Metal Finishing Inc 773 521-0700
2215 S Christiana Ave Chicago (60623) *(G-5445)*
Midwest Metals Inc 618 295-3444
1296 Green Diamond Rd Marissa (62257) *(G-13543)*
Midwest Meter Inc 217 623-4064
200 E Franklin St Edinburg (62531) *(G-8335)*
Midwest Mixing Inc 708 422-8100
5630 Pleasant Blvd Chicago Ridge (60415) *(G-6803)*
Midwest Mktg/Pdctn Mfg Co 217 256-3414
521 Main St Warsaw (62379) *(G-20258)*
Midwest Mobile Canning LLC 815 861-4515
1228 Westport Rdg Crystal Lake (60014) *(G-7229)*
Midwest Model Aircraft Co 773 229-0740
6917 W 59th St Chicago (60638) *(G-5446)*
Midwest Molding Inc 224 208-1110
1560 Hecht Ct Bartlett (60103) *(G-1298)*

Midwest Molding Solutions 309 663-7374
3001 Gill St Bloomington (61704) *(G-2079)*
Midwest Nameplate Corp 708 614-0606
15127 S 73rd Ave Ste H Orland Park (60462) *(G-15968)*
Midwest Nonwovens LLC 618 337-9662
1642 Sauget Business Blvd Sauget (62206) *(G-18395)*
Midwest Oil Co Inc 847 928-9999
9739 Irving Park Rd Schiller Park (60176) *(G-18826)*
Midwest Oil LLC 309 456-3663
135 S Chestnut St Good Hope (61438) *(G-10670)*
Midwest Orthotic & Technology 773 930-3770
7025 Veterans Blvd A Burr Ridge (60527) *(G-2703)*
Midwest Outdoors Ltd 630 887-7722
111 Shore Dr Burr Ridge (60527) *(G-2704)*
Midwest Packaging & Cont Inc 815 633-6800
9718 Forest Hills Rd Machesney Park (61115) *(G-13361)*
Midwest Patterns Inc 217 228-6900
4901 N 12th St Quincy (62305) *(G-16914)*
Midwest Perma-Column Inc 309 589-7949
7407 N Kckapoo Edwards Rd Edwards (61528) *(G-8339)*
Midwest Plastic Products 630 262-1095
1490 W Bernard Dr Ste C Addison (60101) *(G-213)*
Midwest Plastics Services Inc 630 551-4921
6048 Dover Ct Oswego (60543) *(G-16014)*
Midwest Poultry Services LP 217 386-2313
Hwy 45 N Ste 2 Loda (60948) *(G-13030)*
Midwest Power Equipment 815 669-6331
1933 Cherry Hill Rd Joliet (60433) *(G-11904)*
Midwest Press Brake Dies Inc 708 598-3860
7520 W 100th Pl Bridgeview (60455) *(G-2366)*
Midwest Processing Company 217 424-5200
4666 E Faries Pkwy Decatur (62526) *(G-7525)*
Midwest Promotional Group Co 708 563-0600
16w 211 S Frontage Rd Burr Ridge (60527) *(G-2705)*
Midwest Pub Safety Outfitters 866 985-0013
414 Redman Way Sw Poplar Grove (61065) *(G-16782)*
Midwest Rail Junction 815 963-0200
1907 Cumberland St Rockford (61103) *(G-17527)*
Midwest Railcar Corporation (HQ) 618 692-5575
855 S Arbor Vitae Edwardsville (62025) *(G-8371)*
Midwest Reconditioning Div, Bloomington Also called Mickey Truck Bodies Inc *(G-2076)*
Midwest Recumbent Bicycles 618 343-1885
109 W George St Mascoutah (62258) *(G-13604)*
Midwest Recycling Co 815 744-4922
2324 Mound Rd Rockdale (60436) *(G-17268)*
Midwest Remanufacturing LLC 708 496-9100
5836 W 66th St Fl 2 Bedford Park (60638) *(G-1484)*
Midwest Research Labs LLC (PA) 847 283-9176
476 Oakwood Ave Lake Forest (60045) *(G-12273)*
Midwest Saw Inc 630 293-4252
850 Meadowview Xing Ste 4 West Chicago (60185) *(G-20618)*
Midwest Screens LLC 847 557-5015
303 Main St Ste 111 Antioch (60002) *(G-626)*
Midwest Sealing Products Inc 847 459-2202
1001 Commerce Ct Buffalo Grove (60089) *(G-2575)*
Midwest Shared Newsletter 847 933-9498
8621 Gross Point Rd Skokie (60077) *(G-18991)*
Midwest Sign & Lighting Inc 708 365-5555
4910 Wilshire Blvd Country Club Hills (60478) *(G-7042)*
Midwest Signs & Structures Inc (PA) 847 249-8398
4215 Grove Ave Gurnee (60031) *(G-10898)*
Midwest Signworks 815 942-3517
307 Bedford Rd Morris (60450) *(G-14314)*
Midwest Silkscreening Inc 217 892-9596
104 N Century Blvd Rantoul (61866) *(G-16980)*
Midwest Skylite Company Inc 847 214-9505
1505 Gilpen Ave South Elgin (60177) *(G-19167)*
Midwest Skylite Service Inc 847 214-9505
907 Lunt Ave Schaumburg (60193) *(G-18630)*
Midwest Socks LLC 773 283-3952
4120 N Leamington Ave Chicago (60641) *(G-5447)*
Midwest Sport Turf Systems LLC 630 923-8342
10138 Bode St Ste E Plainfield (60585) *(G-16690)*
Midwest Stair Parts 630 723-3991
31w335 Schoger Dr Naperville (60564) *(G-14979)*
Midwest Stitch 815 394-1516
6767 Charles St Rockford (61108) *(G-17528)*
Midwest Stone Sales Inc (PA) 815 254-6600
11926 S Aero Dr Plainfield (60585) *(G-16691)*
Midwest Store Fixtures, University Park Also called Midwest Custom Case Inc *(G-19961)*
Midwest Stucco-Eifs Dist, Addison Also called Ken Matthews & Associates Inc *(G-167)*
Midwest Sun-Ray Lighting & Sig 618 656-2884
4762 E Chain Of Rocks Rd Granite City (62040) *(G-10726)*
Midwest Sun-Ray Ltg & Sign, Granite City Also called Midwest Sun-Ray Lighting & Sig *(G-10726)*
Midwest Swiss Embroideries Co 773 631-7120
5590 N Northwest Hwy Chicago (60630) *(G-5448)*
Midwest Theological Forum Inc 630 739-9750
4340 Cross St 1 Downers Grove (60515) *(G-8057)*
Midwest Tool Inc 773 588-1313
4055 W Peterson Ave # 205 Chicago (60646) *(G-5449)*
Midwest Treasure Detectors 217 223-4769
2408 Cherry St Ste 1 Quincy (62301) *(G-16915)*
Midwest Tropical Entps Inc 847 679-6666
3420 W Touhy Ave Lincolnwood (60712) *(G-12831)*
Midwest Tungsten Service Inc 630 325-1001
540 Executive Dr Willowbrook (60527) *(G-21051)*
Midwest Turned Products LLC 847 551-4482
80 Prairie Pkwy Gilberts (60136) *(G-10362)*
Midwest Ultrasonics Inc 630 434-9458
2000 Harper Rd Darien (60561) *(G-7409)*
Midwest Uncuts Inc 312 664-3131
5585 N Lynch Ave Chicago (60630) *(G-5450)*
Midwest Utility, Burr Ridge Also called STI Holdings Inc *(G-2722)*
Midwest Water Group Inc 866 526-6558
72 East St Ste 1 Crystal Lake (60014) *(G-7230)*
Midwest Wheel Covers Inc 847 609-9980
27175 W Flynn Creek Dr Barrington (60010) *(G-1228)*
Midwest Wire Works LLC (PA) 815 874-1701
4657 Stenstrom Rd Rockford (61109) *(G-17529)*
Midwest Woodcrafters Inc 630 665-0901
26w415 Saint Charles Rd Carol Stream (60188) *(G-3031)*
Midwest-Design Inc 708 615-1572
2350 S 27th Ave Broadview (60155) *(G-2452)*
Midwestern Contractors, Elburn Also called Electric Conduit Construction *(G-8454)*
Midwestern Family Magazine LLC 309 303-7309
3823 N Harmon Ave Peoria (61614) *(G-16477)*
Midwestern Mch Hydraulics Inc 618 246-9440
17265 N Timberline Ln Mount Vernon (62864) *(G-14625)*
Midwestern Pet Foods Inc 309 734-3121
617 S D St Monmouth (61462) *(G-14223)*
Midwestern Rust Proof Inc 773 725-6636
3636 N Kilbourn Ave Chicago (60641) *(G-5451)*
Midwestern Wood Products Co 309 266-9771
1500 W Jefferson St Morton (61550) *(G-14366)*
Mifab Inc (PA) 773 341-3030
1321 W 119th St Chicago (60643) *(G-5452)*
Mifco, Danville Also called McEnglevan Indus Frnc Mfg Inc *(G-7363)*
Migatron Corporation 815 338-5800
935 Dieckman St Ste A Woodstock (60098) *(G-21411)*
Mighty Hook Inc 773 378-1909
1017 N Cicero Ave Chicago (60651) *(G-5453)*
Mighty Mites Awards and Sons 847 297-0035
1297 Rand Rd Des Plaines (60016) *(G-7802)*
Miglio Di Mario Uomo Inc 312 391-0831
436 E 47th St Unit 302 Chicago (60653) *(G-5454)*
Miha Bodytec Inc 833 367-6442
2171 W Executive Dr # 200 Addison (60101) *(G-214)*
Mihalis Marine 773 445-6220
1224 W 91st St Chicago (60620) *(G-5455)*
Mii Inc 630 879-3000
1380 Nagel Blvd Batavia (60510) *(G-1395)*
Mik Tool & Die Co Inc 847 487-4311
1000 Brown St Ste 304 Wauconda (60084) *(G-20377)*
Mikari, Dekalb Also called Southmoor Estates Inc *(G-7705)*
Mike Howerton 217 242-9676
1214 Huntleigh Rd Quincy (62305) *(G-16916)*
Mike Meier & Sons Fence Mfg 847 587-1111
7501 Meyer Rd Ste 1 Spring Grove (60081) *(G-19284)*
Mike Mulcahy Motorsports LLC 630 567-0298
1801 Bruce St Morris (60450) *(G-14315)*
Mike's Hard Beverage Company, Chicago Also called Mark Anthony Brewing Inc *(G-5339)*
Mikes Inc (PA) 618 254-4491
109 Velma Ave South Roxana (62087) *(G-19253)*
Mikes Anodizing Co 773 722-5778
859 N Spaulding Ave Chicago (60651) *(G-5456)*
Mikes Machinery Rebuilders 630 543-6400
125 W Factory Rd Addison (60101) *(G-215)*
Milan Stone Quarry, Milan Also called Collinson Stone Co *(G-14004)*
Milan, Wilbert Vault Co, Milan Also called Wilbert Vault Company *(G-14032)*
Milano Bakery Inc 815 727-2253
433 S Chicago St Joliet (60436) *(G-11905)*
Milano Metals & Recyling, Mount Vernon Also called Shapiro Bros of Illinois Inc *(G-14638)*
Milans Machining & Mfg Co Inc 708 780-6600
1301 S Laramie Ave Cicero (60804) *(G-6867)*
Milco Precision Machining Inc 630 628-5730
730 W Annoreno Dr Addison (60101) *(G-216)*
Miles Bros 618 937-4115
1000 S Jefferson St West Frankfort (62896) *(G-20678)*
Military Medical News 312 368-4860
11 E Adams St Ste 906 Chicago (60603) *(G-5457)*
Milk Design Company 312 563-6455
14150 S Western Ave Posen (60469) *(G-16798)*
Milk Products Holdings N Amer 847 928-1600
9525 Bryn Mawr Ave Rosemont (60018) *(G-18036)*
Milkhouse Diner, Viola Also called Viola Ice Cream Shoppe *(G-20183)*
Mill Creek Mining Inc 309 787-1414
700 4th St W Milan (61264) *(G-14017)*

Mill Products Division, Crystal Lake *Also called Tc Industries Inc* ***(G-7276)***
Mill Tek Metals, Itasca *Also called Millenia Products Group Inc* ***(G-11704)***
Millcraft....618 426-9819
2116 Trico Rd Campbell Hill (62916) ***(G-2817)***
Millenia Metals LLC....630 458-0401
1345 Norwood Ave Itasca (60143) ***(G-11703)***
Millenia Products Group Inc (PA)....630 458-0401
1345 Norwood Ave Itasca (60143) ***(G-11704)***
Millennium Electronics Inc....815 479-9755
300 Millennium Dr Crystal Lake (60012) ***(G-7231)***
Millennium Mold & Tool....847 438-5600
1194 Heather Dr Lake Zurich (60047) ***(G-12433)***
Miller and Company LLC (HQ)....847 696-2400
9550 W Higgins Rd Ste 380 Rosemont (60018) ***(G-18037)***
Miller Container, Rock Island *Also called Liberty Diversified Intl Inc* ***(G-17227)***
Miller Enterprises, Champaign *Also called Miller Roger Weston* ***(G-3322)***
Miller Ervin B, Arthur *Also called Country Workshop* ***(G-849)***
Miller Fabrication LLC....307 358-4777
303 E Wacker Dr Ste 1040 Chicago (60601) ***(G-5458)***
Miller Fertilizer Inc (PA)....217 382-4241
601 W Main St Casey (62420) ***(G-3207)***
Miller Formers Co, McHenry *Also called Mfs Holdings LLC* ***(G-13769)***
Miller Group Multiplex Div, Dupo *Also called Multiplex Display Fixture Co* ***(G-8141)***
Miller Machine....815 845-2508
299 W Stagecoach Trl Scales Mound (61075) ***(G-18421)***
Miller Manufacturing Co Inc....636 343-5700
1610 Design Way Dupo (62239) ***(G-8140)***
Miller Midwestern Die Co....815 338-6686
1076 Lake Ave Woodstock (60098) ***(G-21412)***
Miller Pallet....217 589-4411
162 E Patterson Rd Roodhouse (62082) ***(G-17893)***
Miller Pharmacal Group Inc....800 323-2935
350 Randy Rd Ste 2 Carol Stream (60188) ***(G-3032)***
Miller Products Inc....708 534-5111
825 Central Ave University Park (60484) ***(G-19962)***
Miller Purcell Co Inc....815 485-2142
244 W 3rd Ave New Lenox (60451) ***(G-15043)***
Miller Roger Weston....217 352-0476
2611 W Cardinal Rd Champaign (61822) ***(G-3322)***
Miller Testing Service....618 262-5911
1125 W 3rd St Mount Carmel (62863) ***(G-14479)***
Miller's Ready Mix, S Chicago Hts *Also called Max Miller* ***(G-18124)***
Millers Country Crafts Inc....618 426-3108
150 Millers Country Ln Ava (62907) ***(G-1175)***
Millers Eureka Inc....312 666-9383
2121 W Hubbard St Chicago (60612) ***(G-5459)***
Millers Fertilizer & Feed....217 783-6321
300 E Cedar St Cowden (62422) ***(G-7079)***
Millers Wood Shop, Carrier Mills *Also called Willard Miller* ***(G-3125)***
Milliken & Company....800 241-4826
222 Merchandise Mart Plz # 1149 Chicago (60654) ***(G-5460)***
Milliken & Company....864 473-1601
2501 W Fulton St Chicago (60612) ***(G-5461)***
Milliken Valve Co Inc....217 425-7410
500 W Eldorado St Decatur (62522) ***(G-7526)***
Millpro LLC....630 608-9241
2245 Sequoia Dr Ste 300 Aurora (60506) ***(G-1135)***
Mills Machine Inc....815 273-4707
2416 Jackson St Savanna (61074) ***(G-18409)***
Mills Machining....815 933-9193
295 Stebbings Ct Ste 4 Bradley (60915) ***(G-2287)***
Mills Pallet....773 533-6458
4500 W Roosevelt Rd Chicago (60624) ***(G-5462)***
Millsdale Plant, Elwood *Also called Stepan Company* ***(G-9464)***
Millstadt Rendering Company....618 538-5312
3151 Clover Leaf Schl Rd Belleville (62223) ***(G-1578)***
Millstadt Township....618 476-3592
18 E Harrison St Millstadt (62260) ***(G-14053)***
Millusions, Schaumburg *Also called AM Precision Machine Inc* ***(G-18436)***
Millwood Inc....708 343-7341
5000 Proviso Dr Ste 1 Melrose Park (60163) ***(G-13893)***
Milmour Products, Mount Prospect *Also called Innovative Hess Products LLC* ***(G-14535)***
Milplex Circuits Inc....630 250-1580
1772 W Armitage Ct Addison (60101) ***(G-217)***
Milplex Electronics Inc....630 250-1580
1772 W Armitage Ct Addison (60101) ***(G-218)***
Milton Division, Elmhurst *Also called Nsa (chi) Liquidating Corp* ***(G-9406)***
Milvia....312 527-3403
222 Merchandise Mart Plz 1427a Chicago (60654) ***(G-5463)***
Milwaukee Electric Tool Corp....847 588-3356
6310 W Gross Point Rd Niles (60714) ***(G-15147)***
Mimo Display LLC (PA)....855 937-6466
14048 W Petronella Dr Libertyville (60048) ***(G-12681)***
Mimo Monitors, Libertyville *Also called Mimo Display LLC* ***(G-12681)***
Mimosa Acoustics Inc....217 359-9740
335 N Fremont St Champaign (61820) ***(G-3323)***
Min Sheng Technology Inc....815 569-4496
461 Kerri Ct Schaumburg (60173) ***(G-18631)***
Minarik Drives, South Beloit *Also called American Control Elec LLC* ***(G-19080)***
Minasian Rug Corporation....847 864-1010
1244 Chicago Ave Evanston (60202) ***(G-9553)***
Mince Master, Chicago *Also called 2 M Tool Company Inc* ***(G-3462)***
Mincon Inc....618 435-3404
107 Industrial Park Rd Benton (62812) ***(G-1932)***
Mincon Rockdrills USA, Benton *Also called Mincon Inc* ***(G-1932)***
Mindful Mdispa Mediclinic Pllc....847 922-4768
723 Division St Barrington (60010) ***(G-1229)***
Mindful Mix....847 284-4404
15 Maple Ave Lake Zurich (60047) ***(G-12434)***
Mindseye....618 394-6444
442 S Demazenod Dr Belleville (62223) ***(G-1579)***
Minelab Americas Inc....630 401-8150
123 Ambassador Dr Ste 123 # 123 Naperville (60540) ***(G-14871)***
Miner Elastomer Products Corp....630 232-3000
1200 E State St Geneva (60134) ***(G-10290)***
Mineral Masters Corporation....630 293-7727
130 W Grand Lake Blvd West Chicago (60185) ***(G-20619)***
Mineral Products Inc....618 433-3150
6 Atkins Dr Harrisburg (62946) ***(G-11026)***
Minerallac Company (PA)....630 543-7080
100 Gast Rd Hampshire (60140) ***(G-10979)***
Minerals Technologies Inc....847 851-1500
2870 Forbs Ave Hoffman Estates (60192) ***(G-11435)***
Minerva Sportswear Inc....309 661-2387
608 Iaa Dr Bloomington (61701) ***(G-2080)***
Ming Trading LLC....773 442-2221
2845 W 48th Pl Chicago (60632) ***(G-5464)***
Miniature Injection Molding, Burlington *Also called Veejay Plastics Inc* ***(G-2643)***
Minic Precision Inc....815 675-0451
7706 Industrial Dr Ste K Spring Grove (60081) ***(G-19285)***
Minigrip Inc....845 680-2710
1510 Warehouse Dr Ottawa (61350) ***(G-16061)***
Minimill Technologies Inc....315 857-7107
505 N Lake Shore Dr # 5407 Chicago (60611) ***(G-5465)***
Mining International LLC....815 722-0900
1955 Patterson Rd Joliet (60436) ***(G-11906)***
Minnesota Diversified Pdts Inc....815 539-3106
1101 Lori Ln Mendota (61342) ***(G-13950)***
Minor League Inc....618 548-8040
905 E Main St Salem (62881) ***(G-18347)***
Minority Auto Hdlg Specialists (HQ)....708 757-8758
22401 Sauk Pointe Dr Chicago Heights (60411) ***(G-6759)***
Minova USA Inc....618 993-2611
809 Skyline Dr Marion (62959) ***(G-13522)***
Mint Masters Inc....847 451-1133
9136 Belden Ave Franklin Park (60131) ***(G-10000)***
Minus Nine Technologies....224 399-9393
101 Ambrogio Dr Gurnee (60031) ***(G-10899)***
Minusnine Technologies, Itasca *Also called ICP Industries LLC* ***(G-11669)***
Minute Man Press....847 839-9600
1037 W Golf Rd Hoffman Estates (60169) ***(G-11436)***
Minute Mlcular Diagnostics Inc....847 849-0263
Hogan Blgcal Scnces Bldg Evanston (60208) ***(G-9554)***
Minuteman International Inc (HQ)....630 627-6900
14n845 Us Highway 20 Pingree Grove (60140) ***(G-16622)***
Minuteman International Inc....847 683-5210
14n845 Us Highway 20 Hampshire (60140) ***(G-10980)***
Minuteman Press, Hoffman Estates *Also called Minute Man Press* ***(G-11436)***
Minuteman Press, Champaign *Also called Mmpcu Limited* ***(G-3324)***
Minuteman Press, Naperville *Also called T C W F Inc* ***(G-14925)***
Minuteman Press, Edwardsville *Also called 510 Holdings Company LLC* ***(G-8343)***
Minuteman Press, Fox Lake *Also called Nowuba LLC - Investio Print* ***(G-9750)***
Minuteman Press, Naperville *Also called T F N W Inc* ***(G-14926)***
Minuteman Press, McHenry *Also called Schommer Inc* ***(G-13791)***
Minuteman Press, Crystal Lake *Also called Jeannie Wagner* ***(G-7212)***
Minuteman Press, Evanston *Also called L P M Inc* ***(G-9545)***
Minuteman Press, Joliet *Also called Jsn Printing Inc* ***(G-11888)***
Minuteman Press, Westchester *Also called P P Graphics Inc* ***(G-20707)***
Minuteman Press, Barrington *Also called Gnk Technologies Inc* ***(G-1220)***
Minuteman Press, Chicago *Also called R T P Inc* ***(G-5954)***
Minuteman Press, Deerfield *Also called Jsolo Corp* ***(G-7624)***
Minuteman Press, Wheeling *Also called Rodin Enterprises Inc* ***(G-20976)***
Minuteman Press, Elmhurst *Also called W R S Inc* ***(G-9443)***
Minuteman Press, Lyons *Also called Steve Bortman* ***(G-13315)***
Minuteman Press....708 524-4940
6949 North Ave Oak Park (60302) ***(G-15765)***
Minuteman Press....708 598-4915
8330 W 95th St Apt 1 Hickory Hills (60457) ***(G-11200)***
Minuteman Press....630 584-7383
1577 Nperville Wheaton Rd Naperville (60563) ***(G-14872)***
Minuteman Press Inc....847 577-2411
1324 W Algonquin Rd Arlington Heights (60005) ***(G-776)***
Minuteman Press Intl Inc....630 574-0090
1301 W 22nd St Ste 709 Oak Brook (60523) ***(G-15646)***

A L P H A B E T I C

Minuteman Press Morton Grove 847 470-0212
6038 Dempster St Morton Grove (60053) *(G-14429)*
Minuteman Press of Countryside 708 354-2190
6566 Joliet Rd Countryside (60525) *(G-7064)*
Minuteman Press of Frankfort 779 254-2912
55 Bankview Dr Frankfort (60423) *(G-9817)*
Minuteman Press of Lansing 708 895-0505
17930 Torrence Ave Ste A Lansing (60438) *(G-12509)*
Minuteman Press of Rockford 815 633-2992
5128 N 2nd St Loves Park (61111) *(G-13237)*
Minuteman Press of Waukegan 847 244-6288
3701 Grand Ave Ste A Gurnee (60031) *(G-10900)*
Mio Med Orthopedics Inc 773 477-8991
2502 N Clark St 212 Chicago (60614) *(G-5466)*
Miracapo Pizza Company, Elk Grove Village *Also called Little Lady Foods Inc (G-9096)*
Miracle Press Company 773 722-6176
2951 W Carroll Ave Chicago (60612) *(G-5467)*
Miracle Sealants Company LLC 626 443-6433
11 E Hawthorn Pkwy Vernon Hills (60061) *(G-20074)*
Mirek Cabinets 630 350-8336
1086 Waveland Ave Franklin Park (60131) *(G-10001)*
Mirror-Democrat 815 244-2411
308 N Main St Mount Carroll (61053) *(G-14496)*
Mirus Research 309 828-3100
618 E Lincoln St Normal (61761) *(G-15210)*
Mislich Bros, Pontiac *Also called MBI Tools LLC (G-16775)*
Misselhorn Welding & Machines 618 426-3714
310 S Main St Campbell Hill (62916) *(G-2818)*
Mission Control Systems Inc 847 956-7650
700 Oakton St Elk Grove Village (60007) *(G-9127)*
Mission Popcorn, Chicago *Also called Revolution Companies Inc (G-6019)*
Mission Press Inc 312 455-9501
10265 Franklin Ave Franklin Park (60131) *(G-10002)*
Mission Signs Inc 630 243-6731
1415 Chestnut Xing Lemont (60439) *(G-12572)*
Mister Inc of Chicago 773 342-7200
4215 W Grand Ave Chicago (60651) *(G-5468)*
Mistic Metal Mover Inc 815 875-1371
1160 N 6th St Princeton (61356) *(G-16814)*
Mistica Foods LLC 630 543-5409
50 W Commercial Ave Addison (60101) *(G-219)*
Mitchco Farms LLC 618 382-5032
1239 County Road 1500 N Carmi (62821) *(G-2911)*
Mitchel Home 773 205-9902
3652 N Tripp Ave Chicago (60641) *(G-5469)*
Mitchell Aircraft Products 815 331-8609
2309 N Ringwood Rd McHenry (60050) *(G-13771)*
Mitchell Aircraft Spares Inc 847 516-3773
1160 Alexander Ct Cary (60013) *(G-3179)*
Mitchell Arcft Expendables LLC 847 516-3773
1160 Alexander Ct Cary (60013) *(G-3180)*
Mitchell Black LLC 312 667-4477
1922 N Damen Ave Chicago (60647) *(G-5470)*
Mitchell Printing, Centralia *Also called James Ray Monroe Corporation (G-3236)*
Mitchlls Cndies Ice Creams Inc 708 799-3835
18211 Dixie Hwy Homewood (60430) *(G-11501)*
Mitek Corporation 608 328-5560
1 Mitek Plz Winslow (61089) *(G-21139)*
Mitek Corporation 815 367-3000
1 Mitek Plz Winslow (61089) *(G-21140)*
Mitel Networks Inc 312 479-9000
70 W Madison St Ste 1600 Chicago (60602) *(G-5471)*
Mitsubishi Chemical Advncd Mtr 847 367-0110
1840 Enterprise Ct Libertyville (60048) *(G-12682)*
Mitsubishi Elc Automtn Inc (HQ) 847 478-2100
500 Corporate Woods Pkwy Vernon Hills (60061) *(G-20075)*
Mitsubishi Electric Us Inc 708 354-2900
5218 Dansher Rd Countryside (60525) *(G-7065)*
Mitsubishi Heavy Inds Amer Inc 630 693-4700
1225 N Greenbriar Dr B Addison (60101) *(G-220)*
Mitsubishi Materials USA Corp 847 519-1601
1314 N Plum Grove Rd Schaumburg (60173) *(G-18632)*
Mitsubshi Elevators Escalators, Countryside *Also called Mitsubishi Electric Us Inc (G-7065)*
Mitsutoyo-Kiko USA Inc 847 981-5200
1600 Golf Rd Ste 1200 Rolling Meadows (60008) *(G-17751)*
Mittal Steel USA Inc 312 899-3440
1 S Dearborn St Ste 1800 Chicago (60603) *(G-5472)*
Mittera Chicago, Berkeley *Also called Mittera Illinois LLC (G-1942)*
Mittera Illinois LLC 708 449-8989
5656 Mcdermott Dr Berkeley (60163) *(G-1942)*
Mity Inc (PA) 630 365-5030
700 E North St Ste B Elburn (60119) *(G-8461)*
Miwa Lock Co 630 365-4261
816 Hicks Dr Elburn (60119) *(G-8462)*
Miwon NA 630 568-5850
669 Executive Dr Willowbrook (60527) *(G-21052)*
Mix N Mingle 815 308-5170
124 Cass St Ste 2 Woodstock (60098) *(G-21413)*
Mixing Division, Carmi *Also called Vibracoustic Usa Inc (G-2916)*
Miyano Machinery USA Inc (HQ) 630 766-4141
2316 Touhy Ave Elk Grove Village (60007) *(G-9128)*
Miyanohitec Machinery Inc 847 382-2794
50 Dundee Ln Barrington (60010) *(G-1230)*
Mizkan America Inc (HQ) 847 590-0059
1661 Feehanville Dr # 200 Mount Prospect (60056) *(G-14547)*
Mizkan America Holdings Inc (HQ) 847 590-0059
1661 Feehanville Dr # 300 Mount Prospect (60056) *(G-14548)*
Mizrahi Grill 847 831-1400
215 Skokie Valley Rd Highland Park (60035) *(G-11284)*
Mj Burton Gifts & Engraving, Quincy *Also called M J Burton Engraving Co (G-16908)*
Mj Celco International LLC 847 671-1900
3900 Wesley Ter Schiller Park (60176) *(G-18827)*
Mj Snyder Ironworks Inc 217 826-6440
15640 E National Rd Marshall (62441) *(G-13575)*
Mj Works Hose & Fitting LLC (PA) 708 995-5723
11122 W 189th Pl Bldg C1 Mokena (60448) *(G-14098)*
MJM Graphics 847 234-1802
433 Greenwood Ave Lake Forest (60045) *(G-12274)*
Mjmc Inc 708 596-5200
3111 167th St Hazel Crest (60429) *(G-11135)*
Mjt Design and Prtg Entps Inc 708 240-4323
4219 Butterfield Rd 1a Hillside (60162) *(G-11348)*
MJT Incorporated 708 597-0059
5801 W 117th Pl Alsip (60803) *(G-480)*
Mk Environmental Inc (PA) 630 848-0585
765 Springer Dr Lombard (60148) *(G-13102)*
Mk Signs Inc 773 545-4444
4900 N Elston Ave Ste M Chicago (60630) *(G-5473)*
Mk Systems Incorporated (PA) 847 709-6180
1455 Brummel Ave Elk Grove Village (60007) *(G-9129)*
Mk Test Systems Americas Inc 773 569-3778
22102 N Pepper Rd Ste 116 Lake Barrington (60010) *(G-12161)*
MK Tile Ink 773 964-8905
5851 S Neenah Ave Chicago (60638) *(G-5474)*
Mla Franklin Park Inc 847 451-0279
2925 Lucy Ln Franklin Park (60131) *(G-10003)*
Mlp Seating, Rockdale *Also called J & E Seating LLC (G-17260)*
Mlp Seating Corp 847 956-1700
125 Connell Ave Rockdale (60436) *(G-17269)*
MMC Armory, Mark *Also called Mennies Machine Company (G-13546)*
MMC Precision Holdings Corp 309 266-7176
1021 W Birchwood St Morton (61550) *(G-14367)*
Mmm Uno Corp 773 577-7329
142 Emerald Dr Streamwood (60107) *(G-19586)*
Mmma 309 888-8765
2601 W College Ave Ste A Normal (61761) *(G-15211)*
Mmp, Des Plaines *Also called Montana Metal Products LLC (G-7803)*
Mmpcu Limited 217 355-0500
905 S Neil St Ste B Champaign (61820) *(G-3324)*
Mmt, Chicago *Also called Marketing & Technology Group (G-5340)*
Mmxix Capital Inc 815 441-2647
65 Carriage Hill Dr Sterling (61081) *(G-19520)*
Mni, Evanston *Also called Manufacturers News Inc (G-9549)*
MNP Precision Parts LLC (HQ) 815 391-5256
1111 Samuelson Rd Rockford (61109) *(G-17530)*
Mo-Par City, Oregon *Also called Larry Pontnack (G-15923)*
Mobell Muscle, Chicago *Also called Xmt Solutions LLC (G-6696)*
Mobil Trailer Transport Inc 630 993-1200
223 E Adele Ct Villa Park (60181) *(G-20160)*
Mobile 7 Group Inc 312 600-8952
642 Hickory St Chicago Heights (60411) *(G-6760)*
Mobile Air Inc 847 755-0586
380 Windy Point Dr Glendale Heights (60139) *(G-10476)*
Mobile Endoscopix LLC 847 380-8992
3330 Dundee Rd Ste C1 Northbrook (60062) *(G-15434)*
Mobile Health & Wellness Inc 773 697-9892
1820 W Webster Ave # 206 Chicago (60614) *(G-5475)*
Mobile Mini Inc 708 297-2004
12658 S Winchester Ave # 2 Calumet Park (60827) *(G-2799)*
Mobile Pallet Service Inc 630 231-6597
1300 W Roosevelt Rd West Chicago (60185) *(G-20620)*
Mobile Systems, Elk Grove Village *Also called Parker-Hannifin Corporation (G-9169)*
Mobilehop Technology LLC 312 504-3773
838 W 31st St Unit 3g Chicago (60608) *(G-5476)*
Mobileskin Imaging, Kildeer *Also called Interexpo Ltd (G-12049)*
Mobilia Inc 708 865-0700
1023 Cernan Dr Bellwood (60104) *(G-1634)*
Mobility Center of Chicago, Oakbrook Terrace *Also called Amigo Mobility Center (G-15784)*
Mobility Connection Inc 815 965-8090
4100 E State St Rockford (61108) *(G-17531)*
Mobility Masters, Carol Stream *Also called Midwest Coach Builders Inc (G-3030)*
Mobiloc LLC 773 742-1329
5800 W 117th Pl Alsip (60803) *(G-481)*
Mobis Parts America LLC 630 907-4700
1705 Sequoia Dr Aurora (60506) *(G-1136)*
Mobotrex Inc 847 546-1616
31632 N Ellis Dr Unit 305 Volo (60073) *(G-20204)*

Mod Tech, East Dundee *Also called DTS America Inc* ***(G-8193)***
Modahl & Scott, Bloomington *Also called Southfield Corporation* ***(G-2096)***
Models Plus Inc 847 231-4300
888 E Belvidere Rd # 110 Grayslake (60030) ***(G-10789)***
Modern Abrasive Corp 815 675-2352
2855 N Us Highway 12 Spring Grove (60081) ***(G-19286)***
Modern Aids Inc 847 437-8600
201 Bond St Elk Grove Village (60007) ***(G-9130)***
Modern Card Co, Lincolnwood *Also called K Chae Corp* ***(G-12826)***
Modern Fluid Technology Inc 815 356-0001
93 Berkshire Dr Ste F Crystal Lake (60014) ***(G-7232)***
Modern Gear & Machine Inc 630 350-9173
406 Evergreen Ave Bensenville (60106) ***(G-1854)***
Modern Graphic Systems Inc 773 476-6898
4922 S Western Ave Chicago (60609) ***(G-5477)***
Modern Home Products Corp (PA) 847 395-6556
150 S Ram Rd Antioch (60002) ***(G-627)***
Modern Lighting Tech LLC 312 624-9267
1751 W Grand Ave Chicago (60622) ***(G-5478)***
Modern Luxury Media LLC 312 274-2500
33 W Monroe St Ste 2100 Chicago (60603) ***(G-5479)***
Modern Media Services 847 548-0408
155 Wicks St Unit E Grayslake (60030) ***(G-10790)***
Modern Metal Products, Chicago *Also called Trend Publishing Inc* ***(G-6415)***
Modern Methods Creative Inc 309 263-4100
408 N Nebraska Ave Morton (61550) ***(G-14368)***
Modern Pattern Works Inc 309 676-2157
1100 Sw Washington St Peoria (61602) ***(G-16478)***
Modern Plating Corporation 815 235-1790
701 S Hancock Ave Freeport (61032) ***(G-10127)***
Modern Pltg Coatings Finishes, Freeport *Also called Modern Plating Corporation* ***(G-10127)***
Modern Printing Colors Inc 708 681-5678
1951 W 21st St Broadview (60155) ***(G-2453)***
Modern Printing of Quincy 217 223-1063
2615 Ellington Rd Quincy (62305) ***(G-16917)***
Modern Process Equipment Inc 773 254-3929
3125 S Kolin Ave Chicago (60623) ***(G-5480)***
Modern Silicone Tech Inc (PA) 727 507-9800
101 Schelter Rd Ste 102b Lincolnshire (60069) ***(G-12785)***
Modern Specialties Company 312 648-5800
661 W Lake St Ste 1s Chicago (60661) ***(G-5481)***
Modern Sprout LLC 312 342-2114
1451 N Ashland Ave Chicago (60622) ***(G-5482)***
Modern Trade Communications (PA) 847 674-2200
7836 Frontage Rd Skokie (60077) ***(G-18992)***
Modern Tube LLC (PA) 877 848-3300
193 Rosedale Ct Bloomingdale (60108) ***(G-2001)***
Modineer P-K Tool LLC 773 235-4700
4700 W Le Moyne St Chicago (60651) ***(G-5483)***
Modular Wood Systems Inc 847 251-6401
736 12th St Ste C Wilmette (60091) ***(G-21088)***
Modularhose.com, Lombard *Also called Oak Hill Brands Corp* ***(G-13111)***
Moduslink Corporation 708 496-7800
6112 W 73rd St Bedford Park (60638) ***(G-1485)***
Moeller Ready Mix Inc 217 243-7471
300 Moeller Rd Jacksonville (62650) ***(G-11776)***
Moes River North LLC 312 245-2000
155 W Kinzie St Chicago (60654) ***(G-5484)***
Moesle Meat Company, Chicago *Also called John J Moesle Whl Meats Inc* ***(G-5042)***
Moffat Wire & Display Inc 630 458-8560
324 S La Londe Ave Addison (60101) ***(G-221)***
Moffitt Co 847 678-5450
9347 Seymour Ave Schiller Park (60176) ***(G-18828)***
Mohawk Industries Inc 630 972-8000
969 Veterans Pkwy Ste B Bolingbrook (60490) ***(G-2215)***
Mohawk Spring, Schiller Park *Also called Matthew Warren Inc* ***(G-18821)***
Mohican Petroleum Inc 312 782-6385
21 S Clark St Ste 3980 Chicago (60603) ***(G-5485)***
Moisture Detection Inc 847 426-0464
2200 Stonington Ave Hoffman Estates (60169) ***(G-11437)***
Mold Express Inc 773 766-0874
8142 W Frest Preserve Ave Chicago (60634) ***(G-5486)***
Mold Repair and Manufacturing 815 477-1332
2520 Il Route 176 Ste 5 Crystal Lake (60014) ***(G-7233)***
Mold Seekers 847 650-8025
319 Fairfax Ln Grayslake (60030) ***(G-10791)***
Mold Shields Inc 708 983-5931
15309 Oak Rd Oak Forest (60452) ***(G-15686)***
Mold-Rite Plastics LLC (HQ) 518 561-1812
30 N La Salle St Ste 2425 Chicago (60602) ***(G-5487)***
Mold-Tech Midwest, Carol Stream *Also called Standex International Corp* ***(G-3076)***
Molded Displays 773 892-4098
739 Old Trail Rd Highland Park (60035) ***(G-11285)***
Molding Services Group Inc 847 931-1491
2051 N La Fox St Lowr 1 South Elgin (60177) ***(G-19168)***
Molding Services Illinois Inc 618 395-3888
126 N West St Olney (62450) ***(G-15874)***
Molding Systems Engrg Corp 618 395-3888
126 N West St Olney (62450) ***(G-15875)***
Moldtronics Inc 630 968-7000
703 Rogers St Downers Grove (60515) ***(G-8058)***
Moldworks Inc 815 520-8819
11052 Jasmine Dr Roscoe (61073) ***(G-17918)***
Molex LLC (HQ) 630 969-4550
2222 Wellington Ct Lisle (60532) ***(G-12911)***
Molex LLC 630 969-4550
1750 Country Farm Dr Naperville (60563) ***(G-14873)***
Molex LLC 630 527-4357
2200 Wellington Ct Lisle (60532) ***(G-12912)***
Molex LLC 630 527-4363
575 Veterans Pkwy Ste A Bolingbrook (60440) ***(G-2216)***
Molex LLC 630 512-8787
5224 Katrine Ave Downers Grove (60515) ***(G-8059)***
Molex Connected Entp Solutions, Lisle *Also called Molex LLC* ***(G-12911)***
Molex Electronic Tech LLC (HQ) 630 969-4550
2222 Wellington Ct Lisle (60532) ***(G-12913)***
Molex Inc. Switch Division, Naperville *Also called Molex LLC* ***(G-14873)***
Molex International Inc (HQ) 630 969-4550
2222 Wellington Ct Lisle (60532) ***(G-12914)***
Molex Premise Networks Inc 866 733-6659
2222 Wellington Ct Lisle (60532) ***(G-12915)***
Moline Consumers Co 309 757-8289
200 23rd Ave Moline (61265) ***(G-14162)***
Moline Dispatch Pubg Co LLC, East Moline *Also called Small Nwsppr Group Shred Svcs* ***(G-8241)***
Moline Forge Inc 309 762-5506
4101 4th Ave Moline (61265) ***(G-14163)***
Moline Welding Inc 309 756-0643
3603 78th Ave Milan (61264) ***(G-14018)***
Molino Baking Co 708 385-6616
13030 Western Ave Blue Island (60406) ***(G-2131)***
Molor Products Company 630 375-5999
73 Chippewa Dr Oswego (60543) ***(G-16015)***
Molson Coors Bev Co USA LLC (HQ) 312 496-2700
250 S Wacker Dr Ste 800 Chicago (60606) ***(G-5488)***
Momence Packing Co 815 472-6485
334 W North St Momence (60954) ***(G-14188)***
Momence Pallet Corporation 815 472-6451
11414 E State Route 114 Momence (60954) ***(G-14189)***
Monahan Filaments LLC (HQ) 217 268-4957
215 Egyptian Trl Arcola (61910) ***(G-657)***
Monahan Partners Inc 217 268-5758
200 N Oak St Arcola (61910) ***(G-658)***
Monarch Manufacturing 630 519-4580
118 E Goebel Dr Lombard (60148) ***(G-13103)***
Monarch Mfg Corp Amer 217 728-2552
Hc 32 Box S Sullivan (61951) ***(G-19671)***
Monarch Tool & Die Co 630 530-8886
862 N Industrial Dr Elmhurst (60126) ***(G-9403)***
Monastery Hill Bindery, Chicago *Also called Hertzberg Ernst & Sons* ***(G-4810)***
Monco Fabricators Inc 630 293-0063
645 Joliet St West Chicago (60185) ***(G-20621)***
Monda Window & Door Corp 773 254-8888
4101 W 42nd Pl Chicago (60632) ***(G-5489)***
Mondays Pub, Anna *Also called Gazette-Democrat* ***(G-584)***
Mondelez Global LLC 815 877-8081
5500 Forest Hills Rd Loves Park (61111) ***(G-13238)***
Mondelez Global LLC (HQ) 847 943-4000
3 N Pkwy Ste 300 Deerfield (60015) ***(G-7637)***
Mondelez Global LLC 630 369-1909
1555 W Ogden Ave Naperville (60540) ***(G-14874)***
Mondelez International Inc 815 710-2114
100 Prologis Pkwy Morris (60450) ***(G-14316)***
Mondelez International Inc (PA) 847 943-4000
905 W Fulton Market # 200 Chicago (60607) ***(G-5490)***
Mondelez Intl Holdings LLC (HQ) 800 572-3847
3 Parkway North Blvd # 300 Deerfield (60015) ***(G-7638)***
Mondi Bags Usa LLC 502 361-1371
1198 Arbor Dr Romeoville (60446) ***(G-17856)***
Mondi Romeoville Inc 630 378-9886
1140 Arbor Dr Romeoville (60446) ***(G-17857)***
Monett Metals Inc 773 478-8888
5739 W Howard St Niles (60714) ***(G-15148)***
Money Stretcher, Peoria *Also called Gatehouse Media Ill Holdings* ***(G-16442)***
Monitor Newspaper Inc 618 271-0468
1501 State St East Saint Louis (62205) ***(G-8315)***
Monitor Publishing Inc 773 205-0303
6304 N Nagle Ave Ste B Chicago (60646) ***(G-5491)***
Monitor Sign Co 217 234-2412
316 N Division St Mattoon (61938) ***(G-13651)***
Monitor Technologies LLC 630 365-9403
44w320 Keslinger Rd Elburn (60119) ***(G-8463)***
Monmouth Grain & Dryer, Monmouth *Also called Big Rver Rsrces W Brlngton LLC* ***(G-14214)***
Monmouth Ready Mix Corp 309 734-3211
816 N Henderson St Galesburg (61401) ***(G-10212)***
Monmouth Stone Co (PA) 309 734-7951
1420 N Main St Monmouth (61462) ***(G-14224)***

ALPHABETIC

Monnex International Inc (PA)...847 850-5263
330 Hastings Dr Buffalo Grove (60089) ***(G-2576)***
Monogen Inc...847 573-6700
140 S Dearborn St Ste 420 Chicago (60603) ***(G-5492)***
Monogram Creative Group Inc...312 802-1433
1723 Wildberry Dr Unit C Glenview (60025) ***(G-10590)***
Monogram Etched Crystal, Evanston *Also called Monogram of Evanston Inc* ***(G-9555)***
Monogram of Evanston Inc...847 864-8100
727 Clinton Pl Evanston (60201) ***(G-9555)***
Monolithic Industries Inc...630 985-6009
7613 Woodridge Dr Woodridge (60517) ***(G-21324)***
Monona Holdings LLC (HQ)...630 946-0630
1952 Mc Dowell Rd Ste 207 Naperville (60563) ***(G-14875)***
Monopar Therapeutics Inc (PA)...847 388-0349
1000 Skokie Blvd Ste 350 Wilmette (60091) ***(G-21089)***
Monotype Imaging Inc...847 631-1111
25 Northwest Point Blvd # 525 Elk Grove Village (60007) ***(G-9131)***
Monqui Suds LLC...217 479-0090
907 W Morton Ave Jacksonville (62650) ***(G-11777)***
Monroe Associates Inc...217 665-3898
1545 Cr 375e Bethany (61914) ***(G-1968)***
Monsanto Company...618 249-6150
3421 Us Highway 51 Centralia (62801) ***(G-3239)***
Monsanto Company...815 758-9293
8350 Minnegan Rd Waterman (60556) ***(G-20299)***
Mont Eagle Products Inc (PA)...618 455-3344
219 S Main St Sainte Marie (62459) ***(G-18327)***
Montana Metal Products LLC (HQ)...847 803-6600
25 Howard Ave Des Plaines (60018) ***(G-7803)***
Montauk Chicago Inc...312 951-5688
401 N Wells St Ste 108a Chicago (60654) ***(G-5493)***
Montclare Scientific Glass...847 255-6870
25 N Hickory Ave Arlington Heights (60004) ***(G-777)***
Montefusco Heating Shtmtl Co, Peoria *Also called Montefusco Hvac Inc* ***(G-16479)***
Montefusco Hvac Inc...309 691-7400
2200 W Altorfer Dr Ste D Peoria (61615) ***(G-16479)***
Monterey Mushrooms Inc...815 875-4436
27268 Us Highway 6 Princeton (61356) ***(G-16815)***
Monthly Aspectarian, The, Morton Grove *Also called Lightworks Communcation Inc* ***(G-14422)***
Montrose Glass & Mirror Corp...773 478-6433
3916 W Montrose Ave Fl 1 Chicago (60618) ***(G-5494)***
Monty Burcenski...815 838-0934
1213 S Lincoln St Lockport (60441) ***(G-13014)***
Monument Company, Beardstown *Also called Riverside Memorial Co* ***(G-1450)***
Monumental Art Works...708 389-3038
2152 Vermont St Ste A2 Blue Island (60406) ***(G-2132)***
Moody Bible Inst of Chicago (PA)...312 329-4000
820 N La Salle Dr Chicago (60610) ***(G-5495)***
Moody Bible Inst of Chicago...312 329-2102
210 W Chestnut St Chicago (60610) ***(G-5496)***
Moody Global Ministries, Chicago *Also called Moody Bible Inst of Chicago* ***(G-5495)***
Moody Press A Division of MBI, Chicago *Also called Moody Bible Inst of Chicago* ***(G-5496)***
Moog Inc...770 987-7550
3650 Woodhead Dr Northbrook (60062) ***(G-15435)***
Moog Inc...847 498-0704
3650 Woodhead Dr Northbrook (60062) ***(G-15436)***
Moon Jump Inc...630 983-0953
1750 W Armitage Ct Addison (60101) ***(G-222)***
Moons Industries America Inc...630 833-5940
1113 N Prospect Ave Itasca (60143) ***(G-11705)***
Moor Printing Services Inc...847 687-7287
438 Pine Lake Cir Vernon Hills (60061) ***(G-20076)***
Moore Machine Works...815 625-0536
706 Gregden Shores Dr Sterling (61081) ***(G-19521)***
Moore Memorials...708 636-6532
5960 111th St Chicago Ridge (60415) ***(G-6804)***
Moorket Inc...888 275-0277
430 E 162nd St Ste 486 South Holland (60473) ***(G-19233)***
Moran Graphics Inc...312 226-3900
1017 W Wa Blvd Unit 101 Chicago (60607) ***(G-5497)***
Moran Properties Inc...312 440-1962
1407 N Dearborn St Chicago (60610) ***(G-5498)***
Morcor Industries Inc...224 293-2000
501 Davis Rd Elgin (60123) ***(G-8664)***
Mordern Flow Equipment, Villa Grove *Also called Pauls Machine & Welding Corp* ***(G-20125)***
More Cupcakes LLC...312 951-0001
1 E Delaware Pl Ste 4 Chicago (60611) ***(G-5499)***
Moreno and Sons Inc...815 725-8600
2366 Plainfield Rd Crest Hill (60403) ***(G-7092)***
Morey Industries Inc...708 343-3220
2000 Beach St Broadview (60155) ***(G-2454)***
Morgan Bronze Products Inc...847 526-6000
340 E Il Route 22 Lake Zurich (60047) ***(G-12435)***
Morgan Li LLC (PA)...708 758-5300
383 E 16th St Chicago Heights (60411) ***(G-6761)***
Morgan Ohare Inc...630 543-6780
701 W Factory Rd Addison (60101) ***(G-223)***
Morgan Robt Inc...217 466-4777
1914 S Central Ave Paris (61944) ***(G-16235)***
Moriteq Rubber Co...847 734-0970
710 W Algonquin Rd Arlington Heights (60005) ***(G-778)***
Moriteq USA Contacts, Arlington Heights *Also called Moriteq Rubber Co* ***(G-778)***
Morkes Chocolates, Palatine *Also called Morkes Inc* ***(G-16141)***
Morkes Inc...847 359-3511
1890 N Rand Rd Palatine (60074) ***(G-16141)***
Mormor Incorporated...630 268-0050
119 E Roosevelt Rd Lombard (60148) ***(G-13104)***
Morningfields...847 309-8460
800 Devon Ave Ste 7 Park Ridge (60068) ***(G-16288)***
Morningside Woodcraft...217 268-4313
545 E County Road 200n Arcola (61910) ***(G-659)***
Morrell Incorporated...630 858-4600
340 Windy Point Dr Glendale Heights (60139) ***(G-10477)***
Morris Construction Inc...618 544-8504
Marathon Ave Robinson (62454) ***(G-17120)***
Morris Daily Herald Publisher, Morris *Also called Morris Publishing Company* ***(G-14317)***
Morris Kurtzon Incorporated...773 277-2121
1420 S Talman Ave Chicago (60608) ***(G-5500)***
Morris Magnetics Inc...847 487-0829
1220 N Old Rand Rd Wauconda (60084) ***(G-20378)***
Morris Meat Packing Co Inc...708 865-8566
1406 S 5th Ave Maywood (60153) ***(G-13673)***
Morris Midwest LLC...630 351-1901
68 Congress Cir W Roselle (60172) ***(G-17971)***
Morris Packaging LLC (PA)...309 663-9100
211 N Williamsburg Dr A Bloomington (61704) ***(G-2081)***
Morris Pallet Skids Inc...618 786-2241
15133 Newbern Rd Dow (62022) ***(G-7946)***
Morris Publishing Company...815 942-3221
1802 N Div St Ste 314 Morris (60450) ***(G-14317)***
Morrison Cont Hdlg Solutions, Glenwood *Also called Morrison Timing Screw Company* ***(G-10643)***
Morrison Timing Screw Company...708 756-6660
335 W 194th St Glenwood (60425) ***(G-10643)***
Morrison Weighing Systems Inc...309 799-7311
7605 50th St Milan (61264) ***(G-14019)***
Morrow Shoe and Boot Inc...217 342-6833
320 W Jefferson Ave Effingham (62401) ***(G-8413)***
Morse Automotive Corporation (PA)...773 843-9000
750 W Lake Cook Rd # 480 Buffalo Grove (60089) ***(G-2577)***
Morse Heavy Duty, Buffalo Grove *Also called Morse Automotive Corporation* ***(G-2577)***
Mortgage Market Info Svcs...630 834-7555
53 E Saint Charles Rd Villa Park (60181) ***(G-20161)***
Morton Automatic Electric Co...309 263-7577
641 W David St Morton (61550) ***(G-14369)***
Morton Buildings Inc...217 357-3713
1825 E Us Highway 136 Carthage (62321) ***(G-3140)***
Morton Buildings Inc...630 904-1122
1519 N Il Route 23 Streator (61364) ***(G-19615)***
Morton Buildings Inc...309 936-7282
605 E Henry St Atkinson (61235) ***(G-902)***
Morton Buildings Inc...309 263-3652
25 Erie Ct Morton (61550) ***(G-14370)***
Morton Group Ltd...847 831-2766
1510 Old Deerfield Rd # 20 Highland Park (60035) ***(G-11286)***
Morton Grove Auto Electric, Arlington Heights *Also called Lawrence Maddock* ***(G-768)***
Morton Grove Phrmceuticals Inc...847 967-5600
6451 Main St Morton Grove (60053) ***(G-14430)***
Morton Industries LLC...309 263-2590
70 Commerce Dr Morton (61550) ***(G-14371)***
Morton Intl Inc Adhsves Spclty...815 653-2042
5005 Barnard Mill Rd Ringwood (60072) ***(G-17045)***
Morton Machining, Morton *Also called Marion Tool & Die Inc* ***(G-14364)***
Morton Ready Mix Concrete, Morton *Also called Southfield Corporation* ***(G-14382)***
Morton Salt Inc (HQ)...312 807-2000
444 W Lake St Ste 3000 Chicago (60606) ***(G-5501)***
Morton Suggestion Company LLC...847 255-4770
800 W Central Rd Ste 101 Mount Prospect (60056) ***(G-14549)***
Mosaic Construction...847 504-0177
425 Huehl Rd Bldg 15b Northbrook (60062) ***(G-15437)***
Mosaic Label & Print LLC (PA)...847 904-1375
4346 Di Paolo Ctr Glenview (60025) ***(G-10591)***
Mosaicos Inc...773 777-8453
4948 N Pulaski Rd Chicago (60630) ***(G-5502)***
Mosedale Manufacturing, Franklin Park *Also called Reliance Tool & Mfg Co* ***(G-10035)***
Moss Holding Company (HQ)...847 238-4200
2600 Elmhurst Rd Elk Grove Village (60007) ***(G-9132)***
Moss Inc (PA)...800 341-1557
2600 Elmhurst Rd Elk Grove Village (60007) ***(G-9133)***
Moss Inc...800 341-1557
222 N Maplewood Ave Chicago (60612) ***(G-5503)***
Mossan Inc...857 247-4122
28 Ashburn Ct Unit Z1 Schaumburg (60193) ***(G-18633)***
Most Enterprise Inc...800 792-4669
1007 W Fulton Market Fl 2 Chicago (60607) ***(G-5504)***
Mostardi Platt, Hoffman Estates *Also called Platt G Mostardi* ***(G-11443)***

Mostert & Ferguson Signs 815 485-1212
16249 107th Ave Ste 10 Orland Park (60467) ***(G-15969)***

Motamed Medical Publishing Co 773 761-6667
7141 N Kedzie Ave # 1504 Chicago (60645) ***(G-5505)***

Motec Inc 630 241-9595
555 Rogers St Ste 5 Downers Grove (60515) ***(G-8060)***

Motherboard Gifts & More LLC 847 550-2222
75 Oakwood Rd Lake Zurich (60047) ***(G-12436)***

Motion Access LLC 847 357-8832
775 Nicholas Blvd Elk Grove Village (60007) ***(G-9134)***

Motivequest LLC (HQ) 847 905-6100
200 S Wacker Dr Ste 625 Chicago (60606) ***(G-5506)***

Motor Capacitors Inc 773 774-6666
335 Beinoris Dr Wood Dale (60191) ***(G-21217)***

Motor Coach Inds Intl Inc (HQ) 847 285-2000
200 E Oakton St Des Plaines (60018) ***(G-7804)***

Motor Coach Industries 847 285-2000
200 E Oakton St Des Plaines (60018) ***(G-7805)***

Motor Oil Inc 847 956-7550
2250 Arthur Ave Elk Grove Village (60007) ***(G-9135)***

Motor Parts & Equipment Corp 217 877-7456
3110 N Woodford St Decatur (62526) ***(G-7527)***

Motor Row Development Corp 773 525-3311
2303 S Mich Ave Ste Assoc Chicago (60616) ***(G-5507)***

Motor Sport Marketing Group 618 654-6750
7 Shamrock Blvd Highland (62249) ***(G-11232)***

Motorola International Capital 847 576-5000
1303 E Algonquin Rd Schaumburg (60196) ***(G-18634)***

Motorola Intl Dev Corp (HQ) 847 576-5000
2000 Progress Pkwy Schaumburg (60196) ***(G-18635)***

Motorola Mobility Holdings LLC (HQ) 800 668-6765
222 Merchandise Mart Plz # 1800 Chicago (60654) ***(G-5508)***

Motorola Mobility LLC 847 576-5000
222 Merchandise Mart Plz # 1800 Chicago (60654) ***(G-5509)***

Motorola Mobility LLC (HQ) 847 523-5000
222 Mdse Mart Plz # 1800 Chicago (60654) ***(G-5510)***

Motorola Solutions Inc (PA) 847 576-5000
500 W Monroe St Ste 4400 Chicago (60661) ***(G-5511)***

Motorola Solutions Inc 847 341-3485
2301 W 22nd St Ste 102 Oak Brook (60523) ***(G-15647)***

Motorola Solutions Inc 217 894-6451
1699 E 2950th St Clayton (62324) ***(G-6910)***

Motorola Solutions Inc 847 523-5000
1899 W Winchester Rd Libertyville (60048) ***(G-12683)***

Motorola Solutions Inc 630 308-9394
2100 Progress Pkwy Schaumburg (60196) ***(G-18636)***

Motorola Solutions Inc 630 353-8000
1411 Opus Pl Ste 350 Downers Grove (60515) ***(G-8061)***

Motorola Solutions Inc 847 576-8600
1295 E Algonquin Rd Schaumburg (60196) ***(G-18637)***

Motorola Solutions Inc 847 523-5000
622 N Us Highway 45 Libertyville (60048) ***(G-12684)***

Motorola Solutions Inc 847 540-8815
1155 W Dundee Rd Arlington Heights (60004) ***(G-779)***

Motorola Solutions Inc 847 523-5000
1200 Technology Way Libertyville (60048) ***(G-12685)***

Motorola Solutions Inc 708 476-8226
1100 E Woodfield Rd # 535 Schaumburg (60173) ***(G-18638)***

Motorola Solutions Inc 800 331-6456
2000 Progress Pkwy Schaumburg (60196) ***(G-18639)***

Motorola Solutions Inc 847 576-5000
2520 Galvin Dr Elgin (60124) ***(G-8665)***

Motorsports Publications House 630 699-7629
24334 Blazing Star Ct Plainfield (60585) ***(G-16692)***

Motr Grafx LLC 847 600-5656
225 Larkin Dr Ste 5 Wheeling (60090) ***(G-20942)***

Motus Digital Llc 972 943-0008
131 Cornell Ave Des Plaines (60016) ***(G-7806)***

Moulding & Millwork Midwest, New Lenox *Also called Sauder Industries Limited* ***(G-15057)***

Mouldtec Inc 815 893-0908
8015 Pyott Rd Crystal Lake (60014) ***(G-7234)***

Moultri Cnty Hstrcl/Gnlgcl Sct 217 728-4085
117 E Harrison St Sullivan (61951) ***(G-19672)***

Moultrie County Hardwoods LLC 217 543-2643
1618 Cr 2000n Arthur (61911) ***(G-870)***

Moultrie County Redi-Mix Co 217 728-2334
622 S Worth St Sullivan (61951) ***(G-19673)***

Mount Vernon Iron Works, Mount Vernon *Also called Mt Vernon Iron Works LLC* ***(G-14628)***

Mount Vernon Mills 618 882-6300
1001 Main St Highland (62249) ***(G-11233)***

Mount Vernon Neon Sign Co 618 242-0645
1 Neon Dr Mount Vernon (62864) ***(G-14626)***

Mount Vernon Zone, Mount Vernon *Also called Centralia Press Ltd* ***(G-14601)***

Mountain Graphix LLC 630 681-8300
226 S Westgate Dr Ste A Carol Stream (60188) ***(G-3033)***

Mountain Highway Holdings, Willowbrook *Also called Nyb Process Fans Inc* ***(G-21055)***

Movie Facts Inc (PA) 847 299-9700
1870 Busse Hwy Ste 200 Des Plaines (60016) ***(G-7807)***

Moweaqua Packing Plant 217 768-4714
601 N Main St Moweaqua (62550) ***(G-14652)***

Moxie Apparel LLC 312 243-9040
222 S Morgan St Ste 3c Chicago (60607) ***(G-5512)***

Moz Nutraceuticals LLC 314 315-2541
14358 N Manhattan Ln Mount Vernon (62864) ***(G-14627)***

Mozaics LLC 614 306-1881
5960 N Broadway St Chicago (60660) ***(G-5513)***

Mozaics Snacks, Chicago *Also called Mozaics LLC* ***(G-5513)***

Mp Manufacturing Inc 815 334-1112
13802 Washington St Ste B Woodstock (60098) ***(G-21414)***

Mp Mold Inc 630 613-8086
1480 W Bernard Dr Ste C Addison (60101) ***(G-224)***

Mp Steel Chicago LLC 773 242-0853
5757 W Ogden Ave Ste 4 Chicago (60804) ***(G-5514)***

Mpc Containment Systems LLC (HQ) 773 927-4121
815 W Van Buren St # 520 Chicago (60607) ***(G-5515)***

Mpc Containment Systems LLC 773 927-4120
3820 W 74th St Chicago (60629) ***(G-5516)***

Mpc Global LLC 816 399-4710
1800 E Adams St Springfield (62703) ***(G-19408)***

Mpc Group LLC (PA) 773 927-4120
815 W Van Buren St # 520 Chicago (60607) ***(G-5517)***

Mpc Products Corporation (HQ) 847 673-8300
6300 W Howard St Niles (60714) ***(G-15149)***

Mpc Products Corporation 847 673-8300
6300 W Howard St Niles (60714) ***(G-15150)***

MPD Inc 847 489-7705
325 1st St Libertyville (60048) ***(G-12686)***

Mpd Medical Systems Inc 815 477-0707
602 E Walnut St Watseka (60970) ***(G-20312)***

Mpm Industries, Glen Carbon *Also called Mechanics Planing Mill Inc* ***(G-10390)***

Mpp Sycamore Div 6063, Sycamore *Also called Orora Packaging Solutions* ***(G-19727)***

Mpr Plastics Inc 847 468-9950
1551 Scottsdale Ct # 100 Elgin (60123) ***(G-8666)***

MPS Chicago Inc (HQ) 630 932-9000
1500 Centre Cir Downers Grove (60515) ***(G-8062)***

MPS Chicago Inc 630 932-5583
315 Eisenhower Ln S Bolingbrook (60440) ***(G-2217)***

Mr Auto Electric 217 523-3659
2649 E Cook St Springfield (62703) ***(G-19409)***

Mr Rakesh Avichal 224 735-0505
2649 Greenleaf Ave Elk Grove Village (60007) ***(G-9136)***

Mr T Shirt and Dollar Plus 708 596-9150
75 W 159th St Harvey (60426) ***(G-11093)***

Mr. Pak's, Chicago *Also called Wisepak Foods LLC* ***(G-6650)***

Mr. Rooter Plumbing, Joliet *Also called Ave Inc* ***(G-11825)***

Mrb Roofing Inc 872 814-4430
1018 Samson Dr University Park (60484) ***(G-19963)***

MRC Global (us) Inc 314 231-3400
3672 State Route 111 Granite City (62040) ***(G-10727)***

MRC Polymers Inc (PA) 773 890-9000
3307 S Lawndale Ave Chicago (60623) ***(G-5518)***

Mrgfastman, Highland Park *Also called G-Fast Distribution Inc* ***(G-11264)***

Mri Department, Glenview *Also called Illinois Bone & Joint Inst LLC* ***(G-10559)***

Mri Steel, Hinsdale *Also called Beh IL Sub LLC* ***(G-11364)***

Mrs Fishers Inc 815 964-9114
1231 Fulton Ave Rockford (61103) ***(G-17532)***

Mrs Mike's Potato Chips, Freeport *Also called Altona Co* ***(G-10099)***

Mrs Weavers Salads, Franklin Park *Also called Dean Food Products Company* ***(G-9928)***

Mrs. Fisher's Chips, Rockford *Also called Mrs Fishers Inc* ***(G-17532)***

Mrt Sureway Inc (PA) 847 801-3010
2959 Hart Ct Franklin Park (60131) ***(G-10004)***

Ms, Addison *Also called Metals and Services Inc* ***(G-200)***

Ms Astral Tool, West Chicago *Also called M S Tool & Engineering* ***(G-20610)***

Ms. Bossy Boots, Crystal Lake *Also called Shoelace Inc* ***(G-7265)***

MSA, Westmont *Also called Magnet-Schultz America Inc* ***(G-20756)***

MSC Pre Finish Metals Egv Inc (HQ) 847 439-2210
2250 Pratt Blvd Elk Grove Village (60007) ***(G-9137)***

Mseed Group LLC 847 226-1147
535 W Taft Dr South Holland (60473) ***(G-19234)***

Msf Graphics Inc 847 446-6900
959 Lee St Des Plaines (60016) ***(G-7808)***

MSF&w, Springfield *Also called Ferenbach Marucco Stoddard* ***(G-19366)***

MSI, Saint Charles *Also called Manufactured Specialties Inc* ***(G-18230)***

MSI Green Inc 312 421-6550
1958 W Grand Ave Chicago (60622) ***(G-5519)***

MSI Southland, Lincolnwood *Also called Rutgers Enterprises Inc* ***(G-12841)***

Msm Promotions, Chicago *Also called Maxs Screen Machine Inc* ***(G-5370)***

MSP, Downers Grove *Also called Machine Solution Providers Inc* ***(G-8049)***

Mssc, Collinsville *Also called Marsh Shipping Supply Co LLC* ***(G-6969)***

Mssc LLC 618 343-1006
926 Mcdonough Lake Rd E Collinsville (62234) ***(G-6971)***

MST Div, Bolingbrook *Also called Kps Capital Partners LP* ***(G-2203)***

Msystems Group LLC 630 567-3930
38w426 Mallard Lake Rd Saint Charles (60175) ***(G-18233)***

Mt Vernon Iron Works LLC 618 244-2313
10950 N Cactus Ln Mount Vernon (62864) ***(G-14628)***

ALPHABETIC

Mt Carmel Machine Shop Inc ... 618 262-4591
10011 N 1250th Blvd Mount Carmel (62863) ***(G-14480)***

Mt Carmel Register Co Inc ... 618 262-5144
117 E 4th St Mount Carmel (62863) ***(G-14481)***

MT Case Company ... 630 227-1019
569 N Edgewood Ave Wood Dale (60191) ***(G-21218)***

Mt Containers Inc ... 708 458-9420
6410 W 74th St Ste B Chicago (60638) ***(G-5520)***

Mt Crmel Stblzation Group Inc (PA) ... 618 262-5118
1611 College Dr Mount Carmel (62863) ***(G-14482)***

Mt Greenwood Embroidery ... 773 779-5798
3136 W 111th St Chicago (60655) ***(G-5521)***

Mt Tool and Manufacturing Inc ... 847 985-6211
1118 Lunt Ave Ste E Schaumburg (60193) ***(G-18640)***

Mt Vernon Electric, Mount Vernon *Also called Decatur Industrial Elc Inc* ***(G-14607)***

Mt Vernon Mold Works Inc ... 618 242-6040
15 Industrial Dr Mount Vernon (62864) ***(G-14629)***

MTA USA Corp ... 847 847-5503
501 Lively Blvd Elk Grove Village (60007) ***(G-9138)***

Mte Hydraulics, Rockford *Also called Mechanical Tool & Engrg Co* ***(G-17513)***

Mtech Cnc Machining Inc ... 224 848-0818
925 Telser Rd Lake Zurich (60047) ***(G-12437)***

Mth Enterprises LLC ... 708 498-1100
1 Mth Plz Hillside (60162) ***(G-11349)***

MTI, Elk Grove Village *Also called Marathon Technologies Inc* ***(G-9111)***

Mtm Jostens Inc ... 815 875-1111
615 S 6th St Princeton (61356) ***(G-16816)***

Mtm Recognition Corporation ... 815 875-1111
615 S 6th St Princeton (61356) ***(G-16817)***

MTS Jerseyville Inc ... 618 639-2583
27065 Crystal Lake Rd Jerseyville (62052) ***(G-11794)***

MTS Publishing Co ... 630 955-9750
5229 Cypress Ct Lisle (60532) ***(G-12916)***

Mtx, Winslow *Also called Mitek Corporation* ***(G-21140)***

Mtx/Oaktron, Winslow *Also called Mitek Corporation* ***(G-21139)***

Mucci Kirkpatrick Sheet Metal ... 815 433-3350
1908 Ottawa Ave Ottawa (61350) ***(G-16062)***

Mudlark Papers Inc ... 630 717-7616
1031 Shimer Ct Naperville (60565) ***(G-14876)***

Mueller Co LLC ... 217 423-4471
500 W Eldorado St Decatur (62522) ***(G-7528)***

Mueller Company Plant 4 ... 217 425-7424
1226 E Garfield Ave Decatur (62526) ***(G-7529)***

Mueller Custom Cabinetry Inc ... 815 448-5448
4730 S Old Mazon Rd Mazon (60444) ***(G-13683)***

Mueller Door Company ... 815 385-8550
27100 N Darrell Rd Wauconda (60084) ***(G-20379)***

Mueller Metal Products, Elk Grove Village *Also called Mueller Mfg Corp* ***(G-9139)***

Mueller Mfg Corp (PA) ... 847 640-1666
300 Lively Blvd Elk Grove Village (60007) ***(G-9139)***

Mueller Ornamental Iron Works ... 847 758-9941
655 Lively Blvd Elk Grove Village (60007) ***(G-9140)***

Mueller Service Co LLC (HQ) ... 217 423-4471
500 W Eldorado St Decatur (62522) ***(G-7530)***

Muffys Inc ... 815 433-6839
423 W Madison St Ottawa (61350) ***(G-16063)***

Muhammad Sotavia ... 708 966-2262
9601 165th St Orland Park (60467) ***(G-15970)***

Muhammed Citizens, Mahomet *Also called Illinois Valley Press East* ***(G-13424)***

Muhs Cabinet Creation, Noble *Also called Muhs Funiture Manufacturing* ***(G-15190)***

Muhs Funiture Manufacturing ... 618 723-2590
4808 N Passport Rd Noble (62868) ***(G-15190)***

Muir Omni Graphics Inc (PA) ... 309 673-7034
908 W Main St Peoria (61606) ***(G-16480)***

Mullarkey Associates Inc ... 708 597-5555
8141 185th St Tinley Park (60487) ***(G-19846)***

Mullen Circle Brand Inc ... 847 676-1880
3514 W Touhy Ave Skokie (60076) ***(G-18993)***

Mullen Foods LLC ... 773 716-9001
6740 N Edgebrook Ter Chicago (60646) ***(G-5522)***

Muller Roofing & Construction, Chicago *Also called Ted Muller* ***(G-6336)***

Muller-Pinehurst Dairy Inc ... 815 968-0441
2110 Ogilby Rd Rockford (61102) ***(G-17533)***

Mullins Food Products Inc ... 708 344-3224
2200 S 25th Ave Broadview (60155) ***(G-2455)***

Multax Corporation ... 309 266-9765
424 W Edgewood Ct Morton (61550) ***(G-14372)***

Multi Business Forms, Darien *Also called Multi Print and Digital LLC* ***(G-7410)***

Multi Packaging Solutions Inc ... 773 283-9500
4221 N Normandy Ave Chicago (60634) ***(G-5523)***

Multi Print and Digital LLC ... 630 985-2600
8113 S Lemont Rd Darien (60561) ***(G-7410)***

Multi Swatch Corporation ... 708 344-9440
2600 S 25th Ave Ste Y Broadview (60155) ***(G-2456)***

Multi-Lngua Communications, Northfield *Also called Chicago Mltlingua Graphics Inc* ***(G-15512)***

Multi-State Indus Contrs Inc ... 217 423-4100
2345 E Garfield Ave Decatur (62526) ***(G-7531)***

Multicopy Corp ... 847 446-7015
33207 N Cove Rd Grayslake (60030) ***(G-10792)***

Multifoil Packaging, Elgin *Also called Transcontinental Multifilm Inc* ***(G-8757)***

Multimail Solutions ... 847 516-9977
700 Industrial Dr Cary (60013) ***(G-3181)***

Multimetal Products Corp ... 847 662-9110
3965 Grove Ave Gurnee (60031) ***(G-10901)***

Multiple Metal Production ... 847 679-1510
8030 Lawndale Ave Skokie (60076) ***(G-18994)***

Multiplex Display Fixture Co ... 800 325-3350
1610 Design Way Dupo (62239) ***(G-8141)***

Multiplex Industries Inc ... 630 906-9780
1650 Se River Rd Montgomery (60538) ***(G-14263)***

Multitech Cold Forming LLC ... 630 949-8200
250 Kehoe Blvd Carol Stream (60188) ***(G-3034)***

Multitech Industries ... 815 206-0015
10603 Arabian Trl Woodstock (60098) ***(G-21415)***

Multitech Industries Inc (PA) ... 630 784-9200
250 Kehoe Blvd Carol Stream (60188) ***(G-3035)***

Multitech McHned Cmponents LLC ... 630 949-8200
250 Kehoe Blvd Carol Stream (60188) ***(G-3036)***

Multitech Swiss Machining LLC ... 260 894-4180
350 Village Dr Carol Stream (60188) ***(G-3037)***

Mulvain Woodworks ... 815 248-2305
14578 Center Rd Durand (61024) ***(G-8154)***

Mumford Metal Casting LLC ... 708 345-0400
2801 Lakeside Dr Ste 300 Bannockburn (60015) ***(G-1204)***

Mumford Metal Casting LLC (PA) ... 312 733-2600
2222 S Halsted St Chicago (60608) ***(G-5524)***

Munoz Flour Tortilleria Inc ... 773 523-1837
1707 W 47th St Chicago (60609) ***(G-5525)***

Muntons Malted Ingredients Inc ... 630 812-1600
2505 S Finley Rd Ste 130 Lombard (60148) ***(G-13105)***

Muntz Industries Inc ... 847 949-8280
710 Tower Rd Mundelein (60060) ***(G-14718)***

Murata Electronics N Amer Inc ... 847 330-9200
425 N Martingale Rd # 1540 Schaumburg (60173) ***(G-18641)***

Murdock Company Inc ... 847 566-0050
936 Turret Ct Mundelein (60060) ***(G-14719)***

Murff Enterprises LLC ... 203 685-5556
9331 S Clyde Ave Chicago (60617) ***(G-5526)***

Murnane Packaging Corporation ... 708 449-1200
607 Northwest Ave Northlake (60164) ***(G-15552)***

Murnane Specialties Inc (PA) ... 708 449-1200
607 Northwest Ave Northlake (60164) ***(G-15553)***

Murnane Specialties Inc ... 708 449-1200
1507 Averill Rd Geneva (60134) ***(G-10291)***

Muro Pallets Corp ... 773 640-8606
5208 S Mozart St Chicago (60632) ***(G-5527)***

Murpack, Northlake *Also called Murnane Packaging Corporation* ***(G-15552)***

Murphy USA Inc ... 815 463-9963
431 E Lincoln Hwy New Lenox (60451) ***(G-15044)***

Murphy USA Inc ... 815 337-2440
1265 Lake Ave Woodstock (60098) ***(G-21416)***

Murphy USA Inc ... 847 245-3283
2676 N Il Route 83 Round Lake Beach (60073) ***(G-18091)***

Murphy USA Inc ... 630 801-4950
1927 Us Route 30 Montgomery (60538) ***(G-14264)***

Murphy USA Inc ... 815 936-6144
503 Riverstone Pkwy Kankakee (60901) ***(G-11992)***

Murphy USA Inc ... 815 356-7633
985 Central Park Dr Crystal Lake (60014) ***(G-7235)***

Murphys Pub ... 847 526-1431
110 Slocum Lake Rd Wauconda (60084) ***(G-20380)***

Murphys Sign Studio ... 630 963-0677
29 E Chicago Ave Westmont (60559) ***(G-20762)***

Murray Inc (PA) ... 847 620-7990
400 N Rand Rd North Barrington (60010) ***(G-15287)***

Murray Cabinetry & Tops Inc ... 815 672-6992
407 N Bloomington St Streator (61364) ***(G-19616)***

Murray Custom Cabinetry ... 309 966-0624
4310 N Sheridan Rd Ste A Peoria (61614) ***(G-16481)***

Murray Printing Service Inc ... 847 310-8959
635 Remington Rd Ste F Schaumburg (60173) ***(G-18642)***

Murrihy Pallet Co ... 615 370-7000
1919 W 74th St Chicago (60636) ***(G-5528)***

Murvin & Meier Oil Co ... 847 277-8380
1531 S Grove Ave Unit 203 Barrington (60010) ***(G-1231)***

Murvin & Meir Oil Co ... 618 395-4405
1102 N East St Olney (62450) ***(G-15876)***

Murvin Oil Company ... 618 393-2124
1712 S Whittle Ave Olney (62450) ***(G-15877)***

Musco Sports Lighting LLC ... 630 876-0500
902 Paramount Pkwy Ste A Batavia (60510) ***(G-1396)***

Mushro Machine & Tool Co ... 815 672-5848
819 E Bridge St Streator (61364) ***(G-19617)***

Music Inc. Magazine, Elmhurst *Also called Maher Publications Inc* ***(G-9398)***

Music Plug LLC ... 309 826-5238
33275 E 1700 North Rd Colfax (61728) ***(G-6950)***

Music Solutions........630 759-3033
490 Woodcreek Dr Ste D Bolingbrook (60440) ***(G-2218)***
Mutual Steel, Highland Park *Also called Mutual Svcs Highland Pk Inc* ***(G-11287)***
Mutual Svcs Highland Pk Inc........847 432-3815
2760 Skokie Valley Rd Highland Park (60035) ***(G-11287)***
Mvs Dynalink, Mundelein *Also called Maclen-Fogg Cmpnent Sltons LLC* ***(G-14711)***
Mvs Molding Inc........847 740-7700
701 Long Lake Dr Round Lake (60073) ***(G-18080)***
MW Hopkins & Sons Inc........847 458-1010
9150 Pyott Rd Lake In The Hills (60156) ***(G-12341)***
Mw Industries, Rosemont *Also called Matthew Warren Inc* ***(G-18035)***
Mw Industries Inc........773 539-5600
131 Foster Ave Bensenville (60106) ***(G-1855)***
MWK Rail LLC........815 671-5217
3021 E Stillwater Lndg Urbana (61802) ***(G-19989)***
MWM Express Inc........630 401-0528
6730 107th St Apt 1d Chicago Ridge (60415) ***(G-6805)***
Mwrbents, Mascoutah *Also called Midwest Recumbent Bicycles* ***(G-13604)***
Mwsts, Plainfield *Also called Midwest Sport Turf Systems LLC* ***(G-16690)***
Mww Food Processing USA LLC (HQ)........773 478-9700
2567 Greenleaf Ave Elk Grove Village (60007) ***(G-9141)***
My Bed Inc........800 326-9233
14040 S Shoshoni Dr Lockport (60491) ***(G-13015)***
My Konjac Sponge Inc........630 345-3653
300 Lake View Pl North Barrington (60010) ***(G-15288)***
My Local Beacon Llc........888 482-6691
73 W Monroe St Ste 323 Chicago (60603) ***(G-5529)***
My Own Meals Inc........773 378-6505
5410 W Roosevelt Rd # 301 Chicago (60644) ***(G-5530)***
My Own Meals Inc (PA)........847 948-1118
400 Lake Cook Rd Ste 107 Deerfield (60015) ***(G-7639)***
My Sports Warehouse, Vernon Hills *Also called Wagner International LLC* ***(G-20109)***
My-Lin Manufacturing Co Inc........630 897-4100
820 N Russell Ave Aurora (60506) ***(G-1137)***
Mycogen Seeds, Pontiac *Also called Dow Agrosciences LLC* ***(G-16769)***
Mydent International, Algonquin *Also called Young Mydent LLC* ***(G-399)***
Myeccho LLC........224 639-3068
550 Graceland Ave Apt 11 Des Plaines (60016) ***(G-7809)***
Myers Concrete & Construction........815 732-2591
1100 Bennett Dr Oregon (61061) ***(G-15924)***
Myers Inc........309 725-3710
99999 Route 1 S Varna (61375) ***(G-20033)***
Myerson LLC........312 432-8200
5106 N Ravenswood Ave Chicago (60640) ***(G-5531)***
Myhomeeq LLC........773 328-7034
1741 N Western Ave Chicago (60647) ***(G-5532)***
Mylan Inc........217 424-8400
705 E Eldorado St Decatur (62523) ***(G-7532)***
Mylan Institutional LLC........724 514-1800
4901 Hiawatha Dr Rockford (61103) ***(G-17534)***
Mypowr, Chicago *Also called Stryde Technologies Inc* ***(G-6255)***
Mystic Pizza Food Company, Elk Grove Village *Also called Globus Food Products LLC* ***(G-9018)***
Mzm Manufacturing Inc........815 624-8666
5409 Swanson Ct Roscoe (61073) ***(G-17919)***
N & M Type & Design........630 834-3696
562 S Rex Blvd Elmhurst (60126) ***(G-9404)***
N & S Pattern Co........815 874-6166
4911 Hydraulic Rd Rockford (61109) ***(G-17535)***
N A L, Flora *Also called North American Lighting Inc* ***(G-9686)***
N Bujarski Inc........847 884-1600
725 E Golf Rd Schaumburg (60173) ***(G-18643)***
N E S Traffic Safety........312 603-7444
8770 W Bryn Mawr Ave Chicago (60631) ***(G-5533)***
N G K Spark Plugs, Wood Dale *Also called NGK Spark Plugs (usa) Inc* ***(G-21222)***
N Henry & Son Inc........847 870-0797
900 N Rohlwing Rd Itasca (60143) ***(G-11706)***
N J Tech Inc........847 428-1001
160 Industrial Dr Ste 5 Gilberts (60136) ***(G-10363)***
N K C Inc........630 628-9159
751 W Winthrop Ave Addison (60101) ***(G-225)***
N P D Inc........708 424-6788
4720 W 103rd St Oak Lawn (60453) ***(G-15729)***
N P S, Alsip *Also called New Process Steel LP* ***(G-484)***
N W Horizontal Boring........618 566-9117
8100 Summerfield South Rd Mascoutah (62258) ***(G-13605)***
Nablus Sweets Inc........708 205-6534
4800 N Kedzie Ave Chicago (60625) ***(G-5534)***
Nablus Sweets Inc (PA)........708 529-3911
8320 S Harlem Ave Bridgeview (60455) ***(G-2367)***
Nacme Steel Processing LLC........847 806-7226
1965 Pratt Blvd Elk Grove Village (60007) ***(G-9142)***
Nacme Steel Processing LLC........847 806-7200
429 W 127th St Chicago (60628) ***(G-5535)***
Naco Printing Co Inc........618 664-0423
202 S 2nd St Greenville (62246) ***(G-10839)***
Nader Wholesale Grocers Inc........773 582-1000
3636 W 83rd Pl Chicago (60652) ***(G-5536)***

Nadig Newspapers Inc........773 286-6100
4937 N Milwaukee Ave Chicago (60630) ***(G-5537)***
Naegele Inc........708 388-7766
5661 W 120th St Alsip (60803) ***(G-482)***
Nafisco Inc........815 372-3300
808 Forestwood Dr Romeoville (60446) ***(G-17858)***
Nafm Llc........513 504-4333
1580 S Milwaukee Ave # 505 Libertyville (60048) ***(G-12687)***
Nagano International Corp........847 537-0011
999 Deerfield Pkwy Buffalo Grove (60089) ***(G-2578)***
Nagel-Chase Inc........847 336-4494
2377 N Delany Rd Gurnee (60031) ***(G-10902)***
Nagle Pumps, Chicago Heights *Also called Jn Pump Holdings Inc* ***(G-6753)***
Nagle Pumps, Chicago Heights *Also called Ruthman Pump and Engineering* ***(G-6773)***
Naija Foods, North Aurora *Also called Iya Foods LLC* ***(G-15264)***
Nail Superstore, Franklin Park *Also called Skyline Beauty Supply Inc* ***(G-10047)***
Nak Won Korean Bakery........773 588-8769
3746 W Lawrence Ave Chicago (60625) ***(G-5538)***
Nakano Foods, Mount Prospect *Also called Mizkan America Inc* ***(G-14547)***
Nakano Foods, Mount Prospect *Also called Mizkan America Holdings Inc* ***(G-14548)***
Nal Worldwide Holdings Inc........630 261-3100
1200 N Greenbriar Dr A Addison (60101) ***(G-226)***
Nal.syncreon Addison, Addison *Also called Nal Worldwide Holdings Inc* ***(G-226)***
Nalco Champion, Salem *Also called Championx LLC* ***(G-18334)***
Nalco Holding Company (HQ)........630 305-1000
1601 W Diehl Rd Naperville (60563) ***(G-14877)***
Nalco Wtr Prtrtment Sltons LLC........708 754-2550
320 W 194th St Glenwood (60425) ***(G-10644)***
Nama Graphics E LLC........262 966-3853
15751 Annico Dr Ste 2 Homer Glen (60491) ***(G-11484)***
Namaste Laboratories LLC (HQ)........708 824-1393
310 S Racine Ave Fl 8 Chicago (60607) ***(G-5539)***
Nameonanythingcom LLC........630 545-2642
23w328 Great Western Ave Glen Ellyn (60137) ***(G-10414)***
Nameplate & Panel Technology, Carol Stream *Also called Photo Techniques Corp* ***(G-3046)***
Nameplate Robinson & Precision........847 678-2255
10129 Pacific Ave Franklin Park (60131) ***(G-10005)***
Nampac, Oak Brook *Also called North America Packaging Corp* ***(G-15648)***
Nanas Kitchen Inc........815 363-8500
1313 Old Bay Rd Johnsburg (60051) ***(G-11808)***
Nanco Sales Co Inc........630 892-9820
320 N Highland Ave Aurora (60506) ***(G-1138)***
Nancy J Perkins........815 748-7121
1950 Dekalb Ave Ste D Dekalb (60115) ***(G-7691)***
Nanex LLC........847 501-4787
818 Elm St Uppr 2 Winnetka (60093) ***(G-21134)***
Nano Gas Technologies Inc........847 317-0656
506 Cambridge Cir Deerfield (60015) ***(G-7640)***
Nano Technologies Inc........630 517-8824
1765 Mustang Ct Wheaton (60189) ***(G-20813)***
Nano2 LLC........217 563-2942
106 E State St Nokomis (62075) ***(G-15195)***
Nanochem Solutions Inc (PA)........708 563-9200
1701 Quincy Ave Ste 10 Naperville (60540) ***(G-14878)***
Nanochem Solutions Inc........815 224-8480
5350 Donlar Ave Peru (61354) ***(G-16583)***
Nanocor LLC (HQ)........847 851-1900
2870 Forbs Ave Hoffman Estates (60192) ***(G-11438)***
Nanocytomics LLC........847 467-2868
1801 Maple Ave Ste 19 Evanston (60201) ***(G-9556)***
Nanolube Inc........630 706-1250
9 N Main St Ste 2 Lombard (60148) ***(G-13106)***
Nanophase Technologies Corp........630 771-6747
453 Commerce St Burr Ridge (60527) ***(G-2706)***
Nanophase Technologies Corp (PA)........630 771-6700
1319 Marquette Dr Romeoville (60446) ***(G-17859)***
Nanosphere LLC........847 400-9000
4088 Commercial Ave Northbrook (60062) ***(G-15438)***
Nantpharma LLC........847 243-1200
1300 Chase Ave Elk Grove Village (60007) ***(G-9143)***
Nantsound Inc........847 939-6101
960 N Northwest Hwy Park Ridge (60068) ***(G-16289)***
NAPA Auto Parts, Chicago *Also called Genuine Parts Company* ***(G-4681)***
NAPA Auto Parts, Goreville *Also called Goreville Auto Parts & Mch Sp* ***(G-10680)***
Napa-Decatur Auto Supply, Decatur *Also called Motor Parts & Equipment Corp* ***(G-7527)***
Napco Inc........630 406-1100
1141 N Raddant Rd Batavia (60510) ***(G-1397)***
Napco Brands, Batavia *Also called Napco Inc* ***(G-1397)***
Napersoft Inc........630 420-1515
40 Shuman Blvd Ste 293 Naperville (60563) ***(G-14879)***
Naperville Hanna Andersson........331 250-7100
140 W Jefferson Ave Naperville (60540) ***(G-14880)***
Napier Machine & Welding Inc........217 525-8740
2519 South Grand Ave E Springfield (62703) ***(G-19410)***
Nar-Dar/Kc St Louis, Chicago *Also called Process Supply Company Inc* ***(G-5890)***
Narda Inc........312 648-2300
222 S Riverside Plz Chicago (60606) ***(G-5540)***

ALPHABETIC

Narita Manufacturing Inc...248 345-1777
828 Landmark Dr Belvidere (61008) ***(G-1688)***
Narrative Health Network Inc...312 600-9154
1201 S Prrie Ave Apt 4103 Chicago (60605) ***(G-5541)***
Narvick Bros Construction, Morris *Also called Narvick Bros Lumber Co Inc* ***(G-14318)***
Narvick Bros Lumber Co Inc (PA)...815 942-1173
1037 Armstrong St Morris (60450) ***(G-14318)***
Narvick Bros Lumber Co Inc...815 521-1173
801 Rail Way Ct Minooka (60447) ***(G-14064)***
Narvick Bros Ready Mix, Minooka *Also called Narvick Bros Lumber Co Inc* ***(G-14064)***
Nas Media Group Inc (PA)...312 371-7499
424 Brookwood Ter 2 Olympia Fields (60461) ***(G-15896)***
Nascote Industries Inc (HQ)...618 327-4381
18310 Enterprise Ave Nashville (62263) ***(G-15002)***
Nascote Industries Inc...618 478-2092
17582 Mockingbird Rd Nashville (62263) ***(G-15003)***
Nashville Interior Systems Div, Nashville *Also called Antolin Interiors Usa Inc* ***(G-14994)***
Nashville Memorial Co...618 327-8492
542 E Saint Louis St Nashville (62263) ***(G-15004)***
Nashville News...618 327-3411
211 W Saint Louis St Nashville (62263) ***(G-15005)***
Nashville News, The, Nashville *Also called Nashville News* ***(G-15005)***
Nass Fresco Finishes, Barrington *Also called Fresco Plaster Finishes Inc* ***(G-1219)***
Nataz Specialty Coatings Inc...773 247-7030
3300 W 31st St Chicago (60623) ***(G-5542)***
Natc LLC...815 389-2300
215 Elmwood Ave South Beloit (61080) ***(G-19104)***
Nathan Winston Service Inc...815 758-4545
132 N 3rd St Dekalb (60115) ***(G-7692)***
Nation Inc...847 844-7300
400 Maple Ave Ste B Carpentersville (60110) ***(G-3109)***
Nation Pizza and Foods, Schaumburg *Also called Nation Pizza Products LP* ***(G-18644)***
Nation Pizza Products LP...847 397-3320
601 E Algonquin Rd Schaumburg (60173) ***(G-18644)***
National Aerospace Corp...847 566-5834
28 Sequoia Rd Hawthorn Woods (60047) ***(G-11125)***
National Association Realtors (PA)...800 874-6500
430 N Michigan Ave Lowr 2 Chicago (60611) ***(G-5543)***
National Bathing Products, Romeoville *Also called G K L Corporation* ***(G-17826)***
National Beef Packing Co LLC...312 332-6166
30 N Michigan Ave # 1702 Chicago (60602) ***(G-5544)***
National Beef Packing Intl, Chicago *Also called National Beef Packing Co LLC* ***(G-5544)***
National Binding Sups Eqp Inc...630 801-7600
39w254 Sheldon Ct Geneva (60134) ***(G-10292)***
National Biscuit Company...773 925-0654
7300 S Kedzie Ave Chicago (60629) ***(G-5545)***
National Bus Trader Inc...815 946-2341
9698 W Judson Rd Polo (61064) ***(G-16757)***
National Bus Trader Magazine, Polo *Also called National Bus Trader Inc* ***(G-16757)***
National Bushing & Mfg...847 847-1553
505 Oakwood Rd Ste 240 Lake Zurich (60047) ***(G-12438)***
National Cap and Set Screw Co...815 675-2363
2991 N Us Highway 12 Spring Grove (60081) ***(G-19287)***
National Casein Co...773 846-7300
6112 Woodcreek Ct Burr Ridge (60527) ***(G-2707)***
National Casein Company (PA)...773 846-7300
6112 Woodcreek Ct Burr Ridge (60527) ***(G-2708)***
National Casein New Jersey Inc...773 846-7300
6112 Woodcreek Ct Burr Ridge (60527) ***(G-2709)***
National Coatings Inc (PA)...309 342-4184
604 Us Highway 150 E Galesburg (61401) ***(G-10213)***
National Component Sales Inc...847 439-0333
1229 E Algonquin Rd Jk Arlington Heights (60005) ***(G-780)***
National Concrete Pipe Co (PA)...630 766-3600
11825 Franklin Ave Franklin Park (60131) ***(G-10006)***
National Cycle Inc...708 343-0400
2200 S Maywood Dr Maywood (60153) ***(G-13674)***
National Data Svcs Chicago Inc (HQ)...630 597-9100
900 Kimberly Dr Carol Stream (60188) ***(G-3038)***
National Data-Label Corp...630 616-9595
301 Arthur Ct Bensenville (60106) ***(G-1856)***
National Def Intelligence Inc...312 233-2318
2863 95th St 143-380 Naperville (60564) ***(G-14980)***
National Detroit Inc...815 877-4041
1590 Northrock Ct Rockford (61103) ***(G-17536)***
National Emergency Med ID Inc...847 366-1267
100 Lincolnwood Ct Spring Grove (60081) ***(G-19288)***
National Excelsior Company, Lansing *Also called Goose Island Mfg & Supply Corp* ***(G-12495)***
National Gift Card Corp (PA)...815 477-4288
300 Millennium Dr Crystal Lake (60012) ***(G-7236)***
National Greenhouse Company, Pana *Also called Nexus Corporation* ***(G-16218)***
National Grinding Wheel, Salem *Also called Radiac Abrasives Inc* ***(G-18354)***
National Industrial Coatings, Itasca *Also called ICP Industrial Inc* ***(G-11668)***
National Interchem LLC...708 597-7777
13750 Chatham St Blue Island (60406) ***(G-2133)***
National Jewelers Co., Chicago *Also called Victor Levy Jewelry Co Inc* ***(G-6545)***
National Locksmith Magazine, Norridge *Also called National Publishing Company* ***(G-15241)***
National Machine Repair Inc...708 672-7711
115 W Burville Rd Crete (60417) ***(G-7142)***
National Maint & Repr Inc (HQ)...618 254-7451
401 S Hawthorne St Hartford (62048) ***(G-11036)***
National Material Company LLC...773 468-2800
429 W 127th St Chicago (60628) ***(G-5546)***
National Material Company LLC (HQ)...847 806-7200
1965 Pratt Blvd Elk Grove Village (60007) ***(G-9144)***
National Material LP...773 646-6300
12100 S Stony Island Ave Chicago (60633) ***(G-5547)***
National Material Processing...773 646-6300
12100 S Stony Island Ave # 1 Chicago (60633) ***(G-5548)***
National Metal Works Inc...815 282-5533
916 River Ln Loves Park (61111) ***(G-13239)***
National Metalwares LP (HQ)...630 892-9000
900 N Russell Ave Aurora (60506) ***(G-1139)***
National Micro Systems Inc...312 566-0414
2 E 8th St Ste 100 Chicago (60605) ***(G-5549)***
National Multi Products Co, Lake Forest *Also called Excel Specialty Corp* ***(G-12248)***
National Peace Officers' Press, Troy *Also called R L Allen Industries* ***(G-19919)***
National Porges Radiator Corp...773 224-3000
320 W 83rd St Chicago (60620) ***(G-5550)***
National Power LLC...773 685-2662
4330 W Belmont Ave Chicago (60641) ***(G-5551)***
National Printing Resources, Chicago *Also called Bardash & Bukowski Inc* ***(G-3831)***
National Processing Co-Plant 1, Chicago *Also called Nacme Steel Processing LLC* ***(G-5535)***
National Publishing Company...630 837-2044
7330 W Montrose Ave Norridge (60706) ***(G-15241)***
National Railway Equipment Co...708 388-4781
14400 Robey Ave Ste 2 Dixmoor (60426) ***(G-7884)***
National Railway Equipment Co...618 241-9270
908 Shawnee St Mount Vernon (62864) ***(G-14630)***
National Railway Equipment Co...309 755-6800
300 9th St N Silvis (61282) ***(G-18908)***
National Railway Equipment Co...708 388-6002
14400 Robey Ave Ste 2 Dixmoor (60426) ***(G-7885)***
National Rubber Stamp Co Inc...773 281-6522
5320 N Lowell Ave Apt 311 Chicago (60630) ***(G-5552)***
National Safety Council (PA)...630 285-1121
1121 Spring Lake Dr Itasca (60143) ***(G-11707)***
National School Services Inc...847 438-3859
3254 Mayflower Ln Long Grove (60047) ***(G-13167)***
National Sporting Goods Assn...847 296-6742
3041 Woodcreek Dr Ste 210 Downers Grove (60515) ***(G-8063)***
National Technology Inc...847 506-1300
1101 Carnegie St Rolling Meadows (60008) ***(G-17752)***
National Temp-Trol Products...630 920-1919
667 Executive Dr Willowbrook (60527) ***(G-21053)***
National Tool & Machine Co...618 271-6445
1235 Piggott Ave East Saint Louis (62201) ***(G-8316)***
National Tool & Mfg Co...847 806-9800
563 Rock Road Dr East Dundee (60118) ***(G-8206)***
National Trackwork Inc...630 250-0600
1500 Industrial Dr Itasca (60143) ***(G-11708)***
National Tractor Parts Inc...630 552-4235
12127a Galena Rd Plano (60545) ***(G-16736)***
National Vinegar Co...618 395-1011
203 W South Ave Olney (62450) ***(G-15878)***
National Window Shade Co, Willowbrook *Also called National Temp-Trol Products* ***(G-21053)***
Nationwide Glove Co Inc (PA)...618 252-7192
925 Bauman Ln Harrisburg (62946) ***(G-11027)***
Nationwide News Monitor...312 424-4224
9239 Kilpatrick Ave Skokie (60076) ***(G-18995)***
Nationwide Precision Pdts Corp...585 272-7100
601 N Skokie Hwy Ste A Lake Bluff (60044) ***(G-12197)***
Natl Ktchn and Bath Cabinetry...815 733-8888
1811 W Normantown Rd Romeoville (60446) ***(G-17860)***
Natl Senior Hlth & Fitnes Day, Libertyville *Also called American Custom Publishing* ***(G-12628)***
Natura Products Inc...847 509-5835
3555 Woodhead Dr Northbrook (60062) ***(G-15439)***
Natural Beginnings...773 457-0509
15904 S Selfridge Cir Plainfield (60586) ***(G-16693)***
Natural Choice Corporation...815 874-4444
4601 Interstate Blvd Loves Park (61111) ***(G-13240)***
Natural Distribution Company...630 350-1700
550 Clayton Ct Wood Dale (60191) ***(G-21219)***
Natural Fiber Welding Inc...309 685-3591
801 W Main St Lab B206 Peoria (61606) ***(G-16482)***
Natural Fiber Welding Inc...309 339-7794
6533 N Galena Rd Peoria (61614) ***(G-16483)***
Natural Formulations, Skokie *Also called Formulations Inc* ***(G-18956)***
Natural Gas Pipeline Amer LLC...618 495-2211
7501 Huey Rd Centralia (62801) ***(G-3240)***
Natural Gas Pipeline Amer LLC...815 426-2151
5611 S 12000w Rd Herscher (60941) ***(G-11185)***
Natural Gas Pipeline Amer LLC...618 829-3224
6 Miles N On Elm St Saint Elmo (62458) ***(G-18310)***

Natural Packaging Inc ... 708 246-3420
550 Hillgrove Ave Ste 518 La Grange (60525) *(G-12083)*
Natural Polymers LLC ... 888 563-3111
14438 E North Ave Cortland (60112) *(G-7025)*
Natural Resources Ill Dept ... 618 439-4320
503 E Main St Benton (62812) *(G-1933)*
Natural Stone Inc ... 847 735-1129
611 Rockland Rd Ste 208 Lake Bluff (60044) *(G-12198)*
Naturally Clean, Darien *Also called Chem Free Solutions (G-7403)*
Nature House Inc ... 217 833-2393
30494 State Highway 107 Griggsville (62340) *(G-10850)*
Nature S American Co ... 630 246-4776
665 W North Ave Ste 105 Lombard (60148) *(G-13107)*
Nature's Touch, Northbrook *Also called Agrochem Inc (G-15334)*
Natures American Co ... 630 246-4274
3105 N Ashland Ave Chicago (60657) *(G-5553)*
Natures Appeal Mfg Corp ... 630 880-6222
1788 W Whispering Ct Addison (60101) *(G-227)*
Natures Healing Remedies Inc ... 773 589-9996
7742 W Addison St Chicago (60634) *(G-5554)*
Natures Sources LLC ... 847 663-9168
5665 W Howard St Niles (60714) *(G-15151)*
Naurex Inc ... 847 871-0377
1801 Maple Ave Ste 70 Evanston (60201) *(G-9557)*
Nautic Global Group LLC ... 574 457-5731
333 W Wacker Dr Ste 600 Chicago (60606) *(G-5555)*
Nautilus Medical ... 847 323-1334
1300 S Grove Ave Ste 200 Barrington (60010) *(G-1232)*
Nauvoo Mill & Bakery ... 217 453-6734
1530 Mulholland St Nauvoo (62354) *(G-15014)*
Nauvoo Products Inc ... 217 453-2817
1420 Mulholland St Nauvoo (62354) *(G-15015)*
Navatek Resources Inc ... 847 301-0174
1505 Wright Blvd Schaumburg (60193) *(G-18645)*
Navigator & Journal Register, Grayville *Also called S & R Media LLC (G-10814)*
Navillus Woodworks LLC ... 312 375-2680
2100 N Major Ave Chicago (60639) *(G-5556)*
Navipoint Genomics LLC ... 630 464-8013
2515 Dewes Ln Naperville (60564) *(G-14981)*
Navistar Inc (HQ) ... 331 332-5000
2701 Navistar Dr Lisle (60532) *(G-12917)*
Navistar Inc ... 331 332-5000
2701 Navistar Dr Lisle (60532) *(G-12918)*
Navistar Inc ... 331 332-5000
2700 Haven Ave Joliet (60433) *(G-11907)*
Navistar Inc ... 317 352-4500
10400 W North Ave Melrose Park (60160) *(G-13894)*
Navistar Inc ... 662 494-3421
2701 Navistar Dr Lisle (60532) *(G-12919)*
Navistar Inc ... 708 865-3333
10400 W North Ave 3 Melrose Park (60160) *(G-13895)*
Navistar Defense LLC ... 662 494-3421
2701 Navistar Dr Lisle (60532) *(G-12920)*
Navistar Defense LLC (HQ) ... 708 617-4500
10400 W North Ave Melrose Park (60160) *(G-13896)*
Navistar International Corp (PA) ... 331 332-5000
2701 Navistar Dr Lisle (60532) *(G-12921)*
Navistarsinfosoft Inc ... 877 270-3543
4323 S Emerald Ave Chicago (60609) *(G-5557)*
Navitas Electronics Corp ... 702 293-4670
1200 Internationale Pkwy Woodridge (60517) *(G-21325)*
Navitas Systems LLC (HQ) ... 630 755-7920
1200 Internationale Pkwy # 125 Woodridge (60517) *(G-21326)*
Navitor Inc ... 800 323-0253
7220 W Wilson Ave Harwood Heights (60706) *(G-11106)*
Navman Wireless Holdings LP ... 866 527-9896
2701 Patriot Blvd Ste 200 Glenview (60026) *(G-10592)*
Naylor Automotive Engrg Co Inc ... 773 582-6900
4645 S Knox Ave Chicago (60632) *(G-5558)*
Nazdar Sourceone ... 800 677-4657
5444 East Ave Ste B Countryside (60525) *(G-7066)*
Nb Coatings Inc (HQ) ... 800 323-3224
2701 E 170th St Lansing (60438) *(G-12510)*
Nb Finishing Inc ... 847 364-7500
3131 W Soffel Ave Melrose Park (60160) *(G-13897)*
NBC Meshtec Americas Inc ... 630 293-5454
512 Kingsland Dr Batavia (60510) *(G-1398)*
Nbs Corporation ... 847 860-8856
1501 Tonne Rd Elk Grove Village (60007) *(G-9145)*
Nbs Systems Inc (PA) ... 217 999-3472
1000 S Old Route 66 Mount Olive (62069) *(G-14507)*
Ncab Group Usa Inc ... 630 562-5550
1300 Norwood Ave Itasca (60143) *(G-11709)*
Ncc, Chicago *Also called J T C Inc (G-4995)*
Nci Technology, Oakbrook Terrace *Also called Heng Tuo Usa Inc (G-15802)*
NCM, Glenview *Also called New Century Mfg (G-10594)*
Ncp Commercial, Paxton *Also called Nexstep Commercial Pdts LLC (G-16309)*
ND Fairmont LLC (PA) ... 937 328-3870
1901 S Meyers Rd Ste 600 Oakbrook Terrace (60181) *(G-15810)*
ND Industries Inc ... 847 498-3600
1840 Raymond Dr Northbrook (60062) *(G-15440)*
ND Paper Inc (HQ) ... 513 200-0908
1901 S Meyers Rd Ste 600 Oakbrook Terrace (60181) *(G-15811)*
ND Paper LLC (HQ) ... 937 528-3870
1901 S Meyers Rd Ste 600 Oakbrook Terrace (60181) *(G-15812)*
Nduja Artisans Co ... 312 550-6991
2817 N Harlem Ave Chicago (60707) *(G-5559)*
NE Desktop Software Inc ... 800 211-8332
1100 E Wdfeld Rd Ste 100a Schaumburg (60173) *(G-18646)*
Nea Agora Packing Co ... 312 421-5130
1056 W Taylor St Chicago (60607) *(G-5560)*
Neals Trailer Sales ... 217 792-5136
1670 1100th St Lincoln (62656) *(G-12736)*
Nec Display Solutions Amer Inc (HQ) ... 630 467-3000
3250 Lacey Rd Ste 500 Downers Grove (60515) *(G-8064)*
Neckbone Skunks Logistics & Te ... 312 218-0281
6835 S Dorchester Ave # 1 Chicago (60637) *(G-5561)*
Necta Sweet Inc ... 847 215-9955
1554 Barclay Blvd Buffalo Grove (60089) *(G-2579)*
Need, Bolingbrook *Also called Hussain Shaheen (G-2187)*
Need To Know Inc ... 309 691-3877
1723 W Detweiller Dr Peoria (61615) *(G-16484)*
Needham Shop Inc ... 630 557-9019
46 W 840 Main Kaneville (60144) *(G-11955)*
Nefab Inc ... 705 748-4888
3105 N Ashland Ave 394 Chicago (60657) *(G-5562)*
Nefab Packaging N Centl LLC ... 630 451-5314
1539 Hunter Rd Hanover Park (60133) *(G-11010)*
Nega, Schaumburg *Also called Nippon Electric Glass Amer Inc (G-18649)*
Negative, McHenry *Also called Super Mix Inc (G-13801)*
Negocios Now, Chicago *Also called Nicado Publishing Company Inc (G-5595)*
Negs & Litho Inc ... 847 647-7770
6501 N Avondale Ave Chicago (60631) *(G-5563)*
Nehring Electrical Works Co ... 815 756-2741
1005 E Locust St Dekalb (60115) *(G-7693)*
Neil Enterprises Inc ... 847 549-7627
1000 Woodlands Pkwy Vernon Hills (60061) *(G-20077)*
Neil International Inc (PA) ... 847 549-7627
1000 Woodlands Pkwy Vernon Hills (60061) *(G-20078)*
Neiland Custom Products ... 815 825-2233
400 Il Route 38 Malta (60150) *(G-13430)*
Neiman Bros Co Inc ... 773 463-3000
3322 W Newport Ave Chicago (60618) *(G-5564)*
Neiman Brothers Co, Chicago *Also called Neiman Bros Co Inc (G-5564)*
Neisewander Enterprises Inc (PA) ... 815 288-1431
1101 E River Rd Dixon (61021) *(G-7904)*
Neiweem Industries Inc (PA) ... 847 487-1239
21 Greenview Rd Oakwood Hills (60013) *(G-15821)*
Nekg Holdings Inc ... 815 383-1379
26709 S Kimberly Ln Channahon (60410) *(G-3391)*
Nelco Coil Supply Company ... 847 259-7517
1500 E Ironwood Dr Mount Prospect (60056) *(G-14550)*
Nelsen Steel and Wire LP ... 847 671-9700
9400 Belmont Ave Franklin Park (60131) *(G-10007)*
Nelsen Steel Company, Franklin Park *Also called Nelsen Steel and Wire LP (G-10007)*
Nelson & Lavold Manufacturing ... 312 943-6300
1530 N Halsted St 34 Chicago (60642) *(G-5565)*
Nelson - Harkins Inds Inc ... 773 478-6243
411 E Scranton Ave Lake Bluff (60044) *(G-12199)*
Nelson C D Mfg & Sup Co, Wauconda *Also called C D Nelson Consulting Inc (G-20336)*
Nelson Door Co ... 217 543-3489
2245 Cr 1500e Arthur (61911) *(G-871)*
Nelson Enterprises Inc ... 815 633-1100
5447 Mainsail Dr Roscoe (61073) *(G-17920)*
Nelson Global Products Inc ... 309 263-8914
231 Detroit Ave Morton (61550) *(G-14373)*
Nelson Manufacturing Co Inc ... 815 229-0161
2516 20th St Rockford (61104) *(G-17537)*
Nelson Sash Systems Inc ... 708 385-5815
4650 W 120th St Alsip (60803) *(G-483)*
Nelson Stud Welding Inc ... 708 430-3770
18601 Graphic Ct Tinley Park (60477) *(G-19847)*
Nelson-Whittaker Ltd ... 815 459-6000
8550 Ridgefield Rd Ste C Crystal Lake (60012) *(G-7237)*
Nemera Buffalo Grove LLC (HQ) ... 847 541-7900
600 Deerfield Pkwy Buffalo Grove (60089) *(G-2580)*
Nemera Buffalo Grove LLC ... 847 325-3629
800 Corporate Grove Dr Buffalo Grove (60089) *(G-2581)*
Nemera Buffalo Grove LLC ... 847 325-3628
800 Corporate Grove Dr Buffalo Grove (60089) *(G-2582)*
Nemeth Tool Inc (PA) ... 630 595-0409
143 Murray Dr Wood Dale (60191) *(G-21220)*
Neo Orthotics Inc ... 309 699-0354
100 Park Pl East Peoria (61611) *(G-8279)*
Neolight Labs LLC ... 312 242-1773
34768 N Elm St Ingleside (60041) *(G-11588)*
Neomek Incorporated ... 630 879-5400
241 Oswald Ave Batavia (60510) *(G-1399)*

ALPHABETIC

Neomek Engineering, Batavia *Also called Neomek Incorporated* ***(G-1399)***
Neon Art 773 588-5883
4752 N Avers Ave Chicago (60625) ***(G-5566)***
Neon Crm, Chicago *Also called Neon One LLC* ***(G-5568)***
Neon Design Inc 773 880-5020
519 Howard St Evanston (60202) ***(G-9558)***
Neon Express Signs 773 463-7335
5026 N Broadway St Chicago (60640) ***(G-5567)***
Neon Nights Dj Svc 309 820-9000
2902 Essington St Bloomington (61705) ***(G-2082)***
Neon One LLC 888 860-6366
4545 N Ravenswood Ave 2ndf Chicago (60640) ***(G-5568)***
Neon Prism Electric Sign Co 630 879-1010
1213 Paramount Pkwy Batavia (60510) ***(G-1400)***
Neon Shop Inc 773 227-0303
2247 N Western Ave Chicago (60647) ***(G-5569)***
Neon Street Productions 217 304-4514
409 S Buchanan St Apt 4 Danville (61832) ***(G-7368)***
Neon Works of St Louis, East Alton *Also called Staar Bales Lestarge Inc* ***(G-8171)***
Neopenda Pbc 919 622-2487
965 W Chicago Ave Chicago (60642) ***(G-5570)***
Neopost R Meadows 630 467-0604
1200 N Arlington Hts Rd Itasca (60143) ***(G-11710)***
Neovision Usa Inc 847 533-0541
21720 W Long Grove Rd C33 Deer Park (60010) ***(G-7582)***
Nep Electronics Inc (PA) 630 595-8500
805 Mittel Dr Wood Dale (60191) ***(G-21221)***
Nepaley LLC 224 420-2310
1900 N Austin Ave Chicago (60639) ***(G-5571)***
Neptune USA Inc 847 987-3804
983 W Wise Rd Ste 101 Schaumburg (60193) ***(G-18647)***
Nerd Island Studios LLC 224 619-5361
1347 Ferndale Ave Highland Park (60035) ***(G-11288)***
Nesterowicz & Associates Inc 815 522-4469
313 W Main St Kirkland (60146) ***(G-12064)***
Nestle Beverage Division, Jacksonville *Also called Nestle Usa Inc* ***(G-11778)***
Nestle Chclat Cnfctons A Div N 847 957-7850
3401 Mount Prospect Rd Franklin Park (60131) ***(G-10008)***
Nestle Confections, Franklin Park *Also called Nestle Usa Inc* ***(G-10009)***
Nestle Confections Factory, Bloomington *Also called Nestle Usa Inc* ***(G-2083)***
Nestle Distribution Center, Dekalb *Also called Nestle Usa Inc* ***(G-7694)***
Nestle Pizza Company Inc (HQ) 847 646-2000
1 Kraft Ct Glenview (60025) ***(G-10593)***
Nestle Prepared Foods Company 630 671-3721
601 Wall St Glendale Heights (60139) ***(G-10478)***
Nestle Usa Inc 309 263-2651
216 N Morton Ave Morton (61550) ***(G-14374)***
Nestle Usa Inc 217 243-9175
1111 Carnation Dr Jacksonville (62650) ***(G-11778)***
Nestle Usa Inc 630 773-2090
1445 Norwood Ave Itasca (60143) ***(G-11711)***
Nestle Usa Inc 847 957-7850
3401 Mount Prospect Rd Franklin Park (60131) ***(G-10009)***
Nestle Usa Inc 815 754-2550
800 Nestle Ct Dekalb (60115) ***(G-7694)***
Nestle Usa Inc 309 829-1031
2501 Beich Rd Bloomington (61705) ***(G-2083)***
Netcom Inc 847 537-6300
599 Wheeling Rd Wheeling (60090) ***(G-20943)***
Netgain Motors Inc 630 243-9100
800 S State St Ste 4 Lockport (60441) ***(G-13016)***
Netgear Inc 630 955-0080
1000 E Warrenville Rd Naperville (60563) ***(G-14881)***
Netnotes, Spring Grove *Also called Kuna Corp* ***(G-19282)***
Netranix Enterprise 630 312-8141
336 Pinto Dr Bolingbrook (60440) ***(G-2219)***
Netsuite Inc 312 273-4100
200 N La Salle St # 2000 Chicago (60601) ***(G-5572)***
Nett Industries 847 838-3300
41736 N Lakeview Ter Antioch (60002) ***(G-628)***
Network Harbor Inc 309 633-9118
1230 W Candletree Dr D Peoria (61614) ***(G-16485)***
Network Printing Inc 847 566-4146
109 Alexandra Ct Mundelein (60060) ***(G-14720)***
Neumann Custom Woodworking 847 979-3199
2420 E Oakton St Ste Z Arlington Heights (60005) ***(G-781)***
Neurotherapeutics Pharma Inc 773 444-4180
8750 W Bryn Mawr Ave # 440 Chicago (60631) ***(G-5573)***
Neuses Tools, Rolling Meadows *Also called P K Neuses Incorporated* ***(G-17758)***
Nevco Sports LLC (PA) 618 664-0360
301 E Harris Ave Greenville (62246) ***(G-10840)***
Neveria Michoacana LLC 630 783-3518
132 N Bolingbrook Dr Bolingbrook (60440) ***(G-2220)***
Neverstrip LLC (PA) 708 588-9707
111 S Hinsdale Hinsdale (60521) ***(G-11370)***
Nevin Labs, Chicago *Also called Dentalez Alabama Inc* ***(G-4341)***
New Age Surfaces LLC 630 226-0011
1237 Naperville Dr Romeoville (60446) ***(G-17861)***
New Alliance Production LLC 309 928-3123
1701 N John St Farmer City (61842) ***(G-9656)***
New Archery Products LLC 708 488-2500
7500 Industrial Dr Forest Park (60130) ***(G-9722)***
New C F & I Inc 312 533-3555
200 E Randolph St # 7800 Chicago (60601) ***(G-5574)***
New Century Mfg 847 998-0960
1016 Pleasant Ln Glenview (60025) ***(G-10594)***
New Century Performance Inc 618 466-6383
3704 Riehl Ln Godfrey (62035) ***(G-10658)***
New Century Picture Corp (PA) 773 638-8888
2737 W Fulton St Chicago (60612) ***(G-5575)***
New Chicago Wholesale Bky Inc 847 981-1600
795 Touhy Ave Elk Grove Village (60007) ***(G-9146)***
New Cie Inc 815 224-1485
85 Chartres St La Salle (61301) ***(G-12118)***
New Cie Inc 815 224-1511
3349 Becker Dr Peru (61354) ***(G-16584)***
New City Communications 312 243-8786
770 N Halsted St Ste 183 Chicago (60642) ***(G-5576)***
New City News, Chicago *Also called New City Communications* ***(G-5576)***
New Dimension Models 815 935-1001
105 W Front St Aroma Park (60910) ***(G-840)***
New Dimensions Precision Mac 815 923-8300
6614 S Union Rd Union (60180) ***(G-19941)***
New ERA Cap Co Inc 504 581-2445
106 N Aberdeen St Ste 200 Chicago (60607) ***(G-5577)***
New Gen Aerospace Corp 847 740-2216
290 Park Ave Lake Villa (60046) ***(G-12361)***
New Image Designs 217 498-9830
136 Roanoke Dr Rochester (62563) ***(G-17170)***
New Image Upholstery 630 542-5560
21 Cedar Ct South Elgin (60177) ***(G-19169)***
New Lenox Machine Co Inc 815 584-4866
1200 E Mazon Ave Ste B Dwight (60420) ***(G-8156)***
New Life Printing & Publishing 847 658-4111
1508 S Main St Algonquin (60102) ***(G-382)***
New Life Screen Printing, Orland Park *Also called Spirit Warrior Inc* ***(G-15983)***
New Line Hardwoods Inc 309 657-7621
8727 Arenzville Rd Beardstown (62618) ***(G-1449)***
New Metal Crafts Inc 312 787-6991
6453 N Kilpatrick Ave Lincolnwood (60712) ***(G-12832)***
New Metal Fabrication Corp 618 532-9000
931 S Brookside St Centralia (62801) ***(G-3241)***
New Millenium Directories (PA) 815 626-5737
324 1st Ave Sterling (61081) ***(G-19522)***
New Ngc Inc 847 623-8100
515 E Sea Horse Dr Waukegan (60085) ***(G-20468)***
New Panel Brick Company of Ill 847 696-1686
6959 N Milwaukee Ave Niles (60714) ***(G-15152)***
New Process Steel LP 708 389-3380
5761 W 118th St Alsip (60803) ***(G-484)***
New SBL Inc 773 376-8280
1001 W 45th St Ste B Chicago (60609) ***(G-5578)***
New Specialty Products Inc 773 847-0230
1421 W 47th St Chicago (60609) ***(G-5579)***
New Spin Cycle 773 952-7490
1400 E 47th St Ste A Chicago (60653) ***(G-5580)***
New Star Lighting Company, Chicago *Also called 555 International Inc* ***(G-3476)***
New Step Orthotic Lab Inc 618 208-4444
14 Schiber Ct Maryville (62062) ***(G-13592)***
New Style Cabinets Inc 773 622-3114
1840 N Major Ave Chicago (60639) ***(G-5581)***
New Taste Good Noodle Inc 312 842-8980
2559 S Archer Ave Chicago (60608) ***(G-5582)***
New Triangle Oil Company 618 262-4131
600 Chestnut St Mount Carmel (62863) ***(G-14483)***
New Usn Chicago LLC (PA) 847 635-6772
1804 W Central Rd Mount Prospect (60056) ***(G-14551)***
New Vision Cstm Cabinets Mllwk 847 265-2723
23390 W Apollo Ct Lake Villa (60046) ***(G-12362)***
New Vision Display 224 268-3345
25 S Grove Ave Ste 400 Elgin (60120) ***(G-8667)***
New Vision Print & Marketing 630 406-0509
31w280 Diehl Rd Ste 104 Naperville (60563) ***(G-14882)***
New Wave Express Inc 630 238-3129
842 Foster Ave Bensenville (60106) ***(G-1857)***
New Wave Lax LLC 630 219-3919
10204 Bode St Ste C Plainfield (60585) ***(G-16694)***
New World Products Inc 630 690-5625
494 Mission St Carol Stream (60188) ***(G-3039)***
New World Trnsp Systems 773 509-5931
5895 N Rogers Ave Chicago (60646) ***(G-5583)***
New York & Company Inc 630 232-7693
410 Commons Dr Geneva (60134) ***(G-10293)***
New York & Company Inc 630 783-2910
639 E Boughton Rd Ste 135 Bolingbrook (60440) ***(G-2221)***
New York Blower Company 217 347-3233
1304 W Jaycee Ave Effingham (62401) ***(G-8414)***

ALPHABETIC SECTION
Nidec Motor Corporation

Newby Oil Company Inc 815 756-7688
2270 Oakland Dr Sycamore (60178) ***(G-19725)***
Newby, Wayne Nsp, Sycamore *Also called Newby Oil Company Inc* ***(G-19725)***
Newell, Oak Brook *Also called Levolor Inc* ***(G-15633)***
Newell Brands Inc 815 266-0066
29 E Stephenson St Freeport (61032) ***(G-10128)***
Newell Operating Company (HQ) 815 235-4171
29 E Stephenson St Freeport (61032) ***(G-10129)***
Newera Software Inc 815 784-3345
9505 Wolf Rd Kingston (60145) ***(G-12056)***
Newf LLC (PA) 630 330-5462
608 Driftwood Ct Naperville (60540) ***(G-14883)***
Newhaven Display Intl Inc 847 844-8795
2661 Galvin Ct Elgin (60124) ***(G-8668)***
Newko Proto Type, Palatine *Also called Newko Tool & Engineering Co* ***(G-16142)***
Newko Tool & Engineering Co 847 359-1670
720 S Vermont St Palatine (60067) ***(G-16142)***
Newly Weds Foods Inc (PA) 773 489-7000
4140 W Fullerton Ave Chicago (60639) ***(G-5584)***
Newly Weds Foods Inc 773 628-6900
4849 N Milwaukee Ave # 700 Chicago (60630) ***(G-5585)***
Newly Weds Foods Inc 773 489-7000
2501 N Keeler Ave Chicago (60639) ***(G-5586)***
Newman Welding & Machine Shop 618 435-5591
400 W Bond St Benton (62812) ***(G-1934)***
Newman-Green Inc 630 543-6500
57 W Interstate Rd Addison (60101) ***(G-228)***
Newmax, Elk Grove Village *Also called Fortman & Associates Ltd* ***(G-9005)***
Newmedical Technology Inc 847 412-1000
310 Era Dr Northbrook (60062) ***(G-15441)***
Newovo Plastics LLC 224 535-8183
345 Willard Ave Elgin (60120) ***(G-8669)***
Newport Media Inc 630 551-1651
439 Raintree Dr Oswego (60543) ***(G-16016)***
Newport Pallet 217 662-6577
310 S Main St Georgetown (61846) ***(G-10329)***
Newport Printing Services Inc 847 632-1000
1250 Remington Rd Schaumburg (60173) ***(G-18648)***
News & Letters 312 663-0839
59 E Van Buren St Chicago (60605) ***(G-5587)***
News Gazette, Urbana *Also called News-Gazette Inc* ***(G-19990)***
News Gazette, Champaign *Also called News-Gazette Inc* ***(G-3329)***
News Media Corporation (PA) 815 562-2061
211 E Il Route 38 Rochelle (61068) ***(G-17150)***
News Progress, Sullivan *Also called Best Newspapers In Ill Inc* ***(G-19661)***
News-Gazette Inc 217 373-7450
2006 Round Barn Rd Champaign (61821) ***(G-3325)***
News-Gazette Inc 217 351-5300
2301 S Neil St Champaign (61820) ***(G-3326)***
News-Gazette Inc 217 351-8128
810 Hamilton Dr Champaign (61820) ***(G-3327)***
News-Gazette Inc 217 384-2302
3202 Apollo Dr Champaign (61822) ***(G-3328)***
News-Gazette Inc 217 351-5311
300 W Main St Urbana (61801) ***(G-19990)***
News-Gazette Inc (PA) 217 351-5252
15 E Main St Champaign (61820) ***(G-3329)***
News-Gazette Inc 217 762-2511
118 E Washington St Monticello (61856) ***(G-14282)***
News-Gazette Inc 217 443-8484
2202 Kickapoo Dr Danville (61832) ***(G-7369)***
Newser LLC 312 284-2300
222 N Columbus Dr Lbby 1 Chicago (60601) ***(G-5588)***
Newspaper 7 Days (PA) 847 272-2212
704 S Milwaukee Ave Wheeling (60090) ***(G-20944)***
Newspaper Holding Inc 618 643-2387
200 S Washinton St Ste 1 Mc Leansboro (62859) ***(G-13707)***
Newspaper Holding Inc 217 446-1000
17 W North St Danville (61832) ***(G-7370)***
Newspaper Holding Inc 217 347-7151
201 N Banker St Effingham (62401) ***(G-8415)***
Newspaper National Network 312 644-1142
500 N Michigan Ave # 2210 Chicago (60611) ***(G-5589)***
Newspaper Solutions Inc 773 930-3404
4968 N Milwaukee Ave 1n Chicago (60630) ***(G-5590)***
Newsprint Ink Inc 618 667-3111
507 Ohara Dr Ste 1 Troy (62294) ***(G-19917)***
Newssor Manufacturing Inc 618 259-1174
302 Dry St East Alton (62024) ***(G-8167)***
Newsweb Corporation (PA) 773 975-5727
2401 N Halsted St Chicago (60614) ***(G-5591)***
Newton Broom & Brush Co, Newton *Also called Don Leventhal Group LLC* ***(G-15082)***
Newton Implement Partnership 618 783-8716
9460 E State Highway 33 Newton (62448) ***(G-15087)***
Newton Press Mentor, Newton *Also called Gatehouse Media LLC* ***(G-15083)***
Newton Ready Mix Inc 618 783-8611
8560 N State Highway 130 Newton (62448) ***(G-15088)***
Nex Gen Manufacturing Inc 847 487-7077
1055 N Old Rand Rd Wauconda (60084) ***(G-20381)***

Nexlp Inc 773 383-4114
318 W Adams St Ste 1100a Chicago (60606) ***(G-5592)***
Nexpump Inc 630 365-4639
820 Stover Dr Unit B Elburn (60119) ***(G-8464)***
Nexstep Commercial Pdts LLC 217 379-2377
1450 W Ottawa Rd Paxton (60957) ***(G-16309)***
Next Day Plus, Orland Park *Also called Next Day Toner Supplies Inc* ***(G-15971)***
Next Day Toner Supplies Inc 708 478-1000
11411 183rd St Ste A Orland Park (60467) ***(G-15971)***
Next Gen Manufacturing Inc 847 289-8444
1330 Crispin Dr Ste 205 Elgin (60123) ***(G-8670)***
Next Generation Inc 312 739-0520
13304 Skyline Dr Plainfield (60585) ***(G-16695)***
Next Gerneration 630 261-1477
1052 N Du Page Ave Lombard (60148) ***(G-13108)***
Next Level Metal 636 627-9497
7525c State Route 154 Baldwin (62217) ***(G-1186)***
Nextpoint Inc 773 929-4000
4043 N Ravenswood Ave Chicago (60613) ***(G-5593)***
Nextstep Commercial Products 217 379-2377
1450 W Ottawa Rd Paxton (60957) ***(G-16310)***
Nexus Corporation 217 303-5544
6 Industrial Park Dr Pana (62557) ***(G-16218)***
Nexus Industries Corp 708 673-9289
520 Winston Dr Melrose Park (60160) ***(G-13898)***
Nexus Office Systems Inc 847 836-1095
2250 Point Blvd Ste 125 Elgin (60123) ***(G-8671)***
Nexus Pharmaceuticals Inc 847 996-3790
400 Knightsbridge Pkwy Lincolnshire (60069) ***(G-12786)***
Nexus Supply Consortium Inc 630 649-2868
13g Fernwood Dr Bolingbrook (60440) ***(G-2222)***
NFC Company Inc 773 472-6468
2944 N Leavitt St Chicago (60618) ***(G-5594)***
NFC Suburban, Chicago *Also called NFC Company Inc* ***(G-5594)***
Nfca 708 236-3411
4415 Harrison St Ste 540 Hillside (60162) ***(G-11350)***
NGK Spark Plugs (usa) Inc 630 595-7894
850 Aec Dr Wood Dale (60191) ***(G-21222)***
NGL Crude Logistics LLC 618 274-4306
6 Pitzman Ave Sauget (62201) ***(G-18396)***
NGS Printing Inc 847 741-4411
1400 Crispin Dr Elgin (60123) ***(G-8672)***
Nhanced Semiconductors Inc (PA) 408 759-4060
1415 Bond St Ste 155 Naperville (60563) ***(G-14884)***
Niagara Lasalle Corporation 708 596-2700
16655 S Canal St South Holland (60473) ***(G-19235)***
Nicado Publishing Company Inc 312 593-2557
1522 W Fuller St Apt 2s Chicago (60608) ***(G-5595)***
Nice Card Company 773 467-8450
803 S Aldine Ave Park Ridge (60068) ***(G-16290)***
Niche Interactive Media Inc 312 498-7933
212 W Van Buren St 2s Chicago (60607) ***(G-5596)***
Nichiden USA Corp 224 266-2928
2228 Landmeier Rd Elk Grove Village (60007) ***(G-9147)***
Nicholas Machine & Tool Inc 847 298-2035
7027 Barry St Rosemont (60018) ***(G-18038)***
Nichols Aluminum LLC 847 634-3150
200 Schelter Rd Lincolnshire (60069) ***(G-12787)***
Nichols Net & Twine Inc 618 797-0211
2200 State Route 111 Granite City (62040) ***(G-10728)***
Nickel Composite Coatings Inc 708 563-2780
6454 W 74th St Chicago (60638) ***(G-5597)***
Nickel Putter 312 337-7888
1229 N North Branch St Chicago (60642) ***(G-5598)***
Nickels Electric 309 676-1350
1208 W Smith St Peoria (61605) ***(G-16486)***
Nickels Quarters LLC 630 514-5779
1651 Bolson Dr Downers Grove (60516) ***(G-8065)***
Nicks Emergency Ltg & More 815 780-8327
3003 7th St Peru (61354) ***(G-16585)***
Nicks Metal Fabg & Sons 708 485-1170
9132 47th St Brookfield (60513) ***(G-2489)***
Nicor Gas, Kankakee *Also called Northern Illinois Gas Company* ***(G-11993)***
Nicor Gas, Carthage *Also called Northern Illinois Gas Company* ***(G-3141)***
Nicor Gas, Crystal Lake *Also called Northern Illinois Gas Company* ***(G-7240)***
Nicor Gas, Ottawa *Also called Northern Illinois Gas Company* ***(G-16065)***
Nicor Gas, Joliet *Also called Northern Illinois Gas Company* ***(G-11908)***
Nicor Gas, Mendota *Also called Northern Illinois Gas Company* ***(G-13951)***
Nicor Products, Joliet *Also called American Chute Systems Inc* ***(G-11819)***
Nidec Mobility America Corp (HQ) 630 443-6800
3709 Ohio Ave Saint Charles (60174) ***(G-18234)***
Nidec Motor Corporation 815 444-1229
4218 East Dr Crystal Lake (60012) ***(G-7238)***
Nidec Motor Corporation 847 439-3760
25 Northwest Point Blvd # 900 Elk Grove Village (60007) ***(G-9148)***
Nidec Motor Corporation 847 585-8430
1901 South St Elgin (60123) ***(G-8673)***
Nidec Motor Corporation 847 439-3760
1905 S Mount Prospect Rd Des Plaines (60018) ***(G-7810)***

Nidec-Shimpo America Corp............630 924-7138
175 Wall St Glendale Heights (60139) ***(G-10479)***
Niedermaier Inc (PA)............312 492-9400
55 E Erie St Apt 3306 Chicago (60611) ***(G-5599)***
Niedermaier Furniture, Chicago *Also called Niedermaier Inc* ***(G-5599)***
Nieman & Considine Inc............312 326-1053
2323 S Michigan Ave Chicago (60616) ***(G-5600)***
Niemann Foods Inc............217 222-0190
520 N 24th St Quincy (62301) ***(G-16918)***
Niemann Foods Inc............217 793-4091
3001 S Veterans Pkwy Springfield (62704) ***(G-19411)***
Nienhouse Media, Chicago *Also called CAM Systems* ***(G-4009)***
Niese Walter Machine Mfg Co............773 774-7337
172 Touhy Ct Des Plaines (60018) ***(G-7811)***
Niffty AG Inc............309 343-7447
427 Old Post Rd Galesburg (61401) ***(G-10214)***
Night Vision Corporation............847 677-7611
4324 W Chase Ave Lincolnwood (60712) ***(G-12833)***
Night Vision Specialists LLC............618 614-8626
260 S Rocky Comfort Rd Makanda (62958) ***(G-13429)***
Nijhuis Water Technology Inc............312 466-9900
770 N Halsted St Ste 301 Chicago (60642) ***(G-5601)***
Nike Inc............773 846-5460
8510 S Cottage Grove Ave Chicago (60619) ***(G-5602)***
Nikkin Flux Corp............618 656-2125
512 Phillipena St Edwardsville (62025) ***(G-8372)***
Nikli Fuels Inc............309 363-2425
801 S 2nd St Pekin (61554) ***(G-16347)***
Nikro Industries Inc............630 530-0558
1115 N Ellsworth Ave Villa Park (60181) ***(G-20162)***
Nilan/Primarc Tool & Mold, Hoffman Estates *Also called Nilan/Primarc Tool & Mold Inc* ***(G-11439)***
Nilan/Primarc Tool & Mold Inc............847 885-2300
2125 Stonington Ave Hoffman Estates (60169) ***(G-11439)***
Niles Auto Parts............847 215-2549
20734 N Elizabeth Ave Lincolnshire (60069) ***(G-12788)***
Nimbl Worldwide Inc............303 800-0245
444 N Michigan Ave # 2550 Chicago (60611) ***(G-5603)***
Nimbl, LLC, Chicago *Also called Nimbl Worldwide Inc* ***(G-5603)***
Nimco Corporation............815 459-4200
1000 Nimco Dr Crystal Lake (60014) ***(G-7239)***
Nimlok Co............855 764-6565
9033 Murphy Rd Woodridge (60517) ***(G-21327)***
Nimlok-Chicago, Des Plaines *Also called Exsel Exhibits Inc* ***(G-7762)***
Ninos LLC............708 932-5555
170 Covington Dr Bloomingdale (60108) ***(G-2002)***
Nippon Electric Glass Amer Inc (HQ)............630 285-8500
1515 E Wdfield Rd Ste 720 Schaumburg (60173) ***(G-18649)***
Nippon Sharyo Mfg LLC............815 562-8600
1600 Ritchie Ct Rochelle (61068) ***(G-17151)***
Nique Soul Catering, Broadview *Also called Dominique Graves* ***(G-2430)***
Nis Express Inc (PA)............708 880-4090
7667 W 95th St Ste 300 Hickory Hills (60457) ***(G-11201)***
Nissan............630 957-4360
27w261 North Ave West Chicago (60185) ***(G-20622)***
Nissan Forklift, Marengo *Also called Unicarriers Americas Corp* ***(G-13496)***
Nissei America Inc............847 228-5000
721 Landmeier Rd Elk Grove Village (60007) ***(G-9149)***
Nissha Si-Cal Technologies Inc (PA)............508 898-1800
311 Shore Dr Burr Ridge (60527) ***(G-2710)***
Nissha Usa Inc (HQ)............847 413-2665
1051 Perimeter Dr Ste 600 Schaumburg (60173) ***(G-18650)***
Nisshin Holding Inc............847 290-5100
900 N Michigan Ave # 1820 Chicago (60611) ***(G-5604)***
Nisshin Steel USA, Chicago *Also called Nisshin Holding Inc* ***(G-5604)***
Nite Lite Signs & Balloons Inc............630 953-2866
506 S Westgate St Addison (60101) ***(G-229)***
Nite Owl Prints LLC............630 541-6273
1323 Butterfield Rd # 102 Downers Grove (60515) ***(G-8066)***
Nitek International LLC............847 259-8900
5410 Newport Dr Ste 24 Rolling Meadows (60008) ***(G-17753)***
Nitrex Inc............630 851-5880
1900 Plain Ave Aurora (60502) ***(G-1003)***
Nitrogen Labs Inc............312 504-8134
201 W Lake St Ste 155 Chicago (60606) ***(G-5605)***
Nivelco USA LLC............630 848-2100
1300 Iroquois Ave Naperville (60563) ***(G-14885)***
Nixalite of America Inc............309 755-8771
1025 16th Ave East Moline (61244) ***(G-8235)***
Nnm Manufacturing LLC............815 436-9201
24133 W 143rd St Plainfield (60544) ***(G-16696)***
NNt Enterprises Incorporated............630 875-9600
1320 Norwood Ave Itasca (60143) ***(G-11712)***
No Denial Foods............312 890-5267
1137 W Monroe St Unit 20 Chicago (60607) ***(G-5606)***
No Surrender Inc............773 929-7920
1056 W Belmont Ave Chicago (60657) ***(G-5607)***
Nobert Plating Co (PA)............312 421-4040
340 N Ashland Ave Chicago (60607) ***(G-5608)***
Nobility Corporation............847 677-3204
5404 Touhy Ave Skokie (60077) ***(G-18996)***
Nobleson and Associates, Rockford *Also called Forest City Grinding Inc* ***(G-17419)***
Nogi Brands LLC............312 371-7974
6448 Cambridge Rd Willowbrook (60527) ***(G-21054)***
Noise Barriers LLC............847 843-0500
2001 Kelley Ct Libertyville (60048) ***(G-12688)***
Nokomis Quarry Company............217 563-2011
23311 Taylorville Rd Nokomis (62075) ***(G-15196)***
Nolan Sealants Inc............630 774-5713
1 Bloomingdale Pl Apt 104 Bloomingdale (60108) ***(G-2003)***
NON-FOR PROFIT NATIONAL TRADE, Schaumburg *Also called Associated Equipment Distrs* ***(G-18447)***
Noniprint............773 366-2846
6150 N Milwaukee Ave Chicago (60646) ***(G-5609)***
Noodle Party............773 205-0505
4205 W Lawrence Ave Chicago (60630) ***(G-5610)***
Noodles Factory LLC............312 842-6500
610 W 26th St Chicago (60616) ***(G-5611)***
Noon Hour Food Products Inc (PA)............312 382-1177
215 N Desplaines St Fl 1 Chicago (60661) ***(G-5612)***
Noor International Inc............847 985-2300
2015 Pennsbury Ln Bartlett (60133) ***(G-1256)***
Noor Jewels LLC............847 505-9849
865 N Marshfield Ave # 3 Chicago (60622) ***(G-5613)***
Nooter/Eriksen Inc............636 651-1028
3014 Croatia Dr Columbia (62236) ***(G-6991)***
Nopalina, Waukegan *Also called Salud Natural Entrepreneur Inc* ***(G-20492)***
Nor Service Inc............815 232-8379
215 S State Ave Freeport (61032) ***(G-10130)***
Nordco, Spring Grove *Also called Northern Ordinance Corporation* ***(G-19289)***
Nordco Inc............414 766-2180
107 N Us Hwy 45 Arcola (61910) ***(G-660)***
Nordent Manufacturing Inc............847 437-4780
610 Bonnie Ln Elk Grove Village (60007) ***(G-9150)***
Nordex Usa Inc (HQ)............312 386-4100
300 S Wacker Dr Ste 1400 Chicago (60606) ***(G-5614)***
Nordic A Filtration N Amer Inc............331 457-5289
507 Fairway Dr Naperville (60563) ***(G-14886)***
Nordic Auto Plow LLC............815 353-8267
771 W North Ave West Chicago (60185) ***(G-20623)***
Nordic Plow, West Chicago *Also called Nordic Auto Plow LLC* ***(G-20623)***
Nordmeyer Graphics............815 697-2634
100 Dieter Rd Chebanse (60922) ***(G-3430)***
Nordson Asymtek Inc............760 431-1919
25033 Network Pl Chicago (60673) ***(G-5615)***
Nordson Corporation............815 784-5025
416 Holly Ct Genoa (60135) ***(G-10320)***
Norforge and Machining Inc............309 772-3124
2007 S Madison St Macomb (61455) ***(G-13394)***
Noridge Die & Mold, Bensenville *Also called Quality Plastic Products Inc* ***(G-1879)***
Norix Group Inc............630 231-1331
1800 W Hawthorne Ln Ste N West Chicago (60185) ***(G-20624)***
Norkin Jewelry Co Inc............312 782-7311
55 E Washington St # 203 Chicago (60602) ***(G-5616)***
Norlux, Rolling Meadows *Also called Carmen Matthew LLC* ***(G-17720)***
Normal Cornbelters............309 451-3432
1000 W Raab Rd Normal (61761) ***(G-15212)***
Normalite Newspaper............309 454-5476
1702 W College Ave Ste G Normal (61761) ***(G-15213)***
Norman Filter Company LLC (PA)............708 233-5521
9850 Industrial Dr Bridgeview (60455) ***(G-2368)***
Norman P Moeller............847 991-3933
372 Rolling Wood Ln Apt D Lake Barrington (60010) ***(G-12162)***
Norman Technology, Carol Stream *Also called Ergoseal Inc* ***(G-2981)***
Norridge Jewelry............312 984-1036
29 E Madison St Ste 1202 Chicago (60602) ***(G-5617)***
Nortech Packaging LLC............847 884-1805
101 E State Pkwy Schaumburg (60173) ***(G-18651)***
Nortech, Inc., Schaumburg *Also called Custom Assembly Solutions Inc* ***(G-18501)***
North Amercn Ret Dealers Assn, Chicago *Also called Narda Inc* ***(G-5540)***
North America O M C G Inc............630 860-1016
857 Industrial Dr Ste 1 Bensenville (60106) ***(G-1858)***
North America Packaging Corp............630 845-8726
515 N First St Peotone (60468) ***(G-16555)***
North America Packaging Corp............847 979-1625
2350 Lively Blvd Elk Grove Village (60007) ***(G-9151)***
North America Packaging Corp (HQ)............630 203-4100
1515 W 22nd St Ste 550 Oak Brook (60523) ***(G-15648)***
North American Adhesives, West Chicago *Also called Mapei Corporation* ***(G-20613)***
North American Bear Co Inc (PA)............773 376-3457
1200 W 35th St Chicago (60609) ***(G-5618)***
North American EN Inc............847 952-3680
776 Lunt Ave Elk Grove Village (60007) ***(G-9152)***
North American Enclosures Inc............630 290-7911
1637 Windward Ct Naperville (60563) ***(G-14887)***
North American Fund III LP (PA)............312 332-4950
135 S La Salle St # 3225 Chicago (60603) ***(G-5619)***

North American Gear and Axel, Chicago Also called United States Gear Corporation *(G-6477)*

North American Lighting Inc 217 465-7800
2277 S Main St Paris (61944) *(G-16236)*

North American Lighting Inc (HQ) 217 465-6600
2275 S Main St Paris (61944) *(G-16237)*

North American Lighting Inc 618 548-6249
1875 W Main St Salem (62881) *(G-18348)*

North American Lighting Inc 618 662-4483
20 Industrial Park Flora (62839) *(G-9686)*

North American Press Inc 847 515-3882
12203 Spring Creek Dr Huntley (60142) *(G-11556)*

North American Refining Co 708 762-5117
7601 W 47th St Mc Cook (60525) *(G-13697)*

North American Safety Pdts Inc 815 469-1144
8910 W 192nd St Ste C Mokena (60448) *(G-14099)*

North American Signal Co 847 537-8888
605 Wheeling Rd Wheeling (60090) *(G-20945)*

North Baking, Melrose Park Also called Lewis Brothers Bakeries Inc *(G-13890)*

North Chicago Iron Works Inc 847 689-2000
1305 Morrow Ave North Chicago (60064) *(G-15317)*

North County News Inc 618 282-3803
124 S Main St Red Bud (62278) *(G-16998)*

North Okaw Woodworking 217 856-2178
2409 E County Road 1700n Humboldt (61931) *(G-11524)*

North Point Investments Inc (PA) 312 977-4386
70 W Madison St Ste 3500 Chicago (60602) *(G-5620)*

North Ridge Properties LLC 815 434-7800
927 Fosse Rd Ottawa (61350) *(G-16064)*

North Sails Group LLC 773 489-1308
1665 N Elston Ave Chicago (60642) *(G-5621)*

North Shore Consultants Inc 847 290-1599
613 Thorndale Ave Elk Grove Village (60007) *(G-9153)*

North Shore Distillery LLC 847 574-2499
13990 W Rockland Rd Libertyville (60048) *(G-12689)*

North Shore Printers Inc 847 623-0037
535 S Sheridan Rd Waukegan (60085) *(G-20469)*

North Shore Sign Company 847 816-7020
1925 Industrial Dr Libertyville (60048) *(G-12690)*

North Shore Stairs 847 295-7906
100 N Skokie Hwy Ste D Lake Bluff (60044) *(G-12200)*

North Shore Truck & Equipment 847 887-0200
29800 N Skokie Hwy Ste B Lake Bluff (60044) *(G-12201)*

North Shore Wtr Rclamation Dst 847 623-6060
Dahringer Rd Waukegan (60085) *(G-20470)*

North Star Lighting LLC 708 681-4330
835 N Industrial Dr Elmhurst (60126) *(G-9405)*

North Star Pickle LLC 847 970-5555
968 Donata Ct Lake Zurich (60047) *(G-12439)*

North Star Productions, Campbell Hill Also called Day Star Systems LLC *(G-2814)*

North Star Stamping & Tool Inc 847 658-9400
1264 Industrial Dr Lake In The Hills (60156) *(G-12342)*

North Star Stone Inc 847 996-6850
1840 Industrial Dr # 180 Libertyville (60048) *(G-12691)*

North-West Drapery Service 773 282-7117
4507 N Milwaukee Ave Chicago (60630) *(G-5622)*

Northcape International, Alsip Also called Chicago Wicker & Trading Co *(G-429)*

Northern Division, Crystal Lake Also called Triumph Twist Drill Co Inc *(G-7286)*

Northern Ill Blood Bnk Inc (PA) 815 965-8751
419 N 6th St Rockford (61107) *(G-17538)*

Northern Ill Wilbert Vlt Co, Belvidere Also called Northern Illinois Wilbert Vlt *(G-1689)*

Northern Illinois Gas Company 630 983-8676
2704 Festival Dr Kankakee (60901) *(G-11993)*

Northern Illinois Gas Company 217 357-3105
1375 Buchanan St Carthage (62321) *(G-3141)*

Northern Illinois Gas Company 630 983-8676
300 W Terra Cotta Ave Crystal Lake (60014) *(G-7240)*

Northern Illinois Gas Company 815 433-3850
1629 Champlain St Ottawa (61350) *(G-16065)*

Northern Illinois Gas Company 815 693-3907
3000 E Cass St Joliet (60432) *(G-11908)*

Northern Illinois Gas Company 815 223-8097
169 N 36th Rd Mendota (61342) *(G-13951)*

Northern Illinois Lumber Spc 630 859-3226
1200 S Lake St Montgomery (60538) *(G-14265)*

Northern Illinois Metal Finshg, Rockford Also called K&J Finishing Inc *(G-17478)*

Northern Illinois Mold Corp 847 669-2100
17n520 Adams Dr Dundee (60118) *(G-8130)*

Northern Illinois Pallet Inc 815 236-9242
1285 Wentworth Dr Fox Lake (60020) *(G-9749)*

Northern Illinois Real Estate 630 257-2480
1244 State St Ste 351 Lemont (60439) *(G-12573)*

Northern Illinois University 815 753-1826
310 N 5th St Dekalb (60115) *(G-7695)*

Northern Illinois Wilbert Vlt 815 544-3355
845 E Jackson St Belvidere (61008) *(G-1689)*

Northern Information Tech 800 528-4343
5410 Newport Dr Ste 24 Rolling Meadows (60008) *(G-17754)*

Northern Lighting & Power Inc 708 383-9926
1138 Woodbine Ave Oak Park (60302) *(G-15766)*

Northern Ordinance Corporation 815 675-6400
7806 Industrial Dr Spring Grove (60081) *(G-19289)*

Northern Orgle County Temple, Byron Also called Rock Valley Publishing LLC *(G-2756)*

Northern Pallet and Supply Co (PA) 847 716-1400
464 Central Ave Ste 18 Northfield (60093) *(G-15524)*

Northern Precision Plastic Inc 815 544-8099
6553 Revlon Dr Belvidere (61008) *(G-1690)*

Northern Precision Plastics, Belvidere Also called Northern Precision Plastic Inc *(G-1690)*

Northern Prints, Wheeling Also called RCM Industries Inc *(G-20970)*

Northern Prosthetics 815 226-0444
2629 Charles St Rockford (61108) *(G-17539)*

Northern Star Plating Division, Loves Park Also called Superior Metal Finishing *(G-13268)*

Northfield Block Company (HQ) 847 816-9000
1 Hunt Ct Mundelein (60060) *(G-14721)*

Northfield Block Company 815 941-4100
3400 Bungalow Rd Morris (60450) *(G-14319)*

Northfield Block Company 708 458-8130
5400 W Canal Bank Rd Berwyn (60402) *(G-1957)*

Northfield Holdings LLC 847 755-0700
700 Wiley Farm Ct Schaumburg (60173) *(G-18652)*

Northfield Industries 847 981-7530
160 N Lively Blvd Elk Grove Village (60007) *(G-9154)*

Northgate Technologies Inc 847 608-8900
1591 Scottsdale Ct Elgin (60123) *(G-8674)*

Northlake Industries 847 358-6875
143 W Robertson St Palatine (60067) *(G-16143)*

Northpoint Heating & Air Cond 847 731-1067
1101 Shiloh Blvd Rear 2 Zion (60099) *(G-21521)*

Northrop Grumman Systems Corp 847 259-9600
600 Hicks Rd Rolling Meadows (60008) *(G-17755)*

Northrop Grumman Systems Corp 847 259-9600
1605 Rohlwing Rd Rolling Meadows (60008) *(G-17756)*

Northshore Gardens Ltd 847 672-4391
2925 22nd Pl North Chicago (60064) *(G-15318)*

Northstar Aerospace (usa) Inc 708 728-2000
6006 W 73rd St Bedford Park (60638) *(G-1486)*

Northstar Aerospace Chicago, Bedford Park Also called Heligear Acquisition Co *(G-1471)*

Northstar Custom Cabinetry 708 597-2099
14825 S Mckinley Ave Posen (60469) *(G-16799)*

Northstar Group Inc 847 726-0880
577 Capital Dr Lake Zurich (60047) *(G-12440)*

Northstar Industries Inc 630 446-7800
591 Mitchell Rd Glendale Heights (60139) *(G-10480)*

Northstar Metal Products, Glendale Heights Also called Northstar Industries Inc *(G-10480)*

Northstar Trading LLC 630 312-8434
50 Messner Dr Wheeling (60090) *(G-20946)*

Northtech Work Holding, Schaumburg Also called Kitagawa-Northtech Inc *(G-18588)*

Northwest Frame Company Inc 847 359-0987
252 N Cady Dr Palatine (60074) *(G-16144)*

Northwest Graphics Inc 815 544-3676
4337 S Perryville Rd Cherry Valley (61016) *(G-3444)*

Northwest Marble Products (PA) 630 860-2288
1229 Silver Pine Dr Hoffman Estates (60010) *(G-11473)*

Northwest Mold & Machine Corp 847 690-1501
131 Martin Ln Elk Grove Village (60007) *(G-9155)*

Northwest Pallet Services LLC 815 544-6001
3648 Morreim Dr Belvidere (61008) *(G-1691)*

Northwest Premier Printing 773 736-1882
5421 W Addison St Chicago (60641) *(G-5623)*

Northwest Printing Inc 815 943-7977
20 N Ayer St Harvard (60033) *(G-11061)*

Northwest Products 630 860-2288
1090 Industrial Dr Ste 1 Bensenville (60106) *(G-1859)*

Northwest Publishing LLC 312 329-0600
500 N Dearborn St # 1014 Chicago (60654) *(G-5624)*

Northwest Side Press, Chicago Also called Nadig Newspapers Inc *(G-5537)*

Northwest Snow and Timber Svc, Lombard Also called Northwest Snow Timber Svc Ltd *(G-13109)*

Northwest Snow Timber Svc Ltd 847 778-4998
1321 S School St Lombard (60148) *(G-13109)*

Northwest Tool Co Inc 630 350-4770
342 Evergreen Ave Bensenville (60106) *(G-1860)*

Northwestern Cup & Logo Inc 773 874-8000
41 W 84th St Fl 1 Chicago (60620) *(G-5625)*

Northwestern Flavors LLC 630 231-6111
120 N Aurora St West Chicago (60185) *(G-20625)*

Northwestern Illinois Farmer 815 369-2811
119 W Railroad St Lena (61048) *(G-12607)*

Northwoods Wreaths Company 847 615-9491
450 W Deerpath Lake Forest (60045) *(G-12275)*

Northwstern Globl Hlth Fndtion 214 207-9485
2707 N Lincoln Ave Apt B Chicago (60614) *(G-5626)*

Norton Machine Co 217 748-6115
711 S Chicago St Rossville (60963) *(G-18066)*

Norvida USA Inc 618 282-2992
310 S Vine St Sparta (62286) *(G-19258)*

Norwalk Tank Co, Joliet Also called Nt Liquidating Inc *(G-11909)*

Norway Press Inc 773 846-9422
400 W 76th St Ste 1105 Chicago (60620) *(G-5627)*
Norwood House Press Inc 866 565-2900
6150 N Milwaukee Ave # 2 Chicago (60646) *(G-5628)*
Norwood Industries Inc. 773 788-1508
7001 W 60th St Ste 1 Chicago (60638) *(G-5629)*
Norwood Marketing Systems, Frankfort Also called Illinois Tool Works Inc *(G-9803)*
Norwood Paper, Chicago Also called Norwood Industries Inc *(G-5629)*
Nosco Inc 847 336-4200
1400 Saint Paul Ave Gurnee (60031) *(G-10903)*
Nosco Bridgeview Inc 773 585-2035
8811 S 77th Ave Bridgeview (60455) *(G-2369)*
Nosco Inc (HQ) 847 336-4200
2199 N Delany Rd Gurnee (60031) *(G-10904)*
Nosco Inc 847 360-4874
651 S Mrtn Lther King Jr Waukegan (60085) *(G-20471)*
Noteworthy Group Inc 618 549-2505
2370 N Mcroy Dr Carbondale (62901) *(G-2851)*
Nothing, Gurnee Also called Quality Molding Products LLC *(G-10921)*
Nourishlife LLC 847 234-2334
37 Sherwood Ter Ste 109 Lake Bluff (60044) *(G-12202)*
Nouryon Chemicals LLC 312 544-7000
131 S Dearborn St # 1000 Chicago (60603) *(G-5630)*
Nouryon Functional Chem LLC (HQ) 312 544-7000
131 S Dearborn St # 1000 Chicago (60603) *(G-5631)*
Nouryon Surface Chemistry LLC (HQ) 312 544-7000
131 S Dearborn St # 1000 Chicago (60603) *(G-5632)*
Nouryon USA LLC 312 544-7000
525 W Van Buren St Chicago (60607) *(G-5633)*
Nova Chemicals Inc 815 224-1525
501 Brunner St Peru (61354) *(G-16586)*
Nova Lines Inc 773 322-6262
2314 River Rd Unit 1 River Grove (60171) *(G-17064)*
Nova Metals Inc 630 690-4300
279 Commonwealth Dr Carol Stream (60188) *(G-3040)*
Nova Printing and Litho Co 773 486-8500
1621 E Dogwood Ln Mount Prospect (60056) *(G-14552)*
Nova Solutions Inc (PA) 217 342-7070
421 Industrial Ave Effingham (62401) *(G-8416)*
Nova The Right Solution, Effingham Also called Nova Solutions Inc *(G-8416)*
Nova Wildcat Amerock LLC 815 266-6416
1750 Lincoln Dr Freeport (61032) *(G-10131)*
Nova-Chrome Inc 847 455-8200
3200 Wolf Rd Franklin Park (60131) *(G-10010)*
Novacare Prosthetics Orthotics, Marion Also called Cape Prosthetics-Orthotics Inc *(G-13507)*
Novak Business Forms Inc 630 932-9850
20 Eisenhower Ln N Lombard (60148) *(G-13110)*
Novalex Therapeutics Inc 630 750-9334
43w605 Willow Creek Dr Elburn (60119) *(G-8465)*
Novanta Inc 781 266-5700
106 Marshall Dr Newton (62448) *(G-15089)*
Novapack, Paris Also called Pvc Container Corporation *(G-16241)*
Novaspect Inc (PA) 847 956-8020
1124 Tower Rd Schaumburg (60173) *(G-18653)*
Novation Industries, McHenry Also called W M Plastics Inc *(G-13808)*
Novatronix Inc 630 860-4300
600 Wheat Ln Wood Dale (60191) *(G-21223)*
Novel Electronic Designs Inc 309 224-9945
143 N 3rd St Chillicothe (61523) *(G-6820)*
Novel Products Inc 815 624-4888
3266 Yale Bridge Rd Rockton (61072) *(G-17700)*
Novipax LLC (HQ) 630 686-2735
2215 York Rd Ste 504 Oak Brook (60523) *(G-15649)*
Novo Surgical Inc 877 860-6686
700 Comme Dr Ste 500 No 1 Oak Brook (60523) *(G-15650)*
Novomatic Americas Sales LLC 224 802-2974
1050 E Business Center Dr Mount Prospect (60056) *(G-14553)*
Novum Pharma LLC 877 404-4724
200 S Wacker Dr Ste 3100 Chicago (60606) *(G-5634)*
Now Foods, Roselle Also called Now Health Group Inc *(G-17972)*
Now Foods, Bloomingdale Also called Now Health Group Inc *(G-2004)*
Now Foods, Bloomingdale Also called Now Health Group Inc *(G-2005)*
Now Health Group Inc 888 669-3663
1620 Central Ave Roselle (60172) *(G-17972)*
Now Health Group Inc (PA) 888 669-3663
244 Knollwood Dr Ste 300 Bloomingdale (60108) *(G-2004)*
Now Health Group Inc 630 545-9098
395 Glen Ellyn Rd Bloomingdale (60108) *(G-2005)*
Nowfab 815 675-2916
6413 Johnsburg Rd Spring Grove (60081) *(G-19290)*
Nowuba LLC - Investio Print 833 669-8221
111 Nippersink Rd Fox Lake (60020) *(G-9750)*
Nowuba LLC (PA) 801 510-8086
111 Nippersink Rd Fox Lake (60020) *(G-9751)*
Npc Sealants, Maywood Also called Nu-Puttie Corporation *(G-13676)*
Npi Holding Corp (HQ) 217 391-1229
1500 Taylor Ave Springfield (62703) *(G-19412)*

Npn360 .... 847 215-7300
2801 Lakeside Dr Ste 100 Bannockburn (60015) *(G-1205)*
Npt Automotive Machine Shop 618 233-1344
308 N 44th St Belleville (62226) *(G-1580)*
Nre, Dixmoor Also called National Railway Equipment Co *(G-7885)*
NRR Corp 630 915-8388
705 Deer Trail Ln Oak Brook (60523) *(G-15651)*
Nrtx LLC 224 717-0465
1454 W Melrose St Ste 2 Chicago (60657) *(G-5635)*
NS Precision Lathe Inc. 708 867-5023
519 Lake St Maywood (60153) *(G-13675)*
Nsa (chi) Liquidating Corp 708 728-2000
205 E Bttrfeld Rd Ste 238 Elmhurst (60126) *(G-9406)*
Nsc, Itasca Also called National Safety Council *(G-11707)*
Nsga Retail Focus, Downers Grove Also called National Sporting Goods Assn *(G-8063)*
Nsi, Buffalo Grove Also called Necta Sweet Inc *(G-2579)*
Nsk-America Corporation 847 843-7664
1800 Global Pkwy Hoffman Estates (60192) *(G-11440)*
Nss Exteriors, Alsip Also called Nelson Sash Systems Inc *(G-483)*
Nt Liquidating Inc 815 726-3351
2121 Maple Rd Joliet (60432) *(G-11909)*
Nta Precision Axle Corporation 630 690-6300
795 Kimberly Dr Carol Stream (60188) *(G-3041)*
Ntb, Naperville Also called Tbc Corporation *(G-14927)*
Ntm, East Dundee Also called National Tool & Mfg Co *(G-8206)*
NTN Bearing Corporation 847 298-7500
1805 E University Dr Macomb (61455) *(G-13395)*
NTN USA Corporation (HQ) 847 298-4652
1600 Bishop Ct Mount Prospect (60056) *(G-14554)*
NTN Warehouse, Macomb Also called NTN Bearing Corporation *(G-13395)*
NTN-Bower Corporation 309 833-4541
707 Bower Rd Macomb (61455) *(G-13396)*
NTN-Bower Corporation (HQ) 309 837-0440
711 Bower Rd Macomb (61455) *(G-13397)*
Ntt America Solutions Inc 847 278-6413
1700 E Golf Rd Ste 1100 Schaumburg (60173) *(G-18654)*
Nu Again 630 564-5590
494 E Thornwood Dr Bartlett (60103) *(G-1299)*
Nu Glo Sign Company 847 223-6160
18880 W Gages Lake Rd Grayslake (60030) *(G-10793)*
Nu Vision Media Inc 773 495-5254
1327 W Wa Blvd Ste 102b Chicago (60607) *(G-5636)*
Nu-Art Printing 618 533-9971
614 W Broadway Centralia (62801) *(G-3242)*
Nu-Dell Manufacturing Co Inc (PA) 847 803-4500
400 E Randolph St Chicago (60601) *(G-5637)*
Nu-Dell Plastics, Chicago Also called Nu-Dell Manufacturing Co Inc *(G-5637)*
Nu-Life Inc of Illinois 618 943-4500
Hwy 1 S Lawrenceville (62439) *(G-12536)*
Nu-Metal Products Inc. 815 459-2075
260 E Prairie St Crystal Lake (60014) *(G-7241)*
Nu-Pro Polymers Inc 224 676-1663
555 Allendale Dr Wheeling (60090) *(G-20947)*
Nu-Puttie Corporation 708 681-1040
1208 S 8th Ave Maywood (60153) *(G-13676)*
Nu-Way Electronics Inc 847 437-7120
165 Martin Ln Elk Grove Village (60007) *(G-9156)*
Nu-Way Industries Inc 847 298-7710
555 Howard Ave Des Plaines (60018) *(G-7812)*
Nuair Filter Company LLC 309 888-4331
2219 W College Ave Normal (61761) *(G-15214)*
Nuance Incorporated 207 449-6398
2702 W Chicago Ave Apt 2 Chicago (60622) *(G-5638)*
Nuance Solutions, Chicago Also called Bullen Midwest Inc *(G-3973)*
Nuclear Power Outfitters LLC 630 963-0320
1955 University Ln Lisle (60532) *(G-12922)*
Nucor Corporation 630 887-1400
201 E Ogden Ave Ste 216 Hinsdale (60521) *(G-11371)*
Nucor Steel Kankakee Inc 815 937-3131
1 Nucor Way Bourbonnais (60914) *(G-2266)*
Nucor Tubular Products Inc (HQ) 708 496-0380
6226 W 74th St Chicago (60638) *(G-5639)*
Nucor Tubular Products Inc 815 795-4400
1201 Broadway St Marseilles (61341) *(G-13561)*
Nucurrent Inc 312 575-0388
641 W Lake St Ste 304 Chicago (60661) *(G-5640)*
Nudo Products Inc 217 528-5636
2508 South Grand Ave E Springfield (62703) *(G-19413)*
Nudo Products Inc (HQ) 217 528-5636
1500 Taylor Ave Springfield (62703) *(G-19414)*
Nuestro Queso LLC 815 443-2100
752 N Kent Rd Kent (61044) *(G-12018)*
Nuestro Queso LLC (PA) 224 366-4320
100 S Wacker Dr Ste 1950 Chicago (60606) *(G-5641)*
Nuevos Semana Newspaper 847 991-3939
1180 E Dundee Rd Palatine (60074) *(G-16145)*
Nufarm Americas Inc (HQ) 708 377-1330
11901 S Austin Ave Alsip (60803) *(G-485)*

Nufarm Americas Inc...708 756-2010
220 E 17th St Fl 2 Chicago Heights (60411) *(G-6762)*
Nufarm North American Office, Alsip *Also called Nufarm Americas Inc (G-485)*
Number One, Chicago *Also called Aurora Narinder (G-3774)*
Numerical Control Incorporated...708 389-8140
12325 S Keeler Ave Alsip (60803) *(G-486)*
Numerical Precision, Wheeling *Also called George Industries LLC (G-20904)*
Numeridex Incorporated...847 541-8840
632 Wheeling Rd Wheeling (60090) *(G-20948)*
Nurture Life Inc (PA)...312 517-1888
358 W Ontario St Chicago (60654) *(G-5642)*
Nuseed Americas Inc (HQ)...800 345-3330
11901 S Austin Ave Alsip (60803) *(G-487)*
Nutec Manufacturing, New Lenox *Also called TEC Systems Inc (G-15062)*
Nutheme Sign Company...847 230-0067
2659 Wisconsin Ave Downers Grove (60515) *(G-8067)*
Nutherm International Inc...618 244-6000
501 S 11th St Mount Vernon (62864) *(G-14631)*
Nutraceuticals and Pharma Tls, Oak Brook *Also called Lodaat LLC (G-15637)*
Nutraid Manufacturing...847 214-4860
420 Airport Rd Elgin (60123) *(G-8675)*
Nutrasweet Company (HQ)...312 873-5000
222 Merchandise Mart Plz # 936 Chicago (60654) *(G-5643)*
Nutriad Inc...847 214-4860
201 Flannigan Rd Hampshire (60140) *(G-10981)*
Nutripack LLC...847 537-0102
2210 W 162nd St Markham (60428) *(G-13549)*
Nutritional Institute LLC...847 223-7676
75 Commerce Dr Unit 7010 Grayslake (60030) *(G-10794)*
Nutrivo LLC (PA)...630 270-1700
1785 N Edgelawn Dr Aurora (60506) *(G-1140)*
Nuttall Gear LLC...815 389-6267
449 Gardner St South Beloit (61080) *(G-19105)*
Nuvixa, Urbana *Also called Personify Inc (G-19992)*
Nuway Distributors, Chicago *Also called Doctors Choice Inc (G-4378)*
Nuway Electronics, Elk Grove Village *Also called Nu-Way Electronics Inc (G-9156)*
Nuyen Awning Co...630 892-3995
850 Ridgeway Ave Ste C Aurora (60506) *(G-1141)*
Nvent Electric Public Ltd Co...618 918-3821
115 Harting Dr Centralia (62801) *(G-3243)*
Nxp Usa Inc...847 843-6824
2800 W Higgins Rd Ste 600 Hoffman Estates (60169) *(G-11441)*
Nyb Process Fans Inc (HQ)...630 794-5700
7660 S Quincy St Willowbrook (60527) *(G-21055)*
Nyclo Screw Machine Pdts Inc...815 229-7900
3610 Mansfield St Rockford (61109) *(G-17540)*
Nycor Products Inc...815 727-9883
603 E Washington St Joliet (60433) *(G-11910)*
Nylok LLC...847 674-9680
6465 W Proesel Ave Lincolnwood (60712) *(G-12834)*
Nypro Hanover Park, Hanover Park *Also called Nypro Inc (G-11011)*
Nypro Hanover Park...630 868-3517
401 S Gary Ave Roselle (60172) *(G-17973)*
Nypro Inc...630 671-2000
6325 Muirfield Dr Hanover Park (60133) *(G-11011)*
Nypromold Inc...847 855-2200
955 Tri State Pkwy Gurnee (60031) *(G-10905)*
Nystrom, Chicago *Also called Herff Jones LLC (G-4807)*
O & G Spring & Wire, Chicago *Also called Will Don Corp (G-6627)*
O & I Woodworking...217 543-3155
125 E County Rd 50 E Arthur (61911) *(G-872)*
O & K American Corp (HQ)...773 767-2500
4630 W 55th St Chicago (60632) *(G-5644)*
O & L Machine Inc...815 963-6600
1115 18th Ave Rockford (61104) *(G-17541)*
O & M Electronic Inc...708 203-1947
5451 W 110th St Ste 4 Oak Lawn (60453) *(G-15730)*
O & P Kinetic...815 401-7260
453 S Main St Bourbonnais (60914) *(G-2267)*
O & W Wire Co Inc...773 776-5919
7816 S Oakley Ave Chicago (60620) *(G-5645)*
O Adjust Matic Pump Company...630 766-1490
429 E Potter St Wood Dale (60191) *(G-21224)*
O Brien Bill...630 980-5571
0n175 Alexander Dr Geneva (60134) *(G-10294)*
O C Keckley Company (PA)...847 674-8422
3400 Cleveland St Skokie (60076) *(G-18997)*
O Chilli Frozen Foods Inc...847 562-1991
1251 Shermer Rd Northbrook (60062) *(G-15442)*
O E I, Hoffman Estates *Also called Omron Electronics LLC (G-11442)*
O E M Marketing Inc (PA)...847 985-9490
1015 Lunt Ave Schaumburg (60193) *(G-18655)*
O K Jobbers Inc...217 728-7378
215 S Hamilton St Sullivan (61951) *(G-19674)*
O Signs Inc...312 888-3386
325 N Hoyne Ave Chicago (60612) *(G-5646)*
O'Meara/Brown Publications, Evanston *Also called Lakeland Boating Magazine (G-9546)*
O'Neill Products, Chicago *Also called Butcher Block Furn By Oneill (G-3986)*
O'Reilly Auto Parts, Bridgeview *Also called OReilly Automotive Stores Inc (G-2370)*
O-Cedar Commercial...217 379-2377
131 N Railroad Ave Paxton (60957) *(G-16311)*
O-Donuts Inc (PA)...217 544-4644
227 E Laurel St Springfield (62704) *(G-19415)*
O-Liminator LLC (PA)...630 400-0373
902 S Randall Rd Ste C240 Saint Charles (60174) *(G-18235)*
O.k Jobbers, Sullivan *Also called O K Jobbers Inc (G-19674)*
O2cool LLC...312 951-6700
300 S Riverside Plz Chicago (60606) *(G-5647)*
O2m Technologies LLC...773 910-8533
2242 W Harrison St Ste 20 Chicago (60612) *(G-5648)*
Oag Aviation Worldwide LLC (PA)...630 515-5300
801 Warrenville Rd # 555 Lisle (60532) *(G-12923)*
Oak Court Creations...815 467-7676
202 Oak Ct Minooka (60447) *(G-14065)*
Oak Foundation, Geneva *Also called Oasis International Limited (G-10295)*
Oak Hill Brands Corp...630 922-5010
1013 N Lombard Rd Lombard (60148) *(G-13111)*
Oak Leaf Outdoors Inc...309 691-9653
10216 W Civil Defense Rd Brimfield (61517) *(G-2407)*
Oak Ridge Molded Products, McHenry *Also called Oakridge Products LLC (G-13772)*
Oak State, Wenona *Also called Hearthside Food Solutions LLC (G-20526)*
Oak Technical LLC (PA)...931 455-7011
600 Holiday Plaza Dr # 130 Matteson (60443) *(G-13627)*
Oakland Industries Ltd...847 827-7600
1551 Bishop Ct Mount Prospect (60056) *(G-14555)*
Oakland Noodle Company...217 346-2322
10 W Main St Oakland (61943) *(G-15819)*
Oakley Industrial McHy Inc...847 966-0052
1601 Lunt Ave Elk Grove Village (60007) *(G-9157)*
Oakley Industries Sub Assembly...815 544-6666
2091 Tripp Rd Belvidere (61008) *(G-1692)*
Oakley Signs & Graphics Inc...224 612-5045
471 N 3rd Ave Des Plaines (60016) *(G-7813)*
Oakridge Corporation...630 435-5900
15800 New Ave Lemont (60439) *(G-12574)*
Oakridge Hobbies, Lemont *Also called Oakridge Corporation (G-12574)*
Oakridge Products LLC...815 363-4700
4612 Century Ct McHenry (60050) *(G-13772)*
Oakwood Memorial Park Inc...815 433-0313
2405 Champlain St Ottawa (61350) *(G-16066)*
Oandg Spring and Wire, Chicago *Also called Willdon Corp (G-6628)*
Oasis Audio LLC...630 668-5367
289 S Main Pl Carol Stream (60188) *(G-3042)*
Oasis International Limited...630 326-0045
1770 S Randall Rd Ste A Geneva (60134) *(G-10295)*
Oban Composites LLC...866 607-0284
1300 W Belmont Ave # 311 Chicago (60657) *(G-5649)*
Oberg Medical Products Co LLC...847 965-3030
6150 W Mulford St Niles (60714) *(G-15153)*
Oberg Medical Products Co LLC...847 364-4750
330 Crossen Ave Elk Grove Village (60007) *(G-9158)*
Obermiller Kustom Fabrication, Tonica *Also called Brian D Obermiller (G-19887)*
OBerry Enterprises Inc (PA)...815 728-9480
5306 Bsineil Pkwy Ste 110 Ringwood (60072) *(G-17046)*
Oberweis Dairy Inc...847 368-9060
9 E Dundee Rd Arlington Heights (60004) *(G-782)*
Oberweis Dairy Inc...630 906-6455
2274 Us Highway 30 Oswego (60543) *(G-16017)*
Oberweis Dairy Inc...708 660-1350
124 N Oak Park Ave Oak Park (60301) *(G-15767)*
Oberweis Dairy Inc...630 782-0141
1018 S York St Elmhurst (60126) *(G-9407)*
Oberweis Dairy Inc...847 290-9222
1735 Algonquin Rd Rolling Meadows (60008) *(G-17757)*
Oberweis Dairy Inc...630 801-6100
651 E Roosevelt St Glen Ellyn (60137) *(G-10415)*
Oberweis Ice Cream and Dar Str, Arlington Heights *Also called Oberweis Dairy Inc (G-782)*
Obies Tackle Co Inc...618 234-5638
124 Cardinal Dr Belleville (62221) *(G-1581)*
OBrien Architectural Mtls Inc...773 868-1065
858 W Armitage Ave # 205 Chicago (60614) *(G-5650)*
OBrien Scntfic GL Blowing LLC...217 762-3636
750 W Railroad St Monticello (61856) *(G-14283)*
OBrothers Bakery Inc...847 249-0091
2820 Belvidere Rd Waukegan (60085) *(G-20472)*
Obsidian Mfg Inds Inc...815 962-8700
5015 28th Ave Rockford (61109) *(G-17542)*
Occidental Chemical Corp...630 505-3242
3030 Warrenville Rd # 330 Lisle (60532) *(G-12924)*
Occidental Chemical Corp...773 284-0079
4201 W 69th St Chicago (60629) *(G-5651)*
Occidental Chemical Corp...618 482-6346
520 Monsanto Ave Sauget (62206) *(G-18397)*
Occly LLC...773 969-5080
2835 N Sheffield Ave Chicago (60657) *(G-5652)*
Oce Bruning, Charleston *Also called Oce-Van Der Grinten NV (G-3408)*

ALPHABETIC

(PA)=Parent Co (HQ)=Headquarters (DH)=Div Headquarters
2020 Harris Illinois Industrial Directory
1211

Oce-Van Der Grinten NV....217 348-8111
815 Reasor Dr Charleston (61920) *(G-3408)*
Oceancomm Incorporated....800 757-3266
1431 W Hubbard St Ste 205 Chicago (60642) *(G-5653)*
Oceanic Food Express Inc....847 480-7217
1715 Longvalley Dr Northbrook (60062) *(G-15443)*
Ochem Inc (PA)....847 403-7044
9044 Buckingham Park Dr Des Plaines (60016) *(G-7814)*
Ochem Inc....847 403-7044
2201 W Campbell Park Dr # 34 Chicago (60612) *(G-5654)*
Oci Manufacturing Company, Oregon *Also called ED Etnyre & Co (G-15917)*
Ockerlund Industries Inc....630 620-1269
1555 W Wrightwood Ct Addison (60101) *(G-230)*
Ocs America Inc....630 595-0111
945 Dillon Dr Wood Dale (60191) *(G-21225)*
Octane Motorsports LLC....224 419-5460
3056 Washington St 2b Waukegan (60085) *(G-20473)*
Octapharma Plasma Inc....708 409-0900
17 W North Ave Northlake (60164) *(G-15554)*
Octapharma Plasma Inc....217 546-8605
1770 Wabash Ave Springfield (62704) *(G-19416)*
Octavia Tool & Gage Company....847 913-9233
135 Kelly St Elk Grove Village (60007) *(G-9159)*
Octura Models Inc....847 674-7351
7351 Hamlin Ave Skokie (60076) *(G-18998)*
Ocularis Pharma....708 712-6263
2436 S 6th Ave Riverside (60546) *(G-17087)*
ODaniel Trucking Co....618 382-5371
1249 County Road 1500 N Carmi (62821) *(G-2912)*
Oden Corp....630 416-4543
1119 Wickfield Ct Naperville (60563) *(G-14888)*
Odin Fabrication Inc....630 365-2475
740 Hicks Dr Elburn (60119) *(G-8466)*
Odin Fire Protection District....618 775-8292
100 Perkins St Odin (62870) *(G-15835)*
Odin Foam, Itasca *Also called W S Darley & Co (G-11752)*
Odin Industries, Elburn *Also called Odin Fabrication Inc (G-8466)*
Odin Industries Inc....630 365-2475
740 Hicks Dr Elburn (60119) *(G-8467)*
Odin Technologies LLC....408 309-1925
4660 N Ravenswood Ave Chicago (60640) *(G-5655)*
Odl Inc (PA)....815 434-0655
1304 Starfire Dr Ottawa (61350) *(G-16067)*
Odm Tool & Mfg Co Inc....708 485-6130
9550 Joliet Rd Hodgkins (60525) *(G-11391)*
Odom Tool and Technology Inc....815 895-8545
216 W Page St Sycamore (60178) *(G-19726)*
Odorite International Inc....816 920-5000
320 37th Ave Saint Charles (60174) *(G-18236)*
Odors Away LLC (PA)....888 235-7559
368 Bluff City Blvd Elgin (60120) *(G-8676)*
Odra Inc....847 249-2910
4310 Lee Ave Gurnee (60031) *(G-10906)*
Odum Concrete Products Inc....618 942-4572
201 Rushing Dr Herrin (62948) *(G-11175)*
Odum Concrete Products Inc (PA)....618 993-6211
1800 N Court St Marion (62959) *(G-13523)*
Odwalla Inc....773 687-8667
2837 N Cambridge Ave Chicago (60657) *(G-5656)*
Odx Media LLC....847 868-0548
848 Dodge Ave Evanston (60202) *(G-9559)*
Oec Graphics-Chicago LLC....630 455-6700
7630 S Quincy St Willowbrook (60527) *(G-21056)*
Oei Products Inc....630 377-1121
1041 Georgian Pl Bartlett (60103) *(G-1300)*
Oelze Equipment Company LLC....618 327-9111
11800 County Highway 27 Nashville (62263) *(G-15006)*
Oerlikon Blzers Cating USA Inc....630 208-0958
737 Peyton St Geneva (60134) *(G-10296)*
Oerlikon Blzers Cating USA Inc (HQ)....847 619-5541
1700 E Golf Rd Ste 200 Schaumburg (60173) *(G-18656)*
Oerlikon Blzers Cating USA Inc....847 695-5200
1181 Jansen Farm Ct Elgin (60123) *(G-8677)*
Oetee LLC....630 373-4671
1814 N Lincoln Park W # 1 Chicago (60614) *(G-5657)*
OFallon Pressure Cast Co....618 632-8694
1418 Frontage Rd O Fallon (62269) *(G-15581)*
Off The Press LLC....815 436-9612
16041 S Lincoln Hwy # 103 Plainfield (60586) *(G-16697)*
Offical Helicopter Blue Book, Wauconda *Also called Helivalues (G-20355)*
Office Express Inc....888 526-8438
1555 Sherman Ave 129 Evanston (60201) *(G-9560)*
Office Furniture Parts LLC....708 546-5841
7540 Roosevelt Rd Forest Park (60130) *(G-9723)*
Office of Experience LLC....872 228-5126
125 S Wacker Dr Ste 3000 Chicago (60606) *(G-5658)*
Office of Mines & Minerals, Benton *Also called Natural Resources Ill Dept (G-1933)*
Office of Spcial Dputy Rceiver, Chicago *Also called State of Illinois (G-6235)*
Office Snax Inc....630 789-1783
125 Windsor Dr Ste 105 Oak Brook (60523) *(G-15652)*
OfficeMax North America Inc....815 748-3007
2350 Sycamore Rd Ste E Dekalb (60115) *(G-7696)*
Officenation Inc....847 504-3000
500 Central Ave Northfield (60093) *(G-15525)*
Officers Printing Inc....847 480-4663
710 Landwehr Rd Ste B Northbrook (60062) *(G-15444)*
Offko Tool Inc....815 933-9474
1995 S Kensington Ave Kankakee (60901) *(G-11994)*
Offsprings Inc....773 525-1800
1451 W Webster Ave Chicago (60614) *(G-5659)*
Offworld Designs....815 786-7080
624 W Center St Sandwich (60548) *(G-18378)*
Ofgd Inc....708 283-7101
2401 Lincoln Hwy Olympia Fields (60461) *(G-15897)*
Ogden Foods LLC (PA)....773 277-8207
4320 W Ogden Ave Chicago (60623) *(G-5660)*
Ogden Foods LLC....773 801-0125
4325 W Ogden Ave Chicago (60623) *(G-5661)*
Ogden Metalworks Inc....217 582-2552
301 N Marilyn St Ogden (61859) *(G-15837)*
Ogden Minuteman Inc....773 542-6917
3939 W Ogden Ave Chicago (60623) *(G-5662)*
Ogden Offset Printers Inc....773 284-7797
6150 S Archer Ave Chicago (60638) *(G-5663)*
Ogden Top & Trim Shop Inc....708 484-5422
6609 Ogden Ave Berwyn (60402) *(G-1958)*
Ogle County Life....815 732-2156
311 W Washington St Oregon (61061) *(G-15925)*
Ogle County Newspaper, Oregon *Also called The b F Shaw Printing Co (G-15928)*
Oglesby & Oglesby Gunmakers....217 487-7100
744 W Andrew Rd Springfield (62707) *(G-19417)*
OGorman Son Carpentry Contrs....815 485-8997
1930 Airway Ct New Lenox (60451) *(G-15045)*
Ogwuru Uzoaku....312 286-5593
7022 S Sth Shr Dr Apt 305 Chicago (60649) *(G-5664)*
OHare Precision Metals LLC....847 640-6050
2404 Hamilton Rd Arlington Heights (60005) *(G-783)*
OHare Shell Partners Inc....847 678-1900
4111 Mannheim Rd Schiller Park (60176) *(G-18829)*
OHare Spring Company Inc....847 298-1360
930 Lee St Elk Grove Village (60007) *(G-9160)*
Ohare Spring Company Inc....847 298-1360
2190 Oxford Rd Des Plaines (60018) *(G-7815)*
Ohio Medical, Gurnee *Also called Omc Investors LLC (G-10908)*
Ohio Medical LLC (HQ)....847 855-0500
1111 Lakeside Dr Gurnee (60031) *(G-10907)*
Ohio Pulp Mills Inc (PA)....312 337-7822
737 N Michigan Ave # 1450 Chicago (60611) *(G-5665)*
Ohmite Holding LLC (HQ)....847 258-0300
27501 Bella Vista Pkwy Warrenville (60555) *(G-20243)*
Ohmite Manufacturing, Warrenville *Also called Ohmite Holding LLC (G-20243)*
Ohmx Corporation....847 491-8500
1801 Maple Ave Ste 18 Evanston (60201) *(G-9561)*
Ohrvall Media LLC....630 378-9738
13400 S Route 59 Plainfield (60585) *(G-16698)*
Oi Glass Containers Oi G9....815 673-5120
901 N Shabbona St Streator (61364) *(G-19618)*
Oil and Gas Discoverer LLC....847 877-1257
1910 Browning Ct Highland Park (60035) *(G-11289)*
Oil Filter Recyclers Inc....309 329-2131
Rr 1 Astoria (61501) *(G-894)*
Oil-Dri Corporation America (PA)....312 321-1515
410 N Michigan Ave # 400 Chicago (60611) *(G-5666)*
Oil-Dri Corporation America....618 745-6881
700 Industrial Park Rd Mounds (62964) *(G-14463)*
Oil-Dri Corporation America....312 321-1516
410 N Michigan Aveste 400 Chicago (60611) *(G-5667)*
Ojedas Welding Co....708 595-3799
312 S 3rd Ave Maywood (60153) *(G-13677)*
Okaw Truss Inc....217 543-3371
368 E Sr 133 Arthur (61911) *(G-873)*
Okaw Valley Woodworking LLC....217 543-5180
432 E Sr 133 Arthur (61911) *(G-874)*
Okawville Times....618 243-5563
109 E Walnut St Okawville (62271) *(G-15846)*
Olcott Plastics Inc....630 584-0555
95 N 17th St Saint Charles (60174) *(G-18237)*
Old Capitol Monument Works Inc (PA)....217 324-5673
627 S 6th St Vandalia (62471) *(G-20017)*
Old Chicago Coffee Co., Orland Park *Also called Calutech Inc (G-15944)*
Old Fashioned Meat Co Inc....312 421-4555
920 W Fulton Market Chicago (60607) *(G-5668)*
Old Gary Inc (HQ)....219 648-3000
350 N Orleans St Fl 10 Chicago (60654) *(G-5669)*
Old Heritage Creamery LLC....217 268-4355
222 N County Road 575e Arcola (61910) *(G-661)*
Old Mill Vineyard LLC....309 258-9954
700 Coon Creek Rd Metamora (61548) *(G-13965)*
Old School Timber Works Co....847 918-8626
15409 W Old School Rd Libertyville (60048) *(G-12692)*

Old Style Iron Works Inc 773 265-5787
7843 S Claremont Ave Chicago (60620) ***(G-5670)***
Old Town Oil Evanston 312 787-9595
1924 Central St Evanston (60201) ***(G-9562)***
Old World Global LLC 800 323-5440
4065 Commercial Ave Northbrook (60062) ***(G-15445)***
Old World Inds Holdings LLC 800 323-5440
4065 Commercial Ave Northbrook (60062) ***(G-15446)***
Old World Millworks, Maple Park *Also called C A Larson & Son Inc* ***(G-13461)***
Oldcastle Buildingenvelope Inc 773 523-8400
4161 S Morgan St Chicago (60609) ***(G-5671)***
Oldcastle Buildingenvelope Inc 630 250-7270
2901 Lively Blvd Elk Grove Village (60007) ***(G-9161)***
Oldcastle Infrastructure Inc 309 661-4608
1204 Aurora Way Normal (61761) ***(G-15215)***
Oldcastle Lawn & Garden Inc 618 274-1222
1130 Queeny Ave East Saint Louis (62206) ***(G-8317)***
Oldcastle Lawn & Grdn Midwest, East Saint Louis *Also called Oldcastle Lawn & Garden Inc* ***(G-8317)***
Oldcastle Materials Inc 309 627-2111
2391 60th St Monmouth (61462) ***(G-14225)***
Olde Print Shoppe Inc 618 395-3833
1314 E Main St Olney (62450) ***(G-15879)***
Oldendorf Machining & Fabg 708 946-2498
3041 E Offner Rd Beecher (60401) ***(G-1519)***
Ole Mexican Foods Inc 708 458-3296
5140 W 73rd St Unit A Bedford Park (60638) ***(G-1487)***
Ole Saltys of Rockford Inc 815 637-2447
3131 Summerdale Ave Rockford (61101) ***(G-17543)***
Ole Saltys of Rockford Inc (PA) 815 637-2447
1920 E Riverside Blvd Loves Park (61111) ***(G-13241)***
Olfb Corporation 309 283-0825
2128 5th Ave Moline (61265) ***(G-14164)***
Olin Chlor Alkali Pdts Vinyls 844 238-3445
1001 31st St Downers Grove (60515) ***(G-8068)***
Olin Corporation 618 258-2000
600 Powder Mill Rd East Alton (62024) ***(G-8168)***
Olin Corporation 618 258-2245
15025 State Highway 111 Brighton (62012) ***(G-2402)***
Olin Engineered Systems Inc 618 258-2874
427 N Shamrock St East Alton (62024) ***(G-8169)***
Olivaceto 708 639-4408
77 S La Grange Rd La Grange (60525) ***(G-12084)***
Olive and Vinnies 630 534-6457
449 N Main St Glen Ellyn (60137) ***(G-10416)***
Olive Leclaire Oil Co 888 255-1867
1524 Coral Dr Yorkville (60560) ***(G-21494)***
Olive Mill, The, Geneva *Also called Olive Oil Store Inc* ***(G-10297)***
Olive Oil Market Place 618 304-3769
1018 Richard Dr Godfrey (62035) ***(G-10659)***
Olive Oil Marketplace Inc (PA) 618 304-3769
108 W 3rd St Alton (62002) ***(G-567)***
Olive Oil Store Inc (PA) 630 262-0210
315 James St Geneva (60134) ***(G-10297)***
Olive Oils & More LLC 618 656-4645
1990 Troy Rd Ste A Edwardsville (62025) ***(G-8373)***
Olive Tree Foods Inc 847 872-2762
2439 Galilee Ave Zion (60099) ***(G-21522)***
Olivet Woodworking 773 505-5225
316 Hickory Rd Lake Zurich (60047) ***(G-12441)***
Olney Daily Mail 618 393-2931
206 S Whittle Ave Olney (62450) ***(G-15880)***
Olney Daily Reporter, Olney *Also called Gatehouse Media LLC* ***(G-15862)***
Olney Machine & Design Inc 618 392-6634
4632 E Radio T Olney (62450) ***(G-15881)***
Olon Decoratives, Geneva *Also called Olon Industries Inc (us)* ***(G-10298)***
Olon Industries Inc (us) (HQ) 630 232-4705
411 Union St Geneva (60134) ***(G-10298)***
Olsen Woodwork Co (PA) 847 865-5054
4709 Southhampton Dr Island Lake (60042) ***(G-11610)***
Olson Aluminum Castings Ltd 815 229-3292
2135 15th St Rockford (61104) ***(G-17544)***
Olson Machining Inc 815 675-2900
1804 Holian Dr Spring Grove (60081) ***(G-19291)***
Olson Metal Products LLC (HQ) 847 981-7550
511 W Algonquin Rd Arlington Heights (60005) ***(G-784)***
Olsun Electrics Corporation 815 678-2421
10901 Commercial St Richmond (60071) ***(G-17019)***
Oltenia Inc 773 987-2888
4905 N Opal Ave Norridge (60706) ***(G-15242)***
Oly Ola Edging Inc 630 833-3033
124 E Saint Charles Rd Villa Park (60181) ***(G-20163)***
Olympia Manufacturing Inc 309 387-2633
101 Annie Ln East Peoria (61611) ***(G-8280)***
Olympic Bindery Inc 847 577-8132
1105 N Chestnut Ave Arlington Heights (60004) ***(G-785)***
Olympic Controls Corp 847 742-3566
1250 Crispin Dr Elgin (60123) ***(G-8678)***
Olympic Petroleum Corporation 847 995-0996
1171 Tower Rd Schaumburg (60173) ***(G-18657)***
Olympic Petroleum Corporation (HQ) 708 876-7900
5000 W 41st St Cicero (60804) ***(G-6868)***
Olympic Signs Inc 630 424-6100
1130 N Garfield St Lombard (60148) ***(G-13112)***
Olympic Steel Inc 847 584-4000
1901 Mitchell Blvd Schaumburg (60193) ***(G-18658)***
Olympic Trophy and Awards Co 773 631-9500
5860 N Northwest Hwy Chicago (60631) ***(G-5672)***
Olyola Etching, Villa Park *Also called Oly Ola Edging Inc* ***(G-20163)***
Omaha Grain & Fertilizer, Omaha *Also called Hayden Mills Inc* ***(G-15900)***
OMalley Welding and Fabg 630 553-1604
1209 Badger St Yorkville (60560) ***(G-21495)***
Omar Medical Supplies Inc (PA) 708 922-4276
345 E Wacker Dr Unit 4601 Chicago (60601) ***(G-5673)***
Omar Supplies, Chicago *Also called Omar Medical Supplies Inc* ***(G-5673)***
Omc Investors LLC (HQ) 847 855-6220
1111 Lakeside Dr Gurnee (60031) ***(G-10908)***
Omcg North America, Bensenville *Also called North America O M C G Inc* ***(G-1858)***
Omega Manufacturing LLC 708 345-8505
1037 N 27th Ave Melrose Park (60160) ***(G-13899)***
Omega Moulding North Amer Inc 630 509-2397
1420 Thorndale Ave Elk Grove Village (60007) ***(G-9162)***
Omega Plating Inc 708 389-5410
4704 137th St Crestwood (60418) ***(G-7123)***
Omega Printing Inc 630 595-6344
201 William St Bensenville (60106) ***(G-1861)***
Omega Products Inc 618 939-3445
502 Walnut St Waterloo (62298) ***(G-20293)***
Omega Royal Graphics Inc 847 952-8000
1621 Brummel Ave Elk Grove Village (60007) ***(G-9163)***
Omega Sign & Lighting Inc 630 237-4397
100 W Fay Ave Addison (60101) ***(G-231)***
Omegacom Inc 773 750-4621
5331 N Lincoln Ave Chicago (60625) ***(G-5674)***
Omex Technologies Inc 847 850-5858
300 E Marquardt Dr # 107 Wheeling (60090) ***(G-20949)***
Omg Inc 413 789-0252
300 S Mitchell Ct Addison (60101) ***(G-232)***
Omg Handbags LLC 847 337-9499
2045 W Grand Ave Ste 202 Chicago (60612) ***(G-5675)***
Omiotek Coil Spring Co (PA) 630 495-4056
833 N Ridge Ave Lombard (60148) ***(G-13113)***
Omni Containment Systems LLC 847 468-1772
1501 Commerce Drive Elgin Elgin (60123) ***(G-8679)***
Omni Craft Inc 815 838-1285
411 New Ave Unit 1 Lockport (60441) ***(G-13017)***
Omni Gear and Machine Corp 815 723-4327
90 Bissel St Joliet (60432) ***(G-11911)***
Omni Materials Inc 618 262-5118
1611 College Dr Mount Carmel (62863) ***(G-14484)***
Omni Products Inc (PA) 815 344-3100
3911 W Dayton St McHenry (60050) ***(G-13773)***
Omni Publishing Co 847 483-9668
45 Versailles Ct Wheeling (60090) ***(G-20950)***
Omni Pump Repairs Inc 847 451-0000
9224 Chestnut Ave Franklin Park (60131) ***(G-10011)***
Omni Vision Inc 630 893-1720
2000 Bloomingdale Rd # 245 Glendale Heights (60139) ***(G-10481)***
Omni-Rinse LLC 708 860-3250
738 E Dundee Rd Ste 197 Palatine (60074) ***(G-16146)***
Omni-Tech Systems Inc 309 962-2281
7 Demma Dr Le Roy (61752) ***(G-12540)***
Omnicare Group Inc 708 949-8802
13557 Parkland Ct Homer Glen (60491) ***(G-11485)***
Omnilight Inc 773 696-1602
6501 N Avondale Ave Chicago (60631) ***(G-5676)***
Omnimax International Inc 309 747-2937
17904 E 3100 North Rd Gridley (61744) ***(G-10846)***
Omnimax International Inc 770 449-7066
6235 W 73rd St Bedford Park (60638) ***(G-1488)***
Omnitronix Corporation 630 837-1400
349 Roma Jean Pkwy Streamwood (60107) ***(G-19587)***
Omobono Inc 312 523-2179
325 W Huron St Ste 215 Chicago (60654) ***(G-5677)***
Omron Electronics LLC (HQ) 847 843-7900
2895 Grnspint Pkwy Ste 20 Hoffman Estates (60169) ***(G-11442)***
Omron Global, Saint Charles *Also called Nidec Mobility America Corp* ***(G-18234)***
Omron Healthcare Inc (HQ) 847 680-6200
1925 W Field Ct Lake Forest (60045) ***(G-12276)***
On Paint It Company 219 765-5639
140 Tygert Ln Dekalb (60115) ***(G-7697)***
On Site Mechanical Svcs Inc 708 367-0470
25250 S State St Crete (60417) ***(G-7143)***
On Site Repair Services Inc 815 223-4058
340 Civic Rd La Salle (61301) ***(G-12119)***
On Target Grinding and Mfg 708 418-3905
2250 199th St Ste 3 Lynwood (60411) ***(G-13296)***
On Time Decorations Inc 708 357-6072
1411 S Laramie Ave Cicero (60804) ***(G-6869)***

On Time Envelopes & Printing............630 682-0466
615 Kimberly Dr Carol Stream (60188) *(G-3043)*
On Time Printing and Finishing............708 544-4500
4206 Warren Ave Hillside (60162) *(G-11351)*
On-Cor Frozen Foods LLC (HQ)............630 851-6600
1225 Corp Blvd Ste 300 Aurora (60505) *(G-1142)*
Oncourse Learning, Hoffman Estates *Also called Tegna Inc (G-11468)*
Oncquest............847 682-4703
43323 N Oak Crest Ln Zion (60099) *(G-21523)*
Oncquest Pharma, Zion *Also called Oncquest (G-21523)*
One Accord Unity Nfp............630 649-0793
1886 Marne Rd Bolingbrook (60490) *(G-2223)*
One Earth Energy LLC............217 784-5321
202 Jordan Dr Gibson City (60936) *(G-10341)*
One Way Safety LLC............708 579-0229
418 Shawmut Ave Ste B La Grange (60526) *(G-12085)*
One Way Solutions LLC............847 446-0872
400 Central Ave Ste 320 Northfield (60093) *(G-15526)*
Onefire Media Group Inc............309 740-0345
801 W Main St Peoria Peoria (61606) *(G-16487)*
ONeill Products Inc............312 243-3413
555 W 16th St Chicago (60616) *(G-5678)*
Oneims Printing LLC............773 297-2050
8833 Groil Pt Rd Ste 202 Skokie (60077) *(G-18999)*
Oneplus Systems Inc............847 498-0955
3182 Macarthur Blvd Northbrook (60062) *(G-15447)*
Onetouchpoint Mtn States LLC............303 227-1400
1200 Harger Rd Ste 419 Oak Brook (60523) *(G-15653)*
Onkens Incorporated............309 562-7477
320 E Main St Easton (62633) *(G-8331)*
Online Business Applications, Lisle *Also called Anju Software Inc (G-12866)*
Online Eei, Romeoville *Also called Exex Holding Corporation (G-17820)*
Online Electronics Inc............847 871-1700
1261 Jarvis Ave Elk Grove Village (60007) *(G-9164)*
Online Inc............815 363-8008
4071 W Albany St McHenry (60050) *(G-13774)*
Only 1 Printers Inc............847 947-4119
540 Allendale Dr Ste K Wheeling (60090) *(G-20951)*
Only Child Brewing Company LLC............847 877-9822
1350 Tri State Pkwy # 124 Gurnee (60031) *(G-10909)*
Only For One Printers, Wheeling *Also called Only 1 Printers Inc (G-20951)*
Only One Boutique, Evanston *Also called SRS Global Ret Solutions LLC (G-9577)*
Onoffblock Inc............312 899-6360
2100 Cattleman Dr New Lenox (60451) *(G-15046)*
Onoffblock Inc (PA)............312 899-6360
2100 Cattleman Dr New Lenox (60451) *(G-15047)*
Onsite Woodwork Corporation (PA)............815 633-6400
4100 Rock Valley Pkwy Loves Park (61111) *(G-13242)*
Onsrud Cutter, Waukegan *Also called Lmt Onsrud LP (G-20461)*
Ontario Die USA............630 761-6562
950 Paramount Pkwy Ste 3 Batavia (60510) *(G-1401)*
Onx USA LLC............630 343-8940
1001 Warrenville Rd Lisle (60532) *(G-12925)*
Oostman Fabricating & Wldg Inc............630 241-1315
45 E Chicago Ave Westmont (60559) *(G-20763)*
Opalek Frontier Inc............312 733-2700
1117 W Grand Ave Chicago (60642) *(G-5679)*
Open Hand Self Defense............815 718-3994
200 W North St Morrison (61270) *(G-14346)*
Open Kitchens Inc (PA)............312 666-5334
2121 S Racine Ave Chicago (60608) *(G-5680)*
Open Kitchens Inc............312 666-5334
2141 S Racine Ave Chicago (60608) *(G-5681)*
Open Point Solutions, Chicago *Also called Productive Edge LLC (G-5895)*
Open Waters Seafood Company............847 329-8585
5010 Howard St Skokie (60077) *(G-19000)*
Opex Analytics LLC............847 733-7439
350 N Orleans St 8500n Chicago (60654) *(G-5682)*
Oppidan Spirits, Wheeling *Also called Windy City Distilling Inc (G-21014)*
Opportunity Inc............847 831-9400
1200 Old Skokie Rd Highland Park (60035) *(G-11290)*
Ops 3 LLC............312 243-8265
2201 W Fulton St Chicago (60612) *(G-5683)*
Opsdirt LLC............773 412-1179
948 N Winchester Ave # 3 Chicago (60622) *(G-5684)*
Optech Ortho & Prosth Svcs............708 364-9700
18016 Wolf Rd Orland Park (60467) *(G-15972)*
Optech Ortho & Prosth Svcs (PA)............815 932-8564
119 E Court St Ste 100 Kankakee (60901) *(G-11995)*
Optek, Batavia *Also called Aggresive Motor Sports (G-1342)*
Opti-Sand Incorporated............630 293-1245
31 W 037 North Ave West Chicago (60185) *(G-20626)*
Opti-Vue Inc............630 274-6121
224 James St Bensenville (60106) *(G-1862)*
Optical Systems, Arlington Heights *Also called Vibgyor Optics Inc (G-827)*
Opticent Inc............410 829-7384
600 Davis St Fl 3 Evanston (60201) *(G-9563)*
Opticote Inc............847 678-8900
10455 Seymour Ave Franklin Park (60131) *(G-10012)*
Optimal Automatics Co............847 439-9110
120 Stanley St Elk Grove Village (60007) *(G-9165)*
Optimal Construction Svcs Inc............630 365-5050
843 Shepherd Ln Elburn (60119) *(G-8468)*
Optimas Oe Solutions LLC (HQ)............224 999-1000
2651 Compass Rd Glenview (60026) *(G-10595)*
Optimum Nutrition, Downers Grove *Also called Glanbia Prfmce Ntrtn NA Inc (G-8012)*
Optimus Advantage LLC............847 905-1000
10 S Lasalle Chicago (60606) *(G-5685)*
Optionscity Software Inc............312 605-4500
150 S Wacker Dr Ste 2300 Chicago (60606) *(G-5686)*
Optiva Signs, Chicago *Also called Ilight Technologies Inc (G-4887)*
Opw Fuel MGT Systems Inc (HQ)............708 352-9617
6900 Santa Fe Dr Hodgkins (60525) *(G-11392)*
Opw Fueling Components Inc............708 485-4200
6900 Santa Fe Dr Hodgkins (60525) *(G-11393)*
Opw Fueling Management Systems, Hodgkins *Also called Opw Fueling Components Inc (G-11393)*
Oq 168 NM Propco LLC............312 542-6116
168 N Michigan Ave Chicago (60601) *(G-5687)*
Oquawka Boats and Fabrications............309 867-2213
1312 E State Highway 164 Oquawka (61469) *(G-15906)*
Ora Holdings, Waukegan *Also called Rock-Tred 2 LLC (G-20489)*
Oracle Bigmachines LLC (HQ)............847 572-0300
1405 Lake Cook Rd Deerfield (60015) *(G-7641)*
Oracle Corporation............773 404-9300
980 N Michigan Ave # 1400 Chicago (60611) *(G-5688)*
Oracle Corporation............312 692-5270
330 N Wabash Ave Ste 2400 Chicago (60611) *(G-5689)*
Oracle Corporation............630 931-6400
17th Fl 2 Pierce Pl Flr 17 Itasca (60143) *(G-11713)*
Oracle Corporation............262 957-3000
233 S Wacker Dr Ste 4500 Chicago (60606) *(G-5690)*
Oracle Hcm User Group Inc............312 222-9350
330 N Wabash Ave Ste 2000 Chicago (60611) *(G-5691)*
Oracle Systems Corporation............312 673-5863
3122 Paysphere Circle Chicago (60674) *(G-5692)*
Oracle Systems Corporation............708 409-7800
3 Westbrook Corp Ctr # 900 Westchester (60154) *(G-20706)*
Orange Crush LLC............847 537-7900
571 Wheeling Rd Wheeling (60090) *(G-20952)*
Orange Crush LLC (PA)............708 544-9440
321 Center St Hillside (60162) *(G-11352)*
Orange Crush LLC............847 428-6176
507 Rock Road Dr East Dundee (60118) *(G-8207)*
Orange Crush LLC............630 739-5560
1001 N Independence Blvd Romeoville (60446) *(G-17862)*
Orat Inc............630 567-6728
761 N 17th St Ste 4 Saint Charles (60174) *(G-18238)*
Oratech Inc............217 793-2735
4777 Alex Blvd Springfield (62711) *(G-19418)*
Orbis Rpm LLC............217 876-8655
1781 Hubbard Ave Decatur (62526) *(G-7533)*
Orbis Rpm LLC............312 343-4902
4400 W 45th St Ste C Chicago (60632) *(G-5693)*
Orbit Enterprises Inc............630 469-3405
3525 S Cass Ct Unit T3n Oak Brook (60523) *(G-15654)*
Orbit Machining Company............847 678-1050
9440 Ainslie St Schiller Park (60176) *(G-18830)*
Orbit Room............773 588-8540
2959 N California Ave Chicago (60618) *(G-5694)*
Orbus LLC (PA)............630 226-1155
9033 Murphy Rd Woodridge (60517) *(G-21328)*
Orbus Exhibit & Display Group, Woodridge *Also called Orbus LLC (G-21328)*
Orbus Holdings Inc............630 226-1155
9033 Murphy Rd Woodridge (60517) *(G-21329)*
Orbus Trade Show, Woodridge *Also called Orbus Holdings Inc (G-21329)*
Orchard Hill Cabinetry Inc (PA)............312 829-4300
401 N Western Ave Ste 3 Chicago (60612) *(G-5695)*
Orchard Products Inc............847 818-6760
500 W Huntington Cmns Mount Prospect (60056) *(G-14556)*
Orchid Labs, Downers Grove *Also called Flavorchem Corporation (G-8004)*
Orecx............312 895-5292
1 N La Salle St Ste 1375 Chicago (60602) *(G-5696)*
Orei LLC............847 983-4761
7440 Long Ave Skokie (60077) *(G-19001)*
OReilly Automotive Stores Inc............847 882-4384
38 E Golf Rd Ste C Schaumburg (60173) *(G-18659)*
OReilly Automotive Stores Inc............847 360-0012
2507 Grand Ave Waukegan (60085) *(G-20474)*
OReilly Automotive Stores Inc............708 430-8155
7100 W 87th St Bridgeview (60455) *(G-2370)*
Oreilly's Auto Parts, Waukegan *Also called OReilly Automotive Stores Inc (G-20474)*
Oremus Materials LLC............520 820-2265
16w361 S Frontage Rd # 1 Burr Ridge (60527) *(G-2711)*
Organ Recovery Systems Inc............847 824-2600
1 Pierce Pl Ste 475w Itasca (60143) *(G-11714)*
Organic Looms Inc (PA)............312 832-0900
401 N Wells St Ste 3 Chicago (60654) *(G-5697)*

Organics LLC 847 897-6000
1935 Techny Rd Ste 14 Northbrook (60062) *(G-15448)*
Organized Noise Inc 630 820-9855
231 Raintree Ct Aurora (60504) *(G-1004)*
Organnica Inc 312 925-7272
3437 Maple Ave Berwyn (60402) *(G-1959)*
Organon API, Des Plaines *Also called Aspen API Inc (G-7734)*
Orica Nitrogen, Morris *Also called Orica USA Inc (G-14320)*
Orica USA Inc 815 357-8711
7700 W Dupont Rd Morris (60450) *(G-14320)*
Orient Machining & Welding Inc 708 371-3500
14501 Wood St Ste A Dixmoor (60426) *(G-7886)*
Oriental Kitchen Corporation 312 738-2850
223 N Justine St Chicago (60607) *(G-5698)*
Origami Risk LLC (PA) 312 546-6515
222 N Lasalle St Ste 2125 Chicago (60601) *(G-5699)*
Original Ferrara Bakery, Chicago *Also called Original Ferrara Inc (G-5700)*
Original Ferrara Inc 312 666-2200
2210 W Taylor St Chicago (60612) *(G-5700)*
Original Notolli & Sons, Chicago *Also called George Nottoli & Sons Inc (G-4683)*
Original Shutter Man 773 966-7160
1231 W 74th Pl Chicago (60636) *(G-5701)*
Original Software Inc 630 413-5762
1010 Executive Dr Ste 230 Westmont (60559) *(G-20764)*
Orin Briant Inc 779 206-2800
246 Stone Ct New Lenox (60451) *(G-15048)*
Orinoco Systems LLC (PA) 630 510-0775
300 S Carlton Ave Ste 100 Wheaton (60187) *(G-20814)*
Oriole Enterprises Inc 773 589-9696
7354 W Addison St Chicago (60634) *(G-5702)*
Orion Enterprises, Monmouth *Also called Forman Co Inc (G-14217)*
Orion Metals Co 847 412-9532
3318 Maple Leaf Dr Glenview (60026) *(G-10596)*
Orion Offset, Palatine *Also called Orion Star Corp (G-16147)*
Orion Star Corp 847 776-2300
236 E Northwest Hwy Ste A Palatine (60067) *(G-16147)*
Orion Tool Die & Machine Co 309 526-3303
1400 16th St Orion (61273) *(G-15930)*
Orland Park Bakery Ltd 708 349-8516
14850 S La Grange Rd Orland Park (60462) *(G-15973)*
Orland Precision Machine LLC 815 464-9210
9302 Gulfstream Rd Ste A Frankfort (60423) *(G-9818)*
Orland Sports Ltd 773 685-3711
5610 W Bloomingdale Ave G Chicago (60639) *(G-5703)*
Orlandi Statuary Company 773 489-0303
1801 N Central Park Ave Chicago (60647) *(G-5704)*
Orli Diamonds, Chicago *Also called Steinmetz R (us) Ltd (G-6241)*
Ornament Shop Co Inc 847 559-8844
2139 Claridge Ln Northbrook (60062) *(G-15449)*
Ornament Shop.com, Northbrook *Also called Ornament Shop Co Inc (G-15449)*
Ornamental Iron Shop 618 281-6072
148 Hill Castle Dr Columbia (62236) *(G-6992)*
Orochem Technologies Inc 630 210-8300
340 Shuman Blvd Naperville (60563) *(G-14889)*
Orora North America 630 613-2600
100 E Progress Rd Lombard (60148) *(G-13114)*
Orora Packaging Solutions 815 895-2343
215 Fair St Sycamore (60178) *(G-19727)*
Orora Visual TX LLC 414 423-2200
7400 N Lehigh Ave Niles (60714) *(G-15154)*
Orr Farms, Watseka *Also called Orr Rudolph (G-20313)*
Orr Marketing Corp 847 401-5171
784 Scott Dr Elgin (60123) *(G-8680)*
Orr Rudolph 815 429-3996
2642 E 2300 North Rd Watseka (60970) *(G-20313)*
Orren Pickell Builders Inc 847 572-5200
444 Skokie Blvd Ste 200 Wilmette (60091) *(G-21090)*
Orsolinis Welding & Fabg 773 722-9855
3040 W Carroll Ave Chicago (60612) *(G-5705)*
Orstrom Woodworking Ltd 847 697-1163
1502 Sawgrass Ct Elgin (60123) *(G-8681)*
Ortho Arch Company Inc 847 885-7805
1107 Tower Rd Schaumburg (60173) *(G-18660)*
Ortho Molecular Products Inc (PA) 815 337-0089
1991 Duncan Pl Woodstock (60098) *(G-21417)*
Ortho Seating LLC 773 276-3539
4444 W Ohio St Chicago (60624) *(G-5706)*
Ortho-Clinical Diagnostics Inc 618 281-3882
8 Briarhill Ln Columbia (62236) *(G-6993)*
Orthotech Sports - Med Eqp Inc (PA) 618 942-6611
1211 Weaver Rd Herrin (62948) *(G-11176)*
Ortman Fluid Power Inc 217 277-0321
1400 N 30th St Ste 20 Quincy (62301) *(G-16919)*
Ortman-Mccain Co 312 666-2244
2715 Grant Ave Bellwood (60104) *(G-1635)*
Orvis Company Inc 312 440-0662
142 E Ontario St Ste 1 Chicago (60611) *(G-5707)*
Os Farr, Crystal Lake *Also called Camfil USA Inc (G-7177)*
Osborne Publications Inc 217 422-9702
132 S Water St Ste 424 Decatur (62523) *(G-7534)*
Oscars Foods Inc (PA) 773 622-6822
6125 W Belmont Ave Chicago (60634) *(G-5708)*
OSG Power Tools Inc 630 561-4008
759 Industrial Dr Bensenville (60106) *(G-1863)*
OSG Usa Inc 800 837-2223
620 Stetson Ave Saint Charles (60174) *(G-18239)*
OSG Usa Inc 630 274-2100
759 Industrial Dr Bensenville (60106) *(G-1864)*
Oshkosh Specialty Vehicles Inc (HQ) 708 868-5071
2150 Dolton Rd Calumet City (60409) *(G-2784)*
Oshkosh/Mcnlus Fncl Svcs Prtnr 630 466-5100
490 N Heartland Dr Sugar Grove (60554) *(G-19648)*
OSI Group, West Chicago *Also called OSI Industries LLC (G-20627)*
OSI Group LLC (PA) 630 851-6600
1225 Corp Blvd Ste 300 Aurora (60505) *(G-1143)*
OSI Industries LLC 630 231-9090
711 Industrial Dr West Chicago (60185) *(G-20627)*
OSI Industries LLC (HQ) 630 851-6600
1225 Corp Blvd Ste 105 Aurora (60505) *(G-1144)*
OSI Industries LLC 773 650-4000
4201 S Ashland Ave Chicago (60609) *(G-5709)*
OSI Industries LLC 773 847-2000
4545 S Racine Ave Chicago (60609) *(G-5710)*
OSI International Foods Ltd 630 851-6600
1225 Corp Blvd Ste 300 Aurora (60504) *(G-1005)*
Osmer Woodworking Inc 815 973-5809
406 E Bradshaw St Dixon (61021) *(G-7905)*
Oso Technologies Inc 844 777-2575
722 W Killarney St Urbana (61801) *(G-19991)*
Oso900 Nfp 312 206-4219
6447 N Sacramento Ave Chicago (60645) *(G-5711)*
Ossola Industrials Inc (PA) 618 451-2621
400 A St Ste B Granite City (62040) *(G-10729)*
Ostrom & Co Inc 503 281-6469
28w600 Roosevelt Rd Winfield (60190) *(G-21113)*
Ostrom Glass & Metal Works, Winfield *Also called Ostrom & Co Inc (G-21113)*
Oswego Diamond 630 636-9617
3370 White Oak Dr Oswego (60543) *(G-16018)*
Oswego Vinyl 331 725-4801
288 Devoe Dr Oswego (60543) *(G-16019)*
Ot Systems Limited 630 554-9178
18 W Main St Plano (60545) *(G-16737)*
Otak International Inc 630 373-9229
2080 N 16th Ave Melrose Park (60160) *(G-13900)*
Othernet Inc 773 688-4320
20535 Il 53 Long Grove (60047) *(G-13168)*
Otis Elevator Company 312 454-1616
651 W Washington Blvd 1n Chicago (60661) *(G-5712)*
Otis Elevator Company 618 529-3411
201 W Kennicott St Carbondale (62901) *(G-2852)*
Otr Wheel Engineering Inc 217 223-7705
4400 Kochs Ln Quincy (62305) *(G-16920)*
Ottawa Publishing Co Inc (HQ) 815 433-2000
110 W Jefferson St Ottawa (61350) *(G-16068)*
Ottawa Publishing Co Inc 815 434-3330
300 W Joliet St Ottawa (61350) *(G-16069)*
Otten Construction Co Inc 618 768-4310
786 Old Saint Louis Rd Addieville (62214) *(G-11)*
Otter Creek Sand & Gravel 309 759-4293
4125 N Stoneyard Rd Havana (62644) *(G-11119)*
Otto & Sons Div, Aurora *Also called OSI Industries LLC (G-1144)*
Ottos Canvas Shop 217 543-3307
1749b State Highway 133 Arthur (61911) *(G-875)*
Ottos Drapery Service Inc 773 777-7755
5219 W Cullom Ave Chicago (60641) *(G-5713)*
Otus LLC 312 229-7648
900 N Michigan Ave # 1600 Chicago (60611) *(G-5714)*
Oui Wee Designs, Chicago *Also called Barrett NJide Yvonne (G-3838)*
Outback USA Inc 863 699-2220
5n825 Prairie Springs Dr Saint Charles (60175) *(G-18240)*
Outbound Lighting LLC 314 330-0696
7080 N Mccormick Blvd Lincolnwood (60712) *(G-12835)*
Outbreak Designs 217 370-5418
1458 S Main St South Jacksonville (62650) *(G-19251)*
Outdoor Advertising, Rock Falls *Also called Turnroth Sign Company Inc (G-17198)*
Outdoor Environments LLC 847 325-5000
288 S Buffalo Grove Rd Buffalo Grove (60089) *(G-2583)*
Outdoor Notebook Publishing 630 257-6534
14805 131st St Lemont (60439) *(G-12575)*
Outdoor Power Inc 217 228-9890
2703 Broadway St Quincy (62301) *(G-16921)*
Outdoor Solutions Team Inc 312 446-4220
1315 Southwind Dr Northbrook (60062) *(G-15450)*
Outdoor Space LLC 773 857-5296
3120 N Sheffield Ave # 1 Chicago (60657) *(G-5715)*
Output Medical Inc 630 430-8024
4660 N Ravenswood Ave Chicago (60640) *(G-5716)*
Outre', Evanston *Also called Filmfax Magazine Inc (G-9520)*

A L P H A B E T I C

Outside Plant Magazine, Schaumburg *Also called Practical Communications Inc* ***(G-18681)***
Oval Brand Fire Products, Glendale Heights *Also called Oval Fire Products Corporation* ***(G-10482)***
Oval Fire Products Corporation....630 635-5000
115 W Lake Dr Ste 300 Glendale Heights (60139) ***(G-10482)***
Overgrad Inc....312 324-4952
11 E Adams St Ste 200 Chicago (60603) ***(G-5717)***
Overhead Door Corporation....630 775-9118
295 S Prospect Ave Itasca (60143) ***(G-11715)***
Overnite Protos, Elk Grove Village *Also called Online Electronics Inc* ***(G-9164)***
Overt Press Inc....773 284-0909
4625 W 53rd St Chicago (60632) ***(G-5718)***
Overton Chicago Gear Corp....773 638-0508
2823 W Fulton St Chicago (60612) ***(G-5719)***
Ovis Loader Attachments Inc....618 203-2757
1555 S Wall St Carbondale (62901) ***(G-2853)***
Ovn LLC....646 204-6781
714 Grosse Pointe Cir Vernon Hills (60061) ***(G-20079)***
Ovs LLC....312 428-3548
5419 N Sheridan Rd # 103 Chicago (60640) ***(G-5720)***
Owen Plastics LLC....847 683-2054
150 French Rd Burlington (60109) ***(G-2642)***
Owen Walker....217 285-4012
837 W Adams St Pittsfield (62363) ***(G-16636)***
Owens Corning Sales LLC....815 226-4627
2710 Laude Dr Rockford (61109) ***(G-17545)***
Owens Corning Sales LLC....708 594-6911
5824 S Archer Rd Argo (60501) ***(G-674)***
Owens Corning Sales LLC....708 594-6935
7800 W 59th St Argo (60501) ***(G-675)***
Owens-Brockway Glass Cont Inc....815 672-3141
901 N Shabbona St Streator (61364) ***(G-19619)***
Owens-Corning Fiberglass Tech....708 563-9091
7734 W 59th St Argo (60501) ***(G-676)***
Own The Night App....773 216-0245
1735 N Paulina St Apt 305 Chicago (60622) ***(G-5721)***
Owp Pharmaceuticals Inc....331 871-7424
400 E Diehl Rd Ste 400 # 400 Naperville (60563) ***(G-14890)***
Ox Paperboard LLC....309 346-4118
1525 S 2nd St Pekin (61554) ***(G-16348)***
Oxalo Therapeutics Inc....530 848-3499
1452 E 53rd St Fl 2 Chicago (60615) ***(G-5722)***
Oxbow Carbon LLC....630 257-7751
12308 New Ave Lemont (60439) ***(G-12576)***
Oxbow Midwest, Lemont *Also called Oxbow Carbon LLC* ***(G-12576)***
Oxbow Midwest Calcining LLC....630 257-7751
12308 New Ave Lemont (60439) ***(G-12577)***
Oxxford Clothes Xx Inc (HQ)....312 829-3600
5635 S Archer Ave Unit 2 Chicago (60638) ***(G-5723)***
OXY Chem, Sauget *Also called Occidental Chemical Corp* ***(G-18397)***
Oxytech Systems Inc....847 888-8611
852 Commerce Pkwy Carpentersville (60110) ***(G-3110)***
Ozark Industries, Elgin *Also called John Omalley* ***(G-8634)***
Ozcut Inc....630 605-7398
350 5th St Ste 266 Peru (61354) ***(G-16587)***
Ozinga Bros Inc (PA)....708 326-4200
19001 Old Lagrange Rd # 30 Mokena (60448) ***(G-14100)***
Ozinga Bros Inc....815 332-8198
990 Ecs Way Belvidere (61008) ***(G-1693)***
Ozinga Bros Inc....815 568-2589
9204 S Il Route 23 Marengo (60152) ***(G-13491)***
Ozinga Bros Inc....847 783-6500
30285 N Skokie Hwy Lake Bluff (60044) ***(G-12203)***
Ozinga Bros Inc....847 768-1697
200 Jarvis Ave Des Plaines (60018) ***(G-7816)***
Ozinga Bros Inc....847 783-6500
10500 S Il Route 31 Algonquin (60102) ***(G-383)***
Ozinga Bros Inc....708 326-4200
1750 State St Chicago Heights (60411) ***(G-6763)***
Ozinga Bros Inc....312 432-5700
2525 Oakton St Evanston (60202) ***(G-9564)***
Ozinga Chicago Ready Mix Con....708 479-9050
12660 S Laramie Ave Alsip (60803) ***(G-488)***
Ozinga Chicago Ready Mix Con....312 432-5700
1818 E 103rd St Chicago (60617) ***(G-5724)***
Ozinga Chicago Ready Mix Con....773 862-2817
2001 N Mendell St Chicago (60614) ***(G-5725)***
Ozinga Chicago Ready Mix Con (HQ)....847 447-0353
2255 S Lumber St Chicago (60616) ***(G-5726)***
Ozinga Concrete Products Inc....847 426-0920
2521 Tech Dr Ste 212 Elgin (60124) ***(G-8682)***
Ozinga Concrete Products Inc....708 479-9050
401 Brier Hill Rd Hampshire (60140) ***(G-10982)***
Ozinga Indiana Rdymx Con Inc....708 479-9050
19001 Old Lagrange Rd Mokena (60448) ***(G-14101)***
Ozinga Materials Inc (HQ)....309 364-3401
19001 Old Lagrange Rd Mokena (60448) ***(G-14102)***
Ozinga Ready Mix Concrete Inc....800 786-6382
11701 S Torrence Ave Chicago (60617) ***(G-5727)***
Ozinga Ready Mix Concrete Inc (PA)....708 326-4200
19001 Old Lagrange Rd # 300 Mokena (60448) ***(G-14103)***
Ozinga Rready Mix, Algonquin *Also called Ozinga Bros Inc* ***(G-383)***
Ozinga S Subn Rdymx Con Inc....708 479-3080
18825 Old Lagrange Rd Mokena (60448) ***(G-14104)***
Ozinga S Subn Rdymx Con Inc (HQ)....708 326-4201
19001 Old Lagrange Rd # 300 Mokena (60448) ***(G-14105)***
Ozinga South Suburban RMC, Mokena *Also called Ozinga S Subn Rdymx Con Inc* ***(G-14105)***
Ozonology Inc....847 998-8808
790 W Frontage Rd Ste 522 Northfield (60093) ***(G-15527)***
P & A Driveline & Machine Inc....630 860-7474
292 Devon Ave Ste 18 Bensenville (60106) ***(G-1865)***
P & D Center, Chicago *Also called Americas Community Bankers* ***(G-3675)***
P & D Sign Co....815 224-9220
1708 4th St Peru (61354) ***(G-16588)***
P & G Machine & Tool Inc....618 283-0273
1910 Illini Ave Vandalia (62471) ***(G-20018)***
P & G Machine Shop, Vandalia *Also called P & G Machine & Tool Inc* ***(G-20018)***
P & H Manufacturing Co....217 774-2123
604 S Lodge St Shelbyville (62565) ***(G-18882)***
P & H Pattern Inc....815 795-2449
225 Lincoln St Marseilles (61341) ***(G-13562)***
P & J Technologies....847 995-1108
1356 Saint Claire Pl Schaumburg (60173) ***(G-18661)***
P & L Mark-It Inc (PA)....630 879-7590
291 Oswald Ave Batavia (60510) ***(G-1402)***
P & L Tool & Manufacturing Co....708 754-4777
3624 Union Ave Steger (60475) ***(G-19491)***
P & M Ornamental Ir Works Inc....708 267-2868
1200 N 31st Ave Melrose Park (60160) ***(G-13901)***
P & P Artec Handrail Div, Wood Dale *Also called P & P Artec Inc* ***(G-21226)***
P & P Artec Inc (HQ)....630 860-2990
700 Creel Dr Wood Dale (60191) ***(G-21226)***
P & P Industries Inc (PA)....815 623-3297
2100 Enterprise Dr Sterling (61081) ***(G-19523)***
P & P Press Inc....309 691-8511
6513 N Galena Rd Peoria (61614) ***(G-16488)***
P & S Cochran Printers Inc (PA)....309 691-6668
8325 N Allen Rd Peoria (61615) ***(G-16489)***
P B A Corp....312 666-7370
522 N Western Ave Chicago (60612) ***(G-5728)***
P B R W Enterprises Inc....815 337-5519
12201 Baker Ter Woodstock (60098) ***(G-21418)***
P F Pettibone & Co....815 344-7811
2220 Il Route 176 Crystal Lake (60014) ***(G-7242)***
P H C Enterprises Inc....847 816-7373
222 Hawthorn Vlg Cmns Vernon Hills (60061) ***(G-20080)***
P I X, Chicago *Also called Printing Inc* ***(G-5881)***
P J Repair Service Inc....618 548-5690
108 S Missouri Ave Salem (62881) ***(G-18349)***
P K Neuses Incorporated....847 253-6555
1401 Rohlwing Rd Rolling Meadows (60008) ***(G-17758)***
P L R Sales Inc....217 733-2245
14187 N 850 E Rd Fairmount (61841) ***(G-9644)***
P M Armor Inc....847 797-9940
237 E Prospect Ave Mount Prospect (60056) ***(G-14557)***
P M C, Romeoville *Also called Precision McHned Cmponents Inc* ***(G-17866)***
P M C, Spring Grove *Also called Precision Molded Concepts* ***(G-19294)***
P M Mfg Services Inc....630 553-6924
9626 Lisbon Rd Yorkville (60560) ***(G-21496)***
P M P, Addison *Also called Precision Metal Products Inc* ***(G-251)***
P M S Consolidated....847 364-0011
2400 E Devon Ave Elk Grove Village (60007) ***(G-9166)***
P N K Ventures Inc....630 527-0500
1701 Quincy Ave Ste 24 Naperville (60540) ***(G-14891)***
P P G Mazer Chemicals Group, Gurnee *Also called PPG Industries Inc* ***(G-10913)***
P P Graphics Inc....708 343-2530
1939 S Mannheim Rd Westchester (60154) ***(G-20707)***
P R Manufacturing Co....309 596-2986
2650 85th Ave Viola (61486) ***(G-20181)***
P R S, Jacksonville *Also called Pallet Repair Systems Inc* ***(G-11780)***
P S A, Wauconda *Also called Professional Sales Associates* ***(G-20384)***
P S G, Franklin Park *Also called Prairie State Impressions LLC* ***(G-10023)***
P S Greetings Inc (PA)....708 831-5340
5730 N Tripp Ave Chicago (60646) ***(G-5729)***
P S Greetings Inc....847 673-7255
4901 Main St Skokie (60077) ***(G-19002)***
P T L Manufacturing Inc....618 277-6789
101 Industrial Dr Belleville (62220) ***(G-1582)***
P W C, Schaumburg *Also called Prime Wood Craft Inc* ***(G-18683)***
P W C E, Goodfield *Also called Paul Wever Construction Eqp Co* ***(G-10676)***
P&L Group Ltd of Illinois....833 362-2100
24 E 107th St Chicago (60628) ***(G-5730)***
P-Americas LLC....217 446-0123
211 S Bowman Ave Danville (61832) ***(G-7371)***
P-Americas LLC....847 437-1520
1500 Touhy Ave Elk Grove Village (60007) ***(G-9167)***

P-Americas LLC ... 773 893-2300
1400 W 35th St Chicago (60609) ***(G-5731)***
P-Americas LLC ... 815 939-3123
1525 S Schuyler Ave Kankakee (60901) ***(G-11996)***
P-Americas LLC ... 309 266-2400
801 W Birchwood St Morton (61550) ***(G-14375)***
P-Americas LLC ... 312 821-2266
555 W Monroe St Fl 1 Chicago (60661) ***(G-5732)***
P-Americas LLC ... 773 624-8013
650 W 51st St Chicago (60609) ***(G-5733)***
P-S Business Acquisition Inc ... 616 887-8837
246 Kehoe Blvd Carol Stream (60188) ***(G-3044)***
P.F., Crystal Lake *Also called P F Pettibone & Co* ***(G-7242)***
P.N.a Construction Tech, Itasca *Also called PNa Construction Tech Inc* ***(G-11720)***
P.V.S. Manufacturing Div, Woodstock *Also called Vorteq Woodstock LLC* ***(G-21445)***
Paani Foods Inc ... 312 420-4624
6167 N Broadway St # 300 Chicago (60660) ***(G-5734)***
Paap Printing ... 217 345-6878
507 Jackson Ave Charleston (61920) ***(G-3409)***
Pac Partners LLC ... 773 315-0828
1815 W Berteau Ave Chicago (60613) ***(G-5735)***
Pac Team US Productions LLC ... 773 360-8960
4447 W Armitage Ave Chicago (60639) ***(G-5736)***
Pac-Clad Metal Roofing, Elk Grove Village *Also called Petersen Aluminum Corporation* ***(G-9176)***
Pace Foundation ... 309 691-3553
3528 W Chartwell Rd Peoria (61614) ***(G-16490)***
Pace Industries Inc (PA) ... 312 226-5500
2545 W Polk St Chicago (60612) ***(G-5737)***
Pace Machinery Group Inc ... 630 377-1750
4n944 Old Lafox Rd Wasco (60183) ***(G-20261)***
Pace Print Plus ... 847 381-1720
1010 W Northwest Hwy Barrington (60010) ***(G-1233)***
Pacific Bearing Corp (PA) ... 815 389-5600
6402 E Rockton Rd Roscoe (61073) ***(G-17921)***
Pacific Custom Components Corp ... 815 206-5450
10200 Us Highway 14 Woodstock (60098) ***(G-21419)***
Pacific Cycle Inc ... 618 393-2508
4730 E Radio Tower Ln Olney (62450) ***(G-15882)***
Pacific Ethanol Canton LLC ... 309 347-9200
1300 S 2nd St Pekin (61554) ***(G-16349)***
Pacific Ethanol Pekin LLC ... 309 347-9200
1300 S 2nd St Pekin (61554) ***(G-16350)***
Pacific Granites Inc ... 312 835-7777
17 N State St Ste 1585 Chicago (60602) ***(G-5738)***
Pacific Press, Mount Carmel *Also called Ppt Industrial Machines Inc* ***(G-14485)***
Pacific Press Technologies, Mount Carmel *Also called Ceg Subsidiary LLC* ***(G-14467)***
Packaging By Design, Elgin *Also called Bellen Container Corporation* ***(G-8520)***
Packaging Corporation America ... 847 388-6000
250 S Shaddle Ave Mundelein (60060) ***(G-14722)***
Packaging Corporation America ... 224 404-6616
25 Northwest Point Blvd Elk Grove Village (60007) ***(G-9168)***
Packaging Corporation America (PA) ... 847 482-3000
1 N Field Ct Lake Forest (60045) ***(G-12277)***
Packaging Corporation America ... 708 821-1600
5445 W 73rd St Chicago (60638) ***(G-5739)***
Packaging Corporation America ... 773 378-8700
5230 W Roosevelt Rd Chicago (60644) ***(G-5740)***
Packaging Corporation America ... 708 594-5260
5555 W 73rd St Bedford Park (60638) ***(G-1489)***
Packaging Corporation America ... 618 662-6700
32 Industrial Park Flora (62839) ***(G-9687)***
Packaging Design Corporation ... 630 323-1354
101 Shore Dr Burr Ridge (60527) ***(G-2712)***
Packaging Dynamics, Chicago *Also called Bagcraftpapercon I LLC* ***(G-3814)***
Packaging Personified, Carol Stream *Also called P-S Business Acquisition Inc* ***(G-3044)***
Packaging Printing Specialists, Saint Charles *Also called Labels & Specialty Pdts LLC* ***(G-18223)***
Packaging Systems, Romeoville *Also called Rapak LLC* ***(G-17868)***
Packaging World ... 305 448-6875
330 N Wabash Ave Ste 2401 Chicago (60611) ***(G-5741)***
Packet, Chicago *Also called Paket Corporation* ***(G-5743)***
Packpors, Chicago *Also called Kodiak LLC* ***(G-5116)***
Paco Corporation ... 708 430-2424
9945 Industrial Dr Bridgeview (60455) ***(G-2371)***
PAcrimson Fire Risk Svcs Inc ... 630 424-3400
920 N Ridge Ave Ste C2 Lombard (60148) ***(G-13115)***
Pactiv Intl Holdings Inc (HQ) ... 847 482-2000
1900 W Field Ct Lake Forest (60045) ***(G-12278)***
Pactiv LLC (HQ) ... 847 482-2000
1900 W Field Ct Lake Forest (60045) ***(G-12279)***
Pactiv LLC ... 219 924-4120
1900 W Field Ct Lake Forest (60045) ***(G-12280)***
Pactiv LLC ... 847 482-2000
1900 W Field Ct Lake Forest (60045) ***(G-12281)***
Pactiv LLC ... 708 924-2402
7701 W 79th St Bridgeview (60455) ***(G-2372)***
Pactiv LLC ... 815 469-2112
437 Center Rd Frankfort (60423) ***(G-9819)***
Pactiv LLC ... 630 262-6335
315 Kirk Rd Saint Charles (60174) ***(G-18241)***
Pactiv LLC ... 217 479-1144
2230 E Morton Ave Jacksonville (62650) ***(G-11779)***
Pactiv LLC ... 847 459-8049
777 Wheeling Rd Wheeling (60090) ***(G-20953)***
Pactiv LLC ... 708 496-2900
7207 S Mason Ave Bedford Park (60638) ***(G-1490)***
Pactiv LLC ... 708 496-2900
7200 S Mason Ave Chicago (60638) ***(G-5742)***
Pactiv Molded Products, Lake Forest *Also called Pactiv LLC* ***(G-12280)***
Pactra Corp ... 847 281-0308
2112 Beaver Creek Dr Vernon Hills (60061) ***(G-20081)***
Paddlewheel The, Havana *Also called James G Carter* ***(G-11115)***
Paddock Industries Inc ... 618 277-1580
306 N Main St Smithton (62285) ***(G-19068)***
Paddock Publications Inc (PA) ... 847 427-4300
95 W Algonquin Rd Ste 300 Arlington Heights (60005) ***(G-786)***
Paddock Publications Inc ... 847 608-2700
385 Airport Rd Ste A Elgin (60123) ***(G-8683)***
Paddock Publications Inc ... 847 427-5545
1000 Albion Ave Schaumburg (60193) ***(G-18662)***
Paddock Publications Inc ... 847 680-5800
1795 N Butterfield Rd # 100 Libertyville (60048) ***(G-12693)***
Padma's Plantation, Batavia *Also called Urban Home Furniture & ACC Inc* ***(G-1438)***
Pafco Truck Bodies Inc ... 309 699-4613
1954 E Washington St East Peoria (61611) ***(G-8281)***
Pagepath Technologies Inc ... 630 689-4111
13 E Main St Plano (60545) ***(G-16738)***
Painted Quarter Ridge ... 618 534-9734
948 Possom Rd Ava (62907) ***(G-1176)***
Pak Source Inc ... 309 786-7374
690 Mill St Rock Island (61201) ***(G-17231)***
Paket Corporation ... 773 221-7300
9165 S Lake Shore Dr Chicago (60617) ***(G-5743)***
Pakistan News ... 773 271-6400
6033 N Sheridan Rd Chicago (60660) ***(G-5744)***
Pal Health Technologies Inc ... 309 347-8785
1805 Riverway Dr Pekin (61554) ***(G-16351)***
Pal Health Technologies II, Pekin *Also called PR Manufacturing Entps LLC* ***(G-16354)***
Pal Midwest Ltd (PA) ... 815 965-2981
1030 S Main St Rockford (61101) ***(G-17546)***
Paladin, Oak Brook *Also called Jrb Attachments LLC* ***(G-15628)***
Paladin Brands International H ... 319 378-3696
2211 York Rd Ste 320 Oak Brook (60523) ***(G-15655)***
Palaestra, Macomb *Also called Challenge Publications L T D* ***(G-13388)***
Palapa Coatings Inc ... 847 628-6360
325 Corporate Dr Elgin (60123) ***(G-8684)***
Palatine Welding Company ... 847 358-1075
3848 Berdnick St Rolling Meadows (60008) ***(G-17759)***
Paldo Sign and Display Company ... 708 456-1711
8110 Grand Ave River Grove (60171) ***(G-17065)***
Paleo Prime LLC ... 312 659-6596
2425 W Gnnison St Chicago Chicago (60625) ***(G-5745)***
Paleteria Azteca 2, Chicago *Also called Paleteria Azteca Inc* ***(G-5746)***
Paleteria Azteca Inc ... 773 277-1423
3119 W Cermak Rd Chicago (60623) ***(G-5746)***
Paleteria Carrucel ... 773 310-5749
6317 W Grand Ave Chicago (60639) ***(G-5747)***
Paleteria El Sabor ... 312 243-2308
1639 W 18th St Chicago (60608) ***(G-5748)***
Paleteria El Sabor De Michoacn ... 773 376-3880
2456 W 47th St Chicago (60632) ***(G-5749)***
Palladium Energy Group Inc (HQ) ... 630 410-7900
1200 Internationale Pkwy # 101 Woodridge (60517) ***(G-21330)***
Pallet Repair Systems Inc ... 217 291-0009
2 Eastgate Dr Jacksonville (62650) ***(G-11780)***
Pallet Sales and Recycling ... 314 452-5175
1200 Thistle St Venice (62090) ***(G-20035)***
Pallet Services Inc ... 630 860-9233
13 Brookwood St Bensenville (60106) ***(G-1866)***
Pallet Solution ... 773 837-8677
205 S Bartlett Rd Streamwood (60107) ***(G-19588)***
Pallet Solution Inc ... 618 445-2316
Hwy 130 N Albion (62806) ***(G-351)***
Pallet Wrapz ... 847 729-5850
2009 Johns Dr Glenview (60025) ***(G-10597)***
Pallet Wrapz Inc ... 847 729-5850
2009 Johns Dr Glenview (60025) ***(G-10598)***
Palletmaxx Inc ... 708 385-9595
4818 137th St Ste 1 Crestwood (60418) ***(G-7124)***
Pallets International Holding ... 773 391-7223
500 W Armory Dr South Holland (60473) ***(G-19236)***
Pallets Plus Inc ... 847 318-1853
1000 Cedar St Park Ridge (60068) ***(G-16291)***
Palm International Inc (PA) ... 630 357-1437
1159 Palmetto Ct Ste B Naperville (60540) ***(G-14892)***

ALPHABETIC

Palmyra Modesto Water Comm....217 436-2519
9934 Water Plant Rd Palmyra (62674) ***(G-16180)***
Paltech Enterprises Illinois, Belvidere *Also called M & M Paltech Inc* ***(G-1681)***
Palwaukee Printing Company....847 459-0240
1684 S Wolf Rd Wheeling (60090) ***(G-20954)***
Pam Printers and Publs Inc (PA)....217 222-4030
1012 Vermont St Quincy (62301) ***(G-16922)***
Pamacheyon Publishing Inc....815 395-0101
305 Saint Louis Ave Rockford (61104) ***(G-17547)***
Pamarco Global Graphics Inc....630 879-7300
125 Flinn St Batavia (60510) ***(G-1403)***
Pamarco Global Graphics Inc....847 459-6000
171 E Marquardt Dr Wheeling (60090) ***(G-20955)***
Pamco Printed Tape Label Inc (HQ)....847 803-2200
2200 S Wolf Rd Des Plaines (60018) ***(G-7817)***
Pan America Environmental Inc....815 344-2960
2309 N Ringwood Rd Ste G McHenry (60050) ***(G-13775)***
Pan American Screw Div, Chicago *Also called Marmon Group LLC* ***(G-5342)***
Pan Pac International Inc....847 222-9077
3456 N Ridge Ave Ste 300 Arlington Heights (60004) ***(G-787)***
Pana Limestone Company....217 562-4231
325 N 1600 East Rd Pana (62557) ***(G-16219)***
Pana Monument Co (PA)....217 562-5121
2 N Poplar St Pana (62557) ***(G-16220)***
Pana News Inc (PA)....217 562-2111
205 S Locust St Pana (62557) ***(G-16221)***
Pana News Palladium, Pana *Also called Pana News Inc* ***(G-16221)***
Panache Editions Ltd....847 921-8574
234 Dennis Ln Glencoe (60022) ***(G-10433)***
Panatech Computer Management....847 678-8848
250 Parkway Dr Ste 150 Lincolnshire (60069) ***(G-12789)***
Panatrol Corporation....630 655-4700
161 Tower Dr Ste D Burr Ridge (60527) ***(G-2713)***
Pancon Illinois LLC....630 972-6400
440 Quadrangle Dr Ste A Bolingbrook (60440) ***(G-2224)***
Panda Marketing Group Inc....847 383-5270
451 N Racine Ave Chicago (60642) ***(G-5750)***
Panduit Corp (PA)....708 532-1800
18900 Panduit Dr Tinley Park (60487) ***(G-19848)***
Panduit Corp....815 836-1800
16530 W 163rd St Lockport (60441) ***(G-13018)***
Panek Precision Products Co....847 291-9755
455 Academy Dr Northbrook (60062) ***(G-15451)***
Panel Authority Inc....815 838-0488
24121 W Theodore St Ste 1 Plainfield (60586) ***(G-16699)***
Panelshopnet Inc....630 692-0214
3460 Ohara Ter Naperville (60564) ***(G-14982)***
Panhandle Eastrn Pipe Line LP....217 753-1108
1801 Business Park Dr Springfield (62703) ***(G-19419)***
Pantagraph Printing and Sty Co (PA)....309 829-1071
217 W Jefferson St Bloomington (61701) ***(G-2084)***
Pantagraph Publishing Co....309 451-0006
2551 W College Ave Normal (61761) ***(G-15216)***
Pantagraph Publishing Co (PA)....309 829-9000
301 W Washington St Bloomington (61701) ***(G-2085)***
Panther Products....618 664-1071
102 W Main St Greenville (62246) ***(G-10841)***
Panthervision, West Dundee *Also called Waters Industries Inc* ***(G-20667)***
Panzer Tool Corp....630 519-5214
920 N Ridge Ave Ste A2 Lombard (60148) ***(G-13116)***
Paoli Inc....312 644-5509
222 Merchandise Mart Plz # 380 Chicago (60654) ***(G-5751)***
Paoli, Stephen International, Rockford *Also called Stephen Paoli Mfg Corp* ***(G-17646)***
Pap-R Products Company (PA)....800 637-4937
1 Harry Glynn Dr Martinsville (62442) ***(G-13587)***
Pap-R-Tainer LLC....217 382-4141
1 Harry Glynn Dr Martinsville (62442) ***(G-13588)***
Papa Charlies Inc....773 522-7900
1800 S Kostner Ave Chicago (60623) ***(G-5752)***
Paper....815 584-1901
204 E Chippewa St Dwight (60420) ***(G-8157)***
Paper Graphics Inc....847 276-2727
612 Heathrow Dr Lincolnshire (60069) ***(G-12790)***
Paper Investments LLC (PA)....309 686-3830
1 Sloan St Peoria (61603) ***(G-16491)***
Paper Investments of Illinois, Peoria *Also called Paper Investments LLC* ***(G-16491)***
Paper Machine Services Inc....608 365-8095
7283 Barngate Dr South Beloit (61080) ***(G-19106)***
Paper Moon Recycling Inc....847 548-8875
123 Bluff Ave Grayslake (60030) ***(G-10795)***
Paper or Plastic Inc....815 582-3696
850 Brookforest Ave F Shorewood (60404) ***(G-18898)***
Paper Spot....815 464-8533
11 S White St Ste 201 Frankfort (60423) ***(G-9820)***
Paper Tube LLC....847 477-0563
971 N Milwaukee Ave # 22 Wheeling (60090) ***(G-20956)***
Paper, The, Barry *Also called Debbie Harshman* ***(G-1249)***
Paperworks....630 969-3218
904 62nd St Downers Grove (60516) ***(G-8069)***
Papiros Graphics....773 581-3000
4557 W 59th St Chicago (60629) ***(G-5753)***
Papmpered Pups....815 782-8383
2011 Essington Rd Joliet (60435) ***(G-11912)***
Pappas & Pappas Enterprises, Saint Charles *Also called Form Plastics Company* ***(G-18203)***
Pappone Inc....630 234-4738
2041 W Carroll Ave C214 Chicago (60612) ***(G-5754)***
Papyrus Press Inc....773 342-0700
3441 W Grand Ave Chicago (60651) ***(G-5755)***
Papys Foods Inc....815 385-3313
4131 W Albany St McHenry (60050) ***(G-13776)***
Par Fabricating Co, Blue Island *Also called J & G Fabricating Inc* ***(G-2126)***
Par Golf Supply Inc....847 891-1222
550 Pratt Ave N Schaumburg (60193) ***(G-18663)***
Parade Magazine, Chicago *Also called Parade Publications Inc* ***(G-5756)***
Parade Publications Inc....312 661-1620
500 N Michigan Ave # 910 Chicago (60611) ***(G-5756)***
Paradigm Coatings LLC....847 961-6466
11259 Kiley Dr Huntley (60142) ***(G-11557)***
Paradigm Development Group Inc....847 545-9600
27 W 230 Becher Ave Ste 2 Winfield (60190) ***(G-21114)***
Paradise Group LLC....779 207-9077
67 E Madison St Ste 1603a Chicago (60603) ***(G-5757)***
Paragon International Inc....847 240-2981
1901 N Roselle Rd Ste 711 Schaumburg (60195) ***(G-18664)***
Paragon Manufacturing Inc....708 345-1717
2001 N 15th Ave Melrose Park (60160) ***(G-13902)***
Paragon Mill & Casework Inc....815 388-7453
2819 Jenny Jae Ln Crystal Lake (60012) ***(G-7243)***
Paragon Oil Company Inc....618 244-5541
1726 Broadway St Ste B Mount Vernon (62864) ***(G-14632)***
Paragon Packaging Inc (PA)....707 786-4004
1201 S Prrie Ave Apt 2801 Chicago (60605) ***(G-5758)***
Paragon Print & Mail Prod Inc....630 671-2222
109 Fairfield Way Ste 202 Bloomingdale (60108) ***(G-2006)***
Paragon Spring Company....773 489-6300
4435 W Rice St Ste 45 Chicago (60651) ***(G-5759)***
Paragon Valuation Group, Schaumburg *Also called Paragon International Inc* ***(G-18664)***
Parallel Machine Products Inc....847 359-1012
255 N Woodwork Ln Palatine (60067) ***(G-16148)***
Parallel Solutions LLC....847 708-9227
1251 N Plum Grove Rd # 160 Schaumburg (60173) ***(G-18665)***
Paralleldirect LLC....847 748-2025
103 Schelter Rd Ste 20 Lincolnshire (60069) ***(G-12791)***
Paramount Laminates Inc....630 594-1840
907 N Central Ave Wood Dale (60191) ***(G-21227)***
Paramount Plastics Inc....815 834-4100
140 S Dearborn St Ste 420 Chicago (60603) ***(G-5760)***
Paramount Plastics LLC....815 834-4100
140 S Dearborn St Ste 420 Chicago (60603) ***(G-5761)***
Paramount Sintered Pdts LLP....847 746-8866
1717 Kenosha Rd Zion (60099) ***(G-21524)***
Paramount Truck Body Co Inc....312 666-6441
4929 S Mason Ave Chicago (60638) ***(G-5762)***
Paratech Incorporated (PA)....815 469-3911
1025 Lambrecht Dr Frankfort (60423) ***(G-9821)***
Parathon Recovery Service LLC....630 689-0450
1415 W Diehl Rd Ste 200n Naperville (60563) ***(G-14893)***
Parenti & Raffaelli Ltd....847 253-5550
215 E Prospect Ave Mount Prospect (60056) ***(G-14558)***
Parenti and Raffaelli Ltd....847 204-8116
1401 Feehanville Dr Mount Prospect (60056) ***(G-14559)***
Paris Frozen Foods Inc....217 532-3822
305 Springfield Rd Hillsboro (62049) ***(G-11318)***
Paris Frozen Foods Locker, Hillsboro *Also called Paris Frozen Foods Inc* ***(G-11318)***
Paris Machine & Welding....217 463-2894
13005 Illinois Hwy 133 Paris (61944) ***(G-16238)***
Paris Metal Products LLC....217 465-6321
13571 Il Highway 133 Paris (61944) ***(G-16239)***
Pariso Inc....773 889-4383
1836 N Lockwood Ave Chicago (60639) ***(G-5763)***
Park Electric Motor Service....217 442-1977
1204 N Collett St Danville (61832) ***(G-7372)***
Park Engineering Inc....847 455-1424
9227 Parklane Ave Franklin Park (60131) ***(G-10013)***
Park Industries, Melrose Park *Also called Park Manufacturing Corp Inc* ***(G-13903)***
Park It Bike Racks Company, Batavia *Also called Treetop Marketing Inc* ***(G-1433)***
Park Lawn Association Inc....708 425-7377
5040 W 111th St Oak Lawn (60453) ***(G-15731)***
Park License Service Inc....815 633-5511
6402 N 2nd St Loves Park (61111) ***(G-13243)***
Park Manufacturing Corp Inc....708 345-6090
1819 N 30th Ave Melrose Park (60160) ***(G-13903)***
Park Packing Company Inc....773 254-0100
4107 S Ashland Ave Chicago (60609) ***(G-5764)***
Park Press, South Holland *Also called KB Publishing Inc* ***(G-19226)***
Park Press Inc....708 331-6352
930 E 162nd St South Holland (60473) ***(G-19237)***

ALPHABETIC SECTION
Payne Chauna

Park Printing Inc (PA) 708 430-4878
9903 S Roberts Rd Palos Hills (60465) ***(G-16203)***

Park Products Inc 630 543-2474
409 W Kay Ave Addison (60101) ***(G-233)***

Park View Manufacturing Corp 618 548-9054
2510 S Broadway Ave Salem (62881) ***(G-18350)***

Park-Hio Frged McHned Pdts LLC 708 652-6691
5301 W Roosevelt Rd Chicago (60804) ***(G-5765)***

Park-Ohio Industries Inc 708 652-6691
5301 W Roosevelt Rd Chicago (60804) ***(G-5766)***

Parke & Son Inc 217 875-0572
3523 Rupp Pkwy Decatur (62526) ***(G-7535)***

Parker Fabrication Inc 309 698-8080
3700 N Main St East Peoria (61611) ***(G-8282)***

Parker Fabrication Inc (PA) 309 266-8413
501 E Courtland St Morton (61550) ***(G-14376)***

Parker Hnnfin Elctrnic Contrls, Morton *Also called Parker-Hannifin Corporation* ***(G-14377)***

Parker International Pdts Inc 815 524-5831
650 Forest Edge Dr Vernon Hills (60061) ***(G-20082)***

Parker Metal, Vernon Hills *Also called Parker International Pdts Inc* ***(G-20082)***

Parker Systems Inc 847 726-8600
20989 N Middleton Dr Kildeer (60047) ***(G-12051)***

Parker Tool & Die Co 847 566-2229
20844 W Park Ave Mundelein (60060) ***(G-14723)***

Parker-Hannifin Corporation 216 896-3000
7939 Collection Center Dr Chicago (60693) ***(G-5767)***

Parker-Hannifin Corporation 847 258-6200
850 Arthur Ave Elk Grove Village (60007) ***(G-9169)***

Parker-Hannifin Corporation 847 836-6859
2565 Northwest Pkwy Elgin (60124) ***(G-8685)***

Parker-Hannifin Corporation 708 681-6300
2445 S 25th Ave Broadview (60155) ***(G-2457)***

Parker-Hannifin Corporation 815 636-4100
10711 N 2nd St Machesney Park (61115) ***(G-13362)***

Parker-Hannifin Corporation 847 955-5000
595 Schelter Rd Ste 100 Lincolnshire (60069) ***(G-12792)***

Parker-Hannifin Corporation 630 427-2020
10625 Beaudin Blvd Woodridge (60517) ***(G-21331)***

Parker-Hannifin Corporation 309 266-2200
1651 N Main St Morton (61550) ***(G-14377)***

Parking Systems Inc 847 891-3819
911 Estes Ct Schaumburg (60193) ***(G-18666)***

Parks Industries LLC 618 997-9608
15460 Crabtree School Rd Marion (62959) ***(G-13524)***

Parkway Metal Products Inc 847 789-4000
130 Rawls Rd Des Plaines (60018) ***(G-7818)***

Parkway Printers 217 525-2485
3755 N Dirksen Pkwy Springfield (62707) ***(G-19420)***

Parr Instrument Company (PA) 309 762-7716
211 53rd St Moline (61265) ***(G-14165)***

Parrot Press 773 376-6333
4484 S Archer Ave Chicago (60632) ***(G-5768)***

Parrott and Assoc Formerly, Bloomington *Also called Five Brother Inc* ***(G-2043)***

Parsonics Corp 815 338-6509
935 Dieckman St Ste A Woodstock (60098) ***(G-21420)***

Parsons Company Inc 309 467-9100
1386 State Route 117 Roanoke (61561) ***(G-17104)***

Part Stop Inc 618 377-5238
5120 State Route 140 Bethalto (62010) ***(G-1965)***

Partec Inc 847 678-9520
9301 Belmont Ave Franklin Park (60131) ***(G-10014)***

Partex Marking Systems Inc 630 516-0400
1155 N Main St Lombard (60148) ***(G-13117)***

Parth Consultants Inc 847 758-1400
2385 Hammond Dr Ste 9 Schaumburg (60173) ***(G-18667)***

Parting Line Tool Inc 847 669-0331
11915 Smith Ct Huntley (60142) ***(G-11558)***

Partners Manufacturing Inc 847 352-1080
625 Lunt Ave Schaumburg (60193) ***(G-18668)***

Partners Resource Inc 630 620-9161
831 Woodland Dr Glen Ellyn (60137) ***(G-10417)***

Parts Specialists Inc 708 371-2444
14639 S Short St Posen (60469) ***(G-16800)***

Partscription, Oak Park *Also called Kap Holdings LLC* ***(G-15759)***

Parvin-Clauss Sign Co Inc 866 490-2877
165 Tubeway Dr Carol Stream (60188) ***(G-3045)***

Passco Parts & Electronics, Lansing *Also called Bedford Rakim* ***(G-12485)***

Passion Fruit Drink Inc 708 769-4749
17335 Sterling Ct South Holland (60473) ***(G-19238)***

Pasta Pappone, Chicago *Also called Pappone Inc* ***(G-5754)***

Pastafresh Co 773 745-5888
3418 N Harlem Ave Chicago (60634) ***(G-5769)***

Pastafresh Homemade Pasta, Chicago *Also called Pastafresh Co* ***(G-5769)***

Pastorelli Food Products Inc 312 455-1006
901 W Lake St Chicago (60607) ***(G-5770)***

Pat 24 Inc 708 336-8671
7107 W 79th St Burbank (60459) ***(G-2637)***

Pate Company Inc 630 705-1920
245 Eisenhower Ln S Lombard (60148) ***(G-13118)***

Patel Dishaben 312 880-8746
57 Bright Ridge Dr Schaumburg (60194) ***(G-18669)***

Patientbond LLC 312 445-8751
126 N York St Ste 2 Elmhurst (60126) ***(G-9408)***

Patio Plus 815 433-2399
1624 W Main St Ottawa (61350) ***(G-16070)***

Patko Tool & Manufacturing 630 616-8802
767 Larsen Ct Bensenville (60106) ***(G-1867)***

Patkus Machine Co 815 398-7818
2607 Marshall St Rockford (61109) ***(G-17548)***

Patlin Enterprises Inc 815 675-6606
2907 N Us Highway 12 Spring Grove (60081) ***(G-19292)***

Patricia Jenkins 224 436-7547
40 Washington Cir Lake Forest (60045) ***(G-12282)***

Patrick Cabinetry Inc 630 307-9333
192 Ring Neck Ln Bloomingdale (60108) ***(G-2007)***

Patrick Holdings Inc (PA) 815 874-5300
5894 Sandy Hollow Rd Rockford (61109) ***(G-17549)***

Patrick Impressions LLC 630 257-9336
16135 New Ave Ste 1a Lemont (60439) ***(G-12578)***

Patrick Industries Inc 630 595-0595
1077 Sesame St Franklin Park (60131) ***(G-10015)***

Patrick Manufacturing Inc 847 697-5920
667 N State St Elgin (60123) ***(G-8686)***

Patrin Pharma Inc 800 936-3088
7817 Babb Ave Skokie (60077) ***(G-19003)***

Patriot Fuels Biodiesel LLC 309 935-5700
101 Patriot Way Annawan (61234) ***(G-591)***

Patriot Materials LLC 630 501-0260
750 N Industrial Dr Elmhurst (60126) ***(G-9409)***

Patriot Renewable Fuels LLC 309 935-5700
101 Patriot Way Annawan (61234) ***(G-592)***

Patt Supply Corporation 708 442-3901
8111 47th St Lyons (60534) ***(G-13312)***

Patterson Avenue Tool Company 847 949-8100
6515 High Meadow Ct Long Grove (60047) ***(G-13169)***

Patterson Products 618 723-2688
580 E Antioch Ln Noble (62868) ***(G-15191)***

Patterson Promotions & Prtg 708 430-0224
9208 S Oketo Ave Bridgeview (60455) ***(G-2373)***

Patti Group Incorporated (PA) 630 243-6320
12301 New Ave Ste A Lemont (60439) ***(G-12579)***

Patton Printing and Graphics 217 347-0220
902 W Wabash Ave B Effingham (62401) ***(G-8417)***

Patty Style Shop 618 654-2015
621 Broadway Apt 1 Highland (62249) ***(G-11234)***

Patty's Style Shop, Highland *Also called Patty Style Shop* ***(G-11234)***

Paul & Ron Manufacturing Inc 309 596-2986
2650 85th Ave Viola (61486) ***(G-20182)***

Paul D Burton 309 467-2613
124 N Main St Eureka (61530) ***(G-9484)***

Paul D Metal Products Inc 773 847-1400
2225 W Pershing Rd Chicago (60609) ***(G-5771)***

Paul D Stark & Associates (PA) 630 964-7111
509 Blackburn Ct Downers Grove (60516) ***(G-8070)***

Paul Sisti 773 472-5615
3520 N Lake Shore Dr Chicago (60657) ***(G-5772)***

Paul Sisti Studio, Chicago *Also called Paul Sisti* ***(G-5772)***

Paul Wever Construction Eqp Co 309 965-2005
401 W Martin Dr Goodfield (61742) ***(G-10676)***

Paulette Colson 618 372-8888
518 S Main St Medora (62063) ***(G-13815)***

Paulmar Industries Inc 847 395-2520
39804 N Stonebridge Ct Antioch (60002) ***(G-629)***

Pauls Machine & Welding Corp (PA) 217 832-2541
650 N Sycamore St Villa Grove (61956) ***(G-20125)***

Paulson Press Inc 847 290-0080
904 Cambridge Dr Elk Grove Village (60007) ***(G-9170)***

Paulson's Litho, Elk Grove Village *Also called Paulson Press Inc* ***(G-9170)***

Paveloc Industries Inc 815 568-4700
8302 S Il Route 23 Marengo (60152) ***(G-13492)***

Paver Protector Inc 630 488-0069
57 Railroad St 171 Gilberts (60136) ***(G-10364)***

Paw Office Machines Inc 815 363-9780
816 Madison Ave McHenry (60050) ***(G-13777)***

Pawnee Oil Corporation 217 522-5440
1204 N 5th St Springfield (62702) ***(G-19421)***

Pawz & Klawz 630 257-0245
12263 Walker Rd Lemont (60439) ***(G-12580)***

Paxton Packing LLC 623 707-5604
145 W State St Paxton (60957) ***(G-16312)***

Paxton Ready Mix Inc 217 379-2303
745 N Market St Paxton (60957) ***(G-16313)***

Paylocity Holding Corporation (PA) 847 463-3200
1400 American Ln Schaumburg (60173) ***(G-18670)***

Paylocity Holding Corporation 331 701-7975
27w675 South Ln Naperville (60540) ***(G-14894)***

Payne Chauna 618 580-2584
333 Longview Dr Belleville (62223) ***(G-1583)***

ALPHABETIC

ALPHABETIC SECTION

Payson Casters Inc 847 336-5033
2335 N Delany Rd Gurnee (60031) *(G-10910)*

Pbc Linear, Roscoe Also called Pacific Bearing Corp *(G-17921)*

Pbi Redi Mix & Trucking 217 562-3717
2 N Walnut St Pana (62557) *(G-16222)*

Pc-Tel Inc (PA) 630 372-6800
471 Brighton Ct Bloomingdale (60108) *(G-2008)*

PCA, Lake Forest Also called Packaging Corporation America *(G-12277)*

PCA, Chicago Also called Packaging Corporation America *(G-5740)*

PCA, Flora Also called Packaging Corporation America *(G-9687)*

PCA Central Cal Corrugated LLC (HQ) 847 482-3000
1955 W Field Ct Lake Forest (60045) *(G-12283)*

PCA Chicago Container, Chicago Also called Packaging Corporation America *(G-5739)*

PCA Corrugated and Display LLC (HQ) 847 482-3000
1955 W Field Ct Lake Forest (60045) *(G-12284)*

PCA International Inc (HQ) 847 482-3000
1955 W Field Ct Lake Forest (60045) *(G-12285)*

PCA Tech Center, Mundelein Also called Packaging Corporation America *(G-14722)*

Pcb Express Inc 847 952-8896
600 E Higgins Rd Ste 2c Elk Grove Village (60007) *(G-9171)*

Pcbl Retail Holdings LLC 610 761-4838
5 Revere Dr Ste 206 Northbrook (60062) *(G-15452)*

PCC, Urbana Also called Plastic Container Corporation *(G-19993)*

Pcc Inc (HQ) 708 868-3800
14201 Paxton Ave Calumet City (60409) *(G-2785)*

Pcj II Inc (HQ) 312 829-2250
1143 W Lake St Chicago (60607) *(G-5773)*

Pcnation, Northfield Also called Officenation Inc *(G-15525)*

Pcr Machining, Broadview Also called Precision Cnncting Rod Svc Inc *(G-2458)*

Pcs Nitrogen Inc (HQ) 847 849-4200
1101 Skokie Blvd Ste 400 Northbrook (60062) *(G-15453)*

Pcs Nitrogen Fertilizer LP 847 849-4200
1101 Skokie Blvd Ste 500 Northbrook (60062) *(G-15454)*

Pcs Nitrogen Trinidad Corp 847 849-4200
1101 Skokie Blvd Ste 400 Northbrook (60062) *(G-15455)*

Pcs Ntrgen Frtlzer Oprtons Inc (HQ) 847 849-4200
1101 Skokie Blvd Ste 400 Northbrook (60062) *(G-15456)*

Pcs Phosphate Company Inc (HQ) 847 849-4200
1101 Skokie Blvd Ste 400 Northbrook (60062) *(G-15457)*

Pcs Phosphate Company Inc 815 795-5111
2660 E Us Highway 6 Marseilles (61341) *(G-13563)*

Pcs Sales, Northbrook Also called Pcs Phosphate Company Inc *(G-15457)*

Pdi, Lake Zurich Also called Performance Design Inc *(G-12443)*

Pdoc LLC (HQ) 773 843-8000
3900 W 43rd St Chicago (60632) *(G-5774)*

PDQ Machine Inc 815 282-7575
7909b Burden Rd Ste B Machesney Park (61115) *(G-13363)*

PDQ Tool & Stamping Co 708 841-3000
14901 Greenwood Rd Dolton (60419) *(G-7938)*

Pdss Construction 847 980-6090
7516 Davis St Morton Grove (60053) *(G-14431)*

Pdv Midwest Refining LLC 630 257-7761
135th St New Ave Lemont (60439) *(G-12581)*

Peabody Coal Company 618 758-2395
13101 Zeigler 11 Rd Coulterville (62237) *(G-7033)*

Peabody Coulterville Min LLC 618 758-3597
13101 Zeigler 11 Rd Coulterville (62237) *(G-7034)*

Peabody Energy Corporation 314 342-3400
420 Long Lane Rd Equality (62934) *(G-9470)*

Peabody Midwest Mining LLC 618 276-5006
12250 Mclain Rd Equality (62934) *(G-9471)*

Peaceful Valley Cabinetry 618 584-3615
2090 N 1000th St Flat Rock (62427) *(G-9672)*

Peacock Colors Company Inc 630 628-1960
1000 W National Ave Addison (60101) *(G-234)*

Peacock Printing Inc 618 242-3157
1112 Jordan St Mount Vernon (62864) *(G-14633)*

Peak Computer Systems Inc 618 398-5612
6400 W Main St Ste 1a Belleville (62223) *(G-1584)*

Peak Healthcare Advisors LLC 646 479-0005
4043 N Ravenswood Ave # 225 Chicago (60613) *(G-5775)*

Peak Printing 309 652-3655
110 W Monroe St Blandinsville (61420) *(G-1972)*

Peanut Butter Partners LLC 847 489-5322
564 Crescent Blvd Glen Ellyn (60137) *(G-10418)*

Peapod Digital Labs LLC 800 573-2763
300 S Riverside Plz Chicago (60606) *(G-5776)*

Pearl Bath Bombs Inc 312 661-2881
2850 N Pulaski Rd Unit 10 Chicago (60641) *(G-5777)*

Pearl Design Group LLC 630 295-8401
154 S Bloomingdale Rd # 102 Bloomingdale (60108) *(G-2009)*

Pearl Perfect Inc 847 679-6251
8220 Austin Ave Morton Grove (60053) *(G-14432)*

Pearson Fastener Corporation 815 397-4460
1400 Samuelson Rd Rockford (61109) *(G-17550)*

Pease Plastics, Glenview Also called Acrylic Ventures Inc *(G-10517)*

Pease's Candy Shops, Springfield Also called Peases Inc *(G-19422)*

Peases Inc (PA) 217 523-3721
1701 S State St Springfield (62704) *(G-19422)*

Peases Inc 217 529-2912
4753 Jeffory St Springfield (62703) *(G-19423)*

Peavey, Sauget Also called NGL Crude Logistics LLC *(G-18396)*

Pechiney Cast Plate 847 299-0220
8770 W Bryn Mawr Ave Fl 9 Chicago (60631) *(G-5778)*

Peco Pallet 773 646-0976
9355 S Damen Ave Chicago (60643) *(G-5779)*

Pecora Tool & Die Co Inc 847 524-1275
520 Morse Ave Schaumburg (60193) *(G-18671)*

Pecora Tool Service Inc 847 524-1275
520 Morse Ave Schaumburg (60193) *(G-18672)*

Pecson Distributors LLC 815 342-7977
27543 S Forest View Ln Beecher (60401) *(G-1520)*

Pedco, Villa Park Also called Precision Engineering & Dev Co *(G-20165)*

Peddinghaus Corporation (PA) 815 937-3800
300 N Washington Ave Bradley (60915) *(G-2288)*

Peddinghause, Bradley Also called Structural Steel Systems Limi *(G-2293)*

Peddlers Den Inc 815 498-3429
119 W Market St Somonauk (60552) *(G-19071)*

Pedraza Inc 773 874-9020
7649 S State St Chicago (60619) *(G-5780)*

Peelmaster Medical Packaging, Niles Also called Peelmaster Packaging Corp *(G-15155)*

Peelmaster Packaging Corp 847 966-6161
6153 W Mulford St Niles (60714) *(G-15155)*

Peep Eliminator, Breese Also called Compound Bow Rifle Sight Inc *(G-2301)*

Peeps Inc 708 935-4201
8945 W 103rd St Palos Hills (60465) *(G-16204)*

Peer Chain Company 847 775-4600
2300 Norman Dr Waukegan (60085) *(G-20475)*

Peer Foods Inc (HQ) 773 927-1440
1200 W 35th St Fl 3 Chicago (60609) *(G-5781)*

Peerless 773 294-2667
4855 S Racine Ave Chicago (60609) *(G-5782)*

Peerless America Incorporated 217 342-0400
1201 W Wabash Ave Effingham (62401) *(G-8418)*

Peerless Chain Company 708 339-0545
16650 State St South Holland (60473) *(G-19239)*

Peerless Industries Inc (PA) 630 375-5100
2300 White Oak Cir Aurora (60502) *(G-1006)*

Peerless-Av, Aurora Also called Peerless Industries Inc *(G-1006)*

Peerless-Premier Appliance Co (PA) 618 233-0475
119 S 14th St Belleville (62220) *(G-1585)*

Peg N Reds 618 586-2015
212 S Main St New Lenox (60451) *(G-15049)*

Pegai LLC 312 799-0417
3550 W Montrose Ave # 4 Chicago (60618) *(G-5783)*

Pegasus Mfg Inc 309 342-9337
1382 Enterprise Ave Galesburg (61401) *(G-10215)*

Pekay Machine & Engrg Co Inc 312 829-5530
2520 W Lake St Chicago (60612) *(G-5784)*

Pekin Division, Pekin Also called Hanna Steel Corporation *(G-16336)*

Pekin Hardwood Lumber Co., Pekin Also called Woodworkers Shop Inc *(G-16371)*

Pekin Mill, Pekin Also called Ox Paperboard LLC *(G-16348)*

Pekin Paperboard Company LP 309 346-4118
1525 S 2nd St Pekin (61554) *(G-16352)*

Pekin Sand and Gravel LLC 309 347-8917
13018 E Manito Rd Pekin (61554) *(G-16353)*

Pekin Weldors Inc 309 382-3627
1525 Edgewater Dr North Pekin (61554) *(G-15327)*

Pelco Tool & Mold Inc 630 871-1010
181 Exchange Blvd Glendale Heights (60139) *(G-10483)*

Pelegan Inc 708 442-9797
277 Northwood Rd Riverside (60546) *(G-17088)*

Pelican Holdco LLC (PA) 847 597-2200
1650 Lake Cook Rd Ste 400 Deerfield (60015) *(G-7642)*

Pellegrini Enterprises Inc 815 717-6408
16249 107th Ave Ste 10 Orland Park (60467) *(G-15974)*

Pelstar LLC 708 377-0600
9500 W 55th St Ste C Countryside (60525) *(G-7067)*

Pen At Hand 847 498-9174
4120 Terri Lyn Ln Northbrook (60062) *(G-15458)*

Pengo Products Company, Chicago Also called City Screen Inc *(G-4161)*

Penguin Foods, Rockford Also called M E F Corp *(G-17501)*

Penn Aluminum Intl LLC (HQ) 618 684-2146
1117 N 2nd St Murphysboro (62966) *(G-14756)*

Pennant Foods 708 752-8730
11746 S Austin Ave Alsip (60803) *(G-489)*

Pennasis Group LLC 630 699-8390
610 Oak Crest Dr North Aurora (60542) *(G-15268)*

Pennsylvania Carbon Products, Northbrook Also called Graphtek LLC *(G-15396)*

Penray Companies Inc (PA) 800 323-6329
2651 Warrenville Rd # 300 Downers Grove (60515) *(G-8071)*

Pentair Flow Technologies LLC 630 859-7000
800 Airport Rd North Aurora (60542) *(G-15269)*

Pentair Fltrtion Solutions LLC (HQ) 630 307-3000
1040 Muirfield Dr Hanover Park (60133) *(G-11012)*

Pentegra Systems LLC......630 941-6000
780 W Belden Ave Ste A Addison (60101) ***(G-235)***
Penton Media - Aviation Week, Chicago *Also called Informa Media Inc* ***(G-4916)***
Pentwater Cabinetry, Lombard *Also called Pentwater Furnishing Inc* ***(G-13119)***
Pentwater Furnishing Inc......630 984-4703
920 N Lombard Rd Lombard (60148) ***(G-13119)***
People & Places Newspaper......847 804-6985
4303 Atlantic Ave Schiller Park (60176) ***(G-18831)***
People Against Dirty Mfg Pbc......415 568-4600
720 E 111th St Chicago (60628) ***(G-5785)***
People's Weekly World, Chicago *Also called Long View Publishing Co Inc* ***(G-5255)***
Peopleadmin Inc......877 637-5800
4611 N Ravenswood Ave # 201 Chicago (60640) ***(G-5786)***
Peoples Cmplete Buiding Centre, Watseka *Also called Peoples Coal and Lumber Co* ***(G-20314)***
Peoples Coal and Lumber Co (PA)......815 432-2456
121 S 3rd St Watseka (60970) ***(G-20314)***
Peoria Bearing, Romeoville *Also called Apex Industrial Automation LLC* ***(G-17795)***
Peoria Journal Star Credit Un......309 686-3191
1 News Plz Peoria (61643) ***(G-16492)***
Peoria Journal Star Inc......309 686-3000
1 News Plz Peoria (61643) ***(G-16493)***
Peoria Midwest Equipment Inc......309 454-6800
2150 W College Ave Normal (61761) ***(G-15217)***
Peoria Open M R I......309 692-7674
6708 N Knoxville Ave # 2 Peoria (61614) ***(G-16494)***
Peoria Packing Ltd (PA)......312 226-2600
1307 W Lake St Chicago (60607) ***(G-5787)***
Peoria Packing Ltd......815 465-9824
8372 N 12000e Rd Grant Park (60940) ***(G-10750)***
Peoria Post Inc......309 688-3628
834 E Glen Ave Peoria (61616) ***(G-16495)***
Peoria Wilbert Vault Co Inc......309 383-2882
510 Townhall Rd Metamora (61548) ***(G-13966)***
Peotone Vidette, Peotone *Also called Russell Publications Inc* ***(G-16557)***
Pep Industries Inc......630 833-0404
725 N Wisconsin Ave Villa Park (60181) ***(G-20164)***
Pepperball Technologies, Lake Forest *Also called United Tactical Systems LLC* ***(G-12320)***
Pepperidge Farm Incorporated......708 478-7450
8910 W 192nd St Mokena (60448) ***(G-14106)***
Pepperidge Farm Incorporated......630 241-6372
230 2nd St Downers Grove (60515) ***(G-8072)***
Pepsi Cola Btlg Co Rock Island, Rock Island *Also called AD Huesing Corporation* ***(G-17199)***
Pepsi Cola Gen Bttlers of Lima (HQ)......847 253-1000
3501 Algonquin Rd Ste 700 Rolling Meadows (60008) ***(G-17760)***
Pepsi Mid America......217 826-8118
202 Vine St Marshall (62441) ***(G-13576)***
Pepsi Midamerica, Marion *Also called Crisp Container Corporation* ***(G-13508)***
Pepsi Midamerica Co (PA)......618 997-1377
2605 W Main St Marion (62959) ***(G-13525)***
Pepsi Midamerica Co......618 242-6285
205 N Davidson St Mount Vernon (62864) ***(G-14634)***
Pepsi-Cola Chmpign Urbana Btlr......217 352-4126
1306 W Anthony Dr Champaign (61821) ***(G-3330)***
Pepsi-Cola Metro Btlg Co Inc......847 598-3000
555 W Monroe St Fl 1 Chicago (60661) ***(G-5788)***
Pepsico, Champaign *Also called Pepsi-Cola Chmpign Urbana Btlr* ***(G-3330)***
Pepsico, Springfield *Also called Springfield Pepsi-Cola Btlg Co* ***(G-19453)***
Pepsico, Decatur *Also called Decatur Bottling Co* ***(G-7485)***
Pepsico, Danville *Also called P-Americas LLC* ***(G-7371)***
Pepsico, Elk Grove Village *Also called P-Americas LLC* ***(G-9167)***
Pepsico, Chicago *Also called P-Americas LLC* ***(G-5731)***
Pepsico, Kankakee *Also called P-Americas LLC* ***(G-11996)***
Pepsico, Morton *Also called P-Americas LLC* ***(G-14375)***
Pepsico, Quincy *Also called Refreshment Services Inc* ***(G-16939)***
Pepsico, Springfield *Also called Refreshment Services Inc* ***(G-19432)***
Pepsico, Rolling Meadows *Also called Pepsi Cola Gen Bttlers of Lima* ***(G-17760)***
Pepsico, Chicago *Also called P-Americas LLC* ***(G-5732)***
Pepsico, Decatur *Also called Refreshment Services Inc* ***(G-7541)***
Pepsico, Chicago *Also called P-Americas LLC* ***(G-5733)***
Pepsico......217 443-8607
1703 E Voorhees St Danville (61834) ***(G-7373)***
Pepsico Inc......312 821-1000
555 W Monroe St Fl 1 Chicago (60661) ***(G-5789)***
Pepsico Inc......847 767-2026
617 W Main St Barrington (60010) ***(G-1234)***
Per Race Engines, Plainfield *Also called Precision Engine Rbldrs Inc* ***(G-16704)***
Perdue Pavement Solutions Inc......309 698-9440
3202 E Washington St East Peoria (61611) ***(G-8283)***
Perfect Circle Projectiles LLC......847 367-8960
28101 N Ballard Dr Ste C Lake Forest (60045) ***(G-12286)***
Perfect Clean, Niles *Also called Umf Corporation* ***(G-15184)***
Perfect Desserts LLC......630 579-6100
2605 White Oak Cir Aurora (60502) ***(G-1007)***
Perfect Mold Inc......630 785-6105
1120 W Republic Dr Addison (60101) ***(G-236)***
Perfect Pasta Inc......630 543-8300
31 S Fairbank St Ste B Addison (60101) ***(G-237)***
Perfect Plastic Printing Corp (PA)......630 584-1600
311 Kautz Rd Ste 1 Saint Charles (60174) ***(G-18242)***
Perfect Plastic Printing Corp......630 584-1600
345 Kautz Rd Saint Charles (60174) ***(G-18243)***
Perfect Shutters Inc......815 648-2401
12213 Il Route 173 Hebron (60034) ***(G-11147)***
Perfectclean, Skokie *Also called Umf Corporation* ***(G-19049)***
Perfection Custom Closets & Co......847 647-6461
7183 N Austin Ave Niles (60714) ***(G-15156)***
Perfection Equipment Inc......847 244-7200
4259 Lee Ave Gurnee (60031) ***(G-10911)***
Perfection Plating Inc (PA)......847 593-6506
775 Morse Ave Elk Grove Village (60007) ***(G-9172)***
Perfection Plating Inc......847 593-6506
1521 Morse Ave Elk Grove Village (60007) ***(G-9173)***
Perfection Probes Inc......847 726-8868
24241 W Rose Ave Lake Zurich (60047) ***(G-12442)***
Perfection Spring Stmping Corp......847 437-3900
1449 E Algonquin Rd Mount Prospect (60056) ***(G-14560)***
Perfection Vault Co Inc......217 673-6111
403 N Ladue Rd Woodson (62695) ***(G-21351)***
Perfectvision Mfg Inc......630 226-9890
1 Gateway Ct Ste Aa Bolingbrook (60440) ***(G-2225)***
Perficient Inc......312 291-9035
212 W Superior St Ste 505 Chicago (60654) ***(G-5790)***
Performance Auto Salon Inc......815 468-6882
17 E Sixth St Manteno (60950) ***(G-13453)***
Performance Automotive......618 377-0020
475 S Prairie St Bethalto (62010) ***(G-1966)***
Performance Battery Group Inc......630 293-5505
870 W Hawthorne Ln Ste A West Chicago (60185) ***(G-20628)***
Performance Design Inc......847 719-1535
238 Telser Rd Lake Zurich (60047) ***(G-12443)***
Performance Diesel Service......217 375-4429
7586 E 4200 North Rd Hoopeston (60942) ***(G-11511)***
Performance Finishes Powder......309 631-0664
1622 18th Ave Apt 23 Rock Island (61201) ***(G-17232)***
Performance Gear Systems Inc......630 739-6666
14309 S Route 59 Plainfield (60544) ***(G-16700)***
Performance Industries Inc......972 393-6881
20 Lake Marian Rd Carpentersville (60110) ***(G-3111)***
Performance Lawn & Power......217 857-3717
1311 W Main St Teutopolis (62467) ***(G-19771)***
Performance Mailing & Prtg Inc......847 549-0500
777 N Milwaukee Ave Libertyville (60048) ***(G-12694)***
Performance Manufacturing......630 231-8099
782 W Hawthorne Ln West Chicago (60185) ***(G-20629)***
PERFORMANCE MATERIAL DIVISION, Itasca *Also called Shima American Corporation* ***(G-11732)***
Performance Pattern & Mch Inc......309 676-0907
2421 Sw Adams St Peoria (61602) ***(G-16496)***
Performance Stamping Co Inc......847 426-2233
20 Lake Marian Rd Carpentersville (60110) ***(G-3112)***
Performance Welding LLC......217 412-5722
10333 W Washington St Rd Maroa (61756) ***(G-13554)***
Performitiv LLC......312 307-5716
220 N Green St Ste 6015 Chicago (60607) ***(G-5791)***
Perftech Inc......630 554-0010
251 Airport Rd North Aurora (60542) ***(G-15270)***
Peritus Plastics LLC......815 448-2005
804 Commercial Dr Mazon (60444) ***(G-13684)***
Perkinelmer Inc......331 229-3012
1842 Centre Point Cir Naperville (60563) ***(G-14895)***
Perkinelmer Hlth Sciences Inc......630 969-6000
2200 Warrenville Rd Downers Grove (60515) ***(G-8073)***
Perkinlmer Lf Anlytcal Scences, Downers Grove *Also called Perkinelmer Hlth Sciences Inc* ***(G-8073)***
Perkins Construction......815 233-9655
4872 W Lily Creek Rd Freeport (61032) ***(G-10132)***
Perkins Engines Inc (HQ)......309 578-7364
N4 Ac6160 # 6160 Mossville (61552) ***(G-14461)***
Perkins Enterprise Inc......708 560-3837
15518 S Park Ave South Holland (60473) ***(G-19240)***
Perkins Manfacturing, Bolingbrook *Also called Hovi Industries Incorporated* ***(G-2186)***
Perkins Manufacturing Co......708 482-9500
380 Veterans Pkwy Ste 110 Bolingbrook (60440) ***(G-2226)***
Perkins Pencil Co......708 363-9249
3059 192nd St Lansing (60438) ***(G-12511)***
Perkins Products Inc......708 458-2000
7025 W 66th Pl Bedford Park (60638) ***(G-1491)***
Perle & Sons Jewelers Inc......630 357-3357
8 W Jefferson Ave Naperville (60540) ***(G-14896)***
Perma Graphics Printers......815 485-6955
216 N Marley Rd New Lenox (60451) ***(G-15050)***
Perma-Pipe Inc (HQ)......847 966-1000
6410 W Howard St Niles (60714) ***(G-15157)***
Perma-Pipe Intl Holdings Inc (PA)......847 966-1000
6410 W Howard St Niles (60714) ***(G-15158)***

ALPHABETIC

Permabilt of Illinois, Le Roy *Also called Omni-Tech Systems Inc* ***(G-12540)***
Permalert E S P, Niles *Also called Perma-Pipe Inc* ***(G-15157)***
Permalert Envmtl Spcialty Pdts 847 966-2190
6410 W Howard St Niles (60714) ***(G-15159)***
Permatron Corporation 847 434-1421
2020 Touhy Ave Elk Grove Village (60007) ***(G-9174)***
Permissions Group Inc 847 635-6550
401 S Milwaukee Ave # 180 Wheeling (60090) ***(G-20957)***
Perq/Hci LLC (HQ) 847 268-1600
5600 N River Rd Ste 900 Rosemont (60018) ***(G-18039)***
Perry Adult Living Inc 618 542-5421
1308 Wells Street Rd Du Quoin (62832) ***(G-8123)***
Perry Ellis International Inc 847 678-7108
5220 Fashion Outlets Way # 2265 Rosemont (60018) ***(G-18040)***
Perry Johnson Inc 847 635-0010
10255 W Higgins Rd # 140 Rosemont (60018) ***(G-18041)***
Perry Johnson Consulting, Rosemont *Also called Perry Johnson Inc* ***(G-18041)***
Perryco Inc (PA) 303 652-8282
6920 Webster St Downers Grove (60516) ***(G-8074)***
Perryco Inc 815 436-2431
15507 S Route 59 Plainfield (60544) ***(G-16701)***
Perryco Inc 217 322-3321
110 E Lafayette St Rushville (62681) ***(G-18112)***
Pershing Road Recycle, Chicago *Also called Legacy Vulcan LLC* ***(G-5197)***
Personal Battery Caddy, Oswego *Also called Tools Aviation LLC* ***(G-16028)***
Personalitee's, Prospect Heights *Also called Woolenwear Co* ***(G-16848)***
Personalized Pillows Co 847 226-7393
16783 W Old Orchard Dr Wadsworth (60083) ***(G-20211)***
Personalized Printing Mailing 847 441-2955
5 Lydia Ct South Elgin (60124) ***(G-19170)***
Personalized Threads 815 431-1815
2655 E 1559th Rd Ottawa (61350) ***(G-16071)***
Personify Inc 855 747-9940
212 W Superior St Ste 202 Chicago (60654) ***(G-5792)***
Personify Inc (PA) 217 840-2638
208a W Main St Urbana (61801) ***(G-19992)***
Perspecto Map Company Inc 815 356-1288
367 Cumberland Ln Village of Lakewood (60014) ***(G-20179)***
Perten Instruments Inc 217 585-9440
3200 Robbins Rd Ste 100a Springfield (62704) ***(G-19424)***
Peru Plant, Peru *Also called Pgi Mfg LLC* ***(G-16589)***
Pervasive Health Inc 312 257-2967
1 N La Salle St Ste 1825 Chicago (60602) ***(G-5793)***
Pespico 708 625-3450
7700 W 71st St Bridgeview (60455) ***(G-2374)***
Pet AG, Hampshire *Also called Pet-Ag Inc* ***(G-10983)***
Pet Age Magazine, Chicago *Also called HH Backer Associates Inc* ***(G-4812)***
Pet Celebrations Inc 630 832-6549
269 N Highland Ave Elmhurst (60126) ***(G-9410)***
Pet Factory Inc 847 837-8900
845 E High St Mundelein (60060) ***(G-14724)***
Pet Groom Products Div, Melrose Park *Also called Veeco Manufacturing Inc* ***(G-13925)***
Pet Loader, Belvidere *Also called AWego Enterprises Inc* ***(G-1651)***
Pet-Ag Inc 847 683-2288
180 Ryan Dr Hampshire (60140) ***(G-10983)***
Petairapy LLC 630 377-0348
3820 Ohio Ave Ste 9 Saint Charles (60174) ***(G-18244)***
Petco, Lake Forest *Also called Polyurthane Engrg Tchnques Inc* ***(G-12292)***
Petco Petroleum Corporation (PA) 630 654-1740
108 E Ogden Ave Ste 100 Hinsdale (60521) ***(G-11372)***
Petdine LLC 815 770-0342
New 2 Dogs Way Harvard (60033) ***(G-11062)***
Pete Aj Co 217 825-5822
103 N Jersey St Gillespie (62033) ***(G-10376)***
Pete Frcano Sons Cstm HM Bldrs 847 258-4626
1225 Howard St Elk Grove Village (60007) ***(G-9175)***
Peter Baker & Son Co (PA) 847 362-3663
1349 Rockland Rd Lake Bluff (60044) ***(G-12204)***
Peter Baker & Son Co 815 344-1640
914 W Illinois Rte 120 Mc Henry (60050) ***(G-13705)***
Peter Built 618 337-4000
2350 Sauget Indus Pkwy East Saint Louis (62206) ***(G-8318)***
Peter Fox 847 428-2249
578 Rock Road Dr Ste 4 East Dundee (60118) ***(G-8208)***
Peter Lehman Inc 847 395-7997
40126 N Il Route 83 Antioch (60002) ***(G-630)***
Peter Perella & Co 815 727-4526
600 N Scott St Joliet (60432) ***(G-11913)***
Peter Troost Monument Co 773 585-0242
7200 Archer Rd Justice (60458) ***(G-11953)***
Peters Construction 773 489-5555
3441 W Grand Ave Chicago (60651) ***(G-5794)***
Peters Machine Works Inc 708 496-3005
8277 S 86th Ct Oak Lawn (60458) ***(G-15732)***
Petersburg Observer Co Inc 217 632-2236
235 E Sangamon Ave Petersburg (62675) ***(G-16603)***
Petersburg Painting & Pwr Wshg, Springfield *Also called Petersburg Power Washing Inc* ***(G-19425)***
Petersburg Power Washing Inc 217 415-9013
829 S 11th St Springfield (62703) ***(G-19425)***
Petersen Aluminum Corporation (HQ) 847 228-7150
1005 Tonne Rd Elk Grove Village (60007) ***(G-9176)***
Petersen Finishing Corporation (PA) 847 228-7150
1005 Tonne Rd Elk Grove Village (60007) ***(G-9177)***
Petersen Sand & Gravel Inc 815 344-1060
914 Rand Rd Ste A Lakemoor (60051) ***(G-12473)***
Petersen/Tru-Cut Automotive, Watseka *Also called T & S Business Group LLC* ***(G-20319)***
Peterson Brothers Plastics 773 286-5666
2929 N Pulaski Rd Chicago (60641) ***(G-5795)***
Peterson Dermond Design LLC 414 383-5029
900 Grove St Ste 10 Evanston (60201) ***(G-9565)***
Peterson Elc Panl Mfg Co Inc 708 449-2270
5550 Mcdermott Dr Berkeley (60163) ***(G-1943)***
Peterson Elctr-Msical Pdts Inc 708 388-3311
11601 S Mayfield Ave Alsip (60803) ***(G-490)***
Peterson Farms, Harvard *Also called Bill Peterson* ***(G-11048)***
Peterson Intl Entp Ltd 847 541-3700
504 Glenn Ave Wheeling (60090) ***(G-20958)***
Peterson Manufacturing Company, Plainfield *Also called Nnm Manufacturing LLC* ***(G-16696)***
Petnet Solutions Inc 847 297-3721
200 Howard Ave Ste 240 Des Plaines (60018) ***(G-7819)***
Petote LLC 312 455-0873
2444 W 16th St Ste 4 Chicago (60608) ***(G-5796)***
Petra Manufacturing Co 773 622-1475
6600 W Armitage Ave Chicago (60707) ***(G-5797)***
Petrak Industries Incorporated 815 483-2290
17250 New Lenox Rd Ste 3 Joliet (60433) ***(G-11914)***
Petro Chem Echer Erhardt LLC 773 847-7535
2628 S Sacramento Ave Chicago (60623) ***(G-5798)***
Petro Enterprises Inc 708 425-1551
10242 Ridgeland Ave Chicago Ridge (60415) ***(G-6806)***
Petro Prop Inc 630 910-4738
7948 Highland Ave Downers Grove (60516) ***(G-8075)***
Petro-Chem Industries Div, Chicago *Also called Petro Chem Echer Erhardt LLC* ***(G-5798)***
Petrochem Inc 630 513-6350
333 N Randall Rd Ste 25 Saint Charles (60174) ***(G-18245)***
Petrochem Corp (HQ) 431 205-8122
8600 W Bryn Mawr Ave 800n Chicago (60631) ***(G-5799)***
Petron Oil Production Inc (PA) 618 783-4486
405 E Jourdan St Newton (62448) ***(G-15090)***
Petronics Inc (PA) 608 630-6527
60 Hazelwood Dr Rm 216 Champaign (61820) ***(G-3331)***
Pets Stop, Melrose Park *Also called Sunscape Time Inc* ***(G-13919)***
Pettibone LLC (HQ) 630 353-5000
27501 Bella Vista Pkwy Warrenville (60555) ***(G-20244)***
Pexco LLC (HQ) 847 296-5511
1600 Birchwood Ave Des Plaines (60018) ***(G-7820)***
Pfanstiehl Inc 847 623-0370
1219 Glen Rock Ave Waukegan (60085) ***(G-20476)***
Pfanstiehl Holdings Inc 847 623-0370
1219 Glen Rock Ave Waukegan (60085) ***(G-20477)***
PFC, Lemont *Also called Plastic Film Corp America Inc* ***(G-12583)***
Pfeifer Industries LLC 630 596-9000
2180 Corp Ln Unit 104 Naperville (60563) ***(G-14897)***
Pfizer Inc 630 634-3704
1 Pierce Pl Ste 300e Itasca (60143) ***(G-11716)***
Pfizer Inc 847 778-9237
1101 S State St Apt 1903 Chicago (60605) ***(G-5800)***
Pfizer Inc 224 212-3129
275 N Field Dr Lake Forest (60045) ***(G-12287)***
Pfizer Inc 847 639-3020
2323 Grove Ln Cary (60013) ***(G-3182)***
Pgi Mfg LLC 815 224-7540
4747 Industrial Dr Peru (61354) ***(G-16589)***
Pgi Mfg LLC 815 398-0313
614 Grable St Rockford (61109) ***(G-17551)***
Pgi Mfg LLC 800 821-3475
614 Grable St Rockford (61109) ***(G-17552)***
PH Tool Manufacturing 847 952-9441
1200 Andrea Ln Des Plaines (60018) ***(G-7821)***
Phalanx Training Inc 847 859-9156
617 Grove St Ste A Evanston (60201) ***(G-9566)***
Pharma Logistics 847 388-3104
1050 E High St Mundelein (60060) ***(G-14725)***
Pharma Nature 224 659-0906
537 Radcliffe Ave Des Plaines (60016) ***(G-7822)***
Pharmaceutical Labs and Cons I 630 359-3831
1010 W Fullerton Ave Addison (60101) ***(G-238)***
Pharmacy Services of Rockford, Rockford *Also called Hot Shots Nm LLC* ***(G-17453)***
Pharmacy Solutions, North Chicago *Also called Abbvie Endocrinology Inc* ***(G-15299)***
Pharmacy Store, Kankakee *Also called Riverside Medi-Center Inc* ***(G-11999)***
Pharmanutrients Inc 847 234-2334
37 Sherwood Ter Ste 109 Lake Bluff (60044) ***(G-12205)***
Pharmasyn Inc 847 752-8405
1840 Industrial Dr # 140 Libertyville (60048) ***(G-12695)***

Pharmazz Inc (PA) 630 780-6087
608 Fawell Ct Naperville (60565) **(G-14898)**
Pharmdium Hlthcare Hldings Inc (HQ) 800 523-7749
2 Conway Prk 150 N Lake Forest (60045) **(G-12288)**
Pharmedium Healthcare Corp (HQ) 847 457-2300
150 N Field Dr Ste 350 Lake Forest (60045) **(G-12289)**
Phathom Pharmaceuticals Inc 650 325-5156
2150 E Lake Cook Rd # 800 Buffalo Grove (60089) **(G-2584)**
Pheasant Hollow Winery Inc 618 629-2302
14931 State Highway 37 Whittington (62897) **(G-21021)**
Phelps Industries LLC 815 397-0236
5213 26th Ave Rockford (61109) **(G-17553)**
Phenome Technologies Inc 847 962-1273
7815 N St Louis Ave Skokie (60076) **(G-19004)**
PHI Group Inc 847 824-5610
555 E Business Center Dr Mount Prospect (60056) **(G-14561)**
PHI Optics Inc 217 819-1570
1800 S Oak St Ste 106 Champaign (61820) **(G-3332)**
Phibro Animal Health, Quincy *Also called Prince Agri Products Inc* **(G-16925)**
Philadelphia Gear, Mokena *Also called Timken Gears & Services Inc* **(G-14122)**
Philip Morris USA Inc 847 605-9595
300 N Martingale Rd # 700 Schaumburg (60173) **(G-18673)**
Philip Reinisch Company 312 644-6776
1555 Naperville Wheaton R Naperville (60563) **(G-14899)**
Philip W Weiss Monument Works, Belleville *Also called Weiss Monument Works Inc* **(G-1611)**
Philips Lighting, Roselle *Also called Signify North America Corp* **(G-17989)**
Philips North America LLC 630 585-2000
555 N Commerce St Aurora (60504) **(G-1008)**
Phillip C Cowen 630 208-1848
106 7th Pl Geneva (60134) **(G-10299)**
Phillip Grigalanz 219 628-6706
114 N Washington St Jerseyville (62052) **(G-11795)**
Phillip Rodgers 815 877-5461
5366 Forest Hills Ct Loves Park (61111) **(G-13244)**
Phillips & Johnston Inc 815 778-3355
900 E Commercial St Lyndon (61261) **(G-13287)**
Philmar LLC (PA) 847 282-0204
2502 Deborah Ave Zion (60099) **(G-21525)**
Philos Technologies Inc 630 945-2933
1011 Commerce Ct Buffalo Grove (60089) **(G-2585)**
Phils Auto Body 773 847-7156
833 W 35th St Chicago (60609) **(G-5801)**
Phoebe & Frances 847 446-5480
566 Chestnut St Winnetka (60093) **(G-21135)**
Phoenix Art Woodworks 847 279-1576
500 Harvester Ct Ste 7 Wheeling (60090) **(G-20959)**
Phoenix Binding Corp 847 981-1111
690 Hilltop Dr Itasca (60143) **(G-11717)**
Phoenix Business Solutions LLC 708 388-1330
12543 S Laramie Ave Alsip (60803) **(G-491)**
Phoenix Converting, Itasca *Also called Serene One LLC* **(G-11731)**
Phoenix Converting Inc 630 258-1500
1251 Ardmore Ave Itasca (60143) **(G-11718)**
Phoenix Electric Mfg Co 773 477-8855
3625 N Halsted St Chicago (60613) **(G-5802)**
Phoenix Fabrication & Sup Inc 708 754-5901
481 S Governors Hwy Peotone (60468) **(G-16556)**
Phoenix Graphics Inc 847 699-9520
2375 Magnolia St Des Plaines (60018) **(G-7823)**
Phoenix Graphix 618 531-3664
4513 Swanwick Rice Rd Pinckneyville (62274) **(G-16618)**
Phoenix Industries, Galesburg *Also called Kccdd Inc* **(G-10205)**
Phoenix Industries Inc 708 478-5474
10601 Saint John Dr Mokena (60448) **(G-14107)**
Phoenix Inks and Coatings LLC 630 972-2500
20w267 101st St Lemont (60439) **(G-12582)**
Phoenix Intl Publications Inc 877 277-9441
8501 W Higgins Rd Ste 300 Chicago (60631) **(G-5803)**
Phoenix Leather Goods LLC 815 676-6712
582 Territorial Dr Ste A Bolingbrook (60440) **(G-2227)**
Phoenix Marketing Services 630 616-8000
104 Terrace Dr Mundelein (60060) **(G-14726)**
Phoenix Pckg Mtrls/Phnix Plltt, Westchester *Also called Phoenix Trucking Inc* **(G-20708)**
Phoenix Press Inc 630 833-2281
1001 W Republic Dr Ste 15 Addison (60101) **(G-239)**
Phoenix Services LLC 708 849-3527
13500 S Perry Ave Riverdale (60827) **(G-17074)**
Phoenix Tool Corp 847 956-1886
700 Lunt Ave Elk Grove Village (60007) **(G-9178)**
Phoenix Trading Chicago Inc 847 304-5181
26809 W Lakeridge Dr Lake Barrington (60010) **(G-12163)**
Phoenix Tree Publishing Inc 773 251-0309
5660 N Jersey Ave Chicago (60659) **(G-5804)**
Phoenix Trucking Inc 708 514-2094
3036 Downing Ave Westchester (60154) **(G-20708)**
Phoenix Unlimited Ltd 847 515-1263
11514 Smith Dr Unit D Huntley (60142) **(G-11559)**
Phoenix Welding Co Inc 630 616-1700
9220 Parklane Ave Franklin Park (60131) **(G-10016)**
Phoenix Woodworking Corp 815 338-9338
2000 Duncan Pl Woodstock (60098) **(G-21421)**
Phonak LLC (HQ) 630 821-5000
4520 Weaver Pkwy Ste 1 Warrenville (60555) **(G-20245)**
Phosphate Resource Ptrs 847 739-1200
100 Saunders Rd Ste 300 Lake Forest (60045) **(G-12290)**
Photo Copy Service, Cherry Valley *Also called L & S Label Printing Inc* **(G-3443)**
Photo Graphic Design Service 815 672-4417
124 N Bloomington St Streator (61364) **(G-19620)**
Photo Techniques Corp (PA) 630 690-9360
387 Gundersen Dr Carol Stream (60188) **(G-3046)**
Photon Partners LLC 773 991-9788
3435 N Avers Ave Chicago (60618) **(G-5805)**
Photonicare Inc 866 411-3277
1902 Fox Dr Ste F Champaign (61820) **(G-3333)**
Photosteel, Tilton *Also called Custom Signs On Metal LLC* **(G-19795)**
Php Racengines Inc 847 526-9393
950 N Rand Rd Ste 107 Wauconda (60084) **(G-20382)**
Physician Software Systems LLC 630 717-8192
3333 Warrenville Rd # 200 Lisle (60532) **(G-12926)**
Physicians Record Co Inc 800 323-9268
3000 Ridgeland Ave Berwyn (60402) **(G-1960)**
Piasa Plastics Inc 618 372-7516
615 N Main St Brighton (62012) **(G-2403)**
Piatt County Clerk Recorder, Monticello *Also called County of Piatt* **(G-14280)**
Piatt County Journal Repub, Monticello *Also called News-Gazette Inc* **(G-14282)**
Piatt County Service Co 217 489-2411
1070 Old Us 150 Mansfield (61854) **(G-13442)**
Piatt County Service Co 217 678-5511
878 State Highway 105 Bement (61813) **(G-1714)**
Piccolino Inc 708 259-2072
802 S Clay St Hinsdale (60521) **(G-11373)**
Picis Clinical Solutions Inc 847 993-2200
9500 W Higgins Rd # 1100 Rosemont (60018) **(G-18042)**
Picket Fence Florist, Paxton *Also called Hts Hancock Transcriptions Svc* **(G-16308)**
Pickles Sorrel Inc 773 379-4748
5610 W Taylor St Chicago (60644) **(G-5806)**
Pickling Steel, Waterman *Also called Vision Pickling and Proc Inc* **(G-20301)**
Picture Frame Factory, Franklin Park *Also called Sarj USA Inc* **(G-10043)**
Picture Frame Factory, Franklin Park *Also called Mercurys Green LLC* **(G-9993)**
Picture Frame Fulfillment LLC 708 483-8537
9201 King St Franklin Park (60131) **(G-10017)**
Picture Stone Inc 773 875-5021
1431 W Greenbriar Dr Mount Prospect (60056) **(G-14562)**
Pictures & More 618 662-4572
134 W North Ave Flora (62839) **(G-9688)**
Pictures & More/Shirt Tales, Flora *Also called Pictures & More* **(G-9688)**
Pie Piper, Bensenville *Also called Distinctive Foods LLC* **(G-1787)**
Pie Piper Products, Wheeling *Also called Distinctive Foods LLC* **(G-20879)**
Piece Works Specialists Inc 309 266-7016
300 W Adams St Morton (61550) **(G-14378)**
Pieces of Learning Inc 618 964-9426
1112 N Carbon St Unit A Marion (62959) **(G-13526)**
Piedmont Hardware Brands, Freeport *Also called Nova Wildcat Amerock LLC* **(G-10131)**
Pierce & Stevens Chemical 630 653-3800
245 Kehoe Blvd Carol Stream (60188) **(G-3047)**
Pierce Crandell & Co Inc 847 549-6015
14047 W Petronella Dr # 103 Libertyville (60048) **(G-12696)**
Pierce Distribution Svcs Co, Loves Park *Also called Pierce Packaging Co* **(G-13245)**
Pierce Packaging Co (PA) 815 636-5650
2028 E Riverside Blvd Loves Park (61111) **(G-13245)**
Pierce Packaging Co 815 636-5656
2130 W Townline Rd Peoria (61615) **(G-16497)**
Pierce Packaging Co 815 636-5656
1200 Windsor Rd Loves Park (61111) **(G-13246)**
Piersons Mattress & Furn Co, Peoria *Also called Piersons Mattress Inc* **(G-16498)**
Piersons Mattress Inc 309 637-8455
1034 S Western Ave Peoria (61605) **(G-16498)**
Pietro Carnaghi USA Inc 779 368-0564
3445 Pyramid Dr Rockford (61109) **(G-17554)**
Pike County Concrete Inc 217 285-5548
1503 Kamar Dr Pittsfield (62363) **(G-16637)**
Pike County Express 217 285-5415
129 N Madison St Pittsfield (62363) **(G-16638)**
Pike Press, Pittsfield *Also called Campbell Publishing Co Inc* **(G-16631)**
Pikids, Chicago *Also called Phoenix Intl Publications Inc* **(G-5803)**
Pilkington North America Inc 815 433-0932
300 Center 20th St Ottawa (61350) **(G-16072)**
Pilla Exec Inc 312 882-8263
2447 W 80th St Chicago (60652) **(G-5807)**
Pillar Enterprises Inc 630 966-2566
121 S Lincolnway Ste 103 North Aurora (60542) **(G-15271)**
Pillarhouse USA Inc 847 593-9080
201 Lively Blvd Elk Grove Village (60007) **(G-9179)**
Pillsbury Company LLC 847 541-8888
135 N Arlington Heghts Buffalo Grove (60089) **(G-2586)**

ALPHABETIC

(PA)=Parent Co (HQ)=Headquarters (DH)=Div Headquarters
2020 Harris Illinois Industrial Directory
1223

Pilot Club of Moline 309 792-4102
3603 74th St Moline (61265) *(G-14166)*
Pilot Corporation of America 773 792-1111
1300 Higgins Rd Ste 214 Park Ridge (60068) *(G-16292)*
Pilot Township Road District 815 426-6221
300 E Kankakee Ave Herscher (60941) *(G-11186)*
Pilz Automtn Safety Ltd Partnr 734 354-0272
7021 Solutions Ctr Chicago (60677) *(G-5808)*
Pimco Plastics Inc 815 675-6464
7517 Meyer Rd Spring Grove (60081) *(G-19293)*
Pin Hsiao & Associates LLC 206 818-0155
1040 Sterling Ave Flossmoor (60422) *(G-9700)*
Pin Up Tattoo 815 477-7515
424 W Virginia St Crystal Lake (60014) *(G-7244)*
Pine Environmental Svcs LLC 847 718-1246
1153 N Main St Lombard (60148) *(G-13120)*
Pine Ridge Archery, Wauconda *Also called Du Bro Products Inc (G-20344)*
Pineapple Led Inc 847 255-3710
395 Covington Dr Barrington (60010) *(G-1235)*
Pinehurst Bus Solutions Corp 630 842-6155
26w362 Pinehurst Dr Winfield (60190) *(G-21115)*
Pines Trailer, Kewanee *Also called Great Dane LLC (G-12038)*
Pineview Woodworking, Arthur *Also called Richard Schrock (G-878)*
Pingotopia Inc 847 503-9333
3334 Commercial Ave Northbrook (60062) *(G-15459)*
Pingoworld, Northbrook *Also called Pingotopia Inc (G-15459)*
Pinnacle, Chicago *Also called Myerson LLC (G-5531)*
Pinnacle Exploration Corp 618 395-8100
510 E Lafayette St Olney (62450) *(G-15883)*
Pinnacle Foods Group LLC 618 829-3275
1000 Brewbaker Dr Saint Elmo (62458) *(G-18311)*
Pinnacle Foods Group LLC 731 343-4995
100 W Calumet St Centralia (62801) *(G-3244)*
Pinnacle Wood Products Inc 815 385-0792
1703 S Schroeder Ln McHenry (60050) *(G-13778)*
Pinnakle Technologies Inc 630 352-0070
75 Executive Dr Ste 353 Aurora (60504) *(G-1009)*
Pinney Printing Company 815 626-2727
1991 Industrial Dr Sterling (61081) *(G-19524)*
Pinoy Monthly 847 329-1073
5323 Wright Ter Skokie (60077) *(G-19005)*
Pins & Needles Consingment 217 299-7365
7580 N Pawnee Rd Pawnee (62558) *(G-16305)*
Pintas Cultured Marble 708 385-3360
5859 W 117th Pl Alsip (60803) *(G-492)*
Pinter Sheet Metal Work, Chicago *Also called Delta Metal Products Co (G-4336)*
Pintsch Tiefenbach Us Inc 618 993-8513
810 Skyline Dr Marion (62959) *(G-13527)*
Pio Woodworking Inc 630 628-6900
1130 W Fullerton Ave Addison (60101) *(G-240)*
Pioneer Container McHy Inc 618 533-7833
1674 Woods Ln Centralia (62801) *(G-3245)*
Pioneer Express 217 236-3022
404 W Highway St Perry (62362) *(G-16562)*
Pioneer Forms Inc 773 539-8587
4315 Regency Dr Glenview (60025) *(G-10599)*
Pioneer Grinding & Mfg Co 847 678-6565
10011 Franklin Ave Franklin Park (60131) *(G-10018)*
Pioneer Hi-Bred Intl Inc 309 962-2931
2112 County Road 1600 N Saint Joseph (61873) *(G-18318)*
Pioneer Labels Inc 618 546-5418
7656 E 700th Ave Robinson (62454) *(G-17121)*
Pioneer Newspapers Inc (HQ) 847 486-0600
350 N Orleans St Fl 10 Chicago (60654) *(G-5809)*
Pioneer Newspapers Inc 708 383-3200
1010 Lake St Ste 104 Oak Park (60301) *(G-15768)*
Pioneer Newspapers Inc 630 887-0600
440 E Ogden Ave Ste 2 Hinsdale (60521) *(G-11374)*
Pioneer Plastics Inc 309 365-2951
510 S Spencer St Lexington (61753) *(G-12620)*
Pioneer Powder Coatings LLC 847 671-1100
9240 Belmont Ave Unit B Franklin Park (60131) *(G-10019)*
Pioneer Press, Chicago *Also called Pioneer Newspapers Inc (G-5809)*
Pioneer Press, Chicago *Also called Schaumburg Review (G-6110)*
Pioneer Printing Service Inc 312 337-4283
1340 N Astor St Chicago (60610) *(G-5810)*
Pioneer Pump and Packing Inc 217 791-5293
1501 N 22nd St Decatur (62526) *(G-7536)*
Pioneer Service Inc 630 628-0249
542 W Factory Rd Addison (60101) *(G-241)*
PIP Printing, Peoria *Also called P & S Cochran Printers Inc (G-16489)*
PIP Printing, Glenview *Also called Printing Shop (G-10603)*
PIP Printing, Rockford *Also called Mencarini Enterprises Inc (G-17516)*
PIP Printing Inc 815 464-0075
9218 Corsair Rd Unit 3 Frankfort (60423) *(G-9822)*
Pipeline Trading Systems LLC 312 212-4288
1 S Dearborn St Ste 2100 Chicago (60603) *(G-5811)*
Piper Plastics, Libertyville *Also called Mitsubishi Chemical Advncd Mtr (G-12682)*
Piranha Fabrication, Rockford *Also called Mega Manufacturing Inc (G-17515)*
Piston Automotive LLC 313 541-8789
3458 Morreim Dr Belvidere (61008) *(G-1694)*
Pitchfork Media Inc 773 395-5937
3317 W Fullerton Ave Chicago (60647) *(G-5812)*
Pitney Bowes Inc 312 209-2216
2330 Hammond Dr Ste G Schaumburg (60173) *(G-18674)*
Pitney Bowes Inc 773 755-5808
3640 N Bosworth Ave 3s Chicago (60613) *(G-5813)*
Pitney Bowes Inc 630 435-7500
750 Warrenville Rd # 300 Lisle (60532) *(G-12927)*
Pitney Bowes Inc 800 784-4224
1025 Hilltop Dr Itasca (60143) *(G-11719)*
Pittsfield Mch Tl & Wldg Co 217 656-4000
306 W State St Payson (62360) *(G-16317)*
Pivot Point Beauty School, Chicago *Also called Pivot Point Usa Inc (G-5814)*
Pivot Point Usa Inc (PA) 800 886-4247
8725 W Higgins Rd Ste 700 Chicago (60631) *(G-5814)*
Pivotal Production LLC 773 726-7706
356 E Sutherland St Chicago (60619) *(G-5815)*
Pix North America Inc 855 800-0720
1222 E Voorhees St Danville (61834) *(G-7374)*
Pixel Pushers Incorporated 847 550-6560
1050 Ensell Rd Ste 108 Lake Zurich (60047) *(G-12444)*
Pixie Sparkle, Glenview *Also called Teitelbaum Brothers Inc (G-10630)*
Pjla Music 847 382-3212
22n159 Pepper Rd Barrington (60010) *(G-1236)*
Pk Corporation 847 879-1070
527 Newberry Dr Elk Grove Village (60007) *(G-9180)*
Pknd Llc 773 491-0070
480 N Mcclurg Ct Chicago (60611) *(G-5816)*
Plain & Posh LLC 630 960-0048
1016 Oakfern Ln Darien (60561) *(G-7411)*
Plaindealer, Sparta *Also called McClatchy Newspapers Inc (G-19257)*
Plainfield Signs Inc 815 439-1063
219 W Main St Plainfield (60544) *(G-16702)*
Planet Earth Antifreeze Inc 815 282-2463
6307 Material Ave Loves Park (61111) *(G-13247)*
Planks Apple Butter 217 268-4933
175 N County Road 525e Arcola (61910) *(G-662)*
Planks Cabinet Shop Inc 217 543-2687
1620 State Highway 133 Arthur (61911) *(G-876)*
Plano Holding LLC (HQ) 630 552-3111
431 E South St Plano (60545) *(G-16739)*
Plano Metal Specialties Inc 630 552-8510
320 W State Rte 34 Plano (60545) *(G-16740)*
Plano Molding Company LLC (HQ) 630 552-3111
431 E South St Plano (60545) *(G-16741)*
Plano Molding Company LLC 630 552-9557
510 Duvick Ave Sandwich (60548) *(G-18379)*
Plano Molding Company LLC 815 538-3111
1800 Hume Dr Mendota (61342) *(G-13952)*
Plano Molding Company LLC 815 786-3331
500 Duvick Ave Sandwich (60548) *(G-18380)*
Planos Past Inc 630 552-9119
7050 Burroughs Ave Plano (60545) *(G-16742)*
Plant 06, Nashville *Also called Beelman Ready-Mix Inc (G-14995)*
Plant 2, Hillside *Also called Dynamic Manufacturing Inc (G-11338)*
Plant 4, West Chicago *Also called Graham Packaging Co Europe LLC (G-20590)*
Plant 6, Mc Henry *Also called Peter Baker & Son Co (G-13705)*
Planter Inc 773 637-7777
1820 N Major Ave Chicago (60639) *(G-5817)*
Plantlink, Urbana *Also called Oso Technologies Inc (G-19991)*
Plasma Technology Systems, Elgin *Also called Plasmatreat USA Inc (G-8687)*
Plasmag Pump Div, Mundelein *Also called Murdock Company Inc (G-14719)*
Plasmatreat USA Inc (PA) 847 783-0622
2541 Tech Dr Ste 407 Elgin (60124) *(G-8687)*
Plaspros Inc (PA) 815 430-2300
1143 Ridgeview Dr McHenry (60050) *(G-13779)*
Plaspros Inc 847 639-6492
511 Cove Dr Cary (60013) *(G-3183)*
Plastak Inc 630 466-4100
44w40 Scott Rd Sugar Grove (60554) *(G-19649)*
Plastech Inc 630 595-7222
873 Fairway Dr Bensenville (60106) *(G-1868)*
Plastech Molding Inc 847 398-0355
2222 Foster Ave Wheeling (60090) *(G-20960)*
Plastic Art, Lombard *Also called Specialized Woodwork Inc (G-13131)*
Plastic Binding Laminating Inc 847 573-0375
27885 Irma Lee Cir # 105 Lake Forest (60045) *(G-12291)*
Plastic Container Corporation (PA) 217 352-2722
2508 N Oak St Urbana (61802) *(G-19993)*
Plastic Designs Inc 217 379-9214
1330 S Vermillion St Paxton (60957) *(G-16314)*
Plastic Film Corp America Inc (PA) 630 887-0800
1011 State St Ste 140 Lemont (60439) *(G-12583)*
Plastic Film Corp America Inc 630 697-5635
007 Geneva St Shorewood (60404) *(G-18899)*

Plastic Injection Molding, Saint Charles *Also called Foreman Tool & Mold Corp* ***(G-18201)***
Plastic Packaging Systems, Kankakee *Also called Signode Industrial Group LLC* ***(G-12002)***
Plastic Parts Intl Inc....815 637-9222
1248 Shappert Dr Machesney Park (61115) ***(G-13364)***
Plastic Power Extrusions Corp....847 233-9901
3860 River Rd Schiller Park (60176) ***(G-18832)***
Plastic Products Company Inc....309 762-6532
4610 44th St Moline (61265) ***(G-14167)***
Plastic Services Group....847 368-1444
115 S Wilke Rd Ste 206e Arlington Heights (60005) ***(G-788)***
Plastic Specialists America....847 406-7547
4225 Tiger Lily Ln # 308 Gurnee (60031) ***(G-10912)***
Plastic Specialties & Tech Inc....847 781-2414
119 Commerce Dr Schaumburg (60173) ***(G-18675)***
Plastic Technologies Inc....847 841-8610
1200 Abbott Dr Elgin (60123) ***(G-8688)***
Plasticrest Products Inc....773 826-2163
4519 W Harrison St Chicago (60624) ***(G-5818)***
Plastics....847 931-9391
39w446 Capulet Cir Elgin (60124) ***(G-8689)***
Plastics Color & Compounding....708 868-3800
14201 Paxton Ave Calumet City (60409) ***(G-2786)***
Plastics Color Corp Illinois....708 868-3800
14201 Paxton Ave Calumet City (60409) ***(G-2787)***
Plastics Color-Chip, Calumet City *Also called Pmc Inc* ***(G-2788)***
Plastics D-E-F....312 226-4337
3065 W Armitage Ave Chicago (60647) ***(G-5819)***
Plastics Printing Group Inc....773 473-4481
5414 W Roosevelt Rd Chicago (60644) ***(G-5820)***
Plasticworks Inc....630 543-1750
712 W Winthrop Ave Addison (60101) ***(G-242)***
Plastipak Packaging Inc....217 398-1832
3310 W Springfield Ave Champaign (61822) ***(G-3334)***
Plastipak Packaging Inc....708 385-0721
12325 S Laramie Ave Alsip (60803) ***(G-493)***
Plastival Inc....847 931-4771
1685 Holmes Rd Elgin (60123) ***(G-8690)***
Plastruct Inc....626 912-7017
65 Bradrock Dr Des Plaines (60018) ***(G-7824)***
Plate and Pre-Press Management....847 352-0462
431 Westover Ln Schaumburg (60193) ***(G-18676)***
Platform Technologies....847 357-0435
2200 S Mount Prospect Rd Des Plaines (60018) ***(G-7825)***
Plating International Inc....847 451-2101
11142 Addison Ave Franklin Park (60131) ***(G-10020)***
Platinum Inc....815 385-0910
813 N Lillian St McHenry (60050) ***(G-13780)***
Platinum Tooling Technologies....847 749-0633
16 Piper Ln Ste 129 Prospect Heights (60070) ***(G-16845)***
Platinum Touch Industries LLC....773 775-9988
471 N 3rd Ave Des Plaines (60016) ***(G-7826)***
Platit Inc....847 680-5270
1840 Industrial Dr # 220 Libertyville (60048) ***(G-12697)***
Platt Cases, Chicago *Also called Platt Luggage Inc* ***(G-5821)***
Platt County Service, Bement *Also called Piatt County Service Co* ***(G-1714)***
Platt G Mostardi....630 993-2100
5595 Trillium Blvd Hoffman Estates (60192) ***(G-11443)***
Platt Industrial Control Inc....630 833-4388
3n301 Ellsworth Ave Addison (60101) ***(G-243)***
Platt Luggage Inc....773 838-2000
4051 W 51st St Chicago (60632) ***(G-5821)***
Platts Printing Company....309 228-1069
25 E Fort St Farmington (61531) ***(G-9663)***
Play It Again Sports 11417, Sycamore *Also called Heartland Inspection Company* ***(G-19713)***
Player Sports Ltd....773 764-4111
2956 W Peterson Ave Chicago (60659) ***(G-5822)***
Playground Pointers....952 200-4168
109 S Quincy St Hinsdale (60521) ***(G-11375)***
Playing With Fusion Inc....309 258-7259
31201 State Route 9 Mackinaw (61755) ***(G-13385)***
Plaza Tool & Mold Co....847 537-2320
500 Harvester Ct Ste 2 Wheeling (60090) ***(G-20961)***
Plaze Inc (HQ)....630 628-4240
2651 Warrenville Rd # 300 Downers Grove (60515) ***(G-8076)***
PLC Corp....847 247-1900
220 Baker Rd Lake Bluff (60044) ***(G-12206)***
Pledgemine, Lombard *Also called Businessmine LLC* ***(G-13049)***
Plews Inc (PA)....815 288-3344
1550 Franklin Grove Rd Dixon (61021) ***(G-7906)***
Plews & Edelmann, Dixon *Also called Plews Inc* ***(G-7906)***
Plexus Corp....847 793-4400
2400 Millbrook Dr Buffalo Grove (60089) ***(G-2587)***
Plexus Manufacturing Solutions, Buffalo Grove *Also called Plexus Corp* ***(G-2587)***
Pliant LLC....812 424-2904
1701 Golf Rd Ste 2-900 Rolling Meadows (60008) ***(G-17761)***
Pliant Corp International....847 969-3300
1701 Golf Rd Ste 2-900 Rolling Meadows (60008) ***(G-17762)***
Pliant Investment Inc....847 969-3300
1475 E Wdfield Rd Ste 600 Schaumburg (60173) ***(G-18677)***
Pliant Solutions Corporation....847 969-3300
1475 E Wdfield Rd Ste 600 Schaumburg (60173) ***(G-18678)***
Plibrico Company LLC (PA)....312 337-9000
1935 Techny Rd Ste 16 Northbrook (60062) ***(G-15460)***
Plibrico Refractory Cnstr, Northbrook *Also called Plibrico Company LLC* ***(G-15460)***
Plitek LLC....847 827-6680
69 Rawls Rd Des Plaines (60018) ***(G-7827)***
Plochman Inc....815 468-3434
1333 N Boudreau Rd Manteno (60950) ***(G-13454)***
Plote Construction Inc....847 695-0422
1100 Brandt Dr Hoffman Estates (60192) ***(G-11444)***
Plote Construction Inc (PA)....847 695-9300
1100 Brandt Dr Hoffman Estates (60192) ***(G-11445)***
Plote Inc....847 695-9467
1100 Brandt Dr Hoffman Estates (60192) ***(G-11446)***
Plug Electric LLC....630 788-1018
10538 Ridgeland Ave Apt 3 Chicago Ridge (60415) ***(G-6807)***
Plug Power Inc Ctc....518 782-7700
1160 Naperville Dr Romeoville (60446) ***(G-17863)***
Plum Grove Printers Inc....847 882-4020
2160 Stonington Ave Hoffman Estates (60169) ***(G-11447)***
Plumbing Engineer Magazine, Niles *Also called Tmb Publishing Inc* ***(G-15181)***
Plumrose Usa Inc....732 253-5257
651 W Washington Blvd # 304 Chicago (60661) ***(G-5823)***
Plumrose Usa Inc (HQ)....800 526-4909
1901 Butterfield Rd # 305 Downers Grove (60515) ***(G-8077)***
Plustech Inc....847 490-8130
735 Remington Rd Schaumburg (60173) ***(G-18679)***
Plymouth Tube Company (PA)....630 393-3550
29w 150 Warrenville Rd Warrenville (60555) ***(G-20246)***
Plymouth Tube Company....773 489-0226
4555 W Armitage Ave Chicago (60639) ***(G-5824)***
Plz Aeroscience, Downers Grove *Also called Plaze Inc* ***(G-8076)***
Plz Aeroscience Corporation (PA)....630 628-3000
2651 Warrenville Rd # 300 Downers Grove (60515) ***(G-8078)***
PM Machine Shop....217 854-3504
706 N Broad St Carlinville (62626) ***(G-2883)***
PM Mold Company....847 923-5400
800 Estes Ave Schaumburg (60193) ***(G-18680)***
PM Woodwind Repair Inc....847 869-7049
822 Custer Ave Evanston (60202) ***(G-9567)***
Pma Friction Products Inc....630 406-9119
880 Kingsland Dr Batavia (60510) ***(G-1404)***
Pmb Industries Inc....708 442-4515
8072 53rd St La Grange (60525) ***(G-12086)***
Pmc Inc....708 868-3800
14201 Paxton Ave Calumet City (60409) ***(G-2788)***
PMC Converting Corp....773 481-2269
5080 N Kimberly Ave # 107 Chicago (60630) ***(G-5825)***
PMI Aerospace Inc....815 397-3894
2801 Eastrock Dr Rockford (61109) ***(G-17555)***
PMI Cartoning Inc....847 437-1427
850 Pratt Blvd Elk Grove Village (60007) ***(G-9181)***
PMI Kyoto Packaging Systems, Elk Grove Village *Also called PMI Cartoning Inc* ***(G-9181)***
Pmj Designs, Lake Forest *Also called Patricia Jenkins* ***(G-12282)***
Pmp Americas Inc....815 633-9962
16200 Woodmint Ln South Beloit (61080) ***(G-19107)***
Pmp Fermentation Products Inc....309 637-0400
900 Ne Adams St Peoria (61603) ***(G-16499)***
Pmt, Frankfort *Also called Prime Market Targeting Inc* ***(G-9826)***
Pmt Nuclear....630 887-7700
9341 Adam Don Pkwy Woodridge (60517) ***(G-21332)***
Pmw Holdings Inc (PA)....815 672-0551
1705 N Shabbona St Streator (61364) ***(G-19621)***
PNa Construction Tech Inc (PA)....770 668-9500
1349 W Bryn Mawr Ave Itasca (60143) ***(G-11720)***
Pnc Inc (PA)....815 946-2328
117 E Mason St Polo (61064) ***(G-16758)***
PNC Financial Svcs Group Inc....630 420-8400
1308 S Naper Blvd Naperville (60540) ***(G-14900)***
Pne Usa Inc....773 329-3705
150 N Michigan Ave # 1500 Chicago (60601) ***(G-5826)***
Pneu Fast Company....847 866-8787
2200 Greenleaf St Evanston (60202) ***(G-9568)***
Pneu-Fast, Evanston *Also called Pneu Fast Company* ***(G-9568)***
Pneutech Products, Schaumburg *Also called Fluid-Aire Dynamics Inc* ***(G-18530)***
Png Transport LLC....312 218-8116
3543 S Parnell Ave Apt B Chicago (60609) ***(G-5827)***
PO Food Specialists Ltd....847 517-8315
1800 Huntington Blvd # 610 Hoffman Estates (60169) ***(G-11448)***
Podhalanska LLC....630 247-9256
1304 Oakmont Dr Unit 10 Lemont (60439) ***(G-12584)***
Podiatry Arts Lab, Pekin *Also called Pal Health Technologies Inc* ***(G-16351)***
Podrez Enterprise LLC....815 353-5893
481 Scotland Rd Unit 102 Lakemoor (60051) ***(G-12474)***
Poersch Metal Manufacturing Co....773 722-0890
4027 W Kinzie St Chicago (60624) ***(G-5828)***
Poetry Center....312 899-1229
641 W Lake St Ste 200 Chicago (60661) ***(G-5829)***

ALPHABETIC

Poetry Foundation 312 787-7070
  61 W Superior St Chicago (60654) *(G-5830)*
POETRY MAGAZINE, Chicago Also called Poetry Foundation *(G-5830)*
Poets Study Inc 773 286-1355
  4366 N Elston Ave Chicago (60641) *(G-5831)*
Poggenpohl LLC (PA) 217 229-3411
  31 Sparks St Raymond (62560) *(G-16990)*
Poggenpohl LLC 217 824-2020
  105 N Baughman Rd Taylorville (62568) *(G-19760)*
Poggenpohl Construction & Mtls, Raymond Also called Poggenpohl LLC *(G-16990)*
Poignant Logging 309 246-5647
  857 State Route 26 Lacon (61540) *(G-12133)*
Point Five Packaging LLC 847 531-4787
  9435 River St Schiller Park (60176) *(G-18833)*
Point Ready Mix LLC (PA) 815 578-9100
  5435 Bull Valley Rd # 130 McHenry (60050) *(G-13781)*
Point Unlimited 708 244-7730
  594 Farmview Ct University Park (60484) *(G-19964)*
Pointe International Company 847 550-7001
  446 Valley View Rd Lake Barrington (60010) *(G-12164)*
Pokorney Manufacturing Co 630 458-0406
  45 N Church St Addison (60101) *(G-244)*
Pola Company 847 470-1182
  8901 N Milwaukee Ave A Niles (60714) *(G-15160)*
Polamer Inc 773 774-3600
  6401 N Milwaukee Ave Chicago (60646) *(G-5832)*
Polamer & Parcel Travel Svc, Chicago Also called Polamer Inc *(G-5832)*
Polancics Meats & Tenderloins 815 433-0324
  412 W Norris Dr Ottawa (61350) *(G-16073)*
Polar Container Corporation 847 299-5030
  1050 Entry Dr Bensenville (60106) *(G-1869)*
Polar Paint Systems, Moline Also called Sentry Pool & Chemical Supply *(G-14177)*
Polar Tech Industries Inc (PA) 815 784-9000
  415 E Railroad Ave Genoa (60135) *(G-10321)*
Polaris Genomics Corporation 773 547-2350
  700 E Bus Ctr Dr 105 Mount Prospect (60056) *(G-14563)*
Polaris Laser Laminations LLC 630 444-0760
  2725 Norton Creek Dr B2 West Chicago (60185) *(G-20630)*
Polaris Technology Group, Bloomingdale Also called Endure Holdings Inc *(G-1992)*
Polaroid Store, Northbrook Also called Pcbl Retail Holdings LLC *(G-15452)*
Pole Express Publishing, Chicago Also called Express Publishing Inc *(G-4545)*
Poli-Film America Inc (HQ) 847 453-8104
  1 Elgiloy Dr Hampshire (60140) *(G-10984)*
Polish Your Lf Nail Salon LLC 312 838-1018
  5017 W 14th St Apt 208 Cicero (60804) *(G-6870)*
Politech Inc 847 516-2717
  108 Turkey Run Rd Trout Valley (60013) *(G-19908)*
Poll Enterprises Inc 708 756-1120
  209 Glenwood Rd Chicago Heights (60411) *(G-6764)*
Pollack Service 773 528-8096
  3701 N Ravenswood Ave Chicago (60613) *(G-5833)*
Pollard Bros Mfg Co 773 763-6868
  5504 N Northwest Hwy Chicago (60630) *(G-5834)*
Pollmann North America Inc 815 834-1122
  950 Chicago Tube Dr Romeoville (60446) *(G-17864)*
Polmax LLC 708 843-8300
  12161 S Central Ave Alsip (60803) *(G-494)*
Polonia Book Store Inc 773 481-6968
  4738 N Milwaukee Ave Chicago (60630) *(G-5835)*
Polpress Inc 773 792-1200
  5566 N Northwest Hwy Chicago (60630) *(G-5836)*
Polpress Priniting, Chicago Also called Polpress Inc *(G-5836)*
Poly Compounding LLC 847 488-0683
  1390 Gateway Dr Ste 6 Elgin (60124) *(G-8691)*
Poly Films Inc 708 547-7963
  4101 Washington Blvd Hillside (60162) *(G-11353)*
Poly Plastics Films Corp 815 636-0821
  334 Northway Park Rd # 3 Machesney Park (61115) *(G-13365)*
Poly-Clip Systems, Mundelein Also called Precitec Corporation *(G-14727)*
Poly-Resyn Inc 847 428-4031
  518 Market Loop Ste A West Dundee (60118) *(G-20665)*
Polyair Corporation 773 253-1220
  808 E 113th St Chicago (60628) *(G-5837)*
Polyair Inter Pack Inc 773 995-1818
  808 E 113th St Chicago (60628) *(G-5838)*
Polybilt Body Company LLC (PA) 708 345-8050
  325 Spring Lake Dr Itasca (60143) *(G-11721)*
Polycast 815 648-4438
  10103 Main St Ste B Hebron (60034) *(G-11148)*
Polyconversions Inc 217 893-3330
  3202 Apollo Dr Champaign (61822) *(G-3335)*
Polydesigns Ltd 847 433-9920
  731 Orleans Dr Highland Park (60035) *(G-11291)*
Polyenviro Labs Inc 708 489-0195
  9960 191st St Ste K Mokena (60448) *(G-14108)*
Polyera Corporation 847 677-7517
  8025 Lamon Ave Ste 43 Skokie (60077) *(G-19006)*
Polyform Products Company 847 427-0020
  1901 Estes Ave Elk Grove Village (60007) *(G-9182)*
Polygem, West Chicago Also called Jjc Epoxy Inc *(G-20604)*
Polymax Thrmplstic Elstmers LL 847 316-9900
  3210 N Oak Grove Ave Waukegan (60087) *(G-20478)*
Polymax Tpe, Waukegan Also called Polymax Thrmplstic Elstmers LL *(G-20478)*
Polymer Nation LLC (PA) 847 972-2157
  405 N Oakwood Ave Waukegan (60085) *(G-20479)*
Polynt Composites II LLC (PA) 847 428-2657
  99 E Cottage Ave Carpentersville (60110) *(G-3113)*
Polynt Composites USA Inc 815 942-4600
  6350 E Collins Rd Morris (60450) *(G-14321)*
Polynt Composites USA Inc (HQ) 847 428-2657
  99 E Cottage Ave Carpentersville (60110) *(G-3114)*
Polyone Corporation 815 385-8500
  833 Ridgeview Dr McHenry (60050) *(G-13782)*
Polyone Corporation 815 385-8500
  921 Ridgeview Dr Mchenry (60050) *(G-13783)*
Polyone Corporation 847 364-0011
  2400 E Devon Ave Elk Grove Village (60007) *(G-9183)*
Polyone Corporation 309 364-2154
  1546 County Road 1450 N Henry (61537) *(G-11168)*
Polyone Corporation 630 972-0505
  1252 Windham Pkwy Romeoville (60446) *(G-17865)*
Polyonics Rubber Co 815 765-2033
  100 E Park St Poplar Grove (61065) *(G-16783)*
Polyscience, Niles Also called Preston Industries Inc *(G-15162)*
Polyscience Inc 847 647-0611
  5709 W Howard St Niles (60714) *(G-15161)*
Polysystems Inc (PA) 312 332-2114
  225 W Washington St # 2300 Chicago (60606) *(G-5839)*
Polytec Plastics Inc 630 584-8282
  3730 Stern Ave Saint Charles (60174) *(G-18246)*
Polytech Inc (PA) 806 338-2008
  315 W 23rd St Chicago (60616) *(G-5840)*
Polytech Industries Inc 630 443-6030
  1755 Wallace Ave Saint Charles (60174) *(G-18247)*
Polyurethane Products Corp 630 543-6700
  31 W Industrial Rd Addison (60101) *(G-245)*
Polyurthane Engrg Tchnques Inc (PA) 847 362-1820
  28041 N Bradley Rd Lake Forest (60045) *(G-12292)*
Polyvinyl Record Co 217 403-1752
  717 S Neil St Champaign (61820) *(G-3336)*
Pomona Winery 618 893-2623
  2865 Hickory Ridge Rd Pomona (62975) *(G-16764)*
Pontiac Engraving 630 834-4424
  586 Meyer Rd Bensenville (60106) *(G-1870)*
Pontiac Granite Company Inc 815 842-1384
  906 W North St Pontiac (61764) *(G-16776)*
Pontiac Recyclers Inc 815 844-6419
  15355 E 1830 North Rd Pontiac (61764) *(G-16777)*
Pony Tools, Chicago Also called Adjustable Clamp Company *(G-3546)*
Pool & Pool Oil Productions 618 544-7590
  1724 W Main St Robinson (62454) *(G-17122)*
Pool Center Inc 217 698-7665
  3740 Wabash Ave Ste C Springfield (62711) *(G-19426)*
Pools Welding Inc 309 787-2083
  816 10th Ave W Milan (61264) *(G-14020)*
Pop Box LLC 630 509-2281
  1700 W Irving Park Rd # 302 Chicago (60613) *(G-5841)*
Pop Brands LLC 630 205-7146
  635 N Dearborn St Apt 906 Chicago (60654) *(G-5842)*
Popsugar Inc 312 595-0533
  1 E Wacker Dr Ste 225 Chicago (60601) *(G-5843)*
Popular Pays Inc 435 767-7297
  130 S Jefferson St # 400 Chicago (60661) *(G-5844)*
Popular Ridge Machine Met Cft 618 687-1656
  134 S Jungle Rd Murphysboro (62966) *(G-14757)*
Porcelain Enamel Finishers 312 808-1560
  1530 S State St Apt 1018 Chicago (60605) *(G-5845)*
Porch Electric LLC 815 368-3230
  205 N Main St Lostant (61334) *(G-13177)*
Portable Cmmnctns Spclsts 630 458-1800
  901 W Lake St Addison (60101) *(G-246)*
Porter Athletic Equipment Co 888 277-7778
  601 Mercury Dr Champaign (61822) *(G-3337)*
Porterville Recorder Inc 559 784-5000
  1120 N Carbon St Ste 100 Marion (62959) *(G-13528)*
Portillos Food Service Inc (PA) 630 620-0460
  380 S Rohlwing Rd Addison (60101) *(G-247)*
Portola Packaging LLC 630 515-8383
  1140 31st St Downers Grove (60515) *(G-8079)*
Pos Plus LLC 618 993-7587
  606 N Van Buren St Marion (62959) *(G-13529)*
Pos Plus Solutions, Marion Also called Pos Plus LLC *(G-13529)*
Posh Lash Inc 630 388-6828
  1652 E 53rd St Chicago (60615) *(G-5846)*
Positive Impressions 618 438-7030
  14190 State Highway 34 Benton (62812) *(G-1935)*
Positive Mama Enterprises LLC 618 508-1995
  701 Martha Ln Flora (62839) *(G-9689)*

ALPHABETIC SECTION
Prairie Farms Dairy Inc

Positive Packaging Inc ... 708 560-3028
1100 Hicks Rd Rolling Meadows (60008) ***(G-17763)***
Positive Packaging & Graphics, Rolling Meadows *Also called Positive Packaging Inc* ***(G-17763)***
Positron Corporation (PA) ... 317 576-0183
530 Oakmont Ln Westmont (60559) ***(G-20765)***
Possehl Connector Svcs SC Inc ... 803 366-8316
1521 Morse Ave Elk Grove Village (60007) ***(G-9184)***
Post Press Production Inc (PA) ... 630 860-9833
2601 Lively Blvd Elk Grove Village (60007) ***(G-9185)***
Post-Tribune, Chicago *Also called Old Gary Inc* ***(G-5669)***
Potash Corp Ssktchewan Fla Inc (HQ) ... 847 849-4200
1101 Skokie Blvd Ste 400 Northbrook (60062) ***(G-15461)***
Potash Holding Company Inc ... 847 849-4200
1101 Skokie Blvd Ste 400 Northbrook (60062) ***(G-15462)***
Potentia, Chicago *Also called Corbett Accel Healthcare Grp C* ***(G-4234)***
Pothole Pros ... 847 815-5789
3074 Chalkstone Ave Elgin (60124) ***(G-8692)***
Potomac Corporation (PA) ... 847 259-0546
2063 Foster Ave Wheeling (60090) ***(G-20962)***
Pour It Again Sam Inc ... 708 474-1744
2200 198th Pl Lynwood (60411) ***(G-13297)***
Powbab Inc ... 630 481-6140
1314 Kensington Rd # 3205 Oak Brook (60523) ***(G-15656)***
Powder Coating Specialists ... 708 387-8000
9436 47th St Brookfield (60513) ***(G-2490)***
Powdered Metal Tech LLC ... 630 852-0500
2655 Wisconsin Ave Downers Grove (60515) ***(G-8080)***
Powell Electrical Systems Inc ... 708 409-1200
515 N Railroad Ave Northlake (60164) ***(G-15555)***
Powell Electrical Systems Inc ... 708 409-1200
515 N Railroad Ave Northlake (60164) ***(G-15556)***
Powell Industries Inc ... 708 409-1200
515 N Railroad Ave Northlake (60164) ***(G-15557)***
Powell Tree Care Inc ... 847 364-1181
212 E Devon Ave Elk Grove Village (60007) ***(G-9186)***
Power Distribution Eqp Co Inc ... 847 455-2500
3010 Willow St Franklin Park (60131) ***(G-10021)***
Power Enclosures Inc (PA) ... 309 274-9000
100 S 4th St Chillicothe (61523) ***(G-6821)***
Power Equipment Company ... 815 754-4090
211 W Stephenie Dr Cortland (60112) ***(G-7026)***
Power Graphics & Print Inc ... 847 568-1808
7345 Monticello Ave Skokie (60076) ***(G-19007)***
Power House Tool Inc ... 815 727-6301
626 Nicholson St Joliet (60435) ***(G-11915)***
Power Lube LLC ... 847 806-7022
1461 Busse Rd Elk Grove Village (60007) ***(G-9187)***
Power Partners LLC ... 773 465-8688
1542 W Devon Ave Chicago (60660) ***(G-5847)***
Power Parts Sign Co, Chicago *Also called Ri-Del Mfg Inc* ***(G-6024)***
Power Plant Repair Svcs LLC ... 708 345-8600
80 Kendall Point Dr Oswego (60543) ***(G-16020)***
Power Plant Services, Melrose Park *Also called Alin Machining Company Inc* ***(G-13821)***
Power Planter Inc ... 217 379-2614
931 N 1600e Rd Loda (60948) ***(G-13031)***
Power Plus Products Inc ... 773 788-9794
6410 W 74th St Ste A Bedford Park (60638) ***(G-1492)***
Power Port Products Inc ... 630 628-9102
301 W Interstate Rd Addison (60101) ***(G-248)***
Power Solutions Intl Inc (HQ) ... 630 350-9400
201 Mittel Dr Wood Dale (60191) ***(G-21228)***
Power-Io Inc ... 630 717-7335
537 Braemar Ave Naperville (60563) ***(G-14901)***
Power-Sonic Corporation ... 309 752-7750
1300 19th St Ste 200 East Moline (61244) ***(G-8236)***
Power-Volt Inc (PA) ... 630 628-9999
300 W Factory Rd Addison (60101) ***(G-249)***
Power102jamz ... 312 912-2766
202 S Broadway Ave # 203 Urbana (61801) ***(G-19994)***
Powerboss Inc ... 630 627-6900
14n845 Us Highway 20 Pingree Grove (60140) ***(G-16623)***
Powercoco LLC ... 614 323-5890
1658 N Milwaukee Ave # 546 Chicago (60647) ***(G-5848)***
Powerhouse Ent Inc ... 312 877-4303
2218 W Granville Ave Chicago (60659) ***(G-5849)***
Powerlab Inc ... 815 273-7718
9741 Powerlab Rd Savanna (61074) ***(G-18410)***
Powermaster ... 630 957-4019
1833 Downs Dr West Chicago (60185) ***(G-20631)***
Powermaster Motorsports, West Chicago *Also called Powermaster* ***(G-20631)***
Powernail Company ... 800 323-1653
1300 Rose Rd Lake Zurich (60047) ***(G-12445)***
Powerone Corp ... 630 443-6500
2325 Dean St Ste 200 Saint Charles (60175) ***(G-18248)***
Powerone Environmental, Saint Charles *Also called Powerone Corp* ***(G-18248)***
Powerpath Microproducts Inc ... 847 827-6330
200 Howard Ave Ste 238 Des Plaines (60018) ***(G-7828)***
Powers John ... 309 742-8929
214 S Magnolia St Elmwood (61529) ***(G-9449)***
Powers Paint Shop Inc ... 815 338-3619
1065 Dieckman St Woodstock (60098) ***(G-21422)***
Powers Sports LLC ... 815 436-6769
2425 Von Esch Rd Ste D Plainfield (60586) ***(G-16703)***
Powers Woodworking ... 630 663-9644
6804 Hobson Valley Dr # 117 Woodridge (60517) ***(G-21333)***
Powerschool Group LLC ... 610 867-9200
2290 Collection Center Dr Chicago (60693) ***(G-5850)***
Powersource Generator Rentals ... 847 587-3991
119 Christopher Way Fox Lake (60020) ***(G-9752)***
Powerstop ... 708 442-6761
7950 Joliet Rd Ste 200 Mc Cook (60525) ***(G-13698)***
Powertech Systems ... 847 553-1867
2548 Bluewater Dr Wauconda (60084) ***(G-20383)***
Powertrain Rockford Inc ... 815 633-7460
1200 Windsor Rd Unit 1 Loves Park (61111) ***(G-13248)***
Powervar Inc (HQ) ... 847 596-7000
1450 S Lakeside Dr Waukegan (60085) ***(G-20480)***
Poxypros Inc ... 630 675-5924
4657 Plymouth Ave Yorkville (60560) ***(G-21497)***
Poynting Products Inc ... 708 386-2139
1011 Madison St Oak Park (60302) ***(G-15769)***
Pp3, Elk Grove Village *Also called Post Press Production Inc* ***(G-9185)***
Ppc Flexible Packaging LLC (HQ) ... 847 541-0000
1111 Busch Pkwy Buffalo Grove (60089) ***(G-2588)***
PPG, Elgin *Also called Proven Partners Group LLC* ***(G-8702)***
PPG 4611, O Fallon *Also called PPG Industries Inc* ***(G-15582)***
PPG 5524, Alsip *Also called PPG Industries Inc* ***(G-495)***
PPG 5527, Chicago *Also called PPG Industries Inc* ***(G-5851)***
PPG 5534, Elgin *Also called PPG Industries Inc* ***(G-8693)***
PPG 9449, Westmont *Also called PPG Industries Inc* ***(G-20766)***
PPG Architectural Finishes Inc ... 217 584-1323
S Washington St Meredosia (62665) ***(G-13956)***
PPG Architectural Finishes Inc ... 309 673-3761
404 Sw Adams St Peoria (61602) ***(G-16500)***
PPG Industries, Decatur *Also called Fuyao Glass Illinois Inc* ***(G-7495)***
PPG Industries Inc ... 847 244-3410
3938 Porett Dr Gurnee (60031) ***(G-10913)***
PPG Industries Inc ... 708 597-7044
5151 W 122nd St Alsip (60803) ***(G-495)***
PPG Industries Inc ... 847 742-3340
266 Kimball St Elgin (60120) ***(G-8693)***
PPG Industries Inc ... 618 206-2250
1333 Central Park Dr # 135 O Fallon (62269) ***(G-15582)***
PPG Industries Inc ... 312 666-2277
345 N Morgan St Chicago (60607) ***(G-5851)***
PPG Industries Inc ... 630 960-3600
6136 S Cass Ave Westmont (60559) ***(G-20766)***
PPG Vpn ... 630 907-8910
2570 Orchard Gateway Rd Aurora (60506) ***(G-1145)***
Ppm, Peoria *Also called Performance Pattern & Mch Inc* ***(G-16496)***
Ppt Industrial Machines Inc ... 800 851-3586
714 N Walnut St Mount Carmel (62863) ***(G-14485)***
PQ Corporation ... 815 667-4241
340 E Grove St Utica (61373) ***(G-20006)***
PQ Corporation ... 847 662-8566
1945 N Delany Rd Gurnee (60031) ***(G-10914)***
PQ Ovens, Byron *Also called Dane Industries LLC* ***(G-2752)***
PR Manufacturing Entps LLC ... 309 347-8785
1805 Riverway Dr Pekin (61554) ***(G-16354)***
PR Orthotics & Ot ... 224 470-8550
4711 Golf Rd Ste 1055 Skokie (60076) ***(G-19008)***
Practechal Marketing ... 847 486-8600
1867 Waukegan Rd Glenview (60025) ***(G-10600)***
Practical Baker Inc ... 815 943-6040
600 Chippewa Rd Harvard (60033) ***(G-11063)***
Practical Communications Inc ... 773 754-3250
1900 E Golf Rd Ste 950 Schaumburg (60173) ***(G-18681)***
Practice Management Info Corp ... 800 633-7467
2001 Butterfield Rd # 310 Downers Grove (60515) ***(G-8081)***
Prager Associates ... 309 691-1565
4035 W Tangleoaks Ct Peoria (61615) ***(G-16501)***
Praire State Floor Covering ... 309 253-5982
333 South St Pekin (61554) ***(G-16355)***
Prairie Area Library System (PA) ... 309 799-3155
220 W 23rd Ave Coal Valley (61240) ***(G-6938)***
Prairie Central, Decatur *Also called Southfield Corporation* ***(G-7548)***
Prairie Central Ready Mix ... 217 877-5210
800 E Mckinley Ave Decatur (62526) ***(G-7537)***
Prairie Construction Material, Peoria *Also called Southfield Corporation* ***(G-16527)***
Prairie Display Chicago Inc ... 630 834-8773
758 N Industrial Dr Elmhurst (60126) ***(G-9411)***
Prairie Farms Dairy, Rockford *Also called Muller-Pinehurst Dairy Inc* ***(G-17533)***
Prairie Farms Dairy Inc ... 618 451-5600
1800 Adams St Granite City (62040) ***(G-10730)***

ALPHABETIC

Prairie Farms Dairy Inc ALPHABETIC SECTION

Prairie Farms Dairy Inc 618 457-4167
742 N Illinois Ave Carbondale (62901) ***(G-2854)***
Prairie Fire Glass Inc 217 762-3332
217 W Washington St Monticello (61856) ***(G-14284)***
Prairie Glen Imaging Ctr LLC 847 296-5366
9680 Golf Rd Des Plaines (60016) ***(G-7829)***
Prairie Group Management LLC 708 458-0400
7601 W 79th St Ste 1 Bridgeview (60455) ***(G-2375)***
Prairie Island Inc 630 395-9846
325 Cromwell Ct Westmont (60559) ***(G-20767)***
Prairie Land Mllwrght Svcs Inc 815 538-3085
617 E Us Highway 34 Mendota (61342) ***(G-13953)***
Prairie Manufacturing Inc 815 498-1593
405 E Lafayette St Ste 1 Somonauk (60552) ***(G-19072)***
Prairie Material, Bridgeview *Also called Vcna Prairie Indiana Inc* ***(G-2396)***
Prairie Material, Bridgeview *Also called Cimentos N Votorantim Amer Inc* ***(G-2335)***
Prairie Material 708 458-0400
7601 W 79th St Ste 1 Bedford Park (60455) ***(G-1493)***
Prairie Materials Group 815 207-6750
19515 Ne Frontage Rd Shorewood (60404) ***(G-18900)***
Prairie North Central Mtls, Manteno *Also called Southfield Corporation* ***(G-13457)***
Prairie Profile 618 846-2116
1437 E 1050 Ave Vandalia (62471) ***(G-20019)***
Prairie Pure Cheese 815 568-5000
1405 N State St Marengo (60152) ***(G-13493)***
Prairie Signs Inc 309 452-0463
1215 Warriner St Normal (61761) ***(G-15218)***
Prairie State Graphics Inc 847 801-3100
11100 Addison Ave Franklin Park (60131) ***(G-10022)***
Prairie State Impressions LLC 847 801-3100
11100 Addison Ave Franklin Park (60131) ***(G-10023)***
Prairie State Machine LLC 217 543-3768
71 E Cr 100 N Arthur (61911) ***(G-877)***
Prairie State Screw & Bolt Co 847 858-9551
4219 Kayla Ln Northbrook (60062) ***(G-15463)***
Prairie State Winery (PA) 815 784-4540
222 W Main St Genoa (60135) ***(G-10322)***
Prairie View Farms, Deer Grove *Also called H W Hostetler & Sons* ***(G-7577)***
Prairie Wi-Fl Systems 515 988-3260
935 W Chestnut St Ste 530 Chicago (60642) ***(G-5852)***
Prairie Woodworks Inc 309 378-2418
311 S Lincoln St Downs (61736) ***(G-8112)***
Prairieland Food Products Co 708 396-8826
3750 W 131st St Alsip (60803) ***(G-496)***
Prairieland Fs Inc 309 329-2162
2452 N Bader Rd Astoria (61501) ***(G-895)***
Prairieland Printing 309 647-5425
1237 Peoria St Washington (61571) ***(G-20276)***
Prarieland Printing Spp, Washington *Also called Prairieland Printing* ***(G-20276)***
Prater Industries Inc (HQ) 630 679-3200
2 Sammons Ct Bolingbrook (60440) ***(G-2228)***
Prater-Sterling, Bolingbrook *Also called Prater Industries Inc* ***(G-2228)***
Prater-Sterling, Sterling *Also called Sterling Systems & Controls* ***(G-19536)***
Pratt-Read Tools LLC 815 895-1121
1375 Park Ave Sycamore (60178) ***(G-19728)***
Praxair Inc 847 428-3405
330 Arrowhead Dr Gilberts (60136) ***(G-10365)***
Praxair Inc 708 728-9353
7400 S Central Ave Chicago (60638) ***(G-5853)***
Praxair Inc 309 347-5575
1225 S Front St Pekin (61554) ***(G-16356)***
Praxair Distribution Inc 314 664-7900
9 Judith Ln Cahokia (62206) ***(G-2763)***
Praxsym Inc 217 897-1744
120 S Third St Fisher (61843) ***(G-9667)***
Pre Fnish Mtals Mrrisville Inc 847 439-2211
2250 Pratt Blvd Elk Grove Village (60007) ***(G-9188)***
Pre Pack Machinery Inc 217 352-1010
520 S Country Fair Dr Champaign (61821) ***(G-3338)***
Precious Metal Ref Svcs Inc 847 756-2700
1531 S Grove Ave Unit 104 Barrington (60010) ***(G-1237)***
Precise Digital Printing Inc 847 593-2645
880 Industrial Dr Bensenville (60106) ***(G-1871)***
Precise Finishing Co Inc 847 451-2077
2842 Birch St Franklin Park (60131) ***(G-10024)***
Precise Lapping Grinding Corp 708 615-0240
2041 Janice Ave Melrose Park (60160) ***(G-13904)***
Precise Lser Waterjet Stamping, North Aurora *Also called Precise Stamping Inc* ***(G-15272)***
Precise Products Inc 630 393-9698
3s286 Talbot Ave Warrenville (60555) ***(G-20247)***
Precise Punch Products Co, Rockford *Also called Cdv Corp* ***(G-17339)***
Precise Rotary Die Inc 847 678-0001
9250 Ivanhoe St Schiller Park (60176) ***(G-18834)***
Precise Stamping Inc 630 897-6477
202 Poplar Pl North Aurora (60542) ***(G-15272)***
Precise Technology 847 459-1001
700 Corporate Grove Dr Buffalo Grove (60089) ***(G-2589)***
Precise Tool & Manufacturing, Loves Park *Also called Phillip Rodgers* ***(G-13244)***

Precisepower LLC 847 908-5400
140 E State Pkwy Schaumburg (60173) ***(G-18682)***
Precision Brand Products Inc 630 969-7200
2250 Curtiss St Downers Grove (60515) ***(G-8082)***
Precision Chrome Inc 847 587-1515
105 Precision Rd Fox Lake (60020) ***(G-9753)***
Precision Circuits Inc 630 515-9100
2538 Wisconsin Ave Downers Grove (60515) ***(G-8083)***
Precision Cnncting Rod Svc Inc 708 345-3700
2600 W Cermak Rd Broadview (60155) ***(G-2458)***
Precision Components Inc 630 462-9110
1020 Cedar Ave Ste 215 Saint Charles (60174) ***(G-18249)***
Precision Computer Methods 630 208-8000
801 Drover St Elburn (60119) ***(G-8469)***
Precision Container Inc 618 548-2830
1370 W Main St Salem (62881) ***(G-18351)***
Precision Control Systems 630 521-0234
1980 University Ln Lisle (60532) ***(G-12928)***
Precision Conveyor and Erct Co 779 324-5269
9511 Corsair Rd Ste E Frankfort (60423) ***(G-9823)***
Precision Ctng Tls Svc Mfg Inc 847 901-6800
3222 W Lake Ave Glenview (60026) ***(G-10601)***
Precision Dialogue Inc 773 237-2264
5501 W Grand Ave Chicago (60639) ***(G-5854)***
Precision Dialogue Direct Inc (HQ) 773 237-2264
5501 W Grand Ave Chicago (60639) ***(G-5855)***
Precision Die Cutting & Finish 773 252-5625
4027 W Le Moyne St Chicago (60651) ***(G-5856)***
Precision Dormer, LLC, Elgin *Also called Dormer Pramet LLC* ***(G-8568)***
Precision Drive & Control Inc 815 235-7595
1650 S Galena Ave Freeport (61032) ***(G-10133)***
Precision Dynamics Inc 815 877-1592
5029 Willow Creek Rd Machesney Park (61115) ***(G-13366)***
Precision Engine Rbldrs Inc 815 254-2333
23807 W Andrew Rd Unit A Plainfield (60585) ***(G-16704)***
Precision Engineering & Dev Co 630 834-5956
701 N Iowa Ave Villa Park (60181) ***(G-20165)***
Precision Entps Fndry Mch Inc (PA) 815 797-1000
1000 E Precision Dr Somonauk (60552) ***(G-19073)***
Precision Entps Fndry Mch Inc 815 498-2317
900 E Precision Dr Somonauk (60552) ***(G-19074)***
Precision Finishing Systems In 847 907-4266
682 Chaddick Dr Wheeling (60090) ***(G-20963)***
Precision Forming Stamping Co 773 489-6868
2419 W George St Chicago (60618) ***(G-5857)***
Precision Foundry Tooling Ltd 217 847-3233
160 Hamilton Indus Park Hamilton (62341) ***(G-10960)***
Precision Gage Company 630 655-2121
100 Shore Dr Burr Ridge (60527) ***(G-2714)***
Precision Governors LLC 815 229-5300
1715 Northrock Ct Rockford (61103) ***(G-17556)***
Precision Grinding Inc 847 238-1000
2375 American Ln Elk Grove Village (60007) ***(G-9189)***
Precision Ground 815 578-2613
548 Herbert Rd Ste 2 Lakemoor (60051) ***(G-12475)***
Precision Header Tooling Inc 815 874-9116
3441 Precision Dr Rockford (61109) ***(G-17557)***
Precision Ibc Inc 708 396-0750
13612 Lawler Ave Crestwood (60418) ***(G-7125)***
Precision Inc 847 593-2947
2210 Elmhurst Rd Elk Grove Village (60007) ***(G-9190)***
Precision Industrial Knife 630 350-7898
850 Dillon Dr Wood Dale (60191) ***(G-21229)***
Precision Ink Corporation 847 952-1500
151 Stanley St Elk Grove Village (60007) ***(G-9191)***
Precision Instruments Inc 847 824-4194
1846 Miner St Des Plaines (60016) ***(G-7830)***
Precision Laboratories LLC 847 282-7228
1429 S Shields Dr Waukegan (60085) ***(G-20481)***
Precision Laser Marking Inc 630 628-8575
900 S Kay Ave Addison (60101) ***(G-250)***
Precision Machine and 618 997-8795
410 N Pentecost Dr Marion (62959) ***(G-13530)***
Precision Machine Products 630 860-0861
655 N Central Ave Ste G Wood Dale (60191) ***(G-21230)***
Precision Machining & Tool Co 847 674-7111
7341 Monticello Ave Skokie (60076) ***(G-19009)***
Precision Masters Inc 815 397-3894
2801 Eastrock Dr Rockford (61109) ***(G-17558)***
Precision McHned Cmponents Inc 630 759-5555
1348 Enterprise Dr Romeoville (60446) ***(G-17866)***
Precision Medical Mfg LLC 847 229-1551
852 Seton Ct Wheeling (60090) ***(G-20964)***
Precision Metal Crafters Inc 847 816-3244
1840 Industrial Dr # 340 Libertyville (60048) ***(G-12698)***
Precision Metal Crafts Inc 815 254-2306
12201 Rhea Dr Plainfield (60585) ***(G-16705)***
Precision Metal Products Inc 630 458-0100
1209 W Capitol Dr Addison (60101) ***(G-251)***
Precision Metal Spinning Corp 847 392-5672
1000 Carnegie St Rolling Meadows (60008) ***(G-17764)***

ALPHABETIC SECTION
Press Fuel

Precision Metal Technologies 847 228-6630
2255 Lois Dr Ste 2 Rolling Meadows (60008) ***(G-17765)***
Precision Molded Concepts 815 675-0060
2402 Spring Ridge Dr C Spring Grove (60081) ***(G-19294)***
Precision Oil Field Cnstr, Mount Sterling *Also called Bruce McCullough* ***(G-14589)***
Precision Paper Tube Company (PA) 847 537-4250
1033 Noel Ave Wheeling (60090) ***(G-20965)***
Precision Plastic Ball Co 847 678-2255
10129 Pacific Ave Franklin Park (60131) ***(G-10025)***
Precision Plastic Products 217 784-4920
111 E 8th St Gibson City (60936) ***(G-10342)***
Precision Plating of Quincy 217 223-6590
2611 Locust St Quincy (62301) ***(G-16923)***
Precision Plugging and Sls Inc 618 395-8510
3978 N Elmdale Rd Olney (62450) ***(G-15884)***
Precision Press & Label Inc 630 625-1225
1285 Hamilton Pkwy Itasca (60143) ***(G-11722)***
Precision Printing, Crest Hill *Also called Temper Enterprises Inc* ***(G-7098)***
Precision Printing Inc 630 317-7004
1422 Centre Cir Downers Grove (60515) ***(G-8084)***
Precision Printing Inc 630 737-0075
230 Eisenhower Ln N Lombard (60148) ***(G-13121)***
Precision Prismatic Inc 708 424-0905
10247 Ridgeland Ave Ste 1 Chicago Ridge (60415) ***(G-6808)***
Precision Process Corp 847 640-9820
1401 Brummel Ave Elk Grove Village (60007) ***(G-9192)***
Precision Products Inc 217 735-1590
316 Limit St Lincoln (62656) ***(G-12737)***
Precision Products Mfg Intl 847 299-8500
1400 E Touhy Ave Ste 402 Des Plaines (60018) ***(G-7831)***
Precision Pump & Valve Service, Salem *Also called Duncan Oil Company Inc* ***(G-18336)***
Precision Quincy Ovens LLC 302 602-8738
483 Gardner St South Beloit (61080) ***(G-19108)***
Precision Remanufacturing Inc 773 489-7225
4520 W Fullerton Ave Chicago (60639) ***(G-5858)***
Precision Reproductions Inc 847 724-0182
4316 Regency Dr Glenview (60025) ***(G-10602)***
Precision Resource Inc 847 383-1300
700 Hickory Hill Dr Vernon Hills (60061) ***(G-20083)***
Precision Resource III Div, Vernon Hills *Also called Precision Resource Inc* ***(G-20083)***
Precision Screen Specialties 630 220-1361
3905 Commerce Dr Saint Charles (60174) ***(G-18250)***
Precision Screw Machining Co 773 205-4280
3511 N Kenton Ave Chicago (60641) ***(G-5859)***
Precision Service 618 345-2047
407 W Main St Collinsville (62234) ***(G-6972)***
Precision Service Mtr Inc 630 628-9900
121 W Fullerton Ave Addison (60101) ***(G-252)***
Precision Stamping Pdts Inc 847 678-0800
4848 River Rd Schiller Park (60176) ***(G-18835)***
Precision Steel Warehouse Inc (HQ) 800 323-0740
3500 Wolf Rd Franklin Park (60131) ***(G-10026)***
Precision Tank & Equipment Co (PA) 217 452-7228
3503 Conover Rd Virginia (62691) ***(G-20195)***
Precision Tank & Equipment Co 217 636-7023
25203 Quarry Ave Athens (62613) ***(G-900)***
Precision Tool 815 464-2428
21200 S La Grange Rd Frankfort (60423) ***(G-9824)***
Precision Tool & Die Company 217 864-3371
445 W Main St Mount Zion (62549) ***(G-14649)***
Precision Tool Welding 630 285-9844
991 Oakton St Elk Grove Village (60007) ***(G-9193)***
Precision Truck Products Inc 618 548-9011
2625 S Broadway Ave Salem (62881) ***(G-18352)***
Precision Vision Inc 815 223-2022
1725 Kilkenny Ct Woodstock (60098) ***(G-21423)***
Precision Waterjet Inc 847 462-9381
684 Tek Dr Crystal Lake (60014) ***(G-7245)***
Precision-Tek Mfg, Arlington Heights *Also called Precision-Tek Mfg Inc* ***(G-789)***
Precision-Tek Mfg Inc 847 364-7800
3206 Nordic Rd Arlington Heights (60005) ***(G-789)***
Precitec Corporation 847 949-2800
1000 Tower Rd Mundelein (60060) ***(G-14727)***
Precoat Metals Corp 618 451-0909
25 Northgate Indus Dr Granite City (62040) ***(G-10731)***
Preferred Bus Publications Inc 815 717-6399
1938 E Lincoln Hwy # 216 New Lenox (60451) ***(G-15051)***
Preferred Fasteners Inc 630 510-0200
250 S Westgate Dr Carol Stream (60188) ***(G-3048)***
Preferred Freezer Services of 773 254-9500
4500 W 42nd Pl Chicago (60632) ***(G-5860)***
Preferred Press Inc 630 980-9799
1934 Bentley Ct Ste D Glendale Heights (60139) ***(G-10484)***
Preferred Printing & Graphics 708 547-6880
5815 Saint Charles Rd Berkeley (60163) ***(G-1944)***
Preferred Printing Service 312 421-2343
2343 W Roosevelt Rd Chicago (60608) ***(G-5861)***
Preformance Signs 815 544-5044
6593 Revlon Dr Belvidere (61008) ***(G-1695)***
Pregel America 847 258-3725
915 Busse Rd Elk Grove Village (60007) ***(G-9194)***
Pregis Innovative Packg LLC 847 597-2200
1650 Lake Cook Rd Ste 400 Deerfield (60015) ***(G-7643)***
Pregis LLC (HQ) 847 597-2200
1650 Lake Cook Rd Ste 400 Deerfield (60015) ***(G-7644)***
Pregis LLC 847 597-2200
1650 Lake Cook Rd Ste 400 Deerfield (60015) ***(G-7645)***
Prella Technologies Inc 630 400-0626
11408 Kiley Dr Huntley (60142) ***(G-11560)***
Premcor Incorporated 618 254-7301
201 E Hawthorne St Hartford (62048) ***(G-11037)***
Premier Beverage Solutions LLC 309 369-7117
805 Oakwood Rd East Peoria (61611) ***(G-8284)***
Premier Cdl Training Svcs LLC (PA) 618 797-1725
5529 Dial Dr Ste 4 Granite City (62040) ***(G-10732)***
Premier Fabrication LLC 309 448-2338
303 County Highway 8 Congerville (61729) ***(G-7000)***
Premier Intl Entps Inc 312 857-2200
221 N La Salle St Ste 900 Chicago (60601) ***(G-5862)***
Premier Laundry Technologies, Joliet *Also called L T P LLC* ***(G-11893)***
Premier Lighting and Sup LLC 708 612-9693
4161 166th St Oak Forest (60452) ***(G-15687)***
Premier Manufacturing Corp 847 640-6644
35 W Laura Dr Addison (60101) ***(G-253)***
Premier Metal Works Inc 312 226-7414
1616 S Clinton St Chicago (60616) ***(G-5863)***
Premier Packaging Corp 815 469-7951
9424 Gulfstream Rd Frankfort (60423) ***(G-9825)***
Premier Print Group, Champaign *Also called Premier Printing Illinois Inc* ***(G-3339)***
Premier Printing & Promotions 815 282-3890
1338 Turret Dr Ste B Machesney Park (61115) ***(G-13367)***
Premier Printing and Packg Inc 847 970-9434
1881 Hicks Rd Ste B Rolling Meadows (60008) ***(G-17766)***
Premier Printing Illinois Inc 217 359-2219
3104 Farber Dr Champaign (61822) ***(G-3339)***
Premier Signs Creations Inc 309 637-6890
710 Fayette St Peoria (61603) ***(G-16502)***
Premier Tool & Machine Inc 618 445-9066
330 Industrial Dr Albion (62806) ***(G-352)***
Premier Tool Works, Burr Ridge *Also called Integral Automation Inc* ***(G-2688)***
Premier Travel Media 630 794-0696
621 Plainfield Rd Ste 406 Willowbrook (60527) ***(G-21057)***
Premier Woodworking Concepts 815 334-0888
1016 Rail Dr Woodstock (60098) ***(G-21424)***
Premiere Distillery LLC 847 662-4444
1503 Saint Paul Ave Gurnee (60031) ***(G-10915)***
Premiere Distribution, Evanston *Also called Michele Terrell* ***(G-9551)***
Premiere Motorsports LLC 708 634-0007
16300 S Lincoln Hwy 1 Plainfield (60586) ***(G-16706)***
Premium Converting LLC 708 510-1842
2743 W 36th Pl Unit C Chicago (60632) ***(G-5864)***
Premium Manufacturing Inc 309 787-3882
4608 78th Ave W Rock Island (61201) ***(G-17233)***
Premium Oil Company 815 963-3800
923 Fairview Ct Rockford (61101) ***(G-17559)***
Premium Pallets 217 974-0155
2877 N Dirksen Pkwy Springfield (62702) ***(G-19427)***
Premium Products Inc 630 553-6160
207 Wolf St Yorkville (60560) ***(G-21498)***
Premium Test Equipment Corp 630 400-2681
30 W 270 Butterfield Warrenville (60555) ***(G-20248)***
Premium Wood Products Inc 815 787-3669
436 E Locust St Dekalb (60115) ***(G-7698)***
Prenosis Inc 949 246-3113
3440 S Dearborn St Chicago (60616) ***(G-5865)***
Prereo LLC 800 555-1055
819 S Wabash Ave Ste 606 Chicago (60605) ***(G-5866)***
Pres-On Corporation 630 628-2255
2600 E 107th St Bolingbrook (60440) ***(G-2229)***
Pres-On Tape & Gasket, Bolingbrook *Also called Pres-On Corporation* ***(G-2229)***
Prescott's TV & Appliance, Sterling *Also called Prescotts Inc* ***(G-19525)***
Prescotts Inc 815 626-2996
1910 E 4th St Sterling (61081) ***(G-19525)***
Prescription Plus Ltd (PA) 618 537-6202
753 True Value Dr Lebanon (62254) ***(G-12546)***
Presence Legacy Association 815 741-7555
2000 Glenwood Ave Ste 102 Joliet (60435) ***(G-11916)***
Press A Light Corporation 630 231-6566
300 Industrial Dr West Chicago (60185) ***(G-20632)***
Press America Inc 847 228-0333
661 Fargo Ave Elk Grove Village (60007) ***(G-9195)***
Press Brake Tool and Supply 847 776-9201
850 N Virginia Lake Ct Palatine (60074) ***(G-16149)***
Press Dough Inc 630 243-6900
22 Longwood Way Lemont (60439) ***(G-12585)***
Press Express, Lisle *Also called Cannon Ball Marketing Inc* ***(G-12875)***
Press Fuel 217 546-9606
2501 Wabash Ave Springfield (62704) ***(G-19428)***

ALPHABETIC

Press On Inc 630 628-1630
  53 S Evergreen Ave Addison (60101) *(G-254)*
Press Proof Printing 847 466-7156
  180 S Western Ave Carpentersville (60110) *(G-3115)*
Press Syndication Group LLC 646 325-3221
  4141 N Sacramento Ave Chicago (60618) *(G-5867)*
Press Tech Inc 847 824-4485
  959 Lee St Des Plaines (60016) *(G-7832)*
Pressd Apparel LLC 312 767-1877
  1200 W 35th St 192 Chicago (60609) *(G-5868)*
Presses Inc 708 496-7450
  5360 W 73rd St Bedford Park (60638) *(G-1494)*
Presspage Inc 312 256-9985
  350 N Orleans St Chicago (60654) *(G-5869)*
Pressure Specialist Inc 815 477-0007
  186 Virginia Rd Crystal Lake (60014) *(G-7246)*
Prestige Brands Inc 224 235-4049
  2100 Sanders Rd Northbrook (60062) *(G-15464)*
Prestige Distribution Inc 847 480-7667
  720 Anthony Trl Northbrook (60062) *(G-15465)*
Prestige Motor Works Inc 630 780-6439
  11258 S Route 59 Ste 1 Naperville (60564) *(G-14983)*
Prestige Threaded Products Co, Burr Ridge Also called *Great Lakes Washer Company (G-2677)*
Preston Industries Inc 847 647-0611
  6600 W Touhy Ave Niles (60714) *(G-15162)*
Prestone Pdts Kik Cstomer Pdts, Alsip Also called *Prestone Products Corporation (G-497)*
Prestone Products Corporation 708 371-3000
  13160 S Pulaski Rd Alsip (60803) *(G-497)*
Prestone Products Corporation (HQ) 888 282-8960
  6250 N River Rd Ste 6000 Rosemont (60018) *(G-18043)*
Pretium Packaging LLC 815 224-2633
  4444 Hollerich Dr Peru (61354) *(G-16590)*
Prevention Health Sciences Inc 618 252-6922
  5110 Highway 34 N Raleigh (62977) *(G-16962)*
Prevue Hendyrx, Chicago Also called *Prevue Pet Products Inc (G-5870)*
Prevue Pet Products Inc (PA) 773 722-1052
  224 N Maplewood Ave Chicago (60612) *(G-5870)*
Preziosio Ltd 630 393-0920
  30 W 270 Butterfield Rd D Warrenville (60555) *(G-20249)*
Price Brothers Co 815 389-4800
  4416 Prairie Hill Rd South Beloit (61080) *(G-19109)*
Price Circuits LLC 847 742-4700
  1300 Holmes Rd Elgin (60123) *(G-8694)*
Price Fx Inc 312 763-3121
  150 S Riverside Plz # 422 Chicago (60606) *(G-5871)*
Price Machine Inc 217 892-8958
  1021 County Road 2850 N Dewey (61840) *(G-7874)*
Pride In Graphics Inc (PA) 312 427-2000
  739 S Clark St Fl 2 Chicago (60605) *(G-5872)*
Pride Machine & Tool Co Inc 708 343-7190
  1821 N 30th Ave Melrose Park (60160) *(G-13905)*
Pride Manufacturing, Chicago Also called *Cintas Corporation (G-4151)*
Pride Metal, Watseka Also called *Lyon LLC (G-20309)*
Pride Metal Products, Watseka Also called *Metal Mfg LLC (G-20311)*
Pride Packaging LLC 309 663-9100
  211 N Williamsburg Dr A Bloomington (61704) *(G-2086)*
Prikos & Becker LLC 847 675-3910
  8109 Lawndale Ave Skokie (60076) *(G-19010)*
Prima Donna Salon, Belleville Also called *Payne Chauna (G-1583)*
Prime Blend LLC 866 217-3732
  1300 Pratt Blvd Elk Grove Village (60007) *(G-9196)*
Prime Dental Manufacturing 773 283-2914
  4555 W Addison St Chicago (60641) *(G-5873)*
Prime Devices Corporation 847 729-2550
  11450 German Church Rd Willow Springs (60480) *(G-21027)*
Prime Group Inc 312 922-3883
  122 S Michigan Ave # 2040 Chicago (60603) *(G-5874)*
Prime Group Realty Trust, Chicago Also called *Prime Group Inc (G-5874)*
Prime Industries Inc 630 725-9200
  4611 Main St Ste A Lisle (60532) *(G-12929)*
Prime Label & Packaging LLC 630 227-1300
  501 N Central Ave Wood Dale (60191) *(G-21231)*
Prime Label Group LLC 773 630-8793
  1380 Nagel Blvd Batavia (60510) *(G-1405)*
Prime Market Targeting Inc 815 469-4555
  7777 W Lincoln Hwy Ste A Frankfort (60423) *(G-9826)*
Prime Publishing LLC 847 205-9375
  3400 Dundee Rd Ste 220 Northbrook (60062) *(G-15466)*
Prime Stainless Products LLC 847 678-0800
  4848 River Rd Schiller Park (60176) *(G-18836)*
Prime Systems Inc 630 681-2100
  416 Mission St Carol Stream (60188) *(G-3049)*
Prime Time Sports LLC 847 637-3500
  216 W University Dr Arlington Heights (60004) *(G-790)*
Prime Uv, Carol Stream Also called *Prime Systems Inc (G-3049)*
Prime Vector International LLC 847 348-1060
  349 S Circle Dr Palatine (60067) *(G-16150)*

Prime Wood Craft Inc (HQ) 216 738-2222
  1450 American Ln Ste 700 Schaumburg (60173) *(G-18683)*
Prime Wood Craft Inc 716 803-3425
  1450 American Ln Ste 700 Schaumburg (60173) *(G-18684)*
Primedge Inc (PA) 224 265-6600
  1281 Arthur Ave Elk Grove Village (60007) *(G-9197)*
Primedia Source LLC 630 553-8451
  627 White Oak Way Yorkville (60560) *(G-21499)*
Primo Designs Inc 217 523-6373
  2417 E North Grand Ave B Springfield (62702) *(G-19429)*
Primo Microphone Inc 630 837-6119
  2 Canterbury Ct Streamwood (60107) *(G-19589)*
Primrose Candy Co 800 268-9522
  4111 W Parker Ave Chicago (60639) *(G-5875)*
Prince Agri Products Inc 217 222-8854
  221 S Prince Agri Way St Quincy (62305) *(G-16924)*
Prince Agri Products Inc 217 222-8854
  229 Radio Rd Quincy (62305) *(G-16925)*
Prince Castle LLC (HQ) 630 462-8800
  355 Kehoe Blvd Carol Stream (60188) *(G-3050)*
Prince Fabricators Inc 630 588-0088
  745 N Gary Ave Carol Stream (60188) *(G-3051)*
Prince Fabricators Division, Carol Stream Also called *Prince Fabricators Inc (G-3051)*
Prince Industries Inc (PA) 630 588-0088
  745 N Gary Ave Carol Stream (60188) *(G-3052)*
Prince Industries Shanghai, Carol Stream Also called *Prince Industries Inc (G-3052)*
Prince Minerals Inc 618 285-6558
  Ferrell St Rosiclare (62982) *(G-18065)*
Prince Minerals LLC 646 747-4222
  223 Hampshire St Quincy (62301) *(G-16926)*
Prince Minerals LLC 646 747-4200
  401 N Prince Plz Quincy (62305) *(G-16927)*
Princess Foods Inc 847 933-1820
  8145 Monticello Ave Skokie (60076) *(G-19011)*
Princeton Chemicals Inc 847 975-6210
  988 Princeton Ave Highland Park (60035) *(G-11292)*
Princeton Fast Stop 815 872-0706
  720 N Main St Princeton (61356) *(G-16818)*
Princeton Flighting Corp 815 872-0945
  145 W Progress Dr Princeton (61356) *(G-16819)*
Princeton Industrial Pdts Inc 847 839-8500
  1485 Davis Rd Ste B Elgin (60123) *(G-8695)*
Princeton Ready-Mix Inc 815 875-3359
  533 E Railroad Ave Princeton (61356) *(G-16820)*
Princeton Sealing Wax Co 815 875-1943
  106 W Long St Princeton (61356) *(G-16821)*
Principal Instruments Inc 815 469-8159
  845 Basswood Ln Frankfort (60423) *(G-9827)*
Principal Manufacturing Corp 708 865-7500
  2800 S 19th Ave Broadview (60155) *(G-2459)*
Prinova Solutions LLC (HQ) 630 868-0300
  285 Fullerton Ave Carol Stream (60188) *(G-3053)*
Prinsco Inc 815 635-3131
  111 E Pine St Chatsworth (60921) *(G-3426)*
Print & Design Services LLC 847 317-9001
  2561 Waukegan Rd Bannockburn (60015) *(G-1206)*
Print & Mailing Solutions LLC (PA) 708 544-9400
  1053 N Schmidt Rd Romeoville (60446) *(G-17867)*
Print & Mailing Solutions LLC 708 544-9400
  745 Dillon Dr Wood Dale (60191) *(G-21232)*
Print and Mktg Solutions Group 847 498-9640
  180 N Stetson Ave # 3500 Chicago (60601) *(G-5876)*
Print Butler Inc 312 296-2804
  674 Indian Path Rd Grayslake (60030) *(G-10796)*
Print Express, Chicago Also called *Shree Mahavir Inc (G-6159)*
Print Loop, Elgin Also called *David H Pool (G-8563)*
Print Management Group Inc 847 671-0900
  1253 Pagni Dr Schiller Park (60176) *(G-18837)*
Print Management Partners Inc (PA) 847 699-2999
  701 Lee St Ste 1050 Des Plaines (60016) *(G-7833)*
Print Ninja LLC 877 396-4652
  1603 Orrington Ave # 150 Evanston (60201) *(G-9569)*
Print Service & Dist Assn Psda 312 321-5120
  401 N Michigan Ave Chicago (60611) *(G-5877)*
Print Shop 815 786-8278
  17 E Center St Sandwich (60548) *(G-18381)*
Print Shop of Morris 815 710-5030
  1836 Unit B N Division St Morris (60450) *(G-14322)*
Print Shoppe Inc The Olde, Olney Also called *Olde Print Shoppe Inc (G-15879)*
Print Source For Business Inc 847 356-0190
  38966 N Deep Lake Rd Lake Villa (60046) *(G-12363)*
Print Tech Inc 847 949-5400
  407 Wshington Blvd Unit C Mundelein (60060) *(G-14728)*
Print Turnaround Inc 847 228-1762
  3025 Malmo Dr Arlington Heights (60005) *(G-791)*
Print Xpress 847 677-5555
  8058 Lincoln Ave Skokie (60077) *(G-19012)*
Print-O-Tape Inc 847 362-1476
  755 Tower Rd Mundelein (60060) *(G-14729)*
Printco Printing, Charleston Also called *Stearns Printing of Charleston (G-3414)*

Printcrazy LLC 630 573-1020
209 Glenwood Rd Chicago Heights (60411) ***(G-6765)***
Printed Impressions Inc 773 604-8585
1640 S Ardmore Ave Oakbrook Terrace (60181) ***(G-15813)***
Printed Word Inc 847 328-1511
1807 Central St Evanston (60201) ***(G-9570)***
Printer Connection 217 268-3252
319 S Elm St Arcola (61910) ***(G-663)***
Printers Ink of Paris Inc 217 463-2552
124 W Court St Paris (61944) ***(G-16240)***
Printers Mark 309 732-1174
1512 4th Ave Rock Island (61201) ***(G-17234)***
Printers Row Loft 312 431-1019
732 S Fincl Pl Ste Mgmt Chicago (60605) ***(G-5878)***
Printers Row Press Inc 312 427-7150
739 S Clark St Fl 1 Chicago (60605) ***(G-5879)***
Printers Square Condo Assn 312 765-8794
680 S Federal St Chicago (60605) ***(G-5880)***
Printers The, Paris *Also called Printers Ink of Paris Inc* ***(G-16240)***
Printforce Inc 618 395-7746
1409 E Main St Olney (62450) ***(G-15885)***
PRINTING, Yorkville *Also called Lambert Print Source Llc* ***(G-21491)***
Printing Inc (HQ) 316 265-1201
35 W Wacker Dr Ste 3600 Chicago (60601) ***(G-5881)***
Printing Arts, Broadview *Also called Ripa LLC* ***(G-2464)***
Printing Arts Cmmnications LLC 708 938-1600
2001 W 21st St Broadview (60155) ***(G-2460)***
Printing By Joseph 708 479-2669
19640 S La Grange Rd Mokena (60448) ***(G-14109)***
Printing Circuit Boards 630 543-3453
447 S Vista Ave Addison (60101) ***(G-255)***
Printing Craftsmen of Joliet 815 254-3982
2101 New Port Dr Joliet (60431) ***(G-11917)***
Printing Craftsmen of Pontiac 815 844-7118
509 W Howard St Pontiac (61764) ***(G-16778)***
Printing Dimensions 847 439-7521
1515 S Highland Ave Arlington Heights (60005) ***(G-792)***
Printing Etc Inc 815 562-6151
1135 Lincoln Hwy Rochelle (61068) ***(G-17152)***
Printing Factory, The, Mundelein *Also called Print Tech Inc* ***(G-14728)***
Printing Gallery Inc 773 525-7102
201 W Lake St Chicago (60606) ***(G-5882)***
Printing Impression Direc 815 385-6688
31704 N Clearwater Dr Lakemoor (60051) ***(G-12476)***
Printing On Ashland Inc 773 488-4707
8227 S Ashland Ave Ste 1 Chicago (60620) ***(G-5883)***
Printing Plant 618 529-3115
606 S Illinois Ave Ste 1 Carbondale (62901) ***(G-2855)***
Printing Plus 708 301-3900
15751 Annico Dr Ste 5 Lockport (60491) ***(G-13019)***
Printing Plus of Roselle Inc 630 893-0410
205 E Irving Park Rd Roselle (60172) ***(G-17974)***
Printing Press The, Milan *Also called Whipples Printing Press Inc* ***(G-14031)***
Printing Shop 847 998-6330
1220 Waukegan Rd Glenview (60025) ***(G-10603)***
Printing Source Inc 773 588-2930
8120 River Dr Ste 2 Morton Grove (60053) ***(G-14433)***
Printing System 630 339-5900
1935 Brandon Ct Ste A Glendale Heights (60139) ***(G-10485)***
Printing Works II, The, Elk Grove Village *Also called Printing Works Inc* ***(G-9198)***
Printing Works Inc 847 860-1920
2485 E Devon Ave Elk Grove Village (60007) ***(G-9198)***
Printing You Can Trust 224 676-0482
707 Mallard Ln Deerfield (60015) ***(G-7646)***
Printing/Typesetting, Rolling Meadows *Also called Tri-Tower Printing Inc* ***(G-17782)***
Printjet Corporation 815 877-7511
7816 Burden Rd Machesney Park (61115) ***(G-13368)***
Printmart, Oak Lawn *Also called N P D Inc* ***(G-15729)***
Printmeisters Inc 708 474-8400
3240 Ridge Rd Lansing (60438) ***(G-12512)***
Printninja, Evanston *Also called Print Ninja LLC* ***(G-9569)***
Printpack Inc 847 888-7150
1400 Abbott Dr Elgin (60123) ***(G-8696)***
Printsmart Printing & Graphics 630 434-2000
3024 Hobson Rd Woodridge (60517) ***(G-21334)***
Printsource Plus Inc 708 389-6252
12128 Western Ave Blue Island (60406) ***(G-2134)***
Printwise Inc 630 833-2845
1670 Monticello Ct Unit E Wheaton (60189) ***(G-20815)***
Printworld 815 544-1000
319 S State St Belvidere (61008) ***(G-1696)***
Prinzings of Rockford 815 874-9654
2046 Schell Dr Rockford (61109) ***(G-17560)***
Priority Care, Elgin *Also called First Priority Inc* ***(G-8587)***
Priority One Printing and Mail 217 224-8008
839 Jersey St Quincy (62301) ***(G-16928)***
Priority One Prtg & Mailing, Quincy *Also called Priority One Printing and Mail* ***(G-16928)***
Priority Print 708 485-7080
9433 Ogden Ave Brookfield (60513) ***(G-2491)***
Priority Printing 773 889-6021
6942 W Diversey Ave Chicago (60707) ***(G-5884)***
Priority Promotions, Sycamore *Also called Visual Persuasion Inc* ***(G-19739)***
Prism Commercial Printing Ctrs 773 735-5400
6130 S Pulaski Rd Chicago (60629) ***(G-5885)***
Prism Esolutions Dv Andy Frain 630 820-3820
761 Shoreline Dr Aurora (60504) ***(G-1010)***
Prismatec Inc 847 562-9022
1964 Raymond Dr Northbrook (60062) ***(G-15467)***
Prismier LLC 630 592-4515
1049 Lily Cache Ln Unit B Bolingbrook (60440) ***(G-2230)***
Pristine Water Solutions Inc 847 689-1100
1570 S Lakeside Dr Waukegan (60085) ***(G-20482)***
Pritchard Enterprises Inc 217 832-8588
955 N State Route 130 Camargo (61919) ***(G-2801)***
Priva Mobility Inc 248 410-3702
515 Sheridan Rd Apt 103 Evanston (60202) ***(G-9571)***
Privacy One LLC 312 872-3757
70 W Burton Pl Apt 1205 Chicago (60610) ***(G-5886)***
Private Studios 217 367-3530
705 Western Ave Urbana (61801) ***(G-19995)***
Pro Access Systems Inc (PA) 630 426-0022
116 Paul St Elburn (60119) ***(G-8470)***
Pro Arc Inc 815 877-1804
7440 Forest Hills Rd Loves Park (61111) ***(G-13249)***
Pro Built Tool & Mold Inc 815 436-9088
23839 W Andrew Rd # 103 Plainfield (60585) ***(G-16707)***
Pro Cabinets Inc 618 993-0008
11123 Skyline Dr Marion (62959) ***(G-13531)***
Pro Circle Golf Centers Inc 815 675-2747
1810 N Us Highway 12 Spring Grove (60081) ***(G-19295)***
Pro Circle Golf Driving Range, Spring Grove *Also called Pro Circle Golf Centers Inc* ***(G-19295)***
Pro Energy Trade Inc 312 961-6404
3180 N Lake Shore Dr # 16 Chicago (60657) ***(G-5887)***
Pro Form Industries Inc 815 923-2555
17714 Jefferson St Union (60180) ***(G-19942)***
Pro Fuel Nine Inc 309 867-3375
101 S 8th St Oquawka (61469) ***(G-15907)***
Pro Glass Corporation 630 553-3141
9318 Corneils Rd Bristol (60512) ***(G-2409)***
Pro Graphics Ink 309 647-2526
322 N 15th Ave Canton (61520) ***(G-2831)***
Pro Intercom LLC (PA) 815 680-5205
4500 Us Highway 14 # 400 Crystal Lake (60014) ***(G-7247)***
Pro Machining Inc 815 633-4140
2131 Harlem Rd Loves Park (61111) ***(G-13250)***
Pro Mold & Die, Roselle *Also called Pro-Mold Incorporated* ***(G-17975)***
Pro Patch Systems Inc 847 356-8100
25704 W Lehmann Blvd Lake Villa (60046) ***(G-12364)***
Pro Rep Sale IL 847 382-1592
25560 N Countryside Dr Barrington (60010) ***(G-1238)***
Pro TEC Metal Finishing Corp 773 384-7853
1428 N Kilpatrick Ave Chicago (60651) ***(G-5888)***
Pro Tech Engineering 309 475-2502
129 W Lincoln St Saybrook (61770) ***(G-18419)***
Pro Techmation Inc 815 459-5909
370 E Prairie St Ste 5 Crystal Lake (60014) ***(G-7248)***
Pro Tools & Equipment Inc 847 838-6666
23529 Eagles Nest Rd Antioch (60002) ***(G-631)***
Pro Tuff Decal Inc 815 356-9160
7505 Eastgate Aly Crystal Lake (60014) ***(G-7249)***
Pro Woodworking 708 508-5948
6554 S Menard Ave Bedford Park (60638) ***(G-1495)***
Pro-AM Team Sports LLC 708 995-1511
8940 W 192nd St Ste J Mokena (60448) ***(G-14110)***
Pro-Beam USA, Aurora *Also called Globaltech International LLC* ***(G-972)***
Pro-Beam USA Inc 630 327-6909
13900 S Van Dyke Rd # 106 Plainfield (60544) ***(G-16708)***
Pro-Bilt Buildings LLC 217 532-9331
9181 Illinois Route 127 Hillsboro (62049) ***(G-11319)***
Pro-Fab Inc 309 263-8454
1050 W Jefferson St Ste A Morton (61550) ***(G-14379)***
Pro-Fab Metals Inc 618 283-2986
10949 Us 40 Vandalia (62471) ***(G-20020)***
Pro-Line Safety Products, West Chicago *Also called Pro-Pak Industries Inc* ***(G-20633)***
Pro-Line Winning Ways & Penlan 309 745-8530
2095 Washington Rd Washington (61571) ***(G-20277)***
Pro-Lube of Shelbyville Inc 217 774-4643
1715 W Main St Shelbyville (62565) ***(G-18883)***
Pro-Mold Incorporated 630 893-3594
55 Chancellor Dr Roselle (60172) ***(G-17975)***
Pro-Pak Industries Inc 630 876-1050
1099 Atlantic Dr Ste 1 West Chicago (60185) ***(G-20633)***
Pro-Parts 773 595-5966
4727 S Ingleside Ave # 1 Chicago (60615) ***(G-5889)***
Pro-Qua Inc 630 543-5644
305 W Laura Dr Addison (60101) ***(G-256)***
Pro-Quip Incorporated 708 352-5732
418 Shawmut Ave Ste A La Grange (60526) ***(G-12087)***

ALPHABETIC

Pro-Tech Machining Inc 773 406-9297
301 Eastern Ave Ste B Bensenville (60106) *(G-1872)*
Pro-Tech Metal Specialties Inc 630 279-7094
233 W Diversey Ave Elmhurst (60126) *(G-9412)*
Pro-Tek, Saint Charles *Also called Protek Inc (G-18252)*
Pro-Tek Products Inc 630 293-5100
1755 S Nprvlle Rd Ste 100 Wheaton (60189) *(G-20816)*
Pro-Tran Inc 217 348-9353
1671 Olive Ave Charleston (61920) *(G-3410)*
Pro-Type Printing Inc (PA) 217 379-4715
130 N Market St Paxton (60957) *(G-16315)*
Proalliance Corp 815 207-8556
300 W Front St Ste 203k Harvard (60033) *(G-11064)*
ProAm Sports Products 708 841-4200
435 Adams St Dolton (60419) *(G-7939)*
Proampac Pg Borrower LLC 618 451-0010
20 Central Industrial Dr Granite City (62040) *(G-10733)*
Problend-Eurogerm LLC 847 221-5004
1801 Hicks Rd Ste H Rolling Meadows (60008) *(G-17767)*
Procal Inc 847 219-7257
5721 Highland Dr Palatine (60067) *(G-16151)*
Process and Control Systems 708 293-0557
5836 W 117th Pl Alsip (60803) *(G-498)*
Process Engineering Corp (PA) 815 459-1734
7426 Virginia Rd Crystal Lake (60014) *(G-7250)*
Process Gear, Des Plaines *Also called CF Gear Holdings LLC (G-7742)*
Process Mechanical Inc 630 416-7021
2208 Pontiac Cir Naperville (60565) *(G-14902)*
Process Piping Inc 708 717-0513
18005 Semmler Dr Tinley Park (60487) *(G-19849)*
Process Screw Products Inc 815 864-2220
10 N Shannon Rte Shannon (61078) *(G-18872)*
Process Supply Company Inc (HQ) 312 943-8338
1087 N North Branch St Chicago (60642) *(G-5890)*
Process Systems Inc 217 563-2872
316 E State St Nokomis (62075) *(G-15197)*
Process Technologies Group 630 393-4777
30w106 Butterfield Rd Warrenville (60555) *(G-20250)*
Processed Steel Company 815 459-2400
3703 S Il Route 31 Crystal Lake (60012) *(G-7251)*
Procomm Inc Hoopeston Illinois 815 268-4303
209 W Grant Ave Onarga (60955) *(G-15902)*
Procon General Services Inc 773 227-8258
1035 N Damen Ave Chicago (60622) *(G-5891)*
Procon Pacific LLC 630 575-0551
436 Eisenhower Ln N Lombard (60148) *(G-13122)*
Procraft Engraving Inc 847 673-1500
8241 Christiana Ave Skokie (60076) *(G-19013)*
Procter & Gamble Co 847 936-4621
3500 16th St North Chicago (60064) *(G-15319)*
Procter & Gamble Company 847 375-5400
10275 W Higgins Rd Chicago (60605) *(G-5892)*
Procura, LLC, Schaumburg *Also called Ch Group Holdings Inc (G-18473)*
Producepro Inc (PA) 630 395-9700
9014 Heritage Pkwy # 304 Woodridge (60517) *(G-21335)*
Producers Chemical Company 630 466-4584
1960 Bucktail Ln Sugar Grove (60554) *(G-19650)*
Producers Envmtl Pdts LLC 630 482-5995
1261 N Raddant Rd Batavia (60510) *(G-1406)*
Product Emphasis, Melrose Park *Also called Fixture Hardware Co (G-13867)*
Product Feeding Solutions Inc 630 709-9546
5632 Pleasant Blvd Chicago Ridge (60415) *(G-6809)*
Product Service Craft Inc 630 964-5160
5407 Walnut Ave Downers Grove (60515) *(G-8085)*
Productigear Inc 773 847-4505
1900 W 34th St Chicago (60608) *(G-5893)*
Production Chemical Co Inc 847 455-8450
9381 Schiller Blvd Franklin Park (60131) *(G-10027)*
Production Cutting Services 815 264-3505
9341 State Route 23 Waterman (60556) *(G-20300)*
Production Engineering, Warsaw *Also called Production Manufacturing (G-20259)*
Production Fabg & Stamping Inc 708 755-5468
3311 Butler St S Chicago Hts (60411) *(G-18126)*
Production Manufacturing 217 256-4211
305 Main St Warsaw (62379) *(G-20259)*
Production Press Inc (PA) 217 243-3353
307 E Morgan St Jacksonville (62650) *(G-11781)*
Production Stampings Inc 815 495-2800
1864 N 4253rd Rd Leland (60531) *(G-12549)*
Production Tool Corporation (PA) 773 288-4400
1229 E 74th St Chicago (60619) *(G-5894)*
Productionpro, Villa Park *Also called Manufacturers Alliance Corp (G-20158)*
Productive Displays, Bensenville *Also called Productive Portable Disp Inc (G-1873)*
Productive Edge LLC (PA) 312 561-9000
11 E Illinois St Ste 200 Chicago (60611) *(G-5895)*
Productive Portable Disp Inc 630 458-9100
546 N York Rd Bensenville (60106) *(G-1873)*
Products In Motion Inc 815 213-7251
804 Industrial Park Rd Rock Falls (61071) *(G-17191)*
Productworks LLC 224 406-8810
610 Academy Dr Northbrook (60062) *(G-15468)*
Proell Inc 630 587-2300
2751 Dukane Dr Saint Charles (60174) *(G-18251)*
Professional Freezing Svcs LLC 773 847-7500
7035 W 65th St Chicago (60638) *(G-5896)*
Professional Gem Sciences Inc 312 920-1541
5 S Wabash Ave Ste 315 Chicago (60603) *(G-5897)*
Professional Graphics Inc 815 226-9422
4404 Boeing Dr Rockford (61109) *(G-17561)*
Professional Metal Works LLC 618 539-2214
9 Industrial Dr Freeburg (62243) *(G-10092)*
Professional Meters Inc 815 942-7000
3605 N State Route 47 D Morris (60450) *(G-14323)*
Professional RR Solutions LLC 815 209-7473
6678 Saladino Dr Roscoe (61073) *(G-17922)*
Professional Sales Associates 847 487-1900
1000 Brown St Ste 303 Wauconda (60084) *(G-20384)*
Professnal Mling Prtg Svcs Inc 630 510-1000
269 Commonwealth Dr Carol Stream (60188) *(G-3054)*
Profile Food Ingredients LLC 847 622-1700
1151 Timber Dr Elgin (60123) *(G-8697)*
Profile Network Inc 847 673-0592
4709 Golf Rd Ste 807 Skokie (60076) *(G-19014)*
Profile Plastics Inc (PA) 847 604-5100
65 Waukegan Rd Lake Bluff (60044) *(G-12207)*
Profile Products LLC (HQ) 847 215-1144
750 W Lake Cook Rd # 440 Buffalo Grove (60089) *(G-2590)*
Profile Screens Incorporated 309 543-2082
901 S Water St Havana (62644) *(G-11120)*
Proform 309 676-2535
708 Fayette St Peoria (61603) *(G-16503)*
Proforma 815 534-5461
144 Hickory St Frankfort (60423) *(G-9828)*
Proforma Awards Print & Promot 630 897-9848
403 Burr Oak Dr Oswego (60543) *(G-16021)*
Proforma Business Builders 309 692-6390
810 W Pioneer Pkwy Peoria (61615) *(G-16504)*
Proforma Coml Print Group, Naperville *Also called Sprinter Coml Print Label Corp (G-14988)*
Proforma Quality Business Svcs 847 356-1959
18582 W Judy Dr Gurnee (60031) *(G-10916)*
Proforma-Ppg Inc 847 429-9349
158 Dawson Dr Elgin (60120) *(G-8698)*
Prograf LLC 815 234-4848
119 W Home Ave Villa Park (60181) *(G-20166)*
Prographics-Aka, Rockford *Also called Professional Graphics Inc (G-17561)*
Progress Printing Corporation 773 927-0123
3324 S Halsted St Ste 1 Chicago (60608) *(G-5898)*
Progress Rail Locomotive Inc (HQ) 800 255-5355
9301 W 55th St Mc Cook (60525) *(G-13699)*
Progress Rail Locomotive Inc 708 387-5510
9301 W 55th St Mc Cook (60525) *(G-13700)*
Progress Rail Services Corp 618 451-0072
1900 Missouri Ave Granite City (62040) *(G-10734)*
Progress Rail Services Corp 309 343-6176
618 Us Highway 150 E Galesburg (61401) *(G-10216)*
Progress Rail Services Corp 309 963-4425
5704 E 1700 North Rd Danvers (61732) *(G-7317)*
Progress Reporter Inc 815 472-2000
110 W River St Momence (60954) *(G-14190)*
Progress Reporter Press, Momence *Also called Progress Reporter Inc (G-14190)*
Progressive Bronze Works Inc 773 463-5500
3550 N Spaulding Ave Chicago (60618) *(G-5899)*
Progressive Coating, Chicago *Also called SKW Industries LLC (G-6182)*
Progressive Coating Corp 773 261-8900
900 S Cicero Ave Chicago (60644) *(G-5900)*
Progressive Concepts 630 736-9822
305 S Bartlett Rd Ste D Streamwood (60107) *(G-19590)*
Progressive Environmental Svcs, Barrington *Also called Precious Metal Ref Svcs Inc (G-1237)*
Progressive Model Design, Romeoville *Also called Circuitron Inc (G-17809)*
Progressive Publications Inc 847 697-9181
85 Market St Ste 105 Elgin (60123) *(G-8699)*
Progressive Recovery Inc (PA) 618 286-5000
700 Industrial Dr Dupo (62239) *(G-8142)*
Progressive Sheet Metal Inc 773 376-1155
2850 S Tripp Ave Chicago (60623) *(G-5901)*
Progressive Solutions Corp 847 639-7272
2848 Corporate Pkwy Algonquin (60102) *(G-384)*
Progressive Steel Treating Inc 815 877-2571
922 Lawn Dr Loves Park (61111) *(G-13251)*
Progressive Systems Netwrk Inc 312 382-8383
1500 S Western Ave Ste 19 Chicago (60608) *(G-5902)*
Progressive Turnings Inc 630 898-3072
1680 Mountain St Aurora (60505) *(G-1146)*
Progrssive Cmponents Intl Corp (PA) 847 487-1000
235 Industrial Dr Wauconda (60084) *(G-20385)*
Prointegration Tech LLC 618 409-3233
13348 Koch Rd Highland (62249) *(G-11235)*

ALPHABETIC SECTION

Project Te Inc 217 344-9763
  2209 E University Ave B Urbana (61802) *(G-19996)*
Prolong Tool, West Chicago Also called Dippit Inc *(G-20571)*
Promark Advertising Specialtie 618 483-6025
  4 N Frontage Rd Altamont (62411) *(G-536)*
Promark Associates Inc 847 676-1894
  3856 Oakton St Ste 250 Skokie (60076) *(G-19015)*
Promark International Inc (PA) 630 830-2500
  1268 Humbracht Cir Bartlett (60103) *(G-1301)*
Promier Products Inc 815 223-3393
  350 5th St Ste 266 Peru (61354) *(G-16591)*
Promiz LLC 618 533-3950
  2228 Green Street Rd Centralia (62801) *(G-3246)*
Prommar Plastics Inc 815 770-0555
  1001 W Diggins St Ste 1 Harvard (60033) *(G-11065)*
Promo Answers Inc 708 633-6653
  15943 Blackwater Ct Tinley Park (60477) *(G-19850)*
Promo Corp 773 217-7666
  744 W Algonquin Rd Arlington Heights (60005) *(G-793)*
Promoframes LLC 866 566-7224
  1113 Tower Rd Schaumburg (60173) *(G-18685)*
Promotional Co of Illinois 847 382-0239
  2222 Shetland Rd Inverness (60010) *(G-11603)*
Promotions Plus, Frankfort Also called Sandra E Greene *(G-9836)*
Prompt Motor Rewinding Service 847 675-7155
  7509 Keystone Ave Skokie (60076) *(G-19016)*
Promus Equity Partners LLC (PA) 312 784-3990
  156 N Jefferson St # 300 Chicago (60661) *(G-5903)*
Pronto Signs and Engraving 847 249-7874
  2114 Grand Ave Waukegan (60085) *(G-20483)*
Proofing Technologies Ltd 847 222-7100
  5400 Newport Dr Ste 14 Rolling Meadows (60008) *(G-17768)*
Propane Central, Roberts Also called Dcc Propane LLC *(G-17105)*
Propeller Hr Solutions Inc 312 342-7355
  5350 Wolf Rd Western Springs (60558) *(G-20723)*
Prophet Gear Co 815 537-2002
  46 Grove St Prophetstown (61277) *(G-16834)*
Proquis Inc 847 278-3230
  423 Walnut Ave Elgin (60123) *(G-8700)*
Prosco Inc 847 336-1323
  3901 Grove Ave Gurnee (60031) *(G-10917)*
Proship Inc 312 332-7447
  29 N Wacker Dr Ste 700 Chicago (60606) *(G-5904)*
Prosig, Elk Grove Village Also called Helitune Inc *(G-9032)*
Prospan Manufacturing 847 815-0191
  10013 Norwood St Rosemont (60018) *(G-18044)*
Prospan Manufacturing Co 630 860-1930
  540 Meyer Rd Bensenville (60106) *(G-1874)*
Prospect Grinding Incorporated 847 229-9240
  925 Seton Ct Ste 11 Wheeling (60090) *(G-20966)*
Prosser Construction Co 217 774-5032
  1410 N 1500 East Rd Shelbyville (62565) *(G-18884)*
Prostat Corporation 630 238-8883
  1072 Tower Ln Bensenville (60106) *(G-1875)*
Prosthetic Orthotic Specialist (PA) 309 454-8733
  303 Landmark Dr Ste 5a Normal (61761) *(G-15219)*
Prosthetics Orthotics Han 847 695-6955
  620 S Il Route 31 Ste 7 McHenry (60050) *(G-13784)*
Protactic Golf Enterprises 708 209-1120
  504 River Oaks Dr River Forest (60305) *(G-17054)*
Prote USA LLC 773 576-9079
  7145 N Ionia Ave Chicago (60646) *(G-5905)*
Protec Equipment Resources Inc 847 434-5808
  1501 Wright Blvd Schaumburg (60193) *(G-18686)*
Protect Assoc 847 446-8664
  3215 Commercial Ave Northbrook (60062) *(G-15469)*
Protection Controls Inc 773 763-3110
  7317 Lawndale Ave Skokie (60076) *(G-19017)*
Protective Coatings & Waterpro 708 403-7650
  9320 136th St Orland Park (60462) *(G-15975)*
Protective Door Industries 773 375-0300
  15700 Lathrop Ave Harvey (60426) *(G-11094)*
Protective Products Intl 847 526-1180
  140 Kerry Ln Wauconda (60084) *(G-20386)*
Protectofire, Skokie Also called Protection Controls Inc *(G-19017)*
Protector, The, Woodridge Also called Ecp Incorporated *(G-21297)*
Protectoseal Company (PA) 630 595-0800
  225 Foster Ave Bensenville (60106) *(G-1876)*
Protein2o Inc 646 919-5320
  815 Bonnie Ln Elk Grove Village (60007) *(G-9199)*
Proteinintech Group Inc 312 455-8498
  5400 Pearl St Ste 300 Rosemont (60018) *(G-18045)*
Protek Inc 888 536-5466
  209 S 3rd St Saint Charles (60174) *(G-18252)*
Protepo Ltd (PA) 847 466-1023
  906 Mayfair Ct Elk Grove Village (60007) *(G-9200)*
Protex Products LLC 312 292-1310
  3104 W Touhy Ave Chicago (60645) *(G-5906)*
Protide Pharmaceuticals Inc 847 726-3100
  220 Telser Rd Lake Zurich (60047) *(G-12446)*

Proto Productions Inc 630 628-6626
  840 S Fiene Dr Addison (60101) *(G-257)*
Proto-Cutter Inc 815 232-2300
  101 S Liberty Ave Ste 1 Freeport (61032) *(G-10134)*
Proton Multimedia Inc 847 531-8664
  1485 Davis Rd Ste A Elgin (60123) *(G-8701)*
Prototech Industries Inc 847 223-9808
  1479 Almaden Ln Gurnee (60031) *(G-10918)*
Prototype & Production Co 847 419-1553
  546 Quail Hollow Dr Wheeling (60090) *(G-20967)*
Prototype Equipment Corp 847 596-9000
  1081 S Northpoint Blvd Waukegan (60085) *(G-20484)*
Protus Construction 773 405-9999
  1429 N Oakley Blvd Chicago (60622) *(G-5907)*
Proven Partners Group LLC (HQ) 847 488-1230
  1111 Bowes Rd Elgin (60123) *(G-8702)*
Provena Enterprises Inc (HQ) 708 478-3230
  555 W Court St Ste 414 Kankakee (60901) *(G-11997)*
Provena Randalwood Open Mri 630 587-9917
  110 James St Geneva (60134) *(G-10300)*
Providence Press, Carol Stream Also called Hope Publishing Company *(G-2999)*
Provisur Technologies 312 284-4698
  222 N La Salle St Chicago (60601) *(G-5908)*
Proximity Capital Partners LLC 773 628-7751
  4159 W Montrose Ave Chicago (60641) *(G-5909)*
Prp Wine International Inc 630 995-4500
  1323 Bond St Ste 179 Naperville (60563) *(G-14903)*
Prs Inc 630 620-7259
  434 S Ahrens Ave Lombard (60148) *(G-13123)*
Pru Dent Mfg Inc 847 301-1170
  1929 Wright Blvd Schaumburg (60193) *(G-18687)*
Pruett Enterprises Inc 618 235-6184
  10 E Cleveland Ave Belleville (62220) *(G-1586)*
Pry-Bar Company 815 436-3383
  18542 Nw Frontage Rd Joliet (60404) *(G-11918)*
Pryco Inc (PA) 217 364-4467
  3rd And Garvey Mechanicsburg (62545) *(G-13811)*
Pryde Graphics Plus 630 882-5103
  306 Hubbard Cir Plano (60545) *(G-16743)*
Ps3 Tool Mold & Assembly LLC 630 802-9462
  3850 Swenson Ave Saint Charles (60174) *(G-18253)*
Psa Equity LLC (PA) 847 478-6000
  485 E Half Day Rd Ste 500 Buffalo Grove (60089) *(G-2591)*
PSI, Havana Also called Profile Screens Incorporated *(G-11120)*
PSI Systems North America Inc 630 830-9435
  1243 Humbracht Cir Bartlett (60103) *(G-1302)*
Psimet LLC (PA) 847 871-7005
  612 N Lyle Ave Elgin (60123) *(G-8703)*
PSM Industries Inc 815 337-8800
  925 Dieckman St Woodstock (60098) *(G-21425)*
Psylotech Inc 847 328-7100
  1616 Payne St Evanston (60201) *(G-9572)*
Psyonic Inc 888 779-6642
  60 Hazelwood Dr Champaign (61820) *(G-3340)*
Psytec Inc 815 758-1415
  520 Linden Pl Dekalb (60115) *(G-7699)*
Pt Holdings Inc (PA) 217 691-1733
  2 White Oak Rd Springfield (62711) *(G-19430)*
Ptc Group Holdings Corp 708 757-4747
  475 E 16th St Chicago Heights (60411) *(G-6766)*
Ptc Tubular Products LLC 815 692-4900
  23041 E 800 North Rd Fairbury (61739) *(G-9612)*
Ptc/User Inc 619 417-2050
  330 N Wabash Ave Ste 2000 Chicago (60611) *(G-5910)*
PTG Impax, Warrenville Also called Process Technologies Group *(G-20250)*
Ptm Biolabs Inc 312 802-6843
  2201 W Campbell Park Dr Chicago (60612) *(G-5911)*
Publications International Ltd (PA) 847 676-3470
  8140 Lehigh Ave Morton Grove (60053) *(G-14434)*
Publishers Graphics LLC (PA) 630 221-1850
  140 Della Ct Carol Stream (60188) *(G-3055)*
Publishers Row 847 568-0593
  9001 Keating Ave Skokie (60076) *(G-19018)*
Publishing Properties LLC (HQ) 312 321-2299
  350 N Orleans St Fl 10 Chicago (60654) *(G-5912)*
Pubpal LLC 309 222-5062
  25130 Schuck Rd Washington (61571) *(G-20278)*
Puckered Pickle, Chicago Also called Pickles Sorrel Inc *(G-5806)*
Pullman Company (PA) 847 482-5000
  500 N Field Dr Lake Forest (60045) *(G-12293)*
Pullman Logistics, Chicago Also called Pullman Sugar LLC *(G-5913)*
Pullman Sugar LLC 773 260-9180
  700 E 107th St Chicago (60628) *(G-5913)*
Pullr Holding Company LLC 224 366-2500
  415 E State Pkwy Schaumburg (60173) *(G-18688)*
Pulpulp, Chicago Also called Thrilled LLC *(G-6373)*
Pulsarlube USA Inc 847 593-5300
  1480 Howard St Elk Grove Village (60007) *(G-9201)*
Pulver Inc 847 734-9000
  575 Bennett Rd Elk Grove Village (60007) *(G-9202)*

Pump House — ALPHABETIC SECTION

Pump House 618 216-2404
  1523 E Edwardsville Rd Wood River (62095) *(G-21266)*
Pumpkin Patch Ventures Inc 708 699-4396
  1343 W Grace St Apt 2 Chicago (60613) *(G-5914)*
Punch Products Manufacturing 773 533-2800
  500 S Kolmar Ave Chicago (60624) *(G-5915)*
Purac America Inc 847 634-6330
  111 Barclay Blvd Lincolnshire (60069) *(G-12793)*
Purchasing Services Ltd Inc 618 566-8100
  602 Industrial St Mascoutah (62258) *(G-13606)*
Pure 111 .... 618 558-7888
  923 Far Oaks Dr Caseyville (62232) *(G-3218)*
Pure Alphalt, Chicago *Also called Pure Asphalt Company (G-5916)*
Pure Asphalt Company 773 247-7030
  3455 W 31st Pl Chicago (60623) *(G-5916)*
Pure Element 309 269-7823
  915 33rd Ave Moline (61265) *(G-14168)*
Pure Flo Bottling Inc 815 963-4797
  2430 N Main St Rockford (61103) *(G-17562)*
Pure Lighting LLC 773 770-1130
  1718 W Fullerton Ave Chicago (60614) *(G-5917)*
Pure N Natural Systems Inc 630 372-9681
  519 S Bartlett Rd Streamwood (60107) *(G-19591)*
Pure Processing LLC 877 718-6868
  130 E Saint Charles Rd C Carol Stream (60188) *(G-3056)*
Pure Skin LLC 217 679-6267
  27 Forest Rdg Springfield (62712) *(G-19431)*
Pure Valley, Chicago *Also called Concept Laboratories Inc (G-4214)*
Purecircle USA Inc 866 960-8242
  915 Harger Rd Ste 250 Oak Brook (60523) *(G-15657)*
Pureline Treatment Systems LLC 847 963-8465
  1241 N Ellis St Bensenville (60106) *(G-1877)*
Pures Food Specialties, Broadview *Also called Pures Food Specialties LLC (G-2461)*
Pures Food Specialties LLC 708 344-8884
  2929 S 25th Ave Broadview (60155) *(G-2461)*
Purified Lubricants Inc 708 478-3500
  9629 194th St Mokena (60448) *(G-14111)*
Purina Animal Nutrition LLC 618 283-2291
  1500 Veterans Ave Vandalia (62471) *(G-20021)*
Purina Animal Nutrition LLC 618 478-5555
  17815 Mockingbird Rd Nashville (62263) *(G-15007)*
Purina Mills LLC 618 283-2291
  1500 Veterans Ave Vandalia (62471) *(G-20022)*
Puro Futbol Newspaper 847 858-7493
  4248 Lake Park Ave Gurnee (60031) *(G-10919)*
Purple Clay Pottery, Chicago *Also called BSC Imports Incorporated (G-3970)*
Purple Onyx LLC 708 756-1500
  420 N Orchard Dr Park Forest (60466) *(G-16258)*
Pursuit Beverage Company LLC 888 606-3353
  972 S Northpoint Blvd Waukegan (60085) *(G-20485)*
Puskar Precision Machining Co 847 888-2929
  1610 Cambridge Dr Elgin (60123) *(G-8704)*
Putman Media Inc (PA) 630 467-1301
  1501 E Wdfeld Rd Ste 400n Schaumburg (60173) *(G-18689)*
Putt and Times, Okawville *Also called Okawville Times (G-15846)*
Puzzles Bus Off Solutions Inc 773 891-7688
  47 W Polk St Chicago (60605) *(G-5918)*
Pvc Container Corporation 217 463-6600
  2015 S Main St Paris (61944) *(G-16241)*
Pvh Corp 217 253-3398
  1011 E Southline Rd Tuscola (61953) *(G-19929)*
PVS Chemical Solutions Inc 773 933-8800
  12260 S Carondolet Ave Chicago (60633) *(G-5919)*
PW Masonry Inc 847 573-0510
  1230 Hunters Ln Libertyville (60048) *(G-12699)*
Pw Services LLC 217 672-3225
  390 W North St Warrensburg (62573) *(G-20227)*
Pwf 815 967-0218
  8123 Harrison Rd Rockford (61101) *(G-17563)*
Pyar & Co LLC 312 451-5073
  807 W Dickens Ave Chicago (60614) *(G-5920)*
Pycas Design Innovations LLC 847 656-5000
  602 Hillside Rd Glenview (60025) *(G-10604)*
Pylon Plastics Inc 630 968-6374
  2111 Ogden Ave Lisle (60532) *(G-12930)*
Pyramid Bottling LLC 847 565-9412
  3500 Sunset Ave Waukegan (60087) *(G-20486)*
Pyramid Manufacturing Corp 630 443-0141
  3815 Illinois Ave Saint Charles (60174) *(G-18254)*
Pyramid Sciences Inc 630 974-6110
  9425 S Madison St Burr Ridge (60527) *(G-2715)*
Pyrex, Rosemont *Also called Corelle Brands LLC (G-18010)*
Q C H Incorporated 630 820-5550
  230 Kendall Point Dr Oswego (60543) *(G-16022)*
Q Lotus Holdings Inc 312 379-1800
  520 N Kingsbury St # 1810 Chicago (60654) *(G-5921)*
Q Products 815 498-6356
  814 Lake Holiday Dr Sandwich (60548) *(G-18382)*
Q S F, Alsip *Also called Quality Snack Foods Inc (G-499)*
Q S T, Chicago *Also called Qst Industries Inc (G-5923)*
Q Sales & Leasing LLC 708 331-0094
  16720 Mozart Ave Ste A Hazel Crest (60429) *(G-11136)*
Q SC Design 815 933-6777
  230 E Broadway St Bradley (60915) *(G-2289)*
Qaboss Partners 312 203-4290
  27 N Wacker Dr Ste 155 Chicago (60606) *(G-5922)*
QBF Group Inc 708 781-9580
  18650 Graphic Ct Tinley Park (60477) *(G-19851)*
Qc Finishers Inc 847 678-2660
  10244 Franklin Ave Franklin Park (60131) *(G-10028)*
Qc Powder Inc 630 832-0606
  226 E Sidney Ct Villa Park (60181) *(G-20167)*
Qc Service Associates Inc 309 755-6785
  1300 90th St Ste 110 East Moline (61244) *(G-8237)*
Qcc LLC (PA) 708 867-5400
  7301 W Wilson Ave Harwood Heights (60706) *(G-11107)*
Qcfec LLC 309 517-1158
  4401 44th Ave Moline (61265) *(G-14169)*
Qcircuits Inc (PA) 847 797-6678
  2574 United Ln Elk Grove Village (60007) *(G-9203)*
Qcircuits Inc 618 662-8365
  1 Industrial Park Flora (62839) *(G-9690)*
Qg LLC 217 347-7721
  420 Industrial Ave Effingham (62401) *(G-8419)*
Qg LLC 217 347-7721
  1200 W Niccum Ave Effingham (62401) *(G-8420)*
Qh Inc 708 534-7801
  2412 Bond St University Park (60484) *(G-19965)*
Qmi Security Solutions, Itasca *Also called Qualitas Manufacturing Inc (G-11723)*
Qp Holdings LLC (PA) 847 695-9700
  1000 Davis Rd Elgin (60123) *(G-8705)*
Qse Inc (PA) 815 432-5281
  316 W Hickory St Watseka (60970) *(G-20315)*
Qsrsoft 630 995-9642
  1806 S Highland Ave Lombard (60148) *(G-13124)*
Qst Industries Inc (PA) 312 930-9400
  550 W Adams St Ste 200 Chicago (60661) *(G-5923)*
Qst Industries Inc 312 930-9400
  550 W Adams St Ste 200 Chicago (60661) *(G-5924)*
Qt Info Systems Inc 800 240-8761
  141 W Jackson Blvd # 125 Chicago (60604) *(G-5925)*
Qt Sign Inc 847 524-7950
  1391 Wright Blvd Schaumburg (60193) *(G-18690)*
Qt9 Software, Aurora *Also called Innovative Custom Software Inc (G-983)*
Qti, Elgin *Also called Quality Technology Intl Inc (G-8709)*
Quad Inc (PA) 815 624-8538
  810 Progressive Ln South Beloit (61080) *(G-19110)*
Quad Cities Concrete Pdts LLC 309 787-4919
  636 10th Ave W Milan (61264) *(G-14021)*
Quad Cities Plant, Milan *Also called Chicago Tube and Iron Company (G-14003)*
Quad City Clown Troupe Inc 309 788-1278
  1601 25th St Rock Island (61201) *(G-17235)*
Quad City Engineering Company 309 755-9762
  3650 Morton Dr East Moline (61244) *(G-8238)*
Quad City Hose 563 386-8936
  9707 86th Street Ct W Taylor Ridge (61284) *(G-19747)*
Quad City Press 309 764-8142
  1325 15th St Moline (61265) *(G-14170)*
Quad City Prosthetics Inc (PA) 309 676-2276
  4730 44th St Ste 1 Rock Island (61201) *(G-17236)*
Quad City Ultralight Aircraft 309 764-3515
  3810 34th St Moline (61265) *(G-14171)*
Quad County Fire Equipment 815 832-4475
  37 Main St Saunemin (61769) *(G-18402)*
Quad County Rdymx New Baden, New Baden *Also called Quad-County Ready Mix Corp (G-15022)*
Quad County Ready Mix Swansea 618 257-9530
  300 Old Fullerton Rd Swansea (62226) *(G-19694)*
Quad Cy Prsthetic-Orthotic Lab, Rock Island *Also called Quad City Prosthetics Inc (G-17236)*
Quad Plus LLC (PA) 815 740-0860
  1921 Cherry Hill Rd Joliet (60433) *(G-11919)*
Quad-County Rdymx Centralia, Centralia *Also called Clinton County Materials Corp (G-3226)*
Quad-County Ready Mix Corp (PA) 618 243-6430
  300 W 12th St Okawville (62271) *(G-15847)*
Quad-County Ready Mix Corp 618 588-4656
  7415 State Route 160 New Baden (62265) *(G-15022)*
Quad-County Ready Mix Corp 618 526-7130
  11 S Plum St Breese (62230) *(G-2306)*
Quad-County Ready Mix Corp 618 244-6973
  9240 Sahara Rd Mount Vernon (62864) *(G-14635)*
Quad-County Ready Mix Corp 618 288-4000
  2458 Formosa Rd Troy (62294) *(G-19918)*
Quad-County Ready Mix Corp 618 327-3748
  1050 N Washington St Nashville (62263) *(G-15008)*
Quad-County Ready Mix Corp 618 594-2732
  2090 Washington St Carlyle (62231) *(G-2894)*

Quad-County Ready Mix Corp 618 295-3000
655 Wshngton Cnty Line Rd Marissa (62257) ***(G-13544)***
Quad-County Ready Mix Corp 618 548-2477
3782 Hotze Rd Salem (62881) ***(G-18353)***
Quad-Illinois Inc (PA) 847 836-1115
2760 Spectrum Dr Elgin (60124) ***(G-8706)***
Quad-Metal Inc 630 953-0907
1345 W Fullerton Ave Addison (60101) ***(G-258)***
Quad/Graphics Inc 815 734-4121
404 N Wesley Ave Mount Morris (61054) ***(G-14500)***
Quad/Graphics Inc 815 338-6750
11595 Mcconnell Rd Woodstock (60098) ***(G-21426)***
Quad/Graphics Inc 217 347-7721
420 Industrial Ave Effingham (62401) ***(G-8421)***
Quadramed Corporation 312 396-0700
440 N Wells St Ste 505 Chicago (60654) ***(G-5926)***
Quadrant Medical Corporation 312 800-1294
3500 Thayer Ct Aurora (60504) ***(G-1011)***
Quadrant Tool and Mfg Co 847 352-6977
1720 W Irving Park Rd Schaumburg (60193) ***(G-18691)***
Quaker Oats Company (HQ) 312 821-1000
555 W Monroe St Fl 1 Chicago (60661) ***(G-5927)***
Quaker Oats Company 217 443-4995
1703 E Voorhees St Danville (61834) ***(G-7375)***
Quaker Oats Company 708 458-7090
7700 W 71st St Bridgeview (60455) ***(G-2376)***
Quaker Oats Europe Inc (HQ) 312 821-1000
555 W Monroe St Fl 1 Chicago (60661) ***(G-5928)***
Qualified Innovation Inc 630 556-4136
1016 Airpark Dr Ste B Sugar Grove (60554) ***(G-19651)***
Qualiseal Technology, Harwood Heights *Also called Technetics Group LLC* ***(G-11111)***
Qualiseal Technology LLC 708 887-6080
7319 W Wilson Ave Harwood Heights (60706) ***(G-11108)***
Qualitas Manufacturing Inc (PA) 630 529-7111
1661 Glenlake Ave Itasca (60143) ***(G-11723)***
Qualitek International Inc 630 628-8083
315 S Fairbank St Addison (60101) ***(G-259)***
Qualitek Manufacturing Inc 847 336-7570
4240 Grove Ave Gurnee (60031) ***(G-10920)***
Quality Armature Inc 773 622-3951
5259 W Grand Ave Chicago (60639) ***(G-5929)***
Quality Bags Inc 630 543-9800
575 S Vista Ave Addison (60101) ***(G-260)***
Quality Bakeries LLC 630 553-7377
1750 E Main St Ste 280 Saint Charles (60174) ***(G-18255)***
Quality Blue & Offset Printing 630 759-8035
7 Sunshine Ct Bolingbrook (60490) ***(G-2231)***
Quality Cable & Components Inc 309 695-3435
109 N Madison Ave Wyoming (61491) ***(G-21461)***
Quality Cleaning Fluids Inc 847 451-1190
9216 Grand Ave Franklin Park (60131) ***(G-10029)***
Quality Cnc Incorporated 630 406-0101
801 N Raddant Rd Batavia (60510) ***(G-1407)***
Quality Coating Co 815 875-3228
2955 N Main St Princeton (61356) ***(G-16822)***
Quality Control Corp 708 887-6239
7315 W Wilson Ave Harwood Heights (60706) ***(G-11109)***
Quality Converting Inc 847 669-9094
10611 Wolf Dr Huntley (60142) ***(G-11561)***
Quality Custom Closets 773 307-1105
4304 Di Paolo Ctr Glenview (60025) ***(G-10605)***
Quality Die Casting Co 847 214-8840
1760 Britannia Dr Ste 5 Elgin (60124) ***(G-8707)***
Quality Drilling Service LLP (PA) 937 663-4715
1715 Liberty St Alton (62002) ***(G-568)***
Quality Fabricators Inc (PA) 630 543-0540
1035 W Fullerton Ave Addison (60101) ***(G-261)***
Quality Fastener Products Inc 224 330-3162
1430 Davis Rd Elgin (60123) ***(G-8708)***
Quality Filter Services 618 654-3716
14446 Baumann Rd Highland (62249) ***(G-11236)***
Quality Finishing Service Inc 847 616-0336
1461 Mark St Elk Grove Village (60007) ***(G-9204)***
Quality Glass Block, Morris *Also called Tuminello Enterprizes Inc* ***(G-14335)***
Quality Glass Block & Win Co, Morris *Also called Tuminello Enterprizes Inc* ***(G-14334)***
Quality Hnge A Div Spreme Hnge 708 534-7801
2412 Bond St University Park (60484) ***(G-19966)***
Quality Intgrted Solutions Inc 815 464-4772
18521 Spring Creek Dr Tinley Park (60477) ***(G-19852)***
Quality Iron Works Inc 630 766-0885
449 Evergreen Ave Bensenville (60106) ***(G-1878)***
Quality Lime Company 217 826-2343
14915 N Quality Lime Rd Marshall (62441) ***(G-13577)***
Quality Line, Marshall *Also called Quality Lime Company* ***(G-13577)***
Quality Liquid Feeds Inc 815 224-1553
75 Creve Coeur St La Salle (61301) ***(G-12120)***
Quality Machine 708 499-0021
5530 W 110th St Ste 8 Oak Lawn (60453) ***(G-15733)***
Quality Machine Tool Services 847 776-0073
2385 Hammond Dr Ste 12 Schaumburg (60173) ***(G-18692)***
Quality Metal Finishing Co 815 234-2711
421 N Walnut St Byron (61010) ***(G-2755)***
Quality Metal Products Inc 309 692-8014
7006 N Galena Rd Peoria (61614) ***(G-16505)***
Quality Metal Works Inc 309 379-5311
200 School St Stanford (61774) ***(G-19473)***
Quality Millwork and Trim, Morris *Also called Torblo Inc* ***(G-14333)***
Quality Molding Products LLC 224 286-4555
118 Nations Dr Gurnee (60031) ***(G-10921)***
Quality Neon Service 847 299-2969
1350 Oakwood Ave Ste A Des Plaines (60016) ***(G-7834)***
Quality Optical Inc 773 561-0870
4610 N Lincoln Ave Chicago (60625) ***(G-5930)***
Quality Pallets Inc 217 459-2655
601 Kentucky Ave Windsor (61957) ***(G-21107)***
Quality Paper Inc 847 258-3999
1855 Greenleaf Ave Elk Grove Village (60007) ***(G-9205)***
Quality Plastic Products Inc 630 766-7593
830 Maple Ln Bensenville (60106) ***(G-1879)***
Quality Plating 815 626-5223
406 Oak Ave Sterling (61081) ***(G-19526)***
Quality Plating Works, Belleville *Also called Koderhandt Inc* ***(G-1565)***
Quality Plus 618 779-4931
901 S Old Route 66 Litchfield (62056) ***(G-12974)***
Quality Quickprint Inc 815 439-3430
2405 Caton Farm Rd Joliet (60403) ***(G-11920)***
Quality Quickprint Inc (PA) 815 723-0941
1258 Cronin Ct Lemont (60439) ***(G-12586)***
Quality Quickprint Inc 815 838-1784
909 E 9th St Lockport (60441) ***(G-13020)***
Quality Ready Mix Concrete Co 815 589-2013
1415 14th Ave Fulton (61252) ***(G-10156)***
Quality Ready Mix Concrete Co (PA) 815 772-7181
14849 Lyndon Rd Morrison (61270) ***(G-14347)***
Quality Ready Mix Concrete Co 815 625-0750
13134 Galt Rd Sterling (61081) ***(G-19527)***
Quality Ready Mix Concrete Co 815 288-6416
1569 Franklin Grove Rd Dixon (61021) ***(G-7907)***
Quality Sand Company Inc 618 346-1070
1327 N Bluff Rd Collinsville (62234) ***(G-6973)***
Quality Sealants Inc 815 342-0409
7n131 Willow St Roselle (60172) ***(G-17976)***
Quality Service & Installation 847 352-4000
923 Sharon Ln Schaumburg (60193) ***(G-18693)***
Quality Sleep Shop Inc (PA) 708 246-2224
1519 W 55th St La Grange Highlands (60525) ***(G-12093)***
Quality Snack Foods Inc 708 377-7120
3750 W 131st St Alsip (60803) ***(G-499)***
Quality Sport Nets Inc 618 533-0700
2330 E Calumet St Centralia (62801) ***(G-3247)***
Quality Spraying Screen Prtg 630 584-8324
3815 Illinois Ave Saint Charles (60174) ***(G-18256)***
Quality Surface Mount Inc 630 350-8556
965 Dillon Dr Wood Dale (60191) ***(G-21233)***
Quality Targets 618 245-6515
204 Through St Farina (62838) ***(G-9653)***
Quality Tech Tool Inc 847 690-9643
759 Industrial Dr Bensenville (60106) ***(G-1880)***
Quality Technology Intl Inc 847 649-9300
1707 N Randall Rd Ste 300 Elgin (60123) ***(G-8709)***
Quality Tool & Machine Inc 773 721-8655
8050 S Constance Ave Chicago (60617) ***(G-5931)***
Quality Tool Inc 847 288-9330
9239 Parklane Ave Franklin Park (60131) ***(G-10030)***
Quality Trailer Sales Inc 630 739-2495
1701 N Main St Morton (61550) ***(G-14380)***
Quality Trucking Inc 309 949-2021
5715 Us Highway 6 Colona (61241) ***(G-6977)***
Quam-Nichols Company 773 488-5800
234 E Marquette Rd Ste 1 Chicago (60637) ***(G-5932)***
Quanex Homeshield LLC 815 635-3171
32140 E 830 North Rd Chatsworth (60921) ***(G-3427)***
Quanex Homeshield LLC 815 635-3171
32140 E 830 North Rd Chatsworth (60921) ***(G-3428)***
Quanex Screens LLC 217 463-2233
13323 Illinois Hwy 133 Paris (61944) ***(G-16242)***
Quantum Color Graphics LLC 847 967-3600
6511 Oakton St Morton Grove (60053) ***(G-14435)***
Quantum Corporation 312 372-2857
1 S Wacker Dr Chicago (60606) ***(G-5933)***
Quantum Data, Elgin *Also called Teledyne Lecroy Inc* ***(G-8749)***
Quantum Design Inc (PA) 815 885-1300
7550 Quantum Ct Machesney Park (61011) ***(G-13321)***
Quantum Healing 217 414-2412
809 Timber Ridge Rd Mechanicsburg (62545) ***(G-13812)***
Quantum Marketing LLC 630 257-7012
12305 New Ave Ste H Lemont (60439) ***(G-12587)***
Quantum Packaging, Lemont *Also called Quantum Marketing LLC* ***(G-12587)***
Quantum Polymers Inc 630 834-8427
100 S York St Ste 222 Elmhurst (60126) ***(G-9413)***

ALPHABETIC

Quantum Precision Inc 630 692-1545
385 Wegner Dr West Chicago (60185) ***(G-20634)***
Quantum Sign Corporation 630 466-0372
693 N Heartland Dr Sugar Grove (60554) ***(G-19652)***
Quantum Storage Systems 630 274-6610
2600 United Ln Elk Grove Village (60007) ***(G-9206)***
Quantum Technical Services Inc 815 464-1540
9524 Gulfstream Rd Frankfort (60423) ***(G-9829)***
Quantum Topping Systems, Frankfort *Also called Quantum Technical Services Inc* ***(G-9829)***
Quantum Vision Centers 618 656-7774
3990 N Illinois St Swansea (62226) ***(G-19695)***
Quarter Master Industries Inc 847 540-8999
510 Telser Rd Lake Zurich (60047) ***(G-12447)***
Quarters Concessions Inc 847 343-4864
4064 Stratford Ln Carpentersville (60110) ***(G-3116)***
Quartix Inc 855 913-6663
875 N Michigan Ave # 3100 Chicago (60611) ***(G-5934)***
Quay Corporation Inc (PA) 847 676-4233
7101 N Capitol Dr Lincolnwood (60712) ***(G-12836)***
Queen Pin, Chicago *Also called Broc LLC* ***(G-3961)***
Quen-Tel Communication Svc Inc 815 463-1800
2759 Meadow Path New Lenox (60451) ***(G-15052)***
Quest Integrity 779 205-3068
908 Geneva St Shorewood (60404) ***(G-18901)***
Quest Manufacturing Inc 815 675-2442
2503 Spring Ridge Dr Spring Grove (60081) ***(G-19296)***
Questek Manufacturing Corp 847 428-0300
2570 Technology Dr Elgin (60124) ***(G-8710)***
Questily LLC (PA) 312 636-6657
3619 N Claremont Ave Chicago (60618) ***(G-5935)***
Questily LLC 312 636-6657
2 N La Salle St Fl 14 Chicago (60602) ***(G-5936)***
Quick Building Systems Inc 708 598-6733
9748 S Cambridge Ct Palos Hills (60465) ***(G-16205)***
Quick Lube, Danville *Also called William Ingram* ***(G-7398)***
Quick Nic Juice LLC 815 315-8523
122 Indian Springs Dr # 5 Sandwich (60548) ***(G-18383)***
Quick Print, Lemont *Also called Quality Quickprint Inc* ***(G-12586)***
Quick Print Shoppe 309 694-1204
500 Fondulac Dr East Peoria (61611) ***(G-8285)***
Quick Quality Printing Inc 708 895-5885
17332 Torrence Ave Lansing (60438) ***(G-12513)***
Quick Signs Inc 630 554-7370
424 Treasure Dr Oswego (60543) ***(G-16023)***
Quick Start Pdts & Solutions 815 562-5414
770 Wiscold Dr Rochelle (61068) ***(G-17153)***
Quicker Engineering 815 675-6516
7516 Buena Vis Spring Grove (60081) ***(G-19297)***
Quicker Printers, Chicago *Also called Dos Bro Corp* ***(G-4386)***
Quickprinters 309 833-5250
1120 E Jackson St Macomb (61455) ***(G-13398)***
Quicksilver Mechanical Inc 847 577-1564
3361 N Ridge Ave Arlington Heights (60004) ***(G-794)***
Quiddity Solutions LLC 773 844-2058
6316 N Magnolia Ave Chicago (60660) ***(G-5937)***
Quiet Graphics, Schaumburg *Also called N Bujarski Inc* ***(G-18643)***
Quik Impressions Group Inc 630 495-7845
1385 W Jeffrey Dr Addison (60101) ***(G-262)***
Quikfletch, Forest Park *Also called New Archery Products LLC* ***(G-9722)***
Quikrete Companies LLC 309 346-1184
11150 Garman Rd Pekin (61554) ***(G-16357)***
Quikrete of Peoria, Pekin *Also called Quikrete Companies LLC* ***(G-16357)***
Quiltmaster Inc 847 426-6741
1 S Wisconsin St Carpentersville (60110) ***(G-3117)***
Quinceaneraboutiquecom Inc 779 324-5468
7624 W Saint Francis Rd Frankfort (60423) ***(G-9830)***
Quincy Bow Pro 217 222-2222
3110 Broadway St Quincy (62301) ***(G-16929)***
Quincy Electric & Sign Company 217 223-8404
1324 Spring Lake Cors Quincy (62305) ***(G-16930)***
Quincy Farm Products LLC 217 214-1905
3501 Wisman Ln Quincy (62301) ***(G-16931)***
Quincy Foundry & Pattern Co 217 222-0718
435 S Front St Quincy (62301) ***(G-16932)***
Quincy Herald-Whig LLC 217 223-5100
130 S 5th St Quincy (62301) ***(G-16933)***
Quincy Lab Inc 773 622-2428
1928 N Leamington Ave Chicago (60639) ***(G-5938)***
Quincy Pepsi-Cola Bottling Co 309 833-4263
236 Collins St Macomb (61455) ***(G-13399)***
Quincy Pepsi-Cola Bottling Co (PA) 217 223-8600
1121 Locust St Quincy (62301) ***(G-16934)***
Quincy Ready Mix Co, Quincy *Also called Bleigh Construction Company* ***(G-16866)***
Quincy Socks House 217 506-6106
840 N 36th St Quincy (62301) ***(G-16935)***
Quinn Broom Works Inc 217 923-3181
1527 Il Route 121 Greenup (62428) ***(G-10822)***
Quinn Print Inc 847 823-9100
508 Higgins Rd Park Ridge (60068) ***(G-16293)***

Quintum Technologies Inc 847 348-7730
1821 Walden Office Sq # 200 Schaumburg (60173) ***(G-18694)***
Quipp Inc (PA) 305 623-8700
3700 W Lake Ave Glenview (60026) ***(G-10606)***
Quixote Corporation (HQ) 312 705-8400
70 W Madison St Ste 2350 Chicago (60602) ***(G-5939)***
Quixote Transportation Safety 312 467-6750
70 W Madison St Ste 2350 Chicago (60602) ***(G-5940)***
Quorum Labs LLC 618 525-5600
895 Grayson Rd Eldorado (62930) ***(G-8482)***
Qwik-Tip Inc 847 640-7387
2415 E Higgins Rd Elk Grove Village (60007) ***(G-9207)***
R & B Metal Products Inc 815 338-1890
801 Mchenry Ave Woodstock (60098) ***(G-21427)***
R & B Powder Coatings Inc 773 247-8300
4000 S Bell Ave Chicago (60609) ***(G-5941)***
R & C Auto Supply Corp 815 625-4414
2526 E Lincolnway Sterling (61081) ***(G-19528)***
R & C Castings, Monee *Also called R & C Pattern Works Inc* ***(G-14204)***
R & C Pattern Works Inc 708 331-1882
6370 W Emerald Pkwy # 111 Monee (60449) ***(G-14204)***
R & D Concrete Products Inc 309 787-0264
8002 31st St W Rock Island (61201) ***(G-17237)***
R & D Electronics Inc 847 583-9080
7948 W Oakton St Niles (60714) ***(G-15163)***
R & D Machine LLC 618 282-6262
126 Jackson St Red Bud (62278) ***(G-16999)***
R & D Oil Producers 217 773-9299
709 N Capitol Ave Mount Sterling (62353) ***(G-14592)***
R & E Quality Mfg Co 773 286-6846
7005 W School St Chicago (60634) ***(G-5942)***
R & G Machine Shop Inc 217 342-6622
1303 Parker Ave Effingham (62401) ***(G-8422)***
R & G Spring Co Inc 847 228-5640
1451 Landmeier Rd Ste L Elk Grove Village (60007) ***(G-9208)***
R & H Products Inc 815 744-4110
800 Moen Ave Unit 7 Rockdale (60436) ***(G-17270)***
R & I Ornamental Iron Inc 847 836-6934
96 Center Dr Gilberts (60136) ***(G-10366)***
R & J Ready Mix, Naperville *Also called Concrete 1 Inc* ***(G-14805)***
R & J Systems Inc 630 289-3010
1580 Birch Ave Bartlett (60133) ***(G-1257)***
R & J Trucking and Recycl Inc 708 563-2600
6650 S Oak Park Ave Chicago (60638) ***(G-5943)***
R & L Business Forms Inc 618 939-6535
8603 Gilmore Lake Rd Waterloo (62298) ***(G-20294)***
R & L Ready Mix Inc 618 544-7514
602 N Steel St Robinson (62454) ***(G-17123)***
R & L Signs Inc 708 233-0112
7430 W 90th St Bridgeview (60455) ***(G-2377)***
R & L Truck Service Inc 847 489-7135
39935 N Prairie View Dr Wadsworth (60083) ***(G-20212)***
R & N Components Co 217 543-3495
261 E County Road 600 N Tuscola (61953) ***(G-19930)***
R & N Machine Co 708 841-5555
14020 S Stewart Ave Riverdale (60827) ***(G-17075)***
R & O Specialties Incorporated (HQ) 309 736-8660
120 4th Ave E Milan (61264) ***(G-14022)***
R & P Fuels 630 855-2358
798 Barrington Rd Hoffman Estates (60169) ***(G-11449)***
R & R Bindery Service Inc 217 627-2143
499 Rachel Rd Girard (62640) ***(G-10384)***
R & R Creative Graphics Inc 630 208-4724
111 N Northampton Dr Geneva (60134) ***(G-10301)***
R & R Custom Cabinet Making 847 358-6188
515 S Vermont St Ste B Palatine (60067) ***(G-16152)***
R & R Engines and Parts Inc 630 628-1545
1244 W Capitol Dr Ste 4 Addison (60101) ***(G-263)***
R & R Lithography, River Grove *Also called R N R Photographers Inc* ***(G-17066)***
R & R Machining Inc 217 835-4579
125 Route 138 Benld (62009) ***(G-1718)***
R & R Services Illinois Inc 217 424-2602
800 E Garfield Ave Decatur (62526) ***(G-7538)***
R & S Automotive Inc 847 622-8838
88 Airport Rd Elgin (60123) ***(G-8711)***
R & S Cutterhead Mfg Co 815 678-2611
11401 Commercial St Ste A Richmond (60071) ***(G-17020)***
R & S Screen Printing Inc 815 337-3935
739 Mchenry Ave Woodstock (60098) ***(G-21428)***
R & S Steel Corporation 309 448-2645
301 W Washington St Congerville (61729) ***(G-7001)***
R & T Enterprises, Kewanee *Also called Elm Street Industries Inc* ***(G-12032)***
R & W Machine, Bedford Park *Also called Warner Industries Inc* ***(G-1510)***
R A E Tool and Manufacturing 815 485-2506
1910 Clearing Ct Ste 2 New Lenox (60451) ***(G-15053)***
R A Kerley Ink Engineers Inc (PA) 708 344-1295
2700 S 12th Ave Broadview (60155) ***(G-2462)***
R A Zweig Inc 847 832-9001
2500 Ravine Way Glenview (60025) ***(G-10607)***

R and B Distributors Inc 815 433-6843
1217 Saint Clair St Ottawa (61350) *(G-16074)*
R and R Brokerage Co (PA) 847 438-4600
800 Ela Rd Lake Zurich (60047) *(G-12448)*
R B Engineering, Bartlett *Also called Robert Brysiewicz Incorporated (G-1304)*
R B Evans Co 630 365-3554
808 Hicks Dr Elburn (60119) *(G-8471)*
R B Hayward Company 847 671-0400
9556 River St Schiller Park (60176) *(G-18838)*
R B M Tool Inc 630 422-7065
2545 American Ln Elk Grove Village (60007) *(G-9209)*
R B White Inc 309 452-5816
2011 Eagle Rd Normal (61761) *(G-15220)*
R C Castings Inc 708 331-1882
6370 W Emerald Pkwy # 111 Monee (60449) *(G-14205)*
R C Coil Spring Mfg Co Inc 630 790-3500
490 Mitchell Rd Glendale Heights (60139) *(G-10486)*
R C Industrial Inc 309 230-4631
255 5th Ave W Milan (61264) *(G-14023)*
R C Industries Inc 773 378-1118
1420 N Lamon Ave Chicago (60651) *(G-5944)*
R C Sales & Manufacturing Inc 815 645-8898
5999 N Cox Rd Stillman Valley (61084) *(G-19545)*
R D Niven & Associates Ltd 630 580-6000
955 Kimberly Dr Carol Stream (60188) *(G-3057)*
R D S Co 630 893-2990
158 Covington Dr Bloomingdale (60108) *(G-2010)*
R E I, Richmond *Also called Rodifer Enterprises Inc (G-17021)*
R E Z Packaging Inc 773 247-0800
3735 S Racine Ave Chicago (60609) *(G-5945)*
R Energy LLC 618 382-7313
1001 E Main St Carmi (62821) *(G-2913)*
R G Controls Inc 847 438-3981
512 Rue Chamonix Barrington (60010) *(G-1239)*
R G H & Associates Inc 630 357-5915
1783 S Washington St Naperville (60565) *(G-14904)*
R G Hanson Company Inc (PA) 309 661-9200
211 S Prospect Rd Ste 7 Bloomington (61704) *(G-2087)*
R G Spring Company Inc 847 695-2986
2587 Millennium Dr Ste F Elgin (60124) *(G-8712)*
R H Johnson Oil Co Inc (PA) 630 668-3649
1017 Delles Rd Wheaton (60189) *(G-20817)*
R Hansel & Son Inc 815 784-5500
221 N Sycamore St Genoa (60135) *(G-10323)*
R I Plastics, Tower Hill *Also called Realt Images Inc (G-19894)*
R J Graham Oil Company, Salem *Also called Ronnie Joe Graham (G-18355)*
R J S Silk Screening Co 708 974-3009
10708 S Roberts Rd Palos Hills (60465) *(G-16206)*
R J Van Drunen & Sons Inc (PA) 815 472-3100
300 W 6th St Momence (60954) *(G-14191)*
R J Van Drunen & Sons Inc 830 422-2167
214 Mechanic St Momence (60954) *(G-14192)*
R J Van Drunen & Sons Inc 815 472-3211
3878 N Vincennes Trl Momence (60954) *(G-14193)*
R K J Pallets Inc 708 493-0701
1003 Cernan Dr Bellwood (60104) *(G-1636)*
R K Precision Machine Inc 574 293-0231
12512 S Springfield Ave Alsip (60803) *(G-500)*
R K Products Inc 309 792-1927
3802 Jean St East Moline (61244) *(G-8239)*
R L Allen Industries 618 667-2544
120 Collinsville Rd Ofc Troy (62294) *(G-19919)*
R L D Communications Inc (PA) 312 338-7007
725 S Wells St Fl 4 Chicago (60607) *(G-5946)*
R L Hoener Co 217 223-2190
2923 Gardner Expy Quincy (62305) *(G-16936)*
R L Kolbi Company 847 506-1440
416 W Campus Dr Arlington Heights (60004) *(G-795)*
R L Lewis Industries Inc (PA) 309 353-7670
14215 Towerline Rd Pekin (61554) *(G-16358)*
R L ONeal & Sons Inc 309 458-3350
819 N County Road 3050 Plymouth (62367) *(G-16750)*
R Lamar Academy Inc 309 712-8100
1110 N Orange St Peoria (61606) *(G-16506)*
R M Armstrong & Son Inc 847 669-3988
11006 Bakley St Huntley (60142) *(G-11562)*
R M J Distributing, Belleville *Also called ABM Marking Ltd (G-1526)*
R M Tool & Manufacturing Co 847 888-0433
368 Bluff City Blvd Ste 6 Elgin (60120) *(G-8713)*
R Machining Inc 217 532-2174
705 Elm St Butler (62015) *(G-2749)*
R Maderite Inc 847 785-0875
2306 Commonwealth Ave North Chicago (60064) *(G-15320)*
R Maderite Inc 773 235-1515
1616 N Washtenaw Ave Chicago (60647) *(G-5947)*
R N I Industries Inc 630 860-9147
236 William St Bensenville (60106) *(G-1881)*
R N R Photographers Inc 708 453-1868
8115 Grand Ave River Grove (60171) *(G-17066)*
R O I, Elgin *Also called Rieke Office Interiors Inc (G-8720)*
R P Grollman Co Inc 847 607-0294
1811 Lawrence Ln Highland Park (60035) *(G-11293)*
R P Solutions LLC 773 971-1363
3920 W 68th St Chicago (60629) *(G-5948)*
R Popernik Co Inc 773 434-4300
2313 W 59th St Chicago (60636) *(G-5949)*
R R Donnelley, Mattoon *Also called R R Donnelley & Sons Company (G-13652)*
R R Donnelley, Chicago *Also called RR Donnelley Printing Co LP (G-6072)*
R R Donnelley, Pontiac *Also called R R Donnelley & Sons Company (G-16779)*
R R Donnelley, Elgin *Also called R R Donnelley & Sons Company (G-8714)*
R R Donnelley, Warrenville *Also called R R Donnelley & Sons Company (G-20251)*
R R Donnelley, Lisle *Also called R R Donnelley & Sons Company (G-12931)*
R R Donnelley & Sons Company (PA) 312 326-8000
35 W Wacker Dr Chicago (60601) *(G-5950)*
R R Donnelley & Sons Company 217 258-2675
6821 E County Road 1100n Mattoon (61938) *(G-13652)*
R R Donnelley & Sons Company 847 593-1200
1099 Greenleaf Ave Elk Grove Village (60007) *(G-9210)*
R R Donnelley & Sons Company 309 808-3018
1821 Hovey Ave Normal (61761) *(G-15221)*
R R Donnelley & Sons Company 630 377-2586
1750 Wallace Ave Saint Charles (60174) *(G-18257)*
R R Donnelley & Sons Company 217 935-2113
900 S Cain St Clinton (61727) *(G-6928)*
R R Donnelley & Sons Company 847 393-3000
850 Technology Way Libertyville (60048) *(G-12700)*
R R Donnelley & Sons Company 815 584-2770
801 N Union St Dwight (60420) *(G-8158)*
R R Donnelley & Sons Company 815 844-5181
1600 N Main St Pontiac (61764) *(G-16779)*
R R Donnelley & Sons Company 847 622-1026
168 E Highland Ave Ste 2 Elgin (60120) *(G-8714)*
R R Donnelley & Sons Company 630 322-6268
4101 Winfield Rd Ste 100 Warrenville (60555) *(G-20251)*
R R Donnelley & Sons Company 630 588-5000
750 Warrenville Rd Lisle (60532) *(G-12931)*
R R Donnelley & Sons Company 847 956-4187
2075 Busse Rd Elk Grove Village (60007) *(G-9211)*
R R Donnelley & Sons Company 630 762-7600
3626 Stern Ave Saint Charles (60174) *(G-18258)*
R R Sausage Factory, Chicago *Also called Oriental Kitchen Corporation (G-5698)*
R R Street & Co Inc 773 247-1190
4600 S Tripp Ave Chicago (60632) *(G-5951)*
R R Street & Co Inc (PA) 630 416-4244
184 Shuman Blvd Ste 150 Naperville (60563) *(G-14905)*
R R Street & Co Inc 773 254-1277
2353 S Blue Island Ave Chicago (60608) *(G-5952)*
R S Bacon Veneer Company (PA) 630 323-1414
770 Front St Lisle (60532) *(G-12932)*
R S Bacon Veneer Company 331 777-4762
770 Front St Lisle (60532) *(G-12933)*
R S Corcoran Co 815 485-2156
500 N Vine St New Lenox (60451) *(G-15054)*
R S Cryo Equipment Inc 815 468-6115
629 N Grove St Manteno (60950) *(G-13455)*
R S Owens & Co Inc 773 282-6000
5535 N Lynch Ave Chicago (60630) *(G-5953)*
R T Beverage, Chicago *Also called Balon International Corp (G-3821)*
R T I, Lincolnwood *Also called Research Technology Intl Co (G-12837)*
R T M Precision Machining Inc 630 595-0946
739 Kimberly Dr Carol Stream (60188) *(G-3058)*
R T P Company 618 286-6100
1610 Design Way Ste B Dupo (62239) *(G-8143)*
R T P Inc 312 664-6150
1249 N Clybourn Ave Chicago (60610) *(G-5954)*
R V Designer Collections, Wheeling *Also called Shapco Inc (G-20982)*
R W G Manufacturing Inc 708 755-8035
3309 Holeman Ave Ste 7 S Chicago Hts (60411) *(G-18127)*
R Z Tool Inc 847 647-2350
5691 W Howard St Niles (60714) *(G-15164)*
R&B Foods Inc (HQ) 847 590-0059
1661 Feehanville Dr # 300 Mount Prospect (60056) *(G-14564)*
R&D Lab, Chicago *Also called Soloinsight Inc (G-6198)*
R&M Pallets 773 317-0574
950 Brian Dr Crest Hill (60403) *(G-7093)*
R&R Engineering, Addison *Also called R & R Engines and Parts Inc (G-263)*
R&R Meat Co 270 898-6296
5156 Old Marion Rd Metropolis (62960) *(G-13976)*
R&R Racing of Palm Beach Inc 618 937-6767
15942 Mine 25 Rd Ste 28 West Frankfort (62896) *(G-20679)*
R&R Research Co 847 345-5051
300 N Prospect Manor Ave Mount Prospect (60056) *(G-14565)*
R&R Rf Inc 847 669-3720
1104 E 17th St Rock Falls (61071) *(G-17192)*
R+d Custom Automation Inc 847 395-3330
23411 W Wall St Lake Villa (60046) *(G-12365)*
R-B Industries Inc 847 647-4020
6380 Oakton St Morton Grove (60053) *(G-14436)*

ALPHABETIC

R-K Press Brake Dies Inc......708 371-1756
12512 S Springfield Ave Chicago (60803) ***(G-5955)***
R-M Industries Inc......630 543-3071
38 W Interstate Rd Addison (60101) ***(G-264)***
R-Signs Service and Design Inc......815 722-0283
720 Collins St Ste D Joliet (60432) ***(G-11921)***
R-Squared Construction Inc......815 232-7433
35 N Commercial Ave Freeport (61032) ***(G-10135)***
R-Tech Feeders Inc......815 874-2990
5292 American Rd Rockford (61109) ***(G-17564)***
R. O. I. Systems, Lake Zurich *Also called Return On Inv Systems Inc* ***(G-12449)***
R.E.F. Silk Screen Productions, Evanston *Also called Lochman Ref Silk Screen Co* ***(G-9547)***
R.L. Ringwood, Bedford Park *Also called Ringwood Company* ***(G-1499)***
R/A Hoerr Inc......309 691-8789
9804 W Primrose Edwards (61528) ***(G-8340)***
R/K Industries Inc......847 526-2222
375 Hollow Hill Rd Wauconda (60084) ***(G-20387)***
R2c Performance Products LLC......708 488-8211
605 Tower Rd Mundelein (60060) ***(G-14730)***
Ra Energy Drink Inc......773 503-8574
6816 S Paxton Ave Chicago (60649) ***(G-5956)***
Raajrtna Stinless Wire USA Inc......847 923-8000
1015 W Wise Rd Ste 201 Schaumburg (60193) ***(G-18695)***
Raani Corporation......708 496-1035
5202 W 70th Pl Bedford Park (60638) ***(G-1496)***
Rabbit Tool USA Inc (PA)......309 793-4375
105 9th St Rock Island (61201) ***(G-17238)***
Raber Packing Company......309 673-0721
1320 N Wood Rd Peoria (61604) ***(G-16507)***
Rabine Paving, Byron *Also called Byron Blacktop Inc* ***(G-2751)***
Racconto, Melrose Park *Also called Alm Distributors LLC* ***(G-13823)***
Rachel Switall Mag Group Nfp......773 344-7123
1441b W Wrightwood Ave Chicago (60614) ***(G-5957)***
Racine Paper Box Manufacturing......773 227-3900
3522 W Potomac Ave Chicago (60651) ***(G-5958)***
Rack Builders Inc (PA)......217 214-9482
3809 Dye Rd Quincy (62305) ***(G-16937)***
Rack'ems, Wauconda *Also called Horizon Mfg Entps Inc* ***(G-20358)***
Rackow Polymers Corporation......630 766-3982
475 Thomas Dr Bensenville (60106) ***(G-1882)***
Raco Steel Company......708 339-2958
2100 W 163rd Pl Markham (60428) ***(G-13550)***
RAD Source Technologies Inc......815 477-1291
8411 Pyott Rd Ste 111 Algonquin (60156) ***(G-385)***
Radco Industries Inc (PA)......630 232-7966
700 Kingsland Dr Batavia (60510) ***(G-1408)***
Radiac Abrasives Inc (HQ)......618 548-4200
1015 S College St Salem (62881) ***(G-18354)***
Radiac Abrasives Inc......630 898-0315
101 Kendall Point Dr Oswego (60543) ***(G-16024)***
Radiad Manufacturing......847 678-5808
3543 Martens St Franklin Park (60131) ***(G-10031)***
Radio Controlled Models Inc......847 740-8726
229 E Rollins Rd Round Lake Beach (60073) ***(G-18092)***
Radio Flyer Inc......773 637-7100
6515 W Grand Ave Ste 1 Chicago (60707) ***(G-5959)***
Radio Frequency Systems Inc......800 321-4700
2000 Nperville Wheaton Rd Naperville (60563) ***(G-14906)***
Radionic Hi-Tech Inc......773 804-0100
6625 W Diversey Ave Chicago (60707) ***(G-5960)***
Radionic Industries Inc......773 804-0100
6625 W Diversey Ave Chicago (60707) ***(G-5961)***
Radius Machine & Tool Inc......847 662-7690
4290 Lee Ave Gurnee (60031) ***(G-10922)***
Radius Solutions Incorporated......312 648-0800
150 N Michigan Ave # 300 Chicago (60601) ***(G-5962)***
Radovent Illinois LLC (PA)......847 637-0297
10s187 Schoger Dr Ste 65 Naperville (60564) ***(G-14984)***
Rae Products and Chem Corp (PA)......708 396-1984
11638 S Mayfield Ave Alsip (60803) ***(G-501)***
Rae Supply, Harvey *Also called Brewer Company* ***(G-11080)***
Rah Enterprises Inc......217 223-1970
2630 S Commercial Dr Quincy (62305) ***(G-16938)***
Rahco Rubber Inc......847 298-4200
1633 Birchwood Ave Des Plaines (60018) ***(G-7835)***
Rahmanims Imports Inc (PA)......312 236-2200
5 S Wabash Ave Ste 1211 Chicago (60603) ***(G-5963)***
Rahn Equipment Company......217 431-1232
2400 Georgetown Rd Danville (61832) ***(G-7376)***
Rahn USA Corp......630 851-4220
1005 N Commons Dr Aurora (60504) ***(G-1012)***
Rail Exchange Inc......708 757-3317
1150 State St Chicago Heights (60411) ***(G-6767)***
Railcraft Nexim Design......309 937-2360
12165 N 850th Ave Cambridge (61238) ***(G-2806)***
Raildecks Intermodal......630 442-7676
1311 Palmer St Downers Grove (60516) ***(G-8086)***
Railroad Electronics, Schiller Park *Also called Rex Morioka* ***(G-18839)***
Railshop Inc......847 816-0925
902 Wexford Ct Libertyville (60048) ***(G-12701)***
Railway & Industrial Spc, Crest Hill *Also called Railway & Industrial Svcs Inc* ***(G-7094)***
Railway & Industrial Svcs Inc......815 726-4224
2201 N Center St Crest Hill (60403) ***(G-7094)***
Railway Program Services Inc......708 552-4000
6235 S Oak Park Ave Chicago (60638) ***(G-5964)***
Raimonde Drilling Corp......630 458-0590
770 W Factory Rd Ste A Addison (60101) ***(G-265)***
Rain Cii Carbon LLC......618 544-2193
12187 E 950th Ave Robinson (62454) ***(G-17124)***
Rain Creek Baking Corp......559 347-9960
1 Sexton Dr Glendale Heights (60139) ***(G-10487)***
Rainbo Sports LLC......847 784-9857
790 W Frontage Rd Ste 705 Northfield (60093) ***(G-15528)***
Rainbow Art Inc......312 421-5600
2224 W Grand Ave Chicago (60612) ***(G-5965)***
Rainbow Cleaners......630 789-6989
836 E Ogden Ave Westmont (60559) ***(G-20768)***
Rainbow Colors Inc......847 640-7700
935 Lee St Elk Grove Village (60007) ***(G-9212)***
Rainbow Farms Enterprises Inc......708 534-1070
25715 S Ridgeland Ave Monee (60449) ***(G-14206)***
Rainbow Graphics, Inc., Mundelein *Also called Rainbow Manufacturing Inc* ***(G-14731)***
Rainbow Lighting......847 480-1136
3545 Commercial Ave Northbrook (60062) ***(G-15470)***
Rainbow Manufacturing Inc......847 824-9600
933 Tower Rd Mundelein (60060) ***(G-14731)***
Rainbow Midwest Inc......847 955-9300
300 Corporate Woods Pkwy Vernon Hills (60061) ***(G-20084)***
Rainbow Play Systems Illinois, Vernon Hills *Also called Rainbow Midwest Inc* ***(G-20084)***
Rainbow Printing, Lemont *Also called Patrick Impressions LLC* ***(G-12578)***
Rainbow Signs......815 675-6750
2404 Spring Ridge Dr A Spring Grove (60081) ***(G-19298)***
Rainmaker......847 998-0838
1539 Palmgren Dr Glenview (60025) ***(G-10608)***
Rainmaker Brands, Quincy *Also called Griffard & Associates LLC* ***(G-16887)***
Raised Expectations, Alsip *Also called B Allan Graphics Inc* ***(G-420)***
Rajner Quality Machine Works......847 394-8999
2092 Foster Ave Wheeling (60090) ***(G-20968)***
Raleigh Ready Mix, Raleigh *Also called Gary & Larry Brown Trucking* ***(G-16961)***
Ralph Cody Gravrok......630 628-9570
729 W Fullerton Ave 6f Addison (60101) ***(G-266)***
Ralston Food Sales Inc......314 877-7000
2021 Spring Rd Ste 600 Oak Brook (60523) ***(G-15658)***
Ram Plastic Corp......847 669-8003
1327 10th Ave Rockford (61104) ***(G-17565)***
Ram R-C Models, Round Lake Beach *Also called Radio Controlled Models Inc* ***(G-18092)***
Ram Systems & Communication......847 487-7575
6411 Round Up Rd McHenry (60050) ***(G-13785)***
Ramallah Jewelry, Oak Lawn *Also called Jordan Gold Inc* ***(G-15722)***
Ramar Industries Inc......847 451-0445
9211 Parklane Ave Franklin Park (60131) ***(G-10032)***
Ramco Group LLC......847 639-9899
764 Tek Dr Crystal Lake (60014) ***(G-7252)***
Ramco Tool, Crystal Lake *Also called Ramco Group LLC* ***(G-7252)***
Ramco Tool & Manufacturing Inc......847 639-9899
760 Industrial Dr Ste I Cary (60013) ***(G-3184)***
Ramona Sedivy......630 983-1902
1840 Auburn Ave Naperville (60565) ***(G-14907)***
Rampnow LLC......630 892-7267
2280 Cornell Ave Montgomery (60538) ***(G-14266)***
Rampro Facilities Svcs Corp......224 639-6378
1701 Grand Ave Waukegan (60085) ***(G-20487)***
Ramptech Inc......303 936-3641
6235 S Oak Park Ave Chicago (60638) ***(G-5966)***
Ramptech Inc......708 594-2179
6900 S Central Ave Chicago (60638) ***(G-5967)***
Rams Sheet Metal Equipment Inc......224 788-9900
77 Mcmillen Rd Ste 100 Antioch (60002) ***(G-632)***
Ramsey Welding Inc......618 483-6248
5360 E 900th Ave Altamont (62411) ***(G-537)***
Ramseys Machine Co......217 824-2320
1333 N Webster St Taylorville (62568) ***(G-19761)***
Ramseys News Agency, New Lenox *Also called Peg N Reds* ***(G-15049)***
Rana Meal Solutions LLC......630 581-4100
550 S Spitzer Rd Bartlett (60103) ***(G-1303)***
Rana Meal Solutions LLC (HQ)......630 581-4100
1400 16th St Ste 275 Oak Brook (60523) ***(G-15659)***
Rancilio North America Inc......630 427-1703
11130 Katherines Xing Woodridge (60517) ***(G-21336)***
Rand Diversified Midwest, Edwardsville *Also called Sjd Direct Midwest LLC* ***(G-8375)***
Rand Manufacturing Network Inc......847 299-8884
840 Tanglewood Dr Wheeling (60090) ***(G-20969)***
Rand McNally, Chicago *Also called Rm Acquisition LLC* ***(G-6039)***
Rand McNally & Company (HQ)......847 329-8100
8770 W Bryn Mawr Ave # 1400 Chicago (60631) ***(G-5968)***

ALPHABETIC SECTION
Rdl Marketing Inc

Rand McNally International Co 847 329-8100
8770 W Bryn Mawr Ave # 1400 Chicago (60631) ***(G-5969)***
Randa Accessories, Rosemont *Also called Trafalgar Company LLC* ***(G-18054)***
Randa Accessories Lea Gds LLC (PA) 847 292-8300
5600 N River Rd Ste 500 Rosemont (60018) ***(G-18046)***
Randal Retail Group, Batavia *Also called Randal Wood Displays Inc* ***(G-1409)***
Randal Wood Displays Inc 630 761-0400
507 N Raddant Rd Batavia (60510) ***(G-1409)***
Randall Manufacturing LLC 630 782-0001
722 N Church Rd Elmhurst (60126) ***(G-9414)***
Randall Publications (PA) 847 437-6604
1840 Jarvis Ave Elk Grove Village (60007) ***(G-9213)***
Randall Publishing Inc 847 437-6604
1425 Lunt Ave Elk Grove Village (60007) ***(G-9214)***
Randolph Agricultural Services 309 473-3256
15125 E 625 North Rd Heyworth (61745) ***(G-11190)***
Randolph County Herald Tribune 618 826-2385
1205 Swanwick St Chester (62233) ***(G-3460)***
Randolph Dairy, Chicago *Also called A New Dairy Company* ***(G-3489)***
Randolph Packing Co 630 830-3100
275 Roma Jean Pkwy Streamwood (60107) ***(G-19592)***
Randy Wright & Son Cnstr 217 478-4171
901 E Old 36 Alexander (62601) ***(G-363)***
Randys Exper-Clean 217 423-1975
4925 W Main St Decatur (62522) ***(G-7539)***
Ranger Redi-Mix & Mtls Inc 815 337-2662
1100 Borden Ln Woodstock (60098) ***(G-21429)***
Rankin Publishing Inc 217 268-4959
204 E Main St Arcola (61910) ***(G-664)***
Rantoul Foods LLC 217 892-4178
205 Turner Dr Rantoul (61866) ***(G-16981)***
Rantoul Youth Wrestling 217 377-9523
920 Pinecrest Dr Rantoul (61866) ***(G-16982)***
RAO Design International Inc 847 671-6182
9311 Osceola Ave Morton Grove (60053) ***(G-14437)***
Rapak LLC (HQ) 630 296-2000
1201 Windham Pkwy Ste D Romeoville (60446) ***(G-17868)***
Rapco Building Pdts & Sup Co, Richview *Also called Rapco Ltd* ***(G-17033)***
Rapco Ltd 618 249-6614
405 E 1st South St Richview (62877) ***(G-17033)***
Rapid Circular Press Inc 312 421-5611
526 N Western Ave Chicago (60612) ***(G-5970)***
Rapid Copy & Duplicating Co 312 733-3353
1723 N 25th Ave Melrose Park (60160) ***(G-13906)***
Rapid Displays Inc (HQ) 773 927-5000
4300 W 47th St Chicago (60632) ***(G-5971)***
Rapid Displays Inc 773 884-0900
4100 W 76th St Unit F Chicago (60652) ***(G-5972)***
Rapid Displays Inc 773 927-1500
4300 W 47th St Chicago (60632) ***(G-5973)***
Rapid Electroplating Process 708 344-2504
2901 W Soffel Ave Melrose Park (60160) ***(G-13907)***
Rapid Foods Inc 708 366-0321
1007 Geneva St Shorewood (60404) ***(G-18902)***
Rapid Landscaping Inc 815 740-1000
2031 N Raynor Ave Crest Hill (60403) ***(G-7095)***
Rapid Line Industries Inc 815 727-4362
455 N Ottawa St Ste 1 Joliet (60432) ***(G-11922)***
Rapid Manufacturing Inc 847 458-0888
1320 Chase St Ste 4 Algonquin (60102) ***(G-386)***
Rapid Motion Cnc LLC 224 372-9000
473 Park Ave Ste 100 Lake Villa (60046) ***(G-12366)***
Rapid Pallets Inc 708 259-4016
4631 S Saint Louis Ave Chicago (60632) ***(G-5974)***
Rapid Pallets Inc (PA) 708 424-2306
9700 S Harlem Ave Bridgeview (60455) ***(G-2378)***
Rapid Print 309 673-0826
934 N Bourland Ave Peoria (61606) ***(G-16508)***
Rapid Printing Service, South Holland *Also called David H Vander Ploeg* ***(G-19206)***
Rapid Wash Group Ltd 847 376-8442
622 E Northwest Hwy Des Plaines (60016) ***(G-7836)***
Rapid Wire Forms Inc 773 586-6600
6932 W 62nd St Chicago (60638) ***(G-5975)***
Rapp Cabinets & Woodworks Inc 618 736-2955
501 E Illinois Hwy 142 Dahlgren (62828) ***(G-7309)***
Rare Birds Inc 847 259-7286
321 E Rand Rd Arlington Heights (60004) ***(G-796)***
Rasoi Resturaunt 847 455-8888
15 Clair Ct Roselle (60172) ***(G-17977)***
Rat Worx, Mount Morris *Also called Research and Testing Worx Inc* ***(G-14501)***
Rathje Enterprises Inc (PA) 217 423-2593
1845 N 22nd St Decatur (62526) ***(G-7540)***
Rathje Enterprises Inc 217 443-0022
19 Withner St Danville (61832) ***(G-7377)***
Rational Cooking Systems Inc 224 366-3500
1701 Golf Rd Ste C-Ll Rolling Meadows (60008) ***(G-17769)***
Rauckman High Voltage Sales 618 239-0399
37 Ednick Dr Swansea (62226) ***(G-19696)***
Rauckman Utility Products LLC 618 234-0001
33 Empire Dr Belleville (62220) ***(G-1587)***
Ravago Americas LLC 815 609-4800
24210 W 143rd St Plainfield (60544) ***(G-16709)***
Ravco Incorporated 815 725-9095
1313 Colorado Ave Joliet (60435) ***(G-11923)***
Raven Tree Press LLC 800 323-8270
6213 Factory Rd Ste B Crystal Lake (60014) ***(G-7253)***
Ravens Wood Pharmacy 708 667-0525
4211 N Cicero Ave Chicago (60641) ***(G-5976)***
Ravenscroft Inc 630 513-9911
473 Dunham Rd Ste 209 Saint Charles (60174) ***(G-18259)***
Ravinia Metals, Itasca *Also called Millenia Metals LLC* ***(G-11703)***
Raw Thrills Inc 847 679-8373
5441 Fargo Ave Skokie (60077) ***(G-19019)***
Rawnature5 LLC 312 800-3239
3026 W Carroll Ave Chicago (60612) ***(G-5977)***
Rawson Custom Woodworks LLC 815 332-9222
601 E State St Cherry Valley (61016) ***(G-3445)***
Ray Tool & Engineering Inc 630 587-0000
2440 Production Dr Saint Charles (60174) ***(G-18260)***
Raycar Gear & Machine Company 815 874-3948
6125 11th St Rockford (61109) ***(G-17566)***
Rayco Printing Services Inc 773 545-4545
6025 N Cicero Ave Chicago (60646) ***(G-5978)***
Raydyot US, Franklin Park *Also called Koehler Enterprises Inc* ***(G-9978)***
Rayes Boiler & Welding Ltd 847 675-6655
8252 Christiana Ave Skokie (60076) ***(G-19020)***
Raymond Earl Fine Woodworking 309 565-7661
201 S Main St Hanna City (61536) ***(G-10994)***
Raymond D Wright 618 783-2206
35 Homestead Dr Newton (62448) ***(G-15091)***
Raymundos Food Group LLC 708 344-8400
7424 S Lockwood Ave Bedford Park (60638) ***(G-1497)***
Raynor Garage Door, Dixon *Also called Neisewander Enterprises Inc* ***(G-7904)***
Raynor Garage Doors, Dixon *Also called Raynor Mfg Co* ***(G-7908)***
Raynor Mfg Co (HQ) 815 288-1431
1101 E River Rd Dixon (61021) ***(G-7908)***
Rayovac Corp 815 285-6500
200 E Corporate Dr Dixon (61021) ***(G-7909)***
Rays Countertop Shop Inc 217 483-2514
125 Robb St Glenarm (62536) ***(G-10427)***
Rays Electrical Service LLC 847 214-2944
37w904 Us Highway 20 Elgin (60124) ***(G-8715)***
Rays Machine & Mfg Co Inc 309 699-2121
419 Truck Haven Rd East Peoria (61611) ***(G-8286)***
Rays Power Wshg Svc Peggy Ray 618 939-6306
318 Bradford Ln Waterloo (62298) ***(G-20295)***
Raytech Machining Fabrication 618 932-2511
10925 Mainline Rd West Frankfort (62896) ***(G-20680)***
Raytheon Company 630 295-6394
4110 Winnetka Ave Rolling Meadows (60008) ***(G-17770)***
Raytheon Technologies Corp 630 516-3460
655 W Grand Ave Ste 320 Elmhurst (60126) ***(G-9415)***
Raytheon Technologies Corp 815 226-6000
4747 Harrison Ave Rockford (61108) ***(G-17567)***
Razny Jewelers Ltd (PA) 630 932-4900
1501 W Lake St Ste 1 Addison (60101) ***(G-267)***
Rbc Services, Aurora *Also called McNish Corporation* ***(G-1128)***
Rbj Inc 309 344-5066
796 S Pearl St Galesburg (61401) ***(G-10217)***
Rbp Services 206 238-3526
1116 Liberty St Apt 6 Morris (60450) ***(G-14324)***
Rcc Conveyors Inc 224 338-8841
31632 N Ellis Dr Unit 105 Volo (60073) ***(G-20205)***
Rci, Milan *Also called R C Industrial Inc* ***(G-14023)***
Rcl Electronics 630 834-0156
826 S Iowa Ave Addison (60101) ***(G-268)***
RCM Industries Inc (PA) 847 455-1950
3021 Cullerton St Franklin Park (60131) ***(G-10033)***
RCM Industries Inc 847 455-1950
161 Carpenter Ave Wheeling (60090) ***(G-20970)***
RCM Smith Inc 309 786-8833
507 34th Ave Rock Island (61201) ***(G-17239)***
RCP Publications Inc 773 227-4066
3449 N Sheffield Ave Chicago (60657) ***(G-5979)***
Rd Daily Enterprises 847 872-7632
911 Fulton Ave Winthrop Harbor (60096) ***(G-21142)***
Rd Husemoller Ltd 847 526-5505
1255 Karl Ct Wauconda (60084) ***(G-20388)***
Rda Inc 815 427-8444
400 N 3rd Ave Saint Anne (60964) ***(G-18137)***
Rdc Linear Enterprises LLC 815 547-1106
6593 Revlon Dr Dr1 Belvidere (61008) ***(G-1697)***
RDF Inc 618 273-4141
2909 Richardson St Eldorado (62930) ***(G-8483)***
Rdh Inc of Rockford 815 874-9421
3445 Lonergan Dr Rockford (61109) ***(G-17568)***
Rdi Group Inc 630 773-4900
1025 W Thorndale Ave Itasca (60143) ***(G-11724)***
Rdl Marketing Inc 773 254-7600
2600 W 19th St Chicago (60608) ***(G-5980)***

ALPHABETIC

ALPHABETIC SECTION

RE Met Corp 312 733-6700
2246 W Hubbard St Chicago (60612) *(G-5981)*

RE-Do-It Corp 708 343-7125
1950 Beach St Broadview (60155) *(G-2463)*

Re-Maid Incorporated 815 315-0500
1440 Sylvan Ct Freeport (61032) *(G-10136)*

Re-Source Building Products, Elgin Also called Plastival Inc *(G-8690)*

React Computer Services Inc 630 323-6200
7654 Plaza Ct Willowbrook (60527) *(G-21058)*

READ Worldwide LLC 312 301-6276
116 W Jckson Blvd Ste 106 Chicago (60604) *(G-5982)*

Reader's Digest, Chicago Also called Trusted Media Brands Inc *(G-6439)*

Ready 2 Roll Inc 847 620-9768
96 Mchenry Rd Wheeling (60090) *(G-20971)*

Ready Access Inc 800 621-5045
1815 Arthur Dr West Chicago (60185) *(G-20635)*

Ready Inc 630 501-1352
231 E Fremont Ave Apt 209 Elmhurst (60126) *(G-9416)*

Ready Mix Solutions LLC 618 889-6188
1800 N Court St Marion (62959) *(G-13532)*

Reag Inc 708 344-0875
9007 S Thomas Ave Bridgeview (60455) *(G-2379)*

Reagent Chemical & RES Inc 618 271-8140
1700 S 20th St East Saint Louis (62207) *(G-8319)*

Real Alloy Recycling LLC 708 757-8900
400 E Lincoln Hwy Chicago Heights (60411) *(G-6768)*

Real Estate Communications, Chicago Also called Law Bulletin Publishing Co *(G-5182)*

Real Estate Developer, Chicago Also called Brd Development Group LLC *(G-3947)*

Real Estate News Corp 773 866-9900
3525 W Peterson Ave T10 Chicago (60659) *(G-5983)*

Real Neon Inc 630 543-0995
226 E Adele Ct Villa Park (60181) *(G-20168)*

Real Taste Noodles Mfg Inc 312 738-1893
1838 S Canal St Chicago (60616) *(G-5984)*

Real Times II LLC (PA) 312 225-2400
4445 S Dr Mrtn Lther King Martin Luther King Chicago (60653) *(G-5985)*

Realclearpolitics (PA) 773 255-5846
6160 N Cicero Ave Ste 410 Chicago (60646) *(G-5986)*

Really Useful Boxes Inc 847 238-0444
355 Longview Dr Bloomingdale (60108) *(G-2011)*

Realt Images Inc 217 567-3487
172 Williamsburg Hl A Tower Hill (62571) *(G-19894)*

Realtor Magazine, Chicago Also called National Association Realtors *(G-5543)*

Realty World, Warsaw Also called Midwest Mktg/Pdctn Mfg Co *(G-20258)*

Realwheels Corporation 847 662-7722
3940 Tannahill Dr Gurnee (60031) *(G-10923)*

Ream's Meat Market, Elburn Also called Elburn Market Inc *(G-8451)*

Reason's Locker, Buffalo Prairie Also called Reasons Inc *(G-2626)*

Reasons Inc 309 537-3424
18510 206th Sw Buffalo Prairie (61237) *(G-2626)*

REB Steel Equipment Corp (PA) 773 252-0400
4556 W Grand Ave Chicago (60639) *(G-5987)*

REB Storage Systems Intl, Chicago Also called REB Steel Equipment Corp *(G-5987)*

Reba Machine Corp 630 595-1272
767 N Edgewood Ave Wood Dale (60191) *(G-21234)*

Rebco Machine Specialties Inc 630 852-3419
138 E Quincy St Westmont (60559) *(G-20769)*

Rebechini Studio Inc 847 437-9030
680 Fargo Ave Elk Grove Village (60007) *(G-9215)*

Rebel Inc 618 235-0582
1 Rebel Pkwy Belleville (62226) *(G-1588)*

Rebel Brands LLC 312 804-0009
600 20th St Wilmette (60091) *(G-21091)*

Rebel Screeners Inc 312 525-2670
820 W Jackson Blvd # 400 Chicago (60607) *(G-5988)*

Rebellion Brew Haus 309 524-5219
1525 3rd Avenue A Moline (61265) *(G-14172)*

Reber Welding Service 217 774-3441
142 S Washington St Shelbyville (62565) *(G-18885)*

Rebuilders Enterprises Inc 708 430-0030
9004 S Octavia Ave Bridgeview (60455) *(G-2380)*

Receiving D84v K2 Complex, North Chicago Also called Abbott Laboratories *(G-15291)*

Recendiz Welding Inc 708 205-8759
2626 N 77th Ct Elmwood Park (60707) *(G-9456)*

Reclaimedtablecom 630 834-1929
222 W Stone Rd Villa Park (60181) *(G-20169)*

Reco, Roodhouse Also called Roodhouse Envelope Co *(G-17894)*

Reco of IL Inc 630 898-2010
1669 Dearborn Ave Aurora (60505) *(G-1147)*

Recognitions, Aviston Also called Mhwp *(G-1182)*

Reconserve of Illinois Inc 708 354-4641
6160 River Rd Hodgkins (60525) *(G-11394)*

Recora LLC 630 879-2202
197 Alder Dr North Aurora (60542) *(G-15273)*

Recora Company, North Aurora Also called Calo Corporation *(G-15256)*

Record Inc 312 985-7270
207 E Ohio St Ste 164 Chicago (60611) *(G-5989)*

Record Printing & Publishing, Millstadt Also called Metro Printing & Pubg Inc *(G-14052)*

Recreation Management, Palatine Also called Cab Communications Inc *(G-16097)*

Recsolu Inc 312 517-3200
55 E Monroe St Ste 3600 Chicago (60603) *(G-5990)*

Recycled Paper Greetings Inc 773 348-6410
111 N Canal St Ste 700 Chicago (60606) *(G-5991)*

Recycled Vinyls LLC 847 624-1880
825 S Waukegan Rd Ste A8 Lake Forest (60045) *(G-12294)*

Recycling Solutions Inc 773 617-6955
6348 N Milwaukee Chicago Chicago (60646) *(G-5992)*

Red Bud Industries, Red Bud Also called Red Bud Industries Inc *(G-17000)*

Red Bud Industries Inc 618 282-3801
200 B East Industrial Dr Red Bud (62278) *(G-17000)*

Red Bud Winery Inc 618 282-9463
214 Main St Ruma (62278) *(G-18105)*

Red Center, Northbrook Also called Regional Emergency Dispatch *(G-15471)*

Red Hill Lava Products Inc (PA) 800 528-2765
8002 31st St W Rock Island (61201) *(G-17240)*

Red Parrot Juices, Lemont Also called Key Colony Inc *(G-12568)*

Red River Lumber Inc 708 388-1818
2200 Burr Oak Ave Blue Island (60406) *(G-2135)*

Red Rumi LLC 847 757-8433
1020 Estancia Ln Algonquin (60102) *(G-387)*

Red Wing 217 655-2772
2418 Georgetown Rd Danville (61832) *(G-7378)*

Red-E-Mix LLC 618 654-2166
405 Main St Highland (62249) *(G-11237)*

Red-E-Mix Transportation LLC 618 654-2166
405 Main St Highland (62249) *(G-11238)*

Redbox Workshop Ltd 773 478-7077
3121 N Rockwell St Chicago (60618) *(G-5993)*

Reddi-Pac Inc (PA) 847 657-5222
3700 W Lake Ave Glenview (60026) *(G-10609)*

Redeen Engraving Inc 847 593-6500
670 Chase Ave Elk Grove Village (60007) *(G-9216)*

Redhorse Performance Inc 708 430-1603
9911 S 78th Ave Hickory Hills (60457) *(G-11202)*

Redi-Serve Foods, Aurora Also called On-Cor Frozen Foods LLC *(G-1142)*

Redi-Strip Company Inc 630 529-2442
100 Central Ave Roselle (60172) *(G-17978)*

Redin Parts Inc 815 398-1010
1922 7th St Ste 4d Rockford (61104) *(G-17569)*

Redin Production Machine, Rockford Also called Redin Parts Inc *(G-17569)*

Reds Muffler Shop 217 344-1676
102 W University Ave Urbana (61801) *(G-19997)*

Redshelf Inc 312 878-8586
500 N Dearborn St # 1200 Chicago (60654) *(G-5994)*

Redshelf/Virdocs, Chicago Also called Redshelf Inc *(G-5994)*

Redwood Landings LLC 312 508-4953
1 E Wacker Dr Ste 1100 Chicago (60601) *(G-5995)*

Reed-Union Corporation (PA) 312 644-3200
875 N Michigan Ave # 3718 Chicago (60611) *(G-5996)*

Reedy Industries Inc (PA) 847 729-9450
2440 Ravine Way Ste 200 Glenview (60025) *(G-10610)*

Reef Development Inc 618 842-7711
Rr 3 Fairfield (62837) *(G-9634)*

Reel Mate Mfg Co 708 423-8005
10113 Buell Ct Oak Lawn (60453) *(G-15734)*

Reelchicagocom Enterprises Inc 312 274-9980
5000 N Marine Dr 4d Chicago (60640) *(G-5997)*

Reesha Printing Inc 708 233-6677
7236 W 90th Pl Bridgeview (60455) *(G-2381)*

Reesha Printing & Signs, Bridgeview Also called Reesha Printing Inc *(G-2381)*

Reeves Lure Co 217 864-3493
4165 Shaw Rd Lovington (61937) *(G-13285)*

Refined Haystack Inc 773 627-3534
1959 N Sheffield Ave Chicago (60614) *(G-5998)*

Reflection Software Inc 630 270-1200
900 S Frontenac St # 100 Aurora (60504) *(G-1013)*

Reflections In Glass, Wauconda Also called T J M & Associates Inc *(G-20396)*

Reflejos Publications LLC 847 806-1111
155 E Algonquin Rd Arlington Heights (60005) *(G-797)*

Reflex Fitness Products Inc 309 756-1050
1130 15th Ave W Milan (61264) *(G-14024)*

Refreshment Services Inc (PA) 217 223-8600
1121 Locust St Quincy (62301) *(G-16939)*

Refreshment Services Inc 217 522-8841
1337 E Cook St Springfield (62703) *(G-19432)*

Refreshment Services Inc 217 429-5415
2112 N Brush College Rd Decatur (62526) *(G-7541)*

Refrigerated Dough Division, Downers Grove Also called Earthgrains Refrigertd Dough P *(G-7996)*

Reg Seneca LLC 888 734-8686
614 Shipyard Rd Seneca (61360) *(G-18860)*

Regal Beloit Corporation 844 527-8392
5330 E Rockton Rd Roscoe (61073) *(G-17923)*

Regal Converting Co Inc 630 257-3581
14503 S Gougar Rd Unit 1 Lockport (60491) *(G-13021)*

Regal Cut Stone LLC 773 826-8796
4213 W Chicago Ave Chicago (60651) *(G-5999)*

Regal Cutting Tools, Roscoe *Also called Regal Beloit Corporation* ***(G-17923)***
Regal Cutting Tools Inc.....815 389-3461
5330 E Rockton Rd Roscoe (61073) ***(G-17924)***
Regal Health Foods Intl Inc.....773 252-1044
2701 N Normandy Ave Chicago (60707) ***(G-6000)***
Regal Johnson Co.....630 885-0688
229 Christine Way Bolingbrook (60440) ***(G-2232)***
Regal Linen, Highland *Also called Mount Vernon Mills* ***(G-11233)***
Regal Steel Erectors LLC.....847 888-3500
850 Tollgate Rd Elgin (60123) ***(G-8716)***
Regency Crystal, Wauconda *Also called Amkine Inc* ***(G-20331)***
Regency Custom Woodworking.....815 689-2117
215 E Van Alstyne St Cullom (60929) ***(G-7300)***
Regency Hand Laundry.....773 871-3950
2739 N Racine Ave Chicago (60614) ***(G-6001)***
Regenex Corp.....815 663-2003
1 Wolfer Industrial Park Spring Valley (61362) ***(G-19311)***
Regent Automotive Engineering.....773 889-5744
2107 N Cicero Ave Chicago (60639) ***(G-6002)***
Regent Window Fashions LLC.....773 871-6400
917 W Irving Park Rd Chicago (60613) ***(G-6003)***
Reggios Pizza Inc (PA).....773 933-7927
1001 E 99th St Chicago (60628) ***(G-6004)***
Regional Emergency Dispatch.....847 498-5748
1842 Shermer Rd Northbrook (60062) ***(G-15471)***
Regional Ready Mix LLC.....815 562-1901
15051 E Lind Rd Rochelle (61068) ***(G-17154)***
Register Publishing Co.....618 253-7146
35 S Vine St Harrisburg (62946) ***(G-11028)***
Regunathan & Assoc Inc.....630 653-0387
1490 Jasper Dr Wheaton (60189) ***(G-20818)***
Rehabilitation and Vocational.....618 833-5344
214 W Davie St Anna (62906) ***(G-587)***
Rehkemper & Sons Inc (PA).....618 526-2269
17817 Saint Rose Rd Breese (62230) ***(G-2307)***
Rehling & Associates Inc.....630 941-3560
1010 S Swain Ave Elmhurst (60126) ***(G-9417)***
Rehobot Inc.....815 385-7777
3980 W Albany St Ste 1 McHenry (60050) ***(G-13786)***
Reichel Hardware Company Inc.....630 762-7394
1820 Wallace Ave Ste 122 Saint Charles (60174) ***(G-18261)***
Reichhold Industries Inc.....815 942-4600
6350 E Collins Rd Morris (60450) ***(G-14325)***
Reichhold Industries Inc (PA).....919 990-7500
100 E Cottage Ave Carpentersville (60110) ***(G-3118)***
Reid Communications Inc.....847 741-9700
450 Shepard Dr Ste 11 Elgin (60123) ***(G-8717)***
Reign Print Solutions Inc.....847 590-7091
550 W Campus Dr Arlington Heights (60004) ***(G-798)***
Reilly Communication Group.....630 756-1225
3030 W Salt Creek Ln # 201 Arlington Heights (60005) ***(G-799)***
Reilly Foam Corp.....630 392-2680
920 Frontenac Rd Naperville (60563) ***(G-14908)***
Reina Imaging, Crystal Lake *Also called X-Ray Cassette Repair Co Inc* ***(G-7296)***
Reino Tool & Manufacturing Co.....773 588-5800
3668 N Elston Ave Chicago (60618) ***(G-6005)***
Rejuv-A-Roller LLC.....815 975-9635
2339 Newburg Rd Belvidere (61008) ***(G-1698)***
Rektrix.....773 475-7926
4545 S Ashland Ave Chicago (60609) ***(G-6006)***
Relativity Oda LLC (HQ).....312 263-1177
231 S Lasalle St Fl 8 Flr 8 Chicago (60604) ***(G-6007)***
Relay Services Mfg Corp.....773 252-2700
1300 N Pulaski Rd Ste 12 Chicago (60651) ***(G-6008)***
Relco Locomotives Inc (PA).....630 968-0670
200 S Frontage Rd Burr Ridge (60527) ***(G-2716)***
Reliable Appliance and Ref.....847 581-9520
7443 Emerson St Morton Grove (60053) ***(G-14438)***
Reliable Asphalt Corporation (PA).....773 254-1121
3741 S Pulaski Rd Chicago (60623) ***(G-6009)***
Reliable Autotech Usa LLC.....815 945-7838
600 N Division St Chenoa (61726) ***(G-3434)***
Reliable Container Inc.....630 543-6131
210 S Addison Rd Addison (60101) ***(G-269)***
Reliable Die Service Inc.....708 458-5155
6700 W 74th St Bedford Park (60638) ***(G-1498)***
Reliable Galvanizing Company.....773 651-2500
2541 Queens Way Northbrook (60062) ***(G-15472)***
Reliable Machine Company.....815 968-8803
521 Schauer Ln Rockford (61107) ***(G-17570)***
Reliable Mail Services Inc.....847 677-6245
2733 Langley Cir Glenview (60026) ***(G-10611)***
Reliable Metal Stamping Co Inc.....773 625-1177
9244 Parklane Ave Franklin Park (60131) ***(G-10034)***
Reliable Plating Corporation.....312 421-4747
1538 W Lake St Chicago (60607) ***(G-6010)***
Reliable Sand and Gravel Co.....815 385-5020
2121 S River Rd Ste B McHenry (60051) ***(G-13787)***
Reliance Dental Mfg Co.....708 597-6694
5805 W 117th Pl Alsip (60803) ***(G-502)***
Reliance Gear Corporation.....630 543-6640
205 W Factory Rd Addison (60101) ***(G-270)***
Reliance Graphics Inc.....847 593-6688
2035 S Arlington Hts Rd Arlington Heights (60005) ***(G-800)***
Reliance Specialty Pdts Inc.....847 640-8923
154 Easy St Carol Stream (60188) ***(G-3059)***
Reliance Tool & Mfg Co (PA).....847 695-1235
900 N State St Ste 101 Elgin (60123) ***(G-8718)***
Reliance Tool & Mfg Co.....847 455-4350
11333 W Melrose St Franklin Park (60131) ***(G-10035)***
Reliance Tool Inc.....815 636-2770
946 River Ln Loves Park (61111) ***(G-13252)***
Reliefband Technologies LLC.....877 735-2263
5600 N River Rd Ste 800 Rosemont (60018) ***(G-18047)***
Reliefwatch Inc.....646 678-2336
1425 E 53rd St Fl 2 Flr 2 Chicago (60615) ***(G-6011)***
Relish Labs LLC (HQ).....872 225-2433
433 W Van Buren St 750n Chicago (60607) ***(G-6012)***
Reload Sales Inc.....618 588-2866
418 Plum Ln New Baden (62265) ***(G-15023)***
Relx Inc.....937 247-3469
28544 Network Pl Chicago (60673) ***(G-6013)***
Relx Inc.....309 689-1000
8512 N Allen Rd Peoria (61615) ***(G-16509)***
Relyon Metal Products Co.....847 679-1510
40w885 Chippewa Pass Elgin (60124) ***(G-8719)***
Remark Technologies Inc (PA).....815 985-2972
10944 N State Route 2 Rockford (61102) ***(G-17571)***
Remco Technology Inc.....847 329-8090
7438 Channel Rd Skokie (60076) ***(G-19021)***
Remet Corporation.....480 766-3464
1540 E Dundee Rd Ste 170 Palatine (60074) ***(G-16153)***
Remin Kart A Bag, Joliet *Also called Remin Laboratories Inc* ***(G-11924)***
Remin Laboratories Inc.....815 723-1940
510 Manhattan Rd Joliet (60433) ***(G-11924)***
Remington Industries Inc.....815 385-1987
3521 Chapel Hill Rd Johnsburg (60051) ***(G-11809)***
Remke Industries Inc (PA).....847 541-3780
730 Lakeview Pkwy Vernon Hills (60061) ***(G-20085)***
Remke Printing Inc.....847 520-7300
225 Larkin Dr Ste 7 Wheeling (60090) ***(G-20972)***
Remmers Welding and Machine.....815 689-2765
17809 N 3500 East Rd Cullom (60929) ***(G-7301)***
Remodeler's Supply Center, Chicago *Also called Logan Square Aluminum Sup Inc* ***(G-5249)***
Remuriate LLC (PA).....815 220-5050
122 Marquette St La Salle (61301) ***(G-12121)***
Remuriate Technologies, La Salle *Also called Remuriate LLC* ***(G-12121)***
Renaissance SSP Holdings Inc (HQ).....210 476-8194
272 E Deerpath Ste 350 Lake Forest (60045) ***(G-12295)***
Renew Packaging LLC.....312 421-6699
2444 W 16th St Ste 4r Chicago (60608) ***(G-6014)***
Renishaw Inc (HQ).....847 286-9953
1001 Wesemann Dr Dundee (60118) ***(G-8131)***
Renner & Co.....847 639-4900
160 Chicago St Cary (60013) ***(G-3185)***
Renner Quarries Ltd (PA).....815 288-6699
1700 S Galena Ave Ste 116 Dixon (61021) ***(G-7910)***
Rensel-Chicago Inc (PA).....773 235-2100
2300 N Kilbourn Ave Chicago (60639) ***(G-6015)***
Rentech Development Corp.....815 747-3101
16675 Us Highway 20 W East Dubuque (61025) ***(G-8179)***
Rentech Energy Midwest Corp.....815 747-3101
16675 Us Highway 20 W Upper East Dubuque (61025) ***(G-8180)***
Renu Electronics Private Ltd.....630 879-8412
336 Mckee St Batavia (60510) ***(G-1410)***
Replace Air, Glendale Heights *Also called Schubert Environmental Eqp Inc* ***(G-10492)***
Replay S Disc Cook-Kankaee LLC.....312 371-5018
25526 S Devonshire Ln Monee (60449) ***(G-14207)***
Replogle Globe Partners, Hillside *Also called Herff Jones LLC* ***(G-11341)***
Replogle Globes Partners LLC.....708 593-3995
125 Fencl Ln Hillside (60162) ***(G-11354)***
Reporter Inc (PA).....217 932-5211
216 S Central Ave Casey (62420) ***(G-3208)***
Reporter Money Saver, Mendota *Also called Mendota Reporter* ***(G-13948)***
Repperts Warehouse Office Furn, Anna *Also called Gazette Democrat* ***(G-583)***
Repro-Graphics Inc.....847 439-1775
1900 Arthur Ave Elk Grove Village (60007) ***(G-9217)***
Reprographics (PA).....815 477-1018
26 Crystal Lake Plz Crystal Lake (60014) ***(G-7254)***
Republic Drill.....708 865-7666
2058 N 15th Ave Melrose Park (60160) ***(G-13908)***
Republic Group Inc (PA).....800 288-8888
2301 Ravine Way Glenview (60025) ***(G-10612)***
Republic of Tea Inc.....618 478-5520
11051 N Mockingbird Rd A Nashville (62263) ***(G-15009)***
Republic Oil Co Inc.....618 842-7591
1508 W Delaware St Fairfield (62837) ***(G-9635)***
Republic Systems Inc (HQ).....773 233-6530
9160 S Green St Chicago (60620) ***(G-6016)***

ALPHABETIC

(PA)=Parent Co (HQ)=Headquarters (DH)=Div Headquarters
2020 Harris Illinois
Industrial Directory
1241

Republic Times LLC 618 939-3814
205 W Mill St Waterloo (62298) ***(G-20296)***
Republic Tobacco, Glenview *Also called Top Tobacco LP* ***(G-10633)***
Rescar Companies Inc 618 875-3234
501 Monsanto Ave East Saint Louis (62206) ***(G-8320)***
Research & Technology Center, Libertyville *Also called USG Corporation* ***(G-12721)***
Research and Testing Worx Inc 815 734-7346
112 E Hitt St Mount Morris (61054) ***(G-14501)***
Research Design Inc 708 246-8166
3901 Clausen Ave Western Springs (60558) ***(G-20724)***
Research In Motion Rf Inc 815 444-1095
500 Coventry Ln Ste 260 Crystal Lake (60014) ***(G-7255)***
Research Mannikins Inc 618 426-3456
143 Lupine Ln Ava (62907) ***(G-1177)***
Research Press Company Inc 217 352-3273
2612 N Mattis Ave Champaign (61822) ***(G-3341)***
Research Technology Intl Co (PA) 847 677-3000
4700 W Chase Ave Lincolnwood (60712) ***(G-12837)***
Residential Steel Services 309 448-2900
315 County Highway 8 Congerville (61729) ***(G-7002)***
Residntial Stl Fabricators Inc 847 695-3400
1555 Gilpen Ave South Elgin (60177) ***(G-19171)***
Resin Exchange Inc 630 628-7266
851 S Westgate St Addison (60101) ***(G-271)***
Resin8 Inc 773 551-3633
603 S Fairview Ave Elmhurst (60126) ***(G-9418)***
Resinite Corporation 847 537-4250
1033 Noel Ave Wheeling (60090) ***(G-20973)***
Resins Inc 847 884-0025
2200 W Higgins Rd Ste 204 Hoffman Estates (60169) ***(G-11450)***
Resist-A-Line Industries Inc 815 650-3177
214 Elm St Joliet (60433) ***(G-11925)***
Resolute Industrial LLC (PA) 800 537-9675
298 Messner Dr Wheeling (60090) ***(G-20974)***
Resolution Systems Inc 616 392-8001
1189 Wilmette Ave Wilmette (60091) ***(G-21092)***
Resonance Medical LLC 229 292-2094
222 Merchandise Mart Plz # 1230 Chicago (60654) ***(G-6017)***
Resource Plastics Inc 708 389-3558
5623 W 115th St Alsip (60803) ***(G-503)***
Respa Pharmaceuticals Inc 630 543-3333
625 W Factory Rd Addison (60101) ***(G-272)***
Respect Incorporated 815 806-1907
15555 Tyndall Ct Manhattan (60442) ***(G-13435)***
Respironics Inc 708 923-6200
12515 S 82nd Ave Palos Park (60464) ***(G-16213)***
Response Graphics & EMB LLC 630 364-1471
23900 W Industrial Dr S # 4 Plainfield (60585) ***(G-16710)***
Restorations Unlimited II Inc 847 639-5818
304 Jandus Rd Cary (60013) ***(G-3186)***
Retailer Watch Newsletter, Evanston *Also called S R Bastien Co* ***(G-9573)***
Retmap Inc 312 224-8938
34435 N Bobolink Trl Grayslake (60030) ***(G-10797)***
Retondo Enterprises Inc 630 837-8130
1539 Brandy Pkwy Streamwood (60107) ***(G-19593)***
Rettick Enterprises Inc 309 275-4967
13958 Roberto Rd Ste 1 Bloomington (61705) ***(G-2088)***
Return On Inv Systems Inc 847 726-0081
950 Ensell Rd Lake Zurich (60047) ***(G-12449)***
Reum Corporation 847 625-7386
140 S Dearborn St Ste 420 Chicago (60603) ***(G-6018)***
Revcor Inc (PA) 847 428-4411
251 Edwards Ave Carpentersville (60110) ***(G-3119)***
Revere Metals LLC 708 995-6131
10014 W 190th Pl Mokena (60448) ***(G-14112)***
Review 309 659-2761
910 Albany St Erie (61250) ***(G-9474)***
Review 618 997-2222
1120 N Carbon St Ste 100 Marion (62959) ***(G-13533)***
Review Graphics Inc (PA) 815 623-2570
10760 Main St Roscoe (61073) ***(G-17925)***
Review Printing Co Inc 309 788-7094
1326 40th St Rock Island (61201) ***(G-17241)***
Review, The, Morrison *Also called Wns Publications Inc* ***(G-14349)***
Revlon Inc 847 240-1558
1900 E Golf Rd Ste 900 Schaumburg (60173) ***(G-18696)***
Revolution Brands LLC 847 902-3320
12327 Bartelt Ct Huntley (60142) ***(G-11563)***
Revolution Companies Inc 800 826-4083
332 S Michigan Ave # 1032 Chicago (60604) ***(G-6019)***
Revolutionary Medical Dvcs Inc 520 464-4299
26125 N Riverwoods Blvd # 500 Mettawa (60045) ***(G-13981)***
Rex Carton Company Inc 773 581-4115
7400 Richards Rd Bridgeview (60455) ***(G-2382)***
Rex Gauge Division, Buffalo Grove *Also called Schultes Precision Mfg Inc* ***(G-2596)***
Rex Morioka 847 651-9400
4257 Wesley Ter Schiller Park (60176) ***(G-18839)***
Rex Radiator and Welding Co (PA) 312 421-1531
1440 W 38th St Chicago (60609) ***(G-6020)***
Rex Radiator and Welding Co 630 595-4664
367 Evergreen Ave Bensenville (60106) ***(G-1883)***
Rex Radiator and Welding Co 815 725-6655
14 Meadow Ave Unit 1 Rockdale (60436) ***(G-17271)***
Rex Radiator and Welding Co 847 428-1112
578 Rock Road Dr Ste 5 East Dundee (60118) ***(G-8209)***
Rex Radiator Sales & Dist, Bensenville *Also called Rex Radiator and Welding Co* ***(G-1883)***
Rex Vault Co 618 783-2416
E Rte 33 Newton (62448) ***(G-15092)***
Rex Worldwide Ltd 630 384-9361
280 Shuman Blvd Ste 270 Naperville (60563) ***(G-14909)***
Rexam, Buffalo Grove *Also called Bprex Healthcare Packaging Inc* ***(G-2519)***
Rexnord Industries LLC 630 969-1770
2400 Curtiss St Downers Grove (60515) ***(G-8087)***
Rexroat Sound 309 764-1663
4531 W High St Colona (61241) ***(G-6978)***
Reyco Precision Welding Inc (PA) 847 593-2947
320 E Il Route 22 Lake Zurich (60047) ***(G-12450)***
Reyes Holdings LLC (PA) 847 227-6500
6250 N River Rd Ste 9000 Rosemont (60018) ***(G-18048)***
Reynolds Consumer Products Co, Lake Forest *Also called Reynolds Consumer Products LLC* ***(G-12297)***
Reynolds Consumer Products Inc (HQ) 800 879-5067
1900 W Field Ct Lake Forest (60045) ***(G-12296)***
Reynolds Consumer Products LLC 217 479-1126
500 E Superior Ave Jacksonville (62650) ***(G-11782)***
Reynolds Consumer Products LLC 217 479-1466
2226 E Morton Ave Jacksonville (62650) ***(G-11783)***
Reynolds Consumer Products LLC (HQ) 847 482-3500
1900 W Field Ct Lake Forest (60045) ***(G-12297)***
Reynolds Food Packaging 815 465-2115
304 Ne Main St Grant Park (60940) ***(G-10751)***
Reynolds Food Packaging LLC 847 482-3500
1900 W Field Ct Lake Forest (60045) ***(G-12298)***
Reynolds Holdings Inc 630 739-0110
684 S Phillips Unit 2 Romeoville (60446) ***(G-17869)***
Reynolds Manufacturing Company 309 787-8600
630 4th St W Milan (61264) ***(G-14025)***
Reznik Instrument Co 847 673-3444
7337 Lawndale Ave Skokie (60076) ***(G-19022)***
Rf Ideas Inc (HQ) 847 870-1723
4020 Winnetka Ave Rolling Meadows (60008) ***(G-17771)***
RF Mau Co 847 329-9731
7140 N Lawndale Ave Lincolnwood (60712) ***(G-12838)***
Rf Plastics Co 630 628-6033
406 W Belden Ave Addison (60101) ***(G-273)***
RF Technologies Inc (PA) 618 377-2654
330 Lexington Dr Buffalo Grove (60089) ***(G-2592)***
Rgb Lights Inc 312 421-6080
6045 N Keystone Ave Chicago (60646) ***(G-6021)***
Rgw Candy Company, Atlanta *Also called Amy Wertheim* ***(G-904)***
Rh Preyda Company (PA) 212 880-1477
333 N Michigan Ave # 3000 Chicago (60601) ***(G-6022)***
Rhine Hall 312 243-4313
2010 W Fulton St F104f Chicago (60612) ***(G-6023)***
Rhino Pros 815 235-7767
4223 Autumn Ln Freeport (61032) ***(G-10137)***
Rhino Tool Company 309 853-5555
1134 W South St Kewanee (61443) ***(G-12040)***
Rhinoag Inc 217 784-4261
1020 S Sangamon Ave Gibson City (60936) ***(G-10343)***
RHO Chemical Company Inc 815 727-4791
30 Industry Ave Joliet (60435) ***(G-11926)***
Rhodes/American, Chicago *Also called Global Material Tech Inc* ***(G-4696)***
Rhone-Poulenc Basic Chem Co 708 757-6111
1101 Arnold St Chicago Heights (60411) ***(G-6769)***
Rhopac Fabricated Products LLC 847 362-3300
1819 Industrial Dr Libertyville (60048) ***(G-12702)***
Rhyme or Reason Woodworking 217 678-8301
280 W Moultrie St Bement (61813) ***(G-1715)***
RI Diamonds, Chicago *Also called Rahmanims Imports Inc* ***(G-5963)***
Ri-Del Mfg Inc (PA) 312 829-8720
1754 W Walnut St Chicago (60612) ***(G-6024)***
Riah Hair, Niles *Also called Bee Sales Company* ***(G-15106)***
Ribbon Print Company 847 421-8208
508 Central Ave Ste 208 Highland Park (60035) ***(G-11294)***
Ribbon Print USA, Highland Park *Also called Ribbon Print Company* ***(G-11294)***
Riber Construction Inc 815 584-3337
405 S Old Route 66 Dwight (60420) ***(G-8159)***
Ricar Industries Inc 847 914-9083
2468 Greenview Rd Northbrook (60062) ***(G-15473)***
Rice Chem, Saint Charles *Also called J Stilling Enterprises Inc* ***(G-18217)***
Rice Precision Machining 630 543-7220
475 W Interstate Rd Addison (60101) ***(G-274)***
Rich Industries Inc 630 766-9150
489 Thomas Dr Bensenville (60106) ***(G-1884)***
Rich Products Corporation 815 729-4509
21511 Division St Crest Hill (60403) ***(G-7096)***

Rich Products Corporation.....847 581-1749
6200 W Mulford St Niles (60714) ***(G-15165)***
Rich Products Corporation.....309 886-2465
1902 Cobblestone Washington (61571) ***(G-20279)***
Rich-Law, Olney *Also called Wabash Valley Service Co* ***(G-15893)***
Richard A Anderson.....815 895-5627
1653 W Motel Rd Sycamore (60178) ***(G-19729)***
Richard King and Sons.....815 654-0226
6735 Elm Ave Loves Park (61111) ***(G-13253)***
Richard Schrock.....217 543-3111
41 E Cr 200 N Arthur (61911) ***(G-878)***
Richard Wolf Med Instrs Corp.....847 913-1113
353 Corporate Woods Pkwy Vernon Hills (60061) ***(G-20086)***
Richards & Stehman LLC.....217 522-6801
317 E Monroe St Springfield (62701) ***(G-19433)***
Richards Brick Company (PA).....618 656-0230
234 Springer Ave Edwardsville (62025) ***(G-8374)***
Richards Electric Motor Co (PA).....217 222-7154
2028 Quintron Way Quincy (62305) ***(G-16940)***
Richards Fabulous Finds.....773 943-0710
2545 W North Ave Chicago (60647) ***(G-6025)***
Richards Fine Jewelry & Design.....847 697-4053
321 Randall Rd South Elgin (60177) ***(G-19172)***
Richards Sper Prmium Ice Cream, Chicago *Also called Richards Sper Prmium Ice Cream* ***(G-6026)***
Richards Sper Prmium Ice Cream.....773 614-8999
11033 S Langley Ave Chicago (60628) ***(G-6026)***
Richards-Wilcox, Aurora *Also called Rwi Manufacturing Inc* ***(G-1151)***
Richardson & Edwards Inc.....630 543-1818
303 Hambletonian Dr Oak Brook (60523) ***(G-15660)***
Richardson Electronics Ltd.....630 208-2278
40 W 267 Keslinger Rd Lafox (60147) ***(G-12137)***
Richardson Electronics Ltd (PA).....630 208-2200
40w267 Keslinger Rd Lafox (60147) ***(G-12138)***
Richardson Ironworks LLC.....217 359-3333
313 N Mattis Ave Ste 208 Champaign (61821) ***(G-3342)***
Richardson Manufacturing Co.....217 546-2249
2209 Old Jacksonville Rd Springfield (62704) ***(G-19434)***
Richardson Rfpd Inc (HQ).....630 262-6800
1950 S Batavia Ave # 100 Geneva (60134) ***(G-10302)***
Richardson Seating Corporation.....312 829-4040
2545 W Arthington St Chicago (60612) ***(G-6027)***
Richars's, South Elgin *Also called Richards Fine Jewelry & Design* ***(G-19172)***
Richland County Machine Inc.....618 392-2892
302 N Walnut St Olney (62450) ***(G-15886)***
Rick Styfer.....630 734-3244
200 Lakewood Cir Burr Ridge (60527) ***(G-2717)***
Rickard Bindery, Chicago *Also called Rickard Circular Folding Co* ***(G-6028)***
Rickard Circular Folding Co.....312 243-6300
325 N Ashland Ave Chicago (60607) ***(G-6028)***
Rickard Publishing.....217 482-3276
126 N Tonica St Mason City (62664) ***(G-13613)***
Rico Computers Enterprises Inc.....708 594-7426
7022 W 73rd Pl Chicago (60638) ***(G-6029)***
Rico Industries Inc (PA).....312 427-0313
7000 N Austin Ave Niles (60714) ***(G-15166)***
Rico Industries Tag Express, Niles *Also called Rico Industries Inc* ***(G-15166)***
Ricon Colors Inc.....630 562-9000
675 Wegner Dr West Chicago (60185) ***(G-20636)***
Ricter Corporation.....708 344-3300
999 Commerce Ct Buffalo Grove (60089) ***(G-2593)***
Riddell Inc (HQ).....847 292-1472
1700 E Higgins Rd Ste 500 Des Plaines (60018) ***(G-7837)***
Riddell Sports, Des Plaines *Also called Riddell Inc* ***(G-7837)***
Riddle McIntyre Inc.....312 782-3317
175 N Franklin St Frnt 1 Chicago (60606) ***(G-6030)***
Ride Performance, Lake Forest *Also called Driv Incorporated* ***(G-12245)***
Ridge Road Defense.....630 820-8906
1850 Tall Oaks Dr # 2206 Aurora (60505) ***(G-1148)***
Ridgefield Industries Co LLC.....800 569-0316
8420 Railroad St Crystal Lake (60012) ***(G-7256)***
Rieco-Titan Products Inc.....815 464-7400
965 Lambrecht Dr Frankfort (60423) ***(G-9831)***
Rieke Office Interiors Inc.....847 622-9711
2000 Fox Ln Elgin (60123) ***(G-8720)***
Rietschle Inc.....410 712-4100
1800 Gardner Expy Quincy (62305) ***(G-16941)***
Rifast Systems LLC (PA).....847 933-8330
3600 W Pratt Ave Lincolnwood (60712) ***(G-12839)***
Riggs Beer Company.....217 649-4286
1901 S High Cross Rd Urbana (61802) ***(G-19998)***
Riggs Brothers Auto Interiors, Villa Park *Also called Air Land and Sea Interiors* ***(G-20129)***
Right Angle Tool Division, Bloomington *Also called Rettick Enterprises Inc* ***(G-2088)***
Right Lane Industries LLC (PA).....857 869-4132
222 N La Salle St Ste 705 Chicago (60601) ***(G-6031)***
Right Rail LLC.....630 882-9335
99 Wooden Bridge Dr Yorkville (60560) ***(G-21500)***
Right Way Signs LLC.....773 930-4361
1134 N Homan Ave Chicago (60651) ***(G-6032)***
Right/Pointe LLC (PA).....815 754-5700
234 Harvestore Dr Dekalb (60115) ***(G-7700)***
Righthand Technologies Inc.....773 774-7600
7450 W Wilson Ave Chicago (60706) ***(G-6033)***
Rightway Printing Inc.....630 790-0444
460 Windy Point Dr Glendale Heights (60139) ***(G-10488)***
Rijon Awning, Blue Island *Also called Rijon Manufacturing Company* ***(G-2136)***
Rijon Manufacturing Company.....708 388-2295
13733 Chatham St Blue Island (60406) ***(G-2136)***
Riken Corporation of America (HQ).....847 673-1400
4709 Golf Rd Ste 807 Skokie (60076) ***(G-19023)***
Rilco Fluid Care Inc.....309 788-1854
1320 1st St Rock Island (61201) ***(G-17242)***
Rimtec Corporation.....630 628-0036
211 S Lombard Rd Addison (60101) ***(G-275)***
Rinalli Boat Co Inc.....618 467-8850
3406 W Delmar Ave Godfrey (62035) ***(G-10660)***
Ring Can, Kankakee *Also called Ringwood Containers LP* ***(G-11998)***
Ring Can of Illinois, Rockford *Also called Ring Container Tech LLC* ***(G-17572)***
Ring Container Tech LLC.....217 875-5084
2454 E Hubbard Ave Decatur (62526) ***(G-7542)***
Ring Container Tech LLC.....815 229-9110
4689 Assembly Dr Rockford (61109) ***(G-17572)***
Ring Screw LLC.....815 544-7574
830 E Menomonie St Belvidere (61008) ***(G-1699)***
Ring Sheet Metal Heating & AC.....309 289-4213
213 Grove St Knoxville (61448) ***(G-12069)***
Ring-O-Bliss, Winnetka *Also called Bliss Ring Company Inc* ***(G-21127)***
Ringmaster Mfg.....815 675-4230
8001 Winn Rd Spring Grove (60081) ***(G-19299)***
Ringspann Corporation.....847 678-3581
10550 Anderson Pl Franklin Park (60131) ***(G-10036)***
Ringwood, Decatur *Also called Ring Container Tech LLC* ***(G-7542)***
Ringwood Company.....708 458-6000
6715 W 73rd St Bedford Park (60638) ***(G-1499)***
Ringwood Containers LP.....815 939-7270
1825 American Way Kankakee (60901) ***(G-11998)***
Rinker Boat Company.....574 457-5731
333 W Wacker Dr Ste 600 Chicago (60606) ***(G-6034)***
Ripa LLC.....708 938-1600
2001 W 21st St Broadview (60155) ***(G-2464)***
Riser Machine Corporation.....708 532-2313
1744 Ferro Dr New Lenox (60451) ***(G-15055)***
Risk Never Die Inc.....708 240-4194
1001 W 15th St Unit 222 Chicago (60608) ***(G-6035)***
RITA Corporation (PA).....815 337-2500
850 S Rte 31 Crystal Lake (60014) ***(G-7257)***
Rite Systems East Inc (HQ).....630 293-9174
625 Wegner Dr West Chicago (60185) ***(G-20637)***
Rite-TEC Communications.....815 459-7712
5812 Marietta Dr Crystal Lake (60014) ***(G-7258)***
Riteway Brake Dies Inc.....708 430-0795
7440 W 100th Pl Bridgeview (60455) ***(G-2383)***
Rittal North America LLC (HQ).....847 240-4600
425 N Martingale Rd # 1540 Schaumburg (60173) ***(G-18697)***
Rivalfly National Network LLC.....847 867-8660
320 W Ohio St Chicago (60654) ***(G-6036)***
Rivalus, Aurora *Also called Nutrivo LLC* ***(G-1140)***
River Bend Printing.....217 324-6056
60 Flat School Ln Litchfield (62056) ***(G-12975)***
River Bend Wild Game & Sausage.....217 688-3337
1161 County Road 2400 E Saint Joseph (61873) ***(G-18319)***
River City Enterprises, Peoria *Also called Staffco Inc* ***(G-16528)***
River City Millwork Inc.....800 892-9297
200 Quaker Rd Ste 3 Rockford (61104) ***(G-17573)***
River City Oil LLC.....309 693-2249
3310 W Chartwell Rd Peoria (61614) ***(G-16510)***
River City Sign Company Inc.....309 796-3606
915 1st Ave Silvis (61282) ***(G-18909)***
River Redi Mix Inc.....815 795-2025
2195 E Bluff St Marseilles (61341) ***(G-13564)***
River View Motor Sports Inc.....309 467-4569
1792 Hillside Rd Congerville (61729) ***(G-7003)***
Riverbank Laboratories Inc.....630 232-2207
18 S 8th St Geneva (60134) ***(G-10303)***
Riverbed Technology Inc.....217 344-8091
2100 S Oak St Champaign (61820) ***(G-3343)***
Riverbend Kitchen & Mllwk LLC (PA).....618 462-8955
215 Herbert St Alton (62002) ***(G-569)***
Riverdale Pltg Heat Trting LLC.....708 849-2050
680 W 134th St Riverdale (60827) ***(G-17076)***
Riverfront Machine Inc.....815 663-5000
6 Wolfer Industrial Park Spring Valley (61362) ***(G-19312)***
Riverside Assessments LLC (PA).....800 767-8420
1 Pierce Pl Ste 900w Itasca (60143) ***(G-11725)***
Riverside Bake Shop.....815 385-0044
1309 N Riverside Dr McHenry (60050) ***(G-13788)***
Riverside Chocolate Factory, McHenry *Also called American Convenience Inc* ***(G-13718)***

A L P H A B E T I C

ALPHABETIC SECTION

Riverside Custom Woodworking 815 589-3608
  1225 22nd Ave Fulton (61252) *(G-10157)*
Riverside Graphics Corporation 312 372-3766
  2 N Riverside Plz Ste 365 Chicago (60606) *(G-6037)*
Riverside Medi-Center Inc 815 932-6632
  400 N Wall St Ste 1 Kankakee (60901) *(G-11999)*
Riverside Memorial Co 217 323-1280
  216 W 2nd St Beardstown (62618) *(G-1450)*
Riverside Publishing, Itasca Also called Houghton Mifflin Harcourt Pubg *(G-11667)*
Riverside Spring Company 815 963-3334
  2136 12th St Ste 121 Rockford (61104) *(G-17574)*
Riverside Tool & Die Co 309 689-0104
  1616 W Chanute Rd Ste A Peoria (61615) *(G-16511)*
Riverstone Group Inc 309 787-3141
  601 Us Route 67 N Milan (61264) *(G-14026)*
Riverstone Group Inc 309 787-1415
  Junction Of 280amp Rock Island (61201) *(G-17243)*
Riverstone Group Inc 309 462-3003
  772 175th St Saint Augustine (61474) *(G-18139)*
Riverstone Group Inc 309 933-1123
  1001 N Broadway St Cleveland (61241) *(G-6912)*
Riverstone Group Inc 309 757-8297
  200 23rd Ave Moline (61265) *(G-14173)*
Riverstone Group Inc 309 788-9543
  1603 Mill St Rock Island (61201) *(G-17244)*
Riverton Cabinet Company 815 462-5300
  22000 S Schoolhouse Rd New Lenox (60451) *(G-15056)*
Rivertoncabinets, New Lenox Also called Riverton Cabinet Company *(G-15056)*
Riverview Mfg House SA 815 625-1459
  901 Regan Rd Rock Falls (61071) *(G-17193)*
Riverview Printing Inc 815 987-1425
  99 E State St Rockford (61104) *(G-17575)*
Riviera Tan Products, Godfrey Also called Riviera Tan Spa *(G-10661)*
Riviera Tan Spa 618 466-1012
  5114 Stiritz Ln Godfrey (62035) *(G-10661)*
Rj Cnc Works Inc 847 671-9120
  10134 Pacific Ave Franklin Park (60131) *(G-10037)*
RJ Distributing Co 309 685-2794
  410 High Point Ln East Peoria (61611) *(G-8287)*
Rj Link, Rockford Also called Rj Link International Inc *(G-17576)*
Rj Link International Inc 815 874-8110
  3741 Publishers Dr Rockford (61109) *(G-17576)*
Rj Race Cars Inc 309 343-7575
  300 N Linwood Rd Galesburg (61401) *(G-10218)*
Rj Stuckel Co Inc 800 789-7220
  94 Garlisch Dr Elk Grove Village (60007) *(G-9218)*
Rj45s.com, Saint Charles Also called David Jeskey *(G-18180)*
Rjd Machining LLC 217 684-5100
  244 County Road 1900 E Longview (61852) *(G-13175)*
Rjg Enterprises Ltd 847 752-2065
  888 E Belvidere Rd # 222 Grayslake (60030) *(G-10798)*
Rjm Manufacturing Inc 215 736-3644
  2200 N Mcroy Dr Carbondale (62901) *(G-2856)*
Rjs Silk Screening, Palos Hills Also called R J S Silk Screening Co *(G-16206)*
Rjt Wood Services 815 858-2081
  1653 S Tippett Rd Galena (61036) *(G-10177)*
Rjw Graphics Inc 847 336-4515
  3420 Grand Ave Waukegan (60085) *(G-20488)*
Rk Maintenance Inc 708 429-2215
  17310 Queen Elizabeth Ln Tinley Park (60477) *(G-19853)*
Rkf Enterprises 773 723-7038
  7331 S Michigan Ave Ste 1 Chicago (60619) *(G-6038)*
Rkfd LLC Grua (PA) 815 414-2392
  500 18th Ave Rockford (61104) *(G-17577)*
Rkfd LLC Grua 815 414-2392
  2702 Preston St Rockford (61102) *(G-17578)*
Rkfdcnc, Rockford Also called Chad Mazeika *(G-17343)*
Rkm Enterprises 217 348-5437
  1003 Madison Ave Charleston (61920) *(G-3411)*
RLC Industries Inc 708 837-7300
  715 S 10th Ave La Grange (60525) *(G-12088)*
Rls USA Inc 865 548-1449
  3350 N Ridge Ave Arlington Heights (60004) *(G-801)*
Rm Acquisition LLC (PA) 847 329-8100
  8770 W Bryn Mawr Ave # 1400 Chicago (60631) *(G-6039)*
RM Lucas Co (PA) 773 523-4300
  12400 S Laramie Ave Alsip (60803) *(G-504)*
RM Lucas Co. 773 523-4300
  3211 S Wood St Chicago (60608) *(G-6040)*
Rmb Engineered Products Inc 847 382-0100
  18-1 E Dundee Rd Ste 220 Barrington (60010) *(G-1240)*
RMC Imaging Inc 815 885-4521
  780 Creek Bluff Ln Rockford (61114) *(G-17579)*
Rmf Products Inc 630 879-0020
  1275 Paramount Pkwy Batavia (60510) *(G-1411)*
RMH Enterprises 630 525-5552
  611 Cadillac Dr Wheaton (60187) *(G-20819)*
Rmi Inc 708 756-5640
  211 E Main St Chicago Heights (60411) *(G-6770)*

Rmic, Bensenville Also called Snyder Industries Inc *(G-1895)*
Rmj Distributing, Belleville Also called ABM Marking Services Ltd *(G-1527)*
Rmkc Inc 630 932-0001
  17w608 14th St Oakbrook Terrace (60181) *(G-15814)*
RMS Utility Services, Crystal Lake Also called Midwest Water Group Inc *(G-7230)*
Rmts, Romeoville Also called Roll McHning Tech Slutions Inc *(G-17870)*
Rna Corporation (PA) 708 597-7777
  13750 Chatham St Blue Island (60406) *(G-2137)*
Rnfl Acquisition LLC 651 442-6011
  10 S La Salle St Ste 3300 Chicago (60603) *(G-6041)*
Ro Pal Grinding Inc 815 964-5894
  1916 20th Ave Rockford (61104) *(G-17580)*
Ro-Web Inc 309 688-2155
  4440 N Prospect Rd Ste C Peoria (61616) *(G-16512)*
Road District, Millstadt Also called Millstadt Township *(G-14053)*
Road Ready Signs (PA) 309 828-1007
  1231 N Mason St Bloomington (61701) *(G-2089)*
Road Runner Sports Inc 847 719-8941
  20291 N Rand Rd Ste 105 Palatine (60074) *(G-16154)*
Roadex Carriers Inc 773 454-8772
  446 Irvine Ct Wheeling (60090) *(G-20975)*
Roadsafe Traffic Systems Inc 217 629-7139
  104 Douglas St Riverton (62561) *(G-17089)*
Roanoke Companies Group Inc (HQ) 630 375-0324
  1105 S Frontenac St Aurora (60504) *(G-1014)*
Roanoke Concrete Products Co 309 885-0250
  1675 S 2nd St Pekin (61554) *(G-16359)*
Roanoke Concrete Products Co 309 698-7882
  1275 Spring Bay Rd East Peoria (61611) *(G-8288)*
Roark Oil Field Services Inc 618 382-4703
  1036 County Road 1575 N Carmi (62821) *(G-2914)*
Robal Company Inc 630 393-0777
  30 W 250th Butterfield304 Warrenville (60555) *(G-20252)*
Robbins Construction Sup LLC 708 574-5944
  17043 Annetta Ave Hazel Crest (60429) *(G-11137)*
Robbins Hdd LLC 847 955-0050
  1221 Flex Ct Lake Zurich (60047) *(G-12451)*
Robbins Pallets, Galesburg Also called Rbj Inc *(G-10217)*
Robbins Resource MGT Inc 309 734-8817
  208 S Main St Monmouth (61462) *(G-14226)*
Robert B Scott Ocularists Ltd (PA) 312 782-3558
  111 N Wabash Ave Ste 1620 Chicago (60602) *(G-6042)*
Robert Boldrey 618 592-4892
  8479 N 2250th St Oblong (62449) *(G-15827)*
Robert Bosch LLC 708 865-5415
  2800 S 25th Ave Broadview (60155) *(G-2465)*
Robert Bosch LLC (HQ) 917 421-7209
  2800 S 25th Ave Broadview (60155) *(G-2466)*
Robert Bosch Tool Corporation (HQ) 224 232-2000
  1800 W Central Rd Mount Prospect (60056) *(G-14566)*
Robert Brysiewicz Incorporated 630 289-0903
  956 S Bartlett Rd Ste 261 Bartlett (60103) *(G-1304)*
Robert C Weisheit Co Inc 847 648-4991
  999 Regency Dr Glendale Heights (60139) *(G-10489)*
Robert Davis & Son Inc 815 889-4168
  832 N State Route 1 Milford (60953) *(G-14036)*
Robert Harlan Ernst 217 627-3401
  145 S 2nd St Girard (62640) *(G-10385)*
Robert Higgins 217 337-0734
  405 E Pennsylvania Ave Urbana (61801) *(G-19999)*
Robert Kellerman & Co 847 526-7266
  1000 N Rand Rd Ste 224 Wauconda (60084) *(G-20389)*
Robert L Murphy 708 424-0277
  9545 S Hamlin Ave Evergreen Park (60805) *(G-9598)*
Robert McCormick Tribune Lbrry 847 619-7980
  1400 N Roosevelt Blvd Schaumburg (60173) *(G-18698)*
Robert Swaar 217 968-2232
  25903 Levee St Greenview (62642) *(G-10824)*
Robert-Leslie Publishing LLC 773 935-8358
  4147 N Ravenswood Ave # 301 Chicago (60613) *(G-6043)*
Roberts & Downey Chapel Eqp 217 795-2391
  101 S North St Argenta (62501) *(G-672)*
Roberts Colonial House Inc 708 331-6233
  15960 Suntone Dr South Holland (60473) *(G-19241)*
Roberts Displays, South Holland Also called Roberts Colonial House Inc *(G-19241)*
Roberts Draperies Center Inc 847 255-4040
  504 E Northwest Hwy Mount Prospect (60056) *(G-14567)*
Roberts Electric Company 773 725-7323
  311 N Morgan St Chicago (60607) *(G-6044)*
Roberts Swiss Inc 630 467-9100
  1387 Ardmore Ave Itasca (60143) *(G-11726)*
Robertshaw Controls Company 815 591-2417
  107 N Washington St Hanover (61041) *(G-10997)*
Robertshaw Controls Company (HQ) 630 260-3400
  1222 Hamilton Pkwy Itasca (60143) *(G-11727)*
Robertson Repair 618 895-2593
  Hwy 15 Sims (62886) *(G-18910)*
Robey Packaging Eqp & Svc 708 758-8250
  3236 Rennie Smith Dr Chicago Heights (60411) *(G-6771)*

ALPHABETIC SECTION Rodger Howard

Robin Hood Mat & Quilting Corp (PA) 312 953-2960
4800 S Richmond St Chicago (60632) ***(G-6045)***
Robin L Barnhouse 309 737-5431
1106 120th Ave Joy (61260) ***(G-11947)***
Robinson Daily News, Robinson *Also called Daily Robinson News Inc **(G-17111)***
Robinson Name Plate, Franklin Park *Also called Precision Plastic Ball Co **(G-10025)***
Robinson Production Inc 618 842-6111
108 Ne 7th St Fairfield (62837) ***(G-9636)***
Robinsport LLC 630 724-9280
2613 York Ct Woodridge (60517) ***(G-21337)***
Robis Elections Inc 630 752-0220
1751 S Nprvlle Rd Ste 104 Wheaton (60189) ***(G-20820)***
Robit Inc (HQ) 708 667-7892
639 W Diversey Pkwy # 217 Chicago (60614) ***(G-6046)***
Robko Flock Coating Company 847 272-6202
1935 Stanley St Northbrook (60062) ***(G-15474)***
Robotics Technologies Inc 815 722-7650
20655 Burl Ct Joliet (60433) ***(G-11927)***
Robs Aquatics 708 444-7627
17135 Harlem Ave Tinley Park (60477) ***(G-19854)***
Robuschi Usa Inc 704 424-1018
1800 Gardner Expy Quincy (62305) ***(G-16942)***
ROC Industries Inc 618 277-6044
101 Industrial Dr Belleville (62220) ***(G-1589)***
Roca Inc 312 421-2345
5275 S Archer Ave Chicago (60632) ***(G-6047)***
Rochelle Foods LLC 815 562-4141
1001 S Main St Rochelle (61068) ***(G-17155)***
Rochelle News Leader, Rochelle *Also called Rochelle Newspapers Inc **(G-17156)***
Rochelle News Leader, Rochelle *Also called Rochelle Newspapers Inc **(G-17157)***
Rochelle Newspapers Inc (HQ) 815 562-4171
211 E Illinois Rte 38 Rochelle (61068) ***(G-17156)***
Rochelle Newspapers Inc 815 562-4171
211 E State Route 38 Rochelle (61068) ***(G-17157)***
Rochelle Vault Co 815 562-6484
2119 S Il Route 251 Rochelle (61068) ***(G-17158)***
Rochester Midland Corporation 630 896-8543
2200 Rochester Rd Montgomery (60538) ***(G-14267)***
Rochester Sand & Gravel, Rochester *Also called Legacy Vulcan LLC **(G-17168)***
Rock Falls Div, Rock Falls *Also called Metal Spinners Inc **(G-17189)***
Rock Island Cannon Company 309 786-1507
2408 4th Ave Rock Island (61201) ***(G-17245)***
Rock Island Ready Mixed, Rock Island *Also called Riverstone Group Inc **(G-17244)***
Rock River Arms Inc 309 792-5780
1042 Cleveland Rd Colona (61241) ***(G-6979)***
Rock River Blending 815 968-7860
1515 Cunningham St Rockford (61102) ***(G-17581)***
Rock River Fabrication, Lyndon *Also called Phillips & Johnston Inc **(G-13287)***
Rock River Ready Mix Inc (PA) 815 288-2260
2320 S Galena Ave Dixon (61021) ***(G-7911)***
Rock River Ready Mix Inc 815 438-2510
24261 Prophet Rd Rock Falls (61071) ***(G-17194)***
Rock River Ready Mix Inc 815 625-1139
1905 Mound Hill Rd Dixon (61021) ***(G-7912)***
Rock River Ready-Mix 815 288-2269
2320 S Galena Ave Dixon (61021) ***(G-7913)***
Rock River Sand & Gravel, Rock Falls *Also called Rock River Ready Mix Inc **(G-17194)***
Rock River Times 815 964-9767
128 N Church St Rockford (61101) ***(G-17582)***
ROCK RIVER VALLEY BLOOD CENTER, Rockford *Also called Northern Ill Blood Bnk Inc **(G-17538)***
Rock Road Companies Inc 815 874-2441
801 Beale Ct Rockford (61109) ***(G-17583)***
Rock Solid Imports LLC 331 472-4522
1004 Creekside Cir Naperville (60563) ***(G-14910)***
Rock Tops Inc 708 672-1450
295 W Burville Rd Crete (60417) ***(G-7144)***
Rock Valley Die Sinking Inc 815 874-8560
2457 Baxter Rd Rockford (61109) ***(G-17584)***
Rock Valley Oil & Chemical Co (PA) 815 654-2400
1911 Windsor Rd Loves Park (61111) ***(G-13254)***
Rock Valley Pallet Company 815 654-4850
3511 Mildred Ct Machesney Park (61115) ***(G-13369)***
Rock Valley Publishing LLC (PA) 815 467-6397
7124 Windsor Lake Pkwy # 4 Loves Park (61111) ***(G-13255)***
Rock Valley Publishing LLC 815 234-4821
418 W Blackhawk Dr Byron (61010) ***(G-2756)***
Rock Valley Publishing LLC 815 654-4854
1102 Ann St Durand (61024) ***(G-8155)***
Rock-Tred 2 LLC (PA) 888 762-5873
405 N Oakwood Ave Waukegan (60085) ***(G-20489)***
Rockbridge Casting Inc 618 753-3188
25 State St Rockbridge (62081) ***(G-17255)***
Rockdale Controls Co Inc 815 436-6181
2419 Von Esch Rd Plainfield (60586) ***(G-16711)***
Rockey Mountain Steel Mills, Chicago *Also called New C F & I Inc **(G-5574)***
Rockfon, Chicago *Also called Roxul USA Inc **(G-6068)***
Rockford Acromatic Products, Loves Park *Also called Aircraft Gear Corporation **(G-13185)***
Rockford Air Devices Inc 815 654-3330
1201 Turret Dr Machesney Park (61115) ***(G-13370)***
Rockford Ball Screw Company 815 961-7700
940 Southrock Dr Rockford (61102) ***(G-17585)***
Rockford Blacktop Cnstr Co 815 654-4700
833 Featherstone Rd Rockford (61107) ***(G-17586)***
Rockford Bolt & Steel Co 815 968-0514
126 Mill St Rockford (61101) ***(G-17587)***
Rockford Broach Inc 815 484-0409
4993 27th Ave Rockford (61109) ***(G-17588)***
Rockford Burrall Mch Co Inc 815 877-7428
4520 Shepherd Trl Rockford (61103) ***(G-17589)***
Rockford Carbide Die & Tool 815 394-0645
1920 20th Ave Rockford (61104) ***(G-17590)***
Rockford Cement Products Co 815 965-0537
315 Peoples Ave Rockford (61104) ***(G-17591)***
Rockford Chemical Co 815 544-3476
915 W Perry St Belvidere (61008) ***(G-1700)***
Rockford Commercial Whse Inc 815 623-8400
8105 Burden Rd Machesney Park (61115) ***(G-13371)***
Rockford Drop Forge Company 815 963-9611
2011 10th St Rockford (61104) ***(G-17592)***
Rockford Electric Equipment Co 815 398-4096
2010 Harrison Ave Rockford (61104) ***(G-17593)***
Rockford Foundries Inc 815 965-7243
212 Mill St Rockford (61101) ***(G-17594)***
Rockford Heat Treaters Inc 815 874-0089
4704 American Rd Rockford (61109) ***(G-17595)***
Rockford Jobbing Service Inc 815 398-8661
4955 28th Ave Rockford (61109) ***(G-17596)***
Rockford Linear Actuation 815 986-4400
2111 23rd Ave Rockford (61104) ***(G-17597)***
Rockford Linear Motion LLC 815 961-7900
940 Southrock Dr Rockford (61102) ***(G-17598)***
Rockford Map Publishers Inc 815 708-6324
124 N Water St Ste 10 Rockford (61107) ***(G-17599)***
Rockford Metal Polishing Co 815 282-4448
5700 Industrial Ave Loves Park (61111) ***(G-13256)***
Rockford Molded Products Inc 815 637-0585
5600 Pike Rd Loves Park (61111) ***(G-13257)***
Rockford Newspapers Inc 815 987-1200
99 E State St Rockford (61104) ***(G-17600)***
Rockford Precision Machine 815 873-1018
4729 Hydraulic Rd Rockford (61109) ***(G-17601)***
Rockford Process Control LLC 815 966-2000
2020 7th St Rockford (61104) ***(G-17602)***
Rockford Quality Grinding Inc 815 227-9001
3160 Forest View Rd Rockford (61109) ***(G-17603)***
Rockford Rams Products Inc 815 226-0016
2902 Eastrock Dr Rockford (61109) ***(G-17604)***
Rockford Register Star, Rockford *Also called Rockford Newspapers Inc **(G-17600)***
Rockford Rigging Inc (PA) 309 263-0566
5401 Mainsail Dr Roscoe (61073) ***(G-17926)***
Rockford Rigging Inc 309 263-0566
1480 S Main St Ste A Morton (61550) ***(G-14381)***
Rockford Sand & Gravel Co (HQ) 815 654-4700
5290 Nimtz Rd Loves Park (61111) ***(G-13258)***
Rockford Secondary Co 815 398-0401
2424 Laude Dr Rockford (61109) ***(G-17605)***
Rockford Separators, Rockford *Also called Tomermo Inc **(G-17665)***
Rockford Sewer Co Inc 815 877-9060
6204 Forest Hills Rd Loves Park (61111) ***(G-13259)***
Rockford Systems LLC 815 874-7891
5795 Logistics Pkwy Rockford (61109) ***(G-17606)***
Rockford Tool and Mfg Co 815 398-5876
3023 Eastrock Ct Rockford (61109) ***(G-17607)***
Rockford Toolcraft Inc (PA) 815 398-5507
766 Research Pkwy Rockford (61109) ***(G-17608)***
Rockford Toolcraft Inc 815 398-5507
5455 11th St Rockford (61109) ***(G-17609)***
Rockform Tooling & Machinery (PA) 770 345-4624
2974 Eastrock Dr Rockford (61109) ***(G-17610)***
Rockform Tooling & Machinery 815 398-7650
2974 Eastrock Dr Rockford (61109) ***(G-17611)***
Rockwell Automation Inc 901 367-4220
2802 W Bloomington Rd Champaign (61822) ***(G-3344)***
Rockwell Automation Inc 630 789-5900
4343 Commerce Ct Ste 200 Lisle (60532) ***(G-12934)***
Rockwell Metal Products Inc 773 762-7030
3232 W Cermak Rd Chicago (60623) ***(G-6048)***
Rockwind Venture Partners LLC (PA) 630 881-6664
8500 E State St Rockford (61108) ***(G-17612)***
Rocky Lane Woodworking, Arthur *Also called Willard R Schorck **(G-882)***
Rocky's Advanced Printing, Harrisburg *Also called Graf Ink Printing Inc **(G-11025)***
Rockys Beverages LLC 312 561-3182
1813 Elmdale Ave Glenview (60026) ***(G-10613)***
Rode Welding Inc 847 439-0910
1211 Louis Ave Elk Grove Village (60007) ***(G-9219)***
Rodger Howard 773 481-6990
5951 W Lawrence Ave Chicago (60630) ***(G-6049)***

ALPHABETIC

Rodger Murphy 309 582-2202
103 W Main St Aledo (61231) *(G-359)*

Rodgers Bill Oil Min Bits Svc 618 299-7771
20226 Wabash 20 Ave West Salem (62476) *(G-20688)*

Rodifer Enterprises Inc 815 678-0100
5700 Walnut St Richmond (60071) *(G-17021)*

Rodin Enterprises Inc 847 412-1370
544b W Dundee Rd Wheeling (60090) *(G-20976)*

Rodney J Gieseke 630 830-7063
342 Terrace Dr Bartlett (60103) *(G-1305)*

Rodney Tite Welding 618 845-9072
391 N Locust St Ullin (62992) *(G-19936)*

Roe Machine Inc 618 983-5524
12725 Union Rd West Frankfort (62896) *(G-20681)*

Roeckers Inc 309 693-2929
6523 N Galena Rd Peoria (61614) *(G-16513)*

Roeda Signs Inc 708 333-3021
20530 Stoney Island Ave Chicago Heights (60411) *(G-6772)*

Roentgen Industrial, Bartlett Also called Assurance Technologies Inc *(G-1265)*

Roentgen USA LLC 847 787-0135
3725 25th Ave Schiller Park (60176) *(G-18840)*

Roesch Acquisitions LLC 618 233-2760
100 N 24th St Belleville (62226) *(G-1590)*

Roesers Bakery 773 489-6900
3216 W North Ave Chicago (60647) *(G-6050)*

Roevolution 226 LLC (PA) 773 658-4022
2610 Lake Cook Rd Riverwoods (60015) *(G-17095)*

Rogan Granitindustrie Inc 708 758-0050
6544 Pontiac Dr Indian Head Park (60525) *(G-11577)*

Rogan Granitindustrie Inc (HQ) 708 758-0050
21550 E Lincoln Hwy Lynwood (60411) *(G-13298)*

Roger Burke Jewelers Inc 309 692-0210
4700 N University St 6 Peoria (61614) *(G-16514)*

Roger Cantu & Assocs 630 573-9215
1100 Jorie Blvd Ste 215 Oak Brook (60523) *(G-15661)*

Roger Fritz & Associates Inc 630 355-2614
1113 N Loomis St Naperville (60563) *(G-14911)*

Roger Jolly Skateboards 618 277-7113
28 S 14th St Belleville (62220) *(G-1591)*

Rogers Loose Leaf Co 312 226-1947
1013 Elmdale Rd Glenview (60025) *(G-10614)*

Rogers Metal Services Inc 847 679-4642
7330 Monticello Ave Skokie (60076) *(G-19024)*

Rogers Motorcycle Shop Inc 309 828-3242
2705 S Main St Bloomington (61704) *(G-2090)*

Rogers Precision Machining 815 233-0065
5816 Us Highway 20 W Freeport (61032) *(G-10138)*

Rogers Ready Mix & Mtls Inc (PA) 815 234-8212
8128 N Walnut St Byron (61010) *(G-2757)*

Rogers Ready Mix & Mtls Inc 815 234-8044
201 E Washington St Oregon (61061) *(G-15926)*

Rogers Ready Mix & Mtls Inc 815 874-6626
5510 S Mulford Rd Rockford (61109) *(G-17613)*

Rogers Ready Mix & Mtls Inc 815 389-2223
14615 N 2nd St Roscoe (61073) *(G-17927)*

Rogers Redi-Mix Inc (PA) 618 282-3844
55 E Mill St Ruma (62278) *(G-18106)*

Rogus Tool Inc 847 824-5939
354 N East River Rd Des Plaines (60016) *(G-7838)*

Rohbi Enterprises Inc 708 343-2004
3020 S 25th Ave Broadview (60155) *(G-2467)*

Rohm and Haas Company 815 728-4602
5005 Barnard Mill Rd Ringwood (60072) *(G-17047)*

Rohn Products LLC (PA) 309 697-4400
1 Fairholm Ave Peoria (61603) *(G-16515)*

Rohn Products LLC 309 566-3000
6718 W Plank Rd Ste 2 Peoria (61604) *(G-16516)*

Rohner Engraving Inc 773 244-8343
5410 W Roosevelt Rd # 202 Chicago (60644) *(G-6051)*

Rohner Letterpress Inc 773 248-0800
5410 W Roosevelt Rd # 202 Chicago (60644) *(G-6052)*

Rohner Press, Chicago Also called Rohner Letterpress Inc *(G-6052)*

Roho Inc (HQ) 618 277-9173
100 N Florida Ave Belleville (62221) *(G-1592)*

Roho Inc 618 234-4899
1501 S 74th St Belleville (62223) *(G-1593)*

Rohrer Corporation 847 961-5920
13701 George Bush Ct Huntley (60142) *(G-11564)*

Rohrer Graphic Arts Inc 630 832-3434
491 W Fullerton Ave Elmhurst (60126) *(G-9419)*

Rohrer Litho Inc 630 833-6610
487 W Fullerton Ave Elmhurst (60126) *(G-9420)*

Rolfs Patisserie Inc 847 675-6565
4343 W Touhy Ave Lincolnwood (60712) *(G-12840)*

Roll McHning Tech Slutions Inc 815 372-9100
641 Forestwood Dr Romeoville (60446) *(G-17870)*

Roll Rite Inc 815 645-8600
6549 N Junction Rd Davis Junction (61020) *(G-7426)*

Roll Roll Met Fabricators Inc 773 434-1315
2310 W 58th St Chicago (60636) *(G-6053)*

Roll Source Paper 630 875-0308
900 N Arlington Heights R Itasca (60143) *(G-11728)*

Roll-A-Way Conveyors Inc 847 336-5033
2335 N Delany Rd Gurnee (60031) *(G-10924)*

Roll-Kraft Northern Inc 815 469-0205
9324 Gulfstream Rd Ste 1e Frankfort (60423) *(G-9832)*

Roll-O-Sheets, Rolling Meadows Also called Pliant LLC *(G-17761)*

Rolled Edge Inc 773 283-9500
4221 N Normandy Ave Chicago (60634) *(G-6054)*

Roller Derby Skate Corp (PA) 217 324-3961
311 W Edwards St Litchfield (62056) *(G-12976)*

Rollex Corporation (PA) 847 437-3000
800 Chase Ave Elk Grove Village (60007) *(G-9220)*

Rolling Meadows Brewery LLC 217 725-2492
1660 W Leland Ave Springfield (62704) *(G-19435)*

Rollstock Inc 708 579-3700
600 E Plainfield Rd Countryside (60525) *(G-7068)*

Roma Bakeries Inc 815 964-6737
523 Marchesano Dr Rockford (61102) *(G-17614)*

Roma Packing Co 773 927-7371
2354 S Leavitt St Chicago (60608) *(G-6055)*

Romaine Empire Inc 312 229-0099
2000 W Fulton St Ste F310 Chicago (60612) *(G-6056)*

Roman Holdings Corporation 708 891-0770
824 State St Calumet City (60409) *(G-2789)*

Roman Products LLC 708 891-0770
824 State St Calumet City (60409) *(G-2790)*

Roman Signs 847 381-3425
819 W Northwest Hwy Barrington (60010) *(G-1241)*

Romar Cabinet & Top Co Inc 815 467-4452
23949 S Northern Ill Dr Channahon (60410) *(G-3392)*

Rome Industries Inc (PA) 309 691-7120
1703 W Detweiller Dr Peoria (61615) *(G-16517)*

Rome Metal Mfg Inc 773 287-1755
4612 W Ohio St Chicago (60644) *(G-6057)*

Romed Industries Corporation 847 362-3900
320 E Il Route 22 Lake Zurich (60047) *(G-12452)*

Romel Press Inc 708 343-6090
1747 N 20th Ave Melrose Park (60160) *(G-13909)*

Romero Steel Company Inc 708 216-0001
1300 Main St Melrose Park (60160) *(G-13910)*

Romtech Machining Inc 630 543-7039
755 W Factory Rd Addison (60101) *(G-276)*

Romus Incorporated 414 350-6233
932 Central Ave Roselle (60172) *(G-17979)*

Ron & Pats Pizza Shack 847 395-5005
40338 N Deep Lake Rd Antioch (60002) *(G-633)*

Ron Meyer 847 844-9880
341 Sola Dr Gilberts (60136) *(G-10367)*

Ron Shew Welding & Fabricating, Marion Also called Shew Brothers Inc *(G-13534)*

Ron's Automotive Machine Shop, Sterling Also called R & C Auto Supply Corp *(G-19528)*

Ronald J Nixon 708 748-8130
56 South St Park Forest (60466) *(G-16259)*

Ronald S Lefors Bs Cpo 618 259-1969
214 W Saint Louis Ave East Alton (62024) *(G-8170)*

Roncin Custom Design 847 669-0260
11514 Smith Dr Unit B Huntley (60142) *(G-11565)*

Rondex Products Incorporated 815 226-0452
324 N Gardiner Ave Rockford (61107) *(G-17615)*

Rondout Iron & Metal Co Inc 847 362-2750
1501 Rockland Rd Lake Bluff (60044) *(G-12208)*

Roney Machine Works Inc 618 462-4113
412 Pearl St Alton (62002) *(G-570)*

Ronk Electrical Industries Inc 217 563-8333
106 E State St Nokomis (62075) *(G-15198)*

Ronnie Joe Graham 618 548-5544
420 W Schwartz St Salem (62881) *(G-18355)*

Ronnie P Faber 815 626-4561
2901 Polo Rd Sterling (61081) *(G-19529)*

Roodhouse Envelope Co 217 589-4321
414 S State St Roodhouse (62082) *(G-17894)*

Roodhouse Fire Protection Dst 217 589-5134
1140 S State St Roodhouse (62082) *(G-17895)*

Roof Structures, New Baden Also called Reload Sales Inc *(G-15023)*

Rookie LLC 708 278-1628
545 S Scolville Ave Oak Park (60304) *(G-15770)*

Room Dividers Now LLC 847 224-7900
38 Otis Rd Barrington (60010) *(G-1242)*

Room Place, The, Lombard Also called Trp Acquisition Corp *(G-13147)*

Rooms Redux Chicago Inc 312 835-1192
6033 N Sheridan Rd 25d Chicago (60660) *(G-6058)*

Roosevelt Mobile 630 293-7630
60 W Roosevelt Rd West Chicago (60185) *(G-20638)*

Ropak Central Inc 847 956-0750
1350 Arthur Ave Elk Grove Village (60007) *(G-9221)*

Roper Whitney, Rockford Also called Whitney Roper LLC *(G-17683)*

Roq Innovation LLC 917 770-2403
1616 E 56th St Unit 604 Chicago (60637) *(G-6059)*

Roquette America Inc 630 232-2157
2211 Innovation Dr Geneva (60134) *(G-10304)*

Rorke & Riley Specialty B..........773 929-2522
3712 N Broadway St # 252 Chicago (60613) ***(G-6060)***
Roscoe Glass Co..........815 623-6268
11212 Main St Roscoe (61073) ***(G-17928)***
Roscoe Tool & Manufacturing..........815 633-8808
5339 Stern Dr Roscoe (61073) ***(G-17929)***
Rose Business Forms & Printing..........618 533-3032
125 N Walnut St Centralia (62801) ***(G-3248)***
Rose Custom Builders, Mundelein *Also called Rose Custom Cabinets Inc* ***(G-14732)***
Rose Custom Cabinets Inc..........847 816-4800
408 Washington Blvd Ste C Mundelein (60060) ***(G-14732)***
Rose Packing Co Inc..........708 458-9300
4900 S Major Ave Chicago (60638) ***(G-6061)***
Rose Packing Company Inc..........708 458-9300
4900 S Major Ave Chicago (60638) ***(G-6062)***
Rose Packing Company Inc..........708 458-9300
5656 W 51st St Chicago (60638) ***(G-6063)***
Rose Pallet LLC..........708 333-3000
7647 W 100th Pl Ste D Bridgeview (60455) ***(G-2384)***
Roseland II LLC..........708 479-5010
18410 115th Ave Orland Park (60467) ***(G-15976)***
Roselle Custom Woodwork LLC..........630 980-5655
57 N Garden Ave Roselle (60172) ***(G-17980)***
Rosemount Inc..........217 877-5278
2241 E Hubbard Ave Decatur (62526) ***(G-7543)***
Rosen Printing Services, Chicago *Also called Roshan Ag Inc* ***(G-6064)***
Rosenthal Manufacturing Co Inc..........847 714-0404
1840 Janke Dr Northbrook (60062) ***(G-15475)***
Roses Moulding By Design Inc..........847 549-9200
408 Washington Blvd Ste C Mundelein (60060) ***(G-14733)***
Rosewood Custom Framing LLC..........217 430-7669
2114 S 40th St Quincy (62305) ***(G-16943)***
Rosewood Software Inc..........847 438-2185
1531 N Haven Dr Palatine (60074) ***(G-16155)***
Roshan Ag Inc..........773 267-1635
3525 W Peterson Ave # 120 Chicago (60659) ***(G-6064)***
Rosiclare Quarry, Golconda *Also called Martin Marietta Materials Inc* ***(G-10667)***
Roskuszka & Sons Inc..........630 851-3400
969 N Farnsworth Ave Aurora (60505) ***(G-1149)***
Ross and White Company..........847 516-3900
1090 Alexander Ct Cary (60013) ***(G-3187)***
Ross Designs Ltd..........847 831-7669
210 Skokie Valley Rd # 5 Highland Park (60035) ***(G-11295)***
Ross Oil Co Inc..........618 592-3808
11172 N 450th St Oblong (62449) ***(G-15828)***
Ross-Gage Inc..........708 347-3659
2346 Alexander Ter Homewood (60430) ***(G-11502)***
Rotadyne Precision Mch Roller, Chicago *Also called Rotation Dynamics Corporation* ***(G-6065)***
Rotadyne-Decorative Tech GP, Romeoville *Also called Advanced Graphics Tech Inc* ***(G-17788)***
Rotadyne-Roll Group, Romeoville *Also called Rotation Dynamics Corporation* ***(G-17871)***
Rotary Airlock LLC..........800 883-8955
301 W 3rd St L Sterling (61081) ***(G-19530)***
Rotary Dryer Parts Inc..........217 877-2787
2590 E Federal Dr Ste 508 Decatur (62526) ***(G-7544)***
Rotary Ram Inc..........618 466-2651
3704 Riehl Ln Godfrey (62035) ***(G-10662)***
Rotation Dynamics Corporation..........630 769-9700
6120 S New England Ave Chicago (60638) ***(G-6065)***
Rotation Dynamics Corporation..........773 247-5600
2512 W 24th St Chicago (60608) ***(G-6066)***
Rotation Dynamics Corporation..........630 679-7053
1101 Windham Pkwy Romeoville (60446) ***(G-17871)***
Rotec Industries Inc (PA)..........630 279-3300
270 Industrial Dr Hampshire (60140) ***(G-10985)***
Roth Metal Fabricators Corp..........708 371-8300
3735 W 128th Pl Alsip (60803) ***(G-505)***
Roth Neon Sign Company Inc..........618 942-6378
1100 N 13th St Herrin (62948) ***(G-11177)***
Roth Pump Company (HQ)..........309 787-1791
525 4th St W Milan (61264) ***(G-14027)***
Roth Sign Company, Herrin *Also called Roth Neon Sign Company Inc* ***(G-11177)***
Roth's Pump Co., Milan *Also called Roy E Roth Company* ***(G-14028)***
Rothenberger USA LLC..........800 545-7698
7130 Clinton Rd Loves Park (61111) ***(G-13260)***
Roto Die Company, Lombard *Also called Roto-Die Company Inc* ***(G-13125)***
Roto Spray Manufacturing, Mokena *Also called Rotospray Mfg Inc* ***(G-14113)***
Roto-Die Company Inc..........630 932-8605
1054 N Du Page Ave Lombard (60148) ***(G-13125)***
Rotospray Mfg Inc..........708 478-3307
10315 Aileen Ave Mokena (60448) ***(G-14113)***
Rototime, Hoffman Estates *Also called Fact NA LLC* ***(G-11422)***
Round Lake Pallets Inc..........847 637-6162
740 Sunset Dr Round Lake (60073) ***(G-18081)***
Roundtble Hlthcare Partners LP (PA)..........847 739-3200
272 E Deerpath Ste 350 Lake Forest (60045) ***(G-12299)***
Roundup Food Equipment Div, Carol Stream *Also called A J Antunes & Co* ***(G-2922)***
Rousselle, Bedford Park *Also called Presses Inc* ***(G-1494)***
Rout A Bout Shop Inc..........309 829-0674
619 W Olive St Bloomington (61701) ***(G-2091)***
Rout-A-Bout, Bloomington *Also called Rout A Bout Shop Inc* ***(G-2091)***
Route 45 Wayside..........217 867-2000
101 S Chestnut St Pesotum (61863) ***(G-16599)***
Rovanco Piping Systems Inc..........815 741-6700
20535 Se Frontage Rd Joliet (60431) ***(G-11928)***
ROW Window Company..........815 725-5491
13404 Wood Duck Dr Plainfield (60585) ***(G-16712)***
Rowboat Creative LLC..........773 675-2628
2649 N Kildare Ave # 1 Chicago (60639) ***(G-6067)***
Rowdy Star Custom Creations..........217 497-1789
1936 Delong St Danville (61832) ***(G-7379)***
Rowe Construction Div, Tremont *Also called Cullinan & Sons Inc* ***(G-19895)***
Rowell Pure Water, Herrin *Also called Samuel Rowell* ***(G-11178)***
Rowlar Tool & Die Div, Franklin Park *Also called Associate General Labs Inc* ***(G-9877)***
Roxul USA Inc..........800 323-7164
4849 S Austin Ave Chicago (60638) ***(G-6068)***
Roy E Roth Company (PA)..........309 787-1791
6th Ave And 4th St Milan (61264) ***(G-14028)***
Roy Winnett..........309 367-4867
303 W Pine St Metamora (61548) ***(G-13967)***
Royal Adhesives & Sealants LLC..........815 464-5606
9411 Corsair Rd Frankfort (60423) ***(G-9833)***
Royal Adhesives and Sealants..........815 464-3310
9001 W Fey Dr Frankfort (60423) ***(G-9834)***
Royal Bedding Company Inc (PA)..........847 645-0200
2600 Forbs Ave Hoffman Estates (60192) ***(G-11451)***
Royal Box Group LLC (HQ)..........708 656-2020
1301 S 47th Ave Cicero (60804) ***(G-6871)***
Royal Box Group LLC..........630 543-4464
654 W Factory Rd Addison (60101) ***(G-277)***
Royal Box Group LLC..........708 222-4650
4600 W 12th Pl Cicero (60804) ***(G-6872)***
Royal Brass Inc..........618 439-6341
1202 Route 14 W Benton (62812) ***(G-1936)***
Royal Casting, Chicago *Also called M B Jewelers Inc* ***(G-5299)***
Royal Continental Box Company, Cicero *Also called Royal Box Group LLC* ***(G-6871)***
Royal Corinthian Inc..........630 876-8899
603 Fenton Ln West Chicago (60185) ***(G-20639)***
Royal Crown Tresses LLC..........773 967-8409
20325 Joy Ln Lynwood (60411) ***(G-13299)***
Royal Die & Stamping Co Inc (HQ)..........630 766-2685
125 Mercedes Dr Carol Stream (60188) ***(G-3060)***
Royal Drilling & Producing..........618 966-2221
Hwy 14 Crossville (62827) ***(G-7151)***
Royal Drilling & Production, Crossville *Also called Royal Drilling & Producing* ***(G-7151)***
Royal Envelope Corporation..........773 376-1212
4114 S Peoria St Chicago (60609) ***(G-6069)***
Royal Fabricators Inc..........847 775-7466
38360 N Cashmore Rd Wadsworth (60083) ***(G-20213)***
Royal Fiberglass Pools Inc..........618 266-7089
312 Duncan Ln Dix (62830) ***(G-7882)***
Royal Foods & Flavors Inc..........847 595-9166
2456 American Ln Elk Grove Village (60007) ***(G-9222)***
Royal Haeger Lamp Co..........309 837-9966
1300 W Piper St Macomb (61455) ***(G-13400)***
Royal Kit Bthroom Cabinets Inc (PA)..........847 588-0011
7727 N Milwaukee Ave Niles (60714) ***(G-15167)***
Royal Kitchen & Bath Cabinets, Niles *Also called Royal Kit Bthroom Cabinets Inc* ***(G-15167)***
Royal Machine Works Inc..........815 465-6879
204 N Stanley St Grant Park (60940) ***(G-10752)***
Royal Machining Corporation..........708 338-3387
1617 N 31st Ave Melrose Park (60160) ***(G-13911)***
Royal Oak Farm Inc..........815 648-4141
15908 Hebron Rd Harvard (60033) ***(G-11066)***
Royal Power Solutions, Carol Stream *Also called Royal Die & Stamping Co Inc* ***(G-3060)***
Royal Printing Co, Quincy *Also called DE Asbury Inc* ***(G-16876)***
Royal Publishing Inc..........309 343-4007
311 E Main St Ste 220 Galesburg (61401) ***(G-10219)***
Royal Publishing Inc..........309 797-6630
1530 46th Ave Moline (61265) ***(G-14174)***
Royal Publishing Inc..........815 220-0400
4375 Venture Dr Peru (61354) ***(G-16592)***
Royal Publishing Inc..........309 829-6191
1730 Bradford Ln Ste 185 Normal (61761) ***(G-15222)***
Royal Publishing Co, Galesburg *Also called Royal Publishing Inc* ***(G-10219)***
Royal Smoke Shop..........815 539-3499
1001 Main St Mendota (61342) ***(G-13954)***
Royal Stairs Co..........847 685-9448
98 East Ave Park Ridge (60068) ***(G-16294)***
Royale Innovation Group Ltd..........312 339-1406
794 Willow Ct Itasca (60143) ***(G-11729)***
Royell Communications, Virden *Also called Royer Systems Inc* ***(G-20189)***
Royer Systems Inc..........217 965-3699
427 W Dean St Virden (62690) ***(G-20189)***

ALPHABETIC

RPC Legacy Inc (PA)   ALPHABETIC SECTION

RPC Legacy Inc (PA) 815 966-2000
2020 7th St Rockford (61104) *(G-17616)*

RPI Business Co Inc 773 254-7095
2501 S Rockwell St Chicago (60608) *(G-6070)*

RPI Extrusion Co 708 389-2584
5623 W 115th St Alsip (60803) *(G-506)*

Rpk Technologies Inc 630 595-0911
272 Judson St Bensenville (60106) *(G-1885)*

RPS Engineering Inc 847 931-1950
1300 Crispin Dr Elgin (60123) *(G-8721)*

RPS Products Inc (PA) 847 683-3400
281 Keyes Ave Hampshire (60140) *(G-10986)*

Rpsi, Chicago Also called Railway Program Services Inc *(G-5964)*

Rpt Toner LLC 630 694-0400
475 Supreme Dr Bensenville (60106) *(G-1886)*

RR Defense Systems Inc 773 529-6007
341 Lively Blvd Elk Grove Village (60007) *(G-9223)*

RR Donnelley, Chicago Also called R R Donnelley & Sons Company *(G-5950)*

RR Donnelley, Saint Charles Also called R R Donnelley & Sons Company *(G-18258)*

RR Donnelley & Sons Company 312 236-8000
111 S Wacker Dr Fl 36 Chicago (60606) *(G-6071)*

RR Donnelley Logistics SE 630 672-2500
200 N Gary Ave Roselle (60172) *(G-17981)*

RR Donnelley Printing Co LP 217 235-0561
6821 E County Road 1100n Mattoon (61938) *(G-13653)*

RR Donnelley Printing Co LP (PA) 312 326-8000
35 W Wacker Dr Ste 3650 Chicago (60601) *(G-6072)*

RR Mulch and Soil LLC 708 596-7200
3900 W 167th St Markham (60428) *(G-13551)*

Rrb Fabrication Inc 815 977-5603
5430 Forest Hills Ct Loves Park (61111) *(G-13261)*

Rrp Enterprises Inc 847 455-5674
9510 Fullerton Ave Franklin Park (60131) *(G-10038)*

Rrsr Graphics & Film Corp 708 478-4573
19759 Westminster Dr Mokena (60448) *(G-14114)*

Rs Ductless Technical Support 815 223-7949
227 Bucklin St La Salle (61301) *(G-12122)*

Rs Fuels Inc 773 205-9833
4650 W Lawrence Ave Chicago (60630) *(G-6073)*

RS Owens Div St Regis LLC 773 282-6000
1612 Glenlake Ave Itasca (60143) *(G-11730)*

Rs Used Oil Services Inc 618 781-1717
4559 Wagon Wheel Rd Roxana (62084) *(G-18101)*

Rs Woodworking 815 476-1818
119 N Water St Wilmington (60481) *(G-21101)*

Rsb Fuels Inc 217 999-4409
701 W Main St Mount Olive (62069) *(G-14508)*

RSM International 312 634-3400
1 S Wacker Dr Ste 800 Chicago (60606) *(G-6074)*

Rsn Mailing 314 724-3364
1985 Raintree Trl Collinsville (62234) *(G-6974)*

Rsp, Springfield Also called Habegger Corporation *(G-19377)*

Rsvp Tooling Inc 815 725-3310
227 Airport Dr Joliet (60431) *(G-11929)*

Rt Associates Inc 847 577-0700
385 Gilman Ave Wheeling (60090) *(G-20977)*

RT Blackhawk Mch Pdts Inc 815 389-3632
956 Gardner St South Beloit (61080) *(G-19111)*

Rt Enterprises Inc 847 675-1444
7540 Linder Ave Skokie (60077) *(G-19025)*

Rt Wholesale (PA) 847 678-3663
4242 Old River Rd Ste 1a Schiller Park (60176) *(G-18841)*

RTC Industries Inc 847 640-2400
3101 S Kedzie Ave Apt S Chicago (60623) *(G-6075)*

RTD Hallstar Inc 908 852-6128
120 S Riverside Plz # 1620 Chicago (60606) *(G-6076)*

Rte, Saint Charles Also called Ray Tool & Engineering Inc *(G-18260)*

Rti Surgical Holdings Inc (PA) 386 418-8888
520 Lake Cook Rd Ste 315 Deerfield (60015) *(G-7647)*

Rtm Trend, Elgin Also called Reliance Tool & Mfg Co *(G-8718)*

RTS Packaging LLC 708 338-2800
250 N Mannheim Rd Hillside (60162) *(G-11355)*

RTS Sentry Inc 618 257-7100
4401 N Belt W Belleville (62226) *(G-1594)*

Rubber Stamp Man, Des Plaines Also called Anderson Safford Mkg Graphics *(G-7732)*

Rubicon Technology Inc (PA) 847 295-7000
900 E Green St Bensenville (60106) *(G-1887)*

Rubin Brothers, Inc., Chicago Also called Rubin Nsa Bros LLC *(G-6078)*

Rubin Manufacturing Inc 312 942-1111
2241 S Halsted St Chicago (60608) *(G-6077)*

Rubin Nsa Bros LLC 312 942-1111
2241 S Halsted St Chicago (60608) *(G-6078)*

Rubis Bakery Inc 847 623-4094
1703 Washington St Waukegan (60085) *(G-20490)*

Ruby Automation LLC 815 624-5959
14300 De La Tour Dr South Beloit (61080) *(G-19112)*

Ruby Automation LLC 847 273-9050
1261 Wiley Rd Ste A Schaumburg (60173) *(G-18699)*

Ruby Industrial Tech LLC 317 248-8355
827 N Central Ave Wood Dale (60191) *(G-21235)*

Rucker's Candy, Bridgeport Also called Ruckers Wholesale & Service Co *(G-2315)*

Ruckers Mkin Batch Candies Inc 618 945-7778
777 Rucker St Bridgeport (62417) *(G-2314)*

Ruckers Wholesale & Service Co 618 945-2411
777 E State St Bridgeport (62417) *(G-2315)*

Ruckus Wireless Inc 630 281-3000
2400 Ogden Ave Ste 180 Lisle (60532) *(G-12935)*

Ruco USA Inc 866 373-7912
915 N Central Ave Wood Dale (60191) *(G-21236)*

Rudd Container Corporation 773 847-7600
4600 S Kolin Ave Chicago (60632) *(G-6079)*

Rudin Printing Company Inc 217 528-5111
927 E Jackson St Springfield (62701) *(G-19436)*

Rudon Enterprises Inc 618 457-0441
118 N Illinois Ave Carbondale (62901) *(G-2857)*

Rudy Brenneman 618 317-2329
1117 Puxico Rd Percy (62272) *(G-16560)*

Rukel Management LLC 630 377-8886
1200 Rukel Way Saint Charles (60174) *(G-18262)*

Rumco, Elk Grove Village Also called Matthew Warren Inc *(G-9113)*

Rumshine Distilling LLC 217 446-6960
8 Hodge St Tilton (61832) *(G-19796)*

Runge Enterprises Inc 630 365-2000
1 N 020 Thryselius Dr Elburn (60119) *(G-8472)*

Runge Equipment Inc 618 322-5628
2370 E 475th Ave Mason (62443) *(G-13609)*

Runway Liquidation LLC 574 247-1500
400 Newport Center Dr Northbrook (60062) *(G-15476)*

Runyon Oil Production Inc 618 395-8510
208 Linn St Olney (62450) *(G-15887)*

Runyon Oil Tools Inc 618 395-5045
331 Herman Dr Olney (62450) *(G-15888)*

Rursch Specialties Inc 309 795-1502
16420 132nd St W Reynolds (61279) *(G-17005)*

Rusco Manufacturing Inc 815 654-3930
1304 Anvil Rd Machesney Park (61115) *(G-13372)*

Ruscorr LLC 708 458-5525
5043 W 67th St Bedford Park (60638) *(G-1500)*

Rush Impressions Inc 847 671-0622
3941 25th Ave Schiller Park (60176) *(G-18842)*

Rush Order Signs & Prtg LLC 630 687-7874
1244 W Capitol Dr Ste B Addison (60101) *(G-278)*

Rush Printing On Oak 815 344-8880
1627 Oak Dr McHenry (60050) *(G-13789)*

Rushville Times, Rushville Also called Perryco Inc *(G-18112)*

Russell Brands LLC 309 454-6737
2015 Eagle Rd Normal (61761) *(G-15223)*

Russell Enterprises Inc (PA) 847 692-6050
865 Busse Hwy Park Ridge (60068) *(G-16295)*

Russell Publications Inc 708 258-3473
120 W North St Peotone (60468) *(G-16557)*

Russell Stanley Midwest Inc 630 739-7700
1000 E 107th St Bolingbrook (60440) *(G-2233)*

Russo Wholesale Meat Inc 708 385-0500
12306 S Cicero Ave Alsip (60803) *(G-507)*

Rust-Leum Con Prtction Systems 918 446-6399
11 E Hawthorn Pkwy Vernon Hills (60061) *(G-20087)*

Rust-Oleum (canada) Ltd 847 367-7700
11 E Hawthorn Pkwy Vernon Hills (60061) *(G-20088)*

Rust-Oleum Corporation (HQ) 847 367-7700
11 E Hawthorn Pkwy Vernon Hills (60061) *(G-20089)*

Rust-Oleum Corporation 815 967-4258
615 Buckbee St Rockford (61104) *(G-17617)*

Rustic Woodcrafts 618 584-3912
10510 E 350th Ave Flat Rock (62427) *(G-9673)*

Rusty & Angela Buzzard 217 342-9841
801 N 3rd St 1 Effingham (62401) *(G-8423)*

Rutgers Enterprises Inc (PA) 847 674-7666
6511 W Proesel Ave Lincolnwood (60712) *(G-12841)*

Ruthman Pump and Engineering 708 754-2940
1249 Center Ave Chicago Heights (60411) *(G-6773)*

Rutke Signs and Safety, Westchester Also called Rutke Signs Inc *(G-20709)*

Rutke Signs Inc 708 841-6464
1 Westbrook Corporate Ctr # 300 Westchester (60154) *(G-20709)*

Rutledge Printing Co 708 479-8282
11415 183rd Pl Ste C Orland Park (60467) *(G-15977)*

Ruyle Incorporated 309 674-6644
1325 Ne Bond St Springfield (62703) *(G-19437)*

Ruyle Mechanical Services Inc 309 674-6644
201 Spring St Ste B Peoria (61603) *(G-16518)*

Rv Air Inc 309 657-4300
475 W Interstate Rd Addison (60101) *(G-279)*

Rv Designer Collection, Wheeling Also called Woodbridge Inc *(G-21015)*

Rv Enterprises Ltd 847 509-8710
8926 N Greenwood Ave Niles (60714) *(G-15168)*

Rv6 Performance 630 346-7998
26w148 Waterbury Ct Wheaton (60187) *(G-20821)*

Rw Acquisition, Rockford Also called Whitney Roper Rockford Inc *(G-17684)*

Rw Technologies US LLC 815 444-6887
387 E Congress Pkwy A1 Crystal Lake (60014) ***(G-7259)***
Rw Welding Inc (PA) 847 541-5508
1511 S Princeton Ave Arlington Heights (60005) ***(G-802)***
Rway Plastics Ltd 815 476-5252
30650 S State Route 53 Wilmington (60481) ***(G-21102)***
Rwi Holdings Inc (PA) 630 897-6951
600 S Lake St Aurora (60506) ***(G-1150)***
Rwi Manufacturing Inc 800 277-1699
600 S Lake St Aurora (60506) ***(G-1151)***
RWS Design and Controls Inc 815 654-6000
13979 Willowbrook Rd Roscoe (61073) ***(G-17930)***
Rx Vials USA 630 378-4417
1296 Lakeview Dr Romeoville (60446) ***(G-17872)***
Ryan Manufacturing Inc 815 695-5310
11610 N La Salle Rd Newark (60541) ***(G-15078)***
Ryan Meat Company 773 783-3840
9620 S Millard Ave Evergreen Park (60805) ***(G-9599)***
Ryan Metal Products Inc 815 936-0700
880 N Washington Ave Kankakee (60901) ***(G-12000)***
Ryan Partnership LLC 312 343-2611
343 W Erie St Ste 600 Chicago (60654) ***(G-6080)***
Ryano Resins Inc 630 621-5677
3808 Baybrook Dr Aurora (60504) ***(G-1015)***
Ryans Glass & Metal Inc (PA) 708 430-7790
7549 W 99th Pl Bridgeview (60455) ***(G-2385)***
Ryans Rub LLC 773 573-8939
402 Se 2nd Ave Aledo (61231) ***(G-360)***
Rycoline Products LLC 773 775-6755
5540 N Northwest Hwy Chicago (60630) ***(G-6081)***
Ryeson Corporation (HQ) 847 455-8677
555 Kimberly Dr Carol Stream (60188) ***(G-3061)***
Rylin Media LLC 708 246-7599
5028 Lawn Ave Western Springs (60558) ***(G-20725)***
S & B Finishing Co Inc 773 533-0033
3005 W Franklin Blvd Chicago (60612) ***(G-6082)***
S & B Jig Grinding Inc 815 654-7907
6820 Forest Hills Rd Loves Park (61111) ***(G-13262)***
S & C Electric Company (PA) 773 338-1000
6601 N Ridge Blvd Chicago (60626) ***(G-6083)***
S & D Products Inc 630 372-2325
1390 Schiferl Rd Bartlett (60103) ***(G-1306)***
S & G Iron Works 224 789-7178
2173 Galilee Ave Zion (60099) ***(G-21526)***
S & G Step Tool Inc 773 992-0808
5203 N Rose St Chicago (60656) ***(G-6084)***
S & J Industrial Supply Corp 708 339-1708
16060 Suntone Dr South Holland (60473) ***(G-19242)***
S & J Machine Inc 815 297-1594
2171 E Yellow Creek Rd Freeport (61032) ***(G-10139)***
S & J Woodproducts 815 973-1970
5305 Forest Hills Rd Rockford (61114) ***(G-17618)***
S & K Boring Inc 815 227-4394
3360 Forest View Rd Rockford (61109) ***(G-17619)***
S & K Label Co 630 307-2577
147 Covington Dr Bloomingdale (60108) ***(G-2012)***
S & M Products, Oswego *Also called Aero-Cables Corp* ***(G-15990)***
S & P Farms 309 772-3936
19485 N 1700th Rd Bushnell (61422) ***(G-2746)***
S & R Media LLC 618 375-7502
113 N Middle St Grayville (62844) ***(G-10814)***
S & R Monogramming Inc 630 369-5468
28w600 Roosevelt Rd Winfield (60190) ***(G-21116)***
S & S Heating & Sheet Metal 815 933-1993
222 N Industrial Dr Bradley (60915) ***(G-2290)***
S & S Hinge Company 630 582-9500
210 Covington Dr Bloomingdale (60108) ***(G-2013)***
S & S Maintenance 815 725-9263
1305 Widows Rd Wilmington (60481) ***(G-21103)***
S & S Metal Recyclers Inc 630 844-3344
336 E Sullivan Rd Aurora (60505) ***(G-1152)***
S & S Mfg Solutions LLC 815 838-1960
15509 Weber Rd # 3 Lockport (60446) ***(G-13022)***
S & S Pallet Corp 618 219-3218
1459 State St Granite City (62040) ***(G-10735)***
S & S Welding & Fabrication 847 742-7344
31w377 Spaulding Rd Elgin (60120) ***(G-8722)***
S & W Machine Works Inc 708 597-6043
12623 S Kroll Dr Alsip (60803) ***(G-508)***
S & W Manufacturing Co Inc 630 595-5044
216 Evergreen Ave Bensenville (60106) ***(G-1888)***
S 4 Global Inc 708 325-1236
7300 S Narragansett Ave Bedford Park (60638) ***(G-1501)***
S A, Bensenville *Also called Spytek Aerospace Corporation* ***(G-1898)***
S A Gear Company Inc 708 496-0395
7252 W 66th St Bedford Park (60638) ***(G-1502)***
S A W Co 630 678-5400
376 E Saint Charles Rd # 5 Lombard (60148) ***(G-13126)***
S and K Packaging Incorporated 563 582-8895
120 N Frentress Lake Rd East Dubuque (61025) ***(G-8181)***
S and S Associates Inc 847 584-0033
1016 Bonaventure Dr Elk Grove Village (60007) ***(G-9224)***
S B Liquidating Company 847 758-9500
1100 Touhy Ave Elk Grove Village (60007) ***(G-9225)***
S C C Pumps Inc 847 593-8495
708 W Algonquin Rd Arlington Heights (60005) ***(G-803)***
S C Johnson & Son Inc 312 702-3100
550 W Washington Blvd # 1400 Chicago (60661) ***(G-6085)***
S Carpenter Logging 618 548-6187
3555 Country Ln Salem (62881) ***(G-18356)***
S D Custom Machining 618 544-7007
9094 E 1050th Ave Robinson (62454) ***(G-17125)***
S Flying Inc 618 586-9999
17583 E 500th Ave Palestine (62451) ***(G-16179)***
S G Acquisition Inc 815 624-6501
14392 De La Tour Dr South Beloit (61080) ***(G-19113)***
S G C, Arlington Heights *Also called Scranton Glltte Cmmnctions Inc* ***(G-805)***
S G C, Arlington Heights *Also called SGC Horizon LLC* ***(G-808)***
S G C M Corp 630 953-2428
1s171 Summit Ave Oakbrook Terrace (60181) ***(G-15815)***
S G Nelson & Co 630 668-7900
209 N Hale St Ste 1 Wheaton (60187) ***(G-20822)***
S G S Inc 708 544-6061
900 Ogden Ave Ste 190 Downers Grove (60515) ***(G-8088)***
S Himmelstein and Company 847 843-3300
2490 Pembroke Ave Hoffman Estates (60169) ***(G-11452)***
S I A Electronics, Tilden *Also called Southern Ill Auto Elec Inc* ***(G-19792)***
S I A Inc (PA) 708 361-3100
11743 Southwest Hwy Palos Heights (60463) ***(G-16191)***
S I S, Glendale Heights *Also called Surgical Instrument Service Co* ***(G-10506)***
S L Fixtures Inc 217 423-9907
2222 E Logan St Decatur (62526) ***(G-7545)***
S P Industries Inc 847 228-2851
1455 Elmhurst Rd Elk Grove Village (60007) ***(G-9226)***
S P M, Wheeling *Also called Swiss Precision Machining Inc* ***(G-20995)***
S R Bastien Co 847 858-1175
600 Davis St Rear Evanston (60201) ***(G-9573)***
S R P, Elk Grove Village *Also called Standard Rubber Products Co* ***(G-9252)***
S S I, Romeoville *Also called Supreme Screw Inc* ***(G-17879)***
S V C Printing Co 773 286-2219
3008 N Laramie Ave Chicago (60641) ***(G-6086)***
S Vs Industries Inc 630 408-1083
646 Wainsford Dr Hoffman Estates (60169) ***(G-11453)***
S&J Food Management Corp 630 323-9296
435 E 4th St Hinsdale (60521) ***(G-11376)***
S&K Machine, Rockford *Also called Spencer and Krahn Mch Tl Sls* ***(G-17639)***
S&L Tool Company Inc 847 455-5550
2324 N 17th Ave Franklin Park (60131) ***(G-10039)***
S&R Precision Machine LLC 815 469-6544
9305 Corsair Rd Ste A Frankfort (60423) ***(G-9835)***
S&S Recovery 217 538-2206
227 Baldknob Trl Fillmore (62032) ***(G-9665)***
S+s Inspection Inc 770 493-9332
1234 Hardt Cir Bartlett (60103) ***(G-1307)***
S-P Products Inc 847 593-8595
730 Pratt Blvd Elk Grove Village (60007) ***(G-9227)***
S-P-D Incorporated 847 882-9820
678 S Middleton Ave Palatine (60067) ***(G-16156)***
S. I. Jacobson Mfg. Company, Waukegan *Also called Jacobson Acqstion Holdings LLC* ***(G-20452)***
S.E. P. I., Glendale Heights *Also called Sound Enhancement Products Inc* ***(G-10496)***
S4 Industries Inc 224 699-9674
140 Prairie Lake Rd East Dundee (60118) ***(G-8210)***
SA Industries Inc 847 730-4823
756 N Edgewood Ave Wood Dale (60191) ***(G-21237)***
SA Nat Industrial Cnstr Co Inc 618 246-9402
103 E Perkins Ave Mount Vernon (62864) ***(G-14636)***
Saachi Inc 630 775-1700
364 Jennifer Ln Roselle (60172) ***(G-17982)***
Saasoom LLC 630 561-7300
7n063 Plymouth Ct Saint Charles (60175) ***(G-18263)***
Saati Americas Corporation 847 296-5090
901 E Business Center Dr Mount Prospect (60056) ***(G-14568)***
Saatiprint Div, Mount Prospect *Also called Saati Americas Corporation* ***(G-14568)***
Sab Tool Supply Co (PA) 847 634-3700
730 Corporate Woods Pkwy Vernon Hills (60061) ***(G-20090)***
Sabic Innovative Plas US LLC 815 434-7000
2148 N 2753rd Rd Ottawa (61350) ***(G-16075)***
Sabinas Food Products Inc 312 738-2412
1509 W 18th St Chicago (60608) ***(G-6087)***
Sacco-Camex Inc 630 595-8090
460 Dominic Ct Franklin Park (60131) ***(G-10040)***
Sadannah Group LLC 630 357-2300
426 W 5th Ave Naperville (60563) ***(G-14912)***
Sadelco USA Corp 847 781-8844
1120 Warwick Cir N Hoffman Estates (60169) ***(G-11454)***
SAE Customs Inc 855 723-2878
27764 Volo Village Rd F Round Lake (60073) ***(G-18082)***

ALPHABETIC

Saf-T-Eze, Lombard *Also called Saf-T-Lok International Corp* ***(G-13127)***
Saf-T-Lok International Corp.....630 495-2001
300 Eisenhower Ln N Lombard (60148) ***(G-13127)***
Safco LLC.....847 677-3204
7631 Austin Ave Skokie (60077) ***(G-19026)***
Safe Effective Alternatives.....618 236-2727
6218 Old Saint Louis Rd Belleville (62223) ***(G-1595)***
Safe Fair Food Company LLC.....904 930-4277
1 N La Salle St Ste 2850 Chicago (60602) ***(G-6088)***
Safe Pet Products, Westmont *Also called Kmp Products LLC* ***(G-20754)***
Safe Traffic System Inc.....847 233-0365
6600 N Lincoln Ave Lincolnwood (60712) ***(G-12842)***
Safe Water Technologies Inc.....847 888-6900
996 Bluff City Blvd Elgin (60120) ***(G-8723)***
Safe-Air of Illinois Inc.....708 652-9100
1855 S 54th Ave Cicero (60804) ***(G-6873)***
Safe-T-Quip Corporation.....773 235-2100
2300 N Kilbourn Ave Chicago (60639) ***(G-6089)***
Safeguard 201 Corp.....630 241-0370
1129 Fairview Ave Westmont (60559) ***(G-20770)***
Safeguard Print & Promo, Westmont *Also called Safeguard 201 Corp* ***(G-20770)***
Safemobile Inc.....847 818-1649
3601 Algonquin Rd Ste 320 Rolling Meadows (60008) ***(G-17772)***
Safersonic Us Inc.....847 274-1534
2873 Arlington Ave # 110 Highland Park (60035) ***(G-11296)***
Safety Security Products Co, Lake Bluff *Also called Profile Plastics Inc* ***(G-12207)***
Safety Socket LLC.....224 484-6222
49 Prairie Pkwy Gilberts (60136) ***(G-10368)***
Safety Storage Inc.....217 345-4422
855 N 5th St Charleston (61920) ***(G-3412)***
Safety-Kleen Systems Inc.....618 875-8050
3000 Missouri Ave East Saint Louis (62205) ***(G-8321)***
Safeway Products Inc.....815 226-8322
1810 15th Ave Rockford (61104) ***(G-17620)***
Safeway Services Rockford Inc.....815 986-1504
1310 Samuelson Rd Rockford (61109) ***(G-17621)***
Saffire Grill Co., Rockford *Also called Home Fires Inc* ***(G-17452)***
Safigel, Chicago *Also called Two Tower Frames Inc* ***(G-6448)***
Saga Communications Inc.....248 631-8099
3501 E Sangamon Ave Springfield (62707) ***(G-19438)***
Sagamore Publishing LLC.....217 359-5940
3611 N Staley Rd Ste B Champaign (61822) ***(G-3345)***
Sage Clover.....630 220-9600
26w400 Torrey Pines Ct Winfield (60190) ***(G-21117)***
Sage Products LLC.....815 455-4700
815 Tek Dr Crystal Lake (60014) ***(G-7260)***
Sage Products LLC (HQ).....815 455-4700
3909 Three Oaks Rd Cary (60013) ***(G-3188)***
Sage Products Holdings II LLC.....800 323-2220
3909 Three Oaks Rd Cary (60013) ***(G-3189)***
Sagent Logistics LP.....847 908-1600
1901 N Roselle Rd Ste 450 Schaumburg (60195) ***(G-18700)***
Sagent Pharmaceuticals Inc.....847 908-1600
1901 N Roselle Rd Ste 400 Schaumburg (60195) ***(G-18701)***
Sagent Pharmaceuticals Inc (HQ).....847 908-1600
1901 N Roselle Rd Ste 450 Schaumburg (60195) ***(G-18702)***
Sahara Air Dryers, Sandwich *Also called Henderson Engineering Co Inc* ***(G-18374)***
SAI, Lake Villa *Also called Strategic Applications Inc* ***(G-12368)***
SAI Advanced Pwr Solutions Inc (PA).....708 450-0990
11333 Addison Ave Apt 100 Franklin Park (60131) ***(G-10041)***
Saicor Inc.....630 530-0350
708 N Princeton Ave Villa Park (60181) ***(G-20170)***
Saint Clair Tennis Club, O Fallon *Also called St Clair Tennis Club LLC* ***(G-15584)***
Saint Mary Fuel Company.....773 918-1681
6700 S Ashland Ave Chicago (60636) ***(G-6090)***
Saint Pierre Oil, Newton *Also called St Pierre Oil Company Inc* ***(G-15093)***
Saint Technologies Inc.....815 864-3035
10 N Locust St Shannon (61078) ***(G-18873)***
Saint-Gobain Abrasives Inc.....630 238-3300
200 Fullerton Ave Carol Stream (60188) ***(G-3062)***
Saint-Gobain Abrasives Inc.....630 868-8060
200 Fullerton Ave Carol Stream (60188) ***(G-3063)***
Saints Volo & Olha Uk Cath Par.....312 829-5209
2245 W Superior St Chicago (60612) ***(G-6091)***
Sakamoto Kanagata Usa Inc.....224 856-2008
433 Joseph Dr South Elgin (60177) ***(G-19173)***
Salamander Studios Chicago Inc.....773 379-2211
5410 W Roosevelt Rd # 306 Chicago (60644) ***(G-6092)***
Salatas Smoked Meats.....224 433-1205
1206 N Oakwood Dr McHenry (60050) ***(G-13790)***
Salco Products Inc (PA).....630 783-2570
1385 101st St Ste A Lemont (60439) ***(G-12588)***
Salem Building Materials Inc.....618 548-3221
1217 S Broadway Ave Salem (62881) ***(G-18357)***
Salem Times-Commoner Inc (HQ).....618 548-3330
120 S Broadway Ave Salem (62881) ***(G-18358)***
Sales & Marketing Resources.....847 910-9169
21 Ashcroft Ct Fox River Grove (60021) ***(G-9761)***
Sales Midwest Prtg & Packg Inc.....309 764-5544
426 37th St Moline (61265) ***(G-14175)***
Sales Stretcher Enterprises.....815 223-9681
4920 E 103rd Rd Peru (61354) ***(G-16593)***
Salesforcecom Inc.....312 361-3555
205 W Wacker Dr Fl 22 Chicago (60606) ***(G-6093)***
Salesforcecom Inc.....312 288-3600
111 W Illinois St Chicago (60654) ***(G-6094)***
Salient Hct, Chicago *Also called Am2pat Inc* ***(G-3641)***
Salisbury By Honeywell, Bolingbrook *Also called Salisbury Elec Safety LLC* ***(G-2234)***
Salisbury Elec Safety LLC.....877 406-4501
101 E Crssrads Pkwy Ste A Bolingbrook (60440) ***(G-2234)***
Salman Metal.....630 359-5110
552 W Fay Ave Elmhurst (60126) ***(G-9421)***
Salmons and Brown.....312 929-6756
44 E Superior St 1 Chicago (60611) ***(G-6095)***
Salsa Verde Batavia Inc.....630 425-3521
107 N Batavia Ave Batavia (60510) ***(G-1412)***
Salsedo Press Inc.....773 533-9900
3139 W Chicago Ave Chicago (60622) ***(G-6096)***
Salt Creek Alpacas Inc.....309 530-7904
3605 N 3300 East Rd Farmer City (61842) ***(G-9657)***
Salter Labs, Lake Forest *Also called Salter Medical Holdings Corp* ***(G-12301)***
Salter Labs (HQ).....847 739-3224
272 E Deerpath Ste 302 Lake Forest (60045) ***(G-12300)***
Salter Medical Holdings Corp.....800 421-0024
272 E Deerpath Ste 302 Lake Forest (60045) ***(G-12301)***
Salud Natural Entrepreneur Inc.....224 789-7400
1120 Glen Rock Ave Waukegan (60085) ***(G-20491)***
Salud Natural Entrepreneur Inc (PA).....224 789-7400
1120 Glen Rock Ave Waukegan (60085) ***(G-20492)***
Salud Natural Entrepreneurs, Waukegan *Also called Salud Natural Entrepreneur Inc* ***(G-20491)***
Sam Electronics Worldwide Inc.....847 290-1720
3410 Newport Dr Unit 34 Rolling Meadows (60008) ***(G-17773)***
Sam Solutions Inc.....708 594-0480
5120 S Lawndale Ave Summit Argo (60501) ***(G-19681)***
Samad General Services Inc.....773 593-3332
511 N Addison Rd Ste A Addison (60101) ***(G-280)***
Sambor Stone Ltd.....708 388-0804
15527 La Salle St South Holland (60473) ***(G-19243)***
Same Day Signs.....773 697-4896
2416 W Barry Ave Chicago (60618) ***(G-6097)***
Samecwei Inc.....630 897-7888
205 N Lake St Ste 103 Aurora (60506) ***(G-1153)***
Samel Botros.....847 466-5905
1 Tiffany Pt Ste G1 Bloomingdale (60108) ***(G-2014)***
Sammy USA Corp.....847 364-9787
800 Arthur Ave Elk Grove Village (60007) ***(G-9228)***
Samsung Sign Corp.....847 816-1374
1840 Industrial Dr # 230 Libertyville (60048) ***(G-12703)***
Samtek International Inc.....314 954-4005
10 Emerald Ter Ste C Swansea (62226) ***(G-19697)***
Samuel Son & Co (usa) Inc (HQ).....630 783-8900
1401 Davey Rd Ste 300 Woodridge (60517) ***(G-21338)***
Samuel Packaging Systems Group, Woodridge *Also called Samuel Son & Co (usa) Inc* ***(G-21338)***
Samuel Rowell.....618 942-6970
2817 S Park Ave Herrin (62948) ***(G-11178)***
San Telmo Ltd.....847 842-9115
330 E Main St Fl 2 Barrington (60010) ***(G-1243)***
Sanchem Inc.....312 733-6100
1600 S Canal St Chicago (60616) ***(G-6098)***
Sanco Industries Inc.....847 243-8675
21800 N Andover Rd Kildeer (60047) ***(G-12052)***
Sand Sculpture Co.....815 334-9101
327 S Jefferson St Woodstock (60098) ***(G-21430)***
Sand Valley Sand & Gravel Inc.....217 446-4210
16395 Lewis Rd Danville (61834) ***(G-7380)***
Sand-Rite Manufacturing Co.....312 997-2200
3080 W Soffel Ave Melrose Park (60160) ***(G-13912)***
Sandbagger LLC.....630 876-2400
765 S State Route 83 Elmhurst (60126) ***(G-9422)***
Sandbagger Corp.....630 876-2400
765 S Il Route 83 Elmhurst (60126) ***(G-9423)***
Sandee Manufacturing Co (PA).....847 671-1335
10520 Waveland Ave Franklin Park (60131) ***(G-10042)***
Sandeno Inc.....815 730-9415
2115 Moen Ave Rockdale (60436) ***(G-17272)***
Sanders Inc.....815 634-4611
2250 Wahoo Dr Morris (60450) ***(G-14326)***
Sanderson and Associates.....312 829-4350
400 N Racine Ave Apt 211 Chicago (60642) ***(G-6099)***
Sandes Quynetta.....815 275-4876
752 W American St Apt 5 Freeport (61032) ***(G-10140)***
Sandlock Sandbox LLC.....630 963-9422
1069 Zygmunt Cir Westmont (60559) ***(G-20771)***
Sandmancom Inc.....630 980-7710
399 Wall St Ste B Glendale Heights (60139) ***(G-10490)***

ALPHABETIC SECTION Scars Publications

Sandner Electric Co Inc 618 932-2179
903 E Saint Louis St West Frankfort (62896) **(G-20682)**
Sandra E Greene 815 469-0092
228 N Locust St Frankfort (60423) **(G-9836)**
Sandstrom Products Company (PA) 309 523-2121
224 S Main St Port Byron (61275) **(G-16787)**
Sandstrom Products Company 309 523-2121
218 S High St Port Byron (61275) **(G-16788)**
Sandtech Inc 847 470-9595
7845 Merrimac Ave Morton Grove (60053) **(G-14439)**
Sandvik Inc 847 519-1737
1665 N Penny Ln Schaumburg (60173) **(G-18703)**
Sandvik Crmant Prductivity Ctr, Schaumburg *Also called Sandvik Inc* **(G-18703)**
Sandwich Casting & Machine, Sandwich *Also called Trio Foundry Inc* **(G-18386)**
Sandwich Casting & Machine Div, Montgomery *Also called Trio Foundry Inc* **(G-14272)**
Sandwich Millworks Inc 815 786-2700
700 W Center St Sandwich (60548) **(G-18384)**
Sanford Chemical Co Inc 847 437-3530
1945 Touhy Ave Elk Grove Village (60007) **(G-9229)**
Sangam, Skokie *Also called Princess Foods Inc* **(G-19011)**
Sangamon Valley Sand & Gravel 217 498-7189
102 Maple Ln Rochester (62563) **(G-17171)**
Sangchris Lake State Park, Rochester *Also called Ill Dept Natural Resources* **(G-17167)**
Sango Embroidery 773 582-4354
5220 S Pulaski Rd Chicago (60632) **(G-6100)**
Sanks Machining Inc 618 635-8279
22991 Ruschaupt Rd Staunton (62088) **(G-19477)**
Sansabelt 312 357-5119
101 N Wacker Dr Chicago (60606) **(G-6101)**
Santa Cruz Holdings LLC (PA) 217 821-0304
1307 Kollmeyer Ln Effingham (62401) **(G-8424)**
Santas Best (PA) 847 459-3301
100 N Fairway Dr Ste 120 Vernon Hills (60061) **(G-20091)**
Santec Systems Inc 847 215-8884
2924 Malmo Dr Arlington Heights (60005) **(G-804)**
Santelli Custom Cabinetry 708 771-3884
1531 Forest Ave Apt 3 River Forest (60305) **(G-17055)**
Santucci Enterprises 773 286-5629
6345 W Warwick Ave Chicago (60634) **(G-6102)**
Sanyo Seiki America Corp 630 876-8270
1417 W Fullerton Ave Addison (60101) **(G-281)**
Sap Acquisition Co LLC 847 229-1600
1200 Barclay Blvd Buffalo Grove (60089) **(G-2594)**
Sap America Inc 630 395-2700
3010 Highland Pkwy # 900 Downers Grove (60515) **(G-8089)**
Sapa Extrusions North Amer LLC 877 922-7272
6250 N River Rd Ste 5000 Rosemont (60018) **(G-18049)**
Saporito Finishing Co (PA) 708 222-5300
3119 S Austin Blvd Cicero (60804) **(G-6874)**
Saporito Finishing Co 708 222-5300
3130 S Austin Blvd Chicago (60804) **(G-6103)**
Saputo Cheese USA Inc (HQ) 847 267-1100
1 Overlook Pt Ste 300 Lincolnshire (60069) **(G-12794)**
Saputo Inc 715 755-3485
1 Overlook Pt Ste 300 Lincolnshire (60069) **(G-12795)**
Sara Lee Baking Group 217 585-3462
6100 S 2nd St Springfield (62711) **(G-19439)**
Sara Lee Food & Beverage, Chicago *Also called Hillshire Brands Company* **(G-4820)**
Saratoga Food Specialties, Bolingbrook *Also called Smithfield Packaged Meats Corp* **(G-2243)**
Saratoga Specialties Co Inc 630 833-3810
200 W Wrightwood Ave Elmhurst (60126) **(G-9424)**
Sarco Hydraulics Inc (PA) 217 324-6577
216 N Old Route 66 Litchfield (62056) **(G-12977)**
Sarco Putty Company 773 735-5577
5959 S Knox Ave Chicago (60629) **(G-6104)**
Sarcol 773 533-3000
3050 W Taylor St Chicago (60612) **(G-6105)**
Sardee Industries Inc (PA) 630 824-4200
5100 Academy Dr Ste 400 Lisle (60532) **(G-12936)**
Sarj USA Inc 708 865-9134
9201 King St Franklin Park (60131) **(G-10043)**
Sas Industrial Machinery Inc 847 455-5526
9212 Cherry Ave Franklin Park (60131) **(G-10044)**
Sashe Lux LLC 312 593-1379
835 N Michigan Ave # 6000 Chicago (60611) **(G-6106)**
Sass-N-Class Inc 630 655-2420
19 W 1st St Ste A Hinsdale (60521) **(G-11377)**
Sassy Primitives Ltd 815 385-9302
3202 Lakeside Ct Unit 1 McCullom Lake (60050) **(G-13712)**
Satellink Inc 618 983-5555
724 W 15th St Johnston City (62951) **(G-11812)**
Sato America, Romeoville *Also called Sato Lbling Solutions Amer Inc* **(G-17873)**
Sato Lbling Solutions Amer Inc 630 771-4200
1140 Windham Pkwy Romeoville (60446) **(G-17873)**
Sato Lbling Solutions Amer Inc (PA) 630 771-4200
1140 Windham Pkwy Romeoville (60446) **(G-17874)**
Saturn Electrical Services Inc 630 980-0300
380 Monaco Dr Roselle (60172) **(G-17983)**
Saturn Manufacturing Company 630 860-8474
233 Park St Bensenville (60106) **(G-1889)**
Saturn Sign 847 520-9009
240 Industrial Ln Ste 1 Wheeling (60090) **(G-20978)**
Sauber Manufacturing Company 630 365-6600
10 N Sauber Rd Virgil (60151) **(G-20191)**
Sauber Mfg. Co., Virgil *Also called C S O Corp* **(G-20190)**
Sauder Industries Limited 815 717-2660
2200 W Haven Ave New Lenox (60451) **(G-15057)**
Sauk Valley Community College 815 835-6321
601 W 13th St Sterling (61081) **(G-19531)**
Sauk Valley Container Corp., Sterling *Also called Sterling Box Company Inc* **(G-19534)**
Sauk Valley Gunsmithing 815 441-0260
710 4th Ave Sterling (61081) **(G-19532)**
Sauk Valley Newspaper, Sterling *Also called B F Shaw Printing Company* **(G-19500)**
Sauk Valley Printing 815 284-2222
113 S Peoria Ave Ste 1 Dixon (61021) **(G-7914)**
Sausages By Amy, Chicago *Also called Pcj II Inc* **(G-5773)**
Savage Bros Company 847 981-3000
1825 Greenleaf Ave Elk Grove Village (60007) **(G-9230)**
Savanna Gas and Welding Sups, Savanna *Also called Mills Machine Inc* **(G-18409)**
Savanna Quarry Inc 815 273-4208
9859 Scenic Bluff Rd Savanna (61074) **(G-18411)**
Savanna Times Journal 815 273-2277
121 Main St Savanna (61074) **(G-18412)**
Savanna Times-Journal, Mount Carroll *Also called Mirror-Democrat* **(G-14496)**
Savannah Industries Inc 773 927-3484
3350 W 48th Pl Chicago (60632) **(G-6107)**
Save On Printing Inc 847 922-7855
1451 Landmeier Rd Elk Grove Village (60007) **(G-9231)**
Savencia Cheese USA LLC 815 369-4577
3990 N Sunnyside Rd Lena (61048) **(G-12608)**
Savex Manufacturing Company 630 668-7219
170 Easy St Carol Stream (60188) **(G-3064)**
Savile Rumtini, Bolingbrook *Also called Dtrs Enterprises Inc* **(G-2170)**
Savino Displays Inc 630 574-0777
28 Bradford Ln Hinsdale (60523) **(G-11378)**
Savino Enterprises 708 385-5277
12453 Gregory St Blue Island (60406) **(G-2138)**
Sawier 630 297-8588
7517 Florence Ave Downers Grove (60516) **(G-8090)**
Sawmill Construction Inc 815 937-0037
5265 E 4000n Rd Bourbonnais (60914) **(G-2268)**
Saws International Inc 815 397-0985
4929 Marlin Dr Machesney Park (61115) **(G-13373)**
Saws Unlimited Inc 847 640-7450
494 Bonnie Ln Elk Grove Village (60007) **(G-9232)**
Say Cheese Cake 618 532-6001
421 W Noleman St Centralia (62801) **(G-3249)**
Sazerac North America Inc (HQ) 502 423-5225
75 Remittance Dr # 3312 Chicago (60675) **(G-6108)**
Sb Acquisition, Elmhurst *Also called Sandbagger LLC* **(G-9422)**
Sb Boron, Bellwood *Also called SB Boron Corporation* **(G-1637)**
SB Boron Corporation 708 547-9002
20 Davis Dr Bellwood (60104) **(G-1637)**
SBA, La Grange *Also called Sergio Barajas* **(G-12089)**
SBA Wireless Inc 847 215-8720
1287 Barclay Blvd Ste 200 Buffalo Grove (60089) **(G-2595)**
SBC, Champaign *Also called Am-Don Partnership* **(G-3263)**
SBE Varvit Usa LLC 331 205-7000
1455 Sequoia Dr Ste 101 Aurora (60506) **(G-1154)**
Sbg Illinois, Elgin *Also called Sharp Defense LLC* **(G-8728)**
Sbic America Inc 847 303-5430
205 Travis Ct Apt 304 Schaumburg (60195) **(G-18704)**
SBS Steel Belt Systems USA Inc 847 841-3300
59 Prairie Pkwy Gilberts (60136) **(G-10369)**
SC Aviation Inc 800 416-4176
1433 Lancaster Ave Saint Charles (60174) **(G-18264)**
SC Holdings LLC (HQ) 217 821-0304
1307 Kollmeyer Ln Effingham (62401) **(G-8425)**
SC Industries LLC 407 484-2081
150 N Michigan Ave # 400 Chicago (60601) **(G-6109)**
SC Lighting 630 849-3384
607 W Wise Rd Schaumburg (60193) **(G-18705)**
Sc2 Inc 309 677-5980
200 Carver Ln East Peoria (61611) **(G-8289)**
Sca, River Forest *Also called Scientific Cmpt Assoc Corp* **(G-17056)**
Sca Thermosafe, Arlington Heights *Also called Sonoco Prtective Solutions Inc* **(G-811)**
Scadaware Inc 309 665-0135
2023 Eagle Rd Normal (61761) **(G-15224)**
Scale Railroad Equipment 630 682-9170
23w546 Saint Charles Rd Carol Stream (60188) **(G-3065)**
Scaletta Moloney Armoring (PA) 708 924-0099
6755 S Belt Circle Dr Bedford Park (60638) **(G-1503)**
Scanlab America Inc 630 797-2044
100 Illinois St Ste 200 Saint Charles (60174) **(G-18265)**
Scars Publications 847 281-9070
829 Brian Ct Gurnee (60031) **(G-10925)**

ALPHABETIC

Scf Services LLC 314 436-7559
8 Pitzman Ave Sauget (62201) *(G-18398)*

Schaefer Technologies LLC 630 406-9377
751 N Raddant Rd Batavia (60510) *(G-1413)*

Schaeffer Electric Co (PA) 618 592-3231
400 S Taylor St Oblong (62449) *(G-15829)*

Schafer Gear Works Roscoe LLC 815 874-4327
5466 E Rockton Rd Roscoe (61073) *(G-17931)*

Schaff International LLC 847 438-4560
451 Oakwood Rd Lake Zurich (60047) *(G-12453)*

Schaff Piano Supply, Lake Zurich Also called Schaff International LLC *(G-12453)*

Schaffer Tool & Design Inc 630 876-3800
3555 Stern Ave Saint Charles (60174) *(G-18266)*

Schau Southeast Sushi Inc 630 783-1000
10350 Argonne Dr Ste 400 Woodridge (60517) *(G-21339)*

Schaumburg Review 847 998-3400
350 N Orleans St Fl 10 Chicago (60654) *(G-6110)*

Schaumburg Specialties Co 847 451-0070
550 Albion Ave Ste 30 Schaumburg (60193) *(G-18706)*

Scheck Siress Prosthetics Inc 312 757-5270
1304 E 47th St 204 Chicago (60653) *(G-6111)*

Scheck Siress Prosthetics Inc 630 424-0392
401 Harrison St Oak Park (60304) *(G-15771)*

Scheffler Custom Woodworking 815 284-6564
925 Depot Ave Dixon (61021) *(G-7915)*

Scheiwes Print and Christn Sup, Crescent City Also called Scheiwes Print Shop *(G-7082)*

Scheiwes Print Shop 815 683-2398
407 Main St Crescent City (60928) *(G-7082)*

Schellerer Corporation Inc 630 980-4567
4350 Chandler Dr Hanover Park (60133) *(G-11013)*

Schiele Graphics Inc 847 434-5455
1880 Busse Rd Elk Grove Village (60007) *(G-9233)*

Schiele Group, Elk Grove Village Also called Schiele Graphics Inc *(G-9233)*

Schilke Music Products Inc 708 343-8858
4520 James Pl Melrose Park (60160) *(G-13913)*

Schindler Logistics Center, Chicago Also called Adams Elevator Equipment Co *(G-3538)*

Schirz Concrete Products Inc 217 368-2153
1251-1299 Prairie St Greenfield (62044) *(G-10818)*

Schlesinger Machinery Inc 630 766-4074
820 Maple Ln Bensenville (60106) *(G-1890)*

Schmalz Precast Concrete Mfg 815 747-3939
18363 Us Highway 20 W East Dubuque (61025) *(G-8182)*

Schmid Tool & Engineering Corp 630 333-1733
930 N Villa Ave Villa Park (60181) *(G-20171)*

Schmidt Marking Systems, Niles Also called Geo T Schmidt Inc *(G-15124)*

Schmidt Printing, Woodstock Also called Dale K Brown *(G-21380)*

Schmit Laboratories Inc 773 476-0072
500 Wall St Glendale Heights (60139) *(G-10491)*

Schneider Elc Buildings LLC (HQ) 815 381-5000
839 N Perryville Rd Rockford (61107) *(G-17622)*

Schneider Elc Buildings LLC 815 227-4000
4104 Charles St Rockford (61108) *(G-17623)*

Schneider Elc Holdings Inc (HQ) 717 944-5460
200 N Martingale Rd # 100 Schaumburg (60173) *(G-18707)*

Schneider Electric Relays, Schaumburg Also called SE Relays LLC *(G-18710)*

Schneider Electric Usa Inc 312 697-4770
311 S Wacker Dr Ste 4550 Chicago (60606) *(G-6112)*

Schneider Electric Usa Inc 847 441-2526
200 N Martingale Rd # 1000 Schaumburg (60173) *(G-18708)*

Schneider Graphics Inc 847 550-4310
885 Telser Rd Lake Zurich (60047) *(G-12454)*

Schneider Pipe Organs Inc 217 871-4807
104 S Johnston St Kenney (61749) *(G-12016)*

Schnowske & Sons Trucking Inc 309 937-3323
10507 Illinois Highway 82 Cambridge (61238) *(G-2807)*

Schnuck Markets Inc 618 466-0825
2712 Godfrey Rd Godfrey (62035) *(G-10663)*

Schnucks Pharmacy, Godfrey Also called Schnuck Markets Inc *(G-10663)*

Scholarship Solutions LLC 847 859-5629
200 W Jackson Blvd # 2700 Chicago (60606) *(G-6113)*

Scholastic Inc 630 443-8197
2315 Dean St Ste 600 Saint Charles (60175) *(G-18267)*

Scholastic Inc 630 671-0601
301 S Gary Ave Unit A Roselle (60172) *(G-17984)*

Scholastic Testing Service 630 766-7150
480 Meyer Rd Bensenville (60106) *(G-1891)*

Schold Holdings Inc 708 458-3788
7201 W 64th Pl Chicago (60638) *(G-6114)*

Scholle Ipn Corporation (PA) 708 562-7290
200 W North Ave Northlake (60164) *(G-15558)*

Scholle Packaging, Northlake Also called Scholle Ipn Corporation *(G-15558)*

Scholle Packaging Inc 708 273-3792
120 N Railroad Ave Northlake (60164) *(G-15559)*

Schommer Inc 815 344-1404
3410 W Elm St McHenry (60050) *(G-13791)*

School Town LLC 847 943-9115
1340 Shermer Rd Ste 245 Northbrook (60062) *(G-15477)*

Schools Processing Service, Bensenville Also called Scholastic Testing Service *(G-1891)*

Schrader-Bridgeport Intl Inc 815 288-3344
1550 Franklin Grove Rd Dixon (61021) *(G-7916)*

Schram Enterprises Inc 708 345-2252
5017 W Lake St Melrose Park (60160) *(G-13914)*

Schreck Kitchens, South Elgin Also called Shreck Kitchens *(G-19174)*

Schreder Lighting LLC 847 621-5130
1415 W 22nd St Ste Tower Oak Brook (60523) *(G-15662)*

Schrock Custom Woodworking 217 849-3375
705 Industrial Dr Toledo (62468) *(G-19877)*

Schrocks Sawmill 217 268-3632
59 N County Road 450e Arcola (61910) *(G-665)*

Schrocks Wood Shop 217 773-3842
356 650n Ave Mount Sterling (62353) *(G-14593)*

Schrocks Woodworking 217 578-3259
135 E Cr 800 N Arthur (61911) *(G-879)*

Schroeders Pallet Service Inc 708 371-9046
3500 Burr Oak Ave Blue Island (60406) *(G-2139)*

Schubert Controls Corporation 847 526-8200
1099 Brown St Ste 109 Wauconda (60084) *(G-20390)*

Schubert Environmental Eqp Inc 630 307-9400
2000 Bloomingdale Rd # 115 Glendale Heights (60139) *(G-10492)*

Schuld-Bushnell, Bushnell Also called Bushnell Illinois Tank Co *(G-2738)*

Schulhof Company 773 348-1123
5801 Ami Dr Richmond (60071) *(G-17022)*

Schultes Precision Mfg Inc 847 465-0300
1250 Busch Pkwy Buffalo Grove (60089) *(G-2596)*

Schultz Brothers Inc 630 458-1437
1001 W Republic Dr Ste 11 Addison (60101) *(G-282)*

Schulze & Schulze Inc 618 687-1106
3198 Town Creek Rd Murphysboro (62966) *(G-14758)*

Schulze and Burch Biscuit Co (PA) 773 927-6622
1133 W 35th St Chicago (60609) *(G-6115)*

Schulze and Burch Biscuit Co 708 354-7050
9100 67th St Hodgkins (60525) *(G-11395)*

Schumacher Electric Corp (PA) 847 385-1600
801 E Business Center Dr Mount Prospect (60056) *(G-14569)*

Schumaker Publications Inc 309 365-7105
Rr 2 Box 72a Lexington (61753) *(G-12621)*

Schutt Sports, Litchfield Also called Kranos Corporation *(G-12969)*

Schwab Paper Products Company 815 372-2233
636 Schwab Cir Romeoville (60446) *(G-17875)*

Schwak, Chicago Also called Blue Software LLC *(G-3914)*

Schwanog LLC 847 289-1055
1301 Bowes Rd Ste A Elgin (60123) *(G-8724)*

Schwartz Electrical Co, Pekin Also called T & J Electric Company Inc *(G-16364)*

Schwartz Oilfield Services (PA) 618 532-0232
501 Schwartz Rd Walnut Hill (62893) *(G-20222)*

Schwartz Pickle, Chicago Also called Bay Valley Foods LLC *(G-3847)*

Schwartzkopf Printing Inc 618 463-0747
4121 Humbert Rd Alton (62002) *(G-571)*

Schwarz, Morton Grove Also called Bunzl Retail Services LLC *(G-14393)*

Schwarz Bros Manufacturing Co 309 342-5814
584 E Brooks St Galesburg (61401) *(G-10220)*

Schwebel Printing 618 684-3911
1408 Walnut St Murphysboro (62966) *(G-14759)*

Schweitzer Engrg Labs Inc 847 362-8304
450 Enterprise Pkwy Lake Zurich (60047) *(G-12455)*

Schwider Systems 815 469-2834
7842 W Laurel Dr Frankfort (60423) *(G-9837)*

SCI, Morris Also called Sponge-Cushion Inc *(G-14328)*

SCI, Rockford Also called Spider Company Inc *(G-17640)*

SCI, Elk Grove Village Also called Smith Cooper International Inc *(G-9244)*

SCI Box LLC 618 244-7244
515 S 1st St Mount Vernon (62864) *(G-14637)*

Sciaky Inc 708 594-3841
4915 W 67th St Chicago (60638) *(G-6116)*

Scibor Upholstering & Gallery 708 671-9700
12210 S Harlem Ave Chicago (60643) *(G-6117)*

Science Solutions LLC (PA) 773 261-1197
5000 W Roosevelt Rd Dock29 Chicago (60644) *(G-6118)*

Scientfic Bndery Prdctions Inc 847 329-0510
8052 Monticello Ave # 206 Skokie (60076) *(G-19027)*

Scientific Cmpt Assoc Corp (PA) 708 771-4567
212 Lathrop Ave River Forest (60305) *(G-17056)*

Scientific Colors Inc (PA) 815 741-1391
1401 Mound Rd Rockdale (60436) *(G-17273)*

Scientific Colors Inc 815 744-5650
1550 Mound Rd Rockdale (60436) *(G-17274)*

Scientific Device Lab Inc 847 803-9495
411 Jarvis Ave Des Plaines (60018) *(G-7839)*

Scientific Instruments Inc 847 679-1242
622 Lunt Ave Schaumburg (60193) *(G-18709)*

Scientific Manufacturing Inc 847 414-5658
209 Hilltop Ln Sleepy Hollow (60118) *(G-19062)*

Scientific Metal Treating Co 630 582-0071
106 Chancellor Dr Roselle (60172) *(G-17985)*

Scimatco Office 630 879-1306
770 N Raddant Rd Batavia (60510) *(G-1414)*

ALPHABETIC SECTION

Scimitar Prototyping Inc 630 483-3875
  1529 Bourbon Pkwy Streamwood (60107) *(G-19594)*
Scis Air Security Corporation 847 671-9502
  4321 United Pkwy Schiller Park (60176) *(G-18843)*
Scope, The, Lena Also called Shoppers Guide *(G-12609)*
Scopedawg Optics LLC 618 401-3342
  3115 Lake Ridge Dr Highland (62249) *(G-11239)*
Scorpio Elec Dschrge Machining, Elgin Also called EDM Scorpio Inc *(G-8573)*
Scorpion Graphics Inc 773 927-3203
  3221 W 36th St Chicago (60632) *(G-6119)*
Scot Electrical Products, Aurora Also called Win Technologies Incorporated *(G-1037)*
Scot Forge Company (PA) 815 675-1000
  8001 Winn Rd Spring Grove (60081) *(G-19300)*
Scot Forge Company 847 678-6000
  9394 Belmont Ave Franklin Park (60131) *(G-10045)*
Scot Inc 630 969-0620
  2525 Curtiss St Downers Grove (60515) *(G-8091)*
Scot Industries Inc 630 466-7591
  1961 W Us Highway 30 Sugar Grove (60554) *(G-19653)*
Scotsman Group Inc (HQ) 847 215-4500
  101 Corporate Woods Pkwy Vernon Hills (60061) *(G-20092)*
Scotsman Ice Systems Division, Vernon Hills Also called Scotsman Group Inc *(G-20092)*
Scotsman Industries Inc (HQ) 847 215-4500
  101 Corporate Woods Pkwy Vernon Hills (60061) *(G-20093)*
Scotsman of Los Angeles, Vernon Hills Also called Scotsman Industries Inc *(G-20093)*
Scott County Times, Winchester Also called Campbell Publishing Inc *(G-21104)*
Scott Industrial Blower Co 847 426-8800
  15 W End Dr Gilberts (60136) *(G-10370)*
Scott Janczak 773 545-7233
  6285 N Knox Ave Chicago (60646) *(G-6120)*
Scott Oil, Newton Also called Trojan Oil Inc *(G-15095)*
Scott Petersen & Company, Lombard Also called Specialty Foods Group LLC *(G-13132)*
Scott Petersen Co, Chicago Also called Specialty Foods Group LLC *(G-6213)*
Scott Sawvel 815 543-4136
  6112 Schaumburg Ln Roscoe (61073) *(G-17932)*
Scott's Popcorn & Company, Chicago Also called Scotts Popcorn LLC *(G-6121)*
Scotts Company LLC 815 467-1605
  23580 W Bluff Rd Channahon (60410) *(G-3393)*
Scotts Company LLC 847 777-0700
  700 Eastwood Ln Buffalo Grove (60089) *(G-2597)*
Scotts Exterior Maintenance Co 309 660-3380
  14866 Craig Rd Bloomington (61705) *(G-2092)*
Scotts Popcorn LLC 773 608-9625
  7129 S Euclid Ave Apt 2 Chicago (60649) *(G-6121)*
Scranton Glltte Cmmnctions Inc (PA) 847 391-1000
  3030 W Salt Creek Ln # 201 Arlington Heights (60005) *(G-805)*
Screen Machine Incorporated 847 439-2233
  1025 Criss Cir Elk Grove Village (60007) *(G-9234)*
Screen North Amer Holdings Inc (HQ) 847 870-7400
  5110 Tollview Dr Rolling Meadows (60008) *(G-17774)*
Screen Print Plus Inc 630 236-0260
  8815 Ramm Dr Ste A Naperville (60564) *(G-14985)*
Screen Works, The, Chicago Also called Ops 3 LLC *(G-5683)*
Screentech, Chicago Heights Also called Roeda Signs Inc *(G-6772)*
Screw Machine Engrg Co Inc 773 631-7600
  6425 N Avondale Ave Chicago (60631) *(G-6122)*
Screws Industries Inc 630 539-9200
  301 High Grove Blvd Glendale Heights (60139) *(G-10493)*
Scribe International Division, Bensenville Also called Singer Data Products Inc *(G-1893)*
Scribes Inc 630 654-3800
  7725 S Grant St Ste 1 Burr Ridge (60527) *(G-2718)*
Scrollex Corporation 630 887-8817
  7888 S Quincy St Willowbrook (60527) *(G-21059)*
Scs Absorbent Mfg Inc 502 417-1365
  1086 S Market St Monticello (61856) *(G-14285)*
Scs Company 708 269-2094
  13633 Crestview Ct Crestwood (60418) *(G-7126)*
Sct Alternative Inc 847 215-7488
  1655 Barclay Blvd Buffalo Grove (60089) *(G-2598)*
Scuba Optics Inc 815 625-7272
  1405 8th Ave Rock Falls (61071) *(G-17195)*
Scuba Sports Inc 217 787-3483
  1609 S Macarthur Blvd Springfield (62704) *(G-19440)*
Scv Floorsmith 661 476-5034
  720 Durham Ln Hoffman Estates (60169) *(G-11455)*
Sdb Products, Round Lake Park Also called Small Different Better Inc *(G-18098)*
Sdr Corp 773 638-1800
  4350 W Ohio St Chicago (60624) *(G-6123)*
SE Relays LLC (HQ) 847 441-2540
  200 N Martingale Rd # 100 Schaumburg (60173) *(G-18710)*
SE Steel Inc (PA) 847 350-9618
  43160 N Crawford Rd Antioch (60002) *(G-634)*
Sea Converting Inc 630 694-9178
  895 Sivert Dr Wood Dale (60191) *(G-21238)*
Sea Horse Blinds, Chicago Also called 21st Century Us-Sino Services *(G-3464)*
Sea-Rich Corp 773 261-6633
  5000 W Roosevelt Rd # 104 Chicago (60644) *(G-6124)*

Seabee Supply Co 630 860-1293
  390 E Irving Park Rd Wood Dale (60191) *(G-21239)*
Seaco Data Systems Inc 630 876-2169
  1360 Rolling Oaks Dr Carol Stream (60188) *(G-3066)*
Seadog 773 235-8100
  1500 W Division St Chicago (60642) *(G-6125)*
Seaga Manufacturing Inc (PA) 815 297-9500
  700 Seaga Dr Freeport (61032) *(G-10141)*
Seal Jet Unlimited, Lansing Also called Seals & Components Inc *(G-12514)*
Sealco Industries Inc (PA) 847 741-3101
  1591 Fleetwood Dr Elgin (60123) *(G-8725)*
Sealed Air Corporation 708 352-8700
  7110 Santa Fe Dr Hodgkins (60525) *(G-11396)*
Sealmaster, Rockford Also called Thorworks Industries Inc *(G-17662)*
Sealmaster Inc 847 480-7325
  425 Huehl Rd Bldg 11b Northbrook (60062) *(G-15478)*
Sealmaster Industries, Streamwood Also called JB Enterprises II Inc *(G-19579)*
Sealmaster/Alsip 708 489-0900
  5844 W 117th Pl Alsip (60803) *(G-509)*
Seals & Components Inc 708 895-5222
  17955 Chappel Ave Lansing (60438) *(G-12514)*
Sealtec 630 692-0633
  1551 Aucutt Rd Montgomery (60538) *(G-14268)*
Sealtech, Montgomery Also called Dqm Inc *(G-14243)*
Sealy Mattress Company 630 879-8011
  1030 E Fabyan Pkwy Batavia (60510) *(G-1415)*
Seamcraft International LLC 773 281-5150
  5610 W Bloomingdale Ave # 4 Chicago (60639) *(G-6126)*
Seamless Gutter Corp 630 495-9800
  601 E Saint Charles Rd Lombard (60148) *(G-13128)*
Sean Matthew Innovations Inc 815 455-4525
  314 Lorraine Dr Crystal Lake (60012) *(G-7261)*
Seaport Digital LLC 847 235-2319
  112 Terrace Dr Mundelein (60060) *(G-14734)*
Seaquist Closures LLC 262 363-7191
  265 Exchange Dr Ste 30 Crystal Lake (60014) *(G-7262)*
Seasonal Designs Inc (PA) 847 688-0280
  1595 S Shields Dr Waukegan (60085) *(G-20493)*
Seasonal Magnets 708 499-3235
  3133 W 102nd St Evergreen Park (60805) *(G-9600)*
Seastar Solutions, Litchfield Also called Marine Acquisition Corp *(G-12973)*
Seat Cover Pro LLC 847 990-1506
  100 N Fairway Dr Ste 106 Vernon Hills (60061) *(G-20094)*
Seat Trans Inc 224 522-1007
  620 Joseph St Lake In The Hills (60156) *(G-12343)*
Seba Signs and Printing, Oak Lawn Also called Biron Studio General Svcs Inc *(G-15703)*
Sebens Backhoe Service Inc 217 762-7365
  903 Madison St Monticello (61856) *(G-14286)*
Sebis Direct Inc (PA) 312 243-9300
  6516 W 74th St Bedford Park (60638) *(G-1504)*
SEC Design Technologies Inc 847 680-0439
  1800 Tempel Dr Libertyville (60048) *(G-12704)*
Secon Rubber and Plastics Inc (PA) 618 282-7700
  240 Kaskaskia Dr Red Bud (62278) *(G-17001)*
Second Chance Inc 630 904-5955
  5320 Switch Grass Ln Naperville (60564) *(G-14986)*
Second City Flooring LLC 973 262-3272
  365 N Jefferson St # 2911 Chicago (60661) *(G-6127)*
Second City Prints 630 504-2423
  1521 Hubbard Ave Batavia (60510) *(G-1416)*
Secretary of State Illinois 217 466-5220
  714 Grandview St Paris (61944) *(G-16243)*
Secretary of State Illinois 708 388-9199
  14434 Pulaski Rd Midlothian (60445) *(G-13995)*
Sectional Snow Plow 815 932-7569
  101 N Euclid Ave Bradley (60915) *(G-2291)*
Secure Data Inc 618 726-5225
  640 Pierce Blvd Ste 200 O Fallon (62269) *(G-15583)*
Securecom Inc 219 314-4537
  3338 E 170th St Lansing (60438) *(G-12515)*
Secureslice Inc 800 984-0494
  6300 N Rockwell St Chicago (60659) *(G-6128)*
Security Holdings LLC 309 856-6000
  212 E 1st St Kewanee (61443) *(G-12041)*
Security Locknut LLC 847 970-4050
  999 Forest Edge Dr Vernon Hills (60061) *(G-20095)*
Security Metal Products Corp 630 965-6355
  1741 Kelley Ln Hampshire (60140) *(G-10987)*
Security Metal Products Inc 815 933-3307
  101 Lawn St Bradley (60915) *(G-2292)*
Security Molding Inc 630 543-8607
  255 W Factory Rd Addison (60101) *(G-283)*
Security Systems Group, University Park Also called Federal Signal Corporation *(G-19954)*
Sedecal Usa Inc (HQ) 847 394-6960
  3190 N Kennicott Ave Arlington Heights (60004) *(G-806)*
Sedia Systems Inc (PA) 312 212-8010
  1820 W Hubbard St Ste 300 Chicago (60622) *(G-6129)*
Sedona Inc (HQ) 309 736-4104
  612 Valley View Dr Moline (61265) *(G-14176)*

Sedona Group, The, Moline *Also called Sedona Inc* ***(G-14176)***
See All Industries Inc (PA) 773 927-3232
3623 S Laflin Pl Chicago (60609) ***(G-6130)***
See What You Send Inc 781 780-1483
727 S Dearborn St Apt 912 Chicago (60605) ***(G-6131)***
Seec Trasportation Corp 800 215-4003
190 S Lasalle Ste 2100 Chicago (60603) ***(G-6132)***
Seedburo Equipment Company 312 738-3700
2293 S Mount Prospect Rd Des Plaines (60018) ***(G-7840)***
Seek Design 312 804-6629
1914 Darrow Ave Evanston (60201) ***(G-9574)***
Seek Sustainable Designs, Evanston *Also called Seek Design* ***(G-9574)***
Segerdahl Corp (PA) 847 541-1080
1351 Wheeling Rd Wheeling (60090) ***(G-20979)***
Segerdahl Corp 630 754-7104
401 E South Frontage Rd Bolingbrook (60440) ***(G-2235)***
Segerdahl Corp 847 850-8811
385 Gilman Ave Wheeling (60090) ***(G-20980)***
Segerdahl Graphics Inc 847 541-1080
1351 Wheeling Rd Wheeling (60090) ***(G-20981)***
Seginus Inc 630 800-2795
114 Kirkland Cir Ste B Oswego (60543) ***(G-16025)***
SEI, Bartlett *Also called Senior Holdings Inc* ***(G-1309)***
Seidel Diesel Group 877 373-6659
1 Seidel Ct Bolingbrook (60490) ***(G-2236)***
Seifferts Locker & Meat Proc 618 594-3921
1370 Fairfax St Carlyle (62231) ***(G-2895)***
Seifferts Meat Proc & Lckr, Carlyle *Also called Seifferts Locker & Meat Proc* ***(G-2895)***
Seigles Cabinet Center LLC (PA) 224 535-7034
1331 Davis Rd Elgin (60123) ***(G-8726)***
Seip Service & Supply Inc 618 532-1923
221 E Broadway Ste 101 Centralia (62801) ***(G-3250)***
Sejasmi Corp 586 725-5300
30 N River Rd Ste 102 Des Plaines (60016) ***(G-7841)***
Sek Corporation (PA) 630 762-0606
3925 Stern Ave Saint Charles (60174) ***(G-18268)***
Selah USA Inc 847 758-0702
1501 Jarvis Ave Elk Grove Village (60007) ***(G-9235)***
Selby Implement Company, Quincy *Also called David Taylor* ***(G-16875)***
Selco Industries 708 499-1060
6655 Kitty Ave Chicago Ridge (60415) ***(G-6810)***
Select Screen Prints & EMB 309 829-6511
112 Southgate Dr Bloomington (61704) ***(G-2093)***
Select Snacks Company Inc 773 933-2167
825 E 99th St Chicago (60628) ***(G-6133)***
Select Tool & Die Inc 630 372-0300
1261 Humbracht Cir Ste F Bartlett (60103) ***(G-1308)***
Select Tool & Die Inc 630 980-8458
324 Pinecroft Dr Roselle (60172) ***(G-17986)***
Selective Label & Tabs Inc 630 466-0091
1962 Us Rte 30 Sugar Grove (60554) ***(G-19654)***
Selective Label & Tabs Inc 630 466-0091
1962 W Us Highway 30 Sugar Grove (60554) ***(G-19655)***
Selective Plating Inc 630 543-1380
240 S Lombard Rd Addison (60101) ***(G-284)***
Selee Corporation 847 428-4455
24 W End Dr Gilberts (60136) ***(G-10371)***
Self Pro Motions LLC 847 749-6077
448 E 134th St Chicago (60827) ***(G-6134)***
Self-Cleaning Strainer Co, Elburn *Also called Mity Inc* ***(G-8461)***
Selig S LLC 815 785-2100
342 E Wabash Ave Forrest (61741) ***(G-9735)***
Selig Sealing Holdings Inc (HQ) 815 785-2100
342 E Wabash Ave Forrest (61741) ***(G-9736)***
Selig Sealing Products Inc (HQ) 815 785-2100
342 E Wabash Ave Forrest (61741) ***(G-9737)***
Sellers Commerce LLC 858 345-1212
633 Skokie Blvd Ste 490 Northbrook (60062) ***(G-15479)***
Selnar Inc 309 699-3977
240 Farmdale Rd East Peoria (61611) ***(G-8290)***
Selrok Inc 630 876-8322
1151 Atlantic Dr Ste 2 West Chicago (60185) ***(G-20640)***
Selvaggio Orna & Strl Stl Inc 217 528-4077
1119 W Dorlan Ave Springfield (62702) ***(G-19441)***
Selvaggio Steel, Springfield *Also called Selvaggio Orna & Strl Stl Inc* ***(G-19441)***
Sem Minerals LP (PA) 217 224-8766
3806 Gardner Expy Quincy (62305) ***(G-16944)***
Semblex Corporation 630 833-2880
370 W Carol Ln Elmhurst (60126) ***(G-9425)***
Semler Industries Inc 847 671-5650
3800 Carnation St Franklin Park (60131) ***(G-10046)***
Semper FI Printing LLC 847 640-7737
2420 E Oakton St Ste Q Arlington Heights (60005) ***(G-807)***
Semper/Exeter Paper Company, Bloomingdale *Also called Cellmark Inc* ***(G-1984)***
Senario LLC 847 882-0677
1325 Remington Rd Ste H Schaumburg (60173) ***(G-18711)***
Sendele Wireless Solutions 815 227-4212
1475 Temple Cir Rockford (61108) ***(G-17624)***
Sendra Service Corp 815 462-0061
309 Garnet Dr New Lenox (60451) ***(G-15058)***
Seneca Custom Cabinetry 815 357-1322
2957 Us Highway 6 Seneca (61360) ***(G-18861)***
Seneca Foods Corporation 309 385-4301
606 S Tremont St Princeville (61559) ***(G-16829)***
Seneca Foods Corporation 309 545-2233
7757 Airport Rd Manito (61546) ***(G-13439)***
Seneca Petroleum Co Inc (PA) 708 396-1100
13301 Cicero Ave Crestwood (60418) ***(G-7127)***
Seneca Petroleum Co Inc 630 257-2268
12460 New Ave Lemont (60439) ***(G-12589)***
Seneca Rebuild LLC (HQ) 618 435-9445
11550 N Thompsonville Rd Macedonia (62860) ***(G-13317)***
Seneca Sand & Gravel LLC 630 746-9183
2962 N 2553rd Rd Seneca (61360) ***(G-18862)***
Senior Automotive, Bartlett *Also called Senior PLC* ***(G-1312)***
Senior Care Pharmacy LLC 847 579-0093
1630 Old Deerfield Rd # 202 Highland Park (60035) ***(G-11297)***
Senior Holdings Inc (HQ) 630 837-1811
300 E Devon Ave Bartlett (60103) ***(G-1309)***
Senior News & Time For Ill 217 528-1882
1000 N 1st St Springfield (62702) ***(G-19442)***
Senior Operations LLC 630 837-1811
300 E Devon Ave Bartlett (60103) ***(G-1310)***
Senior Operations LLC (HQ) 630 372-3500
300 E Devon Ave Bartlett (60103) ***(G-1311)***
Senior PLC 630 372-3511
300 E Devon Ave Bartlett (60103) ***(G-1312)***
Senju Comtek Corp 847 549-5690
1322 Armour Blvd Mundelein (60060) ***(G-14735)***
Senn Enterprises Inc (PA) 309 637-1147
1309 W Main St Peoria (61606) ***(G-16519)***
Senn Enterprises Inc 309 673-4384
1829 W Main St Peoria (61606) ***(G-16520)***
Senna Design LLC 847 821-7877
100 Corporate Woods Pkwy Vernon Hills (60061) ***(G-20096)***
Sennco Solutions Inc 815 577-3400
14407 Coil Plus Dr # 101 Plainfield (60544) ***(G-16713)***
Senoplast USA 630 898-0731
75 Executive Dr Ste 129 Aurora (60504) ***(G-1016)***
Sensible Designs Online Inc 708 267-8924
10556 Great Egret Dr Orland Park (60467) ***(G-15978)***
Sensible Products Inc 773 774-7400
7290 W Devon Ave Chicago (60631) ***(G-6135)***
Sensient Flavors 847 645-7002
5115 Sedge Blvd Hoffman Estates (60192) ***(G-11456)***
Sensient Flavors LLC (HQ) 317 243-3521
2800 W Higgins Rd Ste 900 Hoffman Estates (60169) ***(G-11457)***
Sensient Flavors LLC 815 857-3691
25 E Main St Amboy (61310) ***(G-580)***
Sensient Technologies Corp 708 481-0910
810 Carnation Ln Matteson (60443) ***(G-13628)***
Sensio America LLC 877 501-5337
270 Tubeway Dr Carol Stream (60188) ***(G-3067)***
Sensor 21 Inc 847 561-6233
19541 W University Dr Mundelein (60060) ***(G-14736)***
Sensor Synergy 847 353-8200
200 N Fairway Dr Ste 198 Vernon Hills (60061) ***(G-20097)***
Sensormedics Corporation (HQ) 872 757-0114
26125 N Riverwoods Blvd Mettawa (60045) ***(G-13982)***
Sensus LLC 312 379-9463
1435 W Arthur Ave Ste B Chicago (60626) ***(G-6136)***
Sensus Wine, Chicago *Also called Sensus LLC* ***(G-6136)***
Sentinel Emrgncy Solutions LLC (PA) 618 539-3863
502 S Richland St Freeburg (62243) ***(G-10093)***
Sentro Printing Equip N Movers 779 423-0255
332 Harwich Pl Rockton (61072) ***(G-17701)***
Sentry Pool & Chemical Supply 309 797-9721
1529 46th Ave Ste 1 Moline (61265) ***(G-14177)***
Sentry Seasonings Inc 630 530-5370
928 N Church Rd Elmhurst (60126) ***(G-9426)***
Seoclarity 773 831-4500
2800 S River Rd Ste 290 Des Plaines (60018) ***(G-7842)***
Sepire LLC 312 965-2500
7600 S Grant St Ste 2 Burr Ridge (60527) ***(G-2719)***
Septic Solutions Inc 217 925-5992
314 W Center St Dieterich (62424) ***(G-7878)***
Serac Inc (HQ) 630 510-9343
160 E Elk Trl Carol Stream (60188) ***(G-3068)***
Seraph Industries LLC 815 222-9686
1175 Krupke Rd Caledonia (61011) ***(G-2771)***
Serbian Yellow Pages Inc 847 588-0555
7400 N Waukegan Rd # 210 Niles (60714) ***(G-15169)***
Sereen Boats, Rockford *Also called Sereen LLC* ***(G-17625)***
Sereen LLC 386 527-4876
4543 Sable Ln Rockford (61109) ***(G-17625)***
Serene One LLC 630 285-1500
1251 Ardmore Ave Itasca (60143) ***(G-11731)***

Sergio Barajas 708 238-7614
205 Washington Ave La Grange (60525) *(G-12089)*
Serien Manufacturing Inc 815 337-1447
900 S Eastwood Dr Woodstock (60098) *(G-21431)*
Serionix Inc 651 503-3930
730 W Killarney St Urbana (61801) *(G-20000)*
Serious Energy Inc 312 515-4606
1333 N Hickory Ave Chicago (60642) *(G-6137)*
Seritex Inc 201 755-3002
1052 W Republic Dr Addison (60101) *(G-285)*
Serlin Iron & Metal Co Inc 773 227-3826
1810 N Kilbourn Ave Chicago (60639) *(G-6138)*
Serola Biomechanics Inc 815 636-2780
5406 Forest Hills Ct Loves Park (61111) *(G-13263)*
Serra Laser Precision LLC 847 367-0282
2400 Commerce Dr Libertyville (60048) *(G-12705)*
Serrala Solutions US Corp (PA) 650 655-3939
205 N Michigan Ave # 4110 Chicago (60601) *(G-6139)*
Serta Mattress Co, Hoffman Estates *Also called Royal Bedding Company Inc (G-11451)*
Sertech, Batavia *Also called CCL Label (chicago) Inc (G-1363)*
Serv-All Die & Tool Company 815 459-2900
110 Erick St Crystal Lake (60014) *(G-7263)*
Servetech Water Solutions Inc 630 784-9050
112 W Liberty Dr Wheaton (60187) *(G-20823)*
Servi-Sure Corporation 773 271-5900
2020 W Rascher Ave Chicago (60625) *(G-6140)*
Service & Manufacturing Corp 773 287-5500
5414c W Roosevelt Rd C Chicago (60644) *(G-6141)*
Service Auto Supply 309 444-9704
101 N Wood St Washington (61571) *(G-20280)*
Service Center, Alsip *Also called Uesco Industries Inc (G-517)*
Service Cutting & Welding 773 622-8366
2911 N Moody Ave Chicago (60634) *(G-6142)*
Service Envelope Corporation 847 559-0004
1925 Holste Rd Northbrook (60062) *(G-15480)*
Service Industries, LLC, Rolling Meadows *Also called Thomas Packaging LLC (G-17779)*
Service Machine Company Inc 815 654-2310
6205 Material Ave Loves Park (61111) *(G-13264)*
Service Machine Jobs 815 986-3033
1308 Barnes St Rockford (61104) *(G-17626)*
Service Metal Enterprises 630 628-1444
915 W National Ave Addison (60101) *(G-286)*
Service Packaging Design Inc 847 966-6592
6238 Lincoln Ave Morton Grove (60053) *(G-14440)*
Service Pallet LLC 708 458-9100
500 Overland Dr North Aurora (60542) *(G-15274)*
Service Printing Corporation 847 669-9620
11960 Oak Creek Pkwy Huntley (60142) *(G-11566)*
Service Pro Electric Mtr Repr 630 766-1215
690 Industrial Dr Bensenville (60106) *(G-1892)*
Service Sheet Metal Works Inc 773 229-0031
5000 W 73rd St Chicago (60638) *(G-6143)*
Service Stampings of IL Inc 630 894-7880
251 Central Ave Roselle (60172) *(G-17987)*
Service Steel Division, East Moline *Also called Van Pelt Corporation (G-8246)*
Servicenow Inc 630 963-4608
2001 Butterfield Rd # 240 Downers Grove (60515) *(G-8092)*
Sesame Solutions LLC 630 427-3400
279 Beaudin Blvd Bolingbrook (60440) *(G-2237)*
Seshin USA Inc 847 550-5556
333 Enterprise Pkwy Lake Zurich (60047) *(G-12456)*
Sesser Concrete Products Co 618 625-2811
910 S Cockrum St Sesser (62884) *(G-18866)*
Set Screw & Mfg Co 847 717-3700
1210 Saint Charles St Elgin (60120) *(G-8727)*
Sethness Caramel Color, Skokie *Also called Sethness Products Company (G-19028)*
Sethness Products Company (HQ) 847 329-2080
3422 W Touhy Ave Ste 1 Skokie (60076) *(G-19028)*
Settima Usa Inc 630 812-1433
1555 N Mittel Blvd Ste A Wood Dale (60191) *(G-21240)*
Severstal US Holdings II Inc (HQ) 708 756-0400
907 N Elm St Ste 100 Hinsdale (60521) *(G-11379)*
Sew Wright Embroidery Inc 309 691-5780
7810 N University St Peoria (61614) *(G-16521)*
Sewer Equipment Co America 815 835-5566
1590 Dutch Rd Dixon (61021) *(G-7917)*
Sewer Equipment of Canada, Dixon *Also called Sewer Equipment Co America (G-7917)*
Sextant Company 847 680-6550
433 Inverness Dr Gurnee (60031) *(G-10926)*
Sexton Wind Power LLC 224 212-1250
49 Sherwood Ter Ste A Lake Bluff (60044) *(G-12209)*
Seymour of Sycamore Inc (PA) 815 895-9101
917 Crosby Ave Sycamore (60178) *(G-19730)*
SF Contracting LLC 618 926-1477
1030 Hamburg Rd Raleigh (62977) *(G-16963)*
SF Holdings Group LLC 630 543-6682
39 W Official Rd Addison (60101) *(G-287)*
Sfc Chemicals Ltd 847 221-2152
1031 W Bryn Mawr Ave 1a Chicago (60660) *(G-6144)*
Sfc of Illinois Inc 815 745-2100
400 S Railroad St Warren (61087) *(G-20224)*
Sg Screen Graphics Inc 309 699-8513
840 Kennedy Dr Pekin (61554) *(G-16360)*
Sg2 847 779-5500
5250 Old Orchard Rd # 700 Skokie (60077) *(G-19029)*
Sg360, Wheeling *Also called Segerdahl Corp (G-20979)*
Sg360, Wheeling *Also called Segerdahl Corp (G-20980)*
Sg360 A Segerdahl Company 847 465-3368
1990 S 25th Ave Broadview (60155) *(G-2468)*
SGC Horizon LLC 847 391-1000
3030 W Salt Creek Ln Arlington Heights (60005) *(G-808)*
Sge Group, The, Chicago *Also called Deshamusic Inc (G-4344)*
Shaars International Inc 815 315-0717
129 Phelps Ave Ste 901a Rockford (61108) *(G-17627)*
Shade Aire Company 815 623-7597
7511 Grace Dr Roscoe (61073) *(G-17933)*
Shade Aire Decorating, Roscoe *Also called Shade Aire Company (G-17933)*
Shade Brookline Co 773 274-5513
6246 N Broadway St Chicago (60660) *(G-6145)*
Shade Solutions Inc 217 239-0718
1102 County Road 900 N Tolono (61880) *(G-19884)*
Shademaker Products Corp 773 955-0998
7300 S Kimbark Ave Chicago (60619) *(G-6146)*
Shading Solutions Group Inc 630 444-2102
1770 S Randall Rd A172 Geneva (60134) *(G-10305)*
Shadowtech Labs Inc 630 413-4478
760 N Frontage Rd Ste 102 Willowbrook (60527) *(G-21060)*
Shady Creek Vineyard Inc 847 275-7979
1238 N Wellington Dr Palatine (60067) *(G-16157)*
Shakthi Solar Inc 630 842-0893
590 Territorial Dr Ste B Bolingbrook (60440) *(G-2238)*
Shale Lake LLC 618 637-2470
1499 Washington Ave Staunton (62088) *(G-19478)*
Shamrock Labels, Bellwood *Also called Shamrock Scientific (G-1638)*
Shamrock Manufacturing Co Inc 708 331-7776
15920 Suntone Dr South Holland (60473) *(G-19244)*
Shamrock Plastics Inc 309 243-7723
2615 Alta Ln Peoria (61615) *(G-16522)*
Shamrock Scientific 800 323-0249
34 Davis Dr Bellwood (60104) *(G-1638)*
Shamrock Specialty Packaging, Elgin *Also called Quad-Illinois Inc (G-8706)*
Shand & Jurs, Hillside *Also called Gpe Controls Inc (G-11340)*
Shaner Quality Machining Inc 815 985-7209
4935 28th Ave Rockford (61109) *(G-17628)*
Shanin Company 847 676-1200
6454 N Kimball Ave Lincolnwood (60712) *(G-12843)*
Shank Precision Machine Co, Cicero *Also called Cyrus Shank Company (G-6838)*
Shanks Veterinary Equipment 815 225-7700
505 E Old Mill St Milledgeville (61051) *(G-14040)*
Shannon & Sons Welding 630 898-7778
1218 E New York St Aurora (60505) *(G-1155)*
Shannon & Sons Welding Shop, Aurora *Also called Shannon & Sons Welding (G-1155)*
Shannon Industrial Corporation (PA) 815 337-2349
2041 Dillard Ct Woodstock (60098) *(G-21432)*
Shannon Industries Inc 815 338-8960
114 S Shannon Dr Woodstock (60098) *(G-21433)*
Shapco Inc 847 229-1439
602 Wheeling Rd Wheeling (60090) *(G-20982)*
Shape Master Inc 217 582-2638
108 E Main St Ogden (61859) *(G-15838)*
Shape Master Inc 217 469-7027
704 E Lincoln St Saint Joseph (61873) *(G-18320)*
Shape-Master Tool Co 815 522-6186
801 W Main St Kirkland (60146) *(G-12065)*
Shapiro Bros of Illinois Inc 618 244-3168
510 S 6th St Mount Vernon (62864) *(G-14638)*
Share Machine Inc 630 906-1810
2175 Rochester Dr Ste C Aurora (60506) *(G-1156)*
Sharlen Electric Co (PA) 773 721-0700
9101 S Baltimore Ave Chicago (60617) *(G-6147)*
Sharn Enterprises Inc 815 464-9715
540 Aberdeen Rd Frankfort (60423) *(G-9838)*
Sharp Defense LLC 630 205-3502
226 Wing Park Blvd Elgin (60123) *(G-8728)*
Sharp Metal Products 847 439-5393
140 Joey Dr Elk Grove Village (60007) *(G-9236)*
Sharp Trading, Niles *Also called D & J International Inc (G-15115)*
Sharpedge Solutions Inc 630 792-9639
2728 Forgue Dr Ste 106 Naperville (60564) *(G-14987)*
Sharper Image Engravers Inc 630 403-1600
261 Eisenhower Ln S Lombard (60148) *(G-13129)*
Sharprint Promotional Apparel, Chicago *Also called Sharprint Slkscrn & Grphcs (G-6148)*
Sharprint Slkscrn & Grphcs 877 649-2554
4200 W Wrightwood Ave Chicago (60639) *(G-6148)*
Shartega Systems, Chicago *Also called Synergy Technology Group Inc (G-6303)*
Shattuc Cord Specialties Inc 847 360-9500
2340 Ernie Krueger Cir Waukegan (60087) *(G-20494)*

ALPHABETIC

Shaw Contract Group, Chicago *Also called Shaw Industries Group Inc* ***(G-6149)***
Shaw Industries..........847 844-9190
2410 Galvin Dr Elgin (60124) ***(G-8729)***
Shaw Industries Group Inc..........312 467-1331
222 Merchandise Mart Plz Chicago (60654) ***(G-6149)***
Shaw Media, Joliet *Also called Joliet Herald Newspaper* ***(G-11886)***
Shaw Suburban Media Group Inc..........815 459-4040
7717 S Il Route 31 Crystal Lake (60014) ***(G-7264)***
Shawcraft Sign Co..........815 282-4105
7727 Burden Rd Machesney Park (61115) ***(G-13374)***
Shawnee Exploration Partners..........618 382-3223
115 Smith St Carmi (62821) ***(G-2915)***
Shawnee Grapevines LLC..........618 893-9463
5100 Wing Hill Rd Cobden (62920) ***(G-6943)***
Shawnee Stone LLC (PA)..........618 548-1585
202 W Main St Salem (62881) ***(G-18359)***
Shawnee Stone LLC..........618 833-2323
1275 Jonesboro Quarry Rd Anna (62906) ***(G-588)***
Shawnee Winery..........618 658-8400
200 Commercial St Vienna (62995) ***(G-20119)***
Shawnimals LLC..........312 235-2625
2825 W Wellington Ave 1 Chicago (60618) ***(G-6150)***
Shawver Press Inc (PA)..........815 772-4700
120 E Lincolnway Morrison (61270) ***(G-14348)***
Shay Mine No. 1, Carlinville *Also called Macoupin Energy LLC* ***(G-2881)***
Sheas Iron Works Inc..........847 356-2922
735 N Milwaukee Ave A Lake Villa (60046) ***(G-12367)***
Shedrain Corporation..........708 848-5212
715 Lake St Ste 269 Oak Park (60301) ***(G-15772)***
Sheer Graphics Inc..........630 654-4422
47 Chestnut Ave Westmont (60559) ***(G-20772)***
Sheet Metal Connectors Inc..........815 874-4600
5601 Sandy Hollow Rd Rockford (61109) ***(G-17629)***
Sheet Metal Supply Ltd..........847 478-8500
150 Pine St Grayslake (60030) ***(G-10799)***
Sheet Metal Werks Inc (PA)..........847 827-4700
455 E Algonquin Rd Arlington Heights (60005) ***(G-809)***
Shelby Tool & Die Inc..........217 774-2189
813 W South 5th St Shelbyville (62565) ***(G-18886)***
Shelbyville Daily Union, Effingham *Also called Cnhi LLC* ***(G-8391)***
Shell Oil Company..........618 254-7371
200 E Lorena Ave Wood River (62095) ***(G-21267)***
Shell Oil Products U S, Chicago *Also called Equilon Enterprises LLC* ***(G-4523)***
Shelter Systems..........773 281-9270
3729 N Ravenswood Ave Chicago (60613) ***(G-6151)***
Shelving and Bath Unlimited..........815 378-3328
4337 S Perryville Rd # 103 Cherry Valley (61016) ***(G-3446)***
Shenglong Intl Group Corp..........312 388-2345
1939 Waukegan Rd Ste 205 Glenview (60025) ***(G-10615)***
Shepard Medical Products Inc..........630 539-7790
675 E Irving Park Rd # 201 Roselle (60172) ***(G-17988)***
Sheraton Road Lumber..........309 691-0858
6600 N Sheridan Rd Peoria (61614) ***(G-16523)***
Sherman Media Company Inc..........312 335-1962
222 E Wisconsin Ave Ste 7 Lake Forest (60045) ***(G-12302)***
Sherman Plastics Corp (PA)..........630 369-6170
1650 Shore Rd Naperville (60563) ***(G-14913)***
Shermar Industries LLC..........847 378-8073
1245 S Leslie Ln Des Plaines (60018) ***(G-7843)***
Shertwinz Inc..........630 886-5681
1212 S Naper Blvd Ste 119 Naperville (60540) ***(G-14914)***
Sherwin Industries Inc..........815 234-8007
149 S Fox Run Ln Byron (61010) ***(G-2758)***
Sherwin-Williams Company..........847 251-6115
614 Green Bay Rd Kenilworth (60043) ***(G-12015)***
Sherwin-Williams Company..........847 573-0240
1618 S Milwaukee Ave Libertyville (60048) ***(G-12706)***
Sherwin-Williams Company..........217 359-4934
109 E Curtis Rd Savoy (61874) ***(G-18416)***
Sherwin-Williams Company..........630 834-1470
223 N York St Elmhurst (60126) ***(G-9427)***
Sherwin-Williams Company..........618 662-4415
14 Industrial Park Flora (62839) ***(G-9691)***
Sherwin-Williams Company..........847 541-9000
1191 Wheeling Rd Wheeling (60090) ***(G-20983)***
Sherwin-Williams Company..........815 337-0942
631 S Eastwood Dr Woodstock (60098) ***(G-21434)***
Sherwin-Williams Company..........847 478-0677
4194 Il Route 83 Long Grove (60047) ***(G-13170)***
Sherwin-Williams Company..........708 409-4728
10551 W Cermak Rd Westchester (60154) ***(G-20710)***
Sherwin-Williams Company..........815 254-3559
664 S Weber Rd Romeoville (60446) ***(G-17876)***
Sherwin-Williams Company..........773 821-3027
11700 S Cottage Grove Ave Chicago (60628) ***(G-6152)***
Sherwin-Williams Company..........815 987-3700
1215 Nelson Blvd Rockford (61104) ***(G-17630)***
Sherwood Industries Inc..........847 626-0300
7800 N Merrimac Ave Niles (60714) ***(G-15170)***
Sherwood Tool Inc..........815 648-1463
12120 Il Route 173 Hebron (60034) ***(G-11149)***
Shevick Sales Corp..........312 487-2865
5620 W Jarvis Ave Niles (60714) ***(G-15171)***
Shew Brothers Inc..........618 997-4414
812 W Longstreet Rd Marion (62959) ***(G-13534)***
Shews Custom Woodworking..........217 737-5543
1441 1200th St Lincoln (62656) ***(G-12738)***
Shiir LLC..........312 828-0400
208 W Kinzie St Ste 5 Chicago (60654) ***(G-6153)***
Shiir Rugs, Chicago *Also called Shiir LLC* ***(G-6153)***
Shima American Corporation..........630 760-4330
500 Park Blvd Ste 725 Itasca (60143) ***(G-11732)***
Shinn Enterprises..........217 698-3344
3310 W Jefferson St Springfield (62707) ***(G-19443)***
Shipbikes.com, Oak Park *Also called Air Caddy* ***(G-15743)***
Shipbob Inc..........217 819-8539
1260 W Madison St Chicago (60607) ***(G-6154)***
Shipbob Inc (PA)..........844 474-4726
120 N Racine Ave Ste 100 Chicago (60607) ***(G-6155)***
Shipshapes Brands, Park Forest *Also called Imageworks Manufacturing Inc* ***(G-16255)***
Shire Biolife, Bannockburn *Also called Biolife Plasma LLC* ***(G-1197)***
Shire Pharmaceuticals LLC..........224 940-2000
1200 Lakeside Dr Bannockburn (60015) ***(G-1207)***
Shirt Off My Back Cstm Tees MO..........331 999-2399
26 Marnel Rd Montgomery (60538) ***(G-14269)***
Shirt Printing 4u Inc..........708 588-8272
5410 S La Grange Rd Ste 1 Countryside (60525) ***(G-7069)***
Shirt Tales..........309 582-5566
204 Sw 2nd Ave Aledo (61231) ***(G-361)***
Shirts Galore & More..........618 797-9801
4132 Pontoon Rd Granite City (62040) ***(G-10736)***
Sho Pak LLC..........618 876-1597
1226 Bissell St Venice (62090) ***(G-20036)***
Sho Technologies Inc..........217 954-0020
4410 Stonebridge Dr Champaign (61822) ***(G-3346)***
Shockwaves Promotional Apparel, Arlington Heights *Also called G and D Enterprises Inc* ***(G-739)***
Shoelace Inc..........847 854-2500
20505 N Rand Rd Ste 218 Kildeer (60047) ***(G-12053)***
Shoelace Inc (PA)..........847 854-2500
23 N Williams St Crystal Lake (60014) ***(G-7265)***
Shop Espresso Mchs Svcs & Sls, Chicago *Also called Rodger Howard* ***(G-6049)***
Shoppe De Lee Inc..........847 350-0580
2625 American Ln Ste A Elk Grove Village (60007) ***(G-9237)***
Shopper Weekly Publishings, Centralia *Also called Shoppers Weekly Inc* ***(G-3251)***
Shoppers Guide..........815 369-4112
213 S Center St Lena (61048) ***(G-12609)***
Shoppers Planet..........877 232-5435
20915 Cambridge Ln Olympia Fields (60461) ***(G-15898)***
Shoppers Weekly Inc..........618 533-7283
301 E Broadway Centralia (62801) ***(G-3251)***
Shoppertrak Rct Corporation (HQ)..........312 529-5300
233 S Wacker Dr Fl 41 Chicago (60606) ***(G-6156)***
Shoppinggives, Chicago *Also called Niche Interactive Media Inc* ***(G-5596)***
Shopware, Elgin *Also called Angsten Group Inc* ***(G-8511)***
Shore Capital Partners LLC (PA)..........312 348-7580
1 E Wacker Dr Ste 2900 Chicago (60601) ***(G-6157)***
Shoreline Glass Co Inc..........312 829-9500
1 Mth Plz Hillside (60162) ***(G-11356)***
Shoreline Graphics Inc..........847 587-4804
415 Washington St Ingleside (60041) ***(G-11589)***
Shoup Manufacturing Co Inc..........815 933-4439
3 Stuart Dr Kankakee (60901) ***(G-12001)***
Show Off, Roselle *Also called Trim Suits By Show-Off Inc* ***(G-17994)***
Showcase Corporation (PA)..........312 651-3000
233 S Wacker Dr Ste 5150 Chicago (60606) ***(G-6158)***
Shreck Kitchens..........847 695-4154
260 Sundown Rd South Elgin (60177) ***(G-19174)***
Shree Mahavir Inc..........312 408-1080
311 S Wacker Dr Ste 4550 Chicago (60606) ***(G-6159)***
Shree Printing Corp..........773 267-9500
3011 W Irving Park Rd Chicago (60618) ***(G-6160)***
Shuffle Tech International LLC..........312 787-7780
1440 N Kingsbury St # 218 Chicago (60642) ***(G-6161)***
Shulman Brothers Inc..........618 283-3253
101 S 4th St Vandalia (62471) ***(G-20023)***
Shup Tool & Machine Co..........618 931-2596
4158 State Route 162 Granite City (62040) ***(G-10737)***
Shur Co of Illinois..........217 877-8277
3993 E Mueller Ave Decatur (62526) ***(G-7546)***
Shure Elec of Ill Div Shure, Wheeling *Also called Shure Incorporated* ***(G-20984)***
Shure Incorporated..........847 520-4404
995 Chaddick Dr Wheeling (60090) ***(G-20984)***
Shure Products Inc..........773 227-1001
4529 N Ravenswood Ave Chicago (60640) ***(G-6162)***
Shutter Bag USA..........618 967-6247
193 Peachtree Ln Carbondale (62902) ***(G-2858)***

Shutterbooth Specl Evnts By La........618 973-1894
10 Cobblestone Ct Granite City (62040) *(G-10738)*
Shutterview........618 244-0656
9135 N Spring Garden Ln Mount Vernon (62864) *(G-14639)*
Si Enterprises Inc........630 539-9200
301 High Grove Blvd Glendale Heights (60139) *(G-10494)*
Sia, Chicago *Also called Surgical Innovation Assoc Inc (G-6289)*
Sids Well Service........618 375-5411
1007 N Ct Grayville (62844) *(G-10815)*
Sieber Tooling Solutions, Carol Stream *Also called Ergoseal Inc (G-2980)*
Sieber Tooling Solutions Inc........630 462-9370
344 Commerce Dr Carol Stream (60188) *(G-3069)*
Sieden Sticker USA Ltd........312 280-7711
1506 W Grand Ave Apt 3e Chicago (60642) *(G-6163)*
Siegling America, Wood Dale *Also called Forbo Siegling LLC (G-21188)*
Siegwerk Eic LLC........800 728-8200
450 Wegner Dr West Chicago (60185) *(G-20641)*
Sielc Technologies Corporation........847 229-2629
804 Seton Ct Wheeling (60090) *(G-20985)*
Siemens Energy Inc........618 357-6360
4646 White Walnut Rd Pinckneyville (62274) *(G-16619)*
Siemens Hlthcare Dgnostics Inc........847 267-5300
1717 Deerfield Rd Ste 1 Deerfield (60015) *(G-7648)*
Siemens Industry Inc........815 672-2653
810 W Grant St Streator (61364) *(G-19622)*
Siemens Industry Inc........847 520-9084
740 Weidner Rd Apt 203 Buffalo Grove (60089) *(G-2599)*
Siemens Industry Inc (HQ)........847 215-1000
1000 Deerfield Pkwy Buffalo Grove (60089) *(G-2600)*
Siemens Industry Inc........309 664-2460
14 Currency Dr Bloomington (61704) *(G-2094)*
Siemens Industry Inc........847 941-5050
1000 Deerfield Pkwy Buffalo Grove (60089) *(G-2601)*
Siemens Industry Inc........630 444-4316
580 Slawin Ct Saint Charles (60174) *(G-18269)*
Siemens Industry Inc........217 824-6833
1058 E Langleyville Rd Taylorville (62568) *(G-19762)*
Siemens Industry Inc........847 215-1000
887 Deerfield Pkwy Buffalo Grove (60089) *(G-2602)*
Siemens Industry Software Inc........630 437-6700
2001 Butterfield Rd # 630 Downers Grove (60515) *(G-8093)*
Siemens Manufacturing Co Inc (PA)........618 539-3000
410 W Washington St Freeburg (62243) *(G-10094)*
Siemens Manufacturing Co Inc........618 475-3325
500 N Johnson St New Athens (62264) *(G-15021)*
Siemens Med Solutions USA Inc........847 304-7700
2501 N Barrington Rd Schaumburg (60195) *(G-18712)*
Siemens Med Solutions USA Inc........847 304-7700
2501 Barrington Rd Hoffman Estates (60192) *(G-11458)*
Siemens Med Solutions USA Inc........847 793-4429
2500 Millbrook Dr Ste B Buffalo Grove (60089) *(G-2603)*
Siemens Mobility, Buffalo Grove *Also called Siemens Industry Inc (G-2600)*
Siemer Enterprises Inc (PA)........217 857-3171
515 W Main St Teutopolis (62467) *(G-19772)*
Sierra Manufacturing Corp........630 458-8830
480 S Irmen Dr Addison (60101) *(G-288)*
Sierra Pacific Engrg & Pdts, Bolingbrook *Also called SPEP Acquisition Corp (G-2246)*
Sievert Electric Svc & Sls Co........708 771-1600
1230 Hannah Ave Forest Park (60130) *(G-9724)*
Sigan America LLC........815 431-9830
1111 W Mckinley Rd Ottawa (61350) *(G-16076)*
Sigan America Holdings LLC (HQ)........815 431-9830
1111 W Mckinley Rd Ottawa (61350) *(G-16077)*
Sigel Welding........217 844-2412
103 S Main St Sigel (62462) *(G-18907)*
Sigenics Inc (PA)........312 448-8000
3440 S Dearborn St 126s Chicago (60616) *(G-6164)*
Siggs Rigs........847 456-4012
3810 S Oak Knoll Rd Crystal Lake (60012) *(G-7266)*
Sigley Printing & Off Sup Co........618 997-5304
110 N Print Ave Marion (62959) *(G-13535)*
Sigma Coatings Inc........630 628-5305
150 S Church St Ste D Addison (60101) *(G-289)*
Sigma Graphics Inc........815 433-1000
4001 Baker Rd Ottawa (61350) *(G-16078)*
Sigma Tool & Machining........815 874-0500
2324 23rd Ave Rockford (61104) *(G-17631)*
Sigmatron International Inc........847 586-5200
1901 South St Elgin (60123) *(G-8730)*
Sigmatron International Inc (PA)........847 956-8000
2201 Landmeier Rd Elk Grove Village (60007) *(G-9238)*
Sign........630 351-8400
399 Wall St Ste J Glendale Heights (60139) *(G-10495)*
Sign & Banner Express........630 783-9700
540 E Boughton Rd Bolingbrook (60440) *(G-2239)*
Sign A Rama........630 293-7300
946 N Neltnor Blvd # 114 West Chicago (60185) *(G-20642)*
Sign A Rama Inc........630 359-5125
100 E Roosevelt Rd Ste 34 Villa Park (60181) *(G-20172)*
Sign America Inc........773 262-7800
2748 W Devon Ave Chicago (60659) *(G-6165)*
Sign Appeal, Charleston *Also called Rkm Enterprises (G-3411)*
Sign Appeal Inc........847 587-4300
20 E Grand Ave Fox Lake (60020) *(G-9754)*
Sign Authority........630 462-9850
901 W Liberty Dr A Wheaton (60187) *(G-20824)*
Sign Central........847 543-7600
34039 N Hainesville Rd Round Lake (60073) *(G-18083)*
Sign Centre........847 595-7300
2422 Pan Am Blvd Elk Grove Village (60007) *(G-9239)*
Sign City Corp........847 382-3838
28144 W Industrial Ave # 104 Lake Barrington (60010) *(G-12165)*
Sign Contractors........708 795-1761
16w143 Hillside Ln Burr Ridge (60527) *(G-2720)*
Sign Express Inc........708 524-8811
900 S Oak Park Ave Ste 1 Oak Park (60304) *(G-15773)*
Sign Fx........630 466-7446
769 N Heartland Dr Ste E Sugar Grove (60554) *(G-19656)*
Sign Girls Inc........847 336-4002
3608 Grand Ave Ste E Gurnee (60031) *(G-10927)*
Sign Holders Supply, Chicago *Also called Marv-O-Lus Manufacturing Co (G-5353)*
Sign Identity Inc........630 942-1400
415 Taft Ave Ste 1b Glen Ellyn (60137) *(G-10419)*
Sign Max, Schaumburg *Also called CNE Inc (G-18480)*
Sign O Rama........815 744-8702
1107 Essington Rd Joliet (60435) *(G-11930)*
Sign One, Morton Grove *Also called Main Street Visuals Inc (G-14425)*
Sign Outlet Inc........708 824-2222
5516 W Cal Sag Rd Alsip (60803) *(G-510)*
Sign Palace Inc........847 228-7446
68 N Lively Blvd Elk Grove Village (60007) *(G-9240)*
Sign Pro, Quincy *Also called Bick Broadcasting Inc (G-16865)*
Sign Pro of Quincy Inc........217 223-9693
408 N 24th St Quincy (62301) *(G-16945)*
Sign Shop Express........630 964-3500
1015 Maple Ave Ste 1 Downers Grove (60515) *(G-8094)*
Sign Solutions........618 443-6565
1255 W Broadway St Sparta (62286) *(G-19259)*
Sign Team Inc........309 302-0017
5417 180th St N East Moline (61244) *(G-8240)*
Sign-A-Rama, West Chicago *Also called Sign A Rama (G-20642)*
Sign-A-Rama, Gurnee *Also called Sign Girls Inc (G-10927)*
Sign-A-Rama, Grayslake *Also called Signarama (G-10800)*
Sign-A-Rama, Naperville *Also called P N K Ventures Inc (G-14891)*
Sign-A-Rama, Romeoville *Also called Zainab Enterprises Inc (G-17891)*
Sign-A-Rama, Glendale Heights *Also called Sign (G-10495)*
Sign-A-Rama, Skokie *Also called Mark Collins (G-18983)*
Sign-A-Rama, Schaumburg *Also called Cacini Inc (G-18466)*
Sign-A-Rama, Countryside *Also called Vinyl Graphics Inc (G-7077)*
Sign-A-Rama, Lansing *Also called Quick Quality Printing Inc (G-12513)*
Sign-A-Rama, Villa Park *Also called Sign A Rama Inc (G-20172)*
Sign-A-Rama........312 922-0509
1513 S State St Chicago (60605) *(G-6166)*
Sign-A-Rama of Buffalo Grove........847 215-1535
352 Lexington Dr Buffalo Grove (60089) *(G-2604)*
Signa Development Group Inc (PA)........773 418-4506
4641 N Oriole Ave Norridge (60706) *(G-15243)*
Signa Group Inc (PA)........847 386-7639
540 W Frontage Rd # 2105 Northfield (60093) *(G-15529)*
Signal, Chicago *Also called Message Mediums LLC (G-5403)*
Signal Digital Inc (PA)........312 685-1911
222 N La Salle St # 1600 Chicago (60601) *(G-6167)*
Signal Graphics Printing, Mundelein *Also called Sphere Inc (G-14738)*
Signal Lighting Operations, Salem *Also called North American Lighting Inc (G-18348)*
SIGNAL PRESS DIVISION, Evanston *Also called Christian National Womans (G-9505)*
Signalmasters Inc........708 534-3330
26120 S Governors Hwy Monee (60449) *(G-14208)*
Signarama........847 543-4870
888 E Belvidere Rd # 408 Grayslake (60030) *(G-10800)*
Signarama Bolingbrook, Romeoville *Also called Reynolds Holdings Inc (G-17869)*
Signarama Skokie, Skokie *Also called All Signs Inc (G-18914)*
Signature Design & Tailoring........773 375-4915
8027 S Stony Island Ave Chicago (60617) *(G-6168)*
Signature Innovations LLC........847 758-9600
1171 Landmeier Rd Elk Grove Village (60007) *(G-9241)*
Signature Label of Illinois........618 283-5145
2025 N 8th St Vandalia (62471) *(G-20024)*
Signature of Chicago Inc........630 271-1876
8428 Brookridge Rd Downers Grove (60516) *(G-8095)*
Signature Screen Printing Corp........773 866-0070
3508 N Elston Ave Chicago (60618) *(G-6169)*
Signcraft Screenprint Inc........815 777-3030
100 A J Harle Dr Galena (61036) *(G-10178)*
Signcrafters Enterprises Inc........815 648-4484
10714 Il Route 47 Hebron (60034) *(G-11150)*

ALPHABETIC

Signet Sign Company 630 830-8242
608 White Oak Ln Bartlett (60103) ***(G-1313)***
Signify North America Corp 708 307-3000
440 Medinah Rd Roselle (60172) ***(G-17989)***
Signkraft Co 217 787-7105
1215 W Miller St Springfield (62702) ***(G-19444)***
Signode, Bridgeview *Also called Illinois Tool Works Inc* ***(G-2356)***
Signode, Buffalo Grove *Also called Illinois Tool Works Inc* ***(G-2548)***
Signode 800 228-4744
3700 W Lake Ave Glenview (60026) ***(G-10616)***
Signode Consumable Plastics, Glenview *Also called Signode Industrial Group LLC* ***(G-10620)***
Signode Industrial Group LLC 800 862-7997
3624 W Lake Ave Glenview (60026) ***(G-10617)***
Signode Industrial Group LLC (HQ) 847 724-7500
3650 W Lake Ave Glenview (60026) ***(G-10618)***
Signode Industrial Group LLC 815 939-6192
2150 S Us Highway 45 52 Kankakee (60901) ***(G-12002)***
Signode Industrial Group LLC 800 628-6787
3644 W Lake Ave Glenview (60026) ***(G-10619)***
Signode Industrial Group LLC 815 939-0033
2150m S Us Highway 45 52 Kankakee (60901) ***(G-12003)***
Signode Industrial Group LLC 847 724-6100
3680 W Lake Ave Glenview (60026) ***(G-10620)***
Signode Industrial Group LLC 708 371-9050
14153 Western Ave Blue Island (60406) ***(G-2140)***
Signode Intl Holdings LLC (HQ) 800 648-8864
3700 W Lake Ave Glenview (60026) ***(G-10621)***
Signode Midwest Steel 847 657-5385
7701 W 71st St Bridgeview (60455) ***(G-2386)***
Signode Packaging Systems, Glenview *Also called Signode Industrial Group LLC* ***(G-10617)***
Signode Supply Corporation 708 458-7320
7701 W 71st St Bridgeview (60455) ***(G-2387)***
Signs & Wonders Unlimited LLC 847 816-9734
28318 N Oak Ln Libertyville (60048) ***(G-12707)***
Signs and Designs, Naperville *Also called Cutting Edge Graphics Ltd* ***(G-14964)***
Signs By Custom Cutting Inc 630 759-2734
300 Dean Cir Bolingbrook (60440) ***(G-2240)***
Signs By Design, Crestwood *Also called Contempo Autographic & Signs* ***(G-7113)***
Signs By Design 708 599-9970
10330 S Harlem Ave Palos Hills (60465) ***(G-16207)***
Signs By Tomorrow, Plainfield *Also called Jem Solutions Inc* ***(G-16677)***
Signs By Tomorrow, Arlington Heights *Also called G & J Associates Inc* ***(G-738)***
Signs By Tomorrow, Elgin *Also called Signs In Dundee Inc* ***(G-8731)***
Signs Direct Inc 309 820-1070
1703 S Veterans Pkwy Bloomington (61701) ***(G-2095)***
Signs Express, Macomb *Also called Quickprinters* ***(G-13398)***
Signs For Success Inc 847 800-4870
1538 Madison Dr Buffalo Grove (60089) ***(G-2605)***
Signs In Dundee Inc 847 742-9530
1028 Dundee Ave Elgin (60120) ***(G-8731)***
Signs N Such, Caseyville *Also called Joseph D Smithies* ***(G-3216)***
Signs Now, Gurnee *Also called Dewrich Inc* ***(G-10868)***
Signs Now, Elk Grove Village *Also called Elk Grove Signs Inc* ***(G-8973)***
Signs Now, Rockford *Also called Timothy Anderson Corporation* ***(G-17663)***
Signs Now, Peoria *Also called Isates Inc* ***(G-16460)***
Signs Now, Highland Park *Also called Eisendrath Inc* ***(G-11261)***
Signs Now, Mundelein *Also called Campbell Management Services* ***(G-14672)***
Signs Now, Chicago *Also called Churchill Wilmslow Corporation* ***(G-4147)***
Signs Now, Lombard *Also called Jodaat Inc* ***(G-13091)***
Signs Now, Downers Grove *Also called Krick Enterprises Inc* ***(G-8041)***
Signs Now, Naperville *Also called Albright Enterprises Inc* ***(G-14769)***
Signs Now, Geneva *Also called Geneva Sign Corporation* ***(G-10273)***
Signs Now 847 427-0005
1670 Greenleaf Ave Elk Grove Village (60007) ***(G-9242)***
Signs Now 800 356-3373
2525 W Hutchinson St Chicago (60618) ***(G-6170)***
Signs Now Naperville, Naperville *Also called Sadannah Group LLC* ***(G-14912)***
Signs of Distinction Inc 847 520-0787
149 Wheeling Rd Wheeling (60090) ***(G-20986)***
Signs of The Times, Hebron *Also called Signcrafters Enterprises Inc* ***(G-11150)***
Signs Plus 847 489-9009
1216 Rand Rd Des Plaines (60016) ***(G-7844)***
Signs Today Inc 847 934-9777
342 W Colfax St Palatine (60067) ***(G-16158)***
Signscapes Inc 847 719-2610
884 S Rand Rd Ste D Lake Zurich (60047) ***(G-12457)***
Signwise Inc 630 932-3204
1001 W Republic Dr Ste 16 Addison (60101) ***(G-290)***
Signworx Sign & Lighting Co 217 413-2532
1048 Francella Ct Springfield (62702) ***(G-19445)***
Signx Co Inc 847 639-7917
508 Cary Algonquin Rd Cary (60013) ***(G-3190)***
Sika Corporation 815 431-1080
1515 Titanium Dr Ottawa (61350) ***(G-16079)***
Sikora Automation Incorporated 630 833-0298
845 S Westgate St Addison (60101) ***(G-291)***
Sikora Precision Inc 847 468-0900
140 Will Scarlett Ln Elgin (60120) ***(G-8732)***
Silbrico Corporation 708 354-3350
6300 River Rd Hodgkins (60525) ***(G-11397)***
Silent W Communications Inc 630 479-7950
1651 Aucutt Rd Montgomery (60538) ***(G-14270)***
Silesia Flavors Inc 847 645-0270
5250 Prairie Stone Pkwy Hoffman Estates (60192) ***(G-11459)***
Silgan Closures, Champaign *Also called Silgan White Cap LLC* ***(G-3347)***
Silgan Containers LLC 815 562-1250
400 N 15th St Rochelle (61068) ***(G-17159)***
Silgan Containers Mfg Corp 217 283-5501
324 W Main St Hoopeston (60942) ***(G-11512)***
Silgan Containers Mfg Corp 847 336-0552
1301 W Dugdale Rd Waukegan (60085) ***(G-20495)***
Silgan Equipment Company 847 336-0552
1301 W Dugdale Rd Waukegan (60085) ***(G-20496)***
Silgan Plastics LLC 618 662-4471
2 Industrial Park Flora (62839) ***(G-9692)***
Silgan Plastics LLC 815 334-1200
1005 Courtaulds Dr Woodstock (60098) ***(G-21435)***
Silgan Plstic Clsure Solutions, Downers Grove *Also called Silgan White Cap Americas LLC* ***(G-8096)***
Silgan White Cap Americas LLC 630 515-8383
1140 31st St Downers Grove (60515) ***(G-8096)***
Silgan White Cap LLC 217 398-1600
3209 Farber Dr Champaign (61822) ***(G-3347)***
Silicon Control Inc (PA) 847 215-7947
155 N Pfingsten Rd # 360 Deerfield (60015) ***(G-7649)***
Silk Road Logistics Co 773 432-5619
2351 S Cannon Dr Apt G2 Mount Prospect (60056) ***(G-14570)***
Silk Screen Express Inc 708 845-5600
7611 185th St Tinley Park (60477) ***(G-19855)***
Silkworm Inc 618 687-4077
102 S Sezmore Dr Murphysboro (62966) ***(G-14760)***
Silkworm Screen Printing, Murphysboro *Also called Silkworm Inc* ***(G-14760)***
Silver Bell Cnstr & Furn Inc 773 578-9450
1500 S Western Ave Chicago (60608) ***(G-6171)***
Silver Bros Inc 217 283-7751
105 E Washington St Hoopeston (60942) ***(G-11513)***
Silver Line 708 832-9100
1550 Huntington Dr Calumet City (60409) ***(G-2791)***
Silver Line Building Pdts LLC 708 474-9100
16801 Exchange Ave Ste 2 Lansing (60438) ***(G-12516)***
Silver Machine Shop Inc 217 359-5717
713 N Market St Champaign (61820) ***(G-3348)***
Silverlight Cnc Inc 847 450-1099
135 Park Ave Barrington (60010) ***(G-1244)***
Silverline Windows, Lansing *Also called Silver Line Building Pdts LLC* ***(G-12516)***
Sim Partners (HQ) 800 260-3380
141 W Jackson Blvd # 1850 Chicago (60604) ***(G-6172)***
Sim Products, Shumway *Also called Southern Illinois McHy Co Inc* ***(G-18906)***
Simfax Agri-Services, Jerseyville *Also called Associated Agri-Business Inc* ***(G-11786)***
Simfax Agri-Services, Eldred *Also called Associated Agri-Business Inc* ***(G-8487)***
Simformotion LLC (PA) 309 263-7595
316 Sw Washington St # 300 Peoria (61602) ***(G-16524)***
Simion Fabrication Inc 618 724-7331
901 W Egyptian Ave Christopher (62822) ***(G-6826)***
Simon Box Mfg Co 815 722-6661
355 Caton Farm Rd Lockport (60441) ***(G-13023)***
Simon Global Services LLC 773 334-7794
5655 N Clark St Ste 5 Chicago (60660) ***(G-6173)***
Simon Zelikman 847 338-8031
106 Meadow Ln Oakwood Hills (60013) ***(G-15822)***
Simonton Building Products Inc 217 466-2851
13263 Il Highway 133 Paris (61944) ***(G-16244)***
Simonton Hardwood Lumber LLC 618 594-2132
16515 Post Oak Rd Carlyle (62231) ***(G-2896)***
Simonton Windows, Paris *Also called Simonton Building Products Inc* ***(G-16244)***
Simpex Medical Inc 847 757-9928
401 E Prospect Ave Mount Prospect (60056) ***(G-14571)***
Simple Canvas Prints LLC 800 900-4244
471 N 3rd Ave Des Plaines (60016) ***(G-7845)***
Simple Circuits Inc 708 671-9600
12756 S 80th Ave Palos Park (60464) ***(G-16214)***
Simple Mills Inc 312 600-6196
435 N Lasalle St Fl 2 Flr 2 Chicago (60654) ***(G-6174)***
Simple Solutions 618 932-6177
110 E Main St West Frankfort (62896) ***(G-20683)***
Simplement Inc (PA) 702 560-5332
1 Northfield Plz Ste 300 Northfield (60093) ***(G-15530)***
Simplex Inc (PA) 217 483-1600
5300 Rising Moon Rd Springfield (62711) ***(G-19446)***
Simplicity Creative Group, Naperville *Also called Wilton Ww Co* ***(G-14950)***
Simplomatic Manufacturing Co 773 342-7757
1616 Berkley St Ste 100 Elgin (60123) ***(G-8733)***

Simply Salsa LLC (PA) 815 514-3993
12630 W 159th St Homer Glen (60491) *(G-11486)*
Simply Signs 309 849-9016
1001 W Mount Vernon St D Metamora (61548) *(G-13968)*
Simpson Anchor Systems, West Chicago *Also called Simpson Strong-Tie Company Inc* *(G-20643)*
Simpson Strong-Tie Company Inc 630 613-5100
2505 Enterprise Cir West Chicago (60185) *(G-20643)*
Sims Company Inc 618 665-3901
1431 Panther Creek Ln Louisville (62858) *(G-13180)*
Simu Ltd (PA) 708 688-2200
8900 W 50th St Mc Cook (60525) *(G-13701)*
Simulation Technology LLC 630 365-3400
747 Herra St Unit B Elburn (60119) *(G-8473)*
Singer Data Products Inc (PA) 630 860-6500
790 Maple Ln Bensenville (60106) *(G-1893)*
Singer Equities Inc 815 874-5364
5463 International Dr Rockford (61109) *(G-17632)*
Singer Medical Products Inc 630 860-6500
790 Maple Ln Bensenville (60106) *(G-1894)*
Singer Safety Company 773 235-2100
2300 N Kilbourn Ave Chicago (60639) *(G-6175)*
Single Path LLC 708 653-4100
905 Parkview Blvd Lombard (60148) *(G-13130)*
Singles Plus Printing, South Elgin *Also called T & C Graphics Inc* *(G-19175)*
Singleton Pallets Co 708 687-7006
15603 Waverly Ave Oak Forest (60452) *(G-15688)*
Sipi Metals Corp (PA) 773 276-0070
1720 N Elston Ave Chicago (60642) *(G-6176)*
Sir Cooper Inc 630 279-0162
203 W Saint Charles Rd Villa Park (60181) *(G-20173)*
Sir Speedy, Aurora *Also called Samecwei Inc* *(G-1153)*
Sir Speedy, Evanston *Also called William Holloway Ltd* *(G-9588)*
Sir Speedy, Naperville *Also called K & J Phillips Corporation* *(G-14856)*
Sir Speedy, Chicago *Also called Two JS Copies Now Inc* *(G-6447)*
Sir Speedy Print Signs Mktg, Villa Park *Also called E A A Enterprises Inc* *(G-20145)*
Sir Speedy Printing 312 337-0774
1711 N Clybourn Ave Chicago (60614) *(G-6177)*
Sir Speedy Printing Cntr 6129 ....708 349-7789
9412 W 143rd St Orland Park (60462) *(G-15979)*
Sirius Automation Group Inc 847 607-9378
1558 Barclay Blvd Buffalo Grove (60089) *(G-2606)*
Sirius Performance Company LLC 312 909-0775
5 Glenview Rd Glenview (60025) *(G-10622)*
Sisco Corporation (PA) 618 327-3066
1520 S Mill St Nashville (62263) *(G-15010)*
Sisler Dairy Products Company 815 376-2913
102 S Grove St Ohio (61349) *(G-15845)*
Sisler's Ice & Ice Cream Co, Ohio *Also called Sisler Dairy Products Company* *(G-15845)*
Sislers Ice Inc 815 756-6903
274 Harvestore Dr Dekalb (60115) *(G-7701)*
Sister Construction, Monmouth *Also called Oldcastle Materials Inc* *(G-14225)*
Site 933, Elgin *Also called BFI Waste Systems N Amer Inc* *(G-8521)*
SITech Inc 630 761-3640
1101 N Raddant Rd Batavia (60510) *(G-1417)*
Sitexpedite LLC 847 245-2185
430 N Crooked Lake Ln Lindenhurst (60046) *(G-12854)*
Sivco Welding Company 309 944-5171
624 E Prospect St Geneseo (61254) *(G-10247)*
Six Color Print LLC (PA) 847 336-3287
2233 Northwestern Ave B Waukegan (60087) *(G-20497)*
Six Oaks Company 312 343-4037
2033 W 108th Pl Chicago (60643) *(G-6178)*
Sjd Direct Midwest LLC (PA) 618 931-2151
21 Gtewy Cmrc Ctr Dr W Edwardsville (62025) *(G-8375)*
Sjti, Machesney Park *Also called Superior Joining Tech Inc* *(G-13376)*
Sk Express Inc 815 748-4388
310 Dietz Ave Dekalb (60115) *(G-7702)*
Sk Hand Tool LLC 815 895-7701
1600 S Prairie Dr Sycamore (60178) *(G-19731)*
Sk Hynix America Inc 847 925-0196
1920 Thoreau Dr N Schaumburg (60173) *(G-18713)*
Skach Manufacturing Co Inc 847 395-3560
950 Anita Ave Antioch (60002) *(G-635)*
Skandia Inc 800 945-7135
5000 Il 251 Davis Junction (61020) *(G-7427)*
Skelcher Concrete Products 618 457-2930
490 San Diego Rd Carbondale (62901) *(G-2859)*
Skender Construction LLC 312 781-0265
1330 W Fulton St Ste 200 Chicago (60607) *(G-6179)*
Skeptic Distillery Co 708 223-8286
2525 W Le Moyne St Melrose Park (60160) *(G-13915)*
Sketchbook Brewing Co., Evanston *Also called Common Culture Brewing Co* *(G-9506)*
SKF Arspace Sling Slutions Div, Elgin *Also called SKF USA Inc* *(G-8734)*
SKF Automotive Division, Elgin *Also called SKF USA Inc* *(G-8735)*
SKF USA Inc 847 742-0700
900 N State St Elgin (60123) *(G-8734)*
SKF USA Inc 847 742-0700
890 N State St Ste 200 Elgin (60123) *(G-8735)*
SKF USA Inc 847 742-0700
900 N State St Elgin (60123) *(G-8736)*
Ski Seal Coating Inc 708 246-5656
7100 Pleasantdale Dr Countryside (60525) *(G-7070)*
Skild Manufacturing Inc 847 437-1717
160 Bond St Fl 1 Elk Grove Village (60007) *(G-9243)*
Skill-Di Inc 708 544-6080
2655 Harrison St Bellwood (60104) *(G-1639)*
Skilled Plating Corp 773 227-0262
151618 N Kilpatrick Ave Chicago (60651) *(G-6180)*
Skiman Sales Inc 847 888-8200
850 Villa St Elgin (60120) *(G-8737)*
Skin and Laser Aesheptics, Lombard *Also called Aespheptics Medical Ltd* *(G-13037)*
Skinny Souping, Chicago *Also called Ali VS Kitchen LLC* *(G-3606)*
Skokie Millwork Inc 847 673-7868
8108 Lawndale Ave Skokie (60076) *(G-19030)*
Skol Mfg Co 773 878-5959
4444 N Ravenswood Ave Chicago (60640) *(G-6181)*
SKW Industries LLC 773 261-8900
900 S Cicero Ave Chicago (60644) *(G-6182)*
Sky Snacks LLC 217 522-3345
1129 Taintor Rd Springfield (62702) *(G-19447)*
Skybitz Tank Monitoring Corp 312 379-8397
200 S Wacker Dr Ste 1800 Chicago (60606) *(G-6183)*
Skyfly Networks Inc 312 429-4580
1210 E Washington St # 203 Des Plaines (60016) *(G-7846)*
Skyjack Equipment Inc (HQ) 630 797-3299
3451 Swenson Ave Saint Charles (60174) *(G-18270)*
Skyjack Inc 630 262-0005
3451 Swenson Ave Saint Charles (60174) *(G-18271)*
Skyjack Parts & Svc Skyjack, Saint Charles *Also called Skyjack Inc* *(G-18271)*
Skyline 312 300-4700
9200 W 55th St Mc Cook (60525) *(G-13702)*
Skyline Beauty Supply Inc 773 275-6003
3804 Carnation St Franklin Park (60131) *(G-10047)*
Skyline Design Inc 773 278-4660
1240 N Homan Ave Ste 1 Chicago (60651) *(G-6184)*
Skyline Foods, Harvey *Also called Skyline Provisions Inc* *(G-11095)*
Skyline International Inc 847 357-9077
4801 Emerson Ave Ste 202 Palatine (60067) *(G-16159)*
Skyline Printing Sales 847 412-1931
3004 Commercial Ave Northbrook (60062) *(G-15481)*
Skyline Provisions Inc 708 331-1982
374 E 167th St Harvey (60426) *(G-11095)*
Skyline Publishing, Bartonville *Also called Loyalty Publishing Inc* *(G-1334)*
Skyward Promotions Inc 815 969-0909
1140 Charles St Rockford (61104) *(G-17633)*
Skyway Cement Company LLC (PA) 800 643-1808
3020 E 103rd St Chicago (60617) *(G-6185)*
Slack Publications 217 268-4950
736 Dogwood Dr Arcola (61910) *(G-666)*
Slagel Drapery Service 815 692-3834
302 S 8th St Fairbury (61739) *(G-9613)*
Slagel Manufacturing Inc 815 688-3318
2911 N 2700 East Rd Forrest (61741) *(G-9738)*
Slam Door Co, Wheeling *Also called Boom Company Inc* *(G-20863)*
Slaughter Company Inc 847 932-3662
28105 N Keith Dr Lake Forest (60045) *(G-12303)*
Slavish Inc 309 754-8233
309 1st St Matherville (61263) *(G-13615)*
Slee Corporation 773 777-2444
1612 Glenlake Ave Itasca (60143) *(G-11733)*
Sleep On Latex, Niles *Also called Shevick Sales Corp* *(G-15171)*
Sleep6 LLC 844 375-3376
1332 N Halsted St Chicago (60642) *(G-6186)*
Sleepeck Printing Company 708 544-8900
70 W Madison St Ste 2300 Chicago (60602) *(G-6187)*
Sleeping Bear Inc 630 541-7220
5401 Patton Dr Ste 115 Lisle (60532) *(G-12937)*
Sleepy Woodworks 773 779-2990
10644 S Drake Ave Chicago (60655) *(G-6188)*
SLF Motion LLC 217 891-8384
1500 Horse Creek Trl Pawnee (62558) *(G-16306)*
Slick Sugar Inc 815 782-7101
24935 Heritage Oaks Dr Plainfield (60585) *(G-16714)*
Slicksugar.com, Plainfield *Also called Slick Sugar Inc* *(G-16714)*
Slide Products Inc 847 541-7220
430 Wheeling Rd Wheeling (60090) *(G-20987)*
Slidematic Industries Inc 815 986-0500
1303 Samuelson Rd Rockford (61109) *(G-17634)*
Slidematic Products Co 773 545-4213
4520 W Addison St Chicago (60641) *(G-6189)*
Slidemtic Prcsion Cmpnents Inc 815 986-0500
1303 Samuelson Rd Rockford (61109) *(G-17635)*
Slipon Nipple Company 708 345-2525
10849 Kingston St Westchester (60154) *(G-20711)*

ALPHABETIC

Sloan Industries Inc — 630 350-1614
1550 N Michael Dr Wood Dale (60191) *(G-21241)*

Sloan Valve Co Fkp, Franklin Park Also called Sloan Valve Company *(G-10048)*

Sloan Valve Company (PA) — 847 671-4300
10500 Seymour Ave Franklin Park (60131) *(G-10048)*

Slsb LLC — 618 219-4115
2000 Access Rd Madison (62060) *(G-13417)*

Small Different Better Inc — 224 302-5163
30 Porter Dr Round Lake Park (60073) *(G-18098)*

Small Newspaper Group (PA) — 815 937-3300
8 Dearborn Sq Kankakee (60901) *(G-12004)*

Small Nwsppr Group Shred Svcs (HQ) — 309 764-4344
1033 7th St Ste 101 East Moline (61244) *(G-8241)*

Small Nwsppr Group Shred Svcs — 309 757-8377
1033 7th St Ste 101 East Moline (61244) *(G-8242)*

Small Tools Div, Stillman Valley Also called Toolmasters LLC *(G-19547)*

Smalley Steel Ring Co (PA) — 847 537-7600
555 Oakwood Rd Lake Zurich (60047) *(G-12458)*

Smart Choice Mobile Inc (PA) — 708 581-4904
7667 W 95th St Ste 300 Hickory Hills (60457) *(G-11203)*

Smart Controls LLC — 618 394-0300
10000 Saint Clair Ave Fairview Heights (62208) *(G-9648)*

Smart Creations Inc — 847 433-3451
1799 Saint Johns Ave Highland Park (60035) *(G-11298)*

Smart Home Office, Champaign Also called Sho Technologies Inc *(G-3346)*

Smart Inc — 847 464-4160
41w584 Us Highway 20 Hampshire (60140) *(G-10988)*

Smart Living Home & Garden, Libertyville Also called Smart Solar Inc *(G-12708)*

Smart Motion Robotics Inc — 815 895-8550
805 Thornwood Dr Sycamore (60178) *(G-19732)*

Smart Office Services Inc — 773 227-1121
3720 W Chicago Ave Chicago (60651) *(G-6190)*

Smart Pixel Inc — 630 771-0206
590 Territorial Dr Ste B Bolingbrook (60440) *(G-2241)*

Smart Scan Mri LLC — 847 623-4000
350 S Greenleaf St # 401 Gurnee (60031) *(G-10928)*

Smart Solar Inc — 813 343-5770
1203 Loyola Dr Libertyville (60048) *(G-12708)*

Smart Solutions Inc — 630 775-1517
211 Catalpa Ave Itasca (60143) *(G-11734)*

Smart Systems Inc — 630 343-3333
554 Territorial Dr Bolingbrook (60440) *(G-2242)*

Smart-Fab Inc — 855 276-2783
721 Armstrong Dr Buffalo Grove (60089) *(G-2607)*

Smart-Slitters, Northbrook Also called Rosenthal Manufacturing Co Inc *(G-15475)*

Smartbyte Solutions Inc — 847 925-1870
712 W Slippery Rock Dr Palatine (60067) *(G-16160)*

Smartsignal, Lisle Also called GE Intelligent Platforms Inc *(G-12894)*

Smb Toolroom Inc — 309 353-7396
206 Derby St Pekin (61554) *(G-16361)*

SMC Corporation of America — 630 449-0600
858 Meridian Lake Dr F Aurora (60504) *(G-1017)*

Smf Inc (PA) — 309 432-2586
1550 N Industrial Park Rd Minonk (61760) *(G-14055)*

Smh2 Manufacturing LLC — 773 793-6643
2021 W Fulton St K-215 Chicago (60612) *(G-6191)*

Smid Heating & Air — 815 467-0362
23864 W Sussex Dr Channahon (60410) *(G-3394)*

Smile Aromatics Inc — 847 759-0350
2454 E Dempster St # 422 Des Plaines (60016) *(G-7847)*

Smile Lee Faces — 773 376-9999
4197 S Archer Ave Chicago (60632) *(G-6192)*

Smith & Richardson Mfg Co — 630 232-2581
727 May St Geneva (60134) *(G-10306)*

Smith and Son Machine Shop — 217 260-3257
454 County Road 2400 E Broadlands (61816) *(G-2410)*

Smith Bros Engineering, Jerseyville Also called Smith Brothers Fabricating *(G-11796)*

Smith Brothers Converters, Crestwood Also called CC Distributing Services Inc *(G-7110)*

Smith Brothers Fabricating — 618 498-5612
406 Maple Ave Jerseyville (62052) *(G-11796)*

Smith Bucklin & Associates, Chicago Also called API Publishing Services LLC *(G-3711)*

Smith Cooper International Inc — 847 595-7572
2701 Busse Rd Elk Grove Village (60007) *(G-9244)*

Smith Filter Corporation — 309 764-8324
5000 41st Street Ct Moline (61265) *(G-14178)*

Smith Greenhouse & Supplies, Mendota Also called E N P Inc *(G-13940)*

Smith Industrial Rubber & Plas, Rockford Also called Smith Industrial Rubber & Plas *(G-17636)*

Smith Industrial Rubber & Plas, Rockford Also called Singer Equities Inc *(G-17632)*

Smith Industrial Rubber & Plas — 815 874-5364
5463 International Dr Rockford (61109) *(G-17636)*

Smith Power Transmission Co — 773 526-5512
5335 S Western Blvd Ste C Chicago (60609) *(G-6193)*

Smith Welding LLC — 618 829-5414
2238 N 2225 St Saint Elmo (62458) *(G-18312)*

Smith, John Crane, Crystal Lake Also called John Crane Inc *(G-7214)*

Smith-Victor, Bartlett Also called Promark International Inc *(G-1301)*

Smithereen Company — 800 340-1888
7400 N Melvina Ave Niles (60714) *(G-15172)*

Smithereen Company Del (PA) — 847 675-0010
7400 N Melvina Ave Niles (60714) *(G-15173)*

Smithereen Exterminating Co, Niles Also called Smithereen Company Del *(G-15173)*

Smithereen Pest Management, Niles Also called Smithereen Company *(G-15172)*

Smithfeld Pckged Mats Sls Corp — 757 365-3541
4225 Naperville Rd Lisle (60532) *(G-12938)*

Smithfield Food, East Dubuque Also called Smithfield Packaged Meats Corp *(G-8183)*

Smithfield Packaged Meats Corp — 630 993-8763
771 W Crssrads Pkwy Ste A Bolingbrook (60490) *(G-2243)*

Smithfield Packaged Meats Corp — 815 747-8809
18531 Us Highway 20 W East Dubuque (61025) *(G-8183)*

Smithfield Packaged Meats Corp — 309 734-5353
1220 N 6th St Monmouth (61462) *(G-14227)*

Smithfield Packaged Meats Corp — 630 281-5224
4225 Naperville Rd # 600 Lisle (60532) *(G-12939)*

Smiths Medical — 847 383-1400
330 Corporate Woods Pkwy Vernon Hills (60061) *(G-20098)*

Smoco Inc — 618 662-6458
832 W North Ave Ste A1 Flora (62839) *(G-9693)*

Smoke Rite Wood Products — 708 485-8910
3801 Arthur Ave Brookfield (60513) *(G-2492)*

Smolich Bros, Joliet Also called Smolich Brothers Sausage Inc *(G-11931)*

Smolich Brothers Sausage Inc — 815 727-2144
760 Theodore St Joliet (60403) *(G-11931)*

SMR Components, Mundelein Also called Stuart Moore Racing Ltd *(G-14740)*

SMS Group Inc — 708 479-1333
19700 97th Ave Mokena (60448) *(G-14115)*

SMS Technical Services, Mokena Also called SMS Group Inc *(G-14115)*

Smt LLC Group — 630 961-3000
2768 Golfview Rd Naperville (60563) *(G-14915)*

Smt Molding, Naperville Also called Smt LLC Group *(G-14915)*

Smurfit-Stone Container, Galesburg Also called Westrock Cp LLC *(G-10224)*

Snagamon Valley Log Builders — 217 632-7609
21500 Old Farm Ave Petersburg (62675) *(G-16604)*

Snaidero USA — 312 644-6662
222 Mrchnds Mrt Pl 140 Chicago (60654) *(G-6194)*

Snak-King Corp — 815 232-6700
3133 Industrial Dr Freeport (61032) *(G-10142)*

Snap Diagnostics LLC — 847 777-0000
5210 Capitol Dr Wheeling (60090) *(G-20988)*

Snap Edge, Saint Charles Also called Sek Corporation *(G-18268)*

Snap-A-Pleat Drapery System, Dunlap Also called Baker Drapery Corporation *(G-8132)*

SNC Solutions Inc — 217 784-5212
496 N 600e Rd Gibson City (60936) *(G-10344)*

Sneaky Clean LLC — 312 550-9654
5117 Main St Ste B Downers Grove (60515) *(G-8097)*

Sno Gem Inc — 888 766-4367
4800 Metalmaster Dr McHenry (60050) *(G-13792)*

Sno Gem Snow Guards, McHenry Also called Sno Gem Inc *(G-13792)*

Sno-Belt Industries, Woodstock Also called Markham Industry Inc *(G-21408)*

Snow & Graham LLC — 773 665-9000
829 Foxdale Ave Winnetka (60093) *(G-21136)*

Snow Command Incorporated — 708 991-7004
1607 Tina Ln Flossmoor (60422) *(G-9701)*

Snow Control Inc — 708 670-6269
7245 W 151st St Orland Park (60462) *(G-15980)*

Snow Printing LLC — 618 233-0712
6428 Old Saint Louis Rd Belleville (62223) *(G-1596)*

Snow River Products, North Barrington Also called Columbian Home Products LLC *(G-15282)*

Snowball Industries — 773 316-0051
3404 N Harding Ave Chicago (60618) *(G-6195)*

Sns Pharma 427 — 217 527-8408
1501 S Dirksen Pkwy Springfield (62703) *(G-19448)*

Snyder Industries Inc — 630 773-9510
736 Birginal Dr Bensenville (60106) *(G-1895)*

Snyders Lance, Skokie Also called Snyders-Lance Inc *(G-19031)*

Snyders-Lance Inc — 847 581-1818
7661 New Gross Point Rd Skokie (60077) *(G-19031)*

Sobot Tool & Manufacturing Co — 847 480-0560
3975 Commercial Ave Northbrook (60062) *(G-15482)*

Social Qnect LLC — 847 997-0077
666 Dundee Rd Ste 1904 Northbrook (60062) *(G-15483)*

Socialcloak Inc — 650 549-4412
399 Sinsinawa Ave East Dubuque (61025) *(G-8184)*

Socius Ingredients LLC — 847 440-0156
1033 University Pl # 110 Evanston (60201) *(G-9575)*

Sock Obsessed — 847 920-4834
345 E Ohio St Apt 403 Chicago (60611) *(G-6196)*

Sofrito Foods LLC — 224 535-9252
181 S Lincolnway North Aurora (60542) *(G-15275)*

Soft O Soft Inc — 630 741-4414
1701 E Wdfield Rd Ste 215 Schaumburg (60173) *(G-18714)*

Softhaus Ltd — 618 463-1140
518 Beacon St Alton (62002) *(G-572)*

Softlabz Corporation (PA)....847 780-7076
1180 Saint Johns Ave Highland Park (60035) ***(G-11299)***
Softtech LLC....847 809-8801
613 Barberry Trl Fox River Grove (60021) ***(G-9762)***
SOFTWARE FOR SUCCESS, Evanston *Also called Innovations For Learning Inc* ***(G-9539)***
Software Maniacs, Woodstock *Also called P B R W Enterprises Inc* ***(G-21418)***
Softwareidm Inc (PA)....331 218-0001
213 W Wesley St Ste 200 Wheaton (60187) ***(G-20825)***
Soil Chemical Corporation....714 761-3292
3150 N Woodford St Decatur (62526) ***(G-7547)***
Sojuz Ent....847 215-9400
464 Country Club Dr Bensenville (60106) ***(G-1896)***
Sokol and Company....708 482-8250
5315 Dansher Rd Countryside (60525) ***(G-7071)***
Solae....217 784-8261
115 Jordan Dr Gibson City (60936) ***(G-10345)***
Solae....217 784-2085
509 W 1st St Gibson City (60936) ***(G-10346)***
Solae LLC....217 784-8261
124 S Rte 47 Gibson City (60936) ***(G-10347)***
Solar Spring & Wire Forms, Elk Grove Village *Also called Solar Spring Company* ***(G-9245)***
Solar Spring Company....847 437-7838
345 Criss Cir Elk Grove Village (60007) ***(G-9245)***
Solar Traffic Systems Inc....331 318-8500
16135 New Ave Ste 2 Lemont (60439) ***(G-12590)***
Solar Turbines Incorporated....630 527-1700
40 Shuman Blvd Ste 350 Naperville (60563) ***(G-14916)***
Solari and Huntington, Park Ridge *Also called Solari R Mfg Jewelers* ***(G-16296)***
Solari R Mfg Jewelers....847 823-4354
100 1/2 Main St Park Ridge (60068) ***(G-16296)***
Solazyme....309 258-5695
910 Ne Adams St Peoria (61603) ***(G-16525)***
Solberg International Ltd (PA)....630 616-4400
1151 Ardmore Ave Itasca (60143) ***(G-11735)***
Solberg Mfg Inc (PA)....630 616-4400
1151 Ardmore Ave Itasca (60143) ***(G-11736)***
Solberg Mfg Inc....630 773-1363
680 Baker Dr Itasca (60143) ***(G-11737)***
Soldy Manufacturing Inc....847 671-3396
9370 Byron St Schiller Park (60176) ***(G-18844)***
Sole Unique, Aurora *Also called Organized Noise Inc* ***(G-1004)***
Soleo Health Inc....630 478-8240
10210 Werch Dr Ste 202 Woodridge (60517) ***(G-21340)***
Solid Impressions Inc....630 543-7300
26w455 Saint Charles Rd Carol Stream (60188) ***(G-3070)***
Solid Metal Group Inc....708 757-7421
1633 5th Ave Chicago Heights (60411) ***(G-6774)***
Solid State Luminaires LLC....877 775-4733
3609 Swenson Ave Saint Charles (60174) ***(G-18272)***
Solidyne Corporation....847 394-3333
4731 Woodland Ct Rolling Meadows (60008) ***(G-17775)***
Solidyne Corporation....847 394-3333
2155 Stonington Ave # 105 Hoffman Estates (60169) ***(G-11460)***
Sollami Company....618 988-1521
1200 Weaver Rd Herrin (62948) ***(G-11179)***
Solo Cup Operating Corporation....217 384-1800
1505 E Main St Urbana (61802) ***(G-20001)***
Solo Cup Operating Corporation....773 767-3300
7575 S Kostner Ave Ste 3 Chicago (60652) ***(G-6197)***
Solo Foods....800 328-7656
5315 Dansher Rd Countryside (60525) ***(G-7072)***
Solo Laboratories, Broadview *Also called BMC 1092 Inc* ***(G-2421)***
Soloinsight Inc....312 846-6729
1260 W Madison St Chicago (60607) ***(G-6198)***
Solomon Colors Inc (PA)....217 522-3112
4050 Color Plant Rd Springfield (62702) ***(G-19449)***
Solomon Plumbing....847 498-6388
3706 Winnetka Rd Glenview (60026) ***(G-10623)***
Soluble Packaging Solutions, Mount Prospect *Also called New Usn Chicago LLC* ***(G-14551)***
Solublend Technologies LLC....815 534-5778
11487 Amhearst Ct Frankfort (60423) ***(G-9839)***
Solutia Inc....618 482-6536
500 Monsanto Ave Sauget (62206) ***(G-18399)***
Solution 3 Graphics Inc....773 233-3600
10547 S Western Ave Chicago (60643) ***(G-6199)***
Solution Comfortseat, Highland Park *Also called Great Ideas Inc* ***(G-11267)***
Solution Designs Inc....847 680-7788
2042 Laurel Valley Dr Vernon Hills (60061) ***(G-20099)***
Solution Printing & Signs, Springfield *Also called Solution Printing Inc* ***(G-19450)***
Solution Printing Inc....217 529-9700
3135 S 14th St Springfield (62703) ***(G-19450)***
Solutions Manufacturing Inc....847 310-4506
2109 Stonington Ave Hoffman Estates (60169) ***(G-11461)***
Solvay Chemicals Inc....618 274-0755
3500 Missouri Ave East Saint Louis (62205) ***(G-8322)***
Solvay Finance (america) LLC....713 525-6000
23424 Network Pl Chicago (60673) ***(G-6200)***
Solvay USA Inc....708 441-6041
1020 State St Chicago Heights (60411) ***(G-6775)***
Solvay USA Inc....708 371-2000
14000 Seeley Ave Blue Island (60406) ***(G-2141)***
Solvay USA Inc....708 235-7200
24601 Governors Hwy University Park (60484) ***(G-19967)***
Somat Corporation (PA)....800 578-4260
2202 Fox Dr Ste A Champaign (61820) ***(G-3349)***
Somebody's Pub & Grille, Arlington Heights *Also called Be McGonagle Inc* ***(G-704)***
Something Old, Something New, Chicago *Also called No Surrender Inc* ***(G-5607)***
Sommer Products Company Inc....309 697-1216
6523 N Galena Rd Peoria (61614) ***(G-16526)***
Sommers & Fahrenbach Inc....773 478-3033
3301 W Belmont Ave Chicago (60618) ***(G-6201)***
Sommers Fare LLC....877 377-9797
1301 Allanson Rd Mundelein (60060) ***(G-14737)***
Soni Mohnish....312 473-7669
1700 Pratt Ave Des Plaines (60018) ***(G-7848)***
Sonic Manufacturing Corp....847 228-0015
950 Lee St Elk Grove Village (60007) ***(G-9246)***
Sonic Tool Mfg, Elk Grove Village *Also called Sonic Manufacturing Corp* ***(G-9246)***
Sonistic....217 377-9698
60 Hazelwood Dr Ste 230g Champaign (61820) ***(G-3350)***
Sonne Industries LLC....630 235-6734
5s528 Arlington Ave Naperville (60540) ***(G-14917)***
Sono Italiano Corporation....817 472-8903
655 Mulberry St Manteno (60950) ***(G-13456)***
Sonoco Alloyd, Dekalb *Also called Tegrant Alloyd Brands Inc* ***(G-7708)***
Sonoco Corrflex, Bolingbrook *Also called Sonoco Display & Packaging LLC* ***(G-2244)***
Sonoco Display & Packaging LLC....630 972-1990
101 E Crossroads Pkwy Bolingbrook (60440) ***(G-2244)***
Sonoco Display & Packaging LLC....630 789-1111
1111 Pasquinelli Dr # 600 Westmont (60559) ***(G-20773)***
Sonoco Plastics Inc....630 628-5859
1035 W Republic Dr Addison (60101) ***(G-292)***
Sonoco Products Company....630 231-1489
1500 Powis Rd West Chicago (60185) ***(G-20644)***
Sonoco Products Company....847 957-6282
11608 Copenhagen Ct Franklin Park (60131) ***(G-10049)***
Sonoco Protective Solutions....847 398-0110
3930 N Ventura Dr Ste 450 Arlington Heights (60004) ***(G-810)***
Sonoco Prtective Solutions Inc....847 398-0110
3930 N Ventura Dr Ste 450 Arlington Heights (60004) ***(G-811)***
Sonoco Prtective Solutions Inc....717 757-2683
91218 Collection Ctr Dr Chicago (60693) ***(G-6202)***
Sonoco Prtective Solutions Inc....815 787-5244
1401 Pleasant St Dekalb (60115) ***(G-7703)***
Sonoco Prtective Solutions Inc....708 946-3244
30553 S Dixie Hwy Beecher (60401) ***(G-1521)***
Sonoscan Inc....847 437-6400
2149 Pratt Blvd Elk Grove Village (60007) ***(G-9247)***
Sonova USA Inc (HQ)....763 744-3300
750 N Commons Dr Aurora (60504) ***(G-1018)***
Sons Enterprises....847 677-4444
4826 Main St Skokie (60077) ***(G-19032)***
Sony Electronics Inc....630 773-7500
1064 Idaho St Carol Stream (60188) ***(G-3071)***
Sony/Atv Music Publishing LLC....630 739-8129
351 Internationale Dr Bolingbrook (60440) ***(G-2245)***
Soosan USA Inc....224 653-8916
1261 Wiley Rd Ste B Schaumburg (60173) ***(G-18715)***
Sopher Design & Manufacturing....309 699-6419
3312 Meadow Ave East Peoria (61611) ***(G-8291)***
Sorento News, Raymond News, Hillsboro *Also called Hillsboro Journal Inc* ***(G-11316)***
Sorini Manufacturing Corp....773 247-5858
2524 S Blue Island Ave Chicago (60608) ***(G-6203)***
Sorini Ring, Chicago *Also called Sorini Manufacturing Corp* ***(G-6203)***
Sortimat Technology LP....847 925-1234
5655 Meadowbrook Indus Ct Rolling Meadows (60008) ***(G-17776)***
Sortimat Techonology, Rolling Meadows *Also called Ats Sortimat USA LLC* ***(G-17713)***
Sota Service Ctr By Bodinets....608 538-3500
436 E Locust St Dekalb (60115) ***(G-7704)***
Sota Turntable, Dekalb *Also called Sota Service Ctr By Bodinets* ***(G-7704)***
Sotiros Foods Inc....708 371-0002
12560 S Holiday Dr Ste B Alsip (60803) ***(G-511)***
Soudan Metals Company Inc (PA)....773 548-7600
319 W 40th Pl Chicago (60609) ***(G-6204)***
Soul Training Program Inc....312 725-9768
903 S Ashland Ave # 1108 Chicago (60607) ***(G-6205)***
Soul Vegan, Chicago *Also called Stable Foods Inc* ***(G-6225)***
Sound Design Inc....630 548-7000
10104 S Mandel St Ste 1 Plainfield (60585) ***(G-16715)***
Sound Enhancement Products Inc....847 639-4646
100 High Grove Blvd Glendale Heights (60139) ***(G-10496)***
Sound Master & Calvert Systems, Port Byron *Also called Calvert Systems* ***(G-16786)***
Sound Seal Inc....630 844-1999
401 Airport Rd North Aurora (60542) ***(G-15276)***
Sound World Solutions, Park Ridge *Also called Nantsound Inc* ***(G-16289)***

A L P H A B E T I C

Soundgrowler Brewing Company 708 263-0083
8201 183rd St Tinley Park (60487) *(G-19856)*

Source 4-Integrated Business, Chicago Also called Available Business Group Inc *(G-3781)*

Source Software Inc (PA) 815 922-7717
16525 W 159th St 200 Lockport (60441) *(G-13024)*

Source United LLC 847 956-1459
825 Nicholas Blvd Elk Grove Village (60007) *(G-9248)*

Sourcebooks Llc (PA) 630 961-3900
1935 Brookdale Rd Ste 139 Naperville (60563) *(G-14918)*

Sourcennex International Co 847 251-5500
825 Green Bay Rd Ste 240 Wilmette (60091) *(G-21093)*

Sourcing Solutions, Naperville Also called Lessy Messy LLC *(G-14977)*

South Central Fs Inc 618 283-1557
10 Interstate Dr Vandalia (62471) *(G-20025)*

South Central Fs Inc 217 849-2242
708 S Meridian St Toledo (62468) *(G-19878)*

South Chicago Packing LLC (HQ) 708 589-2400
16250 Vincennes Ave South Holland (60473) *(G-19245)*

South Chicago Packing LLC 708 589-2400
945 W 38th St Chicago (60609) *(G-6206)*

South County Publications (PA) 217 438-6155
110 N 5th St Auburn (62615) *(G-907)*

South Florida Test Service Div, Mount Prospect Also called Atlas Material Tstg Tech LLC *(G-14512)*

South Holland Met Finshg Inc 708 235-0842
26100 S Whiting Way Monee (60449) *(G-14209)*

South Midwest Division, Kankakee Also called Legacy Vulcan LLC *(G-11989)*

South Post LLC 815 510-9395
104 E Livingston Rd Streator (61364) *(G-19623)*

South Side Bler Wldg Works Inc 708 478-1714
10811 Minnesota Ct Orland Park (60467) *(G-15981)*

South Side Boiler & Wldg Work, Orland Park Also called South Side Bler Wldg Works Inc *(G-15981)*

South Subn Logistics Sups Corp 312 804-3401
16610 Finch Ave Harvey (60426) *(G-11096)*

South Subn Wldg & Fabg Co Inc 708 385-7160
14022 S Western Ave Posen (60469) *(G-16801)*

South Water Signs LLC 630 333-4900
934 N Church Rd Ste B Elmhurst (60126) *(G-9428)*

South West Oil Inc 815 416-0400
7080 Highland Dr Morris (60450) *(G-14327)*

Southeast Wood Treating Inc 815 562-5007
300 E Avenue G Rochelle (61068) *(G-17160)*

Southern Color Company Inc (HQ) 770 386-4766
2051 Lynch Ave East Saint Louis (62204) *(G-8323)*

Southern Color N.A., East Saint Louis Also called Southern Color Company Inc *(G-8323)*

Southern Graphic Systems LLC 847 695-9515
5500 Pearl St Ste 100 Rosemont (60018) *(G-18050)*

Southern IL Crankshaft Inc 618 282-4100
225 Kaskaskia Dr Red Bud (62278) *(G-17002)*

Southern IL Raceway 618 201-0500
11682 Macie Dr Marion (62959) *(G-13536)*

Southern Ill Auto Elec Inc 618 587-3308
730 N Minnie Ave Tilden (62292) *(G-19792)*

Southern Ill Helicopters LLC 618 997-0101
2405 Black Diamond Dr Marion (62959) *(G-13537)*

Southern Ill Scale & Cnstr Inc 618 723-2303
430 W South Ave Noble (62868) *(G-15192)*

Southern Ill Wilbert Vlt Co 618 942-5845
2221 N Park Ave Herrin (62948) *(G-11180)*

Southern Ill Wine Trail Nfp 618 695-9463
48 E Glendale Rd Golconda (62938) *(G-10668)*

Southern Illinois Crankshafts 618 282-4100
225 Kaskaskia St Ruma (62278) *(G-18107)*

Southern Illinois Material, Buncombe Also called Southern Illinois Power Coop *(G-2628)*

Southern Illinois McHy Co Inc 217 868-5431
6903 E 1600th Ave Shumway (62461) *(G-18906)*

Southern Illinois Miners 618 969-8506
1000 Miners Dr Marion (62959) *(G-13538)*

Southern Illinois Power Coop 618 995-2371
Rr 37 Box N Buncombe (62912) *(G-2628)*

Southern Illinois Redimix Inc (PA) 618 993-3600
11039 Skyline Dr Marion (62959) *(G-13539)*

Southern Illinois State Cont, Nashville Also called Sisco Corporation *(G-15010)*

Southern Illinois Stone Co (HQ) 573 334-5261
4800 State Rte 37 N Buncombe (62912) *(G-2629)*

Southern Illinois Stone Co 618 995-2392
4800 Hwy 37 N Buncombe (62912) *(G-2630)*

Southern Illinois Vault Co Inc 270 554-4436
2221 N Park Ave Herrin (62948) *(G-11181)*

Southern Illinoisan, Marion Also called Lee Enterprises Incorporated *(G-13519)*

Southern Illinoisan, Carbondale Also called Lee Enterprises Incorporated *(G-2849)*

Southern Imperial Inc (HQ) 815 877-7041
1400 Eddy Ave Rockford (61103) *(G-17637)*

Southern Imperial Inc 815 877-7041
7135 Clinton Rd Loves Park (61111) *(G-13265)*

Southern Mold Finishing Inc 618 983-5049
500 Follis Ave Johnston City (62951) *(G-11813)*

Southern Plating Inc 618 983-6350
500 Follis Ave Johnston City (62951) *(G-11814)*

Southern Steel and Wire Inc (HQ) 618 654-2161
1111 6th St Highland (62249) *(G-11240)*

Southern Triangle Oil Co, Mount Carmel Also called New Triangle Oil Company *(G-14483)*

Southern Triangle Oil Company 618 262-4131
600 Chestnut St Mount Carmel (62863) *(G-14486)*

Southern Truss Inc 618 252-8144
5510 Highway 13 W Harrisburg (62946) *(G-11029)*

Southern Wisconsin Metal Fabrc 815 389-3021
4241 Prairie Hill Rd South Beloit (61080) *(G-19114)*

Southfield Corporation 217 875-5455
705 E Mckinley Ave Decatur (62526) *(G-7548)*

Southfield Corporation 708 563-4056
799 S Route 53 Addison (60101) *(G-293)*

Southfield Corporation 309 676-6121
775 W Birchwood St Morton (61550) *(G-14382)*

Southfield Corporation 815 284-3357
1914 White Oak Ln Dixon (61021) *(G-7918)*

Southfield Corporation 217 877-5210
800 E Mckinley Ave Decatur (62526) *(G-7549)*

Southfield Corporation 708 458-0400
7601 W 79th St Oak Lawn (60455) *(G-15735)*

Southfield Corporation 708 458-0400
7601 W 79th St Bridgeview (60455) *(G-2388)*

Southfield Corporation 217 379-3606
100 N 2280e Rd Paxton (60957) *(G-16316)*

Southfield Corporation 815 842-2333
15887 E 1200 North Rd Pontiac (61764) *(G-16780)*

Southfield Corporation 309 829-1087
917 E Grove St Bloomington (61701) *(G-2096)*

Southfield Corporation 309 676-0576
100 W Cass St Peoria (61602) *(G-16527)*

Southfield Corporation 815 468-8700
8215c N Us Highway 45 52 Manteno (60950) *(G-13457)*

Southland Industries Inc 757 543-5701
2345 Waukegan Rd Ste 155 Bannockburn (60015) *(G-1208)*

Southland Painting 833 724-6803
316 Forest Blvd Park Forest (60466) *(G-16260)*

Southland Voice 708 214-8582
1712 S Dixie Hwy Trlr 133 Crete (60417) *(G-7145)*

Southmoor Estates Inc 815 756-1299
1032 S 7th St Dekalb (60115) *(G-7705)*

Southport Records, Chicago Also called Sparrow Sound Design *(G-6209)*

Southtown Star Newspapers 708 633-4800
18312 West Creek Dr Tinley Park (60477) *(G-19857)*

Southwest Denture Center, Oak Lawn Also called Lmpl Management Corporation *(G-15725)*

Southwest Messenger Press Inc 708 388-2425
3840 147th St Midlothian (60445) *(G-13996)*

Southwest Printing Co 708 389-0800
12003 S Pulaski Rd Alsip (60803) *(G-512)*

Southwest Senior, Summit Argo Also called Vondrak Publishing Co Inc *(G-19684)*

Southwest Signs Inc 773 585-3530
5641 W 63rd St Chicago (60638) *(G-6207)*

Southwest Tool & Machine 708 349-4441
15600 116th Ct Orland Park (60467) *(G-15982)*

Southwestern Hearing Centers 618 651-4199
1328 Mercantile Dr Highland (62249) *(G-11241)*

Southwick Machine & Design Co 309 949-2868
21300 Briar Bluff Rd Colona (61241) *(G-6980)*

Southwire, Lincolnshire Also called Coleman Cable LLC *(G-12752)*

Southwire Company LLC 618 662-8341
Eash Rd Flora (62839) *(G-9694)*

Soy City Sock Co Inc 217 762-2157
1086 S Market St Monticello (61856) *(G-14287)*

Sp Industries, Elk Grove Village Also called S P Industries Inc *(G-9226)*

Spacil Construction Co 708 448-3809
6018 W 123rd St Palos Heights (60463) *(G-16192)*

Spaeth Welding Inc 618 588-3596
321 W Missouri St New Baden (62265) *(G-15024)*

Spannagel Tool & Die 630 969-7575
2732 Wisconsin Ave Downers Grove (60515) *(G-8098)*

Spannuth Boiler Co 708 386-1882
264 Madison St Oak Park (60302) *(G-15774)*

Sparrer Sausage Company Inc 773 762-3334
4325 W Ogden Ave Chicago (60623) *(G-6208)*

Sparrow Coffee Roastery 321 648-6415
10330 W Roosevelt Rd # 200 Westchester (60154) *(G-20712)*

Sparrow Sound Design 773 281-8510
3501 N Southport Ave Chicago (60657) *(G-6209)*

Spartaclean, Machesney Park Also called Spartacus Group Inc *(G-13375)*

Spartacus Group Inc 815 637-1574
925 Colonial Dr Machesney Park (61115) *(G-13375)*

Spartan Flame Retardants Inc 815 459-8500
345 E Terra Cotta Ave Crystal Lake (60014) *(G-7267)*

Spartan Light Metal Pdts Inc (PA) 618 443-4346
510 E Mcclurken Ave Sparta (62286) *(G-19260)*

Spartan Light Metal Pdts Inc 618 443-4346
405 E 4th St Sparta (62286) *(G-19261)*

Spartan Petroleum Company 618 262-4197
328 N Market St Mount Carmel (62863) *(G-14487)*
Spartan Products Inc 815 459-8500
345 E Terra Cotta Ave Crystal Lake (60014) *(G-7268)*
Spartan Sheet Metal Inc 773 895-7266
3006 W Bryn Mawr Ave Chicago (60659) *(G-6210)*
Spartanics Ltd 847 394-5700
3605 Edison Pl Rolling Meadows (60008) *(G-17777)*
Sparton Aydin LLC 800 772-7866
425 N Martingale Rd Schaumburg (60173) *(G-18716)*
Sparton Corporation (HQ) 847 762-5800
425 N Martingale Rd # 100 Schaumburg (60173) *(G-18717)*
Sparton Design Services LLC (HQ) 847 762-5800
425 N Martingale Rd # 2050 Schaumburg (60173) *(G-18718)*
Sparton Emt LLC (HQ) 800 772-7866
425 N Martingale Rd Ste 2 Schaumburg (60173) *(G-18719)*
Sparton Onyx Holdings LLC (HQ) 847 762-5800
425 N Martingale Rd Schaumburg (60173) *(G-18720)*
Sparton Parent Inc (PA) 847 762-5800
425 N Martingale Rd Schaumburg (60173) *(G-18721)*
Sparx EDM Inc 847 722-7577
65 Sangra Ct Streamwood (60107) *(G-19595)*
SPD Press Prtg Solutions LLC 773 299-1700
1444 W 37th St Chicago (60609) *(G-6211)*
Speak Out, Lombard *Also called Ea Mackay Enterprises Inc (G-13070)*
Spec Built 312 623-5533
11912 Southwest Hwy Palos Park (60464) *(G-16215)*
Specco Industries Inc 630 257-5060
601 N 5th Ave Kankakee (60901) *(G-12005)*
Specgx LLC 618 664-2111
100 Louis Latzer Dr Greenville (62246) *(G-10842)*
Special Fastener Operations 815 544-6449
1993 Belford North Dr # 102 Belvidere (61008) *(G-1701)*
Special Mine Services Inc (PA) 618 932-2151
11782 Country Club Rd West Frankfort (62896) *(G-20684)*
Special Products Company, Oregon *Also called Speeco Incorporated (G-15927)*
Special Products Division, La Salle *Also called New Cie Inc (G-12118)*
Special Tool Engineering Co 773 767-6690
4539 S Knox Ave Chicago (60632) *(G-6212)*
Specialized Liftruck Svcs LLC 708 552-2705
6650 S Narragansett Ave Bedford Park (60638) *(G-1505)*
Specialized Woodwork Inc 630 627-0450
74 Eisenhower Ln N Lombard (60148) *(G-13131)*
Specially Selected, Skokie *Also called Specialty Selected Ltd (G-19033)*
Specialty Box Corp 630 897-7278
366 Smoketree Bsn Dr Pa North Aurora (60542) *(G-15277)*
Specialty Chemicals, Chicago *Also called Nouryon Chemicals LLC (G-5630)*
Specialty Cnstr Brands Inc (HQ) 630 851-0782
1105 S Frontenac St Aurora (60504) *(G-1019)*
Specialty Crate Factory (PA) 708 756-2100
3320 Louis Sherman Dr Steger (60475) *(G-19492)*
Specialty Enterprises Inc 630 595-7808
1075 Waveland Ave Franklin Park (60131) *(G-10050)*
Specialty Filaments, Arcola *Also called Monahan Filaments LLC (G-657)*
Specialty Foods Group LLC 773 378-1300
4550 W Jackson Blvd Chicago (60624) *(G-6213)*
Specialty Foods Group LLC 630 599-5900
477 E Bttrfeld Rd Ste 410 Lombard (60148) *(G-13132)*
Specialty Graphics Supply Inc 630 584-8202
3875 Commerce Dr Saint Charles (60174) *(G-18273)*
Specialty Nut & Bky Sup Co Inc 630 268-8500
1417 W Jeffrey Dr Addison (60101) *(G-294)*
Specialty Pntg Soda Blastg Inc 815 577-0006
24031 W Winners Circle Ct Plainfield (60585) *(G-16716)*
Specialty Printing Company, Niles *Also called Specialty Promotions Inc (G-15174)*
Specialty Printing Midwest 618 799-8472
1 Gemini Industrial Dr Roxana (62084) *(G-18102)*
Specialty Promotions Inc (PA) 847 588-2580
6019 W Howard St Niles (60714) *(G-15174)*
Specialty Publishing Company 630 933-0844
135 E Saint Charles Rd D Carol Stream (60188) *(G-3072)*
Specialty Screw Corporation 815 969-4100
2801 Huffman Blvd Rockford (61103) *(G-17638)*
Specialty Selected Ltd 847 967-1701
9111 Terminal Ave Skokie (60077) *(G-19033)*
Specialty Tape & Label Co Inc 708 863-3800
7830 47th St Lyons (60534) *(G-13313)*
Specific Press Brake Dies Inc 708 478-1776
9439 Enterprise Dr Mokena (60448) *(G-14116)*
Speco Inc 847 678-4240
3946 Willow St Schiller Park (60176) *(G-18845)*
Spectacle Zoom LLC 504 352-7237
8671 Josephine St Apt A Des Plaines (60016) *(G-7849)*
Spectracrafts Ltd 847 824-4117
931 N Ridge Ave Lombard (60148) *(G-13133)*
Spectral Dynamics Inc 630 595-4288
1549 Ardmore Ave Itasca (60143) *(G-11738)*
Spectroclick Inc 217 356-4829
904 Mayfair Rd Champaign (61821) *(G-3351)*
Spectron Manufacturing 720 879-7605
328 Georgetown Ct Unit C Bloomingdale (60108) *(G-2015)*
Spectrum Brands Inc 815 285-6500
200 E Corporate Dr Dixon (61021) *(G-7919)*
Spectrum Cos International 630 879-8008
336 Mckee St Batavia (60510) *(G-1418)*
Spectrum Machining Co 630 562-9400
776 W Hawthorne Ln West Chicago (60185) *(G-20645)*
Spectrum Media Inc 217 234-2044
921 S 19th St Mattoon (61938) *(G-13654)*
Spectrum Metals Inc 847 969-0887
890 E Higgins Rd Ste 150d Schaumburg (60173) *(G-18722)*
Spectrum Preferred Meats Inc 815 946-3816
6194 W Pines Rd Mount Morris (61054) *(G-14502)*
Spectrum Technologies Intl Ltd 630 961-5244
6368 Greene Rd Woodridge (60517) *(G-21341)*
Speeco Incorporated 303 279-5544
2606 S Illinois Route 2 Oregon (61061) *(G-15927)*
Speed Powder Coatings Inc 630 549-0657
870 W Hawthorne Ln Ste C West Chicago (60185) *(G-20646)*
Speed Tech Technology Inc 847 516-2001
314 Cary Point Dr Cary (60013) *(G-3191)*
Speedotron Corporation 630 246-5001
1268 Humbracht Cir Bartlett (60103) *(G-1314)*
Speedpro Imaging 847 856-8220
1350 Tri State Pkwy Gurnee (60031) *(G-10929)*
Speedpro North Shore 847 983-0095
8246 Kimball Ave Skokie (60076) *(G-19034)*
Speedpro of Dupage 630 812-5080
441 Eisenhower Ln S Lombard (60148) *(G-13134)*
Speedys Quick Print 217 431-0510
44 N Vermilion St Danville (61832) *(G-7381)*
Speidel Applicators, Stanford *Also called Quality Metal Works Inc (G-19473)*
Spell It With Color Inc 630 961-5617
1644 Swallow St Naperville (60565) *(G-14919)*
Spence Monuments Co 217 348-5992
525 W State St Charleston (61920) *(G-3413)*
Spencer and Krahn Mch Tl Sls (PA) 815 282-3300
2621 Springdale Dr Rockford (61114) *(G-17639)*
Spencer Welding Service Inc 847 272-0580
3215 Doolittle Dr Northbrook (60062) *(G-15484)*
SPEP Acquisition Corp 310 608-0693
1 Gateway Ct Ste E Bolingbrook (60440) *(G-2246)*
Spf Supplies Inc 847 454-9081
300 Scott St Elk Grove Village (60007) *(G-9249)*
Spg International LLC 815 233-0022
1555 Il Route 75 E Ste 2 Freeport (61032) *(G-10143)*
Spg Usa Inc 847 439-4949
1726 Wright Blvd Schaumburg (60193) *(G-18723)*
Sphere Inc 847 566-4800
316 Washington Blvd Mundelein (60060) *(G-14738)*
Sphere Laser LLC 317 752-1604
392 38th Ave Saint Charles (60174) *(G-18274)*
Sphere Laser LLC (PA) 317 752-1604
2020 Julia Way McHenry (60051) *(G-13793)*
Spherotech Inc 847 680-8922
27845 Irma Lee Cir # 101 Lake Forest (60045) *(G-12304)*
Sphinx Panel and Door Inc 618 351-9266
317 Locust St Cobden (62920) *(G-6944)*
Spicetec Flavors & Seasonings, Carol Stream *Also called Givaudan Flavors Corporation (G-2992)*
Spider Company Inc (PA) 815 961-8200
2340 11th St Rockford (61104) *(G-17640)*
Spider Company Inc 815 961-8200
2340 11th St Rockford (61104) *(G-17641)*
Spie Tool Co 847 891-6556
1350 Wright Blvd Schaumburg (60193) *(G-18724)*
Spike Nanotech Inc 847 504-6273
1008 Donnington Dr Matteson (60443) *(G-13629)*
Spiked 469 235-8103
1620 Fowler Ave Evanston (60201) *(G-9576)*
Spinball Sports LLC (PA) 314 503-3194
9725 Woods Dr Unit 1015 Skokie (60077) *(G-19035)*
Spinball Sports Products, Skokie *Also called Spinball Sports LLC (G-19035)*
Spinner Medical Products Inc 312 944-8700
900 N Lake Shore Dr Ste 1 Chicago (60611) *(G-6214)*
Spintex Inc 847 608-5411
1439 Holmes Rd Elgin (60123) *(G-8738)*
Spiral Binding of Illinois, Elk Grove Village *Also called S B Liquidating Company (G-9225)*
Spiral-Helix Inc 224 659-7870
500 Industrial Dr Bensenville (60106) *(G-1897)*
Spirax Sarco Inc 630 493-4525
1500 Eisenhower Ln # 600 Lisle (60532) *(G-12940)*
Spirit Brands/ Zoo Piks, Lake Forest *Also called Spirit Foodservice Inc (G-12305)*
Spirit Concepts Inc 708 388-4500
4365 136th Ct Crestwood (60418) *(G-7128)*
Spirit Foodservice Inc 214 634-1393
1900 W Field Ct Lake Forest (60045) *(G-12305)*
Spirit Industries Inc 217 285-4500
39920 274th Ln Griggsville (62340) *(G-10851)*

ALPHABETIC

Spirit Warrior Inc 708 614-0020
15519 S 70th Ct Orland Park (60462) *(G-15983)*

Spirolox Inc 847 719-5900
555 Oakwood Rd Lake Zurich (60047) *(G-12459)*

Spirotherm Inc 630 307-2662
25 N Brandon Dr Glendale Heights (60139) *(G-10497)*

Spitfire Controls, Elgin Also called Sigmatron International Inc *(G-8730)*

Spl Software Alliance LLC 309 266-0304
500 N Morton Ave Morton (61550) *(G-14383)*

Spl-Usa LLC 312 807-2000
123 N Wacker Dr Chicago (60606) *(G-6215)*

Splash Dog Therapy Inc 847 296-4007
42 N Broadway St Des Plaines (60016) *(G-7850)*

Splat Creative Inc 708 567-8412
2150 S Canalport Ave Chicago (60608) *(G-6216)*

Splice Energy Solutions LLC 815 861-8402
2106 Stilling Ln Mchenry (60050) *(G-13794)*

Split Nutrition LLC 855 775-4801
2405 N Shffeld Ave 1446 # 14466 Chicago (60614) *(G-6217)*

Sponge-Cushion Inc 815 942-2300
902 Armstrong St Morris (60450) *(G-14328)*

Spooky Cool Labs LLC 773 577-5555
5515 N Cumberland Ave # 803 Chicago (60656) *(G-6218)*

Spoon River F S, Wataga Also called West Central Fs Inc *(G-20287)*

Sport Connection 630 980-1787
741 E Nerge Rd Roselle (60172) *(G-17990)*

Sport Electronics Inc 847 564-5575
1000 Skokie Blvd Unit 413 Northbrook (60062) *(G-15485)*

Sport Incentives Inc 847 427-8650
1050 Pauly Dr Elk Grove Village (60007) *(G-9250)*

Sport Redi-Mix LLC (PA) 217 355-4222
401 Wilbur Ave Champaign (61822) *(G-3352)*

Sport Redi-Mix LLC 217 892-4222
527 S Tanner St Rantoul (61866) *(G-16983)*

Sportdecals Inc 800 435-6110
2504 Spring Ridge Dr Spring Grove (60081) *(G-19301)*

Sports All Sorts AP & Design 815 756-9910
147 N 2nd St Ste 2 Dekalb (60115) *(G-7706)*

Sports Awards, Chicago Also called Stellar Recognition Inc *(G-6243)*

Sports Corner & Creations, Peoria Also called Waldos Sports Corner Inc *(G-16545)*

Sports Designs & Graphics 217 342-2777
807 S Maple St Effingham (62401) *(G-8426)*

Sports Illustrated For Kids 312 321-7828
303 E Ohio St Ste D Chicago (60611) *(G-6219)*

Sports Profiles Plus, Skokie Also called Profile Network Inc *(G-19014)*

Sports Recreation and AP Inc 815 962-7767
623 E Jefferson St Rockford (61107) *(G-17642)*

Sportscar365, Palos Park Also called John Dagys Media LLC *(G-16212)*

Spot Printing & Office Sups, Oakbrook Terrace Also called S G C M Corp *(G-15815)*

Spot Welding Products Inc 630 238-0880
406 Dominic Ct Franklin Park (60131) *(G-10051)*

Spotlight Graphic Solutions 847 944-9600
1400 Wilkening Rd Schaumburg (60173) *(G-18725)*

Spotlight Graphics, Schaumburg Also called K & M Printing Company Inc *(G-18584)*

Spouts of Water Inc (PA) 303 570-5104
9416 Margail Ave Des Plaines (60016) *(G-7851)*

Spray Foam Direct, Riverwoods Also called Guardian Energy Tech Inc *(G-17091)*

Spraying Systems Co, Glendale Heights Also called Spraying Systems Midwest Inc *(G-10499)*

Spraying Systems Co (PA) 630 665-5000
200 W North Ave Glendale Heights (60139) *(G-10498)*

Spraying Systems Co 630 665-5001
2580 Diehl Rd Ste E Aurora (60502) *(G-1020)*

Spraying Systems Midwest Inc 630 665-5000
N Ave And Schmale Rd Glendale Heights (60139) *(G-10499)*

Spraytech LLC 847 973-9432
89 S Us Highway 12 Fox Lake (60020) *(G-9755)*

Spreader Inc 217 568-7219
2296 County Road 3000 N Gifford (61847) *(G-10348)*

Spring Brook Nature Center 630 773-5572
411 N Prospect Ave Itasca (60143) *(G-11739)*

Spring R-R Corporation 630 543-7445
100 W Laura Dr Addison (60101) *(G-295)*

Spring Specialist Corporation 815 562-7991
14400 E Dutch Rd Kings (61068) *(G-12054)*

Springbox Inc 708 921-9944
2842 Scott Cres Flossmoor (60422) *(G-9702)*

Springcoin Inc (PA) 323 577-9322
20 W Kinzie St Ste 1700 Chicago (60654) *(G-6220)*

Springfield Inc 309 944-5631
420 W Main St Geneseo (61254) *(G-10248)*

Springfield Armory, Geneseo Also called Springfield Inc *(G-10248)*

Springfield Auto Ctr Stor Pool, Springfield Also called Springfield Welding & Auto Bdy *(G-19457)*

Springfield Business Journal, Springfield Also called Springfield Publishers Inc *(G-19455)*

Springfield Coal Company LLC 217 698-3300
3008 Happy Landing Dr Springfield (62711) *(G-19451)*

Springfield Iron & Metal Co 217 544-7131
930 N Wolfe St Springfield (62702) *(G-19452)*

Springfield Pepsi-Cola Btlg Co (PA) 217 522-8841
2900 Singer Ave Springfield (62703) *(G-19453)*

Springfield Plastics Inc 217 438-6167
7300 W State Route 104 Auburn (62615) *(G-908)*

Springfield Printing Inc 217 787-3500
3500 Constitution Dr Springfield (62711) *(G-19454)*

Springfield Publishers Inc 217 726-6600
1118 W Laurel St Springfield (62704) *(G-19455)*

Springfield Sales Assoc Inc 217 529-6987
3513 Tamarak Dr Springfield (62712) *(G-19456)*

Springfield Welding & Auto Bdy 217 523-5365
2720 Holmes Ave Springfield (62704) *(G-19457)*

Springfield Woodworks 217 483-7234
6651 Wesley Chapel Rd Chatham (62629) *(G-3424)*

Sprinkles Confetti 815 304-5974
46 Baker St Kankakee (60901) *(G-12006)*

Sprinter Coml Print Label Corp 630 460-3492
4820 Fesseneva Ln Naperville (60564) *(G-14988)*

Sprout Social Inc (PA) 866 878-3231
131 S Dearborn St Ste 700 Chicago (60603) *(G-6221)*

Spudnik Press Cooperative 312 563-0302
1821 W Hubbard St Ste 302 Chicago (60622) *(G-6222)*

Spurt Inc 847 571-6497
4033 Dana Ct Northbrook (60062) *(G-15486)*

SPX Corporation 847 593-8855
800 Arthur Ave Elk Grove Village (60007) *(G-9251)*

SPX Corporation 815 874-5556
5885 11th St Rockford (61109) *(G-17643)*

SPX Flow US LLC 815 874-5556
5885 11th St Rockford (61109) *(G-17644)*

Spyco Industries Inc 630 655-5900
7029 High Grove Blvd Burr Ridge (60527) *(G-2721)*

Spyco Tool Co, Burr Ridge Also called Spyco Industries Inc *(G-2721)*

Spytek Aerospace Corporation 847 318-7515
450 Frontier Way Ste D Bensenville (60106) *(G-1898)*

Squeegee Brothers Inc (PA) 630 510-9152
398 E Saint Charles Rd Carol Stream (60188) *(G-3073)*

Squibb Tank Company 618 548-0141
1001 S Broadway Ave Salem (62881) *(G-18360)*

Sram LLC (PA) 312 664-8800
1000 W Fulton Market Fl 4 Chicago (60607) *(G-6223)*

Srds, Rosemont Also called Perq/Hci LLC *(G-18039)*

Srh Holdings Inc 847 583-2295
6100 W Howard St Niles (60714) *(G-15175)*

Srj Inc (PA) 630 351-0639
2242 Palmer Dr Schaumburg (60173) *(G-18726)*

Srm, Centreville Also called Steel Rebar Manufacturing LLC *(G-3255)*

Srm Industries Inc (PA) 847 735-0077
1009 S Green Bay Rd Lake Forest (60045) *(G-12306)*

Srmd Solutions LLC 217 925-5773
202 W Center St Dieterich (62424) *(G-7879)*

Srr Manufacturing Services 847 404-3527
205 Tyler Creek St Gilberts (60136) *(G-10372)*

SRS Global Ret Solutions LLC (PA) 773 888-3094
1001 Brown Ave Evanston (60202) *(G-9577)*

Srv Professional Publications 847 330-1260
235 Monson Ct Schaumburg (60173) *(G-18727)*

Ssa Global, Chicago Also called Infor (us) Inc *(G-4914)*

Ssab Sales Inc 630 810-4800
801 Warrenville Rd # 800 Lisle (60532) *(G-12941)*

Ssab Texas Inc 630 810-4800
801 Warrenville Rd # 800 Lisle (60532) *(G-12942)*

Ssi, Newton Also called Newton Ready Mix Inc *(G-15088)*

Ssn LLC 815 978-8729
4875 E Nordic Woods Dr Byron (61010) *(G-2759)*

Sst Forming Roll Inc 847 215-6812
1318 Busch Pkwy Buffalo Grove (60089) *(G-2608)*

St Charles Memorial Works Inc (PA) 630 584-0183
1640 W Main St Saint Charles (60174) *(G-18275)*

St Charles Screw Products Inc 815 943-8060
404 E Park St Harvard (60033) *(G-11067)*

St Charles Stamping Inc 630 584-2029
318 N 4th St Saint Charles (60174) *(G-18276)*

St Clair Tennis Club LLC 618 632-1400
733 Hartman Ln O Fallon (62269) *(G-15584)*

St Imaging Inc 847 501-3344
630 Dundee Rd Ste 210 Northbrook (60062) *(G-15487)*

St John S United Church of, Evanston Also called St Johns United Church Christ *(G-9578)*

St Johns United Church Christ 847 491-6686
1136 Wesley Ave Evanston (60202) *(G-9578)*

St Louis Flexicore Inc 618 531-8691
6351 Collinsville Rd East Saint Louis (62201) *(G-8324)*

St Louis Scrap Trading LLC 618 307-9002
5 Sunset Hills Blvd N Edwardsville (62025) *(G-8376)*

St Louis Screw & Bolt, Madison Also called Slsb LLC *(G-13417)*

St Marys Cement 773 995-5100
12101 S Doty Ave Chicago (60633) *(G-6224)*

ALPHABETIC SECTION
Starline Designs

St Marys Cement Inc (us)....313 842-4600
1914 White Oak Ln Dixon (61021) ***(G-7920)***
St Nicholas Brewing Co (PA)....618 790-9212
12 S Oak St Du Quoin (62832) ***(G-8124)***
St Pierre Oil Company Inc....618 783-4441
102 N Van Buren St Newton (62448) ***(G-15093)***
St. Louis Packaging, East Dundee *Also called Alliance Creative Group Inc* ***(G-8187)***
STA-Rite Ginnie Lou Inc....217 774-3921
245 E South 1st St Shelbyville (62565) ***(G-18887)***
Staar Bales Lestarge Inc....618 259-6366
450 W Saint Louis Ave East Alton (62024) ***(G-8171)***
Stabiloc LLC....586 412-1147
545 Kimberly Dr Carol Stream (60188) ***(G-3074)***
Stable Beginning Corporation....815 745-2100
400 S Railroad St Warren (61087) ***(G-20225)***
Stable Foods Inc....773 793-2547
7130 S Yates Blvd Apt 3 Chicago (60649) ***(G-6225)***
Stadium....312 455-2582
1901 W Madison St 5 Chicago (60612) ***(G-6226)***
Staffco Inc....309 688-3223
3806 N Northwood Ave Peoria (61614) ***(G-16528)***
Stages Construction Inc....773 619-2977
4317 Regency Dr Glenview (60025) ***(G-10624)***
Stagnito Media, Chicago *Also called Stagnito Partners LLC* ***(G-6227)***
Stagnito Partners LLC (HQ)....224 632-8200
8550 W Bryn Mawr Ave # 200 Chicago (60631) ***(G-6227)***
Stahl Lumber Company (PA)....309 695-4331
117 S Galena Ave Wyoming (61491) ***(G-21462)***
Stahl Lumber Company....309 385-2552
117 S Galena Ave Wyoming (61491) ***(G-21463)***
Stahl Ready Concrete, Wyoming *Also called Stahl Lumber Company* ***(G-21463)***
Stahl Ready Mix Concrete, Wyoming *Also called Stahl Lumber Company* ***(G-21462)***
Stained Glass of Peoria....309 674-7929
2215 W Arrowhead Ln Peoria (61604) ***(G-16529)***
Stainless Specialties Inc....618 654-7723
329 Il Route 143 Pocahontas (62275) ***(G-16754)***
Stainless Steel Prod, Deer Grove *Also called Sterling Gear Inc* ***(G-7578)***
Stairs and Rails Inc....708 216-0078
1200 Main St Ste 2 Melrose Park (60160) ***(G-13916)***
Stairsland....708 853-9593
8001 47th St Fl 4 Lyons (60534) ***(G-13314)***
Staley Concrete Co....217 356-9533
4106 Kearns Dr Champaign (61822) ***(G-3353)***
Stampede Meat Inc (HQ)....773 376-4300
7351 S 78th Ave Bridgeview (60455) ***(G-2389)***
Stan-Ed Metal Mfg Co, Chicago *Also called Ed Stan Fabricating Co* ***(G-4449)***
Stancy Woodworking Co Inc....847 526-0252
301 Fern Dr Island Lake (60042) ***(G-11611)***
Stand Fast Group LLC....630 600-0900
710 Kimberly Dr Carol Stream (60188) ***(G-3075)***
Standard Boiler Tank & Testing, Riverdale *Also called JM Industries LLC* ***(G-17072)***
Standard Car Truck Company (HQ)....847 692-6050
6400 Shafer Ct Ste 450 Rosemont (60018) ***(G-18051)***
Standard Car Truck Company....630 860-5511
701 Maple Ln Bensenville (60106) ***(G-1899)***
Standard Condenser Corporation....847 965-2722
5412 Keeney St Morton Grove (60053) ***(G-14441)***
Standard Container Co of Edgar (PA)....847 438-1510
717 N Old Rand Rd Lake Zurich (60047) ***(G-12460)***
Standard Electric Supply Inc....217 239-0800
1904 W Springer Dr Champaign (61821) ***(G-3354)***
Standard Heat Treating LLC....773 242-0853
5757 W Ogden Ave Cicero (60804) ***(G-6875)***
Standard Heat Treating Co Inc....708 447-7504
5757 W Ogden Ave Chicago (60804) ***(G-6228)***
Standard Indus & Auto Eqp Inc....630 289-9500
6211 Church Rd Hanover Park (60133) ***(G-11014)***
Standard Laboratories Inc....618 539-5836
8451 River King Dr Freeburg (62243) ***(G-10095)***
Standard Laboratory, Freeburg *Also called Standard Laboratories Inc* ***(G-10095)***
Standard Lifts & Equipment Inc....414 444-1000
6211 Church Rd Hanover Park (60133) ***(G-11015)***
Standard Machine & Tool Corp....309 762-6431
206 43rd St Moline (61265) ***(G-14179)***
Standard Marble & Granite....773 533-0450
4551 W 5th Ave Chicago (60624) ***(G-6229)***
Standard Perforating & Mfg, Chicago *Also called Accurate Perforating Co Inc* ***(G-3519)***
Standard Precision Grinding Co....708 474-1211
2800 Bernice Rd Ste 1 Lansing (60438) ***(G-12517)***
Standard Provision Co, Shorewood *Also called Rapid Foods Inc* ***(G-18902)***
Standard Refrigeration LLC....608 855-5800
321 Foster Ave Wood Dale (60191) ***(G-21242)***
Standard Register Inc....815 432-4203
112 E Walnut St Ste B Watseka (60970) ***(G-20316)***
Standard Register Inc....630 467-8300
1 Pierce Pl Ste 270c Itasca (60143) ***(G-11740)***
Standard Rubber Products Co....847 593-5630
120 Seegers Ave Elk Grove Village (60007) ***(G-9252)***
Standard Safety Equipment Co....815 363-8565
1407 Ridgeview Dr McHenry (60050) ***(G-13795)***
Standard Sheet Metal Works Inc....309 633-2300
220 N Commerce Pl Peoria (61604) ***(G-16530)***
Standard Truck Parts Inc (PA)....815 726-4486
566 N Chicago St Joliet (60432) ***(G-11932)***
Standard Wire & Steel Works, South Holland *Also called G F Ltd* ***(G-19212)***
Standex International Corp....630 588-0400
279 E Lies Rd Carol Stream (60188) ***(G-3076)***
Stanford Products LLC (HQ)....618 548-2600
1139 S Broadway Ave Salem (62881) ***(G-18361)***
Stange Industrial Group....847 640-8470
494 Bonnie Ln Elk Grove Village (60007) ***(G-9253)***
Stanger Tool & Mold Inc....847 426-5826
2713 Winfield Ln Belvidere (61008) ***(G-1702)***
Stanick Tool Manufacturing Co....847 726-7090
1190 Heather Dr Lake Zurich (60047) ***(G-12461)***
Stanley Black & Decker Inc....630 724-3632
2854 Hitchcock Ave Downers Grove (60515) ***(G-8099)***
Stanley Machining & Tool Corp (PA)....847 426-4560
425 Maple Ave Carpentersville (60110) ***(G-3120)***
Stanley Spring & Stamping Corp....773 777-2600
5050 W Foster Ave Chicago (60630) ***(G-6230)***
Stanron Corporation (PA)....773 777-2600
5050 W Foster Ave Chicago (60630) ***(G-6231)***
Stanron Steel Specialties Div, Chicago *Also called Stanron Corporation* ***(G-6231)***
Stans Sportsworld Inc....217 359-8474
47 E Green St Champaign (61820) ***(G-3355)***
Stanton Wind Energy LLC....312 224-1400
1 S Wacker Dr Ste 1900 Chicago (60606) ***(G-6232)***
Star Cabinetry....773 725-4651
4440 W Belmont Ave Chicago (60641) ***(G-6233)***
Star Cnc Machine Tool Corp....847 437-8300
375 Bennett Rd Elk Grove Village (60007) ***(G-9254)***
Star Cushion Products Inc....618 539-7070
5 Commerce Dr Freeburg (62243) ***(G-10096)***
Star Die Molding Inc....847 766-7952
2741 Katherine Way Elk Grove Village (60007) ***(G-9255)***
Star Energy Corp Inc....618 584-3631
1675 N 1200 Rd Flat Rock (62427) ***(G-9674)***
Star Forge Inc....815 235-7750
1801 S Ihm Blvd Freeport (61032) ***(G-10144)***
Star Freeport Company, Freeport *Also called Forge Group Star LLC* ***(G-10110)***
Star Freeport Company LLC....815 758-6400
1801 S Ihm Blvd Freeport (61032) ***(G-10145)***
Star Industries Inc....708 240-4862
2210 Skokie Valley Rd Highland Park (60035) ***(G-11300)***
Star Industries Intl Div, Highland Park *Also called Star Industries Inc* ***(G-11300)***
Star Lite Mfg....630 595-8338
735 N Edgewood Ave Ste C Wood Dale (60191) ***(G-21243)***
Star Manufacturing Company, Freeport *Also called Star Forge Inc* ***(G-10144)***
Star Media Group....847 674-7827
8200 Niles Center Rd Skokie (60077) ***(G-19036)***
Star Moulding & Trim Company....708 458-1040
6606 W 74th St Bedford Park (60638) ***(G-1506)***
Star Ophthalmic Instrs Inc....630 655-4500
14038 Stonegate Ln Orland Park (60467) ***(G-15984)***
Star Plastics, Broadview *Also called Star Thermoplastic Alloys and* ***(G-2470)***
Star Silkscreen Design Inc....217 877-0804
2281 E Hubbard Ave Decatur (62526) ***(G-7550)***
Star Sleigh....630 858-2576
716 Crescent Blvd Glen Ellyn (60137) ***(G-10420)***
Star Su Fellows Cutter LLC....847 649-1450
5200 Prairie Stone Pkwy Hoffman Estates (60192) ***(G-11462)***
Star Test Dynamometer Inc....309 452-0371
712 Thistlewood Cc Ct Normal (61761) ***(G-15225)***
Star Thermoplastic Alloys and (PA)....708 343-1100
2121 W 21st St Broadview (60155) ***(G-2469)***
Star Thermoplastic Alloys and....708 343-1100
2121 W 21st St Broadview (60155) ***(G-2470)***
Star Thermoplastics, Broadview *Also called Star Thermoplastic Alloys and* ***(G-2469)***
Star-Times Publishing Co Inc....618 635-2000
108 W Main St Staunton (62088) ***(G-19479)***
Starex Inc....847 918-5555
1880 W Winchester Rd # 206 Libertyville (60048) ***(G-12709)***
Starfire Industries LLC....217 721-4165
2109 S Oak St Ste 100 Champaign (61820) ***(G-3356)***
Stark Aire Fluid Bed Dryers, Downers Grove *Also called Paul D Stark & Associates* ***(G-8070)***
Stark County Communications....309 286-4444
101 W Main St Toulon (61483) ***(G-19891)***
Stark Tools and Supply Inc....847 772-8974
1001 Fargo Ave Ste 105 Elk Grove Village (60007) ***(G-9256)***
Starlight Express Coaches Inc....708 388-3365
13720 Kostner Ave Crestwood (60418) ***(G-7129)***
Starlight Software System Inc....309 454-7349
25130 Arrowhead Ln Hudson (61748) ***(G-11519)***
Starline Communications, Rockford *Also called Fred Kennerly* ***(G-17424)***
Starline Designs....773 683-7506
750 E 43rd St Chicago (60653) ***(G-6234)***

ALPHABETIC

Starmont Manufacturing Co 815 939-1041
655 S Harrison Ave Kankakee (60901) *(G-12007)*
Starmont Manufacturing Inc 708 758-2525
640 217th St Chicago Heights (60411) *(G-6776)*
Starnet Digital Publishing, Bloomington *Also called July 25th Corporation (G-2064)*
Starro Precision Products Inc 847 741-9400
1730 Todd Farm Dr Elgin (60123) *(G-8739)*
Start Magazine, Carol Stream *Also called Specialty Publishing Company (G-3072)*
Starview Vineyard, Cobden *Also called Shawnee Grapevines LLC (G-6943)*
State Attorney Appellate 217 782-3397
1021 E North Grand Ave Springfield (62702) *(G-19458)*
State Comptroller Print Shop, Springfield *Also called Financial and Professional Reg (G-19367)*
State Journal Register, The, Springfield *Also called Gatehuse Mdia III Hldngs II In (G-19374)*
State Line Foundries Inc 815 389-3921
13227 N 2nd St Roscoe (61073) *(G-17934)*
State Line International Inc 708 251-5772
18107 Torrence Ave Lansing (60438) *(G-12518)*
State of Illinois 312 836-9500
222 Merchandise Mart Plz # 1450 Chicago (60654) *(G-6235)*
State Street Jewelers Inc 630 232-2085
230 W State St Geneva (60134) *(G-10307)*
Stateline Renewable Fuels LLC 608 931-4634
6 Regent Ct W Buffalo Grove (60089) *(G-2609)*
Stateline Swiss Mfg LLC 815 282-5181
5326 Stern Dr Ste C Roscoe (61073) *(G-17935)*
Stationery Print Shop Inc (PA) 214 256-3583
925 Knollwood Dr Buffalo Grove (60089) *(G-2610)*
Staunton Star Times, Staunton *Also called Star-Times Publishing Co Inc (G-19479)*
Stay Straight Manufacturing 312 226-2137
4145 W Kinzie St Chicago (60624) *(G-6236)*
STC Inc 618 643-2555
1201 W Randolph St Mc Leansboro (62859) *(G-13708)*
STC International, Machesney Park *Also called Rockford Commercial Whse Inc (G-13371)*
Steakhouse Premium, Mount Prospect *Also called Advertising Premiums Inc (G-14509)*
Steam Plant, Chicago *Also called University of Chicago (G-6487)*
Steamgard LLC 847 913-8400
730 Forest Edge Dr Vernon Hills (60061) *(G-20100)*
Stearns Printing of Charleston 217 345-7518
304 8th St Charleston (61920) *(G-3414)*
Stecker Graphics Inc 309 786-4973
2215 4th Ave Rock Island (61201) *(G-17246)*
Steel Construction Svcs Inc 815 678-7509
9618 Keystone Rd Richmond (60071) *(G-17023)*
Steel Fab & Finish, Chicago *Also called Soudan Metals Company Inc (G-6204)*
Steel Fabricating Inc 815 977-5355
2806 22nd St Rockford (61109) *(G-17645)*
Steel Fabrication and Welding 773 343-0731
3200 S 61st Ave Cicero (60804) *(G-6876)*
Steel Management Inc 630 397-5083
716 Natwill Sq Geneva (60134) *(G-10308)*
Steel Rebar Manufacturing LLC 618 920-2748
4926 Church Rd Centreville (62207) *(G-3255)*
Steel Services Enterprises 708 259-1181
17500 Paxton Ave Lansing (60438) *(G-12519)*
Steel Solutions USA 815 432-4938
602 E Walnut St Watseka (60970) *(G-20317)*
Steel Span Inc 815 943-9071
630 W Blackman St Harvard (60033) *(G-11068)*
Steel Tube Institute N Amer 847 461-1701
2516 Waukegan Rd Ste 172 Glenview (60025) *(G-10625)*
Steel Whse Quad Cities LLC 309 756-1089
4305 81st Ave W Rock Island (61201) *(G-17247)*
Steel-Guard Safety Corp 708 589-4588
16520 Vincennes Ave South Holland (60473) *(G-19246)*
Steelcase Inc 312 321-3720
222 Merchandise Mart Plz # 300 Chicago (60654) *(G-6237)*
Steele & Loeber Lumber (HQ) 708 544-8383
801 Mannheim Rd Bellwood (60104) *(G-1640)*
Steelfab Inc 815 935-6540
2045 S Kensington Ave Kankakee (60901) *(G-12008)*
Steelweld Division, Galesburg *Also called Midstate Manufacturing Company (G-10210)*
Steibel License Service 618 233-7555
2704 N Illinois St Ste D Swansea (62226) *(G-19698)*
Stein Inc 815 626-9355
610 Wallace St Sterling (61081) *(G-19533)*
Stein Inc 618 452-0836
2201 Edwardsville Rd Granite City (62040) *(G-10739)*
Stein Steel Mini Services, Sterling *Also called Stein Inc (G-19533)*
Stein Still Mills, Granite City *Also called Stein Inc (G-10739)*
Steinbach Provision Company 773 538-1511
741 W 47th St Chicago (60609) *(G-6238)*
Steiner Electric Company 312 421-7220
2225 W Hubbard St Chicago (60612) *(G-6239)*
Steiner Impressions Inc 815 633-4135
5596 E Riverside Blvd # 2 Loves Park (61111) *(G-13266)*
Steiner Industries Inc 773 588-3444
5801 N Tripp Ave Chicago (60646) *(G-6240)*
Steinmetz R (us) Ltd 312 332-0990
67 E Madison St Ste 1606 Chicago (60603) *(G-6241)*
Stelfast Inc 847 783-0161
2780 Spectrum Dr Elgin (60124) *(G-8740)*
Stellar Blending & Packaging 314 520-7318
1556 Decoma Dr Dupo (62239) *(G-8144)*
Stellar Manufacturing Company 618 823-3761
1647 Sauget Business Blvd Cahokia (62206) *(G-2764)*
Stellar Orthtics Prsthtics LLC 847 410-2751
2401 Ravine Way Ste 301 Glenview (60025) *(G-10626)*
Stellar Performance Mfg LLC 312 951-2311
640 N La Salle Dr Ste 540 Chicago (60654) *(G-6242)*
Stellar Plastics Corporation 630 443-1200
3627 Stern Ave Saint Charles (60174) *(G-18277)*
Stellar Recognition Inc 773 282-8060
5544 W Armstrong Ave Chicago (60646) *(G-6243)*
Stellato Printing Inc 815 280-5664
777 Joyce Rd Joliet (60436) *(G-11933)*
Stellato Printing Inc (PA) 815 280-5664
1801 Jared Dr Crest Hill (60403) *(G-7097)*
Stelmont Inc 847 870-0200
1312 W Northwest Hwy Arlington Heights (60004) *(G-812)*
Steloc Fastener Co 847 459-6200
160 Abbott Dr Wheeling (60090) *(G-20989)*
Stembox, Elgin *Also called TLC Dental Care LLC (G-8755)*
Stenograph LLC (HQ) 630 532-5100
596 W Lamont Rd Elmhurst (60126) *(G-9429)*
Stentech Inc 630 833-4747
853 N Industrial Dr Elmhurst (60126) *(G-9430)*
Stentech-Chicago, Elmhurst *Also called Stentech Inc (G-9430)*
Step One Stairworks Inc 815 286-7464
201 Somonauk Rd Hinckley (60520) *(G-11359)*
Stepac USA Corporation (HQ) 630 296-2000
1201 Windham Pkwy Romeoville (60446) *(G-17877)*
Stepan Company (PA) 847 446-7500
22 W Frontage Rd Northfield (60093) *(G-15531)*
Stepan Company 847 446-7500
22500 Stepan Rd Elwood (60421) *(G-9464)*
Stepan Specialty Products LLC 847 446-7500
22 W Frontage Rd Northfield (60093) *(G-15532)*
Stephen Fossler Company 847 635-7200
1600 E Touhy Ave Des Plaines (60018) *(G-7852)*
Stephen Paoli Mfg Corp 815 965-0621
2531 11th St Rockford (61104) *(G-17646)*
Stephens Pipe & Steel LLC 800 451-2612
603 Oak Crest Dr North Aurora (60542) *(G-15278)*
Stera-Sheen, Wauconda *Also called Rd Husemoller Ltd (G-20388)*
Stereo Optical Company Inc 773 867-0380
8600 W Catalpa Ave Chicago (60656) *(G-6244)*
Stergo Roofing 312 640-9008
172 W Golf Rd Ste 299 Mount Prospect (60056) *(G-14572)*
Sterigenics US LLC 847 855-0727
1003 Lakeside Dr Gurnee (60031) *(G-10930)*
Steris Corporation 847 455-2881
11457 Melrose Ave Ste B Franklin Park (60131) *(G-10052)*
Sterline Bridge, Bensenville *Also called Pureline Treatment Systems LLC (G-1877)*
Sterline Manufacturing Corp 847 244-1234
4000 Porett Dr Ste B Gurnee (60031) *(G-10931)*
Sterling Books Limited 630 325-3853
735 S Oak St Hinsdale (60521) *(G-11380)*
Sterling Box Company Inc 815 626-9657
1980 Eastwood Dr Sterling (61081) *(G-19534)*
Sterling Brands LLC 847 229-1600
555 Allendale Dr Wheeling (60090) *(G-20990)*
Sterling Die Inc 216 267-1300
676 E Fullerton Ave Glendale Heights (60139) *(G-10500)*
Sterling Extract Company Inc 847 451-9728
10929 Franklin Ave Ste V Franklin Park (60131) *(G-10053)*
Sterling Gear Inc 815 438-4327
1582 Hoover Rd Deer Grove (61243) *(G-7578)*
Sterling Mattress Factory, Herrin *Also called Wicoff Inc (G-11182)*
Sterling Multi-Products, Prophetstown *Also called Imh Fabrication Inc (G-16833)*
Sterling Phrm Svcs LLC 618 286-4116
102 Coulter Rd East Carondelet (62240) *(G-8173)*
Sterling Phrm Svcs LLC (PA) 618 286-6060
109 S 2nd St Dupo (62239) *(G-8145)*
Sterling Plating Inc 708 867-6587
4629 N Ronald St Harwood Heights (60706) *(G-11110)*
Sterling RE & Investments, Fox River Grove *Also called Sales & Marketing Resources (G-9761)*
Sterling Site Access Sol (PA) 708 388-2223
501 E 151st St Phoenix (60426) *(G-16609)*
Sterling Spring LLC (PA) 773 582-6464
5432 W 54th St Chicago (60638) *(G-6245)*
Sterling Spring LLC 773 777-4647
7171 W 65th St Bedford Park (60638) *(G-1507)*
Sterling Steel 0530, Sterling *Also called Sterling Steel Company LLC (G-19535)*
Sterling Steel Ball, Sterling *Also called Frantz Manufacturing Company (G-19509)*

Sterling Steel Company LLC 815 548-7000
101 Avenue K Sterling (61081) *(G-19535)*
Sterling Systems & Controls 815 625-0852
24711 Emerson Rd Sterling (61081) *(G-19536)*
Sterling Systems Sales Corp 630 584-3580
3745 Stern Ave Saint Charles (60174) *(G-18278)*
Sterling Tool & Manufacturing 847 304-1800
28080 W Coml Ave Ste 8 Barrington (60010) *(G-1245)*
Sterling Vault Company 815 625-0077
2411 W Lincolnway Sterling (61081) *(G-19537)*
Sterling Wire Products Inc 815 625-3015
804 E 10th St Rock Falls (61071) *(G-17196)*
Sterling-Rock Falls Ready Mix 815 288-3135
1905 Mound Hill Rd Dixon (61021) *(G-7921)*
Sternberg Lanterns Inc (HQ) 847 588-3400
555 Lawrence Ave Roselle (60172) *(G-17991)*
Sternberg Lighting, Roselle *Also called Sternberg Lanterns Inc (G-17991)*
Sterner Screw Machine, Rockford *Also called Jim Sterner Machines (G-17474)*
Stertil Alm Corp 815 673-5546
200 Benchmark Indus Dr Streator (61364) *(G-19624)*
Steuben Township 309 208-7073
374 County Road 850 E Sparland (61565) *(G-19254)*
Steve Bortman 708 442-1669
7937 Ogden Ave Lyons (60534) *(G-13315)*
Steve C Gough 618 529-7423
550 N University Ave Carbondale (62901) *(G-2860)*
Steve Forrest 815 765-9040
290 E Park St Poplar Grove (61065) *(G-16784)*
Steve Janik Cabinetry LLC 630 553-8383
314 N Lake St Ste 3 Aurora (60506) *(G-1157)*
Steve O Inc 847 473-4466
1550 Green Bay Rd North Chicago (60064) *(G-15321)*
Steve Olson Printing & Design, North Chicago *Also called Steve O Inc (G-15321)*
Steven A Zanetis 618 393-2176
1060 W Main St Olney (62450) *(G-15889)*
Steven Brownstein 847 909-6677
5830 Lincoln Ave Unit A Morton Grove (60053) *(G-14442)*
Steven Plastics Inc 847 885-2300
2125 Stonington Ave Hoffman Estates (60169) *(G-11463)*
Stevens Cabinets Inc (PA) 217 857-7100
704 W Main St Teutopolis (62467) *(G-19773)*
Stevens Exhibits & Displays 773 523-3900
3900 S Union Ave Chicago (60609) *(G-6246)*
Stevens Group LLC (PA) 331 209-2100
188 W Indl Dr Ste 428 Elmhurst (60126) *(G-9431)*
Stevens Instrument Company 847 336-9375
111 W Greenwood Ave Waukegan (60087) *(G-20498)*
Stevens Sign Co Inc 708 562-4888
57 E Fullerton Ave Northlake (60164) *(G-15560)*
Stevens Tot-Mate, Teutopolis *Also called Stevens Cabinets Inc (G-19773)*
Stevenson Fabrication Svcs Inc 815 468-7941
680 Mulberry St Manteno (60950) *(G-13458)*
Stevenson Oil Inc 773 237-6185
3200 N Harlem Ave Chicago (60634) *(G-6247)*
Stevenson Paper Co Inc 630 879-5000
1775 Hubbard Ave Batavia (60510) *(G-1419)*
Stewart Brothers Packing Co 217 422-7741
1004 N Country Club Rd Decatur (62521) *(G-7551)*
Stewart Ingrdients Systems Inc 312 254-3539
1843 W Fulton St Chicago (60612) *(G-6248)*
Stewart Producers Inc (PA) 618 244-3754
301 N 27th St Mount Vernon (62864) *(G-14640)*
Stewart S Pritikin Associates, Bartlett *Also called Vision Sales Incorporated (G-1321)*
Stewart Well Service, Mount Vernon *Also called Stewart Producers Inc (G-14640)*
Stewarts Prvate Blend Fods Inc (PA) 773 489-2500
301 Carlton Dr Carol Stream (60188) *(G-3077)*
STI Holdings Inc 630 789-2713
15w700 N Frontage Rd # 140 Burr Ridge (60527) *(G-2722)*
Sticker Dude Inc 815 322-2480
3420 N Richmond Rd Unit A Johnsburg (60051) *(G-11810)*
Stickon Adhesive Inds Inc 847 593-5959
282 Jamie Ln Wauconda (60084) *(G-20391)*
Stickon Packaging Systems, Wauconda *Also called Stickon Adhesive Inds Inc (G-20391)*
Stiglmeier Sausage Co Inc 847 537-9988
619 Chaddick Dr Wheeling (60090) *(G-20991)*
Stikkiworks Co, Glendale Heights *Also called Lectro Stik Corp (G-10466)*
Stine Woodworking LLC 618 885-2229
16376 Bartlett Rd Dow (62022) *(G-7947)*
Stitch By Stitch Incorporated 847 541-2543
65 E Palatine Rd Ste 217 Prospect Heights (60070) *(G-16846)*
Stitch Magic Usa Inc 847 836-5000
785 S 8th St West Dundee (60118) *(G-20666)*
Stitch N Print, Chicago Ridge *Also called G & M Embroidery (G-6795)*
Stitch Plus, Prospect Heights *Also called Stitch By Stitch Incorporated (G-16846)*
Stitch TEC Co Inc (PA) 618 327-8054
887 N Washington St Nashville (62263) *(G-15011)*
Stitchables Embroidery 217 322-3000
416 Silverleaf St Rushville (62681) *(G-18113)*
Stitched Conversation 312 966-1146
404 N Marion St Oak Park (60302) *(G-15775)*
Stitchin Image 815 578-9890
9203 Glacier Rdg Richmond (60071) *(G-17024)*
Stitchmine Custom Embroidery, Glenview *Also called Gcg Corp (G-10548)*
Stm Reader LLC 312 222-6920
350 N Orleans St Chicago (60654) *(G-6249)*
Stockdale Block Systems LLC 815 416-1030
4675 Weitz Rd Morris (60450) *(G-14329)*
Stockton Stainless Inc 815 947-2168
11434 E Willow Rd Stockton (61085) *(G-19550)*
Stockwell Greetings, Chicago *Also called Salamander Studios Chicago Inc (G-6092)*
Stokes Sand & Gravel Inc 815 489-0680
35w160 Butterfield Rd Batavia (60510) *(G-1420)*
Stolle Casper Quar & Contg Co 618 337-5212
2901 Stolle Rd Dupo (62239) *(G-8146)*
Stolp Gore Company 630 904-5180
10101 Bode St Ste A Plainfield (60585) *(G-16717)*
Stone Center Inc 630 971-2060
2127 Ogden Ave Lisle (60532) *(G-12943)*
Stone Design Inc 630 790-5715
598 Mitchell Rd Glendale Heights (60139) *(G-10501)*
Stone Design Inc (PA) 630 790-5715
551 598 Mitchell Rd Glendale Heights (60139) *(G-10502)*
Stone Fabricators Company 847 788-8296
1604 N Clarence Ave Arlington Heights (60004) *(G-813)*
Stone Installation & Maint Inc 630 545-2326
598 Mitchell Rd Glendale Heights (60139) *(G-10503)*
Stone Lighting LLC 312 240-0400
2630 Flossmoor Rd Ste 102 Flossmoor (60422) *(G-9703)*
Stonecasters LLC 847 526-5200
1250 Henri Dr Wauconda (60084) *(G-20392)*
Stonecraft Cast Stone LLC 708 653-1477
3025 Louis Sherman Dr Steger (60475) *(G-19493)*
Stonecrafters Inc 815 363-8730
430 W Wegner Rd Lakemoor (60051) *(G-12477)*
Stonetree Fabrication Inc 618 332-1700
9 Production Pkwy East Saint Louis (62206) *(G-8325)*
Stop & Go International Inc 815 455-9080
3610 Thunderbird Ln Crystal Lake (60012) *(G-7269)*
Stor-Loc, Kankakee *Also called Ryan Metal Products Inc (G-12000)*
Storage Battery Systems LLC 630 221-1700
179 Easy St Carol Stream (60188) *(G-3078)*
Storage Dem Envmtl Consulting, Eola *Also called Asbestos Control & Envmtl Svc (G-9469)*
Store 409 Inc 708 478-5751
9960 191st St Ste E Mokena (60448) *(G-14117)*
Storiant Inc 617 431-8000
70 W Madison St Ste 2300 Chicago (60602) *(G-6250)*
Storms Industries Inc 312 243-7480
1500 S Western Ave Ste 5 Chicago (60608) *(G-6251)*
Stovers Fine Woodworking Inc 630 557-0072
474 Harter Rd Maple Park (60151) *(G-13466)*
Stradis Healthcare, Waukegan *Also called Stradis Medical LLC (G-20499)*
Stradis Medical LLC 847 887-8400
3600 Burwood Dr Waukegan (60085) *(G-20499)*
Strahman Valves Inc 630 208-9343
1n046 Linlar Dr Lafox (60147) *(G-12139)*
Straightline AG Inc 217 963-1270
8990 W Us 36 Harristown (62537) *(G-11033)*
Straightline Erectors Inc 708 430-5426
7812 W 91st St Oak Lawn (60457) *(G-15736)*
Strait-O-Flex 815 965-2625
7372 Kishwaukee Rd Stillman Valley (61084) *(G-19546)*
Strange Engineering Inc 847 663-1701
8300 Austin Ave Morton Grove (60053) *(G-14443)*
Strat-O-Span Buildings Inc (PA) 618 526-4566
7980 Old Us Highway 50 Breese (62230) *(G-2308)*
Strata Exploration Inc 618 842-2610
201 Ne 7th St Fairfield (62837) *(G-9637)*
Strata-Tac Inc 630 879-9388
3980 Swenson Ave Saint Charles (60174) *(G-18279)*
Stratas Foods LLC 217 424-5660
3601 E Division St Decatur (62526) *(G-7552)*
Strateg Telekom, Chicago *Also called Global Technologies I LLC (G-4699)*
Strategic Applications Inc 847 680-9385
278 Park Ave Lake Villa (60046) *(G-12368)*
Strategic Mfg Partner LLC (PA) 262 878-5213
3145 Elder Ct Northbrook (60062) *(G-15488)*
Strathmore Company 630 232-9677
2000 Gary Ln Geneva (60134) *(G-10309)*
Strathmore Press 513 483-3600
2400 E Main St Saint Charles (60174) *(G-18280)*
Strausak Inc 847 281-8550
1295 Armour Blvd Mundelein (60060) *(G-14739)*
Strausbrger Assoc Sls Mktg Inc 630 768-6179
701 Teri Ln Yorkville (60560) *(G-21501)*
Strauss Facter Assoc Inc 847 759-1100
1440 Renaissance Dr Park Ridge (60068) *(G-16297)*
Streamlinx LLC 630 864-3043
387 Shuman Blvd Ste 205w Naperville (60563) *(G-14920)*

ALPHABETIC

Streamwood Plastics Ltd........847 895-9190
979 Lunt Ave Schaumburg (60193) ***(G-18728)***
Streamwood Plating Co........630 830-6363
1545 Brandy Pkwy Streamwood (60107) ***(G-19596)***
Streator Asphalt Inc (HQ)........815 426-2164
104 S Park Rd Herscher (60941) ***(G-11187)***
Streator Asphalt Inc........815 672-8683
1019 E Livingston Rd Streator (61364) ***(G-19625)***
Streator Dependable Mfg, Streator *Also called Streator Industrial Hdlg Inc* ***(G-19626)***
Streator Industrial Hdlg Inc (HQ)........815 672-0551
1705 N Shabbona St Streator (61364) ***(G-19626)***
Streator Machine Company........815 672-2436
504 E Larue St Streator (61364) ***(G-19627)***
Streator Machine Mfg Co, Streator *Also called Streator Machine Company* ***(G-19627)***
Streem & Cleo Communications, Rockford *Also called Cleo Communications Inc* ***(G-17353)***
Street Comedy Records, Chicago *Also called Tony Patterson* ***(G-6390)***
Street Dept, Pekin *Also called City of Pekin* ***(G-16325)***
Street's, Naperville *Also called R R Street & Co Inc* ***(G-14905)***
Streets and Sanitation, Dept, Chicago *Also called City of Chicago* ***(G-4159)***
Streetwise........773 334-6600
4554 N Broadway St # 350 Chicago (60640) ***(G-6252)***
Stretch CHI........773 420-9355
4765 N Lincoln Ave # 207 Chicago (60625) ***(G-6253)***
Strictly Dentures........815 969-0531
3920 E State St Ste 2 Rockford (61108) ***(G-17647)***
Strictly Neon Inc........708 597-1616
4608 137th St Ste D Crestwood (60418) ***(G-7130)***
Strictly Signs, Crestwood *Also called Strictly Neon Inc* ***(G-7130)***
Strictly Stainless Inc........847 885-2890
2108 Stonington Ave Hoffman Estates (60169) ***(G-11464)***
Strikeforce Bowling LLC........800 297-8555
2020 Indian Boundry Dr Melrose Park (60160) ***(G-13917)***
Stripmasters Illinois Inc........618 452-1060
1107 22nd St Granite City (62040) ***(G-10740)***
Stripmasters Services Inc........217 429-0904
2500 N 22nd St Decatur (62526) ***(G-7553)***
Stritzel Awnng Svc/Aurra Tent........630 420-2000
10206 Clow Creek Rd Ste A Plainfield (60585) ***(G-16718)***
Strive Converting Corporation........773 227-6000
4545 W Palmer St Chicago (60639) ***(G-6254)***
Strohm Newspapers Inc........217 826-3600
610 Archer Ave Marshall (62441) ***(G-13578)***
Stromberg Allen and Company........773 847-7131
18504 West Creek Dr Ste A Tinley Park (60477) ***(G-19858)***
Structural Design Corp........847 816-3816
1133 Claridge Dr Libertyville (60048) ***(G-12710)***
Structural Steel Systems Limi........815 937-3800
300 N Washington Ave Bradley (60915) ***(G-2293)***
Structurepoint LLC........847 966-4357
5420 Old Orchard Rd Skokie (60077) ***(G-19037)***
Strut & Supply Inc........847 756-4337
28005 W Commercial Ave Lake Barrington (60010) ***(G-12166)***
Stryco Industries, Peoria *Also called Sommer Products Company Inc* ***(G-16526)***
Stryde Technologies Inc........510 786-8890
300 N Canal St Apt 1505 Chicago (60606) ***(G-6255)***
Stryker Corporation, Cary *Also called Sage Products LLC* ***(G-3188)***
Stryker Corporation........630 616-0606
1360 N Wood Dale Rd Ste B Wood Dale (60191) ***(G-21244)***
Stryker Corporation........847 829-5238
3909 3 Oaks Rd Cary (60013) ***(G-3192)***
Stryker Corporation........312 386-9780
350 N Orleans St Ste 650 Chicago (60654) ***(G-6256)***
Stryker Enterprises LLC........815 975-5167
7307 Edward Dr Loves Park (61111) ***(G-13267)***
Strytech Adhesives........847 509-7566
707 Skokie Blvd Ste 600 Northbrook (60062) ***(G-15489)***
Stuart Hale Company, Chicago *Also called Sdr Corp* ***(G-6123)***
Stuart Moore Racing Ltd........847 949-9100
831 E Orchard St Mundelein (60060) ***(G-14740)***
Stucchi Usa Inc........847 956-9720
1105 Windham Pkwy Romeoville (60446) ***(G-17878)***
Students Publishing Company In........847 491-7206
1999 Sheridan Rd Evanston (60201) ***(G-9579)***
Studio 41, Schaumburg *Also called Logan Square Aluminum Sup Inc* ***(G-18611)***
Studio 41, Lincolnwood *Also called Logan Square Aluminum Sup Inc* ***(G-12828)***
Studio 88 Creative Design LLC........312 288-3955
55 E Monroe St Ste 3800 Chicago (60603) ***(G-6257)***
Studio Moulding........217 523-2101
2650 Colt Rd Springfield (62707) ***(G-19459)***
Studio Out West, Forest Park *Also called Chicago Producers Inc* ***(G-9709)***
Studio Technologies Inc........847 676-9177
7440 Frontage Rd Skokie (60077) ***(G-19038)***
Studley Products Inc (PA)........309 663-2313
903 Morrissey Dr Bloomington (61701) ***(G-2097)***
Stuecklen Manufacturing Co........847 678-5130
10022 Pacific Ave Franklin Park (60131) ***(G-10054)***
Stuhlman Engrg Manfacturin Co, Plainfield *Also called Stuhlman Family LLC* ***(G-16719)***
Stuhlman Family LLC........815 436-2432
12435 S Industrial Dr E Plainfield (60585) ***(G-16719)***
Stuhr Manufacturing Co........815 398-2460
5085 27th Ave Rockford (61109) ***(G-17648)***
Stumpfoll Tool & Mfg........312 733-2632
1713 W Hubbard St Chicago (60622) ***(G-6258)***
Sturdee Metal Products Inc........773 523-3074
1060 Grand Mesa Ave New Lenox (60451) ***(G-15059)***
Sturdi Iron Inc........815 464-1173
22405 S Center Rd Frankfort (60423) ***(G-9840)***
Sturtevant Inc........630 613-8968
959 N Garfield St Lombard (60148) ***(G-13135)***
Sturtevant Richmont, Carol Stream *Also called Ryeson Corporation* ***(G-3061)***
Stutz Company........773 287-1068
4450 W Carroll Ave Chicago (60624) ***(G-6259)***
Style Rite Restaurant Eqp Co........630 628-0940
578 S Vista Ave Addison (60101) ***(G-296)***
Stylenquaza LLC........847 981-0191
750 Pratt Blvd Elk Grove Village (60007) ***(G-9257)***
Stylish Kit Bath Cabinets Corp........773 525-8667
3535 N Lincoln Ave Chicago (60657) ***(G-6260)***
Stylus Mart, Peoria *Also called Techgraphic Solutions Inc* ***(G-16536)***
Stz Industries LLC........773 265-3000
600 N Kilbourn Ave Chicago (60624) ***(G-6261)***
Su Enterprise Inc........847 394-1656
403 N Reuter Dr Arlington Heights (60005) ***(G-814)***
Sub Source Inc........815 968-7800
600 18th Ave Rockford (61104) ***(G-17649)***
Sub-Sem Inc........815 459-4139
473 S Dartmoor Dr Crystal Lake (60014) ***(G-7270)***
Sub-Surface Sign Co Ltd........847 675-6530
7410 Niles Center Rd Skokie (60077) ***(G-19039)***
Subaru of America Inc........630 250-4740
500 Park Blvd Ste 255c Itasca (60143) ***(G-11741)***
Subco Foods of Illinois Inc (PA)........630 231-0003
1150 Commerce Dr West Chicago (60185) ***(G-20647)***
Substrate Technology Inc........815 941-4800
1384 Bungalow Rd Morris (60450) ***(G-14330)***
Suburban Accents Inc........847 776-7474
3701 Berdnick St Ste A Rolling Meadows (60008) ***(G-17778)***
Suburban Drive Line, Villa Park *Also called Suburban Driveline Inc* ***(G-20174)***
Suburban Driveline Inc........630 941-7101
747 W North Ave Villa Park (60181) ***(G-20174)***
Suburban Fabricators Inc........847 729-0866
1119 Depot St Glenview (60025) ***(G-10627)***
Suburban Fix & Installation........847 823-4047
420 S Fairview Ave Park Ridge (60068) ***(G-16298)***
Suburban Indus Tl & Mfg Co........708 597-7788
11606 S Mayfield Ave Alsip (60803) ***(G-513)***
Suburban Industries Inc........630 766-3773
1090 E Green St Franklin Park (60131) ***(G-10055)***
Suburban Laminating Inc........708 389-6106
908 W Lake St Melrose Park (60160) ***(G-13918)***
Suburban Machine & Tool........815 469-2221
8119 189th St Mokena (60448) ***(G-14118)***
Suburban Machine Corporation........847 808-9095
512 Northgate Pkwy Wheeling (60090) ***(G-20992)***
Suburban Metalcraft Inc........847 678-7550
9045 Exchange Ave Franklin Park (60131) ***(G-10056)***
Suburban Plastics Co........708 681-1475
3110 S 26th Ave Broadview (60155) ***(G-2471)***
Suburban Screw Machine Pdts........815 337-0434
16210 Us Highway 14 Woodstock (60098) ***(G-21436)***
Suburban Surgical Co........847 537-9320
275 12th St Ste A Wheeling (60090) ***(G-20993)***
Suburban Welding & Steel LLC........847 678-1264
9820 Franklin Ave Franklin Park (60131) ***(G-10057)***
Subway 25858, Chicago *Also called Sunny Enterprises Inc* ***(G-6274)***
Success Journal Corp........847 583-9000
7848 Foster St Morton Grove (60053) ***(G-14444)***
Success Publishing Group Inc........708 565-2681
310 S Michigan Ave Fl 9 Chicago (60604) ***(G-6262)***
Success Vending Mfg Co LLC........773 262-1685
5128 W Irving Park Rd Chicago (60641) ***(G-6263)***
Sudden Impact Sports, Minier *Also called Laughing Dog Graphics* ***(G-14054)***
Sudholt Sheet Metal Inc........618 228-7351
350 W 4th St Aviston (62216) ***(G-1183)***
Sudpack USA Inc........630 258-4015
937 N Washington St Naperville (60563) ***(G-14921)***
Sue P Knits, Glenview *Also called Sue Peterson* ***(G-10628)***
Sue Peterson........847 730-3035
1100 Raleigh Rd Glenview (60025) ***(G-10628)***
Suez Wts Usa Inc........630 543-8480
333 S Lombard Rd Addison (60101) ***(G-297)***
Suffolk Business Group Inc........847 404-2486
132 N Prospect Ave Bartlett (60103) ***(G-1315)***
Sugar Monkey Cupcakes Inc........630 527-1869
2728 Wild Timothy Rd Naperville (60564) ***(G-14989)***
Sugar River Machine Shop........815 624-0214
667 Progressive Ln South Beloit (61080) ***(G-19115)***

Sugarcreek Woodworking 618 584-3817
1501 N 1300th St Flat Rock (62427) *(G-9675)*
Suhner Manufacturing Inc 847 308-8900
1360 Busch Pkwy Buffalo Grove (60089) *(G-2611)*
Suit Plus More, Hillside *Also called Mjt Design and Prtg Entps Inc (G-11348)*
Sukgyung At Inc 847 298-6570
2400 E Devon Ave Ste 283 Des Plaines (60018) *(G-7853)*
Sullivan Home Health Products 217 532-6366
311 Berry St Hillsboro (62049) *(G-11320)*
Sullivan Tool and Repair Inc 224 856-5867
370 Brook St Unit 3 Elgin (60120) *(G-8741)*
Sullivans Inc 815 331-8347
5508 W Chasefield Cir McHenry (60050) *(G-13796)*
Sultry Satchels Inc 312 810-1081
8159 S Troy St Chicago (60652) *(G-6264)*
Sulzer Midwest Service Center, Joliet *Also called Sulzer Pump Services (us) Inc (G-11934)*
Sulzer Pump Services (us) Inc 815 600-7355
2600 Citys Edge Dr Joliet (60436) *(G-11934)*
Suma America Inc 847 427-7880
2700 Patriot Blvd Ste 250 Glenview (60026) *(G-10629)*
Sumida America Inc 847 545-6700
1251 N Plum Grove Rd # 150 Schaumburg (60173) *(G-18729)*
Sumitomo Machinery Corp Amer 630 752-0200
175 W Lake Dr Glendale Heights (60139) *(G-10504)*
Summer Products, Peoria *Also called Micro Products Company (G-16472)*
Summervlle Consulting Svcs LLC 618 547-7142
8655 Garrett Rd Alma (62807) *(G-404)*
Summit Architectural Mtls LLC 815 934-3484
455 N Campbell Ave Chicago (60612) *(G-6265)*
Summit Graphics Inc 309 799-5100
6810 34th Street Ct Moline (61265) *(G-14180)*
Summit Industries LLC 773 353-4000
7555 N Caldwell Ave Niles (60714) *(G-15176)*
Summit Laboratories Inc 708 333-2995
17010 Halsted St Harvey (60426) *(G-11097)*
Summit Metal Products Inc 630 879-7008
1351 Nagel Blvd Batavia (60510) *(G-1421)*
Summit Plastics Inc 815 578-8700
1207 Adams Dr McHenry (60051) *(G-13797)*
Summit Polymers Inc 269 532-1900
12359 S Burley Ave Chicago (60633) *(G-6266)*
Summit Sheet Metal Specialists 708 458-8622
7325 W 59th St Summit Argo (60501) *(G-19682)*
Summit Signworks Inc 847 870-0937
2265 E Ashbury Ct Arlington Heights (60004) *(G-815)*
Summit Tank & Equipment Co 708 594-3040
7801 W 47th St Mc Cook (60525) *(G-13703)*
Summit Tooling Inc 815 385-7500
1207 Adams Dr McHenry (60051) *(G-13798)*
Summit Window Co Inc 708 594-3200
7719 W 60th Pl Ste 6 Summit Argo (60501) *(G-19683)*
Sumner Press 618 936-2212
216 S Christy Ave Sumner (62466) *(G-19688)*
Sun Ag Inc 815 689-2144
236 S Cherry St Cullom (60929) *(G-7302)*
Sun Ag Inc 309 726-1331
108 N Shiner St Hudson (61748) *(G-11520)*
Sun America, Elk Grove Village *Also called Bell Litho Inc (G-8863)*
Sun Beam Logistics Inc 847 454-5884
630 N Franklin St Apt 618 Chicago (60654) *(G-6267)*
Sun Centre Usa Inc 224 699-9058
930 Pyott Rd Ste 100 Crystal Lake (60014) *(G-7271)*
Sun Chemical Corporation 708 562-0550
135 W Lake St Ste 2 Northlake (60164) *(G-15561)*
Sun Chemical Corporation 815 939-0136
3200 Festival Dr Kankakee (60901) *(G-12009)*
Sun Chemical Corporation 630 513-5348
2445 Production Dr Saint Charles (60174) *(G-18281)*
Sun Coke Energy, Lisle *Also called Sun Coke International Inc (G-12944)*
Sun Coke International Inc (HQ) 630 824-1000
1011 Warrenville Rd # 600 Lisle (60532) *(G-12944)*
Sun Container Inc 417 681-0503
515 S 1st St Mount Vernon (62864) *(G-14641)*
Sun Dome Inc 773 890-5350
3641 S Washtenaw Ave Chicago (60632) *(G-6268)*
Sun Gard Window Fashions, Peoria *Also called Midwest Marketing Distrs Inc (G-16476)*
Sun Graphic Inc 773 775-6755
5540 N Northwest Hwy Chicago (60630) *(G-6269)*
Sun Infrared Technologies Inc 618 632-3013
808 Lakeshore Dr O Fallon (62269) *(G-15585)*
Sun Pattern & Model Inc 630 293-3366
505 Wegner Dr West Chicago (60185) *(G-20648)*
Sun Process Converting Inc 847 593-0447
1660 W Kenneth Dr Mount Prospect (60056) *(G-14573)*
Sun Steel Trading LLC (PA) 614 439-3390
10275 W Higgins Rd # 410 Rosemont (60018) *(G-18052)*
Sun Times News Agency 815 672-1260
56 Sunset Dr Streator (61364) *(G-19628)*
Sun Transformer, Mc Leansboro *Also called STC Inc (G-13708)*
Sun-Times Media LLC 312 222-6920
350 N Orleans St 1000b-1 Chicago (60654) *(G-6270)*
Sun-Times Media Group Inc (HQ) 312 321-3000
30 N Racine Ave Ste 300 Chicago (60607) *(G-6271)*
Sun-Times Media Holdings LLC (HQ) 312 321-2299
350 N Orleans St 1000b-1 Chicago (60654) *(G-6272)*
Sunbelt Plastic Extrusions, Rockford *Also called Southern Imperial Inc (G-17637)*
Sunburst Sportswear Inc (PA) 630 717-8680
95 N Brandon Dr Glendale Heights (60139) *(G-10505)*
Suncast Corporation (PA) 630 879-2050
701 N Kirk Rd Batavia (60510) *(G-1422)*
Suncoke Energy Inc (PA) 630 824-1000
1011 Warrenville Rd # 600 Lisle (60532) *(G-12945)*
Suncoke Energy Partners LP (HQ) 630 824-1000
1011 Warrenville Rd # 600 Lisle (60532) *(G-12946)*
Suncoke Technology and Dev LLC 630 824-1000
1011 Warrenville Rd Fl 6 Lisle (60532) *(G-12947)*
Suncraft Technologies Inc (PA) 630 369-7900
1301 Frontenac Rd Naperville (60563) *(G-14922)*
Sunday Missal Service, Quincy *Also called Pam Printers and Publs Inc (G-16922)*
Sundstrom Pressed Steel Co 773 721-2237
8030 S South Chicago Ave Chicago (60617) *(G-6273)*
Sunemco Technologies Inc 630 369-8947
500 Braemar Ave Naperville (60563) *(G-14923)*
Sung Ji USA Inc 847 956-9400
128 N Lively Blvd Elk Grove Village (60007) *(G-9258)*
Sungard, Chicago *Also called Powerschool Group LLC (G-5850)*
Sunglass Otftters By Snglass H 847 645-0476
5225 Prairie Stone Pkwy Hoffman Estates (60192) *(G-11465)*
Sunny Brook Farm, Campbell Hill *Also called Mast Harness Shop (G-2816)*
Sunny Day Distributing Inc 630 779-8466
76 E Meadow Dr Cortland (60112) *(G-7027)*
Sunny Direct LLC (PA) 630 795-0800
300 E 5th Ave Ste 465 Naperville (60563) *(G-14924)*
Sunny Enterprises Inc 847 219-1045
2811 S Kedzie Ave Chicago (60623) *(G-6274)*
Sunnywood Incorporated 815 675-9777
2750 Barney Ct McHenry (60051) *(G-13799)*
Sunrise AG Service Company 309 538-4287
Rr 1 Kilbourne (62655) *(G-12045)*
Sunrise Digital, Chicago *Also called Sunrise Hitek Service Inc (G-6277)*
Sunrise Distributors Inc 630 400-8786
2411 United Ln Elk Grove Village (60007) *(G-9259)*
Sunrise Electronics Inc 847 357-0500
130 Martin Ln Elk Grove Village (60007) *(G-9260)*
Sunrise Foods, Elk Grove Village *Also called Sunrise Distributors Inc (G-9259)*
Sunrise Futures LLC 312 612-1041
30 S Wacker Dr Ste 1706 Chicago (60606) *(G-6275)*
Sunrise Hitek Group LLC 773 792-8880
5915 N Northwest Hwy Chicago (60631) *(G-6276)*
Sunrise Hitek Service Inc 773 792-8880
5915 N Northwest Hwy Chicago (60631) *(G-6277)*
Sunrise Printing Inc 847 928-1800
9701 Cary Ave Schiller Park (60176) *(G-18846)*
Sunscape Time Inc 708 345-8791
2001 Janice Ave Melrose Park (60160) *(G-13919)*
Sunset Food Mart Inc 847 234-0854
825 S Waukegan Rd Ste A8 Lake Forest (60045) *(G-12307)*
Sunset Halthcare Solutions Inc (PA) 877 578-6738
180 N Michigan Ave # 2000 Chicago (60601) *(G-6278)*
Sunshine Metals Inc 304 422-0090
555 Skokie Blvd Ste 555 # 555 Northbrook (60062) *(G-15490)*
Sunshine Products, Maywood *Also called Mackenzie Johnson (G-13672)*
Sunsource Holdings Inc (PA) 630 317-2700
2301 W Windsor Ct Addison (60101) *(G-298)*
Sunstar Americas Inc (HQ) 847 794-4157
301 E Central Rd Schaumburg (60195) *(G-18730)*
Sunstar Pharmaceutical Inc 773 777-4000
1300 Abbott Dr Elgin (60123) *(G-8742)*
Suntimez Entertainment 630 747-0712
5811 W Roosevelt Rd Cicero (60804) *(G-6877)*
Supalicious Soups Inc 708 491-9738
7251 S Luella Ave Chicago (60649) *(G-6279)*
Suparossa Pizza, Chicago *Also called Biagios Gourmet Foods Inc (G-3880)*
Super Aggregates Inc (HQ) 815 385-8000
5435 Bull Valley Rd # 330 McHenry (60050) *(G-13800)*
Super Life, Chicago *Also called Unicut Corporation (G-6464)*
Super Mix, McHenry *Also called Super Aggregates Inc (G-13800)*
Super Mix Inc (PA) 815 578-9100
5435 Bull Valley Rd # 130 McHenry (60050) *(G-13801)*
Super Mix of Wisconsin Inc 262 859-9000
5435 Bull Valley Rd # 130 McHenry (60050) *(G-13802)*
Super Mix of Wisconsin Inc 815 578-9100
5435 Bull Valley Rd # 130 McHenry (60050) *(G-13803)*
Super Phone Store, Urbana *Also called Robert Higgins (G-19999)*
Super Press Instant Prtg Co, Mount Prospect *Also called Grovak Instant Printing Co (G-14532)*

ALPHABETIC

Super Sign Service ALPHABETIC SECTION

Super Sign Service.....309 829-9241
621 W Olive St Bloomington (61701) ***(G-2098)***
Super Sublimation LLC.....309 256-0184
368 Erie Ave Morton (61550) ***(G-14384)***
Super Target Systems LLC.....800 556-3162
2055 Comprehensive Dr Aurora (60505) ***(G-1158)***
Super-Cut Abrasives, Carol Stream *Also called Saint-Gobain Abrasives Inc* ***(G-3063)***
Super-Dri Corp.....708 599-8700
9707 S 76th Ave Bridgeview (60455) ***(G-2390)***
Superabrasives, Carol Stream *Also called Saint-Gobain Abrasives Inc* ***(G-3062)***
Superheat Fgh Services Inc.....618 251-9450
4767 Signature Industrial Roxana (62084) ***(G-18103)***
Superheat Fgh Services Inc (PA).....708 478-0205
313 Garnet Dr New Lenox (60451) ***(G-15060)***
Superheat Fgh Services Inc (PA).....708 478-0205
313 Garnet Dr New Lenox (60451) ***(G-15061)***
Superior Baking Stone Inc.....815 726-4610
926 Plainfield Rd Joliet (60435) ***(G-11935)***
Superior Biologics II Inc.....847 469-2400
2050 E Algonquin Rd # 606 Schaumburg (60173) ***(G-18731)***
Superior Bumpers Inc.....630 932-4910
920 N Ridge Ave Ste C3 Lombard (60148) ***(G-13136)***
Superior Cabinet Company.....708 658-6613
8904 S Harlem Ave Bridgeview (60455) ***(G-2391)***
Superior Cabinet Supply Inc.....815 464-2700
19800 S Harlem Ave Frankfort (60423) ***(G-9841)***
Superior Coatings Illinois LLC.....309 367-9625
612 Outback Ln Metamora (61548) ***(G-13969)***
Superior Felt & Filtration LLC.....815 331-6382
27709 W Concrete Dr Ingleside (60041) ***(G-11590)***
Superior Findings, Chicago *Also called Masud Jewelers Inc* ***(G-5363)***
Superior Graphite Co (PA).....312 559-2999
10 S Riverside Plz # 1470 Chicago (60606) ***(G-6280)***
Superior Graphite Co.....708 458-0006
6540 S Laramie Ave Chicago (60638) ***(G-6281)***
Superior Graphite Co.....773 890-4100
4201 W 36th St Bldg Rear Chicago (60632) ***(G-6282)***
Superior Health Linens LLC.....630 593-5091
1160 Pierson Dr Ste 104 Batavia (60510) ***(G-1423)***
Superior Home Products Inc.....217 726-9300
3000 Great Northern Springfield (62711) ***(G-19460)***
Superior Industries Inc.....309 346-1742
14425 Wagonseller Rd Pekin (61554) ***(G-16362)***
Superior Joining Tech Inc.....815 282-7581
1260 Turret Dr Machesney Park (61115) ***(G-13376)***
Superior Knife Inc.....847 982-2280
6235 W Howard St Niles (60714) ***(G-15177)***
Superior Metal Finishing.....815 282-8888
962 Industrial Ct Loves Park (61111) ***(G-13268)***
Superior Metal Products Inc.....630 466-1150
1993 Bucktail Ln Sugar Grove (60554) ***(G-19657)***
Superior Metalcraft Inc.....708 418-8940
17655 Chappel Ave Lansing (60438) ***(G-12520)***
Superior Mfg Group - Europe (PA).....708 458-4600
5655 W 73rd St Bestle Par Chicago (60638) ***(G-6283)***
Superior Mobile Home Service.....708 672-7799
3421 E Reichert Dr Crete (60417) ***(G-7146)***
Superior Piling Inc.....708 496-1196
7247 S 78th Ave Ste 2 Bridgeview (60455) ***(G-2392)***
Superior Print Services Inc.....630 257-7012
12305 New Ave Ste H Lemont (60439) ***(G-12591)***
Superior Surgical Instrumen TS.....630 628-8437
602 W Lake Park Dr Addison (60101) ***(G-299)***
Superior Table Pad Co.....773 248-7232
3010 N Oakley Ave Chicago (60618) ***(G-6284)***
Superior Truck Dock Services.....630 978-1697
2431 Angela Ln Aurora (60502) ***(G-1021)***
Superior Water Services Inc.....309 691-9287
5831 N Knoxville Ave Peoria (61614) ***(G-16531)***
Superior Water Systems, Peoria *Also called Superior Water Services Inc* ***(G-16531)***
Superior Welding Inc.....618 544-8822
9172 E 1050th Ave Robinson (62454) ***(G-17126)***
Superior X Ray Tube Company.....815 338-4424
1220 Claussen Dr Woodstock (60098) ***(G-21437)***
Superno2va, Mettawa *Also called Revolutionary Medical Dvcs Inc* ***(G-13981)***
Supertek Scientific LLC.....630 345-3450
15 W Commercial Ave Addison (60101) ***(G-300)***
Supertuf, Edwardsville *Also called Beall Manufacturing Inc* ***(G-8349)***
Supplied Indus Solutions Inc.....618 452-8151
550 Niedringhaus Ave Granite City (62040) ***(G-10741)***
Supply Solutions Network, Byron *Also called Ssn LLC* ***(G-2759)***
Supply Vision Inc.....847 388-0064
171 N Aberdeen St Ste 400 Chicago (60607) ***(G-6285)***
Supportstoreus, Litchfield *Also called Quality Plus* ***(G-12974)***
Supreme Felt & Abrasives Inc.....708 344-0134
1633 S 55th Ave Cicero (60804) ***(G-6878)***
Supreme Frame & Moulding Co.....312 930-9056
652 W Randolph St Chicago (60661) ***(G-6286)***
Supreme Hinge, University Park *Also called Qh Inc* ***(G-19965)***
Supreme Manufacturing Company.....847 297-8212
1755 Birchwood Ave Des Plaines (60018) ***(G-7854)***
Supreme Screw Inc.....630 226-9000
1224 N Independence Blvd Romeoville (60446) ***(G-17879)***
Supreme Screw Products.....708 579-3500
5227 Dansher Rd Countryside (60525) ***(G-7073)***
Supreme Tamale Co.....773 622-3777
1495 Brummel Ave Elk Grove Village (60007) ***(G-9261)***
Sur-Fit Corporation.....815 301-5815
110 Erick St Crystal Lake (60014) ***(G-7272)***
Surcom Industries Inc.....773 378-0736
1017 N Cicero Ave Chicago (60651) ***(G-6287)***
Sure Plus Manufacturing Co.....708 756-3100
185 E 12th St Chicago Heights (60411) ***(G-6777)***
Sure Shine Polishing.....217 853-4888
1455 N Main St Decatur (62526) ***(G-7554)***
Sure-Response Inc.....888 530-5668
1075 N Reed Station Rd Carbondale (62902) ***(G-2861)***
Sure-Way Die Designs Inc (PA).....630 323-0370
414 Lindley Ave Westmont (60559) ***(G-20774)***
Sure-Way Products, Westmont *Also called Sure-Way Die Designs Inc* ***(G-20774)***
Surebond Inc.....630 762-0606
3925 Stern Ave Saint Charles (60174) ***(G-18282)***
Surebonder Adhesives Inc.....847 487-4583
355 Hollow Hill Rd Wauconda (60084) ***(G-20393)***
Surebonder Com Inc.....847 270-0254
23670 W Chardon Rd Grayslake (60030) ***(G-10801)***
Suretint Technologies LLC (PA).....847 509-3625
411 E Bus Ctr Dr Ste 104 Mount Prospect (60056) ***(G-14574)***
Sureway Tool & Engineering Co, Franklin Park *Also called Mrt Sureway Inc* ***(G-10004)***
Surface Finishes, Addison *Also called SF Holdings Group LLC* ***(G-287)***
Surface Manufacturing Company.....815 569-2362
135 S 4th St Capron (61012) ***(G-2837)***
Surface Mining Reclamation Off.....618 463-6460
501 Belle St Ste 216 Alton (62002) ***(G-573)***
Surface Shields Inc (PA).....708 226-9810
8451 183rd Pl Tinley Park (60487) ***(G-19859)***
Surface Solutions Group LLC.....773 427-2084
5492 N Northwest Hwy Chicago (60630) ***(G-6288)***
Surface Solutions Illinois Inc (PA).....708 571-3449
9615 194th Pl Mokena (60448) ***(G-14119)***
Surfacetec Corp.....630 521-0001
471 Podlin Dr Franklin Park (60131) ***(G-10058)***
Surge Clutch & Drive Line Co.....708 331-1352
16145 Thornton Blue Is South Holland (60473) ***(G-19247)***
Surgical Innovation Assoc Inc (PA).....626 372-4884
800 Liberty Dr Chicago (60601) ***(G-6289)***
Surgical Innovation Assoc Inc.....847 548-8499
800 Liberty Dr Libertyville (60048) ***(G-12711)***
Surgical Instrument Service Co.....630 221-1988
151 N Brandon Dr Glendale Heights (60139) ***(G-10506)***
Surgical Instrument Svcs & Sav.....847 646-2000
3 Lakes Dr Northfield (60093) ***(G-15533)***
Surgical Solutions LLC.....847 607-6098
1751 Lake Cook Rd Ste 230 Deerfield (60015) ***(G-7650)***
Surplus Record LLC.....312 372-9077
20 N Wacker Dr Ste 2400 Chicago (60606) ***(G-6290)***
Surrey Books Inc.....847 475-4457
1501 Madison St Evanston (60202) ***(G-9580)***
Suruga USA Corp.....630 628-0989
1717 N Penny Ln Ste 200 Schaumburg (60173) ***(G-18732)***
Survyvn Ltd.....847 977-8665
4613 Glacial Trl Ringwood (60072) ***(G-17048)***
Surya Electronics Inc.....630 858-8000
600 Windy Point Dr Glendale Heights (60139) ***(G-10507)***
Sustainable Innovations Inc.....815 713-1637
1491 S Bell School Rd Rockford (61108) ***(G-17650)***
Sustainable Solutions Amer Led, Chicago *Also called Sustanble Sltions Amer Led LLC* ***(G-6291)***
Sustainable Sourcing LLC.....815 714-8055
19633 S La Grange Rd Mokena (60448) ***(G-14120)***
Sustanable Infrastructures Inc.....815 341-1447
20632 Abbey Dr Frankfort (60423) ***(G-9842)***
Sustanble Sltions Amer Led LLC.....866 323-3494
910 W Van Buren St Ste 6a Chicago (60607) ***(G-6291)***
Suter Company Inc.....815 895-9186
1015 Bethany Rd Sycamore (60178) ***(G-19733)***
Suzlon Wind Energy Corporation.....773 328-5077
2583 Technology Dr Elgin (60124) ***(G-8743)***
Sv Family Evanston LLC.....773 420-6767
6 Martha Ln Evanston (60201) ***(G-9581)***
Swaby Manufacturing Company (PA).....773 626-1400
5420 W Roosevelt Rd 300b Chicago (60644) ***(G-6292)***
Swag Golf, Northbrook *Also called Kuldisak LLC* ***(G-15416)***
Swager & Associates, Bridgeport *Also called Team Energy LLC* ***(G-2316)***
Swagger Foods Corporation.....847 913-1200
900 Corporate Woods Pkwy Vernon Hills (60061) ***(G-20101)***
Swan Analytical Usa Inc.....847 229-1290
225 Larkin Dr Ste 4 Wheeling (60090) ***(G-20994)***

ALPHABETIC SECTION

Swan Surfaces LLC 618 532-5673
 200 Swan Ave Centralia (62801) *(G-3252)*
Swansea Building Products Inc 618 874-6282
 494 N 33rd St East Saint Louis (62205) *(G-8326)*
Swanson Water Treatment Inc 847 680-1113
 509 E Park Ave Ste 101 Libertyville (60048) *(G-12712)*
Swapp Technologies Inc 312 912-1515
 505 N Mcclurg Ct Apt 1505 Chicago (60611) *(G-6293)*
Swarovski North America Ltd 708 364-0090
 288 Orland Square Dr Orland Park (60462) *(G-15985)*
Swarovski North America Ltd 847 680-5150
 116 Hawthorne Shopg Ctr Vernon Hills (60061) *(G-20102)*
Swarovski North America Ltd 847 413-9960
 D344 Woodfield Mall Schaumburg (60173) *(G-18733)*
Swarovski US Holding Limited 847 679-8670
 4999 Old Orchard Ctr B22 Skokie (60077) *(G-19040)*
SWB Inc 847 438-1800
 529 Capital Dr Lake Zurich (60047) *(G-12462)*
Swd Inc 630 543-3003
 910 S Stiles Dr Addison (60101) *(G-301)*
Swebco Mfg Inc 815 636-7160
 7909 Burden Rd Machesney Park (61115) *(G-13377)*
Swedish Food Products, Chicago Also called Noon Hour Food Products Inc *(G-5612)*
Sweet Annies Bakery Inc 708 297-7066
 19710 Governors Hwy Ste 6 Flossmoor (60422) *(G-9704)*
Sweet As Sin, Roscoe Also called Scott Sawvel *(G-17932)*
Sweet Creation By Sheila 708 754-7938
 803 N Rainbow Dr Glenwood (60425) *(G-10645)*
Sweet Manufacturing Corp 847 546-5575
 111 E Chestnut St Apt 36k Chicago (60611) *(G-6294)*
Sweet Solutions LLC 630 364-2843
 25503 W Ruff St Unit A Plainfield (60585) *(G-16720)*
Sweet Specialty Solutions LLC 630 739-9151
 1005 101st St Ste B Lemont (60439) *(G-12592)*
Sweet Thyme Soaps 708 848-0234
 808 S Elmwood Ave Oak Park (60304) *(G-15776)*
Sweetener Supply Corporation 708 484-3455
 2905 Ridgeland Ave Berwyn (60402) *(G-1961)*
Swift Education Systems Inc 312 257-3751
 332 S Michigan Ave # 1032 Chicago (60604) *(G-6295)*
Swift Impressions Inc 312 372-0002
 70 E Lake St Ste 1010 Chicago (60601) *(G-6296)*
Swift Technologies Inc 815 568-8402
 8601 S Hill Rd Marengo (60152) *(G-13494)*
Swifty Print 630 584-9063
 210 W Main St Saint Charles (60174) *(G-18283)*
Swirlcup 847 229-2200
 255 Parkway Dr Ste B Lincolnshire (60069) *(G-12796)*
Swiss Automation Inc 847 381-4405
 1020 W Northwest Hwy Barrington (60010) *(G-1246)*
Swiss E D M Wirecut Inc 847 459-4310
 743 Pinecrest Dr Prospect Heights (60070) *(G-16847)*
Swiss Precision Machining Inc 847 647-7111
 634 Glenn Ave Wheeling (60090) *(G-20995)*
Swiss Products LP 773 394-6480
 4333 W Division St Chicago (60651) *(G-6297)*
Swisslog Consulting, Rolling Meadows Also called Translogic Corporation *(G-17781)*
Swissport Fueling Incorpo 773 203-5419
 5000 W 63rd St Chicago (60638) *(G-6298)*
Swisstronics Corp 708 403-8877
 16308 107th Ave Ste 8 Orland Park (60467) *(G-15986)*
Switchboard Apparatus, Franklin Park Also called SAI Advanced Pwr Solutions Inc *(G-10041)*
Switchcraft Inc (HQ) 773 792-2700
 5555 N Elston Ave Chicago (60630) *(G-6299)*
Switchcraft Holdco Inc (HQ) 773 792-2700
 5555 N Elston Ave Chicago (60630) *(G-6300)*
Switchee Bandz Usa LLC 312 415-1100
 804 Kimballwood Ln Highland Park (60035) *(G-11301)*
Switchee USA, Highland Park Also called Switchee Bandz Usa LLC *(G-11301)*
Swiveloc, Carol Stream Also called Stabiloc LLC *(G-3074)*
Swoon Living, Chicago Also called 3-Switch LLC *(G-3466)*
Sws Industries Inc 904 482-0091
 280 Prairie Ridge Dr Woodstock (60098) *(G-21438)*
Sycamore Precision 815 784-5151
 334 E 1st St Ste 1 Genoa (60135) *(G-10324)*
Sycamore Welding & Fabg Co 815 784-2557
 675 Park Ave Genoa (60135) *(G-10325)*
Symbol Tool Inc 847 674-1080
 8106 Ridgeway Ave Skokie (60076) *(G-19041)*
Symbria Rx Services LLC (PA) 630 981-8000
 7125 Janes Ave Ste 300 Woodridge (60517) *(G-21342)*
Symfact Inc 847 380-4174
 55 W Monroe St Ste 2900 Chicago (60603) *(G-6301)*
Synax Inc 224 352-2927
 1374 Abbott Ct Buffalo Grove (60089) *(G-2612)*
Syndigo LLC 309 690-5231
 1720 W Detweiller Dr Peoria (61615) *(G-16532)*
Synergetic Holdings LLC 309 673-2437
 3012 Sw Adams St Peoria (61602) *(G-16533)*
Synergetic Industries 309 321-8145
 1060 W Jefferson St Morton (61550) *(G-14385)*
Synergy Advnced Phrmctcals Inc 212 297-0020
 300 N La Salle Dr # 4925 Chicago (60654) *(G-6302)*
Synergy Flavors Inc (HQ) 847 487-1011
 1500 Synergy Dr Wauconda (60084) *(G-20394)*
Synergy Flavors NY Company LLC (HQ) 585 232-6648
 1500 Synergy Dr Wauconda (60084) *(G-20395)*
Synergy Mech Solutions Inc 847 437-4500
 55 N Lively Blvd Elk Grove Village (60007) *(G-9262)*
Synergy Mechanical Inc 708 410-1004
 9835 Derby Ln Westchester (60154) *(G-20713)*
Synergy Power Group LLC 618 247-3200
 610 E Illinois Ave Sandoval (62882) *(G-18365)*
Synergy Technology Group Inc 773 305-3500
 1250 W Augusta Blvd # 201 Chicago (60642) *(G-6303)*
Syngenta Seeds LLC 309 478-3686
 18356 Rte 9 Pekin (61554) *(G-16363)*
Synlawn of Chicago, Chicago Also called Outdoor Space LLC *(G-5715)*
Synopsys Inc 847 706-2000
 10 N Martingale Rd # 400 Schaumburg (60173) *(G-18734)*
Synsel Energy Inc 630 516-1284
 445 W Fullerton Ave Elmhurst (60126) *(G-9432)*
Syr Tech Perforating, Glendale Heights Also called United Steel Perforating/ARC *(G-10513)*
Syr-Tech Perforating Co 630 942-7300
 325 Windy Point Dr Glendale Heights (60139) *(G-10508)*
Syracuse Guage, Dixon Also called Schrader-Bridgeport Intl Inc *(G-7916)*
Sysmex America Inc (HQ) 847 996-4500
 577 Aptakisic Rd Lincolnshire (60069) *(G-12797)*
Sysmex Reagents America Inc 847 996-4500
 2 Sysmex Way Mundelein (60060) *(G-14741)*
System Science Corporation 708 214-2264
 1408 W Taylor St Apt 301 Chicago (60607) *(G-6304)*
Systematics Screen Printing 630 521-1123
 1625 Norwood Ave Itasca (60143) *(G-11742)*
Systems & Electronics Inc 847 228-0985
 190 Gordon St Elk Grove Village (60007) *(G-9263)*
Systems By Lar Inc 815 694-3141
 841 E 3000 North Rd Clifton (60927) *(G-6916)*
Systems Equipment Services 708 535-1273
 4314 166th St Oak Forest (60452) *(G-15689)*
Systems Live Ltd 815 455-3383
 6917 Red Barn Rd Crystal Lake (60012) *(G-7273)*
Systems Piping 847 948-1373
 1625 Half Day Rd Deerfield (60015) *(G-7651)*
Systems Unlimited Inc 630 285-0010
 1350 W Bryn Mawr Ave Itasca (60143) *(G-11743)*
Systemslogix LLC 630 784-3113
 140 W Lake Dr Glendale Heights (60139) *(G-10509)*
T & C Graphics Inc 630 532-5050
 645 Stevenson Rd South Elgin (60177) *(G-19175)*
T & C Metal Co 815 459-4445
 378 E Prairie St Crystal Lake (60014) *(G-7274)*
T & D Metal Products LLC (PA) 815 432-4938
 602 E Walnut St Watseka (60970) *(G-20318)*
T & E Auto Haulers, Herscher Also called T & E Enterprises Herscher Inc *(G-11188)*
T & E Enterprises Herscher Inc 815 426-2761
 80 Tobey Dr Herscher (60941) *(G-11188)*
T & H Lemont Inc 708 482-1800
 5118 Dansher Rd Countryside (60525) *(G-7074)*
T & J Electric Company Inc 309 347-2196
 2627 Allentown Rd Pekin (61554) *(G-16364)*
T & J Meatpacking Inc 708 758-6748
 635 Glenwood Dyer Rd Chicago Heights (60411) *(G-6778)*
T & K Precision Grinding 708 450-0565
 1301 Armitage Ave Ste C Melrose Park (60160) *(G-13920)*
T & K Tool & Manufacturing Co 815 338-0954
 2250 S Eastwood Dr Woodstock (60098) *(G-21439)*
T & K Trucking, Caseyville Also called Kevin Robinson *(G-3217)*
T & L Sheet Metal Inc 630 628-7960
 555 S Vista Ave Addison (60101) *(G-302)*
T & S Business Group LLC 815 432-7084
 602 E Walnut St Watseka (60970) *(G-20319)*
T & T Carbide Inc 618 439-7253
 17409 Lowry Ave Logan (62856) *(G-13032)*
T & T Complete Construction 312 929-5352
 205 S Peoria St Apt 1306 Chicago (60607) *(G-6305)*
T & T Distribution Inc 815 223-0715
 304 5th St Peru (61354) *(G-16594)*
T & T Machine Shop 847 244-2020
 4406 Lee Ave Gurnee (60031) *(G-10932)*
T 26 Inc 773 862-1201
 1110 N Milwaukee Ave Chicago (60642) *(G-6306)*
T A E Signals Division, East Hazel Crest Also called Tool Automation Enterprises *(G-8218)*
T A U Inc 708 841-5757
 14075 Lincoln Ave Dolton (60419) *(G-7940)*
T and T Cabinet Co 815 245-6322
 5505 W Chasefield Cir McHenry (60050) *(G-13804)*

T C, Schaumburg *Also called Thiessen Communications Inc* ***(G-18746)***
T C I Vacuum Forming Company 847 622-9100
1620 Cambridge Dr Elgin (60123) ***(G-8744)***
T C W F Inc 630 369-1360
1577 Nperville Wheaton Rd Naperville (60563) ***(G-14925)***
T C4 Inc 618 335-3486
1207 N Carlisle Rd Vandalia (62471) ***(G-20026)***
T D J Group Inc 847 639-1113
760 Industrial Dr Ste A Cary (60013) ***(G-3193)***
T E A M, Elk Grove Village *Also called Team Impressions Inc* ***(G-9266)***
T E C A, Chicago *Also called Thermoelectric Coolg Amer Corp* ***(G-6362)***
T E Q, Huntley *Also called Thermform Engineered Qulty LLC* ***(G-11568)***
T F N W Inc 630 584-7383
1577 Nperville Wheaton Rd Naperville (60563) ***(G-14926)***
T G Automotive 630 916-7818
901 N Ridge Ave Ste 1 Lombard (60148) ***(G-13137)***
T Graphics 618 592-4145
701 S Range St Oblong (62449) ***(G-15830)***
T H Davidson & Co Inc (PA) 815 464-2000
4243 166th St Oak Forest (60452) ***(G-15690)***
T H Davidson & Co Inc 815 941-0280
1350 Bungalow Rd Morris (60450) ***(G-14331)***
T H K Holdings of America LLC (HQ) 847 310-1111
200 Commerce Dr Schaumburg (60173) ***(G-18735)***
T Ham Sign Inc (PA) 618 242-2010
7699 N Goshen Ln Opdyke (62872) ***(G-15905)***
T J Brooks Co 847 680-0350
804 E Park Ave Ste 104 Libertyville (60048) ***(G-12713)***
T J M & Associates Inc 847 382-1993
1160 N Dato Ln Wauconda (60084) ***(G-20396)***
T J Marche Ltd 618 445-2314
11 N 5th St Albion (62806) ***(G-353)***
T J Martin & Co Division, Orland Park *Also called Diagrind Inc* ***(G-15951)***
T J P Investments Inc 309 673-8383
2522 W War Memorial Dr Peoria (61615) ***(G-16534)***
T J S Equipment Inc 618 656-8046
1514 Weber Dr Edwardsville (62025) ***(G-8377)***
T J Van Der Bosch & Associates 815 344-3210
430 W Wegner Rd McHenry (60051) ***(G-13805)***
T K O Waterproof Coating LLP 815 338-2006
427 E Judd St Woodstock (60098) ***(G-21440)***
T L Swint Industries Inc 847 358-3834
2211 Banbury Rd Inverness (60067) ***(G-11598)***
T M I S, Wauconda *Also called Tent Maker Industrial Sup Inc* ***(G-20398)***
T M J, Crystal Lake *Also called TMJ Architectural LLC* ***(G-7283)***
T M T Industries Inc 815 562-0111
770 Wiscold Dr Rochelle (61068) ***(G-17161)***
T P R Resources Inc 630 443-9060
3604 Greenwood Ln Saint Charles (60175) ***(G-18284)***
T R Communications Inc 773 238-3366
10546 S Western Ave Chicago (60643) ***(G-6307)***
T R Machine Inc 815 865-5711
103 Il Route 75 E Ste 100 Davis (61019) ***(G-7419)***
T R Z Motorsports Inc 815 806-0838
25045 S Center Rd Frankfort (60423) ***(G-9843)***
T Renee Productions, Flora *Also called Crusade Enterprises Inc* ***(G-9679)***
T S I, Galena *Also called Technical Sealants Inc* ***(G-10179)***
T Shirtz Etc Inc 815 962-5194
1000 9th St Apt D Rockford (61104) ***(G-17651)***
T T T Inc 630 860-7499
387 Crestwood Rd Wood Dale (60191) ***(G-21245)***
T&D Trucking, Watseka *Also called T & D Metal Products LLC* ***(G-20318)***
T&J Turning Inc 309 738-8762
4 Goembel Dr Colona (61241) ***(G-6981)***
T&L International Mfg/Dist Inc 309 830-7238
25833 Hillcrest Dr Farmer City (61842) ***(G-9658)***
T&T Hydraulics, Peru *Also called T & T Distribution Inc* ***(G-16594)***
T-G Ad Service, Chicago *Also called Mer-Pla Inc* ***(G-5393)***
T-Mobile, Hickory Hills *Also called Smart Choice Mobile Inc* ***(G-11203)***
T-Mobile Usa Inc 847 289-9988
416 Randall Rd South Elgin (60177) ***(G-19176)***
T-P Electric & Manufacturing, Lawrenceville *Also called Tracy Electric Inc* ***(G-12538)***
T-Shirt Factory, The, Galesburg *Also called Go Van Goghs Tee Shirt* ***(G-10198)***
T.S. Shure, Chicago *Also called Shure Products Inc* ***(G-6162)***
T/CCI Manufacturing LLC (PA) 217 423-0066
2120 N 22nd St Decatur (62526) ***(G-7555)***
T/J Fabricators Inc 630 543-2293
2150 W Executive Dr Addison (60101) ***(G-303)***
T2 Cabinets Inc 312 593-1507
1400 W 37th St Chicago (60609) ***(G-6308)***
T2 Site Amenities Incorporated 847 579-9003
1805 Spruce St Highland Park (60035) ***(G-11302)***
T9 Group LLC 847 912-8862
25635 N Stoney Kirk Ct Hawthorn Woods (60047) ***(G-11126)***
Ta Delaware Inc 773 646-6550
12350 S Avenue O Chicago (60633) ***(G-6309)***
Ta Oil Field Service Inc 618 249-9001
27573 State Route 177 Richview (62877) ***(G-17034)***
Taap Corp 224 676-0653
300 Holbrook Dr Wheeling (60090) ***(G-20996)***
Tabbies, Itasca *Also called Xertrex International Inc* ***(G-11755)***
Tablecraft Products Co Inc (PA) 847 855-9000
801 Lakeside Dr Gurnee (60031) ***(G-10933)***
Tacknologies 630 729-9900
10720 Beaudin Blvd Ste A Woodridge (60517) ***(G-21343)***
Tacmina USA Corporation 312 810-8128
105 W Central Rd Schaumburg (60195) ***(G-18736)***
Tactical Lighting Systems Inc 800 705-0518
1001 N Lombard Rd Lombard (60148) ***(G-13138)***
Tadd LLC 847 380-3540
188 Northwest Hwy Cary (60013) ***(G-3194)***
Tads 815 654-3500
10 E Riverside Blvd Loves Park (61111) ***(G-13269)***
Tafco Corporation 847 678-8425
1953 N 17th Ave Melrose Park (60160) ***(G-13921)***
Tag Diamond & Label 630 844-9395
100 Hankes Ave Aurora (60505) ***(G-1159)***
Tag Master Line, Wauconda *Also called Dard Products Inc* ***(G-20341)***
Tag Sales Co Inc 630 990-3434
1000 Jorie Blvd Ste 26 Hinsdale (60523) ***(G-11381)***
Tag Tool Services Incorporated 309 694-2400
3303 N Main St East Peoria (61611) ***(G-8292)***
Tag's Bakery & Pastry Shop, Evanston *Also called Tags Bakery Inc* ***(G-9582)***
Tag-Barton LLC (PA) 217 428-0711
1395 S Taylorville Rd Decatur (62521) ***(G-7556)***
Tagitsold Inc 630 724-1800
1136 Lacebark Ct Darien (60561) ***(G-7412)***
Tagore Technology Inc 847 790-3799
5 E College Dr Ste 200 Arlington Heights (60004) ***(G-816)***
Tags Bakery Inc 847 328-1200
2010 Central St Evanston (60201) ***(G-9582)***
Tahini Empire Inc 773 742-2382
4938 N Elston Ave Chicago (60630) ***(G-6310)***
Tailored Inc 708 387-9854
9520 47th St Ste 2 Brookfield (60513) ***(G-2493)***
Tailored Printing Inc 217 498-1057
4855 Sage Rd Rochester (62563) ***(G-17172)***
Tails Inc 773 564-9300
4410 N Ravenswood Ave # 1 Chicago (60640) ***(G-6311)***
Tailwinds Distillery 630 746-7526
14912 S Eastern Ave Plainfield (60544) ***(G-16721)***
Taisei Lamick USA Inc 847 258-3283
1801 Howard St Elk Grove Village (60007) ***(G-9264)***
Tait Machine Tool Inc 815 932-2011
417 S Schuyler Ave Kankakee (60901) ***(G-12010)***
Taitt Burial Garments 773 483-7424
6649 S Wabash Ave Chicago (60637) ***(G-6312)***
TAKASAGO INTERNATIONAL CORPORATION (U.S.A.), Crystal Lake *Also called Takasago Intl Corp USA* ***(G-7275)***
Takasago Intl Corp USA 815 479-5030
300 Memorial Dr Ste 100 Crystal Lake (60014) ***(G-7275)***
Take Your Mark Sports LLC 708 655-0525
1010 Longmeadow Ln Western Springs (60558) ***(G-20726)***
Takeda 847 902-0659
8 Copperfield Dr Hawthorn Woods (60047) ***(G-11127)***
Takeda Pharmaceuticals USA Inc 847 315-9228
2355 Waukegan Rd Bannockburn (60015) ***(G-1209)***
Takeda Phrmaceuticals Intl Inc 224 554-6500
1200 Lakeside Dr Bannockburn (60015) ***(G-1210)***
Tal-Mar Cstm Met Fbrctors Corp 708 371-0333
4632 138th St Crestwood (60418) ***(G-7131)***
Talaris Inc (HQ) 630 577-1000
3333 Warrenville Rd # 310 Lisle (60532) ***(G-12948)***
Talcott Communications Corp (PA) 312 849-2220
704 N Wells St Fl 2 Chicago (60654) ***(G-6313)***
Talis Biomedical Corporation (PA) 312 589-5000
125 S Clark St Fl 17 Chicago (60603) ***(G-6314)***
Talk-A-Phone LLC 773 539-1100
7530 N Natchez Ave Niles (60714) ***(G-15178)***
Tall Trees Farm, Crystal Lake *Also called Ridgefield Industries Co LLC* ***(G-7256)***
Tallwood 815 786-8186
15751 Burr Oak Rd Plano (60545) ***(G-16744)***
Tally Metals Holdings LLC 773 264-5900
1031 E 103rd St Chicago (60628) ***(G-6315)***
Taloc Usa Inc 847 665-8222
1915 Enterprise Ct Libertyville (60048) ***(G-12714)***
Tam Tav Bakery Inc 773 764-8877
2944 W Devon Ave Chicago (60659) ***(G-6316)***
Tamarack Products Inc 847 526-9333
1071 N Old Rand Rd Wauconda (60084) ***(G-20397)***
Tamms Industries Inc 815 522-3394
3835 Il Route 72 Kirkland (60146) ***(G-12066)***
Tammy Banks 312 280-1388
500 N Michigan Ave # 600 Chicago (60611) ***(G-6317)***
Tammy Smith 618 372-8410
14 Willow Way Brighton (62012) ***(G-2404)***
Tampico Beverages Inc 773 296-0190
2425 W Barry Ave Chicago (60618) ***(G-6318)***

ALPHABETIC SECTION Tc Industries Inc (HQ)

Tampico Beverages Inc (HQ)......773 296-0190
3106 N Campbell Ave Chicago (60618) *(G-6319)*
Tampico Press......312 243-5448
1919 S Blue Island Ave Chicago (60608) *(G-6320)*
Tampoprint Mid-West Corp......312 971-7715
525 W Monroe St Ste 2360 Chicago (60661) *(G-6321)*
Tampotech Decorating Inc......847 515-2968
10901 Union Special Plz Huntley (60142) *(G-11567)*
Tamtam Candy, Addison *Also called Samad General Services Inc (G-280)*
Tanaka Dental Enterprises Inc......847 679-1610
8001 Lincoln Ave Ste 201 Skokie (60077) *(G-19042)*
Tanaka Dental Products Div, Skokie *Also called Tanaka Dental Enterprises Inc (G-19042)*
Tanaka Kikinzoku International, Schaumburg *Also called Tanaka Kknzoku Intrnational Kk (G-18738)*
Tanaka Kikinzoku Intl Amer Inc......224 653-8309
475 N Martingale Rd # 150 Schaumburg (60173) *(G-18737)*
Tanaka Kknzoku Intrnational Kk......224 653-8309
425 N Martingale Rd # 1550 Schaumburg (60173) *(G-18738)*
Tancher Corp......847 668-8765
1493 Vernon Ave Park Ridge (60068) *(G-16299)*
Tandem Industries Inc......630 761-6615
3820 Ohio Ave Ste 16 Saint Charles (60174) *(G-18285)*
Tandem Usa LLC......224 653-8840
518 Lunt Ave Schaumburg (60193) *(G-18739)*
Tane Corporation......847 705-7125
1122 W Partridge Dr Palatine (60067) *(G-16161)*
Tangent Screen Print Inc......773 342-1223
9041 S Albany Ave Evergreen Park (60805) *(G-9601)*
Tangent Systems Inc......847 882-3833
2155 Stnngton Ave Ste 107 Hoffman Estates (60169) *(G-11466)*
Tangent Technologies LLC (PA)......630 264-1110
1001 Sullivan Rd Aurora (60506) *(G-1160)*
Tanis Custom Golf, Matteson *Also called Custom Golf By Tanis (G-13622)*
Tank In A Box LLC......847 624-1234
333 S Wabash Ave Ste 2700 Chicago (60604) *(G-6322)*
Tank Noodle Inc......773 878-2253
4953 N Broadway St Chicago (60640) *(G-6323)*
Tank Wind-Down Corp......815 756-1551
345 Harvestore Dr Dekalb (60115) *(G-7707)*
Tanklink Corporation, Chicago *Also called Skybitz Tank Monitoring Corp (G-6183)*
Tanko Screw Products, Bensenville *Also called L D Redmer Screw Pdts Inc (G-1838)*
Tanko Scrw Prd Corp......708 418-0300
19830 Stoney Island Ave Chicago Heights (60411) *(G-6779)*
Tannery Row LLC......847 840-7647
1515 W Carroll Ave Chicago (60607) *(G-6324)*
Tanvas Inc......773 295-6220
600 W Van Buren St # 710 Chicago (60607) *(G-6325)*
Tanya Shipley......708 476-0433
11344 Abbey Rd Mokena (60448) *(G-14121)*
Tao Trading Corporation......773 764-6542
1420 W Howard St Apt 201 Chicago (60626) *(G-6326)*
Tapco Cutting Tools Inc......815 877-4039
5605 Pike Rd Loves Park (61111) *(G-13270)*
Tapco USA Inc......815 877-4039
5605 Pike Rd Loves Park (61111) *(G-13271)*
Tape Case Ltd......847 299-7880
150 Gaylord St Elk Grove Village (60007) *(G-9265)*
Tar-B Precision Machining Corp......630 521-9771
605 Country Club Dr Ste D Bensenville (60106) *(G-1900)*
Tara International LP......708 354-7050
9100 67th St Hodgkins (60525) *(G-11398)*
Tara Tape, Carbondale *Also called Rjm Manufacturing Inc (G-2856)*
Taranda Specialties Inc......815 469-3041
8746 W Manhattan Monee Rd Frankfort (60423) *(G-9844)*
Target, Palatine *Also called Aimtron Systems LLC (G-16092)*
Target, Rantoul *Also called East Central Communications Co (G-16975)*
Target Laser & Machining Inc......815 963-6706
2433 Fremont St Rockford (61103) *(G-17652)*
Target Plastics Tech Corp......630 545-1776
400 Windy Point Dr Glendale Heights (60139) *(G-10510)*
Targin Sign Systems Inc......630 766-7667
160 W Irving Park Rd Wood Dale (60191) *(G-21246)*
Targun Plastic Co......847 509-9355
899 Skokie Blvd Ste 334 Northbrook (60062) *(G-15491)*
Tarney Inc......773 235-0331
4520 W North Ave Chicago (60639) *(G-6327)*
Tarnow Logistics Inc......773 844-3203
1001 N 16th Ave Melrose Park (60160) *(G-13922)*
Tarps Manufacturing Inc......217 245-6181
1000 State Highway 104 Meredosia (62665) *(G-13957)*
Tarrerias-Bonjean USA Inc......216 217-1726
541 N Fairbanks Ct # 2200 Chicago (60611) *(G-6328)*
Tarte Cupcakery Company......312 898-2103
18509 School St Apt 1d Lansing (60438) *(G-12521)*
Tassos Metal Inc......630 953-1333
950 N Lombard Rd Lombard (60148) *(G-13139)*
Tate & Lyle Americas LLC......217 421-3268
2200 E Eldorado St Decatur (62521) *(G-7557)*
Tate & Lyle Citric Acid, Decatur *Also called Tate Lyle Ingrdnts Amricas LLC (G-7558)*
Tate and Lyle, Heyworth *Also called Tate Lyle Ingrdnts Amricas LLC (G-11191)*
Tate Lyle Ingrdnts Amricas LLC......847 396-7500
5450 Prairie Stone Pkwy Hoffman Estates (60192) *(G-11467)*
Tate Lyle Ingrdnts Amricas LLC (HQ)......217 423-4411
2200 E Eldorado St Decatur (62521) *(G-7558)*
Tate Lyle Ingrdnts Amricas LLC......309 473-2721
702 S Vine St Heyworth (61745) *(G-11191)*
Tatine......312 733-0173
4200 W Diversey Ave Chicago (60639) *(G-6329)*
Tatty Stick LLC......815 905-1023
205 Highpoint Dr Essex (60935) *(G-9476)*
Taubensee Steel & Wire Company (PA)......847 459-5100
600 Diens Dr Wheeling (60090) *(G-20997)*
Tauber Brothers Tool & Die Co......708 867-9100
4701 N Olcott Ave Chicago (60706) *(G-6330)*
Taurus 80 LLC......704 927-2793
5196 27th Ave Rockford (61109) *(G-17653)*
Taurus Cycle......309 454-1565
1 Lafayette Ct Bloomington (61701) *(G-2099)*
Taurus Die Casting LLC......815 316-6160
5196 27th Ave Rockford (61109) *(G-17654)*
Taurus Engraving, Elk Grove Village *Also called Ambrit Inc (G-8820)*
Taurus Safety Products Inc......630 620-7940
39 S Glenview Ave Lombard (60148) *(G-13140)*
Taw Enterprises LLC......618 466-0134
5100 Seminole Ct Godfrey (62035) *(G-10664)*
Tax Collector, Melrose Park *Also called Bost Corporation (G-13835)*
Taycorp Inc (PA)......708 629-0921
5700 W 120th St Alsip (60803) *(G-514)*
Taycorp Inc......630 530-7500
752 N Larch Ave Elmhurst (60126) *(G-9433)*
Taykit Inc......847 888-1150
1175 Davis Rd Elgin (60123) *(G-8745)*
Taylor & Francis Group LLC......630 482-9886
1292 Averill Dr Batavia (60510) *(G-1424)*
Taylor Co Asuess Taylor......815 624-8333
750 N Blackhawk Blvd Rockton (61072) *(G-17702)*
Taylor Coating Sales, Brookfield *Also called Taylor Consultants Inc (G-2495)*
Taylor Coating Sales Inc......708 387-0305
8520 Brookfield Ave Brookfield (60513) *(G-2494)*
Taylor Coml Foodservice Inc (HQ)......815 624-8333
750 N Blackhawk Blvd Rockton (61072) *(G-17703)*
Taylor Coml Foodservice Inc......815 624-8333
98 Autumnwood Dr Rockton (61072) *(G-17704)*
Taylor Communication......309 664-0444
1 Hardman Dr Bloomington (61701) *(G-2100)*
Taylor Communications Inc......309 693-3700
1100 W Glen Ave Ste 300 Peoria (61614) *(G-16535)*
Taylor Communications Inc......217 793-1900
450 S Durkin Dr Ste C Springfield (62704) *(G-19461)*
Taylor Communications Inc......708 560-7600
4849 167th St Ste 201 Oak Forest (60452) *(G-15691)*
Taylor Communications Inc......630 368-0336
900 Jorie Blvd Ste 238 Oak Brook (60523) *(G-15663)*
Taylor Consultants, Brookfield *Also called Taylor Coating Sales Inc (G-2494)*
Taylor Consultants Inc......708 387-0305
8520 Brookfield Ave Brookfield (60513) *(G-2495)*
Taylor Design Inc......815 389-3991
5375 E Rockton Rd Roscoe (61073) *(G-17936)*
Taylor Enterprises Inc......847 367-1032
5510 Fairmont Rd Ste A Libertyville (60048) *(G-12715)*
Taylor Farms Illinois Inc......312 432-6800
200 N Artesian Ave Chicago (60612) *(G-6331)*
Taylor Made Machining Inc......815 339-6267
W Mark Indus Park Rr 71 Mark (61340) *(G-13547)*
Taylor Off Road Racing......815 544-4500
6925 Imron Dr Belvidere (61008) *(G-1703)*
Taylor Pharmacal Co......217 423-9715
1222 W Grand Ave Decatur (62522) *(G-7559)*
Taylor Spring Mfg. Co., Alsip *Also called Taycorp Inc (G-514)*
Taylors Candy Inc......708 371-0332
4855 W 115th St Alsip (60803) *(G-515)*
Tazewell Floor Covering Inc......309 266-6371
419 W Jefferson St Morton (61550) *(G-14386)*
Tazewell Machine Works Inc......309 347-3181
2015 S 2nd St Pekin (61554) *(G-16365)*
Tb Woods Incorporated......815 389-6600
449 Gardner St South Beloit (61080) *(G-19116)*
Tbc Corporation......630 428-2233
915 E Ogden Ave Naperville (60563) *(G-14927)*
Tbc Retail Group Inc......630 692-0232
1971 Hill Ave Montgomery (60538) *(G-14271)*
Tbw Machining Inc......847 524-1501
1030 Morse Ave Schaumburg (60193) *(G-18740)*
Tc Electric Controls LLC......815 213-7680
1741 Industrial Dr # 14 Sterling (61081) *(G-19538)*
Tc Electric Controls LLC (PA)......815 213-7680
1320 Tower Rd Schaumburg (60173) *(G-18741)*
Tc Industries Inc (HQ)......815 459-2401
3703 S Il Route 31 Crystal Lake (60012) *(G-7276)*

ALPHABETIC

Tc Printers, Salem *Also called Salem Times-Commoner Inc* ***(G-18358)***
TCI Companies Inc......309 965-2057
405 State Route 117 Goodfield (61742) ***(G-10677)***
TCI Manufacturing & Eqp Sls, Walnut *Also called Tricon Inds Mfg & Eqp Sls* ***(G-20220)***
Tcr Systems LLC......217 877-5622
4900 N Brush College Rd Decatur (62526) ***(G-7560)***
Tdc Filter......503 521-9988
2 Territorial Ct Bolingbrook (60440) ***(G-2247)***
Tdm Systems Inc......847 605-1269
1901 N Roselle Rd Ste 800 Schaumburg (60195) ***(G-18742)***
Tdr Express Inc......224 805-0070
5231 N Oakview St Apt 3e Chicago (60656) ***(G-6332)***
Tdr Transport, Yorkville *Also called Edward J Warren Jr* ***(G-21481)***
Tds Inc......847 678-2084
9225 Ivanhoe St Schiller Park (60176) ***(G-18847)***
TDS Machining Inc......630 964-0004
8402 Wilmette Ave Ste B Darien (60561) ***(G-7413)***
Tdw Services Inc......815 407-0675
565 Anderson Dr Ste A Romeoville (60446) ***(G-17880)***
Tdw Welding LLC (PA)......217 690-3521
17515 N 400th St Wheeler (62479) ***(G-20833)***
Tdy Industries LLC......847 564-0700
700 Landwehr Rd Northbrook (60062) ***(G-15492)***
Te Connectivity Corporation......847 680-7400
620 S Butterfield Rd Mundelein (60060) ***(G-14742)***
Te Shurt Shop Inc......217 344-1226
711 S Wright St Champaign (61820) ***(G-3357)***
Team Cnc Inc......630 377-2723
761 N 17th St Ste 22 Saint Charles (60174) ***(G-18286)***
Team Cncept Prtg Thrmgrphy Inc......630 653-8326
540 Tower Blvd Carol Stream (60188) ***(G-3079)***
Team Energy LLC (PA)......618 943-1010
Rr 1 Box 197 Bridgeport (62417) ***(G-2316)***
Team Fenex, Sandoval *Also called Synergy Power Group LLC* ***(G-18365)***
Team Impressions Inc......847 357-9270
360 Scott St Elk Grove Village (60007) ***(G-9266)***
Team Play Inc......847 952-7533
201 Crossen Ave Elk Grove Village (60007) ***(G-9267)***
Team Print Inc......815 933-5111
1605 Commerce Dr Bourbonnais (60914) ***(G-2269)***
Team Products Inc......815 244-6100
636 S East St Mount Carroll (61053) ***(G-14497)***
Team Sider Inc......847 767-0107
158 Hastings Ave Highland Park (60035) ***(G-11303)***
Team Technologies Inc......630 406-0678
1119 Lyon Rd Batavia (60510) ***(G-1425)***
Team Technologies Inc......630 937-0380
1300 Nagel Blvd Batavia (60510) ***(G-1426)***
Team Works By Holzhauer Inc......309 745-9924
2168 Washington Rd Washington (61571) ***(G-20281)***
Teamdance Illinois......815 463-9044
215 Fulton St Geneva (60134) ***(G-10310)***
Teasdale Foods Inc......217 283-7771
215 W Washington St Hoopeston (60942) ***(G-11514)***
Tease......630 960-4950
4717 Seeley Ave Downers Grove (60515) ***(G-8100)***
TEC Foods Inc......800 315-8002
4300 W Ohio St Chicago (60624) ***(G-6333)***
TEC Rep Corporation......630 627-9110
1919 S Highland Ave 330a Lombard (60148) ***(G-13141)***
TEC Systems Inc......815 722-2800
908 Garnet Ct New Lenox (60451) ***(G-15062)***
Tech Global Inc......847 532-4882
2759 Pinnacle Dr Elgin (60124) ***(G-8746)***
Tech Global Inc......224 623-2000
2521 Tech Dr Ste 206 Elgin (60124) ***(G-8747)***
Tech Oasis International Inc......847 302-1590
5652 Chapel Hl Gurnee (60031) ***(G-10934)***
Tech Star Design and Mfg......847 290-8676
116 N Lively Blvd Elk Grove Village (60007) ***(G-9268)***
Tech Upgraders......877 324-8940
2007 S 9th Ave Maywood (60153) ***(G-13678)***
Tech-Max Machine Inc......630 875-0054
1170 Ardmore Ave Itasca (60143) ***(G-11744)***
Tech-Tool Enterprise......630 639-9425
100 Monaco Dr Roselle (60172) ***(G-17992)***
Tech-Weld Inc......630 365-3000
801 E North St Elburn (60119) ***(G-8474)***
Techgraphic Solutions Inc......309 693-9400
8824 N Industrial Rd Peoria (61615) ***(G-16536)***
Techmer Pm LLC......630 579-6961
900 Douglas Rd Batavia (60510) ***(G-1427)***
Technatool Inc......847 398-0355
2222 Foster Ave Wheeling (60090) ***(G-20998)***
Technetics Group LLC......708 887-6080
7319 W Wilson Ave Harwood Heights (60706) ***(G-11111)***
Technic Inc......773 262-2662
3265 N Ridge Ave Arlington Heights (60004) ***(G-817)***
Technical Metals Inc......815 692-4643
1301 W Oak St Fairbury (61739) ***(G-9614)***
Technical Ordnance Inc......630 969-0620
2525 Curtiss St Downers Grove (60515) ***(G-8101)***
Technical Power Systems Inc......630 719-1471
4642 Western Ave Lisle (60532) ***(G-12949)***
Technical Propellants Inc......815 942-2900
6440 E Collins Rd Morris (60450) ***(G-14332)***
Technical Sales Midwest Inc......847 855-2457
36149 N Edgewater Ct Gurnee (60031) ***(G-10935)***
Technical Sealants Inc......815 777-9797
11476 Technnical Dr Galena (61036) ***(G-10179)***
Technical Services Intl Inc......708 596-5200
3115 167th St Hazel Crest (60429) ***(G-11138)***
Technical Tool Enterprise......630 893-3390
1550 W Fullerton Ave D Addison (60101) ***(G-304)***
Technicraft Display Graphics, Peoria *Also called Technicraft Supply Co* ***(G-16537)***
Technicraft Supply Co (PA)......309 495-5245
419 Elm St Peoria (61605) ***(G-16537)***
Technics Inc......630 938-4709
1000 W Crossroads Pkwy J Bolingbrook (60490) ***(G-2248)***
Technics Fabrication Inc......630 938-4709
1000 W Crossroads Pkwy Bolingbrook (60490) ***(G-2249)***
Technigraph, Chicago *Also called Alpha Packaging Minnesota Inc* ***(G-3630)***
Technipaq Inc......815 477-1800
975 Lutter Dr Crystal Lake (60014) ***(G-7277)***
Technique Eng Inc......847 816-1870
968 S Northpoint Blvd Waukegan (60085) ***(G-20500)***
Technique Engineering Inc......847 816-1870
968 S Northpoint Blvd Waukegan (60085) ***(G-20501)***
Technisand, Troy Grove *Also called Fairmount Santrol Inc* ***(G-19921)***
Technisand Inc......815 433-2449
776 Centennial Dr Ottawa (61350) ***(G-16080)***
Techno - Grphics Trnsltons Inc......708 331-3333
1451 E 168th St South Holland (60473) ***(G-19248)***
Technocure, Antioch *Also called Pro Tools & Equipment Inc* ***(G-631)***
Technologies Dvlpmnt......815 943-9922
3517 Braberry Ln Crystal Lake (60012) ***(G-7278)***
Technology Assistance USA LLC......773 671-6712
5117 Ne River Rd Unit 1j Chicago (60656) ***(G-6334)***
Technology One Welding Inc......630 871-1296
210 Easy St Ste D Carol Stream (60188) ***(G-3080)***
Technotrans America Inc (HQ)......847 227-9200
1441 E Business Center Dr Mount Prospect (60056) ***(G-14575)***
Technoweld, Chicago *Also called Alberto Daza* ***(G-3597)***
Technox Machine & Mfg Inc......773 745-6800
2619 N Normandy Ave Chicago (60707) ***(G-6335)***
Techny Plastics Corp......847 498-2212
1919 Techny Rd Northbrook (60062) ***(G-15493)***
Techny Precision Mfg Inc......630 543-7065
818 S Westwood Ave Ste C Addison (60101) ***(G-305)***
Technymon Technology USA Inc......630 787-0501
730 N Edgewood Ave Wood Dale (60191) ***(G-21247)***
Techo-Bloc Midwest Corp......877 832-4625
8111 31st St W Rock Island (61201) ***(G-17248)***
Techpol Automation Inc......847 347-4765
2083 Maple St Des Plaines (60018) ***(G-7855)***
Techprint Inc......847 616-0109
2330 Eastern Ave Elk Grove Village (60007) ***(G-9269)***
Tecnova Electronics Inc......847 336-6160
2383 N Delany Rd Waukegan (60087) ***(G-20502)***
Tecstar Mfg Company III Div, Libertyville *Also called Mgs Mfg Group Inc* ***(G-12680)***
Ted Muller......312 435-0978
910 S Michigan Ave # 1612 Chicago (60605) ***(G-6336)***
Tedds Cstm Installations Inc......815 485-6800
21719 S Center Ave Ste A New Lenox (60451) ***(G-15063)***
Tedds Custom Installations, New Lenox *Also called Tedds Cstm Installations Inc* ***(G-15063)***
Teds Shirt Shack Inc......217 224-9705
2811 Bluff Ridge Dr Quincy (62305) ***(G-16946)***
Tee Group Films Inc......815 894-2331
605 N Mn Ave Ladd (61329) ***(G-12134)***
Tee Lee Popcorn Inc......815 864-2363
101 W Badger St Shannon (61078) ***(G-18874)***
Teejet Technologies LLC (HQ)......630 665-5002
1801 Business Park Dr Springfield (62703) ***(G-19462)***
Teenfitnation LLC......847 322-2953
12 Westlake Dr South Barrington (60010) ***(G-19077)***
Teepak Usa LLC......217 446-6460
915 N Michigan Ave Danville (61834) ***(G-7382)***
Tees and Things......708 351-8584
537 W 111th St Chicago (60628) ***(G-6337)***
Tees Ink......815 462-7300
1215 Revere Ct New Lenox (60451) ***(G-15064)***
Teestyler Inc......630 484-3104
4163 Oak Tree Ln Plainfield (60586) ***(G-16722)***
Tegna Inc......847 490-6657
1721 Moon Lake Blvd # 540 Hoffman Estates (60169) ***(G-11468)***
Tegrant Alloyd Brands Inc (HQ)......815 756-8451
1401 Pleasant St Dekalb (60115) ***(G-7708)***
Tegrant Corporation......630 879-0121
1500 Paramount Pkwy Batavia (60510) ***(G-1428)***

ALPHABETIC SECTION
Termax LLC

Tegratecs Development Corp....847 397-0088
1320 Tower Rd Schaumburg (60173) ***(G-18743)***
Teitelbaum Brothers Inc....847 729-3490
1944 Lehigh Ave Ste D Glenview (60026) ***(G-10630)***
Tek Pak Inc (PA)....630 406-0560
1336 Paramount Pkwy Batavia (60510) ***(G-1429)***
Tek Pak Inc....331 901-5570
707 Kautz Rd Saint Charles (60174) ***(G-18287)***
Tek-Cast Inc....630 422-1458
195 Corporate Dr Elgin (60123) ***(G-8748)***
Tekky Toys, Orland Park *Also called Jcw Investments Inc* ***(G-15962)***
Tekmill Inc....217 353-5111
210 Hazelwood Dr Ste 103 Champaign (61822) ***(G-3358)***
Tekni-Plex Inc....217 935-8311
10610 State Highway 10 Clinton (61727) ***(G-6929)***
Tekno Industries Inc (PA)....630 766-6960
1200 Roosevelt Rd Ste 200 Glen Ellyn (60137) ***(G-10421)***
Tektrol LLC....847 857-6076
796 Tek Dr Ste 300 Crystal Lake (60014) ***(G-7279)***
Tekvend, Park Ridge *Also called Advanced Technologies Inc* ***(G-16264)***
Tel Aviv Kosher Bakery, Chicago *Also called Tam Tav Bakery Inc* ***(G-6316)***
Tel-Comm Incorporated....847 593-8480
804 Coventry Cir S Sycamore (60178) ***(G-19734)***
Telco Machine & Manufacturing (PA)....773 725-4441
3957 N Normandy Ave Chicago (60634) ***(G-6338)***
Telco Machine & Manufacturing....773 725-4441
6610 W Dakin St Chicago (60634) ***(G-6339)***
Telcom Innovations Group LLC....630 350-0700
125 N Prospect Ave Itasca (60143) ***(G-11745)***
Tele Guia Spanish TV Guide....708 656-9800
3116 S Austin Blvd Cicero (60804) ***(G-6879)***
Tele Print....630 941-7877
494 E Atwood Ct Elmhurst (60126) ***(G-9434)***
Telecom Audio, Sandwich *Also called Jk Audio Inc* ***(G-18375)***
Teledyne Defense Elec LLC....630 754-3300
10221 Werch Dr Woodridge (60517) ***(G-21344)***
Teledyne Lecroy Inc....847 888-0450
2111 Big Timber Rd Elgin (60123) ***(G-8749)***
Teledyne Monitor Labs Inc....303 792-3300
12497 Collection Ctr Dr Chicago (60693) ***(G-6340)***
Teledyne Storm Microwave, Woodridge *Also called Teledyne Defense Elec LLC* ***(G-21344)***
Teleflex Incorporated....847 259-7400
900 W University Dr Arlington Heights (60004) ***(G-818)***
Teleflex Medical OEM LLC (HQ)....847 596-3100
1425 Tr State Pkwy Ste 12 Gurnee (60031) ***(G-10936)***
Telegartner Inc....630 616-7600
411 Dominic Ct Franklin Park (60131) ***(G-10059)***
Telegraph, The, Alton *Also called Hearst Corporation* ***(G-558)***
Teleguia Inc....708 656-6675
3116 S Austin Blvd Cicero (60804) ***(G-6880)***
Telehealth Sensors LLC....630 879-3101
197 Alder Dr North Aurora (60542) ***(G-15279)***
Telemedicine Solutions LLC....847 519-3500
425 N Martingale Rd # 1250 Schaumburg (60173) ***(G-18744)***
Teletrac Navman US Ltd (HQ)....866 527-9896
2700 Patriot Blvd Ste 200 Glenview (60026) ***(G-10631)***
Teleweld Inc....815 672-4561
502 N Vermillion St Streator (61364) ***(G-19629)***
Telguard, Chicago *Also called Telular Corporation* ***(G-6341)***
Tella Technology Div, Lombard *Also called Tella Tool & Mfg Co* ***(G-13142)***
Tella Tool & Mfg Co (PA)....630 495-0545
1015 N Ridge Ave Ste 1 Lombard (60148) ***(G-13142)***
Tellabs Mexico Inc (HQ)....630 445-5333
1415 W Diehl Rd Naperville (60563) ***(G-14928)***
Tellabs Tg Inc....630 798-8800
1415 W Diehl Rd Naperville (60563) ***(G-14929)***
Tellenar Inc....815 356-8044
727 Tek Dr Crystal Lake (60014) ***(G-7280)***
Telser Lighting Associates LLC....630 800-5312
558 Plate Dr Ste 1 East Dundee (60118) ***(G-8211)***
Telular Corporation (HQ)....800 835-8527
200 S Wacker Dr Ste 1800 Chicago (60606) ***(G-6341)***
Telza Welding Co, Chicago *Also called Telza Welding Inc* ***(G-6342)***
Telza Welding Inc....773 777-4467
1624 N Kilbourn Ave Chicago (60639) ***(G-6342)***
Temco Communications, South Barrington *Also called Temco Japan Co Ltd* ***(G-19078)***
Temco Grinding Inc....815 282-9405
1002 River Ln Loves Park (61111) ***(G-13272)***
Temco Japan Co Ltd....847 359-3277
13 Chipping Campden Dr South Barrington (60010) ***(G-19078)***
Temp Excel Properties LLC....847 844-3845
2520 Vantage Dr Elgin (60124) ***(G-8750)***
Temp-Air Inc....847 931-7700
39 W 107 Highland Ave Elgin (60123) ***(G-8751)***
Tempco Electric Heater Corp (PA)....630 350-2252
607 N Central Ave Wood Dale (60191) ***(G-21248)***
Tempco Products Co....618 544-3175
301 E Tempco Ave Robinson (62454) ***(G-17127)***
Tempel Farms, Chicago *Also called Tempel Holdings Inc* ***(G-6343)***
Tempel Farms, Old Mill Creek *Also called Tempel Holdings Inc* ***(G-15849)***
Tempel Holdings Inc (PA)....773 250-8000
5500 N Wolcott Ave Chicago (60640) ***(G-6343)***
Tempel Holdings Inc....773 250-8000
5454 N Wolcott Ave Chicago (60640) ***(G-6344)***
Tempel Holdings Inc....847 244-5330
17000 W Wadsworth Rd Old Mill Creek (60083) ***(G-15849)***
Tempel Steel Company....847 966-9099
5215 Old Orchard Rd Skokie (60077) ***(G-19043)***
Tempel Steel Company (HQ)....773 250-8000
5500 N Wolcott Ave Chicago (60640) ***(G-6345)***
Temper Enterprises Inc....815 553-0374
2218 Plainfield Rd Ste B Crest Hill (60403) ***(G-7098)***
Temperance Beer Company LLC....847 864-1000
2000 Dempster St Evanston (60202) ***(G-9583)***
Temperature Equipment Corp....847 429-0818
1313 Timber Dr Elgin (60123) ***(G-8752)***
Temperature Equipment Corp....815 229-2935
1818 18th Ave Rockford (61104) ***(G-17655)***
Tempil Inc (HQ)....908 757-8300
1201 Pratt Blvd Elk Grove Village (60007) ***(G-9270)***
Temple Display Ltd....630 851-3331
114 Kirkland Cir Ste C Oswego (60543) ***(G-16026)***
Templegate Publishers....217 522-3353
302 E Adams St Springfield (62701) ***(G-19463)***
Tempo Enterprises Inc....331 903-2786
21 Fountainhead Dr # 201 Westmont (60559) ***(G-20775)***
Temprian Therapeutics Inc....513 374-1180
222 Merchandise Mart Plz Chicago (60654) ***(G-6346)***
Temprite Company....630 293-5910
1555 W Hawthorne Ln 1e West Chicago (60185) ***(G-20649)***
Tempro International Corp....847 677-5370
8343 Niles Center Rd Skokie (60077) ***(G-19044)***
Tempus Labs Inc....312 784-4400
600 W Chicago Ave Ste 510 Chicago (60654) ***(G-6347)***
Tenco Hydro Inc of Illinois....708 387-0700
4620 Forest Ave Brookfield (60513) ***(G-2496)***
Tender Loving Care Inds Inc....847 891-0230
1270 Abbott Dr Elgin (60123) ***(G-8753)***
Tenex Corporation....847 504-0400
230 W Superior St Ste 200 Chicago (60654) ***(G-6348)***
Tenexco Inc....708 771-7870
17w715 Butterfield Rd C Oakbrook Terrace (60181) ***(G-15816)***
Tenggren-Mehl Co Inc....773 763-3290
7019 W Higgins Ave Chicago (60656) ***(G-6349)***
Tennant Company....773 376-7132
1120 W Exchange Ave Chicago (60609) ***(G-6350)***
Tenneco Automobile, Lake Forest *Also called Tenneco Europe Limited* ***(G-12310)***
Tenneco Automotive Oper Co Inc (HQ)....847 482-5000
500 N Field Dr Lake Forest (60045) ***(G-12308)***
Tenneco Automotive Oper Co Inc....847 821-0757
605 Heathrow Dr Lincolnshire (60069) ***(G-12798)***
Tenneco Automotive Rsa Company....847 482-5000
500 N Field Dr Lake Forest (60045) ***(G-12309)***
Tenneco Europe Limited....847 482-5000
500 N Field Dr Lake Forest (60045) ***(G-12310)***
Tenneco Global Holdings Inc (HQ)....847 482-5000
500 N Field Dr Lake Forest (60045) ***(G-12311)***
Tenneco Inc....847 774-1636
7001 N Central Park Ave Lincolnwood (60712) ***(G-12844)***
Tenneco Inc (PA)....847 482-5000
500 N Field Dr Lake Forest (60045) ***(G-12312)***
Tenneco Intl Holdg Corp (HQ)....847 482-5000
500 N Field Dr Lake Forest (60045) ***(G-12313)***
Tent Maker Industrial Sup Inc....847 469-6070
531 Brown St Wauconda (60084) ***(G-20398)***
Tenth and Blake Beer Company (HQ)....312 496-2759
250 S Wacker Dr Ste 800 Chicago (60606) ***(G-6351)***
Tepromark International Inc....847 329-7881
140 S Dearborn St Ste 420 Chicago (60603) ***(G-6352)***
Ter-Son Corporation....309 274-6227
1801 N Logan St Chillicothe (61523) ***(G-6822)***
Tera-Print LLC....224 534-7543
8140 Mccormick Blvd # 13 Skokie (60076) ***(G-19045)***
Teradyne Inc....847 981-0400
715 W Algonquin Rd Ste A Arlington Heights (60005) ***(G-819)***
Terco Inc....630 894-8828
459 Camden Dr Bloomingdale (60108) ***(G-2016)***
Tercor Inc (PA)....773 549-8303
4343 N Claredon Chicago (60613) ***(G-6353)***
Teresa Foods Inc....708 258-6200
116 Main St Peotone (60468) ***(G-16558)***
Teresa Frozen Pizzas, Peotone *Also called Teresa Foods Inc* ***(G-16558)***
Terlato Wine Group Ltd (PA)....847 604-8900
900 Armour Dr Lake Bluff (60044) ***(G-12210)***
Termax LLC (HQ)....847 519-1500
200 Telser Rd Lake Zurich (60047) ***(G-12463)***
Termax LLC....847 519-1500
1155 Rose Rd Ste A Lake Zurich (60047) ***(G-12464)***

ALPHABETIC

(PA)=Parent Co (HQ)=Headquarters (DH)=Div Headquarters
2020 Harris Illinois Industrial Directory
1275

Terra Cotta Holdings Co (PA) 815 459-2400
3703 S Il Route 31 Crystal Lake (60012) ***(G-7281)***
Terra Nitrogen Company LP (HQ) 847 405-2400
4 Parkway North Blvd # 400 Deerfield (60015) ***(G-7652)***
Terra Nitrogen GP Inc (HQ) 847 405-2400
4 Parkway North Blvd # 400 Deerfield (60015) ***(G-7653)***
Terrace Holding Company 708 652-5600
1325 S Cicero Ave Cicero (60804) ***(G-6881)***
Terracycle Regulated Waste LLC 800 909-9709
2200 Ogden Ave Ste 100 Lisle (60532) ***(G-12950)***
Terramac LLC 630 365-4800
724 Hicks Dr Elburn (60119) ***(G-8475)***
Terraneo Merchants Inc 312 753-9134
6525 W Proesel Ave Lincolnwood (60712) ***(G-12845)***
Terrapin Xpress Inc 866 823-7323
7801 W 123rd Pl Palos Heights (60463) ***(G-16193)***
Terrasource Global Corporation 618 641-6985
1 Freedom Dr Belleville (62226) ***(G-1597)***
Terrell Materials Corporation 847 635-8530
10600 W Higgins Rd # 300 Rosemont (60018) ***(G-18053)***
Terry Terri Mulgrew 815 747-6248
521 Montgomery Ave East Dubuque (61025) ***(G-8185)***
Teshurt, Champaign *Also called Te Shurt Shop Inc* ***(G-3357)***
Tesko Enterprises, Norridge *Also called Tesko Welding & Mfg Co* ***(G-15244)***
Tesko Welding & Mfg Co 708 452-0045
7350 W Montrose Ave Norridge (60706) ***(G-15244)***
Tesla Inc 312 733-9780
1053 W Grand Ave Chicago (60642) ***(G-6354)***
Tesla Motors 630 541-1214
50 W Ogden Ave Westmont (60559) ***(G-20776)***
Tesler Company of Illinois Inc 773 522-4400
2312 17th St Franklin Park (60131) ***(G-10060)***
Testa Steel Constructors Inc 815 729-4777
22449 Thomas Dilon Dr Channahon (60410) ***(G-3395)***
Testor Corporation 815 962-6654
615 Buckbee St Rockford (61104) ***(G-17656)***
Tetra Medical Supply Corp 847 647-0590
6364 W Gross Point Rd Niles (60714) ***(G-15179)***
Tetra Pak Inc 847 955-6000
600 Bunker Ct Vernon Hills (60061) ***(G-20103)***
Tetra Pak Materials LP (HQ) 847 955-6000
101 Corporate Woods Pkwy Vernon Hills (60061) ***(G-20104)***
Tewell Bros Machine Inc 217 253-6303
300 N Parke St Tuscola (61953) ***(G-19931)***
Tex Tana Inc (PA) 773 561-9270
2243 W Belmont Ave Ste 1 Chicago (60618) ***(G-6355)***
Tex Trend Inc 847 215-6796
767 Kristy Ln Wheeling (60090) ***(G-20999)***
Texas Instruments Incorporated 630 836-2827
27715 Diehl Rd Warrenville (60555) ***(G-20253)***
Texmac Inc 630 244-4702
224 Terrace Dr Mundelein (60060) ***(G-14743)***
Textron Aviation Inc 630 443-5080
2700 Intl Dr Ste 304 West Chicago (60185) ***(G-20650)***
Textura Corporation (HQ) 866 839-8872
1405 Lake Cook Rd Deerfield (60015) ***(G-7654)***
Texxon Plastics Corporation 630 369-6850
424 Fort Hill Dr Ste 131 Naperville (60540) ***(G-14930)***
Teys (usa) Inc (HQ) 312 492-7163
770 N Halsted St Ste 202 Chicago (60642) ***(G-6356)***
Tezzaron Semiconductor Corp 630 505-0404
1415 Bond St Ste 111 Naperville (60563) ***(G-14931)***
Tfa Signs 773 267-6007
5500 N Kedzie Ave Chicago (60625) ***(G-6357)***
TFC Group LLC 630 559-0808
136 W Commercial Ave Addison (60101) ***(G-306)***
Tfo Group LLC 608 469-7519
2140 W Fulton St Ste F Chicago (60612) ***(G-6358)***
Tft Inc 309 531-2012
31784 E 1400 North Rd Colfax (61728) ***(G-6951)***
Tgm Fabricating Inc 708 533-0857
57 E 24th St Chicago Heights (60411) ***(G-6780)***
Th Foods Inc 702 565-2816
2154 Harlem Rd Loves Park (61111) ***(G-13273)***
Th Foods Inc (HQ) 800 896-2396
2134 Harlem Rd Loves Park (61111) ***(G-13274)***
Th Snyder Company, Danville *Also called Vermilion Millworks LLC* ***(G-7390)***
Thales Visionix Inc 630 375-2008
1444 N Farnsworth Ave # 604 Aurora (60505) ***(G-1161)***
Thanasi Foods LLC 720 570-1065
222 Merchandise Mart Plz # 1300 Chicago (60654) ***(G-6359)***
Thatcher Oaks Inc 630 833-5700
718 N Industrial Dr Elmhurst (60126) ***(G-9435)***
Thatcher Retractbles, Elmhurst *Also called Thatcher Oaks Inc* ***(G-9435)***
The Amateur Athlete Magazine, Niles *Also called Chicago Sports Media Inc* ***(G-15109)***
The b F Shaw Printing Co 815 875-4461
800 Ace Rd Princeton (61356) ***(G-16823)***
The b F Shaw Printing Co 815 732-6166
121 S 4th St Ste A Oregon (61061) ***(G-15928)***
The Calumet Carton Company (PA) 708 331-7910
16920 State St South Holland (60473) ***(G-19249)***
The Chronicle, Hoopeston *Also called Times Republic* ***(G-11515)***
The Curry Companies, Decatur *Also called Curry Ready-Mix of Decatur* ***(G-7479)***
The Daily Record, Lawrenceville *Also called Daily Lawrenceville Record* ***(G-12529)***
The Gem Group, Chicago *Also called Ebonyenergy Publishing Inc Nfp* ***(G-4442)***
The Intec Group Inc (PA) 847 358-0088
666 S Vermont St Palatine (60067) ***(G-16162)***
The Korea Centl Daily Chicago, Rolling Meadows *Also called Joong-Ang Daily News* ***(G-17743)***
The Lifeguard Store Inc 630 548-5500
1212 S Naper Blvd Ste 109 Naperville (60540) ***(G-14932)***
The Master's Shop, Thomasboro *Also called Masters Shop* ***(G-19776)***
The Pantagraph, Bloomington *Also called Hearst Communications Inc* ***(G-2056)***
The Parts House 309 343-0146
343 S Kellogg St Galesburg (61401) ***(G-10221)***
The Pool Center, Dix *Also called Royal Fiberglass Pools Inc* ***(G-7882)***
The Syntek Group Inc 773 279-0131
3415 N Pulaski Rd 23 Chicago (60641) ***(G-6360)***
The Times 815 433-2000
110 W Jefferson St Ottawa (61350) ***(G-16081)***
The United Group Inc 847 816-7100
13700 W Polo Trail Dr Lake Forest (60045) ***(G-12314)***
The Web Cmmnications Group Inc 630 467-0900
105 E Irving Park Rd Itasca (60143) ***(G-11746)***
Theatre In The Park, Jacksonville *Also called Creative Ideas Inc* ***(G-11763)***
Thelen Sand & Gravel Inc (PA) 847 838-8800
28955 W Il Route 173 # 1 Antioch (60002) ***(G-636)***
Thelen Sand & Gravel Inc 847 662-0760
1020 Elizabeth St Waukegan (60085) ***(G-20503)***
THEOSOPHICAL PUBLISHING HOUSE, Wheaton *Also called Theosophical Society In Amer* ***(G-20826)***
Theosophical Society In Amer (PA) 630 665-0130
1926 N Main St Wheaton (60187) ***(G-20826)***
Theosophical Society In Amer 630 665-0123
306 W Geneva Rd Wheaton (60187) ***(G-20827)***
Theosphcal Pubg Hs/Quest Bk Sp, Wheaton *Also called Theosophical Society In Amer* ***(G-20827)***
Ther A Pedic Midwest Inc 309 788-0401
2350 5th St Rock Island (61201) ***(G-17249)***
Therapeutic Envisions Inc 720 323-7032
151 Blueberry Rd Libertyville (60048) ***(G-12716)***
Therapeutic Skin Care 630 244-1833
21w221 Hemstead Rd Lombard (60148) ***(G-13143)***
Therm-O-Web Inc 847 520-5200
770 Glenn Ave Wheeling (60090) ***(G-21000)***
Therma-Kleen Inc 630 718-0212
10212 S Mandel St Ste A Plainfield (60585) ***(G-16723)***
Thermal Care Inc 847 966-2260
5680 W Jarvis Ave Niles (60714) ***(G-15180)***
Thermal Ceramics Inc 217 627-2101
1st & Mound St Girard (62640) ***(G-10386)***
Thermal Industries Inc 800 237-0560
830 Sivert Dr Wood Dale (60191) ***(G-21249)***
Thermal Safe Brands, Arlington Heights *Also called Sonoco Protective Solutions* ***(G-810)***
Thermal Solutions Inc 217 352-7019
1706 Lyndhurst Dr Savoy (61874) ***(G-18417)***
Thermal-Chem, Broadview *Also called Alliance Industries Inc* ***(G-2416)***
Thermal-Tech Systems Inc 630 639-5115
1215 Atlantic Dr West Chicago (60185) ***(G-20651)***
Thermamax Inc 630 340-5682
1207 Bilter Rd Ste 119 Aurora (60502) ***(G-1022)***
Thermatome Corporation 312 772-2201
2242 W Harrison St 201-22 Chicago (60612) ***(G-6361)***
Thermform Engineered Qulty LLC (HQ) 847 669-5291
11320 Main St Huntley (60142) ***(G-11568)***
Thermionics Corp (PA) 800 800-5728
1214 Bunn Ave Ste 5 Springfield (62703) ***(G-19464)***
Thermo Fisher Scientific Inc 847 295-7500
3000 Lakeside Dr Ste 116n Bannockburn (60015) ***(G-1211)***
Thermo Fisher Scientific Inc 815 968-7970
3747 N Meridian Rd Rockford (61101) ***(G-17657)***
Thermo Fisher Scientific Inc 847 381-7050
1230 Hardt Cir Bartlett (60103) ***(G-1316)***
Thermo Mattson, Bannockburn *Also called Thermo Fisher Scientific Inc* ***(G-1211)***
Thermo-Graphic LLC 630 350-2226
301 Arthur Ct Bensenville (60106) ***(G-1901)***
Thermoelectric Coolg Amer Corp 773 342-4900
4048 W Schubert Ave Chicago (60639) ***(G-6362)***
Thermoflex Corp (PA) 847 473-9001
1535 S Lakeside Dr Waukegan (60085) ***(G-20504)***
Thermoflex Corp 847 473-9001
1817-1855 S Waukegan Rd Waukegan (60085) ***(G-20505)***
Thermoplastec Inc 815 873-9288
4755 Colt Rd Rockford (61109) ***(G-17658)***
Thermos LLC (HQ) 847 439-7821
475 N Martingale Rd # 1100 Schaumburg (60173) ***(G-18745)***

Thermosafe, Beecher Also called Sonoco Prtective Solutions Inc **(G-1521)**
Thermosoft International Corp..847 279-3800
  701 Corporate Woods Pkwy Vernon Hills (60061) **(G-20105)**
Thg International Publishing...312 540-3000
  303 E Wacker Dr Chicago (60601) **(G-6363)**
Thia & Co...630 510-9770
  519 W Front St Wheaton (60187) **(G-20828)**
Thiessen Communications Inc..847 884-0980
  1300 Basswood Rd Schaumburg (60173) **(G-18746)**
Think Ink Inc..815 459-4565
  890 Cog Cir Crystal Lake (60014) **(G-7282)**
Think Jerky LLC..917 623-1989
  500 N Michigan Ave # 600 Chicago (60611) **(G-6364)**
Thinkahead, Chicago Also called Ahead Inc **(G-3584)**
Thinkcercacom Inc...224 412-3722
  440 N Wells St Ste 720 Chicago (60654) **(G-6365)**
Third Day Oil & Gas LLC...618 553-5538
  210 S Range St Oblong (62449) **(G-15831)**
Third Wrld Press Fundation Inc..773 651-0700
  7822 S Dobson Ave Chicago (60619) **(G-6366)**
Thirteen Rf Inc..618 687-1313
  10 Alliance Ave Murphysboro (62966) **(G-14761)**
This Week In Chicago Inc..312 943-0838
  222 W Ontario St Ste 420 Chicago (60654) **(G-6367)**
Thk America Inc (HQ)..847 310-1111
  200 Commerce Dr Schaumburg (60173) **(G-18747)**
Thoennes & Thoennes Inc...309 663-4053
  1102 Eastport Dr Ste B Bloomington (61704) **(G-2101)**
Tholeo Design Inc...630 325-3792
  418 Ridge Ave Clarendon Hills (60514) **(G-6901)**
Thomas & Betts Power Solutions, Chicago Also called ABB Power Protection LLC **(G-3501)**
Thomas A Doan..847 864-8772
  2717 Harrison St Evanston (60201) **(G-9584)**
Thomas Electronics Inc...315 923-2051
  330 S La Londe Ave Addison (60101) **(G-307)**
Thomas Engineering Inc (PA)...847 358-5800
  575 W Central Rd Hoffman Estates (60192) **(G-11469)**
Thomas Engineering Inc...815 398-0280
  2500 Harrison Ave Rockford (61108) **(G-17659)**
Thomas Gardner Denver Inc...217 222-5400
  1800 Gardner Expy Quincy (62305) **(G-16947)**
Thomas Glenn Holdings LLC...630 916-8090
  1000 N Main St Lombard (60148) **(G-13144)**
Thomas Monahan Company (PA)...217 268-5771
  202 N Oak St Arcola (61910) **(G-667)**
Thomas Packaging LLC..847 392-1652
  3885 Industrial Ave Rolling Meadows (60008) **(G-17779)**
Thomas Printing & Sty Co...618 435-2801
  301 S Du Quoin St Benton (62812) **(G-1937)**
Thomas Proestler...630 971-0185
  5400 Patton Dr Ste 2c Lisle (60532) **(G-12951)**
Thomas Publishing Printing Div...618 351-6655
  701 W Main St Carbondale (62901) **(G-2862)**
Thomas Pump Company...630 851-9393
  2301 Liberty St Aurora (60502) **(G-1023)**
Thomas Research Products LLC...224 654-8626
  1215 Bowes Rd Ste 1225 Elgin (60123) **(G-8754)**
Thomas Tees Inc..217 488-2288
  210 S Oak St New Berlin (62670) **(G-15025)**
Thomas-Zientz Group Inc...847 395-2363
  925 Carney Ct Antioch (60002) **(G-637)**
Thomason Machine Works Inc (PA)...815 874-8217
  5459 11th St Rockford (61109) **(G-17660)**
Thompson Industries Inc (PA)..815 899-6670
  1018 Crosby Ave Sycamore (60178) **(G-19735)**
Thomson Casual Furniture Co, Galva Also called Dixline Corporation **(G-10230)**
Thomson Industries Inc..815 568-4309
  1300 N State St Marengo (60152) **(G-13495)**
Thomson Quantitative Analytics..847 610-0574
  230 S La Salle St Ste 688 Chicago (60604) **(G-6368)**
Thomson Reuters Corporation...312 288-4654
  1 N Dearborn St Ste 1400 Chicago (60602) **(G-6369)**
Thomson Steel Polishing Corp..773 586-2345
  6150 S New England Ave Chicago (60638) **(G-6370)**
Thoroughbred Plastics LLC..815 985-5116
  129 Phelps Ave Ste 838 Rockford (61108) **(G-17661)**
Thorworks Industries Inc...815 969-0664
  904 7th St Rockford (61104) **(G-17662)**
Thoughtly Corp...772 559-2008
  750 N Rush St Apt 1906 Chicago (60611) **(G-6371)**
Thrall Enterprises Inc (PA)..312 621-8200
  180 N Stetson Ave # 4330 Chicago (60601) **(G-6372)**
Thread & Gage Co Inc...815 675-2305
  3000 N Us Highway 12 Spring Grove (60081) **(G-19302)**
Threads Up Inc...630 595-2297
  461 N Jonathan Dr Apt 201 Palatine (60074) **(G-16163)**
Three Angels Printing Svcs Inc..630 333-4305
  1105 S Westwood Ave Addison (60101) **(G-308)**
Three Castle Press Inc...630 540-0120
  213 Mayfield Dr Streamwood (60107) **(G-19597)**

Three Hands Technologies...847 680-5358
  462 Harrison Ct Vernon Hills (60061) **(G-20106)**
Three JS Industries Inc...847 640-6080
  701 Landmeier Rd Elk Grove Village (60007) **(G-9271)**
Three Penguin Ice, University Park Also called Tinley Ice Company **(G-19968)**
Three R Plastics Inc...815 675-0844
  1801 Holian Dr Spring Grove (60081) **(G-19303)**
Three R Plastics Inc...847 740-2845
  310 W Nippersink Rd Round Lake (60073) **(G-18084)**
Three Star Mfg Co Inc..847 526-2222
  375 Hollow Hill Rd Wauconda (60084) **(G-20399)**
Three Z Printing, Teutopolis Also called Three-Z Printing Co **(G-19774)**
Three-Z Printing Co (PA)...217 857-3153
  902 W Main St Teutopolis (62467) **(G-19774)**
Thrice Publishing Nfp..630 776-0478
  734 Berwick Pl Roselle (60172) **(G-17993)**
Thrift Medical Products...630 857-3548
  1701 Quincy Ave Naperville (60540) **(G-14933)**
Thrift n Swift...847 455-1350
  309 Elmwood Ct Palatine (60067) **(G-16164)**
Thrifty Nckel Amrcn Clssifieds, Champaign Also called Want ADS of Champaign Inc **(G-3368)**
Thrilled LLC..312 404-1929
  555 W Jackson Blvd # 400 Chicago (60661) **(G-6373)**
Thryselius Machining Inc...630 365-9191
  44w480 Keslinger Rd Elburn (60119) **(G-8476)**
Thryselius Stamping Inc..630 232-0795
  28 S 8th St Geneva (60134) **(G-10311)**
Thule Inc..847 455-2420
  7609 Industrial Dr Forest Park (60130) **(G-9725)**
Thule Chicago, Forest Park Also called Thule Inc **(G-9725)**
Thunderbird LLC (PA)..847 718-9300
  1501 Oakton St Elk Grove Village (60007) **(G-9272)**
Thurne USA, Elk Grove Village Also called Mww Food Processing USA LLC **(G-9141)**
Thurow Tool Works Inc..630 377-6403
  41 W 523 Rte 64 Saint Charles (60175) **(G-18288)**
Thybar Corporation (PA)...630 543-5300
  913 S Kay Ave Addison (60101) **(G-309)**
Thycurb Fabricating, Addison Also called Thybar Corporation **(G-309)**
Thyng LLC...312 262-5703
  351 W Hubbard St Ste 510 Chicago (60654) **(G-6374)**
Thyssenkrupp Crankshaft Co LLC (HQ)..................................217 431-0060
  1000 Lynch Rd Danville (61834) **(G-7383)**
Thyssenkrupp Crankshaft Co LLC..217 444-5400
  1200 International Pl Danville (61834) **(G-7384)**
Thyssenkrupp Crankshaft Co LLC..217 444-5500
  75 Walz Crk Danville (61834) **(G-7385)**
Thyssenkrupp North America Inc (HQ)...................................312 525-2800
  111 W Jackson Blvd # 2400 Chicago (60604) **(G-6375)**
Thyssenkrupp Presta Cold Forgi..217 431-4212
  69 Walz Crk Danville (61834) **(G-7386)**
Thyssenkrupp Stainless N Amer, Bannockburn Also called Mexinox USA Inc **(G-1203)**
Thyssnkrupp Prsta Danville LLC..217 444-5500
  75 Walz Crk Danville (61834) **(G-7387)**
TI Gotham Inc...312 321-7833
  303 E Ohio St Fl 22 Chicago (60611) **(G-6376)**
TI International Ltd..847 689-0233
  2260 Commonwealth Ave North Chicago (60064) **(G-15322)**
TI Squared Technologies Inc..541 367-2929
  1019 W Wise Rd Ste 101 Schaumburg (60193) **(G-18748)**
Tia Tynette Designs Inc...219 440-2859
  2600 Troy Cir Olympia Fields (60461) **(G-15899)**
Tianhe Stem Cell Biotechnolgie...630 723-1968
  6398 Holly Ct Lisle (60532) **(G-12952)**
Tibor Machine Products Inc (PA)...708 499-0017
  7400 W 100th Pl Bridgeview (60455) **(G-2393)**
Tibor Machine Products Inc..309 786-3052
  2832 5th St Ste 2 Rock Island (61201) **(G-17250)**
Tickle Asphalt Co Ltd...309 787-1308
  700 4th St W Milan (61264) **(G-14029)**
Ticona Technical Polymers..847 949-1444
  1301 Halifax Dr Mundelein (60060) **(G-14744)**
Tiege Hanley LLC...312 953-4131
  2023 W Carroll Ave C212 Chicago (60612) **(G-6377)**
Tiem Engineering Corporation...630 553-7484
  202 Beaver St Yorkville (60560) **(G-21502)**
Tierneys Signs Inc..847 395-8224
  36701 N Il Route 83 Apt A Lake Villa (60046) **(G-12369)**
Tiesenbach, Marion Also called Hauhinco LP **(G-13514)**
Tifb Media Group Inc...844 862-4391
  7608 Lockwood Ave Burbank (60459) **(G-2638)**
Tiffany Stained Glass Ltd..312 642-0680
  428 Des Plaines Ave Ste 1 Forest Park (60130) **(G-9726)**
Tiger Accessory Group LLC (HQ)...847 821-9630
  6700 Wildlife Way Long Grove (60047) **(G-13171)**
Tiger Drylac USA Inc (HQ)..630 587-2918
  3945 Swenson Ave Saint Charles (60174) **(G-18289)**
Tiger Tool Inc...888 551-4490
  410 Windy Point Dr Glendale Heights (60139) **(G-10511)**

Tiger Tool Supply, Inc., Glendale Heights *Also called Tiger Tool Inc* **(G-10511)**
Tigerflex Corporation........847 439-1766
1551 Pratt Blvd Elk Grove Village (60007) **(G-9273)**
Tighe Publishing Services Inc........773 281-9100
1700 W Irvng Park Rd # 210 Chicago (60613) **(G-6378)**
Tii Technical Educatn Systems........847 428-3085
56 E End Dr Gilberts (60136) **(G-10373)**
Tiller Farms Holdings LLC........224 572-7814
37165 N Green Bay Rd Beach Park (60087) **(G-1444)**
Tillock Steel Supply and Salv, Baldwin *Also called Higman LLC* **(G-1185)**
Tilton Pattern Works Inc........217 442-1502
21204 Rileysburg Rd Danville (61834) **(G-7388)**
Tim Detwiler Enterprises Inc........815 758-9950
1140 S 7th St Dekalb (60115) **(G-7709)**
Tim Snyder........309 657-4764
13520 Winfield Dr Manito (61546) **(G-13440)**
Tim Wallace Ldscp Sup Co Inc (PA)........630 759-6813
1481 W Boughton Rd Bolingbrook (60490) **(G-2250)**
Timber Creek Pallets........217 268-3062
447 E County Road 200n Arcola (61910) **(G-668)**
Timber Industries LLC........815 857-3674
900 Depot Ave Dixon (61021) **(G-7922)**
Timberland Custom Cab & Tops........815 722-0825
1923 Cherry Hill Rd Joliet (60433) **(G-11936)**
Timberline Manufacturing, Downers Grove *Also called Apergy Energy Automation LLC* **(G-7952)**
Timberline Pallet & Skid Inc........309 752-1770
2500 8th Ave East Moline (61244) **(G-8243)**
Timberside Woodworking........217 578-3201
715 N Cr 125 E Arthur (61911) **(G-880)**
Time Embroidery........847 364-4371
2201 Lively Blvd Elk Grove Village (60007) **(G-9274)**
Time Out Chicago Partners Lllp........312 924-9555
247 S State St Fl 17 Chicago (60604) **(G-6379)**
Time Rec Pubg Bbby Mrtin Prdct........618 996-3803
2537 Wards Mill Rd Marion (62959) **(G-13540)**
Time-O-Matic Inc., Danville *Also called Watchfire Signs LLC* **(G-7394)**
Timeless Reflections........815 663-8148
104 E Kansas St Bureau (61315) **(G-2639)**
Timeout Devices Inc........847 729-6543
2718 Covert Rd Glenview (60025) **(G-10632)**
Timepilot Corporation........630 879-6400
340 Mckee St Batavia (60510) **(G-1430)**
Times Energy........773 444-9282
11241 S Natoma Ave Worth (60482) **(G-21456)**
Times Record Company........309 582-5112
219 S College Ave Aledo (61231) **(G-362)**
Times Republic (HQ)........815 432-5227
1492 E Walnut St Watseka (60970) **(G-20320)**
Times Republic........217 283-5111
308 E Main St Hoopeston (60942) **(G-11515)**
Times-Leader, Mc Leansboro *Also called Newspaper Holding Inc* **(G-13707)**
Times-Press Publishing Co........815 673-3771
115 Oak St Streator (61364) **(G-19630)**
Times-Tribune, Troy *Also called Newsprint Ink Inc* **(G-19917)**
Timewell Drainage Pdts & Svcs, Timewell *Also called C & L Tiling Inc* **(G-19797)**
Timken Company........630 679-6756
3155 Book Rd Ste 103 Naperville (60564) **(G-14990)**
Timken Drives LLC (HQ)........815 589-2211
901 19th Ave Fulton (61252) **(G-10158)**
Timken Drives LLC........312 274-9710
875 N Michigan Ave Chicago (60611) **(G-6380)**
Timken Gears & Services Inc........708 720-9400
8529 192nd St Mokena (60448) **(G-14122)**
Timothy Anderson Corporation........815 398-8371
700 20th St Rockford (61104) **(G-17663)**
Timothy Darrey........847 231-2277
1153 Lee St Bldg 223 Des Plaines (60016) **(G-7856)**
Timpte Industries Inc........309 820-1095
2312 W Market St Bloomington (61705) **(G-2102)**
Tin Man Heating & Cooling Inc........630 267-3232
419 Rathbone Ave Aurora (60506) **(G-1162)**
Tin Mans Garage Inc........630 262-0752
39w869 Midan Dr Unit B Elburn (60119) **(G-8477)**
Tin Maung........217 233-1405
1770 E Lake Shore Dr Decatur (62521) **(G-7561)**
Tin Tree Gifts........630 935-8086
2720 Stuart Kaplan Dr Aurora (60503) **(G-1024)**
Tini Martini........773 269-2900
2169 N Milwaukee Ave Chicago (60647) **(G-6381)**
Tinley Ice Company........708 532-8777
450 Central Ave Ste A University Park (60484) **(G-19968)**
Tinney Tool & Machine Co........618 236-7273
815 N Church St Belleville (62220) **(G-1598)**
Tinscape LLC........630 236-7236
1050 Stockton Ct Aurora (60502) **(G-1025)**
Tinsley Steel Inc........618 656-5231
2 Oasis Dr Edwardsville (62025) **(G-8378)**
Tiny Human Food Inc........630 397-9936
5s220 Beau Bien Blvd Naperville (60563) **(G-14934)**
Tips, Yorkville *Also called Titan Injection Parts & Svc* **(G-21503)**
Tisch Granite & Marble, Belleville *Also called Tisch Monuments Inc* **(G-1599)**
Tisch Monuments Inc (PA)........618 233-3017
17 N 3rd St Belleville (62220) **(G-1599)**
Tisco Parts, Rockford *Also called Woods Equipment Company* **(G-17690)**
Tishma Engineering LLC........847 755-1200
850 Pratt Blvd Elk Grove Village (60007) **(G-9275)**
Tishma Technologies, Schaumburg *Also called Nortech Packaging LLC* **(G-18651)**
Tishma Technology LLC........847 884-1805
101 E State Pkwy Schaumburg (60173) **(G-18749)**
Tison & Hall Concrete Products........618 253-7808
210 N Commercial St Harrisburg (62946) **(G-11030)**
Titan Industries Inc........309 440-1010
100 Prspect Dr Deer Crk Deer Creek Deer Creek (61733) **(G-7576)**
Titan Injection Parts & Svc........630 882-8455
204 Beaver St Yorkville (60560) **(G-21503)**
Titan International Inc (PA)........217 228-6011
2701 Spruce St Quincy (62301) **(G-16948)**
Titan Metals Inc........630 752-9700
180 W Lake Dr Glendale Heights (60139) **(G-10512)**
Titan Tire Corporation........217 228-6011
2701 Spruce St Quincy (62301) **(G-16949)**
Titan Tool Company Inc........847 671-0045
10001 Pacific Ave Franklin Park (60131) **(G-10061)**
Titan Tool Works LLC........630 221-1080
615 Kimberly Dr Carol Stream (60188) **(G-3081)**
Titan Tyre Corporation........217 228-6011
3769 Us Highway 20 E Freeport (61032) **(G-10146)**
Titan US LLC........331 212-5953
1585 Beverly Ct Ste 112 Aurora (60502) **(G-1026)**
Titan Wheel Corp Illinois........217 228-6023
2701 Spruce St Quincy (62301) **(G-16950)**
Titanium Inc........847 691-5446
888 E Belvidere Rd # 104 Grayslake (60030) **(G-10802)**
Titanium Insulation Inc........708 932-5927
14533 Turner Ave Midlothian (60445) **(G-13997)**
Titanium Supply Co, Grayslake *Also called Titanium Inc* **(G-10802)**
Titus Tool Company Inc........847 243-8801
11056 Addison Ave Franklin Park (60131) **(G-10062)**
Tivor Machine Products, Chicago Ridge *Also called Lho Enterprises Inc* **(G-6801)**
TJ Assemblies Inc........847 671-0060
511 E Pine Ave Bensenville (60106) **(G-1902)**
Tj Tool Inc........630 543-3595
224 Independence Ln Bloomingdale (60108) **(G-2017)**
Tj Wire Forming Inc........630 628-9209
824 S Kay Ave Addison (60101) **(G-310)**
Tkg Sweeping & Services LLC........847 505-1400
345 N Lakewood Ave Waukegan (60085) **(G-20506)**
Tkk USA Inc (HQ)........847 439-7821
2550 Golf Rd Ste 800 Rolling Meadows (60008) **(G-17780)**
Tks Control Systems Inc........630 554-3020
88 Templeton Dr Oswego (60543) **(G-16027)**
TLC Dental Care LLC........425 442-9000
344 Shadow Hill Dr Elgin (60124) **(G-8755)**
TLC Industries, Elgin *Also called Tender Loving Care Inds Inc* **(G-8753)**
Tlk Industries Inc........847 359-3200
130 Prairie Lake Rd Ste A East Dundee (60118) **(G-8212)**
Tlk Tool & Stamping Inc........224 293-6941
130 Prairie Lake Rd Ste C East Dundee (60118) **(G-8213)**
Tlm Enterprises Inc........815 284-5040
213 W 1st St Dixon (61021) **(G-7923)**
Tls Windsled Inc........815 262-5791
507 W 10th St Belvidere (61008) **(G-1704)**
Tmb Industries Inc........312 280-2565
980 N Michigan Ave # 11400 Chicago (60611) **(G-6382)**
Tmb Publishing Inc........847 564-1127
6201 W Howard St Ste 201 Niles (60714) **(G-15181)**
TMC Services Inc........217 528-2297
920 S Spring St Springfield (62704) **(G-19465)**
Tmf Plastic Solutions LLC........630 552-7575
12127b Galena Rd Plano (60545) **(G-16745)**
Tmf Polymer Solutions Inc (PA)........630 552-7575
12127b Galena Rd Plano (60545) **(G-16746)**
TMI, Norridge *Also called Transformer Manufacturers Inc* **(G-15245)**
TMI, Fairbury *Also called Technical Metals Inc* **(G-9614)**
TMJ Architectural LLC........815 388-7820
430 Everett Ave Crystal Lake (60014) **(G-7283)**
Tml Inc........847 382-1550
223 W Main St Barrington (60010) **(G-1247)**
Tms International LLC........618 451-7840
22nd & Edwardsville Rd Granite City (62040) **(G-10742)**
Tms International LLC........815 939-1178
1 Nucor Way Bourbonnais (60914) **(G-2270)**
Tms International LLC........618 451-9526
2500 E 23rd St Granite City (62040) **(G-10743)**
Tms International LLC........815 939-9460
1 Nucor Way Bourbonnais (60914) **(G-2271)**

Tms Manufacturing Co ... 847 353-8000
3555 W 123rd St Alsip (60803) ***(G-516)***

Tngp, Deerfield *Also called Terra Nitrogen GP Inc* ***(G-7653)***

Tnp Machinery Co Inc ... 708 344-7750
9860 Derby Ln Westchester (60154) ***(G-20714)***

TOA Resource ... 312 317-3957
374 Sandhurst Cir Apt 3 Glen Ellyn (60137) ***(G-10422)***

Toastmaster, Elgin *Also called Middleby Corporation* ***(G-8661)***

Toby Small Engine Repair ... 708 699-6021
22704 Millard Ave Richton Park (60471) ***(G-17031)***

Toco ... 618 257-8626
825 W Main St Belleville (62220) ***(G-1600)***

Todays Advantage Inc ... 618 463-0612
235 E Center Dr Alton (62002) ***(G-574)***

Todays Temptations Inc ... 773 385-5355
1900 N Austin Ave Ste 72 Chicago (60639) ***(G-6383)***

Todd Scanlan ... 217 585-1717
3112 Normandy Rd Springfield (62703) ***(G-19466)***

Toffee Time ... 309 788-2466
2510 22 1/2 Ave Rock Island (61201) ***(G-17251)***

Toggle Inc (PA) ... 323 882-6339
2004 Wattles Dr Chicago (60614) ***(G-6384)***

Toho Technology Inc ... 773 583-7183
4809 N Ravenswood Ave Chicago (60640) ***(G-6385)***

Tolar Group LLC ... 847 662-8000
616 Washington St Waukegan (60085) ***(G-20507)***

Tolar Wstgate Fnrals Crmations, Waukegan *Also called Tolar Group LLC* ***(G-20507)***

Toledo Democrat ... 217 849-2000
116 Court House Sq Toledo (62468) ***(G-19879)***

Toledo Machine & Welding Inc ... 217 849-2251
607 E Illinois Rt 121 Toledo (62468) ***(G-19880)***

Toledo Screw Machine Products ... 815 877-8213
5257 Northrock Dr Rockford (61103) ***(G-17664)***

Tolerance Manufacturing Inc ... 847 244-8836
1435 10th St Waukegan (60085) ***(G-20508)***

Tolerances Grinding Co Inc ... 630 543-6066
1020 W National Ave Addison (60101) ***(G-311)***

Tom Crown Mute Co ... 773 930-4979
4110 N Nashville Ave Chicago (60634) ***(G-6386)***

Tom Tom Tamales & Baking Co, Chicago *Also called Tom Tom Tamales Mfg Co Inc* ***(G-6387)***

Tom Tom Tamales Mfg Co Inc ... 773 523-5675
4750 S Washtenaw Ave Chicago (60632) ***(G-6387)***

Tom Zosel Associates Ltd ... 847 540-6543
3880 Salem Lake Dr Ste B Long Grove (60047) ***(G-13172)***

Tomahawk AG & Industrial LLC ... 309 275-2874
514 Prairie Meadows Dr Heyworth (61745) ***(G-11192)***

Tomahawk Defense ... 773 871-7268
1230 W Altgeld St Chicago (60614) ***(G-6388)***

Tomantron Inc ... 708 532-2456
17942 66th Ave Tinley Park (60477) ***(G-19860)***

Tomcyndi Inc ... 773 847-5400
822 W Exchange Ave Chicago (60609) ***(G-6389)***

Tomenson Machine Works Inc ... 630 377-7670
1150 Powis Rd West Chicago (60185) ***(G-20652)***

Tomermo Inc ... 815 229-5077
5127 28th Ave Rockford (61109) ***(G-17665)***

Tomko Machine Works Inc ... 630 244-0902
20w067 Pleasantdale Dr Lemont (60439) ***(G-12593)***

Tommy Rock, Bloomingdale *Also called Artistries By Tommy Musto Inc* ***(G-1977)***

Tompkins Aluminum Foundry Inc ... 815 438-5578
23876 Prophet Rd Rock Falls (61071) ***(G-17197)***

Toms Signs ... 630 377-8525
6n592 Il Route 25 Saint Charles (60174) ***(G-18290)***

Tomson Railings, Mokena *Also called Tomsons Products Inc* ***(G-14123)***

Tomsons Products Inc (PA) ... 708 479-7030
13210 S 85th Ave Orland Park (60462) ***(G-15987)***

Tomsons Products Inc ... 708 479-7030
18800 Wolf Rd Mokena (60448) ***(G-14123)***

Tondinis Wrecker Service ... 618 997-9884
2200 S Court St Marion (62959) ***(G-13541)***

Tone Products Inc ... 708 681-3660
2129 N 15th Ave Melrose Park (60160) ***(G-13923)***

Tonerhead Inc ... 815 331-3200
3106 N Us Highway 12 Spring Grove (60081) ***(G-19304)***

Tones Brothers, Oakbrook Terrace *Also called Ach Food Companies Inc* ***(G-15780)***

Toni Federici ... 618 244-4842
916 Main St Mount Vernon (62864) ***(G-14642)***

Tonjon Company ... 630 208-1173
1450 Meadows Rd Geneva (60134) ***(G-10312)***

Tony Patterson ... 773 487-4000
623 E 89th St Chicago (60619) ***(G-6390)***

Tony Weishaar ... 217 774-2774
Hwy 16 One 16th Mile E Shelbyville (62565) ***(G-18888)***

Tony's Welding & Repair Svc, Shelbyville *Also called Tony Weishaar* ***(G-18888)***

Tonys Bakery ... 847 599-1590
1117 Washington St Waukegan (60085) ***(G-20509)***

Tonys Welding Service Inc ... 618 532-9353
624 N Elm St Centralia (62801) ***(G-3253)***

Tool Automation Enterprises ... 708 799-6847
1516 175th St Ste A East Hazel Crest (60429) ***(G-8218)***

Tool Engrg Consulting Mfg LLC ... 815 316-2304
2932 Eastrock Dr Rockford (61109) ***(G-17666)***

Tool Form Inc ... 815 654-0035
2102 Margaret Dr Loves Park (61111) ***(G-13275)***

Tool Rite Industries Inc ... 630 406-6161
570 S River St Batavia (60510) ***(G-1431)***

Tool World, Arthur *Also called Doerock Inc* ***(G-853)***

Tool-Masters Tool & Stamp Inc ... 815 465-6830
204 N Stanley St Grant Park (60940) ***(G-10753)***

Toolex Corporation ... 630 458-0001
1204 W Capitol Dr Addison (60101) ***(G-312)***

Tooling Solutions Inc ... 847 472-9940
1515 Commerce Dr Elgin (60123) ***(G-8756)***

Toolmasters LLC (PA) ... 815 968-0961
1204 Milford Ave Rockford (61109) ***(G-17667)***

Toolmasters LLC ... 815 645-2224
206 S Walnut St Stillman Valley (61084) ***(G-19547)***

Tools Aviation LLC ... 630 377-7260
101a Theodore Dr Oswego (60543) ***(G-16028)***

Tools For Industry Inc ... 847 658-0455
812 Oceola Dr Algonquin (60102) ***(G-388)***

Toolweld Inc ... 847 854-8013
1750 Cumberland Pkwy # 8 Algonquin (60102) ***(G-389)***

Tootsie Roll Company Inc ... 773 838-3400
7401 S Cicero Ave Chicago (60629) ***(G-6391)***

Tootsie Roll Industries, Chicago *Also called Tri International Co* ***(G-6417)***

Tootsie Roll Industries Inc (PA) ... 773 838-3400
7401 S Cicero Ave Chicago (60629) ***(G-6392)***

Tootsie Roll Industries LLC (HQ) ... 773 245-4202
7401 S Cicero Ave Chicago (60629) ***(G-6393)***

Tootsie Roll Worldwide Ltd (HQ) ... 773 838-3400
7401 S Cicero Ave Chicago (60629) ***(G-6394)***

Top Ace Inc ... 847 581-0550
8440 Callie Ave Unit 612 Morton Grove (60053) ***(G-14445)***

Top Brass Inc ... 719 539-7242
2700 Missouri Ave Granite City (62040) ***(G-10744)***

Top Brass LLC ... 800 836-4683
2700 Missouri Ave Granite City (62040) ***(G-10745)***

Top Dollar Slots ... 779 210-4884
6590 N Alpine Rd Loves Park (61111) ***(G-13276)***

Top Hat Company Inc (PA) ... 847 256-6565
2407 Birchwood Ln Wilmette (60091) ***(G-21094)***

Top Metal Buyers Inc (PA) ... 314 421-2721
808 Walnut Ave East Saint Louis (62201) ***(G-8327)***

Top Metal Recycling, East Saint Louis *Also called Top Metal Buyers Inc* ***(G-8327)***

Top Notch Silk Screening ... 773 847-6335
3382 S Archer Ave Chicago (60608) ***(G-6395)***

Top Notch Tool & Supply Inc ... 815 633-6295
3175 Tuggle Dr Cherry Valley (61016) ***(G-3447)***

Top Tobacco LP (PA) ... 847 832-9700
2301 Ravine Way Glenview (60025) ***(G-10633)***

Topeka Metal Specialties, Harvey *Also called Lb Steel LLC* ***(G-11092)***

Topgolf International Inc ... 630 595-4653
1001 N Prospect Ave Wood Dale (60191) ***(G-21250)***

Topical Pharmaceuticals Inc ... 630 396-3970
715 W Racquet Club Dr Addison (60101) ***(G-313)***

Topical Pharmaceuticals Inc (PA) ... 630 396-3970
1470 W Bernard Dr Addison (60101) ***(G-314)***

Topilonio, Collinsville *Also called Alao Temitope* ***(G-6953)***

Toppert Jetting Service Inc (PA) ... 309 755-2240
1350 10th St East Moline (61244) ***(G-8244)***

Topweb LLC ... 773 975-0400
5450 N Northwest Hwy Chicago (60630) ***(G-6396)***

Topy America Inc ... 847 350-6399
1200 Mark St Elk Grove Village (60007) ***(G-9276)***

Topy Precision Mfg Inc (HQ) ... 847 228-5902
1375 Lunt Ave Elk Grove Village (60007) ***(G-9277)***

Torblo Inc ... 815 941-2684
7075 Lisbon Rd Morris (60450) ***(G-14333)***

Torgo Inc ... 800 360-5910
2033 Milwaukee Ave # 352 Riverwoods (60015) ***(G-17096)***

Tornado Industries LLC ... 817 551-6507
333 Charles Ct Ste 109 West Chicago (60185) ***(G-20653)***

Tornos Technologies US Corp (PA) ... 630 812-2040
200 Howard Ave Ste 220 Des Plaines (60018) ***(G-7857)***

Torqeedo Inc ... 815 444-8806
171 Erick St Ste A1 Crystal Lake (60014) ***(G-7284)***

Torrence Machine & Tool Co ... 815 469-1850
18830 82nd Ave Mokena (60448) ***(G-14124)***

Torstenson Glass Co ... 773 525-0435
3233 N Sheffield Ave Chicago (60657) ***(G-6397)***

Tortilleria Atotonilco Inc ... 773 523-0800
1850 W 47th St Chicago (60609) ***(G-6398)***

Tortilleria Industries, Chicago *Also called El Popocatapetl Industries Inc* ***(G-4467)***

Tortilleria La Mexicana, Chicago *Also called La Mexicana Tortilleria Inc* ***(G-5148)***

Toshiba America Electronic ... 847 484-2400
2150 E Lake Cook Rd Buffalo Grove (60089) ***(G-2613)***

Total Control Sports Inc......708 486-5800
2000 S 25th Ave Ste C Broadview (60155) ***(G-2472)***
Total Engineered Products Inc......630 543-9006
908 S Westwood Ave Addison (60101) ***(G-315)***
Total Graphics Services Inc......847 675-0800
8343 Niles Center Rd Skokie (60077) ***(G-19046)***
Total Plastics Inc......847 593-5000
505 Busse Rd Elk Grove Village (60007) ***(G-9278)***
Total Print Solutions Inc......630 494-0160
109 Fairfield Way Bloomingdale (60108) ***(G-2018)***
Total Printing Systems, Newton *Also called TPS Enterprises Inc* ***(G-15094)***
Total Titanium Inc......866 208-6446
281 Kennedy Dr Red Bud (62278) ***(G-17003)***
Total Tooling Technology Inc......847 437-5135
1475 Elmhurst Rd Elk Grove Village (60007) ***(G-9279)***
Totalworks Inc......773 489-4313
420 W Huron St Chicago (60654) ***(G-6399)***
Toth Automotive......708 474-5137
1621 Thornton Lansing Rd Lansing (60438) ***(G-12522)***
Touch & Glow, Broadview *Also called Bright Image Corporation* ***(G-2423)***
Touch Quest, Rosemont *Also called Digital Minds Inc* ***(G-18017)***
Touchsensor Technologies LLC......630 221-9000
203 N Gables Blvd Wheaton (60187) ***(G-20829)***
Tough Electric Inc......630 236-8332
717 Jackson St Aurora (60505) ***(G-1163)***
Touhy Diagnostic At Home LLC......847 803-1111
1293 Rand Rd Des Plaines (60016) ***(G-7858)***
Toulon City Water & Sew, Toulon *Also called City of Toulon* ***(G-19890)***
Tour, Litchfield *Also called Roller Derby Skate Corp* ***(G-12976)***
Tour Industries Inc......847 854-9400
1188 Starwood Pass Lake In The Hills (60156) ***(G-12344)***
Tower Atmtive Oprtons USA I LL......773 646-6550
12350 S Avenue O Chicago (60633) ***(G-6400)***
Tower Automotive Chicago, Chicago *Also called Ta Delaware Inc* ***(G-6309)***
Tower Metal Products LP (PA)......847 806-7200
1965 Pratt Blvd Elk Grove Village (60007) ***(G-9280)***
Tower Oil & Technology Co......773 927-6161
4300 S Tripp Ave Chicago (60632) ***(G-6401)***
Tower Plastics Mfg Inc......847 788-1700
181 Shore Ct Ste 2 Burr Ridge (60527) ***(G-2723)***
Tower Printing & Design......630 495-1976
2211 S Highland Ave 5a Lombard (60148) ***(G-13145)***
Tower Rock Stone Company (PA)......618 281-4106
250 W Sand Bank Rd Columbia (62236) ***(G-6994)***
Tower Tool & Engineering Inc......815 654-1115
11052 Raleigh Ct Machesney Park (61115) ***(G-13378)***
Tower Works Inc......630 557-2221
47w543 Perry Rd Maple Park (60151) ***(G-13467)***
Towerleaf LLC......847 985-1937
1680 Wright Blvd Schaumburg (60193) ***(G-18750)***
Towers Holdings, Northfield *Also called Towers Media Holdings Inc* ***(G-15534)***
Towers Media Holdings Inc......312 993-1550
1 Northfield Plz Ste 300 Northfield (60093) ***(G-15534)***
Town Hall Archery, Belleville *Also called Town Hall Sports Inc* ***(G-1601)***
Town Hall Sports Inc......618 235-9881
5901 Cool Sports Rd Belleville (62223) ***(G-1601)***
Town Square Publications LLC......847 427-4633
155 E Arlington Hts Rd Arlington Heights (60005) ***(G-820)***
Towne Machine Tool Company......217 442-4910
1009 Lynch Rd Danville (61834) ***(G-7389)***
Towne Towing Inc......847 705-1710
400 S Vermont St Palatine (60067) ***(G-16165)***
Townley Engrg & Mfg Co Inc......618 273-8271
607 Sutton Rd Eldorado (62930) ***(G-8484)***
Towntees, Wheaton *Also called Kmf Enterprises Inc* ***(G-20808)***
Tox- Pressotechnik LLC......630 447-4600
4250 Weaver Pkwy Warrenville (60555) ***(G-20254)***
Toyal America Inc......630 505-2160
1717 N Naper Blvd Ste 201 Naperville (60563) ***(G-14935)***
Toyal America Inc (HQ)......630 505-2160
17401 Broadway St Lockport (60441) ***(G-13025)***
Toyo Ink International Corp......630 930-5100
710 W Belden Ave Ste B Addison (60101) ***(G-316)***
Toyo Ink International Corp (HQ)......866 969-8696
1225 N Michael Dr Wood Dale (60191) ***(G-21251)***
Toyo Precision U S A, Bloomington *Also called Toyo USA Manufacturing Inc* ***(G-2103)***
Toyo USA Manufacturing Inc......309 827-8836
818 Avalon Way Bloomington (61705) ***(G-2103)***
Toyoda Grinders For Industry, Arlington Heights *Also called Jtekt Toyoda Americas Corp* ***(G-764)***
Toyota Boshoku Illinois LLC......618 943-5300
100 Trim Masters Dr Lawrenceville (62439) ***(G-12537)***
Toyota Tsusho America Inc......847 439-8500
25 Nw Point Boulev Elk Grove Village (60007) ***(G-9281)***
TPC Metals LLC (PA)......330 479-9510
7000 S Adams St Willowbrook (60527) ***(G-21061)***
Tpf Liquidation Co......847 362-0028
28160 Keith Rd Lake Forest (60045) ***(G-12315)***
Tpg Plastics LLC......630 828-2800
7409 S Quincy St Willowbrook (60527) ***(G-21062)***
Tpr America Inc......847 446-5336
10 N Martingale Rd # 145 Schaumburg (60173) ***(G-18751)***
TPS Enterprises Inc......618 783-2978
201 S Gregory Dr Newton (62448) ***(G-15094)***
Tr Chem Solutions LLC......262 865-7228
5250 Grand Ave Ste 14 Gurnee (60031) ***(G-10937)***
Track Group Inc (PA)......877 260-2010
200 E 5th Ave Ste 100 Naperville (60563) ***(G-14936)***
Track My Foreclosures LLC......877 732-8187
107 N State St Ste 1 Monticello (61856) ***(G-14288)***
Track Works LLC......618 731-2375
13790 Frey Acres Dr Highland (62249) ***(G-11242)***
Tracoinsa USA......309 287-7046
108 S Center St Gridley (61744) ***(G-10847)***
Tracy Electric Inc......618 943-6205
1308 Jefferson St Lawrenceville (62439) ***(G-12538)***
Trade Industries......618 643-4321
1020 E Randolph St Mc Leansboro (62859) ***(G-13709)***
Trade Label & Decal (PA)......630 773-0447
1285 Hamilton Pkwy Itasca (60143) ***(G-11747)***
Trade Print Inc......773 625-0792
7748 W Addison St Chicago (60634) ***(G-6402)***
Trade-Mark Coffee Corporation (PA)......847 382-4200
8 Lakeside Ln North Barrington (60010) ***(G-15289)***
Tradebe Environmental Svcs LLC......219 354-2452
1301 W 22nd St Oak Brook (60523) ***(G-15664)***
Trademark Products, Elk Grove Village *Also called S and S Associates Inc* ***(G-9224)***
Tradex International Inc......216 651-4788
21705 W Mississippi Ave Elwood (60421) ***(G-9465)***
Tradin Post Newspaper, Peoria *Also called Peoria Post Inc* ***(G-16495)***
Trading Square Company Inc......630 960-0606
6434 S Cass Ave Westmont (60559) ***(G-20777)***
Traena Inc (PA)......630 605-3087
2158 Pine St 2 Chicago (60602) ***(G-6403)***
Traeyne Corporation......309 936-7878
17982 E 2350th St Atkinson (61235) ***(G-903)***
Trafalgar Company LLC......847 292-8300
5600 N River Rd Ste 500 Rosemont (60018) ***(G-18054)***
Traffco Products LLC......773 374-6645
7731 S South Chicago Ave Chicago (60619) ***(G-6404)***
Traffic Sign Store, The, Bloomington *Also called Road Ready Signs* ***(G-2089)***
Trafficcom (HQ)......773 997-8351
425 W Randolph St Chicago (60606) ***(G-6405)***
Trafficguard Inc......877 727-7347
1730 Afton Rd Ste 1 Sycamore (60178) ***(G-19736)***
Trailers Inc......217 472-6000
1839 Saint Pauls Ch Rd Chapin (62628) ***(G-3396)***
Trailers Machine & Welding, Chapin *Also called Trailers Inc* ***(G-3396)***
Trainor AG Products LLC (PA)......618 614-5770
5380 State Route 146 E Anna (62906) ***(G-589)***
Tramac, Buffalo Grove *Also called Maclean Fastener Services LLC* ***(G-2566)***
Tramco Pump Co......312 243-5800
1428 Sherman Rd Romeoville (60446) ***(G-17881)***
Tramec Hill Fastener, Rock Falls *Also called Hill Holdings Inc* ***(G-17183)***
Trane Technologies Company LLC......630 530-3800
131 W Diversey Ave Elmhurst (60126) ***(G-9436)***
Trane Technologies Company LLC......704 655-4000
15768 Collection Ctr Dr Chicago (60693) ***(G-6406)***
Trane US Inc......630 734-3200
7100 S Madison St Willowbrook (60527) ***(G-21063)***
Trane US Inc......708 532-8004
18452 West Creek Dr Tinley Park (60477) ***(G-19861)***
Trans-Astro, South Beloit *Also called McCleary Inc* ***(G-19101)***
Transagra International Inc (PA)......312 856-1010
155 N Michigan Ave # 720 Chicago (60601) ***(G-6407)***
Transcedar Limited......618 262-4153
916 Empire St Mount Carmel (62863) ***(G-14488)***
Transcend Corp......847 395-6630
90 Mcmillen Rd Antioch (60002) ***(G-638)***
Transcend Orthtics Prosthetics, Burr Ridge *Also called Midwest Orthotic & Technology* ***(G-2703)***
Transcenda Inc......847 705-6670
923 W Sparrow Ct Palatine (60067) ***(G-16166)***
Transcendia Inc (PA)......847 678-1800
9201 Belmont Ave Ste 100a Franklin Park (60131) ***(G-10063)***
Transcendia Inc......847 678-1800
9201 Belmont Ave Ste 100a Franklin Park (60131) ***(G-10064)***
Transco Inc......419 562-1031
200 N La Salle St Lbby 5 Chicago (60601) ***(G-6408)***
Transco Products Inc......312 427-2818
1215 E 12th St Streator (61364) ***(G-19631)***
Transco Railway Products, Chicago *Also called Transco Inc* ***(G-6408)***
Transco Railway Products Inc (HQ)......312 427-2818
200 N La Salle St Lbby 5 Chicago (60601) ***(G-6409)***
Transcontinental Cold Storage, Hillsdale *Also called Tyson Fresh Meats Inc* ***(G-11323)***
Transcontinental Holding Corp (HQ)......773 877-3300
8600 W Bryn Mawr Ave Chicago (60631) ***(G-6410)***

Transcontinental Multifilm Inc (HQ) 847 695-7600
1040 N Mclean Blvd Elgin (60123) *(G-8757)*
Transcontinental Multifilm Inc 847 695-7600
1700 Big Timber Rd Elgin (60123) *(G-8758)*
Transcontinental Tech LLC 877 447-3539
8600 W Bryn Mawr Ave Chicago (60631) *(G-6411)*
Transfer Logistics Inc 773 646-0529
11600 S Burley Ave Chicago (60617) *(G-6412)*
Transformer Manufacturers Inc 708 457-1200
7051 W Wilson Ave Norridge (60706) *(G-15245)*
Transfrmtional Enrgy Solutions 828 226-7821
1418 W King St Decatur (62522) *(G-7562)*
Translogic Corporation 847 392-3700
1951 Rohlwing Rd Ste C Rolling Meadows (60008) *(G-17781)*
Translucent Publishing Corp 312 447-5450
222 W Ontario St Ste 410 Chicago (60654) *(G-6413)*
Transom Symphony Opco LLC 203 951-1919
205 Shellhouse Dr Rantoul (61866) *(G-16984)*
Transomatic Des Plaines LLC 847 625-1500
1500 Rand Rd Des Plaines (60016) *(G-7859)*
Transpac Usa Inc 847 605-1616
1515 E Wdfield Rd Ste 340 Schaumburg (60173) *(G-18752)*
Transparent Container Co Inc 630 543-1818
625 Thomas Dr Bensenville (60106) *(G-1903)*
Transportation Eqp Advisors 847 318-7575
6250 N River Rd Ste 5000 Rosemont (60018) *(G-18055)*
Transportation Tech Industires, Rockford *Also called Gunite Corporation (G-17437)*
Transworld Plastic Films Inc 815 561-7117
150 N 15th St Rochelle (61068) *(G-17162)*
Tranter Phe Inc 217 227-3470
30241 W Frontage Rd Farmersville (62533) *(G-9660)*
Traube Canvas Products Inc 618 281-0696
1727 Bluffview Dr Dupo (62239) *(G-8147)*
Travel Caddy Inc 847 621-7000
11333 Addison Ave Apt 200 Franklin Park (60131) *(G-10065)*
Travel Hammock Inc 847 486-0005
8136 Monticello Ave Skokie (60076) *(G-19047)*
Traveler Printing, Peoria *Also called Elise S Allen (G-16434)*
Travelon, Franklin Park *Also called Travel Caddy Inc (G-10065)*
Traxco Inc 847 669-1545
11416 Kiley Dr Huntley (60142) *(G-11569)*
TRC Environmental Corp 630 953-9046
7521 Brush Hill Dr Burr Ridge (60527) *(G-2724)*
Trd Manufacturing Inc 815 654-7775
10914 N 2nd St Machesney Park (61115) *(G-13379)*
Treasure Keeper Inc 630 761-1500
1355 Paramount Pkwy Batavia (60510) *(G-1432)*
Treasure Keeper X, Batavia *Also called Treasure Keeper Inc (G-1432)*
Treatment Products Ltd 773 626-8888
4701 W Augusta Blvd Chicago (60651) *(G-6414)*
Trebor Enterprises Ltd 815 235-1700
927 W Stephenson St Freeport (61032) *(G-10147)*
Tredegar Film Products Corp 847 438-2111
351 Oakwood Rd Lake Zurich (60047) *(G-12465)*
Tree Towns Reprographics Inc 630 832-0209
1041 S Il Route 83 Elmhurst (60126) *(G-9437)*
Tree Twns Imging Clor Graphics, Elmhurst *Also called Tree Towns Reprographics Inc (G-9437)*
Tree-O Lumber Inc 618 357-2576
5492 Woodhaven Rd Pinckneyville (62274) *(G-16620)*
Treehouse Foods Inc (PA) 708 483-1300
2021 Spring Rd Ste 600 Oak Brook (60523) *(G-15665)*
Treehouse Private Brands Inc 630 455-5265
3250 Lacey Rd Ste 600 Downers Grove (60515) *(G-8102)*
Treehouse Private Brands Inc 815 389-2745
1450 Pate Plaza Dr South Beloit (61080) *(G-19117)*
Treehouse Private Brands Inc (HQ) 314 877-7300
2021 Spring Rd Ste 600 Oak Brook (60523) *(G-15666)*
Treetop Marketing Inc 877 249-0479
717 Main St Batavia (60510) *(G-1433)*
Trekon Company Inc 309 925-7942
115 E South St Tremont (61568) *(G-19899)*
Trellborg Sling Sltions US Inc 630 539-5500
20 N Martingale Rd # 210 Schaumburg (60173) *(G-18753)*
Trellborg Sling Sltions US Inc 630 289-1500
901 Phoenix Lake Ave Streamwood (60107) *(G-19598)*
Trelleborg Slng Slns Strmwd, Streamwood *Also called Trellborg Sling Sltions US Inc (G-19598)*
Tremont Kitchen Tops Inc 309 925-5736
100 N West St Tremont (61568) *(G-19900)*
Trend Publishing Inc 312 654-2300
625 N Michigan Ave # 1050 Chicago (60611) *(G-6415)*
Trend Setters Ltd 309 929-7012
22500 State Route 9 Tremont (61568) *(G-19901)*
Trend Technologies LLC 847 640-2382
737 Fargo Ave Elk Grove Village (60007) *(G-9282)*
Trendler Inc 773 284-6600
4540 W 51st St Chicago (60632) *(G-6416)*
Trendy Screenprinting 815 895-0081
155 E Maplewood Dr Sycamore (60178) *(G-19737)*
Trenton Sun 618 224-9422
19 W Broadway Trenton (62293) *(G-19905)*
Tres Joli Designs Ltd 847 520-3903
634 Wheeling Rd Wheeling (60090) *(G-21001)*
Treudt Corporation 630 293-0500
131 Fremont St West Chicago (60185) *(G-20654)*
Tri Cable Inc 847 815-6082
521 Sandy Ln Libertyville (60048) *(G-12717)*
Tri City Canvas Products Inc (PA) 618 797-1662
3240 W Chain Of Rocks Rd A Granite City (62040) *(G-10746)*
Tri City Sheet Metal 630 232-4255
701 May St Geneva (60134) *(G-10313)*
Tri County Concrete 309 222-4000
2021 E Harvard Ave Peoria (61614) *(G-16538)*
Tri County Journal, Tuscola *Also called Tuscola Journal Incorporated (G-19932)*
Tri County Lift Trucks Inc 847 838-0183
1020 Anita Ave Antioch (60002) *(G-639)*
Tri County Scribe, Augusta *Also called Augusta Eagle (G-909)*
Tri Family Oil Co (PA) 618 654-1137
2103 Saint Michael Ct N Highland (62249) *(G-11243)*
Tri Guards Inc 847 537-8444
80 N Lively Blvd Elk Grove Village (60007) *(G-9283)*
Tri Industries Nfp 773 754-3100
780 Corporate Woods Pkwy Vernon Hills (60061) *(G-20107)*
Tri International Co 773 838-3400
7401 S Cicero Ave Chicago (60629) *(G-6417)*
Tri Kote Inc 618 262-4156
1126 W 3rd St Mount Carmel (62863) *(G-14489)*
Tri Par Die Mold 847 515-3801
12872 Bluebell Ave Huntley (60142) *(G-11570)*
Tri Pro Graphics LLC 309 664-5875
2422 E Washington St # 102 Bloomington (61704) *(G-2104)*
Tri R 224 399-7786
1921 Industrial Dr Libertyville (60048) *(G-12718)*
Tri Sales Co 773 838-3400
7401 S Cicero Ave Chicago (60629) *(G-6418)*
Tri Sales Co 773 838-3400
7401 S Cicero Ave Chicago (60629) *(G-6419)*
Tri Sales Co 773 838-3400
7401 S Cicero Ave Chicago (60629) *(G-6420)*
Tri Sales Co (HQ) 773 838-3400
7401 S Cicero Ave Chicago (60629) *(G-6421)*
Tri Sect Corporation 847 524-1119
717 Morse Ave Schaumburg (60193) *(G-18754)*
Tri Star Cabinet & Top Co Inc (PA) 815 485-2564
1000 S Cedar Rd New Lenox (60451) *(G-15065)*
Tri Star Manufacturing, Schaumburg *Also called Lynda Hervas (G-18615)*
Tri Star Plowing 847 584-5070
876 Asbury Ln Schaumburg (60193) *(G-18755)*
Tri State Acid Co Inc 618 676-1111
110 Industrial Park Clay City (62824) *(G-6908)*
Tri State Aluminum Products 815 877-6081
6300 Forest Hills Rd Loves Park (61111) *(G-13277)*
Tri State Cut Stone & Brick Co, Frankfort *Also called Tri-State Cut Stone Co (G-9845)*
Tri State Recycling Service 708 865-9939
301 W Lake St Frnt 1 Northlake (60164) *(G-15562)*
Tri Systmes, Libertyville *Also called Tri Cable Inc (G-12717)*
Tri Vantage LLC 630 530-5333
957 N Oaklawn Ave Elmhurst (60126) *(G-9438)*
Tri-City Corrugated Inc 630 372-6200
1307 Schiferl Rd Bartlett (60103) *(G-1317)*
Tri-City Gold Exchange Inc 708 331-5995
470 E 147th St Harvey (60426) *(G-11098)*
Tri-City Heat Treat Co Inc 309 786-2689
2020 5th St Rock Island (61201) *(G-17252)*
Tri-City Ready-Mix 618 439-2071
302 E Bond St Benton (62812) *(G-1938)*
Tri-City Sports Inc 217 224-2489
4360 Broadway St Quincy (62305) *(G-16951)*
Tri-Con Materials Inc (PA) 815 872-3206
308 W Railroad Ave Princeton (61356) *(G-16824)*
Tri-County Chemical Inc (PA) 618 273-2071
2441 Public Rd Eldorado (62930) *(G-8485)*
Tri-County Concrete Inc 815 786-2179
331 W Church St Sandwich (60548) *(G-18385)*
Tri-County Truck Tops Inc 847 740-4004
1218 W Rollins Rd Round Lake (60073) *(G-18085)*
Tri-Cunty Wldg Fabrication LLC 217 543-3304
1031 E Columbia St Arthur (61911) *(G-881)*
Tri-Dim Filter Corporation 847 695-5822
999 Raymond St Elgin (60120) *(G-8759)*
Tri-Fin LLC 630 467-0991
79 Bond St Elk Grove Village (60007) *(G-9284)*
Tri-J Machine Works 618 542-2663
546 N Howard St Du Quoin (62832) *(G-8125)*
Tri-Lite Inc 773 384-7765
1642 N Besly Ct Chicago (60642) *(G-6422)*

ALPHABETIC

Tri-Par Die and Mold Corp 630 232-8800
670 Sundown Rd South Elgin (60177) **(G-19177)**
Tri-Part Screw Products Inc 815 654-7311
10739 N 2nd St Machesney Park (61115) **(G-13380)**
Tri-Star Engineering Inc 847 595-3377
2455 Pan Am Blvd Elk Grove Village (60007) **(G-9285)**
Tri-State Alum & Vinyl Pdts, Loves Park *Also called Tri State Aluminum Products* **(G-13277)**
Tri-State Asphalt Emulsions, Elgin *Also called Cgk Enterprises Inc* **(G-8535)**
Tri-State Cut Stone Co 815 469-7550
10333 Vans Dr Frankfort (60423) **(G-9845)**
Tri-State Disposal Inc 708 388-9910
13903 S Ashland Ave Riverdale (60827) **(G-17077)**
Tri-State Food Equipment 217 228-1550
1605 Chestnut St Quincy (62301) **(G-16952)**
Tri-State Producing Developing 618 393-2176
1060 W Main St Olney (62450) **(G-15890)**
Tri-State Tool & Design Inc 217 696-2477
2537 N 2200th Ave Camp Point (62320) **(G-2812)**
Tri-Tech Molding 847 263-7769
21547 W Morton Dr Lake Villa (60046) **(G-12370)**
Tri-Tech Sltons Consulting Inc 847 941-0199
259 N Woodland Dr Mount Prospect (60056) **(G-14576)**
Tri-Tower Printing Inc 847 640-6633
1701 Golf Rd Ste L01 Rolling Meadows (60008) **(G-17782)**
Triad Circuits Inc 847 283-8600
3135 N Oak Grove Ave Waukegan (60087) **(G-20510)**
Triad Controls Inc (PA) 630 443-9320
3715 Swenson Ave Saint Charles (60174) **(G-18291)**
Triad Cutting Tools Svc & Mfg 847 352-0459
1025 Lunt Ave Ste E Schaumburg (60193) **(G-18756)**
Trialco Inc (PA) 708 757-4200
900 E Lincoln Hwy Ste 1 Chicago Heights (60411) **(G-6781)**
Triangle, Skokie *Also called Expercolor Inc* **(G-18953)**
Triangle Concrete Co Inc 309 853-4334
1201 New St Kewanee (61443) **(G-12042)**
Triangle Dies and Supplies Inc (PA) 630 454-3200
1436 Louis Bork Dr Batavia (60510) **(G-1434)**
Triangle Engineered Products, Bensenville *Also called Standard Car Truck Company* **(G-1899)**
Triangle Metals Div, Hoffman Estates *Also called Thomas Engineering Inc* **(G-11469)**
Triangle Metals Division, Rockford *Also called Thomas Engineering Inc* **(G-17659)**
Triangle Printers Inc 847 675-3700
3737 Chase Ave Skokie (60076) **(G-19048)**
Triangle Screen Print Inc 847 678-9200
10353 Franklin Ave Franklin Park (60131) **(G-10066)**
Triangle Technologies Inc 630 736-3318
687 Bonded Pkwy Streamwood (60107) **(G-19599)**
Tribeam Inc 847 409-9497
1323 S Fernandez Ave Arlington Heights (60005) **(G-821)**
Tribune Freedom Center, Chicago *Also called Chicago Tribune Company* **(G-4133)**
Tribune Publishing Company (PA) 312 222-9100
160 N Stetson Ave Chicago (60601) **(G-6423)**
Tribune Publishing Company LLC (HQ) 312 222-9100
435 N Michigan Ave Fl 2 Chicago (60611) **(G-6424)**
Tribune Publishing Company LLC 312 832-6711
435 N Michigan Ave Fl 2 Chicago (60611) **(G-6425)**
Tribus Aerospace Corp 312 876-2683
10 S Wacker Dr Ste 3300 Chicago (60606) **(G-6426)**
Tribus Aerospace LLC (PA) 312 876-7267
10 S Wacker Dr Ste 3300 Chicago (60606) **(G-6427)**
Tricast/Presfore Corporation 815 459-1820
169 Virginia Rd Crystal Lake (60014) **(G-7285)**
Tricel Corporation 847 336-1321
2100 Swanson Ct Gurnee (60031) **(G-10938)**
Trick Percussion Products Inc 847 342-2019
17 E University Dr Arlington Heights (60004) **(G-822)**
Trico Technologies Inc 847 662-9224
209 Ambrogio Dr Gurnee (60031) **(G-10939)**
Tricon Inds Mfg & Eqp Sls 815 379-2090
28524 1250 E St Walnut (61376) **(G-20220)**
Tricon Wear Solutions LLC 708 235-4064
2605 Federal Signal Dr University Park (60484) **(G-19969)**
Tricor Systems Inc 847 742-5542
1650 Todd Farm Dr Elgin (60123) **(G-8760)**
Tricounty, Antioch *Also called Tri County Lift Trucks Inc* **(G-639)**
Tridan International, Danville *Also called Kaydon Acquisition Xii Inc* **(G-7354)**
Trident Industries 847 285-1316
1900 E Golf Rd Schaumburg (60173) **(G-18757)**
Trident Machine Co 815 968-1585
3491 N Meridian Rd Rockford (61101) **(G-17668)**
Trident Manufacturing Inc 847 464-0140
14n2 Prairie St Pingree Grove (60140) **(G-16624)**
Trident Software Corp 847 219-8777
1183 S Scoville Ave Niles (60714) **(G-15182)**
Triezenberg Millwork Co 708 489-9062
4737 138th St Ste 202 Crestwood (60418) **(G-7132)**
Trifab Inc 847 838-2083
606 Longview Dr Antioch (60002) **(G-640)**
Trigon International Corp, Aurora *Also called Trigon International LLC* **(G-1027)**
Trigon International LLC 630 978-9990
4000 Sussex Ave Aurora (60504) **(G-1027)**
Trim Suits By Show-Off Inc 630 894-0100
48 Congress Cir W Roselle (60172) **(G-17994)**
Trim-Rite Food Corporation 847 649-3400
801 Commerce Pkwy Carpentersville (60110) **(G-3121)**
Trim-Tex Inc (PA) 847 679-3000
3700 W Pratt Ave Lincolnwood (60712) **(G-12846)**
Trimaco LLC 919 674-3476
1215 Landmeier Rd Elk Grove Village (60007) **(G-9286)**
Trimark Screen Printing Inc 630 629-2823
710 E Western Ave Ste C Lombard (60148) **(G-13146)**
Trinity Brand Industries Inc 708 482-4980
280 Shore Dr Burr Ridge (60527) **(G-2725)**
Trinity Machined Products Inc 630 876-6992
2560 White Oak Cir Aurora (60502) **(G-1028)**
Trinity Services Inc 815 485-5612
210 Haines Ave New Lenox (60451) **(G-15066)**
Trinket Studios 773 888-3454
3701 N Ravenswood Ave # 206 Chicago (60613) **(G-6428)**
Trio Foundry Inc (PA) 630 892-1676
1985 Aucutt Rd Montgomery (60538) **(G-14272)**
Trio Foundry Inc 815 786-6616
924 W Church St Sandwich (60548) **(G-18386)**
Trio Wire Products Inc 815 469-2148
141 Ontario St Frankfort (60423) **(G-9846)**
Triple B Manufacturing Co Inc 618 566-2888
620 Industrial St Mascoutah (62258) **(G-13607)**
Triple Edge Manufacturing Inc 847 468-9156
320 Production Dr South Elgin (60177) **(G-19178)**
Triple R Graphics, Mokena *Also called Rrr Graphics & Film Corp* **(G-14114)**
Triple Sticks Foods LLC 800 468-3354
9200 W Main St Belleville (62223) **(G-1602)**
Tripp Lite, Chicago *Also called Trippe Manufacturing Company* **(G-6429)**
Trippe Manufacturing Company 773 869-1111
1111 W 35th St Fl 12 Chicago (60609) **(G-6429)**
Triseal Corporation 815 648-2473
11920 Price Rd Hebron (60034) **(G-11151)**
Triseal Worldwide, Hebron *Also called Triseal Corporation* **(G-11151)**
Trisure Closures Worldwide, Carol Stream *Also called American Flange & Mfg Co Inc* **(G-2933)**
Tritech International LLC 847 888-0333
1710 Todd Farm Dr Elgin (60123) **(G-8761)**
Triton Industries Inc (PA) 773 384-3700
1020 N Kolmar Ave Chicago (60651) **(G-6430)**
Triton Manufacturing Co Inc (PA) 708 587-4000
5700 W Triton Way Monee (60449) **(G-14210)**
Triumph Books LLC 800 888-4741
814 N Franklin St Chicago (60610) **(G-6431)**
Triumph Books Corp 312 337-0747
814 N Franklin St Fl 3 Chicago (60610) **(G-6432)**
Triumph Group Inc 312 498-2516
621 Plainfield Rd Ste 309 Willowbrook (60527) **(G-21064)**
Triumph Packaging Georgia LLC 312 251-9600
736 N Western Ave Ste 352 Lake Forest (60045) **(G-12316)**
Triumph Packaging Group 312 251-9600
736 N Western Ave Ste 352 Lake Forest (60045) **(G-12317)**
Triumph Truss & Steel Company 815 522-6000
1250 Larkin Ave Ste 200 Elgin (60123) **(G-8762)**
Triumph Twist Drill Co Inc 815 459-6250
301 Industrial Rd Crystal Lake (60012) **(G-7286)**
Triumph Workplace Solutions, Vernon Hills *Also called Tri Industries Nfp* **(G-20107)**
Trivaeo LLC 760 505-4751
1 Regina Dr Paris (61944) **(G-16245)**
Trivial Development Corp 630 860-2500
1035 Hilltop Dr Itasca (60143) **(G-11748)**
Triwater Holdings LLC 847 457-1812
1915 Windridge Dr Lake Forest (60045) **(G-12318)**
Triwire Inc 815 633-7707
2201 Range Rd Loves Park (61111) **(G-13278)**
Trmg LLP 847 441-4122
790 W Frontage Rd Ste 416 Northfield (60093) **(G-15535)**
Tro Manufacturing Company Inc 847 455-3755
2610 Edgington St Franklin Park (60131) **(G-10067)**
Trodat Usa Inc 847 806-1750
2630 Greenleaf Ave Elk Grove Village (60007) **(G-9287)**
Trojan Oil Inc 618 754-3474
953 N 1300th St Newton (62448) **(G-15095)**
Tronox Incorporated 203 705-3704
2 Washington Ave Madison (62060) **(G-13418)**
Tropar Trophy Manufacturing Co 630 787-1900
839 N Central Ave Wood Dale (60191) **(G-21252)**
Trophies and Awards Plus 708 754-7127
3344 Chicago Rd Ste 3 Steger (60475) **(G-19494)**
Trophies By George 630 497-1212
239 Cedarfield Dr Bartlett (60103) **(G-1318)**
Trophytime Inc 217 351-7958
223 S Locust St Champaign (61820) **(G-3359)**
Trotta Enterprises Inc 312 829-7084
1050 W Hubbard St Chicago (60642) **(G-6433)**

ALPHABETIC SECTION

Trotters Manufacturing Co...217 364-4540
  101 S West St Buffalo (62515) *(G-2501)*
Trottie Publishing Group Inc..708 344-5975
  9930 Derby Ln Ste 102 Westchester (60154) *(G-20715)*
Trouw Nutrition Usa LLC..618 654-2070
  115 Executive Dr Highland (62249) *(G-11244)*
Trouw Nutrition Usa LLC (HQ)..618 654-2070
  115 Executive Dr Highland (62249) *(G-11245)*
Trouw Nutrition Usa LLC..618 654-2070
  1 Ultraway Dr Highland (62249) *(G-11246)*
Trouw Nutrition Usa LLC..618 654-2070
  145 Matter Dr Highland (62249) *(G-11247)*
Troverco Inc (PA)...800 468-3354
  9200 W Main St Ste 1 Belleville (62223) *(G-1603)*
Troy Design & Manufacturing Co...312 692-9706
  3400 E 126th St Chicago (60633) *(G-6434)*
Troy Iron Works, Chicago *Also called Lake Iron Inc (G-5160)*
Troy McDaniel..309 369-6225
  132 Court St Pekin (61554) *(G-16366)*
Trp, Elgin *Also called Thomas Research Products LLC (G-8754)*
Trp Acquisition Corp (PA)...630 261-2380
  1000 N Rohlwing Rd Ste 46 Lombard (60148) *(G-13147)*
Tru Coat Plating and Finishing..708 544-3940
  130 Mannheim Rd Bellwood (60104) *(G-1641)*
Tru Fragrance & Beauty LLC...630 563-4110
  7725 S Quincy St Willowbrook (60527) *(G-21065)*
Tru Grind Inc...847 749-3163
  3803 N Ventura Dr Arlington Heights (60004) *(G-823)*
Tru Line Lithographing Inc (HQ)..262 554-7300
  7400 N Lehigh Ave Niles (60714) *(G-15183)*
Tru Serv Corp..773 695-5674
  8600 W Bryn Mawr Ave Chicago (60631) *(G-6435)*
Tru Vue Inc (HQ)..708 485-5080
  9400 W 55th St Countryside (60525) *(G-7075)*
Tru-Colour Products LLC..630 447-0559
  27575 Ferry Rd Fl 2 Warrenville (60555) *(G-20255)*
Tru-Cut Inc...847 639-2090
  231 Jandus Rd Cary (60013) *(G-3195)*
Tru-Cut Machine Incorporated..815 422-5047
  480 S Oak St Saint Anne (60964) *(G-18138)*
Tru-Cut Production Inc...815 335-2215
  211 W Main St Winnebago (61088) *(G-21121)*
Tru-Cut Tool & Supply Co..708 396-1122
  1480 S Wolf Rd Wheeling (60090) *(G-21002)*
Tru-Machine Co Inc...815 675-6735
  7502 Mayo Ct Unit 3 Spring Grove (60081) *(G-19305)*
Tru-Native Enterprises...630 409-3258
  50 W Commercial Ave Addison (60101) *(G-317)*
Tru-Native N'Genuity, Addison *Also called Tru-Native Enterprises (G-317)*
Tru-Tone Finishing Inc (PA)..630 543-5520
  128 S Lombard Rd Addison (60101) *(G-318)*
Tru-Way Inc...708 562-3690
  36 W Lake St Northlake (60164) *(G-15563)*
Truckers Oil Pros Inc...773 523-8990
  2756 W 35th St Chicago (60632) *(G-6436)*
Trucut, Cary *Also called Horizon Steel Treating Inc (G-3167)*
Trudeau Approved Products Inc..312 924-7230
  3 Grant Sq 332 Hinsdale (60521) *(G-11382)*
True Dimension, Addison *Also called Formar Inc (G-128)*
True Lacrosse LLC...630 359-3857
  131 Eisenhower Ln N Lombard (60148) *(G-13148)*
True Line Mold and Engrg Corp...815 648-2739
  12205 Hansen Rd Hebron (60034) *(G-11152)*
True Royalty Scents...309 992-0688
  2404 N Elmwood Ave Peoria (61604) *(G-16539)*
True Sun Dried Tomatoes, Manteno *Also called Sono Italiano Corporation (G-13456)*
True Value, Lebanon *Also called Prescription Plus Ltd (G-12546)*
True Value Company LLC..847 639-5383
  201 Jandus Rd Cary (60013) *(G-3196)*
True Value Company LLC (HQ)...773 695-5000
  8600 W Bryn Mawr Ave 100s Chicago (60631) *(G-6437)*
True Woods Cabinetry Inc..847 550-1860
  1050 Ensell Rd Ste 100 Lake Zurich (60047) *(G-12466)*
True-Cut Wire EDM Div, Rockford *Also called Industrial Molds Inc (G-17459)*
Trueline Inc..309 378-2571
  7095 Shaffer Dr Downs (61736) *(G-8113)*
Truepad LLC..847 274-6898
  180 N Wabash Ave Ste 730 Chicago (60601) *(G-6438)*
Trufab Group USA LLC (PA)..630 994-3286
  550 Albion Ave Ste 90 Schaumburg (60193) *(G-18758)*
Trugrid.com, Schaumburg *Also called NE Desktop Software Inc (G-18646)*
Trumans Brands LLC..224 302-5605
  30 Porter Dr Round Lake Park (60073) *(G-18099)*
Trump Direct, Decatur *Also called Trump Printing Inc (G-7563)*
Trump Printing Inc..217 429-9001
  1591 N Water St Decatur (62526) *(G-7563)*
Truss Components Inc (PA)...800 678-7877
  607 N Main St Ste 100 Columbia (62236) *(G-6995)*
Truss Slater, Virden *Also called Lumberyard Suppliers Inc (G-20187)*

Trustar Holdings LLC...847 598-8800
  1515 E Wdfield Rd Ste 740 Schaumburg (60173) *(G-18759)*
Trusted Media Brands Inc..312 540-0035
  233 N Michigan Ave # 1740 Chicago (60601) *(G-6439)*
Trustwave Holdings Inc (HQ)...312 750-0950
  70 W Madison St Ste 600 Chicago (60602) *(G-6440)*
Trusty Warns Inc (PA)...630 766-9015
  229 N Central Ave Wood Dale (60191) *(G-21253)*
Truth Labs, Chicago *Also called Perficient Inc (G-5790)*
Truvanity Beauty LLC (PA)..312 778-6499
  55 E Monroe St Ste 3800 Chicago (60603) *(G-6441)*
Trx Express Inc...815 582-3792
  820 Brian Dr Crest Hill (60403) *(G-7099)*
Trx Pubco LLC (HQ)...312 222-9100
  435 N Michigan Ave Chicago (60611) *(G-6442)*
Try Our Pallets Inc..708 343-0166
  37 S 9th Ave Maywood (60153) *(G-13679)*
Tryad Specialties Inc (PA)...630 549-0079
  2015 Dean St Ste 6 Saint Charles (60174) *(G-18292)*
Tryson Metal Stampg & Mfg Inc (PA)......................................630 458-0591
  311 S Stewart Ave Addison (60101) *(G-319)*
Trz Race Cars, Frankfort *Also called T R Z Motorsports Inc (G-9843)*
TSA Processing Chicago Inc...630 860-5900
  520 Thomas Dr Bensenville (60106) *(G-1904)*
TSC Ferrite International, Toledo *Also called TSC Pyroferric International (G-19881)*
TSC Ferrite International, Wadsworth *Also called TSC International Inc (G-20214)*
TSC Ferrite International, Wadsworth *Also called Ferrite International Company (G-20209)*
TSC International Inc...847 249-4900
  39105 Magnetics Blvd Wadsworth (60083) *(G-20214)*
TSC Pyroferric International (PA)..217 849-2230
  507 E Madison Toledo (62468) *(G-19881)*
Tsd Manufacturing Co Inc..630 238-8750
  825 Chase Ave Elk Grove Village (60007) *(G-9288)*
Tsk Mnufacturing Solutions LLC..847 450-4099
  2390 Esplanade Dr 200f Algonquin (60102) *(G-390)*
Tsm Inc...815 544-5012
  6859 Belford Indus Dr Belvidere (61008) *(G-1705)*
Tsm North America Inc...815 372-1600
  1320 Tower Rd Schaumburg (60173) *(G-18760)*
Tst/Impreso Inc..630 775-9555
  450 S Lombard Rd Ste C Addison (60101) *(G-320)*
Tsv Adhesive Systems Inc...815 464-5606
  9411 Corsair Rd Frankfort (60423) *(G-9847)*
TT Technologies Inc...630 851-8200
  2020 E New York St Aurora (60502) *(G-1029)*
Tu-Star Manufacturing Co Inc...815 338-5760
  1200 Cobblestone Way Woodstock (60098) *(G-21441)*
Tube & Pipe Association Intl...815 399-8700
  2135 Point Blvd Elgin (60123) *(G-8763)*
Tube Line Stainless, Carol Stream *Also called Core Pipe Products Inc (G-2967)*
Tuf-Guard, Frankfort *Also called Dunhill Corp (G-9788)*
Tuf-Tite Inc...847 550-1011
  1200 Flex Ct Lake Zurich (60047) *(G-12467)*
Tuff Shed Inc...847 704-1147
  1408 E Northwest Hwy Palatine (60074) *(G-16167)*
Tuftads, Bensenville *Also called Bls Enterprises Inc (G-1754)*
Tukaiz LLC...847 288-4804
  2917 Latoria Ln Franklin Park (60131) *(G-10068)*
Tulip Tree Gardens Co..708 612-7094
  1236 E Eagle Lake Rd Beecher (60401) *(G-1522)*
Tuminello Enterprizes Inc (PA)..815 416-1007
  1347 East St Morris (60450) *(G-14334)*
Tuminello Enterprizes Inc...815 416-1007
  1347 East St Morris (60450) *(G-14335)*
Turasky Meats, Springfield *Also called Y T Packing Co (G-19470)*
Turbine Charging Unit, Bolingbrook *Also called Abb Inc (G-2145)*
Turbo Dry LLC..847 702-4430
  873 N Martin Dr Palatine (60067) *(G-16168)*
Turbo Tool & Mold Co...708 615-1730
  3045 S 26th Ave Broadview (60155) *(G-2473)*
Turf Inc..630 365-3903
  Os 951 953 Green Rd 951 Os Elburn (60119) *(G-8478)*
Turfmapp Inc..703 473-5678
  3550 N Lake Shore Dr Chicago (60657) *(G-6443)*
Turn Key Forging, Elk Grove Village *Also called Klein Tools Inc (G-9078)*
Turnco Inc..708 756-6565
  2200 S Halsted St Chicago Heights (60411) *(G-6782)*
Turnco Products, Chicago Heights *Also called Turnco Inc (G-6782)*
Turner Agward...773 669-8559
  5642 W Div St Ste 212 Chicago (60651) *(G-6444)*
Turner Jct Prtg & Litho Svc...630 293-1377
  850 Meadowview Xing Ste 2 West Chicago (60185) *(G-20655)*
Turnroth Sign Company Inc..815 625-1155
  1207 E Rock Falls Rd Rock Falls (61071) *(G-17198)*
Tuscan Hills Winery LLC..217 347-9463
  2200 Historic Hills Dr Effingham (62401) *(G-8427)*
Tuschall Engineering Co Inc..630 655-9100
  15w700 79th St Unit 1 Burr Ridge (60527) *(G-2726)*

Alphabetic Section

Tuscola Journal Incorporated 217 253-5086
115 W Sale St Tuscola (61953) *(G-19932)*

Tuscola Stone Company 217 253-4705
1199 E Us Highway 36 Tuscola (61953) *(G-19933)*

Tuskin Equipment Corporation 630 466-5590
483 N Heartland Dr Ste F Sugar Grove (60554) *(G-19658)*

Tussey G K Oil Explrtn & Prdc 618 948-2871
4th & Main St Saint Francisville (62460) *(G-18315)*

Tuthill Corporation (PA) 630 382-4900
8500 S Madison St Burr Ridge (60527) *(G-2727)*

Tuu Duc Le Inc (PA) 630 897-6363
110 John St North Aurora (60542) *(G-15280)*

Tuxco Corporation 847 244-2220
4300 Grove Ave Gurnee (60031) *(G-10940)*

Tuxhorn Drapery, Springfield Also called Afar Imports & Interiors Inc *(G-19316)*

Tvh Parts Co 847 223-1000
95 S Rte 83 Grayslake (60030) *(G-10803)*

Tvj Electroforming Division, Chicago Also called Dover Industrial Chrome Inc *(G-4391)*

Tvo Acquisition Corporation (PA) 708 656-4240
2540 S 50th Ave Cicero (60804) *(G-6882)*

Tvp Color Graphics Inc 630 837-3600
230 Roma Jean Pkwy Streamwood (60107) *(G-19600)*

Twain Media Mark Publishing 217 223-7008
617 Broadway St Quincy (62301) *(G-16953)*

Tweeten Fibre Co 312 733-7878
1756 W Hubbard St Chicago (60622) *(G-6445)*

Twin City Awards 309 452-9291
1531 Fort Jesse Rd Ste 5b Normal (61761) *(G-15226)*

Twin City Electric Inc 309 827-0636
1701 Easy St Ste 5 Bloomington (61701) *(G-2105)*

Twin City Tent & Awning Co, Urbana Also called Champaign Cnty Tent & Awng Co *(G-19977)*

Twin City Wood Recycling Corp 309 827-9663
1606 W Oakland Ave Bloomington (61701) *(G-2106)*

Twin Mills Timber & Tie Co Inc 618 932-3662
3268 State Highway 37 West Frankfort (62896) *(G-20685)*

Twin Plex Manufacturing, Wood Dale Also called Hcf Building Corporation *(G-21196)*

Twin States Publishing Co, Watseka Also called Times Republic *(G-20320)*

Twin Supplies Ltd 630 590-5138
1010 Jorie Blvd Ste 124 Oak Brook (60523) *(G-15667)*

Twin Towers Embroidery, Belvidere Also called Twin Towers Marketing *(G-1706)*

Twin Towers Marketing 815 544-5554
1231 Logan Ave Belvidere (61008) *(G-1706)*

Twinplex Manufacturing Co 630 595-2040
840 Lively Blvd Wood Dale (60191) *(G-21254)*

Twinplex Stamping Company, Wood Dale Also called Twinplex Manufacturing Co *(G-21254)*

Twist and Seal, Joliet Also called Midwest Innovative Pdts LLC *(G-11903)*

Twisted Traces Inc 630 345-5400
725 Nicholas Blvd Elk Grove Village (60007) *(G-9289)*

Twistshake LLC 224 419-0086
1070 S Northpoint Blvd Waukegan (60085) *(G-20511)*

Two Brothers Brewing Company 630 393-2337
30w315 Calumet Ave W Warrenville (60555) *(G-20256)*

Two Cards Innovation LLC 815 793-2517
1294 Dixie Trl Rockton (61072) *(G-17705)*

Two Eagles Distillery Llc 773 450-7575
1852 S Elmhurst Rd Mount Prospect (60056) *(G-14577)*

Two Four Seven Metal Laser 847 250-5199
1428 Norwood Ave Itasca (60143) *(G-11749)*

Two J S Sheet Metal Works Inc 773 436-9424
5828 S Oakley Ave Chicago (60636) *(G-6446)*

Two JS Copies Now Inc 847 292-2679
6725 N Northwest Hwy Chicago (60631) *(G-6447)*

Two Rivers Oil & Gas Co Inc 217 773-3356
116 S Capitol Ave Mount Sterling (62353) *(G-14594)*

Two Tower Frames Inc 773 517-0394
3501 N Sthport Ave Chcago Chicago (60657) *(G-6448)*

Two Tribes LLC 847 272-7711
3607 Lawson Rd Glenview (60026) *(G-10634)*

Two Wild Seeds Baking Company 630 797-5350
320 W Main St Saint Charles (60174) *(G-18293)*

Twocanoes Software Inc 630 305-9601
34 W Chicago Ave Ste A Naperville (60540) *(G-14937)*

Twoinspireyou LLC 630 849-8214
39w890 Carney Ln Geneva (60134) *(G-10314)*

Twr Service Corporation 847 923-0692
940 Lunt Ave Schaumburg (60193) *(G-18761)*

Twr3 Inc 847 784-5251
400 Central Ave Ste 306 Northfield (60093) *(G-15536)*

TWT Marketing Inc. 773 274-4470
2719 W Lunt Ave Chicago (60645) *(G-6449)*

Ty Miles Incorporated 708 344-5480
9855 Derby Ln Westchester (60154) *(G-20716)*

Ty Precision Automatics Inc 815 963-9668
2606 Falund St Rockford (61109) *(G-17669)*

Tyler, Thomas A PHD, New Lenox Also called Merit Emplyment Assssment Svcs *(G-15041)*

Tylka Printing Inc 773 767-3775
18400 76th Ave Ste A Tinley Park (60477) *(G-19862)*

Tylu Wireless Technology LLC 312 260-7934
3424 S State St Chicago (60616) *(G-6450)*

Tyrolit Limited 618 548-8314
101 Kendall Point Dr Oswego (60543) *(G-16029)*

Tyson 773 282-2900
3548 N Kostner Ave Chicago (60641) *(G-6451)*

Tyson Foods (HQ) 312 614-6000
400 S Jefferson St Chicago (60607) *(G-6452)*

Tyson Foods Inc 309 658-2291
28424 38th Ave N Hillsdale (61257) *(G-11322)*

Tyson Foods Inc 773 650-4000
4201 S Ashland Ave Chicago (60609) *(G-6453)*

Tyson Fresh Meats Inc 847 836-5550
2170 Point Blvd Ste 300 Elgin (60123) *(G-8764)*

Tyson Fresh Meats Inc 309 658-3377
28424 38th Ave N Hillsdale (61257) *(G-11323)*

Tyson Fresh Meats Inc 309 965-2565
373 Hwy 117 N Goodfield (61742) *(G-10678)*

Tza Consulting, Long Grove Also called Tom Zosel Associates Ltd *(G-13172)*

Tzee Inc 630 857-3425
4343 Commerce Ct Ste 200 Lisle (60532) *(G-12953)*

U G N Inc (HQ) 773 437-2400
18410 Crossing Dr Ste C Tinley Park (60487) *(G-19863)*

U Keep US In Stitches 847 427-8127
1420 S Redwood Dr Mount Prospect (60056) *(G-14578)*

U Mark Inc 618 235-7500
102 Iowa Ave Belleville (62220) *(G-1604)*

U O P Equitec Services Inc 847 391-2000
25 E Algonquin Rd Des Plaines (60016) *(G-7860)*

U R On It 847 382-0182
22172 N Hillview Dr Lake Barrington (60010) *(G-12167)*

U S Co-Tronics Corp 815 692-3204
403 E Locust St Fairbury (61739) *(G-9615)*

U S Colors & Coatings Inc 630 879-8898
1180 Lyon Rd Batavia (60510) *(G-1435)*

U S Filter Products 618 451-1205
3202 W 20th St Granite City (62040) *(G-10747)*

U S Filters 815 932-8154
404 E Broadway St Bradley (60915) *(G-2294)*

U S Free Press LLC 319 524-3802
950 E Us Highway 136 Hamilton (62341) *(G-10961)*

U S Intermodal Inc 708 448-9862
20635 Abbey Woods Ct N # 201 Frankfort (60423) *(G-9848)*

U S Naval Institute 800 233-8764
2427 Bond St University Park (60484) *(G-19970)*

U S Railway Services 708 468-8343
8201 183rd St Ste C Tinley Park (60487) *(G-19864)*

U S Silica Company 800 635-7263
701 Boyce Memorial Dr Ottawa (61350) *(G-16082)*

U S Soy LLC 217 235-1020
2808 Thomason Dr Mattoon (61938) *(G-13655)*

U S Tool & Manufacturing Co 630 953-1000
1335 W Fullerton Ave Addison (60101) *(G-321)*

U S Truck Body-Midwest, Streator Also called Mid-America Truck Corporation *(G-19614)*

U S Weight Inc 618 392-0408
4594 E Radio Tower Ln Olney (62450) *(G-15891)*

U Wash Equipment Co 618 466-9442
116 Northport Dr Alton (62002) *(G-575)*

U-Haul, Washington Also called Service Auto Supply *(G-20280)*

U.S. Architectural Glass & Met, Chicago Also called Glass Management Services Inc *(G-4693)*

U.S.T.H., Wheeling Also called US Tsubaki Holdings Inc *(G-21003)*

Uarco, Watseka Also called Standard Register Inc *(G-20316)*

Uber Technologies Inc 612 600-4737
111 N Canal St Ste 900 Chicago (60606) *(G-6454)*

Uberlube Inc 847 372-3127
2611 Hartzell St Evanston (60201) *(G-9585)*

Uberlube Inc 847 644-4230
8833 Lincolnwood Dr Evanston (60203) *(G-9586)*

Ubipass Inc 312 626-4624
5931 Stewart Dr Apt 1021 Willowbrook (60527) *(G-21066)*

Ucal Holdings Inc (HQ) 847 695-8030
1875 Holmes Rd Elgin (60123) *(G-8765)*

Ucal Systems Inc 847 695-8030
1355 Holmes Rd Elgin (60123) *(G-8766)*

Ucal Systems Inc (HQ) 847 695-8030
1875 Holmes Rd Elgin (60123) *(G-8767)*

Ucc Holdings Corporation (HQ) 847 473-5900
2100 Norman Dr Waukegan (60085) *(G-20512)*

Ucp, Morris Also called Utility Concrete Products LLC *(G-14338)*

Uesco Crane, Alsip Also called Uesco Industries Inc *(G-518)*

Uesco Industries Inc 708 385-7700
5908 W 118th St Alsip (60803) *(G-517)*

Uesco Industries Inc 800 325-8372
5908 W 118th St Alsip (60803) *(G-518)*

Ugly Hookah Tobacco Inc 708 724-9621
5530 W 110th St Ste 10 Oak Lawn (60453) *(G-15737)*

Ugn Automotive, Tinley Park Also called U G N Inc *(G-19863)*

Ugx, Lockport Also called Unlimited Graphix Inc *(G-13026)*

Uhlir Manufacturing Corp 773 376-5289
2642 W Cullerton St Chicago (60608) *(G-6455)*

UIC 312 413-7697
1747 W Roosevelt Rd 145 Chicago (60608) ***(G-6456)***
Uic Inc 815 744-4477
16720 Cherry Creek Ct Joliet (60433) ***(G-11937)***
Uico LLC 630 592-4400
650 W Grand Ave Ste 308 Elmhurst (60126) ***(G-9439)***
Uk Abrasives Inc 847 291-3566
3045 Macarthur Blvd Northbrook (60062) ***(G-15494)***
Uk Sailmakers, Chicago *Also called Nieman & Considine Inc* ***(G-5600)***
Ulla of Finland 773 763-0700
6221 N Leona Ave Chicago (60646) ***(G-6457)***
Ulrich Kaeppler 847 290-0220
1693 Elmhurst Rd Elk Grove Village (60007) ***(G-9290)***
Ultimate Distributing Inc 847 566-2250
436 Morris Ave Mundelein (60060) ***(G-14745)***
Ultimate Machining & Engrg Inc 815 439-8361
14015 S Van Dyke Rd Plainfield (60544) ***(G-16724)***
Ultimate Millwork Inc 773 343-3070
350 Lively Blvd Elk Grove Village (60007) ***(G-9291)***
Ultimate Screen Printing, Mundelein *Also called Ultimate Distributing Inc* ***(G-14745)***
Ultimate Sign Co 773 282-4595
5511 W Pensacola Ave Chicago (60641) ***(G-6458)***
Ultimate Software Group Inc 847 273-1701
9450 Bryn Mawr Ave # 650 Rosemont (60018) ***(G-18056)***
Ultra Packaging Inc 630 595-9820
534 N York Rd Bensenville (60106) ***(G-1905)***
Ultra Play Systems Inc (HQ) 618 282-8200
1675 Locust St Red Bud (62278) ***(G-17004)***
Ultra Polishing 224 769-7140
1320 Holmes Rd Elgin (60123) ***(G-8768)***
Ultra Polishing Inc 630 635-2926
640 Pratt Ave N Schaumburg (60193) ***(G-18762)***
Ultra Seal Lock, Bartlett *Also called Usl Lock Corporation* ***(G-1320)***
Ultra Specialties Incorporated 847 437-8110
1360 Howard St Elk Grove Village (60007) ***(G-9292)***
Ultra Specialty Holdings Inc 847 437-8110
1360 Howard St Elk Grove Village (60007) ***(G-9293)***
Ultra Stamping & Assembly Inc 815 874-9888
4590 Hydraulic Rd Rockford (61109) ***(G-17670)***
Ultra-Metric Tool Co 773 281-4200
2952 N Leavitt St Chicago (60618) ***(G-6459)***
Ultramatic Equipment Co 630 543-4565
848 S Westgate St Addison (60101) ***(G-322)***
Ultrasonic Power Corporation 815 235-6020
239 E Stephenson St Freeport (61032) ***(G-10148)***
Ultrasound Div - Buffalo Grove, Buffalo Grove *Also called Siemens Med Solutions USA Inc* ***(G-2603)***
Ultratech Inc 630 539-3578
251 Covington Dr Bloomingdale (60108) ***(G-2019)***
Umf Corporation 224 251-7822
5721 W Howard St Niles (60714) ***(G-15184)***
Umf Corporation (PA) 847 920-0370
4709 Golf Rd Ste 300a Skokie (60076) ***(G-19049)***
Umphreys McGee Inc 773 880-0024
1530 W Oakdale Ave Chicago (60657) ***(G-6460)***
Umw Inc 847 352-5252
601 Lunt Ave Schaumburg (60193) ***(G-18763)***
Uncommon Elements LLC 847 414-0708
22 Fawn Ridge Dr Oakwood Hills (60013) ***(G-15823)***
Uncommon Radiant 773 640-1674
2826 W Fitch Ave Chicago (60645) ***(G-6461)***
Uncommon Threads, Buffalo Grove *Also called V-Tex Inc* ***(G-2615)***
Underground Devices Inc 847 205-9000
420 Academy Dr Northbrook (60062) ***(G-15495)***
Underwood Dental Laboratories 217 398-0090
301 S 1st St Champaign (61820) ***(G-3360)***
UNI Electric Enterprise Inc 630 372-6312
1889 Seneca Dr Bartlett (60133) ***(G-1258)***
UNI-Ball Corporation 310 505-5926
400 S County Farm Rd # 300 Wheaton (60187) ***(G-20830)***
UNI-Glide, Chicago *Also called Singer Safety Company* ***(G-6175)***
UNI-Glide Corp 773 235-2100
2300 N Kilbourn Ave Chicago (60639) ***(G-6462)***
UNI-Label and Tag Corporation 847 956-8900
1121 Pagni Dr Elk Grove Village (60007) ***(G-9294)***
Unicarriers Americas Corp (HQ) 800 871-5438
240 N Prospect St Marengo (60152) ***(G-13496)***
Unichem, Elgin *Also called Universal Chem & Coatings Inc* ***(G-8769)***
Unichem Corporation 773 376-8872
1201 W 37th St Chicago (60609) ***(G-6463)***
Unichem International Inc 630 302-1469
11530 Smith Dr Huntley (60142) ***(G-11571)***
Unicor, Greenville *Also called Federal Prison Industries* ***(G-10834)***
Unicor, Pekin *Also called Federal Prison Industries* ***(G-16333)***
Unicord Companies, The, Calumet Park *Also called Unicord Corporation* ***(G-2800)***
Unicord Corporation 708 385-7999
12010 S Paulina St Calumet Park (60827) ***(G-2800)***
Unicorn Designs 847 295-5230
659 N Bank Ln Lake Forest (60045) ***(G-12319)***
Unicut Corporation 773 525-4210
1770 W Berteau Ave # 401 Chicago (60613) ***(G-6464)***
Unifab Mfg Inc 630 682-8970
450 Saint Paul Blvd Carol Stream (60188) ***(G-3082)***
Unified Distributors, Arlington Heights *Also called Unified Solutions Corp* ***(G-824)***
Unified Solutions Corp 847 478-9100
3456 N Ridge Ave Ste 200 Arlington Heights (60004) ***(G-824)***
Unified Tool Die & Mfg Co Inc 847 678-3773
9331 Seymour Ave Schiller Park (60176) ***(G-18848)***
Unified Wire and Cable Company 815 748-4876
338 Wurlitzer Dr Dekalb (60115) ***(G-7710)***
Uniflex of America LLC 847 519-1100
1088 National Pkwy Schaumburg (60173) ***(G-18764)***
Unilock 262 742-3890
301 E Sullivan Rd Aurora (60505) ***(G-1164)***
Unilock Chicago Inc (PA) 630 892-9191
301 E Sullivan Rd Aurora (60505) ***(G-1165)***
Unimin Lime Corporation (HQ) 203 966-8880
776 Centennial Dr Ottawa (61350) ***(G-16083)***
Unimode Inc 773 343-6754
11s104 S Jackson St Burr Ridge (60527) ***(G-2728)***
Union Ave Auto Inc 708 754-3899
3236 Union Ave Steger (60475) ***(G-19495)***
Union Banner Publishing Ltd 618 594-3131
17549 County Farm Rd Carlyle (62231) ***(G-2897)***
Union Carbide Corporation 708 396-3000
12840 S Pulaski Rd Alsip (60803) ***(G-519)***
Union Drainage District 618 445-2843
Rr 1 Mount Erie (62446) ***(G-14498)***
Union Foods Inc 201 327-2828
233 N Michigan Ave Chicago (60601) ***(G-6465)***
Union Iron Inc (HQ) 217 429-5148
3550 E Mound Rd Decatur (62521) ***(G-7564)***
Union Special LLC 847 669-5101
1 Union Special Plz Huntley (60142) ***(G-11572)***
Union Street Tin Co 312 379-8200
350 S Northwest Hwy Park Ridge (60068) ***(G-16300)***
Union Tank Car Company (HQ) 312 431-3111
175 W Jackson Blvd # 2100 Chicago (60604) ***(G-6466)***
Union Tank Car Company 815 942-7391
8805 Tabler Rd Morris (60450) ***(G-14336)***
Union Tank Car Company 312 431-3111
175 W Jackson Blvd # 2100 Chicago (60604) ***(G-6467)***
Uniphase Inc 630 584-4747
425 38th Ave Saint Charles (60174) ***(G-18294)***
Unique Assembly & Decorating 630 241-4300
2550 Wisconsin Ave Downers Grove (60515) ***(G-8103)***
Unique Blister Company 630 289-1232
1296 Humbracht Cir Bartlett (60103) ***(G-1319)***
Unique Checkout Systems, Franklin Park *Also called Tesler Company of Illinois Inc* ***(G-10060)***
Unique Concrete Concepts Inc 618 466-0700
26860 State Highway 16 Jerseyville (62052) ***(G-11797)***
Unique Designs 309 454-1226
408 Lumbertown Rd Normal (61761) ***(G-15227)***
Unique Envelope Corporation 773 586-0330
5958 S Oak Park Ave Chicago (60638) ***(G-6468)***
Unique Indoor Comfort 847 362-1910
624 2nd St Libertyville (60048) ***(G-12719)***
Unique Mold & Machine Inc 630 406-8305
1485 Louis Bork Dr Batavia (60510) ***(G-1436)***
Unique Novelty & Manufacturing 217 538-2014
200 S Main St Fillmore (62032) ***(G-9666)***
Unique Novelty Mfg & Sales, Fillmore *Also called Unique Novelty & Manufacturing* ***(G-9666)***
Unique Plastics, Schaumburg *Also called WJ Die Mold Inc* ***(G-18775)***
Unique Product Productions Inc 708 259-1500
22141 Woodbine Rd Richton Park (60471) ***(G-17032)***
Unique Prtrs Lithographers Inc 708 656-8900
5500 W 31st St Cicero (60804) ***(G-6883)***
Unique/Active LLC 708 656-8900
5500 W 31st St Cicero (60804) ***(G-6884)***
Uniquee Tees Inc 309 839-0280
1200 W Main St Ste 25 Peoria (61606) ***(G-16540)***
Unistrut Construction, Addison *Also called Unistrut International Corp* ***(G-323)***
Unistrut International Corp 630 773-3460
2171 W Executive Dr # 100 Addison (60101) ***(G-323)***
Unistrut International Corp (HQ) 800 882-5543
16100 Lathrop Ave Harvey (60426) ***(G-11099)***
Unit Step Company, Colona *Also called Leonards Unit Step of Moline* ***(G-6976)***
Unitech Industries Inc 847 357-8800
1461 Elmhurst Rd Elk Grove Village (60007) ***(G-9295)***
United Adhesives Inc (PA) 224 436-0077
820 Port Clinton Ct E Buffalo Grove (60089) ***(G-2614)***
United Amercn Healthcare Corp (PA) 313 393-4571
303 E Wacker Dr Ste 1040 Chicago (60601) ***(G-6469)***
United American Metals, Chicago *Also called RE Met Corp* ***(G-5981)***
United Animal Health, Rock Falls *Also called Hueber LLC* ***(G-17185)***
United Animal Health Inc 309 747-2196
116 W 2nd St Gridley (61744) ***(G-10848)***

ALPHABETIC

United Awning, Antioch *Also called United Canvas Inc* ***(G-641)***
United Bindery Service 312 243-0240
1845 W Carroll Ave Chicago (60612) ***(G-6470)***
United Canvas Inc 847 395-1470
25434 W Il Route 173 Antioch (60002) ***(G-641)***
United Carborator, Schiller Park *Also called United Remanufacturing Co Inc* ***(G-18851)***
UNITED CARBURATOR, Schiller Park *Also called United Remanufacturing Co Inc* ***(G-18850)***
United Carburator, Schiller Park *Also called United Carburetor Inc* ***(G-18849)***
United Carburetor Inc (PA) 773 777-1223
9550 Soreng Ave Schiller Park (60176) ***(G-18849)***
United Chemi-Con Inc (HQ) 847 696-2000
1701 Golf Rd Ste 1-1200 Rolling Meadows (60008) ***(G-17783)***
United Cmra Binocular Repr LLC 630 595-2525
2525 Busse Rd Elk Grove Village (60007) ***(G-9296)***
United Communications Corp 847 746-1515
2711 Sheridan Rd Ste 202 Zion (60099) ***(G-21527)***
United Communications Corp 847 746-4700
2711 Shrridon Rd Unit 202 Zion (60099) ***(G-21528)***
United Container Corporation 773 342-2200
1350 N Elston Ave Chicago (60642) ***(G-6471)***
United Conveyor Corporation (HQ) 847 473-5900
2100 Norman Dr Waukegan (60085) ***(G-20513)***
United Conveyor Supply Company (HQ) 847 672-5100
2100 Norman Dr Waukegan (60085) ***(G-20514)***
United Craftsmen Ltd 815 626-7802
1500 W 4th St Sterling (61081) ***(G-19539)***
United Electronics Corp Inc 847 671-6034
3615 Wolf Rd Franklin Park (60131) ***(G-10069)***
United Engravers Inc 847 301-3740
618 Pratt Ave N Schaumburg (60193) ***(G-18765)***
United Engraving, Romeoville *Also called Wood Graphics Inc* ***(G-17890)***
United Fence Co Inc 773 924-0773
3617 W 83rd St Chicago (60652) ***(G-6472)***
United Flexible Inc (PA) 815 886-1140
815 Forestwood Dr Romeoville (60446) ***(G-17882)***
United Food Ingredients Inc 630 655-9494
15w700 S Frontage Rd Burr Ridge (60527) ***(G-2729)***
United Gasket Corporation 708 656-3700
1633 S 55th Ave Cicero (60804) ***(G-6885)***
United General Graphics LLC 262 657-5054
7400 N Lehigh Ave Niles (60714) ***(G-15185)***
United Gilsonite Labs Inc 217 243-7878
550 Capitol Way Jacksonville (62650) ***(G-11784)***
United Granite & Marble 815 582-3345
321 Airport Dr Joliet (60431) ***(G-11938)***
United Graphics Llc 217 235-7161
2916 Marshall Ave Mattoon (61938) ***(G-13656)***
United Graphics Mailing Group, Elk Grove Village *Also called United Letter Service Inc* ***(G-9297)***
United Industries Illinois Ltd 847 526-9485
270 Jamie Ln Wauconda (60084) ***(G-20400)***
United Laboratories Inc (PA) 630 377-0900
320 37th Ave Saint Charles (60174) ***(G-18295)***
United Letter Service Inc 312 408-2404
898 Cambridge Dr Elk Grove Village (60007) ***(G-9297)***
United Lithograph Inc 847 803-1700
1670 S River Rd Des Plaines (60018) ***(G-7861)***
United Machine Works Inc 847 352-5252
601 Lunt Ave Schaumburg (60193) ***(G-18766)***
United Maint Wldg & McHy C 708 458-1705
5252 W 73rd St Bedford Park (60638) ***(G-1508)***
United Oil Co 309 378-3049
405 S Seminary St Downs (61736) ***(G-8114)***
United Press Inc 847 482-0597
211 Northampton Ln Lincolnshire (60069) ***(G-12799)***
United Printers Inc 773 376-1955
1540 W 44th St Chicago (60609) ***(G-6473)***
United Rawhide Mfg Co 847 692-2791
1315 Linden Ave Park Ridge (60068) ***(G-16301)***
United Ready Mix Inc (PA) 309 676-3287
1 Leland St Peoria (61602) ***(G-16541)***
United Remanufacturing Co Inc (HQ) 773 777-1223
9550 Soreng Ave Schiller Park (60176) ***(G-18850)***
United Remanufacturing Co Inc 847 678-2233
9550 Soreng Ave Schiller Park (60176) ***(G-18851)***
United Seating & Mobility LLC 309 699-0509
125 Thunderbird Ln Ste 1 East Peoria (61611) ***(G-8293)***
United Skilled Inc 815 874-9696
3412 Precision Dr Rockford (61109) ***(G-17671)***
United Skys LLC 847 546-7776
71 S Wacker Dr Ste 1600 Chicago (60606) ***(G-6474)***
United Spring & Manufacturing 773 384-8464
830 N Pulaski Rd Chicago (60651) ***(G-6475)***
United Standard Industries Inc 847 724-0350
2062 Lehigh Ave Glenview (60026) ***(G-10635)***
United States Audio Corp (PA) 312 316-2929
411 Crabtree Ln Glenview (60025) ***(G-10636)***
United States Audio Corp 312 316-2929
1658 W 35th St Chicago (60609) ***(G-6476)***
United States Filter/Iwt 815 877-3041
4669 Shepherd Trl Rockford (61103) ***(G-17672)***
United States Gear Corporation 773 821-5450
1020 W 119th St Chicago (60643) ***(G-6477)***
United States Gypsum Company (HQ) 312 606-4000
550 W Adams St Ste 1300 Chicago (60661) ***(G-6478)***
United States Steel Corp 618 451-3456
1951 State St Granite City (62040) ***(G-10748)***
United Steel & Fasteners Inc 630 250-0900
1500 Industrial Dr Itasca (60143) ***(G-11750)***
United Steel Perforating/ARC 630 942-7300
325 Windy Point Dr Glendale Heights (60139) ***(G-10513)***
United Systems Incorporated 708 479-1450
9704 194th St Mokena (60448) ***(G-14125)***
United Tactical Systems LLC (PA) 260 478-2500
28101 N Ballard Dr Ste F Lake Forest (60045) ***(G-12320)***
United Tech Arospc Systems, Rockford *Also called Hamilton Sundstrand Corp* ***(G-17440)***
United Tool and Engineering Co 815 389-3021
4095 Prairie Hill Rd South Beloit (61080) ***(G-19118)***
United Toolers of Illinois 779 423-0548
7203 Clinton Rd Loves Park (61111) ***(G-13279)***
United Universal Inds Inc 815 727-4445
20620 Burl Ct Ste 1 Joliet (60433) ***(G-11939)***
United Validation & Com 815 953-6068
1728 E 1700 North Rd Watseka (60970) ***(G-20321)***
United Woodworking Inc 847 352-3066
729 Lunt Ave Schaumburg (60193) ***(G-18767)***
Unitel Technologies Inc 847 297-2265
479 E Bus Ctr Dr Ste 105 Mount Prospect (60056) ***(G-14579)***
Unitex Industries Inc (PA) 708 524-0664
7001 North Ave Ste 2ne Oak Park (60302) ***(G-15777)***
Unitrol Electronics Inc 847 480-0115
702 Landwehr Rd Northbrook (60062) ***(G-15496)***
Unity Envirotech Illinois LLC 309 364-2361
1557 County Road 1400 N Henry (61537) ***(G-11169)***
Unity Hardwoods LLC 708 701-2943
5950 W 66th St Unit C Chicago (60638) ***(G-6479)***
Universal Air Filter Company (HQ) 618 271-7300
1624 Sauget Indus Pkwy East Saint Louis (62206) ***(G-8328)***
Universal Broaching Inc 847 228-1440
1203 Pagni Dr Elk Grove Village (60007) ***(G-9298)***
Universal Chem & Coatings Inc (PA) 847 931-1700
1975 Fox Ln Elgin (60123) ***(G-8769)***
Universal Chem & Coatings Inc 847 297-2001
1124 Elmhurst Rd Elk Grove Village (60007) ***(G-9299)***
Universal Coatings Inc 708 756-7000
3001 Louis Sherman Dr Steger (60475) ***(G-19496)***
Universal Die Cast Corporation 815 633-1702
11500 Summerwood Dr Machesney Park (61115) ***(G-13381)***
Universal Digital Printing 708 389-0133
3314 147th St Midlothian (60445) ***(G-13998)***
Universal Display Products, Des Plaines *Also called Timothy Darrey* ***(G-7856)***
Universal Electric Foundry Inc 312 421-7233
1523 W Hubbard St Chicago (60642) ***(G-6480)***
Universal Feeder Inc 815 633-0752
5299 Irving Blvd Machesney Park (61115) ***(G-13382)***
Universal Holdings Inc 224 353-6198
2800 W Higgins Rd Ste 210 Hoffman Estates (60169) ***(G-11470)***
Universal Hovercraft Amer Inc 815 963-1200
1218 Buchanan St Rockford (61101) ***(G-17673)***
Universal Instrument Company, Lake Barrington *Also called Norman P Moeller* ***(G-12162)***
Universal Lighting & Clg Sup, Chicago *Also called Universal Lighting Corporation* ***(G-6481)***
Universal Lighting Corporation 773 927-2000
3084 S Lock St Chicago (60608) ***(G-6481)***
Universal Metal Hose, South Holland *Also called Hyspan Precision Products Inc* ***(G-19223)***
Universal Mfg Corporation 630 613-7340
18 W 140 Butterfield Rd Oakbrook Terrace (60181) ***(G-15817)***
Universal Overall Company 312 226-3336
1060 W Van Buren St Chicago (60607) ***(G-6482)***
Universal Pallet Inc 815 928-8546
368 S Michigan Ave Bradley (60915) ***(G-2295)***
Universal Scientific Ill Inc 847 228-6464
1512 N Fremont St Ste 103 Chicago (60642) ***(G-6483)***
Universal Trnspt Systems LLC 312 994-2349
474 N Lake Shore Dr # 5805 Chicago (60611) ***(G-6484)***
Universal-Spc Inc 847 742-4400
412 N State St Elgin (60123) ***(G-8770)***
Universial Cat LLC 708 753-8070
111 E 34th St S Chicago Hts (60411) ***(G-18128)***
University of Chicago 773 702-1722
1427 E 60th St Chicago (60637) ***(G-6485)***
University of Chicago 773 702-7000
11030 S Langley Ave Chicago (60628) ***(G-6486)***
University of Chicago 773 702-9780
6101 S Blackstone Ave Chicago (60637) ***(G-6487)***
University of Chicago Press, Chicago *Also called University of Chicago* ***(G-6486)***
University of Illinois 217 333-9350
54 E Gregory Dr Champaign (61820) ***(G-3361)***
University Printing, Bannockburn *Also called B P I Printing & Duplicating* ***(G-1191)***

University Sport Shop, Peoria *Also called Senn Enterprises Inc* ***(G-16519)***
Unknown, Chicago *Also called Praxair Inc* ***(G-5853)***
Unlimited Graphix Inc 630 759-0007
1453 Caton Farm Rd Lockport (60441) ***(G-13026)***
Unlimited Svcs Wisconsin Inc 815 399-0282
10108 Forest Hills Rd Machesney Park (61115) ***(G-13383)***
Unofficial Cardboard Inc 224 565-5391
1115 Walden Ln Deerfield (60015) ***(G-7655)***
Unytite Inc 815 224-2221
1 Unytite Dr Peru (61354) ***(G-16595)***
UOP LLC 708 442-3681
2820 N Southport Ave Chicago (60657) ***(G-6488)***
UOP LLC 847 391-2540
201 W Oakton St Ste 2 Des Plaines (60018) ***(G-7862)***
UOP LLC 708 442-7400
8400 Joliet Rd Ste 100 Mc Cook (60525) ***(G-13704)***
Up At Dawn Inc 773 457-3859
18504 West Creek Dr Tinley Park (60477) ***(G-19865)***
Up North Printing Inc 630 584-8675
1050 W Republic Dr Addison (60101) ***(G-324)***
Up-N-Runnin LLC 217 413-6293
3388 E Boyd Rd Decatur (62526) ***(G-7565)***
Upchurch Ready Mix Concrete 618 235-6222
950 West Blvd Belleville (62221) ***(G-1605)***
Upchurch Ready Mix Concrete 618 286-4808
200 N 2nd St Dupo (62239) ***(G-8148)***
Upcycle Products Inc 815 383-6220
400 E Wapella St Minooka (60447) ***(G-14066)***
Upholstered Walls By Anne Mari 847 202-0642
419 S Rose St Palatine (60067) ***(G-16169)***
Upholstred Walls By Anne Marie, Palatine *Also called Upholstered Walls By Anne Mari* ***(G-16169)***
Upland Concrete 224 699-9909
563 Commonwealth Dr # 1000 East Dundee (60118) ***(G-8214)***
Upm North America, Naperville *Also called Upm-Kymmene Inc* ***(G-14938)***
Upm Raflatac Inc 815 285-6100
101 E Corporate Dr Dixon (61021) ***(G-7924)***
Upm-Kymmene Inc (HQ) 630 922-2500
55 Shuman Blvd Ste 400 Naperville (60563) ***(G-14938)***
Upmerch LLC 847 674-8601
6634 N Minnehaha Ave Lincolnwood (60712) ***(G-12847)***
Upper Limits Midwest Inc 217 679-4315
1205 S 2nd St Ste B Springfield (62704) ***(G-19467)***
Upper Urban Green Prprty Maint 312 218-5903
3135 S Throop St Chicago (60608) ***(G-6489)***
UPS Authorized Retailer 708 354-8772
106 W Calendar Ave La Grange (60525) ***(G-12090)***
UPS Power Management Inc 844 877-2288
4940 S Kilbourn Ave Chicago (60632) ***(G-6490)***
UPS Store 312 372-2727
27 N Wacker Dr Chicago (60606) ***(G-6491)***
UPS Store of Elmhurst, The, Elmhurst *Also called Bb Services LLC* ***(G-9328)***
UPS Stores 2872, The, Chicago *Also called Weary & Baity Inc* ***(G-6594)***
Upshot Putter Company, Aurora *Also called Welding Company of America* ***(G-1168)***
Upstaging Inc (PA) 815 899-9888
821 Park Ave Sycamore (60178) ***(G-19738)***
Ur Inc 630 450-5279
859 Ravinia Ct Batavia (60510) ***(G-1437)***
Urantia Corp 773 248-6616
533 W Diversey Pkwy Chicago (60614) ***(G-6492)***
Urantia Foundation (PA) 773 525-3319
533 W Diversey Pkwy Chicago (60614) ***(G-6493)***
Urban Accents Incorporated 773 528-9515
4043 N Ravenswood Ave # 216 Chicago (60613) ***(G-6494)***
Urban Home Furniture & ACC Inc 630 761-3200
1375 Kingsland Dr Batavia (60510) ***(G-1438)***
Urban Imaging Group Inc 773 961-7500
3246 N Elston Ave Chicago (60618) ***(G-6495)***
Urban Services of America (PA) 847 278-3210
1901 N Roselle Rd Ste 740 Schaumburg (60195) ***(G-18768)***
Urban Wood Goods Ltd 248 310-7668
3815 Grandville Ave Ste C Gurnee (60031) ***(G-10941)***
Urdu Times 773 274-3100
7061 N Kedzie Ave # 1102 Chicago (60645) ***(G-6496)***
Uresil LLC 847 982-0200
5418 Touhy Ave Skokie (60077) ***(G-19050)***
Url Pharmpro LLC 630 888-3820
2500 Molitor Rd Aurora (60502) ***(G-1030)***
Urpoint LLC 773 919-9002
1739 187th St Homewood (60430) ***(G-11503)***
Urway Design and Manufacturing 847 674-7464
8101 Monticello Ave Skokie (60076) ***(G-19051)***
US Acrylic LLC 847 837-4800
1320 Harris Rd Libertyville (60048) ***(G-12720)***
US Adhesives 312 829-7438
1735 W Carroll Ave Chicago (60612) ***(G-6497)***
US Aluminium IL 708 458-9070
5501 W Ogden Ave Chicago (60804) ***(G-6498)***
US Audio, Glenview *Also called United States Audio Corp* ***(G-10636)***
US Borax Inc (HQ) 773 270-6500
200 E Randolph St # 7100 Chicago (60601) ***(G-6499)***
US Catholic Magazine 312 236-7782
205 W Monroe St Fl 9 Chicago (60606) ***(G-6500)***
US Chrome Corp Illinois 815 544-3487
305 Herbert Rd Kingston (60145) ***(G-12057)***
US Conveyor Tech Mfg Inc 309 359-4088
30000 State Route 9 Mackinaw (61755) ***(G-13386)***
US Conveyor Technologies 309 359-4088
30000 State Route 9 Mackinaw (61755) ***(G-13387)***
US Dept Agriculture Forest Svc 618 285-5211
345 Job Corps Rd Golconda (62938) ***(G-10669)***
US Fabg & Mine Svcs Inc 618 983-7850
11196 Illinois Steel Rd Johnston City (62951) ***(G-11815)***
US Fireplace Products Inc 888 290-8181
110 Albrecht Dr Lake Bluff (60044) ***(G-12211)***
US Foods Culinary Eqp Sups LLC (HQ) 847 720-8000
9399 W Higgins Rd # 100 Rosemont (60018) ***(G-18057)***
US Hose Corp (HQ) 815 886-1140
815 Forestwood Dr Romeoville (60446) ***(G-17883)***
US Ignition, Chadwick *Also called Chadwick Manufacturing Ltd* ***(G-3257)***
US International Inc 312 671-9207
1950 W Armitage Ave # 1 Chicago (60622) ***(G-6501)***
US International Supply, Chicago *Also called US International Inc* ***(G-6501)***
US Minerals Inc (PA) 708 623-1935
18635 West Creek Dr Ste 2 Tinley Park (60477) ***(G-19866)***
US Minerals Inc 618 785-2217
11000 Baldwin Rd Baldwin (62217) ***(G-1187)***
US Minerals Inc 217 534-2370
796 Cips Trl Coffeen (62017) ***(G-6945)***
US Oil Morris IL 815 513-3496
105 E Main St Morris (60450) ***(G-14337)***
US Pallett Supply Inc (PA) 618 243-6449
15340 Sawmill Rd Okawville (62271) ***(G-15848)***
US Plating Co Inc 773 522-7300
2136 S Sawyer Ave Chicago (60623) ***(G-6502)***
US Post Co Inc 815 675-9313
2701 N Us Highway 12 A Spring Grove (60081) ***(G-19306)***
US Shredder Castings Group Inc 309 359-3151
4408 N Rockwood Dr Peoria (61615) ***(G-16542)***
US Silica Co, Ottawa *Also called US Silica Holdings Inc* ***(G-16084)***
US Silica Holdings Inc 312 589-7539
200 N La Salle St # 2100 Chicago (60601) ***(G-6503)***
US Silica Holdings Inc 312 291-4400
200 N Lasalle St Ste 2100 Chicago (60601) ***(G-6504)***
US Silica Holdings Inc 815 667-7085
701 Boyce Memorial Dr Ottawa (61350) ***(G-16084)***
US Smokeless Tob Mfg Co LLC 804 274-2000
11601 Copenhagen Ct Franklin Park (60131) ***(G-10070)***
US Soy, Mattoon *Also called U S Soy LLC* ***(G-13655)***
US Standard Sign, Franklin Park *Also called Mandel Metals Inc* ***(G-9984)***
US Tsubaki Holdings Inc (HQ) 847 459-9500
301 E Marquardt Dr Wheeling (60090) ***(G-21003)***
US Tsubaki Power Transm LLC (HQ) 847 459-9500
301 E Marquardt Dr Wheeling (60090) ***(G-21004)***
USA Drives Inc 630 323-1282
7900 S Madison St Burr Ridge (60527) ***(G-2730)***
USA Embroidery 309 692-1391
1605 W Candletree Dr # 102 Peoria (61614) ***(G-16543)***
USA Hoist Company, Chicago *Also called Mid-American Elevator Co Inc* ***(G-5428)***
USA Hoist Company, Joliet *Also called Mid-American Elevator Co Inc* ***(G-11902)***
USA Hoist Company Inc (HQ) 815 740-1890
1000 Sak Dr Unit A Crest Hill (60403) ***(G-7100)***
USA Industrial Export Corp 312 391-5552
707 Skokie Blvd Ste 600 Northbrook (60062) ***(G-15497)***
USA Printworks LLC 815 206-0854
1525 W Lake Shore Dr Woodstock (60098) ***(G-21442)***
USA Star Group of Company 773 456-6677
4403 N Broadway St Chicago (60640) ***(G-6505)***
USA Today, Yorkville *Also called Gannett Stllite Info Ntwrk LLC* ***(G-21484)***
Usa/Docufinish, Yorkville *Also called McKillip Industries Inc* ***(G-21493)***
Usach Technologies , Inc., Elgin *Also called Hardinge Grinding Group Inc* ***(G-8606)***
USG Corporation 847 970-5200
700 N Us Highway 45 Libertyville (60048) ***(G-12721)***
USG Corporation (HQ) 312 436-4000
550 W Adams St Chicago (60661) ***(G-6506)***
Usl Lock Corporation 815 739-4707
241 Windsor Dr Bartlett (60103) ***(G-1320)***
Usmedexport Company 847 749-5520
772 River Walk Dr Wheeling (60090) ***(G-21005)***
Usmss Inc 708 409-9010
2428 Pinecrest Ln Westchester (60154) ***(G-20717)***
USP Holdings Inc 847 604-6100
6250 N Rver Rd Ste 10100 Rosemont (60018) ***(G-18058)***
USspice Mill Inc 773 378-6800
4537 W Fulton St Chicago (60624) ***(G-6507)***
Ust Inc 847 957-5104
11601 Copenhagen Ct Franklin Park (60131) ***(G-10071)***
UTC Aerospace Systems, Rockford *Also called Goodrich Corporation* ***(G-17432)***

ALPHABETIC

UTC Aerospace Systems, Rockford *Also called Hamilton Sundstrand Corp* ***(G-17441)***
UTC Aerospace Systems............877 808-7575
4747 Harrison Ave Rockford (61108) ***(G-17674)***
UTC Railcar Repair Svcs LLC............312 431-5053
161 N Clark St Chicago (60601) ***(G-6508)***
Utica Stone Co Inc............815 667-4690
773 N 27th Rd Utica (61373) ***(G-20007)***
Utica Terminal Inc............217 245-6181
715 N 27th Rd Utica (61373) ***(G-20008)***
Utility Business Media Inc............815 459-1796
360 Memorial Dr Ste 10 Crystal Lake (60014) ***(G-7287)***
Utility Concrete Products LLC............815 416-1000
2495 Bungalow Rd Morris (60450) ***(G-14338)***
UTILITY SAFETY & OPS LEADERSHI, Crystal Lake *Also called Utility Business Media Inc* ***(G-7287)***
Utlx Manufacturing Inc............312 431-3111
175 W Jackson Blvd Chicago (60604) ***(G-6509)***
Utz Quality Foods LLC............309 245-2191
632 N Main St Farmington (61531) ***(G-9664)***
Utz Quality Foods LLC............309 772-2798
110 Industrial Park Rd Bushnell (61422) ***(G-2747)***
Uv Process Supply, Chicago *Also called Con-Trol-Cure Inc* ***(G-4211)***
Uwd Inc............815 316-3080
9135 N 2nd St Ste 100 Roscoe (61073) ***(G-17937)***
Uxm Studio Inc............773 359-1333
707 N Iowa Ave Villa Park (60181) ***(G-20175)***
Uzhavoor Fuels Inc............630 401-6173
707 N Galena Ave Dixon (61021) ***(G-7925)***
V & A Manufacturing............630 595-1072
1054 Fairway Dr Bensenville (60106) ***(G-1906)***
V & C Converters............708 251-5635
3511 Illinois St Lansing (60438) ***(G-12523)***
V & L Enterprises Inc............847 541-1760
422 Mercantile Ct Wheeling (60090) ***(G-21006)***
V & N Concrete Products Inc............815 293-0315
35 Forestwood Dr Romeoville (60446) ***(G-17884)***
V & O Style Jewelers, Chicago *Also called V & O Style Jewelry Mfg Co* ***(G-6510)***
V & O Style Jewelry Mfg Co............312 372-2454
5 S Wabash Ave Ste 415 Chicago (60603) ***(G-6510)***
V & V Supremo Foods Inc (PA)............312 733-5652
2141 S Throop St Chicago (60608) ***(G-6511)***
V A M D Inc............773 631-8400
7035 W Higgins Ave Chicago (60656) ***(G-6512)***
V A Robinson Ltd............773 205-4364
2850 N Pulaski Rd Ste 4r Chicago (60641) ***(G-6513)***
V and F Transformer Corp (PA)............630 497-8070
2475 Millennium Dr Elgin (60124) ***(G-8771)***
V and L Polishing Co............630 543-5999
341 W Interstate Rd Addison (60101) ***(G-325)***
V and L Red Devil Mfg Co............847 215-1377
422 Mercantile Ct Wheeling (60090) ***(G-21007)***
V Brothers Machine Co............708 652-0062
4900 W 16th St Cicero (60804) ***(G-6886)***
V C P Inc............847 658-5090
901 W Algonquin Rd Algonquin (60102) ***(G-391)***
V C P Printing, Algonquin *Also called V C P Inc* ***(G-391)***
V Formusa Co............224 938-9360
2150 Oxford Rd Des Plaines (60018) ***(G-7863)***
V J Dolan & Company Inc............773 237-0100
1830 N Laramie Ave Chicago (60639) ***(G-6514)***
V J I, Bedford Park *Also called Vegetable Juices Inc* ***(G-1509)***
V J Mattson Company............708 479-1990
713 Jennifer Ct New Lenox (60451) ***(G-15067)***
V M I, Elgin *Also called Vecchio Manufacturing of Ill* ***(G-8773)***
V P Anodizing Inc............773 622-9100
1819 N Lorel Ave Chicago (60639) ***(G-6515)***
V W Broaching Service Inc............773 533-9000
3250 W Lake St Chicago (60624) ***(G-6516)***
V&F Transformer, Elgin *Also called V and F Transformer Corp* ***(G-8771)***
V-Tex Inc............847 325-4140
1027 Busch Pkwy Buffalo Grove (60089) ***(G-2615)***
V2 Solutions Inc............312 528-9050
636 Remington Rd Ste B Schaumburg (60173) ***(G-18769)***
Vac Serve Inc............224 766-6445
4240 Oakton St Skokie (60076) ***(G-19052)***
Vac-Matic Corporation (PA)............630 543-4518
2 S Lincoln Ave Addison (60101) ***(G-326)***
Vactor Manufacturing Inc............815 672-3171
1621 S Illinois St Streator (61364) ***(G-19632)***
Vacudyne Incorporated (HQ)............708 757-5200
375 E Joe Orr Rd Chicago Heights (60411) ***(G-6783)***
Vacumet Corp............708 562-7290
200 W North Ave Northlake (60164) ***(G-15564)***
Vada LLC............407 572-4979
3723 N Van Rd Olney (62450) ***(G-15892)***
Vaimo Inc............502 767-9550
20 N Wade Dr Ste 1200 Chicago (60606) ***(G-6517)***
Val Custom Cabinets & Flrg Inc............708 790-8373
240 Evergreen Ave Bensenville (60106) ***(G-1907)***
Val P Enterprises............708 982-6561
12045 S Emerald Ave Chicago (60628) ***(G-6518)***
Val-Matic Valve and Mfg Corp (PA)............630 941-7600
905 S Riverside Dr Elmhurst (60126) ***(G-9440)***
Valaji Pharma Chem, Schaumburg *Also called Patel Dishaben* ***(G-18669)***
Valbruna Stainless Inc............630 871-5524
370 Village Dr Carol Stream (60188) ***(G-3083)***
Valee Inc (PA)............847 364-6464
859 Oakton St Elk Grove Village (60007) ***(G-9300)***
Valent Biosciences LLC (HQ)............800 323-9597
870 Technology Way # 100 Libertyville (60048) ***(G-12722)***
Valent USA, Libertyville *Also called Valent Biosciences LLC* ***(G-12722)***
Valent USA LLC............816 206-3919
1035 County Road 300 E Seymour (61875) ***(G-18869)***
Valentino Vineyards & Winery, Long Grove *Also called Valentino Vineyards Inc* ***(G-13173)***
Valentino Vineyards Inc............847 634-2831
5175 Aptakisic Rd Long Grove (60047) ***(G-13173)***
Valid Secure Solutions LLC............260 633-0728
1011 Warrenville Rd # 450 Lisle (60532) ***(G-12954)***
Valid Usa Inc (HQ)............630 852-8200
1011 Warrenville Rd # 450 Lisle (60532) ***(G-12955)***
Valley Concrete Inc............815 725-2422
19515 Ne Frontage Rd Joliet (60404) ***(G-11940)***
Valley Custom Woodwork Inc............815 544-3939
1626 Industrial Ct Belvidere (61008) ***(G-1707)***
Valley Fastener Group LLC............630 548-5679
5s250 Frontenac Rd Naperville (60563) ***(G-14939)***
Valley Fastener Group LLC............708 343-2496
3302 Bloomingdale Ave Melrose Park (60160) ***(G-13924)***
Valley Fasteners Group, Naperville *Also called Valley Fastener Group LLC* ***(G-14939)***
Valley Meats LLC............309 799-7341
2302 1st St Sr Coal Valley (61240) ***(G-6939)***
Valley Racing Inc............708 946-1440
325 W 323rd St Beecher (60401) ***(G-1523)***
Valley Run Stone Inc............630 553-7974
6369 Whitetail Ridge Ct Yorkville (60560) ***(G-21504)***
Valley View Industries Hc Inc............800 323-9369
13834 Kostner Ave Crestwood (60418) ***(G-7133)***
Valley View Industries Inc (PA)............815 358-2236
7551e 2500 N Rd Cornell (61319) ***(G-7014)***
Valley View Specialties, Crestwood *Also called Valley View Industries Hc Inc* ***(G-7133)***
Valmont Coatings Inc............847 455-0884
10909 Franklin Ave Franklin Park (60131) ***(G-10072)***
Valmont Ctngs Empire Glvnizing, Franklin Park *Also called Valmont Industries Inc* ***(G-10073)***
Valmont Industries Inc............773 625-0354
10909 Franklin Ave Franklin Park (60131) ***(G-10073)***
Valspar............309 743-7133
3560 5th Ave East Moline (61244) ***(G-8245)***
Value Added Services & Tech............847 888-8232
164 Division St Ste 315 Elgin (60120) ***(G-8772)***
Value Engineered Products............708 867-6777
1700 Hicks Rd Rolling Meadows (60008) ***(G-17784)***
Value Lift, Addison *Also called George Hansen & Co Inc* ***(G-139)***
Valve Acquisition, LLC, Elk Grove Village *Also called Advanced Valve Tech LLC* ***(G-8810)***
Van Bergen & Greener, Maywood *Also called Weldon Corporation* ***(G-13680)***
Van Craft Industry of Del Edel (HQ)............708 430-6670
8938 Ridgeland Ave Oak Lawn (60453) ***(G-15738)***
Van Diest Supply Company............815 232-6053
1771 Lincoln Dr Freeport (61032) ***(G-10149)***
Van Drunen Farms, Momence *Also called R J Van Drunen & Sons Inc* ***(G-14191)***
Van Drunen Farms, Momence *Also called R J Van Drunen & Sons Inc* ***(G-14192)***
Van Hessen USA Inc (HQ)............773 376-9200
4420 S Wolcott Ave Chicago (60609) ***(G-6519)***
Van Heusen, Tuscola *Also called Pvh Corp* ***(G-19929)***
Van Leer Containers Inc (HQ)............708 371-4777
4300 W 130th St Alsip (60803) ***(G-520)***
Van Meter Graphx Inc............847 465-0600
970 Seton Ct Wheeling (60090) ***(G-21008)***
Van Meter Mail, Wheeling *Also called Van Meter Graphx Inc* ***(G-21008)***
Van Norman Molding Company LLC............708 430-4343
9615 S 76th Ave Oak Lawn (60455) ***(G-15739)***
Van Pelt Corporation............313 365-3600
2930 Morton Dr East Moline (61244) ***(G-8246)***
Van Stockum Kristine............847 914-0015
827 Woodward Ave Deerfield (60015) ***(G-7656)***
Van Voorst Lumber Company Inc............815 426-2544
1 Center St Union Hill (60969) ***(G-19943)***
Van-Packer Co............309 895-2311
302 Mill St Buda (61314) ***(G-2500)***
Vanart Engineering Company............847 678-6255
3504 River Rd Franklin Park (60131) ***(G-10074)***
Vanco Printers Division, Rockford *Also called Ideal Advertising & Printing* ***(G-17456)***
Vandalia Electric Mtr Svc Inc............618 283-0068
561 Il 185 Vandalia (62471) ***(G-20027)***
Vandalia Ready-Mix, Vandalia *Also called Mid-Illinois Concrete Inc* ***(G-20015)***
Vandalia Sand & Gravel Inc............618 283-4029
Rr 2 Vandalia (62471) ***(G-20028)***

ALPHABETIC SECTION
Vep, Rolling Meadows

Vandee Mfg Co Div, Batavia *Also called Vandeventer Mfg Co Inc* ***(G-1439)***
Vanderbosch Tj & Assoc Inc 815 344-3210
1614 S River Rd McHenry (60051) ***(G-13806)***
Vandeventer Mfg Co Inc 630 879-2511
812 Main St Batavia (60510) ***(G-1439)***
Vanee Foods Company 708 449-7300
5418 Mcdermott Dr Berkeley (60163) ***(G-1945)***
Vanex Color, Mount Vernon *Also called Vanex Inc* ***(G-14643)***
Vanex Inc 618 244-1413
1700 Shawnee St Mount Vernon (62864) ***(G-14643)***
Vanfab Inc 815 426-2544
1 Center St Union Hill (60969) ***(G-19944)***
Vangard Box & Packaging Group, Berwyn *Also called Vangard Distribution Inc* ***(G-1962)***
Vangard Distribution Inc 708 484-9895
2905 Ridgeland Ave Berwyn (60402) ***(G-1962)***
Vangard Distribution Inc (PA) 708 588-8400
9501 Southview Ave Brookfield (60513) ***(G-2497)***
Vanguard Chemical Corporation 312 751-0717
429 W Ohio St Chicago (60654) ***(G-6520)***
Vanguard Defense Group 850 218-4233
3005 Max Ct Island Lake (60042) ***(G-11612)***
Vanguard Tool & Engineering Co 847 981-9595
555 W Carboy Rd Mount Prospect (60056) ***(G-14580)***
Vanities Inc 847 483-0240
212 W University Dr Arlington Heights (60004) ***(G-825)***
Vanlab, Wauconda *Also called Synergy Flavors NY Company LLC* ***(G-20395)***
Vans Inc 718 349-2311
113 N Elizabeth St Chicago (60607) ***(G-6521)***
Vanseal Corporation 618 283-4700
815 Payne Dr Vandalia (62471) ***(G-20029)***
Vantage Corn Processors LLC (HQ) 217 424-5200
4666 E Faries Pkwy Decatur (62526) ***(G-7566)***
Vantage Oleochemicals Inc 773 376-9000
4650 S Racine Ave Chicago (60609) ***(G-6522)***
Vantage Specialties Inc 773 579-5842
3938 Porett Dr Gurnee (60031) ***(G-10942)***
Vantage Specialties Inc (HQ) 773 376-9000
3938 Porett Dr Gurnee (60031) ***(G-10943)***
Vantage Specialties Inc 847 244-3410
4650 S Racine Ave Chicago (60609) ***(G-6523)***
Vapor Bus International, Buffalo Grove *Also called Westinghouse A Brake Tech Corp* ***(G-2622)***
Vapor Bus International, Buffalo Grove *Also called Vapor Corporation* ***(G-2616)***
Vapor Corporation 847 777-6400
1010 Johnson Dr Buffalo Grove (60089) ***(G-2616)***
Vapor Power International LLC (PA) 630 694-5500
551 S County Line Rd Franklin Park (60131) ***(G-10075)***
Var Graphics 708 456-2028
1743 N 75th Ct Elmwood Park (60707) ***(G-9457)***
Varda Graphics, Skokie *Also called Publishers Row* ***(G-19018)***
Varex Imaging Corporation 847 279-5121
3835 Carnation St Franklin Park (60131) ***(G-10076)***
Variable Operations Tech Inc 815 479-8528
1145 Paltronics Ct Crystal Lake (60014) ***(G-7288)***
Varian Medical Systems Inc 847 279-5100
425 Barclay Blvd Lincolnshire (60069) ***(G-12800)***
Varimed Division, Elk Grove Village *Also called UNI-Label and Tag Corporation* ***(G-9294)***
Varn International Inc 630 406-6501
1333 N Kirk Rd Batavia (60510) ***(G-1440)***
Varsity Logistics Inc 650 392-7979
10275 W Higgins Rd # 250 Rosemont (60018) ***(G-18059)***
Varsity Publications Inc 309 353-4570
309 Railroad Ave Pekin (61554) ***(G-16367)***
Varsity Striping & Cnstr Co 217 352-2203
2601 W Cardinal Rd Champaign (61822) ***(G-3362)***
Vas Design Inc 773 794-1368
3356 N Milwaukee Ave Chicago (60641) ***(G-6524)***
Vast, Elgin *Also called Value Added Services & Tech* ***(G-8772)***
Vator Accessories Inc 630 876-8370
1090 Atlantic Dr West Chicago (60185) ***(G-20656)***
Vaughan & Bushnell Mfg Co (PA) 815 648-2446
11414 Maple Ave Hebron (60034) ***(G-11153)***
Vaughan & Bushnell Mfg Co 309 772-2131
201 W Main St Bushnell (61422) ***(G-2748)***
Vaughan Equipment Inc 618 842-3500
1102 S 1st St Fairfield (62837) ***(G-9638)***
Vaughn & Sons Machine Shop 618 842-9048
Hwy 45 Fairfield (62837) ***(G-9639)***
Vault Furniture Inc 734 323-4166
1965 W Pershing Rd Ste 1 Chicago (60609) ***(G-6525)***
Vauto Inc (HQ) 630 590-2000
1901 S Meyers Rd Ste 700 Oakbrook Terrace (60181) ***(G-15818)***
Vaxcel International Co Ltd 630 260-0067
121 E North Ave Carol Stream (60188) ***(G-3084)***
Vcna Praire Yard 1033 ....708 458-0400
3300 S California Ave Chicago (60608) ***(G-6526)***
Vcna Prairie, Pontiac *Also called Southfield Corporation* ***(G-16780)***
Vcna Prairie Inc 312 733-0094
865 N Peoria St Chicago (60642) ***(G-6527)***
Vcna Prairie LLC (PA) 708 458-0400
7601 W 79th St Ste 1 Bridgeview (60455) ***(G-2394)***
Vcna Prairie Illinois Inc 217 398-4346
3208 W Springfield Ave Champaign (61822) ***(G-3363)***
Vcna Prairie Illinois Inc (PA) 708 458-0400
7601 W 79th St Ste 1 Bridgeview (60455) ***(G-2395)***
Vcna Prairie Indiana Inc 708 458-0400
7601 W 79th St Ste 1 Bridgeview (60455) ***(G-2396)***
Vcr Service Center, Flossmoor *Also called Grevan Enterprises Inc* ***(G-9699)***
Veal Tech Inc 630 554-0410
15 Stonehill Rd Oswego (60543) ***(G-16030)***
Vecchio Manufacturing of Ill (PA) 847 742-8429
801d N State St Unit D Elgin (60123) ***(G-8773)***
Vector Custom Fabricating Inc 312 421-5161
2128 W Fulton St Chicago (60612) ***(G-6528)***
Vector Engineering & Mfg Corp 708 474-3900
17506 Chicago Ave Lansing (60438) ***(G-12524)***
Vector Packaging, Oak Brook *Also called Vector USA Inc* ***(G-15668)***
Vector USA Inc (HQ) 800 929-4516
1900 Spring Rd Ste 450 Oak Brook (60523) ***(G-15668)***
Vectorbuilder Inc (PA) 510 552-3632
1010 W 35th St Chicago (60609) ***(G-6529)***
Vee Pak LLC (HQ) 708 482-8881
6710 River Rd Hodgkins (60525) ***(G-11399)***
Vee Pak LLC 708 482-8881
5321 Dansher Rd Countryside (60525) ***(G-7076)***
Veeco Manufacturing Inc 312 666-0900
1930 George St Ste A Melrose Park (60160) ***(G-13925)***
Veejay Plastics Inc 847 683-2954
395 S Main St Burlington (60109) ***(G-2643)***
Veejay Plstic Injction Molding, Burlington *Also called Kunverji Enterprise Corp* ***(G-2641)***
Vees Collectibles, Frankfort *Also called DJB Corporation* ***(G-9786)***
Vega Molded Products Inc 847 428-7761
122 Industrial Dr Gilberts (60136) ***(G-10374)***
Vega Technology & Systems 630 855-5068
7980 Kingsbury Dr Bartlett (60133) ***(G-1259)***
Vega Wave Systems Inc 630 562-9433
1275 W Roosevelt Rd # 104 West Chicago (60185) ***(G-20657)***
Vegetable Juices Inc 708 924-9500
7400 S Narragansett Ave Bedford Park (60638) ***(G-1509)***
Vegter Steel Fabrication, Morrison *Also called American Piping Group Inc* ***(G-14340)***
Vehicle Improvement Pdts Inc 847 395-7250
151 S Ram Rd Antioch (60002) ***(G-642)***
Vej Holdings LLC 630 219-1598
1717 N Naper Blvd Ste 108 Naperville (60563) ***(G-14940)***
Vek Screw Machine Products 630 543-5557
1500 W Wrightwood Ct Addison (60101) ***(G-327)***
Vel-Tye LLC 757 518-5400
23808 W Andrew Rd Ste 3 Plainfield (60585) ***(G-16725)***
Velasquez & Sons Muffler Shop 847 740-6990
507 W Rollins Rd Round Lake Beach (60073) ***(G-18093)***
Velocity Software LLC 800 351-6893
1042 E Maple St Lombard (60148) ***(G-13149)***
Veloflip Inc 847 757-4972
540 W Frontage Rd # 2035 Northfield (60093) ***(G-15537)***
Velsicol Chemical LLC (HQ) 847 813-7888
10400 W Higgins Rd # 303 Rosemont (60018) ***(G-18060)***
Veltex Corporation (PA) 312 235-4014
123 W Madison St Ste 1500 Chicago (60602) ***(G-6530)***
Venetian Monument Company 312 829-9622
527 N Western Ave Chicago (60612) ***(G-6531)***
Vent Fabrics, Chicago *Also called Ventfabrics Inc* ***(G-6534)***
Vent Products Co Inc 773 521-1900
1901 S Kilbourn Ave Chicago (60623) ***(G-6532)***
Vent Ure Air 708 652-7200
1855 S 54th Ave Chicago (60804) ***(G-6533)***
Ventec USA LLC 847 621-2261
720 Lee St Elk Grove Village (60007) ***(G-9301)***
Ventfabrics Inc 773 775-4477
5520 N Lynch Ave Chicago (60630) ***(G-6534)***
Ventura Foods LLC 708 877-5150
201 Armory Dr Thornton (60476) ***(G-19791)***
Venture Design Incorporated 630 369-1148
2250 Allegany Dr Naperville (60565) ***(G-14941)***
Venture Publishing Inc 217 359-5940
1807 N Federal Dr Urbana (61801) ***(G-20002)***
Venturedyne Ltd 708 597-7550
4101 W 126th St Chicago (60803) ***(G-6535)***
Venturedyne Ltd 708 597-7090
4101 W 126th St Alsip (60803) ***(G-521)***
Venus Laboratories Inc (PA) 630 595-1900
111 S Rohlwing Rd Addison (60101) ***(G-328)***
Venus Printing Inc 847 985-7510
549 Morse Ave Schaumburg (60193) ***(G-18770)***
Venus Processing & Storage 847 455-0496
2401 Rose St Franklin Park (60131) ***(G-10077)***
Veolia Water Technologies Inc 815 609-2000
23563 W Main St Plainfield (60544) ***(G-16726)***
Vep, Rolling Meadows *Also called Value Engineered Products* ***(G-17784)***

ALPHABETIC

(PA)=Parent Co (HQ)=Headquarters (DH)=Div Headquarters
2020 Harris Illinois Industrial Directory
1289

Verdasee Solutions Inc ALPHABETIC SECTION

Verdasee Solutions Inc 847 265-9441
17825 W Pond Ridge Cir Gurnee (60031) ***(G-10944)***
Verena Solutions LLC 314 651-1908
965 W Chicago Ave Chicago (60642) ***(G-6536)***
Veritas Steel LLC (PA) 630 423-8708
2300 Cabot Dr Ste 425 Lisle (60532) ***(G-12956)***
Verlo Mat of Skokie-Evanston 847 966-9988
7927 Golf Rd Morton Grove (60053) ***(G-14446)***
Verlo Mattress Factory, Morton Grove *Also called Verlo Mat of Skokie-Evanston* ***(G-14446)***
Verlo Mattress of Lake Geneva 815 455-2570
5150 Northwest Hwy Ste 1 Crystal Lake (60014) ***(G-7289)***
Vermilion Millworks LLC 217 446-8443
611 Oak St Danville (61832) ***(G-7390)***
Vermilion Steel Fabrication 217 442-5300
3295 E Main St Ste A Danville (61834) ***(G-7391)***
Vernon Micheal 217 735-4005
1100 Home Ave Lincoln (62656) ***(G-12739)***
Vernon Township Offices 847 634-4600
3050 N Main St Buffalo Grove (60089) ***(G-2617)***
Verona Rubber Works Inc 815 673-2929
31577 N 1250 East Rd Blackstone (61313) ***(G-1971)***
Verone Publishing Inc 773 866-0811
5421 Ne Rver Rd Apt 1605 Chicago (60656) ***(G-6537)***
Versa Press Inc 309 822-0260
1465 Spring Bay Rd East Peoria (61611) ***(G-8294)***
Versatech LLC 217 342-3500
1609 W Wernsing Ave Ste D Effingham (62401) ***(G-8428)***
Versatile Materials Inc 773 924-3700
600 W 52nd St Chicago (60609) ***(G-6538)***
Versatility Tl Works Mfg Inc 708 389-8909
11532 S Mayfield Ave Alsip (60803) ***(G-522)***
Verson Enterprises Inc 847 364-2600
870 Cambridge Dr Elk Grove Village (60007) ***(G-9302)***
Vertec Biosolvents Inc 630 960-0600
1441 Branding Ave Ste 100 Downers Grove (60515) ***(G-8104)***
Vertex Chemical Corporation 618 286-5207
3101 Carondelet Ave Dupo (62239) ***(G-8149)***
Vertex Consulting Services Inc 313 492-5154
935 N Plum Grove Rd Ste D Schaumburg (60173) ***(G-18771)***
Vertex Fasteners, Des Plaines *Also called Leggett & Platt Incorporated* ***(G-7798)***
Vertex International Inc 312 242-1864
2015 Spring Rd Ste 215 Oak Brook (60523) ***(G-15669)***
Vertical Blinds Factory, Niles *Also called 9161 Corporation* ***(G-15097)***
Vertical Blinds Factory, Chicago *Also called Offsprings Inc* ***(G-5659)***
Vertical Lighting Controls, East Dundee *Also called Telser Lighting Associates LLC* ***(G-8211)***
Vertical Software Inc 309 633-0700
409 Keller St Bartonville (61607) ***(G-1336)***
Vertical Tower Partner 217 819-3040
2626 Midwest Ct Champaign (61822) ***(G-3364)***
Vertical Web Media LLC 312 362-0076
125 S Wacker Dr Ste 1900 Chicago (60606) ***(G-6539)***
Vertiv Group Corporation 630 579-5000
995 Oak Creek Dr Lombard (60148) ***(G-13150)***
Verzenay LLC 817 875-0699
714 New Mexico Trl Elk Grove Village (60007) ***(G-9303)***
Verzenay Patisserie, Elk Grove Village *Also called Verzenay LLC* ***(G-9303)***
Vestergaard Company Inc (PA) 815 759-9102
1721 Oak Dr McHenry (60050) ***(G-13807)***
Vestis Group, Palatine *Also called Consolidated Mill Supply Inc* ***(G-16104)***
Vesuvius Crucible Company (HQ) 217 351-5000
1404 Newton Dr Champaign (61822) ***(G-3365)***
Vesuvius U S A Corporation (HQ) 217 351-5000
1404 Newton Dr Champaign (61822) ***(G-3366)***
Vesuvius U S A Corporation 708 757-7880
333 State St Chicago Heights (60411) ***(G-6784)***
Vesuvius U S A Corporation 217 897-1145
Hwy 136 E Fisher (61843) ***(G-9668)***
Vesuvius U S A Corporation 217 345-7044
955 N 5th St Charleston (61920) ***(G-3415)***
Veteran Greens LLC 773 599-9689
7552 S Union Ave Chicago (60620) ***(G-6540)***
Veteran Roasters, Chicago *Also called Cup O Joe Coffee LLC* ***(G-4284)***
Veteran Wire and Cable LLC 630 327-5849
1135 W National Ave Addison (60101) ***(G-329)***
Veterans Parking Lot Maint 815 245-7584
240 Mchenry Ave Woodstock (60098) ***(G-21443)***
Veterans Print Management 630 816-0853
35 Cherrywood Dr Palos Park (60464) ***(G-16216)***
Vetter CM USA LLC 847 813-5895
10 W Algonquin Rd Des Plaines (60016) ***(G-7864)***
Vfn Fiberglass Inc 630 543-0232
330 W Factory Rd Addison (60101) ***(G-330)***
VG Ates and Welding 847 263-4416
33 Le Baron St Waukegan (60085) ***(G-20515)***
Vg Pallet Inc 815 527-5344
320 E Church St Woodstock (60098) ***(G-21444)***
Vhd Inc 815 544-2169
6833 Irene Rd Belvidere (61008) ***(G-1708)***
Vhrk Food Inc 630 640-6525
810 Bonnie Ln Chicago (60656) ***(G-6541)***
Vl Inc 618 277-8703
1801 N Belt W Ste 4 Belleville (62226) ***(G-1606)***
Via Galante Cement Con In 773 589-9893
3641 N Pittsburgh Ave Chicago (60634) ***(G-6542)***
Via Times News Organization, Chicago *Also called Verone Publishing Inc* ***(G-6537)***
Viakable Manufacturing LLC 815 615-8355
2969 Chartres St La Salle (61301) ***(G-12123)***
Viant Wheeling Inc 847 520-1553
140 E Hintz Rd Wheeling (60090) ***(G-21009)***
Vibgyor Optical Systems Corp 847 818-0788
1140 N Phelps Ave Arlington Heights (60004) ***(G-826)***
Vibgyor Optics Inc 847 818-0788
1140 N Phelps Ave Arlington Heights (60004) ***(G-827)***
Vibra Tech, Glen Ellyn *Also called Vibra-Tech Engineers Inc* ***(G-10423)***
Vibra-Tech Engineers Inc 630 858-0681
777 Roosevelt Rd Ste 110 Glen Ellyn (60137) ***(G-10423)***
Vibracoustic Usa Inc 618 382-5891
1500 E Main St Carmi (62821) ***(G-2916)***
Vibracoustic Usa Inc 618 382-2318
102 Industrial Ave Carmi (62821) ***(G-2917)***
Vic Cook System, Alton *Also called Softhaus Ltd* ***(G-572)***
Vicari Tool & Plastics Inc 847 671-9430
3350 Schierhorn Ct Franklin Park (60131) ***(G-10078)***
Viclarity Inc 201 214-5405
300 N Lasalle St Chicago (60654) ***(G-6543)***
Vicma Tool Co 847 541-0177
505 Harvester Ct Ste J Wheeling (60090) ***(G-21010)***
Vicron Optical Inc 847 412-5530
1020 Milwaukee Ave # 235 Deerfield (60015) ***(G-7657)***
Victaulic Company 630 585-2919
1207 Bilter Rd Ste 103 Aurora (60502) ***(G-1031)***
Victor Consulting 847 267-8012
42 Cumberland Dr 2a Lincolnshire (60069) ***(G-12801)***
Victor Division Dana, Robinson *Also called Dana Sealing Manufacturing LLC* ***(G-17112)***
Victor Envelope Mfg Corp 630 616-2750
301 Arthur Ct Bensenville (60106) ***(G-1908)***
Victor Food Products 773 478-9529
4194 N Elston Ave Chicago (60618) ***(G-6544)***
Victor Levy Jewelry Co Inc 312 782-5297
29 E Madison St Ste 1640 Chicago (60602) ***(G-6545)***
Victor's Food, Chicago *Also called Victor Food Products* ***(G-6544)***
Victoria Amplifier Company 630 369-3527
1504 Newman Ct Naperville (60564) ***(G-14991)***
Victoria Metal Processor Inc 773 633-7497
4836 W Division St Chicago (60651) ***(G-6546)***
Victorias Secret Stores LLC 312 583-0488
1138 S Delano Ct W Chicago (60605) ***(G-6547)***
Victory Division of Planter, Chicago *Also called Planter Inc* ***(G-5817)***
Victory Medical Equipment, Calumet City *Also called Victory Pharmacy Decatur Inc* ***(G-2792)***
Victory Pharmacy Decatur Inc 708 801-9626
1837 River Oaks Dr Calumet City (60409) ***(G-2792)***
Vida Cabinets Inc 847 258-4468
225 Stanley St Elk Grove Village (60007) ***(G-9304)***
Vidasym Inc 847 549-3357
872 S Milwaukee Ave 213 Libertyville (60048) ***(G-12723)***
Video Gaming Technologies Inc 847 776-3516
963 N Carmel Dr Palatine (60074) ***(G-16170)***
Video Refurbishing Svcs Inc 847 844-7366
850 Commerce Pkwy Carpentersville (60110) ***(G-3122)***
Video Surveillance, Oak Lawn *Also called Chicago Cardinal Communication* ***(G-15708)***
Videojet Technologies Inc (HQ) 630 860-7300
1500 N Mittel Blvd Wood Dale (60191) ***(G-21255)***
Vienna Beef Ltd (PA) 773 278-7800
2501 N Damen Ave Chicago (60647) ***(G-6548)***
Vienna Beef Ltd 800 366-3647
1000 W Pershing Rd Chicago (60609) ***(G-6549)***
Vigil Printing Inc 773 794-8808
4415 W Lawrence Ave Chicago (60630) ***(G-6550)***
Vigilanz Corporation 708 383-3008
137 N Oak Park Ave # 329 Oak Park (60301) ***(G-15778)***
Vigo Coal Operating Co Inc 618 262-7022
7790 Highway 15 Mount Carmel (62863) ***(G-14490)***
Viking Awards Inc 630 833-1733
846 N York St Ste A Elmhurst (60126) ***(G-9441)***
Viking Metal Cabinet Co LLC 800 776-7767
420 N Main St Montgomery (60538) ***(G-14273)***
Viking Metal Cabinet Company 630 863-7234
420 N Main St Montgomery (60538) ***(G-14274)***
Viking Mining LLC (HQ) 314 932-6140
Mc1 Mine 11525 N Thmpsn St Macedonia (62860) ***(G-13318)***
Viking Printing & Copying Inc 312 341-0985
53 W Jackson Blvd Lbby Chicago (60604) ***(G-6551)***
Viking Prtg Graphic Forms Inc 630 521-0150
530 E Green St Bensenville (60106) ***(G-1909)***
Villa Foods LLC 815 721-1136
8565 Jamesport Dr Rockford (61108) ***(G-17675)***

Village Hampshire Trtmnt Plant ... 847 683-2064
350 Mill Ave Hampshire (60140) *(G-10989)*
Village Hebron Water Sewage ... 815 648-2353
12007 Prairie Ave Hebron (60034) *(G-11154)*
Village Itasca Nature Center, Itasca *Also called Spring Brook Nature Center (G-11739)*
Village of Burnham ... 708 868-0661
14450 S Manistee Ave Chicago (60633) *(G-6552)*
Village of Mt Zion ... 217 864-4212
433 N State Route 121 Mount Zion (62549) *(G-14650)*
Village Optical Shop ... 847 295-3290
237 Forest View Dr Lake Bluff (60044) *(G-12212)*
Village Press Inc ... 847 362-1856
124 E Church St Libertyville (60048) *(G-12724)*
Village Typographers Inc ... 618 235-6756
1381 Rocky Creek Ct Belleville (62220) *(G-1607)*
Village Vintner Winery Brewry ... 847 658-4900
2380 Esplanade Dr Algonquin (60102) *(G-392)*
Villagers Voice ... 618 378-3094
103 E Main St Norris City (62869) *(G-15251)*
Vilutis and Co Inc ... 815 469-2116
22535 S Center Rd Frankfort (60423) *(G-9849)*
Vim Recyclers LP ... 630 892-2559
920 Rathbone Ave Aurora (60506) *(G-1166)*
Vincent Castillo, Harvard *Also called Cartel Holdings Inc (G-11049)*
Vincit Omnia LLC ... 773 631-4020
7312 N Oriole Ave Chicago (60631) *(G-6553)*
Vincor Ltd (PA) ... 708 534-0008
5652 W Monee Manhattan Rd Monee (60449) *(G-14211)*
Vindee Industries Inc ... 815 469-3300
965 Lambrecht Dr Frankfort (60423) *(G-9850)*
Vins & Vignobles LLC ... 312 375-7656
40 E Northwest Hwy # 211 Mount Prospect (60056) *(G-14581)*
Vintage Modern Collection Inc ... 312 774-8424
1401 E 55th St Apt 606n Chicago (60615) *(G-6554)*
Vintage Roxx, Chicago *Also called Vintage Modern Collection Inc (G-6554)*
Vintaj Natural Brass Co ... 815 776-9300
5140 W Us Highway 20 A Galena (61036) *(G-10180)*
Vinyl Graphics Inc ... 708 579-1234
35 E Plainfield Rd Ste 2 Countryside (60525) *(G-7077)*
Vinyl Life North ... 630 906-9686
661 Dewig Ct North Aurora (60542) *(G-15281)*
Vinylworks Inc ... 815 477-9680
8550 Ridgefield Rd Ste E Crystal Lake (60012) *(G-7290)*
Viobin USA, Monticello *Also called McShares Inc (G-14281)*
Viola Ice Cream Shoppe ... 309 596-2131
1003 13th St Viola (61486) *(G-20183)*
Vipar Heavy Duty Inc (PA) ... 815 788-1700
760 Mcardle Dr Ste D Crystal Lake (60014) *(G-7291)*
Virden Recorder, Virden *Also called Gold Nugget Publications Inc (G-20185)*
Virtu ... 773 235-3790
2034 N Damen Ave Chicago (60647) *(G-6555)*
Virtusense Technologies Inc ... 855 443-5744
801 W Main St Rm B216 Peoria (61606) *(G-16544)*
Vis-O-Graphic Inc ... 630 590-6100
1220 W National Ave Addison (60101) *(G-331)*
Vis-O-Graphic Printing, Addison *Also called Vis-O-Graphic Inc (G-331)*
Viscofan Usa Inc ... 217 444-8000
915 Michigan St Danville (61834) *(G-7392)*
Visimark Inc ... 866 344-7721
521 S County Line Rd Franklin Park (60131) *(G-10079)*
Vision Assessment Corporation ... 847 239-5889
2675 Coyle Ave Elk Grove Village (60007) *(G-9305)*
Vision Engineering Labs (PA) ... 630 350-9470
215 Gateway Rd Bensenville (60106) *(G-1910)*
Vision I Systems ... 312 326-9188
2416 S Canal St Chicago (60616) *(G-6556)*
Vision Intgrted Grphics Group (PA) ... 312 373-6300
208 S Jefferson St Fl 3 Chicago (60661) *(G-6557)*
Vision Intgrted Grphics Group ... 331 318-7800
605 Territorial Dr Ste A Bolingbrook (60440) *(G-2251)*
Vision Machine & Fabrication ... 618 965-3199
1102 N Cherry St Steeleville (62288) *(G-19485)*
Vision Pickling and Proc Inc ... 815 264-7755
9341 State Route 23 Waterman (60556) *(G-20301)*
Vision Sales Incorporated (PA) ... 630 483-1900
1264 Appaloosa Way Bartlett (60103) *(G-1321)*
Vision Signs Inc ... 815 530-0870
2104 Oak Leaf St Unit A Joliet (60436) *(G-11941)*
Vision Wholesale Corp ... 708 496-6015
5620 W 51st St Chicago (60638) *(G-6558)*
Visionary Solutions Inc ... 847 296-9615
129 Rawls Rd Des Plaines (60018) *(G-7865)*
Visiplex Inc ... 847 229-0250
1287 Barclay Blvd Ste 100 Buffalo Grove (60089) *(G-2618)*
Viskase Companies Inc (HQ) ... 630 874-0700
333 E Bttrfeld Rd Ste Lombard (60148) *(G-13151)*
Viskase Corporation (HQ) ... 630 874-0700
333 E Bttrfeld Rd Ste 400 Lombard (60148) *(G-13152)*
Visos Machine Shop & Mfg ... 630 372-3925
686 Bonded Pkwy Streamwood (60107) *(G-19601)*
Vista Outdoor Inc ... 309 693-2746
909 Pacesetter Dr Rantoul (61866) *(G-16985)*
Vista Outdoor Inc ... 217 893-7254
1001 Innovation Rd Rantoul (61866) *(G-16986)*
Vista Woodworking ... 815 922-2297
500 Joyce Rd Unit B Joliet (60436) *(G-11942)*
Visual Imaging, Fulton *Also called Visual Marketing Solutions (G-10159)*
Visual Information Tech Inc ... 217 841-2155
60 Hazelwood Dr Champaign (61820) *(G-3367)*
Visual Marketing Inc ... 312 664-9177
154 W Erie St Chicago (60654) *(G-6559)*
Visual Marketing Solutions ... 815 589-3848
800 20th Ave Fulton (61252) *(G-10159)*
Visual Persuasion Inc ... 815 899-6609
337 E State St Sycamore (60178) *(G-19739)*
Visucom ... 708 460-3001
9910 W 190th St Ste C Mokena (60448) *(G-14126)*
Vita Food Products Inc (PA) ... 312 738-4500
2222 W Lake St Chicago (60612) *(G-6560)*
Vital, Breese *Also called Jlg Innovations Inc (G-2305)*
Vital Care Reps ... 708 342-2680
18470 Thompson Ct Ste 1b Tinley Park (60477) *(G-19867)*
Vital Proteins LLC (PA) ... 224 544-9110
939 W Fulton Market Chicago (60607) *(G-6561)*
Vital Proteins LLC ... 224 544-9110
1201 W Washington Blvd Chicago (60607) *(G-6562)*
Vital Signs Inc (HQ) ... 872 757-0114
26125 N Riverwoods Blvd Mettawa (60045) *(G-13983)*
Vital Signs USA ... 630 832-9600
791 N Industrial Dr Elmhurst (60126) *(G-9442)*
Vital Times ... 847 675-2577
7301 N Lincoln Ave # 190 Lincolnwood (60712) *(G-12848)*
Vitelli Concrete Products Inc ... 708 754-5846
2410 S Halsted St Chicago Heights (60411) *(G-6785)*
Vitesco Technologies Usa LLC ... 847 862-5000
21440 W Lake Cook Rd Deer Park (60010) *(G-7583)*
Vitner Chips, Ottawa *Also called R and B Distributors Inc (G-16074)*
Vivotronix Inc ... 312 536-3130
965 W Chicago Ave Chicago (60642) *(G-6563)*
Vizr Tech LLC ... 312 420-4466
400 N Mcclurg Ct Apt 2906 Chicago (60611) *(G-6564)*
Vlahos Electric Service Dr ... 224 764-2335
1707 N Dale Ave Arlington Heights (60004) *(G-828)*
Vlasici Hardwood Floors Co ... 815 505-4308
1959 Somerset Dr Romeoville (60446) *(G-17885)*
Vlc Solutions LLC ... 630 447-9852
718 Killarney Ct Apt 2b Schaumburg (60193) *(G-18772)*
Vm Electronics LLC ... 847 663-9310
5080 N Kimberly Ave # 110 Chicago (60630) *(G-6565)*
Vm Hoist Crane ... 708 771-1600
1230 Hannah Ave Forest Park (60130) *(G-9727)*
Vma Group Inc ... 847 877-7039
13 Saint Clair Ln Vernon Hills (60061) *(G-20108)*
Vmm USA Unique Master Mod ... 847 537-0867
1042 Inverrary Ln Deerfield (60015) *(G-7658)*
Vo-Tech, Crystal Lake *Also called Variable Operations Tech Inc (G-7288)*
Voco Tool & Mfg Inc ... 708 771-3800
1441 Circle Ave Forest Park (60130) *(G-9728)*
Vodori Inc ... 312 324-3992
171 N Aberdeen St Ste 400 Chicago (60607) *(G-6566)*
Voestalpine Nortrak Inc ... 217 876-9160
690 E Kenwood Ave Decatur (62526) *(G-7567)*
Voestalpine Nortrak Inc ... 708 753-2125
2705 State St Chicago Heights (60411) *(G-6786)*
Voestlpine High Prfmce Mtls Co, Saint Charles *Also called Eifeler Coatings Tech Inc (G-18194)*
Voestlpine Precision Strip LLC ... 847 227-5272
901 Morse Ave Elk Grove Village (60007) *(G-9306)*
Vogel Manufacturing Co Inc ... 217 536-6946
10862 N 1000th Rd Effingham (62401) *(G-8429)*
Vogel/Hill Corporation ... 773 235-6916
3935 W Shakespeare Ave Chicago (60647) *(G-6567)*
Voges Inc (PA) ... 618 233-2760
100 N 24th St Belleville (62226) *(G-1608)*
Voges Inc ... 618 233-2760
502 Chestnut St Evansville (62242) *(G-9590)*
Voice ... 630 966-8642
314 N Lake St Ste 2 Aurora (60506) *(G-1167)*
Volflex Inc ... 708 478-1117
10920 Walnut Ln Ste 1 Mokena (60448) *(G-14127)*
Voltronics Inc ... 773 625-1779
7746 W Addison St Chicago (60634) *(G-6568)*
Vonberg Valve Inc ... 847 259-3800
3800 Industrial Ave Rolling Meadows (60008) *(G-17785)*
Vondrak Publishing Co Inc ... 773 476-4800
7676 W 63rd St Summit Argo (60501) *(G-19684)*
Voodoo Ride LLC ... 312 944-0465
1341 W Fullerton Ave # 255 Chicago (60614) *(G-6569)*
Voris Communication Co Inc (PA) ... 630 898-4268
5656 Mcdermott Dr Berkeley (60163) *(G-1946)*

ALPHABETIC

(PA)=Parent Co (HQ)=Headquarters (DH)=Div Headquarters
2020 Harris Illinois
Industrial Directory
1291

Vorne Industries Inc 630 875-3600
1445 Industrial Dr Itasca (60143) *(G-11751)*
Vorteq Coil Finishers LLC 847 455-7200
11440 W Addison St Franklin Park (60131) *(G-10080)*
Vorteq Woodstock LLC 815 338-6410
15920 Nelson Rd Woodstock (60098) *(G-21445)*
Vortex Media Group Inc 630 717-9541
1118 Knoll Dr Naperville (60565) *(G-14942)*
Vosges Ltd (PA) 773 388-5560
2950 N Oakley Ave Chicago (60618) *(G-6570)*
Vosges Haut Chocolate, Chicago *Also called Vosges Ltd (G-6570)*
Voss Belting & Specialty Co 847 673-8900
6965 N Hamlin Ave Ste 1 Lincolnwood (60712) *(G-12849)*
Voss Electric Inc 708 596-6000
15241 Commercial Ave Harvey (60426) *(G-11100)*
Voss Engineering Inc 847 673-8900
6965 N Hamlin Ave Ste 1 Lincolnwood (60712) *(G-12850)*
Voss Pattern Works Inc 618 233-4242
123 Iowa Ave Belleville (62220) *(G-1609)*
Voss Sandworks Inc 815 795-9366
3460 W Nettle Creek Dr Morris (60450) *(G-14339)*
Voss Sandworks West Inc 815 474-4042
418 N 35th Rd La Salle (61301) *(G-12124)*
Voyager Enterprise Inc 815 436-2431
15507 S Route 59 Plainfield (60544) *(G-16727)*
Voyant Beauty, Hodgkins *Also called Vee Pak LLC (G-11399)*
Voyant Beauty LLC 708 482-8881
6710 River Rd Hodgkins (60525) *(G-11400)*
Voyant Diagnostics Inc 630 456-6340
1600 S Ind Ave Apt 1101 Chicago (60616) *(G-6571)*
Vp Finish, Chicago *Also called Pariso Inc (G-5763)*
VPI Holding Company LLC (PA) 312 255-4800
676 N Michigan Ave Chicago (60611) *(G-6572)*
VPI Holdings Corp (HQ) 770 499-8100
1925 W Field Ct Ste 300 Lake Forest (60045) *(G-12321)*
Vpr Unlimited Inc 708 830-6285
10215 Camden Ln Apt E Bridgeview (60455) *(G-2397)*
Vr Printing Co Inc 630 980-2315
1979 Bloomingdale Rd Glendale Heights (60139) *(G-10514)*
Vrg Controls LLC 844 356-9874
1199 Flex Ct Ste B Lake Zurich (60047) *(G-12468)*
Vrn Welding & Fabrication Inc 847 735-7270
102 Skokie Valley Rd Lake Bluff (60044) *(G-12213)*
Vst America Inc 847 952-3800
85 W Algonquin Rd Ste 210 Arlington Heights (60005) *(G-829)*
Vtsi, Bartlett *Also called Vega Technology & Systems (G-1259)*
Vtw, Alsip *Also called Versatility Tl Works Mfg Inc (G-522)*
Vulcan Construction Mtls LLC 630 955-8500
1000 E Wrrnvlle Rd Ste 10 Naperville (60563) *(G-14943)*
Vulcan Equipment, Forrest *Also called Slagel Manufacturing Inc (G-9738)*
Vulcan Ladder Usa LLC 847 526-6321
675 Seybrooke Ln Crystal Lake (60012) *(G-7292)*
Vulcan Materials Company 847 695-0057
2000 Vulcan Pkwy Bartlett (60103) *(G-1322)*
Vulcan Materials Company 815 899-7204
12502 Lloyd Rd Sycamore (60178) *(G-19740)*
Vvf Illinois Services LLC 630 892-4381
2000 Aucutt Rd Montgomery (60538) *(G-14275)*
Vyaire Company (HQ) 833 327-3284
26125 N Riverwoods Blvd # 1 Mettawa (60045) *(G-13984)*
Vyaire Medical Inc (HQ) 833 327-3284
26125 N Riverwoods Blvd # 1 Mettawa (60045) *(G-13985)*
Vyaire Medical LLC (HQ) 833 327-3284
26125 N Riverwoods Blvd # 1 Mettawa (60045) *(G-13986)*
Vyaire Medical Mx LLC (HQ) 872 757-0114
26125 N Riverwoods Blvd Mettawa (60045) *(G-13987)*
Vyaire Medical Payroll LLC 224 544-5436
26125 N Riverwoods Blvd # 1 Mettawa (60045) *(G-13988)*
Vyse Gelatin LLC 847 678-4780
5010 Rose St Schiller Park (60176) *(G-18852)*
W & K Machining Inc 708 430-9000
4711 W 120th St Alsip (60803) *(G-523)*
W & W Associates Inc 847 719-1760
704 Telser Rd Lake Zurich (60047) *(G-12469)*
W A M Computers International 217 324-6926
211 N State St Litchfield (62056) *(G-12978)*
W A Rice Seed Company 618 498-5538
1108 W Carpenter St Jerseyville (62052) *(G-11798)*
W B Mason Co Inc 888 926-2766
810 Kimberly Dr Carol Stream (60188) *(G-3085)*
W Bozarth Logging 618 658-4016
540 Hillside Ln Vienna (62995) *(G-20120)*
W C S, Saint Charles *Also called R R Donnelley & Sons Company (G-18257)*
W D Mold Finishing Inc 847 678-8449
3923 Wesley Ter Schiller Park (60176) *(G-18853)*
W D W S, Champaign *Also called News-Gazette Inc (G-3326)*
W Diamond Group Corporation (PA) 646 647-2790
901 W Oakton St Des Plaines (60018) *(G-7866)*
W E S Inc 815 436-1732
18530 Nw Frontage Rd Joliet (60404) *(G-11943)*
W G N Flag & Decorating Co 773 768-8076
798488 S Chicago Ave Chicago (60617) *(G-6573)*
W G N Radio Mass Calling 312 591-7200
435 N Michigan Ave Ste 1 Chicago (60611) *(G-6574)*
W H A M, Mason City *Also called Mason City Banner Times (G-13612)*
W H Maze Company (PA) 815 223-1742
1100 Water St Peru (61354) *(G-16596)*
W H Maze Company 815 223-8290
100 Church St Peru (61354) *(G-16597)*
W I C S, Springfield *Also called Wyzz Inc (G-19468)*
W L & J Enterprises Inc 708 946-0999
31745 S Dixie Hwy Beecher (60401) *(G-1524)*
W L Engler Distributing Inc 630 898-5400
4 Gastville St Aurora (60503) *(G-1032)*
W M Plastics Inc 815 578-8888
5151 Bolger Ct McHenry (60050) *(G-13808)*
W N G S Inc 847 451-1224
11415 Melrose Ave Franklin Park (60131) *(G-10081)*
W R B Refinery LLC 618 255-2345
900 S Central Ave Roxana (62084) *(G-18104)*
W R Grace & Co 773 838-3200
4099 W 71st St Chicago (60629) *(G-6575)*
W R Grace & Co 708 458-9700
6051 W 65th St Chicago (60638) *(G-6576)*
W R Grace & Co-Conn 708 458-9700
6051 W 65th St Chicago (60638) *(G-6577)*
W R Grace Construction Pdts, Chicago *Also called W R Grace & Co-Conn (G-6577)*
W R Grace Davison Chemical Div, Chicago *Also called W R Grace & Co (G-6575)*
W R Pabich Mfg Co Inc 773 486-4141
2323 N Knox Ave Chicago (60639) *(G-6578)*
W R S Inc 630 279-0400
675 W Saint Charles Rd Elmhurst (60126) *(G-9443)*
W R Typesetting Co 847 966-8327
8120 River Dr Ste 2 Morton Grove (60053) *(G-14447)*
W S C Inc 312 372-1121
70 W Madison St Ste 2300 Chicago (60602) *(G-6579)*
W S Darley & Co 630 735-3500
325 Spring Lake Dr Itasca (60143) *(G-11752)*
W S Hampshire, Hampshire *Also called Western Slate Company (G-10990)*
W W Barthel & Co 847 392-5643
220 W Campus Dr Ste C Arlington Heights (60004) *(G-830)*
W W Williams Company LLC 309 756-1068
7800 14th St W Rock Island (61201) *(G-17253)*
W-D Tool Engineering Company 773 638-2688
3128 W Grand Ave Chicago (60622) *(G-6580)*
W-F Professional Assoc Inc 847 945-8050
400 Lake Cook Rd Ste 207 Deerfield (60015) *(G-7659)*
W-R Industries Inc 312 733-5200
2715 Grant Ave Bellwood (60104) *(G-1642)*
W. H. Salisbury Elec Safety, Bolingbrook *Also called Honeywell Safety Pdts USA Inc (G-2185)*
W.R. Typesetting Co., Morton Grove *Also called W R Typesetting Co (G-14447)*
W/M Display Group, Chicago *Also called Wiremasters Incorporated (G-6649)*
W/S Packaging Group Inc 847 658-7363
1310 Zange Dr Algonquin (60102) *(G-393)*
Wabash Container Corporation 618 263-3586
1015 W 9th St Mount Carmel (62863) *(G-14491)*
Wabash Mines, Keensburg *Also called Alpha Natural Resources Inc (G-12012)*
Wabash Publishing Co Inc (PA) 312 939-5900
906 S Wabash Ave Chicago (60605) *(G-6581)*
Wabash Valley Service Co 618 393-2971
1201 S Whittle Ave Olney (62450) *(G-15893)*
Wabel Tool Company 217 429-3656
1020 E Eldorado St Decatur (62521) *(G-7568)*
Wabtec, Chicago *Also called Cardwell Westinghouse Company (G-4027)*
Waco, Chicago *Also called Wilkens-Anderson Company (G-6626)*
Waco Manufacturing Co Inc 312 733-0054
2233 W Ferdinand St Chicago (60612) *(G-6582)*
Wag Industries Inc 847 329-8932
4117 Grove St Skokie (60076) *(G-19053)*
Wagenate Entps Holdings LLC 773 503-1306
14331 S Clark St Riverdale (60827) *(G-17078)*
Wagner John 847 564-0017
3004 Commercial Ave Northbrook (60062) *(G-15498)*
Wagner Brass Foundry, Chicago *Also called Bronze Memorial Inc (G-3963)*
Wagner Brass Foundry Inc 773 276-7907
1838 N Elston Ave Chicago (60642) *(G-6583)*
Wagner International LLC 224 619-9247
105 W Townline Rd Ste 160 Vernon Hills (60061) *(G-20109)*
Wagner Midwest Die Supply Inc 630 782-6230
960 N Industrial Dr Ste 8 Elmhurst (60126) *(G-9444)*
Wagner Pump & Supply Co Inc 847 526-8573
809 Lake Shore Dr Wauconda (60084) *(G-20401)*
Wagner Zip-Change Inc 708 681-4100
3100 W Hirsch St Melrose Park (60160) *(G-13926)*

Wagners Custom Wood Design ... 847 487-2788
4035 Roberts Rd Island Lake (60042) ***(G-11613)***
Wagners LLC ... 815 889-4101
2812 E 1100 North Rd Milford (60953) ***(G-14037)***
Wah King Noodle Co Inc (PA) ... 323 268-0222
5770 S Perry Ave Chicago (60621) ***(G-6584)***
Wahl Clipper Corporation (PA) ... 815 625-6525
2900 Locust St Sterling (61081) ***(G-19540)***
Wahl Clipper Corporation ... 815 625-6525
2902 Locust St Sterling (61081) ***(G-19541)***
Waist Up Imprntd Sprtswear LLC ... 847 963-1400
422 S Vermont St Palatine (60067) ***(G-16171)***
Walach Manufacturing Co Inc ... 773 836-2060
5049 W Diversey Ave Chicago (60639) ***(G-6585)***
Walco Tool & Engineering Corp ... 815 834-0225
18954 W Airport Rd Romeoville (60446) ***(G-17886)***
Waldos Sports Corner Inc ... 309 688-2425
1306 E Seiberling Ave Peoria (61616) ***(G-16545)***
Walega Precision Company Inc ... 630 682-5000
205 Kehoe Blvd Ste 3 Carol Stream (60188) ***(G-3086)***
Walern Form Grinding, Rockford *Also called Walern Form Grinding Inc* ***(G-17676)***
Walern Form Grinding Inc ... 815 874-7000
4717 Colt Rd Rockford (61109) ***(G-17676)***
Walgreen Asia Services Sarl (HQ) ... 847 527-4341
4010 Commercial Ave Northbrook (60062) ***(G-15499)***
Walgreen Intl Sarl - US BR, Northbrook *Also called Walgreen Asia Services Sarl* ***(G-15499)***
Walk 4 Life Inc ... 815 439-2340
1981c Wiesbrook Rd Oswego (60543) ***(G-16031)***
Walker's Bluff, Carterville *Also called Cellar LLC* ***(G-3131)***
Walker's Repair Shop, Pittsfield *Also called Owen Walker* ***(G-16636)***
Walker's Supersaver Foods, Charleston *Also called Charleston County Market* ***(G-3399)***
Wallace Enterprises Inc ... 309 496-1230
1812 21st Ave East Moline (61244) ***(G-8247)***
Wallace Industries Inc ... 815 389-8999
530 Eastern Ave South Beloit (61080) ***(G-19119)***
Wallace/Haskin Corp ... 630 789-2882
900 Ogden Ave 181 Downers Grove (60515) ***(G-8105)***
Wallpaperwiz.com, Chicago *Also called Tercor Inc* ***(G-6353)***
Wally's Printing, Aurora *Also called Roskuszka & Sons Inc* ***(G-1149)***
Wallys Precision Machining ... 708 205-2950
1025 N 27th Ave Melrose Park (60160) ***(G-13927)***
Walman Optical Company ... 309 787-0000
1280 11th St W Milan (61264) ***(G-14030)***
Walneck's Cycle Trader, Downers Grove *Also called Walnecks Inc* ***(G-8106)***
Walnecks Inc ... 630 985-2097
7923 Janes Ave Downers Grove (60517) ***(G-8106)***
Walnut Creek Hardwood ... 815 389-3317
851 Doner Dr South Beloit (61080) ***(G-19120)***
Walnut Custom Homes Inc ... 815 379-2151
300 Wyanet Rd Walnut (61376) ***(G-20221)***
Walnut Grove Packaging ... 217 268-5112
578 E County Road 200n Arcola (61910) ***(G-669)***
Walnut St Winery Plus Saunas ... 217 498-9800
309 S Walnut St Rochester (62563) ***(G-17173)***
Walter & Kathy Anczerewicz (PA) ... 708 448-3676
12807 S Harlem Ave Palos Heights (60463) ***(G-16194)***
Walter H Jelly & Co Inc ... 847 455-4235
2822 Birch St Franklin Park (60131) ***(G-10082)***
Walter Lagestee Inc ... 708 957-2974
2345 183rd St Ste 2 Homewood (60430) ***(G-11504)***
Walter Louis Chem & Assoc Inc ... 217 223-2017
530 S 5th St Quincy (62301) ***(G-16954)***
Walter Louis Fluid Tech, Quincy *Also called Walter Louis Chem & Assoc Inc* ***(G-16954)***
Walter Payton Power Eqp LLC (HQ) ... 708 656-7700
930 W 138th St Riverdale (60827) ***(G-17079)***
Walter Tool & Mfg Inc ... 847 697-7230
1535 Commerce Dr Elgin (60123) ***(G-8774)***
Walters Buildings, Fairfield *Also called Jack Walters & Sons Corp* ***(G-9627)***
Walters Distributing Company ... 847 468-0941
1625 Dundee Ave Ste D Elgin (60120) ***(G-8775)***
Walters Metal Fabrication Inc ... 618 931-5551
3660 State Route 111 Granite City (62040) ***(G-10749)***
Walterscheid Inc Woodridge (HQ) ... 630 972-9300
2715 Davey Rd Woodridge (60517) ***(G-21345)***
Walts Food Center, Homewood *Also called Walter Lagestee Inc* ***(G-11504)***
Waltz Brothers Inc ... 847 520-1122
10 W Waltz Dr Wheeling (60090) ***(G-21011)***
Wand Enterprises Inc (PA) ... 847 433-0231
1029 Green Bay Rd Highland Park (60035) ***(G-11304)***
Wand Tool Company, Highland Park *Also called Wand Enterprises Inc* ***(G-11304)***
Wand Tool Enterprise ... 847 433-0231
1029 Green Bay Rd Highland Park (60035) ***(G-11305)***
Wandas Bakery LLC ... 815 900-6268
4409 Greenwood Rd Woodstock (60098) ***(G-21446)***
Wandfluh of America Inc ... 847 566-5700
909 E High St Mundelein (60060) ***(G-14746)***
Wangren Machine, Rolling Meadows *Also called Apex Tool Works Inc* ***(G-17712)***
Want ADS of Champaign Inc (PA) ... 217 356-4804
505 E University Ave C Champaign (61820) ***(G-3368)***
Wanxiang USA Holdings Corp (HQ) ... 847 622-8838
88 Airport Rd Ste 100 Elgin (60123) ***(G-8776)***
Wapro Inc ... 888 927-8677
150 N Michigan Ave Chicago (60601) ***(G-6586)***
Warbler of Illinois Company ... 301 520-0438
3127 Village Office Pl Champaign (61822) ***(G-3369)***
Warcorp, Frankfort *Also called Western Applied Robotics Corp* ***(G-9852)***
Ward Cnc Machining ... 815 637-1490
7480 Forest Hills Rd Loves Park (61111) ***(G-13280)***
Wardzala Industries Inc ... 847 288-9909
9330 Grand Ave Franklin Park (60131) ***(G-10083)***
Warehouse Direct Inc (PA) ... 847 952-1925
2001 S Mount Prospect Rd Des Plaines (60018) ***(G-7867)***
Warehuse Drect Wrkplace Sltons, Des Plaines *Also called Warehouse Direct Inc* ***(G-7867)***
Warfield Electric Company Inc (PA) ... 815 469-4094
175 Industry Ave Frankfort (60423) ***(G-9851)***
Wargaming (usa) Inc (PA) ... 312 258-0500
651 W Washington Blvd # 600 Chicago (60661) ***(G-6587)***
Wargaming West, Chicago *Also called Wargaming (usa) Inc* ***(G-6587)***
Warming Systems ... 800 663-7831
7706 Industrial Dr Unit D Lake Villa (60046) ***(G-12371)***
Warner Harvey Lee Farm Inc ... 217 849-2548
556 County Road 800 E Toledo (62468) ***(G-19882)***
Warner Brothers Inc ... 217 643-7950
1254 County Road 2700 N Rantoul (61866) ***(G-16987)***
Warner Electric Indus Pdts, South Beloit *Also called Warner Electric LLC* ***(G-19122)***
Warner Electric LLC ... 815 547-1106
449 Gardner St South Beloit (61080) ***(G-19121)***
Warner Electric LLC (HQ) ... 815 389-4300
449 Gardner St South Beloit (61080) ***(G-19122)***
Warner Farms, Toledo *Also called Warner Harvey Lee Farm Inc* ***(G-19882)***
Warner Industries Inc ... 708 458-0627
6551 W 74th St Bedford Park (60638) ***(G-1510)***
Warner Offset Inc ... 847 695-9400
640 Stevenson Rd South Elgin (60177) ***(G-19179)***
Warp Bros, Chicago *Also called Flex-O-Glass Inc* ***(G-4605)***
Warphole LLC ... 866 471-6464
364 Pnnsylvnia Ave Ste 20 Glen Ellyn (60137) ***(G-10424)***
Warren Oil MGT Co IL LLC ... 618 997-5951
201 N 4th St Marion (62959) ***(G-13542)***
Warren Service Company ... 618 384-2117
1714 Oak St Carmi (62821) ***(G-2918)***
Warrior Logging & Perforagine ... 618 662-7373
174 Lincoln Rd Flora (62839) ***(G-9695)***
Warrior Well Services Inc ... 618 662-7710
745 Cedardom Dr Flora (62839) ***(G-9696)***
Warthog Inc ... 815 540-7197
2615 Yonge St Rockford (61101) ***(G-17677)***
Warwick Publishing Company ... 630 584-3871
2601 E Main St Saint Charles (60174) ***(G-18296)***
Waseet America ... 708 430-1950
6000 W 79th St Ste 203 Bedford Park (60459) ***(G-1511)***
Washburn Graficolor Inc ... 630 596-0880
1255 E Bailey Rd Naperville (60565) ***(G-14944)***
Washington Courier ... 309 444-3139
100 Ford Ln Washington (61571) ***(G-20282)***
Washington Equipment Company, Eureka *Also called Columbus McKinnon Corporation* ***(G-9478)***
Washington Mills Hennepin Inc ... 815 925-7302
13230 Prairie Indl Pkwy Hennepin (61327) ***(G-11160)***
Washington Woodworking ... 309 339-0913
1514 Willow Dr Washington (61571) ***(G-20283)***
Wasowski Jacek ... 847 693-1878
9a E Dundee Quarter Dr A Palatine (60074) ***(G-16172)***
Wastequip Saint Louis ... 216 292-0625
2701 Converse Ave East Saint Louis (62207) ***(G-8329)***
Watchfire Enterprises Inc (HQ) ... 217 442-0611
1015 Maple St Danville (61832) ***(G-7393)***
Watchfire Signs LLC (HQ) ... 217 442-0611
1015 Maple St Danville (61832) ***(G-7394)***
Watchfire Tech Holdings I Inc (PA) ... 217 442-6971
1015 Maple St Danville (61832) ***(G-7395)***
Watchfire Tech Holdings II Inc (HQ) ... 217 442-0611
1015 Maple St Danville (61832) ***(G-7396)***
Water & Gas Technologies ... 708 829-3254
8046 W 128th Pl Palos Park (60464) ***(G-16217)***
Water Dynamics Inc (PA) ... 630 584-8475
1553 Allen Ln Saint Charles (60174) ***(G-18297)***
Water Environmental Tech, Streamwood *Also called Wet USA Inc* ***(G-19603)***
Water Products Company Ill Inc ... 630 553-0840
1213 Badger St Yorkville (60560) ***(G-21505)***
Water Saver Faucet Co (PA) ... 312 666-5500
701 W Erie St Chicago (60654) ***(G-6588)***
Water Services Company of Ill ... 847 697-6623
390 Sadler Ave Elgin (60120) ***(G-8777)***
Waterco of Central States Inc ... 630 576-4782
1920 S Highland Ave # 113 Lombard (60148) ***(G-13153)***

ALPHABETIC

Waterman Winery & Vineyards...............815 264-3268
11582 Waterman Rd Waterman (60556) *(G-20302)*

Watermat Company, Glen Ellyn *Also called H2o Pod Inc (G-10404)*

Waters Associates, Wood Dale *Also called Waters Technologies Corp (G-21256)*

Waters Industries Inc...............847 783-5900
213 W Main St West Dundee (60118) *(G-20667)*

Waters Technologies Corp...............630 766-6249
1360 N Wood Dale Rd Ste C Wood Dale (60191) *(G-21256)*

Waters Technologies Corp...............508 482-8365
4559 Paysphere Cir Chicago (60674) *(G-6589)*

Waters Wire EDM Service...............630 640-3534
2719 Curtiss St Downers Grove (60515) *(G-8107)*

Waterway Rv LLC Mfg Home...............312 207-1835
2 N Riverside Plz Ste 800 Chicago (60606) *(G-6590)*

Watlow Electric Mfg Co...............314 878-4600
5710 Kenosha St Richmond (60071) *(G-17025)*

Watson Foods Co Inc...............847 245-8404
1711 E Grand Ave Lindenhurst (60046) *(G-12855)*

Watson LLC...............217 824-4440
1900 S Spresser St Taylorville (62568) *(G-19763)*

Watt Global Media, Rockford *Also called Watt Publishing Co (G-17678)*

Watt Publishing Co (PA)...............815 966-5400
401 E State St Fl 3 Rockford (61104) *(G-17678)*

Wattcore Inc...............571 482-6777
6208 Oakton St Morton Grove (60053) *(G-14448)*

Watters Fishmarket, Hamburg *Also called Betty Watters (G-10948)*

Wauconda Tool & Engrg LLC (HQ)...............847 658-4588
821 W Algonquin Rd Algonquin (60102) *(G-394)*

Waukegan Architectural Inc...............847 746-9077
3505 16th St Zion (60099) *(G-21529)*

Waukegan Ready Mix, Waukegan *Also called Thelen Sand & Gravel Inc (G-20503)*

Waukegan Steel LLC...............847 662-2810
1201 Belvidere Rd Waukegan (60085) *(G-20516)*

Waupaca Foundry Inc...............217 347-0600
1500 Heartland Blvd Effingham (62401) *(G-8430)*

Wave Graphics Inc...............217 234-8100
320 N 2nd St Mattoon (61938) *(G-13657)*

Wave Mechanics Neon...............312 829-9283
450 N Leavitt St Chicago (60612) *(G-6591)*

Wave Pads LLC...............224 444-9283
24121 W Theodore St 4-A Plainfield (60586) *(G-16728)*

Waverly Journal...............217 435-9221
130 S Pearl St Waverly (62692) *(G-20523)*

Wavsys LLC...............773 442-0888
2333 N Seeley Ave Chicago (60647) *(G-6592)*

Waxman Candles Inc...............773 929-3000
3044 N Lincoln Ave Chicago (60657) *(G-6593)*

Waxstar Inc...............708 755-3530
3224 Butler St S Chicago Hts (60411) *(G-18129)*

Wayland Ready Mix Concrete Svc...............309 833-2064
816 N Henderson St Galesburg (61401) *(G-10222)*

Waymore Power Co Inc...............618 729-3876
8334 Piasa Rd Piasa (62079) *(G-16610)*

Wayne County Press Inc...............618 842-2662
213 E Main St Fairfield (62837) *(G-9640)*

Wayne County Well Surveys Inc...............618 842-9116
2225 Industrial Dr Fairfield (62837) *(G-9641)*

Wayne Engineering (PA)...............416 943-6271
8242 Christiana Ave Skokie (60076) *(G-19054)*

Wayne Printing Company (PA)...............309 691-2496
7917 N Kckapoo Edwards Rd Edwards (61528) *(G-8341)*

Wayne Printing Company...............309 691-2496
7917 N Kckapoo Edwards Rd Edwards (61528) *(G-8342)*

Wayne Wagoner Printing, Edwards *Also called Wayne Printing Company (G-8342)*

Waypoint Enterprises...............847 551-9213
2328 Stonegate Rd Algonquin (60102) *(G-395)*

Waystar, Chicago *Also called Zirmed Inc (G-6721)*

Wb Tray LLC...............618 918-3821
115 Harting Dr Centralia (62801) *(G-3254)*

Wbt, Centralia *Also called Nvent Electric Public Ltd Co (G-3243)*

Wc Richards, Alsip *Also called Tms Manufacturing Co (G-516)*

WCI, Chicago *Also called Wood Creations Incorporated (G-6665)*

Wcr Inc...............309 697-0389
1610 W Altorfer Dr Peoria (61615) *(G-16546)*

Wctu Press (PA)...............847 864-1396
1730 Chicago Ave Evanston (60201) *(G-9587)*

Wdqn Radio, Du Quoin *Also called E & R Media LLC (G-8119)*

We Are Done LLC...............708 598-7100
8407 S 77th Ave Bridgeview (60455) *(G-2398)*

We Clean...............708 574-2551
5845 Victoria Dr Oak Forest (60452) *(G-15692)*

We Do Tech Americas Inc...............630 217-8723
3333 Warrenville Rd # 200 Lisle (60532) *(G-12957)*

We Innovex Inc...............847 291-3553
3045 Macarthur Blvd Northbrook (60062) *(G-15500)*

We International...............618 549-1784
54 Oakview Rd Carbondale (62901) *(G-2863)*

We Love Soy Inc...............630 629-9667
120 S Fairbank St Unit B Addison (60101) *(G-332)*

We-B-Print Inc...............309 353-8801
1107 N 8th St Pekin (61554) *(G-16368)*

Weakley Printing & Sign Shop...............847 473-4466
1550 Green Bay Rd North Chicago (60064) *(G-15323)*

Wear-Cote International Inc...............309 793-1250
101 10th St Rock Island (61201) *(G-17254)*

Wear-Flex Slings, Chicago *Also called MHS Ltd (G-5419)*

Weary & Baity Inc...............312 943-6197
333 W North Ave Ste F Chicago (60610) *(G-6594)*

Weatherford International LLC...............309 342-5154
961 Abingdon St Galesburg (61401) *(G-10223)*

Weatherford Signs...............618 529-2000
219 Weatherford Ln Carbondale (62902) *(G-2864)*

Weatherguard Buildings...............217 894-6213
1654 E 2950th St Clayton (62324) *(G-6911)*

Weaver Equipment LLC...............618 833-5521
1240 Mount Pleasant Rd Buncombe (62912) *(G-2631)*

Weaver Equitment Co, Buncombe *Also called Weaver Equipment LLC (G-2631)*

Web Printing Control, Arlington Heights *Also called Wpc Machinery Corp (G-836)*

Web Printing Controls, Arlington Heights *Also called Baldwin Technology Company Inc (G-702)*

WEb Production & Fabg Inc...............312 733-6800
448 N Artesian Ave Chicago (60612) *(G-6595)*

Webb-Mason Inc...............630 428-5838
280 Shuman Blvd Ste 200 Naperville (60563) *(G-14945)*

Webe Ink...............618 498-7620
103 Lincoln Ave Jerseyville (62052) *(G-11799)*

Weber Flavors, Wheeling *Also called Edgar A Weber & Company (G-20886)*

Weber Flavors, Wheeling *Also called Edgar A Weber & Company (G-20887)*

Weber Grills, Palatine *Also called Weber-Stephen Products LLC (G-16173)*

Weber Grills, Palatine *Also called Weber-Stephen Products LLC (G-16174)*

Weber Marking Systems Inc (PA)...............847 364-8500
711 W Algonquin Rd Arlington Heights (60005) *(G-831)*

Weber Metal Products Inc...............815 844-3169
10702 E 1400 North Rd Chenoa (61726) *(G-3435)*

Weber Packaging Solutions, Arlington Heights *Also called Weber Marking Systems Inc (G-831)*

Weber Press Inc...............773 561-9815
5746 N Western Ave Chicago (60659) *(G-6596)*

Weber-Stephen Products LLC (PA)...............847 934-5700
1415 S Roselle Rd Palatine (60067) *(G-16173)*

Weber-Stephen Products LLC...............224 836-8536
306 E Helen Rd Palatine (60067) *(G-16174)*

Weber-Stephen Products LLC...............847 669-4900
11811 Oak Creek Pkwy Huntley (60142) *(G-11573)*

Webqa Incorporated (PA)...............630 985-1300
900 S Frontage Rd Ste 110 Woodridge (60517) *(G-21346)*

Websolutions Technology Inc...............630 375-6833
3817 Mccoy Dr Ste 105 Aurora (60504) *(G-1033)*

Webster-Hoff Corporation...............630 858-8030
704 E Fullerton Ave Glendale Heights (60139) *(G-10515)*

Webzonepro.com, Deerfield *Also called Medical ID Fashions Company (G-7636)*

Wec Welding and Machining LLC (HQ)...............847 680-8100
1 Energy Dr Lake Bluff (60044) *(G-12214)*

Wecaretoo, Chicago *Also called TWT Marketing Inc (G-6449)*

Weco Trading Inc (PA)...............847 615-1020
21 N Skokie Hwy Ste 101 Lake Bluff (60044) *(G-12215)*

Wedco Molded Products...............630 455-6711
7409 S Quincy St Willowbrook (60527) *(G-21067)*

Wedding Pages of Chicago, The, Elk Grove Village *Also called Chambers Marketing Options (G-8888)*

Wedgewood...............847 672-4497
4555 W York House Rd Wadsworth (60083) *(G-20215)*

Wedi Corp...............847 357-9815
1160 Pierson Dr Ste 102 Batavia (60510) *(G-1441)*

Wednesday Journal Inc...............708 386-5555
332 S Michigan Ave # 900 Chicago (60604) *(G-6597)*

Wedron Silica Company...............815 433-2449
3450 E 2056th Rd Wedron (60557) *(G-20525)*

Weeb Enterprises LLC...............815 861-2625
770 Peninsula Dr Wauconda (60084) *(G-20402)*

Weekly Extra, Galesburg *Also called Galesburg Register-Mail (G-10193)*

Weekly Journals...............815 459-4040
7717 S Il Route 31 Crystal Lake (60014) *(G-7293)*

Weekly Visitor...............815 845-2328
101 E Burrall Ave Scales Mound (61075) *(G-18422)*

Weeks Seatcovers, Springfield *Also called Bill Weeks Inc (G-19326)*

Wegener Welding LLC...............630 789-0990
16w301 S Frontage Rd Burr Ridge (60527) *(G-2731)*

Wehrle Lumber Co Inc...............618 283-4859
820 E 1900 Ave Vandalia (62471) *(G-20030)*

Wehrli Custom Fabrication...............630 277-8239
300 Harvestore Dr Dekalb (60115) *(G-7711)*

Wehrli Equipment Co Inc...............630 717-4150
1805 High Grove Ln # 117 Naperville (60540) *(G-14946)*

WEI TO Associates Inc...............708 747-6660
224 Early St Park Forest (60466) *(G-16261)*

ALPHABETIC SECTION

WEI-Chuan USA Inc 708 352-8886
   6845 Santa Fe Dr Hodgkins (60525) *(G-11401)*
Weidenmiller Co 630 250-2500
   1464 Industrial Dr Itasca (60143) *(G-11753)*
Weigh Right Automatic Scale Co 815 726-4626
   612a Mills Rd Joliet (60433) *(G-11944)*
Weiland Fast Trac Inc 847 438-7996
   3386 Rfd Long Grove (60047) *(G-13174)*
Weiland Welding Inc 815 580-8079
   4727 Lindbloom Ln Cherry Valley (61016) *(G-3448)*
Weiler Engineering Inc 847 697-4900
   1395 Gateway Dr Elgin (60124) *(G-8778)*
Weiler Rubber Technologies LLC 773 826-8900
   4223 W Lake St Chicago (60624) *(G-6598)*
Weingarten LLC 618 973-1879
   1780 E State Route 15 Belleville (62221) *(G-1610)*
Weiskamp Screen Printing 217 398-8428
   312 S Neil St Champaign (61820) *(G-3370)*
Weiss Monument Works Inc 618 398-1811
   9904 W Main St Belleville (62223) *(G-1611)*
Welch Bros Inc (PA) 847 741-6134
   1050 Saint Charles St Elgin (60120) *(G-8779)*
Welch Bros Inc. 815 547-3000
   1000 Town Hall Rd Belvidere (61008) *(G-1709)*
Welch Packaging Group Inc 815 547-1505
   4133 Newburg Rd Belvidere (61008) *(G-1710)*
Welch Paper, Belvidere Also called Welch Packaging Group Inc *(G-1710)*
Welch Steel Products Inc. 847 741-2623
   333 Hammond Ave Elgin (60120) *(G-8780)*
Weld Cote Metals 888 258-0121
   7720 N Lehigh Ave Niles (60714) *(G-15186)*
Weld Seam Inc 773 588-1012
   875 Lively Blvd Wood Dale (60191) *(G-21257)*
Weld-Rite Service Inc 708 458-6000
   6715 W 73rd St Bedford Park (60638) *(G-1512)*
Weld-Seam, Wood Dale Also called Weld Seam Inc *(G-21257)*
Weldbend Corporation 708 594-1700
   6600 S Harlem Ave Argo (60501) *(G-677)*
Welding By K &K LLC 847 360-1190
   54 Le Baron St Waukegan (60085) *(G-20517)*
Welding Company of America 630 806-2000
   335 E Sullivan Rd Aurora (60505) *(G-1168)*
Welding Fabrication, Loves Park Also called Rrb Fabrication Inc *(G-13261)*
Welding Shop 773 785-1305
   109 W 103rd St Chicago (60628) *(G-6599)*
Welding Specialties 708 798-5388
   17300 Laflin Ave East Hazel Crest (60429) *(G-8219)*
Weldon Corporation 708 343-4700
   1818 Madison St Maywood (60153) *(G-13680)*
Weldstar Company (PA) 630 859-3100
   1750 Mitchell Rd Aurora (60505) *(G-1169)*
Welkins LLC 877 319-3504
   3000 Woodcreek Dr Ste 300 Downers Grove (60515) *(G-8108)*
Wellington Drive Tech US 847 922-5098
   1407 Barclay Blvd Buffalo Grove (60089) *(G-2619)*
Welliver & Sons Inc 815 874-2400
   1540 New Milford Schl Rd Rockford (61109) *(G-17679)*
Wellness Center Usa Inc (PA) 847 925-1885
   2500 W Higgins Rd Ste 770 Hoffman Estates (60169) *(G-11471)*
Wellness Monitoring, Chicago Also called Carematix Inc *(G-4028)*
Wells Janitorial Service Inc 872 226-9983
   11006 S Michigan Ave # 4 Chicago (60628) *(G-6600)*
Wells Lamont Indust Group LLC 800 247-3295
   5215 Old Orchard Rd # 725 Skokie (60077) *(G-19055)*
Wells Pet Stores, Monmouth Also called Midwestern Pet Foods Inc *(G-14223)*
Wells Printing Co, Oak Park Also called Charles Chauncey Wells Inc *(G-15749)*
Wells Sinkware Corp 312 850-3466
   916 W 21st St Chicago (60608) *(G-6601)*
Wells-Gardner Technologies Inc 630 819-8219
   16w 281 S Frontage Rd Burr Ridge (60527) *(G-2732)*
Wellsky Corporation 630 218-2700
   1900 Spring Rd Ste 450 Oak Brook (60523) *(G-15670)*
Wellspring Investments LLC 773 736-1213
   5470 N Elston Ave Chicago (60630) *(G-6602)*
Welsch Ready Mix, Morris Also called T H Davidson & Co Inc *(G-14331)*
Welsch Ready Mix Inc 815 524-1850
   2000 W 135th St Bolingbrook (60490) *(G-2252)*
Welsh Industries Ltd 815 756-1111
   6 Evergreen Cir Dekalb (60115) *(G-7712)*
Wemco Inc 708 388-1980
   11721 S Austin Ave Alsip (60803) *(G-524)*
Wenco Manufacturing Co Inc 630 377-7474
   11n261 Muirhead Rd Elgin (60124) *(G-8781)*
Wendell Adams (PA) 217 345-9587
   1286 W State St Charleston (61920) *(G-3416)*
Wenesco Inc 773 283-3004
   930 W National Ave Addison (60101) *(G-333)*
Wenger Woodcraft 217 578-3440
   676 N County Road 250 E Tuscola (61953) *(G-19934)*
Wengers Springbrook Cheese Inc 815 865-5855
   12805 N Spring Brook Rd Davis (61019) *(G-7420)*
Wenlyn Screw Company Inc 630 766-0050
   810 Maple Ln Bensenville (60106) *(G-1911)*
Wenona Food & Fuel 815 853-4141
   3075 Il Route 17 Wenona (61377) *(G-20527)*
Wenona Index, Henry Also called Henry News Republican *(G-11166)*
Wensco Michigan Corporation 630 333-4440
   936 W Fullerton Ave Addison (60101) *(G-334)*
Werner Co 815 459-6020
   420 E Terra Cotta Ave Crystal Lake (60014) *(G-7294)*
Werner Co 847 455-8001
   555 W Pierce Rd Ste 300 Itasca (60143) *(G-11754)*
Wernze Farms Inc 618 569-4820
   20563 N 400th St Annapolis (62413) *(G-590)*
Wes Tech Printing Graphic 630 520-9041
   1555 W Hawthorne Ln West Chicago (60185) *(G-20658)*
Wes-Tech Inc 847 541-5070
   720 Dartmouth Ln Buffalo Grove (60089) *(G-2620)*
Wes-Tech Automtn Solutions LLC 847 541-5070
   720 Dartmouth Ln Buffalo Grove (60089) *(G-2621)*
Wesco, Chicago Also called Sterling Spring LLC *(G-6245)*
Wesco International Inc 630 513-4864
   737 N Oaklawn Ave Elmhurst (60126) *(G-9445)*
Wescom Products 217 932-5292
   503 Ne 15th St Casey (62420) *(G-3209)*
Wesdar Technologies Inc 630 761-0965
   924 Vineyard Ln Aurora (60502) *(G-1034)*
Wesley-Jessen Corporation Del 847 294-3000
   333 Howard Ave Des Plaines (60018) *(G-7868)*
Wesling Products Inc 773 533-2850
   2912 W Lake St Chicago (60612) *(G-6603)*
West Central Fs Inc 309 375-6904
   686 N Depot Rd Wataga (61488) *(G-20287)*
West Chicago Plastics Corp 708 582-4014
   700 24th Ave Bellwood (60104) *(G-1643)*
West Chicago Printing Company, West Chicago Also called Treudt Corporation *(G-20654)*
West End Tool & Die Inc 815 462-3040
   22020 Howell Dr New Lenox (60451) *(G-15068)*
West Fuels Inc 708 488-8880
   7340 Harrison St Forest Park (60130) *(G-9729)*
West Laboratories Inc 815 935-1630
   1305 Harvard Dr Kankakee (60901) *(G-12011)*
West Liberty Foods LLC 603 679-2300
   750 S Schmidt Rd Bolingbrook (60440) *(G-2253)*
West Loop Salumi Co 312 255-7004
   200 N Jefferson St # 704 Chicago (60661) *(G-6604)*
West Machine Products Inc 847 740-2404
   606 Long Lake Dr Round Lake (60073) *(G-18086)*
West Precision Tool Inc 630 766-8304
   447 Evergreen Ave Bensenville (60106) *(G-1912)*
West Publishing Corporation 312 894-1690
   111 W Jackson Blvd # 1700 Chicago (60604) *(G-6605)*
West Salem Knox County Htchy 618 456-3601
   615 W Church St West Salem (62476) *(G-20689)*
West Side Machine Inc 630 243-1069
   11201 S Boyer St Lemont (60439) *(G-12594)*
West Side Tractor Sales Co 815 961-3160
   3110 Prairie Rd Rockford (61102) *(G-17680)*
West Suburban Journal 708 344-5975
   229 Esprit Ct Bloomingdale (60108) *(G-2020)*
West Suburban Journal News, Westchester Also called Trottie Publishing Group Inc *(G-20715)*
West Suburban Living Magazine, Hillside Also called C2 Publishing Inc *(G-11332)*
West Town Plating Inc 708 652-1600
   5243 W 25th Pl Cicero (60804) *(G-6887)*
West Vly Graphics & Print Inc 630 377-7575
   201 S 3rd St Saint Charles (60174) *(G-18298)*
West Water Inc 312 326-7480
   463 W 24th St Ste 1 Chicago (60616) *(G-6606)*
West Zwick Corp 217 222-0228
   2132 Glenayre Way Quincy (62305) *(G-16955)*
Westell Inc (HQ) 630 898-2500
   750 N Commons Dr Aurora (60504) *(G-1035)*
Westell Technologies Inc (PA) 630 898-2500
   750 N Commons Dr Aurora (60504) *(G-1036)*
Western Analytical Products 800 541-8421
   625 Bunker Ct Vernon Hills (60061) *(G-20110)*
Western Applied Robotics Corp 815 735-6476
   22530 S Center Rd Frankfort (60423) *(G-9852)*
Western Architectural Iron Co 773 463-1500
   3455 N Elston Ave Chicago (60618) *(G-6607)*
Western Consolidated Tech Inc 815 334-3684
   1425 Lake Ave Woodstock (60098) *(G-21447)*
Western Digital Tech Inc 949 672-7000
   15535 Collection Ctr Dr Chicago (60693) *(G-6608)*
Western Illinois Optical Inc 309 837-2000
   909 E Grant St Macomb (61455) *(G-13401)*
Western Ill Agri-Systems Inc 217 746-2144
   1830 E County Road 2100 Burnside (62330) *(G-2646)*

Western Industries Inc (HQ) ALPHABETIC SECTION

Western Industries Inc (HQ) 920 261-0660
1111 Wheeling Rd Wheeling (60090) ***(G-21012)***

Western Lighting Inc 847 451-7200
2349 17th St Franklin Park (60131) ***(G-10084)***

Western Motor Mfg Co 815 986-2214
1211 23rd Ave Rockford (61104) ***(G-17681)***

Western Motor Service Div, Rockford *Also called Forest City Auto Electric Co* ***(G-17418)***

Western Oil & Gas Dev Co 618 544-8646
9234 E 1050th Ave Robinson (62454) ***(G-17128)***

Western Printing Machinery Co (PA) 847 678-1740
9229 Ivanhoe St Schiller Park (60176) ***(G-18854)***

Western Printing Machinery Co 847 678-1740
9228 Ivanhoe St Schiller Park (60176) ***(G-18855)***

Western Railway Devices Corp 847 625-8500
28665 Braeloch Ct Lake Bluff (60044) ***(G-12216)***

Western Railway Equipment, Lake Bluff *Also called Western Railway Devices Corp* ***(G-12216)***

Western Remac Inc (PA) 630 972-7770
1740 Internationale Pkwy Woodridge (60517) ***(G-21347)***

Western Sand & Gravel Co 815 433-1600
4220 Mbl Dr Ottawa (61350) ***(G-16085)***

Western Slate Company (PA) 847 683-4400
365 Keyes Ave Hampshire (60140) ***(G-10990)***

Western Stoneware, Monmouth *Also called Ws Incorporated of Manmouth* ***(G-14228)***

Western Yeast Company Inc 309 274-3160
305 W Ash St Chillicothe (61523) ***(G-6823)***

Western-Cullen-Hayes Inc (PA) 773 254-9600
2700 W 36th Pl Chicago (60632) ***(G-6609)***

Westfalia-Surge Inc 630 759-7346
1354 Enterprise Dr Romeoville (60446) ***(G-17887)***

Westheimer Corp 847 498-9850
100 Oakwood Rd Ste B Lake Zurich (60047) ***(G-12470)***

Westinghouse, Lake Bluff *Also called Wec Welding and Machining LLC* ***(G-12214)***

Westinghouse A Brake Tech Corp 847 777-6400
1010 Johnson Dr Buffalo Grove (60089) ***(G-2622)***

Westmont Engineering Company, Broadview *Also called Morey Industries Inc* ***(G-2454)***

Westmont Metal Mfg LLC 708 343-0214
2350 S 27th Ave Broadview (60155) ***(G-2474)***

Westmore Supply Co 630 627-0278
250 Westmore Meyers Rd Lombard (60148) ***(G-13154)***

Westosha Airport, Antioch *Also called Thelen Sand & Gravel Inc* ***(G-636)***

Westran Thermal Processing LLC 815 634-1001
483 Gardner St South Beloit (61080) ***(G-19123)***

Westrock Cnsmr Packg Group LLC 804 444-1000
1950 N Ruby St Melrose Park (60160) ***(G-13928)***

Westrock Container LLC (PA) 847 239-8800
1101 Skokie Blvd Ste 300 Northbrook (60062) ***(G-15501)***

Westrock Converting LLC 630 783-6700
365 Crossing Rd Bolingbrook (60440) ***(G-2254)***

Westrock Converting LLC 618 709-5284
3101 Westway Dr Edwardsville (62025) ***(G-8379)***

Westrock Cp LLC 309 342-0121
775 S Linwood Rd Galesburg (61401) ***(G-10224)***

Westrock Cp LLC 847 689-4200
1900 Foss Park Ave North Chicago (60064) ***(G-15324)***

Westrock Cp LLC 618 654-2141
501 Zschokke St Highland (62249) ***(G-11248)***

Westrock Cp LLC 630 443-3538
415 37th Ave Saint Charles (60174) ***(G-18299)***

Westrock Cp LLC 708 458-8100
7601 S 78th Ave Bridgeview (60455) ***(G-2399)***

Westrock Cp LLC 773 254-1030
1415 W 44th St Chicago (60609) ***(G-6610)***

Westrock Cp LLC 630 924-0104
965 Muirfield Dr Bartlett (60133) ***(G-1260)***

Westrock Cp LLC 630 384-5200
450 E North Ave Carol Stream (60188) ***(G-3087)***

Westrock Cp LLC 847 625-8284
3145 Central Ave Waukegan (60085) ***(G-20518)***

Westrock Cp LLC 630 655-6951
8170 S Madison St Burr Ridge (60527) ***(G-2733)***

Westrock Cp LLC 312 346-6600
150 N Michigan Ave Chicago (60601) ***(G-6611)***

Westrock Cp LLC 708 458-5288
6131 W 74th St Bedford Park (60638) ***(G-1513)***

Westrock CP LLC 773 264-3516
626 E 111th St Chicago (60628) ***(G-6612)***

Westrock Healthcare, Bartlett *Also called Westrock Mwv LLC* ***(G-1323)***

Westrock Mwv LLC 773 221-9015
9540 S Dorchester Ave Chicago (60628) ***(G-6613)***

Westrock Mwv LLC 217 442-2247
202 Eastgate Dr Danville (61834) ***(G-7397)***

Westrock Mwv LLC 630 289-8537
1534 Stockton Ct Bartlett (60103) ***(G-1323)***

Westrock Rkt LLC 815 756-8913
800 Nestle Ct Dekalb (60115) ***(G-7713)***

Westrock Rkt LLC 312 346-6600
222 N La Salle St Chicago (60601) ***(G-6614)***

Westrock Rkt LLC 630 325-9670
51 Shore Dr Ste 1 Burr Ridge (60527) ***(G-2734)***

Westrock Rkt LLC 630 429-2400
1601 Mountain St Aurora (60505) ***(G-1170)***

Westville Ready Mix Inc 217 267-2082
1409 English St Westville (61883) ***(G-20782)***

Westway Feed Products LLC 309 654-2211
22220 Route 84 N Cordova (61242) ***(G-7011)***

Westway Trading, Cordova *Also called Westway Feed Products LLC* ***(G-7011)***

Westwick Foundry Ltd 815 777-0815
200 S Main St Galena (61036) ***(G-10181)***

Westwood Lands Inc 618 877-4990
4 Caine Dr Madison (62060) ***(G-13419)***

Westwood Machine & Tool Co 815 626-5090
1703 Westwood Dr Sterling (61081) ***(G-19542)***

Wet International Inc 630 540-2113
316 Roma Jean Pkwy Streamwood (60107) ***(G-19602)***

Wet USA Inc 630 540-2113
316 Roma Jean Pkwy Streamwood (60107) ***(G-19603)***

Wevaultcom LLC 877 938-2858
190 Liberty Rd Unit 3 Crystal Lake (60014) ***(G-7295)***

Wex Distributors Inc 847 691-5823
40471 N Bluff Dr Antioch (60002) ***(G-643)***

Wexford Home Corp 847 922-5738
707 Skokie Blvd Northbrook (60062) ***(G-15502)***

Wexford Home Corp 331 225-0979
430 E Plainfield Rd Countryside (60525) ***(G-7078)***

Weyerhaeuser Company 847 439-1111
1800 Nicholas Blvd Elk Grove Village (60007) ***(G-9307)***

Weyerhaeuser Company 815 987-0395
1753 23rd Ave Rockford (61104) ***(G-17682)***

Weyerhaeuser Company 630 778-7070
220 Brookshire Ct Naperville (60540) ***(G-14947)***

Weyerhauser, Naperville *Also called Weyerhaeuser Company* ***(G-14947)***

Wf Machining Product, Darien *Also called Willow Farm Product Inc* ***(G-7414)***

Wgel Radio, Greenville *Also called Bond Broadcasting Inc* ***(G-10828)***

Wgi Innovations Ltd 800 847-8269
431 E South St Plano (60545) ***(G-16747)***

Wgt, Palos Park *Also called Water & Gas Technologies* ***(G-16217)***

Whale Manufacturing Inc 847 357-9192
870 N Ridge Ave Lombard (60148) ***(G-13155)***

Whalen Manufacturing Company 309 836-1438
1270 E Murray St Macomb (61455) ***(G-13402)***

What We Make Inc 331 442-4830
207 Berg St Algonquin (60102) ***(G-396)***

Wheatland Cstm Cbntry Wdwkg LL 630 359-8553
228 W Ridge Rd Villa Park (60181) ***(G-20176)***

Wheatland Tube Company, Chicago *Also called John Maneely Company* ***(G-5043)***

Wheaton Brace, Carol Stream *Also called Wheaton Resource Corp* ***(G-3088)***

Wheaton Cabinetry 815 729-1085
17238 Weber Rd Lockport (60441) ***(G-13027)***

Wheaton Resource Corp 630 690-5795
380 S Schmale Rd Ste 121 Carol Stream (60188) ***(G-3088)***

Wheaton Trophy & Engravers 630 682-4200
107 W Front St Ste 3 Wheaton (60187) ***(G-20831)***

Wheel Worx North LLC 309 346-3535
200 Hanna Dr Pekin (61554) ***(G-16369)***

Wheels & Deals 217 423-6333
170 N Oakdale Blvd Decatur (62522) ***(G-7569)***

Where 2 Get It LLC 224 232-5550
21 S Evergreen Ave 240a Arlington Heights (60005) ***(G-832)***

Wherry Machine & Welding Inc 309 828-5423
11 Carri Dr Bloomington (61705) ***(G-2107)***

Whi Capital Partners (HQ) 312 621-0590
191 N Wacker Dr Ste 1500 Chicago (60606) ***(G-6615)***

Whiner Beer Company, Chicago *Also called Whiner Brewery LLC* ***(G-6616)***

Whiner Brewery LLC 312 810-2271
1400 W 46th St 104 Chicago (60609) ***(G-6616)***

Whipples Printing Press Inc 309 787-3538
2410 119th Avenue Ct W Milan (61264) ***(G-14031)***

Whiskey Acres Distilling Co 815 739-8711
11504 Keslinger Rd Dekalb (60115) ***(G-7714)***

Whitacres Country Oaks Shop 309 726-1305
704 S Broadway St Hudson (61748) ***(G-11521)***

Whitacres Handcrafted, Hudson *Also called Whitacres Country Oaks Shop* ***(G-11521)***

White County Coal LLC (HQ) 618 382-4651
1525 County Rd 1300 N Carmi (62821) ***(G-2919)***

White Diamond Bubbles Hand 773 417-3237
4532 W Madison St Chicago (60624) ***(G-6617)***

White Diamonds Inc 708 868-4006
96 River Oaks Ctr Calumet City (60409) ***(G-2793)***

White Eagle Spring & 773 384-4455
1637 N Lowell Ave Chicago (60639) ***(G-6618)***

White Graphics Inc 630 791-0232
1411 Centre Cir Downers Grove (60515) ***(G-8109)***

White Graphics Printing Svcs 630 629-9300
1411 Centre Cir Downers Grove (60515) ***(G-8110)***

White Jig Grinding 847 888-2260
625 Martin Dr South Elgin (60177) ***(G-19180)***

White Land & Mineral Inc....618 262-5102
526 N Market St Mount Carmel (62863) *(G-14492)*
White Oak Energy LLC....815 824-2182
11827 E 2100 North Rd Carlock (61725) *(G-2888)*
White Oak Resources LLC....618 643-5500
18033 County Road 500 E Dahlgren (62828) *(G-7310)*
White Oak Technology....309 228-4201
524 Wedgewood Ter Germantown Hills (61548) *(G-10334)*
White Racker Co Inc....847 758-1640
420 Lively Blvd Elk Grove Village (60007) *(G-9308)*
White Rhino LLC....309 691-9653
10216 W Civil Defense Rd Brimfield (61517) *(G-2408)*
White Sheet Metal....217 465-3195
303 N Austin St Paris (61944) *(G-16246)*
White Star Silo....618 523-4735
8320 Wesclin Rd Germantown (62245) *(G-10332)*
White Stokes Company Inc....773 254-5000
4433 W Touhy Ave Ste 207 Lincolnwood (60712) *(G-12851)*
White Way Sign & Maint Co....847 391-0200
2722 N Racine Ave Chicago (60614) *(G-6619)*
White Whale LLC....309 303-0028
10639 State St Mossville (61552) *(G-14462)*
Whiteside Drapery Fabricators....847 746-5300
2701 Deborah Ave Ste A Zion (60099) *(G-21530)*
Whiting Corporation (HQ)....800 861-5744
26000 S Whiting Way Ste 1 Monee (60449) *(G-14212)*
Whiting Partners LLC....773 978-8221
8614 S Commercial Ave Chicago (60617) *(G-6620)*
Whitney Foods Inc....773 842-8511
687 Country Ln Glencoe (60022) *(G-10434)*
Whitney Medical Solutions, Niles *Also called Whitney Products Inc* *(G-15187)*
Whitney Products Inc....847 966-6161
5737 W Howard St Niles (60714) *(G-15187)*
Whitney Roper LLC....815 962-3011
2833 Huffman Blvd Rockford (61103) *(G-17683)*
Whitney Roper Rockford Inc....815 962-3011
2833 Huffman Blvd Rockford (61103) *(G-17684)*
Whittl, Chicago *Also called Band of Shoppers Inc* *(G-3824)*
Wholesale For Industrial Beari, Carol Stream *Also called Kgbal Manufacturing LLC* *(G-3009)*
Wholesale Gate Co, Dekalb *Also called Tim Detwiler Enterprises Inc* *(G-7709)*
Wholesale Point Inc....630 986-1700
260 Shore Ct Burr Ridge (60527) *(G-2735)*
Whospoppin Enterprises Inc....312 912-8480
5618 S Indiana Ave Chicago (60637) *(G-6621)*
Whyte Gate Incorporated....847 201-7000
400 S Curran Rd Ste 1 Grayslake (60030) *(G-10804)*
Wicc Ltd....309 444-4125
119 Muller Rd Washington (61571) *(G-20284)*
Wichita Packing Co....312 421-0606
340 N Oakley Blvd Chicago (60612) *(G-6622)*
Wicks Organ Company....618 654-2191
416 Pine St Highland (62249) *(G-11249)*
Wicks Pipe Organ Company, Highland *Also called Wicks Organ Company* *(G-11249)*
Wicoff Inc....618 988-8888
3201 S Park Ave Herrin (62948) *(G-11182)*
Wide Image Incorporated....773 279-9183
1187 Tower Rd Schaumburg (60173) *(G-18773)*
Wiegmann Woodworking....618 248-1300
105 Sugar Creek Ln Damiansville (62215) *(G-7316)*
Wieland Holdings Inc (HQ)....847 537-3990
567 Northgate Pkwy Wheeling (60090) *(G-21013)*
Wieland Rolled Pdts N Amer LLC....630 260-0802
3832 Collection Center Dr Chicago (60693) *(G-6623)*
Wielgus Product Models Inc....312 432-1950
1435 W Fulton St Chicago (60607) *(G-6624)*
Wieman Fuels LP Gas Company....618 632-4015
418 S Belt E Belleville (62220) *(G-1612)*
Wienmar Inc....847 742-9222
1601 N La Fox St South Elgin (60177) *(G-19181)*
Wikoff Color Corporation....847 487-2704
240 Jamie Ln Wauconda (60084) *(G-20403)*
Wikus Saw Technology Corp....630 766-0960
700 W Belden Ave Addison (60101) *(G-335)*
Wil Lan Company, Lockport *Also called Bending Specialists LLC* *(G-12983)*
Wil Son Pallet....217 543-3555
1858 Cr 1300e Sullivan (61951) *(G-19675)*
Wilbert Quincy Vault Co....217 224-8557
4128 Wisman Ln Quincy (62305) *(G-16956)*
Wilbert Vault, Sterling *Also called Sterling Vault Company* *(G-19537)*
Wilbert Vault Company....309 787-5281
636 10th Ave W Milan (61264) *(G-14032)*
Wilcor Solid Surface Inc....888 956-1001
2371 United Ln Elk Grove Village (60007) *(G-9309)*
Wilczak Industrial Parts Inc....847 260-5559
9220 Chestnut Ave Franklin Park (60131) *(G-10085)*
Wildcat Hills....618 273-8600
115 Grayson Ln Eldorado (62930) *(G-8486)*
Wildcat Hlls Cottage Grove Pit, Equality *Also called Peabody Midwest Mining LLC* *(G-9471)*
Wilderness Woodworks LLC....815 210-3751
36931 Irish Ln Custer Park (60481) *(G-7303)*
Wildlife Materials Inc....618 687-3505
1202 Walnut St Murphysboro (62966) *(G-14762)*
Wiliams Interactive LLC....773 961-1920
2718 W Roscoe St Chicago (60618) *(G-6625)*
Wilkens-Anderson Company (PA)....773 384-4433
4525 W Division St Chicago (60651) *(G-6626)*
Wilkos Industries....563 249-6691
3199 School Dr Savanna (61074) *(G-18413)*
Will County Well & Pump Co Inc (PA)....815 485-2413
1200 S Cedar Rd Ste 1a New Lenox (60451) *(G-15069)*
Will Don Corp....773 276-7081
7171 W 65th St Chicago (60638) *(G-6627)*
Will Hamms Stained Glass....847 255-2230
628 N Highland Ave Arlington Heights (60004) *(G-833)*
Willard Miller....618 252-4407
265 Battleford Rd Carrier Mills (62917) *(G-3125)*
Willard R Schorck....217 543-2160
55 E Cr 300 N Arthur (61911) *(G-882)*
Willdon Corp....773 276-7080
7171 W 65th St Chicago (60638) *(G-6628)*
Wille Bros Co (PA)....708 535-4101
11303 Manhattan Monee Rd Monee (60449) *(G-14213)*
Willenborg Hardwood Inds Inc....217 844-2082
15485 E 1900th Ave Effingham (62401) *(G-8431)*
Willert Company....630 860-1620
1144 E Green St Franklin Park (60131) *(G-10086)*
Willetts Winery & Cellar....309 968-7070
105 E Market St Manito (61546) *(G-13441)*
William Badal....815 264-7752
190 W Lincoln Hwy Waterman (60556) *(G-20303)*
William Charles Cnstr Co LLC....815 654-4720
4525 Irene Rd Belvidere (61008) *(G-1711)*
William Dach....815 962-3455
4901 W State St Rockford (61102) *(G-17685)*
William Davis & Co....847 395-6860
488 Donin Dr Antioch (60002) *(G-644)*
William Dudek Manufacturing Co....773 622-2727
4901 W Armitage Ave Chicago (60639) *(G-6629)*
William Frick & Company (PA)....847 918-3700
2600 Commerce Dr Libertyville (60048) *(G-12725)*
William Harris Investors, Chicago *Also called Harris William & Company Inc* *(G-4782)*
William Holloway Ltd....847 866-9520
1800 Dempster St Evanston (60202) *(G-9588)*
William Ingram....217 442-5075
216 S Gilbert St Danville (61832) *(G-7398)*
William J Kline & Co Inc....815 338-2055
425 Borden St Woodstock (60098) *(G-21448)*
William N Pasulka....815 339-6300
15685 State Highway 71 Peru (61354) *(G-16598)*
William R Becker....618 378-3337
760 Route 45 N Norris City (62869) *(G-15252)*
William W Meyer and Sons (PA)....847 918-0111
1700 Franklin Blvd Libertyville (60048) *(G-12726)*
Williams White & Company....309 797-7650
600 River Dr Moline (61265) *(G-14181)*
Williams Electronic Games De (HQ)....773 961-1000
350 N Orleans St Chicago (60654) *(G-6630)*
Williams Electronic Games De....773 961-1000
350 N Orleans St Chicago (60654) *(G-6631)*
Williams Halthcare Systems LLC....847 741-3650
158 N Edison Ave Elgin (60123) *(G-8782)*
Williams Welding Service....217 235-1758
14772 Cooks Mills Rd Humboldt (61931) *(G-11525)*
Williams-Hayward Protective Co, Summit Argo *Also called Willims-Hyward Intl Ctings Inc* *(G-19685)*
Williamson J Hunter & Company....847 441-7888
170 Linden St Winnetka (60093) *(G-21137)*
Willie Washer Mfg Co....847 956-1344
2101 Greenleaf Ave Elk Grove Village (60007) *(G-9310)*
Willims-Hyward Intl Ctings Inc (PA)....708 563-5182
7425 W 59th St Summit Argo (60501) *(G-19685)*
Willims-Hyward Intl Ctings Inc....708 458-0015
7400 W Archer Ave Argo (60501) *(G-678)*
Willis Publishing....618 497-8272
1101 E Pine St Percy (62272) *(G-16561)*
Willis Stein & Partners Manage (PA)....312 422-2400
444 W Lake St Ste 4700 Chicago (60606) *(G-6632)*
Willoughbys Auto & Mch Sp....815 448-2281
615 East St Mazon (60444) *(G-13685)*
Willow Creek Energy LLC (PA)....312 224-1400
1 S Wacker Dr Ste 1900 Chicago (60606) *(G-6633)*
Willow Farm Product Inc....630 395-9246
8193 S Lemont Rd Darien (60561) *(G-7414)*
Willow Farm Products Inc....630 430-7491
20w114 97th St Lemont (60439) *(G-12595)*
Willow Ridge Glass Inc (PA)....630 910-8300
8102 Lemont Rd Ste 100 Woodridge (60517) *(G-21348)*

ALPHABETIC

Willowbrook Sawmill.....618 592-3806
1469 E 1600th Ave Oblong (62449) ***(G-15832)***
Wills Milling and Hardwood Inc.....217 854-9056
9674 Colt Rd Carlinville (62626) ***(G-2884)***
Willy Wonka Candy Factory, Itasca *Also called Nestle Usa Inc* ***(G-11711)***
Wilmar Group LLC.....847 421-6595
818 Larchmont Ln Lake Forest (60045) ***(G-12322)***
Wilmette Screw Products.....773 725-2626
4432 N Elston Ave Chicago (60630) ***(G-6634)***
Wilmington Free Press, Wilmington *Also called G-W Communications Inc* ***(G-21099)***
Wilmouth Machine Works Inc.....618 372-3189
1723 Terpening Rd Brighton (62012) ***(G-2405)***
Wilpro.....618 382-4667
205 Industrial Ave Carmi (62821) ***(G-2920)***
Wilseys Handmade Sweets LLC.....314 504-0851
316 W Park St Edwardsville (62025) ***(G-8380)***
Wilson & Wilson Monument Co.....618 775-6488
406 W Poplar St Odin (62870) ***(G-15836)***
Wilson Kitchens Inc.....618 253-7449
1653 S Feazel St Harrisburg (62946) ***(G-11031)***
Wilson Mfg Screw Mch Pdts.....815 964-8724
4004 Auburn St Rockford (61101) ***(G-17686)***
Wilson Racket Division, Chicago *Also called Wilson Sporting Goods Co* ***(G-6636)***
Wilson Railing & Metal Fabg Co.....847 662-1747
640 Wilson Ave Park City (60085) ***(G-16248)***
Wilson Sporting Goods Co (HQ).....773 714-6400
1 Prudntial Pl 130 E Rndl Chicago (60601) ***(G-6635)***
Wilson Sporting Goods Co.....773 714-6500
8700 W Bryn Mawr Ave Chicago (60631) ***(G-6636)***
Wilson Tool Corporation.....815 226-0147
2401 20th St Rockford (61104) ***(G-17687)***
Wiltek Inc.....630 922-9200
3819 Grassmere Rd Naperville (60564) ***(G-14992)***
Wilton Brands Inc.....815 823-8547
21350 Sw Frontage Rd Joliet (60404) ***(G-11945)***
Wilton Brands LLC (PA).....630 963-7100
535 E Diehl Rd Ste 333 Naperville (60563) ***(G-14948)***
Wilton Holdings Inc.....630 963-7100
2240 75th St Woodridge (60517) ***(G-21349)***
Wilton Industries, Joliet *Also called Wilton Brands Inc* ***(G-11945)***
Wilton Industries, Woodridge *Also called Wilton Holdings Inc* ***(G-21349)***
Wilton Industries Inc (HQ).....630 963-7100
535 E Diehl Rd Ste 333 Naperville (60563) ***(G-14949)***
Wilton Industries Inc.....815 834-9390
1125 Taylor Rd Romeoville (60446) ***(G-17888)***
Wilton Industries Co, Naperville *Also called Wilton Industries Inc* ***(G-14949)***
Wilton Ww Co (PA).....615 501-3000
535 E Diehl Rd Ste 300 Naperville (60563) ***(G-14950)***
Win Soon Chicago Inc.....630 585-7090
190 Kendall Point Dr Oswego (60543) ***(G-16032)***
Win Technologies Incorporated.....630 236-1020
800 S Frontenac St Unit 1 Aurora (60504) ***(G-1037)***
Wincademy Inc.....847 445-7886
34331 N Stonebridge Ln Grayslake (60030) ***(G-10805)***
Winchester Ammunition, East Alton *Also called Olin Corporation* ***(G-8168)***
Winchester Interconnect Rugged (HQ).....708 594-5890
2150 Parkes Dr Broadview (60155) ***(G-2475)***
Winco Finishing Div, South Elgin *Also called Custom Aluminum Products Inc* ***(G-19141)***
Wind Point Partners LP (PA).....312 255-4800
676 N Michigan Ave # 3700 Chicago (60611) ***(G-6637)***
Wind Point Partners Vi LP (HQ).....312 255-4800
676 N Michigan Ave # 3700 Chicago (60611) ***(G-6638)***
Window Coverings, Loves Park *Also called Znl Corporation* ***(G-13284)***
Window Fashion Unlimited, Palatine *Also called Interior Fashions Contract* ***(G-16131)***
Windsong Press Ltd.....847 223-4586
33403 N Greentree Rd Grayslake (60030) ***(G-10806)***
Windsor Systems, Chicago *Also called James Instruments Inc* ***(G-5002)***
Windward Brands LLC.....224 432-5704
2550 Compass Rd Ste G Glenview (60026) ***(G-10637)***
Windwrap LLC.....773 594-1724
6943 N Minnetonka Ave Chicago (60646) ***(G-6639)***
Windy City Cutting Die Inc.....630 521-9410
104 Foster Ave Bensenville (60106) ***(G-1913)***
Windy City Distilling Inc.....312 788-7503
140 Shepard Ave Ste B Wheeling (60090) ***(G-21014)***
Windy City Engineering Inc.....773 254-8113
3244 W 30th St Chicago (60623) ***(G-6640)***
Windy City Fine Framing LLC.....312 455-1213
840 N Milwaukee Ave Chicago (60642) ***(G-6641)***
Windy City Laser Service Inc.....773 995-0188
820 W 120th St Chicago (60643) ***(G-6642)***
Windy City Plastics Inc.....773 533-1099
263 N California Ave Chicago (60612) ***(G-6643)***
Windy City Publishers LLC.....847 925-9434
1051 S Hiddenbrook Trl Palatine (60067) ***(G-16175)***
Windy City RC.....847 818-8354
220 W Rand Rd Arlington Heights (60004) ***(G-834)***
Windy City Silkscreening Inc.....312 842-0030
2715 S Archer Ave Chicago (60608) ***(G-6644)***
Windy City Times, Chicago *Also called Lambda Publications Inc* ***(G-5169)***
Windy Hill Woodworking Inc.....309 275-2415
4 Candle Ridge Rd Towanda (61776) ***(G-19893)***
Windy Polymers Inc.....630 272-7453
3701 Illinois Ave Saint Charles (60174) ***(G-18300)***
Winery At Shale Lake The, Staunton *Also called Shale Lake LLC* ***(G-19478)***
Winery West of Wise.....217 632-6003
14096 State Highway 97 Petersburg (62675) ***(G-16605)***
Winfield Technology Inc.....630 584-0475
53 Stirrup Cup Ct Saint Charles (60174) ***(G-18301)***
Wingfield Manufacturing LLC.....800 637-6712
5811 N High Cross Rd Urbana (61802) ***(G-20003)***
Wings of Roselle LLC.....630 529-5700
840 Lake St Ste 414 Roselle (60172) ***(G-17995)***
Winhere Brake Parts Inc.....630 307-0158
1331 Schiferl Rd Bartlett (60103) ***(G-1324)***
Winlind Skincare LLC.....630 789-9408
80 Burr Ridge Pkwy Burr Ridge (60527) ***(G-2736)***
Winn Star Inc.....618 964-1811
395 S Wolf Creek Rd Fl 1 Carbondale (62902) ***(G-2865)***
Winnebago Foundry Inc.....815 389-3533
132 Blackhawk Blvd South Beloit (61080) ***(G-19124)***
Winner Cutting & Stamping Co.....630 963-1800
1245 Warren Ave Downers Grove (60515) ***(G-8111)***
Winnetka Mews Condominium Assn.....847 501-2770
640 Winnetka Mews Winnetka (60093) ***(G-21138)***
Winnetka Sign Co Inc.....847 473-9378
3338 Berwyn Ave Unit 93 North Chicago (60064) ***(G-15325)***
Winning Colors.....815 462-4810
345 Jan St Unit C Manhattan (60442) ***(G-13436)***
Winning Promotions, Vernon Hills *Also called H & H Graphics LLC* ***(G-20057)***
Winning Stitch.....217 348-8279
725 Windsor Rd Charleston (61920) ***(G-3417)***
Winning Streak Inc.....618 277-8191
1580 Decoma Dr Dupo (62239) ***(G-8150)***
Winpak Heat Seal Corp.....309 477-6600
1821 Riverway Dr Pekin (61554) ***(G-16370)***
Winpak Portion Packaging Inc (HQ).....708 753-5700
1111 Winpak Way Sauk Village (60411) ***(G-18401)***
Winscribe Usa Inc (HQ).....773 399-1608
10 S Lasalle St Chicago (60603) ***(G-6645)***
Winsight LLC (HQ).....312 876-0004
300 S Riverside Plz # 1600 Chicago (60606) ***(G-6646)***
Winslyn Industries.....630 401-8051
777 W Thornwood Dr South Elgin (60177) ***(G-19182)***
Winston Pharmaceuticals Inc (HQ).....847 362-8200
100 N Fairway Dr Ste 134 Vernon Hills (60061) ***(G-20111)***
Winston Privacy Inc.....312 282-0162
311 W Monroe St Chicago (60606) ***(G-6647)***
Wintek Electro-Optics Corp (HQ).....734 477-5480
1132 Waukegan Rd Ste 101 Glenview (60025) ***(G-10638)***
Winters Welding Inc.....773 860-7735
7122 S Seeley Ave Chicago (60636) ***(G-6648)***
Winzeler Inc.....708 867-7971
7355 W Wilson Ave Harwood Heights (60706) ***(G-11112)***
Winzeler Gear, Harwood Heights *Also called Winzeler Inc* ***(G-11112)***
Wirco Inc.....217 398-3200
1700 W Washington St Champaign (61821) ***(G-3371)***
Wire Cloth Filter Mfg, Maywood *Also called Jsn Inc* ***(G-13670)***
Wire Mesh LLC.....815 579-8597
42 Marquette Ave Oglesby (61348) ***(G-15844)***
Wireformers Inc.....847 718-1920
500 W Carboy Rd Mount Prospect (60056) ***(G-14582)***
Wireless Chamberlain Products.....800 282-6225
845 N Larch Ave Elmhurst (60126) ***(G-9446)***
Wireless Express Inc Central.....309 689-9933
4732 N University St Peoria (61614) ***(G-16547)***
Wireless USA, Quincy *Also called Wirelessusa Inc* ***(G-16957)***
Wirelessusa Inc.....217 222-4300
2517 W Schneidman Dr E Quincy (62305) ***(G-16957)***
Wiremasters Incorporated.....773 254-3700
1040 W 40th St 1050 Chicago (60609) ***(G-6649)***
Wiretech Inc.....815 986-9614
521 18th Ave Rockford (61104) ***(G-17688)***
Wirfs Industries Inc.....815 344-0635
4021 Main St McHenry (60050) ***(G-13809)***
Wirtz Bev Ill Metro-Chicago, Cicero *Also called Wirtz Beverage Illinois LLC* ***(G-6888)***
Wirtz Beverage Illinois LLC (PA).....847 228-9000
3333 S Laramie Ave Cicero (60804) ***(G-6888)***
Wis - Pak Inc.....217 224-6800
2400 N 30th St Quincy (62301) ***(G-16958)***
Wis-Pak of Quincy, Quincy *Also called Wis - Pak Inc* ***(G-16958)***
Wiscon Corp (PA).....708 450-0074
2050 N 15th Ave Melrose Park (60160) ***(G-13929)***
Wiscon Corp.....708 450-0074
1931 N 15th Ave Melrose Park (60160) ***(G-13930)***
Wisconsin Cheese, Melrose Park *Also called Wiscon Corp* ***(G-13929)***
Wisconsin Cheese, Melrose Park *Also called Wiscon Corp* ***(G-13930)***

Wisconsin Flameproof Shop, Montgomery *Also called Chicago Flameproof WD Spc Corp* ***(G-14240)***
Wisconsin Wilderness Food Pdts.......847 735-8661
918 Timber Ln Lake Forest (60045) ***(G-12323)***
Wisdom Adhesives LLC (HQ).......847 841-7002
1575 Executive Dr Elgin (60123) ***(G-8783)***
Wisdom Adhesives LLC.......847 841-7002
1500 Scottsdale Ct Elgin (60123) ***(G-8784)***
Wisdom Medical Technology LLC.......630 803-6383
19 Stonehill Rd Oswego (60543) ***(G-16033)***
Wise Co Inc.......618 594-4091
3750 Industrial Dr Carlyle (62231) ***(G-2898)***
Wise Construction Services.......630 553-6350
1107 S Bridge St Ste E Yorkville (60560) ***(G-21506)***
Wise Equipment & Rentals Inc.......847 895-5555
1475 Rodenburg Rd Schaumburg (60193) ***(G-18774)***
Wise Hamlin Plastics, Saint Charles *Also called Wise Plastics Technologies Inc* ***(G-18302)***
Wise Plastics Technologies Inc (PA).......847 697-2840
3810 Stern Ave Saint Charles (60174) ***(G-18302)***
Wise Plastics Technologies Inc.......847 697-2840
1601 W Hawthorne Ln West Chicago (60185) ***(G-20659)***
Wisepak Foods LLC.......773 772-0072
4225 N Pulaski Rd Chicago (60641) ***(G-6650)***
Wish Bone Rescue.......309 212-9210
1007 S Madison St Bloomington (61701) ***(G-2108)***
Wishzing.......217 413-8469
320 S East St Dalton City (61925) ***(G-7315)***
Wisniwski Rchard Stl Rule Dies.......773 282-1144
4422 N Elston Ave Chicago (60630) ***(G-6651)***
Wissmiller & Evans Road Eqp.......309 725-3598
102 S Jeffrey St Cooksville (61730) ***(G-7004)***
Wissmiller Welding, Cooksville *Also called Wissmiller & Evans Road Eqp* ***(G-7004)***
Without A Trace Weaver Inc (PA).......773 588-4922
3344 W Bryn Mawr Ave Chicago (60659) ***(G-6652)***
Witron Intgrated Logistics Inc.......847 398-6130
3721 N Ventura Dr Arlington Heights (60004) ***(G-835)***
Witt Disintegrating Service, Addison *Also called Ralph Cody Gravrok* ***(G-266)***
Witte Kendel Die & Mold.......815 233-9270
657 Youngs Ln Freeport (61032) ***(G-10150)***
Wittenstein Inc.......630 540-5300
1249 Humbracht Cir Bartlett (60103) ***(G-1325)***
Wittenstein Arspc Smlation Inc (PA).......630 540-5300
1249 Humbracht Cir Bartlett (60103) ***(G-1326)***
WJ Die Mold Inc.......847 895-6561
915 Estes Ct Schaumburg (60193) ***(G-18775)***
Wk Drainage, Campbell Hill *Also called Wk Machine* ***(G-2819)***
Wk Machine.......618 426-3423
98 Catalpa Ln Campbell Hill (62916) ***(G-2819)***
Wki, Harrisburg *Also called Wilson Kitchens Inc* ***(G-11031)***
Wm F Meyer Co (PA).......773 772-7272
1855 E New York St Aurora (60502) ***(G-1038)***
Wm Huber Cabinet Works.......773 235-7660
2400 N Campbell Ave Chicago (60647) ***(G-6653)***
Wm W Nugent & Co Inc.......847 673-8109
3440 Cleveland St Skokie (60076) ***(G-19056)***
Wm Wrigley Jr Company (HQ).......312 280-4710
930 W Evergreen Ave Chicago (60642) ***(G-6654)***
Wm Wrigley Jr Company.......312 644-2121
825 W Bluff Rd Romeoville (60446) ***(G-17889)***
Wm Wrigley Jr Company.......312 205-2300
1300 N North Branch St Chicago (60642) ***(G-6655)***
Wm Wrigley Jr Company.......312 644-2121
600 W Chicago Ave Ste 500 Chicago (60654) ***(G-6656)***
WMS Games Inc (HQ).......773 728-2300
350 N Orleans St 2000s Chicago (60654) ***(G-6657)***
WMS Gaming, Chicago *Also called Williams Electronic Games De* ***(G-6631)***
WMS Gaming Inc.......773 961-1747
350 N Orleans St 2000s Chicago (60654) ***(G-6658)***
WMS Gaming Inc (HQ).......773 961-1000
350 N Orleans St 2000s Chicago (60654) ***(G-6659)***
WMS Industries Inc (HQ).......847 785-3000
350 N Orleans St 2000s Chicago (60654) ***(G-6660)***
Wns Publication, Erie *Also called Review* ***(G-9474)***
Wns Publications Inc.......815 772-7244
100 E Main St Morrison (61270) ***(G-14349)***
Wnta Studio Line.......815 874-7861
830 Sandy Hollow Rd Rockford (61109) ***(G-17689)***
Wockhardt Holding Corp.......847 967-5600
6451 Main St Morton Grove (60053) ***(G-14449)***
Wodack Electric Tool Corp.......773 287-9866
4627 W Huron St Chicago (60644) ***(G-6661)***
Wold Printing Services Ltd.......847 546-3110
26639 W Commerce Dr # 402 Volo (60073) ***(G-20206)***
Wolf Cabinetry & Ganite.......847 358-9922
1703 N Rand Rd Palatine (60074) ***(G-16176)***
Wolfam Holdings Corporation.......312 407-0100
120 W Madison St Ste 510 Chicago (60602) ***(G-6662)***
Wolfart Maciej.......312 248-3575
6150 N Hamilton Ave Apt 3 Chicago (60659) ***(G-6663)***
Wolfe Burial Vault Co Inc.......815 697-2012
310 N Oak St Chebanse (60922) ***(G-3431)***
Wolfram Research Inc (PA).......217 398-0700
100 Trade Centre Dr 6th Champaign (61820) ***(G-3372)***
Wolfsword Press.......773 403-1144
7144 N Harlem Ave 325 Chicago (60631) ***(G-6664)***
Wolters Custom Cabinets LLC.......618 282-3158
8204 State Route 3 Evansville (62242) ***(G-9591)***
Wolters Kluwer US Inc (HQ).......847 580-5000
2700 Lake Cook Rd Riverwoods (60015) ***(G-17097)***
Woman Christian Temperance Un, Evanston *Also called Wctu Press* ***(G-9587)***
Wonder Kids Inc.......773 437-8025
1719 Brummel St Evanston (60202) ***(G-9589)***
Wonder Tucky Distillery & Btlg.......224 678-4396
315 E South St Woodstock (60098) ***(G-21449)***
Wonderlic Inc.......847 680-4900
400 Lakeview Pkwy Ste 200 Vernon Hills (60061) ***(G-20112)***
Wonderlin Galleries, Normal *Also called Frame Mart Inc* ***(G-15203)***
Wood & Wire, Mundelein *Also called Ww Displays Inc* ***(G-14747)***
Wood Creations Incorporated (PA).......773 772-1375
3918 W Shakespeare Ave Chicago (60647) ***(G-6665)***
Wood Creations Incorporated.......773 772-1375
4627 W Fullerton Ave Chicago (60639) ***(G-6666)***
Wood Dale Pipe & Supply Co, Wood Dale *Also called O Adjust Matic Pump Company* ***(G-21224)***
Wood Energy Inc.......618 244-1590
3007 Broadway St Mount Vernon (62864) ***(G-14644)***
Wood Graphics Inc.......704 872-5798
1101 Windham Pkwy Romeoville (60446) ***(G-17890)***
Wood River Printing & Pubg Co.......618 254-3134
22 N 1st St Wood River (62095) ***(G-21268)***
Wood Shop.......773 994-6666
441 E 75th St Chicago (60619) ***(G-6667)***
Wood Specialties Incorporated.......217 678-8420
964 E 1100 North Rd Bement (61813) ***(G-1716)***
Woodbridge Inc.......847 229-1741
602 Wheeling Rd Wheeling (60090) ***(G-21015)***
Woodcraft Enterprises Inc.......815 485-2787
1928 Clearing Ct Ste A New Lenox (60451) ***(G-15070)***
Wooded Wonderland.......815 777-1223
610 S Devils Ladder Rd Galena (61036) ***(G-10182)***
Wooden Nickel Pub and Grill.......618 288-2141
171 S Main St Glen Carbon (62034) ***(G-10391)***
Wooden World of Richmond Inc.......815 405-4503
7617 Il Route 31 Richmond (60071) ***(G-17026)***
Woodhaven Woodworks, Springfield *Also called Todd Scanlan* ***(G-19466)***
Woodhead Industries LLC (HQ).......847 353-2500
333 Knightsbridge Pkwy # 200 Lincolnshire (60069) ***(G-12802)***
Woodhead Industries Inc.......847 236-9300
3 Parkway North Blvd Deerfield (60015) ***(G-7660)***
Woodhill Cabinetry Design Inc.......815 431-0545
3381 N State Route 23 Ottawa (61350) ***(G-16086)***
Woodland Engineering Company.......847 362-0110
122 Baker Rd Lake Bluff (60044) ***(G-12217)***
Woodland Fence Forest Pdts Inc.......630 393-2220
3 S 264 Hc 59 Warrenville (60555) ***(G-20257)***
Woodland Foods Ltd (PA).......847 625-8600
3751 Sunset Ave Waukegan (60087) ***(G-20519)***
Woodland Plastics Corp.......630 543-1144
1340 W National Ave Addison (60101) ***(G-336)***
Woodlawn Engineering Co Inc.......630 543-3550
325 W Fay Ave Addison (60101) ***(G-337)***
Woodlogic Custom Millwork Inc.......847 640-4500
505 Bonnie Ln Elk Grove Village (60007) ***(G-9311)***
Woodmac Industries Inc.......708 755-3545
3233 Holeman Ave S Chicago Hts (60411) ***(G-18130)***
Woodrow Todd.......618 838-9105
1502 N Olive Rd Flora (62839) ***(G-9697)***
Woods Equipment Company.......815 732-2141
1818 Elmwood Rd Ste 2 Rockford (61103) ***(G-17690)***
Woods Equipment Company.......815 732-2141
2606 S Il Route 2 Oregon (61061) ***(G-15929)***
Woods Manufacturing Co Inc.......630 595-6620
300 Beinoris Dr Wood Dale (60191) ***(G-21258)***
Woodshop, The, Chicago *Also called Wood Shop* ***(G-6667)***
Woodstock Gardens, Woodstock *Also called Contempo Industries Inc* ***(G-21375)***
Woodstock Independent.......815 338-8040
671 E Calhoun St Woodstock (60098) ***(G-21450)***
Woodstreet Cabinet.......708 995-6077
9951 W 190th St Mokena (60448) ***(G-14128)***
Woodward Inc.......847 673-8300
7320 Linder Ave Skokie (60077) ***(G-19057)***
Woodward Inc.......815 877-7441
1 Woodward Loves Park (61111) ***(G-13281)***
Woodward Inc.......815 877-7441
5001 N 2nd St Loves Park (61111) ***(G-13282)***
Woodward Controls Inc (HQ).......847 673-8300
7320 Linder Ave Skokie (60077) ***(G-19058)***

ALPHABETIC

Woodward Governor Hlth Svcs Tr 815 877-7441
5001 N 2nd St Loves Park (61111) **(G-13283)**
Woodward Mpc, Inc., Niles *Also called Mpc Products Corporation* **(G-15149)**
Woodways Industries LLC....616 956-3070
850 S Wabash Ave Ste 300 Chicago (60605) **(G-6668)**
Woodwind Specialists....217 423-4122
890 W William St Decatur (62522) **(G-7570)**
Woodwork Apts LLC....224 595-9691
124 Linden Ave Streamwood (60107) **(G-19604)**
Woodwork Refined Corporation 708 385-7255
5917 W 115th St Alsip (60803) **(G-525)**
Woodworkers Shop Inc (PA)....309 347-5111
13587 E Manito Rd Pekin (61554) **(G-16371)**
Woodworking Unlimited Inc 630 469-7023
23w450 Burdette Ave Carol Stream (60188) **(G-3089)**
Woodwrights Shoppe Inc 309 360-6603
304 Townhall Rd Metamora (61548) **(G-13970)**
Woodx Lumber Inc 331 979-2171
471 W Wrightwood Ave Elmhurst (60126) **(G-9447)**
Woody's Ems, Kankakee *Also called Metzka Inc* **(G-11991)**
Woogl Corporation....847 806-1160
859 Oakton St Elk Grove Village (60007) **(G-9312)**
Woojin Plaimm Inc....708 606-5536
1693 W Imperial Ct Mount Prospect (60056) **(G-14583)**
Woolenwear Co....847 520-9243
739 Pinecrest Dr Prospect Heights (60070) **(G-16848)**
Wordspace Press Limited....773 292-0292
2259 N Kedzie Blvd Chicago (60647) **(G-6669)**
Work Song Productions, Chicago *Also called LMS Innovations Inc* **(G-5247)**
Workforce On Line, Chicago *Also called Crain Communications Inc* **(G-4258)**
Works In Progress Foundation 847 997-8338
24978 W Lakeview Dr Lake Villa (60046) **(G-12372)**
Workshop (PA) 815 777-2211
706 S West St Galena (61036) **(G-10183)**
Workshop Ltd Inc 708 458-3222
5900 W 51st St Bedford Park (60638) **(G-1514)**
Workspace Lyon Products LLC 630 892-8941
420 N Main St Montgomery (60538) **(G-14276)**
World Book Direct Marketing, Chicago *Also called World Book Inc* **(G-6671)**
World Book Direct Marketing, Chicago *Also called World Book Encyclopedia Del* **(G-6670)**
World Book Encyclopedia Del (HQ)....312 729-5800
180 N La Salle St Ste 900 Chicago (60601) **(G-6670)**
World Book Inc (HQ) 312 729-5800
180 N La Salle St Ste 900 Chicago (60601) **(G-6671)**
World Class Tae Kwon....630 870-9293
627 S Route 59 Aurora (60504) **(G-1039)**
World Class Technologies Inc....312 758-3114
70 E Lake St Ste 600 Chicago (60601) **(G-6672)**
World Class Tool & Machine....815 962-2081
698 Quality Ln South Beloit (61080) **(G-19125)**
World Contract Packagers Inc 815 624-6501
14392 De La Tour Dr South Beloit (61080) **(G-19126)**
World Cup Packaging Inc 815 624-6501
14392 De La Tour Dr South Beloit (61080) **(G-19127)**
World Dryer Corporation 800 323-0701
340 County Line Rd Ste A Bensenville (60106) **(G-1914)**
World Explorer, Kempton *Also called Adventures Unlimited* **(G-12013)**
World Fuel Services Inc 305 428-8000
2458 Paysphere Cir Chicago (60674) **(G-6673)**
World Granite Inc....815 288-3350
1220 S Galena Ave Dixon (61021) **(G-7926)**
World Journal Chinese Daily, Chicago *Also called World Journal LLC* **(G-6675)**
World Journal LLC 312 842-8005
2116 S Archer Ave Chicago (60616) **(G-6674)**
World Journal LLC 312 842-8080
2471 S Archer Ave Ste 1 Chicago (60616) **(G-6675)**
World Library Publications....847 678-9300
3708 River Rd Ste 400 Franklin Park (60131) **(G-10087)**
World of Soul Inc....773 840-4839
9131 S La Salle St Chicago (60620) **(G-6676)**
World Richman Mfg Corp 847 468-8898
2505 Bath Rd Elgin (60124) **(G-8785)**
World Washer & Stamping Inc 630 543-6749
763 W Annoreno Dr Addison (60101) **(G-338)**
World Wide Broach, Arlington Heights *Also called National Component Sales Inc* **(G-780)**
World Wide Rotary Die....630 521-9410
104 Foster Ave Bensenville (60106) **(G-1915)**
Worldcolor Effingham, Effingham *Also called Qg LLC* **(G-8420)**
Worlds Finest Chocolate Inc (PA)....773 847-4600
4801 S Lawndale Ave Chicago (60632) **(G-6677)**
Worlds Printing & Spc Co Ltd....312 565-1401
233 N Michigan Ave Chicago (60601) **(G-6678)**
Worldwide Tiles Ltd Inc 708 389-2992
11708 S Mayfield Ave Alsip (60803) **(G-526)**
Worldwide Trans and Diff Corp....773 930-3447
5663 N Mason Ave Chicago (60646) **(G-6679)**
Worldwide Voltage, Rolling Meadows *Also called Sam Electronics Worldwide Inc* **(G-17773)**
Worth Auto Parts, Worth *Also called Auto Head and Engine Exchange* **(G-21454)**
Worth Steel and Machine Co 708 388-6300
4001 W 123rd St Alsip (60803) **(G-527)**
Worth-Pfaff Innovations Inc (PA)....847 940-9305
444 Lake Cook Rd Ste 17 Deerfield (60015) **(G-7661)**
Wortman Printing Company Inc....217 347-3775
1713 S Banker St Effingham (62401) **(G-8432)**
Wound Rounds, Schaumburg *Also called Telemedicine Solutions LLC* **(G-18744)**
Wow Bao LLC 888 496-9226
230 W Huron St Ste 430 Chicago (60654) **(G-6680)**
Wow Signs Inc 847 910-4405
150 Augusta Dr Deerfield (60015) **(G-7662)**
Wozniak Industries Inc....630 820-4052
2560 White Oak Cir Aurora (60502) **(G-1040)**
Wozniak Industries Inc (PA)....630 954-3400
1901 N Roselle Rd Ste 750 Schaumburg (60195) **(G-18776)**
Wozniak Industries Inc....708 458-1220
5757 W 65th St Bedford Park (60638) **(G-1515)**
Wpc Machinery Corp....630 231-7721
3350 W Salt Creek Ln Arlington Heights (60005) **(G-836)**
Wpg US Holdco LLC (HQ)....312 517-3750
330 N Wabash Ave Ste 3750 Chicago (60611) **(G-6681)**
WPGU-FM, Champaign *Also called Illini Media Co* **(G-3306)**
Wpm, Schiller Park *Also called Western Printing Machinery Co* **(G-18854)**
Wrap & Send Services 847 329-2559
4909 Old Orchard Ctr Skokie (60077) **(G-19059)**
Wrap-On Company LLC....708 496-2150
11756 S Austin Ave Alsip (60803) **(G-528)**
Wrapping Inc....773 871-2898
3600 N Lake Shore Dr Chicago (60613) **(G-6682)**
Wrapports LLC (HQ)....312 321-3000
350 N Orleans St Fl 10 Chicago (60654) **(G-6683)**
Wreck Room Inc 630 530-2166
207 W Saint Charles Rd Villa Park (60181) **(G-20177)**
Wrench 773 609-1698
1208 W Hubbard St Chicago (60642) **(G-6684)**
Wri, Woodridge *Also called Western Remac Inc* **(G-21347)**
Wright Advertising, Cicero *Also called Wright Quick Signs Inc* **(G-6889)**
Wright Metals Inc....847 267-1212
1405 Valley Rd Bannockburn (60015) **(G-1212)**
Wright Quick Signs Inc 708 652-6020
1347 S Laramie Ave Cicero (60804) **(G-6889)**
Wright Technologies Inc....847 439-4150
1380 Howard St Elk Grove Village (60007) **(G-9313)**
Wright Tool & Die Inc....815 669-2020
4829 Prime Pkwy McHenry (60050) **(G-13810)**
Wrightwood Technologies Inc....312 238-9512
3440 S Dearborn St Ste 39 Chicago (60616) **(G-6685)**
Wrigley Manufacturing Co LLC (HQ)....312 644-2121
410 N Michigan Ave Chicago (60611) **(G-6686)**
Wrigley Manufacturing Co LLC 630 553-4800
2800 State Route 47 Yorkville (60560) **(G-21507)**
Wrigley Manufacturing Co LLC....312 644-2121
1452 N Cherry Ave Chicago (60642) **(G-6687)**
Wrigley Midwest, Romeoville *Also called Wm Wrigley Jr Company* **(G-17889)**
Wrigley Sales Company LLC....312 644-2121
410 N Michigan Ave C-1 Chicago (60611) **(G-6688)**
Wrigley's, Chicago *Also called Wm Wrigley Jr Company* **(G-6655)**
Wrigley's, Chicago *Also called Wrigley Manufacturing Co LLC* **(G-6686)**
Wrigley's, Yorkville *Also called Wrigley Manufacturing Co LLC* **(G-21507)**
Wrigley's, Chicago *Also called Wrigley Manufacturing Co LLC* **(G-6687)**
Write Stuff 630 365-4425
5n465 Hazelwood Ct Saint Charles (60175) **(G-18303)**
Written Word Inc....630 671-9803
986 Lake St Ste 108 Roselle (60172) **(G-17996)**
Wrt Inc 847 922-2235
400 Industrial Dr South Elgin (60177) **(G-19183)**
Ws Incorporated of Manmouth (PA) 309 734-2161
220 W Franklin Ave Monmouth (61462) **(G-14228)**
Wsol, Aurora *Also called Websolutions Technology Inc* **(G-1033)**
Wsw Industrial Maintenance 773 721-0675
2701 E 105th St Chicago (60617) **(G-6689)**
Wuebbels Repair & Sales LLC 618 648-2227
505 W Market St Mc Leansboro (62859) **(G-13710)**
Wunderlich Diamond Tool Corp....847 437-9904
1330 Howard St Elk Grove Village (60007) **(G-9314)**
Wurst Kitchen Inc (PA)....630 898-9242
638 2nd Ave Aurora (60505) **(G-1171)**
Ww Displays Inc 847 566-6979
401 Wshington Blvd Ste 10 Mundelein (60060) **(G-14747)**
WW Engineering Company LLC....773 376-9494
4321 W 32nd St Chicago (60623) **(G-6690)**
WW Henry Company LP....815 933-8059
150 Mooney Dr Bourbonnais (60914) **(G-2272)**
WW Timbers Inc (PA)....708 423-9112
10150 Virginia Ave Ste K Chicago Ridge (60415) **(G-6811)**
Www.agrinews-Pubs.com, La Salle *Also called Agri-News Publications Inc* **(G-12100)**
Www.lorainesiogisticsllc.com, Chicago *Also called Loraines Logistics LLC* **(G-5259)**
Www.vltg-Cnvrtr-Transformercom, Roselle *Also called Saachi Inc* **(G-17982)**

Wyckoff Advertising Inc 630 260-2525
1203 E Prairie Ave Wheaton (60187) ***(G-20832)***
Wyldewood Cellars 2 LLC 217 469-9463
218 E Lincoln St Saint Joseph (61873) ***(G-18321)***
Wyman and Company 708 532-9064
17324 Oak Park Ave Tinley Park (60477) ***(G-19868)***
Wyzz Inc 217 753-5620
2680 E Cook St Springfield (62703) ***(G-19468)***
X Hale 847 884-6250
4811 N Olcott Ave # 504 Harwood Heights (60706) ***(G-11113)***
X-Cel Technologies Inc 708 802-7400
7800 Graphic Dr Tinley Park (60477) ***(G-19869)***
X-Cel X-Ray, Crystal Lake *Also called Arquilla Inc* ***(G-7163)***
X-Ray Cassette Repair Co Inc 815 356-8181
6107 Lou St Crystal Lake (60014) ***(G-7296)***
X-Tech Innovations Inc 815 962-4127
424 18th Ave Rockford (61104) ***(G-17691)***
Xact Wire EDM Corp 847 516-0903
720 Industrial Dr Ste 126 Cary (60013) ***(G-3197)***
Xaptum Inc 312 852-1595
541 N Fairbanks Ct # 2200 Chicago (60611) ***(G-6691)***
Xcell International Corp 630 323-0107
16400 103rd St Lemont (60439) ***(G-12596)***
Xco International Incorporated 847 428-2400
1082 Rock Road Ln Ste A East Dundee (60118) ***(G-8215)***
Xd Industries Inc 630 766-2843
244 James St Bensenville (60106) ***(G-1916)***
Xd Industries Inc 847 293-0796
836 E Old Willow Rd Prospect Heights (60070) ***(G-16849)***
Xelerated Inc (PA) 408 222-2500
150 N Michigan Ave # 1950 Chicago (60601) ***(G-6692)***
Xellia Phaceuticals Inc 847 986-7980
34121 N Us Highway 45 # 207 Grayslake (60030) ***(G-10807)***
Xellia Pharmaceuticals USA LLC (HQ) 847 947-0254
2150 E Lake Cook Rd # 101 Buffalo Grove (60089) ***(G-2623)***
Xena International Inc (PA) 630 587-2734
910 S Division Ave Polo (61064) ***(G-16759)***
Xena International Inc 815 946-2626
910 S Division Ave Polo (61064) ***(G-16760)***
Xenesis, New Lenox *Also called Onoffblock Inc* ***(G-15046)***
Xenesis, New Lenox *Also called Onoffblock Inc* ***(G-15047)***
Xenia Mfg Inc (PA) 618 678-2218
1507 Church St Xenia (62899) ***(G-21469)***
Xenia Mfg Inc 618 392-7212
1915 Miller Dr Olney (62450) ***(G-15894)***
Xentris Wireless LLC 844 936-8747
1250 N Greenbriar Dr A Addison (60101) ***(G-339)***
Xeris Pharmaceuticals Inc (PA) 844 445-5704
180 N Lasalle St Ste 1600 Chicago (60601) ***(G-6693)***
Xerox Corporation 630 983-0172
1435 Foxhill Rd Naperville (60563) ***(G-14951)***
Xerox Corporation 630 573-1000
2301 W 22nd St Ste 300 Hinsdale (60523) ***(G-11383)***
Xertrex International Inc (PA) 630 773-4020
1530 Glenlake Ave Itasca (60143) ***(G-11755)***
Xform Power and Eqp Sups LLC 773 260-0209
3023 N Clark St Chicago (60657) ***(G-6694)***
Xingfa USA Corporation 630 305-9097
20 N Martingale Rd # 140 Schaumburg (60173) ***(G-18777)***
Xl Manufacture 773 271-8900
2717 W Lawrence Ave Chicago (60625) ***(G-6695)***
Xlogotech Inc 888 244-5152
1312 W Northwest Hwy Palatine (60067) ***(G-16177)***
Xmt Solutions LLC 703 338-9422
1749 N Wells St Apt 2010 Chicago (60614) ***(G-6696)***
Xomi Instruments Co Ltd 847 660-4614
1463 Pinehurst Dr Vernon Hills (60061) ***(G-20113)***
Xpac, Milan *Also called Export Packaging Co Inc* ***(G-14010)***
Xpress Printing & Copying Co 630 980-9600
147 W Irving Park Rd Roselle (60172) ***(G-17997)***
Xpressigns Inc 888 303-0640
2470 E Oakton St Arlington Heights (60005) ***(G-837)***
Xshredders Inc (PA) 847 205-1875
2855 Shermer Rd Northbrook (60062) ***(G-15503)***
Xtrem Graphix Solutions Inc 217 698-6424
1620 S 5th St Ste A Springfield (62703) ***(G-19469)***
Xtreme Cylinders LLC 877 219-9001
7601 191st St Tinley Park (60487) ***(G-19870)***
Xtreme Dzignz 309 633-9311
4001 Constitution Dr Bartonville (61607) ***(G-1337)***
Xtremedata Inc 847 871-0379
999 N Plaza Dr Ste 570 Schaumburg (60173) ***(G-18778)***
Xttrium Laboratories Inc (PA) 773 268-5800
1200 E Business Center Dr Mount Prospect (60056) ***(G-14584)***
Xylem, Cordova *Also called Melyx Inc* ***(G-7010)***
Xylem Inc 847 966-3700
8200 Austin Ave Morton Grove (60053) ***(G-14450)***
Xylem Lnc 847 966-3700
8200 Austin Ave Morton Grove (60053) ***(G-14451)***
Xylem Water Solutions USA Inc 856 467-3636
9661 194th St Mokena (60448) ***(G-14129)***
Y 2 K Electronics Inc 847 238-9024
2574 United Ln Elk Grove Village (60007) ***(G-9315)***
Y T Packing Co 217 522-3345
1129 Taintor Rd Springfield (62702) ***(G-19470)***
Yamada America Inc 847 228-9063
955 E Algonquin Rd Arlington Heights (60005) ***(G-838)***
Yana House 773 874-7120
7120 S Normal Blvd Chicago (60621) ***(G-6697)***
Yanfeng US Automotive 779 552-7300
775 Logistics Dr Belvidere (61008) ***(G-1712)***
Yankee Mold Inc 815 986-1776
1158 Power Rd Machesney Park (61115) ***(G-13384)***
Yanmar (usa) Inc 847 541-1900
901 Corporate Grove Dr Buffalo Grove (60089) ***(G-2624)***
Yargus Manufacturing Inc 217 826-6352
12285 E Main St Marshall (62441) ***(G-13579)***
Yash Technologies Inc 309 755-0433
841 42nd Ave East Moline (61244) ***(G-8248)***
Yaskawa America Inc (HQ) 847 887-7000
2121 Norman Dr Waukegan (60085) ***(G-20520)***
Yaskawa America Inc 847 887-7909
1297 E Walnut Ave Des Plaines (60016) ***(G-7869)***
Yates Complete Concrete, Edwardsville *Also called David Yates* ***(G-8356)***
Yates Motloid, Elmhurst *Also called Bird-X Inc* ***(G-9334)***
Yazdan Essie 847 675-7916
3730 W Morse Ave Lincolnwood (60712) ***(G-12852)***
Ycl International Inc 630 873-0768
3118 Whispering Oaks Ln Woodridge (60517) ***(G-21350)***
Ye Olde Sign Shoppe 847 228-7446
68 N Lively Blvd Elk Grove Village (60007) ***(G-9316)***
Yeager Jl & Associates Inc 847 283-9162
476 Oakwood Ave Lake Forest (60045) ***(G-12324)***
Yello, Chicago *Also called Recsolu Inc* ***(G-5990)***
Yeomans Pump, Aurora *Also called Grundfos Water Utility Inc* ***(G-976)***
Yer Kiln Me LLC 309 606-9007
108 N 7th St Wyoming (61491) ***(G-21464)***
Yes Packaging, Chicago *Also called Yes Print Management Inc* ***(G-6698)***
Yes Print Management Inc 312 226-4444
3636 S Iron St Chicago (60609) ***(G-6698)***
Yesco Chicago, Addison *Also called Omega Sign & Lighting Inc* ***(G-231)***
Yesimpact 765 413-9667
8202 Ripple Rdg Darien (60561) ***(G-7415)***
Yetter Farm Equipment, Colchester *Also called Yetter Manufacturing Company* ***(G-6948)***
Yetter M Co Inc Emp B Tr 309 776-4111
109 S Mcdonough St Colchester (62326) ***(G-6947)***
Yetter Manufacturing Company 309 833-1445
1270 E Murray St Macomb (61455) ***(G-13403)***
Yetter Manufacturing Company (PA) 309 776-3222
109 S Mcdonough St Colchester (62326) ***(G-6948)***
Yfy Jupiter Inc 312 419-8565
445 N Wells St Ste 401 Chicago (60654) ***(G-6699)***
Yg-1 Tool USA, Vernon Hills *Also called Sab Tool Supply Co* ***(G-20090)***
Yhlsoft Inc 844 829-0039
935 W Chestnut St Chicago (60642) ***(G-6700)***
Yield Management Systems LLC 312 665-1595
2626 N Lakeview Ave # 708 Chicago (60614) ***(G-6701)***
Yield360, Morton *Also called 360 Yield Center LLC* ***(G-14352)***
Yinlun Usa Inc 309 291-0843
77 Commerce Dr Morton (61550) ***(G-14387)***
YKK AP America Inc 630 582-9602
1000 Stevenson Ct Ste 101 Roselle (60172) ***(G-17998)***
YMC Corp 312 842-4900
481 W 26th St Chicago (60616) ***(G-6702)***
Yockey Oil Incorporated 618 393-6236
1043 W Main St Olney (62450) ***(G-15895)***
Yoder John 217 676-3430
2580 N 1500 East Rd Blue Mound (62513) ***(G-2142)***
Yoders Portable Buildings LLC (PA) 618 936-2419
5425 Larkspur Rd Sumner (62466) ***(G-19689)***
Yolanda Lorente Ltd (PA) 773 334-4536
4424 N Ravenswood Ave 1 Chicago (60640) ***(G-6703)***
Yoos Imports, Chicago *Also called Evoys Corp* ***(G-4540)***
York Corrugated Container Corp 630 260-2900
120 W Lake Dr Glendale Heights (60139) ***(G-10516)***
York International Corporation 815 946-2351
3820 S Il Route 26 Polo (61064) ***(G-16761)***
York Spring Co 847 695-5978
1551 N La Fox St South Elgin (60177) ***(G-19184)***
Yorke Printe Shoppe Inc 630 627-4960
930 N Lombard Rd Lombard (60148) ***(G-13156)***
Yoshino America Corporation 708 534-1141
2500 Palmer Ave University Park (60484) ***(G-19971)***
Yotta Pet Products Inc 217 466-4777
1977 S Central Ave Paris (61944) ***(G-16247)***
Young Innovations Inc (HQ) 847 458-5400
2260 Wendt St Algonquin (60102) ***(G-397)***

ALPHABETIC

Young Innovations Inc (PA) ALPHABETIC SECTION

Young Innovations Inc (PA) 847 458-5400
2260 Wendt St Algonquin (60102) ***(G-398)***
Young Mydent LLC 631 434-3190
2260 Wendt St Algonquin (60102) ***(G-399)***
Young Os LLC 847 458-5400
2260 Wendt St Algonquin (60102) ***(G-400)***
Young Shin Honey Farm, Mount Prospect *Also called Ys Health Corporation* ***(G-14585)***
Young Shin USA Limited 847 598-3611
1320 Tower Rd Ste 111 Schaumburg (60173) ***(G-18779)***
Youngberg Industries Inc 815 544-2177
6863 Indy Dr Belvidere (61008) ***(G-1713)***
Your Custom Cabinetry Corp 773 290-7247
1609 N 31st Ave Melrose Park (60160) ***(G-13931)***
Your Images Group Inc 847 437-6688
1300 Basswood Rd Ste 200 Schaumburg (60173) ***(G-18780)***
Your Logo Here 708 258-6666
9525 W Laraway Rd Frankfort (60423) ***(G-9853)***
Your Supply Depot Limited 815 568-4115
207 E Grant Hwy Marengo (60152) ***(G-13497)***
Yourfeel Products Corp 708 596-2150
505 W Taft Dr South Holland (60473) ***(G-19250)***
Ys Health Corporation 847 391-9122
411 Kingston Ct Ste A Mount Prospect (60056) ***(G-14585)***
Yusraa Inc 312 608-1916
14828 Cottage Grove Ave Dolton (60419) ***(G-7941)***
Z & L Machining Inc (PA) 847 623-9500
3140 Central Ave Waukegan (60085) ***(G-20521)***
Z Automation Company 847 483-0120
163 N Archer Ave Mundelein (60060) ***(G-14748)***
Z Print Inc 773 685-4878
5257 N Central Ave Chicago (60630) ***(G-6704)***
Z-Modular LLC 312 275-1600
227 W Monroe St Ste 2600 Chicago (60606) ***(G-6705)***
Z-Patch Inc 618 529-2431
800 W Industrial Park Rd Carbondale (62901) ***(G-2866)***
Z-Tech Inc 815 335-7395
1958 S Winnebago Rd Winnebago (61088) ***(G-21122)***
Zabiha Halal Mt Processors Inc 630 620-5000
1715 W Cortland Ct Addison (60101) ***(G-340)***
Zagone Studios LLC 773 509-0610
4533 W North Ave Melrose Park (60160) ***(G-13932)***
Zaibak Bros (PA) 312 564-5800
207 E Ohio St Ste 374 Chicago (60611) ***(G-6706)***
Zainab Enterprises Inc 630 739-0110
684 Phelps Ave Romeoville (60446) ***(G-17891)***
Zakrose Inc 847 372-7309
2100 N Major Ave Chicago (60639) ***(G-6707)***
Zanetis Oil Company 618 262-4593
319 E 8th St Mount Carmel (62863) ***(G-14493)***
Zantech Inc 309 692-8307
7501 N Harker Dr Peoria (61615) ***(G-16548)***
Zapp Noodle 618 979-8863
1407 W Highway 50 Ste 106 O Fallon (62269) ***(G-15586)***
Zapp Tooling Alloys Inc 847 599-0351
1528 Saint Paul Ave Gurnee (60031) ***(G-10945)***
Zaptel Corporation 847 386-8050
836 S Arlington Hts Rd Elk Grove Village (60007) ***(G-9317)***
Zarc International Inc 309 807-2565
529 S Petri Dr Minonk (61760) ***(G-14056)***
Zaxis Factory Inc 888 299-5516
2150 S Canalport Ave Chicago (60608) ***(G-6708)***
Zb Importing Inc (PA) 708 222-8330
5400 W 35th St Cicero (60804) ***(G-6890)***
Zb Importing Inc 708 222-8330
5400 W 35th St Chicago (60804) ***(G-6709)***
Zebra, Lincolnshire *Also called Zih Corp* ***(G-12808)***
Zebra Outlet 312 416-1518
5750 W Bloomingdale Ave # 1 Chicago (60639) ***(G-6710)***
Zebra Retail Solutions LLC 847 634-6700
3 Overlook Pt Lincolnshire (60069) ***(G-12803)***
Zebra Technologies Corporation (PA) 847 634-6700
3 Overlook Pt Lincolnshire (60069) ***(G-12804)***
Zebra Technologies Corporation 847 793-5911
2550 Millbrook Dr Buffalo Grove (60089) ***(G-2625)***
Zebra Technologies Corporation 630 548-1370
1116 Magenta Ct Naperville (60564) ***(G-14993)***
Zebra Technologies Corporation 847 634-6700
6048 Eagle Way Chicago (60678) ***(G-6711)***
Zebra Technologies Intl LLC (HQ) 847 634-6700
3 Overlook Pt Lincolnshire (60069) ***(G-12805)***
Zedpharma 847 295-1950
602 Academy Woods Dr Lake Forest (60045) ***(G-12325)***
Zegers Inc 708 474-7700
16727 Chicago Ave Lansing (60438) ***(G-12525)***
Zeigler Chrysler Dodge 708 956-7700
6539 Ogden Ave Berwyn (60402) ***(G-1963)***
Zeigler Preowned of Chicago, Berwyn *Also called Zeigler Chrysler Dodge* ***(G-1963)***
Zekelman Industries Inc 773 646-4500
1855 E 122nd St Chicago (60633) ***(G-6712)***
Zekelman Industries Inc (PA) 312 275-1600
227 W Monroe St Ste 2600 Chicago (60606) ***(G-6713)***
Zelda's Sweet Shoppe, Skokie *Also called Zeldaco Ltd* ***(G-19060)***
Zeldaco Ltd (PA) 847 674-0033
4113 Main St Skokie (60076) ***(G-19060)***
Zell Co 312 226-9191
329 W 18th St Ste 507 Chicago (60616) ***(G-6714)***
Zeller + Gmelin Corporation 630 443-8800
3820 Ohio Ave Ste 1 Saint Charles (60174) ***(G-18304)***
Zeller Plastik Usa Inc (HQ) 847 247-7900
1515 Franklin Blvd Libertyville (60048) ***(G-12727)***
Zeman Mfg Co 630 960-2300
1996 University Ln Lisle (60532) ***(G-12958)***
Zen Bakery, MA, Flossmoor *Also called Pin Hsiao & Associates LLC* ***(G-9700)***
Zenb US Inc 312 581-6574
950 W Fulton Market Chicago (60607) ***(G-6715)***
Zendavor Signs & Graphics Inc 309 691-8822
2251 W Altorfer Dr Peoria (61615) ***(G-16549)***
Zender Enterprises Ltd 773 282-2293
3692 N Milwaukee Ave Chicago (60641) ***(G-6716)***
Zender Molding Solutions, Chicago *Also called Zender Enterprises Ltd* ***(G-6716)***
Zenfab, Chicago *Also called Zenith Fabricating Company* ***(G-6717)***
Zenith Electronics Corporation (HQ) 847 941-8000
2000 Millbrook Dr Lincolnshire (60069) ***(G-12806)***
Zenith Fabricating Company 773 622-2601
1928 N Leamington Ave Chicago (60639) ***(G-6717)***
Zero Ground LLC 847 360-9500
2340 Ernie Krueger Cir Waukegan (60087) ***(G-20522)***
Zeta Manufacturing Company 708 301-3766
3549 E Reichert Dr Crete (60417) ***(G-7147)***
ZF Active Safety & Elec US LLC 217 826-3011
902 S 2nd St Marshall (62441) ***(G-13580)***
ZF Chassis Components LLC 773 371-4550
3400 E 126th St Chicago (60633) ***(G-6718)***
ZF Chassis Systems Tuscaloosa, Chicago *Also called ZF Chassis Components LLC* ***(G-6718)***
ZF Industries, Vernon Hills *Also called ZF Services LLC* ***(G-20115)***
ZF North America Inc 847 478-6868
777 Hickory Hill Dr Vernon Hills (60061) ***(G-20114)***
ZF Services LLC 847 478-6868
777 Hickory Hill Dr Vernon Hills (60061) ***(G-20115)***
ZF Services North America, Vernon Hills *Also called ZF North America Inc* ***(G-20114)***
ZF TRW Active Pssive Sfety Tec, Marshall *Also called ZF Active Safety & Elec US LLC* ***(G-13580)***
Zg3 Systems LLC 309 745-3398
25232 Spring Creek Rd Washington (61571) ***(G-20285)***
Zhmin Power, Aurora *Also called Astral Power Systems Inc* ***(G-1055)***
Zic Incorporated (PA) 847 680-8833
1535 Abbott Dr Wheeling (60090) ***(G-21016)***
Ziemer Usa Inc 618 462-9301
620 E 3rd St Alton (62002) ***(G-576)***
Ziglers & Mch & Metalworks LLC 815 255-8200
629 Palmyra Rd Dixon (61021) ***(G-7927)***
Zih Corp 847 634-6700
3 Overlook Pt Lincolnshire (60069) ***(G-12807)***
Zih Corp 847 634-6700
3 Overlook Pt Lincolnshire (60069) ***(G-12808)***
Zim Manufacturing Co 773 622-2500
2275 Sprucewood Ave Des Plaines (60018) ***(G-7870)***
Zimco, Chicago *Also called Zimmerman Brush Co* ***(G-6719)***
Zimmer Smith & Associates Inc 217 788-5800
120 E Scarritt St Ste A Springfield (62704) ***(G-19471)***
Zimmerman Brush Co 773 761-6331
6320 N Whipple St Chicago (60659) ***(G-6719)***
Zimmerman Enterprises Inc (PA) 847 297-3177
1216 Rand Rd Des Plaines (60016) ***(G-7871)***
Zing Enterprises LLC 608 201-9490
83 Templeton Dr Ste G Oswego (60543) ***(G-16034)***
Zirlin Interiors Inc 773 334-5530
5540 N Broadway St Chicago (60640) ***(G-6720)***
Zirmed Inc 312 207-0889
1330 W Fulton Market # 300 Chicago (60607) ***(G-6721)***
Zitropack Ltd 630 543-1016
240 S La Londe Ave Addison (60101) ***(G-341)***
Ziv USA Inc 224 735-3961
5410 Newport Dr Ste 38 Rolling Meadows (60008) ***(G-17786)***
Ziyad Brothers Importing, Cicero *Also called Zb Importing Inc* ***(G-6890)***
Zj Industries Inc (PA) 630 543-6400
125 W Factory Rd Addison (60101) ***(G-342)***
Zmf Inc 603 667-1672
8015 Salisbury Ave Lyons (60534) ***(G-13316)***
Zmf Headphones, Lyons *Also called Zmf Inc* ***(G-13316)***
Znl Corporation 815 654-0870
2120 Harlem Rd Loves Park (61111) ***(G-13284)***
Zoes Mfgco LLC 312 666-4018
168 N Sangamon St Chicago (60607) ***(G-6722)***
Zoetis LLC 708 757-2592
400 State St Chicago Heights (60411) ***(G-6787)***

ALPHABETIC SECTION

Zoia Monument Company 815 338-0358
  222 Washington St Woodstock (60098) *(G-21451)*
Zoll-Dental, Niles *Also called Cislak Manufacturing Inc (G-15110)*
Zookbinders Inc 847 272-5745
  151 S Pfingsten Rd Ste K Deerfield (60015) *(G-7663)*
Zopel Engineering Co., Elk Grove Village *Also called Ultra Specialties Incorporated (G-9292)*
Zorch International Inc 312 751-8010
  223 W Erie St Ste 5nw Chicago (60654) *(G-6723)*
Zorin Material Handling Co (PA) 773 342-3818
  1937 W Wolfram St Chicago (60657) *(G-6724)*

Zotos International Inc 847 390-0984
  10600 W Higgins Rd # 415 Rosemont (60018) *(G-18061)*
Zsi-Foster Inc 800 323-7053
  6571 Solutions Ctr Chicago (60677) *(G-6725)*
Zuchem Inc 312 997-2150
  2242 W Harrison St 201-3 Chicago (60612) *(G-6726)*
Zweibel Worldwide Productions 312 751-0503
  212 W Superior St Ste 200 Chicago (60654) *(G-6727)*
Zzzsock LLC 224 330-7364
  501 N Pine St Mount Prospect (60056) *(G-14586)*

PRODUCT INDEX

• Product categories are listed in alphabetical order.

A

ABRASIVE SAND MINING
ABRASIVES
ABRASIVES: Aluminum Oxide Fused
ABRASIVES: Diamond Powder
ABRASIVES: Polishing Rouge
ABRASIVES: Steel Shot
ABRASIVES: Tungsten Carbide
ACCELERATION INDICATORS & SYSTEM COMPONENTS: Aerospace
ACCELERATORS: Electrostatic Particle
ACCELERATORS: Linear
ACCIDENT INSURANCE CARRIERS
ACCOUNTING SVCS, NEC
ACIDS: Hydrochloric
ACIDS: Inorganic
ACIDS: Sulfuric, Oleum
ACRYLIC RESINS
ACTUATORS: Indl, NEC
ADDITIVE BASED PLASTIC MATERIALS: Plasticizers
ADDRESSING SVCS
ADHESIVES
ADHESIVES & SEALANTS
ADHESIVES: Adhesives, plastic
ADHESIVES: Epoxy
ADULT DAYCARE CENTERS
ADVERTISING AGENCIES
ADVERTISING AGENCIES: Consultants
ADVERTISING COPY WRITING SVCS
ADVERTISING CURTAINS
ADVERTISING DISPLAY PRDTS
ADVERTISING REPRESENTATIVES: Electronic Media
ADVERTISING REPRESENTATIVES: Media
ADVERTISING REPRESENTATIVES: Newspaper
ADVERTISING REPRESENTATIVES: Printed Media
ADVERTISING SPECIALTIES, WHOLESALE
ADVERTISING SVCS, NEC
ADVERTISING SVCS: Billboards
ADVERTISING SVCS: Direct Mail
ADVERTISING SVCS: Display
ADVERTISING SVCS: Outdoor
ADVERTISING SVCS: Poster, Exc Outdoor
ADVERTISING SVCS: Poster, Outdoor
ADVERTISING SVCS: Transit
AERIAL WORK PLATFORMS
AEROSOLS
AGENTS & MANAGERS: Entertainers
AGENTS, BROKERS & BUREAUS: Personal Service
AGRICULTURAL CHEMICALS: Trace Elements
AGRICULTURAL CREDIT INSTITUTIONS
AGRICULTURAL EQPT: BARN, SILO, POULTRY, DAIRY/LIVESTOCK MACH
AGRICULTURAL EQPT: Barn Cleaners
AGRICULTURAL EQPT: Cutters & Blowers, Ensilage
AGRICULTURAL EQPT: Elevators, Farm
AGRICULTURAL EQPT: Fertilizing Machinery
AGRICULTURAL EQPT: Fertilizng, Sprayng, Dustng/Irrigatn Mach
AGRICULTURAL EQPT: Fillers & Unloaders, Silo
AGRICULTURAL EQPT: Grade, Clean & Sort Machines, Fruit/Veg
AGRICULTURAL EQPT: Greens Mowing Eqpt
AGRICULTURAL EQPT: Haying Mach, Mowers, Rakes, Stackers, Etc
AGRICULTURAL EQPT: Loaders, Manure & General Utility
AGRICULTURAL EQPT: Planting Machines
AGRICULTURAL EQPT: Spreaders, Fertilizer
AGRICULTURAL EQPT: Storage Bins, Crop
AGRICULTURAL EQPT: Tractors, Farm
AGRICULTURAL EQPT: Trailers & Wagons, Farm
AGRICULTURAL EQPT: Turf & Grounds Eqpt
AGRICULTURAL EQPT: Turf Eqpt, Commercial
AGRICULTURAL EQPT: Weeding Machines
AGRICULTURAL LIMESTONE: Ground
AGRICULTURAL MACHINERY & EQPT REPAIR
AGRICULTURAL MACHINERY & EQPT: Wholesalers
AIR CLEANING SYSTEMS
AIR CONDITIONERS: Motor Vehicle

AIR CONDITIONING & VENTILATION EQPT & SPLYS: Wholesales
AIR CONDITIONING EQPT
AIR CONDITIONING REPAIR SVCS
AIR CONDITIONING UNITS: Complete, Domestic Or Indl
AIR COOLERS: Metal Plate
AIR CURTAINS
AIR MATTRESSES: Plastic
AIR POLLUTION CONTROL EQPT & SPLYS WHOLESALERS
AIR PURIFICATION EQPT
AIR-CONDITIONING SPLY SVCS
AIRCRAFT & AEROSPACE FLIGHT INSTRUMENTS & GUIDANCE SYSTEMS
AIRCRAFT & HEAVY EQPT REPAIR SVCS
AIRCRAFT ASSEMBLY PLANTS
AIRCRAFT CONTROL SYSTEMS: Electronic Totalizing Counters
AIRCRAFT DEALERS
AIRCRAFT ENG/ENG PART: Extrnl Pwr Unt, Hand Inertia Starter
AIRCRAFT ENGINES & ENGINE PARTS: Airfoils
AIRCRAFT ENGINES & ENGINE PARTS: Mount Parts
AIRCRAFT ENGINES & ENGINE PARTS: Nonelectric Starters
AIRCRAFT ENGINES & ENGINE PARTS: Research & Development, Mfr
AIRCRAFT ENGINES & PARTS
AIRCRAFT EQPT & SPLYS WHOLESALERS
AIRCRAFT FLIGHT INSTRUMENT REPAIR SVCS
AIRCRAFT FUELING SVCS
AIRCRAFT HANGAR OPERATION SVCS
AIRCRAFT LIGHTING
AIRCRAFT MAINTENANCE & REPAIR SVCS
AIRCRAFT PARTS & AUX EQPT: Governors, Propeller Feathering
AIRCRAFT PARTS & AUXILIARY EQPT: Aircraft Training Eqpt
AIRCRAFT PARTS & AUXILIARY EQPT: Assys, Subassemblies/Parts
AIRCRAFT PARTS & AUXILIARY EQPT: Blades, Prop, Metal Or Wood
AIRCRAFT PARTS & AUXILIARY EQPT: Bodies
AIRCRAFT PARTS & AUXILIARY EQPT: Body & Wing Assys & Parts
AIRCRAFT PARTS & AUXILIARY EQPT: Body Assemblies & Parts
AIRCRAFT PARTS & AUXILIARY EQPT: Gears, Power Transmission
AIRCRAFT PARTS & AUXILIARY EQPT: Landing Assemblies & Brakes
AIRCRAFT PARTS & AUXILIARY EQPT: Link Trainers/Trng Mech
AIRCRAFT PARTS & AUXILIARY EQPT: Military Eqpt & Armament
AIRCRAFT PARTS & AUXILIARY EQPT: Refueling Eqpt, In Flight
AIRCRAFT PARTS & AUXILIARY EQPT: Research & Development, Mfr
AIRCRAFT PARTS & EQPT, NEC
AIRCRAFT PARTS WHOLESALERS
AIRCRAFT SEATS
AIRCRAFT SERVICING & REPAIRING
AIRCRAFT: Airplanes, Fixed Or Rotary Wing
AIRLOCKS
ALARMS: Burglar
ALARMS: Fire
ALCOHOL, ETHYL: For Beverage Purposes
ALCOHOL, GRAIN: For Beverage Purposes
ALCOHOL: Ethyl & Ethanol
ALCOHOL: Methyl & Methanol, Synthetic
ALKALIES & CHLORINE
ALL-TERRAIN VEHICLE DEALERS
ALLOYS: Additive, Exc Copper Or Made In Blast Furnaces
ALTERNATORS: Automotive
ALUMINUM
ALUMINUM PRDTS
ALUMINUM: Coil & Sheet
ALUMINUM: Rolling & Drawing
AMMONIA & AMMONIUM SALTS

AMMONIUM NITRATE OR AMMONIUM SULFATE
AMMUNITION
AMMUNITION: Small Arms
AMPLIFIERS
AMPLIFIERS: RF & IF Power
AMUSEMENT & RECREATION SVCS, NEC
AMUSEMENT & RECREATION SVCS: Exhibition & Carnival Op Svcs
AMUSEMENT & RECREATION SVCS: Indoor Or Outdoor Court Clubs
AMUSEMENT & RECREATION SVCS: Scuba & Skin Diving Instruction
AMUSEMENT & RECREATION SVCS: Shooting Range
AMUSEMENT & RECREATION SVCS: Tennis Club, Membership
AMUSEMENT & RECREATION SVCS: Tennis Courts, Non-Member
AMUSEMENT & RECREATION SVCS: Theme Park
AMUSEMENT MACHINES: Coin Operated
AMUSEMENT PARK DEVICES & RIDES
AMUSEMENT PARK DEVICES & RIDES: Carnival Mach & Eqpt, NEC
ANALYZERS: Blood & Body Fluid
ANALYZERS: Coulometric, Indl Process
ANALYZERS: Moisture
ANALYZERS: Network
ANALYZERS: Respiratory
ANATOMICAL SPECIMENS & RESEARCH MATERIAL, WHOLESALE
ANESTHETICS: Bulk Form
ANIMAL BASED MEDICINAL CHEMICAL PRDTS
ANIMAL FEED & SUPPLEMENTS: Livestock & Poultry
ANIMAL FEED: Wholesalers
ANIMAL FOOD & SUPPLEMENTS: Bird Food, Prepared
ANIMAL FOOD & SUPPLEMENTS: Bone Meal
ANIMAL FOOD & SUPPLEMENTS: Dog
ANIMAL FOOD & SUPPLEMENTS: Dog & Cat
ANIMAL FOOD & SUPPLEMENTS: Feed Premixes
ANIMAL FOOD & SUPPLEMENTS: Feed Supplements
ANIMAL FOOD & SUPPLEMENTS: Livestock
ANIMAL FOOD & SUPPLEMENTS: Mineral feed supplements
ANIMAL FOOD & SUPPLEMENTS: Pet, Exc Dog & Cat, Canned
ANIMAL FOOD & SUPPLEMENTS: Pet, Exc Dog & Cat, Dry
ANIMAL FOOD & SUPPLEMENTS: Poultry
ANIMAL FOOD & SUPPLEMENTS: Specialty, Mice & Other Pets
ANIMAL OILS: Medicinal Grade, Refined Or Concentrated
ANNEALING: Metal
ANODIZING SVC
ANTENNAS: Receiving
ANTENNAS: Satellite, Household Use
ANTIBIOTICS
ANTIFREEZE
ANTIHISTAMINE PREPARATIONS
ANTIQUE & CLASSIC AUTOMOBILE RESTORATION
ANTIQUE AUTOMOBILE DEALERS
ANTIQUE FURNITURE RESTORATION & REPAIR
ANTIQUE REPAIR & RESTORATION SVCS, EXC FURNITURE & AUTOS
ANTIQUE SHOPS
ANTISCALING COMPOUNDS, BOILER
ANTISEPTICS, MEDICINAL
APPAREL ACCESS STORES
APPAREL DESIGNERS: Commercial
APPLIANCE CORDS: Household Electrical Eqpt
APPLIANCE PARTS: Porcelain Enameled
APPLIANCES, HOUSEHOLD OR COIN OPERATED: Laundry Dryers
APPLIANCES, HOUSEHOLD: Ice Boxes, Metal Or Wood
APPLIANCES, HOUSEHOLD: Kitchen, Major, Exc Refrigs & Stoves
APPLIANCES, HOUSEHOLD: Laundry Machines, Incl Coin-Operated
APPLIANCES, HOUSEHOLD: Refrigs, Mechanical & Absorption
APPLIANCES, HOUSEHOLD: Sweepers, Electric
APPLIANCES: Household, Refrigerators & Freezers

PRODUCT INDEX

APPLIANCES: Major, Cooking
APPLIANCES: Small, Electric
APPLICATIONS SOFTWARE PROGRAMMING
APPRENTICESHIP TRAINING SCHOOLS
AQUARIUMS & ACCESS: Glass
AQUARIUMS & ACCESS: Plastic
ARCHITECTURAL SVCS
ARMATURE REPAIRING & REWINDING SVC
ARMATURES: Ind
ART & ORNAMENTAL WARE: Pottery
ART DEALERS & GALLERIES
ART DESIGN SVCS
ART GOODS & SPLYS WHOLESALERS
ART GOODS, WHOLESALE
ART MARBLE: Concrete
ART RESTORATION SVC
ART SCHOOL, EXC COMMERCIAL
ARTIFICIAL FLOWERS & TREES
ARTIST'S MATERIALS & SPLYS
ARTISTS' AGENTS & BROKERS
ARTISTS' MATERIALS, WHOLESALE
ARTISTS' MATERIALS: Brushes, Air
ARTISTS' MATERIALS: Chalks, Carpenters', Blackboard, Etc
ARTISTS' MATERIALS: Clay, Modeling
ARTISTS' MATERIALS: Eraser Guides & Shields
ARTISTS' MATERIALS: Ink, Drawing, Black & Colored
ARTISTS' MATERIALS: Lettering Instruments
ARTISTS' MATERIALS: Palettes
ARTISTS' MATERIALS: Pencils & Pencil Parts
ARTISTS' MATERIALS: Wax
ARTWORK: Framed
ASBESTOS PRDTS: Insulation, Molded
ASBESTOS PRDTS: Wick
ASBESTOS PRODUCTS
ASBESTOS REMOVAL EQPT
ASH TRAYS: Stamped Metal
ASPHALT & ASPHALT PRDTS
ASPHALT COATINGS & SEALERS
ASPHALT MIXTURES WHOLESALERS
ASPHALT PLANTS INCLUDING GRAVEL MIX TYPE
ASSEMBLING & PACKAGING SVCS: Cosmetic Kits
ASSEMBLING SVC: Clocks
ASSEMBLING SVC: Plumbing Fixture Fittings, Plastic
ASSOCIATIONS: Bar
ASSOCIATIONS: Business
ASSOCIATIONS: Real Estate Management
ASSOCIATIONS: Trade
ATOMIZERS
AUCTION SVCS: Livestock
AUCTION SVCS: Motor Vehicle
AUDIO & VIDEO EQPT, EXC COMMERCIAL
AUDIO & VIDEO TAPES WHOLESALERS
AUDIO COMPONENTS
AUDIO ELECTRONIC SYSTEMS
AUTO & HOME SUPPLY STORES: Auto & Truck Eqpt & Parts
AUTO & HOME SUPPLY STORES: Automotive Access
AUTO & HOME SUPPLY STORES: Automotive parts
AUTO & HOME SUPPLY STORES: Batteries, Automotive & Truck
AUTO & HOME SUPPLY STORES: Speed Shops, Incl Race Car Splys
AUTO & HOME SUPPLY STORES: Truck Eqpt & Parts
AUTO SPLYS & PARTS, NEW, WHSLE: Exhaust Sys, Mufflers, Etc
AUTOMATIC REGULATING CNTRLS: Liq Lvl, Residential/Comm Heat
AUTOMATIC REGULATING CNTRLS: Steam Press, Residential/ Comm
AUTOMATIC REGULATING CONTROL: Building Svcs Monitoring, Auto
AUTOMATIC REGULATING CONTROLS: AC & Refrigeration
AUTOMATIC REGULATING CONTROLS: Appliance, Exc Air-Cond/Refr
AUTOMATIC REGULATING CONTROLS: Gas Burner, Automatic
AUTOMATIC REGULATING CONTROLS: Gradual Switches, Pneumatic
AUTOMATIC REGULATING CONTROLS: Hydronic Circulator, Auto
AUTOMATIC REGULATING CONTROLS: Incinerator, Residential/Comm
AUTOMATIC REGULATING CONTROLS: Pneumatic Relays, Air-Cond
AUTOMATIC REGULATING CONTROLS: Refrigeration, Pressure

AUTOMATIC REGULATING CTRLS: Damper, Pneumatic Or Electric
AUTOMATIC TELLER MACHINES
AUTOMATIC VENDING MACHINES: Mechanisms & Parts
AUTOMOBILE FABRICS, WHOLESALE
AUTOMOBILE FINANCE LEASING
AUTOMOBILE STORAGE GARAGE
AUTOMOBILES & OTHER MOTOR VEHICLES WHOLESALERS
AUTOMOBILES: Wholesalers
AUTOMOTIVE & TRUCK GENERAL REPAIR SVC
AUTOMOTIVE BODY SHOP
AUTOMOTIVE BODY, PAINT & INTERIOR REPAIR & MAINTENANCE SVC
AUTOMOTIVE DEALERS, NEC
AUTOMOTIVE EMISSIONS TESTING SVCS
AUTOMOTIVE EXHAUST REPAIR SVC
AUTOMOTIVE EXTERIOR REPAIR SVCS
AUTOMOTIVE GLASS REPLACEMENT SHOPS
AUTOMOTIVE LETTERING & PAINTING SVCS
AUTOMOTIVE PAINT SHOP
AUTOMOTIVE PARTS, ACCESS & SPLYS
AUTOMOTIVE PARTS: Plastic
AUTOMOTIVE PRDTS: Rubber
AUTOMOTIVE RADIATOR REPAIR SHOPS
AUTOMOTIVE REPAIR SHOPS: Alternators/Generator, Rebuild/Rpr
AUTOMOTIVE REPAIR SHOPS: Diesel Engine Repair
AUTOMOTIVE REPAIR SHOPS: Electrical Svcs
AUTOMOTIVE REPAIR SHOPS: Engine Rebuilding
AUTOMOTIVE REPAIR SHOPS: Engine Repair
AUTOMOTIVE REPAIR SHOPS: Frame Repair Shops
AUTOMOTIVE REPAIR SHOPS: Machine Shop
AUTOMOTIVE REPAIR SHOPS: Muffler Shop, Sale/Rpr/Installation
AUTOMOTIVE REPAIR SHOPS: Torque Converter Repair
AUTOMOTIVE REPAIR SHOPS: Trailer Repair
AUTOMOTIVE REPAIR SHOPS: Truck Engine Repair, Exc Indl
AUTOMOTIVE REPAIR SVC
AUTOMOTIVE SPLYS & PARTS, NEW, WHOL: Testing Eqpt, Electric
AUTOMOTIVE SPLYS & PARTS, NEW, WHOLESALE: Brakes
AUTOMOTIVE SPLYS & PARTS, NEW, WHOLESALE: Clutches
AUTOMOTIVE SPLYS & PARTS, NEW, WHOLESALE: Engines/Eng Parts
AUTOMOTIVE SPLYS & PARTS, NEW, WHOLESALE: Seat Covers
AUTOMOTIVE SPLYS & PARTS, NEW, WHOLESALE: Splys
AUTOMOTIVE SPLYS & PARTS, NEW, WHOLESALE: Stampings
AUTOMOTIVE SPLYS & PARTS, NEW, WHOLESALE: Testing Eqpt, Eng
AUTOMOTIVE SPLYS & PARTS, NEW, WHOLESALE: Tools & Eqpt
AUTOMOTIVE SPLYS & PARTS, NEW, WHOLESALE: Trailer Parts
AUTOMOTIVE SPLYS & PARTS, NEW, WHOLESALE: Wheels
AUTOMOTIVE SPLYS & PARTS, USED, WHOLESALE
AUTOMOTIVE SPLYS & PARTS, WHOLESALE, NEC
AUTOMOTIVE SPLYS/PARTS, NEW, WHOL: Body Rpr/Paint Shop Splys
AUTOMOTIVE SVCS, EXC REPAIR & CARWASHES: Customizing
AUTOMOTIVE SVCS, EXC REPAIR & CARWASHES: Maintenance
AUTOMOTIVE SVCS, EXC REPAIR: Truck Wash
AUTOMOTIVE SVCS, EXC REPAIR: Washing & Polishing
AUTOMOTIVE SVCS, EXC RPR/CARWASHES: High Perf Auto Rpr/Svc
AUTOMOTIVE TOPS INSTALLATION OR REPAIR: Canvas Or Plastic
AUTOMOTIVE TOWING SVCS
AUTOMOTIVE TRANSMISSION REPAIR SVC
AUTOMOTIVE UPHOLSTERY SHOPS
AUTOMOTIVE WELDING SVCS
AUTOMOTIVE: Bodies
AUTOMOTIVE: Seat Frames, Metal
AUTOMOTIVE: Seating
AUTOTRANSFORMERS: Electric
AVIATION SCHOOL
AWNING REPAIR SHOP

AWNINGS & CANOPIES
AWNINGS & CANOPIES: Awnings, Fabric, From Purchased Matls
AWNINGS & CANOPIES: Canopies, Fabric, From Purchased Matls
AWNINGS & CANOPIES: Fabric
AWNINGS: Fiberglass
AWNINGS: Metal
AXLES

B

BABY FORMULA
BACKHOES
BADGES, WHOLESALE
BADGES: Identification & Insignia
BAGS & CONTAINERS: Textile, Exc Sleeping
BAGS & SACKS: Shipping & Shopping
BAGS: Cellophane
BAGS: Duffle, Canvas, Made From Purchased Mater als
BAGS: Flour, Made From Purchased Materials
BAGS: Food Storage & Frozen Food, Plastic
BAGS: Food Storage & Trash, Plastic
BAGS: Garment & Wardrobe, Plastic Film
BAGS: Paper
BAGS: Paper, Made From Purchased Materials
BAGS: Plastic
BAGS: Plastic & Pliofilm
BAGS: Plastic, Made From Purchased Materials
BAGS: Rubber Or Rubberized Fabric
BAGS: Shipping
BAGS: Textile
BAGS: Trash, Plastic Film, Made From Purchased Materials
BAGS: Vacuum cleaner, Made From Purchased Materials
BAGS: Wardrobe, Closet Access, Made From Purchased Materials
BAIT, FISHING, WHOLESALE
BAKERIES, COMMERCIAL: On Premises Baking Only
BAKERIES: On Premises Baking & Consumption
BAKERY MACHINERY
BAKERY PRDTS, FROZEN: Wholesalers
BAKERY PRDTS: Bagels, Fresh Or Frozen
BAKERY PRDTS: Bakery Prdts, Partially Cooked, Exc frozen
BAKERY PRDTS: Bread, All Types, Fresh Or Frozen
BAKERY PRDTS: Cakes, Bakery, Exc Frozen
BAKERY PRDTS: Cakes, Bakery, Frozen
BAKERY PRDTS: Charlotte Russe, Exc Frozen
BAKERY PRDTS: Cookies
BAKERY PRDTS: Cookies & crackers
BAKERY PRDTS: Crackers
BAKERY PRDTS: Croissants, Frozen
BAKERY PRDTS: Doughnuts, Exc Frozen
BAKERY PRDTS: Doughnuts, Frozen
BAKERY PRDTS: Dry
BAKERY PRDTS: Frozen
BAKERY PRDTS: Rice Cakes
BAKERY PRDTS: Wholesalers
BAKERY: Wholesale Or Wholesale & Retail Combined
BALERS
BALLASTS: Fluorescent
BALLOONS: Hot Air
BALLOONS: Rubber Laminated Metal Foil
BALLOONS: Toy & Advertising, Rubber
BANKS: Commercial, NEC
BANNERS: Fabric
BANQUET HALL FACILITIES
BAR
BARBECUE EQPT
BARGES BUILDING & REPAIR
BARRELS: Shipping, Metal
BARRICADES: Metal
BARS, COLD FINISHED: Steel, From Purchased Hot-Rolled
BARS, PIPES, PLATES & SHAPES: Lead/Lead Alloy Bars, Pipe
BARS, PLATES & SHEETS: Zinc & Zinc Alloy Bars, Plates, Etc
BARS: Cargo, Stabilizing, Metal
BARS: Concrete Reinforcing, Fabricated Steel
BASES, BEVERAGE
BATH SALTS
BATH SHOPS
BATHROOM ACCESS & FITTINGS: Vitreous China & Earthenware
BATHROOM FIXTURES: Plastic
BATTERIES, EXC AUTOMOTIVE: Wholesalers
BATTERIES: Alkaline, Cell Storage

PRODUCT INDEX

BATTERIES: Lead Acid, Storage
BATTERIES: Nickel-Cadmium
BATTERIES: Rechargeable
BATTERIES: Storage
BATTERIES: Wet
BATTERY CASES: Plastic Or Plastics Combination
BATTERY CHARGERS
BATTERY CHARGERS: Storage, Motor & Engine Generator Type
BEARINGS
BEARINGS & PARTS Ball
BEARINGS: Ball & Roller
BEARINGS: Railroad Car Journal
BEARINGS: Roller & Parts
BEAUTY & BARBER SHOP EQPT
BEAUTY & BARBER SHOP EQPT & SPLYS WHOLESALERS
BEAUTY SALONS
BED SHEETING, COTTON
BEDDING, BEDSPREAD, BLANKET/SHEET: Pillowcase, Purchd Mtrl
BEDDING, BEDSPREADS, BLANKETS & SHEETS: Comforters & Quilts
BEDS: Hospital
BEDS: Inflatable
BEDSPREADS & BED SETS, FROM PURCHASED MATERIALS
BEDSPREADS, COTTON
BEEKEEPERS' SPLYS: Honeycomb Foundations
BEER & ALE WHOLESALERS
BEER & ALE, WHOLESALE: Beer & Other Fermented Malt Liquors
BEER PUMP COIL CLEANING & REPAIR SVCS
BEER, WINE & LIQUOR STORES
BEER, WINE & LIQUOR STORES: Beer, Packaged
BEER, WINE & LIQUOR STORES: Wine
BEER, WINE & LIQUOR STORES: Wine & Beer
BELLOWS
BELLOWS ASSEMBLIES: Missiles, Metal
BELTING: Plastic
BELTING: Rubber
BELTS: Seat, Automotive & Aircraft
BENCHES, WORK : Factory
BENCHES: Seating
BENTONITE MINING
BEVERAGE BASES & SYRUPS
BEVERAGE POWDERS
BEVERAGE PRDTS: Brewers' Grain
BEVERAGE PRDTS: Malt Syrup
BEVERAGE PRDTS: Malt, Barley
BEVERAGE PRDTS: Malt, Corn
BEVERAGE STORES
BEVERAGE, NONALCOHOLIC: Iced Tea/Fruit Drink, Bottled/Canned
BEVERAGES, ALCOHOLIC: Ale
BEVERAGES, ALCOHOLIC: Beer
BEVERAGES, ALCOHOLIC: Beer & Ale
BEVERAGES, ALCOHOLIC: Bourbon Whiskey
BEVERAGES, ALCOHOLIC: Brandy & Brandy Spirits
BEVERAGES, ALCOHOLIC: Cocktails
BEVERAGES, ALCOHOLIC: Distilled Liquors
BEVERAGES, ALCOHOLIC: Gin
BEVERAGES, ALCOHOLIC: Liquors, Malt
BEVERAGES, ALCOHOLIC: Near Beer
BEVERAGES, ALCOHOLIC: Rum
BEVERAGES, ALCOHOLIC: Scotch Whiskey
BEVERAGES, ALCOHOLIC: Vodka
BEVERAGES, ALCOHOLIC: Wines
BEVERAGES, BEER & ALE, WHOLESALE: Ale
BEVERAGES, NONALCOHOLIC: Bottled & canned soft drinks
BEVERAGES, NONALCOHOLIC: Carbonated
BEVERAGES, NONALCOHOLIC: Carbonated, Canned & Bottled, Etc
BEVERAGES, NONALCOHOLIC: Cider
BEVERAGES, NONALCOHOLIC: Flavoring extracts & syrups, nec
BEVERAGES, NONALCOHOLIC: Fruit Juices, Concentrtd, Fountain
BEVERAGES, NONALCOHOLIC: Soft Drinks, Canned & Bottled, Etc
BEVERAGES, WINE & DISTILLED ALCOHOLIC, WHOLESALE: Liquor
BEVERAGES, WINE & DISTILLED ALCOHOLIC, WHOLESALE: Neutral Sp

BEVERAGES, WINE & DISTILLED ALCOHOLIC, WHOLESALE: Wine
BIBLE SCHOOL
BICYCLE REPAIR SHOP
BICYCLE SHOPS
BICYCLES, PARTS & ACCESS
BIDETS: Vitreous China
BILLETS: Steel
BILLFOLD INSERTS: Plastic
BILLIARD & POOL TABLES & SPLYS
BILLIARD EQPT & SPLYS WHOLESALERS
BILLING & BOOKKEEPING SVCS
BINDING SVC: Books & Manuals
BINDING SVC: Trade
BIOLOGICAL PRDTS: Blood Derivatives
BIOLOGICAL PRDTS: Coagulation
BIOLOGICAL PRDTS: Exc Diagnostic
BIOLOGICAL PRDTS: Toxin, Viruses/Simlr Substncs, Incl Venom
BIOLOGICAL PRDTS: Vaccines
BIOLOGICAL PRDTS: Veterinary
BLACKBOARDS & CHALKBOARDS
BLACKBOARDS: Slate
BLACKSMITH SHOP
BLADES: Knife
BLADES: Saw, Chain Type
BLADES: Saw, Hand Or Power
BLANKBOOKS & LOOSELEAF BINDERS
BLANKBOOKS: Albums
BLANKBOOKS: Albums, Record
BLANKBOOKS: Ledgers & Ledger Sheets
BLANKBOOKS: Memorandum, Printed
BLANKBOOKS: Passbooks, Bank, Etc
BLANKBOOKS: Scrapbooks
BLANKETS, FROM PURCHASED MATERIALS
BLAST FURNACE & RELATED PRDTS
BLASTING SVC: Sand, Metal Parts
BLINDS & SHADES: Vertical
BLINDS : Window
BLINDS, WOOD
BLOCKS & BRICKS: Concrete
BLOCKS: Drystack Interlocking, Concrete
BLOCKS: Landscape Or Retaining Wall, Concrete
BLOCKS: Paving, Composition
BLOCKS: Paving, Concrete
BLOCKS: Paving, Cut Stone
BLOCKS: Sewer & Manhole, Concrete
BLOCKS: Standard, Concrete Or Cinder
BLOCKS: Tackle, Metal
BLOOD RELATED HEALTH SVCS
BLOWER FILTER UNITS: Furnace Blowers
BLOWERS & FANS
BLOWERS & FANS
BLUEPRINTING SVCS
BOAT BLDG/RPRG: Life Rafts, Noninflatable, Rubber/Plastic
BOAT BUILDING & REPAIR
BOAT BUILDING & REPAIRING: Fiberglass
BOAT BUILDING & REPAIRING: Motorboats, Inboard Or Outboard
BOAT BUILDING & REPAIRING: Pontoons, Exc Aircraft & Inflat
BOAT DEALERS
BOAT DEALERS: Motor
BOAT DEALERS: Outboard
BOAT REPAIR SVCS
BOATS & OTHER MARINE EQPT: Plastic
BOBBINS: Textile Spinning, Made From Purchased Materials
BODIES: Truck & Bus
BODY PARTS: Automobile, Stamped Metal
BOILER & HEATING REPAIR SVCS
BOILER REPAIR SHOP
BOILERS & BOILER SHOP WORK
BOILERS: Low-Pressure Heating, Steam Or Hot Water
BOLTS: Metal
BOOK ENDS, METAL
BOOK STORES
BOOK STORES: Children's
BOOK STORES: College
BOOK STORES: Religious
BOOKING AGENCIES, THEATRICAL
BOOKS, WHOLESALE
BOOKS: Memorandum, Exc Printed, From Purchased Materials
BOOSTERS: Feeder Voltage, Electric
BOOTHS: Spray, Sheet Metal, Prefabricated

BOOTS: Women's
BORATE COMPOUND MINING: Natural
BORING MILL
BOTTLE CAPS & RESEALERS: Plastic
BOTTLED GAS DEALERS: Propane
BOTTLED WATER DELIVERY
BOTTLES: Plastic
BOTTLES: Vacuum
BOWLING CENTERS
BOWLING EQPT & SPLYS
BOX & CARTON MANUFACTURING EQPT
BOXES & CRATES: Rectangular, Wood
BOXES & SHOOK: Nailed Wood
BOXES: Cash & Stamp, Stamped Metal
BOXES: Corrugated
BOXES: Junction, Electric
BOXES: Mail Or Post Office, Collection/Storage, Sheet Metal
BOXES: Outlet, Electric Wiring Device
BOXES: Packing & Shipping, Metal
BOXES: Paperboard, Folding
BOXES: Paperboard, Set-Up
BOXES: Plastic
BOXES: Solid Fiber
BOXES: Stamped Metal
BOXES: Wirebound, Wood
BOXES: Wooden
BRAKES & BRAKE PARTS
BRAKES: Metal Forming
BRAKES: Press
BRASS & BRONZE PRDTS: Die-casted
BRASS FOUNDRY, NEC
BRASS ROLLING & DRAWING
BRASSWORK: Ornamental, Structural
BRAZING SVCS
BRAZING: Metal
BRICK, STONE & RELATED PRDTS WHOLESALERS
BRICKS : Ceramic Glazed, Clay
BRICKS : Paving, Clay
BRICKS: Clay
BRICKS: Concrete
BRIDAL SHOPS
BRIEFCASES
BROACHING MACHINES
BROADCASTING & COMMS EQPT: Antennas, Transmitting/Comms
BROADCASTING & COMMS EQPT: Rcvr-Transmitter Unt, Transceiver
BROADCASTING & COMMUNICATION EQPT: Transmit-Receiver, Radio
BROADCASTING & COMMUNICATIONS EQPT: Cellular Radio Telephone
BROADCASTING & COMMUNICATIONS EQPT: Studio Eqpt, Radio & TV
BROADCASTING & COMMUNICATIONS EQPT: Transmitting, Radio/TV
BROKERS' SVCS
BROKERS, MARINE TRANSPORTATION
BROKERS: Business
BROKERS: Commodity Contracts
BROKERS: Contract Basis
BROKERS: Food
BROKERS: Log & Lumber
BROKERS: Mortgage, Arranging For Loans
BROKERS: Printing
BRONZE FOUNDRY, NEC
BRONZE ROLLING & DRAWING
BROOMS
BROOMS & BRUSHES
BROOMS & BRUSHES: Household Or Indl
BROOMS & BRUSHES: Paint & Varnish
BROOMS & BRUSHES: Paint Rollers
BROOMS & BRUSHES: Push
BROOMS & BRUSHES: Street Sweeping, Hand Or Machine
BRUSHES
BRUSHES & BRUSH STOCK CONTACTS: Electric
BUCKLES & PARTS
BUFFING FOR THE TRADE
BUILDING & OFFICE CLEANING SVCS
BUILDING & STRUCTURAL WOOD MBRS: Timbers, Struct, Lam Lumber
BUILDING & STRUCTURAL WOOD MEMBERS
BUILDING CLEANING & MAINTENANCE SVCS
BUILDING COMPONENT CLEANING SVCS
BUILDING COMPONENTS: Structural Steel
BUILDING INSPECTION SVCS

PRODUCT INDEX

BUILDING MAINTENANCE SVCS, EXC REPAIRS
BUILDING PRDTS & MATERIALS DEALERS
BUILDING PRDTS: Concrete
BUILDING PRDTS: Stone
BUILDINGS & COMPONENTS: Prefabricated Metal
BUILDINGS: Farm & Utility
BUILDINGS: Farm, Prefabricated Or Portable, Wood
BUILDINGS: Mobile, For Commercial Use
BUILDINGS: Portable
BUILDINGS: Prefabricated, Metal
BUILDINGS: Prefabricated, Wood
BUILDINGS: Prefabricated, Wood
BULLETIN BOARDS: Wood
BUMPERS: Motor Vehicle
BURIAL VAULTS, FIBERGLASS
BURIAL VAULTS: Concrete Or Precast Terrazzo
BURNERS: Gas, Domestic
BURNERS: Gas, Indl
BURNERS: Gas-Oil, Combination
BUS BARS: Electrical
BUSES: Wholesalers
BUSINESS & SECRETARIAL SCHOOLS
BUSINESS ACTIVITIES: Non-Commercial Site
BUSINESS COLLEGE OR SCHOOLS
BUSINESS FORMS WHOLESALERS
BUSINESS FORMS: Printed, Continuous
BUSINESS FORMS: Printed, Manifold
BUSINESS FORMS: Unit Sets, Manifold
BUSINESS MACHINE REPAIR, ELECTRIC
BUSINESS SUPPORT SVCS
BUSINESS TRAINING SVCS
BUTADIENE: Indl, Organic, Chemical
BUTTONS

C

CABINETS & CASES: Show, Display & Storage, Exc Wood
CABINETS: Bathroom Vanities, Wood
CABINETS: Entertainment
CABINETS: Entertainment Units, Household, Wood
CABINETS: Factory
CABINETS: Filing, Wood
CABINETS: Kitchen, Metal
CABINETS: Kitchen, Wood
CABINETS: Office, Metal
CABINETS: Office, Wood
CABINETS: Radio & Television, Metal
CABINETS: Show, Display, Etc, Wood, Exc Refrigerated
CABINETS: Television, Plastic
CABLE & OTHER PAY TELEVISION DISTRIBUTION
CABLE & PAY TELEVISION SVCS: Direct Broadcast Satellite
CABLE & PAY TELEVISION SVCS: Subscription
CABLE TELEVISION
CABLE TELEVISION PRDTS
CABLE WIRING SETS: Battery, Internal Combustion Engines
CABLE: Coaxial
CABLE: Fiber
CABLE: Fiber Optic
CABLE: Noninsulated
CABLE: Ropes & Fiber
CABLE: Steel, Insulated Or Armored
CABS: Indl Trucks & Tractors
CAGES: Wire
CALCULATING & ACCOUNTING EQPT
CALENDARS, WHOLESALE
CALIBRATING SVCS, NEC
CALLIGRAPHER
CAMERAS & RELATED EQPT: Photographic
CAMPGROUNDS
CAMSHAFTS
CAN LIDS & ENDS
CANDLE SHOPS
CANDLES
CANDLES: Wholesalers
CANDY & CONFECTIONS: Cake Ornaments
CANDY & CONFECTIONS: Candy Bars, Including Chocolate Covered
CANDY & CONFECTIONS: Chocolate Candy, Exc Solid Chocolate
CANDY & CONFECTIONS: Fruit & Fruit Peel
CANDY & CONFECTIONS: Fudge
CANDY & CONFECTIONS: Jellybeans
CANDY & CONFECTIONS: Marshmallows
CANDY & CONFECTIONS: Popcorn Balls/Other Trtd Popcorn Prdts
CANDY MAKING GOODS & SPLYS, WHOLESALE

CANDY, NUT & CONFECTIONERY STORE: Popcorn, Incl Caramel Corn
CANDY, NUT & CONFECTIONERY STORES: Candy
CANDY, NUT & CONFECTIONERY STORES: Confectionery
CANDY, NUT & CONFECTIONERY STORES: Produced For Direct Sale
CANDY: Chocolate From Cacao Beans
CANDY: Hard
CANDY: Soft
CANES & TRIMMINGS, EXC PRECIOUS METAL
CANNED SPECIALTIES
CANS: Composite Foil-Fiber, Made From Purchased Materials
CANS: Garbage, Stamped Or Pressed Metal
CANS: Metal
CANS: Oil, Metal
CANVAS PRDTS
CANVAS PRDTS, WHOLESALE
CANVAS PRDTS: Air Cushions & Mattresses
CANVAS PRDTS: Convertible Tops, Car/Boat, Fm Purchased Mtrl
CANVAS PRDTS: Shades, Made From Purchased Materials
CAPACITORS & CONDENSERS
CAPACITORS: AC, Motors Or Fluorescent Lamp Ballasts
CAPACITORS: NEC
CAPS & TOPS: Bottle, Stamped Metal
CAPS: Plastic
CAR WASH EQPT
CAR WASHES
CARBIDES
CARBON & GRAPHITE PRDTS, NEC
CARBON BLACK
CARBON PAPER & INKED RIBBONS
CARBON REMOVING SOLVENT
CARBON SPECIALTIES Electrical Use
CARBURETORS
CARDBOARD PRDTS, EXC DIE-CUT
CARDIOVASCULAR SYSTEM DRUGS, EXC DIAGNOSTIC
CARDS, PLASTIC, UNPRINTED, WHOLESALE
CARDS: Color
CARDS: Greeting
CARDS: Identification
CARPET & UPHOLSTERY CLEANING SVCS
CARPETS & RUGS: Tufted
CARPETS, RUGS & FLOOR COVERING
CARPETS: Wilton
CARPORTS: Prefabricated Metal
CARRIER EQPT: Telephone Or Telegraph
CARRYING CASES, WHOLESALE
CARS: Electric
CASES, WOOD
CASES: Attache'
CASES: Carrying
CASES: Jewelry
CASES: Nonrefrigerated, Exc Wood
CASES: Packing, Nailed Or Lock Corner, Wood
CASES: Plastic
CASES: Sample Cases
CASES: Shipping, Nailed Or Lock Corner, Wood
CASH REGISTERS WHOLESALERS
CASINGS: Sheet Metal
CASINO HOTELS & MOTELS
CASKETS & ACCESS
CASKETS WHOLESALERS
CAST STONE: Concrete
CASTERS
CASTINGS GRINDING: For The Trade
CASTINGS: Aerospace, Aluminum
CASTINGS: Aluminum
CASTINGS: Brass, NEC, Exc Die
CASTINGS: Bronze, NEC, Exc Die
CASTINGS: Die, Aluminum
CASTINGS: Die, Copper & Copper Alloy
CASTINGS: Die, Lead & Zinc
CASTINGS: Die, Magnesium & Magnesium-Base Alloy
CASTINGS: Die, Nonferrous
CASTINGS: Die, Titanium
CASTINGS: Die, Zinc
CASTINGS: Ductile
CASTINGS: Gray Iron
CASTINGS: Lead
CASTINGS: Machinery, Aluminum
CASTINGS: Machinery, Copper Or Copper-Base Alloy
CASTINGS: Machinery, Nonferrous, Exc Die or Aluminum Copper
CASTINGS: Precision

CASTINGS: Steel
CASTINGS: Zinc
CAT BOX FILLER
CATALOG & MAIL-ORDER HOUSES
CATALOG SALES
CATALYSTS: Chemical
CATAPULTS
CATCH BASIN COVERS: Concrete
CATERERS
CAULKING COMPOUNDS
CELLULOID PRDTS
CELLULOSE DERIVATIVE MATERIALS
CEMENT & CONCRETE RELATED PRDTS & EQPT: Bituminous
CEMENT ROCK: Crushed & Broken
CEMENT: Clay Refractory
CEMENT: High Temperature, Refractory, Nonclay
CEMENT: Hydraulic
CEMENT: Masonry
CEMENT: Portland
CEMETERIES
CEMETERIES: Real Estate Operation
CEMETERY & FUNERAL DIRECTOR'S EQPT & SPLYS WHOLESALERS
CEMETERY MEMORIAL DEALERS
CERAMIC FIBER
CERAMIC FLOOR & WALL TILE WHOLESALERS
CHAIN: Welded, Made From Purchased Wire
CHAINS: Forged
CHAMBERS: Fumigating, Metal Plate
CHANDELIERS: Commercial
CHANGE MAKING MACHINES
CHARCOAL: Activated
CHASING SVC: Metal
CHASSIS: Automobile Trailer
CHASSIS: Motor Vehicle
CHEESE WHOLESALERS
CHEMICAL ELEMENTS
CHEMICAL PROCESSING MACHINERY & EQPT
CHEMICAL SPLYS FOR FOUNDRIES
CHEMICAL: Sodm Compnds/Salts, Inorg, Exc Rfnd Sodm Chloride
CHEMICALS & ALLIED PRDTS WHOLESALERS, NEC
CHEMICALS & ALLIED PRDTS, WHOL: Food Additives/Preservatives
CHEMICALS & ALLIED PRDTS, WHOL: Gases, Compressed/Liquefied
CHEMICALS & ALLIED PRDTS, WHOLESALE: Aerosols
CHEMICALS & ALLIED PRDTS, WHOLESALE: Alcohols
CHEMICALS & ALLIED PRDTS, WHOLESALE: Chemicals, Indl
CHEMICALS & ALLIED PRDTS, WHOLESALE: Chemicals, Indl & Heavy
CHEMICALS & ALLIED PRDTS, WHOLESALE: Chemicals, Rustproofing
CHEMICALS & ALLIED PRDTS, WHOLESALE: Detergent/Soap
CHEMICALS & ALLIED PRDTS, WHOLESALE: Detergents
CHEMICALS & ALLIED PRDTS, WHOLESALE: Dry Ice
CHEMICALS & ALLIED PRDTS, WHOLESALE: Gelatin
CHEMICALS & ALLIED PRDTS, WHOLESALE: Indl Gases
CHEMICALS & ALLIED PRDTS, WHOLESALE: Oxygen
CHEMICALS & ALLIED PRDTS, WHOLESALE: Plastics Film
CHEMICALS & ALLIED PRDTS, WHOLESALE: Plastics Materials, NEC
CHEMICALS & ALLIED PRDTS, WHOLESALE: Plastics Prdts, NEC
CHEMICALS & ALLIED PRDTS, WHOLESALE: Plastics Sheets & Rods
CHEMICALS & ALLIED PRDTS, WHOLESALE: Polishes, NEC
CHEMICALS & ALLIED PRDTS, WHOLESALE: Polyurethane Prdts
CHEMICALS & ALLIED PRDTS, WHOLESALE: Resins
CHEMICALS & ALLIED PRDTS, WHOLESALE: Resins, Plastics
CHEMICALS & ALLIED PRDTS, WHOLESALE: Resins, Synthetic
CHEMICALS & ALLIED PRDTS, WHOLESALE: Sealants
CHEMICALS & ALLIED PRDTS, WHOLESALE: Silicon Lubricants
CHEMICALS & ALLIED PRDTS, WHOLESALE: Spec Clean/Sanitation
CHEMICALS & ALLIED PRDTS, WHOLESALE: Syn Resin, Rub/Plastic

PRODUCT INDEX

CHEMICALS & OTHER PRDTS DERIVED FROM COKING
CHEMICALS, AGRICULTURE: Wholesalers
CHEMICALS: Agricultural
CHEMICALS: Alcohols
CHEMICALS: Alkali Metals, Lithium, Cesium, Francium/Rubidium
CHEMICALS: Aluminum Compounds
CHEMICALS: Aluminum Sulfate
CHEMICALS: Anhydrous Ammonia
CHEMICALS: Bleaching Powder, Lime Bleaching Compounds
CHEMICALS: Copper Compounds Or Salts, Inorganic
CHEMICALS: Fluorine, Elemental
CHEMICALS: Fuel Tank Or Engine Cleaning
CHEMICALS: High Purity Grade, Organic
CHEMICALS: High Purity, Refined From Technical Grade
CHEMICALS: Hydrogen Peroxide
CHEMICALS: Inorganic, NEC
CHEMICALS: Lead Compounds/Salts, Inorganic, Not Pigments
CHEMICALS: Medicinal
CHEMICALS: Medicinal, Organic, Uncompounded, Bulk
CHEMICALS: Mercury, Redistilled
CHEMICALS: NEC
CHEMICALS: Nonmetallic Compounds
CHEMICALS: Organic, NEC
CHEMICALS: Phosphates, Defluorinated/Ammoniated, Exc Fertlr
CHEMICALS: Potash Alum
CHEMICALS: Potassium Compound/Salt, Exc Hydroxide/Carbonate
CHEMICALS: Reagent Grade, Refined From Technical Grade
CHEMICALS: Sulfur Chloride
CHEMICALS: Sulfur, Incl Rcvrd/Refined, Fm Sour Natural Gas
CHEMICALS: Water Treatment
CHEMICALS: Zinc Chloride
CHEWING GUM
CHICKEN SLAUGHTERING & PROCESSING
CHILDBIRTH PREPARATION CLINIC
CHILDREN'S WEAR STORES
CHIMNEY CAPS: Concrete
CHIMNEY CLEANING SVCS
CHINA & GLASS REPAIR SVCS
CHINA FIRING & DECORATING SVCS, TO INDIVIDUAL ORDER
CHIROPRACTORS' OFFICES
CHLORINE
CHOCOLATE, EXC CANDY FROM BEANS: Chips, Powder, Block, Syrup
CHOCOLATE, EXC CANDY FROM PURCH CHOC: Chips, Powder, Block
CHRISTMAS NOVELTIES, WHOLESALE
CHRISTMAS TREE LIGHTING SETS: Electric
CHROMATOGRAPHY EQPT
CHUCKS
CHURCHES
CHUTES & TROUGHS
CHUTES: Metal Plate
CIGAR & CIGARETTE HOLDERS
CIGARETTE & CIGAR PRDTS & ACCESS
CIGARETTE FILTERS
CIGARETTE STORES
CIRCUIT BOARD REPAIR SVCS
CIRCUIT BOARDS, PRINTED: Television & Radio
CIRCUIT BOARDS: Wiring
CIRCUIT BREAKERS
CIRCUIT BREAKERS: Air
CIRCUITS, INTEGRATED: Hybrid
CIRCUITS: Electronic
CLAIMS ADJUSTING SVCS
CLAMPS & COUPLINGS: Hose
CLAMPS & SHORES: Column
CLAMPS: Ground, Electric-Wiring Devices
CLAMPS: Metal
CLAY MINING, COMMON
CLAYS, EXC KAOLIN & BALL
CLEANING & DESCALING SVC: Metal Prdts
CLEANING & DYEING PLANTS, EXC RUGS
CLEANING COMPOUNDS: Rifle Bore
CLEANING EQPT: Blast, Dustless
CLEANING EQPT: Carpet Sweepers, Exc Household Elec Vacuum
CLEANING EQPT: Commercial
CLEANING EQPT: Dirt Sweeping Units, Indl
CLEANING EQPT: Floor Washing & Polishing, Commercial
CLEANING EQPT: High Pressure

CLEANING OR POLISHING PREPARATIONS, NEC
CLEANING PRDTS: Ammonia, Household
CLEANING PRDTS: Automobile Polish
CLEANING PRDTS: Bleaches, Household, Dry Or Liquid
CLEANING PRDTS: Deodorants, Nonpersonal
CLEANING PRDTS: Disinfectants, Household Or Indl Plant
CLEANING PRDTS: Drain Pipe Solvents Or Cleaners
CLEANING PRDTS: Drycleaning Preparations
CLEANING PRDTS: Floor Waxes
CLEANING PRDTS: Indl Plant Disinfectants Or Deodorants
CLEANING PRDTS: Laundry Preparations
CLEANING PRDTS: Polishing Preparations & Related Prdts
CLEANING PRDTS: Rug, Upholstery/Dry Clng Detergents/Spotters
CLEANING PRDTS: Sanitation Preparations
CLEANING PRDTS: Sanitation Preps, Disinfectants/Deodorants
CLEANING PRDTS: Specialty
CLEANING PRDTS: Window Cleaning Preparations
CLIPPERS: Hair, Human
CLIPS & FASTENERS, MADE FROM PURCHASED WIRE
CLOSURES: Closures, Stamped Metal
CLOSURES: Plastic
CLOTHESPINS: Plastic
CLOTHING & ACCESS STORES
CLOTHING & ACCESS, WOMEN, CHILD & INFANT, WHSLE: Sportswear
CLOTHING & ACCESS, WOMEN, CHILDREN & INFANT, WHOL: Handbags
CLOTHING & ACCESS, WOMEN, CHILDREN & INFANT, WHOL: Uniforms
CLOTHING & ACCESS, WOMEN, CHILDREN/INFANT, WHOL: Outerwear
CLOTHING & ACCESS: Costumes, Masquerade
CLOTHING & ACCESS: Costumes, Theatrical
CLOTHING & ACCESS: Handicapped
CLOTHING & ACCESS: Hospital Gowns
CLOTHING & ACCESS: Men's Miscellaneous Access
CLOTHING & ACCESS: Regalia
CLOTHING & APPAREL STORES: Custom
CLOTHING & FURNISHINGS, MEN'S & BOYS', WHOLESALE: Hats
CLOTHING & FURNISHINGS, MEN'S & BOYS', WHOLESALE: Shirts
CLOTHING & FURNISHINGS, MEN'S & BOYS', WHOLESALE: Umbrellas
CLOTHING & FURNISHINGS, MEN'S & BOYS', WHOLESALE: Uniforms
CLOTHING & FURNISHINGS, MENS & BOYS, WHOL: Sportswear/Work
CLOTHING & FURNISHINGS, MENS & BOYS, WHOLESALE: Apprl Belts
CLOTHING STORES, NEC
CLOTHING STORES: Formal Wear
CLOTHING STORES: Lingerie, Outerwear
CLOTHING STORES: Shirts, Custom Made
CLOTHING STORES: T-Shirts, Printed, Custom
CLOTHING STORES: Uniforms & Work
CLOTHING STORES: Unisex
CLOTHING STORES: Work
CLOTHING/ACCESS, WOMEN, CHILDREN/INFANT, WHOL: Apparel Belt
CLOTHING: Academic Vestments
CLOTHING: Access
CLOTHING: Access, Women's & Misses'
CLOTHING: Anklets & Socks
CLOTHING: Aprons, Harness
CLOTHING: Aprons, Waterproof, From Purchased Materials
CLOTHING: Athletic & Sportswear, Men's & Boys'
CLOTHING: Athletic & Sportswear, Women's & Girls'
CLOTHING: Baker, Barber, Lab/Svc Ind Apparel, Washable, Men
CLOTHING: Band Uniforms
CLOTHING: Bathing Suits & Swimwear, Knit
CLOTHING: Blouses, Women's & Girls'
CLOTHING: Bras & Corsets, Maternity
CLOTHING: Bridal Gowns
CLOTHING: Capes, Exc Fur/Rubber, Womens, Misses & Juniors
CLOTHING: Caps, Baseball
CLOTHING: Children & Infants'
CLOTHING: Children's, Girls'
CLOTHING: Clergy Vestments
CLOTHING: Coats & Suits, Men's & Boys'
CLOTHING: Coats, Overcoats & Vests

CLOTHING: Cold Weather Knit Outerwear, Including Ski Wear
CLOTHING: Collar & Cuff Sets, Knit
CLOTHING: Costumes
CLOTHING: Disposable
CLOTHING: Dresses
CLOTHING: Garments, Indl, Men's & Boys
CLOTHING: Gowns & Dresses, Wedding
CLOTHING: Gowns, Plastic
CLOTHING: Hats & Caps, NEC
CLOTHING: Hats & Caps, Police
CLOTHING: Hats & Caps, Uniform
CLOTHING: Hats & Headwear, Knit
CLOTHING: Hats, Silk
CLOTHING: Hosiery, Pantyhose & Knee Length, Sheer
CLOTHING: Hospital, Men's
CLOTHING: Housecoats, Mens & Womens, From Purchased Mtrls
CLOTHING: Jackets, Field, Military
CLOTHING: Jackets, Tailored Men's & Boys'
CLOTHING: Jeans, Men's & Boys'
CLOTHING: Jerseys, Knit
CLOTHING: Leather & sheep-lined clothing
CLOTHING: Maternity
CLOTHING: Men's & boy's clothing, nec
CLOTHING: Neckwear
CLOTHING: Outerwear, Knit
CLOTHING: Outerwear, Women's & Misses' NEC
CLOTHING: Robes & Dressing Gowns
CLOTHING: Scarves, Men's & Boys'
CLOTHING: Service Apparel, Women's
CLOTHING: Shirts
CLOTHING: Shirts & T-Shirts, Knit
CLOTHING: Shirts, Dress, Men's & Boys'
CLOTHING: Shirts, Sports & Polo, Men's & Boys'
CLOTHING: Socks
CLOTHING: Sportswear, Women's
CLOTHING: Suits, Men's & Boys', From Purchased Materials
CLOTHING: Sweaters & Sweater Coats, Knit
CLOTHING: Sweaters, Men's & Boys'
CLOTHING: T-Shirts & Tops, Knit
CLOTHING: T-Shirts & Tops, Women's & Girls'
CLOTHING: Ties, Neck, Men's & Boys', From Purchased Material
CLOTHING: Trousers & Slacks, Men's & Boys'
CLOTHING: Underwear, Women's & Children's
CLOTHING: Uniforms & Vestments
CLOTHING: Uniforms, Ex Athletic, Women's, Misses' & Juniors'
CLOTHING: Uniforms, Military, Men/Youth, Purchased Materials
CLOTHING: Uniforms, Policemen's, From Purchased Materials
CLOTHING: Uniforms, Team Athletic
CLOTHING: Uniforms, Work
CLOTHING: Warm Weather Knit Outerwear, Including Beachwear
CLOTHING: WarmUp, Jogging & Sweat Suits, Girls' & Children's
CLOTHING: Waterproof Outerwear
CLOTHING: Work, Men's
CLUTCHES OR BRAKES: Electromagnetic
CLUTCHES, EXC VEHICULAR
COAL MINING EXPLORATION & TEST BORING SVC
COAL MINING SERVICES
COAL MINING SVCS: Anthracite, Contract Basis
COAL MINING: Anthracite, Underground
COAL MINING: Bituminous & Lignite Surface
COAL MINING: Bituminous Coal & Lignite-Surface Mining
COAL MINING: Bituminous Underground
COAL MINING: Bituminous, Strip
COAL, MINERALS & ORES, WHOLESALE: Copper Ore
COATED OR PLATED PRDTS
COATERS: High Vacuum, Metal Plate
COATING COMPOUNDS: Tar
COATING SVC
COATING SVC: Aluminum, Metal Prdts
COATING SVC: Hot Dip, Metals Or Formed Prdts
COATING SVC: Metals & Formed Prdts
COATING SVC: Metals, With Plastic Or Resins
COATING SVC: Rust Preventative
COATING SVC: Silicon
COATINGS: Air Curing
COATINGS: Epoxy
COATINGS: Polyurethane
COCKTAIL LOUNGE

PRODUCT INDEX

COFFEE SVCS
COIL WINDING SVC
COILS & ROD: Extruded, Aluminum
COILS & TRANSFORMERS
COILS: Electric Motors Or Generators
COILS: Pipe
COIN-OPERATED LAUNDRY
COINS & TOKENS: Non-Currency
COKE OVEN PRDTS, NEC
COKE OVEN PRDTS: Beehive
COKE: Petroleum
COLLECTION AGENCY, EXC REAL ESTATE
COLLECTOR RINGS: Electric Motors Or Generators
COLLEGES, UNIVERSITIES & PROFESSIONAL SCHOOLS
COLOGNES
COLOR LAKES OR TONERS
COLOR PIGMENTS
COLORS IN OIL, EXC ARTISTS'
COLORS: Pigments, Inorganic
COLORS: Pigments, Organic
COMBS, EXC HARD RUBBER
COMMERCIAL & INDL SHELVING WHOLESALERS
COMMERCIAL & OFFICE BUILDINGS RENOVATION & REPAIR
COMMERCIAL ART & GRAPHIC DESIGN SVCS
COMMERCIAL ART & ILLUSTRATION SVCS
COMMERCIAL CONTAINERS WHOLESALERS
COMMERCIAL EQPT WHOLESALERS, NEC
COMMERCIAL EQPT, WHOLESALE: Bakery Eqpt & Splys
COMMERCIAL EQPT, WHOLESALE: Coffee Brewing Eqpt & Splys
COMMERCIAL EQPT, WHOLESALE: Comm Cooking & Food Svc Eqpt
COMMERCIAL EQPT, WHOLESALE: Display Eqpt, Exc Refrigerated
COMMERCIAL EQPT, WHOLESALE: Neon Signs
COMMERCIAL EQPT, WHOLESALE: Restaurant, NEC
COMMERCIAL EQPT, WHOLESALE: Scales, Exc Laboratory
COMMERCIAL EQPT, WHOLESALE: Store Fixtures & Display Eqpt
COMMERCIAL LAUNDRY EQPT
COMMERCIAL PHOTOGRAPHIC STUDIO
COMMERCIAL PRINTING & NEWSPAPER PUBLISHING COMBINED
COMMERCIAL SECTOR REG, LICENSING & INSP, GOVT: Insurance
COMMODITY CONTRACTS BROKERS, DEALERS
COMMON SAND MINING
COMMUNICATIONS EQPT & SYSTEMS, NEC
COMMUNICATIONS EQPT WHOLESALERS
COMMUNICATIONS EQPT: Microwave
COMMUNICATIONS SVCS
COMMUNICATIONS SVCS: Cellular
COMMUNICATIONS SVCS: Data
COMMUNICATIONS SVCS: Electronic Mail
COMMUNICATIONS SVCS: Facsimile Transmission
COMMUNICATIONS SVCS: Internet Connectivity Svcs
COMMUNICATIONS SVCS: Internet Host Svcs
COMMUNICATIONS SVCS: Online Svc Providers
COMMUNICATIONS SVCS: Proprietary Online Svcs Networks
COMMUNICATIONS SVCS: Signal Enhancement Network Svcs
COMMUNICATIONS SVCS: Telephone Or Video
COMMUNICATIONS SVCS: Telephone, Local
COMMUNICATIONS SVCS: Telephone, Local & Long Distance
COMMUNITY DEVELOPMENT GROUPS
COMPACT LASER DISCS: Prerecorded
COMPACTORS: Trash & Garbage, Residential
COMPOST
COMPRESSORS, AIR CONDITIONING: Wholesalers
COMPRESSORS: Air & Gas
COMPRESSORS: Air & Gas, Including Vacuum Pumps
COMPRESSORS: Refrigeration & Air Conditioning Eqpt
COMPRESSORS: Repairing
COMPUTER & COMPUTER SOFTWARE STORES
COMPUTER & COMPUTER SOFTWARE STORES: Peripheral Eqpt
COMPUTER & COMPUTER SOFTWARE STORES: Personal Computers
COMPUTER & COMPUTER SOFTWARE STORES: Printers & Plotters
COMPUTER & COMPUTER SOFTWARE STORES: Software & Access
COMPUTER & COMPUTER SOFTWARE STORES: Software, Bus/Non-Game
COMPUTER & DATA PROCESSING EQPT REPAIR & MAINTENANCE
COMPUTER & OFFICE MACHINE MAINTENANCE & REPAIR
COMPUTER & SFTWR STORE: Modem, Monitor, Terminal/Disk Drive
COMPUTER DATA ESCROW SVCS
COMPUTER DISKETTES WHOLESALERS
COMPUTER FORMS
COMPUTER GRAPHICS SVCS
COMPUTER INTERFACE EQPT: Indl Process
COMPUTER PERIPHERAL EQPT REPAIR & MAINTENANCE
COMPUTER PERIPHERAL EQPT, NEC
COMPUTER PERIPHERAL EQPT, WHOLESALE
COMPUTER PERIPHERAL EQPT: Graphic Displays, Exc Terminals
COMPUTER PERIPHERAL EQPT: Input Or Output
COMPUTER PROCESSING SVCS
COMPUTER PROGRAMMING SVCS
COMPUTER PROGRAMMING SVCS: Custom
COMPUTER RELATED MAINTENANCE SVCS
COMPUTER RELATED SVCS, NEC
COMPUTER SERVICE BUREAU
COMPUTER SOFTWARE DEVELOPMENT
COMPUTER SOFTWARE DEVELOPMENT & APPLICATIONS
COMPUTER SOFTWARE SYSTEMS ANALYSIS & DESIGN: Custom
COMPUTER SOFTWARE WRITERS
COMPUTER SOFTWARE WRITERS: Freelance
COMPUTER STORAGE DEVICES, NEC
COMPUTER STORAGE UNITS: Auxiliary
COMPUTER SYSTEM SELLING SVCS
COMPUTER SYSTEMS ANALYSIS & DESIGN
COMPUTER TERMINALS
COMPUTER TERMINALS: CRT
COMPUTER TIME-SHARING
COMPUTER TRAINING SCHOOLS
COMPUTER-AIDED DESIGN SYSTEMS SVCS
COMPUTERS, NEC
COMPUTERS, NEC, WHOLESALE
COMPUTERS, PERIPHERALS & SOFTWARE, WHOLESALE: Printers
COMPUTERS, PERIPHERALS & SOFTWARE, WHOLESALE: Software
COMPUTERS, PERIPHERALS/SFTWR, WHOL: Anti-Static Eqpt/Devices
COMPUTERS: Personal
CONCENTRATES, DRINK
CONCENTRATES, FLAVORING, EXC DRINK
CONCRETE BUILDING PRDTS WHOLESALERS
CONCRETE CURING & HARDENING COMPOUNDS
CONCRETE PRDTS
CONCRETE PRDTS, PRECAST, NEC
CONCRETE REINFORCING MATERIAL
CONCRETE: Dry Mixture
CONCRETE: Ready-Mixed
CONDENSERS & CONDENSING UNITS: Air Conditioner
CONDENSERS: Refrigeration
CONDUITS & FITTINGS: Electric
CONDUITS: Concrete
CONFECTIONERY PRDTS WHOLESALERS
CONFECTIONS & CANDY
CONFINEMENT SURVEILLANCE SYS MAINTENANCE & MONITORING SVCS
CONNECTORS & TERMINALS: Electrical Device Uses
CONNECTORS: Cord, Electric
CONNECTORS: Electrical
CONNECTORS: Electronic
CONNECTORS: Power, Electric
CONSERVATION PROGRAMS ADMINISTRATION SVCS
CONSTRUCTION & MINING MACHINERY WHOLESALERS
CONSTRUCTION & ROAD MAINTENANCE EQPT: Drags, Road
CONSTRUCTION EQPT REPAIR SVCS
CONSTRUCTION EQPT: Attachments
CONSTRUCTION EQPT: Attachments, Snow Plow
CONSTRUCTION EQPT: Attachments, Subsoiler, Tractor Mounted
CONSTRUCTION EQPT: Backhoes, Tractors, Cranes & Similar Eqpt
CONSTRUCTION EQPT: Bucket Or Scarifier Teeth
CONSTRUCTION EQPT: Cabs
CONSTRUCTION EQPT: Crane Carriers
CONSTRUCTION EQPT: Cranes
CONSTRUCTION EQPT: Hammer Mills, Port, Incl Rock/Ore Crush
CONSTRUCTION EQPT: Loaders, Shovel, Self-Propelled
CONSTRUCTION EQPT: Rock Crushing Machinery, Portable
CONSTRUCTION EQPT: Roofing Eqpt
CONSTRUCTION EQPT: Tractors
CONSTRUCTION EQPT: Tractors, Crawler
CONSTRUCTION EQPT: Trucks, Off-Highway
CONSTRUCTION EQPT: Wrecker Hoists, Automobile
CONSTRUCTION MATERIALS WHOLESALERS
CONSTRUCTION MATERIALS, WHOL: Concrete/Cinder Bldg Prdts
CONSTRUCTION MATERIALS, WHOLESALE: Aggregate
CONSTRUCTION MATERIALS, WHOLESALE: Air Ducts, Sheet Metal
CONSTRUCTION MATERIALS, WHOLESALE: Architectural Metalwork
CONSTRUCTION MATERIALS, WHOLESALE: Awnings
CONSTRUCTION MATERIALS, WHOLESALE: Block, Concrete & Cinder
CONSTRUCTION MATERIALS, WHOLESALE: Brick, Exc Refractory
CONSTRUCTION MATERIALS, WHOLESALE: Building Stone, Granite
CONSTRUCTION MATERIALS, WHOLESALE: Building Stone, Marble
CONSTRUCTION MATERIALS, WHOLESALE: Building, Exterior
CONSTRUCTION MATERIALS, WHOLESALE: Cement
CONSTRUCTION MATERIALS, WHOLESALE: Ceramic, Exc Refractory
CONSTRUCTION MATERIALS, WHOLESALE: Clay, Exc Refractory
CONSTRUCTION MATERIALS, WHOLESALE: Concrete Mixtures
CONSTRUCTION MATERIALS, WHOLESALE: Doors, Garage
CONSTRUCTION MATERIALS, WHOLESALE: Doors, Sliding
CONSTRUCTION MATERIALS, WHOLESALE: Drywall Materials
CONSTRUCTION MATERIALS, WHOLESALE: Fiberglass Building Mat
CONSTRUCTION MATERIALS, WHOLESALE: Glass
CONSTRUCTION MATERIALS, WHOLESALE: Grain Storage Bins
CONSTRUCTION MATERIALS, WHOLESALE: Gravel
CONSTRUCTION MATERIALS, WHOLESALE: Insulation, Thermal
CONSTRUCTION MATERIALS, WHOLESALE: Joists
CONSTRUCTION MATERIALS, WHOLESALE: Limestone
CONSTRUCTION MATERIALS, WHOLESALE: Lockers
CONSTRUCTION MATERIALS, WHOLESALE: Masons' Materials
CONSTRUCTION MATERIALS, WHOLESALE: Millwork
CONSTRUCTION MATERIALS, WHOLESALE: Molding, All Materials
CONSTRUCTION MATERIALS, WHOLESALE: Pallets, Wood
CONSTRUCTION MATERIALS, WHOLESALE: Paving Materials
CONSTRUCTION MATERIALS, WHOLESALE: Prefabricated Structures
CONSTRUCTION MATERIALS, WHOLESALE: Roof, Asphalt/Sheet Metal
CONSTRUCTION MATERIALS, WHOLESALE: Roofing & Siding Material
CONSTRUCTION MATERIALS, WHOLESALE: Sand
CONSTRUCTION MATERIALS, WHOLESALE: Septic Tanks
CONSTRUCTION MATERIALS, WHOLESALE: Sewer Pipe, Clay
CONSTRUCTION MATERIALS, WHOLESALE: Stone, Crushed Or Broken
CONSTRUCTION MATERIALS, WHOLESALE: Tile & Clay Prdts
CONSTRUCTION MATERIALS, WHOLESALE: Veneer
CONSTRUCTION MATERIALS, WHOLESALE: Windows
CONSTRUCTION MATLS, WHOL: Composite Board Prdts, Woodboard
CONSTRUCTION MATLS, WHOL: Lumber, Rough, Dressed/Finished
CONSTRUCTION MATLS, WHOLESALE: Soil Erosion Cntrl Fabrics

PRODUCT INDEX

CONSTRUCTION MTRLS, WHOL: Exterior Flat Glass, Plate/Window
CONSTRUCTION SAND MINING
CONSTRUCTION SITE PREPARATION SVCS
CONSTRUCTION: Agricultural Building
CONSTRUCTION: Athletic & Recreation Facilities
CONSTRUCTION: Bridge
CONSTRUCTION: Commercial & Institutional Building
CONSTRUCTION: Commercial & Office Building, New
CONSTRUCTION: Condominium
CONSTRUCTION: Drainage System
CONSTRUCTION: Farm Building
CONSTRUCTION: Food Prdts Manufacturing or Packing Plant
CONSTRUCTION: Heavy Highway & Street
CONSTRUCTION: Indl Building & Warehouse
CONSTRUCTION: Indl Building, Prefabricated
CONSTRUCTION: Indl Buildings, New, NEC
CONSTRUCTION: Irrigation System
CONSTRUCTION: Mausoleum
CONSTRUCTION: Multi-Family Housing
CONSTRUCTION: Oil & Gas Pipeline Construction
CONSTRUCTION: Pharmaceutical Manufacturing Plant
CONSTRUCTION: Power & Communication Transmission Tower
CONSTRUCTION: Railroad & Subway
CONSTRUCTION: Residential, Nec
CONSTRUCTION: Retaining Wall
CONSTRUCTION: Scaffolding
CONSTRUCTION: Sewer Line
CONSTRUCTION: Single-Family Housing
CONSTRUCTION: Single-family Housing, New
CONSTRUCTION: Street Surfacing & Paving
CONSTRUCTION: Swimming Pools
CONSTRUCTION: Tennis Court
CONSTRUCTION: Truck & Automobile Assembly Plant
CONSTRUCTION: Tunnel
CONSTRUCTION: Utility Line
CONSTRUCTION: Waste Water & Sewage Treatment Plant
CONSTRUCTION: Water & Sewer Line
CONSTRUCTION: Water Main
CONSULTING SVC: Actuarial
CONSULTING SVC: Business, NEC
CONSULTING SVC: Chemical
CONSULTING SVC: Computer
CONSULTING SVC: Data Processing
CONSULTING SVC: Educational
CONSULTING SVC: Engineering
CONSULTING SVC: Financial Management
CONSULTING SVC: Human Resource
CONSULTING SVC: Management
CONSULTING SVC: Marketing Management
CONSULTING SVC: Motion Picture
CONSULTING SVC: Online Technology
CONSULTING SVC: Sales Management
CONSULTING SVC: Telecommunications
CONSULTING SVCS, BUSINESS: Agricultural
CONSULTING SVCS, BUSINESS: Communications
CONSULTING SVCS, BUSINESS: Energy Conservation
CONSULTING SVCS, BUSINESS: Environmental
CONSULTING SVCS, BUSINESS: Publishing
CONSULTING SVCS, BUSINESS: Safety Training Svcs
CONSULTING SVCS, BUSINESS: Sys Engnrg, Exc Computer/Prof
CONSULTING SVCS, BUSINESS: Systems Analysis & Engineering
CONSULTING SVCS, BUSINESS: Testing, Educational Or Personnel
CONSULTING SVCS: Oil
CONTACT LENSES
CONTAINERS, GLASS: Food
CONTAINERS, GLASS: Medicine Bottles
CONTAINERS, GLASS: Packers' Ware
CONTAINERS: Air Cargo, Metal
CONTAINERS: Cargo, Wood
CONTAINERS: Cargo, Wood & Metal Combination
CONTAINERS: Cargo, Wood & Wood With Metal
CONTAINERS: Corrugated
CONTAINERS: Foil, Bakery Goods & Frozen Foods
CONTAINERS: Food & Beverage
CONTAINERS: Food, Folding, Made From Purchased Materials
CONTAINERS: Food, Liquid Tight, Including Milk
CONTAINERS: Food, Wood Wirebound
CONTAINERS: Frozen Food & Ice Cream
CONTAINERS: Glass

CONTAINERS: Metal
CONTAINERS: Plastic
CONTAINERS: Plywood & Veneer, Wood
CONTAINERS: Sanitary, Food
CONTAINERS: Shipping & Mailing, Fiber
CONTAINERS: Shipping, Wood
CONTAINERS: Wood
CONTAINMENT VESSELS: Reactor, Metal Plate
CONTRACTORS: Access Flooring System Installation
CONTRACTORS: Antenna Installation
CONTRACTORS: Asbestos Removal & Encapsulation
CONTRACTORS: Asphalt
CONTRACTORS: Awning Installation
CONTRACTORS: Boiler & Furnace
CONTRACTORS: Boiler Maintenance Contractor
CONTRACTORS: Boring, Building Construction
CONTRACTORS: Building Eqpt & Machinery Installation
CONTRACTORS: Building Front Installation, Metal
CONTRACTORS: Building Sign Installation & Mntnce
CONTRACTORS: Cable Splicing Svcs
CONTRACTORS: Cable TV Installation
CONTRACTORS: Caisson Drilling
CONTRACTORS: Carpentry Work
CONTRACTORS: Carpentry, Cabinet & Finish Work
CONTRACTORS: Carpentry, Cabinet Building & Installation
CONTRACTORS: Carpentry, Finish & Trim Work
CONTRACTORS: Closed Circuit Television Installation
CONTRACTORS: Commercial & Office Building
CONTRACTORS: Communications Svcs
CONTRACTORS: Computer Installation
CONTRACTORS: Computerized Controls Installation
CONTRACTORS: Concrete
CONTRACTORS: Concrete Breaking, Street & Highway
CONTRACTORS: Concrete Pumping
CONTRACTORS: Concrete Reinforcement Placing
CONTRACTORS: Concrete Structure Coating, Plastic
CONTRACTORS: Construction Site Cleanup
CONTRACTORS: Countertop Installation
CONTRACTORS: Decontamination Svcs
CONTRACTORS: Demolition, Building & Other Structures
CONTRACTORS: Directional Oil & Gas Well Drilling Svc
CONTRACTORS: Dock Eqpt Installation, Indl
CONTRACTORS: Drapery Track Installation
CONTRACTORS: Driveway
CONTRACTORS: Electric Power Systems
CONTRACTORS: Electrical
CONTRACTORS: Electronic Controls Installation
CONTRACTORS: Energy Management Control
CONTRACTORS: Excavating
CONTRACTORS: Excavating Slush Pits & Cellars Svcs
CONTRACTORS: Exterior Wall System Installation
CONTRACTORS: Fence Construction
CONTRACTORS: Fiberglass Work
CONTRACTORS: Fire Detection & Burglar Alarm Systems
CONTRACTORS: Floor Laying & Other Floor Work
CONTRACTORS: Flooring
CONTRACTORS: Fountain Installation
CONTRACTORS: Garage Doors
CONTRACTORS: Gas Field Svcs, NEC
CONTRACTORS: General Electric
CONTRACTORS: Geothermal Drilling
CONTRACTORS: Glass Tinting, Architectural & Automotive
CONTRACTORS: Glass, Glazing & Tinting
CONTRACTORS: Gutters & Downspouts
CONTRACTORS: Heating & Air Conditioning
CONTRACTORS: Heating Systems Repair & Maintenance Svc
CONTRACTORS: Highway & Street Construction, General
CONTRACTORS: Highway & Street Paving
CONTRACTORS: Highway & Street Resurfacing
CONTRACTORS: Highway Sign & Guardrail Construction & Install
CONTRACTORS: Home & Office Intrs Finish, Furnish/Remodel
CONTRACTORS: Hotel, Motel/Multi-Famly Home Renovtn/Remodel
CONTRACTORS: Hydraulic Eqpt Installation & Svcs
CONTRACTORS: Indl Building Renovation, Remodeling & Repair
CONTRACTORS: Insulation Installation, Building
CONTRACTORS: Kitchen & Bathroom Remodeling
CONTRACTORS: Kitchen Cabinet Installation
CONTRACTORS: Land Reclamation
CONTRACTORS: Lighting Conductor Erection
CONTRACTORS: Lighting Syst

CONTRACTORS: Machine Rigging & Moving
CONTRACTORS: Machinery Installation
CONTRACTORS: Marble Installation, Interior
CONTRACTORS: Marble Masonry, Exterior
CONTRACTORS: Masonry & Stonework
CONTRACTORS: Mechanical
CONTRACTORS: Metal Ceiling Construction & Repair Work
CONTRACTORS: Millwrights
CONTRACTORS: Multi-Family Home Remodeling
CONTRACTORS: Nonresidential Building Design & Construction
CONTRACTORS: Oil & Gas Building, Repairing & Dismantling Svc
CONTRACTORS: Oil & Gas Field Geological Exploration Svcs
CONTRACTORS: Oil & Gas Field Geophysical Exploration Svcs
CONTRACTORS: Oil & Gas Field Salt Water Impound/Storing Svc
CONTRACTORS: Oil & Gas Well Casing Cement Svcs
CONTRACTORS: Oil & Gas Well Drilling Svc
CONTRACTORS: Oil & Gas Well Foundation Grading Svcs
CONTRACTORS: Oil & Gas Well On-Site Foundation Building Svcs
CONTRACTORS: Oil & Gas Well Plugging & Abandoning Svcs
CONTRACTORS: Oil & Gas Wells Pumping Svcs
CONTRACTORS: Oil & Gas Wells Svcs
CONTRACTORS: Oil Field Haulage Svcs
CONTRACTORS: Oil Field Lease Tanks: Erectg, Clng/Rprg Svcs
CONTRACTORS: Oil Field Pipe Testing Svcs
CONTRACTORS: Oil/Gas Well Construction, Rpr/Dismantling Svcs
CONTRACTORS: On-Site Welding
CONTRACTORS: Ornamental Metal Work
CONTRACTORS: Painting & Wall Covering
CONTRACTORS: Painting, Commercial
CONTRACTORS: Painting, Indl
CONTRACTORS: Patio & Deck Construction & Repair
CONTRACTORS: Pavement Marking
CONTRACTORS: Pipe Laying
CONTRACTORS: Plumbing
CONTRACTORS: Pollution Control Eqpt Installation
CONTRACTORS: Power Generating Eqpt Installation
CONTRACTORS: Precast Concrete Struct Framing & Panel Placing
CONTRACTORS: Process Piping
CONTRACTORS: Refractory or Acid Brick Masonry
CONTRACTORS: Refrigeration
CONTRACTORS: Rock Removal
CONTRACTORS: Roofing
CONTRACTORS: Roofing & Gutter Work
CONTRACTORS: Safety & Security Eqpt
CONTRACTORS: Sandblasting Svc, Building Exteriors
CONTRACTORS: Screening, Window & Door
CONTRACTORS: Seismograph Survey Svcs
CONTRACTORS: Septic System
CONTRACTORS: Sheet Metal Work, NEC
CONTRACTORS: Sheet metal Work, Architectural
CONTRACTORS: Siding
CONTRACTORS: Single-family Home General Remodeling
CONTRACTORS: Skylight Installation
CONTRACTORS: Solar Energy Eqpt
CONTRACTORS: Sound Eqpt Installation
CONTRACTORS: Spa & Hot Tub Construction & Installation
CONTRACTORS: Steam Cleaning, Building Exterior
CONTRACTORS: Stone Masonry
CONTRACTORS: Storage Tank Erection, Metal
CONTRACTORS: Store Fixture Installation
CONTRACTORS: Structural Iron Work, Structural
CONTRACTORS: Structural Steel Erection
CONTRACTORS: Svc Station Eqpt
CONTRACTORS: Svc Station Eqpt Installation, Maint & Repair
CONTRACTORS: Svc Well Drilling Svcs
CONTRACTORS: Textile Warping
CONTRACTORS: Tile Installation, Ceramic
CONTRACTORS: Underground Utilities
CONTRACTORS: Ventilation & Duct Work
CONTRACTORS: Warm Air Heating & Air Conditioning
CONTRACTORS: Water Intake Well Drilling Svc
CONTRACTORS: Water Well Drilling
CONTRACTORS: Waterproofing
CONTRACTORS: Well Acidizing Svcs

PRODUCT INDEX

CONTRACTORS: Well Bailing, Cleaning, Swabbing & Treating Svc
CONTRACTORS: Well Casings Perforating Svcs
CONTRACTORS: Well Chemical Treating Svcs
CONTRACTORS: Window Treatment Installation
CONTRACTORS: Windows & Doors
CONTRACTORS: Wood Floor Installation & Refinishing
CONTRACTORS: Wrecking & Demolition
CONTROL CIRCUIT DEVICES
CONTROL EQPT: Electric
CONTROL EQPT: Electric Buses & Locomotives
CONTROL EQPT: Noise
CONTROL PANELS: Electrical
CONTROLS & ACCESS: Indl, Electric
CONTROLS & ACCESS: Motor
CONTROLS: Access, Motor
CONTROLS: Adjustable Speed Drive
CONTROLS: Air Flow, Refrigeration
CONTROLS: Automatic Temperature
CONTROLS: Electric Motor
CONTROLS: Environmental
CONTROLS: Numerical
CONTROLS: Relay & Ind
CONTROLS: Thermostats
CONTROLS: Thermostats, Built-in
CONTROLS: Water Heater
CONVENTION & TRADE SHOW SVCS
CONVERTERS: Data
CONVERTERS: Frequency
CONVERTERS: Phase Or Rotary, Electrical
CONVERTERS: Rotary, Electrical
CONVERTERS: Torque, Exc Auto
CONVEYOR SYSTEMS
CONVEYOR SYSTEMS: Belt, General Indl Use
CONVEYOR SYSTEMS: Bucket Type
CONVEYOR SYSTEMS: Bulk Handling
CONVEYOR SYSTEMS: Pneumatic Tube
CONVEYOR SYSTEMS: Robotic
CONVEYORS & CONVEYING EQPT
CONVEYORS: Overhead
COOKING & FOOD WARMING EQPT: Commercial
COOKING & FOODWARMING EQPT: Coffee Brewing
COOKING & FOODWARMING EQPT: Commercial
COOKING & FOODWARMING EQPT: Popcorn Machines, Commercial
COOKING EQPT, HOUSEHOLD: Ranges, Gas
COOKING SCHOOL
COOKING WARE, EXC PORCELAIN ENAMELED
COOKING WARE: Cooking Ware, Porcelain Enameled
COOLERS & ICE CHESTS: Polystyrene Foam
COOLING TOWERS: Metal
COOLING TOWERS: Wood
COPPER ORE MILLING & PREPARATION
COPPER: Blocks
COPPER: Cathodes, Primary
COPPER: Rolling & Drawing
COPY MACHINES WHOLESALERS
CORD & TWINE
CORE WASH OR WAX
CORK & CORK PRDTS
CORK & CORK PRDTS: Bottle
CORK & CORK PRDTS: Insulating Material
CORRECTION FLUID
CORRECTIONAL INSTITUTIONS
CORRUGATED PRDTS: Boxes, Partition, Display Items, Sheet/Pad
COSMETIC PREPARATIONS
COSMETICS & TOILETRIES
COSMETICS WHOLESALERS
COSMETOLOGIST
COSMETOLOGY & PERSONAL HYGIENE SALONS
COSTUME JEWELRY & NOVELTIES: Bracelets, Exc Precious Metals
COSTUME JEWELRY & NOVELTIES: Earrings, Exc Precious Metals
COSTUME JEWELRY & NOVELTIES: Exc Semi & Precious
COSTUME JEWELRY & NOVELTIES: Pins, Exc Precious Metals
COSTUME JEWELRY & NOVELTIES: Rosaries & Sm Religious Items
COSTUME JEWELRY & NOVELTIES: Watchbands, Base Metal
COSTUME JEWELRY/NOVELTS: Cuff-Link/Stud, Exc Prec Metal/Gem
COSTUMES & WIGS STORES

COUNTER & SINK TOPS
COUNTERS & COUNTING DEVICES
COUNTERS OR COUNTER DISPLAY CASES, EXC WOOD
COUNTERS OR COUNTER DISPLAY CASES, WOOD
COUNTING DEVICES: Controls, Revolution & Timing
COUNTING DEVICES: Electromechanical
COUNTING DEVICES: Gauges, Press Temp Corrections Computing
COUNTING DEVICES: Odometers
COUNTING DEVICES: Pedometers
COUNTING DEVICES: Revolution
COUNTING DEVICES: Tachometer, Centrifugal
COUPLINGS, EXC PRESSURE & SOIL PIPE
COUPLINGS: Shaft
COURIER OR MESSENGER SVCS
COURIER SVCS: Air
COURIER SVCS: Ground
COURIER SVCS: Package By Vehicle
COVERS: Automobile Seat
COVERS: Metal Plate
COVERS: Slip Made Of Fabric, Plastic, Etc.
CRACKED CASTING REPAIR SVCS
CRANE & AERIAL LIFT SVCS
CRANES: Indl Plant
CRANES: Indl Truck
CRANES: Locomotive
CRANES: Overhead
CRANKSHAFTS & CAMSHAFTS: Machining
CREATIVE SVCS: Advertisers, Exc Writers
CREDIT CLEARINGHOUSE SVC
CREDIT INST, SHORT-TERM BUSINESS: Financing Dealers
CREDIT INSTITUTIONS, SHORT-TERM BUSINESS: Mercantile Finance
CREMATORIES
CROWNS & CLOSURES
CRUDE PETROLEUM & NATURAL GAS PRODUCTION
CRUDE PETROLEUM & NATURAL GAS PRODUCTION
CRUDE PETROLEUM PRODUCTION
CRUDES: Cyclic, Organic
CRYSTALS
CUBICLES: Electric Switchboard Eqpt
CULTURE MEDIA
CUPS & PLATES: Foamed Plastics
CUPS: Plastic Exc Polystyrene Foam
CURTAIN & DRAPERY FIXTURES: Poles, Rods & Rollers
CURTAIN WALLS: Building, Steel
CUSHIONS & PILLOWS
CUSHIONS & PILLOWS: Bed, From Purchased Materials
CUSHIONS & PILLOWS: Hassocks, Textile, Purchased Materials
CUSHIONS: Textile, Exc Spring & Carpet
CUSTOM COMPOUNDING OF RUBBER MATERIALS
CUSTOMIZING SVCS
CUT STONE & STONE PRODUCTS
CUTLERY
CUTLERY WHOLESALERS
CUTLERY, STAINLESS STEEL
CUTLERY: Table, Exc Metal Handled
CUTOUTS: Distribution
CUTTING SVC: Paper, Exc Die-Cut
CUTTING SVC: Paperboard
CYCLIC CRUDES & INTERMEDIATES
CYCLONES: Indl, Metal Plate
CYLINDER & ACTUATORS: Fluid Power
CYLINDERS: Pressure
CYLINDERS: Pump

D

DAIRY EQPT
DAIRY PRDTS STORE: Ice Cream, Packaged
DAIRY PRDTS STORE: Milk
DAIRY PRDTS STORES
DAIRY PRDTS WHOLESALERS: Fresh
DAIRY PRDTS: Butter
DAIRY PRDTS: Butter Oil
DAIRY PRDTS: Cheese
DAIRY PRDTS: Cream Substitutes
DAIRY PRDTS: Custard, Frozen
DAIRY PRDTS: Dairy Based Desserts, Frozen
DAIRY PRDTS: Dietary Supplements, Dairy & Non-Dairy Based
DAIRY PRDTS: Dips & Spreads, Cheese Based
DAIRY PRDTS: Dips & Spreads, Sour Cream Based
DAIRY PRDTS: Dried Milk
DAIRY PRDTS: Evaporated Milk

DAIRY PRDTS: Fermented & Cultured Milk Prdts
DAIRY PRDTS: Frozen Desserts & Novelties
DAIRY PRDTS: Ice Cream & Ice Milk
DAIRY PRDTS: Ice Cream, Bulk
DAIRY PRDTS: Ice Cream, Packaged, Molded, On Sticks, Etc.
DAIRY PRDTS: Imitation Cheese
DAIRY PRDTS: Milk & Cream, Cultured & Flavored
DAIRY PRDTS: Milk Preparations, Dried
DAIRY PRDTS: Milk, Chocolate
DAIRY PRDTS: Milk, Condensed & Evaporated
DAIRY PRDTS: Milk, Fluid
DAIRY PRDTS: Milk, Processed, Pasteurized, Homogenized/Btld
DAIRY PRDTS: Natural Cheese
DAIRY PRDTS: Powdered Buttermilk
DAIRY PRDTS: Processed Cheese
DAIRY PRDTS: Whey, Powdered
DAIRY PRDTS: Whipped Topping, Dry Mix
DAIRY PRDTS: Yogurt, Exc Frozen
DAIRY PRDTS: Yogurt, Frozen
DATA ENTRY SVCS
DATA PROCESSING & PREPARATION SVCS
DATA PROCESSING SVCS
DECORATIVE WOOD & WOODWORK
DEFENSE SYSTEMS & EQPT
DEGREASING MACHINES
DEHYDRATION EQPT
DELIVERY SVCS, BY VEHICLE
DEMONSTRATION SVCS
DENTAL EQPT
DENTAL EQPT & SPLYS
DENTAL EQPT & SPLYS WHOLESALERS
DENTAL EQPT & SPLYS: Compounds
DENTAL EQPT & SPLYS: Dental Hand Instruments, NEC
DENTAL EQPT & SPLYS: Dental Materials
DENTAL EQPT & SPLYS: Denture Materials
DENTAL EQPT & SPLYS: Enamels
DENTAL EQPT & SPLYS: Laboratory
DENTAL EQPT & SPLYS: Sterilizers
DENTAL EQPT & SPLYS: Teeth, Artificial, Exc In Dental Labs
DENTAL INSTRUMENT REPAIR SVCS
DENTISTS' OFFICES & CLINICS
DENTURE CLEANERS
DEODORANTS: Personal
DEPARTMENT STORES: Army-Navy Goods
DEPARTMENT STORES: Country General
DEPILATORIES, COSMETIC
DERMATOLOGICALS
DERRICKS: Oil & Gas Field
DESIGN SVCS, NEC
DESIGN SVCS: Commercial & Indl
DESIGN SVCS: Computer Integrated Systems
DESIGNS SVCS: Scenery, Theatrical
DETECTION APPARATUS: Electronic/Magnetic Field, Light/Heat
DETECTION EQPT: Magnetic Field
DETECTIVE SVCS
DETECTORS: Water Leak
DETONATORS & DETONATING CAPS
DIAGNOSTIC SUBSTANCES
DIAGNOSTIC SUBSTANCES OR AGENTS: Blood Derivative
DIAGNOSTIC SUBSTANCES OR AGENTS: Enzyme & Isoenzyme
DIAGNOSTIC SUBSTANCES OR AGENTS: In Vitro
DIAGNOSTIC SUBSTANCES OR AGENTS: Microbiology & Virology
DIAGNOSTIC SUBSTANCES OR AGENTS: Radioactive
DIAMONDS, GEMS, WHOLESALE
DIAMONDS: Cutting & Polishing
DIATHERMY EQPT
DIE CUTTING SVC: Paper
DIE SETS: Presses, Metal Stamping
DIES & TOOLS: Special
DIES: Cutting, Exc Metal
DIES: Extrusion
DIES: Paper Cutting
DIES: Plastic Forming
DIES: Steel Rule
DIES: Wire Drawing & Straightening
DIODES: Light Emitting
DIRECT SELLING ESTABLISHMENTS, NEC
DIRECT SELLING ESTABLISHMENTS: Beverage Svcs
DIRECT SELLING ESTABLISHMENTS: Food, Mobile, Exc Coffee-Cart

PRODUCT INDEX

DIRECT SELLING ESTABLISHMENTS: Milk Delivery
DIRECT SELLING ESTABLISHMENTS: Telemarketing
DISINFECTING SVCS
DISK DRIVES: Computer
DISKETTE DUPLICATING SVCS
DISKS & DRUMS Magnetic
DISPENSING EQPT & PARTS, BEVERAGE: Beer
DISPENSING EQPT & PARTS, BEVERAGE: Coolers, Milk/Water, Elec
DISPENSING EQPT & PARTS, BEVERAGE: Fountain/Other Beverage
DISPENSING EQPT & PARTS, BEVERAGE: Fountains, Parts/Access
DISPLAY CASES: Refrigerated
DISPLAY FIXTURES: Showcases, Wood, Exc Refrigerated
DISPLAY FIXTURES: Wood
DISPLAY ITEMS: Corrugated, Made From Purchased Materials
DISPLAY ITEMS: Solid Fiber, Made From Purchased Materials
DISPLAY LETTERING SVCS
DISTILLERS DRIED GRAIN & SOLUBLES
DIVING EQPT STORES
DOCK EQPT & SPLYS, INDL
DOCKS: Marinas, Prefabricated, Wood
DOCKS: Prefabricated Metal
DOCUMENT EMBOSSING SVCS
DOLOMITE: Crushed & Broken
DOOR & WINDOW REPAIR SVCS
DOOR FRAMES: Concrete
DOOR FRAMES: Wood
DOOR MATS: Rubber
DOOR OPERATING SYSTEMS: Electric
DOORS & WINDOWS WHOLESALERS: All Materials
DOORS & WINDOWS: Screen & Storm
DOORS & WINDOWS: Storm, Metal
DOORS: Fire, Metal
DOORS: Folding, Plastic Or Plastic Coated Fabric
DOORS: Garage, Overhead, Metal
DOORS: Garage, Overhead, Wood
DOORS: Glass
DOORS: Hangar, Metal
DOORS: Rolling, Indl Building Or Warehouse, Metal
DOORS: Safe & Vault, Metal
DOORS: Screen, Metal
DOORS: Wooden
DOWELS & DOWEL RODS
DOWNSPOUTS: Sheet Metal
DRAFTING SPLYS WHOLESALERS
DRAFTING SVCS
DRAINAGE PRDTS: Concrete
DRAINING OR PUMPING OF METAL MINES
DRAPERIES & CURTAINS
DRAPERIES & DRAPERY FABRICS, COTTON
DRAPERIES: Plastic & Textile, From Purchased Materials
DRAPERY & UPHOLSTERY STORES: Curtains
DRAPERY & UPHOLSTERY STORES: Draperies
DRAPES & DRAPERY FABRICS, FROM MANMADE FIBER
DRIED FRUITS WHOLESALERS
DRILL BITS
DRILLING MACHINERY & EQPT: Oil & Gas
DRILLING MACHINERY & EQPT: Water Well
DRILLS & DRILLING EQPT: Mining
DRINK MIXES, NONALCOHOLIC: Cocktail
DRINKING FOUNTAINS: Metal, Nonrefrigerated
DRINKING PLACES: Alcoholic Beverages
DRINKING PLACES: Bars & Lounges
DRINKING PLACES: Night Clubs
DRINKING PLACES: Tavern
DRINKING PLACES: Wine Bar
DRINKING WATER COOLERS WHOLESALERS: Mechanical
DRIVE CHAINS: Bicycle Or Motorcycle
DRIVE SHAFTS
DRIVES: High Speed Indl, Exc Hydrostatic
DRIVES: Hydrostatic
DROP CLOTHS: Fabric
DRUG STORES
DRUG TESTING KITS: Blood & Urine
DRUGS & DRUG PROPRIETARIES, WHOLESALE
DRUGS & DRUG PROPRIETARIES, WHOLESALE: Animal Medicines
DRUGS & DRUG PROPRIETARIES, WHOLESALE: Medicinals/Botanicals
DRUGS & DRUG PROPRIETARIES, WHOLESALE: Pharmaceuticals
DRUGS & DRUG PROPRIETARIES, WHOLESALE: Vitamins & Minerals
DRUGS ACTING ON THE CENTRAL NERVOUS SYSTEM & SENSE ORGANS
DRUMS: Brake
DRUMS: Fiber
DRUMS: Magnetic
DRUMS: Shipping, Metal
DRYCLEANING & LAUNDRY SVCS: Commercial & Family
DRYCLEANING EQPT & SPLYS: Commercial
DRYERS & REDRYERS: Indl
DUCTING: Metal Plate
DUCTS: Sheet Metal
DUMBWAITERS
DUMPSTERS: Garbage
DURABLE GOODS WHOLESALERS, NEC
DUST OR FUME COLLECTING EQPT: Indl
DYES & PIGMENTS: Organic
DYNAMOMETERS

E

EARTH SCIENCE SVCS
EARTHS: Ground Or Otherwise Treated
EATING PLACES
ECCLESIASTICAL WARE, NEC
EDUCATIONAL PROGRAM ADMINISTRATION, GOVT: Level Of Govt
EDUCATIONAL SVCS
EDUCATIONAL SVCS, NONDEGREE GRANTING: Continuing Education
ELASTIC BRAID & NARROW WOVEN FABRICS
ELASTOMERS
ELECTRIC FENCE CHARGERS
ELECTRIC MOTOR & GENERATOR AUXILIARY PARTS
ELECTRIC MOTOR REPAIR SVCS
ELECTRIC WATER HEATERS WHOLESALERS
ELECTRICAL APPARATUS & EQPT WHOLESALERS
ELECTRICAL APPLIANCES, TELEVISIONS & RADIOS WHOLESALERS
ELECTRICAL CONSTRUCTION MATERIALS WHOLESALERS
ELECTRICAL CURRENT CARRYING WIRING DEVICES
ELECTRICAL DISCHARGE MACHINING, EDM
ELECTRICAL EQPT & SPLYS
ELECTRICAL EQPT FOR ENGINES
ELECTRICAL EQPT REPAIR & MAINTENANCE
ELECTRICAL EQPT REPAIR SVCS
ELECTRICAL EQPT: Automotive, NEC
ELECTRICAL EQPT: Household
ELECTRICAL GOODS, WHOL: Antennas, Receiving/Satellite Dishes
ELECTRICAL GOODS, WHOLESALE: Alarms & Signaling Eqpt
ELECTRICAL GOODS, WHOLESALE: Batteries, Storage, Indl
ELECTRICAL GOODS, WHOLESALE: Burglar Alarm Systems
ELECTRICAL GOODS, WHOLESALE: Circuit Breakers
ELECTRICAL GOODS, WHOLESALE: Citizens Band Radios
ELECTRICAL GOODS, WHOLESALE: Connectors
ELECTRICAL GOODS, WHOLESALE: Electrical Appliances, Major
ELECTRICAL GOODS, WHOLESALE: Electrical Entertainment Eqpt
ELECTRICAL GOODS, WHOLESALE: Electronic Parts
ELECTRICAL GOODS, WHOLESALE: Fans, Household
ELECTRICAL GOODS, WHOLESALE: Fire Alarm Systems
ELECTRICAL GOODS, WHOLESALE: Flashlights
ELECTRICAL GOODS, WHOLESALE: Generators
ELECTRICAL GOODS, WHOLESALE: High Fidelity Eqpt
ELECTRICAL GOODS, WHOLESALE: Household Appliances, NEC
ELECTRICAL GOODS, WHOLESALE: Light Bulbs & Related Splys
ELECTRICAL GOODS, WHOLESALE: Lighting Fittings & Access
ELECTRICAL GOODS, WHOLESALE: Lighting Fixtures, Comm & Indl
ELECTRICAL GOODS, WHOLESALE: Modems, Computer
ELECTRICAL GOODS, WHOLESALE: Motor Ctrls, Starters & Relays
ELECTRICAL GOODS, WHOLESALE: Motors
ELECTRICAL GOODS, WHOLESALE: Paging & Signaling Eqpt
ELECTRICAL GOODS, WHOLESALE: Panelboards
ELECTRICAL GOODS, WHOLESALE: Radio Parts & Access, NEC
ELECTRICAL GOODS, WHOLESALE: Resistors
ELECTRICAL GOODS, WHOLESALE: Safety Switches
ELECTRICAL GOODS, WHOLESALE: Security Control Eqpt & Systems
ELECTRICAL GOODS, WHOLESALE: Semiconductor Devices
ELECTRICAL GOODS, WHOLESALE: Signaling, Eqpt
ELECTRICAL GOODS, WHOLESALE: Sound Eqpt
ELECTRICAL GOODS, WHOLESALE: Switchboards
ELECTRICAL GOODS, WHOLESALE: Switches, Exc Electronic, NEC
ELECTRICAL GOODS, WHOLESALE: Telephone & Telegraphic Eqpt
ELECTRICAL GOODS, WHOLESALE: Telephone Eqpt
ELECTRICAL GOODS, WHOLESALE: Transformer & Transmission Eqpt
ELECTRICAL GOODS, WHOLESALE: Transformers
ELECTRICAL GOODS, WHOLESALE: Wire & Cable
ELECTRICAL GOODS, WHOLESALE: Wire & Cable, Electronic
ELECTRICAL GOODS, WHOLESALE: Wire & Cable, Power
ELECTRICAL HOUSEHOLD APPLIANCE REPAIR
ELECTRICAL INDL APPARATUS, NEC
ELECTRICAL SPLYS
ELECTRICAL SUPPLIES: Porcelain
ELECTRODES: Indl Process
ELECTRODES: Thermal & Electrolytic
ELECTROLYZING SVC: Steel, Light Gauge
ELECTROMEDICAL EQPT
ELECTROMEDICAL EQPT WHOLESALERS
ELECTROMETALLURGICAL PRDTS
ELECTRON BEAM: Cutting, Forming, Welding
ELECTRON TUBES
ELECTRON TUBES: Cathode Ray
ELECTRON TUBES: Parts
ELECTRON TUBES: Transmitting
ELECTRONIC COMPONENTS
ELECTRONIC DEVICES: Solid State, NEC
ELECTRONIC EQPT REPAIR SVCS
ELECTRONIC LOADS & POWER SPLYS
ELECTRONIC PARTS & EQPT WHOLESALERS
ELECTRONIC SHOPPING
ELECTRONIC TRAINING DEVICES
ELECTROPLATING & PLATING SVC
ELEVATOR: Grain, Storage Only
ELEVATORS & EQPT
ELEVATORS WHOLESALERS
ELEVATORS: Installation & Conversion
EMBALMING FLUID
EMBLEMS: Embroidered
EMBOSSING SVC: Paper
EMBROIDERING & ART NEEDLEWORK FOR THE TRADE
EMBROIDERING SVC
EMBROIDERING SVC: Schiffli Machine
EMBROIDERY ADVERTISING SVCS
EMERGENCY ALARMS
EMPLOYMENT AGENCY SVCS
ENAMELING SVC: Metal Prdts, Including Porcelain
ENAMELS
ENCLOSURES: Electronic
ENCLOSURES: Screen
ENCODERS: Digital
ENCRYPTION EQPT & DEVICES
ENERGY MEASUREMENT EQPT
ENGINE PARTS & ACCESS: Internal Combustion
ENGINE REBUILDING: Diesel
ENGINE REBUILDING: Gas
ENGINEERING SVCS
ENGINEERING SVCS: Aviation Or Aeronautical
ENGINEERING SVCS: Building Construction
ENGINEERING SVCS: Chemical
ENGINEERING SVCS: Civil
ENGINEERING SVCS: Electrical Or Electronic
ENGINEERING SVCS: Energy conservation
ENGINEERING SVCS: Heating & Ventilation
ENGINEERING SVCS: Industrial
ENGINEERING SVCS: Machine Tool Design
ENGINEERING SVCS: Marine
ENGINEERING SVCS: Mechanical
ENGINEERING SVCS: Pollution Control
ENGINEERING SVCS: Professional
ENGINEERING SVCS: Structural
ENGINES: Diesel & Semi-Diesel Or Duel Fuel
ENGINES: Gasoline, NEC
ENGINES: Internal Combustion, NEC

PRODUCT INDEX

ENGINES: Jet Propulsion
ENGINES: Marine
ENGINES: Steam
ENGRAVING SVC, NEC
ENGRAVING SVC: Jewelry & Personal Goods
ENGRAVING SVCS
ENGRAVING: Currency
ENGRAVINGS: Plastic
ENTERTAINERS & ENTERTAINMENT GROUPS
ENTERTAINMENT PROMOTION SVCS
ENTERTAINMENT SVCS
ENVELOPES
ENVELOPES WHOLESALERS
ENVIR QLTY PROG ADMN, GOV: Land, Minl & Wildlif Consv, State
ENZYMES
EPOXY RESINS
EQUIPMENT: Pedestrian Traffic Control
EQUIPMENT: Rental & Leasing, NEC
ESCALATORS: Passenger & Freight
ETCHING & ENGRAVING SVC
ETCHING SVC: Metal
ETCHING SVC: Photochemical
ETHYLENE
ETHYLENE OXIDE
ETHYLENE-PROPYLENE RUBBERS: EPDM Polymers
EXCAVATING EQPT
EXCAVATING MACHINERY & EQPT WHOLESALERS
EXHAUST HOOD OR FAN CLEANING SVCS
EXHAUST SYSTEMS: Eqpt & Parts
EXHIBITORS, AIRLINES, MOTION PICTURE
EXPLOSIVES
EXPLOSIVES, EXC AMMO & FIREWORKS WHOLESALERS
EXTENSION CORDS
EXTERMINATING & FUMIGATING SVCS
EXTRACTS, FLAVORING
EYEGLASSES
EYEGLASSES: Sunglasses
EYELASHES, ARTIFICIAL
EYES & HOOKS Screw
EYES: Artificial

F

FABRIC STORES
FABRICATED METAL PRODUCTS, NEC
FABRICS & CLOTH: Quilted
FABRICS & CLOTHING: Rubber Coated
FABRICS: Alpacas, Mohair, Woven
FABRICS: Apparel & Outerwear, Cotton
FABRICS: Apparel & Outerwear, From Manmade Fiber Or Silk
FABRICS: Awning Stripes, Cotton
FABRICS: Bags & Bagging, Cotton
FABRICS: Bandage Cloth, Cotton
FABRICS: Broadwoven, Cotton
FABRICS: Broadwoven, Synthetic Manmade Fiber & Silk
FABRICS: Broadwoven, Wool
FABRICS: Coated Or Treated
FABRICS: Cotton, Narrow
FABRICS: Fiberglass, Broadwoven
FABRICS: Filter Cloth, Cotton
FABRICS: Furniture Denim
FABRICS: Metallized
FABRICS: Nonwoven
FABRICS: Nylon, Broadwoven
FABRICS: Polypropylene, Broadwoven
FABRICS: Print, Cotton
FABRICS: Resin Or Plastic Coated
FABRICS: Seat Cover, Automobile, Cotton
FABRICS: Shoe Laces, Exc Leather
FABRICS: Stretch, Cotton
FABRICS: Tapestry, Cotton
FABRICS: Trimmings
FABRICS: Trimmings, Textile
FABRICS: Upholstery, Wool
FABRICS: Wall Covering, From Manmade Fiber Or Silk
FABRICS: Weft Or Circular Knit
FABRICS: Woven, Narrow Cotton, Wool, Silk
FACILITIES SUPPORT SVCS
FACSIMILE COMMUNICATION EQPT
FAMILY CLOTHING STORES
FAMILY COUNSELING SVCS
FANS, BLOWING: Indl Or Commercial
FANS, EXHAUST: Indl Or Commercial
FANS, VENTILATING: Indl Or Commercial
FANS: Ceiling

FARM & GARDEN MACHINERY WHOLESALERS
FARM MACHINERY REPAIR SVCS
FARM PRDTS, RAW MATERIAL, WHOLESALE: Tobacco & Tobacco Prdts
FARM PRDTS, RAW MATERIALS, WHOLESALE: Broomcorn
FARM PRDTS, RAW MATERIALS, WHOLESALE: Farm Animals
FARM SPLY STORES
FARM SPLYS WHOLESALERS
FARM SPLYS, WHOLESALE: Beekeeping Splys, Nondurable
FARM SPLYS, WHOLESALE: Feed
FARM SPLYS, WHOLESALE: Fertilizers & Agricultural Chemicals
FARM SPLYS, WHOLESALE: Greenhouse Eqpt & Splys
FARM SPLYS, WHOLESALE: Harness Eqpt
FARM SPLYS, WHOLESALE: Limestone, Agricultural
FARM SPLYS, WHOLESALE: Soil, Potting & Planting
FASTENERS WHOLESALERS
FASTENERS: Metal
FASTENERS: Metal
FASTENERS: Notions, NEC
FASTENERS: Notions, Zippers
FASTENERS: Wire, Made From Purchased Wire
FATTY ACID ESTERS & AMINOS
FAUCETS & SPIGOTS: Metal & Plastic
FEATHERS: Dusters
FEDERAL CROP INSURANCE CORP
FELT PARTS
FELT, WHOLESALE
FELT: Polishing
FENCE POSTS: Iron & Steel
FENCES OR POSTS: Ornamental Iron Or Steel
FENCING DEALERS
FENCING MATERIALS: Plastic
FENCING MATERIALS: Snow Fence, Wood
FENCING MATERIALS: Wood
FENCING: Chain Link
FENDERS: Automobile, Stamped Or Pressed Metal
FERRITES
FERTILIZER, AGRICULTURAL: Wholesalers
FERTILIZERS: NEC
FERTILIZERS: Nitrogen Solutions
FERTILIZERS: Nitrogenous
FERTILIZERS: Phosphatic
FIBER & FIBER PRDTS: Acrylic
FIBER & FIBER PRDTS: Cigarette Tow Cellulosic
FIBER & FIBER PRDTS: Organic, Noncellulose
FIBER & FIBER PRDTS: Polyester
FIBER & FIBER PRDTS: Protein
FIBER & FIBER PRDTS: Synthetic Cellulosic
FIBER & FIBER PRDTS: Vinyl
FIBER OPTICS
FIELD WAREHOUSING SVCS
FILE FOLDERS
FILLERS & SEALERS: Putty
FILLERS & SEALERS: Putty, Wood
FILLERS & SEALERS: Wood
FILM & SHEET: Unsuppported Plastic
FILM BASE: Cellulose Acetate Or Nitrocellulose Plastics
FILM DEVELOPING & PRINTING SVCS
FILM: Motion Picture
FILTER CLEANING SVCS
FILTER ELEMENTS: Fluid & Hydraulic Line
FILTERING MEDIA: Pottery
FILTERS
FILTERS & SOFTENERS: Water, Household
FILTERS & STRAINERS: Pipeline
FILTERS: Air
FILTERS: Air Intake, Internal Combustion Engine, Exc Auto
FILTERS: General Line, Indl
FILTERS: Motor Vehicle
FILTERS: Oil, Internal Combustion Engine, Exc Auto
FILTRATION DEVICES: Electronic
FINANCIAL INVESTMENT ADVICE
FINANCIAL SVCS
FINDINGS & TRIMMINGS: Apparel
FINGERNAILS, ARTIFICIAL
FINISHERS: Concrete & Bituminous, Powered
FINISHING AGENTS
FINISHING AGENTS: Leather
FINISHING SCHOOLS, CHARM & MODELING
FINISHING SVCS
FIRE ARMS, SMALL: Guns Or Gun Parts, 30 mm & Below
FIRE ARMS, SMALL: Machine Guns & Grenade Launchers

FIRE ARMS, SMALL: Machine Guns/Machine Gun Parts, 30mm/below
FIRE ARMS, SMALL: Rifles Or Rifle Parts, 30 mm & below
FIRE DETECTION SYSTEMS
FIRE EXTINGUISHER CHARGES
FIRE EXTINGUISHER SVC
FIRE EXTINGUISHERS, WHOLESALE
FIRE EXTINGUISHERS: Portable
FIRE OR BURGLARY RESISTIVE PRDTS
FIRE PROTECTION EQPT
FIREARMS & AMMUNITION, EXC SPORTING, WHOLESALE
FIREARMS: Large, Greater Than 30mm
FIREARMS: Small, 30mm or Less
FIREFIGHTING APPARATUS
FIREPLACE & CHIMNEY MATERIAL: Concrete
FIREPLACE EQPT & ACCESS
FIREPLACES: Concrete
FIREWOOD, WHOLESALE
FIREWORKS
FISH & SEAFOOD PROCESSORS: Canned Or Cured
FISH & SEAFOOD PROCESSORS: Fresh Or Frozen
FISH & SEAFOOD WHOLESALERS
FISH FOOD
FISHING EQPT: Lures
FISHING EQPT: Nets & Seines
FITTINGS & ASSEMBLIES: Hose & Tube, Hydraulic Or Pneumatic
FITTINGS & SPECIALTIES: Steam
FITTINGS: Pipe
FITTINGS: Pipe, Fabricated
FIXTURES & EQPT: Kitchen, Metal, Exc Cast Aluminum
FIXTURES & EQPT: Kitchen, Porcelain Enameled
FIXTURES: Cut Stone
FLAGS: Fabric
FLAT GLASS: Antique
FLAT GLASS: Building
FLAT GLASS: Picture
FLAT GLASS: Sheet
FLAT GLASS: Skylight
FLAT GLASS: Tempered
FLAT GLASS: Window, Clear & Colored
FLAVORS OR FLAVORING MATERIALS: Synthetic
FLOOR COVERING STORES
FLOOR COVERING STORES: Carpets
FLOOR COVERING STORES: Floor Tile
FLOOR COVERING: Plastic
FLOOR COVERINGS WHOLESALERS
FLOOR COVERINGS: Asphalted-Felt Base, Linoleum Or Carpet
FLOOR COVERINGS: Rubber
FLOOR COVERINGS: Textile Fiber
FLOORING & GRATINGS: Open, Construction Applications
FLOORING: Hard Surface
FLOORING: Hardwood
FLOORING: Rubber
FLORIST TELEGRAPH SVCS
FLORIST: Flowers, Fresh
FLORISTS
FLORISTS' SPLYS, WHOLESALE
FLOWER ARRANGEMENTS: Artificial
FLOWERS: Artificial & Preserved
FLUID METERS & COUNTING DEVICES
FLUID POWER PUMPS & MOTORS
FLUID POWER VALVES & HOSE FITTINGS
FLUORSPAR MINING
FLUXES
FM & AM RADIO TUNERS
FOAM RUBBER
FOAM RUBBER, WHOLESALE
FOAMS & RUBBER, WHOLESALE
FOIL & LEAF: Metal
FOIL OR LEAF: Gold
FOIL, ALUMINUM, HOUSEHOLD, WHOLESALE
FOIL: Aluminum
FOIL: Laminated To Paper Or Other Materials
FOOD CASINGS: Plastic
FOOD COLORINGS
FOOD PRDTS, BREAKFAST: Cereal, Corn Flakes
FOOD PRDTS, BREAKFAST: Cereal, Oatmeal
FOOD PRDTS, CANNED OR FRESH PACK: Fruit Juices
FOOD PRDTS, CANNED OR FRESH PACK: Vegetable Juices
FOOD PRDTS, CANNED, NEC
FOOD PRDTS, CANNED: Applesauce
FOOD PRDTS, CANNED: Baby Food

PRODUCT INDEX

FOOD PRDTS, CANNED: Barbecue Sauce
FOOD PRDTS, CANNED: Beans & Bean Sprouts
FOOD PRDTS, CANNED: Beans, Baked Without Meat
FOOD PRDTS, CANNED: Catsup
FOOD PRDTS, CANNED: Fruit Juices, Fresh
FOOD PRDTS, CANNED: Fruits
FOOD PRDTS, CANNED: Fruits & Fruit Prdts
FOOD PRDTS, CANNED: Italian
FOOD PRDTS, CANNED: Jams, Including Imitation
FOOD PRDTS, CANNED: Jams, Jellies & Preserves
FOOD PRDTS, CANNED: Jellies, Edible, Including Imitation
FOOD PRDTS, CANNED: Maraschino Cherries
FOOD PRDTS, CANNED: Mexican, NEC
FOOD PRDTS, CANNED: Pizza Sauce
FOOD PRDTS, CANNED: Puddings, Exc Meat
FOOD PRDTS, CANNED: Soup, Beef
FOOD PRDTS, CANNED: Soups
FOOD PRDTS, CANNED: Spaghetti & Other Pasta Sauce
FOOD PRDTS, CANNED: Tamales
FOOD PRDTS, CANNED: Tomato Sauce.
FOOD PRDTS, CANNED: Tomatoes
FOOD PRDTS, CANNED: Tortillas
FOOD PRDTS, CANNED: Vegetable Purees
FOOD PRDTS, CANNED: Vegetables
FOOD PRDTS, CANNED: Vegetables
FOOD PRDTS, CONFECTIONERY, WHOLESALE: Candy
FOOD PRDTS, CONFECTIONERY, WHOLESALE: Nuts, Salted/Roasted
FOOD PRDTS, CONFECTIONERY, WHOLESALE: Potato Chips
FOOD PRDTS, CONFECTIONERY, WHOLESALE: Snack Foods
FOOD PRDTS, DAIRY, WHOLESALE: Dried Or Canned
FOOD PRDTS, DAIRY, WHOLESALE: Frozen Dairy Desserts
FOOD PRDTS, FISH & SEAFOOD, WHOLESALE: Fresh
FOOD PRDTS, FISH & SEAFOOD: Chowders, Frozen
FOOD PRDTS, FISH & SEAFOOD: Fish Sticks
FOOD PRDTS, FISH & SEAFOOD: Fish, Canned & Cured
FOOD PRDTS, FISH & SEAFOOD: Fish, Smoked
FOOD PRDTS, FISH & SEAFOOD: Fresh, Prepared
FOOD PRDTS, FISH & SEAFOOD: Fresh/Frozen Chowder, Soup/Stew
FOOD PRDTS, FISH & SEAFOOD: Seafood, Frozen, Prepared
FOOD PRDTS, FROZEN: Breakfasts, Packaged
FOOD PRDTS, FROZEN: Dinners, Packaged
FOOD PRDTS, FROZEN: Ethnic Foods, NEC
FOOD PRDTS, FROZEN: Fruit Juice, Concentrates
FOOD PRDTS, FROZEN: Fruits & Vegetables
FOOD PRDTS, FROZEN: Fruits, Juices & Vegetables
FOOD PRDTS, FROZEN: Lunches, Packaged
FOOD PRDTS, FROZEN: NEC
FOOD PRDTS, FROZEN: Pizza
FOOD PRDTS, FROZEN: Potato Prdts
FOOD PRDTS, FROZEN: Snack Items
FOOD PRDTS, FROZEN: Vegetables, Exc Potato Prdts
FOOD PRDTS, FRUITS & VEG, FRESH, WHOL: Banana Ripening Svc
FOOD PRDTS, MEAT & MEAT PRDTS, WHOLESALE: Cured Or Smoked
FOOD PRDTS, MEAT & MEAT PRDTS, WHOLESALE: Fresh
FOOD PRDTS, WHOLESALE: Baking Splys
FOOD PRDTS, WHOLESALE: Beverage Concentrates
FOOD PRDTS, WHOLESALE: Beverages, Exc Coffee & Tea
FOOD PRDTS, WHOLESALE: Coffee & Tea
FOOD PRDTS, WHOLESALE: Coffee, Green Or Roasted
FOOD PRDTS, WHOLESALE: Condiments
FOOD PRDTS, WHOLESALE: Cookies
FOOD PRDTS, WHOLESALE: Diet
FOOD PRDTS, WHOLESALE: Dried or Canned Foods
FOOD PRDTS, WHOLESALE: Flavorings & Fragrances
FOOD PRDTS, WHOLESALE: Flour
FOOD PRDTS, WHOLESALE: Grain Elevators
FOOD PRDTS, WHOLESALE: Grains
FOOD PRDTS, WHOLESALE: Health
FOOD PRDTS, WHOLESALE: Honey
FOOD PRDTS, WHOLESALE: Natural & Organic
FOOD PRDTS, WHOLESALE: Pasta & Rice
FOOD PRDTS, WHOLESALE: Pizza Splys
FOOD PRDTS, WHOLESALE: Rice, Polished
FOOD PRDTS, WHOLESALE: Salt, Edible
FOOD PRDTS, WHOLESALE: Sauces
FOOD PRDTS, WHOLESALE: Shortening, Vegetable
FOOD PRDTS, WHOLESALE: Soups, Exc Frozen
FOOD PRDTS, WHOLESALE: Specialty
FOOD PRDTS, WHOLESALE: Spices & Seasonings
FOOD PRDTS, WHOLESALE: Water, Distilled
FOOD PRDTS, WHOLESALE: Wheat
FOOD PRDTS: Animal & marine fats & oils
FOOD PRDTS: Baking Soda
FOOD PRDTS: Bran & Middlings, Exc Rice
FOOD PRDTS: Bread Crumbs, Exc Made In Bakeries
FOOD PRDTS: Breakfast Bars
FOOD PRDTS: Cake Fillings, Exc Fruit
FOOD PRDTS: Cereals
FOOD PRDTS: Chewing Gum Base
FOOD PRDTS: Chicken, Processed, Fresh
FOOD PRDTS: Chicken, Processed, Frozen
FOOD PRDTS: Chicken, Processed, NEC
FOOD PRDTS: Cocoa, Butter
FOOD PRDTS: Cocoa, Instant
FOOD PRDTS: Cocoa, Powdered
FOOD PRDTS: Coffee
FOOD PRDTS: Coffee Extracts
FOOD PRDTS: Coffee Roasting, Exc Wholesale Grocers
FOOD PRDTS: Coffee Substitutes
FOOD PRDTS: Compound Shortenings
FOOD PRDTS: Cooking Oils, Refined Vegetable, Exc Corn
FOOD PRDTS: Corn & other vegetable starches
FOOD PRDTS: Corn Chips & Other Corn-Based Snacks
FOOD PRDTS: Corn Meal
FOOD PRDTS: Cottonseed Oil, Cake & Meal
FOOD PRDTS: Cottonseed Oil, Deodorized
FOOD PRDTS: Dessert Mixes & Fillings
FOOD PRDTS: Desserts, Ready-To-Mix
FOOD PRDTS: Dips, Exc Cheese & Sour Cream Based
FOOD PRDTS: Dough, Pizza, Prepared
FOOD PRDTS: Doughs, Frozen Or Refrig From Purchased Flour
FOOD PRDTS: Dressings, Salad, Raw & Cooked Exc Dry Mixes
FOOD PRDTS: Dried & Dehydrated Fruits, Vegetables & Soup Mix
FOOD PRDTS: Duck Slaughtering & Processing
FOOD PRDTS: Edible Oil Prdts, Exc Corn Oil
FOOD PRDTS: Edible fats & oils
FOOD PRDTS: Egg Substitutes, Made From Eggs
FOOD PRDTS: Emulsifiers
FOOD PRDTS: Fat Substitutes
FOOD PRDTS: Fish Meal
FOOD PRDTS: Flour
FOOD PRDTS: Flour & Other Grain Mill Products
FOOD PRDTS: Flour Mixes & Doughs
FOOD PRDTS: Flour, Blended From Purchased Flour
FOOD PRDTS: Flours & Flour Mixes, From Purchased Flour
FOOD PRDTS: Fresh Vegetables, Peeled Or Processed
FOOD PRDTS: Fruit Juices
FOOD PRDTS: Fruit Pops, Frozen
FOOD PRDTS: Fruits, Dehydrated Or Dried
FOOD PRDTS: Gelatin Dessert Preparations
FOOD PRDTS: Gluten Feed
FOOD PRDTS: Granola & Energy Bars, Nonchocolate
FOOD PRDTS: High fructose corn syrup
FOOD PRDTS: Honey
FOOD PRDTS: Horseradish, Exc Sauce
FOOD PRDTS: Ice, Blocks
FOOD PRDTS: Ice, Cubes
FOOD PRDTS: Instant Coffee
FOOD PRDTS: Macaroni Prdts, Dry, Alphabet, Rings Or Shells
FOOD PRDTS: Macaroni, Noodles, Spaghetti, Pasta, Etc
FOOD PRDTS: Malt
FOOD PRDTS: Meat Meal & Tankage, Inedible
FOOD PRDTS: Milled Corn By-Prdts
FOOD PRDTS: Mixes, Bread & Roll From Purchased Flour
FOOD PRDTS: Mixes, Cake, From Purchased Flour
FOOD PRDTS: Mixes, Doughnut From Purchased Flour
FOOD PRDTS: Mixes, Gravy, Dry
FOOD PRDTS: Mixes, Pancake From Purchased Flour
FOOD PRDTS: Mixes, Pizza From Purchased Flour
FOOD PRDTS: Mixes, Sauces, Dry
FOOD PRDTS: Mixes, Seasonings, Dry
FOOD PRDTS: Molasses, Mixed/Blended, Purchased Ingredients
FOOD PRDTS: Mustard, Prepared
FOOD PRDTS: Noodles, Uncooked, Packaged W/Other Ingredients
FOOD PRDTS: Nuts & Seeds
FOOD PRDTS: Oil, Hydrogenated, Edible
FOOD PRDTS: Oils & Fats, Animal
FOOD PRDTS: Olive Oil
FOOD PRDTS: Oriental Noodles
FOOD PRDTS: Pasta, Rice/Potatoes, Uncooked, Pkgd
FOOD PRDTS: Pasta, Uncooked, Packaged With Other Ingredients
FOOD PRDTS: Peanut Butter
FOOD PRDTS: Pickles, Vinegar
FOOD PRDTS: Pizza Doughs From Purchased Flour
FOOD PRDTS: Popcorn, Popped
FOOD PRDTS: Popcorn, Unpopped
FOOD PRDTS: Pork Rinds
FOOD PRDTS: Potato & Corn Chips & Similar Prdts
FOOD PRDTS: Potato Chips & Other Potato-Based Snacks
FOOD PRDTS: Potatoes, Dried
FOOD PRDTS: Poultry Sausage, Lunch Meats/Other Poultry Prdts
FOOD PRDTS: Preparations
FOOD PRDTS: Prepared Meat Sauces Exc Tomato & Dry
FOOD PRDTS: Prepared Sauces, Exc Tomato Based
FOOD PRDTS: Prepared Vegetable Sauces Exc Tomato & Dry
FOOD PRDTS: Raw cane sugar
FOOD PRDTS: Rice, Milled
FOOD PRDTS: Rice, Packaged & Seasoned
FOOD PRDTS: Salads
FOOD PRDTS: Sandwiches
FOOD PRDTS: Seasonings & Spices
FOOD PRDTS: Shortening & Solid Edible Fats
FOOD PRDTS: Soup Mixes
FOOD PRDTS: Soup Mixes, Dried
FOOD PRDTS: Soybean Lecithin
FOOD PRDTS: Soybean Oil, Deodorized
FOOD PRDTS: Soybean Powder
FOOD PRDTS: Soybean Protein Concentrates & Isolates
FOOD PRDTS: Spices, Including Ground
FOOD PRDTS: Starch, Corn
FOOD PRDTS: Starches
FOOD PRDTS: Sugar
FOOD PRDTS: Sugar Syrup From Sugar Beets
FOOD PRDTS: Sugar, Beet
FOOD PRDTS: Sugar, Cane
FOOD PRDTS: Sugar, Granulated Cane, Purchd Raw Sugar/Syrup
FOOD PRDTS: Sugar, Liquid Cane Prdts, Exc Refined
FOOD PRDTS: Sugar, Maple, Indl
FOOD PRDTS: Syrup, Maple
FOOD PRDTS: Syrup, Pancake, Blended & Mixed
FOOD PRDTS: Syrups
FOOD PRDTS: Tea
FOOD PRDTS: Tortilla Chips
FOOD PRDTS: Tortillas
FOOD PRDTS: Turkey, Processed, NEC
FOOD PRDTS: Variety Meats, Poultry
FOOD PRDTS: Vegetable Oil Mills, NEC
FOOD PRDTS: Vegetable Shortenings, Exc Corn Oil
FOOD PRDTS: Vegetables, Dehydrated Or Dried
FOOD PRDTS: Vegetables, Dried or Dehydrated Exc Freeze-Dried
FOOD PRDTS: Vinegar
FOOD PRDTS: Wheat Flour
FOOD PRDTS: Wheat gluten
FOOD PRDTS: Yeast
FOOD PRODUCTS MACHINERY
FOOD STORES: Delicatessen
FOOD STORES: Grocery, Chain
FOOD STORES: Grocery, Independent
FOOD STORES: Supermarkets
FOOD STORES: Supermarkets, Chain
FOOD STORES: Supermarkets, Independent
FOOD WARMING EQPT: Commercial
FOOTWEAR, WHOLESALE: Shoe Access
FOOTWEAR, WHOLESALE: Shoes
FOOTWEAR: Cut Stock
FORESTRY RELATED EQPT
FORGINGS
FORGINGS: Aircraft, Ferrous
FORGINGS: Anchors
FORGINGS: Armor Plate, Iron Or Steel
FORGINGS: Automotive & Internal Combustion Engine
FORGINGS: Bearing & Bearing Race, Nonferrous
FORGINGS: Construction Or Mining Eqpt, Ferrous
FORGINGS: Engine Or Turbine, Nonferrous
FORGINGS: Gear & Chain
FORGINGS: Iron & Steel
FORGINGS: Machinery, Ferrous

PRODUCT INDEX

FORGINGS: Metal, Ornamental, Ferrous
FORGINGS: Nonferrous
FORMS: Concrete, Sheet Metal
FOUNDRIES: Aluminum
FOUNDRIES: Brass, Bronze & Copper
FOUNDRIES: Gray & Ductile Iron
FOUNDRIES: Iron
FOUNDRIES: Nonferrous
FOUNDRIES: Steel
FOUNDRIES: Steel Investment
FOUNDRY MACHINERY & EQPT
FOUNTAIN SUPPLIES WHOLESALERS
FOUNTAINS: Concrete
FRAMES & FRAMING WHOLESALE
FRANCHISES, SELLING OR LICENSING
FREEZERS: Household
FREIGHT FORWARDING ARRANGEMENTS
FREIGHT FORWARDING ARRANGEMENTS: Domestic
FREIGHT TRANSPORTATION ARRANGEMENTS
FRICTION MATERIAL, MADE FROM POWDERED METAL
FRUIT & VEGETABLE MARKETS
FRUIT STANDS OR MARKETS
FRUITS & VEGETABLES WHOLESALERS: Fresh
FRUITS: Artificial & Preserved
FUEL ADDITIVES
FUEL BRIQUETTES OR BOULETS, MADE WITH PETROLEUM BINDER
FUEL DEALERS: Wood
FUEL OIL DEALERS
FUEL TREATING
FUELS: Diesel
FUELS: Ethanol
FUELS: Jet
FULLER'S EARTH MINING
FUND RAISING ORGANIZATION, NON-FEE BASIS
FUNERAL HOME
FUNERAL HOMES & SVCS
FUNGICIDES OR HERBICIDES
FURNACE CASINGS: Sheet Metal
FURNACES & OVENS: Fuel-Fired
FURNACES & OVENS: Indl
FURNITURE & CABINET STORES: Cabinets, Custom Work
FURNITURE & CABINET STORES: Custom
FURNITURE & FIXTURES Factory
FURNITURE PARTS: Metal
FURNITURE REFINISHING SVCS
FURNITURE REPAIR & MAINTENANCE SVCS
FURNITURE STOCK & PARTS: Carvings, Wood
FURNITURE STOCK & PARTS: Dimension Stock, Hardwood
FURNITURE STOCK & PARTS: Frames, Upholstered Furniture, Wood
FURNITURE STOCK & PARTS: Hardwood
FURNITURE STORES
FURNITURE STORES: Cabinets, Kitchen, Exc Custom Made
FURNITURE STORES: Custom Made, Exc Cabinets
FURNITURE STORES: Office
FURNITURE STORES: Outdoor & Garden
FURNITURE UPHOLSTERY REPAIR SVCS
FURNITURE WHOLESALERS
FURNITURE, BARBER & BEAUTY SHOP
FURNITURE, GARDEN: Concrete
FURNITURE, HOUSEHOLD: Wholesalers
FURNITURE, MATTRESSES: Wholesalers
FURNITURE, OFFICE: Wholesalers
FURNITURE, OUTDOOR & LAWN: Wholesalers
FURNITURE, PUBLIC BUILDING: Wholesalers
FURNITURE, WHOLESALE: Bar
FURNITURE, WHOLESALE: Chairs
FURNITURE, WHOLESALE: Lockers
FURNITURE, WHOLESALE: Racks
FURNITURE: Bar furniture
FURNITURE: Bed Frames & Headboards, Wood
FURNITURE: Bedroom, Wood
FURNITURE: Beds, Household, Incl Folding & Cabinet, Metal
FURNITURE: Bedsprings, Assembled
FURNITURE: Bookcases & Stereo Cabinets, Metal
FURNITURE: Bookcases, Office, Wood
FURNITURE: Box Springs, Assembled
FURNITURE: Cabinets & Filing Drawers, Office, Exc Wood
FURNITURE: Cabinets & Vanities, Medicine, Metal
FURNITURE: Cafeteria
FURNITURE: Chairs, Household Upholstered
FURNITURE: Chairs, Household Wood
FURNITURE: Chairs, Household, Metal
FURNITURE: Chairs, Office Exc Wood

FURNITURE: Chairs, Office Wood
FURNITURE: China Closets
FURNITURE: Church
FURNITURE: Church, Cut Stone
FURNITURE: Coffee Tables, Wood
FURNITURE: Desks & Tables, Office, Exc Wood
FURNITURE: Desks, Household, Wood
FURNITURE: Desks, Metal
FURNITURE: Desks, Wood
FURNITURE: Dining Room, Wood
FURNITURE: Fiberglass & Plastic
FURNITURE: Foundations & Platforms
FURNITURE: Garden, Exc Wood, Metal, Stone Or Concrete
FURNITURE: Hammocks, Metal Or Fabric & Metal Combined
FURNITURE: Hospital
FURNITURE: Household, Metal
FURNITURE: Household, NEC
FURNITURE: Household, Upholstered On Metal Frames
FURNITURE: Household, Upholstered, Exc Wood Or Metal
FURNITURE: Household, Wood
FURNITURE: Hydraulic Barber & Beauty Shop Chairs
FURNITURE: Institutional, Exc Wood
FURNITURE: Juvenile, Wood
FURNITURE: Kitchen & Dining Room, Metal
FURNITURE: Laboratory
FURNITURE: Lawn & Garden, Except Wood & Metal
FURNITURE: Lawn, Exc Wood, Metal, Stone Or Concrete
FURNITURE: Lawn, Metal
FURNITURE: Lawn, Wood
FURNITURE: Library
FURNITURE: Living Room, Upholstered On Wood Frames
FURNITURE: Mattresses & Foundations
FURNITURE: Mattresses, Box & Bedsprings
FURNITURE: Mattresses, Innerspring Or Box Spring
FURNITURE: NEC
FURNITURE: Office, Exc Wood
FURNITURE: Office, Wood
FURNITURE: Outdoor, Wood
FURNITURE: Picnic Tables Or Benches, Park
FURNITURE: Rattan
FURNITURE: Restaurant
FURNITURE: School
FURNITURE: Sleep
FURNITURE: Sofa Beds Or Convertible Sofas)
FURNITURE: Stadium
FURNITURE: Stools With Casters, Metal, Exc Home Or Office
FURNITURE: Storage Chests, Household, Wood
FURNITURE: Table Tops, Marble
FURNITURE: Tables & Table Tops, Wood
FURNITURE: Tables, Office, Exc Wood
FURNITURE: Tables, Office, Wood
FURNITURE: Television, Wood
FURNITURE: Unfinished, Wood
FURNITURE: Upholstered
FUSES & FUSE EQPT
FUSES: Electric
Furs

G

GAMBLING: Lotteries
GAMES & TOYS: Air Rifles
GAMES & TOYS: Banks
GAMES & TOYS: Blocks
GAMES & TOYS: Board Games, Children's & Adults'
GAMES & TOYS: Cars, Play, Children's Vehicles
GAMES & TOYS: Child Restraint Seats, Automotive
GAMES & TOYS: Craft & Hobby Kits & Sets
GAMES & TOYS: Doll Carriages & Carts
GAMES & TOYS: Electronic
GAMES & TOYS: Game Machines, Exc Coin-Operated
GAMES & TOYS: Kits, Science, Incl Microscopes/Chemistry Sets
GAMES & TOYS: Models, Automobile & Truck, Toy & Hobby
GAMES & TOYS: Models, Boat & Ship, Toy & Hobby
GAMES & TOYS: Models, Railroad, Toy & Hobby
GAMES & TOYS: Puzzles
GAMES & TOYS: Sleds, Children's
GAMES & TOYS: Strollers, Baby, Vehicle
GAMES & TOYS: Trains & Eqpt, Electric & Mechanical
GAMES & TOYS: Wagons, Coaster, Express & Play, Children's
GARAGE DOOR REPAIR SVCS
GARBAGE CONTAINERS: Plastic
GARBAGE DISPOSERS & COMPACTORS: Commercial
GAS & HYDROCARBON LIQUEFACTION FROM COAL

GAS & OIL FIELD EXPLORATION SVCS
GAS & OIL FIELD SVCS, NEC
GAS FIELD MACHINERY & EQPT
GAS PROCESSING SVC
GAS PRODUCTION & DISTRIBUTION: Mixed Natural & Manufactured
GAS STATIONS
GAS: Refinery
GASES & LIQUIFIED PETROLEUM GASES
GASES: Acetylene
GASES: Carbon Dioxide
GASES: Flourinated Hydrocarbon
GASES: Helium
GASES: Hydrogen
GASES: Indl
GASES: Neon
GASES: Nitrogen
GASES: Oxygen
GASKET MATERIALS
GASKETS
GASKETS & SEALING DEVICES
GASOLINE FILLING STATIONS
GASTROINTESTINAL OR GENITOURINARY SYSTEM DRUGS
GATES: Dam, Metal Plate
GATES: Ornamental Metal
GAUGES
GEARS
GEARS & GEAR UNITS: Reduction, Exc Auto
GEARS: Power Transmission, Exc Auto
GELATIN
GEM STONES MINING, NEC: Natural
GEMSTONE & INDL DIAMOND MINING SVCS
GENEALOGICAL INVESTIGATION SVCS
GENERAL & INDUSTRIAL LOAN INSTITUTIONS
GENERAL COUNSELING SVCS
GENERAL MERCHANDISE, NONDURABLE, WHOLESALE
GENERATING APPARATUS & PARTS: Electrical
GENERATION EQPT: Electronic
GENERATOR REPAIR SVCS
GENERATORS SETS: Steam
GENERATORS: Electric
GENERATORS: Storage Battery Chargers
GENERATORS: Vehicles, Gas-Electric Or Oil-Electric
GERIATRIC SOCIAL SVCS
GIFT SHOP
GIFT, NOVELTY & SOUVENIR STORES: Party Favors
GIFT, NOVELTY & SOUVENIR STORES: Trading Cards, Sports
GIFTS & NOVELTIES: Wholesalers
GLACE, FOR GLAZING FOOD
GLASS & GLASS CERAMIC PRDTS, PRESSED OR BLOWN: Tableware
GLASS FABRICATORS
GLASS PRDTS, FROM PURCHASED GLASS: Art
GLASS PRDTS, FROM PURCHASED GLASS: Glassware
GLASS PRDTS, FROM PURCHASED GLASS: Glassware, Indl
GLASS PRDTS, FROM PURCHASED GLASS: Insulating
GLASS PRDTS, FROM PURCHASED GLASS: Mirrored
GLASS PRDTS, FROM PURCHASED GLASS: Mirrors, Framed
GLASS PRDTS, FROM PURCHASED GLASS: Novelties, Fruit, Etc
GLASS PRDTS, FROM PURCHASED GLASS: Ornaments, Christmas Tree
GLASS PRDTS, FROM PURCHASED GLASS: Sheet, Bent
GLASS PRDTS, FROM PURCHASED GLASS: Windshields
GLASS PRDTS, PRESSED OR BLOWN: Blocks & Bricks
GLASS PRDTS, PRESSED OR BLOWN: Bulbs, Electric Lights
GLASS PRDTS, PRESSED OR BLOWN: Glassware, Art Or Decorative
GLASS PRDTS, PRESSED OR BLOWN: Glassware, Novelty
GLASS PRDTS, PRESSED OR BLOWN: Ornaments, Christmas Tree
GLASS PRDTS, PRESSED OR BLOWN: Scientific Glassware
GLASS PRDTS, PRESSED OR BLOWN: Tubing
GLASS PRDTS, PRESSED/BLOWN: Glassware, Art, Decor/Novelty
GLASS PRDTS, PURCHD GLASS: Furniture Top, Cut, Beveld/Polshd
GLASS PRDTS, PURCHSD GLASS: Ornamental, Cut, Engraved/Décor
GLASS STORE: Leaded Or Stained

PRODUCT INDEX

GLASS STORES
GLASS: Fiber
GLASS: Flat
GLASS: Indl Prdts
GLASS: Insulating
GLASS: Pressed & Blown, NEC
GLASS: Stained
GLASS: Tempered
GLASSWARE STORES
GLASSWARE WHOLESALERS
GLASSWARE: Cut & Engraved
GLASSWARE: Laboratory
GLASSWARE: Laboratory & Medical
GLOBAL POSITIONING SYSTEMS & EQPT
GLOBES, GEOGRAPHICAL
GLOVES & MITTENS DYEING & FINISHING
GLOVES: Fabric
GLOVES: Leather
GLOVES: Leather, Work
GLOVES: Plastic
GLOVES: Safety
GLOVES: Work
GLUE
GO-CART DEALERS
GOLD ORE MINING
GOLD ORES
GOLF CARTS: Powered
GOLF CLUB & EQPT REPAIR SVCS
GOLF DRIVING RANGES
GOLF EQPT
GOLF GOODS & EQPT
GOURMET FOOD STORES
GOVERNMENT, EXECUTIVE OFFICES: Local
GOVERNMENT, EXECUTIVE OFFICES: Mayors'
GOVERNMENT, EXECUTIVE OFFICES: State & Local
GOVERNMENT, GENERAL: Administration
GOVERNORS: Diesel Engine, Pump
GRADING SVCS
GRAIN & FIELD BEANS WHOLESALERS
GRANITE: Crushed & Broken
GRANITE: Cut & Shaped
GRANITE: Dimension
GRAPHIC ARTS & RELATED DESIGN SVCS
GRAPHIC LAYOUT SVCS: Printed Circuitry
GRATINGS: Open Steel Flooring
GRATINGS: Tread, Fabricated Metal
GRAVE MARKERS: Concrete
GRAVEL & PEBBLE MINING
GRAVEL MINING
GREASES & INEDIBLE FATS, RENDERED
GREENHOUSES: Prefabricated Metal
GREETING CARD PAINTING BY HAND
GREETING CARD SHOPS
GREETING CARDS WHOLESALERS
GRILLES & REGISTERS: Ornamental Metal Work
GRINDING SVC: Precision, Commercial Or Indl
GRINDING SVCS: Ophthalmic Lens, Exc Prescription
GRINDSTONES: Artificial
GRIPS OR HANDLES: Rubber
GROCERIES WHOLESALERS, NEC
GROCERIES, GENERAL LINE WHOLESALERS
GROMMETS: Rubber
GROUTING EQPT: Concrete
GUARD SVCS
GUARDRAILS
GUARDS: Machine, Sheet Metal
GUIDED MISSILES & SPACE VEHICLES: Research & Development
GUIDED MISSILES/SPACE VEHICLE PARTS/AUX EQPT: Research/Devel
GUM & WOOD CHEMICALS
GUN PARTS MADE TO INDIVIDUAL ORDER
GUNSMITHS
GUTTERS
GUTTERS: Sheet Metal
GYPSUM BOARD
GYPSUM PRDTS

H

HAIR & HAIR BASED PRDTS
HAIR ACCESS: Rubber
HAIR CARE PRDTS
HAIR CURLERS: Beauty Shop
HAIR NETS
HAIR REPLACEMENT & WEAVING SVCS

HAIR STYLIST: Men
HAIRDRESSERS
HAMPERS: Solid Fiber, Made From Purchased Materials
HAND TOOLS, NEC: Wholesalers
HANDBAG STORES
HANDLES: Brush Or Tool, Plastic
HANDLES: Wood
HANGERS: Garment, Plastic
HARD RUBBER PRDTS, NEC
HARDWARE
HARDWARE & BUILDING PRDTS: Plastic
HARDWARE & EQPT: Stage, Exc Lighting
HARDWARE STORES
HARDWARE STORES: Builders'
HARDWARE STORES: Chainsaws
HARDWARE STORES: Door Locks & Lock Sets
HARDWARE STORES: Pumps & Pumping Eqpt
HARDWARE STORES: Snowblowers
HARDWARE STORES: Tools
HARDWARE STORES: Tools, Hand
HARDWARE STORES: Tools, Power
HARDWARE WHOLESALERS
HARDWARE, WHOLESALE: Bolts
HARDWARE, WHOLESALE: Builders', NEC
HARDWARE, WHOLESALE: Casters & Glides
HARDWARE, WHOLESALE: Chains
HARDWARE, WHOLESALE: Furniture, NEC
HARDWARE, WHOLESALE: Nuts
HARDWARE, WHOLESALE: Power Tools & Access
HARDWARE, WHOLESALE: Screws
HARDWARE, WHOLESALE: Security Devices, Locks
HARDWARE, WHOLESALE: Staples
HARDWARE: Builders'
HARDWARE: Cabinet
HARDWARE: Casket
HARDWARE: Door Opening & Closing Devices, Exc Electrical
HARDWARE: Furniture
HARDWARE: Furniture, Builders' & Other Household
HARDWARE: Luggage
HARDWARE: Plastic
HARDWARE: Rubber
HARNESS ASSEMBLIES: Cable & Wire
HARNESS WIRING SETS: Internal Combustion Engines
HARNESSES, HALTERS, SADDLERY & STRAPS
HEADPHONES: Radio
HEALTH & ALLIED SERVICES, NEC
HEALTH & WELFARE COUNCIL
HEALTH AIDS: Exercise Eqpt
HEALTH AIDS: Vaporizers
HEALTH FOOD & SUPPLEMENT STORES
HEARING AIDS
HEARING TESTING SVCS
HEAT EMISSION OPERATING APPARATUS
HEAT EXCHANGERS
HEAT EXCHANGERS: After Or Inter Coolers Or Condensers, Etc
HEAT TREATING SALTS
HEAT TREATING: Metal
HEATERS: Induction & Dielectric
HEATERS: Space, Exc Electric
HEATERS: Swimming Pool, Electric
HEATING & AIR CONDITIONING EQPT & SPLYS WHOLESALERS
HEATING & AIR CONDITIONING UNITS, COMBINATION
HEATING EQPT & SPLYS
HEATING EQPT: Complete
HEATING EQPT: Induction
HEATING PADS, ELECTRIC
HEATING UNITS & DEVICES: Indl, Electric
HEATING UNITS: Gas, Infrared
HELICOPTERS
HELMETS: Athletic
HELP SUPPLY SERVICES
HIGH ENERGY PARTICLE PHYSICS EQPT
HIGHWAY & STREET MAINTENANCE SVCS
HITCHES: Trailer
HOBBY & CRAFT SPLY STORES
HOBBY SUPPLIES, WHOLESALE
HOBBY, TOY & GAME STORES: Arts & Crafts & Splys
HOBBY, TOY & GAME STORES: Children's Toys & Games, Exc Dolls
HOBBY, TOY & GAME STORES: Hobbies, NEC
HOBBY, TOY & GAME STORES: Toys & Games
HOISTS
HOISTS: Mine

HOLDERS, PAPER TOWEL, GROCERY BAG, ETC: Plastic
HOLDING COMPANIES: Banks
HOLDING COMPANIES: Investment, Exc Banks
HOLDING COMPANIES: Personal, Exc Banks
HOLDING COMPANIES: Public Utility
HOME CENTER STORES
HOME DELIVERY NEWSPAPER ROUTES
HOME ENTERTAINMENT EQPT: Electronic, NEC
HOME ENTERTAINMENT REPAIR SVCS
HOME FOR THE MENTALLY RETARDED
HOME FURNISHINGS WHOLESALERS
HOME HEALTH CARE SVCS
HOME IMPROVEMENT & RENOVATION CONTRACTOR AGENCY
HOMEBUILDERS & OTHER OPERATIVE BUILDERS
HOMEFURNISHING STORE: Bedding, Sheet, Blanket,Spread/Pillow
HOMEFURNISHING STORES: Beddings & Linens
HOMEFURNISHING STORES: Brooms
HOMEFURNISHING STORES: Lighting Fixtures
HOMEFURNISHING STORES: Mirrors
HOMEFURNISHING STORES: Pictures, Wall
HOMEFURNISHING STORES: Pottery
HOMEFURNISHING STORES: Wicker, Rattan, Or Reed
HOMEFURNISHING STORES: Window Furnishings
HOMEFURNISHING STORES: Window Shades, NEC
HOMEFURNISHINGS & SPLYS, WHOLESALE: Decorative
HOMEFURNISHINGS, WHOLESALE: Aluminumware
HOMEFURNISHINGS, WHOLESALE: Blinds, Vertical
HOMEFURNISHINGS, WHOLESALE: Carpets
HOMEFURNISHINGS, WHOLESALE: Draperies
HOMEFURNISHINGS, WHOLESALE: Fireplace Eqpt & Access
HOMEFURNISHINGS, WHOLESALE: Kitchenware
HOMEFURNISHINGS, WHOLESALE: Linens, Table
HOMEFURNISHINGS, WHOLESALE: Wood Flooring
HOMES, MODULAR: Wooden
HOMES: Log Cabins
HONEYCOMB CORE & BOARD: Made From Purchased Materials
HOODS: Range, Sheet Metal
HOOKS: Gate
HORNS: Marine, Electric
HORSESHOES
HOSE: Air Line Or Air Brake, Rubber Or Rubberized Fabric
HOSE: Automobile, Plastic
HOSE: Flexible Metal
HOSE: Heater, Plastic
HOSE: Plastic
HOSE: Rubber
HOSES & BELTING: Rubber & Plastic
HOSPITAL EQPT REPAIR SVCS
HOSPITALS: Medical & Surgical
HOTEL & MOTEL RESERVATION SVCS
HOTELS & MOTELS
HOUSEHOLD APPLIANCE PARTS: Wholesalers
HOUSEHOLD APPLIANCE STORES: Electric
HOUSEHOLD APPLIANCE STORES: Electric Household Appliance, Sm
HOUSEHOLD APPLIANCE STORES: Electric Household, Major
HOUSEHOLD ARTICLES, EXC FURNITURE: Cut Stone
HOUSEHOLD FURNISHINGS, NEC
HOUSEWARE STORES
HOUSEWARES, ELECTRIC, EXC COOKING APPLIANCES & UTENSILS
HOUSEWARES, ELECTRIC: Air Purifiers, Portable
HOUSEWARES, ELECTRIC: Bedcoverings
HOUSEWARES, ELECTRIC: Cooking Appliances
HOUSEWARES, ELECTRIC: Dryers, Hair
HOUSEWARES, ELECTRIC: Dryers, Hand & Face
HOUSEWARES, ELECTRIC: Fans, Desk
HOUSEWARES, ELECTRIC: Fans, Exhaust & Ventilating
HOUSEWARES, ELECTRIC: Heaters, Immersion
HOUSEWARES, ELECTRIC: Heaters, Space
HOUSEWARES, ELECTRIC: Heaters, Tape
HOUSEWARES, ELECTRIC: Heating Units, Electric Appliances
HOUSEWARES, ELECTRIC: Heating, Bsbrd/Wall, Radiant Heat
HOUSEWARES, ELECTRIC: Humidifiers, Household
HOUSEWARES, ELECTRIC: Irons, Household
HOUSEWARES, ELECTRIC: Lighters, Cigarette
HOUSEWARES, ELECTRIC: Massage Machines, Exc Beauty/Barber

PRODUCT INDEX

HOUSEWARES, ELECTRIC: Mixers, Food
HOUSEWARES, ELECTRIC: Radiators
HOUSEWARES, ELECTRIC: Toasters
HOUSEWARES: Bowls, Wood
HOUSEWARES: Dishes, China
HOUSEWARES: Dishes, Plastic
HOUSEWARES: Household & Commercial, Vitreous China
HOUSEWARES: Kettles & Skillets, Cast Iron
HOUSEWARES: Pots & Pans, Glass
HOUSING COMPONENTS: Prefabricated, Concrete
HOUSINGS: Business Machine, Sheet Metal
HOUSINGS: Motor
HOUSINGS: Pressure
HUB CAPS: Automobile, Stamped Metal
HUMIDIFIERS & DEHUMIDIFIERS
HUMIDIFYING EQPT, EXC PORTABLE
HYDRAULIC EQPT REPAIR SVC
HYDRAULIC FLUIDS: Synthetic Based
HYDROPONIC EQPT
Hard Rubber & Molded Rubber Prdts

I

ICE
ICE CREAM & ICES WHOLESALERS
ICE WHOLESALERS
ICE: Dry
IDENTIFICATION PLATES
IDENTIFICATION TAGS, EXC PAPER
IGNEOUS ROCK: Crushed & Broken
IGNITION APPARATUS & DISTRIBUTORS
IGNITION SYSTEMS: Internal Combustion Engine
INCINERATORS
INCUBATORS & BROODERS: Farm
INDL & PERSONAL SVC PAPER WHOLESALERS
INDL & PERSONAL SVC PAPER, WHOL: Bags, Paper/Disp Plastic
INDL & PERSONAL SVC PAPER, WHOL: Boxes, Corrugtd/Solid Fiber
INDL & PERSONAL SVC PAPER, WHOL: Boxes, Paperbrd/Plastic
INDL & PERSONAL SVC PAPER, WHOL: Container, Paper/Plastic
INDL & PERSONAL SVC PAPER, WHOL: Cups, Disp, Plastic/Paper
INDL & PERSONAL SVC PAPER, WHOL: Paper, Wrap/Coarse/Prdts
INDL & PERSONAL SVC PAPER, WHOLESALE: Boxes & Containers
INDL & PERSONAL SVC PAPER, WHOLESALE: Paperboard & Prdts
INDL & PERSONAL SVC PAPER, WHOLESALE: Press Sensitive Tape
INDL & PERSONAL SVC PAPER, WHOLESALE: Shipping Splys
INDL CONTRACTORS: Exhibit Construction
INDL DIAMONDS WHOLESALERS
INDL EQPT SVCS
INDL GASES WHOLESALERS
INDL MACHINERY & EQPT WHOLESALERS
INDL MACHINERY REPAIR & MAINTENANCE
INDL PATTERNS: Foundry Cores
INDL PATTERNS: Foundry Patternmaking
INDL PROCESS INSTR: Transmit, Process Variables
INDL PROCESS INSTRUMENTS: Absorp Analyzers, Infrared, X-Ray
INDL PROCESS INSTRUMENTS: Analyzers
INDL PROCESS INSTRUMENTS: Boiler Controls, Power & Marine
INDL PROCESS INSTRUMENTS: Control
INDL PROCESS INSTRUMENTS: Controllers, Process Variables
INDL PROCESS INSTRUMENTS: Data Loggers
INDL PROCESS INSTRUMENTS: Digital Display, Process Variables
INDL PROCESS INSTRUMENTS: Draft Gauges
INDL PROCESS INSTRUMENTS: Elements, Primary
INDL PROCESS INSTRUMENTS: Indl Flow & Measuring
INDL PROCESS INSTRUMENTS: Level & Bulk Measuring
INDL PROCESS INSTRUMENTS: Manometers
INDL PROCESS INSTRUMENTS: Temperature
INDL PROCESS INSTRUMENTS: Water Quality Monitoring/Cntrl Sys
INDL SALTS WHOLESALERS
INDL SPLYS WHOLESALERS
INDL SPLYS, WHOL: Fasteners, Incl Nuts, Bolts, Screws, Etc
INDL SPLYS, WHOLESALE: Abrasives
INDL SPLYS, WHOLESALE: Adhesives, Tape & Plasters
INDL SPLYS, WHOLESALE: Bearings
INDL SPLYS, WHOLESALE: Bins & Containers, Storage
INDL SPLYS, WHOLESALE: Bottler Splys
INDL SPLYS, WHOLESALE: Cordage
INDL SPLYS, WHOLESALE: Drums, New Or Reconditioned
INDL SPLYS, WHOLESALE: Fasteners & Fastening Eqpt
INDL SPLYS, WHOLESALE: Filters, Indl
INDL SPLYS, WHOLESALE: Gaskets
INDL SPLYS, WHOLESALE: Gaskets & Seals
INDL SPLYS, WHOLESALE: Gears
INDL SPLYS, WHOLESALE: Glass Bottles
INDL SPLYS, WHOLESALE: Pipeline Wrappings, Anti-Corrosive
INDL SPLYS, WHOLESALE: Plastic Bottles
INDL SPLYS, WHOLESALE: Power Transmission, Eqpt & Apparatus
INDL SPLYS, WHOLESALE: Rubber Goods, Mechanical
INDL SPLYS, WHOLESALE: Seals
INDL SPLYS, WHOLESALE: Signmaker Eqpt & Splys
INDL SPLYS, WHOLESALE: Springs
INDL SPLYS, WHOLESALE: Staplers & Tackers
INDL SPLYS, WHOLESALE: Textile Printers' Splys
INDL SPLYS, WHOLESALE: Tools
INDL SPLYS, WHOLESALE: Tools, NEC
INDL SPLYS, WHOLESALE: Valves & Fittings
INDL SPLYS, WHOLESALE: Wheels
INDL TOOL GRINDING SVCS
INDUCTORS
INDUSTRIAL & COMMERCIAL EQPT INSPECTION SVCS
INERTIAL GUIDANCE SYSTEMS
INFORMATION RETRIEVAL SERVICES
INFRARED OBJECT DETECTION EQPT
INGOT, EXTRUSION: Extrusion ingot, aluminum: rolling mills
INGOTS: Steel
INK OR WRITING FLUIDS
INK: Gravure
INK: Letterpress Or Offset
INK: Lithographic
INK: Printing
INK: Screen process
INSECTICIDES
INSECTICIDES & PESTICIDES
INSPECTION & TESTING SVCS
INSTR, MEASURE & CONTROL: Gauge, Oil Pressure & Water Temp
INSTRUMENTS & METERS: Measuring, Electric
INSTRUMENTS, LAB: Refractometers, Exc Indl Process Types
INSTRUMENTS, LAB: Spectroscopic/Optical Properties Measuring
INSTRUMENTS, LABORATORY: Analyzers, Automatic Chemical
INSTRUMENTS, LABORATORY: Blood Testing
INSTRUMENTS, LABORATORY: Infrared Analytical
INSTRUMENTS, LABORATORY: Photomicrographic
INSTRUMENTS, LABORATORY: Ultraviolet Analytical
INSTRUMENTS, MEASURING & CNTRL: Radiation & Testing, Nuclear
INSTRUMENTS, MEASURING & CNTRL: Testing, Abrasion, Etc
INSTRUMENTS, MEASURING & CNTRLG: Aircraft & Motor Vehicle
INSTRUMENTS, MEASURING & CNTRLG: Thermometers/Temp Sensors
INSTRUMENTS, MEASURING & CNTRLNG: Nuclear Instrument Modules
INSTRUMENTS, MEASURING & CNTRLNG: Wind Direction Indicators
INSTRUMENTS, MEASURING & CONTROLLING: Gas Detectors
INSTRUMENTS, MEASURING & CONTROLLING: Gauges, Rain
INSTRUMENTS, MEASURING & CONTROLLING: Surveying & Drafting
INSTRUMENTS, MEASURING & CONTROLLING: Transits, Surveyors'
INSTRUMENTS, MEASURING & CONTROLLING: Ultrasonic Testing
INSTRUMENTS, MEASURING & CONTROLLING: Weather Tracking
INSTRUMENTS, MEASURING/CNTRL: Gauging, Ultrasonic Thickness
INSTRUMENTS, MEASURING/CNTRL: Hydrometers, Exc Indl Process
INSTRUMENTS, MEASURING/CNTRLG: Fare Registers, St Cars/Buses
INSTRUMENTS, MEASURING/CNTRLG: Fire Detect Sys, Non-Electric
INSTRUMENTS, MEASURING/CNTRLG: Fuel Densitometers, Acft Eng
INSTRUMENTS, MEASURING/CNTRLNG: Med Diagnostic Sys, Nuclear
INSTRUMENTS, OPTICAL: Elements & Assemblies, Exc Ophthalmic
INSTRUMENTS, OPTICAL: Lenses, All Types Exc Ophthalmic
INSTRUMENTS, OPTICAL: Mirrors
INSTRUMENTS, OPTICAL: Test & Inspection
INSTRUMENTS, SURGICAL & MED: Cleaning Eqpt, Ultrasonic Med
INSTRUMENTS, SURGICAL & MEDICAL: Blood & Bone Work
INSTRUMENTS, SURGICAL & MEDICAL: Blood Pressure
INSTRUMENTS, SURGICAL & MEDICAL: Blood Transfusion
INSTRUMENTS, SURGICAL & MEDICAL: Cannulae
INSTRUMENTS, SURGICAL & MEDICAL: Catheters
INSTRUMENTS, SURGICAL & MEDICAL: Hemodialysis
INSTRUMENTS, SURGICAL & MEDICAL: Inhalation Therapy
INSTRUMENTS, SURGICAL & MEDICAL: Inhalators
INSTRUMENTS, SURGICAL & MEDICAL: Muscle Exercise, Ophthalmic
INSTRUMENTS, SURGICAL & MEDICAL: Needles, Suture
INSTRUMENTS, SURGICAL & MEDICAL: Ophthalmic
INSTRUMENTS, SURGICAL & MEDICAL: Retinoscopes
INSTRUMENTS, SURGICAL & MEDICAL: Suction Therapy
INSTRUMENTS, SURGICAL/MED: Microsurgical, Exc Electromedical
INSTRUMENTS: Analytical
INSTRUMENTS: Combustion Control, Indl
INSTRUMENTS: Digital Panel Meters, Electricity Measuring
INSTRUMENTS: Elec Lab Stds, Resist, Inductance/Capacitance
INSTRUMENTS: Electrocardiographs
INSTRUMENTS: Electronic, Analog-Digital Converters
INSTRUMENTS: Endoscopic Eqpt, Electromedical
INSTRUMENTS: Eye Examination
INSTRUMENTS: Flow, Indl Process
INSTRUMENTS: Generators Tachometer
INSTRUMENTS: Humidity, Indl Process
INSTRUMENTS: Indicating, Electric
INSTRUMENTS: Indl Process Control
INSTRUMENTS: Laser, Scientific & Engineering
INSTRUMENTS: Liquid Level, Indl Process
INSTRUMENTS: Measurement, Indl Process
INSTRUMENTS: Measuring & Controlling
INSTRUMENTS: Measuring Electricity
INSTRUMENTS: Measuring, Electrical Power
INSTRUMENTS: Measuring, Electrical Quantities
INSTRUMENTS: Medical & Surgical
INSTRUMENTS: Multimeters
INSTRUMENTS: Oscillographs & Oscilloscopes
INSTRUMENTS: Potentiometric
INSTRUMENTS: Radio Frequency Measuring
INSTRUMENTS: Signal Generators & Averagers
INSTRUMENTS: Temperature Measurement, Indl
INSTRUMENTS: Test, Digital, Electronic & Electrical Circuits
INSTRUMENTS: Test, Electrical, Engine
INSTRUMENTS: Test, Electronic & Electric Measurement
INSTRUMENTS: Test, Electronic & Electrical Circuits
INSTRUMENTS: Testing, Semiconductor
INSTRUMENTS: Thermal Conductive, Indl
INSTRUMENTS: Time Code Generators
INSTRUMENTS: Vibration
INSULATION & CUSHIONING FOAM: Polystyrene
INSULATION MATERIALS WHOLESALERS
INSULATION: Fiberglass
INSULATORS & INSULATION MATERIALS: Electrical
INSURANCE AGENTS, NEC
INSURANCE CARRIERS: Life
INSURANCE CLAIM PROCESSING, EXC MEDICAL
INSURANCE INFORMATION & CONSULTING SVCS
INSURANCE PROFESSIONAL STANDARDS SVCS
INSURANCE: Agents, Brokers & Service
INTEGRATED CIRCUITS, SEMICONDUCTOR NETWORKS, ETC
INTERCOMMUNICATION EQPT REPAIR SVCS
INTERCOMMUNICATIONS SYSTEMS: Electric
INTERIOR DECORATING SVCS

PRODUCT INDEX

INTERIOR DESIGN SVCS, NEC
INTERIOR DESIGNING SVCS
INTERMEDIATES Cyclic, Organic
INTRAVENOUS SOLUTIONS
INVENTORY COMPUTING SVCS
INVERTERS: Nonrotating Electrical
INVESTMENT ADVISORY SVCS
INVESTMENT CLUBS
INVESTMENT FIRM: General Brokerage
INVESTMENT FUNDS, NEC
INVESTMENT FUNDS: Open-Ended
INVESTORS, NEC
INVESTORS: Real Estate, Exc Property Operators
IRON & STEEL PRDTS: Hot-Rolled
IRON ORE PREPARATION
IRON ORES
IRON: Sponge
IRONING BOARDS
IRRADIATION EQPT: Nuclear
IRRIGATION SYSTEMS, NEC Water Distribution Or Sply Systems

J

JACKS: Hydraulic
JANITORIAL & CUSTODIAL SVCS
JANITORIAL EQPT & SPLYS WHOLESALERS
JARS: Plastic
JEWELERS' FINDINGS & MATERIALS: Castings
JEWELRY & PRECIOUS STONES WHOLESALERS
JEWELRY APPAREL
JEWELRY FINDINGS & LAPIDARY WORK
JEWELRY REPAIR SVCS
JEWELRY STORES
JEWELRY STORES: Clocks
JEWELRY STORES: Precious Stones & Precious Metals
JEWELRY STORES: Silverware
JEWELRY STORES: Watches
JEWELRY, PREC METAL: Mountings, Pens, Lthr, Etc, Gold/Silver
JEWELRY, PRECIOUS METAL: Cigar & Cigarette Access
JEWELRY, PRECIOUS METAL: Medals, Precious Or Semiprecious
JEWELRY, PRECIOUS METAL: Pearl, Natural Or Cultured
JEWELRY, PRECIOUS METAL: Rings, Finger
JEWELRY, PRECIOUS METAL: Rosaries/Other Sm Religious Article
JEWELRY, PRECIOUS METAL: Settings & Mountings
JEWELRY, WHOLESALE
JEWELRY: Decorative, Fashion & Costume
JEWELRY: Precious Metal
JIGS & FIXTURES
JIGS: Welding Positioners
JOB PRINTING & NEWSPAPER PUBLISHING COMBINED
JOB TRAINING & VOCATIONAL REHABILITATION SVCS
JOINTS & COUPLINGS
JOINTS: Ball Except aircraft & Auto
JOINTS: Expansion
JOINTS: Swivel & Universal, Exc Aircraft & Auto
JOISTS: Long-Span Series, Open Web Steel

K

KAOLIN MINING
KEYBOARDS: Computer Or Office Machine
KITCHEN CABINET STORES, EXC CUSTOM
KITCHEN CABINETS WHOLESALERS
KITCHEN TOOLS & UTENSILS WHOLESALERS
KITCHEN UTENSILS: Bakers' Eqpt, Wood
KITCHEN UTENSILS: Food Handling & Processing Prdts, Wood
KITCHEN UTENSILS: Wooden
KITCHENWARE STORES
KITCHENWARE: Plastic
KITS: Plastic
KNIVES: Agricultural Or indl
KNURLING

L

LABELS: Cotton, Printed
LABELS: Paper, Made From Purchased Materials
LABELS: Woven
LABORATORIES, TESTING: Metallurgical
LABORATORIES, TESTING: Product Testing
LABORATORIES, TESTING: Product Testing, Safety/Performance
LABORATORIES, TESTING: Radiation
LABORATORIES, TESTING: Seed
LABORATORIES, TESTING: Veterinary
LABORATORIES, TESTING: Welded Joint Radiographing
LABORATORIES: Biological Research
LABORATORIES: Biotechnology
LABORATORIES: Commercial Nonphysical Research
LABORATORIES: Dental
LABORATORIES: Dental, Artificial Teeth Production
LABORATORIES: Dental, Crown & Bridge Production
LABORATORIES: Dental, Denture Production
LABORATORIES: Electronic Research
LABORATORIES: Medical
LABORATORIES: Neurological
LABORATORIES: Noncommercial Research
LABORATORIES: Physical Research, Commercial
LABORATORIES: Testing
LABORATORIES: Testing
LABORATORY APPARATUS & FURNITURE
LABORATORY APPARATUS & FURNITURE: Worktables
LABORATORY APPARATUS, EXC HEATING & MEASURING
LABORATORY APPARATUS: Bunsen Burners
LABORATORY APPARATUS: Calibration Tapes, Phy Testing Mach
LABORATORY APPARATUS: Calorimeters
LABORATORY APPARATUS: Freezers
LABORATORY APPARATUS: Laser Beam Alignment Device
LABORATORY APPARATUS: Metal Periphery Dir Rdg Diameter Tape
LABORATORY APPARATUS: Particle Size Reduction
LABORATORY APPARATUS: Pipettes, Hemocytometer
LABORATORY APPARATUS: Sample Preparation Apparatus
LABORATORY APPARATUS: Shakers & Stirrers
LABORATORY CHEMICALS: Organic
LABORATORY EQPT, EXC MEDICAL: Wholesalers
LABORATORY EQPT: Chemical
LABORATORY EQPT: Clinical Instruments Exc Medical
LABORATORY EQPT: Incubators
LABORATORY EQPT: Measuring
LABORATORY EQPT: Sterilizers
LADDER & WORKSTAND COMBINATION ASSEMBLIES: Metal
LADDERS: Metal
LADDERS: Portable, Metal
LAMINATED PLASTICS: Plate, Sheet, Rod & Tubes
LAMINATING MATERIALS
LAMINATING SVCS
LAMP & LIGHT BULBS & TUBES
LAMP BULBS & TUBES, ELEC: Lead-In Wires, From Purchased Wire
LAMP BULBS & TUBES, ELECTRIC: Electric Light
LAMP BULBS & TUBES, ELECTRIC: For Specialized Applications
LAMP BULBS & TUBES/PARTS, ELECTRIC: Generalized Applications
LAMP REPAIR & MOUNTING SVCS
LAMP SHADES: Metal
LAMP STORES
LAMPS: Boudoir, Residential
LAMPS: Desk, Residential
LAMPS: Incandescent, Filament
LAMPS: Table, Residential
LAMPS: Ultraviolet
LAND SUBDIVISION & DEVELOPMENT
LANTERNS
LAPIDARY WORK: Jewel Cut, Drill, Polish, Recut/Setting
LASER SYSTEMS & EQPT
LASERS: Welding, Drilling & Cutting Eqpt
LATH: Expanded Metal
LATHES
LAUNDRY & GARMENT SVCS, NEC: Garment Making, Alter & Repair
LAUNDRY & GARMENT SVCS: Dressmaking, Matl Owned By Customer
LAUNDRY EQPT: Commercial
LAUNDRY EQPT: Household
LAWN & GARDEN EQPT
LAWN & GARDEN EQPT STORES
LAWN & GARDEN EQPT: Blowers & Vacuums
LAWN & GARDEN EQPT: Edgers
LAWN & GARDEN EQPT: Grass Catchers, Lawn Mower
LAWN & GARDEN EQPT: Loaders
LAWN & GARDEN EQPT: Tractors & Eqpt
LAWN MOWER REPAIR SHOP
LEAD & ZINC

LEAD & ZINC ORES
LEAD ORE MINING
LEAD PENCILS & ART GOODS
LEASING & RENTAL SVCS: Computer Hardware, Exc Finance
LEASING & RENTAL SVCS: Cranes & Aerial Lift Eqpt
LEASING & RENTAL: Boats & Ships
LEASING & RENTAL: Computers & Eqpt
LEASING & RENTAL: Construction & Mining Eqpt
LEASING & RENTAL: Medical Machinery & Eqpt
LEASING & RENTAL: Mobile Home Sites
LEASING & RENTAL: Office Machines & Eqpt
LEASING & RENTAL: Trucks, Without Drivers
LEASING: Passenger Car
LEASING: Shipping Container
LEATHER GOODS, EXC FOOTWEAR, GLOVES, LUGGAGE/BELTING, WHOL
LEATHER GOODS: Cases
LEATHER GOODS: Embossed
LEATHER GOODS: Garments
LEATHER GOODS: Harnesses Or Harness Parts
LEATHER GOODS: Key Cases
LEATHER GOODS: NEC
LEATHER GOODS: Personal
LEATHER GOODS: Sewing Cases
LEATHER GOODS: Wallets
LEATHER TANNING & FINISHING
LEATHER: Accessory Prdts
LEATHER: Artificial
LEATHER: Rawhide
LEATHER: Shoe
LEGAL & TAX SVCS
LEGAL COUNSEL & PROSECUTION: Attorney General's Office
LEGAL OFFICES & SVCS
LEGAL SVCS: Taxation Law
LENS COATING: Ophthalmic
LETTERS: Cardboard, Die-Cut, Made From Purchased Materials
LICENSE TAGS: Automobile, Stamped Metal
LIGHT OR HEAT EMISSION OPERATING APPARATUS
LIGHTING EQPT: Area & Sports Luminaries
LIGHTING EQPT: Bicycle Lamps
LIGHTING EQPT: Flashlights
LIGHTING EQPT: Fog Lights
LIGHTING EQPT: Locomotive & Railroad Car Lights
LIGHTING EQPT: Motor Vehicle
LIGHTING EQPT: Motor Vehicle, Flasher Lights
LIGHTING EQPT: Motor Vehicle, NEC
LIGHTING EQPT: Motorcycle Lamps
LIGHTING EQPT: Outdoor
LIGHTING EQPT: Reflectors, Metal, For Lighting Eqpt
LIGHTING EQPT: Strobe Lighting Systems
LIGHTING FIXTURES WHOLESALERS
LIGHTING FIXTURES, NEC
LIGHTING FIXTURES: Airport
LIGHTING FIXTURES: Decorative Area
LIGHTING FIXTURES: Fluorescent, Commercial
LIGHTING FIXTURES: Gas
LIGHTING FIXTURES: Indl & Commercial
LIGHTING FIXTURES: Marine
LIGHTING FIXTURES: Motor Vehicle
LIGHTING FIXTURES: Ornamental, Commercial
LIGHTING FIXTURES: Public
LIGHTING FIXTURES: Residential
LIGHTING FIXTURES: Residential, Electric
LIGHTING FIXTURES: Street
LIME
LIME ROCK: Ground
LIME: Building
LIMESTONE & MARBLE: Dimension
LIMESTONE: Crushed & Broken
LIMESTONE: Cut & Shaped
LIMESTONE: Dimension
LIMESTONE: Ground
LINEN SPLY SVC: Apron
LINENS & TOWELS WHOLESALERS
LINENS: Napkins, Fabric & Nonwoven, From Purchased Materials
LINENS: Tablecloths, From Purchased Materials
LINER BRICK OR PLATES: Sewer Or Tank Lining, Vitrified Clay
LINER STRIPS: Rubber
LINERS & COVERS: Fabric
LINERS & LINING

2020 Harris Illinois
Industrial Directory

1319

PRODUCT INDEX

LININGS: Safe & Vault, Metal
LIQUEFIED PETROLEUM GAS DEALERS
LIQUEFIED PETROLEUM GAS WHOLESALERS
LIQUID CRYSTAL DISPLAYS
LITHOGRAPHIC PLATES
LIVESTOCK WHOLESALERS, NEC
LOADS: Electronic
LOCK & KEY SVCS
LOCKS
LOCKS & LOCK SETS, WHOLESALE
LOCKS: Safe & Vault, Metal
LOCKSMITHS
LOCOMOTIVES & PARTS
LOG SPLITTERS
LOGGING
LOGGING CAMPS & CONTRACTORS
LOGGING: Stump Harvesting
LOGGING: Timber, Cut At Logging Camp
LOGGING: Wood Chips, Produced In The Field
LOOSELEAF BINDERS
LOOSELEAF BINDERS: Library
LOTIONS OR CREAMS: Face
LOTIONS: SHAVING
LOUDSPEAKERS
LOUVERS: Ventilating
LOZENGES: Pharmaceutical
LUBRICANTS: Corrosion Preventive
LUBRICATING EQPT: Indl
LUBRICATING OIL & GREASE WHOLESALERS
LUGGAGE & BRIEFCASES
LUGGAGE & LEATHER GOODS STORES
LUGGAGE & LEATHER GOODS STORES: Leather, Exc Luggage & Shoes
LUGGAGE: Traveling Bags
LUGGAGE: Wardrobe Bags
LUMBER & BLDG MATLS DEALER, RET: Electric Constructn Matls
LUMBER & BLDG MATLS DEALER, RET: Garage Doors, Sell/Install
LUMBER & BLDG MTRLS DEALERS, RET: Doors, Storm, Wood/Metal
LUMBER & BLDG MTRLS DEALERS, RET: Greenhouse Kits, Prefab
LUMBER & BLDG MTRLS DEALERS, RET: Planing Mill Prdts/Lumber
LUMBER & BLDG MTRLS DEALERS, RET: Windows, Storm, Wood/Metal
LUMBER & BUILDING MATERIAL DEALERS, RETAIL: Roofing Material
LUMBER & BUILDING MATERIALS DEALER, RET: Door & Window Prdts
LUMBER & BUILDING MATERIALS DEALER, RET: Masonry Matls/Splys
LUMBER & BUILDING MATERIALS DEALERS, RETAIL: Brick
LUMBER & BUILDING MATERIALS DEALERS, RETAIL: Cement
LUMBER & BUILDING MATERIALS DEALERS, RETAIL: Countertops
LUMBER & BUILDING MATERIALS DEALERS, RETAIL: Sand & Gravel
LUMBER & BUILDING MATERIALS DEALERS, RETAIL: Tile, Ceramic
LUMBER & BUILDING MATERIALS RET DEALERS: Millwork & Lumber
LUMBER & BUILDING MATLS DEALERS, RET: Concrete/Cinder Block
LUMBER & BUILDING MATLS DEALERS, RET: Screens, Door/Window
LUMBER & BUILDING MTRLS DEALERS, RET: Insulation Mtrl, Bldg
LUMBER: Flooring, Dressed, Softwood
LUMBER: Hardboard
LUMBER: Hardwood Dimension
LUMBER: Hardwood Dimension & Flooring Mills
LUMBER: Kiln Dried
LUMBER: Panels, Plywood, Softwood
LUMBER: Piles, Foundation & Marine Construction, Treated
LUMBER: Plywood, Hardwood
LUMBER: Plywood, Hardwood or Hardwood Faced
LUMBER: Plywood, Prefinished, Hardwood
LUMBER: Plywood, Softwood
LUMBER: Resawn, Small Dimension
LUMBER: Treated
LUMBER: Veneer, Hardwood

M

MACHINE GUNS, WHOLESALE
MACHINE PARTS: Stamped Or Pressed Metal
MACHINE SHOPS
MACHINE TOOL ACCESS: Balancing Machines
MACHINE TOOL ACCESS: Boring Attachments
MACHINE TOOL ACCESS: Broaches
MACHINE TOOL ACCESS: Cams
MACHINE TOOL ACCESS: Cutting
MACHINE TOOL ACCESS: Diamond Cutting, For Turning, Etc
MACHINE TOOL ACCESS: Dresser, Abrasive Wheel Or Other
MACHINE TOOL ACCESS: Drill Bushings, Drilling Jig
MACHINE TOOL ACCESS: Drills
MACHINE TOOL ACCESS: Hopper Feed Devices
MACHINE TOOL ACCESS: Knives, Metalworking
MACHINE TOOL ACCESS: Machine Attachments & Access, Drilling
MACHINE TOOL ACCESS: Milling Machine Attachments
MACHINE TOOL ACCESS: Pushers
MACHINE TOOL ACCESS: Rotary Tables
MACHINE TOOL ACCESS: Threading Tools
MACHINE TOOL ACCESS: Tool Holders
MACHINE TOOL ACCESS: Tools & Access
MACHINE TOOL ATTACHMENTS & ACCESS
MACHINE TOOLS & ACCESS
MACHINE TOOLS, METAL CUTTING: Brushing
MACHINE TOOLS, METAL CUTTING: Centering
MACHINE TOOLS, METAL CUTTING: Cutoff
MACHINE TOOLS, METAL CUTTING: Drilling
MACHINE TOOLS, METAL CUTTING: Drilling & Boring
MACHINE TOOLS, METAL CUTTING: Exotic, Including Explosive
MACHINE TOOLS, METAL CUTTING: Grind, Polish, Buff, Lapp
MACHINE TOOLS, METAL CUTTING: Home Workshop
MACHINE TOOLS, METAL CUTTING: Keysetting
MACHINE TOOLS, METAL CUTTING: Lathes
MACHINE TOOLS, METAL CUTTING: Milling, Chemical
MACHINE TOOLS, METAL CUTTING: Numerically Controlled
MACHINE TOOLS, METAL CUTTING: Pipe Cutting & Threading
MACHINE TOOLS, METAL CUTTING: Planers
MACHINE TOOLS, METAL CUTTING: Plasma Process
MACHINE TOOLS, METAL CUTTING: Screw & Thread
MACHINE TOOLS, METAL CUTTING: Tool Replacement & Rpr Parts
MACHINE TOOLS, METAL FORMING: Bending
MACHINE TOOLS, METAL FORMING: Container, Metal Incl Cans
MACHINE TOOLS, METAL FORMING: Crimping, Metal
MACHINE TOOLS, METAL FORMING: Die Casting & Extruding
MACHINE TOOLS, METAL FORMING: Electroforming
MACHINE TOOLS, METAL FORMING: Forming, Metal Deposit
MACHINE TOOLS, METAL FORMING: Headers
MACHINE TOOLS, METAL FORMING: High Energy Rate
MACHINE TOOLS, METAL FORMING: Magnetic Forming
MACHINE TOOLS, METAL FORMING: Marking
MACHINE TOOLS, METAL FORMING: Mechanical, Pneumatic Or Hyd
MACHINE TOOLS, METAL FORMING: Pressing
MACHINE TOOLS, METAL FORMING: Rebuilt
MACHINE TOOLS, METAL FORMING: Robots, Pressing, Extrudg, Etc
MACHINE TOOLS, METAL FORMING: Spring Winding & Forming
MACHINE TOOLS: Metal Cutting
MACHINE TOOLS: Metal Forming
MACHINERY & EQPT FINANCE LEASING
MACHINERY & EQPT, AGRICULTURAL, WHOL: Farm Eqpt Parts/Splys
MACHINERY & EQPT, AGRICULTURAL, WHOLESALE: Agricultural, NEC
MACHINERY & EQPT, AGRICULTURAL, WHOLESALE: Dairy
MACHINERY & EQPT, AGRICULTURAL, WHOLESALE: Farm Implements
MACHINERY & EQPT, AGRICULTURAL, WHOLESALE: Landscaping Eqpt
MACHINERY & EQPT, AGRICULTURAL, WHOLESALE: Lawn
MACHINERY & EQPT, AGRICULTURAL, WHOLESALE: Lawn & Garden
MACHINERY & EQPT, AGRICULTURAL, WHOLESALE: Livestock Eqpt
MACHINERY & EQPT, AGRICULTURAL, WHOLESALE: Tractors
MACHINERY & EQPT, INDL, WHOL: Controlling Instruments/Access
MACHINERY & EQPT, INDL, WHOL: Environ Pollution Cntrl, Air
MACHINERY & EQPT, INDL, WHOLESALE: Chemical Process
MACHINERY & EQPT, INDL, WHOLESALE: Conveyor Systems
MACHINERY & EQPT, INDL, WHOLESALE: Cranes
MACHINERY & EQPT, INDL, WHOLESALE: Drilling Bits
MACHINERY & EQPT, INDL, WHOLESALE: Drilling, Exc Bits
MACHINERY & EQPT, INDL, WHOLESALE: Engines & Parts, Diesel
MACHINERY & EQPT, INDL, WHOLESALE: Engines, Gasoline
MACHINERY & EQPT, INDL, WHOLESALE: Engs & Parts, Air-Cooled
MACHINERY & EQPT, INDL, WHOLESALE: Engs/Transportation Eqpt
MACHINERY & EQPT, INDL, WHOLESALE: Food Manufacturing
MACHINERY & EQPT, INDL, WHOLESALE: Fuel Injection Systems
MACHINERY & EQPT, INDL, WHOLESALE: Heat Exchange
MACHINERY & EQPT, INDL, WHOLESALE: Hoists
MACHINERY & EQPT, INDL, WHOLESALE: Hydraulic Systems
MACHINERY & EQPT, INDL, WHOLESALE: Indl Machine Parts
MACHINERY & EQPT, INDL, WHOLESALE: Instruments & Cntrl Eqpt
MACHINERY & EQPT, INDL, WHOLESALE: Lift Trucks & Parts
MACHINERY & EQPT, INDL, WHOLESALE: Machine Tools & Access
MACHINERY & EQPT, INDL, WHOLESALE: Machine Tools & Metalwork
MACHINERY & EQPT, INDL, WHOLESALE: Measure/Test, Electric
MACHINERY & EQPT, INDL, WHOLESALE: Metal Refining
MACHINERY & EQPT, INDL, WHOLESALE: Packaging
MACHINERY & EQPT, INDL, WHOLESALE: Paint Spray
MACHINERY & EQPT, INDL, WHOLESALE: Petroleum Industry
MACHINERY & EQPT, INDL, WHOLESALE: Plastic Prdts Machinery
MACHINERY & EQPT, INDL, WHOLESALE: Pneumatic Tools
MACHINERY & EQPT, INDL, WHOLESALE: Processing & Packaging
MACHINERY & EQPT, INDL, WHOLESALE: Robots
MACHINERY & EQPT, INDL, WHOLESALE: Safety Eqpt
MACHINERY & EQPT, INDL, WHOLESALE: Sewing
MACHINERY & EQPT, INDL, WHOLESALE: Tanks, Storage
MACHINERY & EQPT, INDL, WHOLESALE: Tapping Attachments
MACHINERY & EQPT, INDL, WHOLESALE: Tool & Die Makers
MACHINERY & EQPT, INDL, WHOLESALE: Water Pumps
MACHINERY & EQPT, WHOLESALE: Blades, Graders, Scrapers, Etc
MACHINERY & EQPT, WHOLESALE: Concrete Processing
MACHINERY & EQPT, WHOLESALE: Construction, General
MACHINERY & EQPT, WHOLESALE: Contractors Materials
MACHINERY & EQPT, WHOLESALE: Masonry
MACHINERY & EQPT, WHOLESALE: Oil Field Eqpt
MACHINERY & EQPT: Electroplating
MACHINERY & EQPT: Farm
MACHINERY & EQPT: Gas Producers, Generators/Other Rltd Eqpt
MACHINERY & EQPT: Liquid Automation
MACHINERY & EQPT: Metal Finishing, Plating Etc
MACHINERY & EQPT: Petroleum Refinery
MACHINERY & EQPT: Vibratory Parts Handling Eqpt
MACHINERY BASES
MACHINERY CLEANING SVCS
MACHINERY, COMMERCIAL LAUNDRY & Drycleaning: Ironers
MACHINERY, COMMERCIAL LAUNDRY: Extractors
MACHINERY, COMMERCIAL LAUNDRY: Washing, Incl Coin-Operated
MACHINERY, EQPT & SUPPLIES: Parking Facility
MACHINERY, FOOD PRDTS: Beverage
MACHINERY, FOOD PRDTS: Confectionery

PRODUCT INDEX

MACHINERY, FOOD PRDTS: Cracker Making
MACHINERY, FOOD PRDTS: Cutting, Chopping, Grinding, Mixing
MACHINERY, FOOD PRDTS: Dies, Biscuit Cutting
MACHINERY, FOOD PRDTS: Food Processing, Smokers
MACHINERY, FOOD PRDTS: Grinders, Commercial
MACHINERY, FOOD PRDTS: Ovens, Bakery
MACHINERY, FOOD PRDTS: Processing, Fish & Shellfish
MACHINERY, FOOD PRDTS: Roasting, Coffee, Peanut, Etc.
MACHINERY, FOOD PRDTS: Sausage Stuffers
MACHINERY, LUBRICATION: Automatic
MACHINERY, MAILING: Canceling
MACHINERY, MAILING: Mailing
MACHINERY, MAILING: Postage Meters
MACHINERY, METALWORKING: Assembly, Including Robotic
MACHINERY, METALWORKING: Coil Winding, For Springs
MACHINERY, METALWORKING: Coiling
MACHINERY, METALWORKING: Cutting & Slitting
MACHINERY, METALWORKING: Rotary Slitters, Metalworking
MACHINERY, OFFICE: Embossing, Store Or Office
MACHINERY, OFFICE: Perforators
MACHINERY, OFFICE: Shorthand
MACHINERY, OFFICE: Time Clocks &Time Recording Devices
MACHINERY, PACKAGING: Canning, Food
MACHINERY, PACKAGING: Carton Packing
MACHINERY, PACKAGING: Packing & Wrapping
MACHINERY, PACKAGING: Vacuum
MACHINERY, PACKAGING: Wrapping
MACHINERY, PAPER INDUSTRY: Coating & Finishing
MACHINERY, PAPER INDUSTRY: Converting, Die Cutting & Stampng
MACHINERY, PAPER INDUSTRY: Cutting
MACHINERY, PAPER INDUSTRY: Pulp Mill
MACHINERY, PRINTING TRADES: Bookbinding Machinery
MACHINERY, PRINTING TRADES: Copy Holders
MACHINERY, PRINTING TRADES: Electrotyping
MACHINERY, PRINTING TRADES: Plates
MACHINERY, PRINTING TRADES: Presses, Envelope
MACHINERY, PRINTING TRADES: Presses, Gravure
MACHINERY, PRINTING TRADES: Printing Trade Parts & Attchts
MACHINERY, SERVICING: Coin-Operated, Exc Dry Clean & Laundry
MACHINERY, SEWING: Bag Seaming & Closing
MACHINERY, SEWING: Sewing & Hat & Zipper Making
MACHINERY, TEXTILE: Creels
MACHINERY, TEXTILE: Dyeing
MACHINERY, TEXTILE: Embroidery
MACHINERY, TEXTILE: Frames, Double & Twisting
MACHINERY, TEXTILE: Knot Tying
MACHINERY, TEXTILE: Printing
MACHINERY, TEXTILE: Silk Screens
MACHINERY, TEXTILE: Spinning
MACHINERY, TEXTILE: Yarn Texturizing
MACHINERY, WOODWORKING: Cabinet Makers'
MACHINERY, WOODWORKING: Furniture Makers
MACHINERY, WOODWORKING: Sanding, Exc Portable Floor Sanders
MACHINERY, WOODWORKING: Saws, Power, Bench & Table
MACHINERY/EQPT, INDL, WHOL: Cleaning, High Press, Sand/Steam
MACHINERY/EQPT, INDL, WHOL: Machinist Precision Measrng Tool
MACHINERY/EQPT, INDL, WHOL: Tool Holder, Incl Chuck/Turret
MACHINERY: Ammunition & Explosives Loading
MACHINERY: Assembly, Exc Metalworking
MACHINERY: Automobile Garage, Frame Straighteners
MACHINERY: Automotive Maintenance
MACHINERY: Automotive Related
MACHINERY: Banking
MACHINERY: Binding
MACHINERY: Blasting, Electrical
MACHINERY: Bottling & Canning
MACHINERY: Brewery & Malting
MACHINERY: Broom Making
MACHINERY: Cement Making
MACHINERY: Concrete Prdts
MACHINERY: Construction
MACHINERY: Cryogenic, Industrial
MACHINERY: Custom
MACHINERY: Deburring
MACHINERY: Die Casting
MACHINERY: Drill Presses
MACHINERY: Electrical Discharge Erosion
MACHINERY: Electronic Component Making
MACHINERY: Electronic Teaching Aids
MACHINERY: Extruding
MACHINERY: Gear Cutting & Finishing
MACHINERY: General, Industrial, NEC
MACHINERY: Glassmaking
MACHINERY: Grinding
MACHINERY: Ice Cream
MACHINERY: Ice Making
MACHINERY: Industrial, NEC
MACHINERY: Kilns
MACHINERY: Knitting
MACHINERY: Labeling
MACHINERY: Lapping
MACHINERY: Metalworking
MACHINERY: Milling
MACHINERY: Mining
MACHINERY: Optical Lens
MACHINERY: Ozone
MACHINERY: Packaging
MACHINERY: Paint Making
MACHINERY: Paper Industry Miscellaneous
MACHINERY: Pharmaciutical
MACHINERY: Photographic Reproduction
MACHINERY: Plastic Working
MACHINERY: Polishing & Buffing
MACHINERY: Printing Presses
MACHINERY: Recycling
MACHINERY: Riveting
MACHINERY: Road Construction & Maintenance
MACHINERY: Rubber Working
MACHINERY: Saw & Sawing
MACHINERY: Semiconductor Manufacturing
MACHINERY: Separation Eqpt, Magnetic
MACHINERY: Service Industry, NEC
MACHINERY: Sheet Metal Working
MACHINERY: Sifting & Screening
MACHINERY: Snow Making
MACHINERY: Specialty
MACHINERY: Textile
MACHINERY: Tire Shredding
MACHINERY: Tobacco Prdts
MACHINERY: Voting
MACHINERY: Wire Drawing
MACHINERY: Woodworking
MACHINES: Forming, Sheet Metal
MACHINISTS' TOOLS & MACHINES: Measuring, Metalworking Type
MACHINISTS' TOOLS: Measuring, Precision
MACHINISTS' TOOLS: Precision
MACHINISTS' TOOLS: Scales, Measuring, Precision
MAGAZINES, WHOLESALE
MAGNESIUM
MAGNETIC INK & OPTICAL SCANNING EQPT
MAGNETIC RESONANCE IMAGING DEVICES: Nonmedical
MAGNETIC SHIELDS, METAL
MAGNETIC TAPE, AUDIO: Prerecorded
MAGNETS: Ceramic
MAGNETS: Permanent
MAIL-ORDER BOOK CLUBS
MAIL-ORDER HOUSE, NEC
MAIL-ORDER HOUSES: Automotive Splys & Eqpt
MAIL-ORDER HOUSES: Books, Exc Book Clubs
MAIL-ORDER HOUSES: Cards
MAIL-ORDER HOUSES: Clothing, Exc Women's
MAIL-ORDER HOUSES: Educational Splys & Eqpt
MAIL-ORDER HOUSES: Electronic Kits & Parts
MAIL-ORDER HOUSES: Fitness & Sporting Goods
MAIL-ORDER HOUSES: Food
MAIL-ORDER HOUSES: Furniture & Furnishings
MAIL-ORDER HOUSES: General Merchandise
MAIL-ORDER HOUSES: Record & Tape, Music Or Video Club
MAIL-ORDER HOUSES: Religious Merchandise
MAIL-ORDER HOUSES: Women's Apparel
MAILBOX RENTAL & RELATED SVCS
MAILING LIST: Management
MAILING SVCS, NEC
MANAGEMENT CONSULTING SVCS: Administrative
MANAGEMENT CONSULTING SVCS: Automation & Robotics
MANAGEMENT CONSULTING SVCS: Business
MANAGEMENT CONSULTING SVCS: Construction Project
MANAGEMENT CONSULTING SVCS: Corporation Organizing
MANAGEMENT CONSULTING SVCS: Food & Beverage
MANAGEMENT CONSULTING SVCS: Foreign Trade
MANAGEMENT CONSULTING SVCS: General
MANAGEMENT CONSULTING SVCS: Hospital & Health
MANAGEMENT CONSULTING SVCS: Industrial & Labor
MANAGEMENT CONSULTING SVCS: Industry Specialist
MANAGEMENT CONSULTING SVCS: Maintenance
MANAGEMENT CONSULTING SVCS: Manufacturing
MANAGEMENT CONSULTING SVCS: Merchandising
MANAGEMENT CONSULTING SVCS: Real Estate
MANAGEMENT CONSULTING SVCS: Retail Trade Consultant
MANAGEMENT CONSULTING SVCS: Training & Development
MANAGEMENT SERVICES
MANAGEMENT SVCS: Administrative
MANAGEMENT SVCS: Business
MANAGEMENT SVCS: Construction
MANAGEMENT SVCS: Hotel Or Motel
MANAGEMENT SVCS: Restaurant
MANHOLES & COVERS: Metal
MANHOLES COVERS: Concrete
MANICURE PREPARATIONS
MANNEQUINS
MANUFACTURED & MOBILE HOME DEALERS
MANUFACTURING INDUSTRIES, NEC
MARBLE, BUILDING: Cut & Shaped
MARINE CARGO HANDLING SVCS
MARINE CARGO HANDLING SVCS: Loading
MARINE HARDWARE
MARINE RELATED EQPT
MARINE SPLY DEALERS
MARINE SPLYS WHOLESALERS
MARKERS
MARKETS: Meat & fish
MARKING DEVICES
MARKING DEVICES: Canceling Stamps, Hand, Rubber Or Metal
MARKING DEVICES: Embossing Seals & Hand Stamps
MARKING DEVICES: Printing Dies, Marking Mach, Rubber/Plastic
MARKING DEVICES: Screens, Textile Printing
MARKING DEVICES: Seal Presses, Notary & Hand
MARKING DEVICES: Stationary Embossers, Personal
MARTIAL ARTS INSTRUCTION
MASQUERADE OR THEATRICAL COSTUMES STORES
MASSAGE MACHINES, ELECTRIC: Barber & Beauty Shops
MASSAGE PARLOR & STEAM BATH SVCS
MASSAGE PARLORS
MASTIC ROOFING COMPOSITION
MATCHES, WHOLESALE
MATERIAL GRINDING & PULVERIZING SVCS NEC
MATERIALS HANDLING EQPT WHOLESALERS
MATERNITY WEAR STORES
MATS & MATTING, MADE FROM PURCHASED WIRE
MATS OR MATTING, NEC: Rubber
MATS, MATTING & PADS: Aircraft, Floor, Exc Rubber Or Plastic
MATS, MATTING & PADS: Nonwoven
MATS, ROOFING: Mineral Wool
MATTRESS STORES
MAUSOLEUMS
MEAL DELIVERY PROGRAMS
MEAT & FISH MARKETS: Freezer Provisioners, Meat
MEAT & MEAT PRDTS WHOLESALERS
MEAT CUTTING & PACKING
MEAT MARKETS
MEAT PRDTS: Boneless Meat, From Purchased Meat
MEAT PRDTS: Boxed Beef, From Slaughtered Meat
MEAT PRDTS: Canned Exc Baby Food, From Slaughtered Meat
MEAT PRDTS: Cooked Meats, From Purchased Meat
MEAT PRDTS: Corned Beef, From Purchased Meat
MEAT PRDTS: Cured Meats, From Purchased Meat
MEAT PRDTS: Frozen
MEAT PRDTS: Hams & Picnics, From Slaughtered Meat
MEAT PRDTS: Lamb, From Slaughtered Meat
MEAT PRDTS: Luncheon Meat, From Purchased Meat
MEAT PRDTS: Meat By-Prdts, From Slaughtered Meat
MEAT PRDTS: Pork, From Slaughtered Meat
MEAT PRDTS: Prepared Beef Prdts From Purchased Beef
MEAT PRDTS: Prepared Pork Prdts, From Purchased Pork
MEAT PRDTS: Roast Beef, From Purchased Meat

PRODUCT INDEX

MEAT PRDTS: Sausage Casings, Natural
MEAT PRDTS: Sausages & Related Prdts, From Purchased Meat
MEAT PRDTS: Sausages, From Purchased Meat
MEAT PRDTS: Sausages, From Slaughtered Meat
MEAT PRDTS: Smoked
MEAT PRDTS: Snack Sticks, Incl Jerky, From Purchased Meat
MEAT PRDTS: Veal, From Slaughtered Meat
MEAT PROCESSED FROM PURCHASED CARCASSES
MEAT PROCESSING MACHINERY
MEATS, PACKAGED FROZEN: Wholesalers
MECHANISMS: Coin-Operated Machines
MEDIA BUYING AGENCIES
MEDIA: Magnetic & Optical Recording
MEDICAL & HOSPITAL EQPT WHOLESALERS
MEDICAL & HOSPITAL SPLYS: Radiation Shielding Garments
MEDICAL & SURGICAL SPLYS: Abdominal Support, Braces/Trusses
MEDICAL & SURGICAL SPLYS: Bandages & Dressings
MEDICAL & SURGICAL SPLYS: Braces, Orthopedic
MEDICAL & SURGICAL SPLYS: Clothing, Fire Resistant & Protect
MEDICAL & SURGICAL SPLYS: Cosmetic Restorations
MEDICAL & SURGICAL SPLYS: Crutches & Walkers
MEDICAL & SURGICAL SPLYS: Drapes, Surgical, Cotton
MEDICAL & SURGICAL SPLYS: Gauze, Surgical
MEDICAL & SURGICAL SPLYS: Gynecological Splys & Appliances
MEDICAL & SURGICAL SPLYS: Infant Incubators
MEDICAL & SURGICAL SPLYS: Ligatures
MEDICAL & SURGICAL SPLYS: Limbs, Artificial
MEDICAL & SURGICAL SPLYS: Models, Anatomical
MEDICAL & SURGICAL SPLYS: Orthopedic Appliances
MEDICAL & SURGICAL SPLYS: Personal Safety Eqpt
MEDICAL & SURGICAL SPLYS: Prosthetic Appliances
MEDICAL & SURGICAL SPLYS: Respiratory Protect Eqpt, Personal
MEDICAL & SURGICAL SPLYS: Splints, Pneumatic & Wood
MEDICAL & SURGICAL SPLYS: Sponges
MEDICAL & SURGICAL SPLYS: Supports, Abdominal, Ankle, Etc
MEDICAL & SURGICAL SPLYS: Technical Aids, Handicapped
MEDICAL & SURGICAL SPLYS: Welders' Hoods
MEDICAL EQPT REPAIR SVCS, NON-ELECTRIC
MEDICAL EQPT: Cardiographs
MEDICAL EQPT: Diagnostic
MEDICAL EQPT: Electromedical Apparatus
MEDICAL EQPT: Heart-Lung Machines, Exc Iron Lungs
MEDICAL EQPT: Laser Systems
MEDICAL EQPT: PET Or Position Emission Tomography Scanners
MEDICAL EQPT: Patient Monitoring
MEDICAL EQPT: Ultrasonic Scanning Devices
MEDICAL EQPT: Ultrasonic, Exc Cleaning
MEDICAL EQPT: X-Ray Apparatus & Tubes, Radiographic
MEDICAL EQPT: X-ray Generators
MEDICAL FIELD ASSOCIATION
MEDICAL SVCS ORGANIZATION
MEDICAL TRAINING SERVICES
MEDICAL X-RAY MACHINES & TUBES WHOLESALERS
MEDICAL, DENTAL & HOSPITAL EQPT, WHOL: Dentists' Prof Splys
MEDICAL, DENTAL & HOSPITAL EQPT, WHOL: Hospital Eqpt & Splys
MEDICAL, DENTAL & HOSPITAL EQPT, WHOL: Hosptl Eqpt/Furniture
MEDICAL, DENTAL & HOSPITAL EQPT, WHOL: Surgical Eqpt & Splys
MEDICAL, DENTAL & HOSPITAL EQPT, WHOLESALE: Artificial Limbs
MEDICAL, DENTAL & HOSPITAL EQPT, WHOLESALE: Dental Lab
MEDICAL, DENTAL & HOSPITAL EQPT, WHOLESALE: Diagnostic, Med
MEDICAL, DENTAL & HOSPITAL EQPT, WHOLESALE: Hearing Aids
MEDICAL, DENTAL & HOSPITAL EQPT, WHOLESALE: Med Eqpt & Splys
MEDICAL, DENTAL & HOSPITAL EQPT, WHOLESALE: Medical Lab
MEDICAL, DENTAL & HOSPITAL EQPT, WHOLESALE: Orthopedic
MEDICAL, DENTAL/HOSPITAL EQPT, WHOL: Tech Aids, Handicapped
MEDITATION THERAPY
MEMBERSHIP ORGANIZATIONS, BUSINESS: Contractors' Association
MEMBERSHIP ORGANIZATIONS, BUSINESS: Merchants' Association
MEMBERSHIP ORGANIZATIONS, NEC: Charitable
MEMBERSHIP ORGANIZATIONS, PROFESSIONAL: Health Association
MEMBERSHIP ORGANIZATIONS, REL: Christian Reformed Church
MEMBERSHIP ORGANIZATIONS, RELIGIOUS: Brethren Church
MEMBERSHIP ORGANIZATIONS, RELIGIOUS: Catholic Church
MEMBERSHIP ORGANIZATIONS, RELIGIOUS: Church Of Christ
MEMBERSHIP ORGANIZATIONS, RELIGIOUS: Nonchurch
MEMBERSHIP ORGANIZATIONS: Reading Rooms/Other Cultural Orgs
MEMBERSHIP ORGS, CIVIC, SOCIAL & FRATERNAL: Condo Assoc
MEMBERSHIP ORGS, CIVIC, SOCIAL/FRAT: Educator's Assoc
MEMBERSHIP SPORTS & RECREATION CLUBS
MEMORIALS, MONUMENTS & MARKERS
MEN'S & BOYS' CLOTHING ACCESS STORES
MEN'S & BOYS' CLOTHING STORES
MEN'S & BOYS' CLOTHING WHOLESALERS, NEC
MEN'S & BOYS' SPORTSWEAR CLOTHING STORES
MEN'S & BOYS' SPORTSWEAR WHOLESALERS
MENTAL HEALTH CLINIC, OUTPATIENT
METAL & STEEL PRDTS: Abrasive
METAL CUTTING SVCS
METAL DETECTORS
METAL FABRICATORS: Architechtural
METAL FABRICATORS: Plate
METAL FABRICATORS: Sheet
METAL FABRICATORS: Structural, Ship
METAL FABRICATORS: Structural, Ship
METAL FINISHING SVCS
METAL MINING SVCS
METAL ORES, NEC
METAL RESHAPING & REPLATING SVCS
METAL SERVICE CENTERS & OFFICES
METAL SPINNING FOR THE TRADE
METAL STAMPING, FOR THE TRADE
METAL STAMPINGS: Ornamental
METAL STAMPINGS: Perforated
METAL TREATING COMPOUNDS
METAL TREATING: Cryogenic
METALS SVC CENTERS & WHOL: Structural Shapes, Iron Or Steel
METALS SVC CENTERS & WHOLESALERS: Bars, Metal
METALS SVC CENTERS & WHOLESALERS: Casting, Rough,Iron/Steel
METALS SVC CENTERS & WHOLESALERS: Copper Prdts
METALS SVC CENTERS & WHOLESALERS: Flat Prdts, Iron Or Steel
METALS SVC CENTERS & WHOLESALERS: Foundry Prdts
METALS SVC CENTERS & WHOLESALERS: Iron & Steel Prdt, Ferrous
METALS SVC CENTERS & WHOLESALERS: Misc Nonferrous Prdts
METALS SVC CENTERS & WHOLESALERS: Nonferrous Sheets, Etc
METALS SVC CENTERS & WHOLESALERS: Pig Iron
METALS SVC CENTERS & WHOLESALERS: Pipe & Tubing, Steel
METALS SVC CENTERS & WHOLESALERS: Rods, Wire, Exc Insulated
METALS SVC CENTERS & WHOLESALERS: Sheets, Metal
METALS SVC CENTERS & WHOLESALERS: Steel
METALS SVC CENTERS & WHOLESALERS: Steel Decking
METALS SVC CENTERS & WHOLESALERS: Tubing, Metal
METALS SVC CENTERS/WHOL: Forms, Steel Concrete Construction
METALS SVC CTRS & WHOLESALERS: Aluminum Bars, Rods, Etc
METALS SVC CTRS & WHOLESALERS: Copper Sheets, Plates, NEC
METALS: Precious NEC
METALS: Precious, Secondary
METALS: Primary Nonferrous, NEC
METALWORK: Miscellaneous
METALWORK: Ornamental
METALWORKING MACHINERY WHOLESALERS
METERING DEVICES: Gasoline Dispensing
METERING DEVICES: Integrating & Totalizing, Gas & Liquids
METERING DEVICES: Water Quality Monitoring & Control Systems
METERS: Audio
METERS: Demand
MGMT CONSULTING SVCS: Matls, Incl Purch, Handle & Invntry
MICA PRDTS
MICROCIRCUITS, INTEGRATED: Semiconductor
MICROFILM SVCS
MICROMETERS
MICROPHONES
MICROPROCESSORS
MICROSCOPES
MICROWAVE COMPONENTS
MICROWAVE OVENS: Household
MILL PRDTS: Structural & Rail
MILLINERY SUPPLIES: Cap Fronts & Visors
MILLINERY SUPPLIES: Veils & Veiling, Bridal, Funeral, Etc
MILLING: Corn Grits & Flakes, For Brewers' Use
MILLING: Grain Cereals, Cracked
MILLING: Grains, Exc Rice
MILLWORK
MINERAL WOOL
MINERAL WOOL INSULATION PRDTS
MINERALS: Ground Or Otherwise Treated
MINERALS: Ground or Treated
MINIATURE GOLF COURSES
MINING EXPLORATION & DEVELOPMENT SVCS
MINING MACHINERY & EQPT WHOLESALERS
MINING MACHINES & EQPT: Augers
MINING MACHINES & EQPT: Bits, Rock, Exc Oil/Gas Field Tools
MINING MACHINES & EQPT: Cleaning, Mineral
MINING MACHINES & EQPT: Crushers, Stationary
MINING MACHINES & EQPT: Loading, Underground, Mobile
MINING MACHINES & EQPT: Mineral Beneficiation
MINING MACHINES & EQPT: Sedimentation, Mineral
MINING MACHINES & EQPT: Stamping Mill Machinery
MIRRORS: Motor Vehicle
MISC FIN INVEST ACT: Shares, RE, Entertain & Eqpt, Sales
MISCELLANEOUS FINANCIAL INVEST ACT: Oil/Gas Lease Brokers
MISSILE GUIDANCE SYSTEMS & EQPT
MISSILES: Guided
MITTENS: Leather
MIXING EQPT
MIXTURES & BLOCKS: Asphalt Paving
MOBILE COMMUNICATIONS EQPT
MOBILE HOME FRAMES
MOBILE HOMES
MOBILE HOMES WHOLESALERS
MOBILE HOMES: Indl Or Commercial Use
MOBILE HOMES: Personal Or Private Use
MODELS
MODELS: General, Exc Toy
MODULES: Computer Logic
MODULES: Solid State
MOLDED RUBBER PRDTS
MOLDING COMPOUNDS
MOLDING SAND MINING
MOLDINGS & TRIM: Metal, Exc Automobile
MOLDINGS & TRIM: Wood
MOLDINGS OR TRIM: Automobile, Stamped Metal
MOLDINGS, ARCHITECTURAL: Plaster Of Paris
MOLDINGS: Picture Frame
MOLDS: Indl
MOLDS: Plastic Working & Foundry
MONASTERIES
MONUMENTS & GRAVE MARKERS, EXC TERRAZZO
MONUMENTS & GRAVE MARKERS, WHOLESALE
MONUMENTS: Concrete
MONUMENTS: Cut Stone, Exc Finishing Or Lettering Only
MOPEDS & PARTS
MOPS: Floor & Dust
MOTION PICTURE & VIDEO PRODUCTION SVCS
MOTION PICTURE & VIDEO PRODUCTION SVCS: Commercials, TV
MOTION PICTURE & VIDEO PRODUCTION SVCS: Educational
MOTION PICTURE DISTRIBUTION SVCS

PRODUCT INDEX

MOTION PICTURE EQPT
MOTION PICTURE PRODUCTION ALLIED SVCS
MOTION PICTURE PRODUCTION SVCS
MOTOR & GENERATOR PARTS: Electric
MOTOR HOMES
MOTOR INN
MOTOR REBUILDING SVCS, EXC AUTOMOTIVE
MOTOR REPAIR SVCS
MOTOR SCOOTERS & PARTS
MOTOR VEHICLE ASSEMBLY, COMPLETE: Ambulances
MOTOR VEHICLE ASSEMBLY, COMPLETE: Autos, Incl Specialty
MOTOR VEHICLE ASSEMBLY, COMPLETE: Bus/Large Spclty Vehicles
MOTOR VEHICLE ASSEMBLY, COMPLETE: Buses, All Types
MOTOR VEHICLE ASSEMBLY, COMPLETE: Fire Department Vehicles
MOTOR VEHICLE ASSEMBLY, COMPLETE: Military Motor Vehicle
MOTOR VEHICLE ASSEMBLY, COMPLETE: Motor Buses
MOTOR VEHICLE ASSEMBLY, COMPLETE: Reconnaissance Cars
MOTOR VEHICLE ASSEMBLY, COMPLETE: Snow Plows
MOTOR VEHICLE ASSEMBLY, COMPLETE: Truck & Tractor Trucks
MOTOR VEHICLE ASSEMBLY, COMPLETE: Truck Tractors, Highway
MOTOR VEHICLE ASSEMBLY, COMPLETE: Wreckers, Tow Truck
MOTOR VEHICLE DEALERS: Automobiles, New & Used
MOTOR VEHICLE DEALERS: Cars, Used Only
MOTOR VEHICLE DEALERS: Trucks, Tractors/Trailers, New & Used
MOTOR VEHICLE PARTS & ACCESS: Air Conditioner Parts
MOTOR VEHICLE PARTS & ACCESS: Axel Housings & Shafts
MOTOR VEHICLE PARTS & ACCESS: Bearings
MOTOR VEHICLE PARTS & ACCESS: Body Components & Frames
MOTOR VEHICLE PARTS & ACCESS: Booster Cables, Jump-Start
MOTOR VEHICLE PARTS & ACCESS: Brakes, Air
MOTOR VEHICLE PARTS & ACCESS: Clutches
MOTOR VEHICLE PARTS & ACCESS: Cylinder Heads
MOTOR VEHICLE PARTS & ACCESS: Electrical Eqpt
MOTOR VEHICLE PARTS & ACCESS: Engines & Parts
MOTOR VEHICLE PARTS & ACCESS: Engs & Trans,Factory, Rebuilt
MOTOR VEHICLE PARTS & ACCESS: Fuel Pumps
MOTOR VEHICLE PARTS & ACCESS: Fuel Systems & Parts
MOTOR VEHICLE PARTS & ACCESS: Gas Tanks
MOTOR VEHICLE PARTS & ACCESS: Gears
MOTOR VEHICLE PARTS & ACCESS: Governors
MOTOR VEHICLE PARTS & ACCESS: Heaters
MOTOR VEHICLE PARTS & ACCESS: Hoods
MOTOR VEHICLE PARTS & ACCESS: Horns
MOTOR VEHICLE PARTS & ACCESS: Instrument Board Assemblies
MOTOR VEHICLE PARTS & ACCESS: Manifolds
MOTOR VEHICLE PARTS & ACCESS: Mufflers, Exhaust
MOTOR VEHICLE PARTS & ACCESS: Oil Pumps
MOTOR VEHICLE PARTS & ACCESS: Thermostats
MOTOR VEHICLE PARTS & ACCESS: Trailer Hitches
MOTOR VEHICLE PARTS & ACCESS: Transmission Housings Or Parts
MOTOR VEHICLE PARTS & ACCESS: Transmissions
MOTOR VEHICLE PARTS & ACCESS: Universal Joints
MOTOR VEHICLE PARTS & ACCESS: Wheel rims
MOTOR VEHICLE PARTS & ACCESS: Wiring Harness Sets
MOTOR VEHICLE RADIOS WHOLESALERS
MOTOR VEHICLE SPLYS & PARTS WHOLESALERS: New
MOTOR VEHICLE SPLYS & PARTS WHOLESALERS: Used
MOTOR VEHICLE: Hardware
MOTOR VEHICLE: Radiators
MOTOR VEHICLE: Shock Absorbers
MOTOR VEHICLE: Steering Mechanisms
MOTOR VEHICLE: Wheels
MOTOR VEHICLES & CAR BODIES
MOTOR VEHICLES, WHOLESALE: Truck bodies
MOTORCYCLE & BICYCLE PARTS: Frames
MOTORCYCLE & BICYCLE PARTS: Gears
MOTORCYCLE ACCESS
MOTORCYCLE DEALERS
MOTORCYCLE PARTS & ACCESS DEALERS
MOTORCYCLE PARTS: Wholesalers
MOTORCYCLE RACING
MOTORCYCLE REPAIR SHOPS
MOTORCYCLES & RELATED PARTS
MOTORS: Electric
MOTORS: Generators
MOTORS: Starting, Automotive & Aircraft
MOTORS: Torque
MOUTHWASHES
MOVING SVC: Local
MOWERS & ACCESSORIES
MULTILITHING SVCS
MUSEUMS
MUSEUMS & ART GALLERIES
MUSIC DISTRIBUTION APPARATUS
MUSIC DISTRIBUTION SYSTEM SVCS
MUSIC RECORDING PRODUCER
MUSIC VIDEO PRODUCTION SVCS
MUSICAL ENTERTAINERS
MUSICAL INSTRUMENT PARTS & ACCESS, WHOLESALE
MUSICAL INSTRUMENT REPAIR
MUSICAL INSTRUMENTS & ACCESS: Carrying Cases
MUSICAL INSTRUMENTS & ACCESS: NEC
MUSICAL INSTRUMENTS & ACCESS: Pipe Organs
MUSICAL INSTRUMENTS & PARTS: Brass
MUSICAL INSTRUMENTS & PARTS: Percussion
MUSICAL INSTRUMENTS & PARTS: Woodwind
MUSICAL INSTRUMENTS & SPLYS STORES
MUSICAL INSTRUMENTS & SPLYS STORES: String instruments
MUSICAL INSTRUMENTS WHOLESALERS
MUSICAL INSTRUMENTS: Bells
MUSICAL INSTRUMENTS: Electric & Electronic
MUSICAL INSTRUMENTS: Guitars & Parts, Electric & Acoustic
MUSICAL INSTRUMENTS: Harmonicas
MUSICAL INSTRUMENTS: Harps & Parts
MUSICAL INSTRUMENTS: Organ Parts & Materials
MUSICAL INSTRUMENTS: Organs
MUSICAL INSTRUMENTS: Violins & Parts

N

NAIL SALONS
NAILS WHOLESALERS
NAILS: Steel, Wire Or Cut
NAME PLATES: Engraved Or Etched
NAMEPLATES
NATIONAL SECURITY FORCES
NATURAL GAS COMPRESSING SVC, On-Site
NATURAL GAS DISTRIBUTION TO CONSUMERS
NATURAL GAS LIQUIDS PRODUCTION
NATURAL GAS LIQUIDS PRODUCTION
NATURAL GAS PRODUCTION
NATURAL GAS TRANSMISSION
NATURAL GAS TRANSMISSION & DISTRIBUTION
NATURAL GASOLINE PRODUCTION
NATURAL LIQUEFIED PETROLEUM GAS PRODUCTION
NATURAL PROPANE PRODUCTION
NAVIGATIONAL SYSTEMS & INSTRUMENTS
NEEDLES
NEPHELINE SYENITE MINING
NETTING: Plastic
NEWS DEALERS & NEWSSTANDS
NEWS FEATURE SYNDICATES
NEWS SYNDICATES
NEWSPAPERS & PERIODICALS NEWS REPORTING SVCS
NEWSPAPERS, WHOLESALE
NEWSSTAND
NICKEL ALLOY
NIPPLES: Rubber
NITRILE RUBBERS: Butadiene-Acrylonitrile
NONAROMATIC CHEMICAL PRDTS
NONCURRENT CARRYING WIRING DEVICES
NONDURABLE GOODS WHOLESALERS, NEC
NONFERROUS: Rolling & Drawing, NEC
NONMETALLIC MINERALS DEVELOPMENT & TEST BORING SVC
NONMETALLIC MINERALS: Support Activities, Exc Fuels
NOTIONS: Button Backs & Parts
NOTIONS: Pins, Hair, Exc Rubber
NOTIONS: Pins, Straight, Steel Or Brass
NOVELTIES
NOVELTIES & SPECIALTIES: Metal
NOVELTIES: Plastic
NOVELTY SHOPS
NOZZLES & SPRINKLERS Lawn Hose
NOZZLES: Fire Fighting
NOZZLES: Spray, Aerosol, Paint Or Insecticide
NUCLEAR REACTORS: Military Or Indl
NURSERIES & LAWN & GARDEN SPLY STORE, RET: Fountain, Outdoor
NURSERIES & LAWN & GARDEN SPLY STORES, RETAIL: Fertilizer
NURSERIES & LAWN & GARDEN SPLY STORES, RETAIL: Lawn Ornament
NURSERIES & LAWN & GARDEN SPLY STORES, RETAIL: Top Soil
NURSERIES & LAWN/GARDEN SPLY STORE, RET: Lawnmowers/Tractors
NURSERIES & LAWN/GARDEN SPLY STORES, RET: Garden Splys/Tools
NURSERIES/LAWN/GARDEN SPLY STORE, RET: Grdn Tractors/Tillers
NURSERY & GARDEN CENTERS
NURSING CARE FACILITIES: Skilled
NUTRITION SVCS
NUTS: Metal

O

OFFICE EQPT WHOLESALERS
OFFICE FIXTURES: Wood
OFFICE FURNITURE REPAIR & MAINTENANCE SVCS
OFFICE MACHINES, NEC
OFFICE SPLY & STATIONERY STORES
OFFICE SPLY & STATIONERY STORES: Office Forms & Splys
OFFICE SPLY & STATIONERY STORES: Writing Splys
OFFICE SPLYS, NEC, WHOLESALE
OFFICES & CLINICS OF DENTISTS: Dental Clinic
OFFICES & CLINICS OF DENTISTS: Group & Corporate Practice
OFFICES & CLINICS OF DOCTORS OF MEDICINE: Dermatologist
OFFICES & CLINICS OF DOCTORS OF MEDICINE: Gynecologist
OFFICES & CLINICS OF DRS OF MEDICINE: Med Clinic, Pri Care
OFFICES & CLINICS OF DRS, MED: Specialized Practitioners
OFFICES & CLINICS OF HEALTH PRACTITIONERS: Physical Therapy
OFFICES & CLINICS OF HEALTH PRACTITIONERS: Speech Therapist
OIL & GAS FIELD EQPT: Drill Rigs
OIL & GAS FIELD MACHINERY
OIL FIELD MACHINERY & EQPT
OIL FIELD SVCS, NEC
OIL TREATING COMPOUNDS
OILS & ESSENTIAL OILS
OILS & GREASES: Blended & Compounded
OILS & GREASES: Lubricating
OILS, ANIMAL OR VEGETABLE, WHOLESALE
OILS: Cutting
OILS: Essential
OILS: Lubricating
OILS: Lubricating
OILS: Mineral, Natural
OILS: Peppermint
OINTMENTS
ON-LINE DATABASE INFORMATION RETRIEVAL SVCS
OPERATOR TRAINING, COMPUTER
OPERATOR: Apartment Buildings
OPERATOR: Nonresidential Buildings
OPHTHALMIC GOODS
OPHTHALMIC GOODS WHOLESALERS
OPHTHALMIC GOODS: Eyewear, Protective
OPHTHALMIC GOODS: Frames & Parts, Eyeglass & Spectacle
OPHTHALMIC GOODS: Goggles, Sun, Safety, Indl, Etc
OPHTHALMIC GOODS: Spectacles
OPTICAL EQPT: Interferometers
OPTICAL GOODS STORES
OPTICAL GOODS STORES: Eyeglasses, Prescription
OPTICAL GOODS STORES: Opticians
OPTICAL INSTRUMENT REPAIR SVCS
OPTICAL INSTRUMENTS & APPARATUS
OPTICAL INSTRUMENTS & LENSES
OPTICAL ISOLATORS
OPTICAL SCANNING SVCS
OPTOMETRISTS' OFFICES
ORDNANCE

PRODUCT INDEX

ORGAN TUNING & REPAIR SVCS
ORGANIZATIONS & UNIONS: Labor
ORGANIZATIONS: Biotechnical Research, Noncommercial
ORGANIZATIONS: Medical Research
ORGANIZATIONS: Professional
ORGANIZATIONS: Religious
ORGANIZATIONS: Safety Research, Noncommercial
ORGANIZATIONS: Scientific Research Agency
ORGANIZATIONS: Veterans' Membership
ORGANIZERS, CLOSET & DRAWER Plastic
ORNAMENTS: Lawn
OSCILLATORS
OSCILLATORS
OSICIZERS: Inorganic
OUTBOARD MOTORS & PARTS
OUTLETS: Electric, Convenience
OUTREACH PROGRAM
OVENS: Cremating
OVENS: Distillation, Charcoal & Coke
OVENS: Infrared
OVENS: Laboratory

P

PACKAGE DESIGN SVCS
PACKAGED FROZEN FOODS WHOLESALERS, NEC
PACKAGING & LABELING SVCS
PACKAGING MATERIALS, INDL: Wholesalers
PACKAGING MATERIALS, WHOLESALE
PACKAGING MATERIALS: Paper
PACKAGING MATERIALS: Paper, Coated Or Laminated
PACKAGING MATERIALS: Paper, Thermoplastic Coated
PACKAGING MATERIALS: Paperboard Backs For Blister/Skin Pkgs
PACKAGING MATERIALS: Plastic Film, Coated Or Laminated
PACKAGING MATERIALS: Polystyrene Foam
PACKAGING MATERIALS: Resinous Impregnated Paper
PACKAGING: Blister Or Bubble Formed, Plastic
PACKING & CRATING SVC
PACKING & CRATING SVCS: Containerized Goods For Shipping
PACKING MATERIALS: Mechanical
PACKING SVCS: Shipping
PACKING: Metallic
PADS: Desk, Exc Paper
PADS: Mattress
PAGERS: One-way
PAGING SVCS
PAILS: Plastic
PAILS: Shipping, Metal
PAINT & PAINTING SPLYS STORE
PAINT STORE
PAINTING SVC: Metal Prdts
PAINTS & ADDITIVES
PAINTS & ALLIED PRODUCTS
PAINTS & VARNISHES: Plastics Based
PAINTS, VARNISHES & SPLYS WHOLESALERS
PAINTS, VARNISHES & SPLYS, WHOLESALE: Colors & Pigments
PAINTS, VARNISHES & SPLYS, WHOLESALE: Paints
PAINTS: Oil Or Alkyd Vehicle Or Water Thinned
PAINTS: Waterproof
PALLET REPAIR SVCS
PALLETS
PALLETS & SKIDS: Wood
PALLETS: Metal
PALLETS: Plastic
PALLETS: Solid Fiber, Made From Purchased Materials
PALLETS: Wood & Metal Combination
PALLETS: Wooden
PANEL & DISTRIBUTION BOARDS & OTHER RELATED APPARATUS
PANEL & DISTRIBUTION BOARDS: Electric
PANELS, CORRUGATED: Plastic
PANELS, FLAT: Plastic
PANELS: Building, Plastic, NEC
PANELS: Building, Wood
PANELS: Control & Metering, Generator
PANELS: Wood
PAPER & BOARD: Die-cut
PAPER & ENVELOPES: Writing, Made From Purchased Materials
PAPER CONVERTING
PAPER MANUFACTURERS: Exc Newsprint
PAPER NAPKINS WHOLESALERS
PAPER PRDTS

PAPER PRDTS: Feminine Hygiene Prdts
PAPER PRDTS: Infant & Baby Prdts
PAPER PRDTS: Pressed & Molded Pulp & Fiber Prdts
PAPER PRDTS: Sanitary
PAPER PRDTS: Sanitary Tissue Paper
PAPER PRDTS: Towels, Napkins/Tissue Paper, From Purchd Mtrls
PAPER PRDTS: Wrappers, Blank, Made From Purchased Materials
PAPER, WHOLESALE: Fine
PAPER, WHOLESALE: Printing
PAPER, WHOLESALE: Writing
PAPER: Absorbent
PAPER: Adhesive
PAPER: Book
PAPER: Business Form
PAPER: Carbon
PAPER: Cardboard
PAPER: Catalog
PAPER: Chemically Treated, Made From Purchased Materials
PAPER: Cigarette
PAPER: Coated & Laminated, NEC
PAPER: Coated, Exc Photographic, Carbon Or Abrasive
PAPER: Filter
PAPER: Gift Wrap
PAPER: Insulation Siding
PAPER: Kraft
PAPER: Lithograph
PAPER: Newsprint
PAPER: Packaging
PAPER: Printer
PAPER: Specialty
PAPER: Tissue
PAPER: Wallpaper
PAPER: Waxed, Made From Purchased Materials
PAPER: Wrapping & Packaging
PAPER: Writing
PAPERBOARD
PAPERBOARD CONVERTING
PAPERBOARD PRDTS: Building Insulating & Packaging
PAPERBOARD PRDTS: Container Board
PAPERBOARD PRDTS: Folding Boxboard
PAPERBOARD PRDTS: Packaging Board
PAPERBOARD: Liner Board
PAPETERIES & WRITING PAPER SETS
PAPIER-MACHE PRDTS, EXC STATUARY & ART GOODS
PARKING LOTS
PARKING LOTS & GARAGES
PARTITIONS & FIXTURES: Except Wood
PARTITIONS: Metal, Ornamental
PARTITIONS: Solid Fiber, Made From Purchased Materials
PARTITIONS: Wood & Fixtures
PARTS: Metal
PASTES: Metal
PATCHING PLASTER: Household
PATENT OWNERS & LESSORS
PATIENT MONITORING EQPT WHOLESALERS
PATTERNS: Indl
PAVERS
PAVING MATERIALS: Prefabricated, Concrete
PAVING MIXTURES
PAYROLL SVCS
PEARLS, WHOLESALE
PEAT GRINDING SVCS
PENCILS & PENS WHOLESALERS
PENS & PARTS: Ball Point
PENS & PENCILS: Mechanical, NEC
PENS: Fountain, Including Desk Sets
PENSION & RETIREMENT PLAN CONSULTANTS
PERFUME: Concentrated
PERFUMES
PERLITE: Processed
PERSONAL & HOUSEHOLD GOODS REPAIR, NEC
PERSONAL CREDIT INSTITUTIONS: Finance Licensed Loan Co's, Sm
PERSONAL DOCUMENT & INFORMATION SVCS
PERSONAL INVESTIGATION SVCS
PERSONAL SHOPPING SVCS
PEST CONTROL IN STRUCTURES SVCS
PESTICIDES WHOLESALERS
PET ACCESS: Collars, Leashes, Etc, Exc Leather
PET COLLARS, LEASHES, MUZZLES & HARNESSES: Leather
PET FOOD WHOLESALERS
PET SPLYS

PET SPLYS WHOLESALERS
PETROLEUM & PETROLEUM PRDTS, WHOL Svc Station Splys, Petro
PETROLEUM & PETROLEUM PRDTS, WHOLESALE Crude Oil
PETROLEUM & PETROLEUM PRDTS, WHOLESALE Fuel Oil
PETROLEUM & PETROLEUM PRDTS, WHOLESALE Petroleum Brokers
PETROLEUM & PETROLEUM PRDTS, WHOLESALE Petroleum Terminals
PETROLEUM & PETROLEUM PRDTS, WHOLESALE: Bulk Stations
PETROLEUM BULK STATIONS & TERMINALS
PETROLEUM PRDTS WHOLESALERS
PETROLEUM REFINERY INSPECTION SVCS
PETS & PET SPLYS, WHOLESALE
PHARMACEUTICAL PREPARATIONS: Adrenal
PHARMACEUTICAL PREPARATIONS: Druggists' Preparations
PHARMACEUTICAL PREPARATIONS: Medicines, Capsule Or Ampule
PHARMACEUTICAL PREPARATIONS: Pills
PHARMACEUTICAL PREPARATIONS: Powders
PHARMACEUTICAL PREPARATIONS: Proprietary Drug PRDTS
PHARMACEUTICAL PREPARATIONS: Solutions
PHARMACEUTICAL PREPARATIONS: Tablets
PHARMACEUTICALS
PHARMACEUTICALS: Medicinal & Botanical Prdts
PHARMACIES & DRUG STORES
PHOSPHATE ROCK MINING
PHOSPHATES
PHOSPHORIC ACID
PHOTOCOPY MACHINES
PHOTOCOPY SPLYS WHOLESALERS
PHOTOCOPYING & DUPLICATING SVCS
PHOTOELECTRIC DEVICES: Magnetic
PHOTOENGRAVING SVC
PHOTOFINISHING LABORATORIES
PHOTOFINISHING LABORATORIES
PHOTOFLASH EQPT
PHOTOGRAPH DEVELOPING & RETOUCHING SVCS
PHOTOGRAPHIC & OPTICAL GOODS EQPT REPAIR SVCS
PHOTOGRAPHIC EQPT & CAMERAS, WHOLESALE
PHOTOGRAPHIC EQPT & SPLYS
PHOTOGRAPHIC EQPT & SPLYS WHOLESALERS
PHOTOGRAPHIC EQPT & SPLYS, WHOLESALE: Motion Picture Camera
PHOTOGRAPHIC EQPT & SPLYS, WHOLESALE: Project, Motion/Slide
PHOTOGRAPHIC EQPT & SPLYS: Blueprint Cloth/Paper, Sensitized
PHOTOGRAPHIC EQPT & SPLYS: Develpg Mach/Eqpt, Still/Motion
PHOTOGRAPHIC EQPT & SPLYS: Graphic Arts Plates, Sensitized
PHOTOGRAPHIC EQPT & SPLYS: Printing Eqpt
PHOTOGRAPHIC EQPT & SPLYS: Printing Frames
PHOTOGRAPHIC EQPT & SPLYS: Toners, Prprd, Not Chem Plnts
PHOTOGRAPHIC EQPT & SPLYS: Tripods, Camera & Projector
PHOTOGRAPHIC EQPT REPAIR SVCS
PHOTOGRAPHIC PEOCESSING CHEMICALS
PHOTOGRAPHY SVCS: Commercial
PHOTOGRAPHY SVCS: Portrait Studios
PHOTOGRAPHY SVCS: Still Or Video
PHOTOTYPESETTING SVC
PHOTOVOLTAIC Solid State
PHYSICAL EXAMINATION & TESTING SVCS
PHYSICAL EXAMINATION SVCS, INSURANCE
PHYSICAL FITNESS CENTERS
PHYSICIANS' OFFICES & CLINICS: Medical doctors
PIANO TUNING & REPAIR SVCS
PICTURE FRAMES: Metal
PICTURE FRAMES: Wood
PICTURE FRAMING SVCS, CUSTOM
PICTURE PROJECTION EQPT
PIECE GOODS & NOTIONS WHOLESALERS
PIECE GOODS, NOTIONS & DRY GOODS, WHOL: Textile Converters
PIECE GOODS, NOTIONS & DRY GOODS, WHOL: Textiles, Woven

PRODUCT INDEX

PIECE GOODS, NOTIONS & DRY GOODS, WHOL: Trimmings, Apparel
PIECE GOODS, NOTIONS & DRY GOODS, WHOLESALE: Fabrics
PIECE GOODS, NOTIONS & DRY GOODS, WHOLESALE: Sewing Access
PIECE GOODS, NOTIONS & OTHER DRY GOODS, WHOL: Flags/Banners
PIECE GOODS, NOTIONS & OTHER DRY GOODS, WHOLESALE: Fabrics
PIECE GOODS, NOTIONS & OTHER DRY GOODS, WHOLESALE: Notions
PIECE GOODS, NOTIONS/DRY GOODS, WHOL: Drapery Mtrl, Woven
PIECE GOODS, NOTIONS/DRY GOODS, WHOL: Fabrics, Synthetic
PIGMENTS, INORGANIC: Zinc Oxide, Zinc Sulfide
PILLOWS: Sponge Rubber
PILLOWS: Stereo
PINS
PINS: Dowel
PIPE & FITTING: Fabrication
PIPE & FITTINGS: Cast Iron
PIPE & TUBES: Aluminum
PIPE & TUBES: Seamless
PIPE CLEANERS
PIPE JOINT COMPOUNDS
PIPE, PRESSURE: Reinforced Concrete
PIPE, SEWER: Concrete
PIPE: Concrete
PIPE: Copper
PIPE: Plastic
PIPE: Seamless Steel
PIPE: Sewer, Cast Iron
PIPE: Sheet Metal
PIPELINE TERMINAL FACILITIES: Independent
PIPELINES: Crude Petroleum
PIPELINES: Natural Gas
PIPELINES: Refined Petroleum
PIPES & TUBES
PIPES & TUBES: Steel
PIPES & TUBES: Welded
PIPES: Steel & Iron
PISTONS & PISTON RINGS
PLANT FOOD, WHOLESALE
PLANT HORMONES
PLANTERS & FLOWER POTS, WHOLESALE
PLANTERS: Plastic
PLANTING MACHINERY & EQPT WHOLESALERS
PLAQUES: Clay, Plaster/Papier-Mache, Factory Production
PLAQUES: Picture, Laminated
PLASMAS
PLASTER & PLASTERBOARD
PLASTER WORK: Ornamental & Architectural
PLASTIC COLORING & FINISHING
PLASTIC FIRE CLAY MINING
PLASTIC PRDTS
PLASTIC PRDTS REPAIR SVCS
PLASTICIZERS, ORGANIC: Cyclic & Acyclic
PLASTICS FILM & SHEET
PLASTICS FILM & SHEET: Polyethylene
PLASTICS FILM & SHEET: Polypropylene
PLASTICS FILM & SHEET: Vinyl
PLASTICS FINISHED PRDTS: Laminated
PLASTICS MATERIAL & RESINS
PLASTICS MATERIALS, BASIC FORMS & SHAPES WHOLESALERS
PLASTICS PROCESSING
PLASTICS SHEET: Packing Materials
PLASTICS: Blow Molded
PLASTICS: Casein
PLASTICS: Extruded
PLASTICS: Finished Injection Molded
PLASTICS: Injection Molded
PLASTICS: Molded
PLASTICS: Polystyrene Foam
PLASTICS: Thermoformed
PLATE WORK: Metalworking Trade
PLATED WARE, ALL METALS
PLATEMAKING SVC: Color Separations, For The Printing Trade
PLATES
PLATES: Aluminum
PLATES: Sheet & Strip, Exc Coated Prdts
PLATES: Steel
PLATES: Truss, Metal
PLATING & FINISHING SVC: Decorative, Formed Prdts
PLATING & POLISHING SVC
PLATING COMPOUNDS
PLATING SVC: Chromium, Metals Or Formed Prdts
PLATING SVC: Electro
PLATING SVC: Gold
PLATING SVC: NEC
PLAYGROUND EQPT
PLEATING & STITCHING FOR TRADE: Permanent Pleating/Pressing
PLEATING & STITCHING SVC
PLUGS: Electric
PLUMBING & HEATING EQPT & SPLY, WHOLESALE: Hydronic Htg Eqpt
PLUMBING & HEATING EQPT & SPLYS WHOLESALERS
PLUMBING & HEATING EQPT & SPLYS, WHOL: Fireplaces, Prefab
PLUMBING & HEATING EQPT & SPLYS, WHOL: Pipe/Fitting, Plastic
PLUMBING & HEATING EQPT & SPLYS, WHOL: Plumbing Fitting/Sply
PLUMBING & HEATING EQPT & SPLYS, WHOL: Water Purif Eqpt
PLUMBING & HEATING EQPT & SPLYS, WHOLESALE: Boilers, Steam
PLUMBING & HEATING EQPT, WHOLESALE: Water Heaters/Purif
PLUMBING FIXTURES
PLUMBING FIXTURES: Brass, Incl Drain Cocks, Faucets/Spigots
PLUMBING FIXTURES: Plastic
PLUMBING FIXTURES: Vitreous
PLUMBING FIXTURES: Vitreous China
POINT OF SALE DEVICES
POLE LINE HARDWARE
POLISHING SVC: Metals Or Formed Prdts
POLYCARBONATE RESINS
POLYMETHYL METHACRYLATE RESINS: Plexiglas
POLYSTYRENE RESINS
POLYTETRAFLUOROETHYLENE RESINS
POLYURETHANE RESINS
POLYVINYL CHLORIDE RESINS
POLYVINYLIDENE CHLORIDE RESINS
POPCORN & SUPPLIES WHOLESALERS
POPULAR MUSIC GROUPS OR ARTISTS
PORCELAIN ENAMELED PRDTS & UTENSILS
POSTERS
POTASH MINING
POTTERY: Laboratory & Indl
POTTING SOILS
POULTRY & POULTRY PRDTS WHOLESALERS
POULTRY & SMALL GAME SLAUGHTERING & PROCESSING
POULTRY SLAUGHTERING & PROCESSING
POWDER: Aluminum Atomized
POWDER: Iron
POWDER: Metal
POWER DISTRIBUTION BOARDS: Electric
POWER GENERATORS
POWER MOWERS WHOLESALERS
POWER SPLY CONVERTERS: Static, Electronic Applications
POWER SUPPLIES: All Types, Static
POWER SUPPLIES: Transformer, Electronic Type
POWER SWITCHING EQPT
POWER TOOLS, HAND: Cartridge-Activated
POWER TOOLS, HAND: Drill Attachments, Portable
POWER TOOLS, HAND: Drills & Drilling Tools
POWER TOOLS, HAND: Grinders, Portable, Electric Or Pneumatic
POWER TOOLS, HAND: Hammers, Portable, Elec/Pneumatic, Chip
POWER TOOLS, HAND: Sanders
POWER TRANSMISSION EQPT WHOLESALERS
POWER TRANSMISSION EQPT: Mechanical
POWER TRANSMISSION EQPT: Vehicle
PRECAST TERRAZZO OR CONCRETE PRDTS
PRECIOUS METALS
PRECIOUS STONES & METALS, WHOLESALE
PRECIOUS STONES WHOLESALERS
PRERECORDED TAPE, CD & RECORD STORE: Record, Disc/Tape
PRERECORDED TAPE, COMPACT DISC & RECORD STORES
PRERECORDED TAPE, COMPACT DISC & RECORD STORES: Compact Disc
PRERECORDED TAPE, COMPACT DISC & RECORD STORES: Records
PRESS CLIPPING SVC
PRESS SVCS
PRESSED & MOLDED PULP PRDTS, NEC: From Purchased Materials
PRESSED FIBER & MOLDED PULP PRDTS, EXC FOOD PRDTS
PRESSES
PRESTRESSED CONCRETE PRDTS
PRIMARY FINISHED OR SEMIFINISHED SHAPES
PRIMARY METAL PRODUCTS
PRINT CARTRIDGES: Laser & Other Computer Printers
PRINTED CIRCUIT BOARDS
PRINTERS & PLOTTERS
PRINTERS' SVCS: Folding, Collating, Etc
PRINTERS: Computer
PRINTERS: Magnetic Ink, Bar Code
PRINTING & BINDING: Book Music
PRINTING & BINDING: Books
PRINTING & BINDING: Textbooks
PRINTING & EMBOSSING: Plastic Fabric Articles
PRINTING & ENGRAVING: Card, Exc Greeting
PRINTING & ENGRAVING: Financial Notes & Certificates
PRINTING & ENGRAVING: Invitation & Stationery
PRINTING & ENGRAVING: Poster & Decal
PRINTING & STAMPING: Fabric Articles
PRINTING & WRITING PAPER WHOLESALERS
PRINTING INKS WHOLESALERS
PRINTING MACHINERY
PRINTING MACHINERY, EQPT & SPLYS: Wholesalers
PRINTING TRADES MACHINERY & EQPT REPAIR SVCS
PRINTING, COMMERCIAL Newspapers, NEC
PRINTING, COMMERCIAL: Announcements, NEC
PRINTING, COMMERCIAL: Business Forms, NEC
PRINTING, COMMERCIAL: Cards, Visiting, Incl Business, NEC
PRINTING, COMMERCIAL: Certificates, Stock, NEC
PRINTING, COMMERCIAL: Coupons, NEC
PRINTING, COMMERCIAL: Decals, NEC
PRINTING, COMMERCIAL: Envelopes, NEC
PRINTING, COMMERCIAL: Imprinting
PRINTING, COMMERCIAL: Invitations, NEC
PRINTING, COMMERCIAL: Labels & Seals, NEC
PRINTING, COMMERCIAL: Letterpress & Screen
PRINTING, COMMERCIAL: Literature, Advertising, NEC
PRINTING, COMMERCIAL: Magazines, NEC
PRINTING, COMMERCIAL: Menus, NEC
PRINTING, COMMERCIAL: Post Cards, Picture, NEC
PRINTING, COMMERCIAL: Promotional
PRINTING, COMMERCIAL: Publications
PRINTING, COMMERCIAL: Ready
PRINTING, COMMERCIAL: Screen
PRINTING, COMMERCIAL: Stationery, NEC
PRINTING, LITHOGRAPHIC: Advertising Posters
PRINTING, LITHOGRAPHIC: Calendars
PRINTING, LITHOGRAPHIC: Color
PRINTING, LITHOGRAPHIC: Decals
PRINTING, LITHOGRAPHIC: Fashion Plates
PRINTING, LITHOGRAPHIC: Forms & Cards, Business
PRINTING, LITHOGRAPHIC: Forms, Business
PRINTING, LITHOGRAPHIC: Letters, Circular Or Form
PRINTING, LITHOGRAPHIC: Maps
PRINTING, LITHOGRAPHIC: Menus
PRINTING, LITHOGRAPHIC: Newspapers
PRINTING, LITHOGRAPHIC: Offset & photolithographic printing
PRINTING, LITHOGRAPHIC: On Metal
PRINTING, LITHOGRAPHIC: Posters
PRINTING, LITHOGRAPHIC: Posters & Decals
PRINTING, LITHOGRAPHIC: Promotional
PRINTING, LITHOGRAPHIC: Transfers, Decalcomania Or Dry
PRINTING, LITHOGRAPHIC: Wrappers
PRINTING: Books
PRINTING: Books
PRINTING: Broadwoven Fabrics. Cotton
PRINTING: Checkbooks
PRINTING: Commercial, NEC
PRINTING: Engraving & Plate
PRINTING: Flexographic
PRINTING: Gravure, Business Form & Card
PRINTING: Gravure, Cards, Exc Greeting
PRINTING: Gravure, Catalogs, No Publishing On-Site

PRODUCT INDEX

PRINTING: Gravure, Circulars
PRINTING: Gravure, Envelopes
PRINTING: Gravure, Job
PRINTING: Gravure, Labels
PRINTING: Gravure, Magazines, No Publishing On-Site
PRINTING: Gravure, Music, Sheet, No Publishing On-Site
PRINTING: Gravure, Post Cards, Picture
PRINTING: Gravure, Promotional
PRINTING: Gravure, Rotogravure
PRINTING: Gravure, Visiting Cards
PRINTING: Laser
PRINTING: Letterpress
PRINTING: Lithographic
PRINTING: Manmade Fiber & Silk, Broadwoven Fabric
PRINTING: Offset
PRINTING: Pamphlets
PRINTING: Photo-Offset
PRINTING: Photolithographic
PRINTING: Roller, Broadwoven Fabrics, Cotton
PRINTING: Roller, Manmade Fiber & Silk, Broadwoven Fabric
PRINTING: Rotogravure
PRINTING: Screen, Broadwoven Fabrics, Cotton
PRINTING: Screen, Fabric
PRINTING: Screen, Manmade Fiber & Silk, Broadwoven Fabric
PRINTING: Thermography
PRODUCT STERILIZATION SVCS
PROFESSIONAL & SEMI-PROFESSIONAL SPORTS CLUBS
PROFESSIONAL EQPT & SPLYS, WHOLESALE: Analytical Instruments
PROFESSIONAL EQPT & SPLYS, WHOLESALE: Bank
PROFESSIONAL EQPT & SPLYS, WHOLESALE: Engineers', NEC
PROFESSIONAL EQPT & SPLYS, WHOLESALE: Optical Goods
PROFESSIONAL EQPT & SPLYS, WHOLESALE: Scientific & Engineerg
PROFESSIONAL INSTRUMENT REPAIR SVCS
PROFESSIONAL SCHOOLS
PROFILE SHAPES: Unsupported Plastics
PROMOTERS OF SHOWS & EXHIBITIONS
PROMOTION SVCS
PROPELLERS: Boat & Ship, Cast
PROPERTY DAMAGE INSURANCE
PROPULSION UNITS: Guided Missiles & Space Vehicles
PROTECTION EQPT: Lightning
PROTECTIVE FOOTWEAR: Rubber Or Plastic
PUBLIC FINANCE, TAXATION & MONETARY POLICY OFFICES
PUBLIC RELATIONS & PUBLICITY SVCS
PUBLIC RELATIONS SVCS
PUBLISHERS: Art Copy
PUBLISHERS: Atlases
PUBLISHERS: Book
PUBLISHERS: Book Clubs, No Printing
PUBLISHERS: Books, No Printing
PUBLISHERS: Catalogs
PUBLISHERS: Comic Books, No Printing
PUBLISHERS: Directories, NEC
PUBLISHERS: Directories, Telephone
PUBLISHERS: Globe Cover Maps
PUBLISHERS: Magazines, No Printing
PUBLISHERS: Maps
PUBLISHERS: Miscellaneous
PUBLISHERS: Music Book
PUBLISHERS: Music Book & Sheet Music
PUBLISHERS: Music, Book
PUBLISHERS: Music, Sheet
PUBLISHERS: Newsletter
PUBLISHERS: Newspaper
PUBLISHERS: Newspapers, No Printing
PUBLISHERS: Pamphlets, No Printing
PUBLISHERS: Periodical Statistical Reports, No Printing
PUBLISHERS: Periodical, With Printing
PUBLISHERS: Periodicals, Magazines
PUBLISHERS: Periodicals, No Printing
PUBLISHERS: Posters
PUBLISHERS: Shopping News
PUBLISHERS: Technical Manuals
PUBLISHERS: Technical Manuals & Papers
PUBLISHERS: Telephone & Other Directory
PUBLISHERS: Textbooks, No Printing
PUBLISHERS: Trade journals, No Printing
PUBLISHING & BROADCASTING: Internet Only
PUBLISHING & PRINTING: Art Copy
PUBLISHING & PRINTING: Book Clubs
PUBLISHING & PRINTING: Book Music
PUBLISHING & PRINTING: Books
PUBLISHING & PRINTING: Catalogs
PUBLISHING & PRINTING: Comic Books
PUBLISHING & PRINTING: Directories, NEC
PUBLISHING & PRINTING: Globe Cover Maps
PUBLISHING & PRINTING: Guides
PUBLISHING & PRINTING: Magazines: publishing & printing
PUBLISHING & PRINTING: Music, Book
PUBLISHING & PRINTING: Newsletters, Business Svc
PUBLISHING & PRINTING: Newspapers
PUBLISHING & PRINTING: Pamphlets
PUBLISHING & PRINTING: Patterns, Paper
PUBLISHING & PRINTING: Periodical Statistical Reports
PUBLISHING & PRINTING: Posters
PUBLISHING & PRINTING: Racing Forms & Programs
PUBLISHING & PRINTING: Shopping News
PUBLISHING & PRINTING: Technical Manuals
PUBLISHING & PRINTING: Textbooks
PUBLISHING & PRINTING: Trade Journals
PUBLISHING & PRINTING: Yearbooks
PULLEYS: Metal
PULLEYS: Power Transmission
PULP MILLS
PULP MILLS: Mech Pulp, Incl Groundwood & Thermomechanical
PULP MILLS: Mechanical & Recycling Processing
PULP MILLS: Wood Based Pulp, NEC
PUMP JACKS & OTHER PUMPING EQPT: Indl
PUMPS
PUMPS & PARTS: Indl
PUMPS & PUMPING EQPT REPAIR SVCS
PUMPS & PUMPING EQPT WHOLESALERS
PUMPS: Domestic, Water Or Sump
PUMPS: Fluid Power
PUMPS: Gasoline, Measuring Or Dispensing
PUMPS: Hydraulic Power Transfer
PUMPS: Measuring & Dispensing
PUMPS: Oil Well & Field
PUMPS: Oil, Measuring Or Dispensing
PUMPS: Vacuum, Exc Laboratory
PUNCHES: Forming & Stamping
PURIFICATION & DUST COLLECTION EQPT
PUSHCARTS
PUSHCARTS & WHEELBARROWS
PYROMETER TUBES

Q

QUARTZ CRYSTAL MINING SVCS
QUILTING SVC & SPLYS, FOR THE TRADE

R

RACE CAR OWNERS
RACE TRACK OPERATION
RACETRACKS
RACEWAYS
RACKS: Bicycle, Automotive
RACKS: Display
RACKS: Magazine, Wood
RACKS: Pallet, Exc Wood
RACKS: Railroad Car, Vehicle Transportation, Steel
RACKS: Trash, Metal Rack
RADAR SYSTEMS & EQPT
RADIATORS: Stationary Engine
RADIO & TELEVISION COMMUNICATIONS EQUIPMENT
RADIO & TELEVISION RECEIVER INSTALLATION SVCS
RADIO & TELEVISION REPAIR
RADIO BROADCASTING & COMMUNICATIONS EQPT
RADIO BROADCASTING MUSIC CHECKERS
RADIO BROADCASTING STATIONS
RADIO COMMUNICATIONS: Airborne Eqpt
RADIO COMMUNICATIONS: Carrier Eqpt
RADIO RECEIVER NETWORKS
RADIO RECEIVING SETS
RADIO REPAIR SHOP, NEC
RADIO, TELEVISION & CONSUMER ELECTRONICS STORES: Eqpt, NEC
RADIO, TV & CONSUMER ELEC STORES: Automotive Sound Eqpt
RADIO, TV & CONSUMER ELEC STORES: High Fidelity Stereo Eqpt
RADIO, TV/CONSUMER ELEC STORES: Antennas, Satellite Dish
RAIL & STRUCTURAL SHAPES: Aluminum rail & structural shapes
RAILINGS: Prefabricated, Metal
RAILINGS: Wood
RAILROAD CAR RENTING & LEASING SVCS
RAILROAD CAR REPAIR SVCS
RAILROAD CARGO LOADING & UNLOADING SVCS
RAILROAD EQPT
RAILROAD EQPT & SPLYS WHOLESALERS
RAILROAD EQPT, EXC LOCOMOTIVES
RAILROAD EQPT: Brakes, Air & Vacuum
RAILROAD EQPT: Cars & Eqpt, Dining
RAILROAD EQPT: Cars & Eqpt, Train, Freight Or Passenger
RAILROAD EQPT: Cars, Maintenance
RAILROAD EQPT: Cars, Motor
RAILROAD EQPT: Cars, Rebuilt
RAILROAD EQPT: Locomotives & Parts, Electric Or Nonelectric
RAILROAD MAINTENANCE & REPAIR SVCS
RAILROAD RELATED EQPT: Ballast Distributors
RAILROAD RELATED EQPT: Railway Track
RAILROADS: Long Haul
RAILS: Elevator, Guide
RAILS: Steel Or Iron
RAMPS: Prefabricated Metal
RAZORS, RAZOR BLADES
REAL ESTATE AGENCIES & BROKERS
REAL ESTATE AGENCIES: Residential
REAL ESTATE AGENTS & MANAGERS
REAL ESTATE FIDUCIARIES' OFFICES
REAL ESTATE INVESTMENT TRUSTS
REAL ESTATE OPERATORS, EXC DEVELOPERS: Commercial/Indl Bldg
REAL ESTATE OPERATORS, EXC DEVELOPERS: Property, Retail
REAMERS
RECLAIMED RUBBER: Reworked By Manufacturing Process
RECORD BLANKS: Phonographic
RECORDING HEADS: Speech & Musical Eqpt
RECORDING TAPE: Video, Blank
RECORDS & TAPES: Prerecorded
RECOVERY SVC: Iron Ore, From Open Hearth Slag
RECOVERY SVCS: Metal
RECREATIONAL CAMPS
RECREATIONAL DEALERS: Campers/Pickup Coaches Truck Mounted
RECREATIONAL SPORTING EQPT REPAIR SVCS
RECREATIONAL VEHICLE DEALERS
RECREATIONAL VEHICLE PARTS & ACCESS STORES
RECREATIONAL VEHICLE REPAIRS
RECTIFIERS: Electrical Apparatus
RECTIFIERS: Electronic, Exc Semiconductor
RECYCLABLE SCRAP & WASTE MATERIALS WHOLESALERS
RECYCLING: Paper
REELS: Cable, Metal
REFINERS & SMELTERS: Aluminum
REFINERS & SMELTERS: Brass, Secondary
REFINERS & SMELTERS: Copper
REFINERS & SMELTERS: Copper, Secondary
REFINERS & SMELTERS: Gold
REFINERS & SMELTERS: Nonferrous Metal
REFINERS & SMELTERS: Tin, Primary
REFINING LUBRICATING OILS & GREASES, NEC
REFINING: Petroleum
REFRACTORIES: Clay
REFRACTORIES: Graphite, Carbon Or Ceramic Bond
REFRACTORIES: Nonclay
REFRACTORY MATERIALS WHOLESALERS
REFRIGERATION & HEATING EQUIPMENT
REFRIGERATION EQPT & SPLYS WHOLESALERS
REFRIGERATION EQPT & SPLYS, WHOLESALE: Beverage Dispensers
REFRIGERATION EQPT & SPLYS, WHOLESALE: Commercial Eqpt
REFRIGERATION EQPT & SPLYS, WHOLESALE: Ice Making Machines
REFRIGERATION EQPT: Complete
REFRIGERATION REPAIR SVCS
REFRIGERATION SVC & REPAIR
REFRIGERATORS & FREEZERS WHOLESALERS
REFUSE SYSTEMS
REGISTERS: Air, Metal
REGULATORS: Generator Voltage
REGULATORS: Line Voltage

PRODUCT INDEX

REGULATORS: Steam Fittings
REGULATORS: Transmission & Distribution Voltage
REHABILITATION CENTER, OUTPATIENT TREATMENT
REHABILITATION CTR, RESIDENTIAL WITH HEALTH CARE INCIDENTAL
REINSURANCE CARRIERS: Accident & Health
RELAYS & SWITCHES: Indl, Electric
RELAYS: Control Circuit, Ind
RELAYS: Electric Power
RELAYS: Electronic Usage
RELIGIOUS SPLYS WHOLESALERS
REMOVERS & CLEANERS
REMOVERS: Paint
RENDERING PLANT
RENT-A-CAR SVCS
RENTAL CENTERS: General
RENTAL CENTERS: Party & Banquet Eqpt & Splys
RENTAL SVCS: Aircraft
RENTAL SVCS: Bicycle & Motorcycle
RENTAL SVCS: Business Machine & Electronic Eqpt
RENTAL SVCS: Carpet & Upholstery Cleaning Eqpt
RENTAL SVCS: Costume
RENTAL SVCS: Electronic Eqpt, Exc Computers
RENTAL SVCS: Floor Maintenance Eqpt
RENTAL SVCS: Live Plant
RENTAL SVCS: Oil Eqpt
RENTAL SVCS: Recreational Vehicle
RENTAL SVCS: Sign
RENTAL SVCS: Sound & Lighting Eqpt
RENTAL SVCS: Tent & Tarpaulin
RENTAL SVCS: Tuxedo
RENTAL SVCS: Video Cassette Recorder & Access
RENTAL SVCS: Work Zone Traffic Eqpt, Flags, Cones, Etc
RENTAL: Video Tape & Disc
REPAIR SERVICES, NEC
REPRODUCTION SVCS: Video Tape Or Disk
RESEARCH & DEVELOPMENT SVCS, COMMERCIAL: Engineering Lab
RESEARCH, DEVELOPMENT & TEST SVCS, COMM: Business Analysis
RESEARCH, DEVELOPMENT & TEST SVCS, COMM: Cmptr Hardware Dev
RESEARCH, DEVELOPMENT & TEST SVCS, COMM: Research, Exc Lab
RESEARCH, DEVELOPMENT & TESTING SVCS, COMM: Agricultural
RESEARCH, DEVELOPMENT & TESTING SVCS, COMM: Research Lab
RESEARCH, DEVELOPMENT & TESTING SVCS, COMMERCIAL: Business
RESEARCH, DEVELOPMENT & TESTING SVCS, COMMERCIAL: Education
RESEARCH, DEVELOPMENT & TESTING SVCS, COMMERCIAL: Energy
RESEARCH, DEVELOPMENT & TESTING SVCS, COMMERCIAL: Medical
RESEARCH, DEVELOPMENT & TESTING SVCS, COMMERCIAL: Physical
RESEARCH, DEVELOPMENT SVCS, COMMERCIAL: Indl Lab
RESEARCH, DVLPT & TEST SVCS, COMM: Mkt Analysis or Research
RESEARCH, DVLPT & TESTING SVCS, COMM: Mkt, Bus & Economic
RESEARCH, DVLPT & TESTING SVCS, COMM: Survey, Mktg
RESIDENTIAL MENTAL HEALTH & SUBSTANCE ABUSE FACILITIES
RESIDENTIAL REMODELERS
RESINS: Custom Compound Purchased
RESISTORS
RESISTORS & RESISTOR UNITS
RESISTORS: Networks
RESPIRATORY SYSTEM DRUGS
RESPIRATORY THERAPY CLINIC
RESTAURANT EQPT REPAIR SVCS
RESTAURANT EQPT: Carts
RESTAURANT EQPT: Food Wagons
RESTAURANT EQPT: Sheet Metal
RESTAURANTS: Delicatessen
RESTAURANTS:Full Svc, American
RESTAURANTS:Full Svc, Barbecue
RESTAURANTS:Full Svc, Chinese
RESTAURANTS:Full Svc, Ethnic Food
RESTAURANTS:Full Svc, Family

RESTAURANTS:Full Svc, Family, Independent
RESTAURANTS:Full Svc, Italian
RESTAURANTS:Full Svc, Mexican
RESTAURANTS:Full Svc, Steak
RESTAURANTS:Limited Svc, Carry-Out Only, Exc Pizza
RESTAURANTS:Limited Svc, Chicken
RESTAURANTS:Limited Svc, Coffee Shop
RESTAURANTS:Limited Svc, Fast-Food, Chain
RESTAURANTS:Limited Svc, Fast-Food, Independent
RESTAURANTS:Limited Svc, Ice Cream Stands Or Dairy Bars
RESTAURANTS:Limited Svc, Pizza
RESTAURANTS:Limited Svc, Pizzeria, Chain
RESTAURANTS:Limited Svc, Pizzeria, Independent
RESTRAINTS
RETAIL BAKERY: Bagels
RETAIL BAKERY: Bread
RETAIL BAKERY: Cakes
RETAIL BAKERY: Doughnuts
RETAIL BAKERY: Pastries
RETAIL LUMBER YARDS
RETAIL STORES, NEC
RETAIL STORES: Air Purification Eqpt
RETAIL STORES: Alarm Signal Systems
RETAIL STORES: Alcoholic Beverage Making Eqpt & Splys
RETAIL STORES: Architectural Splys
RETAIL STORES: Artificial Limbs
RETAIL STORES: Audio-Visual Eqpt & Splys
RETAIL STORES: Awnings
RETAIL STORES: Banners
RETAIL STORES: Batteries, Non-Automotive
RETAIL STORES: Business Machines & Eqpt
RETAIL STORES: Cake Decorating Splys
RETAIL STORES: Canvas Prdts
RETAIL STORES: Christmas Lights & Decorations
RETAIL STORES: Cleaning Eqpt & Splys
RETAIL STORES: Communication Eqpt
RETAIL STORES: Concrete Prdts, Precast
RETAIL STORES: Drafting Eqpt & Splys
RETAIL STORES: Educational Aids & Electronic Training Mat
RETAIL STORES: Electronic Parts & Eqpt
RETAIL STORES: Engine & Motor Eqpt & Splys
RETAIL STORES: Farm Eqpt & Splys
RETAIL STORES: Farm Machinery, NEC
RETAIL STORES: Fire Extinguishers
RETAIL STORES: Flags
RETAIL STORES: Foam & Foam Prdts
RETAIL STORES: Gravestones, Finished
RETAIL STORES: Hair Care Prdts
RETAIL STORES: Hearing Aids
RETAIL STORES: Hospital Eqpt & Splys
RETAIL STORES: Ice
RETAIL STORES: Insecticides
RETAIL STORES: Medical Apparatus & Splys
RETAIL STORES: Mobile Telephones & Eqpt
RETAIL STORES: Monuments, Finished To Custom Order
RETAIL STORES: Motors, Electric
RETAIL STORES: Orthopedic & Prosthesis Applications
RETAIL STORES: Perfumes & Colognes
RETAIL STORES: Pet Food
RETAIL STORES: Photocopy Machines
RETAIL STORES: Picture Frames, Ready Made
RETAIL STORES: Plumbing & Heating Splys
RETAIL STORES: Religious Goods
RETAIL STORES: Rubber Stamps
RETAIL STORES: Safety Splys & Eqpt
RETAIL STORES: Swimming Pools, Above Ground
RETAIL STORES: Telephone & Communication Eqpt
RETAIL STORES: Tents
RETAIL STORES: Tombstones
RETAIL STORES: Typewriters & Business Machines
RETAIL STORES: Vaults & Safes
RETAIL STORES: Water Purification Eqpt
RETAIL STORES: Welding Splys
RETREADING MATERIALS: Tire
REUPHOLSTERY & FURNITURE REPAIR
REUPHOLSTERY SVCS
REWINDING SVCS
RIBBONS & BOWS
RIBBONS: Machine, Inked Or Carbon
RIDING STABLES
RIVETS: Metal
ROAD CONSTRUCTION EQUIPMENT WHOLESALERS
ROBOTS: Assembly Line
ROCK SALT MINING

ROCKETS: Space & Military
RODS: Plastic
RODS: Steel & Iron, Made In Steel Mills
ROLL COVERINGS: Rubber
ROLLING MACHINERY: Steel
ROLLING MILL EQPT: Picklers & Pickling Lines
ROLLING MILL EQPT: Plate
ROLLING MILL MACHINERY
ROLLING MILL ROLLS: Cast Steel
ROLLS & BLANKETS, PRINTERS': Rubber Or Rubberized Fabric
ROLLS & ROLL COVERINGS: Rubber
ROLLS: Rubber, Solid Or Covered
ROOF DECKS
ROOFING MATERIALS: Asphalt
ROOFING MATERIALS: Sheet Metal
ROOM COOLERS: Portable
ROPE
ROTORS: Motor
RUBBER
RUBBER PRDTS
RUBBER PRDTS: Appliance, Mechanical
RUBBER PRDTS: Automotive, Mechanical
RUBBER PRDTS: Mechanical
RUBBER PRDTS: Medical & Surgical Tubing, Extrudd & Lathe-Cut
RUBBER PRDTS: Oil & Gas Field Machinery, Mechanical
RUBBER PRDTS: Silicone
RUBBER PRDTS: Sponge
RUBBER STAMP, WHOLESALE
RUBBER STRUCTURES: Air-Supported
RUGS : Hand & Machine Made
RULERS: Metal
RUST RESISTING

S

SAFES & VAULTS: Metal
SAFETY EQPT & SPLYS WHOLESALERS
SAFETY INSPECTION SVCS
SAILS
SALES PROMOTION SVCS
SALT
SALT & SULFUR MINING
SAMPLE BOOKS
SAND & GRAVEL
SAND MINING
SAND RIDDLES: Hand Sifting Or Screening Apparatus
SAND: Hygrade
SAND: Silica
SANDBLASTING EQPT
SANITARY SVC, NEC
SANITARY SVCS: Chemical Detoxification
SANITARY SVCS: Dead Animal Disposal
SANITARY SVCS: Hazardous Waste, Collection & Disposal
SANITARY SVCS: Incinerator, Operation Of
SANITARY SVCS: Medical Waste Disposal
SANITARY SVCS: Refuse Collection & Disposal Svcs
SANITARY SVCS: Rubbish Collection & Disposal
SANITARY SVCS: Waste Materials, Recycling
SANITARY WARE: Metal
SANITATION CHEMICALS & CLEANING AGENTS
SASHES: Door Or Window, Metal
SATCHELS
SATELLITES: Communications
SAW BLADES
SAWING & PLANING MILLS
SAWING & PLANING MILLS: Custom
SAWS & SAWING EQPT
SCAFFOLDING WHOLESALERS
SCAFFOLDS: Mobile Or Stationary, Metal
SCALE REPAIR SVCS
SCALES & BALANCES, EXC LABORATORY
SCALES: Baby
SCALES: Bathroom
SCALES: Indl
SCALES: Truck
SCANNING DEVICES: Optical
SCHOOL SPLYS, EXC BOOKS: Wholesalers
SCHOOLS: Elementary & Secondary
SCHOOLS: Vocational, NEC
SCIENTIFIC INSTRUMENTS WHOLESALERS
SCRAP & WASTE MATERIALS, WHOLESALE: Auto Wrecking For Scrap
SCRAP & WASTE MATERIALS, WHOLESALE: Ferrous Metal
SCRAP & WASTE MATERIALS, WHOLESALE: Junk & Scrap

PRODUCT INDEX

SCRAP & WASTE MATERIALS, WHOLESALE: Metal
SCRAP & WASTE MATERIALS, WHOLESALE: Nonferrous Metals Scrap
SCRAP & WASTE MATERIALS, WHOLESALE: Paper
SCRAP & WASTE MATERIALS, WHOLESALE: Paper & Cloth Materials
SCREENS: Projection
SCREENS: Window, Metal
SCREENS: Woven Wire
SCREW MACHINE PRDTS
SCREW MACHINES
SCREWS: Metal
SEALANTS
SEALS: Hermetic
SEALS: Oil, Leather
SEALS: Oil, Rubber
SEARCH & DETECTION SYSTEMS, EXC RADAR
SEARCH & NAVIGATION SYSTEMS
SEAT BELTS: Automobile & Aircraft
SEATING: Chairs, Table & Arm
SEATING: Railroad
SEATING: Transportation
SECRETARIAL SVCS
SECURITY CONTROL EQPT & SYSTEMS
SECURITY DEVICES
SECURITY EQPT STORES
SECURITY PROTECTIVE DEVICES MAINTENANCE & MONITORING SVCS
SECURITY SYSTEMS SERVICES
SEEDS & BULBS WHOLESALERS
SEEDS: Coated Or Treated, From Purchased Seeds
SELF-PROPELLED AIRCRAFT DEALER
SEMICONDUCTOR CIRCUIT NETWORKS
SEMICONDUCTOR DEVICES: Wafers
SEMICONDUCTORS & RELATED DEVICES
SENSORS: Infrared, Solid State
SENSORS: Radiation
SENSORS: Temperature For Motor Windings
SEPARATORS: Metal Plate
SEPTIC TANK CLEANING SVCS
SEPTIC TANKS: Concrete
SEWAGE & WATER TREATMENT EQPT
SEWAGE TREATMENT SYSTEMS & EQPT
SEWER CLEANING & RODDING SVC
SEWER CLEANING EQPT: Power
SEWER INSPECTION SVCS
SEWING CONTRACTORS
SEWING MACHINE REPAIR SHOP
SEWING MACHINES & PARTS: Indl
SEWING, NEEDLEWORK & PIECE GOODS STORES
SEWING, NEEDLEWORK & PIECE GOODS STORES: Sewing & Needlework
SEXTANTS
SHADES: Lamp & Light, Residential
SHADES: Window
SHAPES & PILINGS, STRUCTURAL: Steel
SHAPES: Extruded, Aluminum, NEC
SHAPES: Flat, Rolled, Aluminum, NEC
SHEATHING: Asphalt Saturated
SHEET METAL SPECIALTIES, EXC STAMPED
SHEETING: Laminated Plastic
SHEETS & STRIPS: Aluminum
SHEETS: Solid Fiber, Made From Purchased Materials
SHELLAC
SHELTERED WORKSHOPS
SHELVES & SHELVING: Wood
SHELVING, MADE FROM PURCHASED WIRE
SHELVING: Office & Store, Exc Wood
SHIELDS OR ENCLOSURES: Radiator, Sheet Metal
SHIMS: Metal
SHIP BUILDING & REPAIRING: Offshore Sply Boats
SHIP BUILDING & REPAIRING: Rigging, Marine
SHIPBUILDING & REPAIR
SHIPPING AGENTS
SHOCK ABSORBERS: Indl
SHOE & BOOT ACCESS
SHOE MATERIALS: Counters
SHOE MATERIALS: Plastic
SHOE MATERIALS: Quarters
SHOE MATERIALS: Rands
SHOE MATERIALS: Rubber
SHOE MATERIALS: Uppers
SHOE STORES
SHOE STORES: Athletic
SHOE STORES: Boots, Men's
SHOE STORES: Boots, Women's
SHOE STORES: Custom & Orthopedic
SHOE STORES: Men's
SHOE STORES: Orthopedic
SHOES & BOOTS WHOLESALERS
SHOES: Ballet Slippers
SHOES: Canvas, Rubber Soled
SHOES: Men's
SHOES: Men's, Dress
SHOES: Orthopedic, Men's
SHOES: Orthopedic, Women's
SHOES: Plastic Or Rubber
SHOES: Rubber Or Rubber Soled Fabric Uppers
SHOES: Women's
SHOPPING CENTERS & MALLS
SHOT PEENING SVC
SHOWCASES & DISPLAY FIXTURES: Office & Store
SHOWER STALLS: Metal
SHOWER STALLS: Plastic & Fiberglass
SHREDDERS: Indl & Commercial
SHUTTERS, DOOR & WINDOW: Metal
SHUTTERS, DOOR & WINDOW: Plastic
SHUTTERS: Door, Wood
SIDING & STRUCTURAL MATERIALS: Wood
SIDING: Precast Stone
SIDING: Sheet Metal
SIGN LETTERING & PAINTING SVCS
SIGN PAINTING & LETTERING SHOP
SIGNALING APPARATUS: Electric
SIGNALING DEVICES: Sound, Electrical
SIGNALS: Railroad, Electric
SIGNALS: Traffic Control, Electric
SIGNALS: Transportation
SIGNS & ADVERTISING SPECIALTIES
SIGNS & ADVERTISING SPECIALTIES: Artwork, Advertising
SIGNS & ADVERTISING SPECIALTIES: Letters For Signs, Metal
SIGNS & ADVERTISING SPECIALTIES: Novelties
SIGNS & ADVERTISING SPECIALTIES: Scoreboards, Electric
SIGNS & ADVERTISING SPECIALTIES: Signs
SIGNS & ADVERTSG SPECIALTIES: Displays/Cutouts Window/Lobby
SIGNS, ELECTRICAL: Wholesalers
SIGNS, EXC ELECTRIC, WHOLESALE
SIGNS: Electrical
SIGNS: Neon
SILICA MINING
SILICON
SILICON WAFERS: Chemically Doped
SILICONES
SILK SCREEN DESIGN SVCS
SILOS: Concrete, Prefabricated
SILOS: Meal
SILVER ORE MINING
SILVER ORES
SILVERSMITHS
SIMULATORS: Flight
SINKS: Vitreous China
SIRENS: Vehicle, Marine, Indl & Warning
SKIDS: Wood
SKYLIGHTS
SLAB & TILE, ROOFING: Concrete
SLAB & TILE: Precast Concrete, Floor
SLAG: Crushed Or Ground
SLATE: Crushed & Broken
SLAUGHTERING & MEAT PACKING
SLIDES & EXHIBITS: Prepared
SLINGS: Lifting, Made From Purchased Wire
SLOT MACHINES
SMOKE DETECTORS
SNIPS: Tinners'
SNOW PLOWING SVCS
SNOW REMOVAL EQPT: Residential
SOAPS & DETERGENTS
SOAPS & DETERGENTS: Glycerin, Crude Or Refined, From Fats
SOAPS & DETERGENTS: Textile
SOCIAL CLUBS
SOCIAL SVCS, HANDICAPPED
SOCIAL SVCS: Individual & Family
SOFT DRINKS WHOLESALERS
SOFTWARE PUBLISHERS: Application
SOFTWARE PUBLISHERS: Business & Professional
SOFTWARE PUBLISHERS: Computer Utilities
SOFTWARE PUBLISHERS: Education
SOFTWARE PUBLISHERS: Home Entertainment
SOFTWARE PUBLISHERS: NEC
SOFTWARE PUBLISHERS: Operating Systems
SOFTWARE PUBLISHERS: Publisher's
SOFTWARE PUBLISHERS: Word Processing
SOFTWARE TRAINING, COMPUTER
SOIL CONDITIONERS
SOIL TESTING KITS
SOLAR CELLS
SOLAR HEATING EQPT
SOLDERING EQPT: Electrical, Exc Handheld
SOLDERS
SOLENOIDS
SOUND EFFECTS & MUSIC PRODUCTION: Motion Picture
SOUND EQPT: Electric
SOUND RECORDING STUDIOS
SOUND REPRODUCING EQPT
SOYBEAN PRDTS
SPACE VEHICLE EQPT
SPEAKER MONITORS
SPEAKER SYSTEMS
SPEAKERS BUREAU
SPECIAL EVENTS DECORATION SVCS
SPECIALTY FOOD STORES, NEC
SPECIALTY FOOD STORES: Coffee
SPECIALTY FOOD STORES: Dietetic Foods
SPECIALTY FOOD STORES: Dried Fruit
SPECIALTY FOOD STORES: Health & Dietetic Food
SPECIALTY FOOD STORES: Juices, Fruit Or Vegetable
SPECIALTY FOOD STORES: Soft Drinks
SPECIALTY FOOD STORES: Vitamin
SPECULATIVE BUILDERS: Single-Family Housing
SPEED CHANGERS
SPICE & HERB STORES
SPINDLES: Textile
SPOOLS: Indl
SPORTING & ATHLETIC GOODS: Bags, Golf
SPORTING & ATHLETIC GOODS: Bases, Baseball
SPORTING & ATHLETIC GOODS: Basketball Eqpt & Splys, NEC
SPORTING & ATHLETIC GOODS: Bowling Alleys & Access
SPORTING & ATHLETIC GOODS: Bows, Archery
SPORTING & ATHLETIC GOODS: Camping Eqpt & Splys
SPORTING & ATHLETIC GOODS: Dartboards & Access
SPORTING & ATHLETIC GOODS: Decoys, Duck & Other Game Birds
SPORTING & ATHLETIC GOODS: Driving Ranges, Golf, Electronic
SPORTING & ATHLETIC GOODS: Dumbbells & Other Weight Eqpt
SPORTING & ATHLETIC GOODS: Exercising Cycles
SPORTING & ATHLETIC GOODS: Fish & Bait Baskets Or Creels
SPORTING & ATHLETIC GOODS: Fishing Eqpt
SPORTING & ATHLETIC GOODS: Fishing Tackle, General
SPORTING & ATHLETIC GOODS: Game Calls
SPORTING & ATHLETIC GOODS: Gymnasium Eqpt
SPORTING & ATHLETIC GOODS: Hooks, Fishing
SPORTING & ATHLETIC GOODS: Hunting Eqpt
SPORTING & ATHLETIC GOODS: Indian Clubs
SPORTING & ATHLETIC GOODS: Lacrosse Eqpt & Splys, NEC
SPORTING & ATHLETIC GOODS: Masks, Hockey, Baseball, Etc
SPORTING & ATHLETIC GOODS: Pools, Swimming, Exc Plastic
SPORTING & ATHLETIC GOODS: Pools, Swimming, Plastic
SPORTING & ATHLETIC GOODS: Protective Sporting Eqpt
SPORTING & ATHLETIC GOODS: Reels, Fishing
SPORTING & ATHLETIC GOODS: Rods & Rod Parts, Fishing
SPORTING & ATHLETIC GOODS: Shafts, Golf Club
SPORTING & ATHLETIC GOODS: Shuffleboards & Shuffleboard Eqpt
SPORTING & ATHLETIC GOODS: Skateboards
SPORTING & ATHLETIC GOODS: Soccer Eqpt & Splys
SPORTING & ATHLETIC GOODS: Softball Eqpt, Splys
SPORTING & ATHLETIC GOODS: Targets, Archery & Rifle Shooting
SPORTING & ATHLETIC GOODS: Team Sports Eqpt
SPORTING & ATHLETIC GOODS: Track & Field Athletic Eqpt
SPORTING & ATHLETIC GOODS: Water Sports Eqpt
SPORTING & RECREATIONAL GOODS & SPLYS WHOLESALERS

PRODUCT INDEX

SPORTING & RECREATIONAL GOODS, WHOLESALE: Athletic Goods
SPORTING & RECREATIONAL GOODS, WHOLESALE: Bicycle
SPORTING & RECREATIONAL GOODS, WHOLESALE: Boat Access & Part
SPORTING & RECREATIONAL GOODS, WHOLESALE: Diving
SPORTING & RECREATIONAL GOODS, WHOLESALE: Exercise
SPORTING & RECREATIONAL GOODS, WHOLESALE: Fishing
SPORTING & RECREATIONAL GOODS, WHOLESALE: Fishing Tackle
SPORTING & RECREATIONAL GOODS, WHOLESALE: Fitness
SPORTING & RECREATIONAL GOODS, WHOLESALE: Golf
SPORTING CAMPS
SPORTING FIREARMS WHOLESALERS
SPORTING GOODS
SPORTING GOODS STORES, NEC
SPORTING GOODS STORES: Archery Splys
SPORTING GOODS STORES: Bait & Tackle
SPORTING GOODS STORES: Firearms
SPORTING GOODS STORES: Hunting Eqpt
SPORTING GOODS STORES: Martial Arts Eqpt & Splys
SPORTING GOODS STORES: Playground Eqpt
SPORTING GOODS STORES: Skiing Eqpt
SPORTING GOODS STORES: Team sports Eqpt
SPORTING GOODS STORES: Tennis Goods & Eqpt
SPORTING GOODS: Archery
SPORTING GOODS: Hammocks, Fabric, Made From Purchased Mat
SPORTING/ATHLETIC GOODS: Gloves, Boxing, Handball, Etc
SPORTS APPAREL STORES
SPOUTING: Plastic & Fiberglass Reinforced
SPOUTS: Sheet Metal
SPRAYING & DUSTING EQPT
SPRINGS: Coiled Flat
SPRINGS: Cold Formed
SPRINGS: Hot Wound, Exc Wire
SPRINGS: Instrument, Precision
SPRINGS: Leaf, Automobile, Locomotive, Etc
SPRINGS: Mechanical, Precision
SPRINGS: Precision
SPRINGS: Steel
SPRINGS: Torsion Bar
SPRINGS: Wire
SPRINKLING SYSTEMS: Fire Control
SPROCKETS: Power Transmission
STAINLESS STEEL
STAINLESS STEEL WARE
STAIRCASES & STAIRS, WOOD
STAMPING SVC: Book, Gold
STAMPINGS: Automotive
STAMPINGS: Metal
STAPLES
STAPLES, MADE FROM PURCHASED WIRE
STARTERS & CONTROLLERS: Motor, Electric
STARTERS: Electric Motor
STARTERS: Motor
STARTING EQPT: Street Cars
STATIC ELIMINATORS: Ind
STATIONARY & OFFICE SPLYS, WHOLESALE: Looseleaf Binders
STATIONARY & OFFICE SPLYS, WHOLESALE Manifold Business Form
STATIONARY & OFFICE SPLYS, WHOLESALE: Office Filing Splys
STATIONARY & OFFICE SPLYS, WHOLESALE: Stationery
STATIONARY & OFFICE SPLYS, WHOLESALE: Writing Ink
STATIONER'S SUNDRIES: Rubber
STATIONERY & OFFICE SPLYS WHOLESALERS
STATIONERY PRDTS
STATIONERY: Made From Purchased Materials
STATORS REWINDING SVCS
STATUARY & OTHER DECORATIVE PRDTS: Nonmetallic
STATUARY GOODS, EXC RELIGIOUS: Wholesalers
STATUES: Nonmetal
STEEL & ALLOYS: Tool & Die
STEEL FABRICATORS
STEEL MILLS
STEEL SHEET: Cold-Rolled
STEEL WOOL

STEEL, COLD-ROLLED: Flat Bright, From Purchased Hot-Rolled
STEEL, COLD-ROLLED: Strip NEC, From Purchased Hot-Rolled
STEEL, HOT-ROLLED: Sheet Or Strip
STEEL: Cold-Rolled
STEEL: Laminated
STEERING SYSTEMS & COMPONENTS
STENCILS
STENCILS & LETTERING MATERIALS: Die-Cut
STEREOGRAPHS: Photographic Message Svcs
STOCK CAR RACING
STONE: Cast Concrete
STONE: Dimension, NEC
STONE: Quarrying & Processing, Own Stone Prdts
STONES: Abrasive
STONEWARE PRDTS: Pottery
STOOLS: Factory
STORE FIXTURES, EXC REFRIGERATED: Wholesalers
STORE FIXTURES: Exc Wood
STORE FIXTURES: Wood
STORES: Auto & Home Supply
STORES: Drapery & Upholstery
STRADDLE CARRIERS: Mobile
STRAINERS: Line, Piping Systems
STRAPPING
STRAPS: Apparel Webbing
STRAW GOODS
STRAWS: Drinking, Made From Purchased Materials
STRINGING BEADS
STRUCTURAL SUPPORT & BUILDING MATERIAL: Concrete
STUDIOS: Artist
STUDIOS: Artists & Artists' Studios
STUDIOS: Sculptor's
STUDS & JOISTS: Sheet Metal
STYLING SVCS: Wigs
STYRENE RESINS, NEC
SUBPRESSES, METALWORKING
SUGAR SUBSTITUTES: Organic
SUNDRIES & RELATED PRDTS: Medical & Laboratory, Rubber
SUNGLASSES, WHOLESALE
SUNROOMS: Prefabricated Metal
SUPERMARKETS & OTHER GROCERY STORES
SURFACE ACTIVE AGENTS
SURFACE ACTIVE AGENTS: Emulsifiers, Exc Food & Pharmaceuticl
SURFACE ACTIVE AGENTS: Oils & Greases
SURFACE ACTIVE AGENTS: Processing Assistants
SURGICAL & MEDICAL INSTRUMENTS WHOLESALERS
SURGICAL APPLIANCES & SPLYS
SURGICAL APPLIANCES & SPLYS
SURGICAL EQPT: See Also Instruments
SURGICAL IMPLANTS
SURVEYING & MAPPING: Land Parcels
SURVEYING INSTRUMENTS WHOLESALERS
SUSPENSION SYSTEMS: Acoustical, Metal
SVC ESTABLISH EQPT, WHOL: Extermination/Fumigatn Eqpt/Splys
SVC ESTABLISHMENT EQPT & SPLYS WHOLESALERS
SVC ESTABLISHMENT EQPT, WHOL: Cleaning & Maint Eqpt & Splys
SVC ESTABLISHMENT EQPT, WHOL: Concrete Burial Vaults & Boxes
SVC ESTABLISHMENT EQPT, WHOL: Liquor Dispensing Eqpt/Sys
SVC ESTABLISHMENT EQPT, WHOLESALE: Beauty Parlor Eqpt & Sply
SVC ESTABLISHMENT EQPT, WHOLESALE: Cemetery Splys & Eqpt
SVC ESTABLISHMENT EQPT, WHOLESALE: Engraving Eqpt & Splys
SVC ESTABLISHMENT EQPT, WHOLESALE: Firefighting Eqpt
SVC ESTABLISHMENT EQPT, WHOLESALE: Laundry Eqpt & Splys
SVC ESTABLISHMENT EQPT, WHOLESALE: Locksmith Eqpt & Splys
SVC ESTABLISHMENT EQPT, WHOLESALE: Restaurant Splys
SVC ESTABLISHMENT EQPT, WHOLESALE: Taxidermist Tools & Eqpt
SVC ESTABLISHMENT EQPT, WHOLESALE: Voting Machines
SWEEPING COMPOUNDS

SWIMMING POOL & HOT TUB CLEANING & MAINTENANCE SVCS
SWIMMING POOL SPLY STORES
SWIMMING POOLS, EQPT & SPLYS: Wholesalers
SWITCHBOARD OPERATIONS: Private Branch Exchanges
SWITCHBOARDS & PARTS: Power
SWITCHES
SWITCHES: Electric Power
SWITCHES: Electric Power, Exc Snap, Push Button, Etc
SWITCHES: Electronic
SWITCHES: Electronic Applications
SWITCHES: Flow Actuated, Electrical
SWITCHES: Solenoid
SWITCHES: Starting, Fluorescent
SWITCHES: Stepping
SWITCHES: Time, Electrical Switchgear Apparatus
SWITCHGEAR & SWITCHBOARD APPARATUS
SWITCHGEAR & SWITCHGEAR ACCESS, NEC
SWITCHING EQPT: Radio & Television Communications
SYNTHETIC RESIN FINISHED PRDTS, NEC
SYRUPS, DRINK
SYRUPS, FLAVORING, EXC DRINK
SYSTEMS ENGINEERING: Computer Related
SYSTEMS INTEGRATION
SYSTEMS INTEGRATION SVCS: Local Area Network
SYSTEMS INTEGRATION SVCS: Office Computer Automation
SYSTEMS SOFTWARE DEVELOPMENT SVCS

T

TABLE OR COUNTERTOPS, PLASTIC LAMINATED
TABLECLOTHS & SETTINGS
TABLETS: Bronze Or Other Metal
TABLEWARE OR KITCHEN ARTICLES: Whiteware, Fine Semivitreous
TAGS & LABELS: Paper
TAGS: Paper, Blank, Made From Purchased Paper
TAILORS: Custom
TALLOW: Animal
TANK REPAIR & CLEANING SVCS
TANK REPAIR SVCS
TANKS & OTHER TRACKED VEHICLE CMPNTS
TANKS: For Tank Trucks, Metal Plate
TANKS: Fuel, Including Oil & Gas, Metal Plate
TANKS: Lined, Metal
TANKS: Plastic & Fiberglass
TANKS: Standard Or Custom Fabricated, Metal Plate
TANKS: Water, Metal Plate
TANNERIES: Leather
TAPE DRIVES
TAPE MEASURES
TAPE RECERTIFICATION SVCS
TAPE STORAGE UNITS: Computer
TAPE: Instrumentation Type, Blank
TAPE: Rubber
TAPES, ADHESIVE: Masking, Made From Purchased Materials
TAPES, ADHESIVE: Medical
TAPES: Coated Fiberglass, Pipe Sealing Or Insulating
TAPES: Fabric
TAPES: Gummed, Cloth Or Paper Based, From Purchased Matls
TAPES: Magnetic
TAPES: Plastic Coated
TAPES: Pressure Sensitive
TAPES: Pressure Sensitive, Rubber
TAPS
TARPAULINS
TARPAULINS, WHOLESALE
TAX RETURN PREPARATION SVCS
TECHNICAL & TRADE SCHOOLS, NEC
TECHNICAL MANUAL PREPARATION SVCS
TECHNICAL WRITING SVCS
TELECOMMUNICATION EQPT REPAIR SVCS, EXC TELEPHONES
TELECOMMUNICATION SYSTEMS & EQPT
TELECOMMUNICATIONS CARRIERS & SVCS: Wired
TELECOMMUNICATIONS CARRIERS & SVCS: Wireless
TELECONFERENCING SVCS
TELEMARKETING BUREAUS
TELEMETERING EQPT
TELEPHONE ANSWERING SVCS
TELEPHONE BOOTHS, EXC WOOD
TELEPHONE CENTRAL OFFICE EQPT: Dial Or Manual
TELEPHONE EQPT INSTALLATION

PRODUCT INDEX

TELEPHONE EQPT: Modems
TELEPHONE EQPT: NEC
TELEPHONE STATION EQPT & PARTS: Wire
TELEPHONE SVCS
TELEPHONE SWITCHING EQPT
TELEPHONE SWITCHING EQPT: Toll Switching
TELEPHONE: Autotransformers For Switchboards
TELEPHONE: Fiber Optic Systems
TELEPHONE: Headsets
TELEPHONE: Sets, Exc Cellular Radio
TELEPHONES: Sound Powered, Without Battery
TELESCOPES
TELETYPEWRITERS
TELEVISION BROADCASTING & COMMUNICATIONS EQPT
TELEVISION BROADCASTING STATIONS
TELEVISION FILM PRODUCTION SVCS
TELEVISION: Cameras
TELEVISION: Closed Circuit Eqpt
TELEVISION: Monitors
TEMPERING: Metal
TENTS: All Materials
TERMINAL BOARDS
TERRAZZO PRECAST PRDTS
TEST BORING SVCS: Nonmetallic Minerals
TEST KITS: Pregnancy
TESTERS: Battery
TESTERS: Environmental
TESTERS: Hardness
TESTERS: Liquid, Exc Indl Process
TESTERS: Logic Circuit
TESTERS: Physical Property
TESTERS: Water, Exc Indl Process
TESTING SVCS
TEXTILE & APPAREL SVCS
TEXTILE BAGS WHOLESALERS
TEXTILE FABRICATORS
TEXTILE FINISHING: Chem Coat/Treat, Man, Broadwoven, Cotton
TEXTILE FINISHING: Chem Coating/Treating, Broadwoven, Cotton
TEXTILE FINISHING: Chemical Coating Or Treating
TEXTILE FINISHING: Dyeing, Broadwoven, Cotton
TEXTILE FINISHING: Dyeing, Finishing & Printng, Linen Fabric
TEXTILE FINISHING: Embossing, Linen, Broadwoven
TEXTILE PRDTS: Hand Woven & Crocheted
TEXTILE: Finishing, Cotton Broadwoven
TEXTILE: Finishing, Raw Stock NEC
TEXTILE: Goods, NEC
TEXTILES: Flock
TEXTILES: Jute & Flax Prdts
TEXTILES: Linen Fabrics
TEXTILES: Linings, Carpet, Exc Felt
TEXTILES: Mill Waste & Remnant
TEXTILES: Padding & Wadding
THEATRICAL LIGHTING SVCS
THEATRICAL PRODUCERS & SVCS
THEATRICAL SCENERY
THEOLOGICAL SEMINARIES
THERMOCOUPLES
THERMOCOUPLES: Indl Process
THERMOMETERS: Liquid-In-Glass & Bimetal
THERMOMETERS: Medical, Digital
THERMOPLASTIC MATERIALS
THERMOPLASTICS
THERMOSTAT REPAIR SVCS
THREAD: All Fibers
THREAD: Embroidery
THYROID PREPARATIONS
TIES, FORM: Metal
TILE: Brick & Structural, Clay
TILE: Clay, Drain & Structural
TILE: Concrete, Drain
TILE: Terrazzo Or Concrete, Precast
TILE: Wall & Floor, Ceramic
TILE: Wall, Ceramic
TIMING DEVICES: Electronic
TIN
TINPLATE
TIRE CORD & FABRIC
TIRE CORD & FABRIC: Indl, Reinforcing
TIRE DEALERS
TIRE INFLATORS: Hand Or Compressor Operated
TIRE INNER-TUBES
TIRE RECAPPING & RETREADING
TIRE SUNDRIES OR REPAIR MATERIALS: Rubber
TIRES & INNER TUBES
TIRES & TUBES WHOLESALERS
TIRES & TUBES, WHOLESALE: Automotive
TIRES & TUBES, WHOLESALE: Truck
TIRES, USED, WHOLESALE
TIRES: Agricultural, Pneumatic
TIRES: Cushion Or Solid Rubber
TIRES: Indl Vehicles
TIRES: Plastic
TIRES: Truck
TITANIUM MILL PRDTS
TOBACCO & PRDTS, WHOLESALE: Cigars
TOBACCO & TOBACCO PRDTS WHOLESALERS
TOBACCO STORES & STANDS
TOBACCO: Chewing
TOBACCO: Chewing & Snuff
TOBACCO: Cigarettes
TOBACCO: Smoking
TOILET PREPARATIONS
TOILET SEATS: Wood
TOILETRIES, COSMETICS & PERFUME STORES
TOILETRIES, WHOLESALE: Hair Preparations
TOILETRIES, WHOLESALE: Perfumes
TOILETRIES, WHOLESALE: Razor Blades
TOILETRIES, WHOLESALE: Toilet Soap
TOILETRIES, WHOLESALE: Toiletries
TOILETS: Portable Chemical, Plastics
TOLL OPERATIONS
TOLLS: Caulking
TOMBSTONES: Terrazzo Or Concrete, Precast
TOOL & DIE STEEL
TOOL REPAIR SVCS
TOOLS: Carpenters', Including Levels & Chisels, Exc Saws
TOOLS: Hand
TOOLS: Hand, Carpet Layers
TOOLS: Hand, Hammers
TOOLS: Hand, Ironworkers'
TOOLS: Hand, Masons'
TOOLS: Hand, Mechanics
TOOLS: Hand, Plumbers'
TOOLS: Hand, Power
TOOTHPASTES, GELS & TOOTHPOWDERS
TOWELETTES: Premoistened
TOWELS: Knit
TOWERS, SECTIONS: Transmission, Radio & Television
TOYS
TOYS & HOBBY GOODS & SPLYS, WHOL: Toy Novelties & Amusements
TOYS & HOBBY GOODS & SPLYS, WHOLESALE: Arts/Crafts Eqpt/Sply
TOYS & HOBBY GOODS & SPLYS, WHOLESALE: Educational Toys
TOYS & HOBBY GOODS & SPLYS, WHOLESALE: Model Kits
TOYS & HOBBY GOODS & SPLYS, WHOLESALE: Toys & Games
TOYS & HOBBY GOODS & SPLYS, WHOLESALE: Toys, NEC
TOYS & HOBBY GOODS & SPLYS, WHOLESALE: Video Games
TOYS, HOBBY GOODS & SPLYS WHOLESALERS
TOYS: Dolls, Stuffed Animals & Parts
TOYS: Electronic
TOYS: Rubber
TOYS: Video Game Machines
TRADE SHOW ARRANGEMENT SVCS
TRADERS: Commodity, Contracts
TRAILERS & CHASSIS: Camping
TRAILERS & PARTS: Boat
TRAILERS & PARTS: Truck & Semi's
TRAILERS & TRAILER EQPT
TRAILERS: Bodies
TRAILERS: Demountable Cargo Containers
TRAILERS: Semitrailers, Truck Tractors
TRANSDUCERS: Electrical Properties
TRANSFORMERS: Control
TRANSFORMERS: Distribution
TRANSFORMERS: Electric
TRANSFORMERS: Electronic
TRANSFORMERS: Fluorescent Lighting
TRANSFORMERS: Flyback
TRANSFORMERS: Lighting, Street & Airport
TRANSFORMERS: Meters, Electronic
TRANSFORMERS: Power Related
TRANSFORMERS: Specialty
TRANSLATION & INTERPRETATION SVCS
TRANSMISSIONS: Motor Vehicle
TRANSPORTATION AGENTS & BROKERS
TRANSPORTATION BROKERS: Truck
TRANSPORTATION EQPT & SPLYS, WHOL: Aeronautical Eqpt & Splys
TRANSPORTATION EQPT & SPLYS, WHOLESALE: Nav Eqpt & Splys
TRANSPORTATION EQPT & SPLYS, WHOLESALE: Pulleys
TRANSPORTATION EQPT & SPLYS WHOLESALERS, NEC
TRANSPORTATION EQUIPMENT, NEC
TRANSPORTATION SVCS, AIR, NONSCHEDULED: Air Cargo Carriers
TRANSPORTATION SVCS, NEC
TRANSPORTATION SVCS: Airport Limousine, Scheduled Svcs
TRANSPORTATION SVCS: Railroads, Interurban
TRANSPORTATION SVCS: Railroads, Steam
TRANSPORTATION: Air, Scheduled Passenger
TRANSPORTATION: Bus Transit Systems
TRANSPORTATION: Deep Sea Domestic Freight
TRANSPORTATION: Transit Systems, NEC
TRAPS: Animal, Iron Or Steel
TRAPS: Stem
TRAVEL TRAILERS & CAMPERS
TRAVELER ACCOMMODATIONS, NEC
TRAYS: Cable, Metal Plate
TRAYS: Plastic
TRIM: Window, Wood
TROPHIES, NEC
TROPHIES, PLATED, ALL METALS
TROPHIES, WHOLESALE
TROPHIES: Metal, Exc Silver
TROPHY & PLAQUE STORES
TRUCK & BUS BODIES: Automobile Wrecker Truck
TRUCK & BUS BODIES: Beverage Truck
TRUCK & BUS BODIES: Bus Bodies
TRUCK & BUS BODIES: Dump Truck
TRUCK & BUS BODIES: Motor Vehicle, Specialty
TRUCK & BUS BODIES: Tank Truck
TRUCK & BUS BODIES: Truck Cabs, Motor Vehicles
TRUCK & BUS BODIES: Truck Tops
TRUCK & BUS BODIES: Truck, Motor Vehicle
TRUCK & BUS BODIES: Utility Truck
TRUCK & BUS BODIES: Van Bodies
TRUCK & FREIGHT TERMINALS & SUPPORT ACTIVITIES
TRUCK BODIES: Body Parts
TRUCK BODY SHOP
TRUCK FINANCE LEASING
TRUCK GENERAL REPAIR SVC
TRUCK PAINTING & LETTERING SVCS
TRUCK PARTS & ACCESSORIES: Wholesalers
TRUCKING & HAULING SVCS: Coal, Local
TRUCKING & HAULING SVCS: Contract Basis
TRUCKING & HAULING SVCS: Heavy Machinery, Local
TRUCKING & HAULING SVCS: Mobile Homes
TRUCKING & HAULING SVCS: Trailer/Container On Flat Car
TRUCKING, DUMP
TRUCKING: Except Local
TRUCKING: Local, With Storage
TRUCKING: Local, Without Storage
TRUCKS & TRACTORS: Industrial
TRUCKS, INDL: Wholesalers
TRUCKS: Forklift
TRUCKS: Indl
TRUSSES & FRAMING: Prefabricated Metal
TRUSSES: Wood, Floor
TRUSSES: Wood, Roof
TRUST COMPANIES: State Accepting Deposits, Commercial
TRUST MANAGEMENT SVCS: Personal Investment
TUB CONTAINERS: Plastic
TUBE & TUBING FABRICATORS
TUBES: Extruded Or Drawn, Aluminum
TUBES: Hard Rubber
TUBES: Paper
TUBES: Paper Or Fiber, Chemical Or Electrical Uses
TUBES: Steel & Iron
TUBES: Television
TUBES: Vacuum
TUBES: Wrought, Welded Or Lock Joint
TUBING, COLD-DRAWN: Mech Or Hypodermic Sizes, Stainless
TUBING: Copper
TUBING: Electrical Use, Quartz

PRODUCT INDEX

TUBING: Flexible, Metallic
TUBING: Seamless
TUCKING FOR THE TRADE
TURBINES & TURBINE GENERATOR SET UNITS, COMPLETE
TURBINES & TURBINE GENERATOR SET UNITS: Gas, Complete
TURBINES & TURBINE GENERATOR SETS
TURBINES & TURBINE GENERATOR SETS & PARTS
TURBINES: Gas, Mechanical Drive
TURBINES: Hydraulic, Complete
TURBINES: Steam
TURBO-GENERATORS
TURBO-SUPERCHARGERS: Aircraft
TURKEY PROCESSING & SLAUGHTERING
TWINE PRDTS
TYPESETTING SVC
TYPESETTING SVC: Computer
TYPESETTING SVC: Hand Composition
TYPOGRAPHY

U

ULTRASONIC EQPT: Cleaning, Exc Med & Dental
UMBRELLAS & CANES
UNDERGROUND GOLD MINING
UNDERGROUND IRON ORE MINING
UNIFORM STORES
UNISEX HAIR SALONS
UNIT TRAIN LOADING FACILITY, BITUMINOUS OR LIGNITE
UNIVERSITY
UNSUPPORTED PLASTICS: Tile
UPHOLSTERY MATERIAL
UPHOLSTERY WORK SVCS
URANIUM ORE MINING, NEC
USED BOOK STORES
USED CAR DEALERS
USED MERCHANDISE STORES
USED MERCHANDISE STORES: Art Objects, Antique
USED MERCHANDISE STORES: Clothing & Shoes
USED MERCHANDISE STORES: Office Furniture
UTENSILS: Cast Aluminum, Cooking Or Kitchen
UTENSILS: Cast Aluminum, Hospital
UTENSILS: Household, Cooking & Kitchen, Metal
UTENSILS: Household, Metal, Exc Cast
UTILITY TRAILER DEALERS

V

VACUUM CLEANER STORES
VACUUM CLEANERS: Household
VACUUM CLEANERS: Indl Type
VACUUM PUMPS & EQPT: Laboratory
VACUUM SYSTEMS: Air Extraction, Indl
VALUE-ADDED RESELLERS: Computer Systems
VALVE REPAIR SVCS, INDL
VALVES
VALVES & PARTS: Gas, Indl
VALVES & PIPE FITTINGS
VALVES & REGULATORS: Pressure, Indl
VALVES: Aerosol, Metal
VALVES: Aircraft, Control, Hydraulic & Pneumatic
VALVES: Control, Automatic
VALVES: Electrohydraulic Servo, Metal
VALVES: Engine
VALVES: Fire Hydrant
VALVES: Fluid Power, Control, Hydraulic & pneumatic
VALVES: Indl
VALVES: Plumbing & Heating
VALVES: Regulating & Control, Automatic
VALVES: Regulating, Process Control
VALVES: Water Works
VARIETY STORE MERCHANDISE, WHOLESALE
VARIETY STORES
VARNISHES, NEC
VARNISHING SVC: Metal Prdts
VAULTS & SAFES WHOLESALERS
VEHICLES: Children's, Exc Bicycles
VEHICLES: Recreational
VENDING MACHINES & PARTS
VENETIAN BLINDS & SHADES
VENTILATING EQPT: Metal
VENTILATING EQPT: Sheet Metal
VENTURE CAPITAL COMPANIES
VETERINARY PHARMACEUTICAL PREPARATIONS
VETERINARY PRDTS: Instruments & Apparatus
VIDEO & AUDIO EQPT, WHOLESALE

VIDEO CAMERA-AUDIO RECORDERS: Household Use
VIDEO EQPT
VIDEO PRODUCTION SVCS
VIDEO TAPE PRODUCTION SVCS
VINYL RESINS, NEC
VISES: Machine
VISUAL COMMUNICATIONS SYSTEMS
VISUAL EFFECTS PRODUCTION SVCS
VITAMINS: Natural Or Synthetic, Uncompounded, Bulk
VITAMINS: Pharmaceutical Preparations
VOCATIONAL REHABILITATION AGENCY
VOCATIONAL TRAINING AGENCY
VOLCANIC ROCK: Dimension

W

WALLBOARD: Decorated, Made From Purchased Materials
WALLPAPER & WALL COVERINGS
WALLPAPER STORE
WALLS: Curtain, Metal
WAREHOUSE CLUBS STORES
WAREHOUSING & STORAGE FACILITIES, NEC
WAREHOUSING & STORAGE, REFRIGERATED: Cold Storage Or Refrig
WAREHOUSING & STORAGE, REFRIGERATED: Frozen Or Refrig Goods
WAREHOUSING & STORAGE: Bulk St & Termnls, Hire, Petro/Chem
WAREHOUSING & STORAGE: General
WAREHOUSING & STORAGE: General
WAREHOUSING & STORAGE: Household Goods
WAREHOUSING & STORAGE; Miniwarehouse
WAREHOUSING & STORAGE: Refrigerated
WARM AIR HEATING & AC EQPT & SPLYS, WHOL: Dust Collecting
WARM AIR HEATING & AC EQPT & SPLYS, WHOLESALE Air Filters
WARM AIR HEATING & AC EQPT & SPLYS, WHOLESALE Heat Exchgrs
WARM AIR HEATING/AC EQPT/SPLYS, WHOL Warm Air Htg Eqpt/Splys
WASHCLOTHS & BATH MITTS, FROM PURCHASED MATERIALS
WASHERS
WASHERS: Lock
WASHERS: Metal
WASHERS: Plastic
WASHERS: Rubber
WASTE CLEANING SVCS
WATCH REPAIR SVCS
WATCHES
WATCHES & PARTS, WHOLESALE
WATER HEATERS
WATER PURIFICATION EQPT: Household
WATER PURIFICATION PRDTS: Chlorination Tablets & Kits
WATER SOFTENER SVCS
WATER SOFTENING WHOLESALERS
WATER SUPPLY
WATER TREATMENT EQPT: Indl
WATER: Distilled
WATER: Mineral, Carbonated, Canned & Bottled, Etc
WATER: Pasteurized & Mineral, Bottled & Canned
WATER: Pasteurized, Canned & Bottled, Etc
WATERPROOFING COMPOUNDS
WAVEGUIDES & FITTINGS
WAX REMOVERS
WAX Sealing wax
WEATHER STRIPS: Metal
WEAVING MILL, BROADWOVEN FABRICS: Wool Or Similar Fabric
WEIGHING MACHINERY & APPARATUS
WELDING & CUTTING APPARATUS & ACCESS, NEC
WELDING EQPT
WELDING EQPT & SPLYS WHOLESALERS
WELDING EQPT & SPLYS: Arc Welders, Transformer-Rectifier
WELDING EQPT & SPLYS: Resistance, Electric
WELDING EQPT & SPLYS: Wire, Bare & Coated
WELDING EQPT REPAIR SVCS
WELDING EQPT: Electric
WELDING EQPT: Electrical
WELDING MACHINES & EQPT: Ultrasonic
WELDING REPAIR SVC
WELDING SPLYS, EXC GASES: Wholesalers
WELDING TIPS: Heat Resistant, Metal
WELDMENTS

WELL CASINGS: Iron & Steel, Made In Steel Mills
WESTERN APPAREL STORES
WET CORN MILLING
WHEEL & CASTER REPAIR SVCS
WHEELCHAIRS
WHEELS
WHEELS & BRAKE SHOES: Railroad, Cast Iron
WHEELS & GRINDSTONES, EXC ARTIFICIAL: Abrasive
WHEELS & PARTS
WHEELS, GRINDING: Artificial
WHEELS: Abrasive
WHEELS: Disc, Wheelbarrow, Stroller, Etc, Stamped Metal
WHEELS: Railroad Car, Cast Steel
WHEELS: Rolled, Locomotive
WHISTLES
WHITING MINING: Crushed & Broken
WICKER PRDTS
WIG & HAIRPIECE STORES
WINCHES
WIND CHIMES
WINDINGS: Coil, Electronic
WINDMILLS: Electric Power Generation
WINDMILLS: Farm Type
WINDOW & DOOR FRAMES
WINDOW BLIND CLEANING SVCS
WINDOW BLIND REPAIR SVCS
WINDOW CLEANING SVCS
WINDOW FRAMES & SASHES: Plastic
WINDOW FRAMES, MOLDING & TRIM: Vinyl
WINDOW FURNISHINGS WHOLESALERS
WINDOW SCREENING: Plastic
WINDOWS: Frames, Wood
WINDOWS: Storm, Wood
WINDOWS: Wood
WINDSHIELD WIPER SYSTEMS
WINE & DISTILLED ALCOHOLIC BEVERAGES WHOLESALERS
WINE CELLARS, BONDED: Wine, Blended
WIRE
WIRE & CABLE: Aluminum
WIRE & CABLE: Aluminum
WIRE & CABLE: Nonferrous, Automotive, Exc Ignition Sets
WIRE & CABLE: Nonferrous, Building
WIRE & WIRE PRDTS
WIRE CLOTH & WOVEN WIRE PRDTS, MADE FROM PURCHASED WIRE
WIRE FABRIC: Welded Steel
WIRE FENCING & ACCESS WHOLESALERS
WIRE MATERIALS: Aluminum
WIRE MATERIALS: Copper
WIRE MATERIALS: Steel
WIRE PRDTS: Steel & Iron
WIRE ROPE CENTERS
WIRE WINDING OF PURCHASED WIRE
WIRE: Communication
WIRE: Mesh
WIRE: Nonferrous
WIRE: Steel, Insulated Or Armored
WIRE: Wire, Ferrous Or Iron
WOMEN'S & CHILDREN'S CLOTHING WHOLESALERS, NEC
WOMEN'S & GIRLS' SPORTSWEAR WHOLESALERS
WOMEN'S CLOTHING STORES
WOMEN'S CLOTHING STORES: Ready-To-Wear
WOMEN'S FULL & KNEE LENGTH HOSIERY DYEING & FINISHING
WOMEN'S SPECIALTY CLOTHING STORES
WOMEN'S SPORTSWEAR STORES
WOOD EXTRACT PRDTS
WOOD PRDTS
WOOD PRDTS: Barrels & Barrel Parts
WOOD PRDTS: Brackets
WOOD PRDTS: Chair Cane, Rattan Or Reed
WOOD PRDTS: Chicken Coops, Wood, Wirebound
WOOD PRDTS: Door Trim
WOOD PRDTS: Handles, Tool
WOOD PRDTS: Ladders & Stepladders
WOOD PRDTS: Laundry
WOOD PRDTS: Moldings, Unfinished & Prefinished
WOOD PRDTS: Mulch Or Sawdust
WOOD PRDTS: Mulch, Wood & Bark
WOOD PRDTS: Newel Posts
WOOD PRDTS: Outdoor, Structural
WOOD PRDTS: Panel Work
WOOD PRDTS: Planters & Window Boxes

PRODUCT INDEX

WOOD PRDTS: Poles
WOOD PRDTS: Signboards
WOOD PRDTS: Stepladders
WOOD PRDTS: Tackle Blocks
WOOD PRDTS: Trophy Bases
WOOD PRODUCTS: Reconstituted
WOOD SHAVINGS BALES, MULCH TYPE, WHOLESALE
WOOD TREATING: Millwork
WOOD TREATING: Railroad Cross-Ties
WOOD TREATING: Structural Lumber & Timber
WOOD TREATING: Wood Prdts, Creosoted
WOOD-BURNING STOVE STORES
WOODWORK & TRIM: Exterior & Ornamental
WOODWORK & TRIM: Interior & Ornamental
WOODWORK: Carved & Turned
WOODWORK: Interior & Ornamental, NEC
WOODWORK: Ornamental, Cornices, Mantels, Etc.
WORD PROCESSING SVCS
WOVEN WIRE PRDTS, NEC
WREATHS: Artificial
WRENCHES
WRITING FOR PUBLICATION SVCS

X

X-RAY EQPT & TUBES
X-RAY EQPT REPAIR SVCS

PRODUCT SECTION

Product category — **BOXES: Folding**
Edgar & Son Paperboard .... G 999 999-9999
  Yourtown *(G-11480)*
Ready Box Co. .... E 999 999-9999
  Anytown *(G-7097)*

City

Indicates approximate employment figure
A = Over 500 employees, B = 251-500
C = 101-250, D = 51-100, E = 20-50
F = 10-19, G = 3-9

Business phone

Geographic Section entry number where full company information appears.

See footnotes for symbols and codes identification.
- Refer to the Industrial Product Index preceding this section to locate product headings.

ABRASIVE SAND MINING
Fjcj LLC .... F 618 785-2217
  Baldwin *(G-1184)*

ABRASIVES
Abrasic 90 Inc .... E 847 647-5994
  Niles *(G-15098)*
Abrasive .... G 630 893-7800
  Bloomingdale *(G-1973)*
Abrasive-Form LLC .... C 630 220-3437
  Bloomingdale *(G-1974)*
Anchor Abrasives Company .... E 708 444-4300
  Tinley Park *(G-19804)*
Dura Wax Company .... F 815 385-5000
  McHenry *(G-13739)*
Fives Landis Corp .... D 815 389-2251
  South Beloit *(G-19092)*
Harsco Corporation .... F 217 237-4335
  Pawnee *(G-16304)*
Ideal Industries Inc .... C 815 895-1108
  Sycamore *(G-19715)*
K & K Abrasives & Supplies .... F 773 582-9500
  Chicago *(G-5063)*
Meinhardt Diamond Tool Co .... G 773 267-3260
  Chicago *(G-5388)*
Oswego Diamond .... G 630 636-9617
  Oswego *(G-16018)*
Rh Preyda Company .... F 212 880-1477
  Chicago *(G-6022)*
S & J Industrial Supply Corp .... F 708 339-1708
  South Holland *(G-19242)*
Saint-Gobain Abrasives Inc .... C 630 238-3300
  Carol Stream *(G-3062)*
Sand-Rite Manufacturing Co .... E 312 997-2200
  Melrose Park *(G-13912)*
Sandtech Inc .... F 847 470-9595
  Morton Grove *(G-14439)*
Schram Enterprises Inc .... E 708 345-2252
  Melrose Park *(G-13914)*
Tyrolit Limited .... G 618 548-8314
  Oswego *(G-16029)*
Uk Abrasives Inc .... E 847 291-3566
  Northbrook *(G-15494)*
Ultramatic Equipment Co .... E 630 543-4565
  Addison *(G-322)*
US Minerals Inc .... F 708 623-1935
  Tinley Park *(G-19866)*
US Minerals Inc .... F 618 785-2217
  Baldwin *(G-1187)*
US Minerals Inc .... F 217 534-2370
  Coffeen *(G-6945)*
Washington Mills Hennepin Inc .... D 815 925-7302
  Hennepin *(G-11160)*

ABRASIVES: Aluminum Oxide Fused
Global Material Tech Inc .... C 773 247-6000
  Chicago *(G-4696)*
Weld Cote Metals .... G 888 258-0121
  Niles *(G-15186)*

ABRASIVES: Diamond Powder
Engis Corporation .... C 847 808-9400
  Wheeling *(G-20891)*

ABRASIVES: Polishing Rouge
Agsco Corporation .... E 847 520-4455
  Wheeling *(G-20842)*

ABRASIVES: Steel Shot
SBS Steel Belt Systems USA Inc .... F 847 841-3300
  Gilberts *(G-10369)*

ABRASIVES: Tungsten Carbide
Carbco Manufacturing Inc .... F 630 377-1410
  Saint Charles *(G-18164)*

ACCELERATION INDICATORS & SYSTEM COMPONENTS: Aerospace
Kaney Capital LLC .... G 815 986-4359
  Rockford *(G-17480)*
Kaney Group LLC .... F 815 986-4359
  Rockford *(G-17481)*
S Flying Inc .... F 618 586-9999
  Palestine *(G-16179)*
UTC Aerospace Systems .... G 877 808-7575
  Rockford *(G-17674)*
Waltz Brothers Inc .... E 847 520-1122
  Wheeling *(G-21011)*

ACCELERATORS: Electrostatic Particle
Starfire Industries LLC .... E 217 721-4165
  Champaign *(G-3356)*

ACCELERATORS: Linear
Rockford Linear Motion LLC .... G 815 961-7900
  Rockford *(G-17598)*

ACCIDENT INSURANCE CARRIERS
Caterpillar Inc .... B 309 675-6590
  Peoria *(G-16411)*
Caterpillar Inc .... G 309 578-2185
  Mossville *(G-14452)*
Caterpillar Inc .... A 224 551-4000
  Deerfield *(G-7600)*
Caterpillar Inc .... D 309 578-6118
  Mossville *(G-14453)*
Caterpillar Inc .... B 888 614-4328
  Peoria *(G-16407)*

ACCOUNTING SVCS, NEC
Paragon International Inc .... F 847 240-2981
  Schaumburg *(G-18664)*

ACIDS: Hydrochloric
Brainerd Chemical Midwest LLC .... G 918 622-1214
  Danville *(G-7325)*
Remuriate LLC .... G 815 220-5050
  La Salle *(G-12121)*
Xingfa USA Corporation .... F 630 305-9097
  Schaumburg *(G-18777)*

ACIDS: Inorganic
Solvay USA Inc .... E 708 371-2000
  Blue Island *(G-2141)*

ACIDS: Sulfuric, Oleum
Phosphate Resource Ptrs .... A 847 739-1200
  Lake Forest *(G-12290)*

ACRYLIC RESINS
Akrylix Inc .... F 773 869-9005
  Frankfort *(G-9764)*

De Enterprises Inc .... F 708 345-8088
  Broadview *(G-2429)*

ACTUATORS: Indl, NEC
Hamilton Sundstrand Corp .... F 815 226-6000
  Rockford *(G-17440)*

ADDITIVE BASED PLASTIC MATERIALS: Plasticizers
Raytech Machining Fabrication .... E 618 932-2511
  West Frankfort *(G-20680)*

ADDRESSING SVCS
Assemble and Mail Group Inc .... G 309 473-2006
  Heyworth *(G-11189)*
J K Printing & Mailing Inc .... G 847 432-7717
  Highland Park *(G-11276)*

ADHESIVES
A J Adhesives Inc .... G 708 210-1111
  South Holland *(G-19186)*
Aabbitt Adhesives Inc .... D 773 227-2700
  Chicago *(G-3499)*
Aabbitt Adhesives Inc .... E 773 723-6780
  Chicago *(G-3500)*
Adhesive Coating Tech Inc .... F 847 215-8355
  Wheeling *(G-20841)*
Alliance Industries Inc .... F 847 288-9090
  Broadview *(G-2416)*
Bradley Adhsive Applctions Inc .... C 630 443-8424
  Saint Charles *(G-18159)*
Campbell Camie Inc .... E 314 968-3222
  Downers Grove *(G-7963)*
Chicago Adhesive Products .... G 630 978-7766
  Aurora *(G-937)*
Emulsicoat Inc .... F 217 344-7775
  Urbana *(G-19981)*
HB Fuller Adhesives LLC .... E 815 357-6726
  Morris *(G-14307)*
HB Fuller Cnstr Pdts Inc .... C 630 978-7766
  Aurora *(G-978)*
Henkel US Operations Corp .... D 847 468-9200
  Elgin *(G-8613)*
ICP Industrial Inc .... E 630 227-1692
  Itasca *(G-11668)*
ITW Dynatec .... G 847 657-4830
  Glenview *(G-10573)*
Lintec of America Inc .... G 847 229-0547
  Schaumburg *(G-18608)*
Mafomsic Incorporated .... F 630 279-2005
  Elmhurst *(G-9397)*
Mapei Corporation .... D 630 293-5800
  West Chicago *(G-20613)*
Morton Intl Inc Adhsves Spclty .... G 815 653-2042
  Ringwood *(G-17045)*
National Casein New Jersey Inc .... E 773 846-7300
  Burr Ridge *(G-2709)*
North Shore Consultants Inc .... G 847 290-1599
  Elk Grove Village *(G-9153)*
Roman Holdings Corporation .... D 708 891-0770
  Calumet City *(G-2789)*
Roman Products LLC .... E 708 891-0770
  Calumet City *(G-2790)*
Rust-Oleum Corporation .... D 815 967-4258
  Rockford *(G-17617)*
Sandstrom Products Company .... E 309 523-2121
  Port Byron *(G-16787)*
Sanford Chemical Co Inc .... F 847 437-3530
  Elk Grove Village *(G-9229)*

Spartan Products Inc .... F 815 459-8500
Crystal Lake (G-7268)
Strytech Adhesives .... G 847 509-7566
Northbrook (G-15489)
Surebond Inc .... E 630 762-0606
Saint Charles (G-18282)
Surebonder Adhesives Inc .... G 847 487-4583
Wauconda (G-20393)
Surebonder Com Inc .... G 847 270-0254
Grayslake (G-10801)
Testor Corporation .... D 815 962-6654
Rockford (G-17656)
Tsv Adhesive Systems Inc .... E 815 464-5606
Frankfort (G-9847)
US Adhesives .... G 312 829-7438
Chicago (G-6497)
Wisdom Adhesives LLC .... E 847 841-7002
Elgin (G-8783)
WW Henry Company LP .... D 815 933-8059
Bourbonnais (G-2272)

ADHESIVES & SEALANTS

Adco Global Inc .... G 847 282-3485
Lincolnshire (G-12742)
All Weather Courts Inc .... G 217 364-4546
Dawson (G-7428)
Brown Packaging LLC .... F 224 415-3182
Elk Grove Village (G-8871)
Chase Corporation .... E 847 866-8500
Evanston (G-9503)
Chromium Industries Inc .... E 773 287-3716
Chicago (G-4145)
Cohera Medical Inc .... G 602 418-8788
Chicago (G-4196)
Daubert Industries Inc .... F 630 203-6800
Burr Ridge (G-2667)
Dip Seal Plastics Inc .... G 815 398-3533
Rockford (G-17379)
Eco-Pur Solutions LLC .... G 630 917-8789
Chicago (G-4446)
Eco-Pur Solutions LLC .... G 630 226-2300
Romeoville (G-17815)
Emecole Inc .... F 815 372-2493
Romeoville (G-17816)
Fitz Chem LLC .... E 630 467-8383
Itasca (G-11658)
Fontana Associates Inc .... G 888 707-8273
Wauconda (G-20352)
G J Nikolas & Co Inc .... E 708 544-0320
Bellwood (G-1625)
Gardner Asphalt Corporation .... E 800 237-1155
Chicago (G-4659)
Glue Inc .... G 312 451-4018
Chicago (G-4702)
Green Products LLC .... F 815 407-0900
Romeoville (G-17829)
Highland Supply Corporation .... B 618 654-2161
Highland (G-11224)
Illinois Tool Works Inc .... B 847 724-7500
Glenview (G-10560)
Illinois Tool Works Inc .... C 630 372-2150
Bartlett (G-1288)
Illinois Tool Works Inc .... C 847 783-5500
Elgin (G-8621)
J & J Industries Inc .... G 630 595-8878
Mount Prospect (G-14538)
Lectro Stik Corp .... E 630 894-1355
Glendale Heights (G-10466)
Liquitube Industries LLC .... F 618 985-4445
Herrin (G-11174)
Mapei Corporation .... G 630 293-5800
West Chicago (G-20612)
Miller Purcell Co Inc .... G 815 485-2142
New Lenox (G-15043)
Miracle Sealants Company LLC .... E 626 443-6433
Vernon Hills (G-20074)
Morton Salt Inc .... C 312 807-2000
Chicago (G-5501)
Nataz Specialty Coatings Inc .... F 773 247-7030
Chicago (G-5542)
ND Industries Inc .... E 847 498-3600
Northbrook (G-15440)
Nu-Puttie Corporation .... E 708 681-1040
Maywood (G-13676)
Opticote Inc .... E 847 678-8900
Franklin Park (G-10012)
Owens Corning Sales LLC .... E 708 594-6935
Argo (G-675)
Pierce & Stevens Chemical .... G 630 653-3800
Carol Stream (G-3047)
Porcelain Enamel Finishers .... G 312 808-1560
Chicago (G-5845)
PPG Architectural Finishes Inc .... B 217 584-1323
Meredosia (G-13956)
Prime Blend LLC .... F 866 217-3732
Elk Grove Village (G-9196)
Protective Products Intl .... G 847 526-1180
Wauconda (G-20386)
Rhopac Fabricated Products LLC .... E 847 362-3300
Libertyville (G-12702)
Right/Pointe LLC .... D 815 754-5700
Dekalb (G-7700)
RM Lucas Co .... E 773 523-4300
Chicago (G-6040)
RM Lucas Co .... E 773 523-4300
Alsip (G-504)
Royal Adhesives & Sealants LLC .... G 815 464-5606
Frankfort (G-9833)
Rust-Oleum Corporation .... C 847 367-7700
Vernon Hills (G-20089)
Saf-T-Lok International Corp .... E 630 495-2001
Lombard (G-13127)
Sandstrom Products Company .... F 309 523-2121
Port Byron (G-16788)
Sigma Coatings Inc .... G 630 628-5305
Addison (G-289)
Simpson Strong-Tie Company Inc .... E 630 613-5100
West Chicago (G-20643)
Ski Seal Coating Inc .... G 708 246-5656
Countryside (G-7070)
Specialty Cnstr Brands Inc .... F 630 851-0782
Aurora (G-1019)
Spl-Usa LLC .... G 312 807-2000
Chicago (G-6215)
Tape Case Ltd .... E 847 299-7880
Elk Grove Village (G-9265)
Therm-O-Web Inc .... E 847 520-5200
Wheeling (G-21000)
United Gilsonite Labs Inc .... E 217 243-7878
Jacksonville (G-11784)
Universal Chem & Coatings Inc .... E 847 931-1700
Elgin (G-8769)
Universal Chem & Coatings Inc .... E 847 297-2001
Elk Grove Village (G-9299)
Versatile Materials Inc .... G 773 924-3700
Chicago (G-6538)
Vibracoustic Usa Inc .... E 618 382-5891
Carmi (G-2916)
W R Grace & Co-Conn .... F 708 458-9700
Chicago (G-6577)
Wisdom Adhesives LLC .... G 847 841-7002
Elgin (G-8784)

ADHESIVES: Adhesives, plastic

A2 Creative Inc .... G 855 344-5667
Edwardsville (G-8344)

ADHESIVES: Epoxy

Poxypros Inc .... G 630 675-5924
Yorkville (G-21497)
Sika Corporation .... G 815 431-1080
Ottawa (G-16079)
United Adhesives Inc .... G 224 436-0077
Buffalo Grove (G-2614)

ADULT DAYCARE CENTERS

Macon Resources Inc .... C 217 875-1910
Decatur (G-7520)

ADVERTISING AGENCIES

3b Media Inc .... F 312 563-9363
Chicago (G-3467)
Ad Images .... G 847 956-1887
Hoffman Estates (G-11403)
American Tape Measures .... G 312 208-0282
Chicago (G-3670)
Athena Design Group Inc .... E 312 733-2828
Chicago (G-3758)
Baka Vitaliy .... G 773 370-5522
Chicago (G-3817)
Bezarr .... G 651 200-5641
Willowbrook (G-21031)
Blue Software LLC .... D 773 957-1600
Chicago (G-3914)
Catalog Designers Inc .... G 847 228-0025
Elk Grove Village (G-8881)
Communications Resource Inc .... G 630 860-1661
Schaumburg (G-18482)
Del Great Frame Up Systems Inc .... E 847 808-1955
Franklin Park (G-9929)
Early Bird Advertising Inc .... G 847 253-1423
Prospect Heights (G-16839)
Edge Communication .... G 708 749-7818
Berwyn (G-1951)
Edwards Creative Services LLC .... F 309 756-0199
Milan (G-14007)
Geomentum Inc .... B 630 729-7500
Downers Grove (G-8007)
Geomentum Inc .... G 630 729-7500
Downers Grove (G-8008)
Holsolutions Inc .... G 888 847-5467
Frankfort (G-9801)
Ideal Advertising & Printing .... F 815 965-1713
Rockford (G-17456)
Leo Burnett Company Inc .... C 312 220-5959
Chicago (G-5205)
McIntyre & Associates .... G 847 639-8050
Fox Lake (G-9748)
Popular Pays Inc .... G 435 767-7297
Chicago (G-5844)
Promark Advertising Specialtie .... G 618 483-6025
Altamont (G-536)
Self Pro Motions LLC .... G 847 749-6077
Chicago (G-6134)
Wright Quick Signs Inc .... G 708 652-6020
Cicero (G-6889)

ADVERTISING AGENCIES: Consultants

Bpn Chicago .... E 312 799-4100
Chicago (G-3940)
Corbett Accel Healthcare Grp C .... C 312 475-2505
Chicago (G-4234)
Dard Products Inc .... C 847 328-5000
Wauconda (G-20341)
Fanning Communications Inc .... G 708 293-1430
Crestwood (G-7118)
Integrated Media Inc .... F 217 854-6260
Carlinville (G-2877)
Legend Promotions .... G 847 438-3528
Lake Zurich (G-12428)
Mallof Abruzino Nash Mktg Inc .... E 630 929-5200
Carol Stream (G-3020)
Media Unlimited Inc .... G 630 527-0900
Naperville (G-14867)
Phoenix Graphics Inc .... G 847 699-9520
Des Plaines (G-7823)
Prime Market Targeting Inc .... E 815 469-4555
Frankfort (G-9826)
Wyckoff Advertising Inc .... G 630 260-2525
Wheaton (G-20832)

ADVERTISING COPY WRITING SVCS

Bezarr .... G 651 200-5641
Willowbrook (G-21031)

ADVERTISING CURTAINS

Erell Manufacturing Company .... F 847 427-3000
Elk Grove Village (G-8982)

ADVERTISING DISPLAY PRDTS

America Display Inc .... F 708 430-7000
Bridgeview (G-2322)
Assemblers Inc .... C 773 378-3000
Chicago (G-3749)
Bezarr .... G 651 200-5641
Willowbrook (G-21031)
Franklin Display Group Inc .... D 815 544-6676
Belvidere (G-1668)
James Coleman Company .... F 847 963-8100
Rolling Meadows (G-17742)
Orbus Holdings Inc .... D 630 226-1155
Woodridge (G-21329)
Roberts Colonial House Inc .... F 708 331-6233
South Holland (G-19241)

ADVERTISING REPRESENTATIVES: Electronic Media

Global Technologies I LLC .... D 312 255-8350
Chicago (G-4699)
Publishing Properties LLC .... G 312 321-2299
Chicago (G-5912)
Sun-Times Media LLC .... F 312 222-6920
Chicago (G-6270)

PRODUCT SECTION

ADVERTISING REPRESENTATIVES: Media

Movie Facts Inc .... E 847 299-9700
  Des Plaines *(G-7807)*
National School Services Inc .... E 847 438-3859
  Long Grove *(G-13167)*
Powerhouse Ent Inc .... G 312 877-4303
  Chicago *(G-5849)*
Schaumburg Review .... F 847 998-3400
  Chicago *(G-6110)*
Time Rec Pubg Bbby Mrtn Prdct .... G 618 996-3803
  Marion *(G-13540)*
Vondrak Publishing Co Inc .... E 773 476-4800
  Summit Argo *(G-19684)*

ADVERTISING REPRESENTATIVES: Newspaper

Independent Shoppers .... G 309 647-5200
  Lewistown *(G-12616)*
Lee Enterprises Incorporated .... C 618 529-5454
  Carbondale *(G-2849)*

ADVERTISING REPRESENTATIVES: Printed Media

Informa Media Inc .... F 212 204-4200
  Chicago *(G-4916)*

ADVERTISING SPECIALTIES, WHOLESALE

Anbek Inc .... F 815 434-7340
  Ottawa *(G-16039)*
ASap Specialties Inc Del .... G 847 223-7699
  Grayslake *(G-10759)*
Badge-A-Minit Ltd .... E 815 883-8822
  Oglesby *(G-15839)*
Bezarr .... G 651 200-5641
  Willowbrook *(G-21031)*
Brown Wood Products Company .... F 847 673-4780
  Lincolnwood *(G-12814)*
C & E Specialties Inc .... E 815 229-9230
  Rockford *(G-17332)*
Cacini Inc .... G 847 884-1162
  Schaumburg *(G-18466)*
Classique Signs & Engrv Inc .... G 217 228-7446
  Quincy *(G-16872)*
Cloz Companies Inc .... E 773 247-8879
  Skokie *(G-18944)*
Crown Publications Inc .... G 217 893-4856
  Rantoul *(G-16973)*
Edventure Promotions Inc .... G 312 440-1800
  Chicago *(G-4460)*
Flow-Eze Company .... F 815 965-1062
  Rockford *(G-17416)*
Great Ideas Inc .... F 800 611-5515
  Highland Park *(G-11267)*
Image Plus Inc .... G 630 852-4920
  Downers Grove *(G-8028)*
John Parker Advertising Co .... G 217 892-4118
  Rantoul *(G-16979)*
K & L Looseleaf Products Inc .... D 847 357-9733
  Elk Grove Village *(G-9072)*
Kingsbury Enterprises Inc .... G 708 535-7590
  Oak Forest *(G-15685)*
Lee-Wel Printing Corporation .... G 630 682-0935
  Wheaton *(G-20812)*
M C F Printing Company .... G 630 279-0301
  Elmhurst *(G-9396)*
Mbh Promotions Inc .... G 847 634-2411
  Buffalo Grove *(G-2570)*
Perkins Pencil Co .... G 708 363-9249
  Lansing *(G-12511)*
Printers Ink of Paris Inc .... G 217 463-2552
  Paris *(G-16240)*
Printing Plus of Roselle Inc .... G 630 893-0410
  Roselle *(G-17974)*
R & R Creative Graphics Inc .... G 630 208-4724
  Geneva *(G-10301)*
S & R Monogramming Inc .... G 630 369-5468
  Winfield *(G-21116)*
Sign-A-Rama of Buffalo Grove .... G 847 215-1535
  Buffalo Grove *(G-2604)*
Skyward Promotions Inc .... G 815 969-0909
  Rockford *(G-17633)*
Stans Sportsworld Inc .... G 217 359-8474
  Champaign *(G-3355)*
Tryad Specialties Inc .... F 630 549-0079
  Saint Charles *(G-18292)*
Unlimited Graphix Inc .... E 630 759-0007
  Lockport *(G-13026)*

Veltex Corporation .... E 312 235-4014
  Chicago *(G-6530)*
Viking Awards Inc .... G 630 833-1733
  Elmhurst *(G-9441)*

ADVERTISING SVCS, NEC

Embroid ME .... G 815 485-4155
  New Lenox *(G-15033)*
Modern Methods Creative Inc .... G 309 263-4100
  Morton *(G-14368)*

ADVERTISING SVCS: Billboards

Adams Outdoor Advg Ltd Partnr .... E 309 692-2482
  Peoria *(G-16375)*
Link Media Florida LLC .... G 815 224-4742
  La Salle *(G-12117)*
Roman Signs .... G 847 381-3425
  Barrington *(G-1241)*
Wright Quick Signs Inc .... G 708 652-6020
  Cicero *(G-6889)*

ADVERTISING SVCS: Direct Mail

American Litho Incorporated .... A 630 682-0600
  Carol Stream *(G-2934)*
Athena Design Group Inc .... E 312 733-2828
  Chicago *(G-3758)*
Card Prsnlzation Solutions LLC .... E 630 543-2630
  Glendale Heights *(G-10441)*
Communication Technologies Inc .... E 630 384-0900
  Glendale Heights *(G-10444)*
Fgs-IL LLC .... C 630 375-8500
  Aurora *(G-960)*
Flyerinc Corporation .... G 630 655-3400
  Oak Brook *(G-15622)*
Group O Inc .... E 309 736-8100
  Milan *(G-14015)*
Integrated Print Graphics Inc .... C 847 695-6777
  South Elgin *(G-19155)*
Lsc Communications Us LLC .... C 217 235-0561
  Mattoon *(G-13642)*
Mac Graphics Group Inc .... G 630 620-7200
  Oakbrook Terrace *(G-15806)*
National Data Svcs Chicago Inc .... C 630 597-9100
  Carol Stream *(G-3038)*
Psa Equity LLC .... C 847 478-6000
  Buffalo Grove *(G-2591)*
R R Donnelley & Sons Company .... C 312 326-8000
  Chicago *(G-5950)*
RR Donnelley & Sons Company .... C 312 236-8000
  Chicago *(G-6071)*
S R Bastien Co .... F 847 858-1175
  Evanston *(G-9573)*
V C P Inc .... E 847 658-5090
  Algonquin *(G-391)*
Vigil Printing Inc .... G 773 794-8808
  Chicago *(G-6550)*

ADVERTISING SVCS: Display

Animated Advg Techniques Inc .... G 312 372-4694
  Chicago *(G-3698)*
Design Phase Inc .... E 847 473-0077
  Waukegan *(G-20436)*
Duo North America .... G 312 421-7755
  Chicago *(G-4406)*
J Wallace & Associates Inc .... G 630 960-4221
  Downers Grove *(G-8033)*
Johnson Rolan Co Inc .... G 309 674-9671
  Peoria *(G-16464)*
M G M Displays Inc .... G 708 594-3699
  Chicago *(G-5300)*
Schellerer Corporation Inc .... D 630 980-4567
  Hanover Park *(G-11013)*

ADVERTISING SVCS: Outdoor

Communications Resource Inc .... G 630 860-1661
  Schaumburg *(G-18482)*
Edwards Creative Services LLC .... F 309 756-0199
  Milan *(G-14007)*
Turnroth Sign Company Inc .... F 815 625-1155
  Rock Falls *(G-17198)*

ADVERTISING SVCS: Poster, Exc Outdoor

Communications Resource Inc .... G 630 860-1661
  Schaumburg *(G-18482)*

ADVERTISING SVCS: Poster, Outdoor

Nite Lite Signs & Balloons Inc .... G 630 953-2866
  Addison *(G-229)*

ADVERTISING SVCS: Transit

Edwards Creative Services LLC .... F 309 756-0199
  Milan *(G-14007)*

AERIAL WORK PLATFORMS

Skyjack Equipment Inc .... E 630 797-3299
  Saint Charles *(G-18270)*
Skyjack Inc .... G 630 262-0005
  Saint Charles *(G-18271)*
USA Hoist Company Inc .... E 815 740-1890
  Crest Hill *(G-7100)*

AEROSOLS

Chase Products Co .... D 708 865-1000
  Broadview *(G-2425)*
Claire-Sprayway Inc .... D 630 628-3000
  Downers Grove *(G-7973)*
Custom Blending & Pckaging of .... F 618 286-1140
  Dupo *(G-8135)*
K-G Spray-Pak Inc .... G 630 543-7600
  Downers Grove *(G-8036)*
Plz Aeroscience Corporation .... E 630 628-3000
  Downers Grove *(G-8078)*
Slide Products Inc .... F 847 541-7220
  Wheeling *(G-20987)*

AGENTS & MANAGERS: Entertainers

Csiteq Studio LLC .... F 312 265-1509
  Rosemont *(G-18012)*

AGENTS, BROKERS & BUREAUS: Personal Service

Clifford W Estes Co Inc .... F 815 433-0944
  Ottawa *(G-16047)*
County Tool & Die .... G 217 324-6527
  Litchfield *(G-12962)*
M L Rongo Inc .... E 630 540-1120
  Bartlett *(G-1294)*

AGRICULTURAL CHEMICALS: Trace Elements

Sem Minerals LP .... D 217 224-8766
  Quincy *(G-16944)*

AGRICULTURAL CREDIT INSTITUTIONS

Deere & Company .... A 309 765-8000
  Moline *(G-14138)*
John Deere AG Holdings Inc .... G 309 765-8000
  Moline *(G-14152)*

AGRICULTURAL EQPT: BARN, SILO, POULTRY, DAIRY/LIVESTOCK MACH

King Systems Inc .... G 309 879-2668
  Dahinda *(G-7305)*

AGRICULTURAL EQPT: Barn Cleaners

Davis Welding & Manfctg Inc .... F 217 784-5480
  Gibson City *(G-10336)*

AGRICULTURAL EQPT: Cutters & Blowers, Ensilage

Yetter Manufacturing Company .... D 309 776-3222
  Colchester *(G-6948)*

AGRICULTURAL EQPT: Elevators, Farm

Davidson Grain Incorporated .... E 815 384-3208
  Creston *(G-7101)*
Union Iron Inc .... E 217 429-5148
  Decatur *(G-7564)*

AGRICULTURAL EQPT: Fertilizing Machinery

Yargus Manufacturing Inc .... E 217 826-6352
  Marshall *(G-13579)*

Employee Codes: A=Over 500 employees, B=251-500
C=101-250, D=51-100, E=20-50, F=10-19, G=3-9

AGRICULTURAL EQPT: Fertilizng, Sprayng, Dustng/Irrigatn Mach

360 Yield Center LLC ....E....... 309 263-4360
  Morton (G-14352)

AGRICULTURAL EQPT: Fillers & Unloaders, Silo

Dspc Company ....E....... 815 997-1116
  Rockford (G-17387)

AGRICULTURAL EQPT: Grade, Clean & Sort Machines, Fruit/Veg

Prater Industries Inc ....D....... 630 679-3200
  Bolingbrook (G-2228)

AGRICULTURAL EQPT: Greens Mowing Eqpt

Midwest Sport Turf Systems LLC ....F....... 630 923-8342
  Plainfield (G-16690)

AGRICULTURAL EQPT: Haying Mach, Mowers, Rakes, Stackers, Etc

Hoyer Outdoor Equipment Inc ....F....... 618 564-2080
  Brookport (G-2498)
Mathews Company ....D....... 815 459-2210
  Crystal Lake (G-7223)

AGRICULTURAL EQPT: Loaders, Manure & General Utility

Avant Tecno USA Inc ....F....... 847 380-1308
  Arlington Heights (G-700)

AGRICULTURAL EQPT: Planting Machines

Brian Burcar ....G....... 815 856-2271
  Leonore (G-12611)
Dutch Prairie Conveyors ....G....... 618 349-6177
  Shobonier (G-18892)
Innovative Growers Eqp Inc ....E....... 815 991-5010
  Sycamore (G-19717)

AGRICULTURAL EQPT: Spreaders, Fertilizer

Spreader Inc ....G....... 217 568-7219
  Gifford (G-10348)

AGRICULTURAL EQPT: Storage Bins, Crop

Arrows Up Inc ....G....... 847 305-2550
  Arlington Heights (G-696)
Grain Systems Inc ....G....... 888 474-2467
  Assumption (G-890)
Gsi Group LLC ....G....... 217 226-4421
  Assumption (G-891)
Gsi Group LLC ....C....... 217 287-6244
  Taylorville (G-19757)
Gsi Holdings Corp ....G....... 217 226-4421
  Assumption (G-892)

AGRICULTURAL EQPT: Tractors, Farm

Deere & Company ....A....... 309 765-8000
  Moline (G-14138)
John Deere AG Holdings Inc ....G....... 309 765-8000
  Moline (G-14152)

AGRICULTURAL EQPT: Trailers & Wagons, Farm

E Z Trail Inc ....E....... 217 543-3471
  Arthur (G-856)

AGRICULTURAL EQPT: Turf & Grounds Eqpt

Ecoturf Midwest Inc ....G....... 630 350-9500
  Bensenville (G-1793)
Outdoor Space LLC ....E....... 773 857-5296
  Chicago (G-5715)
Woods Equipment Company ....D....... 815 732-2141
  Rockford (G-17690)

AGRICULTURAL EQPT: Turf Eqpt, Commercial

Ideal Turf Inc ....G....... 309 691-3362
  Peoria (G-16455)

Mega Equipment Inc ....G....... 309 764-5310
  Moline (G-14160)

AGRICULTURAL EQPT: Weeding Machines

Quality Metal Works Inc ....G....... 309 379-5311
  Stanford (G-19473)

AGRICULTURAL LIMESTONE: Ground

Central Stone Company ....F....... 309 776-3900
  Colchester (G-6946)
Meyer Material Co Merger Corp ....D....... 815 943-2605
  Harvard (G-11060)
Mining International LLC ....E....... 815 722-0900
  Joliet (G-11906)
Tuscola Stone Company ....F....... 217 253-4705
  Tuscola (G-19933)

AGRICULTURAL MACHINERY & EQPT REPAIR

Birkeys Farm Store Inc ....E....... 217 337-1772
  Urbana (G-19975)
Grower Equipment & Supply Co ....F....... 847 223-3100
  Hainesville (G-10947)

AGRICULTURAL MACHINERY & EQPT: Wholesalers

Bill Chandler Farms ....G....... 618 752-7551
  Noble (G-15188)
Walterscheid Inc Woodridge ....C....... 630 972-9300
  Woodridge (G-21345)
Wpg US Holdco LLC ....B....... 312 517-3750
  Chicago (G-6681)

AIR CLEANING SYSTEMS

Bact Process Systems Inc ....G....... 847 577-0950
  Arlington Heights (G-701)
Heidolph NA LLC ....F....... 224 265-9600
  Wood Dale (G-21197)
Midwest Air Pro Inc ....G....... 773 622-4566
  Chicago (G-5439)
Schubert Environmental Eqp Inc ....F....... 630 307-9400
  Glendale Heights (G-10492)

AIR CONDITIONERS: Motor Vehicle

Bergstrom Inc ....D....... 815 874-7821
  Rockford (G-17322)

AIR CONDITIONING & VENTILATION EQPT & SPLYS: Wholesales

Aen Industries Inc ....F....... 708 758-3000
  Chicago Heights (G-6728)
Anytime Heating & AC ....F....... 630 851-6696
  Naperville (G-14959)
Maxi-Vac Inc ....G....... 630 620-6669
  Elgin (G-8653)
Ruyle Incorporated ....E....... 309 674-6644
  Springfield (G-19437)

AIR CONDITIONING EQPT

Sendra Service Corp ....G....... 815 462-0061
  New Lenox (G-15058)
Voges Inc ....D....... 618 233-2760
  Belleville (G-1608)

AIR CONDITIONING REPAIR SVCS

Evans Heating and Air Inc ....G....... 217 483-8440
  Chatham (G-3420)
White Sheet Metal ....G....... 217 465-3195
  Paris (G-16246)

AIR CONDITIONING UNITS: Complete, Domestic Or Indl

Bergstrom Climate Systems LLC ....B....... 815 874-7821
  Rockford (G-17319)
Goodman Manufacturing Co LP ....G....... 618 234-2781
  Swansea (G-19692)
Honeywell International Inc ....D....... 847 797-4000
  Des Plaines (G-7778)
Lennox Industries Inc ....D....... 630 378-7054
  Romeoville (G-17842)
Ventfabrics Inc ....F....... 773 775-4477
  Chicago (G-6534)

AIR COOLERS: Metal Plate

Diesel Radiator Co ....D....... 708 865-7299
  Melrose Park (G-13852)
Elkay Manufacturing Company ....B....... 815 273-7001
  Savanna (G-18404)

AIR CURTAINS

H D A Fans Inc ....G....... 630 627-2087
  Elk Grove Village (G-9025)

AIR MATTRESSES: Plastic

B & M Plastic Inc ....F....... 847 258-4437
  Franklin Park (G-9880)
Clover Plastics LLC ....G....... 630 473-6488
  West Chicago (G-20564)
Pliant LLC ....A....... 812 424-2904
  Rolling Meadows (G-17761)
Tekni-Plex Inc ....E....... 217 935-8311
  Clinton (G-6929)

AIR POLLUTION CONTROL EQPT & SPLYS WHOLESALERS

Bee Clean Specialties LLC ....F....... 847 451-0844
  Schaumburg (G-18457)

AIR PURIFICATION EQPT

Aen Industries Inc ....F....... 708 758-3000
  Chicago Heights (G-6728)
Altair Corporation ....E....... 847 634-9540
  Lincolnshire (G-12744)
Architectural Fan Coil Inc ....G....... 312 399-1203
  Chicago (G-3729)
Bee Clean Specialties LLC ....F....... 847 451-0844
  Schaumburg (G-18457)
Bofa Americas Inc ....G....... 618 205-5007
  Staunton (G-19474)
Calutech Inc ....G....... 708 614-0228
  Orland Park (G-15944)
Chatham Corporation ....F....... 847 634-5506
  Lincolnshire (G-12749)
Chicago Plastic Systems Inc ....E....... 815 455-4599
  Crystal Lake (G-7181)
Flsmidth Inc ....G....... 309 347-3031
  Pekin (G-16334)
Fuel Tech Inc ....G....... 630 845-4500
  Warrenville (G-20237)
Hydrosil International Ltd ....G....... 847 741-1600
  East Dundee (G-8201)
Mason Engineering & Designing ....E....... 630 595-5000
  Inverness (G-11602)
Met-Pro Technologies LLC ....E....... 630 775-0707
  Wood Dale (G-21215)
Paul D Stark & Associates ....F....... 630 964-7111
  Downers Grove (G-8070)
Petairapy LLC ....G....... 630 377-0348
  Saint Charles (G-18244)
Promark Associates Inc ....G....... 847 676-1894
  Skokie (G-19015)
Revcor Inc ....B....... 847 428-4411
  Carpentersville (G-3119)
Sanders Inc ....E....... 815 634-4611
  Morris (G-14326)
Tdc Filter ....F....... 503 521-9988
  Bolingbrook (G-2247)

AIR-CONDITIONING SPLY SVCS

Caldwell Plumbing Co ....F....... 630 588-8900
  Wheaton (G-20792)

AIRCRAFT & AEROSPACE FLIGHT INSTRUMENTS & GUIDANCE SYSTEMS

Csiteq LLC ....F....... 312 265-1509
  Rosemont (G-18011)
Mpc Products Corporation ....A....... 847 673-8300
  Niles (G-15149)

AIRCRAFT & HEAVY EQPT REPAIR SVCS

Midwest Aero Support Inc ....E....... 815 398-9202
  Machesney Park (G-13360)
P J Repair Service Inc ....F....... 618 548-5690
  Salem (G-18349)
Phoenix Welding Co Inc ....F....... 630 616-1700
  Franklin Park (G-10016)

PRODUCT SECTION

AIRCRAFT PARTS & AUXILIARY EQPT: Gears, Power Transmission

AIRCRAFT ASSEMBLY PLANTS

Aerostars Inc .... G 847 736-8171
  Cary *(G-3145)*
Aerovision Engine Services LLC ...... E 231 799-9000
  Chicago *(G-3576)*
Aviation Services Group Inc .... G 708 425-4700
  Chicago Ridge *(G-6788)*
Boeing International Corp .... E 312 544-2000
  Chicago *(G-3927)*
Calumet Motorsports Inc .... G 708 895-0398
  Lansing *(G-12487)*
Elan Express Inc .... E 815 713-1190
  Rockford *(G-17393)*
Gulfstream Aerospace Corp .... A 630 470-9146
  Naperville *(G-14839)*
Gulfstream Aerospace Corp .... G 815 469-1509
  Frankfort *(G-9798)*
Ibanum Manufacturing LLC .... G 815 262-5373
  Rockford *(G-17455)*
Inav LLC .... F 847 847-3600
  Crystal Lake *(G-7209)*
Jet Aviation St Louis Inc .... D 618 646-8000
  Cahokia *(G-2761)*
Learjet Inc .... B 847 553-0172
  Des Plaines *(G-7797)*
Mitchell Arcft Expendables LLC ...... E 847 516-3773
  Cary *(G-3180)*
Quad City Ultralight Aircraft .... F 309 764-3515
  Moline *(G-14171)*
SC Aviation Inc .... G 800 416-4176
  Saint Charles *(G-18264)*
Tribus Aerospace Corp .... G 312 876-2683
  Chicago *(G-6426)*

AIRCRAFT CONTROL SYSTEMS: Electronic Totalizing Counters

Honeywell International Inc .... A 401 573-6821
  Moline *(G-14149)*
Midwest Aero Support Inc .... E 815 398-9202
  Machesney Park *(G-13360)*

AIRCRAFT DEALERS

Textron Aviation Inc .... G 630 443-5080
  West Chicago *(G-20650)*

AIRCRAFT ENG/ENG PART: Extrnl Pwr Unt, Hand Inertia Starter

Green Apu LLC .... G 310 736-2211
  Lemont *(G-12565)*

AIRCRAFT ENGINES & ENGINE PARTS: Airfoils

Jetpower LLC .... F 847 856-8359
  Gurnee *(G-10889)*

AIRCRAFT ENGINES & ENGINE PARTS: Mount Parts

Danville Metal Stamping Co Inc ...... F 217 446-0647
  Danville *(G-7328)*
Danville Metal Stamping Co Inc ...... F 217 446-0647
  Danville *(G-7329)*

AIRCRAFT ENGINES & ENGINE PARTS: Nonelectric Starters

Essex Electro Engineers Inc .... E 847 891-4444
  Schaumburg *(G-18522)*

AIRCRAFT ENGINES & ENGINE PARTS: Research & Development, Mfr

CTS Electronic Components Inc ...... D 630 577-8800
  Lisle *(G-12882)*
Honeywell International Inc .... A 480 353-3020
  Chicago *(G-4837)*
Innovative Design and RES Inc ...... G 217 322-3907
  Rushville *(G-18111)*

AIRCRAFT ENGINES & PARTS

AAR Corp .... D 630 227-2000
  Wood Dale *(G-21149)*
Acra Products .... G 847 346-9889
  Addison *(G-17)*
Aero-Cables Corp .... G 815 609-6600
  Oswego *(G-15990)*
Aerovision Engine Services LLC ..... E 231 799-9000
  Chicago *(G-3576)*
Aertrade LLC .... G 630 428-4440
  Aurora *(G-910)*
Area Diesel Service Inc .... E 217 854-2641
  Carlinville *(G-2867)*
Arrow Gear Company .... B 630 969-7640
  Downers Grove *(G-7955)*
Chemring Energetic Devices Inc .... C 630 969-0620
  Downers Grove *(G-7968)*
Dynomax Inc .... E 847 680-8833
  Wheeling *(G-20882)*
Dynomax Inc .... B 847 680-8833
  Wheeling *(G-20883)*
GE Ges Inc .... G 815 307-0595
  Ingleside *(G-11583)*
General Machinery & Mfg Co .... F 773 235-3700
  Chicago *(G-4674)*
Heligear Acquisition Co .... C 708 728-2000
  Bedford Park *(G-1471)*
Honeywell .... E 815 235-5500
  Freeport *(G-10115)*
Honeywell .... F 618 546-1671
  Robinson *(G-17117)*
Honeywell International Inc .... F 847 251-3510
  Freeport *(G-10116)*
Honeywell International Inc .... A 630 960-5282
  Darien *(G-7407)*
Honeywell International Inc .... A 630 922-0138
  Naperville *(G-14973)*
Honeywell International Inc .... G 630 554-5342
  Oswego *(G-16007)*
Honeywell International Inc .... D 815 266-3209
  Freeport *(G-10117)*
Honeywell International Inc .... E 847 797-4612
  Des Plaines *(G-7779)*
Honeywell International Inc .... A 401 573-6821
  Moline *(G-14149)*
Honeywell International Inc .... A 847 701-3038
  Palatine *(G-16125)*
Honeywell International Inc .... C 815 663-2011
  Spring Valley *(G-19308)*
Honeywell International Inc .... C 815 777-2780
  Galena *(G-10174)*
Honeywell International Inc .... B 630 377-6580
  Saint Charles *(G-18207)*
Honeywell International Inc .... G 847 634-2802
  Lincolnshire *(G-12771)*
Honeywell International Inc .... A 973 455-2000
  Chicago *(G-4838)*
Honeywell International Inc .... A 309 383-4045
  Metamora *(G-13961)*
Honeywell International Inc .... G 217 431-3710
  Danville *(G-7346)*
I D Rockford Shop Inc .... G 815 335-1150
  Winnebago *(G-21120)*
Midwest Fuel Injction Svc Corp ...... F 847 991-7867
  Palatine *(G-16140)*
Pietro Carnaghi USA Inc .... G 779 368-0564
  Rockford *(G-17554)*
Precoat Metals Corp .... D 618 451-0909
  Granite City *(G-10731)*
Raytheon Technologies Corp .... B 630 516-3460
  Elmhurst *(G-9415)*
Raytheon Technologies Corp .... B 815 226-6000
  Rockford *(G-17567)*
Superior Joining Tech Inc .... E 815 282-7581
  Machesney Park *(G-13376)*
Universal Trnspt Systems LLC .... F 312 994-2349
  Chicago *(G-6484)*
Woodward Inc .... A 815 877-7441
  Loves Park *(G-13282)*

AIRCRAFT EQPT & SPLYS WHOLESALERS

Koerner Aviation Inc .... G 815 932-4222
  Kankakee *(G-11988)*

AIRCRAFT FLIGHT INSTRUMENT REPAIR SVCS

Heligear Acquisition Co .... C 708 728-2000
  Bedford Park *(G-1471)*

AIRCRAFT FUELING SVCS

Jet Aviation St Louis Inc .... D 618 646-8000
  Cahokia *(G-2761)*

AIRCRAFT HANGAR OPERATION SVCS

Thelen Sand & Gravel Inc .... D 847 838-8800
  Antioch *(G-636)*

AIRCRAFT LIGHTING

Astronics Cnnctvity Systems Cr ...... F 847 821-3059
  Waukegan *(G-20419)*

AIRCRAFT MAINTENANCE & REPAIR SVCS

AAR Corp .... D 630 227-2000
  Wood Dale *(G-21149)*
Jme Technologies Inc .... E 815 477-8800
  Crystal Lake *(G-7213)*
Skandia Inc .... D 800 945-7135
  Davis Junction *(G-7427)*

AIRCRAFT PARTS & AUX EQPT: Governors, Propeller Feathering

CEF Industries LLC .... C 630 628-2299
  Addison *(G-65)*

AIRCRAFT PARTS & AUXILIARY EQPT: Aircraft Training Eqpt

Boaleeco Inc .... G 847 428-3085
  Gilberts *(G-10351)*
Frasca International Inc .... C 217 344-9200
  Urbana *(G-19986)*

AIRCRAFT PARTS & AUXILIARY EQPT: Assys, Subassemblies/Parts

CMC Electronics Aurora LLC .... D 630 556-9619
  Sugar Grove *(G-19640)*
Cyn Industries Inc .... F 773 895-4324
  Chicago *(G-4295)*
Hamilton Sundstrand Corp .... A 815 226-6000
  Rockford *(G-17441)*
S I A Inc .... G 708 361-3100
  Palos Heights *(G-16191)*
TI International Ltd .... G 847 689-0233
  North Chicago *(G-15322)*
Woodward Inc .... B 815 877-7441
  Loves Park *(G-13281)*

AIRCRAFT PARTS & AUXILIARY EQPT: Blades, Prop, Metal Or Wood

Prograf LLC .... G 815 234-4848
  Villa Park *(G-20166)*

AIRCRAFT PARTS & AUXILIARY EQPT: Bodies

Jetpower LLC .... F 847 856-8359
  Gurnee *(G-10889)*

AIRCRAFT PARTS & AUXILIARY EQPT: Body & Wing Assys & Parts

Boeing Company .... C 312 544-2000
  Chicago *(G-3925)*
Jsn Inc .... E 708 410-1800
  Maywood *(G-13670)*
Mpc Products Corporation .... A 847 673-8300
  Niles *(G-15149)*
Triumph Group Inc .... C 312 498-2516
  Willowbrook *(G-21064)*

AIRCRAFT PARTS & AUXILIARY EQPT: Body Assemblies & Parts

Brunswick International Ltd .... E 847 735-4700
  Mettawa *(G-13980)*

AIRCRAFT PARTS & AUXILIARY EQPT: Gears, Power Transmission

A J R Industries Inc .... E 847 439-0380
  Elk Grove Village *(G-8791)*
Aircraft Gear Corporation .... D 815 877-7473
  Loves Park *(G-13185)*
Auxitrol SA .... G 815 874-2471
  Rockford *(G-17309)*
Nsa (chi) Liquidating Corp .... F 708 728-2000
  Elmhurst *(G-9406)*

Employee Codes: A=Over 500 employees, B=251-500
C=101-250, D=51-100, E=20-50, F=10-19, G=3-9

AIRCRAFT PARTS & AUXILIARY EQPT: Landing Assemblies & Brakes

Chicago Midway Airport ....G....... 773 838-0600
Chicago (G-4117)

AIRCRAFT PARTS & AUXILIARY EQPT: Link Trainers/Trng Mech

Wittenstein Arspc Smlation Inc ....G....... 630 540-5300
Bartlett (G-1326)

AIRCRAFT PARTS & AUXILIARY EQPT: Military Eqpt & Armament

Bison Aerospace and Def LLC ....G....... 618 795-2678
Savanna (G-18403)
Shadowtech Labs Inc ....G....... 630 413-4478
Willowbrook (G-21060)

AIRCRAFT PARTS & AUXILIARY EQPT: Refueling Eqpt, In Flight

Airport Aviation Professionals ....G....... 773 948-6631
Chicago (G-3589)
Kemell Enterprises LLC ....G....... 618 671-1513
Belleville (G-1561)

AIRCRAFT PARTS & AUXILIARY EQPT: Research & Development, Mfr

Azimuth Cnc Inc ....F....... 815 399-4433
Rockford (G-17310)
Electronica Aviation LLC ....G....... 407 498-1092
Chicago (G-4479)
Thales Visionix Inc ....D....... 630 375-2008
Aurora (G-1161)

AIRCRAFT PARTS & EQPT, NEC

AAR Aircraft & Eng Sls & Lsg ....G....... 630 227-2000
Wood Dale (G-21147)
AAR Allen Services Inc ....D....... 630 227-2410
Wood Dale (G-21148)
AAR Government Services Inc ....E....... 630 227-2000
Wood Dale (G-21150)
AAR Supply Chain Inc ....D....... 630 227-2000
Wood Dale (G-21151)
ACS Parts Group LLC ....G....... 815 211-4707
Park Forest (G-16249)
Aero Aviation Company Inc ....F....... 618 797-6630
Granite City (G-10690)
Air Land and Sea Interiors ....G....... 630 834-1717
Villa Park (G-20129)
American Concorde Systems ....F....... 773 342-9951
Streamwood (G-19561)
American Science and Tech Corp ....G....... 312 433-3800
Chicago (G-3666)
Armstrong Aerospace Inc ....D....... 847 244-4500
Waukegan (G-20418)
Art Technologies Inc ....G....... 773 557-3896
Bensenville (G-1747)
Astronics Cnnctvity Systems Cr ....F....... 847 821-3059
Waukegan (G-20419)
Calport Aviation Company ....G....... 630 588-8091
Bartlett (G-1254)
Certifynation Inc ....G....... 775 237-8439
Elmhurst (G-9342)
Chucking Machine Products Inc ....D....... 847 678-1192
Franklin Park (G-9907)
Direct Aerosystems Inc ....F....... 630 509-2141
Aurora (G-952)
GE Aviation Systems LLC ....C....... 779 203-8100
Loves Park (G-13214)
Goodrich Corporation ....F....... 815 226-5915
Rockford (G-17433)
Gpe Controls Inc ....F....... 708 236-6000
Hillside (G-11340)
Hamilton Sndstrand Space Syste ......G....... 815 226-6000
Rockford (G-17439)
Helitune Inc ....G....... 847 228-0985
Elk Grove Village (G-9032)
Ibanum Manufacturing LLC ....G....... 815 262-5373
Rockford (G-17455)
Ingenium Aerospace LLC ....E....... 815 525-2000
Rockford (G-17460)
Jet X Aerospace LLC ....E....... 630 238-1920
Bensenville (G-1830)
Kellstrom Coml Arospc Inc ....E....... 847 233-5800
Roselle (G-17961)

Logan Actuator Co ....G....... 815 943-9500
Harvard (G-11059)
Makerite Mfg Co Inc ....E....... 815 389-3902
Roscoe (G-17916)
Mitchell Aircraft Products ....G....... 815 331-8609
McHenry (G-13771)
Mitchell Aircraft Spares Inc ....E....... 847 516-3773
Cary (G-3179)
Multax Corporation ....D....... 309 266-9765
Morton (G-14372)
New Gen Aerospace Corp ....G....... 847 740-2216
Lake Villa (G-12361)
Northstar Aerospace (usa) Inc ....F....... 708 728-2000
Bedford Park (G-1486)
Quad City Ultralight Aircraft ....F....... 309 764-3515
Moline (G-14171)
Qualiseal Technology LLC ....E....... 708 887-6080
Harwood Heights (G-11108)
Seginus Inc ....G....... 630 800-2795
Oswego (G-16025)
Skandia Inc ....G....... 800 945-7135
Davis Junction (G-7427)
South Subn Logistics Sups Corp ....G....... 312 804-3401
Harvey (G-11096)
Systems & Electronics Inc ....E....... 847 228-0985
Elk Grove Village (G-9263)
Textron Aviation Inc ....G....... 630 443-5080
West Chicago (G-20650)
Trident Machine Co ....G....... 815 968-1585
Rockford (G-17668)
Vestergaard Company Inc ....G....... 815 759-9102
McHenry (G-13807)
Video Refurbishing Svcs Inc ....E....... 847 844-7366
Carpentersville (G-3122)
Vonberg Valve Inc ....E....... 847 259-3800
Rolling Meadows (G-17785)
Woodward Governor Hlth Svcs Tr .....G....... 815 877-7441
Loves Park (G-13283)

AIRCRAFT PARTS WHOLESALERS

AAR Supply Chain Inc ....D....... 630 227-2000
Wood Dale (G-21151)
Jet Aviation St Louis Inc ....D....... 618 646-8000
Cahokia (G-2761)

AIRCRAFT SEATS

B/E Aerospace Inc ....C....... 561 791-5000
Hanover Park (G-11000)

AIRCRAFT SERVICING & REPAIRING

Jet Aviation St Louis Inc ....D....... 618 646-8000
Cahokia (G-2761)

AIRCRAFT: Airplanes, Fixed Or Rotary Wing

Boeing Company ....C....... 312 544-2000
Chicago (G-3925)
Boeing Company ....G....... 618 746-4062
Scott Afb (G-18856)
Boeing Global Holdings Corp ....C....... 312 544-2000
Chicago (G-3926)
Boeing LTS Inc ....B....... 312 544-2000
Chicago (G-3929)
Southern Ill Helicopters LLC ....G....... 618 997-0101
Marion (G-13537)
Textron Aviation Inc ....G....... 630 443-5080
West Chicago (G-20650)

AIRLOCKS

Rotary Airlock LLC ....E....... 800 883-8955
Sterling (G-19530)

ALARMS: Burglar

All Tech Systems & Install ....G....... 815 609-0685
Plainfield (G-16641)
RF Technologies Inc ....E....... 618 377-2654
Buffalo Grove (G-2592)
Telular Corporation ....D....... 800 835-8527
Chicago (G-6341)

ALARMS: Fire

Global Fire Control Inc ....G....... 309 755-6352
East Moline (G-8227)
Harrington Signal Inc ....E....... 309 762-0731
Moline (G-14148)
Siemens Industry Inc ....D....... 630 444-4316
Saint Charles (G-18269)

ALCOHOL, ETHYL: For Beverage Purposes

Mgpi Processing Inc ....C....... 309 353-3990
Pekin (G-16346)

ALCOHOL, GRAIN: For Beverage Purposes

Tiller Farms Holdings LLC ....G....... 224 572-7814
Beach Park (G-1444)

ALCOHOL: Ethyl & Ethanol

Adkins Energy LLC ....E....... 815 369-9173
Lena (G-12597)
Aventine Rnwble Enrgy Hldngs L .....E....... 309 347-9200
Pekin (G-16324)
Big River Resources Galva LLC ....C....... 309 932-2033
Galva (G-10228)
Center Ethanol Company LLC ....E....... 618 875-3008
Sauget (G-18391)
Illinois River Energy LLC ....D....... 815 561-0650
Rochelle (G-17146)
Mgpi Processing Inc ....C....... 309 353-3990
Pekin (G-16346)
One Earth Energy LLC ....E....... 217 784-5321
Gibson City (G-10341)
Pacific Ethanol Canton LLC ....G....... 309 347-9200
Pekin (G-16349)
Patriot Renewable Fuels LLC ....D....... 309 935-5700
Annawan (G-592)

ALCOHOL: Methyl & Methanol, Synthetic

Marquis Marine Inc ....G....... 815 925-9125
Hennepin (G-11159)

ALKALIES & CHLORINE

Arkema Inc ....C....... 708 385-2188
Alsip (G-418)
Aspen API Inc ....F....... 847 635-0985
Des Plaines (G-7734)
Clorox Manufacturing Company ......C....... 847 229-5500
Wheeling (G-20872)
Coral Chemical Company ....E....... 847 246-6666
Zion (G-21510)
FMC Corporation ....E....... 309 695-2571
Wyoming (G-21459)
KA Steel Chemicals Inc ....E....... 630 257-3900
Downers Grove (G-8037)
Occidental Chemical Corp ....F....... 618 482-6346
Sauget (G-18397)
Olin Chlor Alkali Pdts Vinyls ....G....... 844 238-3445
Downers Grove (G-8068)

ALL-TERRAIN VEHICLE DEALERS

Outdoor Power Inc ....F....... 217 228-9890
Quincy (G-16921)

ALLOYS: Additive, Exc Copper Or Made In Blast Furnaces

Hickman Williams & Company ....F....... 630 574-2150
Palos Heights (G-16188)
Masters & Alloy LLC ....G....... 312 582-1880
Alsip (G-473)
Miller and Company LLC ....E....... 847 696-2400
Rosemont (G-18037)

ALTERNATORS: Automotive

A E Iskra Inc ....G....... 815 874-4022
Rockford (G-17280)
Powermaster ....G....... 630 957-4019
West Chicago (G-20631)

ALUMINUM

Huml Industries Inc ....G....... 847 426-8061
Gilberts (G-10358)
New Century Performance Inc ....G....... 618 466-6383
Godfrey (G-10658)
Penn Aluminum Intl LLC ....C....... 618 684-2146
Murphysboro (G-14756)

ALUMINUM PRDTS

Afco Industries Inc ....C....... 618 742-6469
Olmsted (G-15850)
Al3 Inc ....G....... 847 441-7888
Winnetka (G-21123)
American Alum Extrusion Co LLC ....C....... 815 525-3100
Roscoe (G-17898)

PRODUCT SECTION

ANIMAL FEED & SUPPLEMENTS: Livestock & Poultry

Central Tool Specialities Co...................G..... 630 543-6351
  Addison *(G-66)*
Century Aluminum Company ....C..... 312 696-3101
  Chicago *(G-4059)*
Crown Cork & Seal Usa Inc ....C..... 815 933-9351
  Bradley *(G-2278)*
Custom Aluminum Products Inc ....D..... 847 717-5000
  Genoa *(G-10316)*
Custom Aluminum Products Inc ....B..... 847 717-5000
  South Elgin *(G-19141)*
Durable Inc ....A..... 847 541-4400
  Wheeling *(G-20881)*
Efco Corporation ....E..... 630 378-4720
  Bolingbrook *(G-2171)*
F K Pattern & Foundry Company ....G..... 847 578-5260
  North Chicago *(G-15311)*
Hydro Extrusion Usa LLC ....C..... 877 710-7272
  Rosemont *(G-18027)*
Imageworks Manufacturing Inc ....E..... 708 503-1122
  Park Forest *(G-16255)*
Maytec Inc ....G..... 847 429-0321
  Dundee *(G-8128)*
Metal Impact LLC ....D..... 847 718-0192
  Elk Grove Village *(G-9117)*
Metal Impact South LLC ....F..... 847 718-9300
  Elk Grove Village *(G-9118)*
Monda Window & Door Corp ....E..... 773 254-8888
  Chicago *(G-5489)*
Rotation Dynamics Corporation ....E..... 630 769-9700
  Chicago *(G-6065)*
Sapa Extrusions North Amer LLC ....G..... 877 922-7272
  Rosemont *(G-18049)*
Signa Group Inc ....G..... 847 386-7639
  Northfield *(G-15529)*
Sno Gem Inc ....F..... 888 766-4367
  McHenry *(G-13792)*
Sternberg Lanterns Inc ....C..... 847 588-3400
  Roselle *(G-17991)*
T A U Inc ....G..... 708 841-5757
  Dolton *(G-7940)*
Werner Co ....A..... 847 455-8001
  Itasca *(G-11754)*
William Dach ....F..... 815 962-3455
  Rockford *(G-17685)*

ALUMINUM: Coil & Sheet

Climco Coils Company ....C..... 815 772-3717
  Morrison *(G-14342)*
Sea Converting Inc ....F..... 630 694-9178
  Wood Dale *(G-21238)*

ALUMINUM: Rolling & Drawing

Corus America Inc ....E..... 847 585-2599
  Schaumburg *(G-18491)*
Lapham-Hickey Steel Corp ....C..... 708 496-6111
  Bedford Park *(G-1479)*
Msystems Group LLC ....G..... 630 567-3930
  Saint Charles *(G-18233)*

AMMONIA & AMMONIUM SALTS

Pcs Nitrogen Inc ....D..... 847 849-4200
  Northbrook *(G-15453)*
Pcs Nitrogen Trinidad Corp ....C..... 847 849-4200
  Northbrook *(G-15455)*
Unity Envirotech Illinois LLC ....E..... 309 364-2361
  Henry *(G-11169)*

AMMONIUM NITRATE OR AMMONIUM SULFATE

East Dbque Ntrgn Frtlizers LLC ....C..... 815 747-3101
  East Dubuque *(G-8176)*

AMMUNITION

General Dynamics Corporation ....E..... 618 993-9207
  Marion *(G-13511)*
General Dynamics Ordnance ....C..... 618 985-8211
  Marion *(G-13512)*

AMMUNITION: Small Arms

A & S Arms Inc ....G..... 224 267-5670
  Antioch *(G-593)*
Bison Aerospace and Def LLC ....G..... 618 795-2678
  Savanna *(G-18403)*
Dan Moy ....G..... 217 243-2572
  Jacksonville *(G-11764)*
RR Defense Systems Inc ....F..... 773 529-6007
  Elk Grove Village *(G-9223)*

Vista Outdoor Inc ....D..... 217 893-7254
  Rantoul *(G-16986)*

AMPLIFIERS

Nantsound Inc ....F..... 847 939-6101
  Park Ridge *(G-16289)*
Victoria Amplifier Company ....F..... 630 369-3527
  Naperville *(G-14991)*

AMPLIFIERS: RF & IF Power

Amplivox Sound Systems LLC ....E..... 800 267-5486
  Northbrook *(G-15336)*
Crescend Technologies LLC ....E..... 847 908-5400
  Schaumburg *(G-18494)*

AMUSEMENT & RECREATION SVCS, NEC

Embroid ME ....G..... 815 485-4155
  New Lenox *(G-15033)*

AMUSEMENT & RECREATION SVCS: Exhibition & Carnival Op Svcs

Alpine Amusement Co Inc ....G..... 708 233-9131
  Oak Lawn *(G-15699)*

AMUSEMENT & RECREATION SVCS: Indoor Or Outdoor Court Clubs

Bernard Cffey Vtrans Fundation ....G..... 630 687-0033
  Naperville *(G-14779)*

AMUSEMENT & RECREATION SVCS: Scuba & Skin Diving Instruction

Scuba Sports Inc ....G..... 217 787-3483
  Springfield *(G-19440)*

AMUSEMENT & RECREATION SVCS: Shooting Range

Best Technology Systems Inc ....E..... 815 254-9554
  Plainfield *(G-16644)*

AMUSEMENT & RECREATION SVCS: Tennis Club, Membership

St Clair Tennis Club LLC ....G..... 618 632-1400
  O Fallon *(G-15584)*

AMUSEMENT & RECREATION SVCS: Tennis Courts, Non-Member

St Clair Tennis Club LLC ....G..... 618 632-1400
  O Fallon *(G-15584)*

AMUSEMENT & RECREATION SVCS: Theme Park

Fox Valley Park District ....D..... 630 892-1550
  Aurora *(G-1100)*

AMUSEMENT MACHINES: Coin Operated

B and B Amusement Illinois LLC ....G..... 309 585-2077
  Bloomington *(G-2025)*
Cobraco Manufacturing Inc ....E..... 847 726-5800
  Lake Zurich *(G-12395)*
Design Plus Industries Inc ....F..... 309 697-9778
  Peoria *(G-16430)*
Fun Industries Inc ....F..... 309 755-5021
  East Moline *(G-8226)*
Grand Products Inc ....B..... 800 621-6101
  Elk Grove Village *(G-9020)*
Williams Electronic Games De ....B..... 773 961-1000
  Chicago *(G-6630)*
Williams Electronic Games De ....G..... 773 961-1000
  Chicago *(G-6631)*
WMS Games Inc ....F..... 773 728-2300
  Chicago *(G-6657)*
WMS Industries Inc ....E..... 847 785-3000
  Chicago *(G-6660)*

AMUSEMENT PARK DEVICES & RIDES

Affri Inc ....G..... 224 374-0931
  Wood Dale *(G-21156)*
Atlas Material Tstg Tech LLC ....G..... 773 327-4520
  Chicago *(G-3766)*

County Tool & Die ....G..... 217 324-6527
  Litchfield *(G-12962)*
Diamond Industrial Sales Ltd ....G..... 630 858-3687
  Glen Ellyn *(G-10400)*
Donaldson Company Inc ....C..... 309 667-2885
  New Windsor *(G-15072)*
Dunteman and Co ....G..... 309 772-2166
  Bushnell *(G-2742)*
Lake County Technologies Inc ....F..... 847 977-1330
  East Dundee *(G-8204)*
Playing With Fusion Inc ....G..... 309 258-7259
  Mackinaw *(G-13385)*
R/K Industries Inc ....F..... 847 526-2222
  Wauconda *(G-20387)*
Senior PLC ....G..... 630 372-3511
  Bartlett *(G-1312)*
Threads Up Inc ....G..... 630 595-2297
  Palatine *(G-16163)*

AMUSEMENT PARK DEVICES & RIDES: Carnival Mach & Eqpt, NEC

Alpine Amusement Co Inc ....G..... 708 233-9131
  Oak Lawn *(G-15699)*

ANALYZERS: Blood & Body Fluid

Output Medical Inc ....G..... 630 430-8024
  Chicago *(G-5716)*

ANALYZERS: Coulometric, Indl Process

Uic Inc ....G..... 815 744-4477
  Joliet *(G-11937)*

ANALYZERS: Moisture

Moisture Detection Inc ....G..... 847 426-0464
  Hoffman Estates *(G-11437)*

ANALYZERS: Network

Amerinet of Michigan Inc ....G..... 708 466-0110
  Naperville *(G-14958)*
Brandt Assoc ....G..... 847 362-0556
  Lake Bluff *(G-12174)*
Cyber Tech Corp ....G..... 630 472-3200
  Oak Brook *(G-15615)*
Hipskind Tech Sltons Group Inc ....D..... 630 920-0960
  Oakbrook Terrace *(G-15803)*
Telcom Innovations Group LLC ....E..... 630 350-0700
  Itasca *(G-11745)*

ANALYZERS: Respiratory

IV & Respiratory Care Services ....E..... 618 398-2720
  Belleville *(G-1559)*

ANATOMICAL SPECIMENS & RESEARCH MATERIAL, WHOLESALE

3M Dekalb Distribution ....E..... 815 756-5087
  Dekalb *(G-7664)*

ANESTHETICS: Bulk Form

Janssen Pharmaceuticals Inc ....F..... 312 750-0507
  Chicago *(G-5007)*

ANIMAL BASED MEDICINAL CHEMICAL PRDTS

Animal Center International ....G..... 217 214-0536
  Quincy *(G-16853)*

ANIMAL FEED & SUPPLEMENTS: Livestock & Poultry

Agresearch Inc ....F..... 815 726-0410
  Joliet *(G-11818)*
Archer-Daniels-Midland Company ....E..... 217 342-3986
  Effingham *(G-8385)*
Archer-Daniels-Midland Company ....G..... 618 432-7194
  Patoka *(G-16302)*
Ardent Mills LLC ....E..... 618 826-2371
  Chester *(G-3449)*
B B Milling Co Inc ....G..... 217 376-3131
  Emden *(G-9466)*
Cargill Incorporated ....F..... 618 662-8070
  Flora *(G-9677)*
Cargill Incorporated ....G..... 309 587-8111
  New Boston *(G-15026)*

ANIMAL FEED & SUPPLEMENTS: Livestock & Poultry

Cargill Dry Corn Ingrdnts Inc..................G....... 217 465-5331
  Paris *(G-16226)*
Cloverleaf Feed Co Inc ....G....... 217 589-5010
  Roodhouse *(G-17892)*
Darling Ingredients Inc..............................E....... 708 388-3223
  Blue Island *(G-2117)*
Darling Ingredients Inc..............................E....... 309 476-8111
  Lynn Center *(G-13289)*
Dawes LLC...F....... 847 577-2020
  Arlington Heights *(G-726)*
Effingham Equity..F....... 217 268-5128
  Arcola *(G-648)*
Garver Feeds...E....... 217 422-2201
  Decatur *(G-7496)*
Helfter Enterprises Inc...............................F....... 309 522-5505
  Osco *(G-15988)*
Hueber LLC...F....... 815 393-4879
  Creston *(G-7102)*
Lebanon Seaboard Corporation ....E....... 217 446-0983
  Danville *(G-7358)*
Liberty Feed Mill..F....... 217 645-3441
  Liberty *(G-12623)*
M & W Feed Service...................................G....... 815 858-2412
  Elizabeth *(G-8787)*
Mendota Agri-Products Inc ....E....... 815 539-5633
  Mendota *(G-13946)*
Mgp Ingredients Illinois Inc.......................C....... 309 353-3990
  Pekin *(G-16345)*
Procal Inc...G....... 847 219-7257
  Palatine *(G-16151)*
Purina Animal Nutrition LLC......................G....... 618 283-2291
  Vandalia *(G-20021)*
Purina Animal Nutrition LLC......................E....... 618 478-5555
  Nashville *(G-15007)*
Purina Mills LLC..E....... 618 283-2291
  Vandalia *(G-20022)*
Reconserve of Illinois Inc..........................E....... 708 354-4641
  Hodgkins *(G-11394)*
Trouw Nutrition Usa LLC...........................G....... 618 654-2070
  Highland *(G-11244)*
Trouw Nutrition Usa LLC............................E....... 618 654-2070
  Highland *(G-11245)*
Trouw Nutrition Usa LLC............................E....... 618 654-2070
  Highland *(G-11246)*
Trouw Nutrition Usa LLC............................E....... 618 654-2070
  Highland *(G-11247)*
Veal Tech Inc...G....... 630 554-0410
  Oswego *(G-16030)*
Zoetis LLC..D....... 708 757-2592
  Chicago Heights *(G-6787)*

ANIMAL FEED: Wholesalers

Archer-Daniels-Midland Company ....F....... 815 223-7907
  Peru *(G-16566)*
K-Pro US LLC...G....... 872 529-5776
  O Fallon *(G-15576)*
Pcs Phosphate Company Inc ....E....... 815 795-5111
  Marseilles *(G-13563)*
Shaars International Inc ....G....... 815 315-0717
  Rockford *(G-17627)*
United Animal Health Inc ....E....... 309 747-2196
  Gridley *(G-10848)*

ANIMAL FOOD & SUPPLEMENTS: Bird Food, Prepared

Bill Chandler Farms ....G....... 618 752-7551
  Noble *(G-15188)*
Rare Birds Inc..G....... 847 259-7286
  Arlington Heights *(G-796)*
Siemer Enterprises Inc...............................E....... 217 857-3171
  Teutopolis *(G-19772)*
Wagners Inc..E....... 815 889-4101
  Milford *(G-14037)*

ANIMAL FOOD & SUPPLEMENTS: Bone Meal

K-Pro US LLC...G....... 872 529-5776
  O Fallon *(G-15576)*

ANIMAL FOOD & SUPPLEMENTS: Dog

Lincoln Bark LLC.......................................G....... 800 428-4027
  Chicago *(G-5224)*
Midwestern Pet Foods Inc.........................E....... 309 734-3121
  Monmouth *(G-14223)*
Papmpered Pups...G....... 815 782-8383
  Joliet *(G-11912)*
Pet-Ag Inc..E....... 847 683-2288
  Hampshire *(G-10983)*

Phelps Industries LLC.................................E....... 815 397-0236
  Rockford *(G-17553)*
Yotta Pet Products Inc ....F....... 217 466-4777
  Paris *(G-16247)*

ANIMAL FOOD & SUPPLEMENTS: Dog & Cat

Denta Treet LLC..G....... 618 384-1028
  Mount Vernon *(G-14609)*
Dr & Dr Property Leasing LLC..................G....... 309 965-3200
  Goodfield *(G-10674)*
Evangers Dog and Cat Fd Co Inc ....E....... 847 537-0102
  Markham *(G-13548)*
Kraft Heinz Foods Company....................C....... 847 291-3900
  Northbrook *(G-15415)*
Nutripack LLC..E....... 847 537-0102
  Markham *(G-13549)*
Pet Celebrations Inc ....G....... 630 832-6549
  Elmhurst *(G-9410)*

ANIMAL FOOD & SUPPLEMENTS: Feed Premixes

Furst-Mcness Company ....D....... 800 435-5100
  Freeport *(G-10112)*
Herris Group LLC ....G....... 630 908-7393
  Orland Park *(G-15959)*
Mont Eagle Products Inc..........................G....... 618 455-3344
  Sainte Marie *(G-18327)*

ANIMAL FOOD & SUPPLEMENTS: Feed Supplements

Lafeber Distribution LLC..........................G....... 630 524-4845
  Cornell *(G-7013)*
Nutriad Inc ....E....... 847 214-4860
  Hampshire *(G-10981)*
Pcs Phosphate Company Inc ....E....... 815 795-5111
  Marseilles *(G-13563)*
Pet-Ag Inc..E....... 847 683-2288
  Hampshire *(G-10983)*
Prince Agri Products Inc ....G....... 217 222-8854
  Quincy *(G-16924)*
Prince Agri Products Inc ....E....... 217 222-8854
  Quincy *(G-16925)*
Quality Liquid Feeds Inc ....G....... 815 224-1553
  La Salle *(G-12120)*
Transagra International Inc ....G....... 312 856-1010
  Chicago *(G-6407)*
Westway Feed Products LLC....................F....... 309 654-2211
  Cordova *(G-7011)*

ANIMAL FOOD & SUPPLEMENTS: Livestock

Alfa-Pet Inc...E....... 314 865-0400
  Godfrey *(G-10648)*
Altair Corporation ....E....... 847 634-9540
  Lincolnshire *(G-12744)*
Archer-Daniels-Midland Company ....E....... 217 222-7100
  Quincy *(G-16854)*
B&A Livestock Feed Company LLC..........G....... 618 245-6422
  Farina *(G-9650)*
Grain Densification Intl LLC......................G....... 618 823-5122
  Granite City *(G-10711)*
Griswold Feed Inc ....G....... 815 432-2811
  Watseka *(G-20305)*
Hueber LLC...G....... 815 625-4546
  Rock Falls *(G-17185)*
Kent Nutrition Group Inc ....F....... 815 874-2411
  Rockford *(G-17483)*
Kent Nutrition Group Inc ....F....... 217 323-1216
  Beardstown *(G-1448)*
Morgan Robt Inc..E....... 217 466-4777
  Paris *(G-16235)*
Quincy Farm Products LLC ....F....... 217 214-1905
  Quincy *(G-16931)*
United Animal Health Inc ....E....... 309 747-2196
  Gridley *(G-10848)*
Western Yeast Company Inc ....E....... 309 274-3160
  Chillicothe *(G-6823)*

ANIMAL FOOD & SUPPLEMENTS: Mineral feed supplements

Sem Minerals LP..D....... 217 224-8766
  Quincy *(G-16944)*

ANIMAL FOOD & SUPPLEMENTS: Pet, Exc Dog & Cat, Canned

All-Feed Proc & Packg Inc ....F....... 309 629-0001
  Alpha *(G-405)*
All-Feed Proc & Packg Inc ....G....... 309 932-3119
  Galva *(G-10226)*

ANIMAL FOOD & SUPPLEMENTS: Pet, Exc Dog & Cat, Dry

Petdine LLC..G....... 815 770-0342
  Harvard *(G-11062)*

ANIMAL FOOD & SUPPLEMENTS: Poultry

Lokman Enterprises Inc ....G....... 773 654-0525
  Chicago *(G-5252)*
Tate Lyle Ingrdnts Amricas LLC................G....... 309 473-2721
  Heyworth *(G-11191)*

ANIMAL FOOD & SUPPLEMENTS: Specialty, Mice & Other Pets

Chatham Corporation ....F....... 847 634-5506
  Lincolnshire *(G-12749)*

ANIMAL OILS: Medicinal Grade, Refined Or Concentrated

RITA Corporation ....E....... 815 337-2500
  Crystal Lake *(G-7257)*

ANNEALING: Metal

Progressive Steel Treating Inc..................E....... 815 877-2571
  Loves Park *(G-13251)*
Riverdale Pltg Heat Trting LLC ....E....... 708 849-2050
  Riverdale *(G-17076)*
Rockford Heat Treaters Inc ....E....... 815 874-0089
  Rockford *(G-17595)*

ANODIZING SVC

Accent Metal Finishing Inc........................F....... 847 678-7420
  Schiller Park *(G-18782)*
Ace Anodizing Impregnating Inc ....D....... 708 547-6680
  Hillside *(G-11324)*
Aerospace Metals LLC ....G....... 888 600-7811
  Sauget *(G-18387)*
Aluminum Coil Anodizing Corp.................C....... 630 837-4000
  Streamwood *(G-19560)*
Anodizing Specialists Ltd ....G....... 847 437-9495
  Elk Grove Village *(G-8833)*
Automatic Anodizing Corp.........................E....... 773 478-3304
  Chicago *(G-3777)*
Finishing Company.....................................C....... 630 559-0808
  Addison *(G-122)*
Meto-Grafics Inc..F....... 847 639-0044
  Crystal Lake *(G-7226)*
P B A Corp ....F....... 312 666-7370
  Chicago *(G-5728)*
Petersen Finishing Corporation ....G....... 847 228-7150
  Elk Grove Village *(G-9177)*
Saporito Finishing Co.................................D....... 708 222-5300
  Cicero *(G-6874)*
Saporito Finishing Co.................................E....... 708 222-5300
  Chicago *(G-6103)*

ANTENNAS: Receiving

Molex LLC...A....... 630 969-4550
  Lisle *(G-12911)*
Molex LLC...G....... 630 527-4363
  Bolingbrook *(G-2216)*
Molex Premise Networks Inc ....A....... 866 733-6659
  Lisle *(G-12915)*
Tedds Cstm Installations Inc ....G....... 815 485-6800
  New Lenox *(G-15063)*

ANTENNAS: Satellite, Household Use

Joseph C Rakers...G....... 618 670-6995
  Pocahontas *(G-16752)*
Othernet Inc...G....... 773 688-4320
  Long Grove *(G-13168)*
Perfectvision Mfg Inc ....F....... 630 226-9890
  Bolingbrook *(G-2225)*
Satellink Inc...E....... 618 983-5555
  Johnston City *(G-11812)*

PRODUCT SECTION

ART GOODS, WHOLESALE

ANTIBIOTICS
Zoetis LLC .... D 708 757-2592
 Chicago Heights *(G-6787)*

ANTIFREEZE
Illinois Oil Products Inc .... F 309 788-1896
 Rock Island *(G-17224)*
Planet Earth Antifreeze Inc .... G 815 282-2463
 Loves Park *(G-13247)*
Prestone Products Corporation .... D 708 371-3000
 Alsip *(G-497)*
Prestone Products Corporation .... C 888 282-8960
 Rosemont *(G-18043)*

ANTIHISTAMINE PREPARATIONS
Abbott Products Inc .... B 847 937-6100
 Abbott Park *(G-6)*

ANTIQUE & CLASSIC AUTOMOBILE RESTORATION
GC Laser Systems Inc .... G 844 532-1064
 Forest Park *(G-9719)*
Mike Mulcahy Motorsports LLC .... G 630 567-0298
 Morris *(G-14315)*
Restorations Unlimited II Inc .... G 847 639-5818
 Cary *(G-3186)*

ANTIQUE AUTOMOBILE DEALERS
Heartland Classics Inc .... G 618 783-4444
 Newton *(G-15084)*

ANTIQUE FURNITURE RESTORATION & REPAIR
Lee Armand & Co Ltd .... E 312 455-1200
 Chicago *(G-5194)*

ANTIQUE REPAIR & RESTORATION SVCS, EXC FURNITURE & AUTOS
Tiffany Stained Glass Ltd .... G 312 642-0680
 Forest Park *(G-9726)*

ANTIQUE SHOPS
Seek Design .... G 312 804-6629
 Evanston *(G-9574)*
Stained Glass of Peoria .... G 309 674-7929
 Peoria *(G-16529)*

ANTISCALING COMPOUNDS, BOILER
Global Water Technology Inc .... E 708 349-9991
 South Holland *(G-19215)*

ANTISEPTICS, MEDICINAL
Ortho Molecular Products Inc .... E 815 337-0089
 Woodstock *(G-21417)*

APPAREL ACCESS STORES
Athletic Outfitters Inc .... G 815 942-6696
 Morris *(G-14291)*

APPAREL DESIGNERS: Commercial
Artistic Embroidery Creations .... G 815 385-8854
 McHenry *(G-13721)*
Diamond Icic Corporation .... E 309 269-8652
 Rock Island *(G-17218)*

APPLIANCE CORDS: Household Electrical Eqpt
Best Rep Company Corporation .... G 847 451-6644
 Franklin Park *(G-9886)*
Coles Craft Corporation .... G 630 858-8171
 Glen Ellyn *(G-10398)*

APPLIANCE PARTS: Porcelain Enameled
Voges Inc .... D 618 233-2760
 Belleville *(G-1608)*

APPLIANCES, HOUSEHOLD OR COIN OPERATED: Laundry Dryers
5 Alarm Coin Laundry Inc .... G 815 298-0585
 Rockford *(G-17278)*
Monqui Suds LLC .... G 217 479-0090
 Jacksonville *(G-11777)*

APPLIANCES, HOUSEHOLD: Ice Boxes, Metal Or Wood
Scotsman Industries Inc .... D 847 215-4500
 Vernon Hills *(G-20093)*

APPLIANCES, HOUSEHOLD: Kitchen, Major, Exc Refrigs & Stoves
Appliance Repair .... G 708 456-1020
 Norridge *(G-15230)*
Mic Quality Service Inc .... E 847 778-5676
 Chicago *(G-5422)*
Rampro Facilities Svcs Corp .... G 224 639-6378
 Waukegan *(G-20487)*
Tablecraft Products Co Inc .... D 847 855-9000
 Gurnee *(G-10933)*

APPLIANCES, HOUSEHOLD: Laundry Machines, Incl Coin-Operated
Eastgate Cleaners .... G 630 627-9494
 Lombard *(G-13071)*

APPLIANCES, HOUSEHOLD: Refrigs, Mechanical & Absorption
Sphinx Panel and Door Inc .... G 618 351-9266
 Cobden *(G-6944)*

APPLIANCES, HOUSEHOLD: Sweepers, Electric
Campanella Clg Solutions Inc .... G 847 949-4222
 Mundelein *(G-14671)*

APPLIANCES: Household, Refrigerators & Freezers
Craig Industries Inc .... D 217 228-2421
 Quincy *(G-16873)*
Dover Corporation .... G 212 922-1640
 Downers Grove *(G-7990)*
Flurida Group Inc .... G 310 513-0888
 Naperville *(G-14966)*
H A Phillips & Co .... E 630 377-0050
 Dekalb *(G-7683)*
Tri-State Food Equipment .... G 217 228-1550
 Quincy *(G-16952)*

APPLIANCES: Major, Cooking
Axis International Marketing .... C 847 297-0744
 Des Plaines *(G-7735)*
BR Machine Inc .... F 815 434-0427
 Ottawa *(G-16042)*
Global Contract Mfg Inc .... G 312 432-6200
 Chicago *(G-4695)*
Marshall Middleby Inc .... C 847 741-3300
 Elgin *(G-8649)*
Taylor Coml Foodservice Inc .... F 815 624-8333
 Rockton *(G-17703)*

APPLIANCES: Small, Electric
American Fuel Economy Inc .... G 815 433-3226
 Ottawa *(G-16037)*
Bunn-O-Matic Corporation .... E 562 926-0764
 Springfield *(G-19332)*
Extractor Corporation .... F 847 742-3532
 South Elgin *(G-19144)*
Keating of Chicago Inc .... E 815 569-2324
 Capron *(G-2834)*
Newhaven Display Intl Inc .... F 847 844-8795
 Elgin *(G-8668)*
Tempro International Corp .... G 847 677-5370
 Skokie *(G-19044)*

APPLICATIONS SOFTWARE PROGRAMMING
Civiq Smartscapes LLC .... G 312 300-4776
 Chicago *(G-4165)*

Hybris (us) Corporation .... E 312 265-5010
 Chicago *(G-4861)*
Lightfoot Technologies Inc .... G 331 302-1297
 Naperville *(G-14864)*
Perficient Inc .... F 312 291-9035
 Chicago *(G-5790)*
Qt Info Systems Inc .... F 800 240-8761
 Chicago *(G-5925)*

APPRENTICESHIP TRAINING SCHOOLS
Bandjwet Enterprises Inc .... E 847 797-9250
 Rolling Meadows *(G-17717)*

AQUARIUMS & ACCESS: Glass
Midwest Tropical Entps Inc .... E 847 679-6666
 Lincolnwood *(G-12831)*

AQUARIUMS & ACCESS: Plastic
Midwest Tropical Entps Inc .... E 847 679-6666
 Lincolnwood *(G-12831)*

ARCHITECTURAL SVCS
Fastsigns .... G 847 675-1600
 Lincolnwood *(G-12818)*
Gerald R Page Corporation .... F 847 398-5575
 Prospect Heights *(G-16842)*
Lingle Design Group Inc .... E 815 369-9155
 Lena *(G-12605)*

ARMATURE REPAIRING & REWINDING SVC
Acme Control Service Inc .... E 773 774-9191
 Chicago *(G-3527)*
Cox Electric Motor Service .... G 217 344-2458
 Urbana *(G-19980)*
Flolo Corporation .... G 847 249-0880
 Gurnee *(G-10878)*
Integrated Power Services LLC .... E 708 877-5310
 Thornton *(G-19789)*
Jasiek Motor Rebuilding Inc .... G 815 883-3678
 Oglesby *(G-15842)*
Lawrence Maddock .... F 847 394-1698
 Arlington Heights *(G-768)*
New Cie Inc .... F 815 224-1485
 La Salle *(G-12118)*
New Cie Inc .... E 815 224-1511
 Peru *(G-16584)*
Precision Drive & Control Inc .... G 815 235-7595
 Freeport *(G-10133)*
Rathje Enterprises Inc .... B 217 423-2593
 Decatur *(G-7540)*
Richards Electric Motor Co .... E 217 222-7154
 Quincy *(G-16940)*

ARMATURES: Ind
Active Tool and Machine Inc .... F 708 599-0022
 Oak Lawn *(G-15697)*

ART & ORNAMENTAL WARE: Pottery
In The Attic Inc .... G 847 949-5077
 Mundelein *(G-14699)*

ART DEALERS & GALLERIES
Wood Shop .... G 773 994-6666
 Chicago *(G-6667)*

ART DESIGN SVCS
3-Switch LLC .... G 217 721-4546
 Chicago *(G-3466)*
Fortman & Associates Ltd .... F 847 524-0741
 Elk Grove Village *(G-9005)*
Mk Signs Inc .... E 773 545-4444
 Chicago *(G-5473)*
Targin Sign Systems Inc .... G 630 766-7667
 Wood Dale *(G-21246)*

ART GOODS & SPLYS WHOLESALERS
Sws Industries Inc .... E 904 482-0091
 Woodstock *(G-21438)*

ART GOODS, WHOLESALE
Chase Group LLC .... F 847 564-2000
 Northbrook *(G-15355)*
Wexford Home Corp .... G 331 225-0979
 Countryside *(G-7078)*

ART MARBLE: Concrete

ART MARBLE: Concrete
Blue Pearl Stone Tech LLC ....G....... 708 698-5700
La Grange (G-12073)

ART RESTORATION SVC
GC Laser Systems Inc ....G....... 844 532-1064
Forest Park (G-9719)

ART SCHOOL, EXC COMMERCIAL
Creative Curricula Inc ....G....... 815 363-9419
McHenry (G-13732)

ARTIFICIAL FLOWERS & TREES
Brees Studio Inc...................................F....... 618 687-3331
Murphysboro (G-14752)
Lcg Sales Inc ....D....... 773 378-7455
Chicago (G-5188)

ARTIST'S MATERIALS & SPLYS
Graphic Chemical & Ink Co..................F....... 630 832-6004
Villa Park (G-20149)

ARTISTS' AGENTS & BROKERS
Csiteq Studio LLC................................F....... 312 265-1509
Rosemont (G-18012)
Strictly Stainless Inc.............................G....... 847 885-2890
Hoffman Estates (G-11464)

ARTISTS' MATERIALS, WHOLESALE
James Howard Co................................G....... 815 497-2831
Compton (G-6996)

ARTISTS' MATERIALS: Brushes, Air
Badger Air Brush Co ....D....... 847 678-3104
Franklin Park (G-9883)
Rust-Oleum Corporation ....D....... 815 967-4258
Rockford (G-17617)
Testor Corporation................................D....... 815 962-6654
Rockford (G-17656)

ARTISTS' MATERIALS: Chalks, Carpenters', Blackboard, Etc
Fernandez Windows Corp......................G....... 773 762-2365
Chicago (G-4581)

ARTISTS' MATERIALS: Clay, Modeling
Polyform Products Company ....E....... 847 427-0020
Elk Grove Village (G-9182)

ARTISTS' MATERIALS: Eraser Guides & Shields
Erasermitt Incorporated ....G....... 312 842-2855
Chicago (G-4525)

ARTISTS' MATERIALS: Ink, Drawing, Black & Colored
Hydro Ink Corp ....G....... 847 674-0057
Skokie (G-18967)

ARTISTS' MATERIALS: Lettering Instruments
On Paint It Company.............................G....... 219 765-5639
Dekalb (G-7697)

ARTISTS' MATERIALS: Palettes
Miller Pallet..F....... 217 589-4411
Roodhouse (G-17893)

ARTISTS' MATERIALS: Pencils & Pencil Parts
Stentech Inc...G....... 630 833-4717
Elmhurst (G-9430)

ARTISTS' MATERIALS: Wax
Lectro Stik Corp ....E....... 630 894-1355
Glendale Heights (G-10466)

ARTWORK: Framed
I T C W Inc...B....... 630 305-8849
Naperville (G-14842)
Thrilled LLC ....G....... 312 404-1929
Chicago (G-6373)
Wexford Home Corp ....G....... 331 225-0979
Countryside (G-7078)

ASBESTOS PRDTS: Insulation, Molded
Asbestos Control & Envmtl Svc ....F....... 630 690-0189
Eola (G-9469)

ASBESTOS PRDTS: Wick
Wise Construction Services ....G....... 630 553-6350
Yorkville (G-21506)

ASBESTOS PRODUCTS
Celtic Environmental ....G....... 708 442-5823
Chicago Ridge (G-6789)

ASBESTOS REMOVAL EQPT
Asbestos Control & Envmtl Svc ....F....... 630 690-0189
Eola (G-9469)
Bunn-O-Matic Corporation ....G....... 217 529-6601
Springfield (G-19334)
Towne Towing Inc ....G....... 847 705-1710
Palatine (G-16165)

ASH TRAYS: Stamped Metal
Creative Metal Products ....F....... 773 638-3200
Chicago (G-4264)

ASPHALT & ASPHALT PRDTS
Allied Asphalt Paving Co Inc ....E....... 630 289-6080
Elgin (G-8503)
Arrow Road Construction Co ....C....... 847 437-0700
Elk Grove Village (G-8839)
Asphalt Products Inc ....F....... 618 943-4716
Lawrenceville (G-12527)
Certified Asphalt Paving ....G....... 847 441-5000
Northfield (G-15511)
Cgk Enterprises Inc ....G....... 847 888-1362
Elgin (G-8535)
Charles E Mahoney Company ....E....... 618 235-3355
Swansea (G-19690)
Corrective Asphalt Mtls LLC ....G....... 618 254-3855
South Roxana (G-19252)
Crowley-Sheppard Asphalt Inc..............F....... 708 499-2900
Chicago Ridge (G-6793)
Curran Contracting Company................E....... 815 455-5100
Crystal Lake (G-7189)
Emulsions Inc.......................................G....... 618 943-2615
Lawrenceville (G-12531)
ET Simonds Materials Company ....E....... 618 457-8191
Carbondale (G-2842)
Frank S Johnson & Company Inc..........G....... 847 492-1660
Evanston (G-9522)
Gallagher Asphalt Corporation..............E....... 708 877-7160
Thornton (G-19786)
Geske and Sons Inc ....G....... 815 459-2407
Crystal Lake (G-7203)
Geske and Sons Inc ....F....... 815 459-2407
Crystal Lake (G-7202)
Gorman Brothers Ready Mix Inc ....F....... 618 498-2173
Jerseyville (G-11791)
Illinois Road Contractors Inc.................E....... 217 245-6181
Jacksonville (G-11769)
Illinois Valley Paving Co Inc..................E....... 217 422-1010
Elwin (G-9459)
Louis Marsch Inc..................................E....... 217 526-3723
Morrisonville (G-14351)
Pothole Pros...G....... 847 815-5789
Elgin (G-8692)
Reliable Asphalt Corporation ....E....... 773 254-1121
Chicago (G-6009)
Savanna Quarry Inc ....G....... 815 273-4208
Savanna (G-18411)
Seneca Petroleum Co Inc ....G....... 630 257-2268
Lemont (G-12589)
Sherwin Industries Inc..........................E....... 815 234-8007
Byron (G-2758)
Utica Terminal Inc ....G....... 217 245-6181
Utica (G-20008)

ASPHALT COATINGS & SEALERS
Allied Asphalt Paving Co Inc ....E....... 630 289-6080
Elgin (G-8503)
Atlas Roofing Corporation.....................E....... 309 752-7121
East Moline (G-8222)
Black Rock Milling and Pav Co..............F....... 847 952-0700
Arlington Heights (G-706)
Bonsal American Inc ....D....... 847 678-6220
Franklin Park (G-9891)
Carlisle Syn TEC Inc.............................F....... 618 664-4540
Greenville (G-10829)
Crown Coatings Company ....F....... 630 365-9925
Elburn (G-8448)
Don Anderson Co ....G....... 618 495-2511
Hoffman (G-11402)
Gardner Asphalt Corporation ....E....... 800 237-1155
Chicago (G-4659)
Harsco Corporation ....F....... 217 237-4335
Pawnee (G-16304)
Jax Asphalt Company Inc ....F....... 618 244-0500
Mount Vernon (G-14618)
Lifetime Rooftile Company ....G....... 630 355-7922
Naperville (G-14863)
Miller Purcell Co Inc.............................G....... 815 485-2142
New Lenox (G-15043)
Natazz Specialty Coatings Inc ....F....... 773 247-7030
Chicago (G-5542)
Nu-Puttie Corporation ....E....... 708 681-1040
Maywood (G-13676)
Omnimax International Inc ....E....... 309 747-2937
Gridley (G-10846)
Owens Corning Sales LLC....................B....... 708 594-6911
Argo (G-674)
Owens Corning Sales LLC....................E....... 708 594-6935
Argo (G-675)
Plote Inc ....D....... 847 695-9467
Hoffman Estates (G-11446)
Pure Asphalt Company ....F....... 773 247-7030
Chicago (G-5916)
Sheet Metal Supply Ltd ....E....... 847 478-8500
Grayslake (G-10799)
St Louis Flexicore Inc...........................F....... 618 531-8691
East Saint Louis (G-8324)

ASPHALT MIXTURES WHOLESALERS
Marathon Petroleum Company LP ....G....... 618 829-3288
Saint Elmo (G-18309)

ASPHALT PLANTS INCLUDING GRAVEL MIX TYPE
Chicago Materials Corporation..............E....... 630 257-5600
Lemont (G-12561)
Jordan Services ....G....... 630 416-6701
Lisle (G-12904)
L & N Structures Inc ....E....... 815 426-2164
Herscher (G-11184)
Peter Baker & Son Co ....F....... 815 344-1640
Mc Henry (G-13705)
Streator Asphalt Inc..............................G....... 815 426-2164
Herscher (G-11187)
Streator Asphalt Inc..............................G....... 815 672-8683
Streator (G-19625)

ASSEMBLING & PACKAGING SVCS: Cosmetic Kits
Assemble and Mail Group Inc...............G....... 309 473-2006
Heyworth (G-11189)

ASSEMBLING SVC: Clocks
Instrument Services Inc ....G....... 815 623-2993
Machesney Park (G-13350)

ASSEMBLING SVC: Plumbing Fixture Fittings, Plastic
Sergio Barajas......................................G....... 708 238-7614
La Grange (G-12089)

ASSOCIATIONS: Bar
American Bar Association ....A....... 312 988-5000
Chicago (G-3650)

ASSOCIATIONS: Business
Chester White Swine Rcord Assn ....G....... 309 691-0151
Peoria (G-16421)

PRODUCT SECTION

AUTO & HOME SUPPLY STORES: Batteries, Automotive & Truck

W A M Computers International .... G 217 324-6926
  Litchfield *(G-12978)*

ASSOCIATIONS: Real Estate Management

Belboz Corp .... G 708 856-6099
  Dolton *(G-7933)*

ASSOCIATIONS: Trade

American Supply Association .... F 630 467-0000
  Itasca *(G-11622)*
Associated Equipment Distrs .... E 630 574-0650
  Schaumburg *(G-18447)*
Comptia Learning LLC .... F 630 678-8490
  Downers Grove *(G-7977)*
Fabricators & Mfrs Assn Intl .... E 815 399-8700
  Elgin *(G-8584)*
National Association Realtors .... C 800 874-6500
  Chicago *(G-5543)*
National Sporting Goods Assn .... F 847 296-6742
  Downers Grove *(G-8063)*
Tube & Pipe Association Intl .... D 815 399-8700
  Elgin *(G-8763)*

ATOMIZERS

3dp Unlimited LLC .... G 815 389-5667
  Roscoe *(G-17896)*
3M Dekalb Distribution .... E 815 756-5087
  Dekalb *(G-7664)*
Acme Finishing Company LLC .... F 847 640-7890
  Elk Grove Village *(G-8803)*
DPM Solutions LLC .... G 630 285-1170
  Addison *(G-98)*
Fuyao Glass Illinois Inc .... C 217 864-2392
  Decatur *(G-7495)*
Ihi Turbo America Co .... D 217 774-9571
  Shelbyville *(G-18880)*
Illinois Bottle Mfg Co .... D 847 595-9000
  Elk Grove Village *(G-9040)*
Integrated Industries Inc .... G 773 299-1970
  Chicago *(G-4940)*
Integrated Mfg Tech LLC .... E 618 282-8306
  Red Bud *(G-16996)*
ITW Bldg Components Group .... G 847 634-1900
  Glenview *(G-10571)*
Jr Industries LLC .... F 773 908-5317
  Chicago *(G-5056)*
Kop Industries Corporated Inc .... G 630 930-9516
  Glen Ellyn *(G-10407)*
Lumentum Operations LLC .... G 408 546-5483
  Chicago *(G-5282)*
Mp Manufacturing Inc .... G 815 334-1112
  Woodstock *(G-21414)*
Pegasus Mfg Inc .... F 309 342-9337
  Galesburg *(G-10215)*
Plastic Container Corporation .... D 217 352-2722
  Urbana *(G-19993)*
Potash Holding Company Inc .... G 847 849-4200
  Northbrook *(G-15462)*
Roll-A-Way Conveyors Inc .... F 847 336-5033
  Gurnee *(G-10924)*
Scs Absorbent Mfg Inc .... F 502 417-1365
  Monticello *(G-14285)*
Singer Equities Inc .... F 815 874-5364
  Rockford *(G-17632)*
Smith Industrial Rubber & Plas .... F 815 874-5364
  Rockford *(G-17636)*
Tropar Trophy Manufacturing Co .... E 630 787-1900
  Wood Dale *(G-21252)*
Yetter Manufacturing Company .... E 309 833-1445
  Macomb *(G-13403)*

AUCTION SVCS: Livestock

Banner Publications .... G 309 338-3294
  Cuba *(G-7297)*

AUCTION SVCS: Motor Vehicle

Nissan .... G 630 957-4360
  West Chicago *(G-20622)*

AUDIO & VIDEO EQPT, EXC COMMERCIAL

Aco Inc .... E 773 774-5200
  Chicago *(G-3529)*
Amplivox Sound Systems LLC .... E 800 267-5486
  Northbrook *(G-15336)*
AVI-Spl Employee .... B 847 437-7712
  Schaumburg *(G-18453)*

Bretford Manufacturing Inc .... B 847 678-2545
  Franklin Park *(G-9892)*
Cco Holdings LLC .... G 618 505-3505
  Troy *(G-19912)*
Cco Holdings LLC .... G 618 651-6486
  Highland *(G-11208)*
Chamberlain Manufacturing Corp .... A 630 279-3600
  Oak Brook *(G-15608)*
Elexa Consumer Products Inc .... B 773 794-1300
  Bannockburn *(G-1200)*
G T C Industries Inc .... G 708 369-9815
  Naperville *(G-14832)*
Harman International Inds Inc .... D 847 996-8118
  Vernon Hills *(G-20059)*
Heil Sound Ltd .... F 618 257-3000
  Fairview Heights *(G-9646)*
Identatronics Inc .... E 847 437-2654
  Crystal Lake *(G-7208)*
J P Goldenne Incorporated .... F 847 776-5063
  Palatine *(G-16132)*
James R Chittick .... G 217 446-0925
  Danville *(G-7353)*
Japan Electronic Manufacturers .... F 972 735-0463
  Wilmette *(G-21080)*
Knowles Corporation .... E 630 250-5100
  Itasca *(G-11685)*
Mechanical Music Corp .... F 847 398-5444
  Arlington Heights *(G-775)*
Metronet Integration Inc .... F 312 781-0045
  Chicago *(G-5412)*
Newhaven Display Intl Inc .... E 847 844-8795
  Elgin *(G-8668)*
Northrop Grumman Systems Corp .... A 847 259-9600
  Rolling Meadows *(G-17755)*
Orei LLC .... G 847 983-4761
  Skokie *(G-19001)*
Peterson Intl Entp Ltd .... F 847 541-3700
  Wheeling *(G-20958)*
Robotics Technologies Inc .... E 815 722-7650
  Joliet *(G-11927)*
Signify North America Corp .... E 708 307-3000
  Roselle *(G-17989)*
Sonistic .... G 217 377-9698
  Champaign *(G-3350)*
Sony Electronics Inc .... C 630 773-7500
  Carol Stream *(G-3071)*
Tech Upgraders .... G 877 324-8940
  Maywood *(G-13678)*
Techpol Automation Inc .... G 847 347-4765
  Des Plaines *(G-7855)*
United States Audio Corp .... G 312 316-2929
  Chicago *(G-6476)*
Wireless Chamberlain Products .... E 800 282-6225
  Elmhurst *(G-9446)*

AUDIO & VIDEO TAPES WHOLESALERS

Holsolutions Inc .... G 888 847-5467
  Frankfort *(G-9801)*

AUDIO COMPONENTS

Bose Corporation .... G 630 575-8044
  Hinsdale *(G-11366)*
Bose Corporation .... G 630 585-6654
  Aurora *(G-924)*
Connecteriors LLC .... G 773 549-3333
  Chicago *(G-4218)*
Crystal Partners Inc .... G 847 882-0467
  Schaumburg *(G-18498)*
Mitek Corporation .... C 815 367-3000
  Winslow *(G-21140)*
Sound Enhancement Products Inc .... E 847 639-4646
  Glendale Heights *(G-10496)*
United States Audio Corp .... F 312 316-2929
  Glenview *(G-10636)*

AUDIO ELECTRONIC SYSTEMS

Clearsounds Communications Inc .... F 630 321-2300
  Naperville *(G-14800)*
John Hardy Co .... G 847 864-8060
  Evanston *(G-9542)*
K C Audio .... G 708 636-4928
  Alsip *(G-462)*
Maxxsonics Usa Inc .... E 847 540-7700
  Libertyville *(G-12676)*
Organized Noise Inc .... G 630 820-9855
  Aurora *(G-1004)*
Prescotts Inc .... G 815 626-2996
  Sterling *(G-19525)*

Studio Technologies Inc .... F 847 676-9177
  Skokie *(G-19038)*
Zenith Electronics Corporation .... E 847 941-8000
  Lincolnshire *(G-12806)*

AUTO & HOME SUPPLY STORES: Auto & Truck Eqpt & Parts

Blanke Industries Incorporated .... G 847 487-2780
  Wauconda *(G-20335)*
Genuine Parts Company .... F 630 293-1300
  Chicago *(G-4681)*
Goreville Auto Parts & Mch Sp .... G 618 995-2375
  Goreville *(G-10680)*
Iggys Auto Parts .... F 708 452-9790
  Norridge *(G-15237)*
L & T Services Inc .... G 815 397-6260
  Rockford *(G-17487)*
Motor Parts & Equipment Corp .... E 217 877-7456
  Decatur *(G-7527)*
Rursch Specialties Inc .... G 309 795-1502
  Reynolds *(G-17005)*
Service Auto Supply .... F 309 444-9704
  Washington *(G-20280)*

AUTO & HOME SUPPLY STORES: Automotive Access

Dss Inc .... G 630 587-1169
  Saint Charles *(G-18187)*
Folk Race Cars .... G 815 629-2418
  Durand *(G-8151)*
Heartland Classics Inc .... G 618 783-4444
  Newton *(G-15084)*
Joes Automotive Inc .... G 815 937-9281
  Kankakee *(G-11982)*

AUTO & HOME SUPPLY STORES: Automotive parts

A Len Radiator Shoppe Inc .... G 630 852-5445
  Downers Grove *(G-7948)*
CC Distributing Services Inc .... G 800 931-2668
  Crestwood *(G-7110)*
Donnelly Automotive Machine .... F 217 428-7414
  Decatur *(G-7491)*
Hymans Auto Supply Co .... E 773 978-8221
  Chicago *(G-4864)*
L A Motors Incorporated .... G 773 736-7305
  Chicago *(G-5142)*
Lakenburges Motor Co .... G 618 523-4231
  Germantown *(G-10331)*
Ln Engineering LLC .... F 815 472-2939
  Momence *(G-14187)*
Niles Auto Parts .... G 847 215-2549
  Lincolnshire *(G-12788)*
O K Jobbers Inc .... G 217 728-7378
  Sullivan *(G-19674)*
OReilly Automotive Stores Inc .... G 708 430-8155
  Bridgeview *(G-2370)*
OReilly Automotive Stores Inc .... G 847 882-4384
  Schaumburg *(G-18659)*
OReilly Automotive Stores Inc .... G 847 360-0012
  Waukegan *(G-20474)*
Part Stop Inc .... G 618 377-5238
  Bethalto *(G-1965)*
R & C Auto Supply Corp .... G 815 625-4414
  Sterling *(G-19528)*
Standard Lifts & Equipment Inc .... G 414 444-1000
  Hanover Park *(G-11015)*
Transcedar Limited .... E 618 262-4153
  Mount Carmel *(G-14488)*
Whiting Partners LLC .... G 773 978-8221
  Chicago *(G-6620)*

AUTO & HOME SUPPLY STORES: Batteries, Automotive & Truck

Batteries Plus 287 .... G 630 279-3478
  Villa Park *(G-20132)*
Battery Sales Inc .... G 708 489-6645
  Matteson *(G-13619)*
Gem Equipment & Mfg LLC .... E 309 923-7312
  Roanoke *(G-17101)*
Interstate All Battery Center .... F 217 214-1069
  Quincy *(G-16894)*
Interstate Btry Sys Intl Inc .... G 708 424-2288
  Oak Lawn *(G-15720)*

Employee Codes: A=Over 500 employees, B=251-500
C=101-250, D=51-100, E=20-50, F=10-19, G=3-9

AUTO & HOME SUPPLY STORES: Speed Shops, Incl Race Car Splys

AUTO & HOME SUPPLY STORES: Speed Shops, Incl Race Car Splys

Car Shop Inc .... G		309 797-4188
Moline (G-14135)		
Nelson Enterprises Inc .... G		815 633-1100
Roscoe (G-17920)		
Rj Race Cars Inc .... F		309 343-7575
Galesburg (G-10218)		

AUTO & HOME SUPPLY STORES: Truck Eqpt & Parts

| Area Diesel Service Inc .... E .... 217 854-2641 |
| Carlinville (G-2867) |
| Hypermax Engineering Inc .... F .... 847 428-5655 |
| Gilberts (G-10359) |
| Kleinhoffer Manufacturing Inc .... G .... 815 725-3638 |
| Joliet (G-11890) |
| Mickey Truck Bodies Inc .... F .... 309 827-8227 |
| Bloomington (G-2076) |
| P & A Driveline & Machine Inc .... F .... 630 860-7474 |
| Bensenville (G-1865) |

AUTO SPLYS & PARTS, NEW, WHSLE: Exhaust Sys, Mufflers, Etc

CC Distributing Services Inc .... G 800 931-2668
Crestwood (G-7110)

AUTOMATIC REGULATING CNTRLS: Liq Lvl, Residential/Comm Heat

New Century Mfg .... G 847 998-0960
Glenview (G-10594)

AUTOMATIC REGULATING CNTRLS: Steam Press, Residential/ Comm

Boyleston 21st Century LLC .... G 708 387-2012
Brookfield (G-2479)

AUTOMATIC REGULATING CONTROL: Building Svcs Monitoring, Auto

| Clarios .... E .... 815 397-5147 |
| Rockford (G-17351) |
| Clarios .... F .... 630 871-7700 |
| Carol Stream (G-2961) |
| Dundee Design LLC .... G .... 847 494-2360 |
| East Dundee (G-8194) |
| E George Special Services LLC .... G .... 773 934-7878 |
| Glenwood (G-10640) |
| Schneider Elc Buildings LLC .... B .... 815 381-5000 |
| Rockford (G-17622) |
| Schneider Elc Buildings LLC .... E .... 815 227-4000 |
| Rockford (G-17623) |
| Schneider Elc Holdings Inc .... A .... 717 944-5460 |
| Schaumburg (G-18707) |

AUTOMATIC REGULATING CONTROLS: AC & Refrigeration

| Ademco Inc .... E .... 847 472-2900 |
| Elk Grove Village (G-8807) |
| Hansen Technologies Corp .... D .... 706 335-5551 |
| Burr Ridge (G-2682) |
| Siemens Industry Inc .... D .... 847 520-9084 |
| Buffalo Grove (G-2599) |
| Siemens Industry Inc .... G .... 309 664-2460 |
| Bloomington (G-2094) |
| Siemens Industry Inc .... G .... 847 941-5050 |
| Buffalo Grove (G-2601) |
| Siemens Industry Inc .... D .... 847 215-1000 |
| Buffalo Grove (G-2602) |
| Siemens Industry Inc .... A .... 847 215-1000 |
| Buffalo Grove (G-2600) |
| Temperature Equipment Corp .... G .... 847 429-0818 |
| Elgin (G-8752) |
| Temprite Company .... E .... 630 293-5910 |
| West Chicago (G-20649) |

AUTOMATIC REGULATING CONTROLS: Appliance, Exc Air-Cond/Refr

| Reliable Appliance and Ref .... G .... 847 581-9520 |
| Morton Grove (G-14438) |
| Sonne Industries LLC .... G .... 630 235-6734 |
| Naperville (G-14917) |

AUTOMATIC REGULATING CONTROLS: Gas Burner, Automatic

| Eclipse Inc .... D .... 815 877-3031 |
| Rockford (G-17388) |
| Indesco Oven Products Inc .... G .... 217 622-6345 |
| Petersburg (G-16602) |

AUTOMATIC REGULATING CONTROLS: Gradual Switches, Pneumatic

Intech Industries Inc .... F 847 487-5599
Wauconda (G-20361)

AUTOMATIC REGULATING CONTROLS: Hydronic Circulator, Auto

Jql Technologies Corporation .... F 800 236-9828
Mundelein (G-14705)

AUTOMATIC REGULATING CONTROLS: Incinerator, Residential/Comm

Cdc Enterprises Inc .... G 815 790-4205
Johnsburg (G-11802)

AUTOMATIC REGULATING CONTROLS: Pneumatic Relays, Air-Cond

SMC Corporation of America .... E 630 449-0600
Aurora (G-1017)

AUTOMATIC REGULATING CONTROLS: Refrigeration, Pressure

H A Phillips & Co .... E 630 377-0050
Dekalb (G-7683)

AUTOMATIC REGULATING CTRLS: Damper, Pneumatic Or Electric

| Control Equipment Company Inc ...... F .... 847 891-7500 |
| Schaumburg (G-18487) |
| ITW Motion .... E .... 708 720-0300 |
| Frankfort (G-9809) |

AUTOMATIC TELLER MACHINES

| Asai Chicago .... F .... 708 239-0133 |
| Alsip (G-419) |
| Chase Home Finance .... G .... 630 617-4747 |
| Elmhurst (G-9343) |
| Cummins-Allison Corp .... B .... 800 786-5528 |
| Mount Prospect (G-14523) |
| Diebold Nixdorf Incorporated .... D .... 847 598-3300 |
| Schaumburg (G-18506) |
| Kahuna LLC .... F .... 888 357-8472 |
| Bloomington (G-2066) |
| OHare Shell Partners Inc .... F .... 847 678-1900 |
| Schiller Park (G-18829) |
| PNC Financial Svcs Group Inc .... G .... 630 420-8400 |
| Naperville (G-14900) |

AUTOMATIC VENDING MACHINES: Mechanisms & Parts

Manufctrng-Resourcing Intl Inc .... F 217 821-3733
Shumway (G-18904)

AUTOMOBILE FABRICS, WHOLESALE

Kop Industries Corporated Inc .... G 630 930-9516
Glen Ellyn (G-10407)

AUTOMOBILE FINANCE LEASING

Navistar International Corp .... A 331 332-5000
Lisle (G-12921)

AUTOMOBILE STORAGE GARAGE

Springfield Welding & Auto Bdy .... E 217 523-5365
Springfield (G-19457)

AUTOMOBILES & OTHER MOTOR VEHICLES WHOLESALERS

| Hertz Corporation .... G .... 630 897-0956 |
| Montgomery (G-14247) |
| North Shore Truck & Equipment ...... F .... 847 887-0200 |
| Lake Bluff (G-12201) |

AUTOMOBILES: Wholesalers

Eaton Corporation .... C 815 562-2107
Rochelle (G-17138)

AUTOMOTIVE & TRUCK GENERAL REPAIR SVC

| A Len Radiator Shoppe Inc .... G .... 630 852-5445 |
| Downers Grove (G-7948) |
| Amis Inc .... G .... 708 598-9700 |
| Bridgeview (G-2323) |
| Bi-Phase Technologies LLC .... F .... 952 886-6450 |
| Wood Dale (G-21168) |
| Bring Your Own Auto Parts Inc .... F .... 815 730-6900 |
| Crest Hill (G-7084) |
| California Muffler and Brakes .... G .... 773 776-8990 |
| Chicago (G-4004) |
| Carnaghi Towing & Repair Inc .... F .... 217 446-0333 |
| Tilton (G-19793) |
| Chicago Drive Line Inc .... G .... 708 385-1900 |
| Alsip (G-427) |
| Eden Fuels LLC .... G .... 847 676-9470 |
| Skokie (G-18949) |
| Entrans International LLC .... E .... 618 548-3660 |
| Salem (G-18337) |
| G&G Machine Shop Inc .... G .... 217 892-9696 |
| Rantoul (G-16976) |
| Gerardo and Quintana Auto Elc .... G .... 773 424-0634 |
| Chicago (G-4686) |
| Lakenburges Motor Co .... G .... 618 523-4231 |
| Germantown (G-10331) |
| Larry Pontnack .... G .... 815 732-7751 |
| Oregon (G-15923) |
| Mickey Truck Bodies Inc .... F .... 309 827-8227 |
| Bloomington (G-2076) |
| Mikes Inc .... D .... 618 254-4491 |
| South Roxana (G-19253) |
| Springfield Welding & Auto Bdy .... E .... 217 523-5365 |
| Springfield (G-19457) |
| Zimmerman Enterprises Inc .... F .... 847 297-3177 |
| Des Plaines (G-7871) |

AUTOMOTIVE BODY SHOP

| Kurts Carstar Collision Ctr .... F .... 618 345-4519 |
| Maryville (G-13591) |
| Phils Auto Body .... G .... 773 847-7156 |
| Chicago (G-5801) |
| Springfield Welding & Auto Bdy .... E .... 217 523-5365 |
| Springfield (G-19457) |
| Union Ave Auto Inc .... G .... 708 754-3899 |
| Steger (G-19495) |

AUTOMOTIVE BODY, PAINT & INTERIOR REPAIR & MAINTENANCE SVC

| D D Sales Inc .... E .... 217 857-3196 |
| Teutopolis (G-19768) |
| Folk Race Cars .... G .... 815 629-2418 |
| Durand (G-8151) |
| Winning Colors .... G .... 815 462-4810 |
| Manhattan (G-13436) |

AUTOMOTIVE DEALERS, NEC

Prestige Motor Works Inc .... G 630 780-6439
Naperville (G-14983)

AUTOMOTIVE EMISSIONS TESTING SVCS

Wreck Room Inc .... F 630 530-2166
Villa Park (G-20177)

AUTOMOTIVE EXHAUST REPAIR SVC

| Aledo Welding Enterprises Inc .... G .... 309 582-2019 |
| Aledo (G-354) |
| Bring Your Own Auto Parts Inc .... F .... 815 730-6900 |
| Crest Hill (G-7084) |

AUTOMOTIVE EXTERIOR REPAIR SVCS

Moultri Cnty Hstrcl/Gnlgcl Sct .... F 217 728-4085
Sullivan (G-19672)

AUTOMOTIVE GLASS REPLACEMENT SHOPS

| Glass America Midwest LLC .... G .... 877 743-7237 |
| Elmhurst (G-9366) |
| Illinois Valley Glass & Mirror .... F .... 309 682-6603 |
| Peoria (G-16457) |

Martin Glass Company....F....618 277-1946
Belleville *(G-1571)*
Roscoe Glass Co....G....815 623-6268
Roscoe *(G-17928)*
T G Automotive....E....630 916-7818
Lombard *(G-13137)*

AUTOMOTIVE LETTERING & PAINTING SVCS

Quality Spraying Screen Prtg....E....630 584-8324
Saint Charles *(G-18256)*

AUTOMOTIVE PAINT SHOP

Jorge A Cruz....G....773 722-2828
Chicago *(G-5049)*
Wreck Room Inc....F....630 530-2166
Villa Park *(G-20177)*

AUTOMOTIVE PARTS, ACCESS & SPLYS

A&G Manufacturing Inc....F....815 562-2107
Rochelle *(G-17129)*
Accurate Engine & Machine Inc....G....773 237-4942
Chicago *(G-3517)*
Acd USA Inc....G....929 428-1744
Wood Dale *(G-21154)*
Adient US LLC....C....815 895-2095
Sycamore *(G-19699)*
Air Land and Sea Interiors....G....630 834-1717
Villa Park *(G-20129)*
Aisin Mfg Illinois LLC....D....618 998-8333
Marion *(G-13501)*
Aisin Mfg Illinois LLC....A....618 998-8333
Marion *(G-13502)*
Amerex Corporation....E....309 382-4389
North Pekin *(G-15326)*
Amsoil Inc....G....630 595-8385
Bensenville *(G-1745)*
Android Indstres- Blvidere LLC....C....815 547-3742
Belvidere *(G-1649)*
Anthony Liftgates Inc....C....815 842-3383
Pontiac *(G-16765)*
Antolin Interiors Usa Inc....B....618 327-4416
Nashville *(G-14994)*
Arco Automotive Elec Svc Co....G....708 422-2976
Oak Lawn *(G-15701)*
Area Diesel Service Inc....E....217 854-2641
Carlinville *(G-2867)*
Arrow Gear Company....B....630 969-7640
Downers Grove *(G-7955)*
Auto Meter Products Inc....C....815 895-8141
Sycamore *(G-19702)*
Belvidere Brose Inc....F....779 552-7600
Belvidere *(G-1654)*
Bill Weeks Inc....G....217 523-8735
Springfield *(G-19326)*
Boler Company....C....630 910-2800
Woodridge *(G-21279)*
Boler Ventures LLC....D....630 773-9111
Itasca *(G-11629)*
Borg Warner Automotive - B....E....248 754-9200
Dixon *(G-7891)*
Borg-Warner Automotive Inc....G....815 469-2721
Frankfort *(G-9774)*
Borgwarner Inc....E....248 754-9200
Frankfort *(G-9775)*
Borgwarner Transm Systems Inc....F....708 731-4540
Melrose Park *(G-13834)*
Boyce Industries Inc....F....708 345-0455
Melrose Park *(G-13836)*
Brake Parts Inc LLC....B....815 363-8181
McHenry *(G-13724)*
Brake Parts Inc LLC....G....217 324-2161
Litchfield *(G-12961)*
Brunos Automotive Products....G....630 458-0043
Addison *(G-56)*
C & M Engineering....G....815 932-3388
Bourbonnais *(G-2257)*
Caldwell & Moten LLC....G....773 619-2584
Chicago *(G-4003)*
Cavanaugh Government Group LLC....F....630 210-8668
Bridgeview *(G-2332)*
Central Hydraulics Inc....G....309 527-5238
El Paso *(G-8434)*
Cft Performance Inc....G....618 781-3981
Maryville *(G-13590)*
Champion Laboratories Inc....F....618 445-5407
Albion *(G-348)*
Chucking Machine Products Inc....D....847 678-1192
Franklin Park *(G-9907)*
City Subn Auto Svc Goodyear....G....773 355-5550
Chicago *(G-4162)*
Clark Filter Inc....E....216 896-3000
Chicago *(G-4167)*
CTS Automotive LLC....C....630 577-8800
Lisle *(G-12880)*
Dana....G....419 887-3000
Sterling *(G-19503)*
Dana Incorporated....E....630 271-0001
Lisle *(G-12883)*
Dana Sealing Manufacturing LLC....G....618 544-8651
Robinson *(G-17112)*
Dana Sealing Manufacturing LLC....B....618 544-8651
Robinson *(G-17113)*
Dana Sealing Products LLC....D....630 960-4200
Lisle *(G-12884)*
Danfoss Power Solutions US Co....C....815 233-4200
Freeport *(G-10105)*
David Horton....G....312 917-8610
Chicago *(G-4325)*
Doga USA Corporation....F....847 669-8529
Huntley *(G-11535)*
Driv Automotive Inc....G....847 482-5000
Lake Forest *(G-12244)*
Driv Incorporated....G....857 842-5000
Lake Forest *(G-12245)*
Eakas Corporation....B....815 223-8811
Peru *(G-16575)*
Eaton Corporation....C....815 562-2107
Rochelle *(G-17138)*
Engine Rebuilders & Supply....G....708 338-1113
Stone Park *(G-19554)*
Exress Motor and Lift Parts....G....630 327-2000
Frankfort *(G-9792)*
Ezee Roll Manufacturing Co....G....217 339-2279
Hoopeston *(G-11508)*
Fabricated Metals Co....C....847 718-1300
Elk Grove Village *(G-8994)*
FCA US LLC....G....630 724-2321
Lisle *(G-12890)*
FCA US LLC....A....630 637-3000
Naperville *(G-14828)*
Federal-Mogul Motorparts LLC....A....847 674-7700
Skokie *(G-18954)*
Flex-N-Gate Corporation....A....217 255-5025
Urbana *(G-19983)*
Flex-N-Gate LLC....G....773 437-5686
Chicago *(G-4604)*
Flex-N-Gate LLC....A....217 278-2400
Urbana *(G-19985)*
Fram Group Holdings Inc....A....847 482-2045
Lake Forest *(G-12249)*
Frantz Manufacturing Company....D....815 564-0991
Sterling *(G-19510)*
Gates Corporation....C....309 343-7171
Galesburg *(G-10196)*
Gem Manufacturing Corporation....G....630 458-0014
Naperville *(G-14834)*
Genuine Parts Company....F....630 293-1300
Chicago *(G-4681)*
Glk Enterprises Inc....G....847 395-7368
Antioch *(G-614)*
Grupo Antolin Illinois Inc....C....815 544-8020
Belvidere *(G-1674)*
Gunite Corporation....B....815 964-3301
Rockford *(G-17437)*
Hardy Radiator Repair....F....217 223-8320
Quincy *(G-16889)*
Hd Turbo Llc....G....847 636-7586
Elk Grove Village *(G-9030)*
Hendrickson Holdings LLC....G....630 910-2800
Itasca *(G-11664)*
Hendrickson International Corp....E....630 874-9700
Woodridge *(G-21311)*
Hendrickson Usa LLC....E....630 910-2800
Woodridge *(G-21312)*
Hendrickson Usa LLC....E....630 874-9700
Itasca *(G-11665)*
Hendrickson Usa LLC....C....630 910-2844
Woodridge *(G-21313)*
Hendrickson Usa LLC....D....815 727-4031
Joliet *(G-11877)*
Hoosier Stamping & Mfg Corp....E....618 375-2057
Grayville *(G-10810)*
Hyperaktive Prfmce Solutions....G....847 321-1982
Antioch *(G-615)*
Iggys Auto Parts....F....708 452-9790
Norridge *(G-15237)*
Illinois Tool Works Inc....E....630 993-9990
Elmhurst *(G-9376)*
Illinois Tool Works Inc....C....708 479-7200
Mokena *(G-14091)*
Illinois Tool Works Inc....C....815 448-7300
Mazon *(G-13681)*
Illinois Tool Works Inc....G....708 479-3346
Tinley Park *(G-19838)*
Interstate Power Systems Inc....F....630 871-1111
Carol Stream *(G-3006)*
Interstate Power Systems Inc....D....952 854-2044
Rockford *(G-17470)*
ITW Global Investments LLC....G....847 724-7500
Glenview *(G-10574)*
Jasiek Motor Rebuilding Inc....G....815 883-3678
Oglesby *(G-15842)*
Kackert Enterprises Inc....G....630 898-9339
Aurora *(G-1120)*
Kccdd Inc....D....309 344-2030
Galesburg *(G-10205)*
Kiene Diesel Accessories Inc....E....630 543-7170
Addison *(G-169)*
Kleinhoffer Manufacturing Inc....G....815 725-3638
Joliet *(G-11890)*
Koehler Enterprises Inc....G....847 451-4966
Franklin Park *(G-9978)*
L & M Screw Machine Products....F....630 801-0455
Montgomery *(G-14253)*
Lemfco Inc....E....815 777-0242
Galena *(G-10176)*
Lgb Industries....G....847 639-1691
Cary *(G-3175)*
Line Craft Tool Company Inc....C....630 932-1182
Lombard *(G-13096)*
Lkq Corporation....C....312 621-1950
Chicago *(G-5243)*
Mag Daddy LLC....G....847 719-5600
Wauconda *(G-20371)*
Magna Exteriors America Inc....B....618 327-2136
Nashville *(G-15000)*
Makerite Mfg Co Inc....E....815 389-3902
Roscoe *(G-17916)*
Mann+hummel Filtration Tech....F....800 407-9263
McHenry *(G-13762)*
Mat Holdings Inc....D....847 821-9630
Long Grove *(G-13165)*
Maxim Inc....F....217 544-7015
Springfield *(G-19403)*
Methode Electronics Inc....A....217 357-3941
Carthage *(G-3139)*
Mike Mulcahy Motorsports LLC....G....630 567-0298
Morris *(G-14315)*
Molor Products Company....F....630 375-5999
Oswego *(G-16015)*
Motec Inc....G....630 241-9595
Downers Grove *(G-8060)*
Motor Coach Inds Intl Inc....C....847 285-2000
Des Plaines *(G-7804)*
Motor Parts & Equipment Corp....E....217 877-7456
Decatur *(G-7527)*
Motor Row Development Corp....G....773 525-3311
Chicago *(G-5507)*
Mouldtec Inc....G....815 893-0908
Crystal Lake *(G-7234)*
National Cycle Inc....C....708 343-0400
Maywood *(G-13674)*
Navistar Inc....C....331 332-5000
Lisle *(G-12917)*
Navistar Inc....D....708 865-3333
Melrose Park *(G-13895)*
Navistar International Corp....A....331 332-5000
Lisle *(G-12921)*
Naylor Automotive Engrg Co Inc....F....773 582-6900
Chicago *(G-5558)*
NGK Spark Plugs (usa) Inc....E....630 595-7894
Wood Dale *(G-21222)*
Nidec Mobility America Corp....A....630 443-6800
Saint Charles *(G-18234)*
Nivelco USA LLC....G....630 848-2100
Naperville *(G-14885)*
Ogden Top & Trim Shop Inc....G....708 484-5422
Berwyn *(G-1958)*
Old World Global LLC....G....800 323-5440
Northbrook *(G-15445)*
Old World Inds Holdings LLC....G....800 323-5440
Northbrook *(G-15446)*
Oshkosh Specialty Vehicles Inc....C....708 868-5071
Calumet City *(G-2784)*
Performance Gear Systems Inc....E....630 739-6666
Plainfield *(G-16700)*
Piston Automotive LLC....C....313 541-8789
Belvidere *(G-1694)*

PRODUCT

Employee Codes: A=Over 500 employees, B=251-500
C=101-250, D=51-100, E=20-50, F=10-19, G=3-9

2020 Harris Illinois
Industrial Directory

1345

AUTOMOTIVE PARTS, ACCESS & SPLYS — PRODUCT SECTION

Plews Inc .... C 815 288-3344
  Dixon *(G-7906)*
Pma Friction Products Inc .... D 630 406-9119
  Batavia *(G-1404)*
Pmw Holdings Inc .... G 815 672-0551
  Streator *(G-19621)*
Prestige Motor Works Inc .... G 630 780-6439
  Naperville *(G-14983)*
R2c Performance Products LLC .... F 708 488-8211
  Mundelein *(G-14730)*
Randall Manufacturing LLC .... D 630 782-0001
  Elmhurst *(G-9414)*
RE-Do-It Corp .... G 708 343-7125
  Broadview *(G-2463)*
Realwheels Corporation .... E 847 662-7722
  Gurnee *(G-10923)*
Redhorse Performance Inc .... G 708 430-1603
  Hickory Hills *(G-11202)*
Rj Race Cars Inc .... F 309 343-7575
  Galesburg *(G-10218)*
Robert Bosch LLC .... F 708 865-5415
  Broadview *(G-2465)*
Rogers Motorcycle Shop Inc .... G 309 828-3242
  Bloomington *(G-2090)*
SKF USA Inc .... D 847 742-0700
  Elgin *(G-8736)*
SLF Motion LLC .... G 217 891-8384
  Pawnee *(G-16306)*
Suburban Plastics Co .... E 708 681-1475
  Broadview *(G-2471)*
Sumitomo Machinery Corp Amer .... E 630 752-0200
  Glendale Heights *(G-10504)*
Sure Plus Manufacturing Co .... D 708 756-3100
  Chicago Heights *(G-6777)*
Symbol Tool Inc .... G 847 674-1080
  Skokie *(G-19041)*
T & T Machine Shop .... G 847 244-2020
  Gurnee *(G-10932)*
T J Van Der Bosch & Associates .... E 815 344-3210
  McHenry *(G-13805)*
Tenneco Automotive Oper Co Inc .... C 847 482-5000
  Lake Forest *(G-12308)*
Tenneco Automotive Oper Co Inc .... C 847 821-0757
  Lincolnshire *(G-12798)*
Tenneco Automotive Rsa Company ..... C 847 482-5000
  Lake Forest *(G-12309)*
Tenneco Europe Limited .... G 847 482-5000
  Lake Forest *(G-12310)*
Tenneco Inc .... G 847 774-1636
  Lincolnwood *(G-12844)*
Tesla Inc .... F 312 733-9780
  Chicago *(G-6354)*
Titan Wheel Corp Illinois .... A 217 228-6023
  Quincy *(G-16950)*
Toyo USA Manufacturing Inc .... F 309 827-8836
  Bloomington *(G-2103)*
Toyota Boshoku Illinois LLC .... B 618 943-5300
  Lawrenceville *(G-12537)*
U G N Inc .... D 773 437-2400
  Tinley Park *(G-19863)*
United Gasket Corporation .... D 708 656-3700
  Cicero *(G-6885)*
US Tsubaki Power Transm LLC .... C 847 459-9500
  Wheeling *(G-21004)*
Vehicle Improvement Pdts Inc .... G 847 395-7250
  Antioch *(G-642)*
Vibracoustic Usa Inc .... C 618 382-2318
  Carmi *(G-2917)*
Vipar Heavy Duty Inc .... F 815 788-1700
  Crystal Lake *(G-7291)*
Vitesco Technologies Usa LLC .... G 847 862-5000
  Deer Park *(G-7583)*
Wanxiang USA Holdings Corp .... F 847 622-8838
  Elgin *(G-8776)*
Woodbridge Inc .... F 847 229-1741
  Wheeling *(G-21015)*
Ycl International Inc .... E 630 873-0768
  Woodridge *(G-21350)*
Zeigler Chrysler Dodge .... G 708 956-7700
  Berwyn *(G-1963)*
ZF North America Inc .... C 847 478-6868
  Vernon Hills *(G-20114)*
ZF Services LLC .... B 847 478-6868
  Vernon Hills *(G-20115)*

AUTOMOTIVE PARTS: Plastic

Cjt Automotive Inc .... G 847 671-0800
  Rosemont *(G-18005)*
Creative Conveniences By K&E .... G 847 975-8526
  Lake Zurich *(G-12399)*

Extruded Solutions Inc .... G 630 871-6450
  West Chicago *(G-20580)*
International Automotive Compo .... B 815 544-2102
  Belvidere *(G-1680)*
John Thomas Inc .... E 815 288-2343
  Dixon *(G-7902)*
Kay Manufacturing Company LLC .... C 708 862-6800
  Calumet City *(G-2782)*
Loop Automotive LLC .... E 847 912-9090
  Chicago *(G-5257)*
Magna Exteriors America Inc .... D 779 552-7400
  Belvidere *(G-1683)*
Martinez Management Inc .... E 847 822-7202
  Algonquin *(G-379)*
Prestige Motor Works Inc .... G 630 780-6439
  Naperville *(G-14983)*
Spraytech LLC .... G 847 973-9432
  Fox Lake *(G-9755)*

AUTOMOTIVE PRDTS: Rubber

A Lakin & Sons Inc .... E 773 871-6360
  Montgomery *(G-14229)*
Lakin General Corporation .... D 773 871-6360
  Montgomery *(G-14255)*

AUTOMOTIVE RADIATOR REPAIR SHOPS

A Len Radiator Shoppe Inc .... G 630 852-5445
  Downers Grove *(G-7948)*
Bushnell Welding & Radiator .... G 309 772-9289
  Bushnell *(G-2740)*
Hardy Radiator Repair .... F 217 223-8320
  Quincy *(G-16889)*
Jones Garrison Sons Mch Works .... G 618 847-2161
  Fairfield *(G-9629)*
Rex Radiator and Welding Co .... G 312 421-1531
  Chicago *(G-6020)*
Rex Radiator and Welding Co .... G 630 595-4664
  Bensenville *(G-1883)*
Rex Radiator and Welding Co .... G 815 725-6655
  Rockdale *(G-17271)*
Rex Radiator and Welding Co .... G 847 428-1112
  East Dundee *(G-8209)*

AUTOMOTIVE REPAIR SHOPS: Alternators/Generator, Rebuild/Rpr

Lawrence Maddock .... F 847 394-1698
  Arlington Heights *(G-768)*

AUTOMOTIVE REPAIR SHOPS: Diesel Engine Repair

Gateway Industrial Power Inc .... G 309 821-1035
  Bloomington *(G-2049)*
Waymore Power Co Inc .... F 618 729-3876
  Piasa *(G-16610)*

AUTOMOTIVE REPAIR SHOPS: Electrical Svcs

AB Machine Shop LLC .... G 618 467-6474
  Godfrey *(G-10646)*
David Jeskey .... G 630 659-6337
  Saint Charles *(G-18180)*
Dooley Brothers Plumbing & Htg .... G 309 852-2720
  Kewanee *(G-12031)*
Mr Auto Electric .... G 217 523-3659
  Springfield *(G-19409)*

AUTOMOTIVE REPAIR SHOPS: Engine Rebuilding

Dss Inc .... G 630 587-1169
  Saint Charles *(G-18187)*
Engine Rebuilders & Supply .... G 708 338-1113
  Stone Park *(G-19554)*
Larrys Garage & Machine Shop .... G 815 968-8416
  Rockford *(G-17491)*
Precision Engine Rbldrs Inc .... G 815 254-2333
  Plainfield *(G-16704)*
R & C Auto Supply Corp .... G 815 625-4414
  Sterling *(G-19528)*

AUTOMOTIVE REPAIR SHOPS: Engine Repair

L A Motors Incorporated .... G 773 736-7305
  Chicago *(G-5142)*

Legend Racing Enterprises Inc .... G 847 923-8979
  Schaumburg *(G-18602)*
Mevert Automotive Inc .... G 618 965-9609
  Steeleville *(G-19484)*
OReilly Automotive Stores Inc .... G 847 882-4384
  Schaumburg *(G-18659)*
OReilly Automotive Stores Inc .... G 847 360-0012
  Waukegan *(G-20474)*
Union Ave Auto Inc .... G 708 754-3899
  Steger *(G-19495)*

AUTOMOTIVE REPAIR SHOPS: Frame Repair Shops

Botts Welding and Trck Svc Inc .... E 815 338-0594
  Woodstock *(G-21366)*

AUTOMOTIVE REPAIR SHOPS: Machine Shop

Accurate Engine & Machine Inc .... G 773 237-4942
  Chicago *(G-3517)*
G&G Machine Shop Inc .... G 217 892-9696
  Rantoul *(G-16976)*
H&S Machine & Tools Inc .... G 618 451-0164
  Granite City *(G-10712)*
Jasiek Motor Rebuilding Inc .... G 815 883-3678
  Oglesby *(G-15842)*
Ln Engineering LLC .... F 815 472-2939
  Momence *(G-14187)*
Mac-Weld Inc .... G 618 529-1828
  Carbondale *(G-2850)*
Precision Engine Rbldrs Inc .... G 815 254-2333
  Plainfield *(G-16704)*
Springfield Welding & Auto Bdy .... E 217 523-5365
  Springfield *(G-19457)*
Trailers Inc .... G 217 472-6000
  Chapin *(G-3396)*

AUTOMOTIVE REPAIR SHOPS: Muffler Shop, Sale/Rpr/Installation

Tbc Retail Group Inc .... G 630 692-0232
  Montgomery *(G-14271)*
Velasquez & Sons Muffler Shop .... G 847 740-6990
  Round Lake Beach *(G-18093)*

AUTOMOTIVE REPAIR SHOPS: Torque Converter Repair

Dynamic Manufacturing Inc .... D 708 547-7081
  Hillside *(G-11337)*

AUTOMOTIVE REPAIR SHOPS: Trailer Repair

Bierman Welding Inc .... F 217 342-2050
  Effingham *(G-8389)*
Load Redi Inc .... G 217 784-4200
  Gibson City *(G-10340)*

AUTOMOTIVE REPAIR SHOPS: Truck Engine Repair, Exc Indl

Cummins Dist Holdco Inc .... E 309 787-4300
  Rock Island *(G-17213)*
Midwest Power Equipment .... G 815 669-6331
  Joliet *(G-11904)*

AUTOMOTIVE REPAIR SVC

Acme Auto Electric Co .... G 708 754-5420
  S Chicago Hts *(G-18115)*
Amy Schutt .... G 618 994-7405
  Carrier Mills *(G-3123)*
Arco Automotive Elec Svc Co .... G 708 422-2976
  Oak Lawn *(G-15701)*
Deyco Inc .... G 630 553-5666
  Yorkville *(G-21480)*
Gerardo and Quintana Auto Elc .... G 773 424-0634
  Chicago *(G-4686)*
L A Motors Incorporated .... G 773 736-7305
  Chicago *(G-5142)*
Naylor Automotive Engrg Co Inc .... F 773 582-6900
  Chicago *(G-5558)*
Standard Indus & Auto Eqp Inc .... E 630 289-9500
  Hanover Park *(G-11014)*

PRODUCT SECTION

AUTOMOTIVE SPLYS & PARTS, NEW, WHOL: Testing Eqpt, Electric

Autonomous Stuff LLC..................G....... 309 291-0966
　Morton (G-14353)

AUTOMOTIVE SPLYS & PARTS, NEW, WHOLESALE: Brakes

Brake Parts Inc LLC.....................G....... 217 324-2161
　Litchfield (G-12961)
Performance Manufacturing ....G....... 630 231-8099
　West Chicago (G-20629)
Powerstop....................................G....... 708 442-6761
　Mc Cook (G-13698)

AUTOMOTIVE SPLYS & PARTS, NEW, WHOLESALE: Clutches

Surge Clutch & Drive Line Co.........G....... 708 331-1352
　South Holland (G-19247)

AUTOMOTIVE SPLYS & PARTS, NEW, WHOLESALE: Engines/Eng Parts

DTE Enterprises LLC ....G....... 630 307-9355
　Addison (G-100)
Hendrix Industrial Gastrux Inc........G....... 847 526-1700
　Mundelein (G-14696)
Mac-Weld Inc ....G....... 618 529-1828
　Carbondale (G-2850)
Speed Tech Technology Inc...........G....... 847 516-2001
　Cary (G-3191)
Tpr America Inc ....G....... 847 446-5336
　Schaumburg (G-18751)

AUTOMOTIVE SPLYS & PARTS, NEW, WHOLESALE: Seat Covers

Wise Co Inc.................................G....... 618 594-4091
　Carlyle (G-2898)

AUTOMOTIVE SPLYS & PARTS, NEW, WHOLESALE: Splys

Group O Inc.................................B....... 309 736-8311
　Milan (G-14014)
Joes Automotive Inc.....................G....... 815 937-9281
　Kankakee (G-11982)
R & O Specialties Incorporated .....D....... 309 736-8660
　Milan (G-14022)

AUTOMOTIVE SPLYS & PARTS, NEW, WHOLESALE: Stampings

Versatility TI Works Mfg Inc...........F....... 708 389-8909
　Alsip (G-522)

AUTOMOTIVE SPLYS & PARTS, NEW, WHOLESALE: Testing Eqpt, Eng

Affri Inc ....G....... 224 374-0931
　Wood Dale (G-21156)
Controls Group USA Inc................G....... 847 551-5775
　Elgin (G-8555)

AUTOMOTIVE SPLYS & PARTS, NEW, WHOLESALE: Tools & Eqpt

Fibro Inc......................................F....... 815 229-1300
　Rockford (G-17415)

AUTOMOTIVE SPLYS & PARTS, NEW, WHOLESALE: Trailer Parts

Neals Trailer Sales ....G....... 217 792-5136
　Lincoln (G-12736)
Tri City Canvas Products Inc ....F....... 618 797-1662
　Granite City (G-10746)

AUTOMOTIVE SPLYS & PARTS, NEW, WHOLESALE: Wheels

Otr Wheel Engineering Inc...........E....... 217 223-7705
　Quincy (G-16920)

AUTOMOTIVE SPLYS & PARTS, USED, WHOLESALE

Velasquez & Sons Muffler Shop ....G....... 847 740-6990
　Round Lake Beach (G-18093)

AUTOMOTIVE SPLYS & PARTS, WHOLESALE, NEC

A Len Radiator Shoppe Inc............G....... 630 852-5445
　Downers Grove (G-7948)
Andrews Automotive Company......F....... 773 768-1122
　Chicago (G-3693)
Arco Automotive Elec Svc Co ....G....... 708 422-2976
　Oak Lawn (G-15701)
Boley Tool & Machine Works Inc...C....... 309 694-2722
　East Peoria (G-8254)
Brake Parts Inc India LLC ....G....... 815 363-9000
　McHenry (G-13723)
Driv Automotive Inc......................G....... 847 482-5000
　Lake Forest (G-12244)
Driv Incorporated.........................G....... 857 842-5000
　Lake Forest (G-12245)
Flexitech Inc................................C....... 309 665-0658
　Bloomington (G-2044)
Genuine Parts Company...............F....... 630 293-1300
　Chicago (G-4681)
H & D Motor Service ....G....... 217 342-3262
　Altamont (G-533)
Honeywell International Inc...........A....... 847 391-2000
　Des Plaines (G-7780)
Instrument Services Inc ....G....... 815 623-2993
　Machesney Park (G-13350)
Just Parts Inc ....G....... 815 756-2184
　Cortland (G-7022)
L M C Automotive Inc...................G....... 618 235-5242
　Belleville (G-1567)
Ln Engineering LLC.....................F....... 815 472-2939
　Momence (G-14187)
Loop Automotive LLC ....E....... 847 912-9090
　Chicago (G-5257)
Motor Parts & Equipment Corp ....E....... 217 877-7456
　Decatur (G-7527)
Niles Auto Parts...........................G....... 847 215-2549
　Lincolnshire (G-12788)
O K Jobbers Inc...........................G....... 217 728-7378
　Sullivan (G-19674)
Robert Bosch LLC........................B....... 917 421-7209
　Broadview (G-2466)
Shima American Corporation ....F....... 630 760-4330
　Itasca (G-11732)
Standard Indus & Auto Eqp Inc ....E....... 630 289-9500
　Hanover Park (G-11014)
Suburban Driveline Inc.................G....... 630 941-7101
　Villa Park (G-20174)
Toth Automotive...........................F....... 708 474-5137
　Lansing (G-12522)
United Remanufacturing Co Inc ...E....... 773 777-1223
　Schiller Park (G-18850)
ZF Chassis Components LLC.......B....... 773 371-4550
　Chicago (G-6718)

AUTOMOTIVE SPLYS/PARTS, NEW, WHOL: Body Rpr/Paint Shop Splys

American Industrial Direct LLC .....E....... 800 382-1200
　Elgin (G-8507)
Wreck Room Inc..........................F....... 630 530-2166
　Villa Park (G-20177)

AUTOMOTIVE SVCS, EXC REPAIR & CARWASHES: Customizing

Midwest Marketing Distrs Inc ....F....... 309 688-8858
　Peoria (G-16476)

AUTOMOTIVE SVCS, EXC REPAIR & CARWASHES: Maintenance

Fleetpride Inc..............................F....... 630 455-6881
　Willowbrook (G-21043)
Gz Sign Designs Inc ....G....... 630 307-7446
　Roselle (G-17956)
William Ingram ....G....... 217 442-5075
　Danville (G-7398)

AUTOMOTIVE SVCS, EXC REPAIR: Truck Wash

Dundee Truck & Trlr Works LLC....G....... 224 484-8182
　East Dundee (G-8195)

AUTOMOTIVE SVCS, EXC REPAIR: Washing & Polishing

Mat Holdings Inc ....D....... 847 821-9630
　Long Grove (G-13165)

AUTOMOTIVE SVCS, EXC RPR/CARWASHES: High Perf Auto Rpr/Svc

Continental Auto Systems Inc ....G....... 847 862-5000
　Deer Park (G-7579)
Legend Racing Enterprises Inc ....G....... 847 923-8979
　Schaumburg (G-18602)
Prestige Motor Works Inc.............G....... 630 780-6439
　Naperville (G-14983)

AUTOMOTIVE TOPS INSTALLATION OR REPAIR: Canvas Or Plastic

Bill Weeks Inc..............................G....... 217 523-8735
　Springfield (G-19326)

AUTOMOTIVE TOWING SVCS

Carnaghi Towing & Repair Inc ......F....... 217 446-0333
　Tilton (G-19793)
City Subn Auto Svc Goodyear......G....... 773 355-5550
　Chicago (G-4162)
Tondinis Wrecker Service ....G....... 618 997-9884
　Marion (G-13541)
Towne Towing Inc ....G....... 847 705-1710
　Palatine (G-16165)

AUTOMOTIVE TRANSMISSION REPAIR SVC

Dynamic Manufacturing Inc..........D....... 708 547-7081
　Hillside (G-11337)
Gates Inc.....................................G....... 217 335-2378
　Barry (G-1250)
Powerstop....................................G....... 708 442-6761
　Mc Cook (G-13698)

AUTOMOTIVE UPHOLSTERY SHOPS

Custom Canvas LLC.....................G....... 847 587-0225
　Ingleside (G-11580)
Heartland Classics Inc..................G....... 618 783-4444
　Newton (G-15084)
Ogden Top & Trim Shop Inc.........G....... 708 484-5422
　Berwyn (G-1958)

AUTOMOTIVE WELDING SVCS

Adermanns Welding & Mch & Co ..G....... 217 342-3234
　Effingham (G-8383)
Botts Welding and Trck Svc Inc ...E....... 815 338-0594
　Woodstock (G-21366)
Bushnell Welding & Radiator........G....... 309 772-9289
　Bushnell (G-2740)
Floyds Welding Service................G....... 618 395-2414
　Olney (G-15861)
Higgs Welding LLC.....................G....... 217 925-5999
　Dieterich (G-7876)
Holstein Garage Inc.....................G....... 630 668-0328
　Wheaton (G-20802)
Incline Construction Inc...............G....... 815 577-8881
　Joliet (G-11881)
Larrys Garage & Machine Shop....G....... 815 968-8416
　Rockford (G-17491)
Mark S Machine Shop Inc............G....... 815 895-3955
　Sycamore (G-19724)
Pekin Weldors Inc........................F....... 309 382-3627
　North Pekin (G-15327)
Rex Radiator and Welding Co.......G....... 630 595-4664
　Bensenville (G-1883)
Robert Davis & Son Inc ....G....... 815 889-4168
　Milford (G-14036)
Robertson Repair.........................G....... 618 895-2593
　Sims (G-18910)
Springfield Welding & Auto Bdy ...E....... 217 523-5365
　Springfield (G-19457)
Stockton Stainless Inc..................E....... 815 947-2168
　Stockton (G-19550)
Xd Industries Inc..........................F....... 630 766-2843
　Bensenville (G-1916)

Employee Codes: A=Over 500 employees, B=251-500
C=101-250, D=51-100, E=20-50, F=10-19, G=3-9

AUTOMOTIVE: Bodies

Jorge A Cruz .... G 773 722-2828
 Chicago *(G-5049)*
Kurts Carstar Collision Ctr .... F 618 345-4519
 Maryville *(G-13591)*
Midwest Remanufacturing LLC .... G 708 496-9100
 Bedford Park *(G-1484)*
Phils Auto Body .... G 773 847-7156
 Chicago *(G-5801)*
R & S Automotive Inc .... G 847 622-8838
 Elgin *(G-8711)*
T J Van Der Bosch & Associates .. E 815 344-3210
 McHenry *(G-13805)*
Tenneco Intl Holdg Corp .... F 847 482-5000
 Lake Forest *(G-12313)*
Vanderbosch Tj & Assoc Inc .... G 815 344-3210
 McHenry *(G-13806)*

AUTOMOTIVE: Seat Frames, Metal

John Thomas Inc .... E 815 288-2343
 Dixon *(G-7902)*
Tvh Parts Co .... E 847 223-1000
 Grayslake *(G-10803)*

AUTOMOTIVE: Seating

Clarios .... C 815 288-3859
 Dixon *(G-7893)*
Clarios .... E 309 427-2800
 East Peoria *(G-8261)*
Clarios .... D 630 573-0897
 Oak Brook *(G-15611)*
Clarios .... G 331 212-3800
 Aurora *(G-940)*
Clarios .... D 630 279-0050
 Elmhurst *(G-9347)*
Clarios .... G 630 351-9407
 Bloomingdale *(G-1986)*
Clarios .... F 630 871-7700
 Carol Stream *(G-2961)*
Freedman Seating Company .... C 773 524-3255
 Chicago *(G-4633)*
Johnson Controls Inc .... G 847 549-2350
 Vernon Hills *(G-20068)*
Johnson Controls Inc .... E 847 364-1500
 Arlington Heights *(G-762)*
The United Group Inc .... E 847 816-7100
 Lake Forest *(G-12314)*
Yanfeng US Automotive .... A 779 552-7300
 Belvidere *(G-1712)*

AUTOTRANSFORMERS: Electric

Power-Volt Inc .... D 630 628-9999
 Addison *(G-249)*

AVIATION SCHOOL

Koerner Aviation Inc .... G 815 932-4222
 Kankakee *(G-11988)*

AWNING REPAIR SHOP

Shade Solutions Inc .... F 217 239-0718
 Tolono *(G-19884)*

AWNINGS & CANOPIES

Awnings Over Chicagoland Inc .... G 847 233-0310
 Franklin Park *(G-9879)*
Eclipse Awnings Inc .... F 708 636-3160
 Evergreen Park *(G-9593)*
Shade Solutions Inc .... F 217 239-0718
 Tolono *(G-19884)*

AWNINGS & CANOPIES: Awnings, Fabric, From Purchased Matls

Americana Building Pdts Inc .... D 618 548-2800
 Salem *(G-18328)*
Awnings By Zip Dee Inc .... E 847 640-0460
 Elk Grove Village *(G-8851)*
Berg Industries Inc .... F 815 874-1588
 Rockford *(G-17318)*
Blake Co Inc .... G 815 962-3852
 Rockford *(G-17325)*
Bloomington Tent & Awning Inc ... G 309 828-3411
 Bloomington *(G-2027)*
Brian Robert Awning Co .... G 847 679-1140
 Skokie *(G-18933)*

Champaign Cnty Tent & Awng Co .. E 217 328-5749
 Urbana *(G-19977)*
Chesterfield Awning Co Inc .... F 708 596-4434
 South Holland *(G-19205)*
Evanston Awning Company .... G 847 864-4520
 Evanston *(G-9515)*
Hunzinger Williams Inc .... F 847 381-1878
 Lake Barrington *(G-12151)*
Johnson Seat & Canvas Shop ...... G 815 756-2037
 Cortland *(G-7021)*
Kankakee Tent & Awning Co .... G 815 932-8000
 Kankakee *(G-11986)*
Midwest Awnings Inc .... G 309 762-3339
 Cameron *(G-2808)*
Nuyen Awning Co .... G 630 892-3995
 Aurora *(G-1141)*
Shade Solutions Inc .... F 217 239-0718
 Tolono *(G-19884)*
Stritzel Awnng Svc/Aurra Tent ..... G 630 420-2000
 Plainfield *(G-16718)*
Traube Canvas Products Inc .... F 618 281-0696
 Dupo *(G-8147)*

AWNINGS & CANOPIES: Canopies, Fabric, From Purchased Matls

Shelter Systems .... G 773 281-9270
 Chicago *(G-6151)*

AWNINGS & CANOPIES: Fabric

Eclipse Awnings Inc .... F 708 636-3160
 Evergreen Park *(G-9593)*
Thatcher Oaks Inc .... E 630 833-5700
 Elmhurst *(G-9435)*

AWNINGS: Fiberglass

Acme Awning Co Inc .... G 847 446-0153
 Lake Zurich *(G-12379)*
Glasstek Inc .... G 630 978-9897
 Naperville *(G-14969)*

AWNINGS: Metal

Advance Awnair Corp .... F 708 422-2730
 Orland Park *(G-15934)*
Americana Building Pdts Inc .... D 618 548-2800
 Salem *(G-18328)*
Charles Atwater Assoc Inc .... G 815 678-4813
 Richmond *(G-17011)*
Logan Square Aluminum Sup Inc . D 847 985-1700
 Schaumburg *(G-18611)*
Npi Holding Corp .... G 217 391-1229
 Springfield *(G-19412)*
Nudo Products Inc .... C 217 528-5636
 Springfield *(G-19414)*
Rijon Manufacturing Company ..... G 708 388-2295
 Blue Island *(G-2136)*
Shademaker Products Corp .... G 773 955-0998
 Chicago *(G-6146)*
Tri State Aluminum Products .... F 815 877-6081
 Loves Park *(G-13277)*

AXLES

Boler Company .... F 630 773-9111
 Itasca *(G-11628)*
Chicago Drive Line Inc .... C 708 385-1900
 Alsip *(G-427)*
Mattoon Precision Mfg .... C 217 235-6000
 Mattoon *(G-13645)*
Strange Engineering Inc .... D 847 663-1701
 Morton Grove *(G-14443)*
Thyssenkrupp North America Inc .. E 312 525-2800
 Chicago *(G-6375)*

BABY FORMULA

Abbott Laboratories .... E 800 551-5838
 Chicago *(G-3504)*
Mead Johnson Nutrition Company .. C 312 466-5800
 Chicago *(G-5379)*

BACKHOES

Jcb Inc .... G 912 704-2995
 Aurora *(G-990)*
Sebens Backhoe Service Inc .... G 217 762-7365
 Monticello *(G-14286)*

BADGES, WHOLESALE

Finer Line Inc .... F 847 884-1611
 Itasca *(G-11657)*
P F Pettibone & Co .... G 815 344-7811
 Crystal Lake *(G-7242)*

BADGES: Identification & Insignia

Marking Specialists/Poly .... F 847 793-8100
 Buffalo Grove *(G-2568)*

BAGS & CONTAINERS: Textile, Exc Sleeping

ABG Bag Inc .... F 815 963-9525
 Rockford *(G-17286)*
Amcraft Manufacturing Inc .... F 847 439-4565
 Elk Grove Village *(G-8821)*
Bearse Manufacturing Co .... D 773 235-8710
 Chicago *(G-3857)*
Keeper Thermal Bag Co Inc .... G 630 213-0125
 Bartlett *(G-1292)*
Midwest Linen Recovery LLC .... F 217 675-2766
 Franklin *(G-9856)*

BAGS & SACKS: Shipping & Shopping

Recycling Solutions Inc .... E 773 617-6955
 Chicago *(G-5992)*
Westrock Rkt LLC .... A 312 346-6600
 Chicago *(G-6614)*

BAGS: Cellophane

Keenpac LLC .... F 845 291-8680
 Morton Grove *(G-14417)*
Keenpac LLC .... G 845 291-8680
 Morton Grove *(G-14418)*
Peelmaster Packaging Corp .... E 847 966-6161
 Niles *(G-15155)*

BAGS: Duffle, Canvas, Made From Purchased Materials

Hunter-Nusport Inc .... G 815 254-7520
 Plainfield *(G-16674)*

BAGS: Flour, Made From Purchased Materials

Morris Packaging LLC .... G 309 663-9100
 Bloomington *(G-2081)*
Pride Packaging LLC .... G 309 663-9100
 Bloomington *(G-2086)*

BAGS: Food Storage & Frozen Food, Plastic

Kleer Pak Mfg Co Inc .... E 630 543-0208
 Addison *(G-171)*
Morris Packaging LLC .... G 309 663-9100
 Bloomington *(G-2081)*
Pactiv LLC .... A 847 482-2000
 Lake Forest *(G-12279)*
R Popernik Co Inc .... F 773 434-4300
 Chicago *(G-5949)*
Vej Holdings LLC .... G 630 219-1598
 Naperville *(G-14940)*

BAGS: Food Storage & Trash, Plastic

Pactiv LLC .... C 708 924-2402
 Bridgeview *(G-2372)*
Pactiv LLC .... C 815 469-2112
 Frankfort *(G-9819)*
Pactiv LLC .... C 217 479-1144
 Jacksonville *(G-11779)*

BAGS: Garment & Wardrobe, Plastic Film

Fischer Paper Products Inc .... D 847 395-6060
 Antioch *(G-611)*

BAGS: Paper

Duro Bag Manufacturing Company .. D 708 385-8674
 Alsip *(G-443)*
Graphic Packaging Intl LLC .... C 630 260-6500
 Carol Stream *(G-2994)*
Lexington Leather Goods Co .... F 773 287-5500
 Chicago *(G-5213)*
Mondi Romeoville Inc .... D 630 378-9886
 Romeoville *(G-17857)*
Proampac Pg Borrower LLC .... B 618 451-0010
 Granite City *(G-10733)*

PRODUCT SECTION — BAKERIES, COMMERCIAL: On Premises Baking Only

Waxstar Inc ....G....... 708 755-3530
  S Chicago Hts *(G-18129)*

BAGS: Paper, Made From Purchased Materials

Bag and Barrier Corporation ....G....... 217 849-3271
  Toledo *(G-19874)*
Bagcraftpapercon I LLC ....C....... 620 856-2800
  Chicago *(G-3814)*
Bagmakers Inc ....B....... 815 923-2247
  Union *(G-19937)*
Fischer Paper Products Inc ....D....... 847 395-6060
  Antioch *(G-611)*

BAGS: Plastic

ABG Bag Inc ....F....... 815 963-9525
  Rockford *(G-17286)*
Advanced Custom Shapes ....F....... 618 684-2222
  Murphysboro *(G-14749)*
Bag and Barrier Corporation ....G....... 217 849-3271
  Toledo *(G-19874)*
Bagcraftpapercon I LLC ....C....... 620 856-2800
  Chicago *(G-3814)*
Drumheller Bag Corporation ....D....... 309 676-1006
  Peoria *(G-16431)*
E-Z Products Inc ....F....... 847 551-9199
  Gilberts *(G-10354)*
Envision Inc ....G....... 847 735-0789
  Lake Forest *(G-12246)*
Flex-O-Glass Inc ....C....... 773 261-5200
  Chicago *(G-4605)*
Foodhandler Inc ....F....... 866 931-3613
  Elk Grove Village *(G-9002)*
Highland Supply Corporation ....B....... 618 654-2161
  Highland *(G-11224)*
Isbir Bulk Bag Usa LLC ....G....... 972 722-9200
  Warrenville *(G-20239)*
Kam Group Inc ....F....... 630 679-9668
  Bolingbrook *(G-2200)*
Kapak Company LLC ....G....... 952 541-0730
  Hanover Park *(G-11008)*
Natural Packaging Inc ....G....... 708 246-3420
  La Grange *(G-12083)*
Pactiv Intl Holdings Inc ....G....... 847 482-2000
  Lake Forest *(G-12278)*
Pak Source Inc ....E....... 309 786-7374
  Rock Island *(G-17231)*
Plastics D-E-F ....G....... 312 226-4337
  Chicago *(G-5819)*
Pliant LLC ....A....... 812 424-2904
  Rolling Meadows *(G-17761)*
Pregis LLC ....A....... 847 597-2200
  Deerfield *(G-7645)*
Printpack Inc ....C....... 847 888-7150
  Elgin *(G-8696)*
Recycling Solutions Inc ....E....... 773 617-6955
  Chicago *(G-5992)*
Renew Packaging LLC ....G....... 312 421-6699
  Chicago *(G-6014)*
Reynolds Consumer Products Inc ....A....... 800 879-5067
  Lake Forest *(G-12296)*
Silgan Plastics LLC ....D....... 618 662-4471
  Flora *(G-9692)*
Transcontinental Holding Corp ....G....... 773 877-3300
  Chicago *(G-6410)*
Transcontinental Tech LLC ....G....... 877 447-3539
  Chicago *(G-6411)*
Waxstar Inc ....G....... 708 755-3530
  S Chicago Hts *(G-18129)*

BAGS: Plastic & Pliofilm

Aargus Plastics Inc ....C....... 847 325-4444
  Wheeling *(G-20837)*
Poly Plastics Films Corp ....G....... 815 636-0821
  Machesney Park *(G-13365)*
Pride Packaging LLC ....G....... 309 663-9100
  Bloomington *(G-2086)*
Procon Pacific LLC ....F....... 630 575-0551
  Lombard *(G-13122)*
Quality Bags Inc ....F....... 630 543-9800
  Addison *(G-260)*
Windy Polymers Inc ....G....... 630 272-7453
  Saint Charles *(G-18300)*

BAGS: Plastic, Made From Purchased Materials

Aargus Industries Inc ....G....... 847 325-4444
  Wheeling *(G-20836)*
Bagmakers Inc ....B....... 815 923-2247
  Union *(G-19937)*
Bio Industries Inc ....D....... 847 215-8999
  Wheeling *(G-20859)*
Diamond Cellophane Pdts Inc ....E....... 847 418-3000
  Northbrook *(G-15375)*
Duro Bag Manufacturing Company .....D....... 708 385-8674
  Alsip *(G-443)*
Engineered Materials Inc ....G....... 847 821-8280
  Buffalo Grove *(G-2534)*
Essentra Packaging US Inc ....G....... 704 418-8692
  Westchester *(G-20699)*
Fisher Container Holdings LLC ....G....... 847 541-0000
  Buffalo Grove *(G-2537)*
Jacobson Acqstion Holdings LLC ....C....... 847 623-1414
  Waukegan *(G-20452)*
Laminet Cover Company ....E....... 773 622-6700
  Chicago *(G-5171)*
P-S Business Acquisition Inc ....G....... 616 887-8837
  Carol Stream *(G-3044)*
Polytech Inc ....G....... 806 338-2008
  Chicago *(G-5840)*
Ppc Flexible Packaging LLC ....G....... 847 541-0000
  Buffalo Grove *(G-2588)*
Vilutis and Co Inc ....E....... 815 469-2116
  Frankfort *(G-9849)*

BAGS: Rubber Or Rubberized Fabric

Singer Equities Inc ....F....... 815 874-5364
  Rockford *(G-17632)*
Smith Industrial Rubber & Plas ....F....... 815 874-5364
  Rockford *(G-17636)*
Team Products Inc ....F....... 815 244-6100
  Mount Carroll *(G-14497)*

BAGS: Shipping

Gateway Packaging Company LLC .....G....... 618 451-0010
  Granite City *(G-10709)*
Langston Bag of Peoria LLC ....D....... 309 676-1006
  Peoria *(G-16468)*

BAGS: Textile

Advance Tools LLC ....G....... 630 337-5904
  Glenview *(G-10520)*
Ajr Enterprises Inc ....G....... 630 377-8886
  Saint Charles *(G-18143)*
Block and Company Inc ....C....... 847 537-7200
  Wheeling *(G-20860)*
J Design Works Inc ....G....... 847 812-0891
  Bolingbrook *(G-2196)*
Jarries Shoe Bags ....G....... 773 379-4044
  Chicago *(G-5008)*
Mondi Bags Usa LLC ....C....... 502 361-1371
  Romeoville *(G-17856)*
Omg Handbags LLC ....G....... 847 337-9499
  Chicago *(G-5675)*
Sea-Rich Corp ....G....... 773 261-6633
  Chicago *(G-6124)*

BAGS: Trash, Plastic Film, Made From Purchased Materials

Colonial Bag Corporation ....D....... 630 690-3999
  Carol Stream *(G-2965)*

BAGS: Vacuum cleaner, Made From Purchased Materials

Studley Products Inc ....C....... 309 663-2313
  Bloomington *(G-2097)*

BAGS: Wardrobe, Closet Access, Made From Purchased Materials

Closet Concept ....G....... 217 375-4214
  Milford *(G-14033)*

BAIT, FISHING, WHOLESALE

Outback USA Inc ....G....... 863 699-2220
  Saint Charles *(G-18240)*

BAKERIES, COMMERCIAL: On Premises Baking Only

Ace Bakeries ....F....... 312 225-4973
  Chicago *(G-3521)*
American Kitchen Delights Inc ....D....... 708 210-3200
  Harvey *(G-11073)*
Athenian Foods Co ....F....... 708 343-6700
  Melrose Park *(G-13827)*
Bear-Stewart Corporation ....E....... 773 276-0400
  Chicago *(G-3854)*
Bimbo Bakeries Usa Inc ....G....... 630 469-4579
  Glendale Heights *(G-10438)*
Bimbo Bakeries Usa Inc ....E....... 773 254-3578
  Chicago *(G-3890)*
Butera Finer Foods Inc ....D....... 708 456-5939
  Norridge *(G-15231)*
Campbell Soup Company ....G....... 618 548-3001
  Salem *(G-18333)*
Campbell Soup Company ....C....... 630 241-6200
  Downers Grove *(G-7964)*
Charleston County Market ....D....... 217 345-7031
  Charleston *(G-3399)*
Chateau Food Products Inc ....F....... 708 863-4207
  Chicago *(G-4079)*
Chicago Baking Company ....A....... 630 684-2335
  Darien *(G-7404)*
Chicago Pastry Inc ....D....... 630 529-6161
  Bloomingdale *(G-1985)*
Cositas Cupcakes & More ....G....... 773 992-7088
  Chicago *(G-4244)*
Cub Foods Inc ....C....... 309 689-0140
  Peoria *(G-16428)*
Cupcakeologist LLC ....G....... 630 656-2272
  Woodridge *(G-21290)*
Dinkels Bakery Inc ....E....... 773 281-7300
  Chicago *(G-4362)*
Distinctive Foods LLC ....E....... 847 459-3600
  Bensenville *(G-1787)*
Dominicks Finer Foods Inc ....D....... 630 584-1750
  Saint Charles *(G-18185)*
Donchef Inc ....G....... 224 619-2223
  Chicago *(G-4381)*
Dunajec Bakery & Deli ....F....... 773 585-9611
  Bridgeview *(G-2341)*
Dunbar Systems Inc ....F....... 630 257-2900
  Lemont *(G-12563)*
El Moro De Letran Churros & Ba ....F....... 312 733-3173
  Chicago *(G-4465)*
Enjoy Life Natural Brands LLC ....E....... 773 632-2163
  Chicago *(G-4511)*
Entrust Services LLC ....G....... 630 699-9132
  Naperville *(G-14825)*
Father Marcellos & Son ....C....... 312 654-2565
  Chicago *(G-4567)*
Faustos Bakery ....G....... 847 255-9049
  Arlington Heights *(G-735)*
Flowers Foods Inc ....F....... 618 286-3300
  Dupo *(G-8137)*
Flowers Foods Inc ....F....... 217 347-2308
  Effingham *(G-8400)*
G & K Baking LLC ....G....... 708 741-7260
  Hickory Hills *(G-11196)*
Golosinas El Canto ....G....... 847 625-5103
  Waukegan *(G-20445)*
Gonnella Baking Co ....D....... 630 820-3433
  Aurora *(G-974)*
Gourmet Frog Pastry Shop ....G....... 847 433-7038
  Highland Park *(G-11266)*
Harners Bakery Restaurant ....D....... 630 892-5545
  North Aurora *(G-15263)*
Hearthside Food Solutions LLC ....B....... 815 853-4348
  Wenona *(G-20526)*
Herbs Bakery Inc ....F....... 847 741-0249
  Elgin *(G-8614)*
Hermanitas Cupcakes ....G....... 708 620-9396
  Calumet City *(G-2781)*
Highland Baking Company Inc ....A....... 847 677-2789
  Northbrook *(G-15400)*
Iced ....G....... 217 774-2247
  Shelbyville *(G-18879)*
Jewel Osco Inc ....C....... 773 728-7730
  Chicago *(G-5026)*
Jewel Osco Inc ....C....... 773 784-1922
  Chicago *(G-5027)*
Jewel Osco Inc ....C....... 708 352-0120
  Countryside *(G-7061)*
Jewel Osco Inc ....D....... 630 859-1212
  Aurora *(G-1118)*
Jewel Osco Inc ....C....... 847 677-3331
  Skokie *(G-18970)*

Employee Codes: A=Over 500 employees, B=251-500
C=101-250, D=51-100, E=20-50, F=10-19, G=3-9

BAKERIES, COMMERCIAL: On Premises Baking Only

Jewel Osco Inc .... C 630 584-4594
  Saint Charles (G-18218)
Jewel Osco Inc .... C 847 428-3547
  West Dundee (G-20664)
Jewel Osco Inc .... C 630 355-2172
  Naperville (G-14854)
Jewel Osco Inc .... D 630 226-1892
  Bolingbrook (G-2198)
Jewel Osco Inc .... C 847 296-7786
  Des Plaines (G-7791)
Jewel Osco Inc .... C 815 464-5352
  Frankfort (G-9810)
Kellogg Company .... C 630 941-0300
  Elmhurst (G-9387)
Kerry Inc .... G 847 595-1003
  Elk Grove Village (G-9076)
Korinek & Co Inc .... G 708 652-2870
  Cicero (G-6860)
Kroger Co .... G 309 694-6298
  East Peoria (G-8275)
Kroger Co .... C 815 332-7267
  Rockford (G-17485)
La Dolce Bella Cupcakes .... G 847 987-3738
  Lockport (G-13005)
Leas Baking Company LLC .... G 708 710-3404
  Homer Glen (G-11483)
Leesons Cakes Inc .... G 708 429-1330
  Tinley Park (G-19844)
Lewis Brothers Bakeries Inc .... E 708 531-6435
  Melrose Park (G-13890)
Lucksfood .... G 773 878-7778
  Chicago (G-5277)
Mangel and Co .... F 847 634-0730
  Long Grove (G-13162)
Marzeya Bakery Inc .... G 773 374-7855
  Chicago (G-5357)
Mel-O-Cream Donuts Intl Inc .... D 217 483-1825
  Springfield (G-19404)
Melinda I Rhodes .... G 815 569-2789
  Capron (G-2836)
Michele Baking Company .... F 847 451-9481
  Franklin Park (G-9996)
Milano Bakery Inc .... E 815 727-2253
  Joliet (G-11905)
Nauvoo Mill & Bakery .... G 217 453-6734
  Nauvoo (G-15014)
Niemann Foods Inc .... C 217 222-0190
  Quincy (G-16918)
Niemann Foods Inc .... C 217 793-4091
  Springfield (G-19411)
Original Ferrara Inc .... F 312 666-2200
  Chicago (G-5700)
Orland Park Bakery Ltd .... E 708 349-8516
  Orland Park (G-15973)
Profile Food Ingredients LLC .... E 847 622-1700
  Elgin (G-8697)
Rain Creek Baking Corp .... G 559 347-9960
  Glendale Heights (G-10487)
Riverside Bake Shop .... E 815 385-0044
  McHenry (G-13788)
Roma Bakeries Inc .... F 815 964-6737
  Rockford (G-17614)
Royal Oak Farm Inc .... F 815 648-4141
  Harvard (G-11066)
Schnuck Markets Inc .... C 618 466-0825
  Godfrey (G-10663)
Schulze and Burch Biscuit Co .... B 773 927-6622
  Chicago (G-6115)
Schulze and Burch Biscuit Co .... G 708 354-7050
  Hodgkins (G-11395)
Sprinkles Confetti .... G 815 304-5974
  Kankakee (G-12006)
Sunset Food Mart Inc .... C 847 234-0854
  Lake Forest (G-12307)
Superior Baking Stone Inc .... G 815 726-4610
  Joliet (G-11935)
Sustainable Innovations Inc .... G 815 713-1637
  Rockford (G-17650)
Tags Bakery Inc .... E 847 328-1200
  Evanston (G-9582)
Tam Tav Bakery Inc .... E 773 764-8877
  Chicago (G-6316)
Tarte Cupcakery Company .... G 312 898-2103
  Lansing (G-12521)
Tortilleria Atotonilco Inc .... E 773 523-0800
  Chicago (G-6398)
Two Wild Seeds Baking Company .... G 630 797-5350
  Saint Charles (G-18293)
Up At Dawn Inc .... D 773 457-3859
  Tinley Park (G-19865)

Walter Lagestee Inc .... C 708 957-2974
  Homewood (G-11504)

BAKERIES: On Premises Baking & Consumption

Ace Bakeries .... F 312 225-4973
  Chicago (G-3521)
Athenian Foods Co .... F 708 343-6700
  Melrose Park (G-13827)
Campbell Soup Company .... C 618 548-3001
  Salem (G-18333)
Campbell Soup Company .... C 630 241-6200
  Downers Grove (G-7964)
Chicago Baking Company .... A 630 684-2335
  Darien (G-7404)
Chipita America Inc .... E 708 731-2434
  Westchester (G-20693)
DAmatos Bakery Inc .... G 312 733-6219
  Chicago (G-4309)
Harners Bakery Restaurant .... D 630 892-5545
  North Aurora (G-15263)
Jewel Osco Inc .... C 773 784-1922
  Chicago (G-5027)
Marzeya Bakery Inc .... C 773 374-7855
  Chicago (G-5357)
OBrothers Bakery Inc .... G 847 249-0091
  Waukegan (G-20472)
Original Ferrara Inc .... F 312 666-2200
  Chicago (G-5700)
Pepperidge Farm Incorporated .... G 708 478-7450
  Mokena (G-14106)
Pepperidge Farm Incorporated .... G 630 241-6372
  Downers Grove (G-8072)
Sunset Food Mart Inc .... C 847 234-0854
  Lake Forest (G-12307)
Tam Tav Bakery Inc .... E 773 764-8877
  Chicago (G-6316)
Tortilleria Atotonilco Inc .... E 773 523-0800
  Chicago (G-6398)

BAKERY MACHINERY

Angel Equipment LLC .... G 847 730-3938
  Glenview (G-10524)
CMC America Corporation .... F 815 726-4337
  Joliet (G-11842)
Custom Systems Inc .... G 314 355-4575
  Granite City (G-10702)
Practical Baker Inc .... G 815 943-6040
  Harvard (G-11063)
Precision Service .... G 618 345-2047
  Collinsville (G-6972)

BAKERY PRDTS, FROZEN: Wholesalers

Mel-O-Cream Donuts Intl Inc .... D 217 483-1825
  Springfield (G-19404)

BAKERY PRDTS: Bagels, Fresh Or Frozen

Bimbo Bakehouse LLC .... E 800 550-6810
  Chicago (G-3889)
Bimbo Bakeries Usa Inc .... B 217 235-3181
  Mattoon (G-13631)
New Chicago Wholesale Bky Inc .... E 847 981-1600
  Elk Grove Village (G-9146)

BAKERY PRDTS: Bakery Prdts, Partially Cooked, Exc frozen

Cathys Sweet Creations .... G 815 886-6769
  Plainfield (G-16648)

BAKERY PRDTS: Bread, All Types, Fresh Or Frozen

Anns Bakery Inc .... G 773 384-5562
  Chicago (G-3700)
Charles Cicero Fingerhut .... F 708 652-3643
  Chicago (G-4073)
Gonnella Baking Co .... D 312 733-2020
  Schaumburg (G-18538)
Gonnella Baking Co .... D 312 733-2020
  Schaumburg (G-18539)
Gonnella Frozen Products LLC .... G 847 884-8829
  Schaumburg (G-18540)
Grecian Delight Foods Inc .... C 847 364-1010
  Elk Grove Village (G-9022)
J & J Snack Foods Corp .... C 708 377-0400
  Alsip (G-460)

Zb Importing Inc .... E 708 222-8330
  Chicago (G-6709)
Zb Importing Inc .... D 708 222-8330
  Cicero (G-6890)

BAKERY PRDTS: Cakes, Bakery, Exc Frozen

Auntie Mmmms .... G 217 509-6012
  Camp Point (G-2809)
Callies Cuties Inc .... G 815 566-6885
  Plainfield (G-16646)
Homer Vintage Bakery .... G 217 896-2538
  Homer (G-11476)
Jr Bakery .... E 773 465-6733
  Chicago (G-5055)
Linx Enterprises LLC .... G 224 409-2206
  Chicago (G-5232)
Morningfields .... G 847 309-8460
  Park Ridge (G-16288)
Nak Won Korean Bakery .... G 773 588-8769
  Chicago (G-5538)
National Biscuit Company .... G 773 925-0654
  Chicago (G-5545)
Say Cheese Cake .... G 618 532-6001
  Centralia (G-3249)
Sugar Monkey Cupcakes Inc .... G 630 527-1869
  Naperville (G-14989)
Sweet Annies Bakery Inc .... F 708 297-7066
  Flossmoor (G-9704)

BAKERY PRDTS: Cakes, Bakery, Frozen

Cake Factory .... G 708 897-0872
  Alsip (G-425)
Elis Cheesecake Company .... C 773 205-3800
  Chicago (G-4485)
Kimmykakes Co .... G 312 927-3933
  Chicago (G-5104)
Sweet Creation By Sheila .... G 708 754-7938
  Glenwood (G-10645)
Vienna Beef Ltd .... E 773 278-7800
  Chicago (G-6548)
Wilseys Handmade Sweets LLC .... G 314 504-0851
  Edwardsville (G-8380)

BAKERY PRDTS: Charlotte Russe, Exc Frozen

Dixie Cream Donut Shop .... E 618 937-4866
  West Frankfort (G-20670)

BAKERY PRDTS: Cookies

Aryzta LLC .... D 312 836-2300
  Chicago (G-3745)
Carols Cookies Inc .... G 847 831-4500
  Northbrook (G-15353)
Christian Wolf Inc .... E 618 667-9522
  Bartelso (G-1252)
Cookie Kingdom Inc .... D 815 883-3331
  Oglesby (G-15840)
F C L Kelloggs .... G 815 467-8198
  Minooka (G-14060)
Fortella Company Inc .... G 312 567-9000
  Chicago (G-4622)
Herman Seekamp Inc .... C 630 628-6555
  Addison (G-149)
Keebler Foods Company .... E 630 833-2900
  Elmhurst (G-9386)
Kellogg Company .... C 630 941-0300
  Elmhurst (G-9387)
Matts Cookie Company .... G 847 537-3888
  Wheeling (G-20939)
Paleo Prime LLC .... G 312 659-6596
  Chicago (G-5745)
Pepperidge Farm Incorporated .... G 708 478-7450
  Mokena (G-14106)
Pepperidge Farm Incorporated .... G 630 241-6372
  Downers Grove (G-8072)
Pures Food Specialties LLC .... E 708 344-8884
  Broadview (G-2461)
Snyders-Lance Inc .... G 847 581-1818
  Skokie (G-19031)
Treehouse Private Brands Inc .... C 815 389-2745
  South Beloit (G-19117)
Wex Distributors Inc .... G 847 691-5823
  Antioch (G-643)

BAKERY PRDTS: Cookies & crackers

Campbell Soup Company .... G 618 548-3001
  Salem (G-18333)

Campbell Soup Company .... C 630 241-6200
  Downers Grove (G-7964)
Casa Nostra Bakery Co Inc .... F 847 455-5175
  Franklin Park (G-9899)
Charleston County Market .... D 217 345-7031
  Charleston (G-3399)
Chicago Pastry Inc .... D 630 529-6161
  Bloomingdale (G-1985)
Chipita America Inc .... E 708 731-2434
  Westchester (G-20693)
DAmatos Bakery Inc .... G 312 733-6219
  Chicago (G-4309)
Dinkels Bakery Inc .... E 773 281-7300
  Chicago (G-4362)
Hop Kee Incorporated .... G 312 791-9111
  Chicago (G-4839)
Jewel Osco Inc .... C 847 677-3331
  Skokie (G-18970)
Jewel Osco Inc .... C 630 355-2172
  Naperville (G-14854)
Jr Bakery .... E 773 465-6733
  Chicago (G-5055)
Katys LLC .... G 708 522-9814
  Oak Park (G-15760)
Kroger Co .... G 815 332-7267
  Rockford (G-17485)
Maiers Bakery .... G 847 967-8042
  Morton Grove (G-14424)
Mondelez Global LLC .... B 630 369-1909
  Naperville (G-14874)
Roma Bakeries Inc .... F 815 964-6737
  Rockford (G-17614)
Schulze and Burch Biscuit Co .... B 773 927-6622
  Chicago (G-6115)
Sustainable Innovations Inc .... G 815 713-1637
  Rockford (G-17650)
Tags Bakery Inc .... E 847 328-1200
  Evanston (G-9582)
Walter Lagestee Inc .... C 708 957-2974
  Homewood (G-11504)

BAKERY PRDTS: Crackers

Lofthouse Bakery Products Inc ...... G 630 455-5229
  Downers Grove (G-8047)
Mondelez Global LLC .... C 847 943-4000
  Deerfield (G-7637)
Th Foods Inc .... G 702 565-2816
  Loves Park (G-13273)
Treehouse Private Brands Inc .... F 630 455-5265
  Downers Grove (G-8102)
Treehouse Private Brands Inc .... C 314 877-7300
  Oak Brook (G-15666)

BAKERY PRDTS: Croissants, Frozen

Forno Palese Baking Company ..... F 630 595-5502
  Bartlett (G-1281)
Le Chocolat Du Bouchard LLC ..... G 630 355-5720
  Naperville (G-14861)

BAKERY PRDTS: Doughnuts, Exc Frozen

Amling Donuts Inc .... E 847 426-5327
  Carpentersville (G-3093)
B N K Inc .... G 630 231-5640
  West Chicago (G-20547)
Dimples Donuts .... G 630 406-0303
  Batavia (G-1373)
Dunkin Donuts .... E 708 460-3088
  Orland Park (G-15954)
Express Donuts Enterprise Inc ...... F 630 510-9310
  Wheaton (G-20798)
Herman Seekamp Inc .... C 630 628-6555
  Addison (G-149)
Honey Fluff Doughnuts .... G 708 579-1826
  Countryside (G-7058)
Jay Elka .... F 847 540-7776
  Lake Zurich (G-12426)
O-Donuts Inc .... F 217 544-4644
  Springfield (G-19415)
Walter & Kathy Anczerewicz .... G 708 448-3676
  Palos Heights (G-16194)

BAKERY PRDTS: Doughnuts, Frozen

Herman Seekamp Inc .... C 630 628-6555
  Addison (G-149)
Mel-O-Cream Donuts Intl Inc .... D 217 483-1825
  Springfield (G-19404)

BAKERY PRDTS: Dry

Baily International Inc .... D 618 451-8878
  Granite City (G-10699)
Blissful Brownies Inc .... G 541 308-0226
  Lake Forest (G-12231)
Comwell .... D 618 282-6233
  Red Bud (G-16991)
Griffin Industries LLC .... G 815 357-8200
  Seneca (G-18858)
Hometown Food Company .... F 312 500-7710
  Chicago (G-4835)
Wandas Bakery LLC .... G 815 900-6268
  Woodstock (G-21446)

BAKERY PRDTS: Frozen

Bear-Stewart Corporation .... E 773 276-0400
  Chicago (G-3854)
Earthgrains Refrigertd Dough P .... A 630 455-5200
  Downers Grove (G-7996)
Griffin Industries LLC .... G 815 357-8200
  Seneca (G-18858)
Hillshire Brands Company .... B 312 614-6000
  Chicago (G-4820)
Hostess Brands LLC .... D 773 745-9800
  Chicago (G-4844)
Pepperidge Farm Incorporated ..... G 708 478-7450
  Mokena (G-14106)
Pepperidge Farm Incorporated ..... G 630 241-6372
  Downers Grove (G-8072)
Quality Bakeries LLC .... F 630 553-7377
  Saint Charles (G-18255)
Rich Products Corporation .... A 815 729-4509
  Crest Hill (G-7096)
Rich Products Corporation .... A 309 886-2465
  Washington (G-20279)
Solublend Technologies LLC .... G 815 534-5778
  Frankfort (G-9839)

BAKERY PRDTS: Rice Cakes

Quaker Oats Company .... A 312 821-1000
  Chicago (G-5927)

BAKERY PRDTS: Wholesalers

Athenian Foods Co .... F 708 343-6700
  Melrose Park (G-13827)
Chicago Pastry Inc .... D 630 529-6161
  Bloomingdale (G-1985)
Dinkels Bakery Inc .... E 773 281-7300
  Chicago (G-4362)
Highland Baking Company Inc ...... A 847 677-2789
  Northbrook (G-15400)
Korinek & Co Inc .... G 708 652-2870
  Cicero (G-6860)
Leesons Cakes Inc .... G 708 429-1330
  Tinley Park (G-19844)
Leos Sweet Sensations Inc .... D 773 237-1200
  Chicago (G-5207)
Mangel and Co .... F 847 634-0730
  Long Grove (G-13162)
Mel-O-Cream Donuts Intl Inc .... D 217 483-1825
  Springfield (G-19404)
Milano Bakery Inc .... E 815 727-2253
  Joliet (G-11905)
Molino Baking Co .... G 708 385-6616
  Blue Island (G-2131)
Original Ferrara Inc .... F 312 666-2200
  Chicago (G-5700)
Riverside Bake Shop .... E 815 385-0044
  McHenry (G-13788)
Roma Bakeries Inc .... F 815 964-6737
  Rockford (G-17614)
Tam Tav Bakery Inc .... E 773 764-8877
  Chicago (G-6316)
Tom Tom Tamales Mfg Co Inc .... F 773 523-5675
  Chicago (G-6387)

BAKERY: Wholesale Or Wholesale & Retail Combined

Aryzta LLC .... G 708 757-4671
  Chicago Heights (G-6731)
Bimbo Bakeries Usa Inc .... D 815 626-6797
  Rock Falls (G-17177)
Bimbo Bakeries Usa Inc .... E 309 797-4968
  Moline (G-14134)
Bimbo Qsr Chicago LLC .... F 773 376-4444
  Chicago (G-3891)
Bimbo Qsr Us LLC .... C 740 450-3869
  Chicago (G-3892)
Bion Dillos Baking Co .... E 773 921-8282
  Chicago (G-3896)
Bodines Baking Company .... G 217 853-7707
  Decatur (G-7465)
Bullards Bakery .... G 618 842-6666
  Fairfield (G-9620)
C & C Bakery Inc .... G 773 276-4233
  Chicago (G-3991)
Casa Nostra Bakery Co Inc .... F 847 455-5175
  Franklin Park (G-9899)
Cbc Restaurant Corp .... D 773 463-0665
  Chicago (G-4046)
Chicago Bread Company .... F 630 620-1849
  Addison (G-69)
Chicago Pastry Inc .... C 630 972-0404
  Bolingbrook (G-2156)
Christys Kitchen .... G 815 735-6791
  La Salle (G-12107)
DAmatos Bakery Inc .... G 312 733-6219
  Chicago (G-4309)
Dominos Pastries Inc .... G 773 889-3549
  Hickory Hills (G-11195)
Doughnut Boy .... E 773 463-6328
  Lincolnshire (G-12760)
Folsoms Bakery Inc .... F 815 622-7870
  Rock Falls (G-17181)
Fortuna Baking Company .... G 630 681-3000
  Carol Stream (G-2987)
Gadgetworld Enterprises Inc .... G 773 703-0796
  Chicago (G-4655)
Gold Standard Baking Inc .... C 773 523-2333
  Chicago (G-4712)
Gordon Hann .... E 630 761-1835
  Batavia (G-1381)
Illinois Baking .... G 773 995-7200
  Chicago (G-4888)
Kerry Ingredients & Flavours .... F 847 595-1003
  Elk Grove Village (G-9077)
La Luc Bakery Inc .... G 847 740-0303
  Round Lake (G-18079)
Labaquette Kedzie Inc .... G 773 925-0455
  Chicago (G-5151)
Le Petit Pain Holdings LLC .... C 312 981-3770
  Chicago (G-5189)
Liborio Baking Co Inc .... G 708 452-7222
  River Grove (G-17061)
Maiers Bakery .... G 847 967-8042
  Morton Grove (G-14424)
Mandys Soul Food Kitchen LLC ... F 630 485-7291
  Bolingbrook (G-2209)
Marias Bakery Inc .... G 847 266-0811
  Highwood (G-11309)
Mariegold Bake Shoppe .... G 773 561-1978
  Chicago (G-5335)
Molino Baking Co .... G 708 385-6616
  Blue Island (G-2131)
OBrothers Bakery Inc .... G 847 249-0091
  Waukegan (G-20472)
Pin Hsiao & Associates LLC .... E 206 818-0155
  Flossmoor (G-9700)
Roesers Bakery .... E 773 489-6900
  Chicago (G-6050)
Rolfs Patisserie Inc .... G 847 675-6565
  Lincolnwood (G-12840)
Rubis Bakery Inc .... G 847 623-4094
  Waukegan (G-20490)
Sara Lee Baking Group .... G 217 585-3462
  Springfield (G-19439)
Swirlcup .... G 847 229-2200
  Lincolnshire (G-12796)
Tahini Empire Inc .... G 773 742-2382
  Chicago (G-6310)
Todays Temptations Inc .... F 773 385-5355
  Chicago (G-6383)
Tonys Bakery .... G 847 599-1590
  Waukegan (G-20509)

BALERS

Coyote Transportation Inc .... G 630 204-5729
  Bensenville (G-1779)
Rudy Brenneman .... G 618 317-2329
  Percy (G-16560)

BALLASTS: Fluorescent

Radionic Industries Inc .... C 773 804-0100
  Chicago (G-5961)

BALLOONS: Hot Air
A R B C Inc ....F 815 777-6006
  Galena *(G-10163)*
Strauss Facter Assoc Inc ....G 847 759-1100
  Park Ridge *(G-16297)*

BALLOONS: Rubber Laminated Metal Foil
CTI Industries Corporation ....C 847 382-1000
  Lake Barrington *(G-12146)*

BALLOONS: Toy & Advertising, Rubber
A R B C Inc ....F 815 777-6006
  Galena *(G-10163)*
Boss Balloon Company Inc ....G 309 852-2131
  Kewanee *(G-12022)*
Boss Holdings Inc ....D 309 852-2131
  Kewanee *(G-12023)*
CTI Industries Corporation ....D 800 284-5605
  Lake Zurich *(G-12400)*

BANKS: Commercial, NEC
Chase Home Finance ....G 630 617-4747
  Elmhurst *(G-9343)*

BANNERS: Fabric
Action Advertising Inc ....G 312 791-0660
  Chicago *(G-3534)*
Fabric Images Inc ....D 847 488-9877
  Elgin *(G-8583)*
Precise Digital Printing Inc ....E 847 593-2645
  Bensenville *(G-1871)*

BANQUET HALL FACILITIES
City Living Design Inc ....G 312 335-0711
  Chicago *(G-4156)*
Copper Dock ....G 618 669-2675
  Pocahontas *(G-16751)*
Hidden Lake Winery Ltd ....E 618 228-9111
  Aviston *(G-1179)*

BAR
Bent River Brewing Co ....F 309 797-2722
  Moline *(G-14133)*
Murphys Pub ....G 847 526-1431
  Wauconda *(G-20380)*

BARBECUE EQPT
Apache Supply ....G 708 409-1040
  Bartlett *(G-1264)*
Belson Outdoors LLC ....E 630 897-8489
  Naperville *(G-14778)*
Chadwick Manufacturing Ltd ....G 815 684-5152
  Chadwick *(G-3257)*
Home & Leisure Lifestyles LLC ....G 618 651-0358
  Highland *(G-11227)*
Kalamazoo Outdoor Gourmet LLC ......G 312 423-8770
  Chicago *(G-5077)*
Weber-Stephen Products LLC ....B 847 934-5700
  Palatine *(G-16173)*
Weber-Stephen Products LLC ....F 224 836-8536
  Palatine *(G-16174)*
Weber-Stephen Products LLC ....F 847 669-4900
  Huntley *(G-11573)*

BARGES BUILDING & REPAIR
Midland Manufacturing Corp ....C 847 677-0333
  Skokie *(G-18990)*

BARRELS: Shipping, Metal
Mauser Usa LLC ....F 773 261-2332
  Chicago *(G-5367)*

BARRICADES: Metal
Builders Chicago Corporation ....D 224 654-2122
  Rosemont *(G-18001)*
Energy Absorption Systems Inc ....E 312 467-6750
  Chicago *(G-4506)*
Infrastructure Def Tech LLC ....G 800 379-1822
  Belvidere *(G-1678)*
Nafisco Inc ....F 815 372-3300
  Romeoville *(G-17858)*
North American Safety Pdts Inc ....G 815 469-1144
  Mokena *(G-14099)*

Quixote Transportation Safety ....D 312 467-6750
  Chicago *(G-5940)*
Trafficguard Inc ....G 877 727-7347
  Sycamore *(G-19736)*

BARS, COLD FINISHED: Steel, From Purchased Hot-Rolled
A & A Steel Fabricating Co ....F 708 389-4499
  Posen *(G-16789)*
Corey Steel Company ....C 708 735-8000
  Cicero *(G-6837)*
Krueger and Company ....E 630 833-5650
  Elmhurst *(G-9389)*
Niagara Lasalle Corporation ....C 708 596-2700
  South Holland *(G-19235)*
Taubensee Steel & Wire Company ......C 847 459-5100
  Wheeling *(G-20997)*
Tinsley Steel Inc ....G 618 656-5231
  Edwardsville *(G-8378)*
Worth Steel and Machine Co ....E 708 388-6300
  Alsip *(G-527)*

BARS, PIPES, PLATES & SHAPES: Lead/Lead Alloy Bars, Pipe
Nuclear Power Outfitters LLC ....F 630 963-0320
  Lisle *(G-12922)*

BARS, PLATES & SHEETS: Zinc & Zinc Alloy Bars, Plates, Etc
Midland Industries Inc ....E 312 664-7300
  Chicago *(G-5434)*

BARS: Cargo, Stabilizing, Metal
Black Mountain Products Inc ....G 224 655-5955
  Spring Grove *(G-19268)*
Durabilt Dyvex Inc ....F 708 397-4673
  Broadview *(G-2432)*

BARS: Concrete Reinforcing, Fabricated Steel
Advanced Assembly ....G 630 379-6158
  Streamwood *(G-19559)*
American Classic Rebar Corp ....G 708 225-1010
  South Holland *(G-19192)*
Bohler ....G 630 883-3000
  Elgin *(G-8522)*
Dayton Superior Corporation ....D 815 936-3300
  Kankakee *(G-11963)*
Duroweld Company Inc ....E 847 680-3064
  Lake Bluff *(G-12179)*
J and D Installers Inc ....G 847 288-0783
  Franklin Park *(G-9968)*
Metals and Services Inc ....D 630 627-2900
  Addison *(G-200)*
Rode Welding Inc ....E 847 439-0910
  Elk Grove Village *(G-9219)*
Steel Fabricating Inc ....F 815 977-5355
  Rockford *(G-17645)*
Steel Rebar Manufacturing LLC ....G 618 920-2748
  Centreville *(G-3255)*
Thirteen Rf Inc ....E 618 687-1313
  Murphysboro *(G-14761)*
Vermilion Steel Fabrication ....G 217 442-5300
  Danville *(G-7391)*

BASES, BEVERAGE
Beverage Flavors Intl LLC ....F 773 248-3860
  Chicago *(G-3876)*
Insight Beverages Inc ....G 847 438-1598
  Lake Zurich *(G-12424)*
Insight Beverages Inc ....E 847 438-1598
  Lake Zurich *(G-12425)*
Lansing Wings Inc ....G 708 895-3300
  Lansing *(G-12504)*
Mondelez Global LLC ....C 847 943-4000
  Deerfield *(G-7637)*

BATH SALTS
Oak Court Creations ....G 815 467-7676
  Minooka *(G-14065)*

BATH SHOPS
Stonecrafters Inc ....E 815 363-8730
  Lakemoor *(G-12477)*

BATHROOM ACCESS & FITTINGS: Vitreous China & Earthenware
Coronado Conservation Inc ....G 301 512-4671
  Chicago *(G-4238)*
Wonder Kids Inc ....G 773 437-8025
  Evanston *(G-9589)*

BATHROOM FIXTURES: Plastic
Carstin Brands Inc ....D 217 543-3331
  Arthur *(G-844)*
Northwest Marble Products ....E 630 860-2288
  Hoffman Estates *(G-11473)*

BATTERIES, EXC AUTOMOTIVE: Wholesalers
Batteries Plus 287 ....G 630 279-3478
  Villa Park *(G-20132)*
Battery Sales Inc ....G 708 489-6645
  Matteson *(G-13619)*
Gem Equipment & Mfg LLC ....E 309 923-7312
  Roanoke *(G-17101)*
Interstate All Battery Center ....F 217 214-1069
  Quincy *(G-16894)*
Interstate Btry Sys Intl Inc ....G 708 424-2288
  Oak Lawn *(G-15720)*
Storage Battery Systems LLC ....G 630 221-1700
  Carol Stream *(G-3078)*

BATTERIES: Alkaline, Cell Storage
Duracell Company ....G 203 796-4000
  Chicago *(G-4410)*
Spectrum Brands Inc ....G 815 285-6500
  Dixon *(G-7919)*

BATTERIES: Lead Acid, Storage
Battery Builders LLC ....D 630 851-5800
  Naperville *(G-14961)*
Clarios ....F 630 871-7700
  Carol Stream *(G-2961)*
Exide Technologies LLC ....D 678 566-9000
  Lombard *(G-13075)*

BATTERIES: Nickel-Cadmium
Hubbell Power Systems Inc ....F 618 797-5000
  Edwardsville *(G-8365)*

BATTERIES: Rechargeable
All Cell Technologies LLC ....E 872 281-7606
  Chicago *(G-3607)*
Duracell US Operations Inc ....G 312 469-5266
  Chicago *(G-4412)*
Iterna ....E 630 585-7400
  Aurora *(G-989)*
National Power LLC ....E 773 685-2662
  Chicago *(G-5551)*
Palladium Energy Group Inc ....E 630 410-7900
  Woodridge *(G-21330)*
Technical Power Systems Inc ....E 630 719-1471
  Lisle *(G-12949)*

BATTERIES: Storage
Batteries Plus 287 ....G 630 279-3478
  Villa Park *(G-20132)*
Battery Sales Inc ....G 708 489-6645
  Matteson *(G-13619)*
C & C 1 LLC ....G 630 903-6345
  Elmhurst *(G-9340)*
Clarios LLC ....B 630 232-4270
  Geneva *(G-10260)*
Crown Battery Manufacturing Co ....G 630 530-8060
  Villa Park *(G-20143)*
Duracell Distributing LLC ....G 203 796-4000
  Chicago *(G-4411)*
East Penn Manufacturing Co ....A 610 682-6361
  Naperville *(G-14819)*
Ecolocap Solutions Inc ....G 312 585-6670
  Morton Grove *(G-14403)*
Enersys ....D 630 455-4872
  Lisle *(G-12889)*
Exide Technologies ....G 630 862-2200
  Lombard *(G-13074)*
Firefly International Enrgy Co ....G 309 402-0701
  Peoria *(G-16438)*
Glidepath Power LLC ....G 312 375-6034
  Elmhurst *(G-9367)*

Interstate All Battery Center ....F 217 214-1069
  Quincy *(G-16894)*
Interstate Btry Sys Intl Inc..................G...... 708 424-2288
  Oak Lawn *(G-15720)*
Inventus Power Inc ....C...... 630 410-7900
  Woodridge *(G-21316)*
Inventus Power Holdings Inc..............G...... 630 410-7900
  Woodridge *(G-21318)*
Itta Corporation ....G...... 872 221-4882
  Chicago *(G-4978)*
Navitas Systems LLC ....F...... 630 755-7920
  Woodridge *(G-21326)*
P L R Sales Inc ....G...... 217 733-2245
  Fairmount *(G-9644)*
Performance Battery Group Inc..........G...... 630 293-5505
  West Chicago *(G-20628)*
Rayovac Corp......................................G...... 815 285-6500
  Dixon *(G-7909)*
Storage Battery Systems LLC ....G...... 630 221-1700
  Carol Stream *(G-3078)*
Veteran Wire and Cable LLC ....G...... 630 327-5849
  Addison *(G-329)*

BATTERIES: Wet

Exide Technologies LLC ....D...... 678 566-9000
  Lombard *(G-13075)*

BATTERY CASES: Plastic Or Plastics Combination

Jessup Manufacturing Company ....D...... 815 385-6650
  Mchenry *(G-13753)*

BATTERY CHARGERS

Battery Systems LLC ....G...... 833 487-6937
  Naperville *(G-14777)*
Charles Industries LLC ....D...... 217 932-2068
  Casey *(G-3199)*
Exide Technologies LLC ....D...... 678 566-9000
  Lombard *(G-13075)*
Inventus Power Inc ....C...... 630 410-7900
  Woodridge *(G-21316)*
La Marche Mfg Co ....C...... 847 299-1188
  Des Plaines *(G-7795)*
Master Control Systems Inc ....E...... 847 295-1010
  Lake Bluff *(G-12195)*
Radionic Hi-Tech Inc...........................D...... 773 804-0100
  Chicago *(G-5960)*
Schumacher Electric Corp ....D...... 847 385-1600
  Mount Prospect *(G-14569)*

BATTERY CHARGERS: Storage, Motor & Engine Generator Type

Datasource ....G...... 312 405-9152
  Calumet City *(G-2774)*
Heng Tuo Usa Inc ....G...... 630 317-7672
  Oakbrook Terrace *(G-15802)*
Luon Energy LLC.................................G...... 217 419-2678
  Savoy *(G-18415)*
UPS Power Management Inc..............F...... 844 877-2288
  Chicago *(G-6490)*

BEARINGS

Composite Bearings Mfg......................F...... 630 595-8334
  Wood Dale *(G-21178)*
Technymon Technology USA Inc ....G...... 630 787-0501
  Wood Dale *(G-21247)*

BEARINGS & PARTS Ball

American NTN Bearing Mfg Corp........B...... 847 741-4545
  Elgin *(G-8508)*
American NTN Bearing Mfg Corp........E...... 847 671-5450
  Schiller Park *(G-18785)*
Frantz Manufacturing Company ....D...... 815 625-7063
  Sterling *(G-19509)*
Mechanical Power Inc ....E...... 847 487-0070
  Wauconda *(G-20375)*
NTN USA Corporation ....C...... 847 298-4652
  Mount Prospect *(G-14554)*
Pacific Bearing Corp............................C...... 815 389-5600
  Roscoe *(G-17921)*
Precision Plastic Ball Co ....G...... 847 678-2255
  Franklin Park *(G-10025)*
SKF USA Inc ....D...... 847 742-0700
  Elgin *(G-8736)*
Thomson Industries Inc ....A...... 815 568-4309
  Marengo *(G-13495)*

BEARINGS: Ball & Roller

Bearings Manufacturing Company ......F...... 773 583-6703
  Chicago *(G-3856)*
Ewellix USA LLC ....G...... 618 392-3647
  Olney *(G-15859)*
HRB America Corporation ....G...... 630 513-1800
  Saint Charles *(G-18208)*
NTN-Bower Corporation ....G...... 309 833-4541
  Macomb *(G-13396)*
Roberts Swiss Inc ....E...... 630 467-9100
  Itasca *(G-11726)*
SKF USA Inc ....D...... 847 742-0700
  Elgin *(G-8735)*

BEARINGS: Railroad Car Journal

Lv Ventures Inc ....G...... 312 993-1800
  Chicago *(G-5289)*

BEARINGS: Roller & Parts

Allegion S&S Holding Co Inc...............C...... 815 875-3311
  Princeton *(G-16805)*
Ccty USA Bearing Co ....G...... 847 540-8196
  Lake Zurich *(G-12391)*
Frantz Manufacturing Company ....G...... 815 625-3333
  Sterling *(G-19508)*
NTN Bearing Corporation ....G...... 847 298-7500
  Macomb *(G-13395)*
NTN-Bower Corporation ....G...... 309 837-0440
  Macomb *(G-13397)*
Timken Company ....G...... 630 679-6756
  Naperville *(G-14990)*

BEAUTY & BARBER SHOP EQPT

A Stucki Company ....E...... 618 498-4442
  Jerseyville *(G-11785)*
Alpha Industries Inc ....F...... 847 945-1740
  Deerfield *(G-7584)*
Anfinsen Plastic Moulding Inc ....E...... 630 554-4100
  Oswego *(G-15992)*
Belvedere Usa LLC ....C...... 815 544-3131
  Belvidere *(G-1653)*
Buhrke Industries LLC ....E...... 630 412-2028
  Elk Grove Village *(G-8873)*
Ccar Industries ....E...... 217 345-3300
  Charleston *(G-3397)*
Circle T Manufacturing LLC ....C...... 217 728-4834
  Sullivan *(G-19665)*
Cleats Mfg Inc ....F...... 773 542-0453
  Chicago *(G-4176)*
Clown Global Brands LLC...................G...... 847 564-5950
  Northbrook *(G-15362)*
Conair Corporation ....G...... 203 351-9000
  Rantoul *(G-16972)*
E2 Manufacturing Group LLC ....G...... 224 399-9608
  Waukegan *(G-20439)*
Flight Manufacturing Corp ....G...... 815 876-1616
  Princeton *(G-16809)*
Gillons Inc..E...... 773 531-8900
  Homewood *(G-11495)*
Gilster-Mary Lee Corporation ....G...... 618 826-3102
  Chester *(G-3455)*
Hair Plus Studios LLC ....G...... 530 487-4247
  Chicago *(G-4768)*
Hu-Friedy Mfg Co LLC ....F...... 847 257-4500
  Des Plaines *(G-7781)*
Hue Circle Inc ....G...... 224 567-8116
  Glenview *(G-10558)*
In Aaw Hair Emporium LLC..................G...... 779 227-1450
  Joliet *(G-11880)*
Ironwood Manufacturing Inc ....G...... 630 969-1100
  Naperville *(G-14975)*
Jf Industries Inc ....G...... 773 775-8840
  Chicago *(G-5028)*
Km4 Manufacturing ....G...... 708 924-5150
  Bedford Park *(G-1476)*
Mgn Tool & Mfg Co Inc ....G...... 630 849-3575
  Carol Stream *(G-3027)*
Ozcut Inc..G...... 630 605-7398
  Peru *(G-16587)*
Pru Dent Mfg Inc ....G...... 847 301-1170
  Schaumburg *(G-18687)*
Quad-Illinois Inc ....F...... 847 836-1115
  Elgin *(G-8706)*
Riverside Memorial Co ....G...... 217 323-1280
  Beardstown *(G-1450)*
Riviera Tan Spa ....G...... 618 466-1012
  Godfrey *(G-10661)*
Scimatco Office...................................E...... 630 879-1306
  Batavia *(G-1414)*
Technical Power Systems Inc ....E...... 630 719-1471
  Lisle *(G-12949)*
Trident Industries ....F...... 847 285-1316
  Schaumburg *(G-18757)*
Veeco Manufacturing Inc.....................F...... 312 666-0900
  Melrose Park *(G-13925)*

BEAUTY & BARBER SHOP EQPT & SPLYS WHOLESALERS

Bee Sales Company ....D...... 847 600-4400
  Niles *(G-15106)*
Hue Circle Inc ....G...... 224 567-8116
  Glenview *(G-10558)*

BEAUTY SALONS

D-Orum Corporation ....F...... 773 567-2064
  Chicago *(G-4302)*
Ecoco Inc ....E...... 773 745-7700
  Chicago *(G-4448)*
Glass Artistry ....G...... 847 998-5800
  Northbrook *(G-15394)*
Lab TEC Cosmt By Marzena Inc.........F...... 630 396-3970
  Addison *(G-178)*
Posh Lash Inc......................................G...... 630 388-6828
  Chicago *(G-5846)*

BED SHEETING, COTTON

Alpha Bedding LLC.............................F...... 847 550-5110
  Lake Zurich *(G-12383)*

BEDDING, BEDSPREAD, BLANKET/SHEET: Pillowcase, Purchd Mtrl

Personalized Pillows Co......................G...... 847 226-7393
  Wadsworth *(G-20211)*

BEDDING, BEDSPREADS, BLANKETS & SHEETS: Comforters & Quilts

Quiltmaster Inc....................................E...... 847 426-6741
  Carpentersville *(G-3117)*

BEDS: Hospital

Kci Satellite...G...... 800 664-2602
  Pittsfield *(G-16635)*
Kreg Medical Inc ....C...... 312 829-8904
  Melrose Park *(G-13889)*

BEDS: Inflatable

Aero Products Holdings Inc.................E...... 847 485-3200
  Schaumburg *(G-18429)*

BEDSPREADS & BED SETS, FROM PURCHASED MATERIALS

Tailored Inc ....G...... 708 387-9854
  Brookfield *(G-2493)*
Unitex Industries Inc ....G...... 708 524-0664
  Oak Park *(G-15777)*

BEDSPREADS, COTTON

Dec Art Designs Inc ....G...... 312 329-0553
  Northbrook *(G-15374)*

BEEKEEPERS' SPLYS: Honeycomb Foundations

Dadant & Sons Inc ....D...... 217 847-3324
  Hamilton *(G-10954)*

BEER & ALE WHOLESALERS

Church Street Brewing Co LLC ....F...... 630 438-5725
  Itasca *(G-11636)*

BEER & ALE, WHOLESALE: Beer & Other Fermented Malt Liquors

Dresbach Distributing Co.....................G...... 815 223-0116
  Peru *(G-16574)*
Finchs Beer Company LLC ....G...... 312 929-4773
  Chicago *(G-4588)*
RJ Distributing Co ....E...... 309 685-2794
  East Peoria *(G-8287)*

BEER PUMP COIL CLEANING & REPAIR SVCS

Leaders Bev Consulting Inc..............F....... 312 497-5602
  Chicago (G-5190)

BEER, WINE & LIQUOR STORES

Cub Foods Inc..............................C....... 309 689-0140
  Peoria (G-16428)
Gold Standard Enterprises Inc.......E....... 217 546-1633
  Springfield (G-19375)

BEER, WINE & LIQUOR STORES: Beer, Packaged

Walter Lagestee Inc.....................C....... 708 957-2974
  Homewood (G-11504)

BEER, WINE & LIQUOR STORES: Wine

Bella Terra Winery LLC................F....... 618 658-8882
  Creal Springs (G-7080)
Kickapoo Creek Winery.................G....... 309 495-9463
  Edwards (G-8338)
Mangel and Co..............................E....... 847 459-3100
  Buffalo Grove (G-2567)
Waterman Winery & Vineyards.......G....... 815 264-3268
  Waterman (G-20302)

BEER, WINE & LIQUOR STORES: Wine & Beer

Two Brothers Brewing Company.....G....... 630 393-3377
  Warrenville (G-20256)

BELLOWS

Brock Industrial Services LLC.......E....... 815 730-3350
  Joliet (G-11834)
Commercial Dynamics Inc.............G....... 847 439-5300
  Arlington Heights (G-717)
Flex-Weld Inc...............................D....... 815 334-3662
  Woodstock (G-21387)
James Walker Mfg Co....................E....... 708 754-4020
  Glenwood (G-10641)
Microlution Inc..............................E....... 773 282-6495
  Chicago (G-5424)

BELLOWS ASSEMBLIES: Missiles, Metal

Duraflex Inc..................................E....... 847 462-1007
  Cary (G-3156)

BELTING: Plastic

Chemi-Flex LLC............................E....... 630 627-9650
  Lombard (G-13051)

BELTING: Rubber

Bando Usa Inc..............................E....... 630 773-6600
  Itasca (G-11625)
Voss Belting & Specialty Co...........E....... 847 673-8900
  Lincolnwood (G-12849)

BELTS: Seat, Automotive & Aircraft

Deyco Inc......................................G....... 630 553-5666
  Yorkville (G-21480)
Hooker Custom Harness Inc...........G....... 815 233-5478
  Freeport (G-10119)

BENCHES, WORK : Factory

L & D Group Inc............................B....... 630 892-8941
  Montgomery (G-14252)

BENCHES: Seating

Center-111 W Burnham Wash LLC..E....... 312 368-5320
  Chicago (G-4055)
J C Decaux New York Inc..............E....... 312 456-2999
  Chicago (G-4989)
T2 Site Amenities Incorporated......G....... 847 579-9003
  Highland Park (G-11302)

BENTONITE MINING

Amcol International Corp...............E....... 847 851-1500
  Hoffman Estates (G-11405)
American Colloid Company............E....... 618 452-8143
  Granite City (G-10694)
American Colloid Company............F....... 304 882-2123
  Elgin (G-8506)
American Colloid Company............F....... 800 527-9948
  Arlington Heights (G-690)
American Colloid Company............E....... 847 851-1700
  Hoffman Estates (G-11406)

BEVERAGE BASES & SYRUPS

Passion Fruit Drink Inc..................G....... 708 769-4749
  South Holland (G-19238)

BEVERAGE POWDERS

Compact Industries Inc................C....... 630 513-9600
  Saint Charles (G-18173)
Inside Beverages..........................C....... 847 438-1338
  Lake Zurich (G-12423)
Kraft Foods Asia PCF Svcs LLC.....G....... 847 943-4000
  Deerfield (G-7627)
Kraft Heinz Company.....................C....... 847 646-2000
  Chicago (G-5129)
Kruger North America Inc............F....... 708 851-3670
  Oak Park (G-15761)
Mondelez International Inc..........A....... 847 943-4000
  Chicago (G-5490)
Treehouse Foods Inc...................C....... 708 483-1300
  Oak Brook (G-15665)
Ur Inc..G....... 630 450-5279
  Batavia (G-1437)

BEVERAGE PRDTS: Brewers' Grain

Rolling Meadows Brewery LLC.....G....... 217 725-2492
  Springfield (G-19435)

BEVERAGE PRDTS: Malt Syrup

Alao Temitope..............................F....... 331 454-3333
  Collinsville (G-6953)

BEVERAGE PRDTS: Malt, Barley

Muntons Malted Ingredients Inc....G....... 630 812-1600
  Lombard (G-13105)

BEVERAGE PRDTS: Malt, Corn

Warner Harvey Lee Farm Inc........G....... 217 849-2548
  Toledo (G-19882)

BEVERAGE STORES

Balon International Corp................E....... 773 379-7779
  Chicago (G-3821)
Coca-Cola Refreshments USA Inc.G....... 217 348-1001
  Charleston (G-3400)
Insight Beverages Inc..................E....... 847 438-1598
  Lake Zurich (G-12425)
Jel Sert Co....................................C....... 630 231-7590
  West Chicago (G-20603)

BEVERAGE, NONALCOHOLIC: Iced Tea/Fruit Drink, Bottled/Canned

Home Juice Corp...........................G....... 708 345-5370
  Melrose Park (G-13880)
Lifeway Kefir Shop LLC..................E....... 847 967-1010
  Morton Grove (G-14421)

BEVERAGES, ALCOHOLIC: Ale

Aero Alehouse LLC........................G....... 815 977-5602
  Loves Park (G-13183)
Ale Syndicate Brewers LLC..........G....... 773 340-2337
  Chicago (G-3600)
Church Street Brewing Co LLC.....F....... 630 438-5725
  Itasca (G-11636)
Colleagues of Beer Inc.................G....... 847 727-3318
  Grayslake (G-10762)
Lil Beaver Brewery LLC................F....... 309 808-2590
  Bloomington (G-2071)
Wirtz Beverage Illinois LLC..........G....... 847 228-9000
  Cicero (G-6888)

BEVERAGES, ALCOHOLIC: Beer

Abbey Ridge LLC..........................G....... 618 713-2537
  Pomona (G-16762)
Aldi Inc..F....... 815 877-0861
  Machesney Park (G-13326)
Anheuser-Busch LLC....................G....... 630 512-9002
  Lisle (G-12865)
Blue Island Beer Co......................G....... 708 954-8085
  Blue Island (G-2111)
Bob C Beverages LLC..................G....... 847 520-7582
  Wheeling (G-20861)
Carlyle Brewing Co.......................G....... 815 963-2739
  Rockford (G-17336)
Cicerone Certification Program.....G....... 773 549-4800
  Chicago (G-4150)
Crazy Llama Brewing Co LLC........G....... 779 200-1878
  Roscoe (G-17901)
Crystal Lake Beer Company..........F....... 779 220-9288
  Crystal Lake (G-7187)
Dovetail Brewery Inc.....................E....... 773 683-1414
  Chicago (G-4392)
Emmetts Tavern & Brewing Co.....G....... 630 434-8500
  Downers Grove (G-8000)
Emmetts Tavern & Brewing Co.....G....... 630 480-7181
  Wheaton (G-20797)
Emmetts Tavern & Brewing Co.....F....... 847 359-1533
  Palatine (G-16115)
Emmetts Tavern & Brewing Co.....E....... 847 428-4500
  West Dundee (G-20663)
Excel Bottling Co..........................E....... 618 526-7159
  Breese (G-2302)
Finchs Beer Company LLC..........E....... 312 929-4773
  Chicago (G-4588)
Ginger Windmill Brew LLC............G....... 630 677-2850
  Geneva (G-10274)
Gnome Brew LLC.........................G....... 773 961-7750
  Chicago (G-4707)
Goose Holdings Inc......................E....... 312 226-1119
  Chicago (G-4718)
Great Revivalist Brewing LLC.......F....... 309 944-5466
  Geneseo (G-10243)
Haymarket Brewing Company LLC.G....... 312 638-0700
  Chicago (G-4789)
Hop Brewery LLC..........................G....... 866 724-4677
  Christopher (G-6825)
Lagunitas Brewing Company.........C....... 773 522-1308
  Chicago (G-5159)
Maverick Ales & Lagers LLC........G....... 408 605-1508
  Chicago (G-5368)
Molson Coors Bev Co USA LLC....A....... 312 496-2700
  Chicago (G-5488)
Only Child Brewing Company LLC.G....... 847 877-9822
  Gurnee (G-10909)
Riggs Beer Company....................G....... 217 649-4286
  Urbana (G-19998)
Soundgrowler Brewing Company..G....... 708 263-0083
  Tinley Park (G-19856)
St Nicholas Brewing Co................G....... 618 790-9212
  Du Quoin (G-8124)
Tenth and Blake Beer Company....G....... 312 496-2759
  Chicago (G-6351)

BEVERAGES, ALCOHOLIC: Beer & Ale

Apple Rush Company....................G....... 847 730-5324
  Glenview (G-10527)
Bent River Brewing Co.................F....... 309 797-2722
  Moline (G-14133)
Breakroom Brewery......................G....... 773 564-9534
  Chicago (G-3949)
Burrell Beverage Co.....................E....... 708 581-6953
  Chicago (G-3977)
Common Culture Brewing Co.......F....... 847 584-2331
  Evanston (G-9506)
Drewrys Brewing Company...........G....... 815 385-9115
  McHenry (G-13738)
Gmb Partners LLC........................E....... 773 248-4038
  Chicago (G-4703)
Libertyville Brewing Company......D....... 847 362-6688
  Libertyville (G-12668)
Pac Partners LLC.........................G....... 773 315-0828
  Chicago (G-5735)
Rebellion Brew Haus....................G....... 309 524-5219
  Moline (G-14172)

BEVERAGES, ALCOHOLIC: Bourbon Whiskey

Beam Suntory Inc.........................C....... 312 964-6999
  Chicago (G-3852)
Jim Beam Brands Co....................B....... 847 948-8903
  Deerfield (G-7620)

BEVERAGES, ALCOHOLIC: Brandy & Brandy Spirits

Copper Dock..................................G....... 618 669-2675
  Pocahontas (G-16751)

BEVERAGES, ALCOHOLIC: Cocktails

Company	Code	Phone
Bartesian Corp — Chicago (G-3844)	G	847 302-4467
Cliffords Pub Inc — Palatine (G-16100)	G	847 259-3000
Kats Meow — East Dubuque (G-8177)	G	815 747-2113
North Shore Distillery LLC — Libertyville (G-12689)	G	847 574-2499

BEVERAGES, ALCOHOLIC: Distilled Liquors

Company	Code	Phone
21 Holdings LLC — West Chicago (G-20528)	G	630 876-4886
Angels Share Brands LLC — Chicago (G-3697)	G	312 494-1100
Barnstormer Distilleries — Rockford (G-17313)	G	314 397-1100
Barrel — Chicago (G-3836)	G	312 754-0156
Beam Global Spirits & Wine LLC — Chicago (G-3851)	C	847 948-8888
Black Band LLC — Peoria (G-16393)	G	309 208-0323
Blaum Brothers Distilling Co — Galena (G-10164)	F	815 777-1000
Callison Distributing LLC — Belleville (G-1537)	D	618 277-4300
Copper Fiddle Distilery — Lake Zurich (G-12397)	G	847 847-7613
Crystal Rain Distillery I — Lake Forest (G-12242)	G	224 508-9361
Distillery Geeks Inc — Chicago (G-4368)	G	630 240-7259
Dtrs Enterprises Inc — Bolingbrook (G-2170)	G	630 296-6890
Future Brands LLC — Chicago (G-4645)	C	847 444-1880
Glunz Fmly Winery Cellars Inc — Grayslake (G-10777)	E	847 548-9463
Heaven Hill Distillery Inc — Chicago (G-4796)	G	773 564-9791
Kindred Spirits Distillery — Mendota (G-13944)	G	815 910-7116
Kothe Distilling Tech Inc — Chicago (G-5125)	G	312 878-7766
Koval Inc — Chicago (G-5126)	F	312 878-7988
Koval Inc — Chicago (G-5127)	F	773 944-0089
Let There Be Distillers LLC — Chicago (G-5209)	G	217 741-0392
Makers Mark Distillery Inc — Chicago (G-5320)	G	312 964-6999
Most Enterprise Inc — Chicago (G-5504)	D	800 792-4669
Premiere Distillery LLC — Gurnee (G-10915)	G	847 662-4444
Rumshine Distilling LLC — Tilton (G-19796)	G	217 446-6960
Sazerac North America Inc — Chicago (G-6108)	E	502 423-5225
Skeptic Distillery Co — Melrose Park (G-13915)	G	708 223-8286
Sun Beam Logistics Inc — Chicago (G-6267)	G	847 454-5884
Tailwinds Distillery — Plainfield (G-16721)	G	630 746-7526
Two Eagles Distillery Llc — Mount Prospect (G-14577)	G	773 450-7575
Vincit Omnia LLC — Chicago (G-6553)	G	773 631-4020
Whiskey Acres Distilling Co — Dekalb (G-7714)	F	815 739-8711

BEVERAGES, ALCOHOLIC: Gin

Company	Code	Phone
Diageo North America Inc — Plainfield (G-16656)	E	815 267-4400
Mgp Ingredients Illinois Inc — Pekin (G-16345)	C	309 353-3990
Windy City Distilling Inc — Wheeling (G-21014)	G	312 788-7503

BEVERAGES, ALCOHOLIC: Liquors, Malt

Company	Code	Phone
Dept 28 Inc — Schaumburg (G-18505)	G	847 285-1343
Dj Liquors Inc — Davis Junction (G-7421)	G	815 645-1145

BEVERAGES, ALCOHOLIC: Near Beer

Company	Code	Phone
Metropolitan Brewing LLC — Chicago (G-5413)	G	773 474-6893

BEVERAGES, ALCOHOLIC: Rum

Company	Code	Phone
Apostrophe Brands — Chicago (G-3713)	F	312 832-0300

BEVERAGES, ALCOHOLIC: Scotch Whiskey

Company	Code	Phone
JK Williams Distilling LLC — East Peoria (G-8272)	G	309 839-0591

BEVERAGES, ALCOHOLIC: Vodka

Company	Code	Phone
773 LLC — Chicago (G-3477)	G	312 707-8780
773 LLC — Chicago (G-3478)	G	312 707-8780
Fire & Ice Imports LLC — Morris (G-14305)	G	310 871-1695
Podhalanska LLC — Lemont (G-12584)	G	630 247-9256

BEVERAGES, ALCOHOLIC: Wines

Company	Code	Phone
Acquaviva Winery LLC — Maple Park (G-13459)	G	630 365-0333
Aeries Riverview Winery Inc — Grafton (G-10683)	G	618 786-7477
Aquaviva Winery — Sycamore (G-19701)	G	815 899-4444
August Hill Winery — Peru (G-16567)	G	815 224-8199
Augusthill Winery Co — Utica (G-20005)	G	815 667-5211
Barrington Cardinal Whse LLC — Barrington (G-1213)	G	847 387-3676
Baxter Vineyards — Nauvoo (G-15013)	G	217 453-2528
Bella Terra Winery LLC — Creal Springs (G-7080)	F	618 658-8882
Benessere Vineyard Inc — Oak Brook (G-15596)	G	708 560-9840
Beverage Art Inc — Chicago (G-3875)	G	773 881-9463
Bluffs Vineyard & Winery L L C — Murphysboro (G-14751)	G	618 763-4447
Broken Earth Winery — Long Grove (G-13158)	F	847 383-5052
Cellar LLC — Carterville (G-3131)	G	618 956-9900
Coopers Hawk Intrmdate Hldg LL — Downers Grove (G-7981)	C	708 839-2920
Coopers Hawk Intrmdate Hldg LL — Countryside (G-7048)	F	708 215-5674
Coopers Hawk Production LLC — Countryside (G-7049)	G	708 839-2920
Coopers Hawk Winery — Saint Charles (G-18175)	F	630 940-1000
Coopers Hwk Intermedte Holdng — Woodridge (G-21288)	F	708 215-5674
D C Estate Winery — South Beloit (G-19089)	G	815 218-0573
De Vine Distributors LLC — Chicago (G-4326)	G	773 248-7005
DVine Wine Crafters LLC — Algonquin (G-372)	G	847 658-4900
Famous Fossil Vinyard & Winery — Freeport (G-10107)	G	815 563-4665
Fox Valley Winery Inc — Oswego (G-16005)	G	630 554-0404
Galena Cellars Winery — Galena (G-10169)	E	815 777-3330
Galena Cellars Winery — Galena (G-10170)	E	815 777-3429
Glunz Fmly Winery Cellars Inc — Grayslake (G-10777)	E	847 548-9463
Grafton Winery Inc — Grafton (G-10684)	F	618 786-3001
Hedman Orchard and Vineyard — Alto Pass (G-8399)	G	618 893-4923
Hogg Hollow Winery LLC — Golconda (G-10665)	G	618 695-9463
Katy Lynn Winery LLC — Carbondale (G-2848)	G	618 964-1818
Kickapoo Creek Winery — Edwards (G-8338)	G	309 495-9463
Klehm Family Winery LLC — Hampshire (G-10975)	G	847 609-9997
Lake Hill Winery Inc — Carthage (G-3137)	G	217 357-2675
Lau Nae Winery Inc — Red Bud (G-16997)	G	618 282-9463
Lavender Crest Winery — Colona (G-6975)	E	309 949-2565
Lincoln Heritage Winery LLC — Cobden (G-6942)	G	618 833-3783
Lynfred Winery Inc — Roselle (G-17965)	E	630 529-9463
Main Street Market Roscoe Inc — Roscoe (G-17915)	G	815 623-6328
Mark Anthony Brewing Inc — Chicago (G-5339)	G	312 202-3700
Mary McHelle Winery Vinyrd LLC — Carrollton (G-3127)	F	217 942-6250
Old Mill Vineyard LLC — Metamora (G-13965)	G	309 258-9954
Pheasant Hollow Winery Inc — Whittington (G-21021)	G	618 629-2302
Pomona Winery — Pomona (G-16764)	G	618 893-2623
Pour It Again Sam Inc — Lynwood (G-13297)	G	708 474-1744
Prairie State Winery — Genoa (G-10322)	G	815 784-4540
Prp Wine International Inc — Naperville (G-14903)	F	630 995-4500
Rapid Displays Inc — Chicago (G-5973)	D	773 927-1500
Robert Boldrey — Oblong (G-15827)	G	618 592-4892
Sensus LLC — Chicago (G-6136)	G	312 379-9463
Shawnee Grapevines LLC — Cobden (G-6943)	G	618 893-9463
Shawnee Winery — Vienna (G-20119)	G	618 658-8400
Southern Ill Wine Trail Nfp — Golconda (G-10668)	G	618 695-9463
Terlato Wine Group Ltd — Lake Bluff (G-12210)	E	847 604-8900
Terraneo Merchants Inc — Lincolnwood (G-12845)	G	312 753-9134
Tuscan Hills Winery LLC — Effingham (G-8427)	G	217 347-9463
Valentino Vineyards Inc — Long Grove (G-13173)	G	847 634-2831
Village Vintner Winery Brewry — Algonquin (G-392)	G	847 658-4900
Vins & Vignobles LLC — Mount Prospect (G-14581)	G	312 375-7656
Walnut St Winery Plus Saunas — Rochester (G-17173)	G	217 498-9800
Waterman Winery & Vineyards — Waterman (G-20302)	G	815 264-3268
Weingarten LLC — Belleville (G-1610)	G	618 973-1879
Willetts Winery & Cellar — Manito (G-13441)	G	309 968-7070
Winery West of Wise — Petersburg (G-16605)	G	217 632-6003
Wyldewood Cellars 2 LLC — Saint Joseph (G-18321)	G	217 469-9463

BEVERAGES, BEER & ALE, WHOLESALE: Ale

Company	Code	Phone
Ale Syndicate Brewers LLC — Chicago (G-3600)	G	773 340-2337

BEVERAGES, NONALCOHOLIC: Bottled & canned soft drinks

Company	Code	Phone
American Bottling Company — Champaign (G-3264)	E	217 356-0577
Arbor Private Inv Co LLC — Chicago (G-3718)	G	312 981-3770
Beastman Tea LLC — Edwardsville (G-8350)	G	636 362-4594
Brewers Bottlers & Bev Corp — Chicago (G-3952)	G	773 262-9711
Central State Coca-Cola Peru — Peru (G-16572)	G	815 220-3100
Chicago Bottling Industries — Hoffman Estates (G-11413)	G	847 885-8093
Coca Cola — Carol Stream (G-2963)	G	630 588-8786
Coca Cola Bottling Compan — Rosemont (G-18006)	G	847 227-6766

Employee Codes: A=Over 500 employees, B=251-500
C=101-250, D=51-100, E=20-50, F=10-19, G=3-9

BEVERAGES, NONALCOHOLIC: Bottled & canned soft drinks

Coca-Cola Fleet Service ....G....... 847 600-2279	Pepsi Mid America ....G....... 217 826-8118	Necta Sweet Inc ....E 847 215-9955
Niles (G-15111)	Marshall (G-13576)	Buffalo Grove (G-2579)
Coca-Cola Btlg Wisconsin Del..............B....... 847 647-0200	Pepsi Midamerica Co.............................A....... 618 997-1377	Neiman Bros Co Inc...............................E 773 463-3000
Niles (G-15112)	Marion (G-13525)	Chicago (G-5564)
Coca-Cola Company ....D....... 847 647-0200	Pepsi Midamerica Co.............................B....... 618 242-6285	NFC Company Inc...................................G....... 773 472-6468
Niles (G-15113)	Mount Vernon (G-14634)	Chicago (G-5594)
Coca-Cola Refreshments USA Inc ....C....... 630 513-5247	Pepsi-Cola Chmpign Urbana Btlr ....D....... 217 352-4126	Pepsico Inc..D....... 312 821-1000
Saint Charles (G-18171)	Champaign (G-3330)	Chicago (G-5789)
Coca-Cola Refreshments USA Inc 217 348-1001	Pepsi-Cola Metro Btlg Co Inc..................D....... 847 598-3000	Royal Foods & Flavors Inc.....................F 847 595-9166
Charleston (G-3400)	Chicago (G-5788)	Elk Grove Village (G-9222)
Coca-Cola Refreshments USA Inc ....C....... 708 597-6700	Pepsico ....F 217 443-8607	Sensient Flavors ....C....... 847 645-7002
Alsip (G-433)	Danville (G-7373)	Hoffman Estates (G-11456)
Coca-Cola Refreshments USA Inc ....D....... 847 647-0200	Pepsico Inc..D....... 312 821-1000	Sensient Technologies Corp ....E 708 481-0910
Niles (G-15114)	Chicago (G-5789)	Matteson (G-13628)
Coca-Cola Refreshments USA Inc ....D....... 708 597-4700	Pepsico Inc..B....... 847 767-2026	Tampico Beverages Inc..........................F 773 296-0190
Chicago (G-4188)	Barrington (G-1234)	Chicago (G-6318)
Coca-Cola Refreshments USA Inc ....D....... 309 697-8600	Pespico ....G....... 708 625-3450	Watson LLC ....E 217 824-4440
Bartonville (G-1329)	Bridgeview (G-2374)	Taylorville (G-19763)
Coca-Cola Refreshments USA Inc 217 544-4892	Quincy Pepsi-Cola Bottling Co ....F 309 833-4263	Wm Wrigley Jr Company ....B....... 312 280-4710
Springfield (G-19352)	Macomb (G-13399)	Chicago (G-6654)
Coca-Cola Refreshments USA Inc ....E 217 367-1761	Quincy Pepsi-Cola Bottling Co ....D....... 217 223-8600	
Urbana (G-19978)	Quincy (G-16934)	## BEVERAGES, NONALCOHOLIC: Fruit Juices, Concentrtd, Fountain
Coca-Cola Refreshments USA Inc ....C....... 813 298-1000	Refreshment Services Inc.....................F 217 223-8600	
Rosemont (G-18007)	Quincy (G-16939)	
Coca-Cola Refreshments USA Inc ....C....... 618 542-2101	Refreshment Services Inc.....................E 217 522-8841	Institutional Foods Packing Co ....E 847 904-5250
Du Quoin (G-8117)	Springfield (G-19432)	Glenview (G-10569)
Containers Inc ....G....... 708 442-2000	Refreshment Services Inc.....................E 217 429-5415	Key Colony Inc..G....... 630 783-8572
Lyons (G-13306)	Decatur (G-7541)	Lemont (G-12568)
E & J Gallo Winery 630 505-4000	Rockys Beverages LLC ....F 312 561-3182	
Lisle (G-12886)	Glenview (G-10613)	## BEVERAGES, NONALCOHOLIC: Soft Drinks, Canned & Bottled, Etc
Emmert John ....F 773 292-6580	Springfield Pepsi-Cola Btlg Co ....C....... 217 522-8841	
Chicago (G-4499)	Springfield (G-19453)	
Essen Nutrition Corporation ....E 630 739-6700		American Bottling Company ....B 708 947-5000
Romeoville (G-17817)	## BEVERAGES, NONALCOHOLIC: Carbonated, Canned & Bottled, Etc	Northlake (G-15540)
Fast Forward Energy Inc ....G....... 312 860-0978		American Bottling Company ....E 815 877-7777
Chicago (G-4562)		Loves Park (G-13188)
Florida Fruit Juices Inc........................E 773 586-6200	Balon International Corp ....F 773 379-7779	American Bottling Company ....E 309 693-2777
Chicago (G-4611)	Chicago (G-3821)	Edwards (G-8336)
Flowers Distributing Inc........................E 618 255-1021	Clover Club Bottling Co Inc ....F 773 261-7100	Berner Food & Beverage LLC..............B 815 563-4222
East Alton (G-8165)	Chicago (G-4180)	Dakota (G-7311)
Gold Standard Enterprises Inc ....E 217 546-1633	Heartland Coca-Cola Btlg LLC...............A....... 217 544-4891	Dr Pepper/7 Up Bottling Group.............. 217 585-1496
Springfield (G-19375)	Springfield (G-19380)	Springfield (G-19360)
Great Lakes Coca-Cola Dist LLC.........D....... 847 227-6500	Heartland Coca-Cola Btlg LLC...............A....... 217 223-3336	Egg Cream America Inc........................G....... 847 559-2700
Rosemont (G-18025)	Quincy (G-16890)	Northbrook (G-15381)
Iberia Foods Corp ....G....... 847 678-2200	Heartland Coca-Cola Btlg LLC............... 217 367-1761	Excel Bottling Co ....E 618 526-7159
Bensenville (G-1821)	Urbana (G-19987)	Breese (G-2302)
Kalena LLC ....G....... 773 598-0033	Heartland Coca-Cola Btlg LLC...............A....... 309 697-8600	Gatorade Company ....A....... 312 821-1000
Chicago (G-5078)	Bartonville (G-1332)	Chicago (G-4662)
Key Colony Inc ....G....... 630 783-8572	Heartland Coca-Cola Btlg LLC...............A....... 217 348-1001	Keurig Dr Pepper Inc..............................D....... 708 947-5000
Lemont (G-12568)	Charleston (G-3403)	Northlake (G-15549)
Lee Gilster-Mary Corporation ....D....... 815 472-6456	Vision Wholesale Corp ....G....... 708 496-6015	Keurig Dr Pepper Inc..............................E 815 877-7777
Momence (G-14186)	Chicago (G-6558)	Loves Park (G-13228)
Powercoco LLC ....G....... 614 323-5890	Win Soon Chicago Inc ....G....... 630 585-7090	P-Americas LLC......................................C....... 309 266-2400
Chicago (G-5848)	Oswego (G-16032)	Morton (G-14375)
Pursuit Beverage Company LLC..........G....... 888 606-3353		Pepsi Cola Gen Bttlers of Lima 847 253-1000
Waukegan (G-20485)	## BEVERAGES, NONALCOHOLIC: Cider	Rolling Meadows (G-17760)
Quaker Oats Company ....A....... 312 821-1000		Rorke & Riley Specialty B ....G....... 773 929-2522
Chicago (G-5927)	Eckert Orchards Inc..............................C....... 618 233-0513	Chicago (G-6060)
Quaker Oats Company ....C....... 708 458-7090	Belleville (G-1549)	Royal Crown Tresses LLC.....................G....... 773 967-8409
Bridgeview (G-2376)	Mangel and Co ....E 847 459-3100	Lynwood (G-13299)
Reyes Holdings LLC.............................E 847 227-6500	Buffalo Grove (G-2567)	
Rosemont (G-18048)		## BEVERAGES, WINE & DISTILLED ALCOHOLIC, WHOLESALE: Liquor
Sirius Performance Company LLC.......G....... 312 909-0775	## BEVERAGES, NONALCOHOLIC: Flavoring extracts & syrups, nec	
Glenview (G-10622)		
Wis - Pak Inc..D....... 217 224-6800		Alto Vineyards Limited ....F 618 893-4898
Quincy (G-16958)	Abelei Inc..F 630 859-1410	Alto Pass (G-538)
Wonder Tucky Distillery & Btlg..............G....... 224 678-4396	North Aurora (G-15253)	Callison Distributing LLC......................D....... 618 277-4300
Woodstock (G-21449)	Big Tent Inc..E 708 532-1222	Belleville (G-1537)
	Tinley Park (G-19811)	Jamiel Inc...G....... 217 423-1000
## BEVERAGES, NONALCOHOLIC: Carbonated	Caravan Ingredients Inc ....D....... 708 849-8590	Decatur (G-7510)
	Dolton (G-7935)	
AD Huesing Corporation ....E 309 788-5652	Containers Inc ....G....... 708 442-2000	## BEVERAGES, WINE & DISTILLED ALCOHOLIC, WHOLESALE: Neutral Sp
Rock Island (G-17199)	Lyons (G-13306)	
Crisp Container Corporation ....D....... 618 998-0400	Custom Culinary Inc ....D....... 630 299-0500	
Marion (G-13508)	Oswego (G-16000)	Coca-Cola Refreshments USA Inc ....E 217 544-4892
Decatur Bottling Co ....E 217 429-5415	Dawn Food Products Inc......................C....... 815 933-0600	Springfield (G-19352)
Decatur (G-7485)	Bradley (G-2280)	Vins & Vignobles LLC............................G....... 312 375-7656
Komodo Brands LLC.............................G....... 312 788-2730	Equi-Chem International Inc ....F 630 784-0432	Mount Prospect (G-14581)
Chicago (G-5121)	Carol Stream (G-2979)	
P-Americas LLC......................................E 217 446-0123	FBC Industries Inc.................................G....... 847 839-0880	## BEVERAGES, WINE & DISTILLED ALCOHOLIC, WHOLESALE: Wine
Danville (G-7371)	Rochelle (G-17140)	
P-Americas LLC......................................D....... 847 437-1520	Flavor Concepts Inc..............................F 630 520-9060	
Elk Grove Village (G-9167)	Addison (G-123)	Bella Terra Winery LLC.........................F 618 658-8882
P-Americas LLC......................................B....... 773 893-2300	Flavor Savor Inc ....F 630 868-0350	Creal Springs (G-7080)
Chicago (G-5731)	Carol Stream (G-2985)	Coopers Hawk Intrmdate Hldg LL ....C....... 708 839-2920
P-Americas LLC......................................D....... 815 939-3123	Flavorfocus LLC.....................................D....... 630 520-9060	Downers Grove (G-7981)
Kankakee (G-11996)	Addison (G-124)	Coopers Hawk Intrmdate Hldg LL ....F 708 215-5674
P-Americas LLC......................................D....... 312 821-2266	Gycor International Ltd ....F 630 754-8070	Countryside (G-7048)
Chicago (G-5732)	Woodridge (G-21308)	De Vine Distributors LLC ....G....... 773 248-7005
P-Americas LLC......................................C....... 773 624-8013	Lee Gilster-Mary Corporation ....D....... 618 965-3426	Chicago (G-4326)
Chicago (G-5733)	Steeleville (G-19481)	

PRODUCT SECTION — BINDING SVC: Books & Manuals

Dtrs Enterprises Inc .... G 630 296-6890
 Bolingbrook *(G-2170)*
E & J Gallo Winery .... E 630 505-4000
 Lisle *(G-12886)*
Galena Cellars Winery .... E 815 777-3330
 Galena *(G-10169)*
Lincoln Heritage Winery LLC .... G 618 833-3783
 Cobden *(G-6942)*
RJ Distributing Co .... E 309 685-2794
 East Peoria *(G-8287)*
Terlato Wine Group Ltd .... G 847 604-8900
 Lake Bluff *(G-12210)*

BIBLE SCHOOL

Moody Bible Inst of Chicago .... A 312 329-4000
 Chicago *(G-5495)*

BICYCLE REPAIR SHOP

In The Attic Inc .... G 847 949-5077
 Mundelein *(G-14699)*

BICYCLE SHOPS

Wrench .... G 773 609-1698
 Chicago *(G-6684)*

BICYCLES, PARTS & ACCESS

Brg Sports Inc .... D 224 585-5200
 Des Plaines *(G-7741)*
Joe Hunt .... G 618 392-2000
 Olney *(G-15866)*
Pacific Cycle Inc .... C 618 393-2508
 Olney *(G-15882)*

BIDETS: Vitreous China

BBC Innovation Corporation .... E 847 458-2334
 Crystal Lake *(G-7168)*

BILLETS: Steel

Keystone Consolidated Inds Inc .... E 309 697-7020
 Peoria *(G-16466)*

BILLFOLD INSERTS: Plastic

Classic Fasteners LLC .... G 630 605-0195
 Saint Charles *(G-18170)*

BILLIARD & POOL TABLES & SPLYS

Tweeten Fibre Co .... E 312 733-7878
 Chicago *(G-6445)*

BILLIARD EQPT & SPLYS WHOLESALERS

Brunswick Corporation .... B 847 735-4700
 Mettawa *(G-13979)*

BILLING & BOOKKEEPING SVCS

American Hosp Assn Svcs Del .... E 312 422-2000
 Chicago *(G-3654)*

BINDING SVC: Books & Manuals

11th Street Express Prtg Inc .... F 815 968-0208
 Rockford *(G-17275)*
A A Swift Print Inc .... G 847 301-1122
 Schaumburg *(G-18424)*
A To Z Engraving Co Inc .... G 847 526-7396
 Wauconda *(G-20324)*
ABS Graphics Inc .... C 630 495-2400
 Itasca *(G-11615)*
Accord Carton Co .... C 708 272-3050
 Alsip *(G-410)*
Adams Printing Co .... G 618 529-2396
 Carbondale *(G-2838)*
Adcraft Printers Inc .... F 815 932-6432
 Kankakee *(G-11956)*
All Printing & Graphics Inc .... F 708 450-1512
 Broadview *(G-2415)*
All-Ways Quick Print .... G 708 403-8422
 Orland Park *(G-15938)*
Allegra Network LLC .... G 630 801-9335
 Aurora *(G-1047)*
Allegra Print & Imaging Inc .... G 847 697-1434
 Elgin *(G-8502)*
Alphadigital Inc .... G 708 482-4488
 La Grange *(G-12071)*
AlphaGraphics Printshops .... G 630 964-9600
 Lisle *(G-12861)*

Apple Graphics Inc .... G 630 389-2222
 Batavia *(G-1350)*
Apple Press Inc .... G 815 224-1451
 Peru *(G-16565)*
Arch Printing Inc .... G 630 966-0235
 Aurora *(G-1053)*
Art Bookbinders of America .... E 312 226-4100
 Chicago *(G-3734)*
Avid of Illinois Inc .... F 847 698-2775
 Saint Charles *(G-18152)*
B & B Printing Company .... G 217 285-6072
 Pittsfield *(G-16628)*
B J Plastic Molding Co .... E 630 766-3200
 Franklin Park *(G-9882)*
Bailleu & Bailleu Printing Inc .... G 309 852-2517
 Kewanee *(G-12021)*
Barnaby Inc .... F 815 895-6555
 Aurora *(G-1061)*
Bell Litho Inc .... D 847 952-3300
 Elk Grove Village *(G-8862)*
Benzinger Printing .... G 815 784-6560
 Genoa *(G-10315)*
Biller Press & Manufacturing .... G 847 395-4111
 Antioch *(G-604)*
Branstiter Printing Co .... G 217 245-6533
 Jacksonville *(G-11760)*
Cadore-Miller Printing Inc .... F 708 430-7091
 Hickory Hills *(G-11194)*
Cameron Printing Inc .... G 630 231-3301
 West Chicago *(G-20558)*
Cannon Ball Marketing Inc .... G 630 971-2127
 Lisle *(G-12875)*
Capitol Impressions Inc .... E 309 633-1400
 Peoria *(G-16397)*
Cardinal Colorprint Prtg Corp .... E 630 467-1000
 Itasca *(G-11634)*
Carter Printing Co Inc .... G 217 227-4464
 Farmersville *(G-9659)*
Century Printing .... G 618 632-2486
 O Fallon *(G-15570)*
Challenge Printers .... G 773 252-0212
 Chicago *(G-4067)*
Christopher R Cline Prtg Ltd .... F 847 981-0500
 Elk Grove Village *(G-8897)*
Cifuentes Luis & Nicole Inc .... G 847 490-3660
 Schaumburg *(G-18477)*
Cmb Printing Inc .... E 630 323-1110
 Burr Ridge *(G-2663)*
Commercial Copy Printing Ctr .... F 847 981-8590
 Elk Grove Village *(G-8903)*
Copy Mat Printing .... G 309 452-1392
 Bloomington *(G-2033)*
Copy Service Inc .... G 815 758-1151
 Dekalb *(G-7670)*
Copy-Mor Inc .... E 312 666-4000
 Streamwood *(G-19568)*
Cpr Printing Inc .... F 630 377-8420
 Geneva *(G-10263)*
Craftsmen Printing .... G 217 283-9574
 Hoopeston *(G-11506)*
Crossmark Printing Inc .... F 708 532-8263
 Tinley Park *(G-19819)*
D E Asbury Inc .... F 217 222-0617
 Hamilton *(G-10953)*
D G Brandt Inc .... G 815 942-4064
 Morris *(G-14301)*
D L V Printing Service Inc .... G 773 626-1661
 Chicago *(G-4301)*
Dale K Brown .... G 815 338-0222
 Woodstock *(G-21380)*
Darnall Printing .... G 309 827-7212
 Bloomington *(G-2039)*
Darwill Inc .... C 708 449-7770
 Hillside *(G-11335)*
David H Vander Ploeg .... G 708 331-7700
 South Holland *(G-19206)*
DE Asbury Inc .... E 217 222-0617
 Quincy *(G-16876)*
Deadline Prtg Clor Copying LLC .... G 847 437-9000
 Elk Grove Village *(G-8940)*
Deluxe Johnson .... C 847 635-7200
 Des Plaines *(G-7754)*
Denor Graphics Inc .... F 847 364-1930
 Elk Grove Village *(G-8944)*
Design Graphics Inc .... G 815 462-3323
 Frankfort *(G-9783)*
Diamond Graphics of Berwyn .... G 708 749-2500
 Berwyn *(G-1950)*
DMarv Design Specialty Prtrs .... G 708 389-4420
 Blue Island *(G-2118)*

Donnells Printing & Off Pdts .... G 815 842-6541
 Pontiac *(G-16768)*
E & H Graphic Service Inc .... G 708 748-5656
 Matteson *(G-13623)*
Einstein Crest .... G 847 965-7791
 Niles *(G-15119)*
Elgin Instant Print .... G 847 931-9006
 Elgin *(G-8575)*
Elliott Publishing Inc .... G 217 645-3033
 Liberty *(G-12622)*
F Weber Printing Co Inc .... G 815 468-6152
 Manteno *(G-13447)*
Fast Printing of Joliet Inc .... G 815 723-0080
 Joliet *(G-11864)*
Fastway Printing Inc .... G 847 882-0950
 Schaumburg *(G-18525)*
Fedex Office & Print Svcs Inc .... E 217 355-3400
 Champaign *(G-3292)*
Fedex Office & Print Svcs Inc .... F 847 475-8650
 Evanston *(G-9519)*
Fedex Office & Print Svcs Inc .... G 815 229-0033
 Rockford *(G-17412)*
Fedex Office & Print Svcs Inc .... F 847 329-9464
 Lincolnwood *(G-12819)*
Fedex Office & Print Svcs Inc .... F 847 729-3030
 Glenview *(G-10545)*
Fedex Office & Print Svcs Inc .... E 309 685-4093
 Peoria *(G-16437)*
Fedex Office & Print Svcs Inc .... G 847 459-8008
 Buffalo Grove *(G-2536)*
Fedex Office & Print Svcs Inc .... E 708 452-0149
 Elmwood Park *(G-9452)*
Fedex Office & Print Svcs Inc .... G 847 823-9360
 Park Ridge *(G-16274)*
Fedex Office & Print Svcs Inc .... F 630 894-1800
 Bloomingdale *(G-1995)*
Fedex Office & Print Svcs Inc .... E 847 670-4100
 Arlington Heights *(G-736)*
Fedex Office & Print Svcs Inc .... F 312 670-4460
 Chicago *(G-4577)*
Fernwood Printers Ltd .... G 630 964-9449
 Oak Forest *(G-15678)*
First Impression of Chicago .... G 773 224-3434
 Chicago *(G-4594)*
Fisheye Services Incorporated .... G 773 942-6314
 Chicago *(G-4598)*
Flash Printing Inc .... G 847 288-9101
 Franklin Park *(G-9944)*
Fleetwood Press Inc .... G 708 485-6811
 Brookfield *(G-2483)*
FM Graphic Impressions Inc .... E 630 897-8788
 Aurora *(G-1097)*
Forms Design Plus Coleman Prtg .... G 309 685-6000
 Peoria *(G-16439)*
French Studio Ltd .... G 618 942-5328
 Herrin *(G-11171)*
G F Printing .... G 618 797-0576
 Granite City *(G-10708)*
Gamma Alpha Visual Communicatn .... G 847 956-0633
 Park Ridge *(G-16279)*
Gossett Printing Inc .... G 618 548-2583
 Salem *(G-18341)*
Graphics Group LLC .... D 708 867-5500
 Chicago *(G-4729)*
Grasso Graphics Inc .... G 708 489-2060
 Alsip *(G-449)*
Grovak Instant Printing Co .... G 847 675-2414
 Mount Prospect *(G-14532)*
Hawthorne Press .... G 708 652-9000
 Cicero *(G-6852)*
Hawthorne Press Inc .... G 847 587-0582
 Spring Grove *(G-19275)*
Heart Printing Inc .... G 847 259-2100
 Arlington Heights *(G-748)*
Heritage Press Inc .... G 847 362-9699
 Libertyville *(G-12657)*
Highland Printers .... G 618 654-5880
 Highland *(G-11221)*
House of Graphics .... E 630 682-0810
 Carol Stream *(G-3000)*
Hq Printers Inc .... G 312 782-2020
 Chicago *(G-4857)*
Hub Printing Company Inc .... F 815 562-7057
 Rochelle *(G-17145)*
Ideal Advertising & Printing .... F 815 965-1713
 Rockford *(G-17456)*
Illinois Office Sup Elect Prtg .... E 815 434-0186
 Ottawa *(G-16056)*
Illinois Tool Works Inc .... E 708 720-0300
 Frankfort *(G-9807)*

Employee Codes: A=Over 500 employees, B=251-500
C=101-250, D=51-100, E=20-50, F=10-19, G=3-9

BINDING SVC: Books & Manuals PRODUCT SECTION

Image Print Inc .... G 815 672-1068
Streator (G-19611)
Impression Printing .... F 708 614-8660
Oak Forest (G-15682)
In-Print Graphics Inc .... E 708 396-1010
Oak Forest (G-15683)
Ink Well Printing & Design Ltd .... G 847 923-8060
Schaumburg (G-18559)
Insty Prints Palatine Inc .... F 847 963-0000
Palatine (G-16129)
Instyprints of Waukegan Inc .... G 847 336-5599
Waukegan (G-20449)
Integra Graphics and Forms Inc .... F 708 385-0950
Crestwood (G-7120)
International Graphics & Assoc .... F 630 584-2248
Saint Charles (G-18215)
J & J Mr Quick Print Inc .... G 773 767-7776
Chicago (G-4984)
J D Graphic Co Inc .... E 847 364-4000
Elk Grove Village (G-9063)
Jay Printing .... G 847 934-6103
Palatine (G-16133)
Jeannie Wagner .... G 815 477-2700
Crystal Lake (G-7212)
Joes Printing .... G 773 545-6063
Chicago (G-5034)
Johns-Byrne Company .... D 847 583-3100
Niles (G-15137)
Johnson Press America Inc .... E 815 844-5161
Pontiac (G-16773)
Josco Inc .... G 708 867-7189
Chicago (G-5051)
Jph Enterprises Inc .... G 847 390-0900
Des Plaines (G-7792)
Juskie Printing Corp .... G 630 663-8833
Downers Grove (G-8035)
K & M Printing Company Inc .... D 847 884-1100
Schaumburg (G-18584)
K O G Mfg & Bindery Corp .... F 847 263-5050
Waukegan (G-20453)
Kelly Printing Co Inc .... E 217 443-1792
Danville (G-7355)
Kendall Printing Co .... G 630 553-9200
Yorkville (G-21490)
Kens Quick Print Inc .... F 847 831-4410
Highland Park (G-11277)
Kevin Kewney .... G 217 228-7444
Quincy (G-16899)
Key Printing .... G 815 933-1800
Kankakee (G-11987)
Klein Printing Inc .... G 773 235-2121
Chicago (G-5108)
Klh Printing Corp .... G 847 459-0115
Wheeling (G-20926)
Kwik Print Inc .... G 630 773-3225
Itasca (G-11689)
LAC Enterprises Inc .... G 815 455-5044
Crystal Lake (G-7219)
Lans Printing Inc .... G 708 895-6226
Lynwood (G-13295)
Lasons Label Co .... G 773 775-2606
Chicago (G-5179)
Lee-Wel Printing Corporation .... G 630 682-0935
Wheaton (G-20812)
Leonard Emerson .... G 217 628-3441
Divernon (G-7880)
Lynns Printing Co .... G 618 465-7701
Alton (G-564)
M & G Graphics Inc .... E 773 247-1596
Chicago (G-5295)
M O W Printing Inc .... F 618 345-5525
Collinsville (G-6967)
Macoupin County Enquirer Inc .... E 217 854-2534
Carlinville (G-2879)
Mall Graphic Inc .... F 847 668-7600
Huntley (G-11554)
Marcus Press .... G 630 351-1857
Bloomingdale (G-1999)
Mark Twain Press Inc .... G 847 255-2700
Mundelein (G-14713)
Marquardt Printing Company .... E 630 887-8500
Burr Ridge (G-2698)
Mason City Banner Times .... F 217 482-3276
Mason City (G-13612)
Master Engraving .... G 217 965-5885
Virden (G-20188)
Mattoon Printing Center .... G 217 234-3100
Mattoon (G-13646)
McGrath Press Inc .... E 815 356-5246
Crystal Lake (G-7224)
McHenry Printing Services .... G 815 385-7600
McHenry (G-13765)
Mencarini Enterprises Inc .... F 815 398-9565
Rockford (G-17516)
Merritt & Edwards Corporation .... F 309 828-4741
Bloomington (G-2075)
Metro Printing & Pubg Inc .... F 618 476-9587
Millstadt (G-14052)
Mid Central Printing & Mailing .... F 847 251-4040
Wilmette (G-21087)
Mid City Printing Service .... G 773 777-5400
Chicago (G-5426)
Minuteman Press Inc .... G 847 577-2411
Arlington Heights (G-776)
Minuteman Press Morton Grove .... G 847 470-0212
Morton Grove (G-14429)
Minuteman Press of Rockford .... G 815 633-2992
Loves Park (G-13237)
Modern Printing of Quincy .... F 217 223-1063
Quincy (G-16917)
Mormor Incorporated .... G 630 268-0050
Lombard (G-13104)
Msf Graphics Inc .... G 847 446-6900
Des Plaines (G-7808)
Multicopy Corp .... G 847 446-7015
Grayslake (G-10792)
N Bujarski Inc .... G 847 884-1600
Schaumburg (G-18643)
N P D Inc .... G 708 424-6788
Oak Lawn (G-15729)
New Life Printing & Publishing .... G 847 658-4111
Algonquin (G-382)
Northwest Premier Printing .... G 773 736-1882
Chicago (G-5623)
Northwest Printing Inc .... G 815 943-7977
Harvard (G-11061)
Nu-Art Printing .... G 618 533-9971
Centralia (G-3242)
Off The Press LLC .... G 815 436-9612
Plainfield (G-16697)
Ogden Offset Printers Inc .... G 773 284-7797
Chicago (G-5663)
Olde Print Shoppe Inc .... G 618 395-3833
Olney (G-15879)
On Time Printing and Finishing .... G 708 544-4500
Hillside (G-11351)
P & S Cochran Printers Inc .... E 309 691-6668
Peoria (G-16489)
P H C Enterprises Inc .... G 847 816-7373
Vernon Hills (G-20080)
P P Graphics Inc .... G 708 343-2530
Westchester (G-20707)
Parrot Press .... G 773 376-6333
Chicago (G-5768)
Patrick Impressions LLC .... G 630 257-9336
Lemont (G-12578)
Patton Printing and Graphics .... G 217 347-0220
Effingham (G-8417)
Perma Graphics Printers .... G 815 485-6955
New Lenox (G-15050)
Perryco Inc .... F 815 436-2431
Plainfield (G-16701)
Pinney Printing Company .... F 815 626-2727
Sterling (G-19524)
PIP Printing Inc .... G 815 464-0075
Frankfort (G-9822)
Prairieland Printing .... G 309 647-5425
Washington (G-20276)
Precision Die Cutting & Finish .... G 773 252-5625
Chicago (G-5856)
Preferred Printing Service .... G 312 421-2343
Chicago (G-5861)
Print & Design Services LLC .... G 847 317-9001
Bannockburn (G-1206)
Print Turnaround Inc .... F 847 228-1762
Arlington Heights (G-791)
Printed Word Inc .... G 847 328-1511
Evanston (G-9570)
Printing Inc .... D 316 265-1201
Chicago (G-5881)
Printing By Joseph .... G 708 479-2669
Mokena (G-14109)
Printing Craftsmen of Joliet .... G 815 254-3982
Joliet (G-11917)
Printing Etc Inc .... G 815 562-6151
Rochelle (G-17152)
Printing Plus .... G 708 301-3900
Lockport (G-13019)
Printing Plus of Roselle Inc .... G 630 893-0410
Roselle (G-17974)
Printing Source Inc .... G 773 588-2930
Morton Grove (G-14433)
Printmeisters Inc .... G 708 474-8400
Lansing (G-12512)
Printsource Plus Inc .... G 708 389-6252
Blue Island (G-2134)
Pro-Type Printing Inc .... G 217 379-4715
Paxton (G-16315)
Progress Printing Corporation .... E 773 927-0123
Chicago (G-5898)
Quad City Press .... F 309 764-8142
Moline (G-14170)
Quad/Graphics Inc .... A 815 734-4121
Mount Morris (G-14500)
Quality Quickprint Inc .... F 815 439-3430
Joliet (G-11920)
Quality Quickprint Inc .... F 815 838-1784
Lockport (G-13020)
Quickprinters .... G 309 833-5250
Macomb (G-13398)
Quinn Print Inc .... G 847 823-9100
Park Ridge (G-16293)
R R Donnelley & Sons Company .... A 815 584-2770
Dwight (G-8158)
Rapid Print .... G 309 673-0826
Peoria (G-16508)
Remke Printing Inc .... G 847 520-7300
Wheeling (G-20972)
Reprographics .... G 815 477-1018
Crystal Lake (G-7254)
Review Printing Co Inc .... G 309 788-7094
Rock Island (G-17241)
Rightway Printing Inc .... F 630 790-0444
Glendale Heights (G-10488)
River Bend Printing .... G 217 324-6056
Litchfield (G-12975)
Ro-Web Inc .... G 309 688-2155
Peoria (G-16512)
Robal Company Inc .... F 630 393-0777
Warrenville (G-20252)
Rodin Enterprises Inc .... G 847 412-1370
Wheeling (G-20976)
Rohrer Litho Inc .... G 630 833-6610
Elmhurst (G-9420)
Rose Business Forms & Printing .... G 618 533-3032
Centralia (G-3248)
Rrr Graphics & Film Corp .... G 708 478-4573
Mokena (G-14114)
Rudin Printing Company Inc .... F 217 528-5111
Springfield (G-19436)
Rusty & Angela Buzzard .... G 217 342-9841
Effingham (G-8423)
S B Liquidating Company .... D 847 758-9500
Elk Grove Village (G-9225)
Salem Times-Commoner Inc .... E 618 548-3330
Salem (G-18358)
Samecwei Inc .... G 630 897-7888
Aurora (G-1153)
Scheiwes Print Shop .... G 815 683-2398
Crescent City (G-7082)
Schommer Inc .... G 815 344-1404
McHenry (G-13791)
Schwebel Printing .... G 618 684-3911
Murphysboro (G-14759)
Scientfic Bndery Prdctions Inc .... G 847 329-0510
Skokie (G-19027)
Service Printing Corporation .... G 847 669-9620
Huntley (G-11566)
Shawver Press Inc .... G 815 772-4700
Morrison (G-14348)
Shoreline Graphics Inc .... G 847 587-4804
Ingleside (G-11589)
Shree Mahavir Inc .... G 312 408-1080
Chicago (G-6159)
Shree Printing Corp .... G 773 267-9500
Chicago (G-6160)
Sigley Printing & Off Sup Co .... G 618 997-5304
Marion (G-13535)
Sir Speedy Printing .... G 312 337-0774
Chicago (G-6177)
Sommers & Fahrenbach Inc .... F 773 478-3033
Chicago (G-6201)
Speedys Quick Print .... G 217 431-0510
Danville (G-7381)
Springfield Printing Inc .... G 217 787-3500
Springfield (G-19454)
Stearns Printing of Charleston .... G 217 345-7518
Charleston (G-3414)
Steve Bortman .... G 708 442-1669
Lyons (G-13315)

Swifty Print .... G 630 584-9063
　Saint Charles (G-18283)
T F N W Inc .... G 630 584-7383
　Naperville (G-14926)
Techprint Inc .... F 847 616-0109
　Elk Grove Village (G-9269)
The b F Shaw Printing Co .... E 815 875-4461
　Princeton (G-16823)
Thomas Printing & Sty Co .... G 618 435-2801
　Benton (G-1937)
Tower Printing & Design .... G 630 495-1976
　Lombard (G-13145)
Tree Towns Reprographics Inc .... F 630 832-0209
　Elmhurst (G-9437)
Tri-Tower Printing Inc .... G 847 640-6633
　Rolling Meadows (G-17782)
Tru Line Lithographing Inc .... E 262 554-7300
　Niles (G-15183)
Trump Printing Inc .... F 217 429-9001
　Decatur (G-7563)
United Lithograph Inc .... G 847 803-1700
　Des Plaines (G-7861)
Viking Printing & Copying Inc .... G 312 341-0985
　Chicago (G-6551)
Voris Communication Co Inc .... C 630 898-4268
　Berkeley (G-1946)
Wagner John .... G 847 564-0017
　Northbrook (G-15498)
We-B-Print Inc .... G 309 353-8801
　Pekin (G-16368)
Weakley Printing & Sign Shop .... G 847 473-4466
　North Chicago (G-15323)
West Vly Graphics & Print Inc .... G 630 377-7575
　Saint Charles (G-18298)
William Holloway Ltd .... G 847 866-9520
　Evanston (G-9588)
Wood River Printing & Pubg Co .... G 618 254-3134
　Wood River (G-21268)
Woogl Corporation .... E 847 806-1160
　Elk Grove Village (G-9312)
Wortman Printing Company Inc .... G 217 347-3775
　Effingham (G-8432)

BINDING SVC: Trade

Hopkins Printing & Envelope Co .... F 630 543-8227
　Addison (G-152)
Instant Collating Service Inc .... F 312 243-4703
　Chicago (G-4937)

BIOLOGICAL PRDTS: Blood Derivatives

Csl Behring LLC .... B 815 932-6773
　Bradley (G-2279)
Northern Ill Blood Bnk Inc .... F 815 965-8751
　Rockford (G-17538)

BIOLOGICAL PRDTS: Coagulation

Aspen API Inc .... F 847 635-0985
　Des Plaines (G-7734)

BIOLOGICAL PRDTS: Exc Diagnostic

Abbvie Inc .... C 847 932-7900
　North Chicago (G-15300)
Abbvie US LLC .... G 800 255-5162
　North Chicago (G-15304)
Avexis Inc .... C 847 572-8280
　Bannockburn (G-1190)
Avexis Inc .... C 847 572-8280
　Libertyville (G-12633)
Avexis Inc .... E 847 572-8280
　Libertyville (G-12634)
Bioaffinity Inc .... G 815 988-5077
　Rockford (G-17324)
Biologos Inc .... G 630 801-4740
　Montgomery (G-14234)
Bn National Trail .... G 618 783-8709
　Newton (G-15081)
C & S Chemicals Inc .... G 815 722-6671
　Joliet (G-11837)
Midwest Bio Manufacturing Div .... F 815 542-6417
　Tampico (G-19744)
Proteintech Group Inc .... E 312 455-8498
　Rosemont (G-18045)
Ptm Biolabs Inc .... G 312 802-6843
　Chicago (G-5911)
Quorum Labs LLC .... G 618 525-5600
　Eldorado (G-8482)
Vectorbuilder Inc .... F 510 552-3632
　Chicago (G-6529)

W-R Industries Inc .... G 312 733-5200
　Bellwood (G-1642)

BIOLOGICAL PRDTS: Toxin, Viruses/Simlr Substncs, Incl Venom

Roy Winnett .... G 309 367-4867
　Metamora (G-13967)

BIOLOGICAL PRDTS: Vaccines

Kinesis Vaccines LLC .... G 847 543-7725
　Grayslake (G-10786)

BIOLOGICAL PRDTS: Veterinary

Cislak Manufacturing Inc .... E 847 647-1819
　Niles (G-15110)
Splash Dog Therapy Inc .... G 847 296-4007
　Des Plaines (G-7850)

BLACKBOARDS & CHALKBOARDS

Claridge Products and Eqp Inc .... G 847 991-8822
　Elgin (G-8543)

BLACKBOARDS: Slate

Vecchio Manufacturing of Ill .... F 847 742-8429
　Elgin (G-8773)

BLACKSMITH SHOP

B J Fehr Machine Co .... G 309 923-8691
　Roanoke (G-17099)
Fehring Ornamental Iron Works .... G 217 483-6727
　Rochester (G-17166)

BLADES: Knife

Summerville Consulting Svcs LLC .... G 618 547-7142
　Alma (G-404)

BLADES: Saw, Chain Type

Unicut Corporation .... G 773 525-4210
　Chicago (G-6464)

BLADES: Saw, Hand Or Power

Amv International Inc .... F 815 282-9990
　Loves Park (G-13189)
Contour Saws Inc .... E 800 259-6834
　Des Plaines (G-7749)
Midwest Saw Inc .... G 630 293-4252
　West Chicago (G-20618)
Roentgen USA LLC .... G 847 787-0135
　Schiller Park (G-18840)
Saws Unlimited Inc .... G 847 640-7450
　Elk Grove Village (G-9232)
Tru-Cut Tool & Supply Co .... F 708 396-1122
　Wheeling (G-21002)
Wikus Saw Technology Corp .... E 630 766-0960
　Addison (G-335)

BLANKBOOKS & LOOSELEAF BINDERS

Acco Europe Fin Holdings LLC .... G 800 222-6462
　Lake Zurich (G-12377)
Assemble and Mail Group Inc .... G 309 473-2006
　Heyworth (G-11189)
Bindery Maintenance Services .... G 618 945-7480
　Bridgeport (G-2309)
Post Press Production Inc .... F 630 860-9833
　Elk Grove Village (G-9185)

BLANKBOOKS: Albums

Zookbinders Inc .... D 847 272-5745
　Deerfield (G-7663)

BLANKBOOKS: Albums, Record

George S Music Room .... G 773 767-4676
　Chicago (G-4684)
Polyvinyl Record Co .... G 217 403-1752
　Champaign (G-3336)

BLANKBOOKS: Ledgers & Ledger Sheets

Howard Medical Company .... G 773 278-1440
　Chicago (G-4850)

BLANKBOOKS: Memorandum, Printed

Funeral Register Books Inc .... F 217 627-3235
　Girard (G-10382)

BLANKBOOKS: Passbooks, Bank, Etc

Harris Bmo Bank National Assn .... E 815 886-1900
　Romeoville (G-17830)

BLANKBOOKS: Scrapbooks

Chartwell Studio Inc .... G 847 868-8674
　Chicago (G-4077)
Got 2b Scrappin .... G 217 347-3600
　Effingham (G-8401)
Heart & Soul Memories Inc .... G 847 478-1931
　Buffalo Grove (G-2544)

BLANKETS, FROM PURCHASED MATERIALS

Cotton Goods Manufacturing Co .... F 773 265-0088
　Chicago (G-4247)

BLAST FURNACE & RELATED PRDTS

Gerdau Ameristeel US Inc .... G 800 237-0230
　Chicago (G-4687)
O & K American Corp .... D 773 767-2500
　Chicago (G-5644)

BLASTING SVC: Sand, Metal Parts

Paradigm Coatings LLC .... G 847 961-6466
　Huntley (G-11557)
Specialty Pntg Soda Blastg Inc .... G 815 577-0006
　Plainfield (G-16716)
Stripmasters Services Inc .... G 217 429-0904
　Decatur (G-7553)

BLINDS & SHADES: Vertical

9161 Corporation .... G 847 470-8828
　Niles (G-15097)
Chicago Blind Company .... G 815 553-5525
　Joliet (G-11839)
Hansens Mfrs Win Coverings .... E 815 935-0010
　Bradley (G-2284)
Jack Beall Vertical Service In .... G 847 426-7958
　Abingdon (G-10)
Regent Window Fashions LLC .... G 773 871-6400
　Chicago (G-6003)
Vertical Tower Partner .... G 217 819-3040
　Champaign (G-3364)
Znl Corporation .... G 815 654-0870
　Loves Park (G-13284)

BLINDS : Window

21st Century Us-Sino Services .... G 312 808-9328
　Chicago (G-3464)
A B C Blind Inc .... G 708 877-7100
　Thornton (G-19784)
Carol Andrzejewski .... G 630 369-9711
　Naperville (G-14790)
EZ Blinds and Drapery Inc .... F 708 246-6600
　Westmont (G-20742)
Levolor Inc .... G 800 346-3278
　Oak Brook (G-15633)

BLINDS, WOOD

Aspen Shutters Inc .... G 847 979-0166
　Schaumburg (G-18446)

BLOCKS & BRICKS: Concrete

Artistries By Tommy Musto Inc .... G 630 674-8667
　Bloomingdale (G-1977)
Beelman Ready-Mix Inc .... G 618 247-3866
　Sandoval (G-18362)
Bricks Inc .... F 773 523-5718
　Chicago (G-3953)
Bricks Inc .... G 630 897-6926
　Aurora (G-1066)
Contractors Ready-Mix Inc .... G 217 482-5530
　Mason City (G-13610)
Hamilton Concrete Products Co .... G 217 847-3118
　Hamilton (G-10958)
Lion Concrete Products Inc .... G 630 892-7304
　Montgomery (G-14257)
M & M Exposed Aggregate Co .... G 847 551-1818
　Carpentersville (G-3108)

BLOCKS & BRICKS: Concrete

Meno Stone Co Inc .... E 630 257-9220
  Lemont *(G-12571)*
Midwest Cement Products Inc .... G 815 284-2342
  Woosung *(G-21452)*
Monmouth Ready Mix Corp .... G 309 734-3211
  Galesburg *(G-10212)*
Quikrete Companies LLC .... F 309 346-1184
  Pekin *(G-16357)*
Southfield Corporation .... F 217 875-5455
  Decatur *(G-7548)*
Southfield Corporation .... E 708 458-0400
  Oak Lawn *(G-15735)*
Techo-Bloc Midwest Corp .... F 877 832-4625
  Rock Island *(G-17248)*

BLOCKS: Drystack Interlocking, Concrete

Max-Block Development LLC .... G 773 220-6214
  Chicago *(G-5369)*

BLOCKS: Landscape Or Retaining Wall, Concrete

Mef Construction Inc .... G 847 741-8601
  Elgin *(G-8655)*
R & D Concrete Products Inc .... E 309 787-0264
  Rock Island *(G-17237)*
RR Mulch and Soil LLC .... G 708 596-7200
  Markham *(G-13551)*
Scotts Exterior Maintenance Co .... G 309 660-3380
  Bloomington *(G-2092)*
Valley View Industries Hc Inc .... E 800 323-9369
  Crestwood *(G-7133)*

BLOCKS: Paving, Composition

Clean Sweep Environmental Inc .... G 630 879-8750
  Batavia *(G-1367)*

BLOCKS: Paving, Concrete

Paveloc Industries Inc .... F 815 568-4700
  Marengo *(G-13492)*

BLOCKS: Paving, Cut Stone

Unilock Chicago Inc .... D 630 892-9191
  Aurora *(G-1165)*

BLOCKS: Sewer & Manhole, Concrete

Midwest Water Group Inc .... E 866 526-6558
  Crystal Lake *(G-7230)*

BLOCKS: Standard, Concrete Or Cinder

Building Products Corp .... E 618 233-4427
  Belleville *(G-1536)*
County Materials Corp .... E 217 352-4181
  Champaign *(G-3283)*
Elston Materials LLC .... G 773 235-3100
  Chicago *(G-4490)*
Harvey Cement Products Inc .... F 708 333-1900
  Harvey *(G-11087)*
Lafarge Building Materials Inc .... D 678 746-2000
  Chicago *(G-5155)*
Lafarge North America Inc .... C 773 372-1000
  Chicago *(G-5156)*
Macomb Concrete Products Inc .... G 309 772-3826
  Bushnell *(G-2743)*
Midwest Block and Brick Inc .... E 618 939-7600
  Waterloo *(G-20292)*
Northfield Block Company .... G 708 458-8130
  Berwyn *(G-1957)*
Sesser Concrete Products Co .... F 618 625-2811
  Sesser *(G-18866)*
Swansea Building Products Inc .... G 618 874-6282
  East Saint Louis *(G-8326)*
Terrell Materials Corporation .... E 847 635-8530
  Rosemont *(G-18053)*
Tison & Hall Concrete Products .... F 618 253-7808
  Harrisburg *(G-11030)*

BLOCKS: Tackle, Metal

Durabilt Dyvex Inc .... F 708 397-4673
  Broadview *(G-2432)*

BLOOD RELATED HEALTH SVCS

Lemaitre Vascular Inc .... F 847 462-2191
  Fox River Grove *(G-9760)*
Samel Botros .... G 847 466-5905
  Bloomingdale *(G-2014)*

BLOWER FILTER UNITS: Furnace Blowers

Clean and Science USA Co Ltd .... G 847 461-9292
  Rolling Meadows *(G-17722)*
Filter Friend Z Inc .... G 847 824-4049
  Des Plaines *(G-7765)*
Kap Holdings LLC .... F 708 948-0226
  Oak Park *(G-15759)*

BLOWERS & FANS

Air Source Corp .... G 630 355-7655
  Geneva *(G-10249)*
Air-Drive Inc .... E 847 625-0226
  Lake Forest *(G-12221)*
Basement Dewatering Systems .... F 309 647-0331
  Canton *(G-2821)*
Bce-USA LLC .... G 815 556-8037
  Franklin Park *(G-9884)*
Bost Corporation .... F 708 450-9234
  Melrose Park *(G-13835)*
C P Environmental Inc .... F 630 759-8866
  Romeoville *(G-17801)*
Camfil USA Inc .... D 815 459-6600
  Crystal Lake *(G-7177)*
Catalytic Products Intl Inc .... E 847 438-0334
  Lake Zurich *(G-12390)*
Communication Coil Inc .... E 847 671-1333
  Schiller Park *(G-18795)*
Durable Manufacturing Company .... F 630 766-0398
  Bensenville *(G-1791)*
Dust Patrol Inc .... G 309 676-1161
  Peoria *(G-16432)*
Filtertek Inc .... B 815 648-2410
  Hebron *(G-11143)*
Filtration Group Corporation .... D 512 593-7999
  Oak Brook *(G-15619)*
Filtration Group LLC .... E 815 726-4600
  Joliet *(G-11865)*
Frequency Devices Inc .... F 815 434-7800
  Ottawa *(G-16053)*
G T C Industries Inc .... G 708 369-9815
  Naperville *(G-14832)*
Gardner Denver Inc .... D 770 632-5000
  Quincy *(G-16883)*
Goose Island Mfg & Supply Corp .... G 708 343-4225
  Lansing *(G-12495)*
Henry Technologies Inc .... G 217 483-2406
  Chatham *(G-3421)*
Industrial Fiberglass Inc .... F 708 681-2707
  Melrose Park *(G-13882)*
Jacobs Boiler & Mech Inds Inc .... E 773 385-9900
  Chicago *(G-4998)*
Keating of Chicago Inc .... E 815 569-2324
  Capron *(G-2834)*
Master Manufacturing Co .... F 630 833-7060
  Villa Park *(G-20159)*
Mity Inc .... G 630 365-5030
  Elburn *(G-8461)*
Perma-Pipe Intl Holdings Inc .... E 847 966-1000
  Niles *(G-15158)*
Quality Cleaning Fluids Inc .... G 847 451-1190
  Franklin Park *(G-10029)*
Robko Flock Coating Company .... G 847 272-6202
  Northbrook *(G-15474)*
Tri-Dim Filter Corporation .... E 847 695-5822
  Elgin *(G-8759)*
Turbo Dry LLC .... F 847 702-4430
  Palatine *(G-16168)*
Vent Products Co Inc .... E 773 521-1900
  Chicago *(G-6532)*

BLOWERS & FANS

Df Fan Services Inc .... F 630 876-1495
  West Chicago *(G-20570)*
Jan-Air Inc .... E 815 678-4516
  Richmond *(G-17015)*
Scott Industrial Blower Co .... F 847 426-8800
  Gilberts *(G-10370)*
William W Meyer and Sons .... D 847 918-0111
  Libertyville *(G-12726)*

BLUEPRINTING SVCS

Accurate Repro Inc .... F 630 428-4433
  Naperville *(G-14763)*
Cushing and Company .... E 312 266-8228
  Chicago *(G-4287)*
Decatur Blue Print Company .... G 217 423-7589
  Decatur *(G-7484)*

PRODUCT SECTION

Lake County Press Inc .... C 847 336-4333
  Waukegan *(G-20458)*
Merritt & Edwards Corporation .... F 309 828-4741
  Bloomington *(G-2075)*
Precision Reproductions Inc .... F 847 724-0182
  Glenview *(G-10602)*
Reprographics .... G 815 477-1018
  Crystal Lake *(G-7254)*
Robal Company Inc .... F 630 393-0777
  Warrenville *(G-20252)*
Tree Towns Reprographics Inc .... F 630 832-0209
  Elmhurst *(G-9437)*
UPS Store .... G 312 372-2727
  Chicago *(G-6491)*

BOAT BLDG/RPRG: Life Rafts, Noninflatable, Rubber/Plastic

Wave Pads LLC .... G 224 444-9283
  Plainfield *(G-16728)*

BOAT BUILDING & REPAIR

Air Land and Sea Interiors .... G 630 834-1717
  Villa Park *(G-20129)*
Akema Inc .... G 708 482-3148
  La Grange *(G-12070)*
Chicago Sea Ray Inc .... E 815 385-2720
  Volo *(G-20197)*
Mastercraft Auto Rebuilding .... F 847 487-8787
  Wauconda *(G-20373)*
Nautic Global Group LLC .... G 574 457-5731
  Chicago *(G-5555)*
Scf Services LLC .... E 314 436-7559
  Sauget *(G-18398)*
Union Ave Auto Inc .... G 708 754-3899
  Steger *(G-19495)*

BOAT BUILDING & REPAIRING: Fiberglass

Advocations Inc .... G 815 568-7505
  Woodstock *(G-21356)*
Brunswick Corporation .... B 847 735-4700
  Mettawa *(G-13979)*
Brunswick Family Boat Co Inc .... G 847 735-4700
  Lake Forest *(G-12234)*
Brunswick International Ltd .... E 847 735-4700
  Mettawa *(G-13980)*
Crowleys Yacht Yard Lakeside .... F 773 221-9990
  Chicago *(G-4276)*
Custom Fiberglass of Illinois .... G 309 344-7727
  Galesburg *(G-10189)*
Elite Power Boats Inc .... G 618 654-6292
  Highland *(G-11215)*
Karma Yacht Sales LLC .... G 773 254-0200
  Chicago *(G-5083)*
Leisure Properties LLC .... A 618 937-6426
  West Frankfort *(G-20675)*
Metro East Fiberglass Repair .... G 618 235-9217
  Belleville *(G-1577)*
Oquawka Boats and Fabrications .... G 309 867-2213
  Oquawka *(G-15906)*
Rinalli Boat Co Inc .... G 618 467-8850
  Godfrey *(G-10660)*
Tls Windsled Inc .... G 815 262-5791
  Belvidere *(G-1704)*

BOAT BUILDING & REPAIRING: Motorboats, Inboard Or Outboard

Sereen LLC .... G 386 527-4876
  Rockford *(G-17625)*
Waypoint Enterprises .... G 847 551-9213
  Algonquin *(G-395)*

BOAT BUILDING & REPAIRING: Pontoons, Exc Aircraft & Inflat

Outback USA Inc .... G 863 699-2220
  Saint Charles *(G-18240)*

BOAT DEALERS

Metro East Fiberglass Repair .... G 618 235-9217
  Belleville *(G-1577)*
Nieman & Considine Inc .... F 312 326-1053
  Chicago *(G-5600)*

BOAT DEALERS: Motor

Chicago Sea Ray Inc .... E 815 385-2720
  Volo *(G-20197)*

PRODUCT SECTION

BOTTLED WATER DELIVERY

Karma Yacht Sales LLC .... G 773 254-0200
Chicago (G-5083)

BOAT DEALERS: Outboard

Sereen LLC .... G 386 527-4876
Rockford (G-17625)

BOAT REPAIR SVCS

Accu-Wright Fiberglass Inc .... G 618 337-3318
East Saint Louis (G-8295)
Bee Boat Co Inc .... G 217 379-2605
Paxton (G-16307)
Karma Yacht Sales LLC .... G 773 254-0200
Chicago (G-5083)
Oquawka Boats and Fabrications .... G 309 867-2213
Oquawka (G-15906)

BOATS & OTHER MARINE EQPT: Plastic

Bee Boat Co Inc .... G 217 379-2605
Paxton (G-16307)
Dometic Corporation .... A 847 447-7190
Rosemont (G-18019)

BOBBINS: Textile Spinning, Made From Purchased Materials

TJ Assemblies Inc .... E 847 671-0060
Bensenville (G-1902)

BODIES: Truck & Bus

Caterpillar Inc .... A 217 475-4000
Decatur (G-7471)
Entrans International LLC .... E 618 548-3660
Salem (G-18337)
Independent Antique RAD Mfg .... G 847 458-7400
Algonquin (G-374)
Knapheide Manufacturing Co .... F 217 222-7134
Quincy (G-16901)
Kurts Carstar Collision Ctr .... F 618 345-4519
Maryville (G-13591)
Lmt Inc .... F 217 568-8265
Galva (G-10235)
McLaughlin Body Co .... D 309 762-7755
Moline (G-14159)
Navistar Inc .... B 662 494-3421
Lisle (G-12919)
Navistar International Corp .... A 331 332-5000
Lisle (G-12921)
Pafco Truck Bodies Inc .... F 309 699-4613
East Peoria (G-8281)
Phils Auto Body .... G 773 847-7156
Chicago (G-5801)
Pools Welding Inc .... G 309 787-2083
Milan (G-14020)
R & L Truck Service Inc .... F 847 489-7135
Wadsworth (G-20212)
Summit Tank & Equipment Co .... F 708 594-3040
Mc Cook (G-13703)
Thule Inc .... C 847 455-2420
Forest Park (G-9725)
Triseal Corporation .... E 815 648-2473
Hebron (G-11151)
Wag Industries Inc .... F 847 329-8932
Skokie (G-19053)

BODY PARTS: Automobile, Stamped Metal

Amis Inc .... G 708 598-9700
Bridgeview (G-2323)
Bosch Auto Svc Solutions Inc .... F 815 407-3900
Romeoville (G-17799)
Illinois Tool Works Inc .... G 708 720-3541
Frankfort (G-9808)
ITW Dynatec .... G 847 657-4830
Glenview (G-10573)
Mmma .... F 309 888-8765
Normal (G-15211)
Rhino Pros .... G 815 235-7767
Freeport (G-10137)
Taurus Die Casting LLC .... F 815 316-6160
Rockford (G-17654)
Waupaca Foundry Inc .... C 217 347-0600
Effingham (G-8430)

BOILER & HEATING REPAIR SVCS

Petro Chem Echer Erhardt LLC .... G 773 847-7535
Chicago (G-5798)

BOILER REPAIR SHOP

Atlas Boiler & Welding Company .... G 815 963-3360
Elgin (G-8517)
Cruise Boiler and Repr Co Inc .... F 630 279-7111
Elmhurst (G-9356)
DS Air & Heating Inc .... G 773 826-7411
Chicago (G-4398)
Jacobs Boiler & Mech Inds Inc .... E 773 385-9900
Chicago (G-4998)
Jarvis Welding Co .... G 309 647-0033
Canton (G-2827)
JM Industries LLC .... E 708 849-4700
Riverdale (G-17072)
Pedraza Inc .... F 773 874-9020
Chicago (G-5780)
Rayes Boiler & Welding Ltd .... G 847 675-6655
Skokie (G-19020)
South Side Bler Wldg Works Inc ..... G 708 478-1714
Orland Park (G-15981)
Spannuth Boiler Co .... G 708 386-1882
Oak Park (G-15774)

BOILERS & BOILER SHOP WORK

Hudson Boiler & Tank Company ..... F 312 666-4780
Lockport (G-13001)
M4 Steel LLC .... G 309 222-6027
Washington (G-20274)

BOILERS: Low-Pressure Heating, Steam Or Hot Water

Cruise Boiler and Repr Co Inc .... F 630 279-7111
Elmhurst (G-9356)
DS Air & Heating Inc .... G 773 826-7411
Chicago (G-4398)

BOLTS: Metal

Acme Screw Co .... D 630 665-2200
Wheaton (G-20784)
Agrati USA Corp .... B 708 228-5193
Park Forest (G-16252)
All American Washer Werks Inc ...... E 847 566-9091
Mundelein (G-14661)
Ampex Screw Mfg Inc .... G 847 228-1202
Arlington Heights (G-692)
Aspen Manufacturing Company ...... G 630 495-0922
Addison (G-41)
BBC Fasteners Inc .... E 708 597-9100
Alsip (G-421)
Elite Fasteners Inc .... E 815 397-8848
Rockford (G-17395)
Formed Fastener Mfg Inc .... E 708 496-1219
Bridgeview (G-2348)
J H Botts LLC .... E 815 726-5885
Joliet (G-11883)
Metform LLC .... E 815 273-2201
Mount Carroll (G-14495)
MNP Precision Parts LLC .... C 815 391-5256
Rockford (G-17530)
Pearson Fastener Corporation .... F 815 397-4460
Rockford (G-17550)
Rockford Bolt & Steel Co .... E 815 968-0514
Rockford (G-17587)
Screws Industries Inc .... D 630 539-9200
Glendale Heights (G-10493)
Wenco Manufacturing Co Inc .... E 630 377-7474
Elgin (G-8781)

BOOK ENDS, METAL

Avondale Adventures .... G 773 588-5761
Chicago (G-3789)

BOOK STORES

African-American Images Inc .... F 708 672-4909
Crete (G-7134)
Filmfax Magazine Inc .... G 847 866-7155
Evanston (G-9520)
Graphic Score Book Co Inc .... G 847 823-7482
Park Ridge (G-16281)

BOOK STORES: Children's

Phoenix Intl Publications Inc .... B 877 277-9441
Chicago (G-5803)
Senario LLC .... F 847 882-0677
Schaumburg (G-18711)

BOOK STORES: College

Barnes & Noble College .... E 309 677-2320
Peoria (G-16390)

BOOK STORES: Religious

Polonia Book Store Inc .... G 773 481-6968
Chicago (G-5835)

BOOKING AGENCIES, THEATRICAL

Haute Noir Media Group Inc .... G 312 869-4526
Chicago (G-4787)

BOOKS, WHOLESALE

About Learning Inc .... F 847 487-1800
Wauconda (G-20326)
Art Media Resources Inc .... G 312 663-5351
Chicago (G-3736)
Baker & Taylor LLC .... B 815 802-2444
Momence (G-14183)
Chicago Review Press Inc .... E 312 337-0747
Chicago (G-4126)
Follett School Solutions Inc .... C 815 759-1700
McHenry (G-13745)
P F Pettibone & Co .... E 815 344-7811
Crystal Lake (G-7242)
Psytec Inc .... G 815 758-1415
Dekalb (G-7699)
Research Press Company Inc .... F 217 352-3273
Champaign (G-3341)

BOOKS: Memorandum, Exc Printed, From Purchased Materials

House of Doolittle Ltd .... E 847 228-9591
Arlington Heights (G-751)

BOOSTERS: Feeder Voltage, Electric

Dukane Corporation .... G 630 797-4900
Saint Charles (G-18190)

BOOTHS: Spray, Sheet Metal, Prefabricated

D & R Autochuck Inc .... E 815 394-1744
Rockford (G-17364)
Heartland Fabrication LLC .... G 309 448-2644
Congerville (G-6999)

BOOTS: Women's

Horse Creek Outfitters .... G 217 544-2740
Springfield (G-19382)

BORATE COMPOUND MINING: Natural

US Borax Inc .... C 773 270-6500
Chicago (G-6499)

BORING MILL

Pietro Carnaghi USA Inc .... G 779 368-0564
Rockford (G-17554)

BOTTLE CAPS & RESEALERS: Plastic

Berry Global Inc .... C 847 884-1200
Schaumburg (G-18461)
Berry Global Inc .... C 847 541-7900
Buffalo Grove (G-2515)
Berry Global Inc .... G 630 375-0358
Aurora (G-923)
Berry Global Inc .... E 630 896-6200
Aurora (G-1065)
Jigsaw Solutions Inc .... G 630 926-1948
Romeoville (G-17835)

BOTTLED GAS DEALERS: Propane

Dcc Propane LLC .... G 217 395-2648
Roberts (G-17105)
Ferrellgas LP .... G 815 877-7333
Machesney Park (G-13342)
Outback USA Inc .... G 863 699-2220
Saint Charles (G-18240)

BOTTLED WATER DELIVERY

Ds Services of America Inc .... F 800 322-6272
Rockford (G-17386)
Mautino Distributing Co Inc .... E 815 664-4311
Spring Valley (G-19310)

BOTTLED WATER DELIVERY

Samuel Rowell..................................G........ 618 942-6970
  Herrin *(G-11178)*
Waterco of Central States Inc................C........ 630 576-4782
  Lombard *(G-13153)*

BOTTLES: Plastic

Alpha Packaging Minnesota Inc............G........ 507 454-3830
  Chicago *(G-3630)*
Astro Plastic Containers Inc...................F........ 708 458-7100
  Bolingbrook *(G-2150)*
Container Specialties Inc........................E........ 708 615-1400
  Franklin Park *(G-9914)*
Dana Plastic Container Corp..................G........ 847 670-0650
  Arlington Heights *(G-725)*
Dana Plastic Container Corp..................E........ 630 529-7878
  Schaumburg *(G-18504)*
Graham Packaging Company LP............E........ 630 739-9150
  Woodridge *(G-21306)*
Illinois Bottle Mfg Co..............................D........ 847 595-9000
  Elk Grove Village *(G-9040)*
Inhance Technologies LLC.....................E........ 630 231-7515
  West Chicago *(G-20595)*
Isovac Products LLC..............................G........ 630 679-1740
  Romeoville *(G-17834)*
Logoplaste Chicago LLC........................G........ 815 230-6961
  Plainfield *(G-16684)*
Logoplaste Fort Worth LLC....................G........ 815 230-6961
  Plainfield *(G-16685)*
Logoplaste Racine LLC..........................G........ 815 230-6961
  Plainfield *(G-16686)*
Logoplaste Usa Inc................................D........ 815 230-6961
  Plainfield *(G-16687)*
Oak Hill Brands Corp..............................G........ 630 922-5010
  Lombard *(G-13111)*
Phoenix Unlimited Ltd............................G........ 847 515-1263
  Huntley *(G-11559)*
Plastic Container Corporation................D........ 217 352-2722
  Urbana *(G-19993)*
Plastipak Packaging Inc.........................B........ 217 398-1832
  Champaign *(G-3334)*
Plastipak Packaging Inc.........................C........ 708 385-0721
  Alsip *(G-493)*
Pretium Packaging LLC..........................D........ 815 224-2633
  Peru *(G-16590)*
Pvc Container Corporation.....................C........ 217 463-6600
  Paris *(G-16241)*
Ring Container Tech LLC.......................E........ 217 875-5084
  Decatur *(G-7542)*
Ring Container Tech LLC.......................E........ 815 229-9110
  Rockford *(G-17572)*
Ringwood Containers LP.......................E........ 815 939-7270
  Kankakee *(G-11998)*
Silgan Plastics LLC.................................D........ 618 662-4471
  Flora *(G-9692)*
Twistshake LLC......................................G........ 224 419-0086
  Waukegan *(G-20511)*
Whitney Products Inc.............................F........ 847 966-6161
  Niles *(G-15187)*

BOTTLES: Vacuum

Tkk USA Inc..C........ 847 439-7821
  Rolling Meadows *(G-17780)*

BOWLING CENTERS

Brunswick Corporation...........................B........ 847 735-4700
  Mettawa *(G-13979)*

BOWLING EQPT & SPLYS

Bobs Business Inc..................................G........ 630 238-5790
  Bensenville *(G-1755)*
Bowl-Tronics Enterprises Inc..................G........ 847 741-4500
  Elgin *(G-8523)*

BOX & CARTON MANUFACTURING EQPT

British Converting Solutions...................G........ 630 219-1906
  Elmhurst *(G-9337)*

BOXES & CRATES: Rectangular, Wood

Caisson Inc...E........ 815 547-5925
  Belvidere *(G-1658)*
Chicago Crate Inc...................................G........ 708 380-4716
  Downers Grove *(G-7969)*
D/C Export & Domestic Pkg Inc.............E........ 847 593-4200
  Elk Grove Village *(G-8935)*
Induspac Rtp Inc.....................................E........ 919 484-9484
  Bridgeview *(G-2358)*
Nefab Packaging N Centl LLC................C........ 630 451-5314
  Hanover Park *(G-11010)*
R & H Products Inc.................................G........ 815 744-4110
  Rockdale *(G-17270)*
Specialty Crate Factory..........................G........ 708 756-2100
  Steger *(G-19492)*
Wil Son Pallet...E........ 217 543-3555
  Sullivan *(G-19675)*

BOXES & SHOOK: Nailed Wood

Arrowtech Pallet & Crating....................D........ 815 547-9300
  Belvidere *(G-1650)*
Central Wood Products Inc....................E........ 217 728-4412
  Sullivan *(G-19664)*
Chicago Export Packing Co....................E........ 773 247-8911
  Chicago *(G-4102)*
Community Support Systems.................D........ 217 705-4300
  Teutopolis *(G-19767)*
Dexton Enterprises.................................G........ 309 788-1881
  Rock Island *(G-17217)*
Du-Call Miller Plastics Inc......................F........ 630 964-6020
  Elburn *(G-8450)*
Fca LLC..E........ 309 949-3999
  Coal Valley *(G-6936)*
Fca LLC..E........ 309 385-2588
  Princeville *(G-16827)*
Jordan Paper Box Company...................F........ 773 287-5362
  Chicago *(G-5048)*
Kccdd Inc...G........ 309 344-2030
  Galesburg *(G-10205)*
Nefab Packaging N Centl LLC................C........ 630 451-5314
  Hanover Park *(G-11010)*
Pak Source Inc.......................................E........ 309 786-7374
  Rock Island *(G-17231)*
R & H Products Inc.................................G........ 815 744-4110
  Rockdale *(G-17270)*
Trade Industries.....................................E........ 618 643-4321
  Mc Leansboro *(G-13709)*

BOXES: Cash & Stamp, Stamped Metal

Block and Company Inc..........................C........ 847 537-7200
  Wheeling *(G-20860)*

BOXES: Corrugated

Akers Packaging Service Inc..................D........ 773 731-2900
  Chicago *(G-3594)*
Akers Packaging Solutions Inc...............E........ 217 468-2396
  Oreana *(G-15910)*
All-Pak Manufacturing Corp...................D........ 630 851-5859
  Aurora *(G-1046)*
Alois Box Co Inc....................................E........ 708 681-4090
  Melrose Park *(G-13824)*
American Boxboard LLC.........................E........ 708 924-9810
  Batavia *(G-1348)*
Batavia Container Inc............................C........ 630 879-2100
  Batavia *(G-1355)*
Blackhawk Corrugated LLC....................E........ 844 270-2296
  Carol Stream *(G-2948)*
Box Manufacturing Inc...........................G........ 309 637-6228
  Peoria *(G-16394)*
Box USA...G........ 708 562-6000
  Northlake *(G-15543)*
Cameo Container Corporation................C........ 773 254-1030
  Chicago *(G-4011)*
Cano Container Corporation..................E........ 630 585-7500
  Aurora *(G-934)*
Capitol Carton Company........................E........ 312 563-9690
  Chicago *(G-4017)*
Capitol Carton Company........................E........ 312 491-2220
  Chicago *(G-4018)*
Cascades Plastics Inc............................E........ 450 469-3389
  Aurora *(G-935)*
Compak Inc..E........ 815 399-2699
  Machesney Park *(G-13335)*
Corr-Pak Corporation.............................E........ 708 442-7806
  Mc Cook *(G-13690)*
Cross Container Corporation..................E........ 847 844-3200
  Carpentersville *(G-3099)*
DDN Industries Inc.................................G........ 847 885-8595
  Hoffman Estates *(G-11417)*
Forest Packaging Corporation................E........ 847 981-7000
  Elk Grove Village *(G-9003)*
Georg-Pcific Corrugated IV LLC.............E........ 630 896-3610
  Aurora *(G-967)*
Georgia-Pacific LLC...............................C........ 217 999-2511
  Mount Olive *(G-14503)*
Green Bay Packaging Inc.......................E........ 847 455-2553
  Downers Grove *(G-8014)*
Greif Inc..D........ 217 468-2396
  Oreana *(G-15911)*
H Field & Sons Inc..................................F........ 847 434-0970
  Arlington Heights *(G-745)*
Harris Container Corp............................G........ 630 553-0027
  Yorkville *(G-21488)*
Heritage Packaging LLC.........................E........ 217 735-4406
  Lincoln *(G-12730)*
Ideal Box Co...C........ 708 594-3100
  Chicago *(G-4875)*
Illinois Valley Container Inc....................E........ 815 223-7200
  Peru *(G-16578)*
Inglese Box Co Ltd................................E........ 847 669-1700
  Huntley *(G-11543)*
International Paper Company.................C........ 708 728-8200
  Chicago *(G-4954)*
International Paper Company.................C........ 630 896-2061
  Montgomery *(G-14251)*
International Paper Company.................D........ 708 562-6000
  Northlake *(G-15548)*
International Paper Company.................E........ 217 735-1221
  Lincoln *(G-12731)*
J H H of Illinois Inc.................................F........ 630 293-0739
  West Chicago *(G-20602)*
Kindlon Enterprises Inc..........................G........ 708 367-4000
  Aurora *(G-994)*
Liberty Diversified Intl Inc......................E........ 217 935-8361
  Clinton *(G-6925)*
Liberty Diversified Intl Inc......................C........ 309 787-6161
  Rock Island *(G-17227)*
M and M Box Partition Co......................E........ 773 276-8400
  Chicago *(G-5298)*
Menasha Corp..G........ 630 679-8000
  Bolingbrook *(G-2210)*
Menasha Packaging Company LLC.......G........ 630 263-4547
  Champaign *(G-3320)*
Menasha Packaging Company LLC.......C........ 773 227-6000
  Chicago *(G-5391)*
Menasha Packaging Company LLC.......B........ 312 880-4620
  Chicago *(G-5392)*
Menasha Packaging Company LLC.......F........ 618 931-7805
  Edwardsville *(G-8369)*
Menasha Packaging Company LLC.......C........ 630 236-4011
  Aurora *(G-1130)*
Menasha Packaging Company LLC.......C........ 708 552-8946
  Bridgeview *(G-2362)*
Menasha Packaging Company LLC.......C........ 618 501-6040
  Edwardsville *(G-8370)*
Menasha Packaging Company LLC.......C........ 708 482-7619
  Bolingbrook *(G-2211)*
Menasha Packaging Company LLC.......G........ 773 489-8332
  Northbrook *(G-15432)*
Menasha Packaging Company LLC.......G........ 708 552-8946
  Bridgeview *(G-2363)*
Menasha Packaging Company LLC.......B........ 309 787-1747
  Rock Island *(G-17229)*
Midwest Fibre Products Inc....................E........ 309 596-2955
  Viola *(G-20180)*
Midwest Packaging & Cont Inc..............D........ 815 633-6800
  Machesney Park *(G-13361)*
Murnane Specialties Inc.........................F........ 708 449-1200
  Geneva *(G-10291)*
Nation Inc...E........ 847 844-7300
  Carpentersville *(G-3109)*
Orora North America..............................D........ 630 613-2600
  Lombard *(G-13114)*
Orora Packaging Solutions.....................D........ 815 895-2343
  Sycamore *(G-19727)*
Packaging Corporation America.............F........ 847 388-6000
  Mundelein *(G-14722)*
Packaging Corporation America.............D........ 708 821-1600
  Chicago *(G-5739)*
Packaging Corporation America.............G........ 773 378-8700
  Chicago *(G-5740)*
Packaging Corporation America.............D........ 708 594-5260
  Bedford Park *(G-1489)*
Packaging Corporation America.............G........ 618 662-6700
  Flora *(G-9687)*
Packaging Design Corporation...............E........ 630 323-1354
  Burr Ridge *(G-2712)*
PCA Corrugated and Display LLC..........A........ 847 482-3000
  Lake Forest *(G-12284)*
PCA International Inc.............................G........ 847 482-3000
  Lake Forest *(G-12285)*
Pry-Bar Company...................................F........ 815 436-3383
  Joliet *(G-11918)*
Reliable Container Inc............................E........ 630 543-6131
  Addison *(G-269)*
Rex Carton Company Inc.......................E........ 773 581-4115
  Bridgeview *(G-2382)*

Royal Box Group LLC..........................C....... 708 656-2020
Cicero *(G-6871)*
Royal Box Group LLC..........................E....... 630 543-4464
Addison *(G-277)*
Royal Box Group LLC..........................F....... 708 222-4650
Cicero *(G-6872)*
Rudd Container Corporation................D....... 773 847-7600
Chicago *(G-6079)*
SCI Box LLC...E....... 618 244-7244
Mount Vernon *(G-14637)*
Simon Box Mfg Co.................................G....... 815 722-6661
Lockport *(G-13023)*
Sisco Corporation..................................E....... 618 327-3066
Nashville *(G-15010)*
Stand Fast Group LLC..........................D....... 630 600-0900
Carol Stream *(G-3075)*
Sterling Box Company Inc....................F....... 815 626-9657
Sterling *(G-19534)*
Strive Converting Corporation.............C....... 773 227-6000
Chicago *(G-6254)*
Sun Container Inc.................................G....... 417 681-0503
Mount Vernon *(G-14641)*
Thomas Glenn Holdings LLC................E....... 630 916-8090
Lombard *(G-13144)*
Tri-City Corrugated Inc.........................F....... 630 372-6200
Bartlett *(G-1317)*
United Container Corporation...............E....... 773 342-2200
Chicago *(G-6471)*
Wabash Container Corporation.............E....... 618 263-3586
Mount Carmel *(G-14491)*
Welch Packaging Group Inc.................E....... 815 547-1505
Belvidere *(G-1710)*
Westrock Container LLC........................D....... 847 239-8800
Northbrook *(G-15501)*
Westrock Cp LLC...................................C....... 309 342-0121
Galesburg *(G-10224)*
Westrock Cp LLC...................................C....... 847 689-4200
North Chicago *(G-15324)*
Westrock Cp LLC...................................C....... 618 654-2141
Highland *(G-11248)*
Westrock Cp LLC...................................D....... 708 458-8100
Bridgeview *(G-2399)*
Westrock Cp LLC...................................D....... 630 384-5200
Carol Stream *(G-3087)*
Westrock Rkt LLC...................................C....... 630 429-2400
Aurora *(G-1170)*
York Corrugated Container Corp...........D....... 630 260-2900
Glendale Heights *(G-10516)*

BOXES: Junction, Electric

Appleton Grp LLC...................................C....... 847 268-6000
Rosemont *(G-17999)*

BOXES: Mail Or Post Office, Collection/Storage, Sheet Metal

US Post Co Inc..G....... 815 675-9313
Spring Grove *(G-19306)*

BOXES: Outlet, Electric Wiring Device

Lew Electric Fittings Co.........................F....... 630 665-2075
Carol Stream *(G-3017)*
Midwest-Design Inc.................................G....... 708 615-1572
Broadview *(G-2452)*

BOXES: Packing & Shipping, Metal

Product Service Craft Inc.......................F....... 630 964-5160
Downers Grove *(G-8085)*
Zenith Fabricating Company..................E....... 773 622-2601
Chicago *(G-6717)*

BOXES: Paperboard, Folding

Accord Carton Co....................................C....... 708 272-3050
Alsip *(G-410)*
Americraft Carton....................................G....... 630 225-7311
Oak Brook *(G-15593)*
Arbor Private Inv Co LLC........................G....... 312 981-3770
Chicago *(G-3718)*
Box Form Inc...E....... 773 927-8808
Chicago *(G-3938)*
Capitol Carton Company.........................E....... 312 563-9690
Chicago *(G-4017)*
Colbert Packaging Corporation..............C....... 847 367-5990
Lake Forest *(G-12238)*
Combined Technologies Inc...................G....... 847 968-4855
Libertyville *(G-12645)*
Gpi Midwest LLC.....................................E....... 847 741-0247
Elgin *(G-8599)*
Graphic Packaging Intl LLC...................D....... 618 533-2721
Centralia *(G-3233)*
Graphic Packaging Intl LLC...................B....... 630 260-6500
Carol Stream *(G-2993)*
H Field & Sons Inc..................................F....... 847 434-0970
Arlington Heights *(G-745)*
Impac Group Inc......................................A....... 708 344-9100
Melrose Park *(G-13881)*
Jordan Paper Box Company..................F....... 773 287-5362
Chicago *(G-5048)*
Knight Paper Box Company...................D....... 773 585-2035
Bridgeview *(G-2360)*
Lbp Manufacturing LLC..........................B....... 800 545-6200
Cicero *(G-6863)*
Master Paper Box Company Inc............C....... 773 927-0252
Chicago *(G-5358)*
MB Box Inc..G....... 815 589-3043
Fulton *(G-10155)*
Midwest Fibre Products Inc...................E....... 309 596-2955
Viola *(G-20180)*
Nosco Inc...B....... 847 336-4200
Gurnee *(G-10904)*
Nosco Inc...D....... 847 360-4874
Waukegan *(G-20471)*
P S Greetings Inc....................................C....... 708 831-5340
Chicago *(G-5729)*
Plasticrest Products Inc..........................F....... 773 826-2163
Chicago *(G-5818)*
Racine Paper Box Manufacturing...........E....... 773 227-3900
Chicago *(G-5958)*
Rex Carton Company Inc........................E....... 773 581-4115
Bridgeview *(G-2382)*
Specialty Box Corp..................................F....... 630 897-7278
North Aurora *(G-15277)*
The Calumet Carton Company...............D....... 708 331-7910
South Holland *(G-19249)*
United Press Inc......................................F....... 847 482-0597
Lincolnshire *(G-12799)*
Westrock Cp LLC....................................C....... 309 342-0121
Galesburg *(G-10224)*

BOXES: Paperboard, Set-Up

Armbrust Paper Tubes Inc.......................E....... 773 586-3232
Chicago *(G-3730)*
Bierdeman Box LLC..................................E....... 847 256-0302
Wilmette *(G-21069)*
Colbert Packaging Corporation...............C....... 847 367-5990
Lake Forest *(G-12238)*
Elegant Acquisition LLC..........................D....... 708 652-3400
Cicero *(G-6845)*
International Paper Company..................E....... 708 728-1000
Bedford Park *(G-1473)*
Jordan Paper Box Company....................F....... 773 287-5362
Chicago *(G-5048)*
Master Paper Box Company Inc..............C....... 773 927-0252
Chicago *(G-5358)*
Racine Paper Box Manufacturing.............E....... 773 227-3900
Chicago *(G-5958)*
Reddi-Pac Inc..F....... 847 657-5222
Glenview *(G-10609)*

BOXES: Plastic

Akrylix Inc...F....... 773 869-9005
Frankfort *(G-9764)*
Aptargroup International LLC.................G....... 815 477-0424
Crystal Lake *(G-7161)*
CTS Automotive LLC................................E....... 815 385-9480
McHenry *(G-13734)*
Home Pdts Intl - N Amer Inc...................B....... 773 890-1010
Chicago *(G-4834)*
Plano Holding LLC...................................F....... 630 552-3111
Plano *(G-16739)*
Plano Molding Company LLC..................G....... 630 552-3111
Plano *(G-16741)*
Plasticrest Products Inc...........................F....... 773 826-2163
Chicago *(G-5818)*
Really Useful Boxes Inc...........................F....... 847 238-0444
Bloomingdale *(G-2011)*

BOXES: Solid Fiber

John J Monaco Products Co Inc.............E....... 708 344-3333
Melrose Park *(G-13887)*
Stitch TEC Co Inc....................................G....... 618 327-8054
Nashville *(G-15011)*
The Calumet Carton Company................D....... 708 331-7910
South Holland *(G-19249)*

BOXES: Stamped Metal

Plasticrest Products Inc...........................F....... 773 826-2163
Chicago *(G-5818)*

BOXES: Wirebound, Wood

A & M Wood Products Inc........................G....... 630 323-2555
Burr Ridge *(G-2647)*

BOXES: Wooden

D/C Export & Domestic Pkg Inc..............E....... 847 593-4200
Elk Grove Village *(G-8935)*
Elm Street Industries Inc.........................F....... 309 854-7000
Kewanee *(G-12032)*
Extreme Tools Inc.....................................G....... 630 202-8324
Naperville *(G-14826)*
Ockerlund Industries Inc..........................E....... 630 620-1269
Addison *(G-230)*
Pierce Packaging Co................................F....... 815 636-5650
Loves Park *(G-13245)*
Pierce Packaging Co................................G....... 815 636-5656
Peoria *(G-16497)*
Pierce Packaging Co................................F....... 815 636-5656
Loves Park *(G-13246)*
Specialty Box Corp...................................F....... 630 897-7278
North Aurora *(G-15277)*

BRAKES & BRAKE PARTS

Bpi Holdings International Inc.................C....... 815 363-9000
McHenry *(G-13722)*
Brake Parts Inc India LLC........................G....... 815 363-9000
McHenry *(G-13723)*
Brake Parts Inc LLC..................................C....... 815 363-9000
McHenry *(G-13725)*
Continental Auto Systems Inc..................B....... 847 862-6300
Deer Park *(G-7580)*
Gunite Corporation...................................B....... 815 490-6260
Rockford *(G-17436)*
Honeywell International Inc.....................B....... 269 428-6305
Saint Joseph *(G-18317)*
Mann+hummel Filtration Technol...........G....... 815 759-7744
McHenry *(G-13763)*
Morse Automotive Corporation...............A....... 773 843-9000
Buffalo Grove *(G-2577)*
Performance Manufacturing.....................G....... 630 231-8099
West Chicago *(G-20629)*
Powerstop...G....... 708 442-6761
Mc Cook *(G-13698)*
Rebuilders Enterprises Inc......................G....... 708 430-0030
Bridgeview *(G-2380)*
Robert Bosch LLC....................................B....... 917 421-7209
Broadview *(G-2466)*

BRAKES: Metal Forming

Kipp Manufacturing Company Inc...........F....... 630 768-9051
Wauconda *(G-20366)*

BRAKES: Press

Ceg Subsidiary LLC..................................D....... 618 262-8666
Mount Carmel *(G-14467)*
R-K Press Brake Dies Inc........................F....... 708 371-1756
Chicago *(G-5955)*
Right Lane Industries LLC.......................G....... 857 869-4132
Chicago *(G-6031)*
Riteway Brake Dies Inc...........................F....... 708 430-0795
Bridgeview *(G-2383)*

BRASS & BRONZE PRDTS: Die-casted

G & W Electric Company..........................E....... 708 388-6363
Blue Island *(G-2123)*
Mahoney Foundries Inc...........................E....... 309 784-2311
Vermont *(G-20037)*

BRASS FOUNDRY, NEC

AJ Oster LLC...C....... 630 260-1040
Carol Stream *(G-2929)*
Altman Pattern and Foundry Co..............F....... 773 586-9100
Chicago *(G-3637)*
Calumet Brass Foundry Inc.....................F....... 708 849-3040
Dolton *(G-7934)*
Cast Technologies Inc..............................C....... 309 676-1715
Peoria *(G-16398)*
Illini Foundry Co Inc.................................G....... 309 697-3142
Peoria *(G-16456)*
Tricast/Presfore Corporation...................G....... 815 459-1820
Crystal Lake *(G-7285)*

PRODUCT

Employee Codes: A=Over 500 employees, B=251-500
C=101-250, D=51-100, E=20-50, F=10-19, G=3-9

2020 Harris Illinois
Industrial Directory

1363

BRASS FOUNDRY, NEC

Trio Foundry Inc .... E 630 892-1676
　Montgomery *(G-14272)*

BRASS ROLLING & DRAWING

Global Brass and Copper Inc .... G 502 873-3000
　East Alton *(G-8166)*
Global Brass Cop Holdings Inc .... E 847 240-4700
　Schaumburg *(G-18535)*
Wieland Holdings Inc .... A 847 537-3990
　Wheeling *(G-21013)*

BRASSWORK: Ornamental, Structural

Krum Kreations .... G 815 772-8296
　Morrison *(G-14344)*

BRAZING SVCS

Ehrhardt Tool & Machine LLC .... C 314 436-6900
　Granite City *(G-10704)*

BRAZING: Metal

International Proc Co Amer .... E 847 437-8400
　Elk Grove Village *(G-9058)*
Rogers Metal Services Inc .... E 847 679-4642
　Skokie *(G-19024)*
Standard Heat Treating Co Inc .... D 708 447-7504
　Chicago *(G-6228)*

BRICK, STONE & RELATED PRDTS WHOLESALERS

Clay Vollmar Products Co .... G 847 540-5850
　Lake Zurich *(G-12394)*
Eagle Stone and Brick Inc .... G 618 282-6722
　Red Bud *(G-16993)*
Jackson County Sand & Grav Co .... G 618 763-4711
　Gorham *(G-10682)*
Paveloc Industries Inc .... F 815 568-4700
　Marengo *(G-13492)*
Tri-State Cut Stone Co .... E 815 469-7550
　Frankfort *(G-9845)*

BRICKS : Ceramic Glazed, Clay

Selee Corporation .... E 847 428-4455
　Gilberts *(G-10371)*

BRICKS : Paving, Clay

Arrowhead Brick Pavers Inc .... E 630 393-1584
　Warrenville *(G-20231)*
Complete Lawn and Snow Service ...... F 847 776-7287
　Palatine *(G-16102)*
Northshore Gardens Ltd .... G 847 672-4391
　North Chicago *(G-15318)*
Rapid Landscaping Inc .... G 815 740-1000
　Crest Hill *(G-7095)*

BRICKS: Clay

Richards Brick Company .... D 618 656-0230
　Edwardsville *(G-8374)*

BRICKS: Concrete

Glen-Gery Corporation .... D 815 795-6911
　Marseilles *(G-13555)*
New Panel Brick Company of Ill .... G 847 696-1686
　Niles *(G-15152)*

BRIDAL SHOPS

Casa Di Castronovo Inc .... G 815 962-4731
　Rockford *(G-17338)*
Chambers Marketing Options .... G 847 584-2626
　Elk Grove Village *(G-8888)*
Doris Bridal Boutique .... G 847 433-2575
　Highwood *(G-11306)*
Duckys Formal Wear Inc .... G 309 342-5914
　Galesburg *(G-10191)*
Jane Stodden Bridals .... G 815 223-2091
　La Salle *(G-12116)*
Winning Stitch .... G 217 348-8279
　Charleston *(G-3417)*

BRIEFCASES

J-Industries Inc .... F 815 654-0055
　Loves Park *(G-13220)*
Jacobson Acqstion Holdings LLC .... C 847 623-1414
　Waukegan *(G-20452)*

BROACHING MACHINES

Illinois Broaching Company .... E 847 678-3080
　Schiller Park *(G-18815)*
Inland Broaching and TI Co LLC .... G 847 233-0033
　Elgin *(G-8626)*
Rockford Broach Inc .... F 815 484-0409
　Rockford *(G-17588)*
Universal Broaching Inc .... F 847 228-1440
　Elk Grove Village *(G-9298)*

BROADCASTING & COMMS EQPT: Antennas, Transmitting/Comms

AF Antronics Inc .... G 217 328-0800
　Villa Grove *(G-20121)*
Amphenol T&M Antennas Inc .... F 847 478-5600
　Lincolnshire *(G-12746)*
Antenex Inc .... D 847 839-6910
　Schaumburg *(G-18441)*
Charles Electronics LLC .... G 815 244-7981
　Mount Carroll *(G-14494)*
Innovative AV Systems Inc .... G 312 265-6282
　Elmhurst *(G-9379)*
Nucurrent Inc .... F 312 575-0388
　Chicago *(G-5640)*
Pc-Tel Inc .... C 630 372-6800
　Bloomingdale *(G-2008)*
Research In Motion Rf Inc .... G 815 444-1095
　Crystal Lake *(G-7255)*

BROADCASTING & COMMS EQPT: Rcvr-Transmitter Unt, Transceiver

Portable Cmmnctons Spclsts .... G 630 458-1800
　Addison *(G-246)*

BROADCASTING & COMMUNICATION EQPT: Transmit-Receiver, Radio

Las Systems Inc .... E 847 462-8100
　Woodstock *(G-21404)*
LL Electronics .... G 217 586-6477
　Mahomet *(G-13425)*
Sure-Response Inc 888 530-5668
　Carbondale *(G-2861)*

BROADCASTING & COMMUNICATIONS EQPT: Cellular Radio Telephone

Acp Tower Holdings LLC .... C 800 835-8527
　Chicago *(G-3531)*
Community Advantage Network .... G 847 376-8943
　Des Plaines *(G-7748)*
Gogo LLC .... D 630 647-1400
　Bensenville *(G-1813)*
Gogo LLC .... B 630 647-1400
　Chicago *(G-4711)*
Lemko Corporation .... E 630 948-3025
　Schaumburg *(G-18603)*
Skybitz Tank Monitoring Corp .... E 312 379-8397
　Chicago *(G-6183)*
Xentris Wireless LLC .... G 844 936-8747
　Addison *(G-339)*

BROADCASTING & COMMUNICATIONS EQPT: Studio Eqpt, Radio & TV

Anywave Communication Tech Inc ..... F 847 415-2258
　Vernon Hills *(G-20042)*
Jai-S Record Label .... G 708 351-4279
　Park Forest *(G-16256)*

BROADCASTING & COMMUNICATIONS EQPT: Transmitting, Radio/TV

BEI Electronics LLC .... F 217 224-9600
　Quincy *(G-16863)*

BROKERS' SVCS

Arby Graphic Service Inc .... F 847 763-0900
　Glencoe *(G-10428)*
Integra Graphics and Forms Inc .... F 708 385-0950
　Crestwood *(G-7120)*
Tailored Printing Inc .... G 217 498-1057
　Rochester *(G-17172)*

BROKERS, MARINE TRANSPORTATION

Kabat American Inc .... G 870 739-1430
　Saint Charles *(G-18219)*

BROKERS: Business

Paragon Packaging Inc .... G 707 786-4004
　Chicago *(G-5758)*
Ssn LLC .... G 815 978-8729
　Byron *(G-2759)*

BROKERS: Commodity Contracts

Huyear Trucking Inc .... G 217 854-3551
　Carlinville *(G-2876)*

BROKERS: Contract Basis

Healthy Body LLC .... G 208 409-6602
　Ottawa *(G-16054)*

BROKERS: Food

Chicago Local Foods LLC .... E 312 432-6575
　Chicago *(G-4111)*
Custom Culinary Inc .... D 630 299-0500
　Oswego *(G-16000)*
Far East Food Inc .... G 312 733-1688
　Chicago *(G-4560)*
Hensaal Management Group Inc .... G 312 624-8133
　Chicago *(G-4804)*
Hop Kee Incorporated .... E 312 791-9111
　Chicago *(G-4839)*
Mat Capital LLC .... G 847 821-9630
　Long Grove *(G-13163)*
Pennant Foods .... G 708 752-8730
　Alsip *(G-489)*
Rawnature5 LLC .... F 312 800-3239
　Chicago *(G-5977)*
Sotiros Foods Inc .... G 708 371-0002
　Alsip *(G-511)*
Zaibak Bros .... E 312 564-5800
　Chicago *(G-6706)*

BROKERS: Log & Lumber

Challinor Wood Products Inc .... G 847 256-8828
　Wilmette *(G-21073)*
Sterling Site Access Sol .... C 708 388-2223
　Phoenix *(G-16609)*

BROKERS: Mortgage, Arranging For Loans

Cummins-American Corp .... G 847 299-9550
　Mount Prospect *(G-14524)*

BROKERS: Printing

Galleon Industries Inc .... G 708 478-5444
　Joliet *(G-11867)*
Lighthouse Printing Inc .... G 708 479-7776
　New Lenox *(G-15039)*
Village Press Inc .... G 847 362-1856
　Libertyville *(G-12724)*

BRONZE FOUNDRY, NEC

Intermet Metals Services Inc .... E 847 605-1300
　Schaumburg *(G-18563)*

BRONZE ROLLING & DRAWING

Universal Electric Foundry Inc .... E 312 421-7233
　Chicago *(G-6480)*

BROOMS

Humboldt Broom Company .... G 217 268-3718
　Arcola *(G-652)*
Luco Mop Company .... G 217 235-1992
　Mattoon *(G-13643)*
Quinn Broom Works Inc .... E 217 923-3181
　Greenup *(G-10822)*

BROOMS & BRUSHES

Concorde Laboratories Inc .... G 630 717-5300
　Lisle *(G-12878)*
Don Leventhal Group LLC .... E 618 783-4424
　Newton *(G-15082)*
Federal Prison Industries .... C 309 346-8588
　Pekin *(G-16333)*
Freudenberg Household Pdts LP .... C 630 270-1400
　Aurora *(G-964)*

PRODUCT SECTION

BUILDINGS & COMPONENTS: Prefabricated Metal

Libman Company .... C 217 268-4200		
Arcola *(G-655)*		
Nexstep Commercial Pdts LLC .... G 217 379-2377		
Paxton *(G-16309)*		
Re-Maid Incorporated .... G 815 315-0500		
Freeport *(G-10136)*		
Rejuv-A-Roller LLC .... G 815 975-9635		
Belvidere *(G-1698)*		

BROOMS & BRUSHES: Household Or Indl

E Gornell & Sons Inc .... E 773 489-2330
  Chicago *(G-4423)*
Zimmerman Brush Co .... D 773 761-6331
  Chicago *(G-6719)*

BROOMS & BRUSHES: Paint & Varnish

True Value Company LLC .... E 847 639-5383
  Cary *(G-3196)*
True Value Company LLC .... B 773 695-5000
  Chicago *(G-6437)*

BROOMS & BRUSHES: Paint Rollers

Newell Operating Company .... C 815 235-4171
  Freeport *(G-10129)*

BROOMS & BRUSHES: Push

Jones Software Corp .... G 312 952-0011
  Chicago *(G-5047)*
Sherwin-Williams Company .... G 847 251-6115
  Kenilworth *(G-12015)*

BROOMS & BRUSHES: Street Sweeping, Hand Or Machine

Gosia Cartage Ltd .... G 312 613-8735
  Hodgkins *(G-11389)*
Klm Commercial Sweeping Inc .... G 618 978-9276
  Belleville *(G-1563)*

BRUSHES

Jim Jolly Sales Inc .... G 847 669-7570
  Huntley *(G-11546)*
Team Technologies Inc .... D 630 937-0380
  Batavia *(G-1426)*

BRUSHES & BRUSH STOCK CONTACTS: Electric

J Ream Manufacturing .... G 630 983-6945
  Naperville *(G-14852)*

BUCKLES & PARTS

Linda Levinson Designs Inc .... G 312 951-6943
  Chicago *(G-5226)*

BUFFING FOR THE TRADE

Bucthel Metal Finishing Corp .... F 847 427-8704
  Elk Grove Village *(G-8872)*
Courtesy Metal Polishing .... G 630 832-1862
  Villa Park *(G-20142)*
Master Polishing & Buffing .... G 773 731-3883
  Chicago *(G-5359)*
Metal Images Inc .... G 847 488-9877
  Elgin *(G-8658)*
Rockford Metal Polishing Co .... G 815 282-4448
  Loves Park *(G-13256)*

BUILDING & OFFICE CLEANING SVCS

Petersburg Power Washing Inc .... F 217 415-9013
  Springfield *(G-19425)*

BUILDING & STRUCTURAL WOOD MBRS: Timbers, Struct, Lam Lumber

Cooper Lake Millworks Inc .... G 217 847-2681
  Hamilton *(G-10951)*
Lamboo Technologies LLC .... G 866 966-2999
  Litchfield *(G-12971)*
WW Timbers Inc .... G 708 423-9112
  Chicago Ridge *(G-6811)*

BUILDING & STRUCTURAL WOOD MEMBERS

Central Wood LLC .... G 217 543-2662
  Arcola *(G-646)*
Connor Sports Flooring LLC .... D 847 290-9020
  Bensenville *(G-1775)*
F5d Inc .... G 815 953-9183
  Herscher *(G-11183)*
Strat-O-Span Buildings Inc .... G 618 526-4566
  Breese *(G-2308)*

BUILDING CLEANING & MAINTENANCE SVCS

New Metal Crafts Inc .... E 312 787-6991
  Lincolnwood *(G-12832)*

BUILDING COMPONENT CLEANING SVCS

Averus Usa Inc .... D 800 913-7034
  Elgin *(G-8518)*

BUILDING COMPONENTS: Structural Steel

A Lucas & Sons .... E 309 673-8547
  Peoria *(G-16372)*
Affton Fabg & Wldg Co Inc .... E 314 781-4100
  Sauget *(G-18388)*
Canam Steel Corporation .... G 815 224-9588
  Peru *(G-16569)*
Central Ill Fbrcation Whse Inc .... F 217 367-2323
  Urbana *(G-19976)*
Delta Erectors Inc .... F 708 267-9721
  Villa Park *(G-20144)*
Dietrich Industries Inc .... G 815 207-0110
  Joliet *(G-11855)*
Esi Steel & Fabrication .... F 618 548-3017
  Salem *(G-18338)*
Garbe Iron Works Inc .... E 630 897-5100
  Aurora *(G-1102)*
Gremp Steel Co .... G 708 389-7393
  Posen *(G-16795)*
H & S Mechanical Inc .... D 309 696-7066
  Peoria *(G-16448)*
Integrated Mfg Tech LLC .... E 618 282-8306
  Red Bud *(G-16996)*
Jameson Steel Fabrication Inc .... G 217 354-2205
  Oakwood *(G-15820)*
Kd Steel Incorporated .... G 630 201-1619
  Westmont *(G-20752)*
Kim Gough .... G 309 734-3511
  Monmouth *(G-14221)*
Knoll Steel Inc .... F 815 675-9400
  Spring Grove *(G-19280)*
Max Fire Training Inc .... F 618 210-2079
  Godfrey *(G-10656)*
Mc Kinney Steel & Sales Inc .... E 847 746-3344
  Zion *(G-21520)*
Pro-Fab Metals Inc .... G 618 283-2986
  Vandalia *(G-20020)*
Romero Steel Company Inc .... E 708 216-0001
  Melrose Park *(G-13910)*
Sheas Iron Works Inc .... E 847 356-2922
  Lake Villa *(G-12367)*
Steel Span Inc .... F 815 943-9071
  Harvard *(G-11068)*
Steelfab Inc .... E 815 935-6540
  Kankakee *(G-12008)*
Trifab Inc .... G 847 838-2083
  Antioch *(G-640)*
Walnut Custom Homes Inc .... E 815 379-2151
  Walnut *(G-20221)*
WEb Production & Fabg Inc .... F 312 733-6800
  Chicago *(G-6595)*

BUILDING INSPECTION SVCS

Tuschall Engineering Co Inc .... E 630 655-9100
  Burr Ridge *(G-2726)*

BUILDING MAINTENANCE SVCS, EXC REPAIRS

Equity Concepts Co Inc .... G 815 226-1300
  Rockford *(G-17399)*

BUILDING PRDTS & MATERIALS DEALERS

Advanced Window Corp .... E 773 379-3500
  Chicago *(G-3568)*
Aetna Plywood Inc .... D 708 343-1515
  Maywood *(G-13658)*
Agusta Mill Works .... G 309 787-4616
  Milan *(G-13999)*
Brewer Company .... F 708 339-9000
  Harvey *(G-11080)*
Charles K Eichen .... G 217 854-9751
  Carlinville *(G-2871)*
County Materials Corp .... E 217 352-4181
  Champaign *(G-3283)*
Custom Woodwork & Interiors .... F 217 546-0006
  Springfield *(G-19358)*
E-Z Tree Recycling Inc .... G 773 493-8600
  Chicago *(G-4428)*
Effingham Equity .... F 217 268-5128
  Arcola *(G-648)*
Elston Materials LLC .... G 773 235-3100
  Chicago *(G-4490)*
Franklin Park Building Mtls .... G 847 455-3985
  Franklin Park *(G-9945)*
Gorman Brothers Ready Mix Inc .... F 618 498-2173
  Jerseyville *(G-11791)*
H J Mohr & Sons Company .... F 708 366-0338
  Oak Park *(G-15756)*
J E Tomes & Associates Inc .... F 708 653-5100
  Blue Island *(G-2127)*
Jesse B Holt Inc .... D 618 783-3075
  Newton *(G-15086)*
Peoples Coal and Lumber Co .... F 815 432-2456
  Watseka *(G-20314)*
Petersen Sand & Gravel Inc .... F 815 344-1060
  Lakemoor *(G-12473)*
Southfield Corporation .... E 708 458-0400
  Oak Lawn *(G-15735)*
Stahl Lumber Company .... F 309 695-4331
  Wyoming *(G-21462)*
Van Voorst Lumber Company Inc .... E 815 426-2544
  Union Hill *(G-19943)*
W H Maze Company .... C 815 223-1742
  Peru *(G-16596)*
Welch Bros Inc .... C 847 741-6134
  Elgin *(G-8779)*
Welch Bros Inc .... C 815 547-3000
  Belvidere *(G-1709)*
Windwrap LLC .... G 773 594-1724
  Chicago *(G-6639)*
Wm F Meyer Co .... E 773 772-7272
  Aurora *(G-1038)*
Wooded Wonderland .... G 815 777-1223
  Galena *(G-10182)*

BUILDING PRDTS: Concrete

Cpg International LLC .... D 570 558-8000
  Chicago *(G-4252)*
Great Lakes Lifting .... G 815 931-4825
  Country Club Hills *(G-7039)*
Quick Building Systems Inc .... G 708 598-6733
  Palos Hills *(G-16205)*
Spacil Construction Co .... G 708 448-3809
  Palos Heights *(G-16192)*
Vcna Prairie Inc .... A 312 733-0094
  Chicago *(G-6527)*

BUILDING PRDTS: Stone

Stylenquaza LLC .... G 847 981-0191
  Elk Grove Village *(G-9257)*

BUILDINGS & COMPONENTS: Prefabricated Metal

Alvarez & Marsal Inc .... E 312 601-4220
  Chicago *(G-3639)*
American Deck & Sunroom C .... G 217 586-4840
  Mahomet *(G-13421)*
Atkore International Group Inc .... A 708 339-1610
  Harvey *(G-11075)*
Atkore Intl Holdings Inc .... G 708 225-2051
  Harvey *(G-11076)*
Beh IL Sub LLC .... G 630 616-1850
  Hinsdale *(G-11364)*
Cardinal Enterprises .... G 618 994-4454
  Stonefort *(G-19557)*
Chicago Steel Inc .... E 800 344-3032
  Chicago *(G-4130)*
Craig Industries Inc .... D 217 228-2421
  Quincy *(G-16873)*
D & D Construction Co LLC .... G 217 852-6631
  Dallas City *(G-7312)*
Eagle Companies Inc .... F 309 686-9054
  Chillicothe *(G-6816)*

BUILDINGS & COMPONENTS: Prefabricated Metal

Elfi LLC .... E 815 439-1833
  Chicago (G-4483)
Esi Steel & Fabrication .... F 618 548-3017
  Salem (G-18338)
George Industries LLC .... E 847 394-3610
  Wheeling (G-20904)
Heico Companies LLC .... F 312 419-8220
  Chicago (G-4798)
K & K Storage Barns LLC .... F 618 927-0533
  Ewing (G-9602)
McElroy Metal Mill Inc 217 935-9421
  Clinton (G-6927)
Minority Auto Hdlg Specialists .... F 708 757-8758
  Chicago Heights (G-6759)
Morton Buildings Inc .... G 217 357-3713
  Carthage (G-3140)
Morton Buildings Inc .... F 309 263-3652
  Morton (G-14370)
Optimal Construction Svcs Inc .... G 630 365-5050
  Elburn (G-8468)
Rv6 Performance .... G 630 346-7998
  Wheaton (G-20821)
Steel Span Inc .... F 815 943-9071
  Harvard (G-11068)
Super Target Systems LLC .... G 800 556-3162
  Aurora (G-1158)
White Star Silo .... G 618 523-4735
  Germantown (G-10332)

BUILDINGS: Farm & Utility

Lamka Enterprises Inc .... G 630 659-5965
  Woodstock (G-21402)
Morton Buildings Inc .... F 630 904-1122
  Streator (G-19615)
Tank Wind-Down Corp .... D 815 756-1551
  Dekalb (G-7707)

BUILDINGS: Farm, Prefabricated Or Portable, Wood

Strat-O-Span Buildings Inc .... G 618 526-4566
  Breese (G-2308)
Yoders Portable Buildings LLC .... G 618 936-2419
  Sumner (G-19689)

BUILDINGS: Mobile, For Commercial Use

Carlin Mfg A Div Grs Holdg LLC ..... E 559 276-0123
  Naperville (G-14789)

BUILDINGS: Portable

American Buildings Company .... C 309 527-5420
  El Paso (G-8433)
Arrow Shed LLC .... E 618 526-4546
  Breese (G-2296)
Fehring Ornamental Iron Works ..... G 217 483-6727
  Rochester (G-17166)
Jack Walters & Sons Corp .... E 618 842-2642
  Fairfield (G-9627)
Mobile Mini Inc .... E 708 297-2004
  Calumet Park (G-2799)
Morton Buildings Inc .... F 309 936-7282
  Atkinson (G-902)
Signa Development Group Inc .... G 773 418-4506
  Norridge (G-15243)
Strat-O-Span Buildings Inc .... G 618 526-4566
  Breese (G-2308)

BUILDINGS: Prefabricated, Metal

Associated Group Holdings LLC .... G 312 662-5488
  Chicago (G-3751)
Safety Storage Inc .... D 217 345-4422
  Charleston (G-3412)
US Aluminium IL .... G 708 458-9070
  Chicago (G-6498)

BUILDINGS: Prefabricated, Wood

Cook Sales Inc .... E 618 893-2114
  Cobden (G-6941)
Everlast Portable Buildings .... G 217 543-4080
  Sullivan (G-19666)
Faze Change Produx .... E 217 728-2184
  Sullivan (G-19667)
Lester Building Systems LLC .... E 217 364-8664
  Charleston (G-3406)
Schrocks Wood Shop .... G 217 773-3842
  Mount Sterling (G-14593)
Steel Span Inc .... F 815 943-9071
  Harvard (G-11068)

Tuff Shed Inc .... F 847 704-1147
  Palatine (G-16167)

BUILDINGS: Prefabricated, Wood

Alply Insulated Panels LLC .... G 217 324-6700
  Litchfield (G-12959)
Frederking Construction Co .... G 618 483-5031
  Altamont (G-532)
Gbh Walnut Inc .... D 815 379-2151
  Walnut (G-20218)
Grs Holding LLC .... F 630 355-1660
  Naperville (G-14838)
Kitchens To Go LLC .... E 630 364-3083
  Naperville (G-14858)
Omni-Tech Systems Inc 309 962-2281
  Le Roy (G-12540)

BULLETIN BOARDS: Wood

Vecchio Manufacturing of Ill .... F 847 742-8429
  Elgin (G-8773)

BUMPERS: Motor Vehicle

Cnh Industrial America LLC .... E 309 965-2233
  Goodfield (G-10672)
Flex-N-Gate Corporation .... D 217 442-4018
  Danville (G-7334)
Flex-N-Gate LLC .... B 217 384-6600
  Urbana (G-19984)
Hendrickson International Corp ..... C 815 727-4031
  Joliet (G-11876)
High Impact Fabricating LLC 708 235-8912
  University Park (G-19956)
Magna Exteriors America Inc .... A 618 327-4381
  Nashville (G-14999)
Mendota Welding & Mfg 815 539-6944
  Mendota (G-13949)
Nascote Industries Inc .... A 618 327-4381
  Nashville (G-15002)
Nascote Industries Inc .... C 618 478-2092
  Nashville (G-15003)

BURIAL VAULTS, FIBERGLASS

Greenwood Inc .... F 800 798-4900
  Danville (G-7341)

BURIAL VAULTS: Concrete Or Precast Terrazzo

American Wilbert Vault Corp .... F 773 238-2746
  Chicago (G-3674)
American Wilbert Vault Corp .... E 708 366-3210
  Hillside (G-11327)
American Wilbert Vault Corp .... G 847 824-4415
  Des Plaines (G-7729)
American Wilbert Vault Corp 847 741-3089
  Elgin (G-8509)
C L Vault & Safe Srv 708 237-0039
  Oak Lawn (G-15704)
Classic Metal Vaults 217 826-6302
  Marshall (G-13567)
Doric Products Inc .... D 217 826-6302
  Marshall (G-13570)
Eagle Burial Vault 815 722-8660
  Frankfort (G-9791)
Farmington Wilbert Vault Corp ...... F 309 245-2133
  Farmington (G-9662)
Forsyth Brothers Concrete Pdts 217 548-2770
  Fithian (G-9669)
Hallen Burial Vault Inc 815 544-6138
  Belvidere (G-1676)
J P Vincent & Sons Inc .... G 815 777-2365
  Galena (G-10175)
Kelley Vault Co Inc 217 355-5551
  Champaign (G-3313)
Merz Vault Company Inc .... E 618 548-2859
  Salem (G-18345)
Northern Illinois Wilbert Vlt 815 544-3355
  Belvidere (G-1689)
Oakwood Memorial Park Inc 815 433-0313
  Ottawa (G-16066)
Peoria Wilbert Vault Co Inc .... F 309 383-2882
  Metamora (G-13966)
Perfection Vault Co Inc 217 673-6111
  Woodson (G-21351)
Quad Cities Concrete Pdts LLC ..... G 309 787-4919
  Milan (G-14021)
Rex Vault Co .... F 618 783-2416
  Newton (G-15092)

Schmalz Precast Concrete Mfg ...... G 815 747-3939
  East Dubuque (G-8182)
Slavish Inc .... G 309 754-8233
  Matherville (G-13615)
Southern Ill Wilbert Vlt Co .... F 618 942-5845
  Herrin (G-11180)
Southern Illinois Vault Co Inc 270 554-4436
  Herrin (G-11181)
Sterling Vault Company .... F 815 625-0077
  Sterling (G-19537)
Tanya Shipley 708 476-0433
  Mokena (G-14121)
Wilbert Quincy Vault Co .... G 217 224-8557
  Quincy (G-16956)
Wilbert Vault Company .... F 309 787-5281
  Milan (G-14032)
Wolfe Burial Vault Co Inc .... G 815 697-2012
  Chebanse (G-3431)

BURNERS: Gas, Domestic

Midco International Inc .... E 773 604-8700
  Chicago (G-5433)

BURNERS: Gas, Indl

Eclipse Combustion Inc .... C 815 877-3031
  Rockford (G-17389)

BURNERS: Gas-Oil, Combination

Eclipse Inc .... D 815 877-3031
  Rockford (G-17388)

BUS BARS: Electrical

Schneider Electric Usa Inc .... E 847 441-2526
  Schaumburg (G-18708)
Triton Manufacturing Co Inc .... C 708 587-4000
  Monee (G-14210)

BUSES: Wholesalers

Motor Coach Industries .... G 847 285-2000
  Des Plaines (G-7805)

BUSINESS & SECRETARIAL SCHOOLS

Illinois Inst Cntng Legl Ed .... E 217 787-2080
  Springfield (G-19386)

BUSINESS ACTIVITIES: Non-Commercial Site

4 Elements Company .... G 773 236-2284
  Mundelein (G-14655)
A & S Arms Inc .... G 224 267-5670
  Antioch (G-593)
Abki Tech Service Inc .... F 847 818-8403
  Des Plaines (G-7721)
Above Waves Inc .... G 708 341-9123
  Mokena (G-14068)
Ace Machine & Tool Inc 815 793-5077
  Cortland (G-7015)
Advanced Cstm Enrgy Sltons Inc .... D 312 428-9540
  Chicago (G-3563)
Advanced Robotics Research 630 544-0040
  Naperville (G-14766)
Airport Park and Fly LLC .... G 708 310-2442
  Chicago (G-3590)
Alao Temitope .... F 331 454-3333
  Collinsville (G-6953)
Anchor Mechanical Inc 312 492-6994
  Chicago (G-3691)
Approved Contact LLC .... G 800 449-7137
  Springfield (G-19319)
Armarius Software Inc .... G 630 639-6332
  Aurora (G-914)
Arvamont .... G 630 926-2468
  Hinsdale (G-11361)
Berner Food & Beverage LLC .... B 815 563-4222
  Dakota (G-7311)
BJs Welding Services Etc Co .... G 773 964-5836
  Chicago (G-3905)
Bold Diagnostics LLC .... G 806 543-5743
  Chicago (G-3930)
Bows Arts Inc .... F 847 501-3161
  Glenview (G-10533)
Brokerassist LLC .... G 847 858-2357
  River Forest (G-17050)
Brunet Snow Service Company ..... G 847 846-0037
  Wood Dale (G-21172)

PRODUCT SECTION

BUSINESS FORMS: Printed, Continuous

Buyersvine Inc ....G....... 630 235-6804
  Hinsdale *(G-11367)*
C & B Services ....G....... 847 462-8484
  Cary *(G-3151)*
Caples-El Transport Inc ....G....... 708 300-2727
  Calumet City *(G-2772)*
CHI Home Improvement Mag Inc ....G....... 630 801-7788
  Aurora *(G-1073)*
CJ Drilling Inc ....D....... 847 669-8000
  Dundee *(G-8126)*
Coaching For Excellence LLC ....F....... 708 957-6047
  Country Club Hills *(G-7036)*
Daves Welding Service Inc ....G....... 630 655-3224
  Darien *(G-7405)*
Delta Erectors Inc ....F....... 708 267-9721
  Villa Park *(G-20144)*
Desforte LLC ....G....... 224 301-5364
  Chicago *(G-4343)*
Doxa Enterprises LLC ....G....... 618 515-4470
  East Saint Louis *(G-8305)*
Drywear Apparel LLC ....G....... 847 687-8540
  Kildeer *(G-12046)*
DS Air & Heating Inc ....G....... 773 826-7411
  Chicago *(G-4398)*
Dtrs Enterprises Inc..............................G....... 630 296-6890
  Bolingbrook *(G-2170)*
Edward J Warren Jr ....G....... 630 882-8817
  Yorkville *(G-21481)*
Effective Energy Assoc LLC ....G....... 815 248-9280
  Davis *(G-7417)*
Erasermitt Incorporated ....G....... 312 842-2855
  Chicago *(G-4525)*
Fleming Music Technology Ctr ....G....... 708 316-8662
  Wheaton *(G-20799)*
Franch & Sons Trnsp Inc ....G....... 630 392-3307
  Addison *(G-129)*
Gillons Inc ....E....... 773 531-8900
  Homewood *(G-11495)*
Gld Industries Inc ....G....... 217 390-9594
  Champaign *(G-3296)*
Grier Abrasive Co Inc ....C....... 708 333-6445
  South Holland *(G-19216)*
Griffard & Associates LLC ....G....... 217 316-1732
  Quincy *(G-16887)*
H2o Solutions LLC ....G....... 618 219-2905
  Granite City *(G-10713)*
Haleys Corker Inc ....G....... 708 228-1427
  River Forest *(G-17052)*
Hallmark Cabinet Company ....D....... 708 757-7807
  Minooka *(G-14061)*
Hampster Industries Inc ....G....... 866 280-2287
  Mundelein *(G-14695)*
Healthy-Txt LLC ....G....... 630 945-1787
  Chicago *(G-4794)*
Hearthside Usa Inc ....B....... 978 716-2530
  Downers Grove *(G-8020)*
Heat Systems Instrs Svc Co LLC ....G....... 630 404-6884
  Willowbrook *(G-21046)*
HI Metals LLC ....G....... 312 590-3360
  Winnetka *(G-21130)*
Idevconcepts Inc ....G....... 312 351-1615
  Chicago *(G-4877)*
Illuminight Lighting LLC ....F....... 312 685-4448
  Highland Park *(G-11272)*
Intecells Inc ....G....... 586 612-9811
  Elgin *(G-8627)*
Integrated Lighting Tech Inc ....G....... 630 750-3786
  Bolingbrook *(G-2193)*
Invisio Communications Inc ....G....... 412 327-6578
  Chicago *(G-4965)*
Jds Labs Inc ....G....... 618 550-9359
  Collinsville *(G-6964)*
Jewerly and Beyond ....G....... 312 833-6785
  Schaumburg *(G-18576)*
John Dagys Media LLC ....G....... 708 373-0180
  Palos Park *(G-16212)*
Katys LLC ....G....... 708 522-9814
  Oak Park *(G-15760)*
Kenneth W Templeman ....G....... 847 912-2740
  Volo *(G-20200)*
Legistek Corporation ....G....... 312 399-4891
  Chicago *(G-5201)*
Lexpress Inc ....G....... 773 517-7095
  Prospect Heights *(G-16844)*
Logicon Group LLC ....G....... 618 558-7757
  Millstadt *(G-14049)*
Lokman Enterprises Inc ....G....... 773 654-0525
  Chicago *(G-5252)*
Love Journey Inc ....G....... 773 447-5591
  Chicago *(G-5268)*

Luon Energy LLC ....G....... 217 419-2678
  Savoy *(G-18415)*
M4 Steel LLC ....G....... 309 222-6027
  Washington *(G-20274)*
Made As Intended Inc ....F....... 630 789-3494
  Oak Brook *(G-15639)*
Mef Construction Inc ....G....... 847 741-8601
  Elgin *(G-8655)*
Midwest Mobile Canning LLC ....G....... 815 861-4515
  Crystal Lake *(G-7229)*
Mrb Roofing Inc ....G....... 872 814-4430
  University Park *(G-19963)*
Mullen Foods LLC ....G....... 773 716-9001
  Chicago *(G-5522)*
Music Plug LLC ....G....... 309 826-5238
  Colfax *(G-6950)*
MWK Rail LLC ....G....... 815 671-5217
  Urbana *(G-19989)*
Natures Appeal Mfg Corp ....G....... 630 880-6222
  Addison *(G-227)*
Navistarsinfosoft Inc ....E....... 877 270-3543
  Chicago *(G-5557)*
Neckbone Skunks Logistics & Te ....F....... 312 218-0281
  Chicago *(G-5561)*
Ohrvall Media LLC ....G....... 630 378-9738
  Plainfield *(G-16698)*
Opsdirt LLC ....G....... 773 412-1179
  Chicago *(G-5684)*
Organnica Inc ....G....... 312 925-7272
  Berwyn *(G-1959)*
Osmer Woodworking Inc ....G....... 815 973-5809
  Dixon *(G-7905)*
Oso900 Nfp ....G....... 312 206-4219
  Chicago *(G-5711)*
Paralleldirect LLC ....G....... 847 748-2025
  Lincolnshire *(G-12791)*
Powercoco LLC ....G....... 614 323-5890
  Chicago *(G-5848)*
Pumpkin Patch Ventures Inc ....G....... 708 699-4396
  Chicago *(G-5914)*
Questily LLC ....G....... 312 636-6657
  Chicago *(G-5935)*
Rays Electrical Service LLC ....F....... 847 214-2944
  Elgin *(G-8715)*
Rays Power Wshg Svc Peggy Ray ....G....... 618 939-6306
  Waterloo *(G-20295)*
Rebel Brands LLC ....G....... 312 804-0009
  Wilmette *(G-21091)*
Revolution Brands LLC ....G....... 847 902-3320
  Huntley *(G-11563)*
Rinalli Boat Co Inc ....G....... 618 467-8850
  Godfrey *(G-10660)*
Roq Innovation LLC ....G....... 917 770-2403
  Chicago *(G-6059)*
Royale Innovation Group Ltd ....G....... 312 339-1406
  Itasca *(G-11729)*
S Vs Industries Inc ....G....... 630 408-1083
  Hoffman Estates *(G-11453)*
Saachi Inc ....G....... 630 775-1700
  Roselle *(G-17982)*
Scotts Popcorn LLC ....G....... 773 608-9625
  Chicago *(G-6121)*
Seat Trans Inc ....G....... 224 522-1007
  Lake In The Hills *(G-12343)*
See What You Send Inc ....G....... 781 780-1483
  Chicago *(G-6131)*
Sho Technologies Inc ....G....... 217 954-0020
  Champaign *(G-3346)*
Signa Development Group Inc ....G....... 773 418-4506
  Norridge *(G-15243)*
Southland Voice ....E....... 708 214-8582
  Crete *(G-7145)*
Spinball Sports LLC ....G....... 314 503-3194
  Skokie *(G-19035)*
Split Nutrition LLC ....G....... 855 775-4801
  Chicago *(G-6217)*
Surgical Innovation Assoc Inc ....G....... 626 372-4884
  Chicago *(G-6289)*
T9 Group LLC ....G....... 847 912-8862
  Hawthorn Woods *(G-11126)*
Take Your Mark Sports LLC ....G....... 708 655-0525
  Western Springs *(G-20726)*
Tape Case Ltd ....E....... 847 299-7880
  Elk Grove Village *(G-9265)*
Team Sider Inc ....G....... 847 767-0107
  Highland Park *(G-11303)*
Terrapin Xpress Inc ....G....... 866 823-7323
  Palos Heights *(G-16193)*
Third Day Oil & Gas LLC ....G....... 618 553-5538
  Oblong *(G-15831)*

Transfrmtional Enrgy Solutions ....G....... 828 226-7821
  Decatur *(G-7562)*
Tru-Tone Finishing Inc ....E....... 630 543-5520
  Addison *(G-318)*
Truepad LLC ....F....... 847 274-6898
  Chicago *(G-6438)*
Turfmapp Inc ....G....... 703 473-5678
  Chicago *(G-6443)*
Turner Agward ....G....... 773 669-8559
  Chicago *(G-6444)*
Twoinspireyou LLC ....G....... 630 849-8214
  Geneva *(G-10314)*
Unique Product Productions Inc ....G....... 708 259-1500
  Richton Park *(G-17032)*
Universal Trnspt Systems LLC ....F....... 312 994-2349
  Chicago *(G-6484)*
Urpoint LLC ....G....... 773 919-9002
  Homewood *(G-11503)*
Veteran Greens LLC ....G....... 773 599-9689
  Chicago *(G-6540)*
Vulcan Ladder Usa LLC ....G....... 847 526-6321
  Crystal Lake *(G-7292)*
Weiss Monument Works Inc ....G....... 618 398-1811
  Belleville *(G-1611)*
Wells Janitorial Service Inc ....G....... 872 226-9983
  Chicago *(G-6600)*
Winlind Skincare LLC ....G....... 630 789-9408
  Burr Ridge *(G-2736)*
World of Soul Inc ....G....... 773 840-4839
  Chicago *(G-6676)*
Zorin Material Handling Co ....G....... 773 342-3818
  Chicago *(G-6724)*

BUSINESS COLLEGE OR SCHOOLS

Connies Home Health Care ....G....... 708 790-4000
  Park Forest *(G-16253)*

BUSINESS FORMS WHOLESALERS

Aais Services Corporation ....E....... 630 681-8347
  Lisle *(G-12856)*
Aais Services Corporation ....G....... 630 457-3263
  Lisle *(G-12857)*
Accurate Business Controls Inc ....G....... 815 633-5500
  Machesney Park *(G-13323)*
Allan Brooks & Associates Inc ....F....... 847 537-7500
  Lake Villa *(G-12345)*
Bfc Forms Service Inc ....C....... 630 879-9240
  Batavia *(G-1358)*
C M J Associates Inc ....G....... 708 636-2995
  Oak Lawn *(G-15705)*
Certified Business Forms Inc ....G....... 773 286-8194
  Chicago *(G-4065)*
Designation Inc ....F....... 847 367-9100
  Mundelein *(G-14683)*
Eagle Printing Company ....G....... 309 762-0771
  Moline *(G-14141)*
Excel Forms Inc ....G....... 630 801-1936
  Aurora *(G-1094)*
Forms Design Plus Coleman Prtg ....G....... 309 685-6000
  Peoria *(G-16439)*
Grand Forms & Systems Inc ....F....... 847 259-4600
  Arlington Heights *(G-744)*
Informative Systems Inc ....F....... 217 523-8422
  Springfield *(G-19389)*
Marc Business Forms Inc ....F....... 847 568-9200
  Lincolnwood *(G-12829)*
Medical Records Co ....G....... 847 662-6373
  Waukegan *(G-20465)*
Mid-Central Business Forms ....G....... 309 692-9090
  Peoria *(G-16474)*
Minuteman Press ....G....... 630 584-7383
  Naperville *(G-14872)*
Noor International Inc ....G....... 847 985-2300
  Bartlett *(G-1256)*
Northstar Group Inc ....F....... 847 726-0880
  Lake Zurich *(G-12440)*
R & R Creative Graphics Inc ....G....... 630 208-4724
  Geneva *(G-10301)*
Reign Print Solutions Inc ....G....... 847 590-7091
  Arlington Heights *(G-798)*
Rose Business Forms & Printing ....G....... 618 533-3032
  Centralia *(G-3248)*
United General Graphics LLC ....F....... 262 657-5054
  Niles *(G-15185)*

BUSINESS FORMS: Printed, Continuous

Acco Brands Corporation ....A....... 847 541-9500
  Lake Zurich *(G-12374)*

BUSINESS FORMS: Printed, Continuous

Acco Brands International Inc ....G....... 847 541-9500
  Lake Zurich *(G-12375)*
R R Donnelley & Sons Company ....D....... 847 593-1200
  Elk Grove Village *(G-9210)*
Standard Register Inc ....F....... 815 432-4203
  Watseka *(G-20316)*

BUSINESS FORMS: Printed, Manifold

Acco Brands USA LLC ....B....... 800 222-6462
  Lake Zurich *(G-12376)*
Acco Brands USA LLC ....D....... 847 272-3700
  Lincolnshire *(G-12741)*
American Graphics Network Inc ....F....... 847 729-7220
  Glenview *(G-10522)*
Azusa Inc ....G....... 618 244-6591
  Mount Vernon *(G-14597)*
B & B Printing Company ....G....... 217 285-6072
  Pittsfield *(G-16628)*
Block and Company Inc ....C....... 847 537-7200
  Wheeling *(G-20860)*
Certified Business Forms Inc ....G....... 773 286-8194
  Chicago *(G-4065)*
Ennis Inc ....E....... 815 875-2000
  Princeton *(G-16808)*
Fast Print Shop ....G....... 618 997-1976
  Marion *(G-13510)*
Frank R Walker Company ....G....... 630 613-9312
  Lombard *(G-13079)*
Gem Acquisition Company Inc ....F....... 773 735-3300
  Chicago *(G-4667)*
Genoa Business Forms Inc ....E....... 815 895-2800
  Sycamore *(G-19711)*
Grand Forms & Systems Inc ....G....... 847 259-4600
  Arlington Heights *(G-744)*
Integrated Print Graphics Inc ....C....... 847 695-6777
  South Elgin *(G-19155)*
J Gooch & Associates Inc ....G....... 217 522-7575
  Springfield *(G-19392)*
Kellogg Printing Co ....F....... 309 734-8388
  Monmouth *(G-14220)*
Keneal Industries Inc ....F....... 815 886-1300
  Romeoville *(G-17837)*
M L S Printing Co Inc ....G....... 847 948-8902
  Deerfield *(G-7633)*
M Wells Printing Co ....G....... 312 455-0400
  Chicago *(G-5305)*
Marc Business Forms Inc ....F....... 847 568-9200
  Lincolnwood *(G-12829)*
Midwest Graphic Industries ....F....... 630 509-2972
  Bensenville *(G-1853)*
N Bujarski Inc ....G....... 847 884-1600
  Schaumburg *(G-18643)*
Novak Business Forms Inc ....G....... 630 932-9850
  Lombard *(G-13110)*
Perftech Inc ....E....... 630 554-0010
  North Aurora *(G-15270)*
Physicians Record Co Inc ....D....... 800 323-9268
  Berwyn *(G-1960)*
Proform ....G....... 309 676-2535
  Peoria *(G-16503)*
R R Donnelley & Sons Company ....G....... 847 956-4187
  Elk Grove Village *(G-9211)*
R R Donnelley & Sons Company ....C....... 217 935-2113
  Clinton *(G-6928)*
Shanin Company ....D....... 847 676-1200
  Lincolnwood *(G-12843)*
Springfield Printing Inc ....G....... 217 787-3500
  Springfield *(G-19454)*
Taylor Communications Inc ....G....... 309 693-3700
  Peoria *(G-16535)*
Taylor Communications Inc ....G....... 217 793-1900
  Springfield *(G-19461)*
Taylor Communications Inc ....G....... 708 560-7600
  Oak Forest *(G-15691)*
Taylor Communications Inc ....G....... 630 368-0335
  Oak Brook *(G-15663)*

BUSINESS FORMS: Unit Sets, Manifold

R & L Business Forms Inc ....F....... 618 939-6535
  Waterloo *(G-20294)*

BUSINESS MACHINE REPAIR, ELECTRIC

Ambrit Inc ....G....... 847 593-3301
  Elk Grove Village *(G-8820)*
CDs Office Systems Inc ....D....... 800 367-1508
  Springfield *(G-19343)*
CDs Office Systems Inc ....F....... 630 305-9034
  Springfield *(G-19344)*

Konica Minolta ....G....... 630 893-8238
  Roselle *(G-17962)*
Konica Mnlta Bus Sltons USA In ....E....... 309 671-1360
  Peoria *(G-16467)*
Xerox Corporation ....E....... 630 573-1000
  Hinsdale *(G-11383)*

BUSINESS SUPPORT SVCS

Brahman Spirit Tribe ....F....... 773 957-2828
  Chicago *(G-3942)*
Cubic Group Inc ....G....... 859 494-5834
  Arlington Heights *(G-722)*
Yeager JI & Associates Inc ....G....... 847 283-9162
  Lake Forest *(G-12324)*

BUSINESS TRAINING SVCS

Myeccho LLC ....G....... 224 639-3068
  Des Plaines *(G-7809)*

BUTADIENE: Indl, Organic, Chemical

Equistar Chemicals LP ....E....... 217 253-3311
  Tuscola *(G-19926)*

BUTTONS

Acme Button & Buttonhole Co ....G....... 773 907-8400
  Chicago *(G-3526)*
Just Another Button ....F....... 618 667-8531
  Troy *(G-19916)*

CABINETS & CASES: Show, Display & Storage, Exc Wood

Advert Display Products Inc ....G....... 815 513-5432
  Morris *(G-14290)*
Central Sheet Metal Pdts Inc ....E....... 773 583-2424
  Skokie *(G-18938)*
Diversified Metal Products Inc ....E....... 847 753-9595
  Northbrook *(G-15377)*
HMC Holdings LLC ....F....... 800 874-6625
  Buffalo Grove *(G-2547)*
Industrial Enclosure Corp ....E....... 630 898-7499
  Aurora *(G-1111)*
Kewaunee Scientific Corp ....G....... 847 675-7744
  Highland Park *(G-11278)*
Liam Brex ....G....... 630 848-0222
  Naperville *(G-14862)*
T & D Metal Products LLC ....G....... 815 432-4938
  Watseka *(G-20318)*
Wilson Kitchens Inc ....D....... 618 253-7449
  Harrisburg *(G-11031)*

CABINETS: Bathroom Vanities, Wood

Ability Cabinet Co Inc ....G....... 847 678-6678
  Franklin Park *(G-9859)*
Autumn Woods Ltd ....E....... 630 668-2080
  Carol Stream *(G-2943)*
Creative Cabinets Countertops ....F....... 217 446-6406
  Danville *(G-7327)*
Crestwood Custom Cabinets ....G....... 708 385-3167
  Crestwood *(G-7115)*
Crown Coverings Inc ....E....... 630 546-2959
  Roselle *(G-17949)*
Custom Woodwork & Interiors ....F....... 217 546-0006
  Springfield *(G-19358)*
Der Holtzmacher Ltd ....G....... 815 895-4887
  Sycamore *(G-19706)*
Designers Point Inc ....G....... 224 578-7043
  Rolling Meadows *(G-17726)*
Joliet Cabinet Company Inc ....E....... 815 727-4096
  Lockport *(G-13003)*
Kaufmans Custom Cabinets ....F....... 217 268-4330
  Arcola *(G-653)*
Kunz Carpentry ....G....... 618 224-7892
  Trenton *(G-19904)*
Lacava LLC ....E....... 773 637-9600
  Chicago *(G-5154)*
Pace Industries Inc ....C....... 312 226-5500
  Chicago *(G-5737)*
Regency Custom Woodworking ....F....... 815 689-2117
  Cullom *(G-7300)*
Seigles Cabinet Center LLC ....G....... 224 535-7130
  Elgin *(G-8726)*
Stonetree Fabrication Inc ....E....... 618 332-1700
  East Saint Louis *(G-8325)*
Vanities Inc ....G....... 847 483-0240
  Arlington Heights *(G-825)*

CABINETS: Entertainment

Anderson & Marter Cabinets ....G....... 630 406-9840
  Batavia *(G-1349)*
Cabinets By Custom Craft Inc ....G....... 815 637-4001
  Roscoe *(G-17900)*
Cooper Lake Millworks Inc ....G....... 217 847-2681
  Hamilton *(G-10951)*
Creative Wood Concepts Inc ....G....... 773 384-9960
  Chicago *(G-4268)*
Crestwood Custom Cabinets ....G....... 708 385-3167
  Crestwood *(G-7115)*
Eddie Gapastione ....G....... 708 430-3881
  Bridgeview *(G-2344)*
Elm Street Industries Inc ....F....... 309 854-7000
  Kewanee *(G-12032)*
Grays Cabinet Co ....G....... 618 948-2211
  Saint Francisville *(G-18314)*
HI Tech ....G....... 708 957-4210
  Homewood *(G-11496)*
Midwest Woodcrafters Inc ....G....... 630 665-0901
  Carol Stream *(G-3031)*
Roncin Custom Design ....G....... 847 669-0260
  Huntley *(G-11565)*
Silver Bell Cnstr & Furn Inc ....G....... 773 578-9450
  Chicago *(G-6171)*
Spirit Concepts Inc ....G....... 708 388-4500
  Crestwood *(G-7128)*
Woodhill Cabinetry Design Inc ....G....... 815 431-0545
  Ottawa *(G-16086)*

CABINETS: Entertainment Units, Household, Wood

Der Holtzmacher Ltd ....G....... 815 895-4887
  Sycamore *(G-19706)*
Timberside Woodworking ....G....... 217 578-3201
  Arthur *(G-880)*

CABINETS: Factory

Aline International LLC ....F....... 708 478-2471
  Mokena *(G-14069)*
Anderson & Marter Cabinets ....G....... 630 406-9840
  Batavia *(G-1349)*
Concord Cabinets Inc ....F....... 217 894-6507
  Clayton *(G-6909)*
Custom Wood & Laminate Ltd ....G....... 815 727-4168
  Joliet *(G-11850)*
Fortune Brands Home & SEC Inc ....D....... 847 484-4400
  Deerfield *(G-7610)*
Glenview Custom Cabinets Inc ....G....... 847 345-5754
  Glenview *(G-10551)*
Hylan Design Ltd ....G....... 312 243-7341
  Chicago *(G-4863)*
Perfection Custom Closets & Co ....F....... 847 647-6461
  Niles *(G-15156)*
S L Fixtures Inc ....G....... 217 423-9907
  Decatur *(G-7545)*

CABINETS: Filing, Wood

C-V Cstom Cntrtops Cbinets Inc ....F....... 708 388-5066
  Blue Island *(G-2113)*
Cabinet Gallery LLC ....G....... 618 882-4801
  Highland *(G-11207)*
Ideal Cabinet Solutions Inc ....G....... 618 514-7087
  Alhambra *(G-401)*

CABINETS: Kitchen, Metal

Dpcac LLC ....F....... 630 741-7900
  Itasca *(G-11644)*

CABINETS: Kitchen, Wood

360 Cabinetry Inc ....G....... 630 879-0701
  Batavia *(G-1338)*
A & A Cabinet Creations Inc ....F....... 630 350-1560
  Bensenville *(G-1720)*
Aba Custom Woodworking ....G....... 815 356-9663
  Crystal Lake *(G-7153)*
Action Cabinet Sales Inc ....G....... 847 717-0011
  Elgin *(G-8494)*
ADM Custome Cabinet Chicago ....G....... 773 688-5379
  Chicago *(G-3547)*
Advanced Cabinets Corp ....G....... 847 928-0001
  Franklin Park *(G-9860)*
Aji Custom Cabinets ....G....... 847 312-7847
  McHenry *(G-13716)*
Allie Woodworking ....G....... 847 244-1919
  Waukegan *(G-20413)*

Alm Fine Cabinetry Inc ....G....... 815 562-6667
Rochelle *(G-17131)*

Amberleaf Cabinetry Inc ....F....... 773 247-8282
Chicago *(G-3644)*

American Custom Woodworking ....F....... 847 526-5900
Wauconda *(G-20330)*

Ameriscan Designs Inc ....D....... 773 542-1291
Chicago *(G-3677)*

Anderson & Marter Cabinets ....G....... 630 406-9840
Batavia *(G-1349)*

Architctlly Designed Cabinetry ....G....... 618 248-5931
Albers *(G-343)*

Aurora Line ....G....... 847 670-1600
Arlington Heights *(G-698)*

Autumn Woods Ltd ....G....... 630 868-3535
Wheaton *(G-20789)*

B & B Formica Appliers Inc ....F....... 773 804-1015
Chicago *(G-3804)*

Becker Jules D Wood Products ....G....... 847 526-8002
Wauconda *(G-20334)*

Bell Cabinet & Millwork Co ....G....... 708 425-1200
Palos Hills *(G-16196)*

Benchmark Cabinets & Mllwk Inc ....E....... 309 697-5855
Peoria *(G-16391)*

Birom Cabinetry LLC ....G....... 312 286-7132
Burr Ridge *(G-2657)*

Bolhuis Woodworking Co ....G....... 708 333-5100
Manhattan *(G-13431)*

Brakur Custom Cabinetry Inc ....C....... 630 355-2244
Shorewood *(G-18893)*

Brian Bequette Cabinetry ....G....... 618 670-5427
Staunton *(G-19475)*

Bridgeview Custom Kit Cabinets ....F....... 708 598-1221
Bridgeview *(G-2330)*

Brighton Cabinetry Inc ....F....... 217 235-1978
Mattoon *(G-13633)*

Brighton Cabinetry Inc ....E....... 217 895-3000
Neoga *(G-15016)*

Brown Woodworking ....G....... 815 477-8333
Crystal Lake *(G-7172)*

Byttow Enterprises Inc ....G....... 708 372-4450
Lansing *(G-12486)*

C-V Cstom Cntrtops Cbinets Inc ....F....... 708 388-5066
Blue Island *(G-2113)*

Cabinet Creations Plus ....F....... 847 245-3800
Mundelein *(G-14670)*

Cabinet Stiles Inc ....G....... 630 553-8639
Yorkville *(G-21474)*

Cabinet Wholesale Supply Inc ....G....... 708 536-7090
Tinley Park *(G-19815)*

Cabinetland of Springfield ....G....... 217 523-7253
Springfield *(G-19335)*

Cabinetry Solutions Imprvs LLC ....G....... 630 333-9195
Willowbrook *(G-21033)*

Cabinets & Granite Direct LLC ....F....... 630 588-8886
Carol Stream *(G-2952)*

Cabinets By Custom Craft Inc ....G....... 815 637-4001
Roscoe *(G-17900)*

Cabinets City ....G....... 847 440-3371
Mount Prospect *(G-14518)*

Cabinets Doors and More LLC ....G....... 847 395-6334
Antioch *(G-607)*

Carpenters Millwork Co ....F....... 708 339-7707
South Holland *(G-19204)*

Carpenters Millwork Co ....F....... 708 339-7707
Villa Park *(G-20137)*

Cassini Cabinetry ....G....... 847 244-9755
Waukegan *(G-20426)*

CCC Chicago Cabinet Center LLC ....F....... 855 508-5525
Elk Grove Village *(G-8883)*

Century Kitchen & Bath Inc ....G....... 847 395-3418
Wadsworth *(G-20208)*

Charles N Benner Inc ....E....... 312 829-4300
Chicago *(G-4075)*

Chicago Cabinet & Fixture Co ....G....... 630 616-8071
Bensenville *(G-1768)*

Chicago Cabinet Co ....G....... 708 429-5100
New Lenox *(G-15027)*

Choice Cabinet Chicago ....G....... 630 599-1099
Glendale Heights *(G-10443)*

Complex Woodwork Inc ....G....... 630 651-3637
Joliet *(G-11846)*

Con-Temp Cabinets Inc ....F....... 630 892-7300
North Aurora *(G-15257)*

Contract Industries Inc ....E....... 708 458-8150
Bedford Park *(G-1464)*

Cooper Lake Millworks Inc ....G....... 217 847-2681
Hamilton *(G-10951)*

Counter Craft Inc ....G....... 847 336-8205
Waukegan *(G-20431)*

Creative Designs Kitc ....E....... 773 327-8400
Chicago *(G-4261)*

Crj Cabinets ....G....... 331 303-0326
Chicago *(G-4271)*

Crooked Oak LLC ....G....... 708 344-6955
Broadview *(G-2428)*

Crown Custom Cabinetry Inc ....G....... 815 942-0432
Morris *(G-14300)*

Custom Cabinet Refacers Inc ....G....... 847 695-8800
Elgin *(G-8559)*

Custom Wood Designs Inc ....G....... 708 799-3439
Crestwood *(G-7116)*

Cws Cabinets ....G....... 847 258-4468
Elk Grove Village *(G-8929)*

Daniel M Powers & Assoc Ltd ....D....... 630 685-8400
Bolingbrook *(G-2166)*

Design Woodworks ....G....... 847 566-6603
Mundelein *(G-14682)*

Deuce Development Corp ....G....... 309 353-6324
Pekin *(G-16328)*

Dicks Custom Cabinet Shop ....G....... 815 358-2663
Cornell *(G-7012)*

Donald Kranz ....G....... 847 428-1616
Carpentersville *(G-3101)*

Dpcac LLC ....F....... 630 741-7900
Itasca *(G-11644)*

Dvoraks Creations Inc ....G....... 815 838-2214
Lockport *(G-12991)*

Eddie Gapastione ....G....... 708 430-3881
Bridgeview *(G-2344)*

Edgars Custom Cabinets ....G....... 847 928-0922
Franklin Park *(G-9937)*

Edward Hull Cabinet Shop ....G....... 217 864-3011
Mount Zion *(G-14645)*

Elkay Manufacturing Company ....G....... 800 223-5529
Downers Grove *(G-7999)*

En Pointe Cabinetry LLC ....G....... 847 787-0777
Elk Grove Village *(G-8977)*

Encon Environmental Concepts ....F....... 630 543-1583
Addison *(G-115)*

Euro-Tech Cabinetry Rmdlg Corp ....G....... 815 254-3876
Plainfield *(G-16661)*

F & B Woodworking Inc ....G....... 217 543-2531
Arthur *(G-857)*

Forest City Counter Tops Inc ....F....... 815 633-8602
Loves Park *(G-13212)*

Four Acre Wood Products ....F....... 217 543-2971
Arthur *(G-858)*

Fra-Milco Cabinets Co Inc ....G ....
Frankfort *(G-9795)*

Fraser Millwork Inc ....G....... 708 447-3262
Lyons *(G-13309)*

Garver Inc ....G....... 217 932-2441
Casey *(G-3201)*

Geneva Cabinet Gallery ....G....... 630 232-9500
Geneva *(G-10271)*

Glenview Custom Cabinets Inc ....G....... 847 345-5754
Glenview *(G-10551)*

Gold Seal Cabinets Countertops ....E....... 630 906-0366
Aurora *(G-1104)*

Grays Cabinet Co ....G....... 618 948-2211
Saint Francisville *(G-18314)*

Hansen Custom Cabinet Inc ....G....... 847 356-1100
Lake Villa *(G-12353)*

Hci Cabinetry and Design Inc ....G....... 630 584-0266
Addison *(G-148)*

Helmuth Custom Kitchens LLC ....E....... 217 543-3588
Arthur *(G-862)*

Hester Cabinets & Millwork ....G....... 815 634-4555
Coal City *(G-6933)*

Hickory Street Cabinets ....G....... 618 667-9676
Troy *(G-19915)*

Hidalgo Fine Cabinetry ....G....... 630 753-9323
Naperville *(G-14972)*

Hylan Design Ltd ....G....... 312 243-7341
Chicago *(G-4863)*

I Kustom Cabinets Inc ....G....... 773 343-6858
Highwood *(G-11307)*

Ideal Cabinet Solutions Inc ....G....... 618 514-7087
Alhambra *(G-401)*

J & K Cabinetry Inc ....G....... 847 758-7808
Elk Grove Village *(G-9062)*

J & M Custom Cabinets ....G....... 217 677-2229
La Place *(G-12099)*

J K Custom Countertops ....G....... 630 495-2324
Lombard *(G-13088)*

J M Lustig Custom Cabinets Co ....F....... 217 342-6661
Effingham *(G-8403)*

Janik Custom Millwork Inc ....G....... 708 482-4844
Hodgkins *(G-11390)*

Jk Cabinets Plus LLC ....G....... 952 237-1825
Union *(G-19940)*

Johnson Custom Cabinets ....G....... 815 675-9690
Spring Grove *(G-19278)*

Jones Design Group Ltd ....G....... 630 462-9340
Winfield *(G-21111)*

Juniors Custom Cabinets ....G....... 773 495-6962
Chicago *(G-5059)*

Kabinet Kraft ....F....... 618 395-1047
Olney *(G-15867)*

Kanneberg Custom Kitchens Inc ....G....... 815 654-1110
Machesney Park *(G-13353)*

Kempner Company Inc ....F....... 312 733-1606
Chicago *(G-5095)*

Kit Artisan Cab Refinishers ....G....... 630 922-9714
Plainfield *(G-16680)*

Kitchen & Bath Cabinet Company ....G....... 217 352-1900
Champaign *(G-3314)*

Kitchen Krafters Inc ....G....... 815 675-6061
Spring Grove *(G-19279)*

Km Cabinet Supply ....G....... 312 927-8860
Evergreen Park *(G-9596)*

Koala Cabinets ....G....... 630 818-1289
West Chicago *(G-20606)*

Kowal Custom Cabinet & Furn ....G....... 708 597-3367
Blue Island *(G-2129)*

Krafty Kabinets ....G....... 815 369-5250
Lena *(G-12601)*

Kuche Fine Cabinetry ....G....... 217 342-2244
Effingham *(G-8406)*

L2 Supply DBA Ica Cab Supp Ly ....G....... 773 382-8037
Chicago *(G-5145)*

Lamico Designers Deerfield Inc ....G....... 847 465-8850
Highland Park *(G-11279)*

Living Laminates Inc ....G....... 847 741-2004
Maple Park *(G-13464)*

Luxe Classic Kitchens & Interi ....G....... 630 774-9337
Yorkville *(G-21492)*

Lyko Woodworking & Cnstr ....G....... 773 583-4561
Chicago *(G-5292)*

M & R Custom Millwork Inc ....G....... 815 547-8549
Belvidere *(G-1682)*

Marfa Cabinets Inc ....E....... 847 701-5558
Skokie *(G-18982)*

Markham Cabinet Works Inc ....G....... 708 687-3074
Midlothian *(G-13993)*

Markus Cabinet Manufacturing ....E....... 618 228-7376
Aviston *(G-1181)*

Masco Corporation ....D....... 847 303-3088
Schaumburg *(G-18621)*

Master Cabinets ....G....... 847 639-1323
Cary *(G-3178)*

Masterbrand Cabinets Inc ....B....... 217 543-3311
Arthur *(G-867)*

Masterbrand Cabinets Inc ....G....... 217 543-3466
Arthur *(G-868)*

Masterbrand Cabinets Inc ....G....... 503 241-4964
Arthur *(G-869)*

Masterpiece Cabinetry Design ....G....... 217 258-6880
Mattoon *(G-13644)*

Masters Shop ....G....... 217 643-7826
Thomasboro *(G-19776)*

Mc Laminated Cabinets ....G....... 773 301-0393
Franklin Park *(G-9987)*

Metro Cabinet Refinishers ....G....... 217 498-7174
Rochester *(G-17169)*

Mettes Cabinet Corner Inc ....F....... 217 342-9552
Effingham *(G-8410)*

Mica Furniture Mfg Inc ....G....... 708 430-1150
Addison *(G-203)*

Middletons Mouldings Inc ....D....... 517 278-6610
Schaumburg *(G-18629)*

Midwest Woodcrafters Inc ....G....... 630 665-0901
Carol Stream *(G-3031)*

Millcraft ....G....... 618 426-9819
Campbell Hill *(G-2817)*

Mirek Cabinets ....G....... 630 350-8336
Franklin Park *(G-10001)*

Monarch Mfg Corp Amer ....E....... 217 728-2552
Sullivan *(G-19671)*

Mueller Custom Cabinetry Inc ....G....... 815 448-5448
Mazon *(G-13683)*

Multiplex Display Fixture Co ....E....... 800 325-3350
Dupo *(G-8141)*

Murray Cabinetry & Tops Inc ....G....... 815 672-6992
Streator *(G-19616)*

Murray Custom Cabinetry ....G....... 309 966-0624
Peoria *(G-16481)*

Natl Ktchn and Bath Cabinetry ....G....... 815 733-8888
Romeoville *(G-17860)*

Employee Codes: A=Over 500 employees, B=251-500
C=101-250, D=51-100, E=20-50, F=10-19, G=3-9
2020 Harris Illinois
Industrial Directory
1369

CABINETS: Kitchen, Wood

Neumann Custom Woodworking .... G 847 979-3199
  Arlington Heights *(G-781)*
New Style Cabinets Inc .... G 773 622-3114
  Chicago *(G-5581)*
New Vision Cstm Cabinets Mllwk .... G 847 265-2723
  Lake Villa *(G-12362)*
Northstar Custom Cabinetry .... G 708 597-2099
  Posen *(G-16799)*
Northwest Marble Products .... E 630 860-2288
  Hoffman Estates *(G-11473)*
OGorman Son Carpentry Contrs .... E 815 485-8997
  New Lenox *(G-15045)*
Okaw Valley Woodworking LLC .... F 217 543-5180
  Arthur *(G-874)*
Orchard Hill Cabinetry Inc .... E 312 829-4300
  Chicago *(G-5695)*
Parenti & Raffaelli Ltd .... C 847 253-5550
  Mount Prospect *(G-14558)*
Peaceful Valley Cabinetry .... G 618 584-3615
  Flat Rock *(G-9672)*
Pentwater Furnishing Inc .... F 630 984-4703
  Lombard *(G-13119)*
Perkins Construction .... G 815 233-9655
  Freeport *(G-10132)*
Phoenix Woodworking Corp .... E 815 338-9338
  Woodstock *(G-21421)*
Pintas Cultured Marble .... E 708 385-3360
  Alsip *(G-492)*
Plain & Posh LLC .... G 630 960-0048
  Darien *(G-7411)*
Planks Cabinet Shop Inc .... G 217 543-2687
  Arthur *(G-876)*
Prairie Woodworks Inc .... G 309 378-2418
  Downs *(G-8112)*
Premier Woodworking Concepts .... G 815 334-0888
  Woodstock *(G-21424)*
Pro Cabinets Inc .... G 618 993-0008
  Marion *(G-13531)*
Quality Finishing Service Inc .... G 847 616-0336
  Elk Grove Village *(G-9204)*
R & R Custom Cabinet Making .... G 847 358-6188
  Palatine *(G-16152)*
Rapp Cabinets & Woodworks Inc .... F 618 736-2955
  Dahlgren *(G-7309)*
Rawson Custom Woodworks LLC .... G 815 332-9222
  Cherry Valley *(G-3445)*
Raymond Earl Fine Woodworking .... G 309 565-7661
  Hanna City *(G-10994)*
Richard King and Sons .... G 815 654-0226
  Loves Park *(G-13253)*
Richard Schrock .... G 217 543-3111
  Arthur *(G-878)*
Riverbend Kitchen & Mllwk LLC .... G 618 462-8955
  Alton *(G-569)*
Riverside Custom Woodworking .... G 815 589-3608
  Fulton *(G-10157)*
Riverton Cabinet Company .... E 815 462-5300
  New Lenox *(G-15056)*
Roeckers Inc .... G 309 693-2929
  Peoria *(G-16513)*
Rogan Granitindustrie Inc .... G 708 758-0050
  Lynwood *(G-13298)*
Romar Cabinet & Top Co Inc .... D 815 467-4452
  Channahon *(G-3392)*
Roncin Custom Design .... G 847 669-0260
  Huntley *(G-11565)*
Ronnie P Faber .... G 815 626-4561
  Sterling *(G-19529)*
Royal Fabricators Inc .... F 847 775-7466
  Wadsworth *(G-20213)*
Santelli Custom Cabinetry .... G 708 771-3884
  River Forest *(G-17055)*
Schrock Custom Woodworking .... G 217 849-3375
  Toledo *(G-19877)*
Schrocks Woodworking .... G 217 578-3259
  Arthur *(G-879)*
Seneca Custom Cabinetry .... G 815 357-1322
  Seneca *(G-18861)*
Shews Custom Woodworking .... G 217 737-5543
  Lincoln *(G-12738)*
Shreck Kitchens .... G 847 695-4154
  South Elgin *(G-19174)*
Silver Bell Cnstr & Furn Inc .... G 773 578-9450
  Chicago *(G-6171)*
Sleeping Bear Inc .... G 630 541-7220
  Lisle *(G-12937)*
Snaidero USA .... G 312 644-6662
  Chicago *(G-6194)*
Specialized Woodwork Inc .... G 630 627-0450
  Lombard *(G-13131)*

Stancy Woodworking Co Inc .... F 847 526-0252
  Island Lake *(G-11611)*
Steve Janik Cabinetry LLC .... G 630 553-8383
  Aurora *(G-1157)*
Stylish Kit Bath Cabinets Corp .... G 773 525-8667
  Chicago *(G-6260)*
Superior Cabinet Company .... G 708 658-6613
  Bridgeview *(G-2391)*
Superior Cabinet Supply Inc .... G 815 464-2700
  Frankfort *(G-9841)*
T and T Cabinet Co .... G 815 245-6322
  McHenry *(G-13804)*
T2 Cabinets Inc .... F 312 593-1507
  Chicago *(G-6308)*
Thoennes & Thoennes Inc .... G 309 663-4053
  Bloomington *(G-2101)*
Timberland Custom Cab & Tops .... G 815 722-0825
  Joliet *(G-11936)*
Tremont Kitchen Tops Inc .... G 309 925-5736
  Tremont *(G-19900)*
Tri Star Cabinet & Top Co Inc .... D 815 485-2564
  New Lenox *(G-15065)*
True Woods Cabinetry Inc .... G 847 550-1860
  Lake Zurich *(G-12466)*
Val Custom Cabinets & Flrg Inc .... G 708 790-8373
  Bensenville *(G-1907)*
Vida Cabinets Inc .... G 847 258-4468
  Elk Grove Village *(G-9304)*
Viking Metal Cabinet Co LLC .... D 800 776-7767
  Montgomery *(G-14273)*
Viking Metal Cabinet Company .... D 630 863-7234
  Montgomery *(G-14274)*
Wheatland Cstm Cbntry Wdwkg LL ...... G 630 359-8553
  Villa Park *(G-20176)*
Wheaton Cabinetry .... G 815 729-1085
  Lockport *(G-13027)*
Wilcor Solid Surface Inc .... F 888 956-1001
  Elk Grove Village *(G-9309)*
Wills Milling and Hardwood Inc .... E 217 854-9056
  Carlinville *(G-2884)*
Winslyn Industries .... G 630 401-8051
  South Elgin *(G-19182)*
Wolf Cabinetry & Ganite .... G 847 358-9922
  Palatine *(G-16176)*
Wolters Custom Cabinets LLC .... G 618 282-3158
  Evansville *(G-9591)*
Wood Shop .... G 773 994-6666
  Chicago *(G-6667)*
Wood Specialties Incorporated .... F 217 678-8420
  Bement *(G-1716)*
Woodcraft Enterprises Inc .... G 815 485-2787
  New Lenox *(G-15070)*
Woodhill Cabinetry Design Inc .... G 815 431-0545
  Ottawa *(G-16086)*
Woodstreet Cabinet .... G 708 995-6077
  Mokena *(G-14128)*
Woodways Industries LLC .... E 616 956-3070
  Chicago *(G-6668)*
Your Custom Cabinetry Corp .... G 773 290-7247
  Melrose Park *(G-13931)*

CABINETS: Office, Metal

Accurate Custom Cabinets Inc .... E 630 458-0460
  Addison *(G-15)*

CABINETS: Office, Wood

Accurate Custom Cabinets Inc .... E 630 458-0460
  Addison *(G-15)*
Castle Craft Products Inc .... F 630 279-7494
  Villa Park *(G-20138)*
Cmp Millwork Co .... G 630 832-6462
  Elmhurst *(G-9348)*
Complete Custom Woodworks .... G 309 644-1911
  Coal Valley *(G-6934)*
Grays Cabinet Co .... G 618 948-2211
  Saint Francisville *(G-18314)*
Stay Straight Manufacturing .... G 312 226-2137
  Chicago *(G-6236)*

CABINETS: Radio & Television, Metal

Modular Wood Systems Inc .... G 847 251-6401
  Wilmette *(G-21088)*

CABINETS: Show, Display, Etc, Wood, Exc Refrigerated

Churchill Cabinet Company .... E 708 780-0070
  Cicero *(G-6833)*
Con-Temp Cabinets Inc .... F 630 892-7300
  North Aurora *(G-15257)*
Imperial Kitchens & Bath Inc .... F 708 485-0020
  Brookfield *(G-2486)*
Kewaunee Scientific Corp .... G 847 675-7744
  Highland Park *(G-11278)*
Marcy Enterprises Inc .... G 708 352-7220
  La Grange Park *(G-12098)*
Midwest Display & Mfg Inc .... G 815 962-2199
  Rockford *(G-17526)*
Omni Craft Inc .... G 815 838-1285
  Lockport *(G-13017)*
Randal Wood Displays Inc .... D 630 761-0400
  Batavia *(G-1409)*
Specialized Woodwork Inc .... G 630 627-0450
  Lombard *(G-13131)*
Wilson Kitchens Inc .... D 618 253-7449
  Harrisburg *(G-11031)*
Windy Hill Woodworking Inc .... G 309 275-2415
  Towanda *(G-19893)*

CABINETS: Television, Plastic

Zenith Electronics Corporation .... E 847 941-8000
  Lincolnshire *(G-12806)*

CABLE & OTHER PAY TELEVISION DISTRIBUTION

Cco Holdings LLC .... G 618 505-3505
  Troy *(G-19912)*
Cco Holdings LLC .... G 618 651-6486
  Highland *(G-11208)*
Icon Acquisition Holdings LP .... G 312 751-8000
  Chicago *(G-4872)*

CABLE & PAY TELEVISION SVCS: Direct Broadcast Satellite

Othernet Inc .... G 773 688-4320
  Long Grove *(G-13168)*

CABLE & PAY TELEVISION SVCS: Subscription

Jklein Enterprises Inc .... G 618 664-4554
  Greenville *(G-10836)*

CABLE TELEVISION

Fred Kennerly .... G 815 398-6861
  Rockford *(G-17424)*

CABLE TELEVISION PRDTS

Conquest Sound Inc .... F 708 534-0309
  Manteno *(G-13445)*
Ed Co .... E 708 614-0695
  Tinley Park *(G-19822)*
Fred Kennerly .... G 815 398-6861
  Rockford *(G-17424)*

CABLE WIRING SETS: Battery, Internal Combustion Engines

Appliance Information and Repr .... G 217 698-8858
  Rochester *(G-17163)*
Sk Express Inc .... C 815 748-4388
  Dekalb *(G-7702)*
UNI Electric Enterprise Inc .... G 630 372-6312
  Bartlett *(G-1258)*

CABLE: Coaxial

Andrew New Zealand Inc .... E 708 873-3507
  Orland Park *(G-15940)*
Commscope Technologies LLC .... B 779 435-6000
  Joliet *(G-11845)*
Industrial Wire Cable II Corp .... F 847 726-8910
  Lake Zurich *(G-12422)*
Teledyne Defense Elec LLC .... C 630 754-3300
  Woodridge *(G-21344)*

CABLE: Fiber

Calvert Systems .... G 309 523-3262
  Port Byron *(G-16786)*
Clark Wire & Cable Co Inc .... E 847 949-9944
  Mundelein *(G-14678)*
CT Group Inc .... G 708 466-8277
  Glen Ellyn *(G-10399)*

PRODUCT SECTION
CANDY: Chocolate From Cacao Beans

CABLE: Fiber Optic
Belford Electronics Inc..................E...... 630 705-3020
  Addison *(G-47)*
Ruckus Wireless Inc........................E...... 630 281-3000
  Lisle *(G-12935)*
SITech Inc..F...... 630 761-3640
  Batavia *(G-1417)*

CABLE: Noninsulated
Advantage Components Inc..........E...... 815 725-8644
  Joliet *(G-11817)*
Amsysco Inc....................................E...... 630 296-8383
  Romeoville *(G-17794)*
Industrial Wire & Cable Corp..........E...... 847 726-8910
  Lake Zurich *(G-12421)*
Unistrut International Corp..............C...... 800 882-5543
  Harvey *(G-11099)*

CABLE: Ropes & Fiber
Lehigh Consumer Products LLC.....C...... 630 851-7330
  Aurora *(G-997)*

CABLE: Steel, Insulated Or Armored
Southwire Company LLC.................D...... 618 662-8341
  Flora *(G-9694)*

CABS: Indl Trucks & Tractors
Dfk America Inc..............................G...... 630 324-6793
  Downers Grove *(G-7986)*

CAGES: Wire
Ameriguard Corporation.................G...... 630 986-1900
  Burr Ridge *(G-2652)*
Circle K Industries Inc....................F...... 847 949-0363
  Mundelein *(G-14677)*

CALCULATING & ACCOUNTING EQPT
Business Valuation Group Inc........G...... 312 595-1900
  Chicago *(G-3982)*

CALENDARS, WHOLESALE
Midwest Promotional Group Co......E...... 708 563-0600
  Burr Ridge *(G-2705)*

CALIBRATING SVCS, NEC
Verson Enterprises Inc...................F...... 847 364-2600
  Elk Grove Village *(G-9302)*

CALLIGRAPHER
Little Shop of Papers Ltd...............G...... 847 382-7733
  Barrington *(G-1225)*

CAMERAS & RELATED EQPT: Photographic
Bka Inc..G...... 847 831-3535
  Highland Park *(G-11255)*
Fire CAM..G...... 618 416-8390
  Belleville *(G-1552)*
Moog Inc...C...... 847 498-0704
  Northbrook *(G-15436)*
Robotics Technologies Inc.............E...... 815 722-7650
  Joliet *(G-11927)*

CAMPGROUNDS
Arthur Leo Kuhl..............................G...... 618 752-5473
  Ingraham *(G-11591)*
Wooded Wonderland......................G...... 815 777-1223
  Galena *(G-10182)*

CAMSHAFTS
Thyssnkrupp Prsta Danville LLC....B...... 217 444-5500
  Danville *(G-7387)*

CAN LIDS & ENDS
Boe Intermediate Holding Corp......B...... 773 890-3300
  Chicago *(G-3924)*
Bway Corporation..........................C...... 847 956-0750
  Elk Grove Village *(G-8875)*
Mauser Pckg Sltons Intrmdate I....G...... 770 645-4800
  Oak Brook *(G-15640)*
Silgan Containers Mfg Corp...........C...... 217 283-5501
  Hoopeston *(G-11512)*

CANDLE SHOPS
Edwin Waldmire & Virginia.............G...... 217 498-9375
  Rochester *(G-17165)*
Marley Candles..............................E...... 815 485-6604
  Mokena *(G-14097)*
Waxman Candles Inc.....................G...... 773 929-3000
  Chicago *(G-6593)*

CANDLES
1803 Candles.................................G...... 815 264-3009
  Waterman *(G-20297)*
C Becky & Company Inc................G...... 847 818-1021
  Mount Prospect *(G-14516)*
Candle Crest LLC..........................G...... 815 704-3809
  Rockford *(G-17334)*
Candle Enterprises Inc..................G...... 618 526-8070
  Breese *(G-2300)*
Candle-Licious..............................G...... 847 488-9982
  Morrison *(G-14341)*
Candleart Candle Company Inc....G...... 217 925-5905
  Dieterich *(G-7875)*
Chicago Candle Company.............G...... 773 637-5279
  Chicago *(G-4094)*
Crystal Clear Cndle Design LLC....F...... 847 749-4782
  Arlington Heights *(G-721)*
Heartland Candle Co.....................G...... 815 698-2200
  Ashkum *(G-883)*
Imagine That Candle Co................G...... 708 481-6370
  Matteson *(G-13625)*
Kemis Kollections..........................G...... 773 431-2307
  Chicago *(G-5094)*
Marley Candles..............................E...... 815 485-6604
  Mokena *(G-14097)*
Mondelez Global LLC....................C...... 847 943-4000
  Deerfield *(G-7637)*
Sashe Lux LLC..............................G...... 312 593-1379
  Chicago *(G-6106)*
Sassy Primitives Ltd......................G...... 815 385-9302
  McCullom Lake *(G-13712)*
Tatine...G...... 312 733-0173
  Chicago *(G-6329)*
Waxman Candles Inc....................G...... 773 929-3000
  Chicago *(G-6593)*

CANDLES: Wholesalers
Chicago Candle Company.............G...... 773 637-5279
  Chicago *(G-4094)*

CANDY & CONFECTIONS: Cake Ornaments
White Stokes Company Inc...........E...... 773 254-5000
  Lincolnwood *(G-12851)*

CANDY & CONFECTIONS: Candy Bars, Including Chocolate Covered
Healthful Habits LLC......................G...... 224 489-4256
  West Chicago *(G-20592)*
Jessis Hideout...............................G...... 618 343-4346
  Caseyville *(G-3215)*
Mexicandy Distributor Inc.............G...... 773 847-0024
  Chicago *(G-5414)*
Opalek Frontier Inc........................G...... 312 733-2700
  Chicago *(G-5679)*
Orbit Room....................................G...... 773 588-8540
  Chicago *(G-5694)*

CANDY & CONFECTIONS: Chocolate Candy, Exc Solid Chocolate
Chocolate Potpourri Ltd.................F...... 847 729-8878
  Glenview *(G-10535)*
Morkes Inc.....................................F...... 847 359-3511
  Palatine *(G-16141)*
Tri International Co........................A...... 773 838-3400
  Chicago *(G-6417)*
Zeldaco Ltd...................................E...... 847 674-0033
  Skokie *(G-19060)*

CANDY & CONFECTIONS: Fruit & Fruit Peel
All American Nut & Candy Corp....F...... 630 595-6473
  Wood Dale *(G-21157)*

CANDY & CONFECTIONS: Fudge
Arndts Stores Inc..........................G...... 618 783-2511
  Newton *(G-15080)*
Deli Star Ventures Inc...................F...... 618 233-0400
  Belleville *(G-1544)*

CANDY & CONFECTIONS: Jellybeans
Goelitz Confectionery Company....C...... 847 689-2225
  North Chicago *(G-15313)*

CANDY & CONFECTIONS: Marshmallows
Doumak Inc....................................G...... 800 323-0318
  Bensenville *(G-1788)*
Doumak Inc....................................D...... 847 981-2180
  Elk Grove Village *(G-8953)*
We Love Soy Inc............................G...... 630 629-9667
  Addison *(G-332)*

CANDY & CONFECTIONS: Popcorn Balls/Other Trtd Popcorn Prdts
McCleary Inc..................................C...... 815 389-3053
  South Beloit *(G-19101)*

CANDY MAKING GOODS & SPLYS, WHOLESALE
Cupcake Holdings LLC..................C...... 800 794-5866
  Woodridge *(G-21289)*
Wilton Holdings Inc........................A...... 630 963-7100
  Woodridge *(G-21349)*
Wilton Industries Inc.......................B...... 630 963-7100
  Naperville *(G-14949)*
Wilton Industries Inc.......................F...... 815 834-9390
  Romeoville *(G-17888)*

CANDY, NUT & CONFECTIONERY STORE: Popcorn, Incl Caramel Corn
Creekstone Kettle Works Ltd........F...... 217 246-5355
  Raymond *(G-16988)*
Great American Popcorn Company...G...... 815 777-4116
  Galena *(G-10173)*

CANDY, NUT & CONFECTIONERY STORES: Candy
American Convenience Inc............F...... 815 344-6040
  McHenry *(G-13718)*
Belgian Chocolatier Piron Inc........G...... 847 864-5504
  Evanston *(G-9498)*
Blissful Brownies Inc......................G...... 541 308-0226
  Lake Forest *(G-12231)*
Cora Lee Candies Inc....................F...... 847 724-2754
  Glenview *(G-10538)*
Dekalb Confectionary Inc..............E...... 815 758-5990
  Dekalb *(G-7676)*
Ford Gum & Machine Company Inc..F...... 847 955-0003
  Buffalo Grove *(G-2540)*
Galenas Kandy Kitchen..................G...... 815 777-0241
  Galena *(G-10171)*
Gayety Candy Co Inc....................E...... 708 418-0062
  Lansing *(G-12494)*
Jelly Belly Candy Company...........C...... 847 689-2225
  North Chicago *(G-15315)*
Mitchlls Cndies Ice Creams Inc.....F...... 708 799-3835
  Homewood *(G-11501)*
Morkes Inc.....................................F...... 847 359-3511
  Palatine *(G-16141)*
Opalek Frontier Inc........................G...... 312 733-2700
  Chicago *(G-5679)*
Peases Inc....................................F...... 217 523-3721
  Springfield *(G-19422)*
Samad General Services Inc........G...... 773 593-3332
  Addison *(G-280)*
Vosges Ltd....................................D...... 773 388-5560
  Chicago *(G-6570)*

CANDY, NUT & CONFECTIONERY STORES: Confectionery
Long Grove Confectionery Co......E...... 847 459-3100
  Buffalo Grove *(G-2565)*

CANDY, NUT & CONFECTIONERY STORES: Produced For Direct Sale
Altona Co......................................G...... 815 232-7819
  Freeport *(G-10099)*

CANDY: Chocolate From Cacao Beans
Godiva Chocolatier Inc..................E...... 630 820-5842
  Aurora *(G-973)*

CANDY: Chocolate From Cacao Beans

Morkes Inc .... F 847 359-3511
 Palatine *(G-16141)*
Vosges Ltd .... D 773 388-5560
 Chicago *(G-6570)*

CANDY: Hard

Primrose Candy Co .... C 800 268-9522
 Chicago *(G-5875)*

CANDY: Soft

Ferrara Candy Company .... B 708 366-0500
 Chicago *(G-4582)*
Ferrara Candy Company .... F 630 378-4197
 Bolingbrook *(G-2177)*
Ferrara Candy Company .... F 708 432-4407
 Bellwood *(G-1624)*
Ferrara Candy Company .... B 708 488-1892
 Forest Park *(G-9716)*

CANES & TRIMMINGS, EXC PRECIOUS METAL

Cane Plus .... G 217 522-4035
 Springfield *(G-19336)*

CANNED SPECIALTIES

Archer-Daniels-Midland Company .... E 309 772-2141
 Bushnell *(G-2737)*
Henkel Consumer Goods Inc .... C 630 892-4381
 Montgomery *(G-14246)*
Kraft Heinz Foods Company .... C 847 291-3900
 Northbrook *(G-15415)*
Lee Gilster-Mary Corporation .... D 618 965-3426
 Steeleville *(G-19481)*
Lightlife Foods Inc .... C 413 774-9000
 Elmhurst *(G-9392)*
Lynfred Winery Inc .... E 630 529-9463
 Roselle *(G-17965)*
McShares Inc .... E 217 762-2561
 Monticello *(G-14281)*
Nogi Brands LLC .... G 312 371-7974
 Willowbrook *(G-21054)*
Sofrito Foods LLC .... G 224 535-9252
 North Aurora *(G-15275)*

CANS: Composite Foil-Fiber, Made From Purchased Materials

Polynt Composites II LLC .... G 847 428-2657
 Carpentersville *(G-3113)*

CANS: Garbage, Stamped Or Pressed Metal

Rapid Wash Group Ltd .... G 847 376-8442
 Des Plaines *(G-7836)*

CANS: Metal

All Container Inc .... G 847 677-2100
 Lincolnwood *(G-12813)*
Brockway Standard Inc .... G 773 893-2100
 Chicago *(G-3962)*
Bway Corporation .... C 773 254-8700
 Chicago *(G-3987)*
Central Can Company Inc .... C 773 254-8700
 Chicago *(G-4056)*
Cooler Concepts Inc .... G 815 462-3866
 New Lenox *(G-15029)*
Creative Metal Products .... F 773 638-3200
 Chicago *(G-4264)*
Crown Cork & Seal Usa Inc .... C 708 239-5555
 Alsip *(G-435)*
Crown Cork & Seal Usa Inc .... C 815 933-9351
 Bradley *(G-2278)*
Crown Cork & Seal Usa Inc .... C 708 239-5000
 Alsip *(G-436)*
Crown Cork & Seal Usa Inc .... F 708 385-8670
 Alsip *(G-437)*
Crown Cork & Seal Usa Inc .... D 217 672-3533
 Warrensburg *(G-20226)*
Crown Cork & Seal Usa Inc .... C 217 872-6100
 Decatur *(G-7478)*
Crown Cork & Seal Usa Inc .... E 630 851-7774
 Aurora *(G-946)*
D & B Fabricators & Distrs .... F 630 325-3811
 Lemont *(G-12562)*
Ds Containers Inc .... C 630 406-9600
 Batavia *(G-1375)*

Ideal Fabricators Inc .... F 217 999-7017
 Mount Olive *(G-14505)*
JL Clark LLC .... C 815 961-5609
 Rockford *(G-17476)*
Jlo Metal Products Co A Corp .... D 773 889-6242
 Chicago *(G-5032)*
Justrite Manufacturing Co LLC .... C 800 798-9250
 Deerfield *(G-7625)*
Metraflex Company .... D 312 738-3800
 Chicago *(G-5411)*
Mt Containers Inc .... G 708 458-9420
 Chicago *(G-5520)*
North America Packaging Corp .... F 847 979-1625
 Elk Grove Village *(G-9151)*
Silgan Containers LLC .... D 815 562-1250
 Rochelle *(G-17159)*
Silgan Containers Mfg Corp .... E 847 336-0552
 Waukegan *(G-20495)*
Silgan Equipment Company .... E 847 336-0552
 Waukegan *(G-20496)*
Silgan White Cap LLC .... C 217 398-1600
 Champaign *(G-3347)*
Spiked .... G 469 235-8103
 Evanston *(G-9576)*
Staffco Inc .... G 309 688-3223
 Peoria *(G-16528)*
Willow Farm Product Inc .... G 630 395-9246
 Darien *(G-7414)*

CANS: Oil, Metal

Best Metal Corporation .... E 815 337-0420
 Woodstock *(G-21364)*

CANVAS PRDTS

A B Kelly Inc .... G 847 639-1022
 Cary *(G-3142)*
Acme Awning Co .... G 847 446-0153
 Highland Park *(G-11251)*
Air Land and Sea Interiors .... G 630 834-1717
 Villa Park *(G-20129)*
Albax Inc .... E 630 758-1072
 Elmhurst *(G-9323)*
Brumleve Industries Inc .... F 217 857-3777
 Teutopolis *(G-19764)*
Ed Hill S Custom Canvas .... G 815 476-5042
 Wilmington *(G-21097)*
Environetics Inc .... F 815 838-8331
 Lockport *(G-12993)*
Flex-O-Glass Inc .... C 773 261-5200
 Chicago *(G-4605)*
Haakes Awning .... G 618 529-4808
 Carbondale *(G-2844)*
Jelinek & Sons Inc .... G 630 355-3474
 Plainfield *(G-16676)*
M Putterman & Co LLC .... D 773 927-4120
 Chicago *(G-5304)*
Material Control Inc .... F 630 892-4274
 Batavia *(G-1393)*
Mpc Containment Systems LLC .... D 773 927-4121
 Chicago *(G-5515)*
Mpc Group LLC .... C 773 927-4120
 Chicago *(G-5517)*
Ogden Top & Trim Shop Inc .... G 708 484-5422
 Berwyn *(G-1958)*
Ottos Canvas Shop .... G 217 543-3307
 Arthur *(G-875)*
Rehabilitation and Vocational .... E 618 833-5344
 Anna *(G-587)*
Tri Vantage LLC .... F 630 530-5333
 Elmhurst *(G-9438)*

CANVAS PRDTS, WHOLESALE

Brumleve Industries Inc .... F 217 857-3777
 Teutopolis *(G-19764)*

CANVAS PRDTS: Air Cushions & Mattresses

Sleep6 LLC .... G 844 375-3376
 Chicago *(G-6186)*

CANVAS PRDTS: Convertible Tops, Car/Boat, Fm Purchased Mtrl

Custom Canvas LLC .... G 847 587-0225
 Ingleside *(G-11580)*
United Canvas Inc .... E 847 395-1470
 Antioch *(G-641)*

CANVAS PRDTS: Shades, Made From Purchased Materials

Shading Solutions Group Inc .... G 630 444-2102
 Geneva *(G-10305)*

CAPACITORS & CONDENSERS

Motor Capacitors Inc .... F 773 774-6666
 Wood Dale *(G-21217)*

CAPACITORS: AC, Motors Or Fluorescent Lamp Ballasts

American Electronic Pdts Inc .... F 630 889-9977
 Oak Brook *(G-15592)*
Innovation Plus Power Systems .... F 630 457-1105
 Saint Charles *(G-18213)*

CAPACITORS: NEC

10g LLC .... F 630 754-2400
 Woodridge *(G-21269)*
Aisin Light Metals LLC .... G 618 997-9800
 Marion *(G-13500)*
Bycap Inc .... E 773 561-4976
 Chicago *(G-3988)*
Illinois Capacitor Inc .... B 847 675-1760
 Des Plaines *(G-7783)*
Jbsmwg Corp .... F 847 675-1865
 Lincolnwood *(G-12824)*
Knowles Corporation .... C 630 250-5100
 Itasca *(G-11686)*
Knowles Corporation .... E 630 250-5100
 Itasca *(G-11685)*
Motor Capacitors Inc .... F 773 774-6666
 Wood Dale *(G-21217)*
Murata Electronics N Amer Inc .... G 847 330-9200
 Schaumburg *(G-18641)*
Standard Condenser Corporation .... F 847 965-2722
 Morton Grove *(G-14441)*
United Chemi-Con Inc .... E 847 696-2000
 Rolling Meadows *(G-17783)*

CAPS & TOPS: Bottle, Stamped Metal

Walter H Jelly & Co Inc .... G 847 455-4235
 Franklin Park *(G-10082)*

CAPS: Plastic

Selig S LLC .... G 815 785-2100
 Forrest *(G-9735)*
Selig Sealing Holdings Inc .... F 815 785-2100
 Forrest *(G-9736)*

CAR WASH EQPT

Avw Equipment Company Inc .... E 708 343-7738
 Maywood *(G-13661)*
Big R Car Wash Inc .... G 217 367-4958
 Urbana *(G-19974)*
Brite-O-Matic Mfg Inc .... D 847 956-1100
 Arlington Heights *(G-709)*
Diskin Systems Inc .... G 815 276-7288
 Algonquin *(G-370)*
Enterprises One Stop .... G 773 924-5506
 Chicago *(G-4515)*
Galesburg Manufacturing Co .... E 309 342-3173
 Galesburg *(G-10192)*
Masters Hand Enterprises LLC .... G 312 933-7674
 Chicago *(G-5362)*
Princeton Fast Stop .... F 815 872-0706
 Princeton *(G-16818)*
U Wash Equipment Co .... G 618 466-9442
 Alton *(G-575)*
White Diamond Bubbles Hand .... G 773 417-3237
 Chicago *(G-6617)*

CAR WASHES

Rays Power Wshg Svc Peggy Ray .... G 618 939-6306
 Waterloo *(G-20295)*
Truckers Oil Pros Inc .... F 773 523-8990
 Chicago *(G-6436)*

CARBIDES

Rockform Tooling & Machinery .... E 770 345-4624
 Rockford *(G-17610)*
Schwanog LLC .... F 847 289-1055
 Elgin *(G-8724)*

PRODUCT SECTION

CARBON & GRAPHITE PRDTS, NEC

Aero Industries Inc .... F 800 747-3553
  Harvard (G-11041)
AMS Seals Inc .... G 815 609-4977
  Plainfield (G-16642)
Cabot Corporation .... D 217 253-5752
  Tuscola (G-19925)
Carbon Solutions Group LLC .... F 312 638-9077
  Chicago (G-4025)
Frantz Manufacturing Company .... D 815 625-7063
  Sterling (G-19509)
Graphtek LLC .... F 847 279-1925
  Northbrook (G-15396)
Industrial Graphite Sales LLC .... G 815 943-5502
  Harvard (G-11057)
Kirkman Composites .... G 309 734-5606
  Monmouth (G-14222)
Process Engineering Corp .... F 815 459-1734
  Crystal Lake (G-7250)
Superior Graphite Co .... E 708 458-0006
  Chicago (G-6281)

CARBON BLACK

Cabot Corporation .... D 217 253-5752
  Tuscola (G-19925)

CARBON PAPER & INKED RIBBONS

Dauphin Enterprise Inc .... G 630 893-6300
  Bloomingdale (G-1987)
Illinois Tool Works Inc .... E 708 720-0300
  Frankfort (G-9807)

CARBON REMOVING SOLVENT

Carbon Clean Solutions USA Inc .... G 872 206-0197
  Chicago (G-4024)

CARBON SPECIALTIES Electrical Use

Becker Brothers Graphite Corp .... G 708 410-0700
  Maywood (G-13662)
Rnfl Acquisition LLC .... E 651 442-6011
  Chicago (G-6041)

CARBURETORS

Borgwarner Inc .... C 815 288-1462
  Dixon (G-7892)
United Carburetor Inc .... F 773 777-1223
  Schiller Park (G-18849)
United Remanufacturing Co Inc .... E 773 777-1223
  Schiller Park (G-18850)
United Remanufacturing Co Inc .... F 847 678-2233
  Schiller Park (G-18851)

CARDBOARD PRDTS, EXC DIE-CUT

Integrated Label Corporation .... F 815 874-2500
  Rockford (G-17467)

CARDIOVASCULAR SYSTEM DRUGS, EXC DIAGNOSTIC

Pfizer Inc .... G 847 778-9237
  Chicago (G-5800)

CARDS, PLASTIC, UNPRINTED, WHOLESALE

Universal Holdings Inc .... F 224 353-6198
  Hoffman Estates (G-11470)

CARDS: Color

Color Communications LLC .... G 312 223-0204
  Chicago (G-4204)
Modern Trade Communications .... F 847 674-2200
  Skokie (G-18992)

CARDS: Greeting

Advantage Printing Inc .... G 630 627-7468
  Lombard (G-13036)
Alex Smart Inc .... G 773 244-9275
  Chicago (G-3604)
Cardthartic LLC .... F 217 239-5895
  Champaign (G-3275)
Cook Communications Ministries .... C 847 741-0800
  Elgin (G-8557)
Crest Greetings Inc .... F 708 210-0800
  Chicago (G-4269)

Ggc Corp .... D 847 671-6500
  Schiller Park (G-18810)
Gram Colossal Inc .... G 847 223-5757
  Grayslake (G-10778)
Gue Liquidation Delivery Inc .... G 630 719-7800
  Downers Grove (G-8015)
Harry Otto Printing Company .... F 630 365-6111
  Elburn (G-8455)
K Chae Corp .... F 847 763-0077
  Lincolnwood (G-12826)
Karen Young .... F 312 202-0142
  Chicago (G-5081)
P S Greetings Inc .... C 708 831-5340
  Chicago (G-5729)
P S Greetings Inc .... F 847 673-7255
  Skokie (G-19002)
Recycled Paper Greetings Inc .... E 773 348-6410
  Chicago (G-5991)
Salamander Studios Chicago Inc .... F 773 379-2211
  Chicago (G-6092)
Tukaiz LLC .... F 847 288-4804
  Franklin Park (G-10068)
United Press Inc .... F 847 482-0597
  Lincolnshire (G-12799)

CARDS: Identification

Computhink Inc .... E 630 705-9050
  Lombard (G-13057)
Hemmerle Jr Irvin .... G 630 334-4392
  Naperville (G-14841)
Idemia America Corp .... D 630 551-0792
  Naperville (G-14844)
Identatronics Inc .... E 847 437-2654
  Crystal Lake (G-7208)
Identification Products Mfg Co .... G 847 367-6452
  Lake Forest (G-12264)
Multi Packaging Solutions Inc .... G 773 283-9500
  Chicago (G-5523)
National Emergency Med ID Inc .... G 847 366-1267
  Spring Grove (G-19288)
Perfect Plastic Printing Corp .... C 630 584-1600
  Saint Charles (G-18242)
Psa Equity LLC .... C 847 478-6000
  Buffalo Grove (G-2591)

CARPET & UPHOLSTERY CLEANING SVCS

Duraclean International Inc .... F 847 704-7100
  Arlington Heights (G-730)
Randys Exper-Clean .... G 217 423-1975
  Decatur (G-7539)

CARPETS & RUGS: Tufted

Interfaceflor LLC .... E 312 836-3389
  Chicago (G-4945)

CARPETS, RUGS & FLOOR COVERING

Aspen Carpet Designs .... G 815 483-8501
  Mokena (G-14073)
Baker Avenue Investments Inc .... D 309 427-2500
  Washington (G-20266)
Blachford Investments Inc .... C 630 231-8300
  West Chicago (G-20552)
Ds Production LLC .... G 708 873-3142
  Orland Park (G-15953)
Eagle Carpet Services Ltd .... G 956 971-8560
  Addison (G-109)
East West Martial Arts Sups .... G 773 878-7711
  Chicago (G-4434)
Edward Fields Incorporated .... G 312 644-0400
  Chicago (G-4461)
Interfaceflor LLC .... F 312 822-9640
  Chicago (G-4946)
L & L Flooring LLC .... E 773 935-9314
  Chicago (G-5140)
Milliken & Company .... F 800 241-4826
  Chicago (G-5460)
Minasian Rug Corporation .... G 847 864-1010
  Evanston (G-9553)
Shaw Industries Group Inc .... G 312 467-1331
  Chicago (G-6149)
Shiir LLC .... F 312 828-0400
  Chicago (G-6153)

CARPETS: Wilton

Mohawk Industries Inc .... D 630 972-8000
  Bolingbrook (G-2215)

CASH REGISTERS WHOLESALERS

CARPORTS: Prefabricated Metal

American Steel Carports Inc .... F 800 487-4010
  Kewanee (G-12020)
Americana Building Pdts Inc .... D 618 548-2800
  Salem (G-18328)

CARRIER EQPT: Telephone Or Telegraph

Quen-Tel Communication Svc Inc .... G 815 463-1800
  New Lenox (G-15052)

CARRYING CASES, WHOLESALE

Bearse Manufacturing Co .... D 773 235-8710
  Chicago (G-3857)
Gabriel Enterprises .... G 773 342-8705
  Chicago (G-4654)

CARS: Electric

Park License Service Inc .... G 815 633-5511
  Loves Park (G-13243)
Tesla Inc .... F 312 733-9780
  Chicago (G-6354)

CASES, WOOD

Kunde Woodwork Inc .... G 847 669-2030
  Huntley (G-11549)
Wesling Products Inc .... G 773 533-2850
  Chicago (G-6603)

CASES: Attache'

Jelco Inc .... F 847 459-5207
  Wheeling (G-20920)
McKlein Company LLC .... F 773 235-0600
  Chicago (G-5378)
Platt Luggage Inc .... D 773 838-2000
  Chicago (G-5821)

CASES: Carrying

Custom Case Co Inc .... E 773 585-1164
  Chicago (G-4289)

CASES: Jewelry

Tia Tynette Designs Inc .... G 219 440-2859
  Olympia Fields (G-15899)

CASES: Nonrefrigerated, Exc Wood

Proto Productions Inc .... E 630 628-6626
  Addison (G-257)

CASES: Packing, Nailed Or Lock Corner, Wood

Botkin Lumber Company Inc .... E 217 287-2127
  Taylorville (G-19751)
Chrometec LLC .... G 630 792-8777
  Lombard (G-13053)
Pregis LLC .... D 847 597-2200
  Deerfield (G-7644)

CASES: Plastic

A W Enterprises Inc .... E 708 458-8989
  Bedford Park (G-1452)
Platt Luggage Inc .... D 773 838-2000
  Chicago (G-5821)
Time Rec Pubg Bbby Mrtin Prdct .... G 618 996-3803
  Marion (G-13540)

CASES: Sample Cases

Seamcraft International LLC .... E 773 281-5150
  Chicago (G-6126)
Service & Manufacturing Corp .... E 773 287-5500
  Chicago (G-6141)

CASES: Shipping, Nailed Or Lock Corner, Wood

BP Shipping .... F 630 393-1032
  Naperville (G-14784)
Export Packaging Co Inc .... A 309 756-4288
  Milan (G-14010)

CASH REGISTERS WHOLESALERS

Micros Systems Inc .... F 443 285-6000
  Itasca (G-11702)

Employee Codes: A=Over 500 employees, B=251-500
C=101-250, D=51-100, E=20-50, F=10-19, G=3-9

CASINGS: Sheet Metal

CASINGS: Sheet Metal
Service Metal Enterprises .... G 630 628-1444
  Addison *(G-286)*
Vanfab Inc .... E 815 426-2544
  Union Hill *(G-19944)*

CASINO HOTELS & MOTELS
Diamond Icic Corporation .... E 309 269-8652
  Rock Island *(G-17218)*

CASKETS & ACCESS
Dixline Corporation .... D 309 932-2011
  Galva *(G-10231)*
Hoffman Burial Supplies Inc .... G 708 233-1567
  Bridgeview *(G-2355)*
J Garvin Industries Inc .... G 708 297-7400
  Posen *(G-16796)*
J Garvin Industries Inc .... G 708 297-7400
  Evergreen Park *(G-9595)*
Tolar Group LLC .... E 847 662-8000
  Waukegan *(G-20507)*

CASKETS WHOLESALERS
Hoffman Burial Supplies Inc .... G 708 233-1567
  Bridgeview *(G-2355)*
Red Wing .... G 217 655-2772
  Danville *(G-7378)*

CAST STONE: Concrete
Casey Stone Co .... G 217 857-3425
  Teutopolis *(G-19766)*
Fischer Stone & Materials LLC .... G 815 233-3232
  Freeport *(G-10108)*

CASTERS
Beauticontrol .... G 217 223-0382
  Quincy *(G-16862)*
Caster Warehouse Inc .... F 847 836-5712
  Carpentersville *(G-3097)*
Pan Pac International Inc .... G 847 222-9077
  Arlington Heights *(G-787)*

CASTINGS GRINDING: For The Trade
Absolute Grinding and Mfg .... F 815 964-1999
  Rockford *(G-17289)*
Acme Grinding & Manufacturing .... C 815 323-1380
  Belvidere *(G-1644)*
Action Carbide Grinding Co .... G 847 891-9026
  Schaumburg *(G-18427)*
Asteroid Precision Inc .... D 847 298-8109
  Wheeling *(G-20852)*
B & R Grinding Co .... G 630 595-7789
  Franklin Park *(G-9881)*
Class A Grinding .... G 815 874-2118
  Rockford *(G-17352)*
Conform Industries Inc .... F 630 285-0272
  Schaumburg *(G-18484)*
Empire Hard Chrome Inc .... B 773 762-3156
  Chicago *(G-4500)*
Express Grinding Inc .... G 847 434-5827
  Elk Grove Village *(G-8992)*
Highland Metal Inc .... E 708 544-6641
  Hillside *(G-11342)*
Metro East Manufacturing .... F 618 233-0182
  Swansea *(G-19693)*
OHare Precision Metals LLC .... E 847 640-6050
  Arlington Heights *(G-783)*
Pioneer Grinding & Mfg Co .... G 847 678-6565
  Franklin Park *(G-10018)*
Precision Ground .... F 815 578-2613
  Lakemoor *(G-12475)*
Roll Rite Inc .... G 815 645-8600
  Davis Junction *(G-7426)*
S & B Jig Grinding Inc .... G 815 654-7907
  Loves Park *(G-13262)*
Sterling Tool & Manufacturing .... G 847 304-1800
  Barrington *(G-1245)*
T & K Precision Grinding .... G 708 450-0565
  Melrose Park *(G-13920)*
Walern Form Grinding Inc .... G 815 874-7000
  Rockford *(G-17676)*

CASTINGS: Aerospace, Aluminum
Aerosourcex LLC .... F 314 565-4026
  South Elgin *(G-19130)*

Ceratizit Chicago Holding Inc .... F 847 923-8400
  Schaumburg *(G-18469)*
Martin Tool Works Inc .... F 847 923-8400
  Schaumburg *(G-18619)*

CASTINGS: Aluminum
Alcast Company .... D 309 691-5513
  Peoria *(G-16380)*
Alcast Company .... E 309 691-5513
  Peoria *(G-16381)*
Alcast Company .... F 309 691-5513
  Peoria *(G-16382)*
Altman Pattern and Foundry Co .... F 773 586-9100
  Chicago *(G-3637)*
Atherton Foundry Products Inc .... G 708 849-4615
  Riverdale *(G-17068)*
Cast Technologies Inc .... C 309 676-1715
  Peoria *(G-16398)*
Chester Brass and Aluminum .... F 618 826-2391
  Chester *(G-3451)*
Illini Foundry Co Inc .... G 309 697-3142
  Peoria *(G-16456)*
Louis Meskan Brass Foundry Inc ...... C 773 237-7662
  Chicago *(G-5267)*
Master Foundry Inc .... F 217 223-7396
  Quincy *(G-16911)*
Olson Aluminum Castings Ltd .... E 815 229-3292
  Rockford *(G-17544)*
Precision Entps Fndry Mch Inc .... E 815 498-2317
  Somonauk *(G-19074)*
Rockford Foundries Inc .... F 815 965-7243
  Rockford *(G-17594)*
Tazewell Machine Works Inc .... C 309 347-3181
  Pekin *(G-16365)*
Trio Foundry Inc .... F 815 786-6616
  Sandwich *(G-18386)*
Universal Electric Foundry Inc .... E 312 421-7233
  Chicago *(G-6480)*
Wagner Brass Foundry Inc .... G 773 276-7907
  Chicago *(G-6583)*

CASTINGS: Brass, NEC, Exc Die
Atherton Foundry Products Inc .... G 708 849-4615
  Riverdale *(G-17068)*
Louis Meskan Brass Foundry Inc ...... C 773 237-7662
  Chicago *(G-5267)*
Rockford Foundries Inc .... F 815 965-7243
  Rockford *(G-17594)*
Tilton Pattern Works Inc .... F 217 442-1502
  Danville *(G-7388)*

CASTINGS: Bronze, NEC, Exc Die
Chester Brass and Aluminum .... F 618 826-2391
  Chester *(G-3451)*

CASTINGS: Die, Aluminum
Able Die Casting Corporation .... D 847 678-1991
  Schiller Park *(G-18781)*
Acme Alliance LLC .... E 847 272-9520
  Northbrook *(G-15330)*
Acme Die Casting LLC .... G 847 272-9520
  Northbrook *(G-15331)*
Aluminum Castings Corporation .... E 309 343-8910
  Galesburg *(G-10184)*
American Electronic Pdts Inc .... F 630 889-9977
  Oak Brook *(G-15592)*
Arrow Aluminum Castings Inc .... G 815 338-4480
  Woodstock *(G-21361)*
Belden Energy Solutions Inc .... G 800 235-3361
  Elmhurst *(G-9330)*
Branatt Enterprises LLC .... G 630 632-3532
  Byron *(G-2750)*
Burgess-Norton Mfg Co Inc .... E 630 232-4100
  Geneva *(G-10257)*
Cast Aluminum Solutions LLC .... D 630 482-5325
  Batavia *(G-1362)*
Cast Products Inc .... C 708 457-1500
  Norridge *(G-15232)*
Chicago White Metal Cast Inc .... C 630 595-4424
  Bensenville *(G-1769)*
Craft Die Casting Corporation .... E 773 237-9710
  Chicago *(G-4254)*
Crown Premiums Inc .... F 815 469-8789
  Frankfort *(G-9781)*
Curto-Ligonier Foundries Co .... E 708 345-2250
  Melrose Park *(G-13846)*
Dart Castings Inc .... F 708 388-4914
  Alsip *(G-438)*

Dixline Corporation .... F 309 932-2011
  Galva *(G-10230)*
Dixline Corporation .... D 309 932-2011
  Galva *(G-10231)*
Duro Cast Inc .... G 815 498-2317
  Somonauk *(G-19070)*
Dynacast Inc .... C 847 608-2200
  Elgin *(G-8572)*
Federal Equipment & Svcs Inc .... F 847 731-9002
  Zion *(G-21514)*
G & M Die Casting Company Inc ...... D 630 595-2340
  Wood Dale *(G-21192)*
G & W Electric Company .... E 708 388-6363
  Blue Island *(G-2123)*
Lovejoy Industries Inc .... G 859 873-6828
  Northbrook *(G-15421)*
Mahoney Foundries Inc .... E 309 784-2311
  Vermont *(G-20037)*
Mattoon Precision Mfg .... C 217 235-6000
  Mattoon *(G-13645)*
Monnex International Inc .... E 847 850-5263
  Buffalo Grove *(G-2576)*
OFallon Pressure Cast Co .... G 618 632-8694
  O Fallon *(G-15581)*
Precision Entps Fndry Mch Inc .... G 815 797-1000
  Somonauk *(G-19073)*
Precision Entps Fndry Mch Inc .... E 815 498-2317
  Somonauk *(G-19074)*
Prismier LLC .... E 630 592-4515
  Bolingbrook *(G-2230)*
RCM Industries Inc .... C 847 455-1950
  Franklin Park *(G-10033)*
RCM Industries Inc .... C 847 455-1950
  Wheeling *(G-20970)*
Rockbridge Casting Inc .... G 618 753-3188
  Rockbridge *(G-17255)*
Soldy Manufacturing Inc .... D 847 671-3396
  Schiller Park *(G-18844)*
Spartan Light Metal Pdts Inc .... E 618 443-4346
  Sparta *(G-19260)*
Spartan Light Metal Pdts Inc .... A 618 443-4346
  Sparta *(G-19261)*
Tompkins Aluminum Foundry Inc ...... G 815 438-5578
  Rock Falls *(G-17197)*

CASTINGS: Die, Copper & Copper Alloy
Amcast Inc .... F 630 766-7450
  Bensenville *(G-1741)*

CASTINGS: Die, Lead & Zinc
Mumford Metal Casting LLC .... C 708 345-0400
  Bannockburn *(G-1204)*

CASTINGS: Die, Magnesium & Magnesium-Base Alloy
Chicago White Metal Cast Inc .... C 630 595-4424
  Bensenville *(G-1769)*
Curto-Ligonier Foundries Co .... E 708 345-2250
  Melrose Park *(G-13846)*
Spartan Light Metal Pdts Inc .... E 618 443-4346
  Sparta *(G-19260)*
Spartan Light Metal Pdts Inc .... A 618 443-4346
  Sparta *(G-19261)*

CASTINGS: Die, Nonferrous
American Cast Products Inc .... F 708 895-5152
  Lansing *(G-12484)*
Creative Iron .... G 217 267-7797
  Westville *(G-20779)*
Direct Aerosystems Inc .... F 630 509-2141
  Aurora *(G-952)*
Rockbridge Casting Inc .... G 618 753-3188
  Rockbridge *(G-17255)*

CASTINGS: Die, Titanium
TI Squared Technologies Inc .... F 541 367-2929
  Schaumburg *(G-18748)*

CASTINGS: Die, Zinc
Accucast Inc .... G 815 394-1875
  Rockford *(G-17292)*
Acme Die Casting LLC .... G 847 272-9520
  Northbrook *(G-15331)*
Allied Die Casting Corporation .... E 815 385-9330
  McHenry *(G-13717)*
Chicago Die Casting Mfg Co .... E 847 671-5010
  Franklin Park *(G-9904)*

PRODUCT SECTION

CEMENT: Hydraulic

Condor Tool & Manufacturing ....F 630 628-8200
  Addison *(G-81)*
Congress Drive Inc ....E 972 875-6060
  Wilmette *(G-21074)*
Dart Castings Inc 708 388-4914
  Alsip *(G-438)*
Dynacast LLC ....C 847 608-2200
  Elgin *(G-8572)*
Hub Manufacturing Company Inc.......E 773 252-1373
  Chicago *(G-4859)*
Lovejoy Industries Inc ....G 859 873-6828
  Northbrook *(G-15421)*
Quality Die Casting Co ....F 847 214-8840
  Elgin *(G-8707)*
Quality Metal Finishing Co...................C 815 234-2711
  Byron *(G-2755)*
Serv-All Die & Tool Company ....G 815 459-2900
  Crystal Lake *(G-7263)*
Soldy Manufacturing Inc ....D 847 671-3396
  Schiller Park *(G-18844)*
Taurus Die Casting LLC ....F 815 316-6160
  Rockford *(G-17654)*
Universal Die Cast Corporation ....G 815 633-1702
  Machesney Park *(G-13381)*
Vogel/Hill Corporation ....E 773 235-6916
  Chicago *(G-6567)*

CASTINGS: Ductile

Russell Enterprises Inc ....B 847 692-6050
  Park Ridge *(G-16295)*
Standard Car Truck Company ....E 847 692-6050
  Rosemont *(G-18051)*
Waupaca Foundry Inc..........................C 217 347-0600
  Effingham *(G-8430)*

CASTINGS: Gray Iron

American Electronic Pdts Inc ....F 630 889-9977
  Oak Brook *(G-15592)*
Branchfield Casting Inc ....G 309 932-2278
  Matherville *(G-13614)*
Castwell Products LLC ....C 847 966-5050
  Skokie *(G-18937)*
Charter Dura-Bar Inc ....E 815 338-3900
  Woodstock *(G-21373)*
Charter Dura-Bar Inc ....E 815 338-7800
  Woodstock *(G-21374)*
Decatur Foundry Inc............................D 217 429-5261
  Decatur *(G-7486)*
E Rowe Foundry & Machine Co ....F 217 382-4135
  Martinsville *(G-13583)*
Illini Foundry Co Inc ....G 309 697-3142
  Peoria *(G-16456)*
Kettler Casting Co Inc ....F 618 234-5303
  Belleville *(G-1562)*
Lemfco Inc ....E 815 777-0242
  Galena *(G-10176)*
Meta TEC of Illinois Inc.......................D 309 246-2960
  Lacon *(G-12132)*
State Line Foundries Inc ....D 815 389-3921
  Roscoe *(G-17934)*
Westwick Foundry Ltd ....E 815 777-0815
  Galena *(G-10181)*
Winnebago Foundry Inc ....D 815 389-3533
  South Beloit *(G-19124)*

CASTINGS: Lead

Knock On Metal Inc..............................G 312 372-4569
  Chicago *(G-5111)*

CASTINGS: Machinery, Aluminum

Kabat American Inc ....G 870 739-1430
  Saint Charles *(G-18219)*
Kz Manufacturing Co ....G 708 937-8097
  Mc Cook *(G-13694)*
Nexus Industries Corp.........................G 708 673-9289
  Melrose Park *(G-13898)*
Sonoco Prtective Solutions Inc ....E 815 787-5244
  Dekalb *(G-7703)*

CASTINGS: Machinery, Copper Or Copper-Base Alloy

General Products International ....G 847 458-6357
  Lake In The Hills *(G-12335)*

CASTINGS: Machinery, Nonferrous, Exc Die or Aluminum Copper

Clark Tashaunda ....G 708 247-8274
  Calumet Park *(G-2796)*

CASTINGS: Precision

Accurate Parts Mfg Co ....E 630 616-4125
  Bensenville *(G-1724)*
Impro Industries Usa Inc ....G 630 759-0280
  Bolingbrook *(G-2191)*
Tempco Electric Heater Corp ....B 630 350-2252
  Wood Dale *(G-21248)*

CASTINGS: Steel

Alloys Tech Inc......................................G 708 248-5041
  S Chicago Hts *(G-18116)*
Branchfield Casting Inc ....G 309 932-2278
  Matherville *(G-13614)*
Devco Casting 312 456-0076
  Chicago *(G-4347)*
Universal Electric Foundry Inc ....E 312 421-7233
  Chicago *(G-6480)*

CASTINGS: Zinc

Able Die Casting Corporation ....D 847 678-1991
  Schiller Park *(G-18781)*

CAT BOX FILLER

Jaffee Investment Partnr LP ....C 312 321-1515
  Chicago *(G-4999)*
Oil-Dri Corporation America ....B 312 321-1516
  Chicago *(G-5667)*

CATALOG & MAIL-ORDER HOUSES

Anatomical Worldwide LLC ....G 312 224-4772
  Evanston *(G-9494)*
Aquadine Inc ....G 800 497-3463
  Harvard *(G-11046)*
Narda Inc..F 312 648-2300
  Chicago *(G-5540)*
Need To Know Inc ....G 309 691-3877
  Peoria *(G-16484)*
Northwoods Wreaths Company ....F 847 615-9491
  Lake Forest *(G-12275)*
Tiege Hanley LLC ....G 312 953-4131
  Chicago *(G-6377)*
Your Supply Depot Limited ....G 815 568-4115
  Marengo *(G-13497)*

CATALOG SALES

Orvis Company Inc ....F 312 440-0662
  Chicago *(G-5707)*

CATALYSTS: Chemical

Arcturus Performance Pdts LLC ....G 630 204-0211
  Saint Charles *(G-18147)*
Catalytic Products Intl Inc...................E 847 438-0334
  Lake Zurich *(G-12390)*
Covachem LLC 779 500-0918
  Rockford *(G-17359)*
Gmm Holdings LLC ....F 312 255-9830
  Chicago *(G-4706)*
Merichem Chem Rfinery Svcs LLC ....C 847 285-3850
  Schaumburg *(G-18628)*
Universal Cat LLC ....E 708 753-8070
  S Chicago Hts *(G-18128)*
UOP LLC ....C 708 442-3681
  Chicago *(G-6488)*
UOP LLC ....C 847 391-2540
  Des Plaines *(G-7862)*
W R Grace & Co ....C 773 838-3200
  Chicago *(G-6575)*
Xena International Inc ....E 815 946-2626
  Polo *(G-16760)*

CATAPULTS

Catapult Integrated Svcs LLC ....G 312 216-4460
  Chicago *(G-4042)*

CATCH BASIN COVERS: Concrete

Rockford Cement Products Co............F 815 965-0537
  Rockford *(G-17591)*
V & N Concrete Products Inc ....F 815 293-0315
  Romeoville *(G-17884)*

CATERERS

Biagios Gourmet Foods Inc ....E 708 867-4641
  Chicago *(G-3880)*
Creative Cakes LLC ....E 708 614-9755
  Tinley Park *(G-19817)*
Danziger Kosher Catering Inc.............E 847 982-1818
  Chicago *(G-4316)*
Eickmans Processing Co Inc ....E 815 247-8451
  Seward *(G-18867)*
Gourmet Gorilla Inc ....D 877 219-3663
  Chicago *(G-4720)*
M&M Restaurant Group LLC ....F 773 253-5326
  Chicago *(G-5307)*
Open Kitchens Inc ....E 312 666-5334
  Chicago *(G-5681)*
Rt Wholesale ....D 847 678-3663
  Schiller Park *(G-18841)*
William Badal..G 815 264-7752
  Waterman *(G-20303)*
Zeldaco Ltd 847 674-0033
  Skokie *(G-19060)*

CAULKING COMPOUNDS

Roanoke Companies Group Inc ....D 630 375-0324
  Aurora *(G-1014)*
Sarco Putty Company..........................G 773 735-5577
  Chicago *(G-6104)*

CELLULOID PRDTS

Viskase Companies Inc ....D 630 874-0700
  Lombard *(G-13151)*
Viskase Corporation ....D 630 874-0700
  Lombard *(G-13152)*

CELLULOSE DERIVATIVE MATERIALS

Scholle Ipn Corporation ....F 708 562-7290
  Northlake *(G-15558)*
Vacumet Corp ....F 708 562-7290
  Northlake *(G-15564)*

CEMENT & CONCRETE RELATED PRDTS & EQPT: Bituminous

Wehrli Equipment Co Inc ....F 630 717-4150
  Naperville *(G-14946)*
Wille Bros Co...D 708 535-4101
  Monee *(G-14213)*

CEMENT ROCK: Crushed & Broken

Charleston Stone Company ....E 217 345-6292
  Ashmore *(G-886)*
Elmhurst-Chicago Stone Company ....E 630 983-6410
  Bolingbrook *(G-2173)*
Riverstone Group Inc ....G 309 462-3003
  Saint Augustine *(G-18139)*
St Marys Cement ....G 773 995-5100
  Chicago *(G-6224)*

CEMENT: Clay Refractory

Cimentos N Votorantim Amer Inc ......G 708 458-0400
  Bridgeview *(G-2335)*

CEMENT: High Temperature, Refractory, Nonclay

Ossola Industrials Inc..........................F 618 451-2621
  Granite City *(G-10729)*

CEMENT: Hydraulic

Bonsal American Inc ....D 847 678-6220
  Franklin Park *(G-9891)*
Coal City Redi-Mix Co Inc ....F 815 634-4455
  Coal City *(G-6931)*
Lafarge North America Inc ....E 630 892-1616
  North Aurora *(G-15266)*
Lafarge North America Inc ....E 847 742-6060
  South Elgin *(G-19163)*
Lafarge North America Inc ....E 815 741-2090
  Rockdale *(G-17264)*
Lafarge North America Inc ....E 773 372-1000
  Golconda *(G-10666)*
Lafarge North America Inc ....C 618 543-7541
  Grand Chain *(G-10687)*
Lafarge North America Inc ....F 847 244-3800
  Waukegan *(G-20457)*

CEMENT: Hydraulic

Lafarge North America Inc .... E 773 372-1000
Chicago (G-5157)
Lafarge North America Inc .... G 773 646-5228
Chicago (G-5158)
Southfield Corporation .... C 815 284-3357
Dixon (G-7918)
Sport Redi-Mix LLC .... E 217 355-4222
Champaign (G-3352)
St Marys Cement Inc (us) .... E 313 842-4600
Dixon (G-7920)

CEMENT: Masonry

Illinois Cement Company LLC .... C 815 224-2112
La Salle (G-12113)
Lafarge Building Materials Inc .... D 678 746-2000
Chicago (G-5155)
Promiz LLC .... G 618 533-3950
Centralia (G-3246)
Skyway Cement Company LLC .... E 800 643-1808
Chicago (G-6185)

CEMENT: Portland

Buzzi Unicem USA Inc .... E 815 768-3660
Joliet (G-11835)
Buzzi Unicem USA Inc .... G 610 882-5000
Rock Island (G-17210)
Holcim (us) Inc .... D 773 372-1000
Chicago (G-4827)
Holcim Participations US Inc .... G 773 372-1000
Chicago (G-4828)
Lafarge North America Inc .... C 773 372-1000
Chicago (G-5156)
Lone Star Industries Inc .... G 815 883-3173
Oglesby (G-15843)
Red-E-Mix Transportation LLC .... E 618 654-2166
Highland (G-11238)

CEMETERIES

Rex Vault Co .... F 618 783-2416
Newton (G-15092)

CEMETERIES: Real Estate Operation

Oakwood Memorial Park Inc .... G 815 433-0313
Ottawa (G-16066)

CEMETERY & FUNERAL DIRECTOR'S EQPT & SPLYS WHOLESALERS

Angels Heavenly Funeral Home .... G 773 239-8700
Chicago (G-3696)
Frigid Fluid Company .... E 708 836-1215
Melrose Park (G-13872)
Tolar Group LLC .... E 847 662-8000
Waukegan (G-20507)

CEMETERY MEMORIAL DEALERS

All Saints Monument Co Inc .... G 847 824-1248
Des Plaines (G-7725)
American Monument Co .... G 618 993-8968
Marion (G-13503)
Doh Services Inc .... F 708 331-3811
South Holland (G-19209)
Meier Granite Company .... G 847 678-7300
Franklin Park (G-9989)
Pontiac Granite Company Inc .... F 815 842-1384
Pontiac (G-16776)
Stonecrafters Inc .... E 815 363-8730
Lakemoor (G-12477)

CERAMIC FIBER

Nanophase Technologies Corp .... F 630 771-6747
Burr Ridge (G-2706)
Nanophase Technologies Corp .... D 630 771-6700
Romeoville (G-17859)
Pillar Enterprises Inc .... G 630 966-2566
North Aurora (G-15271)
Thermal Ceramics Inc .... E 217 627-2101
Girard (G-10386)
Thermionics Corp .... F 800 800-5728
Springfield (G-19464)

CERAMIC FLOOR & WALL TILE WHOLESALERS

American Bullnose Co Midw .... G 630 238-1300
Wood Dale (G-21162)

Great Lakes Clay & Supply Inc .... G 224 535-8127
Elgin (G-8601)
MK Tile Ink .... G 773 964-8905
Chicago (G-5474)

CHAIN: Welded, Made From Purchased Wire

Durabilt Dyvex Inc .... F 708 397-4673
Broadview (G-2432)

CHAINS: Forged

Timken Drives LLC .... D 815 589-2211
Fulton (G-10158)
Timken Drives LLC .... G 312 274-9710
Chicago (G-6380)

CHAMBERS: Fumigating, Metal Plate

Pureline Treatment Systems LLC ..... C 847 963-8465
Bensenville (G-1877)

CHANDELIERS: Commercial

Challenger Lighting Co Inc .... E 847 717-4700
Batavia (G-1365)

CHANGE MAKING MACHINES

Singer Data Products Inc .... G 630 860-6500
Bensenville (G-1893)

CHARCOAL: Activated

McClendon Holdings LLC .... G 773 251-2314
Chicago (G-5373)
Plaze Inc .... C 630 628-4240
Downers Grove (G-8076)
Reliance Specialty Pdts Inc .... F 847 640-8923
Carol Stream (G-3059)
Wet International Inc .... E 630 540-2113
Streamwood (G-19602)

CHASING SVC: Metal

Dt Metronic Inc .... G 224 567-8414
Des Plaines (G-7757)

CHASSIS: Automobile Trailer

T & E Enterprises Herscher Inc .... F 815 426-2761
Herscher (G-11188)

CHASSIS: Motor Vehicle

Federal Signal Corporation .... E 708 534-4756
University Park (G-19952)
Federal Signal Corporation .... E 708 534-3400
University Park (G-19954)
Folk Race Cars .... G 815 629-2418
Durand (G-8151)
Taylor Off Road Racing .... G 815 544-4500
Belvidere (G-1703)

CHEESE WHOLESALERS

A New Dairy Company .... E 312 421-1234
Chicago (G-3489)
Cheese Merchants America LLC ..... B 630 221-0580
Bartlett (G-1272)
Nuestro Queso LLC .... E 224 366-4320
Chicago (G-5641)
Randolph Packing Co .... D 630 830-3100
Streamwood (G-19592)
Savencia Cheese USA LLC .... G 815 369-4577
Lena (G-12608)
Wiscon Corp .... E 708 450-0074
Melrose Park (G-13929)

CHEMICAL ELEMENTS

Artisan Element .... G 630 229-5654
Woodridge (G-21276)
Element Events LLC .... G 630 717-2800
Naperville (G-14822)
Elemental Art Jewelry .... G 773 844-4812
Chicago (G-4481)
Elements Group .... G 312 664-2252
Chicago (G-4482)
First Element Solutions .... G 847 691-8381
Mount Prospect (G-14529)
Pure Element .... G 309 269-7823
Moline (G-14168)

CHEMICAL PROCESSING MACHINERY & EQPT

Americhem Systems Inc .... E 630 495-9300
Aurora (G-1050)
D R Sperry & Co .... D 630 892-4361
Aurora (G-1083)
G K Enterprises Inc .... G 708 587-2150
Monee (G-14201)
Innovtive Prcess Applctons LLC ...... G 708 844-6100
Crestwood (G-7119)
Prater Industries Inc .... D 630 679-3200
Bolingbrook (G-2228)
Spf Supplies Inc .... G 847 454-9081
Elk Grove Village (G-9249)
WEI TO Associates Inc .... G 708 747-6660
Park Forest (G-16261)

CHEMICAL SPLYS FOR FOUNDRIES

Chem Trade Global .... G 847 675-2682
Skokie (G-18940)
Mid America Intl Inc .... G 847 635-8303
Glenview (G-10589)
T D J Group Inc .... G 847 639-1113
Cary (G-3193)

CHEMICAL: Sodm Compnds/Salts, Inorg, Exc Rfnd Sodm Chloride

Chicago Salt Company Inc .... G 708 906-4718
River Grove (G-17058)

CHEMICALS & ALLIED PRDTS WHOLESALERS, NEC

A J Funk & Co .... G 847 741-6760
Elgin (G-8489)
Air Products and Chemicals Inc .... D 618 451-0577
Granite City (G-10692)
Airgas Usa LLC .... E 630 231-9260
West Chicago (G-20533)
AmeriGas .... D 708 544-1131
Hillside (G-11328)
Cater Chemical Co .... G 630 980-2300
Roselle (G-17943)
Cedar Concepts Corporation .... E 773 890-5790
Chicago (G-4050)
Chemix Corp .... F 708 754-2150
Glenwood (G-10639)
Colorex Chemical Co Inc .... G 630 238-3124
Bensenville (G-1774)
Delta Products Group Inc .... F 630 357-5544
Aurora (G-1084)
Dumore Supplies Inc .... F 312 949-6260
Chicago (G-4403)
Esma Inc .... G 708 331-0456
South Holland (G-19211)
Gano Welding Supplies Inc .... F 217 345-3777
Charleston (G-3402)
GE Healthcare Holdings Inc .... A 847 398-8400
Arlington Heights (G-741)
GL Downs Inc .... G 618 993-9777
Marion (G-13513)
Henkel US Operations Corp .... D 847 468-9200
Elgin (G-8613)
Hurst Chemical Company .... G 815 964-0451
Rockford (G-17454)
Indorama Vntres USA Hldings LP .... G 847 943-3100
Riverwoods (G-17093)
J B Watts Company Inc .... G 773 643-1855
Chicago (G-4987)
Lee Quigley Company .... G 708 563-1600
Chicago (G-5195)
Liquid Resin International .... E 618 392-3590
Olney (G-15869)
Litho Research Incorporated .... G 630 860-7070
Itasca (G-11695)
McClendon Holdings LLC .... G 773 251-2314
Chicago (G-5373)
North Shore Consultants Inc .... G 847 290-1599
Elk Grove Village (G-9153)
RITA Corporation .... E 815 337-2500
Crystal Lake (G-7257)
Robert B Scott Ocularists Ltd .... E 312 782-3558
Chicago (G-6042)
Rock Valley Oil & Chemical Co .... D 815 654-2400
Loves Park (G-13254)
T9 Group LLC .... G 847 912-8862
Hawthorn Woods (G-11126)

PRODUCT SECTION

CHEMICALS & ALLIED PRDTS, WHOLESALE: Spec Clean/Sanitation

Toyota Tsusho America Inc..............D...... 847 439-8500
  Elk Grove Village (G-9281)
Vanguard Chemical Corporation..........F...... 312 751-0717
  Chicago (G-6520)
Varn International Inc..............E...... 630 406-6501
  Batavia (G-1440)
Wet International Inc..............E...... 630 540-2113
  Streamwood (G-19602)
Xena International Inc..............E...... 815 946-2626
  Polo (G-16760)

CHEMICALS & ALLIED PRDTS, WHOL: Food Additives/Preservatives

Essen Nutrition Corporation..............E...... 630 739-6700
  Romeoville (G-17817)
Pmp Fermentation Products Inc..........E...... 309 637-0400
  Peoria (G-16499)

CHEMICALS & ALLIED PRDTS, WHOL: Gases, Compressed/Liquefied

Lincoln Electric Company..............F...... 630 783-3600
  Bolingbrook (G-2204)
Praxair Distribution Inc..............E...... 314 664-7900
  Cahokia (G-2763)

CHEMICALS & ALLIED PRDTS, WHOLESALE: Aerosols

Diversified CPC Intl Inc..............E...... 815 424-2000
  Channahon (G-3380)
Plaze Inc..............C...... 630 628-4240
  Downers Grove (G-8076)

CHEMICALS & ALLIED PRDTS, WHOLESALE: Alcohols

Illinois Corn Processing LLC..............D...... 309 353-3990
  Pekin (G-16339)
Wirtz Beverage Illinois LLC..............C...... 847 228-9000
  Cicero (G-6888)

CHEMICALS & ALLIED PRDTS, WHOLESALE: Chemicals, Indl

Americo Chemical Products Inc..............E...... 630 588-0830
  Carol Stream (G-2938)
Amtex Chemicals LLC..............G...... 630 268-0085
  Lombard (G-13039)
Emco Chemical Distributors Inc..............F...... 262 427-0400
  North Chicago (G-15310)
Global Water Technology Inc..............E...... 708 349-9991
  South Holland (G-19215)
Hallstar Company..............C...... 312 554-7400
  Chicago (G-4772)
Hallstar Services Corp..............G...... 312 554-7400
  Chicago (G-4773)
Holland Applied Technologies..............E...... 630 325-5130
  Burr Ridge (G-2683)
Innovative Molecular Diagnosti..............G...... 630 845-8246
  Geneva (G-10283)
Interra Global Corporation..............F...... 847 292-8600
  Park Ridge (G-16285)
Producers Chemical Company..............E...... 630 466-4584
  Sugar Grove (G-19650)
Stutz Company..............F...... 773 287-1068
  Chicago (G-6259)
Vantage Oleochemicals Inc..............C...... 773 376-9000
  Chicago (G-6522)
Vantage Specialties Inc..............G...... 847 244-3410
  Chicago (G-6523)

CHEMICALS & ALLIED PRDTS, WHOLESALE: Chemicals, Indl & Heavy

Benetech Inc..............E...... 630 844-1300
  Aurora (G-1063)
Benetech (taiwan) LLC..............G...... 630 844-1300
  Aurora (G-1064)
Fitz Chem LLC..............E...... 630 467-8383
  Itasca (G-11658)
Illini Fs Inc..............G...... 217 442-4737
  Potomac (G-16802)
Magnum International Inc..............G...... 708 889-9999
  Lansing (G-12507)
Mineral Masters Corporation..............F...... 630 293-7727
  West Chicago (G-20619)
T D J Group Inc..............G...... 847 639-1113
  Cary (G-3193)

CHEMICALS & ALLIED PRDTS, WHOLESALE: Chemicals, Rustproofing

Daubert Industries Inc..............F...... 630 203-6800
  Burr Ridge (G-2667)
Ecp Incorporated..............D...... 630 754-4200
  Woodridge (G-21297)

CHEMICALS & ALLIED PRDTS, WHOLESALE: Detergent/Soap

Henkel Consumer Goods Inc..............C...... 630 892-4381
  Montgomery (G-14246)
Vision Wholesale Corp..............G...... 708 496-6015
  Chicago (G-6558)

CHEMICALS & ALLIED PRDTS, WHOLESALE: Detergents

Italmatch Sc LLC..............G...... 708 929-9657
  Bedford Park (G-1474)

CHEMICALS & ALLIED PRDTS, WHOLESALE: Dry Ice

Continental Carbonic Pdts Inc..............E...... 309 346-7515
  Pekin (G-16326)

CHEMICALS & ALLIED PRDTS, WHOLESALE: Gelatin

Al Gelato Chicago LLC..............G...... 847 455-5355
  Franklin Park (G-9864)

CHEMICALS & ALLIED PRDTS, WHOLESALE: Indl Gases

Airgas Usa LLC..............G...... 618 439-7207
  Benton (G-1917)

CHEMICALS & ALLIED PRDTS, WHOLESALE: Oxygen

Little Egypt Gas A & Wldg Sups..............G...... 618 937-2271
  West Frankfort (G-20677)

CHEMICALS & ALLIED PRDTS, WHOLESALE: Plastics Film

Proofing Technologies Ltd..............G...... 847 222-7100
  Rolling Meadows (G-17768)
Protective Products Intl..............G...... 847 526-1180
  Wauconda (G-20386)

CHEMICALS & ALLIED PRDTS, WHOLESALE: Plastics Materials, NEC

Alpha Omega Plastics Company..............D...... 847 956-8777
  Elk Grove Village (G-8817)
Cope Plastics Inc..............G...... 309 787-4465
  East Peoria (G-8263)
Magnum International Inc..............G...... 708 889-9999
  Lansing (G-12507)
Peterson Brothers Plastics..............F...... 773 286-5666
  Chicago (G-5795)
Shannon Industrial Corporation..............F...... 815 337-2349
  Woodstock (G-21432)
Sherman Plastics Corp..............E...... 630 369-6170
  Naperville (G-14913)
Streamwood Plastics Ltd..............G...... 847 895-9190
  Schaumburg (G-18728)

CHEMICALS & ALLIED PRDTS, WHOLESALE: Plastics Prdts, NEC

Ability Plastics Inc..............E...... 708 458-4480
  Justice (G-11949)
Addison Pro Plastics Inc..............G...... 630 543-6770
  Addison (G-21)
AIM Distribution Inc..............F...... 815 986-2770
  Rockford (G-17298)
Azul 3d Inc..............F...... 321 277-7807
  Skokie (G-18926)
Bucktown Polymers..............G...... 312 436-1460
  Chicago (G-3971)
Essentra Corp..............G...... 814 899-7671
  Westchester (G-20697)
Fisher Container Holdings LLC..............G...... 847 541-0000
  Buffalo Grove (G-2537)
Flow-Eze Company..............F...... 815 965-1062
  Rockford (G-17416)
Foodhandler Inc..............F...... 866 931-3613
  Elk Grove Village (G-9002)
Mate Technologies Inc..............F...... 847 289-1010
  Elgin (G-8652)
Midwest Innovative Pdts LLC..............E...... 888 945-4545
  Joliet (G-11903)
Ppc Flexible Packaging LLC..............C...... 847 541-0000
  Buffalo Grove (G-2588)
Reynolds Consumer Products Inc..............A...... 800 879-5067
  Lake Forest (G-12296)
Transcendia Inc..............C...... 847 678-1800
  Franklin Park (G-10063)

CHEMICALS & ALLIED PRDTS, WHOLESALE: Plastics Sheets & Rods

Cope Plastics Inc..............D...... 618 466-0221
  Alton (G-549)
D and K Plastics..............G...... 712 723-5372
  Yorkville (G-21476)
Edmik Inc..............E...... 847 263-0460
  Gurnee (G-10874)
Engineered Plastic Pdts Corp..............E...... 847 952-8400
  Mount Prospect (G-14526)
Plastic Film Corp America Inc..............F...... 630 887-0800
  Lemont (G-12583)
Plastic Film Corp America Inc..............E...... 630 697-5635
  Shorewood (G-18899)

CHEMICALS & ALLIED PRDTS, WHOLESALE: Polishes, NEC

Jacob Hay Company..............G...... 847 215-8880
  Wheeling (G-20918)

CHEMICALS & ALLIED PRDTS, WHOLESALE: Polyurethane Prdts

Guardian Energy Tech Inc..............F...... 800 516-0949
  Riverwoods (G-17091)

CHEMICALS & ALLIED PRDTS, WHOLESALE: Resins

Resin Exchange Inc..............E...... 630 628-7266
  Addison (G-271)
Resins Inc..............G...... 847 884-0025
  Hoffman Estates (G-11450)

CHEMICALS & ALLIED PRDTS, WHOLESALE: Resins, Plastics

Bamberger Polymers Inc..............F...... 630 773-8626
  Itasca (G-11624)
Certified Polymers Inc..............G...... 630 515-0007
  Western Springs (G-20719)
Entec Polymers LLC..............G...... 866 598-8941
  Plainfield (G-16660)
North American Fund III LP..............G...... 312 332-4950
  Chicago (G-5619)
Polyone Corporation..............D...... 630 972-0505
  Romeoville (G-17865)

CHEMICALS & ALLIED PRDTS, WHOLESALE: Resins, Synthetic

M-Prime Company..............E...... 630 834-9400
  Villa Park (G-20157)

CHEMICALS & ALLIED PRDTS, WHOLESALE: Sealants

Rae Products and Chem Corp..............G...... 708 396-1984
  Alsip (G-501)

CHEMICALS & ALLIED PRDTS, WHOLESALE: Silicon Lubricants

Erbeck One Chem & Lab Sup Inc..............G...... 312 203-0078
  Manhattan (G-13432)

CHEMICALS & ALLIED PRDTS, WHOLESALE: Spec Clean/Sanitation

Apco Enterprises Inc..............G...... 708 430-7333
  Bridgeview (G-2324)
Kuna Meat Company Inc..............C...... 618 286-4000
  Dupo (G-8139)

CHEMICALS & ALLIED PRDTS, WHOLESALE: Spec Clean/Sanitation

Quality Cleaning Fluids Inc............G....... 847 451-1190
  Franklin Park *(G-10029)*
United Laboratories Inc..................D....... 630 377-0900
  Saint Charles *(G-18295)*

CHEMICALS & ALLIED PRDTS, WHOLESALE: Syn Resin, Rub/Plastic

Ricon Colors Inc.............................F....... 630 562-9000
  West Chicago *(G-20636)*
Rite Systems East Inc......................E....... 630 293-9174
  West Chicago *(G-20637)*

CHEMICALS & OTHER PRDTS DERIVED FROM COKING

Bluestone Specialty Chem LLC........F....... 815 727-3010
  Joliet *(G-11833)*
Kusmierek Industries Inc.................G....... 708 258-3100
  Peotone *(G-16554)*

CHEMICALS, AGRICULTURE: Wholesalers

Helena Agri-Enterprises LLC..........G....... 217 234-2726
  Mattoon *(G-13636)*
Van Diest Supply Company..............G....... 815 232-6053
  Freeport *(G-10149)*

CHEMICALS: Agricultural

Agriscience Inc................................G....... 212 365-4214
  Peoria *(G-16377)*
Agrofresh Inc...................................C....... 267 317-9135
  Chicago *(G-3583)*
Alpha AG Inc...................................G....... 217 546-2724
  Pleasant Plains *(G-16749)*
Chase Products Co..........................D....... 708 865-1000
  Broadview *(G-2425)*
Claire-Sprayway Inc.........................D....... 630 628-3000
  Downers Grove *(G-7973)*
Clarke Aquatic Services Inc............D....... 630 894-2000
  Saint Charles *(G-18167)*
Dow Agrosciences LLC....................G....... 815 844-3128
  Pontiac *(G-16769)*
Du Pont Delaware Inc.....................G....... 630 285-2700
  Itasca *(G-11645)*
E N P Inc..G....... 800 255-4906
  Mendota *(G-13940)*
FMC Corporation............................E....... 309 695-2571
  Wyoming *(G-21460)*
Harbach Nixon & Willson Inc.........G....... 217 935-8378
  Clinton *(G-6923)*
Isky North America Inc...................G....... 937 641-1368
  Chicago *(G-4972)*
Maplehurst Farms Inc.....................F....... 815 562-8723
  Rochelle *(G-17148)*
Monsanto Company.........................D....... 618 249-6150
  Centralia *(G-3239)*
Monsanto Company.........................D....... 815 758-9293
  Waterman *(G-20299)*
Nufarm Americas Inc......................D....... 708 377-1330
  Alsip *(G-485)*
Nuseed Americas Inc......................E....... 800 345-3330
  Alsip *(G-487)*
Precision Laboratories LLC...........E....... 847 282-7228
  Waukegan *(G-20481)*
Pro-Tek Products Inc.....................G....... 630 293-5100
  Wheaton *(G-20816)*
Smithereen Company.......................D....... 800 340-1888
  Niles *(G-15172)*
Smithereen Company Del................D....... 847 675-0010
  Niles *(G-15173)*
Trainor AG Products LLC...............G....... 618 614-5770
  Anna *(G-589)*
Valent Biosciences LLC..................D....... 800 323-9597
  Libertyville *(G-12722)*
Valent USA LLC..............................F....... 816 206-3919
  Seymour *(G-18869)*
Van Diest Supply Company..............G....... 815 232-6053
  Freeport *(G-10149)*

CHEMICALS: Alcohols

RJ Distributing Co..........................E....... 309 685-2794
  East Peoria *(G-8287)*

CHEMICALS: Alkali Metals, Lithium, Cesium, Francium/Rubidium

Amnetic LLC....................................G....... 877 877-3678
  Des Plaines *(G-7730)*

Bellman-Melcor Holdings Inc..........F....... 708 532-5000
  Tinley Park *(G-19807)*

CHEMICALS: Aluminum Compounds

Illinois Capacitor Inc......................B....... 847 675-1760
  Des Plaines *(G-7783)*
Interra Global Corporation.............F....... 847 292-8600
  Park Ridge *(G-16285)*

CHEMICALS: Aluminum Sulfate

C & S Chemicals Inc.......................G....... 815 722-6671
  Joliet *(G-11837)*
Chemtrade Chemicals US LLC.......E....... 618 274-4363
  East Saint Louis *(G-8301)*

CHEMICALS: Anhydrous Ammonia

CF Industries Inc............................B....... 847 405-2400
  Deerfield *(G-7601)*
Cronus Chemicals LLC..................G....... 312 863-8638
  Chicago *(G-4272)*

CHEMICALS: Bleaching Powder, Lime Bleaching Compounds

Vertex Chemical Corporation.........F....... 618 286-5207
  Dupo *(G-8149)*

CHEMICALS: Copper Compounds Or Salts, Inorganic

American Chemet Corporation........F....... 847 948-0800
  Deerfield *(G-7585)*

CHEMICALS: Fluorine, Elemental

Solvay Chemicals Inc......................E....... 618 274-0755
  East Saint Louis *(G-8322)*

CHEMICALS: Fuel Tank Or Engine Cleaning

Kop-Coat Inc...................................F....... 847 272-2278
  Buffalo Grove *(G-2557)*

CHEMICALS: High Purity Grade, Organic

Covachem LLC.................................F....... 815 714-8421
  Loves Park *(G-13197)*

CHEMICALS: High Purity, Refined From Technical Grade

Chemtech Services Inc....................F....... 815 838-4800
  Lockport *(G-12986)*
Delta Products Group Inc...............F....... 630 357-5544
  Aurora *(G-1084)*
Incon Industries Inc.......................G....... 630 728-4014
  Saint Charles *(G-18211)*
Pharmasyn Inc.................................G....... 847 752-8405
  Libertyville *(G-12695)*

CHEMICALS: Hydrogen Peroxide

Hydrox Chemical Company Inc......D....... 847 468-9400
  Elgin *(G-8618)*
McShares Inc...................................E....... 217 762-2561
  Monticello *(G-14281)*

CHEMICALS: Inorganic, NEC

51 Elements....................................G....... 847 712-5550
  Buffalo Grove *(G-2503)*
Acl Inc...F....... 773 285-0295
  Chicago *(G-3525)*
Advanced Diamond Tech Inc..........E....... 815 293-0900
  Northbrook *(G-15332)*
Alltech Associates Inc....................D....... 773 261-2252
  Chicago *(G-3624)*
Amcol International........................G....... 847 392-4673
  Arlington Heights *(G-689)*
Americo Chemical Products Inc.....E....... 630 588-0830
  Carol Stream *(G-2938)*
Aquion Partners Ltd Partnr............G....... 847 437-9400
  Elk Grove Village *(G-8836)*
Batavia Bio Processing Limited......G....... 630 761-1180
  Batavia *(G-1354)*
Big River Zinc Corporation.............E....... 618 274-5000
  Sauget *(G-18389)*
Boyer Corporation...........................G....... 708 352-2553
  La Grange *(G-12074)*

BP Amoco Chemical Company........B....... 630 420-5111
  Naperville *(G-14782)*
Bullen Midwest Inc..........................E....... 773 785-2300
  Chicago *(G-3973)*
Cabot Corporation...........................E....... 217 253-3370
  Tuscola *(G-19924)*
Cabot McRlectronics Globl Corp....G....... 630 375-6631
  Aurora *(G-930)*
Cabot Microelectronics Corp..........D....... 630 375-6631
  Aurora *(G-931)*
Cabot Microelectronics Corp..........C....... 630 375-6631
  Aurora *(G-933)*
Campbell Camie Inc.........................E....... 314 968-3222
  Downers Grove *(G-7963)*
Carus Corporation...........................D....... 815 223-1565
  La Salle *(G-12105)*
Carus LLC.......................................C....... 815 223-1500
  La Salle *(G-12106)*
Cater Chemical Co..........................G....... 630 980-2300
  Roselle *(G-17943)*
Chemtrade Logistics (us) Inc..........C....... 704 369-2496
  Chicago *(G-4082)*
Condy Holdings LLC.......................G....... 815 223-1500
  Peru *(G-16573)*
Cs Elements LLC............................G....... 219 508-9270
  Chicago *(G-4279)*
Dauber Company Inc.......................E....... 815 442-3569
  Tonica *(G-19888)*
Dow Chemical Company..................E....... 847 439-2240
  Elk Grove Village *(G-8954)*
Dow Chemical Company..................G....... 815 653-2411
  Ringwood *(G-17042)*
Dow Chemical Company..................D....... 815 933-8900
  Kankakee *(G-11966)*
DSM Desotech Inc...........................C....... 847 697-0400
  Elgin *(G-8570)*
E I Du Pont De Nemours & Co.......E....... 847 965-6580
  Morton Grove *(G-14402)*
E I Du Pont De Nemours & Co.......G....... 815 562-7570
  Rochelle *(G-17137)*
Emco Chemical Distributors Inc.....C....... 262 427-0400
  North Chicago *(G-15310)*
Entrust Services LLC.....................G....... 630 699-9132
  Naperville *(G-14825)*
Esma Inc..G....... 708 331-0456
  South Holland *(G-19211)*
Frank Miller & Sons Inc..................E....... 708 201-7200
  Mokena *(G-14083)*
Fusion Chemical Corporation.........G....... 847 656-5285
  Park Ridge *(G-16278)*
Gcp Applied Technologies...............F....... 708 728-2420
  Chicago *(G-4665)*
Gcp Applied Technologies Inc........C....... 617 876-1400
  Bannockburn *(G-1202)*
Gycor International Ltd..................F....... 630 754-8070
  Woodridge *(G-21308)*
Hallstar Company............................E....... 901 948-8663
  Chicago *(G-4771)*
Helena Agri-Enterprises LLC..........F....... 217 382-4241
  Martinsville *(G-13585)*
Helena Agri-Enterprises LLC..........G....... 217 234-2726
  Mattoon *(G-13636)*
Honeywell International Inc............B....... 618 524-2111
  Metropolis *(G-13972)*
Hussain Shaheen.............................G....... 630 405-8009
  Bolingbrook *(G-2187)*
Incon Processing LLC....................E....... 630 305-8556
  Batavia *(G-1385)*
Innophos Inc....................................G....... 773 468-2300
  Chicago *(G-4929)*
J B Watts Company Inc...................G....... 773 643-1855
  Chicago *(G-4987)*
J Stilling Enterprises Inc................G....... 630 584-5050
  Saint Charles *(G-18217)*
JM Huber Corporation.....................E....... 217 224-1100
  Quincy *(G-16895)*
JM Huber Corporation.....................D....... 217 224-1123
  Quincy *(G-16896)*
Kafko International Ltd..................E....... 847 763-0333
  Skokie *(G-18971)*
Klean-Ko Inc....................................D....... 630 620-1860
  Lombard *(G-13092)*
Konzen Chemicals Inc....................F....... 708 878-7636
  Matteson *(G-13626)*
Lonza LLC..D....... 309 697-7200
  Mapleton *(G-13475)*
Maclee Chemical Company Inc......G....... 847 480-0953
  Northbrook *(G-15426)*
Magrabar LLC.................................F....... 847 965-7550
  Morton Grove *(G-14423)*

March Industries Inc ....F 224 654-6500
Hampshire *(G-10978)*
Metal Finishing Research Corp ....F 773 373-0800
Chicago *(G-5404)*
Milliken & Company ....D 864 473-1601
Chicago *(G-5461)*
Minus Nine Technologies ....G 224 399-9393
Gurnee *(G-10899)*
Murdock Company Inc ....G 847 566-0050
Mundelein *(G-14719)*
Nanochem Solutions Inc ....F 708 563-9200
Naperville *(G-14878)*
Nanochem Solutions Inc ....F 815 224-8480
Peru *(G-16583)*
National Interchem LLC ....G 708 597-7777
Blue Island *(G-2133)*
Nikkin Flux Corp ....G 618 656-2125
Edwardsville *(G-8372)*
NNt Enterprises Incorporated ....E 630 875-9600
Itasca *(G-11712)*
Nouryon Chemicals LLC ....C 312 544-7000
Chicago *(G-5630)*
Nouryon USA LLC ....F 312 544-7000
Chicago *(G-5633)*
Occidental Chemical Corp ....G 630 505-3242
Lisle *(G-12924)*
Orica USA Inc ....E 815 357-8711
Morris *(G-14320)*
Perkinelmer Hlth Sciences Inc ....C 630 969-6000
Downers Grove *(G-8073)*
PQ Corporation ....E 815 667-4241
Utica *(G-20006)*
PQ Corporation ....F 847 662-8566
Gurnee *(G-10914)*
Radco Industries Inc ....E 630 232-7966
Batavia *(G-1408)*
Rhone-Poulenc Basic Chem Co ....G 708 757-6111
Chicago Heights *(G-6769)*
Rohm and Haas Company ....F 815 728-4602
Ringwood *(G-17047)*
Sanford Chemical Co Inc ....F 847 437-3530
Elk Grove Village *(G-9229)*
Scholle Ipn Corporation ....F 708 562-7290
Northlake *(G-15558)*
Solvay Finance (america) LLC ....F 713 525-6000
Chicago *(G-6200)*
Solvay USA Inc ....E 708 441-6041
Chicago Heights *(G-6775)*
Spartan Flame Retardants Inc ....F 815 459-8500
Crystal Lake *(G-7267)*
Stellar Manufacturing Company ....D 618 823-3761
Cahokia *(G-2764)*
Toyal America Inc ....G 630 505-2160
Naperville *(G-14935)*
Tr Chem Solutions LLC ....G 262 865-7228
Gurnee *(G-10937)*
Trico Technologies Inc ....G 847 662-9224
Gurnee *(G-10939)*
Uncommon Elements LLC ....G 847 414-0708
Oakwood Hills *(G-15823)*
Universal Chem & Coatings Inc ....E 847 297-2001
Elk Grove Village *(G-9299)*
UOP LLC ....D 708 442-7400
Mc Cook *(G-13704)*
US Borax Inc ....C 773 270-6500
Chicago *(G-6499)*
US Silica Holdings Inc ....C 312 589-7539
Chicago *(G-6503)*
US Silica Holdings Inc ....F 312 291-4400
Chicago *(G-6504)*
US Silica Holdings Inc ....F 815 667-7085
Ottawa *(G-16084)*
Vacumet Corp ....F 708 562-7290
Northlake *(G-15564)*
Velsicol Chemical LLC ....G 847 813-7888
Rosemont *(G-18060)*
Vernon Micheal ....G 217 735-4005
Lincoln *(G-12739)*
W R Grace & Co-Conn ....F 708 458-9700
Chicago *(G-6577)*

CHEMICALS: Lead Compounds/Salts, Inorganic, Not Pigments

Powerlab Inc ....F 815 273-7718
Savanna *(G-18410)*

CHEMICALS: Medicinal

Chemsci Technologies Inc ....G 815 608-9135
Belvidere *(G-1662)*
Covachem LLC ....G 779 500-0918
Rockford *(G-17359)*
Frontida Biopharm Inc ....G 215 620-3527
Aurora *(G-965)*

CHEMICALS: Medicinal, Organic, Uncompounded, Bulk

Dottikon Es America Inc ....G 215 295-2295
Chicago *(G-4387)*
Organnica Inc ....G 312 925-7272
Berwyn *(G-1959)*
UOP LLC ....D 708 442-7400
Mc Cook *(G-13704)*

CHEMICALS: Mercury, Redistilled

Dfg Mercury Corp ....G 847 869-7800
Evanston *(G-9510)*

CHEMICALS: NEC

ABM Marking Ltd ....F 618 277-3773
Belleville *(G-1526)*
Accusol Incorporated ....G 773 283-4686
Oak Lawn *(G-15696)*
Afton Chemical Corporation ....B 618 583-1000
East Saint Louis *(G-8296)*
Alloy Chrome Inc ....G 847 678-2880
Schiller Park *(G-18784)*
American Chemical & Eqp Inc ....G 815 675-9199
Northlake *(G-15541)*
American Colloid Company ....E 618 452-8143
Granite City *(G-10694)*
American Colloid Company ....F 304 882-2123
Elgin *(G-8506)*
American Colloid Company ....E 847 851-1700
Hoffman Estates *(G-11406)*
Americlean Inc ....F 314 741-8901
Wood River *(G-21259)*
Apex Engineering Products Corp ....F 630 820-8888
Aurora *(G-912)*
APL Engineered Materials Inc ....E 217 367-1340
Urbana *(G-19972)*
BASF Corporation ....B 815 932-6751
Kankakee *(G-11959)*
Bird-X Inc ....E 312 226-2473
Elmhurst *(G-9334)*
Black Swan Manufacturing Co ....F 773 227-3700
Chicago *(G-3908)*
Bmi Products Northern Ill Inc ....E 847 395-7110
Antioch *(G-605)*
Bonsal American Inc ....D 847 678-6220
Franklin Park *(G-9891)*
Brite Site Supply Inc ....G 773 772-7300
Chicago *(G-3959)*
Buzz Sales Company Inc ....G 815 459-1170
Crystal Lake *(G-7175)*
C & S Chemicals Inc ....G 815 722-6671
Joliet *(G-11837)*
Cabot Corporation ....D 217 253-5752
Tuscola *(G-19925)*
Campbell Camie Inc ....E 314 968-3222
Downers Grove *(G-7963)*
Cater Chemical Co ....G 630 980-2300
Roselle *(G-17943)*
CCI Manufacturing IL Corp ....E 630 739-0606
Lemont *(G-12559)*
CD Magic Inc ....G 708 582-3496
Roselle *(G-17944)*
Championx LLC ....G 618 740-1279
Salem *(G-18334)*
Chemical Processing & Acc ....G 847 793-2387
Lincolnshire *(G-12750)*
Chemix Corp ....F 708 754-2150
Glenwood *(G-10639)*
Circle Systems Inc ....F 815 286-3271
Hinckley *(G-11357)*
Claire-Sprayway Inc ....D 630 628-3000
Downers Grove *(G-7973)*
CLC Lubricants Company ....E 630 232-7900
Geneva *(G-10261)*
Dayton Superior Corporation ....C 815 936-3300
Kankakee *(G-11964)*
De Enterprises Inc ....F 708 345-8088
Broadview *(G-2429)*
Emerald Polymer Additives LLC ....D 309 364-2311
Henry *(G-11165)*
Enterprise Oil Co ....E 312 487-2025
Chicago *(G-4514)*
Enviro Tech International Inc ....G 708 343-6641
Melrose Park *(G-13865)*
Environmental Specialties Inc ....G 630 860-7070
Itasca *(G-11651)*
Frank Miller & Sons Inc ....E 708 201-7200
Mokena *(G-14083)*
Gelita USA Inc ....G 708 891-8400
Calumet City *(G-2777)*
Getex Corporation ....G 630 993-1300
Aurora *(G-968)*
H-O-H Water Technology Inc ....E 847 358-7400
Palatine *(G-16121)*
Hallstar Company ....E 901 948-8663
Chicago *(G-4771)*
Hawkins Inc ....G 708 258-3797
Peotone *(G-16553)*
Henkel Technology Corporation ....G 708 924-9582
Chicago *(G-4802)*
HIG Chemicals Holdings ....C 773 376-9000
Chicago *(G-4814)*
I W M Corporation ....G 847 695-0700
Elgin *(G-8619)*
Illinois Tool Works Inc ....E 847 350-0193
Elk Grove Village *(G-9043)*
Industrial Specialty Chem Inc ....E 708 339-1313
South Holland *(G-19224)*
Industrial Waste Elimination ....F 312 498-0880
Peoria *(G-16459)*
Interra Global Corporation ....F 847 292-8600
Park Ridge *(G-16285)*
ITW Fluids North America ....G 630 384-0146
Carol Stream *(G-3008)*
Jackson Marking Products Co ....F 618 242-7901
Mount Vernon *(G-14617)*
JM Huber Corporation ....E 217 224-1100
Quincy *(G-16895)*
Klein Tools Inc ....D 847 228-6999
Elk Grove Village *(G-9078)*
Klein Tools Inc ....E 847 821-5500
Lincolnshire *(G-12779)*
Lawter Inc ....E 312 662-5700
Chicago *(G-5185)*
Litho Research Incorporated ....G 630 860-7070
Itasca *(G-11695)*
Magnetic Inspection Lab Inc ....D 847 437-4488
Elk Grove Village *(G-9106)*
Mapei Corporation ....D 630 293-5800
West Chicago *(G-20613)*
Mc Chemical Company ....G 618 965-3668
Steeleville *(G-19483)*
Mc Chemical Company ....E 815 964-7687
Rockford *(G-17511)*
Metal Finishing Research Corp ....F 773 373-0800
Chicago *(G-5404)*
Micro Surface Corporation ....F 815 942-4221
Morris *(G-14312)*
Miller Purcell Co Inc ....G 815 485-2142
New Lenox *(G-15043)*
Mineral Masters Corporation ....F 630 293-7727
West Chicago *(G-20619)*
Miracle Sealants Company LLC ....E 626 443-6433
Vernon Hills *(G-20074)*
Morton Salt Inc ....C 312 807-2000
Chicago *(G-5501)*
Nalco Holding Company ....E 630 305-1000
Naperville *(G-14877)*
Nataz Specialty Coatings Inc ....F 773 247-7030
Chicago *(G-5542)*
Nouryon Surface Chemistry LLC ....E 312 544-7000
Chicago *(G-5632)*
Ochem Inc ....G 847 403-7044
Des Plaines *(G-7814)*
Ochem Inc ....F 847 403-7044
Chicago *(G-5654)*
Polyenviro Labs Inc ....G 708 489-0195
Mokena *(G-14108)*
PQ Corporation ....E 815 667-4241
Utica *(G-20006)*
Pro TEC Metal Finishing Corp ....G 773 384-7853
Chicago *(G-5888)*
Producers Chemical Company ....E 630 466-4584
Sugar Grove *(G-19650)*
Progressive Solutions Corp ....G 847 639-7272
Algonquin *(G-384)*
PVS Chemical Solutions Inc ....E 773 933-8800
Chicago *(G-5919)*
Rust-Oleum Corporation ....C 847 367-7700
Vernon Hills *(G-20089)*
Rycoline Products LLC ....C 773 775-6755
Chicago *(G-6081)*
Sanford Chemical Co Inc ....F 847 437-3530
Elk Grove Village *(G-9229)*

Employee Codes: A=Over 500 employees, B=251-500
C=101-250, D=51-100, E=20-50, F=10-19, G=3-9
2020 Harris Illinois
Industrial Directory
1379

CHEMICALS: NEC

Seymour of Sycamore Inc..................C...... 815 895-9101
  Sycamore (G-19730)
Sika Corporation ....G...... 815 431-1080
  Ottawa (G-16079)
Solazyme ....G...... 309 258-5695
  Peoria (G-16525)
Solvay Chemicals Inc ....E...... 618 274-0755
  East Saint Louis (G-8322)
Solvay USA Inc ....E...... 708 235-7200
  University Park (G-19967)
Specco Industries Inc ....F...... 630 257-5060
  Kankakee (G-12005)
Specialty Cnstr Brands Inc ....E...... 630 851-0782
  Aurora (G-1019)
Technisand Inc ....G...... 815 433-2449
  Ottawa (G-16080)
Tower Oil & Technology Co ....F...... 773 927-6161
  Chicago (G-6401)
United Gilsonite Labs Inc ....E...... 217 243-7878
  Jacksonville (G-11784)
Varn International Inc ....E...... 630 406-6501
  Batavia (G-1440)
W R Grace & Co-Conn ....E...... 708 458-9700
  Chicago (G-6577)
Wenesco Inc ....F...... 773 283-3004
  Addison (G-333)
Wet International Inc ....E...... 630 540-2113
  Streamwood (G-19602)
Wet USA Inc ....G...... 630 540-2113
  Streamwood (G-19603)
Winn Star Inc ....G...... 618 964-1811
  Carbondale (G-2865)

CHEMICALS: Nonmetallic Compounds

Circle Systems Inc ....F...... 815 286-3271
  Hinckley (G-11357)

CHEMICALS: Organic, NEC

Afton Chemical Corporation ....B...... 618 583-1000
  East Saint Louis (G-8296)
Amtex Chemicals LLC ....G...... 630 268-0085
  Lombard (G-13039)
Arvens Technology Inc ....G...... 650 776-5443
  Peoria (G-16387)
Aspen API Inc ....F...... 847 635-0985
  Des Plaines (G-7734)
AST Industries Inc ....F...... 847 455-2300
  Franklin Park (G-9878)
Atmosphere Global LLC ....G...... 630 660-2833
  Chicago (G-3772)
Avatar Corporation ....D...... 708 534-5511
  University Park (G-19947)
BASF Corporation ....B...... 815 932-6751
  Kankakee (G-11959)
BP Amoco Chemical Company ....B...... 630 420-5111
  Naperville (G-14782)
Bullen Midwest Inc ....E...... 773 785-2300
  Chicago (G-3973)
Campbell Camie Inc ....F...... 314 968-3222
  Downers Grove (G-7963)
Cedar Concepts Corporation ....E...... 773 890-5790
  Chicago (G-4050)
Chemtura Corporation ....G...... 309 633-9480
  Mapleton (G-13470)
Clean Motion Inc ....F...... 607 323-1778
  Chicago (G-4173)
Custom Chemical Inc ....G...... 217 529-0878
  Springfield (G-19357)
Dow Chemical Company ....E...... 708 396-3009
  Alsip (G-442)
Dubois Chemicals Group Inc ....G...... 708 458-2000
  Chicago (G-4400)
Dynachem Inc ....D...... 217 662-2136
  Westville (G-20780)
Elevance Rnewable Sciences Inc ....C...... 630 296-8880
  Woodridge (G-21299)
Emerald Biofuels LLC ....G...... 847 420-0898
  Chicago (G-4494)
Emerald One LLC ....G...... 601 529-6793
  Chicago (G-4496)
Entrust Services LLC ....G...... 630 699-9132
  Naperville (G-14825)
Equa Star Chemical Corp ....G...... 815 942-7011
  Morris (G-14303)
Ethyl Corp ....E...... 618 583-1292
  East Saint Louis (G-8307)
Evonik Corporation ....C...... 309 697-6220
  Mapleton (G-13472)
Evonik Corporation ....G...... 630 230-0176
  Burr Ridge (G-2673)

Fci Flavors ....G...... 630 373-1707
  Addison (G-119)
Givaudan Fragrances Corp ....G...... 847 645-7000
  Elgin (G-8596)
Global Water Technology Inc ....E...... 708 349-9991
  South Holland (G-19215)
Green Plains Partners LP ....F...... 618 451-4420
  Madison (G-13413)
Ha-International LLC ....E...... 630 575-5700
  Westmont (G-20744)
Ha-International LLC ....E...... 815 732-3898
  Oregon (G-15922)
Ha-Usa Inc ....G...... 630 575-5700
  Westmont (G-20745)
Hallstar ....G...... 330 945-5292
  Bedford Park (G-1469)
Hallstar Company ....G...... 901 948-8663
  Chicago (G-4771)
Hallstar Company ....D...... 708 594-5947
  Bedford Park (G-1470)
Honeywell International Inc ....B...... 618 524-2111
  Metropolis (G-13972)
Hurst Chemical Company ....G...... 815 964-0451
  Rockford (G-17454)
Hydrox Chemical Company Inc ....D...... 847 468-9400
  Elgin (G-8618)
Indorama Ventures Oxide & Glyl ....E...... 800 365-0794
  Riverwoods (G-17092)
Koppers Industries Inc ....E...... 708 656-5900
  Cicero (G-6859)
Lanzatech Inc ....D...... 630 439-3050
  Skokie (G-18976)
Liquid Resin International ....E...... 618 392-3590
  Olney (G-15869)
Lonza LLC ....D...... 309 697-7200
  Mapleton (G-13475)
Lyondell Chemical Company ....B...... 815 942-7011
  Morris (G-14311)
March Industries Inc ....F...... 224 654-6500
  Hampshire (G-10978)
Merisant Company ....F...... 312 840-6000
  Chicago (G-5396)
Miwon NA ....G...... 630 568-5850
  Willowbrook (G-21052)
National Interchem LLC ....G...... 708 597-7777
  Blue Island (G-2133)
Natures Appeal Mfg Corp ....G...... 630 880-6222
  Addison (G-227)
Nouryon Functional Chem LLC ....D...... 312 544-7000
  Chicago (G-5631)
Nufarm Americas Inc ....E...... 708 377-1330
  Alsip (G-485)
Nutrasweet Company ....G...... 312 873-5000
  Chicago (G-5643)
Penray Companies Inc ....D...... 800 323-6329
  Downers Grove (G-8071)
Pmp Fermentation Products Inc ....E...... 309 637-0400
  Peoria (G-16499)
Polyenviro Labs Inc ....G...... 708 489-0195
  Mokena (G-14108)
PVS Chemical Solutions Inc ....E...... 773 933-8800
  Chicago (G-5919)
Rahn USA Corp ....E...... 630 851-4220
  Aurora (G-1012)
Reg Seneca LLC ....E...... 888 734-8686
  Seneca (G-18860)
RHO Chemical Company Inc ....F...... 815 727-4791
  Joliet (G-11926)
RTD Hallstar Inc ....C...... 908 852-6128
  Chicago (G-6076)
SB Boron Corporation ....G...... 708 547-9002
  Bellwood (G-1637)
Solutia Inc ....A...... 618 482-6536
  Sauget (G-18399)
Solvay Chemicals Inc ....E...... 618 274-0755
  East Saint Louis (G-8322)
Solvay USA Inc ....E...... 708 371-2000
  Blue Island (G-2141)
Standard Rubber Products Co ....E...... 847 593-5630
  Elk Grove Village (G-9252)
Stepan Company ....B...... 847 446-7500
  Elwood (G-9464)
Tate Lyle Ingrdnts Amricas LLC ....G...... 309 473-2721
  Heyworth (G-11191)
Vantage Corn Processors LLC ....B...... 217 424-5200
  Decatur (G-7566)
Vertec Biosolvents Inc ....G...... 630 960-0600
  Downers Grove (G-8104)
Xena International Inc ....E...... 815 946-2626
  Polo (G-16760)

CHEMICALS: Phosphates, Defluorinated/Ammoniated, Exc Fertlr

Innophos Inc ....C...... 708 757-6111
  Chicago Heights (G-6750)
Pcs Phosphate Company Inc ....D...... 847 849-4200
  Northbrook (G-15457)

CHEMICALS: Potash Alum

Potash Corp Ssktchewan Fla Inc ....C...... 847 849-4200
  Northbrook (G-15461)

CHEMICALS: Potassium Compound/Salt, Exc Hydroxide/Carbonate

Carus Group Inc ....D...... 815 223-1500
  Peru (G-16570)
Carus LLC ....D...... 815 223-1500
  Peru (G-16571)

CHEMICALS: Reagent Grade, Refined From Technical Grade

Campbell Science Corp ....F...... 815 962-7415
  Rockford (G-17333)

CHEMICALS: Sulfur Chloride

PVS Chemical Solutions Inc ....E...... 773 933-8800
  Chicago (G-5919)

CHEMICALS: Sulfur, Incl Rcvrd/Refined, Fm Sour Natural Gas

Reagent Chemical & RES Inc ....G...... 618 271-8140
  East Saint Louis (G-8319)

CHEMICALS: Water Treatment

American Technologies Inc ....E...... 630 548-8150
  Naperville (G-14773)
Arch Chemicals Inc ....G...... 630 365-1720
  Elburn (G-8444)
Bromine Systems Inc ....G...... 331 209-9881
  Addison (G-55)
Custom Chemical Inc ....G...... 217 529-0878
  Springfield (G-19357)
Dober Chemical Corp ....C...... 630 410-7300
  Woodridge (G-21294)
Garratt-Callahan Company ....G...... 630 543-4411
  Addison (G-135)
Girard Chemical Company ....G...... 630 293-5886
  Bensenville (G-1811)
Rockford Chemical Co ....G...... 815 544-3476
  Belvidere (G-1700)
RPS Products Inc ....E...... 847 683-3400
  Hampshire (G-10986)
Suez Wts Usa Inc ....E...... 630 543-8480
  Addison (G-297)
Swanson Water Treatment Inc ....G...... 847 680-1113
  Libertyville (G-12712)

CHEMICALS: Zinc Chloride

Tally Metals Holdings LLC ....G...... 773 264-5900
  Chicago (G-6315)

CHEWING GUM

Ford Gum & Machine Company Inc ....F...... 847 955-0003
  Buffalo Grove (G-2540)
Mars Incorporated ....G...... 630 293-9066
  West Chicago (G-20615)
Mid Pack ....G...... 773 626-3500
  Chicago (G-5427)
Mondelez Global LLC ....C...... 847 943-4000
  Deerfield (G-7637)
Wm Wrigley Jr Company ....E...... 312 205-2300
  Chicago (G-6655)
Wrigley Manufacturing Co LLC ....A...... 312 644-2121
  Chicago (G-6686)
Wrigley Manufacturing Co LLC ....B...... 630 553-4800
  Yorkville (G-21507)
Wrigley Manufacturing Co LLC ....A...... 312 644-2121
  Chicago (G-6687)
Wrigley Sales Company LLC ....F...... 312 644-2121
  Chicago (G-6688)

CHICKEN SLAUGHTERING & PROCESSING
Charles Autin Limited .... D 312 432-0888
  Chicago (G-4072)

CHILDBIRTH PREPARATION CLINIC
Cambridge Sensors USA LLC .... G 877 374-4062
  Plainfield (G-16647)

CHILDREN'S WEAR STORES
Initial Choice .... F 847 234-5884
  Lake Forest (G-12267)
Slick Sugar Inc .... G 815 782-7101
  Plainfield (G-16714)

CHIMNEY CAPS: Concrete
Taurus Safety Products Inc .... G 630 620-7940
  Lombard (G-13140)

CHIMNEY CLEANING SVCS
Lindemann Chimney Service Inc .... F 847 918-7994
  Lake Bluff (G-12193)

CHINA & GLASS REPAIR SVCS
Colorsmith Stained GL Studio .... G 708 447-8763
  Riverside (G-17083)
Glass Fx .... G 217 359-0048
  Champaign (G-3295)

CHINA FIRING & DECORATING SVCS, TO INDIVIDUAL ORDER
Besco Awards & Embroidery .... G 847 395-4862
  Antioch (G-603)

CHIROPRACTORS' OFFICES
Serola Biomechanics Inc .... F 815 636-2780
  Loves Park (G-13263)

CHLORINE
Arkema Inc .... C 708 396-3001
  Alsip (G-417)
Champion Packaging & Dist Inc .... C 630 972-0100
  Woodridge (G-21283)

CHOCOLATE, EXC CANDY FROM BEANS: Chips, Powder, Block, Syrup
American Convenience Inc .... F 815 344-6040
  McHenry (G-13718)
Andersons Candy Shop Inc .... F 815 678-6000
  Richmond (G-17009)
Belgian Chocolatier Piron Inc .... G 847 864-5504
  Evanston (G-9498)
Cora Lee Candies Inc .... F 847 724-2754
  Glenview (G-10538)
Dekalb Confectionary Inc .... E 815 758-5990
  Dekalb (G-7676)
Galenas Kandy Kitchen .... G 815 777-0241
  Galena (G-10171)
Gayety Candy Co Inc .... E 708 418-0062
  Lansing (G-12494)
Hershey Company .... G 800 468-1714
  Deerfield (G-7614)
Hershey Company .... A 618 544-3111
  Robinson (G-17116)
John B Sanfilippo & Son Inc .... C 847 289-1800
  Elgin (G-8632)
Mars Chocolate North Amer LLC .... C 630 850-9898
  Burr Ridge (G-2699)
Mars Chocolate North Amer LLC .... A 662 335-8000
  Chicago (G-5347)
Peases Inc .... F 217 529-2912
  Springfield (G-19423)
Worlds Finest Chocolate Inc .... B 773 847-4600
  Chicago (G-6677)

CHOCOLATE, EXC CANDY FROM PURCH CHOC: Chips, Powder, Block
Barry Callebaut USA LLC .... G 312 496-7300
  Chicago (G-3839)
Barry Callebaut USA LLC .... B 312 496-7300
  Chicago (G-3840)
Barry Callebaut USA LLC .... G 312 496-7372
  Robinson (G-17106)

Chocolate Potpourri Ltd .... F 847 729-8878
  Glenview (G-10535)
Mondelez Global LLC .... C 847 943-4000
  Deerfield (G-7637)

CHRISTMAS NOVELTIES, WHOLESALE
Mattarusky Inc .... G 630 469-4125
  Glen Ellyn (G-10412)
Temple Display Ltd .... G 630 851-3331
  Oswego (G-16026)

CHRISTMAS TREE LIGHTING SETS: Electric
American Holiday Lights Inc .... G 630 769-9999
  Woodridge (G-21274)
Santas Best .... F 847 459-3301
  Vernon Hills (G-20091)

CHROMATOGRAPHY EQPT
Dionex Corporation 847 295-7500
  Bannockburn (G-1199)
Waters Technologies Corp .... F 630 766-6249
  Wood Dale (G-21256)
Waters Technologies Corp 508 482-8365
  Chicago (G-6589)

CHUCKS
Electro-Matic Products Co 773 235-4010
  Chicago (G-4477)
Kenyeri Consulting LLC .... G 630 920-3497
  Downers Grove (G-8039)
Kitagawa Usa Inc .... E 847 310-8198
  Schaumburg (G-18587)
Kitagawa-Northtech Inc .... E 847 310-8787
  Schaumburg (G-18588)
LFA Industries Inc .... G 630 762-7391
  Saint Charles (G-18227)
Miyanohitec Machinery Inc .... G 847 382-2794
  Barrington (G-1230)
Reichel Hardware Company Inc .... G 630 762-7394
  Saint Charles (G-18261)

CHURCHES
Interntnal Awkening Ministries .... G 630 653-8616
  Wheaton (G-20806)

CHUTES & TROUGHS
American Chute Systems Inc .... G 815 723-7632
  Joliet (G-11819)

CHUTES: Metal Plate
Columbia Chutes LLC .... G 847 520-5989
  Rockdale (G-17257)
Roth Metal Fabricators Corp .... G 708 371-8300
  Alsip (G-505)

CIGAR & CIGARETTE HOLDERS
MI Vape Co .... F 815 582-3838
  Joliet (G-11901)

CIGARETTE & CIGAR PRDTS & ACCESS
A and T Cigarettes Imports .... G 847 836-9134
  East Dundee (G-8186)

CIGARETTE FILTERS
Essentra Corp .... G 814 899-7671
  Westchester (G-20697)
Essentra Holdings Corp .... G 804 518-0322
  Westchester (G-20698)

CIGARETTE STORES
Hotvapes Ltd .... F 775 468-8273
  Niles (G-15130)

CIRCUIT BOARD REPAIR SVCS
Novatronix Inc .... E 630 860-4300
  Wood Dale (G-21223)

CIRCUIT BOARDS, PRINTED: Television & Radio
Alpha Circuit Corporation .... E 630 617-5555
  Elmhurst (G-9325)

American Controls & Automation .... G 630 293-8841
  West Chicago (G-20537)
Amitron Inc .... C 847 290-9800
  Elk Grove Village (G-8828)
Aurora Circuits Inc .... D 630 978-3830
  Aurora (G-915)
Bandjwet Enterprises Inc .... E 847 797-9250
  Rolling Meadows (G-17717)
Bestproto Inc .... F 224 387-3280
  South Elgin (G-19138)
Circuit Works Corporation .... D 847 283-8600
  Waukegan (G-20428)
Circuit World Inc .... E 630 250-1100
  Itasca (G-11637)
Delta Circuits Inc .... E 630 876-0691
  West Chicago (G-20569)
Eagle Capital Group Inc .... D 847 891-5800
  Schaumburg (G-18512)
Electronic Interconnect Corp .... D 847 364-4848
  Elk Grove Village (G-8971)
Excell Electronics Corporation .... E 847 766-7455
  Elk Grove Village (G-8988)
Light of Mine LLC .... G 312 840-8570
  Chicago (G-5220)
Microsun Electronics Corp .... F 630 410-7900
  Woodridge (G-21323)
Ncab Group Usa Inc .... F 630 562-5550
  Itasca (G-11709)
Online Electronics Inc .... E 847 871-1700
  Elk Grove Village (G-9164)
Paramount Laminates Inc .... G 630 594-1840
  Wood Dale (G-21227)
Parth Consultants Inc .... E 847 758-1400
  Schaumburg (G-18667)
Printing Circuit Boards .... F 630 543-3453
  Addison (G-255)
Quality Surface Mount Inc .... G 630 350-8556
  Wood Dale (G-21233)
United Electronics Corp Inc .... D 847 671-6034
  Franklin Park (G-10069)

CIRCUIT BOARDS: Wiring
American Progressive Circuits .... E 630 495-6900
  Addison (G-34)

CIRCUIT BREAKERS
Allocator Logistics Co .... G 708 339-5678
  South Holland (G-19190)
Boltswitch Inc .... E 815 459-6900
  Crystal Lake (G-7170)
Clark Tashaunda .... G 708 247-8274
  Calumet Park (G-2796)

CIRCUIT BREAKERS: Air
Schneider Electric Usa Inc .... G 312 697-4770
  Chicago (G-6112)

CIRCUITS, INTEGRATED: Hybrid
Hytel Group Inc .... E 847 683-9800
  Hampshire (G-10974)

CIRCUITS: Electronic
Accelerated Assemblies Inc .... E 630 616-6680
  Elk Grove Village (G-8798)
Access Assembly LLC .... G 847 894-1047
  Mundelein (G-14659)
Aimtron Corporation .... D 630 372-7500
  Palatine (G-16091)
Air802 Corporation .... G 630 966-2501
  Oswego (G-15991)
Andrew Technologies Inc .... E 847 520-5770
  Wheeling (G-20849)
ARC-Tronics Inc .... C 847 437-0211
  Elk Grove Village (G-8837)
Aria Corporation .... G 847 327-9000
  Libertyville (G-12630)
B D C Inc .... E 847 741-2233
  Elgin (G-8519)
Bestar Technologies Inc .... G 847 261-2850
  Saint Charles (G-18155)
Blockmaster Electronics Inc .... G 847 956-1680
  Elk Grove Village (G-8869)
C Hofbauer Inc .... G 630 920-1222
  Burr Ridge (G-2659)
C L Greenslade Sales Inc .... G 847 593-3450
  Arlington Heights (G-713)
C R V Electronics Corp .... D 815 675-6500
  Spring Grove (G-19269)

CIRCUITS: Electronic

Cal-Tronics Systems Inc .... E 630 350-0044
  Wood Dale *(G-21174)*
Capital Advanced Technologies .... G 630 690-1696
  Carol Stream *(G-2955)*
Circom Inc .... E 630 595-4460
  Bensenville *(G-1770)*
Cita Technologies LLC .... G 847 419-9118
  Buffalo Grove *(G-2525)*
Cmetrix Inc .... G 630 595-9800
  Wood Dale *(G-21177)*
Continental Assembly Inc .... F 773 472-8004
  Chicago *(G-4226)*
Daesam Corporation .... G 917 653-2000
  Grayslake *(G-10765)*
Dalco Marketing Services .... G 630 961-3366
  Carol Stream *(G-2971)*
De Amertek Corporation Inc .... D 630 572-0800
  Lombard *(G-13063)*
Delta Circuits Inc .... E 630 876-0691
  West Chicago *(G-20569)*
Elan Industries Inc .... F 630 679-2000
  Bolingbrook *(G-2172)*
Four Star Tool Inc .... D 224 735-2419
  Rolling Meadows *(G-17733)*
G T C Industries Inc .... G 708 369-9815
  Naperville *(G-14832)*
Integrated Circuits Research .... G 630 830-9024
  Hanover Park *(G-11007)*
Journey Circuits Inc .... G 630 283-0604
  Schaumburg *(G-18579)*
L I K Inc .... F 630 213-1282
  Streamwood *(G-19583)*
Lace Technologies Inc .... F 630 528-8083
  Addison *(G-180)*
Littelfuse Inc .... A 773 628-1000
  Chicago *(G-5238)*
Loda Electronics Co .... G 217 386-2554
  Loda *(G-13029)*
Matrix Circuits LLC .... G 319 367-5000
  Lake Villa *(G-12360)*
Midwest Aero Support Inc .... E 815 398-9202
  Machesney Park *(G-13360)*
Monnex International Inc .... E 847 850-5263
  Buffalo Grove *(G-2576)*
Murata Electronics N Amer Inc .... G 847 330-9200
  Schaumburg *(G-18641)*
Navatek Resources Inc .... G 847 301-0174
  Schaumburg *(G-18645)*
Navitas Electronics Corp .... E 702 293-4670
  Woodridge *(G-21325)*
Northrop Grumman Systems Corp .... A 847 259-9600
  Rolling Meadows *(G-17755)*
Novel Electronic Designs Inc .... G 309 224-9945
  Chillicothe *(G-6820)*
Polyera Corporation .... E 847 677-7517
  Skokie *(G-19006)*
Precision Circuits Inc .... F 630 515-9100
  Downers Grove *(G-8083)*
Qcircuits Inc .... D 847 797-6678
  Elk Grove Village *(G-9203)*
Richardson Electronics Ltd .... C 630 208-2200
  Lafox *(G-12138)*
Safemobile Inc .... F 847 818-1649
  Rolling Meadows *(G-17772)*
Sigmatron International Inc .... G 847 586-5200
  Elgin *(G-8730)*
Sigmatron International Inc .... G 847 956-8000
  Elk Grove Village *(G-9238)*
Simple Circuits Inc .... G 708 671-9600
  Palos Park *(G-16214)*
Skyline International Inc .... F 847 357-9077
  Palatine *(G-16159)*
Sub-Sem Inc .... E 815 459-4139
  Crystal Lake *(G-7270)*
Tanvas Inc .... G 773 295-6220
  Chicago *(G-6325)*
Tech Star Design and Mfg .... F 847 290-8676
  Elk Grove Village *(G-9268)*
Teejet Technologies LLC .... D 630 665-5002
  Springfield *(G-19462)*
Tvh Parts Co .... E 847 223-1000
  Grayslake *(G-10803)*
Uico LLC .... E 630 592-4400
  Elmhurst *(G-9439)*
Zic Incorporated .... G 847 680-8333
  Wheeling *(G-21016)*

CLAIMS ADJUSTING SVCS

Crawford Heating & Cooling Co .... D 309 788-4573
  Rock Island *(G-17211)*

CLAMPS & COUPLINGS: Hose

American Couplings Co .... G 630 323-4442
  Westmont *(G-20728)*
Capital Rubber Corporation .... F 630 595-6644
  Bensenville *(G-1762)*

CLAMPS & SHORES: Column

Prospan Manufacturing Co .... G 630 860-1930
  Bensenville *(G-1874)*

CLAMPS: Ground, Electric-Wiring Devices

Maclean Senior Industries LLC .... G 630 350-1600
  Wood Dale *(G-21210)*

CLAMPS: Metal

Adjustable Clamp Company .... C 312 666-0640
  Chicago *(G-3546)*
Berens Inc .... G 815 932-0913
  Kankakee *(G-11960)*
Strut & Supply Inc .... G 847 756-4337
  Lake Barrington *(G-12166)*
Value Engineered Products .... E 708 867-6777
  Rolling Meadows *(G-17784)*
Zsi-Foster Inc .... G 800 323-7053
  Chicago *(G-6725)*

CLAY MINING, COMMON

Carpentersville Quarry Inc .... F 847 836-1550
  Carpentersville *(G-3096)*
Oil-Dri Corporation America .... B 312 321-1516
  Chicago *(G-5667)*

CLAYS, EXC KAOLIN & BALL

American Colloid Company .... F 815 547-5369
  Belvidere *(G-1648)*
Oil-Dri Corporation America .... D 618 745-6881
  Mounds *(G-14463)*

CLEANING & DESCALING SVC: Metal Prdts

AAM-Ro Corporation .... F 708 343-5543
  Broadview *(G-2412)*
Ace Metal Refinishers Inc .... G 800 323-7147
  Oak Brook *(G-15588)*
Great Lakes Finishing Eqp Inc .... G 708 345-5300
  South Elgin *(G-19150)*

CLEANING & DYEING PLANTS, EXC RUGS

Eastgate Cleaners .... G 630 627-9494
  Lombard *(G-13071)*
Regency Hand Laundry .... G 773 871-3950
  Chicago *(G-6001)*

CLEANING COMPOUNDS: Rifle Bore

300 Below Inc .... G 217 423-3070
  Decatur *(G-7431)*

CLEANING EQPT: Blast, Dustless

Disa Holding Corp .... G 630 820-3000
  Oswego *(G-16002)*

CLEANING EQPT: Carpet Sweepers, Exc Household Elec Vacuum

Best Way Carpet & Uphl Clg .... G 618 544-8585
  Robinson *(G-17108)*

CLEANING EQPT: Commercial

Detrex Corporation .... G 708 345-3806
  Melrose Park *(G-13849)*
Markham Division 9 Inc .... E 708 503-0657
  Park Forest *(G-16257)*
Meyer Machine & Equipment Inc .... E 847 395-2977
  Antioch *(G-625)*
Minuteman International Inc .... E 630 627-6900
  Pingree Grove *(G-16622)*
Minuteman International Inc .... D 847 683-5210
  Hampshire *(G-10980)*
Producers Envmtl Pdts LLC .... G 630 482-5995
  Batavia *(G-1406)*
Umf Corporation .... G 224 251-7822
  Niles *(G-15184)*
Umf Corporation .... F 847 920-0370
  Skokie *(G-19049)*

CLEANING EQPT: Dirt Sweeping Units, Indl

Tkg Sweeping & Services LLC .... G 847 505-1400
  Waukegan *(G-20506)*

CLEANING EQPT: Floor Washing & Polishing, Commercial

Rays Power Wshg Svc Peggy Ray .... G 618 939-6306
  Waterloo *(G-20295)*
Selrok Inc .... G 630 876-8322
  West Chicago *(G-20640)*
Star Industries Inc .... E 708 240-4862
  Highland Park *(G-11300)*

CLEANING EQPT: High Pressure

Fna Ip Holdings Inc .... D 847 348-1500
  Elk Grove Village *(G-9001)*
James A Freund LLC .... G 630 664-7692
  Oswego *(G-16009)*
Jetin Systems Inc .... F 815 726-4686
  Joliet *(G-11885)*
M & M Pump Co .... G 217 935-2517
  Clinton *(G-6926)*
Ross and White Company .... F 847 516-3900
  Cary *(G-3187)*

CLEANING OR POLISHING PREPARATIONS, NEC

Apco Enterprises Inc .... G 708 430-7333
  Bridgeview *(G-2324)*
Apex Engineering Products Corp .... F 630 820-8888
  Aurora *(G-912)*
Chemical Specialties Mfg Corp .... G 309 697-5400
  Mapleton *(G-13469)*
Claire-Sprayway Inc .... E 630 628-3000
  Downers Grove *(G-7972)*
Colorex Chemical Co Inc .... G 630 238-3124
  Bensenville *(G-1774)*
Coral Chemical Company .... E 847 246-6666
  Zion *(G-21510)*
Duraclean International Inc .... F 847 704-7100
  Arlington Heights *(G-730)*
Floor-Chem Inc .... G 630 789-2152
  Romeoville *(G-17824)*
Houghton International Inc .... F 610 666-4000
  Chicago *(G-4849)*
Kik International Inc .... F 905 660-0444
  Carol Stream *(G-3010)*
Minuteman International Inc .... C 630 627-6900
  Pingree Grove *(G-16622)*
Penray Companies Inc .... D 800 323-6329
  Downers Grove *(G-8071)*
PLC Corp .... G 847 247-1900
  Lake Bluff *(G-12206)*
R E Z Packaging Inc .... F 773 247-0800
  Chicago *(G-5945)*
R R Street & Co Inc .... E 773 247-1190
  Chicago *(G-5951)*
Rycoline Products LLC .... C 773 775-6755
  Chicago *(G-6081)*
Science Solutions LLC .... G 773 261-1197
  Chicago *(G-6118)*
Stellar Blending & Packaging .... F 314 520-7318
  Dupo *(G-8144)*
Tri Sect Corporation .... F 847 524-1119
  Schaumburg *(G-18754)*
Venus Laboratories Inc .... E 630 595-1900
  Addison *(G-328)*

CLEANING PRDTS: Ammonia, Household

Champion Packaging & Dist Inc .... C 630 972-0100
  Woodridge *(G-21283)*
Formulations Inc .... G 847 674-9141
  Skokie *(G-18956)*

CLEANING PRDTS: Automobile Polish

Bumper Scuffs .... G 847 489-7926
  Lake Villa *(G-12347)*
Reed-Union Corporation .... F 312 644-3200
  Chicago *(G-5996)*
Treatment Products Ltd .... E 773 626-8888
  Chicago *(G-6414)*
Voodoo Ride LLC .... G 312 944-0465
  Chicago *(G-6569)*

PRODUCT SECTION — CLOTHING & ACCESS: Men's Miscellaneous Access

CLEANING PRDTS: Bleaches, Household, Dry Or Liquid
- Clorox Hidden Valley Mfg .... F 847 229-5500
  Wheeling *(G-20871)*
- Korex Chicago LLC .... E 708 458-4890
  Chicago *(G-5124)*

CLEANING PRDTS: Deodorants, Nonpersonal
- Odorite International Inc .... F 816 920-5000
  Saint Charles *(G-18236)*

CLEANING PRDTS: Disinfectants, Household Or Indl Plant
- Advanage Diversified Pdts Inc .... F 708 331-8390
  Harvey *(G-11069)*

CLEANING PRDTS: Drain Pipe Solvents Or Cleaners
- Detrex Corporation .... G 708 345-3806
  Melrose Park *(G-13849)*
- Imagination Products Corp .... E 309 274-6223
  Chillicothe *(G-6818)*

CLEANING PRDTS: Drycleaning Preparations
- R R Street & Co Inc .... F 773 254-1277
  Chicago *(G-5952)*

CLEANING PRDTS: Floor Waxes
- Bullen Midwest Inc .... E 773 785-2300
  Chicago *(G-3973)*
- Dura Wax Company .... F 815 385-5000
  McHenry *(G-13739)*
- S C Johnson & Son Inc .... C 312 702-3100
  Chicago *(G-6085)*

CLEANING PRDTS: Indl Plant Disinfectants Or Deodorants
- Interflo Industries Inc .... G 847 228-0606
  Elk Grove Village *(G-9056)*
- Teitelbaum Brothers Inc .... G 847 729-3490
  Glenview *(G-10630)*

CLEANING PRDTS: Laundry Preparations
- Clorox Company .... E 510 271-7000
  Willowbrook *(G-21036)*

CLEANING PRDTS: Polishing Preparations & Related Prdts
- Zoes Mfgco LLC .... F 312 666-4018
  Chicago *(G-6722)*

CLEANING PRDTS: Rug, Upholstery/Dry Clng Detergents/Spotters
- Elco Laboratories Inc .... D 708 534-3000
  Coal City *(G-6932)*
- R R Street & Co Inc .... E 630 416-4244
  Naperville *(G-14905)*

CLEANING PRDTS: Sanitation Preparations
- Bass Brother Incorporated .... G 800 252-1114
  Des Plaines *(G-7736)*
- City of Chicago .... E 312 744-0940
  Chicago *(G-4157)*
- First Ayd Corporation .... D 847 622-0001
  Elgin *(G-8586)*
- Gea Farm Technologies Inc .... C 630 548-8200
  Naperville *(G-14833)*
- Odors Away LLC .... G 888 235-7559
  Elgin *(G-8676)*
- Rd Husemoller Ltd .... F 847 526-5505
  Wauconda *(G-20388)*

CLEANING PRDTS: Sanitation Preps, Disinfectants/Deodorants
- City of Chicago .... E 312 746-6583
  Chicago *(G-4159)*

- Ecolab Inc .... E 815 389-3441
  Roscoe *(G-17905)*
- Sneaky Clean LLC .... G 312 550-9654
  Downers Grove *(G-8097)*

CLEANING PRDTS: Specialty
- 300 Below Inc .... G 217 423-3070
  Decatur *(G-7431)*
- Atm America Corp .... E 800 298-0030
  Chicago *(G-3770)*
- Blue Light Inc .... E 630 400-4539
  Lisle *(G-12873)*
- Boyer Corporation .... F 708 352-2553
  La Grange *(G-12074)*
- Brite Site Supply Inc .... G 773 772-7300
  Chicago *(G-3959)*
- Clifton Chemical Company .... F 815 697-2343
  Chebanse *(G-3429)*
- Creative Metal Products .... F 773 638-3200
  Chicago *(G-4264)*
- Doris Company .... G 224 302-5605
  Round Lake Park *(G-18096)*
- Ecolab Inc .... E 815 729-7334
  Joliet *(G-11857)*
- Ecp Incorporated .... D 630 754-4200
  Woodridge *(G-21297)*
- Fola Community Action Services .... F 773 487-4310
  Chicago *(G-4615)*
- Gfl Environmental Svcs USA Inc .... E 866 579-6900
  Mokena *(G-14088)*
- Pete Frcano Sons Cstm HM Bldrs .... F 847 258-4626
  Elk Grove Village *(G-9175)*
- Procter & Gamble Company .... G 847 375-5400
  Chicago *(G-5892)*
- Scs Company .... E 708 269-2094
  Crestwood *(G-7126)*
- Tiger Accessory Group LLC .... F 847 821-9630
  Long Grove *(G-13171)*
- United Laboratories Inc .... D 630 377-0900
  Saint Charles *(G-18295)*

CLEANING PRDTS: Window Cleaning Preparations
- A J Funk & Co .... G 847 741-6760
  Elgin *(G-8489)*
- Anytime Window Cleaning Inc .... G 773 235-5677
  Chicago *(G-3709)*
- Newby Oil Company Inc .... G 815 756-7688
  Sycamore *(G-19725)*

CLIPPERS: Hair, Human
- Wahl Clipper Corporation .... A 815 625-6525
  Sterling *(G-19540)*
- Wahl Clipper Corporation .... F 815 625-6525
  Sterling *(G-19541)*

CLIPS & FASTENERS, MADE FROM PURCHASED WIRE
- Acco Brands USA LLC .... B 800 222-6462
  Lake Zurich *(G-12376)*
- Acco Brands USA LLC .... D 847 272-3700
  Lincolnshire *(G-12741)*
- Keats Manufacturing Co .... D 847 520-1133
  Wheeling *(G-20923)*
- Manufasteners House Iq Inc .... G 847 705-6538
  Palatine *(G-16138)*
- Precitec Corporation .... D 847 949-2800
  Mundelein *(G-14727)*

CLOSURES: Closures, Stamped Metal
- Sorini Manufacturing Corp .... E 773 247-5858
  Chicago *(G-6203)*

CLOSURES: Plastic
- Aptargroup Inc .... G 847 816-9400
  Libertyville *(G-12629)*
- Aptargroup Inc .... C 815 477-0424
  Crystal Lake *(G-7160)*
- Mold-Rite Plastics LLC .... C 518 561-1812
  Chicago *(G-5487)*
- Portola Packaging LLC .... E 630 515-8383
  Downers Grove *(G-8079)*
- Sun Dome Inc .... F 773 890-5350
  Chicago *(G-6268)*

CLOTHESPINS: Plastic
- Goodco Products LLC .... G 630 258-6384
  Countryside *(G-7055)*

CLOTHING & ACCESS STORES
- Sunglass Otftters By Snglass H .... G 847 645-0476
  Hoffman Estates *(G-11465)*

CLOTHING & ACCESS, WOMEN, CHILD & INFANT, WHSLE: Sportswear
- Select Screen Prints & EMB .... F 309 829-6511
  Bloomington *(G-2093)*

CLOTHING & ACCESS, WOMEN, CHILDREN & INFANT, WHOL: Handbags
- Advance Tools LLC .... G 630 337-5904
  Glenview *(G-10520)*

CLOTHING & ACCESS, WOMEN, CHILDREN & INFANT, WHOL: Uniforms
- Chicago Knitting Mills .... G 773 463-1464
  Northbrook *(G-15358)*

CLOTHING & ACCESS, WOMEN, CHILDREN/INFANT, WHOL: Outerwear
- All In Stitches .... G 309 944-4084
  Geneseo *(G-10238)*
- Anntaylor Retail Inc .... G 309 693-2762
  Peoria *(G-16383)*
- Summit Graphics Inc .... F 309 799-5100
  Moline *(G-14180)*

CLOTHING & ACCESS: Costumes, Masquerade
- Zagone Studios LLC .... E 773 509-0610
  Melrose Park *(G-13932)*

CLOTHING & ACCESS: Costumes, Theatrical
- Custom & Hard To Find Wigs .... F 773 777-0222
  Chicago *(G-4288)*
- Facemakers Inc .... F 815 273-3944
  Savanna *(G-18405)*
- Facemakers Inc .... E 815 273-3944
  Savanna *(G-18406)*

CLOTHING & ACCESS: Handicapped
- Living Royal Inc .... E 312 906-7600
  Wheeling *(G-20934)*
- Roq Innovation LLC .... G 917 770-2403
  Chicago *(G-6059)*

CLOTHING & ACCESS: Hospital Gowns
- Baxter Healthcare Corporation .... E 847 578-4671
  Waukegan *(G-20422)*

CLOTHING & ACCESS: Men's Miscellaneous Access
- Allen Larson .... G 773 454-2210
  Chicago *(G-3614)*
- Anntaylor Retail Inc .... G 309 693-2762
  Peoria *(G-16383)*
- Daniel Bruce LLC .... F 917 583-1538
  Palatine *(G-16108)*
- Four Star Denim and AP LLC .... F 847 707-6365
  Chicago *(G-4626)*
- Gennco International Inc .... F 847 541-3333
  Northbrook *(G-15393)*
- K&G Mens Company Inc .... G 708 349-2579
  Orland Park *(G-15963)*
- New York & Company Inc .... F 630 232-7693
  Geneva *(G-10293)*
- New York & Company Inc .... F 630 783-2910
  Bolingbrook *(G-2221)*
- Nu-Life Inc of Illinois .... G 618 943-4500
  Lawrenceville *(G-12536)*
- Sieden Sticker USA Ltd .... G 312 280-7711
  Chicago *(G-6163)*

Employee Codes: A=Over 500 employees, B=251-500
C=101-250, D=51-100, E=20-50, F=10-19, G=3-9

CLOTHING & ACCESS: Regalia

Pollack Service .... D 773 528-8096
Chicago *(G-5833)*

CLOTHING & APPAREL STORES: Custom

AM Harper Products Inc .... F 312 767-8283
Chicago *(G-3640)*
American Enlightenment LLC .... G 773 687-8996
Chicago *(G-3652)*
American Outfitters Ltd .... E 847 623-3959
Waukegan *(G-20414)*
False Hope Brand Co .... G 312 265-1364
Chicago *(G-4556)*
Fast Lane Threads Custom EMB ..... G 815 544-9898
Belvidere *(G-1667)*

CLOTHING & FURNISHINGS, MEN'S & BOYS', WHOLESALE: Hats

Gabriel Enterprises .... G 773 342-8705
Chicago *(G-4654)*

CLOTHING & FURNISHINGS, MEN'S & BOYS', WHOLESALE: Shirts

Go Van Goghs Tee Shirt .... G 309 342-1112
Galesburg *(G-10198)*
Screen Machine Incorporated .... G 847 439-2233
Elk Grove Village *(G-9234)*

CLOTHING & FURNISHINGS, MEN'S & BOYS', WHOLESALE: Umbrellas

Shedrain Corporation .... G 708 848-5212
Oak Park *(G-15772)*

CLOTHING & FURNISHINGS, MEN'S & BOYS', WHOLESALE: Uniforms

Chicago Knitting Mills .... G 773 463-1464
Northbrook *(G-15358)*
High Performance Entp Inc .... E 773 283-1778
Chicago *(G-4816)*
Vertex International Inc .... G 312 242-1864
Oak Brook *(G-15669)*

CLOTHING & FURNISHINGS, MENS & BOYS, WHOL: Sportswear/Work

Athllete LLC .... F 773 829-3752
Bolingbrook *(G-2151)*
Select Screen Prints & EMB .... F 309 829-6511
Bloomington *(G-2093)*

CLOTHING & FURNISHINGS, MENS & BOYS, WHOLESALE: Apprl Belts

Randa Accessories Lea Gds LLC ..... D 847 292-8300
Rosemont *(G-18046)*

CLOTHING STORES, NEC

Mjt Design and Prtg Entps Inc .... G 708 240-4323
Hillside *(G-11348)*

CLOTHING STORES: Formal Wear

Duckys Formal Wear Inc .... G 309 342-5914
Galesburg *(G-10191)*
Winning Stitch .... G 217 348-8279
Charleston *(G-3417)*

CLOTHING STORES: Lingerie, Outerwear

Victorias Secret Stores LLC .... G 312 583-0488
Chicago *(G-6547)*

CLOTHING STORES: Shirts, Custom Made

Go Van Goghs Tee Shirt .... G 309 342-1112
Galesburg *(G-10198)*

CLOTHING STORES: T-Shirts, Printed, Custom

Academy Screenprinting Awards .... G 309 686-0026
Peoria *(G-16374)*
Camilles of Canton Inc .... G 309 647-7403
Canton *(G-2822)*
Chicago Printing and EMB Inc .... F 630 628-1777
Addison *(G-71)*
Diamond Teez & More LLC .... G 618 579-9876
Alton *(G-552)*
Grey Shirt Guys LLC .... G 800 787-4478
Mascoutah *(G-13597)*
High-5 Printwear Inc .... G 847 818-0081
Arlington Heights *(G-749)*
Hole In The Wall Screen Arts .... G 217 243-9100
Jacksonville *(G-11767)*
Mjt Design and Prtg Entps Inc .... G 708 240-4323
Hillside *(G-11348)*
Peacock Printing Inc .... G 618 242-3157
Mount Vernon *(G-14633)*
Select Screen Prints & EMB .... F 309 829-6511
Bloomington *(G-2093)*
Teds Shirt Shack Inc .... G 217 224-9705
Quincy *(G-16946)*

CLOTHING STORES: Uniforms & Work

Four Star Denim and AP LLC .... F 847 707-6365
Chicago *(G-4626)*
LAC Enterprises Inc .... G 815 455-5044
Crystal Lake *(G-7219)*

CLOTHING STORES: Unisex

Elan Furs .... F 317 255-6100
Morton Grove *(G-14404)*
Icandee LLC .... G 773 754-0493
Chicago *(G-4871)*
No Surrender Inc .... F 773 929-7920
Chicago *(G-5607)*

CLOTHING STORES: Work

Magid Glove Safety Mfg Co LLC ..... B 773 384-2070
Romeoville *(G-17844)*
Mennon Rbr & Safety Pdts Inc .... G 847 678-8250
Schiller Park *(G-18823)*

CLOTHING/ACCESS, WOMEN, CHILDREN/INFANT, WHOL: Apparel Belt

Continent Corp .... G 773 733-1584
Bolingbrook *(G-2158)*

CLOTHING: Academic Vestments

Herff Jones LLC .... C 217 268-4543
Arcola *(G-651)*
Herff Jones LLC .... C 317 612-3705
Hillside *(G-11341)*

CLOTHING: Access

Andrea and ME and ME Too .... G 708 955-3850
Matteson *(G-13618)*
Browns Global Exchange .... D 708 345-0955
Maywood *(G-13664)*
Cayenne Couture Atelier .... G 773 408-4664
Chicago *(G-4045)*
Phoebe & Frances .... F 847 446-5480
Winnetka *(G-21135)*
Sunglass Otftters By Snglass H ...... G 847 645-0476
Hoffman Estates *(G-11465)*

CLOTHING: Access, Women's & Misses'

Daniel Bruce LLC .... F 917 583-1538
Palatine *(G-16108)*
Doughman Don & Assoc .... G 312 321-1011
Chicago *(G-4389)*
Jenny Capp Co .... F 773 217-0057
Chicago *(G-5018)*
Pola Company .... G 847 470-1182
Niles *(G-15160)*

CLOTHING: Anklets & Socks

Felice Hosiery Company Inc .... E 312 922-3710
Chicago *(G-4579)*

CLOTHING: Aprons, Harness

Rock Tops Inc .... G 708 672-1450
Crete *(G-7144)*

CLOTHING: Aprons, Waterproof, From Purchased Materials

Petra Manufacturing Co .... D 773 622-1475
Chicago *(G-5797)*

CLOTHING: Athletic & Sportswear, Men's & Boys'

Athllete LLC .... F 773 829-3752
Bolingbrook *(G-2151)*
BMW Sportswear Inc .... G 773 265-0110
Chicago *(G-3921)*
Choi Brands Inc .... C 773 489-2800
Chicago *(G-4142)*
Cloz Companies Inc .... E 773 247-8879
Skokie *(G-18944)*
Express LLC .... E 708 453-0566
Norridge *(G-15234)*
Pro-AM Team Sports LLC .... F 708 995-1511
Mokena *(G-14110)*
Tfo Group LLC .... G 608 469-7519
Chicago *(G-6358)*
Vista Outdoor Inc .... G 309 693-2746
Rantoul *(G-16985)*

CLOTHING: Athletic & Sportswear, Women's & Girls'

Athllete LLC .... F 773 829-3752
Bolingbrook *(G-2151)*
Libaerty LLC .... G 312 330-2767
Chicago *(G-5216)*
Srh Holdings Inc .... F 847 583-2295
Niles *(G-15175)*

CLOTHING: Baker, Barber, Lab/Svc Ind Apparel, Washable, Men

False Hope Brand Co .... G 312 265-1364
Chicago *(G-4556)*
V-Tex Inc .... E 847 325-4140
Buffalo Grove *(G-2615)*
Woolenwear Co .... F 847 520-9243
Prospect Heights *(G-16848)*

CLOTHING: Band Uniforms

Demoulin Brothers & Company ...... C 618 664-2000
Greenville *(G-10832)*

CLOTHING: Bathing Suits & Swimwear, Knit

The Lifeguard Store Inc .... G 630 548-5500
Naperville *(G-14932)*

CLOTHING: Blouses, Women's & Girls'

Apparel Works Intl LLC .... G 847 778-9559
Lake Bluff *(G-12171)*
Joriki LLC .... G 312 848-1136
Chicago *(G-5050)*
Rubin Nsa Bros LLC .... G 312 942-1111
Chicago *(G-6078)*
Yolanda Lorente Ltd .... E 773 334-4536
Chicago *(G-6703)*

CLOTHING: Bras & Corsets, Maternity

Golda Inc .... C 217 895-3602
Neoga *(G-15017)*

CLOTHING: Bridal Gowns

Doris Bridal Boutique .... G 847 433-2575
Highwood *(G-11306)*

CLOTHING: Capes, Exc Fur/Rubber, Womens, Misses & Juniors

Mademoiselle Inc .... F 773 394-4555
Chicago *(G-5311)*

CLOTHING: Caps, Baseball

Bee Sales Company .... D 847 600-4400
Niles *(G-15106)*

CLOTHING: Children & Infants'

Dino Design Incorporated .... G 773 763-4223
Morton Grove *(G-14400)*

CLOTHING: Children's, Girls'

Bee Sales Company .... D 847 600-4400
Niles *(G-15106)*
Cloz Companies Inc .... E 773 247-8879
Skokie *(G-18944)*

PRODUCT SECTION — CLOTHING: Socks

Laurenceleste Inc................................G....... 708 383-3432
  Oak Park (G-15762)
Little Journeys Limited.....................G....... 847 677-0350
  Skokie (G-18980)
Slick Sugar Inc...................................G....... 815 782-7101
  Plainfield (G-16714)

CLOTHING: Clergy Vestments

American Church Supply ....G....... 847 464-4140
  Saint Charles (G-18145)

CLOTHING: Coats & Suits, Men's & Boys'

Demoulin Brothers & Company............C....... 618 664-2000
  Greenville (G-10832)
W Diamond Group Corporation............A....... 646 647-2790
  Des Plaines (G-7866)

CLOTHING: Coats, Overcoats & Vests

Pro-Pak Industries Inc........................F....... 630 876-1050
  West Chicago (G-20633)

CLOTHING: Cold Weather Knit Outerwear, Including Ski Wear

Five Brother Inc.................................G....... 309 663-6323
  Bloomington (G-2043)

CLOTHING: Collar & Cuff Sets, Knit

Bird Dog Bay Inc................................G....... 312 631-3108
  Chicago (G-3899)

CLOTHING: Costumes

Andy Dallas & Co................................F....... 217 351-5974
  Champaign (G-3265)
Learning Curve International..............E....... 630 573-7200
  Oak Brook (G-15632)
Orr Marketing Corp ....F....... 847 401-5171
  Elgin (G-8680)
Sunnywood Incorporated...................G....... 815 675-9777
  McHenry (G-13799)

CLOTHING: Disposable

Jero Medical Eqp & Sups Inc..............E....... 773 305-4193
  Chicago (G-5022)
Luna Medical Inc................................F....... 800 380-4339
  Chicago (G-5286)
Taitt Burial Garments..........................F....... 773 483-7424
  Chicago (G-6312)

CLOTHING: Dresses

Caroline Rose Inc...............................G....... 708 386-1011
  Oak Park (G-15748)
G-III Apparel Group Ltd ....C....... 630 236-8900
  Aurora (G-966)
Runway Liquidation LLC ....G....... 574 247-1500
  Northbrook (G-15476)
Salmons and Brown ....G....... 312 929-6756
  Chicago (G-6095)
Yolanda Lorente Ltd ....E....... 773 334-4536
  Chicago (G-6703)

CLOTHING: Garments, Indl, Men's & Boys

Apparel Works Intl LLC ....G....... 847 778-9559
  Lake Bluff (G-12171)
Rubin Nsa Bros LLC ....G....... 312 942-1111
  Chicago (G-6078)

CLOTHING: Gowns & Dresses, Wedding

Alyce Designs Inc ....E....... 847 966-6933
  Morton Grove (G-14389)
Casa Di Castronovo Inc......................G....... 815 962-4731
  Rockford (G-17338)
Halanick Enterprises Inc ....E....... 708 403-3334
  Orland Park (G-15958)
Igar Bridal Inc ....G....... 224 318-2337
  Arlington Heights (G-754)
Jane Stodden Bridals ....G....... 815 223-2091
  La Salle (G-12116)

CLOTHING: Gowns, Plastic

Polyconversions Inc ....E....... 217 893-3330
  Champaign (G-3335)

CLOTHING: Hats & Caps, NEC

American Needle Inc..........................E....... 847 215-0011
  Buffalo Grove (G-2511)
Hats For You ....G....... 773 481-1611
  Chicago (G-4785)
Lids Corporation ....G....... 708 873-9606
  Orland Park (G-15965)
Miglio Di Mario Uomo Inc..................G....... 312 391-0831
  Chicago (G-5454)

CLOTHING: Hats & Caps, Police

Midway Cap Company ....E....... 773 384-0911
  Chicago (G-5436)

CLOTHING: Hats & Caps, Uniform

Midway Cap Company ....E....... 773 384-0911
  Chicago (G-5437)
New ERA Cap Co Inc ....B....... 504 581-2445
  Chicago (G-5577)

CLOTHING: Hats & Headwear, Knit

A&B Apparel ....G....... 815 962-5070
  Rockford (G-17281)
Waters Industries Inc.........................E....... 847 783-5900
  West Dundee (G-20667)

CLOTHING: Hats, Silk

Jenny Capp Co....................................F....... 773 217-0057
  Chicago (G-5018)

CLOTHING: Hosiery, Pantyhose & Knee Length, Sheer

Bee Sales Company.............................D....... 847 600-4400
  Niles (G-15106)

CLOTHING: Hospital, Men's

Cintas Corporation ....D....... 708 563-2626
  Chicago (G-4151)
Iguanamed LLC ....G....... 312 546-4182
  Chicago (G-4881)
Most Enterprise Inc............................D....... 800 792-4669
  Chicago (G-5504)
Silk Road Logistics Co ....G....... 773 432-5619
  Mount Prospect (G-14570)

CLOTHING: Housecoats, Mens & Womens, From Purchased Mtrls

Universal Mfg Corporation..................C....... 630 613-7340
  Oakbrook Terrace (G-15817)

CLOTHING: Jackets, Field, Military

Vertex International Inc ....G....... 312 242-1864
  Oak Brook (G-15669)

CLOTHING: Jackets, Tailored Men's & Boys'

Signature Design & Tailoring..............F....... 773 375-4915
  Chicago (G-6168)

CLOTHING: Jeans, Men's & Boys'

Guess Inc...E....... 312 440-9592
  Chicago (G-4749)

CLOTHING: Jerseys, Knit

Russell Brands LLC ....D....... 309 454-6737
  Normal (G-15223)

CLOTHING: Leather & sheep-lined clothing

Keleen Leathers Inc...........................F....... 630 590-5300
  Westmont (G-20753)

CLOTHING: Maternity

Golda Inc..C....... 217 895-3502
  Neoga (G-15017)

CLOTHING: Men's & boy's clothing, nec

Sansabelt...G....... 312 357-5119
  Chicago (G-6101)

CLOTHING: Neckwear

Amazing Mascots................................G....... 727 475-0255
  Chicago (G-3643)
Backyard Bucket Co............................G....... 773 771-0743
  Chicago (G-3813)
Jerjerb LLC ....G....... 917 415-3319
  Chicago (G-5020)
Shertwinz Inc.....................................G....... 630 886-5681
  Naperville (G-14914)

CLOTHING: Outerwear, Knit

Heartfelt Gifts Inc..............................G....... 309 852-2296
  Kewanee (G-12039)

CLOTHING: Outerwear, Women's & Misses' NEC

Anart Inc ....E....... 708 447-0225
  Riverside (G-17080)
Chicago Knitting Mills ....G....... 773 463-1464
  Northbrook (G-15358)
Cintas Corporation ....D....... 708 563-2626
  Chicago (G-4151)
Cloz Companies Inc ....G....... 773 247-8879
  Skokie (G-18944)
Demoulin Brothers & Company............C....... 618 664-2000
  Greenville (G-10832)
Fashahnn Corporation ....G....... 773 994-3132
  Chicago (G-4561)
Gennco International Inc ....F....... 847 541-3333
  Northbrook (G-15393)
James Rosenbaum Co ....G....... 847 859-7660
  Evanston (G-9541)
Marena Marena Two Inc.....................G....... 773 327-0619
  Chicago (G-5331)
Paul Sisti ....G....... 773 472-5615
  Chicago (G-5772)
Yolanda Lorente Ltd ....E....... 773 334-4536
  Chicago (G-6703)

CLOTHING: Robes & Dressing Gowns

Halanick Enterprises Inc ....E....... 708 403-3334
  Orland Park (G-15958)
Herff Jones LLC ....C....... 317 612-3705
  Hillside (G-11341)
Maries Custom Made Choir Robes........G....... 773 826-1214
  Chicago (G-5336)

CLOTHING: Scarves, Men's & Boys'

Trafalgar Company LLC ....G....... 847 292-8300
  Rosemont (G-18054)

CLOTHING: Service Apparel, Women's

Woolenwear Co ....F....... 847 520-9243
  Prospect Heights (G-16848)

CLOTHING: Shirts

Perry Ellis International Inc.................G....... 847 678-7108
  Rosemont (G-18040)
Riddle McIntyre Inc ....G....... 312 782-3317
  Chicago (G-6030)
Salmons and Brown ....G....... 312 929-6756
  Chicago (G-6095)

CLOTHING: Shirts & T-Shirts, Knit

Top Ace Inc ....G....... 847 581-0550
  Morton Grove (G-14445)

CLOTHING: Shirts, Dress, Men's & Boys'

Pvh Corp..F....... 217 253-3398
  Tuscola (G-19929)

CLOTHING: Shirts, Sports & Polo, Men's & Boys'

Drywear Apparel LLC ....G....... 847 687-8540
  Kildeer (G-12046)

CLOTHING: Socks

Bee Sales Company.............................D....... 847 600-4400
  Niles (G-15106)
Emeelys Socks and More....................G....... 847 529-3026
  Chicago (G-4493)
Living Royal ....F....... 312 906-7600
  Wheeling (G-20933)

CLOTHING: Socks

Living Royal Inc .... E 312 906-7600
  Wheeling *(G-20934)*
Midwest Socks LLC .... G 773 283-3952
  Chicago *(G-5447)*
Quincy Socks House .... G 217 506-6106
  Quincy *(G-16935)*
Sock Obsessed .... G 847 920-4834
  Chicago *(G-6196)*
Soy City Sock Co Inc .... F 217 762-2157
  Monticello *(G-14287)*
Zzzsock Inc .... G 224 330-7364
  Mount Prospect *(G-14586)*

CLOTHING: Sportswear, Women's

Caroline Rose Inc .... G 708 386-1011
  Oak Park *(G-15748)*
Laqueus Inc .... F 773 508-1993
  Chicago *(G-5176)*

CLOTHING: Suits, Men's & Boys', From Purchased Materials

Mancillas International Ltd .... F 847 441-7748
  Winnetka *(G-21132)*
Oxxford Clothes Xx Inc .... C 312 829-3600
  Chicago *(G-5723)*

CLOTHING: Sweaters & Sweater Coats, Knit

Chicago Knitting Mills .... G 773 463-1464
  Northbrook *(G-15358)*
Sue Peterson .... G 847 730-3035
  Glenview *(G-10628)*

CLOTHING: Sweaters, Men's & Boys'

Miglio Di Mario Uomo Inc .... G 312 391-0831
  Chicago *(G-5454)*

CLOTHING: T-Shirts & Tops, Knit

Csi Chicago Inc .... G 773 665-2226
  Chicago *(G-4280)*
Derbyteescom .... G 309 264-1033
  Henry *(G-11162)*
M & G Simplicitees .... G 224 372-7426
  Lake Villa *(G-12359)*
Main Street Records .... G 618 244-2737
  Mount Vernon *(G-14623)*
Mr T Shirt and Dollar Plus .... G 708 596-9150
  Harvey *(G-11093)*
NRR Corp .... F 630 915-8388
  Oak Brook *(G-15651)*

CLOTHING: T-Shirts & Tops, Women's & Girls'

Forever Fly LLC .... G 312 981-9161
  Chicago *(G-4619)*

CLOTHING: Ties, Neck, Men's & Boys', From Purchased Material

Corporate Textiles Inc .... G 847 433-4111
  Lincolnwood *(G-12815)*

CLOTHING: Trousers & Slacks, Men's & Boys'

Kanan Fashions Inc .... E 630 240-1234
  Oak Brook *(G-15629)*
Oxxford Clothes Xx Inc .... C 312 829-3600
  Chicago *(G-5723)*

CLOTHING: Underwear, Women's & Children's

Victorias Secret Stores LLC .... G 312 583-0488
  Chicago *(G-6547)*

CLOTHING: Uniforms & Vestments

Midwest Pub Safety Outfitters .... F 866 985-0013
  Poplar Grove *(G-16782)*

CLOTHING: Uniforms, Ex Athletic, Women's, Misses' & Juniors'

Advance Uniform Company .... F 312 922-1797
  Chicago *(G-3559)*

Advantex Inc of Illinois .... D 618 505-0701
  Troy *(G-19910)*
Atlas Uniform Company .... G 312 492-8527
  Chicago *(G-3769)*
Choi Brands Inc .... C 773 489-2800
  Chicago *(G-4142)*
Cintas Corporation .... D 708 563-2626
  Chicago *(G-4151)*
Cintas Corporation No 2 .... G 708 424-4747
  Oak Lawn *(G-15709)*
Iguanamed LLC .... G 312 546-4182
  Chicago *(G-4881)*

CLOTHING: Uniforms, Military, Men/Youth, Purchased Materials

Vertex International Inc .... G 312 242-1864
  Oak Brook *(G-15669)*

CLOTHING: Uniforms, Policemen's, From Purchased Materials

J G Uniforms Inc .... G 773 545-4644
  Chicago *(G-4990)*

CLOTHING: Uniforms, Team Athletic

Athletic Sewing Mfg Co .... E 773 589-0361
  Chicago *(G-3759)*
Curt Smith Sporting Goods Inc .... E 618 233-5177
  Belleville *(G-1541)*
Exclusive Pro Sports Ltd .... E 815 877-8585
  Rockford *(G-17409)*

CLOTHING: Uniforms, Work

Advance Uniform Company .... F 312 922-1797
  Chicago *(G-3559)*
Atlas Uniform Company .... G 312 492-8527
  Chicago *(G-3769)*
Choi Brands Inc .... C 773 489-2800
  Chicago *(G-4142)*
High Performance Entp Inc .... E 773 283-1778
  Chicago *(G-4816)*

CLOTHING: Warm Weather Knit Outerwear, Including Beachwear

Creative Clothing Created 4 U .... G 847 543-0051
  Grayslake *(G-10764)*

CLOTHING: WarmUp, Jogging & Sweat Suits, Girls' & Children's

Trim Suits By Show-Off Inc .... G 630 894-0100
  Roselle *(G-17994)*

CLOTHING: Waterproof Outerwear

Boss Holdings Inc .... D 309 852-2131
  Kewanee *(G-12023)*
Boss Manufacturing Holdings .... F 309 852-2781
  Kewanee *(G-12025)*

CLOTHING: Work, Men's

Ai Ind .... E 773 265-6640
  Chicago *(G-3586)*
Demoulin Brothers & Company .... C 618 664-2000
  Greenville *(G-10832)*
Hot Topic Inc .... G 708 453-1216
  Norridge *(G-15236)*
Magid Glove Safety Mfg Co LLC .... B 773 384-2070
  Romeoville *(G-17844)*
Mennon Rbr & Safety Pdts Inc .... G 847 678-8250
  Schiller Park *(G-18823)*
Mighty Mites Awards and Sons .... G 847 297-0035
  Des Plaines *(G-7802)*
Standard Safety Equipment Co .... E 815 363-8565
  McHenry *(G-13795)*
Universal Overall Company .... E 312 226-3336
  Chicago *(G-6482)*

CLUTCHES OR BRAKES: Electromagnetic

Rimtec Corporation .... F 630 628-0036
  Addison *(G-275)*

CLUTCHES, EXC VEHICULAR

Dyneer Corporation .... B 217 228-6011
  Quincy *(G-16877)*

Marland Clutch .... G 800 216-3515
  South Beloit *(G-19098)*
Ringspann Corporation .... F 847 678-3581
  Franklin Park *(G-10036)*

COAL MINING EXPLORATION & TEST BORING SVC

Freeman United Coal Mining Co .... E 217 698-3300
  Springfield *(G-19371)*
Keyrock Energy LLC .... E 618 982-9710
  Thompsonville *(G-19778)*

COAL MINING SERVICES

Cobra Coal Inc .... E 630 560-1050
  West Chicago *(G-20565)*
Exxon Mobil Corporation .... B 217 854-3291
  Carlinville *(G-2875)*
Fjcj LLC .... F 618 785-2217
  Baldwin *(G-1184)*
Freeman Energy Corporation .... F 217 698-3949
  Springfield *(G-19370)*
Freeman United Coal Mining Co .... C 217 627-2161
  Girard *(G-10381)*
Hamilton County Coal LLC .... B 618 648-2603
  Dahlgren *(G-7307)*
Icg Illinois .... G 217 947-2332
  Elkhart *(G-9318)*
Icg Illinois LLC .... C 217 566-3000
  Williamsville *(G-21023)*
Knight Hawk Coal LLC .... G 618 426-3662
  Percy *(G-16559)*
Knight Hawk Coal LLC .... C 618 497-2768
  Cutler *(G-7304)*
Mach Mining LLC .... G 618 983-3020
  Marion *(G-13520)*
Macoupin Energy LLC .... F 217 854-3291
  Carlinville *(G-2880)*
Macoupin Energy LLC .... G 217 854-3291
  Carlinville *(G-2881)*
Springfield Coal Company LLC .... E 217 698-3300
  Springfield *(G-19451)*
Suncoke Energy Inc .... C 630 824-1000
  Lisle *(G-12945)*
Surface Mining Reclamation Off .... E 618 463-6460
  Alton *(G-573)*
White Oak Resources LLC .... A 618 643-5500
  Dahlgren *(G-7310)*
Wildcat Hills 618 273-8600
  Eldorado *(G-8486)*

COAL MINING SVCS: Anthracite, Contract Basis

Seneca Rebuild LLC .... F 618 435-9445
  Macedonia *(G-13317)*

COAL MINING: Anthracite, Underground

Fabick Mining LLC .... F 618 982-9000
  Norris City *(G-15249)*

COAL MINING: Bituminous & Lignite Surface

Hillsboro Energy LLC .... G 217 532-7310
  Hillsboro *(G-11315)*

COAL MINING: Bituminous Coal & Lignite-Surface Mining

Alpha Natural Resources Inc .... C 618 298-2394
  Keensburg *(G-12012)*
Arch Coal Inc .... F 217 566-3000
  Williamsville *(G-21022)*
Hnrc Dissolution Co .... C 618 758-4501
  Coulterville *(G-7032)*
Keller Group Inc .... B 847 446-7550
  Northfield *(G-15520)*
Peabody Coal Company .... C 618 758-2395
  Coulterville *(G-7033)*
Peabody Coulterville Min LLC .... G 618 758-3597
  Coulterville *(G-7034)*
Peabody Energy Corporation .... G 314 342-3400
  Equality *(G-9470)*
Peabody Midwest Mining LLC .... C 618 276-5006
  Equality *(G-9471)*
Standard Laboratories Inc .... E 618 539-5836
  Freeburg *(G-10095)*
Sun Coke International Inc .... D 630 824-1000
  Lisle *(G-12944)*

PRODUCT SECTION

COATINGS: Epoxy

White County Coal LLC ....D 618 382-4651
 Carmi *(G-2919)*

COAL MINING: Bituminous Underground

Alpha Natural Resources Inc ....C 618 298-2394
 Keensburg *(G-12012)*
American Coal Company ....G 618 268-6311
 Galatia *(G-10161)*
Exxon Mobil Corporation ....B 217 854-3291
 Carlinville *(G-2875)*
Gateway North Mine ....G 618 758-1515
 Coulterville *(G-7031)*
Illinois Fuel Company LLC ....D 618 275-4486
 Herod *(G-11170)*
Jewell Resources Corporation ....G 276 935-8810
 Lisle *(G-12903)*
Keller Group Inc ....B 847 446-7550
 Northfield *(G-15520)*
Knight Hawk Coal LLC ....G 618 426-3662
 Percy *(G-16559)*
Mid-America Carbonates LLC ....D 618 944-6171
 Cave In Rock *(G-3220)*
Sun Coke International Inc ....D 630 824-1000
 Lisle *(G-12944)*

COAL MINING: Bituminous, Strip

Illinois Fuel Company LLC ....D 618 275-4486
 Herod *(G-11170)*
Jader Fuel Co Inc ....G 618 269-3101
 Shawneetown *(G-18875)*

COAL, MINERALS & ORES, WHOLESALE: Copper Ore

American Coal Company ....G 618 268-6311
 Galatia *(G-10161)*

COATED OR PLATED PRDTS

Cobraa Inc ....G 618 228-7380
 Aviston *(G-1178)*

COATERS: High Vacuum, Metal Plate

Starfire Industries LLC ....E 217 721-4165
 Champaign *(G-3356)*

COATING COMPOUNDS: Tar

American Grinders Inc ....G 815 943-4902
 Harvard *(G-11045)*
Brewer Company ....F 708 339-9000
 Harvey *(G-11080)*
Emulsicoat Inc ....F 217 344-7775
 Urbana *(G-19981)*
Sales Stretcher Enterprises ....F 815 223-9681
 Peru *(G-16593)*

COATING SVC

Aggressive Motorsports Inc ....G 847 846-7488
 Batavia *(G-1343)*
Ambrotos Inc ....G 815 355-8217
 Crystal Lake *(G-7159)*
Ecosystem Protective Coatings ......G 815 725-6343
 Joliet *(G-11858)*
Legend Dynamix Inc ....G 847 789-7007
 Antioch *(G-622)*
Midwest Nameplate Corp ....G 708 614-0606
 Orland Park *(G-15968)*
Sc2 Inc ....G 309 677-5980
 East Peoria *(G-8289)*

COATING SVC: Aluminum, Metal Prdts

Finishing Company ....C 630 559-0808
 Addison *(G-122)*
Marie Gere Corporation ....C 847 540-1154
 Lake Zurich *(G-12430)*
Micron Metal Finishing LLC ....G 708 599-0055
 Bridgeview *(G-2364)*
Voges Inc ....D 618 233-2760
 Belleville *(G-1608)*

COATING SVC: Hot Dip, Metals Or Formed Prdts

AAA Galvanizing - Joliet Inc ....E 815 284-5001
 Dixon *(G-7887)*
AAA Galvanizing - Joliet Inc ....D 815 723-5000
 Joliet *(G-11816)*

COATING SVC: Metals & Formed Prdts

AAA Galvanizing - Peoria Inc ....E 309 697-4100
 Peoria *(G-16373)*
Accent Metal Finishing Inc ....F 847 678-7420
 Schiller Park *(G-18782)*
Accurate Finishers ....G 630 543-8575
 Addison *(G-16)*
Advance Enameling Co ....E 773 737-7356
 Chicago *(G-3554)*
Advanced Graphics Tech Inc ....C 817 481-8561
 Romeoville *(G-17788)*
Armoloy of Illinois Inc ....G 815 758-6657
 Dekalb *(G-7666)*
Bfw Coating ....G 847 639-2155
 Cary *(G-3150)*
BL Downey Company LLC ....D 708 345-8000
 Broadview *(G-2420)*
Casting Impregnators Inc ....F 847 455-1000
 Franklin Park *(G-9900)*
Cavero Coatings Company LLC .....G 630 616-2868
 Bensenville *(G-1763)*
Chem Processing Inc ....F 815 965-1037
 Rockford *(G-17347)*
Chem Processing Inc ....D 815 874-8118
 Rockford *(G-17346)*
Clad-Rex Steel LLC ....E 847 455-7373
 Franklin Park *(G-9909)*
Coating Methods Incorporated ....F 847 428-8800
 Carpentersville *(G-3098)*
Commercial Finishes Co Ltd ....E 847 981-9222
 Elk Grove Village *(G-8904)*
Core Finishing Inc ....E 630 521-9635
 Bensenville *(G-1776)*
Creative Powder Coating Inc ....G 815 260-3124
 Crest Hill *(G-7085)*
Curtis Metal Finishing Company ....D 815 633-6693
 Machesney Park *(G-13338)*
Czarnik Precision Grinding Mch .....G 708 229-9639
 Oak Lawn *(G-15711)*
Diamond Spray Painting Inc ....G 630 513-5600
 Saint Charles *(G-18183)*
Dover Industrial Chrome Inc ....G 773 478-2022
 Chicago *(G-4391)*
Downey Investments Inc ....B 708 345-8000
 Broadview *(G-2431)*
E & R Powder Coatings Inc ....G 773 523-9510
 Chicago *(G-4421)*
Enameled Steel and Sign Co ....E 773 481-2270
 Chicago *(G-4504)*
ICP Industrial Inc ....E 630 227-1692
 Itasca *(G-11668)*
ICP Industries LLC ....E 888 672-2123
 Itasca *(G-11669)*
Industrial Cstm Pwdr Cting Inc ....F 217 423-4272
 Decatur *(G-7506)*
J and J Prfrmce Powdr Coating .....G 309 376-4340
 Carlock *(G-2887)*
Jet Finishers Inc ....D 847 718-0501
 Addison *(G-160)*
Jjc Epoxy Inc ....G 630 231-5600
 West Chicago *(G-20604)*
Joseph Kristan ....G 847 731-3131
 Zion *(G-21518)*
Kobac ....G 847 520-6000
 Buffalo Grove *(G-2553)*
Kobelco Advnced Cting Amer Inc ..A 847 520-6000
 Buffalo Grove *(G-2554)*
Krueger and Company ....E 630 833-5650
 Elmhurst *(G-9389)*
Kvf-Quad Corporation ....E 563 529-1916
 East Moline *(G-8231)*
Lo-Ko Performance Coatings ....G 708 424-7863
 Oak Lawn *(G-15726)*
Metokote Corporation ....E 815 223-1190
 Peru *(G-16582)*
Midwest Coatings Inc ....G 815 717-8914
 Bolingbrook *(G-2214)*
Midwest Metal Coatings LLC ....E 618 451-2971
 Granite City *(G-10725)*
MSC Pre Finish Metals Egv Inc ......C 847 439-2210
 Elk Grove Village *(G-9137)*
Oerlikon Blzers Cating USA Inc ......F 630 208-0958
 Geneva *(G-10296)*
Oerlikon Blzers Cating USA Inc ......F 847 619-5541
 Schaumburg *(G-18656)*
Oerlikon Blzers Cating USA Inc ......E 847 695-5200
 Elgin *(G-8677)*
Omega Plating Inc ....F 708 389-5410
 Crestwood *(G-7123)*
Palapa Coatings Inc ....G 847 628-6360
 Elgin *(G-8684)*
Pioneer Powder Coatings LLC ....E 847 671-1100
 Franklin Park *(G-10019)*
Polaris Laser Laminations LLC ......E 630 444-0760
 West Chicago *(G-20630)*
Powder Coating Specialists ....G 708 387-8000
 Brookfield *(G-2490)*
Powers Paint Shop Inc ....G 815 338-3619
 Woodstock *(G-21422)*
Precoat Metals Corp ....D 618 451-0909
 Granite City *(G-10731)*
Progressive Coating Corp ....F 773 261-8900
 Chicago *(G-5900)*
Quality Coating Co ....E 815 875-3228
 Princeton *(G-16822)*
R & B Powder Coatings Inc ....E 773 247-8300
 Chicago *(G-5941)*
Rainbow Art Inc ....F 312 421-5600
 Chicago *(G-5965)*
Ro Pal Grinding Inc ....F 815 964-5894
 Rockford *(G-17580)*
S & B Finishing Co Inc ....D 773 533-0033
 Chicago *(G-6082)*
SKW Industries LLC ....F 773 261-8900
 Chicago *(G-6182)*
Speed Powder Coatings Inc ....G 630 549-0657
 West Chicago *(G-20646)*
Sub Source Inc ....E 815 968-7800
 Rockford *(G-17649)*
Thomson Steel Polishing Corp ....G 773 586-2345
 Chicago *(G-6370)*
Tiger Drylac USA Inc ....F 630 587-2918
 Saint Charles *(G-18289)*
Transco Products Inc ....D 312 427-2818
 Streator *(G-19631)*
Tru-Tone Finishing Inc ....E 630 543-5520
 Addison *(G-318)*
Valmont Coatings Inc ....G 847 455-0884
 Franklin Park *(G-10072)*
Vorteq Woodstock LLC ....E 815 338-6410
 Woodstock *(G-21445)*
Wear-Cote International Inc ....E 309 793-1250
 Rock Island *(G-17254)*
Zegers Inc ....F 708 474-7700
 Lansing *(G-12525)*

COATING SVC: Metals, With Plastic Or Resins

ABC Coating Company III Inc ....E 708 258-9633
 Manteno *(G-13443)*
Britt Industries Inc ....E 847 640-1177
 Arlington Heights *(G-710)*
Epscca ....E 815 568-3020
 Marengo *(G-13484)*
Jet Rack Corp ....E 773 586-2150
 Chicago *(G-5025)*
Metal Impregnating Corp ....G 630 543-3443
 Addison *(G-198)*

COATING SVC: Rust Preventative

Aqua Coat Inc ....G 815 209-0808
 Elgin *(G-8512)*
Superior Coatings Illinois LLC ....F 309 367-9625
 Metamora *(G-13969)*

COATING SVC: Silicon

D N D Coating ....G 309 379-3021
 Stanford *(G-19472)*

COATINGS: Air Curing

Magnum International Inc ....G 708 889-9999
 Lansing *(G-12507)*
Mid-Amrica Prtctive Ctings Inc ....G 630 628-4501
 Addison *(G-208)*
Universal Chem & Coatings Inc .....E 847 931-1700
 Elgin *(G-8769)*

COATINGS: Epoxy

Master Builders LLC ....G 847 249-4080
 Gurnee *(G-10895)*
Mla Franklin Park Inc ....F 847 451-0279
 Franklin Park *(G-10003)*
Neverstrip LLC ....G 708 588-9707
 Hinsdale *(G-11370)*

Employee Codes: A=Over 500 employees, B=251-500
C=101-250, D=51-100, E=20-50, F=10-19, G=3-9

COATINGS: Polyurethane

COATINGS: Polyurethane
- Agi Corp .... F 815 708-0502
  Loves Park *(G-13184)*
- International Paint LLC .... F 847 623-4200
  Waukegan *(G-20450)*
- Rock-Tred 2 LLC .... E 888 762-5873
  Waukegan *(G-20489)*

COCKTAIL LOUNGE
- Libertyville Brewing Company .... D 847 362-6688
  Libertyville *(G-12668)*
- Rumshine Distilling LLC .... G 217 446-6960
  Tilton *(G-19796)*

COFFEE SVCS
- Wolfart Maciej .... G 312 248-3575
  Chicago *(G-6663)*

COIL WINDING SVC
- Mid-America Taping Reeling Inc .... D 630 629-6646
  Glendale Heights *(G-10475)*
- Pillarhouse USA Inc .... F 847 593-9080
  Elk Grove Village *(G-9179)*

COILS & ROD: Extruded, Aluminum
- Peerless America Incorporated .... C 217 342-0400
  Effingham *(G-8418)*

COILS & TRANSFORMERS
- Arnold Engineering Co .... D 815 568-2000
  Marengo *(G-13479)*
- AT&T Corp .... F 312 602-4108
  Chicago *(G-3755)*
- Becker Specialty Corporation .... E 847 766-3555
  Elk Grove Village *(G-8860)*
- Blocksmoy Inc .... F 847 260-9070
  Franklin Park *(G-9889)*
- Charles Industries LLC .... D 217 826-2318
  Marshall *(G-13566)*
- Coilform Company .... E 630 232-8000
  Geneva *(G-10262)*
- Eis .... G 630 530-7500
  Elmhurst *(G-9359)*
- Forest Electric Company .... E 708 681-0180
  Melrose Park *(G-13868)*
- Magnetic Devices Inc .... G 815 459-0077
  Crystal Lake *(G-7222)*
- Muntz Industries Inc .... E 847 949-8280
  Mundelein *(G-14718)*
- North Point Investments Inc .... E 312 977-4386
  Chicago *(G-5620)*
- Power House Tool Inc .... E 815 727-6301
  Joliet *(G-11915)*
- Qcircuits Inc .... E 618 662-8365
  Flora *(G-9690)*
- Qse Inc .... E 815 432-5281
  Watseka *(G-20315)*
- Sam Electronics Worldwide Inc .... F 847 290-1720
  Rolling Meadows *(G-17773)*
- Santucci Enterprises .... G 773 286-5629
  Chicago *(G-6102)*
- Sigmatron International Inc .... G 847 586-5200
  Elgin *(G-8730)*
- Sigmatron International Inc .... G 847 956-8000
  Elk Grove Village *(G-9238)*
- STC Inc .... E 618 643-2555
  Mc Leansboro *(G-13708)*
- Stryde Technologies Inc .... G 510 786-8890
  Chicago *(G-6255)*
- Taycorp Inc .... E 630 530-7500
  Elmhurst *(G-9433)*
- Taycorp Inc .... E 708 629-0921
  Alsip *(G-514)*
- Transformer Manufacturers Inc .... E 708 457-1200
  Norridge *(G-15245)*
- U S Co-Tronics Corp .... E 815 692-3204
  Fairbury *(G-9615)*
- V and F Transformer Corp .... D 630 497-8070
  Elgin *(G-8771)*
- Wattcore Inc .... G 571 482-6777
  Morton Grove *(G-14448)*

COILS: Electric Motors Or Generators
- Calumet Armature and Elc LLC .... E 708 841-6880
  Riverdale *(G-17070)*
- U S Co-Tronics Corp .... E 815 692-3204
  Fairbury *(G-9615)*

COILS: Pipe
- Integrated Mfg Tech LLC .... E 618 282-8306
  Red Bud *(G-16996)*

COIN-OPERATED LAUNDRY
- Lloyd M Hughes Enterprises Inc .... G 773 363-6331
  Chicago *(G-5245)*

COINS & TOKENS: Non-Currency
- Jing MEI Industrial USA Inc .... E 847 671-0800
  Rosemont *(G-18028)*

COKE OVEN PRDTS, NEC
- Suncoke Energy Partners LP .... G 630 824-1000
  Lisle *(G-12946)*

COKE OVEN PRDTS: Beehive
- Prairie Profile .... G 618 846-2116
  Vandalia *(G-20019)*

COKE: Petroleum
- Oxbow Carbon LLC .... E 630 257-7751
  Lemont *(G-12576)*
- Oxbow Midwest Calcining LLC .... D 630 257-7751
  Lemont *(G-12577)*

COLLECTION AGENCY, EXC REAL ESTATE
- Manufctrers Clring Hse Ill Inc .... G 773 545-6300
  Chicago *(G-5327)*
- Quadramed Corporation .... E 312 396-0700
  Chicago *(G-5926)*

COLLECTOR RINGS: Electric Motors Or Generators
- Fulling Motor USA Inc .... G 847 894-6238
  Park Ridge *(G-16277)*

COLLEGES, UNIVERSITIES & PROFESSIONAL SCHOOLS
- Tanaka Dental Enterprises Inc .... F 847 679-1610
  Skokie *(G-19042)*

COLOGNES
- Givaudan Fragrances Corp .... G 847 735-0221
  Lake Forest *(G-12250)*

COLOR LAKES OR TONERS
- Discount Computer Supply Inc .... G 847 883-8743
  Buffalo Grove *(G-2533)*

COLOR PIGMENTS
- Accel Corporation .... E 630 579-6961
  Batavia *(G-1340)*
- Cathay Industries (usa) Inc .... G 219 531-5359
  Bartlett *(G-1271)*
- Kasha Industries Inc .... E 618 375-2511
  Grayville *(G-10811)*
- Kasha Industries Inc .... F 618 375-2511
  Grayville *(G-10812)*

COLORS IN OIL, EXC ARTISTS'
- Finishing Company .... C 630 559-0808
  Addison *(G-122)*

COLORS: Pigments, Inorganic
- Chroma Color Corporation .... C 877 385-8777
  McHenry *(G-13726)*
- Chromium Industries Inc .... E 773 287-3716
  Chicago *(G-4145)*
- Colors For Plastics Inc .... D 847 437-0033
  Elk Grove Village *(G-8901)*
- Fortune International Tech LLC .... G 847 429-9791
  Hoffman Estates *(G-11425)*
- Plastics Color Corp Illinois .... D 708 868-3800
  Calumet City *(G-2787)*
- Polyone Corporation .... D 847 364-0011
  Elk Grove Village *(G-9183)*
- Prince Minerals LLC .... G 646 747-4222
  Quincy *(G-16926)*
- Prince Minerals LLC .... G 646 747-4200
  Quincy *(G-16927)*
- Rust-Oleum Corporation .... C 847 367-7700
  Vernon Hills *(G-20089)*
- Scientific Colors Inc .... C 815 741-1391
  Rockdale *(G-17273)*
- Solomon Colors Inc .... D 217 522-3112
  Springfield *(G-19449)*
- Southern Color Company Inc .... C 770 386-4766
  East Saint Louis *(G-8323)*
- Toyal America Inc .... G 630 505-2160
  Naperville *(G-14935)*
- Toyal America Inc .... G 630 505-2160
  Lockport *(G-13025)*
- Versatile Materials Inc .... G 773 924-3700
  Chicago *(G-6538)*

COLORS: Pigments, Organic
- Apex Colors .... G 219 764-3301
  Chicago *(G-3710)*
- General Press Colors Ltd .... E 630 543-7878
  Chicago *(G-4677)*
- HI Tech Colorants .... G 630 762-0368
  Saint Charles *(G-18206)*
- Nb Coatings Inc .... C 800 323-3224
  Lansing *(G-12510)*
- Rite Systems East Inc .... E 630 293-9174
  West Chicago *(G-20637)*
- Scientific Colors Inc .... C 815 741-1391
  Rockdale *(G-17273)*

COMBS, EXC HARD RUBBER
- Dometic Corporation .... A 847 447-7190
  Rosemont *(G-18019)*

COMMERCIAL & INDL SHELVING WHOLESALERS
- Djr Inc .... F 773 581-5204
  Chicago *(G-4372)*
- REB Steel Equipment Corp .... E 773 252-0400
  Chicago *(G-5987)*
- Rwi Holdings Inc .... G 630 897-6951
  Aurora *(G-1150)*

COMMERCIAL & OFFICE BUILDINGS RENOVATION & REPAIR
- Lamka Enterprises Inc .... G 630 659-5965
  Woodstock *(G-21402)*
- Pete Frcano Sons Cstm HM Bldrs .... F 847 258-4626
  Elk Grove Village *(G-9175)*
- Signa Development Group Inc .... G 773 418-4506
  Norridge *(G-15243)*

COMMERCIAL ART & GRAPHIC DESIGN SVCS
- Active Graphics Inc .... E 708 656-8900
  Cicero *(G-6827)*
- Aloha Document Services Inc .... E 312 542-1300
  Chicago *(G-3626)*
- Athena Design Group Inc .... E 312 733-2828
  Chicago *(G-3758)*
- Burgopak Limited .... E 312 255-0827
  Chicago *(G-3976)*
- Concept One Design Inc .... F 708 807-3111
  Naperville *(G-14804)*
- Custom Direct Inc .... F 630 529-1936
  Roselle *(G-17950)*
- Delta Press Inc .... E 847 671-3200
  Palatine *(G-16111)*
- Digital Prtg & Total Graphics .... G 630 627-7400
  Lombard *(G-13068)*
- Drawn LLC .... E 312 982-0040
  Chicago *(G-4397)*
- Dzro-Bans International Inc .... G 779 324-2740
  Homewood *(G-11492)*
- Expercolor Inc .... E 773 465-3400
  Skokie *(G-18953)*
- F Weber Printing Co Inc .... G 815 468-6152
  Manteno *(G-13447)*
- G T Services of Illionois Inc .... G 309 925-5111
  Tremont *(G-19896)*
- Greco Graphics Inc .... G 217 483-2877
  Glenarm *(G-10425)*

PRODUCT SECTION — COMMERCIAL PRINTING & NEWSPAPER PUBLISHING COMBINED

Haute Noir Media Group Inc .... G 312 869-4526
Chicago *(G-4787)*
Henderson Co Inc .... F 773 628-7216
Chicago *(G-4800)*
L P M Inc .... G 847 866-9777
Evanston *(G-9545)*
Lambert Print Source Llc .... G 630 708-0505
Yorkville *(G-21491)*
Linx Enterprises LLC .... G 224 409-2206
Chicago *(G-5232)*
M M Marketing .... G 815 459-7968
Wauconda *(G-20370)*
Mac Graphics Group Inc .... G 630 620-7200
Oakbrook Terrace *(G-15806)*
McGrath Press Inc .... E 815 356-5246
Crystal Lake *(G-7224)*
Media Unlimited Inc .... G 630 527-0900
Naperville *(G-14867)*
Motr Grafx LLC .... G 847 600-5656
Wheeling *(G-20942)*
P N K Ventures Inc .... G 630 527-0500
Naperville *(G-14891)*
Platts Printing Company .... G 309 228-1069
Farmington *(G-9663)*
Printed Word Inc .... G 847 328-1511
Evanston *(G-9570)*
Rite-TEC Communications .... G 815 459-7712
Crystal Lake *(G-7258)*
S G S Inc .... G 708 544-6061
Downers Grove *(G-8088)*
Shree Printing Corp .... G 773 267-9500
Chicago *(G-6160)*
Viking Awards Inc .... G 630 833-1733
Elmhurst *(G-9441)*

COMMERCIAL ART & ILLUSTRATION SVCS

Mc Adams Multigraphics Inc .... G 630 990-1707
Oak Brook *(G-15641)*
Morton Suggestion Company LLC ...... G 847 255-4770
Mount Prospect *(G-14549)*

COMMERCIAL CONTAINERS WHOLESALERS

Greif Inc .... E 630 753-1859
Naperville *(G-14836)*

COMMERCIAL EQPT WHOLESALERS, NEC

Equipsolutions LLC .... E 630 351-9070
Roselle *(G-17953)*
T J S Equipment Inc .... G 618 656-8046
Edwardsville *(G-8377)*
Tee Lee Popcorn Inc .... E 815 864-2363
Shannon *(G-18874)*

COMMERCIAL EQPT, WHOLESALE: Bakery Eqpt & Splys

Wilton Brands LLC .... B 630 963-7100
Naperville *(G-14948)*

COMMERCIAL EQPT, WHOLESALE: Coffee Brewing Eqpt & Splys

Classic Vending Inc .... E 773 252-7000
Chicago *(G-4171)*

COMMERCIAL EQPT, WHOLESALE: Comm Cooking & Food Svc Eqpt

Ja-T & Associates Inc .... F 773 744-2094
Chicago *(G-4996)*
Style Rite Restaurant Eqp Co .... G 630 628-0940
Addison *(G-296)*
Tri-State Food Equipment .... G 217 228-1550
Quincy *(G-16952)*
Wag Industries Inc .... F 847 329-8932
Skokie *(G-19053)*

COMMERCIAL EQPT, WHOLESALE: Display Eqpt, Exc Refrigerated

Creative Merchandising Systems .... G 847 955-9990
Lincolnshire *(G-12756)*
Exclusively Expo .... D 630 378-4600
Romeoville *(G-17818)*
Iretired LLC .... E 630 285-9500
Itasca *(G-11678)*
Marietta Corporation .... C 773 816-5137
Chicago *(G-5337)*
Richardson Electronics Ltd .... C 630 208-2278
Lafox *(G-12137)*

COMMERCIAL EQPT, WHOLESALE: Neon Signs

Neon Design Inc .... G 773 880-5020
Evanston *(G-9558)*
Signet Sign Company .... G 630 830-8242
Bartlett *(G-1313)*
Staar Bales Lestarge Inc .... G 618 259-6366
East Alton *(G-8171)*

COMMERCIAL EQPT, WHOLESALE: Restaurant, NEC

American Soda Ftn Exch Inc .... F 312 733-5000
Chicago *(G-3668)*
Balton Corporation .... F 773 933-7927
Chicago *(G-3822)*
Co-Rect Products Inc .... E 763 542-9200
Lincolnshire *(G-12751)*
Institutional Equipment Inc .... E 630 771-0990
Bolingbrook *(G-2192)*
NFC Company Inc .... G 773 472-6468
Chicago *(G-5594)*

COMMERCIAL EQPT, WHOLESALE: Scales, Exc Laboratory

Advanced Weighing Systems Inc .... G 630 916-6179
Addison *(G-22)*
Doran Scales Inc .... E 630 879-1200
Saint Charles *(G-18186)*
Fill-Weigh Inc .... G 815 254-4704
Plainfield *(G-16665)*
Florida Metrology LLC .... F 630 833-3800
Villa Park *(G-20147)*

COMMERCIAL EQPT, WHOLESALE: Store Fixtures & Display Eqpt

Advert Display Products Inc .... G 815 513-5432
Morris *(G-14290)*
Duo Usa Incorporated .... G 312 421-7755
Chicago *(G-4407)*
G D S Professional Bus Display .... E 309 829-3298
Bloomington *(G-2047)*
Monogram Creative Group Inc .... G 312 802-1433
Glenview *(G-10590)*
Prairie Display Chicago Inc .... F 630 834-8773
Elmhurst *(G-9411)*
Southern Imperial Inc .... C 815 877-7041
Rockford *(G-17637)*

COMMERCIAL LAUNDRY EQPT

Chicago Dryer Company .... C 773 235-4430
Chicago *(G-4101)*
Ellis Corporation .... D 630 250-9222
Itasca *(G-11648)*

COMMERCIAL PHOTOGRAPHIC STUDIO

Epic Eye .... G 309 210-6212
Grand Ridge *(G-10688)*
Wyckoff Advertising Inc .... G 630 260-2525
Wheaton *(G-20832)*

COMMERCIAL PRINTING & NEWSPAPER PUBLISHING COMBINED

Ada Holding Company Inc .... F 312 440-2897
Chicago *(G-3537)*
Amboy News .... G 815 857-2311
Amboy *(G-578)*
Bar Code Dr Inc .... G 815 547-1001
Cherry Valley *(G-3438)*
Belair Hd Studios LLC .... E 312 254-5188
Chicago *(G-3863)*
Belvidere Daily Republican Co .... E 815 547-0084
Belvidere *(G-1655)*
Benton Evening News Co .... G 618 438-5611
Benton *(G-1919)*
Best Newspapers In Ill Inc .... G 217 728-7381
Sullivan *(G-19661)*
Carroll County Review .... G 815 259-2131
Thomson *(G-19780)*
Central Ill Communications LLC .... F 217 753-2226
Springfield *(G-19345)*
Chicago Jewish News .... F 847 966-0606
Skokie *(G-18941)*
Cnhi LLC .... F 217 774-2161
Effingham *(G-8391)*
Cnlc-Stc Inc .... A 312 321-3000
Chicago *(G-4186)*
Daily Robinson News Inc .... E 618 544-2101
Robinson *(G-17111)*
De Boer & Associates .... G 630 972-1600
Bolingbrook *(G-2167)*
Gatehouse Media LLC .... D 585 598-0030
Oakbrook Terrace *(G-15799)*
Gatehuse Mdia Ill Hldngs II In .... B 217 788-1300
Springfield *(G-19374)*
Herald Newspapers Inc .... E 773 643-8533
Chicago *(G-4806)*
Highland News Leader .... G 618 654-2366
Highland *(G-11220)*
Joong-Ang Daily News .... E 847 228-7200
Rolling Meadows *(G-17743)*
Journal News .... G 217 532-3933
Hillsboro *(G-11317)*
Journal News .... G 217 324-6604
Litchfield *(G-12968)*
Jury Verdict Reporter .... G 312 644-7800
Chicago *(G-5061)*
Kankakee Daily Journal Co LLC .... C 815 937-3300
Kankakee *(G-11985)*
Korea Times Chicago Inc .... E 847 626-0388
Glenview *(G-10580)*
Lee Enterprises Incorporated .... F 309 829-9000
Bloomington *(G-2070)*
Lee Enterprises Incorporated .... G 618 998-8499
Marion *(G-13519)*
Mendota Reporter .... F 815 539-9396
Mendota *(G-13948)*
Nadig Newspapers Inc .... F 773 286-6100
Chicago *(G-5537)*
Nashville News .... F 618 327-3411
Nashville *(G-15005)*
News-Gazette Inc .... B 217 351-5252
Champaign *(G-3329)*
Nowuba LLC .... G 801 510-8086
Fox Lake *(G-9751)*
Ogle County Life .... G 815 732-2156
Oregon *(G-15925)*
Okawville Times .... G 618 243-5563
Okawville *(G-15846)*
Ottawa Publishing Co Inc .... G 815 433-2000
Ottawa *(G-16068)*
Ottawa Publishing Co Inc .... F 815 434-3330
Ottawa *(G-16069)*
Paddock Publications Inc .... B 847 427-4300
Arlington Heights *(G-786)*
Paddock Publications Inc .... C 847 427-5545
Schaumburg *(G-18662)*
Peoria Journal Star Inc .... C 309 686-3000
Peoria *(G-16493)*
Pioneer Newspapers Inc .... G 847 486-0600
Chicago *(G-5809)*
Progress Reporter Inc .... G 815 472-2000
Momence *(G-14190)*
Sun-Times Media Holdings LLC .... E 312 321-2299
Chicago *(G-6272)*
Tegna Inc .... C 847 490-6657
Hoffman Estates *(G-11468)*
The b F Shaw Printing Co .... E 815 875-4461
Princeton *(G-16823)*
The Times .... G 815 433-2000
Ottawa *(G-16081)*
Times Record Company .... E 309 582-5112
Aledo *(G-362)*
Times-Press Publishing Co .... E 815 673-3771
Streator *(G-19630)*
Trenton Sun .... G 618 224-9422
Trenton *(G-19905)*
Trx Pubco LLC .... G 312 222-9100
Chicago *(G-6442)*
Urdu Times .... G 773 274-3100
Chicago *(G-6496)*
Voice .... G 630 966-8642
Aurora *(G-1167)*
Wayne County Press Inc .... E 618 842-2662
Fairfield *(G-9640)*
West Suburban Journal .... G 708 344-5975
Bloomingdale *(G-2020)*
World Journal LLC .... F 312 842-8080
Chicago *(G-6675)*

Employee Codes: A=Over 500 employees, B=251-500
C=101-250, D=51-100, E=20-50, F=10-19, G=3-9

COMMERCIAL SECTOR REG, LICENSING & INSP, GOVT: Insurance

State of Illinois .... C 312 836-9500
  Chicago *(G-6235)*

COMMODITY CONTRACTS BROKERS, DEALERS

J and K Printing .... G 708 229-9558
  Oak Lawn *(G-15721)*

COMMON SAND MINING

Lafarge Aggregates III Inc .... G 847 742-6060
  South Elgin *(G-19162)*
Lafarge Aggregates III Inc .... G 630 365-3600
  Elburn *(G-8457)*
Material Service Corporation .... E 815 942-1830
  Romeoville *(G-17847)*
Reliable Sand and Gravel Co .... G 815 385-5020
  McHenry *(G-13787)*
Southfield Corporation .... G 217 379-3606
  Paxton *(G-16316)*

COMMUNICATIONS EQPT & SYSTEMS, NEC

Extentel Wrless Communications ..... G 847 809-3131
  Inverness *(G-11595)*
Lares Technologies LLC .... G 630 408-4368
  Oswego *(G-16010)*
Neovision Usa Inc .... F 847 533-0541
  Deer Park *(G-7582)*
Quality Service & Installation .... G 847 352-4000
  Schaumburg *(G-18693)*
Securecom Inc .... G 219 314-4537
  Lansing *(G-12515)*
Xomi Instruments Co Ltd .... G 847 660-4614
  Vernon Hills *(G-20113)*

COMMUNICATIONS EQPT WHOLESALERS

Data Comm For Business Inc .... F 217 897-1741
  Dewey *(G-7873)*
David Jeskey .... G 630 659-6337
  Saint Charles *(G-18180)*

COMMUNICATIONS EQPT: Microwave

Andrew International Svcs Corp ..... A 779 435-6000
  Joliet *(G-11823)*
Andrew New Zealand Inc .... E 708 873-3507
  Orland Park *(G-15940)*
Callpod Inc .... F 312 829-2680
  Chicago *(G-4007)*
Commscope Technologies LLC ..... B 779 435-6000
  Joliet *(G-11845)*

COMMUNICATIONS SVCS

Infinite Cnvrgnce Slutions Inc .... G 224 764-3400
  Arlington Heights *(G-758)*
Telcom Innovations Group LLC ..... E 630 350-0700
  Itasca *(G-11745)*
Valid Secure Solutions LLC .... F 260 633-0728
  Lisle *(G-12954)*

COMMUNICATIONS SVCS: Cellular

AT&T Teleholdings Inc .... F 800 288-2020
  Chicago *(G-3756)*
Driver Services .... G 505 267-8686
  Bensenville *(G-1789)*
Gogo LLC .... B 630 647-1400
  Chicago *(G-4711)*
Gogo LLC .... D 630 647-1400
  Bensenville *(G-1813)*
Motorola Mobility LLC .... B 847 523-5000
  Chicago *(G-5510)*
O & M Electronic Inc .... F 708 203-1947
  Oak Lawn *(G-15730)*
T-Mobile Usa Inc .... F 847 289-9988
  South Elgin *(G-19176)*
Tylu Wireless Technology LLC ..... G 312 260-7934
  Chicago *(G-6450)*

COMMUNICATIONS SVCS: Data

Gogo LLC .... B 630 647-1400
  Chicago *(G-4711)*

COMMUNICATIONS SVCS: Electronic Mail

H&R Block Inc .... F 847 566-5557
  Mundelein *(G-14694)*

COMMUNICATIONS SVCS: Facsimile Transmission

Fedex Office & Print Svcs Inc .... G 630 759-5784
  Bolingbrook *(G-2176)*

COMMUNICATIONS SVCS: Internet Connectivity Svcs

Businessmine LLC .... G 630 541-8480
  Lombard *(G-13049)*
Telcom Innovations Group LLC ..... E 630 350-0700
  Itasca *(G-11745)*
Vision I Systems .... G 312 326-9188
  Chicago *(G-6556)*

COMMUNICATIONS SVCS: Internet Host Svcs

Capital Merchant Solutions Inc ...... F 309 452-5990
  Bloomington *(G-2030)*
TWT Marketing Inc .... G 773 274-4470
  Chicago *(G-6449)*

COMMUNICATIONS SVCS: Online Svc Providers

Royer Systems Inc .... G 217 965-3699
  Virden *(G-20189)*
Websolutions Technology Inc .... E 630 375-6833
  Aurora *(G-1033)*
Yamada America Inc .... G 847 228-9063
  Arlington Heights *(G-838)*

COMMUNICATIONS SVCS: Proprietary Online Svcs Networks

Meshplusplus Inc .... G 847 494-6325
  Chicago *(G-5402)*

COMMUNICATIONS SVCS: Signal Enhancement Network Svcs

Csiteq LLC .... F 312 265-1509
  Rosemont *(G-18011)*
GBA Systems Integrators LLC ..... G 913 492-0400
  Moline *(G-14147)*
Hauhinco LP .... E 618 993-5399
  Marion *(G-13514)*
Quixote Corporation .... E 312 705-8400
  Chicago *(G-5939)*
Temco Japan Co Ltd .... G 847 359-3277
  South Barrington *(G-19078)*

COMMUNICATIONS SVCS: Telephone Or Video

Chicago Cardinal Communication ..... F 708 424-1446
  Oak Lawn *(G-15708)*

COMMUNICATIONS SVCS: Telephone, Local

AT&T Teleholdings Inc .... F 800 288-2020
  Chicago *(G-3756)*

COMMUNICATIONS SVCS: Telephone, Local & Long Distance

Zaptel Corporation .... G 847 386-8050
  Elk Grove Village *(G-9317)*

COMMUNITY DEVELOPMENT GROUPS

Kingspan Light & Air LLC .... G 847 816-1060
  Lake Forest *(G-12268)*
Mental Health Ctrs Centl Ill .... D 217 735-1413
  Lincoln *(G-12735)*

COMPACT LASER DISCS: Prerecorded

Cedille Chicago Nfp .... G 773 989-2515
  Chicago *(G-4052)*
Corporate Disk Company .... D 800 634-3475
  McHenry *(G-13730)*
Datasis Corporation .... F 847 427-0909
  Elk Grove Village *(G-8938)*

Delmark Records LLC .... G 773 539-5001
  Chicago *(G-4334)*
Tony Patterson .... G 773 487-4000
  Chicago *(G-6390)*

COMPACTORS: Trash & Garbage, Residential

Belson Outdoors LLC .... E 630 897-8489
  Naperville *(G-14778)*

COMPOST

Better Earth Premium Compost ..... G 309 697-0963
  Peoria *(G-16392)*
Green Earth Technologies Inc ..... G 847 991-0436
  Palatine *(G-16120)*
Green Organics Inc .... F 630 871-0108
  Carol Stream *(G-2995)*
Midwest Intgrted Companies LLC ..... C 847 426-6354
  Gilberts *(G-10361)*
Veteran Greens LLC .... G 773 599-9689
  Chicago *(G-6540)*

COMPRESSORS, AIR CONDITIONING: Wholesalers

A-L-L Equipment Company .... G 815 877-7000
  Loves Park *(G-13181)*
Bridgeport Air Comprsr & Tl Co ..... G 618 945-7163
  Bridgeport *(G-2310)*

COMPRESSORS: Air & Gas

Agro-Chem Inc .... F 309 475-8311
  Saybrook *(G-18418)*
Atlas Copco Compressors LLC ..... F 847 640-6067
  Elk Grove Village *(G-8845)*
Atlas Copco Compressors LLC ..... F 281 590-7500
  Chicago *(G-3762)*
Buell Manufacturing Company ..... G 708 447-6320
  Lyons *(G-13304)*
Corken Inc .... D 405 946-5576
  Lake Bluff *(G-12177)*
Cvp Systems LLC .... D 630 852-1190
  Elgin *(G-8561)*
Fluid-Aire Dynamics Inc .... F 847 678-8388
  Schaumburg *(G-18530)*
Gardner Denver Inc .... D 217 222-5400
  Quincy *(G-16884)*
Gardner Denver Inc .... D 815 875-3321
  Princeton *(G-16810)*
Gardner Denver Nash LLC .... F 331 457-5377
  Naperville *(G-14968)*
Harris Equipment Corporation ...... E 708 343-0866
  Melrose Park *(G-13878)*
Howe Corporation .... G 773 235-0200
  Chicago *(G-4851)*
Idex Corporation .... C 847 498-7070
  Lake Forest *(G-12265)*
Mat Industries LLC .... G 847 821-9630
  Long Grove *(G-13166)*
Nordson Corporation .... E 815 784-5025
  Genoa *(G-10320)*
Ohio Medical LLC .... G 847 855-0500
  Gurnee *(G-10907)*
Ortman-Mccain Co .... G 312 666-2244
  Bellwood *(G-1635)*
Rebuilders Enterprises Inc .... G 708 430-0030
  Bridgeview *(G-2380)*
Rietschle Inc 410 712-4100
  Quincy *(G-16941)*
Ryan Manufacturing Inc .... G 815 695-5310
  Newark *(G-15078)*
Scrollex Corporation .... G 630 887-8817
  Willowbrook *(G-21059)*
Standard Car Truck Company ..... D 630 860-5511
  Bensenville *(G-1899)*
Standard Lifts & Equipment Inc ..... G 414 444-1000
  Hanover Park *(G-11015)*
William W Meyer and Sons .... D 847 918-0111
  Libertyville *(G-12726)*

COMPRESSORS: Air & Gas, Including Vacuum Pumps

Allegion S&S Holding Co Inc .... C 815 875-3311
  Princeton *(G-16805)*
Bridgeport Air Comprsr & Tl Co ..... G 618 945-7163
  Bridgeport *(G-2310)*

PRODUCT SECTION

COMPUTER PERIPHERAL EQPT, NEC

Brock Equipment Company ..... E 815 459-4210
　Woodstock *(G-21367)*
Compressed Air Advisors Inc ..... G 877 247-2381
　Hillside *(G-11334)*
Mat Holdings Inc ..... D 847 821-9630
　Long Grove *(G-13165)*
Resolute Industrial LLC ..... D 800 537-9675
　Wheeling *(G-20974)*
Technology Assistance USA LLC ..... G 773 671-6712
　Chicago *(G-6334)*
Thomas Gardner Denver Inc ..... E 217 222-5400
　Quincy *(G-16947)*
Trane Technologies Company LLC ..... E 704 655-4000
　Chicago *(G-6406)*

COMPRESSORS: Refrigeration & Air Conditioning Eqpt

Buell Manufacturing Company ..... G 708 447-6320
　Lyons *(G-13304)*
Parks Industries LLC ..... F 618 997-9608
　Marion *(G-13524)*
York International Corporation ..... D 815 946-2351
　Polo *(G-16761)*

COMPRESSORS: Repairing

Compressed Air Advisors Inc ..... G 877 247-2381
　Hillside *(G-11334)*
Fluid-Aire Dynamics Inc ..... E 847 678-8388
　Schaumburg *(G-18530)*

COMPUTER & COMPUTER SOFTWARE STORES

Associate Computer Systems ..... G 618 997-3653
　Marion *(G-13505)*
Createasoft Inc ..... F 630 851-9474
　Aurora *(G-943)*
Derbytech Inc ..... E 309 755-2662
　East Moline *(G-8225)*
Friedrich Klatt and Associates ..... G 773 753-1806
　Chicago *(G-4636)*

COMPUTER & COMPUTER SOFTWARE STORES: Peripheral Eqpt

Ahead Inc ..... D 312 924-4492
　Chicago *(G-3584)*
Ahead Data Blue LLC ..... G 866 577-2902
　Chicago *(G-3585)*
Koi Computers Inc ..... G 630 627-8811
　Downers Grove *(G-8040)*
Laser Pro ..... G 847 742-1055
　Elgin *(G-8640)*
Proship Inc ..... G 312 332-7447
　Chicago *(G-5904)*

COMPUTER & COMPUTER SOFTWARE STORES: Personal Computers

Ep Technology Corporation USA ..... D 217 351-7888
　Champaign *(G-3290)*
Rf Ideas Inc ..... D 847 870-1723
　Rolling Meadows *(G-17771)*

COMPUTER & COMPUTER SOFTWARE STORES: Printers & Plotters

Cityblue Technologies LLC ..... F 309 550-5000
　Peoria *(G-16423)*
Digi Trax Corporation ..... E 847 613-2100
　Lincolnshire *(G-12759)*

COMPUTER & COMPUTER SOFTWARE STORES: Software & Access

Bantix Technologies LLC ..... G 630 446-0886
　Glen Ellyn *(G-10396)*
Bishop Engineering Company ..... F 630 305-9538
　Lisle *(G-12872)*
CDI Computers US Corporation ..... G 888 226-5727
　Chicago *(G-4048)*
Information Builders Inc ..... E 630 971-6700
　Schaumburg *(G-18558)*
Tegratecs Development Corp ..... G 847 397-0088
　Schaumburg *(G-18743)*

COMPUTER & COMPUTER SOFTWARE STORES: Software, Bus/Non-Game

David Corporation ..... E 781 587-3008
　Chicago *(G-4324)*
Precision Computer Methods ..... G 630 208-8000
　Elburn *(G-8469)*
Scientific Cmpt Assoc Corp ..... G 708 771-4567
　River Forest *(G-17056)*

COMPUTER & DATA PROCESSING EQPT REPAIR & MAINTENANCE

AR Inet Corp ..... G 603 380-3903
　Aurora *(G-913)*

COMPUTER & OFFICE MACHINE MAINTENANCE & REPAIR

Bc Asi Capital II Inc ..... A 708 534-5575
　University Park *(G-19948)*
Blue Gem Computers Inc ..... G 708 562-5524
　Morris *(G-14295)*
CDs Office Systems Inc ..... D 800 367-1508
　Springfield *(G-19343)*
Computer Svcs & Consulting Inc ..... E 855 482-2267
　Burr Ridge *(G-2666)*
Derbytech Inc ..... E 309 755-2662
　East Moline *(G-8225)*
Ibs Conversions Inc ..... D 630 571-9100
　Oak Brook *(G-15626)*
National Micro Systems Inc ..... E 312 566-0414
　Chicago *(G-5549)*
Pinehurst Bus Solutions Corp ..... G 630 842-6155
　Winfield *(G-21115)*
React Computer Services Inc ..... D 630 323-6200
　Willowbrook *(G-21058)*
Rico Computers Enterprises Inc ..... F 708 594-7426
　Chicago *(G-6029)*
Tech Upgraders ..... G 877 324-8940
　Maywood *(G-13678)*
Xerox Corporation ..... E 630 573-1000
　Hinsdale *(G-11383)*

COMPUTER & SFTWR STORE: Modem, Monitor, Terminal/Disk Drive

Integrity Technologies LLC ..... G 850 240-6089
　Elgin *(G-8628)*

COMPUTER DATA ESCROW SVCS

Secureslice Inc ..... E 800 984-0494
　Chicago *(G-6128)*

COMPUTER DISKETTES WHOLESALERS

Xlogotech Inc ..... G 888 244-5152
　Palatine *(G-16177)*

COMPUTER FORMS

Multi Packaging Solutions Inc ..... G 773 283-9500
　Chicago *(G-5523)*
Nbs Systems Inc ..... E 217 999-3472
　Mount Olive *(G-14507)*

COMPUTER GRAPHICS SVCS

Donnas House of Type Inc ..... G 217 522-5050
　Athens *(G-896)*
E-Intrctive Mktg Solutions Inc ..... G 312 241-1692
　Bridgeview *(G-2342)*
Fanning Communications Inc ..... G 708 293-1430
　Crestwood *(G-7118)*
Holsolutions Inc ..... G 888 847-5467
　Frankfort *(G-9801)*
Integrated Media Inc ..... F 217 854-6260
　Carlinville *(G-2877)*
Syndigo LLC ..... C 309 690-5231
　Peoria *(G-16532)*

COMPUTER INTERFACE EQPT: Indl Process

Creative Controls Systems Inc ..... G 815 629-2358
　Rockton *(G-17696)*
Emac Inc ..... E 618 529-4525
　Carbondale *(G-2841)*
Innovative Werks Inc ..... G 312 767-8618
　Naperville *(G-14848)*
Lake Electronics Inc ..... F 847 201-1270
　Volo *(G-20202)*
Sendele Wireless Solutions ..... G 815 227-4212
　Rockford *(G-17624)*
Sensor Synergy ..... G 847 353-8200
　Vernon Hills *(G-20097)*
Surya Electronics Inc ..... C 630 858-8000
　Glendale Heights *(G-10507)*

COMPUTER PERIPHERAL EQPT REPAIR & MAINTENANCE

Computer Maintenance Inc ..... G 630 953-1555
　Addison *(G-79)*
L P S Express Inc ..... G 217 636-7683
　Springfield *(G-19396)*
Midwest Laser Incorporated ..... G 708 974-0084
　Palos Hills *(G-16202)*

COMPUTER PERIPHERAL EQPT, NEC

Adazon Inc ..... G 847 235-2700
　Lake Forest *(G-12220)*
Ambir Technology Inc ..... G 630 530-5400
　Wood Dale *(G-21161)*
American Digital Corporation ..... E 847 637-4300
　Elk Grove Village *(G-8823)*
Andrew New Zealand Inc ..... E 708 873-3507
　Orland Park *(G-15940)*
Antares Computer Systems Inc ..... G 773 783-8855
　Chicago *(G-3704)*
Automated Systems & Control Co ..... G 847 735-8310
　Lake Bluff *(G-12172)*
Bigtime Fantasy Sports Inc ..... G 630 605-7544
　Lombard *(G-13043)*
Black Box Corporation ..... G 847 439-5000
　Elk Grove Village *(G-8868)*
Black Box Corporation ..... F 312 656-8807
　Tinley Park *(G-19812)*
Bycap Inc ..... E 773 561-4976
　Chicago *(G-3988)*
CDI Computers US Corporation ..... G 888 226-5727
　Chicago *(G-4048)*
CDs Office Systems Inc ..... D 800 367-1508
　Springfield *(G-19343)*
Cobius Halthcare Solutions LLC ..... G 847 656-8700
　Northbrook *(G-15363)*
Commscope Technologies LLC ..... B 779 435-6000
　Joliet *(G-11845)*
Computerprox ..... F 847 516-8560
　Elgin *(G-8548)*
Contemporary Ctrl Systems Inc ..... D 630 963-7070
　Downers Grove *(G-7980)*
Domino Amjet Inc ..... E 847 662-3148
　Gurnee *(G-10869)*
Domino Lasers Inc ..... E 847 855-1364
　Gurnee *(G-10872)*
Dover Corporation ..... C 630 541-1540
　Downers Grove *(G-7989)*
Election Systems & Sftwr LLC ..... F 815 397-8144
　Rockford *(G-17394)*
Epix Inc ..... G 847 465-1818
　Buffalo Grove *(G-2535)*
Gb Marketing Inc ..... F 847 367-0101
　Vernon Hills *(G-20055)*
Hoffman J&M Farm Holdings Inc ..... D 847 671-6280
　Schiller Park *(G-18813)*
Ig US Holdings Inc ..... G 312 884-0179
　Chicago *(G-4879)*
Illinois Tool Works Inc ..... D 618 997-1716
　Marion *(G-13518)*
Illinois Tool Works Inc ..... G 847 724-7500
　Des Plaines *(G-7784)*
Imageworks Manufacturing Inc ..... E 708 503-1122
　Park Forest *(G-16255)*
Micros Systems Inc ..... F 443 285-6000
　Itasca *(G-11702)*
Omex Technologies Inc ..... G 847 850-5858
　Wheeling *(G-20949)*
Omni Vision Inc ..... E 630 893-1720
　Glendale Heights *(G-10481)*
Paradise Group LLC ..... G 779 207-9077
　Chicago *(G-5757)*
Poynting Products Inc ..... G 708 386-2139
　Oak Park *(G-15769)*
Riverbed Technology Inc ..... G 217 344-8091
　Champaign *(G-3343)*
Source Software Inc ..... G 815 922-7717
　Lockport *(G-13024)*
Sparton Aydin LLC ..... G 800 772-7866
　Schaumburg *(G-18716)*
Tech Global Inc ..... F 847 532-4882
　Elgin *(G-8746)*

Employee Codes: A=Over 500 employees, B=251-500
C=101-250, D=51-100, E=20-50, F=10-19, G=3-9

2020 Harris Illinois Industrial Directory

COMPUTER PERIPHERAL EQPT, NEC

Teledyne Lecroy Inc .... E 847 888-0450
  Elgin *(G-8749)*
Timeout Devices Inc .... F 847 729-6543
  Glenview *(G-10632)*
Tomantron Inc .... F 708 532-2456
  Tinley Park *(G-19860)*
Trippe Manufacturing Company .... B 773 869-1111
  Chicago *(G-6429)*
United Universal Inds Inc .... E 815 727-4445
  Joliet *(G-11939)*
Verdasee Solutions Inc .... G 847 265-9441
  Gurnee *(G-10944)*
Xerox Corporation .... E 630 573-1000
  Hinsdale *(G-11383)*
Zebra Retail Solutions LLC .... G 847 634-6700
  Lincolnshire *(G-12803)*
Zebra Technologies Corporation ... D 847 793-5911
  Buffalo Grove *(G-2625)*
Zebra Technologies Corporation ... G 630 548-1370
  Naperville *(G-14993)*

COMPUTER PERIPHERAL EQPT, WHOLESALE

C M F Enterprises Inc .... F 847 526-9499
  Wauconda *(G-20337)*
M & S Technologies Inc .... F 847 763-0500
  Niles *(G-15142)*
Techgraphic Solutions Inc .... F 309 693-9400
  Peoria *(G-16536)*

COMPUTER PERIPHERAL EQPT: Graphic Displays, Exc Terminals

Bishop Image Group Inc .... G 312 735-8153
  Chicago *(G-3900)*
Corporate Graphics Inc .... G 630 762-9000
  Saint Charles *(G-18176)*

COMPUTER PERIPHERAL EQPT: Input Or Output

Oceancomm Incorporated 800 757-3266
  Chicago *(G-5653)*
Scadaware Inc .... F 309 665-0135
  Normal *(G-15224)*

COMPUTER PROCESSING SVCS

Mako Networks Sales & Mktg Inc ... D 847 752-5566
  Elgin *(G-8647)*

COMPUTER PROGRAMMING SVCS

Adept Coalescence LLC .... G 440 503-1808
  Rockford *(G-17295)*
Arxium Inc .... C 847 808-2600
  Buffalo Grove *(G-2513)*
Canon Solutions America Inc .... D 630 351-1227
  Itasca *(G-11633)*
Clutch Systems Inc .... G 815 282-7960
  Machesney Park *(G-13334)*
Creative Controls Systems Inc ..... G 815 629-2358
  Rockton *(G-17696)*
Cyborg Systems Inc .... C 312 279-7000
  Chicago *(G-4293)*
Drawn LLC .... E 312 982-0040
  Chicago *(G-4397)*
Information Builders Inc .... E 630 971-6700
  Schaumburg *(G-18558)*
Innovative Werks Inc .... G 312 767-8618
  Naperville *(G-14848)*
Lattice Incorporated .... E 630 949-3250
  Wheaton *(G-20811)*
Micrograms Inc .... G 815 877-4455
  Rockford *(G-17523)*
National Data Svcs Chicago Inc ... C 630 597-9100
  Carol Stream *(G-3038)*
Pagepath Technologies Inc .... F 630 689-4111
  Plano *(G-16738)*
Poynting Products Inc .... G 708 386-2139
  Oak Park *(G-15769)*
Process and Control Systems ...... F 708 293-0557
  Alsip *(G-498)*
Pycas Design Innovations LLC .... E 847 656-5000
  Glenview *(G-10604)*
Quadramed Corporation .... E 312 396-0700
  Chicago *(G-5926)*
React Computer Services Inc ...... D 630 323-6200
  Willowbrook *(G-21058)*
Reliefwatch Inc .... G 646 678-2336
  Chicago *(G-6011)*
Showcase Corporation .... C 312 651-3000
  Chicago *(G-6158)*
Systems Live Ltd .... G 815 455-3383
  Crystal Lake *(G-7273)*
Thomas A Doan .... G 847 864-8772
  Evanston *(G-9584)*
Thomson Quantitative Analytics ... E 847 610-0574
  Chicago *(G-6368)*
Uxm Studio Inc .... G 773 359-1333
  Villa Park *(G-20175)*
Val P Enterprises .... G 708 982-6561
  Chicago *(G-6518)*
Verdasee Solutions Inc .... G 847 265-9441
  Gurnee *(G-10944)*

COMPUTER PROGRAMMING SVCS: Custom

Abki Tech Service Inc .... F 847 818-8403
  Des Plaines *(G-7721)*
AR Inet Corp .... G 603 380-3903
  Aurora *(G-913)*
Manufacturing Tech Group Inc ..... G 815 966-2300
  Rockford *(G-17504)*

COMPUTER RELATED MAINTENANCE SVCS

7000 Inc .... F 312 800-3612
  Bolingbrook *(G-2143)*
Applus Technologies Inc .... E 312 661-1100
  Chicago *(G-3714)*
Officenation Inc .... E 847 504-3000
  Northfield *(G-15525)*
Palm International Inc .... G 630 357-1437
  Naperville *(G-14892)*
Pinehurst Bus Solutions Corp ...... G 630 842-6155
  Winfield *(G-21115)*

COMPUTER RELATED SVCS, NEC

Adept Coalescence LLC .... G 440 503-1808
  Rockford *(G-17295)*
Joliet Herald Newspaper .... E 815 280-4100
  Joliet *(G-11886)*

COMPUTER SERVICE BUREAU

Abki Tech Service Inc .... F 847 818-8403
  Des Plaines *(G-7721)*
Be Group Inc .... G 312 436-0301
  Chicago *(G-3848)*
Precision Reproductions Inc .... F 847 724-0182
  Glenview *(G-10602)*
W R Typesetting Co .... F 847 966-8327
  Morton Grove *(G-14447)*

COMPUTER SOFTWARE DEVELOPMENT

Access International Inc .... E 312 920-9366
  Chicago *(G-3514)*
Agile Health Technologies Inc ...... E 331 457-5167
  Naperville *(G-14952)*
Anylogic N Amer Ltd Lblty Co ...... F 312 635-3344
  Oakbrook Terrace *(G-15785)*
Applied Systems Inc .... A 708 534-5575
  University Park *(G-19946)*
Bc Asi Capital II Inc .... A 708 534-5575
  University Park *(G-19948)*
Bigtime Fantasy Sports Inc .... G 630 605-7544
  Lombard *(G-13043)*
Bytebin LLC .... G 312 286-0740
  Chicago *(G-3989)*
Catapult Communications Corp ... G 847 884-0048
  Schaumburg *(G-18468)*
CCH Incorporated .... A 847 267-7000
  Riverwoods *(G-17090)*
Chicago Data Solutions Inc .... G 847 370-4609
  Willowbrook *(G-21035)*
Computer Pwr Solutions III Ltd .... E 618 281-8898
  Columbia *(G-6988)*
Document Publishing Group .... E 847 783-0670
  Elgin *(G-8567)*
Flexera Holdings LP .... G 847 466-4000
  Itasca *(G-11659)*
Flexera Software LLC .... A 847 466-4000
  Itasca *(G-11660)*
High Tech Research Inc .... G 847 215-9797
  Deerfield *(G-7615)*
Idevconcepts Inc .... G 312 351-1615
  Chicago *(G-4877)*
Infosys Limited .... E 630 482-5000
  Lisle *(G-12901)*
Innolitica Labs LLC .... G 224 434-1238
  Chicago *(G-4928)*
Intelligrated Systems Inc .... B 630 985-4350
  Woodridge *(G-21315)*
Isoprime Corporation .... G 630 737-0963
  Lisle *(G-12902)*
J S Paluch Co Inc .... C 847 678-9300
  Franklin Park *(G-9969)*
Lemko Corporation .... E 630 948-3025
  Schaumburg *(G-18603)*
Logicgate Inc .... G 312 279-2775
  Chicago *(G-5250)*
Paulmar Industries Inc .... F 847 395-2520
  Antioch *(G-629)*
Prairie Wi-FI Systems .... G 515 988-3260
  Chicago *(G-5852)*
Premier Intl Entps Inc .... E 312 857-2200
  Chicago *(G-5862)*
Productive Edge LLC .... G 312 561-9000
  Chicago *(G-5895)*
Proship Inc .... G 312 332-7447
  Chicago *(G-5904)*
Screen North Amer Holdings Inc ... F 847 870-7400
  Rolling Meadows *(G-17774)*
Stenograph LLC .... G 630 532-5100
  Elmhurst *(G-9429)*
Structurepoint LLC .... G 847 966-4357
  Skokie *(G-19037)*
Tangent Systems Inc .... F 847 882-3833
  Hoffman Estates *(G-11466)*
Vertex Consulting Services Inc ... F 313 492-5154
  Schaumburg *(G-18771)*
Websolutions Technology Inc ...... E 630 375-6833
  Aurora *(G-1033)*

COMPUTER SOFTWARE DEVELOPMENT & APPLICATIONS

Active Simulations Inc .... G 630 747-8393
  Oak Park *(G-15740)*
Aeverie Inc .... G 844 238-3743
  Buffalo Grove *(G-2505)*
Applus Technologies Inc .... E 312 661-1100
  Chicago *(G-3714)*
Cognizant Tech Solutions Corp .... E 630 955-0617
  Lisle *(G-12877)*
Createasoft Inc .... F 630 851-9474
  Aurora *(G-943)*
Daniels Sharpsmart Inc .... E 312 546-8900
  Chicago *(G-4313)*
Digital H2o Inc .... F 847 456-8424
  Chicago *(G-4360)*
E & R Media LLC .... F 618 790-9376
  Du Quoin *(G-8119)*
E-Intrctive Mktg Solutions Inc ..... G 312 241-1692
  Bridgeview *(G-2342)*
Eighty Nine Robotics LLC .... G 512 573-9091
  Chicago *(G-4463)*
Endure Holdings Inc .... G 224 558-1828
  Bloomingdale *(G-1992)*
Follett School Solutions Inc .... C 815 759-1700
  McHenry *(G-13745)*
G2 Crowd Inc .... D 847 748-7559
  Chicago *(G-4652)*
Gatesair Inc .... C 800 622-0022
  Quincy *(G-16886)*
Hologram Inc .... G 716 771-8308
  Chicago *(G-4831)*
Jones Software Corp .... G 312 952-0011
  Chicago *(G-5047)*
Locusview Solutions Inc .... E 312 548-3848
  Chicago *(G-5248)*
Memorable Inc .... G 847 272-8207
  Northbrook *(G-15431)*
Mrb Roofing Inc .... G 872 814-4430
  University Park *(G-19963)*
Next Generation Inc .... G 312 739-0520
  Plainfield *(G-16695)*
Pintsch Tiefenbach Us Inc .... G 618 993-8513
  Marion *(G-13527)*
Professional RR Solutions LLC .... G 815 209-7473
  Roscoe *(G-17922)*
Proquis Inc .... F 847 278-3230
  Elgin *(G-8700)*
Psylotech Inc .... G 847 328-7100
  Evanston *(G-9572)*
Rico Computers Enterprises Inc ... F 708 594-7426
  Chicago *(G-6029)*
Scadaware Inc .... F 309 665-0135
  Normal *(G-15224)*

PRODUCT SECTION
COMPUTERS, PERIPHERALS & SOFTWARE, WHOLESALE: Software

Scholastic Testing Service..............F....... 630 766-7150
  Bensenville *(G-1891)*
Shoppertrak Rct Corporation..............F....... 312 529-5300
  Chicago *(G-6156)*
Synergy Technology Group Inc..............F....... 773 305-3500
  Chicago *(G-6303)*
Traena Inc..............G....... 630 605-3087
  Chicago *(G-6403)*
Trivaeo LLC..............G....... 760 505-4751
  Paris *(G-16245)*
Veloflip Inc..............G....... 847 757-4972
  Northfield *(G-15537)*

COMPUTER SOFTWARE SYSTEMS ANALYSIS & DESIGN: Custom

Ascent Innovations LLC..............E....... 847 572-8000
  Schaumburg *(G-18445)*
Bitsio Inc..............G....... 217 793-2827
  Springfield *(G-19327)*
Cloud 9 Infosystems Inc..............C....... 855 225-6839
  Downers Grove *(G-7974)*
Digi Trax Corporation..............E....... 847 613-2100
  Lincolnshire *(G-12759)*
Elemech Inc..............E....... 630 417-2845
  Aurora *(G-956)*
Emac Inc..............E....... 618 529-4525
  Carbondale *(G-2841)*
Entappia LLC..............G....... 630 546-4531
  Aurora *(G-957)*
Ferenbach Marucco Stoddard..............E....... 217 698-3535
  Springfield *(G-19366)*
Logical Design Solutions Inc..............G....... 630 786-5999
  Naperville *(G-14865)*
Optimus Advantage LLC..............G....... 847 905-1000
  Chicago *(G-5685)*
Orinoco Systems LLC..............F....... 630 510-0775
  Wheaton *(G-20814)*
Peak Computer Systems Inc..............F....... 618 398-5612
  Belleville *(G-1584)*
Phillip Grigalanz..............G....... 219 628-6706
  Jerseyville *(G-11795)*
Pinnakle Technologies Inc..............F....... 630 352-0070
  Aurora *(G-1009)*
Richardson Electronics Ltd..............C....... 630 208-2278
  Lafox *(G-12137)*
Secure Data Inc..............F....... 618 726-5225
  O Fallon *(G-15583)*
Softhaus Ltd..............G....... 618 463-1140
  Alton *(G-572)*
Tempus Labs Inc..............E....... 312 784-4400
  Chicago *(G-6347)*
Tryad Specialties Inc..............F....... 630 549-0079
  Saint Charles *(G-18292)*
Whospoppin Enterprises Inc..............G....... 312 912-8480
  Chicago *(G-6621)*

COMPUTER SOFTWARE WRITERS

Koombea Inc..............G....... 408 786-5290
  Chicago *(G-5123)*
Localfix Solutions LLC..............G....... 312 569-0619
  Winfield *(G-21112)*
Picis Clinical Solutions Inc..............F....... 847 993-2200
  Rosemont *(G-18042)*
Recsolu Inc..............E....... 312 517-3200
  Chicago *(G-5990)*
Western Printing Machinery Co..............E....... 847 678-1740
  Schiller Park *(G-18854)*
Western Printing Machinery Co..............E....... 847 678-1740
  Schiller Park *(G-18855)*

COMPUTER SOFTWARE WRITERS: Freelance

Imaging Systems Inc..............F....... 630 875-1100
  Itasca *(G-11674)*

COMPUTER STORAGE DEVICES, NEC

10th Magnitude LLC..............E....... 224 628-9047
  Chicago *(G-3461)*
Ally Global Corporation..............G....... 773 822-3573
  Chicago *(G-3625)*
Atmark Trading Inc..............E....... 312 933-7907
  Chicago *(G-3771)*
Context Software Systems..............G....... 630 654-0291
  Westmont *(G-20733)*
Das Brothers..............G....... 925 980-6180
  Frankfort *(G-9782)*
Dickson/Unigage Inc..............E....... 630 543-3747
  Addison *(G-92)*
E Mc..............G....... 217 228-1280
  Quincy *(G-16878)*
E N M Company..............D....... 773 775-8400
  Chicago *(G-4425)*
EMC Corporation..............E....... 312 577-0026
  Chicago *(G-4491)*
EMC Corporation..............E....... 312 577-0026
  Chicago *(G-4492)*
EMC Fire Inc..............G....... 480 225-5498
  Channahon *(G-3382)*
File System Labs LLC..............F....... 617 431-4313
  Northbrook *(G-15390)*
Guidance Software Inc..............G....... 847 994-7324
  Chicago *(G-4751)*
Illinoi Eye Surgns/Quantm Visn..............G....... 618 315-6560
  Mount Vernon *(G-14615)*
Interntional Cmpt Concepts Inc..............E....... 847 808-7789
  Northbrook *(G-15407)*
Omobono Inc..............G....... 312 523-2179
  Chicago *(G-5677)*
Pinehurst Bus Solutions Corp..............G....... 630 842-6155
  Winfield *(G-21115)*
Quantum Corporation..............D....... 312 372-2857
  Chicago *(G-5933)*
Quantum Healing..............G....... 217 414-2412
  Mechanicsburg *(G-13812)*
Quantum Marketing LLC..............G....... 630 257-7012
  Lemont *(G-12587)*
Quantum Vision Centers..............G....... 618 656-7774
  Swansea *(G-19695)*
Western Digital Tech Inc..............G....... 949 672-7000
  Chicago *(G-6608)*
Wevaultcom LLC..............G....... 877 938-2858
  Crystal Lake *(G-7295)*

COMPUTER STORAGE UNITS: Auxiliary

International Bus Mchs Corp..............C....... 312 423-6640
  Chicago *(G-4951)*

COMPUTER SYSTEM SELLING SVCS

Karimi Saifuddin..............G....... 630 943-8808
  Plainfield *(G-16678)*

COMPUTER SYSTEMS ANALYSIS & DESIGN

American Digital Corporation..............E....... 847 637-4300
  Elk Grove Village *(G-8823)*
Cronus Technologies Inc..............D....... 847 839-0088
  Schaumburg *(G-18496)*
Polysystems Inc..............D....... 312 332-2114
  Chicago *(G-5839)*
Precision Computer Methods..............G....... 630 208-8000
  Elburn *(G-8469)*

COMPUTER TERMINALS

Grayhill Inc..............G....... 708 482-1411
  Mc Cook *(G-13691)*
Honeywell International Inc..............C....... 815 745-2131
  Warren *(G-20223)*
Lightfoot Technologies Inc..............G....... 331 302-1297
  Naperville *(G-14864)*
Teledyne Lecroy Inc..............E....... 847 888-0450
  Elgin *(G-8749)*

COMPUTER TERMINALS: CRT

Kristel Limited Partnership..............D....... 630 443-1290
  Saint Charles *(G-18222)*

COMPUTER TIME-SHARING

Amoco Technology Company..............C....... 312 861-6000
  Chicago *(G-3682)*
Polysystems Inc..............D....... 312 332-2114
  Chicago *(G-5839)*

COMPUTER TRAINING SCHOOLS

Dmi Information Process Center..............E....... 773 378-2644
  Chicago *(G-4373)*

COMPUTER-AIDED DESIGN SYSTEMS SVCS

C Tri Co..............E....... 309 467-4715
  Eureka *(G-9477)*
Octane Motorsports LLC..............G....... 224 419-5460
  Waukegan *(G-20473)*

COMPUTERS, NEC

Accelerated Assemblies Inc..............E....... 630 616-6680
  Elk Grove Village *(G-8798)*
Ace Pcb Design Inc..............G....... 847 674-8745
  Skokie *(G-18912)*
Alegria Company..............C....... 608 726-2336
  Chicago *(G-3601)*
Fourier Systems Inc..............G....... 708 478-5333
  Homer Glen *(G-11481)*
General Dynmics Mssion Systems..............C....... 703 876-3000
  Chicago *(G-4670)*
Gld Industries Inc..............G....... 217 390-9594
  Champaign *(G-3296)*
High Power Inc..............F....... 773 581-7650
  Chicago *(G-4817)*
ICC Intrntonal Celsius Concept..............G....... 773 993-4405
  Cicero *(G-6853)*
Integrity Technologies LLC..............G....... 850 240-6089
  Elgin *(G-8628)*
Inverom Corporation..............G....... 630 568-5609
  Burr Ridge *(G-2690)*
Jets Computing Inc..............G....... 618 585-6676
  Bunker Hill *(G-2634)*
Js Poole Inc..............F....... 847 241-8441
  Chicago *(G-5057)*
Koi Computers Inc..............G....... 630 627-8811
  Downers Grove *(G-8040)*
Konica Minolta..............G....... 630 893-8238
  Roselle *(G-17962)*
Konica Mnlta Bus Sltons USA In..............E....... 309 671-1360
  Peoria *(G-16467)*
Motorola Solutions Inc..............G....... 847 341-3485
  Oak Brook *(G-15647)*
National Micro Systems Inc..............G....... 312 566-0414
  Chicago *(G-5549)*
Nazdar Sourceone..............G....... 800 677-4657
  Countryside *(G-7066)*
Northrop Grumman Systems Corp..............A....... 847 259-9600
  Rolling Meadows *(G-17755)*
Officenation Inc..............E....... 847 504-3000
  Northfield *(G-15525)*
Ogwuru Uzoaku..............G....... 312 286-5593
  Chicago *(G-5664)*
Perkins Enterprise Inc..............G....... 708 560-3837
  South Holland *(G-19240)*
Pinehurst Bus Solutions Corp..............G....... 630 842-6155
  Winfield *(G-21115)*
Pro-Parts..............G....... 773 595-5966
  Chicago *(G-5889)*
Rico Computers Enterprises Inc..............F....... 708 594-7426
  Chicago *(G-6029)*
RMC Imaging Inc..............G....... 815 885-4521
  Rockford *(G-17579)*
Royer Systems Inc..............G....... 217 965-3699
  Virden *(G-20189)*
Tech Global Inc..............G....... 224 623-2000
  Elgin *(G-8747)*
Texmac Inc..............G....... 630 244-4702
  Mundelein *(G-14743)*
W S C Inc..............G....... 312 372-1121
  Chicago *(G-6579)*

COMPUTERS, NEC, WHOLESALE

Computer Maintenance Inc..............G....... 630 953-1555
  Addison *(G-79)*
Decision Systems Company..............G....... 815 885-3000
  Roscoe *(G-17902)*
Derbytech Inc..............E....... 309 755-2662
  East Moline *(G-8225)*
Illinois Tool Works Inc..............E....... 708 720-0300
  Frankfort *(G-9807)*
Panatech Computer Management..............G....... 847 678-8848
  Lincolnshire *(G-12789)*

COMPUTERS, PERIPHERALS & SOFTWARE, WHOLESALE: Printers

3dp Unlimited LLC..............G....... 815 389-5667
  Roscoe *(G-17896)*
Next Day Toner Supplies Inc..............E....... 708 478-1000
  Orland Park *(G-15971)*

COMPUTERS, PERIPHERALS & SOFTWARE, WHOLESALE: Software

Blue Sky Bio LLC..............F....... 718 376-0422
  Libertyville *(G-12638)*
G2 Crowd Inc..............D....... 847 748-7559
  Chicago *(G-4652)*

COMPUTERS, PERIPHERALS & SOFTWARE, WHOLESALE: Software

Imaging Systems Inc .... F 630 875-1100
  Itasca (G-11674)
Michaels Ross and Cole Inc .... F 630 916-0662
  Oak Brook (G-15644)
Pinnakle Technologies Inc .... F 630 352-0070
  Aurora (G-1009)
Rand McNally & Company .... B 847 329-8100
  Chicago (G-5968)
Relativity Oda LLC .... C 312 263-1177
  Chicago (G-6007)
Thomson Quantitative Analytics .... E 847 610-0574
  Chicago (G-6368)

COMPUTERS, PERIPHERALS/SFTWR, WHOL: Anti-Static Eqpt/Devices

L-Data Corporation .... E 312 552-7855
  Chicago (G-5144)

COMPUTERS: Personal

Antares Computer Systems Inc .... G 773 783-8855
  Chicago (G-3704)
Hp Inc .... B 650 857-1501
  Chicago (G-4853)
Hp Inc .... D 309 664-4000
  Bloomington (G-2060)
Hp Inc .... C 650 857-1501
  Schaumburg (G-18551)
Hp Inc .... E 650 857-1501
  Chicago (G-4854)
Monroe Associates Inc .... G 217 665-3898
  Bethany (G-1968)
Motorola Solutions Inc .... C 847 576-8600
  Schaumburg (G-18637)

CONCENTRATES, DRINK

Amt Group LLC .... D 847 324-4411
  Niles (G-15103)
Ra Energy Drink Inc .... G 773 503-8574
  Chicago (G-5956)
Tampico Beverages Inc .... E 773 296-0190
  Chicago (G-6319)

CONCENTRATES, FLAVORING, EXC DRINK

Jel Sert Co .... C 630 231-7590
  West Chicago (G-20603)

CONCRETE BUILDING PRDTS WHOLESALERS

Carroll Distrg & Cnstr Sup Inc .... G 630 892-4855
  Aurora (G-1070)
CCS Contractor Eqp & Sup Inc .... E 630 393-9020
  Naperville (G-14793)
Macomb Concrete Products Inc .... G 309 772-3826
  Bushnell (G-2743)
Mazel & Co Inc .... F 773 533-1600
  Chicago (G-5372)
Stockdale Block Systems LLC .... G 815 416-1030
  Morris (G-14329)

CONCRETE CURING & HARDENING COMPOUNDS

Advantech Limited .... G 815 289-7678
  Aurora (G-1043)
Colloid Envmtl Tech Co LLC .... C 847 851-1500
  Hoffman Estates (G-11415)
Euclid Chemical Company .... F 815 522-2308
  Kirkland (G-12060)
Master Builders LLC .... G 847 249-4080
  Gurnee (G-10895)
Right/Pointe LLC .... D 815 754-5700
  Dekalb (G-7700)
W R Grace & Co .... F 708 458-9700
  Chicago (G-6576)

CONCRETE PRDTS

A&J Paving Inc .... G 773 889-9133
  Chicago (G-3493)
Abel Vault & Monument Co Inc .... G 309 647-0105
  Canton (G-2820)
Architectural Cast Stone LLC .... G 630 377-4800
  West Chicago (G-20544)
Bricks Inc .... G 630 897-6926
  Aurora (G-1066)
Classical Statuary & Decor .... G 815 462-3408
  New Lenox (G-15028)
Clay Vollmar Products Co .... G 847 540-5850
  Lake Zurich (G-12394)
Concrete Specialities Co Inc .... E 847 608-1200
  Elgin (G-8549)
Contractors Ready-Mix Inc .... F 217 735-2565
  Lincoln (G-12728)
Cortelyou Excavating .... G 309 772-2922
  Bushnell (G-2741)
County Materials Corp .... E 217 352-4181
  Champaign (G-3283)
Custom Stone Works Inc .... E 815 748-2109
  Cortland (G-7018)
Elmhurst-Chicago Stone Company .... F 630 557-2446
  Kaneville (G-11954)
Elmhurst-Chicago Stone Company .... G 630 983-6410
  Bolingbrook (G-2173)
F H Leinweber Co Inc .... G 773 568-7722
  Chicago (G-4548)
Ferber George & Sons .... G 217 733-2184
  Fairmount (G-9643)
Forrest Redi-Mix Inc .... G 815 657-8241
  Forrest (G-9733)
Great Lakes Envmtl Mar Del .... E 312 332-3377
  Chicago (G-4734)
Hamel Tire and Concrete Pdts .... G 618 633-2405
  Hamel (G-10950)
Hamilton Concrete Products Co .... G 217 847-3118
  Hamilton (G-10958)
Hanson Aggregates East LLC .... E 815 398-2300
  Rockford (G-17442)
Holcim (us) Inc .... D 773 372-1000
  Chicago (G-4827)
Holcim Participations US Inc .... G 773 372-1000
  Chicago (G-4828)
Jet Precast & Redimix Inc .... G 618 632-3594
  O Fallon (G-15575)
Lafarge North America Inc .... C 773 372-1000
  Chicago (G-5156)
Legacy Vulcan LLC .... G 773 890-2360
  Chicago (G-5197)
Lion Concrete Products Inc .... G 630 892-7304
  Montgomery (G-14257)
Macomb Concrete Products Inc .... G 309 772-3826
  Bushnell (G-2743)
Material Service Corporation .... E 815 838-2400
  Romeoville (G-17846)
Meyer Material Co Merger Corp .... D 815 943-2605
  Harvard (G-11060)
Mid-Illinois Concrete Inc .... G 618 664-1340
  Greenville (G-10838)
Mid-Illinois Concrete Inc .... E 217 235-5858
  Mattoon (G-13650)
Midwest Cement Products Inc .... G 815 284-2342
  Woosung (G-21452)
Northfield Block Company .... C 847 816-9000
  Mundelein (G-14721)
Northfield Block Company .... G 815 941-4100
  Morris (G-14319)
Northfield Block Company .... G 708 458-8130
  Berwyn (G-1957)
Orlandi Statuary Company .... D 773 489-0303
  Chicago (G-5704)
Ozinga Concrete Products Inc .... E 847 426-0920
  Elgin (G-8682)
Ozinga Ready Mix Concrete Inc .... E 708 326-4200
  Mokena (G-14103)
Prosser Construction Co .... F 217 774-5032
  Shelbyville (G-18884)
Quikrete Companies LLC .... G 309 346-1184
  Pekin (G-16357)
Rochelle Vault Co .... G 815 562-6484
  Rochelle (G-17158)
Southfield Corporation .... F 217 875-5455
  Decatur (G-7548)
Stockdale Block Systems LLC .... G 815 416-1030
  Morris (G-14329)
Stonecraft Cast Stone LLC .... G 708 653-1477
  Steger (G-19493)
Vcna Prairie Indiana Inc .... E 708 458-0400
  Bridgeview (G-2396)

CONCRETE PRDTS, PRECAST, NEC

American Cast Stone .... G 630 291-0250
  Lemont (G-12552)
Architectural Cast Ston .... E 630 377-4800
  West Chicago (G-20543)
Atmi Dynacore LLC .... D 815 838-9492
  Chicago (G-1056)
Atmi Precast Inc .... E 630 897-0577
  Aurora (G-1057)
Atmi Precast Inc .... E 630 897-0577
  Aurora (G-1058)
Avan Precast Concrete Pdts Inc .... F 708 757-6200
  Lynwood (G-13291)
B A Precast Inc .... G 309 645-0639
  Ellisville (G-9320)
Concrete Products .... G 815 339-6395
  Granville (G-10754)
Concrete Specialties Co .... E 847 608-1200
  Elgin (G-8550)
Doty & Sons Concrete Products .... F 815 895-2884
  Sycamore (G-19708)
Ed Bell Investments Inc .... G 618 345-0799
  Belleville (G-1550)
Gary & Larry Brown Trucking .... G 618 268-6377
  Raleigh (G-16961)
Hahn Industries .... G 815 689-2133
  Cullom (G-7299)
Illini Precast .... G 815 795-6161
  Marseilles (G-13557)
Illini Precast LLC .... F 708 562-7700
  Westchester (G-20700)
Imco Precast LLC .... G 217 742-5300
  Springfield (G-19388)
Impact Polymer LLC .... G 847 441-2394
  Northfield (G-15517)
J E Tomes & Associates Inc .... F 708 653-5100
  Blue Island (G-2127)
Kw Precast LLC .... F 708 562-7700
  Westchester (G-20702)
Leonards Unit Step Co .... G 815 744-1263
  Rockdale (G-17265)
Leonards Unit Step of Moline .... G 309 792-9641
  Colona (G-6976)
Lombard Archtctral Prcast Pdts .... E 708 389-1060
  Chicago (G-5253)
Lombard Investment Company .... D 708 389-1060
  Alsip (G-469)
McCann Concrete Products Inc .... E 618 377-3888
  Dorsey (G-7945)
Mid-Illinois Concrete Inc .... G 217 382-6650
  Martinsville (G-13586)
Mid-Illinois Concrete Inc .... F 618 283-1600
  Vandalia (G-20015)
Mid-States Concrete Inds LLC .... D 815 389-2277
  South Beloit (G-19103)
Midwest Perma-Column Inc .... G 309 589-7949
  Edwards (G-8339)
Southern Illinois Redimix Inc .... F 618 993-3600
  Marion (G-13539)
Utility Concrete Products LLC .... E 815 416-1000
  Morris (G-14338)
Van-Packer Co .... E 309 895-2311
  Buda (G-2500)
Vitelli Concrete Products Inc .... G 708 754-5846
  Chicago Heights (G-6785)
Welch Bros Inc .... C 847 741-6134
  Elgin (G-8779)
Welch Bros Inc .... G 815 547-3000
  Belvidere (G-1709)

CONCRETE REINFORCING MATERIAL

Hohmann & Barnard Illinois LLC .... E 773 586-6700
  Chicago Ridge (G-6798)
Mazel & Co Inc .... F 773 533-1600
  Chicago (G-5372)

CONCRETE: Dry Mixture

Bonsal American Inc .... D 847 678-6220
  Franklin Park (G-9891)

CONCRETE: Ready-Mixed

A & L Construction Inc .... E 708 343-1660
  Melrose Park (G-13816)
Advanced On-Site Concrete Inc .... E 773 622-7836
  Chicago (G-3566)
Aggregate Industries MGT Inc .... G 773 372-1000
  Chicago (G-3581)
All American Ready Mix .... F 217 931-2344
  Springfield (G-19317)
Atlas Ready Mix Inc .... G 618 271-0774
  East Saint Louis (G-8297)
Aztec Material Service Corp .... D 773 521-0909
  Chicago (G-3800)
Ballard Bros Inc .... F 217 374-2137
  White Hall (G-21017)
Barnett Redi-Mix Inc .... G 618 276-4298
  Junction (G-11948)

Bee Line Service Inc....G.... 815 233-1812
Freeport (G-10102)
Beelman Ready-Mix Inc....G.... 618 357-6120
Pinckneyville (G-16611)
Beelman Ready-Mix Inc....E.... 618 646-5300
East Saint Louis (G-8299)
Beelman Ready-Mix Inc....G.... 618 244-9600
Mount Vernon (G-14598)
Beelman Ready-Mix Inc....G.... 618 247-3866
Sandoval (G-18362)
Beelman Ready-Mix Inc....G.... 618 478-2044
Nashville (G-14995)
Beelman Ready-Mix Inc....F.... 618 526-0260
Breese (G-2298)
Biochemical Lab....G.... 708 447-3923
Riverside (G-17082)
Bleigh Construction Company....G.... 217 222-5005
Quincy (G-16866)
Blomberg Bros Inc....F.... 618 245-6321
Farina (G-9651)
Bmi Products Northern Ill Inc....E.... 847 395-7110
Antioch (G-605)
Bob Barnett Redi-Mix Inc....E.... 618 252-3581
Harrisburg (G-11020)
Breckenridge Material Company....E.... 618 398-4141
Caseyville (G-3211)
Builders Ready-Mix Co....E.... 847 866-6300
Evanston (G-9501)
Canton Redi-Mix Inc....F.... 309 668-2261
Canton (G-2823)
Canton Redi-Mix Inc....E.... 309 647-0019
Canton (G-2824)
Capitol Ready-Mix Inc....E.... 217 528-1100
Springfield (G-19340)
Cemex Cement Inc....G.... 773 995-5100
Chicago (G-4054)
Charleston Concrete Supply Co....F.... 217 345-6404
Charleston (G-3398)
Chris Dj Mix LLC....G.... 312 725-3838
Chicago (G-4143)
Clinard Ready Mix Inc....E.... 217 773-3965
Mount Sterling (G-14590)
Clinton County Materials Corp....F.... 618 533-4252
Centralia (G-3226)
Coal City Redi-Mix Co Inc....F.... 815 634-4455
Coal City (G-6931)
Community Rady Mix of Pttsfeld....G.... 217 285-5548
Pittsfield (G-16633)
Community Readymix Inc....E.... 217 245-6668
Jacksonville (G-11762)
Concrete 1 Inc....G.... 630 357-1329
Naperville (G-14805)
Concrete Supply LLC....G.... 618 646-5300
East Saint Louis (G-8302)
Concrete Supply Tolono Inc....G.... 217 485-3100
Urbana (G-19979)
Condominiums Northbrook Cort 1....G.... 847 498-1640
Lincolnshire (G-12754)
Continental Materials Corp....F.... 312 541-7200
Chicago (G-4228)
Contractors Concrete....G.... 217 826-2290
Marshall (G-13568)
Contractors Concrete Inc....E.... 217 342-2299
Effingham (G-8394)
Contractors Ready-Mix Inc....G.... 217 482-5530
Mason City (G-13610)
Contractors Ready-Mix Inc....F.... 217 735-2565
Lincoln (G-12728)
Country Stone Inc....E.... 309 787-1744
Milan (G-14005)
County Materials Corp....E.... 217 352-4181
Champaign (G-3283)
Curry Ready Mix of Petersburg....G.... 217 632-2516
Petersburg (G-16601)
Curry Ready-Mix of Decatur....F.... 217 428-7177
Decatur (G-7479)
David Yates....G.... 618 656-7879
Edwardsville (G-8356)
Diamond Ready Mix Inc....F.... 630 355-5414
Naperville (G-14815)
Edwards Acquisition Corp....F.... 309 944-2117
Geneseo (G-10241)
Edwards County Concrete LL....G.... 618 445-2711
Harrisburg (G-11022)
Edwards County Concrete LLC....G.... 618 445-2711
Albion (G-349)
Elmhurst-Chicago Stone Company....E.... 630 832-4000
Elmhurst (G-9360)
Elmhurst-Chicago Stone Company....E.... 630 983-6410
Bolingbrook (G-2173)

Fairfield Ready Mix Inc....G.... 618 842-9462
Fairfield (G-9623)
Fehrenbacher Ready-Mix Inc....G.... 618 395-2306
Olney (G-15860)
Ferber George & Sons....G.... 217 733-2184
Fairmount (G-9643)
Fishstone Studio Inc....G.... 815 276-0299
Crystal Lake (G-7199)
Flora Ready Mix Inc....G.... 618 662-4818
Flora (G-9681)
Fnh Ready Mix Inc....F.... 815 235-1400
Freeport (G-10109)
Forrest Redi-Mix Inc....G.... 815 657-8241
Forrest (G-9733)
Fox Redi-Mix Inc....G.... 217 774-2110
Shelbyville (G-18878)
Franklin Park Building Mtls....G.... 847 455-3985
Franklin Park (G-9945)
Fuller Brothers Ready Mix....G.... 217 532-2422
Hillsboro (G-11312)
Gary & Larry Brown Trucking....G.... 618 268-6377
Raleigh (G-16961)
Goreville Concrete Inc....E.... 618 995-2670
Goreville (G-10681)
Gorman Brothers Ready Mix Inc....F.... 618 498-2173
Jerseyville (G-11791)
Great River Ready Mix Inc....F.... 217 847-3515
Hamilton (G-10956)
Grohne Concrete Products Co....G.... 217 877-4197
Decatur (G-7498)
H J Mohr & Sons Company....F.... 708 366-0338
Oak Park (G-15756)
Hardin Ready Mix Inc....F.... 618 576-9313
Hardin (G-11017)
Herman Bade & Sons....G.... 217 832-9444
Villa Grove (G-20123)
Illini Concrete Inc....F.... 618 235-4141
Belleville (G-1557)
Illini Concrete Inc....G.... 618 398-4141
Caseyville (G-3214)
Illini Ready Mix Inc....G.... 618 833-7321
Anna (G-585)
Illini Ready Mix Inc....G.... 618 734-0287
Carbondale (G-2846)
J W Ossola Company Inc....G.... 815 339-6112
Granville (G-10755)
J&J Ready Mix Inc....G.... 309 676-0579
East Peoria (G-8271)
Jerry Berry Contracting Co....G.... 618 594-3339
Carlyle (G-2891)
Joe Hatzer & Son Inc....E.... 815 673-5571
Streator (G-19612)
Joe Hatzer & Son Inc....G.... 815 672-2161
Streator (G-19613)
JW Ossola Co Inc....G.... 815 339-6113
Granville (G-10756)
Kendall County Concrete Inc....E.... 630 851-9197
Aurora (G-992)
Kienstra-Illinois LLC....F.... 618 251-6345
Wood River (G-21265)
Lafarge Building Materials Inc....D.... 678 746-2000
Chicago (G-5155)
Lafarge North America Inc....C.... 773 372-1000
Chicago (G-5156)
Lahood Construction Inc....E.... 309 699-5080
East Peoria (G-8276)
Langheim Ready Mix Inc....G.... 217 625-2351
Girard (G-10383)
Legacy Vulcan LLC....E.... 847 437-4181
Elk Grove Village (G-9092)
Legacy Vulcan LLC....F.... 217 932-2611
Casey (G-3205)
Legacy Vulcan LLC....F.... 815 726-6900
Joliet (G-11894)
Legacy Vulcan LLC....F.... 630 739-0182
Romeoville (G-17841)
Legacy Vulcan LLC....D.... 708 485-6602
Mc Cook (G-13695)
Legacy Vulcan LLC....E.... 815 436-3535
Plainfield (G-16682)
Material Service Corporation....E.... 815 838-2400
Romeoville (G-17846)
Max Miller....F.... 708 758-7760
S Chicago Hts (G-18124)
Maxheimer Construction Inc....G.... 309 444-4200
Washington (G-20275)
McLean County Asphalt Co....D.... 309 827-6115
Bloomington (G-2072)
Menoni & Mocogni Inc....F.... 847 432-0850
Highland Park (G-11283)

Mertel Gravel Company Inc....F.... 815 223-0468
Peru (G-16581)
Metropolis Ready Mix Inc....E.... 618 524-8221
Metropolis (G-13974)
Meyer Material Co Merger Corp....F.... 847 658-7811
Algonquin (G-381)
Meyer Material Co Merger Corp....E.... 847 824-4111
Elburn (G-8460)
Meyer Material Co Merger Corp....E.... 815 331-7200
Streamwood (G-19585)
Meyer Material Co Merger Corp....E.... 847 689-9200
Lake Bluff (G-12196)
Meyer Material Co Merger Corp....D.... 815 943-2605
Harvard (G-11060)
Mid-Illinois Concrete Inc....E.... 217 235-5858
Mattoon (G-13650)
Mid-Illinois Concrete Inc....G.... 217 345-6404
Charleston (G-3407)
Mid-Illinois Concrete Inc....G.... 217 382-6650
Martinsville (G-13586)
Mid-Illinois Concrete Inc....G.... 618 664-1340
Greenville (G-10838)
Mid-Illinois Concrete Inc....F.... 618 283-1600
Vandalia (G-20015)
Mindful Mix....G.... 847 284-4404
Lake Zurich (G-12434)
Mix N Mingle....G.... 815 308-5170
Woodstock (G-21413)
Moeller Ready Mix Inc....F.... 217 243-7471
Jacksonville (G-11776)
Moline Consumers Co....F.... 309 757-8289
Moline (G-14162)
Monmouth Ready Mix Corp....G.... 309 734-3211
Galesburg (G-10212)
Moultrie County Redi-Mix Co....G.... 217 728-2334
Sullivan (G-19673)
Mt Crmel Stblzation Group Inc....E.... 618 262-5118
Mount Carmel (G-14482)
Myers Concrete & Construction....G.... 815 732-2591
Oregon (G-15924)
Narvick Bros Lumber Co Inc....E.... 815 521-1173
Minooka (G-14064)
Narvick Bros Lumber Co Inc....E.... 815 942-1173
Morris (G-14318)
Newton Ready Mix Inc....F.... 618 783-8611
Newton (G-15088)
ODaniel Trucking Co....D.... 618 382-5371
Carmi (G-2912)
Odum Concrete Products Inc....G.... 618 942-4572
Herrin (G-11175)
Odum Concrete Products Inc....E.... 618 993-6211
Marion (G-13523)
Oldcastle Materials Inc....F.... 309 627-2111
Monmouth (G-14225)
Oremus Materials LLC....G.... 520 820-2265
Burr Ridge (G-2711)
Ozinga Bros Inc....E.... 708 326-4200
Mokena (G-14100)
Ozinga Bros Inc....E.... 815 568-2589
Marengo (G-13491)
Ozinga Bros Inc....E.... 847 783-6500
Lake Bluff (G-12203)
Ozinga Bros Inc....D.... 847 768-1697
Des Plaines (G-7816)
Ozinga Bros Inc....E.... 847 783-6500
Algonquin (G-383)
Ozinga Bros Inc....D.... 708 326-4200
Chicago Heights (G-6763)
Ozinga Bros Inc....D.... 312 432-5700
Evanston (G-9564)
Ozinga Bros Inc....D.... 815 332-8198
Belvidere (G-1693)
Ozinga Chicago Ready Mix Con....E.... 708 479-9050
Alsip (G-488)
Ozinga Chicago Ready Mix Con....E.... 312 432-5700
Chicago (G-5724)
Ozinga Chicago Ready Mix Con....E.... 773 862-2817
Chicago (G-5725)
Ozinga Chicago Ready Mix Con....E.... 847 447-0353
Chicago (G-5726)
Ozinga Concrete Products Inc....G.... 708 479-9050
Hampshire (G-10982)
Ozinga Indiana Rdymx Con Inc....G.... 708 479-9050
Mokena (G-14101)
Ozinga Materials Inc....C.... 309 364-3401
Mokena (G-14102)
Ozinga Ready Mix Concrete Inc....E.... 800 786-6382
Chicago (G-5727)
Ozinga Ready Mix Concrete Inc....E.... 708 326-4200
Mokena (G-14103)

Employee Codes: A=Over 500 employees, B=251-500
C=101-250, D=51-100, E=20-50, F=10-19, G=3-9
2020 Harris Illinois
Industrial Directory
1395

CONCRETE: Ready-Mixed

Ozinga S Subn Rdymx Con Inc ....F 708 479-3080
  Mokena *(G-14104)*
Ozinga S Subn Rdymx Con Inc ....D 708 326-4201
  Mokena *(G-14105)*
Paxton Ready Mix Inc ....G 217 379-2303
  Paxton *(G-16313)*
Pbi Redi Mix & Trucking ....E 217 562-3717
  Pana *(G-16222)*
Peoples Coal and Lumber Co ....F 815 432-2456
  Watseka *(G-20314)*
Pike County Concrete Inc 217 285-5548
  Pittsfield *(G-16637)*
Poggenpohl LLC ....G 217 229-3411
  Raymond *(G-16990)*
Poggenpohl LLC 217 824-2020
  Taylorville *(G-19760)*
Point Ready Mix LLC ....G 815 578-9100
  McHenry *(G-13781)*
Prairie Central Ready Mix ....G 217 877-5210
  Decatur *(G-7537)*
Prairie Group Management LLC ....D 708 458-0400
  Bridgeview *(G-2375)*
Prairie Material ....F 708 458-0400
  Bedford Park *(G-1493)*
Prairie Materials Group 815 207-6750
  Shorewood *(G-18900)*
Princeton Ready-Mix Inc ....F 815 875-3359
  Princeton *(G-16820)*
Quad County Ready Mix Swansea ....G 618 257-9530
  Swansea *(G-19694)*
Quad-County Ready Mix Corp ....F 618 243-6430
  Okawville *(G-15847)*
Quad-County Ready Mix Corp 618 588-4656
  New Baden *(G-15022)*
Quad-County Ready Mix Corp 618 526-7130
  Breese *(G-2306)*
Quad-County Ready Mix Corp ....E 618 244-6973
  Mount Vernon *(G-14635)*
Quad-County Ready Mix Corp ....G 618 288-4000
  Troy *(G-19918)*
Quad-County Ready Mix Corp ....F 618 327-3748
  Nashville *(G-15008)*
Quad-County Ready Mix Corp ....F 618 594-2732
  Carlyle *(G-2894)*
Quad-County Ready Mix Corp ....F 618 548-2477
  Salem *(G-18353)*
Quad-County Ready Mix Corp 618 295-3000
  Marissa *(G-13544)*
Quality Ready Mix Concrete Co ....G 815 589-2013
  Fulton *(G-10156)*
Quality Ready Mix Concrete Co ....F 815 772-7181
  Morrison *(G-14347)*
Quality Ready Mix Concrete Co 815 625-0750
  Sterling *(G-19527)*
Quality Ready Mix Concrete Co ....G 815 288-6416
  Dixon *(G-7907)*
R & L Ready Mix Inc ....F 618 544-7514
  Robinson *(G-17123)*
Ranger Redi-Mix & Mtls Inc ....G 815 337-2662
  Woodstock *(G-21429)*
Rapco Ltd 618 249-6614
  Richview *(G-17033)*
Ready 2 Roll Inc ....G 847 620-9768
  Wheeling *(G-20971)*
Ready Mix Solutions LLC ....G 618 889-6188
  Marion *(G-13532)*
Red-E-Mix LLC ....D 618 654-2166
  Highland *(G-11237)*
Regional Ready Mix LLC ....F 815 562-1901
  Rochelle *(G-17154)*
Riber Construction Inc ....F 815 584-3337
  Dwight *(G-8159)*
River Redi Mix Inc ....G 815 795-2025
  Marseilles *(G-13564)*
Riverstone Group Inc 309 757-8297
  Moline *(G-14173)*
Riverstone Group Inc ....F 309 788-9543
  Rock Island *(G-17244)*
Roanoke Concrete Products Co ....G 309 885-0250
  Pekin *(G-16359)*
Roanoke Concrete Products Co ....F 309 698-7882
  East Peoria *(G-8288)*
Rock River Ready Mix Inc ....G 815 625-1139
  Dixon *(G-7912)*
Rock River Ready-Mix ....E 815 288-2269
  Dixon *(G-7913)*
Rogers Ready Mix & Mtls Inc ....D 815 234-8212
  Byron *(G-2757)*
Rogers Ready Mix & Mtls Inc ....G 815 234-8044
  Oregon *(G-15926)*

Rogers Ready Mix & Mtls Inc ....E 815 874-6626
  Rockford *(G-17613)*
Rogers Ready Mix & Mtls Inc ....F 815 389-2223
  Roscoe *(G-17927)*
Rogers Redi-Mix Inc ....F 618 282-3844
  Ruma *(G-18106)*
Schirz Concrete Products Inc ....F 217 368-2153
  Greenfield *(G-10818)*
Silver Bros Inc ....G 217 283-7751
  Hoopeston *(G-11513)*
Southern Illinois Redimix Inc ....F 618 993-3600
  Marion *(G-13539)*
Southfield Corporation ....D 708 563-4056
  Addison *(G-293)*
Southfield Corporation ....D 309 676-6121
  Morton *(G-14382)*
Southfield Corporation ....C 815 284-3357
  Dixon *(G-7918)*
Southfield Corporation ....F 217 877-5210
  Decatur *(G-7549)*
Southfield Corporation ....D 708 458-0400
  Bridgeview *(G-2388)*
Southfield Corporation ....E 309 829-1087
  Bloomington *(G-2096)*
Southfield Corporation ....E 309 676-0576
  Peoria *(G-16527)*
Southfield Corporation 708 458-0400
  Oak Lawn *(G-15735)*
Sport Redi-Mix LLC ....E 217 892-4222
  Rantoul *(G-16983)*
Stahl Lumber Company ....F 309 695-4331
  Wyoming *(G-21462)*
Stahl Lumber Company ....F 309 385-2552
  Wyoming *(G-21463)*
Staley Concrete Co ....E 217 356-9533
  Champaign *(G-3353)*
Sterling-Rock Falls Ready Mix ....F 815 288-3135
  Dixon *(G-7921)*
Super Mix Inc ....D 815 578-9100
  McHenry *(G-13801)*
Super Mix of Wisconsin Inc ....G 262 859-9000
  McHenry *(G-13802)*
Super Mix of Wisconsin Inc ....F 815 578-9100
  McHenry *(G-13803)*
T H Davidson & Co Inc ....E 815 464-2000
  Oak Forest *(G-15690)*
T H Davidson & Co Inc 815 941-0280
  Morris *(G-14331)*
Thelen Sand & Gravel Inc ....D 847 838-8800
  Antioch *(G-636)*
Tri County Concrete ....G 309 222-4000
  Peoria *(G-16538)*
Tri-City Ready-Mix ....G 618 439-2071
  Benton *(G-1938)*
Tri-County Concrete Inc ....G 815 786-2179
  Sandwich *(G-18385)*
Triangle Concrete Co Inc ....G 309 853-4334
  Kewanee *(G-12042)*
United Ready Mix Inc ....E 309 676-3287
  Peoria *(G-16541)*
Upchurch Ready Mix Concrete ....G 618 235-6222
  Belleville *(G-1605)*
Upchurch Ready Mix Concrete ....G 618 286-4808
  Dupo *(G-8148)*
Upland Concrete 224 699-9909
  East Dundee *(G-8214)*
Valley Concrete Inc 815 725-2422
  Joliet *(G-11940)*
Vcna Praire Yard 1033 ....G 708 458-0400
  Chicago *(G-6526)*
Vcna Prairie LLC ....A 708 458-0400
  Bridgeview *(G-2394)*
Vcna Prairie Illinois Inc ....F 217 398-4346
  Champaign *(G-3363)*
Vcna Prairie Illinois Inc 708 458-0400
  Bridgeview *(G-2395)*
Via Galante Cement Con In ....G 773 589-9893
  Chicago *(G-6542)*
Vulcan Materials Company ....F 847 695-0057
  Bartlett *(G-1322)*
Wayland Ready Mix Concrete Svc ....F 309 833-2064
  Galesburg *(G-10222)*
Welsch Ready Mix Inc ....G 815 524-1850
  Bolingbrook *(G-2252)*
Westmore Supply Co ....F 630 627-0278
  Lombard *(G-13154)*
Westville Ready Mix Inc 217 267-2082
  Westville *(G-20782)*
Winnetka Mews Condominium Assn ....G 847 501-2770
  Winnetka *(G-21138)*

CONDENSERS & CONDENSING UNITS: Air Conditioner

American Event Services LLC ....G 217 709-1811
  Danville *(G-7319)*

CONDENSERS: Refrigeration

Peerless America Incorporated ....C 217 342-0400
  Effingham *(G-8418)*

CONDUITS & FITTINGS: Electric

Anamet Electrical Inc ....C 217 234-8844
  Mattoon *(G-13630)*
Anamet Inc ....G 217 234-8844
  Glen Ellyn *(G-10394)*
Beacon Fas & Components Inc ....E 847 541-0404
  Wheeling *(G-20857)*
Cable Management Products Inc ....G 630 723-0470
  Aurora *(G-929)*
Electri-Flex Company ....D 630 529-2920
  Roselle *(G-17952)*
Electric Conduit Cnstr Co ....C 630 293-4474
  Elburn *(G-8453)*
Electric Conduit Construction ....F 630 859-9310
  Elburn *(G-8454)*
John Maneely Company ....C 773 254-0617
  Chicago *(G-5043)*
Linear Solutions Inc ....G 724 426-6384
  Chicago *(G-5228)*
Minerallac Company ....E 630 543-7080
  Hampshire *(G-10979)*
Panduit Corp ....E 815 836-1800
  Lockport *(G-13018)*
Panduit Corp ....A 708 532-1800
  Tinley Park *(G-19848)*

CONDUITS: Concrete

Electric Conduit Cnstr Co ....C 630 293-4474
  Elburn *(G-8453)*

CONFECTIONERY PRDTS WHOLESALERS

Baldi Candy Co ....E 773 267-5770
  Chicago *(G-3818)*
Chipita America Inc ....E 708 731-2434
  Westchester *(G-20693)*
Combined Technologies Inc ....G 847 968-4855
  Libertyville *(G-12645)*
Frito-Lay North America Inc ....C 708 331-7200
  Oak Forest *(G-15679)*
Select Snacks Company Inc ....D 773 933-2167
  Chicago *(G-6133)*
Thanasi Foods LLC ....E 720 570-1065
  Chicago *(G-6359)*

CONFECTIONS & CANDY

American Convenience Inc ....F 815 344-6040
  McHenry *(G-13718)*
Amy Wertheim ....G 309 830-4361
  Atlanta *(G-904)*
Andersons Candy Shop Inc ....F 815 678-6000
  Richmond *(G-17009)*
Baldi Candy Co ....E 773 267-5770
  Chicago *(G-3818)*
Baldi Candy Co ....D 773 267-5770
  Chicago *(G-3819)*
Belgian Chocolatier Piron Inc ....G 847 864-5504
  Evanston *(G-9498)*
Bobbie Haycraft ....G 217 856-2194
  Humboldt *(G-11522)*
Cambridge Brands Mfg Inc ....G 773 838-3400
  Chicago *(G-4010)*
Capol LLC 224 545-5095
  Deerfield *(G-7599)*
Cellas Confections Inc ....D 773 838-3400
  Chicago *(G-4053)*
Colleens Confection 630 653-2231
  Carol Stream *(G-2964)*
Das Foods LLC ....G 224 715-9289
  Chicago *(G-4320)*
Fannie May Cnfctons Brands Inc ....F 330 494-0833
  Chicago *(G-4558)*
Fattah Trading Company Inc ....G 773 227-2525
  Chicago *(G-4568)*
Ferrara Candy Company ....G 800 323-1768
  Itasca *(G-11655)*
Ferrara Candy Company ....B 630 366-0500
  Forest Park *(G-9715)*

PRODUCT SECTION
CONSTRUCTION & MINING MACHINERY WHOLESALERS

Ferrara Candy Company .... C 507 452-3433
  Chicago *(G-4583)*
Galenas Kandy Kitchen .... G 815 777-0241
  Galena *(G-10171)*
Graziano TI Inc .... E 847 741-1900
  Elgin *(G-8600)*
Hershey Company .... A 618 544-3111
  Robinson *(G-17116)*
Hollingworth Candies Inc .... E 815 838-2275
  Lockport *(G-13000)*
Imaginings 3 Inc .... E 847 647-1370
  Niles *(G-15131)*
Jelly Belly Candy Company .... C 847 689-2225
  North Chicago *(G-15315)*
John B Sanfilippo & Son Inc .... C 847 289-1800
  Elgin *(G-8632)*
Killeen Confectionery LLC .... C 312 804-0009
  Wilmette *(G-21083)*
Long Grove Confectionery Co .... E 847 459-3100
  Buffalo Grove *(G-2565)*
Mars Chocolate North Amer LLC .... A 662 335-8000
  Chicago *(G-5347)*
Mars Chocolate North Amer LLC .... C 630 850-9898
  Burr Ridge *(G-2699)*
Mars Snackfood US .... F 773 637-0659
  Chicago *(G-5348)*
Mederer Group .... G 630 860-4587
  Des Plaines *(G-7801)*
Mondelez Global LLC .... C 815 877-8081
  Loves Park *(G-13238)*
MSI Green Inc .... G 312 421-6550
  Chicago *(G-5519)*
Nestle Chclat Cnfctons A Div N 847 957-7850
  Franklin Park *(G-10008)*
Nestle Usa Inc .... C 630 773-2090
  Itasca *(G-11711)*
Nestle Usa Inc .... D 847 957-7850
  Franklin Park *(G-10009)*
Office Snax Inc 630 789-1783
  Oak Brook *(G-15652)*
Peases Inc .... F 217 523-3721
  Springfield *(G-19422)*
Peases Inc .... F 217 529-2912
  Springfield *(G-19423)*
Princess Foods Inc .... E 847 933-1820
  Skokie *(G-19011)*
Profile Food Ingredients LLC .... E 847 622-1700
  Elgin *(G-8697)*
Rebel Brands LLC 312 804-0009
  Wilmette *(G-21091)*
Ruckers Mkin Batch Candies Inc .... E 618 945-7778
  Bridgeport *(G-2314)*
Ruckers Wholesale & Service Co .... C 618 945-2411
  Bridgeport *(G-2315)*
Samad General Services Inc .... G 773 593-3332
  Addison *(G-280)*
Taylors Candy Inc .... E 708 371-0332
  Alsip *(G-515)*
Toffee Time .... G 309 788-2466
  Rock Island *(G-17251)*
Tootsie Roll Company Inc .... A 773 838-3400
  Chicago *(G-6391)*
Tootsie Roll Industries Inc .... A 773 838-3400
  Chicago *(G-6392)*
Tootsie Roll Industries LLC .... A 773 245-4202
  Chicago *(G-6393)*
Tootsie Roll Worldwide Ltd .... A 773 838-3400
  Chicago *(G-6394)*
Tri Sales Co .... F 773 838-3400
  Chicago *(G-6418)*
Tri Sales Co .... F 773 838-3400
  Chicago *(G-6419)*
Tri Sales Co .... F 773 838-3400
  Chicago *(G-6420)*
Tri Sales Co .... G 773 838-3400
  Chicago *(G-6421)*
Wm Wrigley Jr Company .... B 312 280-4710
  Chicago *(G-6654)*
Wm Wrigley Jr Company .... A 312 644-2121
  Chicago *(G-6656)*
Wrigley Manufacturing Co LLC .... B 630 553-4800
  Yorkville *(G-21507)*
Zb Importing Inc .... D 708 222-8330
  Cicero *(G-6890)*
Zb Importing Inc .... E 708 222-8330
  Chicago *(G-6709)*

CONFINEMENT SURVEILLANCE SYS MAINTENANCE & MONITORING SVCS

Moog Inc .... E 770 987-7550
  Northbrook *(G-15435)*

CONNECTORS & TERMINALS: Electrical Device Uses

Amerline Enterprises Co Inc .... E 847 671-6554
  Schiller Park *(G-18786)*
Central Rubber Company .... E 815 544-2191
  Belvidere *(G-1661)*
Cinch Connectors Inc .... D 630 705-6001
  Lombard *(G-13055)*
David Jeskey .... G 630 659-6337
  Saint Charles *(G-18180)*
Itron Corporation Del .... F 708 222-5320
  Cicero *(G-6857)*
J P Goldenne Incorporated .... F 847 776-5063
  Palatine *(G-16132)*
Molex LLC .... A 630 969-4550
  Lisle *(G-12911)*
Molex LLC .... E 630 527-4363
  Bolingbrook *(G-2216)*
Molex LLC .... F 630 512-8787
  Downers Grove *(G-8059)*
Molex International Inc .... F 630 969-4550
  Lisle *(G-12914)*
Molex Premise Networks Inc .... A 866 733-6659
  Lisle *(G-12915)*
Panduit Corp .... E 815 836-1800
  Lockport *(G-13018)*
Remke Industries Inc .... D 847 541-3780
  Vernon Hills *(G-20085)*
Special Mine Services Inc .... D 618 932-2151
  West Frankfort *(G-20684)*
Woodhead Industries LLC .... B 847 353-2500
  Lincolnshire *(G-12802)*

CONNECTORS: Cord, Electric

Shattuc Cord Specialties Inc .... F 847 360-9500
  Waukegan *(G-20494)*

CONNECTORS: Electrical

Amphenol Eec Inc .... E 773 463-8343
  Des Plaines *(G-7731)*
Eastco Inc .... G 708 499-1701
  Oak Lawn *(G-15714)*
Pancon Illinois LLC .... G 630 972-6400
  Bolingbrook *(G-2224)*
Possehl Connector Svcs SC Inc .... E 803 366-8316
  Elk Grove Village *(G-9184)*
Winchester Interconnect Rugged .... G 708 594-5890
  Broadview *(G-2475)*

CONNECTORS: Electronic

Advantage Components Inc .... E 815 725-8644
  Joliet *(G-11817)*
Aiwa Corporation .... G 305 394-4119
  Chicago *(G-3591)*
Amphenol Corporation .... D 800 944-6446
  Lisle *(G-12863)*
Amphenol Corporation .... G 847 478-5600
  Lincolnshire *(G-12745)*
Amphenol Fiber Optic Products .... E 630 960-1010
  Lisle *(G-12864)*
Belden Energy Solutions Inc .... G 800 235-3361
  Elmhurst *(G-9330)*
C D T Manufacturing Inc .... G 847 679-2361
  Skokie *(G-18935)*
Central Rubber Company .... E 815 544-2191
  Belvidere *(G-1661)*
Cinch Cnnctivity Solutions Inc .... C 630 705-6000
  Lombard *(G-13054)*
Cinch Connectors Inc .... D 630 705-6001
  Lombard *(G-13055)*
Conxall Corporation .... C 630 834-7504
  Villa Park *(G-20141)*
Cord Sets Inc .... G 847 427-1185
  Elk Grove Village *(G-8915)*
CTS Corporation .... C 630 577-8800
  Lisle *(G-12881)*
Data Accessories Inc .... G 847 669-3640
  Huntley *(G-11533)*
David Jeskey .... G 630 659-6337
  Saint Charles *(G-18180)*
Dynomax Inc .... B 847 680-8833
  Wheeling *(G-20883)*
Eastco Inc .... G 708 499-1701
  Oak Lawn *(G-15714)*
Evoys Corp .... G 773 736-4200
  Chicago *(G-4540)*
Gage Applied Technologies LLC .... E 815 838-0005
  Lockport *(G-12995)*
Glenair Inc .... E 847 679-8833
  Lincolnwood *(G-12823)*
Harting Inc of North America .... E 847 741-2700
  Elgin *(G-8608)*
Harting Inc of North America .... E 847 741-1500
  Elgin *(G-8609)*
Harting Manufacturing Inc .... G 847 741-1500
  Elgin *(G-8610)*
Hirose Electric (usa) Inc .... D 630 282-6700
  Downers Grove *(G-8024)*
Industrial Electronic Contrls .... F 815 873-1980
  Rockford *(G-17458)*
Ip Media Holdings .... E 847 714-1177
  Wheeling *(G-20917)*
Konnectronix Inc .... E 847 672-8685
  Waukegan *(G-20456)*
Kylon Midwest .... G 773 699-3640
  Chicago *(G-5139)*
Mac Lean-Fogg Company .... D 847 566-0010
  Mundelein *(G-14710)*
Methode Development Co .... E 708 867-6777
  Chicago *(G-5408)*
Methode Electronics Inc .... B 708 867-6777
  Chicago *(G-5409)*
Methode Electronics Inc .... C 847 577-9545
  Rolling Meadows *(G-17750)*
Methode Electronics Inc .... A 217 357-3941
  Carthage *(G-3139)*
Microway Systems Inc .... E 847 679-8833
  Lincolnwood *(G-12830)*
Molex LLC .... G 630 969-4550
  Naperville *(G-14873)*
Molex LLC .... G 630 527-4357
  Lisle *(G-12912)*
Molex LLC .... F 630 512-8787
  Downers Grove *(G-8059)*
Molex Electronic Tech LLC .... G 630 969-4550
  Lisle *(G-12913)*
Molex International Inc .... F 630 969-4550
  Lisle *(G-12914)*
Newko Tool & Engineering Co .... E 847 359-1670
  Palatine *(G-16142)*
Nobility Corporation .... E 847 677-3204
  Skokie *(G-18996)*
North Ridge Properties LLC .... G 815 434-7800
  Ottawa *(G-16064)*
P K Neuses Incorporated .... E 847 253-6555
  Rolling Meadows *(G-17758)*
Switchcraft Inc .... B 773 792-2700
  Chicago *(G-6299)*
Switchcraft Holdco Inc .... G 773 792-2700
  Chicago *(G-6300)*
Te Connectivity Corporation .... D 847 680-7400
  Mundelein *(G-14742)*
United Universal Inds Inc .... E 815 727-4445
  Joliet *(G-11939)*
Woodhead Industries LLC .... B 847 353-2500
  Lincolnshire *(G-12802)*
Woodhead Industries Inc .... G 847 236-9300
  Deerfield *(G-7660)*

CONNECTORS: Power, Electric

David Jeskey .... G 630 659-6337
  Saint Charles *(G-18180)*

CONSERVATION PROGRAMS ADMINISTRATION SVCS

Natural Resources Ill Dept .... E 618 439-4320
  Benton *(G-1933)*

CONSTRUCTION & MINING MACHINERY WHOLESALERS

Altorfer Power Systems .... G 309 697-1234
  Bartonville *(G-1328)*
C S O Corp .... D 630 365-6600
  Virgil *(G-20190)*
Caterpillar Inc .... F 309 578-4643
  Peoria *(G-16406)*
Hg-Farley Holdings LLC .... F 815 874-1400
  Rockford *(G-17449)*
Hg-Farley Laserlab USA Inc .... G 815 874-1400
  Rockford *(G-17450)*

Employee Codes: A=Over 500 employees, B=251-500
C=101-250, D=51-100, E=20-50, F=10-19, G=3-9

CONSTRUCTION & MINING MACHINERY WHOLESALERS

Mikes Inc..................................D....... 618 254-4491
South Roxana *(G-19253)*
Sauber Manufacturing Company..........D....... 630 365-6600
Virgil *(G-20191)*
Spl Software Alliance LLC ....G....... 309 266-0304
Morton *(G-14383)*
West Side Tractor Sales Co ....E....... 815 961-3160
Rockford *(G-17680)*

CONSTRUCTION & ROAD MAINTENANCE EQPT: Drags, Road

Central Township Road & Bridge ....G....... 618 704-5517
Greenville *(G-10830)*
Mfs Holdings LLC ....E....... 815 385-7700
McHenry *(G-13769)*
Steuben Township ....F....... 309 208-7073
Sparland *(G-19254)*

CONSTRUCTION EQPT REPAIR SVCS

Avant Tecno USA Inc ....F....... 847 380-1308
Arlington Heights *(G-700)*
Braden Rock Bit ....G....... 618 435-4519
Benton *(G-1922)*

CONSTRUCTION EQPT: Attachments

Baird Inc..G....... 217 526-3407
Morrisonville *(G-14350)*
C S O Corp ....D....... 630 365-6600
Virgil *(G-20190)*
Global Track Property USA Inc ....G....... 630 213-6863
Bartlett *(G-1283)*
Paul Wever Construction Eqp Co..........F....... 309 965-2005
Goodfield *(G-10676)*
Podrez Enterprise LLC ....G....... 815 353-5893
Lakemoor *(G-12474)*
Rockford Rigging Inc............................G....... 309 263-0566
Morton *(G-14381)*
Sauber Manufacturing Company..........D....... 630 365-6600
Virgil *(G-20191)*
Woods Equipment Company ....D....... 815 732-2141
Oregon *(G-15929)*

CONSTRUCTION EQPT: Attachments, Snow Plow

Flink Company ....E....... 815 673-4321
Streator *(G-19608)*
Henderson Products Inc ....F....... 847 836-4996
Gilberts *(G-10357)*
Nordic Auto Plow LLC ....G....... 815 353-8267
West Chicago *(G-20623)*
Tim Wallace Ldscp Sup Co Inc ....F....... 630 759-6813
Bolingbrook *(G-2250)*

CONSTRUCTION EQPT: Attachments, Subsoiler, Tractor Mounted

Ovis Loader Attachments Inc ....G....... 618 203-2757
Carbondale *(G-2853)*

CONSTRUCTION EQPT: Backhoes, Tractors, Cranes & Similar Eqpt

Clarke Equipment Company ....G....... 701 241-8700
Woodridge *(G-21285)*
Manitou Americas Inc ....G....... 262 334-9461
Belvidere *(G-1684)*
Mjmc Inc...E....... 708 596-5200
Hazel Crest *(G-11135)*
National Tractor Parts Inc ....E....... 630 552-4235
Plano *(G-16736)*

CONSTRUCTION EQPT: Bucket Or Scarifier Teeth

USA Star Group of Company ....G....... 773 456-6677
Chicago *(G-6505)*

CONSTRUCTION EQPT: Cabs

Bergstrom Elctrfied Systems LL ....G....... 815 874-7821
Rockford *(G-17320)*
Bergstrom Inc.......................................B....... 815 874-7821
Rockford *(G-17321)*
Bergstrom Parts LLC ....G....... 815 874-7821
Rockford *(G-17323)*

CONSTRUCTION EQPT: Crane Carriers

Avanti Motor Carriers Inc ....G....... 630 313-9160
Naperville *(G-14960)*
Lanigan Holdings LLC ....F....... 708 596-5200
Hazel Crest *(G-11132)*
Walter Payton Power Eqp LLC ....E....... 708 656-7700
Riverdale *(G-17079)*

CONSTRUCTION EQPT: Cranes

Uesco Industries Inc ....G....... 708 385-7700
Alsip *(G-517)*

CONSTRUCTION EQPT: Hammer Mills, Port, Incl Rock/Ore Crush

Genesis III Inc......................................E....... 815 537-7900
Prophetstown *(G-16831)*

CONSTRUCTION EQPT: Loaders, Shovel, Self-Propelled

Avant Tecno USA Inc ....F....... 847 380-1308
Arlington Heights *(G-700)*

CONSTRUCTION EQPT: Rock Crushing Machinery, Portable

Flsmidth Pekin LLC ....D....... 309 347-3031
Pekin *(G-16335)*

CONSTRUCTION EQPT: Roofing Eqpt

Illinois Tool Works Inc ....F....... 847 918-6473
Libertyville *(G-12662)*
Machine Solution Providers Inc ....D....... 630 717-7040
Downers Grove *(G-8049)*
Omg Inc..E....... 413 789-0252
Addison *(G-232)*
Rdi Group Inc ....C....... 630 773-4900
Itasca *(G-11724)*
Reload Sales Inc ....E....... 618 588-2866
New Baden *(G-15023)*

CONSTRUCTION EQPT: Tractors

Caterpillar Inc ....B....... 309 675-1000
East Peoria *(G-8256)*
Caterpillar Inc ....B....... 217 475-4355
Decatur *(G-7472)*
Caterpillar Inc ....B....... 217 424-1809
Decatur *(G-7473)*
Caterpillar Inc ....A....... 217 475-4000
Decatur *(G-7471)*

CONSTRUCTION EQPT: Tractors, Crawler

Caterpillar Inc ....B....... 309 675-1000
East Peoria *(G-8255)*
Caterpillar Inc ....A....... 309 578-1615
Mossville *(G-14459)*
Caterpillar Inc ....B....... 309 675-6590
Peoria *(G-16411)*

CONSTRUCTION EQPT: Trucks, Off-Highway

Kress Corporation ....D....... 309 446-3395
Brimfield *(G-2406)*

CONSTRUCTION EQPT: Wrecker Hoists, Automobile

High Point Recovery Company ....G....... 217 821-7777
Toledo *(G-19876)*
S&S Recovery ....G....... 217 538-2206
Fillmore *(G-9665)*

CONSTRUCTION MATERIALS WHOLESALERS

Windwrap LLC......................................G....... 773 594-1724
Chicago *(G-6639)*

CONSTRUCTION MATERIALS, WHOL: Concrete/Cinder Bldg Prdts

Edwards Acquisition Corp ....F....... 309 944-2117
Geneseo *(G-10241)*
Hamilton Concrete Products Co...........G....... 217 847-3118
Hamilton *(G-10958)*
Ozinga Bros Inc....................................D....... 815 332-8198
Belvidere *(G-1693)*
Schirz Concrete Products Inc ....F....... 217 368-2153
Greenfield *(G-10818)*
Upland Concrete ....G....... 224 699-9909
East Dundee *(G-8214)*

CONSTRUCTION MATERIALS, WHOLESALE: Aggregate

Rogers Ready Mix & Mtls Inc ....D....... 815 234-8212
Byron *(G-2757)*

CONSTRUCTION MATERIALS, WHOLESALE: Air Ducts, Sheet Metal

Bisco Enterprise Inc ....F....... 630 628-1831
Schaumburg *(G-18463)*

CONSTRUCTION MATERIALS, WHOLESALE: Architectural Metalwork

Carl Stahl Decrcabl Innovtns I ....F....... 312 474-1100
Burr Ridge *(G-2660)*

CONSTRUCTION MATERIALS, WHOLESALE: Awnings

Acme Awning Co Inc ....G....... 847 446-0153
Lake Zurich *(G-12379)*
Tri State Aluminum Products ....F....... 815 877-6081
Loves Park *(G-13277)*

CONSTRUCTION MATERIALS, WHOLESALE: Block, Concrete & Cinder

Contractors Concrete Inc ....E....... 217 342-2299
Effingham *(G-8394)*

CONSTRUCTION MATERIALS, WHOLESALE: Brick, Exc Refractory

Bricks Inc...G....... 630 897-6926
Aurora *(G-1066)*
Richards Brick Company ....D....... 618 656-0230
Edwardsville *(G-8374)*
Sesser Concrete Products Co ....F....... 618 625-2811
Sesser *(G-18866)*
Stone Center Inc ....G....... 630 971-2060
Lisle *(G-12943)*

CONSTRUCTION MATERIALS, WHOLESALE: Building Stone, Granite

Lansing Cut Stone Co ....F....... 708 474-7515
Lansing *(G-12503)*
Midwest Stone Sales Inc ....F....... 815 254-6600
Plainfield *(G-16691)*

CONSTRUCTION MATERIALS, WHOLESALE: Building Stone, Marble

American Marble & Granite Inc............G....... 815 741-1710
Crest Hill *(G-7083)*
House Granite & Marble Corp ....G....... 847 928-1111
Schiller Park *(G-18814)*
Marble Emporium Inc ....E....... 847 205-4000
Northbrook *(G-15427)*
Northwest Products ....G....... 630 860-2288
Bensenville *(G-1859)*
Stone Design Inc..................................F....... 630 790-5715
Glendale Heights *(G-10501)*
Stone Design Inc..................................E....... 630 790-5715
Glendale Heights *(G-10502)*

CONSTRUCTION MATERIALS, WHOLESALE: Building, Exterior

Arrowtech Pallet & Crating ....D....... 815 547-9300
Belvidere *(G-1650)*
Chicago Flameproof WD Spc Corp .....E....... 630 859-0009
Montgomery *(G-14240)*
Continental Materials Corp ....F....... 312 541-7200
Chicago *(G-4228)*
H J Mohr & Sons Company ....F....... 708 366-0338
Oak Park *(G-15756)*
Illinois Tool Works Inc ....F....... 708 720-7070
Frankfort *(G-9806)*
Logan Square Aluminum Sup Inc ....D....... 847 985-1700
Schaumburg *(G-18611)*

PRODUCT SECTION

CONSTRUCTION MATLS, WHOL: Lumber, Rough, Dressed/Finished

Woodx Lumber Inc ....G....... 331 979-2171
  Elmhurst *(G-9447)*

CONSTRUCTION MATERIALS, WHOLESALE: Cement

Illinois Cement Company LLC ....C....... 815 224-2112
  La Salle *(G-12113)*

CONSTRUCTION MATERIALS, WHOLESALE: Ceramic, Exc Refractory

Nidec-Shimpo America Corp ....E....... 630 924-7138
  Glendale Heights *(G-10479)*

CONSTRUCTION MATERIALS, WHOLESALE: Clay, Exc Refractory

Amcol International Corp ....E....... 847 851-1500
  Hoffman Estates *(G-11405)*

CONSTRUCTION MATERIALS, WHOLESALE: Concrete Mixtures

Advanced On-Site Concrete Inc ....E....... 773 622-7836
  Chicago *(G-3566)*
Material Service Corporation ....E....... 815 838-2400
  Romeoville *(G-17846)*
Rock River Ready Mix Inc ....G....... 815 288-2260
  Dixon *(G-7911)*

CONSTRUCTION MATERIALS, WHOLESALE: Doors, Garage

Bricks Inc ....G....... 630 897-6926
  Aurora *(G-1066)*

CONSTRUCTION MATERIALS, WHOLESALE: Doors, Sliding

Cmp Millwork Co ....G....... 630 832-6462
  Elmhurst *(G-9348)*
Metal Products Sales Corp ....G....... 708 301-6844
  Lockport *(G-13013)*

CONSTRUCTION MATERIALS, WHOLESALE: Drywall Materials

Illinois Fibre Specialty Co ....E....... 773 376-1122
  Chicago *(G-4890)*
Pro Patch Systems Inc ....G....... 847 356-8100
  Lake Villa *(G-12364)*

CONSTRUCTION MATERIALS, WHOLESALE: Fiberglass Building Mat

Npi Holding Corp ....G....... 217 391-1229
  Springfield *(G-19412)*
Nudo Products Inc ....C....... 217 528-5636
  Springfield *(G-19414)*

CONSTRUCTION MATERIALS, WHOLESALE: Glass

Euroview Enterprises LLC ....E....... 630 227-3300
  Elmhurst *(G-9364)*
House of Color ....F....... 708 352-3222
  Countryside *(G-7059)*
Moore Memorials ....F....... 708 636-6532
  Chicago Ridge *(G-6804)*
Shoreline Glass Co Inc ....E....... 312 829-9500
  Hillside *(G-11356)*
Tafco Corporation ....E....... 847 678-8425
  Melrose Park *(G-13921)*

CONSTRUCTION MATERIALS, WHOLESALE: Grain Storage Bins

Arrows Up Inc ....G....... 847 305-2550
  Arlington Heights *(G-696)*

CONSTRUCTION MATERIALS, WHOLESALE: Gravel

Rock River Ready-Mix ....E....... 815 288-2269
  Dixon *(G-7913)*
Western Sand & Gravel Co ....F....... 815 433-1600
  Ottawa *(G-16085)*

CONSTRUCTION MATERIALS, WHOLESALE: Insulation, Thermal

Kalb Corporation ....F....... 309 483-3600
  Oneida *(G-15903)*

CONSTRUCTION MATERIALS, WHOLESALE: Joists

Heckmann Building Products Inc ....E....... 708 865-2403
  Melrose Park *(G-13879)*
Selco Industries ....G....... 708 499-1060
  Chicago Ridge *(G-6810)*

CONSTRUCTION MATERIALS, WHOLESALE: Limestone

Riverstone Group Inc ....F....... 309 933-1123
  Cleveland *(G-6912)*

CONSTRUCTION MATERIALS, WHOLESALE: Lockers

Prestige Distribution Inc ....G....... 847 480-7667
  Northbrook *(G-15465)*

CONSTRUCTION MATERIALS, WHOLESALE: Masons' Materials

Harvey Cement Products Inc ....F....... 708 333-1900
  Harvey *(G-11087)*
Northfield Block Company ....G....... 708 458-8130
  Berwyn *(G-1957)*

CONSTRUCTION MATERIALS, WHOLESALE: Millwork

Kohout Woodwork Inc ....G....... 630 628-6257
  Addison *(G-174)*
Mid-West Millwork Wholesale ....G....... 618 407-5940
  Mascoutah *(G-13603)*
River City Millwork Inc ....D....... 800 892-9297
  Rockford *(G-17573)*
Triezenberg Millwork Co ....G....... 708 489-9062
  Crestwood *(G-7132)*

CONSTRUCTION MATERIALS, WHOLESALE: Molding, All Materials

AGCO Recycling LLC ....F....... 217 224-9048
  Quincy *(G-16851)*
Southern Mold Finishing Inc ....F....... 618 983-5049
  Johnston City *(G-11813)*

CONSTRUCTION MATERIALS, WHOLESALE: Pallets, Wood

F and L Pallets Inc ....G....... 773 364-0798
  Chicago *(G-4547)*
Northern Pallet and Supply Co ....G....... 847 716-1400
  Northfield *(G-15524)*

CONSTRUCTION MATERIALS, WHOLESALE: Paving Materials

Curran Contracting Company ....G....... 815 758-8113
  Dekalb *(G-7671)*

CONSTRUCTION MATERIALS, WHOLESALE: Prefabricated Structures

Morton Buildings Inc ....G....... 217 357-3713
  Carthage *(G-3140)*
Morton Buildings Inc ....F....... 309 936-7282
  Atkinson *(G-902)*

CONSTRUCTION MATERIALS, WHOLESALE: Roof, Asphalt/Sheet Metal

Crown Coatings Company ....F....... 630 365-9925
  Elburn *(G-8448)*
Roxul USA Inc ....A....... 800 323-7164
  Chicago *(G-6068)*

CONSTRUCTION MATERIALS, WHOLESALE: Roofing & Siding Material

Co-Fair Corporation ....E....... 847 626-1500
  Skokie *(G-18945)*

Cofair Products Inc ....G....... 847 626-1500
  Skokie *(G-18946)*
Petersen Aluminum Corporation ....D....... 847 228-7150
  Elk Grove Village *(G-9176)*
TMJ Architectural LLC ....G....... 815 388-7820
  Crystal Lake *(G-7283)*

CONSTRUCTION MATERIALS, WHOLESALE: Sand

Mertel Gravel Company Inc ....F....... 815 223-0468
  Peru *(G-16581)*

CONSTRUCTION MATERIALS, WHOLESALE: Septic Tanks

Septic Solutions Inc ....G....... 217 925-5992
  Dieterich *(G-7878)*

CONSTRUCTION MATERIALS, WHOLESALE: Sewer Pipe, Clay

Clay Vollmar Products Co ....F....... 773 774-1234
  Chicago *(G-4172)*
Kieft Bros Inc ....E....... 630 832-8090
  Elmhurst *(G-9388)*

CONSTRUCTION MATERIALS, WHOLESALE: Stone, Crushed Or Broken

Central Stone Company ....F....... 309 776-3900
  Colchester *(G-6946)*
Gallasi Cut Stone & Marble LLC ....E....... 708 479-9494
  Mokena *(G-14086)*
Galloy and Van Etten Inc ....E....... 773 928-4800
  Chicago *(G-4657)*
Riverstone Group Inc ....E....... 309 787-3141
  Milan *(G-14026)*
Rogers Ready Mix & Mtls Inc ....F....... 815 389-2223
  Roscoe *(G-17927)*
Southern Illinois Stone Co ....E....... 618 995-2392
  Buncombe *(G-2630)*
Southfield Corporation ....E....... 815 842-2333
  Pontiac *(G-16780)*
Southfield Corporation ....E....... 708 458-0400
  Oak Lawn *(G-15735)*
T H Davidson & Co Inc ....E....... 815 464-2000
  Oak Forest *(G-15690)*
Tuscola Stone Company ....F....... 217 253-4705
  Tuscola *(G-19933)*
William Charles Cnstr Co LLC ....G....... 815 654-4720
  Belvidere *(G-1711)*

CONSTRUCTION MATERIALS, WHOLESALE: Tile & Clay Prdts

Worldwide Tiles Ltd Inc ....G....... 708 389-2992
  Alsip *(G-526)*

CONSTRUCTION MATERIALS, WHOLESALE: Veneer

R S Bacon Veneer Company ....C....... 630 323-1414
  Lisle *(G-12932)*

CONSTRUCTION MATERIALS, WHOLESALE: Windows

Climate Guard Design ....G....... 773 873-0000
  Chicago *(G-4178)*
Cmp Millwork Co ....G....... 630 832-6462
  Elmhurst *(G-9348)*
Metal Products Sales Corp ....G....... 708 301-6844
  Lockport *(G-13013)*

CONSTRUCTION MATLS, WHOL: Composite Board Prdts, Woodboard

Fca LLC ....E....... 309 792-3444
  Moline *(G-14145)*

CONSTRUCTION MATLS, WHOL: Lumber, Rough, Dressed/Finished

Aetna Plywood Inc ....D....... 708 343-1515
  Maywood *(G-13658)*
Connor Sports Flooring LLC ....D....... 847 290-9020
  Bensenville *(G-1775)*
Enterprise Pallet Inc ....F....... 815 928-8546
  Bourbonnais *(G-2260)*

Employee Codes: A=Over 500 employees, B=251-500
C=101-250, D=51-100, E=20-50, F=10-19, G=3-9

CONSTRUCTION MATLS, WHOL: Lumber, Rough, Dressed/Finished

Farrow Lumber Co ....G....... 618 734-0255
  Cairo *(G-2767)*
Red River Lumber Inc ....D....... 708 388-1818
  Blue Island *(G-2135)*
Southeast Wood Treating Inc ....F....... 815 562-5007
  Rochelle *(G-17160)*
Sterling Site Access Sol ....C....... 708 388-2223
  Phoenix *(G-16609)*
Toyota Tsusho America Inc ....D....... 847 439-8500
  Elk Grove Village *(G-9281)*
Wooded Wonderland ....G....... 815 777-1223
  Galena *(G-10182)*
Woodworkers Shop Inc ....E....... 309 347-5111
  Pekin *(G-16371)*

CONSTRUCTION MATLS, WHOLESALE: Soil Erosion Cntrl Fabrics

RR Mulch and Soil LLC ....G....... 708 596-7200
  Markham *(G-13551)*

CONSTRUCTION MTRLS, WHOL: Exterior Flat Glass, Plate/Window

T J M & Associates Inc ....G....... 847 382-1993
  Wauconda *(G-20396)*
Torstenson Glass Co ....E....... 773 525-0435
  Chicago *(G-6397)*

CONSTRUCTION SAND MINING

Clear Lake Sand & Gravel Co ....F....... 217 725-6999
  Springfield *(G-19351)*
Jackson County Sand & Grav Co ....G....... 618 763-4711
  Gorham *(G-10682)*
Material Service Corporation ....C....... 708 731-2600
  Westchester *(G-20705)*
Plote Construction Inc ....D....... 847 695-9300
  Hoffman Estates *(G-11445)*
Quality Sand Company Inc ....G....... 618 346-1070
  Collinsville *(G-6973)*
Rock River Ready Mix Inc ....G....... 815 288-2260
  Dixon *(G-7911)*

CONSTRUCTION SITE PREPARATION SVCS

Powell Tree Care Inc ....G....... 847 364-1181
  Elk Grove Village *(G-9186)*

CONSTRUCTION: Agricultural Building

Better Built Buildings ....G....... 217 267-7824
  Westville *(G-20778)*
Morton Buildings Inc ....F....... 630 904-1122
  Streator *(G-19615)*
Morton Buildings Inc ....F....... 309 936-7282
  Atkinson *(G-902)*
West Central Fs Inc ....G....... 309 375-6904
  Wataga *(G-20287)*

CONSTRUCTION: Athletic & Recreation Facilities

Armitage Welding ....G....... 773 772-1442
  Chicago *(G-3731)*
Mef Construction Inc ....G....... 847 741-8601
  Elgin *(G-8655)*

CONSTRUCTION: Bridge

Hillyer Inc ....D....... 309 837-6434
  Macomb *(G-13392)*
Riber Construction Inc ....F....... 815 584-3337
  Dwight *(G-8159)*

CONSTRUCTION: Commercial & Institutional Building

Brd Development Group LLC ....F....... 312 912-7110
  Chicago *(G-3947)*
Chicagoland Metal Fabricators ....G....... 847 260-5320
  Franklin Park *(G-9906)*
Contract Industries Inc ....E....... 708 458-8150
  Bedford Park *(G-1464)*
Creative Designs Kitc ....E....... 773 327-8400
  Chicago *(G-4261)*
D Kersey Construction Co ....G....... 847 919-4980
  Northbrook *(G-15371)*
Frederking Construction Co ....G....... 618 483-5031
  Altamont *(G-532)*
Spannuth Boiler Co ....G....... 708 386-1882
  Oak Park *(G-15774)*

CONSTRUCTION: Commercial & Office Building, New

Blue Yonder Inc ....G....... 630 701-1492
  Naperville *(G-14781)*
Gerald R Page Corporation ....F....... 847 398-5575
  Prospect Heights *(G-16842)*
Global Brass and Copper Inc ....G....... 502 873-3000
  East Alton *(G-8166)*
Global General Contractors LLC ....G....... 708 663-0476
  Tinley Park *(G-19832)*
Morris Construction Inc ....E....... 618 544-8504
  Robinson *(G-17120)*
Skender Construction LLC ....D....... 312 781-0265
  Chicago *(G-6179)*

CONSTRUCTION: Condominium

Global General Contractors LLC ....G....... 708 663-0476
  Tinley Park *(G-19832)*

CONSTRUCTION: Drainage System

Rockford Blacktop Cnstr Co ....D....... 815 654-4700
  Rockford *(G-17586)*

CONSTRUCTION: Farm Building

Greene Welding & Hardware Inc ....E....... 217 375-4244
  East Lynn *(G-8220)*

CONSTRUCTION: Food Prdts Manufacturing or Packing Plant

American Kitchen Delights Inc ....D....... 708 210-3200
  Harvey *(G-11073)*
Balton Corporation ....F....... 773 933-7927
  Chicago *(G-3822)*

CONSTRUCTION: Heavy Highway & Street

Blue Yonder Inc ....G....... 630 701-1492
  Naperville *(G-14781)*
Curran Contracting Company ....E....... 815 455-5100
  Crystal Lake *(G-7189)*
Illinois Valley Paving Co Inc ....E....... 217 422-1010
  Elwin *(G-9459)*
Peter Baker & Son Co ....F....... 815 344-1640
  Mc Henry *(G-13705)*
Schulze & Schulze Inc ....G....... 618 687-1106
  Murphysboro *(G-14758)*
Seneca Petroleum Co Inc ....E....... 708 396-1100
  Crestwood *(G-7127)*
Southern Illinois Stone Co ....F....... 573 334-5261
  Buncombe *(G-2629)*

CONSTRUCTION: Indl Building & Warehouse

Amex Nooter LLC ....F....... 708 429-8300
  Tinley Park *(G-19803)*
I P G Warehouse Ltd ....E....... 773 722-5527
  Chicago *(G-4867)*

CONSTRUCTION: Indl Building, Prefabricated

Morton Buildings Inc ....F....... 309 936-7282
  Atkinson *(G-902)*
Signa Development Group Inc ....G....... 773 418-4506
  Norridge *(G-15243)*

CONSTRUCTION: Indl Buildings, New, NEC

Blue Yonder Inc ....G....... 630 701-1492
  Naperville *(G-14781)*
Gerald R Page Corporation ....F....... 847 398-5575
  Prospect Heights *(G-16842)*
Grs Holding LLC ....F....... 630 355-1660
  Naperville *(G-14838)*
Kelley Construction Inc ....E....... 217 422-1800
  Decatur *(G-7513)*
Silver Bros Inc ....E....... 217 283-7751
  Hoopeston *(G-11513)*

CONSTRUCTION: Irrigation System

C & L Tiling Inc ....D....... 217 773-3357
  Timewell *(G-19797)*

CONSTRUCTION: Mausoleum

St Charles Memorial Works Inc ....G....... 630 584-0183
  Saint Charles *(G-18275)*

CONSTRUCTION: Multi-Family Housing

Frederking Construction Co ....G....... 618 483-5031
  Altamont *(G-532)*
Quality Molding Products LLC ....G....... 224 286-4555
  Gurnee *(G-10921)*

CONSTRUCTION: Oil & Gas Pipeline Construction

Csiteq LLC ....F....... 312 265-1509
  Rosemont *(G-18011)*
Electric Conduit Cnstr Co ....C....... 630 293-4474
  Elburn *(G-8453)*
L & H Company Inc ....F....... 630 571-7200
  Oak Brook *(G-15630)*

CONSTRUCTION: Pharmaceutical Manufacturing Plant

Most Enterprise Inc ....D....... 800 792-4669
  Chicago *(G-5504)*

CONSTRUCTION: Power & Communication Transmission Tower

SNC Solutions Inc ....E....... 217 784-5212
  Gibson City *(G-10344)*
Veteran Wire and Cable LLC ....G....... 630 327-5849
  Addison *(G-329)*

CONSTRUCTION: Railroad & Subway

AR Concepts USA Inc ....G....... 847 392-4608
  Palatine *(G-16093)*

CONSTRUCTION: Residential, Nec

Protective Coatings & Waterpro ....G....... 708 403-7650
  Orland Park *(G-15975)*

CONSTRUCTION: Retaining Wall

Unilock Chicago Inc ....D....... 630 892-9191
  Aurora *(G-1165)*

CONSTRUCTION: Scaffolding

Gilco Real Estate Company ....E....... 847 298-1717
  Des Plaines *(G-7774)*

CONSTRUCTION: Sewer Line

Rockford Blacktop Cnstr Co ....D....... 815 654-4700
  Rockford *(G-17586)*

CONSTRUCTION: Single-Family Housing

Bernard Cffey Vtrans Fundation ....G....... 630 687-0033
  Naperville *(G-14779)*
Chicagoland Metal Fabricators ....G....... 847 260-5320
  Franklin Park *(G-9906)*
Construction Contg Svcs Inc ....F....... 219 779-0900
  Lansing *(G-12489)*
Electric Conduit Cnstr Co ....C....... 630 293-4474
  Elburn *(G-8453)*
Global General Contractors LLC ....G....... 708 663-0476
  Tinley Park *(G-19832)*
Otten Construction Co Inc ....G....... 618 768-4310
  Addieville *(G-11)*
Poggenpohl LLC ....G....... 217 229-3411
  Raymond *(G-16990)*
Poggenpohl LLC ....G....... 217 824-2020
  Taylorville *(G-19760)*
Scheffler Custom Woodworking ....G....... 815 284-6564
  Dixon *(G-7915)*
Stahl Lumber Company ....F....... 309 695-4331
  Wyoming *(G-21462)*

CONSTRUCTION: Single-family Housing, New

Frederking Construction Co ....G....... 618 483-5031
  Altamont *(G-532)*
Jack Ruch Quality Homes Inc ....G....... 309 663-6595
  Bloomington *(G-2063)*
Pete Frcano Sons Cstm HM Bldrs ....F....... 847 258-4626
  Elk Grove Village *(G-9175)*
Peters Construction ....G....... 773 489-5555
  Chicago *(G-5794)*
R-Squared Construction Inc ....G....... 815 232-7433
  Freeport *(G-10135)*

PRODUCT SECTION

Savino Enterprises .... G 708 385-5277
  Blue Island (G-2138)

CONSTRUCTION: Street Surfacing & Paving

A&J Paving Inc .... G 773 889-9133
  Chicago (G-3493)
Advanced Asphalt Co .... E 815 872-9911
  Princeton (G-16804)
Cullinan & Sons Inc .... E 309 925-2711
  Tremont (G-19895)
Geske and Sons Inc .... F 815 459-2407
  Crystal Lake (G-7202)
Hillyer Inc .... D 309 837-6434
  Macomb (G-13392)

CONSTRUCTION: Swimming Pools

Knapheide Manufacturing Co .... E 217 223-1848
  Quincy (G-16902)
Rockford Sewer Co Inc .... G 815 877-9060
  Loves Park (G-13259)
Royal Fiberglass Pools Inc .... D 618 266-7089
  Dix (G-7882)

CONSTRUCTION: Tennis Court

All Weather Courts Inc .... G 217 364-4546
  Dawson (G-7428)
Schulze & Schulze Inc .... G 618 687-1106
  Murphysboro (G-14758)

CONSTRUCTION: Truck & Automobile Assembly Plant

Auto Truck Group LLC .... C 630 860-5600
  Bartlett (G-1267)

CONSTRUCTION: Tunnel

Industrial Controls Inc .... G 630 752-8100
  Geneva (G-10278)

CONSTRUCTION: Utility Line

Cullinan & Sons Inc .... E 309 925-2711
  Tremont (G-19895)
Foltz Welding Ltd .... C 618 432-7777
  Patoka (G-16303)
Mid-America Underground LLC .... E 630 443-9999
  Aurora (G-1134)

CONSTRUCTION: Waste Water & Sewage Treatment Plant

Allendale Gravel Co Inc .... F 618 263-3521
  Allendale (G-402)
Applied Mechanical Tech LLC .... G 815 472-2700
  Momence (G-14182)
Gig Karasek LLC .... F 630 549-0394
  Saint Charles (G-18204)
Supplied Indus Solutions Inc .... E 618 452-8151
  Granite City (G-10741)

CONSTRUCTION: Water & Sewer Line

Kvd Enterprises LLC .... G 618 726-5114
  O Fallon (G-15577)
Mef Construction Inc .... G 847 741-8601
  Elgin (G-8655)

CONSTRUCTION: Water Main

Hillyer Inc .... D 309 837-6434
  Macomb (G-13392)
Lake County Grading Co LLC .... D 847 362-2590
  Libertyville (G-12665)

CONSULTING SVC: Actuarial

Mark S Machine Shop Inc .... G 815 895-3955
  Sycamore (G-19724)
Taloc Usa Inc .... G 847 665-8222
  Libertyville (G-12714)

CONSULTING SVC: Business, NEC

10th Magnitude LLC .... E 224 628-9047
  Chicago (G-3461)
Ada Holding Company Inc .... F 312 440-2897
  Chicago (G-3537)
Advantage Press Inc .... G 630 960-5305
  Lisle (G-12858)

Ascent Innovations LLC .... E 847 572-8000
  Schaumburg (G-18445)
Captains Emporium Inc .... G 773 972-7609
  Chicago (G-4021)
Doxa Enterprises LLC .... G 618 515-4470
  East Saint Louis (G-8305)
Eco-Pur Solutions LLC .... G 630 226-2300
  Romeoville (G-17815)
ESP Properties LLC .... E 312 725-5100
  Chicago (G-4531)
G T C Industries Inc .... G 708 369-9815
  Naperville (G-14832)
Gmb Partners LLC .... E 773 248-4038
  Chicago (G-4703)
High Power Inc .... F 773 581-7650
  Chicago (G-4817)
Honeywell Safety Pdts USA Inc .... C 309 786-7741
  Rock Island (G-17223)
I W M Corporation .... G 847 695-0700
  Elgin (G-8619)
Joe Hunt .... G 618 392-2000
  Olney (G-15866)
K-Pro US LLC .... G 872 529-5776
  O Fallon (G-15576)
Kishknows Inc .... G 708 252-3648
  Richton Park (G-17030)
L T P LLC .... C 815 723-9400
  Joliet (G-11893)
Logicgate Inc .... C 312 279-2775
  Chicago (G-5250)
McIlvaine Co .... E 847 784-0012
  Northfield (G-15522)
Monolithic Industries Inc .... G 630 985-6009
  Woodridge (G-21324)
Motivequest LLC .... F 847 905-6100
  Chicago (G-5506)
Nas Media Group Inc .... G 312 371-7499
  Olympia Fields (G-15896)
North Shore Consultants Inc .... G 847 290-1599
  Elk Grove Village (G-9153)
Nowuba LLC .... G 801 510-8086
  Fox Lake (G-9751)
Paragon International Inc .... F 847 240-2981
  Schaumburg (G-18664)
Perry Johnson Inc .... F 847 635-0010
  Rosemont (G-18041)
Pool Center Inc .... G 217 698-7665
  Springfield (G-19426)
Promark Associates Inc .... F 847 676-1894
  Skokie (G-19015)
Pure Flo Bottling Inc .... G 815 963-4797
  Rockford (G-17562)
Regunathan & Assoc Inc .... G 630 653-0387
  Wheaton (G-20818)
Reign Print Solutions Inc .... G 847 590-7091
  Arlington Heights (G-798)
St Louis Scrap Trading LLC .... G 618 307-9002
  Edwardsville (G-8376)
Strategic Applications Inc .... G 847 680-9385
  Lake Villa (G-12368)
Tighe Publishing Services Inc .... F 773 281-9100
  Chicago (G-6378)
W-F Professional Assoc Inc .... G 847 945-8050
  Deerfield (G-7659)
Weeb Enterprises LLC .... G 815 861-2625
  Wauconda (G-20402)

CONSULTING SVC: Chemical

Vantage Specialties Inc .... G 847 244-3410
  Chicago (G-6523)

CONSULTING SVC: Computer

Advanced Web Technologies LLC .... E 847 985-3833
  South Elgin (G-19129)
Amaitis and Associates Inc .... F 847 428-1269
  Wood Dale (G-21160)
Ascent Innovations LLC .... E 847 572-8000
  Schaumburg (G-18445)
Ats Commercial Group LLC .... F 815 686-2705
  Piper City (G-16625)
Bantix Technologies LLC .... G 630 446-0886
  Glen Ellyn (G-10396)
Buyersvine Inc .... G 630 235-6804
  Hinsdale (G-11367)
Computer Industry Almanac Inc .... G 847 758-1926
  Arlington Heights (G-718)
Computer Pwr Solutions III Ltd .... E 618 281-8898
  Columbia (G-6988)
Comvigo Inc .... G 312 933-3385
  Willowbrook (G-21037)

CONSULTING SVC: Engineering

Createasoft Inc .... F 630 851-9474
  Aurora (G-943)
Entappia LLC .... G 630 546-4531
  Aurora (G-957)
Friedrich Klatt and Associates .... G 773 753-1806
  Chicago (G-4636)
Gld Industries Inc .... G 217 390-9594
  Champaign (G-3296)
Imcp Inc .... G 630 477-8600
  Itasca (G-11675)
Infosys Limited .... E 630 482-5000
  Lisle (G-12901)
Key Resources Inc .... G 800 574-1339
  Lake Villa (G-12357)
Koombea Inc .... G 408 786-5290
  Chicago (G-5123)
Logicgate Inc .... C 312 279-2775
  Chicago (G-5250)
M K Advantage Inc .... F 773 902-5272
  Chicago (G-5302)
Manufacturers News Inc .... D 847 864-7000
  Evanston (G-9549)
Marie Gere Corporation .... C 847 540-1154
  Lake Zurich (G-12430)
Monroe Associates Inc .... G 217 665-3898
  Bethany (G-1968)
National Def Intelligence Inc .... G 312 233-2318
  Naperville (G-14980)
Onx USA LLC .... E 630 343-8940
  Lisle (G-12925)
Pagepath Technologies Inc .... F 630 689-4111
  Plano (G-16738)
Panatech Computer Management .... G 847 678-8848
  Lincolnshire (G-12789)
Premier Intl Entps Inc .... E 312 857-2200
  Chicago (G-5862)
Print Management Partners Inc .... E 847 699-2999
  Des Plaines (G-7833)
Reign Print Solutions Inc .... G 847 590-7091
  Arlington Heights (G-798)
Sedona Inc .... C 309 736-4104
  Moline (G-14176)
Synergy Technology Group Inc .... F 773 305-3500
  Chicago (G-6303)
Tegratecs Development Corp .... G 847 397-0088
  Schaumburg (G-18743)
Vertical Software Inc .... F 309 633-0700
  Bartonville (G-1336)

CONSULTING SVC: Data Processing

Ifs North America Inc .... E 888 437-4968
  Itasca (G-11670)
Pycas Design Innovations LLC .... E 847 656-5000
  Glenview (G-10604)

CONSULTING SVC: Educational

African-American Images Inc .... F 708 672-4909
  Crete (G-7134)
LMS Innovations Inc .... G 312 613-2345
  Chicago (G-5247)
Pieces of Learning Inc .... G 618 964-9426
  Marion (G-13526)

CONSULTING SVC: Engineering

Accelrted Mch Design Engrg LLC ...... E 815 316-6381
  Rockford (G-17290)
Armstrong Aerospace Inc .... D 847 244-4500
  Waukegan (G-20418)
Component Tool & Mfg Co .... F 708 672-6505
  Crete (G-7136)
Control Panels Inc .... F 815 654-6000
  Rockford (G-17357)
Dike-O-Seal Incorporated .... F 773 254-3224
  Chicago (G-4361)
Enders Process Equipment Corp .... G 630 469-3787
  Glendale Heights (G-10449)
Industrial Phrm Resources Inc .... F 630 823-4700
  Bartlett (G-1290)
Kenyeri Consulting LLC .... G 630 920-3497
  Downers Grove (G-8039)
Marie Gere Corporation .... C 847 540-1154
  Lake Zurich (G-12430)
Meyer Systems .... G 815 436-7077
  Joliet (G-11900)
Mid-City Die & Mold Corp .... G 773 278-4844
  Chicago (G-5430)
Most Enterprise Inc .... D 800 792-4669
  Chicago (G-5504)

Employee Codes: A=Over 500 employees, B=251-500
C=101-250, D=51-100, E=20-50, F=10-19, G=3-9

CONSULTING SVC: Engineering

Neomek Incorporated .... F 630 879-5400
  Batavia *(G-1399)*
Silicon Control Inc .... G 847 215-7947
  Deerfield *(G-7649)*
Triangle Technologies Inc .... G 630 736-3318
  Streamwood *(G-19599)*

CONSULTING SVC: Financial Management

Alvarez & Marsal Inc .... E 312 601-4220
  Chicago *(G-3639)*
Lehigh Consumer Products LLC .... C 630 851-7330
  Aurora *(G-997)*

CONSULTING SVC: Human Resource

Merit Emplyment Asssment Svcs .... G 815 320-3680
  New Lenox *(G-15041)*

CONSULTING SVC: Management

7000 Inc .... F 312 800-3612
  Bolingbrook *(G-2143)*
C D Nelson Consulting Inc .... G 847 487-4870
  Wauconda *(G-20336)*
Chad Mazeika .... G 815 298-8118
  Rockford *(G-17343)*
Csiteq LLC .... G 312 265-1509
  Rosemont *(G-18011)*
Datair Employee Benefit Systems .... E 630 325-2600
  Westmont *(G-20734)*
Falex Corporation .... E 630 556-3679
  Sugar Grove *(G-19643)*
Huntley & Associates Inc .... G 224 381-8500
  Lake Zurich *(G-12420)*
I T C W Inc .... B 630 305-8849
  Naperville *(G-14842)*
Identiti Resources Ltd .... E 866 477-4467
  Schaumburg *(G-18554)*
Infogix Inc .... C 630 505-1800
  Naperville *(G-14846)*
Knowledgeshift Inc .... G 630 221-8759
  Wheaton *(G-20809)*
Lenrok Industries Inc .... G 630 628-1946
  Addison *(G-182)*
McClendon Holdings LLC .... G 773 251-2314
  Chicago *(G-5373)*
McIlvaine Co .... E 847 784-0012
  Northfield *(G-15522)*
NFC Company Inc .... G 773 472-6468
  Chicago *(G-5594)*
Parth Consultants Inc .... E 847 758-1400
  Schaumburg *(G-18667)*
Screen North Amer Holdings Inc .... F 847 870-7400
  Rolling Meadows *(G-17774)*
State of Illinois .... C 312 836-9500
  Chicago *(G-6235)*
Vega Technology & Systems .... G 630 855-5068
  Bartlett *(G-1259)*
Ycl International Inc .... E 630 873-0768
  Woodridge *(G-21350)*

CONSULTING SVC: Marketing Management

Allegra Marketing Print Mail .... G 630 790-0444
  Schaumburg *(G-18431)*
Alliance Creative Group Inc .... E 847 885-1800
  East Dundee *(G-8187)*
Arcsec Digital LLC .... G 312 324-4794
  Lake Forest *(G-12225)*
Bendinger Bruce Crtve Comm In .... G 773 871-1179
  Chicago *(G-3866)*
Canright & Paule Inc .... G 888 202-3894
  Chicago *(G-4015)*
Chase Security Systems Inc .... G 773 594-1919
  Chicago *(G-4078)*
Cheetah Digital Inc .... D 312 858-8200
  Chicago *(G-4081)*
Custom Direct Inc .... F 630 529-1936
  Roselle *(G-17950)*
Darwill Inc .... C 708 449-7770
  Hillside *(G-11335)*
E-Intrctive Mktg Solutions Inc .... G 312 241-1692
  Bridgeview *(G-2342)*
Evo Exhibits LLC .... G 630 520-0710
  West Chicago *(G-20577)*
Flyerinc Corporation .... G 630 655-3400
  Oak Brook *(G-15622)*
Forrest Consulting .... G 630 730-9619
  Glen Ellyn *(G-10403)*
Intellisource Inc .... E 847 426-7400
  Elgin *(G-8629)*

Lure Group LLC .... G 630 222-6515
  Bolingbrook *(G-2207)*
M Wells Printing Co .... G 312 455-0400
  Chicago *(G-5305)*
Mittera Illinois LLC .... D 708 449-8989
  Berkeley *(G-1942)*
Multi Print and Digital LLC .... G 630 985-2600
  Darien *(G-7410)*
Orr Marketing Corp .... F 847 401-5171
  Elgin *(G-8680)*
Palm International Inc .... G 630 357-1437
  Naperville *(G-14892)*
Print and Mktg Solutions Group .... E 847 498-9640
  Chicago *(G-5876)*
Print Management Partners Inc .... E 847 699-2999
  Des Plaines *(G-7833)*
Segerdahl Graphics Inc .... B 847 541-1080
  Wheeling *(G-20981)*
Srv Professional Publications .... G 847 330-1260
  Schaumburg *(G-18727)*
Stagnito Partners LLC .... E 224 632-8200
  Chicago *(G-6227)*
Taylor Communication .... C 309 664-0444
  Bloomington *(G-2100)*
The Web Cmmnications Group Inc .... G 630 467-0900
  Itasca *(G-11746)*

CONSULTING SVC: Motion Picture

2nd Cine Inc .... G 773 455-5808
  Elgin *(G-8488)*

CONSULTING SVC: Online Technology

Baka Vitaliy .... G 773 370-5522
  Chicago *(G-3817)*
Nimbl Worldwide Inc .... E 303 800-0245
  Chicago *(G-5603)*
Sunemco Technologies Inc .... G 630 369-8947
  Naperville *(G-14923)*
Titanium Inc .... G 847 691-5446
  Grayslake *(G-10802)*
Wrapports LLC .... F 312 321-3000
  Chicago *(G-6683)*

CONSULTING SVC: Sales Management

Am-Don Partnership .... G 217 355-7750
  Champaign *(G-3263)*
Partners Resource Inc .... G 630 620-9161
  Glen Ellyn *(G-10417)*
Scholastic Inc .... E 630 443-8197
  Saint Charles *(G-18267)*

CONSULTING SVC: Telecommunications

Brahman Spirit Tribe .... F 773 957-2828
  Chicago *(G-3942)*
Driver Services .... G 505 267-8686
  Bensenville *(G-1789)*
Innovative AV Systems Inc .... G 312 265-6282
  Elmhurst *(G-9379)*
Lumentum Operations LLC .... G 408 546-5483
  Chicago *(G-5282)*
Othernet Inc .... G 773 688-4320
  Long Grove *(G-13168)*

CONSULTING SVCS, BUSINESS: Agricultural

Busatis Inc .... G 630 844-9803
  Montgomery *(G-14236)*

CONSULTING SVCS, BUSINESS: Communications

Above Waves Inc .... G 708 341-9123
  Mokena *(G-14068)*
Darwill Inc .... C 708 449-7770
  Hillside *(G-11335)*

CONSULTING SVCS, BUSINESS: Energy Conservation

Clean Energy Renewables LLC .... E 309 797-4844
  Moline *(G-14136)*

CONSULTING SVCS, BUSINESS: Environmental

Blackburn Sampling Inc .... G 309 342-8429
  Galesburg *(G-10185)*

Pan America Environmental Inc .... G 815 344-2960
  McHenry *(G-13775)*
Wet USA Inc .... G 630 540-2113
  Streamwood *(G-19603)*

CONSULTING SVCS, BUSINESS: Publishing

Cade Communications Inc .... G 773 477-7184
  Chicago *(G-4000)*
College Bound Publications .... G 773 262-5810
  Chicago *(G-4201)*
Forrest Consulting .... G 630 730-9619
  Glen Ellyn *(G-10403)*
John C Grafft .... F 847 842-9200
  Lake Barrington *(G-12153)*

CONSULTING SVCS, BUSINESS: Safety Training Svcs

Coaching For Excellence LLC .... F 708 957-6047
  Country Club Hills *(G-7036)*
Utility Business Media Inc .... F 815 459-1796
  Crystal Lake *(G-7287)*

CONSULTING SVCS, BUSINESS: Sys Engnrg, Exc Computer/Prof

AR Inet Corp .... G 603 380-3903
  Aurora *(G-913)*
Braindok LLC .... G 847 877-1586
  Buffalo Grove *(G-2520)*
Innovative Werks Inc .... G 312 767-8618
  Naperville *(G-14848)*
Logical Design Solutions Inc .... G 630 786-5999
  Naperville *(G-14865)*
Prairie Wi-FI Systems .... G 515 988-3260
  Chicago *(G-5852)*
Turner Agward .... G 773 669-8559
  Chicago *(G-6444)*

CONSULTING SVCS, BUSINESS: Systems Analysis & Engineering

Global Tech & Resources Inc .... G 630 364-4260
  Rolling Meadows *(G-17734)*
Haran Ventures LLC .... G 217 239-1628
  Champaign *(G-3299)*
Igt Testing Systems Inc .... G 847 952-2448
  Arlington Heights *(G-755)*

CONSULTING SVCS, BUSINESS: Testing, Educational Or Personnel

Scholastic Testing Service .... F 630 766-7150
  Bensenville *(G-1891)*

CONSULTING SVCS: Oil

Advanced Lubrication Inc .... G 815 932-3288
  Kankakee *(G-11957)*
Howard Energy Corporation .... G 618 263-3000
  Mount Carmel *(G-14473)*
Team Energy LLC .... F 618 943-1010
  Bridgeport *(G-2316)*

CONTACT LENSES

Alcon Vision LLC .... E 312 751-6200
  Chicago *(G-3599)*
Wesley-Jessen Corporation Del .... A 847 294-3000
  Des Plaines *(G-7868)*

CONTAINERS, GLASS: Food

Fri Jado Inc .... G 630 633-7944
  Woodridge *(G-21302)*

CONTAINERS, GLASS: Medicine Bottles

Alexander Technique .... G 847 337-7926
  Evanston *(G-9490)*
Teamdance Illinois .... G 815 463-9044
  Geneva *(G-10310)*

CONTAINERS, GLASS: Packers' Ware

Owens-Brockway Glass Cont Inc .... C 815 672-3141
  Streator *(G-19619)*

CONTAINERS: Air Cargo, Metal

AAR Corp .... D 630 227-2000
  Wood Dale *(G-21149)*

PRODUCT SECTION

CONTAINERS: Plastic

John Bean Technologies Corp ....D....... 312 861-5900
  Chicago *(G-5036)*
Majesty Cases Inc ....E....... 847 546-2558
  Ingleside *(G-11587)*

CONTAINERS: Cargo, Wood

Blue Comet Transport Inc ....G....... 773 617-9512
  Chicago *(G-3913)*

CONTAINERS: Cargo, Wood & Metal Combination

Cimc Leasing Usa Inc ....G....... 630 785-6875
  Oakbrook Terrace *(G-15793)*
Raildecks Intermodal ....G....... 630 442-7676
  Downers Grove *(G-8086)*

CONTAINERS: Cargo, Wood & Wood With Metal

Arrows Up Inc ....G....... 847 305-2550
  Arlington Heights *(G-696)*

CONTAINERS: Corrugated

A Trustworthy Sup Inc ....G....... 773 480-0255
  Chicago *(G-3492)*
APAC Unlimited Inc ....G....... 847 441-4282
  Northfield *(G-15505)*
Armbrust Paper Tubes Inc ....E....... 773 586-3232
  Chicago *(G-3730)*
Combined Technologies Inc ....G....... 847 968-4855
  Libertyville *(G-12645)*
Corrugated Solutions LLC ....G....... 847 220-8348
  Lake Forest *(G-12241)*
Custom Boxes Inc ....F....... 630 364-3944
  Bolingbrook *(G-2162)*
Dexton Enterprises ....G....... 309 788-1881
  Rock Island *(G-17217)*
Elm Street Industries Inc ....F....... 309 854-7000
  Kewanee *(G-12032)*
Fca LLC ....E....... 309 949-3999
  Coal Valley *(G-6936)*
Grafcor Packaging Inc ....F....... 815 639-2380
  Loves Park *(G-13215)*
Graphic Packaging Intl LLC ....B....... 630 260-6500
  Carol Stream *(G-2993)*
International Paper Company ....C....... 630 585-3300
  Aurora *(G-986)*
Jordan Paper Box Company ....F....... 773 287-5362
  Chicago *(G-5048)*
Kodiak LLC ....E....... 248 545-7520
  Chicago *(G-5115)*
Ockerlund Industries Inc ....E....... 630 620-1269
  Addison *(G-230)*
Packaging Corporation America ....C....... 847 482-3000
  Lake Forest *(G-12277)*
Pak Source Inc ....E....... 309 786-7374
  Rock Island *(G-17231)*
PCA Central Cal Corrugated LLC ....G....... 847 482-3000
  Lake Forest *(G-12283)*
Sonoco Products Company ....D....... 630 231-1489
  West Chicago *(G-20644)*
Specialty Box Corp ....F....... 630 897-7278
  North Aurora *(G-15277)*
Vangard Distribution Inc ....G....... 708 484-9895
  Berwyn *(G-1962)*
Vangard Distribution Inc ....G....... 708 588-8400
  Brookfield *(G-2497)*
Westrock Rkt LLC ....E....... 815 756-8913
  Dekalb *(G-7713)*

CONTAINERS: Foil, Bakery Goods & Frozen Foods

Durable Inc ....A....... 847 541-4400
  Wheeling *(G-20881)*
Handi-Foil Corp ....A....... 847 520-1000
  Wheeling *(G-20907)*
Hfa Inc ....A....... 847 520-1000
  Wheeling *(G-20908)*
Q Sales & Leasing LLC ....F....... 708 331-0094
  Hazel Crest *(G-11136)*
R and R Brokerage Co ....C....... 847 438-4600
  Lake Zurich *(G-12448)*

CONTAINERS: Food & Beverage

Amcor Rigid Plastics Usa LLC ....F....... 630 406-3500
  Batavia *(G-1347)*

Ignite Usa LLC ....E....... 312 432-6223
  Chicago *(G-4880)*
Jamiel Inc ....G....... 217 423-1000
  Decatur *(G-7510)*
Kraft Heinz Company ....C....... 847 646-2000
  Chicago *(G-5129)*
Shenglong Intl Group Corp ....G....... 312 388-2345
  Glenview *(G-10615)*
Silgan White Cap Americas LLC ....F....... 630 515-8383
  Downers Grove *(G-8096)*

CONTAINERS: Food, Folding, Made From Purchased Materials

Pactiv LLC ....C....... 630 262-6335
  Saint Charles *(G-18241)*

CONTAINERS: Food, Liquid Tight, Including Milk

International Paper Company ....C....... 217 735-1221
  Lincoln *(G-12731)*

CONTAINERS: Food, Wood Wirebound

Elm Street Industries Inc ....F....... 309 854-7000
  Kewanee *(G-12032)*

CONTAINERS: Frozen Food & Ice Cream

Earthgrains Refrigertd Dough P ....A....... 630 455-5200
  Downers Grove *(G-7996)*

CONTAINERS: Glass

Amcor Phrm Packg USA LLC ....C....... 847 298-5626
  Des Plaines *(G-7726)*
Ardagh Glass Inc ....G....... 847 869-7248
  Evanston *(G-9495)*
Ardagh Glass Inc ....D....... 708 849-4010
  Dolton *(G-7929)*
Ball Foster Glass Container ....G....... 708 849-1500
  Dolton *(G-7932)*
Gerresheimer Glass Inc ....C....... 708 843-4246
  Chicago Heights *(G-6747)*
Glass Haus ....G....... 815 459-5849
  McHenry *(G-13746)*
Kavalierglass North Amer Inc ....F....... 847 364-7303
  Elk Grove Village *(G-9075)*

CONTAINERS: Metal

Central Can Company Inc ....C....... 773 254-8700
  Chicago *(G-4056)*
D & B Fabricators & Distrs ....F....... 630 325-3811
  Lemont *(G-12562)*
Grafcor Packaging Inc ....F....... 815 639-2380
  Loves Park *(G-13215)*
Greif Inc ....E....... 815 935-7575
  Bradley *(G-2283)*
Higgins Bros Inc ....F....... 773 523-0124
  Chicago *(G-4815)*
Liberty Diversified Intl Inc ....E....... 217 935-8361
  Clinton *(G-6925)*
Production Manufacturing ....G....... 217 256-4211
  Warsaw *(G-20259)*
Staffco Inc ....G....... 309 688-3223
  Peoria *(G-16528)*
Van Leer Containers Inc ....C....... 708 371-4777
  Alsip *(G-520)*
Westrock Cp LLC ....C....... 847 689-4200
  North Chicago *(G-15324)*
Woods Equipment Company ....D....... 815 732-2141
  Oregon *(G-15929)*

CONTAINERS: Plastic

Altium Packaging ....C....... 815 943-7828
  Harvard *(G-11042)*
Altium Packaging ....C....... 630 231-7150
  West Chicago *(G-20536)*
Amcor Phrm Packg USA LLC ....C....... 847 298-5626
  Des Plaines *(G-7726)*
Amcor Rigid Packaging Usa LLC ....E....... 630 628-5859
  Addison *(G-29)*
Amcor Rigid Packaging Usa LLC ....D....... 630 773-3235
  Itasca *(G-11621)*
Armbrust Paper Tubes Inc ....E....... 773 586-3232
  Chicago *(G-3730)*
Berry Global Inc ....C....... 815 334-5225
  Woodstock *(G-21363)*

Blackhawk Molding Co Inc ....F....... 630 543-3900
  Addison *(G-52)*
Bli Legacy Inc ....E....... 847 428-6059
  Carpentersville *(G-3095)*
Boe Intermediate Holding Corp ....B....... 773 890-3300
  Chicago *(G-3924)*
Bway Corporation ....C....... 847 956-0750
  Elk Grove Village *(G-8875)*
Bway Corporation ....C....... 773 254-8700
  Chicago *(G-3987)*
CTI Industries Corporation ....C....... 847 382-1000
  Lake Barrington *(G-12146)*
CTI Industries Corporation ....D....... 800 284-5605
  Lake Zurich *(G-12400)*
Flow-Eze Company ....F....... 815 965-1062
  Rockford *(G-17416)*
Gilster-Mary Lee Corporation ....A....... 618 826-2361
  Chester *(G-3456)*
Graham Packaging Co Europe LLC .....A....... 630 293-8616
  West Chicago *(G-20589)*
Graham Packaging Co Europe LLC .....C....... 630 562-5912
  West Chicago *(G-20590)*
Graham Packaging Company LP ....E....... 630 739-9150
  Woodridge *(G-21306)*
Greif Inc ....E....... 815 838-7210
  Lockport *(G-12998)*
Hardwood Line Manufacturing Co ....E....... 773 463-2600
  Chicago *(G-4780)*
Illinois Bottle Mfg Co ....D....... 847 595-9000
  Elk Grove Village *(G-9040)*
Illinois Tool Works Inc ....D....... 217 345-2166
  Charleston *(G-3404)*
International Mold & Prod LLC ....G....... 313 617-5251
  Grayslake *(G-10783)*
Isovac Products LLC ....G....... 630 679-1740
  Romeoville *(G-17834)*
JL Clark LLC ....G....... 815 961-5677
  Rockford *(G-17475)*
JL Clark LLC ....C....... 815 961-5609
  Rockford *(G-17476)*
Jodi Maurer ....G....... 847 961-5347
  Lake In The Hills *(G-12337)*
Jordan Specialty Plastics Inc ....G....... 847 945-5591
  Deerfield *(G-7622)*
Jtec Industries Inc ....E....... 309 698-9301
  East Peoria *(G-8273)*
Leapfrog Product Dev LLC ....F....... 312 229-0089
  Chicago *(G-5192)*
Lee Gilster-Mary Corporation ....G....... 618 826-2361
  Chester *(G-3457)*
Lee Gilster-Mary Corporation ....E....... 618 443-5676
  Sparta *(G-19256)*
Lee Gilster-Mary Corporation ....D....... 815 472-6456
  Momence *(G-14186)*
Mary Lee Packaging Corporation ....E....... 618 826-2361
  Chester *(G-3458)*
Mauser Pckg Sltons Intrmdate I ....G....... 770 645-4800
  Oak Brook *(G-15640)*
MCS Midwest LLC ....G....... 630 393-7402
  Aurora *(G-1129)*
Neomek Incorporated ....F....... 630 879-5400
  Batavia *(G-1399)*
North America Packaging Corp ....E....... 630 203-4100
  Oak Brook *(G-15648)*
Olcott Plastics Inc ....G....... 630 584-0555
  Saint Charles *(G-18237)*
Pactiv LLC ....C....... 217 479-1144
  Jacksonville *(G-11779)*
Paragon Manufacturing Inc ....D....... 708 345-1717
  Melrose Park *(G-13902)*
Petrochem Corp ....G....... 431 205-8122
  Chicago *(G-5799)*
Plano Molding Company LLC ....C....... 630 552-9557
  Sandwich *(G-18379)*
Plano Molding Company LLC ....C....... 815 786-3331
  Sandwich *(G-18380)*
Planos Past Inc ....G....... 630 552-9119
  Plano *(G-16742)*
Plastic Container Corporation ....D....... 217 352-2722
  Urbana *(G-19993)*
Polar Tech Industries Inc ....E....... 815 784-9000
  Genoa *(G-10321)*
Precision Container Inc ....G....... 618 548-2830
  Salem *(G-18351)*
Pylon Plastics Inc ....G....... 630 968-6374
  Lisle *(G-12930)*
RPS Products Inc ....E....... 847 683-3400
  Hampshire *(G-10986)*
Russell Stanley Midwest Inc ....G....... 630 739-7700
  Bolingbrook *(G-2233)*

Employee Codes: A=Over 500 employees, B=251-500
C=101-250, D=51-100, E=20-50, F=10-19, G=3-9

2020 Harris Illinois
Industrial Directory

1403

CONTAINERS: Plastic

Safeway Products Inc ....F 815 226-8322
  Rockford (G-17620)
Silgan Plastics LLC ....C 815 334-1200
  Woodstock (G-21435)
Snyder Industries Inc ....D 630 773-9510
  Bensenville (G-1895)
Solo Cup Operating Corporation ....B 217 384-1800
  Urbana (G-20001)
Transparent Container Co Inc ....D 630 543-1818
  Bensenville (G-1903)
Yoshino America Corporation ....E 708 534-1141
  University Park (G-19971)

CONTAINERS: Plywood & Veneer, Wood

Chicago Floral Planters Inc ....G 708 423-2754
  Chicago Ridge (G-6790)
Midwest Mktg/Pdctn Mfg Co ....G 217 256-3414
  Warsaw (G-20258)
Production Manufacturing ....G 217 256-4211
  Warsaw (G-20259)

CONTAINERS: Sanitary, Food

Pactiv LLC ....C 219 924-4120
  Lake Forest (G-12280)
Pactiv LLC ....C 630 262-6335
  Saint Charles (G-18241)

CONTAINERS: Shipping & Mailing, Fiber

Advantage Structures LLC ....G 773 734-9305
  Chicago (G-3570)
G T Express Ltd ....G 708 338-0303
  River Grove (G-17060)

CONTAINERS: Shipping, Wood

Polamer Inc ....G 773 774-3600
  Chicago (G-5832)

CONTAINERS: Wood

Aetna Plywood Inc ....D 708 343-1515
  Maywood (G-13658)
Central Wood Products Inc ....E 217 728-4412
  Sullivan (G-19664)
Cole Pallet Services Corp ....E 815 758-3226
  Dekalb (G-7668)
Van Voorst Lumber Company Inc ....E 815 426-2544
  Union Hill (G-19943)
Wesling Products Inc ....G 773 533-2850
  Chicago (G-6603)

CONTAINMENT VESSELS: Reactor, Metal Plate

Powerone Corp ....G 630 443-6500
  Saint Charles (G-18248)

CONTRACTORS: Access Flooring System Installation

Imbert Construction Inds Inc ....G 847 588-3170
  Niles (G-15132)
Polymer Nation LLC ....G 847 972-2157
  Waukegan (G-20479)
Rampro Facilities Svcs Corp ....G 224 639-6378
  Waukegan (G-20487)

CONTRACTORS: Antenna Installation

Vincor Ltd ....F 708 534-0008
  Monee (G-14211)

CONTRACTORS: Asbestos Removal & Encapsulation

Husar Abatement Ltd ....F 847 349-9105
  Franklin Park (G-9960)

CONTRACTORS: Asphalt

Aimee M Ford ....G 630 308-9785
  Aurora (G-1044)
Cope & Sons Asphalt ....G 618 462-2207
  Alton (G-548)
Crowley-Sheppard Asphalt Inc ....F 708 499-2900
  Chicago Ridge (G-6793)
Freesen Inc ....E 309 827-4554
  Bloomington (G-2046)
Gunner Energy Corporation ....G 618 237-2829
  Mount Vernon (G-14612)

CONTRACTORS: Awning Installation

Nuyen Awning Co ....G 630 892-3995
  Aurora (G-1141)
Shade Solutions Inc ....F 217 239-0718
  Tolono (G-19884)

CONTRACTORS: Boiler & Furnace

Ed Hartwig Trucking & Excvtg ....G 309 364-3672
  Henry (G-11163)
Hidden Hollow Stables Inc ....G 309 243-7979
  Dunlap (G-8133)
Moultri Cnty Hstrcl/Gnlgcl Sct ....F 217 728-4085
  Sullivan (G-19672)
Resolute Industrial LLC ....D 800 537-9675
  Wheeling (G-20974)
White Sheet Metal ....G 217 465-3195
  Paris (G-16246)

CONTRACTORS: Boiler Maintenance Contractor

Depue Mechanical Inc ....E 815 447-2267
  Depue (G-7716)
Hudson Boiler & Tank Company ....F 312 666-4780
  Lockport (G-13001)

CONTRACTORS: Boring, Building Construction

Mid-America Underground LLC ....E 630 443-9999
  Aurora (G-1134)

CONTRACTORS: Building Eqpt & Machinery Installation

Assa Abloy Entrance Systems US ....F 847 228-5600
  Elk Grove Village (G-8843)
Avenue Metal Manufacturing Co ....F 312 243-3483
  Chicago (G-3785)
Chevron Commercial Inc ....G 618 654-5555
  Highland (G-11209)
Fixture Company ....G 847 214-3100
  Chicago (G-4600)
Great Lakes Mech Svcs Inc ....F 708 672-5900
  Lincolnshire (G-12768)
Kelly Systems Inc ....E 312 733-3224
  Chicago (G-5093)
Patrick Holdings Inc ....F 815 874-5300
  Rockford (G-17549)
Randal Wood Displays Inc ....D 630 761-0400
  Batavia (G-1409)
Siemens Industry Inc ....G 309 664-2460
  Bloomington (G-2094)
Sudholt Sheet Metal Inc ....F 618 228-7351
  Aviston (G-1183)

CONTRACTORS: Building Front Installation, Metal

Delta Erectors Inc ....F 708 267-9721
  Villa Park (G-20144)

CONTRACTORS: Building Sign Installation & Mntnce

Action Advertising Inc ....G 312 791-0660
  Chicago (G-3534)
Ad Deluxe Sign Company Inc ....G 815 556-8469
  Blue Island (G-2109)
All-Right Sign Inc ....F 708 754-6366
  Steger (G-19487)
All-Steel Structures Inc ....E 708 210-1313
  South Holland (G-19189)
American Sign & Lighting Co ....F 847 258-8151
  Chicago (G-3667)
Bella Sign Co ....G 630 539-0343
  Roselle (G-17940)
Bendsen Signs & Graphics Inc ....F 217 877-2345
  Decatur (G-7464)
Best Neon Sign Co ....G 773 586-2700
  Chicago (G-3872)
Demond Signs Inc ....F 618 624-7260
  O Fallon (G-15571)
Friendly Signs Inc ....G 815 933-7070
  Kankakee (G-11973)
Hercl Signs & Service Inc ....F 847 471-4015
  South Elgin (G-19151)
Holland Design Group Inc ....F 847 526-8848
  Wauconda (G-20357)
Hughes & Son Inc ....G 815 459-1887
  Crystal Lake (G-7206)
Image Signs Inc ....F 815 282-4141
  Loves Park (G-13218)
Midwest Sun-Ray Lighting & Sig ....F 618 656-2884
  Granite City (G-10726)
Mk Signs Inc ....E 773 545-4444
  Chicago (G-5473)
Monitor Sign Co ....F 217 234-2412
  Mattoon (G-13651)
North Shore Sign Company ....G 847 816-7020
  Libertyville (G-12690)
Roth Neon Sign Company Inc ....G 618 942-6378
  Herrin (G-11177)
Signet Sign Company ....G 630 830-8242
  Bartlett (G-1313)
Solid Metal Group Inc ....G 708 757-7421
  Chicago Heights (G-6774)
Staar Bales Lestarge Inc ....G 618 259-6366
  East Alton (G-8171)
Strictly Neon Inc ....G 708 597-1616
  Crestwood (G-7130)
T Ham Sign Inc ....E 618 242-2010
  Opdyke (G-15905)

CONTRACTORS: Cable Splicing Svcs

Express Signs & Lighting Maint ....F 815 725-9080
  Shorewood (G-18896)

CONTRACTORS: Cable TV Installation

Jklein Enterprises Inc ....G 618 664-4554
  Greenville (G-10836)

CONTRACTORS: Caisson Drilling

CJ Drilling Inc ....D 847 669-8000
  Dundee (G-8126)

CONTRACTORS: Carpentry Work

Ashland Door Solutions LLC ....G 773 348-5106
  Elk Grove Village (G-8842)
Chicago Steel Inc ....E 800 344-3032
  Chicago (G-4130)
Contract Industries Inc ....E 708 458-8150
  Bedford Park (G-1464)
Craiger Inc ....G 815 479-9660
  Crystal Lake (G-7186)
Ken Young Construction Co ....G 847 358-3026
  Hoffman Estates (G-11433)
Lyko Woodworking & Cnstr ....G 773 583-4561
  Chicago (G-5292)
Perkins Construction ....G 815 233-9655
  Freeport (G-10132)
Peters Construction ....G 773 489-5555
  Chicago (G-5794)
Savino Enterprises ....G 708 385-5277
  Blue Island (G-2138)
Southland Painting ....G 833 724-6803
  Park Forest (G-16260)
Ww Displays Inc ....F 847 566-6979
  Mundelein (G-14747)

CONTRACTORS: Carpentry, Cabinet & Finish Work

Aba Custom Woodworking ....G 815 356-9663
  Crystal Lake (G-7153)
Allie Woodworking ....G 847 244-1919
  Waukegan (G-20413)
Anderson & Marter Cabinets ....G 630 406-9840
  Batavia (G-1349)
Axis Design Architectual Mllwk ....F 630 466-4549
  Sugar Grove (G-19637)
Concord Cabinets Inc ....F 217 894-6507
  Clayton (G-6909)
Cooper Lake Millworks Inc ....G 217 847-2681
  Hamilton (G-10951)
Eiesland Builders Inc ....E 847 998-1731
  Glenview (G-10544)
Greenberg Casework Company Inc ....E 815 624-0288
  South Beloit (G-19096)
L Surges Custom Woodwork ....G 815 774-9663
  Joliet (G-11892)
Orren Pickell Builders Inc ....F 847 572-5200
  Wilmette (G-21090)
Rays Countertop Shop Inc ....F 217 483-2514
  Glenarm (G-10427)
Stairsland ....G 708 853-9593
  Lyons (G-13314)

PRODUCT SECTION — CONTRACTORS: Excavating

Unique Designs .... G 309 454-1226
  Normal *(G-15227)*
Wagners Custom Wood Design .... G 847 487-2788
  Island Lake *(G-11613)*
Wenger Woodcraft .... G 217 578-3440
  Tuscola *(G-19934)*
Wheatland Cstm Cbntry Wdwkg LL ..... G 630 359-8553
  Villa Park *(G-20176)*

CONTRACTORS: Carpentry, Cabinet Building & Installation

Action Cabinet Sales Inc .... G 847 717-0011
  Elgin *(G-8494)*
Baker Elements Inc .... G 630 660-8100
  Oak Park *(G-15746)*
Design Woodworks .... G 847 566-6603
  Mundelein *(G-14682)*
Eddie Gapastione .... G 708 430-3881
  Bridgeview *(G-2344)*
Imperial Kitchens & Bath Inc .... F 708 485-0020
  Brookfield *(G-2486)*
OGorman Son Carpentry Contrs .... E 815 485-8997
  New Lenox *(G-15045)*
Riverton Cabinet Company .... E 815 462-5300
  New Lenox *(G-15056)*
Sleeping Bear Inc .... G 630 541-7220
  Lisle *(G-12937)*

CONTRACTORS: Carpentry, Finish & Trim Work

Masters Shop .... G 217 643-7826
  Thomasboro *(G-19776)*
Robert Harlan Ernst .... G 217 627-3401
  Girard *(G-10385)*

CONTRACTORS: Closed Circuit Television Installation

Quality Intgrted Solutions Inc .... G 815 464-4772
  Tinley Park *(G-19852)*

CONTRACTORS: Commercial & Office Building

Anchor Mechanical Inc .... G 312 492-6994
  Chicago *(G-3691)*
Lombard Investment Company .... D 708 389-1060
  Alsip *(G-469)*
Narvick Bros Lumber Co Inc .... E 815 942-1173
  Morris *(G-14318)*
Poggenpohl LLC .... G 217 229-3411
  Raymond *(G-16990)*
Poggenpohl LLC .... G 217 824-2020
  Taylorville *(G-19760)*

CONTRACTORS: Communications Svcs

Gatesair Inc .... C 800 622-0022
  Quincy *(G-16886)*
Heil Sound Ltd .... F 618 257-3000
  Fairview Heights *(G-9646)*
Jax Asphalt Company Inc .... F 618 244-0500
  Mount Vernon *(G-14618)*

CONTRACTORS: Computer Installation

Data Accessories Inc .... G 847 669-3640
  Huntley *(G-11533)*

CONTRACTORS: Computerized Controls Installation

Innovative Werks Inc .... G 312 767-8618
  Naperville *(G-14848)*

CONTRACTORS: Concrete

All City Brick Staining LLC .... G 312 459-8937
  Chicago *(G-3608)*
Andel Services Inc .... G 630 566-0210
  Aurora *(G-1052)*
Charles E Mahoney Company .... E 618 235-3355
  Swansea *(G-19690)*
Christopher Concrete Products .... G 618 724-2951
  Buckner *(G-2499)*
Hamilton Concrete Products Co .... G 217 847-3118
  Hamilton *(G-10958)*
Herman Bade & Sons .... G 217 832-9444
  Villa Grove *(G-20123)*
Jerry Berry Contracting Co .... G 618 594-3339
  Carlyle *(G-2891)*
Langheim Ready Mix Inc .... G 217 625-2351
  Girard *(G-10383)*
Macon Gc LLC .... D 309 897-8216
  Bradford *(G-2275)*
Myers Concrete & Construction .... G 815 732-2591
  Oregon *(G-15924)*
Prosser Construction Co .... F 217 774-5032
  Shelbyville *(G-18884)*
Rock Road Companies Inc .... F 815 874-2441
  Rockford *(G-17583)*
SNC Solutions Inc .... E 217 784-5212
  Gibson City *(G-10344)*

CONTRACTORS: Concrete Breaking, Street & Highway

Orange Crush LLC .... G 847 537-7900
  Wheeling *(G-20952)*
Orange Crush LLC .... C 708 544-9440
  Hillside *(G-11352)*
Orange Crush LLC .... G 847 428-6176
  East Dundee *(G-8207)*
Orange Crush LLC .... G 630 739-5560
  Romeoville *(G-17862)*

CONTRACTORS: Concrete Pumping

Gary & Larry Brown Trucking .... G 618 268-6377
  Raleigh *(G-16961)*

CONTRACTORS: Concrete Reinforcement Placing

Steel Fabrication and Welding .... G 773 343-0731
  Cicero *(G-6876)*

CONTRACTORS: Concrete Structure Coating, Plastic

Yankee Mold Inc .... G 815 986-1776
  Machesney Park *(G-13384)*

CONTRACTORS: Construction Site Cleanup

Platinum Inc .... G 815 385-0910
  McHenry *(G-13780)*
Stages Construction Inc .... G 773 619-2977
  Glenview *(G-10624)*

CONTRACTORS: Countertop Installation

Carrera Stone Systems of Chica .... E 847 566-2277
  Mundelein *(G-14673)*
Clover Custom Counters Inc .... G 708 598-8912
  Bridgeview *(G-2336)*
Design Plus Industries Inc .... F 309 697-9778
  Peoria *(G-16430)*
Gerali Custom Design Inc .... D 847 760-0500
  Elgin *(G-8593)*
Kitchen Krafters Inc .... G 815 675-6061
  Spring Grove *(G-19279)*
R & R Custom Cabinet Making .... G 847 358-6188
  Palatine *(G-16152)*
Surface Solutions Illinois Inc .... G 708 571-3449
  Mokena *(G-14119)*
Wienmar Inc .... C 847 742-9222
  South Elgin *(G-19181)*
Wilcor Solid Surface Inc .... F 888 956-1001
  Elk Grove Village *(G-9309)*

CONTRACTORS: Decontamination Svcs

Best Technology Systems Inc .... E 815 254-9554
  Plainfield *(G-16644)*

CONTRACTORS: Demolition, Building & Other Structures

Certified Asphalt Paving .... G 847 441-5000
  Northfield *(G-15511)*

CONTRACTORS: Directional Oil & Gas Well Drilling Svc

A and P Directional Drlg LLC .... G 708 715-1192
  Alsip *(G-407)*
A and P Directional Drlg LLC .... G 708 715-1192
  Orland Park *(G-15932)*
Booth Resources Inc .... G 618 662-4955
  Flora *(G-9676)*
C&R Directional Boring .... G 630 458-0055
  Addison *(G-60)*
Coursons Coring & Drilling .... G 618 349-8765
  Saint Peter *(G-18323)*
Crystal Precision Drilling .... G 815 633-5460
  Loves Park *(G-13199)*
Jackson Oil Corporation .... G 618 263-6521
  Mount Carmel *(G-14475)*
Mid-America Underground LLC .... E 630 443-9999
  Aurora *(G-1134)*
Rays Electrical Service LLC .... F 847 214-2944
  Elgin *(G-8715)*
Southern Triangle Oil Company .... F 618 262-4131
  Mount Carmel *(G-14486)*

CONTRACTORS: Dock Eqpt Installation, Indl

Builders Chicago Corporation .... D 224 654-2122
  Rosemont *(G-18001)*
Fix It Fast Ltd .... F 708 401-8320
  Midlothian *(G-13991)*

CONTRACTORS: Drapery Track Installation

Dons Drapery Service .... G 815 385-4759
  McHenry *(G-13737)*

CONTRACTORS: Driveway

Fuller Asphalt & Landscape .... G 618 797-1169
  Granite City *(G-10707)*

CONTRACTORS: Electric Power Systems

Enterprise Service Corporation .... G 773 589-2727
  Des Plaines *(G-7758)*

CONTRACTORS: Electrical

Aemm A Electric .... G 708 403-6700
  Orland Park *(G-15935)*
Carey Electric Co Inc .... G 847 949-9294
  Grayslake *(G-10761)*
Connor Electric Services Inc .... E 630 823-8230
  Schaumburg *(G-18485)*
Cullinan & Sons Inc .... E 309 925-2711
  Tremont *(G-19895)*
Eberhart Sign & Lighting Co .... G 618 656-7256
  Edwardsville *(G-8359)*
Erbes Electric .... G 815 849-5508
  Sublette *(G-19636)*
H & S Mechanical Inc .... D 309 696-7066
  Peoria *(G-16448)*
Heico Companies LLC .... F 312 419-8220
  Chicago *(G-4798)*
Kavanaugh Electric Inc .... G 708 503-1310
  Frankfort *(G-9812)*
Kohns Electric .... G 309 463-2331
  Varna *(G-20032)*
Lightscape Inc .... E 847 247-8800
  Libertyville *(G-12670)*
Marshall Electric Inc .... F 618 382-3932
  Carmi *(G-2910)*
Midwest Sun-Ray Lighting & Sig .... F 618 656-2884
  Granite City *(G-10726)*
Richards Electric Motor Co .... E 217 222-7154
  Quincy *(G-16940)*

CONTRACTORS: Electronic Controls Installation

Humidity 2 Optimization LLC .... F 847 991-7488
  East Dundee *(G-8200)*

CONTRACTORS: Energy Management Control

Abb Inc .... F 630 759-7428
  Bolingbrook *(G-2145)*
Contempary Enrgy Slutions LLC .... F 630 768-3743
  Naperville *(G-14963)*
Global Technologies I LLC .... D 312 255-8350
  Chicago *(G-4699)*
Lightitech LLC .... G 847 910-4177
  Chicago *(G-5222)*
World Fuel Services Inc .... F 305 428-8000
  Chicago *(G-6673)*

CONTRACTORS: Excavating

A E Frasz Inc .... F 630 232-6223
  Elburn *(G-8440)*

CONTRACTORS: Excavating

Company	Section	Phone
Amigoni Construction Roanoke (G-17098)	G	309 923-3701
Certified Asphalt Paving Northfield (G-15511)	G	847 441-5000
Conmat Inc Freeport (G-10104)	E	815 235-2200
Cortelyou Excavating Bushnell (G-2741)	G	309 772-2922
Ed Hartwig Trucking & Excvtg Henry (G-11163)	G	309 364-3672
Gorman Brothers Ready Mix Inc Jerseyville (G-11791)	F	618 498-2173
Hamilton Concrete Products Co Hamilton (G-10958)	G	217 847-3118
Hulse Excavating Flanagan (G-9670)	G	815 796-4106
J W Ossola Company Inc Granville (G-10755)	G	815 339-6112
Jay A Morris Watseka (G-20308)	G	815 432-6440
Jerry Berry Contracting Co Carlyle (G-2891)	G	618 594-3339
Joe Hatzer & Son Inc Streator (G-19612)	E	815 673-5571
Lake County Grading Co LLC Libertyville (G-12665)	D	847 362-2590
Mertel Gravel Company Inc Peru (G-16581)	F	815 223-0468
Mid-America Underground LLC Aurora (G-1134)	E	630 443-9999
Myers Concrete & Construction Oregon (G-15924)	G	815 732-2591
SNC Solutions Inc Gibson City (G-10344)	E	217 784-5212

CONTRACTORS: Excavating Slush Pits & Cellars Svcs

Company	Section	Phone
Ican Clinic LLC Wood River (G-21263)	G	618 254-2273
Toppert Jetting Service Inc East Moline (G-8244)	G	309 755-2240

CONTRACTORS: Exterior Wall System Installation

Company	Section	Phone
Polymer Nation LLC Waukegan (G-20479)	G	847 972-2157

CONTRACTORS: Fence Construction

Company	Section	Phone
Alfredos Iron Works Inc Cortland (G-7017)	E	815 748-1177
Bergeron Group Inc Joliet (G-11830)	E	815 741-1635
GV Welding Inc Chicago (G-4753)		312 863-0071
Industrial Fence Inc Chicago (G-4906)	D	773 521-9900
Invisible Fencing of Quad City Moline (G-14151)	G	309 797-1688
United Fence Co Inc Chicago (G-6472)	G	773 924-0773
William Dach Rockford (G-17685)	F	815 962-3455
Winters Welding Inc Chicago (G-6648)		773 860-7735
Woodland Fence Forest Pdts Inc Warrenville (G-20257)	G	630 393-2220

CONTRACTORS: Fiberglass Work

Company	Section	Phone
Accu-Wright Fiberglass Inc East Saint Louis (G-8295)	G	618 337-3318

CONTRACTORS: Fire Detection & Burglar Alarm Systems

Company	Section	Phone
Accurate Security & Lock Corp Lake In The Hills (G-12326)	G	815 455-0133

CONTRACTORS: Floor Laying & Other Floor Work

Company	Section	Phone
Cullinan & Sons Inc Tremont (G-19895)	E	309 925-2711
F H Leinweber Co Inc Oak Lawn (G-15715)	G	708 424-7000
F H Leinweber Co Inc Chicago (G-4548)		773 568-7722
Grads Inc East Dundee (G-8198)	G	847 426-3904
Intelligent Flrg Systems LLC Saint Charles (G-18214)	G	630 587-1800

CONTRACTORS: Flooring

Company	Section	Phone
Substrate Technology Inc Morris (G-14330)	F	815 941-4800

CONTRACTORS: Fountain Installation

Company	Section	Phone
Fountain Technologies Ltd Wheeling (G-20900)	E	847 537-3677

CONTRACTORS: Garage Doors

Company	Section	Phone
Allied Garage Door Inc Addison (G-27)	E	630 279-0795
Builders Chicago Corporation Rosemont (G-18001)	D	224 654-2122

CONTRACTORS: Gas Field Svcs, NEC

Company	Section	Phone
Harold L Ray Truck & Trctr Svc Cisne (G-6893)	F	618 673-2701

CONTRACTORS: General Electric

Company	Section	Phone
Advanced Enrgy Solutions Group Carterville (G-3128)	F	618 988-0888
Archer General Contg & Fabg Steger (G-19488)	G	708 757-7902
Cable Electric Company Inc Oak Lawn (G-15706)	G	708 458-8900
Clarios Calumet City (G-2773)	D	708 474-1717
Control Panels Inc Rockford (G-17357)	F	815 654-6000
Jf Industries Inc Chicago (G-5028)	G	773 775-8840
K R J Inc Tremont (G-19897)	G	309 925-5123
Phoenix Business Solutions LLC Alsip (G-491)	E	708 388-1330
Rathje Enterprises Inc Decatur (G-7540)	B	217 423-2593
Rathje Enterprises Inc Danville (G-7377)	F	217 443-0022
Rays Electrical Service LLC Elgin (G-8715)	F	847 214-2944
Saturn Electrical Services Inc Roselle (G-17983)	G	630 980-0300
Sharlen Electric Co Chicago (G-6147)	E	773 721-0700
Sievert Electric Svc & Sls Co Forest Park (G-9724)	D	708 771-1600
SNC Solutions Inc Gibson City (G-10344)	E	217 784-5212
T & J Electric Company Inc Pekin (G-16364)	F	309 347-2196
Tracy Electric Inc Lawrenceville (G-12538)	E	618 943-6205
Twin City Electric Inc Bloomington (G-2105)	E	309 827-0636
Twin Supplies Ltd Oak Brook (G-15667)	F	630 590-5138

CONTRACTORS: Geothermal Drilling

Company	Section	Phone
Unique Indoor Comfort Libertyville (G-12719)	F	847 362-1910

CONTRACTORS: Glass Tinting, Architectural & Automotive

Company	Section	Phone
J & J Inc of Illinois Greenview (G-10823)	F	217 306-0787

CONTRACTORS: Glass, Glazing & Tinting

Company	Section	Phone
Botti Studio of Architectural Glenview (G-10532)	E	847 869-5933
Christopher Glass & Aluminum Elmhurst (G-9346)	D	312 256-8500
Circle Studio Stained Glass Highland Park (G-11258)	G	847 432-7249
Euroview Enterprises LLC Elmhurst (G-9364)	E	630 227-3300
Illinois Valley Glass & Mirror Peoria (G-16457)	F	309 682-6603
Shoreline Glass Co Inc Hillside (G-11356)	E	312 829-9500
T J M & Associates Inc Wauconda (G-20396)	G	847 382-1993
Tuminello Enterprizes Inc Morris (G-14334)	G	815 416-1007
Tuminello Enterprizes Inc Morris (G-14335)	G	815 416-1007
Will Hamms Stained Glass Arlington Heights (G-833)	F	847 255-2230
Willow Ridge Glass Inc Woodridge (G-21348)		630 910-8300

CONTRACTORS: Gutters & Downspouts

Company	Section	Phone
GROsse&sons Htg &SHeet Met Inc Lyons (G-13310)	G	708 447-8397
Rebel Inc Belleville (G-1588)	E	618 235-0582

CONTRACTORS: Heating & Air Conditioning

Company	Section	Phone
B A P Enterprises Inc Dolton (G-7931)	G	708 849-0900
Bring Your Own Auto Parts Inc Crest Hill (G-7084)	F	815 730-6900
Clarios Carol Stream (G-2961)	F	630 871-7700
Crawford Heating & Cooling Co Rock Island (G-17211)	D	309 788-4573
D and S Molding & Dctg Inc Rockford (G-17366)	G	815 399-2734
Elk Grove Custom Sheet Metal Elk Grove Village (G-8972)	F	847 352-2845
Ja-T & Associates Inc Chicago (G-4996)	F	773 744-2094
Kool Technologies Inc Streamwood (G-19581)	G	630 483-2256
Mach Mechanical Group LLC Naperville (G-14978)	G	630 674-6224
National Metal Works Inc Loves Park (G-13239)	G	815 282-5533

CONTRACTORS: Heating Systems Repair & Maintenance Svc

Company	Section	Phone
Air Pure LLC Freeport (G-10098)	G	815 275-8990
Atk Services Inc O Fallon (G-15568)	G	618 726-5114
DS Air & Heating Inc Chicago (G-4398)	G	773 826-7411
Smid Heating & Air Channahon (G-3394)	G	815 467-0362

CONTRACTORS: Highway & Street Construction, General

Company	Section	Phone
Air Duct Manufacturing Inc Lisle (G-12859)	G	630 620-9866
Allendale Gravel Co Inc Allendale (G-402)	F	618 263-3521
Ambraw Asphalt Materials Inc Lawrenceville (G-12526)	E	618 943-4716
Charles Sheridan and Sons Evanston (G-9502)	G	847 903-7209
Don Anderson Co Hoffman (G-11402)	G	618 495-2511
L & H Company Inc Oak Brook (G-15630)	F	630 571-7200
Mt Crmel Stblzation Group Inc Mount Carmel (G-14482)	E	618 262-5118
ODaniel Trucking Co Carmi (G-2912)	D	618 382-5371

CONTRACTORS: Highway & Street Paving

Company	Section	Phone
Allied Asphalt Paving Co Inc Elgin (G-8503)	E	630 289-6080
Andel Services Inc Aurora (G-1052)	G	630 566-0210
Arrow Road Construction Co Elk Grove Village (G-8839)	C	847 437-0700
Charles E Mahoney Company Swansea (G-19690)	E	618 235-3355
Corrective Asphalt Mtls LLC South Roxana (G-19252)	G	618 254-3855
Curran Contracting Company Dekalb (G-7671)	G	815 758-8113
Curran Group Inc Crystal Lake (G-7190)	D	815 455-5100
Gallagher Asphalt Corporation Thornton (G-19786)	E	708 877-7160

PRODUCT SECTION
CONTRACTORS: Oil & Gas Well Drilling Svc

Geneva Construction Company .... G 630 892-6536
  North Aurora *(G-15261)*
McLean County Asphalt Co .... D 309 827-6115
  Bloomington *(G-2072)*
Peter Baker & Son Co .... D 847 362-3663
  Lake Bluff *(G-12204)*
Plote Construction Inc .... E 847 695-0422
  Hoffman Estates *(G-11444)*
Plote Construction Inc .... D 847 695-9300
  Hoffman Estates *(G-11445)*
Prosser Construction Co .... F 217 774-5032
  Shelbyville *(G-18884)*
Rock Road Companies Inc .... F 815 874-2441
  Rockford *(G-17583)*
Rockford Blacktop Cnstr Co .... D 815 654-4700
  Rockford *(G-17586)*

CONTRACTORS: Highway & Street Resurfacing

All Weather Courts Inc .... G 217 364-4546
  Dawson *(G-7428)*
G & S Asphalt Inc .... F 217 826-2421
  Marshall *(G-13571)*

CONTRACTORS: Highway Sign & Guardrail Construction & Install

Industrial Fence Inc .... D 773 521-9900
  Chicago *(G-4906)*
Solid Metal Group Inc .... G 708 757-7421
  Chicago Heights *(G-6774)*

CONTRACTORS: Home & Office Intrs Finish, Furnish/Remodel

Baker Avenue Investments Inc .... D 309 427-2500
  Washington *(G-20266)*
Lincoln Office LLC .... D 309 427-2500
  Washington *(G-20273)*
Osmer Woodworking Inc .... G 815 973-5809
  Dixon *(G-7905)*
Systems Unlimited Inc .... C 630 285-0010
  Itasca *(G-11743)*
Woodworking Unlimited Inc .... F 630 469-7023
  Carol Stream *(G-3089)*

CONTRACTORS: Hotel, Motel/Multi-Famly Home Renovtn/Remodel

Illinois Green Cnstr Inc .... F 847 975-2312
  Chicago *(G-4891)*

CONTRACTORS: Hydraulic Eqpt Installation & Svcs

Professional Meters Inc .... C 815 942-7000
  Morris *(G-14323)*
Rehobot Inc .... G 815 385-7777
  McHenry *(G-13786)*
Wandfluh of America Inc .... F 847 566-5700
  Mundelein *(G-14746)*

CONTRACTORS: Indl Building Renovation, Remodeling & Repair

Gcpro LLC .... E 773 764-2776
  Lombard *(G-13082)*
Lamka Enterprises Inc .... G 630 659-5965
  Woodstock *(G-21402)*

CONTRACTORS: Insulation Installation, Building

Rebel Inc .... E 618 235-0582
  Belleville *(G-1588)*

CONTRACTORS: Kitchen & Bathroom Remodeling

Creative Designs Kitc .... E 773 327-8400
  Chicago *(G-4261)*
Lamka Enterprises Inc .... G 630 659-5965
  Woodstock *(G-21402)*
Perkins Construction .... G 815 233-9655
  Freeport *(G-10132)*
Rays Countertop Shop Inc .... F 217 483-2514
  Glenarm *(G-10427)*
Wenger Woodcraft .... G 217 578-3440
  Tuscola *(G-19934)*

CONTRACTORS: Kitchen Cabinet Installation

Hci Cabinetry and Design Inc .... G 630 584-0266
  Addison *(G-148)*

CONTRACTORS: Land Reclamation

SF Contracting LLC .... E 618 926-1477
  Raleigh *(G-16963)*

CONTRACTORS: Lighting Conductor Erection

Harger Inc .... E 847 548-8700
  Grayslake *(G-10780)*

CONTRACTORS: Lighting Syst

L & H Company Inc .... F 630 571-7200
  Oak Brook *(G-15630)*
TCI Companies Inc .... E 309 965-2057
  Goodfield *(G-10677)*

CONTRACTORS: Machine Rigging & Moving

Chicago Flyhouse Incorporated ..... F 773 533-1590
  Chicago *(G-4104)*
New Cie Inc .... E 815 224-1511
  Peru *(G-16584)*

CONTRACTORS: Machinery Installation

Aak Mechanical Inc .... D 217 935-8501
  Clinton *(G-6917)*
Dontech Industries Inc .... F 847 428-8222
  Gilberts *(G-10353)*
Morey Industries Inc .... C 708 343-3220
  Broadview *(G-2454)*
Mww Food Processing USA LLC ... G 773 478-9700
  Elk Grove Village *(G-9141)*
R C Industrial Inc .... G 309 230-4631
  Milan *(G-14023)*
Sardee Industries Inc .... G 630 824-4200
  Lisle *(G-12936)*

CONTRACTORS: Marble Installation, Interior

Acme Marble Co Inc .... G 630 964-7162
  Darien *(G-7399)*
Marble Emporium Inc .... E 847 205-4000
  Northbrook *(G-15427)*
Stonecrafters Inc .... E 815 363-8730
  Lakemoor *(G-12477)*

CONTRACTORS: Marble Masonry, Exterior

Galloy and Van Etten Inc .... E 773 928-4800
  Chicago *(G-4657)*
Standard Marble & Granite .... F 773 533-0450
  Chicago *(G-6229)*

CONTRACTORS: Masonry & Stonework

Surface Solutions Illinois Inc .... G 708 571-3449
  Mokena *(G-14119)*

CONTRACTORS: Mechanical

5h Consulting & Design LLC .... E 618 317-5822
  Ellis Grove *(G-9319)*
Anchor Mechanical Inc .... G 312 492-6994
  Chicago *(G-3691)*
H & S Mechanical Inc .... D 309 696-7066
  Peoria *(G-16448)*
Lake Process Systems Inc .... E 847 381-7663
  Lake Barrington *(G-12157)*
Manhattan Mechanical Svcs LLC .. E 815 478-9940
  Manhattan *(G-13434)*
Miller Roger Weston .... G 217 352-0476
  Champaign *(G-3322)*
R B Hayward Company .... E 847 671-0400
  Schiller Park *(G-18838)*
Schneider Elc Buildings LLC .... B 815 381-5000
  Rockford *(G-17622)*
Schneider Elc Buildings LLC .... E 815 227-4000
  Rockford *(G-17623)*
Schneider Elc Holdings Inc .... A 717 944-5460
  Schaumburg *(G-18707)*
Synergy Mechanical Inc .... G 708 410-1004
  Westchester *(G-20713)*

CONTRACTORS: Metal Ceiling Construction & Repair Work

Polymer Nation LLC .... G 847 972-2157
  Waukegan *(G-20479)*

CONTRACTORS: Millwrights

Key West Metal Industries Inc ..... C 708 371-1470
  Crestwood *(G-7121)*
Macon Gc LLC .... D 309 897-8216
  Bradford *(G-2275)*
Neiweem Industries Inc .... G 847 487-1239
  Oakwood Hills *(G-15821)*

CONTRACTORS: Multi-Family Home Remodeling

Gcpro LLC .... E 773 764-2776
  Lombard *(G-13082)*
Lamka Enterprises Inc .... G 630 659-5965
  Woodstock *(G-21402)*

CONTRACTORS: Nonresidential Building Design & Construction

Chicago Steel Inc .... E 800 344-3032
  Chicago *(G-4130)*

CONTRACTORS: Oil & Gas Building, Repairing & Dismantling Svc

Gholson Pump & Repairs Co ..... G 618 382-4730
  Carmi *(G-2906)*
Samtek International Inc .... G 314 954-4005
  Swansea *(G-19697)*

CONTRACTORS: Oil & Gas Field Geological Exploration Svcs

Howard Energy Corporation .... G 618 263-3000
  Mount Carmel *(G-14473)*

CONTRACTORS: Oil & Gas Field Geophysical Exploration Svcs

Strata Exploration Inc .... G 618 842-2610
  Fairfield *(G-9637)*

CONTRACTORS: Oil & Gas Field Salt Water Impound/Storing Svc

Water & Gas Technologies .... G 708 829-3254
  Palos Park *(G-16217)*

CONTRACTORS: Oil & Gas Well Casing Cement Svcs

Glover Oil Field Service Inc .... F 618 395-3624
  Olney *(G-15863)*

CONTRACTORS: Oil & Gas Well Drilling Svc

Baker Hghes Olfld Oprtions LLC ... F 618 393-2919
  Olney *(G-15854)*
Black Bison Water Services LLC .. E 630 272-5935
  Chicago *(G-3907)*
Dee Drilling Co .... E 618 262-4136
  Mount Carmel *(G-14470)*
Drig Corporation .... D 312 265-1509
  Rosemont *(G-18020)*
Ebers Drilling Co .... G 618 826-5398
  Chester *(G-3454)*
Evergreen Energy LLC .... G 618 384-9295
  Carmi *(G-2905)*
Five P Drilling Inc .... E 618 943-9771
  Bridgeport *(G-2313)*
Glover Oil Field Service Inc ..... F 618 395-3624
  Olney *(G-15863)*
J H Robison & Associates Ltd .. G 847 559-9662
  Northbrook *(G-15408)*
Jerry D Graham Oil .... G 618 548-5540
  Salem *(G-18344)*
Kapp Company LLC .... G 618 676-1000
  Olney *(G-15868)*
Kincaid Oil Producers Inc .... G 618 686-3084
  Louisville *(G-13179)*
Kinoco Inc .... G 618 378-3802
  Norris City *(G-15250)*
Marion Oelze .... G 618 327-9224
  Nashville *(G-15001)*

CONTRACTORS: Oil & Gas Well Drilling Svc

Murvin & Meier Oil Co .... G 847 277-8380
   Barrington *(G-1231)*
Paragon Oil Company Inc .... G 618 244-5541
   Mount Vernon *(G-14632)*
Quality Drilling Service LLP .... G 937 663-4715
   Alton *(G-568)*
Reef Development Inc .... F 618 842-7711
   Fairfield *(G-9634)*
Rodgers Bill Oil Min Bits Svc .... G 618 299-7771
   West Salem *(G-20688)*
Royal Drilling & Producing .... G 618 966-2221
   Crossville *(G-7151)*
Runyon Oil Production Inc .... G 618 395-8510
   Olney *(G-15887)*
Spartan Petroleum Company .... G 618 262-4197
   Mount Carmel *(G-14487)*
Ta Oil Field Service Inc .... G 618 249-9001
   Richview *(G-17034)*
Tussey G K Oil Explrtn & Prdc .... G 618 948-2871
   Saint Francisville *(G-18315)*

CONTRACTORS: Oil & Gas Well Foundation Grading Svcs

Runyon Oil Tools Inc .... G 618 395-5045
   Olney *(G-15888)*

CONTRACTORS: Oil & Gas Well On-Site Foundation Building Svcs

Deep Rock Energy Corporation .... E 618 548-2779
   Kinmundy *(G-12058)*

CONTRACTORS: Oil & Gas Well Plugging & Abandoning Svcs

I D Tool Specialty Company .... G 815 432-2007
   Watseka *(G-20307)*

CONTRACTORS: Oil & Gas Wells Pumping Svcs

Cdg Operations LLC .... G 618 943-8700
   Bridgeport *(G-2311)*
Wilpro .... G 618 382-4667
   Carmi *(G-2920)*

CONTRACTORS: Oil & Gas Wells Svcs

Abner Trucking Co Inc .... G 618 676-1301
   Clay City *(G-6902)*
M & L Well Service Inc .... G 618 395-4538
   Olney *(G-15871)*
Mitchco Farms LLC .... F 618 382-5032
   Carmi *(G-2911)*
Sids Well Service .... G 618 375-5411
   Grayville *(G-10815)*

CONTRACTORS: Oil Field Haulage Svcs

Haggard Well Services Inc .... G 618 262-5060
   Mount Carmel *(G-14471)*

CONTRACTORS: Oil Field Lease Tanks: Erectg, Clng/Rprg Svcs

De Vries International Inc .... E 773 248-6695
   Chicago *(G-4327)*
J B Oil Field Cnstr & Sup .... G 618 936-2350
   Sumner *(G-19687)*

CONTRACTORS: Oil Field Pipe Testing Svcs

Buckeye Partners LP .... G 217 342-2336
   Effingham *(G-8390)*
Foltz Welding Ltd .... C 618 432-7777
   Patoka *(G-16303)*
McNdt Pipeline Ltd .... F 815 467-5200
   Channahon *(G-3388)*
Panhandle Eastrn Pipe Line LP .... E 217 753-1108
   Springfield *(G-19419)*

CONTRACTORS: Oil/Gas Well Construction, Rpr/Dismantling Svcs

1 Heavy Equipment Loading Inc .... F 773 581-7374
   Bedford Park *(G-1451)*
Abundance House Treasure Nfp .... G 312 788-4316
   Chicago *(G-3511)*
Air Pure LLC .... G 815 275-8990
   Freeport *(G-10098)*
Atk Services Inc .... G 618 726-5114
   O Fallon *(G-15568)*
Aurel Construction LLC .... G 312 998-5000
   Chicago *(G-3773)*
Blue Yonder Inc .... G 630 701-1492
   Naperville *(G-14781)*
Construction Contg Svcs Inc .... F 219 779-0900
   Lansing *(G-12489)*
Craftwood Inc .... E 630 758-1740
   Elmhurst *(G-9354)*
Creed Group LLC .... G 708 261-8387
   Matteson *(G-13621)*
Crystatech Inc .... F 847 768-0500
   Des Plaines *(G-7752)*
D Kersey Construction Co .... G 847 919-4980
   Northbrook *(G-15371)*
Finite Resources Ltd .... G 618 252-3733
   Harrisburg *(G-11023)*
First American Restoration Inc .... F 800 209-3609
   Harwood Heights *(G-11105)*
Gcpro LLC .... E 773 764-2776
   Lombard *(G-13082)*
Global General Contractors LLC .... G 708 663-0476
   Tinley Park *(G-19832)*
Invenergy Investment Company L .... G 312 224-1400
   Chicago *(G-4962)*
Ja-T & Associates Inc .... F 773 744-2094
   Chicago *(G-4996)*
Jeff E Allen .... G 217 801-6878
   Springfield *(G-19394)*
Jsq Inc .... G 847 731-8800
   Zion *(G-21519)*
Local 46 Training Program Tr .... G 217 528-4041
   Springfield *(G-19399)*
Luxury Upgrade Inc .... G 773 875-8018
   Arlington Heights *(G-773)*
Mac Construction .... E 618 541-4092
   Millstadt *(G-14050)*
Macon Gc LLC .... D 309 897-8216
   Bradford *(G-2275)*
Matrix North Amercn Cnstr Inc .... G 312 754-6605
   Chicago *(G-5366)*
Mdm Construction Supply LLC .... G 815 847-7340
   Rockford *(G-17512)*
Pool Center Inc .... G 217 698-7665
   Springfield *(G-19426)*
Protus Construction .... G 773 405-9999
   Chicago *(G-5907)*
Seek Design .... G 312 804-6629
   Evanston *(G-9574)*
Stages Construction Inc .... G 773 619-2977
   Glenview *(G-10624)*
T & T Complete Construction .... F 312 929-5352
   Chicago *(G-6305)*

CONTRACTORS: On-Site Welding

1883 Properties Inc .... D 847 537-8800
   Lincolnshire *(G-12740)*
A&S Machining & Welding Inc .... E 708 442-4544
   Mc Cook *(G-13689)*
Alloyweld Inspection Co Inc .... E 630 595-2145
   Bensenville *(G-1738)*
B J Fehr Machine Co .... G 309 923-8691
   Roanoke *(G-17099)*
Bulaw Welding & Engineering Co .... D 630 228-8300
   Itasca *(G-11632)*
Cokel Welding Shop .... G 217 357-3312
   Carthage *(G-3134)*
D W Terry Welding Company .... G 618 433-9722
   Alton *(G-551)*
Daves Welding Service Inc .... G 630 655-3224
   Darien *(G-7405)*
F Vogelmann and Company .... F 815 469-2285
   Frankfort *(G-9793)*
Fabricators Unlimited Inc .... G 847 223-7986
   Grayslake *(G-10772)*
Koenig Machine & Welding Inc .... G 217 228-6538
   Quincy *(G-16904)*
Mevert Automotive Inc .... G 618 965-9609
   Steeleville *(G-19484)*
Paris Machine & Welding .... G 217 463-2894
   Paris *(G-16238)*
Pools Welding Inc .... G 309 787-2083
   Milan *(G-14020)*
Pro Machining Inc .... F 815 633-4140
   Loves Park *(G-13250)*
Pro-Tran Inc .... G 217 348-9353
   Charleston *(G-3410)*
Reyco Precision Welding Inc .... F 847 593-2947
   Lake Zurich *(G-12450)*
Shannon & Sons Welding .... G 630 898-7778
   Aurora *(G-1155)*
Southwick Machine & Design Co .... G 309 949-2868
   Colona *(G-6980)*
Tri-Cunty Wldg Fabrication LLC .... E 217 543-3304
   Arthur *(G-881)*
Wec Welding and Machining LLC .... G 847 680-8100
   Lake Bluff *(G-12214)*
Weld Seam Inc .... F 773 588-1012
   Wood Dale *(G-21257)*
Wissmiller & Evans Road Eqp .... G 309 725-3598
   Cooksville *(G-7004)*

CONTRACTORS: Ornamental Metal Work

European Ornamental Iron Works .... G 630 705-9300
   Addison *(G-117)*
Fehring Ornamental Iron Works .... G 217 483-6727
   Rochester *(G-17166)*
K D Iron Works .... G 847 991-3039
   Palatine *(G-16134)*
Legna Iron Works Inc .... E 630 894-8056
   Roselle *(G-17964)*
Ornamental Iron Shop .... G 618 281-6072
   Columbia *(G-6992)*
Quality Iron Works Inc .... F 630 766-0885
   Bensenville *(G-1878)*
R & I Ornamental Iron Inc .... G 847 836-6934
   Gilberts *(G-10366)*

CONTRACTORS: Painting & Wall Covering

All City Brick Staining LLC .... G 312 459-8937
   Chicago *(G-3608)*
Artistries By Tommy Musto Inc .... G 630 674-8667
   Bloomingdale *(G-1977)*
Brothers Decorating .... G 815 648-2214
   Hebron *(G-11139)*
Jones Design Group Ltd .... G 630 462-9340
   Winfield *(G-21111)*
Southland Painting .... G 833 724-6803
   Park Forest *(G-16260)*

CONTRACTORS: Painting, Commercial

Ace Sandblast Company .... F 773 777-6654
   Chicago *(G-3523)*
Central Illinois Sign Company .... G 217 523-4740
   Springfield *(G-19346)*

CONTRACTORS: Painting, Indl

Metal Prep Services Inc .... G 815 874-7631
   Rockford *(G-17519)*

CONTRACTORS: Patio & Deck Construction & Repair

Bergeron Group Inc .... E 815 741-1635
   Joliet *(G-11830)*
Scotts Exterior Maintenance Co .... G 309 660-3380
   Bloomington *(G-2092)*

CONTRACTORS: Pavement Marking

Varsity Striping & Cnstr Co .... E 217 352-2203
   Champaign *(G-3362)*

CONTRACTORS: Pipe Laying

Lake Process Systems Inc .... E 847 381-7663
   Lake Barrington *(G-12157)*

CONTRACTORS: Plumbing

Ave Inc .... G 815 727-0153
   Joliet *(G-11825)*
F J Murphy & Son Inc .... D 217 787-3477
   Springfield *(G-19364)*
Hamilton Concrete Products Co .... G 217 847-3118
   Hamilton *(G-10958)*
Jupiter Industries Inc .... G 847 925-5120
   Schaumburg *(G-18580)*
Key West Metal Industries Inc .... C 708 371-1470
   Crestwood *(G-7121)*
Kitchen & Bath Gallery .... G 217 214-0310
   Quincy *(G-16900)*
Marvin Schumaker Plbg Inc .... G 815 626-8130
   Sterling *(G-19516)*
Peter Perella & Co .... F 815 727-4526
   Joliet *(G-11913)*
Tane Corporation .... G 847 705-7125
   Palatine *(G-16161)*

PRODUCT SECTION

CONTRACTORS: Pollution Control Eqpt Installation
Elk Grove Custom Sheet Metal............F....... 847 352-2845
  Elk Grove Village *(G-8972)*

CONTRACTORS: Power Generating Eqpt Installation
Mat Holdings Inc................D....... 847 821-9630
  Long Grove *(G-13165)*

CONTRACTORS: Precast Concrete Struct Framing & Panel Placing
Lombard Archtctral Prcast Pdts............E....... 708 389-1060
  Chicago *(G-5253)*
Lombard Investment Company............D....... 708 389-1060
  Alsip *(G-469)*

CONTRACTORS: Process Piping
Stainless Specialties Inc............G....... 618 654-7723
  Pocahontas *(G-16754)*

CONTRACTORS: Refractory or Acid Brick Masonry
V J Mattson Company............D....... 708 479-1990
  New Lenox *(G-15067)*

CONTRACTORS: Refrigeration
Advanced Cooler Inc............G....... 630 443-8933
  Saint Charles *(G-18142)*
Hudson Technologies Inc............E....... 217 373-1414
  Champaign *(G-3304)*
Tracy Electric Inc............E....... 618 943-6205
  Lawrenceville *(G-12538)*

CONTRACTORS: Rock Removal
Civil Constructors Inc............G....... 815 858-2691
  Elizabeth *(G-8786)*

CONTRACTORS: Roofing
Joiner Sheet Metal & Roofg Inc............G....... 618 664-9488
  Highland *(G-11229)*
L R Gregory and Son Inc............E....... 847 247-0216
  Lake Bluff *(G-12191)*
RM Lucas Co............E....... 773 523-4300
  Chicago *(G-6040)*
RM Lucas Co............E....... 773 523-4300
  Alsip *(G-504)*

CONTRACTORS: Roofing & Gutter Work
Cofair Products Inc............G....... 847 626-1500
  Skokie *(G-18946)*

CONTRACTORS: Safety & Security Eqpt
Lane Industries Inc............E....... 847 498-6650
  Northbrook *(G-15417)*
National Safety Council............B....... 630 285-1121
  Itasca *(G-11707)*
Siemens Industry Inc............A....... 847 215-1000
  Buffalo Grove *(G-2600)*

CONTRACTORS: Sandblasting Svc, Building Exteriors
Ace Sandblast Company............F....... 773 777-6654
  Chicago *(G-3523)*
Fox Valley Sandblasting Inc............G....... 630 553-6050
  Yorkville *(G-21483)*
Metal Prep Services Inc............G....... 815 874-7631
  Rockford *(G-17519)*
Stripmasters Illinois Inc............G....... 618 452-1060
  Granite City *(G-10740)*

CONTRACTORS: Screening, Window & Door
Metaltek Fabricating Inc............F....... 708 534-9102
  University Park *(G-19960)*

CONTRACTORS: Seismograph Survey Svcs
Baker Hghes Olfld Oprtions LLC............F....... 618 393-2919
  Olney *(G-15854)*

CONTRACTORS: Septic System
Alternative Wastewater Systems............G....... 630 761-8720
  Batavia *(G-1345)*
Cortelyou Excavating............G....... 309 772-2922
  Bushnell *(G-2741)*
Gary & Larry Brown Trucking............G....... 618 268-6377
  Raleigh *(G-16961)*
Rochelle Vault Co............G....... 815 562-6484
  Rochelle *(G-17158)*
Rockford Sewer Co Inc............G....... 815 877-9060
  Loves Park *(G-13259)*

CONTRACTORS: Sheet Metal Work, NEC
A J Wagner & Son............F....... 773 935-1414
  Wauconda *(G-20323)*
Arrow Sheet Metal Company............E....... 815 455-2019
  Crystal Lake *(G-7164)*
Cleats Mfg Inc............F....... 773 521-0300
  Chicago *(G-4175)*
Elk Grove Custom Sheet Metal............F....... 847 352-2845
  Elk Grove Village *(G-8972)*
Gengler-Lowney Laser Works............F....... 630 801-4840
  Aurora *(G-1103)*
Highland Park Mechanical Inc............G....... 847 269-3863
  Zion *(G-21517)*
Hohlflder A H Shtmtl Htg Coolg............G....... 815 965-9134
  Rockford *(G-17451)*
John J Rickhoff Shtmtl Co Inc............F....... 708 331-2970
  Phoenix *(G-16608)*
Kirby Sheet Metal Works Inc............E....... 773 247-6477
  Chicago *(G-5106)*
Kwm Gutterman Inc............E....... 815 725-9205
  Rockdale *(G-17263)*
S & S Heating & Sheet Metal............G....... 815 933-1993
  Bradley *(G-2290)*
Western Industries Inc............C....... 920 261-0660
  Wheeling *(G-21012)*

CONTRACTORS: Sheet metal Work, Architectural
Hemingway Chimney Inc............G....... 708 333-0355
  South Holland *(G-19219)*
Nesterowicz & Associates Inc............G....... 815 522-4469
  Kirkland *(G-12064)*
Steel Rebar Manufacturing LLC............G....... 618 920-2748
  Centreville *(G-3255)*
Taloc Usa Inc............G....... 847 665-8222
  Libertyville *(G-12714)*

CONTRACTORS: Siding
Boekeloo Heating & Sheet Metal............G....... 708 877-6560
  Thornton *(G-19785)*
Four Seasons Gutter Prote............G....... 309 694-4565
  East Peoria *(G-8268)*
Seamless Gutter Corp............E....... 630 495-9800
  Lombard *(G-13128)*

CONTRACTORS: Single-family Home General Remodeling
Basement Dewatering Systems............F....... 309 647-0331
  Canton *(G-2821)*
Bushnell Locker Service............G....... 309 772-2783
  Bushnell *(G-2739)*
Duhack Lehn & Associates Inc............G....... 815 777-3460
  Galena *(G-10168)*
Gcpro LLC............E....... 773 764-2776
  Lombard *(G-13082)*
Jelinek & Sons Inc............G....... 630 355-3474
  Plainfield *(G-16676)*
Legna Iron Works Inc............E....... 630 894-8056
  Roselle *(G-17964)*
Netranix Enterprise............G....... 630 312-8141
  Bolingbrook *(G-2219)*
Raymond Earl Fine Woodworking............G....... 309 565-7661
  Hanna City *(G-10994)*

CONTRACTORS: Skylight Installation
Ccsi International Inc............E....... 815 544-8385
  Garden Prairie *(G-10236)*
Midwest Skylite Company Inc............E....... 847 214-9505
  South Elgin *(G-19167)*
United Skys LLC............F....... 847 546-7776
  Chicago *(G-6474)*

CONTRACTORS: Solar Energy Eqpt
Advanced Enrgy Solutions Group............F....... 618 988-0888
  Carterville *(G-3128)*
Astral Power Systems Inc............G....... 630 518-1741
  Aurora *(G-1055)*

CONTRACTORS: Sound Eqpt Installation
Pentegra Systems LLC............E....... 630 941-6000
  Addison *(G-235)*
Rexroat Sound............G....... 309 764-1663
  Colona *(G-6978)*

CONTRACTORS: Spa & Hot Tub Construction & Installation
Pure Skin LLC............G....... 217 679-6267
  Springfield *(G-19431)*

CONTRACTORS: Steam Cleaning, Building Exterior
All Seasons Heating & AC............G....... 217 429-2022
  Decatur *(G-7440)*
Therma-Kleen Inc............G....... 630 718-0212
  Plainfield *(G-16723)*

CONTRACTORS: Stone Masonry
Collinsville Ice & Fuel Co............F....... 618 344-3272
  Collinsville *(G-6955)*
Meno Stone Co Inc............E....... 630 257-9220
  Lemont *(G-12571)*
North Star Stone Inc............G....... 847 996-6850
  Libertyville *(G-12691)*

CONTRACTORS: Storage Tank Erection, Metal
JM Industries LLC............E....... 708 849-4700
  Riverdale *(G-17072)*
Matrix Service Inc............F....... 618 466-4862
  Alton *(G-566)*

CONTRACTORS: Store Fixture Installation
Suburban Fix & Installation............G....... 847 823-4047
  Park Ridge *(G-16298)*

CONTRACTORS: Structural Iron Work, Structural
Lamonica Ornamental Iron Works............G....... 773 638-6633
  Chicago *(G-5172)*
North Chicago Iron Works Inc............E....... 847 689-2000
  North Chicago *(G-15317)*
Steel Services Enterprises............E....... 708 259-1181
  Lansing *(G-12519)*

CONTRACTORS: Structural Steel Erection
Advance Iron Works Inc............F....... 708 798-3540
  East Hazel Crest *(G-8216)*
Advance Steel Services Inc............G....... 773 619-2977
  Chicago *(G-3558)*
Aetna Engineering Works Inc............E....... 773 785-0489
  Chicago *(G-3577)*
Alfredos Iron Works Inc............E....... 815 748-1177
  Cortland *(G-7017)*
Atkore International Group Inc............A....... 708 339-1610
  Harvey *(G-11075)*
Atkore Intl Holdings Inc............G....... 708 225-2051
  Harvey *(G-11076)*
Builders Chicago Corporation............D....... 224 654-2122
  Rosemont *(G-18001)*
Chicago Ornamental Iron Inc............E....... 773 321-9635
  Chicago *(G-4121)*
Chicago Steel Inc............E....... 800 344-3032
  Chicago *(G-4130)*
Corsetti Structural Steel Inc............E....... 815 726-0186
  Joliet *(G-11848)*
Fbs Group Inc............F....... 773 229-8675
  Chicago *(G-4569)*
Guardian Construction Pdts Inc............E....... 630 820-8899
  Naperville *(G-14970)*
H & S Mechanical Inc............D....... 309 696-7066
  Peoria *(G-16448)*
Hudson Boiler & Tank Company............F....... 312 666-4780
  Lockport *(G-13001)*
Kd Steel Incorporated............G....... 630 201-1619
  Westmont *(G-20752)*

Employee Codes: A=Over 500 employees, B=251-500
C=101-250, D=51-100, E=20-50, F=10-19, G=3-9

CONTRACTORS: Structural Steel Erection

Lichtnwald - Johnston Ir Works .... E 847 966-1100
　Morton Grove *(G-14419)*
Marqutte Stl Sup Fbrcation Inc .... F 815 433-0178
　Ottawa *(G-16060)*
Mechanical Indus Stl Svcs Inc .... E 815 521-1725
　Channahon *(G-3389)*
Morey Industries Inc .... C 708 343-3220
　Broadview *(G-2454)*
Old Style Iron Works Inc .... G 773 265-5787
　Chicago *(G-5670)*
Regal Steel Erectors LLC .... E 847 888-3500
　Elgin *(G-8716)*
Tuschall Engineering Co Inc .... E 630 655-9100
　Burr Ridge *(G-2726)*
Unistrut International Corp .... C 800 882-5543
　Harvey *(G-11099)*
WEb Production & Fabg Inc .... F 312 733-6800
　Chicago *(G-6595)*

CONTRACTORS: Svc Station Eqpt

Emco Wheaton Usa Inc .... E 217 222-5400
　Quincy *(G-16879)*

CONTRACTORS: Svc Station Eqpt Installation, Maint & Repair

R L Hoener Co .... E 217 223-2190
　Quincy *(G-16936)*

CONTRACTORS: Svc Well Drilling Svcs

TCI Companies Inc .... E 309 965-2057
　Goodfield *(G-10677)*

CONTRACTORS: Textile Warping

Next Gen Manufacturing Inc .... G 847 289-8444
　Elgin *(G-8670)*

CONTRACTORS: Tile Installation, Ceramic

Contempo Marble & Granite Inc .... G 312 455-0022
　Chicago *(G-4225)*
Ford Marble and Tile Inc .... F 618 475-2987
　New Athens *(G-15019)*
MK Tile Ink .... G 773 964-8905
　Chicago *(G-5474)*
Standard Marble & Granite .... F 773 533-0450
　Chicago *(G-6229)*

CONTRACTORS: Underground Utilities

Jklein Enterprises Inc .... G 618 664-4554
　Greenville *(G-10836)*
McLean Subsurface Utility .... G 336 988-2520
　Decatur *(G-7521)*

CONTRACTORS: Ventilation & Duct Work

All Seasons Heating & AC .... G 217 429-2022
　Decatur *(G-7440)*
American Metal Installers & FA .... G 630 993-0812
　Villa Park *(G-20131)*

CONTRACTORS: Warm Air Heating & Air Conditioning

Alton Sheet Metal Corp .... F 618 462-0609
　Alton *(G-543)*
Anytime Heating & AC .... F 630 851-6696
　Naperville *(G-14959)*
Boekeloo Heating & Sheet Metal .... G 708 877-6560
　Thornton *(G-19785)*
Brex-Arlington Incorporated .... F 847 255-6284
　Mount Prospect *(G-14515)*
Eikenberry Sheet Metal Works .... E 815 625-0955
　Sterling *(G-19507)*
Gengler-Lowney Laser Works .... F 630 801-4840
　Aurora *(G-1103)*
GROsse&sons Htg &SHeet Met Inc .... G 708 447-8397
　Lyons *(G-13310)*
Habegger Corporation .... F 309 793-7172
　Rock Island *(G-17221)*
Highland Park Mechanical Inc .... G 847 269-3863
　Zion *(G-21517)*
Hillers Sheet Metal Works .... G 217 532-2595
　Hillsboro *(G-11314)*
Hohlflder A H Shtmtl Htg Coolg .... G 815 965-9134
　Rockford *(G-17451)*
Ibbotson Heating Co .... E 847 253-0866
　Arlington Heights *(G-752)*
J D Refrigeration .... G 618 345-0041
　Collinsville *(G-6963)*
Keil-Forness Comfort Systems .... G 618 233-3039
　Belleville *(G-1560)*
L M Sheet Metal Inc .... E 815 654-1837
　Loves Park *(G-13230)*
L R Gregory and Son Inc .... E 847 247-0216
　Lake Bluff *(G-12191)*
Lemanski Heating & AC .... G 815 232-4519
　Freeport *(G-10125)*
Lizotte Sheet Metal Inc .... G 618 656-3066
　Edwardsville *(G-8368)*
Macari Service Center Inc .... F 217 774-4214
　Shelbyville *(G-18881)*
Merz Air Conditioning and Htg .... E 217 342-2323
　Effingham *(G-8409)*
Montefusco Hvac Inc .... G 309 691-7400
　Peoria *(G-16479)*
Reedy Industries Inc .... F 847 729-9450
　Glenview *(G-10610)*
Ring Sheet Metal Heating & AC .... G 309 289-4213
　Knoxville *(G-12069)*
Ruyle Incorporated .... E 309 674-6644
　Springfield *(G-19437)*
S & S Heating & Sheet Metal .... G 815 933-1993
　Bradley *(G-2290)*
Sudholt Sheet Metal Inc .... G 618 228-7351
　Aviston *(G-1183)*
Tri City Sheet Metal .... G 630 232-4255
　Geneva *(G-10313)*
Unique Indoor Comfort .... F 847 362-1910
　Libertyville *(G-12719)*

CONTRACTORS: Water Intake Well Drilling Svc

Mashburn Well Drilling .... G 217 794-3728
　Maroa *(G-13553)*
Raimonde Drilling Corp .... F 630 458-0590
　Addison *(G-265)*

CONTRACTORS: Water Well Drilling

Coursons Coring & Drilling .... G 618 349-8765
　Saint Peter *(G-18323)*
Kohnens Concrete Products Inc .... E 618 277-2120
　Germantown *(G-10330)*
Mashburn Well Drilling .... G 217 794-3728
　Maroa *(G-13553)*
TCI Companies Inc .... E 309 965-2057
　Goodfield *(G-10677)*
Will County Well & Pump Co Inc .... G 815 485-2413
　New Lenox *(G-15069)*

CONTRACTORS: Waterproofing

Basement Flood Protector Inc .... F 847 438-6770
　Lake Zurich *(G-12387)*
Protective Coatings & Waterpro .... G 708 403-7650
　Orland Park *(G-15975)*
Ted Muller .... G 312 435-0978
　Chicago *(G-6336)*

CONTRACTORS: Well Acidizing Svcs

B & B Tank Truck Construction .... F 618 378-3337
　Norris City *(G-15246)*
Fairfield Acid and Frac Co .... F 618 842-9186
　Fairfield *(G-9622)*
Tri State Acid Co Inc .... F 618 676-1111
　Clay City *(G-6908)*

CONTRACTORS: Well Bailing, Cleaning, Swabbing & Treating Svc

Orr Rudolph .... G 815 429-3996
　Watseka *(G-20313)*

CONTRACTORS: Well Casings Perforating Svcs

Gain Wireline Services Inc .... G 618 842-2914
　Fairfield *(G-9625)*

CONTRACTORS: Well Chemical Treating Svcs

Sims Company Inc .... G 618 665-3901
　Louisville *(G-13180)*

CONTRACTORS: Window Treatment Installation

Energy Solutions Inc .... G 618 465-5404
　Alton *(G-556)*
Regent Window Fashions LLC .... G 773 871-6400
　Chicago *(G-6003)*

CONTRACTORS: Windows & Doors

A Ashland Lock Company .... F 773 348-5106
　Chicago *(G-3485)*
Cofair Products Inc .... G 847 626-1500
　Skokie *(G-18946)*
Doralco Inc .... E 708 388-9324
　Alsip *(G-441)*
Illinois Green Cnstr Inc .... G 847 975-2312
　Chicago *(G-4891)*

CONTRACTORS: Wood Floor Installation & Refinishing

Signature Innovations LLC .... G 847 758-9600
　Elk Grove Village *(G-9241)*

CONTRACTORS: Wrecking & Demolition

Lake County Grading Co LLC .... D 847 362-2590
　Libertyville *(G-12665)*
St Louis Scrap Trading LLC .... G 618 307-9002
　Edwardsville *(G-8376)*

CONTROL CIRCUIT DEVICES

Master Control Systems Inc .... E 847 295-1010
　Lake Bluff *(G-12195)*

CONTROL EQPT: Electric

BTR Controls Inc .... G 847 608-9500
　Elgin *(G-8525)*
Con-Trol-Cure Inc .... F 773 248-0099
　Chicago *(G-4211)*
Control Systems Inc .... G 847 438-6228
　Long Grove *(G-13159)*
Copar Corporation .... E 708 496-1859
　Burbank *(G-2635)*
Don Johns Inc .... G 630 454-4700
　Batavia *(G-1374)*
Dresser LLC .... D 847 437-5940
　Elk Grove Village *(G-8955)*
Elcon Inc .... E 815 467-9500
　Minooka *(G-14059)*
Enercon Engineering Inc .... C 800 218-8831
　East Peoria *(G-8266)*
Joliet Technologies LLC .... G 815 725-9696
　Crest Hill *(G-7089)*
M-1 Tool Works Inc .... E 815 344-1275
　McHenry *(G-13761)*
Machine Control Systems Inc .... G 708 389-2160
　Palos Heights *(G-16190)*
Meyer Systems .... G 815 436-7077
　Joliet *(G-11900)*
Parking Systems Inc .... G 847 891-3819
　Schaumburg *(G-18666)*
Process and Control Systems .... F 708 293-0557
　Alsip *(G-498)*
R & D Electronics Inc .... G 847 583-9080
　Niles *(G-15163)*
Rockdale Controls Co Inc .... F 815 436-6181
　Plainfield *(G-16711)*
Sparton Aydin LLC .... G 800 772-7866
　Schaumburg *(G-18716)*
Spectrum Cos International .... G 630 879-8008
　Batavia *(G-1418)*
Unitrol Electronics Inc .... E 847 480-0115
　Northbrook *(G-15496)*
Win Technologies Incorporated .... E 630 236-1020
　Aurora *(G-1037)*

CONTROL EQPT: Electric Buses & Locomotives

International Supply Co .... D 309 249-6211
　Edelstein *(G-8333)*

CONTROL EQPT: Noise

Blachford Investments Inc .... C 630 231-8300
　West Chicago *(G-20552)*
Rensel-Chicago Inc .... E 773 235-2100
　Chicago *(G-6015)*

PRODUCT SECTION

CONTROLS: Relay & Ind

Sound Seal Inc ....E...... 630 844-1999
  North Aurora (G-15276)
Steel-Guard Safety Corp ....G...... 708 589-4588
  South Holland (G-19246)

CONTROL PANELS: Electrical

Cable Electric Company Inc ....G...... 708 458-8900
  Oak Lawn (G-15706)
Control Panels Inc ....F...... 815 654-6000
  Rockford (G-17357)
Control Works Inc ....G...... 630 444-1942
  Saint Charles (G-18174)
Cymatics Inc ....G...... 630 420-7117
  Naperville (G-14811)
Don Johns Inc ....E...... 630 454-4700
  Batavia (G-1374)
Enercon Engineering Inc ....E...... 800 218-8831
  East Peoria (G-8266)
Engineered Fluid Inc ....C...... 618 533-1351
  Centralia (G-3230)
Excel Ltd Inc ....G...... 847 543-9138
  Grayslake (G-10771)
Inland Tech Holdings LLC ....E...... 618 476-7678
  Millstadt (G-14048)
Its Solar LLC ....E...... 618 476-7678
  Waterloo (G-20291)
Kenyeri Consulting LLC ....G...... 630 920-3497
  Downers Grove (G-8039)
Machine Control Systems Inc ....G...... 708 597-1200
  Alsip (G-471)
Machine Control Systems Inc ....G...... 708 389-2160
  Palos Heights (G-16190)
Morton Automatic Electric Co ....G...... 309 263-7577
  Morton (G-14369)
Panel Authority Inc ....F...... 815 838-0488
  Plainfield (G-16699)
Panelshopnet Inc ....G...... 630 692-0214
  Naperville (G-14982)
Platt Industrial Control Inc ....G...... 630 833-4388
  Addison (G-243)
Prater Industries Inc ....D...... 630 679-3200
  Bolingbrook (G-2228)
Protection Controls Inc ....E...... 773 763-3110
  Skokie (G-19017)
Quantum Design Inc ....D...... 815 885-1300
  Machesney Park (G-13321)
R G Controls Inc ....G...... 847 438-3981
  Barrington (G-1239)
RLC Industries Inc ....G...... 708 837-7300
  La Grange (G-12088)
RWS Design and Controls Inc ....E...... 815 654-6000
  Roscoe (G-17930)
Schubert Controls Corporation ....G...... 847 526-8200
  Wauconda (G-20390)
Venture Design Incorporated ....F...... 630 369-1148
  Naperville (G-14941)

CONTROLS & ACCESS: Indl, Electric

7 Mile Solutions Inc ....E...... 847 588-2280
  Niles (G-15096)
American Control Elec LLC ....G...... 815 624-6950
  South Beloit (G-19080)
Box of Rain Ltd ....G...... 847 640-6996
  Arlington Heights (G-707)
Capable Controls Inc ....D...... 630 860-6514
  Bensenville (G-1761)
Control Designs Inc ....G...... 847 672-9514
  Gurnee (G-10865)
Control Research Inc ....G...... 847 352-4920
  Schaumburg (G-18488)
Electro-Matic Products Co ....F...... 773 235-4010
  Chicago (G-4477)
Fivecubits Inc ....F...... 925 273-1862
  Oak Brook (G-15621)
Harrington Signal Inc ....E...... 309 762-0731
  Moline (G-14148)
I P C Automation Inc ....G...... 815 759-3934
  McHenry (G-13749)
Instrmntation Ctrl Systems Inc ....F...... 630 543-6200
  Roselle (G-17959)
Jtekt Toyoda Americas Corp ....C...... 847 253-0340
  Arlington Heights (G-764)
Justice Manufacturing Inc ....G...... 217 877-2250
  Decatur (G-7512)
Lumenite Control Technology ....F...... 847 455-1450
  Franklin Park (G-9982)
Meister Industries Inc ....G...... 815 623-8919
  Roscoe (G-17917)
Mission Control Systems Inc ....F...... 847 956-7650
  Elk Grove Village (G-9127)

Questek Manufacturing Corp ....D...... 847 428-0300
  Elgin (G-8710)
Value Added Services & Tech ....G...... 847 888-8232
  Elgin (G-8772)

CONTROLS & ACCESS: Motor

Capsonic Automotive Inc ....F...... 847 888-7300
  Elgin (G-8529)
Capsonic Automotive Inc ....F...... 847 888-7300
  Elgin (G-8530)
Capsonic Automotive Inc ....B...... 915 872-3585
  Chicago (G-4020)
Danfoss Inc ....G...... 815 639-8600
  Loves Park (G-13204)
Danfoss LLC ....C...... 888 326-3677
  Loves Park (G-13206)

CONTROLS: Access, Motor

Industrial Controls Inc ....G...... 630 752-8100
  Geneva (G-10278)

CONTROLS: Adjustable Speed Drive

Invektek Llc ....G...... 312 343-0600
  Chicago (G-4961)
Mektronix Technology Inc ....G...... 847 680-3300
  Libertyville (G-12677)

CONTROLS: Air Flow, Refrigeration

Holland Safety Equipment Inc ....G...... 847 680-9930
  Libertyville (G-12659)

CONTROLS: Automatic Temperature

Automatic Building Contrls LLC ....D...... 847 296-4000
  Rolling Meadows (G-17714)
Clarios ....D...... 708 474-1717
  Calumet City (G-2773)
Industrial Thermo Products ....G...... 847 398-8600
  Rolling Meadows (G-17740)
Interactive Bldg Solutions LLC ....F...... 815 724-0525
  Joliet (G-11882)
Precision Control Systems ....D...... 630 521-0234
  Lisle (G-12928)
Professional Freezing Svcs LLC ....G...... 773 847-7500
  Chicago (G-5896)
Siemens Industry Inc ....D...... 630 444-4316
  Saint Charles (G-18269)

CONTROLS: Electric Motor

Bodine Electric Company ....B...... 773 478-3515
  Northfield (G-15509)
Continental Auto Systems Inc ....G...... 847 862-5000
  Deer Park (G-7579)
Four-Most Inc ....G...... 815 282-9788
  Rockford (G-17422)
Industrial Service Solutions ....C...... 917 609-6979
  Chicago (G-4910)

CONTROLS: Environmental

Ademco Inc ....G...... 708 599-1390
  Bridgeview (G-2319)
Automax Corporation ....G...... 630 972-1919
  Woodridge (G-21277)
Baldwin Technology Company Inc ....C...... 618 842-2664
  Fairfield (G-9618)
Beneficial Reuse MGT LLC ....F...... 312 784-0300
  Chicago (G-3867)
Biosynergy Inc ....G...... 847 956-0471
  Elk Grove Village (G-8867)
Candy Manufacturing Company ....F...... 847 588-2639
  Niles (G-15107)
Catalytic Products Intl Inc ....E...... 847 438-0334
  Lake Zurich (G-12390)
Caterpillar Inc ....B...... 815 729-5511
  Joliet (G-11838)
Creative Controls Systems Inc ....G...... 815 629-2358
  Rockton (G-17696)
Danfoss LLC ....G...... 717 261-5000
  Loves Park (G-13205)
Dickson/Unigage Inc ....E...... 630 543-3747
  Addison (G-92)
Dometic Corporation ....A...... 847 447-7190
  Rosemont (G-18019)
Elcon Inc ....E...... 815 467-9500
  Minooka (G-14059)
Global Green Products LLC ....G...... 708 341-3670
  Orland Park (G-15955)

Green Ladder Technologies LLC ....E...... 630 457-1872
  Batavia (G-1382)
Gus Berthold Electric Company ....D...... 312 243-5767
  Chicago (G-4752)
Homecontrolplus Incorporated ....G...... 847 823-8414
  Park Ridge (G-16283)
Mitsubishi Elc Automtn Inc ....C...... 847 478-2100
  Vernon Hills (G-20075)
R & D Electronics Inc ....G...... 847 583-9080
  Niles (G-15163)
Robertshaw Controls Company ....C...... 630 260-3400
  Itasca (G-11727)
Scientific Instruments Inc ....G...... 847 679-1242
  Schaumburg (G-18709)
Solidyne Corporation ....F...... 847 394-3333
  Rolling Meadows (G-17775)
Solidyne Corporation ....F...... 847 394-3333
  Hoffman Estates (G-11460)
Spring Brook Nature Center ....G...... 630 773-5572
  Itasca (G-11739)
Tempro International Corp ....G...... 847 677-5370
  Skokie (G-19044)
Vent Ure Air ....G...... 708 652-7200
  Chicago (G-6533)

CONTROLS: Numerical

Hausermann Controls Co ....F...... 630 543-6688
  Addison (G-147)
Kz Manufacturing Co ....G...... 708 937-8097
  Mc Cook (G-13694)

CONTROLS: Relay & Ind

Advanced Technologies Inc ....G...... 847 329-9875
  Park Ridge (G-16264)
Arens Controls Company LLc ....D...... 847 844-4700
  Arlington Heights (G-694)
Automated Systems & Control Co ....G...... 847 735-8310
  Lake Bluff (G-12172)
Baldwin Technology Company Inc ....C...... 618 842-2664
  Fairfield (G-9618)
Burke Tool & Manufacturing Inc ....G...... 618 542-6441
  Du Quoin (G-8116)
Caterpillar Inc ....B...... 815 729-5511
  Joliet (G-11838)
Chamberlain Manufacturing Corp ....A...... 630 279-3600
  Oak Brook (G-15608)
Control Solutions LLC ....D...... 630 806-7062
  Aurora (G-941)
Control System Innovators Inc ....G...... 847 741-0007
  Elgin (G-8553)
Controllink Incorporated ....E...... 847 622-1100
  Elgin (G-8554)
Creative Controls Systems Inc ....G...... 815 629-2358
  Rockton (G-17696)
Danfoss LLC ....G...... 717 261-5000
  Loves Park (G-13205)
Dgm Electronics Inc ....G...... 815 389-2040
  Roscoe (G-17904)
Domino Engineering Corp ....F...... 217 824-9441
  Taylorville (G-19756)
Eaton Corporation ....C...... 815 562-2107
  Rochelle (G-17138)
Elemech Inc ....E...... 630 417-2845
  Aurora (G-956)
Elenco Electronics Inc ....E...... 847 541-3800
  Wheeling (G-20889)
Enercon Engineering Inc ....D...... 309 694-1418
  East Peoria (G-8267)
Envirnmntal Ctrl Solutions Inc ....G...... 217 793-8966
  Springfield (G-19363)
Flolo Corporation ....G...... 847 249-0880
  Gurnee (G-10878)
Gpe Controls Inc ....F...... 708 236-6000
  Hillside (G-11340)
Grayhill Inc ....G...... 708 482-1411
  Mc Cook (G-13691)
Guardian Consolidated Tech Inc ....G...... 815 334-3600
  Woodstock (G-21392)
Guardian Electric Mfg Co ....D...... 815 334-3600
  Woodstock (G-21393)
Harris Precision Tools Inc ....G...... 708 422-5808
  Chicago Ridge (G-6797)
Harvey Bros Inc ....F...... 309 342-3137
  Galesburg (G-10199)
Hauhinco LP ....E...... 618 993-5399
  Marion (G-13514)
Hella Corporate Center USA Inc ....B...... 734 414-0900
  Flora (G-9682)
Hella Corporate Center USA Inc ....B...... 618 662-4402
  Flora (G-9683)

Employee Codes: A=Over 500 employees, B=251-500
C=101-250, D=51-100, E=20-50, F=10-19, G=3-9

2020 Harris Illinois Industrial Directory

CONTROLS: Relay & Ind

Hella Electronics Corporation ......A...... 618 662-5186
  Flora (G-9684)
Ideal Industries Inc ......C...... 815 895-1108
  Sycamore (G-19715)
Industrial Motion Control LLC ......C...... 847 459-5200
  Wheeling (G-20915)
Industrial Sensing and Safety ......G...... 630 264-8249
  Aurora (G-1112)
K & W Auto Electric ......F...... 217 857-1717
  Teutopolis (G-19770)
Kackert Enterprises Inc ......G...... 630 898-9339
  Aurora (G-1120)
Keonix Corporation ......G...... 847 259-9430
  Arlington Heights (G-765)
Loda Electronics Co ......G...... 217 386-2554
  Loda (G-13029)
Machine Control Systems Inc ......G...... 708 597-1200
  Alsip (G-471)
Magnetrol International Inc ......C...... 630 723-6600
  Aurora (G-1001)
Martin Automatic Inc ......C...... 815 654-4800
  Rockford (G-17505)
Maurey Instrument Corp ......F...... 708 388-9898
  Alsip (G-474)
Methode Electronics Inc ......A...... 217 357-3941
  Carthage (G-3139)
Meto-Grafics Inc ......F...... 847 639-0044
  Crystal Lake (G-7226)
Morton Automatic Electric Co ......G...... 309 263-7577
  Morton (G-14369)
Mpc Products Corporation ......A...... 847 673-8300
  Niles (G-15149)
New Cie Inc ......F...... 815 224-1485
  La Salle (G-12118)
Nidec Mobility America Corp ......A...... 630 443-6800
  Saint Charles (G-18234)
Niles Auto Parts ......G...... 847 215-2549
  Lincolnshire (G-12788)
O C Keckley Company ......E...... 847 674-8422
  Skokie (G-18997)
Olympic Controls Corp ......G...... 847 742-3566
  Elgin (G-8678)
Panatrol Corporation ......E...... 630 655-4700
  Burr Ridge (G-2713)
Pilz Automtn Safety Ltd Partnr ......G...... 734 354-0272
  Chicago (G-5808)
Power-Io Inc ......E...... 630 717-7335
  Naperville (G-14901)
Pro-Quip Incorporated ......F...... 708 352-5732
  La Grange (G-12087)
Process Technologies Group ......G...... 630 393-4777
  Warrenville (G-20250)
Protection Controls Inc ......E...... 773 763-3110
  Skokie (G-19017)
Rockwell Automation Inc ......F...... 901 367-4220
  Champaign (G-3344)
Rockwell Automation Inc ......D...... 630 789-5900
  Lisle (G-12934)
Ruby Automation LLC ......F...... 815 624-5959
  South Beloit (G-19112)
S & C Electric Company ......A...... 773 338-1000
  Chicago (G-6083)
Schneider Elc Buildings LLC ......B...... 815 381-5000
  Rockford (G-17622)
Schneider Elc Holdings Inc ......A...... 717 944-5460
  Schaumburg (G-18707)
Scientific Instruments Inc ......G...... 847 679-1242
  Schaumburg (G-18709)
SE Relays LLC ......G...... 847 441-2540
  Schaumburg (G-18710)
Siemens Industry Inc ......A...... 847 215-1000
  Buffalo Grove (G-2600)
Siemens Industry Inc ......G...... 217 824-6833
  Taylorville (G-19762)
Simplex Inc ......C...... 217 483-1600
  Springfield (G-19446)
Smart Systems Inc ......E...... 630 343-3333
  Bolingbrook (G-2242)
Sparton Onyx Holdings LLC ......G...... 847 762-5800
  Schaumburg (G-18720)
Sterling Systems & Controls ......F...... 815 625-0852
  Sterling (G-19536)
Sumitomo Machinery Corp Amer ......E...... 630 752-0200
  Glendale Heights (G-10504)
Tc Electric Controls LLC ......G...... 815 213-7680
  Sterling (G-19538)
Tc Electric Controls LLC ......G...... 815 213-7680
  Schaumburg (G-18741)
Tomantron Inc ......F...... 708 532-2456
  Tinley Park (G-19860)

Wgi Innovations Ltd ......G...... 800 847-8269
  Plano (G-16747)
Yaskawa America Inc ......C...... 847 887-7000
  Waukegan (G-20520)

CONTROLS: Thermostats

Building Technologies Inc ......G...... 800 743-6367
  Buffalo Grove (G-2521)
Kingfisher Controls LLC ......G...... 425 359-5601
  Illiopolis (G-11574)

CONTROLS: Thermostats, Built-in

Goodrich Sensor Systems ......G...... 847 546-5749
  Round Lake (G-18077)

CONTROLS: Water Heater

A&B Reliable ......G...... 708 228-6148
  Lemont (G-12551)
Lopez Plumbing Systems Inc 773 424-8225
  Chicago (G-5258)
Unitrol Electronics Inc ......E...... 847 480-0115
  Northbrook (G-15496)

CONVENTION & TRADE SHOW SVCS

Be Group Inc ......G...... 312 436-0301
  Chicago (G-3848)
Stagnito Partners LLC ......E...... 224 632-8200
  Chicago (G-6227)

CONVERTERS: Data

Cisco Systems Inc ......B...... 847 678-6600
  Des Plaines (G-7747)
Ibs Conversions Inc ......D...... 630 571-9100
  Oak Brook (G-15626)
Mediarecall Holdings LLC ......E...... 847 513-6710
  Northbrook (G-15430)
Precision Computer Methods ......G...... 630 208-8000
  Elburn (G-8469)
Richardson Electronics Ltd ......G...... 630 208-2278
  Lafox (G-12137)

CONVERTERS: Frequency

Hamilton Sundstrand Corp ......F...... 815 226-6000
  Rockford (G-17440)
Weldon Corporation ......E...... 708 343-4700
  Maywood (G-13680)

CONVERTERS: Phase Or Rotary, Electrical

Ronk Electrical Industries Inc ......E...... 217 563-8333
  Nokomis (G-15198)
Tracy Electric Inc ......E...... 618 943-6205
  Lawrenceville (G-12538)

CONVERTERS: Rotary, Electrical

Ground Cover Industries Inc ......G...... 800 550-4424
  Kildeer (G-12048)

CONVERTERS: Torque, Exc Auto

Dynamic Powertrain Reman LLC ......F...... 708 343-5444
  Melrose Park (G-13858)
Midwest Converters Inc ......F...... 815 229-9808
  Rockford (G-17525)

CONVEYOR SYSTEMS

Deyco Inc ......G...... 630 553-5666
  Yorkville (G-21480)
Ehs Solutions LLC ......E...... 309 282-9121
  Peoria (G-16433)
Ewab Engineering Inc ......E...... 847 247-0015
  Libertyville (G-12649)
Industrial Kinetics Inc ......E...... 630 655-0300
  Downers Grove (G-8031)
Krygier Design Inc ......F...... 620 766-1001
  Wood Dale (G-21205)
Witron Intgrated Logistics Inc ......C...... 847 398-6130
  Arlington Heights (G-835)

CONVEYOR SYSTEMS: Belt, General Indl Use

Duravant LLC ......F...... 630 635-3910
  Downers Grove (G-7995)
Erect - O -Veyor Corporation ......F...... 630 766-1200
  Franklin Park (G-9939)

Forbo Siegling LLC ......F...... 630 595-4031
  Wood Dale (G-21188)
J W Todd Co ......G...... 630 406-5715
  Aurora (G-1114)
Lake Fabrication Inc ......G...... 217 832-2761
  Villa Grove (G-20124)
Rotec Industries Inc ......D...... 630 279-3300
  Hampshire (G-10985)

CONVEYOR SYSTEMS: Bucket Type

Joy Global Underground Min LLC ......E...... 618 242-3650
  Mount Vernon (G-14619)

CONVEYOR SYSTEMS: Bulk Handling

Align Production Systems LLC ......E...... 217 423-6001
  Decatur (G-7439)
GMI Packaging Co ......G...... 734 972-7389
  Chicago (G-4705)
William W Meyer and Sons ......D...... 847 918-0111
  Libertyville (G-12726)

CONVEYOR SYSTEMS: Pneumatic Tube

Bankmark Inc ......F...... 847 683-9834
  Hampshire (G-10963)
Barrington Automation Ltd ......E...... 847 458-0900
  Lake In The Hills (G-12329)
Kelly Systems Inc ......E...... 312 733-3224
  Chicago (G-5093)
Kongskilde Industries Inc ......E...... 309 452-3300
  Normal (G-15207)
Return On Inv Systems Inc ......G...... 847 726-0081
  Lake Zurich (G-12449)
Translogic Corporation ......F...... 847 392-3700
  Rolling Meadows (G-17781)

CONVEYOR SYSTEMS: Robotic

Diversified Fleet MGT Inc ......E...... 815 578-1051
  McHenry (G-13736)
Matrix Design LLC ......D...... 847 841-8260
  Bartlett (G-1296)
Smart Motion Robotics Inc ......E...... 815 895-8550
  Sycamore (G-19732)

CONVEYORS & CONVEYING EQPT

Acro Magnetics Inc ......G...... 815 943-5018
  Harvard (G-11040)
Astec Mobile Screens Inc ......C...... 815 626-6374
  Sterling (G-19498)
Atbc LLC ......G...... 847 648-2822
  Park Ridge (G-16269)
Automated Material Hdlg Svcs ......G...... 630 947-7605
  Batavia (G-1352)
Automatic Feeder Company Inc ......F...... 847 534-2300
  Schaumburg (G-18449)
Avasarala Inc ......G...... 847 969-0630
  Palatine (G-16095)
Barry-Whmller Cont Systems Inc ......C...... 630 759-6800
  Romeoville (G-17798)
Benda Manufacturing Inc ......G...... 708 633-4600
  Tinley Park (G-19808)
Bettendorf Stanford Inc ......D...... 618 548-3555
  Salem (G-18331)
Birnberg Machinery Inc ......G...... 847 673-5242
  Deerfield (G-7597)
Bost Corporation ......E...... 708 344-7023
  Maywood (G-13663)
Canconex Inc ......F...... 847 458-9955
  Algonquin (G-368)
Central Manufacturing Company ......G...... 309 387-6591
  East Peoria (G-8259)
Chicago Can Conveyor Corp ......G...... 708 430-0988
  Bridgeview (G-2334)
Chicago Chain and Transm Co ......E...... 630 482-9000
  Countryside (G-7046)
Cmd Conveyor Inc ......E...... 708 237-0996
  Chicago Ridge (G-6792)
Complete Conveying Svcs LLC ......G...... 815 695-5176
  Newark (G-15075)
Confab Systems Inc ......F...... 708 388-4103
  Posen (G-16792)
Container Hdlg Systems Corp ......E...... 708 482-9900
  Countryside (G-7047)
Container Service Group Inc ......F...... 815 744-8693
  Rockdale (G-17258)
Conveyor Specialties Inc ......G...... 815 727-7638
  Joliet (G-11847)
Conveyor Systems & Engineering ......G...... 847 593-2900
  Arlington Heights (G-720)

Conveyors Plus Inc....................................G....... 708 361-1512
  Orland Park (G-15948)
Dabrico Inc..E....... 815 939-0580
  Bourbonnais (G-2259)
Dematic Corp..F....... 630 852-9200
  Lisle (G-12885)
Diversatech Metalfab LLC........................E....... 309 747-4159
  Gridley (G-10843)
Dspc Company...E....... 815 997-1116
  Rockford (G-17387)
Duravant...G....... 630 635-3910
  Downers Grove (G-7994)
Eaglestone Inc..F....... 630 587-1115
  Saint Charles (G-18192)
Eirich Machines Inc..................................D....... 847 336-2444
  Gurnee (G-10875)
Engineered Plumbing Spc LLC................E....... 630 682-1555
  Joliet (G-11862)
Engineering Products Company..............G....... 815 436-9055
  Plainfield (G-16659)
Forte Automation Systems Inc................E....... 815 316-6247
  Machesney Park (G-13344)
Frantz Manufacturing Company...............D....... 815 564-0991
  Sterling (G-19510)
GE Fairchild Mining Equipment................D....... 618 559-3216
  Du Quoin (G-8121)
Gsi Group LLC..C....... 217 463-1612
  Paris (G-16230)
Icon Co..G....... 630 545-2345
  Glen Ellyn (G-10405)
Illinois Conveyor Service Inc....................G....... 630 469-1300
  Glen Ellyn (G-10406)
Industrial Motion Control LLC..................C....... 847 459-5200
  Wheeling (G-20915)
Intelligrated Systems Inc.........................B....... 630 985-4350
  Woodridge (G-21315)
International Conveyors Amer..................G....... 630 549-4007
  Geneva (G-10284)
K Transco Inc...G....... 630 881-5411
  Lemont (G-12567)
Kamflex Conveyor Corporation................G....... 630 682-1555
  Joliet (G-11889)
Kimco USA Inc...F....... 800 788-1133
  Marshall (G-13574)
L M C Inc..G....... 815 758-3514
  Dekalb (G-7687)
Logicon Group LLC..................................G....... 618 558-7757
  Millstadt (G-14049)
Loop Belt Industries Inc..........................G....... 630 469-1300
  Glen Ellyn (G-10410)
Mallard Handling Solutions LLC..............E....... 815 625-9491
  Sterling (G-19515)
MCR Technologies Group Inc..................G....... 815 622-3181
  Sterling (G-19517)
Mid States Corporation............................E....... 708 754-1760
  S Chicago Hts (G-18125)
Mid-American Elevator Co Inc.................C....... 773 486-6900
  Chicago (G-5428)
Mid-American Elevator Co Inc.................E....... 815 740-1204
  Joliet (G-11902)
Midstates Rail LLC..................................F....... 708 758-7245
  Chicago Heights (G-6758)
Morrison Timing Screw Company.............D....... 708 756-6660
  Glenwood (G-10643)
Payson Casters Inc..................................C....... 847 336-5033
  Gurnee (G-10910)
Pre Pack Machinery Inc...........................G....... 217 352-1010
  Champaign (G-3338)
Precision Conveyor and Erct Co..............F....... 779 324-5269
  Frankfort (G-9823)
Roll-A-Way Conveyors Inc......................F....... 847 336-5033
  Gurnee (G-10924)
RPS Engineering Inc................................F....... 847 931-1950
  Elgin (G-8721)
SA Nat Industrial Cnstr Co Inc................E....... 618 246-9402
  Mount Vernon (G-14636)
Sardee Industries Inc..............................G....... 630 824-4200
  Lisle (G-12936)
SBS Steel Belt Systems USA Inc............F....... 847 841-3300
  Gilberts (G-10369)
Special Tool Engineering Co....................F....... 773 767-6690
  Chicago (G-6212)
Superior Industries Inc............................F....... 309 346-1742
  Pekin (G-16362)
Tracoinsa USA..G....... 309 287-7046
  Gridley (G-10847)
Tricon Inds Mfg & Eqp Sls.......................E....... 815 379-2090
  Walnut (G-20220)
United Conveyor Corporation...................C....... 847 473-5900
  Waukegan (G-20513)

United Conveyor Supply Company..........D....... 847 672-5100
  Waukegan (G-20514)
United Systems Incorporated..................F....... 708 479-1450
  Mokena (G-14125)
US Conveyor Tech Mfg Inc......................E....... 309 359-4088
  Mackinaw (G-13386)
US Conveyor Technologies.....................F....... 309 359-4088
  Mackinaw (G-13387)
V & C Converters.....................................G....... 708 251-5635
  Lansing (G-12523)
Wes-Tech Automtn Solutions LLC...........D....... 847 541-5070
  Buffalo Grove (G-2621)

CONVEYORS: Overhead

Rwi Manufacturing Inc............................C....... 800 277-1699
  Aurora (G-1151)

COOKING & FOOD WARMING EQPT: Commercial

A J Antunes & Co....................................C....... 630 784-1000
  Carol Stream (G-2922)
Keating of Chicago Inc............................E....... 815 569-2324
  Capron (G-2834)
Middleby Corporation...............................E....... 847 741-3300
  Elgin (G-8660)
Omni Containment Systems LLC.............G....... 847 468-1772
  Elgin (G-8679)
Optimal Automatics Co............................G....... 847 439-9110
  Elk Grove Village (G-9165)
Prince Castle LLC....................................C....... 630 462-8800
  Carol Stream (G-3050)
Quantum Technical Services Inc.............E....... 815 464-1540
  Frankfort (G-9829)

COOKING & FOODWARMING EQPT: Coffee Brewing

Bravilor Bonamat LLC.............................F....... 630 423-9400
  Aurora (G-926)
Bunn-O-Matic Corporation.......................G....... 217 529-6601
  Springfield (G-19331)
Bunn-O-Matic Corporation.......................G....... 217 528-8739
  Springfield (G-19333)

COOKING & FOODWARMING EQPT: Commercial

Ali Group North America Corp.................C....... 847 215-6565
  Vernon Hills (G-20040)
Midco International Inc............................E....... 773 604-8700
  Chicago (G-5433)
Middleby Corporation...............................E....... 847 741-3300
  Elgin (G-8661)

COOKING & FOODWARMING EQPT: Popcorn Machines, Commercial

C Cretors & Co..D....... 847 616-6900
  Wood Dale (G-21173)

COOKING EQPT, HOUSEHOLD: Ranges, Gas

Empire Comfort Systems Inc...................C....... 618 233-7420
  Belleville (G-1551)
Peerless-Premier Appliance Co...............C....... 618 233-0475
  Belleville (G-1585)

COOKING SCHOOL

Wilton Brands LLC...................................B....... 630 963-7100
  Naperville (G-14948)

COOKING WARE, EXC PORCELAIN ENAMELED

Crown Brands LLC...................................E....... 224 513-2917
  Lincolnshire (G-12757)

COOKING WARE: Cooking Ware, Porcelain Enameled

Columbian Home Products LLC...............C....... 847 307-8500
  North Barrington (G-15282)

COOLERS & ICE CHESTS: Polystyrene Foam

Tkk USA Inc..C....... 847 439-7821
  Rolling Meadows (G-17780)

COOLING TOWERS: Metal

Amsted Industries Incorporated..............B....... 312 645-1700
  Chicago (G-3685)
Amsted Industries Incorporated..............F....... 312 645-1700
  Chicago (G-3686)
Evapco Inc...E....... 410 756-2600
  Chicago (G-4538)
SPX Corporation......................................C....... 847 593-8855
  Elk Grove Village (G-9251)
SPX Corporation......................................B....... 815 874-5556
  Rockford (G-17643)

COOLING TOWERS: Wood

Mc Mechanical Contractors Inc...............G....... 708 460-0075
  Orland Park (G-15967)

COPPER ORE MILLING & PREPARATION

Ventec USA LLC......................................G....... 847 621-2261
  Elk Grove Village (G-9301)

COPPER: Blocks

Bryan Metals LLC....................................G....... 419 636-4571
  East Alton (G-8163)

COPPER: Cathodes, Primary

Atlas Trade Solutions LLC.......................G....... 618 954-6119
  Belleville (G-1531)

COPPER: Rolling & Drawing

Aurubis Buffalo Inc..................................G....... 630 980-8400
  Bloomingdale (G-1978)
Chicago Hardware and Fix Co.................C....... 847 455-6609
  Franklin Park (G-9905)
Demco Products Inc................................F....... 708 636-6240
  Oak Lawn (G-15713)
Empire Bronze Corp................................F....... 630 916-9722
  Lombard (G-13073)
Fairbanks Wire Corporation....................E....... 847 683-2600
  Hampshire (G-10972)
Kroh-Wagner Inc.....................................E....... 773 252-2031
  Chicago (G-5133)
Olin Corporation......................................G....... 618 258-2245
  Brighton (G-2402)
Technetics Group LLC............................G....... 708 887-6080
  Harwood Heights (G-11111)
Wieland Rolled Pdts N Amer LLC...........G....... 630 260-0802
  Chicago (G-6623)

COPY MACHINES WHOLESALERS

CDs Office Systems Inc..........................D....... 800 367-1508
  Springfield (G-19343)
Konica Minolta...G....... 630 893-8238
  Roselle (G-17962)
Konica Mnlta Bus Sltons USA In.............E....... 309 671-1360
  Peoria (G-16467)

CORD & TWINE

Erin Rope Corporation.............................F....... 708 377-1084
  Blue Island (G-2122)
Obies Tackle Co Inc................................G....... 618 234-5638
  Belleville (G-1581)
Turf Inc..G....... 630 365-3903
  Elburn (G-8478)

CORE WASH OR WAX

Butterfield Color Inc................................E....... 630 906-1980
  Aurora (G-1067)

CORK & CORK PRDTS

Edgewater Products Company Inc.........F....... 708 345-9200
  Melrose Park (G-13860)

CORK & CORK PRDTS: Bottle

Haleys Corker Inc....................................G....... 708 228-1427
  River Forest (G-17052)

CORK & CORK PRDTS: Insulating Material

Cma Inc..E....... 847 848-0674
  Joliet (G-11841)
Cma Inc..D....... 630 551-3100
  Oswego (G-15996)

CORRECTION FLUID

Gillette Company	D	847	689-3111

North Chicago *(G-15312)*

CORRECTIONAL INSTITUTIONS

Federal Prison Industries ....F....... 618 664-6361
  Greenville *(G-10834)*
Federal Prison Industries ....C....... 309 346-8588
  Pekin *(G-16333)*

CORRUGATED PRDTS: Boxes, Partition, Display Items, Sheet/Pad

Blackhawk Courtyards LLC ....G....... 416 298-8101
  Carol Stream *(G-2949)*
D/C Export & Domestic Pkg Inc .....E....... 847 593-4200
  Elk Grove Village *(G-8935)*
J Wallace & Associates Inc ....G....... 630 960-4221
  Downers Grove *(G-8033)*
Murnane Specialties Inc ....E....... 708 449-1200
  Northlake *(G-15553)*
Westrock Rkt LLC ....A....... 312 346-6600
  Chicago *(G-6614)*
Weyerhaeuser Company ....C....... 847 439-1111
  Elk Grove Village *(G-9307)*

COSMETIC PREPARATIONS

A & H Manufacturing Inc ....F....... 630 543-5900
  Addison *(G-13)*
All Dental ....G....... 708 749-0277
  Berwyn *(G-1948)*
Amedico Laboratories LLC ....G....... 347 857-7546
  Oakbrook Terrace *(G-15783)*
Clintex Laboratories Inc ....E....... 773 493-9777
  Chicago *(G-4179)*
Combe Laboratories Inc ....C....... 217 893-4490
  Rantoul *(G-16971)*
Concept Laboratories Inc ....D....... 773 395-7300
  Chicago *(G-4214)*
Delta Laboratories Inc ....G....... 630 351-1798
  Elk Grove Village *(G-8942)*
Emlin Cosmetics Inc ....D....... 630 860-5773
  Bensenville *(G-1796)*
Essential Laser and Skin Inst ....G....... 815 381-7005
  Rockford *(G-17401)*
Geka Manufacturing Corporation ....E....... 224 238-5080
  Elgin *(G-8592)*
Inkjet Inc ....G....... 800 280-3245
  Hoffman Estates *(G-11429)*
Marcy Laboratories Inc ....E....... 630 377-6655
  West Chicago *(G-20614)*
Maynard Inc ....G....... 773 235-5225
  Chicago *(G-5371)*
Mseed Group LLC ....G....... 847 226-1147
  South Holland *(G-19234)*
Revlon Inc ....G....... 847 240-1558
  Schaumburg *(G-18696)*
Rna Corporation ....D....... 708 597-7777
  Blue Island *(G-2137)*
Skyline Beauty Supply Inc ....F....... 773 275-6003
  Franklin Park *(G-10047)*
Vee Pak LLC ....D....... 708 482-8881
  Hodgkins *(G-11399)*
Vee Pak LLC ....E....... 708 482-8881
  Countryside *(G-7076)*

COSMETICS & TOILETRIES

4 Elements Company ....G....... 773 236-2284
  Mundelein *(G-14655)*
Aerosols Danville Inc ....G....... 773 816-5132
  Chicago *(G-3574)*
Aerosols Danville Inc ....B....... 217 442-1400
  Danville *(G-7318)*
Art of Shaving - Fl LLC ....G....... 630 495-7316
  Lombard *(G-13040)*
Art of Shaving - Fl LLC ....G....... 312 527-1604
  Chicago *(G-3737)*
Art of Shaving - Fl LLC ....G....... 630 684-0277
  Oak Brook *(G-15594)*
Avlon Industries Inc ....D....... 708 344-0709
  Melrose Park *(G-13829)*
Bearmoon LLC ....G....... 815 312-2327
  Oregon *(G-15912)*
Belle-Aire Fragrances Inc ....E....... 847 816-3500
  Mundelein *(G-14666)*
Chemquest International Inc ....E....... 630 628-1900
  Addison *(G-68)*

Collagen Usa Inc ....G....... 708 716-0251
  Chicago *(G-4200)*
Common Scents Mom ....G....... 309 389-3216
  Mapleton *(G-13471)*
Conopco Inc ....C....... 773 916-4400
  Chicago *(G-4220)*
Deputante Inc ....G....... 773 545-9531
  Chicago *(G-4342)*
Desforte LLC ....G....... 224 301-5364
  Chicago *(G-4343)*
Eggology Inc ....F....... 818 610-2222
  Pearl City *(G-16319)*
Fareva Morton Grove Inc ....G....... 847 966-0200
  Morton Grove *(G-14406)*
Formulations Inc ....G....... 847 674-9141
  Skokie *(G-18956)*
Garcoa Inc ....B....... 708 905-5118
  Brookfield *(G-2484)*
H N C Products Inc ....E....... 309 319-2151
  Bloomington *(G-2055)*
Handcrafted By Jackie Turbot ....G....... 815 708-7200
  Roscoe *(G-17909)*
Healing Scents ....G....... 815 874-0924
  Rockford *(G-17446)*
Henkel Consumer Goods Inc ....C....... 630 892-4381
  Montgomery *(G-14246)*
Kellyjo Makes Scents ....G....... 618 281-4241
  Columbia *(G-6990)*
Labtec Cosmetics ....G....... 630 359-4569
  Addison *(G-179)*
Lasner Bros Inc ....G....... 773 935-7383
  Chicago *(G-5178)*
Luxis International Inc ....G....... 800 240-1473
  Dekalb *(G-7689)*
Pal Midwest Ltd ....G....... 815 965-2981
  Rockford *(G-17546)*
Pearl Bath Bombs Inc ....F....... 312 661-2881
  Chicago *(G-5777)*
Pivotal Production LLC ....G....... 773 726-7706
  Chicago *(G-5815)*
Princeton Chemicals Inc ....G....... 847 975-6210
  Highland Park *(G-11292)*
Proximity Capital Partners LLC ....F....... 773 628-7751
  Chicago *(G-5909)*
San Telmo Ltd ....G....... 847 842-9115
  Barrington *(G-1243)*
Schmit Laboratories Inc ....E....... 773 476-0072
  Glendale Heights *(G-10491)*
Sigan America LLC ....D....... 815 431-9830
  Ottawa *(G-16076)*
Sigan America Holdings LLC ....G....... 815 431-9830
  Ottawa *(G-16077)*
Spike Nanotech Inc ....G....... 847 504-6273
  Matteson *(G-13629)*
Sunstar Americas Inc ....B....... 847 794-4157
  Schaumburg *(G-18730)*
Suretint Technologies LLC ....G....... 847 509-3625
  Mount Prospect *(G-14574)*
Tiege Hanley LLC ....G....... 312 953-4131
  Chicago *(G-6377)*
Transom Symphony Opco LLC ....C....... 203 951-1919
  Rantoul *(G-16984)*
True Royalty Scents ....G....... 309 992-0688
  Peoria *(G-16539)*
Trumans Brands LLC ....F....... 224 302-5605
  Round Lake Park *(G-18099)*
Voyant Beauty LLC ....G....... 708 482-8881
  Hodgkins *(G-11400)*
W-R Industries Inc ....G....... 312 733-5200
  Bellwood *(G-1642)*
Walgreen Asia Services Sarl ....G....... 847 527-4341
  Northbrook *(G-15499)*

COSMETICS WHOLESALERS

Avlon Industries Inc ....D....... 708 344-0709
  Melrose Park *(G-13829)*
Garcoa Inc ....B....... 708 905-5118
  Brookfield *(G-2484)*

COSMETOLOGIST

Payne Chauna ....G....... 618 580-2584
  Belleville *(G-1583)*

COSMETOLOGY & PERSONAL HYGIENE SALONS

Patty Style Shop ....G....... 618 654-2015
  Highland *(G-11234)*

COSTUME JEWELRY & NOVELTIES: Bracelets, Exc Precious Metals

Medical ID Fashions Company ....G....... 847 404-6789
  Deerfield *(G-7636)*

COSTUME JEWELRY & NOVELTIES: Earrings, Exc Precious Metals

Alessco Inc ....F....... 773 327-7919
  Chicago *(G-3602)*

COSTUME JEWELRY & NOVELTIES: Exc Semi & Precious

Pearl Perfect Inc ....E....... 847 679-6251
  Morton Grove *(G-14432)*

COSTUME JEWELRY & NOVELTIES: Pins, Exc Precious Metals

R S Owens & Co Inc ....B....... 773 282-6000
  Chicago *(G-5953)*

COSTUME JEWELRY & NOVELTIES: Rosaries & Sm Religious Items

Anthos and Co LLC ....G....... 773 744-6813
  Inverness *(G-11594)*

COSTUME JEWELRY & NOVELTIES: Watchbands, Base Metal

JP Leatherworks Inc ....G....... 847 317-9804
  Deerfield *(G-7623)*

COSTUME JEWELRY/NOVELTS: Cuff-Link/Stud, Exc Prec Metal/Gem

Bird Dog Bay Inc ....G....... 312 631-3108
  Chicago *(G-3899)*
Richards Fabulous Finds ....G....... 773 943-0710
  Chicago *(G-6025)*

COSTUMES & WIGS STORES

Custom & Hard To Find Wigs ....F....... 773 777-0222
  Chicago *(G-4288)*

COUNTER & SINK TOPS

All Stone Inc ....G....... 815 529-1754
  Romeoville *(G-17790)*
Brothers Leal LLC ....G....... 708 385-4400
  Alsip *(G-424)*
Counter Craft Inc ....G....... 847 336-8205
  Waukegan *(G-20431)*
Countertop Creations ....F....... 618 736-2700
  Dahlgren *(G-7306)*
Crown Coverings Inc ....E....... 630 546-2959
  Roselle *(G-17949)*
DK Knutsen ....G....... 815 626-4388
  Sterling *(G-19505)*
Graniteworks ....G....... 815 288-3350
  Dixon *(G-7901)*
Kitchen Krafters Inc ....G....... 815 675-6061
  Spring Grove *(G-19279)*
New Age Surfaces LLC ....G....... 630 226-0011
  Romeoville *(G-17861)*
Royal Fabricators Inc ....F....... 847 775-7466
  Wadsworth *(G-20213)*
Stone Fabricators Company ....G....... 847 788-8296
  Arlington Heights *(G-813)*
Surface Solutions Illinois Inc ....G....... 708 571-3449
  Mokena *(G-14119)*

COUNTERS & COUNTING DEVICES

ARC-Tronics Inc ....C....... 847 437-0211
  Elk Grove Village *(G-8837)*
Flodyne Inc ....G....... 630 563-3600
  Hanover Park *(G-11004)*
Nichiden USA Corp ....G....... 224 266-2928
  Elk Grove Village *(G-9147)*
Otak International Inc ....G....... 630 373-9229
  Melrose Park *(G-13900)*
Shoppertrak Rct Corporation ....F....... 312 529-5300
  Chicago *(G-6156)*
Spartanics Ltd ....E....... 847 394-5700
  Rolling Meadows *(G-17777)*

PRODUCT SECTION

CRUDE PETROLEUM & NATURAL GAS PRODUCTION

Tml Inc .... G 847 382-1550
 Barrington *(G-1247)*
Woodward Inc .... F 847 673-8300
 Skokie *(G-19057)*

COUNTERS OR COUNTER DISPLAY CASES, EXC WOOD

Gerali Custom Design Inc .... D 847 760-0500
 Elgin *(G-8593)*
Jbc Holding Co .... G 217 347-7701
 Effingham *(G-8404)*

COUNTERS OR COUNTER DISPLAY CASES, WOOD

Hallmark Cabinet Company .... D 708 757-7807
 Minooka *(G-14061)*
Maxwell Counters Inc .... E 309 928-2848
 Farmer City *(G-9655)*
Murray Cabinetry & Tops Inc .... G 815 672-6992
 Streator *(G-19616)*
Wilcor Solid Surface Inc .... F 888 956-1001
 Elk Grove Village *(G-9309)*

COUNTING DEVICES: Controls, Revolution & Timing

Dynapar Corporation .... C 847 662-2666
 Gurnee *(G-10873)*

COUNTING DEVICES: Electromechanical

Line Group Inc .... E 847 593-6810
 Arlington Heights *(G-769)*
Nep Electronics Inc .... C 630 595-8500
 Wood Dale *(G-21221)*

COUNTING DEVICES: Gauges, Press Temp Corrections Computing

G H Meiser & Co .... E 708 388-7867
 Mokena *(G-14085)*

COUNTING DEVICES: Odometers

O E M Marketing Inc .... F 847 985-9490
 Schaumburg *(G-18655)*

COUNTING DEVICES: Pedometers

Walk 4 Life Inc .... F 815 439-2340
 Oswego *(G-16031)*

COUNTING DEVICES: Revolution

E N M Company .... D 773 775-8400
 Chicago *(G-4425)*

COUNTING DEVICES: Tachometer, Centrifugal

Auto Meter Products Inc .... C 815 895-8141
 Sycamore *(G-19702)*

COUPLINGS, EXC PRESSURE & SOIL PIPE

Flender Corporation .... C 847 931-1990
 Elgin *(G-8588)*
RF Mau Co .... F 847 329-9731
 Lincolnwood *(G-12838)*
Victaulic Company .... B 630 585-2919
 Aurora *(G-1031)*

COUPLINGS: Shaft

Excalbur Pr-Keyed Shafting Inc .... F 800 487-0514
 Wauconda *(G-20349)*
Lovejoy Inc .... C 630 852-0500
 Downers Grove *(G-8048)*
Mathis Energy LLC .... G 309 925-3177
 Tremont *(G-19898)*

COURIER OR MESSENGER SVCS

Keane Inc .... F 847 952-9700
 Mount Prospect *(G-14541)*
Ocs America Inc .... E 630 595-0111
 Wood Dale *(G-21225)*

COURIER SVCS: Air

Hunter Logistics .... G 309 299-7015
 Wataga *(G-20286)*

COURIER SVCS: Ground

Bb Services LLC .... G 630 941-8122
 Elmhurst *(G-9328)*
Lottobot LLC .... G 773 909-6656
 Chicago *(G-5265)*
Open Kitchens Inc .... E 312 666-5334
 Chicago *(G-5681)*

COURIER SVCS: Package By Vehicle

Leg Up LLC .... G 312 282-2725
 Chicago *(G-5196)*

COVERS: Automobile Seat

Bill Weeks Inc .... G 217 523-8735
 Springfield *(G-19326)*

COVERS: Metal Plate

Imbert Construction Inds Inc .... G 847 588-3170
 Niles *(G-15132)*

COVERS: Slip Made Of Fabric, Plastic, Etc.

Ameriguard Corporation .... G 630 986-1900
 Burr Ridge *(G-2652)*

CRACKED CASTING REPAIR SVCS

Franklin Maintenance .... G 815 284-6806
 Dixon *(G-7900)*
Ramsey Welding Inc .... E 618 483-6248
 Altamont *(G-537)*

CRANE & AERIAL LIFT SVCS

Sheas Iron Works Inc .... E 847 356-2922
 Lake Villa *(G-12367)*

CRANES: Indl Plant

Handling Systems Intl Inc .... E 708 352-1213
 Mc Cook *(G-13692)*

CRANES: Indl Truck

CF Solutions Co .... G 630 413-9058
 Schaumburg *(G-18472)*

CRANES: Locomotive

W N G S Inc .... E 847 451-1224
 Franklin Park *(G-10081)*

CRANES: Overhead

Gh Cranes Corporation .... G 815 277-5328
 Frankfort *(G-9797)*
Lanco International Inc .... B 708 596-5200
 Hazel Crest *(G-11131)*
Uesco Industries Inc .... E 800 325-8372
 Alsip *(G-518)*
Whiting Corporation .... C 800 861-5744
 Monee *(G-14212)*

CRANKSHAFTS & CAMSHAFTS: Machining

Chrome Crankshaft Company LLC ..... F 815 725-9030
 Joliet *(G-11840)*
G&D Integrated Mfg LLC .... E 309 284-6700
 Morton *(G-14361)*
Precision Dynamics Inc .... F 815 877-1592
 Machesney Park *(G-13366)*
Regent Automotive Engineering .... G 773 889-5744
 Chicago *(G-6002)*
Riser Machine Corporation .... F 708 532-2313
 New Lenox *(G-15055)*
Southern Illinois Crankshafts .... F 618 282-4100
 Ruma *(G-18107)*

CREATIVE SVCS: Advertisers, Exc Writers

Phoenix Graphix .... G 618 531-3664
 Pinckneyville *(G-16618)*

CREDIT CLEARINGHOUSE SVC

Manufctrers Clring Hse Ill Inc .... G 773 545-6300
 Chicago *(G-5327)*

CREDIT INST, SHORT-TERM BUSINESS: Financing Dealers

Navistar Inc .... C 331 332-5000
 Lisle *(G-12917)*

CREDIT INSTITUTIONS, SHORT-TERM BUSINESS: Mercantile Finance

Caterpillar Inc .... B 309 675-6590
 Peoria *(G-16411)*
Caterpillar Inc .... C 309 578-2185
 Mossville *(G-14452)*

CREMATORIES

Sterling Vault Company .... F 815 625-0077
 Sterling *(G-19537)*

CROWNS & CLOSURES

Alcon Tool & Mfg Co Inc .... F 773 545-8742
 Chicago *(G-3598)*
Amcor Flexibles LLC .... C 224 313-7000
 Buffalo Grove *(G-2510)*
Kile Machine & Tool Inc .... G 217 446-8616
 Danville *(G-7357)*
Kipp Manufacturing Company Inc ...... F 630 768-9051
 Wauconda *(G-20366)*
Precise Technology .... G 847 459-1001
 Buffalo Grove *(G-2589)*
Product Service Craft Inc .... F 630 964-5160
 Downers Grove *(G-8085)*

CRUDE PETROLEUM & NATURAL GAS PRODUCTION

Glover Oil Field Service Inc .... F 618 395-3624
 Olney *(G-15863)*
Murphy USA Inc .... G 815 463-9963
 New Lenox *(G-15044)*
Murphy USA Inc .... F 815 337-2440
 Woodstock *(G-21416)*
Murphy USA Inc .... F 815 936-6144
 Kankakee *(G-11992)*
Oelze Equipment Company LLC .... E 618 327-9111
 Nashville *(G-15006)*
R H Johnson Oil Co Inc .... G 630 668-3649
 Wheaton *(G-20817)*
St Pierre Oil Company Inc .... G 618 783-4441
 Newton *(G-15093)*

CRUDE PETROLEUM & NATURAL GAS PRODUCTION

BP Products North America Inc .... G 630 420-4300
 Naperville *(G-14783)*
Concord Well Service Inc .... G 618 395-4405
 Olney *(G-15858)*
Drig Corporation .... D 312 265-1509
 Rosemont *(G-18020)*
Ensource Inc .... G 312 912-1048
 Chicago *(G-4513)*
Jbl - Alton .... G 618 466-0411
 Alton *(G-561)*
Kerogen Resources Inc .... G 618 382-3114
 Carmi *(G-2908)*
Midwest Oil LLC .... G 309 456-3663
 Good Hope *(G-10670)*
MRC Global (us) Inc .... F 314 231-3400
 Granite City *(G-10727)*
Natural Gas Pipeline Amer LLC .... E 618 495-2211
 Centralia *(G-3240)*
Natural Gas Pipeline Amer LLC .... E 618 829-3224
 Saint Elmo *(G-18310)*
River City Oil LLC .... G 309 693-2249
 Peoria *(G-16510)*
Rodgers Bill Oil Min Bits Svc .... G 618 299-7771
 West Salem *(G-20688)*
Roosevelt Mobile .... G 630 293-7630
 West Chicago *(G-20638)*
Star Energy Corp Inc .... G 618 584-3631
 Flat Rock *(G-9674)*
UOP LLC .... D 708 442-7400
 Mc Cook *(G-13704)*
Warren Oil MGT Co IL LLC .... G 618 997-5951
 Marion *(G-13542)*
Zanetis Oil Company .... G 618 262-4593
 Mount Carmel *(G-14493)*

CRUDE PETROLEUM PRODUCTION

Ashley Oil Co	G	217 932-2112
Casey *(G-3198)*		
B Quad Oil Inc	G	618 656-4419
Edwardsville *(G-8347)*		
Bam Operating Inc	G	254 629-8561
Evanston *(G-9497)*		
Basin Transports	G	618 829-3323
Saint Elmo *(G-18305)*		
Basnett Investments	G	618 842-4040
Fairfield *(G-9619)*		
Belden Enterprises LP	F	618 829-3274
Saint Elmo *(G-18306)*		
Bell Brothers	G	618 544-2157
Robinson *(G-17107)*		
Bi-Petro Inc	E	217 535-0181
Springfield *(G-19325)*		
Booth Resources Inc	G	618 662-4955
Flora *(G-9676)*		
Brehm Oil Inc	F	618 242-4620
Mount Vernon *(G-14600)*		
Brookstone Resources Inc	G	618 382-2893
Carmi *(G-2900)*		
Bruce McCullough	G	217 773-3130
Mount Sterling *(G-14589)*		
Budmark Oil Company Inc	G	618 937-2495
West Frankfort *(G-20669)*		
Carter Anna Brooks LLC	G	618 382-3939
Carmi *(G-2903)*		
Citation Oil & Gas Corp	G	618 676-1044
Clay City *(G-6904)*		
Citation Oil & Gas Corp	E	618 966-2101
Crossville *(G-7150)*		
Collins Brothers Oil Corp	G	618 244-1093
Mount Vernon *(G-14602)*		
Continental Resources III Inc	E	618 242-1717
Mount Vernon *(G-14603)*		
D & Z Exploration Inc	G	618 829-3274
Saint Elmo *(G-18307)*		
D Little Drilling	G	618 943-3721
Saint Francisville *(G-18313)*		
Deep Rock Energy Corporation	F	618 548-2779
Salem *(G-18335)*		
Doran Oil Properties	G	618 283-2460
Vandalia *(G-20010)*		
Duncan Oil Company Inc	G	618 548-2923
Salem *(G-18336)*		
Evans Talaiha	G	618 327-8200
Nashville *(G-14996)*		
Finks Oil Co Inc	G	618 548-5757
Salem *(G-18339)*		
Friend Oil Co	G	618 842-9161
Fairfield *(G-9624)*		
Gulf Coast Exploration Inc	G	847 226-4654
Highland Park *(G-11268)*		
Herman L Loeb LLC	E	618 943-2227
Lawrenceville *(G-12535)*		
Hocking Oil Company Inc	G	618 263-3258
Mount Carmel *(G-14472)*		
Howard Energy Corporation	G	618 263-3000
Mount Carmel *(G-14473)*		
J W Rudy Co Inc	F	618 676-1616
Clay City *(G-6906)*		
Jarvis Drilling Co	G	217 422-3120
Decatur *(G-7511)*		
Jim Haley Oil Production Co	F	618 382-7338
Carmi *(G-2907)*		
L & J Producers Inc	G	217 932-5639
Casey *(G-3204)*		
Lakeshore Operating LLC	E	844 557-4763
Chicago *(G-5165)*		
Lampley Oil Inc	G	618 439-6288
Benton *(G-1931)*		
Lawrence Oil Company Inc	G	618 262-4138
Mount Carmel *(G-14477)*		
Midco Petroleum Inc	G	630 655-2198
Westmont *(G-20760)*		
Mitchco Farms LLC	F	618 382-5032
Carmi *(G-2911)*		
New Triangle Oil Company	G	618 262-4131
Mount Carmel *(G-14483)*		
Pawnee Oil Corporation	F	217 522-5440
Springfield *(G-19421)*		
Petco Petroleum Corporation	G	630 654-1740
Hinsdale *(G-11372)*		
Petron Oil Production Inc	F	618 783-4486
Newton *(G-15090)*		
Phosphate Resource Ptrs	A	847 739-1200
Lake Forest *(G-12290)*		
Pool & Pool Oil Productions	G	618 544-7590
Robinson *(G-17122)*		
R & D Oil Producers	G	217 773-9299
Mount Sterling *(G-14592)*		
Republic Oil Co Inc	G	618 842-7591
Fairfield *(G-9635)*		
Robinson Production Inc	G	618 842-6111
Fairfield *(G-9636)*		
Ronnie Joe Graham	G	618 548-5544
Salem *(G-18355)*		
Ross Oil Co Inc	G	618 592-3808
Oblong *(G-15828)*		
Shawnee Exploration Partners	G	618 382-3223
Carmi *(G-2915)*		
Shulman Brothers Inc	G	618 283-3253
Vandalia *(G-20023)*		
Smoco Inc	G	618 662-6458
Flora *(G-9693)*		
Southern Triangle Oil Company	F	618 262-4131
Mount Carmel *(G-14486)*		
Spartan Petroleum Company	G	618 262-4197
Mount Carmel *(G-14487)*		
Steven A Zanetis	G	618 393-2176
Olney *(G-15889)*		
Team Energy LLC	F	618 943-1010
Bridgeport *(G-2316)*		
Tri Family Oil Co	G	618 654-1137
Highland *(G-11243)*		
Tri-State Producing Developing	G	618 393-2176
Olney *(G-15890)*		
Trojan Oil Inc	G	618 754-3474
Newton *(G-15095)*		
Tussey G K Oil Explrtn & Prdc	G	618 948-2871
Saint Francisville *(G-18315)*		
Two Rivers Oil & Gas Co Inc	G	217 773-3356
Mount Sterling *(G-14594)*		
Western Oil & Gas Dev Co	F	618 544-8646
Robinson *(G-17128)*		
White Land & Mineral Inc	G	618 262-5102
Mount Carmel *(G-14492)*		
William R Becker	F	618 378-3337
Norris City *(G-15252)*		
Wood Energy Inc	G	618 244-1590
Mount Vernon *(G-14644)*		
Yockey Oil Incorporated	G	618 393-6236
Olney *(G-15895)*		

CRUDES: Cyclic, Organic

BP Amoco Chemical Company	B	630 420-5111
Naperville *(G-14782)*		

CRYSTALS

Netcom Inc	C	847 537-6300
Wheeling *(G-20943)*		
Rubicon Technology Inc	E	847 295-7000
Bensenville *(G-1887)*		

CUBICLES: Electric Switchboard Eqpt

J & A Sheet Metal Shop Inc	E	773 276-3739
Chicago *(G-4981)*		

CULTURE MEDIA

3abn	G	618 627-4651
Thompsonville *(G-19777)*		
Amphix Bio Inc	G	720 840-7327
Chicago *(G-3684)*		
Culture Media Supplies Inc	G	630 499-5000
Oswego *(G-15999)*		
Laboratory Media Corporation	F	630 897-8000
Montgomery *(G-14254)*		

CUPS & PLATES: Foamed Plastics

All-Vac Industries Inc	F	847 675-2290
Skokie *(G-18915)*		
Dart Container Corp Illinois	C	630 896-4631
North Aurora *(G-15258)*		

CUPS: Plastic Exc Polystyrene Foam

Northwestern Cup & Logo Inc	G	773 874-8000
Chicago *(G-5625)*		
Solo Cup Operating Corporation	C	773 767-3300
Chicago *(G-6197)*		

CURTAIN & DRAPERY FIXTURES: Poles, Rods & Rollers

Baker Drapery Corporation	G	309 691-3295
Dunlap *(G-8132)*		
Dezign Sewing Inc	G	773 549-4336
Chicago *(G-4349)*		
Dons Drapery Service	G	815 385-4759
McHenry *(G-13737)*		
Draperyland Inc	F	630 521-1000
Wood Dale *(G-21182)*		
House of Atlas LLC	G	847 491-1800
Evanston *(G-9536)*		
J & J Inc of Illinois	F	217 306-0787
Greenview *(G-10823)*		
Logoskirt Corporation	F	773 584-7300
Chicago *(G-5251)*		
Offsprings Inc	G	773 525-1800
Chicago *(G-5659)*		
Ottos Drapery Service Inc	G	773 777-7755
Chicago *(G-5713)*		
Roberts Draperies Center Inc	G	847 255-4040
Mount Prospect *(G-14567)*		
Shade Aire Company	G	815 623-7597
Roscoe *(G-17933)*		
Unitex Industries Inc	G	708 524-0664
Oak Park *(G-15777)*		
Woodbridge Inc	F	847 229-1741
Wheeling *(G-21015)*		
Zirlin Interiors Inc	E	773 334-5530
Chicago *(G-6720)*		

CURTAIN WALLS: Building, Steel

Delta Erectors Inc	F	708 267-9721
Villa Park *(G-20144)*		

CUSHIONS & PILLOWS

Bean Products Inc	E	312 666-3600
Chicago *(G-3853)*		
Eastern Accents Inc	C	773 604-7300
Chicago *(G-4435)*		
Ileesh Products LLC	F	224 424-4682
Vernon Hills *(G-20062)*		
Pyar & Co LLC	G	312 451-5073
Chicago *(G-5920)*		

CUSHIONS & PILLOWS: Bed, From Purchased Materials

American Dawn Inc	G	312 961-2909
Wood Dale *(G-21163)*		
Encompass Group LLC	E	847 680-3388
Mundelein *(G-14686)*		

CUSHIONS & PILLOWS: Hassocks, Textile, Purchased Materials

Peterson Dermond Design LLC	G	414 383-5029
Evanston *(G-9565)*		

CUSHIONS: Textile, Exc Spring & Carpet

American Dawn Inc	G	312 961-2909
Wood Dale *(G-21163)*		

CUSTOM COMPOUNDING OF RUBBER MATERIALS

Verona Rubber Works Inc	F	815 673-2929
Blackstone *(G-1971)*		

CUSTOMIZING SVCS

A J R International Inc	D	800 232-3965
Glendale Heights *(G-10435)*		

CUT STONE & STONE PRODUCTS

Acme Marble Co Inc	G	630 964-7162
Darien *(G-7399)*		
American Marble & Granite Inc	G	815 741-1710
Crest Hill *(G-7083)*		
Arnold Monument Co Inc	G	217 546-2102
Springfield *(G-19320)*		
Atelier Jvnce Stncarving Tiles	G	312 492-7922
Chicago *(G-3757)*		
Beutel Corporation	G	309 786-8134
Rock Island *(G-17207)*		
Cline Concrete Products	F	217 283-5012
Hoopeston *(G-11505)*		

PRODUCT SECTION

CUTLERY (continued)

Clugston Tibbitts Funeral Home ....G...... 309 833-2188
  Macomb *(G-13389)*
Contractors Ready-Mix Inc ....G...... 217 482-5530
  Mason City *(G-13610)*
Country Stone Inc ....E...... 309 787-1744
  Milan *(G-14005)*
Creative Inds Terrazzo Pdts ....G...... 773 235-9088
  Chicago *(G-4263)*
Custom Stone Wrks Acqstion Inc ....G...... 630 669-1119
  Cortland *(G-7019)*
Czarnik Memorials Inc ....G...... 708 458-4443
  Justice *(G-11951)*
Daprato Rigali Studios Inc ....E...... 773 763-5511
  Chicago *(G-4317)*
Dtk Construction Inc ....G...... 312 296-2762
  Wheeling *(G-20880)*
Effingham Monument Co Inc ....G...... 217 857-6085
  Effingham *(G-8397)*
Gallasi Cut Stone & Marble LLC ....E...... 708 479-9494
  Mokena *(G-14086)*
Galloy and Van Etten Inc ....E...... 773 928-4800
  Chicago *(G-4657)*
Gast Monuments Inc ....G...... 773 262-2400
  Chicago *(G-4660)*
Jacksonville Monument Co ....G...... 217 245-2514
  Jacksonville *(G-11772)*
Knauer Industries Ltd ....E...... 815 725-0246
  Joliet *(G-11891)*
Lansing Cut Stone Co ....F...... 708 474-7515
  Lansing *(G-12503)*
Luxury MBL & Gran Design Inc ....G...... 773 656-2125
  Chicago *(G-5288)*
Machine & Design ....G...... 630 858-6416
  Glen Ellyn *(G-10411)*
Material Service Corporation ....E...... 217 732-2117
  Athens *(G-897)*
Meier Granite Company ....G...... 847 678-7300
  Franklin Park *(G-9989)*
Mendota Monument Co ....G...... 815 539-7276
  Mendota *(G-13947)*
Meno Stone Co Inc ....E...... 630 257-9220
  Lemont *(G-12571)*
Moore Memorials ....F...... 708 636-6532
  Chicago Ridge *(G-6804)*
Newton Ready Mix Inc ....F...... 618 783-8611
  Newton *(G-15088)*
Nu-Dell Manufacturing Co Inc ....F...... 847 803-4500
  Chicago *(G-5637)*
Pana Monument Co ....G...... 217 562-5121
  Pana *(G-16220)*
Peter Troost Monument Co ....G...... 773 585-0242
  Justice *(G-11953)*
Regal Cut Stone LLC ....F...... 773 826-8796
  Chicago *(G-5999)*
Spence Monuments Co ....G...... 217 348-5992
  Charleston *(G-3413)*
St Charles Memorial Works Inc ....G...... 630 584-0183
  Saint Charles *(G-18275)*
Stone Center Inc ....G...... 630 971-2060
  Lisle *(G-12943)*
Stone Design Inc ....F...... 630 790-5715
  Glendale Heights *(G-10501)*
Stone Design Inc ....E...... 630 790-5715
  Glendale Heights *(G-10502)*
Stonecasters LLC ....D...... 847 526-5200
  Wauconda *(G-20392)*
Tisch Monuments Inc ....G...... 618 233-3017
  Belleville *(G-1599)*
Unilock ....G...... 262 742-3890
  Aurora *(G-1164)*
Venetian Monument Company ....F...... 312 829-9622
  Chicago *(G-6531)*
Weiss Monument Works Inc ....G...... 618 398-1811
  Belleville *(G-1611)*
Wendell Adams ....E...... 217 345-9587
  Charleston *(G-3416)*
World Granite Inc ....G...... 815 288-3350
  Dixon *(G-7926)*
Worldwide Tiles Ltd Inc ....G...... 708 389-2992
  Alsip *(G-526)*
Zoia Monument Company ....G...... 815 338-0358
  Woodstock *(G-21451)*

CUTLERY

Alps Group Inc ....G...... 815 469-4800
  Chicago *(G-3632)*
Custom Cutting Tools Inc ....G...... 815 986-0320
  Loves Park *(G-13200)*
Estwing Manufacturing Co Inc ....B...... 815 397-9521
  Rockford *(G-17402)*
Harris Precision Tools Inc ....G...... 708 422-5808
  Chicago Ridge *(G-6797)*
Kernel Kutter Inc ....G...... 815 877-1515
  Machesney Park *(G-13354)*
Mega Manufacturing Inc ....G...... 620 663-1127
  Rockford *(G-17515)*
Solo Cup Operating Corporation ....C...... 773 767-3300
  Chicago *(G-6197)*
Superior Knife Inc ....E...... 847 982-2280
  Niles *(G-15177)*
Tarrerias-Bonjean USA Inc ....G...... 216 217-1726
  Chicago *(G-6328)*
Wallace/Haskin Corp ....G...... 630 789-2882
  Downers Grove *(G-8105)*
Whitney Roper LLC ....D...... 815 962-3011
  Rockford *(G-17683)*
Whitney Roper Rockford Inc ....D...... 815 962-3011
  Rockford *(G-17684)*

CUTLERY WHOLESALERS

Primedge Inc ....C...... 224 265-6600
  Elk Grove Village *(G-9197)*

CUTLERY, STAINLESS STEEL

Crown Brands LLC ....E...... 224 513-2917
  Lincolnshire *(G-12757)*

CUTLERY: Table, Exc Metal Handled

Goodco Products LLC ....G...... 630 258-6384
  Countryside *(G-7055)*

CUTOUTS: Distribution

Kms Industries LLC ....G...... 331 225-2671
  Addison *(G-173)*

CUTTING SVC: Paper, Exc Die-Cut

Olympic Bindery Inc ....D...... 847 577-8132
  Arlington Heights *(G-785)*

CUTTING SVC: Paperboard

Diecrafters Inc ....E...... 708 656-3336
  Cicero *(G-6841)*
Global Abrasive Products Inc ....E...... 630 543-9466
  Addison *(G-142)*

CYCLIC CRUDES & INTERMEDIATES

Chroma Color Corporation ....C...... 877 385-8777
  McHenry *(G-13726)*
Colors For Plastics Inc ....D...... 847 437-0033
  Elk Grove Village *(G-8901)*
Miller Purcell Co Inc ....G...... 815 485-2142
  New Lenox *(G-15043)*
Polyone Corporation ....D...... 630 972-0505
  Romeoville *(G-17865)*
S C Johnson & Son Inc ....C...... 312 702-3100
  Chicago *(G-6085)*
Scientific Colors Inc ....C...... 815 744-5650
  Rockdale *(G-17274)*
Southern Color Company Inc ....G...... 770 386-4766
  East Saint Louis *(G-8323)*
Stepan Company ....B...... 847 446-7500
  Elwood *(G-9464)*
U S Colors & Coatings Inc ....G...... 630 879-8898
  Batavia *(G-1435)*

CYCLONES: Indl, Metal Plate

Paul D Stark & Associates ....F...... 630 964-7111
  Downers Grove *(G-8070)*

CYLINDER & ACTUATORS: Fluid Power

Bimba Manufacturing Company ....E...... 708 534-7997
  Manteno *(G-13444)*
Bimba Manufacturing Company ....G...... 815 654-7775
  Machesney Park *(G-13329)*
Blac Inc ....D...... 630 279-6400
  Elmhurst *(G-9335)*
Brake Parts Inc LLC ....G...... 217 324-2161
  Litchfield *(G-12961)*
Dresser Inc ....D...... 847 437-5940
  Elk Grove Village *(G-8955)*
Ergo-Help Inc ....G...... 847 593-0722
  Fox River Grove *(G-9757)*
Gpe Controls Inc ....F...... 708 236-6000
  Hillside *(G-11340)*
Hadady Machining Company Inc ....F...... 708 474-8620
  Lansing *(G-12496)*
Ken Elliott Co ....G...... 618 466-8200
  Godfrey *(G-10654)*
Kitagawa Usa Inc ....E...... 847 310-8198
  Schaumburg *(G-18587)*
Master Hydraulics & Machining ....F...... 847 895-5578
  Schaumburg *(G-18623)*
Mead Fluid Dynamics Inc ....E...... 773 685-6800
  University Park *(G-19959)*
RE-Do-It Corp ....G...... 708 343-7125
  Broadview *(G-2463)*
Sarco Hydraulics Inc ....E...... 217 324-6577
  Litchfield *(G-12977)*
T J Brooks Co ....G...... 847 680-0350
  Libertyville *(G-12713)*
Tuxco Corporation ....F...... 847 244-2220
  Gurnee *(G-10940)*
Walach Manufacturing Co Inc ....F...... 773 836-2060
  Chicago *(G-6585)*

CYLINDERS: Pressure

Hoerbiger-Origa Corporation ....D...... 800 283-1377
  Glendale Heights *(G-10456)*
Maccarb Inc ....G...... 877 427-2499
  Elgin *(G-8645)*
Midwest Hydra-Line Inc ....G...... 309 674-6570
  Peoria *(G-16475)*
Midwest Hydra-Line Inc ....F...... 309 342-6171
  Galesburg *(G-10211)*
Reino Tool & Manufacturing Co ....F...... 773 588-5800
  Chicago *(G-6005)*
Rockford Air Devices Inc ....F...... 815 654-3330
  Machesney Park *(G-13370)*
Rode Welding Inc ....E...... 847 439-0910
  Elk Grove Village *(G-9219)*

CYLINDERS: Pump

Davis Welding & Manfctg Inc ....F...... 217 784-5480
  Gibson City *(G-10336)*
Pokorney Manufacturing Co ....G...... 630 458-0406
  Addison *(G-244)*
Rrp Enterprises Inc ....G...... 847 455-5674
  Franklin Park *(G-10038)*
Trd Manufacturing Inc ....E...... 815 654-7775
  Machesney Park *(G-13379)*

DAIRY EQPT

Gea Farm Technologies Inc ....C...... 630 548-8200
  Naperville *(G-14833)*

DAIRY PRDTS STORE: Ice Cream, Packaged

Al Gelato Chicago LLC ....G...... 847 455-5355
  Franklin Park *(G-9864)*

DAIRY PRDTS STORE: Milk

Oberweis Dairy Inc ....F...... 847 368-9060
  Arlington Heights *(G-782)*
Oberweis Dairy Inc ....E...... 630 906-6455
  Oswego *(G-16017)*
Oberweis Dairy Inc ....E...... 708 660-1350
  Oak Park *(G-15767)*
Oberweis Dairy Inc ....F...... 630 782-0141
  Elmhurst *(G-9407)*
Oberweis Dairy Inc ....F...... 847 290-9222
  Rolling Meadows *(G-17757)*
Oberweis Dairy Inc ....F...... 630 801-6100
  Glen Ellyn *(G-10415)*

DAIRY PRDTS STORES

Wiscon Corp ....E...... 708 450-0074
  Melrose Park *(G-13930)*

DAIRY PRDTS WHOLESALERS: Fresh

Milk Products Holdings N Amer ....C...... 847 928-1600
  Rosemont *(G-18036)*
Prairie Pure Cheese ....G...... 815 568-5000
  Marengo *(G-13493)*

DAIRY PRDTS: Butter

Danish Maid Butter Company ....F...... 773 731-8787
  Chicago *(G-4315)*
Hoogwegt US Inc ....D...... 847 918-8787
  Lake Forest *(G-12254)*
Old Heritage Creamery LLC ....G...... 217 268-4355
  Arcola *(G-661)*

DAIRY PRDTS: Butter Oil

DAIRY PRDTS: Butter Oil
Madison Farms Butter Company ....E 217 854-2547
  Carlinville *(G-2882)*

DAIRY PRDTS: Cheese
Arthur Schuman Inc .... E 847 851-8500
  Elgin *(G-8514)*
Arthur Schuman Midwest LLC .... D 847 851-8500
  Elgin *(G-8515)*
Berner Food & Beverage LLC .... E 815 865-5136
  Rock City *(G-17174)*
Cheese Merchants America LLC .... B 630 221-0580
  Bartlett *(G-1272)*
El Encanto Products Inc .... F 773 940-1807
  Chicago *(G-4464)*
Hoogwegt US Inc .... D 847 918-8787
  Lake Forest *(G-12254)*
Kraft Heinz Foods Company .... C 847 646-2000
  Northfield *(G-15521)*
Kraft Heinz Foods Company .... D 217 378-1900
  Champaign *(G-3315)*
Mondelez Global LLC .... C 847 943-4000
  Deerfield *(G-7637)*
Nuestro Queso LLC .... C 815 443-2100
  Kent *(G-12018)*
Nuestro Queso LLC .... E 224 366-4320
  Chicago *(G-5641)*
Prairie Pure Cheese .... C 815 568-5000
  Marengo *(G-13493)*
Saputo Inc .... E 715 755-3485
  Lincolnshire *(G-12795)*
Savencia Cheese USA LLC .... G 815 369-4577
  Lena *(G-12608)*
V Formusa Co .... F 224 938-9360
  Des Plaines *(G-7863)*
Wiscon Corp .... E 708 450-0074
  Melrose Park *(G-13930)*
Wiscon Corp .... E 708 450-0074
  Melrose Park *(G-13929)*

DAIRY PRDTS: Cream Substitutes
Bay Valley Foods LLC .... D 815 239-2631
  Pecatonica *(G-16321)*
Treehouse Foods Inc .... C 708 483-1300
  Oak Brook *(G-15665)*

DAIRY PRDTS: Custard, Frozen
Gregs Frozen Custard Company .... G 847 837-4175
  Mundelein *(G-14692)*

DAIRY PRDTS: Dairy Based Desserts, Frozen
Baldwin Richardson Foods Co .... G 815 464-9994
  Oakbrook Terrace *(G-15787)*
Profile Food Ingredients LLC .... E 847 622-1700
  Elgin *(G-8697)*

DAIRY PRDTS: Dietary Supplements, Dairy & Non-Dairy Based
Health King Enterprise Inc .... G 312 567-9978
  Chicago *(G-4791)*
Healthy Body LLC .... G 208 409-6602
  Ottawa *(G-16054)*
Liqua Fit Inc .... G 630 965-8067
  Grayslake *(G-10787)*
Saasoom LLC .... G 630 561-7300
  Saint Charles *(G-18263)*
Salud Natural Entrepreneur Inc .... E 224 789-7400
  Waukegan *(G-20491)*
Salud Natural Entrepreneur Inc .... E 224 789-7400
  Waukegan *(G-20492)*
Santa Cruz Holdings LLC .... G 217 821-0304
  Effingham *(G-8424)*
Vital Proteins LLC .... E 224 544-9110
  Chicago *(G-6562)*

DAIRY PRDTS: Dips & Spreads, Cheese Based
Berner Food & Beverage LLC .... B 815 563-4222
  Dakota *(G-7311)*
Handcut Foods LLC .... D 312 239-0381
  Chicago *(G-4776)*
Kraft Heinz Foods Company .... G 412 456-5700
  Chicago *(G-5130)*
Saputo Cheese USA Inc .... D 847 267-1100
  Lincolnshire *(G-12794)*

DAIRY PRDTS: Dips & Spreads, Sour Cream Based
Berner Food & Beverage LLC .... B 815 563-4222
  Dakota *(G-7311)*

DAIRY PRDTS: Dried Milk
Fonterra (usa) Inc .... D 847 928-1600
  Chicago *(G-4616)*

DAIRY PRDTS: Evaporated Milk
Nestle Usa Inc .... C 309 263-2651
  Morton *(G-14374)*
Nestle Usa Inc .... C 217 243-9175
  Jacksonville *(G-11778)*
Nestle Usa Inc .... C 815 754-2550
  Dekalb *(G-7694)*
Nestle Usa Inc .... C 309 829-1031
  Bloomington *(G-2083)*

DAIRY PRDTS: Fermented & Cultured Milk Prdts
Chester Dairy Company Inc .... F 618 826-2394
  Chester *(G-3452)*
Chester Dairy Company Inc .... G 618 826-2395
  Chester *(G-3453)*
Douglas Graybill .... G 815 218-1749
  Freeport *(G-10106)*

DAIRY PRDTS: Frozen Desserts & Novelties
Al Gelato Chicago LLC .... G 847 455-5355
  Franklin Park *(G-9864)*
Creamery Inc .... G 708 479-5706
  Mokena *(G-14077)*
Deja Investments Inc .... D 630 408-9222
  Bolingbrook *(G-2168)*
Delicious Treats LLC .... G 618 410-6722
  East Saint Louis *(G-8303)*
Dianas Bananas Inc .... F 773 638-6800
  Chicago *(G-4353)*
Five Star Desserts and Foods .... G 773 375-5100
  Chicago *(G-4599)*
Gayety Candy Co Inc .... E 708 418-0062
  Lansing *(G-12494)*
Genes Ice Cream Inc .... G 309 846-5925
  Bloomington *(G-2051)*
Icream Group LLC .... G 773 342-2834
  Chicago *(G-4873)*
Kent Precision Foods Group Inc .... E 630 226-0071
  Bolingbrook *(G-2201)*
Lezza Spumoni and Desserts Inc .... E 708 547-5969
  Bellwood *(G-1631)*
Los Mangos .... G 815 630-2611
  Crest Hill *(G-7091)*
ME and Gia Inc .... G 708 583-1111
  Elmwood Park *(G-9454)*
Mitchlls Cndies Ice Creams Inc .... F 708 799-3835
  Homewood *(G-11501)*
Paleteria Carrucel .... G 773 310-5749
  Chicago *(G-5747)*
Paleteria El Sabor .... G 312 243-2308
  Chicago *(G-5748)*
Richards Sper Prmium Ice Cream .... F 773 614-8999
  Chicago *(G-6026)*
Union Foods Inc .... G 201 327-2828
  Chicago *(G-6465)*
Viola Ice Cream Shoppe .... G 309 596-2131
  Viola *(G-20183)*
We Love Soy Inc .... G 630 629-9667
  Addison *(G-332)*

DAIRY PRDTS: Ice Cream & Ice Milk
Muller-Pinehurst Dairy Inc .... C 815 968-0441
  Rockford *(G-17533)*
Roesers Bakery .... E 773 489-6900
  Chicago *(G-6050)*

DAIRY PRDTS: Ice Cream, Bulk
Gyood .... G 773 360-8810
  Chicago *(G-4754)*
Hershey Creamery Company .... F 708 339-4656
  South Holland *(G-19220)*
Homers Ice Cream Inc .... E 847 251-0477
  Wilmette *(G-21078)*
Los Mangos .... G 773 542-1522
  Chicago *(G-5262)*

DAIRY PRDTS: Ice Cream, Packaged, Molded, On Sticks, Etc.
Sisler Dairy Products Company .... G 815 376-2913
  Ohio *(G-15845)*

DAIRY PRDTS: Imitation Cheese
We Love Soy Inc .... G 630 629-9667
  Addison *(G-332)*

DAIRY PRDTS: Milk & Cream, Cultured & Flavored
Socius Ingredients LLC .... F 847 440-0156
  Evanston *(G-9575)*

DAIRY PRDTS: Milk Preparations, Dried
Erie Group International Inc .... D 309 659-2233
  Rochelle *(G-17139)*

DAIRY PRDTS: Milk, Chocolate
Gametime Snacks LLC .... E 309 517-6342
  Milan *(G-14011)*

DAIRY PRDTS: Milk, Condensed & Evaporated
Abbott Laboratories .... A 224 667-6100
  Abbott Park *(G-1)*
Abbott Laboratories .... A 847 932-7900
  North Chicago *(G-15293)*
Corefx Ingredients LLC .... F 773 271-2663
  Orangeville *(G-15908)*
Lifeway Foods Inc .... C 847 967-1010
  Morton Grove *(G-14420)*
Milk Products Holdings N Amer .... C 847 928-1600
  Rosemont *(G-18036)*
MSI Green Inc .... G 312 421-6550
  Chicago *(G-5519)*

DAIRY PRDTS: Milk, Fluid
Bay Valley Foods LLC .... D 815 239-2631
  Pecatonica *(G-16321)*
Berner Food & Beverage LLC .... E 815 865-5136
  Rock City *(G-17174)*
Dean Dairy Fluid LLC .... D 847 669-5508
  Huntley *(G-11534)*
Dean Dairy Ice Cream LLC .... D 815 544-2105
  Belvidere *(G-1665)*
Dean Dairy Ice Cream LLC .... G 937 323-5777
  Franklin Park *(G-9927)*
Dean Food Products Company .... E 847 678-1680
  Franklin Park *(G-9928)*
Deja Investments Inc .... D 630 408-9222
  Bolingbrook *(G-2168)*
Erie Group International Inc .... D 309 659-2233
  Rochelle *(G-17139)*
Kraft Heinz Foods Company .... D 217 378-1900
  Champaign *(G-3315)*
Lifeway Foods Inc .... C 847 967-1010
  Morton Grove *(G-14420)*
Midwest Ice Cream Company LLC .... F 815 544-2105
  Belvidere *(G-1687)*
Rich Products Corporation .... D 847 581-1749
  Niles *(G-15165)*

DAIRY PRDTS: Milk, Processed, Pasteurized, Homogenized/Btld
Dean Dairy Fluid LLC .... D 815 490-5578
  Rockford *(G-17371)*
Dean Dairy Fluid LLC .... C 815 943-7375
  Harvard *(G-11052)*
Dean Dairy Fluid LLC .... G 217 428-6726
  Decatur *(G-7483)*
Dean Dairy Ice Cream LLC .... E 630 879-0800
  Batavia *(G-1372)*
East Side Jersey Dairy Inc .... E 217 854-2547
  Carlinville *(G-2873)*
East Side Jersey Dairy Inc .... G 662 289-3344
  Edwardsville *(G-8358)*

PRODUCT SECTION

DENTAL EQPT & SPLYS

Muller-Pinehurst Dairy Inc .... C 815 968-0441
  Rockford (G-17533)
Oberweis Dairy Inc .... F 847 368-9060
  Arlington Heights (G-782)
Oberweis Dairy Inc .... E 630 906-6455
  Oswego (G-16017)
Oberweis Dairy Inc .... E 708 660-1350
  Oak Park (G-15767)
Oberweis Dairy Inc .... F 630 782-0141
  Elmhurst (G-9407)
Oberweis Dairy Inc .... F 847 290-9222
  Rolling Meadows (G-17757)
Oberweis Dairy Inc .... E 630 801-6100
  Glen Ellyn (G-10415)
Prairie Farms Dairy Inc .... G 618 451-5600
  Granite City (G-10730)
Prairie Farms Dairy Inc .... G 618 457-4167
  Carbondale (G-2854)

DAIRY PRDTS: Natural Cheese

Avanti Foods Company .... E 815 379-2155
  Walnut (G-20216)
Bel Americas Inc .... G 646 454-8220
  Chicago (G-3859)
Bel Brands Usa Inc .... E 312 462-1500
  Chicago (G-3860)
Brewster Cheese Company .... D 815 947-3361
  Stockton (G-19548)
Carl Buddig and Company .... E 708 798-0900
  Homewood (G-11489)
Churny Company Inc .... B 847 646-5500
  Chicago (G-4148)
Conagra Dairy Foods Company .... B 630 848-0975
  Chicago (G-4213)
Kolb-Lena Inc .... D 815 369-4577
  Lena (G-12600)
Kraft Heinz Company .... C 847 646-2000
  Chicago (G-5129)
Mancuso Cheese Company .... F 815 722-2475
  Joliet (G-11897)
Marcoot Jersey Creamery LLC .... F 618 664-1110
  Greenville (G-10837)
Two Tribes LLC .... G 847 272-7711
  Glenview (G-10634)
V & V Supremo Foods Inc .... C 312 733-5652
  Chicago (G-6511)
Wengers Springbrook Cheese Inc .... F 815 865-5855
  Davis (G-7420)

DAIRY PRDTS: Powdered Buttermilk

Hoogwegt US Inc .... D 847 918-8787
  Lake Forest (G-12254)

DAIRY PRDTS: Processed Cheese

Kraft Foods Asia PCF Svcs LLC .... G 847 943-4000
  Deerfield (G-7627)
La Hispamex Food Products Inc .... G 708 780-1808
  Chicago (G-5147)
Mondelez International Inc .... G 815 710-2114
  Morris (G-14316)
Mondelez International Inc .... A 847 943-4000
  Chicago (G-5490)

DAIRY PRDTS: Whey, Powdered

Armada Nutrition LLC .... G 931 451-7808
  Carol Stream (G-2940)

DAIRY PRDTS: Whipped Topping, Dry Mix

Rich Products Corporation .... D 847 581-1749
  Niles (G-15165)

DAIRY PRDTS: Yogurt, Exc Frozen

Lulus Real Froyo .... G 630 299-3854
  Aurora (G-999)
Maple Hill Creamery LLC .... E 518 758-7777
  Deerfield (G-7635)

DAIRY PRDTS: Yogurt, Frozen

A&W Stone Masonry LLC .... G 618 499-7239
  Harrisburg (G-11019)
Amani Froyo LLC .... G 941 744-1111
  Oakbrook Terrace (G-15782)

DATA ENTRY SVCS

Connies Home Health Care .... G 708 790-4000
  Park Forest (G-16253)

Information Resources Inc .... B 312 474-3154
  Bartlett (G-1255)

DATA PROCESSING & PREPARATION SVCS

Imaging Systems Inc .... F 630 875-1100
  Itasca (G-11674)
Innerworkings Inc .... D 312 642-3700
  Chicago (G-4927)
Reprographics .... G 815 477-1018
  Crystal Lake (G-7254)
Sebis Direct Inc .... E 312 243-9300
  Bedford Park (G-1504)
Tempus Labs Inc .... E 312 784-4400
  Chicago (G-6347)
Track Group Inc .... E 877 260-2010
  Naperville (G-14936)
Val P Enterprises .... G 708 982-6561
  Chicago (G-6518)
Vertex Consulting Services Inc .... F 313 492-5154
  Schaumburg (G-18771)

DATA PROCESSING SVCS

Accuity Inc .... B 847 676-9600
  Evanston (G-9486)
Microdynamics Corporation .... C 630 276-0527
  Naperville (G-14870)
Negs & Litho Inc .... F 847 647-7770
  Chicago (G-5563)
Overt Press Inc .... E 773 284-0909
  Chicago (G-5718)

DECORATIVE WOOD & WOODWORK

Aba Custom Woodworking .... G 815 356-9663
  Crystal Lake (G-7153)
All American Wood Register Co .... F 815 356-1000
  Crystal Lake (G-7155)
Barsanti Woodwork Corporation .... E 773 284-6888
  Chicago (G-3842)
Brown Woodworking .... G 815 477-8333
  Crystal Lake (G-7172)
Curtis Woodworking Inc .... G 815 544-3543
  Belvidere (G-1664)
Delleman Associates & Corp .... G 708 345-9520
  Maywood (G-13668)
Dusty Lane Wood Products .... G 618 426-9045
  Campbell Hill (G-2815)
Forest Awards & Engraving .... G 630 595-2242
  Wood Dale (G-21189)
Haight Company .... E 224 407-0763
  Elgin (G-8603)
Herschberger Wood Working .... G 217 543-4075
  Arthur (G-863)
Hexacomb Corporation .... G 847 955-7984
  Buffalo Grove (G-2546)
Jack Ruch Quality Homes Inc .... G 309 663-6595
  Bloomington (G-2063)
Jacobs Reproduction .... G 618 374-2198
  Elsah (G-9458)
Joseph Woodworking Corporation ...... F 847 233-9766
  Schiller Park (G-18816)
Kaufman Woodworking .... G 217 543-3607
  Arthur (G-864)
Kaufmans Custom Cabinets .... F 217 268-4330
  Arcola (G-653)
Kohout Woodwork Inc .... G 630 628-6257
  Addison (G-174)
Little Creek Woodworking .... G 217 543-2815
  Arthur (G-866)
Orren Pickell Builders Inc .... F 847 572-5200
  Wilmette (G-21090)
Powers Woodworking .... G 630 663-9644
  Woodridge (G-21333)
Premium Wood Products Inc .... E 815 787-3669
  Dekalb (G-7698)
R Maderite Inc .... G 773 235-1515
  Chicago (G-5947)
R S Bacon Veneer Company .... C 630 323-1414
  Lisle (G-12932)
Roselle Custom Woodwork LLC .... G 630 980-5655
  Roselle (G-17980)
Silver Line .... G 708 832-9100
  Calumet City (G-2791)
Stancy Woodworking Co Inc .... F 847 526-0252
  Island Lake (G-11611)
Star Cabinetry .... G 773 725-4651
  Chicago (G-6233)
Tender Loving Care Inds Inc .... D 847 891-0230
  Elgin (G-8753)

Tepromark International Inc .... G 847 329-7881
  Chicago (G-6352)
Todd Scanlan .... G 217 585-1717
  Springfield (G-19466)
Woodwind Specialists .... G 217 423-4122
  Decatur (G-7570)

DEFENSE SYSTEMS & EQPT

2nd Amendment Defense Inc .... G 815 218-2847
  Rockford (G-17276)
Bizstarterscom LLC .... G 847 305-4626
  Arlington Heights (G-705)
Black Bear Defense LLC .... G 708 357-7233
  Chicago (G-3906)
Contego Defense Group .... G 630 532-1063
  Woodridge (G-21287)
Ctg Advanced Materials LLC .... E 630 226-9080
  Bolingbrook (G-2161)
Dapper Defense LLC .... G 309 922-9203
  East Peoria (G-8265)
Frostdefense Envirotech Inc .... G 217 979-3052
  Champaign (G-3293)
Guardian Personal Defense Tng .... G 630 272-9811
  Oswego (G-16006)
Illinois Ticket Defense Firm .... G 954 467-1965
  Saint Charles (G-18210)
Kogan Self Defense .... G 847 877-4711
  Buffalo Grove (G-2555)
Lg Innotek USA Inc .... G 847 941-8713
  Lincolnshire (G-12780)
Navistar Defense LLC .... E 708 617-4500
  Melrose Park (G-13896)
Open Hand Self Defense .... G 815 718-3994
  Morrison (G-14346)
Raytheon Company .... B 630 295-6394
  Rolling Meadows (G-17770)
Ridge Road Defense .... G 630 820-8906
  Aurora (G-1148)
Sharp Defense LLC .... G 630 205-3502
  Elgin (G-8728)
Tomahawk Defense .... G 773 871-7268
  Chicago (G-6388)
Vanguard Defense Group .... G 850 218-4233
  Island Lake (G-11612)

DEGREASING MACHINES

Graymills Corporation .... D 773 477-4100
  Broadview (G-2439)
Therma-Kleen Inc .... G 630 718-0212
  Plainfield (G-16723)

DEHYDRATION EQPT

Kitchy Koo Gourmet Co .... G 708 499-5236
  Oak Lawn (G-15723)

DELIVERY SVCS, BY VEHICLE

Lexpress Inc .... G 773 517-7095
  Prospect Heights (G-16844)
Mel Price Company Inc .... F 217 442-9092
  Danville (G-7364)
Tolar Group LLC .... E 847 662-8000
  Waukegan (G-20507)

DEMONSTRATION SVCS

Modern Printing Colors Inc .... F 708 681-5678
  Broadview (G-2453)

DENTAL EQPT

Gc America Inc .... C 708 597-0900
  Alsip (G-446)
Goldman Products Inc .... E 847 526-1166
  Wauconda (G-20354)
Nordent Manufacturing Inc .... E 847 437-4780
  Elk Grove Village (G-9150)
Young Mydent LLC .... F 631 434-3190
  Algonquin (G-399)

DENTAL EQPT & SPLYS

Acquamed Technologies Inc .... G 630 728-4014
  Oswego (G-15989)
Apex Dental Materials Inc .... G 847 719-1133
  Lake Zurich (G-12385)
Artistic Dental Studio Inc .... E 630 679-8686
  Bolingbrook (G-2149)
Bennett Technologies Inc .... F 708 389-9501
  Tinley Park (G-19809)

Employee Codes: A=Over 500 employees, B=251-500
C=101-250, D=51-100, E=20-50, F=10-19, G=3-9

DENTAL EQPT & SPLYS

Ched Markay Inc ....G....... 847 566-3307
  Mundelein *(G-14675)*
Denbur Inc ....G....... 630 986-9667
  Westmont *(G-20735)*
Dental Arts Laboratories Inc ....G....... 309 342-3117
  Galesburg *(G-10190)*
Dental Craft Corp ....F....... 815 385-7132
  Ringwood *(G-17041)*
Dental Crafts Lab Inc ....G....... 815 872-3221
  Princeton *(G-16806)*
Dental Laboratory Inc ....G....... 630 262-3700
  Geneva *(G-10265)*
Dental Technologies Inc ....D....... 847 677-5500
  Lincolnwood *(G-12816)*
Dentalez Alabama Inc ....C....... 773 624-4330
  Chicago *(G-4341)*
Dentsply Sirona Inc ....C....... 847 640-4800
  Elgin *(G-8565)*
Dove Dental Studio ....G....... 847 679-2434
  Niles *(G-15116)*
Duquoin Dental Associates ....G....... 618 542-8832
  Du Quoin *(G-8118)*
Fred Pigg Dental Lab ....G....... 618 439-6829
  Mount Vernon *(G-14611)*
Fricke Dental Manufacturing Co ....G....... 630 540-1900
  Streamwood *(G-19575)*
Gc Manufacturing America LLC ....D....... 708 597-0900
  Alsip *(G-447)*
Healthdentl LLC ....G....... 800 845-5172
  Plainfield *(G-16670)*
Holland Specialty Co ....E....... 309 697-9262
  Peoria *(G-16453)*
J L Lawrence & Co ....G....... 217 235-3622
  Mattoon *(G-13638)*
Lmpl Management Corporation ....G....... 708 636-2443
  Oak Lawn *(G-15725)*
Mandis Dental Laboratory ....G....... 618 345-3777
  Collinsville *(G-6968)*
Odl Inc ....D....... 815 434-0655
  Ottawa *(G-16067)*
Oratech Inc ....E....... 217 793-2735
  Springfield *(G-19418)*
Ortho Arch Company Inc ....E....... 847 885-7805
  Schaumburg *(G-18660)*
Proalliance Corp ....G....... 815 207-8556
  Harvard *(G-11064)*
Sunstar Americas Inc ....B....... 847 794-4157
  Schaumburg *(G-18730)*
Tanaka Dental Enterprises Inc ....F....... 847 679-1610
  Skokie *(G-19042)*
Underwood Dental Laboratories ....F....... 217 398-0090
  Champaign *(G-3360)*
Young Innovations Inc ....D....... 847 458-5400
  Algonquin *(G-397)*
Young Innovations Inc ....D....... 847 458-5400
  Algonquin *(G-398)*
Young Os LLC ....G....... 847 458-5400
  Algonquin *(G-400)*

DENTAL EQPT & SPLYS WHOLESALERS

Omar Medical Supplies Inc ....F....... 708 922-4276
  Chicago *(G-5673)*

DENTAL EQPT & SPLYS: Compounds

Lang Dental Mfg Co Inc ....F....... 847 215-6622
  Wheeling *(G-20929)*

DENTAL EQPT & SPLYS: Dental Hand Instruments, NEC

Cislak Manufacturing Inc ....E....... 847 647-1819
  Niles *(G-15110)*
Hu-Friedy Mfg Co LLC ....C....... 773 975-3975
  Chicago *(G-4858)*
M & N Dental ....G....... 815 678-0036
  Richmond *(G-17017)*

DENTAL EQPT & SPLYS: Dental Materials

Bisco Inc ....D....... 847 534-6000
  Schaumburg *(G-18464)*
Reliance Dental Mfg Co ....G....... 708 597-6694
  Alsip *(G-502)*

DENTAL EQPT & SPLYS: Denture Materials

Astron Dental Corporation ....F....... 847 726-8787
  Lake Zurich *(G-12386)*
Prime Dental Manufacturing ....E....... 773 283-2914
  Chicago *(G-5873)*

DENTAL EQPT & SPLYS: Enamels

James Street Dental P C ....G....... 630 232-9535
  Geneva *(G-10286)*
Smile Lee Faces ....G....... 773 376-9999
  Chicago *(G-6192)*

DENTAL EQPT & SPLYS: Laboratory

Strictly Dentures ....G....... 815 969-0531
  Rockford *(G-17647)*

DENTAL EQPT & SPLYS: Sterilizers

Integrated Medical Tech Inc ....G....... 309 662-3614
  Bloomington *(G-2062)*

DENTAL EQPT & SPLYS: Teeth, Artificial, Exc In Dental Labs

Martin Dental Laboratory Inc ....F....... 708 597-8880
  Lockport *(G-13011)*
Myerson LLC ....G....... 312 432-8200
  Chicago *(G-5531)*

DENTAL INSTRUMENT REPAIR SVCS

Nordent Manufacturing Inc ....E....... 847 437-4780
  Elk Grove Village *(G-9150)*

DENTISTS' OFFICES & CLINICS

Bisco Inc ....D....... 847 534-6000
  Schaumburg *(G-18464)*
Fricke Dental Manufacturing Co ....G....... 630 540-1900
  Streamwood *(G-19575)*

DENTURE CLEANERS

Holland Specialty Co ....E....... 309 697-9262
  Peoria *(G-16453)*

DEODORANTS: Personal

Procter & Gamble Company ....G....... 847 375-5400
  Chicago *(G-5892)*

DEPARTMENT STORES: Army-Navy Goods

Peacock Printing Inc ....G....... 618 242-3157
  Mount Vernon *(G-14633)*

DEPARTMENT STORES: Country General

Reasons Inc ....G....... 309 537-3424
  Buffalo Prairie *(G-2626)*

DEPILATORIES, COSMETIC

Bioelements Inc ....F....... 773 525-3509
  Chicago *(G-3895)*

DERMATOLOGICALS

Therapeutic Skin Care ....G....... 630 244-1833
  Lombard *(G-13143)*

DERRICKS: Oil & Gas Field

David L Kaufman ....F....... 217 543-4190
  Arthur *(G-851)*

DESIGN SVCS, NEC

3rd Coast Imaging Inc ....G....... 312 322-3111
  Chicago *(G-3470)*
4ever Printing Inc ....G....... 847 222-1525
  Arlington Heights *(G-679)*
5h Consulting & Design LLC ....E....... 618 317-5822
  Ellis Grove *(G-9319)*
Concepts Magnet ....G....... 847 253-3351
  Mount Prospect *(G-14520)*
D5 Design Met Fabrication LLC ....G....... 773 770-4705
  Chicago *(G-4303)*
Daxam Inc ....F....... 847 214-1733
  Elgin *(G-8564)*
Heat Seal Tooling Corporation ....G....... 815 626-6009
  Rock Falls *(G-17182)*
Kohler Co ....E....... 847 635-8071
  Glenview *(G-10578)*
Legacy 3d LLC ....F....... 815 727-5454
  Crest Hill *(G-7090)*
M & G Simplicitees ....G....... 224 372-7426
  Lake Villa *(G-12359)*
Manufcture Dsign Innvation Inc ....G....... 773 526-7773
  West Chicago *(G-20611)*
Randal Wood Displays Inc ....D....... 630 761-0400
  Batavia *(G-1409)*
Sadannah Group LLC ....G....... 630 357-2300
  Naperville *(G-14912)*
Spectrum Cos International ....G....... 630 879-8008
  Batavia *(G-1418)*
Splat Creative Inc ....G....... 708 567-8412
  Chicago *(G-6216)*
Sunrise Hitek Service Inc ....E....... 773 792-8880
  Chicago *(G-6277)*
Telcom Innovations Group LLC ....E....... 630 350-0700
  Itasca *(G-11745)*
Tlk Industries Inc ....D....... 847 359-3200
  East Dundee *(G-8212)*
Wesdar Technologies Inc ....G....... 630 761-0965
  Aurora *(G-1034)*

DESIGN SVCS: Commercial & Indl

Active Automation Inc ....F....... 847 427-8100
  Elk Grove Village *(G-8806)*
Corporation Supply Co Inc ....E....... 312 726-3375
  Chicago *(G-4241)*
Device Technologies Inc ....G....... 630 553-7178
  Yorkville *(G-21479)*
E Gornell & Sons Inc ....E....... 773 489-2330
  Chicago *(G-4423)*
M & R Printing Inc ....G....... 847 398-2500
  Rolling Meadows *(G-17749)*
Pmb Industries Inc ....E....... 708 442-4515
  La Grange *(G-12086)*
Scientific Instruments Inc ....G....... 847 679-1242
  Schaumburg *(G-18709)*
Universal Feeder Inc ....G....... 815 633-0752
  Machesney Park *(G-13382)*
William Frick & Company ....E....... 847 918-3700
  Libertyville *(G-12725)*

DESIGN SVCS: Computer Integrated Systems

Adept Coalescence LLC ....G....... 440 503-1808
  Rockford *(G-17295)*
Applus Technologies Inc ....E....... 312 661-1100
  Chicago *(G-3714)*
Ascent Innovations LLC ....E....... 847 572-8000
  Schaumburg *(G-18445)*
Cloud 9 Infosystems Inc ....C....... 855 225-6839
  Downers Grove *(G-7974)*
Controllink Incorporated ....E....... 847 622-1100
  Elgin *(G-8554)*
Drawn LLC ....E....... 312 982-0040
  Chicago *(G-4397)*
GE Intelligent Platforms Inc ....D....... 630 829-4000
  Lisle *(G-12894)*
Infinite Cnvrgnce Slutions Inc ....G....... 224 764-3400
  Arlington Heights *(G-758)*
Isewa LLC ....G....... 847 877-1586
  Buffalo Grove *(G-2551)*
Juniper Networks Inc ....E....... 773 632-1200
  Chicago *(G-5060)*
Koi Computers Inc ....G....... 630 627-8811
  Downers Grove *(G-8040)*
Logicon Group LLC ....G....... 618 558-7757
  Millstadt *(G-14049)*
M13 Inc ....E....... 847 310-1913
  Schaumburg *(G-18617)*
Matrix Circuits LLC ....G....... 319 367-5000
  Lake Villa *(G-12360)*
National School Services Inc ....G....... 847 438-3859
  Long Grove *(G-13167)*
Palm International Inc ....G....... 630 357-1437
  Naperville *(G-14892)*
Pervasive Health Inc ....E....... 312 257-2967
  Chicago *(G-5793)*
Phillip Grigalanz ....G....... 219 628-6706
  Jerseyville *(G-11795)*
Pinehurst Bus Solutions Corp ....G....... 630 842-6155
  Winfield *(G-21115)*
Quadramed Corporation ....E....... 312 396-0700
  Chicago *(G-5926)*
Richardson Electronics Ltd ....C....... 630 208-2200
  Lafox *(G-12138)*
Righthand Technologies Inc ....E....... 773 774-7600
  Chicago *(G-6033)*
Schwider Systems ....G....... 815 469-2834
  Frankfort *(G-9837)*
Val P Enterprises ....G....... 708 982-6561
  Chicago *(G-6518)*

PRODUCT SECTION

DIES & TOOLS: Special

Vertex Consulting Services Inc ....F 313 492-5154
 Schaumburg *(G-18771)*

DESIGNS SVCS: Scenery, Theatrical

Guess Whackit & Hope Inc ....G 773 342-4273
 Chicago *(G-4750)*
Ivan Carlson Associates Inc ....E 312 829-4616
 Chicago *(G-4979)*

DETECTION APPARATUS: Electronic/Magnetic Field, Light/Heat

Checkpoint Systems Inc ....D 630 771-4240
 Romeoville *(G-17806)*
Ecolotech Asl Inc ....G 630 859-0485
 Aurora *(G-1086)*
Graceland Custom Products Inc ....F 630 616-4143
 Bensenville *(G-1815)*
Intex Systems Corp ....G 630 636-6594
 Oswego *(G-16008)*
Smart Pixel Inc ....G 630 771-0206
 Bolingbrook *(G-2241)*

DETECTION EQPT: Magnetic Field

Magnetec Inspection Inc ....F 815 802-1363
 Bradley *(G-2286)*

DETECTIVE SVCS

National Def Intelligence Inc ....G 312 233-2318
 Naperville *(G-14980)*

DETECTORS: Water Leak

CAM Co Inc ....F 630 556-3110
 Big Rock *(G-1969)*

DETONATORS & DETONATING CAPS

Hanley Industries Inc ....D 618 465-8892
 Alton *(G-557)*

DIAGNOSTIC SUBSTANCES

3primedx Inc ....G 312 621-0643
 Chicago *(G-3469)*
Abbott Laboratories ....A 224 667-6100
 Abbott Park *(G-1)*
Abbott Laboratories ....G 800 551-5838
 Lake Forest *(G-12218)*
Abbott Laboratories ....A 847 932-7900
 North Chicago *(G-15293)*
Abbott Molecular Inc ....G 224 361-7800
 Des Plaines *(G-7719)*
Abbott Molecular Inc ....D 224 361-7800
 Des Plaines *(G-7720)*
Amoco Technology Company ....C 312 861-6000
 Chicago *(G-3682)*
Bion Enterprises Ltd ....E 847 544-5044
 Des Plaines *(G-7740)*
Cairo Diagnostic Center ....F 618 734-1500
 Cairo *(G-2765)*
Cooper Equipment Company Inc .....G 708 367-1291
 Crete *(G-7137)*
Innovative Molecular Diagnosti ....G 630 845-8246
 Geneva *(G-10283)*
Ohmx Corporation ....F 847 491-8500
 Evanston *(G-9561)*
Pyramid Sciences Inc ....G 630 974-6110
 Burr Ridge *(G-2715)*
Sysmex Reagents America Inc ....E 847 996-4500
 Mundelein *(G-14741)*

DIAGNOSTIC SUBSTANCES OR AGENTS: Blood Derivative

Baxalta Export Corporation ....C 224 948-2000
 Bannockburn *(G-1193)*
Baxalta US Inc ....F 312 648-2244
 Chicago *(G-3846)*
Baxalta World Trade LLC ....G 224 940-2000
 Bannockburn *(G-1195)*
Baxalta Worldwide LLC ....C 224 948-2000
 Deerfield *(G-7590)*
Baxter Healthcare Corporation ....E 847 578-4671
 Waukegan *(G-20422)*
Baxter International Inc ....A 224 948-2000
 Deerfield *(G-7595)*
Ortho-Clinical Diagnostics Inc ....C 618 281-3882
 Columbia *(G-6993)*

DIAGNOSTIC SUBSTANCES OR AGENTS: Enzyme & Isoenzyme

Bioanalytics Inc ....G 217 649-6820
 Monticello *(G-14278)*

DIAGNOSTIC SUBSTANCES OR AGENTS: In Vitro

Fisher Scientific Company LLC ....G 800 528-0494
 Chicago *(G-4597)*
Glucosentient Inc ....G 217 487-4087
 Champaign *(G-3297)*
Prenosis Inc ....G 949 246-3113
 Chicago *(G-5865)*
Scientific Device Lab Inc ....E 847 803-9495
 Des Plaines *(G-7839)*
Voyant Diagnostics Inc ....G 630 456-6340
 Chicago *(G-6571)*

DIAGNOSTIC SUBSTANCES OR AGENTS: Microbiology & Virology

Ancillary Genomic Systems LLC .....G 765 714-3799
 Chicago *(G-3692)*
Muhammad Sotavia ....G 708 966-2262
 Orland Park *(G-15970)*
Polaris Genomics Corporation ....G 773 547-2350
 Mount Prospect *(G-14563)*
Soul Training Program Inc ....G 312 725-9768
 Chicago *(G-6205)*

DIAGNOSTIC SUBSTANCES OR AGENTS: Radioactive

GE Healthcare Holdings Inc ....A 847 398-8400
 Arlington Heights *(G-741)*
Petnet Solutions Inc ....G 847 297-3721
 Des Plaines *(G-7819)*

DIAMONDS, GEMS, WHOLESALE

Hy Spreckman & Sons Inc ....F 312 236-2173
 Skokie *(G-18966)*
Norkin Jewelry Co Inc ....E 312 782-7311
 Chicago *(G-5616)*
Steinmetz R (us) Ltd ....G 312 332-0990
 Chicago *(G-6241)*

DIAMONDS: Cutting & Polishing

144 International Inc ....F 847 426-8881
 West Dundee *(G-20660)*
Precise Lapping Grinding Corp ....F 708 615-0240
 Melrose Park *(G-13904)*
S G Nelson & Co ....G 630 668-7900
 Wheaton *(G-20822)*
Steinmetz R (us) Ltd ....G 312 332-0990
 Chicago *(G-6241)*

DIATHERMY EQPT

Sullivan Home Health Products ......G 217 532-6366
 Hillsboro *(G-11320)*

DIE CUTTING SVC: Paper

Capital Prtg & Die Cutng Inc ....G 630 896-5520
 Aurora *(G-1069)*
Graphic Arts Finishing Company .....D 708 345-8484
 Melrose Park *(G-13875)*
Intra-Cut Die Cutting Inc ....F 773 775-6228
 Chicago *(G-4960)*
PMC Converting Corp ....G 773 481-2269
 Chicago *(G-5825)*

DIE SETS: Presses, Metal Stamping

Amity Die and Stamping Co ....E 847 680-6600
 Lake Forest *(G-12224)*
Ammentorp Tool Company Inc ....G 847 671-9290
 Franklin Park *(G-9869)*
Atomic Engineering Co ....F 847 228-1387
 Elk Grove Village *(G-8846)*
Barco Stamping Co ....E 630 293-5155
 West Chicago *(G-20549)*
Capitol City Tool & Design ....G 217 544-9250
 Springfield *(G-19339)*
CGR Technologies Inc ....E 847 934-7622
 Palatine *(G-16099)*
Dkb Partners Inc ....G 618 632-6718
 O Fallon *(G-15572)*

Dms Inc ....F 847 726-2828
 Lake Zurich *(G-12403)*
Ehrhardt Tool & Machine LLC ....C 314 436-6900
 Granite City *(G-10704)*
ERA Tool and Manufacturing Co .....E 847 298-6333
 Zion *(G-21513)*
Erva Tool & Die Company ....G 773 533-7806
 Chicago *(G-4528)*
Harig Manufacturing Corp ....E 847 647-9500
 Skokie *(G-18964)*
J F Schroeder Company Inc ....E 847 357-8600
 Arlington Heights *(G-759)*
Jenco Metal Products Inc ....F 847 956-0550
 Mount Prospect *(G-14539)*
PDQ Tool & Stamping Co ....E 708 841-3000
 Dolton *(G-7938)*
Pecora Tool & Die Co Inc ....G 847 524-1275
 Schaumburg *(G-18671)*
Rj Stuckel Co Inc ....E 800 789-7220
 Elk Grove Village *(G-9218)*
Sierra Manufacturing Corp ....G 630 458-8830
 Addison *(G-288)*
Tauber Brothers Tool & Die Co ....E 708 867-9100
 Chicago *(G-6330)*
Wireformers Inc ....E 847 718-1920
 Mount Prospect *(G-14582)*

DIES & TOOLS: Special

3d Industries Inc ....E 630 616-8702
 Bensenville *(G-1719)*
A M Tool & Die ....E 847 398-7530
 Rolling Meadows *(G-17708)*
ABS Tool & Machine Inc ....G 815 968-4630
 Rockford *(G-17288)*
Accu Cast 2 Inc ....F 423 622-4344
 Elgin *(G-8491)*
Accurate Die Cutting Inc ....G 847 437-7215
 Elk Grove Village *(G-8800)*
Action Tool & Mfg Inc ....E 815 874-5775
 Rockford *(G-17294)*
Airo Tool & Manufacturing Inc ....F 815 547-7588
 Belvidere *(G-1647)*
Alpha Products Inc ....G 708 387-1580
 Brookfield *(G-2478)*
Altman Manufacturing Co Inc ....G 630 963-0031
 Lisle *(G-12862)*
Apex Tool Works Inc ....E 847 394-5810
 Rolling Meadows *(G-17712)*
Arrow Engineering Inc ....G 815 397-0862
 Rockford *(G-17307)*
Astro Tool Co Inc ....G 630 876-3402
 West Chicago *(G-20546)*
Austin Tool & Die Co ....D 847 509-5800
 Northbrook *(G-15344)*
Azimuth Cnc Inc ....F 815 399-4433
 Rockford *(G-17310)*
B & D Murray Manufacturing Co .....G 815 568-6176
 Marengo *(G-13481)*
B L I Tool & Die Inc ....E 217 434-9106
 Fowler *(G-9742)*
B Radtke and Sons Inc ....E 847 546-3999
 Round Lake Park *(G-18095)*
Bel-Air Manufacturing Inc ....F 773 276-7550
 Chicago *(G-3862)*
Bennett Metal Products Inc ....D 618 244-1911
 Mount Vernon *(G-14599)*
Bergst Special Tools Inc ....G 630 543-1020
 Addison *(G-48)*
Bi-Link Metal Specialties Inc ....C 630 858-5900
 Bloomingdale *(G-1980)*
Big 3 Precision Products Inc ....E 618 533-3251
 Centralia *(G-3222)*
Binder Tool Inc ....G 847 678-4222
 Franklin Park *(G-9887)*
Bomel Tool Manufacturing Co ....C 708 343-3663
 Broadview *(G-2422)*
Briergate Tool & Engrg Co ....F 630 766-7050
 Bensenville *(G-1756)*
BT & E Co ....G 815 544-6431
 Belvidere *(G-1657)*
Burdzy Tool & Die Co ....G 847 671-6666
 Schiller Park *(G-18790)*
Canny Tool & Mold Corporation .....G 847 548-1573
 Grayslake *(G-10760)*
Cdv Corp ....F 815 397-3903
 Rockford *(G-17339)*
Center Tool Company ....G 847 683-7559
 Hampshire *(G-10966)*
Central Tool Specialities Co ....G 630 543-6351
 Addison *(G-66)*

DIES & TOOLS: Special

Company	Code	Phone
Chelar Tool & Die Inc — Belleville (G-1539)	D	618 234-6550
CII Engineering LLC — Addison (G-74)	G	630 628-8393
Component Tool & Mfg Co — Crete (G-7136)	F	708 672-5505
Correct Tool Inc — Bensenville (G-1777)	F	630 595-6055
County Tool & Die — Litchfield (G-12962)	G	217 324-6527
Custom Cuttingedge Tool Inc — Batavia (G-1370)	G	847 622-0457
Custom Mold Services Inc — Mount Prospect (G-14525)	F	847 364-6589
Cutting Edge Industries Inc — Franklin Park (G-9923)	G	847 678-1777
D & D Manufacturing Inc — Bolingbrook (G-2163)	F	888 300-6869
D & D Tooling and Mfg Inc — Bolingbrook (G-2164)	D	888 300-6869
D & D Tooling Inc — Bolingbrook (G-2165)	C	630 759-0015
D C T/Precision LLC — Decatur (G-7481)	F	217 475-0141
D E Specialty Tool & Mfg Inc — Franklin Park (G-9925)	E	847 678-0004
D M C Mold & Tool Corp — Cary (G-3152)	E	847 639-3098
D S Precision Tool Company — Downers Grove (G-7982)	E	630 627-0696
Daley Automation LLC — Naperville (G-14812)	G	630 384-9900
Davis Machine Company Inc — Joliet (G-11854)	G	815 723-9121
Dec Tool Corp — Saint Charles (G-18181)	E	630 513-9883
Decore Tool & Mfg Inc — Carol Stream (G-2975)	F	630 681-9760
Dice Mold & Engineering Inc — Itasca (G-11642)	E	630 773-3595
Die Darrell — Eureka (G-9480)	G	309 282-9112
Die Specialty Co — La Grange Park (G-12096)	G	312 303-5738
Dies Plus Inc — Carpentersville (G-3100)	F	630 285-1065
Do-Rite Die & Engineering Co — S Chicago Hts (G-18120)	F	708 754-4355
Domeny Tool & Stamping Company — Wauconda (G-20342)	F	847 526-5700
Double M Machine Inc — Fairbury (G-9605)	F	815 692-4676
Dovee Manufacturing Inc — Elgin (G-8569)	F	847 437-8122
E-Lite Tool & Mfg Co — Belleville (G-1548)	F	618 236-1580
East Side Tool & Die Co Inc — Caseyville (G-3212)	F	618 397-1633
Eberle Manufacturing Company — Wheeling (G-20885)	F	847 215-0100
Embeddedkits — Streamwood (G-19572)	G	847 401-7488
Engineering Design & Dev — Morton (G-14359)	E	309 266-6298
Extrusion Tooling Technology — Wauconda (G-20350)	F	847 526-1606
Fabrik Industries Inc — McHenry (G-13743)	B	815 385-9480
Federal Signal Corporation — Oak Brook (G-15618)	D	630 954-2000
Fidelity Tool & Mold Ltd — Batavia (G-1377)	F	630 879-2300
Ford Tool & Machining Inc — Loves Park (G-13211)	D	815 633-5727
Forster Products Inc — Lanark (G-12481)	E	815 493-6360
Forster Tool & Mfg Co Inc — Bensenville (G-1802)	E	630 616-8177
Frankfort Machine & Tools Inc — Frankfort (G-9796)	G	815 469-9902
G & J Hall Tools Inc — Lombard (G-13081)	G	314 968-5040
G & M Die Casting Company Inc — Wood Dale (G-21192)	D	630 595-2340
Gage Grinding Company Inc — Cary (G-3161)	F	847 639-3888
Gage Tool & Manufacturing Inc — Elk Grove Village (G-9010)	G	847 640-1069
General Forging Die Co Inc — Rockford (G-17428)	E	815 874-4224
Genesis Mold Corp — Libertyville (G-12654)	G	847 573-9431
Geo T Schmidt Inc — Niles (G-15124)	D	847 647-7117
George Hansen & Co Inc — Addison (G-139)	F	630 628-8700
Gerhard Designing & Mfg Inc — Bridgeview (G-2349)	E	708 599-4664
Global Tool & Die Inc — Elk Grove Village (G-9016)	G	847 956-1200
H&H Die Manufacturing Inc — Frankfort (G-9799)	G	708 479-6267
Hansels Custom Tech Inc — Sheridan (G-18889)	G	815 496-2345
Header Die and Tool Inc — Rockford (G-17445)	D	815 397-0123
Helm Tool Company Incorporated — Elk Grove Village (G-9033)	E	847 952-9528
HI Prcision Tl Makers McHy Inc — Bensenville (G-1818)	G	630 694-0200
Hill Engineering Inc — Carol Stream (G-2998)	E	630 315-5070
Hoffman Tool Inc — Fairbury (G-9608)	E	815 692-4643
Icon Metalcraft Inc — Wood Dale (G-21200)	C	630 766-5600
Idea Tool & Manufacturing Co — Chicago (G-4874)	E	312 476-1080
Iemco Corporation — Chicago (G-4878)	G	773 728-4400
Imperial Punch & Manufacturing — Rockford (G-17457)	F	815 226-8200
IMS Olson LLC — Downers Grove (G-8030)	D	630 969-9400
Industrial Park Machine & Tool — S Chicago Hts (G-18122)	F	708 754-7080
International Cutting Die Inc — Melrose Park (G-13884)	E	708 343-3333
J & J Carbide & Tool Inc — Alsip (G-459)	E	708 489-0300
J H Benedict Co Inc — East Peoria (G-8270)	D	309 694-3111
J R Mold Inc — Streamwood (G-19578)	G	630 289-2192
Jamco Tool & Cams Inc — Franklin Park (G-9972)	F	847 678-0280
Jasco Tool & Manufacturing — McHenry (G-13751)	G	815 271-5158
JC Tool and Mold Inc — Streamwood (G-19580)	G	630 483-2203
JC Tooling Company Inc — Nashville (G-14998)	F	618 327-9379
Jensen and Son Inc — Sycamore (G-19719)	G	815 895-3855
JM Tool & Die LLC — Bensenville (G-1832)	G	630 616-7776
Kam Tool and Mold — Woodstock (G-21397)	G	815 338-8360
Kazmier Tooling Inc — Chicago (G-5087)	G	773 586-0300
Kenmode Tool and Engrg Inc — Algonquin (G-376)	C	847 658-5041
Kensen Tool & Die Inc — Franklin Park (G-9976)	F	847 455-0150
Ki Machine Tools & Productions — Loves Park (G-13229)	G	815 484-9216
Kleen Cut Tool Inc — Warrenville (G-20240)	G	630 447-7020
Kosmos Tool Inc — Spring Grove (G-19281)	F	815 675-2200
Kreis Tool & Mfg Co Inc — Elgin (G-8639)	E	847 289-3700
Kyowa Industrial Co Ltd USA — Wheeling (G-20927)	F	847 459-3500
L T L Co — Rockford (G-17488)	F	815 874-0913
Lenhardt Tool and Die Company — Alton (G-563)	D	618 462-1075
Lew-El Tool & Manufacturing Co — Chicago (G-5212)	F	773 804-1133
Line Group Inc — Arlington Heights (G-769)	E	847 593-6810
Lion Tool & Die Co — Algonquin (G-377)	F	847 658-8898
Lorette Dies Inc — Elmhurst (G-9393)	G	630 279-9682
M S Tool & Engineering — West Chicago (G-20610)	F	630 876-3437
M-1 Tool Works Inc — McHenry (G-13761)	E	815 344-1275
Manor Tool and Mfg Co — Schiller Park (G-18820)	D	847 678-2020
Marathon Cutting Die Inc — Wheeling (G-20938)	E	847 398-5165
Master Tech Tool Inc — McHenry (G-13764)	G	815 363-4001
McCurdy Tool & Machining Co — Caledonia (G-2770)	D	815 765-2117
Micro Mold Corporation — Addison (G-206)	G	630 628-0777
Micron Engineering Co — Crystal Lake (G-7228)	G	815 455-2888
Mid-States Forging Die-Tool — Rockford (G-17524)	G	815 226-2313
Midwest Machine Tool Inc — Saint Anne (G-18136)	G	815 427-8665
Midwest Press Brake Dies Inc — Bridgeview (G-2366)	F	708 598-3860
Mik Tool & Die Co Inc — Wauconda (G-20377)	G	847 487-4311
Monarch Tool & Die Co — Elmhurst (G-9403)	G	630 530-8886
Mt Vernon Mold Works Inc — Mount Vernon (G-14629)	F	618 242-6040
Natura Products Inc — Northbrook (G-15439)	F	847 509-5835
Newko Tool & Engineering Co — Palatine (G-16142)	G	847 359-1670
Octavia Tool & Gage Company — Elk Grove Village (G-9159)	G	847 913-9233
Odom Tool and Technology Inc — Sycamore (G-19726)	G	815 895-8545
Ontario Die USA — Batavia (G-1401)	F	630 761-6562
P & L Tool & Manufacturing Co — Steger (G-19491)	G	708 754-4777
Panzer Tool Corp — Lombard (G-13116)	G	630 519-5214
Partners Manufacturing Inc — Schaumburg (G-18668)	E	847 352-1080
Pelco Tool & Mold Inc — Glendale Heights (G-10483)	G	630 871-1010
Performance Stamping Co Inc — Carpentersville (G-3112)	E	847 426-2233
Precision Process Corp — Elk Grove Village (G-9192)	E	847 640-9820
Precision Tool & Die Company — Mount Zion (G-14649)	F	217 864-3371
Pro-Tech Metal Specialties Inc — Elmhurst (G-9412)	G	630 279-7094
Procraft Engraving Inc — Skokie (G-19013)	G	847 673-1500
Production Fabg & Stamping Inc — S Chicago Hts (G-18126)	F	708 755-5468
Qualitek Manufacturing Inc — Gurnee (G-10920)	E	847 336-7570
Quality Tool & Machine Inc — Chicago (G-5931)	G	773 721-8655
Radius Machine & Tool Inc — Gurnee (G-10922)	F	847 662-7690
Rapid Manufacturing Inc — Algonquin (G-386)	G	847 458-0888
Ravco Incorporated — Joliet (G-11923)	G	815 725-9095
Ray Tool & Engineering Inc — Saint Charles (G-18260)	E	630 587-0000
Reliable Die Service Inc — Bedford Park (G-1498)	F	708 458-5155
Relyon Metal Products Co — Elgin (G-8719)	G	847 679-1510
Reynolds Manufacturing Company — Milan (G-14025)	E	309 787-8600
Risk Never Die Inc — Chicago (G-6035)	G	708 240-4194
Rockford Tool and Mfg Co — Rockford (G-17607)	F	815 398-5876
Rockford Toolcraft Inc — Rockford (G-17608)	C	815 398-5507
Rockford Toolcraft Inc — Rockford (G-17609)	E	815 398-5507
Roto-Die Company Inc — Lombard (G-13125)	G	630 932-8605
Schwarz Bros Manufacturing Co — Galesburg (G-10220)	G	309 342-5814
Select Die & Tool Inc — Bartlett (G-1308)	G	630 372-0300
Select Tool & Die Inc — Roselle (G-17986)	G	630 980-8458
Serv-All Die & Tool Company — Crystal Lake (G-7263)	D	815 459-2900

PRODUCT SECTION

DISPLAY ITEMS: Corrugated, Made From Purchased Materials

Shelby Tool & Die Inc .... G 217 774-2189
  Shelbyville *(G-18886)*
Shup Tool & Machine Co .... G 618 931-2596
  Granite City *(G-10737)*
Sieber Tooling Solutions Inc .... G 630 462-9370
  Carol Stream *(G-3069)*
Sopher Design & Manufacturing .... G 309 699-6419
  East Peoria *(G-8291)*
Spannagel Tool & Die .... E 630 969-7575
  Downers Grove *(G-8098)*
Specific Press Brake Dies Inc .... F 708 478-1776
  Mokena *(G-14116)*
Standard Machine & Tool Corp .... F 309 762-6431
  Moline *(G-14179)*
Stanick Tool Manufacturing Co .... G 847 726-7090
  Lake Zurich *(G-12461)*
Sterling Die Inc .... G 216 267-1300
  Glendale Heights *(G-10500)*
Summit Tooling Inc .... F 815 385-7500
  McHenry *(G-13798)*
Synergetic Holdings LLC .... F 309 673-2437
  Peoria *(G-16533)*
T & H Lemont Inc .... D 708 482-1800
  Countryside *(G-7074)*
Taylor Design Inc .... G 815 389-3991
  Roscoe *(G-17936)*
Technical Tool Enterprise .... G 630 893-3390
  Addison *(G-304)*
Tella Tool & Mfg Co .... C 630 495-0545
  Lombard *(G-13142)*
Three Star Mfg Co Inc .... G 847 526-2222
  Wauconda *(G-20399)*
Titan Tool Company Inc .... G 847 671-0045
  Franklin Park *(G-10061)*
Tower Tool & Engineering Inc .... F 815 654-1115
  Machesney Park *(G-13378)*
Tri-Par Die and Mold Corp .... E 630 232-8800
  South Elgin *(G-19177)*
Tri-Star Engineering Inc .... E 847 595-3377
  Elk Grove Village *(G-9285)*
Tri-State Tool & Design Inc .... G 217 696-2477
  Camp Point *(G-2812)*
Ultra Polishing Inc .... E 630 635-2926
  Schaumburg *(G-18762)*
Unified Tool Die & Mfg Co Inc .... F 847 678-3773
  Schiller Park *(G-18848)*
United Skilled Inc .... G 815 874-9696
  Rockford *(G-17671)*
United Tool and Engineering Co .... D 815 389-3021
  South Beloit *(G-19118)*
Urway Design and Manufacturing .... G 847 674-7464
  Skokie *(G-19051)*
Vhd Inc .... E 815 544-2169
  Belvidere *(G-1708)*
Wagner Midwest Die Supply Inc .... G 630 782-6230
  Elmhurst *(G-9444)*
West End Tool & Die Inc .... G 815 462-3040
  New Lenox *(G-15068)*
Westwood Machine & Tool Co .... F 815 626-5090
  Sterling *(G-19542)*
WJ Die Mold Inc .... F 847 895-6561
  Schaumburg *(G-18775)*
World Wide Rotary Die .... G 630 521-9410
  Bensenville *(G-1915)*

DIES: Cutting, Exc Metal

Atlas Die LLC .... D 630 351-5140
  Glendale Heights *(G-10436)*

DIES: Extrusion

Best Metal Extrusions Inc .... E 847 981-0797
  Elk Grove Village *(G-8865)*

DIES: Paper Cutting

Best Cutting Die Co .... C 847 675-5522
  Skokie *(G-18929)*

DIES: Plastic Forming

Witte Kendel Die & Mold .... G 815 233-9270
  Freeport *(G-10150)*

DIES: Steel Rule

Alcon Tool & Mfg Co Inc .... F 773 545-8742
  Chicago *(G-3598)*
C & S Steel Rule Die Co Inc .... G 773 254-4027
  Chicago *(G-3994)*
Converting Technology Inc .... D 847 290-0590
  Elk Grove Village *(G-8912)*
Dax Steel Rule Dies Inc .... G 708 448-4436
  Orland Park *(G-15950)*
Die Cut Group Inc .... F 630 629-9211
  Lombard *(G-13065)*
Die Pros Inc .... G 630 543-2025
  Addison *(G-93)*
Die World Steel Rule Dies .... G 815 399-8675
  Rockford *(G-17378)*
Durabuilt Die Corp .... G 847 437-2086
  Elk Grove Village *(G-8958)*
F & S Engraving Inc .... E 847 870-8400
  Mount Prospect *(G-14527)*
Johnson Steel Rule & Die .... G 708 547-1726
  Bellwood *(G-1630)*
Johnson Steel Rule Die Co .... F 773 921-4334
  Chicago *(G-5046)*
Mid-City Die & Mold Corp .... G 773 278-4844
  Chicago *(G-5430)*
Precise Rotary Die Inc .... E 847 678-0001
  Schiller Park *(G-18834)*
Triangle Dies and Supplies Inc .... D 630 454-3200
  Batavia *(G-1434)*
Windy City Cutting Die Inc .... E 630 521-9410
  Bensenville *(G-1913)*

DIES: Wire Drawing & Straightening

Southern Steel and Wire Inc .... G 618 654-2161
  Highland *(G-11240)*

DIODES: Light Emitting

Bare Development Inc .... F 708 352-2273
  Countryside *(G-7044)*
Integrated Lighting Tech Inc .... G 630 750-3786
  Bolingbrook *(G-2193)*
LED Rite LLC .... G 847 683-8000
  Hampshire *(G-10977)*
Luminaid Lab LLC .... G 312 600-8997
  Chicago *(G-5284)*
Lynk Labs Inc .... G 847 783-0123
  Elgin *(G-8643)*
Solid State Luminaires LLC .... G 877 775-4733
  Saint Charles *(G-18272)*
Tech Oasis International Inc .... F 847 302-1590
  Gurnee *(G-10934)*

DIRECT SELLING ESTABLISHMENTS, NEC

Nak Won Korean Bakery .... G 773 588-8769
  Chicago *(G-5538)*

DIRECT SELLING ESTABLISHMENTS: Beverage Svcs

Boombox Beverage LLC .... G 312 607-1038
  Skokie *(G-18930)*

DIRECT SELLING ESTABLISHMENTS: Food, Mobile, Exc Coffee-Cart

Cindys Pocket Kitchen .... G 815 388-8385
  Harvard *(G-11050)*

DIRECT SELLING ESTABLISHMENTS: Milk Delivery

Oberweis Dairy Inc .... F 847 368-9060
  Arlington Heights *(G-782)*
Oberweis Dairy Inc .... E 630 906-6455
  Oswego *(G-16017)*
Oberweis Dairy Inc .... E 708 660-1350
  Oak Park *(G-15767)*
Oberweis Dairy Inc .... F 630 782-0141
  Elmhurst *(G-9407)*
Oberweis Dairy Inc .... F 847 290-9222
  Rolling Meadows *(G-17757)*
Oberweis Dairy Inc .... E 630 801-6100
  Glen Ellyn *(G-10415)*

DIRECT SELLING ESTABLISHMENTS: Telemarketing

Darwill Inc .... C 708 449-7770
  Hillside *(G-11335)*
Evo Exhibits LLC .... G 630 520-0710
  West Chicago *(G-20577)*

DISINFECTING SVCS

Wet International Inc .... E 630 540-2113
  Streamwood *(G-19602)*

DISK DRIVES: Computer

Ckd USA Corporation .... E 847 368-0539
  Schaumburg *(G-18478)*
Xlogotech Inc .... G 888 244-5152
  Palatine *(G-16177)*

DISKETTE DUPLICATING SVCS

Abbey Products LLP .... G 636 922-5577
  Troy *(G-19909)*

DISKS & DRUMS Magnetic

Magna-Flux International .... G 815 623-7634
  Roscoe *(G-17914)*

DISPENSING EQPT & PARTS, BEVERAGE: Beer

Banner Equipment Co .... E 815 941-9600
  Morris *(G-14294)*
Leaders Bev Consulting Inc .... F 312 497-5602
  Chicago *(G-5190)*

DISPENSING EQPT & PARTS, BEVERAGE: Coolers, Milk/Water, Elec

Elkay Manufacturing Company .... C 815 493-8850
  Lanark *(G-12480)*
Elkay Manufacturing Company .... G 800 223-5529
  Downers Grove *(G-7999)*
Haskris Co .... D 847 956-6420
  Elk Grove Village *(G-9028)*

DISPENSING EQPT & PARTS, BEVERAGE: Fountain/Other Beverage

Cornelius Inc .... B 630 539-6850
  Glendale Heights *(G-10445)*
Natural Choice Corporation .... F 815 874-4444
  Loves Park *(G-13240)*
Perfection Equipment Inc .... E 847 244-7200
  Gurnee *(G-10911)*

DISPENSING EQPT & PARTS, BEVERAGE: Fountains, Parts/Access

American Soda Ftn Exch Inc .... F 312 733-5000
  Chicago *(G-3668)*

DISPLAY CASES: Refrigerated

John F Mate Co .... G 847 381-8131
  Lake Barrington *(G-12154)*

DISPLAY FIXTURES: Showcases, Wood, Exc Refrigerated

Redbox Workshop Ltd .... E 773 478-7077
  Chicago *(G-5993)*

DISPLAY FIXTURES: Wood

Duo Usa Incorporated .... G 312 421-7755
  Chicago *(G-4407)*
Laminated Components Inc .... E 815 648-4811
  Hebron *(G-11146)*
Marv-O-Lus Manufacturing Co .... F 773 826-1717
  Chicago *(G-5353)*
Multiplex Display Fixture Co .... E 800 325-3350
  Dupo *(G-8141)*
Pac Team US Productions LLC .... G 773 360-8960
  Chicago *(G-5736)*
Proto Productions Inc .... E 630 628-6626
  Addison *(G-257)*
Ww Displays Inc .... F 847 566-6979
  Mundelein *(G-14747)*

DISPLAY ITEMS: Corrugated, Made From Purchased Materials

Kodiak LLC .... E 773 284-9975
  Chicago *(G-5116)*
Precision Die Cutting & Finish .... G 773 252-5625
  Chicago *(G-5856)*
Sonoco Display & Packaging LLC .... F 630 789-1111
  Westmont *(G-20773)*

DISPLAY ITEMS: Solid Fiber, Made From Purchased Materials

Ameriguard Corporation ....G....... 630 986-1900
  Burr Ridge *(G-2652)*

DISPLAY LETTERING SVCS

Effingham Signs & Graphics ....G....... 217 347-8711
  Effingham *(G-8398)*
Signature Screen Printing Corp ....G....... 773 866-0070
  Chicago *(G-6169)*

DISTILLERS DRIED GRAIN & SOLUBLES

Mega Equipment Inc ....G....... 309 764-5310
  Moline *(G-14160)*
Mid-Oak Distillery Inc ....F....... 708 926-9131
  Posen *(G-16797)*

DIVING EQPT STORES

Scuba Sports Inc ....G....... 217 787-3483
  Springfield *(G-19440)*

DOCK EQPT & SPLYS, INDL

H and D Distribution Inc ....G....... 847 247-2011
  Libertyville *(G-12656)*

DOCKS: Marinas, Prefabricated, Wood

Bitter End Yacht Club Intl ....F....... 312 506-6205
  Chicago *(G-3902)*

DOCKS: Prefabricated Metal

Hadley Capital Fund II LP ....G....... 847 906-5300
  Wilmette *(G-21076)*

DOCUMENT EMBOSSING SVCS

510 Holdings Company LLC ....F....... 618 659-8600
  Edwardsville *(G-8343)*

DOLOMITE: Crushed & Broken

Covia Holdings Corporation ....G....... 618 747-2355
  Tamms *(G-19742)*
Mill Creek Mining Inc ....G....... 309 787-1414
  Milan *(G-14017)*

DOOR & WINDOW REPAIR SVCS

Boom Company Inc ....G....... 847 459-6199
  Wheeling *(G-20863)*

DOOR FRAMES: Concrete

Jgr Commercial Solutions Inc ....G....... 847 669-7010
  Huntley *(G-11545)*

DOOR FRAMES: Wood

Alliance Door and Hardware LLC ....G....... 630 451-7070
  Hillside *(G-11326)*

DOOR MATS: Rubber

Superior Mfg Group - Europe ....G....... 708 458-4600
  Chicago *(G-6283)*

DOOR OPERATING SYSTEMS: Electric

Assa Abloy ACC Door Cntrls Gro ....D....... 704 283-2101
  Franklin Park *(G-9876)*
Assa Abloy Entrance Systems US ......F....... 847 228-5600
  Elk Grove Village *(G-8843)*
Chamberlain Group Inc ....B....... 630 279-3600
  Oak Brook *(G-15606)*
Chamberlain Manufacturing Corp ....A....... 630 279-3600
  Oak Brook *(G-15608)*
Gate Systems Corporation ....G....... 847 731-6700
  Gurnee *(G-10882)*
Kamstra Door Service Inc ....G....... 708 895-9990
  Lansing *(G-12500)*
Mi-Jack Systems & Tech LLC ....F....... 708 596-3780
  Hazel Crest *(G-11134)*
Pro Access Systems Inc ....F....... 630 426-0022
  Elburn *(G-8470)*

DOORS & WINDOWS WHOLESALERS: All Materials

A-Ok Inc ....E....... 815 943-7431
  Harvard *(G-11039)*
Absolute Windows Inc ....E....... 708 599-9191
  Oak Lawn *(G-15693)*
Carpenters Millwork Co ....F....... 708 339-7707
  South Holland *(G-19204)*
Carpenters Millwork Co ....F....... 708 339-7707
  Villa Park *(G-20137)*
Fox Valley Windows LLC ....G....... 630 210-6400
  Aurora *(G-963)*
Kramer Window Co ....G....... 708 343-4780
  Maywood *(G-13671)*
Salem Building Materials Inc ....G....... 618 548-3221
  Salem *(G-18357)*
Specialty Crate Factory ....G....... 708 756-2100
  Steger *(G-19492)*

DOORS & WINDOWS: Screen & Storm

Aluminite of Paris ....G....... 217 463-2233
  Paris *(G-16224)*
Del Storm Products Inc ....F....... 217 446-3377
  Danville *(G-7330)*
Tri State Aluminum Products ....F....... 815 877-6081
  Loves Park *(G-13277)*

DOORS & WINDOWS: Storm, Metal

Allmetal Inc ....E....... 630 766-8500
  Bensenville *(G-1736)*
Kramer Window Co ....G....... 708 343-4780
  Maywood *(G-13671)*
Lang Exterior Inc ....D....... 773 737-4500
  Chicago *(G-5175)*
Tempco Products Co ....D....... 618 544-3175
  Robinson *(G-17127)*

DOORS: Fire, Metal

Fix It Fast Ltd ....F....... 708 401-8320
  Midlothian *(G-13991)*

DOORS: Folding, Plastic Or Plastic Coated Fabric

Mueller Door Company ....E....... 815 385-8550
  Wauconda *(G-20379)*

DOORS: Garage, Overhead, Metal

Builders Chicago Corporation ....D....... 224 654-2122
  Rosemont *(G-18001)*
C B M Plastics Inc ....F....... 217 543-3870
  Arthur *(G-843)*
Hormann LLC ....C....... 630 859-3000
  Montgomery *(G-14248)*
Neisewander Enterprises Inc ....A....... 815 288-1431
  Dixon *(G-7904)*
Overhead Door Corporation ....G....... 630 775-9118
  Itasca *(G-11715)*
Raynor Mfg Co ....A....... 815 288-1431
  Dixon *(G-7908)*

DOORS: Garage, Overhead, Wood

Allied Garage Door Inc ....E....... 630 279-0795
  Addison *(G-27)*
Clopay Building Pdts Co Inc ....G....... 708 346-0901
  Chicago Ridge *(G-6791)*
Micanan Systems Inc ....G....... 630 501-1909
  Addison *(G-204)*
Neisewander Enterprises Inc ....A....... 815 288-1431
  Dixon *(G-7904)*

DOORS: Glass

Clear View Industries Inc ....G....... 815 267-3593
  Plainfield *(G-16652)*
Doralco ....E....... 708 388-9324
  Alsip *(G-441)*

DOORS: Hangar, Metal

Erect-A-Tube Inc ....E....... 815 943-4091
  Harvard *(G-11054)*

DOORS: Rolling, Indl Building Or Warehouse, Metal

Allied Garage Door Inc ....E....... 630 279-0795
  Addison *(G-27)*
Entrematic HPD North Amer Inc ....D....... 847 562-4910
  Mundelein *(G-14687)*
Power-Sonic Corporation ....G....... 309 752-7750
  East Moline *(G-8236)*
Steel-Guard Safety Corp ....G....... 708 589-4588
  South Holland *(G-19246)*

DOORS: Safe & Vault, Metal

Promus Equity Partners LLC ....F....... 312 784-3990
  Chicago *(G-5903)*

DOORS: Screen, Metal

Midwest Screens LLC ....G....... 847 557-5015
  Antioch *(G-626)*
Quanex Screens LLC ....G....... 217 463-2233
  Paris *(G-16242)*

DOORS: Wooden

Accurate Cstm Sash Mllwk Corp ....G....... 708 423-0423
  Oak Lawn *(G-15694)*
Custom Crafted Door Inc ....F....... 309 527-5075
  El Paso *(G-8435)*
Decore-Ative Specialties ....B....... 630 947-6294
  Cary *(G-3155)*
Geo J Rothan Co ....E....... 309 674-5189
  Peoria *(G-16445)*
Harold Prefinished Wood Inc ....F....... 618 548-1414
  Salem *(G-18342)*
Janik Custom Millwork Inc ....G....... 708 482-4844
  Hodgkins *(G-11390)*
Jeld-Wen Inc ....D....... 217 893-4444
  Rantoul *(G-16978)*
Landquist & Son Inc ....E....... 847 674-6600
  Mokena *(G-14094)*
Masonite Corporation ....G....... 630 584-6330
  West Chicago *(G-20616)*
Nelson Door Co ....G....... 217 543-3489
  Arthur *(G-871)*
Overhead Door Corporation ....G....... 630 775-9118
  Itasca *(G-11715)*
Richard King and Sons ....G....... 815 654-0226
  Loves Park *(G-13253)*
Torblo Inc ....G....... 815 941-2684
  Morris *(G-14333)*

DOWELS & DOWEL RODS

Excel Group Holdings Inc ....E....... 630 773-1815
  Itasca *(G-11653)*

DOWNSPOUTS: Sheet Metal

Chicago Mtal Sup Fbrcation Inc ....F....... 773 227-6200
  Chicago *(G-4119)*

DRAFTING SPLYS WHOLESALERS

Numeridex Incorporated ....F....... 847 541-8840
  Wheeling *(G-20948)*

DRAFTING SVCS

Associated Design Inc ....F....... 708 974-9100
  Palos Hills *(G-16195)*

DRAINAGE PRDTS: Concrete

Southern Illinois Stone Co ....F....... 573 334-5261
  Buncombe *(G-2629)*

DRAINING OR PUMPING OF METAL MINES

Ave Inc ....G....... 815 727-0153
  Joliet *(G-11825)*

DRAPERIES & CURTAINS

A B Kelly Inc ....G....... 847 639-1022
  Cary *(G-3142)*
Baker Drapery Corporation ....G....... 309 691-3295
  Dunlap *(G-8132)*
Berg Industries Inc ....F....... 815 874-1588
  Rockford *(G-17318)*
Dezign Sewing Inc ....G....... 773 549-4336
  Chicago *(G-4349)*

PRODUCT SECTION

DRUGS & DRUG PROPRIETARIES, WHOLESALE: Pharmaceuticals

Dons Drapery Service .... G 815 385-4759
  McHenry *(G-13737)*
Drapery Room Inc .... F 708 301-3374
  Homer Glen *(G-11478)*
Draperyland Inc .... F 630 521-1000
  Wood Dale *(G-21182)*
Drexel House of Drapes Inc .... G 618 624-5415
  Belleville *(G-1547)*
Interior Fashions Contract .... G 847 358-6050
  Palatine *(G-16131)*
Logoskirt Corporation .... F 773 584-7300
  Chicago *(G-5251)*
Medline Industries Inc .... G 618 283-4036
  Vandalia *(G-20014)*
Robert Harlan Ernst .... G 217 627-3401
  Girard *(G-10385)*
Roberts Draperies Center Inc .... G 847 255-4040
  Mount Prospect *(G-14567)*
Shade Aire Company .... G 815 623-7597
  Roscoe *(G-17933)*
Tazewell Floor Covering Inc .... F 309 266-6371
  Morton *(G-14386)*
Tenggren-Mehl Co Inc .... G 773 763-3290
  Chicago *(G-6349)*
Tres Joli Designs Ltd .... G 847 520-3903
  Wheeling *(G-21001)*
Zirlin Interiors Inc .... E 773 334-5530
  Chicago *(G-6720)*

DRAPERIES & DRAPERY FABRICS, COTTON

A B C Blind Inc .... G 708 877-7100
  Thornton *(G-19784)*
Annas Draperies & Associates .... G 773 282-1365
  Chicago *(G-3699)*
Drapery Room Inc .... F 708 301-3374
  Homer Glen *(G-11478)*
F & L Drapery Inc .... G 815 932-8997
  Saint Anne *(G-18134)*
Kempco Window Treatments Inc .... E 708 754-4484
  Chicago Heights *(G-6755)*
Robert Harlan Ernst .... G 217 627-3401
  Girard *(G-10385)*

DRAPERIES: Plastic & Textile, From Purchased Materials

A D Specialty Sewing .... G 847 639-0390
  Fox River Grove *(G-9756)*
Aracon Drpery Vntian Blind Ltd .... G 773 252-1281
  Chicago *(G-3717)*
E J Self Furniture .... G 847 394-0899
  Arlington Heights *(G-731)*
North-West Drapery Service .... G 773 282-7117
  Chicago *(G-5622)*
Shade Brookline Co .... F 773 274-5513
  Chicago *(G-6145)*
Slagel Drapery Service .... G 815 692-3834
  Fairbury *(G-9613)*
Tailored Inc .... G 708 387-9854
  Brookfield *(G-2493)*
Unitex Industries Inc .... G 708 524-0664
  Oak Park *(G-15777)*
Whiteside Drapery Fabricators .... F 847 746-5300
  Zion *(G-21530)*

DRAPERY & UPHOLSTERY STORES: Curtains

Annas Draperies & Associates .... G 773 282-1365
  Chicago *(G-3699)*

DRAPERY & UPHOLSTERY STORES: Draperies

Afar Imports & Interiors Inc .... G 217 744-3262
  Springfield *(G-19316)*
Draperyland Inc .... F 630 521-1000
  Wood Dale *(G-21182)*
Drexel House of Drapes Inc .... G 618 624-5415
  Belleville *(G-1547)*
Hansens Mfrs Win Coverings .... E 815 935-0010
  Bradley *(G-2284)*
Roberts Draperies Center Inc .... G 847 255-4040
  Mount Prospect *(G-14567)*
Tres Joli Designs Ltd .... G 847 520-3903
  Wheeling *(G-21001)*

DRAPES & DRAPERY FABRICS, FROM MANMADE FIBER

Robert Harlan Ernst .... G 217 627-3401
  Girard *(G-10385)*

DRIED FRUITS WHOLESALERS

TEC Foods Inc .... E 800 315-8002
  Chicago *(G-6333)*

DRILL BITS

Galaxy Industries Inc .... D 847 639-8580
  Cary *(G-3162)*
Irwin Industrial Tool Company .... C 815 235-4171
  Freeport *(G-10121)*
Mincon Inc .... E 618 435-3404
  Benton *(G-1932)*
Quality Tech Tool Inc .... E 847 690-9643
  Bensenville *(G-1880)*
Tru-Cut Inc .... D 847 639-2090
  Cary *(G-3195)*

DRILLING MACHINERY & EQPT: Oil & Gas

Dover Corporation .... C 630 541-1540
  Downers Grove *(G-7989)*
Oil Filter Recyclers Inc .... E 309 329-2131
  Astoria *(G-894)*

DRILLING MACHINERY & EQPT: Water Well

Azcon Inc .... E 815 548-7000
  Sterling *(G-19499)*
Innerweld Cover Co .... F 847 497-3009
  Mundelein *(G-14701)*
Maass - Midwest Mfg Inc .... E 847 669-5135
  Huntley *(G-11553)*

DRILLS & DRILLING EQPT: Mining

Midwest Machine Tool Inc .... G 815 427-8665
  Saint Anne *(G-18136)*

DRINK MIXES, NONALCOHOLIC: Cocktail

Jo Snow Inc .... G 773 732-3045
  Chicago *(G-5033)*

DRINKING FOUNTAINS: Metal, Nonrefrigerated

Elkay Manufacturing Company .... B 815 273-7001
  Savanna *(G-18404)*

DRINKING PLACES: Alcoholic Beverages

Andrias Food Group Inc .... E 618 632-4866
  O Fallon *(G-15565)*
Father Marcellos & Son .... C 312 654-2565
  Chicago *(G-4567)*
Goose Holdings Inc .... E 312 226-1119
  Chicago *(G-4718)*

DRINKING PLACES: Bars & Lounges

Common Culture Brewing Co .... F 847 584-2337
  Evanston *(G-9506)*
Haymarket Brewing Company LLC .... G 312 638-0700
  Chicago *(G-4789)*

DRINKING PLACES: Night Clubs

Tini Martini .... G 773 269-2900
  Chicago *(G-6381)*

DRINKING PLACES: Tavern

Broken Oar Inc .... G 847 639-9468
  Port Barrington *(G-16785)*

DRINKING PLACES: Wine Bar

Galena Cellars Winery .... E 815 777-3330
  Galena *(G-10169)*

DRINKING WATER COOLERS WHOLESALERS: Mechanical

Natural Choice Corporation .... F 815 874-4444
  Loves Park *(G-13240)*
Superior Water Services Inc .... G 309 691-9287
  Peoria *(G-16531)*

DRIVE CHAINS: Bicycle Or Motorcycle

Wrench .... G 773 609-1698
  Chicago *(G-6684)*

DRIVE SHAFTS

Aluminum Drive Line Products .... G 708 946-9777
  Beecher *(G-1516)*
Dana Driveshaft Mfg LLC .... E 815 626-6700
  Sterling *(G-19504)*
Drive Shaft Unlimited Inc .... G 708 447-2211
  Lyons *(G-13307)*
Johnson Power Ltd .... E 708 345-4300
  Broadview *(G-2445)*
Quarter Master Industries Inc .... E 847 540-8999
  Lake Zurich *(G-12447)*
Suburban Driveline Inc .... G 630 941-7101
  Villa Park *(G-20174)*
Surge Clutch & Drive Line Co .... G 708 331-1352
  South Holland *(G-19247)*

DRIVES: High Speed Indl, Exc Hydrostatic

Arrow Gear Company .... B 630 969-7640
  Downers Grove *(G-7955)*

DRIVES: Hydrostatic

Hydro-Gear Inc .... C 217 728-2581
  Sullivan *(G-19668)*
Kocsis Technologies Inc .... G 708 597-4177
  Alsip *(G-467)*

DROP CLOTHS: Fabric

Chicago Dropcloth Tarpaulin Co .... E 773 588-3123
  Chicago *(G-4100)*

DRUG STORES

Bridgeport Pharmacy Inc .... G 312 791-9000
  Chicago *(G-3956)*
Jewel Osco Inc .... C 847 882-6477
  Hoffman Estates *(G-11432)*
Prescription Plus Ltd .... F 618 537-6202
  Lebanon *(G-12546)*

DRUG TESTING KITS: Blood & Urine

First Step Womens Center .... G 217 523-0100
  Springfield *(G-19369)*

DRUGS & DRUG PROPRIETARIES, WHOLESALE

Medexus Pharma Inc .... G 312 854-0500
  Chicago *(G-5382)*

DRUGS & DRUG PROPRIETARIES, WHOLESALE: Animal Medicines

First Priority Inc .... D 847 531-1215
  Elgin *(G-8587)*

DRUGS & DRUG PROPRIETARIES, WHOLESALE: Medicinals/Botanicals

GE Healthcare Holdings Inc .... A 847 398-8400
  Arlington Heights *(G-741)*
Green Thumb Industries Inc .... F 312 471-6720
  Chicago *(G-4740)*
Upper Limits Midwest Inc .... G 217 679-4315
  Springfield *(G-19467)*

DRUGS & DRUG PROPRIETARIES, WHOLESALE: Pharmaceuticals

Avocet Polymer Tech Inc .... G 773 523-2872
  Chicago *(G-3788)*
Daito Pharmaceuticals Amer Inc .... G 847 205-0800
  Northbrook *(G-15372)*
Espee Biopharma & Finechem LLC .... G 888 851-6667
  Schaumburg *(G-18521)*
Fresenius Kabi Usa Inc .... B 708 450-7500
  Melrose Park *(G-13869)*
Jewel Osco Inc .... C 847 882-6477
  Hoffman Estates *(G-11432)*
Lundbeck LLC .... C 847 282-1000
  Deerfield *(G-7631)*
Owp Pharmaceuticals Inc .... F 331 871-7424
  Naperville *(G-14890)*

Employee Codes: A=Over 500 employees, B=251-500
C=101-250, D=51-100, E=20-50, F=10-19, G=3-9

DRUGS & DRUG PROPRIETARIES, WHOLESALE: Pharmaceuticals

Ravens Wood Pharmacy ....G...... 708 667-0525
  Chicago *(G-5976)*
Sagent Pharmaceuticals Inc ....C...... 847 908-1600
  Schaumburg *(G-18701)*
Sagent Pharmaceuticals Inc ....D...... 847 908-1600
  Schaumburg *(G-18702)*
Symbria Rx Services LLC ....E...... 630 981-8000
  Woodridge *(G-21342)*

DRUGS & DRUG PROPRIETARIES, WHOLESALE: Vitamins & Minerals

Glanbia Performance Ntrtn Inc ....F...... 630 236-0097
  Aurora *(G-970)*
Glanbia Prfmce Ntrtn NA Inc ....C...... 630 236-0097
  Downers Grove *(G-8012)*
Healthy Life Nutraceutics Inc........................G...... 201 253-9053
  Deerfield *(G-7613)*
Hollywood Traders LLC ....G...... 630 943-6461
  Lombard *(G-13085)*
Natures Sources LLC ....G...... 847 663-9168
  Niles *(G-15151)*
Vital Proteins LLC ....C...... 224 544-9110
  Chicago *(G-6561)*

DRUGS ACTING ON THE CENTRAL NERVOUS SYSTEM & SENSE ORGANS

Allergan Inc ....G...... 714 246-4500
  Gurnee *(G-10858)*
Assertio Holdings Inc ....B...... 224 419-7106
  Lake Forest *(G-12227)*
Assertio Therapeutics Inc.............................D...... 224 419-7106
  Lake Forest *(G-12228)*

DRUMS: Brake

Ascent Tranz Group LLC ....G...... 844 424-7347
  Chicago *(G-3747)*
Winhere Brake Parts Inc ....G...... 630 307-0158
  Bartlett *(G-1324)*

DRUMS: Fiber

Fibre Drum Company ....E...... 815 933-3222
  Kankakee *(G-11971)*
Greif Inc ....E...... 630 961-1842
  Naperville *(G-14837)*

DRUMS: Magnetic

Estad Stamping & Mfg Co ....E...... 217 442-4600
  Danville *(G-7331)*

DRUMS: Shipping, Metal

Meyer Steel Drum Inc ....E...... 773 522-3030
  Chicago *(G-5416)*
Meyer Steel Drum Inc ....C...... 773 376-8376
  Chicago *(G-5417)*
Mobile Mini Inc ....E...... 708 297-2004
  Calumet Park *(G-2799)*
Zorin Material Handling Co ....G...... 773 342-3818
  Chicago *(G-6724)*

DRYCLEANING & LAUNDRY SVCS: Commercial & Family

Workshop ....E...... 815 777-2211
  Galena *(G-10183)*

DRYCLEANING EQPT & SPLYS: Commercial

Eminent Technologies LLC ....G...... 630 416-2311
  Naperville *(G-14824)*

DRYERS & REDRYERS: Indl

Henderson Engineering Co Inc ....G...... 815 786-9471
  Sandwich *(G-18374)*
Paul D Stark & Associates ....F...... 630 964-7111
  Downers Grove *(G-8070)*

DUCTING: Metal Plate

Mach Mechanical Group LLC ....G...... 630 674-6224
  Naperville *(G-14978)*

DUCTS: Sheet Metal

Air-Duct Manufacturing Inc ....G...... 630 620-9866
  Aurora *(G-1045)*

Cleats Mfg Inc ....F...... 773 521-0300
  Chicago *(G-4175)*
Crawford Heating & Cooling Co ....D...... 309 788-4573
  Rock Island *(G-17211)*
Daniel & Sons Mech Contrs Inc ....F...... 618 997-2822
  Marion *(G-13509)*
Lindemann Chimney Service Inc ....F...... 847 918-7994
  Lake Bluff *(G-12193)*
Macari Service Center Inc ....F...... 217 774-4214
  Shelbyville *(G-18881)*
Safe-Air of Illinois Inc ....E...... 708 652-9100
  Cicero *(G-6873)*
Sheet Metal Connectors Inc ....F...... 815 874-4600
  Rockford *(G-17629)*
Synergy Mechanical Inc ....G...... 708 410-1004
  Westchester *(G-20713)*

DUMBWAITERS

Otis Elevator Company ....F...... 618 529-3411
  Carbondale *(G-2852)*

DUMPSTERS: Garbage

Captain Hook Inc ....G...... 309 565-7676
  Hanna City *(G-10991)*
Cheap Dumpster For Rent ....G...... 773 770-4334
  Chicago *(G-4080)*
D & P Construction Co Inc ....E...... 773 714-9330
  Chicago *(G-4299)*
Dumpster Dave LLC ....G...... 618 475-3835
  Lenzburg *(G-12610)*
Tri-State Disposal Inc ....E...... 708 388-9910
  Riverdale *(G-17077)*

DURABLE GOODS WHOLESALERS, NEC

AEP Inc ....G...... 618 466-7668
  Alton *(G-542)*

DUST OR FUME COLLECTING EQPT: Indl

Blowers LLC ....E...... 708 594-1800
  Elmhurst *(G-9336)*
Bost Corporation ....E...... 708 344-7023
  Maywood *(G-13663)*
Custom Systems Inc ....G...... 314 355-4575
  Granite City *(G-10702)*
Dekalb Blower Inc ....F...... 630 553-8831
  Yorkville *(G-21478)*
Dustcatchers Inc ....G...... 773 768-1440
  Chicago *(G-4414)*

DYES & PIGMENTS: Organic

Clariant Plas Coatings USA LLC ....D...... 630 562-9700
  West Chicago *(G-20562)*
Polyone Corporation ....D...... 847 364-0011
  Elk Grove Village *(G-9183)*

DYNAMOMETERS

Star Test Dynamometer Inc........................G...... 309 452-0371
  Normal *(G-15225)*

EARTH SCIENCE SVCS

Toppert Jetting Service Inc ....G...... 309 755-2240
  East Moline *(G-8244)*

EARTHS: Ground Or Otherwise Treated

Oil-Dri Corporation America ....D...... 312 321-1515
  Chicago *(G-5666)*

EATING PLACES

Abbey Ridge LLC ....G...... 618 713-2537
  Pomona *(G-16762)*
Aero Alehouse LLC ....G...... 815 977-5602
  Loves Park *(G-13183)*
Amity Packing Company Inc ....C...... 312 942-0270
  Chicago *(G-3680)*
Campeche Restaurant Inc ....G...... 815 776-9950
  Galena *(G-10166)*
Consumers Packing Co Inc ....D...... 708 344-0047
  Melrose Park *(G-13844)*
Coopers Hawk Intrmdate Hldg LL ....C...... 708 839-2920
  Downers Grove *(G-7981)*
Coopers Hawk Intrmdate Hldg LL ....F...... 708 215-5674
  Countryside *(G-7048)*
Copper Dock ....G...... 618 669-2675
  Pocahontas *(G-16751)*

Cornerstone Communications ....E...... 773 989-2087
  Chicago *(G-4236)*
Doreens Pizza Inc ....F...... 708 862-7499
  Calumet City *(G-2775)*
Elis Cheesecake Company ....C...... 773 205-3800
  Chicago *(G-4485)*
Express Donuts Enterprise Inc ....F...... 630 510-9310
  Wheaton *(G-20798)*
Gonnella Baking Co ....D...... 312 733-2020
  Schaumburg *(G-18538)*
Hidden Hollow Stables Inc ....G...... 309 243-7979
  Dunlap *(G-8133)*
Homers Ice Cream Inc ....E...... 847 251-0477
  Wilmette *(G-21078)*
Italia Foods Inc ....C...... 847 397-4479
  Schaumburg *(G-18573)*
Jewel Osco Inc ....C...... 815 464-5352
  Frankfort *(G-9810)*
Kernel Kutter Inc ....E...... 815 877-1515
  Machesney Park *(G-13354)*
Lau Nae Winery Inc ....G...... 618 282-9463
  Red Bud *(G-16997)*
Lynfred Winery Inc ....E...... 630 529-9463
  Roselle *(G-17965)*
Mariegold Bake Shoppe ....G...... 773 561-1978
  Chicago *(G-5335)*
Marion Oelze ....G...... 618 327-9224
  Nashville *(G-15001)*
Meats By Linz Inc ....E...... 708 862-0830
  Calumet City *(G-2783)*
Napco Inc ....G...... 630 406-1100
  Batavia *(G-1397)*
Niemann Foods Inc ....C...... 217 222-0190
  Quincy *(G-16918)*
Niemann Foods Inc ....C...... 217 793-4091
  Springfield *(G-19411)*
Plochman Inc ....E...... 815 468-3434
  Manteno *(G-13454)*
Ron & Pats Pizza Shack ....G...... 847 395-5005
  Antioch *(G-633)*
Royal Oak Farm Inc ....F...... 815 648-4141
  Harvard *(G-11066)*
Schau Southeast Sushi Inc ....E...... 630 783-1000
  Woodridge *(G-21339)*
Schnuck Markets Inc ....C...... 618 466-0825
  Godfrey *(G-10663)*
Union Foods Inc ....G...... 201 327-2828
  Chicago *(G-6465)*

ECCLESIASTICAL WARE, NEC

Empire Bronze Corp ....F...... 630 916-9722
  Lombard *(G-13073)*

EDUCATIONAL PROGRAM ADMINISTRATION, GOVT: Level Of Govt

Max Fire Training Inc ....F...... 618 210-2079
  Godfrey *(G-10656)*

EDUCATIONAL SVCS

Care Education Group Inc ....G...... 708 361-4110
  Palos Park *(G-16208)*
Great Books Foundation ....E...... 312 332-5870
  Chicago *(G-4732)*
Iep Quality Inc ....G...... 217 840-0570
  Champaign *(G-3305)*
LMS Innovations Inc ....C...... 312 613-2345
  Chicago *(G-5247)*
Mold Shields Inc ....G...... 708 983-5931
  Oak Forest *(G-15686)*
Peopleadmin Inc ....E...... 877 637-5800
  Chicago *(G-5786)*
Thinkcercacom Inc ....F...... 224 412-3722
  Chicago *(G-6365)*
Yesimpact ....G...... 765 413-9667
  Darien *(G-7415)*

EDUCATIONAL SVCS, NONDEGREE GRANTING: Continuing Education

National Association Realtors ....C...... 800 874-6500
  Chicago *(G-5543)*

ELASTIC BRAID & NARROW WOVEN FABRICS

Lea & Sachs Inc ....F...... 847 296-8000
  Des Plaines *(G-7796)*

ELASTOMERS

Miner Elastomer Products Corp............E....... 630 232-3000
  Geneva *(G-10290)*

ELECTRIC FENCE CHARGERS

Invisible Fencing of Quad City............G....... 309 797-1688
  Moline *(G-14151)*

ELECTRIC MOTOR & GENERATOR AUXILIARY PARTS

Ruby Automation LLC..........................F....... 815 624-5959
  South Beloit *(G-19112)*
Ruby Automation LLC..........................F....... 847 273-9050
  Schaumburg *(G-18699)*
Torqeedo Inc..G....... 815 444-8806
  Crystal Lake *(G-7284)*

ELECTRIC MOTOR REPAIR SVCS

Accurate Elc Mtr & Pump Co...............G....... 708 448-2792
  Worth *(G-21453)*
Addison Electric Inc..............................E....... 800 517-4871
  Addison *(G-19)*
All Electric Mtr Repr Svc Inc................F....... 773 925-2404
  Chicago *(G-3609)*
Apex Industrial Automation LLC..........G....... 866 924-2808
  Romeoville *(G-17795)*
Armature Motor & Pump Company......G....... 309 829-3600
  East Peoria *(G-8251)*
Avana Electric Motors Inc....................F....... 847 588-0400
  Elk Grove Village *(G-8850)*
Bak Electric..G....... 708 458-3578
  Bridgeview *(G-2327)*
Bellwood Electric Motors Inc...............G....... 708 544-7223
  Bellwood *(G-1615)*
BP Elc Mtrs Pump & Svc Inc................G....... 773 539-4343
  Skokie *(G-18931)*
Calumet Armature and Elc LLC...........E....... 708 841-6880
  Riverdale *(G-17070)*
Cameron Electric Motor Corp..............F....... 312 939-5770
  Chicago *(G-4012)*
Decatur Industrial Elc Inc.....................E....... 217 428-6621
  Decatur *(G-7487)*
Dependable Electric..............................G....... 618 592-3314
  Oblong *(G-15826)*
Dreisilker Electric Motors Inc...............C....... 630 469-7510
  Glen Ellyn *(G-10401)*
Eastland Industries Inc........................G....... 708 547-6500
  Hillside *(G-11339)*
Ebling Electric Company......................F....... 312 455-1885
  Chicago *(G-4441)*
Elmot Inc..G....... 773 791-7039
  Chicago *(G-4489)*
Erbes Electric..G....... 815 849-5508
  Sublette *(G-19636)*
First Electric Motor Shop Inc...............G....... 217 698-0672
  Springfield *(G-19368)*
Flolo Corporation..................................E....... 630 595-1010
  West Chicago *(G-20585)*
Four-Most Inc..G....... 563 323-3233
  Peoria *(G-16440)*
Gem Electric Motor Repair..................G....... 815 756-5317
  Dekalb *(G-7682)*
Goding Electric Company.....................F....... 630 858-7700
  Glendale Heights *(G-10455)*
H & H Motor Service Inc......................G....... 708 652-6100
  Cicero *(G-6850)*
Harvey Bros Inc....................................F....... 309 342-3137
  Galesburg *(G-10199)*
Heise Industries Inc..............................G....... 847 223-2410
  Grayslake *(G-10781)*
Hills Electric Motor Service..................G....... 815 625-0305
  Rock Falls *(G-17184)*
Hopcroft Electric Inc.............................G....... 618 288-7302
  Glen Carbon *(G-10388)*
Iesco Inc...E....... 708 594-1250
  Romeoville *(G-17831)*
Illinois Electric Works Inc.....................E....... 618 451-6900
  Granite City *(G-10717)*
Industrial Service Solutions.................C....... 917 609-6979
  Chicago *(G-4910)*
Inman Electric Motors Inc....................E....... 815 223-2288
  La Salle *(G-12115)*
J & J Electric Motor Repair Sp............G....... 217 529-0015
  Springfield *(G-19391)*
Joes Automotive...................................G....... 815 937-9281
  Kankakee *(G-11982)*
Kankakee Industrial Tech.....................F....... 815 933-6683
  Bradley *(G-2285)*

Lakenburges Motor Co.........................G....... 618 523-4231
  Germantown *(G-10331)*
Lange Electric Inc.................................G....... 217 347-7626
  Effingham *(G-8407)*
Lee Foss Electric Motor Svc................G....... 708 681-5335
  Stone Park *(G-19556)*
M H Electric Motor & Ctrl Corp............G....... 630 393-3736
  Warrenville *(G-20242)*
Metzka Inc...G....... 815 932-6363
  Kankakee *(G-11991)*
Midwest Elc Mtr Inc Danville...............G....... 217 442-5656
  Danville *(G-7367)*
Park Electric Motor Service.................G....... 217 442-1977
  Danville *(G-7372)*
Quality Armature Inc............................G....... 773 622-3951
  Chicago *(G-5929)*
Rockford Electric Equipment Co.........G....... 815 398-4096
  Rockford *(G-17593)*
Sandner Electric Co Inc........................G....... 618 932-2179
  West Frankfort *(G-20682)*
Schaeffer Electric Co............................G....... 618 592-3231
  Oblong *(G-15829)*
Service Pro Electric Mtr Repr..............G....... 630 766-1215
  Bensenville *(G-1892)*
Steiner Electric Company....................E....... 312 421-7220
  Chicago *(G-6239)*
Vandalia Electric Mtr Svc Inc..............G....... 618 283-0068
  Vandalia *(G-20027)*
Voss Electric Inc...................................G....... 708 596-6000
  Harvey *(G-11100)*
Xylem Water Solutions USA Inc..........F....... 856 467-3636
  Mokena *(G-14129)*
Yaskawa America Inc...........................C....... 847 887-7000
  Waukegan *(G-20520)*

ELECTRIC WATER HEATERS WHOLESALERS

Metropolitan Industries Inc..................C....... 815 886-9200
  Romeoville *(G-17851)*

ELECTRICAL APPARATUS & EQPT WHOLESALERS

Ademco Inc..G....... 708 599-1390
  Bridgeview *(G-2319)*
Ademco Inc..E....... 847 472-2900
  Elk Grove Village *(G-8807)*
Arrow Edm Inc.......................................F....... 217 893-4277
  Rantoul *(G-16967)*
Automated Design Corp........................G....... 630 783-1150
  Romeoville *(G-17797)*
C R V Electronics Corp..........................D....... 815 675-6500
  Spring Grove *(G-19269)*
Calumet Armature and Elc LLC...........E....... 708 841-6880
  Riverdale *(G-17070)*
Chicago Chain and Transm Co............E....... 630 482-9000
  Countryside *(G-7046)*
Chicago Technical Sales Inc................G....... 630 889-7121
  Oakbrook Terrace *(G-15792)*
City Screen Inc......................................G....... 773 588-5642
  Chicago *(G-4161)*
Dalco Marketing Services....................G....... 630 961-3366
  Carol Stream *(G-2971)*
Dumore Supplies Inc............................F....... 312 949-6260
  Chicago *(G-4403)*
Eazypower Corporation.......................E....... 773 278-5000
  Chicago *(G-4439)*
Enersys..D....... 630 455-4872
  Lisle *(G-12889)*
Hallmark Industries Inc.........................F....... 847 301-8050
  Streamwood *(G-19577)*
Industrial Controls Inc..........................G....... 630 752-8100
  Geneva *(G-10278)*
Inter-Market Inc.....................................G....... 847 729-5330
  Glenview *(G-10570)*
Min Sheng Technology Inc...................G....... 815 569-4496
  Schaumburg *(G-18631)*
Motor Coach Industries........................G....... 847 285-2000
  Des Plaines *(G-7805)*
New Cie Inc...E....... 815 224-1511
  Peru *(G-16584)*
New Cie Inc...F....... 815 224-1485
  La Salle *(G-12118)*
North Point Investments Inc................G....... 312 977-4386
  Chicago *(G-5620)*
Numeridex Incorporated......................F....... 847 541-8840
  Wheeling *(G-20948)*
Ogwuru Uzoaku.....................................G....... 312 286-5593
  Chicago *(G-5664)*

Panduit Corp...A....... 708 532-1800
  Tinley Park *(G-19848)*
Panduit Corp...E....... 815 836-1800
  Lockport *(G-13018)*
Rockford Electric Equipment Co.........G....... 815 398-4096
  Rockford *(G-17593)*
Special Mine Services Inc....................D....... 618 932-2151
  West Frankfort *(G-20684)*
Standard Electric Supply Inc................G....... 217 239-0800
  Champaign *(G-3354)*
Tent Maker Industrial Sup Inc.............G....... 847 469-6070
  Wauconda *(G-20398)*
V and F Transformer Corp...................D....... 630 497-8070
  Elgin *(G-8771)*
Wesco International Inc.......................G....... 630 513-4864
  Elmhurst *(G-9445)*

ELECTRICAL APPLIANCES, TELEVISIONS & RADIOS WHOLESALERS

AVI-Spl Employee.................................B....... 847 437-7712
  Schaumburg *(G-18453)*
Cco Holdings LLC..................................G....... 618 505-3505
  Troy *(G-19912)*
Cco Holdings LLC..................................G....... 618 651-6486
  Highland *(G-11208)*
Portable Cmmnctons Spclsts...............G....... 630 458-1800
  Addison *(G-246)*

ELECTRICAL CONSTRUCTION MATERIALS WHOLESALERS

Matrix North Amercn Cnstr Inc............G....... 312 754-6605
  Chicago *(G-5366)*

ELECTRICAL CURRENT CARRYING WIRING DEVICES

ABB Power Protection LLC...................F....... 804 236-3300
  Chicago *(G-3501)*
Aco Inc...E....... 773 774-5200
  Chicago *(G-3529)*
Alan Manufacturing Corp.....................G....... 815 568-6836
  Marengo *(G-13478)*
Alcon Tool & Mfg Co Inc.......................F....... 773 545-8742
  Chicago *(G-3598)*
American Bare Conductor Inc.............E....... 815 224-3422
  La Salle *(G-12102)*
Belden Energy Solutions Inc................G....... 800 235-3361
  Elmhurst *(G-9330)*
Connector Concepts Inc......................F....... 847 541-4020
  Mundelein *(G-14680)*
CTS Automotive LLC.............................C....... 630 577-8800
  Lisle *(G-12880)*
Dcx-Chol Enterprises Inc.....................E....... 309 353-4455
  Pekin *(G-16327)*
Dqm Inc..F....... 630 692-0633
  Montgomery *(G-14243)*
Excel Specialty Corp.............................E....... 773 262-7575
  Lake Forest *(G-12248)*
Flex-Weld Inc...D....... 815 334-3662
  Woodstock *(G-21387)*
Gateway Cable Inc................................F....... 630 766-7969
  Lisle *(G-12893)*
General Electric Company...................C....... 309 664-1513
  Bloomington *(G-2050)*
Grayhill Inc...C....... 847 428-6990
  Carpentersville *(G-3102)*
Grayhill Inc...G....... 708 482-1411
  Mc Cook *(G-13691)*
Gus Berthold Electric Company...........D....... 312 243-5767
  Chicago *(G-4752)*
Hauhinco LP..E....... 618 993-5399
  Marion *(G-13514)*
Heil Sound Ltd......................................F....... 618 257-3000
  Fairview Heights *(G-9646)*
Hubbell Incorporated...........................F....... 972 756-1184
  Aurora *(G-1110)*
Ideal Industries Inc..............................C....... 815 895-1108
  Sycamore *(G-19715)*
Ideal Industries Inc..............................C....... 815 895-5181
  Sycamore *(G-19716)*
Ideal Industries Inc..............................C....... 815 895-5181
  Sycamore *(G-19714)*
IL Tool Work..G....... 630 972-6400
  Bolingbrook *(G-2189)*
Illinois Tool Works Inc..........................C....... 847 724-7500
  Des Plaines *(G-7784)*
Inglot Electronics Corp........................D....... 773 286-5881
  Chicago *(G-4921)*

Employee Codes: A=Over 500 employees, B=251-500
C=101-250, D=51-100, E=20-50, F=10-19, G=3-9

2020 Harris Illinois Industrial Directory

Ki Industries Inc ....E 708 449-1990
Berkeley (G-1941)
Leviton Manufacturing Co Inc ....C 630 443-0500
Saint Charles (G-18226)
Lutamar Electrical Assemblies ....E 847 679-5400
Skokie (G-18981)
M E Barber Co Inc ....G 217 428-4591
Decatur (G-7518)
Magnetrol International Inc ....C 630 723-6600
Aurora (G-1001)
Methode Development Co ....D 708 867-6777
Chicago (G-5408)
Methode Electronics Inc ....C 847 577-9545
Rolling Meadows (G-17750)
Methode Electronics Inc ....A 217 357-3941
Carthage (G-3139)
Methode Electronics Inc ....B 708 867-6777
Chicago (G-5409)
Micro West Ltd ....G 630 766-7160
Bensenville (G-1850)
Midwest Fiber Solutions ....G 217 971-7400
Springfield (G-19407)
Mpc Products Corporation ....G 847 673-8300
Niles (G-15150)
Porch Electric LLC ....G 815 368-3230
Lostant (G-13177)
Process Screw Products Inc ....E 815 864-2220
Shannon (G-18872)
Rockford Rigging Inc ....F 309 263-0566
Roscoe (G-17926)
S & C Electric Company ....A 773 338-1000
Chicago (G-6083)
S-P Products Inc ....F 847 593-8595
Elk Grove Village (G-9227)
Safco LLC ....E 847 677-3204
Skokie (G-19026)
Simplex Inc ....C 217 483-1600
Springfield (G-19446)
Skach Manufacturing Co Inc ....E 847 395-3560
Antioch (G-635)
Switchcraft Inc ....B 773 792-2700
Chicago (G-6299)
Switchcraft Holdco Inc ....G 773 792-2700
Chicago (G-6300)
Twin City Electric Inc ....E 309 827-0636
Bloomington (G-2105)
U S Tool & Manufacturing Co ....E 630 953-1000
Addison (G-321)
United Universal Inds Inc ....E 815 727-4445
Joliet (G-11939)
Unlimited Svcs Wisconsin Inc ....E 815 399-0282
Machesney Park (G-13383)
Western-Cullen-Hayes Inc ....D 773 254-9600
Chicago (G-6609)
Woodward Controls Inc ....C 847 673-8300
Skokie (G-19058)

ELECTRICAL DISCHARGE MACHINING, EDM

Abet Industries Corporation ....G 708 482-8282
La Grange Park (G-12094)
Alicona Manufacturing Inc ....G 630 736-2718
Bartlett (G-1263)
EDM Scorpio Inc ....G 847 931-5164
Elgin (G-8573)
Electroform Company ....E 815 633-1113
Machesney Park (G-13341)
Inventive Mfg Inc ....F 847 647-9500
Skokie (G-18969)
Master Cut E D M Inc ....G 847 534-0343
Schaumburg (G-18622)
Xact Wire EDM Corp ....F 847 516-0903
Cary (G-3197)

ELECTRICAL EQPT & SPLYS

AAC Microtec North America Inc ....E 602 284-7997
Columbia (G-6982)
Aemm A Electric ....G 708 403-6700
Orland Park (G-15935)
Agrowtek Inc ....G 847 380-3009
Gurnee (G-10854)
Aim Inc ....G 630 941-0027
Elmhurst (G-9322)
Ambient Lightning and Electric ....G 708 529-3434
Oak Lawn (G-15700)
Associate General Labs Inc ....G 847 678-2717
Franklin Park (G-9877)
Azz Incorporated ....D 815 723-5000
Joliet (G-11826)
Bechara Sim ....F 847 913-9950
Buffalo Grove (G-2514)
Blg McC Enterprises Inc ....E 847 455-0188
Franklin Park (G-9888)
Carey Electric Co Inc ....G 847 949-9294
Grayslake (G-10761)
Cdc Enterprises Inc ....G 815 790-4205
Johnsburg (G-11802)
Cecomp Electronics Inc ....E 847 918-3510
Libertyville (G-12642)
Chamberlain Group Inc ....F 630 705-0300
Addison (G-67)
Chamberlain Group Inc ....E 630 279-3600
Oak Brook (G-15607)
Connor Electric Services Inc ....E 630 823-8230
Schaumburg (G-18485)
Custom Tool Inc ....F 217 465-8538
Paris (G-16228)
Domino Amjet Inc ....E 847 662-3148
Gurnee (G-10869)
E N M Company ....D 773 775-8400
Chicago (G-4425)
East West Martial Arts Sups ....G 773 878-7711
Chicago (G-4434)
Elec Easel ....G 815 444-9700
Crystal Lake (G-7196)
Electri-Flex Company ....D 630 529-2920
Roselle (G-17952)
Electro-Technic Products Inc ....F 773 561-2349
Chicago (G-4478)
Elenco Electronics Inc ....E 847 541-3800
Wheeling (G-20889)
Enginuity Communications Corp ....E 630 444-0778
Saint Charles (G-18198)
Extreme Flight Simulation ....G 224 656-5546
Gurnee (G-10877)
Eztech Manufacturing Inc ....F 630 293-0010
West Chicago (G-20582)
Gerardo and Quintana Auto Elc ....G 773 424-0634
Chicago (G-4686)
Giba Electric ....G 773 685-4420
Chicago (G-4690)
Global Manufacturing ....G 630 908-7633
Willowbrook (G-21045)
Heuft Usa Inc ....F 630 395-9521
Downers Grove (G-8021)
Hopcroft Electric Inc ....G 618 288-7302
Glen Carbon (G-10388)
Hubbell Power Systems Inc ....F 618 797-5000
Edwardsville (G-8365)
IMS Engineered Products LLC ....C 847 391-8100
Des Plaines (G-7787)
Industrial Enclosure Corp ....E 630 898-7499
Aurora (G-1111)
Inventus Power (illinois) LLC ....C 630 410-7900
Woodridge (G-21317)
James J Sandoval ....G 734 717-7555
Lombard (G-13089)
Jardis Industries Inc ....F 630 773-5600
Itasca (G-11681)
Jescorp Inc ....D 847 378-1200
Elk Grove Village (G-9068)
Kavanaugh Electric Inc ....G 708 503-1310
Frankfort (G-9812)
Kaybee Engineering Company Inc ....E 630 968-7100
Westmont (G-20751)
Kohns Electric ....G 309 463-2331
Varna (G-20032)
Lecip Inc ....F 312 626-2525
Bensenville (G-1842)
Lutamar Electrical Assemblies ....E 847 679-5400
Skokie (G-18981)
Magnetrol International Inc ....C 630 723-6600
Aurora (G-1001)
Marmon Engineered Components ....G 312 372-9500
Chicago (G-5341)
Mason Electric ....G 618 457-8900
Carterville (G-3133)
Midwest Tool Inc ....G 773 588-1313
Chicago (G-5449)
Migatron Corporation ....E 815 338-5800
Woodstock (G-21411)
Motor Sport Marketing Group ....E 618 654-6750
Highland (G-11232)
Newhaven Display Intl Inc ....E 847 844-8795
Elgin (G-8668)
Occly LLC ....G 773 969-5080
Chicago (G-5652)
Omron Electronics LLC ....D 847 843-7900
Hoffman Estates (G-11442)
Panduit Corp ....A 708 532-1800
Tinley Park (G-19848)
Panduit Corp ....E 815 836-1800
Lockport (G-13018)
Powertech Systems ....G 847 553-1867
Wauconda (G-20383)
Prime Devices Corporation ....F 847 729-2550
Willow Springs (G-21027)
Protection Controls Inc ....E 773 763-3110
Skokie (G-19017)
Raynor Mfg Co ....A 815 288-1431
Dixon (G-7908)
Roundtble Hlthcare Partners LP ....E 847 739-3200
Lake Forest (G-12299)
Scis Air Security Corporation ....G 847 671-9502
Schiller Park (G-18843)
Sparton Onyx Holdings LLC ....G 847 762-5800
Schaumburg (G-18720)
Spurt Inc ....G 847 571-6497
Northbrook (G-15486)
Standard Electric Supply Inc ....G 217 239-0800
Champaign (G-3354)
Sustanable Infrastructures Inc ....G 815 341-1447
Frankfort (G-9842)
Tenneco Automotive Oper Co Inc ....C 847 482-5000
Lake Forest (G-12308)
Tii Technical Educatn Systems ....G 847 428-3085
Gilberts (G-10373)
Toho Technology Inc ....G 773 583-7183
Chicago (G-6385)
Unified Tool Die & Mfg Co Inc ....F 847 678-3773
Schiller Park (G-18848)
United Universal Inds Inc ....E 815 727-4445
Joliet (G-11939)
Vlahos Electric Service Dr ....G 224 764-2335
Arlington Heights (G-828)
Wesco International Inc ....G 630 513-4864
Elmhurst (G-9445)
Wildlife Materials Inc ....E 618 687-3505
Murphysboro (G-14762)

ELECTRICAL EQPT FOR ENGINES

Aerodyne Incorporated ....G 773 588-2905
Chicago (G-3572)
Amerline Enterprises Co Inc ....E 847 671-6554
Schiller Park (G-18786)
Ark Technologies Inc ....D 630 377-8855
Saint Charles (G-18149)
Egan Wagner Corporation ....G 630 985-8007
Woodridge (G-21298)
Excel Specialty Corp ....E 773 262-7575
Lake Forest (G-12248)
Harvey Bros Inc ....F 309 342-3137
Galesburg (G-10199)
Innovation Specialists Inc ....G 815 372-9001
New Lenox (G-15037)
K & W Auto Electric ....F 217 857-1717
Teutopolis (G-19770)
Kold-Ban International Ltd ....E 847 658-8561
Lake In The Hills (G-12338)
Major Wire Incorporated ....F 708 457-0121
Norridge (G-15239)
Mat Engine Technologies LLC ....G 847 821-9630
Long Grove (G-13164)
MTA USA Corp ....G 847 847-5503
Elk Grove Village (G-9138)
Niles Auto Parts ....G 847 215-2549
Lincolnshire (G-12788)
W W Williams Company LLC ....F 309 756-1068
Rock Island (G-17253)

ELECTRICAL EQPT REPAIR & MAINTENANCE

A J R International Inc ....D 800 232-3965
Glendale Heights (G-10435)
Ad Deluxe Sign Company Inc ....G 815 556-8469
Blue Island (G-2109)
B J Fehr Machine Co ....G 309 923-8691
Roanoke (G-17099)
Caterpillar Globl Min Amer LLC ....D 618 982-9000
Carrier Mills (G-3124)
CB Machine & Tool Corp ....G 847 288-1807
Franklin Park (G-9901)
Century Signs Inc ....F 217 224-7419
Quincy (G-16871)
Clarios ....D 708 474-1717
Calumet City (G-2773)
Cooper Equipment Company Inc ....G 708 367-1291
Crete (G-7137)
Cox Electric Motor Service ....G 217 344-2458
Urbana (G-19980)

PRODUCT SECTION

ELECTRICAL GOODS, WHOLESALE: Motors

FH Ayer Manufacturing Co ....E...... 708 755-0550
  Chicago Heights *(G-6746)*
Industrial Welder Rebuilders ....G...... 708 371-5688
  Alsip *(G-457)*
Integrated Power Services LLC ....E...... 708 877-5310
  Thornton *(G-19789)*
Jacobs Boiler & Mech Inds Inc ....E...... 773 385-9900
  Chicago *(G-4998)*
Midwest Machine Service Inc ....F...... 708 229-1122
  Alsip *(G-479)*
Napier Machine & Welding Inc............G...... 217 525-8740
  Springfield *(G-19410)*
National Machine Repair Inc ....F...... 708 672-7711
  Crete *(G-7142)*
Niese Walter Machine Mfg Co ....G...... 773 774-7337
  Des Plaines *(G-7811)*
S-P-D Incorporated ....G...... 847 882-9820
  Palatine *(G-16156)*
Smart Inc..G...... 847 464-4160
  Hampshire *(G-10988)*
White Way Sign & Maint Co ....C...... 847 391-0200
  Chicago *(G-6619)*

ELECTRICAL EQPT REPAIR SVCS

Huygen Corporation ....F...... 815 455-2200
  Crystal Lake *(G-7207)*

ELECTRICAL EQPT: Automotive, NEC

Ark De Mexico LLC ....B...... 630 240-9483
  Saint Charles *(G-18148)*
Bill West Enterprises Inc ....G...... 217 886-2591
  Jacksonville *(G-11757)*
Carnation Enterprises ....G...... 847 804-5928
  Niles *(G-15108)*
County Packaging Inc ....D...... 708 597-1100
  Crestwood *(G-7114)*
Elc Industries Corp ....E...... 630 851-1616
  Aurora *(G-1088)*
Joes Automotive Inc ....G...... 815 937-9281
  Kankakee *(G-11982)*
Midtronics Inc....................................D...... 630 323-2800
  Willowbrook *(G-21050)*
Plasmatreat USA Inc ....F...... 847 783-0622
  Elgin *(G-8687)*
Southern Ill Auto Elec Inc ....F...... 618 587-3308
  Tilden *(G-19792)*

ELECTRICAL EQPT: Household

Eazypower Corporation ....E...... 773 278-5000
  Chicago *(G-4439)*
Eazypower Corporation ....G...... 773 278-5000
  Chicago *(G-4440)*
Intermountain Electronics Inc ....G...... 618 339-6743
  Centralia *(G-3235)*
Temple Display Ltd ....G...... 630 851-3331
  Oswego *(G-16026)*

ELECTRICAL GOODS, WHOL: Antennas, Receiving/Satellite Dishes

Good Vibes Sound Inc.......................F...... 217 351-0909
  Champaign *(G-3298)*

ELECTRICAL GOODS, WHOLESALE: Alarms & Signaling Eqpt

Siemens Industry Inc ....A...... 847 215-1000
  Buffalo Grove *(G-2600)*

ELECTRICAL GOODS, WHOLESALE: Batteries, Storage, Indl

Clarios LLC ....B...... 630 232-4270
  Geneva *(G-10260)*

ELECTRICAL GOODS, WHOLESALE: Burglar Alarm Systems

Audio Installers Inc...........................F...... 815 969-7500
  Loves Park *(G-13193)*

ELECTRICAL GOODS, WHOLESALE: Circuit Breakers

Chicago Circuits Corporation ....F...... 847 238-1623
  Elk Grove Village *(G-8891)*
Exide Technologies ....G...... 630 862-2200
  Lombard *(G-13074)*

ELECTRICAL GOODS, WHOLESALE: Citizens Band Radios

Wirelessusa Inc ....G...... 217 222-4300
  Quincy *(G-16957)*

ELECTRICAL GOODS, WHOLESALE: Connectors

Harting Inc of North America ....E...... 847 741-1500
  Elgin *(G-8609)*
Omnitronix Corporation ....F...... 630 837-1400
  Streamwood *(G-19587)*

ELECTRICAL GOODS, WHOLESALE: Electrical Appliances, Major

Appliance Repair.................................G...... 708 456-1020
  Norridge *(G-15230)*

ELECTRICAL GOODS, WHOLESALE: Electrical Entertainment Eqpt

Gb Marketing Inc ....F...... 847 367-0101
  Vernon Hills *(G-20055)*
Harman International Inds Inc ....D...... 847 996-8118
  Vernon Hills *(G-20059)*
Prager Associates ....G...... 309 691-1565
  Peoria *(G-16501)*

ELECTRICAL GOODS, WHOLESALE: Electronic Parts

Bea Electro Sales Inc.........................G...... 847 238-1420
  Elk Grove Village *(G-8859)*
Belford Electronics Inc ....E...... 630 705-3020
  Addison *(G-47)*
Bisco Intl Inc......................................G...... 708 544-6308
  Hillside *(G-11331)*
Dytec Midwest Inc ....G...... 847 255-3200
  Rolling Meadows *(G-17728)*
Hirose Electric (usa) Inc ....D...... 630 282-6700
  Downers Grove *(G-8024)*
Huygen Corporation ....F...... 815 455-2200
  Crystal Lake *(G-7207)*
Industrial Electronic Contrls ....F...... 815 873-1980
  Rockford *(G-17458)*
Japan Electronic Manufacturers ....F...... 972 735-0463
  Wilmette *(G-21080)*
Jme Technologies Inc.........................E...... 815 477-8800
  Crystal Lake *(G-7213)*
Marshall Wolf Automation Inc.............E...... 847 658-8130
  Algonquin *(G-378)*
Morrell Incorporated ....F...... 630 858-4600
  Glendale Heights *(G-10477)*
Nep Electronics Inc............................C...... 630 595-8500
  Wood Dale *(G-21221)*
Nidec Mobility America Corp ....A...... 630 443-6800
  Saint Charles *(G-18234)*
Nu-Way Electronics Inc ....E...... 847 437-7120
  Elk Grove Village *(G-9156)*
Omron Electronics LLC ....D...... 847 843-7900
  Hoffman Estates *(G-11442)*
Richardson Electronics Ltd ....C...... 630 208-2200
  Lafox *(G-12138)*

ELECTRICAL GOODS, WHOLESALE: Fans, Household

Df Fan Services Inc............................F...... 630 876-1495
  West Chicago *(G-20570)*

ELECTRICAL GOODS, WHOLESALE: Fire Alarm Systems

Flame Guard Usa LLC ....G...... 815 219-4074
  Vernon Hills *(G-20054)*
Global Fire Control Inc ....G...... 309 755-6352
  East Moline *(G-8227)*

ELECTRICAL GOODS, WHOLESALE: Flashlights

Datasource ....G...... 312 405-9152
  Calumet City *(G-2774)*

ELECTRICAL GOODS, WHOLESALE: Generators

Ees Inc ....G...... 708 343-1800
  Stone Park *(G-19553)*
Industrial Welder Rebuilders ....G...... 708 371-5688
  Alsip *(G-457)*
Kackert Enterprises Inc ....G...... 630 898-9339
  Aurora *(G-1120)*
Lionheart Critical Pow ....E...... 847 291-1413
  Huntley *(G-11552)*
Peoria Midwest Equipment Inc ....G...... 309 454-6800
  Normal *(G-15217)*
Unique Indoor Comfort........................F...... 847 362-1910
  Libertyville *(G-12719)*
Xform Power and Eqp Sups LLC ....G...... 773 260-0209
  Chicago *(G-6694)*

ELECTRICAL GOODS, WHOLESALE: High Fidelity Eqpt

Acoustic Avenue Inc ....F...... 217 544-9810
  Springfield *(G-19315)*

ELECTRICAL GOODS, WHOLESALE: Household Appliances, NEC

Mfp Holding Co ....G...... 312 666-3366
  Chicago *(G-5418)*

ELECTRICAL GOODS, WHOLESALE: Light Bulbs & Related Splys

Advanced Micro Lites Inc....................G...... 630 365-5450
  Elburn *(G-8442)*
Aero-Tech Light Bulb Co ....D...... 847 352-4900
  Schaumburg *(G-18430)*
Omnilight Inc ....G...... 773 696-1602
  Chicago *(G-5676)*
Stone Lighting LLC ....F...... 312 240-0400
  Flossmoor *(G-9703)*

ELECTRICAL GOODS, WHOLESALE: Lighting Fittings & Access

Rgb Lights Inc ....F...... 312 421-6080
  Chicago *(G-6021)*

ELECTRICAL GOODS, WHOLESALE: Lighting Fixtures, Comm & Indl

First Light Inc ....G...... 630 520-0017
  West Chicago *(G-20583)*
Holiday Bright Lights Inc ....G...... 312 226-8281
  Chicago *(G-4830)*
New Metal Crafts Inc..........................E...... 312 787-6991
  Lincolnwood *(G-12832)*

ELECTRICAL GOODS, WHOLESALE: Modems, Computer

Hologram Inc ....G...... 716 771-8308
  Chicago *(G-4831)*

ELECTRICAL GOODS, WHOLESALE: Motor Ctrls, Starters & Relays

Dreisilker Electric Motors Inc ....C...... 630 469-7510
  Glen Ellyn *(G-10401)*
Envirnmntal Ctrl Solutions Inc ....G...... 217 793-8966
  Springfield *(G-19363)*
Midwest Elc Mtr Inc Danville..............G...... 217 442-5656
  Danville *(G-7367)*

ELECTRICAL GOODS, WHOLESALE: Motors

Accurate Elc Mtr & Pump Co ....G...... 708 448-2792
  Worth *(G-21453)*
Addison Electric Inc ....E...... 800 517-4871
  Addison *(G-19)*
Altran Magnetics LLC ....G...... 815 632-3150
  Sterling *(G-19497)*
Avana Electric Motors Inc ....F...... 847 588-0400
  Elk Grove Village *(G-8850)*
Bellwood Electric Motors Inc..............G...... 708 544-7223
  Bellwood *(G-1615)*
Bodine Electric Company ....B...... 773 478-3515
  Northfield *(G-15509)*
BP Elc Mtrs Pump & Svc Inc ....G...... 773 539-4343
  Skokie *(G-18931)*

ELECTRICAL GOODS, WHOLESALE: Motors

Cox Electric Motor Service .... G 217 344-2458
 Urbana *(G-19980)*
Flolo Corporation .... G 847 249-0880
 Gurnee *(G-10878)*
Flolo Corporation .... E 630 595-1010
 West Chicago *(G-20585)*
Four-Most Inc .... G 563 323-3233
 Peoria *(G-16440)*
Gem Electric Motor Repair .... G 815 756-5317
 Dekalb *(G-7682)*
Goding Electric Company .... F 630 858-7700
 Glendale Heights *(G-10455)*
Heise Industries Inc .... G 847 223-2410
 Grayslake *(G-10781)*
Hills Electric Motor Service .... G 815 625-0305
 Rock Falls *(G-17184)*
Hopcroft Electric Inc .... G 618 288-7302
 Glen Carbon *(G-10388)*
Industrial Service Solutions .... C 917 609-6979
 Chicago *(G-4910)*
Inman Electric Motors Inc .... E 815 223-2288
 La Salle *(G-12115)*
J Ream Manufacturing .... G 630 983-6945
 Naperville *(G-14852)*
Kankakee Industrial Tech .... F 815 933-6683
 Bradley *(G-2285)*
Lange Electric Inc .... G 217 347-7626
 Effingham *(G-8407)*
M R Glenn Electric Inc .... E 708 479-9200
 Lockport *(G-13009)*
Metzka Inc .... G 815 932-6363
 Kankakee *(G-11991)*
Park Electric Motor Service .... G 217 442-1977
 Danville *(G-7372)*
Richards Electric Motor Co .... E 217 222-7154
 Quincy *(G-16940)*
Roberts Electric Company .... G 773 725-7323
 Chicago *(G-6044)*
Ruby Automation LLC .... F 847 273-9050
 Schaumburg *(G-18699)*
Sandner Electric Co Inc .... G 618 932-2179
 West Frankfort *(G-20682)*
Spg Usa Inc .... G 847 439-4949
 Schaumburg *(G-18723)*
Union Special LLC .... C 847 669-5101
 Huntley *(G-11572)*
Vandalia Electric Mtr Svc Inc .... G 618 283-0068
 Vandalia *(G-20027)*
Yaskawa America Inc .... C 847 887-7909
 Des Plaines *(G-7869)*
Yaskawa America Inc .... C 847 887-7000
 Waukegan *(G-20520)*

ELECTRICAL GOODS, WHOLESALE: Paging & Signaling Eqpt

Visiplex Inc .... F 847 229-0250
 Buffalo Grove *(G-2618)*

ELECTRICAL GOODS, WHOLESALE: Panelboards

Industrial Electric Svc Inc .... G 708 997-2090
 Bartlett *(G-1289)*

ELECTRICAL GOODS, WHOLESALE: Radio Parts & Access, NEC

Amis Inc .... G 708 598-9700
 Bridgeview *(G-2323)*

ELECTRICAL GOODS, WHOLESALE: Resistors

Ohmite Holding LLC .... E 847 258-0300
 Warrenville *(G-20243)*

ELECTRICAL GOODS, WHOLESALE: Safety Switches

Bircher America Inc .... G 847 952-3730
 Schaumburg *(G-18462)*

ELECTRICAL GOODS, WHOLESALE: Security Control Eqpt & Systems

Ionit Technologies Inc .... E 847 205-9651
 Northfield *(G-15518)*
No Surrender Inc .... F 773 929-7920
 Chicago *(G-5607)*

ELECTRICAL GOODS, WHOLESALE: Semiconductor Devices

Component Sales Incorporated .... F 630 543-9666
 Addison *(G-78)*

ELECTRICAL GOODS, WHOLESALE: Signaling, Eqpt

Autonomous Stuff LLC .... G 309 291-0966
 Morton *(G-14353)*
Nafisco Inc .... F 815 372-3300
 Romeoville *(G-17858)*

ELECTRICAL GOODS, WHOLESALE: Sound Eqpt

Amplivox Sound Systems LLC .... E 800 267-5486
 Northbrook *(G-15336)*
Rexroat Sound .... G 309 764-1663
 Colona *(G-6978)*

ELECTRICAL GOODS, WHOLESALE: Switchboards

Power Distribution Eqp Co Inc .... E 847 455-2500
 Franklin Park *(G-10021)*

ELECTRICAL GOODS, WHOLESALE: Switches, Exc Electronic, NEC

Data Accessories Inc .... G 847 669-3640
 Huntley *(G-11533)*

ELECTRICAL GOODS, WHOLESALE: Telephone & Telegraphic Eqpt

Wescom Products .... G 217 932-5292
 Casey *(G-3209)*

ELECTRICAL GOODS, WHOLESALE: Telephone Eqpt

AT&T Teleholdings Inc .... F 800 288-2020
 Chicago *(G-3756)*
Charles Industries LLC .... D 217 932-5292
 Casey *(G-3200)*
Custom Canvas LLC .... G 847 587-0225
 Ingleside *(G-11580)*
Mako Networks Sales & Mktg Inc .... D 847 752-5566
 Elgin *(G-8647)*

ELECTRICAL GOODS, WHOLESALE: Transformer & Transmission Eqpt

Aldonex Inc .... F 708 547-5663
 Bellwood *(G-1613)*
Custom Millers Supply Inc .... G 309 734-6312
 Monmouth *(G-14216)*
McC Technology Inc .... F 630 377-7200
 Saint Charles *(G-18231)*

ELECTRICAL GOODS, WHOLESALE: Transformers

Signify North America Corp .... E 708 307-3000
 Roselle *(G-17989)*

ELECTRICAL GOODS, WHOLESALE: Wire & Cable

Cable Company .... E 847 437-5267
 Elk Grove Village *(G-8877)*
Hamalot Inc .... E 847 944-1500
 Schaumburg *(G-18542)*
Manu Industries Inc .... F 847 891-6412
 Schaumburg *(G-18618)*
Monona Holdings LLC .... G 630 946-0630
 Naperville *(G-14875)*
Optimas Oe Solutions LLC .... G 224 999-1000
 Glenview *(G-10595)*
Partex Marking Systems Inc .... G 630 516-0400
 Lombard *(G-13117)*
Quality Cable & Components Inc .... E 309 695-3435
 Wyoming *(G-21461)*

ELECTRICAL GOODS, WHOLESALE: Wire & Cable, Electronic

Clark Wire & Cable Co Inc .... E 847 949-9944
 Mundelein *(G-14678)*

ELECTRICAL GOODS, WHOLESALE: Wire & Cable, Power

Pro-Pak Industries Inc .... F 630 876-1050
 West Chicago *(G-20633)*

ELECTRICAL HOUSEHOLD APPLIANCE REPAIR

Appliance Repair .... G 708 456-1020
 Norridge *(G-15230)*

ELECTRICAL INDL APPARATUS, NEC

Divergent Alliance LLC .... G 847 531-0559
 West Dundee *(G-20662)*
Powerone Corp .... G 630 443-6500
 Saint Charles *(G-18248)*

ELECTRICAL SPLYS

Clarios .... E 309 427-2800
 East Peoria *(G-8261)*
Decatur Industrial Elc Inc .... E 217 428-6621
 Decatur *(G-7487)*
Linx Global Mfg LLC .... G 847 910-5303
 Chicago *(G-5233)*
Precision Drive & Control Inc .... E 815 235-7595
 Freeport *(G-10133)*
Rathje Enterprises Inc .... B 217 423-2593
 Decatur *(G-7540)*
Steiner Electric Company .... E 312 421-7220
 Chicago *(G-6239)*
Telegartner Inc .... E 630 616-7600
 Franklin Park *(G-10059)*
Uesco Industries Inc .... E 800 325-8372
 Alsip *(G-518)*

ELECTRICAL SUPPLIES: Porcelain

Dpcac LLC .... E 630 741-7900
 Itasca *(G-11644)*
Ferro Corporation .... C 847 623-0370
 Waukegan *(G-20443)*
Johnson Sign Co .... G 847 678-2092
 Franklin Park *(G-9975)*
Porcelain Enamel Finishers .... G 312 808-1560
 Chicago *(G-5845)*
Senna Design LLC .... G 847 821-7877
 Vernon Hills *(G-20096)*
Voges Inc .... D 618 233-2760
 Belleville *(G-1608)*

ELECTRODES: Indl Process

Mettler-Toledo LLC .... E 630 446-7700
 Aurora *(G-1002)*

ELECTRODES: Thermal & Electrolytic

Starex Inc .... G 847 918-5555
 Libertyville *(G-12709)*

ELECTROLYZING SVC: Steel, Light Gauge

Koderhandt Inc .... G 618 233-4808
 Belleville *(G-1565)*

ELECTROMEDICAL EQPT

Aed Essentials .... G 815 977-5920
 Rockford *(G-17297)*
Arxium Inc .... C 847 808-2600
 Buffalo Grove *(G-2513)*
Barrington Clinical Partners .... G 847 508-9737
 Barrington *(G-1214)*
Domino Lasers Inc .... E 847 855-1364
 Gurnee *(G-10872)*
Henderson Engineering Co Inc .... G 815 786-9471
 Sandwich *(G-18374)*
Interexpo Ltd .... F 847 489-7056
 Kildeer *(G-12049)*
Jones Medical Instrument Co .... E 630 571-1980
 Oak Brook *(G-15627)*
Lifeline Scientific Inc .... E 847 294-0300
 Itasca *(G-11691)*

PRODUCT SECTION

EMBLEMS: Embroidered

Lifewatch Technologies Inc ....D....... 847 720-2100
  Rosemont *(G-18033)*
Medtex Health Services Inc ....G....... 630 789-0330
  Clarendon Hills *(G-6900)*
Metritrack Inc ....G....... 630 607-9311
  Hillside *(G-11347)*
Northgate Technologies Inc ....E....... 847 608-8900
  Elgin *(G-8674)*
Odin Technologies LLC ....G....... 408 309-1925
  Chicago *(G-5655)*
Omex Technologies Inc ....G....... 847 850-5858
  Wheeling *(G-20949)*
Omron Healthcare Inc ....D....... 847 680-6200
  Lake Forest *(G-12276)*
Retmap Inc ....G....... 312 224-8938
  Grayslake *(G-10797)*
Siemens Med Solutions USA Inc ....D....... 847 304-7700
  Hoffman Estates *(G-11458)*
Snap Diagnostics LLC ....F....... 847 777-0000
  Wheeling *(G-20988)*
System Science Corporation ....G....... 708 214-2264
  Chicago *(G-6304)*
Thermatome Corporation ....G....... 312 772-2201
  Chicago *(G-6361)*
Virtusense Technologies Inc ....E....... 855 443-5744
  Peoria *(G-16544)*

ELECTROMEDICAL EQPT WHOLESALERS

Interexpo Ltd ....F....... 847 489-7056
  Kildeer *(G-12049)*
Lifewatch Technologies Inc ....D....... 847 720-2100
  Rosemont *(G-18033)*
Medical Specialties Distrs LLC ....E....... 630 307-6200
  Hanover Park *(G-11009)*

ELECTROMETALLURGICAL PRDTS

Prince Minerals LLC ....G....... 646 747-4222
  Quincy *(G-16926)*
Prince Minerals LLC ....G....... 646 747-4200
  Quincy *(G-16927)*
Tempel Holdings Inc ....F....... 847 244-5330
  Old Mill Creek *(G-15849)*
Tempel Holdings Inc ....A....... 773 250-8000
  Chicago *(G-6343)*

ELECTRON BEAM: Cutting, Forming, Welding

Sciaky Inc ....E....... 708 594-3841
  Chicago *(G-6116)*

ELECTRON TUBES

Dcx-Chol Enterprises Inc ....E....... 309 353-4455
  Pekin *(G-16327)*
Northrop Grumman Systems Corp ....A....... 847 259-9600
  Rolling Meadows *(G-17755)*
Rcl Electronics ....G....... 630 834-0156
  Addison *(G-268)*

ELECTRON TUBES: Cathode Ray

Light of Mine LLC ....G....... 312 840-8570
  Chicago *(G-5220)*
Thomas Electronics Inc ....E....... 315 923-2051
  Addison *(G-307)*

ELECTRON TUBES: Parts

Richardson Electronics Ltd ....C....... 630 208-2200
  Lafox *(G-12138)*

ELECTRON TUBES: Transmitting

F & L Electronics LLC ....F....... 217 586-2132
  Mahomet *(G-13423)*

ELECTRONIC COMPONENTS

C & B Services ....G....... 847 462-8484
  Cary *(G-3151)*
Compu Doc Inc ....G....... 630 554-5800
  Oswego *(G-15997)*
Dynamac Microwave Inc ....G....... 630 543-0033
  Addison *(G-105)*
Grayhill Inc ....G....... 708 482-1411
  Mc Cook *(G-13691)*
Ot Systems Limited ....G....... 630 554-9178
  Plano *(G-16737)*
Seaco Data Systems Inc ....D....... 630 876-2169
  Carol Stream *(G-3066)*

ELECTRONIC DEVICES: Solid State, NEC

Dynawave Corporation ....F....... 630 232-4945
  Geneva *(G-10267)*

ELECTRONIC EQPT REPAIR SVCS

Assa Abloy ACC Door Cntrls Gro ....D....... 704 283-2101
  Franklin Park *(G-9876)*
Bowl-Tronics Enterprises Inc ....G....... 847 741-4500
  Elgin *(G-8523)*
Elcon Inc ....E....... 815 467-9500
  Minooka *(G-14059)*
Murata Electronics N Amer Inc ....E....... 847 330-9200
  Schaumburg *(G-18641)*
Rockford Electric Equipment Co ....G....... 815 398-4096
  Rockford *(G-17593)*

ELECTRONIC LOADS & POWER SPLYS

Advanced Strobe Products Inc ....D....... 708 867-3100
  Chicago *(G-3567)*
Inventus Power (illinois) LLC ....C....... 630 410-7900
  Woodridge *(G-21317)*
Limitless Innovations Inc ....E....... 855 843-4828
  McHenry *(G-13758)*
Power Equipment Company ....E....... 815 754-4090
  Cortland *(G-7026)*
Sumida America Inc ....E....... 847 545-6700
  Schaumburg *(G-18729)*
T&L International Mfg/Dist Inc ....G....... 309 830-7238
  Farmer City *(G-9658)*
VI Inc ....E....... 618 277-8703
  Belleville *(G-1606)*
ZF Active Safety & Elec US LLC ....B....... 217 826-3011
  Marshall *(G-13580)*

ELECTRONIC PARTS & EQPT WHOLESALERS

Ally Global Corporation ....G....... 773 822-3373
  Chicago *(G-3625)*
ASap Specialties Inc Del ....G....... 847 223-7699
  Grayslake *(G-10759)*
Bechara Sim ....F....... 847 913-9950
  Buffalo Grove *(G-2514)*
Cisco Systems Inc ....B....... 847 678-6600
  Des Plaines *(G-7747)*
Communication Coil Inc ....G....... 847 671-1333
  Schiller Park *(G-18795)*
Consolidated Elec Wire & Cable ....D....... 847 455-8830
  Franklin Park *(G-9913)*
Gepco International Inc ....E....... 847 795-9555
  Des Plaines *(G-7773)*
Heuft Usa Inc ....F....... 630 395-9521
  Downers Grove *(G-8021)*
Inglot Electronics Corp ....D....... 773 286-5881
  Chicago *(G-4921)*
Limitless Innovations Inc ....E....... 855 843-4828
  McHenry *(G-13758)*
Pactra Corp ....G....... 847 281-0308
  Vernon Hills *(G-20081)*
Rittal North America LLC ....A....... 847 240-4600
  Schaumburg *(G-18697)*
Standard Electric Supply Inc ....E....... 217 239-0800
  Champaign *(G-3354)*
Sumida America Inc ....E....... 847 545-6700
  Schaumburg *(G-18729)*
Touchsensor Technologies LLC ....B....... 630 221-9000
  Wheaton *(G-20829)*
Unified Solutions Corp ....E....... 847 478-9100
  Arlington Heights *(G-824)*
Vincor Ltd ....F....... 708 534-0008
  Monee *(G-14211)*

ELECTRONIC SHOPPING

Corelle Brands LLC ....C....... 847 233-8600
  Rosemont *(G-18010)*
Four Star Denim and AP LLC ....F....... 847 707-6365
  Chicago *(G-4626)*
Twoinspireyou LLC ....G....... 630 849-8214
  Geneva *(G-10314)*

ELECTRONIC TRAINING DEVICES

Boaleeco Inc ....G....... 847 428-3085
  Gilberts *(G-10351)*
Pipeline Trading Systems LLC ....G....... 312 212-4288
  Chicago *(G-5811)*
Three Hands Technologies ....G....... 847 680-5358
  Vernon Hills *(G-20106)*

Tricor Systems Inc ....E....... 847 742-5542
  Elgin *(G-8760)*

ELECTROPLATING & PLATING SVC

Midwest Power Equipment ....G....... 815 669-6331
  Joliet *(G-11904)*

ELEVATOR: Grain, Storage Only

Gateway Fs Inc ....G....... 618 824-6631
  Venedy *(G-20034)*

ELEVATORS & EQPT

Adams Elevator Equipment Co ....E....... 847 581-2900
  Chicago *(G-3538)*
CJ Anderson & Company ....E....... 708 867-4002
  Harwood Heights *(G-11102)*
D A Matot Inc ....D....... 708 547-1888
  Bellwood *(G-1620)*
Elevator Cable & Supply Co ....E....... 708 338-9700
  Broadview *(G-2433)*
Formula Systems North America ....G....... 847 350-0655
  Elk Grove Village *(G-9004)*
Harris Companies Inc ....F....... 217 578-2231
  Atwood *(G-905)*
Hollister-Whitney Elev Co LLC ....B....... 217 222-0466
  Quincy *(G-16892)*
Integrated Display Systems Inc ....F....... 708 298-9661
  Cicero *(G-6856)*
Kafka Manufacturing Co ....G....... 708 771-0970
  Forest Park *(G-9721)*
Kone Elevator ....C....... 309 764-6771
  Moline *(G-14154)*
Lifts of Illinois Inc ....G....... 309 923-7450
  Roanoke *(G-17103)*
Long Elevator and Mch Co Inc ....D....... 217 629-9648
  Springfield *(G-19400)*
Mitsubishi Electric Us Inc ....E....... 708 354-2900
  Countryside *(G-7065)*
Otis Elevator Company ....D....... 312 454-1616
  Chicago *(G-5712)*
Raytheon Technologies Corp ....B....... 815 226-6000
  Rockford *(G-17567)*
Vator Accessories Inc ....G....... 630 876-8370
  West Chicago *(G-20656)*

ELEVATORS WHOLESALERS

Lifts of Illinois Inc ....G....... 309 923-7450
  Roanoke *(G-17103)*
Otis Elevator Company ....F....... 618 529-3411
  Carbondale *(G-2852)*
Parts Specialists Inc ....G....... 708 371-2444
  Posen *(G-16800)*

ELEVATORS: Installation & Conversion

Colley Elevator Company ....E....... 630 766-7230
  Bensenville *(G-1773)*
Kone Inc ....A....... 630 577-1650
  Lisle *(G-12906)*
Lifts of Illinois Inc ....G....... 309 923-7450
  Roanoke *(G-17103)*
Mid-American Elevator Co Inc ....C....... 773 486-6900
  Chicago *(G-5428)*
Mid-American Elevator Co Inc ....E....... 815 740-1204
  Joliet *(G-11902)*

EMBALMING FLUID

Frigid Fluid Company ....E....... 708 836-1215
  Melrose Park *(G-13872)*

EMBLEMS: Embroidered

Ameri-Tex ....G....... 847 247-0777
  Mundelein *(G-14663)*
Chicago Knitting Mills ....G....... 773 463-1464
  Northbrook *(G-15358)*
Cq Industries Inc ....G....... 630 530-0177
  Elmhurst *(G-9353)*
Fast Lane Threads Custom EMB ....G....... 815 544-9898
  Belvidere *(G-1667)*
Midwest Swiss Embroideries Co ....E....... 773 631-7120
  Chicago *(G-5448)*
Personalized Threads ....G....... 815 431-1815
  Ottawa *(G-16071)*
Stitch Magic Usa Inc ....E....... 847 836-5000
  West Dundee *(G-20666)*
Stitchables Embroidery ....G....... 217 322-3000
  Rushville *(G-18113)*

Employee Codes: A=Over 500 employees, B=251-500
C=101-250, D=51-100, E=20-50, F=10-19, G=3-9

EMBLEMS: Embroidered

Trading Square Company Inc .... G 630 960-0606
Westmont *(G-20777)*
Tryad Specialties Inc .... F 630 549-0079
Saint Charles *(G-18292)*
Welsh Industries Ltd .... E 815 756-1111
Dekalb *(G-7712)*
Winning Stitch .... G 217 348-8279
Charleston *(G-3417)*

EMBOSSING SVC: Paper

Capital Prtg & Die Cutng Inc .... G 630 896-5520
Aurora *(G-1069)*
Capitol Impressions Inc .... E 309 633-1400
Peoria *(G-16397)*
Creative Lithocraft Inc .... F 847 352-7002
Schaumburg *(G-18493)*
H A Friend & Company Inc .... E 847 746-1248
Zion *(G-21516)*
Lasersketch Ltd .... G 630 243-6360
Romeoville *(G-17840)*
Midwest Gold Stampers Inc .... F 773 775-5253
Chicago *(G-5442)*
Redeen Engraving Inc .... G 847 593-6500
Elk Grove Village *(G-9216)*

EMBROIDERING & ART NEEDLEWORK FOR THE TRADE

All In Stitches .... G 309 944-4084
Geneseo *(G-10238)*
ASap Specialties Inc Del .... G 847 223-7699
Grayslake *(G-10759)*
Athletic Outfitters Inc .... G 815 942-6696
Morris *(G-14291)*
B & B Custom TS & Gifts .... G 618 463-0443
Alton *(G-544)*
Barnes & Noble College .... E 309 677-2320
Peoria *(G-16390)*
Camilles of Canton Inc .... G 309 647-7403
Canton *(G-2822)*
Chicago Printing and EMB Inc .... F 630 628-1777
Addison *(G-71)*
Cloz Companies Inc .... E 773 247-8879
Skokie *(G-18944)*
Cubby Hole of Carlinville Inc .... F 217 854-8511
Carlinville *(G-2872)*
Custom Monogramming .... G 815 625-9044
Rock Falls *(G-17180)*
D & J International Inc .... F 847 966-9260
Niles *(G-15115)*
Dpe Incorporated .... G 773 306-0105
Chicago *(G-4394)*
Elegant Embroidery Inc .... G 847 540-8003
Lake Zurich *(G-12407)*
Embroid ME .... G 847 272-9000
Northbrook *(G-15384)*
Embroidea Custom Embroidery .... G 217 698-6422
Springfield *(G-19362)*
Embroidery Services Inc .... G 847 588-2660
Niles *(G-15120)*
Embroidme .... G 847 301-1010
Lake Villa *(G-12349)*
Fielders Choice .... G 618 937-2294
West Frankfort *(G-20671)*
First Impression .... G 815 883-3357
Oglesby *(G-15841)*
Incredible Threads LLC .... G 847 970-0183
Elgin *(G-8624)*
Minor League Inc .... G 618 548-8040
Salem *(G-18347)*
Mt Greenwood Embroidery .... G 773 779-5798
Chicago *(G-5521)*
Nelson Enterprises Inc .... G 815 633-1100
Roscoe *(G-17920)*
Select Screen Prints & EMB .... F 309 829-6511
Bloomington *(G-2093)*
Senn Enterprises Inc .... F 309 637-1147
Peoria *(G-16519)*
Sg Screen Graphics Inc .... G 309 699-8513
Pekin *(G-16360)*
Stans Sportsworld Inc .... G 217 359-8474
Champaign *(G-3355)*
Star Silkscreen Design Inc .... G 217 877-0804
Decatur *(G-7550)*
Stitch By Stitch Incorporated .... G 847 541-2543
Prospect Heights *(G-16846)*
Stitched Conversation .... G 312 966-1146
Oak Park *(G-15775)*
T Graphics .... G 618 592-4145
Oblong *(G-15830)*

T J Marche Ltd .... G 618 445-2314
Albion *(G-353)*
Town Hall Sports Inc .... F 618 235-9881
Belleville *(G-1601)*
Wellspring Investments LLC .... G 773 736-1213
Chicago *(G-6602)*
Winning Streak Inc .... D 618 277-8191
Dupo *(G-8150)*

EMBROIDERING SVC

A B S Embroidery Inc .... G 708 597-7785
Alsip *(G-408)*
A Plus Apparel .... G 815 675-2117
Spring Grove *(G-19262)*
Action Screen Print Inc .... F 630 393-1990
Warrenville *(G-20228)*
All Stars -N- Stitches Inc .... G 618 435-5555
Benton *(G-1918)*
Allstar Embroidery .... G 847 913-1133
Buffalo Grove *(G-2509)*
Artistic Embroidery Creations .... G 815 385-8854
McHenry *(G-13721)*
Bee Designs Embroidery & Scree .... G 815 393-4593
Esmond *(G-9475)*
Bullseye Imprinting & EMB .... G 630 834-8175
Elmhurst *(G-9339)*
C & C Embroidery Inc .... G 815 777-6167
Galena *(G-10165)*
Classic Embroidery Inc .... F 708 485-7034
Chicago *(G-4168)*
D & D Embroidery .... G 309 266-7092
Morton *(G-14357)*
Design Loft Imaging Inc .... G 847 439-2486
Elk Grove Village *(G-8946)*
Digistitch Embroidery & Design .... G 773 229-8630
Chicago *(G-4357)*
Dilars Embroidery & Monograms .... G 815 338-6066
Woodstock *(G-21381)*
Doras Spinning Wheel Inc .... G 618 466-1900
Alton *(G-553)*
Embroidery Experts Inc .... E 847 403-0200
Vernon Hills *(G-20051)*
Ensign Emblem Ltd .... D 217 877-8224
Decatur *(G-7493)*
Essential Creat Chicago Inc .... G 773 238-1700
Chicago *(G-4533)*
Expressions By Christine Inc .... F 217 223-2750
Quincy *(G-16881)*
Femina Sport Inc .... G 630 271-1876
Downers Grove *(G-8002)*
G & M Embroidery .... G 708 636-7005
Chicago Ridge *(G-6795)*
Harlan Vance Company .... F 309 888-4804
Normal *(G-15205)*
Hermans Inc .... E 309 206-4892
Rock Island *(G-17222)*
Hyperstitch .... F 815 568-0590
Marengo *(G-13485)*
I D Togs .... G 618 235-1538
Belleville *(G-1556)*
Illinois Embroidery Service .... G 618 526-8006
Breese *(G-2304)*
Image Plus Inc .... G 630 852-4920
Downers Grove *(G-8028)*
J C Embroidery & Screen Print .... G 630 595-4670
Bensenville *(G-1827)*
Midwest Stitch .... G 815 394-1516
Rockford *(G-17528)*
Pictures & More .... G 618 662-4572
Flora *(G-9688)*
Project Te Inc .... G 217 344-9833
Urbana *(G-19996)*
Reel Mate Mfg Co .... G 708 423-8005
Oak Lawn *(G-15734)*
Sango Embroidery .... G 773 582-4354
Chicago *(G-6100)*
Senn Enterprises Inc .... G 309 673-4384
Peoria *(G-16520)*
Signature of Chicago Inc .... G 630 271-1876
Downers Grove *(G-8095)*
Stitchin Image .... G 815 578-9890
Richmond *(G-17024)*
Time Embroidery .... G 847 364-4371
Elk Grove Village *(G-9274)*
Twin Towers Marketing .... G 815 544-5554
Belvidere *(G-1706)*
U Keep US In Stitches .... G 847 427-8127
Mount Prospect *(G-14578)*
U R On It .... G 847 382-0182
Lake Barrington *(G-12167)*

USA Embroidery .... G 309 692-1391
Peoria *(G-16543)*
Visual Persuasion Inc .... F 815 899-6609
Sycamore *(G-19739)*
Waist Up Imprntd Sprtswear LLC .... G 847 963-1400
Palatine *(G-16171)*
Woolenwear Co .... F 847 520-9243
Prospect Heights *(G-16848)*

EMBROIDERING SVC: Schiffli Machine

Midwest Swiss Embroideries Co .... E 773 631-7120
Chicago *(G-5448)*

EMBROIDERY ADVERTISING SVCS

Ad Images .... G 847 956-1887
Hoffman Estates *(G-11403)*
Ameri-Tex .... G 847 247-0777
Mundelein *(G-14663)*
C & C Sport Stop .... G 618 632-7812
O Fallon *(G-15569)*
C M F Enterprises Inc .... F 847 526-9499
Wauconda *(G-20337)*
Chicago Printing and EMB Inc .... F 630 628-1777
Addison *(G-71)*
Energy Tees .... G 708 771-0000
Forest Park *(G-9713)*
Spirit Warrior Inc .... G 708 614-0020
Orland Park *(G-15983)*
Visual Persuasion Inc .... F 815 899-6609
Sycamore *(G-19739)*
Wagner International LLC .... G 224 619-9247
Vernon Hills *(G-20109)*

EMERGENCY ALARMS

Ademco Inc .... G 708 599-1390
Bridgeview *(G-2319)*
Ademco Inc .... E 847 472-2900
Elk Grove Village *(G-8807)*
Jeron Electronic Systems Inc .... D 773 275-1900
Niles *(G-15136)*
Lumentum Operations LLC .... G 408 546-5483
Chicago *(G-5282)*
Marine Technologies Inc .... E 847 546-9001
Volo *(G-20203)*
Pacific Custom Components Corp .... F 815 206-5450
Woodstock *(G-21419)*
Regional Emergency Dispatch .... F 847 498-5748
Northbrook *(G-15471)*
Siemens Industry Inc .... A 847 215-1000
Buffalo Grove *(G-2600)*
Tri-Lite Inc .... E 773 384-7765
Chicago *(G-6422)*
Wireless Chamberlain Products .... E 800 282-6225
Elmhurst *(G-9446)*

EMPLOYMENT AGENCY SVCS

Dev Base LLC .... E 319 321-3014
Chicago *(G-4346)*
Wesco International Inc .... G 630 513-4864
Elmhurst *(G-9445)*

ENAMELING SVC: Metal Prdts, Including Porcelain

Durable Longlasting .... E 847 350-0113
Elk Grove Village *(G-8957)*

ENAMELS

American Powder Coatings Inc .... E 630 762-0100
Saint Charles *(G-18146)*
Rust-Oleum Corporation .... D 815 967-4258
Rockford *(G-17617)*
Testor Corporation .... D 815 962-6654
Rockford *(G-17656)*
U S Colors & Coatings Inc .... G 630 879-8898
Batavia *(G-1435)*

ENCLOSURES: Electronic

Equipto Electronics Corp .... E 630 897-4691
Aurora *(G-1091)*
G & M Manufacturing Corp .... E 815 455-1900
Crystal Lake *(G-7201)*
Laystrom Manufacturing Co .... D 773 342-4800
Chicago *(G-5186)*
MNP Precision Parts LLC .... C 815 391-5256
Rockford *(G-17530)*

PRODUCT SECTION

ENGINEERING SVCS: Mechanical

New Dimension Models ....G....... 815 935-1001
  Aroma Park *(G-840)*
Perfection Spring Stmping Corp ....D....... 847 437-3900
  Mount Prospect *(G-14560)*
Rittal North America LLC ....A....... 847 240-4600
  Schaumburg *(G-18697)*
Tellenar Inc ....F....... 815 356-8044
  Crystal Lake *(G-7280)*

ENCLOSURES: Screen

Chicago Enclosures ....G....... 708 344-6600
  Melrose Park *(G-13842)*
Singer Safety Company ....F....... 773 235-2100
  Chicago *(G-6175)*

ENCODERS: Digital

Evanston Graphic Imaging Inc ....G....... 847 869-7446
  Evanston *(G-9516)*

ENCRYPTION EQPT & DEVICES

Winston Privacy Inc ....G....... 312 282-0162
  Chicago *(G-6647)*

ENERGY MEASUREMENT EQPT

Bluenrgy LLC ....D....... 802 865-3866
  Chicago *(G-3917)*

ENGINE PARTS & ACCESS: Internal Combustion

Boley Tool & Machine Works Inc ....C....... 309 694-2722
  East Peoria *(G-8254)*
Nelson Enterprises Inc ....G....... 815 633-1100
  Roscoe *(G-17920)*
Tpr America Inc ....G....... 847 446-5336
  Schaumburg *(G-18751)*
Wuebbels Repair & Sales LLC ....G....... 618 648-2227
  Mc Leansboro *(G-13710)*

ENGINE REBUILDING: Diesel

Honeywell International Inc ....A....... 847 391-2000
  Des Plaines *(G-7780)*
L S Diesel Repair Inc ....G....... 217 283-5537
  Hoopeston *(G-11510)*

ENGINE REBUILDING: Gas

C & M Engineering ....G....... 815 932-3388
  Bourbonnais *(G-2257)*
Precision Engine Rbldrs Inc ....G....... 815 254-2333
  Plainfield *(G-16704)*

ENGINEERING SVCS

10g LLC ....F....... 630 754-2400
  Woodridge *(G-21269)*
Art Cnc Machining LLC ....G....... 708 907-3090
  Bridgeview *(G-2325)*
Automated Systems & Control Co ....G....... 847 735-8310
  Lake Bluff *(G-12172)*
Autonomous Stuff LLC ....G....... 309 291-0966
  Morton *(G-14353)*
Bc Asi Capital II Inc ....A....... 708 534-5575
  University Park *(G-19948)*
Charter Dura-Bar Inc ....C....... 815 338-7800
  Woodstock *(G-21374)*
Circom Inc ....E....... 630 595-4460
  Bensenville *(G-1770)*
Deyco Inc ....G....... 630 553-5666
  Yorkville *(G-21480)*
E-Motion LLC ....G....... 815 825-4411
  Fairbury *(G-9606)*
Ehs Solutions LLC ....E....... 309 282-9121
  Peoria *(G-16433)*
Elgin National Industries Inc ....F....... 630 434-7200
  Downers Grove *(G-7998)*
Emac Inc ....E....... 618 529-4525
  Carbondale *(G-2841)*
Engineering Finshg Systems LLC ....F....... 815 893-6090
  Elmhurst *(G-9361)*
Gama Electronics Inc ....F....... 815 356-9600
  Woodstock *(G-21391)*
General Electro Corporation ....F....... 630 595-8989
  Bensenville *(G-1810)*
Ghetzler Aero-Power Corp ....G....... 224 513-5636
  Vernon Hills *(G-20056)*
Global Water Technology Inc ....E....... 708 349-9991
  South Holland *(G-19215)*

H L Clausing Inc ....G....... 847 676-0330
  Skokie *(G-18962)*
Hpd LLC ....C....... 815 609-2032
  Plainfield *(G-16673)*
Icon Mech Cnstr & Engrg LLC ....C....... 618 452-0035
  Granite City *(G-10716)*
IMS Companies LLC ....D....... 847 391-8100
  Des Plaines *(G-7786)*
Innovative Werks Inc ....G....... 312 767-8618
  Naperville *(G-14848)*
Integral Automation Inc ....F....... 630 654-4300
  Burr Ridge *(G-2688)*
International Mold & Prod LLC ....G....... 313 617-5251
  Grayslake *(G-10783)*
Ionit Technologies Inc ....E....... 847 205-9651
  Northfield *(G-15518)*
Kingfisher Controls LLC ....G....... 425 359-5601
  Illiopolis *(G-11574)*
Lake County Tool Works North ....G....... 847 662-4542
  Wadsworth *(G-20210)*
Ln Engineering LLC ....G....... 815 472-2939
  Momence *(G-14187)*
Loda Electronics Co ....G....... 217 386-2554
  Loda *(G-13029)*
Logicon Group LLC ....G....... 618 558-7757
  Millstadt *(G-14049)*
M H Detrick Company ....E....... 708 479-5085
  Frankfort *(G-9814)*
Matrix IV Inc ....E....... 815 338-4500
  Woodstock *(G-21409)*
McLean Subsurface Utility ....G....... 336 988-2520
  Decatur *(G-7521)*
Messer North America Inc ....E....... 630 257-3612
  Lockport *(G-13012)*
Mid-States Concrete Inds LLC ....D....... 815 389-2277
  South Beloit *(G-19103)*
Midwest Control Corp ....F....... 708 599-1331
  Bridgeview *(G-2365)*
Modern Process Equipment Inc ....E....... 773 254-3929
  Chicago *(G-5480)*
Newko Tool & Engineering Co ....E....... 847 359-1670
  Palatine *(G-16142)*
Octane Motorsports LLC ....G....... 224 419-5460
  Waukegan *(G-20473)*
Oso900 Nfp ....G....... 312 206-4219
  Chicago *(G-5711)*
Outbound Lighting LLC ....E....... 314 330-0696
  Lincolnwood *(G-12835)*
Performance Pattern & Mch Inc ....E....... 309 676-0907
  Peoria *(G-16496)*
Plastic Services Group ....G....... 847 368-1444
  Arlington Heights *(G-788)*
Precision Metal Technologies ....F....... 847 228-6630
  Rolling Meadows *(G-17765)*
Royale Innovation Group Ltd ....G....... 312 339-1406
  Itasca *(G-11729)*
S & C Electric Company ....A....... 773 338-1000
  Chicago *(G-6083)*
S Flying Inc ....F....... 618 586-9999
  Palestine *(G-16179)*
SBS Steel Belt Systems USA Inc ....F....... 847 841-3300
  Gilberts *(G-10369)*
Senior PLC ....G....... 630 372-3511
  Bartlett *(G-1312)*
Sigenics Inc ....F....... 312 448-8000
  Chicago *(G-6164)*
SPEP Acquisition Corp ....G....... 310 608-0693
  Bolingbrook *(G-2246)*
Tecnova Electronics Inc ....D....... 847 336-6160
  Waukegan *(G-20502)*
V2 Solutions Inc ....G....... 312 528-9050
  Schaumburg *(G-18769)*
Walters Metal Fabrication Inc ....D....... 618 931-5551
  Granite City *(G-10749)*

ENGINEERING SVCS: Aviation Or Aeronautical

ARINC Incorporated ....E....... 800 633-6882
  O Fallon *(G-15567)*

ENGINEERING SVCS: Building Construction

Brd Development Group LLC ....F....... 312 912-7110
  Chicago *(G-3947)*
Elliott Aviation Arcft Sls Inc ....G....... 309 799-3183
  Milan *(G-14008)*
Global General Contractors LLC ....G....... 708 663-0476
  Tinley Park *(G-19832)*
Matrix North Amercn Cnstr Inc ....G....... 312 754-6605
  Chicago *(G-5366)*

Osmer Woodworking Inc ....G....... 815 973-5809
  Dixon *(G-7905)*
Ozinga Ready Mix Concrete Inc ....E....... 708 326-4200
  Mokena *(G-14103)*
Stages Construction Inc ....G....... 773 619-2977
  Glenview *(G-10624)*

ENGINEERING SVCS: Chemical

Agriscience Inc ....G....... 212 365-4214
  Peoria *(G-16377)*
Gig Karasek LLC ....F....... 630 549-0394
  Saint Charles *(G-18204)*

ENGINEERING SVCS: Civil

Structurepoint LLC ....F....... 847 966-4357
  Skokie *(G-19037)*

ENGINEERING SVCS: Electrical Or Electronic

Aria Corporation ....G....... 847 327-9000
  Libertyville *(G-12630)*
Bishop Engineering Company ....F....... 630 305-9538
  Lisle *(G-12872)*
Calvert Systems ....G....... 309 523-3262
  Port Byron *(G-16786)*
Control Works Inc ....G....... 630 444-1942
  Saint Charles *(G-18174)*
Elemech Inc ....E....... 630 417-2845
  Aurora *(G-956)*
Imagineering Inc ....E....... 847 806-0003
  Elk Grove Village *(G-9047)*
Industrial Controls Inc ....G....... 630 752-8100
  Geneva *(G-10278)*
Lli Architectural Lighting LLC ....F....... 847 412-4880
  Buffalo Grove *(G-2564)*
Online Electronics Inc ....E....... 847 871-1700
  Elk Grove Village *(G-9164)*
Righthand Technologies Inc ....G....... 773 774-7600
  Chicago *(G-6033)*
RWS Design and Controls Inc ....E....... 815 654-6000
  Roscoe *(G-17930)*
Spurt Inc ....G....... 847 571-6497
  Northbrook *(G-15486)*

ENGINEERING SVCS: Energy conservation

Clean Energy Renewables LLC ....E....... 309 797-4844
  Moline *(G-14136)*
Elfi LLC ....E....... 815 439-1833
  Chicago *(G-4483)*

ENGINEERING SVCS: Heating & Ventilation

Honeywell International Inc ....D....... 847 797-4000
  Des Plaines *(G-7778)*

ENGINEERING SVCS: Industrial

Falcon Technologies Inc ....G....... 847 550-1866
  Lake Zurich *(G-12410)*
Gerb Vibration Control Systems ....G....... 630 724-1660
  Lisle *(G-12895)*

ENGINEERING SVCS: Machine Tool Design

All Cnc Solutions Inc ....G....... 847 972-1139
  Skokie *(G-18913)*
Bartell Corporation ....G....... 847 854-3232
  Algonquin *(G-367)*
Design Systems Inc ....E....... 309 263-7706
  Morton *(G-14358)*
Ehrhardt Tool & Machine LLC ....C....... 314 436-6900
  Granite City *(G-10704)*
Ingenious Concepts Inc ....G....... 630 539-8059
  Medinah *(G-13814)*
Matt Pak Inc ....D....... 847 451-4018
  Franklin Park *(G-9985)*
Ramco Group LLC ....F....... 847 639-9899
  Crystal Lake *(G-7252)*
Sloan Industries Inc ....E....... 630 350-1614
  Wood Dale *(G-21241)*

ENGINEERING SVCS: Marine

Great Lakes Envmtl Mar Del ....G....... 312 332-3377
  Chicago *(G-4734)*

ENGINEERING SVCS: Mechanical

Design Technology Inc ....E....... 630 920-1300
  Westmont *(G-20736)*

Employee Codes: A=Over 500 employees, B=251-500
C=101-250, D=51-100, E=20-50, F=10-19, G=3-9

2020 Harris Illinois Industrial Directory

ENGINEERING SVCS: Mechanical

Dynamic Automation Inc .... G 312 782-8555
  Lincolnwood *(G-12817)*
Eighty Nine Robotics LLC .... G 512 573-9091
  Chicago *(G-4463)*
Klapperich Tool Inc .... F 847 608-8471
  South Elgin *(G-19160)*
Langham Engineering .... G 815 223-5250
  Peru *(G-16580)*
Livingston Products Inc .... F 847 808-0900
  Waukegan *(G-20460)*
MEA Inc .... E 847 766-9040
  Elk Grove Village *(G-9114)*
Specialized Liftruck Svcs LLC .... F 708 552-2705
  Bedford Park *(G-1505)*
Technique Engineering Inc .... F 847 816-1870
  Waukegan *(G-20501)*
Titan US LLC .... G 331 212-5953
  Aurora *(G-1026)*
Z-Tech Inc .... G 815 335-7395
  Winnebago *(G-21122)*

ENGINEERING SVCS: Pollution Control

C P Environmental Inc .... F 630 759-8866
  Romeoville *(G-17801)*

ENGINEERING SVCS: Professional

Concept and Design Services .... G 847 259-1675
  Mount Prospect *(G-14519)*
Intratek Inc .... G 847 640-0007
  Elk Grove Village *(G-9059)*
Vibra-Tech Engineers Inc .... G 630 858-0681
  Glen Ellyn *(G-10423)*

ENGINEERING SVCS: Structural

Structural Design Corp .... G 847 816-3816
  Libertyville *(G-12710)*
Versatech LLC .... C 217 342-3500
  Effingham *(G-8428)*

ENGINES: Diesel & Semi-Diesel Or Duel Fuel

Caterpillar Inc .... A 309 578-1615
  Mossville *(G-14459)*
Caterpillar Inc .... B 309 675-6590
  Peoria *(G-16411)*
Caterpillar Inc .... G 309 578-2185
  Mossville *(G-14452)*
Caterpillar Inc .... A 224 551-4000
  Deerfield *(G-7600)*
Caterpillar Inc .... D 309 578-6118
  Mossville *(G-14453)*
Caterpillar Inc .... B 888 614-4328
  Peoria *(G-16407)*
Heavy Quip Incorporated .... F 312 368-7997
  Chicago *(G-4797)*
Navistar Inc .... C 331 332-5000
  Lisle *(G-12917)*
Navistar International Corp .... A 331 332-5000
  Lisle *(G-12921)*

ENGINES: Gasoline, NEC

Speed Tech Technology Inc .... G 847 516-2001
  Cary *(G-3191)*
Unicarriers Americas Corp .... G 800 871-5438
  Marengo *(G-13496)*

ENGINES: Internal Combustion, NEC

American Speed Enterprises .... G 309 764-3601
  Moline *(G-14131)*
Caterpillar Gb LLC .... G 309 675-1000
  Peoria *(G-16403)*
Cummins - Allison Corp .... D 847 299-9550
  Mount Prospect *(G-14521)*
Cummins - Allison Corp .... C 847 299-9550
  Mount Prospect *(G-14522)*
Cummins - Allison Corp .... F 630 833-2285
  Elmhurst *(G-9357)*
Cummins Crosspoint LLC .... G 309 452-4454
  Normal *(G-15201)*
Cummins Dist Holdco Inc .... E 309 787-4300
  Rock Island *(G-17213)*
Cummins Inc .... E 309 787-4300
  Rock Island *(G-17214)*
Cummins Npower LLC .... E 708 579-9222
  Hodgkins *(G-11387)*
Cummins-Allison Corp .... B 800 786-5528
  Mount Prospect *(G-14523)*
Cummins-American Corp .... G 847 299-9550
  Mount Prospect *(G-14524)*
Engine Efficiency Systems LLC .... F 630 590-5241
  Burr Ridge *(G-2670)*
Hunt Charles .... G 217 793-5151
  Springfield *(G-19383)*
Jasiek Motor Rebuilding Inc .... G 815 883-3678
  Oglesby *(G-15842)*
JDM Engines Chicago LLC .... G 214 235-5071
  Elk Grove Village *(G-9066)*
Navistar Inc .... B 317 352-4500
  Melrose Park *(G-13894)*
Npt Automotive Machine Shop .... G 618 233-1344
  Belleville *(G-1580)*
Perkins Engines Inc .... E 309 578-7364
  Mossville *(G-14461)*
Progress Rail Locomotive Inc .... A 800 255-5355
  Mc Cook *(G-13699)*
Progress Rail Locomotive Inc .... F 708 387-5510
  Mc Cook *(G-13700)*
R & C Auto Supply Corp .... G 815 625-4414
  Sterling *(G-19528)*
Waymore Power Co Inc .... F 618 729-3876
  Piasa *(G-16610)*

ENGINES: Jet Propulsion

Chicago Jet Group LLC .... E 630 466-3600
  Sugar Grove *(G-19639)*

ENGINES: Marine

B & M Automotive .... G 309 637-4977
  Peoria *(G-16389)*

ENGINES: Steam

Union Iron Inc .... E 217 429-5148
  Decatur *(G-7564)*

ENGRAVING SVC, NEC

Fresh Concept Enterprises Inc .... G 815 254-7295
  Plainfield *(G-16667)*

ENGRAVING SVC: Jewelry & Personal Goods

Ace Engraving & Specialties Co .... G 815 759-2093
  McHenry *(G-13714)*
Addison Engraving Inc .... G 630 833-9123
  Villa Park *(G-20127)*
Comet Die & Engraving Company .... D 630 833-5600
  Elmhurst *(G-9350)*
Finer Line Inc .... F 847 884-1611
  Itasca *(G-11657)*
Hoeing Die & Mold Engraving .... G 630 543-0006
  Addison *(G-151)*
Johnos Inc .... G 630 897-6929
  Aurora *(G-1119)*
M J Burton Engraving Co .... G 217 223-7273
  Quincy *(G-16908)*
Trophies and Awards Plus .... G 708 754-7127
  Steger *(G-19494)*
Viking Awards Inc .... G 630 833-1733
  Elmhurst *(G-9441)*
Wheaton Trophy & Engravers .... G 630 682-4200
  Wheaton *(G-20831)*

ENGRAVING SVCS

Ambrit Inc .... G 847 593-3301
  Elk Grove Village *(G-8820)*
Amkine Inc .... F 847 526-7088
  Wauconda *(G-20331)*
Benzinger Printing .... G 815 784-6560
  Genoa *(G-10315)*
Bertco Enterprises Inc .... G 618 234-9283
  Belleville *(G-1535)*
C F C Interantional .... G 708 753-0679
  Chicago Heights *(G-6737)*
Engravings Plus .... G 217 784-8426
  Gibson City *(G-10337)*
Finer Line Inc .... F 847 884-1611
  Itasca *(G-11657)*
George Lauterer Corporation .... E 312 913-1881
  Chicago *(G-4682)*
Light Waves LLC .... F 847 251-1622
  Wilmette *(G-21084)*
M J Burton Engraving Co .... G 217 223-7273
  Quincy *(G-16908)*
Nathan Winston Service Inc .... G 815 758-4545
  Dekalb *(G-7692)*
National Rubber Stamp Co Inc .... G 773 281-6522
  Chicago *(G-5552)*
Procraft Engraving Inc .... G 847 673-1500
  Skokie *(G-19013)*
Standex International Corp .... E 630 588-0400
  Carol Stream *(G-3076)*
Trophies By George .... G 630 497-1212
  Bartlett *(G-1318)*
Walnut Creek Hardwood .... G 815 389-3317
  South Beloit *(G-19120)*

ENGRAVING: Currency

Edv Dstrict 7 Clringhouse Vine .... G 312 380-1349
  Chicago *(G-4459)*

ENGRAVINGS: Plastic

A To Z Engraving Co Inc .... G 847 526-7396
  Wauconda *(G-20324)*
Lens Lenticlear Lenticular .... F 630 467-0900
  Elk Grove Village *(G-9093)*

ENTERTAINERS & ENTERTAINMENT GROUPS

Ikan Creations LLC .... G 312 204-7333
  Chicago *(G-4884)*
Linx Enterprises LLC .... G 224 409-2206
  Chicago *(G-5232)*
Windsong Press Ltd .... G 847 223-4586
  Grayslake *(G-10806)*

ENTERTAINMENT PROMOTION SVCS

Deshamusic Inc .... G 818 257-2716
  Chicago *(G-4344)*

ENTERTAINMENT SVCS

Beyond Limits Media Group LLC .... G 773 948-9296
  Chicago *(G-3878)*
Powerhouse Ent Inc .... G 312 877-4303
  Chicago *(G-5849)*

ENVELOPES

American Graphics Network Inc .... F 847 729-7220
  Glenview *(G-10522)*
Diamond Envelope Corporation .... D 630 499-2800
  Aurora *(G-951)*
Federal Envelope Company .... D 630 595-2000
  Bensenville *(G-1799)*
Forest Envelope Company .... E 630 515-1200
  Bolingbrook *(G-2178)*
Gaw-Ohara Envelope Co .... E 773 638-1200
  Chicago *(G-4664)*
Gluetech Inc .... F 847 455-2707
  Wood Dale *(G-21194)*
Graphic Industries Inc .... E 847 357-9870
  South Elgin *(G-19148)*
Managed Marketing Inc .... G 847 279-8260
  Wheeling *(G-20935)*
Office Express Inc .... G 888 526-8438
  Evanston *(G-9560)*
Overt Press Inc .... E 773 284-0909
  Chicago *(G-5718)*
Roodhouse Envelope Co .... D 217 589-4321
  Roodhouse *(G-17894)*
The Calumet Carton Company .... D 708 331-7910
  South Holland *(G-19249)*
Trekon Company Inc .... G 309 925-7942
  Tremont *(G-19899)*
Unique Envelope Corporation .... E 773 586-0330
  Chicago *(G-6468)*

ENVELOPES WHOLESALERS

Envelopes Only Inc .... E 630 213-2500
  Streamwood *(G-19573)*
Office Express Inc .... G 888 526-8438
  Evanston *(G-9560)*

ENVIR QLTY PROG ADMN, GOV: Land, Minl & Wildlif Consv, State

Ill Dept Natural Resources .... G 217 498-9208
  Rochester *(G-17167)*
Ill Dept Natural Resources .... F 217 782-4970
  Springfield *(G-19384)*

PRODUCT SECTION

ENZYMES

Chem Free Solutions ....G....... 630 541-7931
  Darien (G-7403)
Enzyme Mechanisms Conference ....G....... 847 491-5653
  Winnetka (G-21129)
Enzymes Incorporated ....G....... 847 487-5401
  Wauconda (G-20348)
Natures Sources LLC ....G....... 847 663-9168
  Niles (G-15151)

EPOXY RESINS

Corro-Shield International Inc ....F....... 847 298-7770
  Elk Grove Village (G-8916)
Kns Companies Inc ....E....... 630 665-9010
  Carol Stream (G-3013)
Resin8 Inc ....G....... 773 551-3633
  Elmhurst (G-9418)

EQUIPMENT: Pedestrian Traffic Control

Km Enterprises Inc ....F....... 618 204-0888
  Mount Vernon (G-14620)

EQUIPMENT: Rental & Leasing, NEC

Amber Soft Inc ....F....... 630 377-6945
  Lake Barrington (G-12141)
Bloomington Tent & Awning Inc ....G....... 309 828-3411
  Bloomington (G-2027)
Breeze Printing Company ....F....... 217 824-2233
  Taylorville (G-19752)
CCS Contractor Eqp & Sup Inc ....E....... 630 393-9020
  Naperville (G-14793)
Champaign Cnty Tent & Awng Co ....E....... 217 328-5749
  Urbana (G-19977)
Chicago Rivet & Machine Co ....D....... 630 357-8500
  Naperville (G-14798)
Ds Services of America Inc ....C....... 773 586-8600
  Chicago (G-4399)
Essannay Show It Inc ....G....... 312 733-5511
  Chicago (G-4532)
Florida Metrology LLC ....F....... 630 833-3800
  Villa Park (G-20147)
Gilco Real Estate Company ....E....... 847 298-1717
  Des Plaines (G-7774)
Grate Signs Inc ....E....... 815 729-9700
  Joliet (G-11870)
Grs Holding LLC ....F....... 630 355-1660
  Naperville (G-14838)
Hinckley & Schmitt Inc ....A....... 773 586-8600
  Chicago (G-4823)
Mobile Air Inc ....F....... 847 755-0586
  Glendale Heights (G-10476)
Narvick Bros Lumber Co Inc ....E....... 815 942-1173
  Morris (G-14318)
Praxair Distribution Inc ....E....... 314 664-7900
  Cahokia (G-2763)
Resolute Industrial LLC ....D....... 800 537-9675
  Wheeling (G-20974)
True Value Company LLC ....B....... 773 695-5000
  Chicago (G-6437)
Vim Recyclers LP ....C....... 630 892-2559
  Aurora (G-1166)

ESCALATORS: Passenger & Freight

Kone Inc ....A....... 630 577-1650
  Lisle (G-12906)

ETCHING & ENGRAVING SVC

Amex Nooter LLC ....F....... 708 429-8300
  Tinley Park (G-19803)
Bertco Enterprises Inc ....E....... 618 234-9283
  Belleville (G-1535)
Bishops Engrv & Trophy Svc Inc ....G....... 773 777-5014
  Chicago (G-3901)
Crown Trophy ....G....... 309 699-1766
  East Peoria (G-8264)
Iemco Corporation ....G....... 773 728-4400
  Chicago (G-4878)
Meto-Grafics Inc ....F....... 847 639-0044
  Crystal Lake (G-7226)
Monogram of Evanston Inc ....G....... 847 864-8100
  Evanston (G-9555)
Petersburg Power Washing Inc ....F....... 217 415-9013
  Springfield (G-19425)
Safeway Services Rockford Inc ....E....... 815 986-1504
  Rockford (G-17621)

ETCHING SVC: Metal

Etch-Tech Inc ....G....... 630 833-4234
  Elmhurst (G-9363)
Lifetime Creations ....G....... 708 895-2770
  Lansing (G-12505)
Ostrom & Co Inc ....F....... 503 281-6469
  Winfield (G-21113)
Rebechini Studio Inc ....F....... 847 437-9030
  Elk Grove Village (G-9215)

ETCHING SVC: Photochemical

Faspro Technologies Inc ....F....... 847 364-9999
  Elk Grove Village (G-8996)

ETHYLENE

C U Plastic LLC ....G....... 888 957-9993
  Rochelle (G-17133)
Marquis Energy LLC ....D....... 815 925-7300
  Hennepin (G-11158)

ETHYLENE OXIDE

Union Carbide Corporation ....D....... 708 396-3000
  Alsip (G-519)

ETHYLENE-PROPYLENE RUBBERS: EPDM Polymers

Crown Polymers Corporation ....F....... 847 659-0300
  Huntley (G-11532)
Everon Polymers LLC ....G....... 815 681-8800
  Joliet (G-11863)
Liberty Chemical Corp ....G....... 773 657-1282
  Elk Grove Village (G-9094)
Mexichem Specialty Resins Inc ....F....... 309 364-2154
  Henry (G-11167)

EXCAVATING EQPT

Caterpillar Inc ....A....... 630 859-5000
  Montgomery (G-14238)

EXCAVATING MACHINERY & EQPT WHOLESALERS

Birkeys Farm Store Inc ....E....... 217 337-1772
  Urbana (G-19975)

EXHAUST HOOD OR FAN CLEANING SVCS

S C Johnson & Son Inc ....C....... 312 702-3100
  Chicago (G-6085)

EXHAUST SYSTEMS: Eqpt & Parts

CC Distributing Services Inc ....G....... 800 931-2668
  Crestwood (G-7110)
Hendrix Industrial Gastrux Inc ....G....... 847 526-1700
  Mundelein (G-14696)
Maintenance Inc ....G....... 708 598-1390
  La Grange (G-12082)
Parker Fabrication Inc ....E....... 309 266-8413
  Morton (G-14376)

EXHIBITORS, AIRLINES, MOTION PICTURE

Chicago Midway Airport ....G....... 773 838-0600
  Chicago (G-4117)

EXPLOSIVES

Buckley Powder Co ....G....... 217 285-5531
  Pittsfield (G-16629)
Dyno Nobel Inc ....E....... 217 285-5531
  Detroit (G-7872)
Evenson Explosives LLC ....E....... 815 942-5800
  Morris (G-14304)
General Dynamics Ordnance ....C....... 618 985-8211
  Marion (G-13512)
Orica USA Inc ....E....... 815 357-8711
  Morris (G-14320)

EXPLOSIVES, EXC AMMO & FIREWORKS WHOLESALERS

Orica USA Inc ....E....... 815 357-8711
  Morris (G-14320)

EXTENSION CORDS

Appleton Grp LLC ....C....... 847 268-6000
  Rosemont (G-17999)
Power Port Products Inc ....E....... 630 628-9102
  Addison (G-248)

EXTERMINATING & FUMIGATING SVCS

Smithereen Company Del ....D....... 847 675-0010
  Niles (G-15173)

EXTRACTS, FLAVORING

Dennco Inc ....G....... 708 862-0070
  Burnham (G-2645)
Edgar A Weber & Company ....E....... 847 215-1980
  Wheeling (G-20886)
Edgar A Weber & Company ....E....... 847 215-1980
  Wheeling (G-20887)
Edlong Corporation ....D....... 847 439-9230
  Elk Grove Village (G-8969)
Flavorchem Corporation ....D....... 630 932-8100
  Downers Grove (G-8004)
Fona International Inc ....G....... 630 578-8600
  Batavia (G-1380)
Fona International Inc ....G....... 630 578-8600
  Saint Charles (G-18200)
Fona International Inc ....D....... 630 578-8600
  Geneva (G-10269)
Fona Uk Ltd ....C....... 331 442-5779
  Geneva (G-10270)
H B Taylor Co ....E....... 773 254-4805
  Chicago (G-4758)
Interntnal Ingredient Mall LLC ....G....... 630 462-1414
  Geneva (G-10285)
Northwestern Flavors LLC ....E....... 630 231-6111
  West Chicago (G-20625)
Sensient Flavors LLC ....B....... 317 243-3521
  Hoffman Estates (G-11457)
Sensient Flavors LLC ....F....... 815 857-3691
  Amboy (G-580)
Silesia Flavors Inc ....E....... 847 645-0270
  Hoffman Estates (G-11459)
Stepan Company ....B....... 847 446-7500
  Northfield (G-15531)
Sterling Extract Company Inc ....G....... 847 451-9728
  Franklin Park (G-10053)
Synergy Flavors Inc ....D....... 847 487-1011
  Wauconda (G-20394)
Synergy Flavors NY Company LLC ....E....... 585 232-6648
  Wauconda (G-20395)
Wm Wrigley Jr Company ....A....... 312 644-2121
  Chicago (G-6656)

EYEGLASSES

Essilor Laboratories Amer Inc ....E....... 309 787-2727
  Rock Island (G-17219)
Midwest Uncuts Inc ....F....... 312 664-3131
  Chicago (G-5450)
Tammy Smith ....G....... 618 372-8410
  Brighton (G-2404)
Vicron Optical Inc ....F....... 847 412-5530
  Deerfield (G-7657)
Waters Industries Inc ....E....... 847 783-5900
  West Dundee (G-20667)

EYEGLASSES: Sunglasses

Ellison Eyewear Inc ....G....... 312 880-7609
  Chicago (G-4487)
Jim Maui Inc ....G....... 888 666-5905
  Peoria (G-16462)

EYELASHES, ARTIFICIAL

Manhattan Eyelash EXT Sew On ....G....... 847 818-8774
  Arlington Heights (G-774)
Posh Lash Inc ....G....... 630 388-6828
  Chicago (G-5846)

EYES & HOOKS Screw

Southern Imperial Inc ....G....... 815 877-7041
  Loves Park (G-13265)

EYES: Artificial

Dean B Scott ....G....... 630 960-4455
  Downers Grove (G-7984)
Eye Surgeons of Libertyville ....G....... 847 362-3811
  Libertyville (G-12650)

EYES: Artificial

Eyewearplanet Com Inc .... G 847 513-6203
  Northbrook *(G-15387)*
Robert B Scott Ocularists Ltd .... E 312 782-3558
  Chicago *(G-6042)*

FABRIC STORES

A D Specialty Sewing .... G 847 639-0390
  Fox River Grove *(G-9756)*
Duracrest Fabrics .... G 847 350-0030
  Elk Grove Village *(G-8959)*

FABRICATED METAL PRODUCTS, NEC

Adk Products Inc .... G 847 710-0021
  Elk Grove Village *(G-8808)*
Avondale Customs Inc .... G 773 680-4631
  Chicago *(G-3790)*
Custom Fabricators LLC .... F 630 372-4399
  Streamwood *(G-19569)*
Dva Metal Fabrication Inc .... G 224 577-8217
  Mundelein *(G-14684)*
F5d Inc .... G 815 953-9183
  Herscher *(G-11183)*
Forge Group Star LLC .... E 815 758-6400
  Freeport *(G-10110)*
Kenneth W Templeman .... G 847 912-2740
  Volo *(G-20200)*
Lindsay Metal Madness Inc .... G 815 568-4560
  Woodstock *(G-21406)*
Macholl Metal Fabrication .... G 815 597-1908
  Garden Prairie *(G-10237)*
Mc Metals & Fabricating Inc .... G 847 961-5242
  Huntley *(G-11555)*
Robin L Barnhouse .... G 309 737-5431
  Joy *(G-11947)*
Signode Midwest Steel .... G 847 657-5385
  Bridgeview *(G-2386)*
Star Freeport Company LLC .... E 815 758-6400
  Freeport *(G-10145)*
Viking Metal Cabinet Co LLC .... D 800 776-7767
  Montgomery *(G-14273)*

FABRICS & CLOTH: Quilted

Advanced Flexible Mtls LLC .... F 312 961-9231
  Chicago *(G-3564)*
Donghia Showrooms Inc .... G 312 822-0766
  Chicago *(G-4383)*
Rock Tops Inc .... G 708 672-1450
  Crete *(G-7144)*

FABRICS & CLOTHING: Rubber Coated

Custom Product Innovations .... G 618 628-0111
  Lebanon *(G-12545)*
Ljm Equipment Co .... G 847 291-0162
  Northbrook *(G-15420)*

FABRICS: Alpacas, Mohair, Woven

Salt Creek Alpacas Inc .... G 309 530-7904
  Farmer City *(G-9657)*

FABRICS: Apparel & Outerwear, Cotton

Akr Industries Inc .... G 732 998-5662
  Peoria *(G-16379)*
Barrett NJide Yvonne .... F 312 701-3962
  Chicago *(G-3838)*
Chicor Inc .... G 630 953-6154
  Oak Brook *(G-15609)*
Dpe Incorporated .... G 773 306-0105
  Chicago *(G-4394)*
Netranix Enterprise .... E 630 312-8141
  Bolingbrook *(G-2219)*
Rubin Manufacturing Inc .... B 312 942-1111
  Chicago *(G-6077)*

FABRICS: Apparel & Outerwear, From Manmade Fiber Or Silk

Henry-Lee & Company LLC .... F 312 242-2501
  Highland Park *(G-11270)*

FABRICS: Awning Stripes, Cotton

Haakes Awning .... G 618 529-4808
  Carbondale *(G-2844)*

FABRICS: Bags & Bagging, Cotton

Jacobson Acqstion Holdings LLC .... C 847 623-1414
  Waukegan *(G-20452)*

Sea-Rich Corp .... G 773 261-6633
  Chicago *(G-6124)*

FABRICS: Bandage Cloth, Cotton

Tru-Colour Products LLC .... G 630 447-0559
  Warrenville *(G-20255)*

FABRICS: Broadwoven, Cotton

Veltex Corporation .... E 312 235-4014
  Chicago *(G-6530)*

FABRICS: Broadwoven, Synthetic Manmade Fiber & Silk

BP Amoco Chemical Company .... B 630 420-5111
  Naperville *(G-14782)*
Haakes Awning .... G 618 529-4808
  Carbondale *(G-2844)*
Lift-All Company Inc .... E 800 909-1964
  Itasca *(G-11692)*
Loomcraft Textile & Supply Co .... E 847 680-0000
  Vernon Hills *(G-20073)*
MHS Ltd .... F 773 736-3333
  Chicago *(G-5419)*
Ogden Top & Trim Shop Inc .... G 708 484-5422
  Berwyn *(G-1958)*

FABRICS: Broadwoven, Wool

Aurora Spclty Txtles Group Inc .... D 800 864-0303
  Yorkville *(G-21473)*
Modern Specialties Company .... G 312 648-5800
  Chicago *(G-5481)*

FABRICS: Coated Or Treated

Ace Anodizing Impregnating Inc .... D 708 547-6680
  Hillside *(G-11324)*
Advanced Flxble Composites Inc .... D 847 658-3938
  Lake In The Hills *(G-12327)*
Allerton Charter Coach .... G 217 344-2600
  Champaign *(G-3261)*
Brasel Products Inc .... G 630 879-3759
  Batavia *(G-1360)*
Jessup Manufacturing Company .... E 847 362-0961
  Lake Bluff *(G-12190)*
Metal Impregnating Corp .... G 630 543-3443
  Addison *(G-198)*
Stickon Adhesive Inds Inc .... G 847 593-5959
  Wauconda *(G-20391)*

FABRICS: Cotton, Narrow

F Hyman & Co .... G 312 664-3810
  Chicago *(G-4549)*

FABRICS: Fiberglass, Broadwoven

Accu-Wright Fiberglass Inc .... G 618 337-3318
  East Saint Louis *(G-8295)*
Aim LLC .... E 727 544-3000
  Alsip *(G-413)*
Fiberglass Solutions Corp .... G 630 458-0756
  Addison *(G-121)*
Fiberteq LLC .... D 217 431-2111
  Danville *(G-7333)*
Jalaa Fiberglass Inc .... G 217 923-3433
  Greenup *(G-10821)*
Kabert Industries Inc .... C 630 833-2115
  Villa Park *(G-20154)*
Mahans Fiberglass .... G 309 562-7349
  Easton *(G-8330)*

FABRICS: Filter Cloth, Cotton

Hygienic Fabrics & Filters Inc .... G 815 493-2502
  Lanark *(G-12482)*

FABRICS: Furniture Denim

Anees Upholstery .... G 312 243-2919
  Chicago *(G-3695)*
City Living Design Inc .... G 312 335-0711
  Chicago *(G-4156)*

FABRICS: Metallized

J M Fabricating Inc .... G 815 359-2024
  Harmon *(G-11018)*
JAm International Co Ltd .... G 847 827-6391
  Riverwoods *(G-17094)*

Vacumet Corp .... F 708 562-7290
  Northlake *(G-15564)*

FABRICS: Nonwoven

Cowtan and Tout Inc .... F 312 644-0717
  Chicago *(G-4251)*
Fibertex Nonwovens LLC .... A 815 349-3200
  Ingleside *(G-11581)*
Fin North America Holding Inc .... D 815 349-3219
  Ingleside *(G-11582)*
Midwest Nonwovens LLC .... E 618 337-9662
  Sauget *(G-18395)*
Smart-Fab Inc .... G 855 276-2783
  Buffalo Grove *(G-2607)*
Windwrap LLC .... G 773 594-1724
  Chicago *(G-6639)*

FABRICS: Nylon, Broadwoven

Srm Industries Inc .... G 847 735-0077
  Lake Forest *(G-12306)*

FABRICS: Polypropylene, Broadwoven

Kobawala Poly-Pack Inc .... G 312 664-3810
  Naperville *(G-14859)*
Neptune USA Inc .... G 847 987-3804
  Schaumburg *(G-18647)*
Sea-Rich Corp .... G 773 261-6633
  Chicago *(G-6124)*

FABRICS: Print, Cotton

DLS Custom Embroidery Inc .... E 847 593-5957
  Elk Grove Village *(G-8952)*

FABRICS: Resin Or Plastic Coated

Wisdom Adhesives LLC .... E 847 841-7002
  Elgin *(G-8783)*

FABRICS: Seat Cover, Automobile, Cotton

Seat Cover Pro LLC .... G 847 990-1506
  Vernon Hills *(G-20094)*

FABRICS: Shoe Laces, Exc Leather

Shoelace Inc .... G 847 854-2500
  Crystal Lake *(G-7265)*

FABRICS: Stretch, Cotton

Moss Holding Company .... C 847 238-4200
  Elk Grove Village *(G-9132)*

FABRICS: Tapestry, Cotton

Toco .... G 618 257-8626
  Belleville *(G-1600)*

FABRICS: Trimmings

A & R Screening LLC .... F 708 598-2480
  Crestwood *(G-7103)*
Alternative TS .... G 618 257-0230
  Belleville *(G-1529)*
Ambrit Inc .... G 847 593-3301
  Elk Grove Village *(G-8820)*
American Name Plate & Metal De .... E 773 376-1400
  Chicago *(G-3663)*
Art Newvo Incorporated .... G 847 838-0304
  Antioch *(G-600)*
Ashland Screening Corporation .... E 708 758-8800
  Chicago Heights *(G-6732)*
Authority Screenprint & EMB .... G 630 236-0289
  Plainfield *(G-16643)*
B and A Screen Printing .... G 217 762-2632
  Monticello *(G-14277)*
Bailleu & Bailleu Printing Inc .... G 309 852-2517
  Kewanee *(G-12021)*
Bow Brothers Co Inc .... G 217 359-0555
  Champaign *(G-3272)*
Carl Gorr Printing Co .... E 815 338-3191
  Woodstock *(G-21370)*
Color Tone Printing .... G 708 385-1442
  Blue Island *(G-2114)*
Creative Clothing Created 4 U .... G 847 543-0051
  Grayslake *(G-10764)*
Custom Monogramming .... G 815 625-9044
  Rock Falls *(G-17180)*
Custom Telephone Printing Co .... F 815 338-0000
  Woodstock *(G-21379)*

PRODUCT SECTION

FARM PRDTS, RAW MATERIALS, WHOLESALE: Farm Animals

Custom Trophies..G....... 217 422-3353
  Decatur *(G-7480)*
Darnall Printing..G....... 309 827-7212
  Bloomington *(G-2039)*
Desk & Door Nameplate Company.............F....... 815 806-8670
  Frankfort *(G-9785)*
DMarv Design Specialty Prtrs.....................G....... 708 389-4420
  Blue Island *(G-2118)*
Earl Ad Inc..G....... 312 666-7106
  Chicago *(G-4431)*
Fantastic Lettering Inc..............................G....... 773 685-7650
  Chicago *(G-4559)*
G and D Enterprises Inc...........................E....... 847 981-8661
  Arlington Heights *(G-739)*
Gabriel Enterprises....................................G....... 773 342-8705
  Chicago *(G-4654)*
George Lauterer Corporation....................E....... 312 913-1881
  Chicago *(G-4682)*
Go Van Goghs Tee Shirt............................G....... 309 342-1112
  Galesburg *(G-10198)*
Good Impressions Inc...............................G....... 847 831-4317
  Highland Park *(G-11265)*
Graphic Screen Printing Inc......................G....... 708 429-3330
  Orland Park *(G-15957)*
Hazen Display Corporation.......................E....... 815 248-2925
  Davis *(G-7418)*
Hole In The Wall Screen Arts....................G....... 217 243-9100
  Jacksonville *(G-11767)*
Image Plus Inc..G....... 630 852-4920
  Downers Grove *(G-8028)*
J & D Instant Signs...................................G....... 847 965-2800
  Morton Grove *(G-14414)*
Johnson Rolan Co Inc...............................G....... 309 674-9671
  Peoria *(G-16464)*
K and A Graphics Inc................................G....... 847 244-2345
  Gurnee *(G-10890)*
Lee-Wel Printing Corporation....................G....... 630 682-0935
  Wheaton *(G-20812)*
Linda Levinson Designs Inc......................G....... 312 951-6943
  Chicago *(G-5226)*
Lloyd Midwest Graphics............................G....... 815 282-8828
  Machesney Park *(G-13357)*
Lochman Ref Silk Screen Co.....................F....... 847 475-6266
  Evanston *(G-9547)*
Locker Room Screen Printing...................G....... 630 759-2533
  Bolingbrook *(G-2206)*
M Wells Printing Co...................................G....... 312 455-0400
  Chicago *(G-5305)*
Mer-Pla Inc...F....... 847 530-9798
  Chicago *(G-5393)*
Mexacali Silkscreen Inc............................G....... 630 628-9313
  Addison *(G-201)*
Midwest Stitch..G....... 815 394-1516
  Rockford *(G-17528)*
Mighty Mites Awards and Sons.................G....... 847 297-0035
  Des Plaines *(G-7802)*
Minerva Sportswear Inc............................F....... 309 661-2387
  Bloomington *(G-2080)*
Need To Know Inc.....................................G....... 309 691-3877
  Peoria *(G-16484)*
Nu-Art Printing..G....... 618 533-9971
  Centralia *(G-3242)*
Offworld Designs......................................G....... 815 786-7080
  Sandwich *(G-18378)*
Olympic Trophy and Awards Co.................F....... 773 631-9500
  Chicago *(G-5672)*
Paddock Industries Inc.............................F....... 618 277-1580
  Smithton *(G-19068)*
Papyrus Press Inc.....................................F....... 773 342-0700
  Chicago *(G-5755)*
Plastics Printing Group Inc........................F....... 773 473-4481
  Chicago *(G-5820)*
Precision Screen Specialties.....................G....... 630 220-1361
  Saint Charles *(G-18250)*
Priority Print...G....... 708 485-7080
  Brookfield *(G-2491)*
Qst Industries Inc......................................E....... 312 930-9400
  Chicago *(G-5923)*
Qst Industries Inc......................................D....... 312 930-9400
  Chicago *(G-5924)*
Quality Spraying Screen Prtg....................E....... 630 584-4156
  Saint Charles *(G-18256)*
R J S Silk Screening Co............................G....... 708 974-3009
  Palos Hills *(G-16206)*
R R Donnelley & Sons Company..............D....... 630 762-7600
  Saint Charles *(G-18258)*
Rainbow Art Inc..F....... 312 421-5600
  Chicago *(G-5965)*
Rico Industries Inc....................................D....... 312 427-0313
  Niles *(G-15166)*

Ronald J Nixon...G....... 708 748-8130
  Park Forest *(G-16259)*
Scheiwes Print Shop.................................G....... 815 683-2398
  Crescent City *(G-7082)*
Screen Machine Incorporated...................G....... 847 439-2233
  Elk Grove Village *(G-9234)*
Select Screen Prints & EMB......................F....... 309 829-6511
  Bloomington *(G-2093)*
Sg Screen Graphics Inc............................G....... 309 699-8513
  Pekin *(G-16360)*
Shree Mahavir Inc.....................................G....... 312 408-1080
  Chicago *(G-6159)*
Signature Label of Illinois.........................G....... 618 283-5145
  Vandalia *(G-20024)*
Signature Screen Printing Corp.................G....... 773 866-0070
  Chicago *(G-6169)*
Signcraft Screenprint Inc..........................C....... 815 777-3030
  Galena *(G-10178)*
Sport Connection.....................................G....... 630 980-1787
  Roselle *(G-17990)*
Stevens Sign Co Inc.................................G....... 708 562-4888
  Northlake *(G-15560)*
Teds Shirt Shack Inc.................................G....... 217 224-9705
  Quincy *(G-16946)*
Think Ink Inc...G....... 815 459-4565
  Crystal Lake *(G-7282)*
Top Notch Silk Screening..........................G....... 773 847-6335
  Chicago *(G-6395)*
Triangle Screen Print Inc..........................F....... 847 678-9200
  Franklin Park *(G-10066)*
Trimark Screen Printing Inc......................G....... 630 629-2823
  Lombard *(G-13146)*
Ultimate Distributing Inc..........................G....... 847 566-2250
  Mundelein *(G-14745)*
Wagner Zip-Change Inc............................E....... 708 681-4100
  Melrose Park *(G-13926)*
Waldos Sports Corner Inc.........................G....... 309 688-2425
  Peoria *(G-16545)*
Weiskamp Screen Printing........................G....... 217 398-8428
  Champaign *(G-3370)*
Winning Stitch..G....... 217 348-8279
  Charleston *(G-3417)*
Woodbridge Inc..F....... 847 229-1741
  Wheeling *(G-21015)*

FABRICS: Trimmings, Textile

Grant Technologies LLC............................G....... 847 370-9306
  Chicago *(G-4725)*

FABRICS: Upholstery, Wool

EW Bredemeier and Co.............................F....... 773 237-1600
  Chicago *(G-4542)*

FABRICS: Wall Covering, From Manmade Fiber Or Silk

Maya Romanoff Corporation.....................E....... 773 465-6909
  Skokie *(G-18986)*

FABRICS: Weft Or Circular Knit

Chicago Knitting Mills...............................G....... 773 463-1464
  Northbrook *(G-15358)*

FABRICS: Woven, Narrow Cotton, Wool, Silk

Chase Corporation....................................E....... 847 866-8500
  Evanston *(G-9503)*
Harbor Village LLC...................................G....... 773 338-2222
  Chicago *(G-4779)*
Shoelace Inc...G....... 847 854-2500
  Kildeer *(G-12053)*
Technical Sealants Inc..............................F....... 815 777-9797
  Galena *(G-10179)*
UNI-Label and Tag Corporation.................E....... 847 956-8900
  Elk Grove Village *(G-9294)*
Voss Belting & Specialty Co......................E....... 847 673-8900
  Lincolnwood *(G-12849)*

FACILITIES SUPPORT SVCS

Bison Aerospace and Def LLC..................G....... 618 795-2678
  Savanna *(G-18403)*
Pitney Bowes Inc......................................E....... 800 784-4224
  Itasca *(G-11719)*

FACSIMILE COMMUNICATION EQPT

Pitney Bowes Inc......................................E....... 800 784-4224
  Itasca *(G-11719)*

FAMILY CLOTHING STORES

Five Brother Inc..G....... 309 663-6323
  Bloomington *(G-2043)*
Teds Shirt Shack Inc.................................G....... 217 224-9705
  Quincy *(G-16946)*
Thrilled LLC..G....... 312 404-1929
  Chicago *(G-6373)*

FAMILY COUNSELING SVCS

Coaching For Excellence LLC..................F....... 708 957-6047
  Country Club Hills *(G-7036)*

FANS, BLOWING: Indl Or Commercial

Eclipse Inc...D....... 815 877-3031
  Rockford *(G-17388)*
Illinois Blower Inc.....................................D....... 847 639-5500
  Cary *(G-3168)*

FANS, EXHAUST: Indl Or Commercial

Car - Mon Products Inc............................E....... 847 695-9000
  Elgin *(G-8532)*
Reds Muffler Shop....................................G....... 217 344-1676
  Urbana *(G-19997)*

FANS, VENTILATING: Indl Or Commercial

Conservation Technology Ltd..................D....... 847 559-5500
  Northbrook *(G-15366)*
New York Blower Company.......................D....... 217 347-3233
  Effingham *(G-8414)*
Nyb Process Fans Inc...............................G....... 630 794-5700
  Willowbrook *(G-21055)*

FANS: Ceiling

Matthews-Gerbar Ltd................................G....... 847 680-9043
  Libertyville *(G-12674)*
Matthews-Gerbar Ltd................................G....... 847 680-9043
  Libertyville *(G-12675)*

FARM & GARDEN MACHINERY WHOLESALERS

Gsi Group LLC...D....... 618 283-9792
  Vandalia *(G-20012)*
Mega Equipment Inc.................................G....... 309 764-5310
  Moline *(G-14160)*
Michaels Equipment Co.............................G....... 618 524-8560
  Metropolis *(G-13975)*
Srj Inc..F....... 630 351-0639
  Schaumburg *(G-18726)*
Wabash Valley Service Co........................F....... 618 393-2971
  Olney *(G-15893)*

FARM MACHINERY REPAIR SVCS

Greene Welding & Hardware Inc..............E....... 217 375-4244
  East Lynn *(G-8220)*
Lake Fabrication Inc.................................G....... 217 832-2761
  Villa Grove *(G-20124)*
Midwest Machine Tool Inc........................G....... 815 427-8665
  Saint Anne *(G-18136)*
Needham Shop Inc...................................G....... 630 557-9019
  Kaneville *(G-11955)*
Trotters Manufacturing Co........................G....... 217 364-4540
  Buffalo *(G-2501)*

FARM PRDTS, RAW MATERIAL, WHOLESALE: Tobacco & Tobacco Prdts

Ugly Hookah Tobacco Inc.........................G....... 708 724-9621
  Oak Lawn *(G-15737)*
Upper Limits Midwest Inc.........................G....... 217 679-4315
  Springfield *(G-19467)*

FARM PRDTS, RAW MATERIALS, WHOLESALE: Broomcorn

Thomas Monahan Company.....................F....... 217 268-5771
  Arcola *(G-667)*

FARM PRDTS, RAW MATERIALS, WHOLESALE: Farm Animals

Millstadt Rendering Company...................E....... 618 538-5312
  Belleville *(G-1578)*

Employee Codes: A=Over 500 employees, B=251-500
C=101-250, D=51-100, E=20-50, F=10-19, G=3-9

FARM SPLY STORES — PRODUCT SECTION

FARM SPLY STORES

Company	Loc	Phone
Piatt County Service Co — Bement (G-1714)	G	217 678-5511
West Salem Knox County Htchy — West Salem (G-20689)	G	618 456-3601

FARM SPLYS WHOLESALERS

Company	Loc	Phone
Archer-Daniels-Midland Company — Altamont (G-530)	G	618 483-6171
Birkeys Farm Store Inc — Urbana (G-19975)	E	217 337-1772
Brandt Consolidated Inc — Springfield (G-19329)	E	217 547-5800
Brandt Consolidated Inc — Lexington (G-12618)	G	309 365-7201
Cloverleaf Feed Co Inc — Roodhouse (G-17892)	G	217 589-5010
Earnest Earth Agriculture Inc — Lynn Center (G-13290)	G	217 766-4401
Hayden Mills Inc — Omaha (G-15900)	G	618 962-3136
Mont Eagle Products Inc — Sainte Marie (G-18327)	G	618 455-3344
South Central Fs Inc — Vandalia (G-20025)	G	618 283-1557

FARM SPLYS, WHOLESALE: Beekeeping Splys, Nondurable

Company	Loc	Phone
Prairie Profile — Vandalia (G-20019)	G	618 846-2116

FARM SPLYS, WHOLESALE: Feed

Company	Loc	Phone
American Milling Company — Pekin (G-16323)	F	309 347-6888
B B Milling Co Inc — Emden (G-9466)	G	217 376-3131
Effingham Equity — Arcola (G-648)	F	217 268-5128
Furst-Mcness Company — Freeport (G-10112)	D	800 435-5100
Hueber LLC — Creston (G-7102)	F	815 393-4879
Liberty Feed Mill — Liberty (G-12623)	F	217 645-3441
M & W Feed Service — Elizabeth (G-8787)	G	815 858-2412
Siemer Enterprises Inc — Teutopolis (G-19772)	E	217 857-3171
Wabash Valley Service Co — Olney (G-15893)	F	618 393-2971

FARM SPLYS, WHOLESALE: Fertilizers & Agricultural Chemicals

Company	Loc	Phone
Prairieland Fs Inc — Astoria (G-895)	G	309 329-2162

FARM SPLYS, WHOLESALE: Greenhouse Eqpt & Splys

Company	Loc	Phone
Interntional Grnhse Contrs Inc — Danville (G-7352)	E	217 443-0600

FARM SPLYS, WHOLESALE: Harness Eqpt

Company	Loc	Phone
Mast Harness Shop — Campbell Hill (G-2816)	E	217 543-3463

FARM SPLYS, WHOLESALE: Limestone, Agricultural

Company	Loc	Phone
Blomberg Bros Inc — Farina (G-9651)	F	618 245-6321

FARM SPLYS, WHOLESALE: Soil, Potting & Planting

Company	Loc	Phone
RR Mulch and Soil LLC — Markham (G-13551)	G	708 596-7200

FASTENERS WHOLESALERS

Company	Loc	Phone
R-B Industries Inc — Morton Grove (G-14436)	E	847 647-4020

FASTENERS: Metal

Company	Loc	Phone
Ecf Holdings LLC — Northbrook (G-15379)	G	224 723-5524
Gemco — Danville (G-7339)	E	217 446-7900
Hilti Inc — Elmhurst (G-9372)	F	847 364-9818
Topy Precision Mfg Inc — Elk Grove Village (G-9277)	D	847 228-5902

FASTENERS: Metal

Company	Loc	Phone
Cleats Mfg Inc — Chicago (G-4175)	F	773 521-0300
Hunter-Stevens Company Inc — Franklin Park (G-9959)	F	847 671-5014
Illinois Tool Works Inc — Broadview (G-2442)	E	708 681-3891
Metal Mfg LLC — Watseka (G-20311)	C	815 432-4595
Rifast Systems LLC — Lincolnwood (G-12839)	E	847 933-8330
Termax LLC — Lake Zurich (G-12463)	C	847 519-1500
Termax LLC — Lake Zurich (G-12464)	G	847 519-1500
United Steel & Fasteners Inc — Itasca (G-11750)	E	630 250-0900

FASTENERS: Notions, NEC

Company	Loc	Phone
Afi Industries Inc — Carol Stream (G-2927)	E	630 462-0400
Agrati Inc — Park Forest (G-16250)	G	704 747-1200
Ample Supply Company — Sycamore (G-19700)	E	815 895-3500
Anixter Inc — Glenview (G-10525)	E	512 989-4254
Buildex Divison of ITW — Itasca (G-11631)	G	630 595-3500
Ecf Holdings LLC — Northbrook (G-15379)	E	224 723-5524
Engineered Components Co — Elgin (G-8579)	E	847 985-8000
Forest City Technologies Inc — Rockford (G-17420)	E	815 965-5880
Hawk Fastener Services — Alsip (G-456)	F	708 489-2000
Ideal Supply Inc — Huntley (G-11541)	G	847 961-5900
Illinois Tool Works Inc — Glenview (G-10560)	B	847 724-7500
Illinois Tool Works Inc — Bartlett (G-1288)	C	630 372-2150
Illinois Tool Works Inc — Elgin (G-8621)	C	847 783-5500
Inland Fastener Inc — West Chicago (G-20596)	F	630 293-3800
L & M Screw Machine Products — Montgomery (G-14253)	F	630 801-0455
Lhs Inc — Elmhurst (G-9391)	G	630 832-3875
Marmon Industrial LLC — Chicago (G-5344)	G	312 372-9500
Multitech Cold Forming LLC — Carol Stream (G-3034)	E	630 949-8200
Nbs Corporation — Elk Grove Village (G-9145)	G	847 860-8856
Pecson Distributors LLC — Beecher (G-1520)	G	815 342-7977
Safety Socket LLC — Gilberts (G-10368)	E	224 484-6222
Sanco Industries Inc — Kildeer (G-12052)	F	847 243-8675
Supreme Screw Inc — Romeoville (G-17879)	G	630 226-9000

FASTENERS: Notions, Zippers

Company	Loc	Phone
Minigrip Inc — Ottawa (G-16061)	D	845 680-2710

FASTENERS: Wire, Made From Purchased Wire

Company	Loc	Phone
Klimp Industries Inc — Carol Stream (G-3011)	G	630 682-0750
Klimp Industries Inc — Carol Stream (G-3012)	G	630 790-0600

FATTY ACID ESTERS & AMINOS

Company	Loc	Phone
Vantage Oleochemicals Inc — Chicago (G-6522)	C	773 376-9000
Vantage Specialties Inc — Gurnee (G-10943)	D	773 376-9000

FAUCETS & SPIGOTS: Metal & Plastic

Company	Loc	Phone
Elkay Manufacturing Company — Saint Charles (G-18196)	E	630 377-0150
Elkay Manufacturing Company — Downers Grove (G-7999)	G	800 223-5529
Homewerks Worldwide LLC — Lake Bluff (G-12188)	E	224 543-1529
PSI Systems North America Inc — Bartlett (G-1302)	G	630 830-9435
Water Saver Faucet Co — Chicago (G-6588)	C	312 666-5500

FEATHERS: Dusters

Company	Loc	Phone
Modern Specialties Company — Chicago (G-5481)	G	312 648-5800

FEDERAL CROP INSURANCE CORP

Company	Loc	Phone
Associated Agri-Business Inc — Jerseyville (G-11786)	G	618 498-2977
Associated Agri-Business Inc — Eldred (G-8487)	G	618 498-2977

FELT PARTS

Company	Loc	Phone
Filter Technology Inc — Bedford Park (G-1467)	E	773 523-7200
Fourell Corp — Winchester (G-21105)	G	217 742-3186

FELT, WHOLESALE

Company	Loc	Phone
Supreme Felt & Abrasives Inc — Cicero (G-6878)	E	708 344-0134

FELT: Polishing

Company	Loc	Phone
Gilday Services — Antioch (G-613)	G	847 395-0853

FENCE POSTS: Iron & Steel

Company	Loc	Phone
CHS Acquisition Corp — Chicago Heights (G-6743)	C	708 756-5648

FENCES OR POSTS: Ornamental Iron Or Steel

Company	Loc	Phone
Builders Ironworks Inc — Crete (G-7135)	G	708 672-1047
Gemini Steel Inc — Momence (G-14185)	G	815 472-4462
Industrial Fence Inc — Chicago (G-4906)	D	773 521-9900
Iron Castle Inc — Chicago (G-4969)	F	773 890-0575
Kelley Ornamental Iron LLC — Bloomington (G-2067)	F	309 820-7540
Mike Meier & Sons Fence Mfg — Spring Grove (G-19284)	E	847 587-1111
Mueller Ornamental Iron Works — Elk Grove Village (G-9140)	F	847 758-9941
Neiweem Industries Inc — Oakwood Hills (G-15821)	G	847 487-1239
Winters Welding Inc — Chicago (G-6648)	G	773 860-7735

FENCING DEALERS

Company	Loc	Phone
Mike Meier & Sons Fence Mfg — Spring Grove (G-19284)	E	847 587-1111
Ornamental Iron Shop — Columbia (G-6992)	G	618 281-6072
William Dach — Rockford (G-17685)	F	815 962-3455
Woodland Fence Forest Pdts Inc — Warrenville (G-20257)	G	630 393-2220

FENCING MATERIALS: Plastic

Company	Loc	Phone
Plastival Inc — Elgin (G-8690)	B	847 931-4771

PRODUCT SECTION

FILLERS & SEALERS: Wood

FENCING MATERIALS: Snow Fence, Wood
Iron Castle Inc ....F 773 890-0575
  Chicago *(G-4969)*

FENCING MATERIALS: Wood
Bergeron Group Inc ....E 815 741-1635
  Joliet *(G-11830)*
Mike Meier & Sons Fence Mfg ....E 847 587-1111
  Spring Grove *(G-19284)*

FENCING: Chain Link
Master-Halco Inc ....E 618 395-4365
  Olney *(G-15873)*
Stephens Pipe & Steel LLC ....E 800 451-2612
  North Aurora *(G-15278)*

FENDERS: Automobile, Stamped Or Pressed Metal
Gs Custom Works Inc ....G 815 233-4724
  Freeport *(G-10113)*

FERRITES
TSC Pyroferric International ....C 217 849-2230
  Toledo *(G-19881)*

FERTILIZER, AGRICULTURAL: Wholesalers
Brandt Consolidated Inc ....F 217 438-6158
  Auburn *(G-906)*
Brandt Consolidated Inc ....G 217 626-1123
  Farmer City *(G-9654)*
F S Gateway Inc ....G 618 458-6588
  Fults *(G-10160)*
Harbach Gillan & Nixon Inc ....G 217 794-5117
  Maroa *(G-13552)*
Harbach Gillan & Nixon Inc ....G 217 935-8378
  Clinton *(G-6922)*
Huyear Trucking Inc ....G 217 854-3551
  Carlinville *(G-2876)*
Illini Fs Inc ....G 217 442-4737
  Potomac *(G-16802)*
Miller Fertilizer Inc ....G 217 382-4241
  Casey *(G-3207)*
Millers Fertilizer & Feed ....F 217 783-6321
  Cowden *(G-7079)*
Potash Holding Company Inc ....G 847 849-4200
  Northbrook *(G-15462)*
Randolph Agricultural Services ....G 309 473-3256
  Heyworth *(G-11190)*
South Central Fs Inc ....F 217 849-2242
  Toledo *(G-19878)*

FERTILIZERS: NEC
Allerton Supply Company ....F 217 896-2522
  Homer *(G-11475)*
Anp Inc ....G 309 757-0372
  Moline *(G-14132)*
Archer-Daniels-Midland Company ....G 618 483-6171
  Altamont *(G-530)*
Biogreen Organics Inc ....G 847 740-9637
  Volo *(G-20196)*
Brandt Consolidated Inc ....G 217 547-5800
  Springfield *(G-19329)*
Brandt Consolidated Inc ....G 217 626-1123
  Farmer City *(G-9654)*
Brandt Consolidated Inc ....G 309 365-7201
  Lexington *(G-12618)*
Brandt Consolidated Inc ....F 217 438-6158
  Auburn *(G-906)*
E N P Inc ....G 815 539-7471
  Mendota *(G-13941)*
E N P Inc ....G 800 255-4906
  Mendota *(G-13940)*
Enp Investments LLC ....G 815 539-7471
  Mendota *(G-13942)*
Evergreen Fs Inc ....G 815 934-5422
  Cullom *(G-7298)*
F S Gateway Inc ....G 618 458-6588
  Fults *(G-10160)*
Harbach Gillan & Nixon Inc ....F 217 935-8378
  Clinton *(G-6922)*
Hayden Mills Inc ....E 618 962-3136
  Omaha *(G-15900)*
Hyponex Corporation ....E 815 772-2167
  Morrison *(G-14343)*
Kreider Services Incorporated ....D 815 288-6691
  Dixon *(G-7903)*

Lebanon Seaboard Corporation ....E 217 446-0983
  Danville *(G-7358)*
Miller Fertilizer Inc ....G 217 382-4241
  Casey *(G-3207)*
Millers Fertilizer & Feed ....F 217 783-6321
  Cowden *(G-7079)*
Myers Inc ....G 309 725-3710
  Varna *(G-20033)*
Piatt County Service Co ....G 217 678-5511
  Bement *(G-1714)*
Piatt County Service Co ....G 217 489-2411
  Mansfield *(G-13442)*
Prairieland Fs Inc ....G 309 329-2162
  Astoria *(G-895)*
Randolph Agricultural Services ....G 309 473-3256
  Heyworth *(G-11190)*
South Central Fs Inc ....F 217 849-2242
  Toledo *(G-19878)*
South Central Fs Inc ....G 618 283-1557
  Vandalia *(G-20025)*
Van Diest Supply Company ....G 815 232-6053
  Freeport *(G-10149)*
Wabash Valley Service Co ....F 618 393-2971
  Olney *(G-15893)*
West Central Fs Inc ....G 309 375-6904
  Wataga *(G-20287)*

FERTILIZERS: Nitrogen Solutions
Rentech Development Corp ....C 815 747-3101
  East Dubuque *(G-8179)*
Terra Nitrogen Company LP ....G 847 405-2400
  Deerfield *(G-7652)*
Terra Nitrogen GP Inc ....G 847 405-2400
  Deerfield *(G-7653)*

FERTILIZERS: Nitrogenous
Biogreen Organics Inc ....G 847 740-9637
  Volo *(G-20196)*
CF Industries Nitrogen LLC ....B 847 405-2400
  Deerfield *(G-7603)*
Clean Hrbors Es Indus Svcs Inc ....F 708 652-0575
  Cicero *(G-6836)*
E N P Inc ....G 800 255-4906
  Mendota *(G-13940)*
E N P Inc ....G 815 539-7471
  Mendota *(G-13941)*
Farmers Manufacturing Company ....G 618 377-6237
  Dorsey *(G-7944)*
Gateway Fs Inc ....G 618 824-6631
  Venedy *(G-20034)*
Harbach Gillan & Nixon Inc ....F 217 935-8378
  Clinton *(G-6922)*
Harbach Gillan & Nixon Inc ....G 217 794-5117
  Maroa *(G-13552)*
Michel Fertilizer & Equipment ....G 618 242-6000
  Mount Vernon *(G-14624)*
Pcs Nitrogen Fertilizer LP ....F 847 849-4200
  Northbrook *(G-15454)*
Pcs Ntrgen Frtlzer Oprtons Inc ....D 847 849-4200
  Northbrook *(G-15456)*
Potash Corp Ssktchewan Fla Inc ....C 847 849-4200
  Northbrook *(G-15461)*
Rentech Energy Midwest Corp ....G 815 747-3101
  East Dubuque *(G-8180)*
Solution Designs Inc ....G 847 680-7788
  Vernon Hills *(G-20099)*
Sun Ag Inc ....G 309 726-1331
  Hudson *(G-11520)*
Sunrise AG Service Company ....G 309 538-4287
  Kilbourne *(G-12045)*

FERTILIZERS: Phosphatic
CF Industries Holdings Inc ....D 847 405-2400
  Deerfield *(G-7602)*
CF Industries Nitrogen LLC ....B 847 405-2400
  Deerfield *(G-7603)*
Gateway Fs Inc ....G 618 824-6631
  Venedy *(G-20034)*
Occidental Chemical Corp ....F 773 284-0079
  Chicago *(G-5651)*
Pcs Nitrogen Inc ....D 847 849-4200
  Northbrook *(G-15453)*
Pcs Phosphate Company Inc ....D 847 849-4200
  Northbrook *(G-15457)*
Potash Corp Ssktchewan Fla Inc ....C 847 849-4200
  Northbrook *(G-15461)*
Sun Ag Inc ....G 309 726-1331
  Hudson *(G-11520)*

Trainor AG Products LLC ....G 618 614-5770
  Anna *(G-589)*

FIBER & FIBER PRDTS: Acrylic
Acrylic Design Works Inc ....F 773 843-1300
  Chicago *(G-3532)*

FIBER & FIBER PRDTS: Cigarette Tow Cellulosic
Essentra Holdings Corp ....G 804 518-0322
  Westchester *(G-20698)*

FIBER & FIBER PRDTS: Organic, Noncellulose
Gig Karasek LLC ....F 630 549-0394
  Saint Charles *(G-18204)*

FIBER & FIBER PRDTS: Polyester
Fairfield Processing Corp ....E 618 452-8404
  Granite City *(G-10706)*

FIBER & FIBER PRDTS: Protein
RITA Corporation ....E 815 337-2500
  Crystal Lake *(G-7257)*

FIBER & FIBER PRDTS: Synthetic Cellulosic
Higgins Bros Inc ....F 773 523-0124
  Chicago *(G-4815)*

FIBER & FIBER PRDTS: Vinyl
Magnetic Occasions & More Inc ....G 815 462-4141
  New Lenox *(G-15040)*
Vinylworks Inc ....G 815 477-9680
  Crystal Lake *(G-7290)*

FIBER OPTICS
Advanced Fiber Products LLC ....G 847 768-9001
  Des Plaines *(G-7724)*
Elite Fiber Optics LLC ....E 630 225-9454
  Franklin Park *(G-9938)*
Neolight Labs LLC ....G 312 242-1773
  Ingleside *(G-11588)*

FIELD WAREHOUSING SVCS
Adams Elevator Equipment Co ....E 847 581-2900
  Chicago *(G-3538)*

FILE FOLDERS
Acco Brands USA LLC ....B 800 222-6462
  Lake Zurich *(G-12376)*
Warwick Publishing Company ....D 630 584-3871
  Saint Charles *(G-18296)*

FILLERS & SEALERS: Putty
Black Swan Manufacturing Co ....F 773 227-3700
  Chicago *(G-3908)*
Nu-Puttie Corporation ....E 708 681-1040
  Maywood *(G-13676)*
Sarco Putty Company ....G 773 735-5577
  Chicago *(G-6104)*

FILLERS & SEALERS: Putty, Wood
Atlas Putty Products Co ....D 708 429-5858
  Tinley Park *(G-19806)*

FILLERS & SEALERS: Wood
Sherwin-Williams Company ....G 217 359-4934
  Savoy *(G-18416)*
Sherwin-Williams Company ....G 630 834-1470
  Elmhurst *(G-9427)*
Sherwin-Williams Company ....G 847 573-0240
  Libertyville *(G-12706)*
Sherwin-Williams Company ....G 815 337-0942
  Woodstock *(G-21434)*
Sherwin-Williams Company ....G 847 478-0677
  Long Grove *(G-13170)*
Sherwin-Williams Company ....G 708 409-4728
  Westchester *(G-20710)*
Sherwin-Williams Company ....G 815 254-3559
  Romeoville *(G-17876)*

FILM & SHEET: Unsuppported Plastic

Abbott Plastics & Supply Co	E	815 874-8500
Rockford *(G-17285)*		
Amcor Flexibles LLC	C	224 313-7000
Buffalo Grove *(G-2510)*		
Avery Dennison Corporation	D	877 214-0909
Niles *(G-15104)*		
Berry Global Inc	C	847 884-1200
Schaumburg *(G-18461)*		
Berry Global Inc	G	630 375-0358
Aurora *(G-923)*		
Bio Star Films LLC	G	773 254-5959
Chicago *(G-3894)*		
Catalina Coating & Plas Inc	G	847 806-1340
Elk Grove Village *(G-8880)*		
CFC International Inc	G	708 891-3456
Chicago Heights *(G-6739)*		
CFC International Corporation	C	708 323-4131
Chicago Heights *(G-6740)*		
Co-Ordinated Packaging Inc	F	847 559-8877
Bensenville *(G-1772)*		
Custom Films Inc	F	217 826-2326
Marshall *(G-13569)*		
Custom Plastics of Peoria	G	309 697-2888
Bartonville *(G-1331)*		
E-Z Products Inc	F	847 551-9199
Gilberts *(G-10354)*		
Environetics Inc	F	815 838-8331
Lockport *(G-12993)*		
Essentra Holdings Corp	G	804 518-0322
Westchester *(G-20698)*		
Exclusively Expo	D	630 378-4600
Romeoville *(G-17818)*		
Fisher Container Holdings LLC	G	847 541-0000
Buffalo Grove *(G-2537)*		
H H Interantional Inc	G	847 697-7805
Elgin *(G-8602)*		
Highland Supply Corporation	B	618 654-2161
Highland *(G-11224)*		
Jordan Specialty Plastics Inc	G	847 945-5591
Deerfield *(G-7622)*		
Kns Companies Inc	E	630 665-9010
Carol Stream *(G-3013)*		
Midwest Lminating Coatings Inc	E	708 653-9500
Alsip *(G-478)*		
Midwest Marketing Distrs Inc	G	309 663-6972
Bloomington *(G-2078)*		
Midwest Marketing Distrs Inc	F	309 688-8858
Peoria *(G-16476)*		
Minigrip Inc	D	845 680-2710
Ottawa *(G-16061)*		
Orbis Rpm LLC	F	217 876-8655
Decatur *(G-7533)*		
Orbis Rpm LLC	F	312 343-4902
Chicago *(G-5693)*		
Polyair Inter Pack Inc	D	773 995-1818
Chicago *(G-5838)*		
Ppc Flexible Packaging LLC	C	847 541-0000
Buffalo Grove *(G-2588)*		
Reynolds Food Packaging LLC	C	847 482-3500
Lake Forest *(G-12298)*		
Sandee Manufacturing Co	E	847 671-1335
Franklin Park *(G-10042)*		
Senoplast USA	G	630 898-0731
Aurora *(G-1016)*		
Transcontinental Multifilm Inc	G	847 695-7600
Elgin *(G-8758)*		

FILM BASE: Cellulose Acetate Or Nitrocellulose Plastics

W R Grace & Co	C	773 838-3200
Chicago *(G-6575)*		

FILM DEVELOPING & PRINTING SVCS

Pictures & More	G	618 662-4572
Flora *(G-9688)*		

FILM: Motion Picture

Chicago Film Archive Nfp	G	773 478-3799
Chicago *(G-4103)*		
Motus Digital Llc	E	972 943-0008
Des Plaines *(G-7806)*		
Purple Onyx LLC	G	708 756-1500
Park Forest *(G-16258)*		

FILTER CLEANING SVCS

All Seasons Heating & AC	G	217 429-2022
Decatur *(G-7440)*		
GAG Industries Inc	E	847 616-8710
Elk Grove Village *(G-9008)*		

FILTER ELEMENTS: Fluid & Hydraulic Line

Doms Incorporated	E	847 838-6723
Antioch *(G-610)*		
Micron Filter Cartridges Corp	G	630 337-3877
Elmhurst *(G-9402)*		

FILTERING MEDIA: Pottery

Spouts of Water Inc	G	303 570-5104
Des Plaines *(G-7851)*		

FILTERS

Camfil USA Inc	D	815 459-6600
Crystal Lake *(G-7177)*		
Custom Filter LLC	D	630 906-2100
Aurora *(G-948)*		
Filter Monkey LLC	G	630 773-4402
Itasca *(G-11656)*		
Filter Renew Tecnologies	G	815 344-2200
McCullom Lake *(G-13711)*		
Filters To You	G	815 939-0700
Bradley *(G-2281)*		
Flow Pro Products Inc	F	815 836-1900
Romeoville *(G-17825)*		
Fryer To Fuel Inc	G	309 654-2875
Cordova *(G-7006)*		
Gutter Masters	G	309 686-1234
Peoria *(G-16447)*		
H2o Filter Inc	G	630 963-3303
Lisle *(G-12896)*		
Helix International Inc	G	847 709-0666
Itasca *(G-11663)*		
Illinois Tool Works Inc	F	708 720-0300
Frankfort *(G-9803)*		
Inlet & Pipe Protection Inc	G	630 355-3288
Naperville *(G-14974)*		
Intech Industries Inc	F	847 487-5599
Wauconda *(G-20361)*		
Leaffilter North LLC	D	630 595-9605
Wood Dale *(G-21207)*		
Norman Filter Company LLC	D	708 233-5521
Bridgeview *(G-2368)*		
Nsk-America Corporation	F	847 843-7664
Hoffman Estates *(G-11440)*		
Quality Cleaning Fluids Inc	G	847 451-1190
Franklin Park *(G-10029)*		
Smb Toolroom Inc	G	309 353-7396
Pekin *(G-16361)*		
Smith Power Transmission Co	G	773 526-5512
Chicago *(G-6193)*		
U S Filter Products	G	618 451-1205
Granite City *(G-10747)*		
U S Filters	G	815 932-8154
Bradley *(G-2294)*		
United States Filter/Iwt	G	815 877-3041
Rockford *(G-17672)*		
Wm W Nugent & Co Inc	E	847 673-8109
Skokie *(G-19056)*		

FILTERS & SOFTENERS: Water, Household

Amber Soft Inc	F	630 377-6945
Lake Barrington *(G-12141)*		
Amsoil Inc	G	630 595-8385
Bensenville *(G-1745)*		
Aquion Inc	C	847 725-3000
Roselle *(G-17938)*		
Durable Manufacturing Company	F	630 766-0398
Bensenville *(G-1791)*		
J II Inc	D	847 432-8979
Highland Park *(G-11275)*		
Liquitech Inc	E	630 693-0500
Lombard *(G-13097)*		
Marmon Group LLC	D	847 647-8200
Skokie *(G-18984)*		
Pure N Natural Systems Inc	F	630 372-9681
Streamwood *(G-19591)*		
RPS Products Inc	E	847 683-3400
Hampshire *(G-10986)*		

FILTERS & STRAINERS: Pipeline

Csiteq LLC	F	312 265-1509
Rosemont *(G-18011)*		
Mity Inc	G	630 365-5030
Elburn *(G-8461)*		
Perma-Pipe Intl Holdings Inc	E	847 966-1000
Niles *(G-15158)*		
Water Products Company III Inc	E	630 553-0840
Yorkville *(G-21505)*		

FILTERS: Air

American Air Filter Co Inc	D	502 637-0011
Chicago *(G-3647)*		
Clark Filter Inc	E	216 896-3000
Chicago *(G-4167)*		
GAG Industries Inc	E	847 616-8710
Elk Grove Village *(G-9008)*		
Henderson Engineering Co Inc	G	815 786-9471
Sandwich *(G-18374)*		
International Filter Mfg Corp	F	217 324-2303
Litchfield *(G-12966)*		
Lilly Air Systems Co Inc	F	630 773-2225
Itasca *(G-11693)*		
Murdock Company Inc	G	847 566-0050
Mundelein *(G-14719)*		
Nordic A Filtration N Amer Inc	G	331 457-5289
Naperville *(G-14886)*		
Permatron Corporation	E	847 434-1421
Elk Grove Village *(G-9174)*		
Rv Air Inc	G	309 657-4300
Addison *(G-279)*		
Smith Filter Corporation	E	309 764-8324
Moline *(G-14178)*		
Solberg International Ltd	G	630 616-4400
Itasca *(G-11735)*		
Solberg Mfg Inc	D	630 616-4400
Itasca *(G-11736)*		
Solberg Mfg Inc	E	630 773-1363
Itasca *(G-11737)*		
Storms Industries Inc	E	312 243-7480
Chicago *(G-6251)*		
Universal Air Filter Company	E	618 271-7300
East Saint Louis *(G-8328)*		

FILTERS: Air Intake, Internal Combustion Engine, Exc Auto

Bedford Rakim	G	773 749-3086
Lansing *(G-12485)*		
Byrne & Schaefer Inc	G	815 727-5000
Lockport *(G-12985)*		
Clean and Science USA Co Ltd	G	847 461-9292
Rolling Meadows *(G-17722)*		
Daves Auto Repiar	G	630 682-4411
Carol Stream *(G-2973)*		
Donaldson Company Inc	E	815 288-3374
Dixon *(G-7898)*		
Jingdiao North America Inc	F	847 906-8888
Mount Prospect *(G-14540)*		
Tane Corporation	G	847 705-7125
Palatine *(G-16161)*		

FILTERS: General Line, Indl

Arrow Pneumatics Inc	D	708 343-6177
Broadview *(G-2418)*		
Averus Usa Inc	D	800 913-7034
Elgin *(G-8518)*		
Century Filter Products Inc	G	773 477-1790
Chicago *(G-4060)*		
Evoqua Water Technologies LLC	G	618 451-1205
Granite City *(G-10705)*		
Industrial Filter Pump Mfg Co	G	708 656-7800
Cicero *(G-6855)*		
Profile Screens Incorporated	G	309 543-2082
Havana *(G-11120)*		
Robko Flock Coating Company	G	847 272-6202
Northbrook *(G-15474)*		
Tri-Dim Filter Corporation	E	847 695-5822
Elgin *(G-8759)*		

FILTERS: Motor Vehicle

Champion Laboratories Inc	A	618 445-6011
Albion *(G-347)*		
Champion Laboratories Inc	F	618 445-6011
Bannockburn *(G-1198)*		
Jsn Inc	E	708 410-1800
Maywood *(G-13670)*		

PRODUCT SECTION

FISH & SEAFOOD PROCESSORS: Canned Or Cured

FILTERS: Oil, Internal Combustion Engine, Exc Auto

Advanced Fltration Systems Inc .... C 217 351-3073
  Champaign (G-3260)

FILTRATION DEVICES: Electronic

Barnes International Inc .... C 815 964-8661
  Rockford (G-17312)
Cemec Inc .... G 630 495-9696
  Downers Grove (G-7966)
Daly Engineered Filtration Inc .... G 708 355-1550
  Naperville (G-14813)
Erbeck One Chem & Lab Sup Inc .... G 312 203-0078
  Manhattan (G-13432)
Netcom Inc .... C 847 537-6300
  Wheeling (G-20943)
Perma-Pipe Intl Holdings Inc .... E 847 966-1000
  Niles (G-15158)
Te Connectivity Corporation .... D 847 680-7400
  Mundelein (G-14742)

FINANCIAL INVESTMENT ADVICE

American Medical Association .... A 312 464-5000
  Chicago (G-3660)
Envestnet Inc .... C 312 827-2800
  Chicago (G-4518)
Envestnet Inc .... G 866 924-8912
  Chicago (G-4517)

FINANCIAL SVCS

Bezarr .... G 651 200-5641
  Willowbrook (G-21031)
Business Valuation Group Inc .... G 312 595-1900
  Chicago (G-3982)
Envestnet Inc .... G 866 924-8912
  Chicago (G-4517)
Envestnet Inc .... C 312 827-2800
  Chicago (G-4518)
Envestnet Rtrment Slutions LLC .... G 312 827-7957
  Chicago (G-4519)
Lbe Ltd .... G 847 907-4959
  Kildeer (G-12050)
Q Lotus Holdings Inc .... G 312 379-1800
  Chicago (G-5921)

FINDINGS & TRIMMINGS: Apparel

Arbetman & Associates .... G 708 386-8586
  Oak Park (G-15745)

FINGERNAILS, ARTIFICIAL

Crystal Nails McHenry .... G 815 363-5498
  McHenry (G-13733)
Polish Your Lf Nail Salon LLC .... G 312 838-1018
  Cicero (G-6870)

FINISHERS: Concrete & Bituminous, Powered

Anchor Mechanical Inc .... G 312 492-6994
  Chicago (G-3691)

FINISHING AGENTS

Ilf Technologies LLC .... G 630 789-9770
  Willowbrook (G-21047)

FINISHING AGENTS: Leather

ISachs Sons Inc .... F 312 733-2815
  Chicago (G-4971)
Sadelco USA Corp .... G 847 781-8844
  Hoffman Estates (G-11454)
Sanford Chemical Co Inc .... F 847 437-3530
  Elk Grove Village (G-9229)

FINISHING SCHOOLS, CHARM & MODELING

Pivot Point Usa Inc .... C 800 886-4247
  Chicago (G-5814)

FINISHING SVCS

Gmk Finishing .... G 630 837-0568
  Bartlett (G-1284)
Quantum Color Graphics LLC .... C 847 967-3600
  Morton Grove (G-14435)

FIRE ARMS, SMALL: Guns Or Gun Parts, 30 mm & Below

A & S Arms Inc .... G 224 267-5670
  Antioch (G-593)
Art Jewel Enterprises Ltd .... F 630 260-0400
  Carol Stream (G-2941)
D S Arms Incorporated .... E 847 277-7258
  Lake Barrington (G-12147)
Devil Dog Arms Inc .... G 847 790-4004
  Lake Zurich (G-12402)
Fim Engineering LLC .... G 773 880-8841
  Milford (G-14034)
Manticore Arms Inc .... G 630 715-0334
  Elburn (G-8459)
Nelson-Whittaker Ltd .... E 815 459-6000
  Crystal Lake (G-7237)
Northern Ordinance Corporation .... G 815 675-6400
  Spring Grove (G-19289)
Oglesby & Oglesby Gunmakers .... G 217 487-7100
  Springfield (G-19417)
Phalanx Training Inc .... G 847 859-9156
  Evanston (G-9566)
Rock River Arms Inc .... D 309 792-5780
  Colona (G-6979)
Springfield Inc .... C 309 944-5631
  Geneseo (G-10248)

FIRE ARMS, SMALL: Machine Guns & Grenade Launchers

Double Nickel LLC .... G 618 476-3200
  Millstadt (G-14045)

FIRE ARMS, SMALL: Machine Guns/Machine Gun Parts, 30mm/below

Pro Tech Engineering .... G 309 475-2502
  Saybrook (G-18419)

FIRE ARMS, SMALL: Rifles Or Rifle Parts, 30 mm & below

Gregory Martin .... G 815 265-4527
  Gilman (G-10379)

FIRE DETECTION SYSTEMS

Brk Brands Inc .... C 630 851-7330
  Aurora (G-927)

FIRE EXTINGUISHER CHARGES

Rampro Facilities Svcs Corp .... G 224 639-6378
  Waukegan (G-20487)

FIRE EXTINGUISHER SVC

Rampro Facilities Svcs Corp .... G 224 639-6378
  Waukegan (G-20487)

FIRE EXTINGUISHERS, WHOLESALE

Flame Guard Usa LLC .... G 815 219-4074
  Vernon Hills (G-20054)
Quality Intgrted Solutions Inc .... G 815 464-4772
  Tinley Park (G-19852)

FIRE EXTINGUISHERS: Portable

Amerex Corporation .... E 309 382-4389
  North Pekin (G-15326)
Bella Casa .... G 630 455-5900
  Hinsdale (G-11365)
First Alert Inc .... C 630 499-3295
  Aurora (G-962)
Flame Guard Usa LLC .... G 815 219-4074
  Vernon Hills (G-20054)
Oval Fire Products Corporation .... G 630 635-5000
  Glendale Heights (G-10482)

FIRE OR BURGLARY RESISTIVE PRDTS

A - Square Manufacturing Inc .... E 800 628-6720
  Chicago (G-3483)
Flexicraft Industries Inc .... F 312 428-4750
  Chicago (G-4608)
Fotofab LLC .... E 773 463-6211
  Chicago (G-4623)
G & M Metal Fabricators Inc .... D 847 678-6501
  Franklin Park (G-9947)
Group Industries Inc .... E 708 877-6200
  Thornton (G-19788)
Millenia Products Group Inc .... C 630 458-0401
  Itasca (G-11704)
Noise Barriers LLC .... E 847 843-0500
  Libertyville (G-12688)
Solid Metal Group Inc .... G 708 757-7421
  Chicago Heights (G-6774)
Viking Metal Cabinet Company .... D 630 863-7234
  Montgomery (G-14274)

FIRE PROTECTION EQPT

Citizenprime LLC .... G 708 995-1241
  Mokena (G-14075)
Evac Systems Fire & Rescue .... F 309 764-7812
  Moline (G-14143)
PAcrimson Fire Risk Svcs Inc .... G 630 424-3400
  Lombard (G-13115)
Paratech Incorporated .... D 815 469-3911
  Frankfort (G-9821)
Roodhouse Fire Protection Dst .... E 217 589-5134
  Roodhouse (G-17895)

FIREARMS & AMMUNITION, EXC SPORTING, WHOLESALE

D S Arms Incorporated .... E 847 277-7258
  Lake Barrington (G-12147)
Printforce Inc .... G 618 395-7746
  Olney (G-15885)
Shaars International Inc .... G 815 315-0717
  Rockford (G-17627)

FIREARMS: Large, Greater Than 30mm

Devil Dog Arms Inc .... G 847 790-4004
  Lake Zurich (G-12402)
Krebs Custom Inc .... G 847 487-7776
  Wauconda (G-20368)

FIREARMS: Small, 30mm or Less

Bison Aerospace and Def LLC .... G 618 795-2678
  Savanna (G-18403)
Olin Corporation .... C 618 258-2000
  East Alton (G-8168)
RR Defense Systems Inc .... F 773 529-6007
  Elk Grove Village (G-9223)

FIREFIGHTING APPARATUS

Amkus Inc .... E 630 515-1800
  Downers Grove (G-7951)

FIREPLACE & CHIMNEY MATERIAL: Concrete

Tagitsold Inc .... G 630 724-1800
  Darien (G-7412)
US Fireplace Products Inc .... G 888 290-8181
  Lake Bluff (G-12211)

FIREPLACE EQPT & ACCESS

Innerweld Cover Co .... F 847 497-3009
  Mundelein (G-14701)

FIREPLACES: Concrete

Fire Orb LLC .... G 847 454-9198
  Prospect Heights (G-16840)

FIREWOOD, WHOLESALE

Dg Wood Processing .... F 217 543-2128
  Arthur (G-852)
E-Z Tree Recycling Inc .... G 773 493-8600
  Chicago (G-4428)

FIREWORKS

Jamaica Pyrotechnics .... G 217 649-2902
  Philo (G-16606)
Lumina Inc .... G 312 829-8970
  Chicago (G-5283)

FISH & SEAFOOD PROCESSORS: Canned Or Cured

Kraft Heinz Foods Company .... C 847 291-3900
  Northbrook (G-15415)

Employee Codes: A=Over 500 employees, B=251-500
C=101-250, D=51-100, E=20-50, F=10-19, G=3-9

FISH & SEAFOOD PROCESSORS: Canned Or Cured

Sokol and Company .... D 708 482-8250
  Countryside *(G-7071)*

FISH & SEAFOOD PROCESSORS: Fresh Or Frozen

Betty Watters .... G 618 232-1150
  Hamburg *(G-10948)*
Ethos Seafood Group LLC .... D 312 858-3474
  Hodgkins *(G-11388)*
Rich Products Corporation .... D 847 581-1749
  Niles *(G-15165)*
Sudpack USA Inc .... G 630 258-4015
  Naperville *(G-14921)*
Wisepak Foods LLC .... E 773 772-0072
  Chicago *(G-6650)*

FISH & SEAFOOD WHOLESALERS

Ethos Seafood Group LLC .... D 312 858-3474
  Hodgkins *(G-11388)*
Honey Foods Inc .... G 847 989-8186
  Franklin Park *(G-9957)*
Jackson & Partners LLC .... G 630 219-1598
  Naperville *(G-14853)*

FISH FOOD

Aqua-Tech Co .... G 847 383-7075
  Elgin *(G-8513)*
Dr & Dr Property Leasing LLC .... G 309 965-3200
  Goodfield *(G-10674)*
Fish King Inc .... G 773 736-4974
  Chicago *(G-4595)*
Lockport Fish Pantry .... G 815 588-3543
  Lockport *(G-13007)*
Oceanic Food Express Inc .... G 847 480-7217
  Northbrook *(G-15443)*

FISHING EQPT: Lures

Biospawn Lure Co .... G 773 458-0752
  Evanston *(G-9500)*
Cast Industries Inc .... E 217 522-8292
  Springfield *(G-19342)*
Jerrys Tackle and Guns .... G 618 654-3235
  Highland *(G-11228)*
Kayser Lure Corp .... G 217 964-2110
  Ursa *(G-20004)*
Luck E Strike Corporation .... F 630 313-2408
  Geneva *(G-10289)*
Obies Tackle Co Inc .... G 618 234-5638
  Belleville *(G-1581)*
Reeves Lure Co .... G 217 864-3493
  Lovington *(G-13285)*

FISHING EQPT: Nets & Seines

Nichols Net & Twine Inc .... G 618 797-0211
  Granite City *(G-10728)*

FITTINGS & ASSEMBLIES: Hose & Tube, Hydraulic Or Pneumatic

A Len Radiator Shoppe Inc .... G 630 852-5445
  Downers Grove *(G-7948)*
All Type Hydraulics Corp .... G 618 585-4844
  Bunker Hill *(G-2632)*
Hurst Manufacturing Co Inc .... F 309 756-9960
  Milan *(G-14016)*
Hydac Technology Corp .... E 630 545-0800
  Glendale Heights *(G-10458)*
J C Hose & Tube Inc .... G 630 543-4747
  Addison *(G-157)*
Megadyne America LLC .... E 630 752-0500
  Carol Stream *(G-3023)*
Nagano International Corp .... G 847 537-0011
  Buffalo Grove *(G-2578)*
Nanco Sales Co Inc .... G 630 892-9820
  Aurora *(G-1138)*
Quad City Hose .... E 563 386-8936
  Taylor Ridge *(G-19747)*
Royal Brass Inc .... G 618 439-6341
  Benton *(G-1936)*
T & T Distribution Inc .... E 815 223-0715
  Peru *(G-16594)*

FITTINGS & SPECIALTIES: Steam

Flexicraft Industries Inc .... F 312 229-7550
  Chicago *(G-4609)*

Steamgard LLC .... E 847 913-8400
  Vernon Hills *(G-20100)*

FITTINGS: Pipe

Advanced Plbg & Pipe Fitting .... G 618 554-2677
  Newton *(G-15079)*
Dixon Brass .... E 630 323-3716
  Westmont *(G-20738)*
Dvcc Inc .... E 630 323-3105
  Westmont *(G-20739)*
Groovjoint LLC .... G 312 803-2627
  Chicago *(G-4744)*
Mechanical Engineering Pdts .... G 312 421-3375
  Chicago *(G-5380)*
Process Piping Inc .... G 708 717-0513
  Tinley Park *(G-19849)*

FITTINGS: Pipe, Fabricated

Chicago Pipe Bending & Coil Co .... F 773 379-1918
  Chicago *(G-4122)*
Duraflex Inc .... E 847 462-1007
  Cary *(G-3156)*
Illco Inc .... G 815 725-9100
  Joliet *(G-11878)*
Lafox Manufacturing Corp .... G 630 232-0266
  Lafox *(G-12136)*

FIXTURES & EQPT: Kitchen, Metal, Exc Cast Aluminum

Style Rite Restaurant Eqp Co .... G 630 628-0940
  Addison *(G-296)*

FIXTURES & EQPT: Kitchen, Porcelain Enameled

Exclusive Stone .... G 847 593-6963
  Elk Grove Village *(G-8989)*
Fountain Products Inc .... G 630 991-7237
  Elgin *(G-8590)*
Pt Holdings Inc .... G 217 691-1793
  Springfield *(G-19430)*

FIXTURES: Cut Stone

Contemporary Marble Inc .... G 618 281-6200
  Columbia *(G-6989)*

FLAGS: Fabric

George Lauterer Corporation .... E 312 913-1881
  Chicago *(G-4682)*
J C Schultz Enterprises Inc .... D 800 323-9127
  Batavia *(G-1388)*
Seasonal Designs Inc .... E 847 688-0280
  Waukegan *(G-20493)*
W G N Flag & Decorating Co .... F 773 768-8076
  Chicago *(G-6573)*

FLAT GLASS: Antique

Timeless Reflections .... G 815 663-8148
  Bureau *(G-2639)*

FLAT GLASS: Building

Chicago Tempered Glass Inc .... F 773 583-2300
  Chicago *(G-4132)*

FLAT GLASS: Picture

Tru Vue Inc .... C 708 485-5080
  Countryside *(G-7075)*

FLAT GLASS: Sheet

Marsco Glass Products LLC .... D 312 326-4710
  Chicago *(G-5349)*

FLAT GLASS: Skylight

Day Star Systems LLC .... G 618 426-1868
  Campbell Hill *(G-2814)*

FLAT GLASS: Tempered

Euroview Enterprises LLC .... E 630 227-3300
  Elmhurst *(G-9364)*
Willow Ridge Glass Inc .... F 630 910-8300
  Woodridge *(G-21348)*

FLAT GLASS: Window, Clear & Colored

Energy-Glazed Systems Inc .... G 847 223-4500
  Grayslake *(G-10769)*

FLAVORS OR FLAVORING MATERIALS: Synthetic

Givaudan Flavors Corporation .... C 847 608-6200
  Elgin *(G-8595)*
Prinova Solutions LLC .... E 630 868-0300
  Carol Stream *(G-3053)*

FLOOR COVERING STORES

Afar Imports & Interiors Inc .... G 217 744-3262
  Springfield *(G-19316)*
L & L Flooring Inc .... E 773 935-9314
  Chicago *(G-5140)*
Ridgefield Industries Co LLC .... E 800 569-0316
  Crystal Lake *(G-7256)*
Sealmaster Inc .... F 847 480-7325
  Northbrook *(G-15478)*

FLOOR COVERING STORES: Carpets

Riverbend Kitchen & Mllwk LLC .... G 618 462-8955
  Alton *(G-569)*
Tazewell Floor Covering Inc .... F 309 266-6371
  Morton *(G-14386)*

FLOOR COVERING STORES: Floor Tile

MK Tile Ink .... G 773 964-8905
  Chicago *(G-5474)*

FLOOR COVERING: Plastic

Sap Acquisition Co LLC .... E 847 229-1600
  Buffalo Grove *(G-2594)*

FLOOR COVERINGS WHOLESALERS

Corsaw Hardwood Lumber Inc .... F 309 293-2055
  Smithfield *(G-19063)*
Hakwood Inc .... G 630 219-3388
  Naperville *(G-14971)*

FLOOR COVERINGS: Asphalted-Felt Base, Linoleum Or Carpet

Owens Corning Sales LLC .... E 708 594-6935
  Argo *(G-675)*

FLOOR COVERINGS: Rubber

Alessco Inc .... F 773 327-7919
  Chicago *(G-3602)*

FLOOR COVERINGS: Textile Fiber

Protect Assoc .... G 847 446-8664
  Northbrook *(G-15469)*

FLOORING & GRATINGS: Open, Construction Applications

Harris Steel Ulc .... D 815 932-1200
  Bourbonnais *(G-2262)*
Oldcastle Infrastructure Inc .... F 309 661-4608
  Normal *(G-15215)*

FLOORING: Hard Surface

Armstrong Flooring Inc .... B 815 939-2501
  Kankakee *(G-11958)*
Kitchen & Bath Gallery .... G 217 214-0310
  Quincy *(G-16900)*
Surface Shields Inc .... E 708 226-9810
  Tinley Park *(G-19859)*

FLOORING: Hardwood

Connor Sports Flooring LLC .... D 847 290-9020
  Bensenville *(G-1775)*
Flooring Warehouse Direct Inc .... G 815 730-6767
  Homer Glen *(G-11479)*
Grads Inc .... G 847 426-3904
  East Dundee *(G-8198)*
Hakwood Inc .... G 630 219-3388
  Naperville *(G-14971)*
Historic Timber & Plank Inc .... E 618 372-4546
  Brighton *(G-2401)*

PRODUCT SECTION

Ridgefield Industries Co LLC............E...... 800 569-0316
  Crystal Lake (G-7256)
Second City Flooring LLC................G...... 973 262-3272
  Chicago (G-6127)
T J P Investments Inc......................G...... 309 673-8383
  Peoria (G-16534)
Unity Hardwoods LLC.......................F...... 708 701-2943
  Chicago (G-6479)
Vlasici Hardwood Floors Co...............G...... 815 505-4308
  Romeoville (G-17885)

FLOORING: Rubber

Eco-Smart Flooring Company.............G...... 847 404-5032
  Chicago (G-4447)
Monogram Creative Group Inc............G...... 312 802-1433
  Glenview (G-10590)

FLORIST TELEGRAPH SVCS

Gue Liquidation Delivery Inc..............G...... 630 719-7800
  Downers Grove (G-8015)

FLORIST: Flowers, Fresh

Albert F Amling LLC..........................C...... 630 333-1720
  Elmhurst (G-9324)
Mangel and Co..................................E...... 847 459-3100
  Buffalo Grove (G-2567)

FLORISTS

Cub Foods Inc..................................C...... 309 689-0140
  Peoria (G-16428)
Hts Hancock Transcriptions Svc.........E...... 217 379-9241
  Paxton (G-16308)
Kroger Co...C...... 309 694-6298
  East Peoria (G-8275)
Kroger Co...C...... 815 332-7267
  Rockford (G-17485)
Niemann Foods Inc..........................C...... 217 222-0190
  Quincy (G-16918)
Niemann Foods Inc..........................C...... 217 793-4091
  Springfield (G-19411)
Schnuck Markets Inc........................C...... 618 466-0825
  Godfrey (G-10663)
Sunset Food Mart Inc.......................C...... 847 234-0854
  Lake Forest (G-12307)
Walter Lagestee Inc.........................C...... 708 957-2974
  Homewood (G-11504)

FLORISTS' SPLYS, WHOLESALE

Gue Liquidation Delivery Inc..............G...... 630 719-7800
  Downers Grove (G-8015)

FLOWER ARRANGEMENTS: Artificial

Floralstar Enterprises.......................G...... 847 726-0124
  Hawthorn Woods (G-11123)
K M I International Corp....................G...... 630 627-6300
  Addison (G-166)

FLOWERS: Artificial & Preserved

Albert F Amling LLC..........................C...... 630 333-1720
  Elmhurst (G-9324)

FLUID METERS & COUNTING DEVICES

Erdco Engineering Corporation.........E...... 847 328-0550
  Evanston (G-9514)
Langham Engineering........................G...... 815 223-5250
  Peru (G-16580)
Metraflex Company...........................D...... 312 738-3800
  Chicago (G-5411)
Midwest Meter Inc............................E...... 217 623-4064
  Edinburg (G-8335)
Perkinelmer Hlth Sciences Inc..........C...... 630 969-6000
  Downers Grove (G-8073)

FLUID POWER PUMPS & MOTORS

American Electronic Pdts Inc............F...... 630 889-9977
  Oak Brook (G-15592)
Caterpillar Inc...................................B...... 815 729-5511
  Joliet (G-11838)
Central Hydraulics Inc......................G...... 309 527-5238
  El Paso (G-8434)
Danfoss Power Solutions US Co......C...... 815 233-4200
  Freeport (G-10105)
Deltrol Corp.......................................C...... 708 547-0500
  Bellwood (G-1621)

Grand Specialties Co........................F...... 630 629-8000
  Oak Brook (G-15625)
Highland Mch & Screw Pdts Co........D...... 618 654-2103
  Highland (G-11218)
Idex Corporation...............................C...... 847 498-7070
  Lake Forest (G-12265)
Leading Edge Group Inc...................C...... 815 316-3500
  Rockford (G-17492)
Mechanical Engineering Pdts...........G...... 312 421-3375
  Chicago (G-5380)
Parker-Hannifin Corporation.............E...... 216 896-3000
  Chicago (G-5767)
Parker-Hannifin Corporation.............C...... 847 258-6200
  Elk Grove Village (G-9169)
Parker-Hannifin Corporation.............D...... 815 636-4100
  Machesney Park (G-13362)
Parker-Hannifin Corporation.............C...... 309 266-2200
  Morton (G-14377)
Rdh Inc of Rockford.........................F...... 815 874-9421
  Rockford (G-17568)
Rhino Tool Company........................F...... 309 853-5555
  Kewanee (G-12040)
Roberts Electric Company................G...... 773 725-7323
  Chicago (G-6044)
Tomenson Machine Works Inc.........D...... 630 377-7670
  West Chicago (G-20652)
Tramco Pump Co..............................C...... 312 243-5800
  Romeoville (G-17881)
Tuxco Corporation.............................F...... 847 244-2220
  Gurnee (G-10940)
Wes-Tech Inc...................................G...... 847 541-5070
  Buffalo Grove (G-2620)

FLUID POWER VALVES & HOSE FITTINGS

Bristol Hose & Fitting Inc.................E...... 708 492-3456
  Melrose Park (G-13837)
Bristol Transport Inc.........................E...... 708 343-6411
  Melrose Park (G-13838)
Deltrol Corp.......................................C...... 708 547-0500
  Bellwood (G-1621)
Deublin Company...............................C...... 847 689-8600
  Waukegan (G-20437)
Flexitech Inc.....................................C...... 309 665-0658
  Bloomington (G-2044)
Flow Valves International LLC..........G...... 847 866-1188
  Evanston (G-9521)
James Walker Mfg Co.......................E...... 708 754-4020
  Glenwood (G-10641)
Kepner Products Company...............D...... 630 279-1550
  Villa Park (G-20156)
Lsl Precision Machining Inc.............E...... 815 633-4701
  Loves Park (G-13234)
Mac Lean-Fogg Company..................D...... 847 566-0010
  Mundelein (G-14710)
Midwest Hose & Fittings Inc............G...... 815 578-9040
  Johnsburg (G-11807)
Mj Works Hose & Fitting LLC...........G...... 708 995-5723
  Mokena (G-14098)
Plews Inc..C...... 815 288-3344
  Dixon (G-7906)
Reber Welding Service.....................G...... 217 774-3441
  Shelbyville (G-18885)
Rehobot Inc.......................................G...... 815 385-7777
  McHenry (G-13786)
Seals & Components Inc..................G...... 708 895-5222
  Lansing (G-12514)
Standard Truck Parts Inc..................G...... 815 726-4486
  Joliet (G-11932)
Trellborg Sling Sltions US Inc...........D...... 630 289-1500
  Streamwood (G-19598)
Woods Manufacturing Co Inc...........G...... 630 595-6620
  Wood Dale (G-21258)

FLUORSPAR MINING

Hastie Min & Trckg Ltd Partnr..........E...... 618 289-4536
  Cave In Rock (G-3219)

FLUXES

American Metal Chemical Corp........E...... 773 254-1818
  Chicago (G-3661)
Helix Re Inc......................................D...... 415 254-2724
  Chicago (G-4799)
Holland LP..C...... 708 672-2300
  Crete (G-7140)
La-Co Industries Inc.........................C...... 847 956-7600
  Elk Grove Village (G-9082)
Qualitek International Inc..................E...... 630 628-8083
  Addison (G-259)

FM & AM RADIO TUNERS

Wirelessusa Inc................................G...... 217 222-4300
  Quincy (G-16957)

FOAM RUBBER

Dennis Carnes..................................G...... 618 244-1770
  Mount Vernon (G-14608)
Reilly Foam Corp...............................E...... 630 392-2680
  Naperville (G-14908)

FOAM RUBBER, WHOLESALE

Reilly Foam Corp...............................E...... 630 392-2680
  Naperville (G-14908)

FOAMS & RUBBER, WHOLESALE

Fairchild Industries Inc......................E...... 847 550-9580
  Lake Zurich (G-12409)

FOIL & LEAF: Metal

Bagcraftpapercon I LLC....................C...... 620 856-2800
  Chicago (G-3814)
D W Machine Products Inc..............G...... 618 654-2161
  Highland (G-11212)
Highland Supply Corporation...........B...... 618 654-2161
  Highland (G-11224)
Pactiv LLC..E...... 847 482-2000
  Lake Forest (G-12281)
Pactiv LLC..C...... 217 479-1144
  Jacksonville (G-11779)
Tinscape LLC...................................G...... 630 236-7236
  Aurora (G-1025)
Winpak Heat Seal Corp....................D...... 309 477-6600
  Pekin (G-16370)

FOIL OR LEAF: Gold

Kurz Transfer Products LP...............G...... 847 228-0001
  Elk Grove Village (G-9080)

FOIL, ALUMINUM, HOUSEHOLD, WHOLESALE

Reynolds Consumer Products Inc....A...... 800 879-5067
  Lake Forest (G-12296)

FOIL: Aluminum

Midwest Lminating Coatings Inc......E...... 708 653-9500
  Alsip (G-478)
Pactiv LLC..E...... 847 482-2000
  Lake Forest (G-12281)
Reynolds Consumer Products LLC..E...... 217 479-1126
  Jacksonville (G-11782)
Reynolds Consumer Products LLC..G...... 217 479-1466
  Jacksonville (G-11783)
Reynolds Consumer Products LLC..B...... 847 482-3500
  Lake Forest (G-12297)
Reynolds Food Packaging................F...... 815 465-2115
  Grant Park (G-10751)

FOIL: Laminated To Paper Or Other Materials

Intellisource Inc.................................E...... 847 426-7400
  Elgin (G-8629)

FOOD CASINGS: Plastic

Damron Corporation..........................E...... 773 265-2724
  Chicago (G-4310)
Lake Pacific Partners LLC................B...... 312 578-1110
  Chicago (G-5161)
Pactiv LLC..A...... 847 482-2000
  Lake Forest (G-12279)
Pactiv LLC..C...... 815 469-2112
  Frankfort (G-9819)
Teepak Usa LLC................................G...... 217 446-6460
  Danville (G-7382)
Vector USA Inc.................................F...... 800 929-4516
  Oak Brook (G-15668)
Viscofan Usa Inc..............................D...... 217 444-8000
  Danville (G-7392)

FOOD COLORINGS

Kosto Food Products Company........F...... 847 487-2600
  Wauconda (G-20367)
Sethness Products Company...........F...... 847 329-2080
  Skokie (G-19028)

FOOD PRDTS, BREAKFAST: Cereal, Corn Flakes

Kellogg Company .... A 773 995-7200
  Chicago **(G-5091)**
Mary Lee Packaging Corporation ..... E 618 826-2361
  Chester **(G-3458)**

FOOD PRDTS, BREAKFAST: Cereal, Oatmeal

Clover US Holdings LLC .... D 630 967-3600
  Downers Grove **(G-7975)**

FOOD PRDTS, CANNED OR FRESH PACK: Fruit Juices

H J M P Corp .... C 708 345-5370
  Melrose Park **(G-13877)**
Juice Tyme Inc .... F 773 579-1291
  Chicago **(G-5058)**
Odwalla Inc .... E 773 687-8667
  Chicago **(G-5656)**

FOOD PRDTS, CANNED OR FRESH PACK: Vegetable Juices

Fresh Factory .... E 630 580-9038
  Carol Stream **(G-2988)**
Here Holdings LLC .... G 563 723-1008
  Carol Stream **(G-2997)**
Vegetable Juices Inc .... D 708 924-9500
  Bedford Park **(G-1509)**

FOOD PRDTS, CANNED, NEC

AA Superb Food Corporation .... E 773 927-3233
  Chicago **(G-3497)**

FOOD PRDTS, CANNED: Applesauce

Planks Apple Butter .... G 217 268-4933
  Arcola **(G-662)**

FOOD PRDTS, CANNED: Baby Food

Kraft Heinz Foods Company .... G 412 456-5700
  Chicago **(G-5130)**
Nurture Life Inc .... E 312 517-1888
  Chicago **(G-5642)**

FOOD PRDTS, CANNED: Barbecue Sauce

Andrias Food Group Inc .... G 618 632-3118
  O Fallon **(G-15566)**
Andrias Food Group Inc .... E 618 632-4866
  O Fallon **(G-15565)**
Dingo Inc .... G 217 868-5615
  Effingham **(G-8395)**
Legacy Foods Mfg LLC .... F 847 595-9106
  Elk Grove Village **(G-9091)**

FOOD PRDTS, CANNED: Beans & Bean Sprouts

Hop Kee Incorporated .... E 312 791-9111
  Chicago **(G-4839)**

FOOD PRDTS, CANNED: Beans, Baked Without Meat

Earthgrains .... G 630 859-8782
  North Aurora **(G-15259)**

FOOD PRDTS, CANNED: Catsup

Kraft Heinz Foods Company .... E 630 505-0170
  Lisle **(G-12907)**

FOOD PRDTS, CANNED: Fruit Juices, Fresh

Florida Fruit Juices Inc .... E 773 586-6200
  Chicago **(G-4611)**

FOOD PRDTS, CANNED: Fruits

Campbell Soup Company .... G 618 548-3001
  Salem **(G-18333)**
Campbell Soup Company .... C 630 241-6200
  Downers Grove **(G-7964)**
Key Colony Inc .... G 630 783-8572
  Lemont **(G-12568)**
Kraft Heinz Foods Company .... C 847 291-3900
  Northbrook **(G-15415)**

Kraft Heinz Foods Company .... C 847 646-3690
  Glenview **(G-10581)**
Kraft Heinz Foods Company .... B 815 338-7000
  Woodstock **(G-21401)**
La Tropicana Inc .... G 773 476-1107
  Chicago **(G-5150)**
Lawrence Foods Inc .... C 847 437-2400
  Elk Grove Village **(G-9088)**
Lynfred Winery Inc .... E 630 529-9463
  Roselle **(G-17965)**
Mancuso Cheese Company .... F 815 722-2475
  Joliet **(G-11897)**
Mullen Foods LLC .... G 773 716-9001
  Chicago **(G-5522)**
Seneca Foods Corporation .... E 309 545-2233
  Manito **(G-13439)**
V Formusa Co .... F 224 938-9360
  Des Plaines **(G-7863)**
Wisconsin Wilderness Food Pdts ..... G 847 735-8661
  Lake Forest **(G-12323)**

FOOD PRDTS, CANNED: Fruits & Fruit Prdts

MSI Green Inc .... G 312 421-6550
  Chicago **(G-5519)**

FOOD PRDTS, CANNED: Italian

Alm Distributors LLC .... G 708 865-8000
  Melrose Park **(G-13823)**
Pastorelli Food Products Inc .... G 312 455-1006
  Chicago **(G-5770)**

FOOD PRDTS, CANNED: Jams, Including Imitation

Bear-Stewart Corporation .... E 773 276-0400
  Chicago **(G-3854)**
Millers Country Crafts Inc .... G 618 426-3108
  Ava **(G-1175)**

FOOD PRDTS, CANNED: Jams, Jellies & Preserves

Ginas Jams .... G 773 622-1051
  Chicago **(G-4692)**
Kuntry Kettle .... G 618 426-1600
  Ava **(G-1173)**
Margies Brands Inc .... E 773 643-1417
  Chicago **(G-5332)**
Split Nutrition LLC 855 775-4801
  Chicago **(G-6217)**
Treehouse Foods Inc .... C 708 483-1300
  Oak Brook **(G-15665)**

FOOD PRDTS, CANNED: Jellies, Edible, Including Imitation

Stewart Ingrdients Systems Inc .... F 312 254-3539
  Chicago **(G-6248)**

FOOD PRDTS, CANNED: Maraschino Cherries

Clearly Kosher Foods .... F 630 546-2052
  Aurora **(G-1076)**

FOOD PRDTS, CANNED: Mexican, NEC

Mexico Enterprise Corporation .... G 920 568-8900
  Chicago **(G-5415)**
Ole Mexican Foods Inc .... E 708 458-3296
  Bedford Park **(G-1487)**
Quay Corporation Inc .... F 847 676-4233
  Lincolnwood **(G-12836)**

FOOD PRDTS, CANNED: Pizza Sauce

Nation Pizza Products LP .... A 847 397-3320
  Schaumburg **(G-18644)**
Pastorelli Food Products Inc .... G 312 455-1006
  Chicago **(G-5770)**
Russo Wholesale Meat Inc .... G 708 385-0500
  Alsip **(G-507)**

FOOD PRDTS, CANNED: Puddings, Exc Meat

Treehouse Foods Inc .... C 708 483-1300
  Oak Brook **(G-15665)**

FOOD PRDTS, CANNED: Soup, Beef

Vanee Foods Company .... D 708 449-7300
  Berkeley **(G-1945)**

FOOD PRDTS, CANNED: Soups

Essen Nutrition Corporation .... E 630 739-6700
  Romeoville **(G-17817)**
Supalicious Soups Inc .... G 708 491-9738
  Chicago **(G-6279)**

FOOD PRDTS, CANNED: Spaghetti & Other Pasta Sauce

Berner Food & Beverage LLC .... B 815 563-4222
  Dakota **(G-7311)**
Pappone Inc .... G 630 234-4738
  Chicago **(G-5754)**
R&B Foods Inc .... E 847 590-0059
  Mount Prospect **(G-14564)**
Rana Meal Solutions LLC .... G 630 581-4100
  Bartlett **(G-1303)**
Rana Meal Solutions LLC .... G 630 581-4100
  Oak Brook **(G-15659)**
Sokol and Company .... D 708 482-8250
  Countryside **(G-7071)**

FOOD PRDTS, CANNED: Tamales

Castro Foods Wholesale Inc .... E 773 869-0641
  Chicago **(G-4038)**
Supreme Tamale Co .... G 773 622-3777
  Elk Grove Village **(G-9261)**
Tom Tom Tamales Mfg Co Inc .... F 773 523-5675
  Chicago **(G-6387)**

FOOD PRDTS, CANNED: Tomato Sauce.

Kraft Heinz Receivables LLC 847 646-2000
  Chicago **(G-5131)**
Simply Salsa LLC .... G 815 514-3993
  Homer Glen **(G-11486)**

FOOD PRDTS, CANNED: Tomatoes

78 Brand Co .... G 312 344-1602
  Chicago **(G-3479)**
Iya Foods LLC 630 854-7107
  North Aurora **(G-15264)**
Mullins Food Products Inc .... B 708 344-3224
  Broadview **(G-2455)**

FOOD PRDTS, CANNED: Tortillas

Lpz Inc .... G 773 579-6120
  Chicago **(G-5271)**

FOOD PRDTS, CANNED: Vegetable Purees

Hooray Puree Inc .... G 312 515-0266
  Park Ridge **(G-16284)**

FOOD PRDTS, CANNED: Vegetables

Fast Technologies Corp .... G 815 234-4744
  Oregon **(G-15920)**
General Mills Inc .... E 815 544-7399
  Belvidere **(G-1671)**
Seneca Foods Corporation .... E 309 385-4301
  Princeville **(G-16829)**
Stable Foods Inc .... F 773 793-2547
  Chicago **(G-6225)**

FOOD PRDTS, CANNED: Vegetables

Del Monte Foods Inc .... G 309 968-7033
  Manito **(G-13437)**

FOOD PRDTS, CONFECTIONERY, WHOLESALE: Candy

Amy Wertheim .... G 309 830-4361
  Atlanta **(G-904)**
Cora Lee Candies Inc .... F 847 724-2754
  Glenview **(G-10538)**
Nader Wholesale Grocers Inc .... F 773 582-1000
  Chicago **(G-5536)**
Samad General Services Inc .... G 773 593-3332
  Addison **(G-280)**
Vision Wholesale Corp .... G 708 496-6015
  Chicago **(G-6558)**

PRODUCT SECTION

FOOD PRDTS, FRUITS & VEG, FRESH, WHOL: Banana Ripening Svc

FOOD PRDTS, CONFECTIONERY, WHOLESALE: Nuts, Salted/Roasted

Anton-Argires Inc................................G...... 708 388-6250
  Alsip *(G-416)*
Specialty Nut & Bky Sup Co Inc ....G...... 630 268-8500
  Addison *(G-294)*

FOOD PRDTS, CONFECTIONERY, WHOLESALE: Potato Chips

Frito-Lay North America Inc................F...... 815 468-3940
  Manteno *(G-13448)*

FOOD PRDTS, CONFECTIONERY, WHOLESALE: Snack Foods

Dessertwerks Inc..................................G...... 847 487-8239
  Libertyville *(G-12647)*
Hensaal Management Group Inc ....G...... 312 624-8133
  Chicago *(G-4804)*
Laredo Foods Inc..................................E...... 773 762-1500
  Chicago *(G-5177)*

FOOD PRDTS, DAIRY, WHOLESALE: Dried Or Canned

Quay Corporation Inc ....F...... 847 676-4233
  Lincolnwood *(G-12836)*

FOOD PRDTS, DAIRY, WHOLESALE: Frozen Dairy Desserts

Al Gelato Chicago LLC........................G...... 847 455-5355
  Franklin Park *(G-9864)*
Creamery Inc ....G...... 708 479-5706
  Mokena *(G-14077)*

FOOD PRDTS, FISH & SEAFOOD, WHOLESALE: Fresh

Betty Watters..G...... 618 232-1150
  Hamburg *(G-10948)*

FOOD PRDTS, FISH & SEAFOOD: Chowders, Frozen

King Midas Seafood Entps Inc ....G...... 847 566-2192
  Mundelein *(G-14707)*

FOOD PRDTS, FISH & SEAFOOD: Fish Sticks

Orin Briant Inc.....................................G...... 779 206-2800
  New Lenox *(G-15048)*

FOOD PRDTS, FISH & SEAFOOD: Fish, Canned & Cured

Vita Food Products Inc ....D...... 312 738-4500
  Chicago *(G-6560)*

FOOD PRDTS, FISH & SEAFOOD: Fish, Smoked

F&A Specialty Foods Inc ....G...... 312 887-1344
  Chicago *(G-4553)*

FOOD PRDTS, FISH & SEAFOOD: Fresh, Prepared

Dar Enterprises Inc..............................G...... 815 961-8748
  Rockford *(G-17367)*

FOOD PRDTS, FISH & SEAFOOD: Fresh/Frozen Chowder, Soup/Stew

Vanee Foods Company ....D...... 708 449-7300
  Berkeley *(G-1945)*

FOOD PRDTS, FISH & SEAFOOD: Seafood, Frozen, Prepared

Open Waters Seafood Company ....G...... 847 329-8585
  Skokie *(G-19000)*

FOOD PRDTS, FROZEN: Breakfasts, Packaged

Pinnacle Foods Group LLC..................B...... 618 829-3275
  Saint Elmo *(G-18311)*

FOOD PRDTS, FROZEN: Dinners, Packaged

Nestle Prepared Foods Company ....B...... 630 671-3721
  Glendale Heights *(G-10478)*
On-Cor Frozen Foods LLC ....E...... 630 851-6600
  Aurora *(G-1142)*
WEI-Chuan USA Inc ....F...... 708 352-8886
  Hodgkins *(G-11401)*

FOOD PRDTS, FROZEN: Ethnic Foods, NEC

Italia Foods Inc....................................E...... 847 397-4479
  Schaumburg *(G-18573)*
Smh2 Manufacturing LLC ....G...... 773 793-6643
  Chicago *(G-6191)*

FOOD PRDTS, FROZEN: Fruit Juice, Concentrates

Greenwood Associates Inc ....F...... 847 579-5500
  Niles *(G-15127)*
Lx/Jt Intermediate Holdings..................G...... 773 369-2652
  Chicago *(G-5291)*

FOOD PRDTS, FROZEN: Fruits & Vegetables

R J Van Drunen & Sons Inc ....D...... 815 472-3211
  Momence *(G-14193)*
R J Van Drunen & Sons Inc ....D...... 815 472-3100
  Momence *(G-14191)*
R J Van Drunen & Sons Inc ....E...... 830 422-2167
  Momence *(G-14192)*

FOOD PRDTS, FROZEN: Fruits, Juices & Vegetables

Citrus Systems.....................................G...... 608 271-3000
  Downers Grove *(G-7971)*
H J M P Corp.......................................C...... 708 345-5370
  Melrose Park *(G-13877)*
Juice Tyme Inc ....F...... 773 579-1291
  Chicago *(G-5058)*
Key Colony Inc....................................G...... 630 783-8572
  Lemont *(G-12568)*
Kraft Heinz Foods Company ....C...... 847 291-3900
  Northbrook *(G-15415)*
Lawlor Marketing ....G...... 847 357-1080
  Arlington Heights *(G-767)*
Premier Beverage Solutions LLC..........G...... 309 369-7117
  East Peoria *(G-8284)*
Shady Creek Vineyard Inc ....G...... 847 275-7979
  Palatine *(G-16157)*

FOOD PRDTS, FROZEN: Lunches, Packaged

Luvo Usa LLC.....................................E...... 847 485-8595
  Schaumburg *(G-18613)*
Luvo Usa LLC.....................................E...... 847 485-8595
  Schaumburg *(G-18614)*

FOOD PRDTS, FROZEN: NEC

A New Dairy Company........................E...... 312 421-1234
  Chicago *(G-3489)*
Ajinomoto Foods North Amer Inc.........F...... 815 452-2559
  Toluca *(G-19885)*
Aryzta LLC..C...... 815 306-7171
  Romeoville *(G-17796)*
Campbell Soup Company ....G...... 618 548-3001
  Salem *(G-18333)*
Campbell Soup Company ....C...... 630 241-6200
  Downers Grove *(G-7964)*
Chateau Food Products Inc ....F...... 708 863-4207
  Chicago *(G-4079)*
Conagra Brands Inc ....C...... 312 549-5000
  Chicago *(G-4212)*
Conagra Brands Inc ....C...... 630 857-1000
  Naperville *(G-14803)*
Danziger Kosher Catering Inc..............E...... 847 982-1818
  Chicago *(G-4316)*
Distinctive Foods LLC ....D...... 847 459-3600
  Wheeling *(G-20879)*
Distinctive Foods LLC ....E...... 847 459-3600
  Bensenville *(G-1787)*
General Mills Inc.................................E...... 815 544-7399
  Belvidere *(G-1671)*
General Mills Green Giant....................G...... 815 547-5311
  Belvidere *(G-1672)*
Givaudan Flavors Corporation..............C...... 630 682-5600
  Carol Stream *(G-2992)*
Globus Food Products LLC..................G...... 847 378-8221
  Elk Grove Village *(G-9018)*

Gonnella Baking Co.............................D...... 312 733-2020
  Schaumburg *(G-18538)*
Heartland Harvest Inc..........................G...... 815 932-2100
  Kankakee *(G-11975)*
Herman Seekamp Inc...........................C...... 630 628-6555
  Addison *(G-149)*
Kraft Heinz Foods Company ....C...... 847 291-3900
  Northbrook *(G-15415)*
Lezza Spumoni and Desserts Inc ....E...... 708 547-5969
  Bellwood *(G-1631)*
Lucrezia LLC.......................................G...... 630 263-0088
  Naperville *(G-14866)*
McCain Foods Usa Inc ....B...... 920 563-6625
  Oakbrook Terrace *(G-15808)*
O Chilli Frozen Foods Inc....................E...... 847 562-1991
  Northbrook *(G-15442)*
Open Kitchens Inc ....C...... 312 666-5334
  Chicago *(G-5681)*
Paani Foods Inc ....F...... 312 420-4624
  Chicago *(G-5734)*
Pinnacle Foods Group LLC..................C...... 731 343-4995
  Centralia *(G-3244)*
Supreme Tamale Co.............................G...... 773 622-3777
  Elk Grove Village *(G-9261)*

FOOD PRDTS, FROZEN: Pizza

Afs Classico LLC ....E...... 309 786-8833
  Rock Island *(G-17200)*
Avanti Foods Company ....E...... 815 379-2155
  Walnut *(G-20216)*
Balton Corporation ....F...... 773 933-7927
  Chicago *(G-3822)*
Biagios Gourmet Foods Inc..................E...... 708 867-4641
  Chicago *(G-3880)*
Champion Foods LLC..........................G...... 815 648-2725
  Hebron *(G-11140)*
Doreens Pizza Inc ....F...... 708 862-7499
  Calumet City *(G-2775)*
Home Run Inn Frozen Foods Corp........D...... 630 783-9696
  Woodridge *(G-21314)*
Little Lady Foods Inc ....C...... 847 806-1440
  Elk Grove Village *(G-9096)*
McCain Usa Inc ....C...... 800 938-7799
  Oakbrook Terrace *(G-15809)*
Nation Pizza Products LP.....................A...... 847 397-3320
  Schaumburg *(G-18644)*
Nestle Pizza Company Inc ....E...... 847 646-2000
  Glenview *(G-10593)*
Preziosio Ltd ....F...... 630 393-0920
  Warrenville *(G-20249)*
RCM Smith Inc....................................F...... 309 786-8833
  Rock Island *(G-17239)*
Reggios Pizza Inc ....F...... 773 933-7927
  Chicago *(G-6004)*
Teresa Foods Inc..................................F...... 708 258-6200
  Peotone *(G-16558)*

FOOD PRDTS, FROZEN: Potato Prdts

McCain Foods Usa Inc ....B...... 630 955-0400
  Oakbrook Terrace *(G-15807)*
McCain Usa Inc ....C...... 800 938-7799
  Oakbrook Terrace *(G-15809)*

FOOD PRDTS, FROZEN: Snack Items

Hearthside Food Solutions LLC ....E...... 630 967-3600
  Downers Grove *(G-8019)*
Mondelez Intl Holdings LLC................F...... 800 572-3847
  Deerfield *(G-7638)*

FOOD PRDTS, FROZEN: Vegetables, Exc Potato Prdts

General Mills Inc.................................E...... 815 544-7399
  Belvidere *(G-1671)*
McCain Foods Usa Inc ....B...... 920 563-6625
  Oakbrook Terrace *(G-15808)*
NGL Crude Logistics LLC...................F...... 618 274-4306
  Sauget *(G-18396)*

FOOD PRDTS, FRUITS & VEG, FRESH, WHOL: Banana Ripening Svc

Hop Kee Incorporated ....E...... 312 791-9111
  Chicago *(G-4839)*

Employee Codes: A=Over 500 employees, B=251-500
C=101-250, D=51-100, E=20-50, F=10-19, G=3-9

FOOD PRDTS, MEAT & MEAT PRDTS, WHOLESALE: Cured Or Smoked

- Atlantic Beverage Company Inc .... G 847 412-6200
  Northbrook *(G-15342)*
- H & B Hams 618 372-8690
  Brighton *(G-2400)*
- Meats By Linz Inc .... E 708 862-0830
  Calumet City *(G-2783)*

FOOD PRDTS, MEAT & MEAT PRDTS, WHOLESALE: Fresh

- Allens Farm Quality Meats .... G 217 896-2532
  Homer *(G-11474)*
- Amity Packing Company Inc .... C 312 942-0270
  Chicago *(G-3680)*
- B B M Packing Co Inc .... G 312 243-1061
  Chicago *(G-3807)*
- Bkbg Enterprises Inc .... D 847 228-7070
  Carol Stream *(G-2947)*
- Bruss Company .... E 773 282-2900
  Chicago *(G-3969)*
- C & F Packing Co Inc .... C 847 245-2000
  Lake Villa *(G-12348)*
- Columbus Meats Inc .... G 312 829-2480
  Chicago *(G-4207)*
- Consumers Packing Co Inc .... D 708 344-0047
  Melrose Park *(G-13844)*
- Danielson Food Products Inc .... E 773 285-2111
  Chicago *(G-4314)*
- Eickmans Processing Co Inc .... E 815 247-8451
  Seward *(G-18867)*
- Fabbri Sausage Manufacturing .... E 312 829-6363
  Chicago *(G-4554)*
- Grant Park Packing Company Inc .... E 312 421-4096
  Franklin Park *(G-9952)*
- H C Schau & Son Inc .... C 630 783-1000
  Woodridge *(G-21309)*
- Hansen Packing Co .... G 618 498-3714
  Jerseyville *(G-11792)*
- Jones Packing Co .... G 815 943-4488
  Harvard *(G-11058)*
- Kelly Corned Beef Co Chicago .... F 773 588-2882
  Chicago *(G-5092)*
- Korte Meat Processors Inc .... G 618 654-3813
  Highland *(G-11230)*
- Moweaqua Packing Plant .... G 217 768-4714
  Moweaqua *(G-14652)*
- Nea Agora Packing Co .... G 312 421-5130
  Chicago *(G-5560)*
- Old Fashioned Meat Co Inc .... G 312 421-4555
  Chicago *(G-5668)*
- OSI Industries LLC .... B 773 847-2000
  Chicago *(G-5710)*
- Park Packing Company Inc .... E 773 254-0100
  Chicago *(G-5764)*
- Portillos Food Service Inc .... E 630 620-0460
  Addison *(G-247)*
- Rapid Foods Inc .... G 708 366-0321
  Shorewood *(G-18902)*
- Roma Packing Co .... G 773 927-7371
  Chicago *(G-6055)*
- Ryan Meat Company .... G 773 783-3840
  Evergreen Park *(G-9599)*
- Seifferts Locker & Meat Proc .... F 618 594-3921
  Carlyle *(G-2895)*
- Skyline Provisions Inc .... F 708 331-1982
  Harvey *(G-11095)*
- Y T Packing Co .... F 217 522-3345
  Springfield *(G-19470)*

FOOD PRDTS, WHOLESALE: Baking Splys

- Bear-Stewart Corporation .... E 773 276-0400
  Chicago *(G-3854)*
- J R Short Milling Company .... C 800 544-8734
  Kankakee *(G-11979)*
- Wilton Brands LLC .... B 630 963-7100
  Naperville *(G-14948)*

FOOD PRDTS, WHOLESALE: Beverage Concentrates

- Quincy Pepsi-Cola Bottling Co .... F 309 833-4263
  Macomb *(G-13399)*

FOOD PRDTS, WHOLESALE: Beverages, Exc Coffee & Tea

- Atlantic Beverage Company Inc .... G 847 412-6200
  Northbrook *(G-15342)*
- Containers Inc .... G 708 442-2000
  Lyons *(G-13306)*
- Gatorade Company .... A 312 821-1000
  Chicago *(G-4662)*
- Gold Standard Enterprises Inc .... E 217 546-1633
  Springfield *(G-19375)*
- H J M P Corp .... C 708 345-5370
  Melrose Park *(G-13877)*
- Heartland Coca-Cola Btlg LLC .... A 217 544-4891
  Springfield *(G-19380)*
- Heartland Coca-Cola Btlg LLC .... A 217 223-3336
  Quincy *(G-16890)*
- Heartland Coca-Cola Btlg LLC .... A 217 367-1761
  Urbana *(G-19987)*
- Heartland Coca-Cola Btlg LLC .... A 309 697-8600
  Bartonville *(G-1332)*
- Heartland Coca-Cola Btlg LLC .... A 217 348-1001
  Charleston *(G-3403)*

FOOD PRDTS, WHOLESALE: Coffee & Tea

- Bamenda Coffee Company Inc .... G 214 566-8175
  Chicago *(G-3823)*
- Boombox Beverage LLC .... G 312 607-1038
  Skokie *(G-18930)*
- Farmer Bros Co .... G 217 787-7565
  Springfield *(G-19365)*
- Wolfart Maciej .... G 312 248-3575
  Chicago *(G-6663)*

FOOD PRDTS, WHOLESALE: Coffee, Green Or Roasted

- Napco Inc .... E 630 406-1100
  Batavia *(G-1397)*
- Troverco Inc .... E 800 468-3354
  Belleville *(G-1603)*

FOOD PRDTS, WHOLESALE: Condiments

- Clorox Hidden Valley Mfg .... F 847 229-5500
  Wheeling *(G-20871)*
- Dell Cove Spice Co .... G 312 339-8389
  Chicago *(G-4333)*

FOOD PRDTS, WHOLESALE: Cookies

- Blissful Brownies Inc .... G 541 308-0226
  Lake Forest *(G-12231)*
- Carols Cookies Inc .... G 847 831-4500
  Northbrook *(G-15353)*

FOOD PRDTS, WHOLESALE: Diet

- Health King Enterprise Inc .... G 312 567-9978
  Chicago *(G-4791)*

FOOD PRDTS, WHOLESALE: Dried or Canned Foods

- Woodland Foods Ltd .... C 847 625-8600
  Waukegan *(G-20519)*

FOOD PRDTS, WHOLESALE: Flavorings & Fragrances

- Givaudan Fragrances Corp .... G 847 735-0221
  Lake Forest *(G-12250)*

FOOD PRDTS, WHOLESALE: Flour

- Ardent Mills LLC .... E 618 826-2371
  Chester *(G-3449)*
- Neiman Bros Co Inc .... E 773 463-3000
  Chicago *(G-5564)*

FOOD PRDTS, WHOLESALE: Grain Elevators

- ADM Grain Company .... E 217 424-5200
  Decatur *(G-7432)*
- Archer-Daniels-Midland Company .... G 815 539-6219
  Mendota *(G-13937)*
- Archer-Daniels-Midland Company .... E 217 224-1800
  Quincy *(G-16856)*
- Archer-Daniels-Midland Company .... A 312 634-8100
  Chicago *(G-3728)*
- Cargill Dry Corn Ingrdents Inc .... G 217 465-5331
  Paris *(G-16226)*
- F S Gateway Inc .... G 618 458-6588
  Fults *(G-10160)*
- Hueber LLC .... G 815 393-4879
  Creston *(G-7102)*
- Maplehurst Farms Inc .... F 815 562-8723
  Rochelle *(G-17148)*
- South Central Fs Inc .... G 217 849-2242
  Toledo *(G-19878)*

FOOD PRDTS, WHOLESALE: Grains

- Archer-Daniels-Midland Company .... G 217 887-2514
  Hume *(G-11526)*
- Cargill Incorporated .... G 815 942-0932
  Morris *(G-14296)*
- Liberty Feed Mill .... F 217 645-3441
  Liberty *(G-12623)*
- Toyota Tsusho America Inc .... D 847 439-8500
  Elk Grove Village *(G-9281)*
- Western Ill Agri-Systems Inc .... G 217 746-2144
  Burnside *(G-2646)*

FOOD PRDTS, WHOLESALE: Health

- Glanbia Performance Ntrtn Inc .... F 630 236-0097
  Aurora *(G-970)*
- Glanbia Prfmce Ntrtn NA Inc .... C 630 236-0097
  Downers Grove *(G-8012)*

FOOD PRDTS, WHOLESALE: Honey

- Millers Country Crafts Inc .... G 618 426-3108
  Ava *(G-1175)*

FOOD PRDTS, WHOLESALE: Natural & Organic

- Iya Foods LLC .... G 630 854-7107
  North Aurora *(G-15264)*
- Natural Distribution Company .... G 630 350-1700
  Wood Dale *(G-21219)*

FOOD PRDTS, WHOLESALE: Pasta & Rice

- Golden Grain Company .... G 708 458-7020
  Bridgeview *(G-2351)*
- Wah King Noodle Co Inc .... F 323 268-0222
  Chicago *(G-6584)*

FOOD PRDTS, WHOLESALE: Pizza Splys

- Avanti Foods Company .... E 815 379-2155
  Walnut *(G-20216)*
- Grant Park Packing Company Inc .... E 312 421-4096
  Franklin Park *(G-9952)*
- Mancuso Cheese Company .... F 815 722-2475
  Joliet *(G-11897)*
- Randolph Packing Co .... D 630 830-3100
  Streamwood *(G-19592)*
- Russo Wholesale Meat Inc .... G 708 385-0500
  Alsip *(G-507)*

FOOD PRDTS, WHOLESALE: Rice, Polished

- International Golden Foods Inc .... F 630 860-5552
  Bensenville *(G-1823)*
- Sunrise Distributors Inc .... G 630 400-8786
  Elk Grove Village *(G-9259)*

FOOD PRDTS, WHOLESALE: Salt, Edible

- K+s Salt LLC .... G 844 789-3991
  Chicago *(G-5070)*

FOOD PRDTS, WHOLESALE: Sauces

- Andrias Food Group Inc .... E 618 632-4866
  O Fallon *(G-15565)*
- Sokol and Company .... D 708 482-8250
  Countryside *(G-7071)*

FOOD PRDTS, WHOLESALE: Shortening, Vegetable

- Abitec Corporation .... E 217 465-8577
  Paris *(G-16223)*

PRODUCT SECTION

FOOD PRDTS, WHOLESALE: Soups, Exc Frozen

Supalicious Soups Inc .... G 708 491-9738
  Chicago *(G-6279)*

FOOD PRDTS, WHOLESALE: Specialty

American Kitchen Delights Inc .... D 708 210-3200
  Harvey *(G-11073)*
Clearly Kosher Foods .... F 630 546-2052
  Aurora *(G-1076)*
Olive and Vinnies .... G 630 534-6457
  Glen Ellyn *(G-10416)*
Plumrose Usa Inc .... E 800 526-4909
  Downers Grove *(G-8077)*
V & V Supremo Foods Inc .... C 312 733-5652
  Chicago *(G-6511)*
Zb Importing Inc .... D 708 222-8330
  Cicero *(G-6890)*
Zb Importing Inc .... E 708 222-8330
  Chicago *(G-6709)*

FOOD PRDTS, WHOLESALE: Spices & Seasonings

La Criolla Inc .... E 312 243-8882
  Alsip *(G-468)*
Laredo Foods Inc .... E 773 762-1500
  Chicago *(G-5177)*
USspice Mill Inc .... F 773 378-6800
  Chicago *(G-6507)*
Vej Holdings LLC .... G 630 219-1598
  Naperville *(G-14940)*
Vita Food Products Inc .... D 312 738-4500
  Chicago *(G-6560)*

FOOD PRDTS, WHOLESALE: Water, Distilled

Ds Services of America Inc .... C 773 586-8600
  Chicago *(G-4399)*
Hinckley & Schmitt Inc .... A 773 586-8600
  Chicago *(G-4823)*

FOOD PRDTS, WHOLESALE: Wheat

Trainor AG Products LLC .... G 618 614-5770
  Anna *(G-589)*

FOOD PRDTS: Animal & marine fats & oils

Abitec Corporation .... E 217 465-8577
  Paris *(G-16223)*
Ace Grease Service Inc .... G 618 781-1207
  Millstadt *(G-14041)*
Darling Ingredients Inc .... E 309 476-8111
  Lynn Center *(G-13289)*
McShares Inc .... E 217 762-2561
  Monticello *(G-14281)*
Micro Surface Corporation .... F 815 942-4221
  Morris *(G-14312)*
Millstadt Rendering Company .... E 618 538-5312
  Belleville *(G-1578)*
Schnowske & Sons Trucking Inc .... G 309 937-3323
  Cambridge *(G-2807)*
Sdr Corp .... G 773 638-1800
  Chicago *(G-6123)*
Sustainable Sourcing LLC .... F 815 714-8055
  Mokena *(G-14120)*

FOOD PRDTS: Baking Soda

Bellisario Holdings LLC .... G 847 867-2960
  Park Ridge *(G-16270)*

FOOD PRDTS: Bran & Middlings, Exc Rice

Salud Natural Entrepreneur Inc .... E 224 789-7400
  Waukegan *(G-20492)*

FOOD PRDTS: Bread Crumbs, Exc Made In Bakeries

Jbc Holding Co .... G 217 347-7701
  Effingham *(G-8404)*
Newly Weds Foods Inc .... A 773 489-7000
  Chicago *(G-5584)*
Pepperidge Farm Incorporated .... G 708 478-7450
  Mokena *(G-14106)*
Pepperidge Farm Incorporated .... G 630 241-6372
  Downers Grove *(G-8072)*

FOOD PRDTS: Breakfast Bars

CGC Corporation .... D 773 838-3400
  Chicago *(G-4066)*

FOOD PRDTS: Cake Fillings, Exc Fruit

Sokol and Company .... D 708 482-8250
  Countryside *(G-7071)*

FOOD PRDTS: Cereals

General Mills Inc .... D 630 844-1125
  Montgomery *(G-14244)*
General Mills Inc .... B 630 231-1140
  Calumet City *(G-2778)*
General Mills Operations LLC .... G 630 844-1125
  Montgomery *(G-14245)*
Gilster-Mary Lee Corporation .... A 618 826-2361
  Chester *(G-3456)*
Hearthside Food Solutions LLC .... E 630 967-3600
  Downers Grove *(G-8019)*
Kellogg Company .... B 773 254-0900
  Chicago *(G-5090)*
Kellogg Company .... F 217 258-3251
  Mattoon *(G-13640)*
Kraft Foods Asia PCF Svcs LLC .... G 847 943-4000
  Deerfield *(G-7627)*
Kraft Heinz Company .... C 847 646-2000
  Chicago *(G-5129)*
Lee Gilster-Mary Corporation .... G 618 826-2361
  Chester *(G-3457)*
Lee Gilster-Mary Corporation .... E 618 443-5676
  Sparta *(G-19256)*
Mondelez Global LLC .... B 630 369-1909
  Naperville *(G-14874)*
Mondelez International Inc .... G 815 710-2114
  Morris *(G-14316)*
Mondelez International Inc .... A 847 943-4000
  Chicago *(G-5490)*
Quaker Oats Company .... A 312 821-1000
  Chicago *(G-5927)*
Quaker Oats Company .... A 217 443-4995
  Danville *(G-7375)*
Quaker Oats Europe Inc .... E 312 821-1000
  Chicago *(G-5928)*
Ralston Food Sales Inc .... G 314 877-7000
  Oak Brook *(G-15658)*
Treehouse Private Brands Inc .... F 630 455-5265
  Downers Grove *(G-8102)*
Treehouse Private Brands Inc .... G 314 877-7300
  Oak Brook *(G-15666)*

FOOD PRDTS: Chewing Gum Base

Wm Wrigley Jr Company .... C 312 644-2121
  Romeoville *(G-17889)*
Wm Wrigley Jr Company .... B 312 280-4710
  Chicago *(G-6654)*
Wm Wrigley Jr Company .... A 312 644-2121
  Chicago *(G-6656)*

FOOD PRDTS: Chicken, Processed, Fresh

Aspen Foods Inc .... C 312 829-7282
  Park Ridge *(G-16268)*
Jcg Industries Inc .... C 312 829-7282
  Park Ridge *(G-16286)*
New Specialty Products Inc .... E 773 847-0230
  Chicago *(G-5579)*

FOOD PRDTS: Chicken, Processed, Frozen

Lean Protein Team LLC .... G 440 525-1532
  Chicago *(G-5191)*
Love ME Tenders LLC .... G 773 502-8000
  Highland Park *(G-11282)*

FOOD PRDTS: Chicken, Processed, NEC

2000plus Groups Inc .... C 800 939-6268
  Chicago *(G-3463)*

FOOD PRDTS: Cocoa, Butter

Blommer Chocolate Company .... F 800 621-1606
  Chicago *(G-3911)*

FOOD PRDTS: Cocoa, Instant

Inside Beverages .... C 847 438-1338
  Lake Zurich *(G-12423)*
Kruger North America Inc .... F 708 851-3670
  Oak Park *(G-15761)*

FOOD PRDTS: Cocoa, Powdered

Compact Industries Inc .... C 630 513-9600
  Saint Charles *(G-18173)*

FOOD PRDTS: Coffee

Back of Yards Coffee LLC .... G 773 475-6381
  Chicago *(G-3812)*
Bamenda Coffee Company Inc .... G 214 566-8175
  Chicago *(G-3823)*
Big Shoulders Coffee Works .... G 312 888-3042
  Chicago *(G-3882)*
Hillshire Brands Company .... C 847 956-7575
  Elk Grove Village *(G-9035)*
Javamania Coffee Roastery Inc .... G 815 885-4661
  Loves Park *(G-13223)*
Manhattan Island .... G 312 762-5152
  Chicago *(G-5326)*
Napco Inc .... E 630 406-1100
  Batavia *(G-1397)*
Sparrow Coffee Roastery .... G 321 648-6415
  Westchester *(G-20712)*
Trade-Mark Coffee Corporation .... F 847 382-4200
  North Barrington *(G-15289)*
Two Brothers Brewing Company .... G 630 393-2337
  Warrenville *(G-20256)*

FOOD PRDTS: Coffee Extracts

Coffee Brewmasters Usa LLC .... F 773 294-9665
  Buffalo Grove *(G-2526)*
Insight Beverages Inc .... E 847 438-1598
  Lake Zurich *(G-12425)*
Limitless Coffee LLC .... E 630 779-3778
  Chicago *(G-5223)*

FOOD PRDTS: Coffee Roasting, Exc Wholesale Grocers

Art House Coffee LLC .... G 618 659-0571
  Edwardsville *(G-8345)*
Cup O Joe Coffee LLC .... G 877 828-7656
  Chicago *(G-4284)*
Farmer Bros Co .... G 217 787-7565
  Springfield *(G-19365)*
Kraft Foods Asia PCF Svcs LLC .... G 847 943-4000
  Deerfield *(G-7627)*
Kraft Heinz Company .... C 847 646-2000
  Chicago *(G-5129)*
Mondelez International Inc .... G 815 710-2114
  Morris *(G-14316)*
Mondelez International Inc .... A 847 943-4000
  Chicago *(G-5490)*
Stewarts Prvate Blend Fods Inc .... E 773 489-2500
  Carol Stream *(G-3077)*
Wolfart Maciej .... G 312 248-3575
  Chicago *(G-6663)*

FOOD PRDTS: Coffee Substitutes

Kws Cereals Usa LLC .... G 815 200-2666
  Champaign *(G-3316)*

FOOD PRDTS: Compound Shortenings

South Chicago Packing LLC .... D 708 589-2400
  South Holland *(G-19245)*
South Chicago Packing LLC .... D 708 589-2400
  Chicago *(G-6206)*

FOOD PRDTS: Cooking Oils, Refined Vegetable, Exc Corn

Fgfi LLC .... E 708 598-0909
  Countryside *(G-7052)*
Pastorelli Food Products Inc .... G 312 455-1006
  Chicago *(G-5770)*

FOOD PRDTS: Corn & other vegetable starches

Ingredion Incorporated .... A 708 551-2600
  Westchester *(G-20701)*
Tate & Lyle Americas LLC .... C 217 421-3268
  Decatur *(G-7557)*
Tate Lyle Ingrdnts Amricas LLC .... F 847 396-7500
  Hoffman Estates *(G-11467)*

FOOD PRDTS: Corn Chips & Other Corn-Based Snacks

El Popocatapetl Industries Inc..............D....... 773 843-0888
  Chicago *(G-4466)*
Snak-King Corp..C....... 815 232-6700
  Freeport *(G-10142)*

FOOD PRDTS: Corn Meal

Cargill Dry Corn Ingrdents Inc..............G....... 217 465-5331
  Paris *(G-16226)*

FOOD PRDTS: Cottonseed Oil, Cake & Meal

Lee Gilster-Mary Corporation ....C....... 618 533-4808
  Centralia *(G-3237)*

FOOD PRDTS: Cottonseed Oil, Deodorized

O-Liminator LLC......................................G....... 630 400-0373
  Saint Charles *(G-18235)*

FOOD PRDTS: Dessert Mixes & Fillings

Conagra Brands Inc ....C....... 312 549-5000
  Chicago *(G-4212)*
Conagra Brands Inc ....C....... 630 857-1000
  Naperville *(G-14803)*
Creative Contract Packg LLC ....D....... 630 851-6226
  Aurora *(G-944)*
Dennco Inc..G....... 708 862-0070
  Burnham *(G-2645)*
Givaudan Flavors Corporation ....C....... 630 682-5600
  Carol Stream *(G-2992)*
Holton Food Products Company.............F....... 708 352-5599
  La Grange *(G-12078)*
Home Style..G....... 847 455-5000
  Franklin Park *(G-9956)*

FOOD PRDTS: Desserts, Ready-To-Mix

Essen Nutrition Corporation....................E....... 630 739-6700
  Romeoville *(G-17817)*
Jel Sert Co...C....... 630 231-7590
  West Chicago *(G-20603)*
Solo Foods ....G....... 800 328-7656
  Countryside *(G-7072)*

FOOD PRDTS: Dips, Exc Cheese & Sour Cream Based

Chicks and Salsa LLC ....G....... 815 735-6660
  Verona *(G-20116)*
Salsa Verde Batavia Inc ....G....... 630 425-3521
  Batavia *(G-1412)*

FOOD PRDTS: Dough, Pizza, Prepared

Balton Corporation ....F....... 773 933-7927
  Chicago *(G-3822)*
LLC Urban Farmer ....D....... 815 468-7200
  Manteno *(G-13451)*

FOOD PRDTS: Doughs, Frozen Or Refrig From Purchased Flour

Loders Croklaan BV.................................C....... 815 730-5200
  Channahon *(G-3386)*

FOOD PRDTS: Dressings, Salad, Raw & Cooked Exc Dry Mixes

Earthgrains Refrigertd Dough P.............A....... 630 455-5200
  Downers Grove *(G-7996)*
Kraft Foods Asia PCF Svcs LLC.............G....... 847 943-4000
  Deerfield *(G-7627)*
Kraft Heinz Company..............................C....... 847 646-2000
  Chicago *(G-5129)*
Mizkan America Inc.................................E....... 847 590-0059
  Mount Prospect *(G-14547)*
Mondelez International Inc ....A....... 847 943-4000
  Chicago *(G-5490)*
Mullins Food Products Inc ....B....... 708 344-3224
  Broadview *(G-2455)*
Treehouse Private Brands Inc ....F....... 630 455-5265
  Downers Grove *(G-8102)*
Treehouse Private Brands Inc ....C....... 314 877-7300
  Oak Brook *(G-15666)*

FOOD PRDTS: Dried & Dehydrated Fruits, Vegetables & Soup Mix

Ali VS Kitchen LLC ....G....... 312 852-5090
  Chicago *(G-3606)*
Bernard Food Industries Inc..................D....... 847 869-5222
  Evanston *(G-9499)*
Biovie Inc...G....... 978 998-4756
  Chicago *(G-3898)*
Chef Lmt Foods LLC................................E....... 847 279-6490
  Arlington Heights *(G-714)*
Karlin Foods Corp....................................F....... 847 441-8330
  Northfield *(G-15519)*
Kent Precision Foods Group Inc............E....... 630 226-0071
  Bolingbrook *(G-2201)*
Kent Precision Foods Group Inc............F....... 630 226-0071
  Bolingbrook *(G-2202)*
Lightlife Foods Inc ....C....... 413 774-9000
  Elmhurst *(G-9392)*
Pknd Llc ....G....... 773 491-0070
  Chicago *(G-5816)*
R J Van Drunen & Sons Inc ....D....... 815 472-3211
  Momence *(G-14193)*
Swiss Products LP...................................E....... 773 394-6480
  Chicago *(G-6297)*
Woodland Foods Ltd ....C....... 847 625-8600
  Waukegan *(G-20519)*

FOOD PRDTS: Duck Slaughtering & Processing

2000plus Groups Inc..............................G....... 630 528-3220
  Oak Brook *(G-15587)*

FOOD PRDTS: Edible Oil Prdts, Exc Corn Oil

Loders Croklaan BV.................................C....... 815 730-5200
  Channahon *(G-3386)*
Loders Croklaan Usa LLC........................C....... 815 730-5200
  Channahon *(G-3387)*

FOOD PRDTS: Edible fats & oils

Ach Food Companies Inc........................C....... 708 458-8690
  Summit Argo *(G-19676)*
All Fresh Food Products ....G....... 847 864-5030
  Evanston *(G-9491)*
Allfresh Food Products Inc ....F....... 847 869-3100
  Evanston *(G-9492)*
Archer-Daniels-Midland Company ....E....... 217 224-1800
  Quincy *(G-16856)*
Avatar Corporation ....D....... 708 534-5511
  University Park *(G-19947)*
Cargill Incorporated ....F....... 773 375-7255
  Chicago *(G-4030)*
Darling Ingredients Inc ....E....... 217 482-3261
  Mason City *(G-13611)*
Dawn Food Products Inc........................C....... 815 933-0600
  Bradley *(G-2280)*
Midwest Processing Company................D....... 217 424-5200
  Decatur *(G-7525)*
Stratas Foods LLC ....E....... 217 424-5660
  Decatur *(G-7552)*
V Formusa Co ....F....... 224 938-9360
  Des Plaines *(G-7863)*

FOOD PRDTS: Egg Substitutes, Made From Eggs

Eggology Inc..F....... 818 610-2222
  Pearl City *(G-16319)*

FOOD PRDTS: Emulsifiers

E I Du Pont De Nemours & Co ....D....... 815 259-3311
  Thomson *(G-19783)*
FBC Industries Inc ....G....... 847 241-6143
  Schaumburg *(G-18526)*
FBC Industries Inc ....G....... 847 839-0880
  Rochelle *(G-17140)*
Kosto Food Products Company..............F....... 847 487-2600
  Wauconda *(G-20367)*

FOOD PRDTS: Fat Substitutes

Fibergel Technologies Inc ....G....... 847 549-6002
  Mundelein *(G-14688)*

FOOD PRDTS: Fish Meal

K-Pro US LLC...G....... 872 529-5776
  O Fallon *(G-15576)*

FOOD PRDTS: Flour

J R Short Milling Company ....C....... 800 544-8734
  Kankakee *(G-11979)*
McShares Inc...E....... 217 762-2561
  Monticello *(G-14281)*
TEC Foods Inc ....E....... 800 315-8002
  Chicago *(G-6333)*

FOOD PRDTS: Flour & Other Grain Mill Products

ADM Grain Company ....E....... 217 424-5200
  Decatur *(G-7432)*
Agritech Worldwide Inc ....F....... 847 549-6002
  Mundelein *(G-14660)*
American Milling Company ....F....... 309 347-6888
  Pekin *(G-16323)*
Archer-Daniels-Midland Company ....G....... 217 764-3345
  Macon *(G-13404)*
Archer-Daniels-Midland Company ....D....... 217 424-5882
  Decatur *(G-7441)*
Archer-Daniels-Midland Company ....G....... 217 451-8909
  Decatur *(G-7442)*
Archer-Daniels-Midland Company ....G....... 618 238-4800
  Edgewood *(G-8334)*
Archer-Daniels-Midland Company ....C....... 217 424-5236
  Decatur *(G-7443)*
Archer-Daniels-Midland Company ....C....... 309 673-7828
  Peoria *(G-16385)*
Archer-Daniels-Midland Company ....G....... 815 428-7513
  Martinton *(G-13589)*
Archer-Daniels-Midland Company ....G....... 217 419-5100
  Champaign *(G-3267)*
Archer-Daniels-Midland Company ....B....... 800 257-5743
  Decatur *(G-7444)*
Archer-Daniels-Midland Company ....G....... 618 483-6171
  Altamont *(G-530)*
Archer-Daniels-Midland Company ....E....... 309 772-2141
  Bushnell *(G-2737)*
Archer-Daniels-Midland Company ....G....... 815 384-4011
  Rochelle *(G-17132)*
Archer-Daniels-Midland Company ....G....... 815 857-2058
  Amboy *(G-579)*
Archer-Daniels-Midland Company ....G....... 217 676-3811
  Mount Auburn *(G-14464)*
Archer-Daniels-Midland Company ....G....... 217 424-5806
  Decatur *(G-7445)*
Archer-Daniels-Midland Company ....F....... 217 451-4460
  Decatur *(G-7446)*
Archer-Daniels-Midland Company ....E....... 217 424-5413
  Decatur *(G-7447)*
Archer-Daniels-Midland Company ....G....... 217 228-0805
  Quincy *(G-16855)*
Archer-Daniels-Midland Company ....D....... 217 424-5200
  Decatur *(G-7448)*
Archer-Daniels-Midland Company ....G....... 217 754-3300
  Meredosia *(G-13955)*
Archer-Daniels-Midland Company ....G....... 815 538-3771
  Mendota *(G-13936)*
Archer-Daniels-Midland Company ....D....... 217 424-5200
  Decatur *(G-7449)*
Archer-Daniels-Midland Company ....E....... 217 424-5830
  Decatur *(G-7450)*
Archer-Daniels-Midland Company ....D....... 217 451-8169
  Decatur *(G-7451)*
Archer-Daniels-Midland Company ....G....... 815 692-2324
  Fairbury *(G-9603)*
Archer-Daniels-Midland Company ....F....... 815 223-7907
  Peru *(G-16566)*
Archer-Daniels-Midland Company ....E....... 217 424-5660
  Decatur *(G-7452)*
Archer-Daniels-Midland Company ....E....... 217 424-5858
  Decatur *(G-7453)*
Archer-Daniels-Midland Company ....G....... 217 887-2514
  Hume *(G-11526)*
Archer-Daniels-Midland Company ....E....... 217 224-1800
  Quincy *(G-16856)*
Archer-Daniels-Midland Company ....F....... 815 459-1600
  Crystal Lake *(G-7162)*
Archer-Daniels-Midland Company ....D....... 217 424-5785
  Decatur *(G-7455)*
Archer-Daniels-Midland Company ....D....... 217 224-1800
  Quincy *(G-16857)*
Archer-Daniels-Midland Company ....G....... 618 432-7194
  Patoka *(G-16302)*
Archer-Daniels-Midland Company ....F....... 217 451-4481
  Decatur *(G-7456)*
Archer-Daniels-Midland Company ....B....... 217 451-6528
  Decatur *(G-7457)*

PRODUCT SECTION

FOOD PRDTS: Mixes, Pizza From Purchased Flour

Archer-Daniels-Midland Company ....G....... 217 423-2788
  Decatur *(G-7458)*
Archer-Daniels-Midland Company ....D....... 217 224-1875
  Quincy *(G-16858)*
Archer-Daniels-Midland Company ....D....... 217 424-5200
  Decatur *(G-7459)*
Archer-Daniels-Midland Company ....F....... 217 424-5669
  Decatur *(G-7460)*
Ardent Mills LLC ....E....... 618 826-2371
  Chester *(G-3449)*
Bio Fuels By American Farmers ....F....... 561 859-6251
  Benton *(G-1921)*
Dix-Mcguire Commodities - LLC ....G....... 847 496-5320
  Palatine *(G-16112)*
General Mills Inc ....E....... 309 342-9165
  Galesburg *(G-10197)*
Hayden Mills Inc ....E....... 618 962-3136
  Omaha *(G-15900)*
J R Short Milling Company ....C....... 815 937-2633
  Kankakee *(G-11980)*
Nauvoo Mill & Bakery ....G....... 217 453-6734
  Nauvoo *(G-15014)*
New Alliance Production LLC ....E....... 309 928-3123
  Farmer City *(G-9656)*
Pillsbury Company LLC ....G....... 847 541-8888
  Buffalo Grove *(G-2586)*
Problend-Eurogerm LLC ....G....... 847 221-5004
  Rolling Meadows *(G-17767)*
Quaker Oats Company ....A....... 217 443-4995
  Danville *(G-7375)*
Ron & Pats Pizza Shack ....G....... 847 395-5005
  Antioch *(G-633)*
Sunrise Distributors Inc ....G....... 630 400-8786
  Elk Grove Village *(G-9259)*
U S Soy LLC ....F....... 217 235-1020
  Mattoon *(G-13655)*

FOOD PRDTS: Flour Mixes & Doughs

Bear-Stewart Corporation ....E....... 773 276-0400
  Chicago *(G-3854)*
Brolite Products Incorporated ....E....... 630 830-0340
  Bartlett *(G-1270)*
Dawn Food Products Inc ....E....... 815 468-6286
  Manteno *(G-13446)*
Dominos Pizza LLC ....E....... 630 783-0738
  Woodridge *(G-21295)*
Lee Gilster-Mary Corporation ....D....... 618 965-3426
  Steeleville *(G-19481)*
Parke & Son Inc ....G....... 217 875-0572
  Decatur *(G-7535)*
Watson Foods Co Inc ....D....... 847 245-8404
  Lindenhurst *(G-12855)*
Watson LLC ....E....... 217 824-4440
  Taylorville *(G-19763)*

FOOD PRDTS: Flour, Blended From Purchased Flour

Fleetchem LLC ....F....... 708 957-5311
  Flossmoor *(G-9698)*
Gilster-Mary Lee Corporation ....A....... 618 826-2361
  Chester *(G-3456)*
Lee Gilster-Mary Corporation ....G....... 618 826-2361
  Chester *(G-3457)*
Lee Gilster-Mary Corporation ....E....... 618 443-5676
  Sparta *(G-19256)*
Lee Gilster-Mary Corporation ....D....... 815 472-6456
  Momence *(G-14186)*

FOOD PRDTS: Flours & Flour Mixes, From Purchased Flour

Continental Mills Inc ....F....... 800 426-0955
  Chicago *(G-4229)*
Continental Mills Inc ....C....... 217 540-4000
  Effingham *(G-8392)*
Quaker Oats Company ....A....... 312 821-1000
  Chicago *(G-5927)*
Quaker Oats Europe Inc ....G....... 312 821-1000
  Chicago *(G-5928)*

FOOD PRDTS: Fresh Vegetables, Peeled Or Processed

Taylor Farms Illinois Inc ....B....... 312 432-6800
  Chicago *(G-6331)*

FOOD PRDTS: Fruit Juices

Dulce Vida Juice Bar LLC ....G....... 224 236-5045
  Hanover Park *(G-11002)*
Fresh Factory ....E....... 630 580-9038
  Carol Stream *(G-2988)*
Here Holdings LLC ....G....... 563 723-1008
  Carol Stream *(G-2997)*
J J Mata Inc ....G....... 773 750-0643
  Chicago *(G-4991)*
Mautino Distributing Co Inc ....E....... 815 664-4311
  Spring Valley *(G-19310)*
Natural Distribution Company ....G....... 630 350-1700
  Wood Dale *(G-21219)*

FOOD PRDTS: Fruit Pops, Frozen

Jel Sert Co ....C....... 630 231-7590
  West Chicago *(G-20603)*

FOOD PRDTS: Fruits, Dehydrated Or Dried

Graziano TI Inc ....E....... 847 741-1900
  Elgin *(G-8600)*
Handcut Foods LLC ....D....... 312 239-0381
  Chicago *(G-4776)*
Hot Mexican Peppers Inc ....G....... 773 843-9774
  Chicago *(G-4847)*
Red Rumi LLC ....G....... 847 757-8433
  Algonquin *(G-387)*

FOOD PRDTS: Gelatin Dessert Preparations

Raymundos Food Group LLC ....C....... 708 344-8400
  Bedford Park *(G-1497)*

FOOD PRDTS: Gluten Feed

Mgp Ingredients Illinois Inc ....C....... 309 353-3990
  Pekin *(G-16345)*
Mgpi Processing Inc ....C....... 309 353-3990
  Pekin *(G-16346)*

FOOD PRDTS: Granola & Energy Bars, Nonchocolate

Element Bars Inc ....E....... 888 411-3536
  Chicago *(G-4480)*
Nature S American Co ....G....... 630 246-4776
  Lombard *(G-13107)*
Quaker Oats Company ....A....... 312 821-1000
  Chicago *(G-5927)*

FOOD PRDTS: High fructose corn syrup

ADM Holdings LLC ....G....... 217 424-5200
  Decatur *(G-7434)*

FOOD PRDTS: Honey

Ys Health Corporation ....F....... 847 391-9122
  Mount Prospect *(G-14585)*

FOOD PRDTS: Horseradish, Exc Sauce

Fournie Farms Inc ....E....... 618 344-8527
  Collinsville *(G-6961)*

FOOD PRDTS: Ice, Blocks

Collinsville Ice & Fuel Co ....F....... 618 344-3272
  Collinsville *(G-6955)*
Just Ice Inc ....G....... 773 301-7323
  Chicago *(G-5062)*

FOOD PRDTS: Ice, Cubes

Sisler Dairy Products Company ....G....... 815 376-2913
  Ohio *(G-15845)*

FOOD PRDTS: Instant Coffee

Berner Food & Beverage LLC ....B....... 815 563-4222
  Dakota *(G-7311)*
Compact Industries Inc ....C....... 630 513-9600
  Saint Charles *(G-18173)*

FOOD PRDTS: Macaroni Prdts, Dry, Alphabet, Rings Or Shells

Gilster-Mary Lee Corporation ....A....... 618 826-2361
  Chester *(G-3456)*
Golden Grain Company ....G....... 708 458-7020
  Bridgeview *(G-2351)*
Lee Gilster-Mary Corporation ....G....... 618 826-2361
  Chester *(G-3457)*
Lee Gilster-Mary Corporation ....E....... 618 443-5676
  Sparta *(G-19256)*
Lee Gilster-Mary Corporation ....D....... 815 472-6456
  Momence *(G-14186)*

FOOD PRDTS: Macaroni, Noodles, Spaghetti, Pasta, Etc

Baily International Inc ....D....... 773 927-3233
  Chicago *(G-3816)*
Burgess & Burgess Inc ....G....... 847 855-1048
  Gurnee *(G-10863)*
General Mills Inc ....B....... 630 231-1140
  Calumet City *(G-2778)*
Kraft Heinz Foods Company ....D....... 217 378-1900
  Champaign *(G-3315)*
Lee Gilster-Mary Corporation ....B....... 618 965-3449
  Steeleville *(G-19482)*
Lee Gilster-Mary Corporation ....D....... 618 965-3426
  Steeleville *(G-19481)*
Mary Lee Packaging Corporation ....E....... 618 826-2361
  Chester *(G-3458)*
Pastafresh Co ....G....... 773 745-5888
  Chicago *(G-5769)*
Trinity Services Inc ....G....... 815 485-5612
  New Lenox *(G-15066)*

FOOD PRDTS: Malt

Archer-Daniels-Midland Company ....D....... 217 424-5200
  Decatur *(G-7448)*
Archer-Daniels-Midland Company ....A....... 312 634-8100
  Chicago *(G-3728)*

FOOD PRDTS: Meat Meal & Tankage, Inedible

Darling Ingredients Inc ....E....... 217 482-3261
  Mason City *(G-13611)*

FOOD PRDTS: Milled Corn By-Prdts

Cargill Incorporated ....E....... 630 505-7788
  Chicago *(G-4031)*
Gro Alliance LLC ....G....... 217 792-3355
  Mount Pulaski *(G-14587)*

FOOD PRDTS: Mixes, Bread & Roll From Purchased Flour

Dunbar Systems Inc ....F....... 630 257-2900
  Lemont *(G-12563)*
Kerry Inc ....D....... 708 450-3260
  Melrose Park *(G-13888)*

FOOD PRDTS: Mixes, Cake, From Purchased Flour

Inside Beverages ....C....... 847 438-1338
  Lake Zurich *(G-12423)*

FOOD PRDTS: Mixes, Doughnut From Purchased Flour

Joshi Brothers Inc ....E....... 847 895-0200
  Schaumburg *(G-18578)*

FOOD PRDTS: Mixes, Gravy, Dry

Custom Culinary Inc ....D....... 630 928-4898
  Lombard *(G-13061)*
Swiss Products LP ....E....... 773 394-6480
  Chicago *(G-6297)*

FOOD PRDTS: Mixes, Pancake From Purchased Flour

Arro Corporation ....E....... 708 352-7412
  Hodgkins *(G-11385)*
Arro Corporation ....C....... 708 352-8200
  Hodgkins *(G-11384)*
Arro Corporation ....G....... 773 978-1251
  Chicago *(G-3733)*

FOOD PRDTS: Mixes, Pizza From Purchased Flour

Diversfied III Green Works LLC ....D....... 773 544-7777
  Chicago *(G-4369)*
Russo Wholesale Meat Inc ....G....... 708 385-0500
  Alsip *(G-507)*

Employee Codes: A=Over 500 employees, B=251-500
C=101-250, D=51-100, E=20-50, F=10-19, G=3-9

FOOD PRDTS: Mixes, Sauces, Dry

Culinary Co-Pack Inc .... G 847 451-1551
Franklin Park *(G-9920)*
Johnny Vans Smokehouse .... G 773 750-1589
Chicago *(G-5045)*
Swagger Foods Corporation .... E 847 913-1200
Vernon Hills *(G-20101)*

FOOD PRDTS: Mixes, Seasonings, Dry

Char Crust Co Inc .... G 773 528-0600
Chicago *(G-4071)*
Griffith Foods Group Inc .... F 708 371-0900
Alsip *(G-451)*
Griffith Foods Inc .... B 708 371-0900
Alsip *(G-452)*
Griffith Foods Worldwide Inc 708 371-0900
Alsip *(G-453)*
Papys Foods Inc .... E 815 385-3313
McHenry *(G-13776)*
Royal Foods & Flavors Inc .... F 847 595-9166
Elk Grove Village *(G-9222)*
Sono Italiano Corporation 817 472-8903
Manteno *(G-13456)*
Vanee Foods Company .... D 708 449-7300
Berkeley *(G-1945)*

FOOD PRDTS: Molasses, Mixed/Blended, Purchased Ingredients

Sweet Solutions LLC .... G 630 364-2843
Plainfield *(G-16720)*

FOOD PRDTS: Mustard, Prepared

Boetje Foods Inc .... G 309 788-4352
Rock Island *(G-17208)*
Flaherty Incorporated .... G 773 472-8456
Skokie *(G-18955)*
Plochman Inc .... E 815 468-3434
Manteno *(G-13454)*

FOOD PRDTS: Noodles, Uncooked, Packaged W/Other Ingredients

Good World Noodle Inc .... G 312 326-0441
Chicago *(G-4716)*
New Taste Good Noodle Inc .... G 312 842-8980
Chicago *(G-5582)*

FOOD PRDTS: Nuts & Seeds

Anton-Argires Inc .... G 708 388-6250
Alsip *(G-416)*
Arthur/Busse Properties Inc .... F 847 289-1800
Elk Grove Village *(G-8840)*
Graziano Tl Inc .... E 847 741-1900
Elgin *(G-8600)*
Peases Inc .... F 217 529-2912
Springfield *(G-19263)*
Specialty Nut & Bky Sup Co Inc .... G 630 268-8500
Addison *(G-294)*

FOOD PRDTS: Oil, Hydrogenated, Edible

Ach Food Companies Inc .... C 866 386-8282
Oakbrook Terrace *(G-15780)*
Ach Food Companies Inc .... C 866 386-8282
Oakbrook Terrace *(G-15781)*

FOOD PRDTS: Oils & Fats, Animal

Mendota Agri-Products Inc .... E 815 539-5633
Mendota *(G-13946)*

FOOD PRDTS: Olive Oil

Cfc Inc .... D 847 257-8920
Des Plaines *(G-7743)*
Old Town Oil Evanston .... G 312 787-9595
Evanston *(G-9562)*
Olivaceto .... G 708 639-4408
La Grange *(G-12084)*
Olive and Vinnies .... G 630 534-6457
Glen Ellyn *(G-10416)*
Olive Leclaire Oil Co .... G 888 255-1867
Yorkville *(G-21494)*
Olive Oil Market Place .... G 618 304-3769
Godfrey *(G-10659)*
Olive Oil Marketplace Inc .... G 618 304-3769
Alton *(G-567)*

Olive Oils & More LLC .... G 618 656-4645
Edwardsville *(G-8373)*

FOOD PRDTS: Oriental Noodles

Ninos LLC .... E 708 932-5555
Bloomingdale *(G-2002)*
Noodles Factory LLC .... G 312 842-6500
Chicago *(G-5611)*
Oakland Noodle Company .... G 217 346-2322
Oakland *(G-15819)*
Real Taste Noodles Mfg Inc .... G 312 738-1893
Chicago *(G-5984)*
YMC Corp .... F 312 842-4900
Chicago *(G-6702)*

FOOD PRDTS: Pasta, Rice/Potatoes, Uncooked, Pkgd

Leos Gluten Free LLC .... F 847 233-9211
Franklin Park *(G-9981)*
Pastafresh Co .... G 773 745-5888
Chicago *(G-5769)*

FOOD PRDTS: Pasta, Uncooked, Packaged With Other Ingredients

E3 Artisan Inc .... E 815 575-9315
Woodstock *(G-21384)*
Gerard Mitchell Company LLC ..... G 708 205-0828
Yorkville *(G-21485)*
Perfect Pasta Inc .... G 630 543-8300
Addison *(G-237)*
Wah King Noodle Co Inc .... F 323 268-0222
Chicago *(G-6584)*

FOOD PRDTS: Peanut Butter

John B Sanfilippo & Son Inc .... C 847 289-1800
Elgin *(G-8632)*
Peanut Butter Partners LLC .... G 847 489-5322
Glen Ellyn *(G-10418)*

FOOD PRDTS: Pickles, Vinegar

Kraft Heinz Foods Company .... B 815 338-7000
Woodstock *(G-21401)*
North Star Pickle LLC .... F 847 970-5555
Lake Zurich *(G-12439)*

FOOD PRDTS: Pizza Doughs From Purchased Flour

Nation Pizza Products LP .... A 847 397-3320
Schaumburg *(G-18644)*

FOOD PRDTS: Popcorn, Popped

Aunt Ems Gourmet Popcorn Inc ... F 309 447-6612
Deer Creek *(G-7571)*
Creekstone Kettle Works Ltd ...... F 217 246-5355
Raymond *(G-16988)*
Great American Popcorn Company ... G 815 777-4116
Galena *(G-10173)*
Scotts Popcorn LLC .... G 773 608-9625
Chicago *(G-6121)*
Tpf Liquidation Co .... D 847 362-0028
Lake Forest *(G-12315)*

FOOD PRDTS: Popcorn, Unpopped

Cornfields LLC .... C 847 263-7000
Waukegan *(G-20430)*
Gilster-Mary Lee Corporation ...... A 618 826-2361
Chester *(G-3456)*
Great American Popcorn Company ... G 815 777-4116
Galena *(G-10173)*
Lee Gilster-Mary Corporation ...... G 618 826-2361
Chester *(G-3457)*
Lee Gilster-Mary Corporation ...... E 618 443-5676
Sparta *(G-19256)*
Lee Gilster-Mary Corporation 815 472-6456
Momence *(G-14186)*
Tee Lee Popcorn Inc .... E 815 864-2363
Shannon *(G-18874)*
Tpf Liquidation Co .... D 847 362-0028
Lake Forest *(G-12315)*

FOOD PRDTS: Pork Rinds

Benestar Brands LLC .... G 773 254-7400
Chicago *(G-3868)*

Evans Food Group Ltd .... D 773 254-7400
Chicago *(G-4536)*
Evans Foods Inc .... D 773 254-7400
Chicago *(G-4537)*

FOOD PRDTS: Potato & Corn Chips & Similar Prdts

Altona Co .... G 815 232-7819
Freeport *(G-10099)*
Campbell Soup Company .... G 618 548-3001
Salem *(G-18333)*
Campbell Soup Company .... C 630 241-6200
Downers Grove *(G-7964)*
Chipita America Inc .... E 708 731-2434
Westchester *(G-20693)*
Chips Aleeces Pita .... G 309 699-8859
East Peoria *(G-8260)*
Frito-Lay North America Inc .... C 217 532-5040
Hillsboro *(G-11311)*
Hello Delicious Brands LLC .... F 844 845-4544
Northbrook *(G-15399)*
John B Sanfilippo & Son Inc .... C 847 289-1800
Elgin *(G-8632)*
Mozaics LLC .... G 614 306-1881
Chicago *(G-5513)*
Pepsico Inc .... D 312 821-1000
Chicago *(G-5789)*
Prairieland Food Products Co ...... G 708 396-8826
Alsip *(G-496)*
Princess Foods Inc .... E 847 933-1820
Skokie *(G-19011)*
Quality Snack Foods Inc .... D 708 377-7120
Alsip *(G-499)*
R and B Distributors Inc .... G 815 433-6843
Ottawa *(G-16074)*
Safe Fair Food Company LLC .... F 904 930-4277
Chicago *(G-6088)*
Select Snacks Company Inc .... G 773 933-2167
Chicago *(G-6133)*
Tee Lee Popcorn Inc .... E 815 864-2363
Shannon *(G-18874)*
Thanasi Foods LLC .... E 720 570-1065
Chicago *(G-6359)*
Wisconsin Wilderness Food Pdts .. G 847 735-8661
Lake Forest *(G-12323)*

FOOD PRDTS: Potato Chips & Other Potato-Based Snacks

Mrs Fishers Inc .... F 815 964-9114
Rockford *(G-17532)*
Ole Saltys of Rockford Inc .... G 815 637-2447
Rockford *(G-17543)*
Ole Saltys of Rockford Inc .... G 815 637-2447
Loves Park *(G-13241)*
Revolution Companies Inc .... G 800 826-4083
Chicago *(G-6019)*
Utz Quality Foods LLC .... D 309 245-2191
Farmington *(G-9664)*
Utz Quality Foods LLC .... E 309 772-2798
Bushnell *(G-2747)*

FOOD PRDTS: Potatoes, Dried

Bran-Zan Holdings LLC .... F 847 342-0000
Arlington Heights *(G-708)*
Noon Hour Food Products Inc ..... E 312 382-1177
Chicago *(G-5612)*

FOOD PRDTS: Poultry Sausage, Lunch Meats/Other Poultry Prdts

Nduja Artisans Co .... G 312 550-6991
Chicago *(G-5559)*

FOOD PRDTS: Preparations

Abelei Inc .... F 630 859-1410
North Aurora *(G-15253)*
Agritech Worldwide Inc .... F 847 549-6002
Mundelein *(G-14660)*
Ajinomoto Foods North Amer Inc .. C 815 452-2361
Toluca *(G-19886)*
Alexia Foods .... G 312 374-3449
Chicago *(G-3605)*
Altona Co .... G 815 232-7819
Freeport *(G-10099)*
American Tristar Inc .... G 630 262-5500
Geneva *(G-10252)*

PRODUCT SECTION

FOOD PRDTS: Prepared Meat Sauces Exc Tomato & Dry

Company	Emp	Phone
Archer-Daniels-Midland Company Bushnell (G-2737)	E	309 772-2141
Arts Tamales Metamora (G-13958)	G	309 367-2850
Athenian Foods Co Melrose Park (G-13827)	F	708 343-6700
Avani Spices LLC Algonquin (G-366)	G	847 532-1075
Barilla America Inc Northbrook (G-15345)	D	515 956-4400
Bay Valley Foods LLC Chicago (G-3847)	D	773 927-7700
Bear-Stewart Corporation Chicago (G-3854)	E	773 276-0400
Bernard Food Industries Inc Evanston (G-9499)	D	847 869-5222
Cahokia Rice Mc Clure (G-13686)	G	618 661-1060
Canadian Harvest LP Galesburg (G-10187)	F	309 343-7808
Canyon Foods Inc Chicago (G-4016)	G	773 890-9888
Caravan Ingredients Inc Dolton (G-7935)	D	708 849-8590
Chateau Food Products Inc Chicago (G-4079)	F	708 863-4207
Chicago Coml & Consmr Brands Chicago (G-4097)	G	773 484-5771
Christian Wolf Inc Bartelso (G-1252)	G	618 667-9522
Cindys Pocket Kitchen Harvard (G-11050)	G	815 388-8385
Clown Global Brands LLC Northbrook (G-15362)	G	847 564-5950
Culinary Co-Pack Incorporated Franklin Park (G-9921)	G	847 451-1551
Cultor Food Science Danis Thomson (G-19781)	G	815 259-3311
Custom Culinary Inc Oswego (G-16000)	D	630 299-0500
Danisco USA Inc Thomson (G-19782)	G	815 259-3311
Deja Investments Inc Bolingbrook (G-2168)	D	630 408-9222
Delobian Foods Chicago (G-4335)	G	773 564-0913
Dutch American Foods Crete (G-7139)	G	708 304-2648
Ebro Foods Inc Chicago (G-4443)	D	773 696-0150
El-Ranchero Food Products Chicago (G-4474)	E	773 847-9167
Equi-Chem International Inc Carol Stream (G-2979)	F	630 784-0432
Euphoria Catering and Events Aurora (G-1092)	G	630 301-4369
Far East Food Inc Chicago (G-4560)	G	312 733-1688
Father and Son Commercial Chicago (G-4566)	G	773 424-3301
Flaherty Incorporated Skokie (G-18955)	G	773 472-8456
Food Service Kankakee (G-11972)	D	815 933-0725
Fresh Express Incorporated Streamwood (G-19574)	G	630 736-3900
Frito-Lay North America Inc Manteno (G-13448)	F	815 468-3940
Frito-Lay North America Inc Oak Forest (G-15679)	C	708 331-7200
Fruit Fancy Chicago (G-4638)	E	708 724-2613
Futters Nut Butters Hoffman Estates (G-11426)	G	847 540-0565
General Mills Inc Calumet City (G-2778)	B	630 231-1140
Georgies Greek Tasty Food Inc Chicago (G-4685)	G	773 987-1298
Gonnella Baking Co Schaumburg (G-18538)	D	312 733-2020
Good Foods Inc Chicago (G-4715)	F	773 260-9110
Grantco Inc Mundelein (G-14691)	G	941 567-9259
Grecian Delight Foods Inc Elk Grove Village (G-9022)	C	847 364-1010
Griffith Foods Inc Chicago (G-4743)	E	773 523-7509
Gycor International Ltd Woodridge (G-21308)	F	630 754-8070
H C Schau & Son Inc Woodridge (G-21309)	C	630 783-1000
Hearthside Usa LLC Woodridge (G-21310)	F	630 783-1000
Herman Seekamp Inc Addison (G-149)	C	630 628-6555
Holcomb Hollow Mundelein (G-14697)	G	847 837-9123
Hop Kee Incorporated Chicago (G-4839)	E	312 791-9111
Ingredients Golden Hill Chicago (G-4922)	G	773 852-5112
Italia Foods Inc Schaumburg (G-18573)	E	847 397-4479
Ixtapa Foods Chicago (G-4980)	G	773 788-9701
John B Sanfilippo & Son Inc Elgin (G-8633)	C	847 690-8432
JRS J Rettenmaier and Soh Galesburg (G-10203)	F	309 343-7808
K M J Enterprises Inc Gurnee (G-10892)	E	847 688-1200
Kanbo International (us) Inc Lisle (G-12905)	G	630 873-6320
Kent Precision Foods Group Inc Bolingbrook (G-2202)	F	630 226-0071
Kerry Inc Melrose Park (G-13888)	D	708 450-3260
Kraft Heinz Foods Company Aurora (G-1121)	G	630 907-2590
Kraft Heinz Foods Company Glenview (G-10582)	C	847 646-2000
Kraft Heinz Foods Company Granite City (G-10718)	B	618 451-4820
Kraft Heinz Foods Company Champaign (G-3315)	D	217 378-1900
Kruger North America Inc Oak Park (G-15761)	F	708 851-3670
La Criolla Inc Alsip (G-468)	E	312 243-8882
Lancaster Traditions LLC South Barrington (G-19076)	G	847 428-5446
Laredo Foods Inc Chicago (G-5177)	E	773 762-1500
Lawrence Foods Inc Elk Grove Village (G-9088)	C	847 437-2400
Lcv Company East Moline (G-8232)	G	309 738-6452
Lee Gilster-Mary Corporation Steeleville (G-19481)	D	618 965-3426
Liborio Baking Co Inc River Grove (G-17061)	G	708 452-7222
Lightlife Foods Inc Elmhurst (G-9392)	C	413 774-9000
Little Lady Foods Inc Elk Grove Village (G-9096)	C	847 806-1440
Ludis Foods Adams Inc Chicago (G-5278)	G	312 939-2877
Mangel and Co Long Grove (G-13162)	F	847 634-0730
Mareta Ravioli Inc Leonore (G-12612)	F	815 856-2621
Monterey Mushrooms Inc Princeton (G-16815)	G	815 875-4436
My Own Meals Inc Chicago (G-5530)	G	773 378-6505
My Own Meals Inc Deerfield (G-7639)	G	847 948-1118
Necta Sweet Inc Buffalo Grove (G-2579)	E	847 215-9955
Neiman Bros Co Inc Chicago (G-5564)	E	773 463-3000
Nepaley LLC Chicago (G-5571)	G	224 420-2310
Newly Weds Foods Inc Chicago (G-5585)	D	773 628-6900
Newly Weds Foods Inc Chicago (G-5586)	B	773 489-7000
No Denial Foods Chicago (G-5606)	G	312 890-5267
Nutrivo LLC Aurora (G-1140)	E	630 270-1700
O Chilli Frozen Foods Inc Northbrook (G-15442)	E	847 562-1991
On-Cor Frozen Foods LLC Aurora (G-1142)	D	630 851-6600
Open Kitchens Inc Chicago (G-5680)	C	312 666-5334
Open Kitchens Inc Chicago (G-5681)	E	312 666-5334
OSI Group LLC Aurora (G-1143)	D	630 851-6600
Pennant Foods Alsip (G-489)	G	708 752-8730
Pickles Sorrel Inc Chicago (G-5806)	F	773 379-4748
PO Food Specialists Ltd Hoffman Estates (G-11448)	G	847 517-8315
Pop Box LLC Chicago (G-5841)	G	630 509-2281
Pop Brands LLC Chicago (G-5842)	G	630 205-7146
Positive Mama Enterprises LLC Flora (G-9689)	G	618 508-1995
Pregel America Elk Grove Village (G-9194)	G	847 258-3725
Prinova Solutions LLC Carol Stream (G-3053)	E	630 868-0300
Proven Partners Group LLC Elgin (G-8702)	D	847 488-1230
Purac America Inc Lincolnshire (G-12793)	G	847 634-6330
Quaker Oats Company Danville (G-7375)	A	217 443-4995
R J Van Drunen & Sons Inc Momence (G-14193)	D	815 472-3211
Rawnature5 LLC Chicago (G-5977)	F	312 800-3239
Regal Health Foods Intl Inc Chicago (G-6000)	E	773 252-1044
Revolution Brands LLC Huntley (G-11563)	G	847 902-3320
Roma Bakeries Inc Rockford (G-17614)	F	815 964-6737
Rt Wholesale Schiller Park (G-18841)	D	847 678-3663
S&J Food Management Corp Hinsdale (G-11376)	G	630 323-9296
Schau Southeast Sushi Inc Woodridge (G-21339)	E	630 783-1000
Schulze and Burch Biscuit Co Chicago (G-6115)	B	773 927-6622
Sdr Corp Chicago (G-6123)	G	773 638-1800
Simple Mills Inc Chicago (G-6174)	E	312 600-6196
Snak-King Corp Freeport (G-10142)	C	815 232-6700
Solae Gibson City (G-10345)	F	217 784-8261
Sotiros Foods Inc Alsip (G-511)	E	708 371-0002
Stepan Specialty Products LLC Northfield (G-15532)	G	847 446-7500
Subco Foods of Illinois Inc West Chicago (G-20647)	D	630 231-0003
Sweetener Supply Corporation Berwyn (G-1961)	F	708 484-3455
Tara International LP Hodgkins (G-11398)	D	708 354-7050
Teasdale Foods Inc Hoopeston (G-11514)	D	217 283-7771
Teresa Foods Inc Peotone (G-16558)	F	708 258-6200
Th Foods Inc Loves Park (G-13274)	C	800 896-2396
Thomas Proestler Lisle (G-12951)	G	630 971-0185
United Food Ingredients Inc Burr Ridge (G-2729)	G	630 655-9494
Urban Accents Incorporated Chicago (G-6494)	G	773 528-9515
Ventura Foods LLC Thornton (G-19791)	E	708 877-5150
Whitney Foods Inc Glencoe (G-10434)	F	773 842-8511
Wisconsin Wilderness Food Pdts Lake Forest (G-12323)	G	847 735-8661
Xena International Inc Polo (G-16759)	D	630 587-2734
Zaibak Bros Chicago (G-6706)	E	312 564-5800
Zenb US Inc Chicago (G-6715)	G	312 581-6574

FOOD PRDTS: Prepared Meat Sauces Exc Tomato & Dry

Company	Emp	Phone
Andrias Food Group Inc O Fallon (G-15566)	G	618 632-3118

Employee Codes: A=Over 500 employees, B=251-500
C=101-250, D=51-100, E=20-50, F=10-19, G=3-9

2020 Harris Illinois Industrial Directory

FOOD PRDTS: Prepared Meat Sauces Exc Tomato & Dry

Andrias Food Group Inc .... E 618 632-4866
  O Fallon (G-15565)

FOOD PRDTS: Prepared Sauces, Exc Tomato Based

Fgfi LLC .... E 708 598-0909
  Countryside (G-7052)
Foods & Things Inc .... G 618 526-4478
  Breese (G-2303)

FOOD PRDTS: Prepared Vegetable Sauces Exc Tomato & Dry

Simply Salsa LLC .... G 815 514-3993
  Homer Glen (G-11486)

FOOD PRDTS: Raw cane sugar

Westway Feed Products LLC .... F 309 654-2211
  Cordova (G-7011)

FOOD PRDTS: Rice, Milled

Grandma Mauds Inc .... G 773 493-5353
  Chicago (G-4723)
International Golden Foods Inc .... F 630 860-5552
  Bensenville (G-1823)

FOOD PRDTS: Rice, Packaged & Seasoned

Quaker Oats Company .... A 312 821-1000
  Chicago (G-5927)

FOOD PRDTS: Salads

A-Z Sales Inc .... G 630 334-2869
  Chicago (G-3495)
Gotham Greens Pullman LLC .... E 779 379-0307
  Chicago (G-4719)
Suter Company Inc .... C 815 895-9186
  Sycamore (G-19733)

FOOD PRDTS: Sandwiches

Calma Optima Foods .... G 847 962-8329
  Franklin Park (G-9897)
Chicago Oriental Cnstr Inc .... G 312 733-9633
  Chicago (G-4120)
Hearthside Usa LLC .... B 978 716-2530
  Downers Grove (G-8020)
Triple Sticks Foods LLC .... D 800 468-3354
  Belleville (G-1602)
Troverco Inc .... E 800 468-3354
  Belleville (G-1603)

FOOD PRDTS: Seasonings & Spices

Deliteful Taste Foods Inc .... G 708 251-5121
  Lansing (G-12490)
Dell Cove Spice Co .... G 312 339-8389
  Chicago (G-4333)
El Tradicional .... G 773 925-0335
  Chicago (G-4469)
Famar Flavor LLC .... G 708 926-2951
  Crestwood (G-7117)
Granadino Food Services Corp .... G 708 717-2930
  Bridgeview (G-2352)
Hensaal Management Group Inc .... G 312 624-8133
  Chicago (G-4804)
La Espanola Food Dist Corp .... F 312 733-0775
  Chicago (G-5146)
Nanas Kitchen Inc .... G 815 363-8500
  Johnsburg (G-11808)
R J Van Drunen & Sons Inc .... D 815 472-3100
  Momence (G-14191)
R J Van Drunen & Sons Inc .... E 830 422-2167
  Momence (G-14192)
Ryans Rub LLC .... G 773 573-8939
  Aledo (G-360)

FOOD PRDTS: Shortening & Solid Edible Fats

Mahoney Environmental Inc .... E 815 730-2087
  Joliet (G-11896)

FOOD PRDTS: Soup Mixes

Custom Culinary Inc .... D 630 928-4898
  Lombard (G-13061)
TEC Foods Inc .... E 800 315-8002
  Chicago (G-6333)

FOOD PRDTS: Soup Mixes, Dried

Grandma Mauds Inc .... G 773 493-5353
  Chicago (G-4723)
Vanee Foods Company .... D 708 449-7300
  Berkeley (G-1945)

FOOD PRDTS: Soybean Lecithin

Cherith Agro Inc .... G 847 258-3865
  Elk Grove Village (G-8890)

FOOD PRDTS: Soybean Oil, Deodorized

Clarkson Soy Products LLC .... G 217 763-9511
  Cerro Gordo (G-3256)

FOOD PRDTS: Soybean Powder

Devansoy Inc .... G 712 792-9665
  Rock City (G-17175)

FOOD PRDTS: Soybean Protein Concentrates & Isolates

Bunge North America Foundation .... C 217 784-8261
  Gibson City (G-10335)
Syngenta Seeds LLC .... E 309 478-3686
  Pekin (G-16363)

FOOD PRDTS: Spices, Including Ground

Ach Food Companies Inc .... C 866 386-8282
  Oakbrook Terrace (G-15781)
Chicago Coml Consmr Brands LLC .... G 773 488-2639
  Chicago (G-4098)
Josephs Food Products Co Inc .... C 708 338-4090
  Broadview (G-2446)
Sentry Seasonings Inc .... E 630 530-5370
  Elmhurst (G-9426)
USspice Mill Inc .... F 773 378-6800
  Chicago (G-6507)

FOOD PRDTS: Starch, Corn

Ingredion Incorporated .... D 309 550-9136
  Mapleton (G-13473)
Ingredion Incorporated .... C 708 563-2400
  Argo (G-673)

FOOD PRDTS: Starches

Ktm Industries Inc .... G 217 224-5861
  Quincy (G-16905)

FOOD PRDTS: Sugar

Combined Technologies Inc .... G 847 968-4855
  Libertyville (G-12645)
Domino Foods Inc .... F 773 646-2203
  Chicago (G-4380)
Zuchem Inc .... G 312 997-2150
  Chicago (G-6726)

FOOD PRDTS: Sugar Syrup From Sugar Beets

Jo Snow Inc .... G 773 732-3045
  Chicago (G-5033)

FOOD PRDTS: Sugar, Beet

Atlas Trade Solutions LLC .... G 618 954-6119
  Belleville (G-1531)
Lee Gilster-Mary Corporation .... B 618 965-3449
  Steeleville (G-19482)
Merisant Us Inc .... C 815 929-2700
  Chicago (G-5399)
Sweet Specialty Solutions LLC .... E 630 739-9151
  Lemont (G-12592)

FOOD PRDTS: Sugar, Cane

Lee Gilster-Mary Corporation .... B 618 965-3449
  Steeleville (G-19482)
Necta Sweet Inc .... E 847 215-9955
  Buffalo Grove (G-2579)
Pullman Sugar LLC .... E 773 260-9180
  Chicago (G-5913)

FOOD PRDTS: Sugar, Granulated Cane, Purchd Raw Sugar/Syrup

Atlas Trade Solutions LLC .... G 618 954-6119
  Belleville (G-1531)
Domino Foods Inc .... E 773 254-8282
  Chicago (G-4379)

FOOD PRDTS: Sugar, Liquid Cane Prdts, Exc Refined

Nablus Sweets Inc .... E 708 205-6534
  Chicago (G-5534)

FOOD PRDTS: Sugar, Maple, Indl

Hogback Haven Maple Farm .... G 815 291-9440
  Orangeville (G-15909)

FOOD PRDTS: Syrup, Maple

Funks Grove Pure Maple Syrup .... F 309 874-3360
  Shirley (G-18891)

FOOD PRDTS: Syrup, Pancake, Blended & Mixed

Briannas Pancake Cafe .... G 630 365-4770
  Elburn (G-8447)

FOOD PRDTS: Syrups

Margies Brands Inc .... E 773 643-1417
  Chicago (G-5332)
Mary Lee Packaging Corporation .... E 618 826-2361
  Chester (G-3458)

FOOD PRDTS: Tea

Damron Corporation .... E 773 265-2724
  Chicago (G-4310)
Insight Beverages Inc .... E 847 438-1598
  Lake Zurich (G-12425)
Republic of Tea Inc .... G 618 478-5520
  Nashville (G-15009)
Sparrow Coffee Roastery .... G 321 648-6415
  Westchester (G-20712)
Stewarts Prvate Blend Fods Inc .... E 773 489-2500
  Carol Stream (G-3077)

FOOD PRDTS: Tortilla Chips

Azteca Foods Inc .... C 708 563-6600
  Chicago (G-3802)
Donkey Brands LLC .... F 630 251-2007
  Carol Stream (G-2977)
El-Ranchero Food Products .... F 773 843-0430
  Chicago (G-4473)
El-Ranchero Food Products .... E 773 847-9167
  Chicago (G-4474)
Masa Uno Inc .... G 708 749-4866
  Berwyn (G-1956)
McCleary Inc .... C 815 389-3053
  South Beloit (G-19101)

FOOD PRDTS: Tortillas

Azteca Foods Inc .... C 708 563-6600
  Chicago (G-3802)
Castro Foods Wholesale Inc .... E 773 869-0641
  Chicago (G-4038)
El Popocatapetl Industries Inc .... E 312 421-6143
  Chicago (G-4467)
El Valle Florido .... G 630 898-0689
  Aurora (G-1087)
El-Milagro Inc .... B 773 579-6120
  Chicago (G-4470)
El-Milagro Inc .... C 773 650-1614
  Chicago (G-4471)
El-Milagro Inc .... E 773 299-1216
  Chicago (G-4472)
La Mexicana Tortilleria Inc .... E 773 247-5443
  Chicago (G-5148)
Los Gamas Inc .... G 872 829-3514
  Chicago (G-5261)
Munoz Flour Tortilleria Inc .... F 773 523-1837
  Chicago (G-5525)
Sabinas Food Products Inc .... E 312 738-2412
  Chicago (G-6087)
Sunny Day Distributing Inc .... G 630 779-8466
  Cortland (G-7027)

PRODUCT SECTION

FOOD PRDTS: Turkey, Processed, NEC

Gift Check Program 2013 Inc .... G 630 986-5081
  Downers Grove *(G-8011)*

FOOD PRDTS: Variety Meats, Poultry

Handcut Foods LLC .... D 312 239-0381
  Chicago *(G-4776)*

FOOD PRDTS: Vegetable Oil Mills, NEC

Abitec Corporation .... E 217 465-8577
  Paris *(G-16223)*
Bio Fuels By American Farmers .... F 561 859-6251
  Benton *(G-1921)*
Dawn Food Products Inc .... C 815 933-0600
  Bradley *(G-2280)*

FOOD PRDTS: Vegetable Shortenings, Exc Corn Oil

Olive Oil Store Inc .... F 630 262-0210
  Geneva *(G-10297)*

FOOD PRDTS: Vegetables, Dehydrated Or Dried

R J Van Drunen & Sons Inc .... D 815 472-3100
  Momence *(G-14191)*
R J Van Drunen & Sons Inc .... D 830 422-2167
  Momence *(G-14192)*

FOOD PRDTS: Vegetables, Dried or Dehydrated Exc Freeze-Dried

Sono Italiano Corporation .... G 817 472-8903
  Manteno *(G-13456)*

FOOD PRDTS: Vinegar

Consumer Vinegar and Spice .... G 708 354-1144
  La Grange *(G-12076)*
Fleischmanns Vinegar Co Inc .... F 773 523-2817
  Chicago *(G-4602)*
Mizkan America Inc .... E 847 590-0059
  Mount Prospect *(G-14547)*
Mizkan America Holdings Inc .... G 847 590-0059
  Mount Prospect *(G-14548)*
National Vinegar Co .... F 618 395-1011
  Olney *(G-15878)*
Pastorelli Food Products Inc .... G 312 455-1006
  Chicago *(G-5770)*

FOOD PRDTS: Wheat Flour

Archer-Daniels-Midland Company .... E 309 699-9581
  Creve Coeur *(G-7148)*
Archer-Daniels-Midland Company .... G 815 539-6219
  Mendota *(G-13937)*
Archer-Daniels-Midland Company .... G 217 429-3054
  Decatur *(G-7454)*
Archer-Daniels-Midland Company .... A 312 634-8100
  Chicago *(G-3728)*
Mennel Milling Co .... F 217 999-2161
  Mount Olive *(G-14506)*
Roquette America Inc .... F 630 232-2157
  Geneva *(G-10304)*

FOOD PRDTS: Wheat gluten

Enjoy Life Natural Brands LLC .... E 773 632-2163
  Chicago *(G-4511)*

FOOD PRDTS: Yeast

Sensient Technologies Corp .... E 708 481-0910
  Matteson *(G-13628)*

FOOD PRODUCTS MACHINERY

American Metal Installers & FA .... G 630 993-0812
  Villa Park *(G-20131)*
Bakery McHy & Fabrication LLC .... G 815 224-1306
  Peru *(G-16568)*
Beacon Inc .... F 708 544-9900
  Alsip *(G-422)*
Bettendorf Stanford Inc .... D 618 548-3555
  Salem *(G-18331)*
Cartpac Inc .... E 630 283-8979
  Carol Stream *(G-2956)*
Cobatco Inc .... F 309 676-2663
  Peoria *(G-16425)*
Colborne Acquisition Co LLC .... E 847 371-0101
  Lake Forest *(G-12239)*
Comtec Industries Ltd .... G 630 759-9000
  Bolingbrook *(G-2157)*
Cornelius .... B 630 539-6850
  Glendale Heights *(G-10445)*
Corrigan Corporation America .... F 800 462-6478
  Gurnee *(G-10866)*
Crm North America LLC .... G 708 603-3475
  Franklin Park *(G-9919)*
Cvp Systems LLC .... D 630 852-1190
  Elgin *(G-8561)*
D W Ram Manufacturing Co .... E 708 633-7900
  Tinley Park *(G-19821)*
Dontech Industries Inc .... F 847 428-8222
  Gilberts *(G-10353)*
Dover Prtg Identification Inc .... D 630 541-1540
  Downers Grove *(G-7992)*
Eirich Machines Inc .... D 847 336-2444
  Gurnee *(G-10875)*
Felste Co Inc .... G 217 283-4884
  Hoopeston *(G-11509)*
Food Equipment Technologies Co .... E 847 719-3000
  Lake Zurich *(G-12412)*
Formax Inc .... E 708 479-3000
  Mokena *(G-14082)*
G K Enterprises Inc .... G 708 587-2150
  Monee *(G-14201)*
Gold Medal Products Co .... G 630 860-2525
  Bensenville *(G-1814)*
Gsi Group LLC .... D 618 283-9792
  Vandalia *(G-20012)*
Heat and Control Inc .... A 847 381-0290
  Inverness *(G-11601)*
Heat and Control Inc .... D 309 342-5518
  Galesburg *(G-10200)*
Hot Food Boxes Inc .... E 773 533-5912
  Chicago *(G-4846)*
Institutional Equipment Inc .... E 630 771-0990
  Bolingbrook *(G-2192)*
Ives Way Products Inc .... G 847 223-1020
  Grayslake *(G-10784)*
John Bean Technologies Corp .... G 845 340-9727
  Chicago *(G-5035)*
John Bean Technologies Corp .... D 312 861-5900
  Chicago *(G-5036)*
Keating of Chicago Inc .... E 815 569-2324
  Capron *(G-2834)*
Mc Cleary Equipment Inc .... G 815 389-3053
  South Beloit *(G-19100)*
Middleby Worldwide Inc .... E 847 741-3300
  Elgin *(G-8663)*
Naegele Inc .... E 708 388-7766
  Alsip *(G-482)*
Nimco Corporation .... D 815 459-4200
  Crystal Lake *(G-7239)*
Optimal Automatics Co .... G 847 439-9110
  Elk Grove Village *(G-9165)*
Pre Pack Machinery Inc .... G 217 352-1010
  Champaign *(G-3338)*
S G Acquisition Inc .... F 815 624-6501
  South Beloit *(G-19113)*
Sojuz Ent .... G 847 215-9400
  Bensenville *(G-1896)*
Speco Inc .... E 847 678-4240
  Schiller Park *(G-18845)*
Taylor Co Asuess Taylor .... G 815 624-8333
  Rockton *(G-17702)*
Terrace Holding Company .... A 708 652-5600
  Cicero *(G-6881)*
Tetra Pak Materials LP .... D 847 955-6000
  Vernon Hills *(G-20104)*
Vilutis and Co Inc .... E 815 469-2116
  Frankfort *(G-9849)*
Vision Machine & Fabrication .... E 618 965-3199
  Steeleville *(G-19485)*
Wag Industries Inc .... F 847 329-8932
  Skokie *(G-19053)*
Wemco Inc .... F 708 388-1980
  Alsip *(G-524)*
World Cup Packaging Inc .... G 815 624-6501
  South Beloit *(G-19127)*

FOOD STORES: Delicatessen

Andys Deli and Mikolajczyk .... E 773 722-1000
  Chicago *(G-3694)*
Vienna Beef Ltd .... E 773 278-7800
  Chicago *(G-6548)*

FOOD STORES: Grocery, Chain

Niemann Foods Inc .... C 217 222-0190
  Quincy *(G-16918)*

FOOD STORES: Grocery, Independent

AM Ko Oriental Foods .... G 217 398-2922
  Champaign *(G-3262)*
Charleston County Market .... D 217 345-7031
  Charleston *(G-3399)*
George Nottoli & Sons Inc .... G 773 589-1010
  Chicago *(G-4683)*
Koenemann Sausage Co .... G 815 385-6260
  Volo *(G-20201)*
Olive Oil Marketplace Inc .... G 618 304-3769
  Alton *(G-567)*
Sunset Food Mart Inc .... C 847 234-0854
  Lake Forest *(G-12307)*
Walter Lagestee Inc .... C 708 957-2974
  Homewood *(G-11504)*

FOOD STORES: Supermarkets

Cub Foods Inc .... C 309 689-0140
  Peoria *(G-16428)*

FOOD STORES: Supermarkets, Chain

Dominicks Finer Foods Inc .... D 630 584-1750
  Saint Charles *(G-18185)*
Jewel Osco Inc .... C 630 355-2172
  Naperville *(G-14854)*
Jewel Osco Inc .... D 630 226-1892
  Bolingbrook *(G-2198)*
Jewel Osco Inc .... C 773 728-7730
  Chicago *(G-5026)*
Jewel Osco Inc .... C 773 784-1922
  Chicago *(G-5027)*
Jewel Osco Inc .... C 847 296-7786
  Des Plaines *(G-7791)*
Jewel Osco Inc .... C 847 677-3331
  Skokie *(G-18970)*
Jewel Osco Inc .... C 708 352-0120
  Countryside *(G-7061)*
Jewel Osco Inc .... C 630 584-4594
  Saint Charles *(G-18218)*
Jewel Osco Inc .... D 630 859-1212
  Aurora *(G-1118)*
Jewel Osco Inc .... C 815 464-5352
  Frankfort *(G-9810)*
Jewel Osco Inc .... C 847 428-3547
  West Dundee *(G-20664)*
Kroger Co .... C 815 332-7267
  Rockford *(G-17485)*
Kroger Co .... C 309 694-6298
  East Peoria *(G-8275)*
Niemann Foods Inc .... C 217 793-4091
  Springfield *(G-19411)*
Schnuck Markets Inc .... C 618 466-0825
  Godfrey *(G-10663)*

FOOD STORES: Supermarkets, Independent

Butera Finer Foods Inc .... D 708 456-5939
  Norridge *(G-15231)*

FOOD WARMING EQPT: Commercial

Carter Hoffmann LLC .... C 847 362-5500
  Mundelein *(G-14674)*
Taylor Coml Foodservice Inc .... F 815 624-8333
  Rockton *(G-17703)*

FOOTWEAR, WHOLESALE: Shoe Access

Marietta Corporation .... C 773 816-5137
  Chicago *(G-5337)*

FOOTWEAR, WHOLESALE: Shoes

A&B Apparel .... G 815 962-5070
  Rockford *(G-17281)*
Leos Dancewear Inc .... D 773 889-7700
  River Forest *(G-17053)*
Mennon Rbr & Safety Pdts Inc .... G 847 678-8250
  Schiller Park *(G-18823)*

FOOTWEAR: Cut Stock

Painted Quarter Ridge .... G 618 534-9734
  Ava *(G-1176)*
Quarters Concessions Inc .... G 847 343-4864
  Carpentersville *(G-3116)*

FORESTRY RELATED EQPT

FORESTRY RELATED EQPT
Runge Equipment Inc ....G 618 322-5628
  Mason *(G-13609)*

FORGINGS
Allied Gear Co ....G 773 287-8742
  River Forest *(G-17049)*
Anchor-Harvey Components LLC ....D 815 233-3833
  Freeport *(G-10100)*
Andrew McDonald ....G 618 867-2323
  De Soto *(G-7430)*
Arrow Gear Company ....B 630 969-7640
  Downers Grove *(G-7955)*
As 1902 LLC ....D 773 287-0874
  Chicago *(G-3746)*
C & F Forge Company ....E 847 455-6609
  Franklin Park *(G-9895)*
Carmona Gear Cutting ....G 815 963-8236
  Rockford *(G-17337)*
Chicago Hardware and Fix Co ....C 847 455-6609
  Franklin Park *(G-9905)*
Cleveland Hdwr & Forging Co ....D 630 896-9850
  Aurora *(G-1077)*
Cornell Forge Company ....G 708 458-1582
  Chicago *(G-4235)*
E M Glabus Co Inc ....F 630 766-3027
  Bensenville *(G-1792)*
Finkl Steel - Houston LLC ....F 773 975-2540
  Chicago *(G-4593)*
Forge Group Dekalb LLC ....D 815 756-3538
  Dekalb *(G-7678)*
Forge Resources Group LLC ....F 815 758-6400
  Dekalb *(G-7681)*
Forgings & Stampings Inc ....E 815 962-5597
  Rockford *(G-17421)*
Gear & Repair ....G 708 387-0144
  Brookfield *(G-2485)*
General Forging Die Co Inc ....E 815 874-4224
  Rockford *(G-17428)*
Group Industries Inc ....E 708 877-6200
  Thornton *(G-19788)*
Hadley Gear Manufacturing Co ....F 773 722-1030
  Chicago *(G-4765)*
HM Manufacturing Inc ....F 847 487-8700
  Wauconda *(G-20356)*
I Forge Company LLC ....G 815 535-0600
  Rock Falls *(G-17186)*
Jernberg Industries LLC ....C 773 268-3004
  Chicago *(G-5021)*
Jernberg Industries LLC ....C 630 972-7000
  Bolingbrook *(G-2197)*
Kd Steel Incorporated ....G 630 201-1619
  Westmont *(G-20752)*
Kdk Upset Forging Co ....E 708 388-8770
  Blue Island *(G-2128)*
Keller Group Inc ....B 847 446-7550
  Northfield *(G-15520)*
Kz Manufacturing Co ....G 708 937-8097
  Mc Cook *(G-13694)*
Lawndale Forging & Tool Works ....G 773 277-2800
  Chicago *(G-5183)*
Lehigh Consumer Products LLC ....G 630 851-7330
  Aurora *(G-997)*
Liberty Spclity Stels Amer Inc ....G 847 521-6464
  Schaumburg *(G-18606)*
Machine Tool Acc & Mfg Co ....G 773 489-0903
  Chicago *(G-5309)*
Metform LLC ....C 815 273-2201
  Savanna *(G-18407)*
Metform LLC ....G 847 566-0010
  Mundelein *(G-14717)*
Metform LLC ....E 815 273-0230
  Savanna *(G-18408)*
Midwest Brass Forging Co ....E 847 678-7023
  Franklin Park *(G-9998)*
Modern Gear & Machine Inc ....F 630 350-9173
  Bensenville *(G-1854)*
Norforge and Machining Inc ....D 309 772-3124
  Macomb *(G-13394)*
Park-Hio Frged McHned Pdts LLC ....D 708 652-6691
  Chicago *(G-5765)*
Peer Chain Company ....D 847 775-4600
  Waukegan *(G-20475)*
Phoenix Trading Chicago Inc ....G 847 304-5181
  Lake Barrington *(G-12163)*
Productigear Inc ....E 773 847-4505
  Chicago *(G-5893)*
Products In Motion Inc ....G 815 213-7251
  Rock Falls *(G-17191)*

Rail Exchange Inc ....E 708 757-3317
  Chicago Heights *(G-6767)*
Rj Link International Inc ....F 815 874-8110
  Rockford *(G-17576)*
Rkfd LLC Grua ....G 815 414-2392
  Rockford *(G-17577)*
Rkfd LLC Grua ....G 815 414-2392
  Rockford *(G-17578)*
Rockford Drop Forge Company ....D 815 963-9611
  Rockford *(G-17592)*
Rockford Jobbing Service Inc ....G 815 398-8661
  Rockford *(G-17596)*
RT Blackhawk Mch Pdts Inc ....G 815 389-3632
  South Beloit *(G-19111)*
Sbic America Inc ....G 847 303-5430
  Schaumburg *(G-18704)*
Schafer Gear Works Roscoe LLC ....C 815 874-4327
  Roscoe *(G-17931)*
Schmid Tool & Engineering Corp ....E 630 333-1733
  Villa Park *(G-20171)*
Scot Forge Company ....D 847 678-6000
  Franklin Park *(G-10045)*
Star Forge Inc ....D 815 235-7750
  Freeport *(G-10144)*
Sumitomo Machinery Corp Amer ....E 630 752-0200
  Glendale Heights *(G-10504)*
Thyssenkrupp Crankshaft Co LLC ....C 217 444-5400
  Danville *(G-7384)*
Thyssenkrupp Crankshaft Co LLC ....C 217 444-5500
  Danville *(G-7385)*
Tomko Machine Works Inc ....G 630 244-0902
  Lemont *(G-12593)*
US Tsubaki Power Transm LLC ....C 847 459-9500
  Wheeling *(G-21004)*
Welch Steel Products Inc ....F 847 741-2623
  Elgin *(G-8780)*
Wozniak Industries Inc ....C 708 458-1220
  Bedford Park *(G-1515)*
Wozniak Industries Inc ....G 630 954-3400
  Schaumburg *(G-18776)*

FORGINGS: Aircraft, Ferrous
Scot Forge Company ....B 815 675-1000
  Spring Grove *(G-19300)*

FORGINGS: Anchors
Simpson Strong-Tie Company Inc ....E 630 613-5100
  West Chicago *(G-20643)*

FORGINGS: Armor Plate, Iron Or Steel
Malca-Amit North America Inc ....G 312 346-1507
  Chicago *(G-5322)*
Prime Stainless Products LLC ....G 847 678-0800
  Schiller Park *(G-18836)*

FORGINGS: Automotive & Internal Combustion Engine
Dss Inc ....G 630 587-1169
  Saint Charles *(G-18187)*
Thyssenkrupp Crankshaft Co LLC ....C 217 431-0060
  Danville *(G-7383)*

FORGINGS: Bearing & Bearing Race, Nonferrous
Voss Engineering Inc ....E 847 673-8900
  Lincolnwood *(G-12850)*

FORGINGS: Construction Or Mining Eqpt, Ferrous
Chicago Clamp Company ....G 708 343-8311
  Broadview *(G-2426)*
Dayton Superior Corporation ....C 815 936-3300
  Kankakee *(G-11964)*
Illinois Expedited Express Inc ....E 217 926-2171
  Lansing *(G-12498)*

FORGINGS: Engine Or Turbine, Nonferrous
Burgess-Norton Mfg Co Inc ....E 630 232-4100
  Geneva *(G-10257)*
Genacc LLC ....G 309 253-9034
  Peoria *(G-16444)*

FORGINGS: Gear & Chain
Crown Industrial ....G 607 745-8709
  Dixon *(G-7894)*
Emco Gears Inc ....E 847 220-4327
  Elk Grove Village *(G-8975)*
Innovative Rack & Gear Company ....F 630 766-2652
  Wood Dale *(G-21201)*
Loch Precision Technologies ....G 847 438-1400
  Lake Zurich *(G-12429)*
Reag Inc ....E 708 344-0875
  Bridgeview *(G-2379)*
Timken Gears & Services Inc ....F 708 720-9400
  Mokena *(G-14122)*

FORGINGS: Iron & Steel
AC Americos ....F 312 366-2943
  Chicago *(G-3513)*
Advantage Tool and Mold Inc ....G 847 301-9020
  Elk Grove Village *(G-8811)*
C & F Forge Company ....E 847 455-6609
  Franklin Park *(G-9895)*
General Products International ....G 847 458-6357
  Lake In The Hills *(G-12335)*

FORGINGS: Machinery, Ferrous
Elgin Fastener Group LLC ....B 847 465-0048
  Wheeling *(G-20890)*
Mitsutoyo-Kiko USA Inc ....G 847 981-5200
  Rolling Meadows *(G-17751)*

FORGINGS: Metal , Ornamental, Ferrous
Great Lakes Forge Company ....G 773 277-2800
  Chicago *(G-4735)*

FORGINGS: Nonferrous
Acme Screw Co ....F 815 332-7548
  Cherry Valley *(G-3436)*
Jernberg Industries LLC ....C 773 268-3004
  Chicago *(G-5021)*

FORMS: Concrete, Sheet Metal
Carroll Distrg & Cnstr Sup Inc ....G 815 464-0100
  Frankfort *(G-9778)*
Carroll Distrg & Cnstr Sup Inc ....G 630 892-4855
  Aurora *(G-1070)*
Carroll Distrg & Cnstr Sup Inc ....G 630 243-0272
  Lemont *(G-12558)*
Carroll Distrg & Cnstr Sup Inc ....G 815 941-1548
  Morris *(G-14297)*
Carroll Distrg & Cnstr Sup Inc ....G 309 449-6044
  Hopedale *(G-11516)*
Carroll Distrg & Cnstr Sup Inc ....F 630 369-6520
  Naperville *(G-14791)*
CCS Contractor Eqp & Sup Inc ....E 630 393-9020
  Naperville *(G-14793)*
Dayton Superior Corporation ....B 847 391-4700
  Elk Grove Village *(G-8939)*
Forming America Ltd ....E 888 993-1304
  West Chicago *(G-20587)*
Gerdau Ameristeel US Inc ....E 815 547-0400
  Belvidere *(G-1673)*
Luebbers Welding & Mfg Inc ....F 618 594-2489
  Carlyle *(G-2893)*
Roth Metal Fabricators Corp ....G 708 371-8300
  Alsip *(G-505)*
Starmont Manufacturing Co ....G 815 939-1041
  Kankakee *(G-12007)*

FOUNDRIES: Aluminum
Able Die Casting Corporation ....D 847 678-1991
  Schiller Park *(G-18781)*
Acme Die Casting LLC ....G 847 272-9520
  Northbrook *(G-15331)*
Altman & Koehler Foundry ....G 773 373-7737
  Chicago *(G-3636)*
Amcast Inc ....F 630 766-7450
  Bensenville *(G-1741)*
Arrow Aluminum Castings Inc ....G 815 338-4480
  Woodstock *(G-21361)*
Batavia Foundry and Machine Co ....G 630 879-1319
  Batavia *(G-1356)*
Becks Light Gauge Aluminum Co ....F 847 290-9990
  Elk Grove Village *(G-8861)*
Curto-Ligonier Foundries Co ....E 708 345-2250
  Melrose Park *(G-13846)*

D R Sperry & Co ..... D 630 892-4361
Aurora *(G-1083)*
Du Page Precision Products Co ..... D 630 849-2940
Aurora *(G-954)*
Dynacast LLC ..... C 847 608-2200
Elgin *(G-8572)*
Jsp Mold LLC ..... G 815 225-7110
Milledgeville *(G-14039)*
Levelor Corporation ..... G 815 233-8684
Freeport *(G-10126)*
Marble Machine Inc ..... G 217 442-0746
Danville *(G-7362)*
Nelson - Harkins Inds Inc ..... E 773 478-6243
Lake Bluff *(G-12199)*
Quincy Foundry & Pattern Co ..... G 217 222-0718
Quincy *(G-16932)*
R&R Racing of Palm Beach Inc ..... G 618 937-6767
West Frankfort *(G-20679)*
RCM Industries Inc ..... C 847 455-1950
Wheeling *(G-20970)*
Reynolds Manufacturing Company ..... E 309 787-8600
Milan *(G-14025)*
Robert Kellerman & Co ..... G 847 526-7266
Wauconda *(G-20389)*
Spartan Light Metal Pdts Inc ..... E 618 443-4346
Sparta *(G-19260)*
Tompkins Aluminum Foundry Inc ..... G 815 438-5578
Rock Falls *(G-17197)*
Tricast/Presfore Corporation ..... G 815 459-1820
Crystal Lake *(G-7285)*
Trio Foundry Inc ..... E 630 892-1676
Montgomery *(G-14272)*

FOUNDRIES: Brass, Bronze & Copper

Alu-Bra Foundry Inc ..... D 630 766-3112
Bensenville *(G-1740)*
Amcast Inc ..... F 630 766-7450
Bensenville *(G-1741)*
American Bare Conductor Inc ..... E 815 224-3422
La Salle *(G-12102)*
Aurora Metals Division LLC ..... C 630 844-4900
Montgomery *(G-14231)*
Bearing Sales Corporation ..... E 773 282-8686
Chicago *(G-3855)*
Chicago Alum Castings Co Inc ..... G 773 762-3009
Chicago *(G-4087)*
Covey Machine Inc ..... F 773 650-1530
Chicago *(G-4250)*
Creative Iron ..... G 217 267-7797
Westville *(G-20779)*
Excel Foundry & Machine Inc ..... G 309 347-6155
Pekin *(G-16332)*
F Kreutzer & Co ..... G 773 826-5767
Chicago *(G-4550)*
Fiberlink LLC ..... G 312 951-8500
Chicago *(G-4585)*
Imperial Punch & Manufacturing ..... F 815 226-8200
Rockford *(G-17457)*
Kellermann Manufacturing Inc ..... G 847 526-7266
Wauconda *(G-20365)*
Louis Meskan Aluminum & Brass ..... G 773 637-8236
Chicago *(G-5266)*
Mahoney Foundries Inc ..... E 309 784-2311
Vermont *(G-20037)*
Reynolds Manufacturing Company ..... E 309 787-8600
Milan *(G-14025)*
Spot Welding Products Inc ..... F 630 238-0880
Franklin Park *(G-10051)*
Universal Electric Foundry Inc ..... E 312 421-7233
Chicago *(G-6480)*
Wagner Brass Foundry Inc ..... G 773 276-7907
Chicago *(G-6583)*

FOUNDRIES: Gray & Ductile Iron

Amsted Industries Incorporated ..... B 312 645-1700
Chicago *(G-3685)*
Burgess-Norton Mfg Co Inc ..... E 630 232-4100
Geneva *(G-10257)*
Demco Products Inc ..... F 708 636-6240
Oak Lawn *(G-15713)*
E H Baare Corporation ..... C 618 546-1575
Robinson *(G-17114)*
Ej Pierogi ..... F 773 318-3383
Elk Grove Village *(G-8970)*
F J Murphy & Son Inc ..... D 217 787-3477
Springfield *(G-19364)*
Group Industries Inc ..... E 708 877-6200
Thornton *(G-19788)*
Johnston & Jennings Inc ..... G 708 757-5375
Chicago Heights *(G-6754)*

M H Detrick Company ..... E 708 479-5085
Frankfort *(G-9814)*
Ptc Tubular Products LLC ..... C 815 692-4900
Fairbury *(G-9612)*
Reynolds Manufacturing Company ..... E 309 787-8600
Milan *(G-14025)*
Rj Link International Inc ..... F 815 874-8110
Rockford *(G-17576)*
Tmb Industries Inc ..... A 312 280-2565
Chicago *(G-6382)*

FOUNDRIES: Iron

Advanced Pattern Works LLC ..... G 618 346-9039
Collinsville *(G-6952)*
Du Page Precision Products Co ..... D 630 849-2940
Aurora *(G-954)*
M H Detrick Company ..... E 708 479-5085
Frankfort *(G-9814)*
Wirco Inc ..... D 217 398-3200
Champaign *(G-3371)*

FOUNDRIES: Nonferrous

Acme Die Casting LLC ..... G 847 272-9520
Northbrook *(G-15331)*
Altman & Koehler Foundry ..... G 773 373-7737
Chicago *(G-3636)*
Amcast Inc ..... F 630 766-7450
Bensenville *(G-1741)*
Avan Tool & Die Co Inc ..... F 773 287-1670
Chicago *(G-3782)*
Cast Glassworks ..... G 847 831-0222
Highland Park *(G-11257)*
Cast Technologies Inc ..... G 309 674-1402
Peoria *(G-16399)*
Charter Dura-Bar Inc ..... C 815 338-7800
Woodstock *(G-21374)*
Clinkenbeard & Associates Inc ..... E 815 226-0291
South Beloit *(G-19087)*
Curto-Ligonier Foundries Co ..... E 708 345-2250
Melrose Park *(G-13846)*
Dmk Specialties ..... G 815 919-7282
Lockport *(G-12987)*
Du Page Precision Products Co ..... D 630 849-2940
Aurora *(G-954)*
Dynacast LLC ..... C 847 608-2200
Elgin *(G-8572)*
G & W Electric Company ..... E 708 388-6363
Blue Island *(G-2123)*
Illini Foundry Co Inc ..... G 309 697-3142
Peoria *(G-16456)*
Ipsen Inc ..... E 815 239-2385
Pecatonica *(G-16322)*
Kabert Industries Inc ..... C 630 833-2115
Villa Park *(G-20154)*
Kettler Casting Co Inc ..... E 618 234-5303
Belleville *(G-1562)*
Lemfco Inc ..... E 815 777-0242
Galena *(G-10176)*
Libco Industries Inc ..... F 815 623-7677
Roscoe *(G-17912)*
Mahoney Foundries Inc ..... E 309 784-2311
Vermont *(G-20037)*
Marble Machine Inc ..... G 217 442-0746
Danville *(G-7362)*
Master Foundry Inc ..... F 217 223-7396
Quincy *(G-16911)*
Quincy Foundry & Pattern Co ..... G 217 222-0718
Quincy *(G-16932)*
Reynolds Manufacturing Company ..... E 309 787-8600
Milan *(G-14025)*
Robert Kellerman & Co ..... G 847 526-7266
Wauconda *(G-20389)*
Rockbridge Casting Inc ..... G 618 753-3188
Rockbridge *(G-17255)*
Rockford Foundries Inc ..... F 815 965-7243
Rockford *(G-17594)*
Sarcol ..... G 773 533-3000
Chicago *(G-6105)*
Spartan Light Metal Pdts Inc ..... E 618 443-4346
Sparta *(G-19260)*
Tompkins Aluminum Foundry Inc ..... G 815 438-5578
Rock Falls *(G-17197)*
Tricast/Presfore Corporation ..... G 815 459-1820
Crystal Lake *(G-7285)*
Trio Foundry Inc ..... E 815 786-6616
Sandwich *(G-18386)*
Trio Foundry Inc ..... E 630 892-1676
Montgomery *(G-14272)*
Universal Electric Foundry Inc ..... E 312 421-7233
Chicago *(G-6480)*

Wagner Brass Foundry Inc ..... G 773 276-7907
Chicago *(G-6583)*
Wishzing ..... E 217 413-8469
Dalton City *(G-7315)*

FOUNDRIES: Steel

Allquip Co Inc ..... G 309 944-6153
Geneseo *(G-10239)*
Amsted Industries Incorporated ..... G 312 819-1181
Chicago *(G-3687)*
Combined Metals Holding Inc ..... C 708 547-8800
Bellwood *(G-1619)*
Componenta USA LLC ..... G 309 691-7000
Peoria *(G-16426)*
Dee Erectors Inc ..... G 630 327-1185
Downers Grove *(G-7985)*
Du Page Precision Products Co ..... D 630 849-2940
Aurora *(G-954)*
E H Baare Corporation ..... C 618 546-1575
Robinson *(G-17114)*
G S Foundry Mfg ..... G 618 282-4114
Red Bud *(G-16995)*
Illinois Ni Cast LLC ..... G 217 398-3200
Champaign *(G-3307)*
Lmt Usa Inc ..... G 630 969-5412
Waukegan *(G-20462)*
Monett Metals Inc ..... G 773 478-8888
Niles *(G-15148)*
Nisshin Holding Inc ..... G 847 290-5100
Chicago *(G-5604)*
Scot Forge Company ..... D 847 678-6000
Franklin Park *(G-10045)*
T & H Lemont Inc ..... D 708 482-1800
Countryside *(G-7074)*

FOUNDRIES: Steel Investment

Barber Steel Foundry Corp ..... F 231 894-1830
Rosemont *(G-18000)*

FOUNDRY MACHINERY & EQPT

Asta Service Inc ..... G 630 271-0960
Lisle *(G-12869)*
Chatham Corporation ..... F 847 634-5506
Lincolnshire *(G-12749)*
Disa Holding Corp ..... G 630 820-3000
Oswego *(G-16002)*
Hunter Foundry Machinery Corp ..... D 847 397-5110
Schaumburg *(G-18553)*
International Molding Mch Co ..... G 708 354-1380
La Grange Park *(G-12097)*
Pekay Machine & Engrg Co Inc ..... F 312 829-5530
Chicago *(G-5784)*

FOUNTAIN SUPPLIES WHOLESALERS

Fountain Technologies Ltd ..... E 847 537-3677
Wheeling *(G-20900)*

FOUNTAINS: Concrete

Aqua Control Inc ..... E 815 664-4900
Spring Valley *(G-19307)*
Fountain Technologies Ltd ..... E 847 537-3677
Wheeling *(G-20900)*

FRAMES & FRAMING WHOLESALE

Frame House Inc ..... G 708 383-1616
Oak Park *(G-15753)*
Mercurys Green LLC ..... E 708 865-9134
Franklin Park *(G-9993)*
Michels Frame Shop ..... G 847 647-7366
Niles *(G-15145)*
Picture Frame Fulfillment LLC ..... D 708 483-8537
Franklin Park *(G-10017)*
Sarj USA Inc ..... E 708 865-9134
Franklin Park *(G-10043)*
Seshin USA Inc ..... G 847 550-5556
Lake Zurich *(G-12456)*

FRANCHISES, SELLING OR LICENSING

Duraclean International Inc ..... F 847 704-7100
Arlington Heights *(G-730)*
H&R Block Inc ..... F 847 566-5557
Mundelein *(G-14694)*

FREEZERS: Household

Lambright Distributors ..... G 217 543-2083
Arthur *(G-865)*

Employee Codes: A=Over 500 employees, B=251-500
C=101-250, D=51-100, E=20-50, F=10-19, G=3-9
2020 Harris Illinois
Industrial Directory
1455

FREIGHT FORWARDING ARRANGEMENTS

FREIGHT FORWARDING ARRANGEMENTS
GE Transportation Parts LLC .... E 814 875-2755
  Chicago *(G-4666)*
Minority Auto Hdlg Specialists .... F 708 757-8758
  Chicago Heights *(G-6759)*
Most Enterprise Inc .... D 800 792-4669
  Chicago *(G-5504)*

FREIGHT FORWARDING ARRANGEMENTS: Domestic
Driver Services .... G 505 267-8686
  Bensenville *(G-1789)*

FREIGHT TRANSPORTATION ARRANGEMENTS
Corr-Pak Corporation .... E 708 442-7806
  Mc Cook *(G-13690)*
Hunter Logistics .... G 309 299-7015
  Wataga *(G-20286)*
K-Pro US LLC .... G 872 529-5776
  O Fallon *(G-15576)*
Kdm Enterprises LLC .... E 877 591-9768
  Carpentersville *(G-3106)*
Kuchar Combine Performance .... G 217 854-9838
  Carlinville *(G-2878)*

FRICTION MATERIAL, MADE FROM POWDERED METAL
Gpi Manufacturing Inc .... E 847 615-8900
  Lake Bluff *(G-12184)*
PSM Industries Inc .... E 815 337-8800
  Woodstock *(G-21425)*
Webster-Hoff Corporation .... D 630 858-8030
  Glendale Heights *(G-10515)*

FRUIT & VEGETABLE MARKETS
Eckert Orchards Inc .... C 618 233-0513
  Belleville *(G-1549)*
Veteran Greens LLC .... G 773 599-9689
  Chicago *(G-6540)*

FRUIT STANDS OR MARKETS
Bobs Market & Greenhouse .... G 217 442-8155
  Danville *(G-7324)*

FRUITS & VEGETABLES WHOLESALERS: Fresh
Kuna Meat Company Inc .... C 618 286-4000
  Dupo *(G-8139)*
Stable Foods Inc .... F 773 793-2547
  Chicago *(G-6225)*
Veteran Greens LLC .... G 773 599-9689
  Chicago *(G-6540)*

FRUITS: Artificial & Preserved
Midwest Foods Mfg Inc .... E 847 455-4636
  Franklin Park *(G-9999)*

FUEL ADDITIVES
Caibros Americas LLC .... G 312 593-3128
  Highland Park *(G-11256)*
Cartel Holdings Inc .... G 815 334-0250
  Harvard *(G-11049)*
ET Products LLC .... G 800 325-5746
  Burr Ridge *(G-2671)*

FUEL BRIQUETTES OR BOULETS, MADE WITH PETROLEUM BINDER
Chemalloy Company LLC .... E 847 696-2400
  Rosemont *(G-18004)*

FUEL DEALERS: Wood
E-Z Tree Recycling Inc .... G 773 493-8600
  Chicago *(G-4428)*
Powell Tree Care Inc .... G 847 364-1181
  Elk Grove Village *(G-9186)*

FUEL OIL DEALERS
Fedder Oil Co Inc .... G 618 344-0050
  Collinsville *(G-6960)*

Times Energy .... G 773 444-9282
  Worth *(G-21456)*
Westmore Supply Co .... F 630 627-0278
  Lombard *(G-13154)*

FUEL TREATING
Debourg Corp .... G 815 338-7852
  Bull Valley *(G-2627)*
Opw Fueling Components Inc .... G 708 485-4200
  Hodgkins *(G-11393)*

FUELS: Diesel
Blackhawk Biofuels LLC .... E 217 431-6600
  Freeport *(G-10103)*
CP Diesel Inc .... G 815 979-9600
  Cissna Park *(G-6896)*
Drig Corporation .... D 312 265-1509
  Rosemont *(G-18020)*
Patriot Fuels Biodiesel LLC .... F 309 935-5700
  Annawan *(G-591)*
Synsel Energy Inc .... G 630 516-1284
  Elmhurst *(G-9432)*

FUELS: Ethanol
Afs Inc .... F 847 437-2345
  Arlington Heights *(G-684)*
AMP Americas LLC .... E 312 300-6700
  Chicago *(G-3683)*
Austins Saloon & Eatery .... G 847 549-1972
  Libertyville *(G-12632)*
Bala & Anula Fuels Inc .... G 630 766-1807
  Bensenville *(G-1751)*
Big River Prairie Gold LLC .... G 319 753-1100
  Galva *(G-10227)*
Big Rver Rsrces W Brlngton LLC .... G 309 734-8423
  Monmouth *(G-14214)*
Bps Fuels Inc .... G 217 452-7608
  Virginia *(G-20192)*
Breakfast Fuel LLC .... G 847 251-3835
  Wilmette *(G-21072)*
Cheers Food and Fuel 240 .... G 618 995-9153
  Goreville *(G-10679)*
Cheers Food Fuel .... G 618 827-4836
  Dongola *(G-7942)*
Chrisman Fuel .... G 217 463-3400
  Paris *(G-16227)*
Cooper Oil Co .... G 708 349-2893
  Orland Park *(G-15949)*
Ecolocap Solutions Inc .... G 312 585-6670
  Morton Grove *(G-14403)*
Eden Fuels LLC .... G 847 676-9470
  Skokie *(G-18949)*
Executive Performance Fuel LLC .... G 847 364-1933
  Elk Grove Village *(G-8991)*
Freedom Fuel & Food Inc .... G 773 233-5350
  Chicago *(G-4634)*
Friends Fuel .... G 773 434-9387
  Chicago *(G-4637)*
Gateway Fuels Inc .... G 618 248-5000
  Albers *(G-345)*
H&Z Fuel & Food Inc .... G 815 399-9108
  Rockford *(G-17438)*
Harvey Fuels .... G 708 339-0777
  Harvey *(G-11088)*
Havanah Fuel .... G 309 543-2211
  Havana *(G-11114)*
Horizon Fuel Cell Americas .... G 312 316-8050
  Chicago *(G-4841)*
Hucks Food Fuel .... F 618 286-5111
  Dupo *(G-8138)*
Illini Fs Inc .... G 217 442-4737
  Potomac *(G-16802)*
Jagjita Corp .... G 217 374-6016
  White Hall *(G-21019)*
K&H Fuel .... G 815 405-4364
  Frankfort *(G-9811)*
L & W Fuels .... G 815 848-8360
  Fairbury *(G-9611)*
Lakeview Energy LLC .... E 312 386-5897
  Chicago *(G-5167)*
Midtown Fuels .... G 217 347-7191
  Effingham *(G-8411)*
Nikli Fuels Inc .... G 309 363-2425
  Pekin *(G-16347)*
Pro Fuel Nine Inc .... G 309 867-3375
  Oquawka *(G-15907)*
R & P Fuels .... G 630 855-2358
  Hoffman Estates *(G-11449)*

PRODUCT SECTION

Rs Fuels Inc .... F 773 205-9833
  Chicago *(G-6073)*
Rsb Fuels Inc .... G 217 999-4409
  Mount Olive *(G-14508)*
Saint Mary Fuel Company .... G 773 918-1681
  Chicago *(G-6090)*
Stateline Renewable Fuels LLC .... G 608 931-4634
  Buffalo Grove *(G-2609)*
Swissport Fueling Incorpo .... G 773 203-5419
  Chicago *(G-6298)*
Uzhavoor Fuels Inc .... G 630 401-6173
  Dixon *(G-7925)*
Wenona Food & Fuel .... G 815 853-4141
  Wenona *(G-20527)*
West Fuels Inc .... G 708 488-8880
  Forest Park *(G-9729)*
Wieman Fuels LP Gas Company .... G 618 632-4015
  Belleville *(G-1612)*
World Fuel Services Inc .... F 305 428-8000
  Chicago *(G-6673)*

FUELS: Jet
Esi Fuel & Energy Group LLC .... G 716 465-4289
  Collinsville *(G-6959)*

FULLER'S EARTH MINING
Profile Products LLC .... G 847 215-1144
  Buffalo Grove *(G-2590)*

FUND RAISING ORGANIZATION, NON-FEE BASIS
R L Allen Industries .... G 618 667-2544
  Troy *(G-19919)*

FUNERAL HOME
Clugston Tibbitts Funeral Home .... G 309 833-2188
  Macomb *(G-13389)*
Greenwood Inc .... F 800 798-4900
  Danville *(G-7341)*
Keepes Funeral Home Inc .... F 618 262-5200
  Mount Carmel *(G-14476)*

FUNERAL HOMES & SVCS
Merz Vault Company Inc .... E 618 548-2859
  Salem *(G-18345)*
Northern Illinois Wilbert Vlt .... G 815 544-3355
  Belvidere *(G-1689)*
St Charles Memorial Works Inc .... G 630 584-0183
  Saint Charles *(G-18275)*

FUNGICIDES OR HERBICIDES
E I Du Pont De Nemours & Co .... E 309 527-5115
  El Paso *(G-8436)*
Frank Miller & Sons Inc .... E 708 201-7200
  Mokena *(G-14083)*
Pfizer Inc .... D 847 639-3020
  Cary *(G-3182)*
Sanford Chemical Co Inc .... F 847 437-3530
  Elk Grove Village *(G-9229)*

FURNACE CASINGS: Sheet Metal
Goose Island Mfg & Supply Corp .... G 708 343-4225
  Lansing *(G-12495)*
Temp Excel Properties LLC .... G 847 844-3845
  Elgin *(G-8750)*
W L Engler Distributing Inc .... G 630 898-5400
  Aurora *(G-1032)*

FURNACES & OVENS: Fuel-Fired
Burdett Burner Mfg Inc .... G 630 617-5060
  Villa Park *(G-20135)*

FURNACES & OVENS: Indl
Amiberica Inc .... E 773 247-3600
  Chicago *(G-3679)*
Anderson Msnry Refr Spcialists .... G 847 540-8885
  Lake Zurich *(G-12384)*
Campbell International Inc .... E 408 661-0794
  Wauconda *(G-20339)*
Chicago Brick Oven LLC .... G 630 359-4793
  Woodridge *(G-21284)*
Dane Industries LLC .... D 815 234-2811
  Byron *(G-2752)*
Diablo Furnaces LLC .... F 815 636-7502
  Machesney Park *(G-13340)*

PRODUCT SECTION
FURNITURE, OFFICE: Wholesalers

Elgin National Industries Inc..............D....... 314 776-2848
  Raleigh (G-16960)
Fish Oven and Equipment Corp...........E....... 847 526-8686
  Wauconda (G-20351)
Furnace Fixers Inc.................................G....... 630 736-0670
  Streamwood (G-19576)
G & M Fabricating Inc............................G....... 815 282-1744
  Roscoe (G-17907)
Grieve Corporation.................................D....... 847 546-8225
  Round Lake (G-18078)
Heat Systems Instrs Svc Co LLC...........G....... 630 404-6884
  Willowbrook (G-21046)
Henry Technologies Inc..........................G....... 217 483-2406
  Chatham (G-3421)
Infratrol LLC...E....... 779 475-3098
  Byron (G-2753)
Ipsen Inc...E....... 815 239-2385
  Pecatonica (G-16322)
K H Huppert Co......................................G....... 708 339-2020
  South Holland (G-19225)
Magneco/Metrel Inc................................E....... 630 543-6660
  Addison (G-190)
Moffitt Co..G....... 847 678-5450
  Schiller Park (G-18828)
Northpoint Heating & Air Cond...............G....... 847 731-1067
  Zion (G-21521)
Pioneer Express....................................G....... 217 236-3022
  Perry (G-16562)
Precision Quincy Ovens LLC.................E....... 302 602-8738
  South Beloit (G-19108)
Quincy Lab Inc.......................................E....... 773 622-2428
  Chicago (G-5938)
Thermal Solutions Inc............................G....... 217 352-7019
  Savoy (G-18417)
Tks Control Systems Inc.......................F....... 630 554-3020
  Oswego (G-16027)
Westran Thermal Processing LLC.........E....... 815 634-1001
  South Beloit (G-19123)

FURNITURE & CABINET STORES: Cabinets, Custom Work

Ameriscan Designs Inc..........................D....... 773 542-1291
  Chicago (G-3677)
Benchmark Cabinets & Mllwk Inc..........E....... 309 697-5855
  Peoria (G-16391)
Bolhuis Woodworking Co........................G....... 708 333-5100
  Manhattan (G-13431)
Dicks Custom Cabinet Shop...................G....... 815 358-2663
  Cornell (G-7012)
Election Works.......................................G....... 630 232-4030
  Geneva (G-10268)
Encon Environmental Concepts.............F....... 630 543-1583
  Addison (G-115)
Fra-Milco Cabinets Co Inc.....................G
  Frankfort (G-9795)
Glenview Custom Cabinets Inc.............G....... 847 345-5754
  Glenview (G-10551)
Hansen Custom Cabinet Inc..................G....... 847 356-1100
  Lake Villa (G-12353)
Hickory Street Cabinets..........................G....... 618 667-9676
  Troy (G-19915)
Kunz Carpentry......................................G....... 618 224-7892
  Trenton (G-19904)
Rose Custom Cabinets Inc....................E....... 847 816-4800
  Mundelein (G-14732)
Scheffler Custom Woodworking.............G....... 815 284-6564
  Dixon (G-7915)
Unique Designs......................................G....... 309 454-1226
  Normal (G-15227)
Wagners Custom Wood Design.............G....... 847 487-2788
  Island Lake (G-11613)

FURNITURE & CABINET STORES: Custom

Bernhard Woodwork Ltd........................D....... 847 291-1040
  Northbrook (G-15348)
Stonetree Fabrication Inc......................E....... 618 332-1700
  East Saint Louis (G-8325)
Vault Furniture Inc.................................G....... 734 323-4166
  Chicago (G-6525)
Woodwrights Shoppe Inc.......................G....... 309 360-6503
  Metamora (G-13970)

FURNITURE & FIXTURES Factory

3-Switch LLC..G....... 217 721-4546
  Chicago (G-3466)
Akerue Industries LLC...........................E....... 847 395-3300
  Antioch (G-597)
Display Plan Lpdg..................................G....... 773 525-3787
  Chicago (G-4366)

Edsal Manufacturing Co LLC.................A....... 773 475-3000
  Chicago (G-4454)
Edsal Manufacturing Co LLC.................C....... 773 475-3165
  Chicago (G-4455)
Edsal Manufacturing Co LLC.................C....... 773 475-3013
  Chicago (G-4456)
Kewaunee Scientific Corp......................G....... 847 675-7744
  Highland Park (G-11278)
Pollard Bros Mfg Co...............................F....... 773 763-6868
  Chicago (G-5834)
Railcraft Nexim Design..........................G....... 309 937-2360
  Cambridge (G-2806)
Vault Furniture Inc.................................G....... 734 323-4166
  Chicago (G-6525)

FURNITURE PARTS: Metal

Chadwick Manufacturing Ltd.................G....... 815 684-5152
  Chadwick (G-3257)
Trendler Inc..E....... 773 284-6600
  Chicago (G-6416)

FURNITURE REFINISHING SVCS

Doll Furniture Co Inc..............................G....... 309 452-2606
  Normal (G-15202)
Mastercraft Furn Rfnishing Inc...............F....... 773 722-5730
  Chicago (G-5361)

FURNITURE REPAIR & MAINTENANCE SVCS

Gmk Finishing..G....... 630 837-0568
  Bartlett (G-1284)

FURNITURE STOCK & PARTS: Carvings, Wood

Greatlkes Archtctral Mllwrks L...............E....... 312 829-7110
  Chicago (G-4739)
Signature Innovations LLC....................G....... 847 758-9600
  Elk Grove Village (G-9241)

FURNITURE STOCK & PARTS: Dimension Stock, Hardwood

Hardwood Lumber Products Co.............G....... 309 538-4411
  Kilbourne (G-12044)
New Line Hardwoods Inc.......................D....... 309 657-7621
  Beardstown (G-1449)

FURNITURE STOCK & PARTS: Frames, Upholstered Furniture, Wood

Redbox Workshop Ltd...........................E....... 773 478-7077
  Chicago (G-5993)

FURNITURE STOCK & PARTS: Hardwood

Heartland Hardwoods Inc......................E....... 217 844-3312
  Effingham (G-8402)
Riverside Custom Woodworking............G....... 815 589-3608
  Fulton (G-10157)

FURNITURE STORES

Aero Products Holdings Inc...................E....... 847 485-3200
  Schaumburg (G-18429)
Albert Vivo Upholstery Co Inc...............G....... 312 226-7779
  Burr Ridge (G-2651)
B & B Formica Appliers Inc...................F....... 773 804-1015
  Chicago (G-3804)
Caroline Cole Inc...................................F....... 618 233-0600
  Belleville (G-1538)
Coles Appliance & Furn Co....................G....... 773 525-1797
  Chicago (G-4199)
Compx Security Products Inc................D....... 847 234-1864
  Grayslake (G-10763)
Doll Furniture Co Inc..............................G....... 309 452-2606
  Normal (G-15202)
Euromarket Designs Inc........................E....... 847 272-2888
  Northbrook (G-15386)
Hanley Design Inc..................................G....... 309 682-9665
  Peoria (G-16452)
Hylan Design Ltd....................................G....... 312 243-7341
  Chicago (G-4863)
Interior Tectonics LLC............................G....... 312 515-7779
  Chicago (G-4947)
Kaufmans Custom Cabinets..................F....... 217 268-4330
  Arcola (G-653)
Petro Enterprises Inc.............................G....... 708 425-1551
  Chicago Ridge (G-6806)

Piersons Mattress Inc............................G....... 309 637-8455
  Peoria (G-16498)
Railcraft Nexim Design..........................G....... 309 937-2360
  Cambridge (G-2806)
Riverton Cabinet Company....................E....... 815 462-5300
  New Lenox (G-15056)
Romar Cabinet & Top Co Inc................D....... 815 467-4452
  Channahon (G-3392)
Vintage Modern Collection Inc..............G....... 312 774-8424
  Chicago (G-6554)
Whitacres Country Oaks Shop...............F....... 309 726-1305
  Hudson (G-11521)

FURNITURE STORES: Cabinets, Kitchen, Exc Custom Made

Kitchen & Bath Gallery..........................G....... 217 214-0310
  Quincy (G-16900)

FURNITURE STORES: Custom Made, Exc Cabinets

Counter Craft Inc...................................G....... 847 336-8205
  Waukegan (G-20431)
Robert Harlan Ernst...............................G....... 217 627-3401
  Girard (G-10385)
Scibor Upholstering & Gallery...............G....... 708 671-9700
  Chicago (G-6117)

FURNITURE STORES: Office

Athletic & Sports Seating......................G....... 630 837-5566
  Streamwood (G-19563)
Gazette Democrat..................................E....... 618 833-2150
  Anna (G-583)
James Ray Monroe Corporation............F....... 618 532-4575
  Centralia (G-3236)
OfficeMax North America Inc...............E....... 815 748-3007
  Dekalb (G-7696)
W B Mason Co Inc.................................E....... 888 926-2766
  Carol Stream (G-3085)

FURNITURE STORES: Outdoor & Garden

Cabinets Doors and More LLC..............G....... 847 395-6334
  Antioch (G-607)

FURNITURE UPHOLSTERY REPAIR SVCS

Marks Custom Seating...........................G....... 630 980-8270
  Roselle (G-17968)

FURNITURE WHOLESALERS

Petro Enterprises Inc.............................G....... 708 425-1551
  Chicago Ridge (G-6806)
Urban Home Furniture & ACC Inc.........E....... 630 761-3200
  Batavia (G-1438)
Vault Furniture Inc.................................G....... 734 323-4166
  Chicago (G-6525)
Veeco Manufacturing Inc.......................F....... 312 666-0900
  Melrose Park (G-13925)

FURNITURE, BARBER & BEAUTY SHOP

Buff & Go Inc..F....... 773 719-4436
  Chicago (G-3972)

FURNITURE, GARDEN: Concrete

M & M Exposed Aggregate Co..............G....... 847 551-1818
  Carpentersville (G-3108)

FURNITURE, HOUSEHOLD: Wholesalers

Athletic & Sports Seating......................G....... 630 837-5566
  Streamwood (G-19563)
Homewerks Worldwide LLC..................E....... 224 543-1529
  Lake Bluff (G-12188)
Ligo Products Inc...................................E....... 708 478-1800
  Mokena (G-14096)

FURNITURE, MATTRESSES: Wholesalers

Wicoff Inc...G....... 618 988-8888
  Herrin (G-11182)

FURNITURE, OFFICE: Wholesalers

H A Friend & Company Inc....................E....... 847 746-1248
  Zion (G-21516)
Lincoln Office LLC..................................D....... 309 427-2500
  Washington (G-20273)

Employee Codes: A=Over 500 employees, B=251-500
C=101-250, D=51-100, E=20-50, F=10-19, G=3-9

2020 Harris Illinois
Industrial Directory

1457

FURNITURE, OFFICE: Wholesalers

Norix Group Inc..................................E....... 630 231-1331
  West Chicago (G-20624)
Nova Solutions Inc..............................E....... 217 342-7070
  Effingham (G-8416)
Roevolution 226 LLC..........................G....... 773 658-4022
  Riverwoods (G-17095)

FURNITURE, OUTDOOR & LAWN: Wholesalers

Prescription Plus Ltd..........................F....... 618 537-6202
  Lebanon (G-12546)

FURNITURE, PUBLIC BUILDING: Wholesalers

Mfp Holding Co....................................G....... 312 666-3366
  Chicago (G-5418)

FURNITURE, WHOLESALE: Bar

Bar Stool Depotcom............................G....... 815 727-7294
  Joliet (G-11827)

FURNITURE, WHOLESALE: Chairs

Choice Furnishings Inc........................F....... 847 329-0004
  Skokie (G-18942)
Ortho Seating LLC..............................F....... 773 276-3539
  Chicago (G-5706)

FURNITURE, WHOLESALE: Lockers

REB Steel Equipment Corp..................E....... 773 252-0400
  Chicago (G-5987)

FURNITURE, WHOLESALE: Racks

R P Solutions LLC................................G....... 773 971-1363
  Chicago (G-5948)

FURNITURE: Bar furniture

Wag Industries Inc...............................F....... 847 329-8932
  Skokie (G-19053)

FURNITURE: Bed Frames & Headboards, Wood

Custom Window Accents.....................F....... 815 943-7651
  Harvard (G-11051)
Rooms Redux Chicago Inc..................F....... 312 835-1192
  Chicago (G-6058)

FURNITURE: Bedroom, Wood

D D G Inc..G....... 847 412-0277
  Northbrook (G-15370)
Douglas County Wood Products.........G....... 217 543-2888
  Arthur (G-854)

FURNITURE: Beds, Household, Incl Folding & Cabinet, Metal

Durable Design Products Inc..............G....... 708 707-1147
  River Forest (G-17051)

FURNITURE: Bedsprings, Assembled

Leggett & Platt Incorporated...............E....... 630 801-0609
  North Aurora (G-15267)

FURNITURE: Bookcases & Stereo Cabinets, Metal

Metal Box International LLC................C....... 847 455-8500
  Franklin Park (G-9994)

FURNITURE: Bookcases, Office, Wood

Djr Inc..F....... 773 581-5204
  Chicago (G-4372)

FURNITURE: Box Springs, Assembled

Leggett & Platt Incorporated...............D....... 773 907-0261
  Chicago (G-5198)

FURNITURE: Cabinets & Filing Drawers, Office, Exc Wood

IMS Engineered Products LLC..........C....... 847 391-8100
  Des Plaines (G-7787)

Mayline Investments Inc......................G....... 847 948-9340
  Northbrook (G-15428)

FURNITURE: Cabinets & Vanities, Medicine, Metal

Pace Industries Inc..............................C....... 312 226-5500
  Chicago (G-5737)

FURNITURE: Cafeteria

Norix Group Inc....................................E....... 630 231-1331
  West Chicago (G-20624)

FURNITURE: Chairs, Household Upholstered

E J Self Furniture.................................G....... 847 394-0899
  Arlington Heights (G-731)

FURNITURE: Chairs, Household Wood

Athletic & Sports Seating.....................G....... 630 837-5566
  Streamwood (G-19563)
Choice Furnishings Inc........................F....... 847 329-0004
  Skokie (G-18942)

FURNITURE: Chairs, Household, Metal

Duracare Seating Company Inc..........F....... 888 592-1102
  Chicago (G-4409)

FURNITURE: Chairs, Office Exc Wood

Mlp Seating Corp..................................E....... 847 956-1700
  Rockdale (G-17269)
Ortho Seating LLC...............................F....... 773 276-3539
  Chicago (G-5706)

FURNITURE: Chairs, Office Wood

Interstuhl USA Inc................................G....... 312 385-0240
  Chicago (G-4959)

FURNITURE: China Closets

A Closet Wholesaler.............................F....... 312 654-1400
  Chicago (G-3486)

FURNITURE: Church

Atwood-Hamlin Mfg Co Inc..................F....... 815 678-7291
  Richmond (G-17010)
Pep Industries Inc................................F....... 630 833-0404
  Villa Park (G-20164)
Roberts & Downey Chapel Eqp...........G....... 217 795-2391
  Argenta (G-672)

FURNITURE: Church, Cut Stone

Pep Industries Inc................................F....... 630 833-0404
  Villa Park (G-20164)

FURNITURE: Coffee Tables, Wood

Signature Innovations LLC..................G....... 847 758-9600
  Elk Grove Village (G-9241)
Wolfart Maciej......................................G....... 312 248-3575
  Chicago (G-6663)

FURNITURE: Desks & Tables, Office, Exc Wood

Kimball Office Inc.................................F....... 800 349-9827
  Chicago (G-5102)

FURNITURE: Desks, Household, Wood

Whitacres Country Oaks Shop.............F....... 309 726-1305
  Hudson (G-11521)

FURNITURE: Desks, Metal

Groupe Lacasse LLC............................C....... 312 670-9100
  Chicago (G-4745)
L & D Group Inc....................................B....... 630 892-8941
  Montgomery (G-14252)

FURNITURE: Desks, Wood

Gianni Incorporated.............................D....... 708 863-6696
  Cicero (G-6849)
Groupe Lacasse LLC............................C....... 312 670-9100
  Chicago (G-4745)
Systems Unlimited Inc.........................C....... 630 285-0010
  Itasca (G-11743)

FURNITURE: Dining Room, Wood

Dendro Co...G....... 312 772-6836
  Lakemoor (G-12471)

FURNITURE: Fiberglass & Plastic

Patio Plus..G....... 815 433-2399
  Ottawa (G-16070)

FURNITURE: Foundations & Platforms

Pace Foundation..................................E....... 309 691-3553
  Peoria (G-16490)

FURNITURE: Garden, Exc Wood, Metal, Stone Or Concrete

Gensler Gardens Inc............................F....... 815 874-9634
  Davis Junction (G-7424)

FURNITURE: Hammocks, Metal Or Fabric & Metal Combined

Smart Solar Inc....................................F....... 813 343-5770
  Libertyville (G-12708)

FURNITURE: Hospital

Kinsman Enterprises Inc.....................G....... 618 932-3838
  West Frankfort (G-20674)
Mpd Medical Systems Inc...................G....... 815 477-0707
  Watseka (G-20312)

FURNITURE: Household, Metal

Chicago American Mfg LLC.................C....... 773 376-0100
  Chicago (G-4088)
Chicagos Finest Ironworks..................G....... 708 895-4484
  Lansing (G-12488)
European Ornamental Iron Works.......G....... 630 705-9300
  Addison (G-117)
Richardson Ironworks LLC..................G....... 217 359-3333
  Champaign (G-3342)
Viking Metal Cabinet Co LLC...............D....... 800 776-7767
  Montgomery (G-14273)
Viking Metal Cabinet Company...........D....... 630 863-7234
  Montgomery (G-14274)

FURNITURE: Household, NEC

Kozaczka Inc..G....... 224 435-6180
  Arlington Heights (G-766)
Mitchel Home..G....... 773 205-9902
  Chicago (G-5469)
Rustic Woodcrafts................................G....... 618 584-3912
  Flat Rock (G-9673)

FURNITURE: Household, Upholstered On Metal Frames

Tesko Welding & Mfg Co.....................D....... 708 452-0045
  Norridge (G-15244)

FURNITURE: Household, Upholstered, Exc Wood Or Metal

Albert Vivo Upholstery Co Inc..............G....... 312 226-7779
  Burr Ridge (G-2651)
Petro Enterprises Inc...........................G....... 708 425-1551
  Chicago Ridge (G-6806)

FURNITURE: Household, Wood

AB&d Custom Furniture Inc.................E....... 708 922-9061
  Homewood (G-11487)
Aba Custom Woodworking...................G....... 815 356-9663
  Crystal Lake (G-7153)
Allie Woodworking................................G....... 847 244-1919
  Waukegan (G-20413)
Amtab Manufacturing Corp..................D....... 630 301-7600
  Bensenville (G-1746)
Bell Cabinet & Millwork Co..................G....... 708 425-1200
  Palos Hills (G-16196)
Bender Mat Fctry Fton Slepshop.........G....... 217 328-1700
  Urbana (G-19973)
Bill Weeks Inc.......................................G....... 217 523-8735
  Springfield (G-19326)
Broome & Greene Online LLC.............G....... 312 584-1580
  Chicago (G-3964)
Butcher Block Furn By Oneill...............G....... 312 666-9144
  Chicago (G-3986)

PRODUCT SECTION FURNITURE: Mattresses, Box & Bedsprings

Carson Properties Inc .... E 630 832-3322
  Elmhurst *(G-9341)*
Chicago Booth Mfg Inc .... F 773 378-8400
  Chicago *(G-4093)*
Chicago Honeymooners LLC .... G 312 399-5699
  Chicago *(G-4106)*
Chicago Wicker & Trading Co .... E 708 563-2890
  Alsip *(G-429)*
Chicagos Finest Ironworks .... G 708 895-4484
  Lansing *(G-12488)*
City Living Design Inc .... G 312 335-0711
  Chicago *(G-4156)*
Columbia Woodworks Corporation .... F 202 526-2387
  Addison *(G-77)*
Comwell .... D 618 282-6233
  Red Bud *(G-16991)*
Country Workshop .... G 217 543-4094
  Arthur *(G-849)*
Creative Wood Concepts Inc .... G 773 384-9960
  Chicago *(G-4268)*
Custom Designs By Georgio .... F 847 233-0410
  Franklin Park *(G-9922)*
Custom Wood Designs Inc .... G 708 799-3439
  Crestwood *(G-7116)*
Debcor Inc .... G 708 333-2191
  South Holland *(G-19207)*
Dicks Custom Cabinet Shop .... G 815 358-2663
  Cornell *(G-7012)*
Diebolds Cabinet Shop .... G 773 772-3076
  Chicago *(G-4356)*
Eddie Gapastione .... G 708 430-3881
  Bridgeview *(G-2344)*
Fredman Bros Furniture Co Inc .... E 309 674-2011
  Peoria *(G-16441)*
Gavin Woodworking Inc .... G 815 786-2242
  Sandwich *(G-18371)*
Great Spirit Hardwoods LLC .... G 224 801-1969
  East Dundee *(G-8199)*
Green Gables Country Store .... D 309 897-7160
  Bradford *(G-2273)*
Guess Whackit & Hope Inc .... G 773 342-4273
  Chicago *(G-4750)*
Hanley Design Inc .... G 309 682-9665
  Peoria *(G-16452)*
Hylan Design Ltd .... G 312 243-7341
  Chicago *(G-4863)*
Imperial Kitchens & Bath Inc .... F 708 485-0020
  Brookfield *(G-2486)*
Innovative Mktg Solutions Inc .... F 630 227-4300
  Schaumburg *(G-18561)*
International Wood Design Inc .... G 773 227-9270
  Chicago *(G-4956)*
J M Lustig Custom Cabinets Co .... F 217 342-6661
  Effingham *(G-8403)*
Jbc Holding Co .... G 217 347-7701
  Effingham *(G-8404)*
Joliet Cabinet Company Inc .... E 815 727-4096
  Lockport *(G-13003)*
Kaufmans Custom Cabinets .... F 217 268-4330
  Arcola *(G-653)*
Kinser Woodworks .... G 618 549-4540
  Makanda *(G-13428)*
Kowal Custom Cabinet & Furn .... G 708 597-3367
  Blue Island *(G-2129)*
Kunz Carpentry .... G 618 224-7892
  Trenton *(G-19904)*
Laverns Wood Items .... G 217 268-4544
  Arcola *(G-654)*
Legacy Woodwork Inc .... G 847 451-7602
  Franklin Park *(G-9980)*
Leggett & Platt Incorporated .... E 630 801-0609
  North Aurora *(G-15267)*
M Inc .... G 312 853-0512
  Chicago *(G-5301)*
Mamagreen LLC .... G 312 953-3557
  Chicago *(G-5325)*
Master Cabinets .... G 847 639-1323
  Cary *(G-3178)*
Mastercraft Furn Rfnishing Inc .... F 773 722-5730
  Chicago *(G-5361)*
Meier Granite Company .... G 847 678-7300
  Franklin Park *(G-9989)*
Mica Furniture Mfg Inc .... G 708 430-1150
  Addison *(G-203)*
Mobilia Inc .... E 708 865-0700
  Bellwood *(G-1634)*
Morningside Woodcraft .... G 217 268-4313
  Arcola *(G-659)*
Muhs Funiture Manufacturing .... G 618 723-2590
  Noble *(G-15190)*

O & I Woodworking .... G 217 543-3155
  Arthur *(G-872)*
Okaw Valley Woodworking LLC .... F 217 543-5180
  Arthur *(G-874)*
ONeill Products Inc .... G 312 243-3413
  Chicago *(G-5678)*
Patio Plus .... G 815 433-2399
  Ottawa *(G-16070)*
Philip Reinisch Company .... F 312 644-6776
  Naperville *(G-14899)*
Planks Cabinet Shop Inc .... G 217 543-2687
  Arthur *(G-876)*
Prairie Woodworks Inc .... G 309 378-2418
  Downs *(G-8112)*
R Maderite Inc .... G 847 785-0875
  North Chicago *(G-15320)*
Riverside Custom Woodworking .... G 815 589-3608
  Fulton *(G-10157)*
Roncin Custom Design .... G 847 669-0260
  Huntley *(G-11565)*
Rose Custom Cabinets Inc .... G 847 816-4800
  Mundelein *(G-14732)*
Royal Fabricators Inc .... F 847 775-7466
  Wadsworth *(G-20213)*
Shews Custom Woodworking .... G 217 737-5543
  Lincoln *(G-12738)*
Silver Bell Cnstr & Furn Inc .... G 773 578-9450
  Chicago *(G-6171)*
Specialized Woodwork Inc .... G 630 627-0450
  Lombard *(G-13131)*
Spirit Concepts Inc .... G 708 388-4500
  Crestwood *(G-7128)*
Stancy Woodworking Co Inc .... F 847 526-0252
  Island Lake *(G-11611)*
Suburban Laminating Inc .... G 708 389-6106
  Melrose Park *(G-13918)*
United Woodworking Inc .... E 847 352-3066
  Schaumburg *(G-18767)*
Urban Wood Goods Ltd .... F 248 310-7668
  Gurnee *(G-10941)*
Verlo Mattress of Lake Geneva .... G 815 455-2570
  Crystal Lake *(G-7289)*
Waco Manufacturing Co Inc .... F 312 733-0054
  Chicago *(G-6582)*
What We Make Inc .... G 331 442-4830
  Algonquin *(G-396)*
Wicks Organ Company .... E 618 654-2191
  Highland *(G-11249)*
Woodcraft Enterprises Inc .... G 815 485-2787
  New Lenox *(G-15070)*
Wooden World of Richmond Inc .... G 815 405-4503
  Richmond *(G-17026)*
Zakrose Inc .... G 847 372-7309
  Chicago *(G-6707)*

FURNITURE: Hydraulic Barber & Beauty Shop Chairs

Ecologic Industries LLC .... E 847 234-5855
  Waukegan *(G-20441)*
Hagen Manufacturing Inc .... G 224 735-2099
  Wheeling *(G-20906)*

FURNITURE: Institutional, Exc Wood

Abundant Living Christian Ctr .... G 708 896-6181
  Dolton *(G-7928)*
Chicago American Mfg LLC .... C 773 376-0100
  Chicago *(G-4088)*
Chicago Booth Mfg Inc .... F 773 378-8400
  Chicago *(G-4093)*
Claridge Products .... G 847 991-8822
  Elgin *(G-8542)*
Correctional Technologies Inc .... F 630 455-0811
  Willowbrook *(G-21038)*
Fortune Brands Home & SEC Inc .... D 847 484-4400
  Deerfield *(G-7610)*
Hanley Design Inc .... G 309 682-9665
  Peoria *(G-16452)*
Jcdecaux Chicago LLC .... E 312 456-2999
  Chicago *(G-5013)*
Kinsman Enterprises Inc .... G 618 932-3838
  West Frankfort *(G-20674)*
Mfp Holding Co .... G 312 666-3366
  Chicago *(G-5418)*
Nu-Dell Manufacturing Co Inc .... F 847 803-4500
  Chicago *(G-5637)*
Partners Resource Inc .... G 630 620-9161
  Glen Ellyn *(G-10417)*
Patio Plus .... G 815 433-2399
  Ottawa *(G-16070)*
Redbox Workshop Ltd .... E 773 478-7077
  Chicago *(G-5993)*
Sedia Systems Inc .... G 312 212-8010
  Chicago *(G-6129)*
Serious Energy Inc .... E 312 515-4606
  Chicago *(G-6137)*
Stevens Cabinets Inc .... B 217 857-7100
  Teutopolis *(G-19773)*
Vecchio Manufacturing of Ill .... F 847 742-8429
  Elgin *(G-8773)*
Waco Manufacturing Co Inc .... F 312 733-0054
  Chicago *(G-6582)*
Wise Co Inc .... G 618 594-4091
  Carlyle *(G-2898)*

FURNITURE: Juvenile, Wood

Stevens Cabinets Inc .... B 217 857-7100
  Teutopolis *(G-19773)*
Tender Loving Care Inds Inc .... D 847 891-0230
  Elgin *(G-8753)*

FURNITURE: Kitchen & Dining Room, Metal

US Foods Culinary Eqp Sups LLC .... G 847 720-8000
  Rosemont *(G-18057)*

FURNITURE: Laboratory

Kewaunee Scientific Corp .... G 847 675-7744
  Highland Park *(G-11278)*
Prime Industries Inc .... E 630 725-9200
  Lisle *(G-12929)*

FURNITURE: Lawn & Garden, Except Wood & Metal

Bradley Terrace Inc .... G 773 775-6579
  Chicago *(G-3941)*

FURNITURE: Lawn, Exc Wood, Metal, Stone Or Concrete

Suncast Corporation .... A 630 879-2050
  Batavia *(G-1422)*

FURNITURE: Lawn, Metal

Dixline Corporation .... F 309 932-2011
  Galva *(G-10230)*

FURNITURE: Lawn, Wood

Cabinets Doors and More LLC .... G 847 395-6334
  Antioch *(G-607)*

FURNITURE: Library

Harrier Interior Products .... G 847 934-1310
  Palatine *(G-16122)*

FURNITURE: Living Room, Upholstered On Wood Frames

Trp Acquisition Corp .... G 630 261-2380
  Lombard *(G-13147)*

FURNITURE: Mattresses & Foundations

Hospitology Products LLC .... G 630 359-5075
  Addison *(G-153)*
Innocor Inc .... F 630 231-0622
  West Chicago *(G-20597)*
Quality Sleep Shop Inc .... G 708 246-2224
  La Grange Highlands *(G-12093)*
Wicoff Inc .... G 618 988-8888
  Herrin *(G-11182)*

FURNITURE: Mattresses, Box & Bedsprings

Corsicana Bedding LLC .... G 708 331-9000
  Aurora *(G-1080)*
L A Bedding Corp .... G 773 715-9641
  Chicago *(G-5141)*
Leggett & Platt Incorporated .... F 630 851-0101
  Aurora *(G-996)*
Leggett & Platt Incorporated .... D 815 233-0022
  Freeport *(G-10124)*
Leggett & Platt Incorporated .... E 312 529-2053
  Chicago *(G-5199)*
Leggett & Platt Incorporated .... G 800 699-0607
  Chicago *(G-5200)*

Employee Codes: A=Over 500 employees, B=251-500
C=101-250, D=51-100, E=20-50, F=10-19, G=3-9

FURNITURE: Mattresses, Box & Bedsprings

Robin Hood Mat & Quilting Corp..........G....... 312 953-2960
  Chicago *(G-6045)*
Shevick Sales Corp..........G....... 312 487-2865
  Niles *(G-15171)*
Ther A Pedic Midwest Inc..........G....... 309 788-0401
  Rock Island *(G-17249)*
Verlo Mat of Skokie-Evanston..........G....... 847 966-9988
  Morton Grove *(G-14446)*
Verlo Mattress of Lake Geneva..........G....... 815 455-2570
  Crystal Lake *(G-7289)*

FURNITURE: Mattresses, Innerspring Or Box Spring

Bedding Group Inc..........D....... 309 788-0401
  Rock Island *(G-17204)*
Bender Mat Fctry Fton Slepshop..........G....... 217 328-1700
  Urbana *(G-19973)*
Made Rite Bedding Company..........F....... 847 349-5886
  Franklin Park *(G-9983)*
Piersons Mattress Inc..........G....... 309 637-8455
  Peoria *(G-16498)*
Royal Bedding Company Inc..........D....... 847 645-0200
  Hoffman Estates *(G-11451)*

FURNITURE: NEC

Classic Remix..........G....... 312 915-0521
  Chicago *(G-4170)*
K K O Inc..........G....... 815 569-2324
  Capron *(G-2833)*
Lacava..........G....... 773 637-9600
  Chicago *(G-5153)*
Montauk Chicago Inc..........G....... 312 951-5688
  Chicago *(G-5493)*

FURNITURE: Office, Exc Wood

Almacen Inc..........G....... 847 934-7955
  Inverness *(G-11593)*
Baker Avenue Investments Inc..........D....... 309 427-2500
  Washington *(G-20266)*
Bretford Manufacturing Inc..........B....... 847 678-2545
  Franklin Park *(G-9892)*
C-V Cstom Cntrtops Cbinets Inc..........F....... 708 388-5066
  Blue Island *(G-2113)*
Capitol Carton Company..........E....... 312 563-9690
  Chicago *(G-4017)*
Central Radiator Cabinet Co..........G....... 773 539-1700
  Lena *(G-12599)*
Debcor Inc..........G....... 708 333-2191
  South Holland *(G-19207)*
Dirtt Envmtl Solutions Inc..........C....... 312 245-2870
  Chicago *(G-4364)*
Edsal Manufacturing Co LLC..........A....... 773 475-3000
  Chicago *(G-4454)*
Edsal Manufacturing Co LLC..........C....... 773 475-3165
  Chicago *(G-4455)*
Edsal Manufacturing Co LLC..........C....... 773 475-3013
  Chicago *(G-4456)*
Fanmar Inc..........E....... 847 621-2010
  Elk Grove Village *(G-8995)*
Hanley Design Inc..........G....... 309 682-9665
  Peoria *(G-16452)*
Iceberg Enterprises LLC..........F....... 847 685-9500
  Des Plaines *(G-7782)*
Lincoln Office LLC..........D....... 309 427-2500
  Washington *(G-20273)*
Marvel Group Inc..........C....... 773 523-4804
  Chicago *(G-5354)*
Marvel Group Inc..........C....... 773 523-4804
  Chicago *(G-5355)*
Marvel Group Inc..........F....... 773 523-4804
  Chicago *(G-5356)*
Metal Box International LLC..........C....... 847 455-8500
  Franklin Park *(G-9994)*
Niedermaier Inc..........D....... 312 492-9400
  Chicago *(G-5599)*
Paoli Inc..........G....... 312 644-5509
  Chicago *(G-5751)*
Pointe International Company..........F....... 847 550-7001
  Lake Barrington *(G-12164)*
Rome Metal Mfg Inc..........G....... 773 287-1755
  Chicago *(G-6057)*
Steel Solutions USA..........G....... 815 432-4938
  Watseka *(G-20317)*
Steelcase Inc..........F....... 312 321-3720
  Chicago *(G-6237)*
T J Van Der Bosch & Associates..........E....... 815 344-3210
  McHenry *(G-13805)*
Viking Metal Cabinet Co LLC..........D....... 800 776-7767
  Montgomery *(G-14273)*
Viking Metal Cabinet Company..........D....... 630 863-7234
  Montgomery *(G-14274)*
Waco Manufacturing Co Inc..........F....... 312 733-0054
  Chicago *(G-6582)*

FURNITURE: Office, Wood

AB&d Custom Furniture Inc..........E....... 708 922-9061
  Homewood *(G-11487)*
Aba Custom Woodworking..........G....... 815 356-9663
  Crystal Lake *(G-7153)*
Almacen Inc..........G....... 847 934-7955
  Inverness *(G-11593)*
B & B Formica Appliers Inc..........F....... 773 804-1015
  Chicago *(G-3804)*
Bretford Manufacturing Inc..........B....... 847 678-2545
  Franklin Park *(G-9892)*
Crestwood Custom Cabinets..........G....... 708 385-3167
  Crestwood *(G-7115)*
Daniel M Powers & Assoc Ltd..........D....... 630 685-8400
  Bolingbrook *(G-2166)*
Debcor Inc..........G....... 708 333-2191
  South Holland *(G-19207)*
Dendro Co..........G....... 312 772-6836
  Lakemoor *(G-12471)*
Diebolds Cabinet Shop..........G....... 773 772-3076
  Chicago *(G-4356)*
Dirtt Envmtl Solutions Inc..........C....... 312 245-2870
  Chicago *(G-4364)*
Donald Kranz..........G....... 847 428-1616
  Carpentersville *(G-3101)*
Eddie Gapastione..........G....... 708 430-3881
  Bridgeview *(G-2344)*
Global Industries Inc..........F....... 630 681-2818
  Glendale Heights *(G-10454)*
Innovant Inc..........D....... 646 368-6254
  Chicago *(G-4930)*
J K Custom Countertops..........G....... 630 495-2324
  Lombard *(G-13088)*
J M Lustig Custom Cabinets Co..........F....... 217 342-6661
  Effingham *(G-8403)*
Knoll Inc..........E....... 312 454-6920
  Chicago *(G-5112)*
Lacava LLC..........E....... 773 637-9600
  Chicago *(G-5154)*
Magnuson Group Inc..........F....... 630 783-8100
  Woodridge *(G-21320)*
Marcy Enterprises Inc..........G....... 708 352-7220
  La Grange Park *(G-12098)*
Marvel Group Inc..........C....... 773 523-4804
  Chicago *(G-5354)*
Mastercraft Furn Rfnishing Inc..........F....... 773 722-5730
  Chicago *(G-5361)*
Mayline Investments Inc..........G....... 847 948-9340
  Northbrook *(G-15428)*
Mlp Seating Corp..........E....... 847 956-1700
  Rockdale *(G-17269)*
Mobilia Inc..........E....... 708 865-0700
  Bellwood *(G-1634)*
Nova Solutions Inc..........E....... 217 342-7070
  Effingham *(G-8416)*
Office Furniture Parts LLC..........G....... 708 546-5841
  Forest Park *(G-9723)*
Pio Woodworking Inc..........G....... 630 628-6900
  Addison *(G-240)*
Regency Custom Woodworking..........F....... 815 689-2117
  Cullom *(G-7300)*
Rieke Office Interiors Inc..........D....... 847 622-9711
  Elgin *(G-8720)*
Roevolution 226 LLC..........G....... 773 658-4022
  Riverwoods *(G-17095)*
S & J Woodproducts..........G....... 815 973-1970
  Rockford *(G-17618)*
Steelcase Inc..........F....... 312 321-3720
  Chicago *(G-6237)*
Wm Huber Cabinet Works..........E....... 773 235-7660
  Chicago *(G-6653)*
Woodhill Cabinetry Design Inc..........G....... 815 431-0545
  Ottawa *(G-16086)*

FURNITURE: Outdoor, Wood

Five Star Industries Inc..........D....... 618 542-4880
  Du Quoin *(G-8120)*
Urban Home Furniture & ACC Inc..........E....... 630 761-3200
  Batavia *(G-1438)*

FURNITURE: Picnic Tables Or Benches, Park

Belson Outdoors LLC..........E....... 630 897-8489
  Naperville *(G-14778)*

Ill Dept Natural Resources..........G....... 217 498-9208
  Rochester *(G-17167)*

FURNITURE: Rattan

House of Rattan Inc..........E....... 630 627-8160
  Lombard *(G-13086)*

FURNITURE: Restaurant

American Metalcraft Inc..........D....... 800 333-9133
  Franklin Park *(G-9866)*
Buhlwork Design Guild..........G....... 630 325-5340
  Oak Brook *(G-15601)*
Chicago Booth Mfg Inc..........F....... 773 378-8400
  Chicago *(G-4093)*
Contract Industries Inc..........E....... 708 458-8150
  Bedford Park *(G-1464)*
E-J Industries Inc..........G....... 312 226-5023
  Chicago *(G-4427)*
Lena Mercantile..........F....... 815 369-9955
  Lena *(G-12603)*
Urban Wood Goods Ltd..........F....... 248 310-7668
  Gurnee *(G-10941)*

FURNITURE: School

James Howard Co..........G....... 815 497-2831
  Compton *(G-6996)*
Pointe International Company..........F....... 847 550-7001
  Lake Barrington *(G-12164)*
Sage Clover..........G....... 630 220-9600
  Winfield *(G-21117)*
Sandlock Sandbox LLC..........G....... 630 963-9422
  Westmont *(G-20771)*

FURNITURE: Sleep

Ceragem 26th St..........G....... 773 277-0672
  Chicago *(G-4064)*
Fredman Bros Furniture Co Inc..........E....... 309 674-2011
  Peoria *(G-16441)*

FURNITURE: Sofa Beds Or Convertible Sofas)

Homwarehouse..........G....... 224 500-3367
  Des Plaines *(G-7777)*

FURNITURE: Stadium

Irwin Seating Company..........C....... 618 483-6157
  Altamont *(G-534)*
Irwin Telescopic Seating Co..........C....... 618 483-6157
  Altamont *(G-535)*

FURNITURE: Stools With Casters, Metal, Exc Home Or Office

Waco Manufacturing Co Inc..........F....... 312 733-0054
  Chicago *(G-6582)*

FURNITURE: Storage Chests, Household, Wood

Chicagoland Closets LLC..........E....... 630 906-0000
  Aurora *(G-1075)*

FURNITURE: Table Tops, Marble

Patterson Products..........G....... 618 723-2688
  Noble *(G-15191)*
Sambor Stone Ltd..........G....... 708 388-0804
  South Holland *(G-19243)*

FURNITURE: Tables & Table Tops, Wood

E J Self Furniture..........G....... 847 394-0899
  Arlington Heights *(G-731)*

FURNITURE: Tables, Office, Exc Wood

Amtab Manufacturing Corp..........D....... 630 301-7600
  Bensenville *(G-1746)*

FURNITURE: Tables, Office, Wood

Amtab Manufacturing Corp..........D....... 630 301-7600
  Bensenville *(G-1746)*

FURNITURE: Television, Wood

Zenith Electronics Corporation..........E....... 847 941-8000
  Lincolnshire *(G-12806)*

PRODUCT SECTION

FURNITURE: Unfinished, Wood
Churchill Cabinet Company .... E 708 780-0070
  Cicero (G-6833)
Trendler Inc .... E 773 284-6600
  Chicago (G-6416)

FURNITURE: Upholstered
Addison Interiors Company .... G 630 628-1345
  Addison (G-20)
Brusic-Rose Inc .... E 708 458-9900
  Bedford Park (G-1460)
Coles Appliance & Furn Co .... G 773 525-1797
  Chicago (G-4199)
E M C Industry .... E 217 543-2894
  Arthur (G-855)
Groupe Lacasse LLC .... C 312 670-9100
  Chicago (G-4745)
New Image Upholstery .... F 630 542-5560
  South Elgin (G-19169)
Patrick Cabinetry Inc .... G 630 307-9333
  Bloomingdale (G-2007)
Scibor Upholstering & Gallery .... G 708 671-9700
  Chicago (G-6117)
Sherwood Industries Inc .... F 847 626-0300
  Niles (G-15170)
Shoppe De Lee Inc .... G 847 350-0580
  Elk Grove Village (G-9237)
Vintage Modern Collection Inc .... G 312 774-8424
  Chicago (G-6554)
Vinyl Life North .... G 630 906-9686
  North Aurora (G-15281)

FUSES & FUSE EQPT
Littelfuse Inc .... A 773 628-1000
  Chicago (G-5238)

FUSES: Electric
S & C Electric Company .... A 773 338-1000
  Chicago (G-6083)

Furs
Elan Furs .... F 317 255-6100
  Morton Grove (G-14404)

GAMBLING: Lotteries
WMS Industries Inc .... E 847 785-3000
  Chicago (G-6660)

GAMES & TOYS: Air Rifles
Airgun Designs USA Inc .... G 847 520-7507
  Cary (G-3146)

GAMES & TOYS: Banks
Harris Skokie .... G 847 675-6300
  Skokie (G-18965)
Ing Bank Fsb .... G 312 981-1236
  Chicago (G-4920)
Liberty Classics Inc .... G 847 367-1288
  Libertyville (G-12667)

GAMES & TOYS: Blocks
Click-Block Corporation .... E 847 749-1651
  Rolling Meadows (G-17723)

GAMES & TOYS: Board Games, Children's & Adults'
Gift of Games Ltd .... G 847 370-1541
  Grayslake (G-10775)
Paragon Packaging Inc .... G 707 786-4004
  Chicago (G-5758)
Rapid Displays Inc .... C 773 927-5000
  Chicago (G-5971)

GAMES & TOYS: Cars, Play, Children's Vehicles
Quicker Engineering .... G 815 675-6516
  Spring Grove (G-19297)

GAMES & TOYS: Child Restraint Seats, Automotive
Safe Traffic System Inc .... G 847 233-0365
  Lincolnwood (G-12842)

Star Sleigh .... F 630 858-2576
  Glen Ellyn (G-10420)

GAMES & TOYS: Craft & Hobby Kits & Sets
Craft World Inc .... G 800 654-6114
  Loves Park (G-13198)
Edwin Waldmire & Virginia .... G 217 498-9375
  Rochester (G-17165)
Kei Keis Kreation Kafe .... F 708 982-6560
  Hazel Crest (G-11130)
Made By Hands Inc .... G 773 761-4200
  Chicago (G-5310)
Virtu .... G 773 235-3790
  Chicago (G-6555)

GAMES & TOYS: Doll Carriages & Carts
Standard Container Co of Edgar .... E 847 438-1510
  Lake Zurich (G-12460)

GAMES & TOYS: Electronic
Manseemanwant LLC .... G 217 610-8888
  Springfield (G-19402)
Wells-Gardner Technologies Inc .... G 630 819-8219
  Burr Ridge (G-2732)

GAMES & TOYS: Game Machines, Exc Coin-Operated
AGS Partners LLC .... D 630 446-7777
  Itasca (G-11616)
Arkadian Gaming LLC .... G 708 377-5656
  Orland Park (G-15942)
Novomatic Americas Sales LLC .... F 224 802-2974
  Mount Prospect (G-14553)
Powers Sports LLC .... G 815 436-6769
  Plainfield (G-16703)
Video Gaming Technologies Inc .... G 847 776-3516
  Palatine (G-16170)

GAMES & TOYS: Kits, Science, Incl Microscopes/Chemistry Sets
American Science & Surplus Inc .... F 773 763-0313
  Chicago (G-3665)

GAMES & TOYS: Models, Automobile & Truck, Toy & Hobby
Branch Lines Ltd .... G 847 256-4294
  Wilmette (G-21070)

GAMES & TOYS: Models, Boat & Ship, Toy & Hobby
Octura Models Inc .... G 847 674-7351
  Skokie (G-18998)

GAMES & TOYS: Models, Railroad, Toy & Hobby
Accurail Inc .... F 630 365-6400
  Elburn (G-8441)
Huff & Puff Industries Ltd .... G 847 381-8255
  North Barrington (G-15286)
Scale Railroad Equipment .... G 630 682-9170
  Carol Stream (G-3065)

GAMES & TOYS: Puzzles
Hart Puzzles Inc .... G 847 910-2290
  Bensenville (G-1817)
Puzzles Bus Off Solutions Inc .... G 773 891-7688
  Chicago (G-5918)

GAMES & TOYS: Sleds, Children's
Pacific Cycle Inc .... C 618 393-2508
  Olney (G-15882)

GAMES & TOYS: Strollers, Baby, Vehicle
Nelson-Whittaker Ltd .... E 815 459-6000
  Crystal Lake (G-7237)

GAMES & TOYS: Trains & Eqpt, Electric & Mechanical
Lake County C V Joints Inc .... G 847 537-7588
  Wheeling (G-20928)

GAMES & TOYS: Wagons, Coaster, Express & Play, Children's
Narita Manufacturing Inc .... F 248 345-1777
  Belvidere (G-1688)
Oakridge Corporation .... G 630 435-5900
  Lemont (G-12574)

Radio Flyer Inc .... E 773 637-7100
  Chicago (G-5959)

GARAGE DOOR REPAIR SVCS
Builders Chicago Corporation .... D 224 654-2122
  Rosemont (G-18001)

GARBAGE CONTAINERS: Plastic
AAA Trash .... G 618 775-1365
  Odin (G-15833)
Kevs Kans Inc .... G 309 303-3999
  Roanoke (G-17102)
MCS Midwest LLC .... G 314 398-8107
  Granite City (G-10723)
T2 Site Amenities Incorporated .... G 847 579-9003
  Highland Park (G-11302)

GARBAGE DISPOSERS & COMPACTORS: Commercial
Area Disposal Service Inc .... F 217 935-1300
  Clinton (G-6919)
Azcon Inc .... F 815 548-7000
  Sterling (G-19499)
Covington Service Installation .... G 309 376-4921
  Carlock (G-2885)

GAS & HYDROCARBON LIQUEFACTION FROM COAL
Oq 168 NM Propco LLC .... G 312 542-6116
  Chicago (G-5687)

GAS & OIL FIELD EXPLORATION SVCS
Angel Rose Energy LLC .... G 618 392-3700
  Olney (G-15853)
Bell Brothers .... G 618 544-2157
  Robinson (G-17107)
Benchmark Properties Ltd .... G 618 395-7023
  Olney (G-15855)
Citation Oil & Gas Corp .... F 618 548-2331
  Odin (G-15834)
Crawford County Oil LLC .... E 618 544-3493
  Robinson (G-17109)
Digital H2o Inc .... F 847 456-8424
  Chicago (G-4360)
Drig Corporation .... D 312 265-1509
  Rosemont (G-18020)
Energy Group Inc .... E 847 836-2000
  Dundee (G-8127)
Ion Inc .... G 224 875-1313
  Lincolnshire (G-12775)
J H Robison & Associates Ltd .... G 847 559-9662
  Northbrook (G-15408)
L C Neelydrilling Inc .... G 618 544-2726
  Robinson (G-17118)
Lla Exploration Inc .... G 217 623-4096
  Taylorville (G-19758)
Map Oil Co Inc .... G 618 375-7616
  Grayville (G-10813)
Martin Exploration Mgt Co .... G 708 385-6500
  Alsip (G-472)
Mid States Salvage .... G 618 842-6741
  Fairfield (G-9632)
Midco Exploration Inc .... G 630 655-2198
  Westmont (G-20759)
Midwest Oil Co Inc .... G 847 928-9999
  Schiller Park (G-18826)
Mohican Petroleum Inc .... G 312 782-6385
  Chicago (G-5485)
Moran Properties Inc .... G 312 440-1962
  Chicago (G-5498)
Murphy USA Inc .... G 630 801-4950
  Montgomery (G-14264)
Murvin & Meir Oil Co .... G 618 395-4405
  Olney (G-15876)
Murvin Oil Company .... E 618 393-2124
  Olney (G-15877)
Northern Illinois Gas Company .... E 630 983-8676
  Kankakee (G-11993)

Employee Codes: A=Over 500 employees, B=251-500
C=101-250, D=51-100, E=20-50, F=10-19, G=3-9

GAS & OIL FIELD EXPLORATION SVCS

Northern Illinois Gas Company .... F 217 357-3105
  Carthage *(G-3141)*
Northern Illinois Gas Company .... C 630 983-8676
  Crystal Lake *(G-7240)*
Northern Illinois Gas Company .... D 815 433-3850
  Ottawa *(G-16065)*
Northern Illinois Gas Company .... C 815 693-3907
  Joliet *(G-11908)*
Northern Illinois Gas Company .... F 815 223-8097
  Mendota *(G-13951)*
Ofgd Inc .... G 708 283-7101
  Olympia Fields *(G-15897)*
Oil and Gas Discoverer LLC .... F 847 877-1257
  Highland Park *(G-11289)*
Stevenson Oil Inc .... G 773 237-6185
  Chicago *(G-6247)*
Stewart Producers Inc .... G 618 244-3754
  Mount Vernon *(G-14640)*
Tenexco Inc .... G 708 771-7870
  Oakbrook Terrace *(G-15816)*
Third Day Oil & Gas LLC .... G 618 553-5538
  Oblong *(G-15831)*
Times Energy .... G 773 444-9282
  Worth *(G-21456)*
Woodrow Todd .... G 618 838-9105
  Flora *(G-9697)*

GAS & OIL FIELD SVCS, NEC

Evergreen Marathon .... G 708 636-5700
  Evergreen Park *(G-9594)*
R Energy LLC .... G 618 382-7313
  Carmi *(G-2913)*

GAS FIELD MACHINERY & EQPT

Alin Machining Company Inc .... C 708 681-1043
  Melrose Park *(G-13821)*
Mueller Co LLC .... E 217 423-4471
  Decatur *(G-7528)*

GAS PROCESSING SVC

East St Louis Trml & Stor Co .... E 618 271-2185
  East Saint Louis *(G-8306)*

GAS PRODUCTION & DISTRIBUTION: Mixed Natural & Manufactured

Vantage Specialties Inc .... D 773 376-9000
  Gurnee *(G-10943)*

GAS STATIONS

Joe Anthony & Associates .... G 708 935-0804
  Richton Park *(G-17029)*
K & J Synthetic Lubricants .... G 630 628-1011
  Addison *(G-164)*

GAS: Refinery

Shell Oil Company .... C 618 254-7371
  Wood River *(G-21267)*

GASES & LIQUIFIED PETROLEUM GASES

Lub-Tek Petroleum Products .... G 815 741-0414
  Joliet *(G-11895)*
Suma America Inc .... G 847 427-7880
  Glenview *(G-10629)*

GASES: Acetylene

Gano Welding Supplies Inc .... F 217 345-3777
  Charleston *(G-3402)*

GASES: Carbon Dioxide

Continental Carbonic Pdts Inc .... E 217 428-2068
  Decatur *(G-7476)*
Maccarb Inc .... G 877 427-2499
  Elgin *(G-8645)*
Messer LLC .... E 309 353-9717
  Pekin *(G-16344)*

GASES: Flourinated Hydrocarbon

Hudson Technologies Inc .... E 217 373-1414
  Champaign *(G-3304)*
Solvay USA Inc .... E 708 235-7200
  University Park *(G-19967)*

GASES: Helium

Boc Global Helium Inc .... C 630 897-1900
  Montgomery *(G-14235)*
Hands To Work Railroading .... G 708 489-9776
  Alsip *(G-454)*

GASES: Hydrogen

Hydrogen Education Council .... G 630 681-1732
  Wheaton *(G-20805)*
Industrial Gas Products Inc .... G 618 337-1030
  East Saint Louis *(G-8312)*

GASES: Indl

Air Liquide America LP .... G 815 747-6803
  East Dubuque *(G-8175)*
Air Products and Chemicals Inc .... E 618 452-5335
  Granite City *(G-10691)*
Air Products and Chemicals Inc .... E 815 223-2924
  La Salle *(G-12101)*
Air Products and Chemicals Inc .... D 618 451-0577
  Granite City *(G-10692)*
Air Products and Chemicals Inc .... E 815 423-5032
  Channahon *(G-3373)*
Airgas Inc .... F 773 785-3000
  Chicago *(G-3588)*
Airgas Usa LLC .... E 630 231-9260
  West Chicago *(G-20533)*
Airgas Usa LLC .... E 708 354-0813
  Countryside *(G-7043)*
Airgas Usa LLC .... G 618 439-7207
  Benton *(G-1917)*
AmeriGas .... D 708 544-1131
  Hillside *(G-11328)*
Brewer Company .... F 708 339-9000
  Harvey *(G-11080)*
Continental Carbonic Pdts Inc .... E 309 346-7515
  Pekin *(G-16326)*
Diversified CPC Intl Inc .... E 815 424-2000
  Channahon *(G-3380)*
Ilmo Products Company .... E 217 245-2183
  Jacksonville *(G-11770)*
Matheson Tri-Gas Inc .... E 815 727-2202
  Joliet *(G-11899)*
Messer LLC .... F 630 690-3010
  Carol Stream *(G-3024)*
Messer North America Inc .... G 630 897-1900
  Montgomery *(G-14262)*
Messer North America Inc .... E 630 257-3612
  Lockport *(G-13012)*
Praxair Inc .... E 847 428-3405
  Gilberts *(G-10365)*
Praxair Inc .... G 708 728-9353
  Chicago *(G-5853)*
Praxair Inc .... F 309 347-5575
  Pekin *(G-16356)*
Praxair Distribution Inc .... E 314 664-7900
  Cahokia *(G-2763)*
Technical Propellants Inc .... F 815 942-2900
  Morris *(G-14332)*
Weldstar Company .... E 630 859-3100
  Aurora *(G-1169)*

GASES: Neon

Chicago Neon and Sign LLC .... G 708 255-5284
  Brookfield *(G-2480)*
Everbrite LLC .... G 618 242-0645
  Mount Vernon *(G-14610)*
Neon Nights Dj Svc .... G 309 820-9000
  Bloomington *(G-2082)*
Neon Street Productions .... G 217 304-4514
  Danville *(G-7368)*
Quality Neon Service .... G 847 299-2969
  Des Plaines *(G-7834)*
Shinn Enterprises .... G 217 698-3344
  Springfield *(G-19443)*

GASES: Nitrogen

Amer Nitrogen Co .... G 847 681-1068
  Highland Park *(G-11253)*
Matheson Tri-Gas Inc .... F 309 697-1933
  Mapleton *(G-13476)*
Messer LLC .... E 630 515-2576
  Naperville *(G-14869)*
Messer LLC .... E 618 251-5217
  Hartford *(G-11035)*
Nitrogen Labs Inc .... G 312 504-8134
  Chicago *(G-5605)*

GASES: Oxygen

Linde Gas North America LLC .... F 630 857-6460
  Broadview *(G-2449)*
Linde Gas North America LLC .... F 630 257-3108
  Lockport *(G-13006)*
Medicate Dme Inc .... F 618 874-3000
  East Saint Louis *(G-8314)*

GASKET MATERIALS

Pres-On Corporation .... E 630 628-2255
  Bolingbrook *(G-2229)*
Supreme Felt & Abrasives Inc .... E 708 344-0134
  Cicero *(G-6878)*

GASKETS

All Products Gasket .... G 877 255-8700
  Romeoville *(G-17789)*
American Gasket Tech Inc .... D 630 543-1510
  Addison *(G-33)*
Better Gaskets Inc .... E 847 276-7635
  Ingleside *(G-11579)*
Cal-Ill Gasket Co .... F 773 287-9605
  Chicago *(G-4002)*
Chambers Gasket & Mfg Co .... E 773 626-8800
  Chicago *(G-4068)*
Excelsior Inc .... E 815 987-2900
  Rockford *(G-17408)*
Excelsior Inc .... E 815 987-2900
  Rockford *(G-17407)*
Gasket & Seal Fabricators Inc .... E 314 241-3673
  East Saint Louis *(G-8308)*
Gaskoa Inc .... E 708 339-5000
  South Holland *(G-19213)*
Ilpea Industries Inc .... D 309 343-3332
  Galesburg *(G-10201)*
M Cor Inc .... F 630 860-1150
  Bensenville *(G-1846)*
Midwest Sealing Products Inc .... E 847 459-2202
  Buffalo Grove *(G-2575)*
Rhopac Fabricated Products LLC ..... E 847 362-3300
  Libertyville *(G-12702)*
Seals & Components Inc .... G 708 895-5222
  Lansing *(G-12514)*
Standard Rubber Products Co .... E 847 593-5630
  Elk Grove Village *(G-9252)*
Winner Cutting & Stamping Co .... F 630 963-1800
  Downers Grove *(G-8111)*
Woods Manufacturing Co Inc .... G 630 595-6620
  Wood Dale *(G-21258)*

GASKETS & SEALING DEVICES

All American Washer Werks Inc .... E 847 566-9091
  Mundelein *(G-14661)*
Federal-Mogul Motorparts LLC .... E 248 354-7700
  Berwyn *(G-1954)*
Hennig Gasket & Seals Inc .... G 312 243-8270
  Chicago *(G-4803)*
John Crane Inc .... A 312 605-7800
  Chicago *(G-5039)*
John Crane Inc .... G 630 410-4444
  Bolingbrook *(G-2199)*
John Crane Inc .... G 847 967-2400
  Morton Grove *(G-14415)*
L A D Specialties .... G 708 430-1588
  Oak Lawn *(G-15724)*
Punch Products Manufacturing .... E 773 533-2800
  Chicago *(G-5915)*
Qcc LLC .... C 708 867-5400
  Harwood Heights *(G-11107)*
Rutgers Enterprises Inc .... G 847 674-7666
  Lincolnwood *(G-12841)*
Sealtec .... F 630 692-0633
  Montgomery *(G-14268)*
SKF USA Inc .... D 847 742-0700
  Elgin *(G-8736)*
Southland Industries Inc .... E 757 543-5701
  Bannockburn *(G-1208)*
Technetics Group LLC .... G 708 887-6080
  Harwood Heights *(G-11111)*

GASOLINE FILLING STATIONS

BP Products North America Inc .... G 630 420-4300
  Naperville *(G-14783)*
Carnaghi Towing & Repair Inc .... F 217 446-0333
  Tilton *(G-19793)*
Equilon Enterprises LLC .... F 312 733-1849
  Chicago *(G-4523)*

PRODUCT SECTION

GIFTS & NOVELTIES: Wholesalers

Lakenburges Motor Co .... G 618 523-4231
  Germantown (G-10331)
Murphy USA Inc .... G 815 463-9963
  New Lenox (G-15044)
Murphy USA Inc .... F 815 337-2440
  Woodstock (G-21416)
Murphy USA Inc .... G 847 245-3283
  Round Lake Beach (G-18091)
Murphy USA Inc .... F 815 936-6144
  Kankakee (G-11992)

GASTROINTESTINAL OR GENITOURINARY SYSTEM DRUGS

Joseph B Pigato MD Ltd .... G 815 937-2122
  Kankakee (G-11983)

GATES: Dam, Metal Plate

BJs Welding Services Etc Co .... G 773 964-5836
  Chicago (G-3905)

GATES: Ornamental Metal

Tim Detwiler Enterprises Inc .... G 815 758-9950
  Dekalb (G-7709)

GAUGES

Accu-Grind Manufacturing Inc .... F 847 526-2700
  Wauconda (G-20327)
Active Grinding & Mfg Co .... F 708 344-0510
  Broadview (G-2414)
Air Gage Company .... C 847 695-0911
  Elgin (G-8500)
Barcor Inc .... F 847 940-0750
  Bannockburn (G-1192)
Dundick Corporation .... E 708 656-6363
  Cicero (G-6843)
Gage Assembly Co .... G 847 679-5180
  Lincolnwood (G-12820)
K Systems Corporation .... G 708 449-0400
  Hillside (G-11343)
Thread & Gage Co Inc .... G 815 675-2305
  Spring Grove (G-19302)

GEARS

Clark Gear Works Inc .... G 630 561-2320
  Carol Stream (G-2962)
Eduardo Enterprises Inc .... G 708 599-9700
  Bridgeview (G-2345)
Excel Gear Inc .... F 815 623-3414
  Roscoe (G-17906)
J & L Gear Incorporated .... F 630 832-1880
  Villa Park (G-20151)
Ken Elliott Co .... G 618 466-8200
  Godfrey (G-10654)
Process Screw Products Inc .... E 815 864-2220
  Shannon (G-18872)
Raycar Gear & Machine Company . E 815 874-3948
  Rockford (G-17566)

GEARS & GEAR UNITS: Reduction, Exc Auto

Gam Enterprises Inc .... E 847 649-2500
  Mount Prospect (G-14530)
Overton Chicago Gear Corp .... D 773 638-0508
  Chicago (G-5719)

GEARS: Power Transmission, Exc Auto

Allied Gear Co .... G 773 287-8742
  River Forest (G-17049)
American Gear Inc .... F 815 537-5111
  Prophetstown (G-16830)
Engelhardt Gear Co .... E 847 766-7070
  Elk Grove Village (G-8978)
Fact NA LLC .... G 847 421-1125
  Hoffman Estates (G-11422)
Hadley Gear Manufacturing Co ..... F 773 722-1030
  Chicago (G-4765)
LI Gear Inc .... G 630 226-1688
  Romeoville (G-17843)
Martin Sprocket & Gear Inc .... F 847 298-8844
  Des Plaines (G-7800)
Omni Gear and Machine Corp ...... F 815 723-4327
  Joliet (G-11911)
Prophet Gear Co .... E 815 537-2002
  Prophetstown (G-16834)
Reliance Gear Corporation .... D 630 543-6640
  Addison (G-270)

GELATIN

Gelita USA Chicago .... F 708 891-8400
  Calumet City (G-2776)
In3gredients Inc .... G 312 577-4275
  Chicago (G-4904)
Vyse Gelatin LLC .... E 847 678-4780
  Schiller Park (G-18852)

GEM STONES MINING, NEC: Natural

Professional Gem Sciences Inc .... G 312 920-1541
  Chicago (G-5897)

GEMSTONE & INDL DIAMOND MINING SVCS

Diamond Icic Corporation .... E 309 269-8652
  Rock Island (G-17218)

GENEALOGICAL INVESTIGATION SVCS

Moultri Cnty Hstrcl/Gnlgcl Sct .... F 217 728-4085
  Sullivan (G-19672)

GENERAL & INDUSTRIAL LOAN INSTITUTIONS

Knowles Elec Holdings Inc .... A 630 250-5100
  Itasca (G-11687)

GENERAL COUNSELING SVCS

Comwell .... D 618 282-6233
  Red Bud (G-16991)
Kccdd Inc .... D 309 344-2030
  Galesburg (G-10205)

GENERAL MERCHANDISE, NONDURABLE, WHOLESALE

Bee Sales Company .... D 847 600-4400
  Niles (G-15106)
C B E Inc .... G 630 571-2610
  Oak Brook (G-15603)
Corporation Supply Co Inc .... E 312 726-3375
  Chicago (G-4241)
D S Arms Incorporated .... E 847 277-7258
  Lake Barrington (G-12147)

GENERATING APPARATUS & PARTS: Electrical

Ees Inc .... G 708 343-1800
  Stone Park (G-19553)
Mecc Alte Inc .... F 815 344-0530
  McHenry (G-13767)

GENERATION EQPT: Electronic

10g LLC .... F 630 754-2400
  Woodridge (G-21269)
A J R International Inc .... D 800 232-3965
  Glendale Heights (G-10435)
Ametek Inc .... C 847 596-7000
  Waukegan (G-20416)
B&Bimc LLC .... D 815 433-5100
  Ottawa (G-16040)
Charles Industries LLC .... D 847 806-6300
  Schaumburg (G-18474)
Delta-Unibus Corp .... C 708 409-1200
  Northlake (G-15545)
Ees Inc .... G 708 343-1800
  Stone Park (G-19553)
Hauhinco LP .... E 618 993-5399
  Marion (G-13514)
Jf Industries Inc .... G 773 775-8840
  Chicago (G-5028)
Panatrol Corporation .... E 630 655-4700
  Burr Ridge (G-2713)
Powell Electrical Systems Inc .... C 708 409-1200
  Northlake (G-15555)
Powell Electrical Systems Inc .... C 708 409-1200
  Northlake (G-15556)
Powervar Inc .... C 847 596-7000
  Waukegan (G-20480)
Rauckman Utility Products LLC .... F 618 234-0001
  Belleville (G-1587)
Seidel Diesel Group .... D 877 373-6659
  Bolingbrook (G-2236)
Slaughter Company Inc .... E 847 932-3662
  Lake Forest (G-12303)
We International .... G 618 549-1784
  Carbondale (G-2863)

GENERATOR REPAIR SVCS

Lionheart Critical Pow .... E 847 291-1413
  Huntley (G-11552)

GENERATORS SETS: Steam

Alin Machining Company Inc .... C 708 681-1043
  Melrose Park (G-13821)

GENERATORS: Electric

CGprofessional Services Inc .... G 708 389-4110
  Orland Park (G-15947)

GENERATORS: Storage Battery Chargers

Performance Battery Group Inc .... G 630 293-5505
  West Chicago (G-20628)

GENERATORS: Vehicles, Gas-Electric Or Oil-Electric

Advanced Enrgy Solutions Group .. F 618 988-0888
  Carterville (G-3128)
Eco Green Analytics LLC .... G 847 691-1148
  Deerfield (G-7608)

GERIATRIC SOCIAL SVCS

Oakland Noodle Company .... G 217 346-2322
  Oakland (G-15819)

GIFT SHOP

Academy Screenprinting Awards .. G 309 686-0026
  Peoria (G-16374)
Bestpysanky Inc .... G 877 797-2659
  Morton Grove (G-14391)
Enesco LLC .... B 630 875-5300
  Itasca (G-11650)
Euromarket Designs Inc .... A 847 272-2888
  Northbrook (G-15386)
Galena Cellars Winery .... E 815 777-3330
  Galena (G-10169)
Heartfelt Gifts Inc .... G 309 852-2296
  Kewanee (G-12039)
In The Attic Inc .... G 847 949-5077
  Mundelein (G-14699)
Initial Choice .... F 847 234-5884
  Lake Forest (G-12267)
Kickapoo Creek Winery .... G 309 495-9463
  Edwards (G-8338)
Little Shop of Papers Ltd .... G 847 382-7733
  Barrington (G-1225)
M J Burton Engraving Co .... G 217 223-7273
  Quincy (G-16908)
Mangel and Co .... E 847 459-3100
  Buffalo Grove (G-2567)
Marley Candles .... E 815 485-6604
  Mokena (G-14097)
Motherboard Gifts & More LLC .... G 847 550-2222
  Lake Zurich (G-12436)
Royal Oak Farm Inc .... F 815 648-4141
  Harvard (G-11066)
Thia & Co .... G 630 510-9770
  Wheaton (G-20828)
Twin City Awards .... G 309 452-9291
  Normal (G-15226)
Virtu .... G 773 235-3790
  Chicago (G-6555)
Workshop .... E 815 777-2211
  Galena (G-10183)

GIFT, NOVELTY & SOUVENIR STORES: Party Favors

Paper Moon Recycling Inc .... G 847 548-8875
  Grayslake (G-10795)

GIFT, NOVELTY & SOUVENIR STORES: Trading Cards, Sports

Fielders Choice .... G 618 937-2294
  West Frankfort (G-20671)

GIFTS & NOVELTIES: Wholesalers

Afar Imports & Interiors Inc .... G 217 744-3262
  Springfield (G-19316)
Alpha Acrylic Design .... G 847 818-8178
  Arlington Heights (G-687)

Employee Codes: A=Over 500 employees, B=251-500
C=101-250, D=51-100, E=20-50, F=10-19, G=3-9

GIFTS & NOVELTIES: Wholesalers

Award Concepts Inc .... E 630 513-7801
  Saint Charles *(G-18153)*
Bella Casa .... G 630 455-5900
  Hinsdale *(G-11365)*
Bestpysanky Inc .... G 877 797-2659
  Morton Grove *(G-14391)*
C Becky & Company Inc .... G 847 818-1021
  Mount Prospect *(G-14516)*
Fragrance Island Inc .... G 773 488-2700
  Chicago *(G-4628)*
George Lauterer Corporation .... E 312 913-1881
  Chicago *(G-4682)*
Icandee LLC .... G 773 754-0493
  Chicago *(G-4871)*
Morton Suggestion Company LLC .... G 847 255-4770
  Mount Prospect *(G-14549)*
Recycled Paper Greetings Inc .... G 773 348-6410
  Chicago *(G-5991)*

GLACE, FOR GLAZING FOOD

Capol LLC .... G 224 545-5095
  Deerfield *(G-7599)*

GLASS & GLASS CERAMIC PRDTS, PRESSED OR BLOWN: Tableware

Corelle Brands LLC .... C 847 233-8600
  Rosemont *(G-18010)*

GLASS FABRICATORS

Bertco Enterprises Inc .... G 618 234-9283
  Belleville *(G-1535)*
Biomerieux Inc .... E 630 628-6055
  Lombard *(G-13046)*
Boom Company Inc .... G 847 459-6199
  Wheeling *(G-20863)*
Central Illinois Glass & .... G 309 367-4242
  Metamora *(G-13960)*
Ceramic Designs Unlimited .... G 708 758-0690
  Chicago Heights *(G-6738)*
Circle Studio Stained Glass .... G 847 432-7249
  Highland Park *(G-11258)*
Circle Studio Stained Glass .... G 773 588-4848
  Chicago *(G-4152)*
Cristaux Inc .... G 312 778-8800
  Elk Grove Village *(G-8921)*
Engineered Glass Products LLC .... C 312 326-4710
  Chicago *(G-4508)*
Engineered Glass Products LLC .... E 773 843-1964
  Chicago *(G-4507)*
Gerresheimer Glass Inc .... C 708 843-4246
  Chicago Heights *(G-6747)*
Glass Dimensions Inc .... F 708 410-2305
  Melrose Park *(G-13874)*
Glazed Structures Inc .... F 847 223-4560
  Grayslake *(G-10776)*
Legend Dynamix Inc .... G 847 789-7007
  Antioch *(G-622)*
Marsco Glass Products LLC .... D 312 326-4710
  Chicago *(G-5349)*
Martin Glass Company .... F 618 277-1946
  Belleville *(G-1571)*
Metal Products Sales Corp .... G 708 301-6844
  Lockport *(G-13013)*
Montclare Scientific Glass .... G 847 255-6870
  Arlington Heights *(G-777)*
Montrose Glass & Mirror Corp .... G 773 478-6433
  Chicago *(G-5494)*
Mth Enterprises LLC .... D 708 498-1100
  Hillside *(G-11349)*
Nexus Corporation .... E 217 303-5544
  Pana *(G-16218)*
Norman P Moeller .... G 847 991-3933
  Lake Barrington *(G-12162)*
OBrien Scntfic GL Blowing LLC .... G 217 762-3636
  Monticello *(G-14283)*
Oi Glass Containers Oi G9 .... G 815 673-5120
  Streator *(G-19618)*
Pilkington North America Inc .... C 815 433-0932
  Ottawa *(G-16072)*
Precision Screen Specialties .... G 630 220-1361
  Saint Charles *(G-18250)*
River City Millwork Inc .... D 800 892-9297
  Rockford *(G-17573)*
Roscoe Glass Co .... G 815 623-6268
  Roscoe *(G-17928)*
S P Industries Inc .... E 847 228-2851
  Elk Grove Village *(G-9226)*
Shoreline Glass Co Inc .... E 312 829-9500
  Hillside *(G-11356)*

Stained Glass of Peoria .... G 309 674-7929
  Peoria *(G-16529)*
Tafco Corporation .... E 847 678-8425
  Melrose Park *(G-13921)*
Tonjon Company .... F 630 208-1173
  Geneva *(G-10312)*
Torstenson Glass Co .... E 773 525-0435
  Chicago *(G-6397)*
Tuminello Enterprizes Inc .... G 815 416-1007
  Morris *(G-14334)*
Tuminello Enterprizes Inc .... G 815 416-1007
  Morris *(G-14335)*

GLASS PRDTS, FROM PURCHASED GLASS: Art

Lotton Art Glass Co .... G 708 672-1400
  Crete *(G-7141)*
New Century Picture Corp .... E 773 638-8888
  Chicago *(G-5575)*
Specialty Selected Ltd .... G 847 967-1701
  Skokie *(G-19033)*

GLASS PRDTS, FROM PURCHASED GLASS: Glassware

Lead n Glass Tm .... F 847 255-2074
  Wheeling *(G-20930)*
Monogram of Evanston Inc .... G 847 864-8100
  Evanston *(G-9555)*

GLASS PRDTS, FROM PURCHASED GLASS: Glassware, Indl

Enameled Steel and Sign Co .... E 773 481-2270
  Chicago *(G-4504)*

GLASS PRDTS, FROM PURCHASED GLASS: Insulating

Duo Plex Glass Ltd .... G 708 532-4422
  Palos Hills *(G-16200)*
Illinois Valley Glass & Mirror .... F 309 682-6603
  Peoria *(G-16457)*

GLASS PRDTS, FROM PURCHASED GLASS: Mirrored

Lester L Brossard Co .... F 815 338-7825
  Woodstock *(G-21405)*
See All Industries Inc .... F 773 927-3232
  Chicago *(G-6130)*

GLASS PRDTS, FROM PURCHASED GLASS: Mirrors, Framed

Sarj USA Inc .... E 708 865-9134
  Franklin Park *(G-10043)*

GLASS PRDTS, FROM PURCHASED GLASS: Novelties, Fruit, Etc

Bards Products Inc .... E 800 323-5499
  Mundelein *(G-14665)*
Glass Haus .... G 815 459-5849
  McHenry *(G-13746)*
Howw Manufacturing Company Inc .... E 847 382-4380
  Lake Barrington *(G-12150)*
Skyline Design Inc .... D 773 278-4660
  Chicago *(G-6184)*

GLASS PRDTS, FROM PURCHASED GLASS: Ornaments, Christmas Tree

Ornament Shop Co Inc .... D 847 559-8844
  Northbrook *(G-15449)*

GLASS PRDTS, FROM PURCHASED GLASS: Sheet, Bent

Brenda Miller .... G 618 678-2639
  Xenia *(G-21467)*

GLASS PRDTS, FROM PURCHASED GLASS: Windshields

Glass America Midwest LLC .... G 877 743-7237
  Elmhurst *(G-9366)*
Pro Glass Corporation .... G 630 553-3141
  Bristol *(G-2409)*

GLASS PRDTS, PRESSED OR BLOWN: Blocks & Bricks

Lang Exterior Inc .... D 773 737-4500
  Chicago *(G-5175)*
Roth Metal Fabricators Corp .... G 708 371-8300
  Alsip *(G-505)*

GLASS PRDTS, PRESSED OR BLOWN: Bulbs, Electric Lights

Tadd LLC .... F 847 380-3540
  Cary *(G-3194)*

GLASS PRDTS, PRESSED OR BLOWN: Glassware, Art Or Decorative

Amkine Inc .... F 847 526-7088
  Wauconda *(G-20331)*
Finer Line Inc .... F 847 884-1611
  Itasca *(G-11657)*
Libation Container Inc .... G 312 636-7206
  Chicago *(G-5217)*

GLASS PRDTS, PRESSED OR BLOWN: Glassware, Novelty

Hunter Mfg LLP .... D 859 254-7573
  Lake Forest *(G-12262)*

GLASS PRDTS, PRESSED OR BLOWN: Ornaments, Christmas Tree

Mattarusky Inc .... G 630 469-4125
  Glen Ellyn *(G-10412)*

GLASS PRDTS, PRESSED OR BLOWN: Scientific Glassware

OBrien Scntfic GL Blowing LLC .... G 217 762-3636
  Monticello *(G-14283)*
Upper Limits Midwest Inc .... G 217 679-4315
  Springfield *(G-19467)*

GLASS PRDTS, PRESSED OR BLOWN: Tubing

Cleavenger Associates Inc .... G 630 221-0007
  Winfield *(G-21109)*

GLASS PRDTS, PRESSED/BLOWN: Glassware, Art, Decor/Novelty

Altamira Art Glass .... G 708 848-3799
  Oak Park *(G-15744)*
Arttig Art .... G 847 804-8001
  Wheeling *(G-20851)*
For Our Generation Inc .... G 312 282-1257
  Deerfield *(G-7609)*

GLASS PRDTS, PURCHD GLASS: Furniture Top, Cut, Beveld/Polshd

J K Custom Countertops .... G 630 495-2324
  Lombard *(G-13088)*

GLASS PRDTS, PURCHSD GLASS: Ornamental, Cut, Engraved/Décor

Besco Awards & Embroidery .... G 847 395-4862
  Antioch *(G-603)*
Ostrom & Co Inc .... F 503 281-6469
  Winfield *(G-21113)*
Slee Corporation .... E 773 777-2444
  Itasca *(G-11733)*
State Street Jewelers Inc .... F 630 232-2085
  Geneva *(G-10307)*

GLASS STORE: Leaded Or Stained

Stained Glass of Peoria .... G 309 674-7929
  Peoria *(G-16529)*
T J M & Associates Inc .... G 847 382-1993
  Wauconda *(G-20396)*
U R On It .... G 847 382-0182
  Lake Barrington *(G-12167)*

GLASS STORES

Duo Plex Glass Ltd .... G 708 532-4422
  Palos Hills *(G-16200)*

Fuyao Glass Illinois Inc .... C .... 217 864-2392 Decatur *(G-7495)* Martin Glass Company .... F .... 618 277-1946 Belleville *(G-1571)* Montrose Glass & Mirror Corp .... G .... 773 478-6433 Chicago *(G-5494)* Oldcastle Buildingenvelope Inc .... G .... 773 523-8400 Chicago *(G-5671)* Shoreline Glass Co Inc .... E .... 312 829-9500 Hillside *(G-11356)*	**GLASS: Tempered** Oldcastle Buildingenvelope Inc .... G .... 773 523-8400 Chicago *(G-5671)* Oldcastle Buildingenvelope Inc .... E .... 630 250-7270 Elk Grove Village *(G-9161)*	**GLOVES: Plastic** Oak Technical LLC .... G .... 931 455-7011 Matteson *(G-13627)* Tradex International Inc .... D .... 216 651-4788 Elwood *(G-9465)*

GOLF GOODS & EQPT

GLASS: Fiber
Industrial Fiberglass Inc .... F 708 681-2707
Melrose Park *(G-13882)*

GLASS: Flat
Cat I Manufacturing Inc .... C 847 931-8986
South Elgin *(G-19140)*
Duo Plex Glass Ltd .... G 708 532-4422
Palos Hills *(G-16200)*
Engineered Glass Products LLC .... E 773 843-1964
Chicago *(G-4507)*
Fuyao Glass Illinois Inc .... C 217 864-2392
Decatur *(G-7495)*
Glazed Structures Inc .... F 847 223-4560
Grayslake *(G-10776)*
Great Lakes GL & Mirror Corp .... G 847 647-1036
Niles *(G-15126)*
Higgins Glass Studio LLC .... G 708 447-2787
Riverside *(G-17084)*
Montrose Glass & Mirror Corp .... G 773 478-6433
Chicago *(G-5494)*
Pilkington North America Inc .... C 815 433-0932
Ottawa *(G-16072)*
Pontiac Recyclers Inc .... G 815 844-6419
Pontiac *(G-16777)*
Thermal Ceramics Inc .... E 217 627-2101
Girard *(G-10386)*

GLASS: Indl Prdts
Montclare Scientific Glass .... G 847 255-6870
Arlington Heights *(G-777)*
Nippon Electric Glass Amer Inc .... G 630 285-8500
Schaumburg *(G-18649)*

GLASS: Insulating
Lang Exterior Inc .... D 773 737-4500
Chicago *(G-5175)*

GLASS: Pressed & Blown, NEC
Alpha Precision Inc .... F 630 553-7331
Yorkville *(G-21471)*
Barcor Inc .... F 847 940-0750
Bannockburn *(G-1192)*
Corelle Brands Holdings Inc .... D 847 233-8600
Rosemont *(G-18009)*
James R Wilbat Glass Studio .... G 847 940-0015
Deerfield *(G-7618)*
Libbey Inc .... A 630 818-3400
West Chicago *(G-20607)*
Lotton Art Glass Co .... G 708 672-1400
Crete *(G-7141)*
Norman P Moeller .... G 847 991-3933
Lake Barrington *(G-12162)*
Prairie Fire Glass Inc .... G 217 762-3332
Monticello *(G-14284)*
Punch Products Manufacturing .... E 773 533-2800
Chicago *(G-5915)*
Quality Coating Co .... F 815 875-3228
Princeton *(G-16822)*
Thermal Ceramics Inc .... E 217 627-2101
Girard *(G-10386)*

GLASS: Stained
Botti Studio of Architectural .... E 847 869-5933
Glenview *(G-10532)*
Colorsmith Stained GL Studio .... G 708 447-8763
Riverside *(G-17083)*
G & R Stained Glass .... G 847 455-7026
Franklin Park *(G-9948)*
Glass Fx .... G 217 359-0048
Champaign *(G-3295)*
Tiffany Stained Glass Ltd .... G 312 642-0680
Forest Park *(G-9726)*
Will Hamms Stained Glass .... F 847 255-2230
Arlington Heights *(G-833)*

GLASSWARE STORES
Altamira Art Glass .... G 708 848-3799
Oak Park *(G-15744)*
Crystal Cave .... F 847 251-1160
Glenview *(G-10540)*
Higgins Glass Studio LLC .... G 708 447-2787
Riverside *(G-17084)*

GLASSWARE WHOLESALERS
McCracken Label Co .... E 773 581-8860
Chicago *(G-5375)*

GLASSWARE: Cut & Engraved
Art Crystal II Enterprises Inc .... F 630 739-0222
Lyons *(G-13301)*
Crystal Cave .... F 847 251-1160
Glenview *(G-10540)*

GLASSWARE: Laboratory
Supertek Scientific LLC .... G 630 345-3450
Addison *(G-300)*

GLASSWARE: Laboratory & Medical
Pure 111 .... G 618 558-7888
Caseyville *(G-3218)*

GLOBAL POSITIONING SYSTEMS & EQPT
Locusview Solutions Inc .... E 312 548-3848
Chicago *(G-5248)*
Safemobile Inc .... F 847 818-1649
Rolling Meadows *(G-17772)*
STC Inc .... E 618 643-2555
Mc Leansboro *(G-13708)*
Telular Corporation .... D 800 835-8527
Chicago *(G-6341)*

GLOBES, GEOGRAPHICAL
Replogle Globes Partners LLC .... G 708 593-3995
Hillside *(G-11354)*

GLOVES & MITTENS DYEING & FINISHING
Omar Medical Supplies Inc .... F 708 922-4276
Chicago *(G-5673)*

GLOVES: Fabric
Boss Manufacturing Company .... E 309 852-2131
Kewanee *(G-12024)*
Boss Manufacturing Holdings .... F 309 852-2781
Kewanee *(G-12025)*
Illinois Glove Company .... G 847 291-1700
Northbrook *(G-15402)*
Klein Tools Inc .... D 847 228-6999
Elk Grove Village *(G-9078)*
Klein Tools Inc .... E 847 821-5500
Lincolnshire *(G-12779)*
Kunz Glove Co Inc .... E 312 733-8780
Chicago *(G-5136)*
PW Masonry Inc .... G 847 573-0510
Libertyville *(G-12699)*

GLOVES: Leather
Boss Manufacturing Holdings .... F 309 852-2781
Kewanee *(G-12025)*

GLOVES: Leather, Work
Boss Holdings Inc .... D 309 852-2131
Kewanee *(G-12023)*
Kunz Glove Co Inc .... E 312 733-8780
Chicago *(G-5136)*
Magid Glove Safety Mfg Co LLC .... B 773 384-2070
Romeoville *(G-17844)*
Magid Glove Safety Mfg Co LLC .... B 773 384-2070
Chicago *(G-5316)*
Nationwide Glove Co Inc .... D 618 252-7192
Harrisburg *(G-11027)*

GLOVES: Safety
Boss Manufacturing Holdings .... F 309 852-2781
Kewanee *(G-12025)*
Enespro LLC .... G 630 332-2801
Oak Brook *(G-15617)*

GLOVES: Work
Boss Holdings Inc .... D 309 852-2131
Kewanee *(G-12023)*
Lamont Wells Industrial .... G 804 299-2557
Skokie *(G-18975)*
Magid Glove Safety Mfg Co LLC .... B 773 384-2070
Romeoville *(G-17844)*
Magid Glove Safety Mfg Co LLC .... B 773 384-2070
Chicago *(G-5316)*
Nationwide Glove Co Inc .... D 618 252-7192
Harrisburg *(G-11027)*
Wells Lamont Indust Group LLC .... A 800 247-3295
Skokie *(G-19055)*

GLUE
National Casein Co .... D 773 846-7300
Burr Ridge *(G-2707)*
National Casein Company .... D 773 846-7300
Burr Ridge *(G-2708)*

GO-CART DEALERS
Hopkins Saws & Karts Inc .... G 618 756-2778
Belle Rive *(G-1525)*

GOLD ORE MINING
Coeur Mining Inc .... D 312 489-5800
Chicago *(G-4194)*

GOLD ORES
Billy Cash For Gold Inc .... G 773 905-2447
Melrose Park *(G-13831)*

GOLF CARTS: Powered
Brewer Utility Systems Inc .... G 217 224-5975
Quincy *(G-16868)*

GOLF CLUB & EQPT REPAIR SVCS
Custom Golf By Tanis .... G 708 481-4433
Matteson *(G-13622)*

GOLF DRIVING RANGES
Pro Circle Golf Centers Inc .... G 815 675-2747
Spring Grove *(G-19295)*

GOLF EQPT
Amer Sports Company .... B 773 714-6400
Chicago *(G-3646)*
Custom Golf By Tanis .... G 708 481-4433
Matteson *(G-13622)*
EJL Custom Golf Clubs Inc .... G 630 654-8887
Willowbrook *(G-21041)*
Infiniti Golf .... G 630 520-0626
West Chicago *(G-20594)*
Kuldisak LLC .... G 847 772-7412
Northbrook *(G-15416)*
Par Golf Supply Inc .... E 847 891-1222
Schaumburg *(G-18663)*
Pro Circle Golf Centers Inc .... G 815 675-2747
Spring Grove *(G-19295)*

GOLF GOODS & EQPT
Brewer Utility Systems Inc .... G 217 224-5975
Quincy *(G-16868)*
Custom Golf By Tanis .... G 708 481-4433
Matteson *(G-13622)*
EJL Custom Golf Clubs Inc .... G 630 654-8887
Willowbrook *(G-21041)*
Oban Composites LLC .... G 866 607-0284
Chicago *(G-5649)*
Pro Circle Golf Centers Inc .... G 815 675-2747
Spring Grove *(G-19295)*

Employee Codes: A=Over 500 employees, B=251-500
C=101-250, D=51-100, E=20-50, F=10-19, G=3-9

GOURMET FOOD STORES

GOURMET FOOD STORES

Pappone Inc.................................G....... 630 234-4738
  Chicago *(G-5754)*

GOVERNMENT, EXECUTIVE OFFICES: Local

City of Chicago.............................E....... 312 744-0940
  Chicago *(G-4157)*

GOVERNMENT, EXECUTIVE OFFICES: Mayors'

City of Pekin................................F....... 309 477-2325
  Pekin *(G-16325)*

GOVERNMENT, EXECUTIVE OFFICES: State & Local

City of Toulon..............................G....... 309 286-7073
  Toulon *(G-19890)*

GOVERNMENT, GENERAL: Administration

City of Chicago.............................G....... 773 581-8000
  Chicago *(G-4158)*

GOVERNORS: Diesel Engine, Pump

Concentric Itasca Inc....................D....... 630 773-3355
  Itasca *(G-11638)*

GRADING SVCS

Thelen Sand & Gravel Inc.............D....... 847 838-8800
  Antioch *(G-636)*

GRAIN & FIELD BEANS WHOLESALERS

Cargill Incorporated......................G....... 630 739-1746
  Woodridge *(G-21280)*
Effingham Equity...........................F....... 217 268-5128
  Arcola *(G-648)*

GRANITE: Crushed & Broken

Martin Marietta Materials Inc.........F....... 618 285-6267
  Golconda *(G-10667)*
Pacific Granites Inc.......................G....... 312 835-7777
  Chicago *(G-5738)*

GRANITE: Cut & Shaped

AA Rigoni Brothers Inc..................E....... 815 838-9770
  Lockport *(G-12980)*
Carrera Stone Systems of Chica....E....... 847 566-2277
  Mundelein *(G-14673)*
Condor Granites Intl Inc.................G....... 847 635-7214
  Elgin *(G-8551)*
D & H Granite and Marble Sup......E....... 773 869-9988
  Chicago *(G-4297)*
Earth Stone Products III Inc..........G....... 847 671-3000
  Schiller Park *(G-18801)*
Ford Marble and Tile Inc...............F....... 618 475-2987
  New Athens *(G-15019)*
Granite Mountain Inc.....................G....... 708 774-1442
  New Lenox *(G-15036)*
House Granite & Marble Corp.......G....... 847 928-1111
  Schiller Park *(G-18814)*
Midwest Stone Sales Inc...............F....... 815 254-6600
  Plainfield *(G-16691)*
Monumental Art Works..................G....... 708 389-3038
  Blue Island *(G-2132)*
Pontiac Granite Company Inc.......G....... 815 842-1384
  Pontiac *(G-16776)*
Tri-State Cut Stone Co..................G....... 815 469-7550
  Frankfort *(G-9845)*
United Granite & Marble................G....... 815 582-3345
  Joliet *(G-11938)*
Wasowski Jacek............................G....... 847 693-1878
  Palatine *(G-16172)*

GRANITE: Dimension

Blue Pearl Stone Tech LLC............G....... 708 698-5700
  La Grange *(G-12073)*
Picture Stone Inc..........................G....... 773 875-5021
  Mount Prospect *(G-14562)*

GRAPHIC ARTS & RELATED DESIGN SVCS

A To Z Type & Graphic Inc.............G....... 312 587-1887
  Chicago *(G-3491)*

Allied Graphics Inc........................G....... 847 419-8830
  Buffalo Grove *(G-2508)*
Anderson Safford Mkg Graphics....F....... 847 827-8968
  Des Plaines *(G-7732)*
Arcsec Digital LLC.........................G....... 312 324-4794
  Lake Forest *(G-12225)*
ASap Specialties Inc Del................G....... 847 223-7699
  Grayslake *(G-10759)*
Bach & Associates.........................G....... 618 277-1652
  Belleville *(G-1532)*
Baseline Graphics Inc...................G....... 630 964-9566
  Downers Grove *(G-7958)*
Baum Holdings Inc........................G....... 847 488-0650
  South Elgin *(G-19135)*
Bindery & Distribution Service.......G....... 847 550-7000
  South Barrington *(G-19075)*
BT Steelle Investments Inc............G....... 618 410-0534
  Highland *(G-11206)*
Chicago Mltlingua Graphics Inc....F....... 847 386-7187
  Northfield *(G-15512)*
Comet Conection Inc.....................G....... 312 243-5400
  Alsip *(G-434)*
Communications Resource Inc.....G....... 630 860-1661
  Schaumburg *(G-18482)*
Corporate Graphics Inc..................G....... 630 762-9000
  Saint Charles *(G-18176)*
Crosstech Communications Inc....E....... 312 382-0111
  Chicago *(G-4273)*
Daxam Inc......................................F....... 847 214-1733
  Elgin *(G-8564)*
Dicianni Graphics Incorporated.....F....... 630 833-5100
  Addison *(G-91)*
Dixon Graphics Incorporated........G....... 217 351-6100
  Champaign *(G-3285)*
Donnas House of Type Inc............G....... 217 522-5050
  Athens *(G-896)*
Edwards Creative Services LLC....F....... 309 756-0199
  Milan *(G-14007)*
First Impression of Chicago...........G....... 773 224-3434
  Chicago *(G-4594)*
G & G Studios /Broadway Prtg......F....... 815 933-8181
  Bradley *(G-2282)*
Gfx International LLC....................G....... 847 543-7179
  Grayslake *(G-10774)*
Gh Printing Co Inc........................E....... 630 960-4115
  Downers Grove *(G-8010)*
Hopper Graphics Inc.....................G....... 708 489-0459
  Palos Heights *(G-16189)*
Innovtive Design Graphics Corp....G....... 847 475-7772
  Evanston *(G-9540)*
Jamali Kopy Kat Printing Inc.........G....... 708 544-6164
  Bellwood *(G-1629)*
Jans Graphics Inc.........................F....... 312 644-4700
  Chicago *(G-5006)*
Josephs Printing Service...............G....... 847 724-4429
  Glenview *(G-10576)*
Just Your Type Inc.........................G....... 847 864-8890
  Evanston *(G-9543)*
Laser Expressions Ltd...................G....... 847 419-9600
  Buffalo Grove *(G-2559)*
Legend Promotions........................G....... 847 438-3528
  Lake Zurich *(G-12428)*
Lloyd Midwest Graphics.................G....... 815 282-8828
  Machesney Park *(G-13357)*
Lsc Communications Us LLC.......C....... 217 235-0561
  Mattoon *(G-13642)*
Luttrell Engraving Inc....................E....... 708 489-3800
  Alsip *(G-470)*
Meltdown Creative Works Inc........G....... 309 310-1978
  Bloomington *(G-2074)*
Nosco Inc......................................E....... 847 336-4200
  Gurnee *(G-10903)*
Pelegan Inc...................................G....... 708 442-9797
  Riverside *(G-17088)*
Phoenix Marketing Services..........F....... 630 616-8000
  Mundelein *(G-14726)*
Precise Digital Printing Inc............E....... 847 593-2645
  Bensenville *(G-1871)*
Prime Market Targeting Inc...........E....... 815 469-4555
  Frankfort *(G-9826)*
R R Donnelley & Sons Company...C....... 312 326-8000
  Chicago *(G-5950)*
Royal Publishing Inc.....................G....... 309 343-4007
  Galesburg *(G-10219)*
RR Donnelley & Sons Company....C....... 312 236-8000
  Chicago *(G-6071)*
Sadannah Group LLC...................G....... 630 357-2300
  Naperville *(G-14912)*
Sandra E Greene..........................G....... 815 469-0092
  Frankfort *(G-9836)*

Shoreline Graphics Inc..................G....... 847 587-4804
  Ingleside *(G-11589)*
Sign & Banner Express..................G....... 630 783-9700
  Bolingbrook *(G-2239)*
Sommers & Fahrenbach Inc..........F....... 773 478-3033
  Chicago *(G-6201)*
Speedpro Imaging..........................G....... 847 856-8220
  Gurnee *(G-10929)*
T J Marche Ltd...............................G....... 618 445-2314
  Albion *(G-353)*
Van Meter Graphx Inc....................G....... 847 465-0600
  Wheeling *(G-21008)*
Vis-O-Graphic Inc..........................E....... 630 590-6100
  Addison *(G-331)*
Washburn Graficolor Inc................G....... 630 596-0880
  Naperville *(G-14944)*
Wyckoff Advertising Inc.................G....... 630 260-2525
  Wheaton *(G-20832)*
Xtrem Graphix Solutions Inc.........G....... 217 698-6424
  Springfield *(G-19469)*

GRAPHIC LAYOUT SVCS: Printed Circuitry

Laux Grafix Inc..............................E....... 618 337-4558
  East Saint Louis *(G-8313)*

GRATINGS: Open Steel Flooring

WEb Production & Fabg Inc...........F....... 312 733-6800
  Chicago *(G-6595)*

GRATINGS: Tread, Fabricated Metal

Cooper B-Line Inc.........................C....... 618 357-5353
  Pinckneyville *(G-16612)*
Gs Metals Corp..............................C....... 618 357-5353
  Pinckneyville *(G-16617)*
Midwest Cage Company................G....... 815 806-0005
  Frankfort *(G-9816)*
Paco Corporation...........................F....... 708 430-2424
  Bridgeview *(G-2371)*

GRAVE MARKERS: Concrete

Spence Monuments Co.................G....... 217 348-5992
  Charleston *(G-3413)*

GRAVEL & PEBBLE MINING

H & H Stone LLC...........................E....... 815 782-5700
  Bolingbrook *(G-2182)*
Valley Run Stone Inc.....................E....... 630 553-7974
  Yorkville *(G-21504)*

GRAVEL MINING

A E Frasz Inc................................F....... 630 232-6223
  Elburn *(G-8440)*
Allendale Gravel Co Inc.................F....... 618 263-3521
  Allendale *(G-402)*
Amigoni Construction....................G....... 309 923-3701
  Roanoke *(G-17098)*
C & H Gravel C Inc........................G....... 217 857-3425
  Teutopolis *(G-19765)*
Edk Construction Inc....................G....... 630 853-3484
  Darien *(G-7406)*
Elmhurst-Chicago Stone Company......E....... 630 832-4000
  Elmhurst *(G-9360)*
Gregory Gravel Co........................G....... 618 943-2796
  Lawrenceville *(G-12533)*
Hastie Min & Trckg Ltd Partnr.......E....... 618 289-4536
  Cave In Rock *(G-3219)*
Lake County Grading Co LLC.......D....... 847 362-2590
  Libertyville *(G-12665)*
Legacy Vulcan LLC........................F....... 815 895-6501
  Sycamore *(G-19722)*
Petersen Sand & Gravel Inc..........F....... 815 344-1060
  Lakemoor *(G-12473)*
Plote Construction Inc..................E....... 847 695-0422
  Hoffman Estates *(G-11444)*
Prosser Construction Co...............F....... 217 774-5032
  Shelbyville *(G-18884)*
Rock River Ready Mix Inc.............G....... 815 438-2510
  Rock Falls *(G-17194)*
Southfield Corporation...................E....... 309 676-0576
  Peoria *(G-16527)*
Thelen Sand & Gravel Inc.............D....... 847 838-8800
  Antioch *(G-636)*

GREASES & INEDIBLE FATS, RENDERED

Darling Ingredients Inc..................E....... 773 376-5550
  Chicago *(G-4319)*

PRODUCT SECTION　　　　　　　　　　　　　　　　　　　　　　　　　　HAIR CARE PRDTS

Kostelac Grease Service Inc .... E 314 436-7166
　Belleville *(G-1566)*

GREENHOUSES: Prefabricated Metal

Interntional Grnhse Contrs Inc .... E 217 443-0600
　Danville *(G-7352)*
Nexus Corporation .... E 217 303-5544
　Pana *(G-16218)*

GREETING CARD PAINTING BY HAND

Card Dynamix LLC .... C 630 685-4060
　Romeoville *(G-17803)*

GREETING CARD SHOPS

Full Line Printing Inc .... G 312 642-8080
　Chicago *(G-4640)*
Jane Stodden Bridals .... G 815 223-2091
　La Salle *(G-12116)*

GREETING CARDS WHOLESALERS

C Becky & Company Inc .... G 847 818-1021
　Mount Prospect *(G-14516)*
Crest Greetings Inc .... F 708 210-0800
　Chicago *(G-4269)*
Found Inc .... G 773 279-3000
　Chicago *(G-4624)*

GRILLES & REGISTERS: Ornamental Metal Work

Birdsell Machine & Orna Inc .... G 217 243-5849
　Jacksonville *(G-11759)*

GRINDING SVC: Precision, Commercial Or Indl

A J Carbide Grinding .... G 847 675-5112
　Skokie *(G-18911)*
A-B Die Mold Inc .... F 847 658-1199
　Bartlett *(G-1261)*
Abrasive West LLC .... G 630 736-0818
　Bartlett *(G-1262)*
Accu-Grind Manufacturing Inc .... F 847 526-2700
　Wauconda *(G-20327)*
B S Grinding Inc .... G 847 787-0770
　Elk Grove Village *(G-8854)*
BT & E Co .... G 815 544-6431
　Belvidere *(G-1657)*
Century Mold & Tool Co .... E 847 364-5858
　Elk Grove Village *(G-8886)*
Contour Tool Works Inc .... G 847 947-4700
　Palatine *(G-16106)*
Ever Ready Pin & Manufacturing ..... D 815 874-4949
　Rockford *(G-17403)*
Grind Lap Services Inc .... G 630 458-1111
　Addison *(G-143)*
HBm Electro Chemical Company ...... G 708 895-7710
　Lansing *(G-12497)*
Kasha Industries Inc .... E 618 375-2511
　Grayville *(G-10811)*
Nb Finishing Inc .... F 847 364-7500
　Melrose Park *(G-13897)*
Pioneer Service Inc .... E 630 628-0249
　Addison *(G-241)*
Prospect Grinding Incorporated .... G 847 229-9240
　Wheeling *(G-20966)*
Ro Pal Grinding Inc .... F 815 964-5894
　Rockford *(G-17580)*
Sterling Tool & Manufacturing .... G 847 304-1800
　Barrington *(G-1245)*

GRINDING SVCS: Ophthalmic Lens, Exc Prescription

Edgebrook Eyecare .... F 815 397-5959
　Rockford *(G-17390)*

GRINDSTONES: Artificial

C M C Industries Inc .... F 630 377-0530
　Saint Charles *(G-18161)*
Radiac Abrasives Inc .... C 618 548-4200
　Salem *(G-18354)*

GRIPS OR HANDLES: Rubber

Go Steady LLC .... G 630 293-3243
　West Chicago *(G-20588)*

GROCERIES WHOLESALERS, NEC

Ach Food Companies Inc .... C 708 458-8690
　Summit Argo *(G-19676)*
American Bottling Company .... B 708 947-5000
　Northlake *(G-15540)*
Chipita America Inc .... E 708 731-2434
　Westchester *(G-20693)*
Coca-Cola Refreshments USA Inc .... C 630 513-5247
　Saint Charles *(G-18171)*
Coca-Cola Refreshments USA Inc .... C 708 597-6700
　Alsip *(G-433)*
Coca-Cola Refreshments USA Inc .... D 708 597-4700
　Chicago *(G-4188)*
Coca-Cola Refreshments USA Inc .... D 309 697-8600
　Bartonville *(G-1329)*
E & J Gallo Winery 630 505-4000
　Lisle *(G-12886)*
Hillshire Brands Company .... C 847 956-7575
　Elk Grove Village *(G-9035)*
Ixtapa Foods 773 788-9701
　Chicago *(G-4980)*
Jewel Osco Inc .... C 630 584-4594
　Saint Charles *(G-18218)*
Kuna Meat Company Inc .... E 618 286-4000
　Dupo *(G-8139)*
Lee Gilster-Mary Corporation .... E 618 533-4808
　Centralia *(G-3237)*
Lewis Brothers Bakeries Inc .... E 708 531-6435
　Melrose Park *(G-13890)*
Noon Hour Food Products Inc .... E 312 382-1177
　Chicago *(G-5612)*
P-Americas LLC .... E 217 446-0123
　Danville *(G-7371)*
P-Americas LLC .... D 815 939-3123
　Kankakee *(G-11996)*
Sotiros Foods Inc 708 371-0002
　Alsip *(G-511)*
Vienna Beef Ltd .... E 773 278-7800
　Chicago *(G-6548)*

GROCERIES, GENERAL LINE WHOLESALERS

Abitec Corporation .... E 217 465-8577
　Paris *(G-16223)*
Arro Corporation .... G 773 978-1251
　Chicago *(G-3733)*
Arro Corporation .... C 708 352-8200
　Hodgkins *(G-11384)*
Arro Corporation 708 352-7412
　Hodgkins *(G-11385)*
Dzro-Bans International Inc 779 324-2740
　Homewood *(G-11492)*
Ixtapa Foods 773 788-9701
　Chicago *(G-4980)*
Iya Foods LLC .... G 630 854-7107
　North Aurora *(G-15264)*
Koenemann Sausage Co 815 385-6260
　Volo *(G-20201)*
Nader Wholesale Grocers Inc .... F 773 582-1000
　Chicago *(G-5536)*
Simu Ltd .... F 708 688-2200
　Mc Cook *(G-13701)*
Thomas Proestler .... G 630 971-0185
　Lisle *(G-12951)*
V Formusa Co .... F 224 938-9360
　Des Plaines *(G-7863)*

GROMMETS: Rubber

Rahco Rubber Inc .... D 847 298-4200
　Des Plaines *(G-7835)*

GROUTING EQPT: Concrete

Black Lab LLC .... G 440 285-3189
　Serena *(G-18863)*

GUARD SVCS

Embassy Security Group Inc .... E 800 627-1325
　Mokena *(G-14079)*

GUARDRAILS

R P Solutions LLC .... G 773 971-1363
　Chicago *(G-5948)*

GUARDS: Machine, Sheet Metal

Hennig Inc .... G 815 636-9900
　Machesney Park *(G-13347)*

GUIDED MISSILES & SPACE VEHICLES: Research & Development

Branmark Strategy Group LLC .... G 847 849-9080
　Glenview *(G-10534)*

GUIDED MISSILES/SPACE VEHICLE PARTS/AUX EQPT: Research/Devel

Azimuth Cnc Inc .... F 815 399-4433
　Rockford *(G-17310)*
Chemring Energetic Devices .... C 310 784-2100
　Downers Grove *(G-7967)*
Wilson Tool Corporation .... E 815 226-0147
　Rockford *(G-17687)*

GUM & WOOD CHEMICALS

Ryano Resins Inc .... G 630 621-5677
　Aurora *(G-1015)*

GUN PARTS MADE TO INDIVIDUAL ORDER

Oglesby & Oglesby Gunmakers .... G 217 487-7100
　Springfield *(G-19417)*

GUNSMITHS

Krebs Custom Inc .... G 847 487-7776
　Wauconda *(G-20368)*

GUTTERS

Four Seasons Gutter Prote .... G 309 694-4565
　East Peoria *(G-8268)*

GUTTERS: Sheet Metal

American Home Aluminium Co .... G 773 925-9442
　Calumet Park *(G-2794)*
Rollex Corporation .... C 847 437-3000
　Elk Grove Village *(G-9220)*

GYPSUM BOARD

United States Gypsum Company ..... B 312 606-4000
　Chicago *(G-6478)*
USG Corporation .... F 847 970-5200
　Libertyville *(G-12721)*
USG Corporation .... B 312 436-4000
　Chicago *(G-6506)*

GYPSUM PRDTS

Continental Studios Inc .... E 773 542-0309
　Chicago *(G-4230)*
Creative Perky Cuisine LLC .... G 312 870-0282
　Tinley Park *(G-19818)*
New Ngc Inc .... D 847 623-8100
　Waukegan *(G-20468)*
Owens Corning Sales LLC .... D 815 226-4627
　Rockford *(G-17545)*
Patrick Industries Inc .... E 630 595-0595
　Franklin Park *(G-10015)*

HAIR & HAIR BASED PRDTS

Afam Concept Inc .... C 773 838-1336
　Chicago *(G-3578)*
Beachwaver Co .... E 201 751-5625
　Libertyville *(G-12637)*
Hairline Creations Inc .... F 773 282-5454
　Chicago *(G-4769)*
Schmit Laboratories Inc .... E 773 476-0072
　Glendale Heights *(G-10491)*
Truvanity Beauty LLC .... G 312 778-6499
　Chicago *(G-6441)*

HAIR ACCESS: Rubber

Bows Arts Inc .... F 847 501-3161
　Glenview *(G-10533)*

HAIR CARE PRDTS

Anderson Lanette .... G 217 284-6603
　Springfield *(G-19318)*
Biocare Labs Inc .... G 708 496-8657
　Posen *(G-16791)*
Curlmix Inc .... G 773 234-6891
　Chicago *(G-4286)*
Ecoco Inc .... E 773 745-7700
　Chicago *(G-4448)*

Employee Codes: A=Over 500 employees, B=251-500
C=101-250, D=51-100, E=20-50, F=10-19, G=3-9

2020 Harris Illinois
Industrial Directory

1467

HAIR CARE PRDTS

Luster Products Inc .... B 773 579-1800
 Chicago *(G-5287)*
Market Ready Inc .... G 847 689-1000
 Round Lake Park *(G-18097)*
Moorket Inc .... G 888 275-0277
 South Holland *(G-19233)*
Namaste Laboratories LLC .... D 708 824-1393
 Chicago *(G-5539)*
Natural Beginnings .... G 773 457-0509
 Plainfield *(G-16693)*
Raani Corporation .... C 708 496-1035
 Bedford Park *(G-1496)*
Safe Effective Alternatives .... F 618 236-2727
 Belleville *(G-1595)*
Summit Laboratories Inc .... E 708 333-2995
 Harvey *(G-11097)*
VPI Holding Company LLC .... G 312 255-4800
 Chicago *(G-6572)*
Zotos International Inc .... C 847 390-0984
 Rosemont *(G-18061)*

HAIR CURLERS: Beauty Shop

Alliance For Illinois Mfg .... G 773 594-9292
 Chicago *(G-3616)*
Cindys Nail & Hair Care .... G 847 234-0780
 Lake Forest *(G-12237)*

HAIR NETS

Tradex International Inc .... D 216 651-4788
 Elwood *(G-9465)*

HAIR REPLACEMENT & WEAVING SVCS

Payne Chauna .... G 618 580-2584
 Belleville *(G-1583)*

HAIR STYLIST: Men

Abyss Salon Inc .... G 312 880-0263
 Chicago *(G-3512)*

HAIRDRESSERS

Truvanity Beauty LLC .... G 312 778-6499
 Chicago *(G-6441)*

HAMPERS: Solid Fiber, Made From Purchased Materials

Westrock Rkt LLC .... E 630 325-9670
 Burr Ridge *(G-2734)*

HAND TOOLS, NEC: Wholesalers

Advance Equipment Mfg Co ...... F 773 287-8220
 Chicago *(G-3555)*
Doerock Inc .... G 217 543-2101
 Arthur *(G-853)*
Remark Technologies Inc .... G 815 985-2972
 Rockford *(G-17571)*
Rockford Commercial Whse Inc . G 815 623-8400
 Machesney Park *(G-13371)*

HANDBAG STORES

Bag and Barrier Corporation ..... G 217 849-3271
 Toledo *(G-19874)*

HANDLES: Brush Or Tool, Plastic

Altamont Co .... D 800 626-5774
 Thomasboro *(G-19775)*
Phoenix Electric Mfg Co .... E 773 477-8855
 Chicago *(G-5802)*

HANDLES: Wood

Vaughan & Bushnell Mfg Co ..... F 815 648-2446
 Hebron *(G-11153)*

HANGERS: Garment, Plastic

Applied Arts & Sciences Inc ...... G 407 288-8228
 Mokena *(G-14072)*

HARD RUBBER PRDTS, NEC

Voss Belting & Specialty Co ..... E 847 673-8900
 Lincolnwood *(G-12849)*

HARDWARE

9161 Corporation .... G 847 470-8828
 Niles *(G-15097)*
Aco Inc .... E 773 774-5200
 Chicago *(G-3529)*
Advanced Custom Metals Inc ... G 847 803-2090
 Des Plaines *(G-7723)*
Advanced Machine & Engrg Co . C 815 962-6076
 Rockford *(G-17296)*
Afc Cable Systems Inc .... B 508 998-1131
 Harvey *(G-11070)*
Agena Manufacturing Co .... E 630 668-5086
 Carol Stream *(G-2928)*
Alan Manufacturing Corp .... G 815 568-6836
 Marengo *(G-13478)*
Aldon Co .... F 847 623-8800
 Waukegan *(G-20412)*
Allquip Co Inc .... G 309 944-6153
 Geneseo *(G-10239)*
American Partsmith Inc .... G 630 520-0432
 West Chicago *(G-20538)*
Ashland Door Solutions LLC .... G 773 348-5106
 Elk Grove Village *(G-8842)*
Baker Drapery Corporation .... G 309 691-3295
 Dunlap *(G-8132)*
Baron Manufacturing Co LLC ... E 630 628-9110
 Itasca *(G-11626)*
Bella Architectural Products ...... G 708 339-4782
 Harvey *(G-11078)*
Caterpillar Inc .... A 309 578-2473
 Mossville *(G-14456)*
Chas O Larson Co .... E 815 625-0503
 Rock Falls *(G-17179)*
Chicago Car Seal Company ..... G 773 278-9400
 Chicago *(G-4095)*
Chicago Hardware and Fix Co .. G 847 455-6609
 Franklin Park *(G-9905)*
Civiq Smartscapes LLC .... G 312 300-4776
 Chicago *(G-4165)*
Compx International Inc .... G 847 234-1864
 Lake Bluff *(G-12176)*
Congress Drive Inc .... E 972 875-6060
 Wilmette *(G-21074)*
Cooper B-Line Inc .... A 618 654-2184
 Highland *(G-11210)*
Crosby Group LLC .... G 708 333-3005
 Harvey *(G-11081)*
Del Storm Products Inc .... F 217 446-3377
 Danville *(G-7330)*
Du Bro Products Inc .... E 847 526-2136
 Wauconda *(G-20344)*
Dumore Supplies Inc .... F 312 949-6260
 Chicago *(G-4403)*
Dura Operating LLC .... C 815 947-3333
 Stockton *(G-19549)*
Engert Co Inc .... E 847 673-1633
 Skokie *(G-18950)*
Erwin Wiczer Industries Inc ...... G 847 541-9556
 Wheeling *(G-20893)*
Estwing Manufacturing Co Inc .. B 815 397-9521
 Rockford *(G-17402)*
Fenix Manufacturing LLC .... G 815 208-0755
 Fulton *(G-10151)*
Geib Industries Inc .... E 847 455-4550
 Bensenville *(G-1809)*
Hendrickson International Corp . C 815 727-4031
 Joliet *(G-11876)*
Honeywell Safety Pdts USA Inc C 630 343-3731
 Bolingbrook *(G-2185)*
Hyspan Precision Products Inc . E 773 277-0700
 South Holland *(G-19223)*
I Hardware Direct Inc .... G 708 325-0000
 Westmont *(G-20748)*
Industrial Rubber & Sup Entp ... G 217 429-3747
 Decatur *(G-7507)*
Inland Fastener Inc .... F 630 293-3800
 West Chicago *(G-20596)*
Jerome Remien Corporation ..... F 847 806-0888
 Elk Grove Village *(G-9067)*
Kemper Industries .... G 217 826-5712
 Marshall *(G-13573)*
MHS Ltd .... F 773 736-3333
 Chicago *(G-5419)*
Miwa Lock Co .... G 630 365-4261
 Elburn *(G-8462)*
Neisewander Enterprises Inc .... A 815 288-1431
 Dixon *(G-7904)*
Norforge and Machining Inc ..... D 309 772-3124
 Macomb *(G-13394)*
OBerry Enterprises Inc .... G 815 728-9480
 Ringwood *(G-17046)*
Oso900 Nfp .... G 312 206-4219
 Chicago *(G-5711)*
Peerless Industries Inc .... C 630 375-5100
 Aurora *(G-1006)*
Plews Inc .... C 815 288-3344
 Dixon *(G-7906)*
Prater Industries Inc .... D 630 679-3200
 Bolingbrook *(G-2228)*
Precision Brand Products Inc ... E 630 969-7200
 Downers Grove *(G-8082)*
Quality Hnge A Div Spreme Hnge E 708 534-7801
 University Park *(G-19966)*
Reichel Hardware Company Inc G 630 762-7394
 Saint Charles *(G-18261)*
Royal Brass Inc .... E 618 439-6341
 Benton *(G-1936)*
RPC Legacy Inc .... D 815 966-2000
 Rockford *(G-17616)*
S & D Products Inc .... G 630 372-2325
 Bartlett *(G-1306)*
S & S Hinge Company .... E 630 582-9500
 Bloomingdale *(G-2013)*
Seamless Gutter Corp .... G 630 495-9800
 Lombard *(G-13128)*
Shapco Inc .... G 847 229-1439
 Wheeling *(G-20982)*
SPEP Acquisition Corp .... G 310 608-0693
 Bolingbrook *(G-2246)*
Standard Truck Parts Inc .... E 815 726-4486
 Joliet *(G-11932)*
Thermos LLC .... D 847 439-7821
 Schaumburg *(G-18745)*
U S Tool & Manufacturing Co ... E 630 953-1000
 Addison *(G-321)*
Unistrut International Corp .... C 800 882-5543
 Harvey *(G-11099)*
Van Craft Industry of Del Edel .. G 708 430-6670
 Oak Lawn *(G-15738)*
Venturedyne Ltd .... E 708 597-7550
 Chicago *(G-6535)*
William Dudek Manufacturing Co E 773 622-2727
 Chicago *(G-6629)*
Wind Point Partners Vi LP .... G 312 255-4800
 Chicago *(G-6638)*
Woodbridge Inc .... F 847 229-1741
 Wheeling *(G-21015)*
Wozniak Industries Inc .... G 708 458-1220
 Bedford Park *(G-1515)*
Zirlin Interiors Inc .... E 773 334-5530
 Chicago *(G-6720)*

HARDWARE & BUILDING PRDTS: Plastic

Cpg International LLC .... D 570 558-8000
 Chicago *(G-4252)*
Dayton Superior Corporation .... C 815 936-3300
 Kankakee *(G-11964)*
Deslauriers Inc .... E 708 544-4455
 La Grange Park *(G-12095)*
Dike-O-Seal Incorporated .... F 773 254-3224
 Chicago *(G-4361)*
Dukane Ias LLC .... E 630 797-4900
 Saint Charles *(G-18191)*
Entrigue Designs .... G 708 647-6159
 Homewood *(G-11493)*
Fiberglass Innovations LLC ...... F 815 962-9338
 Rockford *(G-17413)*
Illinois Tool Works Inc .... C 708 479-7200
 Mokena *(G-14091)*
Illinois Tool Works Inc .... G 708 479-3346
 Tinley Park *(G-19838)*
Jay Cee Plastic Fabricators ...... F 773 276-1920
 Chicago *(G-5012)*
Kalle USA Inc .... G 847 775-0781
 Gurnee *(G-10893)*
L & P Guarding LLC .... C 708 325-0400
 Bedford Park *(G-1477)*
Nu-Dell Manufacturing Co Inc .. G 847 803-4500
 Chicago *(G-5637)*
Pexco LLC .... C 847 296-5511
 Des Plaines *(G-7820)*
Quixote Corporation .... E 312 705-8400
 Chicago *(G-5939)*
Right Lane Industries LLC .... G 857 869-4132
 Chicago *(G-6031)*
Sno Gem Inc .... F 888 766-4367
 McHenry *(G-13792)*
Specialized Woodwork Inc .... G 630 627-0450
 Lombard *(G-13131)*

PRODUCT SECTION

HARDWARE: Furniture, Builders' & Other Household

Tri Guards Inc .... F 847 537-8444
  Elk Grove Village *(G-9283)*
Tuf-Tite Inc .... F 847 550-1011
  Lake Zurich *(G-12467)*

HARDWARE & EQPT: Stage, Exc Lighting

UIC .... F 312 413-7697
  Chicago *(G-6456)*

HARDWARE STORES

Anixter Inc .... E 512 989-4254
  Glenview *(G-10525)*
Ashland Door Solutions LLC .... G 773 348-5106
  Elk Grove Village *(G-8842)*
Chicago Clamp Company .... G 708 343-8311
  Broadview *(G-2426)*
Continental Midland .... G 708 441-1000
  Calumet Park *(G-2797)*
Dumore Supplies Inc .... F 312 949-6260
  Chicago *(G-4403)*
Four Seasons Ace Hardware .... G 618 439-2101
  Benton *(G-1925)*
Hymans Auto Supply Co .... E 773 978-8221
  Chicago *(G-4864)*
Koson Tool Inc .... G 815 277-2107
  Frankfort *(G-9813)*
March Industries Inc .... F 224 654-6500
  Hampshire *(G-10978)*
Peoples Coal and Lumber Co .... F 815 432-2456
  Watseka *(G-20314)*
Prescription Plus Ltd .... F 618 537-6202
  Lebanon *(G-12546)*
Reasons Inc .... G 309 537-3424
  Buffalo Prairie *(G-2626)*
Whiting Partners LLC .... G 773 978-8221
  Chicago *(G-6620)*
Wille Bros Co .... D 708 535-4101
  Monee *(G-14213)*

HARDWARE STORES: Builders'

A Ashland Lock Company .... F 773 348-5106
  Chicago *(G-3485)*
Greene Welding & Hardware Inc .... E 217 375-4244
  East Lynn *(G-8220)*

HARDWARE STORES: Chainsaws

Outdoor Power Inc .... F 217 228-9890
  Quincy *(G-16921)*
Owen Walker .... G 217 285-4012
  Pittsfield *(G-16636)*

HARDWARE STORES: Door Locks & Lock Sets

Kaser Power Equipment Inc .... G 309 289-2176
  Knoxville *(G-12068)*

HARDWARE STORES: Pumps & Pumping Eqpt

Wagner Pump & Supply Co Inc .... G 847 526-8573
  Wauconda *(G-20401)*

HARDWARE STORES: Snowblowers

Wissmiller & Evans Road Eqp .... G 309 725-3598
  Cooksville *(G-7004)*

HARDWARE STORES: Tools

Correct Tool Inc .... F 630 595-6055
  Bensenville *(G-1777)*
Form Relief Tool Co Inc .... F 815 393-4263
  Davis Junction *(G-7423)*
Line Craft Tool Company Inc .... C 630 932-1182
  Lombard *(G-13096)*
Quality Tech Tool Inc .... E 847 690-9643
  Bensenville *(G-1880)*
Rsvp Tooling Inc .... G 815 725-3310
  Joliet *(G-11929)*
Sab Tool Supply Co .... G 847 634-3700
  Vernon Hills *(G-20090)*
Sport Redi-Mix LLC .... E 217 355-4222
  Champaign *(G-3352)*

HARDWARE STORES: Tools, Hand

Doerock Inc .... G 217 543-2101
  Arthur *(G-853)*

HARDWARE STORES: Tools, Power

Performance Lawn & Power .... G 217 857-3717
  Teutopolis *(G-19771)*

HARDWARE WHOLESALERS

Advance Tools LLC .... G 630 337-5904
  Glenview *(G-10520)*
Champion Chisel Works Inc .... F 815 535-0647
  Rock Falls *(G-17178)*
Continental Midland .... G 708 441-1000
  Calumet Park *(G-2797)*
Engert Co Inc .... E 847 673-1633
  Skokie *(G-18950)*
L & M Hardware Ltd .... G 630 493-1026
  Burr Ridge *(G-2694)*
March Industries Inc .... F 224 654-6500
  Hampshire *(G-10978)*
Mechanics Planing Mill Inc .... E 618 288-3000
  Glen Carbon *(G-10390)*
OBerry Enterprises Inc .... G 815 728-9480
  Ringwood *(G-17046)*
Optimas Oe Solutions LLC .... G 224 999-1000
  Glenview *(G-10595)*
SPEP Acquisition Corp .... G 310 608-0693
  Bolingbrook *(G-2246)*
True Value Company LLC .... E 847 639-5383
  Cary *(G-3196)*
UNI-Glide Corp .... G 773 235-2100
  Chicago *(G-6462)*

HARDWARE, WHOLESALE: Bolts

Beacon Fas & Components Inc .... E 847 541-0404
  Wheeling *(G-20857)*
Sanco Industries Inc .... F 847 243-8675
  Kildeer *(G-12052)*
Slsb LLC .... D 618 219-4115
  Madison *(G-13417)*

HARDWARE, WHOLESALE: Builders', NEC

Beno J Gundlach Company .... E 618 233-1781
  Belleville *(G-1534)*
Fna Ip Holdings Inc .... D 847 348-1500
  Elk Grove Village *(G-9001)*
Hersheys Metal Meister LLC .... E 217 234-4700
  Claremont *(G-6898)*
La Force Inc .... G 630 325-1950
  Willowbrook *(G-21048)*
Simpson Strong-Tie Company Inc .... E 630 613-5100
  West Chicago *(G-20643)*

HARDWARE, WHOLESALE: Casters & Glides

Clark Caster Co .... G 708 366-1913
  Forest Park *(G-9710)*

HARDWARE, WHOLESALE: Chains

Galva Iron and Metal Co Inc .... G 309 932-3450
  Galva *(G-10232)*
Timken Drives LLC .... D 815 589-2211
  Fulton *(G-10158)*

HARDWARE, WHOLESALE: Furniture, NEC

Innovative Components Inc .... E 847 885-9050
  Schaumburg *(G-18560)*

HARDWARE, WHOLESALE: Nuts

Ability Fasteners Inc .... F 847 593-4230
  Elk Grove Village *(G-8795)*

HARDWARE, WHOLESALE: Power Tools & Access

Dun-Rite Tool & Machine Co .... E 815 758-5464
  Cortland *(G-7020)*
Eazypower Corporation .... G 773 278-5000
  Chicago *(G-4440)*

HARDWARE, WHOLESALE: Screws

Air Stamping Inc .... F 217 342-1283
  Effingham *(G-8384)*
Archer Screw Products Inc .... D 847 451-1150
  Franklin Park *(G-9873)*
Cold Headers Inc .... F 773 775-7900
  Chicago *(G-4197)*
Gateway Screw & Rivet Inc .... E 630 539-2232
  Glendale Heights *(G-10452)*
Illinois Tool Works Inc .... B 630 595-3500
  Roselle *(G-17958)*
Komar Screw Corp .... E 847 965-9090
  Niles *(G-15139)*
Lombard Swiss Screw Company .... E 630 576-5096
  Addison *(G-185)*

HARDWARE, WHOLESALE: Security Devices, Locks

Patt Supply Corporation .... F 708 442-3901
  Lyons *(G-13312)*

HARDWARE, WHOLESALE: Staples

ITW Bldg Components Group .... G 847 634-1900
  Glenview *(G-10571)*

HARDWARE: Builders'

Amos Industries Inc .... F 630 393-0606
  Aurora *(G-911)*
Braun Manufacturing Co Inc .... E 847 635-2050
  Mount Prospect *(G-14514)*
Buildingpoint Midwest LLC .... G 855 332-7527
  Plainfield *(G-16645)*
Dormakaba USA Inc .... D 618 965-3491
  Steeleville *(G-19480)*
Graber Building Sup & Hdwr Inc .... G 217 268-3014
  Arcola *(G-650)*
Grand Specialties Co .... F 630 629-8000
  Oak Brook *(G-15625)*
Heckmann Building Products Inc .... E 708 865-2403
  Melrose Park *(G-13879)*
Stanley Black & Decker Inc .... G 630 724-3632
  Downers Grove *(G-8099)*

HARDWARE: Cabinet

Avoca Ridge Ltd .... G 815 692-4772
  Fairbury *(G-9604)*
Nova Wildcat Amerock LLC .... F 815 266-6416
  Freeport *(G-10131)*
Royal Kit Bthroom Cabinets Inc .... F 847 588-0011
  Niles *(G-15167)*
S L Fixtures Inc .... G 217 423-9907
  Decatur *(G-7545)*
Sweet Manufacturing Corp .... E 847 546-5575
  Chicago *(G-6294)*

HARDWARE: Casket

Dixline Corporation .... D 309 932-2011
  Galva *(G-10231)*
Dixline Corporation .... F 309 932-2011
  Galva *(G-10230)*
Estad Stamping & Mfg Co .... E 217 442-4600
  Danville *(G-7331)*
General Machinery & Mfg Co .... F 773 235-3700
  Chicago *(G-4674)*

HARDWARE: Door Opening & Closing Devices, Exc Electrical

MJT Incorporated .... G 708 597-0059
  Alsip *(G-480)*
Rockford Process Control LLC .... C 815 966-2000
  Rockford *(G-17602)*

HARDWARE: Furniture

Compx Security Products Inc .... D 847 234-1864
  Grayslake *(G-10763)*
Focus Marketing Group Inc .... G 815 363-2525
  Johnsburg *(G-11803)*
Haddock Tool & Manufacturing .... G 815 786-2739
  Sandwich *(G-18373)*
Illinois Fibre Specialty Co .... E 773 376-1122
  Chicago *(G-4890)*
Innovative Components Inc .... E 847 885-9050
  Schaumburg *(G-18560)*
Tolerance Manufacturing Inc .... F 847 244-8836
  Waukegan *(G-20508)*

HARDWARE: Furniture, Builders' & Other Household

Allegion S&S Holding Co Inc .... C 815 875-3311
  Princeton *(G-16805)*

HARDWARE: Luggage
Remin Laboratories Inc .... D 815 723-1940
  Joliet (G-11924)

HARDWARE: Plastic
Rand Manufacturing Network Inc .... G 847 299-8884
  Wheeling (G-20969)

HARDWARE: Rubber
Edgewater Products Company Inc .... F 708 345-9200
  Melrose Park (G-13860)
Finzer Holding LLC .... G 847 390-6200
  Des Plaines (G-7768)

HARNESS ASSEMBLIES: Cable & Wire
Advanced Technologies Inc .... G 847 329-9875
  Park Ridge (G-16264)
C & S Electric Specialties .... G 630 406-6170
  Bolingbrook (G-2154)
Capsonic Automotive Inc .... F 847 888-7300
  Elgin (G-8530)
Casco Manufacturing Inc .... E 630 771-9555
  Bolingbrook (G-2155)
Central Industries of Indiana .... G 618 943-2311
  Lawrenceville (G-12528)
Cinch Cnnctivity Solutions Inc .... C 630 705-6000
  Lombard (G-13054)
Delta Design Inc .... F 708 424-9400
  Evergreen Park (G-9592)
Excel Specialty Corp .... E 773 262-7575
  Lake Forest (G-12248)
Flp Industries LLC .... F 847 215-8650
  Wheeling (G-20897)
Gateway Cable Inc .... G 630 766-7969
  Bensenville (G-1808)
Grand Products Inc .... B 800 621-6101
  Elk Grove Village (G-9020)
Hart Electric LLC .... E 815 368-3341
  Lostant (G-13176)
IMS Companies LLC .... D 847 391-8100
  Des Plaines (G-7786)
Ksm Electronics Inc .... C 630 393-9310
  Warrenville (G-20241)
Lodan Electronics Inc .... C 847 398-5311
  Arlington Heights (G-771)
Lynn Electronics Corp .... G 972 412-7240
  Bolingbrook (G-2208)
Manu-TEC of Illinois LLC .... F 630 543-3022
  Addison (G-191)
Millennium Electronics Inc .... D 815 479-9755
  Crystal Lake (G-7231)
Mk Test Systems Americas Inc .... G 773 569-3778
  Lake Barrington (G-12161)
Nep Electronics Inc .... C 630 595-8500
  Wood Dale (G-21221)
Nu-Way Electronics Inc .... E 847 437-7120
  Elk Grove Village (G-9156)
Omnitronix Corporation .... F 630 837-1400
  Streamwood (G-19587)
Partec Inc .... C 847 678-9520
  Franklin Park (G-10014)
Quality Cable & Components Inc .... E 309 695-3435
  Wyoming (G-21461)
Triton Manufacturing Co Inc .... C 708 587-4000
  Monee (G-14210)
Unlimited Svcs Wisconsin Inc .... E 815 399-0282
  Machesney Park (G-13383)
Zero Ground LLC .... F 847 360-9500
  Waukegan (G-20522)

HARNESS WIRING SETS: Internal Combustion Engines
Aeromotive Services Inc .... F 224 535-9220
  Elgin (G-8498)
Midwest Aero Support Inc .... E 815 398-9202
  Machesney Park (G-13360)
Monona Holdings LLC .... G 630 946-0630
  Naperville (G-14875)
Xenia Mfg Inc .... C 618 678-2218
  Xenia (G-21469)
Xenia Mfg Inc .... E 618 392-7212
  Olney (G-15894)

HARNESSES, HALTERS, SADDLERY & STRAPS
Spirit Industries Inc .... G 217 285-4500
  Griggsville (G-10851)

HEADPHONES: Radio
Bem Wireless LLC .... F 815 337-0541
  Schaumburg (G-18460)
Bozki Inc .... G 312 767-2122
  Wheeling (G-20865)
Jds Labs Inc .... G 618 550-9359
  Collinsville (G-6964)

HEALTH & ALLIED SERVICES, NEC
Bundlar LLC .... G 773 839-3976
  Chicago (G-3974)

HEALTH & WELFARE COUNCIL
National Safety Council .... B 630 285-1121
  Itasca (G-11707)

HEALTH AIDS: Exercise Eqpt
Lumos Holdings US Acquisition .... G 847 288-3300
  Rosemont (G-18034)
Miha Bodytec Inc .... G 833 367-6442
  Addison (G-214)
Reflex Fitness Products Inc .... F 309 756-1050
  Milan (G-14024)
Septic Solutions Inc .... G 217 925-5992
  Dieterich (G-7878)
Xmt Solutions LLC .... G 703 338-9422
  Chicago (G-6696)

HEALTH AIDS: Vaporizers
Quick Nic Juice LLC .... F 815 315-8523
  Sandwich (G-18383)
Upper Limits Midwest Inc .... G 217 679-4315
  Springfield (G-19467)

HEALTH FOOD & SUPPLEMENT STORES
Helmuth Custom Kitchens LLC .... E 217 543-3588
  Arthur (G-862)
Relish Labs LLC .... G 872 225-2433
  Chicago (G-6012)

HEARING AIDS
Accutone Hearing Aid Inc .... G 773 545-3279
  Evanston (G-9487)
Beltone Corporation .... C 847 832-3300
  Glenview (G-10530)
Etymotic Research Inc .... E 847 228-0006
  Elk Grove Village (G-8984)
Gohear LLC .... G 847 574-7829
  Lake Forest (G-12252)
Hearing Aid Warehouse Inc .... G 217 431-4700
  Danville (G-7343)
Imhear Corporation .... G 630 395-9628
  Downers Grove (G-8029)
Knowles Electronics LLC .... G 630 250-5100
  Itasca (G-11688)
Mimosa Acoustics Inc .... G 217 359-9740
  Champaign (G-3323)
Phonak LLC .... A 630 821-5000
  Warrenville (G-20245)
SC Industries LLC .... F 407 484-2081
  Chicago (G-6109)
Sonova USA Inc .... C 763 744-3300
  Aurora (G-1018)

HEARING TESTING SVCS
Gohear LLC .... G 847 574-7829
  Lake Forest (G-12252)
Mimosa Acoustics Inc .... G 217 359-9740
  Champaign (G-3323)

HEAT EMISSION OPERATING APPARATUS
Delta-Therm Corporation .... F 847 526-2407
  Crystal Lake (G-7193)

HEAT EXCHANGERS
Pw Services LLC .... G 217 672-3225
  Warrensburg (G-20227)

HEAT EXCHANGERS: After Or Inter Coolers Or Condensers, Etc
Energy Solutions Inc .... G 618 465-5404
  Alton (G-556)
Roney Machine Works Inc .... E 618 462-4113
  Alton (G-570)
Yinlun Usa Inc .... G 309 291-0843
  Morton (G-14387)

HEAT TREATING SALTS
Houghton International Inc .... F 610 666-4000
  Chicago (G-4849)
Philos Technologies Inc .... G 630 945-2933
  Buffalo Grove (G-2585)

HEAT TREATING: Metal
300 Below Inc .... G 217 423-3070
  Decatur (G-7431)
Advanced Heat Treating Inc .... E 815 877-8593
  Loves Park (G-13182)
Advanced Thermal Processing .... G 630 595-9000
  Bensenville (G-1732)
Arrow Gear Company .... B 630 969-7640
  Downers Grove (G-7955)
Beechner Heat Treating Co Inc .... G 815 397-4314
  Rockford (G-17317)
Bodycote Thermal Proc Inc .... D 708 236-5360
  Melrose Park (G-13832)
Bodycote Thermal Proc Inc .... G 630 221-0385
  Glendale Heights (G-10439)
Bonell Manufacturing Company .... E 708 849-1770
  Riverdale (G-17069)
Bulaw Welding & Engineering Co .... D 630 228-8300
  Itasca (G-11632)
Bwt LLC .... E 708 410-8000
  Northlake (G-15544)
Bwt LLC .... G 630 210-4577
  Rockford (G-17331)
CB Machine & Tool Corp .... G 847 288-1807
  Franklin Park (G-9901)
Certified Heat Treating Co .... F 309 693-7711
  Peoria (G-16419)
Chem-Plate Industries Inc .... E 708 345-3588
  Maywood (G-13665)
Chem-Plate Industries Inc .... D 847 640-1600
  Elk Grove Village (G-8889)
Cooley Wire Products Mfg Co .... E 847 678-8585
  Schiller Park (G-18796)
Curtis Metal Finishing Company .... F 815 282-1433
  Machesney Park (G-13337)
Diamond Heat Treat Inc .... E 815 873-1348
  Rockford (G-17377)
Eklund Metal Treating Inc .... E 815 877-7436
  Loves Park (G-13209)
F P M LLC .... C 847 228-2525
  Elk Grove Village (G-8993)
F P M LLC .... D 815 332-4961
  Cherry Valley (G-3440)
Fpm Heat Treating .... F 815 332-4961
  Cherry Valley (G-3441)
General Surface Hardening Inc .... E 312 226-5472
  Chicago (G-4679)
Golfers Family Corporation .... E 815 968-0094
  Rockford (G-17431)
Horizon Steel Treating Inc .... D 847 639-4030
  Cary (G-3167)
Hudapack Mtal Treating III Inc .... E 630 793-1916
  Glendale Heights (G-10457)
Induction Heat Treating Corp .... E 815 477-7788
  Crystal Lake (G-7210)
K V F Company .... E 847 437-5100
  Elk Grove Village (G-9073)
K V F Company .... F 847 437-5019
  Elk Grove Village (G-9074)
Lapham-Hickey Steel Corp .... C 708 496-6111
  Bedford Park (G-1479)
Metals Technology Corporation .... C 630 221-2500
  Carol Stream (G-3025)
Metform LLC .... E 815 273-0230
  Savanna (G-18408)
Mp Steel Chicago LLC .... E 773 242-0853
  Chicago (G-5514)
Nitrex Inc .... E 630 851-5880
  Aurora (G-1003)
Precision Chrome Inc .... E 847 587-1515
  Fox Lake (G-9753)
Precision Metal Technologies .... F 847 228-6630
  Rolling Meadows (G-17765)

R-M Industries Inc .... F 630 543-3071
  Addison (G-264)
Salman Metal .... G 630 359-5110
  Elmhurst (G-9421)
Scientific Metal Treating Co .... E 630 582-0071
  Roselle (G-17985)
Standard Heat Treating LLC .... E 773 242-0853
  Cicero (G-6875)
Superheat Fgh Services Inc .... F 708 478-0205
  New Lenox (G-15060)
Superheat Fgh Services Inc .... F 708 478-0205
  New Lenox (G-15061)
Tc Industries Inc .... C 815 459-2401
  Crystal Lake (G-7276)
Tempel Holdings Inc .... A 773 250-8000
  Chicago (G-6343)
Terra Cotta Holdings Co .... E 815 459-2400
  Crystal Lake (G-7281)
Tri-City Heat Treat Co Inc .... D 309 786-2689
  Rock Island (G-17252)
Wec Welding and Machining LLC .... G 847 680-8100
  Lake Bluff (G-12214)

HEATERS: Induction & Dielectric

IDI Fabrication Inc .... F 630 783-2246
  Lemont (G-12566)

HEATERS: Space, Exc Electric

Empire Comfort Systems Inc .... C 618 233-7420
  Belleville (G-1551)

HEATERS: Swimming Pool, Electric

Superheat Fgh Services Inc .... F 618 251-9450
  Roxana (G-18103)

HEATING & AIR CONDITIONING EQPT & SPLYS WHOLESALERS

Ecolab Inc .... E 815 729-7334
  Joliet (G-11857)
Ecolab Inc .... E 847 350-2229
  Elk Grove Village (G-8968)
Frigel North America Inc .... E 847 540-0160
  East Dundee (G-8196)
Illco Inc .... G 815 725-9100
  Joliet (G-11878)
Lennox Industries Inc .... D 630 378-7054
  Romeoville (G-17842)
Mucci Kirkpatrick Sheet Metal .... G 815 433-3350
  Ottawa (G-16062)
Quality Filter Services .... G 618 654-3716
  Highland (G-11236)

HEATING & AIR CONDITIONING UNITS, COMBINATION

Bernard Cffey Vtrans Fundation .... G 630 687-0033
  Naperville (G-14779)
EZ Comfort Heating & AC .... G 630 289-2020
  Elgin (G-8582)
Synergy Mech Solutions Inc .... G 847 437-4500
  Elk Grove Village (G-9262)

HEATING EQPT & SPLYS

Aldrico Inc .... E 309 695-2311
  Wyoming (G-21457)
All American Wood Register Co .... F 815 356-1000
  Crystal Lake (G-7155)
American Fuel Economy Inc .... G 815 433-3226
  Ottawa (G-16037)
BP Solar International Inc .... A 301 698-4200
  Naperville (G-14785)
Easy Heat Inc .... E 847 268-6000
  Rosemont (G-18022)
Filtran Holdings LLC .... G 847 635-6670
  Des Plaines (G-7766)
Filtran LLC .... C 847 635-6670
  Des Plaines (G-7767)
Goose Island Mfg & Supply Corp .... G 708 343-4225
  Lansing (G-12495)
Grieve Corporation .... D 847 546-8225
  Round Lake (G-18078)
Hardy Radiator Repair .... F 217 223-8320
  Quincy (G-16889)
Industries Publication Inc .... E 630 357-5269
  Lisle (G-12899)
Ipsen Inc .... E 815 239-2385
  Pecatonica (G-16322)

R & D Electronics Inc .... G 847 583-9080
  Niles (G-15163)
Spirotherm Inc .... G 630 307-2662
  Glendale Heights (G-10497)
Sws Industries Inc .... E 904 482-0091
  Woodstock (G-21438)
Tri-State Food Equipment .... G 217 228-1550
  Quincy (G-16952)

HEATING EQPT: Complete

American Fuel Economy Inc .... G 815 433-3226
  Ottawa (G-16037)
Big M Manufacturing LLC .... G 217 824-9372
  Taylorville (G-19750)
Flinn & Dreffein Engrg Co .... E 847 272-6374
  Northbrook (G-15391)
Frigel North America Inc .... E 847 540-0160
  East Dundee (G-8196)
Habegger Corporation .... F 309 793-7172
  Rock Island (G-17221)
Highland Park Mechanical Inc .... G 847 269-3863
  Zion (G-21517)
Industrial Thermo Products .... G 847 398-8600
  Rolling Meadows (G-17740)
Kelco Industries Inc .... G 815 334-3600
  Woodstock (G-21398)
Temperature Equipment Corp .... G 815 229-2935
  Rockford (G-17655)

HEATING EQPT: Induction

Precision Chrome Inc .... E 847 587-1515
  Fox Lake (G-9753)

HEATING PADS, ELECTRIC

Cabot Microelectronics Corp .... D 630 375-6631
  Aurora (G-932)

HEATING UNITS & DEVICES: Indl, Electric

Armil/Cfs Inc .... E 708 339-6810
  South Holland (G-19198)
Calco Controls Inc .... F 847 639-3858
  Crystal Lake (G-7176)
Delta-Therm Corporation .... F 847 526-2407
  Crystal Lake (G-7193)
Hts Chicago Inc .... G 630 352-3690
  Wheaton (G-20804)
Ipsen Inc .... C 815 332-4941
  Cherry Valley (G-3442)
J N Machinery Corp .... G 224 699-9161
  East Dundee (G-8203)
M H Detrick Company .... E 708 479-5085
  Frankfort (G-9814)
McEnglevan Indus Frnc Mfg Inc .... G 217 446-0941
  Danville (G-7363)
Oakley Industrial McHy Inc .... E 847 966-0052
  Elk Grove Village (G-9157)
Tempco Electric Heater Corp .... B 630 350-2252
  Wood Dale (G-21248)
Tempro International Corp .... G 847 677-5370
  Skokie (G-19044)
Titanium Inc .... G 847 691-5446
  Grayslake (G-10802)
Zeman Mfg Co .... E 630 960-2300
  Lisle (G-12958)

HEATING UNITS: Gas, Infrared

Burdett Burner Mfg Inc .... G 630 617-5060
  Villa Park (G-20135)

HELICOPTERS

A & S Helicopters Inc .... G 618 337-2600
  Cahokia (G-2760)
Helivalues .... G 847 487-8258
  Wauconda (G-20355)
Raytheon Technologies Corp .... B 815 226-6000
  Rockford (G-17567)
Ruby Industrial Tech LLC .... E 317 248-8355
  Wood Dale (G-21235)

HELMETS: Athletic

Bell Racing Usa LLC .... G 217 239-5355
  Champaign (G-3271)
Bell Sports Inc .... D 217 893-9300
  Rantoul (G-16968)
Brg Sports Inc .... D 224 585-5200
  Des Plaines (G-7741)

Park View Manufacturing Corp .... D 618 548-9054
  Salem (G-18350)
Riddell Inc .... C 847 292-1472
  Des Plaines (G-7837)

HELP SUPPLY SERVICES

National Emergency Med ID Inc .... G 847 366-1267
  Spring Grove (G-19288)
Wind Point Partners LP .... F 312 255-4800
  Chicago (G-6637)

HIGH ENERGY PARTICLE PHYSICS EQPT

Raytheon Technologies Corp .... B 815 226-6000
  Rockford (G-17567)

HIGHWAY & STREET MAINTENANCE SVCS

Illinois Road Contractors Inc .... E 217 245-6181
  Jacksonville (G-11769)
Louis Marsch Inc .... E 217 526-3723
  Morrisonville (G-14351)

HITCHES: Trailer

Great Lakes Forge Company .... G 773 277-2800
  Chicago (G-4735)
Kerins Industries Inc .... G 630 515-9111
  Darien (G-7408)

HOBBY & CRAFT SPLY STORES

Made By Hands Inc .... G 773 761-4200
  Chicago (G-5310)

HOBBY SUPPLIES, WHOLESALE

Central RC Hobbies .... G 309 686-8004
  Peoria (G-16418)

HOBBY, TOY & GAME STORES: Arts & Crafts & Splys

Smart Creations Inc .... G 847 433-3451
  Highland Park (G-11298)

HOBBY, TOY & GAME STORES: Children's Toys & Games, Exc Dolls

Midwest Rail Junction .... G 815 963-0200
  Rockford (G-17527)

HOBBY, TOY & GAME STORES: Hobbies, NEC

Central RC Hobbies .... G 309 686-8004
  Peoria (G-16418)
Hands To Work Railroading .... G 708 489-9776
  Alsip (G-454)

HOBBY, TOY & GAME STORES: Toys & Games

Enesco LLC .... B 630 875-5300
  Itasca (G-11650)

HOISTS

Columbus McKinnon Corporation .... C 800 548-2930
  Eureka (G-9478)
Columbus McKinnon Corporation .... E 630 783-1195
  Woodridge (G-21286)
Peerless Chain Company .... E 708 339-0545
  South Holland (G-19239)
Ramseys Machine Co .... G 217 824-2320
  Taylorville (G-19761)
Sievert Electric Svc & Sls Co .... D 708 771-1600
  Forest Park (G-9724)

HOISTS: Mine

Logan Actuator Co .... G 815 943-9500
  Harvard (G-11059)

HOLDERS, PAPER TOWEL, GROCERY BAG, ETC: Plastic

C Line Products Inc .... D 847 827-6661
  Mount Prospect (G-14517)
Urpoint LLC .... G 773 919-9002
  Homewood (G-11503)

HOLDERS, PAPER TOWEL, GROCERY BAG, ETC: Plastic

Vision Wholesale Corp .... G 708 496-6015
  Chicago *(G-6558)*

HOLDING COMPANIES: Banks

T H K Holdings of America LLC .... G 847 310-1111
  Schaumburg *(G-18735)*

HOLDING COMPANIES: Investment, Exc Banks

Agrati Inc .... G 704 747-1200
  Park Forest *(G-16250)*
Atkore Intl Holdings Inc .... G 708 225-2051
  Harvey *(G-11076)*
False Hope Brand Co .... G 312 265-1364
  Chicago *(G-4556)*
Fisher Container Holdings LLC .... G 847 541-0000
  Buffalo Grove *(G-2537)*
Hovi Industries Incorporated .... E 815 512-7500
  Bolingbrook *(G-2186)*
Industrial Service Solutions .... G 917 609-6979
  Chicago *(G-4910)*
Lumos Holdings US Acquisition .... G 847 288-3300
  Rosemont *(G-18034)*
Lx/Jt Intermediate Holdings .... G 773 369-2652
  Chicago *(G-5291)*
Madison Inds Holdings LLC .... G 312 277-0156
  Chicago *(G-5313)*
Mat Capital LLC .... G 847 821-9630
  Long Grove *(G-13163)*
Npi Holding Corp .... G 217 391-1229
  Springfield *(G-19412)*
Omc Investors LLC .... G 847 855-6220
  Gurnee *(G-10908)*
Orbus Holdings Inc .... D 630 226-1155
  Woodridge *(G-21329)*
Roevolution 226 LLC .... G 773 658-4022
  Riverwoods *(G-17095)*
Tag-Barton LLC .... G 217 428-0711
  Decatur *(G-7556)*
Thyssenkrupp North America Inc ..... E 312 525-2800
  Chicago *(G-6375)*
Transcontinental Holding Corp .... G 773 877-3300
  Chicago *(G-6410)*
Trx Pubco LLC .... G 312 222-9100
  Chicago *(G-6442)*
VPI Holding Company LLC .... G 312 255-4800
  Chicago *(G-6572)*
Wieland Holdings Inc .... A 847 537-3990
  Wheeling *(G-21013)*
Wpg US Holdco LLC .... B 312 517-3750
  Chicago *(G-6681)*

HOLDING COMPANIES: Personal, Exc Banks

Baker Avenue Investments Inc .... D 309 427-2500
  Washington *(G-20266)*
Condy Holdings LLC .... G 815 223-1500
  Peru *(G-16573)*
Pharmdium Hlthcare Hldings Inc ..... G 800 523-7749
  Lake Forest *(G-12288)*
Pt Holdings Inc .... G 217 691-1793
  Springfield *(G-19270)*
Tally Metals Holdings LLC .... G 773 264-5900
  Chicago *(G-6315)*

HOLDING COMPANIES: Public Utility

Fin North America Holding Inc .... D 815 349-3219
  Ingleside *(G-11582)*

HOME CENTER STORES

Ronnie P Faber .... G 815 626-4561
  Sterling *(G-19529)*

HOME DELIVERY NEWSPAPER ROUTES

Phoenix Press Inc .... G 630 833-2281
  Addison *(G-239)*

HOME ENTERTAINMENT EQPT: Electronic, NEC

Senario LLC .... F 847 882-0677
  Schaumburg *(G-18711)*
William N Pasulka .... G 815 339-6300
  Peru *(G-16598)*

HOME ENTERTAINMENT REPAIR SVCS

Acoustic Avenue Inc .... F 217 544-9810
  Springfield *(G-19315)*
Sota Service Ctr By Bodinets .... G 608 538-3500
  Dekalb *(G-7704)*

HOME FOR THE MENTALLY RETARDED

Community Support Systems .... D 217 705-4300
  Teutopolis *(G-19767)*

HOME FURNISHINGS WHOLESALERS

Amk Enterprises Chicago Inc .... G 312 523-7212
  Chicago *(G-3681)*
Del Great Frame Up Systems Inc .... E 847 808-1955
  Franklin Park *(G-9929)*
Larson-Juhl US LLC .... E 630 307-9700
  Roselle *(G-17963)*

HOME HEALTH CARE SVCS

All Dental .... G 708 749-0277
  Berwyn *(G-1948)*
Connies Home Health Care .... G 708 790-4000
  Park Forest *(G-16253)*

HOME IMPROVEMENT & RENOVATION CONTRACTOR AGENCY

Crosscom Inc .... F 630 871-5500
  Wheaton *(G-20794)*
Ornamental Iron Shop .... G 618 281-6072
  Columbia *(G-6992)*

HOMEBUILDERS & OTHER OPERATIVE BUILDERS

Chicago Steel Inc .... E 800 344-3032
  Chicago *(G-4130)*
Midwest Plastics Services Inc .... G 630 551-4921
  Oswego *(G-16014)*

HOMEFURNISHING STORE: Bedding, Sheet, Blanket, Spread/Pillow

Standard Container Co of Edgar ..... E 847 438-1510
  Lake Zurich *(G-12460)*

HOMEFURNISHING STORES: Beddings & Linens

Eastern Accents Inc .... C 773 604-7300
  Chicago *(G-4435)*

HOMEFURNISHING STORES: Brooms

Luco Mop Company .... G 217 235-1992
  Mattoon *(G-13643)*

HOMEFURNISHING STORES: Lighting Fixtures

Acculight LLC .... G 630 847-1000
  Elk Grove Village *(G-8799)*

HOMEFURNISHING STORES: Mirrors

Montrose Glass & Mirror Corp .... G 773 478-6433
  Chicago *(G-5494)*

HOMEFURNISHING STORES: Pictures, Wall

Picture Frame Fulfillment LLC .... D 708 483-8537
  Franklin Park *(G-10017)*
Supreme Frame & Moulding Co ...... F 312 930-9056
  Chicago *(G-6286)*

HOMEFURNISHING STORES: Pottery

Great Lakes Clay & Supply Inc .... G 224 535-8127
  Elgin *(G-8601)*

HOMEFURNISHING STORES: Wicker, Rattan, Or Reed

House of Rattan Inc .... E 630 627-8160
  Lombard *(G-13086)*
Wise Construction Services .... G 630 553-6350
  Yorkville *(G-21506)*

HOMEFURNISHING STORES: Window Furnishings

9161 Corporation .... G 847 470-8828
  Niles *(G-15097)*
Loomcraft Textile & Supply Co .... E 847 680-0000
  Vernon Hills *(G-20073)*
Offsprings Inc .... G 773 525-1800
  Chicago *(G-5659)*
Regent Window Fashions LLC .... G 773 871-6400
  Chicago *(G-6003)*
Roberts Draperies Center Inc .... G 847 255-4040
  Mount Prospect *(G-14567)*

HOMEFURNISHING STORES: Window Shades, NEC

Midwest Marketing Distrs Inc .... G 309 663-6972
  Bloomington *(G-2078)*
Midwest Marketing Distrs Inc .... F 309 688-8858
  Peoria *(G-16476)*

HOMEFURNISHINGS & SPLYS, WHOLESALE: Decorative

Limitless Innovations Inc .... E 855 843-4828
  McHenry *(G-13758)*
Little Journeys Limited .... G 847 677-0350
  Skokie *(G-18980)*
Mitchell Black LLC .... F 312 667-4477
  Chicago *(G-5470)*
Pingotopia Inc .... F 847 503-9333
  Northbrook *(G-15459)*

HOMEFURNISHINGS, WHOLESALE: Aluminumware

Axis International Marketing .... C 847 297-0744
  Des Plaines *(G-7735)*

HOMEFURNISHINGS, WHOLESALE: Blinds, Vertical

Unitex Industries Inc .... G 708 524-0664
  Oak Park *(G-15777)*

HOMEFURNISHINGS, WHOLESALE: Carpets

Milliken & Company .... F 800 241-4826
  Chicago *(G-5460)*

HOMEFURNISHINGS, WHOLESALE: Draperies

Baker Drapery Corporation .... G 309 691-3295
  Dunlap *(G-8132)*
Dons Drapery Service .... G 815 385-4759
  McHenry *(G-13737)*
Kempco Window Treatments Inc .... E 708 754-4484
  Chicago Heights *(G-6755)*

HOMEFURNISHINGS, WHOLESALE: Fireplace Eqpt & Access

Citizenprime LLC .... G 708 995-1241
  Mokena *(G-14075)*

HOMEFURNISHINGS, WHOLESALE: Kitchenware

Cupcake Holdings LLC .... C 800 794-5866
  Woodridge *(G-21289)*
Kitchen Supply Wholesale .... G 224 603-1208
  Antioch *(G-618)*
Rays Countertop Shop Inc .... F 217 483-2514
  Glenarm *(G-10427)*
Wilton Holdings Inc .... A 630 963-7100
  Woodridge *(G-21349)*
Wilton Industries Inc .... B 630 963-7100
  Naperville *(G-14949)*
Wilton Industries Inc .... F 815 834-9390
  Romeoville *(G-17888)*
Xcell International Corp .... D 630 323-0107
  Lemont *(G-12596)*

HOMEFURNISHINGS, WHOLESALE: Linens, Table

Pyar & Co LLC .... G 312 451-5073
  Chicago *(G-5920)*

PRODUCT SECTIONHOUSEWARES, ELECTRIC: Heaters, Immersion

HOMEFURNISHINGS, WHOLESALE: Wood Flooring

Moultrie County Hardwoods LLC .... G 217 543-2643
  Arthur *(G-870)*
Ridgefield Industries Co LLC .... E 800 569-0316
  Crystal Lake *(G-7256)*
Signature Innovations LLC .... G 847 758-9600
  Elk Grove Village *(G-9241)*

HOMES, MODULAR: Wooden

Csi Manufacturing Inc .... E 309 937-2653
  Cambridge *(G-2804)*
Homeway Homes Inc .... D 309 965-2312
  Deer Creek *(G-7575)*
Z-Modular LLC .... E 312 275-1600
  Chicago *(G-6705)*

HOMES: Log Cabins

Otten Construction Co Inc .... G 618 768-4310
  Addieville *(G-11)*
Snagamon Valley Log Builders .... G 217 632-7609
  Petersburg *(G-16604)*

HONEYCOMB CORE & BOARD: Made From Purchased Materials

Tricel Corporation .... F 847 336-1321
  Gurnee *(G-10938)*

HOODS: Range, Sheet Metal

All Seasons Heating & AC .... G 217 429-2022
  Decatur *(G-7440)*

HOOKS: Gate

Alltec Gates Inc .... G 708 301-9361
  Tinley Park *(G-19801)*

HORNS: Marine, Electric

Buell Manufacturing Company .... G 708 447-6320
  Lyons *(G-13304)*

HORSESHOES

Anvil Acquisition Corp .... F 309 365-8270
  Lexington *(G-12617)*
Moline Forge Inc .... D 309 762-5506
  Moline *(G-14163)*

HOSE: Air Line Or Air Brake, Rubber Or Rubberized Fabric

Flexicraft Industries Inc .... E 312 738-3588
  Chicago *(G-4610)*
Power Port Products Inc .... E 630 628-9102
  Addison *(G-248)*

HOSE: Automobile, Plastic

Bristol Hose & Fitting Inc .... E 708 492-3456
  Melrose Park *(G-13837)*

HOSE: Flexible Metal

Afc Cable Systems Inc .... B 508 998-1131
  Harvey *(G-11070)*
Anamet Inc .... G 217 234-8844
  Glen Ellyn *(G-10394)*
Electri-Flex Company .... D 630 529-2920
  Roselle *(G-17952)*
Flextron Inc .... F 630 543-5995
  Addison *(G-125)*
Manhattan Mechanical Svcs LLC .... E 815 478-9940
  Manhattan *(G-13434)*
Senior Holdings Inc .... D 630 837-1811
  Bartlett *(G-1309)*
Senior Operations LLC .... B 630 372-3500
  Bartlett *(G-1311)*

HOSE: Heater, Plastic

Kanaflex Corporation Illinois .... G 847 634-6100
  Vernon Hills *(G-20069)*

HOSE: Plastic

Tigerflex Corporation .... A 847 439-1766
  Elk Grove Village *(G-9273)*

HOSE: Rubber

Gates Corporation .... C 309 343-7171
  Galesburg *(G-10196)*
Gusco Silicone Rbr & Svcs LLC .... F 773 770-5008
  Aurora *(G-1106)*
Suncast Corporation .... A 630 879-2050
  Batavia *(G-1422)*

HOSES & BELTING: Rubber & Plastic

6965 North Hamlin LLC .... G 847 673-8900
  Lincolnwood *(G-12809)*
Behabelt USA .... G 630 521-9835
  Addison *(G-46)*
Bristol Transport Inc .... E 708 343-6411
  Melrose Park *(G-13838)*
Caterpillar Inc .... A 309 578-2473
  Mossville *(G-14456)*
Flexicraft Industries Inc .... F 312 229-7550
  Chicago *(G-4609)*
Geib Industries Inc .... E 847 455-4550
  Bensenville *(G-1809)*
Industrial Rubber & Sup Entp .... G 217 429-3747
  Decatur *(G-7507)*
Kemper Industries .... G 217 826-5712
  Marshall *(G-13573)*
Kuriyama of America Inc .... D 847 755-0360
  Schaumburg *(G-18594)*
Lanmar Inc .... G 800 233-5520
  Northbrook *(G-15418)*
Megadyne America LLC .... E 630 752-0600
  Carol Stream *(G-3023)*
Pix North America Inc .... F 855 800-0720
  Danville *(G-7374)*
Quad City Hose .... E 563 386-8936
  Taylor Ridge *(G-19747)*
Royal Brass Inc .... G 618 439-6341
  Benton *(G-1936)*
Srj Inc .... F 630 351-0639
  Schaumburg *(G-18726)*
Western Consolidated Tech Inc .... F 815 334-3684
  Woodstock *(G-21447)*

HOSPITAL EQPT REPAIR SVCS

Amity Hospital Services Inc .... G 708 206-3970
  Country Club Hills *(G-7035)*

HOSPITALS: Medical & Surgical

Southwestern Hearing Centers .... G 618 651-4199
  Highland *(G-11241)*

HOTEL & MOTEL RESERVATION SVCS

Bitter End Yacht Club Intl .... F 312 506-6205
  Chicago *(G-3902)*

HOTELS & MOTELS

Raynor Mfg Co .... A 815 288-1431
  Dixon *(G-7908)*

HOUSEHOLD APPLIANCE PARTS: Wholesalers

Ameriguard Corporation .... G 630 986-1900
  Burr Ridge *(G-2652)*

HOUSEHOLD APPLIANCE STORES: Electric

Doctors Choice Inc .... G 312 666-1111
  Chicago *(G-4378)*
Macari Service Center Inc .... F 217 774-4214
  Shelbyville *(G-18881)*
Reasons Inc .... G 309 537-3424
  Buffalo Prairie *(G-2626)*

HOUSEHOLD APPLIANCE STORES: Electric Household Appliance, Sm

Coles Appliance & Furn Co .... G 773 525-1797
  Chicago *(G-4199)*
Heaven Fresh USA Inc .... G 800 642-0367
  Plainfield *(G-16671)*

HOUSEHOLD APPLIANCE STORES: Electric Household, Major

Fna Ip Holdings Inc .... D 847 348-1500
  Elk Grove Village *(G-9001)*

HOUSEHOLD ARTICLES, EXC FURNITURE: Cut Stone

Hollywood Traders LLC .... G 630 943-6461
  Lombard *(G-13085)*
Wienmar Inc .... C 847 742-9222
  South Elgin *(G-19181)*

HOUSEHOLD FURNISHINGS, NEC

A D Specialty Sewing .... G 847 639-0390
  Fox River Grove *(G-9756)*
Caroline Cole Inc .... F 618 233-0600
  Belleville *(G-1538)*
Envision Unlimited .... C 773 651-1100
  Chicago *(G-4521)*
Interior Fashions Contract .... G 847 358-6050
  Palatine *(G-16131)*
Logoskirt Corporation .... F 773 584-7300
  Chicago *(G-5251)*
Qst Industries Inc .... E 312 930-9400
  Chicago *(G-5923)*
Rome Metal Mfg Inc .... G 773 287-1755
  Chicago *(G-6057)*
Slagel Drapery Service .... G 815 692-3834
  Fairbury *(G-9613)*

HOUSEWARE STORES

Al Bar Laboratories Inc .... F 847 251-1218
  Wilmette *(G-21068)*

HOUSEWARES, ELECTRIC, EXC COOKING APPLIANCES & UTENSILS

Baier Home Center .... G 815 457-2300
  Cissna Park *(G-6894)*
Sensible Designs Online Inc .... G 708 267-8924
  Orland Park *(G-15978)*

HOUSEWARES, ELECTRIC: Air Purifiers, Portable

Blueair Inc .... F 888 258-3247
  Chicago *(G-3915)*
Heaven Fresh USA Inc .... G 800 642-0367
  Plainfield *(G-16671)*
Radovent Illinois LLC .... G 847 637-0297
  Naperville *(G-14984)*

HOUSEWARES, ELECTRIC: Bedcoverings

Alpha Bedding LLC .... F 847 550-5110
  Lake Zurich *(G-12383)*

HOUSEWARES, ELECTRIC: Cooking Appliances

Lighthouse Marketing Inc .... G 949 542-4558
  Chicago *(G-5221)*
Mh Equipment Company .... D 217 443-7210
  Danville *(G-7366)*

HOUSEWARES, ELECTRIC: Dryers, Hair

Tonjon Company .... F 630 208-1173
  Geneva *(G-10312)*

HOUSEWARES, ELECTRIC: Dryers, Hand & Face

Taylor Coml Foodservice Inc .... F 815 624-8333
  Rockton *(G-17703)*
World Dryer Corporation .... E 800 323-0701
  Bensenville *(G-1914)*

HOUSEWARES, ELECTRIC: Fans, Desk

O2cool LLC .... E 312 951-6700
  Chicago *(G-5647)*

HOUSEWARES, ELECTRIC: Fans, Exhaust & Ventilating

Winchester Interconnect Rugged .... G 708 594-5890
  Broadview *(G-2475)*

HOUSEWARES, ELECTRIC: Heaters, Immersion

Expo Engineered Inc .... G 708 780-7155
  Cicero *(G-6847)*

Employee Codes: A=Over 500 employees, B=251-500
C=101-250, D=51-100, E=20-50, F=10-19, G=3-9

2020 Harris Illinois Industrial Directory

HOUSEWARES, ELECTRIC: Heaters, Space

High Rise Specialty Products .... G 708 343-9265
Maywood *(G-13669)*

HOUSEWARES, ELECTRIC: Heaters, Tape

Thermosoft International Corp .... E 847 279-3800
Vernon Hills *(G-20105)*

HOUSEWARES, ELECTRIC: Heating Units, Electric Appliances

General Electric Company .... F 708 780-2600
Cicero *(G-6848)*

HOUSEWARES, ELECTRIC: Heating, Bsbrd/Wall, Radiant Heat

Kalb Corporation .... F 309 483-3600
Oneida *(G-15903)*

HOUSEWARES, ELECTRIC: Humidifiers, Household

Bestair Pro .... G 847 683-3400
Hampshire *(G-10964)*

HOUSEWARES, ELECTRIC: Irons, Household

Conair Corporation .... G 203 351-9000
Rantoul *(G-16972)*

HOUSEWARES, ELECTRIC: Lighters, Cigarette

Hotvapes Ltd .... F 775 468-8273
Niles *(G-15130)*

HOUSEWARES, ELECTRIC: Massage Machines, Exc Beauty/Barber

Tifb Media Group Inc .... G 844 862-4391
Burbank *(G-2638)*

HOUSEWARES, ELECTRIC: Mixers, Food

Imh Fabrication Inc .... F 815 537-2381
Prophetstown *(G-16833)*

HOUSEWARES, ELECTRIC: Radiators

Menk Usa LLC .... E 815 626-9730
Sterling *(G-19518)*

HOUSEWARES, ELECTRIC: Toasters

Hamilton Beach Brands Inc .... E 847 252-7036
Inverness *(G-11596)*

HOUSEWARES: Bowls, Wood

Elegant Concepts Ltd .... G 708 456-9590
Elmwood Park *(G-9451)*

HOUSEWARES: Dishes, China

Edwin M Knowles China Company .... F 847 581-8354
Niles *(G-15118)*

HOUSEWARES: Dishes, Plastic

Alpha Acrylic Design .... G 847 818-8178
Arlington Heights *(G-687)*
D&W Fine Pack Holdings LLC .... G 847 378-1200
Wood Dale *(G-21179)*
D&W Fine Pack LLC .... G 800 323-0422
Lake Zurich *(G-12401)*
EMC Innovations Inc .... G 815 741-2546
Joliet *(G-11860)*
Frederics Frame Studio Inc .... F 312 243-2950
Chicago *(G-4632)*
Global Contract Mfg Inc .... G 312 432-6200
Chicago *(G-4695)*
Kitchen Supply Wholesale .... G 224 603-1208
Antioch *(G-618)*
Mat Capital LLC .... G 847 821-9630
Long Grove *(G-13163)*
Mgs Mfg Group Inc .... E 847 968-4335
Libertyville *(G-12680)*
Microthincom Inc .... F 630 543-0501
Bensenville *(G-1851)*

Mid Oaks Investments LLC .... G 847 215-3475
Buffalo Grove *(G-2573)*
Molor Products Company .... F 630 375-5999
Oswego *(G-16015)*
Newell Brands Inc .... D 815 266-0066
Freeport *(G-10128)*
Tenex Corporation .... E 847 504-0400
Chicago *(G-6348)*
Thermform Engineered Qulty LLC .... D 847 669-5291
Huntley *(G-11568)*
US Acrylic LLC .... D 847 837-4800
Libertyville *(G-12720)*

HOUSEWARES: Household & Commercial, Vitreous China

Cornerstone Fdsrvice Group Inc .... G 630 527-8600
Naperville *(G-14808)*

HOUSEWARES: Kettles & Skillets, Cast Iron

Sunrise Distributors Inc .... G 630 400-8786
Elk Grove Village *(G-9259)*

HOUSEWARES: Pots & Pans, Glass

Harris Potteries LP .... G 847 564-5544
Northbrook *(G-15397)*

HOUSING COMPONENTS: Prefabricated, Concrete

Bernard Cffey Vtrans Fundation .... G 630 687-0033
Naperville *(G-14779)*
Englewood Co Op .... G 773 873-1201
Chicago *(G-4510)*

HOUSINGS: Business Machine, Sheet Metal

IMS Engineered Products LLC .... C 847 391-8100
Des Plaines *(G-7787)*
K B Metal Company .... G 309 248-7355
Washburn *(G-20264)*
Prismier LLC .... E 630 592-4515
Bolingbrook *(G-2230)*

HOUSINGS: Motor

Power Enclosures Inc .... F 309 274-9000
Chillicothe *(G-6821)*

HOUSINGS: Pressure

Murdock Company Inc .... G 847 566-0050
Mundelein *(G-14719)*

HUB CAPS: Automobile, Stamped Metal

Marmon Industries LLC .... G 312 372-9500
Chicago *(G-5345)*

HUMIDIFIERS & DEHUMIDIFIERS

Heaven Fresh USA Inc .... G 800 642-0367
Plainfield *(G-16671)*
Pure N Natural Systems Inc .... F 630 372-9681
Streamwood *(G-19591)*

HUMIDIFYING EQPT, EXC PORTABLE

Galmar Enterprises Inc .... G 815 463-9826
New Lenox *(G-15035)*

HYDRAULIC EQPT REPAIR SVC

Central Hydraulics Inc .... G 309 527-5238
El Paso *(G-8434)*
Cylinder Services Inc .... G 630 466-9820
Sugar Grove *(G-19641)*
HBm Electro Chemical Company .... G 708 895-7710
Lansing *(G-12497)*
Master Hydraulics & Machining .... F 847 895-5578
Schaumburg *(G-18623)*
Midwestern Mch Hydraulics Inc .... F 618 246-9440
Mount Vernon *(G-14625)*
RE-Do-It Corp .... G 708 343-7125
Broadview *(G-2463)*
Sarco Hydraulics Inc .... E 217 324-6577
Litchfield *(G-12977)*

HYDRAULIC FLUIDS: Synthetic Based

Houghton International Inc .... F 610 666-4000
Chicago *(G-4849)*

HYDROPONIC EQPT

Modern Sprout LLC .... G 312 342-2114
Chicago *(G-5482)*

Hard Rubber & Molded Rubber Prdts

Dyneer Corporation .... B 217 228-6011
Quincy *(G-16877)*
Weiland Fast Trac Inc .... G 847 438-7996
Long Grove *(G-13174)*

ICE

Carnaghi Towing & Repair Inc .... F 217 446-0333
Tilton *(G-19793)*
Four Seasons Ace Hardware .... G 618 439-2101
Benton *(G-1925)*
Home City Ice .... F 773 622-9400
Chicago *(G-4833)*
Interntnal Ice Bgging Systems .... G 312 633-4000
Glencoe *(G-10431)*
Muller-Pinehurst Dairy Inc .... C 815 968-0441
Rockford *(G-17533)*
Pro Rep Sale IL .... G 847 382-1592
Barrington *(G-1238)*
Sislers Ice Inc .... E 815 756-6903
Dekalb *(G-7701)*
Tinley Ice Company .... E 708 532-8777
University Park *(G-19968)*

ICE CREAM & ICES WHOLESALERS

Jel Sert Co .... C 630 231-7590
West Chicago *(G-20603)*
Mitchlls Cndies Ice Creams Inc .... F 708 799-3835
Homewood *(G-11501)*

ICE WHOLESALERS

Powerone Corp .... G 630 443-6500
Saint Charles *(G-18248)*

ICE: Dry

Dixie Carbonic Inc .... D 217 428-2068
Decatur *(G-7490)*

IDENTIFICATION PLATES

R L Allen Industries .... G 618 667-2544
Troy *(G-19919)*
Zing Enterprises LLC .... G 608 201-9490
Oswego *(G-16034)*

IDENTIFICATION TAGS, EXC PAPER

Bocks Cattle-Identi Co Inc .... G 217 234-6634
Mattoon *(G-13632)*
C H Hanson Company .... D 630 848-2000
Naperville *(G-14786)*
Edmark Visual Identification .... G 800 923-8333
Chicago *(G-4452)*

IGNEOUS ROCK: Crushed & Broken

Gateway Crushing & Screening .... E 618 337-1954
East Saint Louis *(G-8309)*
Monmouth Stone Co .... F 309 734-7951
Monmouth *(G-14224)*

IGNITION APPARATUS & DISTRIBUTORS

Charlotte Louise Tate .... G 773 849-3236
Chicago *(G-4076)*
Nidec Motor Corporation .... D 847 439-3760
Des Plaines *(G-7810)*

IGNITION SYSTEMS: Internal Combustion Engine

Motorola Solutions Inc .... C 847 576-8600
Schaumburg *(G-18637)*

INCINERATORS

Elastec Inc .... C 618 382-2525
Carmi *(G-2904)*
Enders Process Equipment Corp .... G 630 469-3787
Glendale Heights *(G-10449)*
Midco International .... E 773 604-8700
Chicago *(G-5433)*

PRODUCT SECTION

INCUBATORS & BROODERS: Farm

Company	Code	Phone
R Lamar Academy Inc — Peoria (G-16506)	G	309 712-8100

INDL & PERSONAL SVC PAPER WHOLESALERS

Company	Code	Phone
Bunzl Retail Services LLC — Morton Grove (G-14393)	E	847 966-2550
Hollymatic Corporation — Countryside (G-7057)	D	708 579-3700
Nanco Sales Co Inc — Aurora (G-1138)	G	630 892-9820
Qualified Innovation Inc — Sugar Grove (G-19651)	F	630 556-4136
Simu Ltd — Mc Cook (G-13701)	F	708 688-2200
Terrapin Xpress Inc — Palos Heights (G-16193)	G	866 823-7323
TLC Dental Care LLC — Elgin (G-8755)	G	425 442-9000
Tri Pro Graphics LLC — Bloomington (G-2104)	G	309 664-5875

INDL & PERSONAL SVC PAPER, WHOL: Bags, Paper/Disp Plastic

Company	Code	Phone
Poly Plastics Films Corp — Machesney Park (G-13365)	G	815 636-0821
Renew Packaging LLC — Chicago (G-6014)	G	312 421-6699
Sea-Rich Corp — Chicago (G-6124)	G	773 261-6633

INDL & PERSONAL SVC PAPER, WHOL: Boxes, Corrugtd/Solid Fiber

Company	Code	Phone
Georgia-Pacific LLC — Mount Olive (G-14503)	C	217 999-2511
Inglese Box Co Ltd — Huntley (G-11543)	E	847 669-1700
Pry-Bar Company — Joliet (G-11918)	F	815 436-3383
Rudd Container Corporation — Chicago (G-6079)	D	773 847-7600
Westrock Cp LLC — Galesburg (G-10224)	C	309 342-0121

INDL & PERSONAL SVC PAPER, WHOL: Boxes, Paperbrd/Plastic

Company	Code	Phone
Co-Ordinated Packaging Inc — Bensenville (G-1772)	F	847 559-8877

INDL & PERSONAL SVC PAPER, WHOL: Container, Paper/Plastic

Company	Code	Phone
Pactiv LLC — Lake Forest (G-12279)	A	847 482-2000

INDL & PERSONAL SVC PAPER, WHOL: Cups, Disp, Plastic/Paper

Company	Code	Phone
Amic Global Inc — Buffalo Grove (G-2512)	G	847 600-3590

INDL & PERSONAL SVC PAPER, WHOL: Paper, Wrap/Coarse/Prdts

Company	Code	Phone
Abbey Products LLP — Troy (G-19909)	G	636 922-5577
Orora North America — Lombard (G-13114)	D	630 613-2600
Orora Packaging Solutions — Sycamore (G-19727)	D	815 895-2343

INDL & PERSONAL SVC PAPER, WHOLESALE: Boxes & Containers

Company	Code	Phone
H Field & Sons Inc — Arlington Heights (G-745)	F	847 434-0970

INDL & PERSONAL SVC PAPER, WHOLESALE: Paperboard & Prdts

Company	Code	Phone
Roll Source Paper — Itasca (G-11728)	G	630 875-0308

INDL & PERSONAL SVC PAPER, WHOLESALE: Press Sensitive Tape

Company	Code	Phone
Hugh Courtright & Co Ltd — Monee (G-14202)	F	708 534-8400
Strata-Tac Inc — Saint Charles (G-18279)	F	630 879-9388

INDL & PERSONAL SVC PAPER, WHOLESALE: Shipping Splys

Company	Code	Phone
Compak Inc — Machesney Park (G-13335)	E	815 399-2699
Heritage Packaging LLC — Lincoln (G-12730)	E	217 735-4406
Layer Saver LLC — Burr Ridge (G-2696)	G	630 325-7287
Primedia Source LLC — Yorkville (G-21499)	G	630 553-8451
Quad-Illinois Inc — Elgin (G-8706)	F	847 836-1115
Weary & Baity Inc — Chicago (G-6594)	G	312 943-6197

INDL CONTRACTORS: Exhibit Construction

Company	Code	Phone
Proto Productions Inc — Addison (G-257)	E	630 628-6626

INDL DIAMONDS WHOLESALERS

Company	Code	Phone
Diamond Industrial Sales Ltd — Glen Ellyn (G-10400)	G	630 858-3687

INDL EQPT SVCS

Company	Code	Phone
AAA Press Specialists Inc — Arlington Heights (G-681)	F	847 818-1100
BSB International Corp — Bensenville (G-1759)	G	847 791-9272
C P Environmental Inc — Romeoville (G-17801)	F	630 759-8866
Cryogenic Systems Equipment — Blue Island (G-2116)	E	708 385-4216
D & N Deburring Co Inc — Franklin Park (G-9924)	G	847 451-7702
Dover Prtg Identification Inc — Downers Grove (G-7992)	D	630 541-1540
Dumore Supplies Inc — Chicago (G-4403)	F	312 949-6260
Electron Beam Technologies Inc — Kankakee (G-11967)	C	815 935-2211
Elmot Inc — Chicago (G-4489)	G	773 791-7039
Erowa Technology Inc — Arlington Heights (G-733)	F	847 290-0295
Gti Spindle Technology Inc — Bloomington (G-2054)	F	309 820-7887
Industrial Mint Wldg Machining — Chicago (G-4908)	D	773 376-6526
Kelly Systems Inc — Chicago (G-5093)	E	312 733-3224
Meta TEC Development Inc — Lacon (G-12131)	G	309 246-2960
Meyer Machine & Equipment Inc — Antioch (G-625)	E	847 395-2977
North Shore Truck & Equipment — Lake Bluff (G-12201)	F	847 887-0200
Plating International Inc — Franklin Park (G-10020)	F	847 451-2101
Richards Electric Motor Co — Quincy (G-16940)	E	217 222-7154
Sloan Industries Inc — Wood Dale (G-21241)	E	630 350-1614
Stickon Adhesive Inds Inc — Wauconda (G-20391)	G	847 593-5959
Stolp Gore Company — Plainfield (G-16717)	G	630 904-5180
Wehrli Equipment Co Inc — Naperville (G-14946)	F	630 717-4150
Windy City Laser Service Inc — Chicago (G-6642)	G	773 995-0188

INDL GASES WHOLESALERS

Company	Code	Phone
Airgas Inc — Chicago (G-3588)	F	773 785-3000
Airgas Usa LLC — Countryside (G-7043)	E	708 354-0813
American Welding & Gas Inc — Stone Park (G-19551)	E	630 527-2550
Boc Global Helium Inc — Montgomery (G-14235)	C	630 897-1900
Maccarb Inc — Elgin (G-8645)	G	877 427-2499
Messer LLC — Carol Stream (G-3024)	F	630 690-3010

INDL MACHINERY & EQPT WHOLESALERS

Company	Code	Phone
AAM-Ro Corporation — Broadview (G-2412)	F	708 343-5543
Active Automation Inc — Elk Grove Village (G-8806)	F	847 427-8100
Air Mite Devices Inc — Round Lake (G-18067)	E	224 338-0071
Airgas Inc — Chicago (G-3588)	F	773 785-3000
Alfa Controls Inc — Wheeling (G-20844)	G	847 978-9245
Alin Machining Company Inc — Melrose Park (G-13821)	C	708 681-1043
Altak Inc — Bloomingdale (G-1975)	D	630 622-0300
American Specialty Toy — Chicago (G-3669)	G	312 222-0984
Amj Industries Inc — Rockford (G-17302)	F	815 654-9000
Baley Enterprises Inc — Melrose Park (G-13830)	G	708 681-0900
Belden Machine Corporation — Broadview (G-2419)	F	708 344-4600
Century Filter Products Inc — Chicago (G-4060)	G	773 477-1790
Chicago Chain and Transm Co — Countryside (G-7046)	E	630 482-9000
Chicago Heights Star Tool and — Chicago Heights (G-6742)	F	708 758-2525
Chicago Metal Fabricators Inc — Chicago (G-4114)	D	773 523-5755
Clybourn Metal Finishing Co — Chicago (G-4183)	E	773 525-8162
Corrugated Converting Eqp — Centralia (G-3227)	F	618 532-2138
Craftsman Tool & Mold Co — Aurora (G-942)	E	630 851-8700
Custom Blades & Tools Inc — Bensenville (G-1782)	G	630 860-7650
Disa Holding Corp — Oswego (G-16002)	G	630 820-3000
DTS America Inc — East Dundee (G-8193)	E	847 783-0401
EJ Cady & Company — Wheeling (G-20888)	G	847 537-2239
Enerstar Inc — Bensenville (G-1797)	G	847 350-3400
Engineered Abrasives Inc — Alsip (G-445)	E	662 582-4143
Entrans International LLC — Salem (G-18337)	E	618 548-3660
Fill-Weigh Inc — Plainfield (G-16665)	G	815 254-4704
Frantz Manufacturing Company — Sterling (G-19509)	D	815 625-7063
Fusibond Piping Systems Inc — Downers Grove (G-8006)	F	630 969-4488
Hartland Cutting Tools Inc — Cary (G-3166)	F	847 639-9400
Hfo Chicago LLC — Elk Grove Village (G-9034)	F	847 258-2850
Hoerbiger-Origa Corporation — Glendale Heights (G-10456)	D	800 283-1377
Holland Applied Technologies — Burr Ridge (G-2683)	E	630 325-5130
Howard Schwartz — Round Lake Beach (G-18089)	G	847 540-8260
Hugh Courtright & Co Ltd — Monee (G-14202)	F	708 534-8400
Hyster-Yale Group Inc — Danville (G-7348)	E	217 443-7416
I W M Corporation — Elgin (G-8619)	G	847 695-0700
Illinois Oil Products Inc — Rock Island (G-17224)	F	309 788-1896
Inlet & Pipe Protection Inc — Naperville (G-14974)	G	630 355-3288
Intelligrated Systems Inc — Woodridge (G-21315)	B	630 985-4350
Interstate Power Systems Inc — Carol Stream (G-3006)	F	630 871-1111
Interstate Power Systems Inc — Rockford (G-17470)	D	952 854-2044

Employee Codes: A=Over 500 employees, B=251-500
C=101-250, D=51-100, E=20-50, F=10-19, G=3-9

INDL MACHINERY & EQPT WHOLESALERS

ITT Water & Wastewater USA Inc .... F 708 342-0484
  Tinley Park *(G-19840)*
Ives Way Products Inc .... G 847 223-1020
  Grayslake *(G-10784)*
J A K Enterprises Inc .... E 217 422-3881
  Decatur *(G-7509)*
Jamco Products Inc .... D 815 624-0400
  South Beloit *(G-19097)*
Jardis Industries Inc .... E 630 860-5959
  Itasca *(G-11680)*
Jn Pump Holdings Inc .... F 708 754-2940
  Chicago Heights *(G-6753)*
K R Komarek Inc .... E 847 956-0060
  Wood Dale *(G-21203)*
Knapheide Manufacturing Co .... E 217 223-1848
  Quincy *(G-16902)*
L & J Engineering Inc .... E 708 236-6000
  Hillside *(G-11344)*
Lab Ten LLC .... E 815 877-1410
  Machesney Park *(G-13355)*
Lc Holdings of Delaware Inc .... G 847 940-3550
  Deerfield *(G-7629)*
Lewis Paper Place Inc .... G 847 808-1343
  Wheeling *(G-20932)*
Liberty Machinery Company .... F 847 276-2761
  Lincolnshire *(G-12781)*
Litho Research Incorporated .... G 630 860-7070
  Itasca *(G-11695)*
Maac Machinery Co Inc .... E 630 665-1700
  Carol Stream *(G-3019)*
Mab Equipment Company .... G 630 551-4017
  Oswego *(G-16012)*
Mega Equipment Inc .... G 309 764-5310
  Moline *(G-14160)*
Midstate Manufacturing Company ..... C 309 342-9555
  Galesburg *(G-10210)*
Mitsubishi Heavy Inds Amer Inc .... F 630 693-4700
  Addison *(G-220)*
Mity Inc .... G 630 365-5030
  Elburn *(G-8461)*
Mueller Mfg Corp .... E 847 640-1666
  Elk Grove Village *(G-9139)*
Nalco Wtr Prtrtment Sltons LLC .... G 708 754-2550
  Glenwood *(G-10644)*
NBC Meshtec Americas Inc .... E 630 293-5454
  Batavia *(G-1398)*
Newssor Manufacturing Inc .... G 618 259-1174
  East Alton *(G-2830)*
Nidec-Shimpo America Corp .... E 630 924-7138
  Glendale Heights *(G-10479)*
O Adjust Matic Pump Company .... G 630 766-1490
  Wood Dale *(G-21224)*
Prime Devices Corporation .... F 847 729-2550
  Willow Springs *(G-21027)*
Process Mechanical Inc .... G 630 416-7021
  Naperville *(G-14902)*
Prosco Inc .... G 847 336-1323
  Gurnee *(G-10917)*
Proto-Cutter Inc .... F 815 232-2300
  Freeport *(G-10134)*
Rams Sheet Metal Equipment Inc ...... G 224 788-9900
  Antioch *(G-632)*
Randall Publishing Inc .... F 847 437-6604
  Elk Grove Village *(G-9214)*
Red Bud Industries Inc .... C 618 282-3801
  Red Bud *(G-17000)*
Renishaw Inc .... D 847 286-9953
  Dundee *(G-8131)*
Robert Brysiewicz Incorporated .... G 630 289-0903
  Bartlett *(G-1304)*
Smart Motion Robotics Inc .... E 815 895-8550
  Sycamore *(G-19732)*
Stein Inc .... D 618 452-0836
  Granite City *(G-10739)*
Stutz Company .... F 773 287-1068
  Chicago *(G-6259)*
Terco Inc .... E 630 894-8828
  Bloomingdale *(G-2016)*
Thomas Engineering Inc .... D 847 358-5800
  Hoffman Estates *(G-11469)*
Triumph Twist Drill Co Inc .... B 815 459-6250
  Crystal Lake *(G-7286)*
Tru-Cut Tool & Supply Co .... F 708 396-1122
  Wheeling *(G-21002)*
Uesco Industries Inc .... G 708 385-7700
  Alsip *(G-517)*
Ultra Packaging Inc .... G 630 595-9820
  Bensenville *(G-1905)*
Ultramatic Equipment Co .... E 630 543-4565
  Addison *(G-322)*

Wehrli Equipment Co Inc .... F 630 717-4150
  Naperville *(G-14946)*

INDL MACHINERY REPAIR & MAINTENANCE

Action Turbine Repair Svc Inc .... F 708 924-9601
  Summit Argo *(G-19677)*
Alin Machining Company Inc .... C 708 681-1043
  Melrose Park *(G-13821)*
Best Rep Company Corporation .... G 847 451-6644
  Franklin Park *(G-9886)*
Bonell Manufacturing Company .... E 708 849-1770
  Riverdale *(G-17069)*
Bos Machine Tool Services Inc .... F 309 658-2223
  Hillsdale *(G-11321)*
Bourn & Koch Inc .... D 815 965-4013
  Rockford *(G-17328)*
Cartpac Inc .... E 630 283-8979
  Carol Stream *(G-2956)*
Cloos Robotic Welding Inc .... F 847 923-9988
  Schaumburg *(G-18479)*
Commercial Machine Services .... F 847 806-1901
  Elk Grove Village *(G-8905)*
Control Works Inc .... G 630 444-1942
  Saint Charles *(G-18174)*
Dainichi Machinery Inc .... G 630 681-1572
  Carol Stream *(G-2970)*
David Schutte .... G 217 223-5464
  Quincy *(G-16874)*
E & H Graphic Service Inc .... E 708 748-5656
  Matteson *(G-13623)*
Gilday Services .... G 847 395-0853
  Antioch *(G-613)*
Global Maintenance LLC .... E 270 933-1281
  Metropolis *(G-13971)*
Hardinge Grinding Group Inc .... E 847 888-0148
  Elgin *(G-8606)*
Hts Coatings LLC .... E 618 215-8161
  Madison *(G-13414)*
Industrial Instrument Svc Corp .... G 773 581-3355
  Chicago *(G-4907)*
Jingdiao North America Inc .... F 847 906-8888
  Mount Prospect *(G-14540)*
Lipscomb Engineering Inc .... G 630 231-3833
  West Chicago *(G-20608)*
McCloskey Eyman Mlone Mfg Svcs ..... G 309 647-4000
  Canton *(G-2830)*
Mj Snyder Ironworks Inc .... E 217 826-6440
  Marshall *(G-13575)*
Modern Fluid Technology Inc .... G 815 356-0001
  Crystal Lake *(G-7232)*
Patrick Holdings Inc .... F 815 874-5300
  Rockford *(G-17549)*
Pillarhouse USA Inc .... F 847 593-9080
  Elk Grove Village *(G-9179)*
Quality Machine Tool Services .... G 847 776-0073
  Schaumburg *(G-18692)*
Robey Packaging Eqp & Svc .... F 708 758-8250
  Chicago Heights *(G-6771)*
S G Acquisition Inc .... F 815 624-6501
  South Beloit *(G-19113)*
Service Cutting & Welding .... G 773 622-8366
  Chicago *(G-6142)*
Sun Centre Usa Inc .... F 224 699-9058
  Crystal Lake *(G-7271)*
Tonys Welding Service Inc .... G 618 532-9353
  Centralia *(G-3253)*
Total Tooling Technology Inc .... F 847 437-5135
  Elk Grove Village *(G-9279)*
Tox- Pressotechnik LLC .... G 630 447-4600
  Warrenville *(G-20254)*
Uesco Industries Inc .... E 800 325-8372
  Alsip *(G-518)*
Wemco Inc .... F 708 388-1980
  Alsip *(G-524)*
World Cup Packaging Inc .... G 815 624-6501
  South Beloit *(G-19127)*
WW Engineering Company LLC .... F 773 376-9494
  Chicago *(G-6690)*

INDL PATTERNS: Foundry Cores

Cores For You Inc .... E 217 847-3233
  Hamilton *(G-10952)*
Johnson Pattern & Mch Works .... E 815 433-2775
  Ottawa *(G-16057)*
Midstate Core Co .... E 217 429-2673
  Decatur *(G-7523)*

PRODUCT SECTION

INDL PATTERNS: Foundry Patternmaking

Arnette Pattern Co Inc .... E 618 451-7700
  Granite City *(G-10698)*
Olson Aluminum Castings Ltd .... E 815 229-3292
  Rockford *(G-17544)*
Park Products Inc .... G 630 543-2474
  Addison *(G-233)*
Prs Inc .... G 630 620-7259
  Lombard *(G-13123)*

INDL PROCESS INSTR: Transmit, Process Variables

Autrol Corporation of AME .... G 847 874-7545
  Crystal Lake *(G-7166)*
Autrol Corporation of America .... F 847 779-5000
  Schaumburg *(G-18450)*
Landairsea Systems Inc .... F 847 462-8100
  Woodstock *(G-21403)*

INDL PROCESS INSTRUMENTS: Absorp Analyzers, Infrared, X-Ray

Alti LLC .... G 951 505-3148
  Highland Park *(G-11252)*

INDL PROCESS INSTRUMENTS: Analyzers

Electronic System Design Inc .... G 847 358-8212
  Bensenville *(G-1794)*

INDL PROCESS INSTRUMENTS: Boiler Controls, Power & Marine

Fuel Tech Inc .... C 630 845-4500
  Warrenville *(G-20237)*
Innovative Marine Safety Inc .... G 618 254-9470
  Wood River *(G-21264)*

INDL PROCESS INSTRUMENTS: Control

ARI Industries Inc .... D 630 953-9100
  Addison *(G-38)*
Charnor Inc .... D 309 787-2427
  Milan *(G-14002)*
Janco Process Controls Inc .... E 847 526-0800
  Wauconda *(G-20363)*
Modern Fluid Technology Inc .... G 815 356-0001
  Crystal Lake *(G-7232)*
Pullman Company .... G 847 482-5000
  Lake Forest *(G-12293)*
Schneider Elc Buildings LLC .... B 815 381-5000
  Rockford *(G-17622)*
Schneider Elc Holdings Inc .... A 717 944-5460
  Schaumburg *(G-18707)*

INDL PROCESS INSTRUMENTS: Controllers, Process Variables

Mid-American Elevator Co Inc .... C 773 486-6900
  Chicago *(G-5428)*
Mid-American Elevator Co Inc .... E 815 740-1204
  Joliet *(G-11902)*

INDL PROCESS INSTRUMENTS: Data Loggers

Embedor Technologies Inc .... G 202 681-0359
  Champaign *(G-3289)*

INDL PROCESS INSTRUMENTS: Digital Display, Process Variables

Liveone Inc .... G 312 282-2320
  Chicago *(G-5242)*
Tomantron Inc .... F 708 532-2456
  Tinley Park *(G-19860)*

INDL PROCESS INSTRUMENTS: Draft Gauges

Indev Gauging Systems Inc .... G 815 282-4463
  Loves Park *(G-13219)*

INDL PROCESS INSTRUMENTS: Elements, Primary

Principal Instruments Inc .... G 815 469-8159
  Frankfort *(G-9827)*

PRODUCT SECTION

INDL SPLYS, WHOLESALE: Pipeline Wrappings, Anti-Corrosive

INDL PROCESS INSTRUMENTS: Indl Flow & Measuring

Nordson Asymtek Inc .... C 760 431-1919
  Chicago *(G-5615)*

INDL PROCESS INSTRUMENTS: Level & Bulk Measuring

Level Developments Ltd .... G 312 465-1082
  Chicago *(G-5210)*
Magnetrol International Inc .... C 630 723-6600
  Aurora *(G-1001)*

INDL PROCESS INSTRUMENTS: Manometers

Rosemount Inc .... G 217 877-5278
  Decatur *(G-7543)*

INDL PROCESS INSTRUMENTS: Temperature

Dickson/Unigage Inc .... E 630 543-3747
  Addison *(G-92)*
Eclipse Inc .... D 815 877-3031
  Rockford *(G-17388)*
Industrial Thermo Products .... G 847 398-8600
  Rolling Meadows *(G-17740)*

INDL PROCESS INSTRUMENTS: Water Quality Monitoring/Cntrl Sys

Automated Logic Corporation .... F 630 852-1700
  Lisle *(G-12870)*
Azcon Inc .... F 815 548-7000
  Sterling *(G-19499)*
Enerstar Inc .... G 847 350-3400
  Bensenville *(G-1797)*
G-M Services .... G 618 532-2324
  Centralia *(G-3232)*
Pan America Environmental Inc .... G 815 344-2960
  McHenry *(G-13775)*
Village Hampshire Trtmnt Plant .... G 847 683-2064
  Hampshire *(G-10989)*
Village Hebron Water Sewage .... G 815 648-2353
  Hebron *(G-11154)*

INDL SALTS WHOLESALERS

K+s Salt LLC .... G 844 789-3991
  Chicago *(G-5070)*

INDL SPLYS WHOLESALERS

ABM Marking Ltd .... F 618 277-3773
  Belleville *(G-1526)*
Afc Cable Systems Inc .... B 508 998-1131
  Harvey *(G-11070)*
Ajr Enterprises Inc .... C 630 377-8886
  Saint Charles *(G-18143)*
American Industrial Direct LLC .... E 800 382-1200
  Elgin *(G-8507)*
Blastline USA Inc .... G 630 871-0147
  Carol Stream *(G-2951)*
Chase Fasteners Inc .... E 708 345-0335
  Melrose Park *(G-13841)*
Darbe Products Company Inc .... G 630 985-0769
  Woodridge *(G-21292)*
Dixon Brass .... E 630 323-3716
  Westmont *(G-20738)*
Dvcc Inc .... E 630 323-3105
  Westmont *(G-20739)*
Fca LLC .... E 309 949-3999
  Coal Valley *(G-6936)*
Fca LLC .... E 309 385-2588
  Princeville *(G-16827)*
Fca LLC .... E 309 792-3444
  Moline *(G-14145)*
Flexicraft Industries Inc .... F 312 229-7550
  Chicago *(G-4609)*
Graphic Pallet & Transport .... E 630 904-4951
  Plainfield *(G-16669)*
Illinois Tool Works Inc .... C 847 299-2222
  Des Plaines *(G-7785)*
Jacob Hay Company .... G 847 215-8880
  Wheeling *(G-20918)*
Kocour Co .... E 773 847-1111
  Chicago *(G-5114)*
Lamin-Art LLC .... F 800 323-7624
  Schaumburg *(G-18598)*

Litho Research Incorporated .... G 630 860-7070
  Itasca *(G-11695)*
M Cor Inc .... F 630 860-1150
  Bensenville *(G-1846)*
Megadyne America LLC .... E 630 752-0600
  Carol Stream *(G-3023)*
Midwest Cnstr Svcs Inc Peoria .... F 309 697-1000
  Bartonville *(G-1335)*
Omar Medical Supplies Inc .... F 708 922-4276
  Chicago *(G-5673)*
Primedia Source LLC .... G 630 553-8451
  Yorkville *(G-21499)*
Resource Plastics Inc .... D 708 389-3558
  Alsip *(G-503)*
RR Donnelley Printing Co LP .... G 312 326-8000
  Chicago *(G-6072)*
S & J Industrial Supply Corp .... F 708 339-1708
  South Holland *(G-19242)*
Samuel Son & Co (usa) Inc .... D 630 783-8900
  Woodridge *(G-21338)*
Shima American Corporation .... F 630 760-4330
  Itasca *(G-11732)*
Steel-Guard Safety Corp .... E 708 589-4588
  South Holland *(G-19246)*
Superior Mfg Group - Europe .... E 708 458-4600
  Chicago *(G-6283)*
Supplied Indus Solutions Inc .... G 618 452-8151
  Granite City *(G-10741)*
Trane Technologies Company LLC ... E 630 530-3800
  Elmhurst *(G-9436)*
United Remanufacturing Co Inc ...... E 773 777-1223
  Schiller Park *(G-18850)*
Wallace/Haskin Corp .... G 630 789-2882
  Downers Grove *(G-8105)*

INDL SPLYS, WHOL: Fasteners, Incl Nuts, Bolts, Screws, Etc

Classic Fasteners LLC .... G 630 605-0195
  Saint Charles *(G-18170)*
Engineered Components Co .... E 847 985-8000
  Elgin *(G-8579)*
Great Lakes Washer Company .... F 630 887-7447
  Burr Ridge *(G-2677)*
Intech Industries Inc .... F 847 487-5599
  Wauconda *(G-20361)*
Set Screw & Mfg Co .... E 847 717-3700
  Elgin *(G-8727)*

INDL SPLYS, WHOLESALE: Abrasives

Abrasic 90 Inc .... E 847 647-5994
  Niles *(G-15098)*
Agsco Corporation .... E 847 520-4455
  Wheeling *(G-20842)*
Bronson & Bratton Inc .... C 630 986-1815
  Burr Ridge *(G-2658)*
K & K Abrasives & Supplies .... E 773 582-9500
  Chicago *(G-5063)*
Weld Cote Metals .... G 888 258-0121
  Niles *(G-15186)*

INDL SPLYS, WHOLESALE: Adhesives, Tape & Plasters

Adhes Tape Technology Inc .... G 847 496-7949
  Arlington Heights *(G-683)*
C H Hanson Company .... D 630 848-2000
  Naperville *(G-14786)*
Fontana Associates Inc .... G 888 707-8273
  Wauconda *(G-20352)*
Lanmar Inc .... G 800 233-5520
  Northbrook *(G-15418)*
Strata-Tac Inc .... F 630 879-9388
  Saint Charles *(G-18279)*
Tape Case Ltd .... E 847 299-7880
  Elk Grove Village *(G-9265)*

INDL SPLYS, WHOLESALE: Bearings

Bearing Sales Corporation .... E 773 282-8686
  Chicago *(G-3855)*
Ccty USA Bearing Co .... G 847 540-8196
  Lake Zurich *(G-12391)*
Composite Bearings Mfg .... F 630 595-8334
  Wood Dale *(G-21178)*
Group O Inc .... B 309 736-8311
  Milan *(G-14014)*
Headco Industries Inc .... F 847 640-6490
  Elk Grove Village *(G-9031)*

Headco Industries Inc .... G 815 729-4016
  Joliet *(G-11875)*
Inpro/Seal LLC .... C 309 787-8940
  Rock Island *(G-17225)*
Isostatic Industries Inc .... E 773 286-3444
  Chicago *(G-4973)*
NTN USA Corporation .... C 847 298-4652
  Mount Prospect *(G-14554)*
R & O Specialties Incorporated ...... D 309 736-8660
  Milan *(G-14022)*
Voss Engineering Inc .... E 847 673-8900
  Lincolnwood *(G-12850)*

INDL SPLYS, WHOLESALE: Bins & Containers, Storage

Arrows Up Inc .... G 847 305-2550
  Arlington Heights *(G-696)*

INDL SPLYS, WHOLESALE: Bottler Splys

Pepsi-Cola Metro Btlg Co Inc .... D 847 598-3000
  Chicago *(G-5788)*

INDL SPLYS, WHOLESALE: Cordage

Tri Vantage LLC .... F 630 530-5333
  Elmhurst *(G-9438)*

INDL SPLYS, WHOLESALE: Drums, New Or Reconditioned

Higgins Bros Inc .... F 773 523-0124
  Chicago *(G-4815)*
Meyer Steel Drum Inc .... E 773 522-3030
  Chicago *(G-5416)*
Meyer Steel Drum Inc .... C 773 376-8376
  Chicago *(G-5417)*

INDL SPLYS, WHOLESALE: Fasteners & Fastening Eqpt

J B Watts Company Inc .... G 773 643-1855
  Chicago *(G-4987)*

INDL SPLYS, WHOLESALE: Filters, Indl

Bisco Enterprise Inc .... F 630 628-1831
  Schaumburg *(G-18463)*
Filter Kleen Inc .... G 708 447-4666
  Lyons *(G-13308)*
GAG Industries Inc .... E 847 616-8710
  Elk Grove Village *(G-9008)*
Murdock Company Inc .... G 847 566-0050
  Mundelein *(G-14719)*

INDL SPLYS, WHOLESALE: Gaskets

Capital Rubber Corporation .... F 630 595-6644
  Bensenville *(G-1762)*
Plastic Specialties & Tech Inc .... G 847 781-2414
  Schaumburg *(G-18675)*

INDL SPLYS, WHOLESALE: Gaskets & Seals

Hennig Gasket & Seals Inc .... G 312 243-8270
  Chicago *(G-4803)*

INDL SPLYS, WHOLESALE: Gears

Flender Corporation .... C 847 931-1990
  Elgin *(G-8588)*
Gear & Repair .... G 708 387-0144
  Brookfield *(G-2485)*
Illinois Pulley & Gear Inc .... G 847 407-9595
  Schaumburg *(G-18556)*
Omni Gear and Machine Corp .... F 815 723-4327
  Joliet *(G-11911)*
Smith Power Transmission Co .... G 773 526-5512
  Chicago *(G-6193)*

INDL SPLYS, WHOLESALE: Glass Bottles

Libation Container Inc .... G 312 636-7206
  Chicago *(G-5217)*

INDL SPLYS, WHOLESALE: Pipeline Wrappings, Anti-Corrosive

Buckeye Partners LP .... G 217 342-2336
  Effingham *(G-8390)*

Employee Codes: A=Over 500 employees, B=251-500
C=101-250, D=51-100, E=20-50, F=10-19, G=3-9

INDL SPLYS, WHOLESALE: Plastic Bottles

INDL SPLYS, WHOLESALE: Plastic Bottles
Decorative Industries Inc .... E 773 229-0015
  Chicago *(G-4329)*

INDL SPLYS, WHOLESALE: Power Transmission, Eqpt & Apparatus
Chicago Chain and Transm Co .... E 630 482-9000
  Countryside *(G-7046)*
Nidec-Shimpo America Corp .... E 630 924-7138
  Glendale Heights *(G-10479)*
US Tsubaki Holdings Inc .... C 847 459-9500
  Wheeling *(G-21003)*
US Tsubaki Power Transm LLC .... C 847 459-9500
  Wheeling *(G-21004)*

INDL SPLYS, WHOLESALE: Rubber Goods, Mechanical
Accurate Products Incorporated .... E 773 878-2200
  Chicago *(G-3520)*
Allstates Rubber & Tool Corp .... F 708 342-1030
  Tinley Park *(G-19800)*
Industrial Rubber & Sup Entp .... G 217 429-3747
  Decatur *(G-7507)*
ONeill Products Inc .... G 312 243-3413
  Chicago *(G-5678)*

INDL SPLYS, WHOLESALE: Seals
AMS Seals Inc .... G 815 609-4977
  Plainfield *(G-16642)*
Lochman Ref Silk Screen Co .... F 847 475-6266
  Evanston *(G-9547)*
Rt Enterprises Inc .... F 847 675-1444
  Skokie *(G-19025)*

INDL SPLYS, WHOLESALE: Signmaker Eqpt & Splys
Component Products Inc .... E 847 301-1000
  Elmhurst *(G-9352)*
Mich Enterprises Inc .... F 630 616-9000
  Wood Dale *(G-21216)*

INDL SPLYS, WHOLESALE: Springs
Ascent Mfg Co .... E 847 806-6600
  Elk Grove Village *(G-8841)*
Mid-West Spring & Stamping Inc .... G 630 739-3800
  Romeoville *(G-17854)*
R & G Spring Co Inc .... E 847 228-5640
  Elk Grove Village *(G-9208)*

INDL SPLYS, WHOLESALE: Staplers & Tackers
Ample Supply Company .... E 815 895-3500
  Sycamore *(G-19700)*

INDL SPLYS, WHOLESALE: Textile Printers' Splys
Chicago Silk Screen Sup Co Inc .... E 312 666-1213
  Chicago *(G-4129)*
Sg2 .... G 847 779-5500
  Skokie *(G-19029)*

INDL SPLYS, WHOLESALE: Tools
David Linderholm .... G 847 336-3755
  Waukegan *(G-20434)*
General Cutng Tl Svc & Mfg Inc .... F 847 677-8770
  Lincolnwood *(G-12821)*
Imprex International Inc .... G 847 364-4930
  Arlington Heights *(G-756)*
Regal Beloit Corporation .... C 844 527-8392
  Roscoe *(G-17923)*
Tapco USA Inc .... G 815 877-4039
  Loves Park *(G-13271)*
Top Notch Tool & Supply Inc .... G 815 633-6295
  Cherry Valley *(G-3447)*
Universal Broaching Inc .... F 847 228-1440
  Elk Grove Village *(G-9298)*

INDL SPLYS, WHOLESALE: Tools, NEC
Belcar Products Inc .... G 630 462-1950
  Carol Stream *(G-2946)*
Bridgeport Air Comprsr & Tl Co .... G 618 945-7163
  Bridgeport *(G-2310)*

INDL SPLYS, WHOLESALE: Valves & Fittings
Clarios .... D 708 474-1717
  Calumet City *(G-2773)*
Cleavenger Associates Inc .... G 630 221-0007
  Winfield *(G-21109)*
Industrial Pipe and Supply Co .... E 708 652-7511
  Chicago *(G-4909)*
Lewis Process Systems Inc .... F 630 510-8200
  Carol Stream *(G-3018)*
Mj Works Hose & Fitting LLC .... G 708 995-5723
  Mokena *(G-14098)*
O C Keckley Company .... E 847 674-8422
  Skokie *(G-18997)*

INDL SPLYS, WHOLESALE: Wheels
Diagrind Inc .... F 708 460-4333
  Orland Park *(G-15951)*
Hayes Abrasives Inc .... F 217 532-6850
  Hillsboro *(G-11313)*

INDL TOOL GRINDING SVCS
A&W Tool Inc 815 653-1700
  Ringwood *(G-17037)*
Diamond Edge Manufacturing .... G 630 458-1630
  Addison *(G-88)*
Kmp Tool Grinding Inc .... F 847 205-9640
  Northbrook *(G-15413)*
Sterling Tool & Manufacturing .... G 847 304-1800
  Barrington *(G-1245)*

INDUCTORS
Communication Coil Inc .... D 847 671-1333
  Schiller Park *(G-18795)*
Induction Innovations Inc .... G 847 836-6933
  Elgin *(G-8625)*

INDUSTRIAL & COMMERCIAL EQPT INSPECTION SVCS
Dabrico Inc .... E 815 939-0580
  Bourbonnais *(G-2259)*
Locusview Solutions Inc .... E 312 548-3848
  Chicago *(G-5248)*
Nordex Usa Inc .... D 312 386-4100
  Chicago *(G-5614)*
X-Tech Innovations Inc 815 962-4127
  Rockford *(G-17691)*

INERTIAL GUIDANCE SYSTEMS
Engility Corporation .... G 847 583-1216
  Skokie *(G-18951)*
Engility Corporation .... G 708 596-8245
  Harvey *(G-11083)*

INFORMATION RETRIEVAL SERVICES
Sprout Social Inc .... D 866 878-3231
  Chicago *(G-6221)*

INFRARED OBJECT DETECTION EQPT
Epir Technologies Inc .... E 630 771-0203
  Bolingbrook *(G-2175)*

INGOT, EXTRUSION: Extrusion ingot, aluminum: rolling mills
Plastic Power Extrusions Corp .... E 847 233-9901
  Schiller Park *(G-18832)*
Werner Co .... E 815 459-6020
  Crystal Lake *(G-7294)*

INGOTS: Steel
A Finkl & Sons Co .... B 773 975-2510
  Chicago *(G-3488)*

INK OR WRITING FLUIDS
Chicago Ink & Research Co Inc .... G 847 395-1078
  Antioch *(G-608)*
Domino Amjet Inc .... E 847 662-3148
  Gurnee *(G-10869)*
Domino Amjet Inc .... D 847 244-2501
  Gurnee *(G-10870)*
Flint Group US LLC .... F 920 725-0101
  Romeoville *(G-17823)*
Graphic Sciences Inc .... G 630 226-0994
  Bolingbrook *(G-2180)*
I S C America Inc .... G 630 616-1331
  Wood Dale *(G-21199)*
INX International Ink Co .... E 630 681-7200
  West Chicago *(G-20600)*
INX International Ink Co .... E 630 382-1800
  Schaumburg *(G-18571)*
INX International Ink Co .... E 630 681-7100
  West Chicago *(G-20601)*
Modern Printing Colors Inc .... F 708 681-5678
  Broadview *(G-2453)*
Phoenix Inks and Coatings LLC .... F 630 972-2500
  Lemont *(G-12582)*
Siegwerk Eic LLC .... F 800 728-8200
  West Chicago *(G-20641)*
Sun Chemical Corporation .... C 630 513-5348
  Saint Charles *(G-18281)*
Zeller + Gmelin Corporation .... G 630 443-8800
  Saint Charles *(G-18304)*

INK: Gravure
Buzz Sales Company Inc .... G 815 459-1170
  Crystal Lake *(G-7175)*
Graphic Chemical & Ink Co .... F 630 832-6004
  Villa Park *(G-20149)*

INK: Letterpress Or Offset
Central Ink Corporation .... D 630 231-6500
  West Chicago *(G-20560)*

INK: Lithographic
Cudner & OConnor Co .... F 773 826-0200
  Chicago *(G-4283)*
Scientific Colors Inc .... C 815 744-5650
  Rockdale *(G-17274)*

INK: Printing
ABM Marking Ltd .... F 618 277-3773
  Belleville *(G-1526)*
Actega North America Inc .... G 847 690-9310
  Elk Grove Village *(G-8805)*
Alden & Ott Printing Inks Co .... D 847 956-6830
  Arlington Heights *(G-686)*
Alden & Ott Printing Inks Co .... F 847 364-6817
  Mount Prospect *(G-14511)*
CIS Systems Inc .... G 847 827-0747
  Glenview *(G-10537)*
Domino Holdings Inc .... D 847 244-2501
  Gurnee *(G-10871)*
Dots UT Inc .... G 217 390-3286
  Champaign *(G-3286)*
Dynamic Colors Inc .... G 847 721-8834
  Evanston *(G-9512)*
Environmental Inks & Coding .... F 630 231-7313
  West Chicago *(G-20574)*
Environmental Specialties Inc .... G 630 860-7070
  Itasca *(G-11651)*
Flint Group US LLC .... E 630 526-9903
  Batavia *(G-1379)*
Flint Group US LLC .... F 920 725-0101
  Romeoville *(G-17823)*
Flint Group US LLC .... F 618 349-8384
  Saint Peter *(G-18324)*
Hostmann Steinberg Inc .... F 502 968-5961
  Kankakee *(G-11976)*
Hubergroup Usa Inc .... D 815 929-9293
  Rolling Meadows *(G-17737)*
Hurst Chemical Company .... G 815 964-0451
  Rockford *(G-17454)*
Hydro Ink Corp .... G 847 674-0057
  Skokie *(G-18967)*
I C T W Ink .... G 630 893-4658
  Roselle *(G-17957)*
I Q Infinity LLC .... G 773 651-2556
  Chicago *(G-4868)*
I S C America Inc .... G 630 616-1331
  Wood Dale *(G-21199)*
Ink Solutions LLC .... F 847 593-5200
  Elk Grove Village *(G-9052)*
Ink Systems Inc .... G 847 427-2200
  Elk Grove Village *(G-9053)*
Interactive Inks Coatings Corp .... F 847 289-8710
  South Elgin *(G-19157)*
INX Digital International Co .... F 630 382-1800
  Schaumburg *(G-18567)*
INX Group .... G 847 441-0600
  Elk Grove Village *(G-9060)*
INX Group Ltd .... G 708 799-1993
  Homewood *(G-11499)*

PRODUCT SECTION
INSTRUMENTS, MEASURING & CONTROLLING: Ultrasonic Testing

INX Group Ltd .... G 630 382-1800
  Schaumburg *(G-18568)*
INX International Ink Co .... D 630 382-1800
  Schaumburg *(G-18569)*
INX International Ink Co .... F 708 799-1993
  Homewood *(G-11500)*
INX International Ink Co .... E 630 681-7200
  West Chicago *(G-20600)*
INX International Ink Co .... E 708 496-3600
  Chicago *(G-4966)*
INX International Ink Co .... E 800 233-4657
  Schaumburg *(G-18570)*
INX International Ink Co .... E 630 382-1800
  Chicago *(G-4967)*
INX International Ink Co .... F 630 382-1800
  Schaumburg *(G-18571)*
INX International Ink Co .... E 630 681-7100
  West Chicago *(G-20601)*
L P S Express Inc .... G 217 636-7683
  Springfield *(G-19396)*
Laser Technology Group Inc .... G 847 524-4088
  Elk Grove Village *(G-9087)*
Midwest Ink Co .... E 708 345-7177
  Broadview *(G-2451)*
Paper Graphics Inc .... G 847 276-2727
  Lincolnshire *(G-12790)*
Precision Ink Corporation .... F 847 952-1500
  Elk Grove Village *(G-9191)*
Process Supply Company Inc .... G 312 943-8338
  Chicago *(G-5890)*
R A Kerley Ink Engineers Inc .... E 708 344-1295
  Broadview *(G-2462)*
Springbox Inc .... G 708 921-9944
  Flossmoor *(G-9702)*
Sun Chemical Corporation .... C 708 562-0550
  Northlake *(G-15561)*
Sun Chemical Corporation .... D 815 939-0136
  Kankakee *(G-12009)*
Sun Graphic Inc .... D 773 775-6755
  Chicago *(G-6269)*
Thrall Enterprises Inc .... F 312 621-8200
  Chicago *(G-6372)*
Toyo Ink International Corp .... F 630 930-5100
  Addison *(G-316)*
Toyo Ink International Corp .... F 866 969-8696
  Wood Dale *(G-21251)*
U S Colors & Coatings Inc .... G 630 879-8898
  Batavia *(G-1435)*
Wikoff Color Corporation .... G 847 487-2704
  Wauconda *(G-20403)*

INK: Screen process
Kolorcure Corporation .... F 630 879-9050
  Batavia *(G-1389)*

INSECTICIDES
Nufarm Americas Inc .... D 708 756-2010
  Chicago Heights *(G-6762)*
S C Johnson & Son Inc .... C 312 702-3100
  Chicago *(G-6085)*

INSECTICIDES & PESTICIDES
Clarke Group Inc .... C 630 894-2000
  Saint Charles *(G-18168)*
Clarke Mosquito Ctrl Pdts Inc .... C 630 894-2000
  Saint Charles *(G-18169)*
Rdl Marketing Inc .... G 773 254-7600
  Chicago *(G-5980)*
Soil Chemical Corporation .... G 714 761-3292
  Decatur *(G-7547)*

INSPECTION & TESTING SVCS
Research and Testing Worx Inc .... G 815 734-7346
  Mount Morris *(G-14501)*
Sub Source Inc .... E 815 968-7800
  Rockford *(G-17649)*

INSTR, MEASURE & CONTROL: Gauge, Oil Pressure & Water Temp
Alphagage .... G 815 391-6400
  Rockford *(G-17299)*
E-Motion LLC .... G 815 825-4411
  Fairbury *(G-9606)*
Water Services Company of Ill .... G 847 697-6623
  Elgin *(G-8777)*

INSTRUMENTS & METERS: Measuring, Electric
Design Technology Inc .... E 630 920-1300
  Westmont *(G-20736)*
Innovative Sports Training Inc .... G 773 244-6470
  Chicago *(G-4932)*
P K Neuses Incorporated .... G 847 253-6555
  Rolling Meadows *(G-17758)*
S Himmelstein and Company .... E 847 843-3300
  Hoffman Estates *(G-11452)*

INSTRUMENTS, LAB: Refractometers, Exc Indl Process Types
Mettler-Toledo LLC .... E 630 446-7700
  Aurora *(G-1002)*

INSTRUMENTS, LAB: Spectroscopic/Optical Properties Measuring
Omex Technologies Inc .... G 847 850-5858
  Wheeling *(G-20949)*
Talis Biomedical Corporation .... G 312 589-5000
  Chicago *(G-6314)*

INSTRUMENTS, LABORATORY: Analyzers, Automatic Chemical
Alti LLC .... G 951 505-3148
  Highland Park *(G-11252)*

INSTRUMENTS, LABORATORY: Blood Testing
Abbott Laboratories .... A 224 667-6100
  Abbott Park *(G-1)*
Abbott Laboratories .... G 800 551-5838
  Lake Forest *(G-12218)*
Cambridge Sensors USA LLC .... G 877 374-4062
  Plainfield *(G-16647)*

INSTRUMENTS, LABORATORY: Infrared Analytical
Enhanced Plasmonics LLC .... G 904 238-9270
  Evanston *(G-9513)*

INSTRUMENTS, LABORATORY: Photomicrographic
St Imaging Inc .... F 847 501-3344
  Northbrook *(G-15487)*

INSTRUMENTS, LABORATORY: Ultraviolet Analytical
Prime Systems Inc .... E 630 681-2100
  Carol Stream *(G-3049)*

INSTRUMENTS, MEASURING & CNTRL: Radiation & Testing, Nuclear
7 Mile Solutions Inc .... E 847 588-2280
  Niles *(G-15096)*
Gamma Products Inc .... F 708 974-4100
  Palos Hills *(G-16201)*

INSTRUMENTS, MEASURING & CNTRL: Testing, Abrasion, Etc
Controls Group USA Inc .... G 847 551-5775
  Elgin *(G-8555)*
EJ Cady & Company .... G 847 537-2239
  Wheeling *(G-20888)*
Kiene Diesel Accessories Inc .... E 630 543-7170
  Addison *(G-169)*
Kocour Co .... E 773 847-1111
  Chicago *(G-5114)*
Libco Industries Inc .... F 815 623-7677
  Roscoe *(G-17912)*
Schultes Precision Mfg Inc .... D 847 465-0300
  Buffalo Grove *(G-2596)*
Technics Inc .... F 630 938-4709
  Bolingbrook *(G-2248)*

INSTRUMENTS, MEASURING & CNTRLG: Aircraft & Motor Vehicle
Emissions Systems Incorporated .... G 847 669-8044
  Lake In The Hills *(G-12333)*
TRC Environmental Corp .... G 630 953-9046
  Burr Ridge *(G-2724)*

INSTRUMENTS, MEASURING & CNTRLG: Thermometers/Temp Sensors
7000 Inc .... F 312 800-3612
  Bolingbrook *(G-2143)*
Apollo Sensors Inc .... F 630 293-5820
  West Chicago *(G-20542)*
Biosynergy Inc .... G 847 956-0471
  Elk Grove Village *(G-8867)*
Durex International Corp .... B 847 639-5600
  Cary *(G-3157)*
Ewikon Molding Tech Inc .... E 815 874-7270
  Rockford *(G-17405)*
I C Innovations Inc .... E 847 279-7888
  Highland Park *(G-11271)*
Industrial Thermo Products .... G 847 398-8600
  Rolling Meadows *(G-17740)*
Melt Design Inc .... F 630 443-4000
  Saint Charles *(G-18232)*
Watlow Electric Mfg Co .... G 314 878-4600
  Richmond *(G-17025)*

INSTRUMENTS, MEASURING & CNTRLNG: Nuclear Instrument Modules
Coinstar Procurement LLC .... G 630 424-4788
  Oakbrook Terrace *(G-15794)*
Laboratory Technologies Inc .... G 630 365-1000
  Elburn *(G-8456)*
M I E America Inc .... F 847 981-6100
  Elk Grove Village *(G-9102)*

INSTRUMENTS, MEASURING & CNTRLNG: Wind Direction Indicators
Clean Energy Renewables LLC .... E 309 797-4844
  Moline *(G-14136)*

INSTRUMENTS, MEASURING & CONTROLLING: Gas Detectors
D O D Technologies Inc .... E 815 788-5200
  Cary *(G-3153)*
First Alert Inc .... C 630 499-3295
  Aurora *(G-962)*
Honeywell Analytics Inc .... C 847 955-8200
  Lincolnshire *(G-12770)*

INSTRUMENTS, MEASURING & CONTROLLING: Gauges, Rain
Innoquest Inc .... G 815 337-8555
  Woodstock *(G-21396)*

INSTRUMENTS, MEASURING & CONTROLLING: Surveying & Drafting
Germann Instruments Inc .... G 847 329-9999
  Evanston *(G-9524)*
Humboldt Mfg Co .... E 708 456-6300
  Elgin *(G-8617)*
S & W Manufacturing Co Inc .... E 630 595-5044
  Bensenville *(G-1888)*

INSTRUMENTS, MEASURING & CONTROLLING: Transits, Surveyors'
Polmax LLC .... C 708 843-8300
  Alsip *(G-494)*

INSTRUMENTS, MEASURING & CONTROLLING: Ultrasonic Testing
Midwest Ultrasonics Inc .... G 630 434-9458
  Darien *(G-7409)*
Migatron Corporation .... E 815 338-5800
  Woodstock *(G-21411)*
Santec Systems Inc .... F 847 215-8884
  Arlington Heights *(G-804)*
Sonoscan Inc .... D 847 437-6400
  Elk Grove Village *(G-9247)*

Employee Codes: A=Over 500 employees, B=251-500
C=101-250, D=51-100, E=20-50, F=10-19, G=3-9

INSTRUMENTS, MEASURING & CONTROLLING: Ultrasonic Testing

Ultrasonic Power Corporation...............E....... 815 235-6020
  Freeport *(G-10148)*

INSTRUMENTS, MEASURING & CONTROLLING: Weather Tracking

Outdoor Environments LLC...................G....... 847 325-5000
  Buffalo Grove *(G-2583)*

INSTRUMENTS, MEASURING/CNTRL: Gauging, Ultrasonic Thickness

Assurance Technologies Inc ....F....... 630 550-5000
  Bartlett *(G-1265)*
Gpe Controls Inc ....F....... 708 236-6000
  Hillside *(G-11340)*
L & J Holding Company Ltd ....D....... 708 236-6000
  Hillside *(G-11345)*
Trinity Brand Industries Inc ....F....... 708 482-4980
  Burr Ridge *(G-2725)*

INSTRUMENTS, MEASURING/CNTRL: Hydrometers, Exc Indl Process

Norman P Moeller ....G....... 847 991-3933
  Lake Barrington *(G-12162)*

INSTRUMENTS, MEASURING/CNTRLG: Fare Registers, St Cars/Buses

Cubic Trnsp Systems Inc ....G....... 312 257-3242
  Chicago *(G-4282)*

INSTRUMENTS, MEASURING/CNTRLG: Fire Detect Sys, Non-Electric

H S I Fire and Safety Group ....G....... 847 427-8340
  Elk Grove Village *(G-9026)*

INSTRUMENTS, MEASURING/CNTRLG: Fuel Densitometers, Acft Eng

Convergence Fuel Systems LLC ....G....... 970 498-3430
  Loves Park *(G-13195)*

INSTRUMENTS, MEASURING/CNTRLNG: Med Diagnostic Sys, Nuclear

Joseph Ringelstein ....G....... 708 955-7467
  Norridge *(G-15238)*
Siemens Med Solutions USA Inc ....D....... 847 304-7700
  Hoffman Estates *(G-11458)*
Touhy Diagnostic At Home LLC ....F....... 847 803-1111
  Des Plaines *(G-7858)*

INSTRUMENTS, OPTICAL: Elements & Assemblies, Exc Ophthalmic

Kreischer Optics Ltd..............................F....... 815 344-4220
  McHenry *(G-13754)*

INSTRUMENTS, OPTICAL: Lenses, All Types Exc Ophthalmic

Beastgrip Co...G....... 312 283-5283
  Des Plaines *(G-7738)*
Karl Lambrecht Corp ....E....... 773 472-5442
  Chicago *(G-5082)*
Lens Lenticlear Lenticular ....F....... 630 467-0900
  Elk Grove Village *(G-9093)*

INSTRUMENTS, OPTICAL: Mirrors

H L Clausing Inc ....G....... 847 676-0330
  Skokie *(G-18962)*
Tonjon Company ....F....... 630 208-1173
  Geneva *(G-10312)*

INSTRUMENTS, OPTICAL: Test & Inspection

Gaertner Scientific Corp........................E....... 847 673-5006
  Skokie *(G-18958)*
Jme Technologies Inc............................E....... 815 477-8800
  Crystal Lake *(G-7213)*

INSTRUMENTS, SURGICAL & MED: Cleaning Eqpt, Ultrasonic Med

Esma Inc ....G....... 708 331-0456
  South Holland *(G-19211)*

INSTRUMENTS, SURGICAL & MEDICAL: Blood & Bone Work

Avalign Grman Specialty Instrs ....E....... 847 908-0292
  Schaumburg *(G-18451)*
Graymont Prof Pdts Ip LLC ....F....... 312 374-4376
  Chicago *(G-4731)*
Jointechlabs Inc ....G....... 773 954-1076
  Wheeling *(G-20921)*
Life Spine Inc ....D....... 847 884-6117
  Huntley *(G-11551)*
Monogen Inc ....E....... 847 573-6700
  Chicago *(G-5492)*
Murray Inc ....E....... 847 620-7990
  North Barrington *(G-15287)*
Sysmex America Inc ....C....... 847 996-4500
  Lincolnshire *(G-12797)*
Tianhe Stem Cell Biotechnolgie ....F....... 630 723-1968
  Lisle *(G-12952)*

INSTRUMENTS, SURGICAL & MEDICAL: Blood Pressure

Bold Diagnostics LLC............................G....... 806 543-5743
  Chicago *(G-3930)*
Endotronix Inc ....E....... 630 504-2861
  Lisle *(G-12888)*

INSTRUMENTS, SURGICAL & MEDICAL: Blood Transfusion

Baxter World Trade Corporation ....F....... 224 948-2000
  Deerfield *(G-7596)*

INSTRUMENTS, SURGICAL & MEDICAL: Cannulae

Sunset Hlthcare Solutions Inc ....E....... 877 578-6738
  Chicago *(G-6278)*

INSTRUMENTS, SURGICAL & MEDICAL: Catheters

Baxter Healthcare Corporation............E....... 847 578-4671
  Waukegan *(G-20422)*

INSTRUMENTS, SURGICAL & MEDICAL: Hemodialysis

Aksys Ltd ....D....... 847 229-2020
  Lincolnshire *(G-12743)*

INSTRUMENTS, SURGICAL & MEDICAL: Inhalation Therapy

Ltc Holdings Inc ....C....... 847 249-5900
  Waukegan *(G-20464)*

INSTRUMENTS, SURGICAL & MEDICAL: Inhalators

Revolutionary Medical Dvcs Inc ....F....... 520 464-4299
  Mettawa *(G-13981)*

INSTRUMENTS, SURGICAL & MEDICAL: Muscle Exercise, Ophthalmic

Stretch CHI ....G....... 773 420-9355
  Chicago *(G-6253)*

INSTRUMENTS, SURGICAL & MEDICAL: Needles, Suture

Manan Tool & Manufacturing ....A....... 847 637-3333
  Wheeling *(G-20937)*

INSTRUMENTS, SURGICAL & MEDICAL: Ophthalmic

Opticent Inc ....G....... 410 829-7384
  Evanston *(G-9563)*
Stereo Optical Company Inc ....F....... 773 867-0380
  Chicago *(G-6244)*

INSTRUMENTS, SURGICAL & MEDICAL: Retinoscopes

Advanced Retinal Institute Inc.............G....... 617 821-5597
  Oak Park *(G-15742)*

INSTRUMENTS, SURGICAL & MEDICAL: Suction Therapy

Mobile Health & Wellness Inc ....G....... 773 697-9892
  Chicago *(G-5475)*
Precision Products Mfg Intl ....E....... 847 299-8500
  Des Plaines *(G-7831)*

INSTRUMENTS, SURGICAL/MED: Microsurgical, Exc Electromedical

Novo Surgical Inc...................................E....... 877 860-6686
  Oak Brook *(G-15650)*

INSTRUMENTS: Analytical

Abbott Laboratories................................A....... 847 932-7900
  North Chicago *(G-15293)*
Abbott Molecular Inc ....G....... 224 361-7800
  Des Plaines *(G-7719)*
Abbott Molecular Inc ....D....... 224 361-7800
  Des Plaines *(G-7720)*
Ag-Defense Systems Inc ....G....... 309 495-7258
  Peoria *(G-16376)*
Beckman Coulter Inc ....G....... 800 526-3821
  Wood Dale *(G-21167)*
Bio-RAD Laboratories Inc ....B....... 847 699-2217
  Des Plaines *(G-7739)*
Carlson Scientific Inc ....G....... 708 258-6377
  Peotone *(G-16551)*
Cbana Labs Inc ....G....... 217 819-5201
  Champaign *(G-3277)*
Chinchilla Scientific LLC ....G....... 630 645-0600
  Oak Brook *(G-15610)*
EJ Cady & Company ....G....... 847 537-2239
  Wheeling *(G-20888)*
EMD Millipore Corporation ....C....... 815 937-8270
  Kankakee *(G-11968)*
Fisher Scientific Company LLC ....C....... 412 490-8300
  Hanover Park *(G-11003)*
Gaertner Scientific Corp.......................E....... 847 673-5006
  Skokie *(G-18958)*
Hach Company ....C....... 800 227-4224
  Chicago *(G-4763)*
Huygen Corporation ....F....... 815 455-2200
  Crystal Lake *(G-7207)*
Igt Testing Systems Inc ....G....... 847 952-2448
  Arlington Heights *(G-755)*
Illinois Instruments Inc........................E....... 815 344-6212
  Johnsburg *(G-11805)*
Illinois Tool Works Inc ....C....... 847 295-6500
  Lake Bluff *(G-12189)*
Instruments & Technology ....G....... 815 838-5909
  Lockport *(G-13002)*
ISs (usa) Inc ....E....... 217 359-8681
  Champaign *(G-3310)*
Jrd Labs LLC ....G....... 847 818-1076
  Elk Grove Village *(G-9070)*
Kw Fabrication Inc ....G....... 773 294-8584
  Riverside *(G-17086)*
L A M Inc De ....G....... 630 860-9700
  Wood Dale *(G-21206)*
Lachata Design Ltd ....G....... 708 946-2757
  Beecher *(G-1518)*
McCrone Associates Inc ....G....... 630 887-7100
  Westmont *(G-20758)*
Orochem Technologies Inc ....E....... 630 210-8300
  Naperville *(G-14889)*
Parr Instrument Company ....C....... 309 762-7716
  Moline *(G-14165)*
Perkinelmer Inc ....G....... 331 229-3012
  Naperville *(G-14895)*
Quest Integrity.......................................G....... 779 205-3068
  Shorewood *(G-18901)*
Scientific Instruments Inc ....G....... 847 679-1242
  Schaumburg *(G-18709)*
Sensor 21 Inc..G....... 847 561-6233
  Mundelein *(G-14736)*
Sherwood Industries Inc ....F....... 847 626-0300
  Niles *(G-15170)*
Spectroclick Inc ....G....... 217 356-4829
  Champaign *(G-3351)*
Supertek Scientific LLC ....G....... 630 345-3450
  Addison *(G-300)*
Thermo Fisher Scientific Inc................G....... 847 295-7500
  Bannockburn *(G-1211)*
Thermo Fisher Scientific Inc................G....... 815 968-7970
  Rockford *(G-17657)*
Thermo Fisher Scientific Inc................D....... 847 381-7050
  Bartlett *(G-1316)*

PRODUCT SECTION

INSTRUMENTS: Measuring & Controlling

Verson Enterprises Inc ....F 847 364-2600
  Elk Grove Village *(G-9302)*
Western Analytical Products ....G 800 541-8421
  Vernon Hills *(G-20110)*

INSTRUMENTS: Combustion Control, Indl

Benetech Inc ....G 630 806-7888
  Montgomery *(G-14232)*
Benetech Inc ....E 630 844-1300
  Aurora *(G-1063)*
Benetech (taiwan) LLC ....G 630 844-1300
  Aurora *(G-1064)*
Champion Comm Svcs Inc ....G 815 654-8607
  Rockford *(G-17344)*

INSTRUMENTS: Digital Panel Meters, Electricity Measuring

Professional Meters Inc ....C 815 942-7000
  Morris *(G-14323)*

INSTRUMENTS: Elec Lab Stds, Resist, Inductance/Capacitance

Spectral Dynamics Inc ....E 630 595-4288
  Itasca *(G-11738)*

INSTRUMENTS: Electrocardiographs

Lifewatch Corp ....G 847 720-2100
  Rosemont *(G-18031)*
Lifewatch Services Inc ....B 847 720-2100
  Rosemont *(G-18032)*
Universal Holdings Inc ....F 224 353-6198
  Hoffman Estates *(G-11470)*

INSTRUMENTS: Electronic, Analog-Digital Converters

Frequency Devices Inc ....F 815 434-7800
  Ottawa *(G-16053)*
Oso Technologies Inc ....G 844 777-2575
  Urbana *(G-19991)*
Serene One LLC ....F 630 285-1500
  Itasca *(G-11731)*
Suffolk Business Group Inc ....G 847 404-2486
  Bartlett *(G-1315)*

INSTRUMENTS: Endoscopic Eqpt, Electromedical

Cortek Endoscopy Inc ....G 847 526-2266
  Wauconda *(G-20340)*
Mobile Endoscopix LLC ....G 847 380-8992
  Northbrook *(G-15434)*

INSTRUMENTS: Eye Examination

Precision Vision Inc ....G 815 223-2022
  Woodstock *(G-21423)*

INSTRUMENTS: Flow, Indl Process

Erdco Engineering Corporation ....E 847 328-0550
  Evanston *(G-9514)*
Fms USA Inc ....G 847 519-4400
  Hoffman Estates *(G-11424)*

INSTRUMENTS: Generators Tachometer

Sfc of Illinois Inc ....E 815 745-2100
  Warren *(G-20224)*

INSTRUMENTS: Humidity, Indl Process

Harry J Trainor ....G 630 493-1163
  Downers Grove *(G-8017)*
Humidity 2 Optimization LLC ....F 847 991-7488
  East Dundee *(G-8200)*

INSTRUMENTS: Indicating, Electric

Schweitzer Engrg Labs Inc ....D 847 362-8304
  Lake Zurich *(G-12455)*

INSTRUMENTS: Indl Process Control

Active Grinding & Mfg Co ....F 708 344-0510
  Broadview *(G-2414)*
Advanced Technologies Inc ....G 847 329-9875
  Park Ridge *(G-16264)*

Air Gage Company ....C 847 695-0911
  Elgin *(G-8500)*
Ametek Inc ....E 630 621-3121
  Warrenville *(G-20230)*
Auto Meter Products Inc ....C 815 895-8141
  Sycamore *(G-19702)*
Axode Corp ....G 312 578-9897
  Chicago *(G-3796)*
Barcor Inc ....F 847 940-0750
  Bannockburn *(G-1192)*
Caterpillar Inc ....B 815 729-5511
  Joliet *(G-11838)*
Cognex Corporation ....G 630 505-9990
  Naperville *(G-14801)*
Competition Electronics Inc ....G 815 874-8001
  Rockford *(G-17356)*
Danfoss LLC ....C 888 326-3677
  Loves Park *(G-13206)*
Decatur Aeration and Temp ....F 217 733-2800
  Fairmount *(G-9642)*
Dometic Corporation ....A 847 447-7190
  Rosemont *(G-18019)*
E+e Elektronik Corporation ....C 847 490-0520
  Schaumburg *(G-18511)*
Electro-Matic Products Co ....F 773 235-4010
  Chicago *(G-4477)*
Emerson Electric Co ....D 847 585-8300
  Elgin *(G-8578)*
Emerson Electric Co ....E 847 268-6000
  Rosemont *(G-18023)*
Emerson Electric Co ....E 312 803-4321
  Chicago *(G-4497)*
Emerson Electric Co ....G 708 263-6100
  Tinley Park *(G-19824)*
Fisher Controls Intl LLC ....D 847 956-8020
  Chicago *(G-4596)*
Fox Meter Inc ....G 630 968-3635
  Lisle *(G-12892)*
Frequency Devices Inc ....F 815 434-7800
  Ottawa *(G-16053)*
FSI Technologies Inc ....E 630 932-9380
  Lombard *(G-13080)*
Goodrich Corporation ....D 815 226-6000
  Rockford *(G-17432)*
Hadady Machining Company Inc ....F 708 474-8620
  Lansing *(G-12496)*
Hauhinco LP ....E 618 993-5399
  Marion *(G-13514)*
Hexagon Metrology Inc ....G 312 624-8786
  Chicago *(G-4811)*
Hexagon Metrology Inc ....G 847 469-3344
  Elgin *(G-8615)*
Imada Inc ....E 847 562-0834
  Northbrook *(G-15403)*
Instrument & Valve Services Co ....D 708 535-5120
  Oak Forest *(G-15684)*
Instrument & Valve Services Co ....F 281 998-6673
  Chicago *(G-4939)*
Jjs Technical Services ....G 847 999-4313
  Schaumburg *(G-18577)*
Liquid Controls LLC ....C 847 295-1050
  Lake Bluff *(G-12194)*
Liquitech Inc ....E 630 693-0500
  Lombard *(G-13097)*
Lumenite Control Technology ....F 847 455-1450
  Franklin Park *(G-9982)*
Martin Automatic Inc ....C 815 654-4800
  Rockford *(G-17505)*
Master Control Systems Inc ....E 847 295-1010
  Lake Bluff *(G-12195)*
Mech-Tronics Corporation ....D 708 344-9823
  Melrose Park *(G-13891)*
Mid-American Elevator Eqp Co ....E 773 486-6900
  Chicago *(G-5429)*
Millpro LLC ....G 630 608-9241
  Aurora *(G-1135)*
National Micro Systems Inc ....G 312 566-0414
  Chicago *(G-5549)*
Nuance Incorporated ....G 207 449-6398
  Chicago *(G-5638)*
Oakland Industries Ltd ....E 847 827-7600
  Mount Prospect *(G-14555)*
Omron Healthcare Inc ....D 847 680-6200
  Lake Forest *(G-12276)*
Oxytech Systems Inc ....F 847 888-8611
  Carpentersville *(G-3110)*
Perkinelmer Hlth Sciences Inc ....C 630 969-6000
  Downers Grove *(G-8073)*
Process Technologies Group ....G 630 393-4777
  Warrenville *(G-20250)*

Prostat Corporation ....F 630 238-8883
  Bensenville *(G-1875)*
Protection Controls Inc ....E 773 763-3110
  Skokie *(G-19017)*
Robertshaw Controls Company ....E 815 591-2417
  Hanover *(G-10997)*
Robertshaw Controls Company ....C 630 260-3400
  Itasca *(G-11727)*
Ruby Automation LLC ....F 815 624-5959
  South Beloit *(G-19112)*
Schrader-Bridgeport Intl Inc ....G 815 288-3344
  Dixon *(G-7916)*
Semler Industries Inc ....E 847 671-5650
  Franklin Park *(G-10046)*
Silicon Control Inc ....G 847 215-7947
  Deerfield *(G-7649)*
Sun Infrared Technologies Inc ....G 618 632-3013
  O Fallon *(G-15585)*
Superior Graphite Co ....E 708 458-0006
  Chicago *(G-6281)*
Tenco Hydro Inc of Illinois ....G 708 387-0700
  Brookfield *(G-2496)*
Thread & Gage Co Inc ....G 815 675-2305
  Spring Grove *(G-19302)*
Tii Technical Educatn Systems ....G 847 428-3085
  Gilberts *(G-10373)*
Tricor Systems Inc ....E 847 742-5542
  Elgin *(G-8760)*
Yaskawa America Inc ....C 847 887-7000
  Waukegan *(G-20520)*

INSTRUMENTS: Laser, Scientific & Engineering

Amoco Technology Company ....C 312 861-6000
  Chicago *(G-3682)*
Grays Laser & Instrument RPR ....G 618 222-1791
  Smithton *(G-19064)*
Laser Products Industries Inc ....G 877 679-1300
  Romeoville *(G-17839)*

INSTRUMENTS: Liquid Level, Indl Process

Danaher Corporation ....C 815 568-8001
  Marengo *(G-13483)*
Monitor Technologies LLC ....E 630 365-9403
  Elburn *(G-8463)*

INSTRUMENTS: Measurement, Indl Process

Clean Energy Renewables LLC ....E 309 797-4844
  Moline *(G-14136)*
Dadant & Sons Inc ....F 217 852-3324
  Dallas City *(G-7313)*
Fusion Systems Incorporated ....E 630 323-4115
  Burr Ridge *(G-2675)*
Imacc LLC ....G 512 341-8189
  Palatine *(G-16126)*
Metrology Resource Group Inc ....G 815 703-3141
  Rockford *(G-17520)*
Midwest Energy Management Inc ....G 630 759-6007
  Lombard *(G-13101)*
Process Mechanical Inc ....G 630 416-7021
  Naperville *(G-14902)*
T T T Inc ....G 630 860-7499
  Wood Dale *(G-21245)*
Technical Sales Midwest Inc ....G 847 855-2457
  Gurnee *(G-10935)*
Vorne Industries Inc ....E 630 875-3600
  Itasca *(G-11751)*

INSTRUMENTS: Measuring & Controlling

Aixacct Systems Inc ....G 952 303-4077
  Wheaton *(G-20787)*
Amerex Corporation ....E 309 382-4389
  North Pekin *(G-15326)*
Asm Sensors Inc ....F 630 832-3202
  Elmhurst *(G-9326)*
Auto Meter Products Inc ....C 815 895-8141
  Sycamore *(G-19702)*
Aw Dynamometer Inc ....F 815 844-6968
  Pontiac *(G-16766)*
Barcor Inc ....F 847 831-2650
  Highland Park *(G-11254)*
Barcor Inc ....F 847 940-0750
  Bannockburn *(G-1192)*
Binks Industries Inc ....G 630 801-1100
  Montgomery *(G-14233)*
Cabot McRlectronics Polsg Corp ....E 630 543-6682
  Addison *(G-61)*

Employee Codes: A=Over 500 employees, B=251-500
C=101-250, D=51-100, E=20-50, F=10-19, G=3-9

CAM Co Inc F 630 556-3110
Big Rock *(G-1969)*
Cd LLC F 312 275-5747
Chicago *(G-4047)*
Celinco Inc G 815 964-2256
Rockford *(G-17341)*
Centurion Non Destructive Tstg F 630 736-5500
Streamwood *(G-19565)*
Chicago Dial Indicator Company E 847 827-7186
Des Plaines *(G-7744)*
Circle Systems Inc F 815 286-3271
Hinckley *(G-11357)*
Converting Systems Inc G 847 519-0232
Schaumburg *(G-18489)*
CTS Corporation C 630 577-8800
Lisle *(G-12881)*
Deatak Inc F 815 322-2013
McHenry *(G-13735)*
Deere & Company E 309 765-2960
Moline *(G-14140)*
Diehl Metering LLC G 331 204-6540
Naperville *(G-14816)*
Double K Towers Inc G 773 964-3104
Chicago *(G-4388)*
Dual Mfg Co Inc F 773 267-4457
Franklin Park *(G-9933)*
Dynamicsignals LLC E 815 838-0005
Lockport *(G-12992)*
Elcon Inc E 815 467-9500
Minooka *(G-14059)*
Elektro-Physik USA Inc G 847 437-6616
Arlington Heights *(G-732)*
Erdco Engineering Corporation E 847 328-0550
Evanston *(G-9514)*
Fluid Manufacturing Services G 800 458-5262
Lake Bluff *(G-12181)*
Illinois Tool Works Inc E 847 657-5300
Glenview *(G-10562)*
Illinois Tool Works Inc C 847 295-6500
Lake Bluff *(G-12189)*
Industrial Msrment Systems Inc G 630 236-5901
Aurora *(G-981)*
James Instruments Inc F 773 463-6565
Chicago *(G-5002)*
Jones Medical Instrument Co E 630 571-1980
Oak Brook *(G-15627)*
Jordan Industrial Controls Inc E 217 864-4444
Mount Zion *(G-14648)*
Keson Industries Inc E 630 820-4200
Aurora *(G-993)*
L & J Engineering Inc E 708 236-6000
Hillside *(G-11344)*
L A M Inc De G 630 860-9700
Wood Dale *(G-21206)*
Landauer Inc C 708 755-7000
Glenwood *(G-10642)*
Livorsi Marine Inc E 847 548-5900
Grayslake *(G-10788)*
Luster Leaf Products Inc F 815 337-5560
Woodstock *(G-21407)*
Martin Engineering Company C 309 852-2384
Neponset *(G-15018)*
Mech-Tronics Corporation G 708 344-0202
Melrose Park *(G-13892)*
Mitsubishi Elc Automtn Inc C 847 478-2100
Vernon Hills *(G-20075)*
MWM Express Inc G 630 401-0528
Chicago Ridge *(G-6805)*
Omron Healthcare Inc D 847 680-6200
Lake Forest *(G-12276)*
Oneplus Systems Inc E 847 498-0955
Northbrook *(G-15447)*
Parking Systems Inc G 847 891-3819
Schaumburg *(G-18666)*
Parsonics Corp G 815 338-6509
Woodstock *(G-21420)*
Perkinelmer Hlth Sciences Inc C 630 969-6000
Downers Grove *(G-8073)*
Power House Tool Inc E 815 727-6301
Joliet *(G-11915)*
Praxsym Inc F 217 897-1744
Fisher *(G-9667)*
Product Feeding Solutions Inc G 630 709-9546
Chicago Ridge *(G-6809)*
Prostat Corporation F 630 238-8883
Bensenville *(G-1875)*
Psylotech Inc G 847 328-7100
Evanston *(G-9572)*
Reliefband Technologies LLC G 877 735-2263
Rosemont *(G-18047)*
Ryeson Corporation D 847 455-8677
Carol Stream *(G-3061)*
Scientific Instruments Inc G 847 679-1242
Schaumburg *(G-18709)*
Sikora Automation Incorporated G 630 833-0298
Addison *(G-291)*
Somat Corporation E 800 578-4260
Champaign *(G-3349)*
Stevens Instrument Company G 847 336-9375
Waukegan *(G-20498)*
Tektrol LLC F 847 857-6076
Crystal Lake *(G-7279)*
Teledyne Lecroy Inc E 847 888-0450
Elgin *(G-8749)*
Teledyne Monitor Labs Inc F 303 792-3300
Chicago *(G-6340)*
Tempro International Corp G 847 677-5370
Skokie *(G-19044)*
Tricor Systems Inc E 847 742-5542
Elgin *(G-8760)*
Venturedyne Ltd E 708 597-7090
Alsip *(G-521)*
Vibra-Tech Engineers Inc G 630 858-0681
Glen Ellyn *(G-10423)*
Wellness Center Usa Inc F 847 925-1885
Hoffman Estates *(G-11471)*
Wilkens-Anderson Company E 773 384-4433
Chicago *(G-6626)*
Worth-Pfaff Innovations Inc G 847 940-9305
Deerfield *(G-7661)*
Ziv USA Inc G 224 735-3961
Rolling Meadows *(G-17786)*

INSTRUMENTS: Measuring Electricity

Accushim Inc G 708 442-6448
Lyons *(G-13300)*
Acl Inc F 773 285-0295
Chicago *(G-3525)*
Agilent Technologies Inc E 800 227-9770
Chicago *(G-3582)*
Agilent Technologies Inc A 847 690-0431
Arlington Heights *(G-685)*
Air Gage Company C 847 695-0911
Elgin *(G-8500)*
Atlas Material Tstg Tech LLC C 773 327-4520
Mount Prospect *(G-14512)*
B+b Smartworx Inc D 815 433-5100
Ottawa *(G-16041)*
Bolingbrook Communications Inc A 630 759-9500
Lisle *(G-12874)*
C E R Machining & Tooling Ltd G 708 442-9614
Lyons *(G-13305)*
Cobalt Tool & Manufacturing G 630 530-8898
Villa Park *(G-20139)*
Davies Molding LLC C 630 510-8188
Carol Stream *(G-2974)*
Electronic System Design Inc G 847 358-8212
Bensenville *(G-1794)*
Erdco Engineering Corporation E 847 328-0550
Evanston *(G-9514)*
Falex Corporation E 630 556-3679
Sugar Grove *(G-19643)*
Heidenhain Corporation D 847 490-1191
Schaumburg *(G-18545)*
I P C Automation Inc G 815 759-3934
McHenry *(G-13749)*
Illinois Tool Works Inc E 847 657-5300
Glenview *(G-10562)*
Illinois Tool Works Inc C 847 295-6500
Lake Bluff *(G-12189)*
Langham Engineering G 815 223-5250
Peru *(G-16580)*
Lindgren Family LLC G 630 307-7200
Glendale Heights *(G-10469)*
Nidec-Shimpo America Corp E 630 924-7138
Glendale Heights *(G-10479)*
Silicon Control Inc G 847 215-7947
Deerfield *(G-7649)*
Transformer Manufacturers Inc E 708 457-1200
Norridge *(G-15245)*

INSTRUMENTS: Measuring, Electrical Power

Ideal Industries Inc C 815 895-5181
Sycamore *(G-19714)*
Ideal Industries Inc C 815 895-1108
Sycamore *(G-19715)*

INSTRUMENTS: Measuring, Electrical Quantities

F T I Inc E 312 943-4015
Chicago *(G-4552)*

INSTRUMENTS: Medical & Surgical

1 Federal Supply Source Inc G 708 964-2222
Steger *(G-19486)*
Abbott Laboratories A 847 932-7900
North Chicago *(G-15293)*
Abrasive West LLC G 630 736-0818
Bartlett *(G-1262)*
Access Medical Supply Inc G 847 891-6210
Schaumburg *(G-18425)*
Adhereon Corporation G 312 997-5002
Chicago *(G-3545)*
ADM Imaging Inc G 630 834-7100
Wheaton *(G-20786)*
Advanced Cooling Therapy Inc E 888 534-4873
Chicago *(G-3562)*
Aerogenaerogen G 312 624-9598
Chicago *(G-3573)*
AG Industries LLC E 636 349-4466
Chicago *(G-3580)*
Alicona Manufacturing Inc G 630 736-2718
Bartlett *(G-1263)*
Amar Plastics Inc F 630 627-4105
Addison *(G-28)*
Amer Surgical Instruments Inc F 630 986-8032
Westmont *(G-20727)*
Argentum Medical LLC E 888 551-0188
Geneva *(G-10253)*
Arpwave Usa LLC G 773 835-0122
Chicago *(G-3732)*
Avalign Technologies Inc D 855 282-5446
Bannockburn *(G-1189)*
Bandgrip Inc G 844 968-6322
Chicago *(G-3825)*
Bard Brachytherapy Inc E 630 933-7610
Carol Stream *(G-2945)*
Baxalta Export Corporation C 224 948-2000
Bannockburn *(G-1193)*
Baxalta World Trade LLC G 224 940-2000
Bannockburn *(G-1195)*
Baxalta Worldwide LLC C 224 948-2000
Deerfield *(G-7590)*
Baxter Global Holdings II Inc E 224 948-1812
Deerfield *(G-7591)*
Baxter Healthcare Corporation G 847 270-4757
Wonder Lake *(G-21143)*
Baxter Healthcare Corporation C 847 948-3206
Spring Grove *(G-19267)*
Baxter Healthcare Corporation D 847 270-5720
Round Lake *(G-18069)*
Baxter Healthcare Corporation F 847 948-4770
Round Lake *(G-18070)*
Baxter Healthcare Corporation C 847 367-2544
Vernon Hills *(G-20045)*
Baxter Healthcare Corporation B 847 948-2000
Deerfield *(G-7593)*
Baxter Healthcare Corporation B 847 940-6599
Round Lake *(G-18072)*
Baxter Healthcare Corporation B 847 948-2000
Deerfield *(G-7594)*
Baxter International Inc A 224 948-2000
Deerfield *(G-7595)*
Beecken Petty Okeefe & Co LLC A 312 435-0300
Chicago *(G-3858)*
Biosynergy Inc G 847 956-0471
Elk Grove Village *(G-8867)*
Bird Products Corporation G 872 757-0114
Mettawa *(G-13978)*
Brainlab Inc C 800 784-7700
Westchester *(G-20692)*
Briteseed LLC G 206 384-0311
Chicago *(G-3960)*
C & S Chemicals Inc G 815 722-6671
Joliet *(G-11837)*
Cardinal Health Inc B 847 578-4443
Waukegan *(G-20424)*
Cardinal Health 200 LLC E 847 689-8410
Waukegan *(G-20425)*
Carstens Incorporated D 708 669-1500
Chicago *(G-4032)*
Chucking Machine Products Inc D 847 678-1192
Franklin Park *(G-9907)*
Clariance Inc F 773 868-7041
Chicago *(G-4166)*

PRODUCT SECTION

INSTRUMENTS: Test, Electrical, Engine

Coeur Inc ....F 815 648-1093
  Hebron *(G-11141)*
Cook Polymer Technology ....G 309 740-2342
  Canton *(G-2825)*
Covidien Holding Inc 618 664-2111
  Greenville *(G-10831)*
Cr Bard Inc ....D 630 933-7653
  Carol Stream *(G-2968)*
Cryonize ....G 773 935-8803
  Chicago *(G-4278)*
Csl Behring LLC ....B 815 932-6773
  Bradley *(G-2279)*
D-M-S Holdings Inc ....E 515 327-6416
  Waukegan *(G-20433)*
Doctors Choice Inc ....G 312 666-1111
  Chicago *(G-4378)*
Elas Tek Molding Inc ....E 815 675-9012
  Spring Grove *(G-19274)*
Elmed Incorporated ....E 224 353-6446
  Glendale Heights *(G-10448)*
Emergency Medical Instruments ...G 630 365-2001
  Maple Park *(G-13462)*
Eriem Surgical Inc ....G 847 549-1410
  Lake Forest *(G-12247)*
Fetzer Surgical LLC ....G 630 635-2520
  Schaumburg *(G-18527)*
Gema Inc ....F 773 508-6690
  Chicago *(G-4668)*
Global Endoscopy Inc ....G 847 910-5836
  Elk Grove Village *(G-9015)*
Glooko ....G 513 307-0903
  Chicago *(G-4701)*
Good Lite Co ....G 847 841-1145
  Elgin *(G-8598)*
Hearing Screening Assoc LLC 855 550-9427
  Arlington Heights *(G-747)*
Hill-Rom Holdings Inc ....B 312 819-7200
  Chicago *(G-4819)*
Hollister Incorporated ....B 847 680-1000
  Libertyville *(G-12660)*
Hospital Therapy Products Inc ....F 630 766-7101
  Wood Dale *(G-21198)*
Imh Fabrication Inc ....F 815 537-2381
  Prophetstown *(G-16833)*
Inland Midwest Corporation ....E 773 775-2111
  Elmhurst *(G-9378)*
Integrated Medical Tech Inc ....G 309 662-3614
  Bloomington *(G-2062)*
Jones Medical Instrument Co ......E 630 571-1980
  Oak Brook *(G-15627)*
Jstone Inc ....E 847 325-5660
  Mundelein *(G-14706)*
Kdk Upset Forging Co ....E 708 388-8770
  Blue Island *(G-2128)*
Konica Minolta Healthcare ....G 815 893-0691
  Crystal Lake *(G-7218)*
Leica Microsystems Inc ....G 847 405-0123
  Buffalo Grove *(G-2562)*
Lsl Industries Inc ....D 773 878-1100
  Niles *(G-15141)*
Ludwig Medical Inc ....G 217 342-6570
  Effingham *(G-8408)*
Manan Medical Products Inc ......D 847 637-3333
  Wheeling *(G-20936)*
Mc Squared Group Inc ....G 815 322-2485
  Spring Grove *(G-19283)*
Medical Adherence Tech Inc ....G 847 525-6300
  Winnetka *(G-21133)*
Medicate Dme Inc ....F 618 874-3000
  East Saint Louis *(G-8314)*
Medigroup Inc ....G 630 554-5533
  Oswego *(G-16013)*
Medline Industries Inc ....A 847 949-5500
  Northfield *(G-15523)*
Medline Industries Inc ....B 847 949-2056
  Mundelein *(G-14715)*
Medline Industries Inc ....B 847 949-5500
  Waukegan *(G-20466)*
Medtex Health Services Inc ....G 630 789-0330
  Clarendon Hills *(G-6900)*
Medtronic Inc ....F 815 444-2500
  Crystal Lake *(G-7225)*
Medtronic Inc ....E 630 627-6677
  Lombard *(G-13099)*
Minute Mlcular Diagnostics Inc ...G 847 849-0263
  Evanston *(G-9554)*
Nanosphere LLC ....C 847 400-9000
  Northbrook *(G-15438)*
Nemera Buffalo Grove LLC ....C 847 541-7900
  Buffalo Grove *(G-2580)*
Nemera Buffalo Grove LLC ....G 847 325-3629
  Buffalo Grove *(G-2581)*
Nemera Buffalo Grove LLC ....G 847 325-3628
  Buffalo Grove *(G-2582)*
Newmedical Technology Inc ....E 847 412-1000
  Northbrook *(G-15441)*
Nordent Manufacturing Inc ....E 847 437-4780
  Elk Grove Village *(G-9150)*
Oakridge Products LLC ....G 815 363-4700
  McHenry *(G-13772)*
Oberg Medical Products Co LLC ...E 847 364-4750
  Elk Grove Village *(G-9158)*
Ohio Medical LLC ....D 847 855-0500
  Gurnee *(G-10907)*
Omc Investors LLC ....E 847 855-6220
  Gurnee *(G-10908)*
Omnicare Group Inc 708 949-8802
  Homer Glen *(G-11485)*
Omron Healthcare Inc ....D 847 680-6200
  Lake Forest *(G-12276)*
Organ Recovery Systems Inc .....F 847 824-2600
  Itasca *(G-11714)*
Phenome Technologies Inc ....G 847 962-1273
  Skokie *(G-19004)*
Photonicare Inc 866 411-3277
  Champaign *(G-3333)*
Precision Medical Mfg LLC ....F 847 229-1551
  Wheeling *(G-20964)*
Quadrant Medical Corporation 312 800-1294
  Aurora *(G-1011)*
RAD Source Technologies Inc 815 477-1291
  Algonquin *(G-385)*
Resonance Medical LLC ....G 229 292-2094
  Chicago *(G-6017)*
Reznik Instrument Co 847 673-3444
  Skokie *(G-19022)*
Richard Wolf Med Instrs Corp ....C 847 913-1113
  Vernon Hills *(G-20086)*
Riverbank Laboratories Inc ....F 630 232-2207
  Geneva *(G-10303)*
Rti Surgical Holdings Inc ....G 386 418-8888
  Deerfield *(G-7647)*
Salter Labs ....F 847 739-3224
  Lake Forest *(G-12300)*
Salter Medical Holdings Corp 800 421-0024
  Lake Forest *(G-12301)*
Siemens Hlthcare Dgnostics Inc ...C 847 267-5300
  Deerfield *(G-7648)*
Simpex Medical Inc ....G 847 757-9928
  Mount Prospect *(G-14571)*
Smiths Medical 847 383-1400
  Vernon Hills *(G-20098)*
Southwestern Hearing Centers ...G 618 651-4199
  Highland *(G-11241)*
Sparton Onyx Holdings LLC ....G 847 762-5800
  Schaumburg *(G-18720)*
Star Cushion Products Inc ....F 618 539-7070
  Freeburg *(G-10096)*
Star Ophthalmic Instrs Inc ....F 630 655-4500
  Orland Park *(G-15984)*
Stradis Medical LLC 847 887-8400
  Waukegan *(G-20499)*
Stryker Enterprises LLC ....G 815 975-5167
  Loves Park *(G-13267)*
Summit Industries LLC ....D 773 353-4000
  Niles *(G-15176)*
Superior Surgical Instrumen TS ...G 630 628-8437
  Addison *(G-299)*
Supertek Scientific LLC 630 345-3450
  Addison *(G-300)*
Surgical Innovation Assoc Inc 626 372-4884
  Chicago *(G-6289)*
Surgical Innovation Assoc Inc 847 548-8499
  Libertyville *(G-12711)*
Surgical Instrument Svcs & Sav ...G 847 646-2000
  Northfield *(G-15533)*
Surgical Solutions LLC ....C 847 607-6098
  Deerfield *(G-7650)*
Teleflex Incorporated ....D 847 259-7400
  Arlington Heights *(G-818)*
Teleflex Medical OEM LLC ....C 847 596-3100
  Gurnee *(G-10936)*
Thermatome Corporation ....G 312 772-2201
  Chicago *(G-6361)*
Thrift Medical Products 630 857-3548
  Naperville *(G-14933)*
Total Titanium Inc ....E 866 208-6446
  Red Bud *(G-17003)*
United Amercn Healthcare Corp ...E 313 393-4571
  Chicago *(G-6469)*
Varian Medical Systems Inc ....F 847 279-5100
  Lincolnshire *(G-12800)*
Vital Care Reps ....G 708 342-2680
  Tinley Park *(G-19867)*
Vital Signs Inc ....G 872 757-0114
  Mettawa *(G-13983)*
Vyaire Company ....G 833 327-3284
  Mettawa *(G-13984)*
Vyaire Medical Inc ....C 833 327-3284
  Mettawa *(G-13985)*
Vyaire Medical LLC ....G 833 327-3284
  Mettawa *(G-13986)*
Vyaire Medical Mx LLC ....B 872 757-0114
  Mettawa *(G-13987)*
Vyaire Medical Payroll LLC ....E 224 544-5436
  Mettawa *(G-13988)*
Welkins LLC ....G 877 319-3504
  Downers Grove *(G-8108)*
Whitney Products Inc ....F 847 966-6161
  Niles *(G-15187)*
Wholesale Point Inc ....F 630 986-1700
  Burr Ridge *(G-2735)*
Wisdom Medical Technology LLC ...G 630 803-6383
  Oswego *(G-16033)*
Ziemer Usa Inc ....F 618 462-9301
  Alton *(G-576)*
Zimmer Smith & Associates Inc ...F 217 788-5800
  Springfield *(G-19471)*

INSTRUMENTS: Multimeters

Nu Vision Media Inc ....G 773 495-5254
  Chicago *(G-5636)*

INSTRUMENTS: Oscillographs & Oscilloscopes

Elenco Electronics Inc ....E 847 541-3800
  Wheeling *(G-20889)*

INSTRUMENTS: Potentiometric

Maurey Instrument Corp ....F 708 388-9898
  Alsip *(G-474)*

INSTRUMENTS: Radio Frequency Measuring

Haynes-Bent Inc ....F 630 845-3316
  Wilmington *(G-21100)*
Richardson Rfpd Inc ....D 630 262-6800
  Geneva *(G-10302)*

INSTRUMENTS: Signal Generators & Averagers

Adams Elevator Equipment Co ...E 847 581-2900
  Chicago *(G-3538)*

INSTRUMENTS: Temperature Measurement, Indl

Atlas Material Tstg Tech LLC ......C 773 327-4520
  Mount Prospect *(G-14512)*
Durex International Corp ....B 847 639-5600
  Cary *(G-3157)*
Heng Tuo Usa Inc ....G 630 317-7672
  Oakbrook Terrace *(G-15802)*

INSTRUMENTS: Test, Digital, Electronic & Electrical Circuits

Creative Science Activities ....G 847 870-1746
  Prospect Heights *(G-16837)*
Righthand Technologies Inc ....E 773 774-7600
  Chicago *(G-6033)*

INSTRUMENTS: Test, Electrical, Engine

10g LLC ....F 630 754-2400
  Woodridge *(G-21269)*
Protec Equipment Resources Inc ...G 847 434-5808
  Schaumburg *(G-18686)*
Sigmatron International Inc ....G 847 586-5200
  Elgin *(G-8730)*
Sigmatron International Inc ....G 847 956-8000
  Elk Grove Village *(G-9238)*
Stevens Instrument Company ....G 847 336-9375
  Waukegan *(G-20498)*

INSTRUMENTS: Test, Electronic & Electric Measurement

INSTRUMENTS: Test, Electronic & Electric Measurement

Associated Research Inc .... E 847 367-4077
  Lake Forest *(G-12229)*
B T Technology Inc .... G 217 322-3768
  Rushville *(G-18108)*
Dytec Midwest Inc .... G 847 255-3200
  Rolling Meadows *(G-17728)*
Gld Industries Inc .... G 217 390-9594
  Champaign *(G-3296)*
Premium Test Equipment Corp .... G 630 400-2681
  Warrenville *(G-20248)*
Prostat Corporation .... F 630 238-8883
  Bensenville *(G-1875)*
TEC Rep Corporation .... F 630 627-9110
  Lombard *(G-13141)*

INSTRUMENTS: Test, Electronic & Electrical Circuits

Aiknow Inc .... F 312 391-9452
  Naperville *(G-14953)*
Centurion Non Destructive Tstg .... F 630 736-5500
  Streamwood *(G-19565)*
Cymatics Inc .... G 630 420-7117
  Naperville *(G-14811)*
Huygen Corporation .... F 815 455-2200
  Crystal Lake *(G-7207)*
International Electro Magnetic .... G 847 358-4622
  Wheeling *(G-20916)*
Methode Electronics Inc .... B 708 867-6777
  Chicago *(G-5409)*
Monolithic Industries Inc .... G 630 985-6009
  Woodridge *(G-21324)*
Teledyne Lecroy Inc .... E 847 888-0450
  Elgin *(G-8749)*

INSTRUMENTS: Testing, Semiconductor

Sk Hynix America Inc .... G 847 925-0196
  Schaumburg *(G-18713)*
Teradyne Inc .... F 847 981-0400
  Arlington Heights *(G-819)*

INSTRUMENTS: Thermal Conductive, Indl

Controlled Thermal Processing .... G 847 651-5511
  Streamwood *(G-19567)*
Luse Thermal Technologies LLC .... G 630 862-2600
  Aurora *(G-1000)*

INSTRUMENTS: Time Code Generators

Dgm Electronics Inc .... G 815 389-2040
  Roscoe *(G-17904)*

INSTRUMENTS: Vibration

Anamet Inc .... G 217 234-8844
  Glen Ellyn *(G-10394)*
SKF USA Inc .... D 847 742-0700
  Elgin *(G-8736)*

INSULATION & CUSHIONING FOAM: Polystyrene

Ade Inc .... E 773 646-3400
  Chicago *(G-3541)*
Armacell LLC .... D 708 596-9501
  South Holland *(G-19197)*
Carlisle Construction Mtls LLC .... D 847 671-2516
  Franklin Park *(G-9898)*
Eagle Panel System Inc .... G 618 326-7132
  Mulberry Grove *(G-14654)*
Free-Flow Packaging Intl Inc .... E 650 261-5300
  Deerfield *(G-7611)*
K & S Service & Rental Corp .... F 630 279-4292
  Elmhurst *(G-9384)*
Minnesota Diversified Pdts Inc .... E 815 539-3106
  Mendota *(G-13950)*
Pregis LLC .... A 847 597-2200
  Deerfield *(G-7645)*
Punch Products Manufacturing .... G 773 533-2800
  Chicago *(G-5915)*
Remco Technology Inc .... F 847 329-8090
  Skokie *(G-19021)*
Republic Systems Inc .... G 773 233-6530
  Chicago *(G-6016)*

INSULATION MATERIALS WHOLESALERS

Hersheys Metal Meister LLC .... E 217 234-4700
  Claremont *(G-6898)*
Insulators Supply Inc .... G 847 394-2836
  Prospect Heights *(G-16843)*
Meyer Enterprises LLC .... G 309 698-0062
  East Peoria *(G-8278)*

INSULATION: Fiberglass

Atlas Roofing Corporation .... E 309 752-7121
  East Moline *(G-8222)*
Owens-Corning Fiberglass Tech ..... G 708 563-9091
  Argo *(G-676)*

INSULATORS & INSULATION MATERIALS: Electrical

Guardian Energy Tech Inc .... F 800 516-0949
  Riverwoods *(G-17091)*
Illinois Tool Works Inc .... D 815 943-4785
  Lincolnshire *(G-12774)*
Resinite Corporation .... C 847 537-4250
  Wheeling *(G-20973)*
Thermamax Inc .... F 630 340-5682
  Aurora *(G-1022)*

INSURANCE AGENTS, NEC

Gibson Insurance Inc .... G 217 864-4877
  Mount Zion *(G-14646)*

INSURANCE CARRIERS: Life

Gibson Insurance Inc .... G 217 864-4877
  Mount Zion *(G-14646)*

INSURANCE CLAIM PROCESSING, EXC MEDICAL

First American Restoration Inc .... F 800 209-3609
  Harwood Heights *(G-11105)*

INSURANCE INFORMATION & CONSULTING SVCS

Applied Systems Inc .... A 708 534-5575
  University Park *(G-19946)*

INSURANCE PROFESSIONAL STANDARDS SVCS

Aais Services Corporation .... E 630 681-8347
  Lisle *(G-12856)*
Aais Services Corporation .... G 630 457-3263
  Lisle *(G-12857)*

INSURANCE: Agents, Brokers & Service

Frank S Johnson & Company Inc ... G 847 492-1660
  Evanston *(G-9522)*
Vej Holdings LLC .... G 630 219-1598
  Naperville *(G-14940)*

INTEGRATED CIRCUITS, SEMICONDUCTOR NETWORKS, ETC

Analog Devices Inc .... G 847 519-3669
  Schaumburg *(G-18439)*
GBA Systems Integrators LLC .... G 913 492-0400
  Moline *(G-14147)*
Hologram Inc .... G 716 771-8308
  Chicago *(G-4831)*
Microchip Technology Inc .... E 630 285-0071
  Itasca *(G-11701)*
Smart Controls LLC .... G 618 394-0300
  Fairview Heights *(G-9648)*
Tezzaron Semiconductor Corp .... C 630 505-0404
  Naperville *(G-14931)*
Xtremedata Inc .... E 847 871-0379
  Schaumburg *(G-18778)*

INTERCOMMUNICATION EQPT REPAIR SVCS

Portable Cmmnctons Spclsts .... G 630 458-1800
  Addison *(G-246)*

INTERCOMMUNICATIONS SYSTEMS: Electric

Aimtron Systems LLC .... E 262 947-8400
  Palatine *(G-16092)*
AVI-Spl Employee .... B 847 437-7712
  Schaumburg *(G-18453)*
Data Comm For Business Inc .... F 217 897-1741
  Dewey *(G-7873)*
Legrand AV Inc .... G 719 661-8134
  Chicago *(G-5203)*
McC Technology Inc .... G 630 377-7200
  Saint Charles *(G-18231)*
Procomm Inc Hoopeston Illinois .... E 815 268-4303
  Onarga *(G-15902)*
Stenograph LLC .... D 630 532-5100
  Elmhurst *(G-9429)*

INTERIOR DECORATING SVCS

Cleavenger Associates Inc .... G 630 221-0007
  Winfield *(G-21109)*
Lloyd M Hughes Enterprises Inc .... G 773 363-6331
  Chicago *(G-5245)*

INTERIOR DESIGN SVCS, NEC

Afar Imports & Interiors Inc .... G 217 744-3262
  Springfield *(G-19316)*
Amk Enterprises Chicago Inc .... G 312 523-7212
  Chicago *(G-3681)*
Baker Avenue Investments Inc ...... D 309 427-2500
  Washington *(G-20266)*
Botti Studio of Architectural .... E 847 869-5933
  Glenview *(G-10532)*
Buhlwork Design Guild .... G 630 325-5340
  Oak Brook *(G-15601)*
Elliott Aviation Arcft Sls Inc .... G 309 799-3183
  Milan *(G-14008)*
Seek Design .... G 312 804-6629
  Evanston *(G-9574)*
Vintage Modern Collection Inc .... G 312 774-8424
  Chicago *(G-6554)*

INTERIOR DESIGNING SVCS

Draperyland Inc .... F 630 521-1000
  Wood Dale *(G-21182)*
Eastern Accents Inc .... C 773 604-7300
  Chicago *(G-4435)*
Essex Electro Engineers Inc .... E 847 891-4444
  Schaumburg *(G-18522)*
Loyola Paper Company .... E 847 956-7770
  Elk Grove Village *(G-9098)*
Michels Frame Shop .... G 847 647-7366
  Niles *(G-15145)*
Mosaic Construction .... G 847 504-0177
  Northbrook *(G-15437)*
Panache Editions Ltd .... G 847 921-8574
  Glencoe *(G-10433)*
Shade Aire Company .... G 815 623-7597
  Roscoe *(G-17933)*

INTERMEDIATES Cyclic, Organic

Stepan Company .... B 847 446-7500
  Northfield *(G-15531)*

INTRAVENOUS SOLUTIONS

Anritsu Infivis Inc .... E 847 419-9729
  Elk Grove Village *(G-8834)*
Baxalta Export Corporation .... C 224 948-2000
  Bannockburn *(G-1193)*
Baxalta Incorporated .... C 224 940-2000
  Bannockburn *(G-1194)*
Baxalta World Trade LLC .... G 224 940-2000
  Bannockburn *(G-1195)*
Baxter International Inc .... A 224 948-2000
  Deerfield *(G-7595)*
Baxter World Trade Corporation .... F 224 948-2000
  Deerfield *(G-7596)*

INVENTORY COMPUTING SVCS

Paragon International Inc .... F 847 240-2981
  Schaumburg *(G-18664)*

INVERTERS: Nonrotating Electrical

Advanced Enrgy Solutions Group .. F 618 988-0888
  Carterville *(G-3128)*

JEWELRY STORES: Precious Stones & Precious Metals

INVESTMENT ADVISORY SVCS
American Association of Indivi ....E....... 312 280-0170
  Chicago (G-3649)

INVESTMENT CLUBS
Harris William & Company Inc ....E....... 312 621-0590
  Chicago (G-4782)
Neckbone Skunks Logistics & Te ....F....... 312 218-0281
  Chicago (G-5561)
Whi Capital Partners ....G....... 312 621-0590
  Chicago (G-6615)

INVESTMENT FIRM: General Brokerage
Lake Pacific Partners LLC ....B....... 312 578-1110
  Chicago (G-5161)
Wanxiang USA Holdings Corp ....F....... 847 622-8838
  Elgin (G-8776)

INVESTMENT FUNDS, NEC
Mid Oaks Investments LLC ....G....... 847 215-3475
  Buffalo Grove (G-2573)

INVESTMENT FUNDS: Open-Ended
Cpg International LLC ....D....... 570 558-8000
  Chicago (G-4252)
Roundtble Hlthcare Partners LP ....E....... 847 739-3200
  Lake Forest (G-12299)

INVESTORS, NEC
Enp Investments LLC ....G....... 815 539-7471
  Mendota (G-13942)
F & B Woodworking Inc ....G....... 217 543-2531
  Arthur (G-857)
Hadley Capital Fund II LP ....G....... 847 906-5300
  Wilmette (G-21076)
Lv Ventures Inc ....E....... 312 993-1758
  Chicago (G-5290)
Shore Capital Partners LLC ....E....... 312 348-7580
  Chicago (G-6157)
Willis Stein & Partners Manage ....F....... 312 422-2400
  Chicago (G-6632)
Wind Point Partners Vi LP ....E....... 312 255-4800
  Chicago (G-6638)

INVESTORS: Real Estate, Exc Property Operators
Tmb Industries Inc ....A....... 312 280-2565
  Chicago (G-6382)

IRON & STEEL PRDTS: Hot-Rolled
Economy Iron Inc ....F....... 708 343-1777
  Melrose Park (G-13859)
Princeton Flighting Corp ....F....... 815 872-0945
  Princeton (G-16819)
TSA Processing Chicago Inc ....G....... 630 860-5900
  Bensenville (G-1904)

IRON ORE PREPARATION
Idlr USA Inc ....G....... 630 375-0101
  Aurora (G-980)

IRON ORES
Q Lotus Holdings Inc ....G....... 312 379-1800
  Chicago (G-5921)
Regal Converting Co Inc ....F....... 630 257-3581
  Lockport (G-13021)

IRON: Sponge
Connelly-Gpm Inc ....E....... 773 247-7231
  Chicago (G-4219)

IRONING BOARDS
Home Pdts Intl - N Amer Inc ....B....... 773 890-1010
  Chicago (G-4834)
Lake Iron Inc ....G....... 708 870-0546
  Chicago (G-5160)

IRRADIATION EQPT: Nuclear
Starfire Industries LLC ....E....... 217 721-4165
  Champaign (G-3356)

IRRIGATION SYSTEMS, NEC Water Distribution Or Sply Systems
Liquitech Inc ....E....... 630 693-0500
  Lombard (G-13097)

JACKS: Hydraulic
Central Hydraulics Inc ....G....... 309 527-5238
  El Paso (G-8434)
Rehobot Inc ....G....... 815 385-7777
  McHenry (G-13786)
Walach Manufacturing Co Inc ....F....... 773 836-2060
  Chicago (G-6585)

JANITORIAL & CUSTODIAL SVCS
Klean-Ko Inc ....D....... 630 620-1860
  Lombard (G-13092)
Macon Resources Inc ....C....... 217 875-1910
  Decatur (G-7520)
Rampro Facilities Svcs Corp ....G....... 224 639-6378
  Waukegan (G-20487)
Wells Janitorial Service Inc ....G....... 872 226-9983
  Chicago (G-6600)
Workshop ....E....... 815 777-2211
  Galena (G-10183)

JANITORIAL EQPT & SPLYS WHOLESALERS
Brite Site Supply Inc ....G....... 773 772-7300
  Chicago (G-3959)
Dura Wax Company ....F....... 815 385-5000
  McHenry (G-13739)
GL Downs Inc ....G....... 618 993-9777
  Marion (G-13513)
Nanco Sales Co Inc ....G....... 630 892-9820
  Aurora (G-1138)

JARS: Plastic
Xcell International Corp ....D....... 630 323-0107
  Lemont (G-12596)

JEWELERS' FINDINGS & MATERIALS: Castings
M B Jewelers Inc ....G....... 312 853-3490
  Chicago (G-5299)

JEWELRY & PRECIOUS STONES WHOLESALERS
Diamond Icic Corporation ....E....... 309 269-8652
  Rock Island (G-17218)
Edgar H Fey Jewelers Inc ....E....... 708 352-4115
  Naperville (G-14821)
S G Nelson & Co ....G....... 630 668-7900
  Wheaton (G-20822)
Tia Tynette Designs Inc ....G....... 219 440-2859
  Olympia Fields (G-15899)

JEWELRY APPAREL
A G Mitchells Jewelers Ltd ....F....... 847 394-0820
  Arlington Heights (G-680)
Vintaj Natural Brass Co ....G....... 815 776-9300
  Galena (G-10180)

JEWELRY FINDINGS & LAPIDARY WORK
Alex and Ani LLC ....G....... 708 403-4450
  Orland Park (G-15937)
C D Nelson Consulting Inc ....G....... 847 487-4870
  Wauconda (G-20336)
Israel Levy Diamnd Cutters Inc ....E....... 312 368-8540
  Chicago (G-4974)
Micro Lapping & Grinding Co ....E....... 847 455-5446
  Franklin Park (G-9997)

JEWELRY REPAIR SVCS
Diamondaire Corp ....G....... 630 355-7464
  Saint Charles (G-18184)
Emerald City Jewelry Inc ....G....... 217 222-8896
  Quincy (G-16880)
Hustedt Manufacturing Jewelers ....G....... 217 784-8462
  Gibson City (G-10339)
Kaye Lee & Company Inc ....G....... 312 236-9686
  Chicago (G-5086)
Masud Jewelers Inc ....G....... 312 236-0547
  Chicago (G-5363)
Michael P Jones ....G....... 217 787-7457
  Springfield (G-19406)
Norkin Jewelry Co Inc ....E....... 312 782-7311
  Chicago (G-5616)
Rodger Murphy ....G....... 309 582-2202
  Aledo (G-359)
Roger Burke Jewelers Inc ....F....... 309 692-0210
  Peoria (G-16514)
Simon Zelikman ....G....... 847 338-8031
  Oakwood Hills (G-15822)
Unicorn Designs ....G....... 847 295-5230
  Lake Forest (G-12319)
Victor Levy Jewelry Co Inc ....G....... 312 782-5297
  Chicago (G-6545)

JEWELRY STORES
A G Mitchells Jewelers Ltd ....F....... 847 394-0820
  Arlington Heights (G-680)
Emerald City Jewelry Inc ....G....... 217 222-8896
  Quincy (G-16880)
Hakimian Gem Co ....G....... 312 236-6969
  Chicago (G-4770)
Marion Oelze ....G....... 618 327-9224
  Nashville (G-15001)
Rodger Murphy ....G....... 309 582-2202
  Aledo (G-359)

JEWELRY STORES: Clocks
Instrument Services Inc ....G....... 815 623-2993
  Machesney Park (G-13350)

JEWELRY STORES: Precious Stones & Precious Metals
A M Lee Inc ....G....... 847 291-1777
  Northbrook (G-15329)
Alan Rocca Ltd ....E....... 630 323-5800
  Oak Brook (G-15590)
Azteca Jewelry ....G....... 773 929-0796
  Chicago (G-3803)
Burdeens Jewelry Ltd ....G....... 847 459-8980
  Buffalo Grove (G-2522)
Charles Horberg Jewelers Inc ....G....... 312 263-4924
  Chicago (G-4074)
D & M Perlman Fine Jewelry ....G....... 847 426-8881
  West Dundee (G-20661)
Daniels Jewelry & Mfg Co ....G....... 847 998-5222
  Glenview (G-10542)
David Nelson Exquisite Jewelry ....G....... 815 741-4702
  Joliet (G-11852)
Edgar H Fey Jewelers Inc ....E....... 708 352-4115
  Naperville (G-14821)
Eve J Alfille Ltd ....E....... 847 869-7920
  Evanston (G-9518)
Faye Jewellery Chez ....G....... 815 477-1818
  Crystal Lake (G-7198)
Frank S Bender Inc ....G....... 847 441-7370
  Northfield (G-15514)
G Blando Jewelers Inc ....G....... 630 627-7963
  Countryside (G-7053)
H Watson Jewelry Co ....G....... 312 236-1104
  Chicago (G-4761)
Ho Brothers LLC ....G....... 312 854-3008
  Chicago (G-4826)
Jordan Gold Inc ....G....... 708 430-7008
  Oak Lawn (G-15722)
Kaye Lee & Company Inc ....G....... 312 236-9686
  Chicago (G-5086)
Leo A Bachrach Jewelers Inc ....G....... 312 263-3111
  Chicago (G-5204)
Lester Lampert Inc ....E....... 312 944-6888
  Chicago (G-5208)
Perle & Sons Jewelers Inc ....G....... 630 357-3357
  Naperville (G-14896)
Razny Jewelers Ltd ....G....... 630 932-4900
  Addison (G-267)
Richards Fine Jewelry & Design ....G....... 847 697-4053
  South Elgin (G-19172)
Roger Burke Jewelers Inc ....F....... 309 692-0210
  Peoria (G-16514)
Ross Designs Ltd ....G....... 847 831-7669
  Highland Park (G-11295)
Solari R Mfg Jewelers ....G....... 847 823-4354
  Park Ridge (G-16296)
State Street Jewelers Inc ....G....... 630 232-2085
  Geneva (G-10307)
Tri-City Gold Exchange Inc ....F....... 708 331-5995
  Harvey (G-11098)
Unicorn Designs ....G....... 847 295-5230
  Lake Forest (G-12319)

JEWELRY STORES: Silverware

Al Bar Laboratories Inc .... F 847 251-1218
Wilmette *(G-21068)*

JEWELRY STORES: Watches

Tammy Banks .... G 312 280-1388
Chicago *(G-6317)*

JEWELRY, PREC METAL: Mountings, Pens, Lthr, Etc, Gold/Silver

Award Emblem Mfg Co Inc .... F 630 739-0800
Bolingbrook *(G-2153)*

JEWELRY, PRECIOUS METAL: Cigar & Cigarette Access

ISA Chicago .... G 630 317-7169
Carol Stream *(G-3007)*

JEWELRY, PRECIOUS METAL: Medals, Precious Or Semiprecious

Mint Masters Inc .... E 847 451-1133
Franklin Park *(G-10000)*
Park-Ohio Industries Inc .... D 708 652-6691
Chicago *(G-5766)*
R S Owens & Co Inc .... B 773 282-6000
Chicago *(G-5953)*

JEWELRY, PRECIOUS METAL: Pearl, Natural Or Cultured

Barrett NJide Yvonne .... F 312 701-3962
Chicago *(G-3838)*

JEWELRY, PRECIOUS METAL: Rings, Finger

Bliss Ring Company Inc .... F 847 446-3440
Winnetka *(G-21127)*
David Nelson Exquisite Jewelry .... G 815 741-4702
Joliet *(G-11852)*
Fashion Craft Corporation .... E 847 998-0092
Highland Park *(G-11262)*
Herff Jones LLC .... F 815 756-4743
Dekalb *(G-7684)*
Herff Jones LLC .... D 773 463-1144
Chicago *(G-4807)*
Herff Jones LLC .... F 217 351-9500
Champaign *(G-3300)*
Herff Jones LLC .... G 708 425-0130
Oak Lawn *(G-15719)*
Razny Jewelers Ltd .... E 630 932-4900
Addison *(G-267)*
Trebor Enterprises Ltd .... G 815 235-1700
Freeport *(G-10147)*
Victor Levy Jewelry Co Inc .... G 312 782-5297
Chicago *(G-6545)*

JEWELRY, PRECIOUS METAL: Rosaries/Other Sm Religious Article

Kesher Stam .... G 773 973-7826
Chicago *(G-5097)*

JEWELRY, PRECIOUS METAL: Settings & Mountings

Eve J Alfille Ltd .... E 847 869-7920
Evanston *(G-9518)*
Fine Gold Mfg Jewelers .... G 630 323-9600
Hinsdale *(G-11368)*
Hy Spreckman & Sons Inc .... F 312 236-2173
Skokie *(G-18966)*
Kaye Lee & Company Inc .... G 312 236-9686
Chicago *(G-5086)*
Michael P Jones .... G 217 787-7457
Springfield *(G-19406)*
Roger Burke Jewelers Inc .... F 309 692-0210
Peoria *(G-16514)*
S G Nelson & Co .... G 630 668-7900
Wheaton *(G-20822)*

JEWELRY, WHOLESALE

Alomar Inc .... G 312 855-0714
Chicago *(G-3627)*
Azteca Jewelry .... G 773 929-0796
Chicago *(G-3803)*
Charles Horberg Jewelers Inc .... G 312 263-4924
Chicago *(G-4074)*
Diamondaire Corp .... G 630 355-7464
Saint Charles *(G-18184)*
Faye Jewellery Chez .... G 815 477-1818
Crystal Lake *(G-7198)*
Jason Lau Jewelry .... G 312 750-1028
Chicago *(G-5010)*
Rahmanims Imports Inc .... G 312 236-2200
Chicago *(G-5963)*

JEWELRY: Decorative, Fashion & Costume

Acme Button & Buttonhole Co .... G 773 907-8400
Chicago *(G-3526)*
Bee-Jay Industries Inc .... F 708 867-4431
Bloomingdale *(G-1979)*
D & D Sukach Inc .... G 815 895-3377
Sycamore *(G-19704)*
Daniels Jewelry & Mfg Co .... G 847 998-5222
Glenview *(G-10542)*
Diamondaire Corp .... G 630 355-7464
Saint Charles *(G-18184)*
Hustedt Manufacturing Jewelers .... G 217 784-8462
Gibson City *(G-10339)*
Jewerly and Beyond .... G 312 833-6785
Schaumburg *(G-18576)*
Jordan Gold Inc .... G 708 430-7008
Oak Lawn *(G-15722)*
K Fleye Designs .... G 773 531-0716
Chicago *(G-5066)*
Noor Jewels LLC .... G 847 505-9849
Chicago *(G-5613)*
Smart Creations Inc .... G 847 433-3451
Highland Park *(G-11298)*
Solari R Mfg Jewelers .... G 847 823-4354
Park Ridge *(G-16296)*
Sunnywood Incorporated .... G 815 675-9777
McHenry *(G-13799)*
Swarovski North America Ltd .... G 708 364-0090
Orland Park *(G-15985)*
Swarovski North America Ltd .... G 847 680-5150
Vernon Hills *(G-20102)*
Swarovski North America Ltd .... G 847 413-9960
Schaumburg *(G-18733)*
Swarovski US Holding Limited .... G 847 679-8670
Skokie *(G-19040)*

JEWELRY: Precious Metal

A M Lee Inc .... G 847 291-1777
Northbrook *(G-15329)*
Accents By Fred .... G 708 366-9850
Forest Park *(G-9707)*
Alan Rocca Ltd .... E 630 323-5800
Oak Brook *(G-15590)*
Alomar Inc .... G 312 855-0714
Chicago *(G-3627)*
Award Concepts Inc .... E 630 513-7801
Saint Charles *(G-18153)*
Azteca Jewelry .... G 773 929-0796
Chicago *(G-3803)*
Bee-Jay Industries Inc .... F 708 867-4431
Bloomingdale *(G-1979)*
Burdeens Jewelry Ltd .... G 847 459-8980
Buffalo Grove *(G-2522)*
Cabanas Manufacturing Jewelers .... G 312 726-0333
Chicago *(G-3999)*
Casting House Inc .... F 312 782-7160
Chicago *(G-4037)*
Charles Horberg Jewelers Inc .... G 312 263-4924
Chicago *(G-4074)*
Club Jewelry Manufacturing Inc .... G 847 541-0700
Wheeling *(G-20873)*
D & M Perlman Fine Jewelry .... G 847 426-8881
West Dundee *(G-20661)*
Edgar H Fey Jewelers Inc .... E 708 352-4115
Naperville *(G-14821)*
Emerald City Jewelry Inc .... G 217 222-8896
Quincy *(G-16880)*
Empire Corp .... G 630 887-8228
Willowbrook *(G-21042)*
Faye Jewellery Chez .... G 815 477-1818
Crystal Lake *(G-7198)*
Frank S Bender Inc .... G 847 441-7370
Northfield *(G-15514)*
G Blando Jewelers Inc .... G 630 627-7963
Countryside *(G-7053)*
General Design Jewelers Inc .... G 312 201-9047
Chicago *(G-4669)*
H Watson Jewelry Co .... G 312 236-1104
Chicago *(G-4761)*
Hakimian Gem Co .... G 312 236-6969
Chicago *(G-4770)*
Herff Jones LLC .... C 317 612-3705
Hillside *(G-11341)*
Ho Brothers LLC .... G 312 854-3008
Chicago *(G-4826)*
Hustedt Manufacturing Jewelers .... G 217 784-8462
Gibson City *(G-10339)*
Jason Lau Jewelry .... G 312 750-1028
Chicago *(G-5010)*
John Buechner Inc .... G 312 263-2226
Chicago *(G-5038)*
Joseph C Wolf .... G 312 332-3135
Chicago *(G-5053)*
Lana Unlimited Co .... G 312 226-7050
Lake Forest *(G-12272)*
Leo A Bachrach Jewelers Inc .... G 312 263-3111
Chicago *(G-5204)*
Lester Lampert Inc .... E 312 944-6888
Chicago *(G-5208)*
M B Jewelers Inc .... G 312 853-3490
Chicago *(G-5299)*
Made As Intended Inc .... F 630 789-3494
Oak Brook *(G-15639)*
Masud Jewelers Inc .... G 312 236-0547
Chicago *(G-5363)*
Medaowview Ventures II Inc .... E 847 965-1700
Morton Grove *(G-14426)*
Mtm Jostens Inc .... G 815 875-1111
Princeton *(G-16816)*
Mtm Recognition Corporation .... C 815 875-1111
Princeton *(G-16817)*
Norkin Jewelry Co Inc .... E 312 782-7311
Chicago *(G-5616)*
Norridge Jewelry .... G 312 984-1036
Chicago *(G-5617)*
Perle & Sons Jewelers Inc .... G 630 357-3357
Naperville *(G-14896)*
Rahmanims Imports Inc .... G 312 236-2200
Chicago *(G-5963)*
Richards Fine Jewelry & Design .... G 847 697-4053
South Elgin *(G-19172)*
Rodger Murphy .... G 309 582-2202
Aledo *(G-359)*
Ross Designs Ltd .... G 847 831-7669
Highland Park *(G-11295)*
Simon Zelikman .... G 847 338-8031
Oakwood Hills *(G-15822)*
Tri-City Gold Exchange Inc .... F 708 331-5995
Harvey *(G-11098)*
Ulla of Finland .... G 773 763-0700
Chicago *(G-6457)*
Unicorn Designs .... G 847 295-5230
Lake Forest *(G-12319)*
V & O Style Jewelry Mfg Co .... G 312 372-2454
Chicago *(G-6510)*
White Diamonds Inc .... G 708 868-4006
Calumet City *(G-2793)*

JIGS & FIXTURES

Grove Plastic Inc .... F 847 678-8244
Franklin Park *(G-9954)*
K & H Tool Co .... G 630 766-4588
Bensenville *(G-1834)*
Precision Engineering & Dev Co .... E 630 834-5956
Villa Park *(G-20165)*
R & R Machining Inc .... G 217 835-4579
Benld *(G-1718)*
Republic Drill .... G 708 865-7666
Melrose Park *(G-13908)*
Roscoe Tool & Manufacturing .... E 815 633-8808
Roscoe *(G-17929)*

JIGS: Welding Positioners

Alm Positioners Inc .... G 309 787-6200
Rock Island *(G-17201)*

JOB PRINTING & NEWSPAPER PUBLISHING COMBINED

Arthur Graphic Clarion .... G 217 543-2151
Arthur *(G-842)*
Augusta Eagle .... G 217 392-2715
Augusta *(G-909)*
Breeze Printing Company .... F 217 824-2233
Taylorville *(G-19752)*
Bunker Hill Publication .... G 618 585-4411
Bunker Hill *(G-2633)*
Farina News .... G 618 245-6216
Farina *(G-9652)*

PRODUCT SECTION

Freeburg Printing & Publishing.............G....... 618 539-3320
  Freeburg (G-10089)
Golden Prairie News.............................G....... 217 226-3721
  Assumption (G-889)
Kaneland Publications Inc....................F....... 630 365-6446
  Saint Charles (G-18220)
KK Stevens Publishing Co.....................E....... 309 329-2151
  Astoria (G-893)
Liberty Group Publishing......................F....... 309 944-1779
  Geneseo (G-10245)
Mason City Banner Times.....................F....... 217 482-3276
  Mason City (G-13612)
Perryco Inc..G....... 217 322-3321
  Rushville (G-18112)
Rankin Publishing Inc............................F....... 217 268-4959
  Arcola (G-664)
Toledo Democrat..................................G....... 217 849-2000
  Toledo (G-19879)

JOB TRAINING & VOCATIONAL REHABILITATION SVCS

Envision Unlimited................................C....... 773 651-1100
  Chicago (G-4521)
Fulton County Rehabilitation................E....... 309 647-6510
  Canton (G-2826)
Mental Health Ctrs Centl Ill..................D....... 217 735-1413
  Lincoln (G-12735)
Olfb Corporation...................................G....... 309 283-0825
  Moline (G-14164)
Park Lawn Association Inc...................F....... 708 425-7377
  Oak Lawn (G-15731)
Rehabilitation and Vocational..............E....... 618 833-5344
  Anna (G-587)
Simformotion LLC..................................F....... 309 263-7595
  Peoria (G-16524)

JOINTS & COUPLINGS

La Salle Co Esda....................................G....... 815 433-5622
  Ottawa (G-16058)
Rimtec Corporation...............................F....... 630 628-0036
  Addison (G-275)

JOINTS: Ball Except aircraft & Auto

Hyspan Precision Products Inc............E....... 773 277-0700
  South Holland (G-19223)

JOINTS: Expansion

Anamet Inc...G....... 217 234-8844
  Glen Ellyn (G-10394)
Commercial Fabricators Inc..................G....... 708 594-1199
  Bridgeview (G-2337)
Lichtnwald - Johnston Ir Works............E....... 847 966-1100
  Morton Grove (G-14419)
Metraflex Company..............................D....... 312 738-3800
  Chicago (G-5411)
Thybar Corporation...............................E....... 630 543-5300
  Addison (G-309)

JOINTS: Swivel & Universal, Exc Aircraft & Auto

Flex-Weld Inc.......................................D....... 815 334-3662
  Woodstock (G-21387)
NTN USA Corporation...........................C....... 847 298-4652
  Mount Prospect (G-14554)

JOISTS: Long-Span Series, Open Web Steel

Gooder-Henrichsen Company Inc........D....... 708 757-5030
  Chicago Heights (G-6748)

KAOLIN MINING

Huber Carbonates LLC.........................F....... 217 224-8737
  Quincy (G-16893)

KEYBOARDS: Computer Or Office Machine

Art Cnc Machining LLC..........................G....... 708 907-3090
  Bridgeview (G-2325)
Grayhill Inc...B....... 708 354-1040
  La Grange (G-12077)

KITCHEN CABINET STORES, EXC CUSTOM

Cabinets & Granite Direct LLC.............F....... 630 588-8886
  Carol Stream (G-2952)
Edward Hull Cabinet Shop....................G....... 217 864-3011
  Mount Zion (G-14645)

Harts Top and Cabinet Shop................G....... 708 957-4666
  Country Club Hills (G-7040)
Hickory Street Cabinets.......................G....... 618 667-9676
  Troy (G-19915)
Kabinet Kraft.......................................F....... 618 395-1047
  Olney (G-15867)
Markham Cabinet Works Inc................G....... 708 687-3074
  Midlothian (G-13993)
Regency Custom Woodworking............F....... 815 689-2117
  Cullom (G-7300)
Wenger Woodcraft...............................G....... 217 578-3440
  Tuscola (G-19934)
Wilson Kitchens Inc.............................D....... 618 253-7449
  Harrisburg (G-11031)

KITCHEN CABINETS WHOLESALERS

Cabinets & Granite Direct LLC.............F....... 630 588-8886
  Carol Stream (G-2952)
Creative Cabinets Countertops............F....... 217 446-6406
  Danville (G-7327)
Gold Seal Cabinets Countertops..........E....... 630 906-0366
  Aurora (G-1104)
Hci Cabinetry and Design Inc..............G....... 630 584-0266
  Addison (G-148)
Lead n Glass Tm..................................F....... 847 255-2074
  Wheeling (G-20930)
Orren Pickell Builders Inc....................F....... 847 572-5200
  Wilmette (G-21090)
Stonecrafters Inc.................................E....... 815 363-8730
  Lakemoor (G-12477)

KITCHEN TOOLS & UTENSILS WHOLESALERS

R/K Industries Inc................................F....... 847 526-2222
  Wauconda (G-20387)
Superior Knife Inc.................................E....... 847 982-2280
  Niles (G-15177)

KITCHEN UTENSILS: Bakers' Eqpt, Wood

House On The Hill Inc..........................G....... 630 279-4455
  Wheaton (G-20803)
John Joda Post 54................................G....... 815 692-3222
  Fairbury (G-9610)

KITCHEN UTENSILS: Food Handling & Processing Prdts, Wood

Axis Design Architectual Mllwk.............F....... 630 466-4549
  Sugar Grove (G-19637)
Villa Foods LLC....................................G....... 815 721-1136
  Rockford (G-17675)

KITCHEN UTENSILS: Wooden

Magick Woods Inc................................G....... 630 229-0121
  Aurora (G-1126)

KITCHENWARE STORES

Euromarket Designs Inc.......................A....... 847 272-2888
  Northbrook (G-15386)
Kitchen Supply Wholesale...................G....... 224 603-1208
  Antioch (G-618)
Tri-State Food Equipment...................G....... 217 228-1550
  Quincy (G-16952)
US Foods Culinary Eqp Sups LLC........G....... 847 720-8000
  Rosemont (G-18057)

KITCHENWARE: Plastic

Limitless Innovations Inc.....................E....... 855 843-4828
  McHenry (G-13758)
Pactiv LLC..C....... 708 496-2900
  Bedford Park (G-1490)
Pactiv LLC..F....... 708 496-2900
  Chicago (G-5742)

KITS: Plastic

Cpg Newco LLC....................................A....... 877 275-2935
  Chicago (G-4253)
Rust-Oleum Corporation......................D....... 815 967-4258
  Rockford (G-17617)
Testor Corporation...............................D....... 815 962-6654
  Rockford (G-17656)
Universal Hovercraft Amer Inc............F....... 815 963-1200
  Rockford (G-17673)

LABORATORIES: Biotechnology

KNIVES: Agricultural Or indl

Gartech Manufacturing Co...................E....... 217 324-6527
  Litchfield (G-12963)
Precision Industrial Knife.....................G....... 630 350-7898
  Wood Dale (G-21229)

KNURLING

Roll Rite Inc...G....... 815 645-8600
  Davis Junction (G-7426)

LABELS: Cotton, Printed

Sato Lbling Solutions Amer Inc............D....... 630 771-4200
  Romeoville (G-17874)

LABELS: Paper, Made From Purchased Materials

Ameri Label Company...........................F....... 847 895-8000
  Bartlett (G-1253)
Diversfied Lbling Slutions Inc..............C....... 630 625-1225
  Itasca (G-11643)
Hospital Hlth Care Systems Inc...........E....... 708 863-3400
  Lyons (G-13311)
Identi-Graphics Inc..............................E....... 630 801-4845
  Montgomery (G-14250)
Illinois Tag Co......................................G....... 773 626-0542
  Carol Stream (G-3001)
Precision Press & Label Inc.................G....... 630 625-1225
  Itasca (G-11722)
Proampac Pg Borrower LLC.................B....... 618 451-0010
  Granite City (G-10733)
Trade Label & Decal............................G....... 630 773-0447
  Itasca (G-11747)

LABELS: Woven

W & W Associates Inc.........................G....... 847 719-1760
  Lake Zurich (G-12469)

LABORATORIES, TESTING: Metallurgical

Magnetic Inspection Lab Inc................D....... 847 437-4488
  Elk Grove Village (G-9106)

LABORATORIES, TESTING: Product Testing

Skandia Inc..D....... 800 945-7135
  Davis Junction (G-7427)
Superior Joining Tech Inc....................E....... 815 282-7581
  Machesney Park (G-13376)

LABORATORIES, TESTING: Product Testing, Safety/Performance

Atlas Material Tstg Tech LLC...............E....... 773 327-4520
  Chicago (G-3767)
Atlas Material Tstg Tech LLC...............C....... 773 327-4520
  Mount Prospect (G-14512)

LABORATORIES, TESTING: Radiation

Landauer Inc.......................................C....... 708 755-7000
  Glenwood (G-10642)

LABORATORIES, TESTING: Seed

Pioneer Hi-Bred Intl Inc.......................F....... 309 962-2931
  Saint Joseph (G-18318)

LABORATORIES, TESTING: Veterinary

Shaars International Inc......................G....... 815 315-0717
  Rockford (G-17627)

LABORATORIES, TESTING: Welded Joint Radiographing

Jay RS Steel & Welding Inc.................G....... 847 949-9353
  Mundelein (G-14703)

LABORATORIES: Biological Research

Isovac Products LLC............................G....... 630 679-1740
  Romeoville (G-17834)

LABORATORIES: Biotechnology

Jointechlabs Inc..................................G....... 773 954-1076
  Wheeling (G-20921)
Sigenics Inc...F....... 312 448-8000
  Chicago (G-6164)

LABORATORIES: Commercial Nonphysical Research

LABORATORIES: Commercial Nonphysical Research

Group O Inc .... E 309 736-8100
  Milan *(G-14015)*
Night Vision Corporation .... G 847 677-7611
  Lincolnwood *(G-12833)*

LABORATORIES: Dental

Dental Laboratory Inc .... E 630 262-3700
  Geneva *(G-10265)*
J L Lawrence & Co .... G 217 235-3622
  Mattoon *(G-13638)*
Lmpl Management Corporation .... G 708 636-2443
  Oak Lawn *(G-15725)*
Martin Dental Laboratory Inc .... F 708 597-8880
  Lockport *(G-13011)*
Tanaka Dental Enterprises Inc .... F 847 679-1610
  Skokie *(G-19042)*
Underwood Dental Laboratories .... F 217 398-0090
  Champaign *(G-3360)*

LABORATORIES: Dental, Artificial Teeth Production

Odl Inc .... D 815 434-0655
  Ottawa *(G-16067)*

LABORATORIES: Dental, Crown & Bridge Production

Artistic Dental Studio Inc .... E 630 679-8686
  Bolingbrook *(G-2149)*
Bennett Technologies Inc .... F 708 389-9501
  Tinley Park *(G-19809)*
Dental Arts Laboratories Inc .... G 309 342-3117
  Galesburg *(G-10190)*
Dental Crafts Lab Inc .... G 815 872-3221
  Princeton *(G-16806)*
Mandis Dental Laboratory .... G 618 345-3777
  Collinsville *(G-6968)*
Oratech Inc .... E 217 793-2735
  Springfield *(G-19418)*

LABORATORIES: Dental, Denture Production

Dental Craft Corp .... F 815 385-7132
  Ringwood *(G-17041)*
Fred Pigg Dental Lab .... G 618 439-6829
  Mount Vernon *(G-14611)*

LABORATORIES: Electronic Research

Emac Inc .... E 618 529-4525
  Carbondale *(G-2841)*
Imagineering Inc .... E 847 806-0003
  Elk Grove Village *(G-9047)*
Spectrum Cos International .... G 630 879-8008
  Batavia *(G-1418)*
Systems & Electronics Inc .... E 847 228-0985
  Elk Grove Village *(G-9263)*
Tech Star Design and Mfg .... F 847 290-8676
  Elk Grove Village *(G-9268)*
Thales Visionix Inc .... D 630 375-2008
  Aurora *(G-1161)*

LABORATORIES: Medical

Biomerieux Inc .... E 630 628-6055
  Lombard *(G-13046)*
Presence Legacy Association .... F 815 741-7555
  Joliet *(G-11916)*

LABORATORIES: Neurological

Naurex Inc .... G 847 871-0377
  Evanston *(G-9557)*

LABORATORIES: Noncommercial Research

Elliot Inst For Scial Scnces R .... G 217 525-8202
  Springfield *(G-19361)*

LABORATORIES: Physical Research, Commercial

Abbott Products Inc .... B 847 937-6100
  Abbott Park *(G-6)*
Associate General Labs Inc .... G 847 678-2717
  Franklin Park *(G-9877)*
Batavia Bio Processing Limited .... G 630 761-1180
  Batavia *(G-1354)*
Blue Pearl Stone Tech LLC .... G 708 698-5700
  La Grange *(G-12073)*
Cabot Microelectronics Corp .... C 630 375-6631
  Aurora *(G-933)*
Chicago Dscovery Solutions LLC .... G 815 609-2071
  Plainfield *(G-16650)*
Circom Inc .... E 630 595-4460
  Bensenville *(G-1770)*
Dawes LLC .... F 847 577-2020
  Arlington Heights *(G-726)*
Dromont Corporation .... G 404 615-2336
  Palatine *(G-16114)*
DSM Desotech Inc .... C 847 697-0400
  Elgin *(G-8570)*
Epir Technologies Inc .... E 630 771-0203
  Bolingbrook *(G-2175)*
Honeywell International Inc .... D 847 797-4000
  Des Plaines *(G-7778)*
Illinois Foundation Seeds Inc .... F 217 485-6420
  Tolono *(G-19883)*
Incon Processing LLC .... E 630 305-8556
  Batavia *(G-1385)*
INX International Ink Co .... E 630 681-7100
  West Chicago *(G-20601)*
Neopenda Pbc .... G 919 622-2487
  Chicago *(G-5570)*
Pharmasyn Inc .... G 847 752-8405
  Libertyville *(G-12695)*
Provisur Technologies .... G 312 284-4698
  Chicago *(G-5908)*
Silicon Control Inc .... G 847 215-7947
  Deerfield *(G-7649)*
Starfire Industries LLC .... G 217 721-4165
  Champaign *(G-3356)*
Tagore Technology Inc .... F 847 790-3799
  Arlington Heights *(G-816)*
Websolutions Technology Inc .... E 630 375-6833
  Aurora *(G-1033)*
Willims-Hyward Intl Ctings Inc .... F 708 458-0015
  Argo *(G-678)*

LABORATORIES: Testing

Alloyweld Inspection Co Inc .... E 630 595-2145
  Bensenville *(G-1738)*
Fisher Scientific Company LLC .... G 800 528-0494
  Chicago *(G-4597)*
Lifewatch Services Inc .... B 847 720-2100
  Rosemont *(G-18032)*

LABORATORIES: Testing

Agrochem Inc .... F 847 564-1304
  Northbrook *(G-15334)*
Alloyweld Inspection Co Inc .... E 630 595-2145
  Bensenville *(G-1738)*
Associate General Labs Inc .... G 847 678-2717
  Franklin Park *(G-9877)*
Batavia Bio Processing Limited .... G 630 761-1180
  Batavia *(G-1354)*
Biomerieux Inc .... F 630 600-5516
  Lombard *(G-13045)*
Biomerieux Inc .... E 630 628-6055
  Lombard *(G-13046)*
Cemec Inc .... G 630 495-9696
  Downers Grove *(G-7966)*
Centurion Non Destructive Tstg .... F 630 736-5500
  Streamwood *(G-19565)*
FH Ayer Manufacturing Co .... E 708 755-0550
  Chicago Heights *(G-6746)*
Incon Processing LLC .... E 630 305-8556
  Batavia *(G-1385)*
McNdt Pipeline Ltd .... F 815 467-5200
  Channahon *(G-3388)*
Peer Chain Company .... D 847 775-4600
  Waukegan *(G-20475)*
Perten Instruments Inc .... E 217 585-9440
  Springfield *(G-19424)*
Pharmaceutical Labs and Cons I .... G 630 359-3831
  Addison *(G-238)*
Professional Gem Sciences Inc .... G 312 920-1541
  Chicago *(G-5897)*
Sonoscan Inc .... D 847 437-6400
  Elk Grove Village *(G-9247)*
Standard Laboratories Inc .... E 618 539-5836
  Freeburg *(G-10095)*
Unified Solutions Corp .... E 847 478-9100
  Arlington Heights *(G-824)*

LABORATORY APPARATUS & FURNITURE

Atlas Material Tstg Tech LLC .... C 773 327-4520
  Mount Prospect *(G-14512)*
B T Technology Inc .... G 217 322-3768
  Rushville *(G-18108)*
Biosynergy Inc .... G 847 956-0471
  Elk Grove Village *(G-8867)*
David Martin .... G 217 564-2440
  Ivesdale *(G-11756)*
Hcs Hahn Calibration Service .... G 847 567-2500
  Lincolnshire *(G-12769)*
L A M Inc De .... G 630 860-9700
  Wood Dale *(G-21206)*
Laboratory Builders Inc .... G 630 598-0216
  Burr Ridge *(G-2695)*
Leica Microsystems Inc .... C 847 405-0123
  Buffalo Grove *(G-2563)*
Ludwig Medical Inc .... G 217 342-6570
  Effingham *(G-8408)*
Norman P Moeller .... G 847 991-3933
  Lake Barrington *(G-12162)*
OBrien Scntfic GL Blowing LLC .... G 217 762-3636
  Monticello *(G-14283)*
Preston Industries Inc .... C 847 647-0611
  Niles *(G-15162)*
Scientific Instruments Inc .... G 847 679-1242
  Schaumburg *(G-18709)*
Sirius Automation Group Inc .... F 847 607-9378
  Buffalo Grove *(G-2606)*
Wrightwood Technologies Inc .... G 312 238-9512
  Chicago *(G-6685)*

LABORATORY APPARATUS & FURNITURE: Worktables

Suburban Surgical Co .... C 847 537-9320
  Wheeling *(G-20993)*

LABORATORY APPARATUS, EXC HEATING & MEASURING

Celinco Inc .... G 815 964-2256
  Rockford *(G-17341)*
Innovative Projects Lab Inc .... G 847 605-2125
  Schaumburg *(G-18562)*
Labjackscom Inc .... G 847 537-2099
  Deerfield *(G-7628)*

LABORATORY APPARATUS: Bunsen Burners

Humboldt Mfg Co .... E 708 456-6300
  Elgin *(G-8617)*

LABORATORY APPARATUS: Calibration Tapes, Phy Testing Mach

Florida Metrology LLC .... F 630 833-3800
  Villa Park *(G-20147)*
Novel Products Inc .... G 815 624-4888
  Rockton *(G-17700)*

LABORATORY APPARATUS: Calorimeters

Parr Instrument Company .... C 309 762-7716
  Moline *(G-14165)*

LABORATORY APPARATUS: Freezers

Preferred Freezer Services of .... F 773 254-9500
  Chicago *(G-5860)*

LABORATORY APPARATUS: Laser Beam Alignment Device

Amoco Technology Company .... C 312 861-6000
  Chicago *(G-3682)*
Bea Electro Sales Inc .... G 847 238-1420
  Elk Grove Village *(G-8859)*
Scanlab America Inc .... G 630 797-2044
  Saint Charles *(G-18265)*

LABORATORY APPARATUS: Metal Periphery Dir Rdg Diameter Tape

R L Kolbi Company .... F 847 506-1440
  Arlington Heights *(G-795)*

PRODUCT SECTION

LABORATORY APPARATUS: Particle Size Reduction

Innovtive Prcess Applctons LLC .... G 708 844-6100
Crestwood *(G-7119)*

LABORATORY APPARATUS: Pipettes, Hemocytometer

Mettler-Toledo LLC .... E 630 446-7700
Aurora *(G-1002)*

LABORATORY APPARATUS: Sample Preparation Apparatus

Illinois Tool Works Inc .... C 847 295-6500
Lake Bluff *(G-12189)*

LABORATORY APPARATUS: Shakers & Stirrers

Heidolph NA LLC .... F 224 265-9600
Wood Dale *(G-21197)*

LABORATORY CHEMICALS: Organic

Franmar Chemical .... G 309 829-5952
Bloomington *(G-2045)*
Ineos Joliet LLC .... C 815 467-3200
Channahon *(G-3384)*
Tempil Inc .... E 908 757-8300
Elk Grove Village *(G-9270)*

LABORATORY EQPT, EXC MEDICAL: Wholesalers

Culture Media Supplies Inc .... G 630 499-5000
Oswego *(G-15999)*
Fisher Scientific Company LLC .... C 412 490-8300
Hanover Park *(G-11003)*
Flinn Scientific Inc .... C 800 452-1261
Batavia *(G-1378)*
Hugh Courtright & Co Ltd .... F 708 534-8400
Monee *(G-14202)*

LABORATORY EQPT: Chemical

Cubic Group Inc .... G 859 494-5834
Arlington Heights *(G-722)*

LABORATORY EQPT: Clinical Instruments Exc Medical

Dual Mfg Co Inc .... F 773 267-4457
Franklin Park *(G-9933)*
Intermerican Clinical Svcs Inc .... F 773 252-1147
Chicago *(G-4949)*

LABORATORY EQPT: Incubators

1 Federal Supply Source Inc .... G 708 964-2222
Steger *(G-19486)*

LABORATORY EQPT: Measuring

Perten Instruments Inc .... E 217 585-9440
Springfield *(G-19424)*
Supertek Scientific LLC .... G 630 345-3450
Addison *(G-300)*

LABORATORY EQPT: Sterilizers

Amity Hospital Services Inc .... G 708 206-3970
Country Club Hills *(G-7035)*
Sterigenics US LLC .... E 847 855-0727
Gurnee *(G-10930)*

LADDER & WORKSTAND COMBINATION ASSEMBLIES: Metal

Ojedas Welding Co .... G 708 595-3799
Maywood *(G-13677)*

LADDERS: Metal

Innerweld Cover Co .... F 847 497-3009
Mundelein *(G-14701)*
Louisville Ladder Inc .... G 309 692-1895
Peoria *(G-16470)*
Vulcan Ladder Usa LLC .... G 847 526-6321
Crystal Lake *(G-7292)*

LADDERS: Portable, Metal

Werner Co .... E 815 459-6020
Crystal Lake *(G-7294)*

LAMINATED PLASTICS: Plate, Sheet, Rod & Tubes

Ameriscan Designs Inc .... D 773 542-1291
Chicago *(G-3677)*
C Line Products Inc .... D 847 827-6661
Mount Prospect *(G-14517)*
Card Dynamix LLC .... C 630 685-4060
Romeoville *(G-17803)*
Carl Gorr Printing Co .... E 815 338-3191
Woodstock *(G-21370)*
CFC International Inc .... G 708 891-3456
Chicago Heights *(G-6739)*
Coilform Company .... E 630 232-8000
Geneva *(G-10262)*
Cortube Products Co .... G 708 429-6700
Tinley Park *(G-19816)*
Custom Films Inc .... F 217 826-2326
Marshall *(G-13569)*
Dana Plastic Container Corp .... E 630 529-7878
Schaumburg *(G-18504)*
Designed Plastics Inc .... E 630 694-7300
Bensenville *(G-1786)*
E-Jay Plastics Co .... F 630 543-4000
Addison *(G-108)*
Glazed Structures Inc .... F 847 223-4560
Grayslake *(G-10776)*
James Injection Molding Co .... E 847 564-3820
Northbrook *(G-15410)*
John Maneely Company .... C 773 254-0617
Chicago *(G-5043)*
Lakone Company .... D 630 892-4251
Montgomery *(G-14256)*
Photo Techniques Corp .... E 630 690-9360
Carol Stream *(G-3046)*
Pioneer Plastics Inc .... C 309 365-2951
Lexington *(G-12620)*
Pro Glass Corporation .... G 630 553-3141
Bristol *(G-2409)*
R & R Custom Cabinet Making .... G 847 358-6188
Palatine *(G-16152)*
Upm Raflatac Inc .... C 815 285-6100
Dixon *(G-7924)*

LAMINATING MATERIALS

D & K Group Inc .... E 847 956-0160
Elk Grove Village *(G-8931)*
D & K International Inc .... D 847 956-0160
Elk Grove Village *(G-8932)*

LAMINATING SVCS

Bellen Container Corporation .... E 847 741-5600
Elgin *(G-8520)*
Identatronics Inc .... E 847 437-2654
Crystal Lake *(G-7208)*
Sign Identity Inc .... G 630 942-1400
Glen Ellyn *(G-10419)*

LAMP & LIGHT BULBS & TUBES

Aco Inc .... E 773 774-5200
Chicago *(G-3529)*
Advanced Micro Lites Inc .... G 630 365-5450
Elburn *(G-8442)*
Advanced Strobe Products Inc .... D 708 867-3100
Chicago *(G-3567)*
Benko Lamps Ltd .... F 708 458-7965
Bridgeview *(G-2328)*
Cec Industries Ltd .... E 847 821-1199
Lincolnshire *(G-12748)*
Dontech Industries Inc .... F 847 428-8222
Gilberts *(G-10353)*
Eden Park Illumination Inc .... G 217 403-1866
Champaign *(G-3287)*
Keating of Chicago Inc .... E 815 569-2324
Capron *(G-2834)*
Lamp Works Inc .... F 630 871-7663
Carol Stream *(G-3015)*
Lampholders Assemblies Inc .... G 773 205-0005
Chicago *(G-5173)*
Light Matrix Inc .... G 847 590-0856
Palatine *(G-16136)*
Mattson Lamp Plant .... E 217 258-9390
Mattoon *(G-13647)*

LAMPS: Ultraviolet

Modern Lighting Tech LLC .... G 312 624-9267
Chicago *(G-5478)*
North American Lighting Inc .... A 618 548-6249
Salem *(G-18348)*
Royal Haeger Lamp Co .... E 309 837-9966
Macomb *(G-13400)*
Universal Lighting Corporation .... G 773 927-2000
Chicago *(G-6481)*
Vision Engineering Labs .... G 630 350-9470
Bensenville *(G-1910)*
Waters Industries Inc .... E 847 783-5900
West Dundee *(G-20667)*

LAMP BULBS & TUBES, ELEC: Lead-In Wires, From Purchased Wire

Anixter Inc .... C 800 323-8167
Glenview *(G-10526)*

LAMP BULBS & TUBES, ELECTRIC: Electric Light

Acculight LLC .... G 630 847-1000
Elk Grove Village *(G-8799)*
Amglo Kemlite Laboratories Inc .... D 630 238-3031
Bensenville *(G-1744)*

LAMP BULBS & TUBES, ELECTRIC: For Specialized Applications

Santas Best .... F 847 459-3301
Vernon Hills *(G-20091)*

LAMP BULBS & TUBES/PARTS, ELECTRIC: Generalized Applications

Malcolite Corporation .... D 847 562-1350
Deerfield *(G-7634)*
S A W Co .... G 630 678-5400
Lombard *(G-13126)*

LAMP REPAIR & MOUNTING SVCS

Bellows Shoppe .... G 847 446-5533
Winnetka *(G-21126)*

LAMP SHADES: Metal

Lampshade Inc .... F 773 522-2300
Chicago *(G-5174)*

LAMP STORES

Bellows Shoppe .... G 847 446-5533
Winnetka *(G-21126)*
Benko Lamps Ltd .... F 708 458-7965
Bridgeview *(G-2328)*
Rainbow Lighting .... E 847 480-1136
Northbrook *(G-15470)*
Smart Solar Inc .... F 813 343-5770
Libertyville *(G-12708)*

LAMPS: Boudoir, Residential

Stone Lighting LLC .... F 312 240-0400
Flossmoor *(G-9703)*

LAMPS: Desk, Residential

Fli Products LLC .... G 630 520-0017
West Chicago *(G-20584)*

LAMPS: Incandescent, Filament

Aero-Tech Light Bulb Co .... D 847 352-4900
Schaumburg *(G-18430)*
Radionic Hi-Tech Inc .... D 773 804-0100
Chicago *(G-5960)*

LAMPS: Table, Residential

Royal Haeger Lamp Co .... E 309 837-9966
Macomb *(G-13400)*

LAMPS: Ultraviolet

AAA Press Specialists Inc .... F 847 818-1100
Arlington Heights *(G-681)*
Ddk Scientific Corporation .... G 618 235-2849
Belleville *(G-1543)*

LAND SUBDIVISION & DEVELOPMENT

LAND SUBDIVISION & DEVELOPMENT
- **Creative Designs Kitc** .... E 773 327-8400
  Chicago *(G-4261)*
- **Elmer L Larson L C** .... F 815 895-4837
  Sycamore *(G-19710)*
- **Jack Ruch Quality Homes Inc** .... G 309 663-6595
  Bloomington *(G-2063)*
- **Plote Construction Inc** .... D 847 695-9300
  Hoffman Estates *(G-11445)*

LANTERNS
- **Big Beam Emergency Systems Inc** .... E 815 459-6100
  Crystal Lake *(G-7169)*
- **Designed For Just For You** .... G 309 221-2667
  Macomb *(G-13391)*

LAPIDARY WORK: Jewel Cut, Drill, Polish, Recut/Setting
- **Edmund D Schmelzie & Sons** .... G 312 782-7230
  Chicago *(G-4453)*

LASER SYSTEMS & EQPT
- **Domino Lasers Inc** .... E 847 855-1364
  Gurnee *(G-10872)*
- **Laser Energy Systems** .... G 815 282-8200
  Loves Park *(G-13232)*
- **Novanta Inc** .... G 781 266-5700
  Newton *(G-15089)*
- **Sphere Laser LLC** .... F 317 752-1604
  Saint Charles *(G-18274)*
- **Sphere Laser LLC** .... G 317 752-1604
  McHenry *(G-13793)*
- **Videojet Technologies Inc** .... A 630 860-7300
  Wood Dale *(G-21255)*
- **Windy City Laser Service Inc** .... G 773 995-0188
  Chicago *(G-6642)*

LASERS: Welding, Drilling & Cutting Eqpt
- **Alliance Laser Sales Inc** .... E 847 487-1945
  Wauconda *(G-20328)*
- **Allmetal Inc** .... D 630 250-8090
  Itasca *(G-11619)*
- **Bystronic Inc** .... C 847 214-0300
  Hoffman Estates *(G-11410)*
- **HK America Inc** .... G 630 916-0200
  Bartlett *(G-1286)*
- **HK Laser and Systems** .... G 630 916-0200
  Bartlett *(G-1287)*
- **United Amercn Healthcare Corp** ..... E 313 393-4571
  Chicago *(G-6469)*

LATH: Expanded Metal
- **Expanded Metal Products Corp** .... F 773 735-4500
  Chicago *(G-4544)*
- **Metalex LLC** .... C 847 362-5400
  Libertyville *(G-12678)*

LATHES
- **T&J Turning Inc** .... G 309 738-8762
  Colona *(G-6981)*

LAUNDRY & GARMENT SVCS, NEC: Garment Making, Alter & Repair
- **Igar Bridal Inc** .... G 224 318-2337
  Arlington Heights *(G-754)*

LAUNDRY & GARMENT SVCS: Dressmaking, Matl Owned By Customer
- **Paul Sisti** .... G 773 472-5615
  Chicago *(G-5772)*

LAUNDRY EQPT: Commercial
- **Jetin Systems Inc** .... F 815 726-4686
  Joliet *(G-11885)*
- **L T P LLC** .... C 815 723-9400
  Joliet *(G-11893)*
- **New Spin Cycle** .... G 773 952-7490
  Chicago *(G-5580)*
- **Ross and White Company** .... F 847 516-3900
  Cary *(G-3187)*

LAUNDRY EQPT: Household
- **C Streeter Enterprise** .... G 773 858-4388
  Chicago *(G-3995)*
- **Coin Macke Laundry** .... G 847 459-1109
  Wheeling *(G-20874)*
- **Iron-A-Way LLC** .... E 309 266-7232
  Morton *(G-14363)*

LAWN & GARDEN EQPT
- **Beall Manufacturing Inc** .... E 618 307-9589
  Edwardsville *(G-8349)*
- **Contempo Industries Inc** .... D 815 337-6267
  Woodstock *(G-21375)*
- **Echo Incorporated** .... A 847 540-8400
  Lake Zurich *(G-12404)*
- **Echo Incorporated** .... E 847 540-3500
  Lake Zurich *(G-12405)*
- **Grower Equipment & Supply Co** ..... F 847 223-3100
  Hainesville *(G-10947)*
- **Hipro Manufacturing Inc** .... E 815 432-5271
  Watseka *(G-20306)*
- **Hyponex Corporation** .... E 815 772-2167
  Morrison *(G-14343)*
- **Jeffs Small Engine Inc** .... G 630 904-6840
  Plainfield *(G-16675)*
- **Lutz Corp** .... G 800 203-7740
  Normal *(G-15208)*
- **Oldcastle Lawn & Garden Inc** .... F 618 274-1222
  East Saint Louis *(G-8317)*
- **Precision Products Inc** .... C 217 735-1590
  Lincoln *(G-12737)*
- **Ryan Manufacturing Inc** .... G 815 695-5310
  Newark *(G-15078)*
- **Sawier** .... E 630 297-8588
  Downers Grove *(G-8090)*
- **Valley View Industries Hc Inc** .... E 800 323-9369
  Crestwood *(G-7133)*
- **Vaughan & Bushnell Mfg Co** .... F 815 648-2446
  Hebron *(G-11153)*

LAWN & GARDEN EQPT STORES
- **Gentry Small Engine Repair** .... G 217 849-3378
  Toledo *(G-19875)*
- **Wise Equipment & Rentals Inc** .... F 847 895-5555
  Schaumburg *(G-18774)*

LAWN & GARDEN EQPT: Blowers & Vacuums
- **David Taylor** .... E 217 222-6480
  Quincy *(G-16875)*
- **Tuthill Corporation** .... E 630 382-4900
  Burr Ridge *(G-2727)*

LAWN & GARDEN EQPT: Edgers
- **Alpha Omega Profile Extrusion** .... F 847 956-8777
  Elk Grove Village *(G-8818)*

LAWN & GARDEN EQPT: Grass Catchers, Lawn Mower
- **M Martinez Inc** .... G 847 740-6364
  Round Lake Heights *(G-18094)*

LAWN & GARDEN EQPT: Loaders
- **Avant Tecno USA Inc** .... F 847 380-1308
  Arlington Heights *(G-700)*

LAWN & GARDEN EQPT: Tractors & Eqpt
- **Cutting Specialists Inc** .... E 731 352-5351
  Edwardsville *(G-8355)*
- **Deere & Company** .... A 309 765-8000
  Moline *(G-14138)*
- **John Deere AG Holdings Inc** .... G 309 765-8000
  Moline *(G-14152)*

LAWN MOWER REPAIR SHOP
- **Lakenburges Motor Co** .... G 618 523-4231
  Germantown *(G-10331)*
- **Outdoor Power Inc** .... F 217 228-9890
  Quincy *(G-16921)*
- **Peoria Midwest Equipment Inc** .... G 309 454-6800
  Normal *(G-15217)*
- **Wise Equipment & Rentals Inc** .... F 847 895-5555
  Schaumburg *(G-18774)*

LEAD & ZINC
- **Big River Zinc Corporation** .... G 618 274-5000
  Sauget *(G-18389)*
- **Mayco-Granite City Inc** .... E 618 451-4400
  Granite City *(G-10722)*

LEAD & ZINC ORES
- **Big River Zinc Corporation** .... G 618 274-5000
  Sauget *(G-18389)*
- **Midland Coal Company** .... G 309 362-2795
  Trivoli *(G-19907)*

LEAD ORE MINING
- **Ebers Drilling Co** .... G 618 826-5398
  Chester *(G-3454)*

LEAD PENCILS & ART GOODS
- **Alexander Manufacturing Co** .... D 309 728-2224
  Towanda *(G-19892)*
- **Cushing and Company** .... E 312 266-8228
  Chicago *(G-4287)*
- **James Howard Co** .... G 815 497-2831
  Compton *(G-6996)*
- **Moldworks Inc** .... E 815 520-8819
  Roscoe *(G-17918)*
- **Perkins Pencil Co** .... G 708 363-9249
  Lansing *(G-12511)*
- **Plastruct Inc** .... G 626 912-7017
  Des Plaines *(G-7824)*

LEASING & RENTAL SVCS: Computer Hardware, Exc Finance
- **Datasis Corporation** .... F 847 427-0909
  Elk Grove Village *(G-8938)*

LEASING & RENTAL SVCS: Cranes & Aerial Lift Eqpt
- **Bendsen Signs & Graphics Inc** .... F 217 877-2345
  Decatur *(G-7464)*
- **Floyd Steel Erectors Inc** .... F 630 238-8383
  Wood Dale *(G-21187)*
- **Joe Hatzer & Son Inc** .... E 815 673-5571
  Streator *(G-19612)*

LEASING & RENTAL: Boats & Ships
- **Outback USA Inc** .... G 863 699-2220
  Saint Charles *(G-18240)*

LEASING & RENTAL: Computers & Eqpt
- **Essannay Show It Inc** .... G 312 733-5511
  Chicago *(G-4532)*
- **Information Builders Inc** .... E 630 971-6700
  Schaumburg *(G-18558)*
- **Pinehurst Bus Solutions Corp** .... G 630 842-6155
  Winfield *(G-21115)*

LEASING & RENTAL: Construction & Mining Eqpt
- **Altorfer Power Systems** .... G 309 697-1234
  Bartonville *(G-1328)*
- **L & N Structures Inc** .... E 815 426-2164
  Herscher *(G-11184)*
- **Lanco International Inc** .... B 708 596-5200
  Hazel Crest *(G-11131)*
- **Lee Jensen Sales Co Inc** .... E 815 459-0929
  Crystal Lake *(G-7220)*
- **Midwest Cnstr Svcs Inc Peoria** .... F 309 697-1000
  Bartonville *(G-1335)*
- **Patrick Holdings Inc** .... F 815 874-5300
  Rockford *(G-17549)*
- **Rotec Industries Inc** .... G 630 279-3300
  Hampshire *(G-10985)*
- **USA Hoist Company Inc** .... E 815 740-1890
  Crest Hill *(G-7100)*

LEASING & RENTAL: Medical Machinery & Eqpt
- **Hill-Rom Holdings Inc** .... B 312 819-7200
  Chicago *(G-4819)*
- **Rampnow LLC** .... G 630 892-7267
  Montgomery *(G-14266)*

PRODUCT SECTION

LEASING & RENTAL: Mobile Home Sites
Southmoor Estates Inc..................G...... 815 756-1299
Dekalb *(G-7705)*

LEASING & RENTAL: Office Machines & Eqpt
Nexus Supply Consortium Inc...............G...... 630 649-2868
Bolingbrook *(G-2222)*

LEASING & RENTAL: Trucks, Without Drivers
City Subn Auto Svc Goodyear...............G...... 773 355-5550
Chicago *(G-4162)*
Doll Furniture Co Inc..................G...... 309 452-2606
Normal *(G-15202)*
Grs Holding LLC..................F...... 630 355-1660
Naperville *(G-14838)*
Service Auto Supply..................F...... 309 444-9704
Washington *(G-20280)*

LEASING: Passenger Car
Carlease Inc..................F...... 847 714-1414
Northbrook *(G-15352)*
Lgb Industries..................G...... 847 639-1691
Cary *(G-3175)*

LEASING: Shipping Container
Mobile Mini Inc..................E...... 708 297-2004
Calumet Park *(G-2799)*

LEATHER GOODS, EXC FOOTWEAR, GLOVES, LUGGAGE/BELTING, WHOL
Keleen Leathers Inc..................F...... 630 590-5300
Westmont *(G-20753)*
Rico Industries Inc..................D...... 312 427-0313
Niles *(G-15166)*

LEATHER GOODS: Cases
A W Enterprises Inc..................E...... 708 458-8989
Bedford Park *(G-1452)*
Hertzberg Ernst & Sons..................E...... 773 525-3518
Chicago *(G-4810)*

LEATHER GOODS: Embossed
Hertzberg Ernst & Sons..................E...... 773 525-3518
Chicago *(G-4810)*

LEATHER GOODS: Garments
Boston Leather Inc..................E...... 815 622-1635
Sterling *(G-19501)*

LEATHER GOODS: Harnesses Or Harness Parts
Mast Harness Shop..................E...... 217 543-3463
Campbell Hill *(G-2816)*

LEATHER GOODS: Key Cases
Curv Group LLC..................E...... 847 636-0101
Elk Grove Village *(G-8925)*

LEATHER GOODS: NEC
Cocajo Blades & Leather..................G...... 217 370-6634
Franklin *(G-9854)*
Pegai LLC..................G...... 312 799-0417
Chicago *(G-5783)*

LEATHER GOODS: Personal
Plasticrest Products Inc..................F...... 773 826-2163
Chicago *(G-5818)*
Randa Accessories Lea Gds LLC..................D...... 847 292-8300
Rosemont *(G-18046)*
SRS Global Ret Solutions LLC..................G...... 773 888-3094
Evanston *(G-9577)*
World Richman Mfg Corp..................F...... 847 468-8898
Elgin *(G-8785)*

LEATHER GOODS: Sewing Cases
Elegant Acquisition LLC..................D...... 708 652-3400
Cicero *(G-6845)*

LEATHER GOODS: Wallets
J-Industries Inc..................F...... 815 654-0055
Loves Park *(G-13220)*
Rico Industries Inc..................D...... 312 427-0313
Niles *(G-15166)*

LEATHER TANNING & FINISHING
Darling Ingredients Inc..................E...... 618 271-8190
National Stock Yards *(G-15012)*
Tyson Fresh Meats Inc..................F...... 847 836-5550
Elgin *(G-8764)*

LEATHER: Accessory Prdts
Brighton Collectibles LLC..................F...... 847 674-6719
Skokie *(G-18934)*

LEATHER: Artificial
Phoenix Leather Goods LLC..................G...... 815 676-6712
Bolingbrook *(G-2227)*

LEATHER: Rawhide
United Rawhide Mfg Co..................G...... 847 692-2791
Park Ridge *(G-16301)*

LEATHER: Shoe
Zoes Mfgco LLC..................F...... 312 666-4018
Chicago *(G-6722)*

LEGAL & TAX SVCS
CCH Incorporated..................A...... 847 267-7000
Riverwoods *(G-17090)*

LEGAL COUNSEL & PROSECUTION: Attorney General's Office
State Attorney Appellate..................G...... 217 782-3397
Springfield *(G-19458)*

LEGAL OFFICES & SVCS
Alexeter Technologies LLC..................F...... 847 419-1507
Wheeling *(G-20843)*
Education Partners Project Ltd..................G...... 773 675-6643
Chicago *(G-4458)*
Inside Council..................F...... 312 654-3500
Chicago *(G-4935)*
State of Illinois..................C...... 312 836-9500
Chicago *(G-6235)*

LEGAL SVCS: Taxation Law
Vernon Township Offices..................E...... 847 634-4600
Buffalo Grove *(G-2617)*

LENS COATING: Ophthalmic
Opticote Inc..................E...... 847 678-8900
Franklin Park *(G-10012)*

LETTERS: Cardboard, Die-Cut, Made From Purchased Materials
Acco Brands USA LLC..................D...... 847 272-3700
Lincolnshire *(G-12741)*
Mich Enterprises Inc..................F...... 630 616-9000
Wood Dale *(G-21216)*

LICENSE TAGS: Automobile, Stamped Metal
10 4 Irp Inc..................G...... 708 485-1040
Brookfield *(G-2476)*
Aable License Consultants..................G...... 708 836-1235
Broadview *(G-2411)*
City of Danville..................G...... 217 442-1564
Tilton *(G-19794)*
Headly Manufacturing Co..................D...... 708 338-0800
Broadview *(G-2441)*
Macon Resources Inc..................C...... 217 875-1910
Decatur *(G-7520)*
Secretary of State Illinois..................G...... 217 466-5220
Paris *(G-16243)*
Secretary of State Illinois..................G...... 708 388-9199
Midlothian *(G-13995)*
Steibel License Service..................618 233-7555
Swansea *(G-19698)*

LIGHT OR HEAT EMISSION OPERATING APPARATUS
Bring Your Own Auto Parts Inc..................F...... 815 730-6900
Crest Hill *(G-7084)*

LIGHTING EQPT: Area & Sports Luminaries
Microlite Corporation..................G...... 630 876-0500
West Chicago *(G-20617)*
Musco Sports Lighting LLC..................G...... 630 876-0500
Batavia *(G-1396)*

LIGHTING EQPT: Bicycle Lamps
Outbound Lighting LLC..................E...... 314 330-0696
Lincolnwood *(G-12835)*

LIGHTING EQPT: Flashlights
First Alert Inc..................C...... 630 499-3295
Aurora *(G-962)*
First-Light Usa LLC..................F...... 217 687-4048
Seymour *(G-18868)*
Press A Light Corporation..................F...... 630 231-6566
West Chicago *(G-20632)*
Promier Products Inc..................F...... 815 223-3393
Peru *(G-16591)*
Waters Industries Inc..................E...... 847 783-5900
West Dundee *(G-20667)*

LIGHTING EQPT: Fog Lights
Master Fog LLC..................G...... 773 918-9080
Romeoville *(G-17845)*

LIGHTING EQPT: Locomotive & Railroad Car Lights
Esafety Lights LLC..................F...... 800 236-8621
Chicago *(G-4529)*
Progress Rail Locomotive Inc..................A...... 800 255-5355
Mc Cook *(G-13699)*

LIGHTING EQPT: Motor Vehicle
Federal Signal Corporation..................D...... 630 954-2000
Oak Brook *(G-15618)*
L & T Services Inc..................G...... 815 397-6260
Rockford *(G-17487)*
Tiger Accessory Group LLC..................F...... 847 821-9630
Long Grove *(G-13171)*

LIGHTING EQPT: Motor Vehicle, Flasher Lights
Tool Automation Enterprises..................G...... 708 799-6847
East Hazel Crest *(G-8218)*

LIGHTING EQPT: Motor Vehicle, NEC
North American Lighting Inc..................B...... 217 465-7800
Paris *(G-16236)*
North American Lighting Inc..................A...... 217 465-6600
Paris *(G-16237)*
North American Lighting Inc..................A...... 618 548-6249
Salem *(G-18348)*
North American Lighting Inc..................B...... 618 662-4483
Flora *(G-9686)*
Tri-Lite Inc..................E...... 773 384-7765
Chicago *(G-6422)*

LIGHTING EQPT: Motorcycle Lamps
River View Motor Sports Inc..................G...... 309 467-4569
Congerville *(G-7003)*

LIGHTING EQPT: Outdoor
Ecurrent LLC..................G...... 888 815-5786
Wood Dale *(G-21184)*
Hubbell Lighting Inc..................G...... 847 515-3057
Rolling Meadows *(G-17736)*
Lightscape Inc..................E...... 847 247-8800
Libertyville *(G-12670)*

LIGHTING EQPT: Reflectors, Metal, For Lighting Eqpt
Akt Corporation..................G...... 414 475-5020
Elgin *(G-8501)*
Plastic Technologies Inc..................E...... 847 841-8610
Elgin *(G-8688)*

LIGHTING EQPT: Strobe Lighting Systems

LIGHTING EQPT: Strobe Lighting Systems

Esafety Lights LLC .... F 800 236-8621
  Chicago *(G-4529)*

LIGHTING FIXTURES WHOLESALERS

American Holiday Lights Inc .... G 630 769-9999
  Woodridge *(G-21274)*
Dado Lighting LLC .... G 877 323-6584
  Western Springs *(G-20720)*
Eagle High Mast Ltg Co Inc .... G 847 473-3800
  Waukegan *(G-20440)*
Good Earth Lighting Inc .... E 847 808-1133
  Mount Prospect *(G-14531)*
Lbl Lighting LLC .... F 708 755-2100
  Skokie *(G-18978)*
Lumenart Ltd .... G 773 254-0744
  Chicago *(G-5281)*
Microlite Corporation .... G 630 876-0500
  West Chicago *(G-20617)*
Ruckus Wireless Inc .... E 630 281-3000
  Lisle *(G-12935)*
Vaxcel International Co Ltd .... E 630 260-0067
  Carol Stream *(G-3084)*

LIGHTING FIXTURES, NEC

Acuity Brands Lighting Inc .... F 847 827-9880
  Des Plaines *(G-7722)*
Bilt-Rite Metal Products Inc .... E 815 495-2211
  Leland *(G-12547)*
Carmen Matthew LLC .... D 630 784-7500
  Rolling Meadows *(G-17720)*
CU Layer Inc .... G 630 802-7873
  Batavia *(G-1369)*
Cyclops Industrial Inc .... G 815 962-1984
  Rockford *(G-17363)*
D2 Lighting LLC .... G 708 243-9059
  La Grange Highlands *(G-12092)*
David Michael Productions .... F 630 972-9640
  Woodridge *(G-21293)*
Duroweld Company Inc .... E 847 680-3064
  Lake Bluff *(G-12179)*
Eagle High Mast Ltg Co Inc .... G 847 473-3800
  Waukegan *(G-20440)*
Eclipse Lighting Inc .... G 847 916-2623
  Franklin Park *(G-9936)*
Efficient Energy Lighting Inc .... G 630 272-9388
  Saint Charles *(G-18193)*
Elcast Manufacturing Inc .... G 630 628-1992
  Addison *(G-111)*
Est Lighting Inc .... G 847 612-1705
  Richmond *(G-17013)*
Flex Lighting II LLC .... G 312 929-3488
  Chicago *(G-4603)*
Genesis Ltg Managemet Svcs .... F 630 986-3900
  Willowbrook *(G-21044)*
Good Earth Lighting Inc .... E 847 808-1133
  Mount Prospect *(G-14531)*
Hangout Lighting LLC .... G 224 817-4101
  Chicago *(G-4777)*
Illuminight Lighting LLC .... F 312 685-4448
  Highland Park *(G-11272)*
Inliten LLC .... F 847 486-4200
  Glenview *(G-10568)*
Intex Lighting LLC .... G 847 380-2027
  Schaumburg *(G-18566)*
Lampholders Assemblies Inc .... G 773 205-0005
  Chicago *(G-5173)*
Lighting Innovations Inc .... E 630 889-8100
  Saint Charles *(G-18228)*
Lightitech LLC .... G 847 910-4177
  Chicago *(G-5222)*
Lightolier Genlyte Inc .... D 847 364-8250
  Elk Grove Village *(G-9095)*
Litetronics Technologies Inc .... G 708 333-6707
  Chicago *(G-5235)*
Midwest Sign & Lighting Inc .... G 708 365-5555
  Country Club Hills *(G-7042)*
Nicks Emergency Ltg & More .... G 815 780-8327
  Peru *(G-16585)*
North American Signal Co .... E 847 537-8888
  Wheeling *(G-20945)*
Northern Lighting & Power Inc .... G 708 383-9926
  Oak Park *(G-15766)*
Productworks LLC .... F 224 406-8810
  Northbrook *(G-15468)*
Radionic Hi-Tech Inc .... D 773 804-0100
  Chicago *(G-5960)*
SC Lighting .... G 630 849-3384
  Schaumburg *(G-18705)*
Schreder Lighting LLC .... E 847 621-5130
  Oak Brook *(G-15662)*
Spurt Inc .... G 847 571-6497
  Northbrook *(G-15486)*
Sternberg Lanterns Inc .... C 847 588-3400
  Roselle *(G-17991)*
Telser Lighting Associates LLC .... G 630 800-5312
  East Dundee *(G-8211)*
Twin Supplies Ltd .... F 630 590-5138
  Oak Brook *(G-15667)*
Western Lighting Inc .... F 847 451-7200
  Franklin Park *(G-10084)*
Winchester Interconnect Rugged .... G 708 594-5890
  Broadview *(G-2475)*

LIGHTING FIXTURES: Airport

Tactical Lighting Systems Inc .... F 800 705-0518
  Lombard *(G-13138)*

LIGHTING FIXTURES: Decorative Area

Boston Warehouse Trading Corp .... G 630 992-5604
  Aurora *(G-925)*
Group O Inc .... D 309 736-8660
  Milan *(G-14013)*
Sensio America LLC .... G 877 501-5337
  Carol Stream *(G-3067)*

LIGHTING FIXTURES: Fluorescent, Commercial

Louvers International Inc .... E 630 782-9977
  Elmhurst *(G-9394)*
Morris Kurtzon Incorporated .... E 773 277-2121
  Chicago *(G-5500)*
Wallace/Haskin Corp .... G 630 789-2882
  Downers Grove *(G-8105)*
Western Lighting Inc .... F 847 451-7200
  Franklin Park *(G-10084)*

LIGHTING FIXTURES: Gas

Modern Home Products Corp .... E 847 395-6556
  Antioch *(G-627)*

LIGHTING FIXTURES: Indl & Commercial

555 International Inc .... E 773 869-0555
  Chicago *(G-3475)*
555 International Inc .... E 773 847-1400
  Chicago *(G-3474)*
Advanced Specialty Lighting .... C 708 867-3140
  Harwood Heights *(G-11101)*
Afx Inc .... C 847 249-5970
  Waukegan *(G-20410)*
Amerilights Inc .... G 847 219-1476
  Bloomingdale *(G-1976)*
Appleton Grp LLC .... C 847 268-6000
  Rosemont *(G-17999)*
Astral Power Systems Inc .... G 630 518-1741
  Aurora *(G-1055)*
Avtec Inc .... F 618 337-7800
  East Saint Louis *(G-8298)*
Blackjack Lighting .... G 847 941-0588
  Buffalo Grove *(G-2518)*
Blg McC Enterprises Inc .... E 847 455-0188
  Franklin Park *(G-9888)*
Conservation Tech III LLC .... F 847 559-5500
  Northbrook *(G-15365)*
Conservation Technology Ltd .... D 847 559-5500
  Northbrook *(G-15366)*
Contemprary Enrgy Slutions LLC .... F 630 768-3743
  Naperville *(G-14963)*
Cooper Lighting LLC .... D 847 956-8400
  Elk Grove Village *(G-8914)*
Dado Lighting LLC .... G 708 243-9059
  Brookfield *(G-2481)*
Dado Lighting LLC .... G 877 323-6584
  Western Springs *(G-20720)*
Dado Lighting LLC .... G 877 323-6584
  Countryside *(G-7050)*
Dva Mayday Corporation .... G 847 848-7555
  Village of Lakewood *(G-20178)*
Eclipse Lighting Inc .... E 847 260-0333
  Schiller Park *(G-18802)*
Esco Lighting Inc .... F 773 427-7000
  Chicago *(G-4530)*
Eti Solid State Lighting Inc .... E 855 384-7754
  Wheeling *(G-20895)*
First Light Inc .... G 630 520-0017
  West Chicago *(G-20583)*
Fli Products LLC .... G 630 520-0017
  West Chicago *(G-20584)*
Focal Point Lighting Inc .... C 773 247-9494
  Chicago *(G-4613)*
Focal Point LLC .... E 773 247-9494
  Chicago *(G-4614)*
Glamox Aqua Signal Corporation .... F 847 639-6412
  Cary *(G-3165)*
H A Framburg & Company .... E 708 547-5757
  Bellwood *(G-1627)*
Holiday Bright Lights Inc .... G 312 226-8281
  Chicago *(G-4830)*
Jarvis Corp .... E 800 363-1075
  Schaumburg *(G-18575)*
Lamp Co of America Inc .... G 630 584-4001
  Saint Charles *(G-18224)*
Lava World International Inc .... G 630 315-3300
  Carol Stream *(G-3016)*
Led Business Solutions LLC .... F 844 464-5337
  Downers Grove *(G-8043)*
Ledil Inc .... F 815 766-3204
  Sycamore *(G-19721)*
Luxo Corporation .... F 914 345-0067
  Cary *(G-3176)*
North Star Lighting LLC .... D 708 681-4330
  Elmhurst *(G-9405)*
Omnilight Inc .... G 773 696-1602
  Chicago *(G-5676)*
Paul D Metal Products Inc .... G 773 847-1400
  Chicago *(G-5771)*
Pineapple Led Inc .... G 847 255-3710
  Barrington *(G-1235)*
Premier Lighting and Sup LLC .... G 708 612-9693
  Oak Forest *(G-15687)*
Productworks LLC .... F 224 406-8810
  Northbrook *(G-15468)*
Pure Lighting LLC .... G 773 770-1130
  Chicago *(G-5917)*
Rainbow Lighting .... E 847 480-1136
  Northbrook *(G-15470)*
Rgb Lights Inc .... F 312 421-6080
  Chicago *(G-6021)*
S-P Products Inc .... F 847 593-8595
  Elk Grove Village *(G-9227)*
Sustanble Sltions Amer Led LLC .... F 866 323-3494
  Chicago *(G-6291)*
Tri-Lite Inc .... G 773 384-7765
  Chicago *(G-6422)*
Twin Supplies Ltd .... F 630 590-5138
  Oak Brook *(G-15667)*

LIGHTING FIXTURES: Marine

Glamox Aqua Signal Corporation .... F 847 639-6412
  Cary *(G-3165)*

LIGHTING FIXTURES: Motor Vehicle

Elc Industries Corp .... E 630 851-1616
  Aurora *(G-1088)*
Lecip Inc .... F 312 626-2525
  Bensenville *(G-1842)*
Progress Rail Locomotive Inc .... F 708 387-5510
  Mc Cook *(G-13700)*

LIGHTING FIXTURES: Ornamental, Commercial

New Metal Crafts Inc .... E 312 787-6991
  Lincolnwood *(G-12832)*
Sensio America LLC .... G 877 501-5337
  Carol Stream *(G-3067)*
Sternberg Lanterns Inc .... C 847 588-3400
  Roselle *(G-17991)*

LIGHTING FIXTURES: Public

Advanced Cstm Enrgy Sltons Inc .... D 312 428-9540
  Chicago *(G-3563)*

LIGHTING FIXTURES: Residential

Advanced Micro Lites Inc .... G 630 365-5450
  Elburn *(G-8442)*
Afx Inc .... C 847 249-5970
  Waukegan *(G-20410)*
Benko Lamps Ltd .... F 708 458-7965
  Bridgeview *(G-2328)*
Blg McC Enterprises Inc .... E 847 455-0188
  Franklin Park *(G-9888)*
Cooper Lighting LLC .... G 312 595-2770
  Elk Grove Village *(G-8913)*

PRODUCT SECTION

LINERS & LINING

Cooper Lighting LLC ....D........ 847 956-8400
  Elk Grove Village (G-8914)
Eclipse Lighting Inc ....E....... 847 260-0333
  Schiller Park (G-18802)
Elcast Manufacturing Inc ....E....... 630 628-1992
  Addison (G-111)
Fanmar Inc ....E....... 847 621-2010
  Elk Grove Village (G-8995)
Gerber Manufacturing (gm) LLC ....F....... 708 478-0100
  Tinley Park (G-19830)
H A Framburg & Company ....E....... 708 547-5757
  Bellwood (G-1627)
H E Associates Inc ....F....... 630 553-6382
  Yorkville (G-21487)
Intermatic Incorporated ....A....... 815 675-7000
  Spring Grove (G-19276)
Io Lighting LLC ....E....... 847 735-7000
  Vernon Hills (G-20067)
K&I Light Kandi Led Inc ....G....... 773 745-1533
  Chicago (G-5068)
Lamp Co of America Inc ....E....... 630 584-4001
  Saint Charles (G-18224)
Lamp Works Inc ....F....... 630 871-7663
  Carol Stream (G-3015)
Lli Architectural Lighting LLC ....F....... 847 412-4880
  Buffalo Grove (G-2564)
LIIb LLC ....F....... 630 315-3300
  Elk Grove Village (G-9097)
Lumenart Ltd ....G....... 773 254-0744
  Chicago (G-5281)
McKenzie & Keim LLC ....G....... 317 443-6663
  Chicago (G-5377)
Metomic Corporation ....E....... 773 247-4716
  Chicago (G-5410)
Midwest Sun-Ray Lighting & Sig ....F....... 618 656-2884
  Granite City (G-10726)
New Metal Crafts Inc ....E....... 312 787-6991
  Lincolnwood (G-12832)
Pace Industries Inc ....F....... 312 226-5500
  Chicago (G-5737)
Productworks LLC ....F....... 224 406-8810
  Northbrook (G-15468)
Rgb Lights Inc ....F....... 312 421-6080
  Chicago (G-6021)
Sternberg Lanterns Inc ....C....... 847 588-3400
  Roselle (G-17991)
Uncommon Radiant ....G....... 773 640-1674
  Chicago (G-6461)
Vaxcel International Co Ltd ....F....... 630 260-0067
  Carol Stream (G-3084)
Western Lighting Inc ....F....... 847 451-7200
  Franklin Park (G-10084)

LIGHTING FIXTURES: Residential, Electric

Jr Lighting Design Inc ....G....... 708 460-6319
  Tinley Park (G-19842)
Lbl Lighting LLC ....F....... 708 755-2100
  Skokie (G-18978)
Tri-Lite Inc ....E....... 773 384-7765
  Chicago (G-6422)

LIGHTING FIXTURES: Street

City of Pekin ....F....... 309 477-2325
  Pekin (G-16325)

LIME

Lafarge Building Materials Inc ....D....... 678 746-2000
  Chicago (G-5155)

LIME ROCK: Ground

Valley View Industries Inc ....E....... 815 358-2236
  Cornell (G-7014)

LIME: Building

Mineral Products Inc ....G....... 618 433-3150
  Harrisburg (G-11026)

LIMESTONE & MARBLE: Dimension

Architectural Limestone Inc ....F....... 847 623-0100
  Gurnee (G-10861)
JKS Ventures Inc ....F....... 708 345-9344
  Melrose Park (G-13886)

LIMESTONE: Crushed & Broken

Anna Quarries Inc ....E....... 618 833-5121
  Anna (G-581)

Argyle Cut Stone Co ....E....... 847 456-6210
  Des Plaines (G-7733)
Callender Construction Co Inc ....F....... 217 285-2161
  Pittsfield (G-16630)
Central Stone Company ....G....... 217 335-2615
  Barry (G-1248)
Central Stone Company ....G....... 217 327-4300
  Chambersburg (G-3259)
Civil Constructors Inc ....G....... 815 858-2691
  Elizabeth (G-8786)
Collinson Stone Co ....F....... 309 787-7983
  Milan (G-14004)
Columbia Quarry Company ....E....... 618 939-8833
  Waterloo (G-20288)
Conmat Inc ....G....... 815 238-3885
  Galena (G-10167)
Conmat Inc ....G....... 815 235-2200
  Freeport (G-10104)
Elmer L Larson L C ....F....... 815 895-4837
  Sycamore (G-19710)
H&H Crushing Inc ....G....... 309 275-0643
  West Peoria (G-20686)
Hastie Min & Trckg Ltd Partnr ....E....... 618 289-4536
  Cave In Rock (G-3219)
Huyear Trucking Inc ....G....... 217 854-3551
  Carlinville (G-2876)
Kimmaterials Inc ....F....... 618 466-0352
  Godfrey (G-10655)
Legacy Vulcan LLC ....G....... 217 963-2196
  Decatur (G-7516)
Legacy Vulcan LLC ....G....... 847 578-9622
  Lake Bluff (G-12192)
Legacy Vulcan LLC ....F....... 630 904-1100
  Plainfield (G-16683)
Legacy Vulcan LLC ....E....... 815 468-8141
  Manteno (G-13450)
Martha Lacey ....G....... 217 723-4380
  Pearl (G-16318)
Material Service Corporation ....C....... 708 731-2600
  Westchester (G-20705)
Material Service Corporation ....E....... 217 732-2117
  Athens (G-897)
Material Service Corporation ....D....... 708 877-6540
  Thornton (G-19790)
Mid-America Carbonates LLC ....G....... 217 222-3500
  Quincy (G-16913)
Nokomis Quarry Company ....F....... 217 563-2011
  Nokomis (G-15196)
Omni Materials Inc ....E....... 618 262-5118
  Mount Carmel (G-14484)
R L ONeal & Sons Inc ....F....... 309 458-3350
  Plymouth (G-16750)
Riverstone Group Inc ....F....... 309 787-3141
  Milan (G-14026)
Shawnee Stone LLC ....F....... 618 548-1585
  Salem (G-18359)
Shawnee Stone LLC ....G....... 618 833-2323
  Anna (G-588)
Southern Illinois Stone Co ....F....... 573 334-5261
  Buncombe (G-2629)
Southfield Corporation ....E....... 815 842-2333
  Pontiac (G-16780)
Southfield Corporation ....F....... 815 468-8700
  Manteno (G-13457)
Stolle Casper Quar & Contg Co ....E....... 618 337-5212
  Dupo (G-8146)
Tower Rock Stone Company ....F....... 618 281-4106
  Columbia (G-6994)
Tri-State Cut Stone Co ....E....... 815 469-7550
  Frankfort (G-9845)
Utica Stone Co Inc ....G....... 815 667-4690
  Utica (G-20007)
Vulcan Construction Mtls LLC ....E....... 630 955-8500
  Naperville (G-14943)
Vulcan Materials Company ....E....... 815 899-7204
  Sycamore (G-19740)
William Charles Cnstr Co LLC ....G....... 815 654-4720
  Belvidere (G-1711)

LIMESTONE: Cut & Shaped

Argyle Cut Stone Co ....E....... 847 456-6210
  Des Plaines (G-7733)
Liberty Limestone Inc ....G....... 815 385-5011
  McHenry (G-13757)

LIMESTONE: Dimension

Anna Quarries Inc ....E....... 618 833-5121
  Anna (G-581)
Joliet Sand and Gravel Company ....D....... 815 741-2090
  Rockdale (G-17262)

Lafarge Aggregates III Inc ....G....... 847 742-6060
  South Elgin (G-19162)
Lafarge Aggregates III Inc ....G....... 630 365-3600
  Elburn (G-8457)
Material Service Corporation ....D....... 708 485-8211
  Mc Cook (G-13696)
Nokomis Quarry Company ....F....... 217 563-2011
  Nokomis (G-15196)
Pana Limestone Company ....G....... 217 562-4231
  Pana (G-16219)

LIMESTONE: Ground

Calhoun Quarry Incorporated ....F....... 618 396-2229
  Batchtown (G-1442)
Calhoun Quarry Incorporated ....G....... 618 576-9223
  Hardin (G-11016)
Central Limestone Company Inc ....F....... 815 736-6341
  Morris (G-14298)
Central Stone Company ....F....... 217 723-4410
  Pittsfield (G-16632)
Central Stone Company ....F....... 217 224-7330
  Quincy (G-16870)
Gray Quarries Inc ....F....... 217 847-2712
  Hamilton (G-10955)
Iola Quarry Inc ....F....... 217 682-3865
  Mode (G-14067)
Lee Quarry Inc ....G....... 815 547-7141
  Kirkland (G-12063)
Material Service Corporation ....E....... 217 563-2531
  Nokomis (G-15194)
Quality Lime Company ....F....... 217 826-2343
  Marshall (G-13577)
Renner Quarries Ltd ....G....... 815 288-6699
  Dixon (G-7910)
Riverstone Group Inc ....F....... 309 933-1123
  Cleveland (G-6912)
Savanna Quarry Inc ....G....... 815 273-4208
  Savanna (G-18411)
Southern Illinois Stone Co ....F....... 618 995-2392
  Buncombe (G-2630)

LINEN SPLY SVC: Apron

NRR Corp ....F....... 630 915-8388
  Oak Brook (G-15651)

LINENS & TOWELS WHOLESALERS

American Dawn Inc ....G....... 312 961-2909
  Wood Dale (G-21163)

LINENS: Napkins, Fabric & Nonwoven, From Purchased Materials

Ameritex Industries Inc ....F....... 217 324-4044
  Litchfield (G-12960)

LINENS: Tablecloths, From Purchased Materials

Trotta Enterprises Inc ....D....... 312 829-7084
  Chicago (G-6433)

LINER BRICK OR PLATES: Sewer Or Tank Lining, Vitrified Clay

Colloid Envmtl Tech Co LLC ....C....... 847 851-1500
  Hoffman Estates (G-11415)

LINER STRIPS: Rubber

Bls Enterprises Inc ....F....... 630 766-1300
  Bensenville (G-1754)

LINERS & COVERS: Fabric

Creative Covers Inc ....G....... 708 233-6880
  Bridgeview (G-2338)
Polyair Inter Pack Inc ....D....... 773 995-1818
  Chicago (G-5838)
Seamcraft International LLC ....E....... 773 281-5150
  Chicago (G-6126)

LINERS & LINING

Chicago Tank Lining Sales ....G....... 847 328-0500
  Evanston (G-9504)
Resist-A-Line Industries Inc ....G....... 815 650-3177
  Joliet (G-11925)
Tacknologies ....G....... 630 729-9900
  Woodridge (G-21343)

LININGS: Safe & Vault, Metal

Variable Operations Tech Inc................E....... 815 479-8528
Crystal Lake *(G-7288)*

LIQUEFIED PETROLEUM GAS DEALERS

AmeriGas...D....... 708 544-1131
Hillside *(G-11328)*
Mills Machine Inc.............................G....... 815 273-4707
Savanna *(G-18409)*
Zorin Material Handling Co..........G....... 773 342-3818
Chicago *(G-6724)*

LIQUEFIED PETROLEUM GAS WHOLESALERS

AmeriGas...D....... 708 544-1131
Hillside *(G-11328)*
Dcc Propane LLC............................G....... 217 395-2648
Roberts *(G-17105)*
Drig Corporation.............................D....... 312 265-1509
Rosemont *(G-18020)*

LIQUID CRYSTAL DISPLAYS

Global Display Solutions Inc........E....... 815 282-2328
Rockford *(G-17429)*
Innolux Technology USA Inc........G....... 847 490-5315
Hoffman Estates *(G-11430)*
Richardson Electronics Ltd..........C....... 630 208-2278
Lafox *(G-12137)*
Wintek Electro-Optics Corp..........F....... 734 477-5480
Glenview *(G-10638)*

LITHOGRAPHIC PLATES

Autotype Americas Incorporated......G....... 847 818-8262
Rolling Meadows *(G-17715)*
Color Smiths Inc..............................E....... 708 562-0061
Elmhurst *(G-9349)*
Dupli Group Inc...............................F....... 773 549-5285
Chicago *(G-4408)*
Printing Inc.......................................D....... 316 265-1201
Chicago *(G-5881)*

LIVESTOCK WHOLESALERS, NEC

Golden Valley Hardscapes LLC....G....... 309 654-2261
Cordova *(G-7007)*
Tyson Fresh Meats Inc...................F....... 309 965-2565
Goodfield *(G-10678)*

LOADS: Electronic

Consolidated Elec Wire & Cable......D....... 847 455-8830
Franklin Park *(G-9913)*

LOCK & KEY SVCS

Agena Manufacturing Co................E....... 630 668-5086
Carol Stream *(G-2928)*

LOCKS

A Ashland Lock Company...............F....... 773 348-5106
Chicago *(G-3485)*
Eastern Company............................C....... 847 537-1800
Wheeling *(G-20884)*
Fort Lock Corporation....................E....... 708 456-1100
Grayslake *(G-10773)*
Practechal Marketing......................G....... 847 486-8600
Glenview *(G-10600)*

LOCKS & LOCK SETS, WHOLESALE

Eastern Company............................C....... 847 537-1800
Wheeling *(G-20884)*

LOCKS: Safe & Vault, Metal

Jerome Remien Corporation..........F....... 847 806-0888
Elk Grove Village *(G-9067)*

LOCKSMITHS

A Ashland Lock Company...............F....... 773 348-5106
Chicago *(G-3485)*

LOCOMOTIVES & PARTS

GE Transportation Parts LLC........E....... 814 875-2755
Chicago *(G-4666)*
Hadady Corporation........................E....... 219 322-7417
South Holland *(G-19218)*
Locodocs Inc....................................G....... 815 448-2100
Mazon *(G-13682)*
National Railway Equipment Co...C....... 309 755-6800
Silvis *(G-18908)*
National Railway Equipment Co...G....... 618 241-9270
Mount Vernon *(G-14630)*
Relco Locomotives Inc...................D....... 630 968-0670
Burr Ridge *(G-2716)*
Tenneco Intl Holdg Corp................F....... 847 482-5000
Lake Forest *(G-12313)*

LOG SPLITTERS

Brave Products Inc..........................G....... 815 672-0551
Streator *(G-19605)*
Speeco Incorporated.......................C....... 303 279-5544
Oregon *(G-15927)*

LOGGING

Beeman & Sons Inc..........................F....... 217 232-4268
Martinsville *(G-13581)*
Brian Kinney.....................................G....... 309 206-4219
Rock Island *(G-17209)*
Christiansen Sawmill and Log......G....... 815 315-7520
Caledonia *(G-2769)*
Ericson S Log & Lumber Co..........G....... 309 667-2147
New Windsor *(G-15073)*
Frank E Galloway............................G....... 618 948-2578
Sumner *(G-19686)*
G & C Enterprises Inc.....................G....... 618 747-2272
Jonesboro *(G-11946)*
Heartland Hardwoods Inc..............E....... 217 844-3312
Effingham *(G-8402)*
Illiana Real Log Homes Inc...........G....... 815 471-4004
Milford *(G-14035)*
K D Custom Sawing Logging........G....... 309 231-4805
Green Valley *(G-10817)*
Larry Musgrave Logging................G....... 618 842-6386
Fairfield *(G-9630)*
Lonnie Hickam..................................G....... 618 893-4223
Pomona *(G-16763)*
Lte-Little Timber Enterprises........G....... 224 321-0361
Lake Villa *(G-12358)*
Warrior Well Services Inc..............G....... 618 662-7710
Flora *(G-9696)*

LOGGING CAMPS & CONTRACTORS

Big Creek Forestry & Logging L....G....... 217 822-8282
Marshall *(G-13565)*
Bourrette Logging............................G....... 815 591-3761
Hanover *(G-10995)*
Dust Logging LLC............................G....... 217 844-2305
Effingham *(G-8396)*
Jack Shepard Logging....................G....... 618 845-3496
Ullin *(G-19935)*
Kelly & Son Forestry & Log LLC...G....... 815 275-6877
Crystal Lake *(G-7216)*
Poignant Logging............................G....... 309 246-5647
Lacon *(G-12133)*
S Carpenter Logging.......................G....... 618 548-6187
Salem *(G-18356)*
W Bozarth Logging..........................G....... 618 658-4016
Vienna *(G-20120)*
Warrior Logging & Perforagine.....G....... 618 662-7373
Flora *(G-9695)*

LOGGING: Stump Harvesting

Cnv Enterprises Inc.........................G....... 815 405-6762
Plainfield *(G-16653)*

LOGGING: Timber, Cut At Logging Camp

Loneoak Timber & Veneere Co.....G....... 618 426-3065
Ava *(G-1174)*
Tallwood..G....... 815 786-8186
Plano *(G-16744)*

LOGGING: Wood Chips, Produced In The Field

Powell Tree Care Inc.......................G....... 847 364-1181
Elk Grove Village *(G-9186)*

LOOSELEAF BINDERS

Acco Brands Corporation...............A....... 847 541-9500
Lake Zurich *(G-12374)*
Acco Brands International Inc.......G....... 847 541-9500
Lake Zurich *(G-12375)*
Acco Intl Holdings Inc.....................G....... 800 222-6462
Lake Zurich *(G-12378)*
Americas Community Bankers......E....... 312 644-3100
Chicago *(G-3675)*
Beta Pak Inc......................................F....... 708 466-7844
Sugar Grove *(G-19638)*
Counter Cft Svc Systems & Pdts......G....... 630 629-7336
Lombard *(G-13059)*
General Loose Leaf Bindery Inc...G....... 847 244-9700
Chicago *(G-4672)*
Jacobson Acqstion Holdings LLC......C....... 847 623-1414
Waukegan *(G-20452)*
K & L Looseleaf Products Inc........D....... 847 357-9733
Elk Grove Village *(G-9072)*
Protek Inc...G....... 888 536-5466
Saint Charles *(G-18252)*
Simu Ltd...F....... 708 688-2200
Mc Cook *(G-13701)*
Tower Plastics Mfg Inc...................G....... 847 788-1700
Burr Ridge *(G-2723)*

LOOSELEAF BINDERS: Library

J-Industries Inc................................F....... 815 654-0055
Loves Park *(G-13220)*

LOTIONS OR CREAMS: Face

Bethany Pharmacol Co Inc.............G....... 217 665-3395
Bethany *(G-1967)*
Dzro-Bans International Inc...........G....... 779 324-2740
Homewood *(G-11492)*
Jindilli Beverages LLC....................G....... 630 581-5697
Burr Ridge *(G-2692)*
Luxurious Lathers Ltd....................G....... 844 877-7627
Hinsdale *(G-11369)*
Paket Corporation............................E....... 773 221-7300
Chicago *(G-5743)*
RITA Corporation.............................E....... 815 337-2500
Crystal Lake *(G-7257)*

LOTIONS: SHAVING

Moz Nutraceuticals LLC..................E....... 314 315-2541
Mount Vernon *(G-14627)*

LOUDSPEAKERS

Advance Tools LLC..........................G....... 630 337-5904
Glenview *(G-10520)*
Quam-Nichols Company.................C....... 773 488-5800
Chicago *(G-5932)*

LOUVERS: Ventilating

CCL Construction Inc......................G....... 219 237-2911
Homewood *(G-11490)*

LOZENGES: Pharmaceutical

SC Holdings LLC..............................B....... 217 821-0304
Effingham *(G-8425)*

LUBRICANTS: Corrosion Preventive

Castrol Industrial N Amer Inc.........C....... 877 641-1600
Naperville *(G-14792)*
Ivanhoe Industries Inc....................E....... 847 872-3311
Mundelein *(G-14702)*
M R O Solutions LLC.......................E....... 847 588-2480
Niles *(G-15143)*
Trane Technologies Company LLC......E....... 704 655-4000
Chicago *(G-6406)*

LUBRICATING EQPT: Indl

Gaunt Industries Inc........................G....... 847 671-0776
Franklin Park *(G-9949)*
LDI Industries Inc.............................D....... 847 669-7510
Huntley *(G-11550)*
Lsp Industries Inc............................F....... 815 226-8090
Rockford *(G-17497)*
Pulsarlube USA Inc..........................G....... 847 593-5300
Elk Grove Village *(G-9201)*
Standard Indus & Auto Eqp Inc.....E....... 630 289-9500
Hanover Park *(G-11014)*

LUBRICATING OIL & GREASE WHOLESALERS

Famous Lubricants Inc....................G....... 773 268-2555
Chicago *(G-4557)*
Fuchs Corporation...........................G....... 800 323-7755
Harvey *(G-11086)*

PRODUCT SECTION
LUMBER: Hardwood Dimension & Flooring Mills

Jx Nippon Oil & Energy USA Inc ....E...... 847 413-2188
  Schaumburg *(G-18583)*
K & J Synthetic Lubricants ....G...... 630 628-1011
  Addison *(G-164)*
Lubeq Corporation...............................F...... 847 931-1020
  Elgin *(G-8642)*
Motor Oil Inc...F...... 847 956-7550
  Elk Grove Village *(G-9135)*
Petrochem Inc ....G...... 630 513-6350
  Saint Charles *(G-18245)*

LUGGAGE & BRIEFCASES

A W Enterprises Inc...............................E...... 708 458-8989
  Bedford Park *(G-1452)*
Art Jewel Enterprises Ltd......................F...... 630 260-0400
  Carol Stream *(G-2941)*
Du-Call Miller Plastics Inc ....F...... 630 964-6020
  Elburn *(G-8450)*
Ips & Luggage Co Inc ....G...... 630 894-2414
  Roselle *(G-17960)*
LC Industries Inc ....E...... 312 455-0500
  Elk Grove Village *(G-9089)*
Midwest Fibre Products Inc ....E...... 309 596-2955
  Viola *(G-20180)*
Plano Molding Company LLC ....C...... 815 786-3331
  Sandwich *(G-18380)*

LUGGAGE & LEATHER GOODS STORES

Keleen Leathers Inc.............................F...... 630 590-5300
  Westmont *(G-20753)*
Randa Accessories Lea Gds LLC.........D...... 847 292-8300
  Rosemont *(G-18046)*

LUGGAGE & LEATHER GOODS STORES: Leather, Exc Luggage & Shoes

Phoenix Leather Goods LLC..................G...... 815 676-6712
  Bolingbrook *(G-2227)*

LUGGAGE: Traveling Bags

Kingport Industries LLC.........................G...... 847 480-5745
  Northbrook *(G-15412)*
Travel Caddy Inc ....E...... 847 621-7000
  Franklin Park *(G-10065)*

LUGGAGE: Wardrobe Bags

Hartmann...G...... 618 684-6814
  Murphysboro *(G-14755)*

LUMBER & BLDG MATLS DEALER, RET: Electric Constructn Matls

Min Sheng Technology Inc....................G...... 815 569-4496
  Schaumburg *(G-18631)*

LUMBER & BLDG MATLS DEALER, RET: Garage Doors, Sell/Install

Allied Garage Door Inc ....E...... 630 279-0795
  Addison *(G-27)*
Kamstra Door Service Inc ....G...... 708 895-9990
  Lansing *(G-12500)*

LUMBER & BLDG MTRLS DEALERS, RET: Doors, Storm, Wood/Metal

Accurate Cstm Sash Mllwk Corp..........G...... 708 423-0423
  Oak Lawn *(G-15694)*
Barneys Aluminum Specialties ....G...... 815 723-5341
  Joliet *(G-11828)*
Cornerstone Building Products..............G...... 217 543-2829
  Arthur *(G-848)*
Defender Steel Door & Window ....E...... 708 780-7320
  Cicero *(G-6839)*
Metal Products Sales Corp ....G...... 708 301-6844
  Lockport *(G-13013)*

LUMBER & BLDG MTRLS DEALERS, RET: Greenhouse Kits, Prefab

Interntional Grnhse Contrs Inc ....E...... 217 443-0600
  Danville *(G-7352)*

LUMBER & BLDG MTRLS DEALERS, RET: Planing Mill Prdts/Lumber

Lumberyard Suppliers Inc......................E...... 217 965-4911
  Virden *(G-20187)*

Sheraton Road Lumber...........................F...... 309 691-0858
  Peoria *(G-16523)*

LUMBER & BLDG MTRLS DEALERS, RET: Windows, Storm, Wood/Metal

Drexel House of Drapes Inc ....G...... 618 624-5415
  Belleville *(G-1547)*
Tuminello Enterprizes Inc ....G...... 815 416-1007
  Morris *(G-14334)*
Tuminello Enterprizes Inc ....G...... 815 416-1007
  Morris *(G-14335)*

LUMBER & BUILDING MATERIAL DEALERS, RETAIL: Roofing Material

Acme Awning Co....................................G...... 847 446-0153
  Highland Park *(G-11251)*

LUMBER & BUILDING MATERIALS DEALER, RET: Door & Window Prdts

Salem Building Materials Inc ....G...... 618 548-3221
  Salem *(G-18357)*

LUMBER & BUILDING MATERIALS DEALER, RET: Masonry Matls/Splys

Architectural Cast Ston ....E...... 630 377-4800
  West Chicago *(G-20543)*
Beelman Ready-Mix Inc ....G...... 618 478-2044
  Nashville *(G-14995)*
Beelman Ready-Mix Inc ....G...... 618 357-6120
  Pinckneyville *(G-16611)*
Exclusive Stone ....G...... 847 593-6963
  Elk Grove Village *(G-8989)*
Gary & Larry Brown Trucking ....G...... 618 268-6377
  Raleigh *(G-16961)*
Lion Concrete Products Inc ....G...... 630 892-7304
  Montgomery *(G-14257)*
Menoni & Mocogni Inc ....F...... 847 432-0850
  Highland Park *(G-11283)*
Monmouth Ready Mix Corp ....G...... 309 734-3211
  Galesburg *(G-10212)*
Odum Concrete Products Inc ....G...... 618 942-4572
  Herrin *(G-11175)*
Southern Illinois Redimix Inc................F...... 618 993-3600
  Marion *(G-13539)*
Tamms Industries Inc ....D...... 815 522-3394
  Kirkland *(G-12066)*

LUMBER & BUILDING MATERIALS DEALERS, RETAIL: Brick

Bricks Inc...G...... 630 897-6926
  Aurora *(G-1066)*
Glen-Gery Corporation...........................D...... 815 795-6911
  Marseilles *(G-13555)*
Southfield Corporation............................F...... 217 875-5455
  Decatur *(G-7548)*
Tison & Hall Concrete Products ....F...... 618 253-7808
  Harrisburg *(G-11030)*

LUMBER & BUILDING MATERIALS DEALERS, RETAIL: Cement

Contractors Concrete ....G...... 217 826-2290
  Marshall *(G-13568)*
Ozinga Bros Inc.....................................D...... 815 332-8198
  Belvidere *(G-1693)*
Upland Concrete ....G...... 224 699-9909
  East Dundee *(G-8214)*

LUMBER & BUILDING MATERIALS DEALERS, RETAIL: Countertops

Granite Mountain Inc ....G...... 708 774-1442
  New Lenox *(G-15036)*
Rays Countertop Shop Inc ....F...... 217 483-2514
  Glenarm *(G-10427)*
Riverbend Kitchen & Mllwk LLC ....G...... 618 462-8955
  Alton *(G-569)*

LUMBER & BUILDING MATERIALS DEALERS, RETAIL: Sand & Gravel

Quad-County Ready Mix Corp ....G...... 618 295-3000
  Marissa *(G-13544)*
Rockford Sand & Gravel Co ....E...... 815 654-4700
  Loves Park *(G-13258)*

LUMBER & BUILDING MATERIALS DEALERS, RETAIL: Tile, Ceramic

MK Tile Ink...G...... 773 964-8905
  Chicago *(G-5474)*

LUMBER & BUILDING MATERIALS RET DEALERS: Millwork & Lumber

Bailey Hardwoods Inc............................G...... 217 529-6800
  Springfield *(G-19324)*
Bull Valley Hardwood ....G...... 815 701-9400
  Woodstock *(G-21368)*
Bull Valley Hardwood ....G...... 815 701-9400
  Crystal Lake *(G-7174)*
Custom Crafted Door Inc ....F...... 309 527-5075
  El Paso *(G-8435)*
Great Spirit Hardwoods LLC ....G...... 224 801-1969
  East Dundee *(G-8199)*
John Tobin Millwork Co ....G...... 630 832-3780
  Villa Park *(G-20152)*
R Maderite Inc ....G...... 773 235-1515
  Chicago *(G-5947)*
Triezenberg Millwork Co ....G...... 708 489-9062
  Crestwood *(G-7132)*

LUMBER & BUILDING MATLS DEALERS, RET: Concrete/Cinder Block

Beelman Ready-Mix Inc ....F...... 618 526-0260
  Breese *(G-2298)*

LUMBER & BUILDING MATLS DEALERS, RET: Screens, Door/Window

Boom Company Inc ....G...... 847 459-6199
  Wheeling *(G-20863)*

LUMBER & BUILDING MTRLS DEALERS, RET: Insulation Mtrl, Bldg

Insulators Supply Inc.............................G...... 847 394-2836
  Prospect Heights *(G-16843)*

LUMBER: Flooring, Dressed, Softwood

Intelligent Flrg Systems LLC ....G...... 630 587-1800
  Saint Charles *(G-18214)*
K&S International Inc...........................G...... 847 229-0202
  Wheeling *(G-20922)*
Mechanics Planing Mill Inc ....E...... 618 288-3000
  Glen Carbon *(G-10390)*
Oltenia Inc..G...... 773 987-2888
  Norridge *(G-15242)*

LUMBER: Hardboard

Craftmaster Manufacturing Inc.............A...... 800 405-2233
  Chicago *(G-4256)*

LUMBER: Hardwood Dimension

Woodworkers Shop Inc ....E...... 309 347-5111
  Pekin *(G-16371)*
Woodx Lumber Inc.................................G...... 331 979-2171
  Elmhurst *(G-9447)*

LUMBER: Hardwood Dimension & Flooring Mills

Art Jewel Enterprises Ltd......................F...... 630 260-0400
  Carol Stream *(G-2941)*
Bond Brothers Hardwoods ....G...... 618 272-4811
  Ridgway *(G-17035)*
Boyd Sawmill..G...... 618 735-2056
  Dix *(G-7881)*
Builders Warehouse Inc ....G...... 309 672-1760
  Peoria *(G-16395)*
Central Illinois Hardwood ....G...... 309 352-2363
  Green Valley *(G-10816)*
Christiansen Sawmill and Log..............G...... 815 315-7520
  Caledonia *(G-2769)*
Eichen Lumber Co Inc..........................G...... 217 854-9751
  Carlinville *(G-2874)*
Enterprise Pallet Inc ....F...... 815 928-8546
  Bourbonnais *(G-2260)*
Ericson S Log & Lumber Co ....G...... 309 667-2147
  New Windsor *(G-15073)*
G L Beaumont Lumber Company ....F...... 618 423-2323
  Ramsey *(G-16964)*

Employee Codes: A=Over 500 employees, B=251-500
C=101-250, D=51-100, E=20-50, F=10-19, G=3-9

LUMBER: Hardwood Dimension & Flooring Mills

Knapp Industrial Wood .... F 815 657-8854
  Forrest *(G-9734)*
Moultrie County Hardwoods LLC .... G 217 543-2643
  Arthur *(G-870)*
Red River Lumber Inc .... D 708 388-1818
  Blue Island *(G-2135)*
Scv Floorsmith .... G 661 476-5034
  Hoffman Estates *(G-11455)*
Simonton Hardwood Lumber LLC .... F 618 594-2132
  Carlyle *(G-2896)*
Tree-O Lumber Inc .... E 618 357-2576
  Pinckneyville *(G-16620)*
Woodcraft Enterprises Inc .... G 815 485-2787
  New Lenox *(G-15070)*
Wooded Wonderland .... G 815 777-1223
  Galena *(G-10182)*
Woodmac Industries Inc .... F 708 755-3545
  S Chicago Hts *(G-18130)*

LUMBER: Kiln Dried

Cairo Dry Kilns Inc .... E 618 734-1039
  Cairo *(G-2766)*

LUMBER: Panels, Plywood, Softwood

Westrock Cp LLC .... D 312 346-6600
  Chicago *(G-6611)*

LUMBER: Piles, Foundation & Marine Construction, Treated

Brd Development Group LLC .... F 312 912-7110
  Chicago *(G-3947)*

LUMBER: Plywood, Hardwood

Aircraft Plywood Mfg Inc .... G 618 654-6740
  Highland *(G-11204)*
Best Veneer Company LLC .... F 630 541-8312
  Burr Ridge *(G-2655)*
Challinor Wood Products Inc .... G 847 256-8828
  Wilmette *(G-21073)*
Chalon Wood Products Inc .... G 630 243-9793
  Lemont *(G-12560)*
L Land Hardwoods .... G 708 496-9000
  Bedford Park *(G-1478)*
Lumberyard Suppliers Inc .... E 217 965-4911
  Virden *(G-20187)*
Red River Lumber Inc .... D 708 388-1818
  Blue Island *(G-2135)*
Woodcraft Enterprises Inc .... G 815 485-2787
  New Lenox *(G-15070)*

LUMBER: Plywood, Hardwood or Hardwood Faced

Westrock Cp LLC .... D 312 346-6600
  Chicago *(G-6611)*

LUMBER: Plywood, Prefinished, Hardwood

R S Bacon Veneer Company .... G 331 777-4762
  Lisle *(G-12933)*

LUMBER: Plywood, Softwood

Best Veneer Company LLC .... F 630 541-8312
  Burr Ridge *(G-2655)*

LUMBER: Resawn, Small Dimension

Liese Lumber Co Inc .... G 618 234-0105
  Belleville *(G-1568)*

LUMBER: Treated

Chicago Flameproof WD Spc Corp .... E 630 859-0009
  Montgomery *(G-14240)*
Nu Again .... F 630 564-5590
  Bartlett *(G-1299)*
Red River Lumber Inc .... D 708 388-1818
  Blue Island *(G-2135)*

LUMBER: Veneer, Hardwood

R S Bacon Veneer Company .... C 630 323-1414
  Lisle *(G-12932)*

MACHINE GUNS, WHOLESALE

Krebs Custom Inc .... G 847 487-7776
  Wauconda *(G-20368)*

MACHINE PARTS: Stamped Or Pressed Metal

Alcon Tool & Mfg Co Inc .... F 773 545-8742
  Chicago *(G-3598)*
Barrington Automation Ltd .... E 847 458-0900
  Lake In The Hills *(G-12329)*
Blue Chip Mfg LLC .... G 630 553-6321
  Oswego *(G-15993)*
C J Holdings Inc .... G 309 274-3141
  Chillicothe *(G-6815)*
Cicero Plastic Products Inc .... E 815 886-9522
  Romeoville *(G-17808)*
Crystal Precision Drilling .... G 815 633-5460
  Loves Park *(G-13199)*
CSI Cutting Specialist Inc .... D 731 352-5351
  Edwardsville *(G-8353)*
Domeny Tool & Stamping Company ..... F 847 526-5700
  Wauconda *(G-20342)*
Force Manufacturing Inc .... G 847 265-6500
  Lake Villa *(G-12351)*
G T L Technologies Inc .... G 630 469-9818
  Glendale Heights *(G-10451)*
Gem Equipment & Mfg LLC .... E 309 923-7312
  Roanoke *(G-17101)*
Graphic Parts Intl Inc .... F 773 725-4900
  Chicago *(G-4726)*
Headly Manufacturing Co .... D 708 338-0800
  Broadview *(G-2440)*
I C Universal Inc .... G 630 766-1169
  Bensenville *(G-1820)*
Icon Power Roller Inc .... E 630 545-2345
  Marseilles *(G-13556)*
Kay Manufacturing Company LLC .... C 708 862-6800
  Calumet City *(G-2782)*
Kr Machine .... G 815 248-2250
  Durand *(G-8153)*
Kz Manufacturing Co .... G 708 937-8097
  Mc Cook *(G-13694)*
Lorbern Mfg Inc .... E 847 301-8600
  Schaumburg *(G-18612)*
Mark Development Corporation .... C 815 339-2226
  Mark *(G-13545)*
Mercury Products Corp .... C 847 524-4400
  Schaumburg *(G-18627)*
Meridian Parts Inc .... G 630 718-1995
  Naperville *(G-14868)*
Northfield Holdings LLC .... E 847 755-0700
  Schaumburg *(G-18652)*
Patko Tool & Manufacturing .... G 630 616-8802
  Bensenville *(G-1867)*
Pro Machining Inc .... F 815 633-4140
  Loves Park *(G-13250)*
R Hansel & Son Inc .... G 815 784-5500
  Genoa *(G-10323)*
R Z Tool Inc .... F 847 647-2350
  Niles *(G-15164)*
Rail Exchange Inc .... E 708 757-3317
  Chicago Heights *(G-6767)*
Riverfront Machine Inc .... D 815 663-5000
  Spring Valley *(G-19312)*
Rockwell Metal Products Inc .... G 773 762-7030
  Chicago *(G-6048)*
Rursch Specialties Inc .... G 309 795-1502
  Reynolds *(G-17005)*
S & W Manufacturing Co Inc .... E 630 595-5044
  Bensenville *(G-1888)*
S&L Tool Company Inc .... G 847 455-5550
  Franklin Park *(G-10039)*
Technical Metals Inc .... D 815 692-4643
  Fairbury *(G-9614)*
Ucal Holdings Inc .... D 847 695-8030
  Elgin *(G-8765)*
Ucal Systems Inc .... C 847 695-8030
  Elgin *(G-8767)*

MACHINE SHOPS

Advantage Machining Inc .... E 630 897-1220
  Aurora *(G-1042)*
All Cnc Solutions Inc .... G 847 972-1139
  Skokie *(G-18913)*
Art Technologies Inc .... G 773 557-3896
  Bensenville *(G-1747)*
Auto Head and Engine Exchange .... G 708 448-8762
  Worth *(G-21454)*
B A P Enterprises Inc .... G 708 849-0900
  Dolton *(G-7931)*
BSB International Corp .... G 847 791-9272
  Bensenville *(G-1759)*
Carmona Gear Cutting .... G 815 963-8236
  Rockford *(G-17337)*
Cirrus Products LLC .... G 630 501-1881
  Burr Ridge *(G-2662)*
Cope Plastics Inc .... D 618 466-0221
  Alton *(G-549)*
Custom Superfinishing Grinding .... G 847 699-9710
  Rosemont *(G-18016)*
D E Specialty Tool & Mfg Inc .... E 847 678-0004
  Franklin Park *(G-9925)*
DNp Enterprises Inc .... G 630 628-7210
  Addison *(G-95)*
Dynomax Inc .... B 847 680-8833
  Wheeling *(G-20883)*
Eastwood Enterprises Inc .... D 847 940-4008
  Deerfield *(G-7607)*
Geo T Schmidt Inc .... D 847 647-7117
  Niles *(G-15124)*
Goreville Auto Parts & Mch Sp .... E 618 995-2375
  Goreville *(G-10680)*
Gti Spindle Technology Inc .... F 309 820-7887
  Bloomington *(G-2054)*
Hfo Chicago LLC .... F 847 258-2850
  Elk Grove Village *(G-9034)*
Indiana Precision Inc .... F 765 361-0247
  Danville *(G-7351)*
Jdb Machining Inc .... G 708 749-9596
  Forest View *(G-9730)*
Komax Corporation .... D 888 465-6629
  Buffalo Grove *(G-2556)*
Linx Global Mfg LLC .... E 847 910-5303
  Chicago *(G-5233)*
Littell LLC .... E 630 916-6662
  Schaumburg *(G-18609)*
Magnet-Schultz Amer Holdg LLC .... G 630 789-0600
  Westmont *(G-20755)*
Magnet-Schultz America Inc .... G 630 789-0600
  Westmont *(G-20756)*
Milco Precision Machining Inc .... F 630 628-5730
  Addison *(G-216)*
Mk Systems Incorporated .... F 847 709-6180
  Elk Grove Village *(G-9129)*
Octane Motorsports LLC .... G 224 419-5460
  Waukegan *(G-20473)*
P & H Manufacturing Co .... D 217 774-2123
  Shelbyville *(G-18882)*
Precision Metal Crafters Inc .... F 847 816-3244
  Libertyville *(G-12698)*
Pro-Qua Inc .... G 630 543-5644
  Addison *(G-256)*
Rah Enterprises Inc .... G 217 223-1970
  Quincy *(G-16938)*
Research and Testing Worx Inc .... E 815 734-7346
  Mount Morris *(G-14501)*
Southwick Machine & Design Co .... G 309 949-2868
  Colona *(G-6980)*
Swebco Mfg Inc .... E 815 636-7160
  Machesney Park *(G-13377)*
Tag-Barton LLC .... G 217 428-0711
  Decatur *(G-7556)*
Tekmill Inc .... E 217 353-5111
  Champaign *(G-3358)*
Total Titanium Inc .... E 866 208-6446
  Red Bud *(G-17003)*
Traxco Inc .... G 847 669-1545
  Huntley *(G-11569)*
Trinity Machined Products Inc .... E 630 876-6992
  Aurora *(G-1028)*
Trufab Group USA LLC .... E 630 994-3286
  Schaumburg *(G-18758)*
Vek Screw Machine Products .... G 630 543-5557
  Addison *(G-327)*

MACHINE TOOL ACCESS: Balancing Machines

Balanstar Corporation .... F 773 261-5034
  Elk Grove Village *(G-8856)*
Stuhr Manufacturing Co .... F 815 398-2460
  Rockford *(G-17648)*

MACHINE TOOL ACCESS: Boring Attachments

Grove Industrial .... G 815 385-4800
  Johnsburg *(G-11804)*
Machine Tool Acc & Mfg Co .... G 773 489-0903
  Chicago *(G-5309)*

MACHINE TOOL ACCESS: Broaches

Universal Broaching Inc .... F 847 228-1440
  Elk Grove Village *(G-9298)*

PRODUCT SECTION

MACHINE TOOLS & ACCESS

MACHINE TOOL ACCESS: Cams
Sacco-Camex Inc .... G 630 595-8090
  Franklin Park *(G-10040)*

MACHINE TOOL ACCESS: Cutting
Abbco Inc .... E 630 595-7115
  Bensenville *(G-1722)*
Advent Tool & Mfg Inc .... F 847 395-9707
  Antioch *(G-594)*
Alfa Mfg Industries Inc .... E 847 470-9595
  Morton Grove *(G-14388)*
Allkut Tool Incorporated .... G 815 476-9656
  Wilmington *(G-21096)*
Big Kser Precision Tooling Inc .... E 847 228-7660
  Hoffman Estates *(G-11409)*
Circle Cutting Tools Inc .... G 815 398-4153
  Rockford *(G-17350)*
Composite Cutter Tech Inc .... G 847 740-6875
  Volo *(G-20198)*
Craftstech Inc .... E 847 758-3100
  Elk Grove Village *(G-8918)*
D & R Autochuck Inc .... E 815 394-1744
  Rockford *(G-17364)*
D & R Ekstrom Carlson Co .... E 815 394-1744
  Rockford *(G-17365)*
Damen Carbide Tool Company Inc .... E 630 766-7875
  Wood Dale *(G-21181)*
Dynacut Industries Inc .... E 630 462-1900
  Carol Stream *(G-2978)*
Everede Tool Company LLC .... D 623 414-4800
  West Chicago *(G-20575)*
Everede Tool Company LLC .... E 773 467-4200
  West Chicago *(G-20576)*
Federal Signal Corporation .... D 630 954-2000
  Oak Brook *(G-15618)*
Illinois Carbide Tool Co Inc .... F 847 244-1110
  Waukegan *(G-20447)*
Ivan Schwenker .... G 630 543-7798
  Addison *(G-156)*
Kennametal Inc .... F 309 578-1888
  Mossville *(G-14460)*
Kitamura Machinery USA Inc .... F 847 520-7755
  Wheeling *(G-20924)*
Midstates Cutting Tools Inc .... G 630 595-0700
  Bensenville *(G-1852)*
Mitsubishi Materials USA Corp .... F 847 519-1601
  Schaumburg *(G-18632)*
New World Products Inc .... G 630 690-5625
  Carol Stream *(G-3039)*
OSG Usa Inc .... C 630 274-2100
  Bensenville *(G-1864)*
Progrssive Cmponents Intl Corp .... D 847 487-1000
  Wauconda *(G-20385)*
Regal Cutting Tools Inc .... C 815 389-3461
  Roscoe *(G-17924)*
Rockform Tooling & Machinery .... G 815 398-7650
  Rockford *(G-17611)*
Sandtech Inc .... F 847 470-9595
  Morton Grove *(G-14439)*
Spie Tool Co .... E 847 891-6556
  Schaumburg *(G-18724)*
Star Su Fellows Cutter LLC .... D 847 649-1450
  Hoffman Estates *(G-11462)*
Tag Tool Services Incorporated .... E 309 694-2400
  East Peoria *(G-8292)*
Tool Engrg Consulting Mfg LLC .... G 815 316-2304
  Rockford *(G-17666)*
Toolmasters LLC .... E 815 968-0961
  Rockford *(G-17667)*
Triad Cutting Tools Svc & Mfg .... G 847 352-0459
  Schaumburg *(G-18756)*
Triumph Twist Drill Co Inc .... B 815 459-6250
  Crystal Lake *(G-7286)*
Wenco Manufacturing Co Inc .... E 630 377-7474
  Elgin *(G-8781)*

MACHINE TOOL ACCESS: Diamond Cutting, For Turning, Etc
Accu-Cut Diamond Tool Company .... F 708 457-8800
  Norridge *(G-15228)*
Meinhardt Diamond Tool Co .... G 773 267-3260
  Chicago *(G-5388)*
Saint-Gobain Abrasives Inc .... C 630 868-8060
  Carol Stream *(G-3063)*
Shape-Master Tool Co .... E 815 522-6186
  Kirkland *(G-12065)*
Wunderlich Diamond Tool Corp .... F 847 437-9904
  Elk Grove Village *(G-9314)*

MACHINE TOOL ACCESS: Dresser, Abrasive Wheel Or Other
Industrial Diamond Products .... E 847 272-7840
  Northbrook *(G-15405)*

MACHINE TOOL ACCESS: Drill Bushings, Drilling Jig
Acme Industrial Company .... C 847 428-3911
  Carpentersville *(G-3090)*
National Bushing & Mfg .... G 847 847-1553
  Lake Zurich *(G-12438)*

MACHINE TOOL ACCESS: Drills
Brunner & Lay Inc .... C 847 678-3232
  Bensenville *(G-1758)*
Cjt Koolcarb Inc .... C 630 690-5933
  Carol Stream *(G-2960)*
Dormer Pramet LLC .... C 800 877-3745
  Elgin *(G-8568)*
Infinity Tool Mfg LLC .... G 618 439-4042
  Benton *(G-1928)*

MACHINE TOOL ACCESS: Hopper Feed Devices
Custom Feeder Co of Rockford .... E 815 654-2444
  Loves Park *(G-13201)*
Jerhen Industries Inc .... D 815 397-0400
  Rockford *(G-17473)*
Universal Feeder Inc .... G 815 633-0752
  Machesney Park *(G-13382)*

MACHINE TOOL ACCESS: Knives, Metalworking
General Cutng Tl Svc & Mfg Inc .... F 847 677-8770
  Lincolnwood *(G-12821)*

MACHINE TOOL ACCESS: Machine Attachments & Access, Drilling
Chicago Quadrill Co .... G 847 824-4196
  Des Plaines *(G-7745)*

MACHINE TOOL ACCESS: Milling Machine Attachments
Bourn & Bourn Inc .... C 815 965-4013
  Rockford *(G-17327)*

MACHINE TOOL ACCESS: Pushers
Pixel Pushers Incorporated .... G 847 550-6560
  Lake Zurich *(G-12444)*

MACHINE TOOL ACCESS: Rotary Tables
Obsidian Mfg Inds Inc .... F 815 962-8700
  Rockford *(G-17542)*

MACHINE TOOL ACCESS: Threading Tools
Rsvp Tooling Inc .... G 815 725-3310
  Joliet *(G-11929)*

MACHINE TOOL ACCESS: Tool Holders
Haimer Usa LLC .... G 630 833-1500
  Villa Park *(G-20150)*

MACHINE TOOL ACCESS: Tools & Access
2l Technologies LLC .... G 312 526-3900
  Chicago *(G-3465)*
Alcon Tool & Mfg Co Inc .... F 773 545-8742
  Chicago *(G-3598)*
Ammentorp Tool Company Inc .... G 847 671-9290
  Franklin Park *(G-9869)*
Burnex Corporation .... E 815 728-1317
  Ringwood *(G-17040)*
Coordinate Machine Company .... E 630 894-9880
  Roselle *(G-17947)*
G & S Manufacturing Inc .... F 847 674-7666
  Bannockburn *(G-1201)*
Harig Manufacturing Corp .... E 847 647-9500
  Skokie *(G-18964)*
Hilti Inc .... F 847 364-9818
  Elmhurst *(G-9372)*
Pace Machinery Group Inc .... F 630 377-1750
  Wasco *(G-20261)*
Park Products Inc .... G 630 543-2474
  Addison *(G-233)*
Tag Sales Co Inc .... G 630 990-3434
  Hinsdale *(G-11381)*
Thermoplastec Inc .... F 815 873-9288
  Rockford *(G-17658)*

MACHINE TOOL ATTACHMENTS & ACCESS
A J Manufacturing Co Inc .... G 630 832-2828
  Elmhurst *(G-9321)*
Belden Tools Inc .... E 708 344-4600
  Hillside *(G-11329)*
Bertsche Engineering Corp .... F 847 537-8757
  Buffalo Grove *(G-2516)*
Edmik Inc .... E 847 263-0460
  Gurnee *(G-10874)*
Galaxy Sourcing Inc .... G 630 532-5003
  Addison *(G-133)*
H R Slater Co Inc .... F 312 666-1855
  Chicago *(G-4760)*
J & J Carbide & Tool Inc .... E 708 489-0300
  Alsip *(G-459)*
Matheu Tool Works Inc .... G 773 327-9274
  Chicago *(G-5365)*
Mid-West Feeder Inc .... E 815 544-2994
  Belvidere *(G-1686)*
Retondo Enterprises Inc .... G 630 837-8130
  Streamwood *(G-19593)*
S Vs Industries Inc .... G 630 408-1083
  Hoffman Estates *(G-11453)*
Tornos Technologies US Corp .... G 630 812-2040
  Des Plaines *(G-7857)*

MACHINE TOOLS & ACCESS
A R Tech & Tool Inc .... G 708 599-5745
  Bridgeview *(G-2317)*
A&W Tool Inc .... G 815 653-1700
  Ringwood *(G-17037)*
ADS LLC .... D 256 430-3366
  Burr Ridge *(G-2650)*
Advent Tool and Mfg .... F 847 395-9707
  Antioch *(G-595)*
Alliance Tool & Manufacturing .... F 708 345-5444
  Maywood *(G-13660)*
American Machine Tools Inc .... G 773 775-6285
  Chicago *(G-3658)*
Apergy Energy Automation LLC .... E 630 541-1540
  Downers Grove *(G-7952)*
Arrow Engineering Inc .... E 815 397-0862
  Rockford *(G-17307)*
Assurance Technologies Inc .... G 630 550-5000
  Bartlett *(G-1265)*
Atm America Corp .... E 800 298-0030
  Chicago *(G-3770)*
Auto Meter Products Inc .... C 815 895-8141
  Sycamore *(G-19702)*
Autocut Machine Company Inc .... G 815 436-1900
  Elwood *(G-9460)*
Belcar Products Inc .... G 630 462-1950
  Carol Stream *(G-2946)*
Beloit Tool Inc .... E 815 389-2300
  South Beloit *(G-19084)*
Besly Cutting Tools Inc .... E 815 389-2231
  South Beloit *(G-19085)*
Blackhawk Industrial Dist Inc .... F 773 736-9600
  Carol Stream *(G-2950)*
C & C Tooling Inc .... F 630 543-5523
  Addison *(G-57)*
Carbco Manufacturing Inc .... F 630 377-1410
  Saint Charles *(G-18164)*
Celinco Inc .... G 815 964-2256
  Rockford *(G-17340)*
Center Tool Company .... G 847 683-7559
  Hampshire *(G-10966)*
Champion Chisel Works Inc .... F 815 535-0647
  Rock Falls *(G-17178)*
Chicago Hardware and Fix Co .... C 847 455-6609
  Franklin Park *(G-9905)*
Custom Cutting Tools Inc .... G 815 986-0320
  Loves Park *(G-13200)*
Custom Tool Inc .... F 217 465-8538
  Paris *(G-16228)*
David Linderholm .... G 847 336-3755
  Waukegan *(G-20434)*
Delco West LLC .... G 309 799-7543
  Milan *(G-14006)*
Design Systems Inc .... E 309 263-7706
  Morton *(G-14358)*

Employee Codes: A=Over 500 employees, B=251-500
C=101-250, D=51-100, E=20-50, F=10-19, G=3-9

MACHINE TOOLS & ACCESS

PRODUCT SECTION

Die Specialty Co .... G 312 303-5738
   La Grange Park *(G-12096)*
Dmg Mori Usa Inc .... D 847 593-5400
   Hoffman Estates *(G-11419)*
Dynomax Inc .... B 847 680-8833
   Wheeling *(G-20883)*
EJ Cady & Company .... G 847 537-2239
   Wheeling *(G-20888)*
Emtech Machining & Grinding .... G 815 338-1580
   Woodstock *(G-21385)*
Engineering Products Company .... G 815 436-9055
   Plainfield *(G-16659)*
Engis Corporation .... C 847 808-9400
   Wheeling *(G-20891)*
Estwing Manufacturing Co Inc .... B 815 397-9521
   Rockford *(G-17402)*
Fox Machine & Tool Inc .... G 847 357-1845
   Elk Grove Village *(G-9006)*
Fulton Corporation .... D 815 589-3211
   Fulton *(G-10152)*
Gator Products Inc .... G 847 836-0581
   Gilberts *(G-10355)*
Gaylee Corporation Saws .... G 586 803-1100
   South Beloit *(G-19094)*
Greenlee Diamond Tool Co .... E 866 451-3316
   Elk Grove Village *(G-9023)*
Guide Line Industries Inc .... F 815 777-3722
   Scales Mound *(G-18420)*
Hallmark Industries Inc .... F 847 301-8050
   Streamwood *(G-19577)*
Harris Precision Tools Inc .... G 708 422-5808
   Chicago Ridge *(G-6797)*
Hartland Cutting Tools Inc .... F 847 639-9400
   Cary *(G-3166)*
Heidenhain Holding Inc .... G 716 661-1700
   Schaumburg *(G-18546)*
Henry Technologies Inc .... G 217 483-2406
   Chatham *(G-3421)*
Hg-Farley Holdings LLC .... F 815 874-1400
   Rockford *(G-17449)*
Hg-Farley Laserlab USA Inc .... F 815 874-1400
   Rockford *(G-17450)*
Holden Industries Inc .... F 847 940-1500
   Deerfield *(G-7616)*
Ideal Industries Inc .... C 815 895-1108
   Sycamore *(G-19715)*
Illinois Broaching Company .... E 847 678-3080
   Schiller Park *(G-18815)*
Imprex International Inc .... G 847 364-4930
   Arlington Heights *(G-756)*
Industrial Instrument Svc Corp .... G 773 581-3355
   Chicago *(G-4907)*
Ingersoll Cutting Tool Company .... B 815 387-6600
   Rockford *(G-17461)*
Ingersoll Machine Tools Inc .... C 815 987-6000
   Rockford *(G-17462)*
Inland Tool Company .... G 217 792-3206
   Mount Pulaski *(G-14588)*
Intech Industries Inc .... F 847 487-5599
   Wauconda *(G-20361)*
J H Benedict Co Inc .... D 309 694-3111
   East Peoria *(G-8270)*
Jamco Tool & Cams Inc .... F 847 678-0280
   Franklin Park *(G-9972)*
Johnson Pattern & Mch Works .... E 815 433-2775
   Ottawa *(G-16057)*
Jupiter Machine Tool Inc .... G 309 297-1920
   Galesburg *(G-10204)*
K-C Tool Co .... G 630 983-5960
   Naperville *(G-14857)*
Kaydon Acquisition Xii Inc .... E 217 443-3592
   Danville *(G-7354)*
Keonix Corporation .... G 847 259-9430
   Arlington Heights *(G-765)*
Kile Machine & Tool Inc .... G 217 446-8616
   Danville *(G-7357)*
Kmp Tool Grinding Inc .... G 847 205-9640
   Northbrook *(G-15413)*
L & M Screw Machine Products .... F 630 801-0455
   Montgomery *(G-14253)*
Lmt Onsrud LP .... C 847 362-1560
   Waukegan *(G-20461)*
Lmt Usa Inc .... G 630 969-5412
   Waukegan *(G-20462)*
Logan Actuator Co .... G 815 943-9500
   Harvard *(G-11059)*
Logan Graphic Products Inc .... D 847 526-5515
   Wauconda *(G-20369)*
Method Molds Inc .... G 815 877-0191
   Loves Park *(G-13236)*

Midland Manufacturing Corp .... C 847 677-0333
   Skokie *(G-18990)*
Moldtronics Inc .... E 630 968-7000
   Downers Grove *(G-8058)*
NNt Enterprises Incorporated .... E 630 875-9600
   Itasca *(G-11712)*
OSG Usa Inc .... E 800 837-2223
   Saint Charles *(G-18239)*
P K Neuses Incorporated .... G 847 253-6555
   Rolling Meadows *(G-17758)*
PDQ Machine Inc .... G 815 282-7575
   Machesney Park *(G-13363)*
Pontiac Engraving .... G 630 834-4424
   Bensenville *(G-1870)*
Porcelain Enamel Finishers .... G 312 808-1560
   Chicago *(G-5845)*
Precision Brand Products Inc .... E 630 969-7200
   Downers Grove *(G-8082)*
Precision Tool & Die Company .... F 217 864-3371
   Mount Zion *(G-14649)*
Prototype & Production Co .... E 847 419-1553
   Wheeling *(G-20967)*
Rdh Inc of Rockford .... F 815 874-9421
   Rockford *(G-17568)*
Regal Beloit Corporation .... C 844 527-8392
   Roscoe *(G-17923)*
Rockford Jobbing Service Inc .... G 815 398-8661
   Rockford *(G-17596)*
Roll McHning Tech Slutions Inc .... E 815 372-9100
   Romeoville *(G-17870)*
Roll Rite Inc .... G 815 645-8600
   Davis Junction *(G-7426)*
S & J Industrial Supply Corp .... F 708 339-1708
   South Holland *(G-19242)*
S & W Manufacturing Co Inc .... E 630 595-5044
   Bensenville *(G-1888)*
Schaefer Technologies LLC .... G 630 406-9377
   Batavia *(G-1413)*
Sensible Products Inc .... G 773 774-7400
   Chicago *(G-6135)*
Shelby Tool & Die Inc .... G 217 774-2189
   Shelbyville *(G-18886)*
Sollami Company .... G 618 988-1521
   Herrin *(G-11179)*
SWB Inc .... G 847 438-1800
   Lake Zurich *(G-12462)*
Technical Tool Enterprise .... G 630 893-3390
   Addison *(G-304)*
Thermal-Tech Systems Inc .... E 630 639-5115
   West Chicago *(G-20651)*
Thomas Packaging LLC .... F 847 392-1652
   Rolling Meadows *(G-17779)*
Top Notch Tool & Supply Inc .... G 815 633-6295
   Cherry Valley *(G-3447)*
Tox- Pressotechnik LLC .... G 630 447-4600
   Warrenville *(G-20254)*
Tri-Star Engineering Inc .... E 847 595-3377
   Elk Grove Village *(G-9285)*
Vanguard Tool & Engineering Co .... E 847 981-9595
   Mount Prospect *(G-14580)*
West Precision Tool Inc .... F 630 766-8304
   Bensenville *(G-1912)*
Willow Farm Products Inc .... G 630 430-7491
   Lemont *(G-12595)*
Wozniak Industries Inc .... C 708 458-1220
   Bedford Park *(G-1515)*
Yana House .... G 773 874-7120
   Chicago *(G-6697)*
Z-Patch Inc .... E 618 529-2431
   Carbondale *(G-2866)*

MACHINE TOOLS, METAL CUTTING: Brushing

Above & Beyond Black Oxiding .... G 708 345-7100
   Melrose Park *(G-13818)*
It For Whats Inc .... G 847 949-6522
   Hawthorn Woods *(G-11124)*

MACHINE TOOLS, METAL CUTTING: Centering

Stuhr Manufacturing Co .... F 815 398-2460
   Rockford *(G-17648)*

MACHINE TOOLS, METAL CUTTING: Cutoff

Harris Precision Tools Inc .... G 708 422-5808
   Chicago Ridge *(G-6797)*
Huml Industries Inc .... G 847 426-8061
   Gilberts *(G-10358)*

Kiene Diesel Accessories Inc .... E 630 543-7170
   Addison *(G-169)*

MACHINE TOOLS, METAL CUTTING: Drilling

Daito USA Inc .... G 847 437-6788
   Elk Grove Village *(G-8937)*
Star Su Fellows Cutter LLC .... D 847 649-1450
   Hoffman Estates *(G-11462)*

MACHINE TOOLS, METAL CUTTING: Drilling & Boring

Advanced Machine & Engrg Co .... C 815 962-6076
   Rockford *(G-17296)*
Midwest Turned Products LLC .... E 847 551-4482
   Gilberts *(G-10362)*
N W Horizontal Boring .... G 618 566-9117
   Mascoutah *(G-13605)*
Rdh Inc of Rockford .... F 815 874-9421
   Rockford *(G-17568)*
Robbins Hdd LLC .... F 847 955-0050
   Lake Zurich *(G-12451)*
TT Technologies Inc .... D 630 851-8200
   Aurora *(G-1029)*

MACHINE TOOLS, METAL CUTTING: Exotic, Including Explosive

Alliance Tool & Manufacturing .... F 708 345-5444
   Maywood *(G-13660)*
Composite Cutter Tech Inc .... G 847 740-6875
   Volo *(G-20198)*
Tauber Brothers Tool & Die Co .... E 708 867-9100
   Chicago *(G-6330)*

MACHINE TOOLS, METAL CUTTING: Grind, Polish, Buff, Lapp

Hausermann Abrading Process Co .... F 630 543-6688
   Addison *(G-146)*
Lc Holdings of Delaware Inc .... G 847 940-3550
   Deerfield *(G-7629)*
Precision Chrome Inc .... E 847 587-1515
   Fox Lake *(G-9753)*

MACHINE TOOLS, METAL CUTTING: Home Workshop

Air Mite Devices Inc .... E 224 338-0071
   Round Lake *(G-18067)*
B & B Machine Inc .... G 309 786-3279
   Rock Island *(G-17202)*

MACHINE TOOLS, METAL CUTTING: Keysetting

Hoffman J&M Farm Holdings Inc .... D 847 671-6280
   Schiller Park *(G-18813)*

MACHINE TOOLS, METAL CUTTING: Lathes

Dainichi Machinery Inc .... G 630 681-1572
   Carol Stream *(G-2970)*

MACHINE TOOLS, METAL CUTTING: Milling, Chemical

Engineered Mills Inc .... G 847 548-0044
   Grayslake *(G-10770)*

MACHINE TOOLS, METAL CUTTING: Numerically Controlled

Accelrted Mch Design Engrg LLC .... E 815 316-6381
   Rockford *(G-17290)*
Dearborn Tool & Mfg Inc .... E 630 655-1260
   Burr Ridge *(G-2669)*
Miyano Machinery USA Inc .... E 630 766-4141
   Elk Grove Village *(G-9128)*
R B Evans Co .... G 630 365-3554
   Elburn *(G-8471)*
Walter Tool & Mfg Inc .... F 847 697-7230
   Elgin *(G-8774)*

MACHINE TOOLS, METAL CUTTING: Pipe Cutting & Threading

Rabbit Tool USA Inc .... F 309 793-4375
   Rock Island *(G-17238)*

PRODUCT SECTION

MACHINE TOOLS: Metal Cutting

MACHINE TOOLS, METAL CUTTING: Planers

- Bourn & Bourn Inc ....C....... 815 965-4013
  Rockford *(G-17327)*
- Spectrum Metals Inc ....F....... 847 969-0887
  Schaumburg *(G-18722)*

MACHINE TOOLS, METAL CUTTING: Plasma Process

- Electron Beam Technologies Inc............C....... 815 935-2211
  Kankakee *(G-11967)*

MACHINE TOOLS, METAL CUTTING: Screw & Thread

- Cutting Tool Innovations Inc...................G....... 630 766-4839
  Bensenville *(G-1784)*
- Folkerts Manufacturing Inc.....................G....... 815 968-7426
  Rockford *(G-17417)*
- Tvo Acquisition Corporation ....E....... 708 656-4240
  Cicero *(G-6882)*

MACHINE TOOLS, METAL CUTTING: Tool Replacement & Rpr Parts

- Bertsche Engineering Corp ....F....... 847 537-8757
  Buffalo Grove *(G-2516)*
- Bury Industrial Service LLC....................G....... 847 235-2053
  Lake Forest *(G-12235)*
- Condor Machine Tool ....G....... 773 767-5985
  Chicago *(G-4217)*
- Ctc Machine Service Inc.........................G....... 630 876-5120
  West Chicago *(G-20568)*
- Endofix Ltd ....G....... 708 715-3472
  Brookfield *(G-2482)*
- Imago Manufacturing................................G....... 815 333-5272
  Woodstock *(G-21395)*
- Jakes McHning Rbilding Svc Inc.............E....... 630 892-3291
  Aurora *(G-1116)*
- Laser Technologies Inc ....G....... 630 761-1200
  Naperville *(G-14860)*
- M & M Tooling Inc ....G....... 630 595-8834
  Wood Dale *(G-21209)*
- Machine Medics LLC ....G....... 309 633-5454
  Peoria *(G-16471)*
- On Site Repair Services Inc ....F....... 815 223-4058
  La Salle *(G-12119)*
- Prototype & Production Co ....E....... 847 419-1553
  Wheeling *(G-20967)*
- Versatility Tl Works Mfg Inc....................F....... 708 389-8909
  Alsip *(G-522)*
- Walega Precision Company Inc..............G....... 630 682-5000
  Carol Stream *(G-3086)*
- Western Applied Robotics Corp ....G....... 815 735-6476
  Frankfort *(G-9852)*

MACHINE TOOLS, METAL FORMING: Bending

- Giant Globes Inc ....G....... 773 772-2917
  Chicago *(G-4689)*
- Hurst Manufacturing Co Inc....................F....... 309 756-9960
  Milan *(G-14016)*

MACHINE TOOLS, METAL FORMING: Container, Metal Incl Cans

- Ives-Way Products Inc.............................G....... 847 740-0658
  Round Lake Beach *(G-18090)*

MACHINE TOOLS, METAL FORMING: Crimping, Metal

- Elpress Inc...G....... 331 814-2910
  Westmont *(G-20740)*
- MB Corp & Associates ....F....... 847 214-8843
  Elgin *(G-8654)*
- Uniflex of America LLC ....G....... 847 519-1100
  Schaumburg *(G-18764)*

MACHINE TOOLS, METAL FORMING: Die Casting & Extruding

- Cutting Edge Industries Inc ....G....... 847 678-1777
  Franklin Park *(G-9923)*
- Park Engineering Inc................................E....... 847 455-1424
  Franklin Park *(G-10013)*
- Service Machine Jobs ....G....... 815 986-3033
  Rockford *(G-17626)*

MACHINE TOOLS, METAL FORMING: Electroforming

- 10x Microstructures LLC........................G....... 847 215-7448
  Wheeling *(G-20834)*

MACHINE TOOLS, METAL FORMING: Forming, Metal Deposit

- Whitney Roper LLC..................................D....... 815 962-3011
  Rockford *(G-17683)*

MACHINE TOOLS, METAL FORMING: Headers

- First Header Die Inc ....E....... 815 282-5161
  Machesney Park *(G-13343)*
- Precision Header Tooling Inc..................F....... 815 874-9116
  Rockford *(G-17557)*

MACHINE TOOLS, METAL FORMING: High Energy Rate

- Innovate Technologies Inc ....G....... 630 587-4220
  Saint Charles *(G-18212)*

MACHINE TOOLS, METAL FORMING: Magnetic Forming

- A & A Magnetics Inc.................................F....... 815 338-6054
  Woodstock *(G-21352)*

MACHINE TOOLS, METAL FORMING: Marking

- Geo T Schmidt Inc ....D....... 847 647-7117
  Niles *(G-15124)*
- Kwik Mark Inc...G....... 815 363-8268
  McHenry *(G-13755)*
- Marsh Shipping Supply Co LLC ....F....... 618 343-1006
  Collinsville *(G-6969)*
- Rae Products and Chem Corp ....G....... 708 396-1984
  Alsip *(G-501)*

MACHINE TOOLS, METAL FORMING: Mechanical, Pneumatic Or Hyd

- Ajax Tool Works Inc ....D....... 847 455-5420
  Franklin Park *(G-9862)*
- Williams White & Company....................C....... 309 797-7650
  Moline *(G-14181)*

MACHINE TOOLS, METAL FORMING: Pressing

- K R Komarek Inc ....E....... 847 956-0060
  Wood Dale *(G-21203)*
- L M C Inc ....G....... 815 758-3514
  Dekalb *(G-7687)*
- Venturedyne Ltd ....E....... 708 597-7550
  Chicago *(G-6535)*

MACHINE TOOLS, METAL FORMING: Rebuilt

- Kwalyti Tling McHy Rblding Inc..............F....... 630 761-8040
  Batavia *(G-1391)*
- Mikes Machinery Rebuilders...................G....... 630 543-6400
  Addison *(G-215)*
- New Lenox Machine Co Inc....................F....... 815 584-4866
  Dwight *(G-8156)*
- Nor Service Inc..E....... 815 232-8379
  Freeport *(G-10130)*
- Tox- Pressotechnik LLC ....G....... 630 447-4600
  Warrenville *(G-20254)*

MACHINE TOOLS, METAL FORMING: Robots, Pressing, Extrudg, Etc

- Cloos Robotic Welding Inc ....F....... 847 923-9988
  Schaumburg *(G-18479)*

MACHINE TOOLS, METAL FORMING: Spring Winding & Forming

- Accurate Spring Tech Inc ....F....... 815 344-3333
  McHenry *(G-13713)*
- Integral Automation Inc..........................F....... 630 654-4300
  Burr Ridge *(G-2688)*

MACHINE TOOLS: Metal Cutting

- 1883 Properties Inc................................D....... 847 537-8800
  Lincolnshire *(G-12740)*
- A&W Tool Inc ....G....... 815 653-1700
  Ringwood *(G-17037)*
- Abbco Inc..E....... 630 595-7115
  Bensenville *(G-1722)*
- Accu-Cut Dmnd Bore Szing Syste ....F....... 708 457-8800
  Norridge *(G-15229)*
- ADS LLC ....D....... 256 430-3366
  Burr Ridge *(G-2650)*
- American Machine Tools Inc ....G....... 773 775-6285
  Chicago *(G-3658)*
- Atometric Inc..G....... 815 505-2582
  Loves Park *(G-13192)*
- Automatic Production Eqp Inc ....G....... 847 439-1448
  Elk Grove Village *(G-8848)*
- Bavius Technologie Inc ....G....... 847 844-3300
  East Dundee *(G-8188)*
- Belcar Products Inc................................G....... 630 462-1950
  Carol Stream *(G-2946)*
- Belden Machine Corporation ....F....... 708 344-4600
  Broadview *(G-2419)*
- Beverly Shear Mfg Corporation ....G....... 773 233-2063
  Chicago *(G-3877)*
- Bilz Tool Company ....F....... 630 495-3996
  Lombard *(G-13044)*
- Bos Machine Tool Services Inc ....F....... 309 658-2223
  Hillsdale *(G-11321)*
- Bystronic Inc..C....... 847 214-0300
  Hoffman Estates *(G-11410)*
- C D T Manufacturing Inc.........................G....... 847 679-2361
  Skokie *(G-18935)*
- Cavallo Tool Service Inc.........................G....... 630 620-4445
  Addison *(G-64)*
- Cdv Corp ....F....... 815 397-3903
  Rockford *(G-17339)*
- Ceratizit Chicago Holding Inc ....F....... 847 923-8400
  Schaumburg *(G-18469)*
- Ceratizit Chicago Inc ....C....... 847 923-8400
  Schaumburg *(G-18470)*
- Chad Mazeika ....G....... 815 298-8118
  Rockford *(G-17343)*
- Chicago Grinding & Machine Co ....E....... 708 343-4399
  Melrose Park *(G-13843)*
- Circle Cutting Tools Inc..........................G....... 815 398-4153
  Rockford *(G-17350)*
- Custom Cutting Tools Inc.......................G....... 815 986-0320
  Loves Park *(G-13200)*
- Custom Tool Inc ....F....... 217 465-8538
  Paris *(G-16228)*
- Delco West LLC.......................................G....... 309 799-7543
  Milan *(G-14006)*
- Diamond Blast Corporation....................F....... 708 681-2640
  Melrose Park *(G-13850)*
- Diamond Edge Manufacturing................G....... 630 458-1630
  Addison *(G-88)*
- Dmg Charlotte LLC..................................F....... 704 583-1193
  Hoffman Estates *(G-11418)*
- Dmg Mori Usa Inc ....D....... 847 593-5400
  Hoffman Estates *(G-11419)*
- Emhart Teknologies LLC ....F....... 877 364-2781
  Chicago *(G-4498)*
- Engineered Abrasives Inc ....E....... 662 582-4143
  Alsip *(G-445)*
- Engis Corporation....................................C....... 847 808-9400
  Wheeling *(G-20891)*
- Everede Tool Company LLC ....E....... 773 467-4200
  West Chicago *(G-20576)*
- Everede Tool Company LLC ....D....... 623 414-4800
  West Chicago *(G-20575)*
- Express Cutting Tools Inc......................G....... 815 964-0410
  Rockford *(G-17410)*
- Flat-Tech Inc ....C....... 847 364-4333
  Wilmette *(G-21075)*
- Form Relief Tool Co Inc..........................F....... 815 393-4263
  Davis Junction *(G-7423)*
- Graff-Pinkert & Co....................................F....... 708 535-2200
  Oak Forest *(G-15680)*
- Greenlee Tools Inc ....C....... 800 435-0786
  Rockford *(G-17435)*
- Hartland Cutting Tools Inc ....F....... 847 639-9400
  Cary *(G-3166)*
- Hfd Manufacturing Inc ....G....... 847 263-5050
  Waukegan *(G-20446)*
- Hobsource ....G....... 847 229-9120
  Mount Prospect *(G-14533)*
- Holden Industries Inc.............................F....... 847 940-1500
  Deerfield *(G-7616)*

MACHINE TOOLS: Metal Cutting

Company	Section	Phone
Hottinger Bldwin Msrements Inc Champaign *(G-3303)*	E	217 328-5359
Ibanum Manufacturing LLC Rockford *(G-17455)*	G	815 262-5373
Illinois Electro Deburring Co Franklin Park *(G-9961)*	F	847 678-5010
Ingersoll Machine Tools Inc Rockford *(G-17462)*	C	815 987-6000
Ingersoll Prod Systems LLC Rockford *(G-17463)*	D	815 637-8500
J & L Gear Incorporated Villa Park *(G-20151)*	F	630 832-1880
Logan Graphic Products Inc Wauconda *(G-20369)*	D	847 526-5515
Machine Technology Inc Marseilles *(G-13560)*	F	815 795-6818
Magnetrol International Inc Aurora *(G-1001)*		630 723-6600
Manan Tool & Manufacturing Wheeling *(G-20937)*	A	847 637-3333
Master Machine Group Inc Elgin *(G-8650)*	G	847 472-9940
Modern Specialties Company Chicago *(G-5481)*	G	312 648-5800
Nicholas Machine & Tool Inc Rosemont *(G-18038)*		847 298-2035
NNt Enterprises Incorporated Itasca *(G-11712)*	E	630 875-9600
OSG Power Tools Inc Bensenville *(G-1863)*	C	630 561-4008
Peddinghaus Corporation Bradley *(G-2288)*	C	815 937-3800
Pioneer Service Inc Addison *(G-241)*	E	630 628-0249
Ppt Industrial Machines Inc Mount Carmel *(G-14485)*		800 851-3586
Prater Industries Inc Bolingbrook *(G-2228)*	D	630 679-3200
Precision Ctng Tls Svc Mfg Inc Glenview *(G-10601)*	G	847 901-6800
Precision McHned Cmponents Inc Romeoville *(G-17866)*	E	630 759-5555
Precision Tool & Die Company Mount Zion *(G-14649)*	F	217 864-3371
Process Screw Products Inc Shannon *(G-18872)*	E	815 864-2220
Radiac Abrasives Inc Oswego *(G-16024)*		630 898-0315
Ramco Group LLC Crystal Lake *(G-7252)*		847 639-9899
Regal Beloit Corporation Roscoe *(G-17923)*	C	844 527-8392
Reliance Tool & Mfg Co Elgin *(G-8718)*	E	847 695-1235
Reliance Tool & Mfg Co Franklin Park *(G-10035)*		847 455-4350
Roberts Swiss Inc Itasca *(G-11726)*	E	630 467-9100
Roll Rite Inc Davis Junction *(G-7426)*	G	815 645-8600
Rsvp Tooling Inc Joliet *(G-11929)*		815 725-3310
Sacco-Camex Inc Franklin Park *(G-10040)*	G	630 595-8090
Schram Enterprises Inc Melrose Park *(G-13914)*	E	708 345-2252
Serien Manufacturing Inc Woodstock *(G-21431)*		815 337-1447
Service Machine Jobs Rockford *(G-17626)*	G	815 986-3033
Specialty Enterprises Inc Franklin Park *(G-10050)*	E	630 595-7808
Swisstronics Corp Orland Park *(G-15986)*	G	708 403-8877
Synax Inc Buffalo Grove *(G-2612)*	F	224 352-2927
Thread & Gage Co Inc Spring Grove *(G-19302)*	G	815 675-2305
Tiger Tool Inc Glendale Heights *(G-10511)*		888 551-4490
Tooling Solutions Inc Elgin *(G-8756)*		847 472-9940
Tools For Industry Inc Algonquin *(G-388)*	G	847 658-0455
Total Tooling Technology Inc Elk Grove Village *(G-9279)*	F	847 437-5135
Ty Miles Incorporated Westchester *(G-20716)*	E	708 344-5480
Variable Operations Tech Inc Crystal Lake *(G-7288)*	E	815 479-8528
Vaughn & Sons Machine Shop Fairfield *(G-9639)*	G	618 842-9048
We Innovex Inc Northbrook *(G-15500)*	G	847 291-3553
Wec Welding and Machining LLC Lake Bluff *(G-12214)*	G	847 680-8100
West Precision Tool Inc Bensenville *(G-1912)*	F	630 766-8304

MACHINE TOOLS: Metal Forming

Company	Section	Phone
A J Carbide Grinding Skokie *(G-18911)*	G	847 675-5112
Advanced Prototype Molding Palatine *(G-16090)*	G	847 202-4200
Alan Manufacturing Corp Marengo *(G-13478)*	G	815 568-6836
Alco Manufacturing Corp LLC Machesney Park *(G-13325)*	F	815 708-5540
Altman Manufacturing Co Inc Lisle *(G-12862)*	F	630 963-0031
American Machine Tools Inc Chicago *(G-3658)*	G	773 775-6285
Best Brake Die Inc Crestwood *(G-7107)*		708 388-1896
Bohl Machine & Tool Company Milan *(G-14001)*		309 799-5122
Centric Mfg Solutions Inc Chicago *(G-4058)*	G	815 315-9258
Chisholm-Boyd & White Alsip *(G-430)*		708 597-7550
D R Sperry & Co Aurora *(G-1083)*	D	630 892-4361
Dover Europe Inc Downers Grove *(G-7991)*		630 541-1540
Elgalabwater LLC Woodridge *(G-21300)*		630 343-5251
Epcor Industrial Inc Elk Grove Village *(G-8979)*	G	847 545-9212
Formtek Inc Lisle *(G-12891)*	F	630 285-1500
Illinois Tool Works Inc Itasca *(G-11672)*	C	630 595-3500
Infinity Metal Spinning Inc Chicago *(G-4913)*		773 731-4467
Ingenious Concepts Inc Medinah *(G-13814)*		630 539-8059
John J Rickhoff Shtmtl Co Inc Phoenix *(G-16608)*	F	708 331-2970
Komori America Corporation Rolling Meadows *(G-17745)*	D	847 806-9000
Kwm Gutterman Inc Rockdale *(G-17263)*	E	815 725-9205
Littell International Inc Schaumburg *(G-18610)*	E	630 622-4950
Lotus Creative Innovations LLC Compton *(G-6997)*	G	815 440-8999
Madison Capital Partners Corp Chicago *(G-5312)*	G	312 277-0323
Metro Tool Company Skokie *(G-18988)*	G	847 673-6790
Mgb Engineering Company Elk Grove Village *(G-9121)*	E	847 956-7444
Mzm Manufacturing Inc Roscoe *(G-17919)*	G	815 624-8666
Petrak Industries Incorporated Joliet *(G-11914)*	E	815 483-2290
Ppt Industrial Machines Inc Mount Carmel *(G-14485)*	E	800 851-3586
Precision Service Mtr Inc Addison *(G-252)*	F	630 628-9900
Punch Products Manufacturing Chicago *(G-5915)*	E	773 533-2800
Rock Valley Die Sinking Inc Rockford *(G-17584)*	F	815 874-8560
Rsvp Tooling Inc Joliet *(G-11929)*	G	815 725-3310
Sloan Industries Inc Wood Dale *(G-21241)*	E	630 350-1614
Sure-Way Die Designs Inc Westmont *(G-20774)*	F	630 323-0370
Tek-Cast Inc Elgin *(G-8748)*	D	630 422-1458
Versatech LLC Effingham *(G-8428)*	C	217 342-3500
Visimark Inc Franklin Park *(G-10079)*	F	866 344-7721
Wardzala Industries Inc Franklin Park *(G-10083)*	F	847 288-9909
Winchester Interconnect Rugged Broadview *(G-2475)*	G	708 594-5890

MACHINERY & EQPT FINANCE LEASING

Company	Section	Phone
AT&T Teleholdings Inc Chicago *(G-3756)*	F	800 288-2020
Marmon Industrial LLC Chicago *(G-5344)*	G	312 372-9500

MACHINERY & EQPT, AGRICULTURAL, WHOL: Farm Eqpt Parts/Splys

Company	Section	Phone
Shoup Manufacturing Co Inc Kankakee *(G-12001)*	E	815 933-4439

MACHINERY & EQPT, AGRICULTURAL, WHOLESALE: Agricultural, NEC

Company	Section	Phone
Seedburo Equipment Company Des Plaines *(G-7840)*	F	312 738-3700

MACHINERY & EQPT, AGRICULTURAL, WHOLESALE: Dairy

Company	Section	Phone
Gea Farm Technologies Inc Naperville *(G-14833)*	C	630 548-8200

MACHINERY & EQPT, AGRICULTURAL, WHOLESALE: Farm Implements

Company	Section	Phone
Birkeys Farm Store Inc Urbana *(G-19975)*	E	217 337-1772

MACHINERY & EQPT, AGRICULTURAL, WHOLESALE: Landscaping Eqpt

Company	Section	Phone
Corsaw Hardwood Lumber Inc Smithfield *(G-19063)*	F	309 293-2055
Oly Ola Edging Inc Villa Park *(G-20163)*	F	630 833-3033

MACHINERY & EQPT, AGRICULTURAL, WHOLESALE: Lawn

Company	Section	Phone
Siemer Enterprises Inc Teutopolis *(G-19772)*	E	217 857-3171

MACHINERY & EQPT, AGRICULTURAL, WHOLESALE: Lawn & Garden

Company	Section	Phone
Cobraco Manufacturing Inc Lake Zurich *(G-12395)*	E	847 726-5800
Grower Equipment & Supply Co Hainesville *(G-10947)*	F	847 223-3100
Power Equipment Company Cortland *(G-7026)*	E	815 754-4090

MACHINERY & EQPT, AGRICULTURAL, WHOLESALE: Livestock Eqpt

Company	Section	Phone
Gsi Group LLC Paris *(G-16230)*	C	217 463-1612

MACHINERY & EQPT, AGRICULTURAL, WHOLESALE: Tractors

Company	Section	Phone
Woods Equipment Company Oregon *(G-15929)*	D	815 732-2141

MACHINERY & EQPT, INDL, WHOL: Controlling Instruments/Access

Company	Section	Phone
Automax Corporation Woodridge *(G-21277)*	G	630 972-1919
Clarios Calumet City *(G-2773)*	D	708 474-1717
E-Motion LLC Fairbury *(G-9606)*		815 825-4411
Novaspect Inc Schaumburg *(G-18653)*	C	847 956-8020
Pro-Quip Incorporated La Grange *(G-12087)*	F	708 352-5732

MACHINERY & EQPT, INDL, WHOL: Environ Pollution Cntrl, Air

Company	Section	Phone
C P Environmental Inc Romeoville *(G-17801)*	F	630 759-8866
Crawford Heating & Cooling Co Rock Island *(G-17212)*	E	309 794-1000
Enders Process Equipment Corp Glendale Heights *(G-10449)*		630 469-3787

MACHINERY & EQPT, INDL, WHOLESALE: Chemical Process

Benetech Inc .... E 630 844-1300
  Aurora *(G-1063)*
Benetech (taiwan) LLC .... G 630 844-1300
  Aurora *(G-1064)*

MACHINERY & EQPT, INDL, WHOLESALE: Conveyor Systems

Centec Automation Inc .... G 847 791-9430
  Palatine *(G-16098)*
Engineering Products Company .... G 815 436-9055
  Plainfield *(G-16659)*
Entech Fabrications Inc .... G 708 597-5568
  Posen *(G-16794)*
Flsmidth Inc .... G 309 347-3031
  Pekin *(G-16334)*
Franklin Automation Inc .... F 630 466-1900
  Sugar Grove *(G-19645)*
Payson Casters Inc .... C 847 336-5033
  Gurnee *(G-10910)*
Sardee Industries Inc .... G 630 824-4200
  Lisle *(G-12936)*
Siemens Industry Inc .... G 309 664-2460
  Bloomington *(G-2094)*
Visionary Solutions Inc .... G 847 296-9615
  Des Plaines *(G-7865)*

MACHINERY & EQPT, INDL, WHOLESALE: Cranes

Lanco International Inc .... B 708 596-5200
  Hazel Crest *(G-11131)*

MACHINERY & EQPT, INDL, WHOLESALE: Drilling Bits

Bit Brokers International Ltd .... E 618 435-5811
  West Frankfort *(G-20668)*
Rodgers Bill Oil Min Bits Svc .... G 618 299-7771
  West Salem *(G-20688)*
T & T Carbide Inc .... E 618 439-7253
  Logan *(G-13032)*
T & T Distribution Inc .... E 815 223-0715
  Peru *(G-16594)*

MACHINERY & EQPT, INDL, WHOLESALE: Drilling, Exc Bits

Galaxy Industries Inc .... D 847 639-8580
  Cary *(G-3162)*
TT Technologies Inc .... D 630 851-8200
  Aurora *(G-1029)*

MACHINERY & EQPT, INDL, WHOLESALE: Engines & Parts, Diesel

American Diesel Tube Corp .... F 630 628-1830
  Addison *(G-32)*
Area Diesel Service Inc .... E 217 854-2641
  Carlinville *(G-2867)*
Concentric Itasca Inc .... D 630 773-3355
  Itasca *(G-11638)*
Cummins Crosspoint LLC .... G 309 452-4454
  Normal *(G-15201)*
Cummins Npower LLC .... E 708 579-9222
  Hodgkins *(G-11387)*
Du Page Precision Products Co .... D 630 849-2940
  Aurora *(G-954)*
Industrial Welder Rebuilders .... G 708 371-5688
  Alsip *(G-457)*
Midwest Fuel Injction Svc Corp .... F 847 991-7867
  Palatine *(G-16140)*
Yanmar (usa) Inc .... G 847 541-1900
  Buffalo Grove *(G-2624)*

MACHINERY & EQPT, INDL, WHOLESALE: Engines, Gasoline

Kaser Power Equipment Inc .... G 309 289-2176
  Knoxville *(G-12068)*
Owen Walker .... G 217 285-4012
  Pittsfield *(G-16636)*

MACHINERY & EQPT, INDL, WHOLESALE: Engs & Parts, Air-Cooled

Cummins Dist Holdco Inc .... E 309 787-4300
  Rock Island *(G-17213)*

MACHINERY & EQPT, INDL, WHOLESALE: Engs/Transportation Eqpt

Kackert Enterprises Inc .... G 630 898-9339
  Aurora *(G-1120)*

MACHINERY & EQPT, INDL, WHOLESALE: Food Manufacturing

Bc International .... G 847 674-7384
  Skokie *(G-18928)*

MACHINERY & EQPT, INDL, WHOLESALE: Fuel Injection Systems

Caterpillar Inc .... B 815 842-6000
  Pontiac *(G-16767)*

MACHINERY & EQPT, INDL, WHOLESALE: Heat Exchange

Maintenance Inc .... G 708 598-1390
  La Grange *(G-12082)*

MACHINERY & EQPT, INDL, WHOLESALE: Hoists

Handling Systems Intl Inc .... E 708 352-1213
  Mc Cook *(G-13692)*

MACHINERY & EQPT, INDL, WHOLESALE: Hydraulic Systems

Erie Vehicle Company .... F 773 536-6300
  Chicago *(G-4526)*
Flodyne Inc .... G 630 563-3600
  Hanover Park *(G-11004)*
Force America Inc .... F 815 730-3600
  Joliet *(G-11866)*
Geib Industries Inc .... E 847 455-4550
  Bensenville *(G-1809)*
Headco Industries Inc .... F 847 640-6490
  Elk Grove Village *(G-9031)*
Headco Industries Inc .... G 815 729-4016
  Joliet *(G-11875)*
Jrm International Inc .... G 815 282-9330
  Loves Park *(G-13227)*
Master Mechanic Mfg Inc .... G 847 573-3812
  Mundelein *(G-14714)*
Morrell Incorporated .... F 630 858-4600
  Glendale Heights *(G-10477)*
Tetra Pak Inc .... D 847 955-6000
  Vernon Hills *(G-20103)*

MACHINERY & EQPT, INDL, WHOLESALE: Indl Machine Parts

Industrial Phrm Resources Inc .... F 630 823-4700
  Bartlett *(G-1290)*
Meadoweld Machine Inc .... G 815 623-3939
  South Beloit *(G-19102)*
Rjg Enterprises Ltd .... G 847 752-2065
  Grayslake *(G-10798)*

MACHINERY & EQPT, INDL, WHOLESALE: Instruments & Cntrl Eqpt

Process Technologies Group .... G 630 393-4777
  Warrenville *(G-20250)*
S-P-D Incorporated .... G 847 882-9820
  Palatine *(G-16156)*
Worth-Pfaff Innovations Inc .... G 847 940-9305
  Deerfield *(G-7661)*

MACHINERY & EQPT, INDL, WHOLESALE: Lift Trucks & Parts

Bolzoni Auramo Inc .... E 708 957-8809
  Homewood *(G-11488)*
Komatsu Forklift USA LLC .... E 847 437-5800
  Rolling Meadows *(G-17744)*
Manitowoc Lifts and Mfg LLC .... G 815 748-9500
  Dekalb *(G-7690)*
Systems Equipment Services .... G 708 535-1273
  Oak Forest *(G-15689)*
Tvh Parts Co .... E 847 223-1000
  Grayslake *(G-10803)*
Unicarriers Americas Corp .... G 800 871-5438
  Marengo *(G-13496)*

MACHINERY & EQPT, INDL, WHOLESALE: Machine Tools & Access

Abbott Machine Co .... F 618 465-1898
  Alton *(G-540)*
Automatic Production Eqp Inc .... G 847 439-1448
  Elk Grove Village *(G-8848)*
Daito USA Inc .... G 847 437-6788
  Elk Grove Village *(G-8937)*
Erowa Technology Inc .... F 847 290-0295
  Arlington Heights *(G-733)*
Fibro Inc .... F 815 229-1300
  Rockford *(G-17415)*
Kwalyti Tling McHy Rblding Inc .... F 630 761-8040
  Batavia *(G-1391)*
Line Craft Tool Company Inc .... C 630 932-1182
  Lombard *(G-13096)*
Machine Technology Inc .... F 815 795-6818
  Marseilles *(G-13560)*
Madden Ventures Inc .... G 847 487-0644
  Mundelein *(G-14712)*
Rockform Tooling & Machinery .... G 815 398-7650
  Rockford *(G-17611)*
Rsvp Tooling Inc .... G 815 725-3310
  Joliet *(G-11929)*
Spencer and Krahn Mch Tl Sls .... G 815 282-3300
  Rockford *(G-17639)*

MACHINERY & EQPT, INDL, WHOLESALE: Machine Tools & Metalwork

Accushim Inc .... G 708 442-6448
  Lyons *(G-13300)*
Belcar Products Inc .... G 630 462-1950
  Carol Stream *(G-2946)*
Flat-Tech Inc .... G 847 364-4333
  Wilmette *(G-21075)*
J Schneerberger Corp .... G 847 888-3498
  Elgin *(G-8630)*
Jtekt Toyoda Americas Corp .... C 847 253-0340
  Arlington Heights *(G-764)*
Lmt Usa Inc .... G 630 969-5412
  Waukegan *(G-20462)*
Pillarhouse USA Inc .... F 847 593-9080
  Elk Grove Village *(G-9179)*
Powernail Company .... E 800 323-1653
  Lake Zurich *(G-12445)*

MACHINERY & EQPT, INDL, WHOLESALE: Measure/Test, Electric

Dickson/Unigage Inc .... E 630 543-3747
  Addison *(G-92)*
Heidenhain Corporation .... D 847 490-1191
  Schaumburg *(G-18545)*
Heidenhain Holding Inc .... G 716 661-1700
  Schaumburg *(G-18546)*
O E M Marketing Inc .... F 847 985-9490
  Schaumburg *(G-18655)*

MACHINERY & EQPT, INDL, WHOLESALE: Metal Refining

American Chemical & Eqp Inc .... G 815 675-9199
  Northlake *(G-15541)*
Amic Global Inc .... G 847 600-3590
  Buffalo Grove *(G-2512)*
Chemical Processing & Acc .... G 847 793-2387
  Lincolnshire *(G-12750)*

MACHINERY & EQPT, INDL, WHOLESALE: Packaging

Birnberg Machinery Inc .... G 847 673-5242
  Deerfield *(G-7597)*
Cama USA Inc .... G 847 607-8797
  Buffalo Grove *(G-2523)*
Fromm Airpad Inc .... F 630 393-9790
  Warrenville *(G-20236)*
Quad-Illinois Inc .... F 847 836-1115
  Elgin *(G-8706)*
Sun Centre Usa Inc .... F 224 699-9058
  Crystal Lake *(G-7271)*

MACHINERY & EQPT, INDL, WHOLESALE: Packaging

Weary & Baity Inc .... G 312 943-6197
Chicago (G-6594)

MACHINERY & EQPT, INDL, WHOLESALE: Paint Spray

Blastline USA Inc .... G 630 871-0147
Carol Stream (G-2951)

MACHINERY & EQPT, INDL, WHOLESALE: Petroleum Industry

American Welding & Gas Inc .... E 630 527-2550
Stone Park (G-19551)
R L Hoener Co .... E 217 223-2190
Quincy (G-16936)

MACHINERY & EQPT, INDL, WHOLESALE: Plastic Prdts Machinery

Nissei America Inc .... G 847 228-5000
Elk Grove Village (G-9149)
Universal Holdings Inc .... F 224 353-6198
Hoffman Estates (G-11470)

MACHINERY & EQPT, INDL, WHOLESALE: Pneumatic Tools

Don Johns Inc .... E 630 454-4700
Batavia (G-1374)
SMC Corporation of America .... E 630 449-0600
Aurora (G-1017)

MACHINERY & EQPT, INDL, WHOLESALE: Processing & Packaging

Stickon Adhesive Inds Inc .... G 847 593-5959
Wauconda (G-20391)
Tramco Pump Co .... E 312 243-5800
Romeoville (G-17881)
Trane Technologies Company LLC ...... E 630 530-3800
Elmhurst (G-9436)

MACHINERY & EQPT, INDL, WHOLESALE: Robots

Innovative Automation .... G 708 418-8720
Lansing (G-12499)

MACHINERY & EQPT, INDL, WHOLESALE: Safety Eqpt

American Labelmark Company .... C 773 478-0900
Chicago (G-3656)
Fisher Scientific Company LLC .... C 412 490-8300
Hanover Park (G-11003)
Guardian Equipment Inc .... E 312 447-8100
Chicago (G-4747)
John Thomas Inc .... E 815 288-2343
Dixon (G-7902)
Midwest Water Group Inc .... E 866 526-6558
Crystal Lake (G-7230)
National Safety Council .... B 630 285-1121
Itasca (G-11707)
North American Safety Pdts Inc .... E 815 469-1144
Mokena (G-14099)

MACHINERY & EQPT, INDL, WHOLESALE: Sewing

Union Special LLC .... C 847 669-5101
Huntley (G-11572)

MACHINERY & EQPT, INDL, WHOLESALE: Tanks, Storage

Evergreen Tank Solutions Inc .... G 708 235-0487
Monee (G-14198)

MACHINERY & EQPT, INDL, WHOLESALE: Tapping Attachments

Tek Pak Inc .... D 630 406-0560
Batavia (G-1429)

MACHINERY & EQPT, INDL, WHOLESALE: Tool & Die Makers

Patkus Machine Co .... G 815 398-7818
Rockford (G-17548)

Progrssive Cmponents Intl Corp .... D 847 487-1000
Wauconda (G-20385)
Tritech International LLC .... G 847 888-0333
Elgin (G-8761)

MACHINERY & EQPT, INDL, WHOLESALE: Water Pumps

Semler Industries Inc .... E 847 671-5650
Franklin Park (G-10046)
Village of Burnham .... G 708 868-0661
Chicago (G-6552)

MACHINERY & EQPT, WHOLESALE: Blades, Graders, Scrapers, Etc

Nordic Auto Plow LLC .... G 815 353-8267
West Chicago (G-20623)

MACHINERY & EQPT, WHOLESALE: Concrete Processing

CCS Contractor Eqp & Sup Inc .... E 630 393-9020
Naperville (G-14793)

MACHINERY & EQPT, WHOLESALE: Construction, General

Elston Materials LLC .... G 773 235-3100
Chicago (G-4490)
Global Track Property USA Inc .... G 630 213-6863
Bartlett (G-1283)
Grover Welding Company .... G 847 966-3119
Skokie (G-18961)
Jcb Inc .... G 912 704-2995
Aurora (G-990)
Lanigan Holdings LLC .... F 708 596-5200
Hazel Crest (G-11132)
Lee Jensen Sales Co Inc .... G 815 459-0929
Crystal Lake (G-7220)
Otak International Inc .... G 630 373-9229
Melrose Park (G-13900)
Rahn Equipment Company .... G 217 431-1232
Danville (G-7376)
USA Hoist Company Inc .... E 815 740-1890
Crest Hill (G-7100)

MACHINERY & EQPT, WHOLESALE: Contractors Materials

Carroll Distrg & Cnstr Sup Inc .... G 630 243-0272
Lemont (G-12558)
Carroll Distrg & Cnstr Sup Inc .... G 815 941-1548
Morris (G-14297)
Carroll Distrg & Cnstr Sup Inc .... G 309 449-6044
Hopedale (G-11516)
Carroll Distrg & Cnstr Sup Inc .... F 630 369-6520
Naperville (G-14791)
Outdoor Power Inc .... F 217 228-9890
Quincy (G-16921)

MACHINERY & EQPT, WHOLESALE: Masonry

Galaxy Industries Inc .... D 847 639-8580
Cary (G-3162)

MACHINERY & EQPT, WHOLESALE: Oil Field Eqpt

Vaughn & Sons Machine Shop .... G 618 842-9048
Fairfield (G-9639)

MACHINERY & EQPT: Electroplating

Hardwood Line Manufacturing Co ...... E 773 463-2600
Chicago (G-4780)
Rapid Electroplating Process .... G 708 344-2504
Melrose Park (G-13907)
Sterling Systems Sales Corp .... G 630 584-3580
Saint Charles (G-18278)

MACHINERY & EQPT: Farm

A P Livestock Division G S I .... G 217 226-4449
Assumption (G-887)
AGCO Corporation .... G 630 293-9905
West Chicago (G-20532)
AGCO Corporation .... E 630 406-3248
Batavia (G-1341)
Agri-Fab Inc .... F 217 875-7051
Decatur (G-7435)

Alvarez & Marsal Inc .... E 312 601-4220
Chicago (G-3639)
Aqua Control Inc .... E 815 664-4900
Spring Valley (G-19307)
B J Fehr Machine Co .... G 309 923-8691
Roanoke (G-17099)
B T Brown Manufacturing .... G 815 947-3633
Kent (G-12017)
Birkeys Farm Store Inc .... E 217 337-1772
Urbana (G-19975)
Calmer Corn Heads Inc .... E 309 629-9000
Lynn Center (G-13288)
Caterpillar Brazil LLC .... A 309 675-1000
Peoria (G-16400)
Christopher Concrete Products .... G 618 724-2951
Buckner (G-2499)
Circle K Industries Inc .... E 847 949-0363
Mundelein (G-14677)
Cline Concrete Products .... G 217 283-5012
Hoopeston (G-11505)
Cnh America LLC .... F 309 965-2217
Goodfield (G-10671)
Cnh Industrial America LLC .... G 847 263-5793
Waukegan (G-20429)
Cnh Industrial America LLC .... G 309 965-2233
Goodfield (G-10672)
Cnh Industrial America LLC .... C 309 965-2217
Goodfield (G-10673)
Cnh Industrial America LLC .... C 630 887-2233
Burr Ridge (G-2664)
Cnh Industrial Capitl Amer LLC .... E 630 887-2233
Burr Ridge (G-2665)
Crane Quality Equipment LLC .... G 815 258-5375
Clifton (G-6914)
Cutting Specialists Inc .... E 731 352-5351
Edwardsville (G-8355)
D & B Fabricators & Distrs .... F 630 325-3811
Lemont (G-12562)
David Taylor .... E 217 222-6480
Quincy (G-16875)
Dawn Equipment Company Inc .... F 815 899-8000
Sycamore (G-19705)
Deere & Company .... D 309 765-8275
Moline (G-14139)
Demuth Steel Products Inc .... F 815 997-1116
Rockford (G-17373)
Dsi Inc .... G 309 965-5110
Goodfield (G-10675)
Dura Feed Inc .... G 815 395-1115
Loves Park (G-13208)
Farmweld Inc .... E 217 857-6423
Teutopolis (G-19769)
Fehr Cab Interiors .... G 815 692-3355
Fairbury (G-9607)
Genwoods Holdco LLC .... A 815 732-2141
Oregon (G-15921)
Globetec Midwest Partners LLC .... G 847 608-9300
South Elgin (G-19147)
H W Hostetler & Sons .... G 815 438-7816
Deer Grove (G-7577)
Hipro Manufacturing Inc .... G 815 432-5271
Watseka (G-20306)
Hypermax Engineering Inc .... F 847 428-5655
Gilberts (G-10359)
J & J Equipment Inc .... G 309 449-5442
Hopedale (G-11517)
Jdis Dealers .... F 309 765-8000
East Moline (G-8230)
Kongskilde Industries Inc .... F 309 452-3300
Normal (G-15207)
Korhumel Inc .... G 847 330-0335
Schaumburg (G-18590)
Ksem Inc .... G 618 656-5388
Edwardsville (G-8367)
Ksi Conveyor Inc .... D 815 457-2403
Cissna Park (G-6897)
Kunz Engineering Inc .... G 815 539-6954
Mendota (G-13945)
Licon Inc .... G 618 485-2222
Ashley (G-885)
Lmt Inc .... F 217 568-8265
Galva (G-10235)
Manitou Americas Inc .... G 262 334-9461
Belvidere (G-1684)
McLaughlin Body Co .... D 309 762-7755
Moline (G-14159)
Meteer Inc .... G 217 636-7280
Athens (G-898)
Midwest Bio-Systems Inc .... F 815 438-7200
Tampico (G-19745)

PRODUCT SECTION

MACHINERY, MAILING: Postage Meters

MTS Jerseyville Inc..................................G....... 618 639-2583
  Jerseyville (G-11794)
Newton Implement Partnership.............E....... 618 783-8716
  Newton (G-15087)
Niffty AG Inc...G....... 309 343-7447
  Galesburg (G-10214)
Ogden Metalworks Inc.............................F....... 217 582-2552
  Ogden (G-15837)
P & H Manufacturing Co............................D....... 217 774-2123
  Shelbyville (G-18882)
Quality Trucking Inc.................................G....... 309 949-2021
  Colona (G-6977)
R K Products Inc......................................G....... 309 792-1927
  East Moline (G-8239)
Rhinoag Inc..E....... 217 784-4261
  Gibson City (G-10343)
Seedburo Equipment Company ....F....... 312 738-3700
  Des Plaines (G-7840)
Shoup Manufacturing Co Inc...................E....... 815 933-4439
  Kankakee (G-12001)
Sopher Design & Manufacturing..............G....... 309 699-6419
  East Peoria (G-8291)
Speeco Incorporated..............................C....... 303 279-5544
  Oregon (G-15927)
Star Forge Inc...E....... 815 235-7750
  Freeport (G-10144)
Straightline AG Inc..................................G....... 217 963-1270
  Harristown (G-11033)
Tank Wind-Down Corp.............................D....... 815 756-1551
  Dekalb (G-7707)
Trusty Warns Inc.....................................E....... 630 766-9015
  Wood Dale (G-21253)
Weaver Equipment LLC..........................G....... 618 833-5521
  Buncombe (G-2631)
Western Ill Agri-Systems Inc....................G....... 217 746-2144
  Burnside (G-2646)
Whalen Manufacturing Company............G....... 309 836-1438
  Macomb (G-13402)

MACHINERY & EQPT: Gas Producers, Generators/Other Rltd Eqpt

Cleavenger Associates Inc ....G....... 630 221-0007
  Winfield (G-21109)

MACHINERY & EQPT: Liquid Automation

Bowl Doctors Inc.....................................G....... 815 282-6009
  Machesney Park (G-13330)
Component Products Inc ....E....... 847 301-1000
  Elmhurst (G-9352)
DTS America Inc ....G....... 847 783-0401
  East Dundee (G-8193)
Fill-Weigh Inc..G....... 815 254-4704
  Plainfield (G-16665)
Ima Automation Usa Inc ....D....... 815 885-8800
  Loves Park (G-13217)
Online Inc...F....... 815 363-8008
  McHenry (G-13774)
Progressive Recovery Inc......................D....... 618 286-5000
  Dupo (G-8142)
Technics Fabrication Inc........................F....... 630 938-4709
  Bolingbrook (G-2249)

MACHINERY & EQPT: Metal Finishing, Plating Etc

American Metal Coil Works Inc ....G....... 708 562-2645
  Northlake (G-15542)
Amiberica Inc...E....... 773 247-3600
  Chicago (G-3679)
Brown Metal Products Ltd.....................G....... 309 936-7384
  Atkinson (G-901)
Crw Finishing Inc...................................E....... 630 495-4994
  Addison (G-84)
Desco Inc...G....... 847 439-2130
  Elk Grove Village (G-8945)
Fanuc America Corporation...................E....... 847 898-5000
  Hoffman Estates (G-11423)
Meminger Metal Finishing Inc................F....... 309 582-3363
  Aledo (G-358)
Morrell Incorporated..............................F....... 630 858-4600
  Glendale Heights (G-10477)
ROC Industries Inc.................................G....... 618 277-6044
  Belleville (G-1589)
Stutz Company......................................F....... 773 287-1068
  Chicago (G-6259)

MACHINERY & EQPT: Petroleum Refinery

Leonard Associates Inc.........................E....... 815 226-9609
  Rockford (G-17494)
Unitel Technologies Inc.........................F....... 847 297-2265
  Mount Prospect (G-14579)

MACHINERY & EQPT: Vibratory Parts Handling Eqpt

Masterfeed Corporation........................G....... 630 879-1133
  Batavia (G-1392)

MACHINERY BASES

G & M Fabricating Inc.............................G....... 815 282-1744
  Roscoe (G-17907)
Hadady Corporation..............................E....... 219 322-7417
  South Holland (G-19218)
JMS Metals Inc......................................G....... 618 443-1000
  Sparta (G-19255)
Roll Roll Met Fabricators Inc..................E....... 773 434-1315
  Chicago (G-6053)
Tc Industries Inc....................................C....... 815 459-2401
  Crystal Lake (G-7276)
Terra Cotta Holdings Co........................E....... 815 459-2400
  Crystal Lake (G-7281)
Tu-Star Manufacturing Co Inc................G....... 815 338-5760
  Woodstock (G-21441)

MACHINERY CLEANING SVCS

GC Laser Systems Inc...........................G....... 844 532-1064
  Forest Park (G-9719)

MACHINERY, COMMERCIAL LAUNDRY & Drycleaning: Ironers

Cmv Sharper Finish Inc.........................E....... 773 276-4800
  Chicago (G-4185)

MACHINERY, COMMERCIAL LAUNDRY: Extractors

Extractor Corporation............................F....... 847 742-3532
  South Elgin (G-19144)

MACHINERY, COMMERCIAL LAUNDRY: Washing, Incl Coin-Operated

B-Clean Laundromat Inc........................G....... 678 983-5492
  Chicago (G-3809)

MACHINERY, EQPT & SUPPLIES: Parking Facility

Federal Signal Corporation....................D....... 630 954-2000
  Oak Brook (G-15618)
Parking Systems Inc..............................G....... 847 891-3819
  Schaumburg (G-18666)

MACHINERY, FOOD PRDTS: Beverage

Cornelius Renew Inc..............................F....... 309 734-9505
  Monmouth (G-14215)
Entech Fabrications Inc........................G....... 708 597-5568
  Posen (G-16794)
IMI McR Inc..E....... 309 734-6282
  Monmouth (G-14218)
Rodger Howard......................................G....... 773 481-6990
  Chicago (G-6049)

MACHINERY, FOOD PRDTS: Confectionery

Savage Bros Company...........................D....... 847 981-3000
  Elk Grove Village (G-9230)

MACHINERY, FOOD PRDTS: Cracker Making

F & S Engraving Inc...............................E....... 847 870-8400
  Mount Prospect (G-14527)

MACHINERY, FOOD PRDTS: Cutting, Chopping, Grinding, Mixing

Houpt Revolving Cutters Inc..................G....... 618 395-1913
  Olney (G-15865)
Mww Food Processing USA LLC.............G....... 773 478-9700
  Elk Grove Village (G-9141)

MACHINERY, FOOD PRDTS: Dies, Biscuit Cutting

Weidenmiller Co......................................F....... 630 250-2500
  Itasca (G-11753)

MACHINERY, FOOD PRDTS: Food Processing, Smokers

Bbq Smokewagon Inc.............................G....... 309 271-7002
  East Peoria (G-8252)
Home Fires Inc......................................G....... 815 967-4100
  Rockford (G-17452)
R S Cryo Equipment Inc.........................G....... 815 468-6115
  Manteno (G-13455)
Titan Injection Parts & Svc.....................G....... 630 882-8455
  Yorkville (G-21503)

MACHINERY, FOOD PRDTS: Grinders, Commercial

Bauermeister Inc...................................G....... 901 363-0921
  Vernon Hills (G-20043)
Modern Process Equipment Inc ....E....... 773 254-3929
  Chicago (G-5480)
Prater Industries Inc..............................D....... 630 679-3200
  Bolingbrook (G-2228)
Wallace/Haskin Corp..............................G....... 630 789-2882
  Downers Grove (G-8105)

MACHINERY, FOOD PRDTS: Ovens, Bakery

Marshall Middleby Inc............................C....... 847 741-3300
  Elgin (G-8649)
Middleby Corporation............................E....... 847 741-3300
  Elgin (G-8660)
Middleby Corporation............................E....... 847 741-3300
  Elgin (G-8661)
Rational Cooking Systems Inc...............D....... 224 366-3500
  Rolling Meadows (G-17769)

MACHINERY, FOOD PRDTS: Processing, Fish & Shellfish

Gregor Jonsson Associates Inc ....E....... 847 247-4200
  Lake Forest (G-12253)

MACHINERY, FOOD PRDTS: Roasting, Coffee, Peanut, Etc.

Rancilio North America Inc ....E....... 630 427-1703
  Woodridge (G-21336)

MACHINERY, FOOD PRDTS: Sausage Stuffers

Gilberts Craft Sausages LLC..................G....... 630 923-8969
  Wheaton (G-20800)

MACHINERY, LUBRICATION: Automatic

Concep Machine Co Inc........................E....... 847 498-9740
  Northbrook (G-15364)

MACHINERY, MAILING: Canceling

Taloc Usa Inc...G....... 847 665-8222
  Libertyville (G-12714)

MACHINERY, MAILING: Mailing

Direct Mail Equipment Services.............G....... 815 485-7010
  New Lenox (G-15030)
Fluence Automation LLC.......................C....... 847 423-7400
  Arlington Heights (G-737)
Multimail Solutions................................G....... 847 516-9977
  Cary (G-3181)
Pitney Bowes Inc...................................E....... 773 755-5808
  Chicago (G-5813)
Pitney Bowes Inc...................................E....... 800 784-4224
  Itasca (G-11719)

MACHINERY, MAILING: Postage Meters

Pitney Bowes Inc...................................E....... 312 209-2216
  Schaumburg (G-18674)
Pitney Bowes Inc...................................D....... 630 435-7500
  Lisle (G-12927)
Singer Data Products Inc......................G....... 630 860-6500
  Bensenville (G-1893)

Employee Codes: A=Over 500 employees, B=251-500
C=101-250, D=51-100, E=20-50, F=10-19, G=3-9

2020 Harris Illinois Industrial Directory

1503

MACHINERY, METALWORKING: Assembly, Including Robotic

- Accelrted Mch Design Engrg LLC .... E 815 316-6381
  Rockford *(G-17290)*
- Active Automation Inc .... F 847 427-8100
  Elk Grove Village *(G-8806)*
- Advanced Robotics Research .... G 630 544-0040
  Naperville *(G-14766)*
- Advantage Machining Inc .... E 630 897-1220
  Aurora *(G-1042)*
- Amber Engineering and Mfg Co .... D 847 595-6966
  Elk Grove Village *(G-8819)*
- Art Technologies Inc .... G 773 557-3896
  Bensenville *(G-1747)*
- Ats Sortimat USA LLC .... D 847 925-1234
  Rolling Meadows *(G-17713)*
- Bartell Corporation .... G 847 854-3232
  Algonquin *(G-367)*
- Connections .... F 217 553-7920
  Springfield *(G-19353)*
- Custom Assembly Solutions Inc .... F 847 224-5800
  Schaumburg *(G-18501)*
- Hilscher North America Inc .... F 630 505-5301
  Lisle *(G-12898)*
- Jerhen Industries Inc .... D 815 397-0400
  Rockford *(G-17473)*
- Modineer P-K Tool LLC .... E 773 235-4700
  Chicago *(G-5483)*
- Performance Design Inc .... G 847 719-1535
  Lake Zurich *(G-12443)*
- Qc Service Associates Inc .... E 309 755-6785
  East Moline *(G-8237)*
- R+d Custom Automation Inc .... E 847 395-3330
  Lake Villa *(G-12365)*
- Sigmatron International Inc .... E 847 586-5200
  Elgin *(G-8730)*
- Sigmatron International Inc .... E 847 956-8000
  Elk Grove Village *(G-9238)*
- Sortimat Technology LP .... E 847 925-1234
  Rolling Meadows *(G-17776)*
- Tellenar Inc .... F 815 356-8044
  Crystal Lake *(G-7280)*
- Tool Rite Industries Inc .... G 630 406-6161
  Batavia *(G-1431)*
- Wes-Tech Automtn Solutions LLC .... D 847 541-5070
  Buffalo Grove *(G-2621)*

MACHINERY, METALWORKING: Coil Winding, For Springs

- Jardis Industries Inc .... F 630 773-5600
  Itasca *(G-11681)*

MACHINERY, METALWORKING: Coiling

- Remington Industries Inc .... F 815 385-1987
  Johnsburg *(G-11809)*

MACHINERY, METALWORKING: Cutting & Slitting

- Navillus Woodworks LLC .... G 312 375-2680
  Chicago *(G-5556)*

MACHINERY, METALWORKING: Rotary Slitters, Metalworking

- Braner Usa Inc .... E 847 671-6210
  Schiller Park *(G-18789)*

MACHINERY, OFFICE: Embossing, Store Or Office

- Your Supply Depot Limited .... G 815 568-4115
  Marengo *(G-13497)*

MACHINERY, OFFICE: Perforators

- American Perforator Company .... G 815 469-4300
  Frankfort *(G-9766)*
- Cummins - Allison Corp .... D 847 299-9550
  Mount Prospect *(G-14521)*
- Cummins - Allison Corp .... C 847 299-9550
  Mount Prospect *(G-14522)*
- Cummins - Allison Corp .... F 630 833-2285
  Elmhurst *(G-9357)*

MACHINERY, OFFICE: Shorthand

- Stenograph LLC .... D 630 532-5100
  Elmhurst *(G-9429)*

MACHINERY, OFFICE: Time Clocks &Time Recording Devices

- SBA Wireless Inc .... E 847 215-8720
  Buffalo Grove *(G-2595)*

MACHINERY, PACKAGING: Canning, Food

- Econopin .... G 708 599-5002
  Bridgeview *(G-2343)*

MACHINERY, PACKAGING: Carton Packing

- Cartpac Inc .... E 630 283-8979
  Carol Stream *(G-2956)*

MACHINERY, PACKAGING: Packing & Wrapping

- Jescorp Inc .... D 847 378-1200
  Elk Grove Village *(G-9068)*
- John R Nalbach Engrg Co Inc .... E 708 579-9100
  Countryside *(G-7062)*
- Point Five Packaging LLC .... G 847 531-4787
  Schiller Park *(G-18833)*
- Signode Industrial Group LLC .... E 800 628-6787
  Glenview *(G-10619)*
- Sjd Direct Midwest LLC .... G 618 931-2151
  Edwardsville *(G-8375)*

MACHINERY, PACKAGING: Vacuum

- All-Vac Industries Inc .... F 847 675-2290
  Skokie *(G-18915)*
- Henkelman Inc .... G 331 979-2013
  Elmhurst *(G-9371)*
- Middleby Packg Solutions LLC .... E 847 741-3500
  Elgin *(G-8662)*
- Robert L Murphy .... G 708 424-0277
  Evergreen Park *(G-9598)*

MACHINERY, PACKAGING: Wrapping

- Arpac LLC .... C 847 678-9034
  Schiller Park *(G-18787)*

MACHINERY, PAPER INDUSTRY: Coating & Finishing

- Platit Inc .... G 847 680-5270
  Libertyville *(G-12697)*

MACHINERY, PAPER INDUSTRY: Converting, Die Cutting & Stampng

- Midwest Gold Stampers Inc .... F 773 775-5253
  Chicago *(G-5442)*
- United Gasket Corporation .... D 708 656-3700
  Cicero *(G-6885)*

MACHINERY, PAPER INDUSTRY: Cutting

- Rosenthal Manufacturing Co Inc .... E 847 714-0404
  Northbrook *(G-15475)*

MACHINERY, PAPER INDUSTRY: Pulp Mill

- Gt Flow Technology Inc .... G 815 636-9982
  Roscoe *(G-17908)*

MACHINERY, PRINTING TRADES: Bookbinding Machinery

- Klai-Co Idntification Pdts Inc .... E 847 573-0375
  Lake Forest *(G-12270)*
- Smart Inc .... G 847 464-4160
  Hampshire *(G-10988)*
- Southern Illinois McHy Co Inc .... D 217 868-5431
  Shumway *(G-18906)*
- Stolp Gore Company .... G 630 904-5180
  Plainfield *(G-16717)*

MACHINERY, PRINTING TRADES: Copy Holders

- Zebra Outlet .... F 312 416-1518
  Chicago *(G-6710)*

MACHINERY, PRINTING TRADES: Electrotyping

- Vm Electronics LLC .... G 847 663-9310
  Chicago *(G-6565)*

MACHINERY, PRINTING TRADES: Plates

- Aaxis Engravers Inc .... G 224 629-4045
  Bensenville *(G-1721)*
- Anderson & Vreeland-Illinois .... F 847 255-2110
  Arlington Heights *(G-693)*
- Banner Moulded Products .... E 708 452-0033
  River Grove *(G-17057)*
- Bisco Intl Inc .... G 708 544-6308
  Hillside *(G-11331)*
- Brahman Spirit Tribe .... F 773 957-2828
  Chicago *(G-3942)*
- Certus Industries N Amer LLC .... G 847 217-2537
  Crystal Lake *(G-7178)*
- Color Smiths Inc .... E 708 562-0061
  Elmhurst *(G-9349)*
- Luttrell Engraving Inc .... E 708 489-3800
  Alsip *(G-470)*
- Oec Graphics-Chicago LLC .... E 630 455-6700
  Willowbrook *(G-21056)*
- Plate and Pre-Press Management .... G 847 352-0462
  Schaumburg *(G-18676)*
- Premium Converting LLC .... E 708 510-1842
  Chicago *(G-5864)*
- Sharper Image Engravers Inc .... E 630 403-1600
  Lombard *(G-13129)*

MACHINERY, PRINTING TRADES: Presses, Envelope

- Paw Office Machines Inc .... G 815 363-9780
  McHenry *(G-13777)*

MACHINERY, PRINTING TRADES: Presses, Gravure

- Martin Automatic Inc .... C 815 654-4800
  Rockford *(G-17505)*

MACHINERY, PRINTING TRADES: Printing Trade Parts & Attchts

- C & C Printing Controls Inc .... G 630 810-0484
  Downers Grove *(G-7961)*
- Tel-Comm Incorporated .... E 847 593-8480
  Sycamore *(G-19734)*

MACHINERY, SERVICING: Coin-Operated, Exc Dry Clean & Laundry

- Butterfield Cleaners .... G 847 816-7060
  Mundelein *(G-14669)*
- Regency Hand Laundry .... G 773 871-3950
  Chicago *(G-6001)*

MACHINERY, SEWING: Bag Seaming & Closing

- Carlson Sti Inc .... G 630 232-2460
  Elgin *(G-8533)*
- Duravant LLC .... F 630 635-3910
  Downers Grove *(G-7995)*

MACHINERY, SEWING: Sewing & Hat & Zipper Making

- SMS Group Inc .... G 708 479-1333
  Mokena *(G-14115)*

MACHINERY, TEXTILE: Creels

- Manufacturers Alliance Corp .... F 847 696-1600
  Villa Park *(G-20158)*

MACHINERY, TEXTILE: Dyeing

- Innovo Corp .... F 847 616-0063
  Elk Grove Village *(G-9054)*

MACHINERY, TEXTILE: Embroidery

- Barudan America Inc .... G 815 227-1359
  Rockford *(G-17315)*
- Initial Impressions Inc .... G 630 208-9399
  Geneva *(G-10281)*

PRODUCT SECTION — MACHINERY: Construction

Peerless .... G 773 294-2667
 Chicago *(G-5782)*

MACHINERY, TEXTILE: Frames, Double & Twisting

Graphic Screen Fashion Ltd .... F 847 695-5566
 South Elgin *(G-19149)*

MACHINERY, TEXTILE: Knot Tying

Forest Lee LLC .... G 312 379-0032
 Chicago *(G-4618)*

MACHINERY, TEXTILE: Printing

M & R Printing Equipment Inc .... B 630 858-6101
 Roselle *(G-17966)*
M&R Holdings Inc .... C 630 858-6101
 Roselle *(G-17967)*

MACHINERY, TEXTILE: Silk Screens

David H Pool .... G 847 695-5007
 Elgin *(G-8563)*
Modern Graphic Systems Inc .... G 773 476-6898
 Chicago *(G-5477)*
On Time Decorations Inc .... F 708 357-6072
 Cicero *(G-6869)*
Signature Label of Illinois .... G 618 283-5145
 Vandalia *(G-20024)*
Summit Graphics Inc .... F 309 799-5100
 Moline *(G-14180)*

MACHINERY, TEXTILE: Spinning

Natural Fiber Welding Inc .... G 309 685-3591
 Peoria *(G-16482)*

MACHINERY, TEXTILE: Yarn Texturizing

Cargill Incorporated .... F 217 872-7653
 Decatur *(G-7469)*

MACHINERY, WOODWORKING: Cabinet Makers'

Bona Fide Corp .... G 847 970-8693
 Wheeling *(G-20862)*
Bw Exhibits .... G 847 697-9224
 Gilberts *(G-10352)*
Yazdan Essie .... G 847 675-7916
 Lincolnwood *(G-12852)*

MACHINERY, WOODWORKING: Furniture Makers

Coalesse .... F 312 622-6269
 Chicago *(G-4187)*
Constrction Sltons Chicago Inc .... G 630 834-1929
 Villa Park *(G-20140)*
Little Creek Woodworking .... G 217 543-2815
 Arthur *(G-866)*

MACHINERY, WOODWORKING: Sanding, Exc Portable Floor Sanders

Crl Industries Inc .... G 847 940-3550
 Deerfield *(G-7605)*
Lc Holdings of Delaware Inc .... G 847 940-3550
 Deerfield *(G-7629)*
Sand-Rite Manufacturing Co .... G 312 997-2200
 Melrose Park *(G-13912)*

MACHINERY, WOODWORKING: Saws, Power, Bench & Table

White Oak Technology .... G 309 228-4201
 Germantown Hills *(G-10334)*

MACHINERY/EQPT, INDL, WHOL: Cleaning, High Press, Sand/Steam

Fna Ip Holdings Inc .... D 847 348-1500
 Elk Grove Village *(G-9001)*
M & M Pump Co .... G 217 935-2517
 Clinton *(G-6926)*
Therma-Kleen Inc .... G 630 718-0212
 Plainfield *(G-16723)*

MACHINERY/EQPT, INDL, WHOL: Machinist Precision Measrng Tool

Sparx EDM Inc .... G 847 722-7577
 Streamwood *(G-19595)*

MACHINERY/EQPT, INDL, WHOL: Tool Holder, Incl Chuck/Turret

Kenyeri Consulting LLC .... G 630 920-3497
 Downers Grove *(G-8039)*

MACHINERY: Ammunition & Explosives Loading

Black Market Parts Inc .... G 630 562-9400
 West Chicago *(G-20553)*
Top Brass Inc .... G 719 539-7242
 Granite City *(G-10744)*
Top Brass LLC .... F 800 836-4683
 Granite City *(G-10745)*

MACHINERY: Assembly, Exc Metalworking

Apf US Inc 217 304-0027
 Danville *(G-7320)*
Ats Sortimat USA LLC .... D 847 925-1234
 Rolling Meadows *(G-17713)*
Automatic Feeder Company Inc .... F 847 534-2300
 Schaumburg *(G-18449)*
Automation Systems Inc .... E 847 671-9515
 Melrose Park *(G-13828)*
Barrington Automation Ltd .... E 847 458-0900
 Lake In The Hills *(G-12329)*
Boley Tool & Machine Works Inc ...... C 309 694-2722
 East Peoria *(G-8254)*
Centec Automation Inc .... G 847 791-9430
 Palatine *(G-16098)*
Concept and Design Services .... G 847 259-1675
 Mount Prospect *(G-14519)*
CTS Advanced Materials LLC .... E 630 577-8800
 Lisle *(G-12879)*
Diamond Machine Werks Inc .... E 847 437-0665
 Arlington Heights *(G-728)*
Eberle Manufacturing Company .... F 847 215-0100
 Wheeling *(G-20885)*
G & W Technical Corporation .... G 847 487-0990
 Island Lake *(G-11607)*
Leading Americas Inc .... G 815 568-2199
 Hampshire *(G-10976)*
Numerical Control Incorporated .... G 708 389-8140
 Alsip *(G-486)*
Pro Techmation Inc .... G 815 459-5909
 Crystal Lake *(G-7248)*
Trueline Inc .... E 309 378-2571
 Downs *(G-8113)*
Western Slate Company .... D 847 683-4400
 Hampshire *(G-10990)*

MACHINERY: Automobile Garage, Frame Straighteners

American Industrial Direct LLC .... E 800 382-1200
 Elgin *(G-8507)*
McLaughlin Body Co .... D 309 762-7755
 Moline *(G-14159)*
Rapid Line Industries Inc .... F 815 727-4362
 Joliet *(G-11922)*

MACHINERY: Automotive Maintenance

Atlas Maintenance Service Inc .... G 773 486-3386
 Chicago *(G-3764)*
Borgwarner Inc .... F 708 731-4540
 Melrose Park *(G-13833)*
Pro Tools & Equipment Inc .... G 847 838-6666
 Antioch *(G-631)*

MACHINERY: Automotive Related

Ace Machine & Tool Inc .... G 815 793-5077
 Cortland *(G-7015)*
Art Technologies Inc .... G 773 557-3896
 Bensenville *(G-1747)*
Automation Specialist Svcs LLC .... F 847 792-1692
 Hampshire *(G-10962)*
Guzzler Manufacturing Inc .... C 815 672-3171
 Streator *(G-19610)*
Hackett Precision Company Inc .... E 615 227-3136
 Chicago *(G-4764)*

Haussermann Usa LLC .... G 847 272-9850
 Northbrook *(G-15398)*
Heico Holding Inc .... E 630 353-5100
 Warrenville *(G-20238)*
I T R Inc .... E 217 245-4478
 Jacksonville *(G-11768)*
Kps Capital Partners LP .... B 630 972-7000
 Bolingbrook *(G-2203)*
Multitech Industries Inc .... E 630 784-9200
 Carol Stream *(G-3035)*
Multitech McHned Cmponents LLC .. E 630 949-8200
 Carol Stream *(G-3036)*
Nal Worldwide Holdings Inc .... B 630 261-3100
 Addison *(G-226)*
Pettibone LLC .... F 630 353-5000
 Warrenville *(G-20244)*
Pollmann North America Inc .... E 815 834-1122
 Romeoville *(G-17864)*
Rcc Conveyors Inc .... G 224 338-8841
 Volo *(G-20205)*
SBE Varvit Usa LLC .... G 331 205-7000
 Aurora *(G-1154)*
SMC Corporation of America .... E 630 449-0600
 Aurora *(G-1017)*
T & S Business Group LLC .... F 815 432-7084
 Watseka *(G-20319)*
Waupaca Foundry Inc .... C 217 347-0600
 Effingham *(G-8430)*

MACHINERY: Banking

Talaris Inc .... C 630 577-1000
 Lisle *(G-12948)*

MACHINERY: Binding

Acco Brands USA LLC .... E 708 280-4702
 Addison *(G-14)*
Deluxe Stitcher Company Inc .... D 847 455-4400
 Franklin Park *(G-9931)*
Identification Products Mfg Co .... G 847 367-6452
 Lake Forest *(G-12264)*
Klai-Co Idntification Pdts Inc .... E 847 573-0375
 Lake Forest *(G-12270)*
Laminting Bnding Solutions Inc .... G 847 573-0375
 Lake Forest *(G-12271)*
Lane Industries Inc .... F 847 498-6650
 Northbrook *(G-15417)*
Plastic Binding Laminating Inc .... G 847 573-0375
 Lake Forest *(G-12291)*
Sws Industries Inc .... E 904 482-0091
 Woodstock *(G-21438)*

MACHINERY: Blasting, Electrical

Beyond Components West Inc .... G 847 465-0480
 Wheeling *(G-20858)*
Engineered Abrasives Inc .... E 662 582-4143
 Alsip *(G-445)*

MACHINERY: Bottling & Canning

Midwest Mobile Canning LLC .... G 815 861-4515
 Crystal Lake *(G-7229)*

MACHINERY: Brewery & Malting

Whiner Brewery LLC .... G 312 810-2271
 Chicago *(G-6616)*

MACHINERY: Broom Making

Carlson Tool & Machine Company ... F 630 232-2460
 Elgin *(G-8534)*

MACHINERY: Cement Making

Eirich Machines Inc .... D 847 336-2444
 Gurnee *(G-10875)*

MACHINERY: Concrete Prdts

Saint-Gobain Abrasives Inc .... C 630 868-8060
 Carol Stream *(G-3063)*
Substrate Technology Inc .... F 815 941-4800
 Morris *(G-14330)*

MACHINERY: Construction

APL Logistics Americas Ltd .... F 630 783-0200
 Woodridge *(G-21275)*
Associated Professionals .... G 847 931-0095
 Elgin *(G-8516)*

Bigfoot Construction Eqp Inc ....G.... 888 743-7320
Woodstock *(G-21365)*

Blount International Inc ....G.... 800 319-6637
Oregon *(G-15914)*

Brunner & Lay Inc ....C.... 847 678-3232
Bensenville *(G-1758)*

Caterpillar Forest Pdts Inc ....E.... 309 675-1000
Peoria *(G-16401)*

Caterpillar Foundation ....G.... 309 675-4232
Peoria *(G-16402)*

Caterpillar Global Mining LLC ....E.... 618 378-3441
Norris City *(G-15247)*

Caterpillar Inc ....G.... 309 578-2185
Mossville *(G-14452)*

Caterpillar Inc ....A.... 224 551-4000
Deerfield *(G-7600)*

Caterpillar Inc ....B.... 815 729-5511
Joliet *(G-11838)*

Caterpillar Inc ....B.... 309 675-1000
Peoria *(G-16404)*

Caterpillar Inc ....D.... 309 675-2545
East Peoria *(G-8249)*

Caterpillar Inc ....D.... 309 578-6118
Mossville *(G-14453)*

Caterpillar Inc ....E.... 309 675-5681
Peoria *(G-16405)*

Caterpillar Inc ....A.... 309 633-8788
Mapleton *(G-13468)*

Caterpillar Inc ....B.... 309 578-2086
Washington *(G-20268)*

Caterpillar Inc ....F.... 309 675-8327
Edwards *(G-8337)*

Caterpillar Inc ....D.... 304 327-7793
Morton *(G-14355)*

Caterpillar Inc ....B.... 309 266-4294
Mossville *(G-14454)*

Caterpillar Inc ....B.... 903 712-4505
Mossville *(G-14455)*

Caterpillar Inc ....D.... 309 495-9216
East Peoria *(G-8257)*

Caterpillar Inc ....F.... 309 578-4643
Peoria *(G-16406)*

Caterpillar Inc ....B.... 888 614-4328
Peoria *(G-16407)*

Caterpillar Inc ....G.... 309 675-1000
Peoria *(G-16408)*

Caterpillar Inc ....G.... 217 475-4322
Decatur *(G-7474)*

Caterpillar Inc ....A.... 309 578-2473
Mossville *(G-14456)*

Caterpillar Inc ....B.... 309 675-1000
Mossville *(G-14457)*

Caterpillar Inc ....E.... 309 675-3183
East Peoria *(G-8258)*

Caterpillar Inc ....E.... 309 675-1000
Peoria *(G-16409)*

Caterpillar Inc ....B.... 309 675-1000
Peoria *(G-16410)*

Caterpillar Inc ....B.... 217 255-8500
Champaign *(G-3276)*

Caterpillar Intl Lsg LLC ....G.... 309 675-1000
Peoria *(G-16412)*

Caterpillar Luxembourg LLC ....G.... 309 675-1000
Peoria *(G-16413)*

Caterpillar Power Systems Inc ....G.... 309 675-1000
Peoria *(G-16414)*

Caterpillar World Trading Corp ....E.... 309 675-1000
Peoria *(G-16415)*

CPM Co Inc ....E.... 815 385-7700
McHenry *(G-13731)*

CTS Advanced Materials LLC ....E.... 630 577-8800
Lisle *(G-12879)*

D & B Fabricators & Distrs ....F.... 630 325-3811
Lemont *(G-12562)*

Deere & Company ....A.... 309 765-8000
Moline *(G-14138)*

Division 5 Metals Inc ....G.... 815 901-5001
Kirkland *(G-12059)*

Domor Equipment LLC ....E.... 309 467-3483
Eureka *(G-9481)*

Dover Europe Inc ....G.... 630 541-1540
Downers Grove *(G-7991)*

Eirich Machines Inc ....D.... 847 336-2444
Gurnee *(G-10875)*

Gemtar Inc ....G.... 618 548-1353
Salem *(G-18340)*

Heico Companies LLC ....F.... 312 419-8220
Chicago *(G-4798)*

Imh Fabrication Inc ....F.... 815 537-2381
Prophetstown *(G-16833)*

Interstate Mechanical Inc ....G.... 312 961-9291
Chicago *(G-4958)*

John Deere AG Holdings Inc ....G.... 309 765-8000
Moline *(G-14152)*

Jrb Attachments LLC ....G.... 319 378-3696
Oak Brook *(G-15628)*

Koflo Corporation ....F.... 847 516-3700
Cary *(G-3174)*

Komatsu America Corp ....B.... 847 437-5800
Chicago *(G-5120)*

Lanco International Inc ....B.... 708 596-5200
Hazel Crest *(G-11131)*

Lmt Inc ....F.... 217 568-8265
Galva *(G-10235)*

Mi-Jack Products Inc ....B.... 708 596-5200
Hazel Crest *(G-11133)*

Midwest Cnstr Svcs Inc Peoria ....F.... 309 697-1000
Bartonville *(G-1335)*

Midwest Mixing Inc ....G.... 708 422-8100
Chicago Ridge *(G-6803)*

Mj Snyder Ironworks Inc ....G.... 217 826-6440
Marshall *(G-13575)*

Multi-State Indus Contrs Inc ....G.... 217 423-4100
Decatur *(G-7531)*

North Point Investments Inc ....G.... 312 977-4386
Chicago *(G-5620)*

Paladin Brands International H ....G.... 319 378-3696
Oak Brook *(G-15655)*

Prella Technologies Inc ....G.... 630 400-0626
Huntley *(G-11560)*

Rhino Tool Company ....F.... 309 853-5555
Kewanee *(G-12040)*

Ringwood Company ....D.... 708 458-6000
Bedford Park *(G-1499)*

Roadsafe Traffic Systems Inc ....G.... 217 629-7139
Riverton *(G-17089)*

Robbins Construction Sup LLC ....G.... 708 574-5944
Hazel Crest *(G-11137)*

Soosan USA Inc ....G.... 224 653-8916
Schaumburg *(G-18715)*

Spreader Inc ....G.... 217 568-7219
Gifford *(G-10348)*

Technical Services Intl Inc ....G.... 708 596-5200
Hazel Crest *(G-11138)*

Terramac LLC ....G.... 630 365-4800
Elburn *(G-8475)*

Track Works LLC ....G.... 618 781-2375
Highland *(G-11242)*

Tsm North America Inc ....G.... 815 372-1600
Schaumburg *(G-18760)*

US Shredder Castings Group Inc ....G.... 309 359-3151
Peoria *(G-16542)*

W R Grace & Co-Conn ....F.... 708 458-9700
Chicago *(G-6577)*

West Side Tractor Sales Co ....E.... 815 961-3160
Rockford *(G-17680)*

MACHINERY: Cryogenic, Industrial

Cryogenic Systems Equipment ....E.... 708 385-4216
Blue Island *(G-2116)*

MACHINERY: Custom

Acme Industries Inc ....C.... 847 296-3346
Elk Grove Village *(G-8804)*

Air Caster LLC ....E.... 217 877-1237
Decatur *(G-7436)*

All Cut Inc ....G.... 630 910-6505
Darien *(G-7400)*

Argo Manufacturing Co ....F.... 630 377-1750
Wasco *(G-20260)*

Ats Sortimat USA LLC ....D.... 847 925-1234
Rolling Meadows *(G-17713)*

Aura Systems Inc ....E.... 217 423-4100
Decatur *(G-7461)*

Automated Design Corp ....G.... 630 783-1150
Romeoville *(G-17797)*

Automated Mfg Solutions Inc ....F.... 815 477-2428
Crystal Lake *(G-7165)*

Axis Manufacturing Inc ....F.... 847 350-0200
Elk Grove Village *(G-8852)*

Banner Service Corporation ....C.... 630 653-7500
Carol Stream *(G-2944)*

Bbs Automation Chicago Inc ....C.... 630 351-3000
Bartlett *(G-1268)*

Big 3 Precision Products Inc ....C.... 618 533-3251
Centralia *(G-3222)*

C N C Central Inc ....G.... 630 595-1453
Bensenville *(G-1760)*

Concepts and Controls Inc ....F.... 847 478-9296
Buffalo Grove *(G-2527)*

Daley Automation LLC ....G.... 630 384-9900
Naperville *(G-14812)*

Datum Machine Works Inc ....F.... 815 877-8502
Rockford *(G-17369)*

David L Knoche ....G.... 618 466-7120
Godfrey *(G-10651)*

Elastec Inc ....C.... 618 382-2525
Carmi *(G-2904)*

Elburn Metal Stamping Inc ....E.... 630 365-2500
Elburn *(G-8452)*

Excel Machine & Tool ....G.... 815 467-1177
Channahon *(G-3383)*

F N Smith Corporation ....E.... 815 732-2171
Oregon *(G-15919)*

Folk Race Cars ....G.... 815 629-2418
Durand *(G-8151)*

Fox Machine & Tool Inc ....G.... 847 357-1845
Elk Grove Village *(G-9006)*

Franklin Automation Inc ....F.... 630 466-1900
Sugar Grove *(G-19645)*

General Machine and Tool Inc ....G.... 815 727-4342
Lockport *(G-12996)*

Hess Machine Inc ....G.... 618 887-4444
Marine *(G-13498)*

Jbw Machining Inc ....E.... 847 451-0276
Franklin Park *(G-9974)*

Johnson Pattern & Mch Works ....E.... 815 433-2775
Ottawa *(G-16057)*

Kopis Machine Co Inc ....E.... 630 543-4138
Addison *(G-175)*

Livingston Products Inc ....F.... 847 808-0900
Waukegan *(G-20460)*

Meta TEC of Illinois Inc ....D.... 309 246-2960
Lacon *(G-12132)*

Midaco Corporation ....E.... 847 593-8420
Elk Grove Village *(G-9123)*

Orat Inc ....G.... 630 567-6728
Saint Charles *(G-18238)*

Pacific Bearing Corp ....C.... 815 389-5600
Roscoe *(G-17921)*

Park Engineering Inc ....E.... 847 455-1424
Franklin Park *(G-10013)*

Parsons Company Inc ....B.... 309 467-9100
Roanoke *(G-17104)*

Patlin Enterprises Inc ....F.... 815 675-6606
Spring Grove *(G-19292)*

Pgi Mfg LLC ....D.... 800 821-3475
Rockford *(G-17552)*

Pmb Industries Inc ....G.... 708 442-4515
La Grange *(G-12086)*

R G Hanson Company Inc ....F.... 309 661-9200
Bloomington *(G-2087)*

Richland County Machine Inc ....G.... 618 392-2892
Olney *(G-15886)*

Rj Link International Inc ....F.... 815 874-8110
Rockford *(G-17576)*

Rockford Linear Actuation ....G.... 815 986-4400
Rockford *(G-17597)*

Romed Industries Corporation ....G.... 847 362-3900
Lake Zurich *(G-12452)*

Sandbagger LLC ....D.... 630 876-2400
Elmhurst *(G-9422)*

SEC Design Technologies Inc ....F.... 847 680-0439
Libertyville *(G-12704)*

Service Machine Jobs ....G.... 815 986-3033
Rockford *(G-17626)*

Sst Forming Roll Inc ....G.... 847 215-6812
Buffalo Grove *(G-2608)*

Taylor Design Inc ....G.... 815 389-3991
Roscoe *(G-17936)*

Terracycle Regulated Waste LLC ....E.... 800 909-9709
Lisle *(G-12950)*

Tower Tool & Engineering Inc ....F.... 815 654-1115
Machesney Park *(G-13378)*

Triple Edge Manufacturing Inc ....G.... 847 468-9156
South Elgin *(G-19178)*

Tsd Manufacturing Co Inc ....F.... 630 238-8750
Elk Grove Village *(G-9288)*

USA Industrial Export Corp ....G.... 312 391-5552
Northbrook *(G-15497)*

Whale Manufacturing Inc ....G.... 847 357-9192
Lombard *(G-13155)*

X-Tech Innovations Inc ....G.... 815 962-4127
Rockford *(G-17691)*

Z-Tech Inc ....G.... 815 335-7395
Winnebago *(G-21122)*

MACHINERY: Deburring

Crw Finishing Inc ....E.... 630 495-4994
Addison *(G-84)*

PRODUCT SECTION

MACHINERY: Mining (continued on right)

Giant Finishing Inc .... G 708 343-6900
　Addison **(G-140)**
Precise Lapping Grinding Corp .... F 708 615-0240
　Melrose Park **(G-13904)**
Redin Parts Inc .... G 815 398-1010
　Rockford **(G-17569)**
Robert Bosch LLC .... B 917 421-7209
　Broadview **(G-2466)**
Ultramatic Equipment Co .... E 630 543-4565
　Addison **(G-322)**

MACHINERY: Die Casting

Crd Enterprises Inc .... G 847 438-4299
　Lake Zurich **(G-12398)**
Die Cast Machinery LLC .... F 847 360-9170
　Waukegan **(G-20438)**
DJB Corporation .... G 815 469-7533
　Frankfort **(G-9786)**
Kaufman-Worthen Machinery Inc .... G 847 360-9170
　Waukegan **(G-20454)**
Precision Entps Fndry Mch Inc .... G 815 797-1000
　Somonauk **(G-19073)**

MACHINERY: Drill Presses

Midwest Machine Tool Inc .... G 815 427-8665
　Saint Anne **(G-18136)**

MACHINERY: Electrical Discharge Erosion

CTS Advanced Materials LLC .... E 630 577-8800
　Lisle **(G-12879)**
Edmpartscom Inc .... G 630 427-1603
　Lombard **(G-13072)**
J Francis & Assoc .... G 309 697-5931
　Bartonville **(G-1333)**

MACHINERY: Electronic Component Making

Altran Magnetics LLC .... G 815 632-3150
　Sterling **(G-19497)**
CIC North America Inc .... F 847 873-0860
　Rolling Meadows **(G-17721)**
Etel Inc .... G 847 519-3380
　Schaumburg **(G-18524)**
Felix Partners LLC .... G 847 648-8449
　Rolling Meadows **(G-17732)**
Renu Electronics Private Ltd .... G 630 879-8412
　Batavia **(G-1410)**
Rex Morioka .... G 847 651-9400
　Schiller Park **(G-18839)**
Srmd Solutions LLC .... G 217 925-5773
　Dieterich **(G-7879)**

MACHINERY: Electronic Teaching Aids

Spartanics Ltd .... E 847 394-5700
　Rolling Meadows **(G-17777)**

MACHINERY: Extruding

Lens Lenticlear Lenticular .... F 630 467-0900
　Elk Grove Village **(G-9093)**

MACHINERY: Gear Cutting & Finishing

Bourn & Koch Inc .... D 815 965-4013
　Rockford **(G-17328)**
Modern Gear & Machine Inc .... F 630 350-9173
　Bensenville **(G-1854)**
Sterling Gear Inc .... F 815 438-4327
　Deer Grove **(G-7578)**

MACHINERY: General, Industrial, NEC

Aberdon Enterprises .... F 847 228-1300
　Elk Grove Village **(G-8794)**
Dtc Products Inc .... G 630 513-3323
　Saint Charles **(G-18188)**
Rotospray Mfg Inc .... G 708 478-3307
　Mokena **(G-14113)**

MACHINERY: Glassmaking

Bystronic Inc .... C 847 214-0300
　Hoffman Estates **(G-11410)**
Bystronic Mfg Americas LLC .... G 847 214-0300
　Hoffman Estates **(G-11411)**

MACHINERY: Grinding

Blackhawk Industrial Dist Inc .... F 773 736-9600
　Carol Stream **(G-2950)**
Genesis Duragrind Inc .... G 815 625-6500
　Sterling **(G-19512)**
Hardinge Grinding Group Inc .... E 847 888-0148
　Elgin **(G-8606)**
J Schneerberger Corp .... G 847 888-3498
　Elgin **(G-8630)**
Jtekt Toyoda Americas Corp .... G 847 253-0340
　Arlington Heights **(G-763)**
Jtekt Toyoda Americas Corp .... C 847 253-0340
　Arlington Heights **(G-764)**
Kmp Tool Grinding Inc .... G 847 205-9640
　Northbrook **(G-15413)**
Prosco Inc .... G 847 336-1323
　Gurnee **(G-10917)**
Spencer and Krahn Mch Tl Sls .... G 815 282-3300
　Rockford **(G-17639)**

MACHINERY: Ice Cream

HC Duke & Son LLC .... C 309 755-4553
　East Moline **(G-8228)**
Taylor Coml Foodservice Inc .... F 815 624-8333
　Rockton **(G-17703)**
Taylor Coml Foodservice Inc .... A 815 624-8333
　Rockton **(G-17704)**

MACHINERY: Ice Making

Scotsman Group Inc .... D 847 215-4500
　Vernon Hills **(G-20092)**

MACHINERY: Industrial, NEC

H&S Machine & Tools Inc .... G 618 451-0164
　Granite City **(G-10712)**
Pro-Beam USA Inc .... G 630 327-6909
　Plainfield **(G-16708)**
RMH Enterprises .... G 630 525-5552
　Wheaton **(G-20819)**
Titus Tool Company Inc .... G 847 243-8801
　Franklin Park **(G-10062)**

MACHINERY: Kilns

Bailey Business Group .... G 618 548-3566
　Salem **(G-18330)**
Yer Kiln Me LLC .... G 309 606-9007
　Wyoming **(G-21464)**

MACHINERY: Knitting

Initially Ewe .... G 708 246-7777
　Western Springs **(G-20722)**

MACHINERY: Labeling

Bevwrap LLC .... G 773 580-5434
　Elk Grove Village **(G-8866)**
Mii Inc .... F 630 879-3000
　Batavia **(G-1395)**

MACHINERY: Lapping

John Crane Inc .... E 815 459-0420
　Crystal Lake **(G-7214)**
Micro Lapping & Grinding Co .... E 847 455-5446
　Franklin Park **(G-9997)**

MACHINERY: Metalworking

Arcam Cad To Metal Inc .... G 630 357-5700
　Naperville **(G-14774)**
Automation Systems Inc .... E 847 671-9515
　Melrose Park **(G-13828)**
Bavius Technologie Inc .... G 847 844-3300
　East Dundee **(G-8188)**
Bear Machine Tool & Die Inc .... G 815 932-4204
　Bradley **(G-2277)**
Beverly Shear Mfg Corporation .... G 773 233-2063
　Chicago **(G-3877)**
Black Bros Co .... D 815 539-7451
　Mendota **(G-13938)**
Burns Machine Company .... E 815 434-3131
　Ottawa **(G-16044)**
C E R Machining & Tooling Ltd .... G 708 442-9614
　Lyons **(G-13305)**
Crl Industries Inc .... G 847 940-3550
　Deerfield **(G-7605)**
Darda Enterprises Inc .... F 847 270-0410
　Palatine **(G-16109)**
Deluxe Stitcher Company Inc .... D 847 455-4400
　Franklin Park **(G-9931)**
Dmtg North America LLC .... G 815 637-8500
　Rockford **(G-17383)**

MACHINERY: Mining

Dooling Machine Products Inc .... G 618 254-0724
　Hartford **(G-11034)**
Engineered Abrasives Inc .... E 662 582-4143
　Alsip **(G-445)**
Falcon Technologies Inc .... G 847 550-1866
　Lake Zurich **(G-12410)**
Gerhard Designing & Mfg Inc .... E 708 599-4664
　Bridgeview **(G-2349)**
GMC Technologies Inc .... E 847 426-8618
　East Dundee **(G-8197)**
Greenlee Tools Inc .... C 800 435-0786
　Rockford **(G-17435)**
Hansel Walter J & Assoc Inc .... G 815 678-6065
　Richmond **(G-17014)**
Illinois Tool Works Inc .... D 618 997-1716
　Marion **(G-13518)**
Junker Inc .... G 630 231-3770
　West Chicago **(G-20605)**
Kormex Metal Craft Inc .... E 630 953-8856
　Lombard **(G-13093)**
Lane Tool & Mfg Co Inc .... E 847 622-1506
　South Elgin **(G-19166)**
Lc Holdings of Delaware Inc .... G 847 940-3550
　Deerfield **(G-7629)**
Leggett & Platt Incorporated .... D 847 768-6139
　Des Plaines **(G-7798)**
Lipscomb Engineering Inc .... G 630 231-3833
　West Chicago **(G-20608)**
Littell LLC .... E 630 916-6662
　Schaumburg **(G-18609)**
Littell International Inc .... E 630 622-4950
　Schaumburg **(G-18610)**
Magnum Steel Works Inc .... D 618 244-5190
　Mount Vernon **(G-14622)**
Master Machine Craft Inc .... G 815 874-3078
　Rockford **(G-17507)**
Master Manufacturing Co .... F 630 833-7060
　Villa Park **(G-20159)**
Meadoweld Machine Inc .... G 815 623-3939
　South Beloit **(G-19102)**
Medford Aero Arms LLC .... G 773 961-7686
　Chicago **(G-5383)**
Mfw Services Inc .... G 708 522-5879
　South Holland **(G-19232)**
North America O M C G Inc .... G 630 860-1016
　Bensenville **(G-1858)**
Omiotek Coil Spring Co .... D 630 495-4056
　Lombard **(G-13113)**
Precision Tool & Die Company .... F 217 864-3371
　Mount Zion **(G-14649)**
Prototype & Production Co .... E 847 419-1553
　Wheeling **(G-20967)**
Red Bud Industries Inc .... C 618 282-3801
　Red Bud **(G-17000)**
Robert Brysiewicz Incorporated .... G 630 289-0903
　Bartlett **(G-1304)**
Schmid Tool & Engineering Corp .... E 630 333-1733
　Villa Park **(G-20171)**
T & K Tool & Manufacturing Co .... G 815 338-0954
　Woodstock **(G-21439)**
Titan Tool Company Inc .... G 847 671-0045
　Franklin Park **(G-10061)**
Ty Miles Incorporated .... E 708 344-5480
　Westchester **(G-20716)**
Ultramatic Equipment Co .... E 630 543-4565
　Addison **(G-322)**
Variable Operations Tech Inc .... E 815 479-8528
　Crystal Lake **(G-7288)**
Vindee Industries Inc .... G 815 469-3300
　Frankfort **(G-9850)**

MACHINERY: Milling

Extrude Hone LLC .... E 847 669-5355
　Huntley **(G-11536)**
Kpi Machining Inc .... G 815 496-2246
　Sheridan **(G-18890)**
Mid-West Millwork Wholesale .... G 618 407-5940
　Mascoutah **(G-13603)**
United Tool and Engineering Co .... D 815 389-3021
　South Beloit **(G-19118)**

MACHINERY: Mining

Caterpillar Globl Min Amer LLC .... D 618 982-9000
　Carrier Mills **(G-3124)**
Dry Systems Technologies LLC .... E 630 427-2051
　Woodridge **(G-21296)**
Dry Systems Technologies LLC .... F 618 658-3000
　Vienna **(G-20117)**
Elgin Equipment Group LLC .... G 630 434-7200
　Downers Grove **(G-7997)**

Employee Codes: A=Over 500 employees, B=251-500
C=101-250, D=51-100, E=20-50, F=10-19, G=3-9

Elgin National Industries Inc F 630 434-7200
Downers Grove (G-7998)
Freedom Material Resources Inc D 618 937-6415
West Frankfort (G-20672)
G&D Integrated Services Inc E 309 284-6700
Morton (G-14362)
GE Fairchild Mining Equipment D 618 559-3216
Du Quoin (G-8121)
Gundlach Equipment Corporation D 618 233-7208
Belleville (G-1554)
Komatsu America Corp B 847 437-5800
Chicago (G-5120)
Lashcon Inc G 217 742-3186
Winchester (G-21106)
Logan Actuator Co G 815 943-9500
Harvard (G-11059)
Martin Engineering Company C 309 852-2384
Neponset (G-15018)
Profile Screens Incorporated G 309 543-2082
Havana (G-11120)
Roe Machine Inc E 618 983-5524
West Frankfort (G-20681)
Sollami Company E 618 988-1521
Herrin (G-11179)
Terrasource Global Corporation D 618 641-6985
Belleville (G-1597)
Townley Engrg & Mfg Co Inc F 618 273-8271
Eldorado (G-8484)
Viking Mining LLC E 314 932-6140
Macedonia (G-13318)

MACHINERY: Optical Lens

Vst America Inc G 847 952-3800
Arlington Heights (G-829)

MACHINERY: Ozone

Ozonology Inc G 847 998-8808
Northfield (G-15527)

MACHINERY: Packaging

Algus Packaging Inc D 815 756-1881
Dekalb (G-7665)
Alps G 847 437-0665
Arlington Heights (G-688)
American Packaging McHy Inc E 815 337-8580
Woodstock (G-21358)
Ats Sortimat USA LLC D 847 925-1234
Rolling Meadows (G-17713)
Automtic Lquid Pckg Sltons LLC E 847 372-3336
Arlington Heights (G-699)
Barrington Packaging Systems G 847 382-8063
Barrington (G-1215)
Base 2 Marketing and Supply G 847 516-0012
Cary (G-3149)
Birnberg Machinery Inc G 847 673-5242
Deerfield (G-7597)
Bms Manufacturing Company Inc E 309 787-3158
Milan (G-14000)
Bprex Healthcare Packaging Inc D 800 537-0178
Buffalo Grove (G-2519)
Burghof Engineering & Mfg Co E 847 634-0737
Lincolnshire (G-12747)
C N C Central Inc G 630 595-1453
Bensenville (G-1760)
Cama USA Inc G 847 607-8797
Buffalo Grove (G-2523)
Competitive Edge Opportunities G 815 981-4060
Island Lake (G-11605)
Cvp Systems LLC D 630 852-1190
Elgin (G-8561)
David S Smith Hldings Amer Inc F 630 296-2000
Romeoville (G-17813)
Dover Europe Inc G 630 541-1540
Downers Grove (G-7991)
Dover Prtg Identification Inc D 630 541-1540
Downers Grove (G-7992)
Dromont Corporation G 404 615-2336
Palatine (G-16114)
Duravant G 630 635-3910
Downers Grove (G-7994)
Duravant LLC F 630 635-3910
Downers Grove (G-7995)
Eoe Inc F 847 550-1665
Lake Zurich (G-12408)
Fgwa G 630 759-6800
Romeoville (G-17822)
Fromm Airpad Inc F 630 393-9790
Warrenville (G-20236)
Fuji Impulse American Corp G 847 236-9190
Deerfield (G-7612)
Gama Electronics Inc F 815 356-9600
Woodstock (G-21391)
Hearthside USA B 630 845-9400
Bolingbrook (G-2184)
Illinois Tool Works Inc E 847 215-8925
Buffalo Grove (G-2548)
Illinois Tool Works Inc E 217 345-2166
Itasca (G-11673)
Illinois Tool Works Inc D 618 997-1716
Marion (G-13518)
Integrated Packg & Fastener D 847 439-5730
Elk Grove Village (G-9055)
Jon Cagle G 618 559-3578
Carterville (G-3132)
Libco Industries Inc F 815 623-7677
Roscoe (G-17912)
Mamata Enterprises Inc G 941 205-0227
Montgomery (G-14260)
Marsh Shipping Supply Co LLC F 618 343-1006
Collinsville (G-6969)
Martin Automatic Inc C 815 654-4800
Rockford (G-17505)
Mc Brady Engineering Inc F 815 744-8900
Rockdale (G-17267)
Midwest Fillers G 309 567-2957
Havana (G-11118)
Mssc LLC G 618 343-1006
Collinsville (G-6971)
Nafm Llc G 513 504-4333
Libertyville (G-12687)
Nortech Packaging LLC D 847 884-1805
Schaumburg (G-18651)
Oden Corp G 630 416-4543
Naperville (G-14888)
Park Lawn Association Inc F 708 425-7377
Oak Lawn (G-15731)
Pioneer Container McHy Inc G 618 533-7833
Centralia (G-3245)
PMI Cartoning Inc D 847 437-1427
Elk Grove Village (G-9181)
Pre Pack Machinery Inc G 217 352-1010
Champaign (G-3338)
Prototype Equipment Corp D 847 596-9000
Waukegan (G-20484)
Purchasing Services Ltd Inc E 618 566-8100
Mascoutah (G-13606)
Q Products G 815 498-6356
Sandwich (G-18382)
R P Grollman Co Inc G 847 607-0294
Highland Park (G-11293)
Robert Bosch LLC B 917 421-7209
Broadview (G-2466)
Rollstock Inc G 708 579-3700
Countryside (G-7068)
Rosenthal Manufacturing Co Inc E 847 714-0404
Northbrook (G-15475)
S G Acquisition Inc F 815 624-6501
South Beloit (G-19113)
Sardee Industries Inc G 630 824-4200
Lisle (G-12936)
Serac Inc E 630 510-9343
Carol Stream (G-3068)
Signode F 800 228-4744
Glenview (G-10616)
Signode Industrial Group LLC E 800 862-7997
Glenview (G-10617)
Signode Industrial Group LLC E 815 939-6192
Kankakee (G-12002)
Signode Supply Corporation C 708 458-7320
Bridgeview (G-2387)
Small Different Better Inc G 224 302-5163
Round Lake Park (G-18098)
Suburban Machine Corporation E 847 808-9095
Wheeling (G-20992)
Sun Centre Usa Inc F 224 699-9058
Crystal Lake (G-7271)
Taisei Lamick USA Inc F 847 258-3283
Elk Grove Village (G-9264)
Taurus 80 LLC G 704 927-2793
Rockford (G-17653)
Tegrant Alloyd Brands Inc B 815 756-8451
Dekalb (G-7708)
Terco Inc E 630 894-8828
Bloomingdale (G-2016)
Tetra Pak Inc D 847 955-6000
Vernon Hills (G-20103)
Tishma Technology LLC F 847 884-1805
Schaumburg (G-18749)
Triangle Technologies Inc G 630 736-3318
Streamwood (G-19599)
Ultra Packaging Inc G 630 595-9820
Bensenville (G-1905)
Unique Blister Company F 630 289-1232
Bartlett (G-1319)
Weigh Right Automatic Scale Co G 815 726-4626
Joliet (G-11944)
Weiler Engineering Inc D 847 697-4900
Elgin (G-8778)
Winpak Portion Packaging Inc D 708 753-5700
Sauk Village (G-18401)
World Cup Packaging Inc G 815 624-6501
South Beloit (G-19127)
Z Automation Company E 847 483-0120
Mundelein (G-14748)
Zitropack Ltd F 630 543-1016
Addison (G-341)

MACHINERY: Paint Making

Engineering Finshg Systems LLC F 815 893-6090
Elmhurst (G-9361)
Fluid Management Inc B 847 537-0880
Wheeling (G-20898)

MACHINERY: Paper Industry Miscellaneous

Birnberg Machinery Inc G 847 673-5242
Deerfield (G-7597)
Black Bros Co D 815 539-7451
Mendota (G-13938)
Emt International Inc G 630 655-4145
Westmont (G-20741)
Finishers Exchange G 847 462-0533
Fox River Grove (G-9758)
Guerrero Industries LLC G 773 968-8648
Palos Heights (G-16187)
Hfd Manufacturing Inc G 847 263-5050
Waukegan (G-20446)
Keene Technology Inc D 815 624-8989
Machesney Park (G-13320)
Quality Converting Inc G 847 669-9094
Huntley (G-11561)
Quipp Inc F 305 623-8700
Glenview (G-10606)
Ringwood Company D 708 458-6000
Bedford Park (G-1499)
Ultra Packaging Inc G 630 595-9820
Bensenville (G-1905)

MACHINERY: Pharmaciutical

Accelrted Mch Design Engrg LLC E 815 316-6381
Rockford (G-17290)
Asahi Kasei Bioprocess Inc E 847 834-0800
Glenview (G-10528)
Industrial Phrm Resources Inc F 630 823-4700
Bartlett (G-1290)
Kirby Lester LLC D 847 984-3377
Lake Forest (G-12269)
Thomas Engineering Inc D 847 358-5800
Hoffman Estates (G-11469)
Thomas Engineering Inc E 815 398-0280
Rockford (G-17659)
United Validation & Com G 815 953-6068
Watseka (G-20321)

MACHINERY: Photographic Reproduction

George Wilson G 847 342-1111
Prospect Heights (G-16841)

MACHINERY: Plastic Working

Black Bros Co D 815 539-7451
Mendota (G-13938)
Credit Card Systems Inc F 847 459-8320
Wheeling (G-20876)
Cumberland Engrg Entps Inc B 314 727-5550
Schaumburg (G-18500)
Ewikon Molding Tech Inc G 815 874-7270
Rockford (G-17405)
Fast Radius Inc E 866 222-5458
Chicago (G-4563)
Hmt Manufacturing Inc E 847 473-2310
North Chicago (G-15314)
Maac Machinery Co Inc E 630 665-1700
Carol Stream (G-3019)
Mamata Enterprises Inc G 941 205-0227
Montgomery (G-14260)
Mgb Engineering Company E 847 956-7444
Elk Grove Village (G-9121)

PRODUCT SECTION — MAGNETIC RESONANCE IMAGING DEVICES: Nonmedical

Midwest Innovations Inc ....G....... 815 578-1401
  McHenry *(G-13770)*
Prinsco Inc ....E....... 815 635-3131
  Chatsworth *(G-3426)*
RAO Design International Inc ....G....... 847 671-6182
  Morton Grove *(G-14437)*
Tek Pak Inc ....D....... 630 406-0560
  Batavia *(G-1429)*
Tuskin Equipment Corporation ....G....... 630 466-5590
  Sugar Grove *(G-19658)*

MACHINERY: Polishing & Buffing

Glaser USA Inc ....G....... 847 362-7878
  Lake Forest *(G-12251)*

MACHINERY: Printing Presses

A-Korn Roller Inc ....D....... 773 254-5700
  Chicago *(G-3494)*
Cy-Tec Inc ....G....... 815 756-8416
  Dekalb *(G-7674)*
Graphic Innovators Inc ....E....... 847 718-1516
  Elk Grove Village *(G-9021)*
Manroland Goss Web Systems Int ....E....... 630 796-7560
  Woodridge *(G-21321)*
Mmpcu Limited ....G....... 217 355-0500
  Champaign *(G-3324)*
Schlesinger Machinery Inc ....E....... 630 766-4074
  Bensenville *(G-1890)*
Sommers & Fahrenbach Inc ....F....... 773 478-3033
  Chicago *(G-6201)*

MACHINERY: Recycling

All Metal Recycling Company ....G....... 847 530-4825
  Villa Park *(G-20130)*
Americlean Inc ....F....... 314 741-8901
  Wood River *(G-21259)*
Arcoa Group Inc ....E....... 847 693-7519
  Waukegan *(G-20417)*
ER&r Inc ....G....... 847 791-5671
  Northbrook *(G-15385)*
Fortune Metal Midwest LLC ....E....... 630 778-7776
  Sandwich *(G-18370)*
Harris Metals & Recycling ....G....... 217 235-1808
  Mattoon *(G-13635)*
Kuusakoski Philadelphia LLC ....G....... 215 533-8323
  Plainfield *(G-16681)*

MACHINERY: Riveting

Chicago Rivet & Machine Co ....D....... 630 357-8500
  Naperville *(G-14798)*
Ebe Industrial LLC ....F....... 815 379-2400
  Walnut *(G-20217)*

MACHINERY: Road Construction & Maintenance

Bonnell Industries Inc ....D....... 815 284-3819
  Dixon *(G-7890)*
ED Etnyre & Co ....B....... 815 732-2116
  Oregon *(G-15917)*
Etnyre International Ltd ....B....... 815 732-2116
  Oregon *(G-15918)*
Millstadt Township ....G....... 618 476-3592
  Millstadt *(G-14053)*
Pilot Township Road District ....G....... 815 426-6221
  Herscher *(G-11186)*
S & S Maintenance ....G....... 815 725-9263
  Wilmington *(G-21103)*

MACHINERY: Rubber Working

Spectral Dynamics Inc ....E....... 630 595-4288
  Itasca *(G-11738)*

MACHINERY: Saw & Sawing

E H Wachs ....G....... 815 943-4785
  Lincolnshire *(G-12762)*
Meadoweld Machine Inc ....G....... 815 623-3939
  South Beloit *(G-19102)*

MACHINERY: Semiconductor Manufacturing

Precisepower LLC ....E....... 847 908-5400
  Schaumburg *(G-18682)*
R & G Machine Shop Inc ....F....... 217 342-6622
  Effingham *(G-8422)*

MACHINERY: Separation Eqpt, Magnetic

Acro Magnetics Inc ....G....... 815 943-5018
  Harvard *(G-11040)*

MACHINERY: Service Industry, NEC

Glo Heat Treat Services LLC ....G....... 815 601-5728
  Durand *(G-8152)*
Prinzings of Rockford ....G....... 815 874-9654
  Rockford *(G-17560)*
We Clean ....G....... 708 574-2551
  Oak Forest *(G-15692)*

MACHINERY: Sheet Metal Working

Rams Sheet Metal Equipment Inc ....G....... 224 788-9900
  Antioch *(G-632)*
Straightline Erectors Inc ....G....... 708 430-5426
  Oak Lawn *(G-15736)*
Whitney Roper Rockford Inc ....D....... 815 962-3011
  Rockford *(G-17684)*

MACHINERY: Sifting & Screening

Classic Fasteners LLC ....G....... 630 605-0195
  Saint Charles *(G-18170)*

MACHINERY: Snow Making

Brunet Snow Service Company ....G....... 847 846-0037
  Wood Dale *(G-21172)*

MACHINERY: Specialty

Quality Fastener Products Inc ....G....... 224 330-3162
  Elgin *(G-8708)*
Six Oaks Company ....G....... 312 343-4037
  Chicago *(G-6178)*

MACHINERY: Textile

Azul 3d Inc ....F....... 321 277-7807
  Skokie *(G-18926)*
Birnberg Machinery Inc ....G....... 847 673-5242
  Deerfield *(G-7597)*
Forte Automation Systems Inc ....E....... 815 316-6247
  Machesney Park *(G-13344)*
Intecells Inc ....G....... 586 612-9811
  Elgin *(G-8627)*

MACHINERY: Tire Shredding

Gone For Good ....G....... 217 753-0414
  Springfield *(G-19376)*

MACHINERY: Tobacco Prdts

Vacudyne Incorporated ....E....... 708 757-5200
  Chicago Heights *(G-6783)*

MACHINERY: Voting

Election Works ....G....... 630 232-4030
  Geneva *(G-10268)*

MACHINERY: Wire Drawing

C B Ferrari Incorporated ....G....... 847 756-4100
  Lake Barrington *(G-12143)*
Drawing Technology Inc ....G....... 815 877-5133
  Rockford *(G-17385)*
International Technologies Inc ....G....... 847 301-9005
  Schaumburg *(G-18565)*
Rockford Systems LLC ....D....... 815 874-7891
  Rockford *(G-17606)*

MACHINERY: Woodworking

Black Bros Co ....D....... 815 539-7451
  Mendota *(G-13938)*
Doll Furniture Co Inc ....G....... 309 452-2606
  Normal *(G-15202)*
Elliott Aviation Arcft Sls Inc ....G....... 309 799-3183
  Milan *(G-14008)*
Prairie State Machine LLC ....G....... 217 543-3768
  Arthur *(G-877)*
SA Industries Inc ....G....... 847 730-4823
  Wood Dale *(G-21237)*
Total Tooling Technology Inc ....F....... 847 437-5135
  Elk Grove Village *(G-9279)*

MACHINES: Forming, Sheet Metal

Comet Roll & Machine Company ....E....... 630 268-1407
  Saint Charles *(G-18172)*
Mac-Ster Inc ....F....... 847 830-7013
  Addison *(G-187)*

MACHINISTS' TOOLS & MACHINES: Measuring, Metalworking Type

Alpha Swiss Industries Inc ....G....... 815 455-3031
  Crystal Lake *(G-7157)*
Precision Gage Company ....F....... 630 655-2121
  Burr Ridge *(G-2714)*
Ryeson Corporation ....D....... 847 455-8677
  Carol Stream *(G-3061)*

MACHINISTS' TOOLS: Measuring, Precision

Crippa Usa LLC ....G....... 630 659-7720
  Geneva *(G-10264)*
Glen Products ....G....... 847 998-1361
  Glenview *(G-10550)*
Keson Industries Inc ....E....... 630 820-4200
  Aurora *(G-993)*
L S Starrett Co ....G....... 847 816-9999
  Vernon Hills *(G-20070)*
Natc LLC ....F....... 815 389-2300
  South Beloit *(G-19104)*
Precision Masters Inc ....E....... 815 397-3894
  Rockford *(G-17558)*
Roscoe Tool & Manufacturing ....E....... 815 633-8808
  Roscoe *(G-17929)*

MACHINISTS' TOOLS: Precision

Advanced Machine Co Inc ....G....... 773 545-9790
  Chicago *(G-3565)*
Automatic Precision Inc ....E....... 708 867-1116
  Chicago *(G-3778)*
Comet Tool Inc ....E....... 847 956-0126
  Elk Grove Village *(G-8902)*
Con Form Industry Inc ....F....... 847 278-1143
  Schaumburg *(G-18483)*
Forster Products Inc ....E....... 815 493-6360
  Lanark *(G-12481)*
Modineer P-K Tool LLC ....E....... 773 235-4700
  Chicago *(G-5483)*
Pfeifer Industries LLC ....G....... 630 596-9000
  Naperville *(G-14897)*
Reino Tool & Manufacturing Co ....F....... 773 588-5800
  Chicago *(G-6005)*
Team Cnc Inc ....G....... 630 377-2723
  Saint Charles *(G-18286)*
Thomas-Zientz Group Inc ....G....... 847 395-2363
  Antioch *(G-637)*

MACHINISTS' TOOLS: Scales, Measuring, Precision

Metrom LLC (not Llc) ....G....... 847 847-7233
  Lake Zurich *(G-12432)*

MAGAZINES, WHOLESALE

Code Black LLC ....G....... 773 493-4500
  Chicago *(G-4191)*
Sherman Media Company Inc ....G....... 312 335-1962
  Lake Forest *(G-12302)*

MAGNESIUM

Chicago Magnesium ....G....... 708 926-9531
  Dixmoor *(G-7883)*
Elektron N Magnesium Amer Inc ....D....... 618 452-5190
  Madison *(G-13410)*

MAGNETIC INK & OPTICAL SCANNING EQPT

Pos Plus LLC ....F....... 618 993-7587
  Marion *(G-13529)*
Tangent Systems Inc ....F....... 847 882-3833
  Hoffman Estates *(G-11466)*

MAGNETIC RESONANCE IMAGING DEVICES: Nonmedical

Illinois Bone & Joint Inst LLC ....D....... 847 724-4470
  Glenview *(G-10559)*
Imed Glenview ....G....... 847 298-2200
  Glenview *(G-10566)*

MAGNETIC RESONANCE IMAGING DEVICES: Nonmedical

O2m Technologies LLC ....G..... 773 910-8533
  Chicago *(G-5648)*
Peoria Open M R I ....G..... 309 692-7674
  Peoria *(G-16494)*
Prairie Glen Imaging Ctr LLC ....G..... 847 296-5366
  Des Plaines *(G-7829)*
Presence Legacy Association ....F..... 815 741-7555
  Joliet *(G-11916)*
Smart Scan Mri LLC ....G..... 847 623-4000
  Gurnee *(G-10928)*

MAGNETIC SHIELDS, METAL

American Partsmith Inc ....G..... 630 520-0432
  West Chicago *(G-20538)*
JL Clark LLC ....C..... 815 961-5609
  Rockford *(G-17476)*
Laird Technologies Inc ....C..... 847 839-6000
  Schaumburg *(G-18597)*
TSC International Inc ....F..... 847 249-4900
  Wadsworth *(G-20214)*

MAGNETIC TAPE, AUDIO: Prerecorded

Acta Publications ....G..... 773 989-3036
  Chicago *(G-3533)*
Advanced Audio Technology Inc ....G..... 630 665-3344
  Carol Stream *(G-2925)*

MAGNETS: Ceramic

Arnold Magnetic Tech Corp ....E..... 815 568-2000
  Marengo *(G-13480)*

MAGNETS: Permanent

Morris Magnetics Inc ....E..... 847 487-0829
  Wauconda *(G-20378)*

MAIL-ORDER BOOK CLUBS

Caxton Club ....G..... 312 266-8825
  Chicago *(G-4044)*

MAIL-ORDER HOUSE, NEC

D S Arms Incorporated ....E..... 847 277-7258
  Lake Barrington *(G-12147)*
Dinkels Bakery Inc ....E..... 773 281-7300
  Chicago *(G-4362)*
Euromarket Designs Inc ....A..... 847 272-2888
  Northbrook *(G-15386)*
Road Runner Sports Inc ....F..... 847 719-8941
  Palatine *(G-16154)*
Spirit Warrior Inc ....G..... 708 614-0020
  Orland Park *(G-15983)*
Waxman Candles Inc ....G..... 773 929-3000
  Chicago *(G-6593)*

MAIL-ORDER HOUSES: Automotive Splys & Eqpt

American Speed Enterprises ....G..... 309 764-3601
  Moline *(G-14131)*

MAIL-ORDER HOUSES: Books, Exc Book Clubs

Adventures Unlimited ....G..... 815 253-6390
  Kempton *(G-12013)*
World Book Inc ....E..... 312 729-5800
  Chicago *(G-6671)*

MAIL-ORDER HOUSES: Cards

Crest Greetings Inc ....F..... 708 210-0800
  Chicago *(G-4269)*

MAIL-ORDER HOUSES: Clothing, Exc Women's

Freddie Bear Sports ....F..... 708 532-4133
  Tinley Park *(G-19829)*

MAIL-ORDER HOUSES: Educational Splys & Eqpt

C W Publications Inc ....G..... 800 554-5537
  Sterling *(G-19502)*
Flinn Scientific Inc ....C..... 800 452-1261
  Batavia *(G-1378)*

MAIL-ORDER HOUSES: Electronic Kits & Parts

A and T Labs Incorporated ....G..... 630 668-8562
  Wheaton *(G-20783)*

MAIL-ORDER HOUSES: Fitness & Sporting Goods

Top Brass Inc ....G..... 719 539-7242
  Granite City *(G-10744)*
Top Brass LLC ....F..... 800 836-4683
  Granite City *(G-10745)*

MAIL-ORDER HOUSES: Food

Advertising Premiums Inc ....G..... 888 364-9710
  Mount Prospect *(G-14509)*

MAIL-ORDER HOUSES: Furniture & Furnishings

Vault Furniture Inc ....G..... 734 323-4166
  Chicago *(G-6525)*

MAIL-ORDER HOUSES: General Merchandise

Micron Filter Cartridges Corp ....G..... 630 337-3877
  Elmhurst *(G-9402)*

MAIL-ORDER HOUSES: Record & Tape, Music Or Video Club

Marshall Pubg & Promotions ....G..... 224 238-3530
  Barrington *(G-1227)*
Polyvinyl Record Co ....G..... 217 403-1752
  Champaign *(G-3336)*
Sandes Quynetta ....G..... 815 275-4876
  Freeport *(G-10140)*

MAIL-ORDER HOUSES: Religious Merchandise

Bible Truth Publishers Inc ....G..... 630 543-1441
  Addison *(G-49)*

MAIL-ORDER HOUSES: Women's Apparel

Doxa Enterprises LLC ....G..... 618 515-4470
  East Saint Louis *(G-8305)*
Living Royal Inc ....E..... 312 906-7600
  Wheeling *(G-20934)*
Trim Suits By Show-Off Inc ....G..... 630 894-0100
  Roselle *(G-17994)*

MAILBOX RENTAL & RELATED SVCS

UPS Authorized Retailer ....G..... 708 354-8772
  La Grange *(G-12090)*
UPS Store ....G..... 312 372-2727
  Chicago *(G-6491)*

MAILING LIST: Management

American Association of Indivi ......E..... 312 280-0170
  Chicago *(G-3649)*

MAILING SVCS, NEC

Allegra Print & Imaging Inc ....G..... 847 697-1434
  Elgin *(G-8502)*
Alliance Graphics ....G..... 312 280-8000
  Chicago *(G-3617)*
Better News Papers Inc ....G..... 618 566-8282
  Mascoutah *(G-13593)*
Caldwell Letter Service Inc ....E..... 773 847-0708
  Orland Park *(G-15943)*
Calmark Group LLC ....E..... 708 728-0101
  Bedford Park *(G-1461)*
Chicago Tribune Company LLC ....A..... 312 222-3232
  Chicago *(G-4134)*
Cision US Inc ....C..... 312 922-2400
  Chicago *(G-4154)*
Com-Graphics Inc ....D..... 312 226-0900
  Chicago *(G-4208)*
Connies Home Health Care ....G..... 708 790-4000
  Park Forest *(G-16253)*
Consumerbase LLC ....C..... 312 600-8000
  Chicago *(G-4224)*
D G Printing Inc ....E..... 847 397-7779
  Hawthorn Woods *(G-11122)*
Des Plaines Journal Inc ....D..... 847 299-5511
  Des Plaines *(G-7755)*
First String Enterprises Inc ....E..... 708 614-1200
  Tinley Park *(G-19827)*
Great Guy Inc ....G..... 312 203-9872
  Medinah *(G-13813)*
Herald Publications ....F..... 618 566-8282
  Mascoutah *(G-13599)*
Inky Printers ....G..... 815 235-3700
  Freeport *(G-10120)*
Kevron Printing & Design Inc ....G..... 708 229-7725
  Hickory Hills *(G-11199)*
Marketing Card Technology LLC ..D..... 630 985-7900
  Downers Grove *(G-8052)*
Metropolitan Graphic Arts Inc ....E..... 847 566-9502
  Gurnee *(G-10896)*
Mid Central Printing & Mailing ......F..... 847 251-4040
  Wilmette *(G-21087)*
Negs & Litho Inc ....G..... 847 647-7770
  Chicago *(G-5563)*
Practical Communications Inc ......E..... 773 754-3250
  Schaumburg *(G-18681)*
Precision Dialogue Direct Inc ....D..... 773 237-2264
  Chicago *(G-5855)*
Printing Plus ....G..... 708 301-3900
  Lockport *(G-13019)*
Priority One Printing and Mail ....G..... 217 224-8008
  Quincy *(G-16928)*
Professnl Mling Prtg Svcs Inc ....F..... 630 510-1000
  Carol Stream *(G-3054)*
Reliable Mail Services Inc ....F..... 847 677-6245
  Glenview *(G-10611)*
Rsn Mailing ....G..... 314 724-3364
  Collinsville *(G-6974)*
United Letter Service Inc ....F..... 312 408-2404
  Elk Grove Village *(G-9297)*
Van Meter Graphx Inc ....G..... 847 465-0600
  Wheeling *(G-21008)*
Your Images Group Inc ....G..... 847 437-6688
  Schaumburg *(G-18780)*
Zell Co ....G..... 312 226-9191
  Chicago *(G-6714)*

MANAGEMENT CONSULTING SVCS: Administrative

Association Management Center ...D..... 847 375-4700
  Chicago *(G-3753)*

MANAGEMENT CONSULTING SVCS: Automation & Robotics

Active Automation Inc ....F..... 847 427-8100
  Elk Grove Village *(G-8806)*
Concepts and Controls Inc ....F..... 847 478-9296
  Buffalo Grove *(G-2527)*
Eighty Nine Robotics LLC ....G..... 512 573-9091
  Chicago *(G-4463)*
Hydrotec Systems Company Inc ...G..... 815 624-6644
  Tiskilwa *(G-19873)*
Indesco Oven Products Inc ....G..... 217 622-6345
  Petersburg *(G-16602)*
R+d Custom Automation Inc ....E..... 847 395-3330
  Lake Villa *(G-12365)*

MANAGEMENT CONSULTING SVCS: Business

Allen Entertainment Management ..E..... 630 752-0903
  Carol Stream *(G-2931)*
Alligator Rec & Artist MGT Inc ......F..... 773 973-7736
  Chicago *(G-3620)*
Education Partners Project Ltd .....G..... 773 675-6643
  Chicago *(G-4458)*
Media Associates Intl Inc ....G..... 630 260-9063
  Carol Stream *(G-3022)*
National Sporting Goods Assn ......F..... 847 296-6742
  Downers Grove *(G-8063)*
Simplement Inc ....G..... 702 560-5332
  Northfield *(G-15530)*
Tom Zosel Associates Ltd ....D..... 847 540-6543
  Long Grove *(G-13172)*

MANAGEMENT CONSULTING SVCS: Construction Project

First American Restoration Inc ......F..... 800 209-3609
  Harwood Heights *(G-11105)*
Interntional Grnhse Contrs Inc ......E..... 217 443-0600
  Danville *(G-7352)*

PRODUCT SECTION

MANUFACTURING INDUSTRIES, NEC

MANAGEMENT CONSULTING SVCS: Corporation Organizing

Roger Fritz & Associates Inc .... G 630 355-2614
  Naperville (G-14911)

MANAGEMENT CONSULTING SVCS: Food & Beverage

78 Brand Co .... G 312 344-1602
  Chicago (G-3479)

MANAGEMENT CONSULTING SVCS: Foreign Trade

ADS LLC .... D 256 430-3366
  Burr Ridge (G-2650)
Mandus Group LLC .... F 309 786-1507
  Rock Island (G-17228)

MANAGEMENT CONSULTING SVCS: General

Proquis Inc .... F 847 278-3230
  Elgin (G-8700)

MANAGEMENT CONSULTING SVCS: Hospital & Health

Care Education Group Inc .... G 708 361-4110
  Palos Park (G-16208)
Dorenfest Group Ltd .... D 312 464-3000
  Chicago (G-4385)
Globepharm Inc .... G 224 904-3352
  Northbrook (G-15395)
Jero Medical Eqp & Sups Inc .... E 773 305-4193
  Chicago (G-5022)
Quadramed Corporation .... E 312 396-0700
  Chicago (G-5926)

MANAGEMENT CONSULTING SVCS: Industrial & Labor

Private Studios .... G 217 367-3530
  Urbana (G-19995)

MANAGEMENT CONSULTING SVCS: Industry Specialist

Broadcast Electronics Inc .... C 217 224-9600
  Quincy (G-16869)
Modern Fluid Technology Inc .... G 815 356-0001
  Crystal Lake (G-7232)

MANAGEMENT CONSULTING SVCS: Maintenance

New Lenox Machine Co Inc .... F 815 584-4866
  Dwight (G-8156)
Specialized Liftruck Svcs LLC .... F 708 552-2705
  Bedford Park (G-1505)

MANAGEMENT CONSULTING SVCS: Manufacturing

Precision Products Mfg Intl .... E 847 299-8500
  Des Plaines (G-7831)
Tropar Trophy Manufacturing Co .... E 630 787-1900
  Wood Dale (G-21252)

MANAGEMENT CONSULTING SVCS: Merchandising

Action Advertising Inc .... G 312 791-0660
  Chicago (G-3534)

MANAGEMENT CONSULTING SVCS: Real Estate

Nidec Mobility America Corp .... A 630 443-6800
  Saint Charles (G-18234)

MANAGEMENT CONSULTING SVCS: Retail Trade Consultant

Seek Design .... G 312 804-6629
  Evanston (G-9574)

MANAGEMENT CONSULTING SVCS: Training & Development

Be Group Inc .... G 312 436-0301
  Chicago (G-3848)
Coaching For Excellence LLC .... F 708 957-6047
  Country Club Hills (G-7036)
Illumen Studios LLC .... G 847 440-2222
  Grayslake (G-10782)
L C Mold Inc .... E 847 593-5004
  Rolling Meadows (G-17746)
Ohrvall Media LLC .... G 630 378-9738
  Plainfield (G-16698)

MANAGEMENT SERVICES

Alliance Technology MGT Corp .... G 847 574-9752
  Northfield (G-15504)
Barry Callebaut USA LLC .... G 312 496-7300
  Chicago (G-3839)
Blue Yonder Inc .... G 630 701-1492
  Naperville (G-14781)
Deshamusic Inc .... G 818 257-2716
  Chicago (G-4344)
Essentra Packaging US Inc .... G 704 418-8692
  Westchester (G-20699)
Grupo Antolin Illinois Inc .... C 815 544-8020
  Belvidere (G-1674)
Madison Capital Partners Corp .... G 312 277-0323
  Chicago (G-5312)
Natural Gas Pipeline Amer LLC .... F 815 426-2151
  Herscher (G-11185)
Prairie Area Library System .... E 309 799-3155
  Coal Valley (G-6938)
Quantum Color Graphics LLC .... C 847 967-3600
  Morton Grove (G-14435)
Ripa LLC .... G 708 938-1600
  Broadview (G-2464)
Subaru of America Inc .... E 630 250-4740
  Itasca (G-11741)
World Fuel Services Inc .... F 305 428-8000
  Chicago (G-6673)

MANAGEMENT SVCS: Administrative

Barry Callebaut USA LLC .... B 312 496-7300
  Chicago (G-3840)
Charles Industries LLC .... D 217 826-2318
  Marshall (G-13566)
Fanning Communications Inc .... G 708 293-1430
  Crestwood (G-7118)
Moody Bible Inst of Chicago .... E 312 329-2102
  Chicago (G-5496)

MANAGEMENT SVCS: Business

Bailey Business Group .... G 618 548-3566
  Salem (G-18330)
Diversified Fleet MGT Inc .... E 815 578-1051
  McHenry (G-13736)
Secure Data Inc .... F 618 726-5225
  O Fallon (G-15583)
Valley Meats LLC .... E 309 799-7341
  Coal Valley (G-6939)

MANAGEMENT SVCS: Construction

Construction Contg Svcs Inc .... F 219 779-0900
  Lansing (G-12489)
First American Restoration Inc .... F 800 209-3609
  Harwood Heights (G-11105)
Stages Construction Inc .... G 773 619-2977
  Glenview (G-10624)

MANAGEMENT SVCS: Hotel Or Motel

Parker International Pdts Inc .... D 815 524-5831
  Vernon Hills (G-20082)

MANAGEMENT SVCS: Restaurant

Coopers Hawk Intrmdate Hldg LL .... C 708 839-2920
  Downers Grove (G-7981)
Coopers Hawk Intrmdate Hldg LL .... F 708 215-5674
  Countryside (G-7048)

MANHOLES & COVERS: Metal

Ej Usa Inc .... F 815 740-1640
  New Lenox (G-15032)

MANHOLES COVERS: Concrete

Skelcher Concrete Products .... G 618 457-2930
  Carbondale (G-2859)
Unique Concrete Concepts Inc .... F 618 466-0700
  Jerseyville (G-11797)

MANICURE PREPARATIONS

Abyss Salon Inc .... G 312 880-0263
  Chicago (G-3512)
Affirmed LLC .... G 847 550-0170
  Lake Zurich (G-12381)
Be Products Inc .... G 312 201-9669
  Chicago (G-3849)

MANNEQUINS

Orlandi Statuary Company .... D 773 489-0303
  Chicago (G-5704)
Research Mannikins Inc .... F 618 426-3456
  Ava (G-1177)

MANUFACTURED & MOBILE HOME DEALERS

Southmoor Estates Inc .... G 815 756-1299
  Dekalb (G-7705)

MANUFACTURING INDUSTRIES, NEC

3 Goldenstar Inc .... F 847 963-0451
  Palatine (G-16088)
425 Manufacturing .... G 815 873-7066
  Rockford (G-17277)
A Wiley & Associates .... G 815 343-7401
  Ottawa (G-16036)
AAM Manufacturing .... G 708 606-9360
  Bolingbrook (G-2144)
ABC Beverage Mfg Inc .... G 708 449-2600
  Northlake (G-15538)
Advance Manufacturing .... G 618 245-6515
  Farina (G-9649)
Amk Enterprises Chicago Inc .... G 312 523-7212
  Chicago (G-3681)
Apollo Aerosol Industries LLC .... G 770 433-0210
  Downers Grove (G-7953)
AR Industries .... G 630 543-0282
  Addison (G-37)
Atlas Manufacturing .... G 773 327-3005
  Chicago (G-3765)
Axxent Energy Inc .... E 312 288-8640
  Chicago (G-3797)
Baessler Carl Dgn Mfg Rep .... G 779 994-4103
  Crystal Lake (G-7167)
Baker Manufacturing LLC .... G 847 362-3663
  Lake Bluff (G-12173)
Bogart Industries LLC .... G 224 242-4578
  Elburn (G-8446)
Boombox Beverage LLC .... G 312 607-1038
  Skokie (G-18930)
Bork Industries .... G 630 365-5517
  Maple Park (G-13460)
Borse Industries Inc .... G 630 325-1210
  Willowbrook (G-21032)
Bw Industries .... G 630 784-1020
  Winfield (G-21108)
Cargo Support Industries Inc .... G 847 744-0786
  Inverness (G-11599)
Chicago Art Center Co .... G 773 817-2725
  Chicago (G-4091)
Chronx Global Industries Ltd .... G 773 770-5753
  Round Lake (G-18073)
CPM Industries .... G 630 469-8200
  Glendale Heights (G-10446)
Cultivated Energy Group Inc .... G 312 203-8833
  Hebron (G-11142)
Curlee Mfg .... G 847 268-6517
  Rosemont (G-18014)
Custom Karts and More LLC .... G 815 703-6438
  Davis (G-7416)
Diamond Industries LLC .... G 612 859-1210
  Chicago (G-4352)
Diamond Quality Manufacturing .... G 815 521-4184
  Channahon (G-3379)
Dyno Manufacturing Inc .... G 618 451-6609
  Madison (G-13409)
Elite Industries .... G 224 433-6988
  Gurnee (G-10876)
Eyes Forward Innovations Corp .... G 281 755-5826
  West Chicago (G-20581)

Flurry Industries Inc ....G.... 630 882-8361
Yorkville *(G-21482)*
Freitas P Sabah ....G.... 708 386-8934
Oak Park *(G-15754)*
Genetics Development Corp ....G.... 847 283-9780
Lake Bluff *(G-12182)*
Goble Manufacturing Inc ....G.... 217 932-5615
Casey *(G-3202)*
Gpi Prototype & Mfg Svcs LLC ....E.... 847 615-8900
Lake Bluff *(G-12185)*
H V Manufacturing Vanguar ....G.... 847 229-5502
Wheeling *(G-20905)*
Hendrick Manufacturing ....G.... 847 608-2047
Elgin *(G-8611)*
Igd Group LLC ....F.... 630 240-6736
Elmhurst *(G-9374)*
Industrial Tech Centl LLC ....G.... 312 785-2520
Chicago *(G-4911)*
Infamous Industries Inc ....G.... 708 789-2326
Hickory Hills *(G-11198)*
J and J International ....G.... 847 842-8628
Barrington *(G-1222)*
J B Burling Group Ltd ....G.... 773 327-5362
Chicago *(G-4986)*
Jamtec USA LLC ....G.... 224 392-1258
Arlington Heights *(G-760)*
JM Industries LLC ....G.... 708 758-2600
Chicago Heights *(G-6752)*
Knapheide Mfg Co ....E.... 217 223-1848
Quincy *(G-16903)*
Kriese Mfg ....G.... 815 748-2683
Cortland *(G-7023)*
Ledretrofitting Inc ....G.... 815 347-5047
Glen Ellyn *(G-10408)*
Lenze Americas ....G.... 224 653-8119
Glendale Heights *(G-10467)*
Liv Labs Inc ....G.... 630 373-1471
Chicago *(G-5240)*
LMD Industries Inc ....G.... 630 383-9546
Oswego *(G-16011)*
Lumen Technologies Inc ....G.... 708 363-7758
Elmhurst *(G-9395)*
Mac Medical Inc ....F.... 618 719-6757
Belleville *(G-1569)*
Marca Industries Inc ....G.... 773 884-4500
Burbank *(G-2636)*
Masterbolt LLC ....F.... 847 834-5191
Lake In The Hills *(G-12340)*
Matrix Industries Inc ....G.... 847 975-7701
Wauconda *(G-20374)*
Mbs Manufacturing ....G.... 630 227-0300
Franklin Park *(G-9986)*
Midwest Nameplate Corp ....G.... 708 614-0606
Orland Park *(G-15968)*
Mold Repair and Manufacturing ....G.... 815 477-1332
Crystal Lake *(G-7233)*
Monty Burcenski ....G.... 815 838-0934
Lockport *(G-13014)*
Murff Enterprises LLC ....G.... 203 685-5556
Chicago *(G-5526)*
Northfield Industries ....G.... 847 981-7530
Elk Grove Village *(G-9154)*
Northlake Industries ....G.... 847 358-6875
Palatine *(G-16143)*
Northwstern Globl Hlth Fndtion ....G.... 214 207-9485
Chicago *(G-5626)*
Nutraid Manufacturing ....G.... 847 214-4860
Elgin *(G-8675)*
Performance Manufacturing ....G.... 630 231-8099
West Chicago *(G-20629)*
Phoenix Industries Inc ....G.... 708 478-5474
Mokena *(G-14107)*
Platinum Touch Industries LLC ....G.... 773 775-9988
Des Plaines *(G-7826)*
Prime Vector International LLC ....G.... 847 348-1060
Palatine *(G-16150)*
Prospan Manufacturing ....G.... 847 815-0191
Rosemont *(G-18044)*
Prote USA LLC ....G.... 773 576-9079
Chicago *(G-5905)*
Psimet LLC ....G.... 847 871-7005
Elgin *(G-8703)*
Ringmaster Mfg ....G.... 815 675-4230
Spring Grove *(G-19299)*
Riverview Mfg House SA ....G.... 815 625-1459
Rock Falls *(G-17193)*
Roses Moulding By Design Inc ....E.... 847 549-9200
Mundelein *(G-14733)*
S & S Mfg Solutions LLC ....G.... 815 838-1960
Lockport *(G-13022)*
Scientific Manufacturing Inc ....G.... 847 414-5658
Sleepy Hollow *(G-19062)*
Sean Matthew Innovations Inc ....G.... 815 455-4525
Crystal Lake *(G-7261)*
Shaw Industries ....G.... 847 844-9190
Elgin *(G-8729)*
Shermar Industries LLC ....G.... 847 378-8073
Des Plaines *(G-7843)*
Snowball Industries ....G.... 773 316-0051
Chicago *(G-6195)*
Star Freeport Company LLC ....E.... 815 758-6400
Freeport *(G-10145)*
Star Lite Mfg ....G.... 630 595-8338
Wood Dale *(G-21243)*
Synergetic Industries ....G.... 309 321-8145
Morton *(G-14385)*
T P R Resources Inc ....G.... 630 443-9060
Saint Charles *(G-18284)*
Tank In A Box LLC ....G.... 847 624-1234
Chicago *(G-6322)*
Timber Industries LLC ....E.... 815 857-3674
Dixon *(G-7922)*
Tiny Human Food Inc ....G.... 630 397-9936
Naperville *(G-14934)*
Tishma Engineering LLC ....G.... 847 755-1200
Elk Grove Village *(G-9275)*
Trustar Holdings LLC ....G.... 847 598-8800
Schaumburg *(G-18759)*
Two Cards Innovation LLC ....G.... 815 793-2517
Rockton *(G-17705)*
US International Inc ....G.... 312 671-9207
Chicago *(G-6501)*
Utlx Manufacturing Inc ....G.... 312 431-3111
Chicago *(G-6509)*
Visionary Solutions Inc ....G.... 847 296-9615
Des Plaines *(G-7865)*
Waterway Rv LLC Mfg Home ....G.... 312 207-1835
Chicago *(G-6590)*
Western Sand & Gravel Co ....F.... 815 433-1600
Ottawa *(G-16085)*
Wilton Brands Inc ....F.... 815 823-8547
Joliet *(G-11945)*
Wingfield Manufacturing LLC ....G.... 800 637-6712
Urbana *(G-20003)*
Write Stuff ....G.... 630 365-4425
Saint Charles *(G-18303)*
Xd Industries Inc ....G.... 847 293-0796
Prospect Heights *(G-16849)*
Xl Manufacture ....G.... 773 271-8900
Chicago *(G-6695)*
Yetter M Co Inc Emp B Tr ....G.... 309 776-4111
Colchester *(G-6947)*
Zeta Manufacturing Company ....G.... 708 301-3766
Crete *(G-7147)*

MARBLE, BUILDING: Cut & Shaped

Botti Studio of Architectural ....E.... 847 869-5933
Glenview *(G-10532)*
Contempo Marble & Granite Inc ....G.... 312 455-0022
Chicago *(G-4225)*
Marble Emporium Inc ....E.... 847 205-4000
Northbrook *(G-15427)*
Natural Stone Inc ....G.... 847 735-1129
Lake Bluff *(G-12198)*
Northwest Products ....G.... 630 860-2288
Bensenville *(G-1859)*
Pintas Cultured Marble ....E.... 708 385-3360
Alsip *(G-492)*
Standard Marble & Granite ....F.... 773 533-0450
Chicago *(G-6229)*
Stonecrafters Inc ....E.... 815 363-8730
Lakemoor *(G-12477)*
Superior Home Products Inc ....G.... 217 726-9300
Springfield *(G-19460)*

MARINE CARGO HANDLING SVCS

Blue Comet Transport Inc ....G.... 773 617-9512
Chicago *(G-3913)*

MARINE CARGO HANDLING SVCS: Loading

Metropolis Ready Mix Inc ....E.... 618 524-8221
Metropolis *(G-13974)*

MARINE HARDWARE

Custom Stainless Steel Inc ....F.... 618 435-2605
Benton *(G-1924)*
Meyer Engineering Co ....G.... 847 746-1500
Winthrop Harbor *(G-21141)*

MARINE RELATED EQPT

Marine Acquisition Corp ....A.... 217 324-9400
Litchfield *(G-12973)*
Prime Group Inc ....G.... 312 922-3883
Chicago *(G-5874)*

MARINE SPLY DEALERS

Cyn Industries Inc ....F.... 773 895-4324
Chicago *(G-4295)*

MARINE SPLYS WHOLESALERS

Cyn Industries Inc ....F.... 773 895-4324
Chicago *(G-4295)*

MARKERS

Premier Packaging Corp ....G.... 815 469-7951
Frankfort *(G-9825)*
U Mark Inc ....E.... 618 235-7500
Belleville *(G-1604)*

MARKETS: Meat & fish

Hartrich Meats Inc ....G.... 618 455-3172
Sainte Marie *(G-18326)*
Jewel Osco Inc ....C.... 847 428-3547
West Dundee *(G-20664)*
Jewel Osco Inc ....D.... 630 226-1892
Bolingbrook *(G-2198)*
Jewel Osco Inc ....C.... 847 296-7786
Des Plaines *(G-7791)*
Jewel Osco Inc ....C.... 815 464-5352
Frankfort *(G-9810)*
Park Packing Company Inc ....E.... 773 254-0100
Chicago *(G-5764)*
T & J Meatpacking Inc ....D.... 708 758-6748
Chicago Heights *(G-6778)*
V A M D Inc ....G.... 773 631-8400
Chicago *(G-6512)*

MARKING DEVICES

A 1 Marking Products ....G.... 309 762-6096
Moline *(G-14130)*
A To Z Engraving Co Inc ....G.... 847 526-7396
Wauconda *(G-20324)*
Bendsen Signs & Graphics Inc ....F.... 217 877-2345
Decatur *(G-7464)*
Bertco Enterprises Inc ....G.... 618 234-9283
Belleville *(G-1535)*
Iemco Corporation ....G.... 773 728-4400
Chicago *(G-4878)*
Illinois Tool Works Inc ....D.... 618 997-1716
Marion *(G-13518)*
Joes Printing ....G.... 773 545-6063
Chicago *(G-5034)*
K and A Graphics Inc ....G.... 847 244-2345
Gurnee *(G-10890)*
Kellogg Printing Co ....F.... 309 734-8388
Monmouth *(G-14220)*
Keneal Industries Inc ....F.... 815 886-1300
Romeoville *(G-17837)*
Keson Industries Inc ....E.... 630 820-4200
Aurora *(G-993)*
Kiwi Coders Corp ....E.... 847 541-4511
Wheeling *(G-20925)*
Letters Unlimited Inc ....G.... 847 891-7811
Schaumburg *(G-18604)*
Mich Enterprises Inc ....F.... 630 616-9000
Wood Dale *(G-21216)*
Nameplate Robinson & Precision ....G.... 847 678-2255
Franklin Park *(G-10005)*
Nathan Winston Service Inc ....G.... 815 758-4545
Dekalb *(G-7692)*
Navitor Inc ....B.... 800 323-0253
Harwood Heights *(G-11106)*
Nelson - Harkins Inds Inc ....E.... 773 478-6243
Lake Bluff *(G-12199)*
Pro-Pak Industries Inc ....F.... 630 876-1050
West Chicago *(G-20633)*
Professional Sales Associates ....G.... 847 487-1900
Wauconda *(G-20384)*
Pylon Plastics Inc ....G.... 630 968-6374
Lisle *(G-12930)*
Richards & Stehman LLC ....G.... 217 522-6801
Springfield *(G-19433)*
Shawver Press Inc ....G.... 815 772-4700
Morrison *(G-14348)*
Trodat Usa Inc ....E.... 847 806-1750
Elk Grove Village *(G-9287)*

PRODUCT SECTION — MEAT CUTTING & PACKING

Wagner Zip-Change Inc .... E 708 681-4100
  Melrose Park *(G-13926)*
Weakley Printing & Sign Shop .... G 847 473-4466
  North Chicago *(G-15323)*

MARKING DEVICES: Canceling Stamps, Hand, Rubber Or Metal

National Rubber Stamp Co Inc .... G 773 281-6522
  Chicago *(G-5552)*
Take Your Mark Sports LLC .... G 708 655-0525
  Western Springs *(G-20726)*

MARKING DEVICES: Embossing Seals & Hand Stamps

A & E Rubber Stamp Corp .... G 312 575-1416
  Chicago *(G-3481)*
Anderson Safford Mkg Graphics .... F 847 827-8968
  Des Plaines *(G-7732)*
Jackson Marking Products Co .... F 618 242-7901
  Mount Vernon *(G-14617)*
S and S Associates Inc .... G 847 584-0033
  Elk Grove Village *(G-9224)*

MARKING DEVICES: Printing Dies, Marking Mach, Rubber/Plastic

B&H Machine Inc .... F 618 281-3737
  Columbia *(G-6984)*

MARKING DEVICES: Screens, Textile Printing

Blue Monkey Graphics Inc .... G 708 488-9501
  Forest Park *(G-9708)*
Hookset Enterprises LLC .... F 224 374-1935
  Wheeling *(G-20911)*
Village Press Inc .... G 847 362-1856
  Libertyville *(G-12724)*

MARKING DEVICES: Seal Presses, Notary & Hand

Education Partners Project Ltd .... G 773 675-6643
  Chicago *(G-4458)*

MARKING DEVICES: Stationary Embossers, Personal

Promoframes LLC .... G 866 566-7224
  Schaumburg *(G-18685)*

MARTIAL ARTS INSTRUCTION

World Class Tae Kwon .... G 630 870-9293
  Aurora *(G-1039)*

MASQUERADE OR THEATRICAL COSTUMES STORES

Andy Dallas & Co .... F 217 351-5974
  Champaign *(G-3265)*

MASSAGE MACHINES, ELECTRIC: Barber & Beauty Shops

Elia Day Spa .... F 708 535-1450
  Oak Forest *(G-15676)*

MASSAGE PARLOR & STEAM BATH SVCS

Ceragem 26th St .... G 773 277-0672
  Chicago *(G-4064)*

MASSAGE PARLORS

Mobile Health & Wellness Inc .... G 773 697-9892
  Chicago *(G-5475)*

MASTIC ROOFING COMPOSITION

Ted Muller .... G 312 435-0978
  Chicago *(G-6336)*

MATCHES, WHOLESALE

Goodco Products LLC .... G 630 258-6384
  Countryside *(G-7055)*

MATERIAL GRINDING & PULVERIZING SVCS NEC

Kemp Manufacturing Company .... E 309 682-7292
  Peoria *(G-16465)*
Sturtevant Inc .... G 630 613-8968
  Lombard *(G-13135)*

MATERIALS HANDLING EQPT WHOLESALERS

Allquip Co Inc .... G 309 944-6153
  Geneseo *(G-10239)*
Allstates Rubber & Tool Corp .... F 708 342-1030
  Tinley Park *(G-19800)*
Brennan Equipment and Mfg Inc .... D 708 534-5500
  University Park *(G-19950)*
Crane Equipment & Services Inc .... E 309 467-6262
  Eureka *(G-9479)*
Ergo-Help Inc .... G 847 593-0722
  Fox River Grove *(G-9757)*
Illinois Lift Equipment Inc .... E 888 745-0577
  Cary *(G-3169)*
Interlake Mecalux Inc .... B 708 344-9999
  Melrose Park *(G-13883)*
Inverom Corporation .... G 630 568-5609
  Burr Ridge *(G-2690)*
Jcb Inc .... G 912 704-2995
  Aurora *(G-990)*
Lamco Slings & Rigging Inc .... E 309 764-7400
  Moline *(G-14157)*
Material Control Inc .... F 630 892-4274
  Batavia *(G-1393)*
R G Hanson Company Inc .... F 309 661-9200
  Bloomington *(G-2087)*
REB Steel Equipment Corp .... E 773 252-0400
  Chicago *(G-5987)*
Schaumburg Specialties Co .... G 847 451-0070
  Schaumburg *(G-18706)*
W N G S Inc .... E 847 451-1224
  Franklin Park *(G-10081)*

MATERNITY WEAR STORES

Golda Inc .... C 217 895-3602
  Neoga *(G-15017)*

MATS & MATTING, MADE FROM PURCHASED WIRE

Logan Graphic Products Inc .... D 847 526-5515
  Wauconda *(G-20369)*
Simonton Hardwood Lumber LLC .... F 618 594-2132
  Carlyle *(G-2896)*
Tru Vue Inc .... C 708 485-5080
  Countryside *(G-7075)*

MATS OR MATTING, NEC: Rubber

March Industries Inc .... F 224 654-6500
  Hampshire *(G-10978)*

MATS, MATTING & PADS: Aircraft, Floor, Exc Rubber Or Plastic

Skandia Inc .... D 800 945-7135
  Davis Junction *(G-7427)*

MATS, MATTING & PADS: Nonwoven

Lessy Messy LLC .... F 708 790-7589
  Naperville *(G-14977)*
March Industries Inc .... F 224 654-6500
  Hampshire *(G-10978)*

MATS, ROOFING: Mineral Wool

Owens Corning Sales LLC .... B 708 594-6911
  Argo *(G-674)*

MATTRESS STORES

Deborah Zeitler Associates Inc .... G 312 527-3733
  Chicago *(G-4328)*
L & W Bedding Inc .... G 309 762-6019
  Moline *(G-14155)*
Montauk Chicago Inc .... G 312 951-5688
  Chicago *(G-5493)*
Verlo Mat of Skokie-Evanston .... G 847 966-9988
  Morton Grove *(G-14446)*
Verlo Mattress of Lake Geneva .... G 815 455-2570
  Crystal Lake *(G-7289)*

MAUSOLEUMS

J W Reynolds Monument Co Inc .... G 618 833-6014
  Anna *(G-586)*

MEAL DELIVERY PROGRAMS

Balton Corporation .... F 773 933-7927
  Chicago *(G-3822)*
Relish Labs LLC .... G 872 225-2433
  Chicago *(G-6012)*

MEAT & FISH MARKETS: Freezer Provisioners, Meat

Professional Freezing Svcs LLC .... G 773 847-7500
  Chicago *(G-5896)*

MEAT & MEAT PRDTS WHOLESALERS

Advertising Premiums Inc .... G 888 364-9710
  Mount Prospect *(G-14509)*
Ba Le Meat Processing & Whl Co .... F 773 506-2499
  Chicago *(G-3810)*
Branding Iron Holdings Inc .... G 618 337-8400
  Sauget *(G-18390)*
Calihan Pork Processors Inc .... D 309 674-9175
  Peoria *(G-16396)*
Charles Autin Limited .... D 312 432-0888
  Chicago *(G-4072)*
Dreymiller & Kray Inc .... G 847 683-2271
  Hampshire *(G-10969)*
Jbs USA Food Company .... E 217 323-6200
  Beardstown *(G-1447)*
John J Moesle Whl Meats Inc .... F 773 847-4900
  Chicago *(G-5042)*
Kuna Meat Company Inc .... C 618 286-4000
  Dupo *(G-8139)*
Lena AJS Maid Meats .... F 815 369-4522
  Lena *(G-12602)*
New SBL Inc .... E 773 376-8280
  Chicago *(G-5578)*
OSI Industries LLC .... C 630 231-9090
  West Chicago *(G-20627)*
Peoria Packing Ltd .... F 312 226-2600
  Chicago *(G-5787)*
Plumrose Usa Inc .... E 800 526-4909
  Downers Grove *(G-8077)*
Quay Corporation Inc .... G 847 676-4233
  Lincolnwood *(G-12836)*
Russo Wholesale Meat Inc .... G 708 385-0500
  Alsip *(G-507)*
Schau Southeast Sushi Inc .... E 630 783-1000
  Woodridge *(G-21339)*
Smithfield Packaged Meats Corp .... A 309 734-5353
  Monmouth *(G-14227)*
Stiglmeier Sausage Co Inc .... F 847 537-9988
  Wheeling *(G-20991)*
T & J Meatpacking Inc .... D 708 758-6748
  Chicago Heights *(G-6778)*
Tomcyndi Inc .... E 773 847-5400
  Chicago *(G-6389)*
Tru-Native Enterprises .... G 630 409-3258
  Addison *(G-317)*
V A M D Inc .... G 773 631-8400
  Chicago *(G-6512)*
Vej Holdings LLC .... G 630 219-1598
  Naperville *(G-14940)*
Vienna Beef Ltd .... E 773 278-7800
  Chicago *(G-6548)*

MEAT CUTTING & PACKING

Allens Farm Quality Meats .... G 217 896-2532
  Homer *(G-11474)*
Amelio Bros Meats .... G 708 300-2920
  Richton Park *(G-17027)*
Amity Packing Company Inc .... C 312 942-0270
  Chicago *(G-3680)*
Belmont Sausage Company .... E 847 357-1515
  Elk Grove Village *(G-8864)*
Bruss Company .... E 773 282-2900
  Chicago *(G-3969)*
Bushnell Locker Service .... G 309 772-2783
  Bushnell *(G-2739)*
Butterball LLC .... B 800 575-3365
  Montgomery *(G-14237)*
Cargill Meat Solutions Corp .... C 630 739-1746
  Woodridge *(G-21281)*

Employee Codes: A=Over 500 employees, B=251-500
C=101-250, D=51-100, E=20-50, F=10-19, G=3-9

MEAT CUTTING & PACKING

Cass Meats .... G 217 452-3072
 Virginia *(G-20193)*
Chenoa Locker Inc .... G 815 945-7323
 Chenoa *(G-3432)*
Cherry Meat Packers Inc .... E 773 927-1200
 Chicago *(G-4083)*
Chicago Meat Authority Inc .... B 773 254-3811
 Chicago *(G-4113)*
Chicago Premier Meats Inc .... G 773 847-5400
 Chicago *(G-4124)*
City Foods Inc .... C 773 523-1566
 Chicago *(G-4155)*
Consumers Packing Co Inc .... D 708 344-0047
 Melrose Park *(G-13844)*
Country Village Meats .... G 815 849-5532
 Sublette *(G-19635)*
Dawn Food Products Inc .... C 815 933-0600
 Bradley *(G-2280)*
Deer Processing .... F 309 799-5994
 Coal Valley *(G-6935)*
Earlville Cold Stor Lckr LLC .... G 815 246-9469
 Earlville *(G-8160)*
Ed Kabrick Beef Inc .... G 217 656-3263
 Plainville *(G-16729)*
Edgar County Locker Service .... G 217 466-5000
 Paris *(G-16229)*
Eureka Locker Inc .... F 309 467-2731
 Eureka *(G-9482)*
Fabbri Sausage Manufacturing .... E 312 829-6363
 Chicago *(G-4554)*
Farmers Packing Inc .... F 618 445-3822
 Albion *(G-350)*
Farmington Locker/Ice Plant Co .... G 309 245-4621
 Farmington *(G-9661)*
Galloway Como Processing .... G 815 626-0305
 Sterling *(G-19511)*
Golden Locker Inc .... G 217 696-4456
 Camp Point *(G-2811)*
Great Lakes Packing Co Intl .... G 773 927-6660
 Chicago *(G-4737)*
Gurman Food Co .... F 847 837-1100
 Mundelein *(G-14693)*
Hansen Packing Co .... G 618 498-3714
 Jerseyville *(G-11792)*
Hartrich Meats Inc .... G 618 455-3172
 Sainte Marie *(G-18326)*
Honey Foods Inc .... G 847 989-8186
 Franklin Park *(G-9957)*
Jancorp LLC .... G 217 892-4830
 Rantoul *(G-16977)*
Johnsons Processing Plant .... G 815 684-5183
 Chadwick *(G-3258)*
Jones Packing Co .... G 815 943-4488
 Harvard *(G-11058)*
Kelly Corned Beef Co Chicago .... E 773 588-2882
 Chicago *(G-5092)*
Korte Meat Processors Inc .... G 618 654-3813
 Highland *(G-11230)*
Kuna Meat Company Inc .... C 618 286-4000
 Dupo *(G-8139)*
Lake Pacific Partners LLC .... B 312 578-1110
 Chicago *(G-5161)*
Lena AJS Maid Meats .... F 815 369-4522
 Lena *(G-12602)*
Magros Processing .... G 217 438-2880
 Springfield *(G-19401)*
Mangold Networks .... G 224 402-0068
 Elgin *(G-8648)*
Meats By Linz Inc .... E 708 862-0830
 Calumet City *(G-2783)*
Momence Packing Co .... B 815 472-6485
 Momence *(G-14188)*
Morris Meat Packing Co Inc .... G 708 865-8566
 Maywood *(G-13673)*
Moweaqua Packing Plant .... G 217 768-4714
 Moweaqua *(G-14652)*
National Beef Packing Co LLC .... G 312 332-6166
 Chicago *(G-5544)*
Nea Agora Packing Co .... G 312 421-5130
 Chicago *(G-5560)*
New SBL Inc .... E 773 376-8280
 Chicago *(G-5578)*
Oriental Kitchen Corporation .... F 312 738-2850
 Chicago *(G-5698)*
Paris Frozen Foods Inc .... G 217 532-3822
 Hillsboro *(G-11318)*
Park Packing Company Inc .... E 773 254-0100
 Chicago *(G-5764)*
Paxton Packing LLC .... F 623 707-5604
 Paxton *(G-16312)*

Peer Foods Inc .... F 773 927-1440
 Chicago *(G-5781)*
Peoria Packing Ltd .... F 312 226-2600
 Chicago *(G-5787)*
Peoria Packing Ltd .... F 815 465-9824
 Grant Park *(G-10750)*
Raber Packing Company .... E 309 673-0721
 Peoria *(G-16507)*
Reasons Inc .... G 309 537-3424
 Buffalo Prairie *(G-2626)*
Rochelle Foods LLC .... A 815 562-4141
 Rochelle *(G-17155)*
Rose Packing Co Inc .... G 708 458-9300
 Chicago *(G-6061)*
Rose Packing Company Inc .... F 708 458-9300
 Chicago *(G-6063)*
Ryan Meat Company .... G 773 783-3840
 Evergreen Park *(G-9599)*
Saratoga Specialties Co Inc .... G 630 833-3810
 Elmhurst *(G-9424)*
Skyline Provisions Inc .... F 708 331-1982
 Harvey *(G-11095)*
Smithfeld Pckged Mats Sls Corp .... F 757 365-3541
 Lisle *(G-12938)*
Smithfield Packaged Meats Corp ...... C 630 993-8763
 Bolingbrook *(G-2243)*
Smithfield Packaged Meats Corp ...... G 815 747-8809
 East Dubuque *(G-8183)*
Smithfield Packaged Meats Corp ...... A 309 734-5353
 Monmouth *(G-14227)*
Smithfield Packaged Meats Corp ...... E 630 281-5224
 Lisle *(G-12939)*
Specialty Foods Group LLC .... C 773 378-1300
 Chicago *(G-6213)*
Specialty Foods Group LLC .... G 630 599-5900
 Lombard *(G-13132)*
Spectrum Preferred Meats Inc .... D 815 946-3816
 Mount Morris *(G-14502)*
Steinbach Provision Company .... G 773 538-1511
 Chicago *(G-6238)*
Stiglmeier Sausage Co Inc .... F 847 537-9988
 Wheeling *(G-20991)*
Tomcyndi Inc .... E 773 847-5400
 Chicago *(G-6389)*
Tyson .... F 773 282-2900
 Chicago *(G-6451)*
Tyson Fresh Meats Inc .... C 309 658-3377
 Hillsdale *(G-11323)*
Tyson Fresh Meats Inc .... F 309 965-2565
 Goodfield *(G-10678)*
Victor Food Products .... G 773 478-9529
 Chicago *(G-6544)*
Wichita Packing Co .... E 312 421-0606
 Chicago *(G-6622)*
Y T Packing Co .... F 217 522-3345
 Springfield *(G-19470)*
Zabiha Halal Mt Processors Inc .... G 630 620-5000
 Addison *(G-340)*

MEAT MARKETS

Allens Farm Quality Meats .... G 217 896-2532
 Homer *(G-11474)*
Cass Meats .... G 217 452-3072
 Virginia *(G-20193)*
Columbus Meats Inc .... G 312 829-2480
 Chicago *(G-4207)*
Country Village Meats .... G 815 849-5532
 Sublette *(G-19635)*
Cub Foods Inc .... C 309 689-0140
 Peoria *(G-16428)*
Dreymiller & Kray Inc .... G 847 683-2271
 Hampshire *(G-10969)*
Eickmans Processing Co Inc .... E 815 247-8451
 Seward *(G-18867)*
Elburn Market Inc .... G 630 365-6461
 Elburn *(G-8451)*
Farmington Locker/Ice Plant Co .... G 309 245-4621
 Farmington *(G-9661)*
Jones Packing Co .... G 815 943-4488
 Harvard *(G-11058)*
Korte Meat Processors Inc .... G 618 654-3813
 Highland *(G-11230)*
M E F Corp .... F 815 965-8604
 Rockford *(G-17501)*
Moweaqua Packing Plant .... G 217 768-4714
 Moweaqua *(G-14652)*
Nea Agora Packing Co .... G 312 421-5130
 Chicago *(G-5560)*
Peoria Packing Ltd .... F 312 226-2600
 Chicago *(G-5787)*

PRODUCT SECTION

Polancics Meats & Tenderloins .... G 815 433-0324
 Ottawa *(G-16073)*
Raber Packing Company .... E 309 673-0721
 Peoria *(G-16507)*
Seifferts Locker & Meat Proc .... F 618 594-3921
 Carlyle *(G-2895)*
Wurst Kitchen Inc .... G 630 898-9242
 Aurora *(G-1171)*
Y T Packing Co .... F 217 522-3345
 Springfield *(G-19470)*

MEAT PRDTS: Boneless Meat, From Purchased Meat

Chicago Local Foods LLC .... E 312 432-6575
 Chicago *(G-4111)*
Greenridge Farm Inc .... E 847 434-1803
 Elk Grove Village *(G-9024)*
Ogden Foods LLC .... G 773 277-8207
 Chicago *(G-5660)*
Ogden Foods LLC .... G 773 801-0125
 Chicago *(G-5661)*

MEAT PRDTS: Boxed Beef, From Slaughtered Meat

Aurora Packing Company Inc .... C 630 897-0551
 North Aurora *(G-15255)*
Tyson Fresh Meats Inc .... F 847 836-5550
 Elgin *(G-8764)*
Valley Meats LLC .... E 309 799-7341
 Coal Valley *(G-6939)*

MEAT PRDTS: Canned Exc Baby Food, From Slaughtered Meat

Bar-B-Que Industries Inc .... F 773 227-5400
 Chicago *(G-3829)*
Sommers Fare LLC .... E 877 377-9797
 Mundelein *(G-14737)*

MEAT PRDTS: Cooked Meats, From Purchased Meat

Bkbg Enterprises Inc .... D 847 228-7070
 Carol Stream *(G-2947)*

MEAT PRDTS: Corned Beef, From Purchased Meat

Bar-B-Que Industries Inc .... F 773 227-5400
 Chicago *(G-3829)*

MEAT PRDTS: Cured Meats, From Purchased Meat

Dabecca Natural Foods Inc .... C 773 291-1428
 Chicago *(G-4304)*
West Loop Salumi Co .... G 312 255-7004
 Chicago *(G-6604)*

MEAT PRDTS: Frozen

Holten Meat Inc .... D 618 337-8400
 Sauget *(G-18394)*
Vhrk Food Inc .... G 630 640-6525
 Chicago *(G-6541)*

MEAT PRDTS: Hams & Picnics, From Slaughtered Meat

John Hofmeister & Son Inc .... D 773 847-0700
 Chicago *(G-5041)*
Plumrose Usa Inc .... G 732 253-5257
 Chicago *(G-5823)*
Plumrose Usa Inc .... E 800 526-4909
 Downers Grove *(G-8077)*

MEAT PRDTS: Lamb, From Slaughtered Meat

Grecian Delight Foods Inc .... C 847 364-1010
 Elk Grove Village *(G-9022)*
Halsted Packing House Co .... G 312 421-5147
 Chicago *(G-4774)*

MEAT PRDTS: Luncheon Meat, From Purchased Meat

Crawford Sausage Co Inc .... E 773 277-3095
 Chicago *(G-4260)*

PRODUCT SECTION

MEAT PROCESSED FROM PURCHASED CARCASSES

MEAT PRDTS: Meat By-Prdts, From Slaughtered Meat

Best Chicago Meat Company LLC ....F 773 523-8161
  Chicago *(G-3870)*
Stewart Brothers Packing Co ....G....... 217 422-7741
  Decatur *(G-7551)*
T & J Meatpacking Inc ....D....... 708 758-6748
  Chicago Heights *(G-6778)*

MEAT PRDTS: Pork, From Slaughtered Meat

Calihan Pork Processors Inc ....D....... 309 674-9175
  Peoria *(G-16396)*
Grant Park Packing Company Inc ....E 312 421-4096
  Franklin Park *(G-9952)*
J Brodie Meat Products Inc ....F 309 342-1500
  Galesburg *(G-10202)*
Rose Packing Company Inc ....A....... 708 458-9300
  Chicago *(G-6062)*

MEAT PRDTS: Prepared Beef Prdts From Purchased Beef

Charles Autin Limited ....D....... 312 432-0888
  Chicago *(G-4072)*
Farmington Foods Inc ....C....... 708 771-3600
  Forest Park *(G-9714)*
Kronos Foods Corp ....B....... 224 353-5400
  Glendale Heights *(G-10465)*
New Specialty Products Inc ....E 773 847-0230
  Chicago *(G-5579)*
Specialty Foods Group LLC ....G....... 630 599-5900
  Lombard *(G-13132)*
Stampede Meat Inc ....A....... 773 376-4300
  Bridgeview *(G-2389)*
Vienna Beef Ltd ....E 773 278-7800
  Chicago *(G-6548)*

MEAT PRDTS: Prepared Pork Prdts, From Purchased Meat

Bridgford Foods Corporation ....B....... 312 733-0300
  Chicago *(G-3958)*
John J Moesle Whl Meats Inc ....F 773 847-4900
  Chicago *(G-5042)*
Polancics Meats & Tenderloins ....G....... 815 433-0324
  Ottawa *(G-16073)*
Trim-Rite Food Corporation ....C....... 847 649-3400
  Carpentersville *(G-3121)*

MEAT PRDTS: Roast Beef, From Purchased Meat

Greenleaf Foods Spc ....E 800 268-3708
  Elmhurst *(G-9369)*

MEAT PRDTS: Sausage Casings, Natural

Van Hessen USA Inc ....E 773 376-9200
  Chicago *(G-6519)*
Viscofan Usa Inc ....D....... 217 444-8000
  Danville *(G-7392)*

MEAT PRDTS: Sausages & Related Prdts, From Purchased Meat

Ifa International Inc ....F 847 566-0008
  Mundelein *(G-14698)*
Russo Wholesale Meat Inc ....G....... 708 385-0500
  Alsip *(G-507)*

MEAT PRDTS: Sausages, From Purchased Meat

Andys Deli and Mikolajczyk ....E 773 722-1000
  Chicago *(G-3694)*
Bende Inc ....G....... 847 913-0304
  Vernon Hills *(G-20047)*
C & F Packing Co Inc ....C....... 847 245-2000
  Lake Villa *(G-12348)*
Cherry Meat Packers Inc ....E 773 927-1200
  Chicago *(G-4083)*
Elburn Market Inc ....E 630 365-6461
  Elburn *(G-8451)*
Fabbri Sausage Manufacturing ....E 312 829-6363
  Chicago *(G-4554)*
Hillshire Brands Company ....E 847 310-9400
  Schaumburg *(G-18549)*
Makowskis Real Sausage Co ....E 312 842-5330
  Chicago *(G-5321)*

Momence Packing Co ....B....... 815 472-6485
  Momence *(G-14188)*
Oriental Kitchen Corporation ....F 312 738-2850
  Chicago *(G-5698)*
Oscars Foods Inc ....G....... 773 622-6822
  Chicago *(G-5708)*
Papa Charlies Inc ....E 773 522-7900
  Chicago *(G-5752)*
Pcj II Inc ....E 312 829-2250
  Chicago *(G-5773)*
Randolph Packing Co ....D....... 630 830-3100
  Streamwood *(G-19592)*
Roma Packing Co ....G....... 773 927-7371
  Chicago *(G-6055)*
Smolich Brothers Sausage Inc ....G....... 815 727-2144
  Joliet *(G-11931)*
Stiglmeier Sausage Co Inc ....F 847 537-9988
  Wheeling *(G-20991)*
Wurst Kitchen Inc ....G....... 630 898-9242
  Aurora *(G-1171)*

MEAT PRDTS: Sausages, From Slaughtered Meat

Heinkels Packing Company Inc ....E 217 428-4401
  Decatur *(G-7501)*

MEAT PRDTS: Smoked

A New Dairy Company ....E 312 421-1234
  Chicago *(G-3489)*
Carl Buddig and Company ....C....... 708 798-0900
  Homewood *(G-11489)*
Food Purveyors Logistics ....F 630 229-6168
  Naperville *(G-14829)*
Land OFrost Inc ....C....... 708 474-7100
  Lansing *(G-12502)*
Salatas Smoked Meats ....G....... 224 433-1205
  McHenry *(G-13790)*
Sparrer Sausage Company Inc ....C....... 773 762-3334
  Chicago *(G-6208)*

MEAT PRDTS: Snack Sticks, Incl Jerky, From Purchased Meat

Think Jerky LLC ....G....... 917 623-1989
  Chicago *(G-6364)*

MEAT PRDTS: Veal, From Slaughtered Meat

Brown Packing Company Inc ....E 708 849-7990
  South Holland *(G-19202)*

MEAT PROCESSED FROM PURCHASED CARCASSES

Allens Farm Quality Meats ....G....... 217 896-2532
  Homer *(G-11474)*
Amylu Foods LLC ....E 312 829-2250
  Chicago *(G-3689)*
Another Chance Community Dev ....E 773 998-1641
  Chicago *(G-3702)*
Arts Tamales ....G....... 309 367-2850
  Metamora *(G-13958)*
Atlantic Beverage Company Inc ....G....... 847 412-6200
  Northbrook *(G-15342)*
B B M Packing Co Inc ....B....... 312 243-1061
  Chicago *(G-3807)*
Ba Le Meat Processing & Whl Co ....F 773 506-2499
  Chicago *(G-3810)*
Barbecue Select Inc ....F 773 847-0230
  Chicago *(G-3830)*
Belmont Sausage Company ....E 847 357-1515
  Elk Grove Village *(G-8864)*
Bob Evans Farms Inc ....D....... 309 932-2194
  Galva *(G-10229)*
Bobak Sausage Company ....E 773 735-5334
  Chicago *(G-3922)*
Branding Iron Holdings Inc ....G....... 618 337-8400
  Sauget *(G-18390)*
Brown Packing Company Inc ....E 708 849-7990
  South Holland *(G-19202)*
Bruss Company ....E 773 282-2900
  Chicago *(G-3969)*
Carroll County Locker ....G....... 815 493-2370
  Lanark *(G-12478)*
Cass Meats ....G....... 217 452-3072
  Virginia *(G-20193)*
Columbus Meats Inc ....G....... 312 829-2480
  Chicago *(G-4207)*

Conagra Brands Inc ....C....... 312 549-5000
  Chicago *(G-4212)*
Conagra Brands Inc ....C....... 630 857-1000
  Naperville *(G-14803)*
Consumers Packing Co Inc ....D....... 708 344-0047
  Melrose Park *(G-13844)*
Country Village Meats ....G....... 815 849-5532
  Sublette *(G-19635)*
Crown Corned Beef and Foods ....G....... 312 738-0099
  Chicago *(G-4277)*
Danielson Food Products Inc ....E 773 285-2111
  Chicago *(G-4314)*
Dawn Food Products Inc ....C....... 815 933-0600
  Bradley *(G-2280)*
Dons Meat Market ....G....... 309 968-6026
  Manito *(G-13438)*
Dreymiller & Kray Inc ....G....... 847 683-2271
  Hampshire *(G-10969)*
Earlville Cold Stor Lckr LLC ....G....... 815 246-9469
  Earlville *(G-8160)*
Ed Kabrick Beef Inc ....G....... 217 656-3263
  Plainville *(G-16729)*
Edgar County Locker Service ....G....... 217 466-5000
  Paris *(G-16229)*
Eickmans Processing Co Inc ....E 815 247-8451
  Seward *(G-18867)*
Emmel Inc ....G....... 847 254-5178
  Lake In The Hills *(G-12334)*
Eureka Locker Inc ....F 309 467-2731
  Eureka *(G-9482)*
Farmington Locker/Ice Plant Co ....G....... 309 245-4621
  Farmington *(G-9661)*
Freedom Sausage Inc ....F 815 792-8276
  Earlville *(G-8161)*
George Nottoli & Sons Inc ....G....... 773 589-1010
  Chicago *(G-4683)*
Givaudan Flavors Corporation ....C....... 630 682-5600
  Carol Stream *(G-2992)*
Glenmark Industries Ltd ....C....... 773 927-4800
  Chicago *(G-4694)*
Golden Locker Inc ....G....... 217 696-4456
  Camp Point *(G-2811)*
Grecian Delight Foods Inc ....C....... 847 364-1010
  Elk Grove Village *(G-9022)*
Gridley Meat Products LLC ....G....... 309 747-2120
  Gridley *(G-10844)*
H & B Hams ....G....... 618 372-8690
  Brighton *(G-2400)*
Halsted Packing House Co ....G....... 312 421-5147
  Chicago *(G-4774)*
Hansen Packing Co ....G....... 618 498-3714
  Jerseyville *(G-11792)*
Hartrich Meats Inc ....G....... 618 455-3172
  Sainte Marie *(G-18326)*
Hillshire Brands Company ....B....... 312 614-6000
  Chicago *(G-4820)*
Hillshire Brands Company ....A....... 312 614-6000
  Chicago *(G-4821)*
Hillshire Brands Company ....B....... 800 727-2533
  Rochelle *(G-17144)*
Hillshire Brands Company ....G....... 888 317-5867
  Chicago *(G-4822)*
Hillshire Brands Company ....E 312 614-6000
  Downers Grove *(G-8022)*
Hillshire Brands Company ....F 630 991-5100
  Downers Grove *(G-8023)*
Houser Meats ....G....... 217 322-4994
  Rushville *(G-18110)*
J Brodie Meat Products Inc ....F 309 342-1500
  Galesburg *(G-10202)*
Jackson & Partners LLC ....G....... 630 219-1598
  Naperville *(G-14853)*
Johnsons Processing Plant ....G....... 815 684-5183
  Chadwick *(G-3258)*
Jones Packing Co ....G....... 815 943-4488
  Harvard *(G-11058)*
Koenemann Sausage Co ....G....... 815 385-6260
  Volo *(G-20201)*
Korte Meat Processors Inc ....G....... 618 654-3813
  Highland *(G-11230)*
Kraft Foods Asia PCF Svcs LLC ....G....... 847 943-4000
  Deerfield *(G-7627)*
Lake Pacific Partners LLC ....B....... 312 578-1110
  Chicago *(G-5161)*
Lena AJS Maid Meats ....F 815 369-4522
  Lena *(G-12602)*
M E F Corp ....F 815 965-8604
  Rockford *(G-17501)*
Meats By Linz Inc ....E 708 862-0830
  Calumet City *(G-2783)*

Employee Codes: A=Over 500 employees, B=251-500
C=101-250, D=51-100, E=20-50, F=10-19, G=3-9

MEAT PROCESSED FROM PURCHASED CARCASSES

Mistica Foods LLC ....C 630 543-5409
  Addison (G-219)
Mondelez International Inc ....G 815 710-2114
  Morris (G-14316)
Mondelez International Inc ....A 847 943-4000
  Chicago (G-5490)
Morris Meat Packing Co Inc ....G 708 865-8566
  Maywood (G-13673)
Moweaqua Packing Plant 217 768-4714
  Moweaqua (G-14652)
Nea Agora Packing Co 312 421-5130
  Chicago (G-5560)
O Chilli Frozen Foods Inc ....E 847 562-1991
  Northbrook (G-15442)
Old Fashioned Meat Co Inc 312 421-4555
  Chicago (G-5668)
On-Cor Frozen Foods LLC ....E 630 851-6600
  Aurora (G-1142)
OSI Industries LLC ....C 630 231-9090
  West Chicago (G-20627)
OSI Industries LLC ....B 773 847-2000
  Chicago (G-5710)
OSI International Foods Ltd ....D 630 851-6600
  Aurora (G-1005)
Park Packing Company Inc ....E 773 254-0100
  Chicago (G-5764)
Plumrose Usa Inc ....E 800 526-4909
  Downers Grove (G-8077)
Portillos Food Service Inc ....E 630 620-0460
  Addison (G-247)
Powers John 309 742-8929
  Elmwood (G-9449)
R&R Meat Co ....G 270 898-6296
  Metropolis (G-13976)
Rapid Foods Inc ....G 708 366-0321
  Shorewood (G-18902)
Roca Inc ....F 312 421-2345
  Chicago (G-6047)
Rochelle Foods LLC ....A 815 562-4141
  Rochelle (G-17155)
Rose Packing Company Inc ....A 708 458-9300
  Chicago (G-6062)
Ryan Meat Company ....G 773 783-3840
  Evergreen Park (G-9599)
Seifferts Locker & Meat Proc ....F 618 594-3921
  Carlyle (G-2895)
Smithfield Packaged Meats Corp ....A 309 734-5353
  Monmouth (G-14227)
Specialty Foods Group LLC ....C 773 378-1300
  Chicago (G-6213)
Steinbach Provision Company ....G 773 538-1511
  Chicago (G-6238)
T & J Meatpacking Inc ....D 708 758-6748
  Chicago Heights (G-6778)
Tandem Usa LLC ....G 224 653-8840
  Schaumburg (G-18739)
Tomcyndi Inc ....E 773 847-5400
  Chicago (G-6389)
Tyson Foods ....C 312 614-6000
  Chicago (G-6452)
Tyson Fresh Meats Inc ....F 847 836-5550
  Elgin (G-8764)
V A M D Inc 773 631-8400
  Chicago (G-6512)
Vienna Beef Ltd ....F 800 366-3647
  Chicago (G-6549)
William Badal ....G 815 264-7752
  Waterman (G-20303)
Y T Packing Co ....F 217 522-3345
  Springfield (G-19470)

MEAT PROCESSING MACHINERY

Cozzini LLC ....C 773 478-9700
  Elk Grove Village (G-8917)
E-Quip Manufacturing Co ....E 815 464-0053
  Frankfort (G-9790)
Hollymatic Corporation ....D 708 579-3700
  Countryside (G-7057)
Miles Bros ....G 618 937-4115
  West Frankfort (G-20678)
Primedge Inc ....C 224 265-6600
  Elk Grove Village (G-9197)
Rantoul Foods LLC ....B 217 892-4178
  Rantoul (G-16981)
Stephen Paoli Mfg Corp ....F 815 965-0621
  Rockford (G-17646)
TEC Systems Inc ....F 815 722-2800
  New Lenox (G-15062)
Tyson Fresh Meats Inc ....F 847 836-5550
  Elgin (G-8764)

MEATS, PACKAGED FROZEN: Wholesalers

B B M Packing Co Inc ....G 312 243-1061
  Chicago (G-3807)
Bruss Company ....E 773 282-2900
  Chicago (G-3969)
Fabbri Sausage Manufacturing ....E 312 829-6363
  Chicago (G-4554)
Randolph Packing Co ....D 630 830-3100
  Streamwood (G-19592)

MECHANISMS: Coin-Operated Machines

Advanced Technologies Inc ....G 847 329-9875
  Park Ridge (G-16264)
Laurel Metal Products Inc ....E 847 674-0064
  Lincolnwood (G-12827)

MEDIA BUYING AGENCIES

7000 Inc ....F 312 800-3612
  Bolingbrook (G-2143)

MEDIA: Magnetic & Optical Recording

Acro Magnetics Inc ....G 815 943-5018
  Harvard (G-11040)
Bpn Chicago ....E 312 799-4100
  Chicago (G-3940)
Brandmuscle Inc ....G 866 236-8481
  Chicago (G-3946)
Magnetic Occasions & More Inc ....G 815 462-4141
  New Lenox (G-15040)

MEDICAL & HOSPITAL EQPT WHOLESALERS

1 Federal Supply Source Inc ....G 708 964-2222
  Steger (G-19486)
Airgas Usa LLC ....E 708 354-0813
  Countryside (G-7043)
Cardinal Health Inc ....B 847 578-4443
  Waukegan (G-20424)
McClendon Holdings LLC ....G 773 251-2314
  Chicago (G-5373)
Medtex Health Services Inc ....G 630 789-0330
  Clarendon Hills (G-6900)
Revolutionary Medical Dvcs Inc ....F 520 464-4299
  Mettawa (G-13981)
Sage Products LLC ....C 815 455-4700
  Cary (G-3188)
Sage Products Holdings II LLC ....G 800 323-2220
  Cary (G-3189)
Vicron Optical Inc ....F 847 412-5530
  Deerfield (G-7657)

MEDICAL & HOSPITAL SPLYS: Radiation Shielding Garments

Accurate Radiation Shielding ....G 847 639-5533
  Cary (G-3143)
Tradex International Inc ....D 216 651-4788
  Elwood (G-9465)

MEDICAL & SURGICAL SPLYS: Abdominal Support, Braces/Trusses

Milvia ....G 312 527-3403
  Chicago (G-5463)

MEDICAL & SURGICAL SPLYS: Bandages & Dressings

Eln Group LLC ....G 847 477-1496
  Winnetka (G-21128)
Newmedical Technology Inc ....E 847 412-1000
  Northbrook (G-15441)

MEDICAL & SURGICAL SPLYS: Braces, Orthopedic

MD Orthotic Prosthetic Lab Inc ....E 708 387-9700
  Brookfield (G-2488)
Midwest Orthotic & Technology ....G 773 930-3770
  Burr Ridge (G-2703)
O & P Kinetic 815 401-7260
  Bourbonnais (G-2267)
Pal Health Technologies Inc ....D 309 347-8785
  Pekin (G-16351)
Therapeutic Envisions Inc 720 323-7032
  Libertyville (G-12716)

MEDICAL & SURGICAL SPLYS: Clothing, Fire Resistant & Protect

Salisbury Elec Safety LLC ....B 877 406-4501
  Bolingbrook (G-2234)

MEDICAL & SURGICAL SPLYS: Cosmetic Restorations

Cosmedent Inc ....E 312 644-9388
  Chicago (G-4245)
Lemaitre Vascular Inc ....F 847 462-2191
  Fox River Grove (G-9760)

MEDICAL & SURGICAL SPLYS: Crutches & Walkers

Go Steady LLC ....G 630 293-3243
  West Chicago (G-20588)

MEDICAL & SURGICAL SPLYS: Drapes, Surgical, Cotton

Brandt Interiors ....G 847 251-3543
  Wilmette (G-21071)

MEDICAL & SURGICAL SPLYS: Gauze, Surgical

Brasel Products Inc ....G 630 879-3759
  Batavia (G-1360)
Modern Aids Inc ....E 847 437-8600
  Elk Grove Village (G-9130)

MEDICAL & SURGICAL SPLYS: Gynecological Splys & Appliances

Medgyn Products Inc ....D 630 627-4105
  Addison (G-195)

MEDICAL & SURGICAL SPLYS: Infant Incubators

Mhub ....G 773 580-1485
  Chicago (G-5420)

MEDICAL & SURGICAL SPLYS: Ligatures

Star Cushion Products Inc ....F 618 539-7070
  Freeburg (G-10096)

MEDICAL & SURGICAL SPLYS: Limbs, Artificial

D J Peters Orthopedics Ltd ....G 309 664-6930
  Bloomington (G-2037)
Gema Inc ....F 773 508-6690
  Chicago (G-4668)
Hanger Prosthetics & ....G 847 623-6080
  Gurnee (G-10886)
Hanger Prosthetics & ....G 630 820-5656
  Aurora (G-977)
Illiana Orthopedics Inc ....G 708 532-0061
  Tinley Park (G-19836)
Koebers Prosthetic Orthpd Lab ....G 309 676-2276
  Chicago (G-5117)
Psyonic Inc ....G 888 779-6642
  Champaign (G-3340)
Quad City Prosthetics Inc ....F 309 676-2276
  Rock Island (G-17236)
Ronald S Lefors Bs Cpo ....G 618 259-1969
  East Alton (G-8170)
Scheck Siress Prosthetics Inc ....C 630 424-0392
  Oak Park (G-15771)
Tuu Duc Le Inc ....G 630 897-6363
  North Aurora (G-15280)

MEDICAL & SURGICAL SPLYS: Models, Anatomical

Anatomical Worldwide LLC ....G 312 224-4772
  Evanston (G-9494)

MEDICAL & SURGICAL SPLYS: Orthopedic Appliances

Bergmann Orthotic Lab Inc ....G 847 446-3616
  Northfield (G-15508)
Bergmann Orthotic Laboratory ....G 847 729-7923
  Glenview (G-10531)

PRODUCT SECTION

MEDICAL EQPT: Ultrasonic, Exc Cleaning

Company	Code	Phone
Comfort Companies LLC	E	406 522-8560
Belleville (G-1540)		
Daniel Zimmer Associates	F	847 697-9393
North Barrington (G-15283)		
Dreher Orthopedic Industries	G	708 848-4646
Western Springs (G-20721)		
Hanger Prsthtics Orthotics Inc	G	815 744-9944
Joliet (G-11873)		
Howmedica Osteonics Corp	G	309 663-6414
Bloomington (G-2059)		
JP Orthotics	G	217 885-3047
Quincy (G-16898)		
Neo Orthotics Inc	G	309 699-0354
East Peoria (G-8279)		
Northern Prosthetics	G	815 226-0444
Rockford (G-17539)		
Optech Ortho & Prosth Svcs	F	815 932-8564
Kankakee (G-11995)		
PR Manufacturing Entps LLC	E	309 347-8785
Pekin (G-16354)		
Prosthetic Orthotic Specialist	F	309 454-8733
Normal (G-15219)		
Roho Inc	D	618 277-9173
Belleville (G-1592)		
Serola Biomechanics Inc	F	815 636-2780
Loves Park (G-13263)		
Stellar Orthtics Prsthtics LLC	F	847 410-2751
Glenview (G-10626)		
World Class Technologies Inc	G	312 758-3114
Chicago (G-6672)		

MEDICAL & SURGICAL SPLYS: Personal Safety Eqpt

Company	Code	Phone
E&B Exercise LLC	G	844 425-5025
Chicago (G-4426)		
Fall Protection Systems Inc	E	618 452-7000
Madison (G-13411)		
Guardian Equipment Inc	E	312 447-8100
Chicago (G-4747)		
Midwest Water Group Inc	E	866 526-6558
Crystal Lake (G-7230)		
One Way Safety LLC	E	708 579-0229
La Grange (G-12085)		
Plastic Specialists America	G	847 406-7547
Gurnee (G-10912)		
Prointegration Tech LLC	E	618 409-3233
Highland (G-11235)		
R G H & Associates Inc	G	630 357-5915
Naperville (G-14904)		
Standard Safety Equipment Co	E	815 363-8565
McHenry (G-13795)		
Steel-Guard Safety Corp	G	708 589-4588
South Holland (G-19246)		
Steiner Industries Inc	D	773 588-3444
Chicago (G-6240)		
Triad Controls Inc	D	630 443-9320
Saint Charles (G-18291)		
Weeb Enterprises LLC	G	815 861-2625
Wauconda (G-20402)		

MEDICAL & SURGICAL SPLYS: Prosthetic Appliances

Company	Code	Phone
Advanced O&P Solutions	E	708 878-2241
Hickory Hills (G-11193)		
Becks Medical & Indus Gases	F	618 273-9019
Eldorado (G-8479)		
Bioconcepts Inc	G	630 986-0007
Burr Ridge (G-2656)		
David Rotter Prosthetics Ltd	G	815 255-3220
Joliet (G-11853)		
Dental Craft Corp	F	815 385-7132
Ringwood (G-17041)		
Hanger Inc	E	847 695-6955
McHenry (G-13747)		
Hanger Inc	F	708 679-1006
Matteson (G-13624)		
Optech Ortho & Prosth Svcs	G	708 364-9700
Orland Park (G-15972)		
Payne Chauna	G	618 580-2584
Belleville (G-1583)		
Prosthetics Orthotics Han	G	847 695-6955
McHenry (G-13784)		
Research Design Inc	G	708 246-8166
Western Springs (G-20724)		

MEDICAL & SURGICAL SPLYS: Respiratory Protect Eqpt, Personal

Company	Code	Phone
Cornucopia Supply Corp	G	847 532-9365
Morton Grove (G-14397)		
Rondex Products Incorporated	F	815 226-0452
Rockford (G-17615)		

MEDICAL & SURGICAL SPLYS: Splints, Pneumatic & Wood

Company	Code	Phone
Gregory Lamar & Assoc Inc	G	312 595-1545
Chicago (G-4741)		

MEDICAL & SURGICAL SPLYS: Sponges

Company	Code	Phone
Integrated Medical Tech Inc	G	309 662-3614
Bloomington (G-2062)		

MEDICAL & SURGICAL SPLYS: Supports, Abdominal, Ankle, Etc

Company	Code	Phone
New Step Orthotic Lab Inc	F	618 208-4444
Maryville (G-13592)		

MEDICAL & SURGICAL SPLYS: Technical Aids, Handicapped

Company	Code	Phone
Great Ideas Inc	F	800 611-5515
Highland Park (G-11267)		
R W G Manufacturing Inc	G	708 755-8035
S Chicago Hts (G-18127)		

MEDICAL & SURGICAL SPLYS: Welders' Hoods

Company	Code	Phone
Sourcennex International Co	G	847 251-5500
Wilmette (G-21093)		
Tri R	G	224 399-7786
Libertyville (G-12718)		

MEDICAL EQPT REPAIR SVCS, NON-ELECTRIC

Company	Code	Phone
Rampnow LLC	G	630 892-7267
Montgomery (G-14266)		

MEDICAL EQPT: Cardiographs

Company	Code	Phone
Elmed Incorporated	E	224 353-6446
Glendale Heights (G-10448)		

MEDICAL EQPT: Diagnostic

Company	Code	Phone
7000 Inc	F	312 800-3612
Bolingbrook (G-2143)		
Abbott Laboratories	A	224 667-6100
Abbott Park (G-1)		
Abbott Laboratories	G	800 551-5838
Lake Forest (G-12218)		
Abbott Laboratories	G	847 937-6100
North Chicago (G-15294)		
Abbott Laboratories Inc	C	224 668-2076
Abbott Park (G-2)		
Addition Technology Inc	F	847 297-8419
Lombard (G-13035)		
American Biooptics LLC	G	847 467-0628
Evanston (G-9493)		
Avant Diagnostics Inc	G	732 410-9810
Chicago (G-3783)		
Becton Dickinson and Company	G	630 743-2006
Downers Grove (G-7959)		
Carematix Inc	E	312 627-9300
Chicago (G-4028)		
Chronos Imaging LLC	D	630 296-9220
Aurora (G-938)		
Diagnostic Photonics Inc	G	312 320-5478
Chicago (G-4351)		
Feelsure Health Corparation	G	847 823-0137
Park Ridge (G-16275)		
Fisher Scientific Company LLC	G	800 528-0494
Chicago (G-4597)		
Hospira Inc	A	224 212-2000
Lake Forest (G-12259)		
Hospira Inc	C	224 212-6244
Lake Forest (G-12260)		
Hospira Worldwide LLC	G	224 212-2000
Lake Forest (G-12261)		
ISS Medical Inc	G	217 359-3681
Champaign (G-3311)		
Leica Microsystems Inc	C	847 405-0123
Buffalo Grove (G-2563)		
Luminex Corporation	G	847 400-9000
Northbrook (G-15423)		
MD Technologies Inc	F	815 598-3143
Elizabeth (G-8788)		
Mindful Mdispa Mediclinic Pllc	G	847 922-4768
Barrington (G-1229)		
Northgate Technologies Inc	E	847 608-8900
Elgin (G-8674)		
Nrtx LLC	G	224 717-0465
Chicago (G-5635)		
Odin Technologies LLC	G	408 309-1925
Chicago (G-5655)		
Provena Randalwood Open Mri	E	630 587-9917
Geneva (G-10300)		
Sensormedics Corporation	G	872 757-0114
Mettawa (G-13982)		
Siemens Med Solutions USA Inc	D	847 304-7700
Schaumburg (G-18712)		

MEDICAL EQPT: Electromedical Apparatus

Company	Code	Phone
CTS Automotive LLC	C	630 577-8800
Lisle (G-12880)		
General Electric Company	B	847 304-7400
Hoffman Estates (G-11428)		
Healthlight LLC	F	224 231-0342
Schaumburg (G-18544)		
Isovac Products LLC	G	630 679-1740
Romeoville (G-17834)		
Medical Specialties Distrs LLC	E	630 307-6200
Hanover Park (G-11009)		
Vivotronix Inc	G	312 536-3130
Chicago (G-6563)		

MEDICAL EQPT: Heart-Lung Machines, Exc Iron Lungs

Company	Code	Phone
Cardiac Imaging Inc	F	630 834-7100
Oakbrook Terrace (G-15791)		

MEDICAL EQPT: Laser Systems

Company	Code	Phone
Aespheptics Medical Ltd	G	630 416-1400
Lombard (G-13037)		
Dermatique Laser & Skin	F	630 262-2515
Geneva (G-10266)		
Samel Botros	G	847 466-5905
Bloomingdale (G-2014)		

MEDICAL EQPT: PET Or Position Emission Tomography Scanners

Company	Code	Phone
Positron Corporation	E	317 576-0183
Westmont (G-20765)		

MEDICAL EQPT: Patient Monitoring

Company	Code	Phone
7000 Inc	F	312 800-3612
Bolingbrook (G-2143)		
Dupage Chropractic Centre Ltd	G	630 858-9780
Glen Ellyn (G-10402)		
Neopenda Pbc	G	919 622-2487
Chicago (G-5570)		

MEDICAL EQPT: Ultrasonic Scanning Devices

Company	Code	Phone
Apana Inc	G	309 303-4007
Peoria (G-16384)		
Nanocytomics LLC	G	847 467-2868
Evanston (G-9556)		
Smart Scan Mri LLC	G	847 623-4000
Gurnee (G-10928)		
Verena Solutions LLC	G	314 651-1908
Chicago (G-6536)		

MEDICAL EQPT: Ultrasonic, Exc Cleaning

Company	Code	Phone
Amcor Flexibles LLC	F	847 362-9000
Mundelein (G-14662)		
Axiosonic LLC	F	217 342-3412
Effingham (G-8387)		
Ctg Advanced Materials LLC	E	630 226-9080
Bolingbrook (G-2161)		
Keebomed Inc	G	630 888-2888
Mount Prospect (G-14542)		
Victory Pharmacy Decatur Inc	G	708 801-9626
Calumet City (G-2792)		

Employee Codes: A=Over 500 employees, B=251-500
C=101-250, D=51-100, E=20-50, F=10-19, G=3-9

MEDICAL EQPT: X-Ray Apparatus & Tubes, Radiographic

General Electric Company ....C...... 630 588-8853
  Carol Stream *(G-2990)*
Wallace Enterprises Inc ....G...... 309 496-1230
  East Moline *(G-8247)*

MEDICAL EQPT: X-ray Generators

Sedecal Usa Inc ....E...... 847 394-6960
  Arlington Heights *(G-806)*

MEDICAL FIELD ASSOCIATION

American Assn Endodontists ....E...... 312 266-7255
  Chicago *(G-3648)*
American Assn Nurosurgeons Inc .....E...... 847 378-0500
  Rolling Meadows *(G-17710)*
American Cllege Chest Physcans .....D...... 224 521-9800
  Glenview *(G-10521)*
American Medical Association ....A...... 312 464-5000
  Chicago *(G-3660)*
American Soc Plastic Surgeons ....D...... 847 228-9900
  Arlington Heights *(G-691)*
International College Surgeons ....G...... 312 642-6502
  Chicago *(G-4952)*

MEDICAL SVCS ORGANIZATION

Smart Scan Mri LLC ....G...... 847 623-4000
  Gurnee *(G-10928)*
Surgical Solutions LLC ....C...... 847 607-6098
  Deerfield *(G-7650)*

MEDICAL TRAINING SERVICES

Tanaka Dental Enterprises Inc ....F...... 847 679-1610
  Skokie *(G-19042)*

MEDICAL X-RAY MACHINES & TUBES WHOLESALERS

Arquilla Inc ....F...... 815 455-2470
  Crystal Lake *(G-7163)*

MEDICAL, DENTAL & HOSPITAL EQPT, WHOL: Dentists' Prof Splys

Dental Laboratory Inc ....E...... 630 262-3700
  Geneva *(G-10265)*

MEDICAL, DENTAL & HOSPITAL EQPT, WHOL: Hospital Eqpt & Splys

Accurate Radiation Shielding ....G...... 847 639-5533
  Cary *(G-3143)*
C R Kesner Company ....G...... 630 232-8118
  Geneva *(G-10258)*
Omron Healthcare Inc ....D...... 847 680-6200
  Lake Forest *(G-12276)*

MEDICAL, DENTAL & HOSPITAL EQPT, WHOL: Hosptl Eqpt/Furniture

Faxitron X-Ray LLC ....E...... 847 465-9729
  Lincolnshire *(G-12763)*
Mark Industries ....G...... 847 487-8670
  Wauconda *(G-20372)*
Medifix Inc ....G...... 847 965-1898
  Morton Grove *(G-14427)*
Shenglong Intl Group Corp ....G...... 312 388-2345
  Glenview *(G-10615)*
Umf Corporation ....F...... 847 920-0370
  Skokie *(G-19049)*

MEDICAL, DENTAL & HOSPITAL EQPT, WHOL: Surgical Eqpt & Splys

Akorn Inc ....F...... 847 625-1100
  Gurnee *(G-10857)*
Akorn Inc ....C...... 847 279-6100
  Lake Forest *(G-12222)*
Tetra Medical Supply Corp ....F...... 847 647-0590
  Niles *(G-15179)*

MEDICAL, DENTAL & HOSPITAL EQPT, WHOLESALE: Artificial Limbs

Gema Inc ....F...... 773 508-6690
  Chicago *(G-4668)*

O & P Kinetic ....G...... 815 401-7260
  Bourbonnais *(G-2267)*

MEDICAL, DENTAL & HOSPITAL EQPT, WHOLESALE: Dental Lab

Bird-X Inc ....E...... 312 226-2473
  Elmhurst *(G-9334)*

MEDICAL, DENTAL & HOSPITAL EQPT, WHOLESALE: Diagnostic, Med

Carematix Inc ....E...... 312 627-9300
  Chicago *(G-4028)*

MEDICAL, DENTAL & HOSPITAL EQPT, WHOLESALE: Hearing Aids

Gohear LLC ....G...... 847 574-7829
  Lake Forest *(G-12252)*

MEDICAL, DENTAL & HOSPITAL EQPT, WHOLESALE: Med Eqpt & Splys

Brainlab Inc ....C...... 800 784-7700
  Westchester *(G-20692)*
Cino Incorporated ....G...... 630 377-7242
  Saint Charles *(G-18166)*
D-M-S Holdings Inc ....E...... 515 327-6416
  Waukegan *(G-20433)*
Doctors Choice Inc ....G...... 312 666-1111
  Chicago *(G-4378)*
Fenwal Inc ....B...... 800 333-6925
  Lake Zurich *(G-12411)*
General Bandages Inc ....F...... 847 966-8383
  Park Ridge *(G-16280)*
Good Lite Co ....G...... 847 841-1145
  Elgin *(G-8598)*
Howard Medical Company ....G...... 773 278-1440
  Chicago *(G-4850)*
Indilab Inc ....E...... 847 928-1050
  Franklin Park *(G-9962)*
Jero Medical Eqp & Sups Inc ....E...... 773 305-4193
  Chicago *(G-5022)*
Mac Medical Inc ....F...... 618 719-6757
  Belleville *(G-1569)*
Medela LLC ....C...... 800 435-8316
  McHenry *(G-13768)*
Medgyn Products Inc ....D...... 630 627-4105
  Addison *(G-195)*
Mobility Connection Inc ....G...... 815 965-8090
  Rockford *(G-17531)*
Northgate Technologies Inc ....E...... 847 608-8900
  Elgin *(G-8674)*
Richard Wolf Med Instrs Corp ....C...... 847 913-1113
  Vernon Hills *(G-20086)*
Simpex Medical Inc ....G...... 847 757-9928
  Mount Prospect *(G-14571)*
Sullivan Home Health Products ....G...... 217 532-6366
  Hillsboro *(G-11320)*
Upper Limits Midwest Inc ....G...... 217 679-4315
  Springfield *(G-19467)*
Victory Pharmacy Decatur Inc ....G...... 708 801-9626
  Calumet City *(G-2792)*
Wholesale Point Inc ....F...... 630 986-1700
  Burr Ridge *(G-2735)*

MEDICAL, DENTAL & HOSPITAL EQPT, WHOLESALE: Medical Lab

Asahi Kasei Bioprocess Inc ....E...... 847 834-0800
  Glenview *(G-10528)*
Baxter Healthcare Corporation ....E...... 847 578-4671
  Waukegan *(G-20422)*
Scientific Device Lab Inc ....E...... 847 803-9495
  Des Plaines *(G-7839)*
Spraying Systems Co ....F...... 630 665-5001
  Aurora *(G-1020)*

MEDICAL, DENTAL & HOSPITAL EQPT, WHOLESALE: Orthopedic

Serola Biomechanics Inc ....F...... 815 636-2780
  Loves Park *(G-13263)*

MEDICAL, DENTAL/HOSPITAL EQPT, WHOL: Tech Aids, Handicapped

Great Ideas Inc ....F...... 800 611-5515
  Highland Park *(G-11267)*

MEDITATION THERAPY

Mobile Health & Wellness Inc ....G...... 773 697-9892
  Chicago *(G-5475)*

MEMBERSHIP ORGANIZATIONS, BUSINESS: Contractors' Association

Be Group Inc ....G...... 312 436-0301
  Chicago *(G-3848)*
Shading Solutions Group Inc ....G...... 630 444-2102
  Geneva *(G-10305)*

MEMBERSHIP ORGANIZATIONS, BUSINESS: Merchants' Association

Narda Inc ....F...... 312 648-2300
  Chicago *(G-5540)*

MEMBERSHIP ORGANIZATIONS, NEC: Charitable

Spudnik Press Cooperative ....F...... 312 563-0302
  Chicago *(G-6222)*
Yesimpact ....G...... 765 413-9667
  Darien *(G-7415)*

MEMBERSHIP ORGANIZATIONS, PROFESSIONAL: Health Association

Christian Cnty Mntal Hlth Assn ....C...... 217 824-9675
  Taylorville *(G-19753)*

MEMBERSHIP ORGANIZATIONS, REL: Christian Reformed Church

Marantha Wrld Rvval Ministries ....G...... 773 384-7717
  Chicago *(G-5328)*

MEMBERSHIP ORGANIZATIONS, RELIGIOUS: Brethren Church

Church of Brethren Inc ....D...... 847 742-5100
  Elgin *(G-8539)*

MEMBERSHIP ORGANIZATIONS, RELIGIOUS: Catholic Church

Saints Volo & Olha Uk Cath Par ....G...... 312 829-5209
  Chicago *(G-6091)*

MEMBERSHIP ORGANIZATIONS, RELIGIOUS: Church Of Christ

St Johns United Church Christ ....G...... 847 491-6686
  Evanston *(G-9578)*

MEMBERSHIP ORGANIZATIONS, RELIGIOUS: Nonchurch

Baptist General Conference ....D...... 800 323-4215
  Arlington Heights *(G-703)*
Theosophical Society In Amer ....E...... 630 665-0130
  Wheaton *(G-20826)*

MEMBERSHIP ORGANIZATIONS: Reading Rooms/Other Cultural Orgs

Theosophical Society In Amer ....F...... 630 665-0123
  Wheaton *(G-20827)*

MEMBERSHIP ORGS, CIVIC, SOCIAL & FRATERNAL: Condo Assoc

Condominiums Northbrook Cort 1 ....G...... 847 498-1640
  Lincolnshire *(G-12754)*
Winnetka Mews Condominium Assn ...G...... 847 501-2770
  Winnetka *(G-21138)*

MEMBERSHIP ORGS, CIVIC, SOCIAL/FRAT: Educator's Assoc

Illinois Assn Cnty Officials ....F...... 217 585-9065
  Springfield *(G-19385)*
Poetry Center ....G...... 312 899-1229
  Chicago *(G-5829)*
Theosophical Society In Amer ....E...... 630 665-0130
  Wheaton *(G-20826)*
Theosophical Society In Amer ....F...... 630 665-0123
  Wheaton *(G-20827)*

PRODUCT SECTION
METAL FABRICATORS: Architechtural

MEMBERSHIP SPORTS & RECREATION CLUBS
Good Sam Enterprises LLC ...... E 847 229-6720
  Lincolnshire *(G-12767)*

MEMORIALS, MONUMENTS & MARKERS
All Saints Monument Co Inc ...... G 847 824-1248
  Des Plaines *(G-7725)*
Doh Services Inc ...... F 708 331-3811
  South Holland *(G-19209)*
Keepes Funeral Home Inc ...... F 618 262-5200
  Mount Carmel *(G-14476)*
Nashville Memorial Co ...... G 618 327-8492
  Nashville *(G-15004)*

MEN'S & BOYS' CLOTHING ACCESS STORES
Duckys Formal Wear Inc ...... G 309 342-5914
  Galesburg *(G-10191)*
Gcg Corp ...... G 847 298-2285
  Glenview *(G-10548)*
Hugo Boss Usa Inc ...... F 847 517-1461
  Schaumburg *(G-18552)*

MEN'S & BOYS' CLOTHING STORES
A&B Apparel ...... G 815 962-5070
  Rockford *(G-17281)*
Fashahnn Corporation ...... G 773 994-3132
  Chicago *(G-4561)*
Signature Design & Tailoring ...... F 773 375-4915
  Chicago *(G-6168)*

MEN'S & BOYS' CLOTHING WHOLESALERS, NEC
ASap Specialties Inc Del ...... G 847 223-7699
  Grayslake *(G-10759)*
Bird Dog Bay Inc ...... G 312 631-3108
  Chicago *(G-3899)*
Dzro-Bans International Inc ...... G 779 324-2740
  Homewood *(G-11492)*
Mennon Rbr & Safety Pdts Inc ...... G 847 678-8250
  Schiller Park *(G-18823)*
Miglio Di Mario Uomo Inc ...... G 312 391-0831
  Chicago *(G-5454)*

MEN'S & BOYS' SPORTSWEAR CLOTHING STORES
B JS Printables ...... G 618 656-8625
  Edwardsville *(G-8346)*
BMW Sportswear Inc ...... G 773 265-0110
  Chicago *(G-3921)*
Fielders Choice ...... G 618 937-2294
  West Frankfort *(G-20671)*
Johnos Inc ...... G 630 897-6929
  Aurora *(G-1119)*
Minerva Sportswear Inc ...... F 309 661-2387
  Bloomington *(G-2080)*
Te Shurt Shop Inc ...... F 217 344-1226
  Champaign *(G-3257)*

MEN'S & BOYS' SPORTSWEAR WHOLESALERS
American Outfitters Ltd ...... E 847 623-3959
  Waukegan *(G-20414)*
Art-Flo Shirt & Lettering Co ...... E 708 656-5422
  Chicago *(G-3738)*
B and A Screen Printing ...... G 217 762-2632
  Monticello *(G-14277)*
B JS Printables ...... G 618 656-8625
  Edwardsville *(G-8346)*
Hermans Inc ...... E 309 206-4892
  Rock Island *(G-17222)*
Ronald J Nixon ...... G 708 748-8130
  Park Forest *(G-16259)*

MENTAL HEALTH CLINIC, OUTPATIENT
Mental Health Ctrs Centl Ill ...... D 217 735-1413
  Lincoln *(G-12735)*

METAL & STEEL PRDTS: Abrasive
Avec Inc ...... G 815 577-3122
  Aurora *(G-917)*

Higman LLC ...... G 618 785-2545
  Baldwin *(G-1185)*
Severstal US Holdings II Inc ...... E 708 756-0400
  Hinsdale *(G-11379)*

METAL CUTTING SVCS
Accurate Metals Illinois LLC ...... F 815 966-6320
  Rockford *(G-17293)*
Custom Fabricators LLC ...... F 630 372-4399
  Streamwood *(G-19569)*
Laser Plus Technologies LLC ...... G 847 787-9017
  Elk Grove Village *(G-9086)*
Polaris Laser Laminations LLC ...... G 630 444-0760
  West Chicago *(G-20630)*
Production Fabg & Stamping Inc ...... F 708 755-5468
  S Chicago Hts *(G-18126)*
Progress Rail Services Corp ...... E 309 963-4425
  Danvers *(G-7317)*

METAL DETECTORS
Minelab Americas Inc ...... F 630 401-8150
  Naperville *(G-14871)*

METAL FABRICATORS: Architechtural
555 International Inc ...... E 773 847-1400
  Chicago *(G-3474)*
A Touch of Beauty Inc ...... G 708 387-0360
  Brookfield *(G-2477)*
Affton Fabg & Wldg Co Inc ...... G 314 781-4100
  Sauget *(G-18388)*
Aj Welding Services ...... G 708 843-2701
  Chicago *(G-3592)*
Alfredos Iron Works Inc ...... E 815 748-1177
  Cortland *(G-7017)*
Amron Stair Works Inc ...... F 847 426-4800
  Gilberts *(G-10350)*
Anchor Welding & Fabrication ...... G 815 937-1640
  Aroma Park *(G-839)*
AS Fabricating Inc ...... G 618 242-7438
  Mount Vernon *(G-14596)*
Atkore International Group Inc ...... A 708 339-1610
  Harvey *(G-11075)*
Atkore Intl Holdings Inc ...... G 708 225-2051
  Harvey *(G-11076)*
Bailey Hardwoods Inc ...... G 217 529-6800
  Springfield *(G-19324)*
Barker Metalcraft Inc ...... G 773 588-9300
  Chicago *(G-3833)*
Botti Studio of Architectural ...... E 847 869-5933
  Glenview *(G-10532)*
Capitol Wood Works LLC ...... D 217 522-5553
  Springfield *(G-19341)*
Chase Security Systems Inc ...... G 773 594-1919
  Chicago *(G-4078)*
Chicago Metal Rolled Pdts Co ...... D 773 523-5757
  Chicago *(G-4115)*
Chicago Ornamental Iron Inc ...... G 773 321-9635
  Chicago *(G-4121)*
Christopher Glass & Aluminum ...... D 312 256-8500
  Elmhurst *(G-9346)*
City Screen Inc ...... G 773 588-5642
  Chicago *(G-4161)*
Creative Iron ...... G 217 267-7797
  Westville *(G-20779)*
Creative Panel Systems Inc ...... G 630 625-5002
  Itasca *(G-11641)*
Daves Welding Service Inc ...... G 630 655-3224
  Darien *(G-7405)*
DSI Spaceframes Inc ...... E 630 607-0045
  Addison *(G-99)*
Economy Iron Inc ...... F 708 343-1777
  Melrose Park *(G-13859)*
Ed Stan Fabricating Co ...... G 708 863-7668
  Chicago *(G-4449)*
Empire Bronze Corp ...... F 630 916-9722
  Lombard *(G-13073)*
European Ornamental Iron Works ...... G 630 705-9300
  Addison *(G-117)*
Fariss John ...... G 815 433-3803
  Moline *(G-14144)*
Fbs Group Inc ...... F 773 229-8675
  Chicago *(G-4569)*
Fehring Ornamental Iron Works ...... G 217 483-6727
  Rochester *(G-17166)*
G & M Fabricating Inc ...... G 815 282-1744
  Roscoe *(G-17907)*
Gilco Real Estate Company ...... E 847 298-1717
  Des Plaines *(G-7774)*

Goose Island Mfg & Supply Corp ...... G 708 343-4225
  Lansing *(G-12495)*
Iron & Wire LLC ...... G 773 255-2672
  Chicago *(G-4968)*
ITW Blding Cmponents Group Inc ...... E 217 324-0303
  Litchfield *(G-12967)*
J B Metal Works Inc ...... G 847 824-4253
  Des Plaines *(G-7790)*
J C Schultz Enterprises Inc ...... D 800 323-9127
  Batavia *(G-1388)*
J H Botts LLC ...... E 815 726-5885
  Joliet *(G-11883)*
Jack Ruch Quality Homes Inc ...... G 309 663-6595
  Bloomington *(G-2063)*
John F Mate Co ...... G 847 381-8131
  Lake Barrington *(G-12154)*
Kencor Stairs & Woodworking ...... G 630 279-8980
  Villa Park *(G-20155)*
Ki Industries Inc ...... E 708 449-1990
  Berkeley *(G-1941)*
Lamonica Ornamental Iron Works ...... G 773 638-6633
  Chicago *(G-5172)*
Lawndale Forging & Tool Works ...... G 773 277-2800
  Chicago *(G-5183)*
Leggs Manufacturing ...... G 618 842-9847
  Fairfield *(G-9631)*
Legna Iron Works Inc ...... E 630 894-8056
  Roselle *(G-17964)*
Leonards Unit Step of Moline ...... G 309 792-9641
  Colona *(G-6976)*
Lickenbrock & Sons Inc ...... E 618 632-4977
  O Fallon *(G-15578)*
Lizotte Sheet Metal Inc ...... G 618 656-3066
  Edwardsville *(G-8368)*
Mechanical Indus Stl Svcs Inc ...... E 815 521-1725
  Channahon *(G-3389)*
Metal Edge Inc ...... F 708 756-4696
  Romeoville *(G-17850)*
Mj Snyder Ironworks Inc ...... G 217 826-6440
  Marshall *(G-13575)*
Montefusco Hvac Inc ...... G 309 691-7400
  Peoria *(G-16479)*
Nelson - Harkins Inds Inc ...... E 773 478-6243
  Lake Bluff *(G-12199)*
Nicks Metal Fabg & Sons ...... F 708 485-1170
  Brookfield *(G-2489)*
North Chicago Iron Works Inc ...... E 847 689-2000
  North Chicago *(G-15317)*
Old Style Iron Works Inc ...... G 773 265-5787
  Chicago *(G-5670)*
Orsolinis Welding & Fabg ...... F 773 722-9855
  Chicago *(G-5705)*
P & M Ornamental Ir Works Inc ...... F 708 267-2868
  Melrose Park *(G-13901)*
Paul D Metal Products Inc ...... D 773 847-1400
  Chicago *(G-5771)*
Quality Iron Works Inc ...... F 630 766-0885
  Bensenville *(G-1878)*
R & B Metal Products Inc ...... G 815 338-1890
  Woodstock *(G-21427)*
R & I Ornamental Iron Inc ...... E 847 836-6934
  Gilberts *(G-10366)*
Selvaggio Orna & Strl Stl Inc ...... E 217 528-4077
  Springfield *(G-19441)*
Sheas Iron Works Inc ...... G 847 356-2922
  Lake Villa *(G-12367)*
Sno Gem Inc ...... F 888 766-4367
  McHenry *(G-13792)*
South Subn Wldg & Fabg Co Inc ...... G 708 385-7160
  Posen *(G-16801)*
Steel Construction Svcs Inc ...... G 815 678-7509
  Richmond *(G-17023)*
Stevenson Fabrication Svcs Inc ...... G 815 468-7941
  Manteno *(G-13458)*
Summit Architectural Mtls LLC ...... F 815 934-3484
  Chicago *(G-6265)*
Tinsley Steel Inc ...... G 618 656-5231
  Edwardsville *(G-8378)*
Tuschall Engineering Co Inc ...... E 630 655-9100
  Burr Ridge *(G-2726)*
United Fence Co Inc ...... G 773 924-0773
  Chicago *(G-6472)*
Vector Custom Fabricating Inc ...... F 312 421-5161
  Chicago *(G-6528)*
W G N Flag & Decorating Co ...... F 773 768-8076
  Chicago *(G-6573)*
Werner Co ...... A 847 455-8001
  Itasca *(G-11754)*
Western Architectural Iron Co ...... E 773 463-1500
  Chicago *(G-6607)*

Employee Codes: A=Over 500 employees, B=251-500
C=101-250, D=51-100, E=20-50, F=10-19, G=3-9

METAL FABRICATORS: Plate

A & A Steel Fabricating Co F 708 389-4499
Posen *(G-16789)*
Abbey Metal Services Inc F 773 568-0330
Chicago *(G-3502)*
Ae2009 Technologies Inc E 708 331-0025
South Holland *(G-19188)*
Allquip Co Inc G 309 944-6153
Geneseo *(G-10239)*
Anchor Welding & Fabrication G 815 937-1640
Aroma Park *(G-839)*
AS Fabricating Inc G 618 242-7438
Mount Vernon *(G-14596)*
Asco LP F 630 789-2082
Arlington Heights *(G-697)*
Atlas Boiler & Welding Company G 815 963-3360
Elgin *(G-8517)*
Atlas Tool & Die Works Inc D 708 442-1661
Lyons *(G-13302)*
Barker Metalcraft Inc G 773 588-9300
Chicago *(G-3833)*
Beaver Creek Enterprises Inc F 815 723-9455
Joliet *(G-11829)*
BR Machine Inc F 815 434-0427
Ottawa *(G-16042)*
Burns Machine Company E 815 434-1660
Ottawa *(G-16045)*
C J Holdings Inc G 309 274-3141
Chillicothe *(G-6815)*
Cadillac Tank Met Fbrctors Inc E 630 543-2600
Addison *(G-62)*
Central Manufacturing Company G 309 387-6591
East Peoria *(G-8259)*
Certified Tank & Mfg LLC E 217 525-1433
Springfield *(G-19347)*
Chadwick Manufacturing Ltd G 815 684-5152
Chadwick *(G-3257)*
Colfax Welding & Fabricating G 847 359-4433
Palatine *(G-16101)*
Contech Engnered Solutions LLC E 217 529-5461
Springfield *(G-19354)*
Contech Engnered Solutions LLC G 630 573-1110
Oak Brook *(G-15613)*
Corrugated Converting Eqp F 618 532-2138
Centralia *(G-3227)*
Cyclops Welding Co G 815 223-0685
La Salle *(G-12109)*
D & D Manufacturing G 815 339-9100
Hennepin *(G-11157)*
D & K Tanks G 618 553-3186
Robinson *(G-17110)*
Debcor Inc G 708 333-2191
South Holland *(G-19207)*
Dip Seal Plastics Inc G 815 398-3533
Rockford *(G-17379)*
E H Baare Corporation C 618 546-1575
Robinson *(G-17114)*
Ed Stan Fabricating Co G 708 863-7668
Chicago *(G-4449)*
Edmik Inc E 847 263-0460
Gurnee *(G-10874)*
Eirich Machines Inc D 847 336-2444
Gurnee *(G-10875)*
Ekstrom Carlson Fabg Co Inc G 815 226-1511
Rockford *(G-17392)*
Elite Fabrication Inc G 773 274-4474
Chicago *(G-4486)*
Evapco Inc C 217 923-3431
Greenup *(G-10820)*
Fabtek Aero Ltd F 630 552-3622
Sandwich *(G-18369)*
G & M Fabricating Inc G 815 282-1744
Roscoe *(G-17907)*
G K Enterprises Inc G 708 587-2150
Monee *(G-14201)*
Gateway Fabricators Inc G 618 271-5700
East Saint Louis *(G-8310)*
Gpe Controls Inc F 708 236-6000
Hillside *(G-11340)*
H A Phillips & Co E 630 377-0050
Dekalb *(G-7683)*
Howe Corporation E 773 235-0200
Chicago *(G-4851)*
Illinois Rack Enterprises Inc E 815 385-5750
Lakemoor *(G-12472)*
Illinois Tool Works Inc C 708 325-2300
Bridgeview *(G-2356)*
Imperial Steel Tank G 773 779-4284
Chicago *(G-4900)*
J & G Fabricating Inc G 708 385-9147
Blue Island *(G-2126)*
J B Metal Works Inc G 847 824-4253
Des Plaines *(G-7790)*
J H Botts LLC E 815 726-5885
Joliet *(G-11883)*
Jet Rack Corp E 773 586-2150
Chicago *(G-5025)*
Jiffy Metal Products Inc G 773 626-8090
Chicago *(G-5030)*
JT Cullen Co Inc D 815 589-2412
Fulton *(G-10154)*
Lawndale Forging & Tool Works G 773 277-2800
Chicago *(G-5183)*
Lewis Process Systems Inc F 630 510-8200
Carol Stream *(G-3018)*
Lizotte Sheet Metal Inc G 618 656-3066
Edwardsville *(G-8368)*
Lmt Inc F 217 568-8265
Galva *(G-10235)*
Madison Inds Holdings LLC G 312 277-0156
Chicago *(G-5313)*
Mendota Welding & Mfg G 815 539-6944
Mendota *(G-13949)*
Mfi Industries Inc F 708 841-0727
Riverdale *(G-17073)*
Midwest Imperial Steel F 815 469-1072
Oak Lawn *(G-15728)*
Mj Snyder Ironworks Inc G 217 826-6440
Marshall *(G-13575)*
Montefusco Hvac Inc G 309 691-7400
Peoria *(G-16479)*
Mpc Containment Systems LLC G 773 927-4120
Chicago *(G-5516)*
Nalco Wtr Prtrtment Sltons LLC G 708 754-2550
Glenwood *(G-10644)*
Newman Welding & Machine Shop G 618 435-5591
Benton *(G-1934)*
Peerless America Incorporated C 217 342-0400
Effingham *(G-8418)*
Petro Chem Echer Erhardt LLC G 773 847-7535
Chicago *(G-5798)*
Pmt Nuclear G 630 887-7700
Woodridge *(G-21332)*
Pools Welding Inc G 309 787-2083
Milan *(G-14020)*
Precision Tank & Equipment Co D 217 452-7228
Virginia *(G-20195)*
Pryco Inc E 217 364-4467
Mechanicsburg *(G-13811)*
R & B Metal Products Inc E 815 338-1890
Woodstock *(G-21427)*
R-M Industries Inc F 630 543-3071
Addison *(G-264)*
Rayes Boiler & Welding Ltd G 847 675-6655
Skokie *(G-19020)*
Realwheels Corporation E 847 662-7722
Gurnee *(G-10923)*
Rome Metal Mfg Inc G 773 287-1755
Chicago *(G-6057)*
Ross and White Company F 847 516-3900
Cary *(G-3187)*
Shew Brothers Inc G 618 997-4414
Marion *(G-13534)*
Simplex Inc C 217 483-1600
Springfield *(G-19446)*
South Subn Wldg & Fabg Co Inc G 708 385-7160
Posen *(G-16801)*
Squibb Tank Company F 618 548-0141
Salem *(G-18360)*
Staffco Inc G 309 688-3223
Peoria *(G-16528)*
Tank Wind-Down Corp D 815 756-1551
Dekalb *(G-7707)*
Temprite Company E 630 293-5910
West Chicago *(G-20649)*
Tinsley Steel Inc G 618 656-5231
Edwardsville *(G-8378)*
Tranter Phe Inc F 217 227-3470
Farmersville *(G-9660)*
Tricon Wear Solutions LLC E 708 235-4064
University Park *(G-19969)*
Ucc Holdings Corporation E 847 473-5900
Waukegan *(G-20512)*
Unistrut International Corp D 630 773-3460
Addison *(G-323)*
Vapor Power International LLC D 630 694-5500
Franklin Park *(G-10075)*
Wcr Inc E 309 697-0389
Peoria *(G-16546)*
Whiting Corporation C 800 861-5744
Monee *(G-14212)*
Wilkos Industries G 563 249-6691
Savanna *(G-18413)*

METAL FABRICATORS: Sheet

555 International Inc E 773 847-1400
Chicago *(G-3474)*
A & A Steel Fabricating Co F 708 389-4499
Posen *(G-16789)*
A Hartlett & Sons Inc G 815 338-0109
Woodstock *(G-21353)*
A J Wagner & Son F 773 935-1414
Wauconda *(G-20323)*
A&S Machining & Welding Inc E 708 442-4544
Mc Cook *(G-13689)*
Abbott Scott Manufacturing Co E 773 342-7200
Chicago *(G-3505)*
Ablaze Welding & Fabricating G 815 965-0046
Rockford *(G-17287)*
Accu-Fab Incorporated E 847 541-4230
Wheeling *(G-20840)*
Ace Metal Spinning Inc F 708 389-5635
Alsip *(G-412)*
Advanced Custom Metals Inc G 847 803-2090
Des Plaines *(G-7723)*
Aetna Engineering Works Inc E 773 785-0489
Chicago *(G-3577)*
Afc Cable Systems Inc B 508 998-1131
Harvey *(G-11070)*
Agena Manufacturing Co E 630 668-5086
Carol Stream *(G-2928)*
Air Flow Company Inc F 630 628-1138
Addison *(G-25)*
All-Vac Industries Inc F 847 675-2290
Skokie *(G-18915)*
Allmetal Inc E 630 350-2524
Wood Dale *(G-21158)*
Alloy Welding Corp E 708 345-6756
Melrose Park *(G-13822)*
Allquip Co Inc G 309 944-6153
Geneseo *(G-10239)*
American Chute Systems Inc G 815 723-7632
Joliet *(G-11819)*
American Fuel Economy Inc G 815 433-3226
Ottawa *(G-16037)*
American Louver Company G 800 772-0355
Des Plaines *(G-7727)*
American Metal Installers & FA G 630 993-0812
Villa Park *(G-20131)*
American Shtmtl Fabricators F 708 877-7200
South Holland *(G-19194)*
Anchor Welding & Fabrication G 815 937-1640
Aroma Park *(G-839)*
Anytime Heating & AC F 630 851-6696
Naperville *(G-14959)*
Aquarius Metal Products Inc F 847 659-9266
Huntley *(G-11528)*
Arntzen Corporation E 815 334-0788
Woodstock *(G-21360)*
Arrow Sheet Metal Company E 815 455-2019
Crystal Lake *(G-7164)*
Art Wire Works Inc F 708 458-3993
Bedford Park *(G-1457)*
AS Fabricating Inc G 618 242-7438
Mount Vernon *(G-14596)*
Astoria Wire Products Inc D 708 496-9950
Bedford Park *(G-1459)*
B & D Independence Inc E 618 262-7117
Mount Carmel *(G-14465)*
B & J Wire Inc E 877 787-9473
Chicago *(G-3805)*
Barker Metalcraft Inc G 773 588-9300
Chicago *(G-3833)*
Bartec Orb Inc E 773 927-8600
Chicago *(G-3843)*
Beverly Shear Mfg Corporation G 773 233-2063
Chicago *(G-3877)*
Bill West Enterprises Inc G 217 886-2591
Jacksonville *(G-11757)*
Boekeloo Heating & Sheet Metal G 708 877-6560
Thornton *(G-19785)*
Boswell Building Contrs Inc F 630 595-5027
Wood Dale *(G-21171)*
Brex-Arlington Incorporated F 847 255-6284
Mount Prospect *(G-14515)*
Brian Burcar G 815 856-2271
Leonore *(G-12611)*
Busatis Inc G 630 844-9803
Montgomery *(G-14236)*

Company	Code	Phone	Location
Buww Coverings Incorporated	E	815 394-1985	Rockford *(G-17330)*
C J Holdings Inc	G	309 274-3141	Chillicothe *(G-6815)*
C Keller Manufacturing Inc	E	630 833-5593	Villa Park *(G-20136)*
Cgi Automated Mfg Inc	E	815 221-5300	Romeoville *(G-17805)*
Charles Industries LLC	D	217 893-8335	Rantoul *(G-16970)*
Chesterfield Awning Co Inc	F	708 596-4434	South Holland *(G-19205)*
Chicago Metal Rolled Pdts Co	D	773 523-5757	Chicago *(G-4115)*
Chicago Metal Supply Inc	G	773 417-7439	Chicago *(G-4116)*
Chicagoland Metal Fabricators	G	847 260-5320	Franklin Park *(G-9906)*
Chris Industries Inc	E	847 729-9292	Northbrook *(G-15359)*
Christensen Precision Products	G	630 543-6525	Addison *(G-72)*
City Screen Inc	G	773 588-5642	Chicago *(G-4161)*
Classic Sheet Metal Inc	E	630 694-0300	Addison *(G-73)*
Cobra Metal Works Inc	C	847 214-8400	Elgin *(G-8544)*
Colfax Welding & Fabricating	G	847 359-4433	Palatine *(G-16101)*
Control Equipment Company Inc	F	847 891-7500	Schaumburg *(G-18487)*
Cooper B-Line Inc	A	618 654-2184	Highland *(G-11210)*
Corrpak Inc	G	618 758-2755	Coulterville *(G-7030)*
Craftsman Custom Metals LLC	D	847 655-0040	Schiller Park *(G-18797)*
Crown Concepts Corporation	E	815 941-1081	Morris *(G-14299)*
Custom Copper Hoods Inc	G	224 577-9000	Libertyville *(G-12646)*
Custom Fabrications Inc	G	847 531-5912	Elgin *(G-8560)*
Cyclops Welding Co	G	815 223-0685	La Salle *(G-12109)*
D L Sheet Metal	G	708 599-5538	Palos Hills *(G-16199)*
D W Terry Welding Company	G	618 433-9722	Alton *(G-551)*
Dadant & Sons Inc	F	217 852-3324	Dallas City *(G-7313)*
Daniel Mfg Inc	F	309 963-4227	Carlock *(G-2886)*
Daves Welding Service Inc	G	630 655-3224	Darien *(G-7405)*
Delaney Sheet Metal Co	G	847 991-9579	Palatine *(G-16110)*
Depue Mechanical Inc	E	815 447-2267	Depue *(G-7716)*
Diemasters Manufacturing Inc	C	847 640-9900	Elk Grove Village *(G-8950)*
Dometic Corporation	A	847 447-7190	Rosemont *(G-18019)*
Duratrack Inc	E	847 806-0202	Elk Grove Village *(G-8960)*
Duroweld Company Inc	E	847 680-3064	Lake Bluff *(G-12179)*
Dynacoil Inc	E	847 731-3300	Zion *(G-21512)*
Ed Stan Fabricating Co	G	708 863-7668	Chicago *(G-4449)*
Eikenberry Sheet Metal Works	G	815 625-0955	Sterling *(G-19507)*
Ekstrom Carlson Fabg Co Inc	G	815 226-1511	Rockford *(G-17392)*
Elite Manufacturing Tech Inc	C	630 351-5757	Bloomingdale *(G-1991)*
Elk Grove Custom Sheet Metal	F	847 352-2845	Elk Grove Village *(G-8972)*
Emerald Machine Inc	G	773 924-3659	Chicago *(G-4495)*
Enterprise AC & Htg Co	G	708 430-2212	Chicago Ridge *(G-6794)*
Esi Steel & Fabrication	F	618 548-3017	Salem *(G-18338)*
Estes Laser & Mfg Inc	F	847 301-8231	Schaumburg *(G-18523)*
Ezee Roll Manufacturing Co	G	217 339-2279	Hoopeston *(G-11508)*
Eztech Manufacturing Inc	F	630 293-0010	West Chicago *(G-20582)*
F Kreutzer & Co	G	773 826-5767	Chicago *(G-4550)*
F Vogelmann and Company	F	815 469-2285	Frankfort *(G-9793)*
Fabricating Machinery Sales	E	630 350-2266	Wood Dale *(G-21186)*
Fanmar Inc	E	847 621-2010	Elk Grove Village *(G-8995)*
Farmweld Inc	E	217 857-6423	Teutopolis *(G-19769)*
Fbs Group Inc	F	773 229-8675	Chicago *(G-4569)*
Feralloy Corporation	E	503 286-8869	Chicago *(G-4580)*
Floline Archtctral Systems LLC	F	630 922-0550	Plainfield *(G-16666)*
Fulton Metal Works Inc	G	217 476-8223	Ashland *(G-884)*
G & M Fabricating Inc	G	815 282-1744	Roscoe *(G-17907)*
Gcb Metal Building Systems LLC	G	224 268-3792	Elgin *(G-8591)*
General Machinery & Mfg Co	F	773 235-3700	Chicago *(G-4674)*
Gengler-Lowney Laser Works	F	630 801-4840	Aurora *(G-1103)*
Glazed Structures Inc	F	847 223-4560	Grayslake *(G-10776)*
Gma Inc	G	630 595-1255	Bensenville *(G-1812)*
Grimm Metal Fabricators Inc	E	630 792-1710	Lombard *(G-13083)*
GROsse&sons Htg &SHeet Met Inc	G	708 447-8397	Lyons *(G-13310)*
Group Industries Inc	E	708 877-6200	Thornton *(G-19788)*
Helander Metal Spinning Co	E	630 268-9292	Lombard *(G-13084)*
Hendrick Metal Products LLC	D	847 742-7002	Elgin *(G-8612)*
Heritage Sheet Metal Inc	G	847 724-8449	Glenview *(G-10557)*
Highland Mch & Screw Pdts Co	D	618 654-2103	Highland *(G-11218)*
Hogg Welding Inc	G	708 339-0033	Harvey *(G-11089)*
Hohlflder A H Shtmtl Htg Coolg	G	815 965-9134	Rockford *(G-17451)*
Hontech International Corp	F	847 364-9800	Elk Grove Village *(G-9036)*
Hot Food Boxes Inc	E	773 533-5912	Chicago *(G-4846)*
Howler Fabrication & Wldg Inc	E	630 293-9300	West Chicago *(G-20593)*
I F & G Metal Craft Co	G	847 488-0630	South Elgin *(G-19153)*
Ibbotson Heating Co	E	847 253-0866	Arlington Heights *(G-752)*
Illinois Valley Glass & Mirror	F	309 682-6603	Peoria *(G-16457)*
Imh Fabrication Inc	F	815 537-2381	Prophetstown *(G-16833)*
Innotech Manufacturing LLC	E	618 244-6261	Mount Vernon *(G-14616)*
Ironform Holdings Co	B	312 374-4810	Chicago *(G-4970)*
J & G Fabricating Inc	G	708 385-9147	Blue Island *(G-2126)*
J & I Son Tool Company Inc	G	847 455-4200	Franklin Park *(G-9967)*
J & M Fab Metals Inc	G	815 758-0354	Marengo *(G-13486)*
J F Schroeder Company Inc	E	847 357-8600	Arlington Heights *(G-759)*
J K Manufacturing Co	D	708 563-2500	Bedford Park *(G-1475)*
J-TEC Metal Products Inc	F	630 875-1300	Itasca *(G-11679)*
JB Metalfab Mfg Inc	G	630 422-7420	Bensenville *(G-1828)*
John J Rickhoff Shtmtl Co Inc	F	708 331-2970	Phoenix *(G-16608)*
Joiner Sheet Metal & Roofg Inc	G	618 664-9488	Highland *(G-11229)*
JT Cullen Co Inc	D	815 589-2412	Fulton *(G-10154)*
K & K Tool & Die Inc	F	309 829-4479	Bloomington *(G-2065)*
K Three Welding Service Inc	G	708 563-2911	Chicago *(G-5067)*
Kcp Metal Fabrications Inc	E	773 775-0318	Chicago *(G-5088)*
Keil-Forness Comfort Systems	G	618 233-3039	Belleville *(G-1560)*
Kelley Construction Inc	B	217 422-1800	Decatur *(G-7513)*
Kemper Industries	G	217 826-5712	Marshall *(G-13573)*
Kim Gough	G	309 734-3511	Monmouth *(G-14221)*
Kirby Sheet Metal Works Inc	E	773 247-6477	Chicago *(G-5106)*
Kroh-Wagner Inc	E	773 252-2031	Chicago *(G-5133)*
L M Sheet Metal Inc	E	815 654-1837	Loves Park *(G-13230)*
L R Gregory and Son Inc	E	847 247-0216	Lake Bluff *(G-12191)*
Lake Iron Inc	G	708 870-0546	Chicago *(G-5160)*
Lamco Slings & Rigging Inc	E	309 764-7400	Moline *(G-14157)*
Laser Center Corporation	E	630 523-1600	Schaumburg *(G-18601)*
Laystrom Manufacturing Co	D	773 342-4800	Chicago *(G-5186)*
Lemanski Heating & AC	G	815 232-4519	Freeport *(G-10125)*
Lewis Process Systems Inc	F	630 510-8200	Carol Stream *(G-3018)*
Licon Inc	G	618 485-2222	Ashley *(G-885)*
Lizotte Sheet Metal Inc	G	618 656-3066	Edwardsville *(G-8368)*
Lmt Usa Inc	G	630 969-5412	Waukegan *(G-20462)*
Mac Ster Inc	G	847 359-3640	Palatine *(G-16137)*
MB Machine Inc	F	815 864-3555	Shannon *(G-18871)*
Mech-Tronics Corporation	D	708 344-9823	Melrose Park *(G-13891)*
Meco Company LLC	E	217 465-5620	Paris *(G-16234)*
Mendota Welding & Mfg	G	815 539-6944	Mendota *(G-13949)*
Merz Air Conditioning and Htg	E	217 342-2323	Effingham *(G-8409)*
Metal Box International LLC	C	847 455-8500	Franklin Park *(G-9994)*
Metal Spinners Inc	E	815 625-0390	Rock Falls *(G-17189)*
Metal Strip Buiding Products	G	847 742-8500	Itasca *(G-11700)*
Metals and Services Inc	D	630 627-2900	Addison *(G-200)*
Midwest Awnings Inc	G	309 762-3339	Cameron *(G-2808)*
Midwest Skylite Service Inc	G	847 214-9505	Schaumburg *(G-18630)*
Mj Celco International LLC	E	847 671-1900	Schiller Park *(G-18827)*
Mj Snyder Ironworks Inc	G	217 826-6440	Marshall *(G-13575)*
Montana Metal Products LLC	C	847 803-6600	Des Plaines *(G-7803)*
Montefusco Hvac Inc	G	309 691-7400	Peoria *(G-16479)*
Mrt Sureway Inc	D	847 801-3010	Franklin Park *(G-10004)*
Mucci Kirkpatrick Sheet Metal	G	815 433-3350	Ottawa *(G-16062)*
National Metal Works Inc	G	815 282-5533	Loves Park *(G-13239)*
Nature House Inc	D	217 833-2393	Griggsville *(G-10850)*
Nelson Manufacturing Co Inc	F	815 229-0161	Rockford *(G-17537)*
Neomek Incorporated	F	630 879-5400	Batavia *(G-1399)*
Nesterowicz & Associates Inc	G	815 522-4469	Kirkland *(G-12064)*
North American Enclosures Inc	G	630 290-7911	Naperville *(G-14887)*
North Shore Truck & Equipment	F	847 887-0200	Lake Bluff *(G-12201)*
Northstar Industries Inc	C	630 446-7800	Glendale Heights *(G-10480)*

Employee Codes: A=Over 500 employees, B=251-500
C=101-250, D=51-100, E=20-50, F=10-19, G=3-9

2020 Harris Illinois
Industrial Directory

1521

METAL FABRICATORS: Sheet

Company	Section	Phone
Olympia Manufacturing Inc	G	309 387-2633
East Peoria (G-8280)		
Omega Products Inc	G	618 939-3445
Waterloo (G-20293)		
Omnimax International Inc		770 449-7066
Bedford Park (G-1488)		
Parker Fabrication Inc	E	309 266-8413
Morton (G-14376)		
Pep Industries Inc	F	630 833-0404
Villa Park (G-20164)		
Peter Perella & Co	F	815 727-4526
Joliet (G-11913)		
Pittsfield Mch Tl & Wldg Co	G	217 656-4000
Payson (G-16317)		
Pools Welding Inc	G	309 787-2083
Milan (G-14020)		
Powdered Metal Tech LLC	G	630 852-0500
Downers Grove (G-8080)		
Precision Metal Products Inc	F	630 458-0100
Addison (G-251)		
Premier Manufacturing Corp	F	847 640-6644
Addison (G-253)		
Pro-Tech Metal Specialties Inc	E	630 279-7094
Elmhurst (G-9412)		
Pro-Tran Inc	G	217 348-9353
Charleston (G-3410)		
Production Fabg & Stamping Inc	F	708 755-5468
S Chicago Hts (G-18126)		
Production Manufacturing		217 256-4211
Warsaw (G-20259)		
Progressive Sheet Metal Inc		773 376-1155
Chicago (G-5901)		
Quality Fabricators Inc	D	630 543-0540
Addison (G-261)		
Quality Metal Works Inc		309 379-5311
Stanford (G-19473)		
Quanex Homeshield LLC	D	815 635-3171
Chatsworth (G-3427)		
Quicksilver Mechanical Inc	G	847 577-1564
Arlington Heights (G-794)		
R & B Metal Products Inc	E	815 338-1890
Woodstock (G-21427)		
R B White Inc	E	309 452-5816
Normal (G-15220)		
R&R Rf Inc		847 669-3720
Rock Falls (G-17192)		
Rebel Inc	E	618 235-0582
Belleville (G-1588)		
Reliable Autotech Usa LLC	G	815 945-7838
Chenoa (G-3434)		
Remin Laboratories Inc	D	815 723-1940
Joliet (G-11924)		
Rettick Enterprises Inc	G	309 275-4967
Bloomington (G-2088)		
Rogers Precision Machining	F	815 233-0065
Freeport (G-10138)		
Ruyle Mechanical Services Inc	D	309 674-6644
Peoria (G-16518)		
S & S Heating & Sheet Metal	G	815 933-1993
Bradley (G-2290)		
S & S Welding & Fabrication		847 742-7344
Elgin (G-8722)		
Schubert Environmental Eqp Inc	F	630 307-9400
Glendale Heights (G-10492)		
Seamless Gutter Corp	E	630 495-9800
Lombard (G-13128)		
Serra Laser Precision LLC	D	847 367-0282
Libertyville (G-12705)		
Service Sheet Metal Works Inc	F	773 229-0031
Chicago (G-6143)		
Shamrock Manufacturing Co Inc	G	708 331-7776
South Holland (G-19244)		
Shannon & Sons Welding	G	630 898-7778
Aurora (G-1155)		
Sheas Iron Works Inc	E	847 356-2922
Lake Villa (G-12367)		
Sheet Metal Supply Ltd	G	847 478-8500
Grayslake (G-10799)		
Sheet Metal Werks Inc	D	847 827-4700
Arlington Heights (G-809)		
Shew Brothers Inc		618 997-4414
Marion (G-13534)		
Silver Machine Shop Inc	G	217 359-5717
Champaign (G-3348)		
Skol Mfg Co	E	773 878-5959
Chicago (G-6181)		
Smid Heating & Air	G	815 467-0362
Channahon (G-3394)		
South Subn Wldg & Fabg Co Inc	G	708 385-7160
Posen (G-16801)		
Southern Wisconsin Metal Fabrc	F	815 389-3021
South Beloit (G-19114)		
Southwick Machine & Design Co	G	309 949-2868
Colona (G-6980)		
Spartan Sheet Metal Inc	G	773 895-7266
Chicago (G-6210)		
Spiral-Helix Inc	F	224 659-7870
Bensenville (G-1897)		
Star Forge Inc	D	815 235-7750
Freeport (G-10144)		
Steel Services Enterprises	E	708 259-1181
Lansing (G-12519)		
Steel Span Inc	F	815 943-9071
Harvard (G-11068)		
Stuecklen Manufacturing Co	G	847 678-5130
Franklin Park (G-10054)		
Sturdee Metal Products Inc	G	773 523-3074
New Lenox (G-15059)		
Suburban Welding & Steel LLC	F	847 678-1264
Franklin Park (G-10057)		
Sudholt Sheet Metal Inc	G	618 228-7351
Aviston (G-1183)		
Sugar River Machine Shop	E	815 624-0214
South Beloit (G-19115)		
Tandem Industries Inc	G	630 761-6615
Saint Charles (G-18285)		
Tcr Systems LLC	D	217 877-5622
Decatur (G-7560)		
Tesler Company of Illinois Inc	G	773 522-4400
Franklin Park (G-10060)		
Tewell Bros Machine Inc	F	217 253-6303
Tuscola (G-19931)		
Thybar Corporation	E	630 543-5300
Addison (G-309)		
Tin Mans Garage Inc	G	630 262-0752
Elburn (G-8477)		
Tinsley Steel Inc	G	618 656-5231
Edwardsville (G-8378)		
Titan Metals Inc	E	630 752-9700
Glendale Heights (G-10512)		
Tlk Industries Inc	D	847 359-3200
East Dundee (G-8212)		
Tri City Sheet Metal		630 232-4255
Geneva (G-10313)		
Tru-Way Inc	E	708 562-3690
Northlake (G-15563)		
Tu-Star Manufacturing Co Inc	G	815 338-5760
Woodstock (G-21441)		
Two J S Sheet Metal Works Inc	G	773 436-9424
Chicago (G-6446)		
Ultratech Inc	E	630 539-3578
Bloomingdale (G-2019)		
Unifab Mfg Inc	E	630 682-8970
Carol Stream (G-3082)		
Unistrut International Corp	D	630 773-3460
Addison (G-323)		
United Canvas Inc	E	847 395-1470
Antioch (G-641)		
Venus Processing & Storage	D	847 455-0496
Franklin Park (G-10077)		
Viking Metal Cabinet Co LLC	D	800 776-7767
Montgomery (G-14273)		
Viking Metal Cabinet Company		630 863-7234
Montgomery (G-14274)		
Wagner Zip-Change Inc	E	708 681-4100
Melrose Park (G-13926)		
Waukegan Architectural Inc		847 746-9077
Zion (G-21529)		
Welding Specialties	G	708 798-5388
East Hazel Crest (G-8219)		
Western Industries Inc	C	920 261-0660
Wheeling (G-21012)		
White Sheet Metal	G	217 465-3195
Paris (G-16246)		
William Dudek Manufacturing Co	E	773 622-2727
Chicago (G-6629)		
Wiltek Inc	G	630 922-9200
Naperville (G-14992)		
Wirfs Industries Inc	F	815 344-0635
McHenry (G-13809)		
Wozniak Industries Inc	G	630 954-3400
Schaumburg (G-18776)		
Wright Metals Inc	G	847 267-1212
Bannockburn (G-1212)		

METAL FABRICATORS: Structural, Ship

Company	Section	Phone
Solid Metal Group Inc	G	708 757-7421
Chicago Heights (G-6774)		
Industrial Steel Cnstr Inc	C	630 232-7473
Geneva (G-10280)		
Veritas Steel LLC	C	630 423-8708
Lisle (G-12956)		

METAL FINISHING SVCS

Company	Section	Phone
A & B Metal Polishing Inc	F	773 847-1077
Chicago (G-3480)		
A & J Finishers	G	847 352-5408
Schaumburg (G-18423)		
Accurate Metal Finishing Co	G	847 428-7705
Gilberts (G-10349)		
Ace Metal Refinishers Inc	E	630 778-9200
Lombard (G-13034)		
Alliance Specialties Corp		847 487-1945
Wauconda (G-20329)		
Ata Finishing Corp	G	847 677-8560
Skokie (G-18925)		
Bar Processing Corporation	E	708 757-4570
Chicago Heights (G-6733)		
Budding Polishing & Met Finshg	G	708 396-1166
South Holland (G-19203)		
Delta Secondary Inc	E	630 766-1180
Bensenville (G-1785)		
Dixline Corporation	F	309 932-2011
Galva (G-10230)		
Eifeler Coatings Tech Inc	E	630 587-1220
Saint Charles (G-18194)		
Electro-Max Inc	D	847 683-4100
Hampshire (G-10970)		
Enameled Steel and Sign Co	E	773 481-2270
Chicago (G-4504)		
Envirocoat Inc	G	847 673-3649
Skokie (G-18952)		
Expert Metal Finishing Inc	F	708 583-2550
River Grove (G-17059)		
Finished Metals Incorporated	F	773 229-1600
Chicago (G-4591)		
G L Tool and Manufacturing Co	F	630 628-1992
Addison (G-132)		
Gyro Processing Inc	E	800 491-0733
Chicago (G-4755)		
Illinois Electro Deburring Co	F	847 678-5010
Franklin Park (G-9961)		
K V F Company	E	847 437-5100
Elk Grove Village (G-9073)		
K V F Company	F	847 437-5019
Elk Grove Village (G-9074)		
Lee Quigley Company	G	708 563-1600
Chicago (G-5195)		
Main Steel Polishing Co Inc	E	847 916-1220
Elk Grove Village (G-9107)		
Markham Industry Inc	G	815 338-0116
Woodstock (G-21408)		
Neiland Custom Products		815 825-2233
Malta (G-13430)		
Oerlikon Blzers Cating USA Inc	F	847 619-5541
Schaumburg (G-18656)		
Performance Auto Salon Inc	E	815 468-6882
Manteno (G-13453)		
Precision Metal Crafts Inc	G	815 254-2306
Plainfield (G-16705)		
R C Industries Inc	F	773 378-1118
Chicago (G-5944)		
Reliable Plating Corporation	D	312 421-4747
Chicago (G-6010)		
Spider Company Inc	D	815 961-8200
Rockford (G-17641)		
Swd Inc	D	630 543-3003
Addison (G-301)		
Transcend Corp	G	847 395-6630
Antioch (G-638)		
Tri-Fin LLC	E	630 467-0991
Elk Grove Village (G-9284)		
Universal Coatings Inc	G	708 756-7000
Steger (G-19496)		

METAL MINING SVCS

Company	Section	Phone
Caterpillar Inc	A	309 675-6223
Mossville (G-14458)		
Regal Johnson Co	G	630 885-0688
Bolingbrook (G-2232)		
SF Contracting LLC	E	618 926-1477
Raleigh (G-16963)		
Trane Technologies Company LLC	E	630 530-3800
Elmhurst (G-9436)		

METAL ORES, NEC

Alpha Consultings .... G 773 251-0053
Chicago *(G-3628)*

METAL RESHAPING & REPLATING SVCS

Bellows Shoppe .... G 847 446-5533
Winnetka *(G-21126)*
Great Lakes Mech Svcs Inc .... F 708 672-5900
Lincolnshire *(G-12768)*
Jet Rack Corp .... E 773 586-2150
Chicago *(G-5025)*
Ralph Cody Gravrok .... G 630 628-9570
Addison *(G-266)*

METAL SERVICE CENTERS & OFFICES

Alter Trading Corporation .... F 217 223-0156
Quincy *(G-16852)*
Andscot Co Inc .... G 847 455-5800
Franklin Park *(G-9870)*
Central Ill Fbrcation Whse Inc .... F 217 367-2323
Urbana *(G-19976)*
Century Spring Corporation .... G 800 237-5225
Chicago *(G-4062)*
Cerro Flow Products LLC .... C 618 337-6000
Sauget *(G-18392)*
Chicago Tube and Iron Company .... E 815 834-2500
Romeoville *(G-17807)*
Commercial Metals Company .... G 815 928-9600
Kankakee *(G-11961)*
D L Austin Steel Supply Corp .... G 618 345-7200
Collinsville *(G-6957)*
Fairbanks Wire Corporation .... G 847 683-2600
Hampshire *(G-10972)*
Heidtman Steel Products Inc .... D 618 451-0052
Granite City *(G-10714)*
Hickman Williams & Company .... F 630 574-2150
Palos Heights *(G-16188)*
Illinois Tool Works Inc .... E 847 215-8925
Buffalo Grove *(G-2548)*
J C Schultz Enterprises Inc .... D 800 323-9127
Batavia *(G-1388)*
Lindsay Metal Madness Inc .... G 815 568-4560
Woodstock *(G-21406)*
Marmon Holdings Inc .... D 312 372-9500
Chicago *(G-5343)*
Mid-State Industries Oper Inc .... E 217 268-3900
Arcola *(G-656)*
Morgan Bronze Products Inc .... D 847 526-6000
Lake Zurich *(G-12435)*
New Process Steel LP .... D 708 389-3380
Alsip *(G-484)*
Raco Steel Company .... E 708 339-2958
Markham *(G-13550)*
Scot Industries Inc .... D 630 466-7591
Sugar Grove *(G-19653)*
Tempel Holdings Inc .... A 773 250-8000
Chicago *(G-6343)*
Union Tank Car Company .... C 312 431-3111
Chicago *(G-6466)*

METAL SPINNING FOR THE TRADE

Ace Metal Spinning Inc .... F 708 389-5635
Alsip *(G-412)*
Columbia Metal Spinning Co .... D 773 685-2800
Chicago *(G-4206)*
Mayfair Metal Spinning Co Inc .... G 847 358-7450
Palatine *(G-16139)*
Metal Spinners Inc .... E 815 625-0390
Rock Falls *(G-17189)*
Precision Metal Spinning Corp .... E 847 392-5672
Rolling Meadows *(G-17764)*
Spectracrafts Ltd .... G 847 824-4117
Lombard *(G-13133)*
Stuecklen Manufacturing Co .... G 847 678-5130
Franklin Park *(G-10054)*

METAL STAMPING, FOR THE TRADE

Ability Metal Company .... E 847 437-7040
Elk Grove Village *(G-8796)*
Acme Spinning Company Inc .... F 773 927-2711
Chicago *(G-3528)*
Action Tool & Mfg Inc .... E 815 874-5775
Rockford *(G-17294)*
Ada Metal Products Inc .... E 847 673-1190
Lincolnwood *(G-12811)*
Alagor Industries Incorporated .... D 630 766-2910
Bensenville *(G-1734)*
Alan Manufacturing Corp .... G 815 568-6836
Marengo *(G-13478)*
Allied Production Drilling .... F 815 969-0940
Stillman Valley *(G-19544)*
Alpha Products Inc .... E 708 594-3883
Bedford Park *(G-1455)*
American Industrial Company .... F 847 855-9200
Gurnee *(G-10859)*
Amity Die and Stamping Co .... E 847 680-6600
Lake Forest *(G-12224)*
Animated Manufacturing Company .... F 708 333-6688
South Holland *(G-19195)*
Archer Manufacturing Corp .... E 773 585-7181
Chicago *(G-3725)*
Aro Metal Stamping Company Inc .... E 630 351-7676
Wood Dale *(G-21166)*
Ask Products Inc .... D 630 896-4056
Aurora *(G-1054)*
Atlantic Engineering .... G 847 782-1762
Zion *(G-21509)*
Atlas Tool & Die Works Inc .... D 708 442-1661
Lyons *(G-13302)*
Barco Stamping Co .... E 630 293-5155
West Chicago *(G-20549)*
Bel-Air Manufacturing Inc .... F 773 276-7550
Chicago *(G-3862)*
Berny Metal Products Inc .... G 847 742-8500
South Elgin *(G-19137)*
Bi-Link Metal Specialties Inc .... C 630 858-5900
Bloomingdale *(G-1980)*
Bingamn-Prcsion Mtal Spnning C .... E 847 392-5620
Rolling Meadows *(G-17719)*
Braun Manufacturing Co Inc .... E 847 635-2050
Mount Prospect *(G-14514)*
Briergate Tool & Engrg Co .... F 630 766-7050
Bensenville *(G-1756)*
Burnex Corporation .... E 815 728-1317
Ringwood *(G-17040)*
C & C Can Co Inc .... G 312 421-2372
Chicago *(G-3992)*
C & J Metal Products Inc .... F 847 455-0766
Franklin Park *(G-9896)*
C Keller Manufacturing Inc .... E 630 833-5593
Villa Park *(G-20136)*
Cac Corporation .... E 630 221-5200
Carol Stream *(G-2953)*
Carlson Capitol Mfg Co .... F 815 398-3110
Rockford *(G-17335)*
Celco Tool & Engineering Inc .... F 847 671-2520
Schiller Park *(G-18792)*
Century Metal Spinning Co Inc .... E 630 595-3900
Bensenville *(G-1765)*
Chicago Cutting Die Co .... D 847 509-5800
Northbrook *(G-15357)*
Cosmos Manufacturing Inc .... C 708 756-1400
S Chicago Hts *(G-18119)*
Craft Metal Spinning Co .... F 773 685-4700
Chicago *(G-4255)*
Dial Tool Industries Inc .... D 630 543-3600
Addison *(G-87)*
Ed Stan Fabricating Co .... G 708 863-7668
Chicago *(G-4449)*
Elburn Metal Stamping Inc .... E 630 365-2500
Elburn *(G-8452)*
Entropy Cab Solutions Inc USA .... F 630 834-3872
Elmhurst *(G-9362)*
ERA Tool and Manufacturing Co .... E 847 298-6333
Zion *(G-21513)*
Erva Tool & Die Company .... G 773 533-7806
Chicago *(G-4528)*
Estad Stamping & Mfg Co .... E 217 442-4600
Danville *(G-7331)*
Exton Corp .... C 847 391-8100
Des Plaines *(G-7763)*
Fabricators Unlimited Inc .... G 847 223-7986
Grayslake *(G-10772)*
FIC America Corp .... A 630 871-7609
Carol Stream *(G-2984)*
Form-All Spring Stamping Inc .... E 630 595-8833
Bensenville *(G-1800)*
Formco Metal Products Inc .... E 630 766-4441
Wood Dale *(G-21190)*
Fox Valley Stamping Company .... F 847 741-2277
South Elgin *(G-19146)*
G & M Metal Fabricators Inc .... D 847 678-6501
Franklin Park *(G-9947)*
Gilbert Spring Corporation .... E 773 486-6030
Chicago *(G-4691)*
Harig Manufacturing Corp .... E 847 647-9500
Skokie *(G-18964)*
Hcf Building Corporation .... F 630 595-2040
Wood Dale *(G-21196)*
Hpl Stampings Inc .... E 847 540-1400
Lake Zurich *(G-12419)*
Hub Manufacturing Company Inc .... E 773 252-1373
Chicago *(G-4859)*
Hudson Tool & Die Co .... F 847 678-8710
Franklin Park *(G-9958)*
Industrial Park Machine & Tool .... F 708 754-7080
S Chicago Hts *(G-18122)*
International Spring Company .... D 847 470-8170
Morton Grove *(G-14413)*
Interplex Daystar Inc .... D 847 455-2424
Franklin Park *(G-9966)*
J F Schroeder Company Inc .... E 847 357-8600
Arlington Heights *(G-759)*
Jenco Metal Products Inc .... F 847 956-0550
Mount Prospect *(G-14539)*
Jiffy Metal Products Inc .... G 773 626-8090
Chicago *(G-5030)*
Jlo Metal Products Co A Corp .... D 773 889-6242
Chicago *(G-5032)*
Johnson Tool Company .... G 708 453-8600
Huntley *(G-11547)*
Kaiser Mfg Co .... C 773 235-4705
Chicago *(G-5076)*
Kaman Tool Corporation .... G 708 652-9023
Cicero *(G-6858)*
Kenmode Tool and Engrg Inc .... C 847 658-5041
Algonquin *(G-376)*
Kensen Tool & Die Inc .... F 847 455-0150
Franklin Park *(G-9976)*
Kier Mfg Co .... G 630 953-9500
Addison *(G-170)*
Klinck Inc .... E 815 397-3306
Rockford *(G-17484)*
Kosmos Tool Inc .... F 815 675-2200
Spring Grove *(G-19281)*
Larsen Manufacturing LLC .... C 847 970-9600
Mundelein *(G-14709)*
Lewis Spring and Mfg Company .... D 847 588-7030
Niles *(G-15140)*
Line Group Inc .... E 847 593-6810
Arlington Heights *(G-769)*
Lsa United Inc .... C 773 476-7439
Lombard *(G-13098)*
M J Celco Inc .... D 847 671-1900
Schiller Park *(G-18818)*
M Lizen Manufacturing Co .... E 708 755-7213
University Park *(G-19958)*
M Ward Manufacturing Co Inc .... E 847 864-4786
Evanston *(G-9548)*
Major Die & Engineering Co .... F 630 773-3444
Itasca *(G-11696)*
Manor Tool and Mfg Co .... D 847 678-2020
Schiller Park *(G-18820)*
Marengo Tool & Die Works Inc .... E 815 568-7411
Marengo *(G-13489)*
Masonite Corporation .... D 630 584-6330
West Chicago *(G-20616)*
Mengarelli Enterprises Inc .... D 847 272-6980
Northbrook *(G-15433)*
Metalstamp Inc .... E 815 467-7800
Minooka *(G-14063)*
Micromatic Spring Stamping Inc .... E 630 607-0141
Addison *(G-207)*
Midland Stamping and Fabg Corp .... D 847 678-7573
Schiller Park *(G-18825)*
Modineer P-K Tool LLC .... E 773 235-4700
Chicago *(G-5483)*
Mueller Mfg Corp .... E 847 640-1666
Elk Grove Village *(G-9139)*
My-Lin Manufacturing Co Inc .... E 630 897-4100
Aurora *(G-1137)*
Nelson Manufacturing Co Inc .... F 815 229-0161
Rockford *(G-17537)*
North Star Stamping & Tool Inc .... F 847 658-9400
Lake In The Hills *(G-12342)*
Nu-Way Industries Inc .... C 847 298-7710
Des Plaines *(G-7812)*
Odm Tool & Mfg Co Inc .... D 708 485-6130
Hodgkins *(G-11391)*
OHare Spring Company Inc .... E 847 298-1360
Elk Grove Village *(G-9160)*
Olson Metal Products LLC .... F 847 981-7550
Arlington Heights *(G-784)*
Omiotek Coil Spring Co .... D 630 495-4056
Lombard *(G-13113)*
P T L Manufacturing Inc .... E 618 277-6789
Belleville *(G-1582)*

Employee Codes: A=Over 500 employees, B=251-500
C=101-250, D=51-100, E=20-50, F=10-19, G=3-9

2020 Harris Illinois
Industrial Directory

1523

METAL STAMPING, FOR THE TRADE — PRODUCT SECTION

Paragon Spring Company .... E 773 489-6300
  Chicago (G-5759)
Parkway Metal Products Inc .... D 847 789-4000
  Des Plaines (G-7818)
Performance Stamping Co Inc .... E 847 426-2233
  Carpentersville (G-3112)
Precise Stamping Inc .... E 630 897-6477
  North Aurora (G-15272)
Precision Forming Stamping Co .... E 773 489-6868
  Chicago (G-5857)
Precision Resource Inc .... E 847 383-1300
  Vernon Hills (G-20083)
Precision Stamping Pdts Inc .... E 847 678-0800
  Schiller Park (G-18835)
Premier Metal Works Inc .... G 312 226-7414
  Chicago (G-5863)
Principal Manufacturing Corp .... B 708 865-7500
  Broadview (G-2459)
Production Fabg & Stamping Inc ...... F 708 755-5468
  S Chicago Hts (G-18126)
Production Stampings Inc .... G 815 495-2800
  Leland (G-12549)
Radiad Manufacturing .... G 847 678-5808
  Franklin Park (G-10031)
Reliable Machine Company .... E 815 968-8803
  Rockford (G-17570)
Reliable Metal Stamping Co Inc .... F 773 625-1177
  Franklin Park (G-10034)
Reliance Tool & Mfg Co .... E 847 695-1235
  Elgin (G-8718)
Relyon Metal Products Co .... E 847 679-1510
  Elgin (G-8719)
Ri-Del Mfg Inc .... D 312 829-8720
  Chicago (G-6024)
Rich Industries Inc .... E 630 766-9150
  Bensenville (G-1884)
Rijon Manufacturing Company .... G 708 388-2295
  Blue Island (G-2136)
Rj Stuckel Co Inc .... E 800 789-7220
  Elk Grove Village (G-9218)
Rockford Toolcraft Inc .... C 815 398-5507
  Rockford (G-17608)
Sealco Industries Inc .... E 847 741-3101
  Elgin (G-8725)
Service Stampings of IL Inc .... E 630 894-7880
  Roselle (G-17987)
Sharp Metal Products .... G 847 439-5393
  Elk Grove Village (G-9236)
Skill-Di Inc .... F 708 544-6080
  Bellwood (G-1639)
Slidematic Products Co .... E 773 545-4213
  Chicago (G-6189)
St Charles Stamping Inc .... F 630 584-2029
  Saint Charles (G-18276)
Stanley Spring & Stamping Corp ...... D 773 777-2600
  Chicago (G-6230)
Stanron Corporation .... D 773 777-2600
  Chicago (G-6231)
Stumpfoll Tool & Mfg .... G 312 733-2632
  Chicago (G-6258)
Suburban Metalcraft Inc .... E 847 678-7550
  Franklin Park (G-10056)
Superior Metal Products Inc .... F 630 466-1150
  Sugar Grove (G-19657)
Sure-Way Die Designs Inc .... F 630 323-0370
  Westmont (G-20774)
Tauber Brothers Tool & Die Co .... E 708 867-9100
  Chicago (G-6330)
Tempel Holdings Inc .... A 773 250-8000
  Chicago (G-6343)
Tempel Holdings Inc .... A 773 250-8000
  Chicago (G-6344)
Tempel Steel Company .... G 847 966-9099
  Skokie (G-19043)
Tempel Steel Company .... G 773 250-8000
  Chicago (G-6345)
Three Star Mfg Co Inc .... G 847 526-2222
  Wauconda (G-20399)
Thryselius Stamping Inc .... G 630 232-0795
  Geneva (G-10311)
Triton Industries Inc .... C 773 384-3700
  Chicago (G-6430)
Tro Manufacturing Company Inc ..... E 847 455-3755
  Franklin Park (G-10067)
Tryson Metal Stampg & Mfg Inc ...... E 630 458-0591
  Addison (G-319)
Twinplex Manufacturing Co .... F 630 595-2040
  Wood Dale (G-21254)
Ultra Stamping & Assembly Inc .... G 815 874-9888
  Rockford (G-17670)

Unified Tool Die & Mfg Co Inc .... F 847 678-3773
  Schiller Park (G-18848)
Vanart Engineering Company .... E 847 678-6255
  Franklin Park (G-10074)
Vindee Industries Inc .... E 815 469-3300
  Frankfort (G-9850)
Voco Tool & Mfg Inc .... G 708 771-3800
  Forest Park (G-9728)
Wauconda Tool & Engrg LLC .... E 847 658-4588
  Algonquin (G-394)
Western Industries Inc .... C 920 261-0660
  Wheeling (G-21012)
Willie Washer Mfg Co .... C 847 956-1344
  Elk Grove Village (G-9310)
Wireformers Inc .... E 847 718-1920
  Mount Prospect (G-14582)
World Washer & Stamping Inc .... F 630 543-6749
  Addison (G-338)

METAL STAMPINGS: Ornamental

Mj Celco International LLC .... E 847 671-1900
  Schiller Park (G-18827)
T A U Inc .... G 708 841-5757
  Dolton (G-7940)

METAL STAMPINGS: Perforated

Accurate Perforating Co Inc .... D 773 254-3232
  Chicago (G-3519)
H&K Perforating LLC .... E 773 626-1800
  Chicago (G-4762)
Metalex LLC .... C 847 362-5400
  Libertyville (G-12678)

METAL TREATING COMPOUNDS

Fuchs Corporation .... G 800 323-7755
  Harvey (G-11086)
Technic Inc .... G 773 262-2662
  Arlington Heights (G-817)

METAL TREATING: Cryogenic

Controlled Thermal Processing .... G 847 651-5511
  Streamwood (G-19567)
Dippit Inc .... G 630 762-6500
  West Chicago (G-20571)

METALS SVC CENTERS & WHOL: Structural Shapes, Iron Or Steel

American Steel Fabricators Inc .... F 847 807-4200
  Melrose Park (G-13825)
Azcon Inc .... F 815 548-7000
  Sterling (G-19499)
Michelmann Steel Cnstr Co .... E 217 222-0555
  Quincy (G-16912)
Mutual Svcs Highland Pk Inc .... F 847 432-3815
  Highland Park (G-11287)
Van Pelt Corporation .... E 313 365-3600
  East Moline (G-8246)

METALS SVC CENTERS & WHOLESALERS: Bars, Metal

Charter Dura-Bar Inc .... F 815 338-3900
  Woodstock (G-21373)
Lapham-Hickey Steel Corp .... C 708 496-6111
  Bedford Park (G-1479)

METALS SVC CENTERS & WHOLESALERS: Casting, Rough, Iron/Steel

R C Castings Inc .... G 708 331-1882
  Monee (G-14205)

METALS SVC CENTERS & WHOLESALERS: Copper Prdts

Chris Industries Inc .... E 847 729-9292
  Northbrook (G-15359)

METALS SVC CENTERS & WHOLESALERS: Flat Prdts, Iron Or Steel

Feralloy Corporation .... E 503 286-8869
  Chicago (G-4580)
JT Cullen Co Inc .... D 815 589-2412
  Fulton (G-10154)

METALS SVC CENTERS & WHOLESALERS: Foundry Prdts

Asta Service Inc .... G 630 271-0960
  Lisle (G-12869)
Vesuvius Crucible Company .... G 217 351-5000
  Champaign (G-3365)

METALS SVC CENTERS & WHOLESALERS: Iron & Steel Prdt, Ferrous

Millenia Metals LLC .... D 630 458-0401
  Itasca (G-11703)
O Brien Bill .... G 630 980-5571
  Geneva (G-10294)

METALS SVC CENTERS & WHOLESALERS: Misc Nonferrous Prdts

Becks Light Gauge Aluminum Co .... F 847 290-9990
  Elk Grove Village (G-8861)

METALS SVC CENTERS & WHOLESALERS: Nonferrous Sheets, Etc

Harris Metals & Recycling .... G 217 235-1808
  Mattoon (G-13635)

METALS SVC CENTERS & WHOLESALERS: Pig Iron

Miller and Company LLC .... E 847 696-2400
  Rosemont (G-18037)

METALS SVC CENTERS & WHOLESALERS: Pipe & Tubing, Steel

Chicago Pipe Bending & Coil Co ..... F 773 379-1918
  Chicago (G-4122)
Illinois Meter Inc .... G 618 438-6039
  Benton (G-1927)
Stephens Pipe & Steel LLC .... E 800 451-2612
  North Aurora (G-15278)

METALS SVC CENTERS & WHOLESALERS: Rods, Wire, Exc Insulated

Avasarala Inc .... G 847 969-0630
  Palatine (G-16095)

METALS SVC CENTERS & WHOLESALERS: Sheets, Metal

American Metal Mfg Inc .... G 847 651-6097
  Chicago (G-3662)
Custom Plastics of Peoria .... G 309 697-2888
  Bartonville (G-1331)

METALS SVC CENTERS & WHOLESALERS: Steel

A2 Sales LLC .... D 708 924-1200
  Bedford Park (G-1453)
Ameralloy Steel Corporation .... E 847 967-0600
  Morton Grove (G-14390)
American Grinding & Machine Co ... D 773 889-4343
  Chicago (G-3653)
Arntzen Corporation .... E 815 334-0788
  Woodstock (G-21360)
ATI Flat Rlled Pdts Hldngs LLC ...... F 708 974-8801
  Bridgeview (G-2326)
Awerkamp Machine Co .... F 217 222-3490
  Quincy (G-16860)
Banner Service Corporation .... C 630 653-7500
  Carol Stream (G-2944)
Central Illinois Steel Company .... E 217 854-3251
  Carlinville (G-2869)
Galva Iron and Metal Co Inc .... G 309 932-3450
  Galva (G-10232)
Harris Steel Company .... D 708 656-5500
  Cicero (G-6851)
Intermet Metals Services Inc .... E 847 605-1300
  Schaumburg (G-18563)
K-Met Industries Inc .... G 708 534-3300
  Monee (G-14203)
Lexington Steel Corporation .... D 708 594-9200
  Bedford Park (G-1480)
Lickenbrock & Sons Inc .... G 618 632-4977
  O Fallon (G-15578)

M C Steel Inc .... E 847 350-9618
  Antioch (G-623)
Madison Inds Holdings LLC .... G 312 277-0156
  Chicago (G-5313)
Mervis Industries Inc 217 753-1492
  Springfield (G-19405)
Metals and Services Inc .... D 630 627-2900
  Addison (G-200)
Millers Eureka Inc .... F 312 666-9383
  Chicago (G-5459)
Multiplex Industries Inc .... G 630 906-9780
  Montgomery (G-14263)
Olympic Steel Inc .... E 847 584-4000
  Schaumburg (G-18658)
Precision Steel Warehouse Inc .... C 800 323-0740
  Franklin Park (G-10026)
Prime Stainless Products LLC .... G 847 678-0800
  Schiller Park (G-18836)
SE Steel Inc .... G 847 350-9618
  Antioch (G-634)
Soudan Metals Company Inc .... C 773 548-7600
  Chicago (G-6204)
Steel Rebar Manufacturing LLC .... G 618 920-2748
  Centreville (G-3255)
Steel Whse Quad Cities LLC .... G 309 756-1089
  Rock Island (G-17247)
Tricon Wear Solutions LLC .... E 708 235-4064
  University Park (G-19969)

METALS SVC CENTERS & WHOLESALERS: Steel Decking

Advance Steel Services Inc .... G 773 619-2977
  Chicago (G-3558)

METALS SVC CENTERS & WHOLESALERS: Tubing, Metal

Chicago Tube and Iron Company .... E 309 787-4947
  Milan (G-14003)
D & W Mfg Co Inc .... E 773 533-1542
  Chicago (G-4300)
Modern Tube LLC .... G 877 848-3300
  Bloomingdale (G-2001)

METALS SVC CENTERS/WHOL: Forms, Steel Concrete Construction

Deslauriers Inc .... E 708 544-4455
  La Grange Park (G-12095)
Forming America Ltd .... E 888 993-1304
  West Chicago (G-20587)

METALS SVC CTRS & WHOLESALERS: Aluminum Bars, Rods, Etc

Aluminum Coil Anodizing Corp .... C 630 837-4000
  Streamwood (G-19560)
Corey Steel Company .... C 708 735-8000
  Cicero (G-6837)
Mandel Metals Inc .... C 847 455-6606
  Franklin Park (G-9984)
Penn Aluminum Intl LLC .... C 618 684-2146
  Murphysboro (G-14756)

METALS SVC CTRS & WHOLESALERS: Copper Sheets, Plates, NEC

Alconix Usa Inc .... G 847 717-7407
  Elk Grove Village (G-8813)

METALS: Precious NEC

Sunshine Metals Inc .... G 304 422-0090
  Northbrook (G-15490)
Tanaka Kikinzoku Intl Amer Inc .... G 224 653-8309
  Schaumburg (G-18737)
Tanaka Kknzoku Intrnational Kk .... G 224 653-8309
  Schaumburg (G-18738)
TPC Metals LLC .... G 330 479-9510
  Willowbrook (G-21061)

METALS: Precious, Secondary

Enviro-Chem Inc .... G 847 549-7797
  Vernon Hills (G-20052)

METALS: Primary Nonferrous, NEC

AG Medical Systems Inc .... F 847 458-3100
  Lake In The Hills (G-12328)

Big River Zinc Corporation .... G 618 274-5000
  Sauget (G-18389)
Horizon Metals Inc .... E 773 478-8888
  Niles (G-15129)
Materion Brush Inc .... F 630 832-9650
  Elmhurst (G-9400)
Mayco Manufacturing LLC .... E 618 451-4400
  Granite City (G-10721)
Powerlab Inc .... F 815 273-7718
  Savanna (G-18410)
Rockford Rigging Inc .... F 309 263-0566
  Roscoe (G-17926)

METALWORK: Miscellaneous

A & S Steel Specialties Inc .... E 815 838-8188
  Lockport (G-12979)
Affton Fabg & Wldg Co Inc .... E 314 781-4100
  Sauget (G-18388)
All-Steel Structures Inc .... E 708 210-1313
  South Holland (G-19189)
American Steel Fabricators Inc .... F 847 807-4200
  Melrose Park (G-13825)
Bergst Special Tools Inc .... G 630 543-1020
  Addison (G-48)
Chicago Metal Rolled Pdts Co .... D 773 523-5757
  Chicago (G-4115)
Crown Premiums Inc .... F 815 469-8789
  Frankfort (G-9781)
Dixline Corporation .... D 309 932-2011
  Galva (G-10231)
Dixline Corporation .... D 309 932-2011
  Galva (G-10230)
Elfi LLC .... E 815 439-1833
  Chicago (G-4483)
Fabco Enterprises Inc .... G 708 333-4644
  Harvey (G-11084)
Gerdau Ameristeel US Inc .... G 800 237-0230
  Chicago (G-4687)
Gerdau Ameristeel US Inc .... E 815 547-0400
  Belvidere (G-1673)
Glass Management Services Inc .... G 312 462-3257
  Chicago (G-4693)
Gmh Metal Fabrication Inc .... G 309 253-6429
  East Peoria (G-8269)
HI Metals LLC .... G 312 590-3360
  Winnetka (G-21130)
JC Metalcrafters Inc .... G 815 942-9891
  Morris (G-14308)
Kroh-Wagner Inc .... E 773 252-2031
  Chicago (G-5133)
MBI Tools LLC .... G 815 844-0937
  Pontiac (G-16775)
Metal Strip Buiding Products .... G 847 742-8500
  Itasca (G-11700)
MMC Precision Holdings Corp .... A 309 266-7176
  Morton (G-14367)
Nucor Steel Kankakee Inc .... B 815 937-3131
  Bourbonnais (G-2266)
Olin Engineered Systems Inc .... G 618 258-2874
  East Alton (G-8169)
PNa Construction Tech Inc .... F 770 668-9500
  Itasca (G-11720)
Sitexpedite LLC .... E 847 245-2185
  Lindenhurst (G-12854)
Trinity Machined Products Inc .... E 630 876-6992
  Aurora (G-1028)
Van Pelt Corporation .... E 313 365-3600
  East Moline (G-8246)
Weld Seam Inc .... F 773 588-1012
  Wood Dale (G-21257)

METALWORK: Ornamental

Aetna Engineering Works Inc .... E 773 785-0489
  Chicago (G-3577)
Chicagos Finest Iron Works .... F 773 646-4484
  Chicago (G-4138)
Chicagos Finest Ironworks .... G 708 895-4484
  Lansing (G-12488)
Crosstree Inc .... G 773 227-1234
  Chicago (G-4274)
D5 Design Met Fabrication LLC .... G 773 770-4705
  Chicago (G-4303)
Ibarra Group LLC .... G 773 650-0503
  Chicago (G-4870)
Kelley Ornamental Iron LLC .... E 309 697-9870
  East Peoria (G-8274)
King Metal Co .... G 708 388-3845
  Alsip (G-464)
Leonards Unit Step Co .... E 815 744-1263
  Rockdale (G-17265)

P & P Artec Inc .... F 630 860-2990
  Wood Dale (G-21226)
Pep Industries Inc .... F 630 833-0404
  Villa Park (G-20164)
Waukegan Architectural Inc .... G 847 746-9077
  Zion (G-21529)
Waukegan Steel LLC .... E 847 662-2810
  Waukegan (G-20516)

METALWORKING MACHINERY WHOLESALERS

Barnes International Inc .... C 815 964-8661
  Rockford (G-17312)
Crd Enterprises Inc .... G 847 438-4299
  Lake Zurich (G-12398)
Hardinge Grinding Group Inc .... E 847 888-0148
  Elgin (G-8606)
Industrial Instrument Svc Corp .... G 773 581-3355
  Chicago (G-4907)
McLean Manufacturing Company .... G 847 277-9912
  Lake Barrington (G-12160)
Miyano Machinery USA Inc .... E 630 766-4141
  Elk Grove Village (G-9128)
Muntz Industries Inc .... E 847 949-8280
  Mundelein (G-14718)

METERING DEVICES: Gasoline Dispensing

Opw Fuel MGT Systems Inc 708 352-9617
  Hodgkins (G-11392)
Professional Meters Inc .... C 815 942-7000
  Morris (G-14323)

METERING DEVICES: Integrating & Totalizing, Gas & Liquids

Advance Engineering Corp .... E 847 760-9421
  Elgin (G-8496)

METERING DEVICES: Water Quality Monitoring & Control Systems

Bc Enterprises .... G 618 655-0784
  Edwardsville (G-8348)

METERS: Audio

Singer Data Products Inc .... G 630 860-6500
  Bensenville (G-1893)
Singer Medical Products Inc .... G 630 860-6500
  Bensenville (G-1894)

METERS: Demand

Etcon Corp .... F 630 325-6100
  Burr Ridge (G-2672)

MGMT CONSULTING SVCS: Matls, Incl Purch, Handle & Invntry

Mennies Machine Company .... C 815 339-2226
  Mark (G-13546)

MICA PRDTS

GL Downs Inc .... G 618 993-9777
  Marion (G-13513)

MICROCIRCUITS, INTEGRATED: Semiconductor

Zenith Electronics Corporation .... E 847 941-8000
  Lincolnshire (G-12806)

MICROFILM SVCS

Com-Graphics Inc .... D 312 226-0900
  Chicago (G-4208)
Forman Co Inc .... G 309 734-3413
  Monmouth (G-14217)
Microdynamics Corporation .... C 630 276-0527
  Naperville (G-14870)

MICROMETERS

Bradley Machining Inc .... F 630 543-2875
  Addison (G-53)

MICROPHONES

Shure Incorporated .... F 847 520-4404
  Wheeling (G-20984)

MICROPROCESSORS

MICROPROCESSORS

Digital Optics Tech Inc .... G 847 358-2592
   Rolling Meadows *(G-17727)*
Intel Corporation .... D 408 765-8080
   Chicago *(G-4941)*
Intel East .... G 312 725-2014
   Mount Prospect *(G-14536)*
Intelligent SCM LLC .... G 630 625-7229
   Wood Dale *(G-21202)*
Sparton Design Services LLC .... G 847 762-5800
   Schaumburg *(G-18718)*
Sparton Emt LLC .... G 800 772-7866
   Schaumburg *(G-18719)*
Sparton Parent Inc .... G 847 762-5800
   Schaumburg *(G-18721)*

MICROSCOPES

Alicona Corporation .... G 630 372-9900
   Itasca *(G-11618)*
McCrone Associates Inc .... G 630 887-7100
   Westmont *(G-20758)*

MICROWAVE COMPONENTS

Formcraft Tool Company .... F 773 476-8727
   Chicago *(G-4620)*
Teledyne Defense Elec LLC .... C 630 754-3300
   Woodridge *(G-21344)*

MICROWAVE OVENS: Household

Microwave RES & Applications ...... G 630 480-7456
   Carol Stream *(G-3029)*

MILL PRDTS: Structural & Rail

Guardian Construction Pdts Inc .... E 630 820-8899
   Naperville *(G-14970)*
Progress Rail Services Corp .... E 309 963-4425
   Danvers *(G-7317)*
Rmi Inc .... F 708 756-5640
   Chicago Heights *(G-6770)*

MILLINERY SUPPLIES: Cap Fronts & Visors

Gcg Corp .... G 847 298-2285
   Glenview *(G-10548)*

MILLINERY SUPPLIES: Veils & Veiling, Bridal, Funeral, Etc

Angels Heavenly Funeral Home ..... G 773 239-8700
   Chicago *(G-3696)*
Hamsher Lakeside Funerals .... G 847 587-2100
   Fox Lake *(G-9747)*
Toni Federici .... F 618 244-4842
   Mount Vernon *(G-14642)*

MILLING: Corn Grits & Flakes, For Brewers' Use

Temperance Beer Company LLC ... G 847 864-1000
   Evanston *(G-9583)*

MILLING: Grain Cereals, Cracked

Natures American Co .... G 630 246-4274
   Chicago *(G-5553)*

MILLING: Grains, Exc Rice

Kws Cereals Usa LLC .... G 815 200-2666
   Champaign *(G-3316)*

MILLWORK

A and J Development Plus LLC ..... G 630 470-9539
   Plainfield *(G-16639)*
A-Squared Woodworking Inc .... G 773 742-7234
   Bridgeview *(G-2318)*
Ability Cabinet Co Inc .... G 847 678-6678
   Franklin Park *(G-9859)*
Adel Woodworks .... G 815 886-9006
   Romeoville *(G-17787)*
All American Wood Register Co .... F 815 356-1000
   Crystal Lake *(G-7155)*
Allie Woodworking .... G 847 244-1919
   Waukegan *(G-20413)*
American Custom Woodworking ... F 847 526-5900
   Wauconda *(G-20330)*
American Woodworks .... G 630 279-1629
   Sleepy Hollow *(G-19061)*
Americsan Designs Inc .... D 773 542-1291
   Chicago *(G-3677)*
Architectual Woodworking .... G 847 259-3331
   Prospect Heights *(G-16835)*
Architectural Mall Inc .... G 630 543-5253
   Carol Stream *(G-2939)*
Architectural Wdwkg Design Inc .. G 630 810-1604
   Downers Grove *(G-7954)*
Architectural Wood Expressions .. G 708 731-2355
   Stone Park *(G-19552)*
Artisan Millwork LLC .... G 847 417-5236
   Saint Charles *(G-18150)*
Back Forty WD Works & Nurs LLC .... G 618 898-1241
   Johnsonville *(G-11811)*
Baker Elements Inc .... G 630 660-8100
   Oak Park *(G-15746)*
Beloit Pattern Works .... F 815 389-2578
   South Beloit *(G-19083)*
Blueberry Woodworking Inc .... G 773 230-7179
   Franklin Park *(G-9890)*
Bond Brothers Hardwoods .... G 618 272-4811
   Ridgway *(G-17035)*
Brown Woodworking .... G 815 477-8333
   Crystal Lake *(G-7172)*
Byttow Enterprises Inc .... G 708 372-4450
   Lansing *(G-12486)*
C and S Carpentry LLC .... G 224 523-8064
   Elgin *(G-8527)*
CA Custom Woodworking .... G 630 201-6154
   Newark *(G-15074)*
Cabinets Doors and More LLC ...... G 847 395-6334
   Antioch *(G-607)*
Cain Millwork Inc .... D 815 561-9700
   Rochelle *(G-17134)*
Carpenters Millwork Co .... F 708 339-7707
   South Holland *(G-19204)*
Carpenters Millwork Co .... F 708 339-7707
   Villa Park *(G-20137)*
Cervantes/Salgado LLC .... G 630 806-4864
   Montgomery *(G-14239)*
Chicago School Woodworking LLC .... G 773 275-1170
   Chicago *(G-4128)*
Christos Woodworking .... G 708 975-5045
   Alsip *(G-431)*
City Screen Inc .... G 773 588-5642
   Chicago *(G-4161)*
Classic Woodwork Inc .... G 815 356-9000
   Crystal Lake *(G-7182)*
CM Woodwords Inc .... G 847 945-7689
   Deerfield *(G-7604)*
Cmp Millwork Co .... G 630 832-6462
   Elmhurst *(G-9348)*
Contract Industries Inc .... E 708 458-8150
   Bedford Park *(G-1464)*
Cooper Lake Millworks Inc .... G 217 847-2681
   Hamilton *(G-10951)*
Corsaw Hardwood Lumber Inc ..... F 309 293-2055
   Smithfield *(G-19063)*
Crea and Crea .... G 630 292-5625
   Bartlett *(G-1273)*
Creative Millwork LLC .... E 630 762-0002
   Saint Charles *(G-18178)*
Creswell Woodworking CA .... G 847 381-9222
   Woodstock *(G-21378)*
Curtis Woodworking Inc .... G 815 544-3543
   Belvidere *(G-1664)*
Custom Hardwoods LLC .... G 815 784-9974
   Sycamore *(G-19703)*
Custom Wood Creations .... G 618 346-2208
   Collinsville *(G-6956)*
Dandurand Custom Woodworking .... G 708 489-6440
   Posen *(G-16793)*
Daniel M Powers & Assoc Ltd ...... D 630 685-8400
   Bolingbrook *(G-2166)*
Decorators Supply Corporation ... E 773 847-6300
   Chicago *(G-4330)*
Deem Woodworks .... G 217 832-9614
   Villa Grove *(G-20122)*
Del Great Frame Up Systems Inc .... E 847 808-1955
   Franklin Park *(G-9929)*
Demeter Millwork LLC .... F 312 224-4440
   Chicago *(G-4338)*
DLM Manufacturing Inc .... F 815 964-3800
   Rockford *(G-17382)*
Duhack Lehn & Associates Inc .... G 815 777-3460
   Galena *(G-10168)*
Dunigan Custom Woodworking .... G 708 351-5213
   Homewood *(G-11491)*
Eiesland Builders Inc .... E 847 998-1731
   Glenview *(G-10544)*
Elite Custom Woodworking .... G 630 888-4322
   Batavia *(G-1376)*
European Wood Works Inc .... G 773 662-6607
   Carol Stream *(G-2982)*
Fraser Millwork Inc .... G 708 447-3262
   Lyons *(G-13309)*
G & M Woodworking Inc .... G 708 425-4013
   Oak Lawn *(G-15717)*
Gavin Woodworking Inc .... G 815 786-2242
   Sandwich *(G-18371)*
Gc Custom Woodworking LLC ..... G 847 724-7292
   Glenview *(G-10547)*
George Drowne Cabinet Sand ..... G 847 234-1487
   Lake Bluff *(G-12183)*
George Pagels Company .... G 708 478-7036
   Mokena *(G-14087)*
Glass & Wood Work Inc .... G 708 945-9558
   Bridgeview *(G-2350)*
Glendale Woodworking .... G 630 545-1520
   Glendale Heights *(G-10453)*
Gmk Finishing .... G 630 837-0568
   Bartlett *(G-1284)*
Grays Cabinet Co .... G 618 948-2211
   Saint Francisville *(G-18314)*
H & M Woodworks .... G 608 289-3141
   Hamilton *(G-10957)*
Hardwood Connection .... G 815 895-8733
   Sycamore *(G-19712)*
Heartland Hardwoods Inc .... E 217 844-3312
   Effingham *(G-8402)*
Heritage Moulding Inc .... G 630 961-0001
   Plainfield *(G-16672)*
Herner-Geissler Wdwkg Corp ..... D 312 226-3400
   Chicago *(G-4809)*
HK Woodwork .... G 773 964-2468
   Wheeling *(G-20909)*
Hpmillwork LLC .... G 630 220-4387
   Northbrook *(G-15401)*
Hylan Design Ltd .... G 312 243-7341
   Chicago *(G-4863)*
Imperial Store Fixtures Inc .... G 773 348-1137
   Chicago *(G-4901)*
Imperial Woodworking Entps Inc ... E 847 358-6920
   Palatine *(G-16128)*
J Hoffman Lumber Co Inc .... G 815 899-2260
   Sycamore *(G-19718)*
J R Husar Inc .... F 312 243-7888
   Chicago *(G-4994)*
Jay A Morris .... G 815 432-6440
   Watseka *(G-20308)*
Jelinek & Sons Inc .... G 630 355-3474
   Plainfield *(G-16676)*
Jj Wood Working .... G 708 426-6854
   Bridgeview *(G-2359)*
Jlm Woodworking .... G 309 275-8259
   Normal *(G-15206)*
John Tobin Millwork Co .... G 630 832-3780
   Villa Park *(G-20152)*
Kabinet Kraft .... F 618 395-1047
   Olney *(G-15867)*
Kep Woodworking .... G 847 480-9545
   Newark *(G-15077)*
Knotty By Nature .... G 618 610-2481
   Grafton *(G-10685)*
L Surges Custom Woodwork .... G 815 774-9663
   Joliet *(G-11892)*
Lyko Woodworking & Cnstr .... G 773 583-4561
   Chicago *(G-5292)*
M & R Custom Millwork Inc .... G 815 547-8549
   Belvidere *(G-1682)*
Majestic Archtctural Wdwrk Inc .... G 708 240-8484
   Bellwood *(G-1632)*
Master Cabinets .... G 847 639-1323
   Cary *(G-3178)*
May Wood Industries Inc .... F 708 489-1515
   Alsip *(G-475)*
Menard Inc .... C 815 474-6767
   Plano *(G-16734)*
Menard Inc .... D 708 346-9144
   Evergreen Park *(G-9597)*
Menard Inc .... D 715 876-5911
   Plano *(G-16735)*
Merkel Woodworking Inc .... F 630 458-0700
   Addison *(G-197)*
Metal Products Sales Corp .... G 708 301-6844
   Lockport *(G-13013)*
Metrie .... E 815 717-2660
   New Lenox *(G-15042)*
Midwest Architectural Millwork ... G 847 621-2013
   Elk Grove Village *(G-9126)*

PRODUCT SECTION

MIXTURES & BLOCKS: Asphalt Paving

Midwest Woodcrafters Inc ....G...... 630 665-0901
  Carol Stream (G-3031)
Midwestern Wood Products Co ....G...... 309 266-9771
  Morton (G-14366)
Minimill Technologies Inc ....G...... 315 857-7107
  Chicago (G-5465)
Mulvain Woodworks ....G...... 815 248-2305
  Durand (G-8154)
Oetee LLC ....G...... 630 373-4671
  Chicago (G-5657)
Olivet Woodworking ....G...... 773 505-5225
  Lake Zurich (G-12441)
Osmer Woodworking Inc ....G...... 815 973-5809
  Dixon (G-7905)
Paragon Mill & Casework Inc ....F...... 815 388-7453
  Crystal Lake (G-7243)
Parenti and Raffaelli Ltd ....G...... 847 204-8116
  Mount Prospect (G-14559)
Performance Lawn & Power ....G...... 217 857-3717
  Teutopolis (G-19771)
Peters Construction ....G...... 773 489-5555
  Chicago (G-5794)
Phoenix Art Woodworks ....G...... 847 279-1576
  Wheeling (G-20959)
Pinnacle Wood Products Inc ....G...... 815 385-0792
  McHenry (G-13778)
Prairie Woodworks Inc ....G...... 309 378-2418
  Downs (G-8112)
Pro Woodworking ....G...... 708 508-5948
  Bedford Park (G-1495)
R W G Manufacturing Inc ....G...... 708 755-8035
  S Chicago Hts (G-18127)
Ramar Industries Inc ....G...... 847 451-0445
  Franklin Park (G-10032)
Raynor Mfg Co ....A...... 815 288-1431
  Dixon (G-7908)
Reclaimedtablecom ....G...... 630 834-1929
  Villa Park (G-20169)
Rhyme or Reason Woodworking ....G...... 217 678-8301
  Bement (G-1715)
River City Millwork Inc ....D...... 800 892-9297
  Rockford (G-17573)
Rs Woodworking ....G...... 815 476-1818
  Wilmington (G-21101)
Sauder Industries Limited ....E...... 815 717-2660
  New Lenox (G-15057)
Scheffler Custom Woodworking ....G...... 815 284-6564
  Dixon (G-7915)
Skokie Millwork Inc ....G...... 847 673-7868
  Skokie (G-19030)
Sleepy Woodworks ....G...... 773 779-2990
  Chicago (G-6188)
Spec Built ....G...... 312 623-5533
  Palos Park (G-16215)
Stancy Woodworking Co Inc ....F...... 847 526-0252
  Island Lake (G-11611)
Stine Woodworking LLC ....E...... 618 885-2229
  Dow (G-7947)
Stovers Fine Woodworking Inc ....G...... 630 557-0072
  Maple Park (G-13466)
Sugarcreek Woodworking ....G...... 618 584-3817
  Flat Rock (G-9675)
Tree-O Lumber Inc ....E...... 618 357-2576
  Pinckneyville (G-16620)
Tri State Aluminum Products ....F...... 815 877-6081
  Loves Park (G-13277)
Triezenberg Millwork Co ....G...... 708 489-9062
  Crestwood (G-7132)
Ultimate Millwork Inc ....G...... 773 343-3070
  Elk Grove Village (G-9291)
Unimode Inc ....G...... 773 343-6754
  Burr Ridge (G-2728)
Vas Design Inc ....G...... 773 794-1368
  Chicago (G-6524)
Vermilion Millworks LLC ....F...... 217 446-8443
  Danville (G-7390)
Vista Woodworking ....G...... 815 922-2297
  Joliet (G-11942)
Washington Woodworking ....G...... 309 339-0913
  Washington (G-20283)
West Zwick Corp ....G...... 217 222-0228
  Quincy (G-16955)
Wiegmann Woodworking ....F...... 618 248-1300
  Damiansville (G-7316)
Wilderness Woodworks LLC ....G...... 815 210-3751
  Custer Park (G-7303)
Willard R Schorck ....F...... 217 543-2160
  Arthur (G-882)
Wood Creations Incorporated ....G...... 773 772-1375
  Chicago (G-6665)

Wood Creations Incorporated ....G...... 773 772-1375
  Chicago (G-6666)
Wooden World of Richmond Inc ....G...... 815 405-4503
  Richmond (G-17026)
Woodlogic Custom Millwork Inc ....E...... 847 640-4500
  Elk Grove Village (G-9311)
Woodwork Apts LLC ....G...... 224 595-9691
  Streamwood (G-19604)
Woodwork Refined Corporation ....G...... 708 385-7255
  Alsip (G-525)

MINERAL WOOL

J & J Industries Inc ....G...... 630 595-8878
  Mount Prospect (G-14538)
Johns Manville Corporation ....C...... 815 744-1545
  Rockdale (G-17261)
Safe-T-Quip Corporation ....F...... 773 235-2100
  Chicago (G-6089)
Silbrico Corporation ....D...... 708 354-3350
  Hodgkins (G-11397)
Tex Trend Inc ....E...... 847 215-6796
  Wheeling (G-20999)

MINERAL WOOL INSULATION PRDTS

USG Corporation ....F...... 847 970-5200
  Libertyville (G-12721)
USG Corporation ....B...... 312 436-4000
  Chicago (G-6506)

MINERALS: Ground Or Otherwise Treated

Prince Minerals Inc ....F...... 618 285-6558
  Rosiclare (G-18065)

MINERALS: Ground or Treated

Dauber Company Inc ....E...... 815 442-3569
  Tonica (G-19888)
Fairmont Central LLC ....E...... 815 433-2449
  Ottawa (G-16050)
Harsco Corporation ....F...... 217 237-4335
  Pawnee (G-16304)
Imerys Refractory Mnrl USA Inc ....E...... 618 285-6558
  Rosiclare (G-18064)
John Crane Inc ....E...... 815 459-0420
  Crystal Lake (G-7214)
Material Service Corporation ....D...... 708 877-6540
  Thornton (G-19790)
McGill Asphalt Construction Co ....G...... 708 924-1755
  Chicago (G-5376)
Mid River Minerals Inc ....G...... 815 941-7524
  Morris (G-14313)
Mineral Products Inc ....G...... 618 433-3150
  Harrisburg (G-11026)
Minerals Technologies Inc ....F...... 847 851-1500
  Hoffman Estates (G-11435)
Oil-Dri Corporation America ....D...... 618 745-6881
  Mounds (G-14463)
Polyform Products Company ....E...... 847 427-0020
  Elk Grove Village (G-9182)
Sem Minerals LP ....D...... 217 224-8766
  Quincy (G-16944)
Stein Inc ....F...... 815 626-9355
  Sterling (G-19533)

MINIATURE GOLF COURSES

Okawville Times ....G...... 618 243-5563
  Okawville (G-15846)

MINING EXPLORATION & DEVELOPMENT SVCS

Caterpillar Inc ....B...... 309 494-0858
  Aurora (G-1071)
Coeur Capital Inc ....G...... 312 489-5800
  Chicago (G-4193)
Mab Equipment Company ....G...... 630 551-4017
  Oswego (G-16012)

MINING MACHINERY & EQPT WHOLESALERS

Komatsu America Corp ....B...... 847 437-5800
  Chicago (G-5120)
Mpc Global LLC ....G...... 816 399-4710
  Springfield (G-19408)

MINING MACHINES & EQPT: Augers

Hydra Fold Auger Inc ....G...... 217 379-2614
  Loda (G-13028)

MINING MACHINES & EQPT: Bits, Rock, Exc Oil/Gas Field Tools

Braden Rock Bit ....G...... 618 435-4519
  Benton (G-1922)

MINING MACHINES & EQPT: Cleaning, Mineral

O-Cedar Commercial ....G...... 217 379-2377
  Paxton (G-16311)

MINING MACHINES & EQPT: Crushers, Stationary

Drumbeaters of America Inc ....F...... 630 365-5527
  Elburn (G-8449)

MINING MACHINES & EQPT: Loading, Underground, Mobile

Fibro Inc ....F...... 815 229-1300
  Rockford (G-17415)

MINING MACHINES & EQPT: Mineral Beneficiation

Carroll International Corp ....C...... 630 983-5979
  Lake Forest (G-12236)
Centrifugal Services Inc ....D...... 618 268-4850
  Raleigh (G-16959)
Elgin National Industries Inc ....D...... 314 776-2848
  Raleigh (G-16960)

MINING MACHINES & EQPT: Sedimentation, Mineral

Fox International Corp ....F...... 773 465-3634
  Chicago (G-4627)

MINING MACHINES & EQPT: Stamping Mill Machinery

American Equipment & Mch Inc ....D...... 618 533-3857
  Centralia (G-3221)

MIRRORS: Motor Vehicle

Sure Plus Manufacturing Co ....D...... 708 756-3100
  Chicago Heights (G-6777)

MISC FIN INVEST ACT: Shares, RE, Entertain & Eqpt, Sales

Equity Concepts Co Inc ....G...... 815 226-1300
  Rockford (G-17399)

MISCELLANEOUS FINANCIAL INVEST ACT: Oil/Gas Lease Brokers

Vigo Coal Operating Co Inc ....G...... 618 262-7022
  Mount Carmel (G-14490)

MISSILE GUIDANCE SYSTEMS & EQPT

Chemring Energetic Devices Inc ....C...... 630 969-0620
  Downers Grove (G-7968)

MISSILES: Guided

Boeing Company ....C...... 312 544-2000
  Chicago (G-3925)

MITTENS: Leather

Neckbone Skunks Logistics & Te ....F...... 312 218-0281
  Chicago (G-5561)

MIXING EQPT

Fluid Mnagement Operations LLC ....G...... 847 537-0880
  Wheeling (G-20899)

MIXTURES & BLOCKS: Asphalt Paving

Advanced Asphalt Co ....E...... 815 872-9911
  Princeton (G-16804)

Employee Codes: A=Over 500 employees, B=251-500
C=101-250, D=51-100, E=20-50, F=10-19, G=3-9

MIXTURES & BLOCKS: Asphalt Paving

Ambraw Asphalt Materials Inc .... E 618 943-4716
  Lawrenceville *(G-12526)*
Asphalt Mtls DBA Hritg Asp LLC .... G 773 735-2233
  Cicero *(G-6830)*
Bonsal American Inc .... D 847 678-6220
  Franklin Park *(G-9891)*
Chicago Baking Company .... A 630 684-2335
  Darien *(G-7404)*
Christ Bros Products LLC .... G 618 537-6174
  Lebanon *(G-12543)*
Consolidated Paving Inc .... G 309 693-3505
  Peoria *(G-16427)*
Cope & Sons Asphalt .... G 618 462-2207
  Alton *(G-548)*
County Asphalt Inc .... G 618 224-9033
  Trenton *(G-19902)*
Cullinan & Sons Inc .... E 309 925-2711
  Tremont *(G-19895)*
Curran Contracting Company .... G 815 758-8113
  Dekalb *(G-7671)*
Dicks Asphalt Service .... G 815 932-7157
  Kankakee *(G-11965)*
Don Anderson Co .... G 618 495-2511
  Hoffman *(G-11402)*
Dougherty E J Oil & Stone Sup .... G 618 271-4414
  East Saint Louis *(G-8304)*
Emulsicoat Inc .... F 217 344-7775
  Urbana *(G-19981)*
Freesen Inc .... E 309 827-4554
  Bloomington *(G-2046)*
Fuller Asphalt & Landscape .... G 618 797-1169
  Granite City *(G-10707)*
G & S Asphalt Inc .... F 217 826-2421
  Marshall *(G-13571)*
Gardner Asphalt Corporation .... E 800 237-1155
  Chicago *(G-4659)*
General Contractor Inc .... G 618 533-5213
  Sandoval *(G-18364)*
Geneva Construction Company .... G 630 892-6536
  North Aurora *(G-15261)*
Hardscape Outpost LLC .... G 630 551-6105
  North Aurora *(G-15262)*
Hassebrock Asphalt Sealing .... G 618 566-7214
  Mascoutah *(G-13598)*
Hillyer Inc .... D 309 837-6434
  Macomb *(G-13392)*
Jax Asphalt Company Inc .... F 618 244-0500
  Mount Vernon *(G-14618)*
JB Enterprises II Inc .... F 630 372-8300
  Streamwood *(G-19579)*
Lafarge North America Inc .... C 773 372-1000
  Chicago *(G-5156)*
Marathon Petroleum Company LP .... G 618 829-3288
  Saint Elmo *(G-18309)*
Orange Crush LLC .... C 708 544-9440
  Hillside *(G-11352)*
Orange Crush LLC .... G 847 428-6176
  East Dundee *(G-8207)*
Orange Crush LLC .... G 630 739-5560
  Romeoville *(G-17862)*
Orange Crush LLC .... G 847 537-7900
  Wheeling *(G-20952)*
Owens Corning Sales LLC .... E 708 594-6935
  Argo *(G-675)*
Peter Baker & Son Co .... D 847 362-3663
  Lake Bluff *(G-12204)*
Plote Construction Inc .... D 847 695-9300
  Hoffman Estates *(G-11445)*
Plote Inc .... D 847 695-9467
  Hoffman Estates *(G-11446)*
Prosser Construction Co .... F 217 774-5032
  Shelbyville *(G-18884)*
Quikrete Companies LLC .... F 309 346-1184
  Pekin *(G-16357)*
Rock Road Companies Inc .... F 815 874-2441
  Rockford *(G-17583)*
Rockford Blacktop Cnstr Co .... D 815 654-4700
  Rockford *(G-17586)*
Sandeno Inc .... G 815 730-9415
  Rockdale *(G-17272)*
Schulze & Schulze Inc .... G 618 687-1106
  Murphysboro *(G-14758)*
Sealmaster Inc .... F 847 480-7325
  Northbrook *(G-15478)*
Sealmaster/Alsip .... G 708 489-0900
  Alsip *(G-509)*
Srj Inc .... F 630 351-0639
  Schaumburg *(G-18726)*
St Clair Tennis Club LLC .... G 618 632-1400
  O Fallon *(G-15584)*
Streator Asphalt Inc .... G 815 672-8683
  Streator *(G-19625)*
Terry Terri Mulgrew .... G 815 747-6248
  East Dubuque *(G-8185)*
Thorworks Industries Inc .... G 815 969-0664
  Rockford *(G-17662)*
Veterans Parking Lot Maint .... G 815 245-7584
  Woodstock *(G-21443)*

MOBILE COMMUNICATIONS EQPT

Kvh Industries Inc .... E 708 444-2800
  Tinley Park *(G-19843)*
Motorola Mobility Holdings LLC .... F 800 668-6765
  Chicago *(G-5508)*
Motorola Mobility LLC .... B 847 523-5000
  Chicago *(G-5510)*
Motorola Solutions Inc .... C 847 576-8600
  Schaumburg *(G-18637)*
Qaboss Partners .... B 312 203-4290
  Chicago *(G-5922)*
T-Mobile Usa Inc .... F 847 289-9988
  South Elgin *(G-19176)*
Tribeam Inc .... G 847 409-9497
  Arlington Heights *(G-821)*

MOBILE HOME FRAMES

Shur Co of Illinois .... G 217 877-8277
  Decatur *(G-7546)*

MOBILE HOMES

Gerald Graff .... E 312 343-2612
  Lincolnwood *(G-12822)*
Mobil Trailer Transport Inc .... E 630 993-1200
  Villa Park *(G-20160)*
Southmoor Estates Inc .... G 815 756-1299
  Dekalb *(G-7705)*
Superior Mobile Home Service .... G 708 672-7799
  Crete *(G-7146)*

MOBILE HOMES WHOLESALERS

Herman Bade & Sons .... G 217 832-9444
  Villa Grove *(G-20123)*

MOBILE HOMES: Indl Or Commercial Use

Skender Construction LLC .... D 312 781-0265
  Chicago *(G-6179)*

MOBILE HOMES: Personal Or Private Use

Skiman Sales Inc .... G 847 888-8200
  Elgin *(G-8737)*

MODELS

Rock Island Cannon Company .... G 309 786-1507
  Rock Island *(G-17245)*

MODELS: General, Exc Toy

Acme Design Inc .... G 847 841-7400
  Elgin *(G-8492)*
Associated Design Inc .... F 708 974-9100
  Palos Hills *(G-16195)*
Capital Pttern Model Works Inc .... G 630 469-8200
  Glendale Heights *(G-10440)*
Denoyer - Geppert Science Co .... E 800 621-1014
  Skokie *(G-18948)*
E J Kupjack & Associates Inc .... F 847 823-6661
  Chicago *(G-4424)*
Evergreen Scale Models Inc .... F 224 567-8099
  Des Plaines *(G-7761)*
Models Plus Inc .... E 847 231-4300
  Grayslake *(G-10789)*
Paradigm Development Group Inc .... F 847 545-9600
  Winfield *(G-21114)*
Sun Pattern & Model Inc .... E 630 293-3366
  West Chicago *(G-20648)*
Wielgus Product Models Inc .... E 312 432-1950
  Chicago *(G-6624)*

MODULES: Computer Logic

Laird Connectivity Inc .... G 847 839-6000
  Schaumburg *(G-18596)*

MODULES: Solid State

Coinstar Procurement LLC .... G 630 424-4788
  Oakbrook Terrace *(G-15794)*

Inland Tech Holdings LLC .... E 618 476-7678
  Millstadt *(G-14048)*
Touchsensor Technologies LLC .... B 630 221-9000
  Wheaton *(G-20829)*

MOLDED RUBBER PRDTS

Accurate Products Incorporated .... E 773 878-2200
  Chicago *(G-3520)*
Aero Rubber Company Inc .... E 800 662-1009
  Tinley Park *(G-19798)*
American Rubber Mfg Inc .... G 331 551-9600
  Bensenville *(G-1743)*
Aztec Products 217 726-8631
  Springfield *(G-19323)*
Custom Seal & Rubber Products .... G 888 356-2966
  Mount Morris *(G-14499)*
Flexan LLC 224 543-0003
  Lincolnshire *(G-12764)*
Gusco Silicone Rbr & Svcs LLC .... F 773 770-5008
  Aurora *(G-1106)*
Honeywell Safety Pdts USA Inc .... C 630 343-3731
  Bolingbrook *(G-2185)*
Jvi Inc 847 675-1560
  Lincolnwood *(G-12825)*
Kelco Industries Inc .... G 815 334-3600
  Woodstock *(G-21398)*
Loop Attachment Co .... E 847 922-0642
  Chicago *(G-5256)*
Midwest Sealing Products Inc .... E 847 459-2202
  Buffalo Grove *(G-2575)*
Omni Products Inc 815 344-3100
  McHenry *(G-13773)*
Polyonics Rubber Co 815 765-2033
  Poplar Grove *(G-16783)*
Roho Inc .... C 618 234-4899
  Belleville *(G-1593)*
Rutgers Enterprises Inc .... G 847 674-7666
  Lincolnwood *(G-12841)*
Southland Industries Inc .... E 757 543-5701
  Bannockburn *(G-1208)*

MOLDING COMPOUNDS

Acomtech Mold Inc .... G 847 741-3537
  Elgin *(G-8493)*
Advanced Prototype Molding .... G 847 202-4200
  Palatine *(G-16090)*
Akshar Plastic Inc .... E 815 635-3536
  Bloomington *(G-2022)*
Camryn Industries LLC .... G 815 544-1900
  Belvidere *(G-1660)*
Coda Resources Ltd .... F 718 649-1666
  Chicago *(G-4190)*
Lyondllbsell Advnced Plymers I .... E 847 426-3350
  Carpentersville *(G-3107)*
Mossan Inc .... G 857 247-4122
  Schaumburg *(G-18633)*
Sejasmi Corp .... G 586 725-5300
  Des Plaines *(G-7841)*
Snyder Industries Inc .... D 630 773-9510
  Bensenville *(G-1895)*
Underground Devices Inc .... F 847 205-9000
  Northbrook *(G-15495)*
Yankee Mold Inc .... G 815 986-1776
  Machesney Park *(G-13384)*

MOLDING SAND MINING

Husar Abatement Ltd .... F 847 349-9105
  Franklin Park *(G-9960)*
Snyder Industries Inc .... D 630 773-9510
  Bensenville *(G-1895)*

MOLDINGS & TRIM: Metal, Exc Automobile

Group Industries Inc .... E 708 877-6200
  Thornton *(G-19788)*
Kroh-Wagner Inc .... E 773 252-2031
  Chicago *(G-5133)*

MOLDINGS & TRIM: Wood

A & M Wood Products Inc .... G 630 323-2555
  Burr Ridge *(G-2647)*

MOLDINGS OR TRIM: Automobile, Stamped Metal

Kipp Manufacturing Company Inc .... F 630 768-9051
  Wauconda *(G-20366)*

PRODUCT SECTION

MOLDINGS, ARCHITECTURAL: Plaster Of Paris

Quality Molding Products LLC ....G....... 224 286-4555
  Gurnee *(G-10921)*

MOLDINGS: Picture Frame

Artistic Framing Inc ....C....... 847 808-0200
  Wheeling *(G-20850)*
Bravura Moulding Company ....G....... 262 633-1882
  Lake Bluff *(G-12175)*
Custom Framework Inc ....G....... 618 401-8494
  Edwardsville *(G-8354)*
Frame Mart Inc ....G....... 309 452-0658
  Normal *(G-15203)*
Iloilo Custom Framing ....G....... 773 334-2844
  Chicago *(G-4893)*
Larson-Juhl US LLC ....E....... 630 307-9700
  Roselle *(G-17963)*
Northwest Frame Company Inc ....G....... 847 359-0987
  Palatine *(G-16144)*
Nu-Dell Manufacturing Co Inc ....F....... 847 803-4500
  Chicago *(G-5637)*
Rosewood Custom Framing LLC ....G....... 217 430-7669
  Quincy *(G-16943)*
Supreme Frame & Moulding Co ....F....... 312 930-9056
  Chicago *(G-6286)*
Woodmac Industries Inc ....F....... 708 755-3545
  S Chicago Hts *(G-18130)*
Wyman and Company ....G....... 708 532-9064
  Tinley Park *(G-19868)*

MOLDS: Indl

A & C Mold Company Inc ....E....... 630 587-0177
  Saint Charles *(G-18141)*
A-1 Tool Corporation ....D....... 708 345-5000
  Melrose Park *(G-13817)*
A-B Die Mold Inc ....F....... 847 658-1199
  Bartlett *(G-1261)*
Aberdeen Technologies Inc ....F....... 630 665-8590
  Carol Stream *(G-2923)*
Admo Inc ....D....... 847 741-5777
  Elgin *(G-8495)*
Advanced Digital & Mold Inc ....G....... 630 595-8242
  Bensenville *(G-1729)*
Allstar Tool & Molds Inc ....F....... 630 766-0162
  Bensenville *(G-1739)*
ARC Industries Inc ....E....... 847 303-5005
  Schaumburg *(G-18444)*
Assurance Clg Restoration LLC ....F....... 630 444-3600
  Saint Charles *(G-18151)*
Atlas Die LLC ....D....... 630 351-5140
  Glendale Heights *(G-10436)*
B A Die Mold Inc ....F....... 630 978-4747
  Aurora *(G-919)*
Bg Die Mold Inc ....G....... 847 961-5861
  Huntley *(G-11529)*
Cameo Mold Corp ....F....... 630 876-1340
  West Chicago *(G-20557)*
Cardon Mold Finishing Inc ....G....... 630 543-5431
  Addison *(G-63)*
Carroll Industrial Molds Inc ....F....... 815 225-7250
  Milledgeville *(G-14038)*
Challenge Tool Co ....G....... 847 640-8085
  Elk Grove Village *(G-8887)*
Comet Die & Engraving Company ....D....... 630 833-5600
  Elmhurst *(G-9350)*
Complete Mold Polishing Inc ....G....... 630 406-7668
  Batavia *(G-1368)*
Craftsman Tool & Mold Co ....E....... 630 851-8700
  Aurora *(G-942)*
Crystal Die and Mold Inc ....E....... 847 658-6535
  Rolling Meadows *(G-17725)*
Dangios Fine Art Inc ....G....... 773 533-3000
  Chicago *(G-4311)*
Davitz Mold Co Inc ....G....... 847 426-4848
  East Dundee *(G-8191)*
Diamond Tool & Mold Inc ....G....... 630 543-7011
  Addison *(G-90)*
Die Mold Jig Grinding & Mfg ....G....... 847 228-1444
  Elk Grove Village *(G-8949)*
Dragon Die Mold Inc ....G....... 630 836-0699
  Warrenville *(G-20235)*
Elba Tool Co Inc ....F....... 847 895-4100
  Bloomingdale *(G-1990)*
Emerson Industries LLC ....F....... 630 279-0920
  Itasca *(G-11649)*
Ewikon Molding Tech Inc ....G....... 815 874-7250
  Rockford *(G-17405)*
Furnel Inc ....E....... 630 543-0885
  Addison *(G-130)*
Glenwood Tool & Mold Inc ....F....... 630 289-3400
  Bartlett *(G-1282)*
Great Lakes Tool & Mold Inc ....G....... 630 964-7121
  Woodridge *(G-21307)*
Haaker Mold Co Inc ....G....... 847 253-8103
  Arlington Heights *(G-746)*
Heritage Mold Incorporated ....F....... 815 397-1117
  Rockford *(G-17448)*
Illinois Mold Builders Inc ....F....... 847 526-0400
  Wauconda *(G-20359)*
Inc Midwest Die Mold ....G....... 224 353-6417
  Schaumburg *(G-18557)*
Industrial Molded Products ....F....... 847 358-2160
  Mundelein *(G-14700)*
Iplastics LLC ....D....... 309 444-8884
  Washington *(G-20270)*
Jbw Machining Inc ....E....... 847 451-0276
  Franklin Park *(G-9974)*
Jsp Mold LLC ....G....... 815 225-7110
  Milledgeville *(G-14039)*
Kelco Industries Inc ....G....... 815 334-3600
  Woodstock *(G-21398)*
Libco Industries Inc ....F....... 815 623-7677
  Roscoe *(G-17912)*
Magic Mold Removal ....G....... 630 486-0912
  Aurora *(G-1125)*
Manufcture Design Innvation Inc ....G....... 773 526-7773
  West Chicago *(G-20611)*
Marshall Mold Inc ....G....... 630 582-1800
  Glendale Heights *(G-10473)*
Matrix Plastic Products Inc ....D....... 630 595-6144
  Wood Dale *(G-21214)*
Melrose Mold & Machine Co Inc ....G....... 847 233-9970
  Franklin Park *(G-9991)*
Metro Tool Company ....G....... 847 673-6790
  Skokie *(G-18988)*
Millennium Mold & Tool ....G....... 847 438-5600
  Lake Zurich *(G-12433)*
Mold Express Inc ....G....... 773 766-0874
  Chicago *(G-5486)*
Mp Mold Co ....G....... 630 613-8086
  Addison *(G-224)*
Nemeth Tool Inc ....G....... 630 595-0409
  Wood Dale *(G-21220)*
Perfect Mold Inc ....G....... 630 785-6105
  Addison *(G-236)*
Phoenix Tool Corp ....F....... 847 956-1886
  Elk Grove Village *(G-9178)*
Plastic Products Company Inc ....C....... 309 762-6532
  Moline *(G-14167)*
Plaza Tool & Mold Co ....G....... 847 537-2320
  Wheeling *(G-20961)*
Pro Built Tool & Mold Inc ....G....... 815 436-9088
  Plainfield *(G-16707)*
Pro-Mold Incorporated ....D....... 630 893-3594
  Roselle *(G-17975)*
Ps3 Tool Mold & Assembly LLC ....D....... 630 802-9462
  Saint Charles *(G-18253)*
Soldy Manufacturing Inc ....D....... 847 671-3396
  Schiller Park *(G-18844)*
Star Die Molding Inc ....D....... 847 766-7952
  Elk Grove Village *(G-9255)*
Surfacetec Corp ....F....... 630 521-0001
  Franklin Park *(G-10058)*
Vicma Tool Co ....G....... 847 541-0177
  Wheeling *(G-21010)*
Voss Pattern Works Inc ....G....... 618 233-4242
  Belleville *(G-1609)*
Wapro Inc ....G....... 888 927-8677
  Chicago *(G-6586)*
William J Kline & Co Inc ....F....... 815 338-2055
  Woodstock *(G-21448)*
Wirco Inc ....D....... 217 398-3200
  Champaign *(G-3371)*
Zender Enterprises Ltd ....G....... 773 282-2293
  Chicago *(G-6716)*

MOLDS: Plastic Working & Foundry

APT Tool Inc ....G....... 815 337-0051
  Woodstock *(G-21359)*
Chicago Mold Engrg Co Inc ....D....... 630 584-1311
  Saint Charles *(G-18165)*
Hatcher Associates Inc ....F....... 773 252-2171
  Chicago *(G-4784)*
Industrial Modern Pattern ....G....... 847 296-4930
  Elk Grove Village *(G-9050)*
Industrial Molds Inc ....D....... 815 397-2971
  Rockford *(G-17459)*
Janler Corporation ....E....... 773 774-0166
  Chicago *(G-5005)*
Lens Lenticlear Lenticular ....F....... 630 467-0900
  Elk Grove Village *(G-9093)*
Method Molds Inc ....G....... 815 877-0191
  Loves Park *(G-13236)*
Monarch Manufacturing ....G....... 630 519-4580
  Lombard *(G-13103)*
Northern Illinois Mold Corp ....F....... 847 669-2100
  Dundee *(G-8130)*
PM Mold Company ....E....... 847 923-5400
  Schaumburg *(G-18680)*
RAO Design International Inc ....G....... 847 671-6182
  Morton Grove *(G-14437)*
Sterling Tool & Manufacturing ....G....... 847 304-1800
  Barrington *(G-1245)*
Wright Tool & Die Inc ....F....... 815 669-2020
  McHenry *(G-13810)*

MONASTERIES

Marytown ....E....... 847 367-7800
  Libertyville *(G-12673)*

MONUMENTS & GRAVE MARKERS, EXC TERRAZZO

Kowalski Memorials Inc ....G....... 630 462-7226
  Carol Stream *(G-3014)*
Libertyville Monuments ....G....... 641 295-3506
  Libertyville *(G-12669)*
Mariachi Monumental De Mexico ....G....... 520 878-8688
  Chicago *(G-5333)*
Monumental Art Works ....G....... 708 389-3038
  Blue Island *(G-2132)*

MONUMENTS & GRAVE MARKERS, WHOLESALE

Tolar Group LLC ....E....... 847 662-8000
  Waukegan *(G-20507)*

MONUMENTS: Concrete

Bobs Market & Greenhouse ....G....... 217 442-8155
  Danville *(G-7324)*
Elite Monument Co ....G....... 217 532-6080
  Hillsboro *(G-11310)*

MONUMENTS: Cut Stone, Exc Finishing Or Lettering Only

American Monument Co ....G....... 618 993-8968
  Marion *(G-13503)*
Bevel Granite Company Inc ....D....... 708 371-4191
  Indian Head Park *(G-11576)*
J W Reynolds Monument Co Inc ....G....... 618 833-6014
  Anna *(G-586)*
King & Sons Monuments ....G....... 815 786-6321
  Sandwich *(G-18376)*
Old Capitol Monument Works Inc ....G....... 217 324-5673
  Vandalia *(G-20017)*
Rogan Granitindustrie Inc ....G....... 708 758-0050
  Indian Head Park *(G-11577)*
Rogan Granitindustrie Inc ....G....... 708 758-0050
  Lynwood *(G-13298)*
Wilson & Wilson Monument Co ....F....... 618 775-6488
  Odin *(G-15836)*

MOPEDS & PARTS

Monahan Partners Inc ....F....... 217 268-5758
  Arcola *(G-658)*

MOPS: Floor & Dust

Don Leventhal Group LLC ....E....... 618 783-4424
  Newton *(G-15082)*
FHP-Berner USA LP ....E....... 630 270-1400
  Aurora *(G-961)*
Freudenberg Household Pdts LP ....C....... 630 270-1400
  Aurora *(G-964)*
Libman Company ....C....... 217 268-4200
  Arcola *(G-655)*

MOTION PICTURE & VIDEO PRODUCTION SVCS

Csiteq Studio LLC ....F....... 312 265-1509
  Rosemont *(G-18012)*
Linx Enterprises LLC ....G....... 224 409-2206
  Chicago *(G-5232)*

MOTION PICTURE & VIDEO PRODUCTION SVCS

Towers Media Holdings Inc......................D...... 312 993-1550
  Northfield *(G-15534)*

MOTION PICTURE & VIDEO PRODUCTION SVCS: Commercials, TV

Gfx International LLC..............................C...... 847 543-7179
  Grayslake *(G-10774)*

MOTION PICTURE & VIDEO PRODUCTION SVCS: Educational

Learning Seed LLC.................................G...... 847 540-8855
  Chicago *(G-5193)*

MOTION PICTURE DISTRIBUTION SVCS

Csiteq Studio LLC....................................F...... 312 265-1509
  Rosemont *(G-18012)*

MOTION PICTURE EQPT

2nd Cine Inc...G...... 773 455-5808
  Elgin *(G-8488)*
Essannay Show It Inc..............................G...... 312 733-5511
  Chicago *(G-4532)*
Imac Asset Sales Corp.............................G...... 847 741-4622
  Elgin *(G-8622)*
Research Technology Intl Co....................E...... 847 677-3000
  Lincolnwood *(G-12837)*

MOTION PICTURE PRODUCTION ALLIED SVCS

Csiteq Studio LLC....................................F...... 312 265-1509
  Rosemont *(G-18012)*
Personify Inc..G...... 217 840-2638
  Urbana *(G-19992)*
Personify Inc..F...... 855 747-9940
  Chicago *(G-5792)*

MOTION PICTURE PRODUCTION SVCS

Icon Acquisition Holdings LP...................G...... 312 751-8000
  Chicago *(G-4872)*

MOTOR & GENERATOR PARTS: Electric

Alfa Controls Inc......................................G...... 847 978-9245
  Wheeling *(G-20844)*
Alin Machining Company Inc...................C...... 708 681-1043
  Melrose Park *(G-13821)*
Djh Industries Inc.....................................E...... 309 246-8456
  Lacon *(G-12126)*
Encap Technologies Inc...........................F...... 510 337-2700
  Palatine *(G-16116)*
Encap Technologies Inc...........................B...... 510 337-2700
  Palatine *(G-16117)*
Inventus Power (illinois) LLC...................C...... 630 410-7900
  Woodridge *(G-21317)*
Kap Holdings LLC...................................F...... 708 948-0226
  Oak Park *(G-15759)*
Stable Beginning Corporation..................E...... 815 745-2100
  Warren *(G-20225)*

MOTOR HOMES

Liberty Coach Inc....................................D...... 847 578-4600
  North Chicago *(G-15316)*

MOTOR INN

River View Motor Sports Inc...................G...... 309 467-4569
  Congerville *(G-7003)*

MOTOR REBUILDING SVCS, EXC AUTOMOTIVE

Amj Industries Inc....................................F...... 815 654-9000
  Rockford *(G-17302)*
C and C Machine Tool Service................G...... 630 810-0484
  Downers Grove *(G-7962)*
Endeavor Technologies Inc......................E...... 630 562-0300
  Saint Charles *(G-18197)*
Fdf Armature Inc.....................................G...... 630 458-0452
  Addison *(G-120)*
Fontela Electric Incorporated..................F...... 630 932-1600
  Addison *(G-127)*
L A Motors Incorporated..........................G...... 773 736-7305
  Chicago *(G-5142)*
M R Glenn Electric Inc............................E...... 708 479-9200
  Lockport *(G-13009)*

OReilly Automotive Stores Inc..................G...... 847 882-4384
  Schaumburg *(G-18659)*
OReilly Automotive Stores Inc..................G...... 847 360-0012
  Waukegan *(G-20474)*
OReilly Automotive Stores Inc..................G...... 708 430-8155
  Bridgeview *(G-2370)*

MOTOR REPAIR SVCS

Decatur Industrial Elc Inc........................E...... 618 244-1066
  Mount Vernon *(G-14607)*
Fleetpride Inc..F...... 630 455-6881
  Willowbrook *(G-21043)*
Fluid Pump Service Inc............................G...... 847 228-0750
  Elk Grove Village *(G-9000)*
Metroeast Motorsports Inc.......................G...... 618 628-2466
  O Fallon *(G-15580)*

MOTOR SCOOTERS & PARTS

Pruett Enterprises Inc..............................G...... 618 235-6184
  Belleville *(G-1586)*

MOTOR VEHICLE ASSEMBLY, COMPLETE: Ambulances

Light of Mine LLC....................................G...... 312 840-8570
  Chicago *(G-5220)*

MOTOR VEHICLE ASSEMBLY, COMPLETE: Autos, Incl Specialty

Blackjack Customs...................................G...... 847 361-5225
  North Chicago *(G-15307)*
Brunos Automotive Products...................G...... 630 458-0043
  Addison *(G-56)*
Chassis Service Unlimited.......................G...... 847 336-2305
  Waukegan *(G-20427)*
Dakkota Integrated Systems LLC............D...... 517 694-6500
  Chicago *(G-4308)*
FCA US LLC..G...... 630 724-2321
  Lisle *(G-12890)*
Fuji Oozx America Inc..............................G...... 281 888-2247
  Schaumburg *(G-18531)*
High Speed Welding Inc..........................G...... 630 971-8929
  Westmont *(G-20747)*
Innova Uev LLC.......................................F...... 630 568-5609
  Burr Ridge *(G-2687)*
John Beyer Race Cars.............................G...... 773 779-5313
  Chicago *(G-5037)*
Kens Street Rod Repair...........................G...... 815 874-1811
  Rockford *(G-17482)*
Legend Racing Enterprises Inc...............G...... 847 923-8979
  Schaumburg *(G-18602)*
Maxim Inc...F...... 217 544-7015
  Springfield *(G-19403)*
Midwest Coach Builders Inc...................G...... 630 690-1420
  Carol Stream *(G-3030)*
Midwest Hot Rods Inc..............................F...... 815 254-7637
  Plainfield *(G-16689)*
Nippon Sharyo Mfg LLC..........................G...... 815 562-8600
  Rochelle *(G-17151)*
Restorations Unlimited II Inc....................G...... 847 639-5818
  Cary *(G-3186)*
Rj Race Cars Inc.....................................F...... 309 343-7575
  Galesburg *(G-10218)*
T R Z Motorsports Inc..............................G...... 815 806-0838
  Frankfort *(G-9843)*

MOTOR VEHICLE ASSEMBLY, COMPLETE: Bus/Large Spclty Vehicles

Oshkosh Specialty Vehicles Inc...............C...... 708 868-5071
  Calumet City *(G-2784)*

MOTOR VEHICLE ASSEMBLY, COMPLETE: Buses, All Types

Motor Coach Inds Intl Inc........................C...... 847 285-2000
  Des Plaines *(G-7804)*
Motor Coach Industries...........................G...... 847 285-2000
  Des Plaines *(G-7805)*

MOTOR VEHICLE ASSEMBLY, COMPLETE: Fire Department Vehicles

Alexis Fire Equipment Company..............D...... 309 482-6121
  Alexis *(G-364)*
Crete Twp..G...... 708 672-3111
  Crete *(G-7138)*

Federal Signal Corporation......................D...... 630 954-2000
  Oak Brook *(G-15618)*
Odin Fire Protection District....................E...... 618 775-8292
  Odin *(G-15835)*
Sentinel Emrgncy Solutions LLC.............E...... 618 539-3863
  Freeburg *(G-10093)*

MOTOR VEHICLE ASSEMBLY, COMPLETE: Military Motor Vehicle

Navistar Defense LLC..............................G...... 662 494-3421
  Lisle *(G-12920)*

MOTOR VEHICLE ASSEMBLY, COMPLETE: Motor Buses

Liberty Coach Inc....................................D...... 847 578-4600
  North Chicago *(G-15316)*

MOTOR VEHICLE ASSEMBLY, COMPLETE: Reconnaissance Cars

Heartland Classics Inc.............................G...... 618 783-4444
  Newton *(G-15084)*

MOTOR VEHICLE ASSEMBLY, COMPLETE: Snow Plows

Enterprise Service Corporation................G...... 773 589-2727
  Des Plaines *(G-7758)*
Koenig Body & Equipment Inc................E...... 309 673-7435
  West Peoria *(G-20687)*

MOTOR VEHICLE ASSEMBLY, COMPLETE: Truck & Tractor Trucks

Direct Dimension Inc...............................G...... 815 479-1936
  Algonquin *(G-369)*
Hertz Corporation....................................G...... 630 897-0956
  Montgomery *(G-14247)*
Jenner Precision Inc................................F...... 815 692-6655
  Fairbury *(G-9609)*
Navistar Inc...D...... 331 332-5000
  Lisle *(G-12918)*
Navistar Inc...D...... 708 865-3333
  Melrose Park *(G-13895)*
Navistar International Corp......................A...... 331 332-5000
  Lisle *(G-12921)*
Rahn Equipment Company.....................G...... 217 431-1232
  Danville *(G-7376)*

MOTOR VEHICLE ASSEMBLY, COMPLETE: Truck Tractors, Highway

Dierzen-Kewanee Heavy Inds.................D...... 309 853-2316
  Kewanee *(G-12030)*
Long Wolf Express Inc.............................G...... 708 673-1583
  South Holland *(G-19230)*

MOTOR VEHICLE ASSEMBLY, COMPLETE: Wreckers, Tow Truck

Mares Service Inc....................................G...... 708 656-1660
  Cicero *(G-6865)*
Neckbone Skunks Logistics & Te............F...... 312 218-0281
  Chicago *(G-5561)*

MOTOR VEHICLE DEALERS: Automobiles, New & Used

Birkeys Farm Store Inc............................E...... 217 337-1772
  Urbana *(G-19975)*
City Subn Auto Svc Goodyear................G...... 773 355-5550
  Chicago *(G-4162)*
Mitsubishi Elc Automtn Inc......................C...... 847 478-2100
  Vernon Hills *(G-20075)*
Mitsubishi Materials USA Corp................F...... 847 519-1601
  Schaumburg *(G-18632)*
Motor Sport Marketing Group..................E...... 618 654-6750
  Highland *(G-11232)*
Nissan..G...... 630 957-4360
  West Chicago *(G-20622)*
Pilla Exec Inc...G...... 312 882-8263
  Chicago *(G-5807)*
Subaru of America Inc............................E...... 630 250-4740
  Itasca *(G-11741)*
Union Ave Auto Inc..................................G...... 708 754-3899
  Steger *(G-19495)*
Zeigler Chrysler Dodge............................G...... 708 956-7700
  Berwyn *(G-1963)*

PRODUCT SECTION

MOTOR VEHICLE PARTS & ACCESS: Transmissions

MOTOR VEHICLE DEALERS: Cars, Used Only

Metzger Welding Service .... G 217 234-2851
Mattoon *(G-13649)*

MOTOR VEHICLE DEALERS: Trucks, Tractors/Trailers, New & Used

Great Dane LLC .... D 773 254-5533
Kewanee *(G-12038)*

MOTOR VEHICLE PARTS & ACCESS: Air Conditioner Parts

Bison Gear & Engineering Corp .... C 630 377-4327
Saint Charles *(G-18156)*
T/CCI Manufacturing LLC .... D 217 423-0066
Decatur *(G-7555)*

MOTOR VEHICLE PARTS & ACCESS: Axel Housings & Shafts

Power Plus Products Inc .... F 773 788-9794
Bedford Park *(G-1492)*

MOTOR VEHICLE PARTS & ACCESS: Bearings

Nta Precision Axle Corporation .... B 630 690-6300
Carol Stream *(G-3041)*

MOTOR VEHICLE PARTS & ACCESS: Body Components & Frames

Clarios .... D 630 279-0050
Elmhurst *(G-9347)*
Clarios .... F 630 871-7700
Carol Stream *(G-2961)*
Eagle Wings Industries Inc .... B 217 892-4322
Rantoul *(G-16974)*
Mobis Parts America LLC .... B 630 907-4700
Aurora *(G-1136)*
Qwik-Tip Inc .... G 847 640-7387
Elk Grove Village *(G-9207)*
Waltz Brothers Inc .... E 847 520-1122
Wheeling *(G-21011)*

MOTOR VEHICLE PARTS & ACCESS: Booster Cables, Jump-Start

Splice Energy Solutions LLC .... G 815 861-8402
Mchenry *(G-13794)*

MOTOR VEHICLE PARTS & ACCESS: Brakes, Air

Air-X Remanufacturing Corp .... G 708 598-0044
Bridgeview *(G-2320)*
Airbrake Products Inc .... F 708 594-1110
Orland Park *(G-15936)*

MOTOR VEHICLE PARTS & ACCESS: Clutches

Clutch Systems Inc .... G 815 282-7960
Machesney Park *(G-13334)*
Matrix International Ltd .... G 815 389-3771
South Beloit *(G-19099)*
Warner Electric LLC .... C 815 389-4300
South Beloit *(G-19122)*

MOTOR VEHICLE PARTS & ACCESS: Cylinder Heads

Accurate Auto Manufacturing Co .... G 618 244-0727
Mount Vernon *(G-14595)*
Little Egypt Gas A & Wldg Sups .... G 618 937-2271
West Frankfort *(G-20677)*

MOTOR VEHICLE PARTS & ACCESS: Electrical Eqpt

Autonomous Stuff LLC .... G 309 291-0966
Morton *(G-14353)*
Byd Motors Inc .... G 847 590-9002
Arlington Heights *(G-712)*
Just Parts Inc .... G 815 756-2184
Cortland *(G-7022)*

Mr Auto Electric .... G 217 523-3659
Springfield *(G-19409)*

MOTOR VEHICLE PARTS & ACCESS: Engines & Parts

Acme Auto Electric Co .... G 708 754-5420
S Chicago Hts *(G-18115)*
Alloy Tech .... G 217 253-3939
Tuscola *(G-19922)*
American Speed Enterprises .... G 309 764-3601
Moline *(G-14131)*
Andersen Machine & Welding Inc ...... G 815 232-4664
Freeport *(G-10101)*
Borgwarner Inc. .... E 248 754-9200
Bellwood *(G-1617)*
Elgin Industries Inc .... C 847 742-1720
Elgin *(G-8574)*
Engine Solutions Inc .... G 815 979-2312
Rockford *(G-17397)*
Fire Chariot LLC .... G 815 561-3688
Rochelle *(G-17141)*
H R Larke Corp .... G 847 204-2776
Crystal Lake *(G-7204)*
Jordan Industries Inc .... F 847 945-5591
Deerfield *(G-7621)*
K & W Auto Electric .... F 217 857-1717
Teutopolis *(G-19770)*
Larry Pontnack .... G 815 732-7751
Oregon *(G-15923)*
Mercury Products Corp .... C 847 524-4400
Schaumburg *(G-18627)*
Php Racengines Inc .... G 847 526-9393
Wauconda *(G-20382)*
Premiere Motorsports LLC .... G 708 634-0007
Plainfield *(G-16706)*
Tenneco Global Holdings Inc .... G 847 482-5000
Lake Forest *(G-12311)*
Tenneco Inc .... D 847 482-5000
Lake Forest *(G-12312)*
U S Tool & Manufacturing Co .... E 630 953-1000
Addison *(G-321)*
Vogel Manufacturing Co Inc .... G 217 536-6946
Effingham *(G-8429)*
ZF Chassis Components LLC .... B 773 371-4550
Chicago *(G-6718)*

MOTOR VEHICLE PARTS & ACCESS: Engs & Trans, Factory, Rebuilt

DTE Enterprises LLC .... G 630 307-9355
Addison *(G-100)*
R & R Engines and Parts Inc .... G 630 628-1545
Addison *(G-263)*
Transomatic Des Plaines LLC .... G 847 625-1500
Des Plaines *(G-7859)*
Windy City Engineering Inc .... F 773 254-8113
Chicago *(G-6640)*

MOTOR VEHICLE PARTS & ACCESS: Fuel Pumps

Airtex Products LP .... E 618 842-2111
Fairfield *(G-9617)*
Olympic Controls Corp .... E 847 742-3566
Elgin *(G-8678)*

MOTOR VEHICLE PARTS & ACCESS: Fuel Systems & Parts

American Diesel Tube Corp .... F 630 628-1830
Addison *(G-32)*
Bi-Phase Technologies LLC .... F 952 886-6450
Wood Dale *(G-21168)*
Borgwarner Inc. .... C 815 288-1462
Dixon *(G-7892)*
Pryco Inc .... E 217 364-4467
Mechanicsburg *(G-13811)*

MOTOR VEHICLE PARTS & ACCESS: Gas Tanks

Gs Custom Works Inc .... G 815 233-4724
Freeport *(G-10113)*

MOTOR VEHICLE PARTS & ACCESS: Gears

Flender Corporation .... C 847 931-1990
Elgin *(G-8588)*
IMS Companies LLC .... D 847 391-8100
Des Plaines *(G-7786)*

Polar Container Corporation .... G 847 299-5030
Bensenville *(G-1869)*
S A Gear Company Inc .... E 708 496-0395
Bedford Park *(G-1502)*
United States Gear Corporation .... G 773 821-5450
Chicago *(G-6477)*

MOTOR VEHICLE PARTS & ACCESS: Governors

Precision Governors LLC .... E 815 229-5300
Rockford *(G-17556)*

MOTOR VEHICLE PARTS & ACCESS: Heaters

Bergstrom Inc. .... D 815 874-7821
Rockford *(G-17322)*
Bergstrom Inc. .... D 847 394-4013
Joliet *(G-11831)*
Illinois Tool Works Inc .... D 630 993-9990
Elmhurst *(G-9377)*

MOTOR VEHICLE PARTS & ACCESS: Hoods

Vfn Fiberglass Inc .... F 630 543-0232
Addison *(G-330)*

MOTOR VEHICLE PARTS & ACCESS: Horns

Buell Manufacturing Company .... G 708 447-6320
Lyons *(G-13304)*

MOTOR VEHICLE PARTS & ACCESS: Instrument Board Assemblies

Aisin Electronics Illinois LLC .... C 618 997-9800
Marion *(G-13499)*

MOTOR VEHICLE PARTS & ACCESS: Manifolds

Industrial Opprtnity Prtners L .... E 847 556-3460
Evanston *(G-9538)*

MOTOR VEHICLE PARTS & ACCESS: Mufflers, Exhaust

California Muffler and Brakes .... G 773 776-8990
Chicago *(G-4004)*
Crawford Heating & Cooling Co .... E 309 794-1000
Rock Island *(G-17212)*
Velasquez & Sons Muffler Shop .... G 847 740-6990
Round Lake Beach *(G-18093)*

MOTOR VEHICLE PARTS & ACCESS: Oil Pumps

Harbison-Fischer Inc .... G 618 375-3841
Grayville *(G-10808)*

MOTOR VEHICLE PARTS & ACCESS: Thermostats

Transcedar Limited .... E 618 262-4153
Mount Carmel *(G-14488)*

MOTOR VEHICLE PARTS & ACCESS: Trailer Hitches

Great Lakes Forge Company .... G 773 277-2800
Chicago *(G-4735)*
Precision Truck Products Inc .... E 618 548-9011
Salem *(G-18352)*

MOTOR VEHICLE PARTS & ACCESS: Transmission Housings Or Parts

Borgwarner Transm Systems Inc .... B 815 469-7819
Chicago *(G-3936)*
Ucal Holdings Inc .... D 847 695-8030
Elgin *(G-8765)*
Ucal Systems Inc .... C 847 695-8030
Elgin *(G-8767)*

MOTOR VEHICLE PARTS & ACCESS: Transmissions

Bedford Rakim .... G 773 759-3947
South Holland *(G-19199)*

Employee Codes: A=Over 500 employees, B=251-500
C=101-250, D=51-100, E=20-50, F=10-19, G=3-9

2020 Harris Illinois Industrial Directory

MOTOR VEHICLE PARTS & ACCESS: Transmissions

Borgwarner Transm Systems Inc .... A 708 547-2600
 Bellwood (G-1618)
Borgwarner Transm Systems Inc .... B 815 469-2721
 Frankfort (G-9776)
Dynamic Manufacturing Inc .... D 708 343-8753
 Hillside (G-11336)
Dynamic Manufacturing Inc .... D 708 681-0682
 Melrose Park (G-13855)
Dynamic Manufacturing Inc .... D 708 547-7081
 Hillside (G-11337)
Dynamic Manufacturing Inc .... E 708 343-8753
 Melrose Park (G-13856)
Dynamic Manufacturing Inc .... B 708 547-9011
 Hillside (G-11338)
Michelangelo & Donata Burdi .... F 773 427-1437
 Chicago (G-5423)
Walters Distributing Company .... G 847 468-0941
 Elgin (G-8775)

MOTOR VEHICLE PARTS & ACCESS: Universal Joints

Aircraft Gear Corporation .... D 815 877-7473
 Loves Park (G-13185)
Federal-Mogul Motorparts LLC .... C 773 478-0404
 Chicago (G-4571)
Federal-Mogul Motorparts LLC .... E 248 354-7700
 Berwyn (G-1954)
Thyssenkrupp Crankshaft Co LLC .... C 217 444-5500
 Danville (G-7385)
Thyssenkrupp Crankshaft Co LLC .... C 217 431-0060
 Danville (G-7383)

MOTOR VEHICLE PARTS & ACCESS: Wheel rims

Advance Wheel Corporation .... D 773 471-5734
 Chicago (G-3560)

MOTOR VEHICLE PARTS & ACCESS: Wiring Harness Sets

Ark De Mexico LLC .... B 630 240-9483
 Saint Charles (G-18148)
Barcar Manufacturing Inc .... G 630 365-5200
 Elburn (G-8445)
Infinitybox LLC .... G 847 232-1991
 Elk Grove Village (G-9051)

MOTOR VEHICLE RADIOS WHOLESALERS

Audio Installers Inc .... F 815 969-7500
 Loves Park (G-13193)
Robert Bosch LLC .... B 917 421-7209
 Broadview (G-2466)

MOTOR VEHICLE SPLYS & PARTS WHOLESALERS: New

A Lakin & Sons Inc .... E 773 871-6360
 Montgomery (G-14229)
Altco Inc .... D 847 549-0321
 Vernon Hills (G-20041)
Chicago Drive Line Inc .... G 708 385-1900
 Alsip (G-427)
Elgin Industries Inc .... C 847 742-1720
 Elgin (G-8574)
Hella Corporate Center USA Inc .... B 734 414-0900
 Flora (G-9682)
Koehler Enterprises Inc .... G 847 451-4966
 Franklin Park (G-9978)
Mann+hummel Filtration Tech .... F 800 407-9263
 McHenry (G-13762)
Riken Corporation of America .... C 847 673-1400
 Skokie (G-19023)
Tvh Parts Co .... E 847 223-1000
 Grayslake (G-10803)
United Gasket Corporation .... D 708 656-3700
 Cicero (G-6885)

MOTOR VEHICLE SPLYS & PARTS WHOLESALERS: Used

Lkq Corporation .... C 312 621-1950
 Chicago (G-5243)

MOTOR VEHICLE: Hardware

Hymans Auto Supply Co .... E 773 978-8221
 Chicago (G-4864)

Whiting Partners LLC .... G 773 978-8221
 Chicago (G-6620)

MOTOR VEHICLE: Radiators

Caterpillar Inc .... B 815 842-6000
 Pontiac (G-16767)
Independent Antique RAD Mfg .... G 847 458-7400
 Algonquin (G-374)
National Porges Radiator Corp .... F 773 224-3000
 Chicago (G-5550)

MOTOR VEHICLE: Shock Absorbers

Taw Enterprises LLC .... G 618 466-0134
 Godfrey (G-10664)
Tenneco Intl Holdg Corp .... F 847 482-5000
 Lake Forest (G-12313)

MOTOR VEHICLE: Steering Mechanisms

Precision Remanufacturing Inc .... F 773 489-7225
 Chicago (G-5858)
Thyssenkrupp Presta Cold Forgi .... E 217 431-4212
 Danville (G-7386)
United Remanufacturing Co Inc .... E 847 678-2233
 Schiller Park (G-18851)

MOTOR VEHICLE: Wheels

Accuride Corporation .... C 630 568-3914
 Hinsdale (G-11360)
American Vulko Tread Corp .... F 847 956-1300
 Elk Grove Village (G-8826)
American Wheel Corp .... E 708 458-9141
 Chicago (G-3673)
Clement Industries Inc Del .... E 708 458-9141
 Bedford Park (G-1463)
Marmon Industries LLC .... G 312 372-9500
 Chicago (G-5345)
Otr Wheel Engineering Inc .... E 217 223-7705
 Quincy (G-16920)
Titan International Inc .... E 217 228-6011
 Quincy (G-16948)
Topy America Inc .... G 847 350-6399
 Elk Grove Village (G-9276)

MOTOR VEHICLES & CAR BODIES

4x4 Headquarters LLC .... G 217 540-5337
 Effingham (G-8381)
AEP Nvh Opco LLC .... F 708 758-0211
 Chicago Heights (G-6729)
Amerex Corporation .... E 309 382-4389
 North Pekin (G-15326)
Bergstrom Inc .... D 847 394-4013
 Joliet (G-11831)
Bill West Enterprises Inc .... G 217 886-2591
 Jacksonville (G-11757)
ED Etnyre & Co .... B 815 732-2116
 Oregon (G-15917)
Fs Depot Inc .... G 847 468-2350
 University Park (G-19955)
Hopperstad Customs .... G 815 547-7534
 Belvidere (G-1677)
Illinois Sterling Ltd. .... G 847 526-5151
 Wauconda (G-20360)
Mickey Truck Bodies Inc .... F 309 827-8227
 Bloomington (G-2076)
Navistar Inc .... C 331 332-5000
 Lisle (G-12917)
Navistar Inc .... C 331 332-5000
 Joliet (G-11907)
Nissan .... G 630 957-4360
 West Chicago (G-20622)
Oshkosh/Mcnlus Fncl Svcs Prtnr .... G 630 466-5100
 Sugar Grove (G-19648)
R/A Hoerr Inc .... G 309 691-8789
 Edwards (G-8340)
SAE Customs Inc .... G 855 723-2878
 Round Lake (G-18082)
Subaru of America Inc .... E 630 250-4740
 Itasca (G-11741)
Tesla Motors .... G 630 541-1214
 Westmont (G-20776)

MOTOR VEHICLES, WHOLESALE: Truck bodies

Bonnell Industries Inc .... D 815 284-3819
 Dixon (G-7890)
Koenig Body & Equipment Inc .... E 309 673-7435
 West Peoria (G-20687)

Mark S Machine Shop Inc .... G 815 895-3955
 Sycamore (G-19724)

MOTORCYCLE & BICYCLE PARTS: Frames

Colnago America Inc .... G 312 239-6666
 Chicago (G-4202)

MOTORCYCLE & BICYCLE PARTS: Gears

David Taylor .... E 217 222-6480
 Quincy (G-16875)
Sram LLC .... D 312 664-8800
 Chicago (G-6223)

MOTORCYCLE ACCESS

Gs Custom Works Inc .... G 815 233-4724
 Freeport (G-10113)
Industrial Opprtnity Prtners L .... E 847 556-3460
 Evanston (G-9538)
National Cycle Inc .... C 708 343-0400
 Maywood (G-13674)

MOTORCYCLE DEALERS

Decatur Industrial Elc Inc .... E 618 244-1066
 Mount Vernon (G-14607)
Lo-Ko Performance Coatings .... G 708 424-7863
 Oak Lawn (G-15726)
Metroeast Motorsports Inc .... G 618 628-2466
 O Fallon (G-15580)
Valley Racing Inc .... G 708 946-1440
 Beecher (G-1523)
Weiland Fast Trac Inc .... G 847 438-7996
 Long Grove (G-13174)

MOTORCYCLE PARTS & ACCESS DEALERS

Rogers Motorcycle Shop Inc .... G 309 828-3242
 Bloomington (G-2090)
Service Pro Electric Mtr Repr .... G 630 766-1215
 Bensenville (G-1892)
W L & J Enterprises Inc .... G 708 946-0999
 Beecher (G-1524)

MOTORCYCLE PARTS: Wholesalers

Franks Maintenance & Engrg .... G 847 475-1003
 Evanston (G-9523)

MOTORCYCLE RACING

Valley Racing Inc .... G 708 946-1440
 Beecher (G-1523)

MOTORCYCLE REPAIR SHOPS

Metroeast Motorsports Inc .... G 618 628-2466
 O Fallon (G-15580)
Valley Racing Inc .... G 708 946-1440
 Beecher (G-1523)

MOTORCYCLES & RELATED PARTS

Black Magic Customs Inc .... G 815 786-1977
 Sandwich (G-18366)
Chopper Mm LLC .... G 309 875-3544
 Maquon (G-13477)
Kyosei International Corp .... G 847 821-0341
 Buffalo Grove (G-2558)
Taurus Cycle .... G 309 454-1565
 Bloomington (G-2099)
World of Soul Inc .... G 773 840-4839
 Chicago (G-6676)

MOTORS: Electric

Bodine Electric Company .... B 773 478-3515
 Northfield (G-15509)
Broad-Ocean Motor LLC .... E 630 908-4720
 Westmont (G-20730)
Charles R Frontczak .... G 224 392-4151
 Rockford (G-17345)
Ddu Magnetics Inc .... G 708 325-6587
 Lynwood (G-13293)
Digitaldrive Tech .... G 630 510-1580
 Wheaton (G-20796)
Dlt Electric LLC .... F 630 552-4115
 Plano (G-16730)
Forest City Auto Electric Co .... F 815 963-4350
 Rockford (G-17418)
Hallmark Industries Inc .... F 847 301-8050
 Streamwood (G-19577)

PRODUCT SECTION

MUSICAL INSTRUMENTS & ACCESS: NEC

Haran Ventures LLC .... G 217 239-1628
  Champaign *(G-3299)*
Hinetics LLC .... G 217 239-1628
  Champaign *(G-3301)*
Howland Technology Inc .... F 847 965-9808
  Morton Grove *(G-14411)*
Jordan Industries Inc .... F 847 945-5591
  Deerfield *(G-7621)*
L & H Company Inc .... F 630 571-7200
  Oak Brook *(G-15630)*
Moons Industries America Inc .... A 630 833-5940
  Itasca *(G-11705)*
Nidec Motor Corporation .... D 847 439-3760
  Elk Grove Village *(G-9148)*
Roberts Electric Company .... G 773 725-7323
  Chicago *(G-6044)*
Schneider Elc Buildings LLC .... B 815 381-5000
  Rockford *(G-17622)*
Schneider Elc Holdings Inc .... A 717 944-5460
  Schaumburg *(G-18707)*
Scot Inc .... G 630 969-0620
  Downers Grove *(G-8091)*
Sfc of Illinois Inc .... E 815 745-2100
  Warren *(G-20224)*
Spg Usa Inc .... G 847 439-4949
  Schaumburg *(G-18723)*
Warfield Electric Company Inc .... E 815 469-4094
  Frankfort *(G-9851)*
Wodack Electric Tool Corp .... F 773 287-9866
  Chicago *(G-6661)*
Yaskawa America Inc .... C 847 887-7000
  Waukegan *(G-20520)*
Yaskawa America Inc .... C 847 887-7909
  Des Plaines *(G-7869)*

MOTORS: Generators

ABB Motors and Mechanical Inc .... C 630 296-1400
  Bolingbrook *(G-2146)*
Altorfer Power Systems .... G 309 697-1234
  Bartonville *(G-1328)*
American Total Engine Co .... G 847 623-2737
  Ingleside *(G-11578)*
Atlas Copco Compressors LLC .... F 281 590-7500
  Chicago *(G-3762)*
Bison Gear & Engineering Corp .... C 630 377-4327
  Saint Charles *(G-18156)*
Bolingbrook Communications Inc ..... A 630 759-9500
  Lisle *(G-12874)*
Cemec Inc .... G 630 495-9696
  Downers Grove *(G-7966)*
Charles Industries LLC .... D 217 826-2318
  Marshall *(G-13566)*
Coilform Company .... E 630 232-8000
  Geneva *(G-10262)*
Communication Coil Inc .... D 847 671-1333
  Schiller Park *(G-18795)*
Con-Trol-Cure Inc .... F 773 248-0099
  Chicago *(G-4211)*
Encap Technologies Inc .... C 847 202-3443
  Grayslake *(G-10768)*
Engine Rebuilders & Supply .... G 708 338-1113
  Stone Park *(G-19554)*
Federal Prison Industries .... C 309 346-8588
  Pekin *(G-16333)*
Flolo Corporation .... G 847 249-0880
  Gurnee *(G-10878)*
General Manufacturing LLC .... D 708 345-8600
  Melrose Park *(G-13873)*
Hardin Industries LLC .... E 309 246-8456
  Lacon *(G-12127)*
Harvey Bros Inc .... F 309 342-3137
  Galesburg *(G-10199)*
Hopcroft Electric Inc .... G 618 288-7302
  Glen Carbon *(G-10388)*
Illinois Tool Works Inc .... C 847 724-7500
  Des Plaines *(G-7784)*
Industrial Welder Rebuilders .... G 708 371-5688
  Alsip *(G-457)*
Inglot Electronics Corp .... D 773 286-5881
  Chicago *(G-4921)*
Inman Electric Motors Inc .... E 815 223-2288
  La Salle *(G-12115)*
Integrated Power Services LLC .... E 708 877-5310
  Thornton *(G-19789)*
Jardis Industries Inc .... F 630 773-5600
  Itasca *(G-11681)*
Jasiek Motor Rebuilding Inc .... G 815 883-3678
  Oglesby *(G-15842)*
Jomar Electric Coil Mfg Inc .... G 630 279-1494
  Villa Park *(G-20153)*

Kackert Enterprises Inc .... G 630 898-9339
  Aurora *(G-1120)*
Kaybee Engineering Company Inc .... E 630 968-7100
  Westmont *(G-20751)*
Lenhardt Tool and Die Company ...... D 618 462-1075
  Alton *(G-563)*
M R Glenn Electric Inc .... E 708 479-9200
  Lockport *(G-13009)*
Magnetic Coil Manufacturing Co ...... E 630 787-1948
  Wood Dale *(G-21212)*
Magnetic Devices Inc .... G 815 459-0077
  Crystal Lake *(G-7222)*
Maurey Instrument Corp .... F 708 388-9898
  Alsip *(G-474)*
Morrell Incorporated .... F 630 858-4600
  Glendale Heights *(G-10477)*
Mpc Products Corporation .... A 847 673-8300
  Niles *(G-15149)*
Nelco Coil Supply Company .... E 847 259-7517
  Mount Prospect *(G-14550)*
Netgain Motors Inc .... G 630 243-9100
  Lockport *(G-13016)*
Nidec Motor Corporation .... G 815 444-1229
  Crystal Lake *(G-7238)*
North Point Investments Inc .... G 312 977-4386
  Chicago *(G-5620)*
Northrop Grumman Systems Corp ... A 847 259-9600
  Rolling Meadows *(G-17755)*
Powersource Generator Rentals .... G 847 587-3991
  Fox Lake *(G-9752)*
Pre Fnish Mtals Mrrisville Inc .... D 847 439-2211
  Elk Grove Village *(G-9188)*
Progress Rail Locomotive Inc .... A 800 255-5355
  Mc Cook *(G-13699)*
Progress Rail Locomotive Inc .... F 708 387-5510
  Mc Cook *(G-13700)*
Provisur Technologies .... G 312 284-4698
  Chicago *(G-5908)*
Qcircuits Inc .... E 618 662-8365
  Flora *(G-9690)*
Rathje Enterprises Inc .... F 217 443-0022
  Danville *(G-7377)*
Rotary Dryer Parts Inc .... G 217 877-2787
  Decatur *(G-7544)*
Santucci Enterprises .... G 773 286-5629
  Chicago *(G-6102)*
Synergy Power Group LLC .... E 618 247-3200
  Sandoval *(G-18365)*
Teledyne Lecroy Inc .... E 847 888-0450
  Elgin *(G-8749)*
Transformer Manufacturers Inc .... E 708 457-1200
  Norridge *(G-15245)*
Transfrmtional Enrgy Solutions .... G 828 226-7821
  Decatur *(G-7562)*
Ultrasonic Power Corporation .... E 815 235-6020
  Freeport *(G-10148)*
Voss Electric Inc .... G 708 596-6000
  Harvey *(G-11100)*
Wellington Drive Tech US .... G 847 922-5098
  Buffalo Grove *(G-2619)*
Western Motor Mfg Co .... G 815 986-2214
  Rockford *(G-17681)*
Xform Power and Eqp Sups LLC .... G 773 260-0209
  Chicago *(G-6694)*
Xylem Lnc .... G 847 966-3700
  Morton Grove *(G-14451)*

MOTORS: Starting, Automotive & Aircraft

Quick Start Pdts & Solutions .... F 815 562-5414
  Rochelle *(G-17153)*
Robert Bosch LLC .... B 917 421-7209
  Broadview *(G-2466)*

MOTORS: Torque

American Electronic Pdts Inc .... F 630 889-9977
  Oak Brook *(G-15592)*
Brown Line Metal Works LLC .... G 312 884-7644
  Chicago *(G-3968)*

MOUTHWASHES

Prevention Health Sciences Inc .... G 618 252-6922
  Raleigh *(G-16962)*

MOVING SVC: Local

Backyard Creations .... G 217 836-5678
  Petersburg *(G-16600)*
Gosia Cartage Ltd .... G 312 613-8735
  Hodgkins *(G-11389)*

MOWERS & ACCESSORIES

Hevco Industries .... G 708 344-1342
  Aurora *(G-1109)*
Mag MO Systems .... F 815 625-0125
  Sterling *(G-19514)*
Mat Holdings Inc .... D 847 821-9630
  Long Grove *(G-13165)*
Up-N-Runnin LLC .... G 217 413-6293
  Decatur *(G-7565)*
Yanmar (usa) Inc .... G 847 541-1900
  Buffalo Grove *(G-2624)*

MULTILITHING SVCS

Tri-Tower Printing Inc .... G 847 640-6633
  Rolling Meadows *(G-17782)*

MUSEUMS

International College Surgeons .... G 312 642-6502
  Chicago *(G-4952)*

MUSEUMS & ART GALLERIES

Antioch Fine Arts Foundation .... G 847 838-2274
  Antioch *(G-599)*
Fox Valley Park District .... D 630 892-1550
  Aurora *(G-1100)*
Sand Sculpture Co .... G 815 334-9101
  Woodstock *(G-21430)*

MUSIC DISTRIBUTION APPARATUS

Billinium Records LLC .... G 800 651-8059
  Chicago *(G-3887)*
Linx Enterprises LLC .... G 224 409-2206
  Chicago *(G-5232)*

MUSIC DISTRIBUTION SYSTEM SVCS

Deshamusic Inc .... G 818 257-2716
  Chicago *(G-4344)*

MUSIC RECORDING PRODUCER

Bailey Business Group .... G 618 548-3566
  Salem *(G-18330)*
Drag City .... G 312 455-1015
  Chicago *(G-4396)*
Linx Enterprises LLC .... G 224 409-2206
  Chicago *(G-5232)*

MUSIC VIDEO PRODUCTION SVCS

Ikan Creations LLC .... G 312 204-7333
  Chicago *(G-4884)*

MUSICAL ENTERTAINERS

Fleming Music Technology Ctr .... G 708 316-8662
  Wheaton *(G-20799)*
Kaelco Entrmt Holdings Inc .... G 217 600-7815
  Champaign *(G-3312)*
Time Rec Pubg Bbby Mrtin Prdct .... G 618 996-3803
  Marion *(G-13540)*

MUSICAL INSTRUMENT PARTS & ACCESS, WHOLESALE

Pjla Music .... G 847 382-3212
  Barrington *(G-1236)*

MUSICAL INSTRUMENT REPAIR

Schilke Music Products Inc .... E 708 343-8858
  Melrose Park *(G-13913)*

MUSICAL INSTRUMENTS & ACCESS: Carrying Cases

Mechanical Music Corp .... F 847 398-5444
  Arlington Heights *(G-775)*

MUSICAL INSTRUMENTS & ACCESS: NEC

American Plating & Mfg Co .... F 773 890-4907
  Chicago *(G-3664)*
Analog Outfitters Inc .... G 217 202-6134
  Rantoul *(G-16966)*
Intelligent Instrument Sy .... G 630 323-3911
  Burr Ridge *(G-2689)*
Lothson Guitars .... G 815 756-2031
  Dekalb *(G-7688)*

Employee Codes: A=Over 500 employees, B=251-500
C=101-250, D=51-100, E=20-50, F=10-19, G=3-9

MUSICAL INSTRUMENTS & ACCESS: NEC

Mechanical Music Corp ....F 847 398-5444
 Arlington Heights *(G-775)*
Peterson Elctr-Msical Pdts Inc ....E 708 388-3311
 Alsip *(G-490)*
Schaff International LLC ....E 847 438-4560
 Lake Zurich *(G-12453)*
Schilke Music Products Inc ....E 708 343-8858
 Melrose Park *(G-13913)*
Suntimez Entertainment ....G 630 747-0712
 Cicero *(G-6877)*
Tom Crown Mute Co 773 930-4979
 Chicago *(G-6386)*
Umphreys McGee Inc 773 880-0024
 Chicago *(G-6460)*
Westheimer Corp 847 498-9850
 Lake Zurich *(G-12470)*

MUSICAL INSTRUMENTS & ACCESS: Pipe Organs

Buzard Pipe Organ Builders LLC ....F 217 352-1955
 Champaign *(G-3273)*
Wicks Organ Company ....E 618 654-2191
 Highland *(G-11249)*

MUSICAL INSTRUMENTS & PARTS: Brass

Pjla Music ....G 847 382-3212
 Barrington *(G-1236)*

MUSICAL INSTRUMENTS & PARTS: Percussion

Fugate Inc ....G 309 472-6830
 Morton *(G-14360)*
Trick Percussion Products Inc ....G 847 342-2019
 Arlington Heights *(G-822)*

MUSICAL INSTRUMENTS & PARTS: Woodwind

North Okaw Woodworking ....G 217 856-2178
 Humboldt *(G-11524)*

MUSICAL INSTRUMENTS & SPLYS STORES

3b Media Inc ....F 312 563-9363
 Chicago *(G-3467)*
Fugate Inc ....G 309 472-6830
 Morton *(G-14360)*
Gibson Brands Inc ....E 800 544-2766
 Elgin *(G-8594)*

MUSICAL INSTRUMENTS & SPLYS STORES: String instruments

Demont Guitars LLC ....G 347 433-6668
 Oswego *(G-16001)*
Lothson Guitars ....G 815 756-2031
 Dekalb *(G-7688)*
Lyon & Healy Holding Corp ....E 312 786-1881
 Chicago *(G-5294)*

MUSICAL INSTRUMENTS WHOLESALERS

Antigua Casa Sherry-Brener ....G 773 737-1711
 Joliet *(G-11824)*
Demont Guitars LLC ....G 347 433-6668
 Oswego *(G-16001)*
Mechanical Music Corp ....F 847 398-5444
 Arlington Heights *(G-775)*
PM Woodwind Repair Inc ....G 847 869-7049
 Evanston *(G-9567)*

MUSICAL INSTRUMENTS: Bells

Century Mallet Instr Svc LLC ....G 773 248-7733
 Chicago *(G-4061)*

MUSICAL INSTRUMENTS: Electric & Electronic

Schneider Pipe Organs Inc ....G 217 871-4807
 Kenney *(G-12016)*

MUSICAL INSTRUMENTS: Guitars & Parts, Electric & Acoustic

Demont Guitars LLC ....G 347 433-6668
 Oswego *(G-16001)*
Gibson Brands Inc ....E 800 544-2766
 Elgin *(G-8594)*

Music Solutions ....F 630 759-3033
 Bolingbrook *(G-2218)*

MUSICAL INSTRUMENTS: Harmonicas

Harrison Harmonicas LLC ....G 312 379-9427
 Chicago *(G-4783)*

MUSICAL INSTRUMENTS: Harps & Parts

Lyon & Healy Harps Inc ....G 312 786-1881
 Chicago *(G-5293)*
Lyon & Healy Holding Corp ....E 312 786-1881
 Chicago *(G-5294)*

MUSICAL INSTRUMENTS: Organ Parts & Materials

Daves Electronic Service ....F 217 283-5010
 Hoopeston *(G-11507)*

MUSICAL INSTRUMENTS: Organs

Berghaus Pipe Organ Builders ....E 708 544-4052
 Bellwood *(G-1616)*
C P O Inc ....G 630 898-7733
 Aurora *(G-1068)*
Fabry Inc ....G 847 395-1919
 Fox Lake *(G-9746)*
Hammond Suzuki Usa Inc ....E 630 543-0277
 Addison *(G-145)*

MUSICAL INSTRUMENTS: Violins & Parts

Mathew Lucante Violins LLC ....G 773 320-2997
 Skokie *(G-18985)*
Village of Burnham ....G 708 868-0661
 Chicago *(G-6552)*

NAIL SALONS

Cindys Nail & Hair Care ....G 847 234-0780
 Lake Forest *(G-12237)*

NAILS WHOLESALERS

Sales Stretcher Enterprises ....F 815 223-9681
 Peru *(G-16593)*

NAILS: Steel, Wire Or Cut

Estad Stamping & Mfg Co ....E 217 442-4600
 Danville *(G-7331)*
Illinois Tool Works Inc ....G 847 821-2170
 Vernon Hills *(G-20065)*
L & J Industrial Staples Inc ....G 815 864-3337
 Shannon *(G-18870)*
W H Maze Company ....C 815 223-1742
 Peru *(G-16596)*
W H Maze Company ....D 815 223-8290
 Peru *(G-16597)*

NAME PLATES: Engraved Or Etched

Durable Engravers Inc ....E 630 766-6420
 Franklin Park *(G-9934)*
Forest Awards & Engraving ....G 630 595-2242
 Wood Dale *(G-21189)*
Mobile Air Inc ....F 847 755-0586
 Glendale Heights *(G-10476)*
Nameplate Robinson & Precision ....G 847 678-2255
 Franklin Park *(G-10005)*
National Rubber Stamp Co Inc ....G 773 281-6522
 Chicago *(G-5552)*
Photo Techniques Corp ....E 630 690-9360
 Carol Stream *(G-3046)*
Porcelain Enamel Finishers ....G 312 808-1560
 Chicago *(G-5845)*

NAMEPLATES

American Name Plate & Metal De ....E 773 376-1400
 Chicago *(G-3663)*
Cypress Multigraphics LLC ....E 708 633-1166
 Tinley Park *(G-19820)*
Gabel & Schubert Bronze ....F 773 878-6800
 Chicago *(G-4653)*
Signcraft Screenprint Inc ....C 815 777-3030
 Galena *(G-10178)*

NATIONAL SECURITY FORCES

Dla Document Services ....F 618 256-4686
 Scott Air Force Base *(G-18857)*

NATURAL GAS COMPRESSING SVC, On-Site

ANR Pipeline Company ....G 309 667-2158
 New Windsor *(G-15071)*

NATURAL GAS DISTRIBUTION TO CONSUMERS

La Quinta Gas Pipeline Company ....G 217 430-6781
 Quincy *(G-16906)*
Northern Illinois Gas Company ....E 630 983-8676
 Kankakee *(G-11993)*
Northern Illinois Gas Company ....F 217 357-3105
 Carthage *(G-3141)*
Northern Illinois Gas Company ....C 630 983-8676
 Crystal Lake *(G-7240)*
Northern Illinois Gas Company ....D 815 433-3850
 Ottawa *(G-16065)*
Northern Illinois Gas Company ....C 815 693-3907
 Joliet *(G-11908)*
Northern Illinois Gas Company ....F 815 223-8097
 Mendota *(G-13951)*

NATURAL GAS LIQUIDS PRODUCTION

Aux Sable Liquid Products LP ....E 815 941-5800
 Morris *(G-14292)*
Aux Sable Midstream LLC ....E 815 941-5800
 Morris *(G-14293)*

NATURAL GAS LIQUIDS PRODUCTION

Enterprise Products Company ....G 708 534-6266
 Monee *(G-14197)*
Ferrellgas LP ....G 815 877-7333
 Machesney Park *(G-13342)*
FMC Technologies Inc ....G 312 803-4321
 Chicago *(G-4612)*

NATURAL GAS PRODUCTION

Gas Depot Inc ....G 847 581-0303
 Morton Grove *(G-14409)*
La Quinta Gas Pipeline Company ....G 217 430-6781
 Quincy *(G-16906)*
Midco Production Co Inc ....G 630 655-2198
 Westmont *(G-20761)*
Natural Gas Pipeline Amer LLC ....F 815 426-2151
 Herscher *(G-11185)*

NATURAL GAS TRANSMISSION

Natural Gas Pipeline Amer LLC ....E 618 495-2211
 Centralia *(G-3240)*
Natural Gas Pipeline Amer LLC ....E 618 829-3224
 Saint Elmo *(G-18310)*

NATURAL GAS TRANSMISSION & DISTRIBUTION

Northern Illinois Gas Company ....E 630 983-8676
 Kankakee *(G-11993)*
Northern Illinois Gas Company ....F 217 357-3105
 Carthage *(G-3141)*
Northern Illinois Gas Company ....C 630 983-8676
 Crystal Lake *(G-7240)*
Northern Illinois Gas Company ....D 815 433-3850
 Ottawa *(G-16065)*
Northern Illinois Gas Company ....C 815 693-3907
 Joliet *(G-11908)*

NATURAL GASOLINE PRODUCTION

15679 Wadsworth Inc ....G 847 662-4561
 Wadsworth *(G-20207)*

NATURAL LIQUEFIED PETROLEUM GAS PRODUCTION

C4 Petrolum Transport Inc ....G 815 690-0356
 Romeoville *(G-17802)*

NATURAL PROPANE PRODUCTION

Dcc Propane LLC ....G 217 395-2648
 Roberts *(G-17105)*

NAVIGATIONAL SYSTEMS & INSTRUMENTS

Auxitrol SA ....G 815 874-2471
 Rockford *(G-17309)*
Brunswick International Ltd ....E 847 735-4700
 Mettawa *(G-13980)*

PRODUCT SECTION

NURSERIES & LAWN & GARDEN SPLY STORES, RETAIL: Fertilizer

Cedar Elec Holdings Corp .... G 630 862-7282
  Chicago (G-4051)
Kvh Industries Inc .... E 708 444-2800
  Tinley Park (G-19843)
Measurement Devices US LLC .... F 281 646-0050
  Dundee (G-8129)
Quartix Inc .... F 855 913-6663
  Chicago (G-5934)
Teletrac Navman US Ltd .... E 866 527-9896
  Glenview (G-10631)

NEEDLES

Newell Operating Company .... C 815 235-4171
  Freeport (G-10129)

NEPHELINE SYENITE MINING

Covia Holdings Corporation .... G 618 747-2355
  Tamms (G-19742)

NETTING: Plastic

Shannon Industries Inc .... G 815 338-8960
  Woodstock (G-21433)

NEWS DEALERS & NEWSSTANDS

Bureau Valley Chief .... G 815 646-4731
  Tiskilwa (G-19871)

NEWS FEATURE SYNDICATES

Chicago Tribune Company LLC .... A 312 222-3232
  Chicago (G-4134)

NEWS SYNDICATES

Sun Times News Agency .... G 815 672-1260
  Streator (G-19628)

NEWSPAPERS & PERIODICALS NEWS REPORTING SVCS

Central Ill Communications LLC .... F 217 753-2226
  Springfield (G-19345)

NEWSPAPERS, WHOLESALE

Ocs America Inc .... E 630 595-0111
  Wood Dale (G-21225)

NEWSSTAND

Daily Egyptian Siu Newspaper .... D 618 536-3311
  Carbondale (G-2840)
Herald Whig Quincy .... G 217 222-7600
  Quincy (G-16891)
Ocs America Inc .... E 630 595-0111
  Wood Dale (G-21225)

NICKEL ALLOY

Alloy Rod Products Inc .... G 815 562-8200
  Aurora (G-1048)
Continuous Cast Alloys LLC .... F 815 562-8200
  Rochelle (G-17136)
Daniel J Nickel & Assocs PC .... G 312 345-1850
  Chicago (G-4312)
Double Nickel Holdings LLC .... G 618 476-3200
  Millstadt (G-14046)
Nickel Putter .... G 312 337-7888
  Chicago (G-5598)
Nickels Electric .... G 309 676-1350
  Peoria (G-16486)
Nickels Quarters LLC .... G 630 514-5779
  Downers Grove (G-8065)
Wooden Nickel Pub and Grill .... G 618 288-2141
  Glen Carbon (G-10391)

NIPPLES: Rubber

Slipon Nipple Company .... G 708 345-2525
  Westchester (G-20711)

NITRILE RUBBERS: Butadiene-Acrylonitrile

Tradex International Inc .... D 216 651-4788
  Elwood (G-9465)

NONAROMATIC CHEMICAL PRDTS

Indilab Inc .... E 847 928-1050
  Franklin Park (G-9962)

NONCURRENT CARRYING WIRING DEVICES

Aco Inc .... E 773 774-5200
  Chicago (G-3529)
Chase Corporation .... F 630 752-3622
  Wheaton (G-20793)
Chicago Switchboard Co Inc .... E 630 833-2266
  Elmhurst (G-9345)
Eaton Corporation .... A 217 732-3131
  Lincoln (G-12729)
Excel Specialty Corp .... E 773 262-7575
  Lake Forest (G-12248)
Methode Development Co .... D 708 867-6777
  Chicago (G-5408)
Questek Manufacturing Corp .... D 847 428-0300
  Elgin (G-8710)
Taurus Safety Products Inc .... G 630 620-7940
  Lombard (G-13140)
Vertiv Group Corporation .... E 630 579-5000
  Lombard (G-13150)

NONDURABLE GOODS WHOLESALERS, NEC

Hollywood Traders LLC .... G 630 943-6461
  Lombard (G-13085)
Modern Methods Creative Inc .... G 309 263-4100
  Morton (G-14368)

NONFERROUS: Rolling & Drawing, NEC

American/Jebco Corporation .... C 847 455-3150
  Cicero (G-6829)
Cooper B-Line Inc .... A 618 654-2184
  Highland (G-11210)
Dupage Products Group .... D 630 969-7200
  Downers Grove (G-7993)
Guardian Rollform LLC .... E 847 382-8074
  Lake Barrington (G-12148)
Hadley Gear Manufacturing Co .... F 773 722-1030
  Chicago (G-4765)
Indium Corporation of America .... G 847 439-9134
  Elk Grove Village (G-9049)
Lawrence Brand Shot .... G 618 798-6112
  Granite City (G-10719)
Mat Holdings Inc .... D 847 821-9630
  Long Grove (G-13165)
Suburban Industries Inc .... F 630 766-3773
  Franklin Park (G-10055)
Tinsley Steel Inc .... G 618 656-5231
  Edwardsville (G-8378)
Townley Engrg & Mfg Co Inc .... F 618 273-8271
  Eldorado (G-8484)
V and L Red Devil Mfg Co .... E 847 215-1377
  Wheeling (G-21007)
Wagner Zip-Change Inc .... E 708 681-4100
  Melrose Park (G-13926)

NONMETALLIC MINERALS DEVELOPMENT & TEST BORING SVC

Pennasis Group LLC .... G 630 699-8390
  North Aurora (G-15268)

NONMETALLIC MINERALS: Support Activities, Exc Fuels

Harsco Corporation .... G 309 347-1962
  Pekin (G-16337)
Hastie Mining & Trucking .... G 618 285-3600
  Rosiclare (G-18063)
Illinois Valley Minerals LLC .... G 815 442-8402
  Tonica (G-19889)
Vigo Coal Operating Co Inc .... G 618 262-7022
  Mount Carmel (G-14490)

NOTIONS: Button Backs & Parts

Matchless Parisian Novelty Inc .... G 773 924-1515
  Chicago (G-5364)

NOTIONS: Pins, Hair, Exc Rubber

STA-Rite Ginnie Lou Inc .... F 217 774-3921
  Shelbyville (G-18887)

NOTIONS: Pins, Straight, Steel Or Brass

Aerofast Inc .... E 630 668-6575
  Carol Stream (G-2926)

NOVELTIES

Creative Werks LLC .... E 630 860-2222
  Bartlett (G-1274)
Creative Werks LLC .... E 630 860-2222
  Elk Grove Village (G-8920)
M & A Grocery .... G 708 749-9786
  Stickney (G-19543)
Ramona Sedivy .... G 630 983-1902
  Naperville (G-14907)
Slagel Manufacturing Inc .... E 815 688-3318
  Forrest (G-9738)

NOVELTIES & SPECIALTIES: Metal

Lynda Hervas .... G 847 985-1690
  Schaumburg (G-18615)
Metal Strip Buiding Products .... G 847 742-8500
  Itasca (G-11700)
Midland Stamping and Fabg Corp .... D 847 678-7573
  Schiller Park (G-18825)
Progressive Bronze Works Inc .... E 773 463-5500
  Chicago (G-5899)
Renner & Co .... F 847 639-4900
  Cary (G-3185)
Wiremasters Incorporated .... E 773 254-3700
  Chicago (G-6649)

NOVELTIES: Plastic

Adams Apple Distributing LP .... E 847 832-9900
  Glenview (G-10518)
Spirit Foodservice Inc .... C 214 634-1393
  Lake Forest (G-12305)

NOVELTY SHOPS

Andy Dallas & Co .... F 217 351-5974
  Champaign (G-3265)
Budget Signs .... F 618 259-4460
  Wood River (G-21260)

NOZZLES & SPRINKLERS Lawn Hose

Leyden Lawn Sprinklers .... E 630 665-5520
  Glen Ellyn (G-10409)
Suncast Corporation .... A 630 879-2050
  Batavia (G-1422)

NOZZLES: Fire Fighting

Max Fire Training Inc .... F 618 210-2079
  Godfrey (G-10656)

NOZZLES: Spray, Aerosol, Paint Or Insecticide

Lechler Inc .... D 630 377-6611
  Saint Charles (G-18225)
Spraying Systems Co .... A 630 665-5000
  Glendale Heights (G-10498)
Spraying Systems Co .... F 630 665-5001
  Aurora (G-1020)
Spraying Systems Midwest Inc .... G 630 665-5000
  Glendale Heights (G-10499)

NUCLEAR REACTORS: Military Or Indl

Spectrum Technologies Intl Ltd .... G 630 961-5244
  Woodridge (G-21341)

NURSERIES & LAWN & GARDEN SPLY STORE, RET: Fountain, Outdoor

Smart Solar Inc .... F 813 343-5770
  Libertyville (G-12708)

NURSERIES & LAWN & GARDEN SPLY STORES, RETAIL: Fertilizer

Allerton Supply Company .... F 217 896-2522
  Homer (G-11475)
Piatt County Service Co .... G 217 489-2411
  Mansfield (G-13442)
Piatt County Service Co .... G 217 678-5511
  Bement (G-1714)
Sun Ag Inc .... G 309 726-1331
  Hudson (G-11520)

Employee Codes: A=Over 500 employees, B=251-500
C=101-250, D=51-100, E=20-50, F=10-19, G=3-9

2020 Harris Illinois Industrial Directory

1535

NURSERIES & LAWN & GARDEN SPLY STORES, RETAIL: Lawn Ornament

NURSERIES & LAWN & GARDEN SPLY STORES, RETAIL: Lawn Ornament

In The Attic Inc ....G....... 847 949-5077
  Mundelein *(G-14699)*

NURSERIES & LAWN & GARDEN SPLY STORES, RETAIL: Top Soil

Markman Peat Corp ....E....... 815 772-4014
  Morrison *(G-14345)*
RR Mulch and Soil LLC ....G....... 708 596-7200
  Markham *(G-13551)*

NURSERIES & LAWN/GARDEN SPLY STORE, RET: Lawnmowers/Tractors

Gibson Insurance Inc ....G....... 217 864-4877
  Mount Zion *(G-14646)*
Hoyer Outdoor Equipment Inc ....F....... 618 564-2080
  Brookport *(G-2498)*
Lakenburges Motor Co ....G....... 618 523-4231
  Germantown *(G-10331)*
Outdoor Power Inc ....F....... 217 228-9890
  Quincy *(G-16921)*
Owen Walker ....G....... 217 285-4012
  Pittsfield *(G-16636)*
Peoria Midwest Equipment Inc ....G....... 309 454-6800
  Normal *(G-15217)*
West Side Tractor Sales Co ....E....... 815 961-3160
  Rockford *(G-17680)*

NURSERIES & LAWN/GARDEN SPLY STORES, RET: Garden Splys/Tools

Albert F Amling LLC ....C....... 630 333-1720
  Elmhurst *(G-9324)*
Gds Enterprises ....G....... 217 543-3681
  Arthur *(G-859)*
Kaser Power Equipment Inc ....G....... 309 289-2176
  Knoxville *(G-12068)*

NURSERIES/LAWN/GARDEN SPLY STORE, RET: Grdn Tractors/Tillers

Service Auto Supply ....F....... 309 444-9704
  Washington *(G-20280)*

NURSERY & GARDEN CENTERS

Tim Wallace Ldscp Sup Co Inc ....F....... 630 759-6813
  Bolingbrook *(G-2250)*
West Central Fs Inc ....G....... 309 375-6904
  Wataga *(G-20287)*

NURSING CARE FACILITIES: Skilled

McKnights Long Term Care News ..G....... 847 559-2884
  Northbrook *(G-15429)*
Willims-Hyward Intl Ctings Inc ....F....... 708 458-0015
  Argo *(G-678)*

NUTRITION SVCS

Wellness Center Usa Inc ....F....... 847 925-1885
  Hoffman Estates *(G-11471)*

NUTS: Metal

Aztech Engineering Inc ....E....... 630 236-3200
  Aurora *(G-918)*
Century Fasteners & Mch Co Inc ....F....... 773 463-3900
  Skokie *(G-18939)*
Folkerts Manufacturing Inc ....G....... 815 968-7426
  Rockford *(G-17417)*
Hill Holdings Inc ....E....... 815 625-6600
  Rock Falls *(G-17183)*
Locknut Technology Inc ....F....... 630 628-5330
  Addison *(G-184)*
Mac Lean-Fogg Company ....D....... 847 566-0010
  Mundelein *(G-14710)*
Maclen-Fogg Cmpnent Sltons LLC ..E....... 248 853-2525
  Mundelein *(G-14711)*
Security Locknut LLC ....E....... 847 970-4050
  Vernon Hills *(G-20095)*
Slidematic Industries Inc ....C....... 815 986-0500
  Rockford *(G-17634)*

OFFICE EQPT WHOLESALERS

Carnation Enterprises ....G....... 847 804-5928
  Niles *(G-15108)*

CDs Office Systems Inc ....F....... 217 351-5046
  Champaign *(G-3278)*
CDs Office Systems Inc ....F....... 630 305-9034
  Springfield *(G-19344)*
H A Friend & Company Inc ....E....... 847 746-1248
  Zion *(G-21516)*
Klai-Co Idntification Pdts Inc ....E....... 847 573-0375
  Lake Forest *(G-12270)*
Komori America Corporation ....D....... 847 806-9000
  Rolling Meadows *(G-17745)*
Next Day Toner Supplies Inc ....E....... 708 478-1000
  Orland Park *(G-15971)*
Officenation Inc ....E....... 847 504-3000
  Northfield *(G-15525)*
Sws Industries Inc ....E....... 904 482-0091
  Woodstock *(G-21438)*
Xerox Corporation ....E....... 630 573-1000
  Hinsdale *(G-11383)*

OFFICE FIXTURES: Wood

Contract Industries Inc ....E....... 708 458-8150
  Bedford Park *(G-1464)*
Hanley Design Inc ....G....... 309 682-9665
  Peoria *(G-16452)*
Hire-Nelson Company Inc ....E....... 630 543-9400
  Addison *(G-150)*

OFFICE FURNITURE REPAIR & MAINTENANCE SVCS

Gavin Woodworking Inc ....G....... 815 786-2242
  Sandwich *(G-18371)*

OFFICE MACHINES, NEC

Ives Way Products Inc ....G....... 847 223-1020
  Grayslake *(G-10784)*
Neopost R Meadows ....G....... 630 467-0604
  Itasca *(G-11710)*

OFFICE SPLY & STATIONERY STORES

A 1 Marking Products ....G....... 309 762-6096
  Moline *(G-14130)*
Ashleys Inc ....G....... 630 794-0804
  Hinsdale *(G-11362)*
CDs Office Systems Inc ....F....... 630 305-9034
  Springfield *(G-19344)*
W/S Packaging Group Inc ....G....... 847 658-7363
  Algonquin *(G-393)*

OFFICE SPLY & STATIONERY STORES: Office Forms & Splys

Capitol Impressions Inc ....E....... 309 633-1400
  Peoria *(G-16397)*
Copy Service Inc ....G....... 815 758-1151
  Dekalb *(G-7670)*
Corporation Supply Co Inc ....E....... 312 726-3375
  Chicago *(G-4241)*
Dans Printing & Off Sups Inc ....F....... 708 687-3055
  Oak Forest *(G-15674)*
Donnells Printing & Off Pdts ....G....... 815 842-6541
  Pontiac *(G-16768)*
Fast Print Shop ....G....... 618 997-1976
  Marion *(G-13510)*
Gazette Democrat ....E....... 618 833-2150
  Anna *(G-583)*
Gold Nugget Publications Inc ....E....... 217 965-3355
  Virden *(G-20185)*
Hub Printing Company Inc ....F....... 815 562-7057
  Rochelle *(G-17145)*
James Ray Monroe Corporation ......F....... 618 532-4575
  Centralia *(G-3236)*
Jds Printing Inc ....G....... 630 208-1195
  Glendale Heights *(G-10463)*
Merritt & Edwards Corporation ....F....... 309 828-4741
  Bloomington *(G-2075)*
Mid-Central Business Forms ....G....... 309 692-9090
  Peoria *(G-16474)*
OfficeMax North America Inc ....E....... 815 748-3007
  Dekalb *(G-7696)*
R R Donnelley & Sons Company ....D....... 847 593-1200
  Elk Grove Village *(G-9210)*
R R Donnelley & Sons Company ....G....... 847 956-4187
  Elk Grove Village *(G-9211)*
Reign Print Solutions Inc ....G....... 847 590-7091
  Arlington Heights *(G-798)*
Ro-Web Inc ....G....... 309 688-2155
  Peoria *(G-16512)*

Selnar Inc ....G....... 309 699-3977
  East Peoria *(G-8290)*
Sigley Printing & Off Sup Co ....G....... 618 997-5304
  Marion *(G-13535)*
Supreme Screw Inc ....G....... 630 226-9000
  Romeoville *(G-17879)*
W B Mason Co Inc ....,.E....... 888 926-2766
  Carol Stream *(G-3085)*
Write Stuff ....G....... 630 365-4425
  Saint Charles *(G-18303)*
Xertrex International Inc ....E....... 630 773-4020
  Itasca *(G-11755)*

OFFICE SPLY & STATIONERY STORES: Writing Splys

A & E Rubber Stamp Corp ....G....... 312 575-1416
  Chicago *(G-3481)*

OFFICE SPLYS, NEC, WHOLESALE

Bar Codes Inc ....D....... 800 351-9962
  Chicago *(G-3828)*
Graphic Source Group Inc ....G....... 847 854-2670
  Lake In The Hills *(G-12336)*
H A Friend & Company Inc ....G....... 847 746-1248
  Zion *(G-21516)*
J M Printers Inc ....F....... 815 727-1579
  Crest Hill *(G-7087)*
Klai-Co Idntification Pdts Inc ....E....... 847 573-0375
  Lake Forest *(G-12270)*
Lewis Paper Place Inc ....G....... 847 808-1343
  Wheeling *(G-20932)*
Officenation Inc ....E....... 847 504-3000
  Northfield *(G-15525)*
Primedia Source LLC ....G....... 630 553-8451
  Yorkville *(G-21499)*
Rehabilitation and Vocational ....E....... 618 833-5344
  Anna *(G-587)*
S G C M Corp ....G....... 630 953-2428
  Oakbrook Terrace *(G-15815)*
Unlimited Graphix Inc ....E....... 630 759-0007
  Lockport *(G-13026)*
Warehouse Direct Inc ....C....... 847 952-1925
  Des Plaines *(G-7867)*

OFFICES & CLINICS OF DENTISTS: Dental Clinic

Dove Dental Studio ....G....... 847 679-2434
  Niles *(G-15116)*
Indilab Inc ....E....... 847 928-1050
  Franklin Park *(G-9962)*
Lmpl Management Corporation ....G....... 708 636-2443
  Oak Lawn *(G-15725)*

OFFICES & CLINICS OF DENTISTS: Group & Corporate Practice

TLC Dental Care LLC ....G....... 425 442-9000
  Elgin *(G-8755)*

OFFICES & CLINICS OF DOCTORS OF MEDICINE: Dermatologist

Michael A Greenberg MD Ltd ....F....... 847 364-4717
  Elk Grove Village *(G-9122)*

OFFICES & CLINICS OF DOCTORS OF MEDICINE: Gynecologist

Samel Botros ....G....... 847 466-5905
  Bloomingdale *(G-2014)*

OFFICES & CLINICS OF DRS OF MEDICINE: Med Clinic, Pri Care

First Step Womens Center ....G....... 217 523-0100
  Springfield *(G-19369)*

OFFICES & CLINICS OF DRS, MED: Specialized Practitioners

Dean Prsthtic Orthtic Svcs Ltd ....G....... 847 475-7080
  Evanston *(G-9508)*

OFFICES & CLINICS OF HEALTH PRACTITIONERS: Physical Therapy

Deborah Morris Gulbrandson Pt .....F....... 847 639-4140
  Cary *(G-3154)*

PRODUCT SECTION

OILS: Lubricating

OFFICES & CLINICS OF HEALTH PRACTITIONERS: Speech Therapist

Janelle Publications Inc ....G........ 815 756-2300
   Dekalb *(G-7686)*

OIL & GAS FIELD EQPT: Drill Rigs

H & H Drilling Co ....G........ 618 529-3697
   Carbondale *(G-2843)*

OIL & GAS FIELD MACHINERY

Arid Technologies Inc ....E........ 630 681-8500
   Wheaton *(G-20788)*
Bartec Orb Inc ....E........ 773 927-8600
   Chicago *(G-3843)*
Royal Brass Inc ....G........ 618 439-6341
   Benton *(G-1936)*
Trusty Warns Inc ....E........ 630 766-9015
   Wood Dale *(G-21253)*
U O P Equitec Services Inc ....A........ 847 391-2000
   Des Plaines *(G-7860)*

OIL FIELD MACHINERY & EQPT

Big Als Machines Inc ....G........ 618 963-2619
   Enfield *(G-9468)*
Gemtar Inc ....G........ 618 548-1353
   Salem *(G-18340)*
Pro Energy Trade Inc ....E........ 312 961-6404
   Chicago *(G-5887)*
Squibb Tank Company ....F........ 618 548-0141
   Salem *(G-18360)*

OIL FIELD SVCS, NEC

Armstrong Tool LLC ....G........ 618 382-4184
   Carmi *(G-2899)*
B & B Equipment ....F........ 217 562-2511
   Assumption *(G-888)*
Baker Hghes Olfld Oprtions LLC ....G........ 618 393-2919
   Olney *(G-15854)*
Baker Petrolite LLC ....F........ 618 966-3688
   Crossville *(G-7149)*
Bangert Casing Pulling Corp ....G........ 618 676-1411
   Clay City *(G-6903)*
Baseline Services Inc ....G........ 618 678-2753
   Xenia *(G-21466)*
Campbell Energy LLC ....G........ 618 382-3939
   Carmi *(G-2901)*
Clinton Oil Corp ....G........ 815 356-1124
   Crystal Lake *(G-7183)*
Concord Oil & Gas Corporation ....E........ 618 393-2124
   Olney *(G-15857)*
Cross Oil & Well Service Inc ....F........ 618 592-4609
   Oblong *(G-15825)*
Duncan Oil Company Inc ....G........ 618 548-2923
   Salem *(G-18336)*
Fedder Oil Co Inc ....G........ 618 344-0050
   Collinsville *(G-6960)*
Feller Oilfield Service Inc ....F........ 618 267-5650
   Saint Elmo *(G-18308)*
Franklin Well Services Inc ....D........ 812 494-2800
   Lawrenceville *(G-12532)*
Gunner Energy Corporation ....G........ 618 237-2829
   Mount Vernon *(G-14612)*
Harris Drilling Fluids Inc ....G........ 618 395-7395
   Olney *(G-15864)*
Kincaid Oil Producers Inc ....G........ 618 686-3084
   Louisville *(G-13179)*
Les Wilson Inc ....G........ 618 382-4667
   Carmi *(G-2909)*
M & I Acid Company Inc ....G........ 618 676-1638
   Clay City *(G-6907)*
M & L Well Service Inc ....E........ 618 393-7144
   Olney *(G-15870)*
M & S Oil Well Cementing Co ....G........ 618 262-7962
   Mount Carmel *(G-14478)*
Mid-States Services LLC ....F........ 618 842-4726
   Fairfield *(G-9633)*
Oelze Equipment Company LLC ....E........ 618 327-9111
   Nashville *(G-15006)*
P J Repair Service Inc ....F........ 618 548-5690
   Salem *(G-18349)*
Pinnacle Exploration Corp ....G........ 618 395-8100
   Olney *(G-15883)*
Precision Plugging and Sls Inc ....F........ 618 395-8510
   Olney *(G-15884)*
Pro-Lube of Shelbyville Inc ....G........ 217 774-4643
   Shelbyville *(G-18883)*
Purified Lubricants Inc ....E........ 708 478-3500
   Mokena *(G-14111)*
Roark Oil Field Services Inc ....G........ 618 382-4703
   Carmi *(G-2914)*
Schwartz Oilfield Services ....F........ 618 532-0232
   Walnut Hill *(G-20222)*
Seip Service & Supply Inc ....F........ 618 532-1923
   Centralia *(G-3250)*
Ta Oil Field Service Inc ....G........ 618 249-9001
   Richview *(G-17034)*
Tdw Services Inc ....F........ 815 407-0675
   Romeoville *(G-17880)*
Tri Kote Inc ....G........ 618 262-4156
   Mount Carmel *(G-14489)*
United Oil Co ....G........ 309 378-3049
   Downs *(G-8114)*
Warren Service Company ....G........ 618 384-2117
   Carmi *(G-2918)*
Wayne County Well Surveys Inc ....F........ 618 842-9116
   Fairfield *(G-9641)*

OIL TREATING COMPOUNDS

Afton Chemical Corporation ....E........ 708 728-1546
   Bedford Park *(G-1454)*
Penray Companies Inc ....D........ 800 323-6329
   Downers Grove *(G-8071)*

OILS & ESSENTIAL OILS

Fragrance Island Inc ....G........ 773 488-2700
   Chicago *(G-4628)*

OILS & GREASES: Blended & Compounded

Calumet Refining LLC ....F........ 708 832-2463
   Burnham *(G-2644)*
CLC Lubricants Company ....E........ 630 232-7900
   Geneva *(G-10261)*
Clean Harbors Wichita LLC ....G........ 815 675-1272
   Spring Grove *(G-19270)*
Comet Supply Inc ....G........ 309 444-2712
   Washington *(G-20269)*
Ecli Products LLC ....E........ 630 449-5000
   Aurora *(G-955)*
Harris Lubricants ....G........ 708 849-1935
   Dolton *(G-7936)*
Illinois Oil Products Inc ....F........ 309 788-1896
   Rock Island *(G-17224)*
Konzen Chemicals Inc ....F........ 708 878-7636
   Matteson *(G-13626)*
Motor Oil Inc ....F........ 847 956-7550
   Elk Grove Village *(G-9135)*
Mullen Circle Brand Inc ....F........ 847 676-1880
   Skokie *(G-18993)*
Perkins Products Inc ....E........ 708 458-2000
   Bedford Park *(G-1491)*
Premium Oil Company ....F........ 815 963-3800
   Rockford *(G-17559)*
Rock Valley Oil & Chemical Co ....D........ 815 654-2400
   Loves Park *(G-13254)*
Truckers Oil Pros Inc ....F........ 773 523-8990
   Chicago *(G-6436)*

OILS & GREASES: Lubricating

Ameriflon Ltd ....G........ 847 541-6000
   Wheeling *(G-20848)*
Amsoil Inc ....G........ 630 595-8385
   Bensenville *(G-1745)*
Avatar Corporation ....D........ 708 534-5511
   University Park *(G-19947)*
Bioblend Lubricants Intl ....G........ 630 227-1800
   Joliet *(G-11832)*
Boyer Corporation ....G........ 708 352-2553
   La Grange *(G-12074)*
Campbell Camie Inc ....E........ 314 968-3222
   Downers Grove *(G-7963)*
Cargill Incorporated ....F........ 773 374-3808
   Chicago *(G-4029)*
Cargill Incorporated ....F........ 773 375-7255
   Chicago *(G-4030)*
Castrol Industrial N Amer Inc ....C........ 877 641-1600
   Naperville *(G-14792)*
Chemix Corp ....F........ 708 754-2150
   Glenwood *(G-10639)*
Chemtool Inc ....F........ 815 459-1250
   Crystal Lake *(G-7179)*
Chemtool Incorporated ....G........ 815 389-0250
   Rockton *(G-17695)*
Claire-Sprayway Inc ....D........ 630 628-3000
   Downers Grove *(G-7973)*
Darling Ingredients Inc ....E........ 217 482-3261
   Mason City *(G-13611)*
Enterprise Oil Co ....E........ 312 487-2025
   Chicago *(G-4514)*
Famous Lubricants Inc ....G........ 773 268-2555
   Chicago *(G-4557)*
Filter Kleen Inc ....G........ 708 447-4666
   Lyons *(G-13308)*
Fuchs Corporation ....G........ 800 323-7755
   Harvey *(G-11086)*
Havoline Xpress Lube LLC ....G........ 847 221-5724
   Palatine *(G-16123)*
Ideas Inc ....G........ 630 620-2010
   Lombard *(G-13087)*
Ideas Inc ....G........ 708 596-1055
   Harvey *(G-11090)*
Italmatch Sc LLC ....G........ 708 929-9657
   Bedford Park *(G-1474)*
Jx Nippon Oil & Energy Lubrica ....F........ 847 413-2188
   Schaumburg *(G-18582)*
K & J Synthetic Lubricants ....G........ 630 628-1011
   Addison *(G-164)*
Kostelac Grease Service Inc ....E........ 314 436-7166
   Belleville *(G-1566)*
Lub-Tek Petroleum Products ....G........ 815 741-0414
   Joliet *(G-11895)*
Midwest Recycling Co ....G........ 815 744-4922
   Rockdale *(G-17268)*
Nalco Holding Company ....E........ 630 305-1000
   Naperville *(G-14877)*
Olympic Petroleum Corporation ....G........ 847 995-0996
   Schaumburg *(G-18657)*
Pdv Midwest Refining LLC ....A........ 630 257-7761
   Lemont *(G-12581)*
Polyenviro Labs Inc ....G........ 708 489-0195
   Mokena *(G-14108)*
Rilco Fluid Care Inc ....E........ 309 788-1854
   Rock Island *(G-17242)*
Rs Used Oil Services Inc ....G........ 618 781-1717
   Roxana *(G-18101)*
Sandstrom Products Company ....F........ 309 523-2121
   Port Byron *(G-16788)*
Shima American Corporation ....G........ 630 760-4330
   Itasca *(G-11732)*
Spartacus Group Inc ....F........ 815 637-1574
   Machesney Park *(G-13375)*
Superior Graphite Co ....G........ 708 458-0006
   Chicago *(G-6281)*
Tower Oil & Technology Co ....E........ 773 927-6161
   Chicago *(G-6401)*
Uberlube Inc ....G........ 847 372-3127
   Evanston *(G-9585)*

OILS, ANIMAL OR VEGETABLE, WHOLESALE

Archer-Daniels-Midland Company ......D........ 217 224-1875
   Quincy *(G-16858)*
Vantage Specialties Inc ....G........ 847 244-3410
   Chicago *(G-6523)*

OILS: Cutting

Chemtool Incorporated ....C........ 815 957-4140
   Rockton *(G-17694)*
Chemtool Incorporated ....D........ 815 459-1250
   Crystal Lake *(G-7180)*
Illini Coolant Management Corp ....G........ 847 966-1079
   Morton Grove *(G-14412)*
Mistic Metal Mover Inc ....G........ 815 875-1371
   Princeton *(G-16814)*

OILS: Essential

Arbor Products ....G........ 847 653-6210
   Park Ridge *(G-16267)*
Super-Dri Corp ....G........ 708 599-8700
   Bridgeview *(G-2390)*

OILS: Lubricating

Lamson Oil Company ....G........ 815 226-8090
   Rockford *(G-17490)*
Power Lube LLC ....G........ 847 806-7022
   Elk Grove Village *(G-9187)*

OILS: Lubricating

Atm America Corp ....E........ 800 298-0030
   Chicago *(G-3770)*
CAM Tek Lubricants Inc ....G........ 708 477-3000
   Orland Park *(G-15945)*

OILS: Lubricating

Gtx Inc .... G 847 699-7421
  Des Plaines *(G-7775)*
High Performance Lubr LLC .... F 815 468-3535
  Manteno *(G-13449)*
Huels Oil Company .... F 877 338-6277
  Carlyle *(G-2890)*
Jx Nippon Oil & Energy USA Inc .... E 847 413-2188
  Schaumburg *(G-18583)*
Loves Travel Stops .... E 618 931-1575
  Granite City *(G-10720)*
Nanolube Inc .... G 630 706-1250
  Lombard *(G-13106)*
Olympic Petroleum Corporation .... D 708 876-7900
  Cicero *(G-6868)*
William Ingram .... G 217 442-5075
  Danville *(G-7398)*

OILS: Mineral, Natural

Tatty Stick LLC .... G 815 905-1023
  Essex *(G-9476)*

OILS: Peppermint

Wm Wrigley Jr Company .... B 312 280-4710
  Chicago *(G-6654)*
Wm Wrigley Jr Company .... A 312 644-2121
  Chicago *(G-6656)*

OINTMENTS

Blistex Inc .... C 630 571-2870
  Oak Brook *(G-15598)*
Blistex Inc .... G 630 571-2870
  Oak Brook *(G-15599)*

ON-LINE DATABASE INFORMATION RETRIEVAL SVCS

AR Inet Corp .... G 603 380-3903
  Aurora *(G-913)*
Calutech Inc .... G 708 614-0228
  Orland Park *(G-15944)*
Informa Media Inc .... F 212 204-4200
  Chicago *(G-4916)*

OPERATOR TRAINING, COMPUTER

Friedrich Klatt and Associates .... G 773 753-1806
  Chicago *(G-4636)*
Mbm Business Assistance Inc .... G 217 398-6600
  Champaign *(G-3318)*

OPERATOR: Apartment Buildings

Christopher Concrete Products .... G 618 724-2951
  Buckner *(G-2499)*
Patty Style Shop .... G 618 654-2015
  Highland *(G-11234)*

OPERATOR: Nonresidential Buildings

D D G Inc .... G 847 412-0277
  Northbrook *(G-15370)*
Upper Urban Green Prprty Maint .... G 312 218-5903
  Chicago *(G-6489)*

OPHTHALMIC GOODS

Asico LLC .... F 630 986-8032
  Westmont *(G-20729)*
C & S Chemicals Inc .... G 815 722-6671
  Joliet *(G-11837)*
Clear Sight Inc .... G 630 323-3590
  Westmont *(G-20732)*
First Look Wholesale Lab Inc .... G 618 462-9042
  Wood River *(G-21261)*
Illmo R/X Service .... F 217 877-1192
  Decatur *(G-7505)*
Innova Systems Inc .... G 630 920-8880
  Burr Ridge *(G-2686)*
M & S Technologies Inc .... F 847 763-0500
  Niles *(G-15142)*
Night Vision Corporation .... G 847 677-7611
  Lincolnwood *(G-12833)*
Quality Optical Inc .... G 773 561-0870
  Chicago *(G-5930)*
Scuba Optics Inc .... G 815 625-7272
  Rock Falls *(G-17195)*
Village Optical Shop .... G 847 295-3290
  Lake Bluff *(G-12212)*
Vision Assessment Corporation .... G 847 239-5889
  Elk Grove Village *(G-9305)*

Walman Optical Company .... E 309 787-0000
  Milan *(G-14030)*

OPHTHALMIC GOODS WHOLESALERS

Asico LLC .... F 630 986-8032
  Westmont *(G-20729)*
Illmo R/X Service .... F 217 877-1192
  Decatur *(G-7505)*
Two Tower Frames Inc .... G 773 517-0394
  Chicago *(G-6448)*
Western Ilinois Optical Inc .... G 309 837-2000
  Macomb *(G-13401)*

OPHTHALMIC GOODS: Eyewear, Protective

Independent Eyewear Mfg LLC .... D 847 537-0008
  Vernon Hills *(G-20066)*

OPHTHALMIC GOODS: Frames & Parts, Eyeglass & Spectacle

Western Ilinois Optical Inc .... G 309 837-2000
  Macomb *(G-13401)*

OPHTHALMIC GOODS: Goggles, Sun, Safety, Indl, Etc

One Way Safety LLC .... E 708 579-0229
  La Grange *(G-12085)*

OPHTHALMIC GOODS: Spectacles

Spectacle Zoom LLC .... G 504 352-7237
  Des Plaines *(G-7849)*

OPTICAL EQPT: Interferometers

PHI Optics Inc .... G 217 819-1570
  Champaign *(G-3332)*

OPTICAL GOODS STORES

Eyelation Inc .... F 888 308-4703
  Tinley Park *(G-19826)*

OPTICAL GOODS STORES: Eyeglasses, Prescription

Edgebrook Eyecare .... F 815 397-5959
  Rockford *(G-17390)*
Quality Optical Inc .... G 773 561-0870
  Chicago *(G-5930)*

OPTICAL GOODS STORES: Opticians

J A K Enterprises Inc .... G 217 422-3881
  Decatur *(G-7509)*
Village Optical Shop .... G 847 295-3290
  Lake Bluff *(G-12212)*

OPTICAL INSTRUMENT REPAIR SVCS

Cortek Endoscopy Inc .... G 847 526-2266
  Wauconda *(G-20340)*

OPTICAL INSTRUMENTS & APPARATUS

Inprentus Inc .... F 217 239-9862
  Champaign *(G-3308)*
Intra Action Corp. .... E 708 547-6644
  Bellwood *(G-1628)*
Laurel Industries Inc .... E 847 432-8204
  Highland Park *(G-11281)*
Leica Microsystems Inc .... C 847 405-0123
  Buffalo Grove *(G-2563)*

OPTICAL INSTRUMENTS & LENSES

4 U Optical .... G 847 459-8598
  Buffalo Grove *(G-2502)*
Abet Technologies LLC .... F 847 682-5541
  Evanston *(G-9485)*
Cabot McRlectronics Polsg Corp .... E 630 543-6682
  Addison *(G-61)*
Cipp Robotics LLC .... G 815 202-6628
  La Salle *(G-12108)*
Elmed Incorporated .... E 224 353-6446
  Glendale Heights *(G-10448)*
Fjw Optical Systems Inc .... F 847 358-2500
  Palatine *(G-16119)*
Illinois Tool Works Inc .... C 847 295-6500
  Lake Bluff *(G-12189)*

J A K Enterprises Inc .... G 217 422-3881
  Decatur *(G-7509)*
Kollmorgen Corp .... G 815 568-8001
  Marengo *(G-13488)*
Leica McRosystems Holdings Inc .... F 800 248-0123
  Buffalo Grove *(G-2561)*
Leica Microsystems Inc .... G 847 405-0123
  Buffalo Grove *(G-2562)*
Lockwood Custom Optics Inc .... G 217 684-2170
  Philo *(G-16607)*
Night Vision Specialists LLC .... G 618 614-8626
  Makanda *(G-13429)*
Omex Technologies Inc .... G 847 850-5858
  Wheeling *(G-20949)*
Opti-Vue Inc .... G 630 274-6121
  Bensenville *(G-1862)*
Precision Vision Inc .... G 815 223-2022
  Woodstock *(G-21423)*
Quality Optical Inc .... G 773 561-0870
  Chicago *(G-5930)*
Scopedawg Optics LLC .... E 618 401-3342
  Highland *(G-11239)*
Strausbrger Assoc Sls Mktg Inc .... G 630 768-6179
  Yorkville *(G-21501)*
Two Tower Frames Inc .... G 773 517-0394
  Chicago *(G-6448)*
Vega Technology & Systems .... G 630 855-5068
  Bartlett *(G-1259)*
Vibgyor Optical Systems Corp .... E 847 818-0788
  Arlington Heights *(G-826)*
Vibgyor Optics Inc .... E 847 818-0788
  Arlington Heights *(G-827)*
Wayne Engineering .... G 416 943-6271
  Skokie *(G-19054)*

OPTICAL ISOLATORS

Jql Technologies Corporation .... F 800 236-9828
  Mundelein *(G-14705)*

OPTICAL SCANNING SVCS

Illinois Bone & Joint Inst LLC .... D 847 724-4470
  Glenview *(G-10559)*

OPTOMETRISTS' OFFICES

Eye Surgeons of Libertyville .... G 847 362-3811
  Libertyville *(G-12650)*

ORDNANCE

General Dynamics Ordnance .... C 618 985-8211
  Marion *(G-13512)*
United Tactical Systems LLC .... E 260 478-2500
  Lake Forest *(G-12320)*

ORGAN TUNING & REPAIR SVCS

Berghaus Pipe Organ Builders .... E 708 544-4052
  Bellwood *(G-1616)*
Buzard Pipe Organ Builders LLC .... F 217 352-1955
  Champaign *(G-3273)*
C P O Inc .... G 630 898-7733
  Aurora *(G-1068)*
Daves Electronic Service .... F 217 283-5010
  Hoopeston *(G-11507)*
Fabry Inc .... G 847 395-1919
  Fox Lake *(G-9746)*
Schneider Pipe Organs Inc .... G 217 871-4807
  Kenney *(G-12016)*

ORGANIZATIONS & UNIONS: Labor

Local 46 Training Program Tr .... G 217 528-4041
  Springfield *(G-19399)*

ORGANIZATIONS: Biotechnical Research, Noncommercial

Proteintech Group Inc .... E 312 455-8498
  Rosemont *(G-18045)*

ORGANIZATIONS: Medical Research

Clarus Therapeutics Inc .... G 847 562-4300
  Northbrook *(G-15361)*
Murray Inc .... E 847 620-7990
  North Barrington *(G-15287)*

ORGANIZATIONS: Professional

American Association of Indivi .... E 312 280-0170
  Chicago *(G-3649)*

PRODUCT SECTION

American Soc HM Inspectors Inc .... F 847 759-2820
  Des Plaines *(G-7728)*
Associated Equipment Distrs .... E 630 574-0650
  Schaumburg *(G-18447)*

ORGANIZATIONS: Religious

Central Ill Communications LLC .... F 217 753-2226
  Springfield *(G-19345)*
Chicago Jewish News .... F 847 966-0606
  Skokie *(G-18941)*
Christian National Womans .... G 847 864-1396
  Evanston *(G-9505)*
Christian Specialized Services .... G 217 546-7338
  Springfield *(G-19350)*
Christian Wolf Inc .... G 618 667-9522
  Bartelso *(G-1252)*
Cook Communications Ministries .... C 847 741-0800
  Elgin *(G-8557)*
Crusade Enterprises Inc .... G 618 662-4461
  Flora *(G-9679)*
Evang Lthn Ch Dr Mrtn Luth KG .... F 773 380-2540
  Chicago *(G-4535)*
Moody Bible Inst of Chicago .... A 312 329-4000
  Chicago *(G-5495)*
Paddock Industries Inc .... F 618 277-1580
  Smithton *(G-19068)*
Templegate Publishers .... G 217 522-3353
  Springfield *(G-19463)*
Urantia Corp .... F 773 248-6616
  Chicago *(G-6492)*
Urantia Foundation .... E 773 525-3319
  Chicago *(G-6493)*

ORGANIZATIONS: Safety Research, Noncommercial

Microwave RES & Applications .... G 630 480-7456
  Carol Stream *(G-3029)*

ORGANIZATIONS: Scientific Research Agency

Advanced Robotics Research .... G 630 544-0040
  Naperville *(G-14766)*

ORGANIZATIONS: Veterans' Membership

John Joda Post 54 .... G 815 692-3222
  Fairbury *(G-9610)*

ORGANIZERS, CLOSET & DRAWER Plastic

Bannon Enterprises Inc .... G 847 529-9265
  Geneva *(G-10254)*
Quality Custom Closets .... G 773 307-1105
  Glenview *(G-10605)*

ORNAMENTS: Lawn

Rome Industries Inc .... G 309 691-7120
  Peoria *(G-16517)*

OSCILLATORS

Connor-Winfield Corp .... C 630 851-4722
  Aurora *(G-1079)*

OSCILLATORS

FSI Technologies Inc .... E 630 932-9380
  Lombard *(G-13080)*
Radio Controlled Models Inc .... G 847 740-8726
  Round Lake Beach *(G-18092)*

OSICIZERS: Inorganic

Indorama Vntres USA Hldings LP .... G 847 943-3100
  Riverwoods *(G-17093)*

OUTBOARD MOTORS & PARTS

Brunswick Corporation .... B 847 735-4700
  Mettawa *(G-13979)*
Brunswick International Ltd .... E 847 735-4700
  Mettawa *(G-13980)*

OUTLETS: Electric, Convenience

Dollar Express .... G 815 399-9719
  Rockford *(G-17384)*

OUTREACH PROGRAM

Cornerstone Community Outreach .... F 773 506-4904
  Chicago *(G-4237)*

OVENS: Cremating

Aquagreen Dispositions LLC .... G 708 606-0211
  Monee *(G-14196)*
Aquagreen Dispositions LLC .... G 708 606-0211
  South Holland *(G-19196)*

OVENS: Distillation, Charcoal & Coke

Uic Inc .... G 815 744-4477
  Joliet *(G-11937)*

OVENS: Infrared

Maintenance Inc .... G 708 598-1390
  La Grange *(G-12082)*

OVENS: Laboratory

Aalborg Company .... G 708 246-8858
  Western Springs *(G-20718)*
Grieve Corporation .... D 847 546-8225
  Round Lake *(G-18078)*
Quincy Lab Inc .... E 773 622-2428
  Chicago *(G-5938)*

PACKAGE DESIGN SVCS

Bar Code Graphics Inc .... F 312 664-0700
  Chicago *(G-3827)*
Cornerstone Communications .... E 773 989-2087
  Chicago *(G-4236)*
Forest Packaging Corporation .... E 847 981-7000
  Elk Grove Village *(G-9003)*
Mii Inc .... G 630 879-3000
  Batavia *(G-1395)*
Pelican Holdco LLC .... F 847 597-2200
  Deerfield *(G-7642)*

PACKAGED FROZEN FOODS WHOLESALERS, NEC

Doreens Pizza Inc .... F 708 862-7499
  Calumet City *(G-2775)*
Ed Kabrick Beef Inc .... G 217 656-3263
  Plainville *(G-16729)*
Great Lakes Coca-Cola Dist LLC .... D 847 227-6500
  Rosemont *(G-18025)*
Jackson & Partners LLC .... G 630 219-1598
  Naperville *(G-14853)*
Koch Meat Co Inc .... B 847 384-5940
  Chicago *(G-5113)*
Lena AJS Maid Meats .... F 815 369-4522
  Lena *(G-12602)*
Paani Foods Inc .... F 312 420-4624
  Chicago *(G-5734)*
Reyes Holdings LLC .... E 847 227-6500
  Rosemont *(G-18048)*
Simu Ltd .... F 708 688-2200
  Mc Cook *(G-13701)*
WEI-Chuan USA Inc .... F 708 352-8886
  Hodgkins *(G-11401)*

PACKAGING & LABELING SVCS

Alltemated Inc .... D 847 394-5800
  Wheeling *(G-20845)*
Assemblers Inc .... C 773 378-3000
  Chicago *(G-3749)*
Bankier Companies Inc .... E 847 647-6565
  Niles *(G-15105)*
Bli Legacy Inc .... E 847 428-6059
  Carpentersville *(G-3095)*
Clifton Chemical Company .... F 815 697-2343
  Chebanse *(G-3429)*
Compact Industries Inc .... C 630 513-9600
  Saint Charles *(G-18173)*
Corr-Pak Corporation .... E 708 442-7806
  Mc Cook *(G-13690)*
County Packaging Inc .... D 708 597-1100
  Crestwood *(G-7114)*
Eagle Express Mail LLC .... G 618 377-6245
  Bethalto *(G-1964)*
Emco Chemical Distributors Inc .... C 262 427-0400
  North Chicago *(G-15310)*
Essentra Corp .... G 814 899-7671
  Westchester *(G-20697)*

PACKAGING MATERIALS, WHOLESALE

Fedex Corporation .... F 847 918-7730
  Vernon Hills *(G-20053)*
Fedex Office & Print Svcs Inc .... F 312 341-9644
  Chicago *(G-4573)*
Fedex Office & Print Svcs Inc .... F 312 755-0325
  Chicago *(G-4574)*
Fedex Office & Print Svcs Inc .... F 312 595-0768
  Chicago *(G-4575)*
Fedex Office & Print Svcs Inc .... F 312 663-1149
  Chicago *(G-4576)*
General Assembly & Mfg Corp .... E 847 516-6462
  Cary *(G-3163)*
Lee Gilster-Mary Corporation .... B 618 965-3449
  Steeleville *(G-19482)*
Leos Gluten Free LLC .... G 847 233-9211
  Franklin Park *(G-9981)*
M-Prime Company .... E 630 834-9400
  Villa Park *(G-20157)*
Marietta Corporation .... C 773 816-5137
  Chicago *(G-5337)*
Midwest Packaging & Cont Inc .... D 815 633-6800
  Machesney Park *(G-13361)*
New Usn Chicago LLC .... D 847 635-6772
  Mount Prospect *(G-14551)*
Paket Corporation .... E 773 221-7300
  Chicago *(G-5743)*
Papys Foods Inc .... E 815 385-3313
  McHenry *(G-13776)*
Park Lawn Association Inc .... F 708 425-7377
  Oak Lawn *(G-15731)*
Patt Supply Corporation .... F 708 442-3901
  Lyons *(G-13312)*
Phoenix Unlimited Ltd .... G 847 515-1263
  Huntley *(G-11559)*
R & R Creative Graphics Inc .... G 630 208-4724
  Geneva *(G-10301)*
Randolph Packing Co .... D 630 830-3100
  Streamwood *(G-19592)*
RPS Products Inc .... E 847 683-3400
  Hampshire *(G-10986)*
Schmit Laboratories Inc .... E 773 476-0072
  Glendale Heights *(G-10491)*
Service Packaging Design Inc .... G 847 966-6592
  Morton Grove *(G-14440)*
Stellar Blending & Packaging .... F 314 520-7318
  Dupo *(G-8144)*
Sunstar Pharmaceutical Inc .... D 773 777-4000
  Elgin *(G-8742)*
Tara International LP .... D 708 354-7050
  Hodgkins *(G-11398)*
Taylors Candy Inc .... E 708 371-0332
  Alsip *(G-515)*
Treatment Products Ltd .... E 773 626-8888
  Chicago *(G-6414)*
Unified Solutions Corp .... E 847 478-9100
  Arlington Heights *(G-824)*
Vegetable Juices Inc .... D 708 924-9500
  Bedford Park *(G-1509)*
Wisconsin Wilderness Food Pdts .... G 847 735-8661
  Lake Forest *(G-12323)*

PACKAGING MATERIALS, INDL: Wholesalers

Sherwood Industries Inc .... F 847 626-0300
  Niles *(G-15170)*
Titan US LLC .... G 331 212-5953
  Aurora *(G-1026)*

PACKAGING MATERIALS, WHOLESALE

Acme Finishing Company LLC .... F 847 640-7890
  Elk Grove Village *(G-8803)*
All-Pak Manufacturing Corp .... D 630 851-5859
  Aurora *(G-1046)*
Alliance Creative Group Inc .... E 847 885-1800
  East Dundee *(G-8187)*
Americo Chemical Products Inc .... E 630 588-0830
  Carol Stream *(G-2938)*
Fromm Airpad Inc .... F 630 393-9790
  Warrenville *(G-20236)*
Illinois Tool Works Inc .... E 217 345-2166
  Itasca *(G-11673)*
Isbir Bulk Bag Usa LLC .... G 972 722-9200
  Warrenville *(G-20239)*
Midpoint Packaging LLC .... G 630 613-9922
  Downers Grove *(G-8056)*
Morton Group Ltd .... E 847 831-2766
  Highland Park *(G-11286)*
Pak Source Inc .... E 309 786-7374
  Rock Island *(G-17231)*
Pelican Holdco LLC .... F 847 597-2200
  Deerfield *(G-7642)*

Employee Codes: A=Over 500 employees, B=251-500
C=101-250, D=51-100, E=20-50, F=10-19, G=3-9

PACKAGING MATERIALS, WHOLESALE

Pregis Innovative Packg LLC .... E 847 597-2200
  Deerfield (G-7643)
S and K Packaging Incorporated .... G 563 582-8895
  East Dubuque (G-8181)
S Vs Industries Inc .... G 630 408-1083
  Hoffman Estates (G-11453)
Signode Intl Holdings LLC .... F 800 648-8864
  Glenview (G-10621)
Stickon Adhesive Inds Inc .... E 847 593-5959
  Wauconda (G-20391)

PACKAGING MATERIALS: Paper

Allegra Print & Imaging Inc .... G 847 697-1434
  Elgin (G-8502)
American Graphics Network Inc .... F 847 729-7220
  Glenview (G-10522)
American Name Plate & Metal De .... E 773 376-1400
  Chicago (G-3663)
Applied Products Inc .... E 815 633-3825
  Machesney Park (G-13327)
Arbor Private Inv Co LLC .... G 312 981-3770
  Chicago (G-3718)
Arcadia Press Inc .... F 847 451-6390
  Franklin Park (G-9872)
Avery Dnnson Ret Info Svcs LLC .... G 626 304-2000
  Chicago (G-3787)
B & B Printing Company .... G 217 285-6072
  Pittsfield (G-16628)
Bagcraftpapercon I LLC .... C 620 856-2800
  Chicago (G-3814)
Bagcraftpapercon II LLC .... A 773 843-8000
  Chicago (G-3815)
Bema Inc .... D 630 279-7800
  Elmhurst (G-9331)
Bucktown Polymers .... G 312 436-1460
  Chicago (G-3971)
Burgopak Limited .... E 312 255-0827
  Chicago (G-3976)
Daubert Cromwell LLC .... E 708 293-7750
  Alsip (G-439)
Deco Adhesive Pdts 1985 Ltd .... E 847 472-2100
  Elk Grove Village (G-8941)
Dresbach Distributing Co .... G 815 223-0116
  Peru (G-16574)
Ennis Inc .... E 815 875-2000
  Princeton (G-16808)
Flex-O-Glass Inc .... E 815 288-1424
  Dixon (G-7899)
General Packaging Products Inc .... D 312 226-5611
  Chicago (G-4675)
H S Crocker Company Inc .... D 847 669-3600
  Huntley (G-11538)
Hanlon Group Ltd .... G 773 525-3666
  Chicago (G-4778)
Illinois Tag Co .... E 773 626-0542
  Carol Stream (G-3001)
Label Graphics Co Inc .... F 815 648-2478
  Hebron (G-11145)
Labels & Specialty Pdts LLC .... E 630 513-8060
  Saint Charles (G-18223)
Labels Unlimited Incorporated .... E 773 523-7500
  Chicago (G-5152)
Lasons Label Co .... G 773 775-2606
  Chicago (G-5179)
Miller Products Inc .... E 708 534-5111
  University Park (G-19962)
Miracle Press Company .... F 773 722-6176
  Chicago (G-5467)
Multi Packaging Solutions Inc .... G 773 283-9500
  Chicago (G-5523)
No Surrender Inc .... F 773 929-7920
  Chicago (G-5607)
Noor International Inc .... E 847 985-2300
  Bartlett (G-1256)
Nosco Inc .... G 847 360-4874
  Waukegan (G-20471)
Odra Inc .... G 847 249-2910
  Gurnee (G-10906)
Pelican Holdco LLC .... F 847 597-2200
  Deerfield (G-7642)
Perryco Inc .... F 815 436-2431
  Plainfield (G-16701)
Phoenix Converting Inc .... D 630 258-1500
  Itasca (G-11718)
Photo Techniques Corp .... E 630 690-9360
  Carol Stream (G-3046)
Pioneer Labels Inc .... C 618 546-5418
  Robinson (G-17121)
Preferred Printing Service .... G 312 421-2343
  Chicago (G-5861)

Pregis Innovative Packg LLC .... E 847 597-2200
  Deerfield (G-7643)
Pregis LLC .... A 847 597-2200
  Deerfield (G-7645)
Prime Label & Packaging LLC .... D 630 227-1300
  Wood Dale (G-21231)
Prime Label Group LLC .... G 773 630-8793
  Batavia (G-1405)
Printpack Inc .... C 847 888-7150
  Elgin (G-8696)
R R Donnelley & Sons Company .... D 630 762-7600
  Saint Charles (G-18258)
RTC Industries Inc .... D 847 640-2400
  Chicago (G-6075)
Seshin USA Inc .... G 847 550-5556
  Lake Zurich (G-12456)
Signature Label of Illinois .... G 618 283-5145
  Vandalia (G-20024)
Stepac USA Corporation .... G 630 296-2000
  Romeoville (G-17877)
Stephen Fossler Company .... D 847 635-7200
  Des Plaines (G-7852)
TLC Dental Care LLC .... G 425 442-9000
  Elgin (G-8755)
Triumph Packaging Georgia LLC .... E 312 251-9600
  Lake Forest (G-12316)
Triumph Packaging Group .... E 312 251-9600
  Lake Forest (G-12317)
UNI-Label and Tag Corporation .... E 847 956-8900
  Elk Grove Village (G-9294)
Westrock Cnsmr Packg Group LLC ...... A 804 444-1000
  Melrose Park (G-13928)

PACKAGING MATERIALS: Paper, Coated Or Laminated

Hexacomb Corporation .... G 847 955-7984
  Buffalo Grove (G-2546)
Midwest Lminating Coatings Inc .... E 708 653-9500
  Alsip (G-478)
Nation Inc .... E 847 844-7300
  Carpentersville (G-3109)
Pdoc LLC .... C 773 843-8000
  Chicago (G-5774)
Selig Sealing Products Inc .... G 815 785-2100
  Forrest (G-9737)
Tetra Pak Inc .... D 847 955-6000
  Vernon Hills (G-20103)
Xshredders Inc .... D 847 205-1875
  Northbrook (G-15503)

PACKAGING MATERIALS: Paper, Thermoplastic Coated

MEI LLC .... G 630 285-1505
  Itasca (G-11699)
Signode Industrial Group LLC .... E 847 724-6100
  Glenview (G-10620)

PACKAGING MATERIALS: Paperboard Backs For Blister/Skin Pkgs

Pure Skin LLC .... G 217 679-6267
  Springfield (G-19431)

PACKAGING MATERIALS: Plastic Film, Coated Or Laminated

Acorn Diversified Inc .... F 708 478-1051
  Orland Park (G-15933)
Amcor Flexibles LLC .... C 224 313-7000
  Buffalo Grove (G-2510)
Ampac Flexicon LLC .... E 630 439-3160
  Hanover Park (G-10998)
Ampac Flexicon LLC .... G 952 541-0730
  Hanover Park (G-10999)
Ampac Flexicon LLC .... D 847 639-3530
  Cary (G-3147)
AZ Plastics Inc .... G 773 679-0988
  Chicago (G-3798)
AZ Plastics Inc .... E 773 679-0988
  Chicago (G-3799)
Elite Extrusion Technology Inc .... G 630 485-2020
  Saint Charles (G-18195)
Farm Plastic Supply Inc .... G 312 625-1024
  Itasca (G-11654)
Fisher Container Holdings LLC .... G 847 541-0000
  Buffalo Grove (G-2537)
Iam Acquisition LLC .... E 847 259-7800
  Wheeling (G-20912)

PRODUCT SECTION

Morcor Industries Inc .... G 224 293-2000
  Elgin (G-8664)
Petra Manufacturing Co .... D 773 622-1475
  Chicago (G-5797)
Polyair Inter Pack Inc .... D 773 995-1818
  Chicago (G-5838)
Ppc Flexible Packaging LLC .... C 847 541-0000
  Buffalo Grove (G-2588)
Pro-Pak Industries Inc .... F 630 876-1050
  West Chicago (G-20633)
Quality Bags Inc .... G 630 543-9800
  Addison (G-260)
Rapak LLC .... C 630 296-2000
  Romeoville (G-17868)
Winpak Portion Packaging Inc .... D 708 753-5700
  Sauk Village (G-18401)
World Contract Packagers Inc .... G 815 624-6501
  South Beloit (G-19126)

PACKAGING MATERIALS: Polystyrene Foam

Co-Ordinated Packaging Inc .... F 847 559-8877
  Bensenville (G-1772)
Cushioneer Inc .... D 815 748-5505
  Dekalb (G-7673)
Custom Foam Works Inc .... G 618 920-2810
  Troy (G-19913)
Elongated Plastics Inc .... E 224 456-0559
  Northbrook (G-15382)
Epe Industries Usa Inc .... F 800 315-0336
  Elk Grove Village (G-8980)
Free-Flow Packaging Intl Inc .... D 708 589-6500
  Homewood (G-11494)
Grafcor Packaging Inc .... F 815 963-1300
  Rockford (G-17434)
Illinois Tool Works Inc .... E 217 345-2166
  Itasca (G-11673)
Layer Saver LLC .... G 630 325-7287
  Burr Ridge (G-2696)
Mailbox Plus .... E 847 577-1737
  Mount Prospect (G-14545)
Midpoint Packaging LLC .... G 630 613-9922
  Downers Grove (G-8056)
Polar Tech Industries Inc .... E 815 784-9000
  Genoa (G-10321)
Polyair Inter Pack Inc .... D 773 995-1818
  Chicago (G-5838)
Positive Packaging Inc .... G 708 560-3028
  Rolling Meadows (G-17763)
Sales Midwest Prtg & Packg Inc .... G 309 764-5544
  Moline (G-14175)
Sealed Air Corporation .... D 708 352-8700
  Hodgkins (G-11396)
Silgan Equipment Company .... E 847 336-0552
  Waukegan (G-20496)
Sonoco Display & Packaging LLC .... D 630 972-1990
  Bolingbrook (G-2244)
Sonoco Protective Solutions .... E 847 398-0110
  Arlington Heights (G-810)
Sonoco Prtective Solutions Inc .... F 717 757-2683
  Chicago (G-6202)
Tri Pro Graphics LLC .... G 309 664-5875
  Bloomington (G-2104)
Volflex Inc .... E 708 478-1117
  Mokena (G-14127)
Wrap & Send Services .... E 847 329-2559
  Skokie (G-19059)
Wrapping Inc .... G 773 871-2898
  Chicago (G-6682)

PACKAGING MATERIALS: Resinous Impregnated Paper

Signode Industrial Group LLC .... E 847 724-7500
  Glenview (G-10618)
Signode Intl Holdings LLC .... F 800 648-8864
  Glenview (G-10621)

PACKAGING: Blister Or Bubble Formed, Plastic

Algus Packaging Inc .... D 815 756-1881
  Dekalb (G-7665)
Polyair Corporation .... G 773 253-1220
  Chicago (G-5837)
Rohrer Corporation .... D 847 961-5920
  Huntley (G-11564)
Tegrant Alloyd Brands Inc .... B 815 756-8451
  Dekalb (G-7708)
Wind Point Partners LP .... F 312 255-4800
  Chicago (G-6637)

PRODUCT SECTION — PAINTS & ALLIED PRODUCTS

PACKING & CRATING SVC
Atlas Putty Products Co..................D....... 708 429-5858
  Tinley Park (G-19806)
D/C Export & Domestic Pkg Inc..........E....... 847 593-4200
  Elk Grove Village (G-8935)
Smart Motion Robotics Inc...............E....... 815 895-8550
  Sycamore (G-19732)

PACKING & CRATING SVCS: Containerized Goods For Shipping
Weyerhaeuser Company....................G....... 815 987-0395
  Rockford (G-17682)

PACKING MATERIALS: Mechanical
CFC International Corporation...........C....... 708 323-4131
  Chicago Heights (G-6740)
Innovative Automation...................G....... 708 418-8720
  Lansing (G-12499)
Vangard Distribution Inc................G....... 708 484-9895
  Berwyn (G-1962)
Vangard Distribution Inc................G....... 708 588-8400
  Brookfield (G-2497)

PACKING SVCS: Shipping
Chicago Export Packing Co...............E....... 773 247-8911
  Chicago (G-4102)
Eagle Express Mail LLC..................G....... 618 377-6245
  Bethalto (G-1964)
Export Packaging Co Inc.................A....... 309 756-4288
  Milan (G-14010)
Fca LLC.................................E....... 309 792-3444
  Moline (G-14145)
Kafko International Ltd.................E....... 847 763-0333
  Skokie (G-18971)
Pierce Packaging Co.....................F....... 815 636-5650
  Loves Park (G-13245)
Pierce Packaging Co.....................G....... 815 636-5656
  Peoria (G-16497)
Pierce Packaging Co.....................G....... 815 636-5656
  Loves Park (G-13246)
Tiem Engineering Corporation............F....... 630 553-7484
  Yorkville (G-21502)

PACKING: Metallic
Union Street Tin Co.....................G....... 312 379-8200
  Park Ridge (G-16300)

PADS: Desk, Exc Paper
G & M Industries Inc....................G....... 618 344-6655
  Collinsville (G-6962)

PADS: Mattress
Innocor Foam Tech W Chcago LLC..........E....... 732 945-6222
  West Chicago (G-20598)
L & W Bedding Inc.......................G....... 309 762-6019
  Moline (G-14155)

PAGERS: One-way
Visiplex Inc............................F....... 847 229-0250
  Buffalo Grove (G-2618)

PAGING SVCS
Chicago Cardinal Communication..........F....... 708 424-1446
  Oak Lawn (G-15708)

PAILS: Plastic
North America Packaging Corp............C....... 630 845-8726
  Peotone (G-16555)

PAILS: Shipping, Metal
Arrows Up Inc...........................G....... 847 305-2550
  Arlington Heights (G-696)
Cleveland Steel Container Corp..........E....... 708 258-0700
  Peotone (G-16552)

PAINT & PAINTING SPLYS STORE
Sherwin-Williams Company................C....... 618 662-4415
  Flora (G-9691)
Tercor Inc..............................G....... 773 549-8303
  Chicago (G-6353)
Wm F Meyer Co...........................E....... 773 772-7272
  Aurora (G-1038)

PAINT STORE
PPG Architectural Finishes Inc..........G....... 309 673-3761
  Peoria (G-16500)
Sherwin-Williams Company................G....... 847 251-6115
  Kenilworth (G-12015)
Sherwin-Williams Company................G....... 847 573-0240
  Libertyville (G-12706)
Sherwin-Williams Company................G....... 815 337-0942
  Woodstock (G-21434)
Sherwin-Williams Company................G....... 847 478-0677
  Long Grove (G-13170)
Sherwin-Williams Company................G....... 708 409-4728
  Westchester (G-20710)
Sherwin-Williams Company................G....... 815 254-3559
  Romeoville (G-17876)
Sherwin-Williams Company................D....... 773 821-3027
  Chicago (G-6152)

PAINTING SVC: Metal Prdts
Drs Electrostatic Painting..............G....... 708 681-5535
  Bellwood (G-1623)
Group O Inc.............................B....... 309 736-8311
  Milan (G-14014)
Industrial Finishing Inc................F....... 847 451-4230
  Franklin Park (G-9963)
Material Sciences Corporation...........E....... 847 439-2210
  Elk Grove Village (G-9112)
Qc Finishers Inc........................E....... 847 678-2660
  Franklin Park (G-10028)
R & O Specialties Incorporated..........D....... 309 736-8660
  Milan (G-14022)
Reliable Autotech Usa LLC...............G....... 815 945-7838
  Chenoa (G-3434)
Specialty Pntg Soda Blastg Inc..........G....... 815 577-0006
  Plainfield (G-16716)
Willis Stein & Partners Manage..........F....... 312 422-2400
  Chicago (G-6632)

PAINTS & ADDITIVES
3d Printer Experience LLC...............G....... 312 896-3399
  Chicago (G-3468)
Alpha Coating Technologies LLC..........E....... 630 268-8787
  West Chicago (G-20535)
Autonomic Materials Inc.................F....... 217 863-2023
  Champaign (G-3270)
Behr Process Corporation................D....... 630 289-6247
  Bartlett (G-1269)
Behr Process Corporation................D....... 708 753-0136
  Chicago Heights (G-6734)
Behr Process Corporation................D....... 708 753-1820
  Lynwood (G-13292)
Behr Process Corporation................C....... 708 757-6350
  Chicago Heights (G-6735)
Carbit Corporation......................D....... 312 280-2300
  Chicago (G-4023)
Finishes Unlimited Inc..................F....... 630 466-4881
  Sugar Grove (G-19644)
Gibraltar Chemical Works Inc............F....... 708 333-0600
  South Holland (G-19214)
National Coatings Inc...................E....... 309 342-4184
  Galesburg (G-10213)
Sherwin-Williams Company................D....... 847 541-9000
  Wheeling (G-20983)
Sherwin-Williams Company................E....... 815 987-3700
  Rockford (G-17630)
Sherwin-Williams Company................D....... 773 821-3027
  Chicago (G-6152)
Tru Serv Corp...........................F....... 773 695-5674
  Chicago (G-6435)
True Value Company LLC..................G....... 847 639-5383
  Cary (G-3196)
True Value Company LLC..................B....... 773 695-5000
  Chicago (G-6437)
Willims-Hyward Intl Ctings Inc..........E....... 708 563-5182
  Summit Argo (G-19685)

PAINTS & ALLIED PRODUCTS
Accurate Color Compounding Inc..........E....... 630 978-1227
  Aurora (G-1041)
Acm Inc.................................G....... 847 473-1991
  North Chicago (G-15305)
Akzo Nobel Coatings Inc.................F....... 312 544-7057
  Chicago (G-3595)
Alliance Industries Inc.................F....... 847 288-9090
  Broadview (G-2416)
Ata Finishing Corp......................G....... 847 677-8560
  Skokie (G-18925)
Automatic Anodizing Corp................E....... 773 478-3304
  Chicago (G-3777)
Basement Dewatering Systems.............F....... 309 647-0331
  Canton (G-2821)
Chase Corporation.......................E....... 847 866-8500
  Evanston (G-9503)
Chase Products Co.......................D....... 708 865-1000
  Broadview (G-2425)
Chemix Corp.............................F....... 708 754-2150
  Glenwood (G-10639)
Chicago Aerosol LLC.....................D....... 708 598-7100
  Bridgeview (G-2333)
Chromium Industries Inc.................E....... 773 287-3716
  Chicago (G-4145)
Clariant Plas Coatings USA LLC..........D....... 630 562-9700
  West Chicago (G-20562)
Coatings International Inc..............E....... 847 455-1400
  Franklin Park (G-9912)
Contract Transportation Sys Co..........C....... 217 342-5757
  Effingham (G-8393)
D and R Tech............................G....... 224 353-6693
  Schaumburg (G-18503)
Dip Seal Plastics Inc...................G....... 815 398-3533
  Rockford (G-17379)
DSM Desotech Inc........................C....... 847 697-0400
  Elgin (G-8570)
Endura Paint Chicago....................G....... 815 630-5083
  Joliet (G-11861)
F H Leinweber Co Inc....................E....... 773 568-7722
  Chicago (G-4548)
Hallstar Company........................E....... 708 594-5947
  Bedford Park (G-1470)
If Walls Could Talk.....................G....... 847 219-5527
  South Elgin (G-19154)
Inhance Technologies LLC................G....... 630 231-7515
  West Chicago (G-20595)
Jet Rack Corp...........................E....... 773 586-2150
  Chicago (G-5025)
Jfb Hart Coatings Inc...................F....... 630 783-1917
  Downers Grove (G-8034)
JR Edwrds Brshes Rollers Inc............E....... 815 933-3742
  Kankakee (G-11984)
Kns Companies Inc.......................E....... 630 665-9010
  Carol Stream (G-3013)
Lawter Inc..............................E....... 312 662-5700
  Chicago (G-5185)
Mate Technologies Inc...................F....... 847 289-1010
  Elgin (G-8652)
Metro Paint Supplies....................G....... 708 385-7701
  Midlothian (G-13994)
Miller Purcell Co Inc...................G....... 815 485-2142
  New Lenox (G-15043)
Morton Salt Inc.........................C....... 312 807-2000
  Chicago (G-5501)
Nataz Specialty Coatings Inc............F....... 773 247-7030
  Chicago (G-5542)
Nfca....................................G....... 708 236-3411
  Hillside (G-11350)
Owens Corning Sales LLC.................E....... 708 594-6935
  Argo (G-675)
Penray Companies Inc....................D....... 800 323-6329
  Downers Grove (G-8071)
Plastics Color Corp Illinois............D....... 708 868-3800
  Calumet City (G-2787)
Pmc Inc.................................G....... 708 868-3800
  Calumet City (G-2788)
Polymer Nation LLC......................G....... 847 972-2157
  Waukegan (G-20479)
Polyone Corporation.....................D....... 847 364-0011
  Elk Grove Village (G-9183)
Polyone Corporation.....................D....... 630 972-0505
  Romeoville (G-17865)
Porcelain Enamel Finishers..............G....... 312 808-1560
  Chicago (G-5845)
PPG Architectural Finishes Inc..........G....... 309 673-3761
  Peoria (G-16500)
PPG Industries Inc......................G....... 847 244-3410
  Gurnee (G-10913)
PPG Industries Inc......................G....... 708 597-7044
  Alsip (G-495)
PPG Industries Inc......................E....... 847 742-3340
  Elgin (G-8693)
PPG Industries Inc......................G....... 618 206-2250
  O Fallon (G-15582)
PPG Industries Inc......................E....... 312 666-2277
  Chicago (G-5851)
PPG Industries Inc......................G....... 630 960-3600
  Westmont (G-20766)
PPG Vpn.................................G....... 630 907-8910
  Aurora (G-1145)

PAINTS & ALLIED PRODUCTS

Premium Products Inc .... F 630 553-6160
  Yorkville *(G-21498)*
Prescription Plus Ltd .... F 618 537-6202
  Lebanon *(G-12546)*
Quality Coating Co .... F 815 875-3228
  Princeton *(G-16822)*
R C Industries Inc .... F 773 378-1118
  Chicago *(G-5944)*
Rdl Marketing Inc .... G 773 254-7600
  Chicago *(G-5980)*
Reichhold Industries Inc .... G 815 942-4600
  Morris *(G-14325)*
Rust-Oleum (canada) Ltd .... B 847 367-7700
  Vernon Hills *(G-20088)*
Sandstrom Products Company .... E 309 523-2121
  Port Byron *(G-16787)*
Sandstrom Products Company .... F 309 523-2121
  Port Byron *(G-16788)*
Sherwin-Williams Company .... C 618 662-4415
  Flora *(G-9691)*
Tamms Industries Inc .... D 815 522-3394
  Kirkland *(G-12066)*
Taylor Coating Sales Inc .... G 708 387-0305
  Brookfield *(G-2494)*
Taylor Consultants Inc .... G 708 387-0305
  Brookfield *(G-2495)*
Tennant Company .... E 773 376-7132
  Chicago *(G-6350)*
Tms Manufacturing Co .... E 847 353-8000
  Alsip *(G-516)*
Universal Chem & Coatings Inc ..... E 847 297-2001
  Elk Grove Village *(G-9299)*
Valspar .... G 309 743-7133
  East Moline *(G-8245)*
Voges Inc .... D 618 233-2760
  Belleville *(G-1608)*
We Are Done LLC .... E 708 598-7100
  Bridgeview *(G-2398)*
Willims-Hyward Intl Ctings Inc .... F 708 458-0015
  Argo *(G-678)*
Yourfeel Products Corp .... G 708 596-2150
  South Holland *(G-19250)*

PAINTS & VARNISHES: Plastics Based

Nb Coatings Inc .... C 800 323-3224
  Lansing *(G-12510)*
Rust-Leum Con Prtction Systems ... E 918 446-6399
  Vernon Hills *(G-20087)*

PAINTS, VARNISHES & SPLYS WHOLESALERS

Federal Equipment & Svcs Inc .... F 847 731-9002
  Zion *(G-21514)*
Global Material Tech Inc 773 247-6000
  Chicago *(G-4696)*
PPG Architectural Finishes Inc ...... G 309 673-3761
  Peoria *(G-16500)*
Sherwin-Williams Company .... G 217 359-4934
  Savoy *(G-18416)*
Sherwin-Williams Company .... G 630 834-1470
  Elmhurst *(G-9427)*
Sherwin-Williams Company .... G 847 573-0240
  Libertyville *(G-12706)*
Sherwin-Williams Company .... G 815 337-0942
  Woodstock *(G-21434)*
Sherwin-Williams Company .... G 847 478-0677
  Long Grove *(G-13170)*
Sherwin-Williams Company .... G 708 409-4728
  Westchester *(G-20710)*
Sherwin-Williams Company .... G 815 254-3559
  Romeoville *(G-17876)*
Sherwin-Williams Company .... D 773 821-3027
  Chicago *(G-6152)*

PAINTS, VARNISHES & SPLYS, WHOLESALE: Colors & Pigments

Fortune International Tech LLC ...... G 847 429-9791
  Hoffman Estates *(G-11425)*
Southern Color Company Inc .... G 770 386-4766
  East Saint Louis *(G-8323)*

PAINTS, VARNISHES & SPLYS, WHOLESALE: Paints

Akzo Nobel Coatings Inc .... E 630 792-1619
  Lombard *(G-13038)*
Hymans Auto Supply Co .... E 773 978-8221
  Chicago *(G-4864)*

Metro Paint Supplies .... G 708 385-7701
  Midlothian *(G-13994)*
United Gilsonite Labs Inc .... E 217 243-7878
  Jacksonville *(G-11784)*
Whiting Partners LLC .... G 773 978-8221
  Chicago *(G-6620)*
Wm F Meyer Co .... E 773 772-7272
  Aurora *(G-1038)*

PAINTS: Oil Or Alkyd Vehicle Or Water Thinned

Akzo Nobel Coatings Inc .... E 630 792-1619
  Lombard *(G-13038)*
Akzo Nobel Coatings Inc .... F 847 623-4200
  Waukegan *(G-20411)*
Seymour of Sycamore Inc .... C 815 895-9101
  Sycamore *(G-19730)*
Vanex Inc .... E 618 244-1413
  Mount Vernon *(G-14643)*

PAINTS: Waterproof

Rust-Oleum Corporation .... C 847 367-7700
  Vernon Hills *(G-20089)*

PALLET REPAIR SVCS

Cardinal Pallet Co .... E 773 725-5387
  Chicago *(G-4026)*
Commercial Pallet Inc .... E 312 226-6699
  Chicago *(G-4209)*
Lake Street Pallets .... G 773 889-2266
  Chicago *(G-5162)*
Mills Pallet .... F 773 533-6458
  Chicago *(G-5462)*
Murrihy Pallet Co .... E 615 370-7000
  Chicago *(G-5528)*
Round Lake Pallets Inc .... G 847 637-6162
  Round Lake *(G-18081)*

PALLETS

3v Pallet .... G 708 333-1113
  Lansing *(G-12483)*
Amerigreen Pallets .... G 309 698-3463
  East Peoria *(G-8250)*
ASAP Pallets Inc .... G 630 917-0180
  Bellwood *(G-1614)*
Champion Wood Pallets Inc .... G 630 801-8036
  Aurora *(G-1072)*
Chicago Heights Pallets Co .... F 708 757-7641
  Chicago Heights *(G-6741)*
Corr-Pak Corporation .... E 708 442-7806
  Mc Cook *(G-13690)*
Diaz Pallets II Corporation .... G 630 340-3736
  Aurora *(G-1085)*
G & S Pallets .... G 630 574-2741
  Oak Brook *(G-15623)*
Glitter Your Pallet .... G 708 516-8494
  Homer Glen *(G-11482)*
Great Lakes Lumber and Pallet ..... G 773 243-6839
  Park Ridge *(G-16282)*
Hope Pallet Inc .... G 815 412-4606
  Rockdale *(G-17259)*
J&A Pallets Service Inc .... F 708 333-6601
  Chicago Heights *(G-6751)*
Joseph B Krisher .... G 618 677-2016
  Mascoutah *(G-13600)*
Muro Pallets Corp .... G 773 640-8606
  Chicago *(G-5527)*
Newport Pallet .... G 217 662-6577
  Georgetown *(G-10329)*
Pallet Wrapz .... F 847 729-5850
  Glenview *(G-10597)*
Pallets International Holding .... G 773 391-7223
  South Holland *(G-19236)*
Peco Pallet .... G 773 646-0976
  Chicago *(G-5779)*
R&M Pallets .... G 773 317-0574
  Crest Hill *(G-7093)*
Rock Valley Pallet Company .... G 815 654-4850
  Machesney Park *(G-13369)*

PALLETS & SKIDS: Wood

355 Pallet Service .... G 773 431-6688
  Addison *(G-12)*
Aldon Co .... F 847 623-8800
  Waukegan *(G-20412)*
Commercial Pallet Inc .... E 312 226-6699
  Chicago *(G-4209)*

PRODUCT SECTION

Community Support Systems .... D 217 705-4300
  Teutopolis *(G-19767)*
Comwell .... D 618 282-6233
  Red Bud *(G-16991)*
Fca LLC .... E 309 385-2588
  Princeville *(G-16827)*
Fulton County Rehabilitation .... E 309 647-6510
  Canton *(G-2826)*
Hammer Enterprises Inc .... F 217 662-8225
  Georgetown *(G-10328)*
J & J Quality Pallets Inc .... G 618 262-6426
  Mount Carmel *(G-14474)*
Lake Street Pallets .... G 773 889-2266
  Chicago *(G-5162)*
Lottus Inc .... G 847 691-9464
  Glenview *(G-10585)*
Mental Health Ctrs Centl Ill .... D 217 735-1413
  Lincoln *(G-12735)*
Northwest Pallet Services LLC ..... A 815 544-6001
  Belvidere *(G-1691)*
Pak Source Inc .... E 309 786-7374
  Rock Island *(G-17231)*
Prime Wood Craft Inc .... G 716 803-3425
  Schaumburg *(G-18684)*
R & H Products Inc .... G 815 744-4110
  Rockdale *(G-17270)*
R & R Services Illinois Inc .... G 217 424-2602
  Decatur *(G-7538)*
Simonton Hardwood Lumber LLC .. F 618 594-2132
  Carlyle *(G-2896)*
Trade Industries .... E 618 643-4321
  Mc Leansboro *(G-13709)*
Twin City Wood Recycling Corp .... G 309 827-9663
  Bloomington *(G-2106)*
Universal Pallet Inc .... G 815 928-8546
  Bradley *(G-2295)*

PALLETS: Metal

Chicago Pallet Service Inc .... E 847 439-8330
  Maywood *(G-13666)*
Marcells Pallet Inc .... G 773 265-1200
  Chicago *(G-5329)*
Midaco Corporation .... E 847 593-8420
  Elk Grove Village *(G-9123)*

PALLETS: Plastic

Chem-Tainer Industries Inc .... G 630 932-7778
  Lombard *(G-13050)*
Fuji Yusoki Kogyo Co Ltd .... G 425 522-0722
  Elk Grove Village *(G-9007)*
Greif Inc .... E 815 935-7575
  Bradley *(G-2283)*
Illinois Tool Works Inc .... E 630 773-9300
  Itasca *(G-11671)*
Plastipak Packaging Inc .... B 217 398-1832
  Champaign *(G-3334)*
Plastipak Packaging Inc .... C 708 385-0721
  Alsip *(G-493)*

PALLETS: Solid Fiber, Made From Purchased Materials

Wehrle Lumber Co Inc .... F 618 283-4859
  Vandalia *(G-20030)*

PALLETS: Wood & Metal Combination

Dexton Enterprises .... G 309 788-1881
  Rock Island *(G-17217)*

PALLETS: Wooden

3v Pallet .... G 708 620-7790
  South Holland *(G-19185)*
815 Pallets Inc .... E 815 678-0012
  Richmond *(G-17006)*
A & F Pallet Service Inc .... F 773 767-9500
  Chicago *(G-3482)*
AA Pallet Inc .... E 773 536-3699
  Chicago *(G-3496)*
ADP Pallet Inc .... F 773 638-3800
  Chicago *(G-3551)*
Advance Pallet Incorporated .... E 847 697-5700
  South Elgin *(G-19128)*
AGCO Recycling LLC .... F 217 224-9048
  Quincy *(G-16851)*
All Pallet Service .... G 618 451-7545
  Granite City *(G-10693)*
American Pallet Co Inc .... D 847 662-5525
  Waukegan *(G-20415)*

PANELS: Building, Wood

American Pallet Industries Inc............F...... 815 678-0680
  Richmond (G-17008)
Arrowtech Pallet & Crating ....D...... 815 547-9300
  Belvidere (G-1650)
ASAP Pallets Inc..............................G...... 630 350-7689
  Franklin Park (G-9875)
Ash Pallet Management Inc.............D...... 847 473-5700
  Antioch (G-601)
Bach Timber & Pallet Inc..................G...... 815 885-3774
  Caledonia (G-2768)
Best Pallet Company LLC..................F...... 815 637-1500
  Loves Park (G-13194)
Best Pallet Company LLC..................F...... 312 242-4009
  Chicago (G-3873)
Botkin Lumber Company Inc............E...... 217 287-2127
  Taylorville (G-19751)
Brothers Pallets Co..........................G...... 773 306-2695
  Chicago (G-3966)
Buckeye Diamond Logistics Inc........G...... 630 236-1174
  Aurora (G-928)
Cardinal Pallet Co............................E...... 773 725-5387
  Chicago (G-4026)
Central States Pallets......................G...... 217 494-2710
  Chatham (G-3418)
Central Wood Products Inc...............E...... 217 728-4412
  Sullivan (G-19664)
Chicago Pallet Service Inc................E...... 847 439-8754
  Elk Grove Village (G-8892)
Chicago Pallet Service II Inc.............E...... 847 439-8330
  Elk Grove Village (G-8893)
City Wide Pallet...............................G...... 773 891-2561
  Chicago (G-4163)
Cole Pallet Services Corp.................E...... 815 758-3226
  Dekalb (G-7668)
Corsaw Hardwood Lumber Inc.........F...... 309 293-2055
  Smithfield (G-19063)
Craft Pallet Inc.................................G...... 618 437-5382
  INA (G-11575)
Crate and Pallet Packg Co LLC.......E...... 217 679-2681
  Springfield (G-19355)
Crossroad Crating & Pallet..............G...... 815 657-8409
  Forrest (G-9732)
Crystal Lake Pallets........................G...... 815 526-3637
  Crystal Lake (G-7188)
D & G Pallet Service Inc..................F...... 773 265-8470
  Chicago (G-4296)
D and D Pallets................................F...... 630 800-1102
  Aurora (G-1082)
Darios Pallets Corp..........................E...... 312 421-3413
  Chicago (G-4318)
Dg Wood Processing.........................F...... 217 543-2128
  Arthur (G-852)
Direct Pallet Inc...............................E...... 847 697-1019
  Elgin (G-8566)
Dixon Pallet Service.........................G...... 773 238-9569
  Chicago (G-4370)
Eam Pallets......................................G...... 708 333-0596
  Harvey (G-11082)
Earthwise Recycled Pallet................G...... 618 286-6015
  Dupo (G-8136)
Edgar Pallets...................................G...... 773 454-8919
  Chicago (G-4450)
Edison Pallet & Wood Products........G...... 630 653-3416
  Winfield (G-21110)
Eds Pallet Services Inc.....................F...... 618 248-5386
  Albers (G-344)
Enterprise Pallet Inc........................F...... 815 928-8546
  Bourbonnais (G-2260)
Equustock LLC..................................F...... 866 962-4686
  Loves Park (G-13210)
Export Packaging Co Inc..................A...... 309 756-4288
  Milan (G-14010)
F and L Pallets Inc...........................G...... 773 364-0798
  Chicago (G-4547)
Fca LLC..G...... 309 792-3444
  Moline (G-14145)
Four Season Pallets Inc...................G...... 708 940-5545
  Harvey (G-11085)
General Pallet..................................G...... 773 660-8550
  Chicago (G-4676)
Georgetown Wood and Pallet Co.....E...... 217 662-2563
  Georgetown (G-10327)
Graphic Pallet & Transport..............E...... 630 904-4951
  Plainfield (G-16669)
Great Lakes Lbr & Pallet Inc...........G...... 773 243-6839
  Chicago (G-4736)
Gueros Pallets Inc............................G...... 312 523-5561
  Chicago (G-4748)
Hardwood Lumber Products Co.......G...... 309 538-4411
  Kilbourne (G-12044)

Hart - Clayton Inc.............................F...... 217 525-1610
  Springfield (G-19378)
Harvey Pallets Inc...........................C...... 708 293-1831
  Blue Island (G-2125)
Hill Top Pallet..................................G...... 618 426-9810
  Ava (G-1172)
HMM Pallets Inc..............................G...... 773 927-3448
  Chicago Heights (G-6749)
Ht Lumber & Crates Inc..................F...... 847 683-0200
  Hampshire (G-10973)
Ifco...G...... 630 226-0650
  Bolingbrook (G-2188)
Illinois Pallets Inc...........................G...... 773 640-9228
  Willow Springs (G-21026)
Industrial Pallets LLC......................G...... 708 351-8783
  Glendale Heights (G-10461)
Jjm Products LLC.............................G...... 630 319-9325
  Westmont (G-20750)
Jose Pallets....................................G...... 773 376-8320
  Chicago (G-5052)
Kccdd Inc...D...... 309 344-2030
  Galesburg (G-10205)
Kirk Wood Products Inc...................E...... 309 829-6661
  Bloomington (G-2068)
Kirkwood Crates LLC.......................G...... 651 373-5945
  Kirkwood (G-12067)
Kryder Wood Products LLC..............F...... 815 494-1208
  Rockford (G-17486)
Lakeland Pallets Inc........................G...... 616 949-9515
  Geneva (G-10288)
Los Primos Pallets Inc.....................G...... 773 418-3584
  Chicago (G-5263)
M & M Paltech Inc...........................D...... 630 350-7890
  Belvidere (G-1681)
M and M Pallet Inc..........................G...... 708 272-4447
  Blue Island (G-2130)
Malvaes Solutions Incorporated......G...... 773 823-1034
  Chicago (G-5324)
McKean Pallet Co............................G...... 309 246-7543
  Lacon (G-12130)
Midland Wood Products...................G...... 618 344-5640
  Collinsville (G-6970)
Mills Pallet......................................F...... 773 533-6458
  Chicago (G-5462)
Millwood Inc.....................................F...... 708 343-7341
  Melrose Park (G-13893)
Mobile Pallet Service Inc.................F...... 630 231-6597
  West Chicago (G-20620)
Momence Pallet Corporation...........E...... 815 472-6451
  Momence (G-14189)
Morris Pallet Skids Inc.....................F...... 618 786-2241
  Dow (G-7946)
Murrihy Pallet Co............................G...... 615 370-7000
  Chicago (G-5528)
Nefab Packaging N Centl LLC.........C...... 630 451-5314
  Hanover Park (G-11010)
Northern Illinois Pallet Inc..............G...... 815 236-9242
  Fox Lake (G-9749)
Northern Pallet and Supply Co........G...... 847 716-1400
  Northfield (G-15524)
One Way Solutions LLC....................G...... 847 446-0872
  Northfield (G-15526)
Pallet Sales and Recycling...............F...... 314 452-5175
  Venice (G-20035)
Pallet Services Inc...........................G...... 630 860-9233
  Bensenville (G-1866)
Pallet Solution................................G...... 773 837-8677
  Streamwood (G-19588)
Pallet Solution Inc...........................E...... 618 445-2316
  Albion (G-351)
Pallet Wrapz Inc..............................G...... 847 729-5850
  Glenview (G-10598)
Palletmaxx Inc.................................G...... 708 385-9595
  Crestwood (G-7124)
Pallets Plus Inc................................G...... 847 318-1853
  Park Ridge (G-16291)
Piece Works Specialists Inc.............F...... 309 266-7016
  Morton (G-14378)
Premium Pallets...............................G...... 217 974-0155
  Springfield (G-19427)
Prime Wood Craft Inc......................E...... 216 738-2222
  Schaumburg (G-18683)
Quality Pallets Inc...........................E...... 217 459-2655
  Windsor (G-21107)
R K J Pallets Inc..............................F...... 708 493-0701
  Bellwood (G-1636)
Rapid Pallets Inc..............................F...... 708 259-4016
  Chicago (G-5974)
Rapid Pallets Inc..............................E...... 708 424-2306
  Bridgeview (G-2378)

Rbj Inc...F...... 309 344-5066
  Galesburg (G-10217)
Robbins Resource MGT Inc..............E...... 309 734-8817
  Monmouth (G-14226)
Rose Pallet LLC...............................G...... 708 333-3000
  Bridgeview (G-2384)
Round Lake Pallets Inc....................G...... 847 637-6162
  Round Lake (G-18081)
RPI Business Co Inc.........................G...... 773 254-7095
  Chicago (G-6070)
S & S Pallet Corp.............................E...... 618 219-3218
  Granite City (G-10735)
Schroeders Pallet Service Inc.........F...... 708 371-9046
  Blue Island (G-2139)
Service Pallet LLC..........................G...... 708 458-9100
  North Aurora (G-15274)
Singleton Pallets Co........................G...... 708 687-7006
  Oak Forest (G-15688)
Sterling Site Access Sol..................C...... 708 388-2223
  Phoenix (G-16609)
Steve Forrest..................................F...... 815 765-9040
  Poplar Grove (G-16784)
Timber Creek Pallets.......................G...... 217 268-3062
  Arcola (G-668)
Timberline Pallet & Skid Inc............F...... 309 752-1770
  East Moline (G-8243)
Try Our Pallets Inc..........................G...... 708 343-0166
  Maywood (G-13679)
US Pallett Supply Inc......................E...... 618 243-6449
  Okawville (G-15848)
Vg Pallet Inc....................................G...... 815 527-5344
  Woodstock (G-21444)
Walnut Grove Packaging..................G...... 217 268-5112
  Arcola (G-669)
Wil Son Pallet..................................E...... 217 543-3555
  Sullivan (G-19675)
Workshop Ltd Inc.............................G...... 708 458-3222
  Bedford Park (G-1514)

PANEL & DISTRIBUTION BOARDS & OTHER RELATED APPARATUS

Agnes & Chris Gulik.........................G...... 847 931-9641
  Elgin (G-8499)
Marshall Electric Inc........................F...... 618 382-3932
  Carmi (G-2910)
Midwest Control Corp......................F...... 708 599-1331
  Bridgeview (G-2365)

PANEL & DISTRIBUTION BOARDS: Electric

AKD Controls Inc..............................G...... 815 633-4586
  Machesney Park (G-13324)
G & F Manufacturing Co Inc............E...... 708 424-4170
  Oak Lawn (G-15716)
General Electric Company................C...... 309 664-1513
  Bloomington (G-2050)
Industrial Electric Svc Inc................G...... 708 997-2090
  Bartlett (G-1289)
Kinney Electrical Mfg Co..................D...... 847 742-9600
  Elgin (G-8636)
Marshall Wolf Automation Inc.........E...... 847 658-8130
  Algonquin (G-378)

PANELS, CORRUGATED: Plastic

Andrews Automotive Company.........F...... 773 768-1122
  Chicago (G-3693)

PANELS, FLAT: Plastic

Sek Corporation...............................E...... 630 762-0606
  Saint Charles (G-18268)

PANELS: Building, Plastic, NEC

Crane Composites Inc.....................B...... 815 467-8600
  Channahon (G-3376)
Crane Composites Inc.....................D...... 630 378-9580
  Bolingbrook (G-2159)
Crane Composites Inc.....................C...... 815 467-1437
  Channahon (G-3377)

PANELS: Building, Wood

McDonnell Components Inc..............D...... 815 547-9555
  Belvidere (G-1685)
R & N Components Co.....................G...... 217 543-3495
  Tuscola (G-19930)

PANELS: Control & Metering, Generator

A C Gentrol Inc .... E 309 274-5486
 Chillicothe *(G-6812)*
Simplex Inc .... C 217 483-1600
 Springfield *(G-19446)*

PANELS: Wood

Klaman Hardwood .... G 217 972-7888
 Decatur *(G-7514)*
R-Squared Construction Inc .... G 815 232-7433
 Freeport *(G-10135)*
Walnut Creek Hardwood .... G 815 389-3317
 South Beloit *(G-19120)*

PAPER & BOARD: Die-cut

11th Street Express Prtg Inc .... F 815 968-0208
 Rockford *(G-17275)*
Ade Inc .... E 773 646-3400
 Chicago *(G-3541)*
Andrews Converting LLC .... E 708 352-2555
 La Grange *(G-12072)*
Animated Advg Techniques Inc .... G 312 372-4694
 Chicago *(G-3698)*
B Allan Graphics Inc .... F 708 396-1704
 Alsip *(G-420)*
Business Forms Finishing Svc .... G 773 229-0230
 Chicago *(G-3979)*
Butler Bros Steel Rule Die Co .... G 815 630-4629
 Shorewood *(G-18894)*
Carson Printing Inc .... G 847 836-0900
 East Dundee *(G-8189)*
Creative Label Inc .... D 847 956-6960
 Elk Grove Village *(G-8919)*
Deco Adhesive Pdts 1985 Ltd .... E 847 472-2100
 Elk Grove Village *(G-8941)*
Delta Press Inc .... E 847 671-3200
 Palatine *(G-16111)*
Gpi Midwest LLC .... E 847 741-0247
 Elgin *(G-8599)*
Impression Printing .... F 708 614-8660
 Oak Forest *(G-15682)*
Lee-Wel Printing Corporation .... G 630 682-0935
 Wheaton *(G-20812)*
M S A Printing Co .... G 847 593-5699
 Elk Grove Village *(G-9103)*
M Wells Printing Co .... G 312 455-0400
 Chicago *(G-5305)*
McGrath Press Inc .... E 815 356-5246
 Crystal Lake *(G-7224)*
Midwest Cortland Inc .... E 847 671-0376
 Addison *(G-209)*
Midwest Index Inc .... D 847 995-8425
 Addison *(G-210)*
Plastics Printing Group Inc .... F 773 473-4481
 Chicago *(G-5820)*
Potomac Corporation .... C 847 259-0546
 Wheeling *(G-20962)*
Precision Die Cutting & Finish .... G 773 252-5625
 Chicago *(G-5856)*
Pry-Bar Company .... F 815 436-3383
 Joliet *(G-11918)*
Racine Paper Box Manufacturing .... E 773 227-3900
 Chicago *(G-5958)*
Rapid Displays Inc .... C 773 927-5000
 Chicago *(G-5971)*
Review Printing Co Inc .... G 309 788-7094
 Rock Island *(G-17241)*
Rhopac Fabricated Products LLC .... E 847 362-3300
 Libertyville *(G-12702)*
Rohrer Corporation .... D 847 961-5920
 Huntley *(G-11564)*
Ross-Gage Inc .... E 708 347-3659
 Homewood *(G-11502)*
RTS Packaging LLC .... C 708 338-2800
 Hillside *(G-11355)*
Sales Midwest Prtg & Packg Inc .... G 309 764-5544
 Moline *(G-14175)*
Stevenson Paper Co Inc .... G 630 879-5000
 Batavia *(G-1419)*
Village Press Inc .... G 847 362-1856
 Libertyville *(G-12724)*
Weber Marking Systems Inc .... B 847 364-8500
 Arlington Heights *(G-831)*
Young Shin USA Limited .... G 847 598-3611
 Schaumburg *(G-18779)*

PAPER & ENVELOPES: Writing, Made From Purchased Materials

Dove Foundation .... G 312 217-3683
 Chicago *(G-4390)*

PAPER CONVERTING

All Weather Products Co LLC .... F 847 981-0386
 Elk Grove Village *(G-8814)*
Ar-En Party Printers Inc .... E 847 673-7390
 Skokie *(G-18923)*
Corydon Converting Company Inc ...... F 630 898-9896
 Naperville *(G-14809)*
Corydon Converting Company Inc ...... E 630 983-1900
 Aurora *(G-1081)*
Dietzgen Corporation .... F 217 348-8111
 Charleston *(G-3401)*
Gro-Mar Industries Inc .... F 708 343-5901
 Melrose Park *(G-13876)*
I M M Inc .... F 773 767-3700
 Chicago *(G-4866)*
Lewis Paper Place Inc .... G 847 808-1343
 Wheeling *(G-20932)*
Norwood Industries Inc .... F 773 788-1508
 Chicago *(G-5629)*
RTS Packaging LLC .... C 708 338-2800
 Hillside *(G-11355)*
Seabee Supply Co .... G 630 860-1293
 Wood Dale *(G-21239)*
Signode Industrial Group LLC .... E 815 939-0033
 Kankakee *(G-12003)*
Signode Industrial Group LLC .... E 708 371-9050
 Blue Island *(G-2140)*
Trimaco LLC .... E 919 674-3476
 Elk Grove Village *(G-9286)*

PAPER MANUFACTURERS: Exc Newsprint

Alsip Minimill LLC .... E 708 625-0098
 Alsip *(G-414)*
Amcor Flexibles LLC .... C 224 313-7000
 Buffalo Grove *(G-2510)*
Boise White Paper LLC .... F 847 482-3000
 Lake Forest *(G-12232)*
Boise White Paper LLC .... F 208 805-1424
 Lake Forest *(G-12233)*
Colorkraft Roll Products Inc .... E 217 382-4967
 Martinsville *(G-13582)*
Danco Converting .... G 630 949-8112
 Carol Stream *(G-2972)*
Georgia-Pacific LLC .... G 815 423-9990
 Elwood *(G-9463)*
Hollingsworth & Vose Company .... G 847 222-9228
 Arlington Heights *(G-750)*
Illinois Tool Works Inc .... G 847 657-4639
 Glenview *(G-10561)*
International Paper Company .... F 618 233-5460
 Belleville *(G-1558)*
International Paper Company .... C 815 398-2100
 Rockford *(G-17469)*
International Paper Company .... F 630 449-7200
 Aurora *(G-985)*
International Paper Company .... F 630 653-3500
 Carol Stream *(G-3005)*
International Paper Company .... E 847 390-1300
 Des Plaines *(G-7788)*
International Paper Company .... C 847 228-7227
 Elk Grove Village *(G-9057)*
International Paper Company .... G 630 585-3400
 Aurora *(G-987)*
International Paper Company .... G 630 250-1300
 Itasca *(G-11677)*
Kdm Enterprises LLC .... E 877 591-9768
 Carpentersville *(G-3106)*
ND Paper Inc .... G 513 200-0908
 Oakbrook Terrace *(G-15811)*
ND Paper LLC .... F 937 528-3870
 Oakbrook Terrace *(G-15812)*
Packaging Corporation America .... G 224 404-6616
 Elk Grove Village *(G-9168)*
Pactiv Intl Holdings Inc .... G 847 482-2000
 Lake Forest *(G-12278)*
Paper Investments LLC .... G 309 686-3830
 Peoria *(G-16491)*
Paper Machine Services Inc .... G 608 365-8095
 South Beloit *(G-19106)*
Pontiac Recyclers Inc .... G 815 844-6419
 Pontiac *(G-16777)*
Roll Source Paper .... G 630 875-0308
 Itasca *(G-11728)*
Tst/Impreso Inc .... G 630 775-9555
 Addison *(G-320)*
Upm-Kymmene Inc .... D 630 922-2500
 Naperville *(G-14938)*
Westrock Cp LLC .... G 847 625-8284
 Waukegan *(G-20518)*
Weyerhaeuser Company .... G 815 987-0395
 Rockford *(G-17682)*

PAPER NAPKINS WHOLESALERS

Welch Packaging Group Inc .... E 815 547-1505
 Belvidere *(G-1710)*

PAPER PRDTS

Identco West LLC .... G 815 385-0011
 Ingleside *(G-11585)*
K & N Laboratories Inc .... F 708 482-3240
 La Grange *(G-12081)*

PAPER PRDTS: Feminine Hygiene Prdts

Barrington Company .... G 815 933-3233
 Bradley *(G-2276)*
Johnson & Johnson .... G 847 640-5400
 Elk Grove Village *(G-9069)*
Sonoco Prtective Solutions Inc .... E 708 946-3244
 Beecher *(G-1521)*

PAPER PRDTS: Infant & Baby Prdts

Kimberly-Clark Corporation .... D 312 371-5166
 Deerfield *(G-7626)*
Kimberly-Clark Corporation .... C 815 886-7872
 Romeoville *(G-17838)*
Kimberly-Clark Corporation .... G 847 885-1050
 Chicago *(G-5103)*
Kimberly-Clark Corporation .... E 708 409-8500
 Northlake *(G-15550)*

PAPER PRDTS: Pressed & Molded Pulp & Fiber Prdts

Pactiv LLC .... C 217 479-1144
 Jacksonville *(G-11779)*

PAPER PRDTS: Sanitary

Dude Products Inc .... G 800 898-7304
 Chicago *(G-4401)*
Procter & Gamble Co .... G 847 936-4621
 North Chicago *(G-15319)*
Wells Janitorial Service Inc .... G 872 226-9983
 Chicago *(G-6600)*

PAPER PRDTS: Sanitary Tissue Paper

Dude Products Inc .... G 800 898-7304
 Chicago *(G-4401)*
Kimberly-Clark Corporation .... D 312 371-5166
 Deerfield *(G-7626)*
Kimberly-Clark Corporation .... C 815 886-7872
 Romeoville *(G-17838)*
Kimberly-Clark Corporation .... G 847 885-1050
 Chicago *(G-5103)*
Kimberly-Clark Corporation .... E 708 409-8500
 Northlake *(G-15550)*

PAPER PRDTS: Towels, Napkins/Tissue Paper, From Purchd Mtrls

EPS Solutions Incorporated .... A 815 206-0868
 Woodstock *(G-21386)*
Evergreen Manufacturing Inc .... E 217 382-5108
 Martinsville *(G-13584)*
Procter & Gamble Company .... G 847 375-5400
 Chicago *(G-5892)*

PAPER PRDTS: Wrappers, Blank, Made From Purchased Materials

Pap-R Products Company .... D 800 637-4937
 Martinsville *(G-13587)*

PAPER, WHOLESALE: Fine

Graphic Chemical & Ink Co .... F 630 832-6004
 Villa Park *(G-20149)*

PRODUCT SECTION

PAPER, WHOLESALE: Printing

Allprint Inc .... G 847 726-0658
  Hawthorn Woods (G-11121)
CIS Systems Inc 847 827-0747
  Glenview (G-10537)
Midland Paper Company .... C 847 777-2700
  Wheeling (G-20941)
Proofing Technologies Ltd .... G 847 222-7100
  Rolling Meadows (G-17768)

PAPER, WHOLESALE: Writing

Roll Source Paper .... G 630 875-0308
  Itasca (G-11728)

PAPER: Absorbent

Evolution Sorbent Products LLC ...... G 630 293-8055
  West Chicago (G-20578)
Evolution Sorbent Products LLC ...... F 630 293-8055
  West Chicago (G-20579)

PAPER: Adhesive

Acco Brands Corporation .... A 847 541-9500
  Lake Zurich (G-12374)
Acco Brands International Inc 847 541-9500
  Lake Zurich (G-12375)
Chase Corporation .... E 847 866-8500
  Evanston (G-9503)
Citadel Specialty Products Inc .... G 630 820-4134
  Aurora (G-939)
H S Crocker Company Inc .... D 847 669-3600
  Huntley (G-11538)
Holden Industries Inc .... F 847 940-1500
  Deerfield (G-7616)
Nosco Inc .... D 847 360-4874
  Waukegan (G-20471)
Primedia Source LLC .... G 630 553-8451
  Yorkville (G-21499)
Punch Products Manufacturing ...... E 773 533-2800
  Chicago (G-5915)
Service Packaging Design Inc .... G 847 966-6592
  Morton Grove (G-14440)
Zebra Technologies Corporation .... B 847 634-6700
  Lincolnshire (G-12804)
Zih Corp .... G 847 634-6700
  Lincolnshire (G-12807)

PAPER: Book

Transpac Usa Inc 847 605-1616
  Schaumburg (G-18752)

PAPER: Business Form

Advantage Printing Inc .... G 630 627-7468
  Lombard (G-13036)
Essentra Packaging US Inc .... G 704 418-8692
  Westchester (G-20699)

PAPER: Carbon

Shoppers Planet .... F 877 232-5435
  Olympia Fields (G-15898)

PAPER: Cardboard

Campus Cardboard .... G 847 373-7673
  Northbrook (G-15351)
Campus Cardboard .... G 847 251-2594
  Skokie (G-18936)
Jsc Products Inc .... G 847 290-9520
  Elk Grove Village (G-9071)
Unofficial Cardboard Inc .... G 224 565-5391
  Deerfield (G-7655)

PAPER: Catalog

Master Mechanic Mfg Inc .... G 847 573-3812
  Mundelein (G-14714)

PAPER: Chemically Treated, Made From Purchased Materials

Channeled Resources Inc .... E 312 733-4200
  Chicago (G-4069)
Daubert Vci Inc .... F 630 203-6800
  Burr Ridge (G-2668)

PAPER: Cigarette

Essentra Corp .... G 814 899-7671
  Westchester (G-20697)

PAPER: Coated & Laminated, NEC

Advanced Web Technologies LLC ... E 847 985-3833
  South Elgin (G-19129)
American Name Plate & Metal De .. E 773 376-1400
  Chicago (G-3663)
Arcadia Press Inc .... F 847 451-6390
  Franklin Park (G-9872)
Avery Dennison Corporation .... D 877 214-0909
  Niles (G-15104)
Avery Dennison Rfid Company ...... F 626 304-2000
  Chicago (G-3786)
Basswood Associates Inc .... F 312 240-9400
  Chicago (G-3845)
Bisco Intl Inc 708 544-6308
  Hillside (G-11331)
Brasel Products Inc .... G 630 879-3759
  Batavia (G-1360)
Classique Signs & Engrv Inc .... G 217 228-7446
  Quincy (G-16872)
Condor Labels Inc .... G 708 429-0707
  Palos Park (G-16209)
Cushing and Company .... E 312 266-8228
  Chicago (G-4287)
Fedex Office & Print Svcs Inc .... F 847 329-9464
  Lincolnwood (G-12819)
Fedex Office & Print Svcs Inc .... E 309 685-4093
  Peoria (G-16437)
Gallas Label & Decal .... F 773 775-1000
  Chicago (G-4656)
General Laminating Company .... G 847 639-8770
  Cary (G-3164)
Highland Supply Corporation .... B 618 654-2161
  Highland (G-11224)
Hollymatic Corporation .... D 708 579-3700
  Countryside (G-7057)
Hugh Courtright & Co Ltd .... F 708 534-8400
  Monee (G-14202)
Identco International Corp .... D 815 385-0011
  Ingleside (G-11584)
J & D Instant Signs 847 965-2800
  Morton Grove (G-14414)
Keneal Industries Inc .... F 815 886-1300
  Romeoville (G-17837)
Knight Prtg & Litho Svc Ltd 847 487-7700
  Island Lake (G-11609)
Label Tek Inc .... F 630 820-8499
  Aurora (G-995)
Lasons Label Co .... G 773 775-2606
  Chicago (G-5179)
Line Craft Inc .... F 630 932-1182
  Lombard (G-13095)
M & R Graphics Inc .... F 708 534-6621
  University Park (G-19957)
Mich Enterprises Inc .... F 630 616-9000
  Wood Dale (G-21216)
Midwest Lminating Coatings Inc ... E 708 653-9500
  Alsip (G-478)
National Data-Label Corp .... E 630 616-9595
  Bensenville (G-1856)
Noor International Inc .... G 847 985-2300
  Bartlett (G-1256)
Pioneer Labels Inc .... C 618 546-5418
  Robinson (G-17121)
Plitek LLC .... D 847 827-6680
  Des Plaines (G-7827)
Preferred Printing Service .... G 312 421-2343
  Chicago (G-5861)
Printing Etc Inc .... G 815 562-6151
  Rochelle (G-17152)
Protex Products LLC 312 292-1310
  Chicago (G-5906)
Qualified Innovation Inc .... F 630 556-4136
  Sugar Grove (G-19651)
Sheer Graphics Inc .... G 630 654-4422
  Westmont (G-20772)
Signature Label of Illinois .... G 618 283-5145
  Vandalia (G-20024)
Signcraft Screenprint Inc .... C 815 777-3030
  Galena (G-10178)
Stephen Fossler Company .... D 847 635-7200
  Des Plaines (G-7852)
Upm Raflatac Inc .... C 815 285-6100
  Dixon (G-7924)
Voss Belting & Specialty Co .... E 847 673-8900
  Lincolnwood (G-12849)

PAPER: Wallpaper

William Holloway Ltd .... G 847 866-9520
  Evanston (G-9588)

PAPER: Coated, Exc Photographic, Carbon Or Abrasive

Avery Dennison Corporation .... C 847 824-7450
  Mount Prospect (G-14513)

PAPER: Filter

Ahlstrm-Munksjo Filtration LLC ..... D 217 824-9611
  Taylorville (G-19748)
Bunn-O-Matic Corporation .... E 562 926-0764
  Springfield (G-19332)

PAPER: Gift Wrap

Found Inc .... G 773 279-3000
  Chicago (G-4624)
Mudlark Papers Inc .... E 630 717-7616
  Naperville (G-14876)

PAPER: Insulation Siding

Meyer Enterprises LLC .... G 309 698-0062
  East Peoria (G-8278)

PAPER: Kraft

Westrock Rkt LLC .... A 312 346-6600
  Chicago (G-6614)

PAPER: Lithograph

Voyager Enterprise Inc .... G 815 436-2431
  Plainfield (G-16727)

PAPER: Newsprint

Westrock Cp LLC .... D 312 346-6600
  Chicago (G-6611)

PAPER: Packaging

Deines-Nitz Solutions LLC .... E 309 658-9985
  Erie (G-9472)
Kapstone Kraft Paper Corp .... F 252 533-6000
  Northbrook (G-15411)
Matt Pak Inc .... D 847 451-4018
  Franklin Park (G-9985)
Midland Paper Company .... C 847 777-2700
  Wheeling (G-20941)
Simu Ltd .... F 708 688-2200
  Mc Cook (G-13701)

PAPER: Printer

Brahman Spirit Tribe .... F 773 957-2828
  Chicago (G-3942)
Frankenstitch Promotions LLC ...... F 847 459-4840
  Wheeling (G-20901)
International Paper Company .... C 217 735-1221
  Lincoln (G-12731)
K C Printing Services Inc .... F 847 382-8822
  Lake Barrington (G-12156)
Lambert Print Source Llc .... G 630 708-0505
  Yorkville (G-21491)
Mii Inc .... F 630 879-3000
  Batavia (G-1395)
Proofing Technologies Ltd .... G 847 222-7100
  Rolling Meadows (G-17768)

PAPER: Specialty

IVEX Specialty Paper LLC .... E 309 686-3830
  Peoria (G-16461)
Midwest Converting Inc .... D 708 924-1510
  Bedford Park (G-1483)

PAPER: Tissue

Amic Global Inc .... G 847 600-3590
  Buffalo Grove (G-2512)

PAPER: Wallpaper

Brothers Decorating .... G 815 648-2214
  Hebron (G-11139)
Chartwell Studio Inc .... G 847 868-8674
  Chicago (G-4077)
Cowtan and Tout Inc .... F 312 644-0717
  Chicago (G-4251)

PAPER: Waxed, Made From Purchased Materials

Waxstar Inc .... G 708 755-3530
S Chicago Hts (G-18129)

PAPER: Wrapping & Packaging

Ripa LLC .... G 708 938-1600
Broadview (G-2464)
S and K Packaging Incorporated ...... G 563 582-8895
East Dubuque (G-8181)
W/S Packaging Group Inc .... G 847 658-7363
Algonquin (G-393)

PAPER: Writing

Cellmark Inc .... G 630 775-9500
Bloomingdale (G-1984)
Pen At Hand .... G 847 498-9174
Northbrook (G-15458)

PAPERBOARD

Armbrust Paper Tubes Inc .... E 773 586-3232
Chicago (G-3730)
Capitol Carton Company .... E 312 563-9690
Chicago (G-4017)
Caraustar Industries Inc .... E 773 308-7622
Chicago (G-4022)
Grafcor Packaging Inc .... F 815 639-2380
Loves Park (G-13215)
Logan Graphic Products Inc .... D 847 526-5515
Wauconda (G-20369)
Mac American Corporation .... G 847 277-9450
Barrington (G-1226)
Midwest Cortland Inc .... E 847 671-0376
Addison (G-209)
PCA Central Cal Corrugated LLC ... G 847 482-3000
Lake Forest (G-12283)
Pekin Paperboard Company LP ..... E 309 346-4118
Pekin (G-16352)
RTS Packaging LLC .... C 708 338-2800
Hillside (G-11355)
Signode Industrial Group LLC .... E 815 939-0033
Kankakee (G-12003)
Sonoco Products Company .... D 630 231-1489
West Chicago (G-20644)
Stevenson Paper Co Inc .... G 630 879-5000
Batavia (G-1419)
Tegrant Corporation .... G 630 879-0121
Batavia (G-1428)
The Calumet Carton Company ..... D 708 331-7910
South Holland (G-19249)
TMC Services Inc .... G 217 528-2297
Springfield (G-19465)
Westrock Converting LLC .... E 630 783-6700
Bolingbrook (G-2254)
Westrock Cp LLC .... D 630 443-3538
Saint Charles (G-18299)
Westrock Cp LLC .... E 630 924-0104
Bartlett (G-1260)
Westrock Cp LLC .... G 847 625-8284
Waukegan (G-20518)
Westrock Cp LLC .... D 708 458-5288
Bedford Park (G-1513)
Westrock Cp LLC .... C 309 342-0121
Galesburg (G-10224)
Westrock CP LLC .... G 773 264-3516
Chicago (G-6612)

PAPERBOARD CONVERTING

Crescent Cardboard Company LLC .... C 888 293-3956
Wheeling (G-20877)
General Laminating Company ...... G 847 639-8770
Cary (G-3164)
Linn West Paper Company .... G 773 561-3839
Chicago (G-5231)
Loyola Paper Company .... E 847 956-7770
Elk Grove Village (G-9098)
Potomac Corporation .... C 847 259-0546
Wheeling (G-20962)
Quality Paper Inc .... F 847 258-3999
Elk Grove Village (G-9205)
Schwab Paper Products Company .... E 815 372-2233
Romeoville (G-17875)
Stanford Products LLC .... E 618 548-2600
Salem (G-18361)

PAPERBOARD PRDTS: Building Insulating & Packaging

Terrapin Xpress Inc .... G 866 823-7323
Palos Heights (G-16193)

PAPERBOARD PRDTS: Container Board

Ox Paperboard LLC .... E 309 346-4118
Pekin (G-16348)
Packaging Corporation America ... C 847 482-3000
Lake Forest (G-12277)
Westrock Rkt LLC .... A 312 346-6600
Chicago (G-6614)

PAPERBOARD PRDTS: Folding Boxboard

Gpi Midwest LLC .... E 847 741-0247
Elgin (G-8599)
Graphic Packaging Corporation .... C 847 451-7400
Franklin Park (G-9953)
Graphic Packaging Intl LLC .... B 630 260-6500
Carol Stream (G-2993)
Graphic Packaging Intl LLC .... C 630 260-6500
Carol Stream (G-2994)

PAPERBOARD PRDTS: Packaging Board

Barrington Packaging Systems ..... G 847 382-8063
Barrington (G-1215)
Igd Display LLC .... F 630 916-0700
Downers Grove (G-8027)
Rjg Enterprises Ltd .... G 847 752-2065
Grayslake (G-10798)

PAPERBOARD: Liner Board

Westrock Cp LLC .... G 773 254-1030
Chicago (G-6610)
Westrock Cp LLC .... D 312 346-6600
Chicago (G-6611)
Westrock Mwv LLC .... G 773 221-9015
Chicago (G-6613)
Westrock Mwv LLC .... E 217 442-2247
Danville (G-7397)
Westrock Mwv LLC .... C 630 289-8537
Bartlett (G-1323)

PAPETERIES & WRITING PAPER SETS

Discount Computer Supply Inc ..... G 847 883-8743
Buffalo Grove (G-2533)

PAPIER-MACHE PRDTS, EXC STATUARY & ART GOODS

Franch & Sons Trnsp Inc .... G 630 392-3307
Addison (G-129)

PARKING LOTS

Clean Sweep Environmental Inc ... G 630 879-8750
Batavia (G-1367)

PARKING LOTS & GARAGES

Airport Park and Fly LLC .... G 708 310-2442
Chicago (G-3590)

PARTITIONS & FIXTURES: Except Wood

Accurate Partitions Corp .... G 708 442-6801
Burr Ridge (G-2649)
Alessco Inc .... F 773 327-7919
Chicago (G-3602)
Apex Wire Products Company Inc .... F 847 671-1830
Franklin Park (G-9871)
Armbrust Paper Tubes Inc .... E 773 586-3232
Chicago (G-3730)
Art Wire Works Inc .... F 708 458-3993
Bedford Park (G-1457)
Bar Stool Depotcom .... G 815 727-7294
Joliet (G-11827)
Bel Mar Wire Products Inc .... F 773 342-3800
Chicago (G-3861)
Bilt-Rite Metal Products Inc .... E 815 495-2211
Leland (G-12547)
C-V Cstom Cntrtops Cbinets Inc .... F 708 388-5066
Blue Island (G-2113)
Cameo Container Corporation ..... C 773 254-1030
Chicago (G-4011)
Capitol Carton Company .... E 312 563-9690
Chicago (G-4017)
Capitol Wood Works LLC .... D 217 522-5553
Springfield (G-19341)
Carl Stahl Decrcabl Innovtns I ..... F 312 474-1100
Burr Ridge (G-2660)
Chicago American Mfg LLC .... C 773 376-0100
Chicago (G-4088)
Colony Display LLC .... E 847 426-5300
Elgin (G-8545)
Consolidated Displays Co Inc ...... G 630 851-8666
Oswego (G-15998)
Creative Metal Products .... F 773 638-3200
Chicago (G-4264)
Crown Metal Manufacturing Co ... C 630 279-9800
Elmhurst (G-9355)
DAmico Associates Inc .... G 847 291-7446
Northbrook (G-15373)
Fleetwood Fixtures .... G 773 271-3390
Chicago (G-4601)
Forest City Counter Tops Inc .... F 815 633-8602
Loves Park (G-13212)
Harder Signs Inc .... F 815 874-7777
Rockford (G-17443)
IMS Engineered Products LLC ..... G 847 391-8100
Des Plaines (G-7787)
Inter-Market Inc .... G 847 729-5330
Glenview (G-10570)
Interlake Mecalux Inc .... C 815 844-7191
Pontiac (G-16772)
Interlake Mecalux Inc .... B 708 344-9999
Melrose Park (G-13883)
Iretired LLC .... G 630 285-9500
Itasca (G-11678)
Ivan Carlson Associates Inc .... E 312 829-4616
Chicago (G-4979)
Klein Tools Inc .... D 847 228-6999
Elk Grove Village (G-9078)
Klein Tools Inc .... E 847 821-5500
Lincolnshire (G-12779)
LL Display Group Ltd .... E 847 982-0231
Chicago (G-5244)
Lyon LLC .... C 815 432-4595
Watseka (G-20309)
Lyon LLC .... E 217 465-6321
Paris (G-16232)
Lyon Workspace Products Inc ..... G 630 892-8941
Montgomery (G-14259)
Metal Box International LLC .... C 847 455-8500
Franklin Park (G-9994)
Middletons Mouldings Inc .... D 517 278-6610
Schaumburg (G-18629)
Midwest Custom Case Inc .... C 708 672-2900
University Park (G-19961)
Multiplex Display Fixture Co .... E 800 325-3350
Dupo (G-8141)
Rome Metal Mfg Inc .... G 773 287-1755
Chicago (G-6057)
Royal Fabricators Inc .... F 847 775-7466
Wadsworth (G-20213)
RTC Industries Inc .... D 847 640-2400
Chicago (G-6075)
Rwi Holdings Inc .... F 630 897-6951
Aurora (G-1150)
West Zwick Corp .... G 217 222-0228
Quincy (G-16955)
Wind Point Partners Vi LP .... G 312 255-4800
Chicago (G-6638)
Ww Displays Inc .... F 847 566-6979
Mundelein (G-14747)

PARTITIONS: Metal, Ornamental

Armstrong World Industries Inc ... E 847 362-8720
Libertyville (G-12631)

PARTITIONS: Solid Fiber, Made From Purchased Materials

Westrock Converting LLC .... E 618 709-5284
Edwardsville (G-8379)

PARTITIONS: Wood & Fixtures

Abitzy Inc .... F 847 659-9228
Wood Dale (G-21152)
Action Cabinet Sales Inc .... G 847 717-0011
Elgin (G-8494)
Allie Woodworking .... G 847 244-1919
Waukegan (G-20413)
Anderson & Marter Cabinets ...... G 630 406-9840
Batavia (G-1349)
Axis Display Group Inc .... G 513 342-1884
South Beloit (G-19082)

PRODUCT SECTION

B & B Formica Appliers Inc......F......773 804-1015
Chicago *(G-3804)*
Bards Products Inc......E......800 323-5499
Mundelein *(G-14665)*
Bolhuis Woodworking Co......G......708 333-5100
Manhattan *(G-13431)*
Brakur Custom Cabinetry Inc......C......630 355-2244
Shorewood *(G-18893)*
C-V Cstom Cntrtops Cbinets Inc......F......708 388-5066
Blue Island *(G-2113)*
Capitol Wood Works LLC......D......217 522-5553
Springfield *(G-19341)*
Chicago Booth Mfg Inc......F......773 378-8400
Chicago *(G-4093)*
Colony Display LLC......E......847 426-5300
Elgin *(G-8545)*
Contempo Marble & Granite Inc......G......312 455-0022
Chicago *(G-4225)*
Cooper Lake Millworks Inc......G......217 847-2681
Hamilton *(G-10951)*
Custom Window Accents......F......815 943-7651
Harvard *(G-11051)*
Custom Woodwork & Interiors......F......217 546-0006
Springfield *(G-19358)*
Der Holtzmacher Ltd......G......815 895-4887
Sycamore *(G-19706)*
Design Woodworks......G......847 566-6603
Mundelein *(G-14682)*
Dpcac LLC......F......630 741-7900
Itasca *(G-11644)*
Eddie Gapastione......G......708 430-3881
Bridgeview *(G-2344)*
Fra-Milco Cabinets Co Inc......G
Frankfort *(G-9795)*
Gerali Custom Design Inc......D......847 760-0500
Elgin *(G-8593)*
Glenview Custom Cabinets Inc......G......847 345-5754
Glenview *(G-10551)*
Hansen Custom Cabinet Inc......G......847 356-1100
Lake Villa *(G-12353)*
Hickory Street Cabinets......G......618 667-9676
Troy *(G-19915)*
Hylan Design Ltd......G......312 243-7341
Chicago *(G-4863)*
J K Custom Countertops......G......630 495-2324
Lombard *(G-13088)*
Janik Custom Millwork Inc......G......708 482-4844
Hodgkins *(G-11390)*
Jbc Holding Co......G......217 347-7701
Effingham *(G-8404)*
John F Mate Co......G......847 381-8131
Lake Barrington *(G-12154)*
Kabinet Kraft......F......618 395-1047
Olney *(G-15867)*
Laminated Designs Countertops......G......815 877-7222
Machesney Park *(G-13356)*
M & R Custom Millwork Inc......G......815 547-8549
Belvidere *(G-1682)*
Meier Granite Company......G......847 678-7300
Franklin Park *(G-9989)*
Miller Manufacturing Co Inc......D......636 343-5700
Dupo *(G-8140)*
Nelson - Harkins Inds Inc......E......773 478-6243
Lake Bluff *(G-12199)*
Northwest Marble Products......E......630 860-2288
Hoffman Estates *(G-11473)*
OGorman Son Carpentry Contrs......E......815 485-8997
New Lenox *(G-15045)*
Perfection Custom Closets & Co......F......847 647-6461
Niles *(G-15156)*
Rays Countertop Shop Inc......F......217 483-2514
Glenarm *(G-10427)*
Regency Custom Woodworking......F......815 689-2117
Cullom *(G-7300)*
Roncin Custom Design......G......847 669-0260
Huntley *(G-11565)*
Suburban Fabricators Inc......G......847 729-0866
Glenview *(G-10627)*
Suburban Laminating Inc......G......708 389-6106
Melrose Park *(G-13918)*
Swan Surfaces LLC......C......618 532-5673
Centralia *(G-3252)*
Unistrut International Corp......D......630 773-3460
Addison *(G-323)*
Wind Point Partners Vi LP......G......312 255-4800
Chicago *(G-6638)*
Woodhill Cabinetry Design Inc......G......815 431-0545
Ottawa *(G-16086)*

PARTS: Metal

Amag Manufacturing Inc......G......773 667-5184
Chicago *(G-3642)*
BR Concepts International Inc......G......847 674-9481
Skokie *(G-18932)*
Component Parts Company......G......815 477-2323
Crystal Lake *(G-7184)*
Nuair Filter Company LLC......G......309 888-4331
Normal *(G-15214)*
Quest Manufacturing Inc......C......815 675-2442
Spring Grove *(G-19296)*

PASTES: Metal

Senju Comtek Corp......G......847 549-5690
Mundelein *(G-14735)*

PATCHING PLASTER: Household

Rda Inc......F......815 427-8444
Saint Anne *(G-18137)*

PATENT OWNERS & LESSORS

3b Media Inc......F......312 563-9363
Chicago *(G-3467)*

PATIENT MONITORING EQPT WHOLESALERS

Lifewatch Corp......G......847 720-2100
Rosemont *(G-18031)*
Lifewatch Services Inc......B......847 720-2100
Rosemont *(G-18032)*

PATTERNS: Indl

Advanced Pattern Works LLC......G......618 346-9039
Collinsville *(G-6952)*
Alang Pattern Inc......G......773 722-9481
Cicero *(G-6828)*
Beloit Pattern Works......F......815 389-2578
South Beloit *(G-19083)*
Cambridge Pattern Works......G......309 937-5370
Cambridge *(G-2803)*
Capital Pttern Model Works Inc......G......630 469-8200
Glendale Heights *(G-10440)*
Carroll Industrial Molds Inc......F......815 225-7250
Milledgeville *(G-14038)*
Chem-Cast Ltd......C......217 443-5532
Danville *(G-7326)*
Clinkenbeard & Associates Inc......E......815 226-0291
South Beloit *(G-19087)*
Curto-Ligonier Foundries Co......E......708 345-2250
Melrose Park *(G-13846)*
Jls Industries Inc......G......630 261-9445
Lombard *(G-13090)*
Jsp Mold LLC......G......815 225-7110
Milledgeville *(G-14039)*
Kerrigan Industries Inc......G......847 251-8994
Wilmette *(G-21082)*
Koswell Pattern Works Inc......G......708 757-5225
Lynwood *(G-13294)*
Master Foundry Inc......F......217 223-7396
Quincy *(G-16911)*
Microtek Pattern Inc......G......217 428-0433
Decatur *(G-7522)*
Midwest Patterns Inc......C......217 228-6900
Quincy *(G-16914)*
Modern Pattern Works Inc......G......309 676-2157
Peoria *(G-16478)*
N & S Pattern Co......F......815 874-6166
Rockford *(G-17535)*
P & H Pattern Inc......G......815 795-2449
Marseilles *(G-13562)*
Precision Entps Fndry Mch Inc......G......815 797-1000
Somonauk *(G-19073)*
Precision Foundry Tooling Ltd......F......217 847-3233
Hamilton *(G-10960)*
Quincy Foundry & Pattern Co......G......217 222-0718
Quincy *(G-16932)*
R & C Pattern Works Inc......G......708 331-1882
Monee *(G-14204)*
R C Castings Inc......G......708 331-1882
Monee *(G-14205)*
Rockbridge Casting Inc......G......618 753-3188
Rockbridge *(G-17255)*
Spectron Manufacturing......G......720 879-7605
Bloomingdale *(G-2015)*
Sun Pattern & Model Inc......E......630 293-3366
West Chicago *(G-20648)*
Tilton Pattern Works Inc......F......217 442-1502
Danville *(G-7388)*
Voss Pattern Works Inc......G......618 233-4242
Belleville *(G-1609)*

PAVERS

Paver Protector Inc......G......630 488-0069
Gilberts *(G-10364)*

PAVING MATERIALS: Prefabricated, Concrete

Peter Baker & Son Co......D......847 362-3663
Lake Bluff *(G-12204)*
Tickle Asphalt Co Ltd......G......309 787-1308
Milan *(G-14029)*

PAVING MIXTURES

Byron Blacktop Inc......G......815 234-2225
Byron *(G-2751)*

PAYROLL SVCS

Willis Stein & Partners Manage......F......312 422-2400
Chicago *(G-6632)*

PEARLS, WHOLESALE

Pearl Bath Bombs Inc......F......312 661-2881
Chicago *(G-5777)*
Pearl Perfect Inc......E......847 679-6251
Morton Grove *(G-14432)*

PEAT GRINDING SVCS

Markman Peat Corp......E......815 772-4014
Morrison *(G-14345)*

PENCILS & PENS WHOLESALERS

C H Hanson Company......D......630 848-2000
Naperville *(G-14786)*

PENS & PARTS: Ball Point

Eversharp Pen Company......E......847 366-5030
Franklin Park *(G-9940)*
Fayco Enterprises Inc......C......618 283-0638
Vandalia *(G-20011)*

PENS & PENCILS: Mechanical, NEC

Alexander Manufacturing Co......D......309 728-2224
Towanda *(G-19892)*
Essentra Holdings Corp......G......804 518-0322
Westchester *(G-20698)*
Gillette Company......D......847 689-3111
North Chicago *(G-15312)*
Perkins Pencil Co......G......708 363-9249
Lansing *(G-12511)*
Pilot Corporation of America......G......773 792-1111
Park Ridge *(G-16292)*
UNI-Ball Corporation......G......310 505-5926
Wheaton *(G-20830)*

PENS: Fountain, Including Desk Sets

Icandee LLC......G......773 754-0493
Chicago *(G-4871)*

PENSION & RETIREMENT PLAN CONSULTANTS

Envestnet Rtrment Slutions LLC......G......312 827-7957
Chicago *(G-4519)*

PERFUME: Concentrated

Lab TEC Cosmt By Marzena Inc......F......630 396-3970
Addison *(G-178)*

PERFUMES

A&B Apparel......G......815 962-5070
Rockford *(G-17281)*
Michael Christopher Ltd......G......815 308-5018
Woodstock *(G-21410)*
Smile Aromatics Inc......E......847 759-0350
Des Plaines *(G-7847)*
Takasago Intl Corp USA......G......815 479-5030
Crystal Lake *(G-7275)*
Tru Fragrance & Beauty LLC......E......630 563-4110
Willowbrook *(G-21065)*

PERLITE: Processed

Phoenix Services LLC .... G 708 849-3527
  Riverdale *(G-17074)*

PERSONAL & HOUSEHOLD GOODS REPAIR, NEC

Globe Union Group Inc .... D 630 679-1420
  Woodridge *(G-21304)*
Kaser Power Equipment Inc .... G 309 289-2176
  Knoxville *(G-12068)*

PERSONAL CREDIT INSTITUTIONS: Finance Licensed Loan Co's, Sm

Russell Enterprises Inc .... B 847 692-6050
  Park Ridge *(G-16295)*

PERSONAL DOCUMENT & INFORMATION SVCS

Source Software Inc .... G 815 922-7717
  Lockport *(G-13024)*

PERSONAL INVESTIGATION SVCS

National Def Intelligence Inc .... G 312 233-2318
  Naperville *(G-14980)*

PERSONAL SHOPPING SVCS

Mjt Design and Prtg Entps Inc .... G 708 240-4323
  Hillside *(G-11348)*

PEST CONTROL IN STRUCTURES SVCS

Smithereen Company .... D 800 340-1888
  Niles *(G-15172)*

PESTICIDES WHOLESALERS

Lebanon Seaboard Corporation .... E 217 446-0983
  Danville *(G-7358)*

PET ACCESS: Collars, Leashes, Etc, Exc Leather

AWego Enterprises Inc .... G 815 765-1957
  Belvidere *(G-1651)*

PET COLLARS, LEASHES, MUZZLES & HARNESSES: Leather

Seat Cover Pro LLC .... G 847 990-1506
  Vernon Hills *(G-20094)*

PET FOOD WHOLESALERS

Frito-Lay North America Inc .... C 708 331-7200
  Oak Forest *(G-15679)*
Garver Feeds .... E 217 422-2201
  Decatur *(G-7496)*
Lafeber Distribution LLC .... G 630 524-4845
  Cornell *(G-7013)*
Pet Factory Inc .... C 847 837-8900
  Mundelein *(G-14724)*

PET SPLYS

Ameriguard Corporation .... G 630 986-1900
  Burr Ridge *(G-2652)*
Andrew C Arnold .... G 815 220-0282
  Peru *(G-16564)*
Aquadine Inc .... G 800 497-3463
  Harvard *(G-11046)*
AWego Enterprises Inc .... G 815 765-1957
  Belvidere *(G-1651)*
Bentleys Pet Stuff LLC .... G 847 793-0500
  Long Grove *(G-13157)*
Bentleys Pet Stuff LLC .... G 773 857-7600
  Chicago *(G-3869)*
Bone A Fide Pet Grooming .... G 217 872-0907
  Decatur *(G-7467)*
Boss Manufacturing Holdings .... G 309 852-2131
  Kewanee *(G-12026)*
Boss Pet Products Inc .... G 216 332-0832
  Kewanee *(G-12027)*
Dal Acres West Kennel .... G 217 793-3647
  Springfield *(G-19359)*
DMJ Group Inc .... G 847 322-7533
  Algonquin *(G-371)*
Dura-Crafts Corp .... F 815 464-3561
  Frankfort *(G-9789)*
GM Partners .... G 847 895-7627
  Schaumburg *(G-18536)*
Hunter Mfg LLP .... D 859 254-7573
  Lake Forest *(G-12262)*
Keys Manufacturing Company Inc ..... E 217 465-4001
  Paris *(G-16231)*
Kmp Products LLC .... G 630 956-0438
  Westmont *(G-20754)*
Luxury Living Inc .... G 847 845-3863
  Cary *(G-3177)*
Ming Trading LLC .... G 773 442-2221
  Chicago *(G-5464)*
Molor Products Company .... F 630 375-5999
  Oswego *(G-16015)*
Nature House Inc .... D 217 833-2393
  Griggsville *(G-10850)*
Pawz & Klawz .... G 630 257-0245
  Lemont *(G-12580)*
Pet Factory Inc .... G 847 837-8900
  Mundelein *(G-14724)*
Petote LLC .... G 312 455-0873
  Chicago *(G-5796)*
Prevue Pet Products Inc .... G 773 722-1052
  Chicago *(G-5870)*
Robs Aquatics .... G 708 444-7627
  Tinley Park *(G-19854)*
Sunscape Time Inc .... G 708 345-8791
  Melrose Park *(G-13919)*
Vim Recyclers LP .... C 630 892-2559
  Aurora *(G-1166)*
Whyte Gate Incorporated .... F 847 201-7000
  Grayslake *(G-10804)*
Wish Bone Rescue .... G 309 212-9210
  Bloomington *(G-2108)*

PET SPLYS WHOLESALERS

Midwestern Pet Foods Inc .... E 309 734-3121
  Monmouth *(G-14223)*
Prevue Pet Products Inc .... E 773 722-1052
  Chicago *(G-5870)*
Wagners LLC .... E 815 889-4101
  Milford *(G-14037)*

PETROLEUM & PETROLEUM PRDTS, WHOL Svc Station Splys, Petro

R L Hoener Co .... E 217 223-2190
  Quincy *(G-16936)*

PETROLEUM & PETROLEUM PRDTS, WHOLESALE Crude Oil

Lakeshore Operating LLC .... E 844 557-4763
  Chicago *(G-5165)*

PETROLEUM & PETROLEUM PRDTS, WHOLESALE Fuel Oil

Huels Oil Company .... F 877 338-6277
  Carlyle *(G-2890)*
R H Johnson Oil Co Inc .... G 630 668-3649
  Wheaton *(G-20817)*

PETROLEUM & PETROLEUM PRDTS, WHOLESALE Petroleum Brokers

South Central Fs Inc .... F 217 849-2242
  Toledo *(G-19878)*

PETROLEUM & PETROLEUM PRDTS, WHOLESALE Petroleum Terminals

Bi-Petro Inc .... E 217 535-0181
  Springfield *(G-19325)*

PETROLEUM & PETROLEUM PRDTS, WHOLESALE: Bulk Stations

AMP Americas LLC .... E 312 300-6700
  Chicago *(G-3683)*
Newby Oil Company Inc .... G 815 756-7688
  Sycamore *(G-19725)*
Premium Oil Company .... F 815 963-3800
  Rockford *(G-17559)*
South Central Fs Inc .... G 618 283-1557
  Vandalia *(G-20025)*

PETROLEUM BULK STATIONS & TERMINALS

BP America Inc .... A 630 420-5111
  Warrenville *(G-20232)*
BP Products North America Inc .... G 630 420-4300
  Naperville *(G-14783)*
Drig Corporation .... D 312 265-1509
  Rosemont *(G-18020)*
Effingham Equity .... F 217 268-5128
  Arcola *(G-648)*
Pdv Midwest Refining LLC .... A 630 257-7761
  Lemont *(G-12581)*
Wabash Valley Service Co .... F 618 393-2971
  Olney *(G-15893)*

PETROLEUM PRDTS WHOLESALERS

BP Products North America Inc .... D 312 594-7689
  Chicago *(G-3939)*
Dougherty E J Oil & Stone Sup .... G 618 271-4414
  East Saint Louis *(G-8304)*
Marathon Petroleum Company LP ..... A 618 544-2121
  Robinson *(G-17119)*
Marathon Petroleum Company LP ..... G 618 829-3288
  Saint Elmo *(G-18309)*
Ross Oil Co Inc .... G 618 592-3808
  Oblong *(G-15828)*
Tower Oil & Technology Co .... E 773 927-6161
  Chicago *(G-6401)*

PETROLEUM REFINERY INSPECTION SVCS

Rain Cii Carbon LLC .... E 618 544-2193
  Robinson *(G-17124)*

PETS & PET SPLYS, WHOLESALE

Lafeber Distribution LLC .... G 630 524-4845
  Cornell *(G-7013)*

PHARMACEUTICAL PREPARATIONS: Adrenal

Aidarex Pharmaceuticals LLC .... G 800 657-4724
  Libertyville *(G-12626)*
Bridgeport Pharmacy Inc .... G 312 791-9000
  Chicago *(G-3956)*
Nantpharma LLC .... C 847 243-1200
  Elk Grove Village *(G-9143)*
Pharmdium Hlthcare Hldings Inc ...... G 800 523-7749
  Lake Forest *(G-12288)*

PHARMACEUTICAL PREPARATIONS: Druggists' Preparations

Aardvark Pharma LLC .... E 630 248-2380
  Oakbrook Terrace *(G-15779)*
Abbott Laboratories .... A 847 735-0573
  Mettawa *(G-13977)*
Abbott Laboratories .... A 847 937-6100
  Des Plaines *(G-7718)*
Abbott Laboratories .... G 800 551-5838
  Lake Forest *(G-12218)*
Abbott Laboratories .... A 224 667-6100
  Abbott Park *(G-1)*
Abbott Universal LLC .... G 224 667-6100
  Abbott Park *(G-7)*
Abbvie Inc .... C 847 932-7900
  North Chicago *(G-15300)*
Abbvie Inc .... D 847 932-7900
  North Chicago *(G-15301)*
Alva/MCO Phrmcal Companies Inc ... E 847 663-0700
  Niles *(G-15101)*
Espee Biopharma & Finechem LLC ... G 224 355-5950
  Schaumburg *(G-18520)*
Hospira Inc .... C 224 212-6244
  Lake Forest *(G-12260)*
International Drug Dev Cons .... G 847 634-9586
  Long Grove *(G-13160)*
Novalex Therapeutics Inc .... G 630 750-9334
  Elburn *(G-8465)*
Ocularis Pharma .... G 708 712-6263
  Riverside *(G-17087)*
Owp Pharmaceuticals Inc .... F 331 871-7424
  Naperville *(G-14890)*
Riverside Medi-Center Inc .... G 815 932-6632
  Kankakee *(G-11999)*
Sagent Pharmaceuticals Inc .... C 847 908-1600
  Schaumburg *(G-18701)*
Sagent Pharmaceuticals Inc .... D 847 908-1600
  Schaumburg *(G-18702)*

Sfc Chemicals Ltd......G...... 847 221-2152
Chicago *(G-6144)*
Soleo Health Inc......G...... 630 478-8240
Woodridge *(G-21340)*

PHARMACEUTICAL PREPARATIONS: Medicines, Capsule Or Ampule

Abbott Laboratories......A...... 847 935-8130
Gurnee *(G-10852)*
Access Medical Supply Inc......G...... 847 891-6210
Schaumburg *(G-18425)*
East West Intergrated Therapys......G...... 815 788-0574
Crystal Lake *(G-7195)*

PHARMACEUTICAL PREPARATIONS: Pills

Am2pat Inc......G...... 847 726-9443
Chicago *(G-3641)*
Ashland ABC Choice Inc......G...... 773 488-7800
Chicago *(G-3748)*
Black Start Labs Inc......G...... 630 444-1800
Saint Charles *(G-18157)*
Roundtble Hlthcare Partners LP......E...... 847 739-3200
Lake Forest *(G-12299)*

PHARMACEUTICAL PREPARATIONS: Powders

Athenex Pharmaceutical Div LLC......F...... 847 922-8041
Schaumburg *(G-18448)*
Meridian Laboratories Inc......G...... 847 808-0081
Buffalo Grove *(G-2572)*
Sukgyung At Inc......G...... 847 298-6570
Des Plaines *(G-7853)*

PHARMACEUTICAL PREPARATIONS: Proprietary Drug PRDTS

Aeropharm Technology LLC......G...... 847 937-6100
North Chicago *(G-15306)*
Hospira Inc......A...... 224 212-2000
Lake Forest *(G-12259)*
Vital Proteins LLC......C...... 224 544-9110
Chicago *(G-6561)*

PHARMACEUTICAL PREPARATIONS: Solutions

Amphix Bio Inc......G...... 720 840-7327
Chicago *(G-3684)*
Bio Ascend LLC......G...... 888 476-9129
Chicago *(G-3893)*
Winlind Skincare LLC......G...... 630 789-9408
Burr Ridge *(G-2736)*

PHARMACEUTICAL PREPARATIONS: Tablets

Acura Pharmaceuticals Inc......F...... 847 705-7709
Palatine *(G-16089)*
Sunstar Pharmaceutical Inc......D...... 773 777-4000
Elgin *(G-8742)*

PHARMACEUTICALS

A-S Medication Solutions LLC......D...... 847 680-3515
Libertyville *(G-12624)*
Abbott Health Products Inc......D...... 847 937-6100
North Chicago *(G-15290)*
Abbott Laboratories......A...... 224 330-0271
Libertyville *(G-12625)*
Abbott Laboratories......A...... 847 937-2210
Chicago *(G-3503)*
Abbott Laboratories......E...... 847 938-3220
Waukegan *(G-20406)*
Abbott Laboratories......A...... 847 937-6100
North Chicago *(G-15291)*
Abbott Laboratories......E...... 847 937-6100
Waukegan *(G-20407)*
Abbott Laboratories......G...... 224 361-7129
Elk Grove Village *(G-8793)*
Abbott Laboratories......D...... 847 938-4196
North Chicago *(G-15292)*
Abbott Laboratories......A...... 847 932-7900
North Chicago *(G-15293)*
Abbott Laboratories......F...... 312 944-0660
Bannockburn *(G-1188)*
Abbott Laboratories......F...... 847 855-9217
Gurnee *(G-10853)*
Abbott Laboratories......G...... 847 937-6100
North Chicago *(G-15294)*
Abbott Laboratories......C...... 847 937-6100
Waukegan *(G-20408)*
Abbott Laboratories Inc......C...... 224 668-2076
Abbott Park *(G-2)*
Abbott Laboratories Intl Co......F...... 847 937-6100
North Chicago *(G-15295)*
Abbott Laboratories PCF Ltd......F...... 847 937-6100
North Chicago *(G-15296)*
Abbott Laboratories Svcs Corp......G...... 708 937-6100
North Chicago *(G-15297)*
Abbott Labs Hlth Care Tr......G...... 224 667-6100
Abbott Park *(G-3)*
Abbott Nutrition Mfg Inc......G...... 614 624-6083
Abbott Park *(G-4)*
Abbott Point of Care Inc......C...... 847 937-6100
Abbott Park *(G-5)*
Abbott-Abbvie Multiple Employe......G...... 847 473-2053
North Chicago *(G-15298)*
Abbvie......G...... 847 946-8753
Mundelein *(G-14658)*
Abbvie......G...... 847 548-1016
Grayslake *(G-10758)*
Abbvie Endocrinology Inc......F...... 888 857-0668
North Chicago *(G-15299)*
Abbvie Inc......G...... 847 367-7621
Vernon Hills *(G-20038)*
Abbvie Inc......D...... 847 937-4566
Abbott Park *(G-9)*
Abbvie Inc......E...... 847 473-4787
Waukegan *(G-20409)*
Abbvie Inc......G...... 847 938-2042
North Chicago *(G-15302)*
Abbvie US LLC......G...... 800 255-5162
North Chicago *(G-15304)*
Abraxis Bioscience LLC......G...... 310 437-7715
Elk Grove Village *(G-8797)*
Abraxis Bioscience LLC......G...... 310 883-1300
Melrose Park *(G-13819)*
Accelerated Pharma Inc......G...... 773 517-0789
Burr Ridge *(G-2648)*
Adello Biologics LLC......G...... 312 620-1500
Chicago *(G-3542)*
Aechem Scientific Corporation......G...... 630 364-5106
Naperville *(G-14768)*
Ajinomoto Food Ingredients LLC......G...... 773 714-1436
Itasca *(G-11617)*
Akorn Inc......F...... 847 625-1100
Gurnee *(G-10857)*
Akorn Inc......C...... 847 279-6100
Lake Forest *(G-12222)*
Akorn Inc......C...... 217 428-1100
Decatur *(G-7437)*
Akorn Inc......C...... 217 423-9715
Decatur *(G-7438)*
Akorn Inc......G...... 847 279-6166
Vernon Hills *(G-20039)*
Akorn Pharmaceuticals......G...... 800 932-5676
Lake Forest *(G-12223)*
Altathera Pharmaceuticals LLC......F...... 312 445-8900
Chicago *(G-3635)*
American Phrm Partners Inc......F...... 847 969-2700
Schaumburg *(G-18438)*
App Pharmaceuticals Inc......G...... 847 969-2700
Schaumburg *(G-18442)*
Apser Laboratory Inc......D...... 630 543-3333
Addison *(G-36)*
Archer-Daniels-Midland Company......D...... 217 424-5200
Decatur *(G-7459)*
Aspen API Inc......F...... 847 635-0985
Des Plaines *(G-7734)*
Astellas Pharma Global Dev Inc......C...... 224 205-8800
Northbrook *(G-15337)*
Astellas Pharma Inc......E...... 800 695-4321
Northbrook *(G-15338)*
Astellas Pharma Us Inc......B...... 800 888-7704
Northbrook *(G-15339)*
Astellas RES Inst Amer LLC......F...... 847 933-7400
Skokie *(G-18924)*
Astellas Scntfic Med Affirs In......C...... 224 205-5452
Northbrook *(G-15340)*
Astellas US Holding Inc......E...... 224 205-8800
Northbrook *(G-15341)*
Astellas US LLC......C...... 800 888-7704
Deerfield *(G-7587)*
Astellas US Technologies Inc......B...... 847 317-8800
Deerfield *(G-7588)*
Avexis......G...... 847 964-9948
Deerfield *(G-7589)*
Avocet Polymer Tech Inc......G...... 773 523-2872
Chicago *(G-3788)*
B & H Biotechnologies LLC......G...... 630 915-3227
Willowbrook *(G-21030)*
Baxalta US Inc......D...... 847 948-2000
Round Lake *(G-18068)*
Baxalta Worldwide LLC......C...... 224 948-2000
Deerfield *(G-7590)*
Baxter Global Holdings II Inc......E...... 224 948-1812
Deerfield *(G-7591)*
Baxter Healthcare Corporation......B...... 847 522-8600
Vernon Hills *(G-20044)*
Baxter Healthcare Corporation......A...... 224 270-6300
Round Lake *(G-18071)*
Bayer Corporation......G...... 847 725-6320
Elk Grove Village *(G-8858)*
Bella Pharmaceuticals Inc......G...... 847 722-1692
Glenview *(G-10529)*
Bimeda Animal Health Inc......G...... 630 928-0361
Oakbrook Terrace *(G-15788)*
Bio-Bridge Science Inc......E...... 630 328-0213
Oakbrook Terrace *(G-15789)*
Biolife Plasma LLC......F...... 224 940-7611
Bannockburn *(G-1197)*
Blistex Global Inc......G...... 630 571-2870
Oak Brook *(G-15597)*
BMC 1092 Inc......E...... 708 544-2200
Broadview *(G-2421)*
Brian K Wattleworth......G...... 847 356-2103
Lake Villa *(G-12346)*
Capstone Dev Svcs Co LLC......G...... 847 999-0131
Rosemont *(G-18002)*
Capstone Therapeutics Corp......G...... 602 286-5520
Alsip *(G-426)*
Catalent Pharma Solutions LLC......D...... 815 338-9500
Woodstock *(G-21371)*
Catalent Pharma Solutions Inc......C...... 815 338-9500
Woodstock *(G-21372)*
Celerity Pharmaceuticals LLC......G...... 847 999-0131
Rosemont *(G-18003)*
Celgene Corporation......F...... 908 673-9000
Melrose Park *(G-13840)*
Cg Nutritionals Inc......G...... 224 667-6100
North Chicago *(G-15309)*
Chem Rx - Chicago LLC......G...... 708 449-7600
Hillside *(G-11333)*
Chicago Dscovery Solutions LLC......G...... 815 609-2071
Plainfield *(G-16650)*
Clarus Therapeutics Inc......G...... 847 562-4300
Northbrook *(G-15361)*
Coretechs Corp......F...... 847 295-3720
Lake Forest *(G-12240)*
Cour Pharmaceuticals Dev......G...... 773 621-3241
Northbrook *(G-15367)*
Curatek Pharmaceuticals LLC......G...... 702 215-5700
Elk Grove Village *(G-8924)*
Daito Pharmaceuticals Amer Inc......G...... 847 205-0800
Northbrook *(G-15372)*
Daniels Sharpsmart Inc......E...... 312 546-8900
Chicago *(G-4313)*
Denovx LLC......G...... 910 333-6689
Chicago *(G-4340)*
Dental Technologies Inc......D...... 847 677-5500
Lincolnwood *(G-12816)*
Dr Earles LLC......G...... 312 225-7200
Chicago *(G-4395)*
Elim Pdtric Phrmaceuticals Inc......G...... 412 266-5968
Rolling Meadows *(G-17729)*
Elim Pdtric Phrmaceuticals Inc......E...... 412 266-5968
Schaumburg *(G-18517)*
Elim Pdtric Phrmaceuticals Inc......G...... 412 266-5968
Rolling Meadows *(G-17730)*
Elorac Inc......F...... 847 362-8200
Vernon Hills *(G-20050)*
Emalex Biosciences LLC......G...... 847 715-0577
Northbrook *(G-15383)*
Espee Biopharma & Finechem LLC......G...... 888 851-6667
Schaumburg *(G-18521)*
Eton Pharmaceuticals Inc......F...... 847 787-7361
Deer Park *(G-7581)*
Frazier Management LLC......G...... 815 484-8900
Rockford *(G-17423)*
Fresenius Kabi LLC......D...... 847 550-2300
Lake Zurich *(G-12413)*
Fresenius Kabi LLC......E...... 630 350-7150
Bensenville *(G-1805)*
Fresenius Kabi Pharm......G...... 847 550-2300
Lake Zurich *(G-12414)*
Fresenius Kabi Usa Inc......C...... 708 410-4761
Melrose Park *(G-13870)*
Fresenius Kabi Usa Inc......C...... 708 345-6170
Melrose Park *(G-13871)*

PHARMACEUTICALS — PRODUCT SECTION

Fresenius Kabi Usa Inc .... B 708 450-7500
  Melrose Park (G-13869)
Fresenius Kabi Usa LLC .... A 847 550-2300
  Lake Zurich (G-12415)
Fresenius Kabi Usa LLC .... E 847 983-7100
  Skokie (G-18957)
Fresenius Kabi Usa LLC .... E 847 550-2300
  Lake Zurich (G-12416)
GE Healthcare Inc .... D 774 249-6290
  Arlington Heights (G-742)
Genentech Inc .... G 650 225-1045
  Libertyville (G-12653)
Global Medical Services LLC .... G 847 460-8086
  Plainfield (G-16668)
Global Pharma Device Solutions ..... G 708 212-5801
  Chicago (G-4698)
Globepharm Inc .... G 224 904-3352
  Northbrook (G-15395)
Hepalink USA Inc .... G 630 206-1788
  Chicago (G-4805)
Horizon Medicines LLC .... C 224 383-3110
  Lake Forest (G-12255)
Horizon Pharma Inc .... C 224 383-3000
  Lake Forest (G-12256)
Horizon Phrma Rheumatology LLC .. F 224 383-3000
  Lake Forest (G-12257)
Horizon Therapeutics Usa Inc .... E 224 383-3000
  Deerfield (G-7617)
Horizon Therapeutics Usa Inc .... F 312 332-1401
  Chicago (G-4842)
Horizon Therapeutics Usa Inc .... E 224 383-3000
  Lake Forest (G-12258)
Hot Shots Nm LLC .... G 815 484-0500
  Rockford (G-17453)
Hznp Usa Inc .... F 224 383-3000
  Lake Forest (G-12263)
Illinois Tool Works Inc .... E 847 593-8811
  Elk Grove Village (G-9042)
Inheris Biopharma Inc .... D 415 482-5652
  Chicago (G-4924)
Iria Pharma Inc .... G 217 979-1417
  Champaign (G-3309)
Iterative Therapeutics Inc .... G 773 455-7203
  Chicago (G-4976)
Iterum Therapeutics US Limited ..... G 312 763-3975
  Chicago (G-4977)
Jdp Therapeutics LLC .... G 847 739-0490
  Deerfield (G-7619)
Johnson & Johnson .... D 815 282-5671
  Loves Park (G-13226)
Johnson Matthey Inc .... E 630 268-6300
  Oakbrook Terrace (G-15804)
Kashiv Biosciences LLC .... G 908 895-1576
  Chicago (G-5084)
Kastle Therapeutics LLC .... G 312 883-5695
  Chicago (G-5085)
Lodaat LLC .... D 630 852-7544
  Downers Grove (G-8046)
Lundbeck LLC .... C 847 282-1000
  Deerfield (G-7631)
Lundbeck Pharmaceuticals LLC ...... A 847 282-1000
  Deerfield (G-7632)
Mab Pharmacy Inc .... G 773 342-5878
  Chicago (G-5308)
Medefil Inc .... D 630 682-4600
  Glendale Heights (G-10474)
Medexus Pharma Inc .... G 312 854-0500
  Chicago (G-5382)
Medicate Pharmacy Inc .... G 618 482-2002
  Cahokia (G-2762)
Meitheal Pharmaceuticals Inc .... G 773 951-6542
  Chicago (G-5389)
Melinta Subsidiary Corp .... E 203 624-5606
  Lincolnshire (G-12783)
Melinta Subsidiary Corp .... F 203 624-5606
  Lincolnshire (G-12784)
Meridian Healthcare .... G 815 633-5326
  Rockford (G-17517)
Mgp Holding Corp .... B 847 967-5600
  Morton Grove (G-14428)
Midwest Biofluids Inc .... G 630 790-9708
  Glen Ellyn (G-10413)
Midwest Research Labs LLC .... G 847 283-9176
  Lake Forest (G-12273)
Miller Pharmacal Group Inc .... G 800 323-2935
  Carol Stream (G-3032)
Monopar Therapeutics Inc .... G 847 388-0349
  Wilmette (G-21089)
Morton Grove Phrmceuticals Inc .... B 847 967-5600
  Morton Grove (G-14430)

Mylan Inc .... G 217 424-8400
  Decatur (G-7532)
Mylan Institutional LLC .... E 724 514-1800
  Rockford (G-17534)
Naurex Inc .... G 847 871-0377
  Evanston (G-9557)
Neurotherapeutics Pharma Inc .... G 773 444-4180
  Chicago (G-5573)
Nexus Pharmaceuticals Inc .... D 847 996-3790
  Lincolnshire (G-12786)
Novum Pharma LLC .... F 877 404-4724
  Chicago (G-5634)
Oncquest .... G 847 682-4703
  Zion (G-21523)
Organics LLC .... G 847 897-6000
  Northbrook (G-15448)
Oxalo Therapeutics Inc .... G 530 848-3499
  Chicago (G-5722)
Pal Midwest Ltd .... G 815 965-2981
  Rockford (G-17546)
Patel Dishaben .... G 312 880-8746
  Schaumburg (G-18669)
Patrin Pharma Inc .... E 800 936-3088
  Skokie (G-19003)
Pfanstiehl Inc .... E 847 623-0370
  Waukegan (G-20476)
Pfanstiehl Holdings Inc .... E 847 623-0370
  Waukegan (G-20477)
Pfizer Inc .... C 630 634-3704
  Itasca (G-11716)
Pfizer Inc .... G 224 212-3129
  Lake Forest (G-12287)
Pharma Logistics .... D 847 388-3104
  Mundelein (G-14725)
Pharma Nature .... G 224 659-0906
  Des Plaines (G-7822)
Pharmaceutical Labs and Cons I .... G 630 359-3831
  Addison (G-238)
Pharmanutrients Inc .... G 847 234-2334
  Lake Bluff (G-12205)
Pharmazz Inc .... G 630 780-6087
  Naperville (G-14898)
Pharmedium Healthcare Corp .... E 847 457-2300
  Lake Forest (G-12289)
Phathom Pharmaceuticals Inc .... F 650 325-5156
  Buffalo Grove (G-2584)
Powbab Inc .... G 630 481-6140
  Oak Brook (G-15656)
Power Partners LLC .... G 773 465-8688
  Chicago (G-5847)
Prestige Brands Inc .... G 224 235-4049
  Northbrook (G-15464)
Protide Pharmaceuticals Inc .... G 847 726-3100
  Lake Zurich (G-12446)
Ravens Wood Pharmacy .... G 708 667-0525
  Chicago (G-5976)
Renaissance SSP Holdings Inc ..... G 210 476-8194
  Lake Forest (G-12295)
Respa Pharmaceuticals Inc .... E 630 543-3333
  Addison (G-272)
Rls USA Inc .... A 865 548-1449
  Arlington Heights (G-801)
Sagent Logistics LP .... F 847 908-1600
  Schaumburg (G-18700)
Senior Care Pharmacy LLC .... G 847 579-0093
  Highland Park (G-11297)
Shire Pharmaceuticals LLC .... G 224 940-2000
  Bannockburn (G-1207)
Siemens Med Solutions USA Inc ... F 847 793-4429
  Buffalo Grove (G-2603)
Sns Pharma 427 .... G 217 527-8408
  Springfield (G-19448)
Specgx LLC .... E 618 664-2111
  Greenville (G-10842)
Sterling Phrm Svcs LLC .... F 618 286-4116
  East Carondelet (G-8173)
Sterling Phrm Svcs LLC .... G 618 286-6060
  Dupo (G-8145)
Strategic Applications Inc .... G 847 680-9385
  Lake Villa (G-12368)
Superior Biologics II Inc .... G 847 469-2400
  Schaumburg (G-18731)
Sustainable Innovations Inc .... G 815 713-1637
  Rockford (G-17650)
Symbria Rx Services LLC .... E 630 981-8000
  Woodridge (G-21342)
Synergy Advnced Phrmctcals Inc .. B 212 297-0020
  Chicago (G-6302)
Takeda .... G 847 902-0659
  Hawthorn Woods (G-11127)

Takeda Pharmaceuticals USA Inc ... G 847 315-9228
  Bannockburn (G-1209)
Takeda Phrmaceuticals Intl Inc .... A 224 554-6500
  Bannockburn (G-1210)
Taylor Pharmacal Co .... G 217 423-9715
  Decatur (G-7559)
Temprian Therapeutics Inc .... G 513 374-1180
  Chicago (G-6346)
Topical Pharmaceuticals Inc .... F 630 396-3970
  Addison (G-313)
Topical Pharmaceuticals Inc .... F 630 396-3970
  Addison (G-314)
Url Pharmpro LLC .... G 630 888-3820
  Aurora (G-1030)
Vetter CM USA LLC .... G 847 813-5895
  Des Plaines (G-7864)
VPI Holdings Corp .... G 770 499-8100
  Lake Forest (G-12321)
Wellness Center Usa Inc .... F 847 925-1885
  Hoffman Estates (G-11471)
Winston Pharmaceuticals Inc .... G 847 362-8200
  Vernon Hills (G-20111)
Wockhardt Holding Corp .... B 847 967-5600
  Morton Grove (G-14449)
Xellia Pharaceuticals Inc .... E 847 986-7980
  Grayslake (G-10807)
Xellia Pharmaceuticals USA LLC ... G 847 947-0254
  Buffalo Grove (G-2623)
Xeris Pharmaceuticals Inc .... E 844 445-5704
  Chicago (G-6693)
Xttrium Laboratories Inc .... D 773 268-5800
  Mount Prospect (G-14584)
Yeager JI & Associates Inc .... G 847 283-9162
  Lake Forest (G-12324)
Zedpharma .... G 847 295-1950
  Lake Forest (G-12325)
Zoetis LLC .... D 708 757-2592
  Chicago Heights (G-6787)

PHARMACEUTICALS: Medicinal & Botanical Prdts

Bean Products Inc .... E 312 666-3600
  Chicago (G-3853)
Biomerieux Inc .... F 630 600-5516
  Lombard (G-13045)
Biomerieux Inc .... E 630 628-6055
  Lombard (G-13046)
Chemblend of America LLC .... F 630 521-1600
  Bensenville (G-1767)
Daito Pharmaceuticals Amer Inc .... G 847 205-0800
  Northbrook (G-15372)
Dawes LLC .... F 847 577-2020
  Arlington Heights (G-726)
GE Healthcare Holdings Inc .... A 847 398-8400
  Arlington Heights (G-741)
GE Healthcare Inc .... E 630 595-6642
  Wood Dale (G-21193)
Green Thumb Industries Inc .... F 312 471-6720
  Chicago (G-4740)
Jewel Osco Inc .... C 847 882-6477
  Hoffman Estates (G-11432)
Lonza LLC .... D 309 697-7200
  Mapleton (G-13475)
Oil-Dri Corporation America .... D 312 321-1515
  Chicago (G-5666)
Orchard Products Inc .... G 847 818-6760
  Mount Prospect (G-14556)
Vidasym Inc .... G 847 549-3357
  Libertyville (G-12723)

PHARMACIES & DRUG STORES

Dominicks Finer Foods Inc .... D 630 584-1750
  Saint Charles (G-18185)
Jewel Osco Inc .... C 630 355-2172
  Naperville (G-14854)
Jewel Osco Inc .... D 630 226-1892
  Bolingbrook (G-2198)
Jewel Osco Inc .... C 847 296-7786
  Des Plaines (G-7791)
Kroger Co .... C 309 694-6298
  East Peoria (G-8275)
Kroger Co .... C 815 332-7267
  Rockford (G-17485)
Ravens Wood Pharmacy .... G 708 667-0525
  Chicago (G-5976)
Schnuck Markets Inc .... C 618 466-0825
  Godfrey (G-10663)
Soleo Health Inc .... G 630 478-8240
  Woodridge (G-21340)

PRODUCT SECTION
PHOTOGRAPHIC EQPT & SPLYS WHOLESALERS

Sunset Food Mart Inc .... C 847 234-0854
  Lake Forest (G-12307)
Walter Lagestee Inc .... C 708 957-2974
  Homewood (G-11504)

PHOSPHATE ROCK MINING

Pcs Phosphate Company Inc .... D 847 849-4200
  Northbrook (G-15457)
Phosphate Resource Ptrs .... A 847 739-1200
  Lake Forest (G-12290)

PHOSPHATES

Innophos Inc .... G 773 468-2300
  Chicago (G-4929)
Innophos Inc .... C 708 757-6111
  Chicago Heights (G-6750)

PHOSPHORIC ACID

CF Industries Inc .... B 847 405-2400
  Deerfield (G-7601)
Phosphate Resource Ptrs .... A 847 739-1200
  Lake Forest (G-12290)

PHOTOCOPY MACHINES

Nexus Office Systems Inc .... F 847 836-1095
  Elgin (G-8671)
Xerox Corporation .... E 630 573-1000
  Hinsdale (G-11383)

PHOTOCOPY SPLYS WHOLESALERS

Next Day Toner Supplies Inc .... E 708 478-1000
  Orland Park (G-15971)

PHOTOCOPYING & DUPLICATING SVCS

11th Street Express Prtg Inc .... F 815 968-0208
  Rockford (G-17275)
A A Swift Print Inc .... G 847 301-1122
  Schaumburg (G-18424)
Alphadigital Inc .... G 708 482-4488
  La Grange (G-12071)
AlphaGraphics Printshops .... G 630 964-9600
  Lisle (G-12861)
Art Bookbinders of America .... E 312 226-4100
  Chicago (G-3734)
Balsley Printing Inc .... F 815 624-7515
  Rockton (G-17693)
Bb Services LLC .... G 630 941-8122
  Elmhurst (G-9328)
Century Printing .... G 618 632-2486
  O Fallon (G-15570)
Comet Conection Inc .... G 312 243-5400
  Alsip (G-434)
Copy Express Inc .... F 815 338-7161
  Woodstock (G-21377)
Copy Mat Printing .... G 309 452-1392
  Bloomington (G-2033)
Copy Service Inc .... G 815 758-1151
  Dekalb (G-7670)
Copyset Shop Inc .... G 847 768-2679
  Des Plaines (G-7751)
Elgin Instant Print .... G 847 931-9006
  Elgin (G-8575)
Fast Printing of Joliet Inc .... G 815 723-0080
  Joliet (G-11864)
Fedex Ground Package Sys Inc .... G 800 463-3339
  Glendale Heights (G-10450)
Fedex Office & Print Svcs Inc .... F 847 475-8650
  Evanston (G-9519)
Fedex Office & Print Svcs Inc .... F 815 229-0033
  Rockford (G-17412)
Fedex Office & Print Svcs Inc .... F 847 329-9464
  Lincolnwood (G-12819)
Fedex Office & Print Svcs Inc .... E 217 355-3400
  Champaign (G-3292)
Fedex Office & Print Svcs Inc .... E 847 729-3030
  Glenview (G-10545)
Fedex Office & Print Svcs Inc .... E 309 685-4093
  Peoria (G-16437)
Fedex Office & Print Svcs Inc .... G 847 459-8008
  Buffalo Grove (G-2536)
Fedex Office & Print Svcs Inc .... E 708 452-0149
  Elmwood Park (G-9452)
Fedex Office & Print Svcs Inc .... G 847 823-9360
  Park Ridge (G-16274)
Fedex Office & Print Svcs Inc .... F 630 894-1800
  Bloomingdale (G-1995)

Fedex Office & Print Svcs Inc .... E 847 670-4100
  Arlington Heights (G-736)
Fedex Office & Print Svcs Inc .... F 312 670-4460
  Chicago (G-4577)
Fedex Office & Print Svcs Inc .... F 312 341-9644
  Chicago (G-4573)
Fedex Office & Print Svcs Inc .... F 312 755-0325
  Chicago (G-4574)
Fedex Office & Print Svcs Inc .... F 312 595-0768
  Chicago (G-4575)
Fedex Office & Print Svcs Inc .... F 312 663-1149
  Chicago (G-4576)
Fedex Office & Print Svcs Inc .... G 847 670-7283
  Mount Prospect (G-14528)
Fedex Office & Print Svcs Inc .... G 630 759-5784
  Bolingbrook (G-2176)
Hafner Printing Co Inc .... F 312 362-0120
  Chicago (G-4767)
Henry Printing Inc .... G 618 529-3040
  Carbondale (G-2845)
Hq Printers Inc .... G 312 782-2020
  Chicago (G-4857)
In-Print Graphics Inc .... E 708 396-1010
  Oak Forest (G-15683)
Jamali Kopy Kat Printing Inc .... G 708 544-6164
  Bellwood (G-1629)
Jph Enterprises Inc .... G 847 390-0900
  Des Plaines (G-7792)
Key Printing .... G 815 933-1800
  Kankakee (G-11987)
Klein Printing Inc .... G 773 235-2121
  Chicago (G-5108)
Kram Digital Solutions Inc .... G 312 222-0431
  Glenview (G-10583)
L & S Label Printing Inc .... G 815 964-6753
  Cherry Valley (G-3443)
L P M Inc .... G 847 866-9777
  Evanston (G-9545)
Media Unlimited Inc .... G 630 527-0900
  Naperville (G-14867)
Merrill Corporation .... C 312 386-2200
  Chicago (G-5400)
National Gift Card Corp .... E 815 477-4288
  Crystal Lake (G-7236)
PIP Printing Inc .... G 815 464-0075
  Frankfort (G-9822)
Platts Printing Company .... G 309 228-1069
  Farmington (G-9663)
Poll Enterprises Inc .... F 708 756-1120
  Chicago Heights (G-6764)
Prairieland Printing .... G 309 647-5425
  Washington (G-20276)
Print & Design Services LLC .... G 847 317-9001
  Bannockburn (G-1206)
Printing Plus of Roselle Inc .... G 630 893-0410
  Roselle (G-17974)
Printmeisters Inc .... G 708 474-8400
  Lansing (G-12512)
Priority One Printing and Mail .... G 217 224-8008
  Quincy (G-16928)
Quality Blue & Offset Printing .... G 630 759-8035
  Bolingbrook (G-2231)
Quality Quickprint Inc .... G 815 723-0941
  Lemont (G-12586)
Quality Quickprint Inc .... F 815 838-1784
  Lockport (G-13020)
Rapid Copy & Duplicating Co .... G 312 733-3353
  Melrose Park (G-13906)
Rapid Print .... G 309 673-0826
  Peoria (G-16508)
Ro-Web Inc .... G 309 688-2155
  Peoria (G-16512)
Rudin Printing Company Inc .... F 217 528-5111
  Springfield (G-19436)
S G S Inc .... G 708 544-6061
  Downers Grove (G-8088)
Samecwei Inc .... G 630 897-7888
  Aurora (G-1153)
Sheer Graphics Inc .... G 630 654-4422
  Westmont (G-20772)
Shree Printing Corp .... G 773 267-9500
  Chicago (G-6160)
Smart Office Services Inc .... G 773 227-1121
  Chicago (G-6190)
Speedys Quick Print .... G 217 431-5010
  Danville (G-7381)
Tvp Color Graphics Inc .... G 630 837-3600
  Streamwood (G-19600)
United Lithograph Inc .... G 847 803-1700
  Des Plaines (G-7861)

Valee Inc .... G 847 364-6464
  Elk Grove Village (G-9300)
Viking Printing & Copying Inc .... G 312 341-0985
  Chicago (G-6551)
We-B-Print Inc .... G 309 353-8801
  Pekin (G-16368)
William Holloway Ltd .... G 847 866-9520
  Evanston (G-9588)

PHOTOELECTRIC DEVICES: Magnetic

Seasonal Magnets .... G 708 499-3235
  Evergreen Park (G-9600)

PHOTOENGRAVING SVC

Graphic Engravers Inc .... E 630 595-0400
  Bensenville (G-1816)

PHOTOFINISHING LABORATORIES

Trend Setters Ltd .... F 309 929-7012
  Tremont (G-19901)

PHOTOFINISHING LABORATORIES

Kroger Co .... C 815 332-7267
  Rockford (G-17485)

PHOTOFLASH EQPT

Speedotron Corporation .... G 630 246-5001
  Bartlett (G-1314)

PHOTOGRAPH DEVELOPING & RETOUCHING SVCS

Tree Towns Reprographics Inc .... F 630 832-0209
  Elmhurst (G-9437)

PHOTOGRAPHIC & OPTICAL GOODS EQPT REPAIR SVCS

Screen North Amer Holdings Inc .... F 847 870-7400
  Rolling Meadows (G-17774)

PHOTOGRAPHIC EQPT & CAMERAS, WHOLESALE

Promoframes LLC .... G 866 566-7224
  Schaumburg (G-18685)

PHOTOGRAPHIC EQPT & SPLYS

9 Dots Solutions LLC .... G 877 919-9349
  Mundelein (G-14656)
A Division of A&A Studios Inc .... F 312 278-1144
  Chicago (G-3487)
ARX Nimbus LLC .... G 888 422-6584
  Chicago (G-3744)
AVI-Spl Employee .... B 847 437-7712
  Schaumburg (G-18453)
Bretford Manufacturing Inc .... B 847 678-2545
  Franklin Park (G-9892)
CDs Office Systems Inc .... D 800 367-1508
  Springfield (G-19343)
Fujifilm Elctrnic Mtls USA Inc .... G 312 924-5800
  Hanover Park (G-11006)
Innovatech It Svc Solutions .... G 815 484-9940
  Rockford (G-17464)
Koll Ltd .... G 224 544-5418
  Mundelein (G-14708)
Paulmar Industries Inc .... F 847 395-2520
  Antioch (G-629)
Poersch Metal Manufacturing Co .... F 773 722-0890
  Chicago (G-5828)
Rmf Products Inc .... G 630 879-0020
  Batavia (G-1411)
Seaport Digital LLC .... G 847 235-2319
  Mundelein (G-14734)
Wesling Products Inc .... G 773 533-2850
  Chicago (G-6603)
Xerox Corporation .... D 630 983-0172
  Naperville (G-14951)

PHOTOGRAPHIC EQPT & SPLYS WHOLESALERS

Beastgrip Co .... G 312 283-5283
  Des Plaines (G-7738)
Fujifilm Elctrnic Mtls USA Inc .... G 312 924-5800
  Hanover Park (G-11006)

Employee Codes: A=Over 500 employees, B=251-500
C=101-250, D=51-100, E=20-50, F=10-19, G=3-9

2020 Harris Illinois Industrial Directory

PHOTOGRAPHIC EQPT & SPLYS, WHOLESALE: Motion Picture Camera — PRODUCT SECTION

PHOTOGRAPHIC EQPT & SPLYS, WHOLESALE: Motion Picture Camera
- 2nd Cine Inc .... G 773 455-5808
  Elgin *(G-8488)*

PHOTOGRAPHIC EQPT & SPLYS, WHOLESALE: Project, Motion/Slide
- AVI-Spl Employee .... B 847 437-7712
  Schaumburg *(G-18453)*

PHOTOGRAPHIC EQPT & SPLYS: Blueprint Cloth/Paper, Sensitized
- Cushing and Company .... E 312 266-8228
  Chicago *(G-4287)*

PHOTOGRAPHIC EQPT & SPLYS: Develpg Mach/Eqpt, Still/Motion
- Kinetic BEI LLC .... F 847 888-8060
  South Elgin *(G-19159)*

PHOTOGRAPHIC EQPT & SPLYS: Graphic Arts Plates, Sensitized
- Base-Line II Inc .... G 847 336-8403
  Gurnee *(G-10862)*
- Letter-Rite Express LLC .... F 847 678-1100
  Aurora *(G-998)*
- Norvida USA Inc .... G 618 282-2992
  Sparta *(G-19258)*
- Rotation Dynamics Corporation ...... E 630 769-9700
  Chicago *(G-6065)*
- Screen North Amer Holdings Inc ... F 847 870-7400
  Rolling Meadows *(G-17774)*

PHOTOGRAPHIC EQPT & SPLYS: Printing Eqpt
- Brahman Spirit Tribe .... F 773 957-2828
  Chicago *(G-3942)*
- Clover Imaging Group LLC .... B 815 431-8100
  Ottawa *(G-16048)*
- Clover Technologies Group LLC ... A 866 734-6548
  Hoffman Estates *(G-11414)*
- Team Play Inc .... F 847 952-7533
  Elk Grove Village *(G-9267)*

PHOTOGRAPHIC EQPT & SPLYS: Printing Frames
- Trend Setters Ltd .... F 309 929-7012
  Tremont *(G-19901)*

PHOTOGRAPHIC EQPT & SPLYS: Toners, Prprd, Not Chem Plnts
- Alpha Laser of Chicago .... G 708 478-0464
  Mokena *(G-14070)*
- Funk Family Holdings Corp .... G 847 276-2700
  Buffalo Grove *(G-2541)*
- Laser Pro .... G 847 742-1055
  Elgin *(G-8640)*
- Midwest Laser Incorporated .... G 708 974-0084
  Palos Hills *(G-16202)*
- Tri Industries Nfp .... E 773 754-3100
  Vernon Hills *(G-20107)*

PHOTOGRAPHIC EQPT & SPLYS: Tripods, Camera & Projector
- Ishot Products Inc .... G 312 497-4190
  Bolingbrook *(G-2195)*
- Promark International Inc .... D 630 830-2500
  Bartlett *(G-1301)*

PHOTOGRAPHIC EQPT REPAIR SVCS
- United Cmra Binocular Repr LLC .. E 630 595-2525
  Elk Grove Village *(G-9296)*

PHOTOGRAPHIC PEOCESSING CHEMICALS
- Lochman Ref Silk Screen Co .... F 847 475-6266
  Evanston *(G-9547)*

PHOTOGRAPHY SVCS: Commercial
- Atlantis Entp Investments Inc ...... G 432 237-0404
  Chicago *(G-3761)*
- B D Enterprises .... G 618 462-5861
  Alton *(G-545)*
- Belair Hd Studios LLC .... E 312 254-5188
  Chicago *(G-3863)*
- Custom Direct Inc .... F 630 529-1936
  Roselle *(G-17950)*
- Early Bird Advertising Inc .... G 847 253-1423
  Prospect Heights *(G-16839)*
- G & G Studios /Broadway Prtg .... F 815 933-8181
  Bradley *(G-2282)*
- Gfx International LLC .... C 847 543-7179
  Grayslake *(G-10774)*

PHOTOGRAPHY SVCS: Portrait Studios
- Concept One Design Inc .... F 708 807-3111
  Naperville *(G-14804)*
- Fedex Office & Print Svcs Inc ...... E 217 355-3400
  Champaign *(G-3292)*

PHOTOGRAPHY SVCS: Still Or Video
- French Studio Ltd .... G 618 942-5328
  Herrin *(G-11171)*
- Haute Noir Media Group Inc .... G 312 869-4526
  Chicago *(G-4787)*

PHOTOTYPESETTING SVC
- Composition One Inc .... E 630 588-1900
  Roselle *(G-17946)*

PHOTOVOLTAIC Solid State
- Bold Renewables Holdings LLC ... G 541 312-3832
  Chicago *(G-3931)*

PHYSICAL EXAMINATION & TESTING SVCS
- Lifewatch Corp .... G 847 720-2100
  Rosemont *(G-18031)*

PHYSICAL EXAMINATION SVCS, INSURANCE
- Lifewatch Services Inc .... B 847 720-2100
  Rosemont *(G-18032)*

PHYSICAL FITNESS CENTERS
- Focus Health and Fitness LLC ..... G 847 975-8687
  Woodstock *(G-21389)*

PHYSICIANS' OFFICES & CLINICS: Medical doctors
- Medbot Inc .... G 213 200-6658
  Chicago *(G-5381)*
- Pal Health Technologies Inc .... D 309 347-8785
  Pekin *(G-16351)*
- Vlahos Electric Service Dr .... G 224 764-2335
  Arlington Heights *(G-828)*

PIANO TUNING & REPAIR SVCS
- Century Mallet Instr Svc LLC ...... G 773 248-7733
  Chicago *(G-4061)*

PICTURE FRAMES: Metal
- Abct Corporation .... G 773 427-1010
  Lincolnwood *(G-12810)*
- All Right Sales Inc .... G 773 558-4800
  West Chicago *(G-20534)*
- Artistic Framing Inc .... C 847 808-0200
  Wheeling *(G-20850)*
- Framery 618 656-5749
  Edwardsville *(G-8363)*
- Frederics Frame Studio Inc .... F 312 243-2950
  Chicago *(G-4632)*
- Supreme Frame & Moulding Co .. F 312 930-9056
  Chicago *(G-6286)*

PICTURE FRAMES: Wood
- Borns Picture Frames .... G 630 876-1709
  West Chicago *(G-20554)*
- Colbert Custom Framing Inc .... F 630 717-1448
  Naperville *(G-14802)*
- Frame House Inc .... G 708 383-1616
  Oak Park *(G-15753)*
- Frank A Edmunds & Co Inc .... F 773 586-2772
  Chicago *(G-4629)*
- Frederics Frame Studio Inc .... F 312 243-2950
  Chicago *(G-4632)*
- House of Color .... F 708 352-3222
  Countryside *(G-7059)*
- Lee Armand & Co Ltd .... E 312 455-1200
  Chicago *(G-5194)*
- Mercurys Green LLC 708 865-9134
  Franklin Park *(G-9993)*
- Michels Frame Shop .... G 847 647-7366
  Niles *(G-15145)*
- New Century Picture Corp .... E 773 638-8888
  Chicago *(G-5575)*
- Oso900 Nfp .... G 312 206-4219
  Chicago *(G-5711)*
- Picture Frame Fulfillment LLC .... D 708 483-8537
  Franklin Park *(G-10017)*
- Sarj USA Inc .... E 708 865-9134
  Franklin Park *(G-10043)*
- Windy City Fine Framing LLC 312 455-1213
  Chicago *(G-6641)*
- Wood Shop .... G 773 994-6666
  Chicago *(G-6667)*

PICTURE FRAMING SVCS, CUSTOM
- Arndt Enterprise Ltd .... G 847 234-5736
  Lake Forest *(G-12226)*
- Mercurys Green LLC .... E 708 865-9134
  Franklin Park *(G-9993)*
- Sarj USA Inc .... E 708 865-9134
  Franklin Park *(G-10043)*
- Supreme Frame & Moulding Co .. F 312 930-9056
  Chicago *(G-6286)*

PICTURE PROJECTION EQPT
- Dukane Corporation .... C 630 797-4900
  Saint Charles *(G-18189)*
- Good Vibes Sound Inc .... F 217 351-0909
  Champaign *(G-3298)*

PIECE GOODS & NOTIONS WHOLESALERS
- Adazon Inc 847 235-2700
  Lake Forest *(G-12220)*
- Avlon Industries Inc .... D 708 344-0709
  Melrose Park *(G-13829)*

PIECE GOODS, NOTIONS & DRY GOODS, WHOL: Textile Converters
- V-Tex Inc .... E 847 325-4140
  Buffalo Grove *(G-2615)*

PIECE GOODS, NOTIONS & DRY GOODS, WHOL: Textiles, Woven
- Advantex Inc of Illinois .... D 618 505-0701
  Troy *(G-19910)*
- American Dawn Inc .... G 312 961-2909
  Wood Dale *(G-21163)*
- Toyota Tsusho America Inc .... D 847 439-8500
  Elk Grove Village *(G-9281)*

PIECE GOODS, NOTIONS & DRY GOODS, WHOL: Trimmings, Apparel
- Phoenix Graphix .... G 618 531-3664
  Pinckneyville *(G-16618)*

PIECE GOODS, NOTIONS & DRY GOODS, WHOLESALE: Fabrics
- Loomcraft Textile & Supply Co ... E 847 680-0000
  Vernon Hills *(G-20073)*

PIECE GOODS, NOTIONS & DRY GOODS, WHOLESALE: Sewing Access
- Marietta Corporation .... C 773 816-5137
  Chicago *(G-5337)*
- Union Special LLC .... C 847 669-5101
  Huntley *(G-11572)*
- Wilton Ww Co .... E 615 501-3000
  Naperville *(G-14950)*

PRODUCT SECTION

PIPELINES: Crude Petroleum

PIECE GOODS, NOTIONS & OTHER DRY GOODS, WHOL: Flags/Banners

Seasonal Designs Inc ....E 847 688-0280
Waukegan *(G-20493)*

PIECE GOODS, NOTIONS & OTHER DRY GOODS, WHOLESALE: Fabrics

C H Hanson Company ....D 630 848-2000
Naperville *(G-14786)*
Illinois Fibre Specialty Co ....E 773 376-1122
Chicago *(G-4890)*
NBC Meshtec Americas Inc ....E 630 293-5454
Batavia *(G-1398)*

PIECE GOODS, NOTIONS & OTHER DRY GOODS, WHOLESALE: Notions

Sullivans Inc ....F 815 331-8347
McHenry *(G-13796)*

PIECE GOODS, NOTIONS/DRY GOODS, WHOL: Drapery Mtrl, Woven

Exclusively Expo ....D 630 378-4600
Romeoville *(G-17818)*
Kempco Window Treatments Inc............E 708 754-4484
Chicago Heights *(G-6755)*

PIECE GOODS, NOTIONS/DRY GOODS, WHOL: Fabrics, Synthetic

Strata-Tac Inc ....F 630 879-9388
Saint Charles *(G-18279)*

PIGMENTS, INORGANIC: Zinc Oxide, Zinc Sulfide

American Chemet Corporation ....F 847 948-0800
Deerfield *(G-7585)*

PILLOWS: Sponge Rubber

Caroline Cole Inc ....F 618 233-0600
Belleville *(G-1538)*
Davis Athletic Equipment Co ....F 708 563-9006
Bedford Park *(G-1466)*
Right Lane Industries LLC ....G 857 869-4132
Chicago *(G-6031)*

PILLOWS: Stereo

Pyar & Co LLC ....G 312 451-5073
Chicago *(G-5920)*

PINS

Arrow Pin and Products Inc ....F 708 755-7575
S Chicago Hts *(G-18117)*
Burgess-Norton Mfg Co Inc ....B 630 232-4100
Geneva *(G-10256)*
Hadady Corporation ....E 219 322-7417
South Holland *(G-19218)*
Pin Up Tattoo ....G 815 477-7515
Crystal Lake *(G-7244)*
Pins & Needles Consignment ....G 217 299-7365
Pawnee *(G-16305)*

PINS: Dowel

Dayton Superior Corporation ....E 219 476-4106
Kankakee *(G-11962)*
Dayton Superior Corporation ....C 815 936-3300
Kankakee *(G-11964)*
Suburban Industries Inc ....F 630 766-3773
Franklin Park *(G-10055)*

PIPE & FITTING: Fabrication

ADS LLC ....D 256 430-3366
Burr Ridge *(G-2650)*
American Diesel Tube Corp ....F 630 628-1830
Addison *(G-32)*
American Piping Products Inc ....E 708 339-1753
South Holland *(G-19193)*
Anamet Electrical Inc ....C 217 234-8844
Mattoon *(G-13630)*
Anvil International LLC ....F 708 534-1414
Tinley Park *(G-19805)*
Anvil International Inc ....E 603 418-2800

Arntzen Corporation ....E 815 334-0788
Woodstock *(G-21360)*
Art Wire Works Inc ....F 708 458-3993
Bedford Park *(G-1457)*
Cerro Flow Products LLC ....C 618 337-6000
Sauget *(G-18392)*
Chicago Metal Fabricators Inc ....D 773 523-5755
Chicago *(G-4114)*
Chicago Metal Rolled Pdts Co ....D 773 523-5757
Chicago *(G-4115)*
Chicago Tube and Iron Company ....E 309 787-4947
Milan *(G-14003)*
Deublin Company ....C 847 689-8600
Waukegan *(G-20437)*
E H Wachs ....E 815 943-4785
Lincolnshire *(G-12761)*
Flex-Weld Inc ....D 815 334-3662
Woodstock *(G-21387)*
Flexicraft Industries Inc ....E 312 738-3588
Chicago *(G-4610)*
Flexicraft Industries Inc ....E 312 428-4750
Chicago *(G-4608)*
Gateway Fbrction Solutions LLC ....E 618 612-3170
Waterloo *(G-20290)*
Geib Industries Inc ....E 847 455-4550
Bensenville *(G-1809)*
Gerlin Inc ....G 630 653-5232
Carol Stream *(G-2991)*
Global Maintenance LLC ....G 270 933-1281
Metropolis *(G-13971)*
Howe Corporation ....E 773 235-0200
Chicago *(G-4851)*
Hub Manufacturing Company Inc ....E 773 252-1373
Chicago *(G-4859)*
Hyspan Precision Products Inc ....E 773 277-0700
South Holland *(G-19223)*
Icon Mech Cnstr & Engrg LLC ....C 618 452-0035
Granite City *(G-10716)*
Industrial Pipe and Supply Co ....E 708 652-7511
Chicago *(G-4909)*
James L Tracey Co ....F 630 907-8999
Aurora *(G-1117)*
John Maneely Company ....C 773 254-0617
Chicago *(G-5043)*
Machine Tool Acc & Mfg Co ....G 773 489-0903
Chicago *(G-5309)*
Manufactured Specialties Inc ....F 630 444-1992
Saint Charles *(G-18230)*
Monco Fabricators Inc ....G 630 293-0063
West Chicago *(G-20621)*
Morris Construction Inc ....E 618 544-8504
Robinson *(G-17120)*
National Metalwares LP ....C 630 892-9000
Aurora *(G-1139)*
Peerless America Incorporated ....C 217 342-0400
Effingham *(G-8418)*
Perma-Pipe Inc ....E 847 966-1000
Niles *(G-15157)*
Permalert Envmtl Spcialty Pdts..............G 847 966-2190
Niles *(G-15159)*
Scot Industries Inc ....D 630 466-7591
Sugar Grove *(G-19653)*
Service Sheet Metal Works Inc ....F 773 229-0031
Chicago *(G-6143)*
Shew Brothers Inc ....E 618 997-4414
Marion *(G-13534)*
Supplied Indus Solutions Inc ....G 618 452-8151
Granite City *(G-10741)*
Tesko Welding & Mfg Co ....D 708 452-0045
Norridge *(G-15244)*
Weatherford International LLC ....E 309 342-5154
Galesburg *(G-10223)*

PIPE & FITTINGS: Cast Iron

USP Holdings Inc ....A 847 604-6100
Rosemont *(G-18058)*

PIPE & TUBES: Aluminum

JM Circle Enterprise Inc ....G 708 946-3333
Beecher *(G-1517)*
Midwest Model Aircraft Co ....F 773 229-0740
Chicago *(G-5446)*

PIPE & TUBES: Seamless

Illinois Meter Inc ....G 618 438-6039
Benton *(G-1927)*
Maruichi Leavitt Pipe Tube LLC ....G 800 532-8488
Chicago *(G-5351)*

Maruichi Leavitt Pipe Tube LLC..............C 773 239-7700
Chicago *(G-5352)*
United Flexible Inc ....F 815 886-1140
Romeoville *(G-17882)*

PIPE CLEANERS

Enz (usa) Inc ....G 630 692-7880
Aurora *(G-958)*
Imagination Products Corp ....E 309 274-6223
Chillicothe *(G-6818)*

PIPE JOINT COMPOUNDS

AST Industries Inc ....F 847 455-2300
Franklin Park *(G-9878)*
Black Swan Manufacturing Co ....F 773 227-3700
Chicago *(G-3908)*
Essentra Corp ....G 814 899-7671
Westchester *(G-20697)*

PIPE, PRESSURE: Reinforced Concrete

Forterra Pressure Pipe Inc ....E 815 389-4800
South Beloit *(G-19093)*

PIPE, SEWER: Concrete

National Concrete Pipe Co ....E 630 766-3600
Franklin Park *(G-10006)*

PIPE: Concrete

Elmhurst-Chicago Stone Company.........E 630 832-4000
Elmhurst *(G-9360)*
Graber Concrete Pipe Company ....E 630 894-5950
Bloomingdale *(G-1996)*

PIPE: Copper

Ems Industrial and Service Co ....E 815 678-2700
Richmond *(G-17012)*
Marmon Holdings Inc ....D 312 372-9500
Chicago *(G-5343)*

PIPE: Plastic

Advanced Drainage Systems Inc ....F 815 539-2160
Mendota *(G-13933)*
Atkore Rmcp Inc ....G 708 339-1610
Harvey *(G-11077)*
Blackburn Sampling Inc ....G 309 342-8429
Galesburg *(G-10185)*
Eastern Illinois Clay Company ....F 815 427-8144
Saint Anne *(G-18133)*
Fusibond Piping Systems Inc ....F 630 969-4488
Downers Grove *(G-8006)*
General Products International ....G 847 458-6357
Lake In The Hills *(G-12335)*
Nt Liquidating Inc ....E 815 726-3351
Joliet *(G-11909)*

PIPE: Seamless Steel

Gerlin Inc ....G 630 653-5232
Carol Stream *(G-2991)*
John Maneely Company ....C 773 254-0617
Chicago *(G-5043)*
Zekelman Industries Inc ....E 312 275-1600
Chicago *(G-6713)*

PIPE: Sewer, Cast Iron

Fast Pipe Lining Inc ....G 815 712-8646
La Salle *(G-12111)*

PIPE: Sheet Metal

Metal Culverts Inc ....E 309 543-2271
Havana *(G-11117)*

PIPELINE TERMINAL FACILITIES: Independent

Kw Precast LLC ....F 708 562-7700
Westchester *(G-20702)*

PIPELINES: Crude Petroleum

BP America Inc ....A 630 420-5111
Warrenville *(G-20232)*
BP Products North America Inc ....G 630 420-4300
Naperville *(G-14783)*

PIPELINES: Natural Gas

ANR Pipeline Company .... G 309 667-2158
  New Windsor (G-15071)
Natural Gas Pipeline Amer LLC .... F 815 426-2151
  Herscher (G-11185)

PIPELINES: Refined Petroleum

BP America Inc .... A 630 420-5111
  Warrenville (G-20232)
BP Products North America Inc .... G 630 420-4300
  Naperville (G-14783)

PIPES & TUBES

Bevstream Corp .... G 630 761-0060
  Batavia (G-1357)
Service Sheet Metal Works Inc .... F 773 229-0031
  Chicago (G-6143)

PIPES & TUBES: Steel

Addison Precision Tech LLC .... G 773 626-4747
  Chicago (G-3540)
Advanced Valve Tech LLC .... E 847 364-3700
  Elk Grove Village (G-8810)
American Diesel Tube Corp .... F 630 628-1830
  Addison (G-32)
Arntzen Corporation .... G 815 334-0788
  Woodstock (G-21360)
Atkore International Inc .... E 708 339-1610
  Harvey (G-11074)
B & B Fabrications LLC .... G 217 620-3210
  Sullivan (G-19660)
Basor Electric Inc .... G 618 476-6300
  Millstadt (G-14043)
Basor Electric Inc .... G 618 476-6300
  Millstadt (G-14044)
Bull Moose Tube Company .... D 708 757-7700
  Chicago Heights (G-6736)
Chicago Tube and Iron Company .... E 815 834-2500
  Romeoville (G-17807)
Coda Resources Ltd .... F 718 649-1666
  Chicago (G-4189)
CSM Tube Usa Inc .... G 847 640-6447
  Elk Grove Village (G-8923)
D D G Inc .... G 847 412-0277
  Northbrook (G-15370)
Durabilt Dyvex Inc .... F 708 397-4673
  Broadview (G-2432)
E & H Tubing Inc .... F 773 522-3100
  Chicago (G-4419)
Epix Tube Co Inc .... E 630 844-0960
  Aurora (G-1090)
Evraz Inc NA .... D 312 533-3555
  Chicago (G-4541)
Forterra Pressure Pipe Inc .... E 815 389-4800
  South Beloit (G-19093)
Gateway Fbrction Solutions LLC .... G 618 612-3170
  Waterloo (G-20290)
Harris William & Company Inc .... E 312 621-0590
  Chicago (G-4782)
Illinois Ni Cast LLC .... G 217 398-3200
  Champaign (G-3307)
Kuhn Special Steel N Amer Inc .... E 262 788-9358
  Chicago (G-5135)
Lapham-Hickey Steel Corp .... C 708 496-6111
  Bedford Park (G-1479)
Leading Edge Group Inc .... C 815 316-3500
  Rockford (G-17492)
Legacy International Assoc LLC .... G 847 823-1602
  Park Ridge (G-16287)
Lex Holding Co .... G 708 594-9200
  Oak Brook (G-15634)
M C Steel Inc .... E 847 350-9618
  Antioch (G-623)
National Metalwares LP .... C 630 892-9000
  Aurora (G-1139)
Nelson Global Products Inc .... F 309 263-8914
  Morton (G-14373)
Nucor Tubular Products Inc .... D 815 795-4400
  Marseilles (G-13561)
Ptc Group Holdings Corp .... D 708 757-4747
  Chicago Heights (G-6766)
Ptc Tubular Products LLC .... G 815 692-4900
  Fairbury (G-9612)
Roll McHning Tech Slutions Inc .... E 815 372-9100
  Romeoville (G-17870)
Structural Steel Systems Limi .... F 815 937-3800
  Bradley (G-2293)

Whi Capital Partners .... G 312 621-0590
  Chicago (G-6615)
Zapp Tooling Alloys Inc .... G 847 599-0351
  Gurnee (G-10945)
Zekelman Industries Inc .... G 773 646-4500
  Chicago (G-6712)

PIPES & TUBES: Welded

Allied Tube & Conduit Corp .... A 708 339-1610
  Harvey (G-11071)
Hanna Steel Corporation .... C 309 478-3800
  Pekin (G-16336)

PIPES: Steel & Iron

5h Consulting & Design LLC .... E 618 317-5822
  Ellis Grove (G-9319)
Franks Maintenance & Engrg .... G 847 475-1003
  Evanston (G-9523)
Ssab Sales Inc .... F 630 810-4800
  Lisle (G-12941)

PISTONS & PISTON RINGS

Burgess-Norton Mfg Co Inc .... B 630 232-4100
  Geneva (G-10256)

PLANT FOOD, WHOLESALE

Wabash Valley Service Co .... F 618 393-2971
  Olney (G-15893)

PLANT HORMONES

Agrochem Inc .... F 847 564-1304
  Northbrook (G-15334)
Gdm Seeds Inc .... F 317 752-6783
  Gibson City (G-10338)

PLANTERS & FLOWER POTS, WHOLESALE

T2 Site Amenities Incorporated .... G 847 579-9003
  Highland Park (G-11302)

PLANTERS: Plastic

Consolidated Foam Inc .... F 847 850-5011
  Buffalo Grove (G-2528)
H E Associates Inc .... F 630 553-6382
  Yorkville (G-21487)

PLANTING MACHINERY & EQPT WHOLESALERS

John Rietveld Farms LLC .... E 815 936-9800
  Bourbonnais (G-2264)

PLAQUES: Clay, Plaster/Papier-Mache, Factory Production

Budget Signs .... F 618 259-4460
  Wood River (G-21260)

PLAQUES: Picture, Laminated

Gabel & Schubert Bronze .... F 773 878-6800
  Chicago (G-4653)
H Hal Kramer Co .... G 847 441-0213
  Northfield (G-15516)
R S Owens & Co Inc .... B 773 282-6000
  Chicago (G-5953)
Rudon Enterprises Inc .... G 618 457-0441
  Carbondale (G-2857)
Stellar Recognition Inc .... D 773 282-8060
  Chicago (G-6243)

PLASMAS

Baxter Healthcare Corporation .... C 800 422-9837
  Deerfield (G-7592)
Csl Plasma Inc .... E 708 343-8845
  Melrose Park (G-13845)
Grifols Shared Svcs N Amer Inc .... F 309 827-3031
  Bloomington (G-2053)
Octapharma Plasma Inc .... G 708 409-0900
  Northlake (G-15554)
Octapharma Plasma Inc .... G 217 546-8605
  Springfield (G-19416)
West Laboratories Inc .... E 815 935-1630
  Kankakee (G-12011)

PLASTER & PLASTERBOARD

Ken Matthews & Associates Inc .... G 630 628-6470
  Addison (G-167)

PLASTER WORK: Ornamental & Architectural

Continental Studios Inc .... E 773 542-0309
  Chicago (G-4230)
Decorators Supply Corporation .... E 773 847-6300
  Chicago (G-4330)

PLASTIC COLORING & FINISHING

Chroma Color Corporation .... C 877 385-8777
  McHenry (G-13726)
Unique Assembly & Decorating .... E 630 241-4300
  Downers Grove (G-8103)

PLASTIC FIRE CLAY MINING

Entec Polymers LLC .... G 866 598-8941
  Plainfield (G-16660)

PLASTIC PRDTS

Advangene Consumables Inc .... G 847 295-2539
  Lake Bluff (G-12168)
AEP Inc .... G 618 466-7668
  Alton (G-542)
Alltech Plastics Inc .... G 847 352-2309
  Schaumburg (G-18434)
APAC II LLC .... G 618 426-1338
  Campbell Hill (G-2813)
Epp Composites Inc .... G 847 612-3495
  Bloomingdale (G-1994)
Fiberglass Innovations LLC .... G 815 962-3727
  Rockford (G-17414)
Laminarp .... E 847 884-9298
  Schaumburg (G-18599)
Paper or Plastic Inc .... G 815 582-3696
  Shorewood (G-18898)
Plaspros Inc .... G 847 639-6492
  Cary (G-3183)
Railshop Inc .... G 847 816-0925
  Libertyville (G-12701)
Rx Vials USA .... G 630 378-4417
  Romeoville (G-17872)
Seaquist Closures LLC .... C 262 363-7191
  Crystal Lake (G-7262)
Ticona Technical Polymers .... G 847 949-1444
  Mundelein (G-14744)

PLASTIC PRDTS REPAIR SVCS

Chicago Mold Engrg Co Inc .... D 630 584-1311
  Saint Charles (G-18165)
Meta-Meg Tool Corporation .... G 847 742-3600
  Elgin (G-8656)

PLASTICIZERS, ORGANIC: Cyclic & Acyclic

Hallstar Company .... C 312 554-7400
  Chicago (G-4772)
Hallstar Services Corp .... G 312 554-7400
  Chicago (G-4773)

PLASTICS FILM & SHEET

Alpha Industries MGT Inc .... D 773 359-8000
  Chicago (G-3629)
Cast Films Inc .... F 847 808-0363
  Wheeling (G-20869)
Clear Pack Company .... C 847 957-6282
  Franklin Park (G-9911)
Clorox Company .... C 510 271-7000
  Willowbrook (G-21036)
Flex-O-Glass Inc .... C 773 261-5200
  Chicago (G-4605)
Flex-O-Glass Inc .... G 773 379-7878
  Chicago (G-4606)
Flex-O-Glass Inc .... E 815 288-1424
  Dixon (G-4607)
Huntsman Expndable Polymers Lc .... C 815 224-5463
  Peru (G-16577)
Midwest Canvas Corp .... C 773 287-4400
  Chicago (G-5440)
Pliant LLC .... A 812 424-2904
  Rolling Meadows (G-17761)
Pliant Corp International .... G 847 969-3300
  Rolling Meadows (G-17762)

PRODUCT SECTION — PLASTICS MATERIAL & RESINS

Company	Code	Phone
Pliant Investment Inc — Schaumburg (G-18677)	G	847 969-3300
Pliant Solutions Corporation — Schaumburg (G-18678)	E	847 969-3300
Printpack Inc — Elgin (G-8696)	C	847 888-7150
Protective Products Intl — Wauconda (G-20386)	G	847 526-1180
Realt Images Inc — Tower Hill (G-19894)	G	217 567-3487
Right Lane Industries LLC — Chicago (G-6031)	G	857 869-4132
Sonoco Products Company — Franklin Park (G-10049)	C	847 957-6282
Transcenda Inc — Palatine (G-16166)	G	847 705-6670
Transcendia Inc — Franklin Park (G-10063)	C	847 678-1800
Transworld Plastic Films Inc — Rochelle (G-17162)	F	815 561-7117

PLASTICS FILM & SHEET: Polyethylene

Company	Code	Phone
Aargus Plastics Inc — Wheeling (G-20837)	C	847 325-4444
Berry Global Films LLC — Alsip (G-423)	D	708 239-4619
Cadillac Products Packaging Co — Paris (G-16225)	C	217 463-1444
Highland Mfg & Sls Co — Highland (G-11219)	D	618 654-2161
Poli-Film America Inc — Hampshire (G-10984)	D	847 453-8104
Poly Films Inc — Hillside (G-11353)	G	708 547-7963
Signode Industrial Group LLC — Glenview (G-10619)	E	800 628-6787
Tee Group Films Inc — Ladd (G-12134)	D	815 894-2331
Tredegar Film Products Corp — Lake Zurich (G-12465)	C	847 438-2111

PLASTICS FILM & SHEET: Polypropylene

Company	Code	Phone
Cosmo Films Inc — Addison (G-82)	E	317 790-9547
Kw Plastics — Chicago (G-5138)	F	708 757-5140
Neptune USA Inc — Schaumburg (G-18647)	G	847 987-3804

PLASTICS FILM & SHEET: Vinyl

Company	Code	Phone
A B Kelly Inc — Cary (G-3142)	G	847 639-1022
C M F Enterprises Inc — Wauconda (G-20337)	F	847 526-9499
Clear Focus Imaging Inc — Franklin Park (G-9910)	E	707 544-7990
Letters Unlimited Inc — Schaumburg (G-18604)	G	847 891-7811
Morton Group Ltd — Highland Park (G-11286)	G	847 831-2766
Sun Process Converting Inc — Mount Prospect (G-14573)	D	847 593-0447
Thermal Industries Inc — Wood Dale (G-21249)	E	800 237-0560
Tradex International Inc — Elwood (G-9465)	D	216 651-4788

PLASTICS FINISHED PRDTS: Laminated

Company	Code	Phone
American Louver Company — Skokie (G-18918)	C	847 470-0400
American Name Plate & Metal De — Chicago (G-3663)	E	773 376-1400
B & B Formica Appliers Inc — Chicago (G-3804)	F	773 804-1015
Blaige — Chicago (G-3909)	G	312 337-5200
Catalina Coating & Plas Inc — Elk Grove Village (G-8880)	F	847 806-1340
Credit Card Systems Inc — Wheeling (G-20876)	F	847 459-8320
Custom Plastics of Peoria — Bartonville (G-1331)	G	309 697-2888
Field Ventures LLC — Northbrook (G-15389)	D	847 509-2250
Idemia America Corp — Naperville (G-14844)	D	630 551-0792
Npi Holding Corp — Springfield (G-19412)	G	217 391-1229
Nudo Products Inc — Springfield (G-19413)	C	217 528-5636
Nudo Products Inc — Springfield (G-19414)	C	217 528-5636
Nypro Hanover Park — Roselle (G-17973)	G	630 868-3517
Rainbow Colors Inc — Elk Grove Village (G-9212)	F	847 640-7700
Suburban Laminating Inc — Melrose Park (G-13918)	G	708 389-6106
Transcendia Inc — Franklin Park (G-10064)	E	847 678-1800
Unique Designs — Normal (G-15227)	G	309 454-1226
Vecchio Manufacturing of Ill — Elgin (G-8773)	F	847 742-8429

PLASTICS MATERIAL & RESINS

Company	Code	Phone
Aabbitt Adhesives Inc — Chicago (G-3499)	D	773 227-2700
Ade Inc — Chicago (G-3541)	E	773 646-3400
Advanced Polymer Alloys LLC — Carpentersville (G-3091)	G	847 836-8119
Akzo Nobel Coatings Inc — Lombard (G-13038)	E	630 792-1619
Amcor Flexibles LLC — Buffalo Grove (G-2510)	C	224 313-7000
Americas Styrenics LLC — Channahon (G-3374)	D	815 418-6403
Ameriflon Ltd — Wheeling (G-20848)	G	847 541-6000
Amsty — Channahon (G-3375)	G	815 418-6430
Atlas Fibre Company — Northbrook (G-15343)	D	847 674-1234
Atsp Innovations Inc — Champaign (G-3269)	G	217 778-4400
BASF Corporation — Kankakee (G-11959)	B	815 932-6751
Brinkman Company Inc — Bensenville (G-1757)	G	630 595-3640
Carver Plastic Products Inc — La Grange (G-12075)	G	708 588-0081
Cope Plastics Inc — East Peoria (G-8263)	G	309 787-4465
Crown Premiums Inc — Frankfort (G-9781)	F	815 469-8789
Dip Seal Plastics Inc — Rockford (G-17379)	G	815 398-3533
Dow Chemical Company — Channahon (G-3381)	C	815 423-5921
Dow Chemical Company — Elk Grove Village (G-8954)	E	847 439-2240
Dow Chemical Company — Ringwood (G-17042)	C	815 653-2411
Dow Chemical Company — Kankakee (G-11966)	D	815 933-8900
DSM Desotech Inc — Elgin (G-8570)	C	847 697-0400
Dynachem Inc — Westville (G-20780)	D	217 662-2136
Eastman Chemical Company — Sauget (G-18393)	F	618 482-6409
Ecologic LLC — Oakbrook Terrace (G-15797)	F	630 869-0495
Elevator Cable & Supply Co — Broadview (G-2433)	E	708 338-9700
Emerald Performance Mtls LLC — Henry (G-11164)	E	309 364-2311
Ems Acrylics & Silk Screener — Chicago (G-4502)	F	773 777-5656
Evergreen Scale Models Inc — Des Plaines (G-7761)	F	224 567-8099
Excelsior Inc — Rockford (G-17407)	E	815 987-2900
F5d Inc — Herscher (G-11183)	G	815 953-9183
Fabritek LLC — Naperville (G-14827)	G	630 983-0211
Fitz Chem LLC — Itasca (G-11658)	E	630 467-8383
Flex-O-Glass Inc — Dixon (G-7899)	E	815 288-1424
Gallagher Corporation — Gurnee (G-10881)	D	847 249-3440
Hanlon Group Ltd — Chicago (G-4778)	G	773 525-3666
Hexion Inc — Bedford Park (G-1472)	E	708 728-8834
Huntsman Expndable Polymers Lc — Peru (G-16577)	C	815 224-5463
ID Additives Inc — La Grange (G-12079)	G	708 588-0081
Ineos Americas LLC — Naperville (G-14845)	G	630 857-7463
Ineos Americas LLC — Lisle (G-12900)	G	630 857-7000
Ineos Styrolution America LLC — Channahon (G-3385)	G	815 423-5541
Ineos Styrolution America LLC — Aurora (G-982)	G	630 820-9500
Innocor Foam Tech W Chcago LLC — West Chicago (G-20598)	E	732 945-6222
Innovative Hess Products LLC — Mount Prospect (G-14535)	B	847 676-3260
J L M Plastics Corporation — Joliet (G-11884)	F	815 722-0066
J6 Polymers LLC — Genoa (G-10319)	G	815 517-1179
Jasch North America Company — Loves Park (G-13222)	G	815 282-4463
Kastalon Inc — Alsip (G-463)	D	708 389-2210
Ko-Polymer Inc — Elgin (G-8638)	F	847 742-7700
Lanxess Solutions US Inc — Mapleton (G-13474)	F	309 633-9480
Lyondell Chemical Company — Morris (G-14311)	B	815 942-7011
Mapei Corporation — West Chicago (G-20613)	G	630 293-5800
Maxwell Counters Inc — Farmer City (G-9655)	E	309 928-2848
Mega Polymers Inc — Romeoville (G-17849)	F	815 230-0092
Minova USA Inc — Marion (G-13522)	D	618 993-2611
Nanocor LLC — Hoffman Estates (G-11438)	E	847 851-1900
National Casein Co — Burr Ridge (G-2707)	D	773 846-7300
Nu-Pro Polymers Inc — Wheeling (G-20947)	G	224 676-1663
Oly Ola Edging Inc — Villa Park (G-20163)	F	630 833-3033
Owens Corning Sales LLC — Rockford (G-17545)	D	815 226-4627
P M S Consolidated — Elk Grove Village (G-9166)	G	847 364-0011
Pcc Inc — Calumet City (G-2785)	E	708 868-3800
Pintas Cultured Marble — Alsip (G-492)	E	708 385-3360
Plastics Color & Compounding — Calumet City (G-2786)	D	708 868-3800
Poly Compounding LLC — Elgin (G-8691)	E	847 488-0683
Poly-Resyn Inc — West Dundee (G-20665)	F	847 428-4031
Polybilt Body Company LLC — Itasca (G-11721)	E	708 345-8050
Polyconversions Inc — Champaign (G-3335)	E	217 893-3330
Polyform Products Company — Elk Grove Village (G-9182)	E	847 427-0020
Polynt Composites USA Inc — Morris (G-14321)	G	815 942-4600
Polyone Corporation — Romeoville (G-17865)	D	630 972-0505
Polyurethane Products Corp — Addison (G-245)	E	630 543-6700
PPG Architectural Finishes Inc — Meredosia (G-13956)	B	217 584-1323
Quantum Polymers Inc — Elmhurst (G-9413)	G	630 834-8427
R T P Company — Dupo (G-8143)	G	618 286-6100
Ravago Americas LLC — Plainfield (G-16709)	E	815 609-4800
Recycled Vinyls LLC — Lake Forest (G-12294)	E	847 624-1880
Reichhold Industries Inc — Morris (G-14325)	E	815 942-4600
Reichhold Industries Inc — Carpentersville (G-3118)	E	919 990-7500
Resin Exchange Inc — Addison (G-271)	E	630 628-7266
Rhopac Fabricated Products LLC — Libertyville (G-12702)	E	847 362-3300

Employee Codes: A=Over 500 employees, B=251-500, C=101-250, D=51-100, E=20-50, F=10-19, G=3-9

2020 Harris Illinois Industrial Directory

PLASTICS MATERIAL & RESINS

PRODUCT SECTION

Sabic Innovative Plas US LLC .... B 815 434-7000
  Ottawa *(G-16075)*
Savannah Industries Inc .... G 773 927-3484
  Chicago *(G-6107)*
Serionix Inc .... G 651 503-3930
  Urbana *(G-20000)*
Sherman Plastics Corp .... E 630 369-6170
  Naperville *(G-14913)*
Solvay USA Inc .... E 708 235-7200
  University Park *(G-19967)*
Standard Rubber Products Co .... E 847 593-5630
  Elk Grove Village *(G-9252)*
Stellar Performance Mfg LLC .... E 312 951-2311
  Chicago *(G-6242)*
Stepan Company .... B 847 446-7500
  Elwood *(G-9464)*
Sunemco Technologies Inc .... G 630 369-8947
  Naperville *(G-14923)*
Tangent Technologies LLC .... C 630 264-1110
  Aurora *(G-1160)*
Targun Plastic Co .... G 847 509-9355
  Northbrook *(G-15491)*
Techmer Pm LLC .... F 630 579-6961
  Batavia *(G-1427)*
Technique Eng Inc .... F 847 816-1870
  Waukegan *(G-20500)*
Texxon Plastics Corporation .... G 630 369-6850
  Naperville *(G-14930)*
Thermoflex Corp .... F 847 473-9001
  Waukegan *(G-20504)*
Thermoflex Corp .... F 847 473-9001
  Waukegan *(G-20505)*
Total Plastics Inc .... F 847 593-5000
  Elk Grove Village *(G-9278)*
United Gilsonite Labs Inc .... E 217 243-7878
  Jacksonville *(G-11784)*
Wilcor Solid Surface Inc .... F 888 956-1001
  Elk Grove Village *(G-9309)*

PLASTICS MATERIALS, BASIC FORMS & SHAPES WHOLESALERS

Atlas Fibre Company .... D 847 674-1234
  Northbrook *(G-15343)*
Bach Plastic Works Inc .... G 847 680-4342
  Libertyville *(G-12635)*
Catalina Coating & Plas Inc .... F 847 806-1340
  Elk Grove Village *(G-8880)*
Hanlon Group Ltd .... G 773 525-3666
  Chicago *(G-4778)*
Lamin-Art LLC .... F 800 323-7624
  Schaumburg *(G-18598)*
Ramar Industries Inc .... G 847 451-0445
  Franklin Park *(G-10032)*
Total Plastics Inc .... F 847 593-5000
  Elk Grove Village *(G-9278)*

PLASTICS PROCESSING

Ace Plastic Inc .... F 815 635-3737
  Chatsworth *(G-3425)*
Acrylic Service Inc .... G 630 543-0336
  Addison *(G-18)*
Acrylic Ventures Inc .... F 847 901-4440
  Glenview *(G-10517)*
C R Plastics Inc .... G 847 541-3601
  Wheeling *(G-20867)*
Cicero Plastic Products Inc .... E 815 886-9522
  Romeoville *(G-17808)*
Cmt International Inc .... G 618 549-1829
  Murphysboro *(G-14754)*
D & D Manufacturing .... G 815 339-9100
  Hennepin *(G-11157)*
D&W Fine Pack LLC .... B 215 362-1501
  Wood Dale *(G-21180)*
Dss Rapak Inc .... G 630 296-2000
  Romeoville *(G-17814)*
Ems Acrylics & Silk Screener .... F 773 777-5656
  Chicago *(G-4502)*
Engineered Plastic Pdts Corp .... E 847 952-8400
  Mount Prospect *(G-14526)*
H&K Perforating LLC .... F 773 626-1800
  Chicago *(G-4762)*
Hazen Display Corporation .... E 815 248-2925
  Davis *(G-7418)*
Heathrow Scientific LLC .... F 847 816-5070
  Vernon Hills *(G-20060)*
Heritage Products Corporation .... G 847 419-8835
  Buffalo Grove *(G-2545)*
Johnson Bag Co Inc .... F 847 438-2424
  Wauconda *(G-20364)*

M Putterman & Co LLC .... D 773 927-4120
  Chicago *(G-5304)*
Mac Lean-Fogg Company .... D 847 566-0010
  Mundelein *(G-14710)*
Material Control Inc .... F 630 892-4274
  Batavia *(G-1393)*
Mpc Group LLC .... C 773 927-4120
  Chicago *(G-5517)*
Northstar Trading LLC .... E 630 312-8434
  Wheeling *(G-20946)*
Pactiv Intl Holdings Inc .... G 847 482-2000
  Lake Forest *(G-12278)*
Plano Metal Specialties Inc .... F 630 552-8510
  Plano *(G-16740)*
Plastic Film Corp America Inc .... F 630 887-0800
  Lemont *(G-12583)*
Plastic Film Corp America Inc .... G 630 697-5635
  Shorewood *(G-18899)*
Plastruct Inc .... D 626 912-7017
  Des Plaines *(G-7824)*
Plitek LLC .... F 847 827-6680
  Des Plaines *(G-7827)*
Polydesigns Ltd .... G 847 433-9920
  Highland Park *(G-11291)*
R C Sales & Manufacturing Inc .... G 815 645-8898
  Stillman Valley *(G-19545)*
Resource Plastics Inc .... D 708 389-3558
  Alsip *(G-503)*
Scholle Ipn Corporation .... F 708 562-7290
  Northlake *(G-15558)*
Scholle Packaging Inc .... G 708 273-3792
  Northlake *(G-15559)*
Simplomatic Manufacturing Co .... E 773 342-7757
  Elgin *(G-8733)*
Team Technologies Inc .... D 630 937-0380
  Batavia *(G-1426)*
Tex Trend Inc .... G 847 215-6796
  Wheeling *(G-20999)*
Thermo-Graphic LLC .... E 630 350-2226
  Bensenville *(G-1901)*
Tredegar Film Products Corp .... C 847 438-2111
  Lake Zurich *(G-12465)*
Trellborg Sling Sltions US Inc .... F 630 539-5500
  Schaumburg *(G-18753)*
Vac-Matic Corporation .... G 630 543-4518
  Addison *(G-326)*

PLASTICS SHEET: Packing Materials

G-P Manufacturing Co Inc .... E 847 473-9001
  Waukegan *(G-20444)*
Scholle Ipn Corporation .... F 708 562-7290
  Northlake *(G-15558)*
Sisco Corporation .... E 618 327-3066
  Nashville *(G-15010)*
Transcontinental Multifilm Inc .... D 847 695-7600
  Elgin *(G-8757)*
Unique Blister Company .... F 630 289-1232
  Bartlett *(G-1319)*
Vacumet Corp .... F 708 562-7290
  Northlake *(G-15564)*

PLASTICS: Blow Molded

CTS Automotive LLC .... C 630 577-8800
  Lisle *(G-12880)*
Ring Container Tech LLC .... E 217 875-5084
  Decatur *(G-7542)*
Ropak Central Inc .... D 847 956-0750
  Elk Grove Village *(G-9221)*
Tpg Plastics LLC .... G 630 828-2800
  Willowbrook *(G-21062)*

PLASTICS: Casein

Midwest Innovative Pdts LLC .... E 888 945-4545
  Joliet *(G-11903)*

PLASTICS: Extruded

Cal-Ill Gasket Co .... F 773 287-9605
  Chicago *(G-4002)*
Corplex Usa LLC .... E 630 755-3132
  Romeoville *(G-17811)*
Custom Plastics Inc .... C 847 439-6770
  Elk Grove Village *(G-8926)*
Davies Molding LLC .... C 630 510-8188
  Carol Stream *(G-2974)*
E & T Plastic Mfg Co Inc .... F 630 628-9048
  Addison *(G-107)*
Fasteners For Retail Inc .... C 847 296-5511
  Des Plaines *(G-7764)*

Nissei America Inc .... G 847 228-5000
  Elk Grove Village *(G-9149)*
Npi Holding Corp .... G 217 391-1229
  Springfield *(G-19412)*
Nudo Products Inc .... G 217 528-5636
  Springfield *(G-19414)*
Plastic Services Group .... G 847 368-1444
  Arlington Heights *(G-788)*
Ravenscroft Inc .... G 630 513-9911
  Saint Charles *(G-18259)*
RPI Extrusion Co .... G 708 389-2584
  Alsip *(G-506)*
Sandee Manufacturing Co .... E 847 671-1335
  Franklin Park *(G-10042)*
Seals & Components Inc .... G 708 895-5222
  Lansing *(G-12514)*
Trim-Tex Inc .... D 847 679-3000
  Lincolnwood *(G-12846)*

PLASTICS: Finished Injection Molded

Accubow LLC .... G 815 250-0607
  Peru *(G-16563)*
Advanced Molding Tech Inc .... D 815 334-3600
  Woodstock *(G-21354)*
Applied Polymer System Inc .... G 847 301-1712
  Schaumburg *(G-18443)*
Aptargroup Inc .... E 847 462-3900
  McHenry *(G-13719)*
Aztec Plastic Company .... E 312 733-0900
  Chicago *(G-3801)*
B J Plastic Molding Co .... E 630 766-3200
  Franklin Park *(G-9882)*
B J Plastic Molding Co .... E 630 766-8750
  Bensenville *(G-1750)*
Capsonic Group LLC .... B 847 888-7264
  Elgin *(G-8531)*
Central Molded Products LLC .... F 773 622-4000
  Chicago *(G-4057)*
Classic Midwest Die Mold Inc .... F 773 227-8000
  Chicago *(G-4169)*
Cutn Edge Cstm Fabrication LLC .... G 779 774-4991
  Machesney Park *(G-13339)*
D and S Molding & Dctg Inc .... G 815 399-2734
  Rockford *(G-17366)*
Designed Plastics Inc .... E 630 694-7300
  Bensenville *(G-1786)*
Dimension Molding Corporation .... G 630 628-0777
  Addison *(G-94)*
Dura Operating LLC .... C 815 947-3333
  Stockton *(G-19549)*
Elas Tek Molding Inc .... E 815 675-9012
  Spring Grove *(G-19274)*
Elgin Molded Plastics Inc .... D 847 931-2455
  Elgin *(G-8576)*
Energy Absorption Systems Inc .... E 312 467-6750
  Chicago *(G-4506)*
Forreston Tool Inc .... F 815 938-3626
  Forreston *(G-9740)*
Four Star Tool Inc .... D 224 735-2419
  Rolling Meadows *(G-17733)*
Fox Valley Molding Inc .... C 630 552-3176
  Plano *(G-16731)*
Global Packaging Dev LLC .... F 847 209-3270
  Chicago *(G-4697)*
ICI Fiberite .... G 708 403-3788
  Orland Park *(G-15960)*
Illinois Electro Deburring Co .... F 847 678-5010
  Franklin Park *(G-9961)*
Illinois Tool Works Inc .... B 847 724-7500
  Glenview *(G-10560)*
Illinois Tool Works Inc .... C 630 372-2150
  Bartlett *(G-1288)*
Illinois Tool Works Inc .... C 708 720-2600
  Frankfort *(G-9805)*
Illinois Tool Works Inc .... D 630 787-3298
  Elk Grove Village *(G-9041)*
Illinois Tool Works Inc .... C 630 315-2150
  Carol Stream *(G-3003)*
Illinois Tool Works Inc .... G 708 479-3346
  Tinley Park *(G-19837)*
Illinois Tool Works Inc .... B 847 724-6100
  Glenview *(G-10563)*
Illinois Tool Works Inc .... C 847 783-5500
  Elgin *(G-8621)*
Illinois Tool Works Inc .... D 847 724-7500
  Buffalo Grove *(G-2549)*
Illinois Tool Works Inc .... D 847 657-4022
  Glenview *(G-10565)*
Illinois Tool Works Inc .... B 630 595-3500
  Roselle *(G-17958)*

Insertech International Inc ....E 847 416-6184
Cary *(G-3172)*
Ironwood Industries Inc ....D 847 362-8681
Libertyville *(G-12664)*
ITW Covid Security Group Inc ....F 847 724-7500
Glenview *(G-10572)*
ITW International Holdings LLC ....F 847 724-7500
Glenview *(G-10575)*
K B Tool Inc ....G 630 595-4340
Bensenville *(G-1835)*
Klein Plastics Company LLC ....D 616 863-9900
Lincolnshire *(G-12777)*
Knight Plastics LLC ....C 815 334-1240
Woodstock *(G-21400)*
Mako Mold Corporation ....G 630 377-9010
Saint Charles *(G-18229)*
Makray Manufacturing Company ....E 708 456-7100
Norridge *(G-15240)*
Mark Power International ....F 815 877-5984
Machesney Park *(G-13358)*
Medplast Group Inc ....B 630 706-5500
Oak Brook *(G-15642)*
Mpr Plastics Inc ....E 847 468-9950
Elgin *(G-8666)*
Neil Enterprises Inc ....D 847 549-7627
Vernon Hills *(G-20077)*
Neil International Inc ....C 847 549-7627
Vernon Hills *(G-20078)*
Odra Inc ....G 847 249-2910
Gurnee *(G-10906)*
Parting Line Tool Inc ....F 847 669-0331
Huntley *(G-11558)*
Peeps Inc ....G 708 935-4201
Palos Hills *(G-16204)*
Pimco Plastics Inc ....G 815 675-6464
Spring Grove *(G-19293)*
Plaspros Inc ....C 815 430-2300
McHenry *(G-13779)*
Plastic Products Company Inc ....C 309 762-6532
Moline *(G-14167)*
Qp Holdings LLC ....G 847 695-9700
Elgin *(G-8705)*
Quixote Transportation Safety ....D 312 467-6750
Chicago *(G-5940)*
Reum Corporation ....C 847 625-7386
Chicago *(G-6018)*
Revcor Inc ....B 847 428-4411
Carpentersville *(G-3119)*
Stanger Tool & Mold Inc ....G 847 426-5826
Belvidere *(G-1702)*
Sullivan Tool and Repair Inc ....G 224 856-5867
Elgin *(G-8741)*
Sun Pattern & Model Inc ....E 630 293-3366
West Chicago *(G-20648)*
Thoroughbred Plastics LLC ....G 815 985-5116
Rockford *(G-17661)*
Van Norman Molding Company LLC ....E 708 430-4343
Oak Lawn *(G-15739)*
Wedco Molded Products ....G 630 455-6711
Willowbrook *(G-21067)*
Western Industries Inc ....C 920 261-0660
Wheeling *(G-21012)*

PLASTICS: Injection Molded

A P L Plastics ....G 773 265-1370
Chicago *(G-3490)*
Abbacus Injection Molding Inc ....E 815 637-9222
Machesney Park *(G-13322)*
Able American Plastics Inc ....F 815 678-4646
Richmond *(G-17007)*
Acco Brands USA LLC ....B 800 222-6462
Lake Zurich *(G-12376)*
Acco Brands USA LLC ....D 847 272-3700
Lincolnshire *(G-12741)*
Admo Inc ....D 847 741-5777
Elgin *(G-8495)*
Advance Plastic Corp ....F 773 637-5922
Chicago *(G-3556)*
Advantech Plastics LLC ....D 815 338-8383
Woodstock *(G-21355)*
AGS Technology Inc ....E 847 534-6600
Batavia *(G-1344)*
All Rite Industries Inc ....E 847 540-0300
Lake Zurich *(G-12382)*
All Star Injection Molders Inc ....G 630 978-4046
Naperville *(G-14956)*
All West Plastics Inc ....D 847 395-8830
Antioch *(G-598)*
Alliance Plastics ....G 888 643-1432
Bensenville *(G-1735)*
Allmetal Inc ....D 630 250-8090
Itasca *(G-11619)*
Allmetal Inc ....F 630 766-1407
Bensenville *(G-1737)*
Alpha Omega Plastics Company ....D 847 956-8777
Elk Grove Village *(G-8817)*
Alpha Star Tool and Mold Inc ....F 815 455-2802
Crystal Lake *(G-7156)*
American Acrylics Inc ....G 847 674-7800
Skokie *(G-18917)*
American Flange & Mfg Co Inc ....E 630 665-7900
Carol Stream *(G-2933)*
American Gasket Tech Inc ....D 630 543-1510
Addison *(G-33)*
American Molding Tech Inc ....E 847 437-6900
Elk Grove Village *(G-8824)*
Apollo Plastics Corporation ....D 773 282-9222
Chicago *(G-3712)*
Armin Molding Corp ....E 847 742-1864
South Elgin *(G-19133)*
Arnel Industries Inc ....E 630 543-6500
Addison *(G-39)*
Bankier Companies Inc ....E 847 647-6565
Niles *(G-15105)*
Baps Investors Group LLC ....E 847 818-8444
Rolling Meadows *(G-17718)*
Bay Plastics ....F 847 299-2045
Des Plaines *(G-7737)*
Box Enclsres Assembly Svcs Inc ....G 847 932-4700
Libertyville *(G-12639)*
Camis Mold & Tool Co ....G 847 593-6620
Elk Grove Village *(G-8878)*
Cell Parts Manufacturing Co ....G 847 669-9690
Huntley *(G-11530)*
Centech Plastics Inc ....C 847 364-4433
Elk Grove Village *(G-8884)*
Century Mold & Tool Co ....E 847 364-5858
Elk Grove Village *(G-8886)*
Chatham Plastics Inc ....G 217 483-1481
Chatham *(G-3419)*
Chemtech Plastics Inc ....D 630 503-6000
Elgin *(G-8537)*
Cim-Tech Plastics Inc ....F 847 350-0900
Elk Grove Village *(G-8898)*
Classic Molding Co Inc ....D 847 671-7888
Schiller Park *(G-18794)*
Commercial Plastics Company ....C 847 566-1700
Mundelein *(G-14679)*
Component Plastics Inc ....D 847 695-9200
Elgin *(G-8546)*
Condor Tool & Manufacturing ....F 630 628-8200
Addison *(G-81)*
Conwed Plas Acquisition V LLC ....D 630 293-3737
West Chicago *(G-20567)*
Cortina Companies Inc ....E 847 455-2800
Franklin Park *(G-9916)*
Cortina Tool & Molding Co ....C 847 455-2800
Franklin Park *(G-9917)*
Cosmos Plastics Company ....E 847 451-1307
Franklin Park *(G-9918)*
Creative Concepts Fabrication ....F 630 940-0500
Saint Charles *(G-18177)*
Crestwood Industries Inc ....F 847 680-9088
Mundelein *(G-14681)*
Crystal Die and Mold Inc ....E 847 658-6535
Rolling Meadows *(G-17725)*
Custom Coating Innovations Inc ....F 618 808-0500
Lebanon *(G-12544)*
Custom Plastics Inc ....F 847 439-6770
Elk Grove Village *(G-8927)*
D & M Custom Injection M ....D 847 683-2054
Burlington *(G-2640)*
Dice Mold & Engineering Inc ....E 630 773-3595
Itasca *(G-11642)*
Dirk Vander Noot ....G 224 558-1878
Prospect Heights *(G-16838)*
Dordan Manufacturing Company ....E 815 334-0087
Woodstock *(G-21382)*
DRG Molding & Pad Printing Inc ....F 847 223-3398
Round Lake Beach *(G-18088)*
Drp Solutions Inc ....G 815 782-2014
Plainfield *(G-16657)*
Drummond Industries Inc ....E 773 637-1264
Bensenville *(G-1790)*
E & C Custom Plastic Inc ....E 630 543-3325
Addison *(G-106)*
E-Z Rotational Molder Inc ....G 847 806-1327
Elk Grove Village *(G-8966)*
Eco-Tech Plastics LLC ....E 262 539-3811
Northbrook *(G-15380)*
Electroform Company ....E 815 633-1113
Machesney Park *(G-13341)*
Enginred Molding Solutions Inc ....E 815 363-9600
McHenry *(G-13741)*
Essentra Corp ....G 814 899-7671
Westchester *(G-20697)*
Evans Tool & Manufacturing ....G 630 897-8656
Aurora *(G-1093)*
F & R Plastics Inc ....G 847 336-1330
Waukegan *(G-20442)*
Fabrik Industries Inc ....B 815 385-9480
McHenry *(G-13743)*
Fapme ....G 815 624-8538
South Beloit *(G-19090)*
Filtertek Inc ....B 815 648-2410
Hebron *(G-11143)*
First Amrcn Plstic Mlding Entp ....D 815 624-8538
South Beloit *(G-19091)*
Flex-N-Gate Corporation ....G 217 442-4018
Danville *(G-7335)*
Flexan LLC ....F 773 685-6446
Chicago *(G-4607)*
Flextronics Intl USA Inc ....D 847 383-1529
Buffalo Grove *(G-2538)*
Flotek Inc ....G 815 943-6816
Harvard *(G-11055)*
Foreman Tool & Mold Corp ....E 630 377-6389
Saint Charles *(G-18201)*
Foreman Tool and Mold ....G 630 377-6389
Saint Charles *(G-18202)*
Foremost Plastic Pdts Co Inc ....E 708 452-5300
Elmwood Park *(G-9453)*
Form Plastics Company ....D 630 443-1400
Saint Charles *(G-18203)*
Formco Plastics Inc ....F 630 860-7998
Bensenville *(G-1801)*
Furnel Inc ....E 630 543-0885
Addison *(G-130)*
GAim Plastics Incorporated ....F 630 350-9500
Bensenville *(G-1806)*
Gayton Group Inc ....G 847 233-0509
Schiller Park *(G-18809)*
Glo-Mold Inc ....F 847 671-1762
Schiller Park *(G-18811)*
Gord Industrial Plastics Inc ....F 815 786-9494
Sandwich *(G-18372)*
Han-Win Products Inc ....E 630 897-1591
Aurora *(G-1107)*
Hansen Plastics Corp ....D 847 741-4510
Elgin *(G-8604)*
Hansen Plastics Corp ....G 847 741-4510
Elgin *(G-8605)*
Hi-Tech Polymers Inc ....F 815 282-2272
Loves Park *(G-13216)*
Hoffer Plastics Corporation ....B 847 741-5740
South Elgin *(G-19152)*
Hpi North America Inc ....G 773 890-8927
Chicago *(G-4856)*
Husky Injection Molding ....F 708 479-9049
Mokena *(G-14089)*
Id3 Inc ....F 847 734-9781
Arlington Heights *(G-753)*
Illinois Tool Works Inc ....D 708 720-0300
Frankfort *(G-9804)*
Illinois Tool Works Inc ....D 708 720-7800
Richton Park *(G-17028)*
Illinois Tool Works Inc ....C 847 299-2222
Des Plaines *(G-7785)*
Illinois Tool Works Inc ....C 815 448-7300
Mazon *(G-13681)*
Indiana Precision Inc ....F 765 361-0247
Danville *(G-7351)*
Innovative Components Inc ....E 847 885-9050
Schaumburg *(G-18560)*
Inplex Custom Extruders LLC ....D 847 827-7046
Naperville *(G-14849)*
Insertech LLC ....D 847 516-6184
Cary *(G-3171)*
Intergrted Thrmforming Systems ....F 630 906-6895
Aurora *(G-1113)*
Intermolding Technology LLC ....F 847 376-8517
Schaumburg *(G-18564)*
Intrepid Molding Inc ....E 847 526-9477
Wauconda *(G-20362)*
Iplastics LLC ....D 309 444-8884
Washington *(G-20270)*
Itasca Plastics Inc ....E 630 443-4446
Saint Charles *(G-18216)*
Ivp Plastics of Missouri LLC ....F 309 444-8884
Washington *(G-20271)*

PRODUCT

Employee Codes: A=Over 500 employees, B=251-500
C=101-250, D=51-100, E=20-50, F=10-19, G=3-9

2020 Harris Illinois
Industrial Directory

1557

J C Products Inc....G.... 847 208-9616
Algonquin (G-375)
James Injection Molding Co....E.... 847 564-3820
Northbrook (G-15410)
Janler Corporation....E.... 773 774-0166
Chicago (G-5005)
Jdi Mold and Tool LLC....F.... 815 759-5646
Johnsburg (G-11806)
K & S Manufacturing Co Inc....F.... 815 232-7519
Freeport (G-10123)
Ki Industries Inc....E.... 708 449-1990
Berkeley (G-1941)
Kunverji Enterprise Corp....F.... 847 683-2954
Burlington (G-2641)
L C Mold Inc....E.... 847 593-5004
Rolling Meadows (G-17746)
L&P Plastics....G.... 618 594-3692
Carlyle (G-2892)
Legacy Plastics Inc....G.... 815 226-3013
Rockford (G-17493)
Leroys Plastic Co Inc....F.... 630 898-7006
Aurora (G-1123)
Lewis Acquisition Corp....D.... 773 486-5660
Addison (G-183)
Lincoln Generating Fcilty LLC....G.... 815 478-3799
Manhattan (G-13433)
Mac Plastics Manufacturing Inc....E.... 618 392-3010
Olney (G-15872)
Magenta LLC....D.... 773 777-5050
Lockport (G-13010)
Makray Manufacturing Company....D.... 847 260-5408
Schiller Park (G-18819)
Manufacturers Custom Products....G.... 630 988-5055
Woodridge (G-21322)
Marathon Manufacturing Inc....E.... 630 543-6262
Addison (G-192)
Master Molded Products LLC....C.... 847 695-9700
Elgin (G-8651)
Mastermolding Inc....E.... 815 741-1230
Joliet (G-11898)
Mate Technologies Inc....F.... 847 289-1010
Elgin (G-8652)
Matrix Plastic Products Inc....D.... 630 595-6144
Wood Dale (G-21214)
Maxon Plastics Inc....G.... 630 761-3667
Batavia (G-1394)
Mega Corporation....E.... 847 985-1900
Schaumburg (G-18626)
Met Plastics....G.... 847 228-5070
Elk Grove Village (G-9115)
Met2plastic LLC....E.... 847 228-5070
Elk Grove Village (G-9116)
Mgs Group North America Inc....D.... 847 371-1158
Libertyville (G-12679)
Micron Mold & Mfg Inc....G.... 630 871-9531
Carol Stream (G-3028)
Mid-America Plastic Company....E.... 815 938-3110
Forreston (G-9741)
Midland Plastics Inc....E.... 262 938-7000
Roselle (G-17970)
Midwest Molding Inc....D.... 224 208-1110
Bartlett (G-1298)
Midwest Molding Solutions....F.... 309 663-7374
Bloomington (G-2079)
Midwest Plastic Products....G.... 630 262-1095
Addison (G-213)
Midwest Plastics Services Inc....G.... 630 551-4921
Oswego (G-16014)
Molding Services Illinois Inc....E.... 618 395-3888
Olney (G-15874)
Molding Systems Engrg Corp....E.... 618 395-3888
Olney (G-15875)
MPD Inc....E.... 847 489-7705
Libertyville (G-12686)
Mvs Molding Inc....G.... 847 740-7700
Round Lake (G-18080)
Navitor Inc....B.... 800 323-0253
Harwood Heights (G-11106)
Newovo Plastics LLC....G.... 224 535-8183
Elgin (G-8669)
North American Fund III LP....G.... 312 332-4950
Chicago (G-5619)
Northern Precision Plastic Inc....E.... 815 544-8099
Belvidere (G-1690)
Nypro Inc....E.... 630 671-2000
Hanover Park (G-11011)
Nypromold Inc....C.... 847 855-2200
Gurnee (G-10905)
Owen Plastics LLC....E.... 847 683-2054
Burlington (G-2642)
P & P Industries Inc....D.... 815 623-3297
Sterling (G-19523)
Paramount Plastics Inc....D.... 815 834-4100
Chicago (G-5760)
Peacock Colors Company Inc....E.... 630 628-1960
Addison (G-234)
Peritus Plastics LLC....E.... 815 448-2005
Mazon (G-13684)
Piasa Plastics Inc....G.... 618 372-7516
Brighton (G-2403)
Plastech Inc....F.... 630 595-7222
Bensenville (G-1868)
Plastech Molding Inc....G.... 847 398-0355
Wheeling (G-20960)
Plastic Parts Intl Inc....E.... 815 637-9222
Machesney Park (G-13364)
Plasticworks Inc....F.... 630 543-1750
Addison (G-242)
Plustech Inc....G.... 847 490-8130
Schaumburg (G-18679)
Pnc Inc....D.... 815 946-2328
Polo (G-16758)
Polytec Plastics Inc....E.... 630 584-8282
Saint Charles (G-18246)
Polytech Industries Inc....E.... 630 443-6030
Saint Charles (G-18247)
Powerpath Microproducts Inc....G.... 847 827-6330
Des Plaines (G-7828)
Precision Molded Concepts....F.... 815 675-0060
Spring Grove (G-19294)
Precision Plastic Products....G.... 217 784-4920
Gibson City (G-10342)
Prismier LLC....E.... 630 592-4515
Bolingbrook (G-2230)
Process Systems Inc....G.... 217 563-2872
Nokomis (G-15197)
Prommar Plastics Inc....G.... 815 770-0555
Harvard (G-11065)
Q C H Incorporated....D.... 630 820-5550
Oswego (G-16022)
Quad Inc....E.... 815 624-8538
South Beloit (G-19110)
Quality Plastic Products Inc....G.... 630 766-7593
Bensenville (G-1879)
R N I Industries Inc....E.... 630 860-9147
Bensenville (G-1881)
Rackow Polymers Corporation....E.... 630 766-3982
Bensenville (G-1882)
Ram Plastic Corp....G.... 847 669-8003
Rockford (G-17565)
Rensel-Chicago Inc....E.... 773 235-2100
Chicago (G-6015)
Rf Plastics Co....G.... 630 628-6033
Addison (G-273)
Rockford Molded Products Inc....D.... 815 637-0585
Loves Park (G-13257)
Rway Plastics Ltd....F.... 815 476-5252
Wilmington (G-21102)
S4 Industries Inc....F.... 224 699-9674
East Dundee (G-8210)
Safe-T-Quip Corporation....F.... 773 235-2100
Chicago (G-6089)
Sakamoto Kanagata Usa Inc....G.... 224 856-2008
South Elgin (G-19173)
Security Molding Inc....F.... 630 543-8607
Addison (G-283)
Shamrock Plastics Inc....E.... 309 243-7723
Peoria (G-16522)
Shape Master Inc....G.... 217 582-2638
Ogden (G-15838)
Sikora Precision Inc....G.... 847 468-0900
Elgin (G-8732)
Smt LLC Group....E.... 630 961-3000
Naperville (G-14915)
Sparx EDM Inc....G.... 847 722-7577
Streamwood (G-19595)
Spintex Inc....G.... 847 608-5411
Elgin (G-8738)
Springfield Plastics Inc....E.... 217 438-6167
Auburn (G-908)
Star Die Molding Inc....D.... 847 766-7952
Elk Grove Village (G-9255)
Stellar Plastics Corporation....D.... 630 443-1200
Saint Charles (G-18277)
Steven Plastics Inc....E.... 847 885-2300
Hoffman Estates (G-11463)
Summit Plastics Inc....G.... 815 578-8700
McHenry (G-13797)
Summit Polymers Inc....G.... 269 532-1900
Chicago (G-6266)
Survyvn Ltd....G.... 847 977-8665
Ringwood (G-17048)
T L Swint Industries Inc....G.... 847 358-3834
Inverness (G-11598)
Target Plastics Tech Corp....D.... 630 545-1776
Glendale Heights (G-10510)
Technatool Inc....G.... 847 398-0355
Wheeling (G-20998)
Techny Plastics Corp....E.... 847 498-2212
Northbrook (G-15493)
Tek Pak Inc....G.... 331 901-5570
Saint Charles (G-18287)
Thermal-Tech Systems Inc....E.... 630 639-5115
West Chicago (G-20651)
Three R Plastics Inc....F.... 815 675-0844
Spring Grove (G-19303)
Three R Plastics Inc....G.... 847 740-2845
Round Lake (G-18084)
Thurow Tool Works Inc....G.... 630 377-6403
Saint Charles (G-18288)
Tmf Plastic Solutions LLC....D.... 630 552-7575
Plano (G-16745)
Tmf Polymer Solutions Inc....G.... 630 552-7575
Plano (G-16746)
Tri Par Die Mold....G.... 847 515-3801
Huntley (G-11570)
Trident Manufacturing Inc....E.... 847 464-0140
Pingree Grove (G-16624)
True Line Mold and Engrg Corp....E.... 815 648-2739
Hebron (G-11152)
Tsk Mnufacturing Solutions LLC....G.... 847 450-4099
Algonquin (G-390)
Ucal Holdings Inc....D.... 847 695-8030
Elgin (G-8765)
Ucal Systems Inc....C.... 847 695-8030
Elgin (G-8767)
Uniphase Inc....E.... 630 584-4747
Saint Charles (G-18294)
Uwd Inc....F.... 815 316-3080
Roscoe (G-17937)
Veejay Plastics Inc....F.... 847 683-2954
Burlington (G-2643)
Vega Molded Products Inc....G.... 847 428-7761
Gilberts (G-10374)
W M Plastics Inc....D.... 815 578-8888
McHenry (G-13808)
Wesdar Technologies Inc....G.... 630 761-0965
Aurora (G-1034)
West Chicago Plastics Corp....G.... 708 582-4014
Bellwood (G-1643)
Wise Plastics Technologies Inc....C.... 847 697-2840
Saint Charles (G-18302)
Wise Plastics Technologies Inc....G.... 847 697-2840
West Chicago (G-20659)
Woodland Engineering Company....G.... 847 362-0110
Lake Bluff (G-12217)
Woodland Plastics Corp....E.... 630 543-1144
Addison (G-336)
Woojin Plaimm Inc....F.... 708 606-5536
Mount Prospect (G-14583)
Yankee Mold Inc....G.... 815 986-1776
Machesney Park (G-13384)
Zeller Plastik Usa Inc....D.... 847 247-7900
Libertyville (G-12727)
Zender Enterprises Ltd....G.... 773 282-2293
Chicago (G-6716)

PLASTICS: Molded

Aberdeen Technologies Inc....F.... 630 665-8590
Carol Stream (G-2923)
Advanced Prototype Molding....G.... 847 202-4200
Palatine (G-16090)
Advert Display Products Inc....G.... 815 513-5432
Morris (G-14290)
Amtec Molded Products Inc....E.... 815 226-0187
Elgin (G-8510)
Anfinsen Plastic Moulding Inc....E.... 630 554-4100
Oswego (G-15992)
BJ Mold & Die Inc....G.... 630 595-1797
Wood Dale (G-21170)
Blackhawk Molding Co Inc....C.... 630 628-6218
Addison (G-51)
Centro Inc....G.... 309 751-9700
East Moline (G-8224)
Chicago Molding Outlet....G.... 773 471-6870
Chicago (G-4118)
Custom Blow Molding....G.... 630 820-9700
Aurora (G-947)
Dove Products Inc....E.... 815 727-4683
Lockport (G-12989)

PRODUCT SECTION

PLATES

Dti Molding Technologies Inc ....D	630 543-3600	
Addison (G-101)		
E A M & J Inc ....E	847 622-9200	
Lake Bluff (G-12180)		
E-Jay Plastics Co ....F	630 543-4000	
Addison (G-108)		
Elgin Die Mold Co ....D	847 464-0140	
Pingree Grove (G-16621)		
Hawk Molding Inc ....G	224 523-2888	
Harvard (G-11056)		
Hbp Inc ....D	815 235-3000	
Freeport (G-10114)		
I TW Deltar Insert Molded Pdts ....G	847 593-8811	
Elk Grove Village (G-9039)		
Inland Plastics Inc ....G	815 933-3500	
Kankakee (G-11977)		
Intec-Mexico LLC ....B	847 358-0088	
Palatine (G-16130)		
J and K Molding ....G	224 276-3355	
Volo (G-20199)		
K H M Plastics Inc ....E	847 249-4910	
Gurnee (G-10891)		
Lakone Company ....D	630 892-4251	
Montgomery (G-14256)		
Lordahl Manufacturing Co ....D	847 244-0448	
Long Grove (G-13161)		
Matrix IV Inc ....E	815 338-4500	
Woodstock (G-21409)		
Midwest Blow Molding LLC ....G	618 283-9223	
Vandalia (G-20016)		
Molded Displays ....G	773 892-4098	
Highland Park (G-11285)		
Molding Services Group Inc ....E	847 931-1491	
South Elgin (G-19168)		
Moldtronics Inc ....E	630 968-7000	
Downers Grove (G-8058)		
Monahan Filaments LLC ....D	217 268-4957	
Arcola (G-657)		
Plano Molding Company LLC C	815 538-3111	
Mendota (G-13952)		
Plastic Designs Inc ....E	217 379-9214	
Paxton (G-16314)		
Plastics ....G	847 931-9391	
Elgin (G-8689)		
Pretium Packaging LLC ....D	815 224-2633	
Peru (G-16590)		
Resins Inc ....G	847 884-0025	
Hoffman Estates (G-11450)		
Riken Corporation of America C	847 673-1400	
Skokie (G-19023)		
Scimitar Prototyping Inc ....G	630 483-3875	
Streamwood (G-19594)		
Sherwood Tool Inc ....F	815 648-1463	
Hebron (G-11149)		
Silgan Plastics LLC ....D	618 662-4471	
Flora (G-9692)		
Spinner Medical Products Inc ....B	312 944-8700	
Chicago (G-6214)		
Studio Moulding ....G	217 523-2101	
Springfield (G-19459)		
T C I Vacuum Forming Company ....E	847 622-9100	
Elgin (G-8744)		
Team Technologies Inc ....F	630 406-0678	
Batavia (G-1425)		
The Intec Group Inc C	847 358-0088	
Palatine (G-16162)		
Trend Technologies LLC C	847 640-2382	
Elk Grove Village (G-9282)		
Tri-Par Die and Mold Corp ....E	630 232-8800	
South Elgin (G-19177)		
Tri-Tech Molding ....G	847 263-7769	
Lake Villa (G-12370)		
Winzeler Inc ....E	708 867-7971	
Harwood Heights (G-11112)		

PLASTICS: Polystyrene Foam

All Foam Products ....G	847 913-9341
Buffalo Grove (G-2507)	
Atlas Roofing Corporation ....E	309 752-7121
East Moline (G-8222)	
Blachford Investments Inc C	630 231-8300
West Chicago (G-20552)	
Dart Container Corp Illinois ....G	800 367-2877
Lincolnshire (G-12758)	
Dow Chemical Company C	815 423-5921
Channahon (G-3381)	
Duraco Specialty Tapes LLC ....D	866 800-0775
Forest Park (G-9712)	
Engineered Foam Solutions Inc ....G	708 769-4130
South Holland (G-19210)	
Excelsior Inc ....E	815 987-2900
Rockford (G-17407)	
Innocor Foam Technologies LLC ....F	630 293-0780
West Chicago (G-20599)	
Meadoworks LLC ....F	847 640-8580
Schaumburg (G-18625)	
Owens Corning Sales LLC ....D	815 226-4627
Rockford (G-17545)	
Pres-On Corporation ....E	630 628-2255
Bolingbrook (G-2229)	
Quality Pallets Inc ....E	217 459-2655
Windsor (G-21107)	
Tek Pak Inc ....D	630 406-0560
Batavia (G-1429)	
Thermos LLC ....E	847 439-7821
Schaumburg (G-18745)	
W R Grace & Co-Conn ....F	708 458-9700
Chicago (G-6577)	
Wave Pads LLC ....G	224 444-9283
Plainfield (G-16728)	

PLASTICS: Thermoformed

Clear Pack Company C	847 957-6282
Franklin Park (G-9911)	
D & J Plastics Inc ....G	847 534-0601
Roselle (G-17951)	
Du-Call Miller Plastics Inc ....F	630 964-6020
Elburn (G-8450)	
Dunham Designs Inc ....G	815 462-0100
New Lenox (G-15031)	
Gmt Inc ....E	847 697-8161
Elgin (G-8597)	
Greenwood Inc ....E	217 431-6034
Danville (G-7342)	
Greenwood Inc ....F	800 798-4900
Danville (G-7341)	
Innovative Plastech Inc ....D	630 232-1808
Batavia (G-1386)	
Jordan Industries Inc ....F	847 945-5591
Deerfield (G-7621)	
Mercury Plastics Inc ....E	888 884-1864
Chicago (G-5394)	
Pactiv LLC ....B	847 459-8049
Wheeling (G-20953)	
Profile Plastics Inc ....D	847 604-5100
Lake Bluff (G-12207)	
Ricon Colors Inc ....F	630 562-9000
West Chicago (G-20636)	
Sonoco Products Company C	847 957-6282
Franklin Park (G-10049)	

PLATE WORK: Metalworking Trade

Ameralloy Steel Corporation ....E	847 967-0600
Morton Grove (G-14390)	
Faspro Technologies Inc C	847 392-9500
Arlington Heights (G-734)	

PLATED WARE, ALL METALS

Fusion Tech Integrated Inc ....D	309 774-4275
Roseville (G-18062)	

PLATEMAKING SVC: Color Separations, For The Printing Trade

Blooming Color Inc ....D	630 705-9200
Lombard (G-13047)	
Chicago Prepress Color Inc ....G	708 385-3465
Midlothian (G-13990)	
Excel Color Corporation ....G	847 734-1270
Elk Grove Village (G-8985)	
Expercolor Inc ....E	773 465-3400
Skokie (G-18953)	
Graphic Arts Studio Inc ....E	847 381-1105
Barrington (G-1221)	
Henderson Co Inc ....F	773 628-7216
Chicago (G-4800)	
M & G Graphics Inc ....E	773 247-1596
Chicago (G-5295)	
Panda Marketing Group Inc ....E	847 383-5270
Chicago (G-5750)	

PLATES

Apr Graphics Inc ....G	847 329-7800
Skokie (G-18922)	
B Allan Graphics Inc ....F	708 396-1704
Alsip (G-420)	
Banner Moulded Products ....E	708 452-0033
River Grove (G-17057)	
Brilliant Color Corp ....G	847 367-3300
Libertyville (G-12640)	
C F C Interarnational ....G	708 753-0679
Chicago Heights (G-6737)	
Cardinal Colorprint Prtg Corp ....E	630 467-1000
Itasca (G-11634)	
Carson Printing Inc ....G	847 836-0900
East Dundee (G-8189)	
Chromium Industries Inc ....E	773 287-3716
Chicago (G-4145)	
Commercial Copy Printing Ctr ....F	847 981-8590
Elk Grove Village (G-8903)	
Cpr Printing Inc ....F	630 377-8420
Geneva (G-10263)	
Creative Label Inc ....D	847 956-6960
Elk Grove Village (G-8919)	
Crossmark Printing Inc ....F	708 532-8263
Tinley Park (G-19819)	
Crosstech Communications Inc ....E	312 382-0111
Chicago (G-4273)	
Delta Press Inc ....G	847 671-3200
Palatine (G-16111)	
Eugene Ewbank ....G	630 705-0400
Oswego (G-16004)	
Graphic Image Corporation ....F	312 829-7800
Orland Park (G-15956)	
Hurst Chemical Company ....G	815 964-0451
Rockford (G-17454)	
Iemco Corporation ....G	773 728-4400
Chicago (G-4878)	
Impression Printing ....F	708 614-8660
Oak Forest (G-15682)	
Instyprints of Waukegan Inc ....G	847 336-5599
Waukegan (G-20449)	
J D Graphic Co Inc ....E	847 364-4000
Elk Grove Village (G-9063)	
Jph Enterprises Inc ....G	847 390-0900
Des Plaines (G-7792)	
Lasons Label Co ....G	773 775-2606
Chicago (G-5179)	
Lloyd Midwest Graphics ....G	815 282-8828
Machesney Park (G-13357)	
Luttrell Engraving Inc ....E	708 489-3800
Alsip (G-470)	
M L S Printing Co Inc ....G	847 948-8902
Deerfield (G-7633)	
M S A Printing Co ....G	847 593-5699
Elk Grove Village (G-9103)	
Marcus Press ....G	630 351-1857
Bloomingdale (G-1999)	
Multicopy Corp ....G	847 446-7015
Grayslake (G-10792)	
N Bujarski Inc ....G	847 884-1600
Schaumburg (G-18643)	
Naco Printing Co Inc ....G	618 664-0423
Greenville (G-10839)	
Oec Graphics-Chicago LLC ....E	630 455-6700
Willowbrook (G-21056)	
Pamarco Global Graphics Inc ....G	630 879-7300
Batavia (G-1403)	
Pamarco Global Graphics Inc ....F	847 459-6000
Wheeling (G-20955)	
Precision Die Cutting & Finish ....G	773 252-5625
Chicago (G-5856)	
Prime Market Targeting Inc ....E	815 469-4555
Frankfort (G-9826)	
Priority Printing ....F	773 889-6021
Chicago (G-5884)	
Rohrer Graphic Arts Inc ....F	630 832-3434
Elmhurst (G-9419)	
Rohrer Litho Inc ....G	630 833-6610
Elmhurst (G-9420)	
Rotation Dynamics Corporation ....E	630 769-9700
Chicago (G-6065)	
Rotation Dynamics Corporation ....D	773 247-5600
Chicago (G-6066)	
Servi-Sure Corporation ....G	773 271-5900
Chicago (G-6140)	
Sharper Image Engravers Inc ....E	630 403-1600
Lombard (G-13129)	
Southern Graphic Systems LLC ....E	847 695-9515
Rosemont (G-18050)	
Sunrise Hitek Service Inc ....E	773 792-8880
Chicago (G-6277)	
The b F Shaw Printing Co ....E	815 875-4461
Princeton (G-16823)	
Tru Line Lithographing Inc ....E	262 554-7300
Niles (G-15183)	
Village Press Inc ....G	847 362-1856
Libertyville (G-12724)	

Employee Codes: A=Over 500 employees, B=251-500
C=101-250, D=51-100, E=20-50, F=10-19, G=3-9

PLATES

PRODUCT SECTION

West Vly Graphics & Print Inc .... G 630 377-7575
  Saint Charles *(G-18298)*
Woogl Corporation .... E 847 806-1160
  Elk Grove Village *(G-9312)*

PLATES: Aluminum

Pechiney Cast Plate .... C 847 299-0220
  Chicago *(G-5778)*

PLATES: Sheet & Strip, Exc Coated Prdts

Mexinox USA Inc .... D 224 533-6700
  Bannockburn *(G-1203)*

PLATES: Steel

Evraz Inc NA .... D 312 533-3555
  Chicago *(G-4541)*
Mittal Steel USA Inc .... F 312 899-3440
  Chicago *(G-5472)*
Seraph Industries LLC .... G 815 222-9686
  Caledonia *(G-2771)*

PLATES: Truss, Metal

ITW Blding Cmponents Group Inc .... E 217 324-0303
  Litchfield *(G-12967)*

PLATING & FINISHING SVC: Decorative, Formed Prdts

Classic Metal Company Inc .... G 815 252-0104
  Mendota *(G-13939)*

PLATING & POLISHING SVC

American Plating & Mfg Co .... F 773 890-4907
  Chicago *(G-3664)*
Arnold Monument Co Inc .... G 217 546-2102
  Springfield *(G-19320)*
Baroque Silversmith Inc .... C 312 357-2813
  Chicago *(G-3835)*
Bellows Shoppe .... G 847 446-5533
  Winnetka *(G-21126)*
Cardon Mold Finishing Inc .... G 630 543-5431
  Addison *(G-63)*
Celinco Inc .... G 815 964-2256
  Rockford *(G-17341)*
Chem-Plate Industries Inc .... D 847 640-1600
  Elk Grove Village *(G-8889)*
Chemix Corp .... F 708 754-2150
  Glenwood *(G-10639)*
Chemtool Incorporated .... D 815 459-1250
  Crystal Lake *(G-7180)*
Circle Studio Stained Glass .... G 847 432-7249
  Highland Park *(G-11258)*
Circle Studio Stained Glass .... G 773 588-4848
  Chicago *(G-4152)*
Clybourn 1200 .... G 312 477-7442
  Chicago *(G-4182)*
Comwell .... D 618 282-6233
  Red Bud *(G-16991)*
Cooley Wire Products Mfg Co .... E 847 678-8585
  Schiller Park *(G-18796)*
Curtis Metal Finishing Company .... D 815 633-6693
  Machesney Park *(G-13338)*
D & N Deburring Co Inc .... G 847 451-7702
  Franklin Park *(G-9924)*
Diamond Spray Painting Inc .... G 630 513-5600
  Saint Charles *(G-18183)*
Dixline Corporation .... D 309 932-2011
  Galva *(G-10231)*
Durr - All Corporation .... G 815 943-1032
  Harvard *(G-11053)*
Dynomax Inc .... B 847 680-8833
  Wheeling *(G-20883)*
Engis Corporation .... C 847 808-9400
  Wheeling *(G-20891)*
Feralloy Corporation .... E 503 286-8869
  Chicago *(G-4580)*
Formulations Inc .... G 847 674-9141
  Skokie *(G-18956)*
Fox Valley Sandblasting Inc .... G 630 553-6050
  Yorkville *(G-21483)*
Glass Fx .... G 217 359-0048
  Champaign *(G-3295)*
Heidtman Steel Products Inc .... D 618 451-0052
  Granite City *(G-10714)*
International Proc Co Amer .... E 847 437-8400
  Elk Grove Village *(G-9058)*
Interntional Metal Finshg Svcs .... G 815 234-5254
  Byron *(G-2754)*

Irmko Tool Works Inc .... E 630 350-7550
  Bensenville *(G-1825)*
Krueger and Company .... E 630 833-5650
  Elmhurst *(G-9389)*
Magnetic Inspection Lab Inc .... D 847 437-4488
  Elk Grove Village *(G-9106)*
Meminger Metal Finishing Inc .... F 309 582-3363
  Aledo *(G-358)*
Metokote Corporation .... E 815 223-1190
  Peru *(G-16582)*
Micro Surface Corporation .... F 815 942-4221
  Morris *(G-14312)*
Midwest Galvanizing Inc .... F 773 434-2682
  Chicago *(G-5441)*
Nb Finishing Inc .... F 847 364-7500
  Melrose Park *(G-13897)*
Performance Finishes Powder .... G 309 631-0664
  Rock Island *(G-17232)*
Polyenviro Labs Inc .... G 708 489-0195
  Mokena *(G-14108)*
Possehl Connector Svcs SC Inc .... E 803 366-8316
  Elk Grove Village *(G-9184)*
Powers Paint Shop Inc .... G 815 338-3619
  Woodstock *(G-21422)*
Pro TEC Metal Finishing Corp .... G 773 384-7853
  Chicago *(G-5888)*
Production Chemical Co Inc .... E 847 455-8450
  Franklin Park *(G-10027)*
Rainbow Art Inc .... F 312 421-5600
  Chicago *(G-5965)*
Redi-Strip Company Inc .... G 630 529-2442
  Roselle *(G-17978)*
Riverdale Pltg Heat Trting LLC .... E 708 849-2050
  Riverdale *(G-17076)*
Scot Industries Inc .... D 630 466-7591
  Sugar Grove *(G-19653)*
Surcom Industries Inc .... G 773 378-0736
  Chicago *(G-6287)*
Ultra Polishing Inc .... E 630 635-2926
  Schaumburg *(G-18762)*
Universal-Spc Inc .... G 847 742-4400
  Elgin *(G-8770)*
Vision Pickling and Proc Inc .... F 815 264-7755
  Waterman *(G-20301)*
Wear-Cote International Inc .... E 309 793-1250
  Rock Island *(G-17254)*
White Racker Co Inc .... G 847 758-1640
  Elk Grove Village *(G-9308)*

PLATING COMPOUNDS

Plating International Inc .... F 847 451-2101
  Franklin Park *(G-10020)*
Stutz Company .... F 773 287-1068
  Chicago *(G-6259)*

PLATING SVC: Chromium, Metals Or Formed Prdts

Alloy Chrome Inc .... G 847 678-2880
  Schiller Park *(G-18784)*
Capron Mfg Co .... D 815 569-2301
  Capron *(G-2832)*
Chromium Industries Inc .... E 773 287-3716
  Chicago *(G-4145)*
Chromium Industries LLC .... E 773 287-3716
  Chicago *(G-4146)*
Custom Chrome & Polishing .... G 618 885-9499
  Jerseyville *(G-11789)*
Ej Somerville Plating Co .... G 708 345-5100
  Melrose Park *(G-13862)*
Ellwood Group Inc .... F 815 725-9030
  Joliet *(G-11859)*
HBm Electro Chemical Company .... G 708 895-7710
  Lansing *(G-12497)*
Precision Chrome Inc .... E 847 587-1515
  Fox Lake *(G-9753)*
R&R Research Co .... F 847 345-5051
  Mount Prospect *(G-14565)*
Surface Manufacturing Company .... F 815 569-2362
  Capron *(G-2837)*
Tru Coat Plating and Finishing .... F 708 544-3940
  Bellwood *(G-1641)*
Wood Graphics Inc .... G 704 872-5798
  Romeoville *(G-17890)*

PLATING SVC: Electro

A and R Custom Chrome .... G 708 728-1005
  Chicago *(G-3484)*
Al Bar Laboratories Inc .... F 847 251-1218
  Wilmette *(G-21068)*

Ameriplate Inc .... E 815 744-8585
  Joliet *(G-11821)*
Arlington Plating Company .... C 847 359-1490
  Palatine *(G-16094)*
Bellwood Industries Inc .... G 773 522-1002
  Chicago *(G-3864)*
Berge Plating Works Inc .... G 309 788-2831
  Rock Island *(G-17206)*
California Technical Pltg Corp .... E 818 365-8205
  Chicago *(G-4005)*
Cardinal Plating Solutions Inc .... G 309 582-6215
  Aledo *(G-355)*
Castle Metal Finishing Corp .... F 847 678-6041
  Schiller Park *(G-18791)*
Chem Processing Inc .... D 815 874-8118
  Rockford *(G-17346)*
Chem Processing Inc .... F 815 965-1037
  Rockford *(G-17347)*
Chicago Anodizing Company .... D 773 533-3737
  Chicago *(G-4090)*
Chris Plating Inc .... E 847 729-9271
  Northbrook *(G-15360)*
Cody Metal Finishing Inc .... F 773 252-2026
  Chicago *(G-4192)*
Custom Hard Chrome Service Co .... E 847 759-1420
  Rosemont *(G-18015)*
De Kalb Plating Co Inc .... G 815 756-6112
  Dekalb *(G-7675)*
Decatur Plating & Mfg Co .... E 217 422-8514
  Decatur *(G-7488)*
Dover Industrial Chrome Inc .... G 773 478-2022
  Chicago *(G-4391)*
Duro-Chrome Industries Inc .... E 847 487-2900
  Wauconda *(G-20345)*
Electronic Plating Co .... E 708 652-8100
  Cicero *(G-6844)*
Empire Hard Chrome Inc .... B 773 762-3156
  Chicago *(G-4500)*
Empire Hard Chrome Inc .... C 312 226-7548
  Chicago *(G-4501)*
En-Chro Plating Inc .... E 708 450-1250
  Melrose Park *(G-13864)*
General Plating Co Inc .... G 630 543-0088
  Addison *(G-138)*
Hausner Hard - Chrome Inc .... E 847 439-6010
  Elk Grove Village *(G-9029)*
Imperial Plating Company III .... E 773 586-3500
  Chicago *(G-4899)*
Industrial Hard Chrome Ltd .... C 630 208-7000
  Geneva *(G-10279)*
J & M Plating Inc .... C 815 964-4975
  Rockford *(G-17471)*
James Precious Metals Plating .... F 773 774-8700
  Chicago *(G-5003)*
Jensen Plating Works Inc .... F 773 252-7733
  Chicago *(G-5019)*
Jvk Precision Hard Chrome Inc .... G 630 628-0810
  Addison *(G-162)*
K & P Industries Inc .... G 630 628-6676
  Addison *(G-165)*
K&J Finishing Inc .... F 815 965-9655
  Rockford *(G-17478)*
Krel Laboratories Inc .... F 773 826-4487
  Chicago *(G-5132)*
M & B Services Ltd Inc .... E 217 463-2162
  Paris *(G-16233)*
Metal Arts Finishing Inc .... E 630 892-6744
  Aurora *(G-1132)*
Metal Finishing Pros Corp .... G 630 883-8339
  Elgin *(G-8657)*
Mexicali Hard Chrome Corp .... E 630 543-0646
  Addison *(G-202)*
Midwestern Rust Proof Inc .... D 773 725-6636
  Chicago *(G-5451)*
Mikes Anodizing Co .... E 773 722-5778
  Chicago *(G-5456)*
Modern Plating Corporation .... D 815 235-1790
  Freeport *(G-10127)*
Morgan Ohare Inc .... D 630 543-6780
  Addison *(G-223)*
MSC Pre Finish Metals Egv Inc .... C 847 439-2210
  Elk Grove Village *(G-9137)*
Nobert Plating Co .... G 312 421-4040
  Chicago *(G-5608)*
Nova-Chrome Inc .... F 847 455-8200
  Franklin Park *(G-10010)*
Pariso Inc .... F 773 889-4383
  Chicago *(G-5763)*
Perfection Plating Inc .... D 847 593-6506
  Elk Grove Village *(G-9172)*

PRODUCT SECTION — PLUMBING FIXTURES

Perfection Plating Inc .... D 847 593-6506
 Elk Grove Village *(G-9173)*
Precise Finishing Co Inc .... E 847 451-2077
 Franklin Park *(G-10024)*
Precision Plating of Quincy .... G 217 223-6590
 Quincy *(G-16923)*
Selective Plating Inc .... E 630 543-1380
 Addison *(G-284)*
Skilled Plating Corp .... G 773 227-0262
 Chicago *(G-6180)*
South Holland Met Finshg Inc .... D 708 235-0842
 Monee *(G-14209)*
TFC Group LLC .... D 630 559-0808
 Addison *(G-306)*
Three JS Industries Inc .... F 847 640-6080
 Elk Grove Village *(G-9271)*
Twr Service Corporation .... F 847 923-0692
 Schaumburg *(G-18761)*
Unitech Industries Inc .... F 847 357-8800
 Elk Grove Village *(G-9295)*
US Chrome Corp Illinois .... E 815 544-3487
 Kingston *(G-12057)*
V P Anodizing Inc .... G 773 622-9100
 Chicago *(G-6515)*
Victoria Metal Processor Inc .... G 773 633-7497
 Chicago *(G-6546)*

PLATING SVC: Gold

Plating International Inc .... F 847 451-2101
 Franklin Park *(G-10020)*

PLATING SVC: NEC

Aaro Roller Corp .... G 815 398-7655
 Rockford *(G-17283)*
Ace Plating Company .... E 773 927-2711
 Chicago *(G-3522)*
Advanced Galvanics .... G 630 422-5157
 Bensenville *(G-1730)*
Advanced Graphics Tech Inc .... C 817 481-8561
 Romeoville *(G-17788)*
All-Brite Anodizing Co Inc .... E 708 562-0502
 Northlake *(G-15539)*
Archer Tinning & Re-Tinning Co .... G 773 927-7240
 Chicago *(G-3727)*
Belmont Plating Works Inc .... C 847 678-0200
 Franklin Park *(G-9885)*
Chem-Plate Industries Inc .... E 708 345-3588
 Maywood *(G-13665)*
Chromold Plating Inc .... G 815 344-8644
 McHenry *(G-13727)*
Ciske & Dresch .... G 630 251-9200
 Batavia *(G-1366)*
Cmp Associates Inc .... F 847 956-1313
 Elk Grove Village *(G-8900)*
Craftsman Pltg & Tinning Corp .... E 773 477-1040
 Chicago *(G-4257)*
Deep Coat LLC .... E 630 466-1505
 Sugar Grove *(G-19642)*
Diamond Plating Company Inc .... E 618 451-7740
 Madison *(G-13408)*
Dyna-Burr Chicago Inc .... F 708 250-6744
 Northlake *(G-15546)*
Forest Plating Co .... G 708 366-2071
 Forest Park *(G-9717)*
Gateway Fbrction Solutions LLC .... G 618 612-3170
 Waterloo *(G-20290)*
Gatto Industrial Platers Inc .... C 773 287-0100
 Chicago *(G-4663)*
Griffin Plating Co Inc .... G 773 342-5181
 Chicago *(G-4742)*
Grove Plating Company Inc .... F 847 639-7651
 Fox River Grove *(G-9759)*
International Plating Svc LLC .... F 619 734-2335
 Franklin Park *(G-9965)*
International Silver Plating .... G 847 835-0705
 Glencoe *(G-10430)*
J D Plating Works Inc .... G 847 662-6484
 Waukegan *(G-20451)*
Manner Plating Inc .... G 815 877-7791
 Loves Park *(G-13235)*
Marjan Inc .... G 630 906-0053
 Montgomery *(G-14261)*
Masters Plating Co Inc .... G 815 226-8846
 Rockford *(G-17508)*
Midwest Metal Finishing Inc .... G 773 521-0700
 Chicago *(G-5445)*
North American EN Inc .... F 847 952-3680
 Elk Grove Village *(G-9152)*
Omega Plating Inc .... F 708 389-5410
 Crestwood *(G-7123)*

Plano Metal Specialties Inc .... F 630 552-8510
 Plano *(G-16740)*
Quality Plating .... G 815 626-5223
 Sterling *(G-19526)*
Southern Plating Inc .... G 618 983-6350
 Johnston City *(G-11814)*
Sterling Plating Inc .... E 708 867-6587
 Harwood Heights *(G-11110)*
Streamwood Plating Co .... G 630 830-6363
 Streamwood *(G-19596)*
Superior Metal Finishing .... F 815 282-8888
 Loves Park *(G-13268)*
Ultra Polishing .... G 224 769-7140
 Elgin *(G-8768)*
US Plating Co Inc .... F 773 522-7300
 Chicago *(G-6502)*
West Town Plating Inc .... E 708 652-1600
 Cicero *(G-6887)*

PLAYGROUND EQPT

International Wood Products .... G 630 530-6164
 Aurora *(G-988)*
Rainbow Midwest Inc .... G 847 955-9300
 Vernon Hills *(G-20084)*

PLEATING & STITCHING FOR TRADE: Permanent Pleating/Pressing

Acme Button & Buttonhole Co .... G 773 907-8400
 Chicago *(G-3526)*

PLEATING & STITCHING SVC

Art-Flo Shirt & Lettering Co .... E 708 656-5422
 Chicago *(G-3738)*
Award Emblem Mfg Co Inc .... F 630 739-0800
 Bolingbrook *(G-2153)*
B JS Printables .... G 618 656-8625
 Edwardsville *(G-8346)*
C & C Sport Stop .... G 618 632-7812
 O Fallon *(G-15569)*
Creative Clothing Created 4 U .... G 847 543-0051
 Grayslake *(G-10764)*
Custom Enterprises .... G 618 439-6626
 Benton *(G-1923)*
Dabel Incorporated .... G 217 398-3389
 Champaign *(G-3284)*
Fitness Wear Inc .... G 847 486-1704
 Glenview *(G-10546)*
G and D Enterprises Inc .... E 847 981-8661
 Arlington Heights *(G-739)*
Initial Choice .... F 847 234-5884
 Lake Forest *(G-12267)*
Johnos Inc .... G 630 897-6929
 Aurora *(G-1119)*
Keneal Industries Inc .... F 815 886-1300
 Romeoville *(G-17837)*
Minerva Sportswear Inc .... F 309 661-2387
 Bloomington *(G-2080)*
Need To Know Inc .... G 309 691-3877
 Peoria *(G-16484)*
Ronald J Nixon .... G 708 748-8130
 Park Forest *(G-16259)*
S & R Monogramming Inc .... G 630 369-5468
 Winfield *(G-21116)*
Second Chance Inc .... F 630 904-5955
 Naperville *(G-14986)*
Triangle Screen Print Inc .... F 847 678-9200
 Franklin Park *(G-10066)*
Trimark Screen Printing Inc .... G 630 629-2823
 Lombard *(G-13146)*
Ultimate Distributing Inc .... G 847 566-2250
 Mundelein *(G-14745)*
Waldos Sports Corner Inc .... G 309 688-2425
 Peoria *(G-16545)*
Wilton Ww Co .... E 615 501-3000
 Naperville *(G-14950)*

PLUGS: Electric

Appleton Grp LLC .... C 847 268-6000
 Rosemont *(G-17999)*
Leviton Manufacturing Co Inc .... B 630 350-2656
 Bensenville *(G-1844)*
Plug Electric LLC .... G 630 788-1018
 Chicago Ridge *(G-6807)*

PLUMBING & HEATING EQPT & SPLY, WHOLESALE: Hydronic Htg Eqpt

K & S Service & Rental Corp .... F 630 279-4292
 Elmhurst *(G-9384)*

PLUMBING & HEATING EQPT & SPLYS WHOLESALERS

Clarios .... D 708 474-1717
 Calumet City *(G-2773)*
Cortube Products Co .... G 708 429-6700
 Tinley Park *(G-19816)*
Dumore Supplies Inc .... F 312 949-6260
 Chicago *(G-4403)*
Imperial Mfg Group Inc .... F 618 465-3133
 Alton *(G-559)*
Jacobs Boiler & Mech Inds Inc .... E 773 385-9900
 Chicago *(G-4998)*
Liquitech Inc .... E 630 693-0500
 Lombard *(G-13097)*
Lordahl Manufacturing Co .... D 847 244-0448
 Long Grove *(G-13161)*
Schulhof Company .... F 773 348-1123
 Richmond *(G-17022)*
Wagner Pump & Supply Co Inc .... G 847 526-8573
 Wauconda *(G-20401)*
Wm F Meyer Co .... E 773 772-7272
 Aurora *(G-1038)*

PLUMBING & HEATING EQPT & SPLYS, WHOL: Fireplaces, Prefab

Bricks Inc .... G 630 897-6926
 Aurora *(G-1066)*

PLUMBING & HEATING EQPT & SPLYS, WHOL: Pipe/Fitting, Plastic

Advanced Valve Tech LLC .... E 847 364-3700
 Elk Grove Village *(G-8810)*

PLUMBING & HEATING EQPT & SPLYS, WHOL: Plumbing Fitting/Sply

Bristol Hose & Fitting Inc .... E 708 492-3456
 Melrose Park *(G-13837)*
J C Hose & Tube Inc .... G 630 543-4747
 Addison *(G-157)*
Jim Jolly Sales Inc .... G 847 669-7570
 Huntley *(G-11546)*
Rothenberger USA LLC 800 545-7698
 Loves Park *(G-13260)*
Stz Industries LLC .... E 773 265-3000
 Chicago *(G-6261)*

PLUMBING & HEATING EQPT & SPLYS, WHOL: Water Purif Eqpt

Arbortech Corporation .... G 847 462-1111
 Johnsburg *(G-11801)*
Gehrke Technology Group Inc .... F 847 498-7320
 Wauconda *(G-20353)*
International Water Werks Inc .... G 847 669-1902
 Huntley *(G-11544)*
Servetech Water Solutions Inc .... G 630 784-9050
 Wheaton *(G-20823)*
Waterco of Central States Inc .... C 630 576-4782
 Lombard *(G-13153)*
Wilton Industries Inc .... F 815 834-9390
 Romeoville *(G-17888)*

PLUMBING & HEATING EQPT & SPLYS, WHOLESALE: Boilers, Steam

Rockford Chemical Co .... G 815 544-3476
 Belvidere *(G-1700)*

PLUMBING & HEATING EQPT, WHOLESALE: Water Heaters/Purif

Nalco Wtr Prtrtment Sltons LLC .... G 708 754-2550
 Glenwood *(G-10644)*

PLUMBING FIXTURES

Anderson Copper & Brass Co LLC .... E 708 535-9030
 Frankfort *(G-9767)*
Black Swan Manufacturing Co .... F 773 227-3700
 Chicago *(G-3908)*

Employee Codes: A=Over 500 employees, B=251-500
C=101-250, D=51-100, E=20-50, F=10-19, G=3-9

PLUMBING FIXTURES

Caldwell Plumbing Co ....F 630 588-8900
  Wheaton *(G-20792)*
Deks North America Inc ....G 312 219-2110
  Chicago *(G-4331)*
Elkay Manufacturing Company ....B 708 681-1880
  Broadview *(G-2434)*
G B Holdings Inc ....C 773 265-3000
  Chicago *(G-4648)*
Guardian Equipment Inc ....E 312 447-8100
  Chicago *(G-4747)*
Hydrology Inc ....G 312 832-9000
  Chicago *(G-4862)*
Iodon Inc ....G 708 799-4062
  Country Club Hills *(G-7041)*
Ki Industries Inc ....E 708 449-1990
  Berkeley *(G-1941)*
Kieft Bros Inc ....E 630 832-8090
  Elmhurst *(G-9388)*
Kohler Co ....D 847 734-1777
  Huntley *(G-11548)*
Lacava LLC ....E 773 637-9600
  Chicago *(G-5154)*
Lavell General Handyman Svcs ....G 773 691-3101
  Chicago *(G-5181)*
Mifab Inc ....E 773 341-3030
  Chicago *(G-5452)*
Royale Innovation Group Ltd ....G 312 339-1406
  Itasca *(G-11729)*
Schulhof Company ....F 773 348-1123
  Richmond *(G-17022)*
Sloan Valve Company ....D 847 671-4300
  Franklin Park *(G-10048)*
Stz Industries LLC ....E 773 265-3000
  Chicago *(G-6261)*
White Racker Co Inc ....E 847 758-1640
  Elk Grove Village *(G-9308)*

PLUMBING FIXTURES: Brass, Incl Drain Cocks, Faucets/Spigots

Cfpg Ltd ....C 630 679-1420
  Woodridge *(G-21282)*
Couplings Company Inc ....F 847 634-8990
  Lincolnshire *(G-12755)*
Globe Union Group Inc ....D 630 679-1420
  Woodridge *(G-21304)*
Isenberg Bath Corporation ....G 972 510-5916
  Bensenville *(G-1826)*
Sterline Manufacturing Corp ....E 847 244-1234
  Gurnee *(G-10931)*

PLUMBING FIXTURES: Plastic

BCI Acrylic Inc ....E 847 963-8827
  Libertyville *(G-12636)*
Danze Inc ....D 630 754-0277
  Woodridge *(G-21291)*
Industrial Fiberglass Inc ....F 708 681-2707
  Melrose Park *(G-13882)*
Jalaa Fiberglass Inc ....G 217 923-3433
  Greenup *(G-10821)*
Lordahl Manufacturing Co ....E 847 244-0448
  Waukegan *(G-20463)*
Pure Processing LLC ....C 877 718-6868
  Carol Stream *(G-3056)*
Staffco Inc ....G 309 688-3223
  Peoria *(G-16528)*
T J Van Der Bosch & Associates ....E 815 344-3210
  McHenry *(G-13805)*

PLUMBING FIXTURES: Vitreous

Elkay Manufacturing Company ....B 708 681-1880
  Broadview *(G-2434)*
Kohler Co ....D 847 734-1777
  Huntley *(G-11548)*
Lacava LLC ....E 773 637-9600
  Chicago *(G-5154)*
Sterline Manufacturing Corp ....E 847 244-1234
  Gurnee *(G-10931)*
Swan Surfaces LLC ....C 618 532-5673
  Centralia *(G-3252)*

PLUMBING FIXTURES: Vitreous China

Cfpg Ltd ....C 630 679-1420
  Woodridge *(G-21282)*
Gerber Plumbing Fixtures LLC ....D 630 679-1420
  Woodridge *(G-21303)*
Globe Union Group Inc ....D 630 679-1420
  Woodridge *(G-21304)*

POINT OF SALE DEVICES

Barcodesource Inc ....G 630 545-9590
  Glen Ellyn *(G-10397)*
Creative Merchandising Systems ....G 847 955-9990
  Lincolnshire *(G-12756)*
Micros Systems Inc ....F 443 285-6000
  Itasca *(G-11702)*
Pos Plus LLC ....F 618 993-7587
  Marion *(G-13529)*

POLE LINE HARDWARE

Maclean Senior Industries LLC ....G 630 350-1600
  Wood Dale *(G-21210)*

POLISHING SVC: Metals Or Formed Prdts

AAA Mold Finishers Inc ....G 773 775-3977
  Chicago *(G-3498)*
Able Electropolishing Co Inc ....D 773 277-1600
  Chicago *(G-3510)*
Aggresive Motor Sports ....G 630 761-1550
  Batavia *(G-1342)*
B & T Polishing Co ....E 847 658-6415
  Chicago *(G-3806)*
Bales Mold Service Inc ....E 630 852-4665
  Downers Grove *(G-7957)*
Barron Metal Finishing LLC ....F 815 962-8053
  Rockford *(G-17314)*
Clybourn Metal Finishing Co ....E 773 525-8162
  Chicago *(G-4183)*
Cornerstone Polishing Company ....G 618 777-2754
  Ozark *(G-16087)*
Deal Mold Polishing Inc ....G 815 363-8200
  Crystal Lake *(G-7192)*
E and J Polishing and Buffing ....G 773 569-0661
  Chicago *(G-4422)*
Finishing Touch Inc ....F 773 774-7349
  Chicago *(G-4592)*
Metco Treating and Dev Co ....D 773 277-1600
  Chicago *(G-5407)*
Sure Shine Polishing ....G 217 853-4888
  Decatur *(G-7554)*
T M T Industries Inc ....E 815 562-0111
  Rochelle *(G-17161)*
Thomson Steel Polishing Corp ....G 773 586-2345
  Chicago *(G-6370)*
V and L Polishing Co ....G 630 543-5999
  Addison *(G-325)*
W D Mold Finishing Inc ....G 847 678-8449
  Schiller Park *(G-18853)*

POLYCARBONATE RESINS

MRC Polymers Inc ....D 773 890-9000
  Chicago *(G-5518)*

POLYMETHYL METHACRYLATE RESINS: Plexiglas

Amcol Hlth Buty Solutions Inc ....F 847 851-1300
  Hoffman Estates *(G-11404)*

POLYSTYRENE RESINS

Flint Hills Resources LP ....G 815 224-5232
  Peru *(G-16576)*
Nova Chemicals Inc ....D 815 224-1525
  Peru *(G-16586)*
Novipax LLC ....F 630 686-2735
  Oak Brook *(G-15649)*
Spherotech Inc ....E 847 680-8922
  Lake Forest *(G-12304)*

POLYTETRAFLUOROETHYLENE RESINS

Senior Holdings Inc ....D 630 837-1811
  Bartlett *(G-1309)*
Voss Belting & Specialty Co ....E 847 673-8900
  Lincolnwood *(G-12849)*

POLYURETHANE RESINS

Custom Films Inc ....F 217 826-2326
  Marshall *(G-13569)*
Huntsman International LLC ....D 815 653-1500
  Ringwood *(G-17044)*
Kunz Industries Inc ....G 708 596-7717
  South Holland *(G-19229)*
Natural Polymers LLC ....G 888 563-3111
  Cortland *(G-7025)*

POLYNT COMPOSITES

Polynt Composites USA Inc ....C 847 428-2657
  Carpentersville *(G-3114)*
Stepan Company ....B 847 446-7500
  Northfield *(G-15531)*

POLYVINYL CHLORIDE RESINS

Drum Manufacturing ....F 217 923-5625
  Greenup *(G-10819)*

POLYVINYLIDENE CHLORIDE RESINS

Polycast ....F 815 648-4438
  Hebron *(G-11148)*

POPCORN & SUPPLIES WHOLESALERS

Creekstone Kettle Works Ltd ....F 217 246-5355
  Raymond *(G-16988)*
Tee Lee Popcorn Inc ....E 815 864-2363
  Shannon *(G-18874)*

POPULAR MUSIC GROUPS OR ARTISTS

Deshamusic Inc ....G 818 257-2716
  Chicago *(G-4344)*
Sandes Quynetta ....G 815 275-4876
  Freeport *(G-10140)*

PORCELAIN ENAMELED PRDTS & UTENSILS

Porcelain Enamel Finishers ....G 312 808-1560
  Chicago *(G-5845)*
Roesch Acquisitions LLC ....D 618 233-2760
  Belleville *(G-1590)*
Senna Design LLC ....E 847 821-7877
  Vernon Hills *(G-20096)*

POSTERS

Gfx International LLC ....C 847 543-7179
  Grayslake *(G-10774)*

POTASH MINING

Pcs Phosphate Company Inc ....D 847 849-4200
  Northbrook *(G-15457)*

POTTERY: Laboratory & Indl

Ipsen Inc ....E 815 239-2385
  Pecatonica *(G-16322)*

POTTING SOILS

Country Stone Inc ....E 309 787-1744
  Milan *(G-14005)*
Earnest Earth Agriculture Inc ....G 217 766-4401
  Lynn Center *(G-13290)*

POULTRY & POULTRY PRDTS WHOLESALERS

Jackson & Partners LLC ....G 630 219-1598
  Naperville *(G-14853)*
Kuna Meat Company Inc ....C 618 286-4000
  Dupo *(G-8139)*

POULTRY & SMALL GAME SLAUGHTERING & PROCESSING

Central Illinois Poultry Proc ....F 217 543-2937
  Arthur *(G-845)*
Grant Park Packing Company Inc ....E 312 421-4096
  Franklin Park *(G-9952)*
Hillshire Brands Company ....E 312 614-6000
  Downers Grove *(G-8022)*
Koch Meat Co Inc ....B 847 384-5940
  Chicago *(G-5113)*
Koch Poultry ....G 847 455-0902
  Franklin Park *(G-9977)*
Tru-Native Enterprises ....G 630 409-3258
  Addison *(G-317)*
Tyson Foods Inc ....F 309 658-2291
  Hillsdale *(G-11322)*
Tyson Foods Inc ....F 773 650-4000
  Chicago *(G-6453)*

POULTRY SLAUGHTERING & PROCESSING

Galloway Como Processing ....G 815 626-0305
  Sterling *(G-19511)*

PRODUCT SECTION — PRERECORDED TAPE, COMPACT DISC & RECORD STORES

Midwest Poultry Services LP .... D 217 386-2313
  Loda *(G-13030)*

POWDER: Aluminum Atomized

National Material Company LLC .... E 847 806-7200
  Elk Grove Village *(G-9144)*

POWDER: Iron

Connelly-Gpm Inc .... E 773 247-7231
  Chicago *(G-4219)*
Mt Vernon Iron Works LLC .... G 618 244-2313
  Mount Vernon *(G-14628)*

POWDER: Metal

Burgess-Norton Mfg Co Inc .... B 630 232-4100
  Geneva *(G-10256)*
Dva Metal Fabrication Inc .... G 224 577-8217
  Elk Grove Village *(G-8961)*
Finish Line USA Inc .... F 847 608-7800
  Elgin *(G-8585)*
Midwest Finishers Pwdrctng 217 536-9098
  Effingham *(G-8412)*
Nanophase Technologies Corp .... D 630 771-6700
  Romeoville *(G-17859)*
Nanophase Technologies Corp .... F 630 771-6747
  Burr Ridge *(G-2706)*
Toyal America Inc 630 505-2160
  Naperville *(G-14935)*
Toyal America Inc .... D 630 505-2160
  Lockport *(G-13025)*

POWER DISTRIBUTION BOARDS: Electric

Rauckman High Voltage Sales .... G 618 239-0399
  Swansea *(G-19696)*

POWER GENERATORS

Becsis LLC .... G 630 400-6454
  South Elgin *(G-19136)*
Ghetzler Aero-Power Corp .... G 224 513-5636
  Vernon Hills *(G-20056)*
Lionheart Critical Pow .... E 847 291-1413
  Huntley *(G-11552)*
Wagenate Entps Holdings LLC .... G 773 503-1306
  Riverdale *(G-17078)*

POWER MOWERS WHOLESALERS

Amerisun Inc .... F 800 791-9458
  Itasca *(G-11623)*
Rahn Equipment Company .... G 217 431-1232
  Danville *(G-7376)*

POWER SPLY CONVERTERS: Static, Electronic Applications

Bias Power Inc .... G 847 419-9180
  Buffalo Grove *(G-2517)*
Pintsch Tiefenbach Us Inc .... G 618 993-8513
  Marion *(G-13527)*

POWER SUPPLIES: All Types, Static

Aerotronic Controls Co .... F 847 228-6504
  Chicago *(G-3575)*
Electronic Design & Mfg Inc .... D 847 550-1912
  Lake Zurich *(G-12406)*
Essex Electro Engineers Inc .... E 847 891-4444
  Schaumburg *(G-18522)*
Hubbell Power Systems Inc .... F 618 797-5000
  Edwardsville *(G-8365)*
Ikonix Group Inc .... G 847 367-4671
  Lake Forest *(G-12266)*
Power-Volt Inc .... D 630 628-9999
  Addison *(G-249)*

POWER SUPPLIES: Transformer, Electronic Type

Datasource .... G 312 405-9152
  Calumet City *(G-2774)*
Power-Volt Inc .... D 630 628-9999
  Addison *(G-249)*
Schumacher Electric Corp .... D 847 385-1600
  Mount Prospect *(G-14569)*
Starfire Industries LLC .... E 217 721-4165
  Champaign *(G-3356)*

POWER SWITCHING EQPT

Ronk Electrical Industries Inc .... E 217 563-8333
  Nokomis *(G-15198)*

POWER TOOLS, HAND: Cartridge-Activated

Robert Bosch Tool Corporation .... A 224 232-2000
  Mount Prospect *(G-14566)*
Sierra Manufacturing Corp .... G 630 458-8830
  Addison *(G-288)*

POWER TOOLS, HAND: Drill Attachments, Portable

Chicago Quadrill Co .... G 847 824-4196
  Des Plaines *(G-7745)*
Stange Industrial Group .... G 847 640-8470
  Elk Grove Village *(G-9253)*

POWER TOOLS, HAND: Drills & Drilling Tools

Groff Testing Corporation .... G 815 939-1153
  Kankakee *(G-11974)*
Pgi Mfg LLC .... G 815 398-0313
  Rockford *(G-17551)*

POWER TOOLS, HAND: Grinders, Portable, Electric Or Pneumatic

Rockford Commercial Whse Inc .... G 815 623-8400
  Machesney Park *(G-13371)*

POWER TOOLS, HAND: Hammers, Portable, Elec/Pneumatic, Chip

Brunner & Lay Inc .... C 847 678-3232
  Bensenville *(G-1758)*

POWER TOOLS, HAND: Sanders

National Detroit Inc .... E 815 877-4041
  Rockford *(G-17536)*

POWER TRANSMISSION EQPT WHOLESALERS

Harger Inc .... E 847 548-8700
  Grayslake *(G-10780)*
Regal Beloit Corporation .... C 844 527-8392
  Roscoe *(G-17923)*
Sumitomo Machinery Corp Amer .... E 630 752-0200
  Glendale Heights *(G-10504)*
US Tsubaki Power Transm LLC .... C 847 459-9500
  Wheeling *(G-21004)*

POWER TRANSMISSION EQPT: Mechanical

Active Tool and Machine Inc .... F 708 599-0022
  Oak Lawn *(G-15697)*
Allied-Locke Industries Inc 800 435-7752
  Dixon *(G-7888)*
Arrow Gear Company .... B 630 969-7640
  Downers Grove *(G-7955)*
Aurora Bearing Company .... B 630 897-8941
  Montgomery *(G-14230)*
Bearing Sales Corporation .... E 773 282-8686
  Chicago *(G-3855)*
Borgwarner Transm Systems Inc .... A 708 547-2600
  Bellwood *(G-1618)*
Cobalt Chains Inc .... F 309 698-9250
  East Peoria *(G-8262)*
Deublin Company .... C 847 689-8600
  Waukegan *(G-20437)*
Federal-Mogul Motorparts LLC .... C 773 478-0404
  Chicago *(G-4571)*
Forbo Siegling LLC .... F 630 595-4031
  Wood Dale *(G-21188)*
Frantz Manufacturing Company .... D 815 564-0991
  Sterling *(G-19510)*
Grayslake Feed Sales Inc .... G 847 223-4855
  Grayslake *(G-10779)*
Industrial Motion Control LLC .... C 847 459-5200
  Wheeling *(G-20915)*
Innovative Mag Drive LLC .... G 630 543-4240
  Chicago *(G-4931)*
Innovative Mag-Drive LLC .... F 630 543-4240
  Addison *(G-155)*
J T C Inc .... F 773 292-9262
  Chicago *(G-4995)*
Kgbal Manufacturing LLC .... G 312 841-3545
  Carol Stream *(G-3009)*
Martin Sprocket & Gear Inc .... F 847 298-8844
  Des Plaines *(G-7800)*
Metal Ceramics Inc .... G 847 678-2293
  Franklin Park *(G-9995)*
Nagel-Chase Inc .... G 847 336-4494
  Gurnee *(G-10902)*
Naylor Automotive Engrg Co Inc .... F 773 582-6900
  Chicago *(G-5558)*
Peer Chain Company .... D 847 775-4600
  Waukegan *(G-20475)*
Process Screw Products Inc .... E 815 864-2220
  Shannon *(G-18872)*
Productigear Inc .... E 773 847-4505
  Chicago *(G-5893)*
Raycar Gear & Machine Company .... E 815 874-3948
  Rockford *(G-17566)*
Reliance Gear Corporation .... D 630 543-6640
  Addison *(G-270)*
Rexnord Industries LLC .... D 630 969-1770
  Downers Grove *(G-8087)*
Rockford Jobbing Service Inc .... G 815 398-8661
  Rockford *(G-17596)*
S&R Precision Machine LLC .... F 815 469-6544
  Frankfort *(G-9835)*
SKF USA Inc .... D 847 742-0700
  Elgin *(G-8736)*
Surge Clutch & Drive Line Co .... G 708 331-1352
  South Holland *(G-19247)*
Tb Woods Incorporated .... D 815 389-6600
  South Beloit *(G-19116)*
Walterscheid Inc Woodridge .... C 630 972-9300
  Woodridge *(G-21345)*
Worldwide Trans and Diff Corp .... G 773 930-3447
  Chicago *(G-6679)*
Wpg US Holdco LLC .... B 312 517-3750
  Chicago *(G-6681)*

POWER TRANSMISSION EQPT: Vehicle

HM Manufacturing Inc .... F 847 487-8700
  Wauconda *(G-20356)*

PRECAST TERRAZZO OR CONCRETE PRDTS

Component Precast Supply Inc .... G 630 483-2900
  West Chicago *(G-20566)*
Connelly-Gpm Inc .... E 773 247-7231
  Chicago *(G-4219)*
Details Etc .... F 708 932-5543
  Mokena *(G-14078)*
Kienstra Pipe & Precast LLC .... E 618 482-3283
  Madison *(G-13416)*
Terrell Materials Corporation .... E 847 635-8530
  Rosemont *(G-18053)*

PRECIOUS METALS

Horizon Metals Inc .... E 773 478-8888
  Niles *(G-15129)*
IL International LLC .... G 773 276-0070
  Chicago *(G-4886)*

PRECIOUS STONES & METALS, WHOLESALE

John Buechner Inc .... G 312 263-2226
  Chicago *(G-5038)*
Masud Jewelers Inc .... G 312 236-0547
  Chicago *(G-5363)*
TPC Metals LLC 330 479-9510
  Willowbrook *(G-21061)*

PRECIOUS STONES WHOLESALERS

Hakimian Gem Co .... G 312 236-6969
  Chicago *(G-4770)*

PRERECORDED TAPE, CD & RECORD STORE: Record, Disc/Tape

Bezarr .... G 651 200-5641
  Willowbrook *(G-21031)*

PRERECORDED TAPE, COMPACT DISC & RECORD STORES

3b Media Inc .... F 312 563-9363
  Chicago *(G-3467)*

Employee Codes: A=Over 500 employees, B=251-500
C=101-250, D=51-100, E=20-50, F=10-19, G=3-9

PRERECORDED TAPE, COMPACT DISC & RECORD STORES

Music Solutions ....F....... 630 759-3033
  Bolingbrook *(G-2218)*

PRERECORDED TAPE, COMPACT DISC & RECORD STORES: Compact Disc

Delmark Records LLC ....G....... 773 539-5001
  Chicago *(G-4334)*

PRERECORDED TAPE, COMPACT DISC & RECORD STORES: Records

Polyvinyl Record Co ....G....... 217 403-1752
  Champaign *(G-3336)*

PRESS CLIPPING SVC

Cision US Inc ....C....... 312 922-2400
  Chicago *(G-4154)*

PRESS SVCS

Elite Die & Finishing Inc ....G....... 708 389-4848
  Tinley Park *(G-19823)*

PRESSED & MOLDED PULP PRDTS, NEC: From Purchased Materials

Midland Davis Corporation ....D....... 309 277-1617
  Moline *(G-14161)*

PRESSED FIBER & MOLDED PULP PRDTS, EXC FOOD PRDTS

Lucky Games Inc ....F....... 773 549-9051
  Northbrook *(G-15422)*
Oce-Van Der Grinten NV ....E....... 217 348-8111
  Charleston *(G-3408)*
Protex Products LLC ....G....... 312 292-1310
  Chicago *(G-5906)*

PRESSES

Bourn & Bourn Inc ....C....... 815 965-4013
  Rockford *(G-17327)*
Hersheys Metal Meister LLC ....E....... 217 234-4700
  Claremont *(G-6898)*
K & S Precision Metals Co ....G....... 773 586-8503
  Chicago *(G-5065)*
Mechanical Tool & Engrg Co ....C....... 815 397-4701
  Rockford *(G-17513)*

PRESTRESSED CONCRETE PRDTS

Price Brothers Co ....D....... 815 389-4800
  South Beloit *(G-19109)*

PRIMARY FINISHED OR SEMIFINISHED SHAPES

Multitech Industries ....G....... 815 206-0015
  Woodstock *(G-21415)*
Works In Progress Foundation ....G....... 847 997-8338
  Lake Villa *(G-12372)*

PRIMARY METAL PRODUCTS

Direct Selling Strategies ....G....... 847 993-3188
  Rosemont *(G-18018)*
Hall Fabrication Inc ....G....... 217 322-2212
  Rushville *(G-18109)*
Lindsay Metal Madness Inc ....G....... 815 568-4560
  Woodstock *(G-21406)*
Orion Metals Co ....G....... 847 412-9532
  Glenview *(G-10596)*
Phillip C Cowen ....E....... 630 208-1848
  Geneva *(G-10299)*

PRINT CARTRIDGES: Laser & Other Computer Printers

Active Office Solutions ....F....... 773 539-3333
  Chicago *(G-3536)*
Aim Graphic Machinery Ltd ....F....... 847 215-8000
  Buffalo Grove *(G-2506)*
Alternative TS ....G....... 618 257-0230
  Belleville *(G-1529)*
Cartridge World Decatur ....G....... 217 875-0465
  Decatur *(G-7470)*
Ink Stop Inc ....G....... 847 478-0631
  Buffalo Grove *(G-2550)*

Next Day Toner Supplies Inc ....E....... 708 478-1000
  Orland Park *(G-15971)*
Rpt Toner LLC ....E....... 630 694-0400
  Bensenville *(G-1886)*
Tonerhead Inc ....E....... 815 331-3200
  Spring Grove *(G-19304)*
Troy McDaniel ....G....... 309 369-6225
  Pekin *(G-16366)*

PRINTED CIRCUIT BOARDS

Accelerated Assemblies Inc ....E....... 630 616-6680
  Elk Grove Village *(G-8798)*
Accutrace Inc ....F....... 847 290-9900
  Elk Grove Village *(G-8801)*
Advanced Electronics Inc ....D....... 630 293-3300
  West Chicago *(G-20531)*
Aerotronic Controls Co ....F....... 847 228-6504
  Chicago *(G-3575)*
Allfavor Technologies Inc ....G....... 630 913-4263
  Schaumburg *(G-18432)*
Alpha Pcb Designs Inc ....G....... 773 631-5543
  Chicago *(G-3631)*
American Circuit Services Inc ....F....... 847 895-0500
  Elk Grove Village *(G-8822)*
American Circuit Systems Inc ....E....... 630 543-4450
  Addison *(G-30)*
American Precision Elec Inc ....D....... 630 510-8080
  Carol Stream *(G-2936)*
American Standard Circuits Inc ....E....... 630 639-5444
  West Chicago *(G-20539)*
Ampel Incorporated ....E....... 847 952-1900
  Elk Grove Village *(G-8829)*
Answer Call ....G....... 773 573-6369
  Chicago *(G-3703)*
ARC-Tronics Inc ....C....... 847 437-0211
  Elk Grove Village *(G-8837)*
Asg-Uniaero ....G....... 773 941-5053
  Dolton *(G-7930)*
Astral Power Systems Inc ....G....... 630 518-1741
  Aurora *(G-1055)*
Aurora Circuits LLC ....D....... 630 978-3830
  Aurora *(G-916)*
Bandjwet Enterprises Inc ....G....... 847 797-9250
  Rolling Meadows *(G-17716)*
Bartec Orb Inc ....E....... 773 927-8600
  Chicago *(G-3843)*
Benchmark Electronics Inc ....B....... 309 822-8587
  Metamora *(G-13959)*
Bishop Engineering Company ....F....... 630 305-9538
  Lisle *(G-12872)*
Brigitflex Inc ....E....... 847 741-1452
  Elgin *(G-8524)*
Camtek Inc ....D....... 309 661-0348
  Bloomington *(G-2029)*
Cck Automations Inc ....E....... 217 243-6040
  Jacksonville *(G-11761)*
Chicago Circuits Corporation ....F....... 847 238-1623
  Elk Grove Village *(G-8891)*
Circom Inc ....E....... 630 595-4460
  Bensenville *(G-1770)*
Circuit Engineering LLC ....E....... 847 806-7777
  Elk Grove Village *(G-8899)*
Circuitronics ....E....... 630 668-5407
  Elgin *(G-8540)*
Creative Hi-Tech Ltd ....E....... 224 653-4000
  Schaumburg *(G-18492)*
Daves Electronic Service ....F....... 217 283-5010
  Hoopeston *(G-11507)*
Delta Precision Circuits Inc ....E....... 847 758-8000
  Elk Grove Village *(G-8943)*
Ecmc Inc ....E....... 847 352-5015
  Schaumburg *(G-18514)*
Edgo Technical Sales Inc ....G....... 630 961-8398
  Naperville *(G-14965)*
Elcon Inc ....E....... 815 467-9500
  Minooka *(G-14059)*
Electro-Circuits Inc ....E....... 630 339-3389
  Schaumburg *(G-18516)*
Electronic Design & Mfg Inc ....D....... 847 550-1912
  Lake Zurich *(G-12406)*
Electronic Resources Corp ....G....... 331 225-3450
  Addison *(G-112)*
Emerge Technology Group LLC ....G....... 224 603-2161
  Lake Villa *(G-12350)*
Excel Electro Assembly Inc ....G....... 847 621-2500
  Elk Grove Village *(G-8986)*
Fine Circuits Inc ....F....... 630 213-8700
  Bartlett *(G-1280)*
Galaxy Circuits Inc ....E....... 630 462-1010
  Carol Stream *(G-2989)*

General Electro Corporation ....F....... 630 595-8989
  Bensenville *(G-1810)*
Get A Quote For Your Pcb ....G....... 847 952-1900
  Elk Grove Village *(G-9014)*
Hytel Group Inc ....E....... 847 683-9800
  Hampshire *(G-10974)*
Illinois Tool Works Inc ....G....... 630 825-7900
  Glendale Heights *(G-10460)*
Image Circuit Inc ....G....... 847 622-3300
  Elk Grove Village *(G-9045)*
Imagineering Inc ....E....... 847 806-0003
  Elk Grove Village *(G-9047)*
International Control Svcs Inc ....C....... 217 422-6700
  Decatur *(G-7508)*
Intratek Inc ....G....... 847 640-0007
  Elk Grove Village *(G-9059)*
Journey Circuits Inc ....G....... 630 283-0604
  Schaumburg *(G-18579)*
K Trox Sales Inc ....G....... 815 568-1521
  Marengo *(G-13487)*
Kay & Cee ....G....... 773 425-9169
  Calumet Park *(G-2798)*
King Circuit ....E....... 630 629-7300
  Schaumburg *(G-18586)*
Landmeier Corp ....E....... 847 709-2823
  Elk Grove Village *(G-9083)*
M-Wave Controls LLC ....E....... 630 562-5550
  Glendale Heights *(G-10470)*
M-Wave International LLC ....E....... 630 562-5550
  Glendale Heights *(G-10471)*
Manu Industries Inc ....E....... 847 891-6412
  Schaumburg *(G-18618)*
Manu-TEC of Illinois LLC ....F....... 630 543-3022
  Addison *(G-191)*
Mega Circuit Inc ....D....... 630 543-8460
  Addison *(G-196)*
Mektronix Technology Inc ....G....... 847 680-3300
  Libertyville *(G-12677)*
Methode Development Co ....D....... 708 867-6777
  Chicago *(G-5408)*
Methode Electronics Inc ....B....... 708 867-6777
  Chicago *(G-5409)*
Meyer Electronic Mfg Svcs Inc ....G....... 309 808-4100
  Normal *(G-15209)*
Michele Terrell ....G....... 312 305-0876
  Evanston *(G-9551)*
Micro Circuit Inc ....F....... 630 628-5760
  Addison *(G-205)*
Milplex Circuits Inc ....C....... 630 250-1580
  Addison *(G-217)*
Milplex Electronics Inc ....E....... 630 250-1580
  Addison *(G-218)*
Mr Rakesh Avichal ....G....... 224 735-0505
  Elk Grove Village *(G-9136)*
National Technology Inc ....E....... 847 506-1300
  Rolling Meadows *(G-17752)*
Novatronix Inc ....E....... 630 860-4300
  Wood Dale *(G-21223)*
Patriot Materials LLC ....G....... 630 501-0260
  Elmhurst *(G-9409)*
Pcb Express Inc ....G....... 847 952-8896
  Elk Grove Village *(G-9171)*
Plexus Corp ....B....... 847 793-4400
  Buffalo Grove *(G-2587)*
Price Circuits LLC ....E....... 847 742-4700
  Elgin *(G-8694)*
Qcircuits Inc ....D....... 847 797-6678
  Elk Grove Village *(G-9203)*
Qcircuits Inc ....E....... 618 662-8365
  Flora *(G-9690)*
Rw Technologies US LLC ....F....... 815 444-6887
  Crystal Lake *(G-7259)*
Siemens Manufacturing Co Inc ....C....... 618 539-3000
  Freeburg *(G-10094)*
Siemens Manufacturing Co Inc ....C....... 618 475-3325
  New Athens *(G-15021)*
Sigmatron International Inc ....G....... 847 586-5200
  Elgin *(G-8730)*
Sigmatron International Inc ....G....... 847 956-8000
  Elk Grove Village *(G-9238)*
Sparton Corporation ....B....... 847 762-5800
  Schaumburg *(G-18717)*
Sparton Design Services LLC ....G....... 847 762-5800
  Schaumburg *(G-18718)*
Sparton Parent Inc ....E....... 847 762-5800
  Schaumburg *(G-18721)*
Srr Manufacturing Services ....G....... 847 404-3527
  Gilberts *(G-10372)*
Sunrise Electronics Inc ....E....... 847 357-0500
  Elk Grove Village *(G-9260)*

PRODUCT SECTION — PRINTING MACHINERY

Surya Electronics Inc .... C 630 858-8000
  Glendale Heights (G-10507)
Taranda Specialties Inc .... G 815 469-3041
  Frankfort (G-9844)
Tecnova Electronics Inc .... D 847 336-6160
  Waukegan (G-20502)
The Syntek Group Inc .... G 773 279-0131
  Chicago (G-6360)
Triad Circuits Inc .... E 847 283-8600
  Waukegan (G-20510)
Twisted Traces Inc .... G 630 345-5400
  Elk Grove Village (G-9289)
Universal Scientific III Inc .... G 847 228-6464
  Chicago (G-6483)
Wand Enterprises Inc .... F 847 433-0231
  Highland Park (G-11304)
Y 2 K Electronics Inc .... F 847 238-9024
  Elk Grove Village (G-9315)

PRINTERS & PLOTTERS

Hafner Duplicating Company .... G 312 362-0120
  Chicago (G-4766)
John Harland Company .... G 815 293-4350
  Romeoville (G-17836)
Yfy Jupiter Inc .... E 312 419-8565
  Chicago (G-6699)

PRINTERS' SVCS: Folding, Collating, Etc

3dp Unlimited LLC .... G 815 389-5667
  Roscoe (G-17896)
Stromberg Allen and Company .... E 773 847-7131
  Tinley Park (G-19858)
Tag Diamond & Label .... E 630 844-9395
  Aurora (G-1159)

PRINTERS: Computer

Lexmark International Inc .... E 847 318-5700
  Rosemont (G-18030)
Sg2 .... G 847 779-5500
  Skokie (G-19029)
Singer Data Products Inc .... E 630 860-6500
  Bensenville (G-1893)

PRINTERS: Magnetic Ink, Bar Code

Bar Codes Inc .... D 800 351-9962
  Chicago (G-3828)
Barcodesource Inc .... G 630 545-9590
  Glen Ellyn (G-10397)
Printjet Corporation .... F 815 877-7511
  Machesney Park (G-13368)
Zebra Technologies Corporation .... B 847 634-6700
  Lincolnshire (G-12804)
Zebra Technologies Corporation .... B 847 634-6700
  Chicago (G-6711)
Zebra Technologies Intl LLC .... G 847 634-6700
  Lincolnshire (G-12805)
Zih Corp .... G 847 634-6700
  Lincolnshire (G-12807)
Zih Corp .... E 847 634-6700
  Lincolnshire (G-12808)

PRINTING & BINDING: Book Music

Sandes Quynetta .... G 815 275-4876
  Freeport (G-10140)

PRINTING & BINDING: Books

Finishing Group .... G 847 884-4890
  Schaumburg (G-18528)
Lsc Communications Us LLC .... C 217 235-0561
  Mattoon (G-13642)
R R Donnelley & Sons Company .... B 630 588-5000
  Lisle (G-12931)
R R Donnelley & Sons Company .... A 312 326-8000
  Chicago (G-5950)
RR Donnelley & Sons Company .... C 312 236-8000
  Chicago (G-6071)
Tvp Color Graphics Inc .... G 630 837-3600
  Streamwood (G-19600)

PRINTING & BINDING: Textbooks

Rsn Mailing .... G 314 724-3364
  Collinsville (G-6974)

PRINTING & EMBOSSING: Plastic Fabric Articles

American Graphic Systems Inc .... E 708 614-7007
  Tinley Park (G-19802)
Fast Lane Threads Custom EMB .... G 815 544-9898
  Belvidere (G-1667)
Fresh Concept Enterprises Inc .... G 815 254-7295
  Plainfield (G-16667)
Marketing Card Technology LLC .... D 630 985-7900
  Downers Grove (G-8052)
Petra Manufacturing Co .... D 773 622-1475
  Chicago (G-5797)

PRINTING & ENGRAVING: Card, Exc Greeting

Poets Study Inc .... G 773 286-1355
  Chicago (G-5831)

PRINTING & ENGRAVING: Financial Notes & Certificates

Financial Graphic Services Inc .... D 708 343-0448
  Broadview (G-2437)
Printforce Inc .... G 618 395-7746
  Olney (G-15885)

PRINTING & ENGRAVING: Invitation & Stationery

All She Wrote .... F 773 529-0100
  Chicago (G-3612)
Artistry Engraving & Embossing .... G 773 775-4888
  Chicago (G-3741)
Duckys Formal Wear Inc .... G 309 342-5914
  Galesburg (G-10191)
Invitation Creations Inc .... G 847 432-4441
  Highland Park (G-11274)
Little Shop of Papers Ltd .... G 847 382-7733
  Barrington (G-1225)
Managed Marketing Inc .... G 847 279-8260
  Wheeling (G-20935)
Master Engraving .... G 217 965-5885
  Virden (G-20188)
Thia & Co .... G 630 510-9770
  Wheaton (G-20828)

PRINTING & ENGRAVING: Poster & Decal

Blooming Color Inc .... D 630 705-9200
  Lombard (G-13047)
Concept One Design Inc .... F 708 807-3111
  Naperville (G-14804)
Signs In Dundee Inc .... G 847 742-9530
  Elgin (G-8731)

PRINTING & STAMPING: Fabric Articles

Action Screen Print Inc .... F 630 393-1990
  Warrenville (G-20228)
Adolph Kiefer & Associates LLC .... D 309 451-5858
  Bloomington (G-2021)
Diemasters Manufacturing Inc .... C 847 640-9900
  Elk Grove Village (G-8950)
Pressd Apparel LLC .... G 312 767-1877
  Chicago (G-5868)
Signs In Dundee Inc .... G 847 742-9530
  Elgin (G-8731)
Super Sublimation LLC .... G 309 256-0184
  Morton (G-14384)
Unique Assembly & Decorating .... E 630 241-4300
  Downers Grove (G-8103)

PRINTING & WRITING PAPER WHOLESALERS

J P Printing Inc .... G 773 626-5222
  Chicago (G-4993)
K C Printing Services Inc .... F 847 382-8822
  Lake Barrington (G-12156)
Progressive Systems Netwrk Inc .... G 312 382-8383
  Chicago (G-5902)
Upm-Kymmene Inc .... D 630 922-2500
  Naperville (G-14938)

PRINTING INKS WHOLESALERS

CIS Systems Inc .... G 847 827-0747
  Glenview (G-10537)
Dyco-TEC Products Ltd .... G 630 837-6410
  Bartlett (G-1275)
Sun Chemical Corporation .... C 630 513-5348
  Saint Charles (G-18281)
Zeller + Gmelin Corporation .... G 630 443-8800
  Saint Charles (G-18304)

PRINTING MACHINERY

2m Control Systems Inc .... G 630 709-6225
  West Chicago (G-20529)
4I Technologies Inc .... A 815 431-8100
  Ottawa (G-16035)
Accu-Chem Industries Inc .... C 708 344-0900
  Melrose Park (G-13820)
Advance World Trade Inc .... D 773 777-7100
  Chicago (G-3561)
Altair Corporation .... E 847 634-9540
  Lincolnshire (G-12744)
Azul 3d Inc .... F 321 277-7807
  Skokie (G-18926)
Baldwin OXY-Dry Corporation .... D 630 595-3651
  Addison (G-45)
Baldwin Technology Company Inc .... C 618 842-2664
  Fairfield (G-9618)
Baldwin Technology Company Inc .... C 618 842-2664
  Arlington Heights (G-702)
Bst North America Inc .... E 630 833-9900
  Elmhurst (G-9338)
C CN Chicago Corp .... C 847 671-3319
  Addison (G-58)
Central Graphics Corp .... F 630 759-1696
  Romeoville (G-17804)
Chatham Corporation .... F 847 634-5506
  Lincolnshire (G-12749)
Cleveland Folder Service .... G 847 782-5850
  Gurnee (G-10864)
Container Graphics Corp .... E 847 584-0299
  Schaumburg (G-18486)
D & K Custom Machine Design .... E 847 956-4757
  Elk Grove Village (G-8930)
D & K Group Inc .... E 847 956-0160
  Elk Grove Village (G-8931)
Distribution Enterprises Inc .... F 847 582-9276
  Lake Forest (G-12243)
Dms Inc .... F 847 726-2828
  Lake Zurich (G-12403)
Domino Amjet Inc .... D 847 244-2501
  Gurnee (G-10870)
Ebway Industries Inc .... E 630 860-5959
  Itasca (G-11646)
Emt International Inc .... G 630 655-4145
  Westmont (G-20741)
Environmental Specialties Inc .... G 630 860-7070
  Itasca (G-11651)
Global Web Systems Inc .... F 630 782-9690
  Elk Grove Village (G-9017)
H R Slater Co Inc .... F 312 666-1855
  Chicago (G-4760)
I S C America Inc .... G 630 616-1331
  Wood Dale (G-21199)
Ilf Technologies LLC .... F 630 759-1776
  Cicero (G-6854)
Imtran Industries Inc .... G 630 752-4000
  Carol Stream (G-3004)
Intersol Industries Inc .... E 630 238-0385
  Bensenville (G-1824)
Jardis Industries Inc .... E 630 860-5959
  Itasca (G-11680)
Kiwi Coders Corp .... E 847 541-4511
  Wheeling (G-20925)
Komori America Corporation .... D 847 806-9000
  Rolling Meadows (G-17745)
Laser Reproductions Inc .... E 847 410-0397
  Skokie (G-18977)
M & R Printing Equipment Inc .... B 630 858-6101
  Roselle (G-17966)
Manroland Inc .... E 630 920-2000
  Westmont (G-20757)
Midwest Index Inc .... D 847 995-8425
  Addison (G-210)
Milans Machining & Mfg Co Inc .... D 708 780-6600
  Cicero (G-6867)
Nama Graphics E LLC .... G 262 966-3853
  Homer Glen (G-11484)
Ortman-Mccain Co .... G 312 666-2244
  Bellwood (G-1635)
Pamarco Global Graphics Inc .... E 630 879-7300
  Batavia (G-1403)
Pamarco Global Graphics Inc .... F 847 459-6000
  Wheeling (G-20955)

Employee Codes: A=Over 500 employees, B=251-500
C=101-250, D=51-100, E=20-50, F=10-19, G=3-9

2020 Harris Illinois Industrial Directory

1565

PRINTING MACHINERY

Polyurathane Engrg Tchnques Inc............E...... 847 362-1820
  Lake Forest *(G-12292)*
Precision Screen Specialties.................G...... 630 220-1361
  Saint Charles *(G-18250)*
Resinite Corporation...........................C...... 847 537-4250
  Wheeling *(G-20973)*
Rotation Dynamics Corporation.............D...... 773 247-5600
  Chicago *(G-6066)*
Rycoline Products LLC ....C...... 773 775-6755
  Chicago *(G-6081)*
Saati Americas Corporation..................F...... 847 296-5090
  Mount Prospect *(G-14568)*
Sopher Design & Manufacturing.............G...... 309 699-6419
  East Peoria *(G-8291)*
Special Tool Engineering Co..................F...... 773 767-6690
  Chicago *(G-6212)*
Tamarack Products Inc........................E...... 847 526-9333
  Wauconda *(G-20397)*
Technotrans America Inc......................E...... 847 227-9200
  Mount Prospect *(G-14575)*
Thermal Care Inc.................................C...... 847 966-2260
  Niles *(G-15180)*
Weber Marking Systems Inc.................B...... 847 364-8500
  Arlington Heights *(G-831)*
Western Printing Machinery Co.............E...... 847 678-1740
  Schiller Park *(G-18854)*
Western Printing Machinery Co.............E...... 847 678-1740
  Schiller Park *(G-18855)*
Wpc Machinery Corp............................E...... 630 231-7721
  Arlington Heights *(G-836)*

PRINTING MACHINERY, EQPT & SPLYS: Wholesalers

AAA Press Specialists Inc.....................F...... 847 818-1100
  Arlington Heights *(G-681)*
Advance World Trade Inc....................D...... 773 777-7100
  Chicago *(G-3561)*
Anderson & Vreeland-Illinois.................F...... 847 255-2110
  Arlington Heights *(G-693)*
Autotype Americas Incorporated............G...... 847 818-8262
  Rolling Meadows *(G-17715)*
C and C Machine Tool Service...............G...... 630 810-0484
  Downers Grove *(G-7962)*
Distribution Enterprises Inc..................F...... 847 582-9276
  Lake Forest *(G-12243)*
Domino Holdings Inc...........................D...... 847 244-2501
  Gurnee *(G-10871)*
Emt International Inc............................G...... 630 655-4145
  Westmont *(G-20741)*
Graphic Innovators Inc........................E...... 847 718-1516
  Elk Grove Village *(G-9021)*
Identatronics Inc..................................E...... 847 437-2654
  Crystal Lake *(G-7208)*
Jardis Industries Inc............................F...... 630 773-5600
  Itasca *(G-11681)*
Laser Reproductions Inc.......................E...... 847 410-0397
  Skokie *(G-18977)*
M & R Printing Equipment Inc..............B...... 630 858-6101
  Roselle *(G-17966)*
Manroland Goss Web Systems Int.........E...... 630 796-7560
  Woodridge *(G-21321)*
Manroland Inc......................................E...... 630 920-2000
  Westmont *(G-20757)*
Menges Roller Co Inc..........................E...... 847 487-8877
  Wauconda *(G-20376)*
Professional Sales Associates...............G...... 847 487-1900
  Wauconda *(G-20384)*
Prograf LLC...G...... 815 234-4848
  Villa Park *(G-20166)*
Schlesinger Machinery Inc....................G...... 630 766-4074
  Bensenville *(G-1890)*
Smart Inc...G...... 847 464-4160
  Hampshire *(G-10988)*
Tampotech Decorating Inc...................F...... 847 515-2968
  Huntley *(G-11567)*
Wikoff Color Corporation......................G...... 847 487-2704
  Wauconda *(G-20403)*

PRINTING TRADES MACHINERY & EQPT REPAIR SVCS

Mah Machine Company.........................C...... 708 656-1826
  Cicero *(G-6864)*
Tlm Enterprises Inc...............................G...... 815 284-5040
  Dixon *(G-7923)*
Wpc Machinery Corp............................E...... 630 231-7721
  Arlington Heights *(G-836)*

PRINTING, COMMERCIAL Newspapers, NEC

Henry News Republican.......................G...... 309 364-3250
  Henry *(G-11166)*
Osborne Publications Inc......................G...... 217 422-9702
  Decatur *(G-7534)*

PRINTING, COMMERCIAL: Announcements, NEC

Bass-Mollett Publishers Inc..................D...... 618 664-3141
  Greenville *(G-10826)*

PRINTING, COMMERCIAL: Business Forms, NEC

Available Business Group Inc...............D...... 773 247-4141
  Chicago *(G-3781)*
Connies Home Health Care...................G...... 708 790-4000
  Park Forest *(G-16253)*
Data Com PLD Inc................................G...... 708 267-5657
  Willow Springs *(G-21025)*
Grand Forms & Systems Inc..................F...... 847 259-4600
  Arlington Heights *(G-744)*
Kara Graphics Inc.................................G...... 630 964-8122
  Woodridge *(G-21319)*
MidAmerican Prtg Systems Inc..............E...... 312 663-4720
  Schiller Park *(G-18824)*
Noor International Inc...........................G...... 847 985-2300
  Bartlett *(G-1256)*
OfficeMax North America Inc...............E...... 815 748-3007
  Dekalb *(G-7696)*
Pioneer Forms Inc...............................G...... 773 539-8587
  Glenview *(G-10599)*
Productive Portable Disp Inc..................G...... 630 458-9100
  Bensenville *(G-1873)*
W W Barthel & Co................................G...... 847 392-5643
  Arlington Heights *(G-830)*

PRINTING, COMMERCIAL: Cards, Visiting, Incl Business, NEC

Ace Printing Co....................................G...... 618 259-2711
  East Alton *(G-8162)*

PRINTING, COMMERCIAL: Certificates, Stock, NEC

Corporation Supply Co Inc....................E...... 312 726-3375
  Chicago *(G-4241)*

PRINTING, COMMERCIAL: Coupons, NEC

Gallimore Industries Inc........................F...... 847 356-3331
  Lake Villa *(G-12352)*

PRINTING, COMMERCIAL: Decals, NEC

Central Decal Company Inc..................D...... 630 325-9892
  Burr Ridge *(G-2661)*
Great Display Company Llc..................F...... 309 821-1037
  Bloomington *(G-2052)*
P & L Mark-It Inc...................................E...... 630 879-7590
  Batavia *(G-1402)*
Sportdecals Inc....................................D...... 800 435-6110
  Spring Grove *(G-19301)*
Winnetka Sign Co Inc............................G...... 847 473-9378
  North Chicago *(G-15325)*

PRINTING, COMMERCIAL: Envelopes, NEC

Americas Community Bankers................E...... 312 644-3100
  Chicago *(G-3675)*
Forest Envelope Company....................E...... 630 515-1200
  Bolingbrook *(G-2178)*
J & J Express Envelopes Inc..................G...... 847 253-7146
  South Elgin *(G-19158)*
Victor Envelope Mfg Corp.....................C...... 630 616-2750
  Bensenville *(G-1908)*

PRINTING, COMMERCIAL: Imprinting

Elite Impressions & Graphics.................G...... 847 695-3730
  South Elgin *(G-19143)*
Excel Glass Inc....................................G...... 847 801-5200
  Schiller Park *(G-18807)*
Rainbow Art Inc....................................F...... 312 421-5600
  Chicago *(G-5965)*

PRINTING, COMMERCIAL: Invitations, NEC

Sass-N-Class Inc..................................G...... 630 655-2420
  Hinsdale *(G-11377)*

PRINTING, COMMERCIAL: Labels & Seals, NEC

A-Flex Label LLC.................................G...... 630 325-7265
  Willowbrook *(G-21028)*
Abbott Label Inc....................................E...... 630 773-3614
  Itasca *(G-11614)*
American Label Company.....................G...... 630 830-4444
  Schaumburg *(G-18437)*
AT&I Resources LLC...........................F...... 918 925-0154
  Addison *(G-42)*
Bar Code Graphics Inc..........................F...... 312 664-0700
  Chicago *(G-3827)*
Delta Label Inc......................................G...... 618 233-8984
  Belleville *(G-1545)*
Healthcare Labels Inc............................F...... 847 382-3993
  North Barrington *(G-15284)*
Heartland Labels Inc.............................E...... 217 826-8324
  Marshall *(G-13572)*
Jordan Industries Inc............................F...... 847 945-5591
  Deerfield *(G-7621)*
Label Design..G...... 815 462-4949
  Mokena *(G-14093)*
Label Printers LP..................................D...... 630 897-6970
  Aurora *(G-1122)*
M & R Graphics Inc...............................F...... 708 534-6621
  University Park *(G-19957)*
Master Tape Printers Inc......................E...... 773 283-8273
  Chicago *(G-5360)*
Mosaic Label & Print LLC......................G...... 847 904-1375
  Glenview *(G-10591)*
National Data-Label Corp.......................E...... 630 616-9595
  Bensenville *(G-1856)*
Primedia Source LLC...........................G...... 630 553-8451
  Yorkville *(G-21499)*
S & K Label Co.....................................G...... 630 307-2577
  Bloomingdale *(G-2012)*
Sato Lbling Solutions Amer Inc..............F...... 630 771-4200
  Romeoville *(G-17873)*
Sato Lbling Solutions Amer Inc..............D...... 630 771-4200
  Romeoville *(G-17874)*
Schultz Brothers Inc..............................G...... 630 458-1437
  Addison *(G-282)*
Selective Label & Tabs Inc....................F...... 630 466-0091
  Sugar Grove *(G-19654)*
Shamrock Scientific..............................E...... 800 323-0249
  Bellwood *(G-1638)*
Stephen Fossler Company....................D...... 847 635-7200
  Des Plaines *(G-7852)*
Team Impressions Inc..........................F...... 847 357-9270
  Elk Grove Village *(G-9266)*
Tiem Engineering Corporation...............F...... 630 553-7484
  Yorkville *(G-21502)*
UNI-Label and Tag Corporation.............E...... 847 956-8900
  Elk Grove Village *(G-9294)*

PRINTING, COMMERCIAL: Letterpress & Screen

American Graphic Systems Inc............E...... 708 614-7007
  Tinley Park *(G-19802)*
Continent Corp.....................................G...... 773 733-1584
  Bolingbrook *(G-2158)*
G Y Industries LLC...............................F...... 708 210-0800
  Chicago *(G-4651)*
Gsipc LLC..D...... 630 325-8181
  Burr Ridge *(G-2678)*
McGrath Press Inc................................G...... 815 356-5246
  Crystal Lake *(G-7224)*
Meltdown Creative Works Inc...............G...... 309 310-1978
  Bloomington *(G-2074)*
Platts Printing Company.......................G...... 309 228-1069
  Farmington *(G-9663)*
Ready Inc...F...... 630 501-1352
  Elmhurst *(G-9416)*
Te Shurt Shop Inc................................F...... 217 344-1226
  Champaign *(G-3357)*

PRINTING, COMMERCIAL: Literature, Advertising, NEC

Bizbash Media Inc................................G...... 312 436-2525
  Chicago *(G-3904)*
Calmark Group LLC.............................E...... 708 728-0101
  Bedford Park *(G-1461)*

PRODUCT SECTION

PRINTING, COMMERCIAL: Screen

Dixon Graphics Incorporated ....G....... 217 351-6100
  Champaign *(G-3285)*
Freddie Bear Sports ....F....... 708 532-4133
  Tinley Park *(G-19829)*
Mjt Design and Prtg Entps Inc ....G....... 708 240-4323
  Hillside *(G-11348)*
Mortgage Market Info Svcs ....E....... 630 834-7555
  Villa Park *(G-20161)*

PRINTING, COMMERCIAL: Magazines, NEC

Central IL Business Magazine ....G....... 217 351-5281
  Champaign *(G-3279)*
Time Out Chicago Partners Lllp ....F....... 312 924-9555
  Chicago *(G-6379)*

PRINTING, COMMERCIAL: Menus, NEC

Rick Styfer ....G....... 630 734-3244
  Burr Ridge *(G-2717)*
Simu Ltd ....F....... 708 688-2200
  Mc Cook *(G-13701)*

PRINTING, COMMERCIAL: Post Cards, Picture, NEC

3rd Coast Imaging Inc ....G....... 312 322-3111
  Chicago *(G-3470)*

PRINTING, COMMERCIAL: Promotional

Belboz Corp ....G....... 708 856-6099
  Dolton *(G-7933)*
Chicago Printing and EMB Inc ....F....... 630 628-1777
  Addison *(G-71)*
Color Communications LLC ....G....... 773 638-1400
  Chicago *(G-4203)*
Great Guy Inc ....G....... 312 203-9872
  Medinah *(G-13813)*
Greco Graphics Inc ....G....... 217 483-2877
  Glenarm *(G-10425)*
M Wells Printing Co ....G....... 312 455-0400
  Chicago *(G-5305)*
Master Marketing Intl Inc ....E....... 630 653-5525
  Carol Stream *(G-3021)*
Mc Adams Multigraphics Inc ....G....... 630 990-1707
  Oak Brook *(G-15641)*
Motr Grafx LLC ....G....... 847 600-5656
  Wheeling *(G-20942)*
Pelegan Inc ....G....... 708 442-9797
  Riverside *(G-17088)*
R L Allen Industries ....G....... 618 667-2544
  Troy *(G-19919)*
Rv Enterprises Ltd ....F....... 847 509-8710
  Niles *(G-15168)*
USA Printworks LLC ....E....... 815 206-0854
  Woodstock *(G-21442)*
Warehouse Direct Inc ....C....... 847 952-1925
  Des Plaines *(G-7867)*
Zorch International Inc ....E....... 312 751-8010
  Chicago *(G-6723)*

PRINTING, COMMERCIAL: Publications

Beslow Associates Inc ....G....... 847 559-2703
  Northbrook *(G-15349)*
Independent Shoppers ....G....... 309 647-5200
  Lewistown *(G-12616)*
Mac Graphics Group Inc ....G....... 630 620-7200
  Oakbrook Terrace *(G-15806)*
McKnights Long Term Care News ....G....... 847 559-2884
  Northbrook *(G-15429)*
Prismatec Inc ....G....... 847 562-9022
  Northbrook *(G-15467)*
Reid Communications Inc ....E....... 847 741-9700
  Elgin *(G-8717)*
Strathmore Press ....E....... 513 483-3600
  Saint Charles *(G-18280)*
Town Square Publications LLC ....G....... 847 427-4633
  Arlington Heights *(G-820)*

PRINTING, COMMERCIAL: Ready

Batavia Instant Print ....G....... 630 262-0370
  West Chicago *(G-20550)*
T F N W Inc ....G....... 630 584-7383
  Naperville *(G-14926)*

PRINTING, COMMERCIAL: Screen

A & R Screening LLC ....F....... 708 598-2480
  Crestwood *(G-7103)*
A-Creations Inc ....G....... 630 541-5801
  Woodridge *(G-21272)*
Ad Images ....G....... 847 956-1887
  Hoffman Estates *(G-11403)*
Advance Press Sign Inc ....G....... 630 833-1600
  Villa Park *(G-20128)*
Aim Screen Printing Supply LLC ....G....... 630 357-4293
  Naperville *(G-14954)*
All Stars -N- Stitches Inc ....G....... 618 435-5555
  Benton *(G-1918)*
American Bell Screen Prtg Co ....G....... 815 623-5522
  Roscoe *(G-17899)*
American Graphics Network Inc ....F....... 847 729-7220
  Glenview *(G-10522)*
American Outfitters Ltd ....E....... 847 623-3959
  Waukegan *(G-20414)*
American Sportswear Inc ....G....... 630 859-8998
  Aurora *(G-1049)*
Amy Schutt ....G....... 618 994-7405
  Carrier Mills *(G-3123)*
Arch Printing ....G....... 630 896-6610
  North Aurora *(G-15254)*
Arena Sports Usa Inc ....F....... 847 809-7268
  McHenry *(G-13720)*
Artisan Handprints Inc ....G....... 773 725-1799
  Chicago *(G-3740)*
Artline Screen Printing Inc ....G....... 815 963-8125
  Rockford *(G-17308)*
Artwear ....G....... 618 234-5522
  Belleville *(G-1530)*
Ashland Screening Corporation ....E....... 708 758-8800
  Chicago Heights *(G-6732)*
Athletic Image ....G....... 217 347-7377
  Effingham *(G-8386)*
Authority Screenprint & EMB ....G....... 630 236-0289
  Plainfield *(G-16643)*
B Creative Screen Print Co ....G....... 815 806-3037
  Frankfort *(G-9769)*
B D Enterprises ....G....... 618 462-5861
  Alton *(G-545)*
Babbletees ....G....... 815 780-1953
  Chicago *(G-3811)*
Bailleu & Bailleu Printing Inc ....G....... 309 852-2517
  Kewanee *(G-12021)*
Baker La Russo ....G....... 630 788-5108
  Naperville *(G-14776)*
Bee Designs Embroidery & Scree ......G....... 815 393-4593
  Esmond *(G-9475)*
Benzinger Printing ....G....... 815 784-6560
  Genoa *(G-10315)*
Bes Designs & Associates Inc ....G....... 217 443-4619
  Danville *(G-7323)*
Bobs Tshirt Store ....G....... 618 567-1730
  Mascoutah *(G-13594)*
C & E Specialties Inc ....E....... 815 229-9230
  Rockford *(G-17332)*
Campus Sportswear Incorporated .....F....... 217 344-0944
  Champaign *(G-3274)*
Cara ANAM Enterprises Inc ....G....... 630 587-8700
  Saint Charles *(G-18163)*
Carl Gorr Printing Co ....E....... 815 338-3191
  Woodstock *(G-21370)*
Chii Clothing Company ....E....... 312 243-8304
  Chicago *(G-4139)*
Classic Screen Printing Inc ....F....... 708 771-9355
  Forest Park *(G-9711)*
Cloz Companies Inc ....E....... 773 247-8879
  Skokie *(G-18944)*
Colvin Printing ....G....... 708 331-4580
  Blue Island *(G-2115)*
Creative Pig Minds Designwear ....G....... 815 968-7447
  Rockford *(G-17360)*
CTI/Usa Inc ....G....... 847 258-1000
  Carol Stream *(G-2969)*
Custom Screen Printing ....G....... 217 543-3691
  Arthur *(G-850)*
D L V Printing Service Inc ....F....... 773 626-1661
  Chicago *(G-4301)*
Decal Solutions Unlimited Inc ....G....... 847 590-5405
  Arlington Heights *(G-727)*
Decal Works LLC ....E....... 815 784-4000
  Kingston *(G-12055)*
Decorative Industries Inc ....E....... 773 229-0015
  Chicago *(G-4329)*
Den Graphix Inc ....F....... 309 962-2000
  Le Roy *(G-12539)*
Diamond Screen Process Inc ....G....... 847 439-6200
  Elk Grove Village *(G-8948)*
Display Link Inc ....G....... 815 968-0778
  Rockford *(G-17380)*
DMarv Design Specialty Prtrs ....G....... 708 389-4420
  Blue Island *(G-2118)*
Dolls Lettering Inc ....G....... 815 467-8000
  Minooka *(G-14057)*
Dpe Incorporated ....G....... 773 306-0105
  Chicago *(G-4394)*
E & H Graphic Service Inc ....G....... 708 748-5656
  Matteson *(G-13623)*
E K Kuhn Inc ....G....... 815 899-9211
  Sycamore *(G-19709)*
Eagle Screen Print Inds Inc ....F....... 708 579-0454
  Countryside *(G-7051)*
Earl Ad Inc ....G....... 312 666-7106
  Chicago *(G-4431)*
Elegant Embroidery Inc ....G....... 847 540-8003
  Lake Zurich *(G-12407)*
Embroid ME ....G....... 815 485-4155
  New Lenox *(G-15033)*
Energy Tees ....G....... 708 771-0000
  Forest Park *(G-9713)*
Eternal Quality Group ....G....... 309 799-3800
  Milan *(G-14009)*
Etlon Enterprises ....G....... 847 258-5265
  Elk Grove Village *(G-8983)*
F-C Enterprises Inc ....G....... 815 254-7295
  Plainfield *(G-16663)*
Fantastic Lettering Inc ....G....... 773 685-7650
  Chicago *(G-4559)*
Flow-Eze Company ....F....... 815 965-1062
  Rockford *(G-17416)*
G and D Enterprises Inc ....E....... 847 981-8661
  Arlington Heights *(G-739)*
Galleon Industries Inc ....G....... 708 478-5444
  Joliet *(G-11867)*
Game Day Incentives Inc ....G....... 630 854-0581
  Naperville *(G-14967)*
Gateway Impressions ....G....... 618 505-7544
  Troy *(G-19914)*
Golf Tee Printers Inc ....G....... 973 328-4008
  Schaumburg *(G-18537)*
Good Impressions Inc ....G....... 847 831-4317
  Highland Park *(G-11265)*
Graphic Screen Printing Inc ....G....... 708 429-3330
  Orland Park *(G-15957)*
H & H Graphics LLC ....E....... 847 383-6285
  Vernon Hills *(G-20057)*
H & H Graphics Illinois Inc ....E....... 847 383-6285
  Vernon Hills *(G-20058)*
H & H Printing ....G....... 847 866-9520
  Evanston *(G-9529)*
Hairy Ant Inc ....G....... 630 338-7194
  Saint Charles *(G-18205)*
Hazen Display Corporation ....E....... 815 248-2925
  Davis *(G-7418)*
High-5 Printwear Inc ....G....... 847 818-0081
  Arlington Heights *(G-749)*
Hole In The Wall Screen Arts ....G....... 217 243-9100
  Jacksonville *(G-11767)*
Image Plus Inc ....G....... 630 852-4920
  Downers Grove *(G-8028)*
Impro International Inc ....G....... 847 398-3870
  Arlington Heights *(G-757)*
Ink Your Wear Inc ....G....... 708 329-4444
  Riverside *(G-17085)*
Inkn Tees ....G....... 847 244-2266
  Waukegan *(G-20448)*
Inkorporated Designs ....G....... 217 965-4653
  Virden *(G-20186)*
J & J Silk Screening ....G....... 773 838-9000
  Chicago *(G-4985)*
Jdl Graphics ....G....... 815 401-1120
  Saint Anne *(G-18135)*
JLJ Corp ....G....... 847 726-9795
  Lake Zurich *(G-12427)*
Joliet Pattern Works Inc ....D....... 815 726-5373
  Crest Hill *(G-7088)*
K and A Graphics Inc ....G....... 847 244-2345
  Gurnee *(G-10890)*
Kevron Printing & Design Inc ......G....... 708 229-7725
  Hickory Hills *(G-11199)*
Kmf Enterprises Inc ....G....... 630 858-2210
  Wheaton *(G-20808)*
Lambert Print Source Llc ....G....... 630 708-0505
  Yorkville *(G-21491)*
Landmarx Screen Printing ....F....... 217 223-4601
  Quincy *(G-16907)*
Lans Printing Inc ....G....... 708 895-6226
  Lynwood *(G-13295)*
Larry & Myra Stone ....G....... 847 433-0540
  Highland Park *(G-11280)*

Employee Codes: A=Over 500 employees, B=251-500
C=101-250, D=51-100, E=20-50, F=10-19, G=3-9

Laughing Dog Graphics ....G....... 309 392-3330
Minier (G-14054)
Legacy Prints ....G....... 815 946-9112
Polo (G-16756)
Lighthouse Printing Inc ....G....... 708 479-7776
New Lenox (G-15039)
Lloyd Midwest Graphics ....G....... 815 282-8828
Machesney Park (G-13357)
Locker Room Screen Printing ....G....... 630 759-2533
Bolingbrook (G-2206)
Logo Wear Unlimited Inc ....G....... 309 367-2333
Metamora (G-13962)
Logo Works ....G....... 815 942-4700
Morris (G-14310)
Ltb Graphics Inc ....G....... 630 238-1754
Wood Dale (G-21208)
Martin Stees LLC ....G....... 630 664-6273
Aurora (G-1127)
McKillip Industries Inc ....E....... 815 439-1050
Yorkville (G-21493)
Melon Ink Screen Print ....G....... 847 726-0003
Lake Zurich (G-12431)
Meto-Grafics Inc ....F....... 847 639-0044
Crystal Lake (G-7226)
Mexacali Silkscreen Inc ....G....... 630 628-9313
Addison (G-201)
Mid State Graphics ....G....... 309 772-3843
Bushnell (G-2745)
Midwest Silkscreening Inc ....G....... 217 892-9596
Rantoul (G-16980)
Minerva Sportswear Inc ....F....... 309 661-2387
Bloomington (G-2080)
Msf Graphics Inc ....G....... 847 446-6900
Des Plaines (G-7808)
Muir Omni Graphics Inc ....E....... 309 673-7034
Peoria (G-16480)
Multi Packaging Solutions Inc ....G....... 773 283-9500
Chicago (G-5523)
NBC Meshtec Americas Inc ....E....... 630 293-5454
Batavia (G-1398)
New Image Designs ....G....... 217 498-9830
Rochester (G-17170)
Newport Printing Services Inc ....G....... 847 632-1000
Schaumburg (G-18648)
Next Gerneration ....F....... 630 261-1477
Lombard (G-13108)
Offworld Designs ....G....... 815 786-7080
Sandwich (G-18378)
Olympic Trophy and Awards Co ....F....... 773 631-9500
Chicago (G-5672)
Orland Sports Ltd ....G....... 773 685-3711
Chicago (G-5703)
Orora Visual TX LLC ....E....... 414 423-2200
Niles (G-15154)
Outbreak Designs ....G....... 217 370-5418
South Jacksonville (G-19251)
Pamco Printed Tape Label Inc ....C....... 847 803-2200
Des Plaines (G-7817)
Panther Products ....G....... 618 664-1071
Greenville (G-10841)
Papyrus Press Inc ....F....... 773 342-0700
Chicago (G-5755)
Phoenix Graphics Inc ....G....... 847 699-9520
Des Plaines (G-7823)
Phoenix Marketing Services ....F....... 630 616-8000
Mundelein (G-14726)
Photo Techniques Corp ....E....... 630 690-9360
Carol Stream (G-3046)
Plastics Printing Group Inc ....F....... 773 473-4481
Chicago (G-5820)
Positive Impressions ....G....... 618 438-7030
Benton (G-1935)
Precision Screen Specialties ....G....... 630 220-1361
Saint Charles (G-18250)
Primo Designs Inc ....F....... 217 523-6373
Springfield (G-19429)
Pro Tuff Decal Inc ....E....... 815 356-9160
Crystal Lake (G-7249)
Proell Inc ....G....... 630 587-2300
Saint Charles (G-18251)
Project Te Inc ....G....... 217 344-9833
Urbana (G-19996)
Promark Advertising Specialtie ....G....... 618 483-6025
Altamont (G-536)
R & S Screen Printing Inc ....G....... 815 337-3935
Woodstock (G-21428)
Response Graphics & EMB LLC ....G....... 630 364-1471
Plainfield (G-16710)
Roeda Signs Inc ....E....... 708 333-3021
Chicago Heights (G-6772)
Ruco USA Inc ....E....... 866 373-7912
Wood Dale (G-21236)
Scheiwes Print Shop ....G....... 815 683-2398
Crescent City (G-7082)
Scorpion Graphics Inc ....F....... 773 927-3203
Chicago (G-6119)
Selah USA Inc ....G....... 847 758-0702
Elk Grove Village (G-9235)
Select Screen Prints & EMB ....F....... 309 829-6511
Bloomington (G-2093)
Self Pro Motions LLC ....G....... 847 749-6077
Chicago (G-6134)
Seritex Inc ....G....... 201 755-3002
Addison (G-285)
Sew Wright Embroidery Inc ....G....... 309 691-5780
Peoria (G-16521)
Sg Screen Graphics Inc ....G....... 309 699-8513
Pekin (G-16360)
Sharprint Slkscrn & Grphcs ....D....... 877 649-2554
Chicago (G-6148)
Shirt Off My Back Cstm Tees MO ....G....... 331 999-2399
Montgomery (G-14269)
Shirt Printing 4u Inc ....G....... 708 588-8272
Countryside (G-7069)
Shirt Tales ....G....... 309 582-5566
Aledo (G-361)
Shirts Galore & More ....G....... 618 797-9801
Granite City (G-10736)
Silk Screen Express Inc ....F....... 708 845-5600
Tinley Park (G-19855)
Silkworm Inc ....D....... 618 687-4077
Murphysboro (G-14760)
Skyline ....G....... 312 300-4700
Mc Cook (G-13702)
Spirit Warrior Inc ....G....... 708 614-0020
Orland Park (G-15983)
Sports All Sorts AP & Design ....G....... 815 756-9910
Dekalb (G-7706)
Sports Designs & Graphics ....E....... 217 342-2777
Effingham (G-8426)
Sports Recreation and AP Inc ....G....... 815 962-7767
Rockford (G-17642)
Squeegee Brothers Inc ....F....... 630 510-9152
Carol Stream (G-3073)
Ssn LLC ....G....... 815 978-8729
Byron (G-2759)
Stellato Printing Inc ....F....... 815 280-5664
Joliet (G-11933)
Sunburst Sportswear Inc ....F....... 630 717-8680
Glendale Heights (G-10505)
Systematics Screen Printing ....F....... 630 521-1123
Itasca (G-11742)
T Graphics ....G....... 618 592-4145
Oblong (G-15830)
T Shirtz Etc Inc ....G....... 815 962-5194
Rockford (G-17651)
Tailored Printing Inc ....G....... 217 498-1057
Rochester (G-17172)
Tease ....G....... 630 960-4950
Downers Grove (G-8100)
Tees and Things ....G....... 708 351-8584
Chicago (G-6337)
Tees Ink ....G....... 815 462-7300
New Lenox (G-15064)
Teestyler Inc ....G....... 630 484-3104
Plainfield (G-16722)
Thermo-Graphic LLC ....E....... 630 350-2226
Bensenville (G-1901)
Think Ink Inc ....G....... 815 459-4565
Crystal Lake (G-7282)
Toms Signs ....G....... 630 377-8525
Saint Charles (G-18290)
Trendy Screenprinting ....G....... 815 895-0081
Sycamore (G-19737)
Tri Star Plowing ....G....... 847 584-5070
Schaumburg (G-18755)
Tri-City Sports Inc ....G....... 217 224-2489
Quincy (G-16951)
Triangle Screen Print Inc ....F....... 847 678-9200
Franklin Park (G-10066)
Trimark Screen Printing Inc ....G....... 630 629-2823
Lombard (G-13146)
Ultimate Distributing Inc ....G....... 847 566-2250
Mundelein (G-14745)
Unique Assembly & Decorating ....E....... 630 241-4300
Downers Grove (G-8103)
Usmss Inc ....G....... 708 409-9010
Westchester (G-20717)
Wagner International LLC ....G....... 224 619-9247
Vernon Hills (G-20109)
Waist Up Imprntd Sprtswear LLC ....G....... 847 963-1400
Palatine (G-16171)
Wave Graphics Inc ....G....... 217 234-8100
Mattoon (G-13657)
Webe Ink ....G....... 618 498-7620
Jerseyville (G-11799)
Weiskamp Screen Printing ....G....... 217 398-8428
Champaign (G-3370)
Winning Streak Inc ....D....... 618 277-8191
Dupo (G-8150)
Woolenwear Co ....F....... 847 520-9243
Prospect Heights (G-16848)
Workshop ....E....... 815 777-2211
Galena (G-10183)
Wortman Printing Company Inc ....G....... 217 347-3775
Effingham (G-8432)
Xtreme Dzignz ....G....... 309 633-9311
Bartonville (G-1337)
Your Logo Here ....G....... 708 258-6666
Frankfort (G-9853)

PRINTING, COMMERCIAL: Stationery, NEC

Merrill Fine Arts Engrv Inc ....D....... 312 786-6300
Chicago (G-5401)
Rohner Engraving Inc ....G....... 773 244-8343
Chicago (G-6051)

PRINTING, LITHOGRAPHIC: Advertising Posters

Phoenix Business Solutions LLC ....E....... 708 388-1330
Alsip (G-491)
Urban Imaging Group Inc ....G....... 773 961-7500
Chicago (G-6495)

PRINTING, LITHOGRAPHIC: Calendars

Custom Calendar Corp ....G....... 708 547-6191
Lombard (G-13060)
House of Doolittle Ltd ....E....... 847 228-9591
Arlington Heights (G-751)
Warwick Publishing Company ....D....... 630 584-3871
Saint Charles (G-18296)

PRINTING, LITHOGRAPHIC: Color

Allprint Inc ....G....... 847 726-0658
Hawthorn Woods (G-11121)
Amric Resources ....G....... 309 664-0391
Bloomington (G-2024)
Brilliant Color Corp ....G....... 847 367-3300
Libertyville (G-12640)
Excel Forms Inc ....G....... 630 801-1936
Aurora (G-1094)
Klh Printing Corp ....G....... 847 459-0115
Wheeling (G-20926)
MPS Chicago Inc ....C....... 630 932-9000
Downers Grove (G-8062)
Northstar Group Inc ....F....... 847 726-0880
Lake Zurich (G-12440)
Qg LLC ....B....... 217 347-7721
Effingham (G-8419)
Tera-Print LLC ....G....... 224 534-7543
Skokie (G-19045)
Triangle Printers Inc ....E....... 847 675-3700
Skokie (G-19048)

PRINTING, LITHOGRAPHIC: Decals

CDI Corp ....E....... 773 205-2960
Chicago (G-4049)
Cypress Multigraphics LLC ....E....... 708 633-1166
Tinley Park (G-19820)
Service Packaging Design Inc ....G....... 847 966-6592
Morton Grove (G-14440)

PRINTING, LITHOGRAPHIC: Fashion Plates

Proform ....G....... 309 676-2535
Peoria (G-16503)

PRINTING, LITHOGRAPHIC: Forms & Cards, Business

Blooming Color Inc ....D....... 630 705-9200
Lombard (G-13047)
Corporate Business Card Ltd ....E....... 847 455-5760
Franklin Park (G-9915)
D E Signs & Storage LLC ....G....... 618 939-8050
Waterloo (G-20289)

PRODUCT SECTION

PRINTING: Commercial, NEC

International Graphics & Assoc ....F 630 584-2248
  Saint Charles (G-18215)
Novak Business Forms Inc ....E 630 932-9850
  Lombard (G-13110)

PRINTING, LITHOGRAPHIC: Forms, Business

Ennis Inc ....E 815 875-2000
  Princeton (G-16808)
Hansen Printing Co Inc ....E 708 599-1500
  Bridgeview (G-2353)
Hq Printers Inc ....G 312 782-2020
  Chicago (G-4857)
Integrated Print Graphics Inc ....C 847 695-6777
  South Elgin (G-19155)
Integrated Print Graphics Inc ....C 847 888-2880
  South Elgin (G-19156)
J J Collins Sons Inc ....F 630 960-2525
  Downers Grove (G-8032)
J J Collins Sons Inc ....D 217 345-7606
  Charleston (G-3405)

PRINTING, LITHOGRAPHIC: Letters, Circular Or Form

RR Donnelley Printing Co LP ....A 217 235-0561
  Mattoon (G-13653)

PRINTING, LITHOGRAPHIC: Maps

Trafficcom ....G 773 997-8351
  Chicago (G-6405)

PRINTING, LITHOGRAPHIC: Menus

Alliance Investment Corp ....F 847 933-0400
  Skokie (G-18916)
Hertzberg Ernst & Sons ....E 773 525-3518
  Chicago (G-4810)
Rick Styfer ....G 630 734-3244
  Burr Ridge (G-2717)

PRINTING, LITHOGRAPHIC: Newspapers

New City Communications ....E 312 243-8786
  Chicago (G-5576)
Newsweb Corporation ....E 773 975-5727
  Chicago (G-5591)

PRINTING, LITHOGRAPHIC: Offset & photolithographic printing

Decatur Blue Print Company ....G 217 423-7589
  Decatur (G-7484)
DMarv Design Specialty Prtrs ....G 708 389-4420
  Blue Island (G-2118)
Fortman & Associates Ltd ....F 847 524-0741
  Elk Grove Village (G-9005)
Impossible Objects Inc ....F 847 400-9582
  Northbrook (G-15404)
Promoframes LLC ....G 866 566-7224
  Schaumburg (G-18685)
Screen Machine Incorporated ....G 847 439-2233
  Elk Grove Village (G-9234)

PRINTING, LITHOGRAPHIC: On Metal

Adams Printing Co ....G 618 529-2396
  Carbondale (G-2838)
American Inks and Coatings Co ....G 630 226-0994
  Romeoville (G-17793)
Bros Lithographing Company ....G 312 666-0919
  Chicago (G-3965)
Carson Printing Inc ....G 847 836-0900
  East Dundee (G-8189)
Catalina Graphics Inc ....G 773 973-7780
  Chicago (G-4039)
Dun-Wel Lithograph Co Inc ....G 773 327-8811
  Chicago (G-4404)
JL Clark LLC ....C 815 961-5609
  Rockford (G-17476)
Keneal Industries Inc ....F 815 886-1300
  Romeoville (G-17837)
Lakeside Lithography LLC ....E 312 243-3001
  Chicago (G-5166)
Little Village Printing Inc ....G 708 749-4414
  Berwyn (G-1955)
Merrill Fine Arts Engrv Inc ....D 312 786-6300
  Chicago (G-5401)
Nature House Inc ....D 217 833-2393
  Griggsville (G-10850)

Paul D Burton ....G 309 467-2613
  Eureka (G-9484)
Printed Word Inc ....G 847 328-1511
  Evanston (G-9570)
Rohrer Graphic Arts Inc ....F 630 832-3434
  Elmhurst (G-9419)
Saints Volo & Olha Uk Cath Par ....G 312 829-5209
  Chicago (G-6091)
Treudt Corporation ....G 630 293-0500
  West Chicago (G-20654)
Tru Line Lithographing Inc ....E 262 554-7300
  Niles (G-15183)
Turner Jct Prtg & Litho Svc ....G 630 293-1377
  West Chicago (G-20655)
Willert Corporation ....G 630 860-1620
  Franklin Park (G-10086)

PRINTING, LITHOGRAPHIC: Posters

Morton Suggestion Company LLC ....G 847 255-4770
  Mount Prospect (G-14549)

PRINTING, LITHOGRAPHIC: Posters & Decals

Media Unlimited Inc ....G 630 527-0900
  Naperville (G-14867)
Signs In Dundee Inc ....G 847 742-9530
  Elgin (G-8731)

PRINTING, LITHOGRAPHIC: Promotional

American Slide-Chart Co ....D 630 665-3333
  Carol Stream (G-2937)
Communication Technologies Inc ....E 630 384-0900
  Glendale Heights (G-10444)
Daxam Inc ....F 847 214-1733
  Elgin (G-8564)
Flyerinc Corporation ....G 630 655-3400
  Oak Brook (G-15622)
Proforma Quality Business Svcs ....G 847 356-1959
  Gurnee (G-10916)
The Web Cmmnications Group Inc ......G 630 467-0900
  Itasca (G-11746)
Warehouse Direct Inc ....C 847 952-1925
  Des Plaines (G-7867)

PRINTING, LITHOGRAPHIC: Transfers, Decalcomania Or Dry

Howard Custom Transfers Inc ....E 847 695-8195
  Elgin (G-8616)

PRINTING, LITHOGRAPHIC: Wrappers

Lithotype Company Inc ....F 630 771-1920
  Bolingbrook (G-2205)

PRINTING: Books

Bible Students Publications ....G 630 595-0984
  Bensenville (G-1753)

PRINTING: Books

Advocate Print Shop ....E 847 390-3594
  Mount Prospect (G-14510)
Andover Junction Publications ....G 815 538-3060
  Mendota (G-13935)
Award/Visionps Inc ....G 331 318-7800
  Chicago (G-3791)
Baker & Taylor LLC ....B 815 802-2444
  Momence (G-14183)
Beslow Associates Inc ....G 847 559-2703
  Northbrook (G-15349)
Bostic Publishing Company ....G 773 551-7065
  Chicago (G-3937)
Charles C Thomas Publisher ....G 217 789-8980
  Springfield (G-19348)
Cook Communications Ministries ....C 847 741-0800
  Elgin (G-8557)
Creasey Printing Services Inc ....G 217 787-1055
  Springfield (G-19356)
Greek Art Printing & Pubg Co ....G 847 724-8860
  Glenview (G-10553)
Hopper Graphics Inc ....G 708 489-0459
  Palos Heights (G-16189)
In-Print Graphics Inc ....E 708 396-1010
  Oak Forest (G-15683)
Ink Spots Prtg & Meida Design ....G 708 754-1300
  Homewood (G-11498)

Interntnal Awakening Ministries ....G 630 653-8616
  Wheaton (G-20806)
Johnson Press America Inc ....E 815 844-5161
  Pontiac (G-16773)
Kellogg Printing Co ....F 309 734-8388
  Monmouth (G-14220)
Kjellberg Printing ....F 630 653-2244
  Wheaton (G-20807)
KK Stevens Publishing Co ....E 309 329-2151
  Astoria (G-893)
Lsc Communications Inc ....C 773 272-9200
  Chicago (G-5272)
Lsc Communications Inc ....G 217 258-2832
  Mattoon (G-13641)
Lsc Communications Mm LLC ....F 815 844-1819
  Chicago (G-5273)
Lsc Communications Us LLC ....B 844 572-5720
  Chicago (G-5274)
Marty Gannon ....E 847 895-1059
  Schaumburg (G-18620)
Pantagraph Printing and Sty Co ....F 309 829-1071
  Bloomington (G-2084)
Printers Row Press Inc ....E 312 427-7150
  Chicago (G-5879)
Quad/Graphics Inc ....A 815 734-4121
  Mount Morris (G-14500)
R R Donnelley & Sons Company ....A 815 844-5181
  Pontiac (G-16779)
R R Donnelley & Sons Company ....A 815 584-2770
  Dwight (G-8158)
Roger Fritz & Associates Inc ....G 630 355-2614
  Naperville (G-14911)
University of Chicago ....E 773 702-7000
  Chicago (G-6486)
Vision Intgrted Grphics Group ....C 331 318-7800
  Bolingbrook (G-2251)
Wold Printing Services Ltd ....G 847 546-3110
  Volo (G-20206)

PRINTING: Broadwoven Fabrics. Cotton

Grey Shirt Guys LLC ....G 800 787-4478
  Mascoutah (G-13597)

PRINTING: Checkbooks

Carousel Checks Inc ....F 708 613-2452
  Palos Hills (G-16197)
Deluxe Corporation ....C 847 635-7200
  Des Plaines (G-7753)

PRINTING: Commercial, NEC

A Corporate Printing Service ....F 630 515-0432
  Woodridge (G-21271)
Aaction Printing ....G 951 788-5111
  Pittsfield (G-16627)
Abbey Copying Support Svcs Inc ....G 618 466-3300
  Godfrey (G-10647)
ABC Imaging of Washington ....E 312 253-0040
  Chicago (G-3508)
ABS Graphics Inc ....C 630 495-2400
  Itasca (G-11615)
Accord Carton Co ....C 708 272-3050
  Alsip (G-410)
Acj Partners LLC ....G 630 745-1335
  Chicago (G-3524)
Active Graphics Inc ....E 708 656-8900
  Cicero (G-6827)
Ad Works Inc ....G 217 342-9688
  Effingham (G-8382)
Ajs Premier Printing Inc ....G 847 838-6350
  Antioch (G-596)
Allan Brooks & Associates Inc ....F 847 537-7500
  Lake Villa (G-12345)
Allegra Marketing Print Mail ....G 630 790-0444
  Schaumburg (G-18431)
Alliance Envelope & Print LLC ....G 847 446-4079
  Winnetka (G-21124)
Allied Graphics Inc ....G 847 419-8830
  Buffalo Grove (G-2508)
Allprint Graphics Inc ....G 847 519-9898
  Schaumburg (G-18433)
Alphabet Shop Inc ....E 847 888-3150
  Elgin (G-8505)
Alta Vista Solutions Inc ....F 312 473-3050
  Chicago (G-3634)
Altco Inc ....D 847 549-0321
  Vernon Hills (G-20041)
American Litho Incorporated ....A 630 682-0600
  Carol Stream (G-2934)

Employee Codes: A=Over 500 employees, B=251-500
C=101-250, D=51-100, E=20-50, F=10-19, G=3-9

Apple Press Inc ....G.... 815 224-1451 Peru *(G-16565)*

Arcadia Press Inc ....F.... 847 451-6390 Franklin Park *(G-9872)*

Arjay Instant Printing ....G.... 847 438-9059 Mundelein *(G-14664)*

Art-Flo Shirt & Lettering Co ....E.... 708 656-5422 Chicago *(G-3738)*

Associated Design Inc ....F.... 708 974-9100 Palos Hills *(G-16195)*

Augusta Label Corp ....G.... 630 537-1961 Burr Ridge *(G-2653)*

Award/Visionps Inc ....G.... 331 318-7800 Chicago *(G-3791)*

B & B Printing Company ....G.... 217 285-6072 Pittsfield *(G-16628)*

B Allan Graphics Inc ....F.... 708 396-1704 Alsip *(G-420)*

Bagcraftpapercon I LLC ....C.... 620 856-2800 Chicago *(G-3814)*

Bally Foil Graphics Inc ....G.... 847 427-1509 Elk Grove Village *(G-8857)*

Barnaby Inc ....F.... 815 895-6555 Aurora *(G-1061)*

Belmonte Printing Co ....G.... 847 352-8841 Schaumburg *(G-18458)*

Biller Press & Manufacturing ....G.... 847 395-4111 Antioch *(G-604)*

Blazing Color Inc ....G.... 618 826-3001 Chester *(G-3450)*

Boree Unlimited LLC ....G.... 773 498-6591 Chicago *(G-3935)*

Branstiter Printing Co ....G.... 217 245-6533 Jacksonville *(G-11760)*

Brooke Graphics LLC ....E.... 847 593-1300 Elk Grove Village *(G-8870)*

BT Steelle Investments Inc ....G.... 618 410-0534 Highland *(G-11206)*

Business Cards Etc ....G.... 847 470-8848 Morton Grove *(G-14394)*

C F C Interantional ....G.... 708 753-0679 Chicago Heights *(G-6737)*

C2 Imaging LLC ....E.... 312 238-3800 Chicago *(G-3996)*

Campbell Publishing Inc ....E.... 217 742-3313 Winchester *(G-21104)*

Cannon Ball Marketing Inc ....G.... 630 971-2127 Lisle *(G-12875)*

Card Prsnlzation Solutions LLC ....E.... 630 543-2630 Glendale Heights *(G-10441)*

Carson Printing Inc ....G.... 847 836-0900 East Dundee *(G-8189)*

Castle-Printech Inc ....G.... 815 758-5484 Dekalb *(G-7667)*

Catalog Designers Inc ....G.... 847 228-0025 Elk Grove Village *(G-8881)*

Cavco Printers ....G.... 618 988-8011 Energy *(G-9467)*

CDs Office Systems Inc ....F.... 217 351-5046 Champaign *(G-3278)*

Century Printing ....G.... 618 632-2486 O Fallon *(G-15570)*

Challenge Printers ....G.... 773 252-0212 Chicago *(G-4067)*

Cherry Street Printing & Award ....G.... 618 252-6814 Harrisburg *(G-11021)*

Chicago Envelope Inc ....E.... 630 668-0400 Carol Stream *(G-2957)*

Chicago Print Partners LLC ....F.... 312 525-2015 Addison *(G-70)*

Churchill Wilmslow Corporation ....G.... 312 759-8911 Chicago *(G-4147)*

Cifuentes Luis & Nicole Inc ....G.... 847 490-3660 Schaumburg *(G-18477)*

Cityblue Technologies LLC ....F.... 309 550-5000 Peoria *(G-16423)*

Classique Signs & Engrv Inc ....G.... 217 228-7446 Quincy *(G-16872)*

Cliffe Printing Company ....G.... 708 345-1665 Maywood *(G-13667)*

Clyde Printing Company ....F.... 773 847-5900 Chicago *(G-4184)*

Com-Graphics Inc ....D.... 312 226-0900 Chicago *(G-4208)*

Corporate Business Card Ltd ....E.... 847 455-5760 Franklin Park *(G-9915)*

Corwin Printing ....G.... 618 263-3936 Mount Carmel *(G-14469)*

Craftsmen Printing ....G.... 217 283-9574 Hoopeston *(G-11506)*

Crest Greetings Inc ....F.... 708 210-0800 Chicago *(G-4269)*

Crown Publications Inc ....G.... 217 893-4856 Rantoul *(G-16973)*

D G Printing Inc ....E.... 847 397-7779 Hawthorn Woods *(G-11122)*

Darwill Inc ....C.... 708 449-7770 Hillside *(G-11335)*

Datasite Global Corporation ....C.... 312 263-3524 Chicago *(G-4321)*

Deluxe Corporation ....C.... 847 635-7200 Des Plaines *(G-7753)*

Deluxe Printing ....G.... 312 225-0061 Chicago *(G-4337)*

Design Graphics Inc ....G.... 815 462-3323 Frankfort *(G-9783)*

Diamond Web Printing LLC ....F.... 630 663-0351 Downers Grove *(G-7987)*

Digital Hub LLC ....E.... 312 943-6161 Berkeley *(G-1940)*

Digital Prtg & Total Graphics ....G.... 630 627-7400 Lombard *(G-13068)*

Domino Amjet Inc ....E.... 847 662-3148 Gurnee *(G-10869)*

Donald J Leventhal ....G.... 309 662-8080 Bloomington *(G-2040)*

Donnells Printing & Off Pdts ....G.... 815 842-6541 Pontiac *(G-16768)*

Drake Envelope Printing Co ....G.... 217 374-2772 White Hall *(G-21018)*

Eagle Express Mail LLC ....G.... 618 377-6245 Bethalto *(G-1964)*

Edwards Creative Services LLC ....F.... 309 756-0199 Milan *(G-14007)*

Elite Die & Finishing Inc ....G.... 708 389-4848 Tinley Park *(G-19823)*

Elliott Publishing Inc ....G.... 217 645-3033 Liberty *(G-12622)*

Emsur USA LLC ....E.... 847 367-8787 Elk Grove Village *(G-8976)*

Envision Graphics LLC ....D.... 630 825-1200 Bloomingdale *(G-1993)*

Ethan Company Incorporated ....G.... 815 715-2283 Shorewood *(G-18895)*

Eugene Ewbank ....G.... 630 705-0400 Oswego *(G-16004)*

F & S Engraving Inc ....E.... 847 870-8400 Mount Prospect *(G-14527)*

Fast Print Shop ....G.... 618 997-1976 Marion *(G-13510)*

Father & Daughters Printing ....G.... 708 749-8286 Berwyn *(G-1953)*

Fedex Ground Package Sys Inc ....G.... 800 463-3339 Glendale Heights *(G-10450)*

Fedex Office & Print Svcs Inc ....G.... 630 759-5784 Bolingbrook *(G-2176)*

Fedex Office & Print Svcs Inc ....G.... 847 670-7283 Mount Prospect *(G-14528)*

Fedex Office & Print Svcs Inc ....E.... 217 355-3400 Champaign *(G-3292)*

Fedex Office & Print Svcs Inc ....E.... 309 685-4093 Peoria *(G-16437)*

Fedex Office & Print Svcs Inc ....E.... 708 452-0149 Elmwood Park *(G-9452)*

Fedex Office & Print Svcs Inc ....F.... 312 670-4460 Chicago *(G-4577)*

Fgs Inc ....F.... 312 421-3060 Chicago *(G-4584)*

Fine Arts Engraving Co ....G.... 800 688-4400 Chicago *(G-4589)*

Fine Line Printing ....G.... 773 582-9709 Chicago *(G-4590)*

First Impression ....G.... 815 883-3357 Oglesby *(G-15841)*

First Impression of Chicago ....G.... 773 224-3434 Chicago *(G-4594)*

Fisheye Services Incorporated ....G.... 773 942-6314 Chicago *(G-4598)*

Fleetwood Press Inc ....G.... 708 485-6811 Brookfield *(G-2483)*

Fort Dearborn Company ....C.... 773 774-4321 Niles *(G-15121)*

Forte Print Corporation ....G.... 773 391-0105 Chicago *(G-4621)*

Freeport Press Inc ....G.... 815 232-1181 Freeport *(G-10111)*

Frye-Williamson Press Inc ....E.... 217 522-7744 Springfield *(G-19372)*

G F Printing ....G.... 618 797-0576 Granite City *(G-10708)*

G Force Labels & Printing Inc ....F.... 630 552-8911 Plano *(G-16733)*

Golden Prairie News ....G.... 217 226-3721 Assumption *(G-889)*

Graphic Press Inc ....G.... 847 272-6000 Morton Grove *(G-14410)*

Graphics Group LLC ....D.... 708 867-5500 Chicago *(G-4729)*

Griffin John ....G.... 708 301-2316 Lockport *(G-12999)*

Hafner Printing Co Inc ....F.... 312 362-0120 Chicago *(G-4767)*

Hastings Printing ....G.... 217 253-5086 Tuscola *(G-19927)*

Hawthorne Press ....G.... 708 652-9000 Cicero *(G-6852)*

Heart Printing Inc ....G.... 847 259-2100 Arlington Heights *(G-748)*

Hermitage Group Inc ....E.... 773 561-3773 Chicago *(G-4808)*

Hillsboro Journal Inc ....E.... 217 532-3933 Hillsboro *(G-11316)*

Hopper Graphics Inc ....G.... 708 489-0459 Palos Heights *(G-16189)*

Howard Press Printing Inc ....G.... 708 345-7437 Northlake *(G-15547)*

Hub Printing Company Inc ....F.... 815 562-7057 Rochelle *(G-17145)*

ID Label Inc ....E.... 847 265-1200 Lake Villa *(G-12355)*

Iemco Corporation ....G.... 773 728-4400 Chicago *(G-4878)*

Illinois Office Sup Elect Prtg ....E.... 815 434-0186 Ottawa *(G-16056)*

Illinois Tag Co ....E.... 773 626-0542 Carol Stream *(G-3001)*

Impressive Impressions ....G.... 312 432-0501 Chicago *(G-4902)*

Imtran Industries Inc ....D.... 630 752-4000 Carol Stream *(G-3004)*

In Color Graphics Coml Prtg ....F.... 847 697-0003 Elgin *(G-8623)*

Integra Graphics and Forms Inc ....F.... 708 385-0950 Crestwood *(G-7120)*

Joes Printing ....G.... 773 545-6063 Chicago *(G-5034)*

Johnson Printing ....G.... 630 595-8815 Bensenville *(G-1833)*

Jph Enterprises Inc ....G.... 847 390-0900 Des Plaines *(G-7792)*

Kellogg Printing Co ....F.... 309 734-8388 Monmouth *(G-14220)*

Kelly Printing Co Inc ....E.... 217 443-1792 Danville *(G-7355)*

Kens Quick Print Inc ....F.... 847 831-4410 Highland Park *(G-11277)*

Kevin Kewney ....G.... 217 228-7444 Quincy *(G-16899)*

Knight Prtg & Litho Svc Ltd ....G.... 847 487-7700 Island Lake *(G-11609)*

Korea Times ....D.... 847 626-0388 Glenview *(G-10579)*

Kwik Print Inc ....G.... 630 773-3225 Itasca *(G-11689)*

Label Tek Inc ....F.... 630 820-8499 Aurora *(G-995)*

Laninver USA Inc ....G.... 847 367-8787 Elk Grove Village *(G-9084)*

Larsen Envelope Co Inc ....E.... 847 952-9020 Elk Grove Village *(G-9085)*

Lee-Wel Printing Corporation ....G.... 630 682-0935 Wheaton *(G-20812)*

Legend Promotions ....G.... 847 438-3528 Lake Zurich *(G-12428)*

Liberty Group Publishing ....G.... 309 937-3303 Cambridge *(G-2805)*

Lighthouse Marketing Services ....G.... 630 482-9900 Elburn *(G-8458)*

Lincolnshire Printing Inc ....G.... 815 578-0740 McHenry *(G-13759)*

Lithuanian Catholic Press ....E.... 773 585-9500 Chicago *(G-5236)*

M & G Graphics Inc ....E.... 773 247-1596 Chicago *(G-5295)*

M L S Printing Co Inc ....G.... 847 948-8902 Deerfield *(G-7633)*

Macoupin County Enquirer Inc ....E.... 217 854-2534 Carlinville *(G-2879)*

Maro Carton Inc ....G.... 708 649-9982 Bellwood *(G-1633)*

PRINTING: Commercial, NEC

Mason City Banner Times ....F 217 482-3276
  Mason City (G-13612)
Mattoon Printing Center ....G 217 234-3100
  Mattoon (G-13646)
Mbh Promotions Inc ....G 847 634-2411
  Buffalo Grove (G-2570)
McHenry Printing Services ....G 815 385-7600
  McHenry (G-13765)
Merrill Corporation ....C 312 386-2200
  Chicago (G-5400)
Mi-Te Fast Printers Inc ....G 312 236-3278
  Glencoe (G-10432)
Mid City Printing Service ....G 773 777-5400
  Chicago (G-5426)
Midwest Labels and Decals Inc ....G 630 543-7556
  Addison (G-211)
Miller Products Inc ....E 708 534-5111
  University Park (G-19962)
Minuteman Press ....G 630 584-7383
  Naperville (G-14872)
Minuteman Press Inc ....G 847 577-2411
  Arlington Heights (G-776)
MJM Graphics ....G 847 234-1802
  Lake Forest (G-12274)
Modern Methods Creative Inc ....G 309 263-4100
  Morton (G-14368)
Moor Printing Services Inc ....G 847 687-7287
  Vernon Hills (G-20076)
Moss Inc ....G 800 341-1555
  Elk Grove Village (G-9133)
Moss Inc ....D 800 341-1557
  Chicago (G-5503)
MPS Chicago Inc ....E 630 932-5583
  Bolingbrook (G-2217)
National Data Svcs Chicago Inc .....C 630 597-9100
  Carol Stream (G-3038)
Nbs Systems Inc ....E 217 999-3472
  Mount Olive (G-14507)
Nissha Usa Inc ....E 847 413-2665
  Schaumburg (G-18650)
Northwest Premier Printing ....G 773 736-1882
  Chicago (G-5623)
Northwestern Illinois Farmer ....G 815 369-2811
  Lena (G-12607)
Norway Press Inc ....G 773 846-9422
  Chicago (G-5627)
Nosco Inc ....D 847 360-4874
  Waukegan (G-20471)
Nu-Art Printing ....G 618 533-9971
  Centralia (G-3242)
Oec Graphics-Chicago LLC ....E 630 455-6700
  Willowbrook (G-21056)
Ottawa Publishing Co Inc ....F 815 434-3330
  Ottawa (G-16069)
P H C Enterprises Inc ....G 847 816-7373
  Vernon Hills (G-20080)
Pana News Inc ....F 217 562-2111
  Pana (G-16221)
Pantagraph Printing and Sty Co .....F 309 829-1071
  Bloomington (G-2084)
Parker Systems Inc ....G 847 726-8600
  Kildeer (G-12051)
Patrick Impressions LLC ....G 630 257-9336
  Lemont (G-12578)
Pcbl Retail Holdings LLC ....G 610 761-4838
  Northbrook (G-15452)
Peddlers Den Inc ....G 815 498-3429
  Somonauk (G-19071)
Perryco Inc ....F 815 436-2431
  Plainfield (G-16701)
Pete Aj Co ....G 217 825-5822
  Gillespie (G-10376)
PHI Group Inc ....C 847 824-5610
  Mount Prospect (G-14561)
Pioneer Printing Service Inc ....G 312 337-4283
  Chicago (G-5810)
Platform Technologies ....G 847 357-0435
  Des Plaines (G-7825)
Pontiac Engraving ....G 630 834-4424
  Bensenville (G-1870)
Premier Printing & Promotions ....F 815 282-3890
  Machesney Park (G-13367)
Premier Printing Illinois Inc ....D 217 359-2219
  Champaign (G-3339)
Print Management Partners Inc ......E 847 699-2999
  Des Plaines (G-7833)
Print Shop of Morris ....G 815 710-5030
  Morris (G-14322)
Printer Connection ....G 217 268-3252
  Arcola (G-663)

Printing Craftsmen of Joliet ....G 815 254-3982
  Joliet (G-11917)
Printing Gallery Inc ....G 773 525-7102
  Chicago (G-5882)
Printing System ....G 630 339-5900
  Glendale Heights (G-10485)
Printmeisters Inc ....G 708 474-8400
  Lansing (G-12512)
Printsource Plus Inc ....G 708 389-6252
  Blue Island (G-2134)
Printworld ....G 815 544-1000
  Belvidere (G-1696)
Priority Print ....G 708 485-7080
  Brookfield (G-2491)
Pryde Graphics Plus ....G 630 882-5103
  Plano (G-16743)
Publishers Graphics LLC ....E 630 221-1850
  Carol Stream (G-3055)
Qg LLC ....D 217 347-7721
  Effingham (G-8420)
Quad/Graphics Inc ....A 815 338-6750
  Woodstock (G-21426)
Quad/Graphics Inc ....A 815 734-4121
  Mount Morris (G-14500)
Quality Blue & Offset Printing ....G 630 759-8035
  Bolingbrook (G-2231)
Quickprinters ....G 309 833-5250
  Macomb (G-13398)
R R Donnelley & Sons Company ....C 312 326-8000
  Chicago (G-5950)
R R Donnelley & Sons Company ....E 217 258-2675
  Mattoon (G-13652)
R R Donnelley & Sons Company ....E 847 622-1026
  Elgin (G-8714)
R R Donnelley & Sons Company ....A 815 584-2770
  Dwight (G-8158)
Rapid Circular Press Inc ....F 312 421-5611
  Chicago (G-5970)
Remke Printing Inc ....G 847 520-7300
  Wheeling (G-20972)
Renishaw Inc ....D 847 286-9953
  Dundee (G-8131)
Review Printing Co Inc ....G 309 788-7094
  Rock Island (G-17241)
Ripa LLC ....G 708 938-1600
  Broadview (G-2464)
Robal Company Inc ....F 630 393-0777
  Warrenville (G-20252)
Rodin Enterprises Inc ....G 847 412-1370
  Wheeling (G-20976)
Rose Business Forms & Printing ...G 618 533-3032
  Centralia (G-3248)
Roshan Ag Inc ....G 773 267-1635
  Chicago (G-6064)
Rowboat Creative LLC ....F 773 675-2628
  Chicago (G-6067)
Royal Envelope Corporation ....D 773 376-1212
  Chicago (G-6069)
RR Donnelley & Sons Company .....C 312 236-8000
  Chicago (G-6071)
RR Donnelley Logistics SE ....F 630 672-2500
  Roselle (G-17981)
Rsn Mailing ....G 314 724-3364
  Collinsville (G-6974)
Rt Associates Inc ....D 847 577-0700
  Wheeling (G-20977)
Rusty & Angela Buzzard ....G 217 342-9841
  Effingham (G-8423)
Samecwei Inc ....G 630 897-7888
  Aurora (G-1153)
Scribes Inc ....G 630 654-3800
  Burr Ridge (G-2718)
Selective Label & Tabs Inc ....G 630 466-0091
  Sugar Grove (G-19655)
Sentro Printing Equip N Movers .....G 779 423-0255
  Rockton (G-17701)
Sepire LLC ....E 312 965-2500
  Burr Ridge (G-2719)
Service Envelope Corporation ....E 847 559-0004
  Northbrook (G-15480)
Shanin Company ....D 847 676-1200
  Lincolnwood (G-12843)
Shawver Press Inc ....G 815 772-4700
  Morrison (G-14348)
Sheer Graphics Inc ....G 630 654-4422
  Westmont (G-20772)
Shree Mahavir Inc ....G 312 408-1080
  Chicago (G-6159)
Sigley Printing & Off Sup Co ....G 618 997-5304
  Marion (G-13535)

Sir Cooper Inc ....G 630 279-0162
  Villa Park (G-20173)
Skyline Printing Sales ....G 847 412-1931
  Northbrook (G-15481)
Southwest Printing Co ....G 708 389-0800
  Alsip (G-512)
Spectrum Media Inc ....G 217 234-2044
  Mattoon (G-13654)
Speedpro Imaging ....G 847 856-8220
  Gurnee (G-10929)
Spotlight Graphic Solutions ....G 847 944-9600
  Schaumburg (G-18725)
Star-Times Publishing Co Inc ....G 618 635-2000
  Staunton (G-19479)
Stellar Recognition Inc ....D 773 282-8060
  Chicago (G-6243)
Sunny Direct LLC ....G 630 795-0800
  Naperville (G-14924)
Sunrise Hitek Service Inc ....E 773 792-8880
  Chicago (G-6277)
Swifty Print ....G 630 584-9063
  Saint Charles (G-18283)
Taylor Communication ....C 309 664-0444
  Bloomington (G-2100)
Team Cncept Prtg Thrmgrphy Inc ..E 630 653-8326
  Carol Stream (G-3079)
Technicraft Supply Co ....G 309 495-5245
  Peoria (G-16537)
Techprint Inc ....F 847 616-0109
  Elk Grove Village (G-9269)
Teds Shirt Shack Inc ....G 217 224-9705
  Quincy (G-16946)
Temper Enterprises Inc ....G 815 553-0374
  Crest Hill (G-7098)
The b F Shaw Printing Co ....E 815 875-4461
  Princeton (G-16823)
Thomas Publishing Printing Div ......G 618 351-6655
  Carbondale (G-2862)
Times Republic ....E 815 432-5227
  Watseka (G-20320)
Toledo Democrat ....G 217 849-2000
  Toledo (G-19879)
Tree Towns Reprographics Inc ......F 630 832-0209
  Elmhurst (G-9437)
Tri-Tower Printing Inc ....G 847 640-6633
  Rolling Meadows (G-17782)
Tru Line Lithographing Inc ....E 262 554-7300
  Niles (G-15183)
Unique Envelope Corporation ....E 773 586-0330
  Chicago (G-6468)
Uniquee Tees Inc ....G 309 839-0280
  Peoria (G-16540)
United Engravers Inc ....E 847 301-3740
  Schaumburg (G-18765)
Universal Digital Printing ....G 708 389-0133
  Midlothian (G-13998)
UPS Authorized Retailer ....G 708 354-8772
  La Grange (G-12090)
Valee Inc ....G 847 364-6464
  Elk Grove Village (G-9300)
Valid Secure Solutions LLC ....F 260 633-0728
  Lisle (G-12954)
Village Press Inc ....G 847 362-1856
  Libertyville (G-12724)
Vision Intgrted Grphics Group ....C 331 318-7800
  Bolingbrook (G-2251)
Vr Printing Co Inc ....G 630 980-2315
  Glendale Heights (G-10514)
Wagner John ....G 847 564-0017
  Northbrook (G-15498)
Wes Tech Printing Graphic ....G 630 520-9041
  West Chicago (G-20658)
White Graphics Printing Svcs ....G 630 629-9300
  Downers Grove (G-8110)
Wide Image Incorporated ....G 773 279-9183
  Schaumburg (G-18773)
William Holloway Ltd ....G 847 866-9520
  Evanston (G-9588)
Wold Printing Services Ltd ....G 847 546-3110
  Volo (G-20206)
Wolters Kluwer US Inc ....E 847 580-5000
  Riverwoods (G-17097)
Wood River Printing & Pubg Co .....G 618 254-3134
  Wood River (G-21268)
Your Images Group Inc ....G 847 437-6688
  Schaumburg (G-18780)
Zell Co ....G 312 226-9191
  Chicago (G-6714)

Employee Codes: A=Over 500 employees, B=251-500
C=101-250, D=51-100, E=20-50, F=10-19, G=3-9

PRINTING: Engraving & Plate

Motherboard Gifts & More LLC............G...... 847 550-2222
  Lake Zurich *(G-12436)*

PRINTING: Flexographic

Bellen Container Corporation............E...... 847 741-5600
  Elgin *(G-8520)*
Bunzl Retail Services LLC............E...... 847 966-2550
  Morton Grove *(G-14393)*
Condor Labels Inc............G...... 708 429-0707
  Palos Park *(G-16209)*
Custom Graphics Inc............E...... 309 633-0850
  Bartonville *(G-1330)*
Flexografix Inc............F...... 630 350-0100
  Carol Stream *(G-2986)*
General Packaging Products Inc............D...... 312 226-5611
  Chicago *(G-4675)*
Identi-Graphics Inc............G...... 630 801-4845
  Montgomery *(G-14250)*
Labels & Specialty Pdts LLC............E...... 630 513-8060
  Saint Charles *(G-18223)*
Labels Unlimited Incorporated............E...... 773 523-7500
  Chicago *(G-5152)*
Prime Label & Packaging LLC............D...... 630 227-1300
  Wood Dale *(G-21231)*
Quality Bags Inc............F...... 630 543-9800
  Addison *(G-260)*
R Popernik Co Inc............F...... 773 434-4300
  Chicago *(G-5949)*
Var Graphics............G...... 708 456-2028
  Elmwood Park *(G-9457)*

PRINTING: Gravure, Business Form & Card

National Gift Card Corp............E...... 815 477-4288
  Crystal Lake *(G-7236)*
Proforma-Ppg Inc............G...... 847 429-9349
  Elgin *(G-8698)*
Tst/Impreso Inc............G...... 630 775-9555
  Addison *(G-320)*

PRINTING: Gravure, Cards, Exc Greeting

Marketing Card Technology LLC............D...... 630 985-7900
  Downers Grove *(G-8052)*

PRINTING: Gravure, Catalogs, No Publishing On-Site

Lsc Communications Us LLC............C...... 217 235-0561
  Mattoon *(G-13642)*
Precision Dialogue Inc............C...... 773 237-2264
  Chicago *(G-5854)*
R R Donnelley & Sons Company............C...... 312 326-8000
  Chicago *(G-5950)*

PRINTING: Gravure, Circulars

KI Watch Service Inc............G...... 847 368-8780
  Bartlett *(G-1293)*

PRINTING: Gravure, Envelopes

Unique Envelope Corporation............E...... 773 586-0330
  Chicago *(G-6468)*

PRINTING: Gravure, Job

Donnells Printing & Off Pdts............G...... 815 842-6541
  Pontiac *(G-16768)*

PRINTING: Gravure, Labels

American Labelmark Company............C...... 773 478-0900
  Chicago *(G-3656)*
Arcadia Press Inc............F...... 847 451-6390
  Franklin Park *(G-9872)*
Field Holdings LLC............D...... 847 509-2250
  Northbrook *(G-15388)*
Label Tek Inc............F...... 630 820-8499
  Aurora *(G-995)*
Pioneer Labels Inc............G...... 618 546-5418
  Robinson *(G-17121)*

PRINTING: Gravure, Magazines, No Publishing On-Site

Cook Communications Minis............D...... 847 741-5168
  Elgin *(G-8556)*
Cucchi-BLT America Inc............G...... 224 829-1400
  Lake In The Hills *(G-12331)*

PRINTING: Gravure, Music, Sheet, No Publishing On-Site

Rogers Loose Leaf Co............F...... 312 226-1947
  Glenview *(G-10614)*

PRINTING: Gravure, Post Cards, Picture

Pingotopia Inc............F...... 847 503-9333
  Northbrook *(G-15459)*

PRINTING: Gravure, Promotional

Frankenstitch Promotions LLC............F...... 847 459-4840
  Wheeling *(G-20901)*

PRINTING: Gravure, Rotogravure

C2 Imaging LLC............E...... 312 238-3800
  Chicago *(G-3996)*
Diversfied Lbling Slutions Inc............C...... 630 625-1225
  Itasca *(G-11643)*
Graphic Industries Inc............E...... 847 357-9870
  South Elgin *(G-19148)*
Illinois Tool Works Inc............D...... 630 752-4000
  Carol Stream *(G-3002)*
Integrated Media Inc............F...... 217 854-6260
  Carlinville *(G-2877)*
International Graphics & Assoc............F...... 630 584-2248
  Saint Charles *(G-18215)*
Qg LLC............D...... 217 347-7721
  Effingham *(G-8420)*
Quad/Graphics Inc............A...... 815 734-4121
  Mount Morris *(G-14500)*
R R Donnelley & Sons Company............G...... 309 808-3018
  Normal *(G-15221)*
R R Donnelley & Sons Company............E...... 847 622-1026
  Elgin *(G-8714)*
R R Donnelley & Sons Company............B...... 630 588-5000
  Lisle *(G-12931)*
RR Donnelley & Sons Company............C...... 312 236-8000
  Chicago *(G-6071)*
RR Donnelley Printing Co LP............A...... 217 235-0561
  Mattoon *(G-13653)*
Standard Register Inc............F...... 630 467-8300
  Itasca *(G-11740)*
White Graphics Printing Svcs............G...... 630 629-9300
  Downers Grove *(G-8110)*
Xpress Printing & Copying Co............G...... 630 980-9600
  Roselle *(G-17997)*

PRINTING: Gravure, Visiting Cards

Chicago Producers Inc............F...... 312 226-6900
  Forest Park *(G-9709)*

PRINTING: Laser

Aloha Document Services Inc............E...... 312 542-1300
  Chicago *(G-3626)*
Document Publishing Group............E...... 847 783-0670
  Elgin *(G-8567)*
Ink Spots Prtg & Meida Design............G...... 708 754-1300
  Homewood *(G-11498)*
Microdynamics Corporation............C...... 630 276-0527
  Naperville *(G-14870)*
Sebis Direct Inc............E...... 312 243-9300
  Bedford Park *(G-1504)*
Tst/Impreso Inc............G...... 630 775-9555
  Addison *(G-320)*

PRINTING: Letterpress

Art-Craft Printers............G...... 847 455-2201
  Franklin Park *(G-9874)*
Bond Brothers & Co............F...... 708 442-5510
  Lyons *(G-13303)*
C E Dienberg Printing Company............G...... 708 848-4406
  Oak Park *(G-15747)*
Carter Printing Co Inc............G...... 217 227-4464
  Farmersville *(G-9659)*
Color Tone Printing............G...... 708 385-1442
  Blue Island *(G-2114)*
Color4............F...... 847 996-6880
  Libertyville *(G-12644)*
Crossmark Printing Inc............G...... 708 754-4000
  Chicago Heights *(G-6745)*
D & R Press............G...... 708 452-0500
  Elmwood Park *(G-9450)*
D G Brandt Inc............G...... 815 942-4064
  Morris *(G-14301)*
Dale K Brown............G...... 815 338-5006
  Woodstock *(G-21380)*
Dans Printing & Off Sups Inc............F...... 708 687-3055
  Oak Forest *(G-15674)*
Duo Graphics............G...... 847 228-7080
  Elk Grove Village *(G-8956)*
Evanston Graphic Imaging Inc............G...... 847 869-7446
  Evanston *(G-9516)*
F Weber Printing Co Inc............G...... 815 468-6152
  Manteno *(G-13447)*
Falcon Press Inc............G...... 815 455-9099
  Crystal Lake *(G-7197)*
Faulstich Printing Company Inc............G...... 217 442-4994
  Danville *(G-7332)*
FM Graphic Impressions Inc............G...... 630 897-8788
  Aurora *(G-1097)*
Freeburg Printing & Publishing............G...... 618 539-3320
  Freeburg *(G-10089)*
Gallas Label & Decal............F...... 773 775-1000
  Chicago *(G-4656)*
George Press Inc............G...... 217 324-2242
  Litchfield *(G-12964)*
Granja & Sons Printing............F...... 773 762-3840
  Chicago *(G-4724)*
Greek Art Printing & Pubg Co............G...... 847 724-8860
  Glenview *(G-10553)*
Hal Mather & Sons Incorporated............G...... 815 338-4000
  Woodstock *(G-21394)*
Harry Otto Printing Company............F...... 630 365-6111
  Elburn *(G-8455)*
Highland Journal Printing Inc............G...... 618 654-4131
  Highland *(G-11217)*
Ideal Advertising & Printing............F...... 815 965-1713
  Rockford *(G-17456)*
Impression Printing............F...... 708 614-8660
  Oak Forest *(G-15682)*
J S Printing Inc............G...... 847 678-6300
  Franklin Park *(G-9970)*
Keneal Industries Inc............F...... 815 886-1300
  Romeoville *(G-17837)*
Kjellberg Printing............F...... 630 653-2244
  Wheaton *(G-20807)*
Klh Printing Corp............G...... 847 459-0115
  Wheeling *(G-20926)*
Kon Printing Inc............G...... 630 879-2211
  Batavia *(G-1390)*
Lasons Label Co............G...... 773 775-2606
  Chicago *(G-5179)*
Lazare Printing Co Inc............G...... 773 871-2500
  Chicago *(G-5187)*
Lsc Communications Us LLC............C...... 217 235-0561
  Mattoon *(G-13642)*
M S A Printing Co............G...... 847 593-5699
  Elk Grove Village *(G-9103)*
McCracken Label Co............E...... 773 581-8860
  Chicago *(G-5375)*
Modern Printing of Quincy............F...... 217 223-1063
  Quincy *(G-16917)*
Olde Print Shoppe Inc............G...... 618 395-3833
  Olney *(G-15879)*
Overt Press Inc............E...... 773 284-0909
  Chicago *(G-5718)*
Paul D Burton............G...... 309 467-2613
  Eureka *(G-9484)*
Peacock Printing Inc............G...... 618 242-3157
  Mount Vernon *(G-14633)*
Petersburg Observer Co Inc............G...... 217 632-2236
  Petersburg *(G-16603)*
Physicians Record Co Inc............D...... 800 323-9268
  Berwyn *(G-1960)*
Preferred Printing Service............G...... 312 421-2343
  Chicago *(G-5861)*
Printing Craftsmen of Pontiac............G...... 815 844-7118
  Pontiac *(G-16778)*
Progress Printing Corporation............F...... 773 927-0123
  Chicago *(G-5898)*
R N R Photographers Inc............G...... 708 453-1868
  River Grove *(G-17066)*
R R Donnelley & Sons Company............B...... 630 588-5000
  Lisle *(G-12931)*
S V C Printing Co............G...... 773 286-2219
  Chicago *(G-6086)*
Schwebel Printing............G...... 618 684-3911
  Murphysboro *(G-14759)*
Stromberg Allen and Company............E...... 773 847-7131
  Tinley Park *(G-19858)*
Tampico Press............G...... 312 243-5448
  Chicago *(G-6320)*
Thomas Printing & Sty Co............G...... 618 435-2801
  Benton *(G-1937)*
Three Castle Press Inc............G...... 630 540-0120
  Streamwood *(G-19597)*

Washington Courier ....F 309 444-3139
Washington *(G-20282)*
Weakley Printing & Sign Shop ....G 847 473-4466
North Chicago *(G-15323)*
Weber Press Inc ....G 773 561-9815
Chicago *(G-6596)*

PRINTING: Lithographic

360 Digital Print Inc ....G 630 682-3601
Carol Stream *(G-2921)*
3d Printer Experience LLC ....G 312 896-3399
Chicago *(G-3468)*
510 Holdings Company LLC ....F 618 659-8600
Edwardsville *(G-8343)*
Ad Works Inc ....G 217 342-9688
Effingham *(G-8382)*
Addvalue2print LLC ....G 847 551-1570
Wood Dale *(G-21155)*
Advantage Printing Inc ....G 630 627-7468
Lombard *(G-13036)*
Advocate ....G 815 694-2122
Clifton *(G-6913)*
Ajs Premier Printing Inc ....G 847 838-6350
Antioch *(G-596)*
Alliance Creative Group Inc ....E 847 885-1800
East Dundee *(G-8187)*
Allied Graphics Inc ....G 847 419-8830
Buffalo Grove *(G-2508)*
Allprint Graphics Inc ....G 847 519-9898
Schaumburg *(G-18433)*
Alphadigital Inc ....G 708 482-4488
La Grange *(G-12071)*
AlphaGraphics Printshops ....G 630 964-9600
Lisle *(G-12861)*
Amboy News ....G 815 857-2311
Amboy *(G-578)*
American Litho Incorporated ....A 630 682-0600
Carol Stream *(G-2934)*
Apple Press Inc ....G 815 224-1451
Peru *(G-16565)*
Apprize Promotional Pdts Inc ....G 630 468-2043
Oakbrook Terrace *(G-15786)*
Arbor Private Inv Co LLC ....G 312 981-3770
Chicago *(G-3718)*
Arby Graphic Service Inc ....F 847 763-0900
Glencoe *(G-10428)*
Art Newvo Incorporated ....G 847 838-0304
Antioch *(G-600)*
Arthur Graphic Clarion ....G 217 543-2151
Arthur *(G-842)*
Arthur R Baker Inc ....G 708 301-4828
Homer Glen *(G-11477)*
Astro Printing Inc ....G 773 436-0500
Chicago *(G-3754)*
Athena Design Group Inc ....E 312 733-2828
Chicago *(G-3758)*
Atlantis Entp Investments Inc ....G 432 237-0404
Chicago *(G-3761)*
Automated Forms & Graphics Inc ....G 630 887-9811
Lockport *(G-12982)*
Avid of Illinois Inc ....F 847 698-2775
Saint Charles *(G-18152)*
Award/Visionps Inc ....G 331 318-7800
Chicago *(G-3791)*
B F Shaw Printing Company ....G 815 625-3600
Sterling *(G-19500)*
B P I Printing & Duplicating ....F 773 327-7300
Chicago *(G-3808)*
Bach & Associates ....G 618 277-1652
Belleville *(G-1532)*
Bardash & Bukowski Inc ....G 312 829-2080
Chicago *(G-3831)*
Barrel Maker Printing ....G 773 490-3065
Chicago *(G-3837)*
Basswood Associates Inc ....F 312 240-9400
Chicago *(G-3845)*
Batavia Instant Print ....G 630 262-0370
West Chicago *(G-20550)*
Beans Printing Inc ....G 217 223-5555
Quincy *(G-16861)*
Belmonte Printing Co ....G 847 352-8841
Schaumburg *(G-18458)*
Benton Evening News Co ....G 618 438-5611
Benton *(G-1919)*
Benzinger Printing ....G 815 784-6560
Genoa *(G-10315)*
Bitforms Inc ....G 630 595-6800
Wood Dale *(G-21169)*
Bluegrass Enterprises LLC ....G 630 544-3781
Saint Charles *(G-18158)*
Bmt Prnting Crtgraph Espclists ....G 773 646-4700
Chicago *(G-3920)*
Bond Brothers & Co ....F 708 442-5510
Lyons *(G-13303)*
Bridge Printing & Promotional ....F 847 776-0200
Roselle *(G-17941)*
Bridge Printing & Promotional ....F 312 929-1456
Chicago *(G-3954)*
Brokers Print Mail Rsource Inc ....G 708 532-9900
Tinley Park *(G-19813)*
Buhl Press ....E 708 449-8989
Berkeley *(G-1939)*
Burstan Inc ....G 847 787-0380
Elk Grove Village *(G-8874)*
Business Card Systems Inc ....F 815 877-0990
Machesney Park *(G-13331)*
Business Cards Tomorrow ....F 815 877-0990
Machesney Park *(G-13332)*
C2 Imaging LLC ....E 847 439-7834
Elk Grove Village *(G-8876)*
Cambrdg Printing Corp ....G 630 510-2100
Carol Stream *(G-2954)*
Campbell Publishing Inc ....E 217 742-3313
Winchester *(G-21104)*
Card Prsnlzation Solutions LLC ....E 630 543-2630
Glendale Heights *(G-10441)*
Carey Color Inc ....G 630 761-2605
West Chicago *(G-20559)*
CDs Office Systems Inc ....F 630 305-9034
Springfield *(G-19344)*
Central Illinois Newspapers ....G 217 935-3171
Clinton *(G-6920)*
Century Printing ....G 618 632-2486
O Fallon *(G-15570)*
Charles C Thomas Publisher ....G 217 789-8980
Springfield *(G-19348)*
Chicago Mltlingua Graphics Inc ....F 847 386-7187
Northfield *(G-15512)*
Chicago Printers Guild ....G 303 819-6197
Chicago *(G-4125)*
Chicago Sun-Times Features Inc ....A 312 321-3000
Chicago *(G-4131)*
Child Evngelism Fellowship Inc ....E 630 983-7708
Naperville *(G-14799)*
Christopher Wagner ....G 630 205-9200
Oswego *(G-15995)*
Cifuentes Luis & Nicole Inc ....G 847 490-3660
Schaumburg *(G-18477)*
Clark Printing & Marketing ....G 217 363-5300
Champaign *(G-3280)*
Clear Print Inc ....G 815 795-6225
Ottawa *(G-16046)*
Colvin Printing ....G 708 331-4580
Blue Island *(G-2115)*
Consulate General Lithuania ....G 312 397-0382
Chicago *(G-4223)*
Corporate Print Source Inc ....G 847 724-1150
Glenview *(G-10539)*
Corporation Supply Co Inc ....E 312 726-3375
Chicago *(G-4241)*
Corps Levl Ventures Inc ....F 312 846-1441
Chicago *(G-4242)*
Creasey Printing Services Inc ....G 217 787-1055
Springfield *(G-19356)*
Crli Acceptance Corp ....G 847 940-1500
Deerfield *(G-7606)*
Cynlar Inc ....G 630 820-2200
Aurora *(G-949)*
D E Asbury Inc ....F 217 222-0617
Hamilton *(G-10953)*
D G Brandt Inc ....G 815 942-4064
Morris *(G-14301)*
D L V Printing Service Inc ....F 773 626-1661
Chicago *(G-4301)*
Damy Corp ....F 847 233-0515
Schiller Park *(G-18798)*
Dark Matter Printing ....G 217 791-4059
Decatur *(G-7482)*
Dean Printing Systems ....G 847 526-9545
Fox Lake *(G-9745)*
Debbie Harshman ....G 217 335-2112
Barry *(G-1249)*
Deluxe Johnson ....C 847 635-7200
Des Plaines *(G-7754)*
Deluxe Printing ....G 312 225-0061
Chicago *(G-4337)*
Des Plaines Journal Inc ....D 847 299-5511
Des Plaines *(G-7755)*
Designation Inc ....F 847 367-9100
Mundelein *(G-14683)*
Dg Digital Printing ....G 815 961-0000
Rockford *(G-17374)*
Di Stefani T Shirt Printing ....G 618 282-2380
Red Bud *(G-16992)*
Diamond Envelope Corporation ....D 630 499-2800
Aurora *(G-951)*
Dla Document Services ....F 618 256-4686
Scott Air Force Base *(G-18857)*
Donnelley Financial LLC ....B 844 866-4337
Chicago *(G-4384)*
Donnelley Financial LLC ....G 630 963-9494
Warrenville *(G-20234)*
Donnells Printing & Off Pdts ....G 815 842-6541
Pontiac *(G-16768)*
Double Image Press Inc ....F 630 893-6777
Glendale Heights *(G-10447)*
Doubletake Marketing Inc ....G 845 598-3175
Evanston *(G-9511)*
Dps Digital Print Svc ....G 847 836-7734
East Dundee *(G-8192)*
Drake Envelope Printing Co ....G 217 374-2772
White Hall *(G-21018)*
Dsr Screenprinting ....G 630 855-2790
Streamwood *(G-19571)*
Dupli Group Inc ....F 773 549-5285
Chicago *(G-4408)*
E & H Graphic Service Inc ....G 708 748-5656
Matteson *(G-13623)*
E A A Enterprises Inc ....G 630 279-0150
Villa Park *(G-20145)*
East Central Communications Co ....E 217 892-9613
Rantoul *(G-16975)*
Edwardsville Publishing Co ....D 618 656-4700
Edwardsville *(G-8361)*
Elise S Allen ....G 309 673-2613
Peoria *(G-16434)*
Elliott Publishing Inc ....G 217 645-3033
Liberty *(G-12622)*
Envelopes Only Inc ....E 630 213-2500
Streamwood *(G-19573)*
Essentra Packaging US Inc ....G 704 418-8692
Westchester *(G-20699)*
Eugene Ewbank ....G 630 705-0400
Oswego *(G-16004)*
Faith Printing ....G 217 675-2191
Franklin *(G-9855)*
Fedex Corporation ....F 847 918-7730
Vernon Hills *(G-20053)*
Fedex Office & Print Svcs Inc ....F 312 341-9644
Chicago *(G-4573)*
Fedex Office & Print Svcs Inc ....F 312 755-0325
Chicago *(G-4574)*
Fedex Office & Print Svcs Inc ....F 312 595-0768
Chicago *(G-4575)*
Fedex Office & Print Svcs Inc ....F 312 663-1149
Chicago *(G-4576)*
Fedex Office & Print Svcs Inc ....F 630 894-1800
Bloomingdale *(G-1995)*
Fgs-IL LLC ....C 630 375-8500
Aurora *(G-960)*
Fidelity Bindery Company ....E 708 343-6833
Broadview *(G-2435)*
Financial and Professional Reg ....G 217 782-2127
Springfield *(G-19367)*
Fine Line Printing ....G 773 582-9709
Chicago *(G-4590)*
Fisheye Services Incorporated ....G 773 942-6314
Chicago *(G-4598)*
Flocon Inc ....G 815 527-7990
Woodstock *(G-21388)*
Forcerl ....G 847 432-7588
Highland Park *(G-11263)*
Foundry Printers Row Crossfit ....G 312 566-7201
Chicago *(G-4625)*
Full Court Press Inc ....G 773 779-1135
Chicago *(G-4639)*
G T Services of Illionois Inc ....G 309 925-5111
Tremont *(G-19896)*
Galesburg Register-Mail ....C 309 343-7181
Galesburg *(G-10193)*
Gamma Alpha Visual Communicatn ....G 847 956-0633
Park Ridge *(G-16279)*
Gatehouse Media LLC ....B 217 788-1300
Springfield *(G-19373)*
Gazette Printing Co ....G 309 389-2811
Glasford *(G-10387)*
George Press Inc ....G 217 324-2242
Litchfield *(G-12964)*
George Vaggelatos ....G 847 361-3880
Itasca *(G-11661)*

Employee Codes: A=Over 500 employees, B=251-500
C=101-250, D=51-100, E=20-50, F=10-19, G=3-9

Gnk Technologies Inc ....G 847 382-1185
Barrington *(G-1220)*

Golden Prairie News ....G 217 226-3721
Assumption *(G-889)*

Goose Printing Co ....G 847 673-1414
Evanston *(G-9525)*

Graf Ink Printing Inc ....G 618 273-4231
Harrisburg *(G-11025)*

Grand Forms & Systems Inc ....F 847 259-4600
Arlington Heights *(G-744)*

Grand Printing & Graphics Inc ....F 312 218-6780
Chicago *(G-4722)*

Granja & Sons Printing ....F 773 762-3840
Chicago *(G-4724)*

Graphic Arts Studio Inc ....E 847 381-1105
Barrington *(G-1221)*

Graphic Source Group Inc ....G 847 854-2670
Lake In The Hills *(G-12336)*

Graphics 255 LLC ....F 312 266-9266
Chicago *(G-4728)*

Hammond Printing ....G 847 724-1539
Glenview *(G-10555)*

Hard Reset Printing Inc ....G 773 850-9277
Joliet *(G-11874)*

Harlan Vance Company ....F 309 888-4804
Normal *(G-15205)*

Harrison Martha Print Studio ....G 949 290-8630
Crystal Lake *(G-7205)*

Hawthorne Press ....G 708 652-9000
Cicero *(G-6852)*

Heavenly Enterprises ....G 773 783-2981
Hickory Hills *(G-11197)*

Henderson Family ....G 309 236-6783
Aledo *(G-357)*

Hermitage Group Inc ....E 773 561-3773
Chicago *(G-4808)*

Hillsboro Journal Inc ....E 217 532-3933
Hillsboro *(G-11316)*

Holden Industries Inc ....F 847 940-1500
Deerfield *(G-7616)*

Howard Press Printing Inc ....G 708 345-7437
Northlake *(G-15547)*

Howlan Inc ....G 847 478-1760
Vernon Hills *(G-20061)*

Hts Hancock Transcriptions Svc ....E 217 379-9241
Paxton *(G-16308)*

Huetone Imprints Inc ....G 630 694-9610
Elk Grove Village *(G-9038)*

In Color Graphics Coml Prtg ....F 847 697-0003
Elgin *(G-8623)*

Ink Spots Prtg & Meida Design ....G 708 754-1300
Homewood *(G-11498)*

Ink Well ....G 618 398-1427
Fairview Heights *(G-9647)*

Innerworkings Inc ....D 312 642-3700
Chicago *(G-4927)*

Innovtive Design Graphics Corp ....G 847 475-7772
Evanston *(G-9540)*

Instyprints of Waukegan Inc ....G 847 336-5599
Waukegan *(G-20449)*

Integra Graphics and Forms Inc ....F 708 385-0950
Crestwood *(G-7120)*

Integra Print & Data Services ....G 708 337-6265
Libertyville *(G-12663)*

Integrity Prtg McHy Svcs LLC ....G 847 834-9484
Hoffman Estates *(G-11431)*

Intersports Screen Printing ....G 773 489-7383
Chicago *(G-4957)*

Jamether Incorporated ....G 815 444-9971
Crystal Lake *(G-7211)*

Jans Graphics Inc ....F 312 644-4700
Chicago *(G-5006)*

Jeannie Wagner ....G 815 477-2700
Crystal Lake *(G-7212)*

Jem Associates Ltd ....G 847 808-8377
Chicago *(G-5016)*

Jjm Printing Inc ....G 815 499-3067
Sterling *(G-19513)*

Johnson Press America Inc ....E 815 844-5161
Pontiac *(G-16773)*

Johnsons Screen Printing ....G 630 262-8210
Geneva *(G-10287)*

Jsn Printing Inc ....G 815 582-4014
Joliet *(G-11888)*

Jsolo Corp ....G 847 964-9188
Deerfield *(G-7624)*

K & J Phillips Corporation ....G 630 355-0660
Naperville *(G-14856)*

Keane Inc ....F 847 952-9700
Mount Prospect *(G-14541)*

Kevin Kewney ....G 217 228-7444
Quincy *(G-16899)*

Key Printing ....G 815 933-1800
Kankakee *(G-11987)*

Kingsbury Enterprises Inc ....G 708 535-7590
Oak Forest *(G-15685)*

Kjellberg Printing ....F 630 653-2244
Wheaton *(G-20807)*

KK Stevens Publishing Co ....E 309 329-2151
Astoria *(G-893)*

Krueger International Inc ....F 312 467-6850
Chicago *(G-5134)*

L P M Inc ....G 847 866-9777
Evanston *(G-9545)*

Lakes Reg Prtg & Graphics LLC ....G 847 838-5838
Antioch *(G-620)*

Lee Enterprises Incorporated ....C 618 529-5454
Carbondale *(G-2849)*

Legend Promotions ....G 847 438-3528
Lake Zurich *(G-12428)*

Lith Liqure ....G 847 458-5180
Lake In The Hills *(G-12339)*

Lithuanian Catholic Press ....E 773 585-9500
Chicago *(G-5236)*

Lloyd Midwest Graphics ....G 815 282-8828
Machesney Park *(G-13357)*

Lsk Import ....G 847 342-8447
Chicago *(G-5275)*

Lucmia Enterprises Inc ....G 800 785-3157
River Grove *(G-17062)*

Lure Group LLC ....G 630 222-6515
Bolingbrook *(G-2207)*

Lutheran General Printing Svcs ....G 847 298-8040
Mount Prospect *(G-14544)*

Lyle James ....G 217 675-2191
Jacksonville *(G-11774)*

M C F Printing Company ....G 630 279-0301
Elmhurst *(G-9396)*

M M Marketing ....G 815 459-7968
Wauconda *(G-20370)*

M Wells Printing Co ....G 312 455-0400
Chicago *(G-5305)*

M13 Inc ....E 847 310-1913
Schaumburg *(G-18617)*

Mac Graphics Group Inc ....G 630 620-7200
Oakbrook Terrace *(G-15806)*

Marc Business Forms Inc ....F 847 568-9200
Lincolnwood *(G-12829)*

Marjo Graphics Inc ....G 847 367-1305
Libertyville *(G-12672)*

Marking Specialists/Poly ....F 847 793-8100
Buffalo Grove *(G-2568)*

Martinez Printing LLC ....G 773 732-8108
Chicago *(G-5350)*

Marty Gannon ....E 847 895-1059
Schaumburg *(G-18620)*

Mason City Banner Times ....F 217 482-3276
Mason City *(G-13612)*

Medical Records Co ....G 847 662-6373
Waukegan *(G-20465)*

Menus To Go ....G 630 483-0848
Streamwood *(G-19584)*

Merritt & Edwards Corporation ....F 309 828-4741
Bloomington *(G-2075)*

Meyercord Revenue Inc ....E 630 682-6200
Carol Stream *(G-3026)*

MGA Innovation Inc ....G 847 672-9947
Gurnee *(G-10897)*

Mgsolutions Inc ....G 630 530-2005
Elmhurst *(G-9401)*

Mich Enterprises Inc ....F 630 616-9000
Wood Dale *(G-21216)*

Michael Burza ....G 815 909-0233
Cortland *(G-7024)*

Microdynamics Corporation ....C 630 276-0527
Naperville *(G-14870)*

Mid-Central Business Forms ....G 309 692-9090
Peoria *(G-16474)*

Midwest Outdoors Ltd ....E 630 887-7722
Burr Ridge *(G-2704)*

Midwest Sign & Lighting Inc ....G 708 365-5555
Country Club Hills *(G-7042)*

Minute Man Press ....G 847 839-9600
Hoffman Estates *(G-11436)*

Minuteman Press ....G 708 524-4940
Oak Park *(G-15765)*

Minuteman Press ....G 708 598-4915
Hickory Hills *(G-11200)*

Minuteman Press ....G 630 584-7383
Naperville *(G-14872)*

Minuteman Press Inc ....G 847 577-2411
Arlington Heights *(G-776)*

Minuteman Press Intl Inc ....G 630 574-0090
Oak Brook *(G-15646)*

Minuteman Press Morton Grove ....G 847 470-0212
Morton Grove *(G-14429)*

Minuteman Press of Countryside ....G 708 354-2190
Countryside *(G-7064)*

Minuteman Press of Frankfort ....G 779 254-2912
Frankfort *(G-9817)*

Minuteman Press of Lansing ....G 708 895-0505
Lansing *(G-12509)*

Minuteman Press of Rockford ....G 815 633-2992
Loves Park *(G-13237)*

Minuteman Press of Waukegan ....G 847 244-6288
Gurnee *(G-10900)*

Mittera Illinois LLC ....D 708 449-8989
Berkeley *(G-1942)*

Mmpcu Limited ....G 217 355-0500
Champaign *(G-3324)*

Moran Graphics Inc ....E 312 226-3900
Chicago *(G-5497)*

Mormor Incorporated ....G 630 268-0050
Lombard *(G-13104)*

Motr Grafx LLC ....G 847 600-5656
Wheeling *(G-20942)*

Mountain Graphix LLC ....F 630 681-8300
Carol Stream *(G-3033)*

Nameonanythingcom LLC ....G 630 545-2642
Glen Ellyn *(G-10414)*

Need To Know Inc ....G 309 691-3877
Peoria *(G-16484)*

NGS Printing Inc ....E 847 741-4411
Elgin *(G-8672)*

Nissha Si-Cal Technologies Inc ....E 508 898-1800
Burr Ridge *(G-2710)*

Nissha Usa Inc ....E 847 413-2665
Schaumburg *(G-18650)*

Nite Owl Prints LLC ....G 630 541-6273
Downers Grove *(G-8066)*

North County News Inc ....G 618 282-3803
Red Bud *(G-16998)*

Northwest Graphics Inc ....G 815 544-3676
Cherry Valley *(G-3444)*

Nosco Inc ....E 847 336-4200
Gurnee *(G-10903)*

Nosco Bridgeview Inc ....D 773 585-2035
Bridgeview *(G-2369)*

Nosco Inc ....B 847 336-4200
Gurnee *(G-10904)*

Nosco Inc ....D 847 360-4874
Waukegan *(G-20471)*

Nowuba LLC - Investio Print ....G 833 669-8221
Fox Lake *(G-9750)*

Oneims Printing LLC ....G 773 297-2050
Skokie *(G-18999)*

Onetouchpoint Mtn States LLC ....G 303 227-1400
Oak Brook *(G-15653)*

Oriole Enterprises Inc ....G 773 589-9696
Chicago *(G-5702)*

Ottawa Publishing Co Inc ....C 815 433-2000
Ottawa *(G-16068)*

Overt Press Inc ....E 773 284-0909
Chicago *(G-5718)*

P H C Enterprises Inc ....G 847 816-7373
Vernon Hills *(G-20080)*

P P Graphics Inc ....G 708 343-2530
Westchester *(G-20707)*

Pamco Printed Tape Label Inc ....C 847 803-2200
Des Plaines *(G-7817)*

Pap-R Products Company ....D 800 637-4937
Martinsville *(G-13587)*

Pap-R-Tainer LLC ....G 217 382-4141
Martinsville *(G-13588)*

Perfect Plastic Printing Corp ....D 630 584-1600
Saint Charles *(G-18243)*

Perryco Inc ....F 815 436-2431
Plainfield *(G-16701)*

Petersburg Observer Co Inc ....G 217 632-2236
Petersburg *(G-16603)*

Phoenix Press Inc ....G 630 833-2281
Addison *(G-239)*

Poets Study Inc ....G 773 286-1355
Chicago *(G-5831)*

Prairieland Printing ....G 309 647-5425
Washington *(G-20276)*

Precision Press & Label Inc ....G 630 625-1225
Itasca *(G-11722)*

Precision Printing Inc ....G 630 737-0075
Lombard *(G-13121)*

PRODUCT SECTION — PRINTING: Offset

Precision Reproductions Inc .... F   847 724-0182
  Glenview (G-10602)
Press Proof Printing .... G   847 466-7156
  Carpentersville (G-3115)
Print & Design Services LLC .... G   847 317-9001
  Bannockburn (G-1206)
Print & Mailing Solutions LLC .... G   708 544-9400
  Romeoville (G-17867)
Print & Mailing Solutions LLC .... G   708 544-9400
  Wood Dale (G-21232)
Print and Mktg Solutions Group .... E   847 498-9640
  Chicago (G-5876)
Print Butler Inc .... F   312 296-2804
  Grayslake (G-10796)
Print Service & Dist Assn Psda .... G   312 321-5120
  Chicago (G-5877)
Printcrazy LLC .... G   630 573-1020
  Chicago Heights (G-6765)
Printers Square Condo Assn .... G   312 765-8794
  Chicago (G-5880)
Printing Inc .... D   316 265-1201
  Chicago (G-5881)
Printing Works Inc .... G   847 860-1920
  Elk Grove Village (G-9198)
Printwise Inc .... G   630 833-2845
  Wheaton (G-20815)
Priority One Printing and Mail .... G   217 224-8008
  Quincy (G-16928)
Pro Graphics Ink .... G   309 647-2526
  Canton (G-2831)
Professnal Mling Prtg Svcs Inc .... F   630 510-1000
  Carol Stream (G-3054)
Proforma Awards Print & Promot .... G   630 897-9848
  Oswego (G-16021)
Promo Answers Inc .... G   708 633-6653
  Tinley Park (G-19850)
Qst Industries Inc .... E   312 930-9400
  Chicago (G-5923)
Quad/Graphics Inc .... A   815 734-4121
  Mount Morris (G-14500)
Quad/Graphics Inc .... A   815 338-6750
  Woodstock (G-21426)
R R Donnelley & Sons Company C   630 377-2586
  Saint Charles (G-18257)
R R Donnelley & Sons Company C   217 935-2113
  Clinton (G-6928)
R R Donnelley & Sons Company .... A   815 584-2770
  Dwight (G-8158)
R R Donnelley & Sons Company .... A   815 844-5181
  Pontiac (G-16779)
R R Donnelley & Sons Company .... A   630 322-6268
  Warrenville (G-20251)
R R Donnelley & Sons Company .... D   630 762-7600
  Saint Charles (G-18258)
R T P Inc .... G   312 664-6150
  Chicago (G-5954)
Reign Print Solutions Inc .... G   847 590-7091
  Arlington Heights (G-798)
Rektrix .... G   773 475-7926
  Chicago (G-6006)
Reliable Mail Services Inc .... F   847 677-6245
  Glenview (G-10611)
Review Printing Co Inc .... G   309 788-7094
  Rock Island (G-17241)
Rockford Newspapers Inc .... B   815 987-1200
  Rockford (G-17600)
Rodin Enterprises Inc .... G   847 412-1370
  Wheeling (G-20976)
Rrr Graphics & Film Corp .... G   708 478-4573
  Mokena (G-14114)
Rt Associates Inc .... D   847 577-0700
  Wheeling (G-20977)
Rush Order Signs & Prtg LLC .... G   630 687-7874
  Addison (G-278)
Safeguard 201 Corp .... G   630 241-0370
  Westmont (G-20770)
Salem Times-Commoner Inc .... E   618 548-3330
  Salem (G-18358)
Samecwei Inc .... G   630 897-7888
  Aurora (G-1153)
Save On Printing Inc .... G   847 922-7855
  Elk Grove Village (G-9231)
Schommer Inc .... G   815 344-1404
  McHenry (G-13791)
Screen Print Plus Inc .... G   630 236-0260
  Naperville (G-14985)
Second City Prints .... G   630 504-2423
  Batavia (G-1416)
Selnar Inc .... G   309 699-3977
  East Peoria (G-8290)

Sg Screen Graphics Inc .... G   309 699-8513
  Pekin (G-16360)
Sheer Graphics Inc .... G   630 654-4422
  Westmont (G-20772)
Shoreline Graphics Inc .... G   847 587-4804
  Ingleside (G-11589)
Signcraft Screenprint Inc C   815 777-3030
  Galena (G-10178)
Signs Today Inc .... G   847 934-9777
  Palatine (G-16158)
Simple Canvas Prints LLC .... G   800 900-4244
  Des Plaines (G-7845)
Sir Speedy Printing .... G   312 337-0774
  Chicago (G-6177)
Sir Speedy Printing Cntr 6129 .... G   708 349-7789
  Orland Park (G-15979)
Small Newspaper Group C   815 937-3300
  Kankakee (G-12004)
Small Nwsppr Group Shred Svcs ...... G   309 764-4344
  East Moline (G-8241)
Smart Office Services Inc .... G   773 227-1121
  Chicago (G-6190)
Sons Enterprises .... F   847 677-4444
  Skokie (G-19032)
Specialty Printing Midwest .... G   618 799-8472
  Roxana (G-18102)
Splat Creative Inc .... G   708 567-8412
  Chicago (G-6216)
Springfield Printing Inc .... G   217 787-3500
  Springfield (G-19454)
Sprinter Coml Print Label Corp .... G   630 460-3492
  Naperville (G-14988)
State Attorney Appellate .... G   217 782-3397
  Springfield (G-19458)
Stationery Print Shop Inc .... G   214 256-3583
  Buffalo Grove (G-2610)
Steve Bortman .... G   708 442-1669
  Lyons (G-13315)
Studio 88 Creative Design LLC .... G   312 288-3955
  Chicago (G-6257)
Sunrise Hitek Service Inc .... E   773 792-8880
  Chicago (G-6277)
T C W F Inc .... E   630 369-1360
  Naperville (G-14925)
T F N W Inc .... G   630 584-7383
  Naperville (G-14926)
Tangent Screen Print Inc .... F   773 342-1223
  Evergreen Park (G-9601)
Taylor Communication C   309 664-0444
  Bloomington (G-2100)
Team Cncept Prtg Thrmgrphy Inc ...... E   630 653-8326
  Carol Stream (G-3079)
Techprint Inc .... F   847 616-0109
  Elk Grove Village (G-9269)
The b F Shaw Printing Co .... E   815 875-4461
  Princeton (G-16823)
Three Angels Printing Svcs Inc .... F   630 333-4305
  Addison (G-308)
Three Castle Press Inc .... G   630 540-0120
  Streamwood (G-19597)
Times Record Company .... E   309 582-5112
  Aledo (G-362)
Times Republic .... E   815 432-5227
  Watseka (G-20320)
Toledo Democrat .... E   217 849-2000
  Toledo (G-19879)
Total Print Solutions Inc .... G   630 494-0160
  Bloomingdale (G-2018)
Tower Printing & Design .... G   630 495-1976
  Lombard (G-13145)
Trade Print Inc .... G   773 625-0792
  Chicago (G-6402)
Trenton Sun .... G   618 224-9422
  Trenton (G-19905)
Two JS Copies Now Inc .... G   847 292-2679
  Chicago (G-6447)
United General Graphics LLC .... F   262 657-5054
  Niles (G-15185)
University of Illinois .... E   217 333-9350
  Champaign (G-3361)
Unlimited Graphix Inc .... E   630 759-0007
  Lockport (G-13026)
Upmerch LLC .... G   847 674-8601
  Lincolnwood (G-12847)
Valid Usa Inc .... G   630 852-8200
  Lisle (G-12955)
Vision Intgrted Grphics Group .... E   312 373-6300
  Chicago (G-6557)
Vision Intgrted Grphics Group C   331 318-7800
  Bolingbrook (G-2251)

Voris Communication Co Inc C   630 898-4268
  Berkeley (G-1946)
W B Mason Co Inc .... E   888 926-2766
  Carol Stream (G-3085)
W R S Inc .... G   630 279-0400
  Elmhurst (G-9443)
W W Barthel & Co .... G   847 392-5643
  Arlington Heights (G-830)
Weary & Baity Inc .... G   312 943-6197
  Chicago (G-6594)
Webb-Mason Inc .... F   630 428-5838
  Naperville (G-14945)
Westrock Mwv LLC .... E   217 442-2247
  Danville (G-7397)
William Holloway Ltd .... G   847 866-9520
  Evanston (G-9588)
Wortman Printing Company Inc .... G   217 347-3775
  Effingham (G-8432)
Wyckoff Advertising Inc .... G   630 260-2525
  Wheaton (G-20832)
Yes Print Management Inc .... G   312 226-4444
  Chicago (G-6698)

PRINTING: Manmade Fiber & Silk, Broadwoven Fabric

Insignia Design Ltd .... G   301 254-9221
  Rolling Meadows (G-17741)

PRINTING: Offset

11th Street Express Prtg Inc .... F   815 968-0208
  Rockford (G-17275)
A & B Printing Service Inc .... G   217 789-9034
  Springfield (G-19313)
A A Swift Print Inc .... G   847 301-1122
  Schaumburg (G-18424)
A-Reliable Printing .... G   630 790-2525
  Glen Ellyn (G-10392)
Abbotts Minute Printing Inc .... G   708 339-6010
  South Holland (G-19187)
ABC Business Forms Inc .... F   773 774-8282
  Chicago (G-3507)
Able Printing Service Inc .... G   708 788-7115
  Berwyn (G-1947)
ABS Graphics Inc C   630 495-2400
  Itasca (G-11615)
Accurate Business Controls Inc .... G   815 633-5500
  Machesney Park (G-13323)
Accurate Printing Inc .... G   708 824-0058
  Midlothian (G-13989)
Ace Graphics Inc .... E   630 357-2244
  Naperville (G-14764)
Active Graphics Inc .... E   708 656-8900
  Cicero (G-6827)
Adcraft Printers Inc .... F   815 932-6432
  Kankakee (G-11956)
Adrenaline Prints .... G   618 277-9600
  Belleville (G-1528)
Advance Quick Print .... G   708 848-2200
  Oak Park (G-15741)
Ah Tensor International LLC .... E   630 739-9600
  Woodridge (G-21273)
Aires Press Inc .... G   847 698-6813
  Park Ridge (G-16265)
Alisun Inc .... G   708 571-3451
  Westchester (G-20691)
All Printing & Graphics Inc .... G   773 553-3049
  Chicago (G-3611)
All Printing & Graphics Inc .... F   708 450-1512
  Broadview (G-2415)
All-Ways Quick Print .... G   708 403-8422
  Orland Park (G-15938)
Allegra Network LLC .... G   331 253-2775
  Romeoville (G-17791)
Allegra Network LLC .... G   630 801-9335
  Aurora (G-1047)
Allegra Print & Imaging .... F   630 963-9100
  Lisle (G-12860)
Allegra Print & Imaging Inc .... G   847 697-1434
  Elgin (G-8502)
Alliance Graphics .... G   312 280-8000
  Chicago (G-3617)
Alliance Printing Inc .... G   630 613-9529
  Addison (G-26)
Allied Printing Inc .... G   773 334-5200
  Chicago (G-3619)
Alwan Printing Inc .... F   708 598-9600
  Bridgeview (G-2321)
America Printing Inc .... G   847 229-8358
  Wheeling (G-20846)

Employee Codes: A=Over 500 employees, B=251-500
C=101-250, D=51-100, E=20-50, F=10-19, G=3-9

2020 Harris Illinois Industrial Directory

PRINTING: Offset

Company	Col	Phone
American Labelmark Company	C	773 478-0900
Chicago (G-3656)		
American Litho Incorporated	B	630 462-1700
Carol Stream (G-2935)		
Anikam Inc		708 385-0200
Alsip (G-415)		
Apple Graphics Inc		630 389-2222
Batavia (G-1350)		
Arbor Printing & Graphics Inc	G	630 969-2277
Lisle (G-12867)		
Arch Printing Inc		630 966-0235
Aurora (G-1053)		
Arla Graphics Inc	G	847 470-0005
Deerfield (G-7586)		
Art-Craft Printers		847 455-2201
Franklin Park (G-9874)		
Artpol Printing Inc		773 622-0498
Chicago (G-3742)		
Aspen Printing Services LLC		630 357-3203
Naperville (G-14775)		
Associated Printers Inc	G	847 548-8929
Antioch (G-602)		
Aurora Fastprint Inc	G	630 896-5980
Aurora (G-1059)		
Available Business Group Inc	D	773 247-4141
Chicago (G-3781)		
Azusa Inc	G	618 244-6591
Mount Vernon (G-14597)		
B & B Printing Company		217 285-6072
Pittsfield (G-16628)		
B Allan Graphics Inc	F	708 396-1704
Alsip (G-420)		
B P I Printing & Duplicating	E	773 822-0111
Bannockburn (G-1191)		
Babak Inc		312 419-8686
Oak Forest (G-15672)		
Bailleu & Bailleu Printing Inc	G	309 852-2517
Kewanee (G-12021)		
Bally Foil Graphics Inc		847 427-1509
Elk Grove Village (G-8857)		
Balsley Printing Inc	F	815 624-7515
Rockton (G-17692)		
Balsley Printing Inc	F	815 624-7515
Rockton (G-17693)		
Barnaby Inc		815 895-6555
Aurora (G-1061)		
Bass Company LLC		618 526-7211
Breese (G-2297)		
Bat Business Services Inc	G	630 801-9335
Aurora (G-1062)		
Beardsley Printery Inc		309 788-4041
Rock Island (G-17203)		
Bell Litho Inc	D	847 952-3300
Elk Grove Village (G-8862)		
Bell Litho Inc		847 290-9300
Elk Grove Village (G-8863)		
Belrock Printing Inc		815 547-1096
Belvidere (G-1652)		
Berland Printing Inc	E	773 702-1999
Bannockburn (G-1196)		
Best Advertising Spc & Prtg	G	708 448-1110
Worth (G-21455)		
Best In Printing Inc	G	630 833-7366
Elmhurst (G-9332)		
Bfc Forms Service Inc	C	630 879-9240
Batavia (G-1358)		
Bfc Print		630 879-9240
Batavia (G-1359)		
Biller Press & Manufacturing	G	847 395-4111
Antioch (G-604)		
Bloomington Offset Process Inc	D	309 662-3395
Bloomington (G-2026)		
Blue Island Newspaper Prtg Inc	D	708 333-1006
Harvey (G-11079)		
Bopi	G	312 320-1109
Bloomington (G-2028)		
Branstiter Printing Co	G	217 245-6533
Jacksonville (G-11760)		
Breaker Press Co Inc	G	773 927-1666
Chicago (G-3948)		
Breese Publishing Co Inc	G	618 526-7211
Breese (G-2299)		
Budget Printing Center	G	618 655-1636
Edwardsville (G-8351)		
Bureau Valley Chief	G	815 646-4731
Tiskilwa (G-19871)		
Button Man Printing Inc	G	630 549-0438
Saint Charles (G-18160)		
C & L Printing Company	F	312 235-0380
Chicago (G-3993)		
C E Dienberg Printing Company	G	708 848-4406
Oak Park (G-15747)		
C F C Interantional	G	708 753-0679
Chicago Heights (G-6737)		
C L Graphics Marketing Inc	E	815 455-0900
South Elgin (G-19139)		
C M J Associates Inc	G	708 636-2995
Oak Lawn (G-15705)		
Cadore-Miller Printing Inc	F	708 430-7091
Hickory Hills (G-11194)		
Caldwell Letter Service Inc	E	773 847-0708
Orland Park (G-15943)		
Cameron Printing Inc	G	630 231-3301
West Chicago (G-20558)		
Cannon Ball Marketing Inc	G	630 971-2127
Lisle (G-12875)		
Capital Prtg & Die Cutng Inc	G	630 896-5520
Aurora (G-1069)		
Capitol Impressions Inc	E	309 633-1400
Peoria (G-16397)		
Cardinal Colorprint Prtg Corp	E	630 467-1000
Itasca (G-11634)		
Carter Printing Co Inc	G	217 227-4464
Farmersville (G-9659)		
Cavco Printers	G	618 988-8011
Energy (G-9467)		
CCL Label (chicago) Inc	E	630 406-9991
Batavia (G-1363)		
Central Printers & Graphics	G	773 586-3711
Bedford Park (G-1462)		
Cenveo Worldwide Limited	D	636 240-5817
Chicago (G-4063)		
Challenge Printers	G	773 252-0212
Chicago (G-4067)		
Charles Chauncey Wells Inc	G	708 524-0695
Oak Park (G-15749)		
Cherokee Printing & Svcs Inc	G	847 566-6116
Mundelein (G-14676)		
CHI-Town Printing Inc	G	773 577-2500
Chicago (G-4085)		
Chicago Press Corporation	E	773 276-1500
Elk Grove Village (G-8894)		
Chicago Print Group Inc	G	312 251-1962
Calumet Park (G-2795)		
Christopher R Cline Prtg Ltd	F	847 981-0500
Elk Grove Village (G-8897)		
Chromatech Printing Inc	F	847 699-0333
Des Plaines (G-7746)		
Classic Color Inc	C	708 484-0000
Broadview (G-2427)		
Classic Printery Inc	G	847 546-6555
Hainesville (G-10946)		
Classic Printing Co Inc	G	217 428-1733
Decatur (G-7475)		
Classic Prtg Thermography Inc	G	630 595-7765
Wood Dale (G-21176)		
Clementi Printing Inc	G	773 622-0795
Chicago (G-4177)		
Cliffe Printing Company	G	708 345-1665
Maywood (G-13667)		
Clyde Printing Company	F	773 847-5900
Chicago (G-4184)		
Cmb Printing Inc	F	630 323-1110
Burr Ridge (G-2663)		
Color Tone Printing		708 385-1442
Blue Island (G-2114)		
Comet Conection Inc		312 243-5400
Alsip (G-434)		
Commercial Copy Printing Ctr	F	847 981-8590
Elk Grove Village (G-8903)		
Commercial Prtg of Rockford	G	815 965-4759
Rockford (G-17355)		
Component Sales Incorporated	F	630 543-9666
Addison (G-78)		
Concept Printers	G	708 481-2430
Chicago Heights (G-6744)		
Concord Printing Inc	G	847 734-1616
Elk Grove Village (G-8908)		
Concorde Prtg Dgtal Imging Inc	G	312 552-3006
Chicago (G-4216)		
Consolidated Carqueville Prtg	G	630 246-6451
Streamwood (G-19566)		
Consolidated Printing Co Inc	F	773 631-2800
Elk Grove Village (G-8909)		
Continental Web Press Inc	C	630 773-1903
Itasca (G-11639)		
Continental Web Press KY Inc	D	630 773-1903
Itasca (G-11640)		
Cook JV Printing	F	708 799-0007
Country Club Hills (G-7037)		
Copies Overnight Inc	E	630 690-2000
Carol Stream (G-2966)		
Copy Mat Printing	G	309 452-1392
Bloomington (G-2033)		
Copy-Mor Inc	E	312 666-4000
Streamwood (G-19568)		
Copyco Printing Inc	E	847 824-4400
Rosemont (G-18008)		
Corporate Graphics America Inc	F	773 481-2100
Chicago (G-4239)		
Corwin Printing		618 263-3936
Mount Carmel (G-14469)		
Cpg Printing & Graphics	G	309 820-1392
Bloomington (G-2034)		
Cpr Printing Inc		630 377-8420
Geneva (G-10263)		
Craftsmen Printing	G	217 283-9574
Hoopeston (G-11506)		
Creative Graphic Arts Inc		847 498-2678
Northbrook (G-15368)		
Creative Lithocraft Inc		847 352-7002
Schaumburg (G-18493)		
Creative Prtg & Smart Ideas	G	773 481-6522
Chicago (G-4265)		
Crossmark Printing Inc	F	708 532-8263
Tinley Park (G-19819)		
Crosswind Printing		847 356-1009
Lindenhurst (G-12853)		
Crown Publications Inc		217 893-4856
Rantoul (G-16973)		
Curtis 1000 Inc		309 663-0325
Bloomington (G-2036)		
Custom Telephone Printing Co	F	815 338-0000
Woodstock (G-21379)		
D & D Business Inc		630 935-3522
Willowbrook (G-21040)		
D & D Printing Inc	G	708 425-2080
Oak Lawn (G-15712)		
D & R Press		708 452-0500
Elmwood Park (G-9450)		
Dale K Brown		815 338-0222
Woodstock (G-21380)		
Dallas Corporation	F	630 322-8000
Downers Grove (G-7983)		
Dandelion Distributors Inc		815 675-9800
Grayslake (G-10766)		
Dans Printing & Off Sups Inc	F	708 687-3055
Oak Forest (G-15674)		
Darnall Printing	G	309 827-7212
Bloomington (G-2039)		
David H Vander Ploeg		708 331-7700
South Holland (G-19206)		
DE Asbury Inc	E	217 222-0617
Quincy (G-16876)		
Deadline Prtg Clor Copying LLC		847 437-9000
Elk Grove Village (G-8940)		
Denor Graphics Inc	F	847 364-1130
Elk Grove Village (G-8944)		
Des Plaines Printing LLC	F	847 465-3300
Buffalo Grove (G-2532)		
Design Graphics Inc	G	815 462-3323
Frankfort (G-9783)		
Design On Time	G	815 464-5750
Frankfort (G-9784)		
Di-Carr Printing Company		708 863-0069
Cicero (G-6840)		
Diamond Graphics of Berwyn	G	708 749-2500
Berwyn (G-1950)		
Diamond Web Printing LLC	F	630 663-0351
Downers Grove (G-7987)		
Diaz Printing	G	773 887-3366
Chicago (G-4354)		
Dicianni Graphics Incorporated	F	630 833-5100
Addison (G-91)		
Digital Printing & Total Graph	G	630 627-7400
Lombard (G-13067)		
Diversified Print Group	G	630 893-8920
Bloomingdale (G-1989)		
Dixon Direct LLC	F	815 284-2211
Dixon (G-7896)		
Dixon Graphics Incorporated	G	217 351-6100
Champaign (G-3285)		
Dos Bro Corp	G	773 334-1919
Chicago (G-4386)		
DOT Sharper Printing Inc	G	847 581-9033
Morton Grove (G-14401)		
Douglas Press Inc	C	800 323-0705
Bellwood (G-1622)		
Dreamwrks Grphic Cmmnctons LLC	D	847 679-6710
Glenview (G-10543)		

Duo Graphics G 847 228-7080
Elk Grove Village *(G-8956)*
Dynagraphics Incorporated E 217 876-9950
Decatur *(G-7492)*
E&D Printing Services Inc G 815 609-8222
Plainfield *(G-16658)*
E-Intrctive Mktg Solutions Inc G 312 241-1692
Bridgeview *(G-2342)*
Eagle Printing Company G 309 762-0771
Moline *(G-14141)*
Ed Garvey and Company D 847 647-1900
Niles *(G-15117)*
Elgin Instant Print G 847 931-9006
Elgin *(G-8575)*
Evanston Graphic Imaging Inc G 847 869-7446
Evanston *(G-9516)*
Expri Publishing & Printing G 773 274-5955
Chicago *(G-4546)*
F Weber Printing Co Inc G 815 468-6152
Manteno *(G-13447)*
Falcon Press Inc G 815 455-9099
Crystal Lake *(G-7197)*
Far West Print Solutions LLC G 630 879-9500
North Aurora *(G-15260)*
Fast Print Shop G 618 997-1976
Marion *(G-13510)*
Fast Printing of Joliet Inc G 815 723-0080
Joliet *(G-11864)*
Fastway Printing Inc G 847 882-0950
Schaumburg *(G-18525)*
Faulstich Printing Company Inc G 217 442-4994
Danville *(G-7332)*
FCL Graphics Inc C 708 867-5500
Harwood Heights *(G-11104)*
Fernwood Printers Ltd G 630 964-9449
Oak Forest *(G-15678)*
Fgs Inc F 312 421-3060
Chicago *(G-4584)*
Fidelity Print Cmmncations LLC E 708 343-6833
Broadview *(G-2436)*
Fisher Printing Inc C 708 598-1500
Bridgeview *(G-2346)*
Five Star Printing Inc G 217 965-3355
Virden *(G-20184)*
FL 1 F 847 956-9400
Elk Grove Village *(G-8999)*
Flash Printing Inc G 847 288-9101
Franklin Park *(G-9944)*
Fleetwood Press Inc G 708 485-6811
Brookfield *(G-2483)*
Flow-Eze Company F 815 965-1062
Rockford *(G-17416)*
FM Graphic Impressions Inc E 630 897-8788
Aurora *(G-1097)*
Forest Printing Co F 708 366-5100
Forest Park *(G-9718)*
Forms Design Plus Coleman Prtg G 309 685-6000
Peoria *(G-16439)*
Forms Press Inc G 815 455-4466
Crystal Lake *(G-7200)*
Franks Dgtal Prtg Off Sups Inc G 630 892-2511
Aurora *(G-1101)*
Frye-Williamson Press Inc E 217 522-7744
Springfield *(G-19372)*
Full Line Printing Inc G 312 642-8080
Chicago *(G-4640)*
G & G Studios /Broadway Prtg F 815 933-8181
Bradley *(G-2282)*
G F Printing G 618 797-0576
Granite City *(G-10708)*
Gallas Label & Decal F 773 775-1000
Chicago *(G-4656)*
Gannon Graphics G 847 895-1043
Schaumburg *(G-18533)*
Gemini Digital Inc G 630 894-9430
Roselle *(G-17954)*
General Converting Inc D 630 378-9800
Bolingbrook *(G-2179)*
Genoa Business Forms Inc E 815 895-2800
Sycamore *(G-19711)*
Gerard Printing Company G 847 437-6442
Elk Grove Village *(G-9013)*
Gh Printing Co Inc G 630 663-0351
Downers Grove *(G-8009)*
Gh Printing Co Inc E 630 960-4115
Downers Grove *(G-8010)*
Good News Printing G 708 389-1127
Palos Heights *(G-16185)*
Gossett Printing Inc G 618 548-2583
Salem *(G-18341)*
Grace Enterprises Inc G 847 423-2100
Chicago *(G-4721)*
Grace Printing and Mailing E 847 423-2100
Skokie *(G-18960)*
Graphic Arts Services Inc E 630 629-7770
Villa Park *(G-20148)*
Graphic Image Corporation F 312 829-7800
Orland Park *(G-15956)*
Graphic Packaging Corporation C 847 451-7400
Franklin Park *(G-9953)*
Graphic Partners Inc E 847 872-9445
Zion *(G-21515)*
Graphic Promotions Inc F 815 726-3288
Shorewood *(G-18897)*
Graphicmark Inc G 708 293-1200
Alsip *(G-448)*
Graphics 2000 Inc F 630 920-0022
Burr Ridge *(G-2676)*
Graphics Group LLC D 708 867-5500
Chicago *(G-4729)*
Grasso Graphics Inc G 708 489-2060
Alsip *(G-449)*
Great Impressions Inc G 847 367-6725
Libertyville *(G-12655)*
Greek Art Printing & Pubg Co G 847 724-8860
Glenview *(G-10553)*
Grovak Instant Printing Co G 847 675-2414
Mount Prospect *(G-14532)*
Grphic Richards Communications F 708 547-6000
Bellwood *(G-1626)*
Hafner Printing Co Inc F 312 362-0120
Chicago *(G-4767)*
Hako Minuteman Inc G 630 627-6900
Addison *(G-144)*
Hal Mather & Sons Incorporated E 815 338-4000
Woodstock *(G-21394)*
Harry Otto Printing Company F 630 365-6111
Elburn *(G-8455)*
Hawthorne Press Inc G 847 587-0582
Spring Grove *(G-19275)*
Heart Printing Inc G 847 259-2100
Arlington Heights *(G-748)*
Hempel Group Inc G 630 389-2222
Batavia *(G-1383)*
Henry Printing Inc G 618 529-3040
Carbondale *(G-2845)*
Heritage Press Inc G 847 362-9699
Libertyville *(G-12657)*
Heritage Printing G 815 537-2372
Prophetstown *(G-16832)*
Higgins Quick Print G 847 635-7700
Des Plaines *(G-7776)*
Highland Printers G 618 654-5880
Highland *(G-11221)*
Holland Printing Inc F 708 596-9000
South Holland *(G-19222)*
House of Graphics E 630 682-0810
Carol Stream *(G-3000)*
Hub Printing Company Inc F 815 562-7057
Rochelle *(G-17145)*
Hunt Enterprises Inc G 708 354-8464
Oak Forest *(G-15681)*
Huston-Patterson Corporation D 217 429-5161
Decatur *(G-7503)*
Ideal Advertising & Printing F 815 965-1713
Rockford *(G-17456)*
Illiana Financial Inc F 630 941-3838
Elmhurst *(G-9375)*
Illini Digital Printing Co G 618 271-6622
East Saint Louis *(G-8311)*
Illinois Office Sup Elect Prtg E 815 434-0186
Ottawa *(G-16056)*
Illinois Printing Services Inc G 217 728-2786
Sullivan *(G-19669)*
Image Pact Printing E 708 460-6070
Tinley Park *(G-19839)*
Image Print Inc G 815 672-1068
Streator *(G-19611)*
Impact Prtrs & Lithographers E 847 981-9676
Elk Grove Village *(G-9048)*
Impress Printing & Design Inc G 815 730-9440
Joliet *(G-11879)*
Impression Printing F 708 614-8660
Oak Forest *(G-15682)*
Impressions Count Printing F 847 395-2445
Antioch *(G-616)*
In-Print Graphics Inc E 708 396-1010
Oak Forest *(G-15683)*
Informative Systems Inc F 217 523-8422
Springfield *(G-19389)*
Ink Enterprises Inc G 815 547-5515
Belvidere *(G-1679)*
Ink Spot Printing G 773 528-0288
Chicago *(G-4926)*
Ink Spot Silk Screen G 847 724-6234
Glenview *(G-10567)*
Ink Well Printing & Design Ltd G 847 923-8060
Schaumburg *(G-18559)*
Inky Printers G 815 235-3700
Freeport *(G-10120)*
Innova Print Fulfillment Inc G 630 845-3215
Geneva *(G-10282)*
Insty Prints Palatine Inc F 847 963-0000
Palatine *(G-16129)*
Integrated Graphics Inc E 630 482-6100
Batavia *(G-1387)*
Intel Printing Inc G 708 343-1144
Broadview *(G-2444)*
Inter Solutions Co G 773 657-4437
Chicago *(G-4942)*
Irving Press Inc E 847 595-6650
Elk Grove Village *(G-9061)*
J & J Mr Quick Print Inc G 773 767-7776
Chicago *(G-4984)*
J and K Printing G 708 229-9558
Oak Lawn *(G-15721)*
J D Graphic Co Inc E 847 364-4000
Elk Grove Village *(G-9063)*
J Gooch & Associates Inc G 217 522-7575
Springfield *(G-19392)*
J K Printing & Mailing Inc G 847 432-7717
Highland Park *(G-11276)*
J M Printers Inc F 815 727-1579
Crest Hill *(G-7087)*
J Oshana & Son Printing G 773 283-8311
Chicago *(G-4992)*
J S Printing Inc G 847 678-6300
Franklin Park *(G-9970)*
Jade Screen Printing G 618 463-2325
Alton *(G-560)*
Jamali Kopy Kat Printing Inc G 708 544-6164
Bellwood *(G-1629)*
James Ray Monroe Corporation F 618 532-4575
Centralia *(G-3236)*
James W Smith Printing Company E 847 244-6486
Gurnee *(G-10888)*
Janssen Avenue Boys Inc G 630 627-0202
North Aurora *(G-15265)*
Jarr Printing Co F 815 363-5435
McHenry *(G-13750)*
Jay Printing G 847 934-6103
Palatine *(G-16133)*
Jds Printing Inc G 630 208-1195
Glendale Heights *(G-10463)*
Joes Printing G 773 545-6063
Chicago *(G-5034)*
John S Swift Company Inc E 847 465-3300
Buffalo Grove *(G-2552)*
Johns-Byrne Company D 847 583-3100
Niles *(G-15137)*
Johnsbyrne Graphic Tech Corp G 847 583-3100
Niles *(G-15138)*
Johnson Printing G 630 595-8815
Bensenville *(G-1833)*
Josco Inc G 708 867-7189
Chicago *(G-5051)*
Josephs Printing Service G 847 724-4429
Glenview *(G-10576)*
Jost & Kiefer Printing Company E 217 222-5145
Quincy *(G-16897)*
Jph Enterprises Inc G 847 390-0900
Des Plaines *(G-7792)*
July 25th Corporation F 309 664-6444
Bloomington *(G-2064)*
Juskie Printing Corp G 630 663-8833
Downers Grove *(G-8035)*
K & M Printing Company Inc D 847 884-1100
Schaumburg *(G-18584)*
K & S Printing Services G 815 899-2923
Sycamore *(G-19720)*
K Chae Corp F 847 763-0077
Lincolnwood *(G-12826)*
KB Publishing Inc D 708 331-6352
South Holland *(G-19226)*
KB Publishing Inc E 708 331-6352
South Holland *(G-19227)*
Kellogg Printing Co F 309 734-8388
Monmouth *(G-14220)*
Kelly Printing Co Inc E 217 443-1792
Danville *(G-7355)*

Employee Codes: A=Over 500 employees, B=251-500
C=101-250, D=51-100, E=20-50, F=10-19, G=3-9
2020 Harris Illinois
Industrial Directory
1577

PRINTING: Offset | PRODUCT SECTION

Kelvyn Press Inc D 708 343-0448
Broadview *(G-2448)*
Kelvyn Press Inc E 630 585-8160
Aurora *(G-991)*
Kendall Printing Co G 630 553-9200
Yorkville *(G-21490)*
Kenilworth Press Incorporated G 847 256-5210
Wilmette *(G-21081)*
Kens Quick Print Inc F 847 831-4410
Highland Park *(G-11277)*
Kestler Digital Printing Inc F 773 581-5918
Chicago *(G-5098)*
Keystone Printing & Publishing G 815 678-2591
Richmond *(G-17016)*
Keystone Printing Services G 773 622-7210
Chicago *(G-5099)*
Kingery Printing Company C 217 347-5151
Effingham *(G-8405)*
Klein Printing Inc G 773 235-2121
Chicago *(G-5108)*
Km Press Incorporated G 618 277-1222
Belleville *(G-1564)*
Knight Prtg & Litho Svc Ltd G 847 487-7700
Island Lake *(G-11609)*
Kon Printing Inc G 630 879-2211
Batavia *(G-1390)*
Kram Digital Solutions Inc G 312 222-0431
Glenview *(G-10583)*
Kwik Print Inc G 630 773-3225
Itasca *(G-11689)*
L & S Label Printing Inc G 815 964-6753
Cherry Valley *(G-3443)*
Labels Unlimited Incorporated E 773 523-7500
Chicago *(G-5152)*
Lambert Print Source Llc G 630 708-0505
Yorkville *(G-21491)*
Lans Printing Inc G 708 895-6226
Lynwood *(G-13295)*
Lazare Printing Co Inc G 773 871-2500
Chicago *(G-5187)*
Lee-Wel Printing Corporation G 630 682-0935
Wheaton *(G-20812)*
Leonard A Unes Printing Co G 309 674-4942
Peoria *(G-16469)*
Leonard Emerson G 217 628-3441
Divernon *(G-7880)*
Less Cost Copy Center Inc G 618 345-3121
Collinsville *(G-6965)*
Lincoln Printers Inc G 217 732-3121
Lincoln *(G-12733)*
Lincoln Square Printing G 773 334-9030
Chicago *(G-5225)*
Lincolnshire Printing Inc G 815 578-0740
McHenry *(G-13759)*
Litho Type LLC E 708 895-3720
Lansing *(G-12506)*
Lithographic Industries Inc E 773 921-7955
Broadview *(G-2450)*
Lsc Communications Us LLC C 217 235-0561
Mattoon *(G-13642)*
Luke Graphics Inc F 773 775-6733
Chicago *(G-5279)*
Luxon Printing Inc F 630 293-7710
West Chicago *(G-20609)*
Lynns Printing Co G 618 465-7701
Alton *(G-564)*
M & R Printing Inc G 847 398-2500
Rolling Meadows *(G-17749)*
M L S Printing Co Inc G 847 948-8902
Deerfield *(G-7633)*
M O W Printing Inc F 618 345-5525
Collinsville *(G-6967)*
M S A Printing Co G 847 593-5699
Elk Grove Village *(G-9103)*
Macoupin County Enquirer Inc E 217 854-2534
Carlinville *(G-2879)*
Madden Communications Inc C 630 787-2200
Wood Dale *(G-21211)*
Madden Communications Inc E 630 784-4325
Bloomingdale *(G-1998)*
Makkah Printing G 630 980-2315
Glendale Heights *(G-10472)*
Mall Graphic Inc F 847 668-7600
Huntley *(G-11554)*
Mallof Abruzino Nash Mktg Inc E 630 929-5200
Carol Stream *(G-3020)*
Mar Graphics D 618 935-2111
Valmeyer *(G-20009)*
Marcus Press G 630 351-1857
Bloomingdale *(G-1999)*
Mark Twain Press Inc G 847 255-2700
Mundelein *(G-14713)*
Marnic Inc G 309 343-1418
Galesburg *(G-10208)*
Marquardt Printing Company E 630 887-8500
Burr Ridge *(G-2698)*
Master Graphics LLC D 815 562-5800
Rochelle *(G-17149)*
Mattoon Printing Center G 217 234-3100
Mattoon *(G-13646)*
Maximum Prtg & Graphics Inc F 630 737-0270
Downers Grove *(G-8053)*
Mc Adams Multigraphics Inc G 630 990-1707
Oak Brook *(G-15641)*
McGrath Press Inc E 815 356-5246
Crystal Lake *(G-7224)*
McHenry Printing Services G 815 385-7600
McHenry *(G-13765)*
McIntyre & Associates G 847 639-8050
Fox Lake *(G-9748)*
Meck Print G 708 358-0600
Oak Park *(G-15764)*
Mencarini Enterprises Inc F 815 398-9565
Rockford *(G-17516)*
Metro Printing & Pubg Inc F 618 476-9587
Millstadt *(G-14052)*
Metropolitan Graphic Arts Inc E 847 566-9502
Gurnee *(G-10896)*
Metropolitan Printers G 309 694-1114
East Peoria *(G-8277)*
Mi-Te Fast Printers Inc G 312 236-3278
Glencoe *(G-10432)*
Mi-Te Fast Printers Inc E 312 236-8352
Chicago *(G-5421)*
Microprint Inc G 630 969-1710
Romeoville *(G-17852)*
Mid Central Printing & Mailing F 847 251-4040
Wilmette *(G-21087)*
Mid City Printing Service G 773 777-5400
Chicago *(G-5426)*
MidAmerican Prtg Systems Inc E 312 663-4720
Schiller Park *(G-18824)*
Midwest Graphic Industries F 630 509-2972
Bensenville *(G-1853)*
Miracle Press Company F 773 722-6176
Chicago *(G-5467)*
Mission Press Inc G 312 455-9501
Franklin Park *(G-10002)*
MJM Graphics G 847 234-1802
Lake Forest *(G-12274)*
Modern Media Services F 847 548-0408
Grayslake *(G-10790)*
Modern Printing of Quincy F 217 223-1063
Quincy *(G-16917)*
Msf Graphics Inc G 847 446-6900
Des Plaines *(G-7808)*
Mt Carmel Register Co Inc E 618 262-5144
Mount Carmel *(G-14481)*
Multicopy Corp G 847 446-7015
Grayslake *(G-10792)*
Murray Printing Service Inc G 847 310-8959
Schaumburg *(G-18642)*
N Bujarski Inc G 847 884-1600
Schaumburg *(G-18643)*
N P D Inc G 708 424-6788
Oak Lawn *(G-15729)*
Naco Printing Co Inc G 618 664-0423
Greenville *(G-10839)*
Nancy J Perkins G 815 748-7121
Dekalb *(G-7691)*
Negs & Litho Inc G 847 647-7770
Chicago *(G-5563)*
Network Printing Inc G 847 566-4146
Mundelein *(G-14720)*
New Life Printing & Publishing G 847 658-4111
Algonquin *(G-382)*
New Vision Print & Marketing G 630 406-0509
Naperville *(G-14882)*
Noniprint G 773 366-2846
Chicago *(G-5609)*
North Shore Printers Inc F 847 623-0037
Waukegan *(G-20469)*
Northwest Premier Printing G 773 736-1882
Chicago *(G-5623)*
Northwest Printing Inc G 815 943-7977
Harvard *(G-11061)*
Nova Printing and Litho Co F 773 486-8500
Mount Prospect *(G-14552)*
Npn360 E 847 215-7300
Bannockburn *(G-1205)*
Nu-Art Printing G 618 533-9971
Centralia *(G-3242)*
Off The Press LLC G 815 436-9612
Plainfield *(G-16697)*
Officers Printing Inc G 847 480-4663
Northbrook *(G-15444)*
Ogden Minuteman Inc G 773 542-6917
Chicago *(G-5662)*
Ogden Offset Printers Inc G 773 284-7797
Chicago *(G-5663)*
Olde Print Shoppe Inc G 618 395-3833
Olney *(G-15879)*
Omega Printing Inc E 630 595-6344
Bensenville *(G-1861)*
Omega Royal Graphics Inc F 847 952-8000
Elk Grove Village *(G-9163)*
On Time Envelopes & Printing G 630 682-0466
Carol Stream *(G-3043)*
On Time Printing and Finishing G 708 544-4500
Hillside *(G-11351)*
Only 1 Printers Inc F 847 947-4119
Wheeling *(G-20951)*
Orion Star Corp F 847 776-2300
Palatine *(G-16147)*
Oswego Vinyl G 331 725-4801
Oswego *(G-16019)*
P & P Press Inc E 309 691-8511
Peoria *(G-16488)*
P & S Cochran Printers Inc E 309 691-6668
Peoria *(G-16489)*
P F Pettibone & Co G 815 344-7811
Crystal Lake *(G-7242)*
Paap Printing G 217 345-6878
Charleston *(G-3409)*
Pace Print Plus G 847 381-1720
Barrington *(G-1233)*
Palwaukee Printing Company G 847 459-0240
Wheeling *(G-20954)*
Pana News Inc F 217 562-2111
Pana *(G-16221)*
Pantagraph Printing and Sty Co F 309 829-1071
Bloomington *(G-2084)*
Papiros Graphics G 773 581-3000
Chicago *(G-5753)*
Papyrus Press Inc F 773 342-0700
Chicago *(G-5755)*
Paragon Print & Mail Prod Inc G 630 671-2222
Bloomingdale *(G-2006)*
Park Press Inc F 708 331-6352
South Holland *(G-19237)*
Park Printing Inc G 708 430-4878
Palos Hills *(G-16203)*
Parkway Printers G 217 525-2485
Springfield *(G-19420)*
Parrot Press G 773 376-6333
Chicago *(G-5768)*
Patrick Impressions LLC G 630 257-9336
Lemont *(G-12578)*
Patterson Promotions & Prtg G 708 430-0224
Bridgeview *(G-2373)*
Patton Printing and Graphics G 217 347-0220
Effingham *(G-8417)*
Paulson Press Inc E 847 290-0080
Elk Grove Village *(G-9170)*
Peacock Printing Inc G 618 242-3157
Mount Vernon *(G-14633)*
Peak Printing G 309 652-3655
Blandinsville *(G-1972)*
Perfect Plastic Printing Corp C 630 584-1600
Saint Charles *(G-18242)*
Performance Mailing & Prtg Inc G 847 549-0500
Libertyville *(G-12694)*
Perma Graphics Printers G 815 485-6955
New Lenox *(G-15050)*
Personalized Printing Mailing G 847 441-2955
South Elgin *(G-19170)*
Photo Graphic Design Service G 815 672-4417
Streator *(G-19620)*
Physicians Record Co Inc D 800 323-9268
Berwyn *(G-1960)*
Pinney Printing Company F 815 626-2727
Sterling *(G-19524)*
Pioneer Printing Service Inc G 312 337-4283
Chicago *(G-5810)*
PIP Printing Inc G 815 464-0075
Frankfort *(G-9822)*
Platts Printing Company G 309 228-1069
Farmington *(G-9663)*
Plum Grove Printers Inc E 847 882-4020
Hoffman Estates *(G-11447)*

Poll Enterprises Inc ....F....... 708 756-1120
Chicago Heights *(G-6764)*
Polpress Inc........G....... 773 792-1200
Chicago *(G-5836)*
Power Graphics & Print Inc........G....... 847 568-1808
Skokie *(G-19007)*
Precision Dialogue Direct Inc........D....... 773 237-2264
Chicago *(G-5855)*
Precision Printing Inc........G....... 630 317-7004
Downers Grove *(G-8084)*
Preferred Press Inc........G....... 630 980-9799
Glendale Heights *(G-10484)*
Preferred Printing & Graphics........G....... 708 547-6880
Berkeley *(G-1944)*
Preferred Printing Service........G....... 312 421-2343
Chicago *(G-5861)*
Premier Printing and Packg Inc........G....... 847 970-9434
Rolling Meadows *(G-17766)*
Premier Printing Illinois Inc........D....... 217 359-2219
Champaign *(G-3339)*
Press America Inc........E....... 847 228-0333
Elk Grove Village *(G-9195)*
Press Tech Inc........F....... 847 824-4485
Des Plaines *(G-7832)*
Pride In Graphics Inc........F....... 312 427-2000
Chicago *(G-5872)*
Print Management Group Inc........G....... 847 671-0900
Schiller Park *(G-18837)*
Print Ninja LLC........G....... 877 396-4652
Evanston *(G-9569)*
Print Shop........G....... 815 786-8278
Sandwich *(G-18381)*
Print Source For Business Inc........G....... 847 356-0190
Lake Villa *(G-12363)*
Print Tech Inc........F....... 847 949-5400
Mundelein *(G-14728)*
Print Turnaround Inc........F....... 847 228-1762
Arlington Heights *(G-791)*
Print Xpress........G....... 847 677-5555
Skokie *(G-19012)*
Printed Impressions Inc........G....... 773 604-8585
Oakbrook Terrace *(G-15813)*
Printers Ink of Paris Inc........G....... 217 463-2552
Paris *(G-16240)*
Printers Mark........G....... 309 732-1174
Rock Island *(G-17234)*
Printers Row Loft........G....... 312 431-1019
Chicago *(G-5878)*
Printers Row Press Inc........E....... 312 427-7150
Chicago *(G-5879)*
Printforce Inc........G....... 618 395-7746
Olney *(G-15885)*
Printing Arts Cmmnications LLC........E....... 708 938-1600
Broadview *(G-2460)*
Printing By Joseph........G....... 708 479-2669
Mokena *(G-14109)*
Printing Craftsmen of Joliet........G....... 815 254-3982
Joliet *(G-11917)*
Printing Craftsmen of Pontiac........G....... 815 844-7118
Pontiac *(G-16778)*
Printing Dimensions........G....... 847 439-7521
Arlington Heights *(G-792)*
Printing Etc Inc........G....... 815 562-6151
Rochelle *(G-17152)*
Printing Impression Direc........G....... 815 385-6688
Lakemoor *(G-12476)*
Printing On Ashland Inc........G....... 773 488-4707
Chicago *(G-5883)*
Printing Plant........G....... 618 529-3115
Carbondale *(G-2855)*
Printing Plus........G....... 708 301-3900
Lockport *(G-13019)*
Printing Plus of Roselle Inc........G....... 630 893-0410
Roselle *(G-17974)*
Printing Shop........G....... 847 998-6330
Glenview *(G-10603)*
Printing Source Inc........G....... 773 588-2930
Morton Grove *(G-14433)*
Printing You Can Trust........G....... 224 676-0482
Deerfield *(G-7646)*
Printmeisters Inc........G....... 708 474-8400
Lansing *(G-12512)*
Printsmart Printing & Graphics........G....... 630 434-2000
Woodridge *(G-21334)*
Printsource Plus Inc........G....... 708 389-6252
Blue Island *(G-2134)*
Priority Print........G....... 708 485-7080
Brookfield *(G-2491)*
Priority Printing........G....... 773 889-6021
Chicago *(G-5884)*
Prism Commercial Printing Ctrs........G....... 773 735-5400
Chicago *(G-5885)*
Pro-Type Printing Inc........G....... 217 379-4715
Paxton *(G-16315)*
Production Press Inc........E....... 217 243-3353
Jacksonville *(G-11781)*
Professional Graphics Inc........E....... 815 226-9422
Rockford *(G-17561)*
Proforma........G....... 815 534-5461
Frankfort *(G-9828)*
Proforma Business Builders........G....... 309 692-6390
Peoria *(G-16504)*
Progress Printing Corporation........E....... 773 927-0123
Chicago *(G-5898)*
Progressive Systems Netwrk Inc........G....... 312 382-8383
Chicago *(G-5902)*
Promo Corp........G....... 773 217-7666
Arlington Heights *(G-793)*
Provena Enterprises Inc........E....... 708 478-3230
Kankakee *(G-11997)*
QBF Group Inc........G....... 708 781-9580
Tinley Park *(G-19851)*
Quad City Press........F....... 309 764-8142
Moline *(G-14170)*
Quad/Graphics Inc........F....... 217 347-7721
Effingham *(G-8421)*
Quality Blue & Offset Printing........G....... 630 759-8035
Bolingbrook *(G-2231)*
Quality Quickprint Inc........F....... 815 439-3430
Joliet *(G-11920)*
Quality Quickprint Inc........G....... 815 723-0941
Lemont *(G-12586)*
Quality Quickprint Inc........F....... 815 838-1784
Lockport *(G-13020)*
Quantum Color Graphics LLC........C....... 847 967-3600
Morton Grove *(G-14435)*
Quick Print Shoppe........G....... 309 694-1204
East Peoria *(G-8285)*
Quickprinters........G....... 309 833-5250
Macomb *(G-13398)*
Quik Impressions Group Inc........E....... 630 495-7845
Addison *(G-262)*
Quinn Print Inc........G....... 847 823-9100
Park Ridge *(G-16293)*
R & R Creative Graphics Inc........G....... 630 208-4724
Geneva *(G-10301)*
R N R Photographers Inc........G....... 708 453-1868
River Grove *(G-17066)*
R R Donnelley & Sons Company........C....... 312 326-8000
Chicago *(G-5950)*
Rainbow Manufacturing Inc........E....... 847 824-9600
Mundelein *(G-14731)*
Rapid Circular Press Inc........F....... 312 421-5611
Chicago *(G-5970)*
Rapid Copy & Duplicating Co........G....... 312 733-3353
Melrose Park *(G-13906)*
Rapid Print........G....... 309 673-0826
Peoria *(G-16508)*
Rayco Printing Services Inc........G....... 773 545-4545
Chicago *(G-5978)*
Reesha Printing Inc........G....... 708 233-6677
Bridgeview *(G-2381)*
Reliance Graphics Inc........G....... 847 593-6688
Arlington Heights *(G-800)*
Remke Printing Inc........G....... 847 520-7300
Wheeling *(G-20972)*
Repro-Graphics Inc........D....... 847 439-1775
Elk Grove Village *(G-9217)*
Review Graphics Inc........G....... 815 623-2570
Roscoe *(G-17925)*
Ribbon Print Company........G....... 847 421-8208
Highland Park *(G-11294)*
Richardson & Edwards Inc........E....... 630 543-1818
Oak Brook *(G-15660)*
Rightway Printing Inc........F....... 630 790-0444
Glendale Heights *(G-10488)*
River Bend Printing........G....... 217 324-6056
Litchfield *(G-12975)*
Riverside Graphics Corporation........G....... 312 372-3766
Chicago *(G-6037)*
Riverview Printing Inc........G....... 815 987-1425
Rockford *(G-17575)*
Ro-Web Inc........G....... 309 688-2155
Peoria *(G-16512)*
Rohner Letterpress Inc........F....... 773 248-0800
Chicago *(G-6052)*
Rohrer Litho Inc........G....... 630 833-6610
Elmhurst *(G-9420)*
Romel Press Inc........G....... 708 343-6090
Melrose Park *(G-13909)*
Rose Business Forms & Printing........G....... 618 533-3032
Centralia *(G-3248)*
Roskuszka & Sons Inc........F....... 630 851-3400
Aurora *(G-1149)*
RR Donnelley Printing Co LP........G....... 312 326-8000
Chicago *(G-6072)*
Rudin Printing Company Inc........F....... 217 528-5111
Springfield *(G-19436)*
Rush Impressions Inc........G....... 847 671-0622
Schiller Park *(G-18842)*
Rush Printing On Oak........G....... 815 344-8880
McHenry *(G-13789)*
Rusty & Angela Buzzard........G....... 217 342-9841
Effingham *(G-8423)*
Rutledge Printing Co........F....... 708 479-8282
Orland Park *(G-15977)*
S G C M Corp........G....... 630 953-2428
Oakbrook Terrace *(G-15815)*
S G S Inc........G....... 708 544-6061
Downers Grove *(G-8088)*
Sales Midwest Prtg & Packg Inc........G....... 309 764-5544
Moline *(G-14175)*
Salsedo Press Inc........F....... 773 533-9900
Chicago *(G-6096)*
Savino Enterprises........G....... 708 385-5277
Blue Island *(G-2138)*
Scheiwes Print Shop........G....... 815 683-2398
Crescent City *(G-7082)*
Schiele Graphics Inc........D....... 847 434-5455
Elk Grove Village *(G-9233)*
Schneider Graphics Inc........E....... 847 550-4310
Lake Zurich *(G-12454)*
Schwartzkopf Printing Inc........F....... 618 463-0747
Alton *(G-571)*
Schwebel Printing........G....... 618 684-3911
Murphysboro *(G-14759)*
Segerdahl Corp........C....... 847 541-1080
Wheeling *(G-20979)*
Segerdahl Corp........D....... 630 754-7104
Bolingbrook *(G-2235)*
Segerdahl Corp........D....... 847 850-8811
Wheeling *(G-20980)*
Segerdahl Graphics Inc........B....... 847 541-1080
Wheeling *(G-20981)*
Semper Fl Printing LLC........G....... 847 640-7737
Arlington Heights *(G-807)*
Service Printing Corporation........G....... 847 669-9620
Huntley *(G-11566)*
Sg360 A Segerdahl Company........F....... 847 465-3368
Broadview *(G-2468)*
Shanin Company........D....... 847 676-1200
Lincolnwood *(G-12843)*
Shawver Press Inc........G....... 815 772-4700
Morrison *(G-14348)*
Shree Mahavir Inc........G....... 312 408-1080
Chicago *(G-6159)*
Shree Printing Corp........G....... 773 267-9500
Chicago *(G-6160)*
Sigley Printing & Off Sup Co........G....... 618 997-5304
Marion *(G-13535)*
Sigma Graphics Inc........F....... 815 433-1000
Ottawa *(G-16078)*
Simple Solutions........G....... 618 932-6177
West Frankfort *(G-20683)*
Six Color Print LLC........F....... 847 336-3287
Waukegan *(G-20497)*
Sleepeck Printing Company........C....... 708 544-8900
Chicago *(G-6187)*
Snow Printing LLC........G....... 618 233-0712
Belleville *(G-1596)*
Solid Impressions Inc........G....... 630 543-7300
Carol Stream *(G-3070)*
Solution 3 Graphics Inc........F....... 773 233-3600
Chicago *(G-6199)*
Solution Printing Inc........G....... 217 529-9700
Springfield *(G-19450)*
Sommers & Fahrenbach Inc........F....... 773 478-3033
Chicago *(G-6201)*
Southwest Printing Co........G....... 708 389-0800
Alsip *(G-512)*
SPD Press Prtg Solutions LLC........G....... 773 299-1700
Chicago *(G-6211)*
Specialty Promotions Inc........C....... 847 588-2580
Niles *(G-15174)*
Speedys Quick Print........G....... 217 431-0510
Danville *(G-7381)*
Spell It With Color Inc........G....... 630 961-5617
Naperville *(G-14919)*
Sphere Inc........G....... 847 566-4800
Mundelein *(G-14738)*

PRODUCT

Employee Codes: A=Over 500 employees, B=251-500
C=101-250, D=51-100, E=20-50, F=10-19, G=3-9

2020 Harris Illinois
Industrial Directory

1579

PRINTING: Offset

Stecker Graphics Inc .... G ... 309 786-4973
  Rock Island *(G-17246)*
Steiner Impressions Inc .... G ... 815 633-4135
  Loves Park *(G-13266)*
Stellato Printing Inc .... G ... 815 280-5664
  Crest Hill *(G-7097)*
Steve O Inc .... G ... 847 473-4466
  North Chicago *(G-15321)*
Stevens Group LLC .... E ... 331 209-2100
  Elmhurst *(G-9431)*
Strathmore Company .... E ... 630 232-9677
  Geneva *(G-10309)*
Stromberg Allen and Company .... E ... 773 847-7131
  Tinley Park *(G-19858)*
Suncraft Technologies Inc .... C ... 630 369-7900
  Naperville *(G-14922)*
Sung Ji USA Inc .... G ... 847 956-9400
  Elk Grove Village *(G-9258)*
Sunrise Hitek Group LLC .... E ... 773 792-8880
  Chicago *(G-6276)*
Sunrise Printing Inc .... F ... 847 928-1800
  Schiller Park *(G-18846)*
Superior Print Services Inc .... G ... 630 257-7012
  Lemont *(G-12591)*
Swift Impressions Inc .... G ... 312 372-0002
  Chicago *(G-6296)*
Swifty Print .... G ... 630 584-9063
  Saint Charles *(G-18283)*
T & C Graphics Inc .... E ... 630 532-5050
  South Elgin *(G-19175)*
Tampico Press .... G ... 312 243-5448
  Chicago *(G-6320)*
Tampoprint Mid-West Corp .... G ... 312 971-7715
  Chicago *(G-6321)*
Taykit Inc .... E ... 847 888-1150
  Elgin *(G-8745)*
Tele Print .... G ... 630 941-7877
  Elmhurst *(G-9434)*
Temper Enterprises Inc .... G ... 815 553-0374
  Crest Hill *(G-7098)*
Thiessen Communications Inc .... E ... 847 884-0980
  Schaumburg *(G-18746)*
Thomas Printing & Sty Co .... G ... 618 435-2801
  Benton *(G-1937)*
Thomas Tees Inc .... G ... 217 488-2288
  New Berlin *(G-15025)*
Three-Z Printing Co .... B ... 217 857-3153
  Teutopolis *(G-19774)*
Thrift n Swift .... G ... 847 455-1350
  Palatine *(G-16164)*
Tlm Enterprises Inc .... G ... 815 284-5040
  Dixon *(G-7923)*
TOA Resource .... G ... 312 317-3957
  Glen Ellyn *(G-10422)*
Topweb LLC .... E ... 773 975-0400
  Chicago *(G-6396)*
Total Graphics Services Inc .... G ... 847 675-0800
  Skokie *(G-19046)*
TPS Enterprises Inc .... E ... 618 783-2978
  Newton *(G-15094)*
Tree Towns Reprographics Inc .... F ... 630 832-0209
  Elmhurst *(G-9437)*
Tri-Tower Printing Inc .... G ... 847 640-6633
  Rolling Meadows *(G-17782)*
Trump Printing Inc .... F ... 217 429-9001
  Decatur *(G-7563)*
Tvp Color Graphics Inc .... G ... 630 837-3600
  Streamwood *(G-19600)*
Tylka Printing Inc .... G ... 773 767-3775
  Tinley Park *(G-19862)*
Unique Prtrs Lithographers Inc .... D ... 708 656-8900
  Cicero *(G-6883)*
Unique/Active LLC .... E ... 708 656-8900
  Cicero *(G-6884)*
United Graphics Llc .... C ... 217 235-7161
  Mattoon *(G-13656)*
United Letter Service Inc .... F ... 312 408-2404
  Elk Grove Village *(G-9297)*
United Lithograph Inc .... G ... 847 803-1700
  Des Plaines *(G-7861)*
United Press Inc .... F ... 847 482-0597
  Lincolnshire *(G-12799)*
United Printers Inc .... G ... 773 376-1955
  Chicago *(G-6473)*
Up North Printing Inc .... G ... 630 584-8675
  Addison *(G-324)*
V C P Inc .... E ... 847 658-5090
  Algonquin *(G-391)*
Valee Inc .... G ... 847 364-6464
  Elk Grove Village *(G-9300)*

Van Meter Graphx Inc .... G ... 847 465-0600
  Wheeling *(G-21008)*
Venus Printing Inc .... G ... 847 985-7510
  Schaumburg *(G-18770)*
Versa Press Inc .... C ... 309 822-0260
  East Peoria *(G-8294)*
Veterans Print Management .... G ... 630 816-0853
  Palos Park *(G-16216)*
Vigil Printing Inc .... G ... 773 794-8808
  Chicago *(G-6550)*
Viking Printing & Copying Inc .... G ... 312 341-0985
  Chicago *(G-6551)*
Viking Prtg Graphic Forms Inc .... F ... 630 521-0150
  Bensenville *(G-1909)*
Village Press Inc .... G ... 847 362-1856
  Libertyville *(G-12724)*
Vis-O-Graphic Inc .... E ... 630 590-6100
  Addison *(G-331)*
Wagner John .... G ... 847 564-0017
  Northbrook *(G-15498)*
Warner Offset Inc .... E ... 847 695-9400
  South Elgin *(G-19179)*
Washburn Graficolor Inc .... G ... 630 596-0880
  Naperville *(G-14944)*
Wayne Printing Company .... E ... 309 691-2496
  Edwards *(G-8341)*
Wayne Printing Company .... E ... 309 691-2496
  Edwards *(G-8342)*
We-B-Print Inc .... G ... 309 353-8801
  Pekin *(G-16368)*
Weakley Printing & Sign Shop .... G ... 847 473-4466
  North Chicago *(G-15323)*
Weber Press Inc .... G ... 773 561-9815
  Chicago *(G-6596)*
West Vly Graphics & Print Inc .... G ... 630 377-7575
  Saint Charles *(G-18298)*
Whipples Printing Press Inc .... G ... 309 787-3538
  Milan *(G-14031)*
White Graphics Inc .... F ... 630 791-0232
  Downers Grove *(G-8109)*
Willis Publishing .... F ... 618 497-8272
  Percy *(G-16561)*
Wold Printing Services Ltd .... G ... 847 546-3110
  Volo *(G-20206)*
Wood River Printing & Pubg Co .... G ... 618 254-3134
  Wood River *(G-21268)*
Woogl Corporation .... E ... 847 806-1160
  Elk Grove Village *(G-9312)*
Yorke Printe Shoppe Inc .... E ... 630 627-4960
  Lombard *(G-13156)*
Z Print Inc .... G ... 773 685-4878
  Chicago *(G-6704)*

PRINTING: Pamphlets

Wctu Press .... G ... 847 864-1396
  Evanston *(G-9587)*

PRINTING: Photo-Offset

Copy Express Inc .... F ... 815 338-7161
  Woodstock *(G-21377)*
Einstein Crest .... G ... 847 965-7791
  Niles *(G-15119)*

PRINTING: Photolithographic

French Studio Ltd .... G ... 618 942-5328
  Herrin *(G-11171)*

PRINTING: Roller, Broadwoven Fabrics, Cotton

Frankenstitch Promotions LLC .... F ... 847 459-4840
  Wheeling *(G-20901)*

PRINTING: Roller, Manmade Fiber & Silk, Broadwoven Fabric

Starline Designs .... G ... 773 683-7506
  Chicago *(G-6234)*

PRINTING: Rotogravure

General Packaging Products Inc .... D ... 312 226-5611
  Chicago *(G-4675)*
RR Donnelley Printing Co LP .... G ... 312 326-8000
  Chicago *(G-6072)*

PRINTING: Screen, Broadwoven Fabrics, Cotton

Holy Cow Sports Incorporated .... F ... 630 852-9001
  Downers Grove *(G-8025)*
Player Sports Ltd .... G ... 773 764-4111
  Chicago *(G-5822)*
Proell Inc .... G ... 630 587-2300
  Saint Charles *(G-18251)*
Top Notch Silk Screening .... G ... 773 847-6335
  Chicago *(G-6395)*

PRINTING: Screen, Fabric

American Enlightenment LLC .... G ... 773 687-8996
  Chicago *(G-3652)*
Art-Flo Shirt & Lettering Co .... E ... 708 656-5422
  Chicago *(G-3738)*
B & B Custom TS & Gifts .... G ... 618 463-0443
  Alton *(G-544)*
B JS Printables .... G ... 618 656-8625
  Edwardsville *(G-8346)*
Bobbi Screen Printing .... G ... 773 847-8200
  Chicago *(G-3923)*
Breedlove Sporting Goods Inc .... F ... 309 852-2434
  Kewanee *(G-12028)*
Breedlove Sporting Goods Inc .... F ... 309 852-2434
  Kewanee *(G-12029)*
C & C Sport Stop .... G ... 618 632-7812
  O Fallon *(G-15569)*
Cubby Hole of Carlinville Inc .... F ... 217 854-8511
  Carlinville *(G-2872)*
Custom Enterprises .... G ... 618 439-6626
  Benton *(G-1923)*
Custom Towels Inc .... G ... 618 539-5005
  Freeburg *(G-10088)*
Dabel Incorporated .... G ... 217 398-3389
  Champaign *(G-3284)*
Diamond Teez & More LLC .... G ... 618 579-9876
  Alton *(G-552)*
Enterprise Signs Inc .... G ... 708 691-1273
  Blue Island *(G-2121)*
Excel Screen Prtg & EMB Inc .... D ... 847 801-5200
  Schiller Park *(G-18808)*
Fitness Wear Inc .... G ... 847 486-1704
  Glenview *(G-10546)*
Ikan Creations LLC .... G ... 312 204-7333
  Chicago *(G-4884)*
Maxs Screen Machine Inc .... G ... 773 878-4949
  Chicago *(G-5370)*
Navitor Inc .... B ... 800 323-0253
  Harwood Heights *(G-11106)*
Rebel Screeners Inc .... D ... 312 525-2670
  Chicago *(G-5988)*
Stans Sportsworld Inc .... G ... 217 359-8474
  Champaign *(G-3355)*
Star Silkscreen Design Inc .... G ... 217 877-0804
  Decatur *(G-7550)*
Team Works By Holzhauer Inc .... G ... 309 745-9924
  Washington *(G-20281)*
Wellspring Investments LLC .... G ... 773 736-1213
  Chicago *(G-6602)*
Windy City Silkscreening Inc .... E ... 312 842-0030
  Chicago *(G-6644)*

PRINTING: Screen, Manmade Fiber & Silk, Broadwoven Fabric

David H Pool .... G ... 847 695-5007
  Elgin *(G-8563)*
Image Plus Inc .... G ... 630 852-4920
  Downers Grove *(G-8028)*
Jdl Graphics Inc .... G ... 815 694-2979
  Clifton *(G-6915)*
Peacock Printing Inc .... G ... 618 242-3157
  Mount Vernon *(G-14633)*
Ultimate Distributing Inc .... G ... 847 566-2250
  Mundelein *(G-14745)*

PRINTING: Thermography

Business Cards Tomorrow .... F ... 815 877-0990
  Machesney Park *(G-13332)*
First String Enterprises Inc .... E ... 708 614-1200
  Tinley Park *(G-19827)*
Klein Printing Inc .... G ... 773 235-2121
  Chicago *(G-5108)*
Wolfam Holdings Corporation .... G ... 312 407-0100
  Chicago *(G-6662)*

PRODUCT SECTION

PRODUCT STERILIZATION SVCS
Sterigenics US LLC..............................E....... 847 855-0727
 Gurnee (G-10930)

PROFESSIONAL & SEMI-PROFESSIONAL SPORTS CLUBS
Profile Network Inc..............................E....... 847 673-0592
 Skokie (G-19014)

PROFESSIONAL EQPT & SPLYS, WHOLESALE: Analytical Instruments
Cbana Labs Inc...................................G....... 217 819-5201
 Champaign (G-3277)
Mettler-Toledo LLC..............................E....... 630 446-7700
 Aurora (G-1002)

PROFESSIONAL EQPT & SPLYS, WHOLESALE: Bank
Block and Company Inc........................C....... 847 537-7200
 Wheeling (G-20860)
Laboratory Media Corporation..............F....... 630 897-8000
 Montgomery (G-14254)

PROFESSIONAL EQPT & SPLYS, WHOLESALE: Engineers', NEC
Decatur Blue Print Company.................G....... 217 423-7589
 Decatur (G-7484)
Ghetzler Aero-Power Corp...................G....... 224 513-5636
 Vernon Hills (G-20056)

PROFESSIONAL EQPT & SPLYS, WHOLESALE: Optical Goods
Illinois Tool Works Inc..........................C....... 847 295-6500
 Lake Bluff (G-12189)
Leica McRosystems Holdings Inc........F....... 800 248-0123
 Buffalo Grove (G-2561)
Opti-Vue Inc.......................................G....... 630 274-6121
 Bensenville (G-1862)
Vibgyor Optics Inc..............................E....... 847 818-0788
 Arlington Heights (G-827)

PROFESSIONAL EQPT & SPLYS, WHOLESALE: Scientific & Engineerg
Cushing and Company.........................E....... 312 266-8228
 Chicago (G-4287)

PROFESSIONAL INSTRUMENT REPAIR SVCS
Dadum Inc...G....... 847 541-7851
 Buffalo Grove (G-2530)
Fugate Inc...G....... 309 472-6830
 Morton (G-14360)
Jero Medical Eqp & Sups Inc...............E....... 773 305-4193
 Chicago (G-5022)
Mettler-Toledo LLC..............................E....... 630 446-7700
 Aurora (G-1002)
Numerical Control Incorporated...........G....... 708 389-8140
 Alsip (G-486)
Otis Elevator Company........................F....... 618 529-3411
 Carbondale (G-2852)
Water Services Company of Ill............G....... 847 697-6623
 Elgin (G-8777)

PROFESSIONAL SCHOOLS
Moody Bible Inst of Chicago................A....... 312 329-4000
 Chicago (G-5495)

PROFILE SHAPES: Unsupported Plastics
Abbott Plastics & Supply Co................E....... 815 874-8500
 Rockford (G-17285)
Atlas Fibre Company...........................D....... 847 674-1234
 Northbrook (G-15343)
Custom Films Inc................................F....... 217 826-2326
 Marshall (G-13569)
Custom Plastics of Peoria....................G....... 309 697-2888
 Bartonville (G-1331)
Engineered Plastic Systems LLC........F....... 800 480-2327
 Elgin (G-8580)
Essentra Holdings Corp.......................G....... 804 518-0322
 Westchester (G-20698)
Flex-O-Glass Inc.................................C....... 773 261-5200
 Chicago (G-4605)
Flex-O-Glass Inc.................................G....... 773 379-7878
 Chicago (G-4606)
Flex-O-Glass Inc.................................E....... 815 288-1424
 Dixon (G-7899)
Resinite Corporation............................C....... 847 537-4250
 Wheeling (G-20973)
Sandee Manufacturing Co...................E....... 847 671-1335
 Franklin Park (G-10042)
Shape Master Inc................................G....... 217 469-7027
 Saint Joseph (G-18320)
Sonoco Plastics Inc.............................F....... 630 628-5859
 Addison (G-292)
Streamwood Plastics Ltd.....................G....... 847 895-9190
 Schaumburg (G-18728)

PROMOTERS OF SHOWS & EXHIBITIONS
Area Marketing Inc..............................G....... 815 806-8844
 Frankfort (G-9768)
Horizon Downing LLC.........................E....... 815 758-6867
 Dekalb (G-7685)

PROMOTION SVCS
Artistic Embroidery Creations..............G....... 815 385-8854
 McHenry (G-13721)
David H Pool..G....... 847 695-5007
 Elgin (G-8563)
Lanigan Holdings LLC.........................F....... 708 596-5200
 Hazel Crest (G-11132)
Progressive Systems Netwrk Inc........G....... 312 382-8383
 Chicago (G-5902)
Terlato Wine Group Ltd.......................E....... 847 604-8900
 Lake Bluff (G-12210)

PROPELLERS: Boat & Ship, Cast
Petro Prop Inc.....................................G....... 630 910-4738
 Downers Grove (G-8075)
Propeller Hr Solutions Inc....................G....... 312 342-7355
 Western Springs (G-20723)

PROPERTY DAMAGE INSURANCE
Gcpro LLC...E....... 773 764-2776
 Lombard (G-13082)
Navistar Inc...C....... 331 332-5000
 Lisle (G-12917)

PROPULSION UNITS: Guided Missiles & Space Vehicles
Atks Inc...G....... 715 914-0395
 Chicago (G-3760)
Boeing Company.................................C....... 312 544-2000
 Chicago (G-3925)

PROTECTION EQPT: Lightning
Cutshaw Instls Inc...............................G....... 847 426-9208
 East Dundee (G-8190)
Harger Inc...E....... 847 548-8700
 Grayslake (G-10780)

PROTECTIVE FOOTWEAR: Rubber Or Plastic
Boss Manufacturing Company.............E....... 309 852-2131
 Kewanee (G-12024)
Plastic Specialists America..................G....... 847 406-7547
 Gurnee (G-10912)

PUBLIC FINANCE, TAXATION & MONETARY POLICY OFFICES
Financial and Professional Reg............G....... 217 782-2127
 Springfield (G-19367)

PUBLIC RELATIONS & PUBLICITY SVCS
Caduceus Communications Inc...........G....... 773 549-4800
 Chicago (G-4001)
Sanderson and Associates..................F....... 312 829-4350
 Chicago (G-6099)

PUBLIC RELATIONS SVCS
Canright & Paule Inc...........................G....... 888 202-3894
 Chicago (G-4015)
Cision Ltd..E....... 866 639-5087
 Chicago (G-4153)
Forrest Consulting...............................G....... 630 730-9619
 Glen Ellyn (G-10403)

PUBLISHERS: Art Copy
Chesley Limited..................................G....... 847 562-9292
 Northbrook (G-15356)

PUBLISHERS: Atlases
World Book Inc....................................E....... 312 729-5800
 Chicago (G-6671)

PUBLISHERS: Book
American Hosp Assn Svcs Del............E....... 312 422-2000
 Chicago (G-3654)
American Labelmark Company............C....... 773 478-0900
 Chicago (G-3656)
American Supply Association..............F....... 630 467-0000
 Itasca (G-11622)
Anonymous Press Inc.........................G....... 509 779-4094
 Chicago (G-3701)
Arthur Coyle Press...............................G....... 773 465-8418
 Chicago (G-3739)
Bendinger Bruce Crtve Comm In........G....... 773 871-1179
 Chicago (G-3866)
Bestwords Org Corp............................G....... 618 939-4324
 Columbia (G-6985)
Brainworx Studio.................................F....... 773 743-8200
 Chicago (G-3944)
Broken Oar Inc....................................G....... 847 639-9468
 Port Barrington (G-16785)
Brown & Miller Literary Assoc.............G....... 312 922-3063
 Chicago (G-3967)
C W Publications Inc..........................G....... 800 554-5537
 Sterling (G-19502)
Carus Publishing Company.................F....... 312 701-1720
 Chicago (G-4034)
Castlegate Publishers Inc...................G....... 847 382-6420
 Barrington (G-1216)
Christian National Womans.................G....... 847 864-1396
 Evanston (G-9505)
City of Chicago....................................G....... 773 581-8000
 Chicago (G-4158)
Coaching For Excellence LLC............F....... 708 957-6047
 Country Club Hills (G-7036)
Continental Sales Inc..........................G....... 847 381-6530
 Barrington (G-1218)
Contractors Register Inc.....................F....... 630 519-3480
 Lombard (G-13058)
Cook Communications Minis...............D....... 847 741-5168
 Elgin (G-8556)
Cornerstone Community Outreach.....F....... 773 506-4904
 Chicago (G-4237)
Creative Curricula Inc.........................G....... 815 363-9419
 McHenry (G-13732)
Crystal Productions Co.......................F....... 847 657-8144
 Northbrook (G-15369)
Damien Corporation............................G....... 630 369-3549
 Naperville (G-14814)
Doxa Enterprises LLC........................G....... 618 515-4470
 East Saint Louis (G-8305)
Ebonyenergy Publishing Inc Nfp.........G....... 773 851-5159
 Chicago (G-4442)
Ebooks2go..G....... 847 598-1145
 Schaumburg (G-18513)
Foundation Lithuanian Minor...............G....... 630 969-1316
 Downers Grove (G-8005)
Gary Grimm & Associates Inc............G....... 217 357-3401
 Carthage (G-3136)
Greek Art Printing & Pubg Co..............G....... 847 724-8860
 Glenview (G-10553)
Green Around Sills LLC.....................G....... 847 868-8957
 Evanston (G-9527)
Highlight of Chicago Bress..................G....... 773 944-0085
 Chicago (G-4818)
Hmh Sports LLC.................................G....... 773 330-3789
 Evanston (G-9532)
Houghton Mifflin Harcourt...................E....... 928 467-9599
 Geneva (G-10275)
Houghton Mifflin Harcourt Co..............G....... 630 467-6049
 Itasca (G-11666)
Houghton Mifflin Harcourt Co..............G....... 303 504-9312
 Geneva (G-10276)
Houghton Mifflin Harcourt Co..............G....... 800 225-5425
 Evanston (G-9533)
How To Be Good For Santa Inc..........G....... 281 961-4002
 North Barrington (G-15285)
Human Factor RES Group Inc...........G....... 618 476-3200
 Millstadt (G-14047)

PUBLISHERS: Book

- IB Source Inc .... G 312 698-7062
  Chicago (G-4869)
- Illinois Inst Cntng Legl Ed .... E 217 787-2080
  Springfield (G-19386)
- Kishknows Inc .... G 708 252-3648
  Richton Park (G-17030)
- Koza .... G 773 646-0958
  Chicago (G-5128)
- Literacy Resources LLC .... G 708 366-5947
  Oak Park (G-15763)
- Michael A Greenberg MD Ltd .... F 847 364-4717
  Elk Grove Village (G-9122)
- Monitor Publishing Inc .... G 773 205-0303
  Chicago (G-5491)
- Moody Bible Inst of Chicago .... E 312 329-2102
  Chicago (G-5496)
- Nature House Inc .... D 217 833-2393
  Griggsville (G-10850)
- Ohrvall Media LLC .... G 630 378-9738
  Plainfield (G-16698)
- Pamacheyon Publishing Inc .... G 815 395-0101
  Rockford (G-17547)
- Poetry Center .... G 312 899-1229
  Chicago (G-5829)
- Practice Management Info Corp ..... E 800 633-7467
  Downers Grove (G-8081)
- Press Syndication Group LLC .... G 646 325-3221
  Chicago (G-5867)
- Preston Industries Inc .... C 847 647-0611
  Niles (G-15162)
- Putman Media Inc .... D 630 467-1301
  Schaumburg (G-18689)
- Raven Tree Press LLC .... G 800 323-8270
  Crystal Lake (G-7253)
- Rite-TEC Communications .... G 815 459-7712
  Crystal Lake (G-7258)
- Riverside Assessments LLC .... G 800 767-8420
  Itasca (G-11725)
- Shure Products Inc .... F 773 227-1001
  Chicago (G-6162)
- Sterling Books Limited .... G 630 325-3853
  Hinsdale (G-11380)
- Theosophical Society In Amer .... G 630 665-0123
  Wheaton (G-20827)
- Theosophical Society In Amer .... E 630 665-0130
  Wheaton (G-20826)
- Thg International Publishing .... E 312 540-3000
  Chicago (G-6363)
- Trade Print Inc .... G 773 625-0792
  Chicago (G-6402)
- Triumph Books LLC .... G 800 888-4741
  Chicago (G-6431)
- U S Naval Institute .... G 800 233-8764
  University Park (G-19970)
- Urantia Corp .... F 773 248-6616
  Chicago (G-6492)
- West Publishing Corporation .... D 312 894-1690
  Chicago (G-6605)
- Windy City Publishers LLC .... G 847 925-9434
  Palatine (G-16175)

PUBLISHERS: Book Clubs, No Printing

- Caxton Club .... G 312 266-8825
  Chicago (G-4044)

PUBLISHERS: Books, No Printing

- Acta Publications .... G 773 989-3036
  Chicago (G-3533)
- Adventures Unlimited .... G 815 253-6390
  Kempton (G-12013)
- African-American Images Inc .... F 708 672-4909
  Crete (G-7134)
- Agate Publishing Inc .... G 847 475-4457
  Evanston (G-9488)
- AJS Publications .... G 847 526-5027
  Island Lake (G-11604)
- Albert Whitman & Company .... E 847 232-2800
  Park Ridge (G-16266)
- Allegro Publishing Inc .... G 847 565-9083
  Chicago (G-3613)
- American Association of Indivi ...... E 312 280-0170
  Chicago (G-3649)
- American Bar Association .... A 312 988-5000
  Chicago (G-3650)
- American Catholic Press Inc .... F 708 331-5485
  South Holland (G-19191)
- Art Media Resources Inc .... G 312 663-5351
  Chicago (G-3736)
- Arvamont .... G 630 926-2468
  Hinsdale (G-11361)

- Audio Tech Bus Bk Summaries ...... G 630 734-0500
  Oak Brook (G-15595)
- Baptist General Conference .... D 800 323-4215
  Arlington Heights (G-703)
- Barks Publications Inc .... F 312 321-9440
  Chicago (G-3834)
- Bolchazy-Carducci Publishers .... F 847 526-4344
  Mundelein (G-14668)
- Catalyst Chicago .... G 312 427-4830
  Chicago (G-4040)
- Charles C Thomas Publisher .... G 217 789-8980
  Springfield (G-19348)
- Chicago Review Press Inc .... E 312 337-0747
  Chicago (G-4126)
- Christianica Center .... G 847 657-3818
  Glenview (G-10536)
- Computer Industry Almanac Inc .... G 847 758-1926
  Arlington Heights (G-718)
- Cupcake Holdings LLC .... C 800 794-5866
  Woodridge (G-21289)
- Curbside Splendor .... G 224 515-6512
  Chicago (G-4285)
- Elliot Inst For Scial Scnces R .... G 217 525-8202
  Springfield (G-19361)
- Empowered Press LLC .... G 630 400-3127
  Oswego (G-16003)
- Encyclopaedia Britannica Inc .... C 312 347-7000
  Chicago (G-4505)
- Frank R Walker Company .... G 630 613-9312
  Lombard (G-13079)
- Great Books Foundation .... E 312 332-5870
  Chicago (G-4732)
- H G Acquisition Corp .... G 630 382-1000
  Burr Ridge (G-2679)
- Helivalues .... G 847 487-8258
  Wauconda (G-20355)
- Holder Publishing Corporation ...... G 309 828-7533
  Bloomington (G-2058)
- Houghton Mifflin Harcourt Pubg ... B 630 467-6095
  Itasca (G-11667)
- Houghton Mifflin Harcourt Pubg ... B 847 869-2300
  Evanston (G-9534)
- Information Usa Inc .... G 312 943-6288
  Chicago (G-4919)
- Intervrsity Chrstn Fllwshp/Usa .... D 630 734-4000
  Westmont (G-20749)
- Kidsbooks LLC .... F 773 509-0707
  Chicago (G-5101)
- Manufctrers Clring Hse III Inc .... G 773 545-6300
  Chicago (G-5327)
- Marytown .... E 847 367-7800
  Libertyville (G-12673)
- Midpoint Trade Books Inc .... F 212 727-0190
  Chicago (G-5435)
- Midwest Theological Forum Inc .... G 630 739-9750
  Downers Grove (G-8057)
- Moody Bible Inst of Chicago .... A 312 329-4000
  Chicago (G-5495)
- National Bus Trader Inc .... F 815 946-2341
  Polo (G-16757)
- Oasis Audio LLC .... G 630 668-5367
  Carol Stream (G-3042)
- Oasis International Limited .... G 630 326-0045
  Geneva (G-10295)
- Permissions Group Inc .... G 847 635-6550
  Wheeling (G-20957)
- Pieces of Learning Inc .... G 618 964-9426
  Marion (G-13526)
- Pivot Point Usa Inc .... C 800 886-4247
  Chicago (G-5814)
- Polonia Book Store Inc .... G 773 481-6968
  Chicago (G-5835)
- Psytec Inc .... G 815 758-1415
  Dekalb (G-7699)
- Publications International Ltd .... B 847 676-3470
  Morton Grove (G-14434)
- Research Press Company Inc .... F 217 352-3273
  Champaign (G-3341)
- Sagamore Publishing LLC .... G 217 359-5940
  Champaign (G-3345)
- Scholastic Inc .... E 630 443-8197
  Saint Charles (G-18267)
- Sourcebooks Llc .... D 630 961-3900
  Naperville (G-14918)
- Students Publishing Company In .. G 847 491-7206
  Evanston (G-9579)
- Surrey Books Inc .... G 847 475-4457
  Evanston (G-9580)
- Taylor Enterprises Inc .... G 847 367-1032
  Libertyville (G-12715)

- Templegate Publishers .... G 217 522-3353
  Springfield (G-19463)
- Third Wrld Press Fundation Inc ..... F 773 651-0700
  Chicago (G-6366)
- Thomson Reuters Corporation ...... D 312 288-4654
  Chicago (G-6369)
- Triumph Books Corp .... E 312 337-0747
  Chicago (G-6432)
- Twain Media Mark Publishing .... G 217 223-7008
  Quincy (G-16953)
- University of Chicago .... B 773 702-1722
  Chicago (G-6485)
- Urantia Foundation .... F 773 525-3319
  Chicago (G-6493)
- Venture Publishing Inc .... G 217 359-5940
  Urbana (G-20002)
- Wilton Holdings Inc .... A 630 963-7100
  Woodridge (G-21349)
- Wilton Industries Inc .... B 630 963-7100
  Naperville (G-14949)
- Wilton Industries Inc .... F 815 834-9390
  Romeoville (G-17888)
- Windsong Press Ltd .... G 847 223-4586
  Grayslake (G-10806)
- Wolters Kluwer US Inc .... E 847 580-5000
  Riverwoods (G-17097)

PUBLISHERS: Catalogs

- Catalog Designers Inc .... G 847 228-0025
  Elk Grove Village (G-8881)
- R R Donnelley & Sons Company ... C 847 393-3000
  Libertyville (G-12700)
- Totalworks Inc .... G 773 489-4313
  Chicago (G-6399)
- Van Meter Graphx Inc .... G 847 465-0600
  Wheeling (G-21008)

PUBLISHERS: Comic Books, No Printing

- American Assn Endodontists .... E 312 266-7255
  Chicago (G-3648)

PUBLISHERS: Directories, NEC

- Aerodine Magazine .... G 847 358-4355
  Inverness (G-11592)
- B A I Publishers .... G 847 537-1300
  Wheeling (G-20854)
- Creative Directory Inc .... G 773 427-7777
  Chicago (G-4262)
- Edge Communication .... G 708 749-7818
  Berwyn (G-1951)
- Food Service Publishing Co .... F 847 699-3300
  Des Plaines (G-7772)
- G R Leonard & Co Inc .... E 847 797-8101
  Arlington Heights (G-740)
- Halper Publishing Company .... G 847 542-9793
  Evanston (G-9530)
- Law Bulletin Publishing Co .... F 847 883-9100
  Buffalo Grove (G-2560)
- Luby Publishing Inc .... F 312 341-1110
  Chicago (G-5276)
- Manufacturers News Inc .... D 847 864-7000
  Evanston (G-9549)
- Modern Trade Communications .... F 847 674-2200
  Skokie (G-18992)
- Perq/Hci LLC .... D 847 268-1600
  Rosemont (G-18039)

PUBLISHERS: Directories, Telephone

- AT&T Teleholdings Inc .... F 800 288-2020
  Chicago (G-3756)

PUBLISHERS: Globe Cover Maps

- Rockford Map Publishers Inc .... F 815 708-6324
  Rockford (G-17599)

PUBLISHERS: Magazines, No Printing

- 3 Point Ink LLC .... G 618 664-1550
  Greenville (G-10825)
- American Bar Association .... A 312 988-5000
  Chicago (G-3650)
- American Catholic Press Inc .... F 708 331-5485
  South Holland (G-19191)
- American Inquiry LLC .... G 312 922-1910
  Chicago (G-3655)
- American Library Association .... E 312 280-5718
  Chicago (G-3657)

PRODUCT SECTION — PUBLISHERS: Miscellaneous

Company	Emp	Phone
Antigua Casa Sherry-Brener, Joliet (G-11824)	G	773 737-1711
Applied Tech Publications Inc, Willowbrook (G-21029)	F	847 382-8100
Associated Publications Inc, Chicago (G-3752)	F	312 266-8680
At Home Magazine, Champaign (G-3268)	G	217 351-5282
Barks Publications Inc, Chicago (G-3834)	F	312 321-9440
Be Group Inc, Chicago (G-3848)	G	312 436-0301
Bhs Media LLC, Chicago (G-3879)	E	312 701-0000
Bible Truth Publishers Inc, Addison (G-49)	G	630 543-1441
BNP Media Inc, Deerfield (G-7598)	C	847 205-5660
C2 Publishing Inc, Hillside (G-11332)	F	630 834-4994
Central Illinois Bus Publs Inc, Peoria (G-16416)	G	309 683-3060
Central Illinois Homes Guide, Peoria (G-16417)	G	309 688-6419
Chas Levy Circulating Co, Lisle (G-12876)	G	630 353-2500
Chester White Swine Rcord Assn, Peoria (G-16421)	G	309 691-0151
Chicago Agent Magazine, Chicago (G-4086)	G	773 296-6001
Chicago and Suburbs, Chicago (G-4089)	G	773 306-3787
Chicago Boating Publications, Chicago (G-4092)	G	312 266-8400
Chicago Sports Media Inc, Niles (G-15109)	G	847 676-1900
Christian Century, Chicago (G-4144)	F	312 263-7510
Christianity Today Intl, Carol Stream (G-2959)	C	630 260-6200
Church of Brethren Inc, Elgin (G-8539)	D	847 742-5100
Community Magazine Group, Chicago (G-4210)	G	312 880-0370
Concierge Preferred, Chicago (G-4215)	G	312 360-1770
Construction Bus Media LLC, Palatine (G-16105)	G	847 359-6493
Country Journal Publishing Co, Decatur (G-7477)	F	217 877-9660
Crain Communications Inc, Chicago (G-4258)	E	312 649-5200
Crain Communications Inc, Chicago (G-4259)	C	312 649-5200
CSP Information Group Inc, Oak Brook (G-15614)	E	630 574-5075
Dadant & Sons Inc, Hamilton (G-10954)	D	217 847-3324
Dow Jones & Company Inc, Chicago (G-4393)	D	312 580-1023
Earl G Graves Pubg Co Inc, Chicago (G-4432)	G	312 274-0682
Ensembleiq Inc, Kildeer (G-12047)	G	847 438-7357
Entrepreneur Media Inc, Chicago (G-4516)	G	312 923-0818
ESP Properties LLC, Chicago (G-4531)	E	312 725-5100
Evang Lthn Ch Dr Mrtn Luth KG, Chicago (G-4535)	F	773 380-2540
Evanston Woman Magazine, Evanston (G-9517)	G	847 722-5654
Filmfax Magazine Inc, Evanston (G-9520)	G	847 866-7155
Gary Grimm & Associates Inc, Carthage (G-3136)	G	217 357-3401
Global Telephony Magazine, Chicago (G-4700)	G	312 840-8405
Good Sam Enterprises LLC, Lincolnshire (G-12767)	E	847 229-6720
Grandstand Publishing LLC, Gurnee (G-10883)	G	847 491-6440
Halper Publishing Company, Evanston (G-9530)	G	847 542-9793
Healthleaders Inc, Chicago (G-4793)	E	312 932-0848
Hearst Corporation, Chicago (G-4795)	E	312 984-5100
Highpoint Publishing Inc, O Fallon (G-15573)	G	928 717-0100
Homewood-Flossmoor Chronicle, Homewood (G-11497)	G	630 728-2661
Homnay Magazine, Chicago (G-4836)	G	773 334-6655
Ideal Media LLC, Chicago (G-4876)	D	312 456-2822
Imagination Publishing LLC, Chicago (G-4894)	E	312 887-1000
Informa Business Media Inc, Chicago (G-4915)	D	312 595-1080
Informa Media Inc, Chicago (G-4916)	F	212 204-4200
Institute For Public Affairs, Chicago (G-4938)	F	773 772-0100
Irish Dancing Magazine, Elmhurst (G-9381)	G	630 279-7521
Jinny Corp, Chicago (G-5031)	G	773 588-7200
John C Grafft, Lake Barrington (G-12153)	F	847 842-9200
Lakeland Boating Magazine, Evanston (G-9546)	G	312 276-0610
Lakeside Publishing Co LLC, Gurnee (G-10894)	G	847 491-6440
Lambda Publications Inc, Chicago (G-5169)	F	773 871-7610
Lithuanian Press Inc, Chicago (G-5237)	G	773 776-3399
M I T Financial Group Inc, Northbrook (G-15425)	E	847 205-3000
Maher Publications Inc, Elmhurst (G-9398)	F	630 941-2030
Mariah Media Inc, Chicago (G-5334)	G	312 222-1100
Marketing & Technology Group, Chicago (G-5340)	E	312 266-3311
Mediatec Publishing Inc, Chicago (G-5386)	E	312 676-9900
Medical Liability Monitor Inc, Elmwood Park (G-9455)	G	312 944-7900
Modern Luxury Media LLC, Chicago (G-5479)	E	312 274-2500
National Bus Trader Inc, Polo (G-16757)	F	815 946-2341
National Publishing Company, Norridge (G-15241)	F	630 837-2044
National Sporting Goods Assn, Downers Grove (G-8063)	F	847 296-6742
Northwest Publishing LLC, Chicago (G-5624)	G	312 329-0600
Outdoor Notebook Publishing, Lemont (G-12575)	F	630 257-6534
Packaging World, Chicago (G-5741)	G	305 448-6875
Parade Publications Inc, Chicago (G-5756)	F	312 661-1620
Poetry Foundation, Chicago (G-5830)	E	312 787-7070
Profile Network Inc, Skokie (G-19014)	E	847 673-0592
Progressive Publications Inc, Elgin (G-8699)	G	847 697-9181
Publications International Ltd, Morton Grove (G-14434)	B	847 676-3470
Quad/Graphics Inc, Woodstock (G-21426)	A	815 338-6750
Randall Publications, Elk Grove Village (G-9213)	F	847 437-6604
Randall Publishing Inc, Elk Grove Village (G-9214)	F	847 437-6604
Real Estate News Corp, Chicago (G-5983)	G	773 866-9900
Reelchicagocom Enterprises Inc, Chicago (G-5997)	G	312 274-9980
Rookie LLC, Oak Park (G-15770)	G	708 278-1628
Royal Publishing Inc, Normal (G-15222)	G	309 829-6191
Sherman Media Company Inc, Lake Forest (G-12302)	G	312 335-1962
Specialty Publishing Company, Carol Stream (G-3072)	E	630 933-0844
Sports Illustrated For Kids, Chicago (G-6219)	G	312 321-7828
Stagnito Partners LLC, Chicago (G-6227)	E	224 632-8200
Talcott Communications Corp, Chicago (G-6313)	E	312 849-2220
Thg International Publishing, Chicago (G-6363)	E	312 540-3000
This Week In Chicago Inc, Chicago (G-6367)	G	312 943-0838
TI Gotham Inc, Chicago (G-6376)	G	312 321-7833
Tmb Publishing Inc, Niles (G-15181)	G	847 564-1127
Trmg LLP, Northfield (G-15535)	F	847 441-4122
Trusted Media Brands Inc, Chicago (G-6439)	E	312 540-0035
US Catholic Magazine, Chicago (G-6500)	G	312 236-7782
Utility Business Media Inc, Crystal Lake (G-7287)	F	815 459-1796
Verone Publishing Inc, Chicago (G-6537)	G	773 866-0811
Walnecks Inc, Downers Grove (G-8106)	G	630 985-2097
Watt Publishing Co, Rockford (G-17678)	E	815 966-5400
Winsight LLC, Chicago (G-6646)	C	312 876-0004

PUBLISHERS: Maps

Company	Emp	Phone
Rand McNally & Company, Chicago (G-5968)	B	847 329-8100
Rand McNally International Co, Chicago (G-5969)	C	847 329-8100

PUBLISHERS: Miscellaneous

Company	Emp	Phone
24land Express Inc, Elk Grove Village (G-8789)	G	630 766-2424
Affectionately Yours Ent, Matteson (G-13616)	G	708 275-6333
Aj Auto, Schiller Park (G-18783)	G	847 678-8200
AJS Ministry, Matteson (G-13617)	G	773 403-4166
Allured Publishing Corporation, Carol Stream (G-2932)	E	630 653-2155
Am-Don Partnership, Champaign (G-3263)	G	217 355-7750
Anash Educational Institute, Chicago (G-3690)	G	773 338-7704
Angle Press Inc, Rolling Meadows (G-17711)	G	847 439-6388
Art In Print Review, Chicago (G-3735)	G	773 697-9478
Avenir Publishing Inc, Chicago (G-3784)	E	872 228-2830
Avondale Adventures, Chicago (G-3789)	G	773 588-5761
Award/Visionps Inc, Chicago (G-3791)	G	331 318-7800
Baka Vitaliy, Chicago (G-3817)	G	773 370-5522
Ball Publishing, West Chicago (G-20548)	F	630 208-9080
Ballotready Inc, Chicago (G-3820)	G	301 706-0708
Bass-Mollett Publishers Inc, Greenville (G-10826)	D	618 664-3141
Bendinger Bruce Crtve Comm In, Chicago (G-3866)	G	773 871-1179
Biz 3 Publicity, Chicago (G-3903)	G	773 342-3331
Brilliant Color Corp, Libertyville (G-12640)	G	847 367-3300
Bureau of National Affairs Inc, Chicago (G-3975)	G	773 775-8801
C and H Publishing Co, Sesser (G-18865)	G	618 625-2711
C W Publications Inc, Sterling (G-19502)	G	800 554-5537
Cade Communications Inc, Chicago (G-4000)	G	773 477-7184
Cambridge Business Publishers, Westmont (G-20731)	G	630 321-0173
Ceg Subsidiary LLC, Mount Carmel (G-14468)	G	618 262-8666
Central Illinois Homes Guide, Peoria (G-16417)	G	309 688-6419
Chicago Sports Media Inc, Niles (G-15109)	G	847 676-1900
Christian Specialized Services, Springfield (G-19350)	G	217 546-7338
Cision US Inc, Chicago (G-4154)	C	312 922-2400
City Press Juice & Bottle, Chicago (G-4160)	G	773 360-7226

Employee Codes: A=Over 500 employees, B=251-500, C=101-250, D=51-100, E=20-50, F=10-19, G=3-9

PUBLISHERS: Miscellaneous

Common Ground Publishing LLC......E... 217 721-6839
  Champaign *(G-3281)*
Communications Resource Inc...........G... 630 860-1661
  Schaumburg *(G-18482)*
Cottage Door Press LLC.....................F... 224 228-6000
  Rolling Meadows *(G-17724)*
Cross Express Company......................G... 847 439-7457
  Elk Grove Village *(G-8922)*
Crystal L Smith.....................................G... 773 817-2797
  Evanston *(G-9507)*
Damien Corporation.............................G... 630 369-3549
  Naperville *(G-14814)*
Delair Publishing Company Inc...........C... 708 345-7000
  Melrose Park *(G-13847)*
Devils Due Publishing.........................G... 773 412-6427
  Chicago *(G-4348)*
Dino Publishing LLC............................G... 312 822-9266
  Chicago *(G-4363)*
Doody Enterprises Inc........................G... 312 239-6226
  Oak Park *(G-15751)*
Dramatic Publishing Company............F... 815 338-7170
  Woodstock *(G-21383)*
Ea Mackay Enterprises Inc.................E... 630 627-7010
  Lombard *(G-13070)*
Eagle Publications Inc........................E... 618 345-5400
  Fairview Heights *(G-9645)*
Earthcomber LLC.................................F... 708 366-1600
  Oak Park *(G-15752)*
Element Collection..............................G... 217 898-5175
  Allerton *(G-403)*
Exclusive Publications Inc.................G... 847 963-0400
  Hoffman Estates *(G-11421)*
Farm Week..E... 309 557-3140
  Bloomington *(G-2042)*
Fire House Press.................................G... 217 864-2864
  Decatur *(G-7494)*
Fisher Printing Inc..............................C... 708 598-1500
  Bridgeview *(G-2346)*
Food Service Publishing Co...............G... 847 699-3300
  Park Ridge *(G-16276)*
Frank R Walker Company....................G... 630 613-9312
  Lombard *(G-13079)*
Fresh Facs...G... 618 357-9697
  Pinckneyville *(G-16614)*
Funny Valentine Press Inc.................G... 773 769-6552
  Chicago *(G-4643)*
Gatehouse Media III Holdings.............G... 585 598-0030
  Peoria *(G-16442)*
Glorius Renditions...............................G... 815 315-0177
  Leaf River *(G-12542)*
Gophercentral.....................................G... 708 478-4500
  Tinley Park *(G-19834)*
Graphic Communicators Inc...............G... 708 385-7550
  Palos Heights *(G-16186)*
Graphic Press......................................G... 312 909-6100
  Chicago *(G-4727)*
Hancock County Shopper....................G... 217 847-6628
  Hamilton *(G-10959)*
Health Administration Press...............D... 312 424-2800
  Chicago *(G-4790)*
Heartland Publications Inc.................G... 217 529-9506
  Springfield *(G-19381)*
Heritage Products Corporation...........G... 847 419-8835
  Buffalo Grove *(G-2545)*
Hermitage Group Inc..........................E... 773 561-3773
  Chicago *(G-4808)*
Holder Publishing Corporation...........G... 309 828-7533
  Bloomington *(G-2058)*
Holsolutions Inc..................................G... 888 847-5467
  Frankfort *(G-9801)*
Holt Publications Inc..........................G... 618 654-6206
  Highland *(G-11226)*
Hope Publishing Company..................F... 630 665-3200
  Carol Stream *(G-2999)*
How To Be Good For Santa Inc.........G... 281 961-4002
  North Barrington *(G-15285)*
I P G Warehouse Ltd..........................E... 773 722-5527
  Chicago *(G-4867)*
Imedia Network Inc.............................G... 847 331-1774
  Chicago *(G-4896)*
Inter-State Studio & Pubg Co............E... 815 874-0342
  Rockford *(G-17468)*
J C Communications Company..........G... 312 236-5122
  Chicago *(G-4988)*
J S Paluch Co Inc................................C... 847 678-9300
  Franklin Park *(G-9969)*
Janelle Publications Inc....................G... 815 756-2300
  Dekalb *(G-7686)*
JAS Express Inc..................................G... 847 836-7984
  Union *(G-19939)*

Java Express.......................................G... 217 525-2430
  Springfield *(G-19393)*
John C Grafft......................................F... 847 842-9200
  Lake Barrington *(G-12153)*
Joong-Ang Daily News.........................E... 847 228-7200
  Rolling Meadows *(G-17743)*
Kae Dj Publishing................................G... 773 233-2609
  Chicago *(G-5074)*
Keane Gillette Publishing LLC............G... 630 279-7521
  Elmhurst *(G-9385)*
L A M Inc De.......................................G... 630 860-9700
  Wood Dale *(G-21206)*
Labelquest Inc....................................E... 630 833-9400
  Elmhurst *(G-9390)*
Lampe Publications............................G... 309 741-9790
  Elmwood *(G-9448)*
Line of Advance Nfp...........................G... 312 768-0043
  Chicago *(G-5227)*
Loyalty Publishing Inc........................E... 309 693-0840
  Bartonville *(G-1334)*
Loyola Press..E... 800 621-1008
  Chicago *(G-5269)*
Luna Azul Communications Inc.........E... 773 616-0007
  Deerfield *(G-7630)*
Lyre Glass Press LLC.........................G... 847 834-9643
  Glenview *(G-10586)*
M & G Graphics Inc...........................G... 773 247-1596
  Chicago *(G-5295)*
M M Marketing....................................G... 815 459-7968
  Wauconda *(G-20370)*
Marshall Pubg & Promotions..............G... 224 238-3530
  Barrington *(G-1227)*
McX Press...G... 630 784-4325
  Bloomingdale *(G-2000)*
Mendota Reporter...............................F... 815 539-9396
  Mendota *(G-13948)*
Merit Emplyment Asssment Svcs......G... 815 320-3680
  New Lenox *(G-15041)*
Midwest Shared Newsletter...............G... 847 933-9498
  Skokie *(G-18991)*
Motorsports Publications House........G... 630 699-7629
  Plainfield *(G-16692)*
New Wave Express Inc.......................G... 630 238-3129
  Bensenville *(G-1857)*
Nice Card Company............................G... 773 467-8450
  Park Ridge *(G-16290)*
North American Press Inc.................G... 847 515-3882
  Huntley *(G-11556)*
Northern Illinois University................F... 815 753-1826
  Dekalb *(G-7695)*
Norwood House Press Inc.................G... 866 565-2900
  Chicago *(G-5628)*
Olney Daily Mail..................................E... 618 393-2931
  Olney *(G-15880)*
Omegacom Inc....................................G... 773 750-4621
  Chicago *(G-5674)*
Omni Publishing Co............................G... 847 483-9668
  Wheeling *(G-20950)*
Paddock Publications Inc..................E... 847 680-5800
  Libertyville *(G-12693)*
Palm International Inc.......................G... 630 357-1437
  Naperville *(G-14892)*
Pam Printers and Publs Inc..............F... 217 222-4030
  Quincy *(G-16922)*
Phoenix Tree Publishing Inc.............G... 773 251-0309
  Chicago *(G-5804)*
Pierce Crandell & Co Inc..................G... 847 549-6015
  Libertyville *(G-12696)*
Popsugar Inc.......................................G... 312 595-0533
  Chicago *(G-5843)*
Preferred Bus Publications Inc.........G... 815 717-6399
  New Lenox *(G-15051)*
Premier Travel Media.........................G... 630 794-0696
  Willowbrook *(G-21057)*
Press Dough Inc.................................G... 630 243-6900
  Lemont *(G-12585)*
Press Fuel..G... 217 546-9606
  Springfield *(G-19428)*
Press On Inc.......................................G... 630 628-1630
  Addison *(G-254)*
Prime Publishing LLC.........................E... 847 205-9375
  Northbrook *(G-15466)*
Publishers Row...................................F... 847 568-0593
  Skokie *(G-19018)*
R L Allen Industries...........................G... 618 667-2544
  Troy *(G-19919)*
R R Donnelley & Sons Company........A... 815 584-2770
  Dwight *(G-8158)*
Rapid Circular Press Inc...................F... 312 421-5611
  Chicago *(G-5970)*

READ Worldwide LLC..........................G... 312 301-6276
  Chicago *(G-5982)*
Redshelf Inc..F... 312 878-8586
  Chicago *(G-5994)*
Reid Communications Inc..................G... 847 741-9700
  Elgin *(G-8717)*
Rickard Publishing..............................G... 217 482-3276
  Mason City *(G-13613)*
Rm Acquisition LLC............................C... 847 329-8100
  Chicago *(G-6039)*
Robert-Leslie Publishing LLC.............G... 773 935-8358
  Chicago *(G-6043)*
Roger Fritz & Associates Inc............G... 630 355-2614
  Naperville *(G-14911)*
Royal Publishing Inc..........................F... 309 797-6630
  Moline *(G-14174)*
RR Donnelley Logistics SE................F... 630 672-2500
  Roselle *(G-17981)*
Scars Publications.............................G... 847 281-9070
  Gurnee *(G-10925)*
Scholastic Testing Service................F... 630 766-7150
  Bensenville *(G-1891)*
Schumaker Publications Inc..............G... 309 365-7105
  Lexington *(G-12621)*
Simon Global Services LLC...............G... 773 334-7794
  Chicago *(G-6173)*
Simple Solutions................................G... 618 932-6177
  West Frankfort *(G-20683)*
Spudnik Press Cooperative................F... 312 563-0302
  Chicago *(G-6222)*
St Johns United Church Christ..........G... 847 491-6686
  Evanston *(G-9578)*
Starlight Express Coaches Inc..........G... 708 388-3365
  Crestwood *(G-7129)*
Sunrise Hitek Service Inc..................E... 773 792-8880
  Chicago *(G-6277)*
Syndigo LLC..C... 309 690-5231
  Peoria *(G-16532)*
Tele Guia Spanish TV Guide..............E... 708 656-9800
  Cicero *(G-6879)*
Thomas Publishing Printing Div.........G... 618 351-6655
  Carbondale *(G-2862)*
Thrice Publishing Nfp.........................G... 630 776-0478
  Roselle *(G-17993)*
Tighe Publishing Services Inc...........F... 773 281-9100
  Chicago *(G-6378)*
Translucent Publishing Corp..............F... 312 447-5450
  Chicago *(G-6413)*
Trend Publishing Inc..........................E... 312 654-2300
  Chicago *(G-6415)*
U S Free Press LLC............................G... 319 524-3802
  Hamilton *(G-10961)*
Varsity Publications Inc....................G... 309 353-4570
  Pekin *(G-16367)*
Vision Intgrted Grphics Group...........C... 331 318-7800
  Bolingbrook *(G-2251)*
Vondrak Publishing Co Inc................E... 773 476-4800
  Summit Argo *(G-19684)*
W-F Professional Assoc Inc..............G... 847 945-8050
  Deerfield *(G-7659)*
Want ADS of Champaign Inc.............G... 217 356-4804
  Champaign *(G-3368)*
We Do Tech Americas Inc.................F... 630 217-8723
  Lisle *(G-12957)*
Wireless Express Inc Central............G... 309 689-9933
  Peoria *(G-16547)*
Wolfsword Press..................................G... 773 403-1144
  Chicago *(G-6664)*
Wonderlic Inc......................................D... 847 680-4900
  Vernon Hills *(G-20112)*
Wordspace Press Limited..................G... 773 292-0292
  Chicago *(G-6669)*
World Book Encyclopedia Del............C... 312 729-5800
  Chicago *(G-6670)*
World Library Publications.................C... 847 678-9300
  Franklin Park *(G-10087)*
Worlds Printing & Spc Co Ltd............G... 312 565-1401
  Chicago *(G-6678)*

PUBLISHERS: Music Book

3b Media Inc.......................................F... 312 563-9363
  Chicago *(G-3467)*
Antigua Casa Sherry-Brener..............G... 773 737-1711
  Joliet *(G-11824)*
Hope Publishing Company..................F... 630 665-3200
  Carol Stream *(G-2999)*

PUBLISHERS: Music Book & Sheet Music

Deshamusic Inc..................................G... 818 257-2716
  Chicago *(G-4344)*

Sony/Atv Music Publishing LLC............E 630 739-8129
Bolingbrook *(G-2245)*

PUBLISHERS: Music, Book

LMS Innovations Inc..............................G....... 312 613-2345
Chicago *(G-5247)*

PUBLISHERS: Music, Sheet

Kaelco Entrmt Holdings Inc....................G....... 217 600-7815
Champaign *(G-3312)*

PUBLISHERS: Newsletter

American Custom Publishing................G....... 847 816-8660
Libertyville *(G-12628)*
Elliot Inst For Scial Scnces R................G....... 217 525-8202
Springfield *(G-19361)*
Imagination Publishing LLC..................E 312 887-1000
Chicago *(G-4894)*

PUBLISHERS: Newspaper

Always Faithful Dog Traning..................G....... 630 696-2572
Saint Charles *(G-18144)*
Baier Publishing Company....................G....... 815 457-2245
Cissna Park *(G-6895)*
Beacon Solutions Inc............................F 303 513-0469
Chicago *(G-3850)*
Bond Broadcasting Inc...........................F 618 664-3300
Greenville *(G-10828)*
Boone County Shopper Inc.....................F 815 544-2166
Belvidere *(G-1656)*
Chicago Weekly......................................G....... 773 702-7718
Chicago *(G-4136)*
Chinese American News........................G....... 312 225-5600
Chicago *(G-4141)*
Dancyn Recovery Systems....................G....... 309 829-5450
Bloomington *(G-2038)*
Danny Fender...G....... 618 665-3135
Louisville *(G-13178)*
Debbie Harshman...................................G....... 217 335-2112
Barry *(G-1249)*
Dennis Kellogg Ofc................................G....... 773 588-3421
Chicago *(G-4339)*
Dmi Information Process Center...........E 773 378-2644
Chicago *(G-4373)*
E & L Communication.............................G....... 773 890-1656
Chicago *(G-4420)*
E & R Media LLC....................................F 618 790-9376
Du Quoin *(G-8119)*
Eisenhower High School - Blue.............G....... 708 385-6815
Blue Island *(G-2120)*
Elise S Allen...G....... 309 673-2613
Peoria *(G-16434)*
Ethnic Media LLC...................................G....... 224 676-0778
Wheeling *(G-20894)*
Forrest Consulting.................................G....... 630 730-9619
Glen Ellyn *(G-10403)*
Fox Valley Park District..........................D....... 630 892-1550
Aurora *(G-1100)*
Friends Pyramid State Park Inc.............F 618 318-3992
Pinckneyville *(G-16615)*
Gannett Stllite Info Ntwrk LLC..............D....... 847 839-1700
Hoffman Estates *(G-11427)*
Gazette-Democrat..................................E 618 833-2158
Anna *(G-584)*
Geomentum Inc.......................................B....... 630 729-7500
Downers Grove *(G-8007)*
Geomentum Inc.......................................G....... 630 729-7500
Downers Grove *(G-8008)*
Hancock County Shopper.......................G....... 217 847-6628
Hamilton *(G-10959)*
Henry News Republican.........................G....... 309 364-3250
Henry *(G-11166)*
Horizon Publications (2003)..................G....... 618 993-1711
Marion *(G-13516)*
Hpc of Pennsylvania Inc.........................D....... 618 993-1711
Marion *(G-13517)*
India Tribune Ltd Corporation...............F 773 588-5077
Chicago *(G-4905)*
International News.................................G....... 773 283-8323
Chicago *(G-4953)*
Kaages News Service.............................G....... 847 529-7199
Chicago *(G-5073)*
Korea Times...D....... 847 626-0388
Glenview *(G-10579)*
Lambda Publications Inc........................F 773 871-7610
Chicago *(G-5169)*
Launch Press...G....... 773 669-8372
Lombard *(G-13094)*
Liberty Group Publishing.......................G....... 309 937-3303
Cambridge *(G-2805)*
Mahoney Publishing Inc.........................G....... 815 369-5384
Lena *(G-12606)*
Naperville Hanna Andersson.................G....... 331 250-7100
Naperville *(G-14880)*
New City Communications.....................E 312 243-8786
Chicago *(G-5576)*
Newspaper National Network................G....... 312 644-1142
Chicago *(G-5589)*
Nicado Publishing Company Inc...........G....... 312 593-2557
Chicago *(G-5595)*
Nuevos Semana Newspaper..................G....... 847 991-3939
Palatine *(G-16145)*
Pantagraph Publishing Co.....................G....... 309 451-0006
Normal *(G-15216)*
Peg N Reds..G....... 618 586-2015
New Lenox *(G-15049)*
Peoria Post Inc.......................................F 309 688-3628
Peoria *(G-16495)*
Publishing Properties LLC....................G....... 312 321-2299
Chicago *(G-5912)*
Puro Futbol Newspaper.........................G....... 847 858-7493
Gurnee *(G-10919)*
RCP Publications Inc.............................G....... 773 227-4066
Chicago *(G-5979)*
Review..G....... 618 997-2222
Marion *(G-13533)*
Schaumburg Review..............................F 847 998-3400
Chicago *(G-6110)*
Sun-Times Media LLC...........................F 312 222-6920
Chicago *(G-6270)*
T R Communications Inc.......................F 773 238-3366
Chicago *(G-6307)*
United Communications Corp...............C 847 746-1515
Zion *(G-21527)*
United Communications Corp...............E 847 746-4700
Zion *(G-21528)*
Vernon Township Offices......................E 847 634-4600
Buffalo Grove *(G-2617)*
Village of Mt Zion..................................G....... 217 864-4212
Mount Zion *(G-14650)*
W G N Radio Mass Calling....................G....... 312 591-7200
Chicago *(G-6574)*
Weekly Visitor..G....... 815 845-2328
Scales Mound *(G-18422)*
Wheels & Deals......................................G....... 217 423-6333
Decatur *(G-7569)*
Wyzz Inc...D....... 217 753-5620
Springfield *(G-19468)*

PUBLISHERS: Newspapers, No Printing

22nd Century Media..............................G....... 847 272-4565
Northbrook *(G-15328)*
22nd Century Media..............................E 708 326-9170
Orland Park *(G-15931)*
All Star Publishing..................................G....... 630 428-1515
Naperville *(G-14772)*
Altamont News.......................................G....... 618 483-6176
Altamont *(G-529)*
Americn Foreign Lang Newspaper........E 312 368-4815
Chicago *(G-3676)*
Beardstown Newspapers Inc................G....... 217 323-1010
Beardstown *(G-1445)*
Better News Papers Inc.........................G....... 618 483-6176
Altamont *(G-531)*
Bond & Fayette County Shopper...........G....... 618 664-4566
Greenville *(G-10827)*
Bureau Valley Chief...............................G....... 815 646-4731
Tiskilwa *(G-19871)*
Campbell Publishing Inc........................E 217 742-3313
Winchester *(G-21104)*
Carbondale Night Life...........................F 618 549-2799
Carbondale *(G-2839)*
Carterville Courier.................................G....... 618 985-6187
Carterville *(G-3130)*
Central Illinois Newspapers..................G....... 217 935-3171
Clinton *(G-6920)*
Centralia Morning Sentinel....................D....... 618 532-5601
Centralia *(G-3224)*
Centralia Press Ltd................................D....... 618 532-5604
Centralia *(G-3225)*
Centralia Press Ltd................................F 618 246-2000
Mount Vernon *(G-14601)*
Chicago Crusader News Group............G....... 773 752-2500
Chicago *(G-4099)*
Daily Lawrenceville Record..................F 618 943-2331
Lawrenceville *(G-12529)*
Daily Lawrenceville Record..................G....... 618 544-2101
Lawrenceville *(G-12530)*
Delavan Times.......................................G....... 309 244-7111
Delavan *(G-7715)*
Democrat Message...............................G....... 217 773-3371
Mount Sterling *(G-14591)*
Des Plaines Journal Inc........................D....... 847 299-5511
Des Plaines *(G-7755)*
Dow Jones & Company Inc...................D....... 312 580-1023
Chicago *(G-4393)*
Ea Mackay Enterprises Inc...................E 630 627-7010
Lombard *(G-13070)*
Eagle Publications Inc..........................E 618 345-5400
Fairview Heights *(G-9645)*
Food Service Publishing Co.................F 847 699-3300
Des Plaines *(G-7772)*
Fox Valley Labor News Inc....................G....... 630 897-4022
Aurora *(G-1099)*
G-W Communications Inc.....................G....... 815 476-7966
Wilmington *(G-21099)*
Gatehouse Media LLC..........................E 618 393-2931
Olney *(G-15862)*
Gatehouse Media III Holdings...............G....... 585 598-0030
Peoria *(G-16442)*
Gazette...E 815 777-0105
Galena *(G-10172)*
Gazette Printing Co...............................G....... 309 389-2811
Glasford *(G-10387)*
German American Nat Congress..........F 773 561-9181
Chicago *(G-4688)*
Gilman Star Inc......................................G....... 815 265-7332
Gilman *(G-10378)*
Gold Nugget Publications Inc................E 217 965-3355
Virden *(G-20185)*
Greene Jersey Shoppers.......................G....... 217 942-3626
Carrollton *(G-3126)*
Greenville Advocate Inc........................G....... 618 664-3144
Greenville *(G-10835)*
Henderson Hancock Quill Inc................G....... 309 924-1871
Stronghurst *(G-19634)*
Heritage Media Svcs Co of Ill...............G....... 708 594-9340
Summit Argo *(G-19679)*
Hillsboro Journal Inc.............................E 217 532-3933
Hillsboro *(G-11316)*
Illini Media Co..B....... 217 337-8300
Champaign *(G-3306)*
Independent News.................................G....... 217 662-6001
Danville *(G-7350)*
John Dagys Media LLC.........................G....... 708 373-0180
Palos Park *(G-16212)*
Journal Standard...................................G....... 815 232-1171
Freeport *(G-10122)*
Lacon Home Journal..............................G....... 309 246-2865
Lacon *(G-12128)*
Lawndale Press Inc................................F 708 656-6900
Cicero *(G-6862)*
Lee Enterprises Incorporated...............C 618 529-5454
Carbondale *(G-2849)*
Liberty Group Publishing.......................G....... 618 937-2850
West Frankfort *(G-20676)*
Litchfield News Herald Inc....................F 217 324-2121
Litchfield *(G-12972)*
Lithuanian Catholic Press.....................E 773 585-9500
Chicago *(G-5236)*
Marion Star..G....... 618 997-7827
Marion *(G-13521)*
Martin Publishing Co..............................G....... 309 647-9501
Canton *(G-2828)*
Martin Publishing Co..............................E 309 543-2000
Havana *(G-11116)*
Martin Publishing Co..............................F 309 647-9501
Canton *(G-2829)*
McClatchy Newspapers Inc...................F 618 443-2145
Sparta *(G-19257)*
Messenger...G....... 618 235-9601
Belleville *(G-1576)*
Monitor Newspaper Inc..........................G....... 618 271-0468
East Saint Louis *(G-8315)*
News & Letters.......................................G....... 312 663-0839
Chicago *(G-5587)*
Newspaper Holding Inc..........................G....... 618 643-2387
Mc Leansboro *(G-13707)*
Newspaper Holding Inc..........................E 217 446-1000
Danville *(G-7370)*
Normalite Newspaper.............................F 309 454-5476
Normal *(G-15213)*
North County News Inc..........................G....... 618 282-3803
Red Bud *(G-16998)*
Ocs America Inc....................................E 630 595-0111
Wood Dale *(G-21225)*
Ovn LLC...G....... 646 204-6781
Vernon Hills *(G-20079)*

Employee Codes: A=Over 500 employees, B=251-500
C=101-250, D=51-100, E=20-50, F=10-19, G=3-9

2020 Harris Illinois
Industrial Directory

1585

PRODUCT

Paper ....E 815 584-1901
Dwight (G-8157)
Perryco Inc ....F 815 436-2431
Plainfield (G-16701)
Petersburg Observer Co Inc ....G 217 632-2236
Petersburg (G-16603)
Porterville Recorder Inc ....G 559 784-5000
Marion (G-13528)
Rachel Switall Mag Group Nfp ....G 773 344-7123
Chicago (G-5957)
Real Times II LLC ....G 312 225-2400
Chicago (G-5985)
Record Inc ....G 312 985-7270
Chicago (G-5989)
Refined Haystack Inc ....G 773 627-3534
Chicago (G-5998)
Republic Times LLC ....G 618 939-3814
Waterloo (G-20296)
Review ....G 309 659-2761
Erie (G-9474)
Rochelle Newspapers Inc ....E 815 562-4171
Rochelle (G-17156)
Rock Valley Publishing LLC ....E 815 467-6397
Loves Park (G-13255)
Rock Valley Publishing LLC ....G 815 234-4821
Byron (G-2756)
Rock Valley Publishing LLC ....F 815 654-4854
Durand (G-8155)
Shoppers Guide ....G 815 369-4112
Lena (G-12609)
South County Publications ....F 217 438-6155
Auburn (G-907)
Southwest Messenger Press Inc ....E 708 388-2425
Midlothian (G-13996)
Star Media Group ....G 847 674-7827
Skokie (G-19036)
Star-Times Publishing Co Inc ....G 618 635-2000
Staunton (G-19479)
Stark County Communications ....G 309 286-4444
Toulon (G-19891)
Steven Brownstein ....G 847 909-6677
Morton Grove (G-14442)
Students Publishing Company In ....G 847 491-7206
Evanston (G-9579)
Sumner Press ....G 618 936-2212
Sumner (G-19688)
Times Republic ....E 815 432-5227
Watseka (G-20320)
Tuscola Journal Incorporated ....G 217 253-5086
Tuscola (G-19932)
Vital Times ....G 847 675-2577
Lincolnwood (G-12848)
Vondrak Publishing Co Inc ....E 773 476-4800
Summit Argo (G-19684)
Want ADS of Champaign Inc ....G 217 356-4804
Champaign (G-3368)
Washington Courier ....F 309 444-3139
Washington (G-20282)
Willis Publishing ....F 618 497-8272
Percy (G-16561)
Wns Publications Inc ....E 815 772-7244
Morrison (G-14349)
World Journal LLC ....F 312 842-8005
Chicago (G-6674)

PUBLISHERS: Pamphlets, No Printing

Eagle Forum ....G 618 462-5415
Alton (G-554)
Good News Publishers ....E 630 682-4300
Wheaton (G-20801)
Media Associates Intl Inc ....F 630 260-9063
Carol Stream (G-3022)
Movie Facts Inc ....E 847 299-9700
Des Plaines (G-7807)
Need To Know Inc ....G 309 691-3877
Peoria (G-16484)
S R Bastien Co ....F 847 858-1175
Evanston (G-9573)

PUBLISHERS: Periodical Statistical Reports, No Printing

M & B Supply Inc ....F 309 944-3206
Geneseo (G-10246)
Pierce Crandell & Co Inc ....G 847 549-6015
Libertyville (G-12696)

PUBLISHERS: Periodical, With Printing

API Publishing Services LLC ....E 312 644-6610
Chicago (G-3711)
Cook Communications Ministries ....C 847 741-0800
Elgin (G-8557)
National Association Realtors ....C 800 874-6500
Chicago (G-5543)

PUBLISHERS: Periodicals, Magazines

Abc Inc ....E 312 980-1000
Chicago (G-3506)
American Assn Nurosurgeons Inc ....E 847 378-0500
Rolling Meadows (G-17710)
American Cllege Chest Physcans ....D 224 521-9800
Glenview (G-10521)
American Hosp Assn Svcs Del ....E 312 422-2000
Chicago (G-3654)
American Soc Plastic Surgeons ....D 847 228-9900
Arlington Heights (G-691)
Anderson House Foundation ....G 630 461-7254
Glen Ellyn (G-10395)
Bowtie Inc ....G 630 515-9493
Lombard (G-13048)
Business Insurance ....F 877 812-1587
Chicago (G-3980)
Caduceus Communications Inc ....G 773 549-4800
Chicago (G-4001)
CAM Systems ....G 800 208-3244
Chicago (G-4009)
Care Education Group Inc ....G 708 361-4110
Palos Park (G-16208)
Chambers Marketing Options ....G 847 584-2626
Elk Grove Village (G-8888)
Cook Communications Minis ....D 847 741-5168
Elgin (G-8556)
Corbett Accel Healthcare Grp C ....C 312 475-2505
Chicago (G-4234)
Cornerstone Communications ....E 773 989-2087
Chicago (G-4236)
Cosmopolitan Foot Care ....G 312 984-5111
Chicago (G-4246)
Eagle Forum ....G 618 462-5415
Alton (G-554)
Express Publishing Inc ....G 773 725-6218
Chicago (G-4545)
Food Service Publishing Co ....F 847 699-3300
Des Plaines (G-7772)
Frank R Walker Company ....G 630 613-9312
Lombard (G-13079)
Gazette ....E 815 777-0105
Galena (G-10172)
Gemworld International Inc ....G 847 657-0555
Glenview (G-10549)
Icd Publications Inc ....G 847 913-8295
Lincolnshire (G-12773)
Icon Acquisition Holdings LP ....G 312 751-8000
Chicago (G-4872)
Illini Media Co ....B 217 337-8300
Champaign (G-3306)
Inside Track Trading ....G 630 585-9218
Aurora (G-984)
J S Paluch Co Inc ....C 847 678-9300
Franklin Park (G-9969)
Keystone Printing & Publishing ....G 815 678-2591
Richmond (G-17016)
Korea Times ....D 847 626-0388
Glenview (G-10579)
Lawrence Rgan Cmmnications Inc ....E 312 960-4100
Chicago (G-5184)
Lightworks Communcation Inc ....G 847 966-1110
Morton Grove (G-14422)
Lithuanian Catholic Press ....E 773 585-9500
Chicago (G-5236)
Liturgical Conference ....G 847 866-3875
Wilmette (G-21085)
Meredith Corp ....D 312 580-1623
Chicago (G-5395)
Metro Printing & Pubg Inc ....F 618 476-9587
Millstadt (G-14052)
Monitor Publishing Inc ....G 773 205-0303
Chicago (G-5491)
Moody Bible Inst of Chicago ....E 312 329-2102
Chicago (G-5496)
MTS Publishing Co ....F 630 955-9750
Lisle (G-12916)
New Life Printing & Publishing ....G 847 658-4111
Algonquin (G-382)
Rbp Services ....G 206 238-3526
Morris (G-14324)
RCP Publications Inc ....G 773 227-4066
Chicago (G-5979)
Relx Inc ....F 937 247-3469
Chicago (G-6013)
Relx Inc ....E 309 689-1000
Peoria (G-16509)
RSM International ....G 312 634-3400
Chicago (G-6074)
S R Bastien Co ....F 847 858-1175
Evanston (G-9573)
Sanderson and Associates ....F 312 829-4350
Chicago (G-6099)
Surplus Record LLC ....F 312 372-9077
Chicago (G-6290)
Techgraphic Solutions Inc ....F 309 693-9400
Peoria (G-16536)
Tegna Inc ....C 847 490-6657
Hoffman Estates (G-11468)
Theosophical Society In Amer ....E 630 665-0130
Wheaton (G-20826)
Theosophical Society In Amer ....F 630 665-0123
Wheaton (G-20827)
Tribune Publishing Company LLC ....D 312 832-6711
Chicago (G-6425)
Tube & Pipe Association Intl ....D 815 399-8700
Elgin (G-8763)

PUBLISHERS: Periodicals, No Printing

Art In Print Review ....G 773 697-9478
Chicago (G-3735)
Baptist General Conference ....D 800 323-4215
Arlington Heights (G-703)
Cube Tomato Inc ....G 224 653-2655
Schaumburg (G-18499)
Cupcake Holdings LLC ....C 800 794-5866
Woodridge (G-21289)
Damien Corporation ....G 630 369-3549
Naperville (G-14814)
Financial Publishing Svcs Co ....F 847 501-4120
Northfield (G-15513)
India Tribune Ltd Corporation ....F 773 588-5077
Chicago (G-4905)
International College Surgeons ....G 312 642-6502
Chicago (G-4952)
Mediatec Publishing Inc ....G 510 834-0100
Chicago (G-5387)
National Safety Council ....B 630 285-1121
Itasca (G-11707)
One Accord Unity Nfp ....G 630 649-0793
Bolingbrook (G-2223)
Pitchfork Media Inc ....E 773 395-5937
Chicago (G-5812)
Rochelle Newspapers Inc ....E 815 562-4171
Rochelle (G-17156)
University of Chicago ....B 773 702-1722
Chicago (G-6485)
Wilton Holdings Inc ....A 630 963-7100
Woodridge (G-21349)
Wilton Industries Inc ....B 630 963-7100
Naperville (G-14949)
Wilton Industries Inc ....F 815 834-9390
Romeoville (G-17888)

PUBLISHERS: Posters

Panache Editions Ltd ....G 847 921-8574
Glencoe (G-10433)

PUBLISHERS: Shopping News

Beardstown Newspapers Inc ....G 217 323-1010
Beardstown (G-1445)
Boone County Shopper Inc ....F 815 544-2166
Belvidere (G-1656)
Peoria Post Inc ....F 309 688-3628
Peoria (G-16495)
Shoppers Weekly Inc ....F 618 533-7283
Centralia (G-3251)

PUBLISHERS: Technical Manuals

Custom Design Services & Assoc ....F 815 226-9747
Rockford (G-17362)
Mcllvaine Co ....E 847 784-0012
Northfield (G-15522)
Techno - Grphics Trnsltons Inc ....E 708 331-3333
South Holland (G-19248)

PUBLISHERS: Technical Manuals & Papers

About Learning Inc ....F 847 487-1800
Wauconda (G-20326)
Canright & Paule Inc ....G 888 202-3894
Chicago (G-4015)
Gantec Pubg Solutions LLC ....F 847 598-1144
Schaumburg (G-18534)

PRODUCT SECTION

PUBLISHING & PRINTING: Magazines: publishing & printing

PUBLISHERS: Telephone & Other Directory

AT&T Corp .... C 630 693-5000
  Lombard (G-13041)
Consumerbase LLC .... C 312 600-8000
  Chicago (G-4224)
Havas Barn .... G 312 640-6800
  Chicago (G-4788)
New Millenium Directories .... E 815 626-5737
  Sterling (G-19522)
Serbian Yellow Pages Inc .... F 847 588-0555
  Niles (G-15169)
TWT Marketing Inc .... G 773 274-4470
  Chicago (G-6449)

PUBLISHERS: Textbooks, No Printing

A Trustworthy Sup Source Inc .... G 773 480-0255
  Chicago (G-3492)
Goodheart-Willcox Company Inc .... D 708 687-0315
  Tinley Park (G-19833)
Gordon Burke John Publisher .... G 847 866-8625
  Evanston (G-9526)
Houghton Mifflin Harcourt Pubg .... B 708 869-2300
  Evanston (G-9535)
LMS Innovations Inc .... G 312 613-2345
  Chicago (G-5247)
Marantha Wrld Rvval Ministries .... G 773 384-7717
  Chicago (G-5328)
Motamed Medical Publishing Co .... G 773 761-6667
  Chicago (G-5505)
National School Services Inc .... E 847 438-3859
  Long Grove (G-13167)
Respect Incorporated .... G 815 806-1907
  Manhattan (G-13435)
Scholastic Inc .... E 630 671-0601
  Roselle (G-17984)
World Book Inc .... E 312 729-5800
  Chicago (G-6671)

PUBLISHERS: Trade journals, No Printing

Aais Services Corporation .... E 630 681-8347
  Lisle (G-12856)
Aais Services Corporation .... G 630 457-3263
  Lisle (G-12857)
Aana Publishing Inc .... G 847 692-7050
  Park Ridge (G-16262)
Allured Publishing Corporation .... E 630 653-2155
  Carol Stream (G-2932)
American City Bus Journals Inc .... G 312 873-2200
  Chicago (G-3651)
American Medical Association .... A 312 464-5000
  Chicago (G-3660)
American Soc HM Inspectors Inc .... F 847 759-2820
  Des Plaines (G-7728)
Associated Equipment Distrs .... E 630 574-0650
  Schaumburg (G-18447)
Banner Publications .... G 309 338-3294
  Cuba (G-7297)
Dorenfest Group Ltd .... D 312 464-3000
  Chicago (G-4385)
Fabricators & Mfrs Assn Intl .... E 815 399-8700
  Elgin (G-8584)
Fma Communicatons Inc .... D 815 227-8284
  Elgin (G-8589)
HH Backer Associates Inc .... F 312 578-1818
  Chicago (G-4812)
Hw Holdco LLC .... D 773 824-2400
  Rosemont (G-18026)
Industrial Market Place .... E 847 676-1900
  Niles (G-15133)
Inside Council .... F 312 654-3500
  Chicago (G-4935)
Luby Publishing Inc .... F 312 341-1110
  Chicago (G-5276)
Mdm Communications Inc .... G 708 582-9667
  Skokie (G-18987)
Modern Trade Communications .... F 847 674-2200
  Skokie (G-18992)
Practical Communications Inc .... E 773 754-3250
  Schaumburg (G-18681)
Putman Media Inc .... D 630 467-1301
  Schaumburg (G-18689)
R L D Communications Inc .... F 312 338-7007
  Chicago (G-5946)
Sagamore Publishing LLC .... F 217 359-5940
  Champaign (G-3345)
Scranton Glltte Cmmnctions Inc .... G 847 391-1000
  Arlington Heights (G-805)
SGC Horizon LLC .... G 847 391-1000
  Arlington Heights (G-808)

Transportation Eqp Advisors .... D 847 318-7575
  Rosemont (G-18055)
Vertical Web Media LLC .... E 312 362-0076
  Chicago (G-6539)
Wolters Kluwer US Inc .... E 847 580-5000
  Riverwoods (G-17097)

PUBLISHING & BROADCASTING: Internet Only

2bald Inc .... G 815 403-8870
  Johnsburg (G-11800)
Arcsec Digital LLC .... G 312 324-4794
  Lake Forest (G-12225)
Band of Shoppers Inc .... G 312 857-4250
  Chicago (G-3824)
Beyond Limits Media Group LLC .... G 773 948-9296
  Chicago (G-3878)
Cammun LLC .... G 312 628-1201
  Chicago (G-4013)
Elliott Jsj & Associates Inc .... G 847 242-0412
  Glencoe (G-10429)
Fully Equipped Inc .... G 312 978-9936
  Chicago (G-4641)
Haute Noir Media Group Inc .... G 312 869-4526
  Chicago (G-4787)
Hill Reporter LLC .... G 309 532-4794
  El Paso (G-8438)
HP Interactive Inc .... G 773 681-4440
  Chicago (G-4855)
Hunting Network LLC .... G 847 659-8200
  Huntley (G-11540)
L C Inn Partners .... F 309 743-0800
  Moline (G-14156)
Mindseye .... G 618 394-6444
  Belleville (G-1579)
Odx Media LLC .... G 847 868-0548
  Evanston (G-9559)
Prereo LLC .... G 800 555-1055
  Chicago (G-5866)
Qt Info Systems Inc .... F 800 240-8761
  Chicago (G-5925)
Sim Partners .... E 800 260-3380
  Chicago (G-6172)
Vortex Media Group Inc .... G 630 717-9541
  Naperville (G-14942)
Zaptel Corporation .... G 847 386-8050
  Elk Grove Village (G-9317)

PUBLISHING & PRINTING: Art Copy

Chase Group LLC .... F 847 564-2000
  Northbrook (G-15355)
Creative Ideas Inc .... G 217 245-1378
  Jacksonville (G-11763)

PUBLISHING & PRINTING: Book Clubs

Rookie LLC .... G 708 278-1628
  Oak Park (G-15770)

PUBLISHING & PRINTING: Book Music

Carus Publishing Company .... G 603 924-7209
  Chicago (G-4033)
Do You See What I See Entertai .... G 773 612-1269
  Chicago (G-4375)

PUBLISHING & PRINTING: Books

Advantage Press Inc .... G 630 960-5305
  Lisle (G-12858)
Bookends Publishing .... G 312 988-1500
  Chicago (G-3934)
CCH Incorporated .... A 847 267-7000
  Riverwoods (G-17090)
Cook Communications Ministries .... C 847 741-0800
  Elgin (G-8557)
Crown Kandy Enterprise Ltd .... F 708 580-6494
  Westchester (G-20696)
Dasher Dependable Reindeer LLC ...... G 630 513-7737
  Saint Charles (G-18179)
Final Call Inc .... D 773 602-1230
  Chicago (G-4587)
Gorman & Associates .... G 309 691-9087
  Peoria (G-16446)
Grace and Truth .... G 217 442-1120
  Danville (G-7340)
Graphic Score Book Co Inc .... G 847 823-7382
  Park Ridge (G-16281)
Multi Packaging Solutions Inc .... G 773 283-9500
  Chicago (G-5523)

Nexus Supply Consortium Inc .... G 630 649-2868
  Bolingbrook (G-2222)
Phoenix Intl Publications Inc .... B 877 277-9441
  Chicago (G-5803)
Springfield Printing Inc .... G 217 787-3500
  Springfield (G-19454)
Taylor & Francis Group LLC .... G 630 482-9886
  Batavia (G-1424)

PUBLISHING & PRINTING: Catalogs

Creasey Printing Services Inc .... G 217 787-1055
  Springfield (G-19356)
Mediatec Publishing Inc .... E 312 676-9900
  Chicago (G-5386)
Ryan Partnership LLC .... F 312 343-2611
  Chicago (G-6080)

PUBLISHING & PRINTING: Comic Books

Genesis Comics Group .... G 312 544-7473
  Chicago (G-4680)
Kiss ME Comix .... G 773 982-8334
  Chicago (G-5107)

PUBLISHING & PRINTING: Directories, NEC

F M Aquisition Corp .... G 773 728-8351
  Chicago (G-4551)
Wolters Kluwer US Inc .... E 847 580-5000
  Riverwoods (G-17097)

PUBLISHING & PRINTING: Globe Cover Maps

Where 2 Get It LLC .... F 224 232-5550
  Arlington Heights (G-832)

PUBLISHING & PRINTING: Guides

Law Bulletin Publishing Co .... C 312 644-2763
  Chicago (G-5182)
Oag Aviation Worldwide LLC .... G 630 515-5300
  Lisle (G-12923)

PUBLISHING & PRINTING: Magazines: publishing & printing

Ada Holding Company Inc .... F 312 440-2897
  Chicago (G-3537)
Alali Enterprises Inc .... G 630 827-9231
  Carol Stream (G-2930)
Allen Entertainment Management ...... E 630 752-0903
  Carol Stream (G-2931)
American Custom Publishing .... G 847 816-8660
  Libertyville (G-12628)
American Trade Magazines LLC .... G 312 497-7707
  Chicago (G-3671)
Andover Junction Publications .... G 815 538-3060
  Mendota (G-13935)
Area Marketing Inc .... G 815 806-8844
  Frankfort (G-9768)
Cap Today .... F 847 832-7377
  Northfield (G-15510)
Challenge Publications L T D .... G 309 421-0392
  Macomb (G-13388)
CHI Home Improvement Mag Inc .... G 630 801-7788
  Aurora (G-1073)
Code Black LLC .... G 773 493-4500
  Chicago (G-4191)
College Bound Publications .... G 773 262-5810
  Chicago (G-4201)
Dobinski Marketing .... G 773 248-5880
  Chicago (G-4376)
Fanning Communications Inc .... G 708 293-1430
  Crestwood (G-7118)
Futures Magazine Inc .... G 312 846-4600
  Chicago (G-4646)
Gail McGrath & Associates Inc .... F 847 770-4620
  Northbrook (G-15392)
Half Price Bks Rec Mgzines Inc .... E 847 588-2286
  Niles (G-15128)
Home School Enrichment Inc .... G 309 347-1392
  Pekin (G-16338)
Hotel Amerika .... G 219 508-9418
  Chicago (G-4848)
Ink Spots Prtg & Meida Design .... G 708 754-1300
  Homewood (G-11498)
Instrumentalists Inc .... F 847 446-5000
  Northbrook (G-15406)
Lsc Communications Inc .... C 773 272-9200
  Chicago (G-5272)

Employee Codes: A=Over 500 employees, B=251-500
C=101-250, D=51-100, E=20-50, F=10-19, G=3-9

Lsc Communications Mm LLC ....F 815 844-1819
Chicago *(G-5273)*
Lsc Communications Us LLC ....A 815 844-5181
Pontiac *(G-16774)*
Lsc Communications Us LLC ....B 844 572-5720
Chicago *(G-5274)*
Magazine Plus ....G 773 281-4106
Chicago *(G-5314)*
Metal Center News ....F 630 571-1067
Oak Brook *(G-15643)*
Midwest Outdoors Ltd ....E 630 887-7722
Burr Ridge *(G-2704)*
Midwestern Family Magazine LLC ....G 309 303-7309
Peoria *(G-16477)*
Northern Illinois Real Estate ....G 630 257-2480
Lemont *(G-12573)*
P&L Group Ltd of Illinois ....F 833 362-2100
Chicago *(G-5730)*
Rankin Publishing Inc ....F 217 268-4959
Arcola *(G-664)*
Reilly Communication Group ....F 630 756-1225
Arlington Heights *(G-799)*
Rylin Media LLC ....G 708 246-7599
Western Springs *(G-20725)*
Silent W Communications Inc ....G 630 479-7950
Montgomery *(G-14270)*
Tails Inc ....F 773 564-9300
Chicago *(G-6311)*
Willis Stein & Partners Manage ....F 312 422-2400
Chicago *(G-6632)*

PUBLISHING & PRINTING: Music, Book

Fleming Music Technology Ctr ....G 708 316-8662
Wheaton *(G-20799)*
G I A Publications Inc ....E 708 496-3800
Chicago *(G-4650)*

PUBLISHING & PRINTING: Newsletters, Business Svc

Arthur Coyle Press ....G 773 465-8418
Chicago *(G-3739)*
Businessmine LLC ....G 630 541-8480
Lombard *(G-13049)*
Cab Communications Inc ....G 847 963-8740
Palatine *(G-16097)*
Debbie Harshman ....G 217 335-2112
Barry *(G-1249)*
Financial Publishing Svcs Co ....F 847 501-4120
Northfield *(G-15513)*
Knighthouse Media Inc ....C 312 676-1100
Chicago *(G-5110)*
Nas Media Group Inc ....G 312 371-7499
Olympia Fields *(G-15896)*
Paperworks ....G 630 969-3218
Downers Grove *(G-8069)*
T R Communications Inc ....F 773 238-3366
Chicago *(G-6307)*

PUBLISHING & PRINTING: Newspapers

Advantage News ....G 618 463-0612
Alton *(G-541)*
Advocate ....G 815 694-2122
Clifton *(G-6913)*
Agri-News Publications Inc ....D 815 223-2558
La Salle *(G-12100)*
Arcola Record Herald ....G 217 268-4950
Arcola *(G-645)*
B F Shaw Printing Company ....G 815 625-3600
Sterling *(G-19500)*
Bar Stool Depotcom ....G 815 727-7294
Joliet *(G-11827)*
Belleville News Democrat ....C 618 239-2552
Belleville *(G-1533)*
Benton Gazette ....G 618 438-6397
Benton *(G-1920)*
Better News Papers Inc ....G 618 566-8282
Mascoutah *(G-13593)*
Blue Island Sun ....G 708 388-9033
Blue Island *(G-2112)*
Breese Publishing Co Inc ....G 618 526-7211
Breese *(G-2299)*
Bulletin ....G 618 553-9764
Oblong *(G-15824)*
C & C Publications ....G 815 723-0325
Joliet *(G-11836)*
Cambridge Chronicle ....G 309 937-3303
Cambridge *(G-2802)*
Campbell Publishing Co Inc ....F 618 498-1234
Jerseyville *(G-11788)*
Campbell Publishing Co Inc ....G 217 285-2345
Pittsfield *(G-16631)*
Carmi Times ....F 618 382-4176
Carmi *(G-2902)*
Catholic Press Assn of The US ....G 312 380-6789
Chicago *(G-4043)*
Central Newspaper Incorporated ....G 630 416-4191
Naperville *(G-14795)*
Chgo Daily Law Bulletin ....G 217 525-6735
Springfield *(G-19349)*
Chicago ....G 847 437-7700
Arlington Heights *(G-715)*
Chicago Chinese Times ....G 630 717-4567
Naperville *(G-14796)*
Chicago Citizen Newsppr Group ....F 773 783-1251
Chicago *(G-4096)*
Chicago Group Acquisition LLC ....G 312 755-0720
Chicago *(G-4105)*
Chicago Sun-Times Features Inc ....A 312 321-3000
Chicago *(G-4131)*
Chicago Tribune Company ....G 312 222-3232
Chicago *(G-4133)*
Chicago Tribune Company LLC ....A 312 222-3232
Chicago *(G-4134)*
China Journal Inc ....G 312 326-3228
Chicago *(G-4140)*
Chronicle Newspapers Inc ....G 630 845-5247
Geneva *(G-10259)*
Clinton Journal ....G 309 242-3900
Bloomington *(G-2032)*
Coal City Courant ....G 815 634-0315
Coal City *(G-6930)*
Crain Communications Inc ....C 312 649-5200
Chicago *(G-4259)*
Czech American TV Herald ....G 708 813-0028
Willowbrook *(G-21039)*
Daily Dollar Savings LLC ....G 860 883-0351
Morton Grove *(G-14398)*
Daily Egyptian Siu Newspaper ....D 618 536-3311
Carbondale *(G-2840)*
Daily Fastner ....G 847 907-9830
Palatine *(G-16107)*
Daily General LLC ....G 217 273-0719
Chicago *(G-4305)*
Daily Kratom ....G 815 768-7104
Joliet *(G-11851)*
Daily Money Matters LLC ....G 847 729-8393
Glenview *(G-10541)*
Daily News Condominium Assn ....E 312 492-8526
Chicago *(G-4306)*
Daily News Tribune Inc ....C 815 223-2558
La Salle *(G-12110)*
Daily Whale ....G 312 787-5204
Chicago *(G-4307)*
Democrat Company Corp ....G 217 357-2149
Carthage *(G-3135)*
Desi Talk LLC ....G 212 675-7515
Chicago *(G-4345)*
District 97 ....G 708 289-7064
Oak Park *(G-15750)*
Dixon Telegraph ....G 815 284-2224
Dixon *(G-7897)*
Dow Jones & Company Inc ....E 618 651-2300
Highland *(G-11214)*
East Central Communications Co ....E 217 892-9613
Rantoul *(G-16975)*
Edwardsville Publishing Co ....D 618 656-4700
Edwardsville *(G-8361)*
Effingham Ttplis News Rport In ....G 217 342-5583
Effingham *(G-8399)*
El Dia Newspaper ....G 708 956-7282
Berwyn *(G-1952)*
El Paso Journal ....G 309 527-8595
El Paso *(G-8437)*
El Sol Dechicago Newspaper ....G 773 235-7655
Chicago *(G-4468)*
Elliott Publishing Inc ....G 217 645-3033
Liberty *(G-12622)*
Elliott Publishing Inc ....G 217 593-6515
Camp Point *(G-2810)*
Examiner Publications Inc ....G 630 830-4145
Bartlett *(G-1279)*
Experimental Aircraft Examiner ....G 847 226-0777
Cary *(G-3158)*
Farm Week ....E 309 557-3140
Bloomington *(G-2042)*
Final Call Inc ....D 773 602-1230
Chicago *(G-4587)*
Fra No 3800 W Division ....G 708 338-0690
Stone Park *(G-19555)*
Free Press Newspapers ....E 815 476-7966
Wilmington *(G-21098)*
Galesburg Register-Mail ....C 309 343-7181
Galesburg *(G-10193)*
Ganji Klames ....G 773 478-9000
Skokie *(G-18959)*
Gannett Stllite Info Ntwrk LLC ....C 630 629-1280
Yorkville *(G-21484)*
Gatehouse Media LLC ....F 309 852-2181
Kewanee *(G-12035)*
Gatehouse Media LLC ....G 618 783-2324
Newton *(G-15083)*
Gatehouse Media LLC ....B 217 788-1300
Springfield *(G-19373)*
Gatehouse Media LLC ....E 618 937-2850
West Frankfort *(G-20673)*
Gatehouse Media LLC ....E 815 842-1153
Pontiac *(G-16771)*
Gatehouse Media LLC ....E 618 253-7146
Harrisburg *(G-11024)*
Gatehouse Media - Wstn Ill Div ....G 309 299-6135
Galesburg *(G-10195)*
Gazette Democrat ....E 618 833-2150
Anna *(G-583)*
Gmd Mobile Pressure Wshg Svcs ....G 773 826-1903
Chicago *(G-4704)*
Golda House ....G 773 927-0140
Chicago *(G-4713)*
Golf Gazette ....G 815 838-0184
Lockport *(G-12997)*
Hardschellreport ....G 773 972-2500
Evanston *(G-9531)*
Hearst Communications Inc ....C 309 829-9000
Bloomington *(G-2056)*
Hearst Corporation ....G 618 463-2500
Alton *(G-558)*
Hearst Corporation ....G 217 245-6121
Jacksonville *(G-11766)*
Heartland News ....G 217 856-2332
Humboldt *(G-11523)*
Herald Mount Olive ....G 217 999-3941
Mount Olive *(G-14504)*
Herald Publications ....F 618 566-8282
Mascoutah *(G-13599)*
Herald Whig Quincy ....G 217 222-7600
Quincy *(G-16891)*
Hl India ....G 773 552-6083
Chicago *(G-4813)*
Horizon Publications Inc ....C 618 993-1711
Marion *(G-13515)*
Illinois Newspaper In Educatn ....F 847 427-4388
Springfield *(G-19387)*
Illinois Valley Press East ....G 217 586-2512
Mahomet *(G-13424)*
India Bulletin Inc ....G 847 674-7941
Skokie *(G-18968)*
Indiana Agri-News Inc ....G 317 726-5391
La Salle *(G-12114)*
Inn Intl Newspaper Network ....G 309 764-5314
Moline *(G-14150)*
Joliet Herald Newspaper ....E 815 280-4100
Joliet *(G-11886)*
Journal of Banking and Fin ....G 618 203-9074
Glen Carbon *(G-10389)*
Kathleen A Badasch ....G 618 462-5881
Alton *(G-562)*
Kendall County Record ....E 630 553-7034
Yorkville *(G-21489)*
Kerala Express Newspaper ....G 773 465-5359
Chicago *(G-5096)*
Knockout LLC Evanston ....G 224 714-3007
Evanston *(G-9544)*
Korea Tribune Inc ....G 847 956-9101
Mount Prospect *(G-14543)*
Korean Media Group LLC ....F 847 391-4112
Northbrook *(G-15414)*
La Raza Chicago Inc ....E 312 870-7000
Chicago *(G-5149)*
Lee Enterprises Incorporated ....E 309 743-0800
Moline *(G-14158)*
Lee Enterprises Incorporated ....C 217 421-6920
Decatur *(G-7515)*
Leroy E Ritzert ....G 815 737-8210
Capron *(G-2835)*
Liberty Suburban Chicago ....G 630 368-1100
Oak Brook *(G-15635)*
Lincolndailynewscom ....G 217 732-7443
Lincoln *(G-12734)*
Live Daily LLC ....G 312 286-6706
Chicago *(G-5241)*

PRODUCT SECTION

PUBLISHING & PRINTING: Textbooks

Long View Publishing Co Inc ....F 773 446-9920
  Chicago (G-5255)
Los Angles Tmes Cmmnctions LLC .....G ... 312 467-4670
  Chicago (G-5260)
Macoupin County Enquirer Inc ....E 217 854-2534
  Carlinville (G-2879)
Marengo Union Times ....G 815 568-5400
  Marengo (G-13490)
Marshall County Publishing Co ....G 309 246-2865
  Lacon (G-12129)
McClatchy Newspapers Inc ....B 618 239-2624
  Belleville (G-1574)
McClatchy Newspapers Inc ....D 618 654-2366
  Highland (G-11231)
McDonough County Shopper Inc ....G 309 833-2114
  Macomb (G-13393)
McDonough Democrat Inc ....F 309 772-2129
  Bushnell (G-2744)
Military Medical News ....E 312 368-4860
  Chicago (G-5457)
Mirror-Democrat ....G 815 244-2411
  Mount Carroll (G-14496)
Morris Publishing Company ....G 815 942-3221
  Morris (G-14317)
Mt Carmel Register Co Inc ....E 618 262-5144
  Mount Carmel (G-14481)
Nationwide News Monitor ....G 312 424-4224
  Skokie (G-18995)
News Media Corporation ....E 815 562-2061
  Rochelle (G-17150)
News-Gazette Inc ....G 217 373-7450
  Champaign (G-3325)
News-Gazette Inc ....E 217 351-5300
  Champaign (G-3326)
News-Gazette Inc ....G 217 351-8128
  Champaign (G-3327)
News-Gazette Inc ....G 217 384-2302
  Champaign (G-3328)
News-Gazette Inc ....G 217 351-5311
  Urbana (G-19990)
News-Gazette Inc ....G 217 762-2511
  Monticello (G-14282)
News-Gazette Inc ....G 217 443-8484
  Danville (G-7369)
Newser LLC ....G 312 284-2300
  Chicago (G-5588)
Newspaper 7 Days ....G 847 272-2212
  Wheeling (G-20944)
Newspaper Holding Inc ....D 217 347-7151
  Effingham (G-8415)
Newspaper Solutions Inc ....F 773 930-3404
  Chicago (G-5590)
Newsprint Ink Inc ....F 618 667-3111
  Troy (G-19917)
Northwestern Illinois Farmer ....G 815 369-2811
  Lena (G-12607)
Old Gary Inc ....F 219 648-3000
  Chicago (G-5669)
Osborne Publications Inc ....G 217 422-9702
  Decatur (G-7534)
Paddock Publications Inc ....C 847 608-2700
  Elgin (G-8683)
Paddock Publications Inc ....E 847 680-5800
  Libertyville (G-12693)
Pakistan News ....G 773 271-6400
  Chicago (G-5744)
Pana News Inc ....F 217 562-2111
  Pana (G-16221)
Pantagraph Publishing Co ....F 309 829-9000
  Bloomington (G-2085)
People & Places Newspaper ....G 847 804-6985
  Schiller Park (G-18831)
Peoria Journal Star Credit Un ....G 309 686-3191
  Peoria (G-16492)
Perryco Inc ....E 303 652-8282
  Downers Grove (G-8074)
Pike County Express ....F 217 285-5415
  Pittsfield (G-16638)
Pilot Club of Moline ....F 309 792-4102
  Moline (G-14166)
Pinoy Monthly ....G 847 329-1073
  Skokie (G-19005)
Pioneer Newspapers Inc ....E 708 383-3200
  Oak Park (G-15768)
Pioneer Newspapers Inc ....E 630 887-0600
  Hinsdale (G-11374)
Quad City Clown Troupe Inc ....G 309 788-1278
  Rock Island (G-17235)
Quincy Herald-Whig LLC ....F 217 223-5100
  Quincy (G-16933)

Randolph County Herald Tribune ....F 618 826-2385
  Chester (G-3460)
Rantoul Youth Wrestling ....G 217 377-9523
  Rantoul (G-16982)
Rd Daily Enterprises ....G 847 872-7632
  Winthrop Harbor (G-21142)
Realclearpolitics ....F 773 255-5846
  Chicago (G-5986)
Redwood Landings LLC ....G 312 508-4953
  Chicago (G-5995)
Reflejos Publications LLC ....E 847 806-1111
  Arlington Heights (G-797)
Register Publishing Co ....E 618 253-7146
  Harrisburg (G-11028)
Reporter Inc ....E 217 932-5211
  Casey (G-3208)
Robert McCormick Tribune Lbrry ......G 847 619-7980
  Schaumburg (G-18698)
Rochelle Newspapers Inc ....E 815 562-4171
  Rochelle (G-17157)
Rock River Times ....F 815 964-9767
  Rockford (G-17582)
Rockford Newspapers Inc ....B 815 987-1200
  Rockford (G-17600)
Rodney J Gieseke ....G 630 830-7063
  Bartlett (G-1305)
Russell Publications Inc ....E 708 258-3473
  Peotone (G-16557)
S & R Media LLC ....F 618 375-7502
  Grayville (G-10814)
Salem Times-Commoner Inc ....E 618 548-3330
  Salem (G-18358)
Sauk Valley Community College ....G 815 835-6321
  Sterling (G-19531)
Sauk Valley Gunsmithing ....G 815 441-0260
  Sterling (G-19532)
Sauk Valley Printing ....G 815 284-2222
  Dixon (G-7914)
Savanna Times Journal ....G 815 273-2277
  Savanna (G-18412)
Senior News & Time For Ill ....G 217 528-1882
  Springfield (G-19442)
Shaw Suburban Media Group Inc .....G 815 459-4040
  Crystal Lake (G-7264)
Slack Publications ....G 217 268-4950
  Arcola (G-666)
Small Newspaper Group ....C 815 937-3300
  Kankakee (G-12004)
Small Nwsppr Group Shred Svcs .....G 309 764-4344
  East Moline (G-8241)
Small Nwsppr Group Shred Svcs .....G 309 757-8377
  East Moline (G-8242)
South Post LLC ....G 815 510-9395
  Streator (G-19623)
Southland Voice ....E 708 214-8582
  Crete (G-7145)
Southtown Star Newspapers ....G 708 633-4800
  Tinley Park (G-19857)
Springfield Publishers Inc ....G 217 726-6600
  Springfield (G-19455)
Stadium ....G 312 455-2582
  Chicago (G-6226)
Stm Reader LLC ....G 312 222-6920
  Chicago (G-6249)
Streetwise ....F 773 334-6600
  Chicago (G-6252)
Strohm Newspapers Inc ....G 217 826-3600
  Marshall (G-13578)
Success Journal Corp ....G 847 583-9000
  Morton Grove (G-14444)
Sun Times News Agency ....G 815 672-1260
  Streator (G-19628)
Sun-Times Media Group Inc ....D 312 321-3000
  Chicago (G-6271)
Sv Family Evanston LLC ....G 773 420-6767
  Evanston (G-9581)
Teleguia Inc ....E 708 656-6675
  Cicero (G-6880)
The b F Shaw Printing Co ....G 815 732-6166
  Oregon (G-15928)
Times Republic ....G 217 283-5111
  Hoopeston (G-11515)
Tini Martini ....G 773 269-2900
  Chicago (G-6381)
Todays Advantage Inc ....F 618 463-0612
  Alton (G-574)
Tribune Publishing Company ....C 312 222-9100
  Chicago (G-6423)
Tribune Publishing Company LLC .....E 312 222-9100
  Chicago (G-6424)

Tribune Publishing Company LLC .....D 312 832-6711
  Chicago (G-6425)
Trottie Publishing Group Inc ....G 708 344-5975
  Westchester (G-20715)
Union Banner Publishing Ltd ....G 618 594-3131
  Carlyle (G-2897)
US Oil Morris IL ....G 815 513-3496
  Morris (G-14337)
Villagers Voice ....G 618 378-3094
  Norris City (G-15251)
Waseet America ....G 708 430-1950
  Bedford Park (G-1511)
Waverly Journal ....G 217 435-9221
  Waverly (G-20523)
Wednesday Journal Inc ....D 708 386-5555
  Chicago (G-6597)
Weekly Journals ....G 815 459-4040
  Crystal Lake (G-7293)
Wnta Studio Line ....G 815 874-7861
  Rockford (G-17689)
Woodstock Independent ....G 815 338-8040
  Woodstock (G-21450)
Wrapports LLC ....F 312 321-3000
  Chicago (G-6683)
Zweibel Worldwide Productions ....F 312 751-0503
  Chicago (G-6727)

PUBLISHING & PRINTING: Pamphlets

Blooming Color Inc ....D 630 705-9200
  Lombard (G-13047)
J S Paluch Co Inc ....C 847 678-9300
  Franklin Park (G-9969)
Rohrer Graphic Arts Inc ....F 630 832-3434
  Elmhurst (G-9419)
Royal Publishing Inc ....G 309 343-4007
  Galesburg (G-10219)
Royal Publishing Inc ....G 815 220-0400
  Peru (G-16592)

PUBLISHING & PRINTING: Patterns, Paper

Multi Print and Digital LLC ....G 630 985-2600
  Darien (G-7410)
Phoenix Press Inc ....G 630 833-2281
  Addison (G-239)

PUBLISHING & PRINTING: Periodical Statistical Reports

CCH Incorporated ....A 847 267-7000
  Riverwoods (G-17090)

PUBLISHING & PRINTING: Posters

Frankenstitch Promotions LLC ....F 847 459-4840
  Wheeling (G-20901)

PUBLISHING & PRINTING: Racing Forms & Programs

Wabash Publishing Co Inc ....G 312 939-5900
  Chicago (G-6581)

PUBLISHING & PRINTING: Shopping News

Liberty Group Publishing ....F 309 944-1779
  Geneseo (G-10245)

PUBLISHING & PRINTING: Technical Manuals

Bishop Engineering Company ....F 630 305-9538
  Lisle (G-12872)
Rs Ductless Technical Support ....G 815 223-7949
  La Salle (G-12122)

PUBLISHING & PRINTING: Textbooks

Houghton Mifflin Harcourt Pubg ....C 630 208-5704
  Geneva (G-10277)
Linmore Publishing Co ....G 847 382-7606
  Barrington (G-1224)
Medical Memories LLC ....G 847 478-0078
  Buffalo Grove (G-2571)
Perry Johnson Inc ....F 847 635-0010
  Rosemont (G-18041)
Success Publishing Group Inc ....F 708 565-2681
  Chicago (G-6262)

Employee Codes: A=Over 500 employees, B=251-500
C=101-250, D=51-100, E=20-50, F=10-19, G=3-9

PUBLISHING & PRINTING: Trade Journals

Association Management Center ....D 847 375-4700
  Chicago *(G-3753)*
Johnson Press America Inc ....E 815 844-5161
  Pontiac *(G-16773)*
Medtext Inc ....G 630 325-3277
  Burr Ridge *(G-2702)*
Narda Inc ....F 312 648-2300
  Chicago *(G-5540)*

PUBLISHING & PRINTING: Yearbooks

Illini Media Co ....B 217 337-8300
  Champaign *(G-3306)*

PULLEYS: Metal

HM Manufacturing Inc ....F 847 487-8700
  Wauconda *(G-20356)*
Nagel-Chase Inc ....G 847 336-4494
  Gurnee *(G-10902)*

PULLEYS: Power Transmission

Chicago Die Casting Mfg Co ....E 847 671-5010
  Franklin Park *(G-9904)*
Illinois Pulley & Gear Inc ....G 847 407-9595
  Schaumburg *(G-18556)*
Prophet Gear Co ....E 815 537-2002
  Prophetstown *(G-16834)*

PULP MILLS

BFI Waste Systems N Amer Inc ....E 847 429-7370
  Elgin *(G-8521)*
Buster Services Inc ....E 773 247-2070
  Chicago *(G-3983)*
C & M Recycling Inc ....E 847 578-1066
  North Chicago *(G-15308)*
Cicero Iron Metal & Paper Inc ....G 708 863-8601
  Cicero *(G-6834)*
International Paper Company ....E 630 250-1300
  Itasca *(G-11677)*
International Paper Company ....C 217 735-1221
  Lincoln *(G-12731)*
Lake Area Disposal Service Inc ....E 217 522-9271
  Springfield *(G-19397)*
Weyerhaeuser Company ....D 630 778-7070
  Naperville *(G-14947)*

PULP MILLS: Mech Pulp, Incl Groundwood & Thermomechanical

Kaskaskia Mechanical Insul Co ....G 618 768-4526
  Mascoutah *(G-13601)*

PULP MILLS: Mechanical & Recycling Processing

Coyote Transportation Inc ....G 630 204-5729
  Bensenville *(G-1779)*
Paper Moon Recycling Inc ....G 847 548-8875
  Grayslake *(G-10795)*
Tradebe Environmental Svcs LLC .....G 219 354-2452
  Oak Brook *(G-15664)*

PULP MILLS: Wood Based Pulp, NEC

Westrock Cp LLC ....D 312 346-6600
  Chicago *(G-6611)*

PUMP JACKS & OTHER PUMPING EQPT: Indl

Grundfos Water Utility Inc ....D 630 236-5500
  Aurora *(G-976)*
Metropolitan Industries Inc ....C 815 886-9200
  Romeoville *(G-17851)*
Park Engineering Inc ....E 847 455-1424
  Franklin Park *(G-10013)*
Roy E Roth Company ....G 309 787-1791
  Milan *(G-14028)*
Townley Engrg & Mfg Co Inc ....F 618 273-8271
  Eldorado *(G-8484)*

PUMPS

A-L-L Equipment Company ....G 815 877-7000
  Loves Park *(G-13181)*
Action Pump Co ....F 847 516-3636
  Cary *(G-3144)*
Advanced Seal Technology Inc ....E 815 861-4010
  Ringwood *(G-17038)*
Allegion S&S Holding Co Inc ....C 815 875-3311
  Princeton *(G-16805)*
Apergy Energy Automation LLC ....E 630 541-1540
  Downers Grove *(G-7952)*
Aptargroup Inc ....B 847 639-2124
  Cary *(G-3148)*
Aqua Control Inc ....E 815 664-4900
  Spring Valley *(G-19307)*
Automax Corporation ....G 630 972-1919
  Woodridge *(G-21277)*
Canada Organization & Dev LLC .....G 630 743-2563
  Downers Grove *(G-7965)*
Century Fasteners & Mch Co Inc ......F 773 463-3900
  Skokie *(G-18939)*
Cool Fluidics Inc ....G 815 861-4063
  Woodstock *(G-21376)*
Corken Inc ....D 405 946-5576
  Lake Bluff *(G-12177)*
CTS Advanced Materials LLC ....E 630 577-8800
  Lisle *(G-12879)*
Dover Pmps Prcess Sltons Sgmen ...E 630 487-2240
  Oakbrook Terrace *(G-15796)*
Emco Wheaton Usa Inc ....E 217 222-5400
  Quincy *(G-16879)*
Engineered Fluid Inc ....C 618 533-1351
  Centralia *(G-3230)*
Engineered Fluid Inc ....D 618 533-1351
  Centralia *(G-3231)*
Evac North America Inc ....E 815 654-8300
  Cherry Valley *(G-3439)*
FH Ayer Manufacturing Co ....E 708 755-0550
  Chicago Heights *(G-6746)*
Flow Control US Holding Corp ....F 630 307-3000
  Hanover Park *(G-11005)*
Flowserve Corporation ....E 630 762-4100
  West Chicago *(G-20586)*
Flowserve Corporation ....E 630 543-4240
  Addison *(G-126)*
Flowserve Corporation ....E 630 435-9596
  Lombard *(G-13076)*
Flowserve US Inc ....D 630 783-1468
  Woodridge *(G-21301)*
Fluid Handling LLC ....B 773 267-1600
  Morton Grove *(G-14408)*
Fna Ip Holdings Inc ....D 847 348-1500
  Elk Grove Village *(G-9001)*
Fura Inc ....G 847 451-0000
  Franklin Park *(G-9946)*
Goulds Pumps LLC ....F 708 563-1220
  Bedford Park *(G-1468)*
Graymills Corporation ....D 773 477-4100
  Broadview *(G-2439)*
Grundfos CBS Inc ....F 331 401-0057
  Aurora *(G-975)*
Heidolph NA LLC ....F 224 265-9600
  Wood Dale *(G-21197)*
Hidrostal LLC ....F 630 240-6271
  Aurora *(G-979)*
ITT Water & Wastewater USA Inc ....F 708 342-0484
  Tinley Park *(G-19840)*
Lubeq Corporation ....F 847 931-1020
  Elgin *(G-8642)*
Mechanical Engineering Pdts ....G 312 421-3375
  Chicago *(G-5380)*
Midwest Fuel Injction Svc Corp ....F 847 991-7867
  Palatine *(G-16140)*
O Adjust Matic Pump Company ....G 630 766-1490
  Wood Dale *(G-21224)*
Pentair Flow Technologies LLC ....C 630 859-7000
  North Aurora *(G-15269)*
Pump House ....G 618 216-2404
  Wood River *(G-21266)*
Roth Pump Company ....E 309 787-1791
  Milan *(G-14027)*
S C C Pumps Inc ....F 847 593-8495
  Arlington Heights *(G-803)*
Sielc Technologies Corporation ....G 847 229-2629
  Wheeling *(G-20985)*
Spirax Sarco Inc ....F 630 493-4525
  Lisle *(G-12940)*
Sulzer Pump Services (us) Inc ....F 815 600-7355
  Joliet *(G-11934)*
Thomas Pump Company ....F 630 851-9393
  Aurora *(G-1023)*
Trane Technologies Company LLC ..E 704 655-4000
  Chicago *(G-6406)*
Trusty Warns Inc ....E 630 766-9015
  Wood Dale *(G-21253)*
Tuthill Corporation ....E 630 382-4900
  Burr Ridge *(G-2727)*
Wagner Pump & Supply Co Inc ....G 847 526-8573
  Wauconda *(G-20401)*
Xylem Inc ....D 847 966-3700
  Morton Grove *(G-14450)*
Yamada America Inc ....E 847 228-9063
  Arlington Heights *(G-838)*

PUMPS & PARTS: Indl

Ergoseal Inc ....E 630 462-9600
  Carol Stream *(G-2981)*
Guzzler Manufacturing Inc ....C 815 672-3171
  Streator *(G-19610)*
Idex Corporation ....C 847 498-7070
  Lake Forest *(G-12265)*
Inman Electric Motors Inc ....E 815 223-2288
  La Salle *(G-12115)*
Jn Pump Holdings Inc ....F 708 754-2940
  Chicago Heights *(G-6753)*
Johnson Pumps America Inc ....E 847 671-7867
  Rockford *(G-17477)*
March Manufacturing Inc ....D 847 729-5300
  Glenview *(G-10587)*
Murdock Company Inc ....G 847 566-0050
  Mundelein *(G-14719)*
Omni Pump Repairs Inc ....F 847 451-0000
  Franklin Park *(G-10011)*
R S Corcoran Co ....E 815 485-2156
  New Lenox *(G-15054)*
Ruthman Pump and Engineering ......G 708 754-2940
  Chicago Heights *(G-6773)*
Tramco Pump Co ....E 312 243-5800
  Romeoville *(G-17881)*
Tuskin Equipment Corporation ....G 630 466-5590
  Sugar Grove *(G-19658)*
W S Darley & Co ....F 630 735-3500
  Itasca *(G-11752)*

PUMPS & PUMPING EQPT REPAIR SVCS

Accurate Elc Mtr & Pump Co ....G 708 448-2792
  Worth *(G-21453)*
All Electric Mtr Repr Svc Inc ....F 773 925-2404
  Chicago *(G-3609)*
Basement Flood Protector Inc ....F 847 438-6770
  Lake Zurich *(G-12387)*
Fluid Pump Service Inc ....G 847 228-0750
  Elk Grove Village *(G-9000)*
Metropolitan Industries Inc ....C 815 886-9200
  Romeoville *(G-17851)*
Omni Pump Repairs Inc ....F 847 451-0000
  Franklin Park *(G-10011)*

PUMPS & PUMPING EQPT WHOLESALERS

A-L-L Equipment Company ....G 815 877-7000
  Loves Park *(G-13181)*
All Electric Mtr Repr Svc Inc ....F 773 925-2404
  Chicago *(G-3609)*
Coe Equipment Inc ....G 217 498-7200
  Rochester *(G-17164)*
Fluid Pump Service Inc ....G 847 228-0750
  Elk Grove Village *(G-9000)*
Grundfos Water Utility Inc ....D 630 236-5500
  Aurora *(G-976)*
Johnson Pumps America Inc ....E 847 671-7867
  Rockford *(G-17477)*
Murdock Company Inc ....G 847 566-0050
  Mundelein *(G-14719)*
Pump House ....G 618 216-2404
  Wood River *(G-21266)*
Roy E Roth Company ....G 309 787-1791
  Milan *(G-14028)*
Thomas Pump Company ....F 630 851-9393
  Aurora *(G-1023)*
Wagner Pump & Supply Co Inc ....G 847 526-8573
  Wauconda *(G-20401)*
Yamada America Inc ....E 847 228-9063
  Arlington Heights *(G-838)*

PUMPS: Domestic, Water Or Sump

Basement Flood Protector Inc ....F 847 438-6770
  Lake Zurich *(G-12387)*
Gardner Denver Inc ....E 800 231-3628
  Quincy *(G-16885)*
Georgetown Waste Water ....G 217 662-2525
  Georgetown *(G-10326)*
Nexpump Inc ....G 630 365-4639
  Elburn *(G-8464)*
S-P-D Incorporated ....G 847 882-9820
  Palatine *(G-16156)*

PRODUCT SECTION

Swaby Manufacturing Company ....G...... 773 626-1400
  Chicago (G-6292)
Tacmina USA Corporation.................G...... 312 810-8128
  Schaumburg (G-18736)
Unique Indoor Comfort........................F...... 847 362-1910
  Libertyville (G-12719)

PUMPS: Fluid Power

Ifh Group Inc ....D...... 800 435-7003
  Rock Falls (G-17187)
Ifh Group Inc ....G...... 815 380-2367
  Galt (G-10225)
Parker-Hannifin Corporation..............C...... 847 955-5000
  Lincolnshire (G-12792)

PUMPS: Gasoline, Measuring Or Dispensing

Franklin Fueling Systems Inc ....F...... 207 283-0156
  Chicago (G-4631)
Tuthill Corporation ....E...... 630 382-4900
  Burr Ridge (G-2727)

PUMPS: Hydraulic Power Transfer

Brock Equipment Company ....E...... 815 459-4210
  Woodstock (G-21367)
Bucher Hydraulics Inc ....G...... 847 429-0700
  Elgin (G-8526)
Mandus Group LLC ....F...... 309 786-1507
  Rock Island (G-17228)
Mechanical Tool & Engrg Co ....C...... 815 397-4701
  Rockford (G-17513)
Mechanical Tool & Engrg Co ....C...... 815 397-4701
  Rockford (G-17514)
Rehobot Inc ....G...... 815 385-7777
  McHenry (G-13786)
Settima Usa Inc ....G...... 630 812-1433
  Wood Dale (G-21240)

PUMPS: Measuring & Dispensing

Cornelius Inc ....B...... 630 539-6850
  Glendale Heights (G-10445)
Dover Corporation ....C...... 630 541-1540
  Downers Grove (G-7989)
Dromont Corporation ....G...... 404 615-2336
  Palatine (G-16114)
Gfi Innovations LLC ....G...... 847 263-9000
  Antioch (G-612)
March Manufacturing Inc ....D...... 847 729-5300
  Glenview (G-10587)

PUMPS: Oil Well & Field

Gas Compression Systems Inc ....F...... 630 766-6049
  Bensenville (G-1807)

PUMPS: Oil, Measuring Or Dispensing

Standard Lifts & Equipment Inc ....G...... 414 444-1000
  Hanover Park (G-11015)

PUMPS: Vacuum, Exc Laboratory

J/B Industries Inc ....D...... 630 851-9444
  Aurora (G-1115)

PUNCHES: Forming & Stamping

Accurate Grinding Co Inc ....G...... 708 371-1887
  Posen (G-16790)
Emt International Inc ....G...... 630 655-4145
  Westmont (G-20741)
Ever Ready Pin & Manufacturing ......D...... 815 874-4949
  Rockford (G-17403)

PURIFICATION & DUST COLLECTION EQPT

Bisco Enterprise Inc ....F...... 630 628-1831
  Schaumburg (G-18463)
Donaldson Company Inc ....E...... 815 288-3374
  Dixon (G-7898)
Robuschi Usa Inc ....G...... 704 424-1018
  Quincy (G-16942)

PUSHCARTS

Smart Solar Inc ....F...... 813 343-5770
  Libertyville (G-12708)

PUSHCARTS & WHEELBARROWS

Brennan Equipment and Mfg Inc ......D...... 708 534-5500
  University Park (G-19950)

PYROMETER TUBES

C & L Manufacturing Entps ....G...... 618 465-7623
  Alton (G-546)

QUARTZ CRYSTAL MINING SVCS

Covia Holdings Corporation ....G...... 618 747-2355
  Tamms (G-19742)

QUILTING SVC & SPLYS, FOR THE TRADE

Quiltmaster Inc ....E...... 847 426-6741
  Carpentersville (G-3117)

RACE CAR OWNERS

R/A Hoerr Inc ....E...... 309 691-8789
  Edwards (G-8340)

RACE TRACK OPERATION

Lanigan Holdings LLC ....F...... 708 596-5200
  Hazel Crest (G-11132)

RACETRACKS

Mike Mulcahy Motorsports LLC ....G...... 630 567-0298
  Morris (G-14315)

RACEWAYS

Dells Raceway Park Inc ....G...... 815 494-0074
  Roscoe (G-17903)
Southern IL Raceway ....G...... 618 201-0500
  Marion (G-13536)
Windy City RC ....G...... 847 818-8354
  Arlington Heights (G-834)

RACKS: Bicycle, Automotive

Treetop Marketing Inc ....G...... 877 249-0479
  Batavia (G-1433)

RACKS: Display

Astoria Wire Products Inc ....D...... 708 496-9950
  Bedford Park (G-1459)
B-O-F Corporation ....E...... 630 585-0020
  Aurora (G-921)
Bunzl Retail LLC ....F...... 847 733-1469
  Morton Grove (G-14392)
Illinois Rack Enterprises Inc ....E...... 815 385-5750
  Lakemoor (G-12472)
Jet Rack Corp ....E...... 773 586-2150
  Chicago (G-5025)
John H Best & Sons Inc ....E...... 309 932-2124
  Galva (G-10234)
Keystone Display Inc ....G...... 815 648-2456
  Hebron (G-11144)
Material Control Systems Inc ....D...... 309 523-3774
  East Moline (G-8233)
Material Control Systems Inc ....G...... 309 654-9031
  Cordova (G-7009)
Nycor Products Inc ....G...... 815 727-9883
  Joliet (G-11910)
Rack Builders Inc ....G...... 217 214-9482
  Quincy (G-16937)
Ryan Metal Products Inc ....E...... 815 936-0700
  Kankakee (G-12000)
Yetter Manufacturing Company ....D...... 309 776-3222
  Colchester (G-6948)

RACKS: Magazine, Wood

Innovative Fix Solutions LLC ....D...... 815 395-8500
  Rockford (G-17466)

RACKS: Pallet, Exc Wood

Room Dividers Now LLC ....G...... 847 224-7900
  Barrington (G-1242)

RACKS: Railroad Car, Vehicle Transportation, Steel

Ireco LLC ....F...... 630 741-0155
  Elmhurst (G-9380)

RACKS: Trash, Metal Rack

Ideal Fabricators Inc ....F...... 217 999-7017
  Mount Olive (G-14505)

RADIO & TELEVISION COMMUNICATIONS EQUIPMENT

RADAR SYSTEMS & EQPT

Motorola Solutions Inc ....C...... 847 576-8600
  Schaumburg (G-18637)

RADIATORS: Stationary Engine

Diesel Radiator Co ....C...... 800 345-9244
  Melrose Park (G-13851)
Diesel Radiator Co ....D...... 708 865-7299
  Melrose Park (G-13852)

RADIO & TELEVISION COMMUNICATIONS EQUIPMENT

Ale USA Inc ....G...... 630 713-5194
  Naperville (G-14770)
Allcom Products Illinois LLC ....E...... 847 468-8830
  South Elgin (G-19131)
Andrew Systems Inc ....E...... 708 873-3855
  Orland Park (G-15941)
AVI-Spl Employee ....B...... 847 437-7712
  Schaumburg (G-18453)
Cco Holdings LLC ....G...... 618 505-3505
  Troy (G-19912)
Cco Holdings LLC ....G...... 618 651-6486
  Highland (G-11208)
Coleman Cable LLC ....D...... 847 672-2300
  Lincolnshire (G-12753)
Colt Technology Services LLC ....F...... 312 465-2484
  Chicago (G-4205)
Commscope Inc North Carolina ....C...... 779 435-6000
  Joliet (G-11843)
Commscope Connectivity LLC ....F...... 779 435-6000
  Joliet (G-11844)
Commscope Solutions Intl Inc ....G...... 828 324-2200
  Westchester (G-20695)
Commscope Technologies LLC ....G...... 847 397-6307
  Schaumburg (G-18481)
D W Ram Manufacturing Co ....E...... 708 633-7900
  Tinley Park (G-19821)
Driver Services ....G...... 505 267-8686
  Bensenville (G-1789)
Easy Trac Gps Inc ....G...... 630 359-5804
  Chicago (G-4436)
Elite Rf LLC ....E...... 847 592-6350
  Hoffman Estates (G-11420)
FSI Technologies Inc ....E...... 630 932-9380
  Lombard (G-13080)
Gatesair Inc ....G...... 800 622-0022
  Quincy (G-16886)
Gogo Intermediate Holdings LLC .....G...... 630 647-1400
  Chicago (G-4710)
Heil Sound Ltd ....F...... 618 257-3000
  Fairview Heights (G-9646)
Huawei Technologies USA Inc ....G...... 425 463-8275
  Rolling Meadows (G-17735)
Inclusion Solutions LLC ....G...... 847 869-2500
  Evanston (G-9537)
Jklein Enterprises Inc ....G...... 618 664-4554
  Greenville (G-10836)
L3 Technologies Inc ....F...... 212 697-1111
  Rolling Meadows (G-17747)
Langham Engineering ....G...... 815 223-5250
  Peru (G-16580)
Latino Arts & Communications ....G...... 773 501-0029
  Chicago (G-5180)
Motorola Intl Dev Corp ....E...... 847 576-5000
  Schaumburg (G-18635)
Motorola Mobility LLC ....F...... 847 576-5000
  Chicago (G-5509)
Motorola Solutions Inc ....G...... 847 341-3485
  Oak Brook (G-15647)
Motorola Solutions Inc ....G...... 217 894-6451
  Clayton (G-6910)
Motorola Solutions Inc ....E...... 847 523-5000
  Libertyville (G-12683)
Motorola Solutions Inc ....C...... 630 308-9394
  Schaumburg (G-18636)
Motorola Solutions Inc ....G...... 630 353-8000
  Downers Grove (G-8061)
Motorola Solutions Inc ....G...... 847 523-5000
  Libertyville (G-12684)
Motorola Solutions Inc ....C...... 847 540-8815
  Arlington Heights (G-779)
Motorola Solutions Inc ....G...... 847 523-5000
  Libertyville (G-12685)
Motorola Solutions Inc ....C...... 708 476-8226
  Schaumburg (G-18638)
Motorola Solutions Inc ....C...... 800 331-6456
  Schaumburg (G-18639)

Employee Codes: A=Over 500 employees, B=251-500
C=101-250, D=51-100, E=20-50, F=10-19, G=3-9

RADIO & TELEVISION COMMUNICATIONS EQUIPMENT

Motorola Solutions Inc ....C...... 847 576-5000
  Elgin *(G-8665)*
Othernet Inc ....G...... 773 688-4320
  Long Grove *(G-13168)*
Radio Frequency Systems Inc ....E...... 800 321-4700
  Naperville *(G-14906)*
Ram Systems & Communication ....G...... 847 487-7575
  McHenry *(G-13785)*
Ruckus Wireless Inc ....E...... 630 281-3000
  Lisle *(G-12935)*
Spectrum Cos International ....G...... 630 879-8008
  Batavia *(G-1418)*
Studio Technologies Inc ....F...... 847 676-9177
  Skokie *(G-19038)*
Switchcraft Inc ....B...... 773 792-2700
  Chicago *(G-6299)*
Switchcraft Holdco Inc ....G...... 773 792-2700
  Chicago *(G-6300)*
Talk-A-Phone LLC ....D...... 773 539-1100
  Niles *(G-15178)*
Twr3 Inc ....G...... 847 784-5251
  Northfield *(G-15536)*

RADIO & TELEVISION RECEIVER INSTALLATION SVCS

Jklein Enterprises Inc ....G...... 618 664-4554
  Greenville *(G-10836)*

RADIO & TELEVISION REPAIR

A J R International Inc ....D...... 800 232-3965
  Glendale Heights *(G-10435)*

RADIO BROADCASTING & COMMUNICATIONS EQPT

BEI Holding Corporation ....G...... 217 224-9600
  Quincy *(G-16864)*
Broadcast Electronics Inc ....C...... 217 224-9600
  Quincy *(G-16869)*
Motorola Solutions Inc ....C...... 847 576-5000
  Chicago *(G-5511)*
Northrop Grumman Systems Corp ..A...... 847 259-9600
  Rolling Meadows *(G-17755)*
Progressive Concepts ....G...... 630 736-9822
  Streamwood *(G-19590)*
Temco Japan Co Ltd ....G...... 847 359-3277
  South Barrington *(G-19078)*

RADIO BROADCASTING MUSIC CHECKERS

Power102jamz ....G...... 312 912-2766
  Urbana *(G-19994)*

RADIO BROADCASTING STATIONS

Abc Inc ....E...... 312 980-1000
  Chicago *(G-3506)*
Bond Broadcasting Inc ....F...... 618 664-3300
  Greenville *(G-10828)*
E & R Media LLC ....F...... 618 790-9376
  Du Quoin *(G-8119)*
Illini Media Co ....B...... 217 337-8300
  Champaign *(G-3306)*
Moody Bible Inst of Chicago ....A...... 312 329-4000
  Chicago *(G-5495)*
W G N Radio Mass Calling ....G...... 312 591-7200
  Chicago *(G-6574)*
Wnta Studio Line ....G...... 815 874-7861
  Rockford *(G-17689)*

RADIO COMMUNICATIONS: Airborne Eqpt

Boeing Company ....C...... 312 544-2000
  Chicago *(G-3925)*
Boeing Irving Company ....A...... 312 544-2000
  Chicago *(G-3928)*

RADIO COMMUNICATIONS: Carrier Eqpt

Invisio Communications Inc ....G...... 412 327-6578
  Chicago *(G-4965)*

RADIO RECEIVER NETWORKS

Iheartcommunications Inc ....E...... 312 255-5100
  Chicago *(G-4882)*
Isco International Inc ....G...... 630 283-3100
  Schaumburg *(G-18572)*
Saga Communications Inc ....G...... 248 631-8099
  Springfield *(G-19438)*

State of Illinois ....C...... 312 836-9500
  Chicago *(G-6235)*

RADIO RECEIVING SETS

Othernet Inc ....G...... 773 688-4320
  Long Grove *(G-13168)*

RADIO REPAIR SHOP, NEC

Midtronics Inc ....D...... 630 323-2800
  Willowbrook *(G-21050)*

RADIO, TELEVISION & CONSUMER ELECTRONICS STORES: Eqpt, NEC

Coles Appliance & Furn Co ....G...... 773 525-1797
  Chicago *(G-4199)*

RADIO, TV & CONSUMER ELEC STORES: Automotive Sound Eqpt

Elm Street Industries Inc ....F...... 309 854-7000
  Kewanee *(G-12032)*

RADIO, TV & CONSUMER ELEC STORES: High Fidelity Stereo Eqpt

Bose Corporation ....G...... 630 575-8044
  Hinsdale *(G-11366)*
Bose Corporation ....G...... 630 585-6654
  Aurora *(G-924)*
Good Vibes Sound Inc ....F...... 217 351-0909
  Champaign *(G-3298)*
Sound Design Inc ....G...... 630 548-7000
  Plainfield *(G-16715)*

RADIO, TV/CONSUMER ELEC STORES: Antennas, Satellite Dish

Jklein Enterprises Inc ....G...... 618 664-4554
  Greenville *(G-10836)*

RAIL & STRUCTURAL SHAPES: Aluminum rail & structural shapes

Meyer Metal Systems Inc ....F...... 847 468-0500
  Elgin *(G-8659)*

RAILINGS: Prefabricated, Metal

K Three Welding Service Inc ....G...... 708 563-2911
  Chicago *(G-5067)*
Patrick Holdings Inc ....F...... 815 874-5300
  Rockford *(G-17549)*

RAILINGS: Wood

Middletons Mouldings Inc ....D...... 517 278-6610
  Schaumburg *(G-18629)*

RAILROAD CAR RENTING & LEASING SVCS

Chicago Freight Car Leasing Co ....D...... 847 318-8000
  Schaumburg *(G-18475)*
Marmon Holdings Inc ....D...... 312 372-9500
  Chicago *(G-5343)*
Marmon Industrial LLC ....D...... 312 372-9500
  Chicago *(G-5344)*
Union Tank Car Company ....C...... 312 431-3111
  Chicago *(G-6466)*
UTC Railcar Repair Svcs LLC ....A...... 312 431-5053
  Chicago *(G-6508)*

RAILROAD CAR REPAIR SVCS

Freight Car Services Inc ....B...... 217 443-4106
  Danville *(G-7336)*
Transco Railway Products Inc ....G...... 312 427-2818
  Chicago *(G-6409)*
Union Tank Car Company ....C...... 312 431-3111
  Chicago *(G-6466)*
UTC Railcar Repair Svcs LLC ....A...... 312 431-5053
  Chicago *(G-6508)*

RAILROAD CARGO LOADING & UNLOADING SVCS

Bison Gear & Engineering Corp .....C...... 630 377-4327
  Saint Charles *(G-18156)*
Blue Comet Transport Inc ....G...... 773 617-9512
  Chicago *(G-3913)*

Global Technologies I LLC ....D...... 312 255-8350
  Chicago *(G-4699)*
Quad-Illinois Inc ....F...... 847 836-1115
  Elgin *(G-8706)*
Robinsport LLC ....G...... 630 724-9280
  Woodridge *(G-21337)*

RAILROAD EQPT

A & S Steel Specialties Inc ....E...... 815 838-8188
  Lockport *(G-12979)*
Aldon Co ....F...... 847 623-8800
  Waukegan *(G-20412)*
Alliance Wheel Services LLC ....G...... 309 444-4334
  Washington *(G-20265)*
Amsted Rail Company Inc ....D...... 312 258-8000
  Chicago *(G-3688)*
Amsted Rail Company Inc ....A...... 618 452-2111
  Granite City *(G-10695)*
Amsted Rail Company Inc ....B...... 618 225-6463
  Granite City *(G-10696)*
Anchor Brake Shoe Company LLC ..F...... 630 293-1110
  West Chicago *(G-20541)*
Clark Industrial Prpts Inc ....G...... 815 265-7210
  Gilman *(G-10377)*
Fugiel Railroad Supply Corp ....G...... 847 516-6862
  Cary *(G-3160)*
Holden America II LLC ....G...... 708 552-4070
  Chicago *(G-4829)*
Holland LP ....G...... 708 672-2300
  Crete *(G-7140)*
Illini Castings LLC ....F...... 217 446-6365
  Danville *(G-7349)*
Maclean Fastener Services LLC ....G...... 847 353-8402
  Buffalo Grove *(G-2566)*
Meadoweld Machine Inc ....G...... 815 623-3939
  South Beloit *(G-19102)*
Midland Railway Supply Inc ....E...... 618 467-6305
  Godfrey *(G-10657)*
Midwest Railcar Corporation ....E...... 618 692-5575
  Edwardsville *(G-8371)*
MWK Rail LLC ....G...... 815 671-5217
  Urbana *(G-19989)*
National Railway Equipment Co ....D...... 708 388-4781
  Dixmoor *(G-7884)*
National Railway Equipment Co ....E...... 708 388-6002
  Dixmoor *(G-7885)*
National Trackwork Inc ....E...... 630 250-0600
  Itasca *(G-11708)*
Nordco Inc ....E...... 414 766-2180
  Arcola *(G-660)*
Pintsch Tiefenbach Us Inc ....E...... 618 993-8513
  Marion *(G-13527)*
Progress Rail Services Corp ....E...... 618 451-0072
  Granite City *(G-10734)*
Progress Rail Services Corp ....F...... 309 343-6176
  Galesburg *(G-10216)*
Ramptech Inc ....E...... 303 936-3641
  Chicago *(G-5966)*
Ramptech Inc ....E...... 708 594-2179
  Chicago *(G-5967)*
Right Rail LLC ....G...... 630 882-9335
  Yorkville *(G-21500)*
Salco Products Inc ....D...... 630 783-2570
  Lemont *(G-12588)*
Transco Railway Products Inc ....G...... 312 427-2818
  Chicago *(G-6409)*
Voestalpine Nortrak Inc ....D...... 217 876-9160
  Decatur *(G-7567)*
Voestalpine Nortrak Inc ....D...... 708 753-2125
  Chicago Heights *(G-6786)*
Wallace Industries Inc ....G...... 815 389-8999
  South Beloit *(G-19119)*
Western Railway Devices Corp ......G...... 847 625-8500
  Lake Bluff *(G-12216)*
Western-Cullen-Hayes Inc ....D...... 773 254-9600
  Chicago *(G-6609)*
Whiting Corporation ....C...... 800 861-5744
  Monee *(G-14212)*
Willims-Hyward Intl Ctings Inc ......F...... 708 458-0015
  Argo *(G-678)*

RAILROAD EQPT & SPLYS WHOLESALERS

Anchor Brake Shoe Company LLC ..F...... 630 293-1110
  West Chicago *(G-20541)*
Fugiel Railroad Supply Corp ....G...... 847 516-6862
  Cary *(G-3160)*
Midland Railway Supply Inc ....E...... 618 467-6305
  Godfrey *(G-10657)*
National Railway Equipment Co ....G...... 618 241-9270
  Mount Vernon *(G-14630)*

PRODUCT SECTION

National Railway Equipment Co .... C 309 755-6800
  Silvis (G-18908)
Railway & Industrial Svcs Inc .... C 815 726-4224
  Crest Hill (G-7094)
Relco Locomotives Inc .... D 630 968-0670
  Burr Ridge (G-2716)
Salco Products Inc .... D 630 783-2570
  Lemont (G-12588)
Western Railway Devices Corp .... G 847 625-8500
  Lake Bluff (G-12216)

RAILROAD EQPT, EXC LOCOMOTIVES

Teleweld Inc .... F 815 672-4561
  Streator (G-19629)

RAILROAD EQPT: Brakes, Air & Vacuum

Standard Car Truck Company .... D 630 860-5511
  Bensenville (G-1899)

RAILROAD EQPT: Cars & Eqpt, Dining

Amsted Industries Incorporated .... B 312 645-1700
  Chicago (G-3685)
Cardwell Westinghouse Company .... D 773 483-7575
  Chicago (G-4027)
Eagle Freight Inc .... G 708 202-0651
  Franklin Park (G-9935)
Kevin Robinson .... G 618 410-3083
  Caseyville (G-3217)
Prairie Island Inc .... G 630 395-9846
  Westmont (G-20767)
Russell Enterprises Inc .... B 847 692-6050
  Park Ridge (G-16295)
Standard Car Truck Company .... E 847 692-6050
  Rosemont (G-18051)

RAILROAD EQPT: Cars & Eqpt, Train, Freight Or Passenger

Freightcar America Inc .... D 800 458-2235
  Chicago (G-4635)
Narita Manufacturing Inc .... F 248 345-1777
  Belvidere (G-1688)
Nis Express Inc .... G 708 880-4090
  Hickory Hills (G-11201)
Seec Trasportation Corp .... G 800 215-4003
  Chicago (G-6132)
Union Tank Car Company .... C 312 431-3111
  Chicago (G-6466)
Union Tank Car Company .... G 815 942-7391
  Morris (G-14336)
Union Tank Car Company .... C 312 431-3111
  Chicago (G-6467)

RAILROAD EQPT: Cars, Maintenance

Creative RIcar Mktg Svcs II LL .... G 773 396-1114
  Chicago (G-4266)
Creative RIcar Mktg Svcs II LL .... G 773 396-1114
  Chicago (G-4267)

RAILROAD EQPT: Cars, Motor

Marmon Holdings Inc .... D 312 372-9500
  Chicago (G-5343)
Marmon Industrial LLC .... G 312 372-9500
  Chicago (G-5344)

RAILROAD EQPT: Cars, Rebuilt

Freight Car Services Inc .... B 217 443-4106
  Danville (G-7336)
Gateway Rail Services Inc .... F 618 451-0100
  Madison (G-13412)
Illinois Transit Assembly Corp .... F 618 451-0100
  Madison (G-13415)
Jaix Leasing Company .... G 312 928-0850
  Chicago (G-5000)
Railway & Industrial Svcs Inc .... C 815 726-4224
  Crest Hill (G-7094)
Railway Program Services Inc .... G 708 552-4000
  Chicago (G-5964)
Rescar Companies Inc .... G 618 875-3234
  East Saint Louis (G-8320)
UTC Railcar Repair Svcs LLC .... A 312 431-5053
  Chicago (G-6508)

RAILROAD EQPT: Locomotives & Parts, Electric Or Nonelectric

Amfab LLC .... G 630 783-2570
  Lemont (G-12553)
Precision Screw Machining Co .... F 773 205-4280
  Chicago (G-5859)
Professional RR Solutions LLC .... G 815 209-7473
  Roscoe (G-17922)
Rail Exchange Inc .... E 708 757-3317
  Chicago Heights (G-6767)

RAILROAD MAINTENANCE & REPAIR SVCS

Progress Rail Services Corp .... E 309 963-4425
  Danvers (G-7317)

RAILROAD RELATED EQPT: Ballast Distributors

Lamination Specialties LLC .... E 312 243-2181
  Oak Brook (G-15631)

RAILROAD RELATED EQPT: Railway Track

Metrom Rail LLC .... E 855 943-8726
  Crystal Lake (G-7227)
Mineral Products Inc .... G 618 433-3150
  Harrisburg (G-11026)
Teleweld Inc .... F 815 672-4561
  Streator (G-19629)
U S Railway Services .... G 708 468-8343
  Tinley Park (G-19864)

RAILROADS: Long Haul

Hauhinco LP .... E 618 993-5399
  Marion (G-13514)

RAILS: Elevator, Guide

Otis Elevator Company .... D 312 454-1616
  Chicago (G-5712)

RAILS: Steel Or Iron

Illinois Engineered Pdts Inc .... E 312 850-3710
  Chicago (G-4889)

RAMPS: Prefabricated Metal

Rampnow LLC .... G 630 892-7267
  Montgomery (G-14266)
Tandem Industries Inc .... G 630 761-6615
  Saint Charles (G-18285)

RAZORS, RAZOR BLADES

Art of Shaving - Fl LLC .... G 630 495-7316
  Lombard (G-13040)
Art of Shaving - Fl LLC .... G 312 527-1604
  Chicago (G-3737)
Art of Shaving - Fl LLC .... G 630 684-0277
  Oak Brook (G-15594)
Edgewell Per Care Brands LLC .... B 708 544-5550
  Melrose Park (G-13861)
Gillette Company .... D 847 689-3111
  North Chicago (G-15312)
Procter & Gamble Company .... G 847 375-5400
  Chicago (G-5892)

REAL ESTATE AGENCIES & BROKERS

Equity Concepts Co Inc .... G 815 226-1300
  Rockford (G-17399)

REAL ESTATE AGENCIES: Residential

Midwest Mktg/Pdctn Mfg Co .... G 217 256-3414
  Warsaw (G-20258)

REAL ESTATE AGENTS & MANAGERS

Basement Dewatering Systems .... F 309 647-0331
  Canton (G-2821)
Brokerassist LLC .... G 847 858-2357
  River Forest (G-17050)
Digital Realty Inc .... E 630 428-7979
  Naperville (G-14817)
John C Grafft .... F 847 842-9200
  Lake Barrington (G-12153)
State of Illinois .... C 312 836-9500
  Chicago (G-6235)

Terra Cotta Holdings Co .... E 815 459-2400
  Crystal Lake (G-7281)

REAL ESTATE FIDUCIARIES' OFFICES

Caterpillar Inc .... A 224 551-4000
  Deerfield (G-7600)
Caterpillar Inc .... D 309 578-6118
  Mossville (G-14453)
Caterpillar Inc .... B 888 614-4328
  Peoria (G-16407)

REAL ESTATE INVESTMENT TRUSTS

Pilla Exec Inc .... G 312 882-8263
  Chicago (G-5807)

REAL ESTATE OPERATORS, EXC DEVELOPERS: Commercial/Indl Bldg

Galena Cellars Winery .... E 815 777-3330
  Galena (G-10169)
Grs Holding LLC .... F 630 355-1660
  Naperville (G-14838)
Ican Clinic LLC .... C 618 254-2273
  Wood River (G-21263)
Kitchens To Go LLC .... E 630 364-3083
  Naperville (G-14858)
MEI Realty Ltd .... G 847 358-5000
  Inverness (G-11597)
Parker International Pdts Inc .... D 815 524-5831
  Vernon Hills (G-20082)

REAL ESTATE OPERATORS, EXC DEVELOPERS: Property, Retail

Sign Centre .... G 847 595-7300
  Elk Grove Village (G-9239)

REAMERS

Precision Header Tooling Inc .... F 815 874-9116
  Rockford (G-17557)
Proto-Cutter Inc .... F 815 232-2300
  Freeport (G-10134)
Vhd Inc .... E 815 544-2169
  Belvidere (G-1708)

RECLAIMED RUBBER: Reworked By Manufacturing Process

RDF Inc .... F 618 273-4141
  Eldorado (G-8483)

RECORD BLANKS: Phonographic

Alligator Rec & Artist MGT Inc .... F 773 973-7736
  Chicago (G-3620)

RECORDING HEADS: Speech & Musical Eqpt

Sandes Quynetta .... G 815 275-4876
  Freeport (G-10140)

RECORDING TAPE: Video, Blank

Jvc Advanced Media USA Inc .... G 630 237-2439
  Schaumburg (G-18581)

RECORDS & TAPES: Prerecorded

Abbey Products LLP .... G 636 922-5577
  Troy (G-19909)
B D C Inc .... E 847 741-2233
  Elgin (G-8519)
BRANCh .... G 312 213-0138
  Chicago (G-3945)
Chicago Producers Inc .... F 312 226-6900
  Forest Park (G-9709)
Crusade Enterprises Inc .... G 618 662-4461
  Flora (G-9679)
Csiteq Studio LLC .... F 312 265-1509
  Rosemont (G-18012)
Drag City .... G 312 455-1015
  Chicago (G-4396)
Ev Interactive LLC .... G 847 907-4689
  Palatine (G-16118)
Fultonworks LLC .... G 312 544-9639
  Chicago (G-4642)
Lmno Technologies LLC .... G 773 418-2875
  Chicago (G-5246)
Modular Wood Systems Inc .... G 847 251-6401
  Wilmette (G-21088)

RECORDS & TAPES: Prerecorded

Private Studios..G........ 217 367-3530
 Urbana (G-19995)
Qsrsoft..G........ 630 995-9642
 Lombard (G-13124)
Replay S Disc Cook-Kankaee LLC........F........ 312 371-5018
 Monee (G-14207)
Sparrow Sound Design.............................G........ 773 281-8510
 Chicago (G-6209)
Towers Media Holdings Inc....................D........ 312 993-1550
 Northfield (G-15534)
United Cmra Binocular Repr LLC...........E........ 630 595-2525
 Elk Grove Village (G-9296)

RECOVERY SVC: Iron Ore, From Open Hearth Slag

Forge Resources Group LLC....................C........ 815 758-6400
 Dekalb (G-7679)
Forge Resources Group LLC....................C........ 815 758-6400
 Dekalb (G-7680)
Forge Resources Group LLC....................F........ 815 758-6400
 Dekalb (G-7681)
Mueller Company Plant 4..........................G........ 217 425-7424
 Decatur (G-7529)
Stein Inc...D........ 618 452-0836
 Granite City (G-10739)

RECOVERY SVCS: Metal

Borders Metals Recovery........................G........ 217 586-2501
 Mahomet (G-13422)
Precious Metal Ref Svcs Inc...................G........ 847 756-2700
 Barrington (G-1237)
Sunshine Metals Inc.................................G........ 304 422-0090
 Northbrook (G-15490)

RECREATIONAL CAMPS

I94 Rv LLC..F........ 847 395-9500
 Russell (G-18114)
Shale Lake LLC.......................................G........ 618 637-2470
 Staunton (G-19478)

RECREATIONAL DEALERS: Campers/Pickup Coaches Truck Mounted

Merritt Farm Equipment Inc....................G........ 217 746-5331
 Carthage (G-3138)

RECREATIONAL SPORTING EQPT REPAIR SVCS

Automated Design Corp............................G........ 630 783-1150
 Romeoville (G-17797)
Crown Gym Mats Inc................................F........ 847 381-8282
 Lake Barrington (G-12145)

RECREATIONAL VEHICLE DEALERS

Metroeast Motorsports Inc.......................G........ 618 628-2466
 O Fallon (G-15580)

RECREATIONAL VEHICLE PARTS & ACCESS STORES

Good Sam Enterprises LLC.....................E........ 847 229-6720
 Lincolnshire (G-12767)

RECREATIONAL VEHICLE REPAIRS

Merritt Farm Equipment Inc....................G........ 217 746-5331
 Carthage (G-3138)

RECTIFIERS: Electrical Apparatus

Electro-Matic Products Co........................F........ 773 235-4010
 Chicago (G-4477)

RECTIFIERS: Electronic, Exc Semiconductor

Ipr Systems Inc..G........ 708 385-7500
 Alsip (G-458)

RECYCLABLE SCRAP & WASTE MATERIALS WHOLESALERS

Galva Iron and Metal Co Inc...................G........ 309 932-3450
 Galva (G-10232)

RECYCLING: Paper

Better Earth LLC..G........ 844 243-6333
 Chicago (G-3874)

Better Earth Premium Compost..............G........ 309 697-0963
 Peoria (G-16392)
J & I Resources LLC................................E........ 773 436-4028
 Chicago (G-4983)
M J Kull LLC...G........ 217 246-5952
 Lerna (G-12614)
ND Fairmont LLC.......................................G........ 937 328-3870
 Oakbrook Terrace (G-15810)
Ohio Pulp Mills Inc...................................F........ 312 337-7822
 Chicago (G-5665)
Profile Products LLC.................................E........ 847 215-1144
 Buffalo Grove (G-2590)
R & J Trucking and Recycl Inc................F........ 708 563-2600
 Chicago (G-5943)
Regenex Corp..F........ 815 663-2003
 Spring Valley (G-19311)
Tri State Recycling Service.....................E........ 708 865-9939
 Northlake (G-15562)

REELS: Cable, Metal

Pmp Americas Inc....................................F........ 815 633-9962
 South Beloit (G-19107)

REFINERS & SMELTERS: Aluminum

Allied Metal Co..E........ 312 225-2800
 Chicago (G-3618)
National Material Company LLC.............G........ 773 468-2800
 Chicago (G-5546)
National Material Company LLC.............E........ 847 806-7200
 Elk Grove Village (G-9144)
Pontiac Recyclers Inc..............................G........ 815 844-6419
 Pontiac (G-16777)
Tower Metal Products LP........................G........ 847 806-7200
 Elk Grove Village (G-9280)
Trialco Inc..E........ 708 757-4200
 Chicago Heights (G-6781)

REFINERS & SMELTERS: Brass, Secondary

H Kramer & Co..C........ 312 226-6600
 Chicago (G-4759)
Sipi Metals Corp.......................................C........ 773 276-0070
 Chicago (G-6176)

REFINERS & SMELTERS: Copper

Cerro Flow Products LLC........................C........ 618 337-6000
 Sauget (G-18392)
Mahoney Foundries Inc...........................E........ 309 784-2311
 Vermont (G-20037)
Spot Welding Products Inc.....................F........ 630 238-0880
 Franklin Park (G-10051)

REFINERS & SMELTERS: Copper, Secondary

Global Brass and Copper Inc..................G........ 502 873-3000
 East Alton (G-8166)
Global Brass Cop Holdings Inc...............E........ 847 240-4700
 Schaumburg (G-18535)
Wieland Holdings Inc................................A........ 847 537-3990
 Wheeling (G-21013)

REFINERS & SMELTERS: Gold

Sipi Metals Corp.......................................C........ 773 276-0070
 Chicago (G-6176)

REFINERS & SMELTERS: Nonferrous Metal

Abco Metals Corporations........................F........ 773 881-1504
 Chicago (G-3509)
Alter Trading Corporation........................F........ 309 697-6161
 Bartonville (G-1327)
Alter Trading Corporation........................F........ 217 223-0156
 Quincy (G-16852)
Archer Metal & Paper Co.........................F........ 773 585-3030
 Chicago (G-3726)
Belson Steel Center Scrap Inc................E........ 815 932-7416
 Bourbonnais (G-2256)
BFI Waste Systems N Amer Inc..............E........ 847 429-7370
 Elgin (G-8521)
Big River Zinc Corporation.......................G........ 618 274-5000
 Sauget (G-18389)
Branchfield Casting Inc...........................G........ 309 932-2278
 Matherville (G-13614)
C & M Recycling Inc.................................E........ 847 578-1066
 North Chicago (G-15308)
C&R Scrap Iron & Metal..........................G........ 847 459-9815
 Wheeling (G-20868)
Cicero Iron Metal & Paper Inc.................G........ 708 863-8601
 Cicero (G-6834)

D R Sperry & Co.......................................D........ 630 892-4361
 Aurora (G-1083)
Dels Metal Co...F........ 309 788-1993
 Rock Island (G-17216)
Elg Metals Inc...E........ 773 374-1500
 Chicago (G-4484)
Fox Valley Iron & Metal Corp..................F........ 630 897-5907
 Aurora (G-1098)
Galva Iron and Metal Co Inc...................G........ 309 932-3450
 Galva (G-10232)
GM Scrap Metals......................................G........ 618 259-8570
 Cottage Hills (G-7028)
International Proc Co Amer....................E........ 847 437-8400
 Elk Grove Village (G-9058)
Lake Area Disposal Service Inc..............E........ 217 522-9271
 Springfield (G-19397)
Lemont Scrap Processing.......................G........ 630 257-6532
 Lemont (G-12569)
M Buckman & Son Co..............................G........ 815 663-9411
 Spring Valley (G-19309)
Mahoney Foundries Inc...........................E........ 309 784-2311
 Vermont (G-20037)
Mervis Industries Inc..............................G........ 217 235-5575
 Mattoon (G-13648)
Mervis Industries Inc..............................G........ 217 753-1492
 Springfield (G-19405)
Metal Management Inc............................E........ 773 721-1100
 Chicago (G-5405)
Metal Management Inc............................E........ 773 489-1800
 Chicago (G-5406)
Midland Davis Corporation.......................D........ 309 277-1617
 Moline (G-14161)
Midstate Salvage Corp.............................G........ 217 824-6047
 Taylorville (G-19759)
Midwest Fiber Inc Decatur.......................G........ 217 424-9460
 Decatur (G-7524)
Real Alloy Recycling LLC..........................D........ 708 757-8900
 Chicago Heights (G-6768)
Rondout Iron & Metal Co Inc..................G........ 847 362-2750
 Lake Bluff (G-12208)
S & S Metal Recyclers Inc.......................F........ 630 844-3344
 Aurora (G-1152)
Serlin Iron & Metal Co Inc.......................F........ 773 227-3826
 Chicago (G-6138)
Shapiro Bros of Illinois Inc.....................G........ 618 244-3168
 Mount Vernon (G-14638)
Springfield Iron & Metal Co.....................G........ 217 544-7131
 Springfield (G-19452)
T & C Metal Co...G........ 815 459-4445
 Crystal Lake (G-7274)
Tms International LLC.............................G........ 815 939-9460
 Bourbonnais (G-2271)
Top Metal Buyers Inc...............................F........ 314 421-2721
 East Saint Louis (G-8327)
Waukegan Architectural Inc....................G........ 847 746-9077
 Zion (G-21529)
Weco Trading Inc.....................................G........ 847 615-1020
 Lake Bluff (G-12215)

REFINERS & SMELTERS: Tin, Primary

RE Met Corp..G........ 312 733-6700
 Chicago (G-5981)

REFINING LUBRICATING OILS & GREASES, NEC

Houghton International Inc.....................F........ 610 666-4000
 Chicago (G-4849)
Lsp Industries Inc....................................F........ 815 226-8090
 Rockford (G-17497)
Lube Rite..G........ 217 267-7766
 Westville (G-20781)
Marathon Petroleum Company LP..........A........ 618 544-2121
 Robinson (G-17119)
Safety-Kleen Systems Inc.......................G........ 618 875-8050
 East Saint Louis (G-8321)

REFINING: Petroleum

4200 Kirchoff Corp...................................G........ 773 551-1541
 Rolling Meadows (G-17707)
Airgas Inc..F........ 773 785-3000
 Chicago (G-3588)
BP America Inc...A........ 630 420-5111
 Warrenville (G-20232)
BP Products North America Inc..............D........ 312 594-7689
 Chicago (G-3939)
Citation Oil & Gas Corp...........................E........ 618 966-2101
 Crossville (G-7150)
Citgo Petroleum Corporation..................G........ 847 818-1800
 Downers Grove (G-7970)

PRODUCT SECTION

REGISTERS: Air, Metal

Equilon Enterprises LLC .... F 312 733-1849
  Chicago *(G-4523)*
Exxonmobil Pipeline Company ..... F 815 423-5571
  Elwood *(G-9462)*
Koppers Industries Inc .... E 708 656-5900
  Cicero *(G-6859)*
Matheson Tri-Gas Inc .... E 815 727-2202
  Joliet *(G-11899)*
Murphy USA Inc .... G 847 245-3283
  Round Lake Beach *(G-18091)*
Murphy USA Inc .... G 815 356-7633
  Crystal Lake *(G-7235)*
Pdv Midwest Refining LLC .... A 630 257-7761
  Lemont *(G-12581)*
Premcor Incorporated .... G 618 254-7301
  Hartford *(G-11037)*
Raymond D Wright .... G 618 783-2206
  Newton *(G-15091)*
South West Oil Inc .... F 815 416-0400
  Morris *(G-14327)*
W R B Refinery LLC .... E 618 255-2345
  Roxana *(G-18104)*

REFRACTORIES: Clay

Bmi Products Northern Ill Inc ...... E 847 395-7110
  Antioch *(G-605)*
Great Lakes Clay & Supply Inc .... G 224 535-8127
  Elgin *(G-8601)*
Harbisonwalker Intl Inc .... G 708 474-5350
  Calumet City *(G-2779)*
Holland Manufacturing Corp .... E 708 849-1000
  Dolton *(G-7937)*
Thermal Ceramics Inc .... E 217 627-2101
  Girard *(G-10386)*
V J Mattson Company .... D 708 479-1990
  New Lenox *(G-15067)*

REFRACTORIES: Graphite, Carbon Or Ceramic Bond

Vesuvius U S A Corporation .... D 708 757-7880
  Chicago Heights *(G-6784)*
Vesuvius U S A Corporation .... C 217 897-1145
  Fisher *(G-9668)*
Vesuvius U S A Corporation .... C 217 345-7044
  Charleston *(G-3415)*

REFRACTORIES: Nonclay

Advanced Refr Instllation Tech .... F 847 741-3105
  Elgin *(G-8497)*
Gardner Asphalt Corporation ...... E 800 237-1155
  Chicago *(G-4659)*
Ipsen Inc .... E 815 239-2385
  Pecatonica *(G-16322)*
M H Detrick Company .... E 708 479-5085
  Frankfort *(G-9814)*
Magneco Inc .... D 630 543-6660
  Addison *(G-188)*
Magneco Inc .... G 630 543-6660
  Addison *(G-189)*
Miller Purcell Co Inc .... G 815 485-2142
  New Lenox *(G-15043)*
Plibrico Company LLC .... F 312 337-9000
  Northbrook *(G-15460)*
Vesuvius Crucible Company .... G 217 351-5000
  Champaign *(G-3365)*
Vesuvius U S A Corporation .... C 217 351-5000
  Champaign *(G-3366)*

REFRACTORY MATERIALS WHOLESALERS

Anderson Msnry Refr Spcialists .. G 847 540-8885
  Lake Zurich *(G-12384)*
Armil/Cfs Inc .... E 708 339-6810
  South Holland *(G-19198)*
Vesuvius U S A Corporation .... C 217 351-5000
  Champaign *(G-3366)*
Vesuvius U S A Corporation .... C 217 345-7044
  Charleston *(G-3415)*

REFRIGERATION & HEATING EQUIPMENT

Amsted Industries Incorporated .. B 312 645-1700
  Chicago *(G-3685)*
Bevstream Corp .... G 630 761-0060
  Batavia *(G-1357)*
Cerro Flow Products LLC .... C 618 337-6000
  Sauget *(G-18392)*
Chill Passion .... G 847 778-6121
  Schaumburg *(G-18476)*
Cisco Heating & Cooling .... G 309 637-6809
  Peoria *(G-16422)*
Clarios .... F 630 871-7700
  Carol Stream *(G-2961)*
Commercial Rfrgn Centl Ill Inc .... E 217 235-5016
  Mattoon *(G-13634)*
Continental Materials Corp .... F 312 541-7200
  Chicago *(G-4228)*
Danfoss LLC .... G 717 261-5000
  Loves Park *(G-13205)*
Dover Corporation .... C 630 541-1540
  Downers Grove *(G-7989)*
Elkay Manufacturing Company ... B 708 681-1880
  Broadview *(G-2434)*
Elkay Manufacturing Company ... B 815 273-7001
  Savanna *(G-18404)*
Gateway Industrial Power Inc ..... G 309 821-1035
  Bloomington *(G-2049)*
Goose Island Mfg & Supply Corp G 708 343-4225
  Lansing *(G-12495)*
H A Phillips & Co .... E 630 377-0050
  Dekalb *(G-7683)*
Habegger Corporation .... G 217 789-4328
  Springfield *(G-19377)*
Hohlflder A H Shtmtl Htg Coolg .. G 815 965-9134
  Rockford *(G-17451)*
ICC Intrntonal Celsius Concept .. G 773 993-4405
  Cicero *(G-6853)*
Illinois Tool Works Inc .... B 847 724-7500
  Glenview *(G-10560)*
Illinois Tool Works Inc .... C 630 372-2150
  Bartlett *(G-1288)*
Illinois Tool Works Inc .... C 847 783-5500
  Elgin *(G-8621)*
J D Refrigeration .... G 618 345-0041
  Collinsville *(G-6963)*
John Bean Technologies Corp ... D 312 861-5900
  Chicago *(G-5036)*
Kackert Enterprises Inc .... G 630 898-9339
  Aurora *(G-1120)*
Kap Holdings LLC .... F 708 948-0226
  Oak Park *(G-15759)*
Kkt Chillers Inc .... E 847 734-1600
  Wood Dale *(G-21204)*
Kool Technologies Inc .... G 630 483-2256
  Streamwood *(G-19581)*
Maid O Mist LLC .... E 773 685-7300
  Chicago *(G-5319)*
Marvin Schumaker Plbg Inc .... G 815 626-8130
  Sterling *(G-19516)*
Micro Matic Usa Inc .... F 815 968-7557
  Machesney Park *(G-13359)*
Polyscience Inc .... D 847 647-0611
  Niles *(G-15161)*
Quality Filter Services .... G 618 654-3716
  Highland *(G-11236)*
Raytheon Technologies Corp ..... B 815 226-6000
  Rockford *(G-17567)*
Ring Sheet Metal Heating & AC . G 309 289-4213
  Knoxville *(G-12069)*
Rukel Management LLC .... A 630 377-8886
  Saint Charles *(G-18262)*
Ruyle Incorporated .... E 309 674-6644
  Springfield *(G-19437)*
Standard Refrigeration LLC .... D 608 855-5800
  Wood Dale *(G-21242)*
Temp-Air Inc .... F 847 931-7700
  Elgin *(G-8751)*
Thermal Care Inc .... C 847 966-2260
  Niles *(G-15180)*
Thermoelectric Coolg Amer Corp G 773 342-4900
  Chicago *(G-6362)*
Trane US Inc .... C 630 734-3200
  Willowbrook *(G-21063)*
Trane US Inc .... G 708 532-8004
  Tinley Park *(G-19861)*

REFRIGERATION EQPT & SPLYS WHOLESALERS

Hansen Technologies Corp .... D 706 335-5551
  Burr Ridge *(G-2682)*
Marcy Enterprises Inc .... G 708 352-7220
  La Grange Park *(G-12098)*
Parker-Hannifin Corporation ...... E 708 681-6300
  Broadview *(G-2457)*

REFRIGERATION EQPT & SPLYS, WHOLESALE: Beverage Dispensers

Banner Equipment Co .... E 815 941-9600
  Morris *(G-14294)*

REFRIGERATION EQPT & SPLYS, WHOLESALE: Commercial Eqpt

Advanced Cooler Inc .... G 630 443-8933
  Saint Charles *(G-18142)*
Evapco Inc .... C 217 923-3431
  Greenup *(G-10820)*
Intrntnal Ice Bgging Systems .... G 312 633-4000
  Glencoe *(G-10431)*
Reedy Industries Inc .... F 847 729-9450
  Glenview *(G-10610)*

REFRIGERATION EQPT & SPLYS, WHOLESALE: Ice Making Machines

Sislers Ice Inc .... E 815 756-6903
  Dekalb *(G-7701)*
Voges Inc .... F 618 233-2760
  Evansville *(G-9590)*

REFRIGERATION EQPT: Complete

Advanced Cooler Inc .... G 630 443-8933
  Saint Charles *(G-18142)*
Henry Technologies Inc .... D 217 483-2406
  Chatham *(G-3422)*
Henry Technologies Inc .... G 217 483-2406
  Chatham *(G-3421)*
Howe Corporation .... E 773 235-0200
  Chicago *(G-4851)*
Marshall Middleby Inc .... C 847 741-3300
  Elgin *(G-8649)*
Scotsman Industries Inc .... D 847 215-4500
  Vernon Hills *(G-20093)*
Taylor Coml Foodservice Inc ..... F 815 624-8333
  Rockton *(G-17703)*

REFRIGERATION REPAIR SVCS

Advanced Cooler Inc .... G 630 443-8933
  Saint Charles *(G-18142)*

REFRIGERATION SVC & REPAIR

Kool Technologies Inc .... G 630 483-2256
  Streamwood *(G-19581)*
Lambright Distributors .... G 217 543-2083
  Arthur *(G-865)*
Mucci Kirkpatrick Sheet Metal ... G 815 433-3350
  Ottawa *(G-16062)*

REFRIGERATORS & FREEZERS WHOLESALERS

Professional Freezing Svcs LLC G 773 847-7500
  Chicago *(G-5896)*

REFUSE SYSTEMS

Abco Metals Corporations .... F 773 881-1504
  Chicago *(G-3509)*
Alter Trading Corporation .... F 217 223-0156
  Quincy *(G-16852)*
Archer Metal & Paper Co .... F 773 585-3030
  Chicago *(G-3726)*
C & M Recycling Inc .... E 847 578-1066
  North Chicago *(G-15308)*
Darling Ingredients Inc .... E 217 482-3261
  Mason City *(G-13611)*
Kostelac Grease Service Inc ..... E 314 436-7166
  Belleville *(G-1566)*
Midwest Fiber Inc Decatur .... E 217 424-9460
  Decatur *(G-7524)*
Safety-Kleen Systems Inc .... G 618 875-8050
  East Saint Louis *(G-8321)*
T & C Metal Co .... G 815 459-4445
  Crystal Lake *(G-7274)*
Top Metal Buyers Inc .... F 314 421-2721
  East Saint Louis *(G-8327)*
Try Our Pallets Inc .... G 708 343-0166
  Maywood *(G-13679)*

REGISTERS: Air, Metal

Hart & Cooley Inc .... C 630 665-5549
  Carol Stream *(G-2996)*

Employee Codes: A=Over 500 employees, B=251-500
C=101-250, D=51-100, E=20-50, F=10-19, G=3-9

REGULATORS: Generator Voltage

Saturn Electrical Services Inc..........G...... 630 980-0300
Roselle *(G-17983)*

REGULATORS: Line Voltage

Intermatic Incorporated..................A...... 815 675-7000
Spring Grove *(G-19276)*

REGULATORS: Steam Fittings

Dresser LLC..................................D...... 847 437-5940
Elk Grove Village *(G-8955)*
Pressure Specialist Inc..................E...... 815 477-0007
Crystal Lake *(G-7246)*

REGULATORS: Transmission & Distribution Voltage

American Cips...............................G...... 618 393-5641
Olney *(G-15852)*

REHABILITATION CENTER, OUTPATIENT TREATMENT

Macon Resources Inc.....................C...... 217 875-1910
Decatur *(G-7520)*

REHABILITATION CTR, RESIDENTIAL WITH HEALTH CARE INCIDENTAL

Five Star Industries Inc...................D...... 618 542-4880
Du Quoin *(G-8120)*
Fulton County Rehabilitation............E...... 309 647-6510
Canton *(G-2826)*

REINSURANCE CARRIERS: Accident & Health

American Medical Association..........A...... 312 464-5000
Chicago *(G-3660)*

RELAYS & SWITCHES: Indl, Electric

American Controls & Automation......G...... 630 293-8841
West Chicago *(G-20537)*
Autotech Tech Ltd Partnr.................E...... 563 359-7501
Chicago *(G-3780)*
Italvibras Usa Inc............................G...... 815 872-1350
Princeton *(G-16811)*
Light of Mine LLC...........................G...... 312 840-8570
Chicago *(G-5220)*
Mpc Products Corporation...............G...... 847 673-8300
Niles *(G-15150)*
Woodward Controls Inc..................C...... 847 673-8300
Skokie *(G-19058)*

RELAYS: Control Circuit, Ind

Essex Electro Engineers Inc............E...... 847 891-4444
Schaumburg *(G-18522)*
Littelfuse Inc..................................E...... 773 628-1000
Chicago *(G-5239)*
Microware Inc................................G...... 847 943-9113
Glenview *(G-10588)*

RELAYS: Electric Power

Tough Electric Inc...........................G...... 630 236-8332
Aurora *(G-1163)*

RELAYS: Electronic Usage

Deltrol Corp....................................C...... 708 547-0500
Bellwood *(G-1621)*
Kelco Industries Inc........................G...... 815 334-3600
Woodstock *(G-21398)*
Relay Services Mfg Corp................F...... 773 252-2700
Chicago *(G-6008)*

RELIGIOUS SPLYS WHOLESALERS

American Church Supply.................G...... 847 464-4140
Saint Charles *(G-18145)*

REMOVERS & CLEANERS

Creekside Exterior Solutions............G...... 618 326-7654
Mulberry Grove *(G-14653)*
Dunamis International.....................G...... 773 504-5733
Chicago *(G-4405)*
Midwest Ground Effects..................G...... 708 516-5874
Plainfield *(G-16688)*

Petrochem Inc................................G...... 630 513-6350
Saint Charles *(G-18245)*
Sectional Snow Plow......................E...... 815 932-7569
Bradley *(G-2291)*
Snow Command Incorporated..........G...... 708 991-7004
Flossmoor *(G-9701)*
Snow Control Inc............................G...... 708 670-6269
Orland Park *(G-15980)*

REMOVERS: Paint

Custom Chemical Inc......................G...... 217 529-0878
Springfield *(G-19357)*

RENDERING PLANT

Ace Grease Service Inc..................G...... 618 337-0974
Millstadt *(G-14042)*
Chaos Ai Art LLC............................G...... 847 274-9158
Chicago *(G-4070)*
MW Hopkins & Sons Inc.................G...... 847 458-1010
Lake In The Hills *(G-12341)*
South Chicago Packing LLC............D...... 708 589-2400
Chicago *(G-6206)*

RENT-A-CAR SVCS

Hertz Corporation...........................G...... 630 897-0956
Montgomery *(G-14247)*

RENTAL CENTERS: General

Pre Pack Machinery Inc..................G...... 217 352-1010
Champaign *(G-3338)*

RENTAL CENTERS: Party & Banquet Eqpt & Splys

Associated Attractions Entps...........F...... 773 376-1900
Chicago *(G-3750)*
Wise Equipment & Rentals Inc........F...... 847 895-5555
Schaumburg *(G-18774)*

RENTAL SVCS: Aircraft

AAR Corp..D...... 630 227-2000
Wood Dale *(G-21149)*

RENTAL SVCS: Bicycle & Motorcycle

Service Pro Electric Mtr Repr..........G...... 630 766-1215
Bensenville *(G-1892)*

RENTAL SVCS: Business Machine & Electronic Eqpt

Pitney Bowes Inc............................E...... 312 209-2216
Schaumburg *(G-18674)*
Pitney Bowes Inc............................D...... 630 435-7500
Lisle *(G-12927)*
Pitney Bowes Inc............................E...... 800 784-4224
Itasca *(G-11719)*

RENTAL SVCS: Carpet & Upholstery Cleaning Eqpt

Best Way Carpet & Uphl Clg...........G...... 618 544-8585
Robinson *(G-17108)*

RENTAL SVCS: Costume

Andy Dallas & Co............................F...... 217 351-5974
Champaign *(G-3265)*

RENTAL SVCS: Electronic Eqpt, Exc Computers

Prairie Wi-FI Systems.....................G...... 515 988-3260
Chicago *(G-5852)*

RENTAL SVCS: Floor Maintenance Eqpt

Gilday Services...............................G...... 847 395-0853
Antioch *(G-613)*

RENTAL SVCS: Live Plant

Albert F Amling LLC........................C...... 630 333-1720
Elmhurst *(G-9324)*

RENTAL SVCS: Oil Eqpt

Purified Lubricants Inc....................E...... 708 478-3500
Mokena *(G-14111)*

Runyon Oil Tools Inc.......................G...... 618 395-5045
Olney *(G-15888)*

RENTAL SVCS: Recreational Vehicle

Bella Terra Winery LLC...................F...... 618 658-8882
Creal Springs *(G-7080)*

RENTAL SVCS: Sign

Ron Meyer......................................G...... 847 844-9880
Gilberts *(G-10367)*

RENTAL SVCS: Sound & Lighting Eqpt

Rexroat Sound................................G...... 309 764-1663
Colona *(G-6978)*

RENTAL SVCS: Tent & Tarpaulin

Berg Industries Inc..........................F...... 815 874-1588
Rockford *(G-17318)*
Kankakee Tent & Awning Co...........G...... 815 932-8000
Kankakee *(G-11986)*
Stritzel Awnng Svc/Aurra Tent........E...... 630 420-2000
Plainfield *(G-16718)*

RENTAL SVCS: Tuxedo

Duckys Formal Wear Inc.................G...... 309 342-5914
Galesburg *(G-10191)*

RENTAL SVCS: Video Cassette Recorder & Access

Video Gaming Technologies Inc......G...... 847 776-3516
Palatine *(G-16170)*

RENTAL SVCS: Work Zone Traffic Eqpt, Flags, Cones, Etc

John Thomas Inc............................E...... 815 288-2343
Dixon *(G-7902)*

RENTAL: Video Tape & Disc

Schnuck Markets Inc......................C...... 618 466-0825
Godfrey *(G-10663)*
Vincor Ltd.......................................F...... 708 534-0008
Monee *(G-14211)*

REPAIR SERVICES, NEC

Ashland Door Solutions LLC...........G...... 773 348-5106
Elk Grove Village *(G-8842)*
Mold Repair and Manufacturing......G...... 815 477-1332
Crystal Lake *(G-7233)*
On Site Mechanical Svcs Inc..........F...... 708 367-0470
Crete *(G-7143)*
Pro-Beam USA Inc.........................G...... 630 327-6909
Plainfield *(G-16708)*

REPRODUCTION SVCS: Video Tape Or Disk

Towers Media Holdings Inc.............D...... 312 993-1550
Northfield *(G-15534)*
United Cmra Binocular Repr LLC....E...... 630 595-2525
Elk Grove Village *(G-9296)*

RESEARCH & DEVELOPMENT SVCS, COMMERCIAL: Engineering Lab

Knowles Elec Holdings Inc..............A...... 630 250-5100
Itasca *(G-11687)*

RESEARCH, DEVELOPMENT & TEST SVCS, COMM: Business Analysis

Createasoft Inc...............................F...... 630 851-9474
Aurora *(G-943)*

RESEARCH, DEVELOPMENT & TEST SVCS, COMM: Cmptr Hardware Dev

Digital Optics Tech Inc....................G...... 847 358-2592
Rolling Meadows *(G-17727)*
Eighty Nine Robotics LLC...............G...... 512 573-9091
Chicago *(G-4463)*

RESEARCH, DEVELOPMENT & TEST SVCS, COMM: Research, Exc Lab

CCH Incorporated .... A 847 267-7000
  Riverwoods *(G-17090)*
Etymotic Research Inc .... E 847 228-0006
  Elk Grove Village *(G-8984)*
Park View Manufacturing Corp .... D 618 548-9054
  Salem *(G-18350)*
T D J Group Inc .... G 847 639-1113
  Cary *(G-3193)*

RESEARCH, DEVELOPMENT & TESTING SVCS, COMM: Agricultural

Dow Agrosciences LLC .... G 815 844-3128
  Pontiac *(G-16769)*

RESEARCH, DEVELOPMENT & TESTING SVCS, COMM: Research Lab

Sonoscan Inc .... D 847 437-6400
  Elk Grove Village *(G-9247)*
Tricor Systems Inc .... E 847 742-5542
  Elgin *(G-8760)*

RESEARCH, DEVELOPMENT & TESTING SVCS, COMMERCIAL: Business

Information Resources Inc .... G 312 474-3380
  Chicago *(G-4917)*

RESEARCH, DEVELOPMENT & TESTING SVCS, COMMERCIAL: Education

Education Partners Project Ltd .... G 773 675-6643
  Chicago *(G-4458)*
Steve C Gough .... G 618 529-7423
  Carbondale *(G-2860)*

RESEARCH, DEVELOPMENT & TESTING SVCS, COMMERCIAL: Energy

300 Below Inc .... G 217 423-3070
  Decatur *(G-7431)*
Firefly International Enrgy Co .... G 309 402-0701
  Peoria *(G-16438)*
Wagenate Entps Holdings LLC .... G 773 503-1306
  Riverdale *(G-17078)*

RESEARCH, DEVELOPMENT & TESTING SVCS, COMMERCIAL: Medical

Medexus Pharma Inc .... G 312 854-0500
  Chicago *(G-5382)*

RESEARCH, DEVELOPMENT & TESTING SVCS, COMMERCIAL: Physical

Atsp Innovations Inc .... G 217 778-4400
  Champaign *(G-3269)*

RESEARCH, DEVELOPMENT SVCS, COMMERCIAL: Indl Lab

Fabricators Unlimited Inc .... G 847 223-7986
  Grayslake *(G-10772)*

RESEARCH, DVLPT & TEST SVCS, COMM: Mkt Analysis or Research

Information Resources Inc .... A 312 474-8900
  Chicago *(G-4918)*
McIlvaine Co .... E 847 784-0012
  Northfield *(G-15522)*

RESEARCH, DVLPT & TESTING SVCS, COMM: Mkt, Bus & Economic

Palm International Inc .... G 630 357-1437
  Naperville *(G-14892)*

RESEARCH, DVLPT & TESTING SVCS, COMM: Survey, Mktg

Screen North Amer Holdings Inc .... F 847 870-7400
  Rolling Meadows *(G-17774)*

RESIDENTIAL MENTAL HEALTH & SUBSTANCE ABUSE FACILITIES

Kreider Services Incorporated .... D 815 288-6691
  Dixon *(G-7903)*

RESIDENTIAL REMODELERS

Illinois Green Cnstr Inc .... F 847 975-2312
  Chicago *(G-4891)*
Kep Woodworking .... G 847 480-9545
  Newark *(G-15077)*
Lamka Enterprises Inc .... G 630 659-5965
  Woodstock *(G-21402)*
Osmer Woodworking Inc .... G 815 973-5809
  Dixon *(G-7905)*
Perkins Construction .... G 815 233-9655
  Freeport *(G-10132)*

RESINS: Custom Compound Purchased

Aabbitt Adhesives Inc .... D 773 227-2700
  Chicago *(G-3499)*
Ameriflon Ltd .... G 847 541-6000
  Wheeling *(G-20848)*
Antek Madison Plastics USA Ltd .... F 773 933-0900
  Chicago *(G-3705)*
Azul 3d Inc .... F 321 277-7807
  Skokie *(G-18926)*
Bach Plastic Works Inc .... G 847 680-4342
  Libertyville *(G-12635)*
Bulk Molding Compounds Inc .... D 630 377-1065
  West Chicago *(G-20556)*
Enbarr LLC .... G 630 217-2101
  Bartlett *(G-1278)*
Lyondell Chemical Company .... B 815 942-7011
  Morris *(G-14311)*
M-Prime Company .... E 630 834-9400
  Villa Park *(G-20157)*
Mervis Industries Inc .... C 217 442-5300
  Danville *(G-7365)*
Parker-Hannifin Corporation .... D 847 836-6859
  Elgin *(G-8685)*
Polyone Corporation .... D 630 972-0505
  Romeoville *(G-17865)*
Polyone Corporation .... D 815 385-8500
  McHenry *(G-13782)*
Polyone Corporation .... F 815 385-8500
  Mchenry *(G-13783)*
Shannon Industrial Corporation .... F 815 337-2349
  Woodstock *(G-21432)*
Standard Rubber Products Co .... E 847 593-5630
  Elk Grove Village *(G-9252)*
Ticona Technical Polymers .... G 847 949-1444
  Mundelein *(G-14744)*

RESISTORS

Elematec USA Corporation .... G 858 527-1700
  Itasca *(G-11647)*
Maurey Instrument Corp .... F 708 388-9898
  Alsip *(G-474)*
Mpc Products Corporation .... A 847 673-8300
  Niles *(G-15149)*
Voltronics Inc .... F 773 625-1779
  Chicago *(G-6568)*

RESISTORS & RESISTOR UNITS

Heico Companies LLC .... G 847 258-0300
  Elmhurst *(G-9370)*
Ohmite Holding LLC .... E 847 258-0300
  Warrenville *(G-20243)*

RESISTORS: Networks

CTS Corporation .... C 630 577-8800
  Lisle *(G-12881)*
Methode Electronics Inc .... B 708 867-6777
  Chicago *(G-5409)*

RESPIRATORY SYSTEM DRUGS

Abbvie Respiratory LLC .... G 847 937-6100
  North Chicago *(G-15303)*

RESPIRATORY THERAPY CLINIC

IV & Respiratory Care Services .... E 618 398-2720
  Belleville *(G-1559)*

RESTAURANT EQPT REPAIR SVCS

American Soda Ftn Exch Inc .... F 312 733-5000
  Chicago *(G-3668)*
Precision Service .... G 618 345-2047
  Collinsville *(G-6972)*

RESTAURANT EQPT: Carts

M L Rongo Inc .... E 630 540-1120
  Bartlett *(G-1294)*
Precision Service .... G 618 345-2047
  Collinsville *(G-6972)*

RESTAURANT EQPT: Food Wagons

Haute Diggity Dawgs .... G 773 801-0195
  Chicago *(G-4786)*
Powerhouse Ent Inc .... G 312 877-4303
  Chicago *(G-5849)*

RESTAURANT EQPT: Sheet Metal

Avenue Metal Manufacturing Co .... F 312 243-3483
  Chicago *(G-3785)*
Ready Access Inc .... E 800 621-5045
  West Chicago *(G-20635)*
Stainless Specialties Inc .... G 618 654-7723
  Pocahontas *(G-16754)*

RESTAURANTS: Delicatessen

Ifa International Inc .... F 847 566-0008
  Mundelein *(G-14698)*

RESTAURANTS: Full Svc, American

Libertyville Brewing Company .... D 847 362-6688
  Libertyville *(G-12668)*

RESTAURANTS: Full Svc, Barbecue

Jessis Hideout .... G 618 343-4346
  Caseyville *(G-3215)*

RESTAURANTS: Full Svc, Chinese

Wow Bao LLC .... D 888 496-9226
  Chicago *(G-6680)*

RESTAURANTS: Full Svc, Ethnic Food

El Moro De Letran Churros & Ba .... F 312 733-3173
  Chicago *(G-4465)*

RESTAURANTS: Full Svc, Family

Mandys Soul Food Kitchen LLC .... F 630 485-7291
  Bolingbrook *(G-2209)*
Two Brothers Brewing Company .... G 630 393-2337
  Warrenville *(G-20256)*

RESTAURANTS: Full Svc, Family, Independent

Bbq Smokewagon Inc .... G 309 271-7002
  East Peoria *(G-8252)*
Harners Bakery Restaurant .... D 630 892-5545
  North Aurora *(G-15263)*

RESTAURANTS: Full Svc, Italian

Father Marcellos & Son .... C 312 654-2565
  Chicago *(G-4567)*
Top Dollar Slots .... G 779 210-4884
  Loves Park *(G-13276)*

RESTAURANTS: Full Svc, Mexican

El-Milagro Inc .... B 773 579-6120
  Chicago *(G-4470)*
El-Milagro Inc .... C 773 650-1614
  Chicago *(G-4471)*
Los Mangos .... G 815 630-2611
  Crest Hill *(G-7091)*

RESTAURANTS: Full Svc, Steak

Andrias Food Group Inc .... E 618 632-4866
  O Fallon *(G-15565)*

RESTAURANTS:Limited Svc, Carry-Out Only, Exc Pizza

RESTAURANTS:Limited Svc, Carry-Out Only, Exc Pizza

Romaine Empire Inc .... D 312 229-0099
Chicago (G-6056)

RESTAURANTS:Limited Svc, Chicken

Emmetts Tavern & Brewing Co .... G 630 434-8500
Downers Grove (G-8000)
Emmetts Tavern & Brewing Co .... G 630 480-7181
Wheaton (G-20797)
Emmetts Tavern & Brewing Co .... F 847 359-1533
Palatine (G-16115)
Emmetts Tavern & Brewing Co .... E 847 428-4500
West Dundee (G-20663)

RESTAURANTS:Limited Svc, Coffee Shop

Briannas Pancake Cafe .... G 630 365-4770
Elburn (G-8447)
Javamania Coffee Roastery Inc .... G 815 885-4661
Loves Park (G-13223)
Joshi Brothers Inc .... E 847 895-0200
Schaumburg (G-18578)
Trenton Sun .... G 618 224-9422
Trenton (G-19905)
Wolfart Maciej .... G 312 248-3575
Chicago (G-6663)

RESTAURANTS:Limited Svc, Fast-Food, Chain

M E F Corp .... F 815 965-8604
Rockford (G-17501)

RESTAURANTS:Limited Svc, Fast-Food, Independent

Homer Vintage Bakery .... G 217 896-2538
Homer (G-11476)

RESTAURANTS:Limited Svc, Ice Cream Stands Or Dairy Bars

B N K Inc .... G 630 231-5640
West Chicago (G-20547)
G K Enterprises Inc .... G 708 587-2150
Monee (G-14201)
Gayety Candy Co Inc .... E 708 418-0062
Lansing (G-12494)
Mitchlls Cndies Ice Creams Inc .... F 708 799-3835
Homewood (G-11501)
Walter & Kathy Anczerewicz .... G 708 448-3676
Palos Heights (G-16194)

RESTAURANTS:Limited Svc, Pizza

Balton Corporation .... F 773 933-7927
Chicago (G-3822)

RESTAURANTS:Limited Svc, Pizzeria, Chain

Dominos Pizza LLC .... E 630 783-0738
Woodridge (G-21295)

RESTAURANTS:Limited Svc, Pizzeria, Independent

Reggios Pizza Inc .... D 773 933-7927
Chicago (G-6004)

RESTRAINTS

E-Z Cuff Inc .... G 847 549-1550
Libertyville (G-12648)

RETAIL BAKERY: Bagels

Bimbo Bakeries Usa Inc .... B 217 235-3181
Mattoon (G-13631)

RETAIL BAKERY: Bread

Anns Bakery Inc .... G 773 384-5562
Chicago (G-3700)
Chicago Pastry Inc .... D 630 529-6161
Bloomingdale (G-1985)
Dinkels Bakery Inc .... E 773 281-7300
Chicago (G-4362)
Milano Bakery Inc .... E 815 727-2253
Joliet (G-11905)

Riverside Bake Shop .... E 815 385-0044
McHenry (G-13788)
Roma Bakeries Inc .... F 815 964-6737
Rockford (G-17614)

RETAIL BAKERY: Cakes

Herbs Bakery Inc .... F 847 741-0249
Elgin (G-8614)
Le Chocolat Du Bouchard LLC .... G 630 355-5720
Naperville (G-14861)
Leesons Cakes Inc .... G 708 429-1330
Tinley Park (G-19844)
More Cupcakes LLC .... G 312 951-0001
Chicago (G-5499)
Orland Park Bakery Ltd .... E 708 349-8516
Orland Park (G-15973)
Tags Bakery Inc .... E 847 328-1200
Evanston (G-9582)
Wilton Brands LLC .... B 630 963-7100
Naperville (G-14948)

RETAIL BAKERY: Doughnuts

B N K Inc .... G 630 231-5640
West Chicago (G-20547)
Dimples Donuts .... G 630 406-0303
Batavia (G-1373)
Dixie Cream Donut Shop .... E 618 937-4866
West Frankfort (G-20670)
Dunkin Donuts .... E 708 460-3088
Orland Park (G-15954)
Express Donuts Enterprise Inc .... F 630 510-9310
Wheaton (G-20798)
Honey Fluff Doughnuts .... G 708 579-1826
Countryside (G-7058)
Jay Elka .... F 847 540-7776
Lake Zurich (G-12426)
O-Donuts Inc .... F 217 544-4644
Springfield (G-19415)
Union Foods Inc .... G 201 327-2828
Chicago (G-6465)
Walter & Kathy Anczerewicz .... G 708 448-3676
Palos Heights (G-16194)

RETAIL BAKERY: Pastries

Nablus Sweets Inc .... E 708 205-6534
Chicago (G-5534)
Nablus Sweets Inc .... E 708 529-3911
Bridgeview (G-2367)
Verzenay LLC .... G 817 875-0699
Elk Grove Village (G-9303)

RETAIL LUMBER YARDS

Alexander Lumber Co .... G 815 754-1000
Cortland (G-7016)
Autumn Mill .... G 217 795-3399
Argenta (G-671)
Co-Fair Corporation .... E 847 626-1500
Skokie (G-18945)
Corsaw Hardwood Lumber Inc .... F 309 293-2055
Smithfield (G-19063)
Engineered Plastic Systems LLC .... F 800 480-2327
Elgin (G-8580)
Liese Lumber Co Inc .... G 618 234-0105
Belleville (G-1568)
Narvick Bros Lumber Co Inc .... E 815 942-1173
Morris (G-14318)
Red River Lumber Inc .... D 708 388-1818
Blue Island (G-2135)
Skokie Millwork Inc .... G 847 673-7868
Skokie (G-19030)
Woodworkers Shop Inc .... E 309 347-5111
Pekin (G-16371)

RETAIL STORES, NEC

Hearing Aid Warehouse Inc .... G 217 431-4700
Danville (G-7343)
James J Sandoval .... G 734 717-7555
Lombard (G-13089)
Lasersketch Ltd .... F 630 243-6360
Romeoville (G-17840)
Val P Enterprises .... G 708 982-6561
Chicago (G-6518)

RETAIL STORES: Air Purification Eqpt

Calutech Inc .... G 708 614-0228
Orland Park (G-15944)

PRODUCT SECTION

Compressed Air Advisors Inc .... G 877 247-2381
Hillside (G-11334)

RETAIL STORES: Alarm Signal Systems

Sound Design Inc .... G 630 548-7000
Plainfield (G-16715)

RETAIL STORES: Alcoholic Beverage Making Eqpt & Splys

MCR Technologies Group Inc .... G 815 622-3181
Sterling (G-19517)
Prairie Profile .... G 618 846-2116
Vandalia (G-20019)
Wilson Railing & Metal Fabg Co .... G 847 662-1747
Park City (G-16248)

RETAIL STORES: Architectural Splys

Arthur R Baker Inc .... G 708 301-4828
Homer Glen (G-11477)

RETAIL STORES: Artificial Limbs

Cape Prosthetics-Orthotics Inc .... G 618 457-4692
Marion (G-13507)

RETAIL STORES: Audio-Visual Eqpt & Splys

Fred Kennerly .... G 815 398-6861
Rockford (G-17424)
Innovative AV Systems Inc .... G 312 265-6282
Elmhurst (G-9379)

RETAIL STORES: Awnings

Blake Co Inc .... G 815 962-3852
Rockford (G-17325)
Bloomington Tent & Awning Inc .... G 309 828-3411
Bloomington (G-2027)
Chesterfield Awning Co Inc .... F 708 596-4434
South Holland (G-19205)
Eclipse Awnings Inc .... F 708 636-3160
Evergreen Park (G-9593)
Haakes Awning .... G 618 529-4808
Carbondale (G-2844)
Kankakee Tent & Awning Co .... G 815 932-8000
Kankakee (G-11986)
Midwest Awnings Inc .... G 309 762-3339
Cameron (G-2808)
Nuyen Awning Co .... G 630 892-3995
Aurora (G-1141)
Shade Solutions Inc .... F 217 239-0718
Tolono (G-19884)

RETAIL STORES: Banners

All Stars -N- Stitches Inc .... G 618 435-5555
Benton (G-1918)
Evo Exhibits LLC .... G 630 520-0710
West Chicago (G-20577)
Image Signs Inc .... F 815 282-4141
Loves Park (G-13218)

RETAIL STORES: Batteries, Non-Automotive

National Power LLC .... E 773 685-2662
Chicago (G-5551)

RETAIL STORES: Business Machines & Eqpt

Buff & Go Inc .... F 773 719-4436
Chicago (G-3972)
CDs Office Systems Inc .... D 800 367-1508
Springfield (G-19343)
CDs Office Systems Inc .... F 630 305-9034
Springfield (G-19344)
Dans Printing & Off Sups Inc .... F 708 687-3055
Oak Forest (G-15674)
Klai-Co Idntification Pdts Inc .... E 847 573-0375
Lake Forest (G-12270)

RETAIL STORES: Cake Decorating Splys

Wilton Brands LLC .... B 630 963-7100
Naperville (G-14948)

RETAIL STORES: Canvas Prdts

Evanston Awning Company .... G 847 864-4520
Evanston (G-9515)

PRODUCT SECTION   RETAIL STORES: Rubber Stamps

RETAIL STORES: Christmas Lights & Decorations
Datasource ....G..... 312 405-9152
  Calumet City *(G-2774)*

RETAIL STORES: Cleaning Eqpt & Splys
Delta Products Group Inc ....F..... 630 357-5544
  Aurora *(G-1084)*

RETAIL STORES: Communication Eqpt
Portable Cmmnctons Spclsts ....G..... 630 458-1800
  Addison *(G-246)*
Procomm Inc Hoopeston Illinois ....E..... 815 268-4303
  Onarga *(G-15902)*

RETAIL STORES: Concrete Prdts, Precast
Ozinga Ready Mix Concrete Inc ....E..... 708 326-4200
  Mokena *(G-14103)*
Stockdale Block Systems LLC ....G..... 815 416-1030
  Morris *(G-14329)*

RETAIL STORES: Drafting Eqpt & Splys
Tree Towns Reprographics Inc ....F..... 630 832-0209
  Elmhurst *(G-9437)*

RETAIL STORES: Educational Aids & Electronic Training Mat
Follett School Solutions Inc ....C..... 815 759-1700
  McHenry *(G-13745)*
LMS Innovations Inc ....G..... 312 613-2345
  Chicago *(G-5247)*

RETAIL STORES: Electronic Parts & Eqpt
Delta Design Inc ....F..... 708 424-9400
  Evergreen Park *(G-9592)*
Eazypower Corporation ....E..... 773 278-5000
  Chicago *(G-4439)*
Rams Sheet Metal Equipment Inc ....G..... 224 788-9900
  Antioch *(G-632)*

RETAIL STORES: Engine & Motor Eqpt & Splys
Jones Garrison Sons Mch Works ....G..... 618 847-2161
  Fairfield *(G-9629)*

RETAIL STORES: Farm Eqpt & Splys
Jenkins Displays Co ....G..... 618 335-3874
  Vandalia *(G-20013)*
Jenner Precision Inc ....F..... 815 692-6655
  Fairbury *(G-9609)*
Michaels Equipment Co ....G..... 618 524-8560
  Metropolis *(G-13975)*

RETAIL STORES: Farm Machinery, NEC
Alpha AG Inc ....G..... 217 546-2724
  Pleasant Plains *(G-16749)*

RETAIL STORES: Fire Extinguishers
Oval Fire Products Corporation ....G..... 630 635-5000
  Glendale Heights *(G-10482)*

RETAIL STORES: Flags
W G N Flag & Decorating Co ....F..... 773 768-8076
  Chicago *(G-6573)*

RETAIL STORES: Foam & Foam Prdts
A D Specialty Sewing ....G..... 847 639-0390
  Fox River Grove *(G-9756)*
Polyair Corporation ....G..... 773 253-1220
  Chicago *(G-5837)*

RETAIL STORES: Gravestones, Finished
Effingham Monument Co Inc ....G..... 217 857-6085
  Effingham *(G-8397)*
Moore Memorials ....F..... 708 636-6532
  Chicago Ridge *(G-6804)*
Weiss Monument Works Inc ....G..... 618 398-1811
  Belleville *(G-1611)*
Wilson & Wilson Monument Co ....F..... 618 775-6488
  Odin *(G-15836)*

RETAIL STORES: Hair Care Prdts
Art of Shaving - Fl LLC ....G..... 630 495-7316
  Lombard *(G-13040)*
Art of Shaving - Fl LLC ....G..... 312 527-1604
  Chicago *(G-3737)*
Art of Shaving - Fl LLC ....G..... 630 684-0277
  Oak Brook *(G-15594)*
Truvanity Beauty LLC ....G..... 312 778-6499
  Chicago *(G-6441)*

RETAIL STORES: Hearing Aids
Phonak LLC ....A..... 630 821-5000
  Warrenville *(G-20245)*

RETAIL STORES: Hospital Eqpt & Splys
Amity Hospital Services Inc ....G..... 708 206-3970
  Country Club Hills *(G-7035)*

RETAIL STORES: Ice
Sislers Ice Inc ....E..... 815 756-6903
  Dekalb *(G-7701)*

RETAIL STORES: Insecticides
Piatt County Service Co ....G..... 217 489-2411
  Mansfield *(G-13442)*

RETAIL STORES: Medical Apparatus & Splys
Carematix Inc ....E..... 312 627-9300
  Chicago *(G-4028)*
Cornucopia Supply Corp ....G..... 847 532-9365
  Morton Grove *(G-14397)*
Interexpo Ltd ....F..... 847 489-7056
  Kildeer *(G-12049)*
Medline Industries Inc ....A..... 847 949-5500
  Northfield *(G-15523)*
Ortho Arch Company Inc ....E..... 847 885-7805
  Schaumburg *(G-18660)*

RETAIL STORES: Mobile Telephones & Eqpt
Firefly Mobile Inc ....E..... 305 538-2777
  Schaumburg *(G-18529)*
Unified Solutions Corp ....E..... 847 478-9100
  Arlington Heights *(G-824)*

RETAIL STORES: Monuments, Finished To Custom Order
Abel Vault & Monument Co Inc ....G..... 309 647-0105
  Canton *(G-2820)*
Arnold Monument Co Inc ....G..... 217 546-2102
  Springfield *(G-19320)*
Beutel Corporation ....G..... 309 786-8134
  Rock Island *(G-17207)*
Bevel Granite Company Inc ....D..... 708 371-4191
  Indian Head Park *(G-11576)*
Czarnik Memorials Inc ....G..... 708 458-4443
  Justice *(G-11951)*
Gast Monuments Inc ....G..... 773 262-2400
  Chicago *(G-4660)*
J P Vincent & Sons Inc ....G..... 815 777-2365
  Galena *(G-10175)*
J W Reynolds Monument Co Inc ....G..... 618 833-6014
  Anna *(G-586)*
Jacksonville Monument Co ....G..... 217 245-2514
  Jacksonville *(G-11772)*
Mendota Monument Co ....G..... 815 539-7276
  Mendota *(G-13947)*
Old Capitol Monument Works Inc ....G..... 217 324-5673
  Vandalia *(G-20017)*
Pana Monument Co ....G..... 217 562-5121
  Pana *(G-16220)*
Peter Troost Monument Co ....G..... 773 585-0242
  Justice *(G-11953)*
Riverside Memorial Co ....G..... 217 323-1280
  Beardstown *(G-1450)*
St Charles Memorial Works Inc ....G..... 630 584-0183
  Saint Charles *(G-18275)*
Tisch Monuments Inc ....G..... 618 233-3017
  Belleville *(G-1599)*
Wendell Adams ....E..... 217 345-9587
  Charleston *(G-3416)*
Zoia Monument Company ....G..... 815 338-0358
  Woodstock *(G-21451)*

RETAIL STORES: Motors, Electric
Accurate Elc Mtr & Pump Co ....G..... 708 448-2792
  Worth *(G-21453)*
All Electric Mtr Repr Svc Inc ....F..... 773 925-2404
  Chicago *(G-3609)*
Bak Electric ....G..... 708 458-3578
  Bridgeview *(G-2327)*
BP Elc Mtrs Pump & Svc Inc ....G..... 773 539-4343
  Skokie *(G-18931)*
Dependable Electric ....G..... 618 592-3314
  Oblong *(G-15826)*
First Electric Motor Shop Inc ....G..... 217 698-0672
  Springfield *(G-19368)*
Goding Electric Company ....F..... 630 858-7700
  Glendale Heights *(G-10455)*
Hills Electric Motor Service ....G..... 815 625-0305
  Rock Falls *(G-17184)*
M H Electric Motor & Ctrl Corp ....G..... 630 393-3736
  Warrenville *(G-20242)*
Midwest Elc Mtr Inc Danville ....G..... 217 442-5656
  Danville *(G-7367)*
New Cie Inc ....G..... 815 224-1511
  Peru *(G-16584)*

RETAIL STORES: Orthopedic & Prosthesis Applications
Hanger Prosthetics & ....G..... 847 623-6080
  Gurnee *(G-10886)*
Hanger Prosthetics & ....G..... 630 820-5656
  Aurora *(G-977)*
Prosthetic Orthotic Specialist ....F..... 309 454-8733
  Normal *(G-15219)*
Research Design Inc ....G..... 708 246-8166
  Western Springs *(G-20724)*
Ronald S Lefors Bs Cpo ....G..... 618 259-1969
  East Alton *(G-8170)*
Wheaton Resource Corp ....G..... 630 690-5795
  Carol Stream *(G-3088)*

RETAIL STORES: Perfumes & Colognes
Aurora Narinder ....G..... 773 275-2100
  Chicago *(G-3774)*

RETAIL STORES: Pet Food
Garver Feeds ....E..... 217 422-2201
  Decatur *(G-7496)*

RETAIL STORES: Photocopy Machines
CDs Office Systems Inc ....F..... 217 351-5046
  Champaign *(G-3278)*

RETAIL STORES: Picture Frames, Ready Made
Colbert Custom Framing Inc ....F..... 630 717-1448
  Naperville *(G-14802)*
Frame House Inc ....G..... 708 383-1616
  Oak Park *(G-15753)*
Frame Mart Inc ....G..... 309 452-0658
  Normal *(G-15203)*
Heartfelt Gifts Inc ....G..... 309 852-2296
  Kewanee *(G-12039)*
Michels Frame Shop ....G..... 847 647-7366
  Niles *(G-15145)*
Technicraft Supply Co ....G..... 309 495-5245
  Peoria *(G-16537)*

RETAIL STORES: Plumbing & Heating Splys
Stz Industries LLC ....E..... 773 265-3000
  Chicago *(G-6261)*

RETAIL STORES: Religious Goods
Anthos and Co LLC ....G..... 773 744-6813
  Inverness *(G-11594)*
Scheiwes Print Shop ....G..... 815 683-2398
  Crescent City *(G-7082)*

RETAIL STORES: Rubber Stamps
Benzinger Printing ....G..... 815 784-6560
  Genoa *(G-10315)*
S and S Associates Inc ....G..... 847 584-0033
  Elk Grove Village *(G-9224)*

Employee Codes: A=Over 500 employees, B=251-500
C=101-250, D=51-100, E=20-50, F=10-19, G=3-9

RETAIL STORES: Safety Splys & Eqpt

Midwest Pub Safety Outfitters ....F 866 985-0013
 Poplar Grove *(G-16782)*
North American Safety Pdts Inc ....G 815 469-1144
 Mokena *(G-14099)*
Oei Products Inc ....G 630 377-1121
 Bartlett *(G-1300)*
Protectoseal Company ....C 630 595-0800
 Bensenville *(G-1876)*
Rutke Signs Inc ....G 708 841-6464
 Westchester *(G-20709)*

RETAIL STORES: Swimming Pools, Above Ground

Evergreen Pool & Spa LLC ....G 618 247-3555
 Sandoval *(G-18363)*
Rockford Sewer Co Inc ....G 815 877-9060
 Loves Park *(G-13259)*

RETAIL STORES: Telephone & Communication Eqpt

Custom Canvas LLC ....G 847 587-0225
 Ingleside *(G-11580)*
Mako Networks Sales & Mktg Inc ....D 847 752-5566
 Elgin *(G-8647)*

RETAIL STORES: Tents

Sawier ....E 630 297-8588
 Downers Grove *(G-8090)*
Wise Equipment & Rentals Inc ....F 847 895-5555
 Schaumburg *(G-18774)*

RETAIL STORES: Tombstones

Venetian Monument Company ....F 312 829-9622
 Chicago *(G-6531)*

RETAIL STORES: Typewriters & Business Machines

James Ray Monroe Corporation ....F 618 532-4575
 Centralia *(G-3236)*

RETAIL STORES: Vaults & Safes

Promus Equity Partners LLC ....F 312 784-3990
 Chicago *(G-5903)*

RETAIL STORES: Water Purification Eqpt

Amber Soft Inc ....F 630 377-6945
 Lake Barrington *(G-12141)*
Mar Cor Purification Inc ....G 630 435-1017
 Downers Grove *(G-8051)*
Nalco Wtr Prtrtment Sltons LLC ....G 708 754-2550
 Glenwood *(G-10644)*
Samuel Rowell ....G 618 942-6970
 Herrin *(G-11178)*
Waterco of Central States Inc ....C 630 576-4782
 Lombard *(G-13153)*

RETAIL STORES: Welding Splys

American Welding & Gas Inc ....E 630 527-2550
 Stone Park *(G-19551)*
Micro Products Company ....G 309 697-1216
 Peoria *(G-16473)*
Steel-Guard Safety Corp ....G 708 589-4588
 South Holland *(G-19246)*

RETREADING MATERIALS: Tire

Jireh Inc ....F 217 335-3276
 Barry *(G-1251)*

REUPHOLSTERY & FURNITURE REPAIR

A B Kelly Inc ....G 847 639-1022
 Cary *(G-3142)*
Custom Wood Designs Inc ....G 708 799-3439
 Crestwood *(G-7116)*
North Sails Group LLC ....G 773 489-1308
 Chicago *(G-5621)*
United Canvas Inc ....E 847 395-1470
 Antioch *(G-641)*

REUPHOLSTERY SVCS

Air Land and Sea Interiors ....G 630 834-1717
 Villa Park *(G-20129)*
Albert Vivo Upholstery Co Inc ....G 312 226-7779
 Burr Ridge *(G-2651)*
Bill Weeks Inc ....G 217 523-8735
 Springfield *(G-19326)*
Brandt Interiors ....G 847 251-3543
 Wilmette *(G-21071)*
Robert Harlan Ernst ....G 217 627-3401
 Girard *(G-10385)*
Scibor Upholstering & Gallery ....G 708 671-9700
 Chicago *(G-6117)*
Waco Manufacturing Co Inc ....F 312 733-0054
 Chicago *(G-6582)*
Zirlin Interiors Inc ....E 773 334-5530
 Chicago *(G-6720)*

REWINDING SVCS

Tracy Electric Inc ....E 618 943-6205
 Lawrenceville *(G-12538)*

RIBBONS & BOWS

Stellar Recognition Inc ....D 773 282-8060
 Chicago *(G-6243)*

RIBBONS: Machine, Inked Or Carbon

Allen Paper Company ....G 312 454-4500
 Chicago *(G-3615)*

RIDING STABLES

Hidden Hollow Stables Inc ....G 309 243-7979
 Dunlap *(G-8133)*

RIVETS: Metal

Accurate Rivet Manufacturing ....G 630 766-3401
 Wood Dale *(G-21153)*
Chicago Rivet & Machine Co ....D 630 357-8500
 Naperville *(G-14798)*
Multitech Cold Forming LLC ....E 630 949-8200
 Carol Stream *(G-3034)*

ROAD CONSTRUCTION EQUIPMENT WHOLESALERS

Wissmiller & Evans Road Eqp ....G 309 725-3598
 Cooksville *(G-7004)*

ROBOTS: Assembly Line

Accelrted Mch Design Engrg LLC ....E 815 316-6381
 Rockford *(G-17290)*
Fanuc America Corporation ....E 847 898-5000
 Hoffman Estates *(G-11423)*
G&K-Vijuk Intern Corp ....G 630 530-2203
 Elmhurst *(G-9365)*
ICC Intrntonal Celsius Concept ....G 773 993-4405
 Cicero *(G-6853)*
Innovative Industrial Svcs LLC ....F 309 527-2035
 El Paso *(G-8439)*
Linear Kinetics Inc ....G 630 365-0075
 Maple Park *(G-13463)*
State Line International Inc ....G 708 251-5772
 Lansing *(G-12518)*
Tampotech Decorating Inc ....G 847 515-2968
 Huntley *(G-11567)*

ROCK SALT MINING

Chicago Salt Company Inc ....G 708 906-4718
 River Grove *(G-17058)*

ROCKETS: Space & Military

National Def Intelligence Inc ....G 312 233-2318
 Naperville *(G-14980)*

RODS: Plastic

Advanced Plastic Corp ....D 847 674-2070
 Lincolnwood *(G-12812)*
G-P Manufacturing Co Inc ....E 847 473-9001
 Waukegan *(G-20444)*

RODS: Steel & Iron, Made In Steel Mills

Beh IL Corp ....G 630 616-1850
 Hinsdale *(G-11363)*
Grab Brothers Ir Works Co Corp ....F 847 288-1055
 Franklin Park *(G-9951)*
Sterling Steel Company LLC ....B 815 548-7000
 Sterling *(G-19535)*

ROLL COVERINGS: Rubber

Finzer Roller Inc ....E 410 939-1850
 Des Plaines *(G-7769)*
Finzer Roller Inc ....E 812 829-1455
 Des Plaines *(G-7771)*
Industrial Roller Co ....F 618 234-0740
 Smithton *(G-19066)*
Menges Roller Co Inc ....E 847 487-8877
 Wauconda *(G-20376)*

ROLLING MACHINERY: Steel

Fkm Usa LLC ....F 815 469-2473
 Frankfort *(G-9794)*
Frame Material Supply Inc ....G 309 362-2323
 Trivoli *(G-19906)*

ROLLING MILL EQPT: Picklers & Pickling Lines

Vision Pickling and Proc Inc ....F 815 264-7755
 Waterman *(G-20301)*

ROLLING MILL EQPT: Plate

Lb Metals LLC ....C 708 331-2600
 Harvey *(G-11091)*

ROLLING MILL MACHINERY

Bonell Manufacturing Company ....E 708 849-1770
 Riverdale *(G-17069)*
Chicago Roll Co Inc ....E 630 627-8888
 Lombard *(G-13052)*
Combined Metals Chicago LLC ....F 847 683-0500
 Hampshire *(G-10967)*
Leading Edge Group Inc ....C 815 316-3500
 Rockford *(G-17492)*
Littell LLC ....E 630 916-6662
 Schaumburg *(G-18609)*
Nor Service Inc ....E 815 232-8379
 Freeport *(G-10130)*
Nucor Steel Kankakee Inc ....B 815 937-3131
 Bourbonnais *(G-2266)*
Worth Steel and Machine Co ....E 708 388-6300
 Alsip *(G-527)*

ROLLING MILL ROLLS: Cast Steel

Ameri Rolls and Guides 815 588-0486
 Lockport *(G-12981)*
Arcelormittal USA LLC ....C 312 899-3400
 Chicago *(G-3722)*
Arcelormittal USA LLC ....B 312 346-0300
 Chicago *(G-3723)*
Metal Resources Intl LLC ....F 847 806-7200
 Elk Grove Village *(G-9119)*
US Tsubaki Power Transm LLC ....C 847 459-9500
 Wheeling *(G-21004)*

ROLLS & BLANKETS, PRINTERS': Rubber Or Rubberized Fabric

Day International Group Inc ....D 630 406-6501
 Batavia *(G-1371)*
Lochman Ref Silk Screen Co ....F 847 475-6266
 Evanston *(G-9547)*
Rotation Dynamics Corporation ....E 630 679-7053
 Romeoville *(G-17871)*

ROLLS & ROLL COVERINGS: Rubber

Finzer Roller Inc ....E 847 390-6200
 Des Plaines *(G-7770)*
Industrial Roller Co ....F 618 234-0740
 Smithton *(G-19067)*
Pamarco Global Graphics Inc ....F 847 459-6000
 Wheeling *(G-20955)*

ROLLS: Rubber, Solid Or Covered

Hydac Rubber Manufacturing ....E 618 233-2129
 Smithton *(G-19065)*

ROOF DECKS

Castle Metal Products Corp ....G 847 806-4540
 Glendale Heights *(G-10442)*
Corrugated Metals Inc ....F 815 323-1310
 Belvidere *(G-1663)*
Epic Metals Corporation ....G 847 803-6411
 Des Plaines *(G-7759)*

PRODUCT SECTION

Pate Company Inc..................................E....... 630 705-1920
Lombard *(G-13118)*

ROOFING MATERIALS: Asphalt

Co-Fair Corporation..............................E....... 847 626-1500
Skokie *(G-18945)*
Cofair Products Inc...............................G....... 847 626-1500
Skokie *(G-18946)*
Cornerstone Building Products.............G....... 217 543-2829
Arthur *(G-848)*
Crosscom Inc...F....... 630 871-5500
Wheaton *(G-20794)*
Decatur Ras LLC...................................G....... 217 433-2794
Decatur *(G-7489)*
Deks North America Inc........................G....... 312 219-2110
Chicago *(G-4331)*
Jesus People USA Full Gos..................G....... 773 989-2083
Chicago *(G-5023)*
Jura Films North America LLC..............G....... 630 261-1226
Addison *(G-161)*
Karnak Midwest LLC............................F....... 708 338-3388
Broadview *(G-2447)*
Lakefront Roofing Supply......................E....... 773 509-0400
Chicago *(G-5163)*
Mrb Roofing Inc.....................................G....... 872 814-4430
University Park *(G-19963)*
RM Lucas Co...E....... 773 523-4300
Alsip *(G-504)*
TMJ Architectural LLC..........................G....... 815 388-7820
Crystal Lake *(G-7283)*
Vada LLC...F....... 407 572-4979
Olney *(G-15892)*

ROOFING MATERIALS: Sheet Metal

Berridge Manufacturing Company.........G....... 630 231-7495
West Chicago *(G-20551)*
J Mac Metals Inc....................................G....... 309 932-3001
Galva *(G-10233)*
Omnimax International Inc....................E....... 309 747-2937
Gridley *(G-10846)*
Petersen Aluminum Corporation...........D....... 847 228-7150
Elk Grove Village *(G-9176)*
Pro-Bilt Buildings LLC...........................F....... 217 532-9331
Hillsboro *(G-11319)*

ROOM COOLERS: Portable

Cardinal Construction Co......................G....... 618 842-5553
Fairfield *(G-9621)*

ROPE

All Gear Inc...G....... 847 564-9016
Northbrook *(G-15335)*

ROTORS: Motor

American Rotors Inc..............................E....... 847 263-1300
Gurnee *(G-10860)*
Marmon Industries LLC.........................G....... 312 372-9500
Chicago *(G-5345)*
Nidec Motor Corporation.......................B....... 847 585-8430
Elgin *(G-8673)*

RUBBER

Allstates Rubber & Tool Corp...............F....... 708 342-1030
Tinley Park *(G-19800)*
Bamberger Polymers Inc......................G....... 630 773-8626
Itasca *(G-11624)*
Crown Polymers LLC...........................G....... 847 683-0800
Hampshire *(G-10968)*
Custom Seal & Rubber Products.........G....... 888 356-2966
Mount Morris *(G-14499)*
Elas Tek Molding Inc............................E....... 815 675-9012
Spring Grove *(G-19274)*
Excelsior Inc...E....... 815 987-2900
Rockford *(G-17407)*
Hallstar Company..................................D....... 708 594-5947
Bedford Park *(G-1470)*
Honeywell Safety Pdts USA Inc..........C....... 630 343-3731
Bolingbrook *(G-2185)*
Modern Silicone Tech Inc.....................F....... 727 507-9800
Lincolnshire *(G-12785)*
Moriteq Rubber Co................................F....... 847 734-0970
Arlington Heights *(G-778)*
Morton Salt Inc......................................C....... 312 807-2000
Chicago *(G-5501)*
Nauvoo Products Inc.............................F....... 217 453-2817
Nauvoo *(G-15015)*
Parker-Hannifin Corporation..................C....... 630 427-2020
Woodridge *(G-21331)*
Plastic Specialties & Tech Inc..............G....... 847 781-2414
Schaumburg *(G-18675)*
Polymax Thrmplstic Elstmers LL..........E....... 847 316-9900
Waukegan *(G-20478)*
Star Thermoplastic Alloys and..............F....... 708 343-1100
Broadview *(G-2470)*
T9 Group LLC.......................................G....... 847 912-8862
Hawthorn Woods *(G-11126)*
Vibracoustic Usa Inc.............................E....... 618 382-5891
Carmi *(G-2916)*
Weiler Rubber Technologies LLC.........G....... 773 826-8900
Chicago *(G-6598)*

RUBBER PRDTS

Pro Form Industries Inc........................G....... 815 923-2555
Union *(G-19942)*
Rehling & Associates Inc......................G....... 630 941-3560
Elmhurst *(G-9417)*

RUBBER PRDTS: Appliance, Mechanical

Calumet Rubber Corp............................G....... 773 536-6350
Chicago *(G-4008)*

RUBBER PRDTS: Automotive, Mechanical

Andrews Automotive Company.............F....... 773 768-1122
Chicago *(G-3693)*
Kokoku Rubber Inc................................G....... 847 517-6770
Schaumburg *(G-18589)*
Mac Lean-Fogg Company......................D....... 847 566-0010
Mundelein *(G-14710)*
Wreck Room Inc....................................F....... 630 530-2166
Villa Park *(G-20177)*

RUBBER PRDTS: Mechanical

All-State Industries Inc..........................D....... 847 350-0460
Elk Grove Village *(G-8815)*
Aztec Products......................................G....... 217 726-8631
Springfield *(G-19323)*
Custom Seal & Rubber Products.........G....... 888 356-2966
Mount Morris *(G-14499)*
Elk Grove Rubber & Plastic Co............F....... 630 543-5656
Addison *(G-113)*
Excelsior Inc...E....... 815 987-2900
Rockford *(G-17407)*
Fairchild Industries Inc..........................E....... 847 550-9580
Lake Zurich *(G-12409)*
Finzer Roller Inc....................................E....... 410 939-1850
Des Plaines *(G-7769)*
Finzer Roller Inc....................................E....... 812 829-1455
Des Plaines *(G-7771)*
Fmi LLC...D....... 847 350-1535
Lincolnshire *(G-12765)*
Industrial Roller Co................................F....... 618 234-0740
Smithton *(G-19066)*
James Walker Mfg Co..........................E....... 708 754-4020
Glenwood *(G-10641)*
Louis J Hansen Enterprises Inc............F....... 630 956-3765
Aurora *(G-1124)*
Modern Silicone Tech Inc.....................F....... 727 507-9800
Lincolnshire *(G-12785)*
Nilan/Primarc Tool & Mold Inc..............F....... 847 885-2300
Hoffman Estates *(G-11439)*
Rotation Dynamics Corporation............D....... 773 247-5600
Chicago *(G-6066)*
Rt Enterprises Inc..................................F....... 847 675-1444
Skokie *(G-19025)*
Sage Products LLC..............................G....... 815 455-4700
Crystal Lake *(G-7260)*
Sanyo Seiki America Corp....................F....... 630 876-2670
Addison *(G-281)*
Smart Solutions Inc...............................G....... 630 775-1517
Itasca *(G-11734)*
Standard Rubber Products Co.............E....... 847 593-5630
Elk Grove Village *(G-9252)*
Systems By Lar Inc..............................G....... 815 694-3141
Clifton *(G-6916)*
Vibracoustic Usa Inc.............................E....... 618 382-5891
Carmi *(G-2916)*
Vibracoustic Usa Inc.............................C....... 618 382-2318
Carmi *(G-2917)*
Weiland Fast Trac Inc...........................G....... 847 438-7996
Long Grove *(G-13174)*

SALES PROMOTION SVCS

RUBBER PRDTS: Medical & Surgical Tubing, Extrudd & Lathe-Cut

Adora Bella Medspa LLC......................G....... 779 206-8331
Chicago *(G-3550)*

RUBBER PRDTS: Oil & Gas Field Machinery, Mechanical

GC Laser Systems Inc..........................G....... 844 532-1064
Forest Park *(G-9719)*

RUBBER PRDTS: Silicone

Advanced Prototype Molding................G....... 847 202-4200
Palatine *(G-16090)*
Voss Belting & Specialty Co................E....... 847 673-8900
Lincolnwood *(G-12849)*

RUBBER PRDTS: Sponge

Duraco Specialty Tapes LLC................D....... 866 800-0775
Forest Park *(G-9712)*
Hst Materials Inc...................................F....... 847 640-1803
Elk Grove Village *(G-9037)*
Jessup Manufacturing Company...........E....... 847 362-0961
Lake Bluff *(G-12190)*
Sponge-Cushion Inc..............................D....... 815 942-2300
Morris *(G-14328)*
Standard Rubber Products Co.............E....... 847 593-5630
Elk Grove Village *(G-9252)*

RUBBER STAMP, WHOLESALE

Bertco Enterprises Inc..........................G....... 618 234-9283
Belleville *(G-1535)*

RUBBER STRUCTURES: Air-Supported

Arizon Strctures Worldwide LLC..........E....... 618 451-7250
Granite City *(G-10697)*

RUGS: Hand & Machine Made

Organic Looms Inc................................G....... 312 832-0900
Chicago *(G-5697)*

RULERS: Metal

Lorette Dies Inc.....................................G....... 630 279-9682
Elmhurst *(G-9393)*

RUST RESISTING

Chemtool Incorporated..........................C....... 815 957-4140
Rockton *(G-17694)*
Chemtool Incorporated..........................D....... 815 459-1250
Crystal Lake *(G-7180)*
Daubert Industries Inc..........................F....... 630 203-6800
Burr Ridge *(G-2667)*
Ecp Incorporated...................................D....... 630 754-4200
Woodridge *(G-21297)*
Sanchem Inc...E....... 312 733-6100
Chicago *(G-6098)*

SAFES & VAULTS: Metal

First Alert Inc...C....... 630 499-3295
Aurora *(G-962)*
Talaris Inc...C....... 630 577-1000
Lisle *(G-12948)*

SAFETY EQPT & SPLYS WHOLESALERS

National Emergency Med ID Inc...........G....... 847 366-1267
Spring Grove *(G-19288)*

SAFETY INSPECTION SVCS

One Way Safety LLC............................E....... 708 579-0229
La Grange *(G-12085)*

SAILS

Nieman & Considine Inc.......................F....... 312 326-1053
Chicago *(G-5600)*
North Sails Group LLC........................G....... 773 489-1308
Chicago *(G-5621)*

SALES PROMOTION SVCS

Icd Publications Inc...............................G....... 847 913-8295
Lincolnshire *(G-12773)*

SALT

SALT

K+s Montana Holdings LLC .... G 312 807-2000
  Chicago *(G-5069)*
K+s Salt LLC .... G 844 789-3991
  Chicago *(G-5070)*

SALT & SULFUR MINING

Morton Salt Inc .... C 312 807-2000
  Chicago *(G-5501)*

SAMPLE BOOKS

Multi Swatch Corporation .... D 708 344-9440
  Broadview *(G-2456)*

SAND & GRAVEL

Aggregate Materials Company .... G 815 747-2430
  East Dubuque *(G-8174)*
Beverly Materials LLC .... G 847 695-9300
  Hoffman Estates *(G-11407)*
Bluemastiff Group LLC .... G 708 704-3529
  Chicago *(G-3916)*
Carlyle Sand & Gravel Ltd .... G 618 594-8263
  Carlyle *(G-2889)*
Consolidated Materials Inc .... G 815 568-1538
  Marengo *(G-13482)*
Consolidated Materials Inc .... F 847 658-4342
  Crystal Lake *(G-7185)*
Contractors Ready-Mix Inc .... G 217 482-5530
  Mason City *(G-13610)*
County Materials Corp .... E 217 352-4181
  Champaign *(G-3283)*
Covia Holdings Corporation .... G 618 747-2355
  Tamms *(G-19742)*
Cullinan & Sons Inc .... G 309 925-2711
  Tremont *(G-19895)*
Edge Capital Group Inc .... F 773 295-4774
  Chicago *(G-4451)*
Elmer L Larson L C .... G 815 895-4837
  Sycamore *(G-19710)*
Elmhurst-Chicago Stone Company .... F 630 557-2446
  Kaneville *(G-11954)*
Elmhurst-Chicago Stone Company .... E 630 983-6410
  Bolingbrook *(G-2173)*
Empire Acoustical Systems Inc .... E 815 261-0072
  Princeton *(G-16807)*
Fairmount Santrol Inc .... F 815 587-4410
  Ottawa *(G-16052)*
Fairmount Santrol Inc .... E 815 538-2645
  Troy Grove *(G-19921)*
FML Terminal Logistics LLC .... G 815 433-2449
  Wedron *(G-20524)*
Galena Road Gravel Inc .... E 309 274-6388
  Chillicothe *(G-6817)*
H & H Services Inc .... F 618 633-2837
  Hamel *(G-10949)*
Joliet Sand and Gravel Company .... D 815 741-2090
  Rockdale *(G-17262)*
Lafarge Aux Sable LLC .... G 815 941-1423
  Morris *(G-14309)*
Lafarge North America Inc .... C 773 372-1000
  Chicago *(G-5156)*
Legacy Vulcan LLC .... E 815 468-8141
  Manteno *(G-13450)*
Legacy Vulcan LLC .... E 815 937-7928
  Kankakee *(G-11989)*
Legacy Vulcan LLC .... E 217 498-7263
  Rochester *(G-17168)*
Legacy Vulcan LLC .... G 217 963-2196
  Harristown *(G-11032)*
Lt Construction .... G 815 243-6807
  Rockford *(G-17498)*
Material Service Corporation .... E 815 838-3420
  Romeoville *(G-17848)*
Material Service Corporation .... E 847 658-4559
  Algonquin *(G-380)*
Material Service Corporation .... E 708 447-1100
  Westchester *(G-20704)*
Material Service Corporation .... E 815 838-2400
  Romeoville *(G-17846)*
May Sand and Gravel Inc .... G 815 338-4761
  Wonder Lake *(G-21145)*
Menoni & Mocogni Inc .... F 847 432-0850
  Highland Park *(G-11283)*
Mertel Gravel Company Inc .... F 815 223-0468
  Peru *(G-16581)*
Mid-America Sand & Gravel .... G 217 355-1307
  Urbana *(G-19988)*
Newton Ready Mix Inc .... F 618 783-8611
  Newton *(G-15088)*
Otter Creek Sand & Gravel .... F 309 759-4293
  Havana *(G-11119)*
Pdss Construction .... F 847 980-6090
  Morton Grove *(G-14431)*
Pekin Sand and Gravel LLC .... G 309 347-8917
  Pekin *(G-16353)*
Plote Inc .... D 847 695-9467
  Hoffman Estates *(G-11446)*
Randy Wright & Son Cnstr .... G 217 478-4171
  Alexander *(G-363)*
Rockford Blacktop Cnstr Co .... D 815 654-4700
  Rockford *(G-17586)*
Rockford Sand & Gravel Co .... E 815 654-4700
  Loves Park *(G-13258)*
Rogers Ready Mix & Mtls Inc .... F 815 389-2223
  Roscoe *(G-17927)*
Rogers Ready Mix & Mtls Inc .... D 815 234-8212
  Byron *(G-2757)*
Rogers Redi-Mix Inc .... F 618 282-3844
  Ruma *(G-18106)*
Sand Valley Sand & Gravel Inc .... G 217 446-4210
  Danville *(G-7380)*
Sangamon Valley Sand & Gravel .... G 217 498-7189
  Rochester *(G-17171)*
Seneca Sand & Gravel LLC .... G 630 746-9183
  Seneca *(G-18862)*
Stokes Sand & Gravel Inc .... G 815 489-0680
  Batavia *(G-1420)*
Thelen Sand & Gravel Inc .... F 847 662-0760
  Waukegan *(G-20503)*
Tri-Con Materials Inc .... E 815 872-3206
  Princeton *(G-16824)*
Vandalia Sand & Gravel Inc .... F 618 283-4029
  Vandalia *(G-20028)*
Voss Sandworks Inc .... G 815 795-9366
  Morris *(G-14339)*
Voss Sandworks West Inc .... G 815 474-4042
  La Salle *(G-12124)*
Wayland Ready Mix Concrete Svc .... F 309 833-2064
  Galesburg *(G-10222)*

SAND MINING

Buckner Sand Co .... G 630 653-3700
  Wheaton *(G-20791)*
Mel Price Company Inc .... F 217 442-9092
  Danville *(G-7364)*
Mid-America Sand & Gravel .... G 217 586-4536
  Mahomet *(G-13426)*
Opti-Sand Incorporated .... G 630 293-1245
  West Chicago *(G-20626)*
Riverstone Group Inc .... G 309 787-1415
  Rock Island *(G-17243)*
Super Aggregates Inc .... G 815 385-8000
  McHenry *(G-13800)*

SAND RIDDLES: Hand Sifting Or Screening Apparatus

Sandbagger Corp .... F 630 876-2400
  Elmhurst *(G-9423)*

SAND: Hygrade

Clifford W Estes Co Inc .... F 815 433-0944
  Ottawa *(G-16047)*
Covia Holdings Corporation .... D 815 732-2121
  Oregon *(G-15916)*
Covia Holdings Corporation .... E 203 966-8880
  Ottawa *(G-16049)*
Fairmount Santrol Inc .... F 815 433-2449
  Ottawa *(G-16051)*
Spectron Manufacturing .... G 720 879-7605
  Bloomingdale *(G-2015)*
Unimin Lime Corporation .... F 203 966-8880
  Ottawa *(G-16083)*
Wedron Silica Company .... G 815 433-2449
  Wedron *(G-20525)*

SAND: Silica

Covia Holdings Corporation .... G 815 539-6734
  Troy Grove *(G-19920)*
U S Silica Company .... G 800 635-7263
  Ottawa *(G-16082)*

SANDBLASTING EQPT

Blastline USA Inc .... G 630 871-0147
  Carol Stream *(G-2951)*

SANITARY SVC, NEC

Best Technology Systems Inc .... E 815 254-9554
  Plainfield *(G-16644)*

SANITARY SVCS: Chemical Detoxification

Rock Valley Oil & Chemical Co .... D 815 654-2400
  Loves Park *(G-13254)*

SANITARY SVCS: Dead Animal Disposal

Millstadt Rendering Company .... E 618 538-5312
  Belleville *(G-1578)*

SANITARY SVCS: Hazardous Waste, Collection & Disposal

Drumbeaters of America Inc .... F 630 365-5527
  Elburn *(G-8449)*
Precious Metal Ref Svcs Inc .... G 847 756-2700
  Barrington *(G-1237)*

SANITARY SVCS: Incinerator, Operation Of

Anderson Msnry Refr Spcialists .... G 847 540-8885
  Lake Zurich *(G-12384)*

SANITARY SVCS: Medical Waste Disposal

Daniels Sharpsmart Inc .... E 312 546-8900
  Chicago *(G-4313)*

SANITARY SVCS: Refuse Collection & Disposal Svcs

Darling Ingredients Inc .... E 708 388-3223
  Blue Island *(G-2117)*
Decatur Ras LLC .... G 217 433-2794
  Decatur *(G-7489)*
Tri-State Disposal Inc .... E 708 388-9910
  Riverdale *(G-17077)*

SANITARY SVCS: Rubbish Collection & Disposal

BFI Waste Systems N Amer Inc .... E 847 429-7370
  Elgin *(G-8521)*

SANITARY SVCS: Waste Materials, Recycling

Ace Plastic Inc .... F 815 635-3737
  Chatsworth *(G-3425)*
Agriscience Inc .... G 212 365-4214
  Peoria *(G-16377)*
Alter Trading Corporation .... F 309 697-6161
  Bartonville *(G-1327)*
Bio Industries Inc .... D 847 215-8999
  Wheeling *(G-20859)*
D & P Construction Co Inc .... E 773 714-9330
  Chicago *(G-4299)*
Dels Metal Co .... F 309 788-1993
  Rock Island *(G-17216)*
Gfl Environmental Svcs USA Inc .... E 866 579-6900
  Mokena *(G-14088)*
GM Scrap Metals .... G 618 259-8570
  Cottage Hills *(G-7028)*
Greencycle of Indiana Inc .... G 847 441-6606
  Northfield *(G-15515)*
Kreider Services Incorporated .... D 815 288-6691
  Dixon *(G-7903)*
Lake Area Disposal Service Inc .... E 217 522-9271
  Springfield *(G-19397)*
Liberty Tire Recycling LLC .... G 773 871-6360
  Chicago *(G-5218)*
Malvaes Solutions Incorporated .... G 773 823-1034
  Chicago *(G-5324)*
Mervis Industries Inc .... G 217 753-1492
  Springfield *(G-19405)*
Midwest Recycling Co .... E 815 744-4922
  Rockdale *(G-17268)*
Pontiac Recyclers Inc .... G 815 844-6419
  Pontiac *(G-16777)*
RDF Inc .... F 618 273-4141
  Eldorado *(G-8483)*
S & S Metal Recyclers Inc .... F 630 844-3344
  Aurora *(G-1152)*
Twin City Wood Recycling Corp .... G 309 827-9663
  Bloomington *(G-2106)*

PRODUCT SECTION

SANITARY WARE: Metal

Kohler Co .... E 630 323-7674
Burr Ridge *(G-2693)*
Kohler Co .... D 847 734-1777
Huntley *(G-11548)*
Swan Surfaces LLC .... C 618 532-5673
Centralia *(G-3252)*

SANITATION CHEMICALS & CLEANING AGENTS

Acl Inc .... F 773 285-0295
Chicago *(G-3525)*
Aerosols Danville Inc .... B 217 442-1400
Danville *(G-7318)*
Calumet Refining LLC .... F 708 832-2463
Burnham *(G-2644)*
Cater Chemical Co .... G 630 980-2300
Roselle *(G-17943)*
Chemix Corp .... F 708 754-2150
Glenwood *(G-10639)*
Chemtool Incorporated .... C 815 957-4140
Rockton *(G-17694)*
Chemtool Incorporated .... D 815 459-1250
Crystal Lake *(G-7180)*
Circle K Industries Inc .... F 847 949-0363
Mundelein *(G-14677)*
Claire-Sprayway Inc .... D 630 628-3000
Downers Grove *(G-7973)*
CLC Lubricants Company .... E 630 232-7900
Geneva *(G-10261)*
Clorox Manufacturing Company ... C 847 229-5500
Wheeling *(G-20872)*
Concept Laboratories Inc .... D 773 395-7300
Chicago *(G-4214)*
Consolidated Chem Works Ltd ... E 312 226-6150
Chicago *(G-4222)*
Damco Products Inc .... G 618 452-4700
Madison *(G-13407)*
Danko Industries .... G 630 882-6070
Yorkville *(G-21477)*
Dober Chemical Corp .... C 630 410-7300
Woodridge *(G-21294)*
Ecolab Inc .... G 847 350-2229
Elk Grove Village *(G-8967)*
Ecolab Inc .... E 847 350-2229
Elk Grove Village *(G-8968)*
Gea Farm Technologies Inc ..... E 630 369-8100
Romeoville *(G-17828)*
Getex Corporation .... G 630 993-1300
Aurora *(G-968)*
Henkel Consumer Goods Inc ... C 630 892-4381
Montgomery *(G-14246)*
Hurst Chemical Company .... G 815 964-0451
Rockford *(G-17454)*
Jacob Hay Company .... G 847 215-8880
Wheeling *(G-20918)*
K-Technology Inc .... G 708 458-4890
Chicago *(G-5072)*
Kafko International Ltd .... E 847 763-0333
Skokie *(G-18971)*
Kocour Co .... E 773 847-1111
Chicago *(G-5114)*
Lundmark Inc .... F 630 628-1199
Addison *(G-186)*
Mackenzie Johnson .... G 630 244-2367
Maywood *(G-13672)*
Oil-Dri Corporation America .... D 618 745-6881
Mounds *(G-14463)*
Premium Oil Company .... F 815 963-3800
Rockford *(G-17559)*
Princeton Sealing Wax Co .... G 815 875-1943
Princeton *(G-16821)*
Protective Products Intl .... F 847 526-1180
Wauconda *(G-20386)*
Rainbow Cleaners .... G 630 789-6989
Westmont *(G-20768)*
Rochester Midland Corporation ... E 630 896-8543
Montgomery *(G-14267)*
Rock-Tred 2 LLC .... E 888 762-5873
Waukegan *(G-20489)*
Rust-Oleum Corporation .... C 847 367-7700
Vernon Hills *(G-20089)*
Sandstrom Products Company ... E 309 523-2121
Port Byron *(G-16787)*
Sandstrom Products Company ... F 309 523-2121
Port Byron *(G-16788)*
Umf Corporation .... G 224 251-7822
Niles *(G-15184)*
Umf Corporation .... F 847 920-0370
Skokie *(G-19049)*
Vanguard Chemical Corporation ... F 312 751-0717
Chicago *(G-6520)*

SASHES: Door Or Window, Metal

Custom Aluminum Products Inc ... B 847 717-5000
South Elgin *(G-19141)*
YKK AP America Inc .... F 630 582-9602
Roselle *(G-17998)*

SATCHELS

Sultry Satchels Inc .... G 312 810-1081
Chicago *(G-6264)*

SATELLITES: Communications

Advance Technologies Inc .... G 815 297-1771
Freeport *(G-10097)*
Bolingbrook Communications Inc ... A 630 759-9500
Lisle *(G-12874)*
Hi-Def Communications .... G 217 258-6679
Mattoon *(G-13637)*
Metro Service Center .... G 618 524-8583
Metropolis *(G-13973)*
Prime Time Sports LLC .... F 847 637-3500
Arlington Heights *(G-790)*
Vincor Ltd .... F 708 534-0008
Monee *(G-14211)*

SAW BLADES

Allkut Tool Incorporated .... G 815 476-9656
Wilmington *(G-21096)*
Contour Saws Inc .... D 800 259-6834
Des Plaines *(G-7750)*
Custom Blades & Tools Inc ..... G 630 860-7650
Bensenville *(G-1782)*
Estwing Manufacturing Co Inc ... B 815 397-9521
Rockford *(G-17402)*
Jaeger Saw and Cutter Inc ...... G 815 963-0313
Rockford *(G-17472)*
Milwaukee Electric Tool Corp ... B 847 588-3356
Niles *(G-15147)*
R & S Cutterhead Mfg Co .... F 815 678-2611
Richmond *(G-17020)*
S & J Industrial Supply Corp ... F 708 339-1708
South Holland *(G-19242)*
Saws International Inc .... E 815 397-0985
Machesney Park *(G-13373)*
Wallace/Haskin Corp .... G 630 789-2882
Downers Grove *(G-8105)*

SAWING & PLANING MILLS

Alstat Wood Products .... F 618 684-5167
Murphysboro *(G-14750)*
Autumn Mill .... G 217 795-3399
Argenta *(G-671)*
Bach Timber & Pallet Inc .... G 815 885-3774
Caledonia *(G-2768)*
Bailey Business Group .... G 618 548-3566
Salem *(G-18330)*
Bond Brothers Hardwoods ...... G 618 272-4811
Ridgway *(G-17035)*
Boyd Sawmill .... G 618 735-2056
Dix *(G-7881)*
Bull Valley Hardwood .... G 815 701-9400
Woodstock *(G-21368)*
Bull Valley Hardwood .... G 815 701-9400
Crystal Lake *(G-7174)*
Carpenters Millwork Co .... F 708 339-7707
South Holland *(G-19204)*
Carpenters Millwork Co .... F 708 339-7707
Villa Park *(G-20137)*
Charles Horn Lumber Company ... F 708 339-7397
Cicero *(G-6832)*
Charles K Eichen .... G 217 854-9751
Carlinville *(G-2871)*
Christiansen Sawmill and Log ... G 815 315-7520
Caledonia *(G-2769)*
Clarence Hancock Sawmill Inc ... G 618 854-2232
Noble *(G-15189)*
Corsaw Hardwood Lumber Inc ... F 309 293-2055
Smithfield *(G-19063)*
Crooked Trails Sawmill .... G 618 244-1547
Opdyke *(G-15904)*
Darrell Fickas .... G 618 599-3632
Mount Vernon *(G-14605)*
E-Z Tree Recycling Inc .... G 773 493-8600
Chicago *(G-4428)*
Eichen Lumber Co Inc .... G 217 854-9751
Carlinville *(G-2874)*
Ericson S Log & Lumber Co .... G 309 667-2147
New Windsor *(G-15073)*
Five Star Pallets Inc .... G 847 613-8488
McHenry *(G-13744)*
Forestech Wood Products .... G 217 279-3659
West Union *(G-20690)*
Francis L Morris .... G 618 676-1724
Clay City *(G-6905)*
Fraser Millwork Inc .... G 708 447-3262
Lyons *(G-13309)*
G L Beaumont Lumber Company ... F 618 423-2323
Ramsey *(G-16964)*
Goodale Corporation .... G 312 421-9663
Chicago *(G-4717)*
Goodman Sawmill .... G 309 547-3597
Lewistown *(G-12615)*
Heartland Hardwoods Inc .... E 217 844-3312
Effingham *(G-8402)*
J M Lustig Custom Cabinets Co ... F 217 342-6661
Effingham *(G-8403)*
Jefferies Orchard Sawmill .... G 217 487-7582
Springfield *(G-19395)*
Kirkland Sawmill Inc .... G 815 522-6150
Kirkland *(G-12062)*
Kniffen Brothers Sawmill .... G 618 629-2437
Whittington *(G-21020)*
Koppers Industries Inc .... E 309 343-5157
Galesburg *(G-10206)*
Larry Musgrave Logging .... G 618 842-6386
Fairfield *(G-9630)*
M D Harmon Inc .... F 618 662-8925
Xenia *(G-21468)*
Marvin Suckow .... G 618 483-5570
Mason *(G-13608)*
Mulvain Woodworks .... G 815 248-2305
Durand *(G-8154)*
Old School Timber Works Co ... G 847 918-8626
Libertyville *(G-12692)*
Paulette Colson .... F 618 372-8888
Medora *(G-13815)*
Red River Lumber Inc .... D 708 388-1818
Blue Island *(G-2135)*
Rjt Wood Services .... G 815 858-2081
Galena *(G-10177)*
Sawmill Construction Inc .... G 815 937-0037
Bourbonnais *(G-2268)*
Schrocks Sawmill .... G 217 268-3632
Arcola *(G-665)*
Simonton Hardwood Lumber LLC ... F 618 594-2132
Carlyle *(G-2896)*
Towerleaf LLC .... G 847 985-1937
Schaumburg *(G-18750)*
Tree-O Lumber Inc .... E 618 357-2576
Pinckneyville *(G-16620)*
Triezenberg Millwork Co .... G 708 489-9062
Crestwood *(G-7132)*
Tronox Incorporated .... E 203 705-3704
Madison *(G-13418)*
Westrock Cp LLC .... G 630 655-6951
Burr Ridge *(G-2733)*
Willenborg Hardwood Inds Inc ... F 217 844-2082
Effingham *(G-8431)*
Willowbrook Sawmill .... G 618 592-3806
Oblong *(G-15832)*
Woodcraft Enterprises Inc ...... G 815 485-2787
New Lenox *(G-15070)*
Wooded Wonderland .... G 815 777-1223
Galena *(G-10182)*

SAWING & PLANING MILLS: Custom

Farrow Lumber Co .... G 618 734-0255
Cairo *(G-2767)*

SAWS & SAWING EQPT

Decatur Custom Tool Inc .... G 618 244-4078
Mount Vernon *(G-14606)*
Ed Hartwig Trucking & Excvtg ... G 309 364-3672
Henry *(G-11163)*
Gentry Small Engine Repair .... G 217 849-3378
Toledo *(G-19875)*
Gibson Insurance Inc .... G 217 864-4877
Mount Zion *(G-14646)*
Hopkins Saws & Karts Inc ...... G 618 756-2778
Belle Rive *(G-1525)*
Kaser Power Equipment Inc .... G 309 289-2176
Knoxville *(G-12068)*
Kevins Small Engine Repair .... G 309 897-2026
Bradford *(G-2274)*

Employee Codes: A=Over 500 employees, B=251-500
C=101-250, D=51-100, E=20-50, F=10-19, G=3-9

SAWS & SAWING EQPT

Michaels Equipment Co .... G 618 524-8560
  Metropolis *(G-13975)*
Outdoor Power Inc .... F 217 228-9890
  Quincy *(G-16921)*
Owen Walker .... G 217 285-4012
  Pittsfield *(G-16636)*
Peoria Midwest Equipment Inc .... G 309 454-6800
  Normal *(G-15217)*
Saws Unlimited Inc .... G 847 640-7450
  Elk Grove Village *(G-9232)*

SCAFFOLDING WHOLESALERS

Designed Eqp Acquisition Corp .... E 847 647-5000
  Elk Grove Village *(G-8947)*
Gilco Real Estate Company .... E 847 298-1717
  Des Plaines *(G-7774)*

SCAFFOLDS: Mobile Or Stationary, Metal

Designed Eqp Acquisition Corp .... E 847 647-5000
  Elk Grove Village *(G-8947)*
Werner Co .... E 815 459-6020
  Crystal Lake *(G-7294)*

SCALE REPAIR SVCS

Florida Metrology LLC .... F 630 833-3800
  Villa Park *(G-20147)*
Southern Ill Scale & Cnstr Inc .... G 618 723-2303
  Noble *(G-15192)*

SCALES & BALANCES, EXC LABORATORY

Brian Burcar .... G 815 856-2271
  Leonore *(G-12611)*
E Rowe Foundry & Machine Co ...... D 217 382-4135
  Martinsville *(G-13583)*
EJ Cady & Company .... G 847 537-2239
  Wheeling *(G-20888)*
Glenview Systems Inc .... F 847 724-2691
  Glenview *(G-10552)*
International Rd Dynamics Corp ..... E 815 675-1430
  Spring Grove *(G-19277)*
Medela LLC .... C 800 435-8316
  McHenry *(G-13768)*
Meto-Grafics Inc .... F 847 639-0044
  Crystal Lake *(G-7226)*
Pelstar LLC .... E 708 377-0600
  Countryside *(G-7067)*

SCALES: Baby

Heng Tuo Usa Inc .... G 630 317-7672
  Oakbrook Terrace *(G-15802)*

SCALES: Bathroom

Lllb LLC .... F 630 315-3300
  Elk Grove Village *(G-9097)*
Newell Operating Company .... C 815 235-4171
  Freeport *(G-10129)*

SCALES: Indl

Advanced Weighing Systems Inc .... G 630 916-6179
  Addison *(G-22)*
Belt-Way Scales Inc .... E 815 625-5573
  Rock Falls *(G-17176)*
Doran Scales Inc .... E 630 879-1200
  Saint Charles *(G-18186)*
G & H Balancer Service .... G 773 509-1988
  Chicago *(G-4647)*
Howard Schwartz .... G 847 540-8260
  Round Lake Beach *(G-18089)*
Mettler-Toledo LLC .... E 630 446-7700
  Aurora *(G-1002)*

SCALES: Truck

Southern Ill Scale & Cnstr Inc .... G 618 723-2303
  Noble *(G-15192)*

SCANNING DEVICES: Optical

Applus Technologies Inc .... E 312 661-1100
  Chicago *(G-3714)*
Bowe Bell + Hwell Scanners LLC ... E 847 675-7600
  Wheeling *(G-20864)*
Dennis Wright .... G 847 816-6110
  Vernon Hills *(G-20049)*
Digital Check Corp .... E 847 446-2285
  Northbrook *(G-15376)*

Spartanics Ltd .... E 847 394-5700
  Rolling Meadows *(G-17777)*

SCHOOL SPLYS, EXC BOOKS: Wholesalers

Debcor Inc .... G 708 333-2191
  South Holland *(G-19207)*

SCHOOLS: Elementary & Secondary

READ Worldwide LLC .... G 312 301-6276
  Chicago *(G-5982)*

SCHOOLS: Vocational, NEC

Associated Design Inc .... F 708 974-9100
  Palos Hills *(G-16195)*

SCIENTIFIC INSTRUMENTS WHOLESALERS

Fox International Corp .... F 773 465-3634
  Chicago *(G-4627)*
Uic Inc .... G 815 744-4477
  Joliet *(G-11937)*
Wilkens-Anderson Company .... E 773 384-4433
  Chicago *(G-6626)*

SCRAP & WASTE MATERIALS, WHOLESALE: Auto Wrecking For Scrap

Lkq Corporation .... C 312 621-1950
  Chicago *(G-5243)*
Springfield Iron & Metal Co .... G 217 544-7131
  Springfield *(G-19452)*

SCRAP & WASTE MATERIALS, WHOLESALE: Ferrous Metal

Alter Trading Corporation .... F 217 223-0156
  Quincy *(G-16852)*
Azcon Inc .... F 815 548-7000
  Sterling *(G-19499)*
Belson Steel Center Scrap Inc .... E 815 932-7416
  Bourbonnais *(G-2256)*
Cicero Iron Metal & Paper Inc .... G 708 863-8601
  Cicero *(G-6834)*
Fox Valley Iron & Metal Corp .... F 630 897-5907
  Aurora *(G-1098)*
GM Scrap Metals .... G 618 259-8570
  Cottage Hills *(G-7028)*
Illini Castings LLC .... F 217 446-6365
  Danville *(G-7349)*
Lemont Scrap Processing .... G 630 257-6532
  Lemont *(G-12569)*
M Buckman & Son Co .... G 815 663-9411
  Spring Valley *(G-19309)*
Mervis Industries Inc .... C 217 442-5300
  Danville *(G-7365)*
Mervis Industries Inc .... F 217 235-5575
  Mattoon *(G-13648)*
Metal Management Inc .... F 773 721-1100
  Chicago *(G-5405)*
Metal Management Inc .... F 773 489-1800
  Chicago *(G-5406)*
Midstate Salvage Corp .... G 217 824-6047
  Taylorville *(G-19759)*
Rondout Iron & Metal Co Inc .... E 847 362-2750
  Lake Bluff *(G-12208)*
Serlin Iron & Metal Co Inc .... F 773 227-3826
  Chicago *(G-6138)*
Weco Trading Inc .... G 847 615-1020
  Lake Bluff *(G-12215)*

SCRAP & WASTE MATERIALS, WHOLESALE: Junk & Scrap

Nelson Manufacturing Co Inc .... F 815 229-0161
  Rockford *(G-17537)*
Top Metal Buyers Inc .... F 314 421-2721
  East Saint Louis *(G-8327)*
Vim Recyclers LP .... C 630 892-2559
  Aurora *(G-1166)*

SCRAP & WASTE MATERIALS, WHOLESALE: Metal

Abco Metals Corporations .... F 773 881-1504
  Chicago *(G-3509)*
Alter Trading Corporation .... F 309 828-6084
  Bloomington *(G-2023)*
Archer Metal & Paper Co .... F 773 585-3030
  Chicago *(G-3726)*

C&R Scrap Iron & Metal .... G 847 459-9815
  Wheeling *(G-20868)*
Dels Metal Co .... F 309 788-1993
  Rock Island *(G-17216)*
Lake Area Disposal Service Inc ..... E 217 522-9271
  Springfield *(G-19397)*
Mervis Industries Inc .... E 217 753-1492
  Springfield *(G-19405)*
Midland Davis Corporation .... D 309 277-1617
  Moline *(G-14161)*
Pontiac Recyclers Inc .... G 815 844-6419
  Pontiac *(G-16777)*

SCRAP & WASTE MATERIALS, WHOLESALE: Nonferrous Metals Scrap

Midland Industries Inc .... E 312 664-7300
  Chicago *(G-5434)*
T & C Metal Co .... G 815 459-4445
  Crystal Lake *(G-7274)*

SCRAP & WASTE MATERIALS, WHOLESALE: Paper

C & M Recycling Inc .... E 847 578-1066
  North Chicago *(G-15308)*
Midwest Fiber Inc Decatur .... E 217 424-9460
  Decatur *(G-7524)*

SCRAP & WASTE MATERIALS, WHOLESALE: Paper & Cloth Materials

Buster Services Inc .... E 773 247-2070
  Chicago *(G-3983)*

SCREENS: Projection

AV Stumpfl Usa Corp .... F 630 359-0999
  Elmhurst *(G-9327)*
Ops 3 LLC .... G 312 243-8265
  Chicago *(G-5683)*
Rensel-Chicago Inc .... E 773 235-2100
  Chicago *(G-6015)*

SCREENS: Window, Metal

Climate Guard Design .... G 773 873-0000
  Chicago *(G-4178)*
Thermal Industries Inc .... E 800 237-0560
  Wood Dale *(G-21249)*

SCREENS: Woven Wire

City Screen Inc .... G 773 588-5642
  Chicago *(G-4161)*

SCREW MACHINE PRDTS

A E Micek Engineering Corp .... E 847 455-8181
  Franklin Park *(G-9857)*
Abbco Inc .... E 630 595-7115
  Bensenville *(G-1722)*
Abbott Interfast LLC .... D 847 459-6200
  Wheeling *(G-20838)*
Abbott Scott Manufacturing Co ...... E 773 342-7200
  Chicago *(G-3505)*
Ability Fasteners Inc .... F 847 593-4230
  Elk Grove Village *(G-8795)*
Accumation Inc .... F 815 455-6250
  Crystal Lake *(G-7154)*
Acme Screw Co .... F 815 332-7548
  Cherry Valley *(G-3436)*
Afco Products Incorporated .... E 847 299-1055
  Lake Zurich *(G-12380)*
Afi Industries Inc .... E 630 462-0400
  Carol Stream *(G-2927)*
Alert Screw Products Corp .... G 847 587-1360
  Fox Lake *(G-9744)*
Alpha Swiss Industries Inc .... G 815 455-3031
  Crystal Lake *(G-7157)*
AM Swiss Screw Mch Pdts Inc ...... F 847 468-9300
  South Elgin *(G-19132)*
American Machine Pdts & Svcs ..... G 708 743-9088
  Mokena *(G-14071)*
American Screw Machine Co .... G 847 455-4308
  Franklin Park *(G-9868)*
American/Jebco Corporation .... C 847 455-3150
  Cicero *(G-6829)*
Ampex Screw Mfg Inc .... G 847 228-1202
  Arlington Heights *(G-692)*
Archer Engineering Company .... G 773 247-3501
  Darien *(G-7402)*

PRODUCT SECTION — SCREW MACHINE PRDTS

Company	Code	Phone
Astro-Craft Inc — Spring Grove (G-19265)	E	815 675-1500
Automatic Precision Inc — Chicago (G-3778)	E	708 867-1116
Automatic Swiss Corporation — Addison (G-43)	E	630 543-3888
Automation Systems Inc — Melrose Park (G-13828)	E	847 671-9515
Autonamic Corporation — Spring Grove (G-19266)		815 675-6300
Autonetics Inc — Carpentersville (G-3094)	F	847 426-8525
Avan Tool & Die Co Inc — Chicago (G-3782)	F	773 287-1670
Avanti Engineering Inc — Glendale Heights (G-10437)	F	630 260-1333
B Radtke and Sons Inc — Round Lake Park (G-18095)	G	847 546-3999
Bal-Craft Screw Machine Co — Elk Grove Village (G-8855)		847 398-7688
Bare Metals Inc — Chicago (G-3832)		773 583-1100
Begoun Inc — Elmhurst (G-9329)		630 617-0200
Bensenville Screw Products — Bensenville (G-1752)		630 860-5222
Bradley Machining Inc — Addison (G-53)	F	630 543-2875
Bridgestone Company Inc — Wheeling (G-20866)	E	847 325-5172
Calcon Machine Inc — Leland (G-12548)	G	815 495-9227
Calumet Screw Machine Products — Mokena (G-14074)	D	708 479-1660
Camco Manufacturing Inc — Crestwood (G-7108)	F	708 597-4288
Camcraft Inc — Hanover Park (G-11001)	C	630 582-6001
Central Autmtc Screw Pdts Inc — Bensenville (G-1764)		630 766-7966
Century Automatics LLC — Huntley (G-11531)	G	847 515-1188
Charter Precision LLC — Elgin (G-8536)	D	847 214-8400
Chase Fasteners Inc — Melrose Park (G-13841)	E	708 345-0335
Chicago Rivet & Machine Co — Naperville (G-14798)	D	630 357-8500
Composite Cutter Tech Inc — Volo (G-20198)	G	847 740-6875
Continental Midland — Calumet Park (G-2797)	G	708 441-1000
Continental Screws Mch Pdts — Wheeling (G-20875)	E	847 459-7766
Contour Screw Products Inc — Arlington Heights (G-719)	E	847 357-1190
CP Screw Machine Products — Bensenville (G-1780)	F	630 766-2313
Demco Products Inc — Oak Lawn (G-15713)	F	708 636-6240
Devon Precision Machine Pdts — Franklin Park (G-9932)	F	847 233-9700
Dune Manufacturing Company — Melrose Park (G-13854)	F	708 681-2905
E J Basler Co — Schiller Park (G-18800)	D	847 678-8880
Ella Engineering Incorporated — Elk Grove Village (G-8974)	G	847 354-4767
Empire Screw Manufacturing Co — Villa Park (G-20146)	F	630 833-7060
Engineered Plastic Pdts Corp — Mount Prospect (G-14526)	E	847 952-8400
F and F Screw Products — Rockford (G-17411)	G	815 968-7330
Flexicraft Industries Inc — Chicago (G-4610)	E	312 738-3588
Formar Inc — Addison (G-128)	F	630 543-1151
Forster Tool & Mfg Co Inc — Bensenville (G-1802)	E	630 616-8177
Francis Screw Products Co Inc — Niles (G-15122)	G	847 647-9462
Franklin Screw Products Inc — Genoa (G-10317)	G	815 784-8500
Fsp LLC — Gurnee (G-10880)	G	773 992-2600
G & E Automatic — Machesney Park (G-13345)	G	815 654-7766
Gage Manufacturing Inc — Elk Grove Village (G-9009)	F	847 228-7300
General Engineering Works — Addison (G-136)	E	630 543-8000
Greg Screw Machine Products — Wood Dale (G-21195)	G	630 694-8875
H & M Thread Rolling Co Inc — Franklin Park (G-9955)	G	847 451-1570
Hi-Tech Welding Services Inc — Bensenville (G-1819)	G	630 595-8160
Highland Mch & Screw Pdts Co — Highland (G-11218)	D	618 654-2103
Highland Metal Inc — Hillside (G-11342)	E	708 544-6641
I D Rockford Shop Inc — Winnebago (G-21120)	G	815 335-1150
Illinois Tool Works Inc — Machesney Park (G-13348)	E	815 654-1510
Illinois Tool Works Inc — Elgin (G-8620)	E	847 741-7900
J N R Custo-Matic Screw Inc — Glendale Heights (G-10462)	D	630 260-1333
JB Mfg & Screw Machine — Burr Ridge (G-2691)	G	630 850-6978
JB Mfg & Screw Machine PR — Franklin Park (G-9973)	G	847 451-0892
Jedi Corporation — McHenry (G-13752)	G	815 344-5334
Jim Sterner Machines — Rockford (G-17474)	G	815 962-8983
Kenent Screw Machine Products — Rockton (G-17699)	F	815 624-7216
L & W Tool & Screw Mch Pdts — Itasca (G-11690)	E	847 238-1212
L D Redmer Screw Pdts Inc — Bensenville (G-1838)	D	630 787-0504
Lab Ten LLC — Machesney Park (G-13355)	E	815 877-1410
Lafox Screw Products Inc — South Elgin (G-19164)	G	847 695-1732
Lakeside Screw Products Inc — Addison (G-181)	C	630 495-1606
Lakeview Prcsion Machining Inc — South Elgin (G-19165)	F	847 742-7170
Lawrence Screw Products Inc — Lincoln (G-12732)	G	217 735-1230
Lombard Swiss Screw Company — Addison (G-185)	E	630 576-5096
Lsl Precision Machining Inc — Loves Park (G-13234)	E	815 633-4701
Mac Lean-Fogg Company — Mundelein (G-14710)	D	847 566-0010
Magnet-Schultz Amer Holdg LLC — Westmont (G-20755)	F	630 789-0600
Magnet-Schultz America Inc — Westmont (G-20756)	D	630 789-0600
Magnus Screw Products Co — Chicago (G-5318)		773 889-2344
Makerite Mfg Co Inc — Roscoe (G-17916)	E	815 389-3902
Masters Yates Inc — Rockford (G-17509)	G	815 227-9585
McHenry Screw Products Inc — McHenry (G-13766)	G	815 344-4638
Meaden Precision — Burr Ridge (G-2700)	G	630 655-0888
Meaden Precision Machined Pdts — Burr Ridge (G-2701)	D	630 655-0888
Meador Industries Inc — Franklin Park (G-9988)	E	847 671-5042
Metomic Corporation — Chicago (G-5410)	E	773 247-4716
Micro Craft Manufacturing Co — Skokie (G-18989)	F	847 679-2022
Micro Screw Machine Co Inc — Rockford (G-17522)	G	815 397-2115
Midway Machine Products & Svcs — Elk Grove Village (G-9125)	G	847 860-8180
Minic Precision Inc — Spring Grove (G-19285)	F	815 675-0451
Monnex International Inc — Buffalo Grove (G-2576)		847 850-5263
Multitech Cold Forming LLC — Carol Stream (G-3034)	E	630 949-8200
Multitech Swiss Machining LLC — Carol Stream (G-3037)		260 894-4180
National Cap and Set Screw Co — Spring Grove (G-19287)	F	815 675-2363
National Cycle Inc — Maywood (G-13674)	C	708 343-0400
Nelson & Lavold Manufacturing — Chicago (G-5565)		312 943-6300
Nu-Metal Products Inc — Crystal Lake (G-7241)	F	815 459-2075
Nyclo Screw Machine Pdts Inc — Rockford (G-17540)	F	815 229-7900
Oberg Medical Products Co LLC — Niles (G-15153)	D	847 965-3030
Panek Precision Products Co — Northbrook (G-15451)	C	847 291-9755
Pioneer Service Inc — Addison (G-241)	E	630 628-0249
Precise Products Inc — Warrenville (G-20247)	E	630 393-9698
Precision McHned Cmponents Inc — Romeoville (G-17866)	E	630 759-5555
Precision Screw Machining Co — Chicago (G-5859)	F	773 205-4280
Precision Steel Warehouse Inc — Franklin Park (G-10026)	C	800 323-0740
Precision-Tek Mfg Inc — Arlington Heights (G-789)	E	847 364-7800
Preferred Fasteners Inc — Carol Stream (G-3048)		630 510-0200
Princeton Industrial Pdts Inc — Elgin (G-8695)	F	847 839-8500
Process Screw Products Inc — Shannon (G-18872)	E	815 864-2220
Progressive Turnings Inc — Aurora (G-1146)	F	630 898-3072
Qcc LLC — Harwood Heights (G-11107)	C	708 867-5400
Quality Control Corp — Harwood Heights (G-11109)	F	708 887-6239
Quantum Precision Inc — West Chicago (G-20634)	E	630 692-1545
R & N Machine Co — Riverdale (G-17075)	F	708 841-5555
R B Evans Co — Elburn (G-8471)	G	630 365-3554
Reino Tool & Manufacturing Co — Chicago (G-6005)	F	773 588-5800
RF Mau Co — Lincolnwood (G-12838)		847 329-9731
Roberts Swiss Inc — Itasca (G-11726)		630 467-9100
S & W Manufacturing Co Inc — Bensenville (G-1888)	E	630 595-5044
Saturn Manufacturing Company — Bensenville (G-1889)	G	630 860-8474
Screw Machine Engrg Co Inc — Chicago (G-6122)		773 631-7600
Screws Industries Inc — Glendale Heights (G-10493)	D	630 539-9200
Security Locknut LLC — Vernon Hills (G-20095)	E	847 970-4050
Special Fastener Operations — Belvidere (G-1701)	G	815 544-6449
Specialty Screw Corporation — Rockford (G-17638)	C	815 969-4100
St Charles Screw Products Inc — Harvard (G-11067)	G	815 943-8060
Suburban Screw Machine Pdts — Woodstock (G-21436)	G	815 337-0434
Supreme Manufacturing Company — Des Plaines (G-7854)	E	847 297-8212
Supreme Screw Products — Countryside (G-7073)		708 579-3500
Swebco Mfg Inc — Machesney Park (G-13377)	E	815 636-7160
Swiss Automation Inc — Barrington (G-1246)	D	847 381-4405
Swisstronics Corp — Orland Park (G-15986)	G	708 403-8877
Tanko Scrw Prd Corp — Chicago Heights (G-6779)	G	708 418-0300
Toledo Screw Machine Products — Rockford (G-17664)	G	815 877-8213
Tri-Part Screw Products Inc — Machesney Park (G-13380)	E	815 654-7311
Turnco Inc — Chicago Heights (G-6782)	G	708 756-6565
Ty Precision Automatics Inc — Rockford (G-17669)	F	815 963-9668
Ucal Systems Inc — Elgin (G-8766)	D	847 695-8030
V and L Red Devil Mfg Co — Wheeling (G-21007)	E	847 215-1377
Vandeventer Mfg Co Inc — Batavia (G-1439)	E	630 879-2511
Vanguard Tool & Engineering Co — Mount Prospect (G-14580)	E	847 981-9595

Employee Codes: A=Over 500 employees, B=251-500
C=101-250, D=51-100, E=20-50, F=10-19, G=3-9

SCREW MACHINE PRDTS

Vek Screw Machine Products ....G...... 630 543-5557
  Addison *(G-327)*
Weber Metal Products Inc ....F...... 815 844-3169
  Chenoa *(G-3435)*
Wenlyn Screw Company Inc ....G...... 630 766-0050
  Bensenville *(G-1911)*
Wilmette Screw Products ....G...... 773 725-2626
  Chicago *(G-6634)*
Wilson Mfg Screw Mch Pdts ....F...... 815 964-8724
  Rockford *(G-17686)*

SCREW MACHINES

Dynamic Automation Inc ....G...... 312 782-8555
  Lincolnwood *(G-12817)*
Rodifer Enterprises Inc ....G...... 815 678-0100
  Richmond *(G-17021)*

SCREWS: Metal

Afi Industries Inc ....E...... 630 462-0400
  Carol Stream *(G-2927)*
Agrati - Park Forest LLC ....C...... 708 228-5193
  Park Forest *(G-16251)*
American/Jebco Corporation ....C...... 847 455-3150
  Cicero *(G-6829)*
Brynolf Manufacturing Inc ....E...... 815 873-8878
  Rockford *(G-17329)*
Chase Fasteners Inc ....E...... 708 345-0335
  Melrose Park *(G-13841)*
Dml Distribution Inc ....F...... 630 839-9041
  Schaumburg *(G-18509)*
Fastron Co ....G...... 630 766-5000
  Melrose Park *(G-13866)*
Gateway Screw & Rivet Inc ....E...... 630 539-2232
  Glendale Heights *(G-10452)*
Geocyn Company Inc ....E...... 331 213-2851
  Naperville *(G-14835)*
Hadley Gear Manufacturing Co ....F...... 773 722-1030
  Chicago *(G-4765)*
Illinois Tool Works Inc ....F...... 815 654-1510
  Machesney Park *(G-13349)*
Inland Fastener Inc ....F...... 630 293-3800
  West Chicago *(G-20596)*
Jeffrey Jae Inc ....E...... 847 808-2002
  Wheeling *(G-20919)*
Klinck Inc ....E...... 815 397-3306
  Rockford *(G-17484)*
Komar Screw Corp ....E...... 847 965-9090
  Niles *(G-15139)*
Matthew Warren Inc ....E...... 847 364-5000
  Elk Grove Village *(G-9113)*
National Cap and Set Screw Co ....F...... 815 675-2363
  Spring Grove *(G-19287)*
Nylok LLC ....D...... 847 674-9680
  Lincolnwood *(G-12834)*
Parker International Pdts Inc ....D...... 815 524-5831
  Vernon Hills *(G-20082)*
Prairie State Screw & Bolt Co ....F...... 847 858-9551
  Northbrook *(G-15463)*
Semblex Corporation ....E...... 630 833-2880
  Elmhurst *(G-9425)*
Si Enterprises Inc ....G...... 630 539-9200
  Glendale Heights *(G-10494)*
Skach Manufacturing Co Inc ....E...... 847 395-3560
  Antioch *(G-635)*
Thread & Gage Co Inc ....G...... 815 675-2305
  Spring Grove *(G-19302)*
Valley Fastener Group LLC ....F...... 708 343-2496
  Melrose Park *(G-13924)*
Wenlyn Screw Company Inc ....G...... 630 766-0050
  Bensenville *(G-1911)*

SEALANTS

Dental Sealants & More ....G...... 309 692-6435
  Peoria *(G-16429)*
F H Leinweber Co Inc ....G...... 708 424-7000
  Oak Lawn *(G-15715)*
F H Leinweber Co Inc ....E...... 773 568-7722
  Chicago *(G-4548)*
JW Sealants Inc ....G...... 630 398-1010
  Bartlett *(G-1291)*
La-Co Industries Inc ....C...... 847 956-7600
  Elk Grove Village *(G-9082)*
Maximum Sealants LLC ....G...... 815 985-7183
  Rockford *(G-17510)*
Nolan Sealants Inc ....G...... 630 774-5713
  Bloomingdale *(G-2003)*
Quality Sealants Inc ....G...... 815 342-0409
  Roselle *(G-17976)*

Royal Adhesives and Sealants ....G...... 815 464-3310
  Frankfort *(G-9834)*

SEALS: Hermetic

Big Joes Sealcoati ....G...... 630 935-7032
  Lisle *(G-12871)*
Chicago Cardinal Communication ....F...... 708 424-1446
  Oak Lawn *(G-15708)*

SEALS: Oil, Leather

James Walker Mfg Co ....E...... 708 754-4020
  Glenwood *(G-10641)*
Triseal Corporation ....E...... 815 648-2473
  Hebron *(G-11151)*

SEALS: Oil, Rubber

Advantage Seal Inc ....F...... 630 226-0200
  Bolingbrook *(G-2147)*

SEARCH & DETECTION SYSTEMS, EXC RADAR

Blaxtair Inc ....G...... 312 299-5590
  Chicago *(G-3910)*
Electro-Technic Products Inc ....F...... 773 561-2349
  Chicago *(G-4478)*
Marine Technologies Inc ....E...... 847 546-9001
  Volo *(G-20203)*
MidAmerican Technology Inc ....G...... 815 496-2400
  Serena *(G-18864)*

SEARCH & NAVIGATION SYSTEMS

Acl Inc ....F...... 773 285-0295
  Chicago *(G-3525)*
Andrew New Zealand Inc ....E...... 708 873-3507
  Orland Park *(G-15940)*
ARINC Incorporated ....E...... 800 633-6882
  O Fallon *(G-15567)*
Boeing Company ....C...... 312 544-2000
  Chicago *(G-3925)*
Bolingbrook Communications Inc ....A...... 630 759-9500
  Lisle *(G-12874)*
CAM Co Inc ....F...... 630 556-3110
  Big Rock *(G-1969)*
CEF Industries LLC ....C...... 630 628-2299
  Addison *(G-65)*
D W Terry Welding Company ....G...... 618 433-9722
  Alton *(G-551)*
FSI Technologies Inc ....E...... 630 932-9380
  Lombard *(G-13080)*
Graceland Ferray Products ....G...... 847 258-3828
  Arlington Heights *(G-743)*
Ihi Terrasun Solutions Inc ....G...... 312 878-8532
  Chicago *(G-4883)*
L A M Inc De ....G...... 630 860-9700
  Wood Dale *(G-21206)*
Learjet Inc ....B...... 847 553-0172
  Des Plaines *(G-7797)*
Lockheed Martin Corporation ....G...... 618 628-0700
  O Fallon *(G-15579)*
Motorola Solutions Inc ....G...... 847 341-3485
  Oak Brook *(G-15647)*
National Aerospace Corp ....G...... 847 566-5834
  Hawthorn Woods *(G-11125)*
Navman Wireless Holdings LP ....D...... 866 527-9896
  Glenview *(G-10592)*
Northrop Grumman Systems Corp ....D...... 847 259-9600
  Rolling Meadows *(G-17756)*
Oceancomm Incorporated ....G...... 800 757-3266
  Chicago *(G-5653)*
Research In Motion Rf Inc ....G...... 815 444-1095
  Crystal Lake *(G-7255)*
Trident Machine Co ....G...... 815 968-1585
  Rockford *(G-17668)*
Winn Star Inc ....G...... 618 964-1811
  Carbondale *(G-2865)*

SEAT BELTS: Automobile & Aircraft

Deyco Inc ....G...... 630 553-5666
  Yorkville *(G-21480)*
Hooker Custom Harness Inc ....G...... 815 233-5478
  Freeport *(G-10119)*

SEATING: Chairs, Table & Arm

Tao Trading Corporation ....G...... 773 764-6542
  Chicago *(G-6326)*

SEATING: Railroad

Inter Swiss Ltd ....F...... 773 379-0400
  Chicago *(G-4943)*

SEATING: Transportation

Fbsa LLC ....G...... 773 524-2440
  Chicago *(G-4570)*

SECRETARIAL SVCS

CCH Incorporated ....A...... 847 267-7000
  Riverwoods *(G-17090)*

SECURITY CONTROL EQPT & SYSTEMS

Azilsa Inc ....E...... 312 919-1741
  Schaumburg *(G-18455)*
Blustor Pmc Inc ....G...... 312 265-3058
  Chicago *(G-3919)*
Calx Trading Corporation ....E...... 630 456-6721
  Naperville *(G-14962)*
Chase Security Systems Inc ....G...... 773 594-1919
  Chicago *(G-4078)*
Checkpoint Systems Inc ....D...... 630 771-4240
  Romeoville *(G-17806)*
Engineered SEC & Sound Inc ....G...... 630 876-8853
  West Chicago *(G-20573)*
Maco-Sys LLC ....F...... 779 888-3260
  Rockford *(G-17502)*
Marbil Enterprises Inc ....G...... 618 257-1810
  Belleville *(G-1570)*
Moog Inc ....E...... 770 987-7550
  Northbrook *(G-15435)*
Nitek International LLC ....G...... 847 259-8900
  Rolling Meadows *(G-17753)*
P & J Technologies ....G...... 847 995-1108
  Schaumburg *(G-18661)*
Sennco Solutions Inc ....E...... 815 577-3400
  Plainfield *(G-16713)*
Tylu Wireless Technology LLC ....G...... 312 260-7934
  Chicago *(G-6450)*

SECURITY DEVICES

Accurate Security & Lock Corp ....G...... 815 455-0133
  Lake In The Hills *(G-12326)*
CTS of Illinois Inc ....G...... 630 892-2355
  Montgomery *(G-14242)*
Duvas USA Limited ....G...... 312 266-1420
  Chicago *(G-4415)*
Interior Tectonics LLC ....G...... 312 515-7779
  Chicago *(G-4947)*
Lt Security Inc ....E...... 630 348-8088
  Elk Grove Village *(G-9099)*
Midwest Treasure Detectors ....G...... 217 223-4769
  Quincy *(G-16915)*
Mobiloc LLC ....G...... 773 742-1329
  Alsip *(G-481)*
Quality Intgrted Solutions Inc ....G...... 815 464-4772
  Tinley Park *(G-19852)*
Rf Ideas Inc ....D...... 847 870-1723
  Rolling Meadows *(G-17771)*
RTS Sentry Inc ....F...... 618 257-7100
  Belleville *(G-1594)*
Stabiloc LLC ....G...... 586 412-1147
  Carol Stream *(G-3074)*
Tri Cable Inc ....G...... 847 815-6082
  Libertyville *(G-12717)*
Unique Product Productions Inc ....G...... 708 259-1500
  Richton Park *(G-17032)*
Usl Lock Corporation ....G...... 815 739-4707
  Bartlett *(G-1320)*

SECURITY EQPT STORES

Lt Security Inc ....E...... 630 348-8088
  Elk Grove Village *(G-9099)*
Netranix Enterprise ....E...... 630 312-8141
  Bolingbrook *(G-2219)*
Printforce Inc ....G...... 618 395-7746
  Olney *(G-15885)*

SECURITY PROTECTIVE DEVICES MAINTENANCE & MONITORING SVCS

Ep Technology Corporation USA ....D...... 217 351-7888
  Champaign *(G-3290)*

PRODUCT SECTION

SEWING, NEEDLEWORK & PIECE GOODS STORES

SECURITY SYSTEMS SERVICES

AT&T Teleholdings Inc ....F 800 288-2020
  Chicago *(G-3756)*
Busways LLC ....G 617 697-2009
  Chicago *(G-3984)*
CTS of Illinois Inc ....G 630 892-2355
  Montgomery *(G-14242)*
Double Nickel LLC ....G 618 476-3200
  Millstadt *(G-14045)*
Hipskind Tech Sltons Group Inc .....D 630 920-0960
  Oakbrook Terrace *(G-15803)*
Honeywell International Inc ....D 847 797-4000
  Des Plaines *(G-7778)*
Quantum Color Graphics LLC ....C 847 967-3600
  Morton Grove *(G-14435)*
Siemens Industry Inc ....A 847 215-1000
  Buffalo Grove *(G-2600)*

SEEDS & BULBS WHOLESALERS

Dow Agrosciences LLC ....G 815 844-3128
  Pontiac *(G-16769)*
Michel Fertilizer & Equipment ....G 618 242-6000
  Mount Vernon *(G-14624)*
New Alliance Production LLC ....E 309 928-3123
  Farmer City *(G-9656)*
Pioneer Hi-Bred Intl Inc ....F 309 962-2931
  Saint Joseph *(G-18318)*

SEEDS: Coated Or Treated, From Purchased Seeds

Gateway Seed Company Inc ....G 618 327-8000
  Nashville *(G-14997)*
Quality Technology Intl Inc ....E 847 649-9300
  Elgin *(G-8709)*

SELF-PROPELLED AIRCRAFT DEALER

AAR Corp ....D 630 227-2000
  Wood Dale *(G-21149)*

SEMICONDUCTOR CIRCUIT NETWORKS

Methode Electronics Inc ....B 708 867-6777
  Chicago *(G-5409)*
Microlink Devices Inc ....D 847 588-3001
  Niles *(G-15146)*
Nhanced Semiconductors Inc ....F 408 759-4060
  Naperville *(G-14884)*

SEMICONDUCTOR DEVICES: Wafers

Akhan Semiconductor Inc ....G 847 855-8400
  Gurnee *(G-10856)*
Sigenics Inc ....F 312 448-8000
  Chicago *(G-6164)*

SEMICONDUCTORS & RELATED DEVICES

Accelerated Assemblies Inc ....E 630 616-6680
  Elk Grove Village *(G-8798)*
Altera Corporation ....G 847 240-0313
  Schaumburg *(G-18435)*
Angela Yang Chingjui ....G 630 724-0596
  Darien *(G-7401)*
B+b Smartworx Inc ....D 815 433-5100
  Ottawa *(G-16041)*
Broadcom Corporation ....G 773 965-1600
  Lake Barrington *(G-12142)*
Brocade Cmmnctions Systems LLC ....F 630 273-5530
  Schaumburg *(G-18465)*
Chicago Pixels SRC ....G 312 513-7949
  Chicago *(G-4123)*
Convergent Bill Ete Ort T ....G 847 387-4059
  Hoffman Estates *(G-11416)*
Csi2d Inc ....G 312 282-7407
  Hoffman Estates *(G-11472)*
CTS Automotive LLC ....C 630 577-8800
  Lisle *(G-12880)*
CTS Corporation ....C 630 577-8800
  Lisle *(G-12881)*
Dover Corporation ....C 630 541-1540
  Downers Grove *(G-7989)*
Effimax Solar ....G 217 550-2422
  Champaign *(G-3288)*
Epir Inc ....G 630 842-4486
  Bolingbrook *(G-2174)*
Epiworks Inc ....D 217 373-1590
  Champaign *(G-3291)*
FSI Technologies Inc ....E 630 932-9380
  Lombard *(G-13080)*

General Lattice Inc ....G 312 374-3158
  Chicago *(G-4671)*
General Products International ......G 847 458-6357
  Lake In The Hills *(G-12335)*
Interplex Daystar Inc ....D 847 455-2424
  Franklin Park *(G-9966)*
Ipr Systems Inc ....G 708 385-7500
  Alsip *(G-458)*
JAD Group Inc ....G 847 223-1804
  Grayslake *(G-10785)*
Linear Technology LLC ....G 847 925-0860
  Schaumburg *(G-18607)*
Micron Technology Inc ....G 208 368-4000
  Chicago *(G-5425)*
Motorola International Capital ....G 847 576-5000
  Schaumburg *(G-18634)*
Motorola Solutions Inc ....C 847 576-8600
  Schaumburg *(G-18637)*
Motorola Solutions Inc ....G 847 341-3485
  Oak Brook *(G-15647)*
New Vision Display ....G 224 268-3345
  Elgin *(G-8667)*
Nxp Usa Inc ....B 847 843-6824
  Hoffman Estates *(G-11441)*
Plug Power Inc Ctc ....G 518 782-7700
  Romeoville *(G-17863)*
Tagore Technology Inc ....F 847 790-3799
  Arlington Heights *(G-816)*
Tempro International Corp ....G 847 677-5370
  Skokie *(G-19044)*
Toshiba America Electronic ....G 847 484-2400
  Buffalo Grove *(G-2613)*
Value Engineered Products ....E 708 867-6777
  Rolling Meadows *(G-17784)*
Vega Wave Systems Inc ....G 630 562-9433
  West Chicago *(G-20657)*
Wilmar Group LLC ....G 847 421-6595
  Lake Forest *(G-12322)*
Xelerated Inc ....G 408 222-2500
  Chicago *(G-6692)*
Xylem Lnc ....G 847 966-3700
  Morton Grove *(G-14451)*
Yash Technologies Inc ....E 309 755-0433
  East Moline *(G-8248)*

SENSORS: Infrared, Solid State

Drs Ntwork Imaging Systems LLC ....G 214 215-5960
  Bolingbrook *(G-2169)*
Epir Technologies Inc ....E 630 771-0203
  Bolingbrook *(G-2175)*
Telehealth Sensors LLC ....E 630 879-3101
  North Aurora *(G-15279)*

SENSORS: Radiation

Capsonic Automotive Inc ....F 847 888-7300
  Elgin *(G-8530)*

SENSORS: Temperature For Motor Windings

Crandall Stats and Sensors Inc ....E 815 316-8600
  Machesney Park *(G-13336)*

SEPARATORS: Metal Plate

S+s Inspection Inc ....G 770 493-9332
  Bartlett *(G-1307)*

SEPTIC TANK CLEANING SVCS

Clay Vollmar Products Co ....G 847 540-5850
  Lake Zurich *(G-12394)*
Unique Concrete Concepts Inc .....F 618 466-0700
  Jerseyville *(G-11797)*

SEPTIC TANKS: Concrete

Christopher Concrete Products .....G 618 724-2951
  Buckner *(G-2499)*
Clay Vollmar Products Co ....F 773 774-1234
  Chicago *(G-4172)*
Cline Concrete Products ....F 217 283-5012
  Hoopeston *(G-11505)*
Hardin Ready Mix Inc ....F 618 576-9313
  Hardin *(G-11017)*
Hinckley Concrete Products Co ....G 815 286-3235
  Hinckley *(G-11358)*
Kieft Bros Inc ....E 630 832-8090
  Elmhurst *(G-9388)*
Kohnens Concrete Products Inc ...F 618 277-2120
  Germantown *(G-10330)*

Nt Liquidating Inc ....E 815 726-3351
  Joliet *(G-11909)*
Rockford Sewer Co Inc ....G 815 877-9060
  Loves Park *(G-13259)*

SEWAGE & WATER TREATMENT EQPT

Alternative Wastewater Systems ...G 630 761-8720
  Batavia *(G-1345)*
Carlinville Waste Water Plants ......G 217 854-6506
  Carlinville *(G-2868)*
City of Toulon ....G 309 286-7073
  Toulon *(G-19890)*
Culligan International Company ....C 847 430-2800
  Rosemont *(G-18013)*
Dontech Industries Inc ....F 847 428-8222
  Gilberts *(G-10353)*
Evac North America Inc ....E 815 654-8300
  Cherry Valley *(G-3439)*
Heico Companies LLC ....F 312 419-8220
  Chicago *(G-4798)*
Holden Industries Inc ....F 847 940-1500
  Deerfield *(G-7616)*
Industrial Specialty Chem Inc ....E 708 339-1313
  South Holland *(G-19224)*
McDowell Inc ....G 309 467-2335
  Eureka *(G-9483)*
Siemens Industry Inc ....G 815 672-2653
  Streator *(G-19622)*

SEWAGE TREATMENT SYSTEMS & EQPT

North Shore Wtr Rclamation Dst ...E 847 623-6060
  Waukegan *(G-20470)*

SEWER CLEANING & RODDING SVC

Ave Inc ....G 815 727-0153
  Joliet *(G-11825)*
Coe Equipment Inc ....G 217 498-7200
  Rochester *(G-17164)*
Hovi Industries Incorporated ....E 815 512-7500
  Bolingbrook *(G-2186)*
Rockford Sewer Co Inc ....G 815 877-9060
  Loves Park *(G-13259)*
Toppert Jetting Service Inc ....G 309 755-2240
  East Moline *(G-8244)*

SEWER CLEANING EQPT: Power

Coe Equipment Inc ....G 217 498-7200
  Rochester *(G-17164)*
Dml LLC ....G 630 231-8873
  West Chicago *(G-20572)*
Inlet & Pipe Protection Inc ....G 630 355-3288
  Naperville *(G-14974)*
Sewer Equipment Co America .....C 815 835-5566
  Dixon *(G-7917)*
Toppert Jetting Service Inc ....G 309 755-2240
  East Moline *(G-8244)*

SEWER INSPECTION SVCS

Midwest Water Group Inc ....E 866 526-6558
  Crystal Lake *(G-7230)*
Toppert Jetting Service Inc ....G 309 755-2240
  East Moline *(G-8244)*

SEWING CONTRACTORS

Choi Brands Inc ....C 773 489-2800
  Chicago *(G-4142)*
H & H Fabric Cutters ....G 773 772-1904
  Chicago *(G-4757)*

SEWING MACHINE REPAIR SHOP

Union Special LLC ....C 847 669-5101
  Huntley *(G-11572)*

SEWING MACHINES & PARTS: Indl

Union Special LLC ....C 847 669-5101
  Huntley *(G-11572)*

SEWING, NEEDLEWORK & PIECE GOODS STORES

Bearse Manufacturing Co ....D 773 235-8710
  Chicago *(G-3857)*

Employee Codes: A=Over 500 employees, B=251-500
C=101-250, D=51-100, E=20-50, F=10-19, G=3-9

SEWING, NEEDLEWORK & PIECE GOODS STORES: Sewing & Needlework

SEWING, NEEDLEWORK & PIECE GOODS STORES: Sewing & Needlework
Embroid ME .... G 815 485-4155
  New Lenox *(G-15033)*

SEXTANTS
Sextant Company .... G 847 680-6550
  Gurnee *(G-10926)*

SHADES: Lamp & Light, Residential
Astral Power Systems Inc .... G 630 518-1741
  Aurora *(G-1055)*
McAteers Wholesale .... G 618 233-3400
  Belleville *(G-1573)*

SHADES: Window
Chicago Shade Makers Inc .... G 708 597-5590
  Alsip *(G-428)*
Custom Window Accents .... F 815 943-7651
  Harvard *(G-11051)*
National Temp-Trol Products .... G 630 920-1919
  Willowbrook *(G-21053)*
Shade Brookline Co .... F 773 274-5513
  Chicago *(G-6145)*

SHAPES & PILINGS, STRUCTURAL: Steel
Accurate Metals Illinois LLC .... F 815 966-6320
  Rockford *(G-17293)*
Advance Steel Services Inc .... G 773 619-2977
  Chicago *(G-3558)*
Alter Trading Corporation .... F 309 828-6084
  Bloomington *(G-2023)*
Gerald R Page Corporation .... F 847 398-5575
  Prospect Heights *(G-16842)*
Marqutte Stl Sup Fbrcation Inc .... F 815 433-0178
  Ottawa *(G-16060)*
Matcon Manufacturing Inc .... F 309 755-1020
  Cordova *(G-7008)*
Residential Steel Services .... G 309 448-2900
  Congerville *(G-7002)*
Residntial Stl Fabricators Inc .... E 847 695-3400
  South Elgin *(G-19171)*
Superior Piling Inc .... G 708 496-1196
  Bridgeview *(G-2392)*

SHAPES: Extruded, Aluminum, NEC
Nichols Aluminum LLC .... C 847 634-3150
  Lincolnshire *(G-12787)*
Plymouth Tube Company .... E 630 393-3550
  Warrenville *(G-20246)*
Plymouth Tube Company .... D 773 489-0226
  Chicago *(G-5824)*

SHAPES: Flat, Rolled, Aluminum, NEC
Kibar Americas Inc .... G 312 285-2553
  Chicago *(G-5100)*

SHEATHING: Asphalt Saturated
American Asp Surfc Recycl Inc .... F 708 448-9540
  Orland Park *(G-15939)*
Perdue Pavement Solutions Inc .... F 309 698-9440
  East Peoria *(G-8283)*

SHEET METAL SPECIALTIES, EXC STAMPED
Aero Metals Alliance Inc .... F 225 236-1441
  Northbrook *(G-15333)*
Angle Metal Manufacturing Co .... G 847 437-8666
  Elk Grove Village *(G-8831)*
Belvin J & F Sheet Metal Co .... G 312 666-5222
  Chicago *(G-3865)*
Central Sheet Metal Pdts Inc .... E 773 583-2424
  Skokie *(G-18938)*
D & J Metalcraft Company Inc .... F 773 878-6446
  Chicago *(G-4298)*
EMR Manufacturing Inc .... E 630 766-3366
  Wood Dale *(G-21185)*
Exton Corp .... C 847 391-8100
  Des Plaines *(G-7763)*
Fab Werks Inc .... E 815 724-0317
  Crest Hill *(G-7086)*
G Branch Corp .... D 630 458-1909
  Addison *(G-131)*
Genesis Inc .... D 630 351-4400
  Roselle *(G-17955)*
GLC Industries Inc .... E 630 628-5870
  Addison *(G-141)*
Hennessy Sheet Metal .... G 708 754-6342
  S Chicago Hts *(G-18121)*
Hpl Stampings Inc .... E 847 540-1400
  Lake Zurich *(G-12419)*
Icon Metalcraft Inc .... C 630 766-5600
  Wood Dale *(G-21200)*
ILmachine Company Inc .... F 847 243-9900
  Wheeling *(G-20913)*
IMS Companies LLC .... D 847 391-8100
  Des Plaines *(G-7786)*
International Source Solutions .... G 847 251-8265
  Wilmette *(G-21079)*
Key West Metal Industries Inc .... C 708 371-1470
  Crestwood *(G-7121)*
Kier Mfg Co .... G 630 953-9500
  Addison *(G-170)*
Kormex Metal Craft Inc .... E 630 953-8856
  Lombard *(G-13093)*
L/J Fabricators Inc .... E 815 397-9099
  Rockford *(G-17489)*
Marcres Manufacturing Inc .... E 847 439-1808
  Mount Prospect *(G-14546)*
Metal-Rite Inc .... F 708 656-3832
  Cicero *(G-6866)*
Midwest Manufacturing & Distrg .... F 773 866-1010
  Chicago *(G-5443)*
Nova Metals Inc .... F 630 690-4300
  Carol Stream *(G-3040)*
Nu-Way Industries Inc .... C 847 298-7710
  Des Plaines *(G-7812)*
Odin Fabrication Inc .... F 630 365-2475
  Elburn *(G-8466)*
Odin Industries Inc .... F 630 365-2475
  Elburn *(G-8467)*
Peter Lehman Inc .... G 847 395-7997
  Antioch *(G-630)*
Prince Fabricators Inc .... E 630 588-0088
  Carol Stream *(G-3051)*
Pyramid Manufacturing Corp .... D 630 443-0141
  Saint Charles *(G-18254)*
Quad-Metal Inc .... G 630 953-0907
  Addison *(G-258)*
Rome Metal Mfg Inc .... G 773 287-1755
  Chicago *(G-6057)*
Summit Sheet Metal Specialists ...... F 708 458-8622
  Summit Argo *(G-19682)*
T & L Sheet Metal Inc .... E 630 628-7960
  Addison *(G-302)*
T/J Fabricators Inc .... D 630 543-2293
  Addison *(G-303)*
Tassos Metal Inc .... E 630 953-1333
  Lombard *(G-13139)*
Tella Tool & Mfg Co .... C 630 495-0545
  Lombard *(G-13142)*
Thomas Engineering Inc .... E 815 398-0280
  Rockford *(G-17659)*
Vent Products Co Inc .... E 773 521-1900
  Chicago *(G-6532)*
Woodlawn Engineering Co Inc .... E 630 543-3550
  Addison *(G-337)*

SHEETING: Laminated Plastic
Acco Brands Corporation .... A 847 541-9500
  Lake Zurich *(G-12374)*
Acco Brands International Inc .... G 847 541-9500
  Lake Zurich *(G-12375)*
Diamond Cellophane Pdts Inc .... E 847 418-3000
  Northbrook *(G-15375)*
Mak Design Group Incorporated .... G 847 682-4504
  Countryside *(G-7063)*
Olon Industries Inc (us) .... E 630 232-4705
  Geneva *(G-10298)*
Sun Process Converting Inc .... D 847 593-0447
  Mount Prospect *(G-14573)*
Technologies Dvlpmnt .... G 815 943-9922
  Crystal Lake *(G-7278)*

SHEETS & STRIPS: Aluminum
Arconic Corporation .... D 217 431-3800
  Danville *(G-7321)*
Howmet Aerospace Inc .... C 773 581-7200
  Chicago *(G-4852)*
Howmet Aerospace Inc .... C 217 324-4469
  Litchfield *(G-12965)*
Howmet Aerospace Inc .... C 309 674-0065
  Peoria *(G-16454)*
J-TEC Metal Products Inc .... F 630 875-1300
  Itasca *(G-11679)*

Security Metal Products Inc .... G 815 933-3307
  Bradley *(G-2292)*

SHEETS: Solid Fiber, Made From Purchased Materials
Corrugated Supplies Co LLC .... E 708 458-5525
  Bedford Park *(G-1465)*
Glass Haus .... G 815 459-5849
  McHenry *(G-13746)*
Ruscorr LLC .... E 708 458-5525
  Bedford Park *(G-1500)*

SHELLAC
Belzona Gateway Inc .... G 888 774-2984
  Caseyville *(G-3210)*

SHELTERED WORKSHOPS
Community Support Systems .... D 217 705-4300
  Teutopolis *(G-19767)*
Five Star Industries Inc .... D 618 542-4880
  Du Quoin *(G-8120)*
Kccdd Inc .... D 309 344-2030
  Galesburg *(G-10205)*
Kreider Services Incorporated .... D 815 288-6691
  Dixon *(G-7903)*
Media Associates Intl Inc .... F 630 260-9063
  Carol Stream *(G-3022)*
Workshop .... G 815 777-2211
  Galena *(G-10183)*

SHELVES & SHELVING: Wood
Quantum Storage Systems .... G 630 274-6610
  Elk Grove Village *(G-9206)*

SHELVING, MADE FROM PURCHASED WIRE
B & J Wire Inc .... E 877 787-9473
  Chicago *(G-3805)*

SHELVING: Office & Store, Exc Wood
Echelon Capital LLC .... G 312 263-0263
  Chicago *(G-4445)*
Edsal Manufacturing Co LLC .... A 773 475-3000
  Chicago *(G-4454)*
Edsal Manufacturing Co LLC .... A 773 475-3165
  Chicago *(G-4455)*
Edsal Manufacturing Co LLC .... C 773 475-3013
  Chicago *(G-4456)*
Imperial Store Fixtures Inc .... G 773 348-1137
  Chicago *(G-4901)*
L & D Group Inc .... B 630 892-8941
  Montgomery *(G-14252)*
Lyon LLC .... C 630 892-8941
  Montgomery *(G-14258)*
R B White Inc .... E 309 452-5816
  Normal *(G-15220)*
REB Steel Equipment Corp .... E 773 252-0400
  Chicago *(G-5987)*
Workspace Lyon Products LLC .... B 630 892-8941
  Montgomery *(G-14276)*

SHIELDS OR ENCLOSURES: Radiator, Sheet Metal
Central Radiator Cabinet Co .... G 773 539-1700
  Lena *(G-12599)*

SHIMS: Metal
Gaskoa Inc .... E 708 339-5000
  South Holland *(G-19213)*
Precision Brand Products Inc .... E 630 969-7200
  Downers Grove *(G-8082)*
Precision Steel Warehouse Inc .... C 800 323-0740
  Franklin Park *(G-10026)*

SHIP BUILDING & REPAIRING: Offshore Sply Boats
Rinker Boat Company .... E 574 457-5731
  Chicago *(G-6034)*

SHIP BUILDING & REPAIRING: Rigging, Marine
Chicago Flyhouse Incorporated .... F 773 533-1590
  Chicago *(G-4104)*

PRODUCT SECTION

SHIPBUILDING & REPAIR
Full Circle Shipyard LLC .... G 630 343-2264
  Lemont *(G-12564)*
Mikes Inc .... D 618 254-4491
  South Roxana *(G-19253)*
National Maint & Repr Inc .... C 618 254-7451
  Hartford *(G-11036)*
Williamson J Hunter & Company .. G 847 441-7888
  Winnetka *(G-21137)*

SHIPPING AGENTS
UPS Store .... G 312 372-2727
  Chicago *(G-6491)*

SHOCK ABSORBERS: Indl
Egd Manufacturing Inc .... G 815 964-2900
  Rockford *(G-17391)*

SHOE & BOOT ACCESS
Hanigs Footwear Inc .... F 773 248-1977
  Wilmette *(G-21077)*
Red Wing .... G 217 655-2772
  Danville *(G-7378)*

SHOE MATERIALS: Counters
Counter .... G 312 666-5335
  Chicago *(G-4249)*
Counter-Intelligence .... G 708 974-3326
  Palos Hills *(G-16198)*
Curt Herrmann Construction Inc .... G 815 748-0531
  Dekalb *(G-7672)*
Rays Countertop Shop Inc .... F 217 483-2514
  Glenarm *(G-10427)*

SHOE MATERIALS: Plastic
Boss Manufacturing Holdings .... F 309 852-2781
  Kewanee *(G-12025)*

SHOE MATERIALS: Quarters
Fifth Quarter .... G 618 346-6659
  Saint Jacob *(G-18316)*

SHOE MATERIALS: Rands
D R Walters .... G 618 926-6337
  Norris City *(G-15248)*

SHOE MATERIALS: Rubber
Morrow Shoe and Boot Inc .... G 217 342-6833
  Effingham *(G-8413)*

SHOE MATERIALS: Uppers
Upper Urban Green Prprty Maint .. G 312 218-5903
  Chicago *(G-6489)*

SHOE STORES
Crocs Inc .... F 630 820-3572
  Aurora *(G-945)*
Hanigs Footwear Inc .... F 773 248-1977
  Wilmette *(G-21077)*
Red Wing .... G 217 655-2772
  Danville *(G-7378)*

SHOE STORES: Athletic
Athletic Outfitters Inc .... G 815 942-6696
  Morris *(G-14291)*
Foot Locker Retail Inc .... G 630 678-0155
  Lombard *(G-13078)*
Road Runner Sports Inc .... F 847 719-8941
  Palatine *(G-16154)*

SHOE STORES: Boots, Men's
Pryco Inc .... E 217 364-4467
  Mechanicsburg *(G-13811)*

SHOE STORES: Boots, Women's
Morrow Shoe and Boot Inc .... G 217 342-6833
  Effingham *(G-8413)*

SHOE STORES: Custom & Orthopedic
London Shoe Shop & Western Wr .. G 618 345-9570
  Collinsville *(G-6966)*

Springfield Sales Assoc Inc .... G 217 529-6987
  Springfield *(G-19456)*

SHOE STORES: Men's
BMW Sportswear Inc .... G 773 265-0110
  Chicago *(G-3921)*
Lids Corporation .... G 708 873-9606
  Orland Park *(G-15965)*
Mennon Rbr & Safety Pdts Inc ...... G 847 678-8250
  Schiller Park *(G-18823)*

SHOE STORES: Orthopedic
New Step Orthotic Lab Inc .... F 618 208-4444
  Maryville *(G-13592)*

SHOES & BOOTS WHOLESALERS
Vertex International Inc .... G 312 242-1864
  Oak Brook *(G-15669)*

SHOES: Ballet Slippers
Patricia Jenkins .... G 224 436-7547
  Lake Forest *(G-12282)*

SHOES: Canvas, Rubber Soled
Vans Inc .... F 718 349-2311
  Chicago *(G-6521)*

SHOES: Men's
Leos Dancewear Inc .... D 773 889-7700
  River Forest *(G-17053)*
London Shoe Shop & Western Wr .. G 618 345-9570
  Collinsville *(G-6966)*

SHOES: Men's, Dress
Barrett NJide Yvonne .... F 312 701-3962
  Chicago *(G-3838)*

SHOES: Orthopedic, Men's
Springfield Sales Assoc Inc .... G 217 529-6987
  Springfield *(G-19456)*

SHOES: Orthopedic, Women's
Springfield Sales Assoc Inc .... G 217 529-6987
  Springfield *(G-19456)*

SHOES: Plastic Or Rubber
Honeywell Safety Pdts USA Inc .... C 309 786-7741
  Rock Island *(G-17223)*
Leos Dancewear Inc .... D 773 889-7700
  River Forest *(G-17053)*
Nike Inc .... E 773 846-5460
  Chicago *(G-5602)*
Polyconversions Inc .... E 217 893-3330
  Champaign *(G-3335)*
Standard Safety Equipment Co .... E 815 363-8565
  McHenry *(G-13795)*

SHOES: Rubber Or Rubber Soled Fabric Uppers
Crocs Inc .... F 630 820-3572
  Aurora *(G-945)*

SHOES: Women's
Leos Dancewear Inc .... D 773 889-7700
  River Forest *(G-17053)*

SHOPPING CENTERS & MALLS
Mfp Holding Co .... G 312 666-3366
  Chicago *(G-5418)*

SHOT PEENING SVC
Ace Sandblast Company .... F 773 777-6654
  Chicago *(G-3523)*
Axletech International .... D 773 264-1234
  Chicago *(G-3795)*
Metal Improvement Company LLC .. E 630 543-4950
  Addison *(G-199)*
Metal Improvement Company LLC .. E 630 620-6808
  Lombard *(G-13100)*

SHOWCASES & DISPLAY FIXTURES: Office & Store
Acrylic Service Inc .... G 630 543-0336
  Addison *(G-18)*
Bark Project Management Inc ...... G 630 964-5876
  Woodridge *(G-21278)*
Igd Display LLC .... F 630 916-0700
  Downers Grove *(G-8027)*
Innovative Mktg Solutions Inc ...... F 630 227-4300
  Schaumburg *(G-18561)*
Inventive Display Group LLC .... F 847 588-1100
  Niles *(G-15134)*
Murray Cabinetry & Tops Inc .... G 815 672-6992
  Streator *(G-19616)*
Schaumburg Specialties Co .... G 847 451-0070
  Schaumburg *(G-18706)*
Wiremasters Incorporated .... E 773 254-3700
  Chicago *(G-6649)*

SHOWER STALLS: Metal
T J M & Associates Inc .... G 847 382-1993
  Wauconda *(G-20396)*
Wedi Corp .... E 847 357-9815
  Batavia *(G-1441)*

SHOWER STALLS: Plastic & Fiberglass
Swan Surfaces LLC .... C 618 532-5673
  Centralia *(G-3252)*

SHREDDERS: Indl & Commercial
Cutting Edge Document Dstrctn .... F 630 620-0193
  Lombard *(G-13062)*
Dun-Rite Tool & Machine Co .... E 815 758-5464
  Cortland *(G-7020)*
Lane Industries Inc .... E 847 498-6650
  Northbrook *(G-15417)*

SHUTTERS, DOOR & WINDOW: Metal
Chicagone Developers Inc .... E 773 783-2105
  Chicago *(G-4137)*
Qualitas Manufacturing Inc .... D 630 529-7111
  Itasca *(G-11723)*
Shutter Bag USA .... G 618 967-6247
  Carbondale *(G-2858)*
Shutterbooth Specl Evnts By La .... G 618 973-1894
  Granite City *(G-10738)*
Shutterview .... G 618 244-0656
  Mount Vernon *(G-14639)*

SHUTTERS, DOOR & WINDOW: Plastic
Perfect Shutters Inc .... E 815 648-2401
  Hebron *(G-11147)*
Qualitas Manufacturing Inc .... D 630 529-7111
  Itasca *(G-11723)*

SHUTTERS: Door, Wood
Original Shutter Man .... G 773 966-7160
  Chicago *(G-5701)*

SIDING & STRUCTURAL MATERIALS: Wood
Backyard Creations .... G 217 836-5678
  Petersburg *(G-16600)*
Boise Cascade Company .... E 618 491-7030
  Granite City *(G-10700)*
Lamboo Inc .... E 866 966-2999
  Litchfield *(G-12970)*
Mesic Vale LLC .... F 309 335-8521
  Galesburg *(G-10209)*
Png Transport LLC .... G 312 218-8116
  Chicago *(G-5827)*
Weatherguard Buildings .... G 217 894-6213
  Clayton *(G-6911)*

SIDING: Precast Stone
North Star Stone Inc .... G 847 996-6850
  Libertyville *(G-12691)*

SIDING: Sheet Metal
Lakefront Roofing Supply .... E 773 509-0400
  Chicago *(G-5163)*
Litt Aluminium & Shtmtl Co .... G 708 366-4720
  Westchester *(G-20703)*
Metal Sales Manufacturing Corp .. E 309 787-1200
  Rock Island *(G-17230)*

Employee Codes: A=Over 500 employees, B=251-500
C=101-250, D=51-100, E=20-50, F=10-19, G=3-9

RPS Engineering Inc....F....847 931-1950
Elgin (G-8721)
Vorteq Coil Finishers LLC....E....847 455-7200
Franklin Park (G-10080)

SIGN LETTERING & PAINTING SVCS

Central Illinois Sign Company....G....217 523-4740
Springfield (G-19346)
Muir Omni Graphics Inc....E....309 673-7034
Peoria (G-16480)
P N K Ventures Inc....G....630 527-0500
Naperville (G-14891)

SIGN PAINTING & LETTERING SHOP

Distinctive SIGns& The Neon Ex....G....847 245-7159
Grayslake (G-10767)
E Z Sign Co Inc....G....815 469-4080
Oak Forest (G-15675)
Enterprise Signs Inc....G....708 691-1273
Blue Island (G-2121)
Grate Signs Inc....E....815 729-9700
Joliet (G-11870)
Harder Signs Inc....F....815 874-7777
Rockford (G-17443)
Hughes & Son Inc....G....815 459-1887
Crystal Lake (G-7206)
J & D Instant Signs....G....847 965-2800
Morton Grove (G-14414)
Johnson Sign Co....G....847 678-2092
Franklin Park (G-9975)
Lettermen Signage Inc....G....708 479-5161
Mokena (G-14095)
Midwest Signworks....G....815 942-3517
Morris (G-14314)
Parvin-Clauss Sign Co Inc....E....866 490-2877
Carol Stream (G-3045)
Qc Finishers Inc....E....847 678-2660
Franklin Park (G-10028)
Rutke Signs Inc....G....708 841-6464
Westchester (G-20709)
Sign Centre....G....847 595-7300
Elk Grove Village (G-9239)
Sign Palace Inc....G....847 228-7446
Elk Grove Village (G-9240)
Signs Today Inc....G....847 934-9777
Palatine (G-16158)
Stevens Sign Co Inc....G....708 562-4888
Northlake (G-15560)

SIGNALING APPARATUS: Electric

Nafisco Inc....F....815 372-3300
Romeoville (G-17858)

SIGNALING DEVICES: Sound, Electrical

Jk Audio Inc....F....815 786-2929
Sandwich (G-18375)

SIGNALS: Railroad, Electric

AR Concepts USA Inc....G....847 392-4608
Palatine (G-16093)
Signalmasters Inc....F....708 534-3330
Monee (G-14208)
Tool Automation Enterprises....G....708 799-6847
East Hazel Crest (G-8218)
Western-Cullen-Hayes Inc....D....773 254-9600
Chicago (G-6609)

SIGNALS: Traffic Control, Electric

John Thomas Inc....E....815 288-2343
Dixon (G-7902)
Mobotrex Inc....G....847 546-1616
Volo (G-20204)
N E S Traffic Safety....F....312 603-7444
Chicago (G-5533)
Traffco Products LLC....G....773 374-6645
Chicago (G-6404)

SIGNALS: Transportation

Gretta Transportation Inc....E....252 202-7714
Westmont (G-20743)
Lecip Inc....F....312 626-2525
Bensenville (G-1842)

SIGNS & ADVERTISING SPECIALTIES

A & E Rubber Stamp Corp....G....312 575-1416
Chicago (G-3481)
A 1 Trophies Awards & Engrv....G....630 837-6000
Streamwood (G-19558)
A Plus Signs Inc....G....708 534-2030
Monee (G-14194)
A To Z Engraving Co Inc....G....847 526-7396
Wauconda (G-20324)
Accurate Repro Inc....F....630 428-4433
Naperville (G-14763)
Action Graphics and Signs Inc....G....618 939-5755
Columbia (G-6983)
Ad Special TZ Inc....G....847 845-6767
Buffalo Grove (G-2504)
Adams Outdoor Advg Ltd Partnr....E....309 692-2482
Peoria (G-16375)
Addison Engraving Inc....G....630 833-9123
Villa Park (G-20127)
Addison Pro Plastics Inc....G....630 543-6770
Addison (G-21)
Adnama Inc....G....312 922-0509
Chicago (G-3549)
Advance Press Sign Inc....G....630 833-1600
Villa Park (G-20128)
Advertising Premiums Inc....G....888 364-9710
Mount Prospect (G-14509)
Albright Enterprises Inc....G....630 357-2300
Naperville (G-14769)
Alex Displays & Co....F....312 829-2948
Chicago (G-3603)
Alexander Manufacturing Co....D....309 728-2224
Towanda (G-19892)
Alexander Signs & Designs Inc....G....815 933-3100
Bourbonnais (G-2255)
All Signs & Wonders Co....G....630 232-9019
Geneva (G-10250)
All Signs Inc....G....847 324-5500
Skokie (G-18914)
Allied Die Casting Corporation....E....815 385-9330
McHenry (G-13717)
Altco Inc....D....847 549-0321
Vernon Hills (G-20041)
Anbek Inc....G....815 672-6087
La Salle (G-12103)
Anbek Inc....F....815 223-0734
La Salle (G-12104)
Antlia Displays LLC....G....773 353-2223
Chicago (G-3706)
Antolak Management Co Inc....G....312 464-1800
Chicago (G-3707)
Arrow Sign Company Inc....G....630 620-9803
Addison (G-40)
Arrow Signs....G....618 466-0818
Godfrey (G-10650)
Art Wire Works Inc....F....708 458-3993
Bedford Park (G-1457)
Artisan Graphics Co....G....847 841-9200
Streamwood (G-19562)
Associated Attractions Entps....F....773 376-1900
Chicago (G-3750)
Athena Design Group Inc....E....312 733-2828
Chicago (G-3758)
Atlantis Entp Investments Inc....G....432 237-0404
Chicago (G-3761)
Authentic Street Signs Inc....G....618 349-8878
Saint Peter (G-18322)
Award Emblem Mfg Co Inc....F....630 739-0800
Bolingbrook (G-2153)
Awnings Express....G....773 579-1437
Chicago (G-3793)
Azusa Inc....G....618 244-6591
Mount Vernon (G-14597)
Bannerville USA Inc....F....630 455-0304
Burr Ridge (G-2654)
Bards Products Inc....E....800 323-5499
Mundelein (G-14665)
Bella Sign Co....G....630 539-0343
Roselle (G-17940)
Bendsen Signs & Graphics Inc....F....217 877-2345
Decatur (G-7464)
Best Advertising Spc & Prtg....G....708 448-1110
Worth (G-21455)
Bick Broadcasting Inc....G....217 223-9693
Quincy (G-16865)
Biron Studio General Svcs Inc....G....708 229-2600
Oak Lawn (G-15703)
Blue Diamond Athletic Disp Inc....G....847 414-9971
Downers Grove (G-7960)
Cacini Inc....G....847 884-1162
Schaumburg (G-18466)
Campbell Management Services....G....847 566-9020
Mundelein (G-14672)
Canham Graphics....G....217 585-5085
Springfield (G-19337)
Captivating Signs LLC....G....630 470-6161
Naperville (G-14788)
Castino & Associates Inc....G....847 291-7446
Northbrook (G-15354)
Central State Finds....G....630 359-4706
Elk Grove Village (G-8885)
Chicago I and D Services Inc....G....312 623-8071
Chicago (G-4107)
Chicago Scenic Studios Inc....D....312 274-9900
Chicago (G-4127)
Chicago Sign & Light Company....G....630 407-0802
Carol Stream (G-2958)
Churchill Wilmslow Corporation....G....312 759-8911
Chicago (G-4147)
CJ Signs....G....309 676-9999
Peoria (G-16424)
Cks Signs Inc....G....847 423-3456
Skokie (G-18943)
Classic Midwest Die Mold Inc....F....773 227-8000
Chicago (G-4169)
Classique Signs & Engrv Inc....G....217 228-7446
Quincy (G-16872)
Cnc Graphics....G....630 766-6308
Bensenville (G-1771)
Cook Fabrication Signs Graphic....G....309 360-3805
Deer Creek (G-7573)
Crown Publications Inc....G....217 893-4856
Rantoul (G-16973)
Crown Trophy....G....309 699-1766
East Peoria (G-8264)
CST Sign & Manufacturing LLC....G....312 222-0020
Chicago (G-4281)
Cubby Hole of Carlinville Inc....F....217 854-8511
Carlinville (G-2872)
Custom Enterprises....G....618 439-6626
Benton (G-1923)
Custom Telephone Printing Co....F....815 338-0000
Woodstock (G-21379)
Custom Trophies....G....217 422-3353
Decatur (G-7480)
Cutting Edge Graphics....G....630 717-9233
Plainfield (G-16654)
Cutting Edge Graphics Ltd....G....630 717-9233
Naperville (G-14964)
D E Signs & Storage LLC....G....618 939-8050
Waterloo (G-20289)
D&J Arlington Heights Inc....G....847 577-8200
Arlington Heights (G-724)
DAmico Associates Inc....G....847 291-7446
Northbrook (G-15373)
Dard Products Inc....C....847 328-5000
Wauconda (G-20341)
Darnall Printing....G....309 827-7212
Bloomington (G-2039)
Dazzling Displays Inc....F....708 262-6340
Morris (G-14302)
DE Asbury Inc....E....217 222-0617
Quincy (G-16876)
Decal Solutions Unlimited Inc....G....847 590-5405
Arlington Heights (G-727)
Designovations Inc....G....815 645-8598
Loves Park (G-13207)
Designs Unlimited....G....618 357-6728
Pinckneyville (G-16613)
Dewrich Inc....G....847 249-7445
Gurnee (G-10868)
Diamond Sign Design....G....630 543-4900
Addison (G-89)
Dicke Tool Company....D....630 969-0050
Downers Grove (G-7988)
Dickey Sign Co....G....618 797-1262
Granite City (G-10703)
Digital Artz LLC....G....618 651-1500
Highland (G-11213)
Digital Edge Signs Inc....G....847 838-4760
Antioch (G-609)
Digital Factory Tech Inc....E....513 560-4074
Chicago (G-4358)
Digital Greensigns Inc....G....312 624-8550
Chicago (G-4359)
Digital Minds Inc....G....847 430-3390
Rosemont (G-18017)
Display Signs & Design....G....800 782-1558
Chicago (G-4367)
Distinctive SIGns& The Neon Ex....G....847 245-7159
Grayslake (G-10767)
Diva Dream Signs....G....618 201-4348
Christopher (G-6824)

PRODUCT SECTION — SIGNS & ADVERTISING SPECIALTIES

Company	Code	Phone
Divine Signs Inc — Schaumburg (G-18507)	G	847 534-9220
E A A Enterprises Inc — Villa Park (G-20145)	G	630 279-0150
East Bank Neon Inc — Collinsville (G-6958)	G	618 345-9517
Edventure Promotions Inc — Chicago (G-4460)	G	312 440-1800
Effingham Signs & Graphics — Effingham (G-8398)	G	217 347-8711
Eisendrath Inc — Highland Park (G-11261)	G	847 432-3899
Elk Grove Signs Inc — Elk Grove Village (G-8973)	G	847 427-0005
Enchanted Signs of Rockford — Rockford (G-17396)	G	815 874-5100
Engravings Plus — Gibson City (G-10337)	G	217 784-8426
Enterprise Signs Inc — Blue Island (G-2121)	G	708 691-1273
Exclusively Expo — Romeoville (G-17819)	F	630 378-4600
Exex Holding Corporation — Romeoville (G-17820)	G	815 703-7295
Exsel Exhibits Inc — Des Plaines (G-7762)	F	847 647-1012
Fast Signs — Chicago (G-4564)	G	773 698-8115
Fast Signs — Mokena (G-14080)	G	815 730-7828
Fast Signs 590 — Kankakee (G-11970)	G	815 937-1855
Fastsigns — Chicago (G-4565)	G	312 344-1765
Fastsigns — Elk Grove Village (G-8997)	G	847 981-1965
Fastsigns — Oakbrook Terrace (G-15798)	G	630 932-0001
Fastsigns — Lincolnwood (G-12818)	G	847 675-1600
Fastsigns — Libertyville (G-12651)	G	847 680-7446
Fastsigns LLC — Downers Grove (G-8001)	G	630 541-8901
Fastsigns International — Morton Grove (G-14407)	G	847 967-7222
Federal Signal Corporation — University Park (G-19953)	D	708 534-3400
Fedex Office & Print Svcs Inc — Peoria (G-16437)	E	309 685-4093
Fedex Office & Print Svcs Inc — Arlington Heights (G-736)	E	847 670-4100
FM Graphic Impressions Inc — Aurora (G-1097)	E	630 897-8788
Forest Awards & Engraving — Wood Dale (G-21189)	G	630 595-2242
Fourth Quarter Holdings Inc — Gurnee (G-10879)	G	847 249-7445
Frank O Carlson & Co Inc — Chicago (G-4630)	F	773 847-6900
Freedom Design & Decals Inc — Mokena (G-14084)	G	815 806-8172
Friendly Signs Inc — Kankakee (G-11973)	G	815 933-7070
G & J Associates Inc — Arlington Heights (G-738)	G	847 255-0123
G and D Enterprises Inc — Arlington Heights (G-739)	E	847 981-8661
G D S Professional Bus Display — Bloomington (G-2047)	E	309 829-3298
Gaytan Signs & Co Inc — Joliet (G-11868)	G	815 726-2975
Geebees Inc — Peoria (G-16443)	G	309 682-5300
General Motor Sign — Round Lake (G-18076)	G	847 546-0424
Geneva Sign Corporation — Geneva (G-10273)	G	630 262-1700
George Lauterer Corporation — Chicago (G-4682)	E	312 913-1881
Grimco Inc — Bolingbrook (G-2181)	F	630 530-7756
Gz Sign Designs Inc — Roselle (G-17956)	G	630 307-7446
Haus Sign Incorporated — Bridgeview (G-2354)	G	708 598-8740
Heavy Hitters LLC — Calumet City (G-2780)	G	630 258-2991
Heffner Designs — Naperville (G-14840)	F	630 854-2852
Hercl Signs & Service Inc — South Elgin (G-19151)	G	847 471-4015
Heritage Signs Ltd — Libertyville (G-12658)	G	847 549-1942
Hermann Gene Signs & Service — Mount Vernon (G-14613)	G	618 244-3681
Heron Bay Inc — Bloomington (G-2057)	G	309 661-1300
Holland Design Group Inc — Wauconda (G-20357)	F	847 526-8848
Holmes Associates Inc — Gurnee (G-10887)	G	847 336-4515
House of Doolittle Ltd — Arlington Heights (G-751)	G	847 228-9591
Hughes & Son Inc — Crystal Lake (G-7206)	G	815 459-1887
ID Sign and Lighting Inc — Montgomery (G-14249)	G	630 844-3565
Ideal Box Co — Chicago (G-4875)	C	708 594-3100
Idek Graphics LLC — Elmhurst (G-9373)	G	630 530-1232
Identiti Resources Ltd — Schaumburg (G-18554)	E	866 477-4467
Idot North Side Sign Shop — Schaumburg (G-18555)	G	847 705-4033
Ilight Technologies Inc — Chicago (G-4887)	F	312 876-8630
Image Fx Corp — Burr Ridge (G-2685)	G	630 655-2850
Imagecare Maintenance Svcs LLC — Rolling Meadows (G-17739)	F	847 631-3306
Images Alive Ltd — Highland Park (G-11273)	G	847 498-5550
Imageworks Manufacturing Inc — Park Forest (G-16255)	E	708 503-1122
Infinity Communications Group — Countryside (G-7060)	F	708 352-1086
Insignia Design Ltd — Rolling Meadows (G-17741)	G	301 254-9221
Interstate Graphics Inc — Machesney Park (G-13351)	E	815 877-6777
Isates Inc — Peoria (G-16460)	G	309 691-8822
Its A Sign — Oak Park (G-15758)	G	708 848-7446
Ivan Carlson Associates Inc — Chicago (G-4979)	E	312 829-4616
J & B Signs Inc — Chicago (G-4982)	G	312 640-8181
J & D Instant Signs — Morton Grove (G-14414)	G	847 965-2800
Jacobson Acqstion Holdings LLC — Waukegan (G-20452)	C	847 623-1414
Jamali Kopy Kat Printing Inc — Bellwood (G-1629)	G	708 544-6164
James D Ahern Company — Chicago (G-5001)	F	773 254-0717
JAS Dahern Signs — Chicago (G-5009)	G	773 254-0717
Jem Solutions Inc — Plainfield (G-16677)	G	815 436-0880
Joans Trophy & Plaque Co — Peoria (G-16463)	E	309 674-6500
Jodaat Inc — Lombard (G-13091)	G	630 916-7776
John Cornbleet Inc — Naperville (G-14855)	G	630 357-3278
John Omalley — Elgin (G-8634)	G	847 924-8670
John Parker Advertising Co — Rantoul (G-16979)	G	217 892-4118
Johnson Sign Co — Franklin Park (G-9975)	G	847 678-2092
Jonem Grp Inc DBA Sign A Rama — Lake Barrington (G-12155)	G	224 848-4620
Joseph D Smithies — Caseyville (G-3216)	G	618 632-6141
Kane Graphical Corporation — Chicago (G-5080)	E	773 384-1200
Kdn Signs Inc — Bensenville (G-1837)	F	847 721-3848
Kellys Sign Shop — Danville (G-7356)	G	217 477-0167
Keystone Display Inc — Hebron (G-11144)	D	815 648-2456
Keystone Printing & Publishing — Richmond (G-17016)	G	815 678-2591
Kornick Enterprises LLC — Schaumburg (G-18591)	G	847 884-1162
Krick Enterprises Inc — Downers Grove (G-8041)	G	630 515-1085
L & C Imaging Inc — Bloomington (G-2069)	G	309 829-1802
Lakeview Sign Co — Chicago (G-5168)	G	773 698-8104
Lambert Print Source Llc — Yorkville (G-21491)	G	630 708-0505
Legacy 3d LLC — Crest Hill (G-7090)	F	815 727-5454
Leo Burnett Company Inc — Chicago (G-5205)	C	312 220-5959
Leos Sign — Chicago (G-5206)	G	773 227-2460
Lettermen Signage Inc — Mokena (G-14095)	G	708 479-5161
Letters Unlimited Inc — Schaumburg (G-18604)	G	847 891-7811
Light Waves LLC — Wilmette (G-21084)	F	847 251-1622
Lightning Graphic — Roscoe (G-17913)	G	815 623-1937
Lincolnland Archtctral Grphics — Glenarm (G-10426)	G	217 629-9009
Link Media Florida LLC — La Salle (G-12117)	G	815 224-4742
Lonelino Sign Company Inc — Jacksonville (G-11773)	G	217 243-2444
M & R Media Inc — Schaumburg (G-18616)	G	847 884-6300
Magnetic Signs — Chicago (G-5317)	G	773 476-6551
Main Street Visuals Inc — Morton Grove (G-14425)	G	847 869-7446
Mark Collins — Skokie (G-18983)	G	847 324-5500
Mark Your Space Inc — Bartlett (G-1295)	G	630 289-7082
Marking Specialists/Poly — Buffalo Grove (G-2568)	F	847 793-8100
Massey Grafix — Watseka (G-20310)	G	815 644-4620
Matrex Exhibits Inc — Addison (G-193)	D	630 628-2233
Maxs Screen Machine Inc — Chicago (G-5370)	G	773 878-4949
Mbm Business Assistance Inc — Champaign (G-3318)	G	217 398-6600
Meagher Sign & Graphics Inc — Flora (G-9685)	G	618 662-7446
Meltdown Creative Works Inc — Bloomington (G-2074)	G	309 310-1978
Mersigns — Belleville (G-1575)	G	618 234-4450
Metal Box International LLC — Franklin Park (G-9994)	C	847 455-8500
Mich Enterprises Inc — Wood Dale (G-21216)	F	630 616-9000
Michael Reggis Clark — Centralia (G-3238)	G	618 533-3841
Midway Displays Inc — Bedford Park (G-1482)	E	708 563-2323
Midwest Nameplate Corp — Orland Park (G-15968)	G	708 614-0606
Midwest Sign & Lighting Inc — Country Club Hills (G-7042)	G	708 365-5555
Midwest Signs & Structures Inc — Gurnee (G-10898)	G	847 249-8398
Midwest Signworks — Morris (G-14314)	G	815 942-3517
Midwest Sun-Ray Lighting & Sig — Granite City (G-10726)	F	618 656-2884
Minerva Sportswear Inc — Bloomington (G-2080)	F	309 661-2387
Mission Signs Inc — Lemont (G-12572)	G	630 243-6731
Murphys Sign Studio — Westmont (G-20762)	G	630 963-0677
N Bujarski Inc — Schaumburg (G-18643)	G	847 884-1600
Nafisco Inc — Romeoville (G-17858)	F	815 372-3300
Nameplate Robinson & Precision — Franklin Park (G-10005)	G	847 678-2255
Nathan Winston Service Inc — Dekalb (G-7692)	G	815 758-4545
Neil International Inc — Vernon Hills (G-20078)	C	847 549-7627
Neon Design Inc — Evanston (G-9558)	G	773 880-5020

Employee Codes: A=Over 500 employees, B=251-500
C=101-250, D=51-100, E=20-50, F=10-19, G=3-9

SIGNS & ADVERTISING SPECIALTIES

Neon Express Signs .... G 773 463-7335
Chicago *(G-5567)*
Newport Printing Services Inc .... G 847 632-1000
Schaumburg *(G-18648)*
Nimlok Co .... G 855 764-6565
Woodridge *(G-21327)*
Nite Lite Signs & Balloons Inc .... G 630 953-2866
Addison *(G-229)*
Nordmeyer Graphics .... G 815 697-2634
Chebanse *(G-3430)*
Noteworthy Group Inc .... G 618 549-2505
Carbondale *(G-2851)*
Nu-Art Printing .... G 618 533-9971
Centralia *(G-3242)*
Nu-Dell Manufacturing Co Inc .... F 847 803-4500
Chicago *(G-5637)*
Nycor Products Inc .... G 815 727-9883
Joliet *(G-11910)*
Oakley Signs & Graphics Inc .... F 224 612-5045
Des Plaines *(G-7813)*
Ogden Offset Printers Inc .... G 773 284-7797
Chicago *(G-5663)*
Olympic Trophy and Awards Co .... F 773 631-9500
Chicago *(G-5672)*
Orbit Enterprises Inc .... G 630 469-3405
Oak Brook *(G-15654)*
Orbus LLC .... C 630 226-1155
Woodridge *(G-21328)*
Outdoor Solutions Team Inc .... E 312 446-4220
Northbrook *(G-15450)*
P & D Sign Co .... G 815 224-9220
Peru *(G-16588)*
P & L Mark-It Inc .... E 630 879-7590
Batavia *(G-1402)*
P N K Ventures Inc .... G 630 527-0500
Naperville *(G-14891)*
Paddock Industries Inc .... F 618 277-1530
Smithton *(G-19068)*
Parvin-Clauss Sign Co Inc .... E 866 490-2877
Carol Stream *(G-3045)*
Photo Techniques Corp .... E 630 690-9360
Carol Stream *(G-3046)*
Platts Printing Company .... G 309 228-1069
Farmington *(G-9663)*
Prairie Display Chicago Inc .... F 630 834-8773
Elmhurst *(G-9411)*
Preformance Signs .... G 815 544-5044
Belvidere *(G-1695)*
Premier Signs Creations Inc .... G 309 637-6890
Peoria *(G-16502)*
Prime Market Targeting Inc .... E 815 469-4555
Frankfort *(G-9826)*
Printing Plus of Roselle Inc .... G 630 893-0410
Roselle *(G-17974)*
Pry-Bar Company .... F 815 436-3383
Joliet *(G-11918)*
Q SC Design .... G 815 933-6777
Bradley *(G-2289)*
Qt Sign Inc .... G 847 524-7950
Schaumburg *(G-18690)*
Quantum Sign Corporation .... F 630 466-0372
Sugar Grove *(G-19652)*
Quick Quality Printing Inc .... G 708 895-5885
Lansing *(G-12513)*
R D Niven & Associates Ltd .... E 630 580-6000
Carol Stream *(G-3057)*
R-Signs Service and Design Inc .... G 815 722-0283
Joliet *(G-11921)*
Realt Images Inc .... G 217 567-3487
Tower Hill *(G-19894)*
Rico Industries Inc .... D 312 427-0313
Niles *(G-15166)*
Rjw Graphics Inc .... G 847 336-4515
Waukegan *(G-20488)*
Rkm Enterprises .... G 217 348-5437
Charleston *(G-3411)*
Rmkc Inc .... G 630 932-0001
Oakbrook Terrace *(G-15814)*
Ron Meyer .... G 847 844-9880
Gilberts *(G-10367)*
Rowdy Star Custom Creations .... G 217 497-1789
Danville *(G-7379)*
Rutke Signs Inc .... G 708 841-6464
Westchester *(G-20709)*
S and S Associates Inc .... G 847 584-0033
Elk Grove Village *(G-9224)*
S D Custom Machining .... G 618 544-7007
Robinson *(G-17125)*
Sadannah Group LLC .... G 630 357-2300
Naperville *(G-14912)*

Same Day Signs .... G 773 697-4896
Chicago *(G-6097)*
Samsung Sign Corp .... G 847 816-1374
Libertyville *(G-12703)*
Sandee Manufacturing Co .... E 847 671-1335
Franklin Park *(G-10042)*
Sandra E Greene .... G 815 469-0092
Frankfort *(G-9836)*
Schellerer Corporation Inc .... D 630 980-4567
Hanover Park *(G-11013)*
Service Sheet Metal Works Inc .... F 773 229-0031
Chicago *(G-6143)*
Sharn Enterprises Inc .... E 815 464-9715
Frankfort *(G-9838)*
Shawcraft Sign Co .... G 815 282-4105
Machesney Park *(G-13374)*
Sign .... G 630 351-8400
Glendale Heights *(G-10495)*
Sign A Rama .... G 630 293-7300
West Chicago *(G-20642)*
Sign A Rama Inc .... G 630 359-5125
Villa Park *(G-20172)*
Sign Appeal Inc .... G 847 587-4300
Fox Lake *(G-9754)*
Sign Authority .... G 630 462-9850
Wheaton *(G-20824)*
Sign Centre .... G 847 595-7300
Elk Grove Village *(G-9239)*
Sign Contractors .... G 708 795-1761
Burr Ridge *(G-2720)*
Sign Express Inc .... G 708 524-8811
Oak Park *(G-15773)*
Sign Fx .... G 630 466-7446
Sugar Grove *(G-19656)*
Sign Girls Inc .... G 847 336-4002
Gurnee *(G-10927)*
Sign Palace Inc .... G 847 228-7446
Elk Grove Village *(G-9240)*
Sign Pro of Quincy Inc .... G 217 223-9693
Quincy *(G-16945)*
Sign Solutions .... G 618 443-6565
Sparta *(G-19259)*
Sign Team Inc .... G 309 302-0017
East Moline *(G-8240)*
Sign-A-Rama .... G 312 922-0509
Chicago *(G-6166)*
Sign-A-Rama of Buffalo Grove .... G 847 215-1535
Buffalo Grove *(G-2604)*
Signarama .... G 847 543-4870
Grayslake *(G-10800)*
Signature Screen Printing Corp .... G 773 866-0070
Chicago *(G-6169)*
Signkraft Co .... G 217 787-7105
Springfield *(G-19444)*
Signs By Custom Cutting Inc .... G 630 759-2734
Bolingbrook *(G-2240)*
Signs In Dundee Inc .... G 847 742-9530
Elgin *(G-8731)*
Signs Now .... G 847 427-0005
Elk Grove Village *(G-9242)*
Signs Now .... G 800 356-3373
Chicago *(G-6170)*
Signs of Distinction Inc .... G 847 520-0787
Wheeling *(G-20986)*
Signs Plus .... G 847 489-9009
Des Plaines *(G-7844)*
Signs Today Inc .... G 847 934-9777
Palatine *(G-16158)*
Signx Co Inc .... G 847 639-7917
Cary *(G-3190)*
Simply Signs .... G 309 849-9016
Metamora *(G-13968)*
Skyward Promotions Inc .... G 815 969-0909
Rockford *(G-17633)*
Southwest Signs Inc .... G 773 585-3530
Chicago *(G-6207)*
Specialty Graphics Supply Inc .... G 630 584-8202
Saint Charles *(G-18273)*
Speedpro North Shore .... G 847 983-0095
Skokie *(G-19034)*
Speedpro of Dupage .... G 630 812-5080
Lombard *(G-13134)*
Stans Sportsworld Inc .... G 217 359-8474
Champaign *(G-3355)*
Stecker Graphics Inc .... G 309 786-4973
Rock Island *(G-17246)*
Stevens Sign Co Inc .... G 708 562-4888
Northlake *(G-15560)*
Sticker Dude Inc .... G 815 322-2480
Johnsburg *(G-11810)*

Store 409 Inc .... F 708 478-5751
Mokena *(G-14117)*
Suburban Accents Inc .... G 847 776-7474
Rolling Meadows *(G-17778)*
Summit Signworks Inc .... G 847 870-0937
Arlington Heights *(G-815)*
Syndigo LLC .... C 309 690-5231
Peoria *(G-16532)*
T Graphics .... G 618 592-4145
Oblong *(G-15830)*
T Ham Sign Inc .... E 618 242-2010
Opdyke *(G-15905)*
T J Marche Ltd .... G 618 445-2314
Albion *(G-353)*
Technicraft Supply Co .... G 309 495-5245
Peoria *(G-16537)*
Teds Shirt Shack Inc .... G 217 224-9705
Quincy *(G-16946)*
Tierneys Signs Inc .... G 847 395-8224
Lake Villa *(G-12369)*
Timothy Anderson Corporation .... F 815 398-8371
Rockford *(G-17663)*
Timothy Darrey .... G 847 231-2277
Des Plaines *(G-7856)*
Trophytime Inc .... G 217 351-7958
Champaign *(G-3359)*
Twin City Awards .... G 309 452-9291
Normal *(G-15226)*
Unistrut International Corp .... D 630 773-3460
Addison *(G-323)*
Varsity Striping & Cnstr Co .... E 217 352-2203
Champaign *(G-3362)*
Vindee Industries Inc .... G 815 469-3300
Frankfort *(G-9850)*
Vinyl Graphics Inc .... G 708 579-1234
Countryside *(G-7077)*
Vision Signs Inc .... G 815 530-0870
Joliet *(G-11941)*
Visual Marketing Solutions .... G 815 589-3848
Fulton *(G-10159)*
Visucom .... G 708 460-3001
Mokena *(G-14126)*
Vital Signs USA .... G 630 832-9600
Elmhurst *(G-9442)*
W G N Flag & Decorating Co .... F 773 768-8076
Chicago *(G-6573)*
Walnut Creek Hardwood .... G 815 389-3317
South Beloit *(G-19120)*
Weakley Printing & Sign Shop .... G 847 473-4466
North Chicago *(G-15323)*
Weiskamp Screen Printing .... G 217 398-8428
Champaign *(G-3370)*
Willdon Corp .... E 773 276-7080
Chicago *(G-6628)*
Windy City Plastics Inc .... G 773 533-1099
Chicago *(G-6643)*
Wiremasters Incorporated .... E 773 254-3700
Chicago *(G-6649)*
Wright Quick Signs Inc .... G 708 652-6020
Cicero *(G-6889)*
Xpressigns Inc .... G 888 303-0640
Arlington Heights *(G-837)*
Xtrem Graphix Solutions Inc .... G 217 698-6424
Springfield *(G-19469)*
Zainab Enterprises Inc .... G 630 739-0110
Romeoville *(G-17891)*
Zendavor Signs & Graphics Inc .... G 309 691-8822
Peoria *(G-16549)*
Zimmerman Enterprises Inc .... F 847 297-3177
Des Plaines *(G-7871)*

SIGNS & ADVERTISING SPECIALTIES:
Artwork, Advertising

Blu Prime Inc .... G 800 709-5413
Chicago *(G-3912)*
Chicago Show Inc .... E 847 955-0200
Buffalo Grove *(G-2524)*
Color Communications LLC .... G 312 223-0204
Chicago *(G-4204)*
Corpro Screen Tech Inc .... G 815 633-1201
Loves Park *(G-13196)*
Horizon Downing LLC .... E 815 758-6867
Dekalb *(G-7685)*
M G M Displays Inc .... G 708 594-3699
Chicago *(G-5300)*
Mekanism Inc .... F 415 908-4000
Chicago *(G-5390)*
Navitor Inc .... B 800 323-0253
Harwood Heights *(G-11106)*

SIGNS, EXC ELECTRIC, WHOLESALE

PRODUCT SECTION

SIGNS & ADVERTISING SPECIALTIES: Letters For Signs, Metal

Company	Code	Phone
A Trustworthy Sup Source Inc	G	773 480-0255
Chicago (G-3492)		
Desk & Door Nameplate Company	F	815 806-8670
Frankfort (G-9785)		
Wagner Zip-Change Inc	E	708 681-4100
Melrose Park (G-13926)		

SIGNS & ADVERTISING SPECIALTIES: Novelties

Company	Code	Phone
B W M Global	G	847 785-1355
Waukegan (G-20421)		
Bee-Jay Industries Inc	F	708 867-4431
Bloomingdale (G-1979)		
Budget Signs	F	618 259-4460
Wood River (G-21260)		
C M F Enterprises Inc	F	847 526-9499
Wauconda (G-20337)		
Concepts Magnet	G	847 253-3351
Mount Prospect (G-14520)		
Flow-Eze Company	F	815 965-1062
Rockford (G-17416)		
Fun Incorporated	F	773 745-3837
Wheeling (G-20902)		
Gemini Industries Inc	D	618 251-3352
Roxana (G-18100)		
Ken Young Construction Co	G	847 358-3026
Hoffman Estates (G-11433)		
Midwest Promotional Group Co	E	708 563-0600
Burr Ridge (G-2705)		
Promotional Co of Illinois	G	847 382-0239
Inverness (G-11603)		
Stellar Recognition Inc	D	773 282-8060
Chicago (G-6243)		

SIGNS & ADVERTISING SPECIALTIES: Scoreboards, Electric

Company	Code	Phone
Nevco Sports LLC	D	618 664-0360
Greenville (G-10840)		

SIGNS & ADVERTISING SPECIALTIES: Signs

Company	Code	Phone
A & J Signs	F	815 476-0128
Wilmington (G-21095)		
Ability Plastics Inc	E	708 458-4480
Justice (G-11949)		
Academy Screenprinting Awards	G	309 686-0026
Peoria (G-16374)		
Ace Sign Co	E	217 522-8417
Springfield (G-19314)		
Advertising Products Inc	G	847 758-0415
Elk Grove Village (G-8812)		
All-Right Sign Inc	F	708 754-6366
Steger (G-19487)		
All-Steel Structures Inc	F	708 210-1313
South Holland (G-19189)		
AM Ko Oriental Foods	G	217 398-2922
Champaign (G-3262)		
Barry Signs Inc	G	773 327-1183
Chicago (G-3841)		
Boatman Signs	G	618 548-6567
Salem (G-18332)		
Briscoe Signs LLC	G	630 529-1616
Roselle (G-17942)		
Color Signs	G	847 368-0101
Arlington Heights (G-716)		
Contempo Autographic & Signs	G	708 371-5499
Crestwood (G-7113)		
Corporate Sign Systems Inc	F	847 882-6100
Roselle (G-17948)		
Custom Sign Consultants Inc	G	312 533-2302
Chicago (G-4292)		
Custom Signs On Metal LLC	G	217 443-5347
Tilton (G-19795)		
E B G B Inc	G	847 228-9333
Elk Grove Village (G-8962)		
E K Kuhn Inc	G	815 899-9211
Sycamore (G-19709)		
E Z Sign Co Inc	G	815 469-4080
Oak Forest (G-15675)		
Graymon Graphics Inc	G	773 737-0176
Chicago (G-4730)		
Heiman Sign Studio	G	815 397-6909
Rockford (G-17447)		
In Sight Sign Company Inc	G	773 267-4002
Chicago (G-4903)		
Janis Plastics Inc	D	847 838-5500
Antioch (G-617)		
K and A Graphics Inc	G	847 244-2345
Gurnee (G-10890)		
Ksem Inc	G	618 656-5388
Edwardsville (G-8367)		
Laux Grafix Inc	G	618 337-4558
East Saint Louis (G-8313)		
Legible Signs Group Corp	F	815 654-0100
Loves Park (G-13233)		
Lena Sign Shop	G	815 369-9090
Lena (G-12604)		
Lettering Specialists Inc	F	847 674-3414
Skokie (G-18979)		
Mmxix Capital Inc	D	815 441-2647
Sterling (G-19520)		
Nelson - Harkins Inds Inc	E	773 478-6243
Lake Bluff (G-12199)		
Nutheme Sign Company	G	847 230-0067
Downers Grove (G-8067)		
O Signs Inc	G	312 888-3386
Chicago (G-5646)		
Peterson Brothers Plastics	F	773 286-5666
Chicago (G-5795)		
Plainfield Signs Inc	G	815 439-1063
Plainfield (G-16702)		
Procon General Services Inc	G	773 227-8258
Chicago (G-5891)		
Pronto Signs and Engraving	F	847 249-7874
Waukegan (G-20483)		
Quick Signs Inc	G	630 554-7370
Oswego (G-16023)		
R & L Signs Inc	G	708 233-0112
Bridgeview (G-2377)		
Road Ready Signs	F	309 828-1007
Bloomington (G-2089)		
Roeda Signs Inc	E	708 333-3021
Chicago Heights (G-6772)		
Roth Neon Sign Company Inc	G	618 942-6378
Herrin (G-11177)		
Saturn Sign	G	847 520-9009
Wheeling (G-20978)		
Savino Displays Inc	G	630 574-0777
Hinsdale (G-11378)		
Sign & Banner Express	G	630 783-9700
Bolingbrook (G-2239)		
Sign America Inc	G	773 262-7800
Chicago (G-6165)		
Sign Identity Inc	G	630 942-1400
Glen Ellyn (G-10419)		
Sign O Rama	G	815 744-8702
Joliet (G-11930)		
Sign Shop Express	G	630 964-3500
Downers Grove (G-8094)		
Signcrafters Enterprises Inc	G	815 648-4484
Hebron (G-11150)		
Signs By Design	G	708 599-9970
Palos Hills (G-16207)		
Signs Direct Inc	F	309 820-1070
Bloomington (G-2095)		
Signscapes Inc	G	847 719-2610
Lake Zurich (G-12457)		
Signwise Inc	G	630 932-3204
Addison (G-290)		
South Water Signs LLC	E	630 333-4900
Elmhurst (G-9428)		
Stelmont Inc	G	847 870-0200
Arlington Heights (G-812)		
Sub-Surface Sign Co Ltd	F	847 675-6530
Skokie (G-19039)		
Targin Sign Systems Inc	G	630 766-7667
Wood Dale (G-21246)		
Toms Signs	G	630 377-8525
Saint Charles (G-18290)		
Turnroth Sign Company Inc	F	815 625-1155
Rock Falls (G-17198)		
Ultimate Sign Co	G	773 282-4595
Chicago (G-6458)		
West Zwick Corp	G	217 222-0228
Quincy (G-16955)		
Western Remac Inc	E	630 972-7770
Woodridge (G-21347)		
William Frick & Company	E	847 918-3700
Libertyville (G-12725)		
Ye Olde Sign Shoppe	G	847 228-7446
Elk Grove Village (G-9316)		

SIGNS & ADVERTSG SPECIALTIES: Displays/Cutouts Window/Lobby

Company	Code	Phone
Accurate Metal Fabricating LLC	D	773 235-0400
Chicago (G-3518)		
Acrylic Service Inc	G	630 543-0336
Addison (G-18)		
AMD Industries Inc	D	708 863-8900
Oak Brook (G-15591)		
Benchmarc Display Incorporated	E	847 541-2828
Vernon Hills (G-20046)		
Bish Creative Display Inc	E	847 438-1500
Lake Zurich (G-12388)		
Braeside Holdings LLC	E	847 395-8500
Antioch (G-606)		
Consolidated Displays Co Inc	G	630 851-8666
Oswego (G-15998)		
Derse Inc	D	847 473-2149
Waukegan (G-20435)		
Design Phase Inc	E	847 473-0077
Waukegan (G-20436)		
Display Link Inc	G	815 968-0778
Rockford (G-17380)		
Hazen Display Corporation	E	815 248-2925
Davis (G-7418)		
J R Fridrich Inc	F	847 439-1554
Elk Grove Village (G-9064)		
Joliet Pattern Works Inc	D	815 726-5373
Crest Hill (G-7088)		
K-Display Corp	F	773 586-2042
Chicago (G-5071)		
McKernin Exhibits Inc	F	708 333-4500
South Holland (G-19231)		
Mer-Pla Inc	F	847 530-9798
Chicago (G-5393)		
Mercury Plastics Inc	E	888 884-1864
Chicago (G-5394)		
Patt Supply Corporation	F	708 442-3901
Lyons (G-13312)		
RTC Industries Inc	D	847 640-2400
Chicago (G-6075)		
Stevens Exhibits & Displays	F	773 523-3900
Chicago (G-6246)		
Thermo-Graphic LLC	E	630 350-2226
Bensenville (G-1901)		
Visual Marketing Inc	E	312 664-9177
Chicago (G-6559)		

SIGNS, ELECTRICAL: Wholesalers

Company	Code	Phone
Frankenstitch Promotions LLC	F	847 459-4840
Wheeling (G-20901)		
Quantum Sign Corporation	F	630 466-0372
Sugar Grove (G-19652)		
Roth Neon Sign Company Inc	G	618 942-6378
Herrin (G-11177)		

SIGNS, EXC ELECTRIC, WHOLESALE

Company	Code	Phone
All Signs & Wonders Co	G	630 232-9019
Geneva (G-10250)		
Budget Signs	F	618 259-4460
Wood River (G-21260)		
C H Hanson Company	D	630 848-2000
Naperville (G-14786)		
Fedex Corporation	F	847 918-7730
Vernon Hills (G-20053)		
Fedex Ground Package Sys Inc	G	800 463-3339
Glendale Heights (G-10450)		
Fedex Office & Print Svcs Inc	F	312 341-9644
Chicago (G-4573)		
Fedex Office & Print Svcs Inc	F	312 755-0325
Chicago (G-4574)		
Fedex Office & Print Svcs Inc	F	312 595-0768
Chicago (G-4575)		
Fedex Office & Print Svcs Inc	G	630 759-5784
Bolingbrook (G-2176)		
Fedex Office & Print Svcs Inc	F	312 663-1149
Chicago (G-4576)		
Fedex Office & Print Svcs Inc	G	847 670-7283
Mount Prospect (G-14528)		
Frankenstitch Promotions LLC	F	847 459-4840
Wheeling (G-20901)		
GL Downs Inc	G	618 993-9777
Marion (G-13513)		
Precise Digital Printing Inc	E	847 593-2645
Bensenville (G-1871)		
Q SC Design	G	815 933-6777
Bradley (G-2289)		
Sign A Rama	G	630 293-7300
West Chicago (G-20642)		

Sign Centre....G.... 847 595-7300
Elk Grove Village *(G-9239)*
Signet Sign Company....G.... 630 830-8242
Bartlett *(G-1313)*
Wagner Zip-Change Inc....E.... 708 681-4100
Melrose Park *(G-13926)*

SIGNS: Electrical

All-American Sign Co Inc....E.... 708 422-2203
Oak Lawn *(G-15698)*
Alphabet Shop Inc....E.... 847 888-3150
Elgin *(G-8505)*
American Sign & Lighting Co....E.... 847 258-8151
Chicago *(G-3667)*
Anbek Inc....F.... 815 434-7340
Ottawa *(G-16039)*
Arrow Signs....F.... 618 466-0818
Godfrey *(G-10649)*
Art & Son Sign Inc....F.... 847 526-7205
Wauconda *(G-20332)*
Arts & Letters Marshall Signs....G.... 773 927-4442
Chicago *(G-3743)*
Aubrey Sign Co Inc....G.... 630 482-9901
Batavia *(G-1351)*
Baum Holdings Inc....G.... 847 488-0650
South Elgin *(G-19135)*
Bright Light Sign Company Inc....G.... 847 550-8902
Lake Zurich *(G-12389)*
Cachera and Klemm Inc....G.... 217 876-7446
Decatur *(G-7468)*
Central Illinois Sign Company....G.... 217 523-4740
Springfield *(G-19346)*
Chicago Sign Group....G.... 847 899-9021
Vernon Hills *(G-20048)*
CNE Inc....G.... 847 534-7135
Schaumburg *(G-18480)*
Comet Neon....G.... 630 668-6366
Lombard *(G-13056)*
Corporate Identification Solut....E.... 773 763-9600
Chicago *(G-4240)*
Demond Signs Inc....F.... 618 624-7260
O Fallon *(G-15571)*
Design Group Signage Corp....F.... 847 390-0350
Des Plaines *(G-7756)*
Eberhart Sign & Lighting Co....G.... 618 656-7256
Edwardsville *(G-8359)*
Express Signs & Lighting Maint....F.... 815 725-9080
Shorewood *(G-18896)*
G M Sign Inc....D.... 847 546-0424
Round Lake *(G-18075)*
Galesburg Sign & Lighting....G.... 309 342-9798
Galesburg *(G-10194)*
Grate Signs Inc....E.... 815 729-9700
Joliet *(G-11870)*
Hanover Displays Inc....F.... 773 334-9934
Elk Grove Village *(G-9027)*
HM Witt & Co....E.... 773 250-5000
Chicago *(G-4824)*
Image Signs Inc....F.... 815 282-4141
Loves Park *(G-13218)*
Impact Signs & Graphics Inc....G.... 708 469-7178
La Grange *(G-12080)*
Integrity Sign Company....F.... 708 532-5038
Mokena *(G-14092)*
Jenkins Displays Co....G.... 618 335-3874
Vandalia *(G-20013)*
Keyesport Manufacturing Inc....G.... 618 749-5510
Keyesport *(G-12043)*
Kieffer Holding Co....G.... 877 543-3337
Lincolnshire *(G-12776)*
Lange Sign Group....G.... 815 747-2448
East Dubuque *(G-8178)*
Monitor Sign Co....F.... 217 234-2412
Mattoon *(G-13651)*
Neon Art....G.... 773 588-5883
Chicago *(G-5566)*
North Shore Sign Company....E.... 847 816-7020
Libertyville *(G-12690)*
Olympic Signs Inc....E.... 630 424-6100
Lombard *(G-13112)*
Paldo Sign and Display Company....G.... 708 456-1711
River Grove *(G-17065)*
Pellegrini Enterprises Inc....G.... 815 717-6408
Orland Park *(G-15974)*
Prairie Signs Inc....F.... 309 452-0463
Normal *(G-15218)*
Quincy Electric & Sign Company....F.... 217 223-8404
Quincy *(G-16930)*
Rainbow Signs....F.... 815 675-6750
Spring Grove *(G-19298)*
Rebechini Studio Inc....F.... 847 437-9030
Elk Grove Village *(G-9215)*
Right Way Signs LLC....G.... 773 930-4361
Chicago *(G-6032)*
Sign Central....G.... 847 543-7600
Round Lake *(G-18083)*
Sign City Corp....G.... 847 382-3838
Lake Barrington *(G-12165)*
Signet Sign Company....G.... 630 830-8242
Bartlett *(G-1313)*
Signworx Sign & Lighting Co....G.... 217 413-2532
Springfield *(G-19445)*
Solar Traffic Systems Inc....G.... 331 318-8500
Lemont *(G-12590)*
Strictly Neon Inc....G.... 708 597-1616
Crestwood *(G-7130)*
Super Sign Service....F.... 309 829-9241
Bloomington *(G-2098)*
T & J Electric Company Inc....F.... 309 347-2196
Pekin *(G-16364)*
Tfa Signs....G.... 773 267-6007
Chicago *(G-6357)*
Watchfire Enterprises Inc....E.... 217 442-0611
Danville *(G-7393)*
Watchfire Signs LLC....B.... 217 442-0611
Danville *(G-7394)*
Watchfire Tech Holdings I Inc....G.... 217 442-6971
Danville *(G-7395)*
Watchfire Tech Holdings II Inc....G.... 217 442-0611
Danville *(G-7396)*
Weatherford Signs....G.... 618 529-2000
Carbondale *(G-2864)*
Western Lighting Inc....F.... 847 451-7200
Franklin Park *(G-10084)*
White Way Sign & Maint Co....C.... 847 391-0200
Chicago *(G-6619)*

SIGNS: Neon

Ad Deluxe Sign Company Inc....G.... 815 556-8469
Blue Island *(G-2109)*
Best Neon Sign Co....G.... 773 586-2700
Chicago *(G-3872)*
Century Signs Inc....F.... 217 224-7419
Quincy *(G-16871)*
Clover Signs....G.... 773 588-2828
Chicago *(G-4181)*
Dgs Import LLC....E.... 800 211-9646
Chicago *(G-4350)*
Doyle Signs Inc....D.... 630 543-9490
Addison *(G-97)*
Harder Signs Inc....F.... 815 874-7777
Rockford *(G-17443)*
Herrmann Signs & Service....G.... 618 246-6537
Mount Vernon *(G-14614)*
Icon Identity Solutions Inc....C.... 847 364-2250
Rolling Meadows *(G-17738)*
Mk Signs Inc....E.... 773 545-4444
Chicago *(G-5473)*
Mostert & Ferguson Signs....G.... 815 485-1212
Orland Park *(G-15969)*
Mount Vernon Neon Sign Co....C.... 618 242-0645
Mount Vernon *(G-14626)*
Neon Prism Electric Sign Co....G.... 630 879-1010
Batavia *(G-1400)*
Neon Shop Inc....G.... 773 227-0303
Chicago *(G-5569)*
Nu Glo Sign Company....F.... 847 223-6160
Grayslake *(G-10793)*
Omega Sign & Lighting Inc....E.... 630 237-4397
Addison *(G-231)*
Real Neon Inc....F.... 630 543-0995
Villa Park *(G-20168)*
Roman Signs....G.... 847 381-3425
Barrington *(G-1241)*
Rout A Bout Shop Inc....G.... 309 829-0674
Bloomington *(G-2091)*
Shinn Enterprises....G.... 217 698-3344
Springfield *(G-19443)*
Sign Outlet Inc....G.... 708 824-2222
Alsip *(G-510)*
Signs For Success Inc....F.... 847 800-4870
Buffalo Grove *(G-2605)*
Staar Bales Lestarge Inc....G.... 618 259-6366
East Alton *(G-8171)*
Wave Mechanics Neon....G.... 312 829-9283
Chicago *(G-6591)*
Wow Signs Inc....G.... 847 910-4405
Deerfield *(G-7662)*

SILICA MINING

Covia Holdings Corporation....G.... 618 747-2355
Tamms *(G-19742)*
Covia Holdings Corporation....E.... 618 747-2338
Tamms *(G-19743)*

SILICON

Jmjocs LLC....G.... 708 769-7981
Chicago Ridge *(G-6800)*

SILICON WAFERS: Chemically Doped

Dauber Company Inc....E.... 815 442-3569
Tonica *(G-19888)*

SILICONES

AB Specialty Silicones LLC....D.... 908 273-8015
Waukegan *(G-20405)*
ICP Industrial Inc....E.... 630 227-1692
Itasca *(G-11668)*
Uberlube Inc....G.... 847 644-4230
Evanston *(G-9586)*

SILK SCREEN DESIGN SVCS

American Outfitters Ltd....E.... 847 623-3959
Waukegan *(G-20414)*
C M F Enterprises Inc....F.... 847 526-9499
Wauconda *(G-20337)*
Chicago Printing and EMB Inc....F.... 630 628-1777
Addison *(G-71)*
Corr-Pak Corporation....E.... 708 442-7806
Mc Cook *(G-13690)*
Custom Trophies....G.... 217 422-3353
Decatur *(G-7480)*
Ems Acrylics & Silk Screener....F.... 773 777-5656
Chicago *(G-4502)*
Essential Creat Chicago Inc....G.... 773 238-1700
Chicago *(G-4533)*
Go Van Goghs Tee Shirt....G.... 309 342-1112
Galesburg *(G-10198)*
Johnson Sign Co....G.... 847 678-2092
Franklin Park *(G-9975)*
Kane Graphical Corporation....E.... 773 384-1200
Chicago *(G-5080)*
Midwest Promotional Group Co....E.... 708 563-0600
Burr Ridge *(G-2705)*
Midwest Silkscreening Inc....G.... 217 892-9596
Rantoul *(G-16980)*
Mt Greenwood Embroidery....G.... 773 779-5798
Chicago *(G-5521)*
R J S Silk Screening Co....G.... 708 974-3009
Palos Hills *(G-16206)*
Signature Screen Printing Corp....G.... 773 866-0070
Chicago *(G-6169)*
Sunburst Sportswear Inc....F.... 630 717-8680
Glendale Heights *(G-10505)*
Team Print Inc....F.... 815 933-5111
Bourbonnais *(G-2269)*

SILOS: Concrete, Prefabricated

White Star Silo....G.... 618 523-4735
Germantown *(G-10332)*

SILOS: Meal

Dspc Company....E.... 815 997-1116
Rockford *(G-17387)*

SILVER ORE MINING

Coeur Mining Inc....D.... 312 489-5800
Chicago *(G-4194)*

SILVER ORES

Callahan Mining Corporation....D.... 312 489-5800
Chicago *(G-4006)*
Coeur Rochester Inc....G.... 312 661-2436
Chicago *(G-4195)*

SILVERSMITHS

Baroque Silversmith Inc....G.... 312 357-2813
Chicago *(G-3835)*

SIMULATORS: Flight

Wittenstein Arspc Smlation Inc....G.... 630 540-5300
Bartlett *(G-1326)*

PRODUCT SECTION

SINKS: Vitreous China

Wells Sinkware Corp .... G 312 850-3466
  Chicago (G-6601)

SIRENS: Vehicle, Marine, Indl & Warning

Federal Signal Corporation .... D 630 954-2000
  Oak Brook (G-15618)
Lund Industries Inc .... E 847 459-1460
  Northbrook (G-15424)
North American Signal Co .... E 847 537-8888
  Wheeling (G-20945)

SKIDS: Wood

Caisson Inc .... E 815 547-5925
  Belvidere (G-1658)

SKYLIGHTS

A D Skylights Inc .... G 847 854-2900
  Algonquin (G-365)
Imperial Glass Structures Co .... F 847 253-6150
  Wheeling (G-20914)
Midwest Skylite Company Inc .... E 847 214-9505
  South Elgin (G-19167)
United Skys LLC .... F 847 546-7776
  Chicago (G-6474)

SLAB & TILE, ROOFING: Concrete

Lifetime Rooftile Company .... G 630 355-7922
  Naperville (G-14863)

SLAB & TILE: Precast Concrete, Floor

Euro Marble Supply Ltd .... F 847 233-0700
  Schiller Park (G-18806)
St Louis Flexicore Inc .... F 618 531-8691
  East Saint Louis (G-8324)

SLAG: Crushed Or Ground

Beelman Slag Sales .... B 618 452-8120
  Madison (G-13405)
Tms International LLC .... D 618 451-7840
  Granite City (G-10742)
Tms International LLC .... G 815 939-9460
  Bourbonnais (G-2271)

SLATE: Crushed & Broken

Mid Illinois Quarry Company .... G 217 932-2611
  Casey (G-3206)

SLAUGHTERING & MEAT PACKING

Eickmans Processing Co Inc .... E 815 247-8451
  Seward (G-18867)
God Family Country LLC .... F 217 285-6487
  Pittsfield (G-16634)
Graized LLC .... G 815 615-1012
  Moweaqua (G-14651)
Jbs USA Food Company .... E 217 323-6200
  Beardstown (G-1447)
Main Street Market Roscoe Inc .... G 815 623-6328
  Roscoe (G-17915)
Teys (usa) Inc .... G 312 492-7163
  Chicago (G-6356)

SLIDES & EXHIBITS: Prepared

Evo Exhibits LLC .... G 630 520-0710
  West Chicago (G-20577)

SLINGS: Lifting, Made From Purchased Wire

Alloy Sling Chains Inc .... D 708 647-4900
  East Hazel Crest (G-8217)
Lamco Slings & Rigging Inc .... E 309 764-7400
  Moline (G-14157)
Lee Jensen Sales Co Inc .... E 815 459-0929
  Crystal Lake (G-7220)
Lift-All Company Inc .... E 800 909-1964
  Itasca (G-11692)
Marcal Rope & Rigging Inc .... E 618 462-0151
  Alton (G-565)

SLOT MACHINES

Top Dollar Slots .... G 779 210-4884
  Loves Park (G-13276)
WMS Gaming Inc .... C 773 961-1747
  Chicago (G-6658)

WMS Gaming Inc .... A 773 961-1000
  Chicago (G-6659)

SMOKE DETECTORS

First Alert Inc .... C 630 499-3295
  Aurora (G-962)

SNIPS: Tinners'

Irwin Industrial Tool Company .... C 815 235-4171
  Freeport (G-10121)

SNOW PLOWING SVCS

Complete Lawn and Snow Service .... F 847 776-7287
  Palatine (G-16102)
Geske and Sons Inc .... F 815 459-2407
  Crystal Lake (G-7202)
Northwest Snow Timber Svc Ltd .... G 847 778-4998
  Lombard (G-13109)
Powell Tree Care Inc .... G 847 364-1181
  Elk Grove Village (G-9186)
Tri Star Plowing .... G 847 584-5070
  Schaumburg (G-18755)

SNOW REMOVAL EQPT: Residential

Amerisun Inc .... F 800 791-9458
  Itasca (G-11623)
Randys Exper-Clean .... G 217 423-1975
  Decatur (G-7539)

SOAPS & DETERGENTS

A & H Manufacturing Inc .... F 630 543-5900
  Addison (G-13)
Aerosols Danville Inc .... G 773 816-5132
  Chicago (G-3574)
Aerosols Danville Inc .... B 217 442-1400
  Danville (G-7318)
Afton Chemical Corporation .... B 618 583-1000
  East Saint Louis (G-8296)
Atm America Corp .... E 800 298-0030
  Chicago (G-3770)
Avatar Corporation .... D 708 534-5511
  University Park (G-19947)
Blachford Corporation .... E 815 464-2100
  Frankfort (G-9773)
Black Swan Manufacturing Co .... F 773 227-3700
  Chicago (G-3908)
Blast Products Inc .... G 618 452-4700
  Madison (G-13406)
Cater Chemical Co .... G 630 980-2300
  Roselle (G-17943)
Cedar Concepts Corporation .... E 773 890-5790
  Chicago (G-4050)
Chemstation Chicago LLC .... E 630 279-2857
  Elmhurst (G-9344)
Chemtool Incorporated .... C 815 957-4140
  Rockton (G-17694)
Chemtool Incorporated .... D 815 459-1250
  Crystal Lake (G-7180)
Combe Laboratories Inc .... C 217 893-4490
  Rantoul (G-16971)
Dairy Dynamics LLC .... F 847 758-7300
  Elk Grove Village (G-8936)
Damco Products Inc .... G 618 452-4700
  Madison (G-13407)
Ecolab Inc .... G 708 496-5378
  Palos Heights (G-16183)
Ecp Incorporated .... D 630 754-4200
  Woodridge (G-21297)
First Ayd Corporation .... D 847 622-0001
  Elgin (G-8586)
Floor-Chem Inc .... G 630 789-2152
  Romeoville (G-17824)
Formulations Inc .... G 847 674-9141
  Skokie (G-18956)
Gea Farm Technologies Inc .... E 630 369-8100
  Romeoville (G-17828)
Henkel Consumer Goods Inc .... D 847 426-4552
  Chicago (G-4801)
Interflo Industries Inc .... G 847 228-0606
  Elk Grove Village (G-9056)
Karimi Saifuddin .... G 630 943-8808
  Plainfield (G-16678)
Korex Chicago LLC .... E 708 458-4890
  Chicago (G-5124)
Nader Wholesale Grocers Inc .... F 773 582-1000
  Chicago (G-5536)
Nataz Specialty Coatings Inc .... F 773 247-7030
  Chicago (G-5542)

People Against Dirty Mfg Pbc .... D 415 568-4600
  Chicago (G-5785)
PLC Corp .... G 847 247-1900
  Lake Bluff (G-12206)
Progressive Solutions Corp .... G 847 639-7272
  Algonquin (G-384)
Rock River Blending .... G 815 968-7860
  Rockford (G-17581)
Scott Sawvel .... G 815 543-4136
  Roscoe (G-17932)
Standard Indus & Auto Eqp Inc .... E 630 289-9500
  Hanover Park (G-11014)
Sweet Thyme Soaps .... G 708 848-0234
  Oak Park (G-15776)
Tri Sect Corporation .... F 847 524-1119
  Schaumburg (G-18754)
Venus Laboratories Inc .... E 630 595-1900
  Addison (G-328)
Vvf Illinois Services LLC .... B 630 892-4381
  Montgomery (G-14275)
Westfalia-Surge Inc .... G 630 759-7346
  Romeoville (G-17887)
Wet International Inc .... E 630 540-2113
  Streamwood (G-19602)

SOAPS & DETERGENTS: Glycerin, Crude Or Refined, From Fats

Vantage Oleochemicals Inc .... C 773 376-9000
  Chicago (G-6522)

SOAPS & DETERGENTS: Textile

AM Harper Products Inc .... F 312 767-8283
  Chicago (G-3640)
Ashley Lauren .... G 847 733-9470
  Evanston (G-9496)

SOCIAL CLUBS

German American Nat Congress .... F 773 561-9181
  Chicago (G-4688)

SOCIAL SVCS, HANDICAPPED

Envision Unlimited .... C 773 651-1100
  Chicago (G-4521)
Perry Adult Living Inc .... G 618 542-5421
  Du Quoin (G-8123)

SOCIAL SVCS: Individual & Family

American Soc Plastic Surgeons .... D 847 228-9900
  Arlington Heights (G-691)

SOFT DRINKS WHOLESALERS

Clover Club Bottling Co Inc .... F 773 261-7100
  Chicago (G-4180)
Excel Bottling Co .... E 618 526-7159
  Breese (G-2302)
Great Lakes Coca-Cola Dist LLC .... D 847 227-6500
  Rosemont (G-18025)
Nader Wholesale Grocers Inc .... F 773 582-1000
  Chicago (G-5536)
P-Americas LLC .... C 309 266-2400
  Morton (G-14375)
P-Americas LLC .... D 312 821-2266
  Chicago (G-5732)
Pepsi Cola Gen Bttlers of Lima .... G 847 253-1000
  Rolling Meadows (G-17760)

SOFTWARE PUBLISHERS: Application

Abki Tech Service Inc .... F 847 818-8403
  Des Plaines (G-7721)
Accuity Inc .... B 847 676-9600
  Evanston (G-9486)
Airport Park and Fly LLC .... G 708 310-2442
  Chicago (G-3590)
Alliance Technology MGT Corp .... G 847 574-9752
  Northfield (G-15504)
Amoco Technology Company .... C 312 861-6000
  Chicago (G-3682)
Appsanity Advisory LLC .... G 847 638-1172
  Winnetka (G-21125)
Aprimo US LLC .... D 877 794-8556
  Chicago (G-3715)
Aqueous Solutions LLC .... F 217 531-1206
  Champaign (G-3266)
Ascent Innovations LLC .... E 847 572-8000
  Schaumburg (G-18445)

Askric LLC ....G.... 309 360-3125
Germantown Hills *(G-10333)*
Axiomatics Inc ....F.... 312 374-3443
Chicago *(G-3794)*
Big Game Software LLC ....F.... 630 592-8082
Elmhurst *(G-9333)*
Brokerassist LLC ....G.... 847 858-2357
River Forest *(G-17050)*
Busways LLC ....G.... 617 697-2009
Chicago *(G-3984)*
Buyersvine Inc ....G.... 630 235-6804
Hinsdale *(G-11367)*
Bytebin LLC ....G.... 312 286-0740
Chicago *(G-3989)*
Ca Inc ....G.... 312 201-8557
Chicago *(G-3998)*
Carlease Inc ....F.... 847 714-1414
Northbrook *(G-15352)*
Champion Medical Tech Inc ....E.... 866 803-3720
Lake Zurich *(G-12392)*
Cheetah Digital Inc ....D.... 312 858-8200
Chicago *(G-4081)*
Chewy Software LLC ....G.... 773 935-2627
Chicago *(G-4084)*
Chicago Data Solutions Inc ....G.... 847 370-4609
Willowbrook *(G-21035)*
Chwey Software LLC ....E.... 773 525-6445
Chicago *(G-4149)*
Cityzenith LLC ....F.... 312 883-5554
Chicago *(G-4164)*
Cliqster LLC ....G.... 847 732-1457
Highland Park *(G-11259)*
Comvigo Inc ....G.... 312 933-3385
Willowbrook *(G-21037)*
Cozent LLC ....G.... 630 781-2822
Naperville *(G-14810)*
Createasoft Inc ....F.... 630 851-9474
Aurora *(G-943)*
Crowdmatrix Fx LLC ....G.... 312 329-1170
Chicago *(G-4275)*
Crowdsource Solutions Inc ....G.... 855 276-9376
Swansea *(G-19691)*
Cunningham Electronics Corp ....G.... 618 833-7775
Anna *(G-582)*
Delante Group Inc ....G.... 312 493-4371
Chicago *(G-4332)*
Earshot Inc ....F.... 773 383-1798
Chicago *(G-4433)*
Effici Inc ....G.... 401 584-2266
Schaumburg *(G-18515)*
Endure Holdings Inc ....G.... 224 558-1828
Bloomingdale *(G-1992)*
Enrollment Rx LLC ....F.... 847 233-0088
Schiller Park *(G-18804)*
Entience ....G.... 217 649-2590
Urbana *(G-19982)*
Ep Technology Corporation USA ....D.... 217 351-7888
Champaign *(G-3290)*
Epazz Inc ....G.... 312 955-8161
Wheeling *(G-20892)*
Focus Health and Fitness LLC ....G.... 847 975-8687
Woodstock *(G-21389)*
Foster Learning LLC ....G.... 618 656-6836
Edwardsville *(G-8362)*
Glidera Inc ....G.... 773 350-4000
Elmhurst *(G-9368)*
Go Mango Interactive Corp ....G.... 224 214-9528
Mundelein *(G-14690)*
H&R Block Inc ....F.... 847 566-5557
Mundelein *(G-14694)*
Healthcare Research LLC ....F.... 773 592-3508
Chicago *(G-4792)*
Healthy-Txt LLC ....G.... 630 945-1787
Chicago *(G-4794)*
Hucuai LLC ....G.... 312 608-6101
Chicago *(G-4860)*
Idevconcepts Inc ....G.... 312 351-1615
Chicago *(G-4877)*
Illinois Assn Cnty Officials ....F.... 217 585-9065
Springfield *(G-19385)*
Imaging Systems Inc ....F.... 630 875-1100
Itasca *(G-11674)*
Infiniscene Inc ....G.... 630 567-0452
Chicago *(G-4912)*
Innolitica Labs LLC ....G.... 224 434-1238
Chicago *(G-4928)*
Intravation Inc ....G.... 847 299-6423
Des Plaines *(G-7789)*
Isewa LLC ....G.... 847 877-1586
Buffalo Grove *(G-2551)*
Janitor Ltd ....G.... 773 936-3389
Chicago *(G-5004)*
Konveau Inc ....G.... 312 476-9385
Chicago *(G-5122)*
Lexray LLC ....F.... 630 664-6740
Downers Grove *(G-8044)*
Lottobot LLC ....G.... 773 909-6656
Chicago *(G-5265)*
M&M Restaurant Group LLC ....F.... 773 253-5326
Chicago *(G-5307)*
Manscore LLC ....G.... 630 297-7502
Downers Grove *(G-8050)*
Memorable Inc ....G.... 847 272-8207
Northbrook *(G-15431)*
Microsoft Corporation ....E.... 847 864-4777
Evanston *(G-9552)*
Microsoft Corporation ....D.... 630 725-4000
Downers Grove *(G-8055)*
Microsoft Corporation ....D.... 309 665-0113
Bloomington *(G-2077)*
Microsoft Corporation ....D.... 708 409-4759
Northlake *(G-15551)*
Mosaic Construction ....G.... 847 504-0177
Northbrook *(G-15437)*
Music Plug LLC ....G.... 309 826-5238
Colfax *(G-6950)*
Narrative Health Network Inc ....G.... 312 600-9154
Chicago *(G-5541)*
Nautilus Medical ....G.... 847 323-1334
Barrington *(G-1232)*
Nextpoint Inc ....E.... 773 929-4000
Chicago *(G-5593)*
Ntt America Solutions Inc ....F.... 847 278-6413
Schaumburg *(G-18654)*
Onefire Media Group Inc ....E.... 309 740-0345
Peoria *(G-16487)*
Optimus Advantage LLC ....G.... 847 905-1000
Chicago *(G-5685)*
Orinoco Systems LLC ....F.... 630 510-0775
Wheaton *(G-20814)*
Own The Night App ....G.... 773 216-0245
Chicago *(G-5721)*
Patientbond LLC ....E.... 312 445-8751
Elmhurst *(G-9408)*
Pearl Bath Bombs Inc ....F.... 312 661-2881
Chicago *(G-5777)*
Perficient Inc ....F.... 312 291-9035
Chicago *(G-5790)*
Performitiv LLC ....G.... 312 307-5716
Chicago *(G-5791)*
Personify Inc ....F.... 855 747-9940
Chicago *(G-5792)*
Physician Software Systems LLC ....F.... 630 717-8192
Lisle *(G-12926)*
Playground Pointers ....G.... 952 200-4168
Hinsdale *(G-11375)*
Polysystems Inc ....D.... 312 332-2114
Chicago *(G-5839)*
Power102jamz ....G.... 312 912-2766
Urbana *(G-19994)*
Presspage Inc ....G.... 312 256-9985
Chicago *(G-5869)*
Priva Mobility Inc ....G.... 248 410-3702
Evanston *(G-9571)*
Privacy One LLC ....G.... 312 872-3757
Chicago *(G-5886)*
Producepro Inc ....G.... 630 395-9700
Woodridge *(G-21335)*
Ptc/User Inc ....G.... 619 417-2050
Chicago *(G-5910)*
Pumpkin Patch Ventures Inc ....G.... 708 699-4396
Chicago *(G-5914)*
Pycas Design Innovations LLC ....E.... 847 656-5000
Glenview *(G-10604)*
Reliefwatch Inc ....G.... 646 678-2336
Chicago *(G-6011)*
Roger Cantu & Assocs ....G.... 630 573-9215
Oak Brook *(G-15661)*
Rosewood Software Inc ....G.... 847 438-2185
Palatine *(G-16155)*
Scholarship Solutions LLC ....F.... 847 859-5629
Chicago *(G-6113)*
Secure Data Inc ....F.... 618 726-5225
O Fallon *(G-15583)*
See What You Send Inc ....G.... 781 780-1483
Chicago *(G-6131)*
Sellers Commerce LLC ....F.... 858 345-1212
Northbrook *(G-15479)*
Serrala Solutions US Corp ....G.... 650 655-3939
Chicago *(G-6139)*
Signal Digital Inc ....E.... 312 685-1911
Chicago *(G-6167)*
Signs & Wonders Unlimited LLC ....G.... 847 816-9734
Libertyville *(G-12707)*
Smartbyte Solutions Inc ....G.... 847 925-1870
Palatine *(G-16160)*
Social Qnect LLC ....G.... 847 997-0077
Northbrook *(G-15483)*
Softtech LLC ....G.... 847 809-8801
Fox River Grove *(G-9762)*
Soloinsight Inc ....F.... 312 846-6729
Chicago *(G-6198)*
Spooky Cool Labs LLC ....E.... 773 577-5555
Chicago *(G-6218)*
Swapp Technologies Inc ....G.... 312 912-1515
Chicago *(G-6293)*
Synopsys Inc ....F.... 847 706-2000
Schaumburg *(G-18734)*
Systems Live Ltd ....G.... 815 455-3383
Crystal Lake *(G-7273)*
Thinkcercacom Inc ....F.... 224 412-3722
Chicago *(G-6365)*
Thoughtly Corp ....G.... 772 559-2008
Chicago *(G-6371)*
Thyng LLC ....G.... 312 262-5703
Chicago *(G-6374)*
Trinket Studios ....G.... 773 888-3454
Chicago *(G-6428)*
Twocanoes Software Inc ....G.... 630 305-9601
Naperville *(G-14937)*
Uber Technologies Inc ....C.... 612 600-4737
Chicago *(G-6454)*
Ubipass Inc ....G.... 312 626-4624
Willowbrook *(G-21066)*
Uxm Studio Inc ....G.... 773 359-1333
Villa Park *(G-20175)*
V2 Solutions Inc ....G.... 312 528-9050
Schaumburg *(G-18769)*
Veloflip Inc ....G.... 847 757-4972
Northfield *(G-15537)*
Viclarity Inc ....G.... 201 214-5405
Chicago *(G-6543)*
Vizr Tech LLC ....G.... 312 420-4466
Chicago *(G-6564)*
Wargaming (usa) Inc ....E.... 312 258-0500
Chicago *(G-6587)*
Webqa Incorporated ....D.... 630 985-1300
Woodridge *(G-21346)*
World Class Tae Kwon ....G.... 630 870-9293
Aurora *(G-1039)*
Wow Bao LLC ....D.... 888 496-9226
Chicago *(G-6680)*
Xaptum Inc ....G.... 312 852-1595
Chicago *(G-6691)*
Yesimpact ....G.... 765 413-9667
Darien *(G-7415)*

SOFTWARE PUBLISHERS: Business & Professional

4degrees AV Inc ....G.... 903 253-7398
Chicago *(G-3472)*
A Trustworthy Sup Source Inc ....G.... 773 480-0255
Chicago *(G-3492)*
Access International Inc ....E.... 312 920-9366
Chicago *(G-3514)*
Accuware Incorporated ....F.... 630 858-8409
Glen Ellyn *(G-10393)*
Adaptive Testing Tech Inc ....F.... 312 878-6490
Chicago *(G-3539)*
Adesso Solutions LLC ....F.... 847 342-1095
Rolling Meadows *(G-17709)*
Aeverie Inc ....G.... 844 238-3743
Buffalo Grove *(G-2505)*
Agile Health Technologies Inc ....E.... 331 457-5167
Naperville *(G-14952)*
Ahead Inc ....D.... 312 924-4492
Chicago *(G-3584)*
Ahead Data Blue LLC ....G.... 866 577-2902
Chicago *(G-3585)*
Anju Software Inc ....E.... 630 243-9810
Lisle *(G-12866)*
Applied Systems Inc ....A.... 708 534-5575
University Park *(G-19946)*
AR Inet Corp ....G.... 603 380-3903
Aurora *(G-913)*
Ariba Inc ....G.... 630 649-7600
Lisle *(G-12868)*
Ats Communications Netwrk Corp ....G.... 309 673-6733
Peoria *(G-16388)*

Bdna Corporation ....D....... 650 625-9530
Itasca *(G-11627)*
Bighand Inc ....F....... 312 893-5906
Chicago *(G-3884)*
Blue Software LLC ....D....... 773 957-1600
Chicago *(G-3914)*
Brevity LLC ....F....... 949 250-0701
Chicago *(G-3951)*
Bundlar LLC ....G....... 773 839-3976
Chicago *(G-3974)*
Business Systems Consultants ....F....... 312 553-1253
Chicago *(G-3981)*
Call Potential LLC ....F....... 877 552-2557
Naperville *(G-14787)*
Capital Merchant Solutions Inc ....F....... 309 452-5990
Bloomington *(G-2030)*
Catalytic Inc ....E....... 844 787-4268
Chicago *(G-4041)*
CDK Global Inc ....A....... 847 397-1700
Hoffman Estates *(G-11412)*
Centrex Technologies LLC ....G....... 800 768-0700
Oak Brook *(G-15605)*
Chartnet Technologies Inc ....F....... 630 385-4100
Yorkville *(G-21475)*
Cloud 9 Infosystems Inc ....C....... 855 225-6839
Downers Grove *(G-7974)*
Compusystems Inc ....C....... 708 344-9070
Downers Grove *(G-7978)*
Computerized Fleet Analysis ....G....... 630 543-1410
Addison *(G-80)*
Condata Global Inc ....E....... 708 390-2500
Mokena *(G-14076)*
Configure One Inc ....E....... 630 368-9950
Oak Brook *(G-15612)*
Conscisys Corp ....E....... 630 810-4444
Downers Grove *(G-7979)*
Coorens Communications Inc ....G....... 773 235-8688
Chicago *(G-4233)*
Credit & Management Systems ....F....... 618 654-3500
Highland *(G-11211)*
Crestwood Associates LLC ....F....... 847 394-8820
Schaumburg *(G-18495)*
Cyborg Systems Inc ....C....... 312 279-7000
Chicago *(G-4293)*
Datair Employee Beneft Systems ....E....... 630 325-2600
Westmont *(G-20734)*
Digi Trax Corporation ....E....... 847 613-2100
Lincolnshire *(G-12759)*
Ecd-Network LLC ....G....... 917 670-0821
Chicago *(G-4444)*
Eighty Nine Robotics LLC ....G....... 512 573-9091
Chicago *(G-4463)*
Elitegen Corp ....F....... 630 637-6917
Naperville *(G-14823)*
EMC Corporation ....D....... 630 505-3273
Lisle *(G-12887)*
Envestnet Rtrment Slutions LLC ....G....... 312 827-7957
Chicago *(G-4519)*
Equilibrium Contact Center Inc ....G....... 888 708-1405
Rockford *(G-17398)*
Evention LLC ....E....... 773 733-4256
Chicago *(G-4539)*
Fibroblast Inc ....F....... 800 396-6463
Chicago *(G-4586)*
Fivecubits Inc ....G....... 630 749-4182
Oak Brook *(G-15620)*
Floydware LLC ....G....... 630 469-1078
Lombard *(G-13077)*
Forecast 5 Analytics Inc ....E....... 630 955-7500
Naperville *(G-14830)*
Friedrich Klatt and Associates ....G....... 773 753-1806
Chicago *(G-4636)*
G2 Crowd Inc ....D....... 847 748-7559
Chicago *(G-4652)*
Gather Voices Inc ....G....... 312 476-9465
Chicago *(G-4661)*
Genisys Decision Corporation ....G....... 708 524-5100
Oak Park *(G-15755)*
Guidance Software Inc ....G....... 847 994-7324
Chicago *(G-4751)*
Havi Global Solutions LLC ....B....... 630 493-7400
Downers Grove *(G-8018)*
Hybris (us) Corporation ....E....... 312 265-5010
Chicago *(G-4861)*
Imanage LLC ....C....... 312 667-7000
Chicago *(G-4895)*
Infogix Inc ....C....... 630 505-1800
Naperville *(G-14846)*
Infor (us) Inc ....D....... 312 279-1245
Chicago *(G-4914)*
Information Resources Inc ....A....... 312 474-8900
Chicago *(G-4918)*
Innovative Custom Software Inc ....G....... 630 892-5022
Aurora *(G-983)*
Inrule Technology Inc ....E....... 312 648-1800
Chicago *(G-4933)*
Intermedix Holdings Inc ....G....... 312 324-7820
Chicago *(G-4948)*
Jellyvision Inc ....D....... 312 266-0606
Chicago *(G-5015)*
Koombea Inc ....G....... 408 786-5290
Chicago *(G-5123)*
Kronos Incorporated ....F....... 847 969-6501
Schaumburg *(G-18592)*
L Street Collaborative LLC ....F....... 630 243-5783
Chicago *(G-5143)*
Lattice Incorporated ....E....... 630 949-3250
Wheaton *(G-20811)*
Legal Files Software Inc ....E....... 217 726-6000
Springfield *(G-19398)*
Legistek Corporation ....G....... 312 399-4891
Chicago *(G-5201)*
Liders LLC ....G....... 312 873-1112
Chicago *(G-5219)*
Localfix Solutions LLC ....G....... 312 569-0619
Winfield *(G-21112)*
Logical Design Solutions Inc ....G....... 630 786-5999
Naperville *(G-14865)*
Logicgate Inc ....C....... 312 279-2775
Chicago *(G-5250)*
Lonelybrand LLC ....G....... 312 880-7506
Chicago *(G-5254)*
Mediafly Inc ....E....... 312 281-5175
Chicago *(G-5384)*
Metamation Inc ....F....... 775 826-1717
Hoffman Estates *(G-11434)*
Motivequest LLC ....F....... 847 905-6100
Chicago *(G-5506)*
My Local Beacon Llc ....G....... 888 482-6691
Chicago *(G-5529)*
Myeccho LLC ....G....... 224 639-3068
Des Plaines *(G-7809)*
Nanex LLC ....G....... 847 501-4787
Winnetka *(G-21134)*
Napersoft Inc ....F....... 630 420-1515
Naperville *(G-14879)*
Navipoint Genomics LLC ....G....... 630 464-8013
Naperville *(G-14981)*
Neon One LLC ....E....... 888 860-6366
Chicago *(G-5568)*
Newera Software Inc ....G....... 815 784-3345
Kingston *(G-12056)*
Next Generation Inc ....G....... 312 739-0520
Plainfield *(G-16695)*
Niche Interactive Media Inc ....F....... 312 498-7933
Chicago *(G-5596)*
Office of Experience LLC ....G....... 872 228-5126
Chicago *(G-5658)*
Onx USA LLC ....E....... 630 343-8940
Lisle *(G-12925)*
Opex Analytics LLC ....E....... 847 733-7439
Chicago *(G-5682)*
Oracle Corporation ....B....... 773 404-9300
Chicago *(G-5688)*
Oracle Corporation ....C....... 312 692-5270
Chicago *(G-5689)*
Oracle Corporation ....B....... 630 931-6400
Itasca *(G-11713)*
Oracle Corporation ....B....... 262 957-3000
Chicago *(G-5690)*
Origami Risk LLC ....E....... 312 546-6515
Chicago *(G-5699)*
Pagepath Technologies Inc ....F....... 630 689-4111
Plano *(G-16738)*
Panatech Computer Management ....G....... 847 678-8848
Lincolnshire *(G-12789)*
Paragon International Inc ....F....... 847 240-2981
Schaumburg *(G-18664)*
Peapod Digital Labs LLC ....G....... 800 573-2763
Chicago *(G-5776)*
Perry Johnson Inc ....F....... 847 635-0010
Rosemont *(G-18041)*
Pervasive Health Inc ....G....... 312 257-2967
Chicago *(G-5793)*
Phillip Grigalanz ....G....... 219 628-6706
Jerseyville *(G-11795)*
Popular Pays Inc ....G....... 435 767-7297
Chicago *(G-5844)*
Proship Inc ....G....... 312 332-7447
Chicago *(G-5904)*
Quiddity Solutions LLC ....G....... 773 844-2058
Chicago *(G-5937)*
Radius Solutions Incorporated ....F....... 312 648-0800
Chicago *(G-5962)*
Recsolu Inc ....E....... 312 517-3200
Chicago *(G-5990)*
Reflection Software Inc ....E....... 630 270-1200
Aurora *(G-1013)*
Relativity Oda LLC ....C....... 312 263-1177
Chicago *(G-6007)*
Rivalfly National Network LLC ....G....... 847 867-8660
Chicago *(G-6036)*
Robis Elections Inc ....F....... 630 752-0220
Wheaton *(G-20820)*
Salesforcecom Inc ....G....... 312 361-3555
Chicago *(G-6093)*
Salesforcecom Inc ....F....... 312 288-3600
Chicago *(G-6094)*
Scientific Cmpt Assoc Corp ....G....... 708 771-4567
River Forest *(G-17056)*
Sct Alternative Inc ....F....... 847 215-7488
Buffalo Grove *(G-2598)*
Secureslice Inc ....E....... 800 984-0494
Chicago *(G-6128)*
Sedona Inc ....C....... 309 736-4104
Moline *(G-14176)*
Showcase Corporation ....C....... 312 651-3000
Chicago *(G-6158)*
Siemens Industry Software Inc ....E....... 630 437-6700
Downers Grove *(G-8093)*
Simplement Inc ....G....... 702 560-5332
Northfield *(G-15530)*
Storiant Inc ....E....... 617 431-8000
Chicago *(G-6250)*
Streamlinx LLC ....F....... 630 864-3043
Naperville *(G-14920)*
Su Enterprise Inc ....G....... 847 394-1656
Arlington Heights *(G-814)*
Supply Vision Inc ....G....... 847 388-0064
Chicago *(G-6285)*
Systemslogix LLC ....G....... 630 784-3113
Glendale Heights *(G-10509)*
Tempus Labs Inc ....E....... 312 784-4400
Chicago *(G-6347)*
Thomas A Doan ....G....... 847 864-8772
Evanston *(G-9584)*
Timepilot Corporation ....G....... 630 879-6400
Batavia *(G-1430)*
Tom Zosel Associates Ltd ....D....... 847 540-6543
Long Grove *(G-13172)*
Track My Foreclosures LLC ....G....... 877 782-8187
Monticello *(G-14288)*
Traena Inc ....G....... 630 605-3087
Chicago *(G-6403)*
Trivaeo LLC ....G....... 760 505-4751
Paris *(G-16245)*
Truepad LLC ....F....... 847 274-6898
Chicago *(G-6438)*
Vaimo Inc ....G....... 502 767-9550
Chicago *(G-6517)*
Varsity Logistics Inc ....E....... 650 392-7979
Rosemont *(G-18059)*
Vauto Inc ....E....... 630 590-2000
Oakbrook Terrace *(G-15818)*
Velocity Software LLC ....F....... 800 351-6893
Lombard *(G-13149)*
Vertical Software Inc ....F....... 309 633-0700
Bartonville *(G-1336)*
Vodori Inc ....D....... 312 324-3992
Chicago *(G-6566)*
Whospoppin Enterprises Inc ....G....... 312 912-8480
Chicago *(G-6621)*
Yhlsoft Inc ....F....... 844 829-0039
Chicago *(G-6700)*

SOFTWARE PUBLISHERS: Computer Utilities

BMC Software Inc ....E....... 331 777-8700
Oakbrook Terrace *(G-15790)*
Energy Services Group LLC ....G....... 630 581-4840
Oak Brook *(G-15616)*
Lbe Ltd ....G....... 847 907-4959
Kildeer *(G-12050)*
Orbit Enterprises Inc ....G....... 630 469-3405
Oak Brook *(G-15654)*
Zirmed Inc ....E....... 312 207-0889
Chicago *(G-6721)*

Employee Codes: A=Over 500 employees, B=251-500
C=101-250, D=51-100, E=20-50, F=10-19, G=3-9
2020 Harris Illinois
Industrial Directory
1617

SOFTWARE PUBLISHERS: Education

Above Waves Inc ....G.... 708 341-9123
Mokena *(G-14068)*
Active Simulations Inc ....G.... 630 747-8393
Oak Park *(G-15740)*
Brainware Company ....G.... 773 250-6465
Chicago *(G-3943)*
C W Publications Inc ....G.... 800 554-5537
Sterling *(G-19502)*
Capsim MGT Simulations Inc ....E.... 312 477-7200
Chicago *(G-4019)*
Classroom Technologies LLC ....F.... 708 548-1642
Frankfort *(G-9780)*
Cleartrial LLC ....F.... 877 206-4846
Chicago *(G-4174)*
Comptia Learning LLC ....F.... 630 678-8490
Downers Grove *(G-7977)*
Digital Ignite LLC ....F.... 630 317-7904
Lombard *(G-13066)*
Education Equity Inc ....B.... 800 339-7985
Chicago *(G-4457)*
Follett School Solutions Inc ....C.... 815 759-1700
McHenry *(G-13745)*
Goeducation LLC ....G.... 312 800-1838
Chicago *(G-4709)*
Gtx Surgery Inc ....G.... 847 920-8489
Evanston *(G-9528)*
Humaginarium LLC ....G.... 312 788-7719
Oak Park *(G-15757)*
Iep Quality Inc ....G.... 217 840-0570
Champaign *(G-3305)*
Illumen Studios LLC ....G.... 847 440-2222
Grayslake *(G-10782)*
Jones Software Corp ....G.... 312 952-0011
Chicago *(G-5047)*
L-Data Corporation ....E.... 312 552-7855
Chicago *(G-5144)*
Lutheran Church-Missouri Synod ....E.... 630 607-0300
Oak Brook *(G-15638)*
Nerd Island Studios LLC ....G.... 224 619-5361
Highland Park *(G-11288)*
Otus LLC ....E.... 312 229-7648
Chicago *(G-5714)*
Overgrad Inc ....G.... 312 324-4952
Chicago *(G-5717)*
Peopleadmin Inc ....E.... 877 637-5800
Chicago *(G-5786)*
Prairie Wi-Fi Systems ....G.... 515 988-3260
Chicago *(G-5852)*
Questily LLC ....G.... 312 636-6657
Chicago *(G-5935)*
Questily LLC ....G.... 312 636-6657
Chicago *(G-5936)*
Swift Education Systems Inc ....G.... 312 257-3751
Chicago *(G-6295)*
Teenfitnation LLC ....G.... 847 322-2953
South Barrington *(G-19077)*
Victor Consulting ....G.... 847 267-8012
Lincolnshire *(G-12801)*
Wincademy Inc ....G.... 847 445-7886
Grayslake *(G-10805)*

SOFTWARE PUBLISHERS: Home Entertainment

Independent Network Tv LLC ....G.... 312 953-8508
Forest Park *(G-9720)*
Liaison Home Automation LLC ....G.... 888 279-1235
Decatur *(G-7517)*

SOFTWARE PUBLISHERS: NEC

3vue LLC ....G.... 630 796-7441
Woodridge *(G-21270)*
4c Insights Inc ....F.... 602 881-9127
Chicago *(G-3471)*
A M P Software Inc ....G.... 630 240-5922
Elk Grove Village *(G-8792)*
Acp Tower Holdings LLC ....C.... 800 835-8527
Chicago *(G-3531)*
Acresso Software Inc ....G.... 408 642-3865
Schaumburg *(G-18426)*
Adams Telephone Co-Operative ....E.... 217 224-9566
Quincy *(G-16850)*
Adept Coalescence LLC ....G.... 440 503-1808
Rockford *(G-17295)*
Adeptia Inc ....E.... 312 229-1727
Chicago *(G-3543)*
Adflow Networks ....G.... 866 423-3569
Chicago *(G-3544)*
Aerial Intelligence Inc ....F.... 312 914-1259
Chicago *(G-3571)*
Aginity Inc ....D.... 224 307-2656
Evanston *(G-9489)*
Ahead Inc ....A.... 312 753-7967
Oak Brook *(G-15589)*
Akamai Technologies Inc ....E.... 312 893-7900
Chicago *(G-3593)*
Allscripts Healthcare LLC ....G.... 312 506-1200
Chicago *(G-3621)*
Allscripts Holdings LLC ....G.... 800 334-8534
Chicago *(G-3622)*
Allscrpts Hlthcare Sltions Inc ....C.... 800 334-8534
Chicago *(G-3623)*
Amada America Inc ....G.... 877 262-3287
Itasca *(G-11620)*
Amariko Inc ....G.... 630 734-1000
Clarendon Hills *(G-6899)*
Angsten Group Inc ....G.... 888 222-7126
Elgin *(G-8511)*
Anylogic N Amer Ltd Lblty Co ....F.... 312 635-3344
Oakbrook Terrace *(G-15785)*
Approved Contact LLC ....G.... 800 449-7137
Springfield *(G-19319)*
Aptean Inc ....F.... 773 975-3100
Chicago *(G-3716)*
Armarius Software Inc ....G.... 630 639-6332
Aurora *(G-914)*
Associate Computer Systems ....G.... 618 997-3653
Marion *(G-13505)*
Associated Agri-Business Inc ....G.... 618 498-2977
Jerseyville *(G-11786)*
Associated Agri-Business Inc ....G.... 618 498-2977
Eldred *(G-8487)*
Auto Injury Solutions Inc ....E.... 312 229-2704
Chicago *(G-3775)*
Autonomous Stuff LLC ....G.... 309 291-0966
Morton *(G-14353)*
Avaya Inc ....F.... 847 885-3598
Schaumburg *(G-18452)*
Bantix Technologies LLC ....G.... 630 446-0886
Glen Ellyn *(G-10396)*
Banyan Technologies Inc ....G.... 312 967-9885
Chicago *(G-3826)*
Barcodesource Inc ....G.... 630 545-9590
Glen Ellyn *(G-10397)*
Bc Asi Capital II Inc ....A.... 708 534-5575
University Park *(G-19948)*
Beacon Annuity Solutions LLC ....G.... 847 864-5447
Northfield *(G-15507)*
Bi Software Inc ....G.... 224 622-4706
Hoffman Estates *(G-11408)*
Bigtime Software Inc ....E.... 312 346-4646
Chicago *(G-3885)*
Bitsio Inc ....G.... 217 793-2827
Springfield *(G-19327)*
Braindok LLC ....G.... 847 877-1586
Buffalo Grove *(G-2520)*
Brechts Database Solutions ....G.... 618 654-6960
Highland *(G-11205)*
Bridgeline Digital Inc ....G.... 312 784-5720
Chicago *(G-3955)*
Capers North America LLC ....F.... 708 995-7500
Willowbrook *(G-21034)*
Cassetica Software Inc ....G.... 312 546-3668
Chicago *(G-4035)*
Catapult Communications Corp ....G.... 847 884-0048
Schaumburg *(G-18468)*
Ch Group Holdings Inc ....G.... 888 428-6614
Schaumburg *(G-18473)*
Cision Ltd ....E.... 866 639-5087
Chicago *(G-4153)*
Clean Coders LLC ....G.... 847 370-4098
Libertyville *(G-12643)*
Cleo Communications Inc ....E.... 815 654-8110
Rockford *(G-17353)*
Cognizant Tech Solutions Corp ....E.... 630 955-0617
Lisle *(G-12877)*
Comdata Inc ....G.... 630 847-6988
Somonauk *(G-19069)*
Common Goal Systems Inc ....E.... 630 592-4200
Elmhurst *(G-9351)*
Computer Maintenance Inc ....G.... 630 953-1555
Addison *(G-79)*
Computer Pwr Solutions Ill Ltd ....E.... 618 281-8898
Columbia *(G-6988)*
Computing Integrity Inc ....G.... 217 355-4469
Champaign *(G-3282)*
Connelly & Associates ....E.... 847 372-5001
Palatine *(G-16103)*
Conor Sports LLC ....G.... 847 903-6639
Chicago *(G-4221)*
Convr Enterprises Inc ....E.... 888 507-9733
Schaumburg *(G-18490)*
Datafordummies ....G.... 618 421-2323
Flat Rock *(G-9671)*
Datix (usa) Inc ....G.... 312 724-7776
Chicago *(G-4322)*
David Corporation ....E.... 781 587-3008
Chicago *(G-4324)*
Dell Software Inc ....D.... 630 836-0503
Buffalo Grove *(G-2531)*
Devnet Incorporated ....E.... 815 899-6850
Sycamore *(G-19707)*
Digital Minds Inc ....G.... 847 430-3390
Rosemont *(G-18017)*
Digital Realty Inc ....E.... 630 428-7979
Naperville *(G-14817)*
Docket Technologies Inc ....G.... 415 489-0127
Chicago *(G-4377)*
Drawn LLC ....E.... 312 982-0040
Chicago *(G-4397)*
Dynami Solutions LLC ....G.... 618 363-2771
Edwardsville *(G-8357)*
Easy Ware Corp ....G.... 773 755-7732
Chicago *(G-4437)*
Eatsee Inc ....G.... 312 846-1492
Chicago *(G-4438)*
Electronics Boutique Amer Inc ....G.... 618 465-3125
Alton *(G-555)*
Embassy Security Group Inc ....E.... 800 627-1325
Mokena *(G-14079)*
Embedur Systems Inc ....G.... 847 749-3665
Rolling Meadows *(G-17731)*
Emx Digital LLC ....G.... 212 792-6810
Chicago *(G-4503)*
Entappia LLC ....G.... 630 546-4531
Aurora *(G-957)*
Envestnet Inc ....G.... 866 924-8912
Chicago *(G-4517)*
Envestnet Inc ....C.... 312 827-2800
Chicago *(G-4518)*
Environmental Systems Res Inst ....G.... 312 609-0966
Chicago *(G-4520)*
Equisoft Inc ....G.... 815 629-2789
Winnebago *(G-21119)*
Equity Concepts Co Inc ....G.... 815 226-1300
Rockford *(G-17399)*
Eyelation Inc ....F.... 888 308-4703
Tinley Park *(G-19826)*
Ferenbach Marucco Stoddard ....E.... 217 698-3535
Springfield *(G-19366)*
Fleetwood Press Inc ....G.... 708 485-6811
Brookfield *(G-2483)*
Flexera Holdings LP ....G.... 847 466-4000
Itasca *(G-11659)*
Flexera Software LLC ....A.... 847 466-4000
Itasca *(G-11660)*
Fresh Software Solutions LLC ....G.... 630 995-4350
Naperville *(G-14831)*
Friedman Corporation ....E.... 847 948-7180
Rosemont *(G-18024)*
GE Intelligent Platforms Inc ....D.... 630 829-4000
Lisle *(G-12894)*
Global Tech & Resources Inc ....G.... 630 364-4260
Rolling Meadows *(G-17734)*
Govqa Inc ....F.... 630 985-1300
Woodridge *(G-21305)*
Great Software Laboratory Inc ....G.... 630 655-8905
Chicago *(G-4738)*
Help/Systems LLC ....G.... 847 605-1311
Schaumburg *(G-18547)*
Hera Cnsltng Interntnl Opratn ....F.... 630 515-8819
Lisle *(G-12897)*
High Tech Research Inc ....F.... 847 215-9797
Deerfield *(G-7615)*
Hyperera Inc ....F.... 312 842-2288
Chicago *(G-4865)*
I2c LLC ....G.... 630 281-2330
Naperville *(G-14843)*
Ifs North America Inc ....E.... 888 437-4968
Itasca *(G-11670)*
Imcp Inc ....G.... 630 477-8600
Itasca *(G-11675)*
Industrial Finance Systems ....G.... 847 592-0200
Itasca *(G-11676)*
Industrial Phrm Resources Inc ....F.... 630 823-4700
Bartlett *(G-1290)*
Infinite Cnvrgnce Slutions Inc ....G.... 224 764-3400
Arlington Heights *(G-758)*

Informatica LLC G 360 393-7576
Naperville *(G-14847)*
Information Builders Inc E 630 971-6700
Schaumburg *(G-18558)*
Information Resources Inc G 312 474-3380
Chicago *(G-4917)*
Information Resources Inc B 312 474-3154
Bartlett *(G-1255)*
Infosys Limited E 630 482-5000
Lisle *(G-12901)*
Injury Sciences LLC F 210 691-0674
Chicago *(G-4925)*
Innovations For Learning Inc G 800 975-3452
Evanston *(G-9539)*
Innovative SEC Systems Inc F 217 355-6308
Savoy *(G-18414)*
Instana Inc G 415 340-2777
Chicago *(G-4936)*
Intel Corporation D 408 765-8080
Chicago *(G-4941)*
Ironsafe LLC G 877 297-1833
Naperville *(G-14851)*
Isoprime Corporation G 630 737-0963
Lisle *(G-12902)*
Jlg Innovations Inc G 618 363-2323
Breese *(G-2305)*
Juniper Networks Inc E 773 632-1200
Chicago *(G-5060)*
K-Tron Inc G 708 460-2128
Orland Park *(G-15964)*
Kana Software Inc G 312 447-5600
Chicago *(G-5079)*
Kinaxis Corp F 613 592-5780
Chicago *(G-5105)*
King of Software Inc G 847 354-8745
Des Plaines *(G-7793)*
Ksr Software LLC G 847 705-0100
Palatine *(G-16135)*
Larsen & Toubro Infotech Ltd G 847 303-3900
Schaumburg *(G-18600)*
Linkedhealth Solutions F 312 600-6684
Chicago *(G-5230)*
Liquidfire G 312 376-7448
Chicago *(G-5234)*
Loadsys Consulting Inc G 708 873-1750
Bourbonnais *(G-2265)*
LP Software Inc G 708 361-4310
Orland Park *(G-15966)*
Manufacturing Tech Group Inc G 815 966-2300
Rockford *(G-17504)*
Marin Software Incorporated G 312 267-2083
Chicago *(G-5338)*
McConnell Chase Software Works G 312 540-1508
Chicago *(G-5374)*
Mealplot Inc G 217 419-2681
Champaign *(G-3319)*
Mediaocean F 312 676-4646
Chicago *(G-5385)*
Message Mediums LLC F 312 566-4300
Chicago *(G-5403)*
Michaels Ross and Cole Inc F 630 916-0662
Oak Brook *(G-15644)*
Micrograms Inc G 815 877-4455
Rockford *(G-17523)*
Mike Howerton G 217 242-9676
Quincy *(G-16916)*
Mirus Research E 309 828-3100
Normal *(G-15210)*
Mobilehop Technology LLC G 312 504-3773
Chicago *(G-5476)*
Moduslink Corporation E 708 496-7800
Bedford Park *(G-1485)*
Monotype Imaging Inc F 847 631-1111
Elk Grove Village *(G-9131)*
Myhomeeq LLC G 773 328-7034
Chicago *(G-5532)*
Navistarsinfosoft Inc E 877 270-3543
Chicago *(G-5557)*
NE Desktop Software Inc F 800 211-8332
Schaumburg *(G-18646)*
Netsuite Inc F 312 273-4100
Chicago *(G-5572)*
Network Harbor Inc G 309 633-9118
Peoria *(G-16485)*
Newport Media Inc G 630 551-1651
Oswego *(G-16016)*
Nexlp Inc F 773 383-4114
Chicago *(G-5592)*
Nimbl Worldwide Inc E 303 800-0245
Chicago *(G-5603)*
Novaspect Inc C 847 956-8020
Schaumburg *(G-18653)*
Onoffblock Inc F 312 899-6360
New Lenox *(G-15046)*
Onoffblock Inc F 312 899-6360
New Lenox *(G-15047)*
Optionscity Software Inc G 312 605-4500
Chicago *(G-5686)*
Oracle Bigmachines LLC D 847 572-0300
Deerfield *(G-7641)*
Oracle Hcm User Group Inc G 312 222-9350
Chicago *(G-5691)*
Oracle Systems Corporation G 312 673-5863
Chicago *(G-5692)*
Oracle Systems Corporation D 708 409-7800
Westchester *(G-20706)*
Orecx F 312 895-5292
Chicago *(G-5696)*
Original Software Inc E 630 413-5762
Westmont *(G-20764)*
P B R W Enterprises Inc G 815 337-5519
Woodstock *(G-21418)*
Parallel Solutions LLC G 847 708-9227
Schaumburg *(G-18665)*
Parathon Recovery Service LLC G 630 689-0450
Naperville *(G-14893)*
Paylocity Holding Corporation C 847 463-3200
Schaumburg *(G-18670)*
Paylocity Holding Corporation C 331 701-7975
Naperville *(G-14894)*
Peak Computer Systems Inc F 618 398-5612
Belleville *(G-1584)*
Personify Inc G 217 840-2638
Urbana *(G-19992)*
Picis Clinical Solutions Inc F 847 993-2200
Rosemont *(G-18042)*
Pinnakle Technologies Inc F 630 352-0070
Aurora *(G-1009)*
Pitney Bowes Inc E 800 784-4224
Itasca *(G-11719)*
Politech Inc G 847 516-2717
Trout Valley *(G-19908)*
Powerschool Group LLC F 610 867-9200
Chicago *(G-5850)*
Premier Intl Entps Inc E 312 857-2200
Chicago *(G-5862)*
Price Fx Inc G 312 763-3121
Chicago *(G-5871)*
Prism Esolutions Dv Andy Frain F 630 820-3820
Aurora *(G-1010)*
Productive Edge LLC D 312 561-9000
Chicago *(G-5895)*
Proquis Inc F 847 278-3230
Elgin *(G-8700)*
Protepo Ltd G 847 466-1023
Elk Grove Village *(G-9200)*
Pubpal LLC G 309 222-5062
Washington *(G-20278)*
Quadramed Corporation E 312 396-0700
Chicago *(G-5926)*
R & J Systems Inc G 630 289-3010
Bartlett *(G-1257)*
React Computer Services Inc D 630 323-6200
Willowbrook *(G-21058)*
Sales & Marketing Resources G 847 910-9169
Fox River Grove *(G-9761)*
Sap America Inc E 630 395-2700
Downers Grove *(G-8089)*
School Town LLC G 847 943-9115
Northbrook *(G-15477)*
Schwider Systems G 815 469-2834
Frankfort *(G-9837)*
Seoclarity F 773 831-4500
Des Plaines *(G-7842)*
Servicenow Inc G 630 963-4608
Downers Grove *(G-8092)*
Sharpedge Solutions Inc F 630 792-9639
Naperville *(G-14987)*
Shipbob Inc B 217 819-8539
Chicago *(G-6154)*
Shipbob Inc F 844 474-4726
Chicago *(G-6155)*
Single Path LLC E 708 653-4100
Lombard *(G-13130)*
Soft O Soft Inc E 630 741-4414
Schaumburg *(G-18714)*
Softhaus Ltd G 618 463-1140
Alton *(G-572)*
Softlabz Corporation G 847 780-7076
Highland Park *(G-11299)*
Softwareidm Inc G 331 218-0001
Wheaton *(G-20825)*
Spl Software Alliance LLC G 309 266-0304
Morton *(G-14383)*
Springcoin Inc G 323 577-9322
Chicago *(G-6220)*
Sprout Social Inc D 866 878-3231
Chicago *(G-6221)*
Starlight Software System Inc G 309 454-7349
Hudson *(G-11519)*
Sunrise Futures LLC G 312 612-1041
Chicago *(G-6275)*
Swift Technologies Inc G 815 568-8402
Marengo *(G-13494)*
Symfact Inc E 847 380-4174
Chicago *(G-6301)*
Synergy Technology Group Inc F 773 305-3500
Chicago *(G-6303)*
Tegratecs Development Corp G 847 397-0088
Schaumburg *(G-18743)*
Telemedicine Solutions LLC F 847 519-3500
Schaumburg *(G-18744)*
Textura Corporation C 866 839-8872
Deerfield *(G-7654)*
Thomson Quantitative Analytics E 847 610-0574
Chicago *(G-6368)*
Torgo Inc G 800 360-5910
Riverwoods *(G-17096)*
Tri-Tech Sltons Consulting Inc G 847 941-0199
Mount Prospect *(G-14576)*
Trident Software Corp G 847 219-8777
Niles *(G-15182)*
Trustwave Holdings Inc G 312 750-0950
Chicago *(G-6440)*
Turfmapp Inc G 703 473-5678
Chicago *(G-6443)*
Tzee Inc G 630 857-3425
Lisle *(G-12953)*
Ultimate Software Group Inc E 847 273-1701
Rosemont *(G-18056)*
Usmedexport Company G 847 749-5520
Wheeling *(G-21005)*
Val P Enterprises G 708 982-6561
Chicago *(G-6518)*
Vertex Consulting Services Inc F 313 492-5154
Schaumburg *(G-18771)*
Vigilanz Corporation E 708 383-3008
Oak Park *(G-15778)*
Vision I Systems G 312 326-9188
Chicago *(G-6556)*
Visual Information Tech Inc G 217 841-2155
Champaign *(G-3367)*
Vlc Solutions LLC D 630 447-9852
Schaumburg *(G-18772)*
W A M Computers International G 217 324-6926
Litchfield *(G-12978)*
Wavsys LLC F 773 442-0888
Chicago *(G-6592)*
Websolutions Technology Inc E 630 375-6833
Aurora *(G-1033)*
Wellsky Corporation G 630 218-2700
Oak Brook *(G-15670)*
Winscribe Usa Inc F 773 399-1608
Chicago *(G-6645)*
Wolfram Research Inc C 217 398-0700
Champaign *(G-3372)*
Written Word Inc G 630 671-9803
Roselle *(G-17996)*
Yield Management Systems LLC G 312 665-1595
Chicago *(G-6701)*

SOFTWARE PUBLISHERS: Operating Systems

Computer Svcs & Consulting Inc E 855 482-2267
Burr Ridge *(G-2666)*
Decision Systems Company G 815 885-3000
Roscoe *(G-17902)*
Designa Access Corporation E 630 891-3105
Westmont *(G-20737)*
Dev Base LLC E 319 321-3014
Chicago *(G-4346)*
Forte Incorporated G 815 224-8300
La Salle *(G-12112)*
Hostforweb Incorporated G 312 343-4678
Chicago *(G-4845)*
Key Resources Inc G 800 574-1339
Lake Villa *(G-12357)*
Prairie Area Library System E 309 799-3155
Coal Valley *(G-6938)*

SOFTWARE PUBLISHERS: Operating Systems

Turner Agward.................................G....... 773 669-8559
  Chicago *(G-6444)*

SOFTWARE PUBLISHERS: Publisher's

4ever Printing Inc...........................G....... 847 222-1525
  Arlington Heights *(G-679)*
American Labelmark Company......C....... 773 478-0900
  Chicago *(G-3656)*
Arvamont..G....... 630 926-2468
  Hinsdale *(G-11361)*
Computhink Inc................................E....... 630 705-9050
  Lombard *(G-13057)*
Epublishing Inc.................................G....... 312 768-6800
  Chicago *(G-4522)*
Family Time Computing Inc............F....... 309 664-1742
  Bloomington *(G-2041)*
Innerworkings Inc............................D....... 312 642-3700
  Chicago *(G-4927)*
Invisible Institute..............................G....... 415 669-4691
  Chicago *(G-4964)*
John Galt Development Inc............G....... 312 701-9026
  Chicago *(G-5040)*
Knowledgeshift Inc..........................G....... 630 221-8759
  Wheaton *(G-20809)*
Mobile 7 Group Inc..........................G....... 312 600-8952
  Chicago Heights *(G-6760)*
Socialcloak Inc.................................G....... 650 549-4412
  East Dubuque *(G-8184)*
Srv Professional Publications.........G....... 847 330-1260
  Schaumburg *(G-18727)*
Structurepoint LLC..........................F....... 847 966-4357
  Skokie *(G-19037)*

SOFTWARE PUBLISHERS: Word Processing

Automated Insights Inc....................C....... 919 442-8865
  Chicago *(G-3776)*

SOFTWARE TRAINING, COMPUTER

Bitsio Inc..G....... 217 793-2827
  Springfield *(G-19327)*
Braindok LLC...................................G....... 847 877-1586
  Buffalo Grove *(G-2520)*
Ifs North America Inc......................E....... 888 437-4968
  Itasca *(G-11670)*
Proquis Inc.......................................F....... 847 278-3230
  Elgin *(G-8700)*
Reliefwatch Inc.................................G....... 646 678-2336
  Chicago *(G-6011)*

SOIL CONDITIONERS

Farmers Manufacturing Company..G....... 618 377-6237
  Dorsey *(G-7944)*

SOIL TESTING KITS

Luster Leaf Products Inc................F....... 815 337-5560
  Woodstock *(G-21407)*

SOLAR CELLS

Amoco Technology Company.........C....... 312 861-6000
  Chicago *(G-3682)*
BP Solar International Inc...............A....... 301 698-4200
  Naperville *(G-14785)*
Shakthi Solar Inc.............................G....... 630 842-0893
  Bolingbrook *(G-2238)*

SOLAR HEATING EQPT

Dva Mayday Corporation.................G....... 847 848-7555
  Village of Lakewood *(G-20178)*
Polyair Inter Pack Inc......................D....... 773 995-1818
  Chicago *(G-5838)*

SOLDERING EQPT: Electrical, Exc Handheld

Wenesco Inc....................................F....... 773 283-3004
  Addison *(G-333)*

SOLDERS

Alpha Assembly Solutions Inc.......C....... 847 426-4241
  Elgin *(G-8504)*
Kester LLC.......................................G....... 630 616-6882
  Itasca *(G-11683)*
Kester LLC.......................................D....... 630 616-4000
  Itasca *(G-11684)*

SOLENOIDS

Guardian Electric Mfg Co...............D....... 815 334-3600
  Woodstock *(G-21393)*
Weldon Corporation........................E....... 708 343-4700
  Maywood *(G-13680)*

SOUND EFFECTS & MUSIC PRODUCTION: Motion Picture

Ikan Creations LLC.........................G....... 312 204-7333
  Chicago *(G-4884)*
Kaelco Entrmt Holdings Inc...........G....... 217 600-7815
  Champaign *(G-3312)*

SOUND EQPT: Electric

Sound Design Inc............................G....... 630 548-7000
  Plainfield *(G-16715)*
Victoria Amplifier Company...........F....... 630 369-3527
  Naperville *(G-14991)*

SOUND RECORDING STUDIOS

Ken Young Construction Co..........G....... 847 358-3026
  Hoffman Estates *(G-11433)*

SOUND REPRODUCING EQPT

Knowles Elec Holdings Inc............A....... 630 250-5100
  Itasca *(G-11687)*
Rexroat Sound.................................G....... 309 764-1663
  Colona *(G-6978)*
Zmf Inc...G....... 603 667-1672
  Lyons *(G-13316)*

SOYBEAN PRDTS

Archer-Daniels-Midland Company.G....... 815 539-6219
  Mendota *(G-13937)*
Archer-Daniels-Midland Company.E....... 217 424-5858
  Decatur *(G-7453)*
Archer-Daniels-Midland Company.A....... 312 634-8100
  Chicago *(G-3728)*
Archer-Daniels-Midland Company.E....... 217 224-1800
  Quincy *(G-16856)*
Cargill Incorporated.........................E....... 309 827-7100
  Bloomington *(G-2031)*
Incobrasa Industries Ltd................C....... 815 265-4803
  Gilman *(G-10380)*
Pioneer Hi-Bred Intl Inc..................F....... 309 962-2931
  Saint Joseph *(G-18318)*
Solae..G....... 217 784-2085
  Gibson City *(G-10346)*
Solae LLC..C....... 217 784-8261
  Gibson City *(G-10347)*

SPACE VEHICLE EQPT

AAC Microtec North America Inc..E....... 602 284-7997
  Columbia *(G-6982)*
Spytek Aerospace Corporation......G....... 847 318-7515
  Bensenville *(G-1898)*

SPEAKER MONITORS

Guys Hi-Def Inc...............................G....... 708 261-7487
  Joliet *(G-11872)*

SPEAKER SYSTEMS

Acoustic Avenue Inc......................F....... 217 544-9810
  Springfield *(G-19315)*
Alumapro Inc...................................G....... 224 569-3650
  Huntley *(G-11527)*
Bem Wireless LLC..........................F....... 815 337-0541
  Schaumburg *(G-18460)*
Hammond Suzuki Usa Inc.............E....... 630 543-0277
  Addison *(G-145)*
Mitek Corporation............................C....... 608 328-5560
  Winslow *(G-21139)*
SBA Wireless Inc............................E....... 847 215-8720
  Buffalo Grove *(G-2595)*

SPEAKERS BUREAU

Perry Johnson Inc...........................F....... 847 635-0010
  Rosemont *(G-18041)*

SPECIAL EVENTS DECORATION SVCS

Anthos and Co LLC.........................G....... 773 744-6813
  Inverness *(G-11594)*

Mediatec Publishing Inc.................E....... 312 676-9900
  Chicago *(G-5386)*

SPECIALTY FOOD STORES, NEC

Supalicious Soups Inc....................G....... 708 491-9738
  Chicago *(G-6279)*

SPECIALTY FOOD STORES: Coffee

Big Shoulders Coffee Works..........G....... 312 888-3042
  Chicago *(G-3882)*
Wolfart Maciej..................................G....... 312 248-3575
  Chicago *(G-6663)*

SPECIALTY FOOD STORES: Dietetic Foods

Health King Enterprise Inc............G....... 312 567-9978
  Chicago *(G-4791)*

SPECIALTY FOOD STORES: Dried Fruit

Think Jerky LLC...............................G....... 917 623-1989
  Chicago *(G-6364)*

SPECIALTY FOOD STORES: Health & Dietetic Food

AM Ko Oriental Foods.....................G....... 217 398-2922
  Champaign *(G-3262)*
Ottos Canvas Shop.........................G....... 217 543-3307
  Arthur *(G-875)*

SPECIALTY FOOD STORES: Juices, Fruit Or Vegetable

Mangel and Co.................................F....... 847 634-0730
  Long Grove *(G-13162)*

SPECIALTY FOOD STORES: Soft Drinks

Homer Vintage Bakery....................G....... 217 896-2538
  Homer *(G-11476)*

SPECIALTY FOOD STORES: Vitamin

Natures Sources LLC.....................G....... 847 663-9168
  Niles *(G-15151)*
Vital Proteins LLC...........................E....... 224 544-9110
  Chicago *(G-6562)*

SPECULATIVE BUILDERS: Single-Family Housing

Plote Construction Inc....................D....... 847 695-9300
  Hoffman Estates *(G-11445)*

SPEED CHANGERS

Diequa Corporation.........................E....... 630 980-1133
  Bloomingdale *(G-1988)*
Productigear Inc..............................E....... 773 847-4505
  Chicago *(G-5893)*

SPICE & HERB STORES

Andrias Food Group Inc.................E....... 618 632-4866
  O Fallon *(G-15565)*
Dell Cove Spice Co.........................G....... 312 339-8389
  Chicago *(G-4333)*
Sunrise Distributors Inc.................G....... 630 400-8786
  Elk Grove Village *(G-9259)*

SPINDLES: Textile

Lmk Technologies LLC...................D....... 815 433-1275
  Ottawa *(G-16059)*

SPOOLS: Indl

Christian Cnty Mntal Hlth Assn.....C....... 217 824-9675
  Taylorville *(G-19753)*
Gavin Woodworking Inc.................G....... 815 786-2242
  Sandwich *(G-18371)*

SPORTING & ATHLETIC GOODS: Bags, Golf

Hunter-Nusport Inc..........................G....... 815 254-7520
  Plainfield *(G-16674)*

SPORTING & RECREATIONAL GOODS & SPLYS WHOLESALERS

SPORTING & ATHLETIC GOODS: Bases, Baseball
- Normal Cornbelters .... G 309 451-3432
  Normal *(G-15212)*
- Southern Illinois Miners .... F 618 969-8506
  Marion *(G-13538)*

SPORTING & ATHLETIC GOODS: Basketball Eqpt & Splys, NEC
- Allied Scoring Tables Inc .... G 815 654-8807
  Loves Park *(G-13187)*

SPORTING & ATHLETIC GOODS: Bowling Alleys & Access
- Flora Bowl .... G 618 662-4561
  Flora *(G-9680)*
- Illinois State Usbc Wba .... G 309 827-6355
  Bloomington *(G-2061)*
- James G Carter .... G 309 543-2634
  Havana *(G-11115)*
- Qcfec LLC .... G 309 517-1158
  Moline *(G-14169)*

SPORTING & ATHLETIC GOODS: Bows, Archery
- Quincy Bow Pro .... G 217 222-2222
  Quincy *(G-16929)*

SPORTING & ATHLETIC GOODS: Camping Eqpt & Splys
- Coleman Company Inc .... C 316 832-2653
  Chicago *(G-4198)*

SPORTING & ATHLETIC GOODS: Dartboards & Access
- Arachnid 360 LLC .... E 815 654-0212
  Loves Park *(G-13190)*

SPORTING & ATHLETIC GOODS: Decoys, Duck & Other Game Birds
- Mallardtone Game Calls .... G 309 798-2481
  Taylor Ridge *(G-19746)*

SPORTING & ATHLETIC GOODS: Driving Ranges, Golf, Electronic
- Topgolf International Inc .... G 630 595-4653
  Wood Dale *(G-21250)*

SPORTING & ATHLETIC GOODS: Dumbbells & Other Weight Eqpt
- Orthotech Sports - Med Eqp Inc .... F 618 942-6611
  Herrin *(G-11176)*
- U S Weight Inc .... E 618 392-0408
  Olney *(G-15891)*

SPORTING & ATHLETIC GOODS: Exercising Cycles
- Kps Capital Partners LP .... A 847 288-3300
  Franklin Park *(G-9979)*

SPORTING & ATHLETIC GOODS: Fish & Bait Baskets Or Creels
- Perry Adult Living Inc .... G 618 542-5421
  Du Quoin *(G-8123)*

SPORTING & ATHLETIC GOODS: Fishing Eqpt
- Donaldson & Associates Inc .... G 708 633-1090
  Lockport *(G-12988)*
- Frabill Inc .... E 630 552-9426
  Plano *(G-16732)*
- Jack & Lidias Resort Inc .... G 847 356-1389
  Lake Villa *(G-12356)*
- White Rhino LLC .... G 309 691-9653
  Brimfield *(G-2408)*
- White Whale LLC .... G 309 303-0028
  Mossville *(G-14462)*

SPORTING & ATHLETIC GOODS: Fishing Tackle, General
- Bob Folder Lures Co .... F 217 787-1116
  Springfield *(G-19328)*
- Orvis Company Inc .... F 312 440-0662
  Chicago *(G-5707)*
- Plastech .... F 630 595-7222
  Bensenville *(G-1868)*

SPORTING & ATHLETIC GOODS: Game Calls
- Dj Illinois River Valley Calls .... G 309 348-2112
  Pekin *(G-16330)*

SPORTING & ATHLETIC GOODS: Gymnasium Eqpt
- Brunswick Corporation .... B 847 288-3300
  Franklin Park *(G-9894)*
- Crown Gym Mats Inc .... F 847 381-8282
  Lake Barrington *(G-12145)*
- Moreno and Sons Inc .... G 815 725-8600
  Crest Hill *(G-7092)*
- Porter Athletic Equipment Co .... G 888 277-7778
  Champaign *(G-3337)*

SPORTING & ATHLETIC GOODS: Hooks, Fishing
- Siggs Rigs .... G 847 456-4012
  Crystal Lake *(G-7266)*

SPORTING & ATHLETIC GOODS: Hunting Eqpt
- Oak Leaf Outdoors Inc .... F 309 691-9653
  Brimfield *(G-2407)*

SPORTING & ATHLETIC GOODS: Indian Clubs
- Rasoi Resturaunt .... G 847 455-8888
  Roselle *(G-17977)*

SPORTING & ATHLETIC GOODS: Lacrosse Eqpt & Splys, NEC
- Lax Shop .... G 847 945-8529
  Highwood *(G-11308)*
- True Lacrosse LLC .... G 630 359-3857
  Lombard *(G-13148)*

SPORTING & ATHLETIC GOODS: Masks, Hockey, Baseball, Etc
- Kranos Corporation .... C 217 324-3978
  Litchfield *(G-12969)*

SPORTING & ATHLETIC GOODS: Pools, Swimming, Exc Plastic
- David Hall .... E 309 797-9721
  Moline *(G-14137)*
- Evergreen Pool & Spa LLC .... G 618 247-3555
  Sandoval *(G-18363)*
- Mullarkey Associates Inc .... F 708 597-5555
  Tinley Park *(G-19846)*
- Royal Fiberglass Pools Inc .... D 618 266-7089
  Dix *(G-7882)*

SPORTING & ATHLETIC GOODS: Pools, Swimming, Plastic
- Midwest Canvas Corp .... C 773 287-4400
  Chicago *(G-5440)*
- Sentry Pool & Chemical Supply .... E 309 797-9721
  Moline *(G-14177)*

SPORTING & ATHLETIC GOODS: Protective Sporting Eqpt
- Vista Outdoor Inc .... G 309 693-2746
  Rantoul *(G-16985)*

SPORTING & ATHLETIC GOODS: Reels, Fishing
- Brunswick International Ltd .... E 847 735-4700
  Mettawa *(G-13980)*

SPORTING & ATHLETIC GOODS: Rods & Rod Parts, Fishing
- Custom Rods By Grandt Ltd .... G 847 577-0848
  Arlington Heights *(G-723)*

SPORTING & ATHLETIC GOODS: Shafts, Golf Club
- Golfco Inc .... E 773 777-7877
  Chicago *(G-4714)*
- Protactic Golf Enterprises .... F 708 209-1120
  River Forest *(G-17054)*

SPORTING & ATHLETIC GOODS: Shuffleboards & Shuffleboard Eqpt
- Shuffle Tech International LLC .... G 312 787-7780
  Chicago *(G-6161)*

SPORTING & ATHLETIC GOODS: Skateboards
- Bluetown Skateboard Co LLC .... G 312 718-4786
  Chicago *(G-3918)*
- Roger Jolly Skateboards .... G 618 277-7113
  Belleville *(G-1591)*

SPORTING & ATHLETIC GOODS: Soccer Eqpt & Splys
- Headball Inc .... G 618 628-2656
  Belleville *(G-1555)*

SPORTING & ATHLETIC GOODS: Softball Eqpt, Splys
- Total Control Sports Inc .... G 708 486-5800
  Broadview *(G-2472)*

SPORTING & ATHLETIC GOODS: Targets, Archery & Rifle Shooting
- Reagent Chemical & RES Inc .... G 618 271-8140
  East Saint Louis *(G-8319)*

SPORTING & ATHLETIC GOODS: Team Sports Eqpt
- Mettle Sports LLC .... G 312 757-6373
  Evanston *(G-9550)*
- Peak Healthcare Advisors LLC .... G 646 479-0005
  Chicago *(G-5775)*
- Pro-AM Team Sports LLC .... F 708 995-1511
  Mokena *(G-14110)*

SPORTING & ATHLETIC GOODS: Track & Field Athletic Eqpt
- Davis Athletic Equipment Co .... F 708 563-9006
  Bedford Park *(G-1466)*
- Litania Sports Group Inc .... C 217 367-8438
  Champaign *(G-3317)*

SPORTING & ATHLETIC GOODS: Water Sports Eqpt
- Ccsi International Inc .... E 815 544-8385
  Garden Prairie *(G-10236)*
- H2o Pod Inc .... G 630 240-1769
  Glen Ellyn *(G-10404)*
- Polyair Inter Pack Inc .... D 773 995-1818
  Chicago *(G-5838)*

SPORTING & RECREATIONAL GOODS & SPLYS WHOLESALERS
- Obies Tackle Co Inc .... G 618 234-5638
  Belleville *(G-1581)*
- Oso900 Nfp .... G 312 206-4219
  Chicago *(G-5711)*
- Player Sports Ltd .... G 773 764-4111
  Chicago *(G-5822)*
- Wilson Sporting Goods Co .... B 773 714-6400
  Chicago *(G-6635)*

Employee Codes: A=Over 500 employees, B=251-500
C=101-250, D=51-100, E=20-50, F=10-19, G=3-9

SPORTING & RECREATIONAL GOODS, WHOLESALE: Athletic Goods

SPORTING & RECREATIONAL GOODS, WHOLESALE: Athletic Goods

Athletic Specialties Inc .... G		847 487-7880
Wauconda (G-20333)		
Curt Smith Sporting Goods Inc .... E		618 233-5177
Belleville (G-1541)		
East West Martial Arts Sups .... G		773 878-7711
Chicago (G-4434)		
Riddell Inc C		847 292-1472
Des Plaines (G-7837)		

SPORTING & RECREATIONAL GOODS, WHOLESALE: Bicycle

Joe Hunt .... G		618 392-2000
Olney (G-15866)		
Outbound Lighting LLC .... E		314 330-0696
Lincolnwood (G-12835)		

SPORTING & RECREATIONAL GOODS, WHOLESALE: Boat Access & Part

Albax Inc .... E		630 758-1072
Elmhurst (G-9323)		
Custom Stainless Steel Inc .... F		618 435-2605
Benton (G-1924)		
Ottos Canvas Shop .... G		217 543-3307
Arthur (G-875)		

SPORTING & RECREATIONAL GOODS, WHOLESALE: Diving

Scuba Sports Inc .... G		217 787-3483
Springfield (G-19440)		

SPORTING & RECREATIONAL GOODS, WHOLESALE: Exercise

Septic Solutions Inc .... G		217 925-5992
Dieterich (G-7878)		

SPORTING & RECREATIONAL GOODS, WHOLESALE: Fishing

Donaldson & Associates Inc .... G		708 633-1090
Lockport (G-12988)		
Jerrys Tackle and Guns .... G		618 654-3235
Highland (G-11228)		

SPORTING & RECREATIONAL GOODS, WHOLESALE: Fishing Tackle

Bob Folder Lures Co .... F		217 787-1116
Springfield (G-19328)		
Outback USA Inc		863 699-2220
Saint Charles (G-18240)		

SPORTING & RECREATIONAL GOODS, WHOLESALE: Fitness

E&B Exercise LLC		844 425-5025
Chicago (G-4426)		
Orthotech Sports - Med Eqp Inc .... F		618 942-6611
Herrin (G-11176)		

SPORTING & RECREATIONAL GOODS, WHOLESALE: Golf

Par Golf Supply Inc .... E		847 891-1222
Schaumburg (G-18663)		

SPORTING CAMPS

Lakeshore Lacrosse LLC .... G		773 350-4356
Wheaton (G-20810)		

SPORTING FIREARMS WHOLESALERS

Airgun Designs USA Inc .... G		847 520-7507
Cary (G-3146)		
Devil Dog Arms Inc .... G		847 790-4004
Lake Zurich (G-12402)		

SPORTING GOODS

All American Athletics Ltd .... G		815 432-8326
Watseka (G-20304)		
Altamont Co .... D		800 626-5774
Thomasboro (G-19775)		
Andrew C Arnold .... G		815 220-0282
Peru (G-16564)		
Athletic Specialties Inc .... G		847 487-7880
Wauconda (G-20333)		
Best Technology Systems Inc .... E		815 254-9554
Plainfield (G-16644)		
Big Dog Treestand Inc .... G		309 263-6800
Morton (G-14354)		
Big Game Gut Glove .... G		847 544-8806
Frankfort (G-9771)		
Bodysmart USA Inc .... G		630 682-9701
Wheaton (G-20790)		
Bowlero Corp .... D		847 473-2600
Waukegan (G-20423)		
Brg Sports Inc .... F		217 892-4704
Rantoul (G-16969)		
Brunswick Corporation .... B		847 735-4700
Mettawa (G-13979)		
BSN Sports LLC .... G		217 788-0914
Springfield (G-19330)		
C6 Agility LLC .... G		734 548-0008
Chicago (G-3997)		
Castillo Leather Goods .... G		773 491-0018
Oak Lawn (G-15707)		
City Sports & Stage Door Dance .... E		708 687-9950
Oak Forest (G-15673)		
Compound Bow Rifle Sight Inc .... G		618 526-4427
Breese (G-2301)		
Crooked Creek Outdoors .... G		309 837-3000
Macomb (G-13390)		
Dark Speed Works .... G		312 772-3275
Wheaton (G-20795)		
Dinger Bats LLC .... G		618 272-7250
Ridgway (G-17036)		
Empire Comfort Systems Inc C		618 233-7420
Belleville (G-1551)		
Enjoylife Inc .... G		847 966-3377
Morton Grove (G-14405)		
Flex Court International Inc .... F		309 852-0899
Kewanee (G-12033)		
Geneva Running Outfitters LLC .... G		331 248-0221
Geneva (G-10272)		
Gill Athletics .... G		217 367-8438
Champaign (G-3294)		
Heartland Inspection Company .... G		630 788-3607
Sycamore (G-19713)		
Hunter Mfg LLP .... D		859 254-7573
Lake Forest (G-12262)		
Iler Brands Inc .... G		314 799-3833
O Fallon (G-15574)		
L L Bean Inc .... G		847 568-3600
Skokie (G-18974)		
Nameplate Robinson & Precision .... G		847 678-2255
Franklin Park (G-10005)		
New Wave Lax LLC .... G		630 219-3919
Plainfield (G-16694)		
Nichols Net & Twine Inc .... G		618 797-0211
Granite City (G-10728)		
Oban Composites LLC .... G		866 607-0284
Chicago (G-5649)		
Oso900 Nfp .... G		312 206-4219
Chicago (G-5711)		
Pritchard Enterprises Inc .... G		217 832-8588
Camargo (G-2801)		
ProAm Sports Products .... G		708 841-4200
Dolton (G-7939)		
Quality Targets		618 245-6515
Farina (G-9653)		
Road Runner Sports Inc .... F		847 719-8941
Palatine (G-16154)		
Roller Derby Skate Corp .... E		217 324-3961
Litchfield (G-12976)		
Scuba Sports Inc .... G		217 787-3483
Springfield (G-19440)		
Spinball Sports LLC .... G		314 503-3194
Skokie (G-19035)		
Strikeforce Bowling LLC .... E		800 297-8555
Melrose Park (G-13917)		
Superior Table Pad Co .... G		773 248-7232
Chicago (G-6284)		
Ultra Play Systems Inc .... E		618 282-8200
Red Bud (G-17004)		
Wagner International LLC .... G		224 619-9247
Vernon Hills (G-20109)		
Warphole LLC .... G		866 471-6464
Glen Ellyn (G-10424)		
Warthog Inc .... G		815 540-7197
Rockford (G-17677)		
Welkins LLC .... G		877 319-3504
Downers Grove (G-8108)		
Wilson Sporting Goods Co C		773 714-6500
Chicago (G-6636)		
Wilson Sporting Goods Co .... B		773 714-6400
Chicago (G-6635)		
Woodland Fence Forest Pdts Inc .... G		630 393-2220
Warrenville (G-20257)		
World Class Technologies Inc .... E		312 758-3114
Chicago (G-6672)		
Zarc International Inc .... F		309 807-2565
Minonk (G-14056)		

SPORTING GOODS STORES, NEC

Airgun Designs USA Inc .... G		847 520-7507
Cary (G-3146)		
Art Jewel Enterprises Ltd .... F		630 260-0400
Carol Stream (G-2941)		
Bee Designs Embroidery & Scree .... G		815 393-4593
Esmond (G-9475)		
Breedlove Sporting Goods Inc .... F		309 852-2434
Kewanee (G-12028)		
Breedlove Sporting Goods Inc .... F		309 852-2434
Kewanee (G-12029)		
C & C Sport Stop .... G		618 632-7812
O Fallon (G-15569)		
Custom Rods By Grandt Ltd .... G		847 577-0848
Arlington Heights (G-723)		
Johnos Inc .... G		630 897-6929
Aurora (G-1119)		
Orvis Company Inc .... F		312 440-0662
Chicago (G-5707)		
Promark Advertising Specialtie .... G		618 483-6025
Altamont (G-536)		
Quincy Bow Pro .... G		217 222-2222
Quincy (G-16929)		
Rock River Arms Inc .... D		309 792-5780
Colona (G-6979)		
Tri-City Sports Inc .... G		217 224-2489
Quincy (G-16951)		
Winning Streak Inc .... G		618 277-8191
Dupo (G-8150)		

SPORTING GOODS STORES: Archery Splys

Freddie Bear Sports .... F		708 532-4133
Tinley Park (G-19829)		
Town Hall Sports Inc .... F		618 235-9881
Belleville (G-1601)		

SPORTING GOODS STORES: Bait & Tackle

Jerrys Tackle and Guns .... G		618 654-3235
Highland (G-11228)		

SPORTING GOODS STORES: Firearms

Devil Dog Arms Inc .... G		847 790-4004
Lake Zurich (G-12402)		
Oglesby & Oglesby Gunmakers .... G		217 487-7100
Springfield (G-19417)		

SPORTING GOODS STORES: Hunting Eqpt

Midwest Pub Safety Outfitters .... F		866 985-0013
Poplar Grove (G-16782)		

SPORTING GOODS STORES: Martial Arts Eqpt & Splys

East West Martial Arts Sups .... G		773 878-7711
Chicago (G-4434)		

SPORTING GOODS STORES: Playground Eqpt

Rainbow Midwest Inc .... G		847 955-9300
Vernon Hills (G-20084)		
Sandlock Sandbox LLC .... G		630 963-9422
Westmont (G-20771)		
Woodland Fence Forest Pdts Inc .... G		630 393-2220
Warrenville (G-20257)		

SPORTING GOODS STORES: Skiing Eqpt

Chicago Sea Ray Inc .... E		815 385-2720
Volo (G-20197)		

SPORTING GOODS STORES: Team sports Eqpt

Minor League Inc .... G		618 548-8040
Salem (G-18347)		

PRODUCT SECTION

Waldos Sports Corner Inc .... G 309 688-2425
Peoria **(G-16545)**

SPORTING GOODS STORES: Tennis Goods & Eqpt

St Clair Tennis Club LLC .... G 618 632-1400
O Fallon **(G-15584)**

SPORTING GOODS: Archery

Bowtree Inc .... G 217 430-8884
Quincy **(G-16867)**
Burt Coyote Co .... F 309 358-1602
Yates City **(G-21470)**
New Archery Products LLC .... D 708 488-2500
Forest Park **(G-9722)**
Prototech Industries Inc .... G 847 223-9808
Gurnee **(G-10918)**

SPORTING GOODS: Hammocks, Fabric, Made From Purchased Mat

Travel Hammock Inc .... G 847 486-0005
Skokie **(G-19047)**

SPORTING/ATHLETIC GOODS: Gloves, Boxing, Handball, Etc

Boss Manufacturing Holdings .... F 309 852-2781
Kewanee **(G-12025)**

SPORTS APPAREL STORES

Chicago Sea Ray Inc .... E 815 385-2720
Volo **(G-20197)**
Fielders Choice .... G 618 937-2294
West Frankfort **(G-20671)**
Senn Enterprises Inc .... F 309 637-1147
Peoria **(G-16519)**
Sport Connection .... G 630 980-1787
Roselle **(G-17990)**
Tri-City Sports Inc .... G 217 224-2489
Quincy **(G-16951)**
U R On It .... G 847 382-0182
Lake Barrington **(G-12167)**
Windy City Silkscreening Inc .... E 312 842-0030
Chicago **(G-6644)**

SPOUTING: Plastic & Fiberglass Reinforced

Kipp Manufacturing Company Inc .... F 630 768-9051
Wauconda **(G-20366)**

SPOUTS: Sheet Metal

Kipp Manufacturing Company Inc .... F 630 768-9051
Wauconda **(G-20366)**

SPRAYING & DUSTING EQPT

Rpk Technologies Inc .... G 630 595-0911
Bensenville **(G-1885)**

SPRINGS: Coiled Flat

Casey Spring Co Inc .... F 708 867-8949
Park Ridge **(G-16272)**
Matthew Warren Inc .... E 847 349-5760
Rosemont **(G-18035)**
Omiotek Coil Spring Co .... D 630 495-4056
Lombard **(G-13113)**

SPRINGS: Cold Formed

A J Kay Co .... F 224 475-0370
Mundelein **(G-14657)**
Lew-El Tool & Manufacturing Co .... F 773 804-1133
Chicago **(G-5212)**

SPRINGS: Hot Wound, Exc Wire

Alco Spring Industries Inc .... D 708 755-0438
Chicago Heights **(G-6730)**

SPRINGS: Instrument, Precision

Ark Technologies Inc .... D 630 377-8855
Saint Charles **(G-18149)**
International Spring Company .... D 847 470-8170
Morton Grove **(G-14413)**
Lewis Spring and Mfg Company .... D 847 588-7030
Niles **(G-15140)**

SPRINGS: Leaf, Automobile, Locomotive, Etc

Boler Company .... F 630 773-9111
Itasca **(G-11628)**

SPRINGS: Mechanical, Precision

Capitol Coil Inc .... F 847 891-1390
Schaumburg **(G-18467)**
Form-All Spring Stamping Inc .... E 630 595-8833
Bensenville **(G-1800)**
Gerb Vibration Control Systems .... G 630 724-1660
Lisle **(G-12895)**
Jackson Spring & Mfg Co .... D 847 952-8850
Elk Grove Village **(G-9065)**
Kaylen Industries Inc .... D 847 671-6767
Schiller Park **(G-18817)**
Matthew Warren Inc .... G 847 671-6767
Schiller Park **(G-18821)**
OHare Spring Company Inc .... E 847 298-1360
Elk Grove Village **(G-9160)**
Solar Spring Company .... C 847 437-7838
Elk Grove Village **(G-9245)**
Spring Specialist Corporation .... G 815 562-7991
Kings **(G-12054)**
White Eagle Spring & .... F 773 384-4455
Chicago **(G-6618)**

SPRINGS: Precision

Ascent Mfg Co .... E 847 806-6600
Elk Grove Village **(G-8841)**
Perfection Spring Stmping Corp .... D 847 437-3900
Mount Prospect **(G-14560)**

SPRINGS: Steel

All Rite Spring Co .... D 815 675-1350
Spring Grove **(G-19263)**
Burnex Corporation .... E 815 728-1317
Ringwood **(G-17040)**
Capitol Coil Inc .... F 847 891-1390
Schaumburg **(G-18467)**
Dudek & Bock Spring Mfg Co .... C 773 379-4100
Chicago **(G-4402)**
High-Life Products Inc .... G 847 991-9449
Palatine **(G-16124)**
Highland Spring & Specialty .... F 618 654-3831
Highland **(G-11223)**
Johnson Tool Company .... G 708 453-8600
Huntley **(G-11547)**
Kdk Upset Forging Co .... E 708 388-8770
Blue Island **(G-2128)**
Khc Corporation .... E 815 337-7630
Woodstock **(G-21399)**
Lewis Spring and Mfg Company .... D 847 588-7030
Niles **(G-15140)**
Mid-West Spring & Stamping Inc .... G 630 739-3800
Romeoville **(G-17854)**
Mw Industries Inc .... D 773 539-5600
Bensenville **(G-1855)**
R & G Spring Co Inc .... G 847 228-5640
Elk Grove Village **(G-9208)**
Smalley Steel Ring Co .... C 847 537-7600
Lake Zurich **(G-12458)**
Spirolox Inc .... B 847 719-5900
Lake Zurich **(G-12459)**
Spring Specialist Corporation .... G 815 562-7991
Kings **(G-12054)**
Stanley Spring & Stamping Corp .... D 773 777-2600
Chicago **(G-6230)**
United Spring & Manufacturing .... E 773 384-8464
Chicago **(G-6475)**
William Dudek Manufacturing Co .... E 773 622-2727
Chicago **(G-6629)**

SPRINGS: Torsion Bar

Gilbert Spring Corporation .... E 773 486-6030
Chicago **(G-4691)**
Mid-West Spring & Stamping Inc .... G 630 739-3800
Romeoville **(G-17853)**
Mid-West Spring Mfg Co .... C 630 739-3800
Romeoville **(G-17855)**
Spring R-R Corporation .... E 630 543-7445
Addison **(G-295)**

SPRINGS: Wire

A J Kay Co .... F 224 475-0370
Mundelein **(G-14657)**
All American Spring Stamping .... G 847 928-9468
Franklin Park **(G-9865)**
All Rite Spring Co .... D 815 675-1350
Spring Grove **(G-19263)**
All Rite Spring Company .... F 815 675-1350
Spring Grove **(G-19264)**
Available Spring and Mfg Co .... G 847 520-4854
Wheeling **(G-20853)**
Century Spring Corporation .... G 800 237-5225
Chicago **(G-4062)**
CFC Wire Forms Inc .... E 630 879-7575
Batavia **(G-1364)**
Classic Products Inc .... E 815 344-0051
McHenry **(G-13728)**
David V Michals .... D 847 671-6767
Schiller Park **(G-18799)**
Highland Spring & Specialty .... F 618 654-3831
Highland **(G-11223)**
Innocor Foam Tech W Chcago LLC .... E 732 945-6222
West Chicago **(G-20598)**
JD Norman Industries Inc .... D 630 458-3700
Addison **(G-159)**
Johnson Tool Company .... G 708 453-8600
Huntley **(G-11547)**
Lew-El Tool & Manufacturing Co .... F 773 804-1133
Chicago **(G-5212)**
M Lizen Manufacturing Co .... E 708 755-7213
University Park **(G-19958)**
Majestic Spring Inc .... F 847 593-8887
Elk Grove Village **(G-9108)**
Master Spring & Wire Form Co .... E 708 453-2570
Itasca **(G-11698)**
Micromatic Spring Stamping Inc .... E 630 607-0141
Addison **(G-207)**
Mid-West Spring & Stamping Inc .... G 630 739-3800
Romeoville **(G-17853)**
Mid-West Spring & Stamping Inc .... G 630 739-3800
Romeoville **(G-17854)**
Mid-West Spring Mfg Co .... C 630 739-3800
Romeoville **(G-17855)**
Mw Industries Inc .... D 773 539-5600
Bensenville **(G-1855)**
Ohare Spring Company Inc .... E 847 298-1360
Des Plaines **(G-7815)**
Paragon Spring Company .... E 773 489-6300
Chicago **(G-5759)**
Patrick Manufacturing Inc .... E 847 697-5920
Elgin **(G-8686)**
R & G Spring Co Inc .... G 847 228-5640
Elk Grove Village **(G-9208)**
R C Coil Spring Mfg Co Inc .... E 630 790-3500
Glendale Heights **(G-10486)**
R G Spring Company Inc .... G 847 695-2986
Elgin **(G-8712)**
Riverside Spring Company .... G 815 963-3334
Rockford **(G-17574)**
Sanco Industries Inc .... F 847 243-8675
Kildeer **(G-12052)**
Schaff International LLC .... E 847 438-4560
Lake Zurich **(G-12453)**
Smalley Steel Ring Co .... C 847 537-7600
Lake Zurich **(G-12458)**
Spirolox Inc .... B 847 719-5900
Lake Zurich **(G-12459)**
Stanley Spring & Stamping Corp .... D 773 777-2600
Chicago **(G-6230)**
Sterling Spring LLC .... D 773 582-6464
Chicago **(G-6245)**
Sterling Spring LLC .... E 773 777-4647
Bedford Park **(G-1507)**
Taycorp Inc .... E 708 629-0921
Alsip **(G-514)**
United Spring & Manufacturing .... E 773 384-8464
Chicago **(G-6475)**
Willdon Corp .... E 773 276-7080
Chicago **(G-6628)**
York Spring Co .... E 847 695-5978
South Elgin **(G-19184)**

SPRINKLING SYSTEMS: Fire Control

Fire Systems Holdings Inc .... F 708 333-4130
Mokena **(G-14081)**
Flame Guard Usa LLC .... G 815 219-4074
Vernon Hills **(G-20054)**
Industrial Pipe and Supply Co .... E 708 652-7511
Chicago **(G-4909)**
Rainmaker .... G 847 998-0838
Glenview **(G-10608)**
Systems Piping .... G 847 948-1373
Deerfield **(G-7651)**

SPROCKETS: Power Transmission

Allied Gear Co ....G.... 773 287-8742
River Forest *(G-17049)*
E N M Company ....D.... 773 775-8400
Chicago *(G-4425)*
Galaxy Sourcing Inc ....G.... 630 532-5003
Addison *(G-133)*
Hadley Gear Manufacturing Co ....F.... 773 722-1030
Chicago *(G-4765)*

STAINLESS STEEL

ATI Flat Rlled Pdts Hldngs LLC ....F.... 708 974-8801
Bridgeview *(G-2326)*
Bruder Tank Inc ....E.... 217 292-9058
Sullivan *(G-19662)*
Commercial Stainless Svcs Inc ....F.... 847 349-1560
Elk Grove Village *(G-8906)*
Elg Metals Inc ....E.... 773 374-1500
Chicago *(G-4484)*
Joe Zsido Sales & Design Inc ....E.... 618 435-2605
Benton *(G-1929)*
Marias Chicken ATI Atihan ....G.... 847 699-3113
Niles *(G-15144)*
Omega Products Inc ....G.... 618 939-3445
Waterloo *(G-20293)*
Raco Steel Company ....E.... 708 339-2958
Markham *(G-13550)*
Strictly Stainless Inc ....G.... 847 885-2890
Hoffman Estates *(G-11464)*
United Toolers of Illinois ....F.... 779 423-0548
Loves Park *(G-13279)*
Valbruna Stainless Inc ....F.... 630 871-5524
Carol Stream *(G-3083)*

STAINLESS STEEL WARE

Nelson-Whittaker Ltd ....E.... 815 459-6000
Crystal Lake *(G-7237)*
Omni-Rinse LLC ....G.... 708 860-3250
Palatine *(G-16146)*

STAIRCASES & STAIRS, WOOD

Amron Stair Works Inc ....F.... 847 426-4800
Gilberts *(G-10350)*
Bailey Hardwoods Inc ....G.... 217 529-6800
Springfield *(G-19324)*
Custom Railz & Stairz Inc ....G.... 773 592-7210
Chicago *(G-4291)*
Designed Stairs Inc ....E.... 815 786-2021
Sandwich *(G-18367)*
Kencor Stairs & Woodworking ....G.... 630 279-8980
Villa Park *(G-20155)*
Lake Shore Stair Co Inc ....E.... 815 363-7777
Ingleside *(G-11586)*
Riverside Custom Woodworking ....G.... 815 589-3608
Fulton *(G-10157)*
Stairsland ....G.... 708 853-9593
Lyons *(G-13314)*

STAMPING SVC: Book, Gold

Creative Label Inc ....D.... 847 956-6960
Elk Grove Village *(G-8919)*
Midwest Gold Stampers Inc ....F.... 773 775-5253
Chicago *(G-5442)*

STAMPINGS: Automotive

Borgwarner Inc ....C.... 815 288-1462
Dixon *(G-7892)*
Borgwarner Transm Systems Inc ....A.... 708 547-2600
Bellwood *(G-1618)*
Clay Cnty Rhbilitation Ctr Inc ....F.... 618 662-6607
Flora *(G-9678)*
Ford Motor Company ....A.... 708 757-5700
Ford Heights *(G-9706)*
G & M Manufacturing Corp ....E.... 815 455-1900
Crystal Lake *(G-7201)*
Inland Tool Company ....E.... 217 792-3206
Mount Pulaski *(G-14588)*
Jahm Inc ....F.... 847 647-7650
Niles *(G-15135)*
Laystrom Manufacturing Co ....D.... 773 342-4800
Chicago *(G-5186)*
Mercury Products Corp ....C.... 847 524-4400
Schaumburg *(G-18627)*
MNP Precision Parts LLC ....C.... 815 391-5256
Rockford *(G-17530)*
Perfection Spring Stmping Corp ....D.... 847 437-3900
Mount Prospect *(G-14560)*
Plastic Technologies Inc ....E.... 847 841-8610
Elgin *(G-8688)*
T R Z Motorsports Inc ....G.... 815 806-0838
Frankfort *(G-9843)*
Topy Precision Mfg Inc ....D.... 847 228-5902
Elk Grove Village *(G-9277)*
Tower Atmtive Oprtons USA I LL ....B.... 773 646-6550
Chicago *(G-6400)*
Troy Design & Manufacturing Co ....G.... 312 692-9706
Chicago *(G-6434)*
Tsm Inc ....G.... 815 544-5012
Belvidere *(G-1705)*

STAMPINGS: Metal

Abbott Scott Manufacturing Co ....E.... 773 342-7200
Chicago *(G-3505)*
Accurate Wire Strip Frming Inc ....F.... 630 260-1000
Carol Stream *(G-2924)*
Ace Plating Company ....E.... 773 927-2711
Chicago *(G-3522)*
Advanced Custom Metals Inc ....G.... 847 803-2090
Des Plaines *(G-7723)*
Agri-Fab Inc ....G.... 217 728-8388
Sullivan *(G-19659)*
All American Spring Stamping ....G.... 847 928-9468
Franklin Park *(G-9865)*
All American Washer Werks Inc ....E.... 847 566-9091
Mundelein *(G-14661)*
American Partsmith Inc ....G.... 630 520-0432
West Chicago *(G-20538)*
Ammentorp Tool Company Inc ....G.... 847 671-9290
Franklin Park *(G-9869)*
Angle Tool Company ....G.... 847 593-7572
Elk Grove Village *(G-8832)*
Apex Wire Products Company Inc ....F.... 847 671-1830
Franklin Park *(G-9871)*
Ark Technologies Inc ....D.... 630 377-8855
Saint Charles *(G-18149)*
Ascent Mfg Co ....E.... 847 806-6600
Elk Grove Village *(G-8841)*
Astoria Wire Products Inc ....D.... 708 496-9950
Bedford Park *(G-1459)*
Austin Tool & Die Co ....D.... 847 509-5800
Northbrook *(G-15344)*
Available Spring and Mfg Co ....G.... 847 520-4854
Wheeling *(G-20853)*
B & D Murray Manufacturing Co ....G.... 815 568-6176
Marengo *(G-13481)*
B Radtke and Sons Inc ....G.... 847 546-3999
Round Lake Park *(G-18095)*
Bellota Agrsltions Tls USA LLC ....E.... 309 787-2491
Rock Island *(G-17205)*
Big 3 Precision Products Inc ....C.... 618 533-3251
Centralia *(G-3222)*
Bilt-Rite Metal Products Inc ....E.... 815 495-2211
Leland *(G-12547)*
Bomel Tool Manufacturing Co ....C.... 708 343-3663
Broadview *(G-2422)*
Borgwarner Transm Systems Inc ....A.... 708 547-2600
Bellwood *(G-1618)*
Buhrke Industries LLC ....B.... 847 981-7550
Arlington Heights *(G-711)*
C E R Machining & Tooling Ltd ....G.... 708 442-9614
Lyons *(G-13305)*
Cardinal Engineering Inc ....G.... 309 342-7474
Galesburg *(G-10188)*
Central Radiator Cabinet Co ....G.... 773 539-1700
Lena *(G-12599)*
Central Tool Specialities Co ....G.... 630 543-6351
Addison *(G-66)*
Chicago Car Seal Company ....G.... 773 278-9400
Chicago *(G-4095)*
Chicago Metal Fabricators Inc ....D.... 773 523-5755
Chicago *(G-4114)*
Coda Resources Ltd ....F.... 718 649-1666
Chicago *(G-4190)*
Component Tool & Mfg Co ....F.... 708 672-5505
Crete *(G-7136)*
Craftsman Custom Metals LLC ....D.... 847 655-0040
Schiller Park *(G-18797)*
Cs Legacy Corp ....E.... 847 741-3101
Elgin *(G-8558)*
D & B Fabricators & Distrs ....F.... 630 325-3811
Lemont *(G-12562)*
D & J Machine Shop Inc ....G.... 815 472-6057
Momence *(G-14184)*
Dadum Inc ....G.... 847 541-7851
Buffalo Grove *(G-2530)*
Delta Metal Products Co ....G.... 773 745-9220
Chicago *(G-4336)*
Desk & Door Nameplate Company ....F.... 815 806-8670
Frankfort *(G-9785)*
Diemasters Manufacturing Inc ....C.... 847 640-9900
Elk Grove Village *(G-8950)*
Dixline Corporation ....F.... 309 932-2011
Galva *(G-10230)*
Dixline Corporation ....D.... 309 932-2011
Galva *(G-10231)*
Dkb Partners Inc ....G.... 618 632-6718
O Fallon *(G-15572)*
Dovee Manufacturing Inc ....F.... 847 437-8122
Elgin *(G-8569)*
Dudek & Bock Spring Mfg Co ....C.... 773 379-4100
Chicago *(G-4402)*
E H Baare Corporation ....C.... 618 546-1575
Robinson *(G-17114)*
Ems Industrial and Service Co ....E.... 815 678-2700
Richmond *(G-17012)*
Equinox Group Inc ....F.... 312 226-7002
Chicago *(G-4524)*
Erickson Tool & Machine Co ....G.... 815 397-2653
Rockford *(G-17400)*
Fabricating Machinery Sales ....E.... 630 350-2266
Wood Dale *(G-21186)*
Fanmar Inc ....E.... 847 621-2010
Elk Grove Village *(G-8995)*
Ford Motor Company ....A.... 708 757-5700
Ford Heights *(G-9706)*
Forster Tool & Mfg Co Inc ....E.... 630 616-8177
Bensenville *(G-1802)*
Four Star Tool Inc ....D.... 224 735-2419
Rolling Meadows *(G-17733)*
General Machinery & Mfg Co ....F.... 773 235-3700
Chicago *(G-4674)*
Global Brass and Copper Inc ....G.... 502 873-3000
East Alton *(G-8166)*
Global Brass Cop Holdings Inc ....E.... 847 240-4700
Schaumburg *(G-18535)*
Haddock Tool & Manufacturing ....G.... 815 786-2739
Sandwich *(G-18373)*
Harrington King Prforating Inc ....C.... 773 626-1800
Chicago *(G-4781)*
Highland Southern Wire Inc ....G.... 618 654-2161
Highland *(G-11222)*
Hoosier Stamping & Mfg Corp ....E.... 618 375-2057
Grayville *(G-10810)*
Illinois Tool Works Inc ....F.... 708 681-3891
Broadview *(G-2443)*
Illinois Tool Works Inc ....C.... 847 299-2222
Des Plaines *(G-7785)*
Imh Fabrication Inc ....F.... 815 537-2381
Prophetstown *(G-16833)*
IMS Companies LLC ....D.... 847 391-8100
Des Plaines *(G-7786)*
IMS Engineered Products LLC ....C.... 847 391-8100
Des Plaines *(G-7787)*
IMS Olson LLC ....D.... 630 969-9400
Downers Grove *(G-8030)*
Industrial Enclosure Corp ....E.... 630 898-7499
Aurora *(G-1111)*
Inland Tool Company ....E.... 217 792-3206
Mount Pulaski *(G-14588)*
Integrity Manufacturing Inc ....G.... 815 514-8230
Romeoville *(G-17832)*
Integrity Metals LLC ....E.... 630 963-4126
Romeoville *(G-17833)*
Ironform Holdings Co ....B.... 312 374-4810
Chicago *(G-4970)*
J-TEC Metal Products Inc ....F.... 630 875-1300
Itasca *(G-11679)*
Jahm Inc ....F.... 847 647-7650
Niles *(G-15135)*
Jason Incorporated ....C.... 630 627-7000
Addison *(G-158)*
JD Norman Industries Inc ....D.... 630 458-3700
Addison *(G-159)*
Jsn Inc ....E.... 708 410-1800
Maywood *(G-13670)*
Kaskaskia Tool and Machine Inc ....E.... 618 475-3301
New Athens *(G-15020)*
Kipp Manufacturing Company Inc ....F.... 630 768-9051
Wauconda *(G-20366)*
Kleen Cut Tool Inc ....G.... 630 447-7020
Warrenville *(G-20240)*
Klein Tools Inc ....D.... 847 228-6999
Elk Grove Village *(G-9078)*
Klein Tools Inc ....E.... 847 821-5500
Lincolnshire *(G-12779)*
Lakeview Metals Inc ....D.... 847 838-9800
Antioch *(G-621)*

PRODUCT SECTION — STEEL FABRICATORS

Lew-El Tool & Manufacturing Co.........F.......773 804-1133
  Chicago *(G-5212)*
Marlboro Wire Ltd.........................E.......217 224-7989
  Quincy *(G-16910)*
Mid-West Spring & Stamping Inc.........G.......630 739-3800
  Romeoville *(G-17853)*
Midwest Nameplate Corp................G.......708 614-0606
  Orland Park *(G-15968)*
Milans Machining & Mfg Co Inc..........D.......708 780-6600
  Cicero *(G-6867)*
Millenia Metals LLC.....................D.......630 458-0401
  Itasca *(G-11703)*
Millenia Products Group Inc.............C.......630 458-0401
  Itasca *(G-11704)*
Mint Masters Inc........................E.......847 451-1133
  Franklin Park *(G-10000)*
Mity Inc................................G.......630 365-5030
  Elburn *(G-8461)*
Moline Welding Inc.....................F.......309 756-0643
  Milan *(G-14018)*
Natura Products Inc....................F.......847 509-5835
  Northbrook *(G-15439)*
Navitor Inc............................B.......800 323-0253
  Harwood Heights *(G-11106)*
Newko Tool & Engineering Co............E.......847 359-1670
  Palatine *(G-16142)*
Octavia Tool & Gage Company............G.......847 913-9233
  Elk Grove Village *(G-9159)*
Offko Tool Inc.........................G.......815 933-9474
  Kankakee *(G-11994)*
Paddock Industries Inc.................F.......618 277-1580
  Smithton *(G-19068)*
Park Manufacturing Corp Inc............F.......708 345-6090
  Melrose Park *(G-13903)*
PDQ Tool & Stamping Co.................E.......708 841-3000
  Dolton *(G-7938)*
Pecora Tool Service Inc................G.......847 524-1275
  Schaumburg *(G-18672)*
Plano Molding Company LLC..............C.......815 538-3111
  Mendota *(G-13952)*
Precision Metal Technologies...........F.......847 228-6630
  Rolling Meadows *(G-17765)*
Prikos & Becker LLC....................D.......847 675-3910
  Skokie *(G-19010)*
Prismier LLC...........................E.......630 592-4515
  Bolingbrook *(G-2230)*
Pro-Tech Metal Specialties Inc.........E.......630 279-7094
  Elmhurst *(G-9412)*
R B White Inc..........................E.......309 452-5816
  Normal *(G-15220)*
R C Coil Spring Mfg Co Inc.............E.......630 790-3500
  Glendale Heights *(G-10486)*
Realwheels Corporation.................E.......847 662-7722
  Gurnee *(G-10923)*
Rockford Toolcraft Inc.................E.......815 398-5507
  Rockford *(G-17609)*
Royal Die & Stamping Co Inc............C.......630 766-2685
  Carol Stream *(G-3060)*
Runge Enterprises Inc..................G.......630 365-2000
  Elburn *(G-8472)*
Service Sheet Metal Works Inc..........F.......773 229-0031
  Chicago *(G-6143)*
Simplomatic Manufacturing Co...........E.......773 342-7757
  Elgin *(G-8733)*
Spannagel Tool & Die...................E.......630 969-7575
  Downers Grove *(G-8098)*
Starmont Manufacturing Co..............G.......815 939-1041
  Kankakee *(G-12007)*
Starmont Manufacturing Inc.............F.......708 758-2525
  Chicago Heights *(G-6776)*
Sweet Manufacturing Corp...............E.......847 546-5575
  Chicago *(G-6294)*
Syr-Tech Perforating Co................E.......630 942-7300
  Glendale Heights *(G-10508)*
T H K Holdings of America LLC..........G.......847 310-1111
  Schaumburg *(G-18735)*
Ta Delaware Inc........................E.......773 646-6550
  Chicago *(G-6309)*
Tarney Inc.............................E.......773 235-0331
  Chicago *(G-6327)*
Tj Wire Forming Inc....................G.......630 628-9209
  Addison *(G-310)*
Tlk Tool & Stamping Inc................G.......224 293-6941
  East Dundee *(G-8213)*
Tool Automation Enterprises............G.......708 799-6847
  East Hazel Crest *(G-8218)*
Trinity Machined Products Inc..........E.......630 876-6992
  Aurora *(G-1028)*
Trio Wire Products Inc.................G.......815 469-2148
  Frankfort *(G-9846)*
Tru-Way Inc............................E.......708 562-3690
  Northlake *(G-15563)*
Tu-Star Manufacturing Co Inc...........G.......815 338-5760
  Woodstock *(G-21441)*
Tvh Parts Inc..........................E.......847 223-1000
  Grayslake *(G-10803)*
United Tool and Engineering Co.........D.......815 389-3021
  South Beloit *(G-19118)*
Voges Inc..............................F.......618 233-2760
  Evansville *(G-9590)*
Wardzala Industries Inc................F.......847 288-9909
  Franklin Park *(G-10083)*
Wenco Manufacturing Co Inc.............E.......630 377-7474
  Elgin *(G-8781)*
Wieland Holdings Inc...................A.......847 537-3990
  Wheeling *(G-21013)*
William Dudek Manufacturing Co.........E.......773 622-2727
  Chicago *(G-6629)*
Wozniak Industries Inc.................C.......630 820-4052
  Aurora *(G-1040)*
Wozniak Industries Inc.................G.......630 954-3400
  Schaumburg *(G-18776)*
ZF Active Safety & Elec US LLC.........B.......217 826-3011
  Marshall *(G-13580)*

STAPLES

L & J Industrial Staples Inc...........G.......815 864-3337
  Shannon *(G-18870)*

STAPLES, MADE FROM PURCHASED WIRE

Illinois Tool Works Inc................G.......847 821-2170
  Vernon Hills *(G-20065)*
Minerallac Company.....................E.......630 543-7080
  Hampshire *(G-10979)*

STARTERS & CONTROLLERS: Motor, Electric

Jordan Industries Inc..................F.......847 945-5591
  Deerfield *(G-7621)*

STARTERS: Electric Motor

General Electric Company...............C.......309 664-1513
  Bloomington *(G-2050)*

STARTERS: Motor

A E Iskra Inc..........................G.......815 874-4022
  Rockford *(G-17280)*

STARTING EQPT: Street Cars

Bill West Enterprises Inc..............G.......217 886-2591
  Jacksonville *(G-11757)*

STATIC ELIMINATORS: Ind

Ksm Electronics Inc....................C.......630 393-9310
  Warrenville *(G-20241)*

STATIONARY & OFFICE SPLYS, WHOLESALE: Looseleaf Binders

Harlan Vance Company...................F.......309 888-4804
  Normal *(G-15205)*

STATIONARY & OFFICE SPLYS, WHOLESALE: Manifold Business Form

Dallas Corporation.....................F.......630 322-8000
  Downers Grove *(G-7983)*

STATIONARY & OFFICE SPLYS, WHOLESALE: Office Filing Splys

Dauphin Enterprise Inc.................G.......630 893-6300
  Bloomingdale *(G-1987)*

STATIONARY & OFFICE SPLYS, WHOLESALE: Stationery

Allen Paper Company....................G.......312 454-4500
  Chicago *(G-3615)*
Allied Graphics Inc....................G.......847 419-8830
  Buffalo Grove *(G-2508)*

STATIONARY & OFFICE SPLYS, WHOLESALE: Writing Ink

Toyo Ink International Corp............F.......866 969-8696
  Wood Dale *(G-21251)*

STATIONER'S SUNDRIES: Rubber

James Ray Monroe Corporation...........F.......618 532-4575
  Centralia *(G-3236)*

STATIONERY & OFFICE SPLYS WHOLESALERS

A Trustworthy Sup Source Inc...........G.......773 480-0255
  Chicago *(G-3492)*
Block and Company Inc..................C.......847 537-7200
  Wheeling *(G-20860)*
Corporation Supply Co Inc..............E.......312 726-3375
  Chicago *(G-4241)*
Icandee LLC............................F.......773 754-0493
  Chicago *(G-4871)*
LAC Enterprises Inc....................G.......815 455-5044
  Crystal Lake *(G-7219)*
Write Stuff............................G.......630 365-4425
  Saint Charles *(G-18303)*

STATIONERY PRDTS

Assemble and Mail Group Inc............G.......309 473-2006
  Heyworth *(G-11189)*
Carl Manufacturing USA Inc.............F.......847 884-2842
  Itasca *(G-11635)*
Mudlark Papers Inc.....................G.......630 717-7616
  Naperville *(G-14876)*

STATIONERY: Made From Purchased Materials

Chicago Contract Bridge Assn...........G.......630 355-5560
  Naperville *(G-14797)*

STATORS REWINDING SVCS

Prompt Motor Rewinding Service.........G.......847 675-7155
  Skokie *(G-19016)*
Warfield Electric Company Inc..........E.......815 469-4094
  Frankfort *(G-9851)*

STATUARY & OTHER DECORATIVE PRDTS: Nonmetallic

Espe Manufacturing Co..................F.......847 678-8950
  Schiller Park *(G-18805)*

STATUARY GOODS, EXC RELIGIOUS: Wholesalers

Lion Concrete Products Inc.............G.......630 892-7304
  Montgomery *(G-14257)*

STATUES: Nonmetal

Daprato Rigali Studios Inc.............E.......773 763-5511
  Chicago *(G-4317)*

STEEL & ALLOYS: Tool & Die

Clawmounts Mfg Inc.....................G.......708 525-7552
  University Park *(G-19951)*
Ergoseal Inc...........................G.......630 462-9370
  Carol Stream *(G-2980)*
Finkl Steel - Houston LLC..............F.......773 975-2540
  Chicago *(G-4593)*
Processed Steel Company................B.......815 459-2400
  Crystal Lake *(G-7251)*
R M Tool & Manufacturing Co............G.......847 888-0433
  Elgin *(G-8713)*
Tj Tool Inc............................F.......630 543-3595
  Bloomingdale *(G-2017)*
Tritech International LLC..............G.......847 888-0333
  Elgin *(G-8761)*

STEEL FABRICATORS

555 Design Fabrication MGT Inc.........G.......773 869-0555
  Chicago *(G-3473)*
A & A Steel Fabricating Co.............F.......708 389-4499
  Posen *(G-16789)*
A & B Metal Polishing Inc..............F.......773 847-1077
  Chicago *(G-3480)*

Employee Codes: A=Over 500 employees, B=251-500
C=101-250, D=51-100, E=20-50, F=10-19, G=3-9

A & S Steel Specialties Inc E 815 838-8188
Lockport *(G-12979)*
AAA Galvanizing - Joliet Inc E 815 284-5001
Dixon *(G-7887)*
Aak Mechanical Inc D 217 935-8501
Clinton *(G-6917)*
Ablaze Welding & Fabricating G 815 965-0046
Rockford *(G-17287)*
Accurate Fabricators Inc G 618 451-1886
Granite City *(G-10689)*
Accurate Metal Fabricating LLC D 773 235-0400
Chicago *(G-3518)*
Ace Metal Crafts Company C 847 455-1010
Bensenville *(G-1726)*
Acro Tech Corporation G 630 408-2248
Wheaton *(G-20785)*
Adams Steel Service Inc E 815 385-9100
McHenry *(G-13715)*
Addison Steel Inc G 847 998-9445
Glenview *(G-10519)*
Adermanns Welding & Mch & Co G 217 342-3234
Effingham *(G-8383)*
Advance Iron Works Inc F 708 798-3540
East Hazel Crest *(G-8216)*
Advanced Custom Metals Inc G 847 803-2090
Des Plaines *(G-7723)*
Advanced Steel Fabrication G 847 956-6565
Elk Grove Village *(G-8809)*
Ae2009 Technologies Inc E 708 331-0025
South Holland *(G-19188)*
Aetna Engineering Works Inc E 773 785-0489
Chicago *(G-3577)*
Alfredos Iron Works Inc E 815 748-1177
Cortland *(G-7017)*
All Metal Solutions Inc G 312 483-4178
Chicago *(G-3610)*
Alloy Specialties Inc F 815 586-4728
Blackstone *(G-1970)*
Allquip Co Inc G 309 944-6153
Geneseo *(G-10239)*
Allstate Metal Fabricators Inc G 630 860-1500
Wood Dale *(G-21159)*
Alton Sheet Metal Corp F 618 462-0609
Alton *(G-543)*
Altra Division 5 Llc F 708 534-1100
University Park *(G-19945)*
American Piping Group Inc D 815 772-7470
Morrison *(G-14340)*
American Steel Services Inc F 815 774-0677
Joliet *(G-11820)*
Anchor Welding & Fabrication G 815 937-1640
Aroma Park *(G-839)*
Andersen Machine & Welding Inc G 815 232-4664
Freeport *(G-10101)*
Andscot Co Inc G 847 455-5800
Franklin Park *(G-9870)*
Archer General Contg & Fabg G 708 757-7902
Steger *(G-19488)*
Architectural Metals LLC F 815 654-2370
Loves Park *(G-13191)*
Arcorp Structures LLC E 773 791-1648
Riverside *(G-17081)*
Arcosa Wind Towers Inc F 217 935-7900
Clinton *(G-6918)*
Area Fabricators G 217 455-3426
Coatsburg *(G-6940)*
Arlington Strl Stl Co Inc E 847 577-2200
Arlington Heights *(G-695)*
Armor Contract Mfg Inc E 847 981-9800
Elk Grove Village *(G-8838)*
Arnette Pattern Co Inc E 618 451-7700
Granite City *(G-10698)*
AS Fabricating Inc G 618 242-7438
Mount Vernon *(G-14596)*
Aspen Industries Inc F 630 238-0611
Bensenville *(G-1748)*
Atkore International Group Inc A 708 339-1610
Harvey *(G-11075)*
Atkore Intl Holdings Inc G 708 225-2051
Harvey *(G-11076)*
B & B Fabrications LLC G 217 620-3210
Sullivan *(G-19660)*
Bending Specialists LLC E 815 726-6281
Lockport *(G-12983)*
Bi State Steel Co G 309 755-0668
East Moline *(G-8223)*
Biewer Fabricating Inc G 630 530-8922
Villa Park *(G-20134)*
Binzel Industries LLC G 847 506-0003
Lockport *(G-12984)*
Birdco Fabricators Inc G 217 408-8744
Jacksonville *(G-11758)*
Birdsell Machine & Orna Inc G 217 243-5849
Jacksonville *(G-11759)*
BR Machine Inc F 815 434-0427
Ottawa *(G-16042)*
Bridge City Mechanical Inc F 309 944-4873
Geneseo *(G-10240)*
Bridgeport Steel Sales Inc F 312 326-4800
Chicago *(G-3957)*
Btd Manufacturing Inc F 309 444-1268
Washington *(G-20267)*
Byus Steel Inc E 630 879-2200
Batavia *(G-1361)*
C Keller Manufacturing Inc E 630 833-5593
Villa Park *(G-20136)*
Catapult Global LLC F 847 364-8149
Elk Grove Village *(G-8882)*
Cem LLC D 708 333-3761
Barrington *(G-1217)*
Central Illinois Steel Company E 217 854-3251
Carlinville *(G-2869)*
Central Steel Fabricators E 708 652-2037
Broadview *(G-2424)*
Cervones Welding Service Inc G 847 985-6865
Schaumburg *(G-18471)*
CFS Crtive Fbrction Sltons LLC G 309 264-3946
Peoria *(G-16420)*
Challenger Fabricators Inc G 815 704-0077
South Beloit *(G-19086)*
Charter Dura-Bar Inc C 815 338-7800
Woodstock *(G-21374)*
Chicago Grinding & Machine Co E 708 343-4399
Melrose Park *(G-13843)*
Chicago Metal Fabricators Inc D 773 523-5755
Chicago *(G-4114)*
Chicago Metal Rolled Pdts Co D 773 523-5757
Chicago *(G-4115)*
Chicagoland Metal Fabricators G 847 260-5320
Franklin Park *(G-9906)*
Circle Metal Specialties Inc E 708 597-1700
Alsip *(G-432)*
CJ Drilling Inc D 847 669-8000
Dundee *(G-8126)*
Clarkwestern Dietrich Building E 815 561-2360
Rochelle *(G-17135)*
Cokel Dj Welding Bay & Muffler G 309 385-4567
Princeville *(G-16825)*
Comet Fabricating & Welding Co E 815 229-0468
Rockford *(G-17354)*
Commercial Metals Company G 815 928-9600
Kankakee *(G-11961)*
Conley Steel Inc G 630 393-1193
Warrenville *(G-20233)*
Cooper B-Line Inc A 618 654-2184
Highland *(G-11210)*
Corsetti Structural Steel Inc E 815 726-0186
Joliet *(G-11848)*
Covey Machine Inc F 773 650-1530
Chicago *(G-4250)*
Creative Iron G 217 267-7797
Westville *(G-20779)*
Crest Metal Craft Inc G 773 978-0950
Chicago *(G-4270)*
Custom Fabricators LLC F 773 814-2757
Streamwood *(G-19570)*
Custom Fbrication Coatings Inc D 618 452-9540
Granite City *(G-10701)*
Custom Feeder Co of Rockford E 815 654-2444
Loves Park *(G-13201)*
Cyclops Welding Co G 815 223-0685
La Salle *(G-12109)*
D & M Welding Inc G 708 233-6080
Bridgeview *(G-2339)*
D L Austin Steel Supply Corp G 618 345-7200
Collinsville *(G-6957)*
D5 Design Met Fabrication LLC G 773 770-4705
Chicago *(G-4303)*
David Architectural Metals Inc E 773 376-3200
Chicago *(G-4323)*
Dayton Superior Corporation D 815 936-3300
Kankakee *(G-11963)*
Delta Structures Inc F 630 694-8700
Lombard *(G-13064)*
Dicke Tool Company D 630 969-0050
Downers Grove *(G-7988)*
DSI Spaceframes Inc E 630 607-0045
Addison *(G-99)*
E B Inc F 815 758-6646
De Kalb *(G-7429)*
East Moline Sheet Metal Co G 309 755-1422
Moline *(G-14142)*
EC Harms Met Fabricators Inc F 309 385-2132
Princeville *(G-16826)*
Ed Stan Fabricating Co G 708 863-7668
Chicago *(G-4449)*
Ekstrom Carlson Fabg Co Inc G 815 226-1511
Rockford *(G-17392)*
Emco Metals LLC F 312 925-1553
Cicero *(G-6846)*
Engineered Iron Works Inc F 773 887-5701
Chicago *(G-4509)*
Ermak Usa Inc F 847 640-7765
Des Plaines *(G-7760)*
European Ornamental Iron Works G 630 705-9300
Addison *(G-117)*
Ex-Cell Kaiser LLC E 847 451-0451
Franklin Park *(G-9941)*
Exo Fabrication Inc G 630 501-1136
Addison *(G-118)*
F Kreutzer & Co G 773 826-5767
Chicago *(G-4550)*
F Vogelmann and Company F 815 469-2285
Frankfort *(G-9793)*
Fabco Enterprises Inc G 708 333-4644
Harvey *(G-11084)*
Fabricated Metal Systems Inc G 815 886-6200
Romeoville *(G-17821)*
Fabricating & Welding Corp E 773 928-2050
Chicago *(G-4555)*
Fanmar Inc E 847 621-2010
Elk Grove Village *(G-8995)*
Fbs Group Inc F 773 229-8675
Chicago *(G-4569)*
Fehring Ornamental Iron Works G 217 483-6727
Rochester *(G-17166)*
First Stage Fabrication Inc G 618 282-8320
Red Bud *(G-16994)*
Flex-Weld Inc D 815 334-3662
Woodstock *(G-21387)*
Floyd Steel Erectors Inc F 630 238-8383
Wood Dale *(G-21187)*
Funk Linko Group Inc G 708 757-7421
Monee *(G-14200)*
Fusion Fabrication G 815 214-9148
Lockport *(G-12994)*
G & F Manufacturing Co Inc E 708 424-4170
Oak Lawn *(G-15716)*
G & M Fabricating Inc G 815 282-1744
Roscoe *(G-17907)*
Gallon Industries Inc E 630 628-1020
Addison *(G-134)*
Gemini Steel Inc G 815 472-4462
Momence *(G-14185)*
Gerdau Ameristeel US Inc E 815 547-0400
Belvidere *(G-1673)*
Gma Inc G 630 595-1255
Bensenville *(G-1812)*
Go To Steel Inc G 773 814-3017
Norridge *(G-15235)*
Great Lakes Precision Tube Inc E 630 859-8940
Aurora *(G-1105)*
Great Lakes Stair & Steel Inc G 708 430-2323
Chicago Ridge *(G-6796)*
Greg Lambert Construction E 815 468-7361
Bourbonnais *(G-2261)*
Grimm Metal Fabricators Inc E 630 792-1710
Lombard *(G-13083)*
Grover Welding Company G 847 966-3119
Skokie *(G-18961)*
Gsi Group LLC C 217 463-1612
Paris *(G-16230)*
H3 Group LLC F 309 222-6027
Peoria *(G-16450)*
Hamilton Fbrcation Stl Sup Inc G 618 466-0012
Godfrey *(G-10652)*
Harmony Metal Fabrication Inc E 847 426-8900
Gilberts *(G-10356)*
Heartland Fabrication LLC G 309 448-2644
Congerville *(G-6999)*
Holden Industries Inc F 847 940-1500
Deerfield *(G-7616)*
Huntley & Associates Inc G 224 381-8500
Lake Zurich *(G-12420)*
Hyspan Precision Products Inc E 773 277-0700
South Holland *(G-19223)*
Ideal Fabricators Inc F 217 999-7017
Mount Olive *(G-14505)*
Igm Solutions Inc E 847 918-1790
Libertyville *(G-12661)*

(G-0000) Company's Geographic Section entry number

PRODUCT SECTION — STEEL FABRICATORS

Company	Code	Phone
Industrial Mint Wldg Machining	D	773 376-6526
Chicago (G-4908)		
ITW Blding Cmponents Group Inc	E	217 324-0303
Litchfield (G-12967)		
J & G Fabricating Inc	G	708 385-9147
Blue Island (G-2126)		
J B Metal Works Inc	G	847 824-4253
Des Plaines (G-7790)		
J H Botts LLC	E	815 726-5885
Joliet (G-11883)		
J&A Mtchell Stl Fbricators Inc	G	815 939-2144
Kankakee (G-11981)		
Jalor Company	G	847 202-1172
Elgin (G-8631)		
James Walker Mfg Co	E	708 754-4020
Glenwood (G-10641)		
Jarvis Welding Co	G	309 647-0033
Canton (G-2827)		
Jay RS Steel & Welding Inc	G	847 949-9353
Mundelein (G-14703)		
JB & S Machining	G	815 258-4007
Bourbonnais (G-2263)		
Jet Industries Inc	E	773 586-8900
Chicago (G-5024)		
Jhelsa Metal Polsg Fabrication	G	773 385-6628
Chicago (G-5029)		
K & K Iron Works LLC	G	773 619-6899
Chicago (G-5064)		
K & K Iron Works LLC	D	708 924-0000
Mc Cook (G-13693)		
K Three Welding Service Inc	G	708 563-2911
Chicago (G-5067)		
K-Met Industries Inc	F	708 534-3300
Monee (G-14203)		
Kelco Construction Inc	G	773 853-2974
Chicago (G-5089)		
Kemper Industries	G	217 826-5712
Marshall (G-13573)		
Keystone Bar Products Inc	E	708 753-1200
Chicago Heights (G-6756)		
King Metal Co	G	708 388-3845
Alsip (G-464)		
Kingery Steel Fabricators Inc	E	708 474-6665
Lansing (G-12501)		
Kmk Metal Fabricators Inc	E	618 224-2000
Trenton (G-19903)		
Kroh-Wagner Inc	E	773 252-2031
Chicago (G-5133)		
Ksem Inc	G	618 656-5388
Edwardsville (G-8367)		
Kso Metalfab Inc	E	630 372-1200
Streamwood (G-19582)		
Kure Steel Inc	G	815 836-8027
Lockport (G-13004)		
Laser Plus Technologies LLC	G	847 787-9017
Elk Grove Village (G-9086)		
Laystrom Manufacturing Co	D	773 342-4800
Chicago (G-5186)		
Leroys Welding & Fabg Inc	F	847 215-6151
Wheeling (G-20931)		
Lesker Company Inc	E	708 343-2277
Bensenville (G-1843)		
Liberty Machinery Company	F	847 276-2761
Lincolnshire (G-12781)		
Lickenbrock & Sons Inc	G	618 632-4977
O Fallon (G-15578)		
Linear Kinetics Inc	G	630 365-0075
Maple Park (G-13463)		
Littell International Inc	E	630 622-4950
Schaumburg (G-18610)		
Lizotte Sheet Metal Inc	G	618 656-3066
Edwardsville (G-8368)		
Lockport Steel Fabricators LLC	D	815 726-6281
Lockport (G-13008)		
Loeffel Steel Products Inc	E	847 382-6770
Lake Barrington (G-12158)		
LPI Worldwide Inc	G	773 826-8600
Chicago (G-5270)		
Mace Iron Works Inc	E	708 479-2456
Frankfort (G-9815)		
Mapes & Sprowl LLC	G	847 364-0055
Elk Grove Village (G-9109)		
Marco Lighting Components Inc	F	312 829-6900
Chicago (G-5330)		
Marqutte Stl Sup Fbrcation Inc	F	815 433-0178
Ottawa (G-16060)		
Martin Steel Fabrication Inc	G	618 410-7066
Mascoutah (G-13602)		
Matcor Mtal Fbrication III Inc	E	309 263-1707
Morton (G-14365)		
McCloud Mtlwrks Indus Svcs Inc	G	618 713-2318
Chester (G-3459)		
McLaughlin Body Co	C	309 736-6105
East Moline (G-8234)		
McLaughlin Body Co	D	309 762-7755
Moline (G-14159)		
Mdt Customs LLC	G	573 316-5995
Mc Clure (G-13687)		
Mechanical Indus Stl Svcs Inc	E	815 521-1725
Channahon (G-3389)		
Meno Stone Co Inc	E	630 257-9220
Lemont (G-12571)		
Metal Tech Inc	E	630 529-7400
Roselle (G-17969)		
Metals & Metals LLC	G	630 866-4200
Bolingbrook (G-2213)		
Metaltek Fabricating Inc	F	708 534-9102
University Park (G-19960)		
Metamora Industries LLC	E	309 367-2368
Metamora (G-13964)		
Michelmann Steel Cnstr Co	E	217 222-0555
Quincy (G-16912)		
Midwest Metals Inc	G	618 295-3444
Marissa (G-13543)		
Miller Fabrication LLC	D	307 358-4777
Chicago (G-5458)		
Mj Snyder Ironworks Inc	G	217 826-6440
Marshall (G-13575)		
Mobile Mini Inc	E	708 297-2004
Calumet Park (G-2799)		
Mold Shields Inc	G	708 983-5931
Oak Forest (G-15686)		
Moline Welding Inc	F	309 756-0643
Milan (G-14018)		
Montefusco Hvac Inc	G	309 691-7400
Peoria (G-16479)		
Morey Industries Inc	C	708 343-3220
Broadview (G-2454)		
Morris Construction Inc	E	618 544-8504
Robinson (G-17120)		
Morton Industries LLC	A	309 263-2590
Morton (G-14371)		
Mutual Svcs Highland Pk Inc	F	847 432-3815
Highland Park (G-11287)		
National Cycle Inc	C	708 343-0400
Maywood (G-13674)		
National Machine Repair Inc	F	708 672-7711
Crete (G-7142)		
Neiweem Industries Inc	G	847 487-1239
Oakwood Hills (G-15821)		
New Metal Fabrication Corp	E	618 532-9000
Centralia (G-3241)		
Newman Welding & Machine Shop	G	618 435-5591
Benton (G-1934)		
Next Level Metal	G	636 627-9497
Baldwin (G-1186)		
Nicks Metal Fabg & Sons	F	708 485-1170
Brookfield (G-2489)		
Nnm Manufacturing LLC	E	815 436-9201
Plainfield (G-16696)		
North Chicago Iron Works Inc	E	847 689-2000
North Chicago (G-15317)		
Nowfab	G	815 675-2916
Spring Grove (G-19290)		
OBrien Architectural Mtls Inc	F	773 868-1065
Chicago (G-5650)		
Okaw Truss Inc	B	217 543-3371
Arthur (G-873)		
Old Style Iron Works Inc	G	773 265-5787
Chicago (G-5670)		
Olympic Steel Inc	E	847 584-4000
Schaumburg (G-18658)		
OMalley Welding and Fabg	G	630 553-1604
Yorkville (G-21495)		
Onkens Incorporated	F	309 562-7477
Easton (G-8331)		
Oostman Fabricating & Wldg Inc	F	630 241-1315
Westmont (G-10308)		
Orsolinis Welding & Fabg	F	773 722-9855
Chicago (G-5705)		
Paco Corporation	F	708 430-2424
Bridgeview (G-2371)		
Pallet Repair Systems Inc	F	217 291-0009
Jacksonville (G-11780)		
Parkway Metal Products Inc	D	847 789-4000
Des Plaines (G-7818)		
Patrick Holdings Inc	F	815 874-5300
Rockford (G-17549)		
Paul Wever Construction Eqp Co	F	309 965-2005
Goodfield (G-10676)		
Performance Industries Inc	E	972 393-6881
Carpentersville (G-3111)		
Phoenix Fabrication & Sup Inc	G	708 754-5901
Peotone (G-16556)		
Phoenix Welding Co Inc	F	630 616-1700
Franklin Park (G-10016)		
Pittsfield Mch Tl & Wldg Co	G	217 656-4000
Payson (G-16317)		
Pools Welding Inc	G	309 787-2083
Milan (G-14020)		
Premier Fabrication LLC	C	309 448-2338
Congerville (G-7000)		
Pro-Fab Inc	E	309 263-8454
Morton (G-14379)		
Pro-Tech Metal Specialties Inc	G	630 279-7094
Elmhurst (G-9412)		
Pro-Tran Inc	G	217 348-9353
Charleston (G-3410)		
Professional Metal Works LLC	F	618 539-2214
Freeburg (G-10092)		
R & B Metal Products Inc	G	815 338-1890
Woodstock (G-21427)		
R C Industrial Inc	G	309 230-4631
Milan (G-14023)		
Rail Exchange Inc	E	708 757-3317
Chicago Heights (G-6767)		
Reber Welding Service	G	217 774-3441
Shelbyville (G-18885)		
Rex Worldwide Ltd	G	630 384-9361
Naperville (G-14909)		
Ri-Del Mfg Inc	D	312 829-8720
Chicago (G-6024)		
Ricar Industries Inc	G	847 914-9083
Northbrook (G-15473)		
Roth Metal Fabricators Corp	G	708 371-8300
Alsip (G-505)		
Rrb Fabrication Inc	F	815 977-5603
Loves Park (G-13261)		
S & S Welding & Fabrication	G	847 742-7344
Elgin (G-8722)		
Selvaggio Orna & Strl Stl Inc	E	217 528-4077
Springfield (G-19441)		
Senior Operations LLC	B	630 372-3500
Bartlett (G-1311)		
Shamrock Manufacturing Co Inc	G	708 331-7776
South Holland (G-19244)		
Sheet Metal Supply Ltd	G	847 478-8500
Grayslake (G-10799)		
Shew Brothers Inc	G	618 997-4414
Marion (G-13534)		
Silver Machine Shop Inc	G	217 359-5717
Champaign (G-3348)		
Simion Fabrication Inc	G	618 724-7331
Christopher (G-6826)		
Sivco Welding Company	G	309 944-5171
Geneseo (G-10247)		
Skyjack Equipment Inc	E	630 797-3299
Saint Charles (G-18270)		
Smf Inc	C	309 432-2586
Minonk (G-14055)		
Smith Brothers Fabricating	G	618 498-5612
Jerseyville (G-11796)		
South Subn Wldg & Fabg Co Inc	G	708 385-7160
Posen (G-16801)		
Spectracrafts Ltd	G	847 824-4117
Lombard (G-13133)		
Spg International LLC	F	815 233-0022
Freeport (G-10143)		
Spider Company Inc	D	815 961-8200
Rockford (G-17640)		
Stairs and Rails Inc	G	708 216-0078
Melrose Park (G-13916)		
Standard Sheet Metal Works Inc	E	309 633-2300
Peoria (G-16530)		
Steel Construction Svcs Inc	G	815 678-7509
Richmond (G-17023)		
Steel Management Inc	G	630 397-5083
Geneva (G-10308)		
Stevenson Fabrication Svcs Inc	G	815 468-7941
Manteno (G-13458)		
Strat-O-Span Buildings Inc	G	618 526-4566
Breese (G-2308)		
Structural Design Corp	G	847 816-3816
Libertyville (G-12710)		
Sturdee Metal Products Inc	G	773 523-3074
New Lenox (G-15059)		
Sturdi Iron Inc	G	815 464-1173
Frankfort (G-9840)		
Summit Metal Products Inc	G	630 879-7008
Batavia (G-1421)		

Employee Codes: A=Over 500 employees, B=251-500
C=101-250, D=51-100, E=20-50, F=10-19, G=3-9

STEEL FABRICATORS

Sundstrom Pressed Steel Co................E 773 721-2237
  Chicago (G-6273)
Superior Joining Tech Inc....................E 815 282-7581
  Machesney Park (G-13376)
Superior Metalcraft Inc.........................F 708 418-8940
  Lansing (G-12520)
Sycamore Welding & Fabg Co.............G 815 784-2557
  Genoa (G-10325)
Taylor Off Road Racing........................G 815 544-4500
  Belvidere (G-1703)
Testa Steel Constructors Inc...............F 815 729-4777
  Channahon (G-3395)
Tgm Fabricating Inc.............................G 708 533-0857
  Chicago Heights (G-6780)
Tinsley Steel Inc...................................G 618 656-5231
  Edwardsville (G-8378)
Titan Industries Inc..............................G 309 440-1010
  Deer Creek (G-7576)
Tower Works Inc...................................F 630 557-2221
  Maple Park (G-13467)
Transco Inc...C 419 562-1031
  Chicago (G-6408)
Tri-Cunty Wldg Fabrication LLC..........E 217 543-3304
  Arthur (G-881)
Triton Industries Inc............................C 773 384-3700
  Chicago (G-6430)
Ultra Stamping & Assembly Inc..........E 815 874-9888
  Rockford (G-17670)
Unistrut International Corp.................C 800 882-5543
  Harvey (G-11099)
Unistrut International Corp.................D 630 773-3460
  Addison (G-323)
United Industries Illinois Ltd..............G 847 526-9485
  Wauconda (G-20400)
United Steel Perforating/ARC............F 630 942-7300
  Glendale Heights (G-10513)
United Tactical Systems LLC..............E 260 478-2500
  Lake Forest (G-12320)
US Fabg & Mine Svcs Inc....................G 618 983-7850
  Johnston City (G-11815)
V A Robinson Ltd..................................E 773 205-4364
  Chicago (G-6513)
Valmont Industries Inc........................D 773 625-0354
  Franklin Park (G-10073)
Van Pelt Corporation............................E 313 365-3600
  East Moline (G-8246)
Vent Products Co Inc...........................E 773 521-1900
  Chicago (G-6532)
Voges Inc...D 618 233-2760
  Belleville (G-1608)
Walters Metal Fabrication Inc............D 618 931-5551
  Granite City (G-10749)
Waukegan Steel LLC............................E 847 662-2810
  Waukegan (G-20516)
Wehrli Custom Fabrication..................F 630 277-8239
  Dekalb (G-7711)
Weld-Rite Service Inc..........................E 708 458-6000
  Bedford Park (G-1512)
Westmont Metal Mfg LLC....................F 708 343-0214
  Broadview (G-2474)
Wherry Machine & Welding Inc..........G 309 828-5423
  Bloomington (G-2107)
Whiting Corporation.............................C 800 861-5744
  Monee (G-14212)
Willow Farm Products Inc..................G 630 430-7491
  Lemont (G-12595)
Wilmouth Machine Works Inc.............F 618 372-3189
  Brighton (G-2405)
Wrt Inc..G 847 922-2235
  South Elgin (G-19183)
Wsw Industrial Maintenance..............F 773 721-0675
  Chicago (G-6689)
Youngberg Industries Inc...................D 815 544-2177
  Belvidere (G-1713)

STEEL MILLS

A & A Steel Fabricating Co..................F 708 389-4499
  Posen (G-16789)
AK Steel Corporation............................B 815 267-3838
  Plainfield (G-16640)
Aldon Co...F 847 623-8800
  Waukegan (G-20412)
Arcelormittal Intl Amer LLC.................B 312 899-3400
  Chicago (G-3719)
Arcelormittal USA Inc..........................G 312 899-3500
  Chicago (G-3721)
Arcelormittal USA LLC.........................B 312 346-0300
  Chicago (G-3723)
Archer Metal & Paper Co.....................F 773 585-3030
  Chicago (G-3726)
Arntzen Corporation.............................E 815 334-0788
  Woodstock (G-21360)
Bar Processing Corporation................E 708 757-4570
  Chicago Heights (G-6733)
Cambridge Pattern Works...................G 309 937-5370
  Cambridge (G-2803)
Chicago Metal Fabricators Inc............D 773 523-5755
  Chicago (G-4114)
Chicago Pipe Bending & Coil Co........F 773 379-1918
  Chicago (G-4122)
Chromium Industries Inc....................E 773 287-3716
  Chicago (G-4145)
Combined Metals Holding Inc............C 708 547-8800
  Bellwood (G-1619)
Commercial Metals Company.............G 815 928-9600
  Kankakee (G-11961)
Consolidated Mill Supply Inc..............G 847 706-6715
  Palatine (G-16104)
Covey Machine Inc..............................F 773 650-1530
  Chicago (G-4250)
D R Sperry & Co...................................D 630 892-4361
  Aurora (G-1083)
Feralloy Corporation............................E 503 286-8869
  Chicago (G-4580)
Fox Valley Iron & Metal Corp..............F 630 897-5907
  Aurora (G-1098)
Heidtman Steel Products Inc.............D 618 451-0052
  Granite City (G-10714)
Illinois Weld & Machine Inc................F 309 565-0533
  Hanna City (G-10992)
Industrial Pipe and Supply Co............E 708 652-7511
  Chicago (G-4909)
Jacobs Boiler & Mech Inds Inc...........E 773 385-9900
  Chicago (G-4998)
Jamco Products Inc............................D 815 624-0400
  South Beloit (G-19097)
John Maneely Company.......................C 773 254-0617
  Chicago (G-5043)
Lawndale Forging & Tool Works.........G 773 277-2800
  Chicago (G-5183)
Lexington Steel Corporation...............D 708 594-9200
  Bedford Park (G-1480)
Mc Chemical Company........................E 815 964-7687
  Rockford (G-17511)
Middletown Coke Company LLC.........G 630 284-1755
  Lisle (G-12910)
Multiplex Industries Inc......................G 630 906-9780
  Montgomery (G-14263)
Nacme Steel Processing LLC.............G 847 806-7226
  Elk Grove Village (G-9142)
Nacme Steel Processing LLC.............D 847 806-7200
  Chicago (G-5535)
National Material Processing.............G 773 646-6300
  Chicago (G-5548)
Nelsen Steel and Wire LP...................D 847 671-9700
  Franklin Park (G-10007)
New C F & I Inc....................................A 312 533-3555
  Chicago (G-5574)
Nucor Corporation................................G 630 887-1400
  Hinsdale (G-11371)
Nucor Steel Kankakee Inc..................B 815 937-3131
  Bourbonnais (G-2266)
Olympic Steel Inc.................................E 847 584-4000
  Schaumburg (G-18658)
P B A Corp...F 312 666-7370
  Chicago (G-5728)
Penn Aluminum Intl LLC......................C 618 684-2146
  Murphysboro (G-14756)
Production Cutting Services..............D 815 264-3505
  Waterman (G-20300)
Rain Cii Carbon LLC.............................E 618 544-2193
  Robinson (G-17124)
Shapiro Bros of Illinois Inc.................E 618 244-3168
  Mount Vernon (G-14638)
Ssab Texas Inc....................................G 630 810-4800
  Lisle (G-12942)
St Louis Scrap Trading LLC................G 618 307-9002
  Edwardsville (G-8376)
Steel Whse Quad Cities LLC..............G 309 756-1089
  Rock Island (G-17247)
Stein Inc..D 618 452-0836
  Granite City (G-10739)
Sun Coke International Inc.................G 630 824-1000
  Lisle (G-12944)
Suncoke Energy Inc.............................G 630 824-1000
  Lisle (G-12945)
Suncoke Technology and Dev LLC.....G 630 824-1000
  Lisle (G-12947)
Tdy Industries LLC...............................D 847 564-0700
  Northbrook (G-15492)

PRODUCT SECTION

Titan International Inc........................C 217 228-6011
  Quincy (G-16948)
Tms International LLC........................G 815 939-1178
  Bourbonnais (G-2270)
Tms International LLC........................G 618 451-9526
  Granite City (G-10743)
Tomko Machine Works Inc..................G 630 244-0902
  Lemont (G-12593)
United States Steel Corp....................D 618 451-3456
  Granite City (G-10748)
Venus Processing & Storage..............G 847 455-0496
  Franklin Park (G-10077)
Voestalpine Nortrak Inc......................G 708 753-2125
  Chicago Heights (G-6786)
Westwood Lands Inc............................G 618 877-4990
  Madison (G-13419)

STEEL SHEET: Cold-Rolled

New Process Steel LP..........................D 708 389-3380
  Alsip (G-484)

STEEL WOOL

Global Material Tech Inc.....................C 847 495-4700
  Buffalo Grove (G-2542)
Superior Joining Tech Inc...................E 815 282-7581
  Machesney Park (G-13376)

STEEL, COLD-ROLLED: Flat Bright, From Purchased Hot-Rolled

Arcelormittal Riverdale LLC................B 708 849-8803
  Riverdale (G-17067)

STEEL, COLD-ROLLED: Strip NEC, From Purchased Hot-Rolled

Sandvik Inc...D 847 519-1737
  Schaumburg (G-18703)

STEEL, HOT-ROLLED: Sheet Or Strip

National Material LP............................E 773 646-6300
  Chicago (G-5547)
Revere Metals LLC...............................G 708 995-6131
  Mokena (G-14112)

STEEL: Cold-Rolled

Arcelormittal Hennepin LLC................C 815 925-2311
  Hennepin (G-11156)
Arcelormittal USA LLC.........................B 312 346-0300
  Chicago (G-3723)
Bonell Manufacturing Company..........E 708 849-1770
  Riverdale (G-17069)
Chase Fasteners Inc...........................E 708 345-0335
  Melrose Park (G-13841)
Combined Metals Chicago LLC...........F 847 683-0500
  Hampshire (G-10967)
Design Manufacturing & Eqp Co........F 217 824-9219
  Taylorville (G-19755)
Expandable Habitats............................. ...... 815 624-6784
  Rockton (G-17697)
Gartech Manufacturing Co..................E 217 324-6527
  Litchfield (G-12963)
Geocyn Company Inc..........................E 331 213-2851
  Naperville (G-14835)
Harris Steel Company.........................D 708 656-5500
  Cicero (G-6851)
Lapham-Hickey Steel Corp.................C 708 496-6111
  Bedford Park (G-1479)
Madison Inds Holdings LLC................G 312 277-0156
  Chicago (G-5313)
Mid-State Industries Oper Inc............E 217 268-3900
  Arcola (G-656)
Multiplex Industries Inc......................G 630 906-9780
  Montgomery (G-14263)
Multitech Industries............................G 815 206-0015
  Woodstock (G-21415)
Phillip C Cowen...................................E 630 208-1848
  Geneva (G-10299)
Ptc Group Holdings Corp....................D 708 757-4747
  Chicago Heights (G-6766)
Rockford Secondary Co.......................G 815 398-0401
  Rockford (G-17605)
Screws Industries Inc.........................G 630 539-9200
  Glendale Heights (G-10493)
Skach Manufacturing Co Inc..............E 847 395-3560
  Antioch (G-635)
Soudan Metals Company Inc..............C 773 548-7600
  Chicago (G-6204)

Tempel Holdings Inc .... A 773 250-8000
 Chicago *(G-6343)*

STEEL: Laminated

Filter Technology Inc .... E 773 523-7200
 Bedford Park *(G-1467)*
Lamination Specialties LLC .... G 773 254-7500
 Chicago *(G-5170)*
Lamination Specialties LLC .... E 312 243-2181
 Oak Brook *(G-15631)*
MSC Pre Finish Metals Egv Inc .... C 847 439-2210
 Elk Grove Village *(G-9137)*
Polaris Laser Laminations LLC .... E 630 444-0760
 West Chicago *(G-20630)*

STEERING SYSTEMS & COMPONENTS

Tuxco Corporation .... F 847 244-2220
 Gurnee *(G-10940)*
United Carburetor Inc .... E 773 777-1223
 Schiller Park *(G-18849)*
United Remanufacturing Co Inc .... E 773 777-1223
 Schiller Park *(G-18850)*

STENCILS

ABM Marking Services Ltd .... G 618 277-3773
 Belleville *(G-1527)*
C H Hanson Company .... D 630 848-2000
 Naperville *(G-14786)*
Chicago Silk Screen Sup Co Inc .... E 312 666-1213
 Chicago *(G-4129)*
Custom Cut Stencil Company Inc .... G 618 277-5077
 Belleville *(G-1542)*
U Mark Inc .... E 618 235-7500
 Belleville *(G-1604)*

STENCILS & LETTERING MATERIALS: Die-Cut

Sign Centre .... G 847 595-7300
 Elk Grove Village *(G-9239)*

STEREOGRAPHS: Photographic Message Svcs

Sport Electronics Inc .... G 847 564-5575
 Northbrook *(G-15485)*

STOCK CAR RACING

Bill West Enterprises Inc .... G 217 886-2591
 Jacksonville *(G-11757)*

STONE: Cast Concrete

Eagle Stone and Brick Inc .... G 618 282-6722
 Red Bud *(G-16993)*
Stone Installation & Maint Inc .... G 630 545-2326
 Glendale Heights *(G-10503)*

STONE: Dimension, NEC

Columbia Quarry Company .... E 618 281-7631
 Columbia *(G-6987)*
Gary Galassi and Sons Inc .... E 815 886-3906
 Romeoville *(G-17827)*
Ill Dept Natural Resources .... F 217 782-4970
 Springfield *(G-19384)*
Stolle Casper Quar & Contg Co .... E 618 337-5212
 Dupo *(G-8146)*
Tri-State Cut Stone Co .... E 815 469-7550
 Frankfort *(G-9845)*
Wendell Adams .... E 217 345-9587
 Charleston *(G-3416)*

STONE: Quarrying & Processing, Own Stone Prdts

Brombereks Flagstone Co Inc .... G 630 257-0686
 Lemont *(G-12557)*
Material Service Corporation .... E 847 658-4559
 Algonquin *(G-380)*
Material Service Corporation .... E 708 447-1100
 Westchester *(G-20704)*

STONES: Abrasive

Rock Solid Imports LLC .... G 331 472-4522
 Naperville *(G-14910)*

STONEWARE PRDTS: Pottery

Ws Incorporated of Manmouth .... F 309 734-2161
 Monmouth *(G-14228)*

STOOLS: Factory

Sport Incentives Inc .... F 847 427-8650
 Elk Grove Village *(G-9250)*

STORE FIXTURES, EXC REFRIGERATED: Wholesalers

Daniel M Powers & Assoc Ltd .... D 630 685-8400
 Bolingbrook *(G-2166)*

STORE FIXTURES: Exc Wood

Marmon Retail Technologies Co .... F 312 332-0317
 Chicago *(G-5346)*
Tesko Welding & Mfg Co .... D 708 452-0045
 Norridge *(G-15244)*

STORE FIXTURES: Wood

Ability Cabinet Co Inc .... G 847 678-6678
 Franklin Park *(G-9859)*
Bernhard Woodwork Ltd .... D 847 291-1040
 Northbrook *(G-15348)*
Castle Craft Products Inc .... F 630 279-7494
 Villa Park *(G-20138)*
Daniel M Powers & Assoc Ltd .... D 630 685-8400
 Bolingbrook *(G-2166)*
Dunhill Corp .... F 815 806-8600
 Frankfort *(G-9788)*
Imperial Woodworking Company .... D 847 221-2107
 Palatine *(G-16127)*
Marmon Retail Technologies Co .... F 312 332-0317
 Chicago *(G-5346)*
Olsen Woodwork Co .... G 847 865-5054
 Island Lake *(G-11610)*
Schrock Custom Woodworking .... G 217 849-3375
 Toledo *(G-19877)*

STORES: Auto & Home Supply

Arco Automotive Elec Svc Co .... G 708 422-2976
 Oak Lawn *(G-15701)*
Coating Specialty Inc .... G 708 754-3311
 S Chicago Hts *(G-18118)*
Entrans International LLC .... E 618 548-3660
 Salem *(G-18337)*
Galva Iron and Metal Co Inc .... G 309 932-3450
 Galva *(G-10232)*
Mag Daddy LLC .... G 847 719-5600
 Wauconda *(G-20371)*
Murphy USA Inc .... G 815 356-7633
 Crystal Lake *(G-7235)*
Smart Systems Inc .... E 630 343-3333
 Bolingbrook *(G-2242)*
Stop & Go International Inc .... G 815 455-9080
 Crystal Lake *(G-7269)*
T G Automotive .... E 630 916-7818
 Lombard *(G-13137)*
Xylem Water Solutions USA Inc .... F 856 467-3636
 Mokena *(G-14129)*

STORES: Drapery & Upholstery

F & L Drapery Inc .... G 815 932-8997
 Saint Anne *(G-18134)*
Loomcraft Textile & Supply Co .... E 847 680-0000
 Vernon Hills *(G-20073)*

STRADDLE CARRIERS: Mobile

Blue Nile Trucking LLC .... G 618 215-1077
 East Saint Louis *(G-8300)*

STRAINERS: Line, Piping Systems

Flexicraft Industries Inc .... F 312 428-4750
 Chicago *(G-4608)*
Key West Metal Industries Inc .... C 708 371-1470
 Crestwood *(G-7121)*
Spirax Sarco Inc .... F 630 493-4525
 Lisle *(G-12940)*

STRAPPING

Illinois Tool Works Inc .... C 708 458-7320
 Bridgeview *(G-2357)*
Illinois Tool Works Inc .... E 847 215-8925
 Buffalo Grove *(G-2548)*
Illinois Tool Works Inc .... B 847 724-7500
 Glenview *(G-10560)*
Illinois Tool Works Inc .... C 630 372-2150
 Bartlett *(G-1288)*
Illinois Tool Works Inc .... C 847 783-5500
 Elgin *(G-8621)*
McLean Manufacturing Company .... G 847 277-9912
 Lake Barrington *(G-12160)*
Samuel Son & Co (usa) Inc .... D 630 783-8900
 Woodridge *(G-21338)*

STRAPS: Apparel Webbing

Phoenix Graphix .... G 618 531-3664
 Pinckneyville *(G-16618)*

STRAW GOODS

Mat Capital LLC .... G 847 821-9630
 Long Grove *(G-13163)*

STRAWS: Drinking, Made From Purchased Materials

Best Diamond Plastics LLC .... F 773 336-3485
 Chicago *(G-3871)*

STRINGING BEADS

State Street Jewelers Inc .... F 630 232-2085
 Geneva *(G-10307)*

STRUCTURAL SUPPORT & BUILDING MATERIAL: Concrete

Aimee M Ford .... G 630 308-9785
 Aurora *(G-1044)*
Kingspan Light & Air LLC .... G 847 816-1060
 Lake Forest *(G-12268)*
Royal Corinthian Inc .... E 630 876-8899
 West Chicago *(G-20639)*

STUDIOS: Artist

Circle Studio Stained Glass .... G 773 588-4848
 Chicago *(G-4152)*

STUDIOS: Artists & Artists' Studios

Chase Group LLC .... F 847 564-2000
 Northbrook *(G-15355)*

STUDIOS: Sculptor's

Rebechini Studio Inc .... F 847 437-9030
 Elk Grove Village *(G-9215)*

STUDS & JOISTS: Sheet Metal

Expanded Metal Products Corp .... F 773 735-4500
 Chicago *(G-4544)*

STYLING SVCS: Wigs

Hairline Creations Inc .... F 773 282-5454
 Chicago *(G-4769)*

STYRENE RESINS, NEC

BP Amoco Chemical Company .... B 630 420-5111
 Naperville *(G-14782)*

SUBPRESSES, METALWORKING

Flores Precision Products .... G 630 264-2222
 Aurora *(G-1096)*

SUGAR SUBSTITUTES: Organic

Merisant Foreign Holdings I .... F 312 840-6000
 Chicago *(G-5397)*
Merisant Us Inc .... B 312 840-6000
 Chicago *(G-5398)*
Merisant Us Inc .... C 815 929-2700
 Chicago *(G-5399)*
Necta Sweet Inc .... E 847 215-9955
 Buffalo Grove *(G-2579)*
Purecircle USA Inc .... E 866 960-8242
 Oak Brook *(G-15657)*

SUNDRIES & RELATED PRDTS: Medical & Laboratory, Rubber

Fenwal Inc .... B 800 333-6925
  Lake Zurich (G-12411)
Safersonic Us Inc .... G 847 274-1534
  Highland Park (G-11296)
Shepard Medical Products Inc .... G 630 539-7790
  Roselle (G-17988)
Shore Capital Partners LLC .... E 312 348-7580
  Chicago (G-6157)
Superior Bumpers Inc .... G 630 932-4910
  Lombard (G-13136)

SUNGLASSES, WHOLESALE

Jim Maui Inc .... G 888 666-5905
  Peoria (G-16462)

SUNROOMS: Prefabricated Metal

Illinois Green Cnstr Inc .... F 847 975-2312
  Chicago (G-4891)

SUPERMARKETS & OTHER GROCERY STORES

Clown Global Brands LLC .... G 847 564-5950
  Northbrook (G-15362)
Elburn Market Inc .... E 630 365-6461
  Elburn (G-8451)
Hartrich Meats Inc .... G 618 455-3172
  Sainte Marie (G-18326)
Lewis Brothers Bakeries Inc .... E 708 531-6435
  Melrose Park (G-13890)
McCain Usa Inc .... C 800 938-7799
  Oakbrook Terrace (G-15809)

SURFACE ACTIVE AGENTS

Aerosols Danville Inc .... B 217 442-1400
  Danville (G-7318)
Avatar Corporation .... D 708 534-5511
  University Park (G-19947)
Cedar Concepts Corporation .... E 773 890-5790
  Chicago (G-4050)
Custom Blending & Pckaging of .... F 618 286-1140
  Dupo (G-8135)
Solvay USA Inc .... E 708 371-2000
  Blue Island (G-2141)
Sun Ag Inc .... G 815 689-2144
  Cullom (G-7302)
Union Drainage District .... G 618 445-2843
  Mount Erie (G-14498)
Vantage Specialties Inc .... F 773 579-5842
  Gurnee (G-10942)
Vantage Specialties Inc .... G 847 244-3410
  Chicago (G-6523)

SURFACE ACTIVE AGENTS: Emulsifiers, Exc Food & Pharmaceuticl

Ivanhoe Industries Inc .... E 847 872-3311
  Mundelein (G-14702)

SURFACE ACTIVE AGENTS: Oils & Greases

Griffin Industries LLC .... G 815 357-8200
  Seneca (G-18858)

SURFACE ACTIVE AGENTS: Processing Assistants

Houghton International Inc .... F 610 666-4000
  Chicago (G-4849)

SURGICAL & MEDICAL INSTRUMENTS WHOLESALERS

Avalign Technologies Inc .... D 855 282-5446
  Bannockburn (G-1189)
Hearing Screening Assoc LLC .... G 855 550-9427
  Arlington Heights (G-747)
Landauer Inc .... C 708 755-7000
  Glenwood (G-10642)
Mc Squared Group Inc .... G 815 322-2485
  Spring Grove (G-19283)
Medline Industries Inc .... A 847 949-5500
  Northfield (G-15523)
Sysmex America Inc .... C 847 996-4500
  Lincolnshire (G-12797)

SURGICAL APPLIANCES & SPLYS

20 20 Medical Systems Inc .... G 815 455-7161
  Crystal Lake (G-7152)
Baxalta Export Corporation .... C 224 948-2000
  Bannockburn (G-1193)
Baxalta World Trade LLC .... G 224 940-2000
  Bannockburn (G-1195)
Baxalta Worldwide LLC .... C 224 948-2000
  Deerfield (G-7590)
Baxter Healthcare Corporation .... E 847 578-4671
  Waukegan (G-20422)
Baxter International Inc .... A 224 948-2000
  Deerfield (G-7595)
Cast21 Inc .... G 847 772-8547
  Chicago (G-4036)
Lsl Industries Inc .... D 773 878-1100
  Nifes (G-15141)
MAC Medical Inc .... C 618 476-3550
  Millstadt (G-14051)
Sage Products LLC .... C 815 455-4700
  Cary (G-3188)
Sage Products Holdings II LLC .... G 800 323-2220
  Cary (G-3189)
Surgical Instrument Service Co .... F 630 221-1988
  Glendale Heights (G-10506)
Teleflex Incorporated .... D 847 259-7400
  Arlington Heights (G-818)
Tetra Medical Supply Corp .... F 847 647-0590
  Niles (G-15179)

SURGICAL APPLIANCES & SPLYS

1 Federal Supply Source Inc .... G 708 964-2222
  Steger (G-19486)
Advanced Bionics LLC .... G 708 946-3406
  Warrenville (G-20229)
Argentum Medical LLC .... E 888 551-0188
  Geneva (G-10253)
Artistic Dental Studio Inc .... E 630 679-8686
  Bolingbrook (G-2149)
Bionic Chicago .... G 773 698-6269
  Chicago (G-3897)
C & S Chemicals Inc .... G 815 722-6671
  Joliet (G-11837)
C R Kesner Company .... G 630 232-8118
  Geneva (G-10258)
Cape Prosthetics-Orthotics Inc .... G 618 457-4692
  Marion (G-13507)
Dabir Surfaces Inc .... F 708 867-6777
  Harwood Heights (G-11103)
Dean Prsthtic Orthtic Svcs Ltd .... G 847 475-7080
  Evanston (G-9508)
Deborah Morris Gulbrandson Pt .... F 847 639-4140
  Cary (G-3154)
Dura-Crafts Corp .... F 815 464-3561
  Frankfort (G-9789)
East West Martial Arts Sups .... G 773 878-7711
  Chicago (G-4434)
Ecomed Solutions LLC .... E 866 817-7114
  Mundelein (G-14685)
Elginex Corporation .... G 815 786-8406
  Sandwich (G-18368)
Elmed Incorporated .... E 224 353-6446
  Glendale Heights (G-10448)
Firm of John Dickinson .... D 847 680-1000
  Libertyville (G-12652)
Hanger Prosthetics & .... G 217 429-6656
  Decatur (G-7499)
Hanger Prosthetics & .... G 630 986-0007
  Burr Ridge (G-2680)
Hanger Prosthetics & .... G 630 986-0007
  Burr Ridge (G-2681)
Hanger Prsthetcs & Ortho Inc .... G 309 585-2349
  Normal (G-15204)
Hanger Prsthetcs & Ortho Inc .... G 217 429-6656
  Decatur (G-7500)
Hanger Prsthtics Orthotics Inc .... G 309 637-6581
  Peoria (G-16451)
Hanger Prsthtics Orthtics E In .... G 618 997-1451
  Herrin (G-11172)
Hollister Incorporated .... B 847 680-1000
  Libertyville (G-12660)
Honeywell Safety Pdts USA Inc .... C 630 343-3731
  Bolingbrook (G-2185)
Kinsman Enterprises Inc .... G 618 932-3838
  West Frankfort (G-20674)
Lester L Brossard Co .... F 815 338-7825
  Woodstock (G-21405)
Logan Actuator Co .... G 815 943-9500
  Harvard (G-11059)
M2m Enterprises LLC .... G 847 899-7565
  Elgin (G-8644)
Magid Glove Safety Mfg Co LLC .... B 773 384-2070
  Romeoville (G-17844)
Manan Medical Products Inc .... D 847 637-3333
  Wheeling (G-20936)
Mandis Dental Laboratory .... G 618 345-3777
  Collinsville (G-6968)
Medbot Inc .... G 213 200-6658
  Chicago (G-5381)
Medline Industries Inc .... G 847 949-5500
  Waukegan (G-20466)
Merry Walker Corporation .... G 847 837-9580
  Mundelein (G-14716)
Microguide Inc .... G 630 964-3335
  Downers Grove (G-8054)
Mio Med Orthopedics Inc .... G 773 477-8991
  Chicago (G-5466)
Opportunity Inc .... D 847 831-9400
  Highland Park (G-11290)
PR Orthotics & Ot .... G 224 470-8550
  Skokie (G-19008)
Pres-On Corporation .... E 630 628-2255
  Bolingbrook (G-2229)
Punch Products Manufacturing .... G 773 533-2800
  Chicago (G-5915)
Quincy Lab Inc .... E 773 622-2428
  Chicago (G-5938)
Respironics Inc .... C 708 923-6200
  Palos Park (G-16213)
Robert B Scott Ocularists Ltd .... E 312 782-3558
  Chicago (G-6042)
Rti Surgical Holdings Inc .... F 386 418-8888
  Deerfield (G-7647)
Scheck Siress Prosthetics Inc .... G 312 757-5270
  Chicago (G-6111)
Steris Corporation .... F 847 455-2881
  Franklin Park (G-10052)
Trigon International LLC .... D 630 978-9990
  Aurora (G-1027)
Welkins LLC .... G 877 319-3504
  Downers Grove (G-8108)
Wheaton Resource Corp .... G 630 690-5795
  Carol Stream (G-3088)
Whitney Products Inc .... F 847 966-6161
  Niles (G-15187)
Williams Halthcare Systems LLC .... D 847 741-3650
  Elgin (G-8782)

SURGICAL EQPT: See Also Instruments

3M Company .... B 309 654-2291
  Cordova (G-7005)
Advanced Microderm Inc .... E 630 980-3300
  Schaumburg (G-18428)
Anchor Products Company .... E 630 543-9124
  Addison (G-35)
Aplicare Products LLC .... G 847 949-5500
  Northfield (G-15506)
Eldest Daughter LLC .... G 949 677-7385
  Chicago (G-4476)
Endofix Ltd .... G 708 715-3472
  Brookfield (G-2482)
Medifix Inc .... G 847 965-1898
  Morton Grove (G-14427)
Stryker Corporation .... G 630 616-0606
  Wood Dale (G-21244)
Stryker Corporation .... G 847 829-5238
  Cary (G-3192)
Stryker Corporation .... B 312 386-9780
  Chicago (G-6256)
Uresil LLC .... E 847 982-0200
  Skokie (G-19050)
Viant Wheeling Inc .... G 847 520-1553
  Wheeling (G-21009)

SURGICAL IMPLANTS

Blue Sky Bio LLC .... F 718 376-0422
  Libertyville (G-12638)

SURVEYING & MAPPING: Land Parcels

Locusview Solutions Inc .... E 312 548-3848
  Chicago (G-5248)
McLean Subsurface Utility .... G 336 988-2520
  Decatur (G-7521)

SURVEYING INSTRUMENTS WHOLESALERS

Measurement Devices US LLC .... F 281 646-0050
  Dundee (G-8129)

SUSPENSION SYSTEMS: Acoustical, Metal

M & D Industries Inc .... E 847 362-8720
  Libertyville *(G-12671)*
Roxul USA Inc .... A 800 323-7164
  Chicago *(G-6068)*

SVC ESTABLISH EQPT, WHOL: Extermination/Fumigatn Eqpt/Splys

Bird-X Inc .... E 312 226-2473
  Elmhurst *(G-9334)*

SVC ESTABLISHMENT EQPT & SPLYS WHOLESALERS

Wet International Inc .... E 630 540-2113
  Streamwood *(G-19602)*

SVC ESTABLISHMENT EQPT, WHOL: Cleaning & Maint Eqpt & Splys

Imagination Products Corp .... E 309 274-6223
  Chillicothe *(G-6818)*
Lindemann Chimney Service Inc .... F 847 918-7994
  Lake Bluff *(G-12193)*
O Brien Bill .... G 630 980-5571
  Geneva *(G-10294)*
Umf Corporation .... G 224 251-7822
  Niles *(G-15184)*
Warehouse Direct Inc .... C 847 952-1925
  Des Plaines *(G-7867)*

SVC ESTABLISHMENT EQPT, WHOL: Concrete Burial Vaults & Boxes

Southern Ill Wilbert Vlt Co .... F 618 942-5845
  Herrin *(G-11180)*
Wilbert Quincy Vault Co .... G 217 224-8557
  Quincy *(G-16956)*

SVC ESTABLISHMENT EQPT, WHOL: Liquor Dispensing Eqpt/Sys

Don Johns Inc .... E 630 454-4700
  Batavia *(G-1374)*

SVC ESTABLISHMENT EQPT, WHOLESALE: Beauty Parlor Eqpt & Sply

Elia Day Spa .... F 708 535-1450
  Oak Forest *(G-15676)*
Lasner Bros Inc .... G 773 935-7383
  Chicago *(G-5178)*
Pivot Point Usa Inc .... C 800 886-4247
  Chicago *(G-5814)*
Skyline Beauty Supply Inc .... F 773 275-6003
  Franklin Park *(G-10047)*

SVC ESTABLISHMENT EQPT, WHOLESALE: Cemetery Splys & Eqpt

Kowalski Memorials Inc .... G 630 462-7226
  Carol Stream *(G-3014)*

SVC ESTABLISHMENT EQPT, WHOLESALE: Engraving Eqpt & Splys

Ambrit Inc .... G 847 593-3301
  Elk Grove Village *(G-8820)*
Finer Line Inc .... F 847 884-1611
  Itasca *(G-11657)*
Motherboard Gifts & More LLC .... G 847 550-2222
  Lake Zurich *(G-12436)*
Your Supply Depot Limited .... G 815 568-4115
  Marengo *(G-13497)*

SVC ESTABLISHMENT EQPT, WHOLESALE: Firefighting Eqpt

Flame Guard Usa LLC .... G 815 219-4074
  Vernon Hills *(G-20054)*
Vertex International Inc .... G 312 242-1864
  Oak Brook *(G-15669)*

SVC ESTABLISHMENT EQPT, WHOLESALE: Laundry Eqpt & Splys

Chicago Dryer Company .... C 773 235-4430
  Chicago *(G-4101)*

Storms Industries Inc .... E 312 243-7480
  Chicago *(G-6251)*

SVC ESTABLISHMENT EQPT, WHOLESALE: Locksmith Eqpt & Splys

Hoffman J&M Farm Holdings Inc .... D 847 671-6280
  Schiller Park *(G-18813)*

SVC ESTABLISHMENT EQPT, WHOLESALE: Restaurant Splys

American Metalcraft Inc .... D 800 333-9133
  Franklin Park *(G-9866)*
Grant Park Packing Company Inc .... E 312 421-4096
  Franklin Park *(G-9952)*

SVC ESTABLISHMENT EQPT, WHOLESALE: Taxidermist Tools & Eqpt

Research Mannikins Inc .... F 618 426-3456
  Ava *(G-1177)*
Walnut Creek Hardwood .... G 815 389-3317
  South Beloit *(G-19120)*

SVC ESTABLISHMENT EQPT, WHOLESALE: Voting Machines

Election Works .... G 630 232-4030
  Geneva *(G-10268)*

SWEEPING COMPOUNDS

Frank Miller & Sons Inc .... E 708 201-7200
  Mokena *(G-14083)*
Jaffee Investment Partnr LP .... C 312 321-1515
  Chicago *(G-4999)*
Oil-Dri Corporation America .... D 312 321-1515
  Chicago *(G-5666)*

SWIMMING POOL & HOT TUB CLEANING & MAINTENANCE SVCS

Petersburg Power Washing Inc .... F 217 415-9013
  Springfield *(G-19425)*
Pool Center Inc .... G 217 698-7665
  Springfield *(G-19426)*
Savino Enterprises .... G 708 385-5277
  Blue Island *(G-2138)*

SWIMMING POOL SPLY STORES

Newby Oil Company Inc .... G 815 756-7688
  Sycamore *(G-19725)*
Sentry Pool & Chemical Supply .... E 309 797-9721
  Moline *(G-14177)*

SWIMMING POOLS, EQPT & SPLYS: Wholesalers

Adolph Kiefer & Associates LLC .... D 309 451-5858
  Bloomington *(G-2021)*
Evergreen Pool & Spa LLC .... G 618 247-3555
  Sandoval *(G-18363)*
Newby Oil Company Inc .... G 815 756-7688
  Sycamore *(G-19725)*

SWITCHBOARD OPERATIONS: Private Branch Exchanges

Chicago Tribune Company LLC .... A 312 222-3232
  Chicago *(G-4134)*

SWITCHBOARDS & PARTS: Power

Chicago Switchboard Co Inc .... E 630 833-2266
  Elmhurst *(G-9345)*
Gus Berthold Electric Company .... D 312 243-5767
  Chicago *(G-4752)*
Illinois Switchboard Corp .... F 630 543-0910
  Addison *(G-154)*
Peterson Elc Panl Mfg Co Inc .... F 708 449-2270
  Berkeley *(G-1943)*
Power Distribution Eqp Co Inc .... E 847 455-2500
  Franklin Park *(G-10021)*
SAI Advanced Pwr Solutions Inc .... D 708 450-0990
  Franklin Park *(G-10041)*

SWITCHES

Bright Image Corporation .... D 708 449-5656
  Broadview *(G-2423)*

Chicago Freight Car Leasing Co .... D 847 318-8000
  Schaumburg *(G-18475)*
Emerge Technology Group LLC .... G 224 603-2161
  Lake Villa *(G-12350)*
Grayhill Inc .... B 708 354-1040
  La Grange *(G-12077)*
Honeywell International Inc .... C 815 745-2131
  Warren *(G-20223)*

SWITCHES: Electric Power

Crane Dorray Corporation .... G 630 893-7553
  Addison *(G-83)*
Grayhill Inc .... B 708 354-1040
  La Grange *(G-12077)*
ICT Power USA Inc .... F 630 313-4941
  Saint Charles *(G-18209)*

SWITCHES: Electric Power, Exc Snap, Push Button, Etc

Calo Corporation .... E 630 879-2202
  North Aurora *(G-15256)*
Emerge Technology Group LLC .... G 224 603-2161
  Lake Villa *(G-12350)*
General Electric Company .... E 630 334-0054
  Oak Brook *(G-15624)*
Grayhill Inc .... B 708 354-1040
  La Grange *(G-12077)*
Honeywell International Inc .... D 815 235-5500
  Freeport *(G-10118)*
Recora LLC .... E 630 879-2202
  North Aurora *(G-15273)*
Texas Instruments Incorporated .... D 630 836-2827
  Warrenville *(G-20253)*

SWITCHES: Electronic

Central Rubber Company .... E 815 544-2191
  Belvidere *(G-1661)*
Chicago Technical Sales Inc .... G 630 889-7121
  Oakbrook Terrace *(G-15792)*
CTS Corporation .... C 630 577-8800
  Lisle *(G-12881)*
Grayhill Inc .... C 847 428-6990
  Carpentersville *(G-3102)*
Grayhill Inc .... B 708 354-1040
  La Grange *(G-12077)*
Illinois Tool Works Inc .... C 847 724-7500
  Des Plaines *(G-7784)*
Kraus & Naimer Inc .... G 847 298-2450
  Des Plaines *(G-7794)*
Molex LLC .... F 630 512-8787
  Downers Grove *(G-8059)*
Molex International Inc .... F 630 969-4550
  Lisle *(G-12914)*
Motec Inc .... G 630 241-9595
  Downers Grove *(G-8060)*
Peterson Elctr-Msical Pdts Inc .... E 708 388-3311
  Alsip *(G-490)*
Relay Services Mfg Corp .... F 773 252-2700
  Chicago *(G-6008)*
Skyfly Networks Inc .... G 312 429-4580
  Des Plaines *(G-7846)*
Switchcraft Inc .... B 773 792-2700
  Chicago *(G-6299)*
Switchcraft Holdco Inc .... G 773 792-2700
  Chicago *(G-6300)*
Switchee Bandz Usa LLC .... G 312 415-1100
  Highland Park *(G-11301)*
Woodhead Industries LLC .... B 847 353-2500
  Lincolnshire *(G-12802)*

SWITCHES: Electronic Applications

CTS Automotive LLC .... C 630 577-8800
  Lisle *(G-12880)*
CTS Automotive LLC .... E 815 385-9480
  McHenry *(G-13734)*
Robert Higgins .... D 217 337-0734
  Urbana *(G-19999)*

SWITCHES: Flow Actuated, Electrical

Warming Systems .... G 800 663-7831
  Lake Villa *(G-12371)*
Warner Electric LLC .... E 815 547-1106
  South Beloit *(G-19121)*

SWITCHES: Solenoid

FSI Technologies Inc .... E 630 932-9380
  Lombard *(G-13080)*

SWITCHES: Solenoid

Intersol Industries Inc..................F 630 238-0385
  Bensenville *(G-1824)*
Knowles Elec Holdings Inc..............A 630 250-5100
  Itasca *(G-11687)*
Magnet-Schultz Amer Holdg LLC ....F 630 789-0600
  Westmont *(G-20755)*
Magnet-Schultz America Inc ....D 630 789-0600
  Westmont *(G-20756)*

SWITCHES: Starting, Fluorescent

Radionic Hi-Tech Inc..................D 773 804-0100
  Chicago *(G-5960)*

SWITCHES: Stepping

Bircher America Inc..................G 847 952-3730
  Schaumburg *(G-18462)*

SWITCHES: Time, Electrical Switchgear Apparatus

Control Solutions LLC ....D 630 806-7062
  Aurora *(G-941)*
Nutherm International Inc ....E 618 244-6000
  Mount Vernon *(G-14631)*

SWITCHGEAR & SWITCHBOARD APPARATUS

Automated Systems & Control Co ......G 847 735-8310
  Lake Bluff *(G-12172)*
E N M Company........................D 773 775-8400
  Chicago *(G-4425)*
Eaton Corporation ....A 217 732-3131
  Lincoln *(G-12729)*
Elcon Inc ....E 815 467-9500
  Minooka *(G-14059)*
Elenco Electronics Inc................E 847 541-3800
  Wheeling *(G-20889)*
Emac Inc ....E 618 529-4525
  Carbondale *(G-2841)*
Enercon Engineering Inc...............D 309 694-1418
  East Peoria *(G-8267)*
Fixture Company ....G 847 214-3100
  Chicago *(G-4600)*
GE Zenith Controls Inc................G 773 299-6600
  Oakbrook Terrace *(G-15800)*
Grayhill Inc ....G 708 482-1411
  Mc Cook *(G-13691)*
Illinois Tool Works Inc...............C 847 724-7500
  Des Plaines *(G-7784)*
Inman Electric Motors Inc ....E 815 223-2288
  La Salle *(G-12115)*
Langham Engineering ....G 815 223-5250
  Peru *(G-16580)*
Lumenite Control Technology ....F 847 455-1450
  Franklin Park *(G-9982)*
Methode Electronics Inc...............A 217 357-3941
  Carthage *(G-3139)*
Meto-Grafics Inc ....F 847 639-0044
  Crystal Lake *(G-7226)*
Mitsubishi Elc Automtn Inc............C 847 478-2100
  Vernon Hills *(G-20075)*
Motec Inc ....G 630 241-9595
  Downers Grove *(G-8060)*
Mpc Products Corporation ....G 847 673-8300
  Niles *(G-15150)*
New Cie Inc ....F 815 224-1485
  La Salle *(G-12118)*
Numerical Control Incorporated ....G 708 389-8140
  Alsip *(G-486)*
Oakland Industries Ltd ....E 847 827-7600
  Mount Prospect *(G-14555)*
Product Service Craft Inc.............F 630 964-5160
  Downers Grove *(G-8085)*
Schneider Electric Usa Inc............E 847 441-2526
  Schaumburg *(G-18708)*
Switchcraft Inc ....B 773 792-2700
  Chicago *(G-6299)*
Switchcraft Holdco ....G 773 792-2700
  Chicago *(G-6300)*
Venturedyne Ltd ....E 708 597-7550
  Chicago *(G-6535)*
Woodward Controls Inc.................C 847 673-8300
  Skokie *(G-19058)*
Xylem Lnc ....G 847 966-3700
  Morton Grove *(G-14451)*

SWITCHGEAR & SWITCHGEAR ACCESS, NEC

Appleton Grp LLC ....C 847 268-6000
  Rosemont *(G-17999)*
Custom Power Products Inc ....G 309 249-2704
  Edelstein *(G-8332)*
Hubbell Power Systems Inc ....E 618 797-5000
  Edwardsville *(G-8366)*

SWITCHING EQPT: Radio & Television Communications

Heico Companies LLC ....F 312 419-8220
  Chicago *(G-4798)*

SYNTHETIC RESIN FINISHED PRDTS, NEC

Certified Polymers Inc ....G 630 515-0007
  Western Springs *(G-20719)*
Custom Films Inc ....F 217 826-2326
  Marshall *(G-13569)*
Werner Co ....E 815 459-6020
  Crystal Lake *(G-7294)*

SYRUPS, DRINK

A Barr Ftn Beverage Sls & Svc ....D 708 442-2000
  Lemont *(G-12550)*
Coca-Cola Refreshments USA Inc ....C 618 542-2101
  Du Quoin *(G-8117)*
Culinary Co-Pack Incorporated ....E 847 451-1551
  Franklin Park *(G-9921)*
Tone Products Inc ....E 708 681-3660
  Melrose Park *(G-13923)*

SYRUPS, FLAVORING, EXC DRINK

White Stokes Company Inc ....E 773 254-5000
  Lincolnwood *(G-12851)*

SYSTEMS ENGINEERING: Computer Related

Abki Tech Service Inc ....F 847 818-8403
  Des Plaines *(G-7721)*
Braindok LLC ....G 847 877-1586
  Buffalo Grove *(G-2520)*
Converting Systems Inc ....G 847 519-0232
  Schaumburg *(G-18489)*
Turner Agward ....G 773 669-8559
  Chicago *(G-6444)*

SYSTEMS INTEGRATION SVCS

Agile Health Technologies Inc ....E 331 457-5167
  Naperville *(G-14952)*
Cdc Enterprises Inc ....G 815 790-4205
  Johnsburg *(G-11802)*
GE Transportation Parts LLC ....E 814 875-2755
  Chicago *(G-4666)*
Ntt America Solutions Inc ....F 847 278-6413
  Schaumburg *(G-18654)*
R+d Custom Automation Inc.............E 847 395-3330
  Lake Villa *(G-12365)*
Trustwave Holdings Inc................G 312 750-0950
  Chicago *(G-6440)*

SYSTEMS INTEGRATION SVCS: Local Area Network

Csiteq LLC ....F 312 265-1509
  Rosemont *(G-18011)*
National Def Intelligence Inc ....G 312 233-2318
  Naperville *(G-14980)*

SYSTEMS INTEGRATION SVCS: Office Computer Automation

Logical Design Solutions Inc..........G 630 786-5999
  Naperville *(G-14865)*
Progressive Systems Netwrk Inc ....G 312 382-8383
  Chicago *(G-5902)*
Srmd Solutions LLC ....G 217 925-5773
  Dieterich *(G-7879)*

SYSTEMS SOFTWARE DEVELOPMENT SVCS

American Controls & Automation ....G 630 293-8841
  West Chicago *(G-20537)*
Automated Insights Inc ....C 919 442-8865
  Chicago *(G-3776)*
Cleo Communications Inc ....E 815 654-8110
  Rockford *(G-17353)*
Computer Pwr Solutions III Ltd ....E 618 281-8898
  Columbia *(G-6988)*
Datasis Corporation ....F 847 427-0909
  Elk Grove Village *(G-8938)*
Evention LLC ....E 773 733-4256
  Chicago *(G-4539)*
Key Resources Inc ....G 800 574-1339
  Lake Villa *(G-12357)*
Orinoco Systems LLC ....G 630 510-0775
  Wheaton *(G-20814)*
Proquis Inc ....F 847 278-3230
  Elgin *(G-8700)*
Recsolu Inc ....G 312 517-3200
  Chicago *(G-5990)*
Smartbyte Solutions Inc...............G 847 925-1870
  Palatine *(G-16160)*
Tylu Wireless Technology LLC ....G 312 260-7934
  Chicago *(G-6450)*
Vaimo Inc ....G 502 767-9550
  Chicago *(G-6517)*
Whospoppin Enterprises Inc ....G 312 912-8480
  Chicago *(G-6621)*

TABLE OR COUNTERTOPS, PLASTIC LAMINATED

All-Style Custom Tops ....G 708 532-6606
  Tinley Park *(G-19799)*
Clover Custom Counters Inc ....G 708 598-8912
  Bridgeview *(G-2336)*
Forest City Counter Tops Inc ....F 815 633-8602
  Loves Park *(G-13212)*
Harts Top and Cabinet Shop ....G 708 957-4666
  Country Club Hills *(G-7040)*
Markham Cabinet Works Inc ....G 708 687-3074
  Midlothian *(G-13993)*
R & R Custom Cabinet Making ....G 847 358-6188
  Palatine *(G-16152)*
Valley Custom Woodwork Inc ....E 815 544-3939
  Belvidere *(G-1707)*

TABLECLOTHS & SETTINGS

Van Stockum Kristine ....G 847 914-0015
  Deerfield *(G-7656)*

TABLETS: Bronze Or Other Metal

Bronze Memorial Inc...................G 773 276-7972
  Chicago *(G-3963)*

TABLEWARE OR KITCHEN ARTICLES: Whiteware, Fine Semivitreous

Antioch Fine Arts Foundation ....G 847 838-2274
  Antioch *(G-599)*

TAGS & LABELS: Paper

Deco Adhesive Pdts 1985 Ltd ....E 847 472-2100
  Elk Grove Village *(G-8941)*
Oei Products Inc ....G 630 377-1121
  Bartlett *(G-1300)*
Service Packaging Design Inc ....G 847 966-6592
  Morton Grove *(G-14440)*
Xertrex International Inc ....E 630 773-4020
  Itasca *(G-11755)*

TAGS: Paper, Blank, Made From Purchased Paper

Bag Tags Inc ....F 847 983-4732
  Skokie *(G-18927)*
Tag Diamond & Label ....E 630 844-9395
  Aurora *(G-1159)*
Zebra Technologies Corporation ....B 847 634-6700
  Lincolnshire *(G-12804)*

TAILORS: Custom

Riddle McIntyre Inc ....G 312 782-3317
  Chicago *(G-6030)*

TALLOW: Animal

Darling Ingredients Inc ....E 618 271-8190
  National Stock Yards *(G-15012)*

TANK REPAIR & CLEANING SVCS

Chicago Tank Lining Sales .... G 847 328-0500
  Evanston *(G-9504)*
Matrix Service Inc .... F 618 466-4862
  Alton *(G-566)*
Pro-Tran Inc .... G 217 348-9353
  Charleston *(G-3410)*

TANK REPAIR SVCS

Summit Tank & Equipment Co .... F 708 594-3040
  Mc Cook *(G-13703)*

TANKS & OTHER TRACKED VEHICLE CMPNTS

Bruder Tank Inc .... E 217 292-9058
  Sullivan *(G-19662)*
Chelsea Framing Products Inc .... G 847 550-5556
  Lake Zurich *(G-12393)*
Navistar Defense LLC .... E 708 617-4500
  Melrose Park *(G-13896)*
Protectoseal Company .... C 630 595-0800
  Bensenville *(G-1876)*

TANKS: For Tank Trucks, Metal Plate

Arthur Custom Tank LLC .... G 217 543-4022
  Arthur *(G-841)*
Brenner Tank Services LLC .... G 773 468-6390
  Chicago *(G-3950)*
Bruder Tank Inc .... E 217 292-9058
  Sullivan *(G-19662)*
Pro-Tran Inc .... G 217 348-9353
  Charleston *(G-3410)*

TANKS: Fuel, Including Oil & Gas, Metal Plate

Alum-I-Tank Inc .... F 800 652-6630
  Harvard *(G-11043)*
Alum-I-Tank Inc .... E 815 943-6649
  Harvard *(G-11044)*
Ameropan Oil Corp .... F 773 847-4400
  Chicago *(G-3678)*
Ifh Group Inc .... D 800 435-7003
  Rock Falls *(G-17187)*
Ifh Group Inc .... G 815 380-2367
  Galt *(G-10225)*
Western Industries Inc .... C 920 261-0660
  Wheeling *(G-21012)*

TANKS: Lined, Metal

Mt Carmel Machine Shop Inc .... F 618 262-4591
  Mount Carmel *(G-14480)*

TANKS: Plastic & Fiberglass

Chicago Plastic Systems Inc .... E 815 455-4599
  Crystal Lake *(G-7181)*
Duratech Corporation .... G 618 533-8891
  Centralia *(G-3229)*
Eagle Plastics & Supply Inc .... G 708 331-6232
  Chicago *(G-4430)*
Fiberbasin Inc .... F 630 978-0705
  Aurora *(G-1095)*
Jalaa Fiberglass Inc .... G 217 923-3433
  Greenup *(G-10821)*

TANKS: Standard Or Custom Fabricated, Metal Plate

Amex Nooter LLC .... F 708 429-8300
  Tinley Park *(G-19803)*
CB&i LLC .... G 815 936-5440
  Bourbonnais *(G-2258)*
Eastland Fabrication LLC .... G 815 493-8399
  Lanark *(G-12479)*
Fabricated Products Co Inc .... F 630 898-6460
  Aurora *(G-959)*
G E Mathis Company .... D 773 586-3800
  Chicago *(G-4649)*
Illinois Oil Marketing Eqp Inc .... E 309 347-1819
  Pekin *(G-16340)*
Illinois Oil Marketing Eqp Inc .... F 217 935-5107
  Clinton *(G-6924)*
JM Industries LLC .... E 708 849-4700
  Riverdale *(G-17072)*
Lake Process Systems Inc .... E 847 381-7663
  Lake Barrington *(G-12157)*
Luebbers Welding & Mfg Inc .... F 618 594-2489
  Carlyle *(G-2893)*
Manchester Tank & Equipment Co .... E 217 224-7600
  Quincy *(G-16909)*
Matrix Service Inc .... F 618 466-4862
  Alton *(G-566)*
Mid-State Tank Co Inc .... D 217 728-8383
  Sullivan *(G-19670)*
Precision Tank & Equipment Co .... F 217 636-7023
  Athens *(G-900)*
R L Hoener Co .... E 217 223-2190
  Quincy *(G-16936)*
Tech-Weld Inc .... F 630 365-3000
  Elburn *(G-8474)*
WW Engineering Company LLC .... F 773 376-9494
  Chicago *(G-6690)*

TANKS: Water, Metal Plate

Kohnens Concrete Products Inc .... E 618 277-2120
  Germantown *(G-10330)*
Melters and More .... G 815 419-2043
  Chenoa *(G-3433)*
Precision Ibc Inc .... F 708 396-0750
  Crestwood *(G-7125)*

TANNERIES: Leather

Tannery Row LLC .... G 847 840-7647
  Chicago *(G-6324)*

TAPE DRIVES

Amaitis and Associates Inc .... F 847 428-1269
  Wood Dale *(G-21160)*

TAPE MEASURES

American Tape Measures .... G 312 208-0282
  Chicago *(G-3670)*

TAPE RECERTIFICATION SVCS

Kishknows Inc .... G 708 252-3648
  Richton Park *(G-17030)*

TAPE STORAGE UNITS: Computer

Numeridex Incorporated .... F 847 541-8840
  Wheeling *(G-20948)*

TAPE: Instrumentation Type, Blank

Imperial Technical Services .... F 708 403-1564
  Orland Park *(G-15961)*

TAPE: Rubber

Adhes Tape Technology Inc .... G 847 496-7949
  Arlington Heights *(G-683)*

TAPES, ADHESIVE: Masking, Made From Purchased Materials

Budnick Converting Inc .... C 618 281-8090
  Columbia *(G-6986)*

TAPES, ADHESIVE: Medical

General Bandages Inc .... F 847 966-8383
  Park Ridge *(G-16280)*

TAPES: Coated Fiberglass, Pipe Sealing Or Insulating

Technical Sealants Inc .... F 815 777-9797
  Galena *(G-10179)*

TAPES: Fabric

Adhes Tape Technology Inc .... G 847 496-7949
  Arlington Heights *(G-683)*

TAPES: Gummed, Cloth Or Paper Based, From Purchased Matls

Prairie State Graphics Inc .... D 847 801-3100
  Franklin Park *(G-10022)*

TAPES: Magnetic

Acta Publications .... G 773 989-3036
  Chicago *(G-3533)*

TAPES: Plastic Coated

Lanmar Inc .... G 800 233-5520
  Northbrook *(G-15418)*

TAPES: Pressure Sensitive

Continental Datalabel Inc .... C 847 742-1600
  Elgin *(G-8552)*
Intertape Polymer Corp .... D 618 549-2131
  Carbondale *(G-2847)*
Labels Unlimited Incorporated .... E 773 523-7500
  Chicago *(G-5152)*
Print-O-Tape Inc .... E 847 362-1476
  Mundelein *(G-14729)*
Rjm Manufacturing Inc .... D 215 736-3644
  Carbondale *(G-2856)*
Specialty Tape & Label Co Inc .... E 708 863-3800
  Lyons *(G-13313)*
Tek Pak Inc .... D 630 406-0560
  Batavia *(G-1429)*

TAPES: Pressure Sensitive, Rubber

Winfield Technology Inc .... F 630 584-0475
  Saint Charles *(G-18301)*

TAPS

Tapco Cutting Tools Inc .... G 815 877-4039
  Loves Park *(G-13270)*
Tapco USA Inc .... G 815 877-4039
  Loves Park *(G-13271)*

TARPAULINS

M Mauritzon & Company Inc .... E 773 235-6000
  Chicago *(G-5303)*
Tarps Manufacturing Inc .... F 217 245-6181
  Meredosia *(G-13957)*
Tri City Canvas Products Inc .... F 618 797-1662
  Granite City *(G-10746)*

TARPAULINS, WHOLESALE

Midwest Awnings Inc .... G 309 762-3339
  Cameron *(G-2808)*
Shur Co of Illinois .... G 217 877-8277
  Decatur *(G-7546)*

TAX RETURN PREPARATION SVCS

H&R Block Inc .... F 847 566-5557
  Mundelein *(G-14694)*

TECHNICAL & TRADE SCHOOLS, NEC

Russell Enterprises Inc .... B 847 692-6050
  Park Ridge *(G-16295)*

TECHNICAL MANUAL PREPARATION SVCS

Amerinet of Michigan Inc .... G 708 466-0110
  Naperville *(G-14958)*
Custom Design Services & Assoc .... F 815 226-9747
  Rockford *(G-17362)*
M & B Supply Inc .... F 309 944-3206
  Geneseo *(G-10246)*

TECHNICAL WRITING SVCS

Fanning Communications Inc .... G 708 293-1430
  Crestwood *(G-7118)*

TELECOMMUNICATION EQPT REPAIR SVCS, EXC TELEPHONES

Sitexpedite LLC .... E 847 245-2185
  Lindenhurst *(G-12854)*
Unified Solutions Corp .... E 847 478-9100
  Arlington Heights *(G-824)*

TELECOMMUNICATION SYSTEMS & EQPT

Alltemated Inc .... D 847 394-5800
  Wheeling *(G-20845)*
Cml Technologies Inc .... G 708 450-1911
  Westchester *(G-20694)*
Coleman Cable LLC .... D 847 672-2300
  Lincolnshire *(G-12753)*
Coriant North America LLC .... A 630 798-8800
  Naperville *(G-14806)*
Coriant Operations Inc .... E 630 798-8800
  Naperville *(G-14807)*

TELECOMMUNICATION SYSTEMS & EQPT

Cronus Technologies Inc .... D 847 839-0088
  Schaumburg (G-18496)
D & S Communications Inc .... D 847 628-4195
  Elgin (G-8562)
Etcon Corp .... F 630 325-6100
  Burr Ridge (G-2672)
HI Tech .... G 708 957-4210
  Homewood (G-11496)
Medical Cmmnctions Systems Inc ...... G 708 895-4500
  Lansing (G-12508)
Primo Microphone Inc .... G 630 837-6119
  Streamwood (G-19589)
Quintum Technologies Inc .... F 847 348-7730
  Schaumburg (G-18694)
Stellar Manufacturing Company .... D 618 823-3761
  Cahokia (G-2764)
Tekno Industries Inc .... F 630 766-6960
  Glen Ellyn (G-10421)
Tellabs Tg Inc .... G 630 798-8800
  Naperville (G-14929)
Unified Solutions Corp .... E 847 478-9100
  Arlington Heights (G-824)
Vertiv Group Corporation .... E 630 579-5000
  Lombard (G-13150)
Westell Inc .... G 630 898-2500
  Aurora (G-1035)
Wireless Chamberlain Products .... E 800 282-6225
  Elmhurst (G-9446)

TELECOMMUNICATIONS CARRIERS & SVCS: Wired

Cutting Edge Communications .... G 815 788-9419
  Crystal Lake (G-7191)
D & S Communications Inc .... D 847 628-4195
  Elgin (G-8562)
Global Technologies I LLC .... D 312 255-8350
  Chicago (G-4699)
Gogo LLC .... B 630 647-1400
  Chicago (G-4711)
Gogo LLC .... G 630 647-1400
  Bensenville (G-1813)
Westell Technologies Inc .... E 630 898-2500
  Aurora (G-1036)

TELECOMMUNICATIONS CARRIERS & SVCS: Wireless

D & S Communications Inc .... D 847 628-4195
  Elgin (G-8562)
Portable Cmmnctons Spclsts .... G 630 458-1800
  Addison (G-246)
Vincor Ltd .... F 708 534-0008
  Monee (G-14211)

TELECONFERENCING SVCS

Innovative AV Systems Inc .... G 312 265-6282
  Elmhurst (G-9379)
Westell Technologies Inc .... E 630 898-2500
  Aurora (G-1036)

TELEMARKETING BUREAUS

Communication Technologies Inc ...... E 630 384-0900
  Glendale Heights (G-10444)

TELEMETERING EQPT

Meshplusplus Inc .... G 847 494-6325
  Chicago (G-5402)

TELEPHONE ANSWERING SVCS

Group O Inc .... E 309 736-8100
  Milan (G-14015)
Hamilton Sundstrand Corp .... A 815 226-6000
  Rockford (G-17441)

TELEPHONE BOOTHS, EXC WOOD

Enclosures Inc .... G 847 678-2020
  Schiller Park (G-18803)

TELEPHONE CENTRAL OFFICE EQPT: Dial Or Manual

Kuna Corp .... G 815 675-0140
  Spring Grove (G-19282)

TELEPHONE EQPT INSTALLATION

Audio Installers Inc .... F 815 969-7500
  Loves Park (G-13193)
Medical Cmmnctions Systems Inc ...... G 708 895-4500
  Lansing (G-12508)

TELEPHONE EQPT: Modems

Motorola Solutions Inc .... C 847 576-5000
  Chicago (G-5511)
Motorola Solutions Inc .... C 847 576-8600
  Schaumburg (G-18637)
Netgear Inc .... G 630 955-0080
  Naperville (G-14881)
Ruckus Wireless Inc .... E 630 281-3000
  Lisle (G-12935)

TELEPHONE EQPT: NEC

A T Products Inc .... G 815 943-3590
  Harvard (G-11038)
American Comm & Networks .... E 630 241-2800
  Downers Grove (G-7950)
Best-Tronics Mfg Inc .... C 708 802-9677
  Tinley Park (G-19810)
Charles Industries LLC .... D 847 806-6300
  Schaumburg (G-18474)
Charles Industries LLC .... D 217 826-2318
  Marshall (G-13566)
Charles Industries LLC .... D 217 932-2068
  Casey (G-3199)
Charles Industries LLC .... D 217 932-5292
  Casey (G-3200)
Elanza Technologies Inc .... E 312 396-4187
  Chicago (G-4475)
Elexa Consumer Products Inc .... B 773 794-1300
  Bannockburn (G-1200)
Mako Networks Sales & Mktg Inc ..... D 847 752-5566
  Elgin (G-8647)
Mitel Networks Inc .... F 312 479-9000
  Chicago (G-5471)
Parts Specialists Inc .... G 708 371-2444
  Posen (G-16800)
Pentegra Systems LLC .... E 630 941-6000
  Addison (G-235)
Precision Components Inc .... D 630 462-9110
  Saint Charles (G-18249)
Tancher Corp .... F 847 668-8765
  Park Ridge (G-16299)
Tellabs Mexico Inc .... F 630 445-5333
  Naperville (G-14928)
Wescom Products .... G 217 932-5292
  Casey (G-3209)
Westell Technologies Inc .... E 630 898-2500
  Aurora (G-1036)

TELEPHONE STATION EQPT & PARTS: Wire

Sandmancom Inc .... G 630 980-7710
  Glendale Heights (G-10490)

TELEPHONE SVCS

Crosscom Inc .... F 630 871-5500
  Wheaton (G-20794)

TELEPHONE SWITCHING EQPT

Olfb Corporation .... G 309 283-0825
  Moline (G-14164)

TELEPHONE SWITCHING EQPT: Toll Switching

Charles Industries LLC .... D 217 893-8335
  Rantoul (G-16970)

TELEPHONE: Autotransformers For Switchboards

AT&T Corp .... F 312 602-4108
  Chicago (G-3755)

TELEPHONE: Fiber Optic Systems

Advantage Optics Inc .... F 630 548-9870
  Naperville (G-14767)
Axon Telecom LLC .... E 618 278-4606
  Dorsey (G-7943)
Connor-Winfield Corp .... D 630 499-2121
  Aurora (G-1078)
Cutting Edge Communications .... G 815 788-9419
  Crystal Lake (G-7191)
Elite Fiber Optics LLC .... E 630 225-9454
  Franklin Park (G-9938)
Excel Photonics Inc .... G 732 829-2667
  Elk Grove Village (G-8987)
IL Green Pastures Fiber Co-Op .... G 815 751-0887
  Kirkland (G-12061)
Ledcor Construction Inc .... F 630 916-1200
  Oakbrook Terrace (G-15805)
Photon Partners LLC .... G 773 991-9788
  Chicago (G-5805)

TELEPHONE: Headsets

O & M Electronic Inc .... F 708 203-1947
  Oak Lawn (G-15730)

TELEPHONE: Sets, Exc Cellular Radio

Firefly Mobile Inc .... E 305 538-2777
  Schaumburg (G-18529)
Smart Choice Mobile Inc .... F 708 581-4904
  Hickory Hills (G-11203)

TELEPHONES: Sound Powered, Without Battery

Datasource .... G 312 405-9152
  Calumet City (G-2774)

TELESCOPES

Astro-Physics Inc .... F 815 282-1513
  Machesney Park (G-13328)

TELETYPEWRITERS

T 26 Inc .... G 773 862-1201
  Chicago (G-6306)

TELEVISION BROADCASTING & COMMUNICATIONS EQPT

Big Ten Network Services LLC .... D 312 329-3666
  Chicago (G-3883)
Cable Company .... E 847 437-5267
  Elk Grove Village (G-8877)
Dtv Innovations LLC .... F 847 919-3550
  Elgin (G-8571)
Wireless Chamberlain Products .... E 800 282-6225
  Elmhurst (G-9446)
Zenith Electronics Corporation .... E 847 941-8000
  Lincolnshire (G-12806)

TELEVISION BROADCASTING STATIONS

Wyzz Inc .... D 217 753-5620
  Springfield (G-19468)

TELEVISION FILM PRODUCTION SVCS

Midwest Outdoors Ltd .... E 630 887-7722
  Burr Ridge (G-2704)

TELEVISION: Cameras

Forest City Satellite .... G 815 639-0500
  Davis Junction (G-7422)

TELEVISION: Closed Circuit Eqpt

Checkpoint Systems Inc .... D 630 771-4240
  Romeoville (G-17806)
Kokes Kid Zone .... G 217 483-4615
  Chatham (G-3423)
Northern Information Tech .... F 800 528-4343
  Rolling Meadows (G-17754)

TELEVISION: Monitors

Omni Vision Inc .... E 630 893-1720
  Glendale Heights (G-10481)

TEMPERING: Metal

Morgan Ohare Inc .... D 630 543-6780
  Addison (G-223)

TENTS: All Materials

Kastelic Canvas Inc .... G 815 436-8160
  Plainfield (G-16679)

PRODUCT SECTION

TERMINAL BOARDS
Lutamar Electrical Assemblies ....E....... 847 679-5400
Skokie *(G-18981)*

TERRAZZO PRECAST PRDTS
Creative Inds Terrazzo Pdts ....G....... 773 235-9088
Chicago *(G-4263)*

TEST BORING SVCS: Nonmetallic Minerals
Natural Resources III Dept ....E....... 618 439-4320
Benton *(G-1933)*
Raimonde Drilling Corp ....F....... 630 458-0590
Addison *(G-265)*

TEST KITS: Pregnancy
Aid For Women Northern Lk Cnty ....F....... 847 249-2700
Gurnee *(G-10855)*
Fox Valley Pregnancy Center ....G....... 847 697-0200
South Elgin *(G-19145)*
Guardian Angel Outreach ....G....... 815 672-4567
Streator *(G-19609)*

TESTERS: Battery
ABM Marking Services Ltd ....G....... 618 277-3773
Belleville *(G-1527)*
Auto Meter Products Inc ....C....... 815 895-8141
Sycamore *(G-19702)*
Greenlee Textron Inc ....C....... 815 784-5127
Genoa *(G-10318)*
Midtronics Inc ....D....... 630 323-2800
Willowbrook *(G-21050)*

TESTERS: Environmental
Alexeter Technologies LLC ....F....... 847 419-1507
Wheeling *(G-20843)*
Blanke Industries Incorporated ....G....... 847 487-2780
Wauconda *(G-20335)*
Mk Environmental Inc ....G....... 630 848-0585
Lombard *(G-13102)*
Pine Environmental Svcs LLC ....G....... 847 718-1246
Lombard *(G-13120)*
Standard Safety Equipment Co ....E....... 815 363-8565
McHenry *(G-13795)*
Warbler of Illinois Company ....G....... 301 520-0438
Champaign *(G-3369)*

TESTERS: Hardness
Rockford Rams Products Inc ....G....... 815 226-0016
Rockford *(G-17604)*
Romus Incorporated ....G....... 414 350-6233
Roselle *(G-17979)*

TESTERS: Liquid, Exc Indl Process
EMD Millipore Corporation ....B....... 815 932-9017
Kankakee *(G-11969)*

TESTERS: Logic Circuit
Integral Automation Inc ....F....... 630 654-4300
Burr Ridge *(G-2688)*

TESTERS: Physical Property
Falex Corporation ....E....... 630 556-3679
Sugar Grove *(G-19643)*
Hamilton Maurer Intl Inc ....G....... 713 468-6805
Hudson *(G-11518)*
Holmes Bros Inc ....E....... 217 442-1430
Danville *(G-7345)*
Perfection Probes Inc ....G....... 847 726-8868
Lake Zurich *(G-12442)*

TESTERS: Water, Exc Indl Process
Swan Analytical Usa Inc ....F....... 847 229-1290
Wheeling *(G-20994)*

TESTING SVCS
Adaptive Testing Tech Inc ....F....... 312 878-6490
Chicago *(G-3539)*
Ddu Magnetics Inc ....G....... 708 325-6587
Lynwood *(G-13293)*
H L Clausing Inc ....G....... 847 676-0330
Skokie *(G-18962)*

TEXTILE & APPAREL SVCS
Allstar Embroidery ....G....... 847 913-1933
Buffalo Grove *(G-2509)*
False Hope Brand Co ....G....... 312 265-1364
Chicago *(G-4556)*
Jenny Capp Co ....F....... 773 217-0057
Chicago *(G-5018)*
Meridian Industries Inc ....D....... 630 892-7651
Aurora *(G-1131)*
Unique Novelty & Manufacturing ....G....... 217 538-2014
Fillmore *(G-9666)*

TEXTILE BAGS WHOLESALERS
NRR Corp ....F....... 630 915-8388
Oak Brook *(G-15651)*
Sea-Rich Corp ....G....... 773 261-6633
Chicago *(G-6124)*

TEXTILE FABRICATORS
Duracrest Fabrics ....G....... 847 350-0030
Elk Grove Village *(G-8959)*
Girlygirl ....G....... 708 633-7290
Tinley Park *(G-19831)*
Heiman Sign Studio ....G....... 815 397-6909
Rockford *(G-17447)*
Vel-Tye LLC ....G....... 757 518-5400
Plainfield *(G-16725)*

TEXTILE FINISHING: Chem Coat/Treat, Man, Broadwoven, Cotton
Saati Americas Corporation ....F....... 847 296-5090
Mount Prospect *(G-14568)*

TEXTILE FINISHING: Chem Coating/Treating, Broadwoven, Cotton
Saati Americas Corporation ....F....... 847 296-5090
Mount Prospect *(G-14568)*

TEXTILE FINISHING: Chemical Coating Or Treating
B and A Screen Printing ....G....... 217 762-2632
Monticello *(G-14277)*

TEXTILE FINISHING: Dyeing, Broadwoven, Cotton
Meridian Industries Inc ....D....... 630 892-7651
Aurora *(G-1131)*

TEXTILE FINISHING: Dyeing, Finishing & Printng, Linen Fabric
Chicago Dye Works ....G....... 847 931-7968
Elgin *(G-8538)*

TEXTILE FINISHING: Embossing, Linen, Broadwoven
Mount Vernon Mills ....G....... 618 882-6300
Highland *(G-11233)*

TEXTILE PRDTS: Hand Woven & Crocheted
Tex Trend Inc ....E....... 847 215-6796
Wheeling *(G-20999)*

TEXTILE: Finishing, Cotton Broadwoven
Aurora Spclty Txtles Group Inc ....D....... 800 864-0303
Yorkville *(G-21473)*
Charles H Luck Envelope Inc ....F....... 847 451-1500
Franklin Park *(G-9903)*
Murphys Pub ....G....... 847 526-1431
Wauconda *(G-20380)*
Toyota Tsusho America Inc ....D....... 847 439-8500
Elk Grove Village *(G-9281)*

TEXTILE: Finishing, Raw Stock NEC
Fas-Trak Industries Inc ....G....... 708 570-0650
Monee *(G-14199)*

TEXTILE: Goods, NEC
Advantex Inc ....G....... 618 505-0701
Troy *(G-19911)*

THERMOMETERS: Medical, Digital

Deelone Distributing Inc ....G....... 309 788-1444
Rock Island *(G-17215)*
Glenraven Inc ....G....... 847 515-1321
Huntley *(G-11537)*
Lorton Group LLC ....G....... 844 352-5089
Wilmette *(G-21086)*
Sustainable Innovations Inc ....G....... 815 713-1637
Rockford *(G-17650)*

TEXTILES: Flock
Cellusuede Products Inc ....E....... 815 964-8619
Rockford *(G-17342)*

TEXTILES: Jute & Flax Prdts
Tex Tana Inc ....G....... 773 561-9270
Chicago *(G-6355)*

TEXTILES: Linen Fabrics
American Dawn Inc ....G....... 312 961-2909
Wood Dale *(G-21163)*
Superior Health Linens LLC ....D....... 630 593-5091
Batavia *(G-1423)*

TEXTILES: Linings, Carpet, Exc Felt
Shiir LLC ....F....... 312 828-0400
Chicago *(G-6153)*

TEXTILES: Mill Waste & Remnant
Federal Prison Industries ....F....... 618 664-6361
Greenville *(G-10834)*

TEXTILES: Padding & Wadding
Novipax LLC ....F....... 630 686-2735
Oak Brook *(G-15649)*

THEATRICAL LIGHTING SVCS
Upstaging Inc ....C....... 815 899-9888
Sycamore *(G-19738)*

THEATRICAL PRODUCERS & SVCS
Dramatic Publishing Company ....F....... 815 338-7170
Woodstock *(G-21383)*

THEATRICAL SCENERY
Big City Sets Inc ....G....... 312 421-3210
Chicago *(G-3881)*
Chicago Scenic Studios Inc ....D....... 312 274-9900
Chicago *(G-4127)*
Consolidated Displays Co Inc ....G....... 630 851-8666
Oswego *(G-15998)*
Illumivation Studios LLC ....G....... 312 261-5561
Chicago *(G-4892)*
Interesting Products Inc ....G....... 773 265-1100
Chicago *(G-4944)*

THEOLOGICAL SEMINARIES
Baptist General Conference ....D....... 800 323-4215
Arlington Heights *(G-703)*

THERMOCOUPLES
C & L Manufacturing Entps ....G....... 618 465-7623
Alton *(G-546)*
Tempco Electric Heater Corp ....B....... 630 350-2252
Wood Dale *(G-21248)*

THERMOCOUPLES: Indl Process
Tempro International Corp ....G....... 847 677-5370
Skokie *(G-19044)*
Xco International Incorporated ....F....... 847 428-2400
East Dundee *(G-8215)*

THERMOMETERS: Liquid-In-Glass & Bimetal
Lcr Hallcrest Llc ....E....... 847 998-8580
Glenview *(G-10584)*

THERMOMETERS: Medical, Digital
Avalign Technologies Inc ....D....... 855 282-5446
Bannockburn *(G-1189)*

Employee Codes: A=Over 500 employees, B=251-500
C=101-250, D=51-100, E=20-50, F=10-19, G=3-9

2020 Harris Illinois Industrial Directory

THERMOPLASTIC MATERIALS

THERMOPLASTIC MATERIALS
Italmatch Sc LLC .... G 708 929-9657
  Bedford Park *(G-1474)*
Polymax Thrmplstic Elstmers LL .... E 847 316-9900
  Waukegan *(G-20478)*
Polyone Corporation .... D 815 385-8500
  McHenry *(G-13782)*
Polyone Corporation .... F 815 385-8500
  Mchenry *(G-13783)*
Polyone Corporation .... C 309 364-2154
  Henry *(G-11168)*
Recycling Solutions Inc .... E 773 617-6955
  Chicago *(G-5992)*
Star Thermoplastic Alloys and .... E 708 343-1100
  Broadview *(G-2469)*
Star Thermoplastic Alloys and .... F 708 343-1100
  Broadview *(G-2470)*

THERMOPLASTICS
Atlas Fibre Company .... D 847 674-1234
  Northbrook *(G-15343)*
Lamin-Art LLC .... F 800 323-7624
  Schaumburg *(G-18598)*

THERMOSTAT REPAIR SVCS
Acme Control Service Inc .... E 773 774-9191
  Chicago *(G-3527)*

THREAD: All Fibers
Advent Tool & Mfg Inc .... F 847 395-9707
  Antioch *(G-594)*
Machine Tool Acc & Mfg Co .... G 773 489-0903
  Chicago *(G-5309)*

THREAD: Embroidery
Greco Graphics Inc .... G 217 483-2877
  Glenarm *(G-10425)*
Team Print Inc .... F 815 933-5111
  Bourbonnais *(G-2269)*

THYROID PREPARATIONS
Abbvie Holdings Inc .... D 847 937-7632
  Abbott Park *(G-8)*

TIES, FORM: Metal
National Tool & Mfg Co .... D 847 806-9800
  East Dundee *(G-8206)*

TILE: Brick & Structural, Clay
Building Products Corp .... E 618 233-4427
  Belleville *(G-1536)*

TILE: Clay, Drain & Structural
C & L Tiling Inc .... D 217 773-3357
  Timewell *(G-19797)*
Coon Run Drainage & Levee Dst .... G 217 248-5511
  Arenzville *(G-670)*

TILE: Concrete, Drain
Hulse Excavating .... G 815 796-4106
  Flanagan *(G-9670)*

TILE: Terrazzo Or Concrete, Precast
MK Tile Ink .... G 773 964-8905
  Chicago *(G-5474)*

TILE: Wall & Floor, Ceramic
Mosaicos Inc .... G 773 777-8453
  Chicago *(G-5502)*

TILE: Wall, Ceramic
Curran Group Inc .... D 815 455-5100
  Crystal Lake *(G-7190)*

TIMING DEVICES: Electronic
Competition Electronics Inc .... G 815 874-8001
  Rockford *(G-17356)*
Connor-Winfield Corp .... C 630 851-4722
  Aurora *(G-1079)*
E N M Company .... D 773 775-8400
  Chicago *(G-4425)*

Las Systems Inc .... E 847 462-8100
  Woodstock *(G-21404)*
USA Drives Inc .... E 630 323-1282
  Burr Ridge *(G-2730)*

TIN
Arcelormittal USA LLC .... B 312 346-0300
  Chicago *(G-3723)*
Pat 24 Inc .... G 708 336-8671
  Burbank *(G-2637)*
Tin Man Heating & Cooling Inc .... E 630 267-3232
  Aurora *(G-1162)*
Tin Maung .... G 217 233-1405
  Decatur *(G-7561)*
Tin Tree Gifts .... G 630 935-8086
  Aurora *(G-1024)*

TINPLATE
Sun Steel Trading LLC .... G 614 439-3390
  Rosemont *(G-18052)*

TIRE CORD & FABRIC
Mc Chemical Company .... G 618 965-3668
  Steeleville *(G-19483)*

TIRE CORD & FABRIC: Indl, Reinforcing
Advanced Flxble Composites Inc .... D 847 658-3938
  Lake In The Hills *(G-12327)*

TIRE DEALERS
American Tire Distributors .... G 708 680-5150
  La Grange Highlands *(G-12091)*
Bridgestone Americas .... E 309 452-4411
  Normal *(G-15200)*
City Subn Auto Svc Goodyear .... G 773 355-5550
  Chicago *(G-4162)*
Goodyear Tire & Rubber Company .... G 815 389-8222
  South Beloit *(G-19095)*
Hamel Tire and Concrete Pdts .... G 618 633-2405
  Hamel *(G-10950)*
Trotters Manufacturing Co .... G 217 364-4540
  Buffalo *(G-2501)*

TIRE INFLATORS: Hand Or Compressor Operated
G H Meiser & Co .... E 708 388-7867
  Mokena *(G-14085)*

TIRE INNER-TUBES
Goodyear Tire & Rubber Company .... G 815 389-8222
  South Beloit *(G-19095)*

TIRE RECAPPING & RETREADING
Jireh Inc .... F 217 335-3276
  Barry *(G-1251)*

TIRE SUNDRIES OR REPAIR MATERIALS: Rubber
Kraly Tire Repair Materials .... G 708 863-5981
  Cicero *(G-6861)*

TIRES & INNER TUBES
American Tire Distributors .... G 708 680-5150
  La Grange Highlands *(G-12091)*
Atturo Tire Corp 855 632-8031
  Waukegan *(G-20420)*
Best Designs Inc .... F 618 985-4445
  Carterville *(G-3129)*
Bridgestone Americas .... E 309 452-4411
  Normal *(G-15200)*
C&C Sealants .... F 708 717-0686
  Elgin *(G-8528)*
Continental Tire Americas LLC .... D 618 242-7100
  Mount Vernon *(G-14604)*
Continental Tire Americas LLC .... G 618 246-2585
  Mascoutah *(G-13596)*
Dealer Tire LLC .... G 847 671-0683
  Franklin Park *(G-9926)*
Joseph Coppolino .... G 773 735-8647
  Chicago *(G-5054)*
Liberty Tire Recycling LLC .... G 773 871-6360
  Chicago *(G-5218)*
Otr Wheel Engineering Inc .... E 217 223-7705
  Quincy *(G-16920)*

Stop & Go International Inc .... G 815 455-9080
  Crystal Lake *(G-7269)*
Tbc Retail Group Inc .... G 630 692-0232
  Montgomery *(G-14271)*
Titan Tire Corporation .... B 217 228-6011
  Quincy *(G-16949)*
Titan Tyre Corporation 217 228-6011
  Freeport *(G-10146)*

TIRES & TUBES WHOLESALERS
American Tire Distributors .... G 708 680-5150
  La Grange Highlands *(G-12091)*
Dealer Tire LLC .... G 847 671-0683
  Franklin Park *(G-9926)*
Hamel Tire and Concrete Pdts .... G 618 633-2405
  Hamel *(G-10950)*
Liberty Tire Recycling LLC .... G 773 871-6360
  Chicago *(G-5218)*

TIRES & TUBES, WHOLESALE: Automotive
Custom Millers Supply Inc .... G 309 734-6312
  Monmouth *(G-14216)*

TIRES & TUBES, WHOLESALE: Truck
D N D Coating .... G 309 379-3021
  Stanford *(G-19472)*

TIRES, USED, WHOLESALE
A Lakin & Sons Inc .... E 773 871-6360
  Montgomery *(G-14229)*
Lakin General Corporation .... D 773 871-6360
  Montgomery *(G-14255)*

TIRES: Agricultural, Pneumatic
Titan International Inc .... C 217 228-6011
  Quincy *(G-16948)*

TIRES: Cushion Or Solid Rubber
Dyneer Corporation .... B 217 228-6011
  Quincy *(G-16877)*
Tbc Corporation .... G 630 428-2233
  Naperville *(G-14927)*

TIRES: Indl Vehicles
Ameroc Export Inc .... G 818 961-6169
  Glenview *(G-10523)*

TIRES: Plastic
Circle Caster Engineering Co .... G 847 455-2206
  Franklin Park *(G-9908)*

TIRES: Truck
Nova Lines Inc .... G 773 322-6262
  River Grove *(G-17064)*

TITANIUM MILL PRDTS
AWI / Titanium .... G 708 263-9970
  Oak Forest *(G-15671)*
Dj Titanium .... G 312 823-2963
  Chicago *(G-4371)*
Titanium Insulation Inc .... G 708 932-5927
  Midlothian *(G-13997)*

TOBACCO & PRDTS, WHOLESALE: Cigars
Itg Brands LLC .... G 217 529-5746
  Springfield *(G-19390)*

TOBACCO & TOBACCO PRDTS WHOLESALERS
8 Electronic Cigarette Inc .... G 630 708-6803
  Saint Charles *(G-18140)*
Nader Wholesale Grocers Inc .... F 773 582-1000
  Chicago *(G-5536)*

TOBACCO STORES & STANDS
Magazine Plus .... G 773 281-4106
  Chicago *(G-5314)*

TOBACCO: Chewing
Paramount Plastics LLC .... D 815 834-4100
  Chicago *(G-5761)*

PRODUCT SECTION

TOBACCO: Chewing & Snuff

Diamond Wholesale Group Inc ....G....... 708 529-7495
Bridgeview *(G-2340)*
Inter-Continental Trdg USA Inc ....D....... 847 640-1777
Mount Prospect *(G-14537)*
Ust Inc ....G....... 847 957-5104
Franklin Park *(G-10071)*

TOBACCO: Cigarettes

8 Electronic Cigarette Inc ....G....... 630 708-6803
Saint Charles *(G-18140)*
Cigtechs ....F....... 630 855-6513
Roselle *(G-17945)*
Itg Brands LLC ....G....... 217 529-5746
Springfield *(G-19390)*
Philip Morris USA Inc ....D....... 847 605-9595
Schaumburg *(G-18673)*
Royal Smoke Shop ....G....... 815 539-3499
Mendota *(G-13954)*

TOBACCO: Smoking

Having A Good Time ....G....... 847 330-8460
Schaumburg *(G-18543)*
Paralleldirect LLC ....G....... 847 748-2025
Lincolnshire *(G-12791)*
Republic Group Inc ....G....... 800 288-8888
Glenview *(G-10612)*
Top Tobacco LP ....G....... 847 832-9700
Glenview *(G-10633)*
Ugly Hookah Tobacco Inc ....G....... 708 724-9621
Oak Lawn *(G-15737)*
US Smokeless Tob Mfg Co LLC ....F....... 804 274-2000
Franklin Park *(G-10070)*

TOILET PREPARATIONS

Cedar Concepts Corporation ....E....... 773 890-5790
Chicago *(G-4050)*
Gillette Company ....D....... 847 689-3111
North Chicago *(G-15312)*

TOILET SEATS: Wood

Liftseat Corporation ....E....... 630 424-2840
Oak Brook *(G-15636)*

TOILETRIES, COSMETICS & PERFUME STORES

AM Harper Products Inc ....F....... 312 767-8283
Chicago *(G-3640)*
Luxurious Lathers Ltd ....G....... 844 877-7627
Hinsdale *(G-11369)*
Proximity Capital Partners LLC ....F....... 773 628-7751
Chicago *(G-5909)*
Winlind Skincare LLC ....G....... 630 789-9408
Burr Ridge *(G-2736)*

TOILETRIES, WHOLESALE: Hair Preparations

Safe Effective Alternatives ....F....... 618 236-2727
Belleville *(G-1595)*

TOILETRIES, WHOLESALE: Perfumes

Aurora Narinder ....G....... 773 275-2100
Chicago *(G-3774)*

TOILETRIES, WHOLESALE: Razor Blades

Art of Shaving - Fl LLC ....G....... 630 495-7316
Lombard *(G-13040)*
Art of Shaving - Fl LLC ....G....... 312 527-1604
Chicago *(G-3737)*
Art of Shaving - Fl LLC ....G....... 630 684-0277
Oak Brook *(G-15594)*

TOILETRIES, WHOLESALE: Toilet Soap

4 Elements Company ....G....... 773 236-2284
Mundelein *(G-14655)*

TOILETRIES, WHOLESALE: Toiletries

1 Federal Supply Source Inc ....G....... 708 964-2222
Steger *(G-19486)*
Marietta Corporation ....C....... 773 816-5137
Chicago *(G-5337)*
Pearl Bath Bombs Inc ....F....... 312 661-2881
Chicago *(G-5777)*
Riviera Tan Spa ....G....... 618 466-1012
Godfrey *(G-10661)*

TOILETS: Portable Chemical, Plastics

Urban Services of America ....G....... 847 278-3210
Schaumburg *(G-18768)*

TOLL OPERATIONS

Ace Plastic Inc ....F....... 815 635-3737
Chatsworth *(G-3425)*

TOLLS: Caulking

Marmon Holdings Inc ....D....... 312 372-9500
Chicago *(G-5343)*

TOMBSTONES: Terrazzo Or Concrete, Precast

Elmos Tombstone Service ....G....... 773 643-0200
Chicago *(G-4488)*

TOOL & DIE STEEL

Automation Design & Mfg Inc ....G....... 630 896-4206
Aurora *(G-1060)*
Contour Tool Works Inc ....G....... 847 947-4700
Palatine *(G-16106)*
Craftsman Custom Metals LLC ....D....... 847 655-0040
Schiller Park *(G-18797)*
Fabricating Machinery Sales ....E....... 630 350-2266
Wood Dale *(G-21186)*
HI Tek Tool & Machining Inc ....G....... 847 836-6422
Algonquin *(G-373)*
Keats Manufacturing Co ....D....... 847 520-1133
Wheeling *(G-20923)*
Mt Tool and Manufacturing Inc ....G....... 847 985-6211
Schaumburg *(G-18640)*
Multiple Metal Production ....G....... 847 679-1510
Skokie *(G-18994)*
Offko Tool Inc ....G....... 815 933-9474
Kankakee *(G-11994)*
Precise Stamping Inc ....E....... 630 897-6477
North Aurora *(G-15272)*
R & E Quality Mfg Co ....G....... 773 286-6846
Chicago *(G-5942)*
Waters Wire EDM Service ....G....... 630 640-3534
Downers Grove *(G-8107)*

TOOL REPAIR SVCS

Allkut Tool Incorporated ....G....... 815 476-9656
Wilmington *(G-21096)*
Ivan Schwenker ....G....... 630 543-7798
Addison *(G-156)*
Rotospray Mfg Inc ....G....... 708 478-3307
Mokena *(G-14113)*

TOOLS: Carpenters', Including Levels & Chisels, Exc Saws

Dasco Pro Inc ....D....... 815 962-3727
Rockford *(G-17368)*

TOOLS: Hand

A To Z Tool Inc ....G....... 630 787-0478
Villa Park *(G-20126)*
Adel Tool Co LLP ....G....... 708 867-8530
Park Ridge *(G-16263)*
Adjustable Clamp Company ....C....... 312 666-0640
Chicago *(G-3546)*
Advance Equipment Mfg Co ....F....... 773 287-8220
Chicago *(G-3555)*
Ajax Tool Works Inc ....D....... 847 455-5420
Franklin Park *(G-9862)*
Aldon Co ....F....... 847 623-8800
Waukegan *(G-20412)*
Brian Burcar ....G....... 815 856-2271
Leonore *(G-12611)*
C K North America Inc ....F....... 815 524-4246
Romeoville *(G-17800)*
Chicago Grinding & Machine Co ......E....... 708 343-4399
Melrose Park *(G-13843)*
Doerock Inc ....G....... 217 543-2101
Arthur *(G-853)*
E J Welch Co Inc ....F....... 847 238-0100
Elk Grove Village *(G-8964)*
Ergo-Help Inc ....G....... 847 593-0722
Fox River Grove *(G-9757)*
Gaither Tool Co ....G....... 217 245-0545
Jacksonville *(G-11765)*
Gaunt Industries Inc ....G....... 847 671-0776
Franklin Park *(G-9949)*
H E Associates Inc ....F....... 630 553-6382
Yorkville *(G-21487)*
H R Slater Co Inc ....F....... 312 666-1855
Chicago *(G-4760)*
H&H Die Manufacturing Inc ....G....... 708 479-6267
Frankfort *(G-9799)*
Hydra Fold Auger Inc ....G....... 217 379-2614
Loda *(G-13028)*
Hyponex Corporation ....E....... 815 772-2167
Morrison *(G-14343)*
I D Rockford Shop Inc ....G....... 815 335-1150
Winnebago *(G-21120)*
Ideal Industries Inc ....C....... 815 895-1108
Sycamore *(G-19715)*
Illinois Tool Works Inc ....E....... 847 634-1900
Vernon Hills *(G-20064)*
Illinois Tool Works Inc ....E....... 847 821-2170
Vernon Hills *(G-20065)*
Illinois Tool Works Inc ....E....... 563 422-5686
Glenview *(G-10564)*
K-C Tool Co ....G....... 630 983-5960
Naperville *(G-14857)*
Klein Tools Inc ....B....... 847 821-5500
Lincolnshire *(G-12778)*
Klein Tools Inc ....G....... 847 249-4930
Waukegan *(G-20455)*
Klein Tools Inc ....D....... 847 228-6999
Elk Grove Village *(G-9078)*
Klein Tools Inc ....E....... 847 821-5500
Lincolnshire *(G-12779)*
Lawndale Forging & Tool Works ....G....... 773 277-2800
Chicago *(G-5183)*
Line Group Inc ....E....... 847 593-6810
Arlington Heights *(G-769)*
Link Tools Intl (usa) Inc ....G....... 773 549-3000
Chicago *(G-5229)*
Lmt Onsrud LP ....C....... 847 362-1560
Waukegan *(G-20461)*
Luster Leaf Products Inc ....F....... 815 337-5560
Woodstock *(G-21407)*
Modern Specialties Company ....G....... 312 648-5800
Chicago *(G-5481)*
Nextstep Commercial Products ....G....... 217 379-2377
Paxton *(G-16310)*
P K Neuses Incorporated ....G....... 847 253-6555
Rolling Meadows *(G-17758)*
Patterson Avenue Tool Company ......G....... 847 949-8100
Long Grove *(G-13169)*
Power House Tool Inc ....E....... 815 727-6301
Joliet *(G-11915)*
Power Planter Inc ....G....... 217 379-2614
Loda *(G-13031)*
Precision Products Inc ....C....... 217 735-1590
Lincoln *(G-12737)*
Precision Tool ....F....... 815 464-2428
Frankfort *(G-9824)*
Pullr Holding Company LLC ....E....... 224 366-2500
Schaumburg *(G-18688)*
Ravco Incorporated ....G....... 815 725-9095
Joliet *(G-11923)*
Remark Technologies Inc ....G....... 815 985-2972
Rockford *(G-17571)*
Rhino Tool Company ....F....... 309 853-5555
Kewanee *(G-12040)*
Ryeson Corporation ....D....... 847 455-8677
Carol Stream *(G-3061)*
S & G Step Tool Inc ....G....... 773 992-0808
Chicago *(G-6084)*
Sab Tool Supply Co ....G....... 847 634-3700
Vernon Hills *(G-20090)*
Stark Tools and Supply Inc ....G....... 847 772-8974
Elk Grove Village *(G-9256)*
Stuhr Manufacturing Co ....F....... 815 398-2460
Rockford *(G-17648)*
Sws Industries Inc ....E....... 904 482-0091
Woodstock *(G-21438)*
Thread & Gage Co Inc ....G....... 815 675-2305
Spring Grove *(G-19302)*
Tuxco Corporation ....F....... 847 244-2220
Gurnee *(G-10940)*
Wenco Manufacturing Co Inc ....E....... 630 377-7474
Elgin *(G-8781)*
Whitney Roper LLC ....D....... 815 962-3011
Rockford *(G-17683)*
Whitney Roper Rockford Inc ....D....... 815 962-3011
Rockford *(G-17684)*

Employee Codes: A=Over 500 employees, B=251-500
C=101-250, D=51-100, E=20-50, F=10-19, G=3-9

TOOLS: Hand

Woodland Engineering Company ....G...... 847 362-0110
Lake Bluff *(G-12217)*

TOOLS: Hand, Carpet Layers

Beno J Gundlach Company ....E...... 618 233-1781
Belleville *(G-1534)*

TOOLS: Hand, Hammers

Bit Brokers International Ltd ....E...... 618 435-5811
West Frankfort *(G-20668)*
Dobratz Sales Company Inc.................G...... 224 569-3081
Lake In The Hills *(G-12332)*
Estwing Manufacturing Co Inc ....B...... 815 397-9521
Rockford *(G-17402)*
Ironwood Manufacturing Inc.................G...... 630 969-1100
Naperville *(G-14975)*
Lsp Industries Inc ....F...... 815 226-8090
Rockford *(G-17497)*
Proton Multimedia Inc............................G...... 847 531-8664
Elgin *(G-8701)*
Vaughan & Bushnell Mfg Co ....F...... 815 648-2446
Hebron *(G-11153)*

TOOLS: Hand, Ironworkers'

Builders Ironworks Inc ....G...... 708 754-4092
Steger *(G-19489)*

TOOLS: Hand, Masons'

Galaxy Industries Inc ....D...... 847 639-8580
Cary *(G-3162)*

TOOLS: Hand, Mechanics

Northern Ordinance Corporation...........G...... 815 675-6400
Spring Grove *(G-19289)*
Toby Small Engine Repair.....................G...... 708 699-6021
Richton Park *(G-17031)*
Zim Manufacturing Co ....E...... 773 622-2500
Des Plaines *(G-7870)*

TOOLS: Hand, Plumbers'

Fitzpatrick Bros Inc................................G...... 217 592-3500
Quincy *(G-16882)*
Hand Tool America.................................G...... 847 947-2866
Buffalo Grove *(G-2543)*
Rothenberger USA LLC..........................D...... 800 545-7698
Loves Park *(G-13260)*

TOOLS: Hand, Power

A J Horne Inc..G...... 630 231-8686
West Chicago *(G-20530)*
Ajax Tool Works Inc..............................D...... 847 455-5420
Franklin Park *(G-9862)*
Allegion S&S Holding Co Inc................C...... 815 875-3311
Princeton *(G-16805)*
Ally Global Corporation..........................G...... 773 822-3373
Chicago *(G-3625)*
Black & Decker Corporation ....F...... 630 521-1097
Addison *(G-50)*
Champion Chisel Works Inc ....F...... 815 535-0647
Rock Falls *(G-17178)*
Custom Cutting Tools Inc......................G...... 815 986-0320
Loves Park *(G-13200)*
Damen Carbide Tool Company Inc.......E...... 630 766-7875
Wood Dale *(G-21181)*
Estwing Manufacturing Co Inc ....B...... 815 397-9521
Rockford *(G-17402)*
Federal Prison Industries.......................C...... 309 346-8588
Pekin *(G-16333)*
Gator Products Inc.................................G...... 847 836-0581
Gilberts *(G-10355)*
Greenlee Tools Inc.................................C...... 800 435-0786
Rockford *(G-17435)*
Harris Precision Tools Inc.....................G...... 708 422-5808
Chicago Ridge *(G-6797)*
I T W Ramset...G...... 630 825-7900
Glendale Heights *(G-10459)*
Illinois Tool Works Inc..........................D...... 847 634-1900
Vernon Hills *(G-20063)*
Illinois Tool Works Inc..........................E...... 847 634-1900
Vernon Hills *(G-20064)*
Industrial Instrument Svc Corp ....G...... 773 581-3355
Chicago *(G-4907)*
Ivan Schwenker.......................................G...... 630 543-7798
Addison *(G-156)*
K-C Tool Co..G...... 630 983-5960
Naperville *(G-14857)*
Link Tools Intl (usa) Inc.........................G...... 773 549-3000
Chicago *(G-5229)*
Milwaukee Electric Tool Corp ....B...... 847 588-3356
Niles *(G-15147)*
NNt Enterprises Incorporated ....E...... 630 875-9600
Itasca *(G-11712)*
Powernail Company.................................G...... 800 323-1653
Lake Zurich *(G-12445)*
R & S Cutterhead Mfg Co ....F...... 815 678-2611
Richmond *(G-17020)*
Ralph Cody Gravrok...............................G...... 630 628-9570
Addison *(G-266)*
Rdh Of Rockford.....................................G...... 815 874-9421
Rockford *(G-17568)*
Rhino Tool Company...............................F...... 309 853-5555
Kewanee *(G-12040)*
S & J Industrial Supply Corp ....F...... 708 339-1708
South Holland *(G-19242)*
Sollami Company ....E...... 618 988-1521
Herrin *(G-11179)*
Suhner Manufacturing Inc.....................G...... 847 308-8900
Buffalo Grove *(G-2611)*
T & T Carbide Inc...................................G...... 618 439-7253
Logan *(G-13032)*
Tapco USA Inc..G...... 815 877-4039
Loves Park *(G-13271)*
Technical Tool Enterprise.....................G...... 630 893-3390
Addison *(G-304)*
Toolmasters LLC.....................................F...... 815 645-2224
Stillman Valley *(G-19547)*
Total Tooling Technology Inc.................F...... 847 437-5135
Elk Grove Village *(G-9279)*
Triumph Twist Drill Co Inc....................B...... 815 459-6250
Crystal Lake *(G-7286)*
Tru-Cut Inc...D...... 847 639-2090
Cary *(G-3195)*
Unicut Corporation..................................G...... 773 525-4210
Chicago *(G-6464)*
Wallace/Haskin Corp.............................G...... 630 789-2882
Downers Grove *(G-8105)*
Welliver & Sons Inc...............................E...... 815 874-2400
Rockford *(G-17679)*
Whitney Roper LLC.................................D...... 815 962-3011
Rockford *(G-17683)*
Whitney Roper Rockford Inc.................D...... 815 962-3011
Rockford *(G-17684)*
Wodack Electric Tool Corp ....F...... 773 287-9866
Chicago *(G-6661)*

TOOTHPASTES, GELS & TOOTHPOWDERS

Sunstar Pharmaceutical Inc..................D...... 773 777-4000
Elgin *(G-8742)*

TOWELETTES: Premoistened

Body Wipe Corporation..........................G...... 847 687-9321
Mundelein *(G-14667)*
New Usn Chicago LLC..........................D...... 847 635-6772
Mount Prospect *(G-14551)*

TOWELS: Knit

Intelex Usa LLC.....................................G...... 844 927-6437
East Dundee *(G-8202)*
Tiger Accessory Group LLC ....F...... 847 821-9630
Long Grove *(G-13171)*

TOWERS, SECTIONS: Transmission, Radio & Television

Rohn Products LLC ....D...... 309 697-4400
Peoria *(G-16515)*
Rohn Products LLC ....E...... 309 566-3000
Peoria *(G-16516)*
SNC Solutions Inc..................................E...... 217 784-5212
Gibson City *(G-10344)*

TOYS

Aeromax Industries Inc.........................G...... 847 756-4085
Lake Barrington *(G-12140)*
Amav Enterprises Ltd ....G...... 630 761-3077
Batavia *(G-1346)*
American Specialty Toy.........................G...... 312 222-0984
Chicago *(G-3669)*
Aqua Golf Inc...G...... 217 824-2097
Taylorville *(G-19749)*
Chicago Contract Bridge Assn ....G...... 630 355-5560
Naperville *(G-14797)*
Cino Incorporated...................................G...... 630 377-7242
Saint Charles *(G-18166)*
E J Kupjack & Associates Inc...............G...... 847 823-6661
Chicago *(G-4424)*
Fun Incorporated....................................E...... 773 745-3837
Wheeling *(G-20902)*
Kaskey Kids Inc.....................................G...... 847 441-3092
Winnetka *(G-21131)*
Kato USA Inc..G...... 847 781-9500
Schaumburg *(G-18585)*
Kd-Kidz Dlight Interactive LLC ....G...... 630 724-0223
Downers Grove *(G-8038)*
Lego Systems Inc ....G...... 312 202-0946
Chicago *(G-5202)*
Pro-Line Winning Ways & Penlan.........G...... 309 745-8530
Washington *(G-20277)*
Racine Paper Box Manufacturing.........E...... 773 227-3900
Chicago *(G-5958)*
Rust-Oleum Corporation........................D...... 815 967-4258
Rockford *(G-17617)*
Shure Products Inc................................F...... 773 227-1001
Chicago *(G-6162)*
Sunnywood Incorporated........................G...... 815 675-9777
McHenry *(G-13799)*
Testor Corporation..................................D...... 815 962-6654
Rockford *(G-17656)*
Vmm USA Unique Master Mod ....G...... 847 537-0867
Deerfield *(G-7658)*

TOYS & HOBBY GOODS & SPLYS, WHOL: Toy Novelties & Amusements

Jcw Investments Inc ....G...... 708 478-7323
Orland Park *(G-15962)*
Urpoint LLC..G...... 773 919-9002
Homewood *(G-11503)*

TOYS & HOBBY GOODS & SPLYS, WHOLESALE: Arts/Crafts Eqpt/Sply

Chartwell Studio Inc ....G...... 847 868-8674
Chicago *(G-4077)*
Freitas P Sabah ....G...... 708 386-8934
Oak Park *(G-15754)*
Multi Packaging Solutions Inc..............G...... 773 283-9500
Chicago *(G-5523)*
Virtu..G...... 773 235-3790
Chicago *(G-6555)*

TOYS & HOBBY GOODS & SPLYS, WHOLESALE: Educational Toys

Learning Curve International ....E...... 630 573-7200
Oak Brook *(G-15632)*
Learning Resources Inc ....D...... 847 573-8400
Vernon Hills *(G-20072)*
Sage Clover ....G...... 630 220-9600
Winfield *(G-21117)*

TOYS & HOBBY GOODS & SPLYS, WHOLESALE: Model Kits

Accurail Inc..F...... 630 365-6400
Elburn *(G-8441)*
Midwest Rail Junction...........................G...... 815 963-0200
Rockford *(G-17527)*

TOYS & HOBBY GOODS & SPLYS, WHOLESALE: Toys & Games

Trivial Development Corp......................E...... 630 860-2500
Itasca *(G-11748)*

TOYS & HOBBY GOODS & SPLYS, WHOLESALE: Toys, NEC

First & Main Inc.....................................E...... 630 587-1000
Saint Charles *(G-18199)*

TOYS & HOBBY GOODS & SPLYS, WHOLESALE: Video Games

Gamestop Inc...G...... 773 568-0457
Chicago *(G-4658)*

TOYS, HOBBY GOODS & SPLYS WHOLESALERS

Enesco LLC..B...... 630 875-5300
Itasca *(G-11650)*
Kd-Kidz Dlight Interactive LLC ....G...... 630 724-0223
Downers Grove *(G-8038)*

PRODUCT SECTION

TOYS: Dolls, Stuffed Animals & Parts
Enesco LLC .... B 630 875-5300
  Itasca *(G-11650)*
Unique Novelty & Manufacturing .... G 217 538-2014
  Fillmore *(G-9666)*

TOYS: Electronic
Circuitron Inc .... G 815 886-9010
  Romeoville *(G-17809)*
Jcw Investments Inc .... G 708 478-7323
  Orland Park *(G-15962)*
Petronics Inc .... G 608 630-6527
  Champaign *(G-3331)*

TOYS: Rubber
Enesco LLC .... B 630 875-5300
  Itasca *(G-11650)*

TOYS: Video Game Machines
Gamestop Inc .... G 773 568-0457
  Chicago *(G-4658)*
Gamestop Corp .... G 618 258-8611
  Wood River *(G-21262)*
Raw Thrills Inc .... D 847 679-8373
  Skokie *(G-19019)*
Wiliams Interactive LLC .... C 773 961-1920
  Chicago *(G-6625)*

TRADE SHOW ARRANGEMENT SVCS
Associated Equipment Distrs .... E 630 574-0650
  Schaumburg *(G-18447)*
Chambers Marketing Options .... G 847 584-2626
  Elk Grove Village *(G-8888)*
HH Backer Associates Inc .... F 312 578-1818
  Chicago *(G-4812)*
Matrex Exhibits Inc .... D 630 628-2233
  Addison *(G-193)*
Stevens Exhibits & Displays .... E 773 523-3900
  Chicago *(G-6246)*

TRADERS: Commodity, Contracts
K-Pro US LLC .... G 872 529-5776
  O Fallon *(G-15576)*

TRAILERS & CHASSIS: Camping
Arthur Leo Kuhl .... G 618 752-5473
  Ingraham *(G-11591)*

TRAILERS & PARTS: Boat
Knight Bros Inc .... E 618 439-9626
  Benton *(G-1930)*

TRAILERS & PARTS: Truck & Semi's
A & S Steel Specialties Inc .... E 815 838-8188
  Lockport *(G-12979)*
Advanced Mobility & .... E 708 235-2800
  Monee *(G-14195)*
Barrington Financial Services .... G 847 404-1767
  Lake In The Hills *(G-12330)*
Barron 2m Inc .... G 847 219-3650
  Schaumburg *(G-18456)*
Classic Roadliner Corporation .... G 708 769-0666
  Justice *(G-11950)*
D D Sales Inc .... G 217 857-3196
  Teutopolis *(G-19768)*
Dolche Truckload Corp .... G 800 719-4921
  Palatine *(G-16113)*
Dundee Truck & Trlr Works LLC ..... G 224 484-8182
  East Dundee *(G-8195)*
Entrans International LLC .... E 618 548-3660
  Salem *(G-18337)*
Fleetpride Inc .... C 708 430-2081
  Bridgeview *(G-2347)*
Great Dane LLC .... D 773 254-5533
  Chicago *(G-4733)*
Groovy Logistics Inc .... G 847 946-1491
  Joliet *(G-11871)*
Hunter Logistics .... G 309 299-7015
  Wataga *(G-20286)*
Jhb Group Inc .... G 657 888-3473
  Cary *(G-3173)*
Load Redi Inc .... G 217 784-4200
  Gibson City *(G-10340)*
Maple Park Trucking Inc .... G 815 899-1958
  Maple Park *(G-13465)*

Matt Snell and Sons .... G 618 695-3555
  Vienna *(G-20118)*
Mickey Truck Bodies Inc .... F 309 827-8227
  Bloomington *(G-2076)*
Midland Manufacturing Corp .... C 847 677-0333
  Skokie *(G-18990)*
Mmm Uno Corp .... G 773 577-7329
  Streamwood *(G-19586)*
Pk Corporation .... G 847 879-1070
  Elk Grove Village *(G-9180)*
Roadex Carriers Inc .... G 773 454-8772
  Wheeling *(G-20975)*
Robert Davis & Son Inc .... G 815 889-4168
  Milford *(G-14036)*
Seat Trans Inc .... G 224 522-1007
  Lake In The Hills *(G-12343)*
Summit Tank & Equipment Co .... F 708 594-3040
  Mc Cook *(G-13703)*
U S Intermodal Inc .... E 708 448-9862
  Frankfort *(G-9848)*
Vaughan Equipment Inc .... G 618 842-3500
  Fairfield *(G-9638)*

TRAILERS & TRAILER EQPT
Advance Metalworking Company ..... E 309 853-3387
  Kewanee *(G-12019)*
Custom Millers Supply Inc .... G 309 734-6312
  Monmouth *(G-14216)*
Grs Holding LLC .... F 630 355-1660
  Naperville *(G-14838)*
New World Trnsp Systems .... C 773 509-5931
  Chicago *(G-5583)*
Synergy Power Group LLC .... E 618 247-3200
  Sandoval *(G-18365)*
Triple B Manufacturing Co Inc .... G 618 566-2888
  Mascoutah *(G-13607)*
Wise Equipment & Rentals Inc .... F 847 895-5555
  Schaumburg *(G-18774)*

TRAILERS: Bodies
Imperial Group Mfg Inc .... B 615 325-9224
  Chicago *(G-4897)*
Paramount Truck Body Co Inc .... E 312 666-6441
  Chicago *(G-5762)*
Peter Built .... E 618 337-4000
  East Saint Louis *(G-8318)*

TRAILERS: Demountable Cargo Containers
Great Dane LLC .... B 309 854-0407
  Kewanee *(G-12037)*

TRAILERS: Semitrailers, Truck Tractors
Azcon Inc .... F 815 548-7000
  Sterling *(G-19499)*
Great Dane LLC .... C 309 854-0407
  Kewanee *(G-12036)*
Great Dane LLC .... D 773 254-5533
  Kewanee *(G-12038)*
Quality Trailer Sales Inc .... G 630 739-2495
  Morton *(G-14380)*
STI Holdings Inc .... F 630 789-2713
  Burr Ridge *(G-2722)*
Timpte Industries Inc .... D 309 820-1095
  Bloomington *(G-2102)*

TRANSDUCERS: Electrical Properties
Knowles Elec Holdings Inc .... A 630 250-5100
  Itasca *(G-11687)*
Knowles Electronics LLC .... C 630 250-5100
  Itasca *(G-11688)*

TRANSFORMERS: Control
Micron Industries Corporation .... C 630 516-1222
  Oak Brook *(G-15645)*
Micron Industries Corporation .... D 815 380-2222
  Sterling *(G-19519)*

TRANSFORMERS: Distribution
Invenergy Wind Fin Co III LLC .... G 312 224-1400
  Chicago *(G-4963)*
Powell Industries Inc .... G 708 409-1200
  Northlake *(G-15557)*
Thomas Research Products LLC .... F 224 654-8626
  Elgin *(G-8754)*

TRANSFORMERS: Power Related

TRANSFORMERS: Electric
Hubbell Power Systems Inc .... F 618 797-5000
  Edwardsville *(G-8365)*
Orei LLC .... G 847 983-4761
  Skokie *(G-19001)*
Wicc Ltd .... D 309 444-4125
  Washington *(G-20284)*

TRANSFORMERS: Electronic
Charles Industries LLC .... D 847 806-6300
  Schaumburg *(G-18474)*
Inglot Electronics Corp .... D 773 286-5881
  Chicago *(G-4921)*
Ipr Systems Inc .... G 708 385-7500
  Alsip *(G-458)*
Lenco Electronics Inc .... E 815 344-2900
  McHenry *(G-13756)*
MEI Realty Ltd .... G 847 358-5000
  Inverness *(G-11597)*

TRANSFORMERS: Fluorescent Lighting
Dex Blue Corp .... F 847 916-7744
  Morton Grove *(G-14399)*

TRANSFORMERS: Flyback
Gsg Industries .... F 618 544-7976
  Robinson *(G-17115)*

TRANSFORMERS: Lighting, Street & Airport
Peterson Elc Panl Mfg Co Inc .... F 708 449-2270
  Berkeley *(G-1943)*

TRANSFORMERS: Meters, Electronic
Cymatics Inc .... G 630 420-7117
  Naperville *(G-14811)*

TRANSFORMERS: Power Related
Coiltechnic Inc .... F 815 675-9260
  Spring Grove *(G-19271)*
Communication Coil Inc .... D 847 671-1333
  Schiller Park *(G-18795)*
Dresser LLC .... D 847 437-5940
  Elk Grove Village *(G-8955)*
Equus Power I LP .... G 847 908-2878
  Schaumburg *(G-18519)*
Forest Electric Company .... E 708 681-0180
  Melrose Park *(G-13868)*
Gsg Industries .... F 618 544-7976
  Robinson *(G-17115)*
Inglot Electronics Corp .... D 773 286-5881
  Chicago *(G-4921)*
Ipr Systems Inc .... G 708 385-7500
  Alsip *(G-458)*
Lenco Electronics Inc .... E 815 344-2900
  McHenry *(G-13756)*
Magnetic Coil Manufacturing Co ..... E 630 787-1948
  Wood Dale *(G-21212)*
Magnetic Devices Inc .... G 815 459-0077
  Crystal Lake *(G-7222)*
Methode Development Co .... D 708 867-6777
  Chicago *(G-5408)*
Micron Engineering Co .... G 815 455-2888
  Crystal Lake *(G-7228)*
Mitsubishi Elc Automtn Inc .... C 847 478-2100
  Vernon Hills *(G-20075)*
Newhaven Display Intl Inc .... E 847 844-8795
  Elgin *(G-8668)*
Pactra Corp .... G 847 281-0308
  Vernon Hills *(G-20081)*
Power House Tool Inc .... E 815 727-6301
  Joliet *(G-11915)*
Precision Components Inc .... D 630 462-9110
  Saint Charles *(G-18249)*
Saachi Inc .... G 630 775-1700
  Roselle *(G-17982)*
Simplex Inc .... C 217 483-1600
  Springfield *(G-19446)*
Storage Battery Systems LLC .... G 630 221-1700
  Carol Stream *(G-3078)*
TLC Dental Care LLC .... G 425 442-9000
  Elgin *(G-8755)*
U S Co-Tronics Corp .... E 815 692-3204
  Fairbury *(G-9615)*

Employee Codes: A=Over 500 employees, B=251-500
C=101-250, D=51-100, E=20-50, F=10-19, G=3-9

TRANSFORMERS: Specialty

TRANSFORMERS: Specialty
- Aldonex Inc .... F 708 547-5663
  Bellwood *(G-1613)*
- Ferrite International Company .... E 847 249-4900
  Wadsworth *(G-20209)*
- Olsun Electrics Corporation .... G 815 678-2421
  Richmond *(G-17019)*
- Relay Services Mfg Corp .... F 773 252-2700
  Chicago *(G-6008)*
- Transformer Manufacturers Inc .... E 708 457-1200
  Norridge *(G-15245)*
- V and F Transformer Corp .... D 630 497-8070
  Elgin *(G-8771)*

TRANSLATION & INTERPRETATION SVCS
- Chicago Mltlingua Graphics Inc .... F 847 386-7187
  Northfield *(G-15512)*
- Techno - Grphics Trnsltons Inc .... E 708 331-3333
  South Holland *(G-19248)*

TRANSMISSIONS: Motor Vehicle
- Gray Machine & Welding Inc .... F 309 788-2501
  Rock Island *(G-17220)*
- Midwest Converters Inc .... F 815 229-9808
  Rockford *(G-17525)*
- Powertrain Rockford Inc .... C 815 633-7460
  Loves Park *(G-13248)*
- Wpg US Holdco LLC .... B 312 517-3750
  Chicago *(G-6681)*

TRANSPORTATION AGENTS & BROKERS
- Icg Illinois .... G 217 947-2332
  Elkhart *(G-9318)*

TRANSPORTATION BROKERS: Truck
- Amcol International Corp .... E 847 851-1500
  Hoffman Estates *(G-11405)*

TRANSPORTATION EPQT & SPLYS, WHOL: Aeronautical Eqpt & Splys
- Direct Aerosystems Inc .... F 630 509-2141
  Aurora *(G-952)*

TRANSPORTATION EPQT & SPLYS, WHOLESALE: Nav Eqpt & Splys
- Cedar Elec Holdings Corp .... G 630 862-7282
  Chicago *(G-4051)*

TRANSPORTATION EPQT & SPLYS, WHOLESALE: Pulleys
- Illinois Pulley & Gear Inc .... G 847 407-9595
  Schaumburg *(G-18556)*

TRANSPORTATION EQPT & SPLYS WHOLESALERS, NEC
- Hella Corporate Center USA Inc .... B 734 414-0900
  Flora *(G-9682)*
- UTC Railcar Repair Svcs LLC .... A 312 431-5053
  Chicago *(G-6508)*
- Voestalpine Nortrak Inc .... D 708 753-2125
  Chicago Heights *(G-6786)*

TRANSPORTATION EQUIPMENT, NEC
- IPC Group Purchasing .... G 630 276-5485
  Naperville *(G-14850)*
- Loraines Logistics LLC .... G 800 839-6943
  Chicago *(G-5259)*

TRANSPORTATION SVCS, AIR, NONSCHEDULED: Air Cargo Carriers
- Bison Aerospace and Def LLC .... G 618 795-2678
  Savanna *(G-18403)*

TRANSPORTATION SVCS, NEC
- Priva Mobility Inc .... G 248 410-3702
  Evanston *(G-9571)*

TRANSPORTATION SVCS: Airport Limousine, Scheduled Svcs
- Driver Services .... G 505 267-8686
  Bensenville *(G-1789)*

TRANSPORTATION SVCS: Railroads, Interurban
- U S Railway Services .... G 708 468-8343
  Tinley Park *(G-19864)*

TRANSPORTATION SVCS: Railroads, Steam
- Covia Holdings Corporation .... G 618 747-2355
  Tamms *(G-19742)*

TRANSPORTATION: Air, Scheduled Passenger
- Hunter Logistics .... G 309 299-7015
  Wataga *(G-20286)*

TRANSPORTATION: Bus Transit Systems
- Zimmerman Enterprises Inc .... F 847 297-3177
  Des Plaines *(G-7871)*

TRANSPORTATION: Deep Sea Domestic Freight
- BP America Inc .... A 630 420-5111
  Warrenville *(G-20232)*

TRANSPORTATION: Transit Systems, NEC
- Polmax LLC .... C 708 843-8300
  Alsip *(G-494)*

TRAPS: Animal, Iron Or Steel
- L & M Hardware Ltd .... G 630 493-1026
  Burr Ridge *(G-2694)*

TRAPS: Stem
- Lilly Industries Inc .... F 630 773-2222
  Itasca *(G-11694)*
- Spirax Sarco Inc .... F 630 493-4525
  Lisle *(G-12940)*

TRAVEL TRAILERS & CAMPERS
- A & S Steel Specialties Inc .... E 815 838-8188
  Lockport *(G-12979)*
- Boyd Spotting Inc .... G 217 669-2418
  Cisco *(G-6891)*
- Brumleve Industries Inc .... F 217 857-3777
  Teutopolis *(G-19764)*
- Davison Co Ltd .... G 815 966-2905
  Rockford *(G-17370)*
- Dedicated Tcs LLC .... F 815 467-9560
  Channahon *(G-3378)*
- I94 Rv LLC .... F 847 395-9500
  Russell *(G-18114)*
- Lakeshore Lacrosse LLC .... G 773 350-4356
  Wheaton *(G-20810)*
- Rieco-Titan Products Inc .... E 815 464-7400
  Frankfort *(G-9831)*
- Travel Caddy Inc .... E 847 621-7000
  Franklin Park *(G-10065)*

TRAVELER ACCOMMODATIONS, NEC
- Jack & Lidias Resort Inc .... G 847 356-1389
  Lake Villa *(G-12356)*
- Lane Industries Inc .... E 847 498-6650
  Northbrook *(G-15417)*

TRAYS: Cable, Metal Plate
- Cablofil Inc .... B 618 566-3230
  Mascoutah *(G-13595)*
- Cooper B-Line Inc .... A 618 654-2184
  Highland *(G-11210)*
- Wb Tray LLC .... G 618 918-3821
  Centralia *(G-3254)*

TRAYS: Plastic
- Newell Operating Company .... C 815 235-4171
  Freeport *(G-10129)*

TRIM: Window, Wood
- Ideal Cabinet Solutions Inc .... G 618 514-7087
  Alhambra *(G-401)*

TROPHIES, NEC
- All American Trophy King Inc .... F 708 597-2121
  Crestwood *(G-7105)*
- AMG International Inc .... G 847 439-1001
  Elk Grove Village *(G-8827)*
- Budget Signs .... F 618 259-4460
  Wood River *(G-21260)*
- Captains Emporium Inc .... G 773 972-7609
  Chicago *(G-4021)*
- Mint Masters Inc .... E 847 451-1133
  Franklin Park *(G-10000)*
- Mtm Recognition Corporation .... C 815 875-1111
  Princeton *(G-16817)*
- Trophies By George .... G 630 497-1212
  Bartlett *(G-1318)*

TROPHIES, PLATED, ALL METALS
- RS Owens Div St Regis LLC .... D 773 282-6000
  Itasca *(G-11730)*
- Rudon Enterprises Inc .... G 618 457-0441
  Carbondale *(G-2857)*
- Stellar Recognition Inc .... D 773 282-8060
  Chicago *(G-6243)*

TROPHIES, WHOLESALE
- A 1 Trophies Awards & Engrv .... G 630 837-6000
  Streamwood *(G-19558)*
- All American Trophy King Inc .... F 708 597-2121
  Crestwood *(G-7105)*
- B D Enterprises .... G 618 462-5861
  Alton *(G-545)*
- Bishops Engrv & Trophy Svc Inc .... G 773 777-5014
  Chicago *(G-3901)*
- Classique Signs & Engrv Inc .... G 217 228-7446
  Quincy *(G-16872)*
- Joans Trophy & Plaque Co .... E 309 674-6500
  Peoria *(G-16463)*
- Johnos Inc .... G 630 897-6929
  Aurora *(G-1119)*

TROPHIES: Metal, Exc Silver
- Afar Imports & Interiors Inc .... G 217 744-3262
  Springfield *(G-19316)*
- American Trophy & Award Co Inc .... G 312 939-3252
  Chicago *(G-3672)*
- Awards and More Inc .... G 773 581-7771
  Chicago *(G-3792)*
- Mighty Mites Awards and Sons .... G 847 297-0035
  Des Plaines *(G-7802)*
- Planter Inc .... D 773 637-7777
  Chicago *(G-5817)*
- R S Owens & Co Inc .... B 773 282-6000
  Chicago *(G-5953)*
- Voss Pattern Works Inc .... G 618 233-4242
  Belleville *(G-1609)*

TROPHY & PLAQUE STORES
- A 1 Trophies Awards & Engrv .... G 630 837-6000
  Streamwood *(G-19558)*
- Academy Screenprinting Awards .... G 309 686-0026
  Peoria *(G-16374)*
- All American Trophy King Inc .... F 708 597-2121
  Crestwood *(G-7105)*
- Athletic Outfitters Inc .... G 815 942-6696
  Morris *(G-14291)*
- Award Emblem Mfg Co Inc .... F 630 739-0800
  Bolingbrook *(G-2153)*
- Awards and More Inc .... G 773 581-7771
  Chicago *(G-3792)*
- Budget Signs .... F 618 259-4460
  Wood River *(G-21260)*
- Camilles of Canton Inc .... G 309 647-7403
  Canton *(G-2822)*
- Classique Signs & Engrv Inc .... G 217 228-7446
  Quincy *(G-16872)*
- Crown Trophy .... G 309 699-1766
  East Peoria *(G-8264)*
- Custom Trophies .... G 217 422-3353
  Decatur *(G-7480)*
- Fielders Choice .... G 618 937-2294
  West Frankfort *(G-20671)*
- Finer Line Inc .... F 847 884-1611
  Itasca *(G-11657)*

PRODUCT SECTION

TRUCKING: Local, Without Storage

Joans Trophy & Plaque Co ....E 309 674-6500
  Peoria (G-16463)
Minor League Inc ....G 618 548-8040
  Salem (G-18347)
Signs Today Inc ....G 847 934-9777
  Palatine (G-16158)
Town Hall Sports Inc ....F 618 235-9881
  Belleville (G-1601)
Trophies and Awards Plus ....G 708 754-7127
  Steger (G-19494)
Trophies By George ....G 630 497-1212
  Bartlett (G-1318)
Trophytime Inc ....G 217 351-7958
  Champaign (G-3359)
Twin City Awards ....G 309 452-9291
  Normal (G-15226)
U R On It ....G 847 382-0182
  Lake Barrington (G-12167)
Walnut Creek Hardwood ....G 815 389-3317
  South Beloit (G-19120)
Wheaton Trophy & Engravers ....G 630 682-4200
  Wheaton (G-20831)

TRUCK & BUS BODIES: Automobile Wrecker Truck

Imperial Oil Inc ....G 773 866-1235
  Chicago (G-4898)
Tondinis Wrecker Service ....G 618 997-9884
  Marion (G-13541)

TRUCK & BUS BODIES: Beverage Truck

Mickey Truck Bodies Inc ....F 309 827-8227
  Bloomington (G-2076)

TRUCK & BUS BODIES: Bus Bodies

Motor Coach Inds Intl Inc ....C 847 285-2000
  Des Plaines (G-7804)

TRUCK & BUS BODIES: Dump Truck

C I F Industries Inc ....E 618 635-2010
  Staunton (G-19476)

TRUCK & BUS BODIES: Motor Vehicle, Specialty

Quad County Fire Equipment ....G 815 832-4475
  Saunemin (G-18402)

TRUCK & BUS BODIES: Tank Truck

Bruder Tank Inc ....E 217 292-9058
  Sullivan (G-19662)

TRUCK & BUS BODIES: Truck Cabs, Motor Vehicles

Campbell International Inc ....E 408 661-0794
  Wauconda (G-20339)
Robinsport LLC ....G 630 724-9280
  Woodridge (G-21337)

TRUCK & BUS BODIES: Truck Tops

Tri-County Truck Tops Inc ....G 847 740-4004
  Round Lake (G-18085)

TRUCK & BUS BODIES: Truck, Motor Vehicle

C S O Corp ....D 630 365-6600
  Virgil (G-20190)
Dierzen Trailer Co ....D 815 695-5291
  Newark (G-15076)
Donermen LLC ....G 773 430-2828
  Chicago (G-4382)
Erie Vehicle Company ....F 773 536-6300
  Chicago (G-4526)
Gvw Group LLC ....G 847 681-8417
  Highland Park (G-11269)
Jarco Inc ....E 888 681-3660
  Salem (G-18343)
Paramount Truck Body Co Inc ....E 312 666-6441
  Chicago (G-5762)
Sauber Manufacturing Company ....D 630 365-6600
  Virgil (G-20191)

TRUCK & BUS BODIES: Utility Truck

City Utility Equipment ....F 815 254-6673
  Plainfield (G-16651)

TRUCK & BUS BODIES: Van Bodies

Mid-America Truck Corporation ....D 815 672-3211
  Streator (G-19614)

TRUCK & FREIGHT TERMINALS & SUPPORT ACTIVITIES

East St Louis Trml & Stor Co ....E 618 271-2185
  East Saint Louis (G-8306)
Hunter Logistics ....G 309 299-7015
  Wataga (G-20286)

TRUCK BODIES: Body Parts

ATI Oldco Inc ....C 630 860-5600
  Bartlett (G-1266)
Auto Truck Group LLC ....C 630 860-5600
  Bartlett (G-1267)
Herr Display Vans Inc ....G 708 755-7926
  Sauk Village (G-18400)
Newf LLC ....G 630 330-5462
  Naperville (G-14883)

TRUCK BODY SHOP

Mickey Truck Bodies Inc ....F 309 827-8227
  Bloomington (G-2076)
Roll-A-Way Conveyors Inc ....F 847 336-5033
  Gurnee (G-10924)

TRUCK FINANCE LEASING

Navistar Inc ....C 331 332-5000
  Lisle (G-12917)

TRUCK GENERAL REPAIR SVC

Botts Welding and Trck Svc Inc ....E 815 338-0594
  Woodstock (G-21366)
D D Sales Inc ....E 217 857-3196
  Teutopolis (G-19768)
Dundee Truck & Trlr Works LLC ....G 224 484-8182
  East Dundee (G-8195)
Holstein Garage Inc ....G 630 668-0328
  Wheaton (G-20802)
National Tractor Parts Inc ....E 630 552-4235
  Plano (G-16736)
North Shore Truck & Equipment ....F 847 887-0200
  Lake Bluff (G-12201)
Rex Radiator and Welding Co ....G 847 428-1112
  East Dundee (G-8209)
Wirfs Industries Inc ....F 815 344-0635
  McHenry (G-13809)

TRUCK PAINTING & LETTERING SVCS

Canham Graphics ....G 217 585-5085
  Springfield (G-19337)
Dierzen-Kewanee Heavy Inds ....D 309 853-2316
  Kewanee (G-12030)
E K Kuhn Inc ....G 815 899-9211
  Sycamore (G-19709)
Enterprise Signs Inc ....G 708 691-1273
  Blue Island (G-2121)
Image Signs Inc ....F 815 282-4141
  Loves Park (G-13218)
Paldo Sign and Display Company ......G 708 456-1711
  River Grove (G-17065)
Schellerer Corporation Inc ....D 630 980-4567
  Hanover Park (G-11013)
Sign Central ....G 847 543-7600
  Round Lake (G-18083)

TRUCK PARTS & ACCESSORIES: Wholesalers

Bonnell Industries Inc ....D 815 284-3819
  Dixon (G-7890)
Botts Welding and Trck Svc Inc ....E 815 338-0594
  Woodstock (G-21366)
Fleetpride Inc ....C 708 430-2081
  Bridgeview (G-2347)
L & T Services Inc ....G 815 397-6260
  Rockford (G-17487)
P & A Driveline & Machine Inc ....F 630 860-7474
  Bensenville (G-1865)
Salco Products Inc ....D 630 783-2570
  Lemont (G-12588)
Standard Truck Parts Inc ....G 815 726-4486
  Joliet (G-11932)

TRUCKING & HAULING SVCS: Coal, Local

ODaniel Trucking Co ....D 618 382-5371
  Carmi (G-2912)

TRUCKING & HAULING SVCS: Contract Basis

Caples-El Transport Inc ....G 708 300-2727
  Calumet City (G-2772)

TRUCKING & HAULING SVCS: Heavy Machinery, Local

Harold L Ray Truck & Trctr Svc ....F 618 673-2701
  Cisne (G-6893)

TRUCKING & HAULING SVCS: Mobile Homes

Mobil Trailer Transport Inc ....E 630 993-1200
  Villa Park (G-20160)

TRUCKING & HAULING SVCS: Trailer/Container On Flat Car

Jtec Industries Inc ....E 309 698-9301
  East Peoria (G-8273)

TRUCKING, DUMP

Callender Construction Co Inc ....F 217 285-2161
  Pittsfield (G-16630)
Conmat Inc ....E 815 235-2200
  Freeport (G-10104)
Myers Concrete & Construction ....G 815 732-2591
  Oregon (G-15924)
Thelen Sand & Gravel Inc ....D 847 838-8800
  Antioch (G-636)

TRUCKING: Except Local

Amcol International Corp ....E 847 851-1500
  Hoffman Estates (G-11405)
CJ Drilling Inc ....D 847 669-8000
  Dundee (G-8126)
Ed Hartwig Trucking & Excvtg ....G 309 364-3672
  Henry (G-11163)
Hunter Logistics ....G 309 299-7015
  Wataga (G-20286)
Illinois Road Contractors Inc ....E 217 245-6181
  Jacksonville (G-11769)
Pdv Midwest Refining LLC ....A 630 257-7761
  Lemont (G-12581)
Phoenix Trucking Inc ....G 708 514-2094
  Westchester (G-20708)
Tyson Fresh Meats Inc ....F 847 836-5550
  Elgin (G-8764)
Valley View Industries Inc ....E 815 358-2236
  Cornell (G-7014)

TRUCKING: Local, With Storage

Coyote Transportation Inc ....G 630 204-5729
  Bensenville (G-1779)
Kraft Heinz Foods Company ....D 217 378-1900
  Champaign (G-3315)

TRUCKING: Local, Without Storage

Abner Trucking Co Inc ....G 618 676-1301
  Clay City (G-6902)
Archer-Daniels-Midland Company .....D 217 424-5882
  Decatur (G-7441)
BFI Waste Systems N Amer Inc ....E 847 429-7370
  Elgin (G-8521)
Blomberg Bros Inc ....F 618 245-6321
  Farina (G-9651)
Bob Barnett Redi-Mix Inc ....E 618 252-3581
  Harrisburg (G-11020)
Bristol Transport Inc ....E 708 343-6411
  Melrose Park (G-13838)
C & H Gravel C Inc ....G 217 857-3425
  Teutopolis (G-19765)
Davidson Grain Incorporated ....E 815 384-3208
  Creston (G-7101)
Fuller Asphalt & Landscape ....G 618 797-1169
  Granite City (G-10707)
Geske and Sons Inc ....F 815 459-2407
  Crystal Lake (G-7202)
Gorman Brothers Ready Mix Inc ....F 618 498-2173
  Jerseyville (G-11791)
Hastie Min & Trckg Ltd Partnr ....E 618 289-4536
  Cave In Rock (G-3219)

TRUCKING: Local, Without Storage PRODUCT SECTION

Huyear Trucking Inc....G....217 854-3551
Carlinville (G-2876)
J W Rudy Co Inc....F....618 676-1616
Clay City (G-6906)
James Randall....G....309 444-8765
Washington (G-20272)
Jax Asphalt Company Inc....F....618 244-0500
Mount Vernon (G-14618)
Jay A Morris....G....815 432-6440
Watseka (G-20308)
Maplehurst Farms Inc....F....815 562-8723
Rochelle (G-17148)
Metropolis Ready Mix Inc....E....618 524-8221
Metropolis (G-13974)
National Concrete Pipe Co....E....630 766-3600
Franklin Park (G-10006)
R & J Trucking and Recycl Inc....F....708 563-2600
Chicago (G-5943)
Rd Daily Enterprises....G....847 872-7632
Winthrop Harbor (G-21142)
Robinsport LLC....G....630 724-9280
Woodridge (G-21337)
Southfield Corporation....E....309 829-1087
Bloomington (G-2096)
Upchurch Ready Mix Concrete....G....618 235-6222
Belleville (G-1605)
Valley View Industries Inc....E....815 358-2236
Cornell (G-7014)

TRUCKS & TRACTORS: Industrial

Align Production Systems LLC....E....217 423-6001
Decatur (G-7439)
All-Vac Industries Inc....F....847 675-2290
Skokie (G-18915)
As Lawn & Land LLC....G....309 246-5012
Lacon (G-12125)
Big Lift LLC....E....630 916-2600
Lombard (G-13042)
Caldwell & Moten LLC....G....773 619-2584
Chicago (G-4003)
Caterpillar Inc....A....630 859-5000
Montgomery (G-14238)
Centralia Machine & Fab Inc....G....618 533-9010
Centralia (G-3223)
Chevron Commercial Inc....G....618 654-5555
Highland (G-11209)
Clark Caster Co....G....708 366-1913
Forest Park (G-9710)
Conveyors Plus Inc....G....708 361-1512
Orland Park (G-15948)
ED Etnyre & Co....B....815 732-2116
Oregon (G-15917)
Elgin Sweeper Company....B....847 741-5370
Elgin (G-8577)
Freight Car Services Inc....B....217 443-4106
Danville (G-7336)
Green Valley Mfg Ill Inc....E....217 864-4125
Mount Zion (G-14647)
H & B Machine Corporation....G....312 829-4850
Chicago (G-4756)
H R Slater Co Inc....F....312 666-1855
Chicago (G-4760)
Handling Systems Intl Inc....E....708 352-1213
Mc Cook (G-13692)
Henderson Products Inc....G....847 515-3482
Huntley (G-11539)
Hyster-Yale Group Inc....E....217 443-7416
Danville (G-7348)
Illinois Lift Equipment Inc....E....888 745-0577
Cary (G-3169)
It Transportation Company....F....773 383-5073
Chicago (G-4975)
J W Todd Co....G....630 406-5715
Aurora (G-1114)
Jcb Inc....G....912 704-2995
Aurora (G-990)
Lanco International Inc....B....708 596-5200
Hazel Crest (G-11131)
Littell LLC....E....630 916-6662
Schaumburg (G-18609)
M&J Hauling Inc....G....312 342-6596
Chicago (G-5306)
Marvel Industries Incorporated....G....847 325-2930
Buffalo Grove (G-2569)
MHS Ltd....F....773 736-3333
Chicago (G-5419)
New Cie Inc....E....815 224-1511
Peru (G-16584)
Phoenix Trucking Inc....G....708 514-2094
Westchester (G-20708)
Pools Welding Inc....G....309 787-2083
Milan (G-14020)
Premier Cdl Training Svcs LLC....G....618 797-1725
Granite City (G-10732)
Sardee Industries Inc....G....630 824-4200
Lisle (G-12936)
STI Holdings Inc....F....630 789-2713
Burr Ridge (G-2722)
Synergy Power Group LLC....E....618 247-3200
Sandoval (G-18365)
T & E Enterprises Herscher Inc....F....815 426-2761
Herscher (G-11188)
Tewell Bros Machine Inc....F....217 253-6303
Tuscola (G-19931)
Tomahawk AG & Industrial LLC....E....309 275-2874
Heyworth (G-11192)
Triple B Manufacturing Co Inc....G....618 566-2888
Mascoutah (G-13607)
Universal Feeder Inc....G....815 633-0752
Machesney Park (G-13382)
Vactor Manufacturing Inc....A....815 672-3171
Streator (G-19632)
William W Meyer and Sons....D....847 918-0111
Libertyville (G-12726)

TRUCKS, INDL: Wholesalers

Hovi Industries Incorporated....E....815 512-7500
Bolingbrook (G-2186)

TRUCKS: Forklift

F and S Enterprises Plainfield....G....815 439-9655
Plainfield (G-16662)
Grant J Grapperhaus....G....618 410-4428
Highland (G-11216)
KG Lift Inc....G....815 908-1855
Addison (G-168)
Komatsu Forklift USA LLC....E....847 437-5800
Rolling Meadows (G-17744)
Manitex International Inc....E....708 430-7500
Bridgeview (G-2361)
Mh Equipment Company....D....217 443-7210
Danville (G-7366)
Pwf....G....815 967-0218
Rockford (G-17563)
Specialized Liftruck Svcs LLC....F....708 552-2705
Bedford Park (G-1505)
Systems Equipment Services....G....708 535-1273
Oak Forest (G-15689)
Tri County Lift Trucks Inc....G....847 838-0183
Antioch (G-639)

TRUCKS: Indl

Aidar Express Inc....G....773 757-3447
Chicago (G-3587)
Always There Express Corp....E....773 931-3744
Romeoville (G-17792)
Bo Inc....F....312 459-0013
Countryside (G-7045)
C C P Express Inc....G....773 315-0317
Berwyn (G-1949)
Dicom Transportation Group LP....G....312 255-4800
Chicago (G-4355)
Edward J Warren Jr....G....630 882-8817
Yorkville (G-21481)
Kta Trucking Services Inc....G....224 788-8312
Antioch (G-619)
Lexpress Inc....G....773 517-7095
Prospect Heights (G-16844)
Lion Trans Group Inc....G....970 402-8073
Rolling Meadows (G-17748)
Platinum Inc....G....815 385-0910
McHenry (G-13780)
Tarnow Logistics Inc....G....773 844-3203
Melrose Park (G-13922)
Tdr Express Inc....G....224 805-0070
Chicago (G-6332)
Trx Express Inc....G....815 582-3792
Crest Hill (G-7099)
Yusraa Inc....G....312 608-1916
Dolton (G-7941)

TRUSSES & FRAMING: Prefabricated Metal

Chicago Panel & Truss Inc....E....630 870-1300
Aurora (G-1074)
Unistrut International Corp....C....800 882-5543
Harvey (G-11099)

TRUSSES: Wood, Floor

Alexander Lumber Co....G....815 754-1000
Cortland (G-7016)
Lumberyard Suppliers Inc....E....217 965-4911
Virden (G-20187)
Okaw Truss Inc....B....217 543-3371
Arthur (G-873)
Rehkemper & Sons Inc....E....618 526-2269
Breese (G-2307)

TRUSSES: Wood, Roof

Anderson Truss Company....G....618 982-9228
Pittsburg (G-16626)
Atlas Building Components Inc....E....618 639-0222
Jerseyville (G-11787)
Atlas Components Inc....E....815 332-4904
Cherry Valley (G-3437)
Bear Creek Truss Inc....E....217 543-3329
Tuscola (G-19923)
Central Illinois Truss....F....309 447-6644
Deer Creek (G-7572)
Central Illinois Truss....G....309 266-8787
Morton (G-14356)
Jesse B Holt Inc....D....618 783-3075
Newton (G-15086)
Southern Truss Inc....E....618 252-8144
Harrisburg (G-11029)
Triumph Truss & Steel Company....F....815 522-6000
Elgin (G-8762)
Truss Components Inc....F....800 678-7877
Columbia (G-6995)

TRUST COMPANIES: State Accepting Deposits, Commercial

Harris Bmo Bank National Assn....E....815 886-1900
Romeoville (G-17830)

TRUST MANAGEMENT SVCS: Personal Investment

Jaffee Investment Partnr LP....C....312 321-1515
Chicago (G-4999)

TUB CONTAINERS: Plastic

R and R Brokerage Co....C....847 438-4600
Lake Zurich (G-12448)

TUBE & TUBING FABRICATORS

Acrofab....G....630 350-7941
Bensenville (G-1727)
Alconix Usa Inc....G....847 717-7407
Elk Grove Village (G-8813)
Alert Tubing Fabricators Inc....G....815 633-5065
Loves Park (G-13186)
Bessco Tube Bending Pipe Fabg....G....708 339-3977
South Holland (G-19201)
Boyce Industries Inc....F....708 345-0455
Melrose Park (G-13836)
Cain Tubular Products Inc....G....630 584-5330
Saint Charles (G-18162)
Chicago Tube and Iron Company....E....815 834-2500
Romeoville (G-17807)
Cortube Products Co....G....708 429-6700
Tinley Park (G-19816)
D & W Mfg Co Inc....E....773 533-1542
Chicago (G-4300)
Dove Steel Inc....F....815 588-3772
Lockport (G-12990)
Fulton Metal Works Inc....G....217 476-8223
Ashland (G-884)
Leading Edge Group Inc....C....815 316-3500
Rockford (G-17492)
Metamora Industries LLC....E....309 367-2368
Metamora (G-13964)
Parker Fabrication Inc....G....309 698-8080
East Peoria (G-8282)
Parker Fabrication Inc....E....309 266-8413
Morton (G-14376)
Pekay Machine & Engrg Co Inc....F....312 829-5530
Chicago (G-5784)
Ptc Tubular Products LLC....C....815 692-4900
Fairbury (G-9612)
Sharlen Electric Co....E....773 721-0700
Chicago (G-6147)
Solid Metal Group Inc....G....708 757-7421
Chicago Heights (G-6774)

PRODUCT SECTION

Strait-O-Flex ....G...... 815 965-2625
  Stillman Valley (G-19546)
Tech-Weld Inc ....F...... 630 365-3000
  Elburn (G-8474)
Vindee Industries Inc ....E...... 815 469-3300
  Frankfort (G-9850)
Zeman Mfg Co ....E...... 630 960-2300
  Lisle (G-12958)

TUBES: Extruded Or Drawn, Aluminum

Penn Aluminum Intl LLC ....C...... 618 684-2146
  Murphysboro (G-14756)

TUBES: Hard Rubber

Traeyne Corporation ....G...... 309 936-7878
  Atkinson (G-903)

TUBES: Paper

Armbrust Paper Tubes Inc ....E...... 773 586-3232
  Chicago (G-3730)
Caraustar Industrial and Con ......D...... 217 323-5225
  Beardstown (G-1446)
Chicago Mailing Tube Company ..E...... 312 243-6050
  Chicago (G-4112)
Illiana Cores Inc ....E...... 618 586-9800
  Palestine (G-16178)
Rolled Edge Inc ....E...... 773 283-9500
  Chicago (G-6054)

TUBES: Paper Or Fiber, Chemical Or Electrical Uses

Precision Paper Tube Company ..C...... 847 537-4250
  Wheeling (G-20965)

TUBES: Steel & Iron

Korhumel Inc ....G...... 847 330-0335
  Schaumburg (G-18590)
Metal-Matic Inc ....C...... 708 594-7553
  Bedford Park (G-1481)
Modern Tube LLC ....G...... 877 848-3300
  Bloomingdale (G-2001)
Phillips & Johnston Inc ....F...... 815 778-3355
  Lyndon (G-13287)
Ptc Tubular Products LLC ....G...... 815 692-4900
  Fairbury (G-9612)
SE Steel Inc ....G...... 847 350-9618
  Antioch (G-634)

TUBES: Television

King S Court Exterior ....G...... 630 904-4305
  Naperville (G-14976)
Zenith Electronics Corporation ...E...... 847 941-8000
  Lincolnshire (G-12806)

TUBES: Vacuum

Futaba Corporation of America ...F...... 847 884-1444
  Schaumburg (G-18532)

TUBES: Wrought, Welded Or Lock Joint

Metal-Matic Inc ....C...... 708 594-7553
  Bedford Park (G-1481)
Nucor Tubular Products Inc ....D...... 708 496-0380
  Chicago (G-5639)

TUBING, COLD-DRAWN: Mech Or Hypodermic Sizes, Stainless

Kroh-Wagner Inc ....E...... 773 252-2031
  Chicago (G-5133)

TUBING: Copper

Cerro Flow Products LLC ....C...... 618 337-6000
  Sauget (G-18392)
Midwest Model Aircraft Co ....F...... 773 229-0740
  Chicago (G-5446)

TUBING: Electrical Use, Quartz

Ghp Group Inc ....E...... 847 324-5900
  Niles (G-15125)

TUBING: Flexible, Metallic

RF Mau Co ....F...... 847 329-9731
  Lincolnwood (G-12838)

TUBING: Seamless

Arcelrmttal N Amer Hldings LLC ...A...... 312 899-3400
  Chicago (G-3724)
Atlas Holding Inc ....F...... 773 646-4500
  Chicago (G-3763)
Atlas Tube (chicago) LLC ....D...... 312 275-1672
  Chicago (G-3768)
Plymouth Tube Company ....E...... 630 393-3550
  Warrenville (G-20246)
Plymouth Tube Company ....D...... 773 489-0226
  Chicago (G-5824)

TUCKING FOR THE TRADE

Alternative TS ....G...... 618 257-0230
  Belleville (G-1529)
James Randall ....G...... 309 444-8765
  Washington (G-20272)

TURBINES & TURBINE GENERATOR SET UNITS, COMPLETE

Kliux Energies Intl Inc ....E...... 312 985-7717
  Chicago (G-5109)

TURBINES & TURBINE GENERATOR SET UNITS: Gas, Complete

A P S Gas Turbine Inc ....G...... 708 262-2939
  Alsip (G-409)
Caterpillar Inc ....A...... 309 578-1615
  Mossville (G-14459)
Caterpillar Inc ....B...... 309 675-6590
  Peoria (G-16411)
Caterpillar Inc ....A...... 309 578-2185
  Mossville (G-14452)
Caterpillar Inc ....A...... 224 551-4000
  Deerfield (G-7600)
Caterpillar Inc ....D...... 309 578-6118
  Mossville (G-14453)
Caterpillar Inc ....B...... 888 614-4328
  Peoria (G-16407)
Pietro Carnaghi USA Inc ....G...... 779 368-0564
  Rockford (G-17554)
Solar Turbines Incorporated ....E...... 630 527-1700
  Naperville (G-14916)

TURBINES & TURBINE GENERATOR SETS

Abb Inc ....F...... 630 759-7428
  Bolingbrook (G-2145)
Acciona Windpower N Amer LLC ...G...... 319 643-9463
  Chicago (G-3515)
Action Turbine Repair Svc Inc ....F...... 708 924-9601
  Summit Argo (G-19677)
Alturdyne Power Systems LLC ...G...... 619 440-5531
  Chicago (G-3638)
Angel Wind Energy Inc ....G...... 815 471-2020
  Onarga (G-15901)
Area Diesel Service Inc ....E...... 217 854-2641
  Carlinville (G-2867)
B N Blance Enrgy Solutions LLC ...G...... 847 287-7466
  Palatine (G-16096)
Catching Hydraulics Co Ltd ....E...... 708 344-2334
  Melrose Park (G-13839)
Gds Enterprises ....G...... 217 543-3681
  Arthur (G-859)
Invenergy ....G...... 815 795-4964
  Marseilles (G-13558)
ITT Water & Wastewater USA Inc ...F...... 708 342-0484
  Tinley Park (G-19840)
Laser Technologies Inc ....C...... 630 761-1200
  Naperville (G-14860)
Mainstream Renewable Power ...G...... 815 379-2784
  Walnut (G-20219)
Marty Lundeen ....G...... 630 250-8917
  Itasca (G-11697)
Nooter/Eriksen Inc ....G...... 636 651-1028
  Columbia (G-6991)
Nordex Usa Inc ....D...... 312 386-4100
  Chicago (G-5614)
Pne Usa Inc ....G...... 773 329-3705
  Chicago (G-5826)
Power Solutions Intl Inc ....C...... 630 350-9400
  Wood Dale (G-21228)
Rebuilders Enterprises Inc ....G...... 708 430-0030
  Bridgeview (G-2380)
Siemens Energy Inc ....C...... 618 357-6360
  Pinckneyville (G-16619)
Suzlon Wind Energy Corporation ...G...... 773 328-5077
  Elgin (G-8743)
Xylem Lnc ....G...... 847 966-3700
  Morton Grove (G-14451)

TURBINES & TURBINE GENERATOR SETS & PARTS

Broadwind Energy Inc ....E...... 708 780-4800
  Cicero (G-6831)
Rockwind Venture Partners LLC ...G...... 630 881-6664
  Rockford (G-17612)

TURBINES: Gas, Mechanical Drive

Power Plant Repair Svcs LLC ....D...... 708 345-8600
  Oswego (G-16020)

TURBINES: Hydraulic, Complete

Sur-Fit Corporation ....E...... 815 301-5815
  Crystal Lake (G-7272)

TURBINES: Steam

Energy Parts Solutions Inc ....F...... 224 653-9412
  Schaumburg (G-18518)
University of Chicago ....F...... 773 702-9780
  Chicago (G-6487)

TURBO-GENERATORS

Michael Wilton Cstm Homes Inc ...G...... 630 508-1200
  Willowbrook (G-21049)

TURBO-SUPERCHARGERS: Aircraft

Ihi Turbo America Co ....D...... 217 774-9571
  Shelbyville (G-18880)

TURKEY PROCESSING & SLAUGHTERING

Kauffman Poultry Farms Inc ....F...... 815 264-3470
  Waterman (G-20298)
West Liberty Foods LLC ....B...... 603 679-2300
  Bolingbrook (G-2253)

TWINE PRDTS

Unicord Corporation ....E...... 708 385-7999
  Calumet Park (G-2800)

TYPESETTING SVC

A To Z Type & Graphic Inc ....G...... 312 587-1887
  Chicago (G-3491)
Adcraft Printers Inc ....F...... 815 932-6432
  Kankakee (G-11956)
All-Ways Quick Print ....G...... 708 403-8422
  Orland Park (G-15938)
Allegra Print & Imaging Inc ....G...... 847 697-1434
  Elgin (G-8502)
Alphadigital Inc ....G...... 708 482-4488
  La Grange (G-12071)
AlphaGraphics Printshops ....G...... 630 964-9600
  Lisle (G-12861)
Amboy News ....G...... 815 857-2311
  Amboy (G-578)
American Graphics Network Inc ...F...... 847 729-7220
  Glenview (G-10522)
Apple Graphics Inc ....G...... 630 389-2222
  Batavia (G-1350)
Apple Press Inc ....G...... 815 224-1451
  Peru (G-16565)
Apr Graphics Inc ....G...... 847 329-7800
  Skokie (G-18922)
Arby Graphic Service Inc ....F...... 847 763-0900
  Glencoe (G-10428)
Arcadia Press Inc ....F...... 847 451-6390
  Franklin Park (G-9872)
Arch Printing Inc ....G...... 630 966-0235
  Aurora (G-1053)
Artistry Engraving & Embossing ...G...... 773 775-4888
  Chicago (G-3741)
Avid of Illinois Inc ....F...... 847 698-2775
  Saint Charles (G-18152)
Azusa Inc ....G...... 618 244-6591
  Mount Vernon (G-14597)
B & B Printing Company ....G...... 217 285-6072
  Pittsfield (G-16628)
B Allan Graphics Inc ....F...... 708 396-1704
  Alsip (G-420)
Babak Inc ....G...... 312 419-8686
  Oak Forest (G-15672)
Bailleu & Bailleu Printing Inc ......G...... 309 852-2517
  Kewanee (G-12021)

Employee Codes: A=Over 500 employees, B=251-500
C=101-250, D=51-100, E=20-50, F=10-19, G=3-9

TYPESETTING SVC — PRODUCT SECTION

Company	Code	Phone
Bally Foil Graphics Inc — Elk Grove Village (G-8857)	G	847 427-1509
Banner Publications — Cuba (G-7297)		309 338-3294
Barnaby Inc — Aurora (G-1061)	F	815 895-6555
Baseline Graphics Inc — Downers Grove (G-7958)	G	630 964-9566
Belmonte Printing Co — Schaumburg (G-18458)	G	847 352-8841
Benzinger Printing — Genoa (G-10315)		815 784-6560
Beslow Associates Inc — Northbrook (G-15349)		847 559-2703
Biller Press & Manufacturing — Antioch (G-604)	G	847 395-4111
Blazing Color Inc — Chester (G-3450)		618 826-3001
Bond Brothers & Co — Lyons (G-13303)	F	708 442-5510
Branstiter Printing Co — Jacksonville (G-11760)		217 245-6533
Budget Printing Center — Edwardsville (G-8351)		618 655-1636
Cameron Printing Inc — West Chicago (G-20558)		630 231-3301
Cardinal Colorprint Prtg Corp — Itasca (G-11634)	E	630 467-1000
Carson Printing Inc — East Dundee (G-8189)		847 836-0900
Carter Printing Co Inc — Farmersville (G-9659)		217 227-4464
Century Printing — O Fallon (G-15570)		618 632-2486
Challenge Printers — Chicago (G-4067)	G	773 252-0212
Chicago Citizen Newsppr Group — Chicago (G-4096)	F	773 783-1251
Chicago Mltlingua Graphics Inc — Northfield (G-15512)	F	847 386-7187
Christopher R Cline Prtg Ltd — Elk Grove Village (G-8897)	F	847 981-0500
Cifuentes Luis & Nicole Inc — Schaumburg (G-18477)	G	847 490-3660
Clementi Printing Inc — Chicago (G-4177)	G	773 622-0795
Clyde Printing Company — Chicago (G-4184)	F	773 847-5900
Cmb Printing Inc — Burr Ridge (G-2663)	F	630 323-1110
Color Smiths Inc — Elmhurst (G-9349)	E	708 562-0061
Commercial Copy Printing Ctr — Elk Grove Village (G-8903)	F	847 981-8590
Communications Resource Inc — Schaumburg (G-18482)	G	630 860-1661
Copy Express Inc — Woodstock (G-21377)	F	815 338-7161
Copy Mat Printing — Bloomington (G-2033)	G	309 452-1392
Copy Service Inc — Dekalb (G-7670)	G	815 758-1151
Copy-Mor Inc — Streamwood (G-19568)	E	312 666-4000
Copyset Shop Inc — Des Plaines (G-7751)	G	847 768-2679
Corwin Printing — Mount Carmel (G-14469)		618 263-3936
Cpr Printing Inc — Geneva (G-10263)	F	630 377-8420
Craftsmen Printing — Hoopeston (G-11506)	G	217 283-9574
Creative Image Inc — Hazel Crest (G-11128)		708 647-2860
Crossmark Printing Inc — Tinley Park (G-19819)	F	708 532-8263
Custom Direct Inc — Roselle (G-17950)	F	630 529-1936
D E Asbury Inc — Hamilton (G-10953)	F	217 222-0617
D L V Printing Service Inc — Chicago (G-4301)	F	773 626-1661
Dale K Brown — Woodstock (G-21380)	G	815 338-0222
Darnall Printing — Bloomington (G-2039)	G	309 827-7212
David H Vander Ploeg — South Holland (G-19206)	G	708 331-7700
DE Asbury Inc — Quincy (G-16876)	E	217 222-0617
Deluxe Johnson — Des Plaines (G-7754)	C	847 635-7200
Denor Graphics Inc — Elk Grove Village (G-8944)	F	847 364-1130
Des Plaines Journal Inc — Des Plaines (G-7755)	D	847 299-5511
Design Graphics Inc — Frankfort (G-9783)	G	815 462-3323
Diamond Graphics of Berwyn — Berwyn (G-1950)	G	708 749-2500
Donnas House of Type Inc — Athens (G-896)	G	217 522-5050
Donnells Printing & Off Pdts — Pontiac (G-16768)	G	815 842-6541
Dupli Group Inc — Chicago (G-4408)	F	773 549-5285
E & H Graphic Service Inc — Matteson (G-13623)	G	708 748-5656
Edwardsville Publishing Co — Edwardsville (G-8361)	D	618 656-4700
Einstein Crest — Niles (G-15119)	G	847 965-7791
Elgin Instant Print — Elgin (G-8575)	G	847 931-9006
Everything Xclusive — Peoria (G-16436)	G	309 370-7450
F Weber Printing Co Inc — Manteno (G-13447)	G	815 468-6152
Fedex Office & Print Svcs Inc — Evanston (G-9519)	F	847 475-8650
Fedex Office & Print Svcs Inc — Rockford (G-17412)	F	815 229-0033
Fedex Office & Print Svcs Inc — Lincolnwood (G-12819)	F	847 329-9464
Fedex Office & Print Svcs Inc — Glenview (G-10545)	E	847 729-3030
Fedex Office & Print Svcs Inc — Buffalo Grove (G-2536)	G	847 459-8008
Fedex Office & Print Svcs Inc — Elmwood Park (G-9452)	E	708 452-0149
Fedex Office & Print Svcs Inc — Park Ridge (G-16274)	G	847 823-9360
Fedex Office & Print Svcs Inc — Bloomingdale (G-1995)	G	630 894-1800
Fedex Office & Print Svcs Inc — Chicago (G-4577)	F	312 670-4460
Fedex Office & Print Svcs Inc — Peoria (G-16437)	E	309 685-4093
Fine Line Printing — Chicago (G-4590)	G	773 582-9709
First Impression of Chicago — Chicago (G-4594)	G	773 224-3434
Fisheye Services Incorporated — Chicago (G-4598)	G	773 942-6314
Flash Printing Inc — Franklin Park (G-9944)	G	847 288-9101
Fleetwood Press Inc — Brookfield (G-2483)	G	708 485-6811
FM Graphic Impressions Inc — Aurora (G-1097)	E	630 897-8788
French Studio Ltd — Herrin (G-11171)	G	618 942-5328
G F Printing — Granite City (G-10708)		618 797-0576
Gamma Alpha Visual Communicatn — Park Ridge (G-16279)	G	847 956-0633
Gatehouse Media LLC — Springfield (G-19373)	B	217 788-1300
Gazette Printing Co — Glasford (G-10387)	G	309 389-2811
Gorman & Associates — Peoria (G-16446)	G	309 691-9087
Gossett Printing Inc — Salem (G-18341)	G	618 548-2583
Graphic Image Corporation — Orland Park (G-15956)	F	312 829-7800
Graphics Group LLC — Chicago (G-4729)	D	708 867-5500
Grasso Graphics Inc — Alsip (G-449)	G	708 489-2060
Gsipc LLC — Burr Ridge (G-2678)	D	630 325-8181
Hawthorne Press Inc — Spring Grove (G-19275)	G	847 587-0582
Heart Printing Inc — Arlington Heights (G-748)	G	847 259-2100
Heritage Media Svcs Co of Ill — Summit Argo (G-19679)	G	708 594-9340
Heritage Press Inc — Libertyville (G-12657)	G	847 362-9699
Heritage Printing — Prophetstown (G-16832)	G	815 537-2372
Highland Printers — Highland (G-11221)	G	618 654-5880
House of Graphics — Carol Stream (G-3000)	E	630 682-0810
Hq Printers Inc — Chicago (G-4857)		312 782-2020
Hub Printing Company Inc — Rochelle (G-17145)	F	815 562-7057
Huston-Patterson Corporation — Decatur (G-7503)	D	217 429-5161
Ideal Advertising & Printing — Rockford (G-17456)	F	815 965-1713
Illinois Office Sup Elect Prtg — Ottawa (G-16056)	E	815 434-0186
Image Print Inc — Streator (G-19611)	G	815 672-1068
Informative Systems Inc — Springfield (G-19389)	F	217 523-8422
Ink Spot Printing — Chicago (G-4926)	G	773 528-0288
Inky Printers — Freeport (G-10120)	G	815 235-3700
Innovtive Design Graphics Corp — Evanston (G-9540)	G	847 475-7772
Insty Prints Palatine Inc — Palatine (G-16129)	G	847 963-0000
Instyprints of Waukegan Inc — Waukegan (G-20449)	G	847 336-5599
International Graphics & Assoc — Saint Charles (G-18215)	F	630 584-2248
J & J Mr Quick Print Inc — Chicago (G-4984)	G	773 767-7776
J Oshana & Son Printing — Chicago (G-4992)	G	773 283-8311
J P Printing Inc — Chicago (G-4993)	G	773 626-5222
James Ray Monroe Corporation — Centralia (G-3236)	F	618 532-4575
Jay Printing — Palatine (G-16133)	G	847 934-6103
Jds Printing Inc — Glendale Heights (G-10463)	G	630 208-1195
Jeannie Wagner — Crystal Lake (G-7212)		815 477-2700
Johns-Byrne Company — Niles (G-15137)	D	847 583-3100
Johnson Press America Inc — Pontiac (G-16773)	E	815 844-5161
Josco Inc — Chicago (G-5051)		708 867-7189
Josephs Printing Service — Glenview (G-10576)	G	847 724-4429
Jph Enterprises Inc — Des Plaines (G-7792)	G	847 390-0900
July 25th Corporation — Bloomington (G-2064)	F	309 664-6444
Just Your Type Inc — Evanston (G-9543)	G	847 864-8890
K & M Printing Company Inc — Schaumburg (G-18584)	D	847 884-1100
Kelly Printing Co Inc — Danville (G-7355)	E	217 443-1792
Kendall Printing Co — Yorkville (G-21490)	G	630 553-9200
Kenilworth Press Incorporated — Wilmette (G-21081)	G	847 256-5210
Kens Quick Print Inc — Highland Park (G-11277)	F	847 831-4410
Kevin Kewney — Quincy (G-16899)		217 228-7444
KK Stevens Publishing Co — Astoria (G-893)	E	309 329-2151
Klein Printing Inc — Chicago (G-5108)	G	773 235-2121
Klh Printing Corp — Wheeling (G-20926)	G	847 459-0115
Korea Times — Glenview (G-10579)	D	847 626-0388
LAC Enterprises Inc — Crystal Lake (G-7219)		815 455-5044
Lake County Press Inc — Waukegan (G-20458)	C	847 336-4333
Lans Printing Inc — Lynwood (G-13295)	G	708 895-6226
Laser Expressions Ltd — Buffalo Grove (G-2559)	G	847 419-9600
Legend Promotions — Lake Zurich (G-12428)	G	847 438-3528

PRODUCT SECTION — TYPESETTING SVC

Company	Code	Phone
Leonard Emerson — Divernon (G-7880)	G	217 628-3441
Lithuanian Catholic Press — Chicago (G-5236)	E	773 585-9500
Lloyd Midwest Graphics — Machesney Park (G-13357)	G	815 282-8828
Lynns Printing Co — Alton (G-564)	G	618 465-7701
M & R Printing Inc — Rolling Meadows (G-17749)	G	847 398-2500
M M Marketing — Wauconda (G-20370)	G	815 459-7968
M O W Printing Inc — Collinsville (G-6967)	F	618 345-5525
Macoupin County Enquirer Inc — Carlinville (G-2879)	E	217 854-2534
Marcus Press — Bloomingdale (G-1999)	G	630 351-1857
Mark Twain Press Inc — Mundelein (G-14713)	G	847 255-2700
Mason City Banner Times — Mason City (G-13612)	F	217 482-3276
Mattoon Printing Center — Mattoon (G-13646)	G	217 234-3100
Mc Adams Multigraphics Inc — Oak Brook (G-15641)	G	630 990-1707
McGrath Press Inc — Crystal Lake (G-7224)	E	815 356-5246
McHenry Printing Services — McHenry (G-13765)	G	815 385-7600
Mencarini Enterprises Inc — Rockford (G-17516)	F	815 398-9565
Metro Printing & Pubg Inc — Millstadt (G-14052)	F	618 476-9587
Metropolitan Graphic Arts Inc — Gurnee (G-10896)	E	847 566-9502
Mid City Printing Service — Chicago (G-5426)	G	773 777-5400
Midwest Outdoors Ltd — Burr Ridge (G-2704)	E	630 887-7722
Minuteman Press — Naperville (G-14872)	G	630 584-7383
Minuteman Press of Rockford — Loves Park (G-13237)	G	815 633-2992
Minuteman Press of Waukegan — Gurnee (G-10900)	G	847 244-6288
Mormor Incorporated — Lombard (G-13104)	G	630 268-0050
Multicopy Corp — Grayslake (G-10792)	G	847 446-7015
N & M Type & Design — Elmhurst (G-9404)	G	630 834-3696
N Bujarski Inc — Schaumburg (G-18643)	G	847 884-1600
N P D Inc — Oak Lawn (G-15729)	G	708 424-6788
Negs & Litho Inc — Chicago (G-5563)	G	847 647-7770
New City Communications — Chicago (G-5576)	E	312 243-8786
New Life Printing & Publishing — Algonquin (G-382)	G	847 658-4111
Northwest Premier Printing — Chicago (G-5623)	G	773 736-1882
Northwest Printing Inc — Harvard (G-11061)	G	815 943-7977
Nu-Art Printing — Centralia (G-3242)	G	618 533-9971
Off The Press LLC — Plainfield (G-16697)	G	815 436-9612
Okawville Times — Okawville (G-15846)	G	618 243-5563
Olde Print Shoppe Inc — Olney (G-15879)	G	618 395-3833
Omni Craft Inc — Lockport (G-13017)	G	815 838-1285
On Time Printing and Finishing — Hillside (G-11351)	G	708 544-4500
Osborne Publications Inc — Decatur (G-7534)	G	217 422-9702
P & S Cochran Printers Inc — Peoria (G-16489)	E	309 691-6668
P H C Enterprises Inc — Vernon Hills (G-20080)	G	847 816-7373
P P Graphics Inc — Westchester (G-20707)	G	708 343-2530
Papyrus Press Inc — Chicago (G-5755)	F	773 342-0700
Park Printing Inc — Palos Hills (G-16203)	G	708 430-4878
Patrick Impressions LLC — Lemont (G-12578)	G	630 257-9336
Patton Printing and Graphics — Effingham (G-8417)	G	217 347-0220
Perma Graphics Printers — New Lenox (G-15050)	G	815 485-6955
Perryco Inc — Plainfield (G-16701)	F	815 436-2431
Photo Graphic Design Service — Streator (G-19620)	G	815 672-4417
PIP Printing Inc — Frankfort (G-9822)	G	815 464-0075
Poets Study Inc — Chicago (G-5831)	G	773 286-1355
Preferred Printing Service — Chicago (G-5861)	G	312 421-2343
Prime Market Targeting Inc — Frankfort (G-9826)	E	815 469-4555
Print & Design Services LLC — Bannockburn (G-1206)	G	847 317-9001
Print Turnaround Inc — Arlington Heights (G-791)	F	847 228-1762
Printed Impressions Inc — Oakbrook Terrace (G-15813)	G	773 604-8585
Printed Word Inc — Evanston (G-9570)	G	847 328-1511
Printing Inc — Chicago (G-5881)	D	316 265-1201
Printing By Joseph — Mokena (G-14109)	G	708 479-2669
Printing Craftsmen of Joliet — Joliet (G-11917)	G	815 254-3982
Printing Etc Inc — Rochelle (G-17152)	G	815 562-6151
Printing Plus of Roselle Inc — Roselle (G-17974)	G	630 893-0410
Printing Source Inc — Morton Grove (G-14433)	G	773 588-2930
Printmeisters Inc — Lansing (G-12512)	G	708 474-8400
Printsource Plus Inc — Blue Island (G-2134)	G	708 389-6252
Pro-Type Printing Inc — Paxton (G-16315)	G	217 379-4715
Progress Printing Corporation — Chicago (G-5898)	E	773 927-0123
Quad City Press — Moline (G-14170)	F	309 764-8142
Quality Quickprint Inc — Joliet (G-11920)	F	815 439-3430
Quality Quickprint Inc — Lockport (G-13020)	F	815 838-1784
Quickprinters — Macomb (G-13398)	G	309 833-5250
Quinn Print Co — Park Ridge (G-16293)	G	847 823-9100
R N R Photographers Inc — River Grove (G-17066)	G	708 453-1868
Rapid Circular Press Inc — Chicago (G-5970)	F	312 421-5611
Remke Printing Inc — Wheeling (G-20972)	G	847 520-7300
Reprographics — Crystal Lake (G-7254)	G	815 477-1018
Review Graphics Inc — Roscoe (G-17925)	G	815 623-2570
Review Printing Co Inc — Rock Island (G-17241)	G	309 788-7094
Rightway Printing Inc — Glendale Heights (G-10488)	F	630 790-0444
Rite-TEC Communications — Crystal Lake (G-7258)	G	815 459-7712
River Bend Printing — Litchfield (G-12975)	G	217 324-6056
Ro-Web Inc — Peoria (G-16512)	G	309 688-2155
Rodin Enterprises Inc — Wheeling (G-20976)	G	847 412-1370
Rohrer Graphic Arts Inc — Elmhurst (G-9419)	F	630 832-3434
Rohrer Litho Inc — Elmhurst (G-9420)	G	630 833-6610
Rose Business Forms & Printing — Centralia (G-3248)	G	618 533-3032
Rrr Graphics & Film Corp — Mokena (G-14114)	G	708 478-4573
Rt Associates Inc — Wheeling (G-20977)	D	847 577-0700
Rudin Printing Company Inc — Springfield (G-19436)	F	217 528-5111
Rusty & Angela Buzzard — Effingham (G-8423)	G	217 342-9841
Salem Times-Commoner Inc — Salem (G-18358)	E	618 548-3330
Samecwei Inc — Aurora (G-1153)	G	630 897-7888
Schiele Graphics Inc — Elk Grove Village (G-9233)	D	847 434-5455
Schommer Inc — McHenry (G-13791)	G	815 344-1404
Schwebel Printing — Murphysboro (G-14759)	G	618 684-3911
Shawver Press Inc — Morrison (G-14348)	G	815 772-4700
Sheer Graphics Inc — Westmont (G-20772)	G	630 654-4422
Shoreline Graphics Inc — Ingleside (G-11589)	G	847 587-4804
Shree Mahavir Inc — Chicago (G-6159)	G	312 408-1080
Shree Printing Corp — Chicago (G-6160)	G	773 267-9500
Sigley Printing & Off Sup Co — Marion (G-13535)	G	618 997-5304
Sir Speedy Printing — Chicago (G-6177)	G	312 337-0774
Small Newspaper Group — Kankakee (G-12004)	C	815 937-3300
Solid Impressions Inc — Carol Stream (G-3070)	G	630 543-7300
Sommers & Fahrenbach Inc — Chicago (G-6201)	F	773 478-3033
Sons Enterprises — Skokie (G-19032)	F	847 677-4444
Speedys Quick Print — Danville (G-7381)	G	217 431-0510
Stearns Printing of Charleston — Charleston (G-3414)	G	217 345-7518
Steve Bortman — Lyons (G-13315)	G	708 442-1669
Swifty Print — Saint Charles (G-18283)	G	630 584-9063
T F N W Inc — Naperville (G-14926)	G	630 584-7383
T R Communications Inc — Chicago (G-6307)	F	773 238-3366
The b F Shaw Printing Co — Princeton (G-16823)	E	815 875-4461
Times Record Company — Aledo (G-362)	E	309 582-5112
Times Republic — Watseka (G-20320)	G	815 432-5227
Tlm Enterprises Inc — Dixon (G-7923)	G	815 284-5040
Toledo Democrat — Toledo (G-19879)	G	217 849-2000
Tower Printing & Design — Lombard (G-13145)	G	630 495-1976
Trenton Sun — Trenton (G-19905)	G	618 224-9422
Tru Line Lithographing Inc — Niles (G-15183)	E	262 554-7300
Trump Printing Inc — Decatur (G-7563)	F	217 429-9001
United Lithograph Inc — Des Plaines (G-7861)	G	847 803-1700
V C P Inc — Algonquin (G-391)	E	847 658-5090
Valee Inc — Elk Grove Village (G-9300)	G	847 364-6464
Viking Printing & Copying Inc — Chicago (G-6551)	G	312 341-0985
Voris Communication Co Inc — Berkeley (G-1946)	C	630 898-4268
W R Typesetting Co — Morton Grove (G-14447)	F	847 966-8327
Wagner John — Northbrook (G-15498)	G	847 564-0017
Washburn Graficolor Inc — Naperville (G-14944)	G	630 596-0880
Weakley Printing & Sign Shop — North Chicago (G-15323)	G	847 473-4466
Weber Press Inc — Chicago (G-6596)	G	773 561-9815
Westrock Mwv LLC — Danville (G-7397)	E	217 442-2247
Woogl Corporation — Elk Grove Village (G-9312)	E	847 806-1160
World Journal LLC — Chicago (G-6674)	F	312 842-8005

Employee Codes: A=Over 500 employees, B=251-500, C=101-250, D=51-100, E=20-50, F=10-19, G=3-9

2020 Harris Illinois Industrial Directory

Wortman Printing Company Inc ....G....... 217 347-3775
  Effingham *(G-8432)*

TYPESETTING SVC: Computer

Breaker Press Co Inc ....G....... 773 927-1666
  Chicago *(G-3948)*
Early Bird Advertising Inc 847 253-1423
  Prospect Heights *(G-16839)*
Print Xpress ....G....... 847 677-5555
  Skokie *(G-19012)*
Tri-Tower Printing Inc ....G....... 847 640-6633
  Rolling Meadows *(G-17782)*

TYPESETTING SVC: Hand Composition

11th Street Express Prtg Inc ....F....... 815 968-0208
  Rockford *(G-17275)*

TYPOGRAPHY

Crosstech Communications Inc ....E....... 312 382-0111
  Chicago *(G-4273)*
Henderson Co Inc ....F....... 773 628-7216
  Chicago *(G-4800)*
JD Pro Productions Inc ....G....... 708 485-2126
  Brookfield *(G-2487)*
Village Typographers Inc ....G....... 618 235-6756
  Belleville *(G-1607)*

ULTRASONIC EQPT: Cleaning, Exc Med & Dental

Fisa North America Inc ....G....... 847 593-2080
  Elk Grove Village *(G-8998)*
Maxi-Vac Inc ....G....... 630 620-6669
  East Dundee *(G-8205)*

UMBRELLAS & CANES

Shedrain Corporation ....G....... 708 848-5212
  Oak Park *(G-15772)*

UNDERGROUND GOLD MINING

Global Technologies I LLC ....D....... 312 255-8350
  Chicago *(G-4699)*

UNDERGROUND IRON ORE MINING

Global Technologies I LLC ....D....... 312 255-8350
  Chicago *(G-4699)*

UNIFORM STORES

Advance Uniform Company ....F....... 312 922-1797
  Chicago *(G-3559)*
Atlas Uniform Company ....G....... 312 492-8527
  Chicago *(G-3769)*
Johnos Inc ....G....... 630 897-6929
  Aurora *(G-1119)*
Waldos Sports Corner Inc ....G....... 309 688-2425
  Peoria *(G-16545)*

UNISEX HAIR SALONS

Curran Group Inc ....D....... 815 455-5100
  Crystal Lake *(G-7190)*
Neckbone Skunks Logistics & Te .....F....... 312 218-0281
  Chicago *(G-5561)*

UNIT TRAIN LOADING FACILITY, BITUMINOUS OR LIGNITE

Interminal Services ....E....... 773 978-8129
  Chicago *(G-4950)*

UNIVERSITY

University of Chicago ....E....... 773 702-7000
  Chicago *(G-6486)*
University of Chicago ....F....... 773 702-9780
  Chicago *(G-6487)*

UNSUPPORTED PLASTICS: Tile

Perfect Circle Projectiles LLC ....F....... 847 367-8960
  Lake Forest *(G-12286)*

UPHOLSTERY MATERIAL

A D Specialty Sewing ....G....... 847 639-0390
  Fox River Grove *(G-9756)*

UPHOLSTERY WORK SVCS

A D Specialty Sewing ....G....... 847 639-0390
  Fox River Grove *(G-9756)*
Addison Interiors Company ....G....... 630 628-1345
  Addison *(G-20)*
Anees Upholstery ....G....... 312 243-2919
  Chicago *(G-3695)*
Fehr Cab Interiors ....G....... 815 692-3355
  Fairbury *(G-9607)*

URANIUM ORE MINING, NEC

Phosphate Resource Ptrs ....A....... 847 739-1200
  Lake Forest *(G-12290)*

USED BOOK STORES

Half Price Bks Rec Mgzines Inc ....E....... 847 588-2286
  Niles *(G-15128)*

USED CAR DEALERS

Competitive Edge Opportunities ....G....... 815 981-4060
  Island Lake *(G-11605)*

USED MERCHANDISE STORES

Donald J Leventhal ....G....... 309 662-8080
  Bloomington *(G-2040)*

USED MERCHANDISE STORES: Art Objects, Antique

International Silver Plating ....G....... 847 835-0705
  Glencoe *(G-10430)*

USED MERCHANDISE STORES: Clothing & Shoes

Entrigue Designs 708 647-6159
  Homewood *(G-11493)*

USED MERCHANDISE STORES: Office Furniture

Rieke Office Interiors Inc ....D....... 847 622-9711
  Elgin *(G-8720)*

UTENSILS: Cast Aluminum, Cooking Or Kitchen

Newell Operating Company ....C....... 815 235-4171
  Freeport *(G-10129)*
Rome Industries Inc ....G....... 309 691-7120
  Peoria *(G-16517)*

UTENSILS: Cast Aluminum, Hospital

Bio Services Inc ....G....... 630 808-2125
  Hillside *(G-11330)*

UTENSILS: Household, Cooking & Kitchen, Metal

Corelle Brands Holdings Inc ....D....... 847 233-8600
  Rosemont *(G-18009)*

UTENSILS: Household, Metal, Exc Cast

Kernel Kutter Inc ....G....... 815 877-1515
  Machesney Park *(G-13354)*

UTILITY TRAILER DEALERS

Knight Bros Inc ....E....... 618 439-9626
  Benton *(G-1930)*

VACUUM CLEANER STORES

Campanella Clg Solutions Inc ....G....... 847 949-4222
  Mundelein *(G-14671)*

VACUUM CLEANERS: Household

Dyson Inc ....G....... 847 995-8010
  Schaumburg *(G-18510)*
Dyson Inc ....D....... 312 469-5950
  Chicago *(G-4416)*
Dyson B2b Inc ....E....... 312 469-5950
  Chicago *(G-4417)*
Dyson Direct Inc ....G....... 312 469-5950
  Chicago *(G-4418)*
Lee Sauzek ....G....... 618 539-5815
  Freeburg *(G-10091)*
Wodack Electric Tool Corp ....F....... 773 287-9866
  Chicago *(G-6661)*

VACUUM CLEANERS: Indl Type

Advanage Diversified Pdts Inc ....F....... 708 331-8390
  Harvey *(G-11069)*
American Vacuum Company ....G....... 847 674-8383
  Niles *(G-15102)*
Bissell Inc ....G....... 815 423-1300
  Elwood *(G-9461)*
Nikro Industries Inc ....F....... 630 530-0558
  Villa Park *(G-20162)*
Powerboss Inc ....C....... 630 627-6900
  Pingree Grove *(G-16623)*
Tornado Industries LLC ....D....... 817 551-6507
  West Chicago *(G-20653)*
William W Meyer and Sons ....D....... 847 918-0111
  Libertyville *(G-12726)*

VACUUM PUMPS & EQPT: Laboratory

Gardner Denver Inc ....E....... 847 676-8800
  Niles *(G-15123)*
Leybold USA Inc ....E....... 724 327-5700
  Chicago *(G-5214)*
Vac Serve Inc ....G....... 224 766-6445
  Skokie *(G-19052)*

VACUUM SYSTEMS: Air Extraction, Indl

Demarco Industrial Vacuum Corp .....G....... 815 344-2222
  Crystal Lake *(G-7194)*
Fna Ip Holdings Inc ....D....... 847 348-1500
  Elk Grove Village *(G-9001)*

VALUE-ADDED RESELLERS: Computer Systems

CDI Computers US Corporation ....G....... 888 226-5727
  Chicago *(G-4048)*
Computer Svcs & Consulting Inc ......E....... 855 482-2267
  Burr Ridge *(G-2666)*
David Corporation ....E....... 781 587-3008
  Chicago *(G-4324)*
Hipskind Tech Sltons Group Inc ....D....... 630 920-0960
  Oakbrook Terrace *(G-15803)*
Paragon International Inc ....F....... 847 240-2981
  Schaumburg *(G-18664)*
Swift Technologies Inc ....G....... 815 568-8402
  Marengo *(G-13494)*
Techno - Grphics Trnsltons Inc ....E....... 708 331-3333
  South Holland *(G-19248)*

VALVE REPAIR SVCS, INDL

Extreme Force Valve Inc ....G....... 618 494-5795
  Jerseyville *(G-11790)*

VALVES

Extreme Force Valve Inc ....G....... 618 494-5795
  Jerseyville *(G-11790)*
Hantemp Corporation ....G....... 630 537-1049
  Westmont *(G-20746)*
Milliken Valve Co Inc ....G....... 217 425-7410
  Decatur *(G-7526)*
Mueller Co LLC ....E....... 217 423-4471
  Decatur *(G-7528)*
Research and Testing Worx Inc ....G....... 815 734-7346
  Mount Morris *(G-14501)*

VALVES & PARTS: Gas, Indl

Corken Inc ....D....... 405 946-5576
  Lake Bluff *(G-12177)*
Emerson Process Management ....D....... 708 535-5120
  Oak Forest *(G-15677)*
Henry Technologies Inc ....G....... 217 483-2406
  Chatham *(G-3421)*

VALVES & PIPE FITTINGS

ADS LLC ....D....... 256 430-3366
  Burr Ridge *(G-2650)*
Aquatrol Inc ....F....... 630 365-2363
  Elburn *(G-8443)*
Arnel Industries Inc ....E....... 630 543-6500
  Addison *(G-39)*
B&B Machining Incorporated ....F....... 630 898-3009
  Aurora *(G-920)*

PRODUCT SECTION — VARNISHES, NEC

Company	Code	Phone
Barrington Automation Ltd	E	847 458-0900
Lake In The Hills *(G-12329)*		
Bi-Torq Valve Automation Inc	G	630 208-9343
Lafox *(G-12135)*		
Caterpillar Inc	B	815 729-5511
Joliet *(G-11838)*		
Chicago Pipe Bending & Coil Co	F	773 379-1918
Chicago *(G-4122)*		
Control Equipment Company Inc	F	847 891-7500
Schaumburg *(G-18487)*		
Couplings Company Inc	F	847 634-8990
Lincolnshire *(G-12755)*		
Deltrol Corp	C	708 547-0500
Bellwood *(G-1621)*		
Deublin Company	C	847 689-8600
Waukegan *(G-20437)*		
Dresser LLC	D	847 437-5940
Elk Grove Village *(G-8955)*		
Eclipse Inc	D	815 877-3031
Rockford *(G-17388)*		
Emerson Process Management	D	708 535-5120
Oak Forest *(G-15677)*		
Evsco Inc	F	847 362-7068
McHenry *(G-13742)*		
Flexicraft Industries Inc	E	312 738-3588
Chicago *(G-4610)*		
Henry Technologies Inc	G	217 483-2406
Chatham *(G-3421)*		
Hoosier Stamping & Mfg Corp	E	618 375-2057
Grayville *(G-10810)*		
Intech Industries Inc	F	847 487-5599
Wauconda *(G-20361)*		
Keckley Manufacturing Company	E	847 674-8422
Skokie *(G-18972)*		
Kelco Industries Inc	G	815 334-3600
Woodstock *(G-21398)*		
Kepner Products Company	D	630 279-1550
Villa Park *(G-20156)*		
Lewis Process Systems Inc	F	630 510-8200
Carol Stream *(G-3018)*		
Lilly Industries Inc	F	630 773-2222
Itasca *(G-11694)*		
M CA Chicago	C	312 384-1220
Burr Ridge *(G-2697)*		
Mead Fluid Dynamics Inc	E	773 685-6800
University Park *(G-19959)*		
Metraflex Company	D	312 738-3800
Chicago *(G-5411)*		
Midland Manufacturing Corp	C	847 677-0333
Skokie *(G-18990)*		
Mity Inc	G	630 365-5030
Elburn *(G-8461)*		
Newman-Green Inc	D	630 543-6500
Addison *(G-228)*		
O C Keckley Company	E	847 674-8422
Skokie *(G-18997)*		
Oso Technologies Inc	G	844 777-2575
Urbana *(G-19991)*		
Pokorney Manufacturing Co	G	630 458-0406
Addison *(G-244)*		
Pro-Quip Incorporated	F	708 352-5732
La Grange *(G-12087)*		
Process Screw Products Inc	E	815 864-2220
Shannon *(G-18872)*		
Sloan Valve Company	D	847 671-4300
Franklin Park *(G-10048)*		
Smith Cooper International Inc	D	847 595-7572
Elk Grove Village *(G-9244)*		
Spreader Inc	E	217 568-7219
Gifford *(G-10348)*		
SPX Flow US LLC	G	815 874-5556
Rockford *(G-17644)*		
Strahman Valves Inc	E	630 208-9343
Lafox *(G-12139)*		
Vonberg Valve Inc	E	847 259-3800
Rolling Meadows *(G-17785)*		

VALVES & REGULATORS: Pressure, Indl

Company	Code	Phone
Keckley Manufacturing Company	E	847 674-8422
Skokie *(G-18972)*		
O C Keckley Company	E	847 674-8422
Skokie *(G-18997)*		
SMC Corporation of America	E	630 449-0600
Aurora *(G-1017)*		

VALVES: Aerosol, Metal

Company	Code	Phone
1776 Fabrication LLC	G	773 895-7590
Wood Dale *(G-21146)*		
American Metal Mfg Inc	G	847 651-6097
Chicago *(G-3662)*		

Company	Code	Phone
Aptargroup Inc	B	847 639-2124
Cary *(G-3148)*		
Aptargroup Inc	G	847 816-9400
Libertyville *(G-12629)*		
Aptargroup Inc	C	815 477-0424
Crystal Lake *(G-7160)*		
Newman-Green Inc	D	630 543-6500
Addison *(G-228)*		

VALVES: Aircraft, Control, Hydraulic & Pneumatic

Company	Code	Phone
Ckd USA Corporation	E	847 368-0539
Schaumburg *(G-18478)*		
Robertshaw Controls Company	C	630 260-3400
Itasca *(G-11727)*		
Vonberg Valve Inc	E	847 259-3800
Rolling Meadows *(G-17785)*		

VALVES: Control, Automatic

Company	Code	Phone
Flexicraft Industries Inc	F	312 428-4750
Chicago *(G-4608)*		
Val-Matic Valve and Mfg Corp	C	630 941-7600
Elmhurst *(G-9440)*		

VALVES: Electrohydraulic Servo, Metal

Company	Code	Phone
Crane Nuclear Inc	E	630 226-4900
Bolingbrook *(G-2160)*		
MEA Inc	E	847 766-9040
Elk Grove Village *(G-9114)*		

VALVES: Engine

Company	Code	Phone
Helio Precision Products Inc	E	585 697-5434
Lake Bluff *(G-12186)*		
Helio Precision Products Inc	C	847 473-1300
Lake Bluff *(G-12187)*		

VALVES: Fire Hydrant

Company	Code	Phone
Midwest Innovative Tech Inc	G	618 740-0074
Salem *(G-18346)*		

VALVES: Fluid Power, Control, Hydraulic & pneumatic

Company	Code	Phone
Delta Power Company	D	815 397-6628
Rockford *(G-17372)*		
Fluid Logic Inc	G	847 459-2202
Buffalo Grove *(G-2539)*		
Hydraforce Inc	A	847 793-2300
Lincolnshire *(G-12772)*		
Kocsis Technologies Inc	F	708 597-4177
Alsip *(G-466)*		
Kocsis Technologies Inc	G	708 597-4177
Alsip *(G-467)*		
Marmon Industrial LLC	G	312 372-9500
Chicago *(G-5344)*		
Mead Fluid Dynamics Inc	E	773 685-6800
University Park *(G-19959)*		
Rotary Ram Inc	E	618 466-2651
Godfrey *(G-10662)*		
SMC Corporation of America	E	630 449-0600
Aurora *(G-1017)*		
Vrg Controls LLC	E	844 356-9874
Lake Zurich *(G-12468)*		
Wandfluh of America Inc	F	847 566-5700
Mundelein *(G-14746)*		

VALVES: Indl

Company	Code	Phone
Advanced Valve Tech LLC	E	877 489-4909
Blue Island *(G-2110)*		
Aptargroup Inc	B	847 639-2124
Cary *(G-3148)*		
Aquatrol Inc	F	630 365-2363
Elburn *(G-8443)*		
Chicago Valves & Controls LLC	C	312 637-3551
Elk Grove Village *(G-8895)*		
Cyrus Shank Company	F	331 212-5488
Aurora *(G-950)*		
Cyrus Shank Company	E	708 652-2700
Cicero *(G-6838)*		
Deltrol Corp	C	708 547-0500
Bellwood *(G-1621)*		
Emerson Automation Solutions	G	309 946-5205
Geneseo *(G-10242)*		
Engineered Fluid Inc	C	618 533-1351
Centralia *(G-3230)*		

Company	Code	Phone
Evsco Inc	F	847 362-7068
McHenry *(G-13742)*		
Flexicraft Industries Inc	E	312 738-3588
Chicago *(G-4610)*		
Flocon Inc	E	815 444-1500
Cary *(G-3159)*		
General Assembly & Mfg Corp	E	847 516-6462
Cary *(G-3163)*		
Gpe Controls Inc	F	708 236-6000
Hillside *(G-11340)*		
H A Phillips & Co	E	630 377-0050
Dekalb *(G-7683)*		
Henry Pratt Company LLC	G	620 208-8100
Decatur *(G-7502)*		
Homewerks Worldwide LLC	E	224 543-1529
Lake Bluff *(G-12188)*		
Hydra-Stop LLC	E	708 389-5111
Burr Ridge *(G-2684)*		
L & J Holding Company Ltd	D	708 236-6000
Hillside *(G-11345)*		
Midland Manufacturing Corp	C	847 677-0333
Skokie *(G-18990)*		
Mueller Service Co LLC	E	217 423-4471
Decatur *(G-7530)*		
Parker-Hannifin Corporation	E	708 681-6300
Broadview *(G-2457)*		
Pioneer Pump and Packing Inc	F	217 791-5293
Decatur *(G-7536)*		
Rebuilders Enterprises Inc	G	708 430-0030
Bridgeview *(G-2380)*		
Rhino Tool Company	F	309 853-5555
Kewanee *(G-12040)*		
Schrader-Bridgeport Intl Inc	G	815 288-3344
Dixon *(G-7916)*		
Sycamore Precision	D	815 784-5151
Genoa *(G-10324)*		
USP Holdings Inc	A	847 604-6100
Rosemont *(G-18058)*		
Vonberg Valve Inc	E	847 259-3800
Rolling Meadows *(G-17785)*		

VALVES: Plumbing & Heating

Company	Code	Phone
Catching Hydraulics Co Ltd	E	708 344-2334
Melrose Park *(G-13839)*		
Dooley Brothers Plumbing & Htg	G	309 852-2720
Kewanee *(G-12031)*		
J/B Industries Inc	D	630 851-9444
Aurora *(G-1115)*		
Solomon Plumbing	G	847 498-6388
Glenview *(G-10623)*		
Wrap-On Company LLC	E	708 496-2150
Alsip *(G-528)*		

VALVES: Regulating & Control, Automatic

Company	Code	Phone
Strahman Valves Inc	E	630 208-9343
Lafox *(G-12139)*		
Western Industries Inc	C	920 261-0660
Wheeling *(G-21012)*		

VALVES: Regulating, Process Control

Company	Code	Phone
Honeywell Analytics Inc	C	847 955-8200
Lincolnshire *(G-12770)*		

VALVES: Water Works

Company	Code	Phone
Ergo-Tech Incorporated	G	630 773-2222
Itasca *(G-11652)*		
Henry Pratt Company LLC	C	630 844-4000
Aurora *(G-1108)*		
Midwest Water Group Inc	E	866 526-6558
Crystal Lake *(G-7230)*		

VARIETY STORE MERCHANDISE, WHOLESALE

Company	Code	Phone
Adams Apple Distributing LP	E	847 832-9900
Glenview *(G-10518)*		
All Right Sales Inc	G	773 558-4800
West Chicago *(G-20534)*		

VARIETY STORES

Company	Code	Phone
State Line International Inc	G	708 251-5772
Lansing *(G-12518)*		

VARNISHES, NEC

Company	Code	Phone
Alvar Inc	F	309 248-7523
Washburn *(G-20262)*		

Employee Codes: A=Over 500 employees, B=251-500
C=101-250, D=51-100, E=20-50, F=10-19, G=3-9

VARNISHES, NEC

Federated Paint Mfg Co .... F 708 345-4848
  Chicago *(G-4572)*
United Gilsonite Labs Inc .... E 217 243-7878
  Jacksonville *(G-11784)*

VARNISHING SVC: Metal Prdts

Nickel Composite Coatings Inc .... E 708 563-2780
  Chicago *(G-5597)*

VAULTS & SAFES WHOLESALERS

Diebold Nixdorf Incorporated .... D 847 598-3300
  Schaumburg *(G-18506)*

VEHICLES: Children's, Exc Bicycles

Henes Usa Inc .... D 312 448-6130
  Glenview *(G-10556)*

VEHICLES: Recreational

Howland Technology Inc .... F 847 965-9808
  Morton Grove *(G-14411)*
M & C Powersports .... G 207 713-3128
  Kankakee *(G-11990)*
Scaletta Moloney Armoring .... C 708 924-0099
  Bedford Park *(G-1503)*

VENDING MACHINES & PARTS

Classic Vending Inc .... E 773 252-7000
  Chicago *(G-4171)*
Lucky Yuppy Puppy Co .... G 847 437-7879
  Arlington Heights *(G-772)*
Partec Inc .... C 847 678-9520
  Franklin Park *(G-10014)*
Seaga Manufacturing Inc .... D 815 297-9500
  Freeport *(G-10141)*
Singer Data Products Inc .... G 630 860-6500
  Bensenville *(G-1893)*
Success Vending Mfg Co LLC .... E 773 262-1685
  Chicago *(G-6263)*

VENETIAN BLINDS & SHADES

Aracon Drpery Vntian Blind Ltd .... G 773 252-1281
  Chicago *(G-3717)*
Bills Shade & Blind Service .... G 773 493-5000
  Chicago *(G-3888)*

VENTILATING EQPT: Metal

Carroll International Corp .... C 630 983-5979
  Lake Forest *(G-12236)*
Demco Inc .... F 708 345-4822
  Melrose Park *(G-13848)*
Evans Heating and Air Inc .... G 217 483-8440
  Chatham *(G-3420)*
Imperial Mfg Group Inc .... F 618 465-3133
  Alton *(G-559)*
R B Hayward Company .... E 847 671-0400
  Schiller Park *(G-18838)*

VENTILATING EQPT: Sheet Metal

Air Vent Inc .... G 309 692-6969
  Peoria *(G-16378)*

VENTURE CAPITAL COMPANIES

Beecken Petty Okeefe & Co LLC .... A 312 435-0300
  Chicago *(G-3858)*
Wind Point Partners LP .... F 312 255-4800
  Chicago *(G-6637)*

VETERINARY PHARMACEUTICAL PREPARATIONS

First Priority Inc .... D 847 531-1215
  Elgin *(G-8587)*
Hydrox Chemical Company Inc .... D 847 468-9400
  Elgin *(G-8618)*
Shaars International Inc .... G 815 315-0717
  Rockford *(G-17627)*

VETERINARY PRDTS: Instruments & Apparatus

American Medical Industries .... G 847 918-9800
  Lake Bluff *(G-12169)*
Shanks Veterinary Equipment .... G 815 225-7700
  Milledgeville *(G-14040)*

VIDEO & AUDIO EQPT, WHOLESALE

Abbey Products LLP .... G 636 922-5577
  Troy *(G-19909)*
Good Vibes Sound Inc .... F 217 351-0909
  Champaign *(G-3298)*
Innovative AV Systems Inc .... G 312 265-6282
  Elmhurst *(G-9379)*
Peerless Industries Inc .... C 630 375-5100
  Aurora *(G-1006)*
Shure Incorporated .... F 847 520-4404
  Wheeling *(G-20984)*

VIDEO CAMERA-AUDIO RECORDERS: Household Use

Alexander Brewster LLC .... G 618 346-8580
  Collinsville *(G-6954)*
Epic Eye .... G 309 210-6212
  Grand Ridge *(G-10688)*
Fire CAM .... G 618 416-8390
  Belleville *(G-1552)*
Fire CAM LLC .... G 618 416-8390
  Belleville *(G-1553)*

VIDEO EQPT

Prager Associates .... G 309 691-1565
  Peoria *(G-16501)*

VIDEO PRODUCTION SVCS

Bible Students Publications .... G 630 595-0984
  Bensenville *(G-1753)*

VIDEO TAPE PRODUCTION SVCS

Andover Junction Publications .... G 815 538-3060
  Mendota *(G-13935)*
C W Publications Inc .... G 800 554-5537
  Sterling *(G-19502)*
Crystal Productions Co .... F 847 657-8144
  Northbrook *(G-15369)*
Cupcake Holdings LLC .... C 800 794-5866
  Woodridge *(G-21289)*
Perry Johnson Inc .... F 847 635-0010
  Rosemont *(G-18041)*
Pieces of Learning Inc .... G 618 964-9426
  Marion *(G-13526)*
Wilton Holdings Inc .... A 630 963-7100
  Woodridge *(G-21349)*
Wilton Industries Inc .... B 630 963-7100
  Naperville *(G-14949)*
Wilton Industries Inc .... F 815 834-9390
  Romeoville *(G-17888)*

VINYL RESINS, NEC

Jakes World Design .... G 217 348-3043
  Lerna *(G-12613)*

VISES: Machine

Adjustable Clamp Company .... C 312 666-0640
  Chicago *(G-3546)*
Jrm International Inc .... G 815 282-9330
  Loves Park *(G-13227)*
Midwest Machine Tool Inc .... G 815 427-8665
  Saint Anne *(G-18136)*

VISUAL COMMUNICATIONS SYSTEMS

Track Group Inc .... E 877 260-2010
  Naperville *(G-14936)*
Western Remac Inc .... E 630 972-7770
  Woodridge *(G-21347)*

VISUAL EFFECTS PRODUCTION SVCS

Intellisource Inc .... E 847 426-7400
  Elgin *(G-8629)*

VITAMINS: Natural Or Synthetic, Uncompounded, Bulk

Bright Brain .... F 844 272-4645
  Bloomingdale *(G-1982)*
Glanbia Performance Ntrtn Inc .... E 630 256-7445
  Aurora *(G-969)*
Glanbia Performance Ntrtn Inc .... F 630 236-0097
  Aurora *(G-970)*
Glanbia Performance Ntrtn Inc .... D 800 336-2183
  Aurora *(G-971)*
Glanbia Prfmce Ntrtn NA Inc .... C 630 236-0097
  Downers Grove *(G-8012)*
Nutritional Institute LLC .... G 847 223-7676
  Grayslake *(G-10794)*
Ys Health Corporation .... F 847 391-9122
  Mount Prospect *(G-14585)*

VITAMINS: Pharmaceutical Preparations

Mead Johnson Nutrition Company ...... C 312 466-5800
  Chicago *(G-5379)*
Trudeau Approved Products Inc .... G 312 924-7230
  Hinsdale *(G-11382)*

VOCATIONAL REHABILITATION AGENCY

Clay Cnty Rhbilitation Ctr Inc .... F 618 662-6607
  Flora *(G-9678)*

VOCATIONAL TRAINING AGENCY

Trade Industries .... E 618 643-4321
  Mc Leansboro *(G-13709)*

VOLCANIC ROCK: Dimension

Red Hill Lava Products Inc .... G 800 528-2765
  Rock Island *(G-17240)*

WALLBOARD: Decorated, Made From Purchased Materials

Stevens Cabinets Inc .... B 217 857-7100
  Teutopolis *(G-19773)*
Wexford Home Corp .... G 847 922-5738
  Northbrook *(G-15502)*

WALLPAPER & WALL COVERINGS

Mitchell Black LLC .... F 312 667-4477
  Chicago *(G-5470)*
Tercor Inc .... G 773 549-8303
  Chicago *(G-6353)*

WALLPAPER STORE

Afar Imports & Interiors Inc .... G 217 744-3262
  Springfield *(G-19316)*
Roberts Draperies Center Inc .... G 847 255-4040
  Mount Prospect *(G-14567)*

WALLS: Curtain, Metal

Chicago Ornamental Iron Inc .... E 773 321-9635
  Chicago *(G-4121)*
Harmon Inc .... E 630 759-8060
  Bolingbrook *(G-2183)*
Ltc Holdings Inc .... C 847 249-5900
  Waukegan *(G-20464)*

WAREHOUSE CLUBS STORES

Vermilion Steel Fabrication .... G 217 442-5300
  Danville *(G-7391)*

WAREHOUSING & STORAGE FACILITIES, NEC

Hurst Chemical Company .... G 815 964-0451
  Rockford *(G-17454)*
M-Prime Company .... E 630 834-9400
  Villa Park *(G-20157)*
Unistrut International Corp .... D 630 773-3460
  Addison *(G-323)*

WAREHOUSING & STORAGE, REFRIGERATED: Cold Storage Or Refrig

Bushnell Locker Service .... G 309 772-2783
  Bushnell *(G-2739)*
Carroll County Locker .... G 815 493-2370
  Lanark *(G-12478)*

WAREHOUSING & STORAGE, REFRIGERATED: Frozen Or Refrig Goods

Edgar County Locker Service .... G 217 466-5000
  Paris *(G-16229)*
Eickmans Processing Co Inc .... E 815 247-8451
  Seward *(G-18867)*
Eureka Locker Inc .... F 309 467-2731
  Eureka *(G-9482)*

Korte Meat Processors Inc..................G....... 618 654-3813
Highland *(G-11230)*

WAREHOUSING & STORAGE: Bulk St & Termnls, Hire, Petro/Chem

East St Louis Trml & Stor Co ....E....... 618 271-2185
East Saint Louis *(G-8306)*

WAREHOUSING & STORAGE: General

Bunn-O-Matic Corporation ....E....... 562 926-0764
Springfield *(G-19332)*
Chicago Export Packing Co ....E....... 773 247-8911
Chicago *(G-4102)*
Chicago Tube and Iron Company ....E....... 309 787-4947
Milan *(G-14003)*
Dallas Corporation ....F....... 630 322-8000
Downers Grove *(G-7983)*
Glanbia Performance Ntrtn Inc ....E....... 630 256-7445
Aurora *(G-969)*
Great Guy Inc ....G....... 312 203-9872
Medinah *(G-13813)*
Hallstar Company ....E....... 901 948-8663
Chicago *(G-4771)*
Horizon Downing LLC ....E....... 815 758-6867
Dekalb *(G-7685)*
Lordahl Manufacturing Co ....D....... 847 244-0448
Long Grove *(G-13161)*
Myers Concrete & Construction ....G....... 815 732-2591
Oregon *(G-15924)*
Thermal Ceramics Inc ....E....... 217 627-2101
Girard *(G-10386)*
Vee Pak LLC ....D....... 708 482-8881
Hodgkins *(G-11399)*
Zoetis LLC ....D....... 708 757-2592
Chicago Heights *(G-6787)*

WAREHOUSING & STORAGE: General

Americas Community Bankers ....E....... 312 644-3100
Chicago *(G-3675)*
Arro Corporation ....C....... 708 352-8200
Hodgkins *(G-11384)*
Arro Corporation ....E....... 708 352-7412
Hodgkins *(G-11385)*
Arro Corporation ....G....... 773 978-1251
Chicago *(G-3733)*
Corr-Pak Corporation ....E....... 708 442-7806
Mc Cook *(G-13690)*
D E Signs & Storage LLC ....G....... 618 939-8050
Waterloo *(G-20289)*
Dynamic Manufacturing Inc ....E....... 708 343-8753
Melrose Park *(G-13857)*
Hyster-Yale Group Inc ....E....... 217 443-7416
Danville *(G-7348)*
Kurz Transfer Products LP ....G....... 847 228-0001
Elk Grove Village *(G-9080)*
Mech-Tronics Corporation ....G....... 708 344-0202
Melrose Park *(G-13892)*
Monnex International Inc ....E....... 847 850-5263
Buffalo Grove *(G-2576)*
Northwest Pallet Services LLC ....A....... 815 544-6001
Belvidere *(G-1691)*
Pinnacle Foods Group LLC ....B....... 618 829-3275
Saint Elmo *(G-18311)*
Polmax LLC ....C....... 708 843-8300
Alsip *(G-494)*
Randal Wood Displays Inc ....D....... 630 761-0400
Batavia *(G-1409)*
Shapiro Bros of Illinois Inc ....E....... 618 244-3168
Mount Vernon *(G-14638)*
Stitch TEC Co Inc ....G....... 618 327-8054
Nashville *(G-15011)*
Venus Processing & Storage ....D....... 847 455-0496
Franklin Park *(G-10077)*

WAREHOUSING & STORAGE: Household Goods

GM Partners ....G....... 847 895-7627
Schaumburg *(G-18536)*

WAREHOUSING & STORAGE: Miniwarehouse

Form Relief Tool Co Inc ....F....... 815 393-4263
Davis Junction *(G-7423)*

WAREHOUSING & STORAGE: Refrigerated

Metropolis Ready Mix Inc ....E....... 618 524-8221
Metropolis *(G-13974)*

WARM AIR HEATING & AC EQPT & SPLYS, WHOL: Dust Collecting

Dust Patrol Inc.....................................G....... 309 676-1161
Peoria *(G-16432)*

WARM AIR HEATING & AC EQPT & SPLYS, WHOLESALE Air Filters

Bisco Enterprise Inc ....F....... 630 628-1831
Schaumburg *(G-18463)*
Clean and Science USA Co Ltd ....G....... 847 461-9292
Rolling Meadows *(G-17722)*
Nuair Filter Company LLC ....G....... 309 888-4331
Normal *(G-15214)*
Pure N Natural Systems Inc ....F....... 630 372-9681
Streamwood *(G-19591)*
Rv Air Inc ....G....... 309 657-4300
Addison *(G-279)*
Sentry Pool & Chemical Supply ....E....... 309 797-9721
Moline *(G-14177)*

WARM AIR HEATING & AC EQPT & SPLYS, WHOLESALE Heat Exchgrs

Pw Services LLC ....G....... 217 672-3225
Warrensburg *(G-20227)*
Yinlun Usa Inc ....G....... 309 291-0843
Morton *(G-14387)*

WARM AIR HEATING/AC EQPT/SPLYS, WHOL Warm Air Htg Eqpt/Splys

Bird-X Inc ....E....... 312 226-2473
Elmhurst *(G-9334)*
Goose Island Mfg & Supply Corp ....G....... 708 343-4225
Lansing *(G-12495)*
Habegger Corporation ....F....... 309 793-7172
Rock Island *(G-17221)*
Temp Excel Properties LLC ....G....... 847 844-3845
Elgin *(G-8750)*
W L Engler Distributing Inc ....G....... 630 898-5400
Aurora *(G-1032)*

WASHCLOTHS & BATH MITTS, FROM PURCHASED MATERIALS

My Konjac Sponge Inc........................F....... 630 345-3653
North Barrington *(G-15288)*

WASHERS

Illinois Tool Works Inc ....F....... 708 681-3891
Broadview *(G-2443)*
Laundry Services Company ....G....... 630 327-9329
Downers Grove *(G-8042)*

WASHERS: Lock

Saint Technologies Inc ....G....... 815 864-3035
Shannon *(G-18873)*

WASHERS: Metal

Freeway-Rockford Inc ....E....... 815 397-6425
Rockford *(G-17425)*
Gaskoa Inc ....E....... 708 339-5000
South Holland *(G-19213)*
Great Lakes Washer Company ....F....... 630 887-7447
Burr Ridge *(G-2677)*
Maxi-Vac Inc ....G....... 630 620-6669
Elgin *(G-8653)*
Willie Washer Mfg Co ....C....... 847 956-1344
Elk Grove Village *(G-9310)*

WASHERS: Plastic

Monda Window & Door Corp ....E....... 773 254-8888
Chicago *(G-5489)*

WASHERS: Rubber

Excelsior Inc ....E....... 815 987-2900
Rockford *(G-17407)*

WASTE CLEANING SVCS

Midwest Intgrted Companies LLC ....C....... 847 426-6354
Gilberts *(G-10361)*

WATCH REPAIR SVCS

A G Mitchells Jewelers Ltd ....F....... 847 394-0820
Arlington Heights *(G-680)*
State Street Jewelers Inc ....F....... 630 232-2085
Geneva *(G-10307)*

WATCHES

Hampden Corporation ....E....... 312 583-3000
Chicago *(G-4775)*
KI Watch Service Inc ....G....... 847 368-8780
Bartlett *(G-1293)*

WATCHES & PARTS, WHOLESALE

Gennco International Inc ....F....... 847 541-3333
Northbrook *(G-15393)*

WATER HEATERS

Unique Indoor Comfort ....F....... 847 362-1910
Libertyville *(G-12719)*

WATER PURIFICATION EQPT: Household

H2o Solutions LLC ....G....... 618 219-2905
Granite City *(G-10713)*
Mullarkey Associates Inc ....F....... 708 597-5555
Tinley Park *(G-19846)*
Natural Choice Corporation ....F....... 815 874-4444
Loves Park *(G-13240)*
Pentair Fltrtion Solutions LLC ....E....... 630 307-3000
Hanover Park *(G-11012)*
Superior Water Services Inc ....G....... 309 691-9287
Peoria *(G-16531)*
Walter Louis Chem & Assoc Inc ....F....... 217 223-2017
Quincy *(G-16954)*
William N Pasulka ....G....... 815 339-6300
Peru *(G-16598)*

WATER PURIFICATION PRDTS: Chlorination Tablets & Kits

Mar Cor Purification Inc ....G....... 630 435-1017
Downers Grove *(G-8051)*

WATER SOFTENER SVCS

American Watersource LLC ....E....... 630 778-9900
Naperville *(G-14957)*
Superior Water Services Inc ....G....... 309 691-9287
Peoria *(G-16531)*
Water Dynamics Inc ....G....... 630 584-8475
Saint Charles *(G-18297)*

WATER SOFTENING WHOLESALERS

Superior Water Services Inc ....G....... 309 691-9287
Peoria *(G-16531)*

WATER SUPPLY

Chicago Waterjet Inc ....G....... 847 350-1898
Elk Grove Village *(G-8896)*
Gehrke Technology Group Inc ....F....... 847 498-7320
Wauconda *(G-20353)*

WATER TREATMENT EQPT: Indl

Advanced Ozone Tech Inc ....F....... 630 964-1300
Downers Grove *(G-7949)*
Ambi-Design Incorporated ....G....... 815 964-7568
Rockford *(G-17300)*
American Watersource LLC ....G....... 630 778-9900
Naperville *(G-14957)*
Applied Mechanical Tech LLC ....G....... 815 472-2700
Momence *(G-14182)*
Arbortech Corporation ....G....... 847 462-1111
Johnsburg *(G-11801)*
C2 Water Inc ....G....... 312 550-1159
Kenilworth *(G-12014)*
Carney Flow Technics LLC ....G....... 815 277-2600
Frankfort *(G-9777)*
Charger Water Conditioning Inc ....F....... 847 967-9558
Morton Grove *(G-14395)*
Chemical Pump ....G....... 815 464-1908
Frankfort *(G-9779)*

WATER TREATMENT EQPT: Indl

City of Edwardsville .... G		618 692-7053
Edwardsville *(G-8352)*		
D R Sperry & Co .... D		630 892-4361
Aurora *(G-1083)*		
Dubois Chemicals Inc .... D		847 457-1813
Rosemont *(G-18021)*		
Earthwise Environmental Inc .... G		630 475-3070
Wood Dale *(G-21183)*		
Ecodyne Water Treatment LLC .. E		630 961-5043
Naperville *(G-14820)*		
Ellis Corporation .... D		630 250-9222
Itasca *(G-11648)*		
Equipsolutions LLC .... E		630 351-9070
Roselle *(G-17953)*		
Evoqua Water Technologies LLC ..E		815 921-8325
Rockford *(G-17404)*		
Evoqua Water Technologies LLC ..E		618 451-1205
Granite City *(G-10705)*		
Extol Hydro Technologies Inc .... F		708 717-4371
Palos Park *(G-16210)*		
Gehrke Technology Group Inc .... F		847 498-7320
Wauconda *(G-20353)*		
Gillespie City Water .... G		217 839-3279
Gillespie *(G-10375)*		
H-O-H Water Technology Inc ..... G		847 358-7400
Palatine *(G-16121)*		
Heat Transfer Laboratories .... G		708 715-4300
Oakbrook Terrace *(G-15801)*		
Hpd LLC C		815 609-2032
Plainfield *(G-16673)*		
Hydrotec Systems Company Inc .. G		815 624-6644
Tiskilwa *(G-19873)*		
Illinois Water Tech Inc .... E		815 636-8884
Roscoe *(G-17911)*		
International Water Werks Inc .. G		847 669-1902
Huntley *(G-11544)*		
Marmon Holdings Inc .... D		312 372-9500
Chicago *(G-5343)*		
Marmon Industrial LLC .... G		312 372-9500
Chicago *(G-5344)*		
McNish Corporation .... D		630 892-7921
Aurora *(G-1128)*		
Microplasma Ozone Tech Inc .... F		217 693-7950
Champaign *(G-3321)*		
Midwest Water Group Inc .... G		866 526-6558
Crystal Lake *(G-7230)*		
Nano Gas Technologies Inc .... G		847 317-0656
Deerfield *(G-7640)*		
Nano2 LLC .... G		217 563-2942
Nokomis *(G-15195)*		
Nijhuis Water Technology Inc .... G		312 466-9900
Chicago *(G-5601)*		
Palmyra Modesto Water Comm .. G		217 436-2519
Palmyra *(G-16180)*		
Pristine Water Solutions Inc ...... F		847 689-1100
Waukegan *(G-20482)*		
Pureline Treatment Systems LLC ..C		847 963-8465
Bensenville *(G-1877)*		
Regunathan & Assoc Inc .... G		630 653-0387
Wheaton *(G-20818)*		
Safe Water Technologies Inc ...... G		847 888-6900
Elgin *(G-8723)*		
Servetech Water Solutions Inc .. G		630 784-9050
Wheaton *(G-20823)*		
Triwater Holdings LLC .... G		847 457-1812
Lake Forest *(G-12318)*		
Veolia Water Technologies Inc .. E		815 609-2000
Plainfield *(G-16726)*		
Water Dynamics Inc .... G		630 584-8475
Saint Charles *(G-18297)*		
Waterco of Central States Inc C		630 576-4782
Lombard *(G-13153)*		
Will County Well & Pump Co Inc .. G		815 485-2413
New Lenox *(G-15069)*		

WATER: Distilled

Samuel Rowell .... G		618 942-6970
Herrin *(G-11178)*		

WATER: Mineral, Carbonated, Canned & Bottled, Etc

Clearly Kosher Foods .... F		630 546-2052
Aurora *(G-1076)*		
Ds Services of America Inc .... F		800 322-6272
Rockford *(G-17386)*		
Ds Services of America Inc .... E		815 469-7100
Frankfort *(G-9787)*		
Protein2o Inc		646 919-5320
Elk Grove Village *(G-9199)*		
Pyramid Bottling LLC .... G		847 565-9412
Waukegan *(G-20486)*		
Team Sider Inc .... G		847 767-0107
Highland Park *(G-11303)*		

WATER: Pasteurized & Mineral, Bottled & Canned

Henderson Water District .... G		618 498-6418
Jerseyville *(G-11793)*		
West Water Inc .... G		312 326-7480
Chicago *(G-6606)*		

WATER: Pasteurized, Canned & Bottled, Etc

Amwell .... F		630 898-6900
Aurora *(G-1051)*		
Ds Services of America Inc C		773 586-8600
Chicago *(G-4399)*		
Hinckley & Schmitt Inc .... A		773 586-8600
Chicago *(G-4823)*		
Pure Flo Bottling Inc .... G		815 963-4797
Rockford *(G-17562)*		
Tst/Impreso Inc .... G		630 775-9555
Addison *(G-320)*		

WATERPROOFING COMPOUNDS

T K O Waterproof Coating LLP .... G		815 338-2006
Woodstock *(G-21440)*		
Tamms Industries Inc .... D		815 522-3394
Kirkland *(G-12066)*		
Ted Muller .... G		312 435-0978
Chicago *(G-6336)*		

WAVEGUIDES & FITTINGS

Andrew New Zealand Inc .... E		708 873-3507
Orland Park *(G-15940)*		
Commscope Technologies LLC .... B		779 435-6000
Joliet *(G-11845)*		

WAX REMOVERS

Fox Valley Chemical Company .... G		815 653-2660
Ringwood *(G-17043)*		

WAX Sealing wax

Princeton Sealing Wax Co .... G		815 875-1943
Princeton *(G-16821)*		
Remet Corporation .... E		480 766-3464
Palatine *(G-16153)*		

WEATHER STRIPS: Metal

Dorbin Metal Strip Mfg Co .... F		708 656-2333
Cicero *(G-6842)*		

WEAVING MILL, BROADWOVEN FABRICS: Wool Or Similar Fabric

Without A Trace Weaver Inc .... F		773 588-4922
Chicago *(G-6652)*		

WEIGHING MACHINERY & APPARATUS

Morrison Weighing Systems Inc .. G		309 799-7311
Milan *(G-14019)*		

WELDING & CUTTING APPARATUS & ACCESS, NEC

Associate General Labs Inc .... G		847 678-2717
Franklin Park *(G-9877)*		
Kriese Mfg .... G		815 748-2683
Cortland *(G-7023)*		

WELDING EQPT

Adams Steel Service Inc .... E		815 385-9100
McHenry *(G-13715)*		
Airgas Inc .... F		773 785-3000
Chicago *(G-3588)*		
Airgas Usa LLC .... E		630 231-9260
West Chicago *(G-20533)*		
D & G Welding Supply Company .. G		815 675-9890
Spring Grove *(G-19272)*		
Ezee Roll Manufacturing Co .... G		217 339-2279
Hoopeston *(G-11508)*		
Industrial Welder Rebuilders ...... G		708 371-5688
Alsip *(G-457)*		
Littell International Inc .... E		630 622-4950
Schaumburg *(G-18610)*		
Reber Welding Service .... G		217 774-3441
Shelbyville *(G-18885)*		

WELDING EQPT & SPLYS WHOLESALERS

Airgas Usa LLC .... G		618 439-7207
Benton *(G-1917)*		
Airgas Usa LLC .... E		630 231-9260
West Chicago *(G-20533)*		
Gano Welding Supplies Inc .... F		217 345-3777
Charleston *(G-3402)*		
Herrmann Ultrasonics Inc .... E		630 626-1626
Bartlett *(G-1285)*		
Ilmo Products Company .... E		217 245-2183
Jacksonville *(G-11770)*		
Lickenbrock & Sons Inc .... G		618 632-4977
O Fallon *(G-15578)*		
Mac-Weld Inc .... G		618 529-1828
Carbondale *(G-2850)*		
Matheson Tri-Gas Inc .... F		309 697-1933
Mapleton *(G-13476)*		
Matheson Tri-Gas Inc .... E		815 727-2202
Joliet *(G-11899)*		
Praxair Distribution Inc .... E		314 664-7900
Cahokia *(G-2763)*		
Shew Brothers Inc .... G		618 997-4414
Marion *(G-13534)*		
Spot Welding Products Inc .... F		630 238-0880
Franklin Park *(G-10051)*		
Weldstar Company .... E		630 859-3100
Aurora *(G-1169)*		

WELDING EQPT & SPLYS: Arc Welders, Transformer-Rectifier

Linz Electric Inc .... F		847 595-1473
Northbrook *(G-15419)*		

WELDING EQPT & SPLYS: Resistance, Electric

Automation International Inc ...... D		217 446-9500
Danville *(G-7322)*		
Spot Welding Products Inc .... F		630 238-0880
Franklin Park *(G-10051)*		

WELDING EQPT & SPLYS: Wire, Bare & Coated

Electron Beam Technologies Inc .. C		815 935-2211
Kankakee *(G-11967)*		

WELDING EQPT REPAIR SVCS

Barton Manufacturing LLC .... F		217 428-0726
Decatur *(G-7463)*		
Globaltech International LLC ...... G		630 327-6909
Aurora *(G-972)*		
Industrial Welder Rebuilders ...... G		708 371-5688
Alsip *(G-457)*		
Pekin Weldors Inc .... F		309 382-3627
North Pekin *(G-15327)*		

WELDING EQPT: Electric

American Vacuum Company .... G		847 674-8383
Niles *(G-15102)*		
Fanuc America Corporation .... E		847 898-5000
Hoffman Estates *(G-11423)*		
Globaltech International LLC ...... G		630 327-6909
Aurora *(G-972)*		
Micro Products Company .... G		309 697-1216
Peoria *(G-16473)*		
Sommer Products Company Inc .. D		309 697-1216
Peoria *(G-16526)*		

WELDING EQPT: Electrical

Min Sheng Technology Inc .... G		815 569-4496
Schaumburg *(G-18631)*		

WELDING MACHINES & EQPT: Ultrasonic

Dukane Corporation C		630 797-4900
Saint Charles *(G-18189)*		
Herrmann Ultrasonics Inc .... E		630 626-1626
Bartlett *(G-1285)*		

WELDING REPAIR SVC

A&S Machining & Welding Inc .... E 708 442-4544
  Mc Cook *(G-13689)*
Ability Welding Service Inc .... G 630 595-3737
  Bensenville *(G-1723)*
Ablaze Welding & Fabricating 815 965-0046
  Rockford *(G-17287)*
Abzenco Welding Inc 630 234-8021
  Batavia *(G-1339)*
Accurate Auto Manufacturing Co ..... G 618 244-0727
  Mount Vernon *(G-14595)*
Adams Steel Service Inc .... E 815 385-9100
  McHenry *(G-13715)*
Advanced Welding Ltd .... F 708 205-4559
  Addison *(G-23)*
Affordable Welding Us Inc .... G 773 374-2000
  Chicago *(G-3579)*
Aileys 3 Welding .... G 815 683-2181
  Crescent City *(G-7081)*
Alberto Daza .... F 773 638-9880
  Chicago *(G-3597)*
Aledo Welding Enterprises Inc .... G 309 582-2019
  Aledo *(G-354)*
All Metal Machine 815 389-0168
  South Beloit *(G-19079)*
All Pro Welding Services Inc .... G 217 586-5383
  Mahomet *(G-13420)*
Allans Welding & Machine Inc .... G 618 392-3708
  Olney *(G-15851)*
Allied Welding Inc .... E 309 274-6227
  Chillicothe *(G-6813)*
Alloy Welding Corp .... E 708 345-6756
  Melrose Park *(G-13822)*
Alloyweld Inspection Co Inc .... G 630 595-2145
  Bensenville *(G-1738)*
American Grinding & Machine Co .... D 773 889-4343
  Chicago *(G-3653)*
American Machining & Wldg Inc ...... E 773 586-2585
  Chicago *(G-3659)*
American Metal Installers & FA .... G 630 993-0812
  Villa Park *(G-20131)*
American Welding & Gas Inc .... E 630 527-2550
  Stone Park *(G-19551)*
Anchor Welding & Fabrication 815 937-1640
  Aroma Park *(G-839)*
Andel Services Inc 630 566-0210
  Aurora *(G-1052)*
Andersen Machine & Welding Inc .... G 815 232-4664
  Freeport *(G-10101)*
Apollo Machine & Manufacturing 847 677-6444
  Skokie *(G-18921)*
Armitage Welding 773 772-1442
  Chicago *(G-3731)*
Arndt Enterprise Ltd 847 234-5736
  Lake Forest *(G-12226)*
AS Fabricating Inc 618 242-7438
  Mount Vernon *(G-14596)*
Ascent Mfg Co .... E 847 806-6600
  Elk Grove Village *(G-8841)*
Assured Welding Service Inc .... G 847 671-1414
  West Chicago *(G-20545)*
Atlas Boiler & Welding Company ..... G 815 963-3360
  Elgin *(G-8517)*
Ats Sortimat USA LLC .... D 847 925-1234
  Rolling Meadows *(G-17713)*
Awerkamp Machine Co .... E 217 222-3480
  Quincy *(G-16859)*
B & W Machine Company Inc .... G 847 364-4500
  Elk Grove Village *(G-8853)*
B J Fehr Machine Co .... G 309 923-8691
  Roanoke *(G-17099)*
B T Brown Manufacturing .... G 815 947-3633
  Kent *(G-12017)*
Bales Mold Service Inc .... E 630 852-4665
  Downers Grove *(G-7957)*
Baley Enterprises Inc .... G 708 681-0900
  Melrose Park *(G-13830)*
Barton Manufacturing LLC .... F 217 428-0726
  Decatur *(G-7463)*
Bc Welding Inc .... G 708 258-0076
  Peotone *(G-16550)*
Bear Machine Tool & Die Inc .... G 815 932-4204
  Bradley *(G-2277)*
Bear Mtal Wldg Fabrication Inc .... G 630 261-9353
  Villa Park *(G-20133)*
Beaver Creek Enterprises Inc .... F 815 723-9455
  Joliet *(G-11829)*
Beesing Welding & Eqp Repr .... G 815 732-7552
  Oregon *(G-15913)*

Bellinis Custom Welding and A .... G 815 284-4175
  Dixon *(G-7889)*
Bessler Welding Inc .... F 309 699-6224
  East Peoria *(G-8253)*
Bi State Steel Co .... G 309 755-0668
  East Moline *(G-8223)*
Bierman Welding Inc .... F 217 342-2050
  Effingham *(G-8389)*
Bill Welding & Fabrication LLC .... G 312 871-2623
  Chicago *(G-3886)*
Brian D Obermiller .... G 815 830-3100
  Tonica *(G-19887)*
Bulaw Welding & Engineering Co ... D 630 228-8300
  Itasca *(G-11632)*
Burgess Manufacturing Inc .... F 847 680-1724
  Libertyville *(G-12641)*
Burke Tool & Manufacturing Inc ...... G 618 542-6441
  Du Quoin *(G-8116)*
Burns Machine Company .... E 815 434-3131
  Ottawa *(G-16044)*
C & B Welders Inc .... G 773 722-0097
  Chicago *(G-3990)*
C E R Machining & Tooling Ltd .... G 708 442-9614
  Lyons *(G-13305)*
C I F Industries Inc .... E 618 635-2010
  Staunton *(G-19476)*
C J Holdings Inc .... G 309 274-3141
  Chillicothe *(G-6815)*
C Keller Manufacturing Inc .... E 630 833-5593
  Villa Park *(G-20136)*
Carrolls Welding & Fabrication .... G 217 728-8720
  Sullivan *(G-19663)*
Casward Tool Works Inc .... G 773 486-4900
  Orland Park *(G-15946)*
CB Machine & Tool Corp .... G 847 288-1807
  Franklin Park *(G-9901)*
Certiweld Inc .... G 708 389-0148
  Crestwood *(G-7111)*
Cervones Welding Service Inc .... G 847 985-6865
  Schaumburg *(G-18471)*
Chicago Tube and Iron Company .... E 815 834-2500
  Romeoville *(G-17807)*
Cokel Dj Welding Bay & Muffler ...... G 309 385-4567
  Princeville *(G-16825)*
Cokel Welding Shop .... G 217 357-3312
  Carthage *(G-3134)*
Colfax Welding & Fabricating .... G 847 359-4433
  Palatine *(G-16101)*
Comers Welding Service Inc .... G 630 892-0168
  Montgomery *(G-14241)*
Comet Fabricating & Welding Co .... E 815 229-0468
  Rockford *(G-17354)*
Commercial Machine Services .... F 847 806-1901
  Elk Grove Village *(G-8905)*
Component Tool & Mfg Co .... F 708 672-5505
  Crete *(G-7136)*
Concept Industries Inc .... G 847 258-3545
  Elk Grove Village *(G-8907)*
Connell Mc Machine & Welding ...... G 815 868-2275
  Mc Connell *(G-13688)*
Coras Welding Shop Inc .... G 815 672-7950
  Streator *(G-19606)*
Corrugated Converting Eqp .... F 618 532-2138
  Centralia *(G-3227)*
County Tool & Die .... G 217 324-6527
  Litchfield *(G-12962)*
Cr Welding Met Fabrication Inc .... G 224 789-7825
  Gurnee *(G-10867)*
Custom Fabricators LLC .... F 630 372-4399
  Streamwood *(G-19569)*
Cyclops Welding Co .... G 815 223-0685
  La Salle *(G-12109)*
Cylinder Services Inc .... G 630 466-9820
  Sugar Grove *(G-19641)*
D & H Precision Tooling Co .... G 815 653-9611
  Wonder Lake *(G-21144)*
D & M Welding Inc .... G 708 233-6080
  Bridgeview *(G-2339)*
D M Manufacturing 2 Inc .... G 618 455-3550
  Sainte Marie *(G-18325)*
D N Welding & Fabricating Inc .... G 847 244-6410
  Waukegan *(G-20432)*
D W Terry Welding Company .... G 618 433-9722
  Alton *(G-551)*
Daniel Mfg Inc .... F 309 963-4227
  Carlock *(G-2886)*
Darnell Welding .... G 618 945-9538
  Bridgeport *(G-2312)*
Daves Welding Service Inc .... G 630 655-3224
  Darien *(G-7405)*

David Schutte .... G 217 223-5464
  Quincy *(G-16874)*
Device Technologies Inc .... G 630 553-7178
  Yorkville *(G-21479)*
Dons Welding .... G 847 526-1177
  Wauconda *(G-20343)*
Dooling Machine Products Inc .... G 618 254-0724
  Hartford *(G-11034)*
Du Page Welding Inc .... G 630 543-8511
  Addison *(G-103)*
Duroweld Company Inc .... E 847 680-3064
  Lake Bluff *(G-12179)*
Dyers Machine Service Inc .... G 708 496-8100
  Summit Argo *(G-19678)*
E & E Machine & Engineering Co ... G 708 841-5208
  Riverdale *(G-17071)*
Eagle Machine Company .... G 312 243-7407
  Chicago *(G-4429)*
Edward F Data .... G 708 597-0158
  Alsip *(G-444)*
Edwardsville Mch & Wldg Co Inc .... G 618 656-5145
  Edwardsville *(G-8360)*
Eenigenburg Mfg Inc .... G 708 474-0850
  Lansing *(G-12492)*
Ekstrom Carlson Fabg Co Inc .... G 815 226-1511
  Rockford *(G-17392)*
Emerald Machine Inc .... G 773 924-3659
  Chicago *(G-4495)*
Emv Welding Inc .... G 630 264-0893
  Aurora *(G-1089)*
Erva Tool & Die Company .... G 773 533-7806
  Chicago *(G-4528)*
Estructuras Inc .... F 773 522-2200
  Chicago *(G-4534)*
Eton Machine Co Ltd .... G 847 426-3380
  Elgin *(G-8581)*
Eveready Welding Service Inc .... G 708 532-2432
  Tinley Park *(G-19825)*
Extreme Welding & Machine Serv ... G 618 272-7237
  Eldorado *(G-8481)*
F Vogelmann and Company .... G 815 469-2285
  Frankfort *(G-9793)*
Fabco Enterprises Inc .... G 708 333-4644
  Harvey *(G-11084)*
Fabricating & Welding Corp .... E 773 928-2050
  Chicago *(G-4555)*
Fast Forward Welding Inc .... G 815 254-1901
  Plainfield *(G-16664)*
Fehring Ornamental Iron Works ...... G 217 483-6727
  Rochester *(G-17166)*
Folk Race Cars .... G 815 629-2418
  Durand *(G-8151)*
Force Manufacturing Inc .... G 847 265-6500
  Lake Villa *(G-12351)*
Franks Ideal Welding Inc .... G 708 344-4409
  Broadview *(G-2438)*
Fred Stollenwerk .... G 309 852-3794
  Kewanee *(G-12034)*
Gengler-Lowney Laser Works .... F 630 801-4840
  Aurora *(G-1103)*
Gma Inc .... G 630 595-1255
  Bensenville *(G-1812)*
Golden Hydraulic & Machine .... G 708 597-4265
  Blue Island *(G-2124)*
Graham Welding Inc .... G 217 422-1423
  Decatur *(G-7497)*
Great Lakes Mech Svcs Inc .... F 708 672-5900
  Lincolnshire *(G-12768)*
Greens Machine Shop .... G 618 532-4631
  Centralia *(G-3234)*
Gridley Welding Inc .... G 309 747-2325
  Gridley *(G-10845)*
Grimm Metal Fabricators Inc .... E 630 792-1710
  Lombard *(G-13083)*
Grover Welding Company .... G 847 966-3119
  Skokie *(G-18961)*
GV Welding Inc .... G 312 863-0071
  Chicago *(G-4753)*
H & H Services Inc .... F 618 633-2837
  Hamel *(G-10949)*
Halter Machine Shop Inc .... G 618 943-2224
  Lawrenceville *(G-12534)*
Harbor Manufacturing Inc .... D 708 543-1740
  Frankfort *(G-9800)*
Hattan Tool Company .... G 708 597-9308
  Alsip *(G-455)*
Hedricks Welding & Fabrication ...... G 217 846-3230
  Foosland *(G-9705)*
Heiss Welding Inc .... F 815 434-1838
  Ottawa *(G-16055)*

Employee Codes: A=Over 500 employees, B=251-500
C=101-250, D=51-100, E=20-50, F=10-19, G=3-9

WELDING REPAIR SVC — PRODUCT SECTION

Hfr Precision Machining Inc .... E 630 556-4325
 Sugar Grove (G-19646)
High Speed Welding Inc .... G 630 971-8929
 Westmont (G-20747)
Hofmeister Welding Inc .... G 217 407-4091
 Griggsville (G-10849)
Hogg Welding Inc .... G 708 339-0033
 Harvey (G-11089)
Holshouser Machine & Tool Inc .... G 618 451-0164
 Granite City (G-10715)
Hts Coatings LLC .... G 618 215-8161
 Madison (G-13414)
Hutton Welding Service Inc .... G 217 932-5585
 Casey (G-3203)
ILmachine Company Inc .... G 847 243-9900
 Wheeling (G-20913)
Industrial Mint Wldg Machining .... D 773 376-6526
 Chicago (G-4908)
Industrial Welding Inc .... F 815 535-9300
 Rock Falls (G-17188)
J & B Welding LLC .... F 309 887-4151
 Fulton (G-10153)
J & I Son Tool Company Inc .... G 847 455-4200
 Franklin Park (G-9967)
J & M Fab Metals Inc .... G 815 758-0354
 Marengo (G-13486)
J B Metal Works Inc .... G 847 824-4253
 Des Plaines (G-7790)
Jacksonville Machine Inc .... D 217 243-1119
 Jacksonville (G-11771)
Jacob Chambliss .... G 618 731-6632
 Dahlgren (G-7308)
Jacobs Boiler & Mech Inds Inc .... E 773 385-9900
 Chicago (G-4998)
Jakes McHning Rbilding Svc Inc .... E 630 892-3291
 Aurora (G-1116)
Jarvis Welding Co .... G 309 647-0033
 Canton (G-2827)
Jasiek Motor Rebuilding Inc .... G 815 883-3678
 Oglesby (G-15842)
Jav Machine Craft Inc .... G 708 867-8608
 Chicago (G-5011)
Jayne Excavating & Welding LLC ..... G 618 553-1149
 Newton (G-15085)
Jet Industries Inc .... E 773 586-8900
 Chicago (G-5024)
Jim Cokel Welding .... G 309 734-5063
 Monmouth (G-14219)
Joint Field Services Inc .... G 815 795-3714
 Marseilles (G-13559)
JW Welding .... G 618 228-7213
 Aviston (G-1180)
K & K Tool & Die Inc .... F 309 829-4479
 Bloomington (G-2065)
K & P Welding .... G 217 536-5245
 Watson (G-20322)
K D Welding Inc .... G 815 591-3545
 Hanover (G-10996)
K Three Welding Service Inc .... G 708 563-2911
 Chicago (G-5067)
Karly Iron Works Inc .... G 815 477-3430
 Crystal Lake (G-7215)
Kemper Industries .... G 217 826-5712
 Marshall (G-13573)
Kenneth W Templeman .... G 847 912-2740
 Volo (G-20200)
Kim Gough .... G 309 734-3511
 Monmouth (G-14221)
Koerner Aviation Inc .... G 815 932-4222
 Kankakee (G-11988)
Kopp Welding Inc .... G 847 593-2070
 Elk Grove Village (G-9079)
Ksem Inc .... G 618 656-5388
 Edwardsville (G-8367)
Lake Fabrication Inc .... G 217 832-2761
 Villa Grove (G-20124)
Laystrom Manufacturing Co .... D 773 342-4800
 Chicago (G-5186)
Lee Brothers Welding Inc .... G 309 342-6017
 Galesburg (G-10207)
Legna Iron Works Inc .... E 630 894-8056
 Roselle (G-17964)
Leroys Welding & Fabg Inc .... F 847 215-6151
 Wheeling (G-20763)
Lewis Process Systems Inc .... F 630 510-8200
 Carol Stream (G-3018)
Linne Machine Company Inc .... G 217 446-5746
 Danville (G-7359)
Luebbers Welding & Mfg Inc .... G 618 594-2489
 Carlyle (G-2893)

M & F Fabrication & Welding .... G 217 457-2221
 Concord (G-6998)
M & J Manufacturing Co Inc .... F 847 364-6066
 Elk Grove Village (G-9100)
M & M Welding Inc .... G 815 895-3955
 Sycamore (G-19723)
Magnetic Inspection Lab Inc .... D 847 437-4488
 Elk Grove Village (G-9106)
Mark Lahey .... G 217 243-4433
 Jacksonville (G-11775)
Marlboro Wire Ltd .... E 217 224-7989
 Quincy (G-16910)
Mason Welding Inc .... G 708 755-0621
 S Chicago Hts (G-18123)
Matrix Machine & Tool Mfg .... G 708 452-8707
 River Grove (G-17063)
MB Machine Inc .... F 815 864-3555
 Shannon (G-18871)
McCloskey Eyman Mlone Mfg Svcs .. G 309 647-4000
 Canton (G-2830)
McFarland Welding and Machine ..... G 618 627-2838
 Thompsonville (G-19779)
Meadoweld Machine Inc .... G 815 623-3939
 South Beloit (G-19102)
Melrose Mold & Machine Co Inc ...... G 847 233-9970
 Franklin Park (G-9991)
Mendota Welding & Mfg .... G 815 539-6944
 Mendota (G-13949)
Merritt Farm Equipment Inc .... G 217 746-5331
 Carthage (G-3138)
Meteer Manufacturing Co .... G 217 636-8109
 Athens (G-899)
Method Molds Inc .... G 815 877-0191
 Loves Park (G-13236)
Metzger Welding Service .... G 217 234-2851
 Mattoon (G-13649)
Mevert Automotive Inc .... G 618 965-9609
 Steeleville (G-19484)
Mfw Services Inc .... G 708 522-5879
 South Holland (G-19232)
Micro Products Company .... E 630 406-9550
 Peoria (G-16472)
Midway Machine & Tool Co Inc .... G 708 385-3450
 Alsip (G-477)
Mihalis Marine .... G 773 445-6220
 Chicago (G-5455)
Milans Machining & Mfg Co Inc .... D 708 780-6600
 Cicero (G-6867)
Millers Eureka Inc .... F 312 666-9383
 Chicago (G-5459)
Misselhorn Welding & Machines ...... G 618 426-3714
 Campbell Hill (G-2818)
Moline Welding Inc .... F 309 756-0643
 Milan (G-14018)
Mt Vernon Mold Works Inc .... E 618 242-6040
 Mount Vernon (G-14629)
Mushro Machine & Tool Co .... F 815 672-5848
 Streator (G-19617)
Napier Machine & Welding Inc .... G 217 525-8740
 Springfield (G-19410)
National Tool & Machine Co .... F 618 271-6445
 East Saint Louis (G-8316)
Natural Fiber Welding Inc .... E 309 339-7794
 Peoria (G-16483)
Neals Trailer Sales .... G 217 792-5136
 Lincoln (G-12736)
Needham Shop Inc .... G 630 557-9019
 Kaneville (G-11955)
Nehring Electrical Works Co .... C 815 756-2741
 Dekalb (G-7693)
Nelson Stud Welding Inc .... G 708 430-3770
 Tinley Park (G-19847)
Newman Welding & Machine Shop .. G 618 435-5591
 Benton (G-1934)
North Shore Truck & Equipment ...... F 847 887-0200
 Lake Bluff (G-12201)
Norton Machine Co .... G 217 748-6115
 Rossville (G-18066)
Odom Tool and Technology Inc .... G 815 895-8545
 Sycamore (G-19726)
On Site Mechanical Svcs Inc .... F 708 367-0470
 Crete (G-7143)
Oostman Fabricating & Wldg Inc ..... F 630 241-1315
 Westmont (G-20763)
Orient Machining & Welding Inc ...... E 708 371-3500
 Dixmoor (G-7886)
Orsolinis Welding & Fabg .... F 773 722-9855
 Chicago (G-5705)
P & G Machine & Tool Inc .... G 618 283-0273
 Vandalia (G-20018)

Palatine Welding Company .... E 847 358-1075
 Rolling Meadows (G-17759)
Parker Fabrication Inc .... E 309 266-8413
 Morton (G-14376)
Patkus Machine Co .... G 815 398-7818
 Rockford (G-17548)
Pauls Machine & Welding Corp .... D 217 832-2541
 Villa Grove (G-20125)
Pedraza Inc .... F 773 874-9020
 Chicago (G-5780)
Performance Welding LLC .... G 217 412-5722
 Maroa (G-13554)
Phoenix Welding Co Inc .... F 630 616-1700
 Franklin Park (G-10016)
PM Woodwind Repair Inc .... G 847 869-7049
 Evanston (G-9567)
Precision Tool Welding .... G 630 285-9844
 Elk Grove Village (G-9193)
Pro Arc Inc .... E 815 877-1804
 Loves Park (G-13249)
Pro-Fab Metals Inc .... G 618 283-2986
 Vandalia (G-20020)
Production Fabg & Stamping Inc .... F 708 755-5468
 S Chicago Hts (G-18126)
Production Manufacturing .... G 217 256-4211
 Warsaw (G-20259)
Professional Metal Works LLC .... F 618 539-2214
 Freeburg (G-10092)
Quality Metal Works Inc .... G 309 379-5311
 Stanford (G-19473)
Quality Tool & Machine Inc .... G 773 721-8655
 Chicago (G-5931)
R & R Machining Inc .... G 217 835-4579
 Benld (G-1718)
R Machining Inc .... G 217 532-2174
 Butler (G-2749)
R-M Industries Inc .... F 630 543-3071
 Addison (G-264)
Ramseys Machine Co .... G 217 824-2320
 Taylorville (G-19761)
Rapco Ltd .... G 618 249-6614
 Richview (G-17033)
Reber Welding Service .... G 217 774-3441
 Shelbyville (G-18885)
Recendiz Welding Inc .... G 708 205-8759
 Elmwood Park (G-9456)
Reco of IL Inc .... G 630 898-2010
 Aurora (G-1147)
Regal Steel Erectors LLC .... G 847 888-3500
 Elgin (G-8716)
Rex Radiator and Welding Co .... G 847 428-1112
 East Dundee (G-8209)
Rex Radiator and Welding Co .... G 312 421-1531
 Chicago (G-6020)
Rex Radiator and Welding Co .... G 815 725-6655
 Rockdale (G-17271)
Ri-Del Mfg Inc .... D 312 829-8720
 Chicago (G-6024)
Rk Maintenance Inc .... G 708 429-2215
 Tinley Park (G-19853)
Rockford Precision Machine .... F 815 873-1018
 Rockford (G-17601)
Rodney Tite Welding .... G 618 845-9072
 Ullin (G-19936)
Rw Welding Inc .... G 847 541-5508
 Arlington Heights (G-802)
S & S Welding & Fabrication .... G 847 742-7344
 Elgin (G-8722)
S & W Manufacturing Co Inc .... G 630 595-5044
 Bensenville (G-1888)
S D Custom Machining .... G 618 544-7007
 Robinson (G-17125)
Service Cutting & Welding .... G 773 622-8366
 Chicago (G-6142)
Service Sheet Metal Works Inc .... F 773 229-0031
 Chicago (G-6143)
Shanks Veterinary Equipment .... G 815 225-7700
 Milledgeville (G-14040)
Shannon & Sons Welding .... G 630 898-7778
 Aurora (G-1155)
Sheas Iron Works Inc .... E 847 356-2922
 Lake Villa (G-12367)
Shup Tool & Machine Co .... G 618 931-2596
 Granite City (G-10737)
Sigel Welding .... G 217 844-2412
 Sigel (G-18907)
Silver Machine Shop Inc .... G 217 359-5717
 Champaign (G-3348)
Sivco Welding Company .... G 309 944-5171
 Geneseo (G-10247)

PRODUCT SECTION — WHEELS: Rolled, Locomotive

Smith Welding LLC ....G...... 618 829-5414
  Saint Elmo (G-18312)
South Side Bler Wldg Works Inc ....G...... 708 478-1714
  Orland Park (G-15981)
South Subn Wldg & Fabg Co Inc ....G...... 708 385-7160
  Posen (G-16801)
Southwick Machine & Design Co ....G...... 309 949-2868
  Colona (G-6980)
Spaeth Welding Inc ....F...... 618 588-3596
  New Baden (G-15024)
Spannuth Boiler Co ....G...... 708 386-1882
  Oak Park (G-15774)
Special Tool Engineering Co ....F...... 773 767-6690
  Chicago (G-6212)
Spencer Welding Service Inc ....G...... 847 272-0580
  Northbrook (G-15484)
Steel Services Enterprises ....E...... 708 259-1181
  Lansing (G-12519)
Stevenson Fabrication Svcs Inc ....G...... 815 468-7941
  Manteno (G-13458)
Stuhlman Family LLC ....G...... 815 436-2432
  Plainfield (G-16719)
Suburban Welding & Steel LLC ....F...... 847 678-1264
  Franklin Park (G-10057)
Superior Joining Tech Inc ....G...... 815 282-7581
  Machesney Park (G-13376)
Superior Welding Inc ....F...... 618 544-8822
  Robinson (G-17126)
Tait Machine Tool Inc ....G...... 815 932-2011
  Kankakee (G-12010)
Taylor Design Inc ....G...... 815 389-3991
  Roscoe (G-17936)
Taylor Off Road Racing ....G...... 815 544-4500
  Belvidere (G-1703)
Tdw Welding LLC ....G...... 217 690-3521
  Wheeler (G-20833)
Technology One Welding Inc ....G...... 630 871-1296
  Carol Stream (G-3080)
Telza Welding Inc ....G...... 773 777-4467
  Chicago (G-6342)
Tewell Bros Machine Inc ....F...... 217 253-6303
  Tuscola (G-19931)
Titan Tool Works LLC ....F...... 630 221-1080
  Carol Stream (G-3081)
Toledo Machine & Welding Inc ....G...... 217 849-2251
  Toledo (G-19880)
Tomko Machine Works Inc ....G...... 630 244-0902
  Lemont (G-12593)
Tony Weishaar ....G...... 217 774-2774
  Shelbyville (G-18888)
Tonys Welding Service Inc ....G...... 618 532-9353
  Centralia (G-3253)
Toolweld Inc ....G...... 847 854-8013
  Algonquin (G-389)
Torrence Machine & Tool Co ....G...... 815 469-1850
  Mokena (G-14124)
Trailers Inc ....G...... 217 472-6000
  Chapin (G-3396)
Tri-Cunty Wldg Fabrication LLC ....E...... 217 543-3304
  Arthur (G-881)
Trotters Manufacturing Co ....G...... 217 364-4540
  Buffalo (G-2501)
United Machine Works Inc ....G...... 847 352-5252
  Schaumburg (G-18766)
United Maint Wldg & McHy C ....F...... 708 458-1705
  Bedford Park (G-1508)
United Tool and Engineering Co ....D...... 815 389-3021
  South Beloit (G-19118)
Universal Broaching Inc ....F...... 847 228-1440
  Elk Grove Village (G-9298)
US Dept Agriculture Forest Svc ....G...... 618 285-5211
  Golconda (G-10669)
V Brothers Machine Co ....E...... 708 652-0062
  Cicero (G-6886)
Vaughn & Sons Machine Shop ....G...... 618 842-9048
  Fairfield (G-9639)
VG Ates and Welding ....G...... 847 263-4416
  Waukegan (G-20515)
Vindee Industries Inc ....E...... 815 469-3300
  Frankfort (G-9850)
Vrn Welding & Fabrication Inc ....G...... 847 735-7270
  Lake Bluff (G-12213)
Walco Tool & Engineering Corp ....D...... 815 834-0225
  Romeoville (G-17886)
Wardzala Industries Inc ....F...... 847 288-9909
  Franklin Park (G-10083)
Warner Brothers Inc ....G...... 217 643-7950
  Rantoul (G-16987)
WEb Production & Fabg Inc ....F...... 312 733-6800
  Chicago (G-6595)

Wegener Welding LLC ....F...... 630 789-0990
  Burr Ridge (G-2731)
Weiland Welding Inc ....G...... 815 580-8079
  Cherry Valley (G-3448)
Weld-Rite Service Inc ....E...... 708 458-6000
  Bedford Park (G-1512)
Welding By K &K LLC ....G...... 847 360-1190
  Waukegan (G-20517)
Welding Company of America ....E...... 630 806-2000
  Aurora (G-1168)
Welding Shop ....G...... 773 785-1305
  Chicago (G-6599)
Welding Specialties ....G...... 708 798-5388
  East Hazel Crest (G-8219)
Wemco Inc ....F...... 708 388-1980
  Alsip (G-524)
West End Tool & Die Inc ....G...... 815 462-3040
  New Lenox (G-15068)
Wherry Machine & Welding Inc ....G...... 309 828-5423
  Bloomington (G-2107)
Williams Welding Service ....G...... 217 235-1758
  Humboldt (G-11525)
Wirfs Industries Inc ....F...... 815 344-0635
  McHenry (G-13809)
Wissmiller & Evans Road Eqp ....G...... 309 725-3598
  Cooksville (G-7004)

WELDING SPLYS, EXC GASES: Wholesalers

Lincoln Electric Company ....F...... 630 783-3600
  Bolingbrook (G-2204)

WELDING TIPS: Heat Resistant, Metal

American Machine ....G...... 815 539-6558
  Mendota (G-13934)
Orient Machining & Welding Inc ....E...... 708 371-3500
  Dixmoor (G-7886)
Two Four Seven Metal Laser ....G...... 847 250-5199
  Itasca (G-11749)
Welding Company of America ....E...... 630 806-2000
  Aurora (G-1168)

WELDMENTS

Ablaze Welding & Fabricating ....G...... 815 965-0046
  Rockford (G-17287)
Ryan Manufacturing Inc ....G...... 815 695-5310
  Newark (G-15078)

WELL CASINGS: Iron & Steel, Made In Steel Mills

Ptc Group Holdings Corp ....D...... 708 757-4747
  Chicago Heights (G-6766)

WESTERN APPAREL STORES

Horse Creek Outfitters ....G...... 217 544-2740
  Springfield (G-19382)

WET CORN MILLING

ADM Holdings LLC ....G...... 217 422-7281
  Decatur (G-7433)
ADM Holdings LLC ....G...... 312 634-8100
  Chicago (G-3548)
Archer-Daniels-Midland Company .....A...... 312 634-8100
  Chicago (G-3728)
Bio Fuels By American Farmers ....F...... 561 859-6251
  Benton (G-1921)
Ingredion Incorporated ....G...... 708 551-2600
  Chicago (G-4923)
Ingredion Incorporated ....C...... 708 728-3535
  Summit Argo (G-19680)
Lee Gilster-Mary Corporation ....D...... 815 472-6456
  Momence (G-14186)
Tate Lyle Ingrdnts Amricas LLC ....A...... 217 423-4411
  Decatur (G-7558)
Tate Lyle Ingrdnts Amricas LLC ....G...... 309 473-2721
  Heyworth (G-11191)

WHEEL & CASTER REPAIR SVCS

Kunz Industries Inc ....G...... 708 596-7717
  South Holland (G-19229)

WHEELCHAIRS

B & D Independence Inc ....E...... 618 262-7117
  Mount Carmel (G-14465)
Duroweld Company Inc ....E...... 847 680-3064
  Lake Bluff (G-12179)

G & M Industries Inc ....G...... 618 344-6655
  Collinsville (G-6962)
Heart 4 Heart Inc ....G...... 217 544-2699
  Springfield (G-19379)
Hogg Welding Inc ....G...... 708 339-0033
  Harvey (G-11089)
Mobility Connection Inc ....G...... 815 965-8090
  Rockford (G-17531)
United Seating & Mobility LLC ....G...... 309 699-0509
  East Peoria (G-8293)

WHEELS

Caster Warehouse Inc ....F...... 847 836-5712
  Carpentersville (G-3097)
Forza Customs ....G...... 708 474-6625
  Lansing (G-12493)
Hoosier Stamping & Mfg Corp ....G...... 812 426-2778
  Grayville (G-10809)
Midwest Wheel Covers Inc ....G...... 847 609-9980
  Barrington (G-1228)
Wheel Worx North LLC ....G...... 309 346-3535
  Pekin (G-16369)

WHEELS & BRAKE SHOES: Railroad, Cast Iron

Anchor Brake Shoe Company LLC .....G...... 630 293-1110
  West Chicago (G-20540)
Anchor Brake Shoe Company LLC .....F...... 630 293-1110
  West Chicago (G-20541)

WHEELS & GRINDSTONES, EXC ARTIFICIAL: Abrasive

Abrasive Technology Inc ....E...... 847 888-7100
  Elgin (G-8490)

WHEELS & PARTS

Autospec Inc ....G...... 773 254-2288
  Chicago (G-3779)
Oakley Industries Sub Assembly ....F...... 815 544-6666
  Belvidere (G-1692)
T G Automotive ....E...... 630 916-7818
  Lombard (G-13137)
Tbc Retail Group Inc ....G...... 630 692-0232
  Montgomery (G-14271)

WHEELS, GRINDING: Artificial

A Wheels Inc ....G...... 847 699-7000
  Des Plaines (G-7717)
Radiac Abrasives Inc ....E...... 630 898-0315
  Oswego (G-16024)

WHEELS: Abrasive

Abrasive Rubber Wheel Co ....F...... 847 587-0900
  Fox Lake (G-9743)
Diagrind Inc ....F...... 708 460-4333
  Orland Park (G-15951)
Grier Abrasive Co Inc ....C...... 708 333-6445
  South Holland (G-19216)
Hayes Abrasives Inc ....F...... 217 532-6850
  Hillsboro (G-11313)
Modern Abrasive Corp ....D...... 815 675-2352
  Spring Grove (G-19286)
Saint-Gobain Abrasives Inc ....C...... 630 868-8060
  Carol Stream (G-3063)

WHEELS: Disc, Wheelbarrow, Stroller, Etc, Stamped Metal

Livingston Innovations LLC ....G...... 847 808-0900
  Waukegan (G-20459)

WHEELS: Railroad Car, Cast Steel

Amsted Industries Incorporated ....B...... 312 645-1700
  Chicago (G-3685)
Colson Group Holdings LLC ....E...... 630 613-2941
  Oakbrook Terrace (G-15795)
Evraz Inc NA ....D...... 312 533-3555
  Chicago (G-4541)

WHEELS: Rolled, Locomotive

Adams Elevator Equipment Co ....E...... 847 581-2900
  Chicago (G-3538)

Employee Codes: A=Over 500 employees, B=251-500
C=101-250, D=51-100, E=20-50, F=10-19, G=3-9

WHISTLES

Burke Whistles Inc .... G 618 534-7953
Murphysboro *(G-14753)*

WHITING MINING: Crushed & Broken

Macklin Inc .... F 815 562-4803
Rochelle *(G-17147)*

WICKER PRDTS

Standard Container Co of Edgar .... E 847 438-1510
Lake Zurich *(G-12460)*

WIG & HAIRPIECE STORES

Hairline Creations Inc .... F 773 282-5454
Chicago *(G-4769)*

WINCHES

Allegion S&S Holding Co Inc .... C 815 875-3311
Princeton *(G-16805)*
Mega Equipment Inc .... G 309 764-5310
Moline *(G-14160)*

WIND CHIMES

River City Sign Company Inc .... G 309 796-3606
Silvis *(G-18909)*

WINDINGS: Coil, Electronic

Altran Corp .... E 815 455-5650
Crystal Lake *(G-7158)*
Coilcraft Incorporated .... D 815 288-7051
Oregon *(G-15915)*
Magnetic Coil Manufacturing Co .... E 630 787-1948
Wood Dale *(G-21212)*
Michele Terrell .... G 312 305-0876
Evanston *(G-9551)*
Nelco Coil Supply Company .... E 847 259-7517
Mount Prospect *(G-14550)*
Olympic Controls Corp .... E 847 742-3566
Elgin *(G-8678)*
Pnc Inc .... D 815 946-2328
Polo *(G-16758)*
Qcircuits Inc .... E 847 797-6678
Elk Grove Village *(G-9203)*

WINDMILLS: Electric Power Generation

Arcosa Wind Towers Inc .... F 217 935-7900
Clinton *(G-6918)*
Awem Corporation .... G 217 670-1451
Springfield *(G-19322)*
Crescent Ridge LLC .... G 815 646-4119
Tiskilwa *(G-19872)*
Lakeview Energy LLC .... E 312 386-5897
Chicago *(G-5167)*
Sexton Wind Power LLC .... G 224 212-1250
Lake Bluff *(G-12209)*
Stanton Wind Energy LLC .... F 312 224-1400
Chicago *(G-6232)*
White Oak Energy LLC .... G 815 824-2182
Carlock *(G-2888)*
Willow Creek Energy LLC .... G 312 224-1400
Chicago *(G-6633)*

WINDMILLS: Farm Type

Lakeview Energy LLC .... E 312 386-5897
Chicago *(G-5167)*

WINDOW & DOOR FRAMES

A-Ok Inc .... E 815 943-7431
Harvard *(G-11039)*
Advantage Manufacturing Inc .... F 773 626-2200
Chicago *(G-3569)*
Alliance Door and Hardware LLC .... G 630 451-7070
Hillside *(G-11326)*
Anchor Welding & Fabrication .... F 815 937-1640
Aroma Park *(G-839)*
Centor North America Inc .... E 630 957-1000
Aurora *(G-936)*
Charles Sheridan and Sons .... G 847 903-7209
Evanston *(G-9502)*
Continental Window South Inc .... F 773 767-1300
Chicago *(G-4232)*
Efco Corporation .... E 630 378-4720
Bolingbrook *(G-2171)*
La Force Inc .... G 630 325-1950
Willowbrook *(G-21048)*
La Force Inc .... E 847 415-5107
Vernon Hills *(G-20071)*
Logan Square Aluminum Sup Inc .... D 847 985-1700
Schaumburg *(G-18611)*
Logan Square Aluminum Sup Inc .... F 847 676-4767
Lincolnwood *(G-12828)*
Logan Square Aluminum Sup Inc .... C 773 278-3600
Chicago *(G-5249)*
Nelson Sash Systems Inc .... G 708 385-5815
Alsip *(G-483)*
Salem Building Materials Inc .... G 618 548-3221
Salem *(G-18357)*
Summit Window Co Inc .... G 708 594-3200
Summit Argo *(G-19683)*

WINDOW BLIND CLEANING SVCS

Drexel House of Drapes Inc .... G 618 624-5415
Belleville *(G-1547)*

WINDOW BLIND REPAIR SVCS

Shade Brookline Co .... F 773 274-5513
Chicago *(G-6145)*

WINDOW CLEANING SVCS

James A Freund LLC .... G 630 664-7692
Oswego *(G-16009)*

WINDOW FRAMES & SASHES: Plastic

Advanced Window Corp .... E 773 379-3500
Chicago *(G-3568)*
Ilpea Industries Inc .... D 309 343-3332
Galesburg *(G-10201)*
Simonton Building Products Inc .... B 217 466-2851
Paris *(G-16244)*
Tempco Products Co .... D 618 544-3175
Robinson *(G-17127)*

WINDOW FRAMES, MOLDING & TRIM: Vinyl

Blackfriars Corp .... G 818 597-3754
Northbrook *(G-15350)*
Continental Window and GL Corp .... E 773 794-1600
Chicago *(G-4231)*
Fox Valley Windows LLC .... G 630 210-6400
Aurora *(G-963)*
Herschberger Window Inc .... G 217 543-2106
Tuscola *(G-19928)*

WINDOW FURNISHINGS WHOLESALERS

EZ Blinds and Drapery Inc .... F 708 246-6600
Westmont *(G-20742)*
Shapco Inc .... G 847 229-1439
Wheeling *(G-20982)*

WINDOW SCREENING: Plastic

Silver Line Building Pdts LLC .... B 708 474-9100
Lansing *(G-12516)*

WINDOWS: Frames, Wood

ROW Window Company .... G 815 725-5491
Plainfield *(G-16712)*

WINDOWS: Storm, Wood

J&E Storm Services Inc .... G 630 401-3793
Tinley Park *(G-19841)*

WINDOWS: Wood

Monda Window & Door Corp .... E 773 254-8888
Chicago *(G-5489)*

WINDSHIELD WIPER SYSTEMS

Taap Corp .... F 224 676-0653
Wheeling *(G-20996)*

WINE & DISTILLED ALCOHOLIC BEVERAGES WHOLESALERS

Emmetts Tavern & Brewing Co .... G 630 434-8500
Downers Grove *(G-8000)*
Emmetts Tavern & Brewing Co .... G 630 480-7181
Wheaton *(G-20797)*
Emmetts Tavern & Brewing Co .... F 847 359-1533
Palatine *(G-16115)*
Emmetts Tavern & Brewing Co .... E 847 428-4500
West Dundee *(G-20663)*

WINE CELLARS, BONDED: Wine, Blended

Blue Sky Vineyard .... G 618 995-9463
Makanda *(G-13427)*
Shale Lake LLC .... G 618 637-2470
Staunton *(G-19478)*

WIRE

Accurate Wire Strip Frming Inc .... F 630 260-1000
Carol Stream *(G-2924)*
Aif Inc .... E 630 495-0077
Addison *(G-24)*
Aspen Guard LLC .... G 708 325-0400
Bedford Park *(G-1458)*
Central Wire Inc .... C 800 435-8317
Union *(G-19938)*
E H Baare Corporation .... C 618 546-1575
Robinson *(G-17114)*
Highland Wire Inc .... F 618 654-2161
Highland *(G-11225)*
Major Wire Incorporated .... F 708 457-0121
Norridge *(G-15239)*
Vision Sales Incorporated .... G 630 483-1900
Bartlett *(G-1321)*
W R Pabich Mfg Co Inc .... G 773 486-4141
Chicago *(G-6578)*

WIRE & CABLE: Aluminum

All Line Inc .... G 630 820-1800
Naperville *(G-14955)*

WIRE & CABLE: Aluminum

Conex Cable LLC .... E 800 877-8089
Dekalb *(G-7669)*
Nehring Electrical Works Co .... C 815 756-2741
Dekalb *(G-7693)*
Viakable Manufacturing LLC .... G 815 615-8355
La Salle *(G-12123)*

WIRE & CABLE: Nonferrous, Automotive, Exc Ignition Sets

Emerge Technology Group LLC .... G 224 603-2161
Lake Villa *(G-12350)*

WIRE & CABLE: Nonferrous, Building

Essex Group Inc .... D 630 628-7841
Addison *(G-116)*
General Cable Industries Inc .... C 618 542-4761
Du Quoin *(G-8122)*
Lake Copper Conductors LLC .... E 847 378-7006
Bensenville *(G-1841)*
Sterling Brands LLC .... E 847 229-1600
Wheeling *(G-20990)*

WIRE & WIRE PRDTS

A J Kay Co .... F 224 475-0370
Mundelein *(G-14657)*
Accurate Wire Strip Frming Inc .... F 630 260-1000
Carol Stream *(G-2924)*
Acme Wire Products LLC .... E 708 345-4430
Broadview *(G-2413)*
Acorn Wire and Iron Works LLC .... E 312 243-6414
Chicago *(G-3530)*
Action Electric Sales Co Inc .... D 773 539-1800
Chicago *(G-3535)*
Agena Manufacturing Co .... E 630 668-5086
Carol Stream *(G-2928)*
Alagor Industries Incorporated .... D 630 766-2910
Bensenville *(G-1734)*
Alecto Industries Inc .... E 708 344-1488
Maywood *(G-13659)*
Allform Manufacturing Co .... G 847 680-0144
Libertyville *(G-12627)*
Altak Inc .... D 630 622-0300
Bloomingdale *(G-1975)*
Amag Manufacturing Inc .... G 773 667-5184
Chicago *(G-3642)*
Ammeraal Beltech Inc .... D 847 673-6720
Skokie *(G-18920)*
Androck Hardware Corporation .... F 815 229-1144
Rockford *(G-17305)*
Archer Wire International Corp .... C 708 563-1700
Bedford Park *(G-1456)*

PRODUCT SECTION

WIRE PRDTS: Steel & Iron

Armstrong/Alar Inc .... G 847 808-8885
  Prospect Heights *(G-16836)*
Ascent Mfg Co .... E 847 806-6600
  Elk Grove Village *(G-8841)*
Astoria Wire Products Inc .... D 708 496-9950
  Bedford Park *(G-1459)*
Atkore International Group Inc .... A 708 339-1610
  Harvey *(G-11075)*
Atkore Intl Holdings Inc .... G 708 225-2051
  Harvey *(G-11076)*
Available Spring and Mfg Co .... G 847 520-4854
  Wheeling *(G-20853)*
Bel Mar Wire Products Inc .... F 773 342-3800
  Chicago *(G-3861)*
Bergeron Group Inc .... E 815 741-1635
  Joliet *(G-11830)*
Bristar .... E 847 678-5000
  Franklin Park *(G-9893)*
C & J Metal Products Inc .... F 847 455-0766
  Franklin Park *(G-9896)*
C R V Electronics Corp .... D 815 675-6500
  Spring Grove *(G-19269)*
Cal-Ill Gasket Co .... F 773 287-9605
  Chicago *(G-4002)*
Capitol Coil Inc .... F 847 891-1390
  Schaumburg *(G-18467)*
Casey Spring Co Inc .... F 708 867-8949
  Park Ridge *(G-16272)*
Cda Industries Inc .... G 630 357-7654
  Naperville *(G-14794)*
CFC Wire Forms Inc .... G 630 879-7575
  Batavia *(G-1364)*
Chas O Larson Co .... E 815 625-0503
  Rock Falls *(G-17179)*
Chicago Car Seal Company .... G 773 278-9400
  Chicago *(G-4095)*
Chicago Hardware and Fix Co .... C 847 455-6609
  Franklin Park *(G-9905)*
Chicagos Finest Ironworks 708 895-4484
  Lansing *(G-12488)*
Contractors Ready-Mix Inc .... G 217 482-5530
  Mason City *(G-13610)*
Cutting Edge Industries Inc .... G 847 678-1777
  Franklin Park *(G-9923)*
D & S Wire Inc .... F 847 766-5520
  Elk Grove Village *(G-8934)*
Darbe Products Company Inc .... G 630 985-0769
  Woodridge *(G-21292)*
Dayton Superior Corporation .... C 815 936-3300
  Kankakee *(G-11964)*
Dove Industries Inc .... F 618 234-4509
  Belleville *(G-1546)*
Dudek & Bock Spring Mfg Co .... C 773 379-4100
  Chicago *(G-4402)*
E H Baare Corporation 618 546-1575
  Robinson *(G-17114)*
Economy Iron Inc 708 343-1777
  Melrose Park *(G-13859)*
Elite Wireworks Corporation .... F 630 837-9100
  Bartlett *(G-1277)*
European Ornamental Iron Works ...... G 630 705-9300
  Addison *(G-117)*
Expandable Habitats .... G 815 624-6784
  Rockton *(G-17697)*
Fbs Group Inc .... F 773 229-8675
  Chicago *(G-4569)*
Fixture Displays .... G 630 296-4190
  Downers Grove *(G-8003)*
Fortune Rope & Metal Co Inc .... G 630 787-9715
  Bensenville *(G-1803)*
Franklin Display Group Inc .... G 815 544-5300
  Belvidere *(G-1669)*
Franklin Wire Works Inc .... G 815 544-6676
  Belvidere *(G-1670)*
Gall Machine Co .... F 708 352-2800
  Countryside *(G-7054)*
Guide Line Industries Inc .... F 815 777-3722
  Scales Mound *(G-18420)*
Hamalot Inc .... E 847 944-1500
  Schaumburg *(G-18542)*
Hohmann & Barnard Inc .... G 773 586-6700
  Chicago Ridge *(G-6799)*
Hudson Tool & Die Co .... F 847 678-8710
  Franklin Park *(G-9958)*
Innovation Specialists Inc .... G 815 372-9001
  New Lenox *(G-15037)*
Innovative Fix Solutions LLC .... F 815 395-8500
  Rockford *(G-17465)*
Jason Incorporated .... C 630 627-7000
  Addison *(G-158)*

JD Norman Industries Inc .... D 630 458-3700
  Addison *(G-159)*
John Sakash Company Inc .... E 630 833-3940
  Elmhurst *(G-9383)*
Johnson Tool Company .... G 708 453-8600
  Huntley *(G-11547)*
Keystone Consolidated Inds Inc .... E 309 697-7020
  Peoria *(G-16466)*
L & P Guarding LLC .... C 708 325-0400
  Bedford Park *(G-1477)*
Lake Cable LLC .... C 888 518-8086
  Bensenville *(G-1840)*
Letraw Manufacturing LLC 815 987-9670
  Rockford *(G-17496)*
Lew-El Tool & Manufacturing Co .... F 773 804-1133
  Chicago *(G-5212)*
Lewis Spring and Mfg Company .... D 847 588-7030
  Niles *(G-15140)*
Lift-All Company Inc .... E 630 534-6860
  Glendale Heights *(G-10468)*
Marlboro Wire Ltd .... F 217 224-7989
  Quincy *(G-16910)*
Master Spring & Wire Form Co .... E 708 453-2570
  Itasca *(G-11698)*
Master-Halco Inc .... E 618 395-4365
  Olney *(G-15873)*
MHS Ltd .... F 773 736-3333
  Chicago *(G-5419)*
Mid-States Wire Proc Corp .... F 773 379-3775
  Chicago *(G-5431)*
Midwest Tungsten Service Inc .... E 630 325-1001
  Willowbrook *(G-21051)*
Midwest Wire Works LLC .... F 815 874-1701
  Rockford *(G-17529)*
Moffat Wire & Display Inc 630 458-8560
  Addison *(G-221)*
Nixalite of America Inc .... F 309 755-8771
  East Moline *(G-8235)*
Nvent Electric Public Ltd Co .... G 618 918-3821
  Centralia *(G-3243)*
Paragon Spring Company .... E 773 489-6300
  Chicago *(G-5759)*
Partex Marking Systems Inc .... G 630 516-0400
  Lombard *(G-13117)*
Perfection Spring Stmping Corp .... D 847 437-3900
  Mount Prospect *(G-14560)*
Precision Forming Stamping Co .... E 773 489-6868
  Chicago *(G-5857)*
Precision Steel Warehouse Inc .... C 800 323-0740
  Franklin Park *(G-10026)*
Rapid Wire Forms Inc .... G 773 586-6600
  Chicago *(G-5975)*
Reino Tool & Manufacturing Co .... F 773 588-5800
  Chicago *(G-6005)*
Remin Laboratories Inc .... D 815 723-1940
  Joliet *(G-11924)*
Riverside Spring Company .... G 815 963-3334
  Rockford *(G-17574)*
Rockford Rigging Inc .... F 309 263-0566
  Roscoe *(G-17926)*
Sanco Industries Inc .... F 847 243-8675
  Kildeer *(G-12052)*
Schaff International LLC .... E 847 438-4560
  Lake Zurich *(G-12453)*
Solar Spring Company .... C 847 437-7838
  Elk Grove Village *(G-9245)*
Spring Specialist Corporation .... G 815 562-7991
  Kings *(G-12054)*
Sterling Wire Products Inc .... G 815 625-3015
  Rock Falls *(G-17196)*
The Parts House .... G 309 343-0146
  Galesburg *(G-10221)*
Trio Wire Products Inc .... G 815 469-2148
  Frankfort *(G-9846)*
Wardzala Industries Inc .... F 847 288-9909
  Franklin Park *(G-10083)*
White Eagle Spring & .... F 773 384-4455
  Chicago *(G-6618)*
Will Don Corp .... D 773 276-7081
  Chicago *(G-6627)*
Willdon Corp 773 276-7080
  Chicago *(G-6628)*
William Dach .... F 815 962-3455
  Rockford *(G-17685)*
William Dudek Manufacturing Co 773 622-2727
  Chicago *(G-6629)*
Wire Mesh LLC .... G 815 579-8597
  Oglesby *(G-15844)*
Wireformers Inc .... E 847 718-1920
  Mount Prospect *(G-14582)*

Wiremasters Incorporated .... E 773 254-3700
  Chicago *(G-6649)*
Woodland Fence Forest Pdts Inc .... G 630 393-2220
  Warrenville *(G-20257)*

WIRE CLOTH & WOVEN WIRE PRDTS, MADE FROM PURCHASED WIRE

Jsn Inc .... E 708 410-1800
  Maywood *(G-13670)*

WIRE FABRIC: Welded Steel

Blue Ridge Forge Inc .... G 309 274-5377
  Chillicothe *(G-6814)*

WIRE FENCING & ACCESS WHOLESALERS

United Fence Co Inc .... G 773 924-0773
  Chicago *(G-6472)*
Vision Sales Incorporated .... G 630 483-1900
  Bartlett *(G-1321)*

WIRE MATERIALS: Aluminum

Southwire Company LLC .... D 618 662-8341
  Flora *(G-9694)*

WIRE MATERIALS: Copper

American Bare Conductor Inc .... E 815 224-3422
  La Salle *(G-12102)*
Industrial Wire Cable II Corp .... F 847 726-8910
  Lake Zurich *(G-12422)*
Nehring Electrical Works Co .... C 815 756-2741
  Dekalb *(G-7693)*

WIRE MATERIALS: Steel

Ace Custom Upholstery & Rod Sp 618 842-2913
  Fairfield *(G-9616)*
Allform Manufacturing Co .... G 847 680-0144
  Libertyville *(G-12627)*
Apex Wire Products Company Inc ..... F 847 671-1830
  Franklin Park *(G-9871)*
Arcelormittal South Chicago 312 899-3300
  Chicago *(G-3720)*
Berens Inc .... G 815 935-3237
  Saint Anne *(G-18132)*
C & L Manufacturing Entps 618 465-7623
  Alton *(G-546)*
Combined Metals Chicago LLC .... F 847 683-0500
  Hampshire *(G-10967)*
Dayton Superior Corporation .... E 219 476-4106
  Kankakee *(G-11962)*
Dayton Superior Corporation .... C 815 936-3300
  Kankakee *(G-11964)*
Excel Specialty Corp .... E 773 262-7575
  Lake Forest *(G-12248)*
Gerdau Ameristeel US Inc .... G 800 237-0230
  Chicago *(G-4687)*
Hamalot Inc .... E 847 944-1500
  Schaumburg *(G-18542)*
Hohmann & Barnard Illinois LLC 773 586-6700
  Chicago Ridge *(G-6798)*
Ifastgroupe Usa LLC .... G 450 658-7148
  Downers Grove *(G-8026)*
Mapes & Sprowl Steel LLC .... G 800 777-1025
  Elk Grove Village *(G-9110)*
Powernail Company .... E 800 323-1653
  Lake Zurich *(G-12445)*
Raajrtna Stinless Wire USA Inc .... F 847 923-8000
  Schaumburg *(G-18695)*
Reino Tool & Manufacturing Co .... F 773 588-5800
  Chicago *(G-6005)*
Rockford Rigging Inc .... F 309 263-0566
  Roscoe *(G-17926)*
The Parts House .... G 309 343-0146
  Galesburg *(G-10221)*
William Dach .... F 815 962-3455
  Rockford *(G-17685)*
Wiretech Inc .... G 815 986-9614
  Rockford *(G-17688)*

WIRE PRDTS: Steel & Iron

Central Wire Inc .... C 800 435-8317
  Union *(G-19938)*
CFC Wire Forms Inc .... G 630 879-7575
  Batavia *(G-1364)*
Highland Southern Wire Inc .... G 618 654-2161
  Highland *(G-11222)*

WIRE PRDTS: Steel & Iron

O & W Wire Co Inc .... F 773 776-5919
  Chicago (G-5645)
Paragon Spring Company .... E 773 489-6300
  Chicago (G-5759)
S 4 Global Inc .... G 708 325-1236
  Bedford Park (G-1501)
Southern Steel and Wire Inc .... G 618 654-2161
  Highland (G-11240)
Steel Fabrication and Welding .... G 773 343-0731
  Cicero (G-6876)
Tj Wire Forming Inc .... E 630 628-9209
  Addison (G-310)

WIRE ROPE CENTERS

Mighty Hook Inc .... E 773 378-1909
  Chicago (G-5453)

WIRE WINDING OF PURCHASED WIRE

Jenco Metal Products Inc .... F 847 956-0550
  Mount Prospect (G-14539)
OHare Spring Company Inc .... E 847 298-1360
  Elk Grove Village (G-9160)

WIRE: Communication

Andrew Corporation .... E 779 435-6000
  Joliet (G-11822)
Central Rubber Company .... E 815 544-2191
  Belvidere (G-1661)
Coleman Cable LLC .... D 847 672-2300
  Lincolnshire (G-12753)
Gepco International Inc .... E 847 795-9555
  Des Plaines (G-7773)
Live Wire & Cable Co .... G 847 577-5483
  Arlington Heights (G-770)
Molex LLC .... A 630 969-4550
  Lisle (G-12911)
Molex LLC .... G 630 527-4363
  Bolingbrook (G-2216)
Molex LLC .... F 630 512-8787
  Downers Grove (G-8059)
Molex International Inc .... F 630 969-4550
  Lisle (G-12914)
Molex Premise Networks Inc .... A 866 733-6659
  Lisle (G-12915)
Pro Intercom LLC .... G 815 680-5205
  Crystal Lake (G-7247)
Woodhead Industries LLC .... B 847 353-2500
  Lincolnshire (G-12802)

WIRE: Mesh

G F Ltd .... E 708 333-8300
  South Holland (G-19212)

WIRE: Nonferrous

Amerline Enterprises Co Inc .... E 847 671-6554
  Schiller Park (G-18786)
ARI Industries Inc .... D 630 953-9100
  Addison (G-38)
Axon Cable Inc .... F 847 230-7813
  Schaumburg (G-18454)
C & L Manufacturing Entps .... G 618 465-7623
  Alton (G-546)
C R V Electronics Corp .... G 815 675-6500
  Spring Grove (G-19269)
Cable X-Perts Inc .... G 800 828-3340
  Woodstock (G-21369)
Charles Industries LLC .... D 217 826-2318
  Marshall (G-13566)
Chase Security Systems Inc .... G 773 594-1919
  Chicago (G-4078)
Chicago Car Seal Company .... G 773 278-9400
  Chicago (G-4095)
Circom Inc .... E 630 595-4460
  Bensenville (G-1770)
Coleman Cable LLC .... D 847 672-2300
  Lincolnshire (G-12752)
Data Cable Technologies Inc .... F 630 226-5600
  Romeoville (G-17812)
Erin Rope Corporation .... F 708 377-1084
  Blue Island (G-2122)
Excel Specialty Corp .... E 773 262-7575
  Lake Forest (G-12248)
Heil Sound Ltd .... F 618 257-3000
  Fairview Heights (G-9646)
Industrial Wire & Cable Corp .... E 847 726-8910
  Lake Zurich (G-12421)
Major Wire Incorporated .... F 708 457-0121
  Norridge (G-15239)

Methode Development Co .... D 708 867-6777
  Chicago (G-5408)
P M Mfg Services Inc .... G 630 553-6924
  Yorkville (G-21496)
Unified Wire and Cable Company .... E 815 748-4876
  Dekalb (G-7710)
United Universal Inds Inc .... E 815 727-4445
  Joliet (G-11939)

WIRE: Steel, Insulated Or Armored

Fairbanks Wire Corporation .... G 847 683-2600
  Hampshire (G-10972)
Krueger and Company .... E 630 833-5650
  Elmhurst (G-9389)
Taubensee Steel & Wire Company .... C 847 459-5100
  Wheeling (G-20997)

WIRE: Wire, Ferrous Or Iron

Heico Companies LLC .... F 312 419-8220
  Chicago (G-4798)
National Material Company LLC .... E 847 806-7200
  Elk Grove Village (G-9144)

WOMEN'S & CHILDREN'S CLOTHING WHOLESALERS, NEC

ASap Specialties Inc Del .... G 847 223-7699
  Grayslake (G-10759)
Dzro-Bans International Inc .... G 779 324-2740
  Homewood (G-11492)
Leos Dancewear Inc .... D 773 889-7700
  River Forest (G-17053)
New York & Company Inc .... F 630 232-7693
  Geneva (G-10293)
New York & Company Inc .... F 630 783-2910
  Bolingbrook (G-2221)
SRS Global Ret Solutions LLC .... G 773 888-3094
  Evanston (G-9577)

WOMEN'S & GIRLS' SPORTSWEAR WHOLESALERS

American Outfitters Ltd .... E 847 623-3959
  Waukegan (G-20414)
Art-Flo Shirt & Lettering Co .... E 708 656-5422
  Chicago (G-3738)
B and A Screen Printing .... E 217 762-2632
  Monticello (G-14277)
B JS Printables .... G 618 656-8625
  Edwardsville (G-8346)
Hermans Inc .... E 309 206-4892
  Rock Island (G-17222)
Screen Machine Incorporated .... G 847 439-2233
  Elk Grove Village (G-9234)

WOMEN'S CLOTHING STORES

Fashahnn Corporation .... G 773 994-3132
  Chicago (G-4561)
Mjt Design and Prtg Entps Inc .... G 708 240-4323
  Hillside (G-11348)
Signature Design & Tailoring .... F 773 375-4915
  Chicago (G-6168)
SRS Global Ret Solutions LLC .... G 773 888-3094
  Evanston (G-9577)

WOMEN'S CLOTHING STORES: Ready-To-Wear

A&B Apparel .... G 815 962-5070
  Rockford (G-17281)
Express LLC .... E 708 453-0566
  Norridge (G-15234)
Four Star Denim and AP LLC .... F 847 707-6365
  Chicago (G-4626)

WOMEN'S FULL & KNEE LENGTH HOSIERY DYEING & FINISHING

Felice Hosiery Co Inc .... G 312 922-3710
  Chicago (G-4578)

WOMEN'S SPECIALTY CLOTHING STORES

Anntaylor Retail Inc .... G 309 693-2762
  Peoria (G-16383)
New York & Company Inc .... F 630 232-7693
  Geneva (G-10293)
New York & Company Inc .... F 630 783-2910
  Bolingbrook (G-2221)

WOMEN'S SPORTSWEAR STORES

B JS Printables .... G 618 656-8625
  Edwardsville (G-8346)

WOOD EXTRACT PRDTS

Bradley Smoker USA Inc .... F 309 343-1124
  Galesburg (G-10186)

WOOD PRDTS

Frame Game .... G 573 754-2385
  Pleasant Hill (G-16748)
Jones Wood Products .... G 618 826-2682
  Rockwood (G-17706)
Mhwp .... G 618 228-7600
  Aviston (G-1182)
Quality Plus .... F 618 779-4931
  Litchfield (G-12974)
Smoke Rite Wood Products .... G 708 485-8910
  Brookfield (G-2492)
Wedgewood .... G 847 672-4497
  Wadsworth (G-20215)

WOOD PRDTS: Barrels & Barrel Parts

Upcycle Products Inc .... G 815 383-6220
  Minooka (G-14066)

WOOD PRDTS: Brackets

Benchmark Cabinets & Mllwk Inc .... E 309 697-5855
  Peoria (G-16391)

WOOD PRDTS: Chair Cane, Rattan Or Reed

Springfield Woodworks .... G 217 483-7234
  Chatham (G-3424)

WOOD PRDTS: Chicken Coops, Wood, Wirebound

Heritage Structures Inc .... F 618 895-8028
  Mc Leansboro (G-13706)

WOOD PRDTS: Door Trim

Four Acre Wood Products .... F 217 543-2971
  Arthur (G-858)

WOOD PRDTS: Handles, Tool

Illinois Tool Works Inc .... F 708 720-7070
  Frankfort (G-9806)

WOOD PRDTS: Ladders & Stepladders

Crown Brands LLC .... E 224 513-2917
  Lincolnshire (G-12757)

WOOD PRDTS: Laundry

Danlee Wood Products Inc .... G 815 938-9016
  Forreston (G-9739)

WOOD PRDTS: Moldings, Unfinished & Prefinished

Agusta Mill Works .... G 309 787-4616
  Milan (G-13999)
Central Wood LLC .... G 217 543-2662
  Arcola (G-646)
Douglas County Mil Moldings .... G 217 268-4689
  Arcola (G-647)
Omega Moulding North Amer Inc .... G 630 509-2397
  Elk Grove Village (G-9162)
Sandwich Millworks Inc .... G 815 786-2700
  Sandwich (G-18384)
Star Moulding & Trim Company .... E 708 458-1040
  Bedford Park (G-1506)

WOOD PRDTS: Mulch Or Sawdust

Golden Valley Hardscapes LLC .... G 309 654-2261
  Cordova (G-7007)
Greencycle of Indiana Inc .... G 847 441-6606
  Northfield (G-15515)

WOOD PRDTS: Mulch, Wood & Bark

Country Stone Inc .... E 309 787-1744
  Milan (G-14005)
E-Z Tree Recycling Inc .... G 773 493-8600
  Chicago (G-4428)

PRODUCT SECTION

Illinois Wood Fiber Products ....G....... 847 836-6176
  Carpentersville *(G-3105)*
Melyx Inc..F....... 309 654-2551
  Cordova *(G-7010)*
Rainbow Farms Enterprises Inc ....G....... 708 534-1070
  Monee *(G-14206)*
RR Mulch and Soil LLC ....G....... 708 596-7200
  Markham *(G-13551)*

WOOD PRDTS: Newel Posts

C A Larson & Son Inc ....E....... 847 717-6010
  Maple Park *(G-13461)*

WOOD PRDTS: Outdoor, Structural

Deborah Zeitler Associates Inc ....G....... 312 527-3733
  Chicago *(G-4328)*
Griffard & Associates LLC ....G....... 217 316-1732
  Quincy *(G-16887)*
IMC Outdoor Living...........................G....... 314 373-1171
  Godfrey *(G-10653)*

WOOD PRDTS: Panel Work

Wagners Custom Wood Design........G....... 847 487-2788
  Island Lake *(G-11613)*

WOOD PRDTS: Planters & Window Boxes

T2 Site Amenities Incorporated ....G....... 847 579-9003
  Highland Park *(G-11302)*

WOOD PRDTS: Poles

Better Built Buildings ....G....... 217 267-7824
  Westville *(G-20778)*

WOOD PRDTS: Signboards

Reynolds Holdings Inc ....G....... 630 739-0110
  Romeoville *(G-17869)*
Shawcraft Sign Co ....G....... 815 282-4105
  Machesney Park *(G-13374)*
Wensco Michigan Corporation ....F....... 630 333-4440
  Addison *(G-334)*

WOOD PRDTS: Stepladders

Werner Co...E....... 815 459-6020
  Crystal Lake *(G-7294)*

WOOD PRDTS: Tackle Blocks

Midwest Lifting Products Inc ....G....... 214 356-7102
  Granite City *(G-10724)*

WOOD PRDTS: Trophy Bases

A & M Products Company ....G....... 815 875-2667
  Princeton *(G-16803)*

WOOD PRODUCTS: Reconstituted

Blue Ridge Fiberboard ....G....... 800 233-8721
  Hampshire *(G-10965)*
Claridge Products and Eqp Inc.........G....... 847 991-8822
  Elgin *(G-8543)*
Jeld-Wen Inc ....C....... 312 544-5041
  Chicago *(G-5014)*

WOOD SHAVINGS BALES, MULCH TYPE, WHOLESALE

M & M Paltech Inc ....D....... 630 350-7890
  Belvidere *(G-1681)*

WOOD TREATING: Millwork

Willard Miller....................................G....... 618 252-4407
  Carrier Mills *(G-3125)*

WOOD TREATING: Railroad Cross-Ties

Midwest Intgrted Companies LLC ....C....... 847 426-6354
  Gilberts *(G-10361)*

WOOD TREATING: Structural Lumber & Timber

John A Biewer Lumber Company......F....... 815 357-6792
  Seneca *(G-18859)*

Northern Illinois Lumber Spc............E....... 630 859-3226
  Montgomery *(G-14265)*
Northwest Snow Timber Svc Ltd......G....... 847 778-4998
  Lombard *(G-13109)*
Southeast Wood Treating Inc ....F....... 815 562-5007
  Rochelle *(G-17160)*

WOOD TREATING: Wood Prdts, Creosoted

Tronox Incorporated.........................E....... 203 705-3704
  Madison *(G-13418)*

WOOD-BURNING STOVE STORES

Hoyer Outdoor Equipment Inc..........F....... 618 564-2080
  Brookport *(G-2498)*

WOODWORK & TRIM: Exterior & Ornamental

Orstrom Woodworking Ltd ....G....... 847 697-1163
  Elgin *(G-8681)*

WOODWORK & TRIM: Interior & Ornamental

Blue Chip Construction Inc..............F....... 630 208-5254
  Geneva *(G-10255)*
Brown Wood Products Company .....F....... 847 673-4780
  Lincolnwood *(G-12814)*
Craiger Inc ....G....... 815 479-9660
  Crystal Lake *(G-7186)*
Der Holtzmacher Ltd ....G....... 815 895-4887
  Sycamore *(G-19706)*
Doctors Interior Plantscaping...........F....... 708 333-3323
  South Holland *(G-19208)*
Gingerich Custom Woodworking ......F....... 217 578-3491
  Arthur *(G-860)*
Greatlkes Archtctral Mllwrks L ....E....... 312 829-7110
  Chicago *(G-4739)*
Kempner Company Inc ....F....... 312 733-1606
  Chicago *(G-5095)*
Wm Huber Cabinet Works................E....... 773 235-7660
  Chicago *(G-6653)*
Woodcraft Enterprises Inc ....G....... 815 485-2787
  New Lenox *(G-15070)*

WOODWORK: Carved & Turned

Aph Custom Wood & Metal Pdts .....G....... 708 410-1274
  Broadview *(G-2417)*
Brown Wood Products Company .....F....... 847 673-4780
  Lincolnwood *(G-12814)*
Equustock LLC.................................F....... 866 962-4686
  Loves Park *(G-13210)*

WOODWORK: Interior & Ornamental, NEC

Becker Jules D Wood Products........G....... 847 526-8002
  Wauconda *(G-20334)*
Bernhard Woodwork Ltd ....D....... 847 291-1040
  Northbrook *(G-15348)*
Extreme Woodworking Inc ....G....... 224 338-8179
  Round Lake *(G-18074)*
Historic Timber & Plank Inc ....E....... 618 372-4546
  Brighton *(G-2401)*
Navillus Woodworks LLC ....G....... 312 375-2680
  Chicago *(G-5556)*
Onsite Woodwork Corporation.........C....... 815 633-6400
  Loves Park *(G-13242)*
Parenti & Raffaelli Ltd......................C....... 847 253-5550
  Mount Prospect *(G-14558)*
Pio Woodworking Inc ....G....... 630 628-6900
  Addison *(G-240)*
Woodwrights Shoppe Inc.................G....... 309 360-6603
  Metamora *(G-13970)*

WOODWORK: Ornamental, Cornices, Mantels, Etc.

Botti Studio of Architectural ....E....... 847 869-5933
  Glenview *(G-10532)*
Custom Window Accents ....F....... 815 943-7651
  Harvard *(G-11051)*

WORD PROCESSING SVCS

Negs & Litho Inc...............................G....... 847 647-7770
  Chicago *(G-5563)*

WOVEN WIRE PRDTS, NEC

Apex Wire Products Company Inc ...F....... 847 671-1830
  Franklin Park *(G-9871)*
Art Wire Works Inc ....F....... 708 458-3993
  Bedford Park *(G-1457)*
Burnex Corporation ....E....... 815 728-1317
  Ringwood *(G-17040)*
Cooley Wire Products Mfg Co ....E....... 847 678-8585
  Schiller Park *(G-18796)*
Highland Southern Wire Inc.............G....... 618 654-2161
  Highland *(G-11222)*
Park Manufacturing Corp Inc ....F....... 708 345-6090
  Melrose Park *(G-13903)*
Southern Steel and Wire Inc ....G....... 618 654-2161
  Highland *(G-11240)*
Wirco Inc..D....... 217 398-3200
  Champaign *(G-3371)*

WREATHS: Artificial

Northwoods Wreaths Company ....E....... 847 615-9491
  Lake Forest *(G-12275)*
Twoinspireyou LLC ....G....... 630 849-8214
  Geneva *(G-10314)*

WRENCHES

Durabilt Dyvex Inc............................F....... 708 397-4673
  Broadview *(G-2432)*
M E Barber Co Inc............................G....... 217 428-4591
  Decatur *(G-7518)*
Precision Instruments Inc ....D....... 847 824-4194
  Des Plaines *(G-7830)*
Sk Hand Tool LLC ....F....... 815 895-7701
  Sycamore *(G-19731)*

WRITING FOR PUBLICATION SVCS

Canright & Paule Inc........................G....... 888 202-3894
  Chicago *(G-4015)*
Rite-TEC Communications...............G....... 815 459-7712
  Crystal Lake *(G-7258)*

X-RAY EQPT & TUBES

7 Mile Solutions Inc ....E....... 847 588-2280
  Niles *(G-15096)*
Abbott Laboratories..........................A....... 847 932-7900
  North Chicago *(G-15293)*
Arquilla Inc ....F....... 815 455-2470
  Crystal Lake *(G-7163)*
Assurance Technologies Inc ....F....... 630 550-5000
  Bartlett *(G-1265)*
Brand X-Ray Company ....F....... 630 543-5331
  Addison *(G-54)*
Faxitron X-Ray LLC ....E....... 847 465-9729
  Lincolnshire *(G-12763)*
Gama Electronics Inc ....F....... 815 356-9600
  Woodstock *(G-21391)*
Lixi Inc..G....... 630 620-4646
  Downers Grove *(G-8045)*
Mark Industries ....G....... 847 487-8670
  Wauconda *(G-20372)*
Material Control Inc ....F....... 630 892-4274
  Batavia *(G-1393)*
Medical Radiation Concepts............G....... 630 289-1515
  Bartlett *(G-1297)*
Midmark Corporation ....D....... 800 643-6275
  Buffalo Grove *(G-2574)*
Philips North America LLC ....C....... 630 585-2000
  Aurora *(G-1008)*
Poersch Metal Manufacturing Co ....F....... 773 722-0890
  Chicago *(G-5828)*
Superior X Ray Tube Company ....G....... 815 338-4424
  Woodstock *(G-21437)*
Varex Imaging Corporation ....D....... 847 279-5121
  Franklin Park *(G-10076)*
X-Ray Cassette Repair Co Inc..........E....... 815 356-8181
  Crystal Lake *(G-7296)*

X-RAY EQPT REPAIR SVCS

X-Ray Cassette Repair Co Inc..........E....... 815 356-8181
  Crystal Lake *(G-7296)*